The Naval Institute Guide to

COMBAT FLEETS

OF THE WORLD, 15TH EDITION

The Naval Institute Guide to

COMBAT FLEETS OF THE WORLD, 15TH EDITION

THEIR SHIPS, AIRCRAFT, AND SYSTEMS

Eric Wertheim

NAVAL INSTITUTE PRESS
Annapolis, Maryland

Naval Institute Press
291 Wood Road
Annapolis, MD 21402

ISBN-13: 978-1-59114-955-2
ISSN: 1057-4581

Printed in the United States of America on acid-free paper

14 13 12 11 10 09 08 07 9 8 7 6 5 4 3 2
First printing

For two of my closest friends:
my brother Robert and my sister Caryn

CONTENTS

SOURCES AND ACKNOWLEDGMENTS

All information in *Combat Fleets* has been derived from unclassified, open-source publications and from correspondence received from around the world. Official sources from many navies and nations have been consulted, but for some fleets, such as North Korea, data must be estimated out of necessity.

As with the previous edition of *Combat Fleets,* special recognition needs to be made here of A. D. Baker III, my predecessor, who served as editor of the *Naval Institute's Guide to Combat Fleets of the World* from 1977 through 2002. I feel fortunate that Mr. Baker continues to offer his opinions on maritime events, and I am indebted to him for his sound and sage advice as I labored daily to keep the nation's premier naval reference book up to date. Yet another vital contributor to the 15th edition of *Combat Fleets of the World* has been Samuel Loring Morison. Readers will undoubtedly appreciate Sam's many hours of research and fact-checking, during which time he earned the title 'Combat Fleets Senior Researcher' many times over. Sam's decades of experience in the field of naval publishing also provided a useful sounding board when editorial changes and decisions were required. The late John Anthony served in a similar capacity for the United Kingdom chapter of the book, and though colleagues mourn his passing, his spirit lives on through John's work on the United Kingdom chapter of *Combat Fleets.*

The editors of France's *Flottes de Combat,* Bernard Prézelin, and Germany's *Weyers Flottentaschenbuch,* Werner Globke, deserve my most sincere thanks here as well. These two international naval experts have unselfishly shared information and illustrations for use in *Combat Fleets* while working hard on new editions of their own outstanding reference books.

Other publications of particular value as sources for (and checks on) information for this edition have been the following periodicals: AFCEA's *SIGNAL* magazine, *The Almanac of Seapower; Defense News; Flight International; Intelligence, Surveillance and Reconnaissance Journal; Jane's Defence Weekly; Jane's International Defence Review; Jane's Navy International; Marine News; Maritime Reporter and Engineering News; Naval Aviation News; Navy Times; Navy Today; Okrety Wojenne; Proceedings of the U.S. Naval Institute; Preview: The Journal of the Defence Procurement Agency; Sea Power; Sea Technology; Seawaves Magazine* (on-line); *Ships of the World; Surface Warfare; Undersea Technology; Undersea Warfare; Warships International Fleet Review; WorkBoat;* and *Work Boat International.* The latest editions of our sister references, *Flottes de Combat, Jane's Fighting Ships,* and *Weyers Flottentaschenbuch,* edited by Bernard Prézelin, Commodore Stephen Saunders, and Werner Globke, respectively, were frequently consulted as well. This edition has continued to make considerable use of official online websites maintained by navies and defenses forces around the globe as well as websites maintained by private individuals that been consulted on a regular basis. I am also indebted to the International Institute for Strategic Studies in London for their excellent statistical reference, *The Military Balance 2005-06,* from which the vast majority of maritime personnel data was derived for this edition of *Combat Fleets.*

Others who have contributed to this edition include: Thomas B. Allen, who offered excellent publishing and literary advice; Captain Massimo A. Annati of the Italian Navy; A. D. Baker III, arguably the world's leading expert on international navies and editor of *Combat Fleets* from 1977–2002, for his words of encouragement and editorial advice; Dr. Ted Barna; Reginaldo J. da Silva Bacchi, for his input on Brazilian and South American navies; Andrew Bahjat, for his expertise on naval aviation; Frank Behling, contributor of timely and superb digital photography; Sumeet Bhatia, General Manager of the UPS Store in Springfield, Virginia for his office's assistance with handling nearly all of the mail addressed to *Combat Fleets* – which can at times be a daunting challenge; Larry Bond, wargamer and bestselling author; Curt Borgenstam Jr., for his fine photos and information about the Swedish Navy; Ignacio Jose Amendolara Bourdette, an unparalleled source for Argentine photography and news; Dr. Maurizio Brescia, historian of the ships of the Italian Navy; Jim Brooke, former Commander General of the Naval Order of the United States for his strong support of *Combat Fleets of the World;* Tom Bullock, for his calm words of advice, especially useful during deadline crunches and other crises; R. J. "Jo" Bunce, former Director of New Zealand's Naval Reputation Management office, for photos, data and the excellent publication *Navy Today;* Richard R. "Rick" Burgess, managing editor of *Sea Power* and contributing editor to *Proceedings* and *Naval Aviation News,* for his CHINFO news updates and assistance with the U.S. Navy aviation section; Camil Busquets i Vilanova, for timely information about Spanish Navy programs and for superbly composed color photography; Rob Cabo, for excellent ship photos, very useful news, and cheerful support from the Netherlands; George and Janine Cornecelli, co-founders of the Mkt. Group, for their insightful thoughts on marketing to the defense industry; Christopher P. Cavas, naval warfare correspondent at *Defense News,* for his many useful e-mails and news items; Marion P. "Blade" Chapman, for engineering acumen and his encyclopedic knowledge of naval equipment fits; Raymond Cheung; Jaroslaw Cislak, for sharing his vast knowledge of the Polish Navy and for providing many fine photos; Douglas A. Cromby, for excellent photography and contributions; Paul Cropper, whose *Russian Military News* was a vital source of naval events in Russia and elsewhere; Dave Cullen for his excellent photography from the United Kingdom; Patrick D'Agostino; Steven Daskal for his informative e-mail updates on defense and technical matters; Gary Davies of Maritime Photographic, one of England's premier naval photography sources; Rear Admiral Samuel P. DeBow Jr., Director of Marine and Aviation Operations at NOAA, for his patience in detailing the latest NOAA developments over a NOUS buffet lunch; Commander Maxim Degtyarev, Assistant Naval Attaché at the Russian Embassy in Washington, D.C. for his insight and assistance understanding Russian naval culture and organization; Leo Dirkx; Ralph Dunn, editor of DERA's *Preview;* Ralph Edwards, for superb photography and knowledgeable commentary; Dipl.-Ing. Hartmut Ehlers, prolific photographer and diligent researcher on the navies of the former Warsaw Pact and elsewhere; Daniel Ferro, for his helpful information on Gibraltar; Frank Findler, for much excellent photography; Dr. Stephen Flynn at the Council on Foreign Relations for his assistance with Homeland Security and Coast Guard issues; Derek Fox, for his first-rate maritime photography; Dr. Zvonimir Freivogel, for photos and detailed information about the Croatian and Federal Yugoslav navies; Dr. Norman Friedman, author of the *Naval Institute Guide to World Naval Weapons Systems;* Stephen Friske, creative web and graphics specialist and founder of Friske Graphics (www.friskegraphics.com) for his assistance with digital imagery and design of the Combat Fleets web site; Cdr Craig Fulton, Staff Officer Submarines, British Naval Staff at the British Embassy in Washington, D.C.; Commander Howard Furness, Assistant Naval Attaché at the Australian Embassy in Washington, for his assistance with updating the Australian Navy chapter; Ross Gillett, Australia's prolific author on naval subjects; Paul Ginnane, for photos of naval auxiliaries; Werner Globke, editor of *Weyers Flottentaschenbuch,* for advice and encouragement and the generous sharing of data and illustrations; John Gourley, for some finely detailed digital views of naval equipment and naval ships; Luciano Grazioli, for hard-to-find photos and information on naval events in Italy; Tomasz Grotnik, for his unique artwork and multi-view line-drawings, many of them exclusive to this edition of *Combat Fleets;* John D. Gresham; Cdr. Alvin H. Grobmeier, USN (Ret.), who provided numerous detailed and authoritative lists of small-craft in U.S. service as well as frequent naval news from around the world; Dr. Eric Grove; Keith Henderson, editor of *Jane's Marine Propulsion,* for his friendship and assistance on maritime propulsion issues; Carlos Hernández González, for invaluable help with the Colombian and Venezuelan navies and for forwarding a large number of photos, both his own and those of the members of the FAV Club; Commander John D. Hooper, USCG, for his strong support of *Combat Fleets* through his leadership in the National Capital Commandery of the Naval Order of the United States; Vic Jeffery, command public relations officer, RAN, Rockingham, for supplying useful information on the RAN and the superb photography taken by the RAN's staff photographers in Western Australia; Margaret Mitchell-Jones, Communications Director at Integrated Coast Guard Systems Deep Water; Mitsuhiro Kadota, for excellent photographs of ships and craft from Japan; Stefan Karpinski for his excellent photography; Cdr. Hans Karr, German Navy ret., now on the editorial staff of *Magazin der Bundeswehr,* for assistance with the Germany chapter of this book, interesting details of naval designs and many useful photos; Richard Kaye; Commander Fred Keating, Assistant Naval Attaché and Senior Technical Officer at the New Zealand Embassy in Washington, for his assistance with my inquiries concerning the status of New Zealand's naval forces; Commander and Mrs. Thomas Kiss, for their friendship, encouragement, and naval expertise; Tohru Kizu, editor of *Ships of the World;* A. A. de Kruijf, for his news updates, timely photos from the Netherlands and patience assisting me with the intricacies of the Dutch language via e-mail; Col. Jürg Kürsener, for excellent photos from his interesting travels; Dr. Eric Labs, Principal Analyst for Naval Forces and Weapons at the Congressional Budget Office; Donna Larocque, marketing department, Marinette Marine, for informative press releases and excellent photos; Boris Lemachko, whose numerous photos of the Russian and Ukrainian navies are absolutely unique; Professor Carlos Lopez for his helpful information on the Chilean and South American navies; Edward Lundquist; Jaroslaw Malinowski, editor of the fine Polish naval periodical *Okrety Wojenne,* for information about Eastern European and Asian navies; Colonel Paul Manley, USAFR (Ret.); Lieutenant Colonel Nick Mansolillo, USAFR; Mike Markowitz at the Center For Naval Analysis, for forwarding many useful articles that may otherwise have been overlooked; Paolo Marsan, for his own fine photos and those of Guy Schaeffer and others; Carlo Martinelli, for a number of excellent photos from the Mediterranean area; Stefan Marx, for his helpful information and expertise on the Latvian navy; Captain Victor Emmanuel Martir, Naval Attaché at the Embassy of the Philippines in Washington, D.C., for his insight into the unique issues facing Philippine naval forces; Mritunjoy Mazumdar, co-proprietor of the highly informative Indian Navy website (www.bharat-rakshak.com/navy/), for detailed information about the Indian Navy and numerous fine photos and drawings; Jim McIngvale, Director of Communications at Northrop Grumman Ship Systems; Edward McDonnell, for his excellent photography from the Middle East and around the world; Erin J. McMunigal, for her assistance with Coast Guard digital photography and nationally recognized expertise in the field of maritime law; Gorka L. Martinez Mezo; Ted Minter, faithful correspondent on the U.S. Navy; Martin Mokrus, a contributor of excellent-quality photos; Julio Montes, for extensive data and many fine photos of Central American ships and craft; Brian Morrison, Warships & Marine Corps Museum, International, Australia, for many absolutely superb warship photos; John Mortimer, who has sent many fine warship photos; Michael Nitz, for his suburb digital photography and news updates from Germany; Takatoshi Okano, for an excellent selection of photos of Japanese Maritime Self-Defense Force and Coast Guard ships and craft; Ron O'Rourke at the Congressional Research Service, for his advice and insightful knowledge on the world's navies; Robert Painter; Steve Pegge; Jeffery Perin of Swiftships shipbuilders; Susan Pierter, director, communications, Bath Iron Works; IJsbrand Plokker, for excellent photography from Europe; Beverly Polmar, for her kind hospitality while working with and visiting the Polmar family; Norman Polmar, friend, mentor and author of dozens of naval books and references, including the *Naval Institute Guide to Ships and Aircraft of the U.S. Fleet,* for providing much useful information and advice; Bernard Prézelin, the generous and energetic editor of our sister publication, *Flottes de Combat,* for news of naval developments worldwide and hundreds of his excellent photos; Fred H. Rainbow, Vice President of Education for AFCEA International and Executive Director of the AFCEA Educational Foundation, for continued strong support on this project, for which I am grateful; Bram Risseeuw, correspondent on the Netherlands, Irish, and South American navies—and others; Eivind Rodlie, for numerous photos of Norwegian units; Capitán de Corbeta John Rodriguez Asti, Peruvian Navy, for providing officially sanctioned photography and data about his navy; Tagg Rogers at Silvership Shipbuilders; Brooks A. Rowlett, for forwarding numerous useful items of naval interest from the Internet; James Ruehrmund, Col. USAFR (Ret.); Neil Ruenzel, Director of Communications at General Dynamics Electric Boat; Neill Rush; Jens Salzmann, for photography of German and Danish naval vessels; Jim Sanderson, for fine photos from the United Kingdom and California; Commodore Sawhney, Indian Naval Attaché, for assistance with the Indian Navy chapter and his gracious invitation to come aboard INS *Tarangini;* Marcin Schiele, for information about Polish and Russian-designed warships; George R. Schneider, for a vast number of excellent photos of U.S., South American, and other naval ships and craft—as well as Herculean labors at making sense of the U.S. Navy and U.S. Coast Guard small craft fleet lists; Mr. A. Scrimali, for his excellent photography; Alexandre Sheldon-Duplaix, for his useful information and photos along with his in-depth knowledge and expertise on warships, particularly concerning the Chinese Navy; Dave Shirlaw, editor of Canada's excellent and indispensable online naval daily Internet report, *Seawaves Magazine* (www.seawaves.com); Capt. Piet Sinke, not only for photos but also for useful information pulled from the Internet and from his own travels; Adam Smigielski, for interesting and informative naval news and correspondence; David Smith, for his superb photography direct from England; Leslie Kohlbry Smith at Workskiff boat builders; Ben Stans, for his useful information and photography; Chris Sattler, for many fine photos from Australia and the Pacific region; H. M. Steel; Jeff Steelman, Director of Naval Programs Strategy and Business Development at Thales, North America; Major Bobby Straight, USMC (Ret.), whose Marine intelligence background proved useful when examining hard-to-interpret naval photography; James B. Stricker, NOAA engineer; Ben Sullivan, for his fine digital photography CDs from the U.K.; Arjun Sarup, for his useful information from around the globe; Beata Swierzy of the public relations department at Blohm Voss; Guy Ames Stitt and his team of naval analysts and advisors at AMI International in Bremerton, Washington, for their excellent input on how to make this reference as user-friendly as possible; Geoffrey Till; Andrew C. Toppan and the Haze Gray and Underway warship database on the Internet (www.hazegray.org); Sarah J. Turgeon, Bath Iron Works; Captain Stefano Vignani, Port Captain Corps, Italian Navy, for data and illustrations on "CP" craft; Leo Van Ginderen, for many fine photos sent almost daily via e-mail; Jasper Van Raemdonck, for current data about the Belgian and NATO Navies; Cdr. Erwin Weissmann, former Assistant Naval Attaché at the German Embassy in Washington, D.C., for his assistance with German and European naval matters; Mike Welsford, for photos of the highest quality; Dinca Wertheim and Jean-Pierre Voncken, for their assistance with the Netherlands and Belgium chapters; Lt. Rick Wester, USCG Public Affairs; Dr. David F. Winkler of the Naval Historical Foundation; Seth Winnick, communications specialist at the Coast Guard's Deepwater Program, for quick answers on the Project Deepwater; Michael Winter, for his always excellent photography; Dieter Wolf, for a great many of his superb photographs; Michael Worley, Vice President of Naval Marine Programs at Rolls-Royce North America; Christopher C. Wright III, editor of *Warship International;* Marian Wright, for excellent photos taken at Portsmouth, U.K.; Commander Yao Jianhong and his predecessor Captain Zhang Junshe, Assistant Naval Attachés at the Embassy of the People's Republic of China in Washington, D.C., for helping providing a better understanding of Chinese naval culture and history; Teresa Yasutis, President of Clarity Communications (www.claritycommunicationsinc.com), for her assistance publicizing *Combat Fleets of the World* and its editor; Cem D. Yaylali, for photography from the Bosporus and news of the Turkish Navy; W. Michael Young, for fine photography from the San Diego area; Aeriell Youngbar, for her photographic expertise; and Steven J. Zaloga, for some very useful photos and brochures. To all those others who helped as well but could not for various reasons be named here, my deepest thanks.

Sandy Adams provided top-notch service as this edition's production manager, directing every aspect of the book's production from chapter due dates to illustration changes to page-proof corrections. Her service proved priceless and she is undoubtedly among the best in the industry. The efforts put in by Therese Boyd and Judy Loeven were also exceptional as they worked from the sidelines as copy editor and proofreader, having to put up with more than their fair share of my very messy handwriting. ATLIS Graphics assisted with compiling the extensive index. Tom Harnish, director of sales at the Naval Institute, was always quick to answer my sales and marketing questions and help with promotions, while Susan Artigiani worked to make sure that readers and the media were aware of our existence. Additionally, designer Brian Barth did a fantastic job with this edition's excellent cover. Robert Timberg, veteran journalist and Editor-in-Chief of USNI *Proceedings* Magazine, often lent me a reporter's ear when I had a question or problem and offered much advice based on his many years as a correspondent for the *Baltimore Sun*. Jim Caiella also deserves much credit here as well, Mr. Caiella serves ably and expertly as editor of my monthly "Combat Fleets" column in *Proceedings* magazine and is himself an excellent source for computer-generated naval and technical artwork, for which I am truly appreciative.

Additionally, at the Naval Institute Tom Cutler provided some invaluable insight into the publishing industry and Jacquelyn Day,

Liese Doherty, Judy Heise, Carol Parkinson, and Brian Walker were always available to answer whatever *Combat Fleets*– related questions or requests I might have during the course of compiling this book. Special thanks also go to Major General Tom Wilkerson, USMC (Ret.), the CEO and Publisher of the United States Naval Institute, for continuing to support *Combat Fleets.* My sincerest thanks also go to my colleagues and supervisors at Science Applications International Corporation (SAIC), including Robert "Mike" Maxwell, Thomas "Fuzzy" Thurston, Gordon Kage, Paul McClure, and Vernon Guidry, each of whom offered much encouragement and flexibility while I balanced my work at SAIC with my writing for the Naval Institute.

Of course my family also deserves great thanks, including Abraham, Marilyn, Caryn, Robert, Amy, Toby and Nora Wertheim—they all had to spend a great deal of time hearing about and, in their own way, helping with this latest edition of *Combat Fleets of the World.*

Combat Fleets is normally published every two years, but the work of revision is continuous. Anyone with information to update or correct the book or with photographs that could be used to illustrate the next edition is urged to contact the editor via the Naval Institute Press, 291 Wood Road, Annapolis, Maryland, 21402-5035. The editor can also be reached via e-mail at: combatfleets@yahoo.com or by fax at: (703) 644-9653. Dates and location data on the back of all photographs are highly desirable, and all illustrations used will be credited to the contributors. With your help, *Combat Fleets* will remain as accurate, thorough, and timely as possible.

Please visit our Combat Fleets website (www.combatfleets.com) for additional information and updates.

Eric Wertheim
5 January 2007

INTRODUCTION: WORLD NAVIES IN REVIEW

The high cost of building and maintaining today's modern warships continues to merge with an understanding that friendly fleets often work best cooperatively. This realization is reflected both in the types of warships now being built and in an ever-growing trend toward interoperability. Through initiatives like the "1,000 Ship Navy," a global maritime network proposed to help prevent terrorism and to provide humanitarian natural disaster relief, navies are becoming more relevant than ever. A new collaborative spirit has been generating optimism in a domain where single ships often cost billions of dollars, yet even the smallest of navies have vital contributions to offer.

This review of the world's navies is arranged by region, with maritime nations discussed alphabetically in each subheading.

Australia and Asia

With a number of new high-profile programs in development, Australia aims to remain an important player in Asian maritime affairs, and if current plans come to pass, their navy appears to be in good shape for dealing with the ongoing changes in the region. Though not without its setbacks, Australia is working across the board to ensure its fleet stays relevant.

With plans and expectations high for the Australian Air Warfare destroyer program, the navy expects a government green-light decision on the project in early 2007. If given final approval, the first vessel, *Hobart,* will enter service in 2013 and will be followed by *Brisbane* in 2014 and sister *Sydney* in 2016. The destroyers will join eight Anzac (MEKO-200 ANZ) -class frigates, the last of which, *Perth,* was fully operational by early 2007. The submarine community also has something to look forward to as upgrade plans to the *Collins*-class submarine were announced in October 2006. Improvements to the class are expected to include electronic warfare, communications, and periscope modernizations. On a smaller scale, additional *Armidale*-class patrol boats continue to be delivered, with 13 units expected to be operational by 2007; two additional boats are on order. In the air, Australia plans to retire their Sea King helicopter fleet early, as efforts to purchase and replace them with NH-90 helicopters have been accelerated. More immediately, however, SH-2G Super SeaSprite helicopters are now ready for service, following five years of delays.

Facing the requirement for new sealift capacity, discussion and planning are under way, with a simple monohull design appearing to be the preferred solution. The new sealift program and its associated vessels are planned to enter service between 2016 and 2018, though as with all dates so far in the future, some slippage can be expected. The Australian Navy's *Appleleaf*-class underway replenishment oiler HMAS *Westralia* returned from her last overseas deployment in April 2006 and was decommissioned in September. *Westralia*'s replacement, *Sirius,* entered service soon thereafter. Next on the slate for Australian maritime capabilities is a new amphibious assault ship program. A request for tenders occurred in the spring of 2006 and Thales and Tenix shipyards both submitted bids for the contract.

In Bangladesh, the government assumed operational control over one of the nation's largest private shipyards due to its financial difficulties, while in Brunei, analysts are awaiting the results of a drawn-out International Court of Justice arbitration decision to determine who is to blame for Brunei's rejection of British-built frigates that were completed and ready for delivery in 2005.

The capabilities and confidence of the Chinese Navy continue to grow at rates unparalleled in the rest of the world during the previous 10-year period. Experts are divided, however, as to whether this rate of expansion and growth will continue or if it has, in fact, reached a plateau. From a big-picture perspective, work on China's project 094 nuclear-powered ballistic-missile submarine, sometimes referred to as the Jin-class, continues and many analysts estimate that the class will be ready for service in 2008. Until that time, the older *Xia*-class nuclear-powered submarine sails on, albeit locally and close to Chinese home waters. The first two of up to 12 Type 093 Chin-class nuclear-powered attack submarines have begun to enter service, and though it may be some time before the new boats are fully operational, they will undoubtedly have a big impact on the fleet in years to come. Two new diesel-powered attack submarines of the Yuan-class (Type 041) are also apparently now in service, and these join 14 Song-class submarines, the last of which entered service by 2006.

During 2006, China's first Project 051C and third Project 052C destroyers were delivered and the third and fourth Russian-built *Sovremennyy*-class destroyers entered service. Although China was the single largest recipient of Russian arms in 2006, the number and variety of Russian arms exports to China are expected to drop as the domestic Chinese arms and naval industries are catching up to their global counterparts. As an example of this, China recently offered its older Ming- and Song-class submarines for sale on the export market along with new C-602 naval cruise missiles. It remains difficult to gauge the amount of money spent on the naval and defense budget, though multiplying China's publicly released defense figures by a factor of three or four is often suggested.

China's third Russian built *Sovremenny*-class destroyer, *Taizhou*, entered service in 2006 Bernard Prézelin

As the capabilities of its surface fleet continue to expand, China is also looking to expand its amphibious warfare capability and in late 2006 announced plans to purchase six 540-ton *Zubr* amphibious landing hovercraft, similar in principle, though larger, than U.S. Landing Craft Air Cushion (LCAC) vessels. Perhaps most illustrative of the dramatic increase in Chinese naval activities was an incident in the autumn of 2006 when a Chinese Song-class diesel-powered submarine surfaced undetected within five miles of the USS *Kitty Hawk* Carrier Strike Group operating in international waters. Though this incident may well have been an accident reflecting the loss of U.S. Navy antisubmarine warfare expertise and capabilities, the incident is worrisome and would likely not have occurred a decade ago.

In India, meanwhile, construction continues on the 40,000-ton *Vikrant*-class Air Defense Ship aircraft carrier, with plans to launch the vessel in 2009 or 2010. A Russian shipyard is also refurbishing the carrier, ex-*Admiral Gorshkov,* since renamed *Vikramaditya*. Plans call for *Vikramaditya* to replace India's long-serving carrier *Viraat* by 2008. With these new ships, India hopes to enhance its capabilities and power projection through naval aviation. India is also looking to purchase new long-range maritime-patrol aircraft, most likely from the United States or Russia. India has also expressed interest in retired Sea King antisubmarine helicopters from the United States. In October they rejected an offer to buy Sea Harrier fighters from the United Kingdom due to price and technology transfer issues.

As India moves to modernize and increase its blue-water presence, a number of older vessels are being decommissioned while new warships continue to enter service. Though a severe spare-parts shortage exists (20% of India's ships and 35% of its submarines are reportedly inoperable), funding appears to be in good shape as a 44% increase in the naval budget is projected under India's five-year defense plan. In addition to increasing logistics and repair capabilities, the fleet hopes to acquire a number of new warships, including three *Bangalore* (Project 15A)-class destroyers in 2008 and three additional Russian-built *Talwar*-class frigates that were ordered in the summer of 2006. The new *Talwar* frigates will be armed with the Brahmos antiship missile and, when delivered by 2011, are to join three older sisters already in service. Also under construction are two new *Shivalik* (Project 17)-class frigates, due to commission by 2008.

While work starts up in Mumbai on India's six Scorpène-class submarines due to enter service between 2012 and 2018, India is also considering a modified variant of the Russian Amur-class submarine that could be fitted with an air-independent propulsion system. Progress on the mysterious and long-planned Advanced Technology Vessel (ATV) nuclear-powered submarine program apparently continues as well, with scientists reported to have completed development of the ATV's nuclear propulsion plant during the summer of 2006. Efforts to boost Indian amphibious and expeditionary capabilities are part of a renewed emphasis on littoral warfare and power projection stemming from a new naval doctrine adopted in 2004. In line with this new doctrine is the recent acquisition of the retired amphibious ship ex-*Trenton,* acquired from the U.S. Navy and transferred to India in January 2007. Work on a new class of Tank Landing Ships is also continuing and first of the class, *Shardul,* entered service in 2006, with *Kesari* to follow in 2007 and sister *Airavat* due for delivery in 2008. India's small combatant forces continue to expand their capabilities as well, and 2006 saw the eighth Israeli Super Dvora Mk II patrol boat enter service. A class of eight new construction coastal minehunters, to be built at Goa shipyard, is also in the works for service entry around 2010.

In Indonesia the military is in the process of reorganizing its forces. Current plans call for consolidation of fleet commands from three down to two. Two new *Diponegoro*-class corvettes are due to commission in 2007, and two more are expected to follow in 2008–9. New amphibious transport docks are also under construction with two *Tanjung Dalpele*–class LPDs planned to be delivered by late 2007 and another of the class to enter service in 2008.

In Japan, although the defense budget has been falling for more than four years, hopes remain high for several new classes of warship. Three improved *Oyashio*-class attack submarines are under varying degrees of construction and due to enter service between 2009 and 2011. The new submarines will join 10 of the original *Oyashio*-class boats, the newest of which will join the fleet in 2008. A new type of 13,500-ton helicopter-carrying destroyer is in the works and up to four of the ships are planned to replace the *Shirane* and *Haruna* classes. The Japanese *Kongo*-class guided-missile destroyers delivered in the 1990s have proven popular and two improved units were laid down in 2005 and 2006 for delivery in 2007 and 2008. Missile defense and naval aviation were also high on the list of Japanese Maritime Self Defense Force priorities with orders for SM-3 block 1A missiles approved for transfer from the United States in June 2006 and deliveries of the first EH101 helicopters arriving for fleet use.

In Malaysia, the first two of six MEKO-100 RMN-class patrol ships, *Kadah* and *Pahang,* have now been delivered. Four additional units may prove unaffordable, calling into question the stated goals of a 27-unit class by around 2020. Aside from the desire for 27 MEKO-100s, the biggest investment for the Malaysian fleet remains the two Scorpène-class submarines on order for delivery by 2009. In an attempt to prepare for the arrival of the new submarines, Malaysian naval leaders have been looking overseas for assistance with submarine training and safety in hopes of avoiding costly or dangerous errors common to new submarine programs.

In February 2006, Dutch shipbuilder Merwede launched New Zealand's new Multi Role Vessel (MRV) amphibious warship, the largest part of New Zealand's Project Protector naval modernization program. Displacing 9,000 tons, the MRV is based on a civilian-use roll-on/roll-off ferry. The MRV is expected to enter service with New Zealand in April 2007 and can transport up to 250 troops along with one SH-2G Super SeaSprite and four NH-90 helicopters. The Project Protector program also includes two Offshore Patrol Vessels (OPV) being built in Melbourne, Australia, the first of which was launched in November of 2006, and four smaller Inshore Patrol Vessels (IPV) built at Whangarei, New Zealand. In total, the project calls for seven ships and will markedly improve New Zealand's maritime capabilities and ability to contribute to international exercises and operations.

New Zealand's new Multi Role Vessel (MRV) amphibious warship forms the largest part of the Project Protector naval modernization program Rob Cabo

As Pakistan expands its naval force, it aims for wide-ranging improvements. Four modern F-22P frigates are on order from China, and in April 2006 the option for a fifth unit of the class was exercised with deliveries of the first four expected between 2008 and 2013 and the fifth unit several years later. Work is also under way to upgrade the submarine force with a third French-designed Agusta-90B–class submarine, *Hamza,* being built at Karachi Naval Shipyard for delivery around 2008. The final *Jalalat*-class guided-missile patrol craft entered full operational service in 2006 and two Kaan (MRTP33) fast-attack craft were ordered from Turkey in August for delivery in 2008. As Pakistan's warships modernize, so too does its naval aviation fleet. The Naval Air Arm now consists of 10 P-3C Orion maritime patrol aircraft, with eight purchased during 2006–7. In order to keep an appropriate force mix and balance, the Pakistani Marine Corps will also be expanding.

In the Philippines, the Army has announced plans to acquire between 18 and 30 new short-range fast transport craft that are capable of traveling at 25 knots and can carry 150 troops for operations between islands. In Singapore efforts are underway to merge two naval squadrons into a single unit that would operate amphibious ships and fast attack craft. Two ex-Swedish *Vastergotland*-class submarines ordered from Sweden in 2005 remain on schedule to join Singapore's fleet in 2010. The *Formidable*-class frigate *Steadfast,* third of six sisters, began sea trials in 2006, while the first of the class completed similar trials in July. Three additional units, *Tenacious, Stalwart,* and *Supreme,* are planned for delivery in 2007, 2008, and 2009 respectively.

South Korea's first of three Type 214 submarines was launched in the spring of 2006. Four of a total six KDX-II–class destroyers had been delivered by early 2007 with two addition units planned for commissioning by 2008. The new KDX-III destroyers are also progressing smoothly and the first of the class is scheduled for delivery late in 2008. Plans are also in the works to develop a new frigate intended to replace the current nine-ship *Ulsan* class by 2015.

Taiwan received the second set of modernized ex-U.S. Navy *Kidd*-class guided missile destroyers by late 2006. The destroyers are the most advanced warships in Taiwan's fleet and are arguably more powerful than any ships now in service with the Chinese People's Liberation Army Navy across the Taiwan Strait. The *Kidd*-class warships were extensively refitted during their three-year reactivation overhauls performed at Detyens Shipyard in South Carolina.

Taiwan, however, appears no closer than it was five years ago to acquiring new diesel-powered submarines promised it by the Bush administration in 2001. Although some reports have indicated that the class could be built using Japanese submarine technology and designs, this is most likely just another shot in the dark for a program that appears to be moving at the speed of seeping lava.

Thailand's normally close ties with the West were jeopardized in September 2006 when its military chief overthrew the prime minister in a surprise coup. Though the lasting impact on Thailand's maritime forces and the country as a whole have yet to be determined, there appears to be a concerted effort on the part of western nations to press for a return to democracy while working to maintain some degree of normalcy. As such, plans continue in preparation for 2007's annual multinational Cobra Gold exercises in which Thailand remains the key player. Little in the way of growth, however, is planned for the Thai navy, other than an occasional addition to the patrol fleet, which most recently gained two small 1,500-ton Chinese patrol ships built in Shanghai and delivered in 2005 and 2006.

Europe

On the European continent, Belgium continues to make the most of cuts in the Netherlands and announced the purchase of two retired Royal Dutch Navy *Karel Doorman*–class frigates, which are due to enter service in 2007–8. The retired Dutch frigates will serve as replacements for the two remaining *Welingen*-class ships, which are, despite upgrades, nearing the end of their useful service lives and will likely be transferred abroad.

In Denmark, the Thales-Netherlands Smart-L radar was recently chosen to equip the three new 5,000-ton "Patrol Ship" frigates intended to replace the *Niels Juel*–class corvettes that have been in service since the early 1980s. The new ships will supplement two multipurpose Flexible Support Ships that entered service in 2004 and 2005. Also under construction for Denmark are a number of different patrol craft, including 100-ton Mk I class and 180-ton Mk II designs being built domestically.

In Estonia, naval forces continue to grow in capabilities if not in numbers, particularly involving noncombatants, auxiliaries, and mine-countermeasures vessels. In September of 2006, Estonia announced the purchase of three ex-U.K. Royal Navy *Sandown*-class minehunters, concluding negotiations that had been ongoing since January 2006. Finland is also working to expand its mine-countermeasures force and in late 2006 it announced an order for three mine-warfare craft based on an Italian design. The new Finnish mine-warfare vessels are due to enter service between 2010 and 2012 and will ironically join a capable fleet of minelaying craft now in service. In June 2006 the fourth and final *Hamina* (Rauma 2000) -class guided-missile patrol boat was delivered to the Finnish Navy. Built by Aker Shipyard in Rauma, the *Pori* joined sisters *Hamina, Tornio,* and *Hanko,* which entered service between 1998 and 2005. All four boats can now carry the South African Denel-Kentron Umkhonto Infra-red point defense vertical launched surface-to-air missile system. Other ongoing modernizations in the Finnish fleet include upgrades to the two *Hämeenmaa*-class minelayers. *Hämeenmaa* and *Uusimaa,* to be completed by Aker in 2007.

In France, some major decisions have yet to be made concerning a second aircraft carrier dubbed the PA2. A large degree of commonality exists between the design for the PA2 and the new British *Queen Elizabeth*–class aircraft carriers, particularly regarding vessel superstructure. Though the French parliament authorized the carrier in 2003, most recent news has been negative. As the addition of weight, complexity, and cost have increased, so has the likelihood of program cancellation. Experts now predict the PA2 has only a 50% chance of surviving upcoming budget reviews. Optimistic carrier supporters, however, hope to have the PA2 operational before the beginning of carrier *Charles de Gaulle*'s refueling and comprehensive overhaul, scheduled to begin in 2015.

Work continues on the new FREMM (Frègates Europèennes Multi-mission) class with 17 French frigates currently planned. Eight of the warships are being built to an antisubmarine warfare configuration and nine are planned as land-attack cruise-missile variants. In 2006 a version of the General Electric LM 2500 gas turbine was selected as the class's power source, with two turbines supplying the propulsion for each warship. The first of the class is expected to enter service by 2011 with the seventeenth planned for the end of 2014. Due to budget cuts in 2006, the decision was made to cancel a third and forth unit of the more expensive *Forbin*-class Horizon guided-missile destroyer. The lead ship of the *Forbin* class was launched in 2005 and is expected to be fully operational by early 2008. In July 2006 the second of the class, *Chevalier Paul,* was launched at DCN's Lorient shipyard.

France's first Horizon-class destroyer, *Forbin* was launched in 2005 and is expected to be fully operational by early 2008 Bernard Prézelin

The *Mistral,* first of a new class of helicopter-carrying landing ships, became fully operational in 2006, with sister *Tonnerre* completing the final phases of fitting out in preparation for operational service with the French Navy. Both ships displace over 21,000 tons full load and will make a major contribution to French power projection capabilities.

Submariners also had reason to celebrate in France with announcement that the navy plans to purchase six new Barracuda-class submarines. The boats, the first of which are expected in service between 2014 and 2016, will replace the six *Améthyste*-class submarines now in use. Meanwhile, testing continues on the new French M-51 submarine-launched ballistic missile (SLBM) intended to replace the M-45 currently in use aboard France's nuclear-powered ballistic-missile submarine force.

In neighboring Germany, several different classes of advanced warships are under design and construction. In 2006 the third and forth Type 212 air-independent propulsion–equipped submarines were delivered and in September Germany announced the decision to purchase two additional Type 212 boats, providing an eventual total of six. Work on the *Braunschweig*-class (K-130) corvettes continues with the first and second units launching this past year. Both are due to enter service in 2007; current plans call for all five of the class to deliver by the end of 2008. Work on the Type K-130s is divided among several shipyards, with sections of each warship constructed at different locations and then brought together at a lead yard for final assembly. Though the navy is itself downsizing, the fleet is also moving to enhance its blue-water and expeditionary focus. Germany has also begun to express interest in outfitting their new *Sachsen*-class guided-missile frigates with a Ballistic Missile Defense capability. Plans for Germany's new 5,500-ton F-125–class frigates appear to be on track, with the first of the class expected in service sometime between 2011 and 2013.

Service entry for Greece's first Type 214–class submarine, *Papanikolis,* has been delayed after several major problems were uncovered; primary among these were reported flaws in the submarine's air-independent propulsion system. The defects may cause slippage of planned delivery and operational dates for sister submarines *Pipinos, Matrozos,* and *Katsonis,* all three of which remain under varying stages of construction. Greece has announced plans to launch a new frigate program and design bids for the program will likely come from successful Dutch and German designs. Plans are also in the works to upgrade Greece's MEKO-200–class frigates during the next decade.

Greek submarine *Papanikolis* has yet to enter service after major problems were reportedly uncovered in the vessel Michael Nitz

A new Italian amphibious battalion was formed in 2006 and will consist of joint forces from both the Italian Army and Navy. Additional restructuring can also be expected as a new defense strategy was unveiled in January 2006. Italy's newest aircraft carrier, the *Cavour,* is expected in service in 2007 and will certainly add a powerful punch, joining the smaller carrier *Giuseppe Garibaldi,* in service since 1985. On the submarine front, four Type 212 submarines are planned for service, with the first two, *Salvatore Todaro* and *Scire,* having entered service in 2006. Work continues on Italy's two Project Horizon destroyers, *Andrea Doria* and *Caio Duilio,* which are expected in service during 2007 and 2009 respectively. One of the largest ongoing programs is the joint French-Italian FREMM frigate program with Italian plans to purchase 10 units, six of which are being configured as land-attack assets and four intended primarily for antisubmarine warfare.

The Netherlands was the first European navy to begin serious investigation into a providing a ballistic-missile defense role for its *De Zeven Provinciën*–class guided-missile frigates. Equipped with the Smart-L radar system, a BMD capability could, if funded, greatly increase the usefulness and flexibility of these already excellent warships. During June 2006, the Dutch patrol and support vessel *Pelikaan* entered service with the Royal Netherlands Navy. Designed to serve as support ship in the Netherlands Antilles, the *Pelikaan* was built at Damen Shipyards in Galati, Romania, and replaced an older ship with the same name.

As the importance of expeditionary warfare has not been lost on the Dutch, *Johan de Witt,* an enhanced version of the successful *Rotterdam*-class amphibious transport ship, began trials in September 2006. The new ship is unique for the Netherlands because it is capable of serving as a marine component command ship during joint and multinational operations, allowing it to play an important command role in future operations and exercises. All these new capabilities have in many ways been paid for by cutbacks elsewhere in the force and *Karel Doorman*–class frigates continue their slow retirement from the ranks, deemed excess due to budgetary constraints.

Though Norway's defense budget was reduced in 2007, its navy actually received a funding increase. The first Norwegian Aegis-equipped warship, frigate *Fridtjof Nansen,* began sea trials early in 2006 and entered service in March of that year. A second unit of the class, *Roald Amundsen,* had also been delivered by late 2006. Part of operational assessments for this class includes conducting life-fire Aegis testing with the Evolved Sea Sparrow missile, a unique weapons combination that proved successful during trials. Though Norway continues to clash with shipbuilder Navantia over payment for the frigate program, these financial problems mar an otherwise successful effort. On 30 October, the second *Skjold*-class air-cushion guided-missile patrol boat was launched and the warship is expected to enter service in February 2008. Though new production is important, keeping older platforms and airplanes like the Air Force's P-3 maritime patrol aircraft operational remains high on the priority list, and in August plans were announced to upgrade the fleet of four P-3Cs for continued operation through 2030.

As Poland works to modernize its fleet, the navy continues to retire many older cold war era vessels, though there is also a concerted effort to breathe new life into warships that may otherwise be considered a bit long in the tooth. Poland's military leaders choose Sweden's Saab RBS-15 Mk3 missile to arm its *Orkan*-class ships and hopes remain high to enhance the weapons fits aboard two second-hand *Oliver Hazard Perry*–class frigates and *Kobbins*-class submarines. Unfortunately, progress toward many other Polish Navy goals has been slow. A proposed mine-countermeasures–ship program known as the Kormoran class remains on hold and progress on the four MEKO A-100-class frigates remains slow. The first unit was laid down in 2001 and is planned to commission in 2007.

Sweden's Saab RBS-15 Mk3 missile will arm Poland's *Orkan*-class patrol craft J. Cislak

In Portugal, another NATO nation struggles to meet its maritime needs in the face of budget realities. Portugal aims to replace its aging *Daphne*-class submarines with two Air-independent propulsion–capable German Type 209 boats ordered in 2004, and two improved *Baptiste de Andrade*–class patrol ships are also on order, expected to join two recently delivered units.

Romanian continues efforts to upgrade their Type 22 frigates, *Regele Ferdinand* and *Regina Marina,* transferred from the United Kingdom in 2004–5.

There has been much ongoing naval construction in Russia, but many of the ships being built do not serve much chance of making it into operational service due to persistent funding shortages. Prime examples of the apparent spike in shipyard productivity can be found in keel laying or launchings of vessels like new Project 22350 frigates, *Borei*-class nuclear-powered ballistic-missile submarines, *Severodvinsk*-class nuclear-powered attack submarines, Lada-class submarines, and *Steregushchiy*-class corvettes—all of which benefited from increased shipyard production in the past year. During this same time, Russia announced that its ninth planned Oscar II–class submarine, the *Volgorad,* would not be commissioned into service as its funding was needed elsewhere. While Russia's shipyards have also kept busy building ships for China, India, and other navies, several trading partners are beginning to acquire the skills required to build larger, more advanced warships on their own. Thus it may only be a matter of time before exports to China and India begin to wane, though perhaps new markets in places like Venezuela and Iran will keep Russian shipyards afloat.

Spain is now reaping the efforts of technical and financial investments made more than a decade ago in the *Álvaro de Bazán* class of Aegis guided-missile frigates. By January 2006, the fourth unit of the class, *Méndez Nuñez,* was conducting sea trials. A fifth unit was ordered in 2005 and is expected to enter service by 2012; a sixth unit is also expected. Also on order are four BPC-47 patrol ships, which displace nearly 3,000 tons when fully loaded. The BPC-47 program calls for four of the units to begin entering service by 2008, with an additional six on order. The Spanish submarine community will receive a boost when its four new S 80 submarines begin to enter service around 2011. The keel for at least one of the class is due to be laid down in 2007. The submarines, being built by Navantia, will be fitted with an air-independent propulsion system, the first such submarines to carry AIP in Spanish service. Perhaps the most high profile of all Spanish warships is the new 27,000-ton "strategic protection" and amphibious-assault ship, recently named *Juan Carlos I,* which is scheduled to commission in early 2009. The new ship displaces a full 10,000 tons more than Spain's aircraft carrier *Príncipe de Asturias* and can carry 1,200 troops or function as a second mini-aircraft carrier for Spanish EAV-8B Harrier jets and helicopters.

Sweden continues to invest in advanced hull designs and technology and these investments have begun paying dividends. *Karlstad,* the last of five *Visby*-class combatants, was launched in August 2006 and, though hampered by numerous delays, the class promises to live up to its unique design and multipurpose intentions.

In Turkey, efforts to complete eight locally built Type 209/1400 submarines continues with the last of the class, *Ikikci Inönü,* to enter service in 2008. Orders for 17 additional S-70B Seahawk helicopters were placed late in 2006, reflecting the importance of maritime aviation and the desire for enough helicopters aboard Turkish Navy surface ships. Deliveries of the new Seahawks will begin in 2009, and bring to 24 the total planned for Turkish naval service. Future budget priorities can also be found in efforts to bring the proposed *Heybeliada* (MIL-GEM)-class corvette program to fruition. Seven of the class are planned and it is hoped that lead unit *Heybeliada* will begin entering service around 2014. In addition to these programs, air-independent propulsion–capable submarines sit high atop the Turkish naval wish list.

Between heavy involvement in Iraq, Afghanistan, and naval operations around the world, the British Royal Navy has had a difficult year making ends meet. Though belt-tightening measures have been under way for years, additional cuts go so deep that many fear an irreversible degradation in capabilities. In July the First Sea Lord announced that force projection and maritime security were two primary roles for the Royal Navy, yet attempting to find the right force mix has proven quite vexing.

In the submarine community, older submarines are being retired early to make way for the new *Astute*-class boats that have been delayed for a multitude of reasons. In 2006 *Swiftsure*-class submarines *Sovereign* and *Spartan* were retired and *Superb* is due to retire by 2008. Debate continues on the affordability of the new aircraft carrier program, though first of the class, *Queen Elizabeth,* is now expected in service in 2014 and *Prince of Wales* in 2017.

On the surface-combatant front, work on the Type 45 destroyers is progressing, though delays continue to be cause for concern. The first of the class, *Daring,* was launched in January 2006, and by midyear, reports surfaced that instead of the eight currently planned, only six may eventually be built. In December 2006 the actual delivery date for the destroyers was pushed back by seven months to accommodate rapidly rising program costs. The destroyers are to begin entering service by 2010. Smaller patrol ships appear to be faring better as work on the River-class is considered a success and a fourth, modified unit of the class, *Clyde,* joined the fleet in 2006 via a lease agreement and serves as Falkland Islands patrol ship, replacing the Castle-class.

Concerning amphibious-warfare capability, the first two *Largs Bay*–class dock landing ships, *Largs Bay* and *Lyme Bay,* are now complete with both 16,000-ton warships expected to be fully operational by 2007.

Royal Navy aviation capabilities suffered a difficult blow in 2006 when the last remaining Sea Harrier FA.2 fighters were retired. Though partially replaced by the Royal Air Force GR.7/GR.9, the radar-equipped Sea Harriers and their AMRAAM beyond-visual-range missiles will be sorely missed. Maritime patrol and helicopters fared better in 2006 than did the Sea Harrier community, with full production of the Nimrod MRA.4 approved in July 2006. Current plans call for the MRA.4 aircraft to be delivered by 2012. Thirty Future Lynx naval helicopters were also ordered in June 2006 with deliveries planned to start in 2015.

Though still in its infancy, the Royal Navy plans to replace its older Royal Fleet Auxiliaries under the MARS (Military Afloat Reach and Sustainability) program. In the not-too-distant future, the U.K. Ministry of Defense hopes to down-select to a single bidder capable of ably managing procurement, construction, and support of the MARS program for decades to come.

Middle East and Africa

Construction of three guided-missile patrol craft for Egypt is under way by VT Halter Marine in the United Kingdom, with the class expected to begin delivery in 2007. Late in 2006 three Rolling Airframe Missile launchers were reportedly ordered to arm the craft. During the spring of 2006, the United States offered two *Osprey*-class minehunting vessels to Egypt, and delivery of the ships is expected in 2007.

Iran continued saber rattling throughout the past year and twice conducted substantial air, land, sea, and undersea war game exercises in and around the Persian Gulf. While the lack of stability in neighboring Iraq remains a major question in the world, Iraqi maritime forces have begun to piece themselves together and appear to be in paradoxically adequate shape. With a current force of around 700 to 800 sailors and 200 marines, the force has made major gains since the Iraqi Coastal Defense forces stood up in 2004 with little more than 200 trainees. Additionally the force is expected to take delivery of more than a dozen new small patrol boats during 2007–8, though understandably, several locally built small craft are facing delays.

Iran's P-3 Orions reportedly played an active role in their recent wargames and exercises
Canadian DND

Israel had a difficult year in 2006 and was forced to reexamine its tactics and strategies as a result of lackluster performance battling against Hezbollah militants in Lebanon. During fighting, the Israeli missile corvette *Hanit* was caught with its guard down and struck by a terrorist antiship missile that inflicted substantial, though reparable, damage. There have been some interesting developments for the Israeli submarine force with two air-independent propulsion–capable submarines ordered from Germany. The new submarines, modified and lengthened versions of the Israeli *Dolphin* class, are to cost about $1.2 billion in total, with one-third of the cost paid by Germany. Delivery of the new AIP-equipped boats can be expected around 2010. An option for a third new submarine may be exercised at a later date. With an emphasis on antiterrorism duties, the Israeli Navy recently ordered six defender boats from the United States in addition to a number of smaller boats. Three Super Dvora Mk III patrol boats were delivered in September 2006 and these join three others already in service. On the international cooperation front, Israeli forces have recently joined North Atlantic Treaty Organization vessels in the Mediterranean Sea to assist with Operation Active Endeavor counterterrorism duties.

In Kuwait, 12 new 27-mm guns were ordered to equip each of the new Mk V-C Pegasus-class Special Operations Craft, the first of which are expected to enter service in 2007. The class is a slightly modified variant of those used by U.S. Navy SEAL Teams. As trade becomes more normalized with Libya, discussions are now under way with the Thales Group to examine upgrading Libya's aging Combattante-II–class guided-missile patrol craft.

By early 2006, the African nation of Nigeria had acquired their first Defender-class response boats from U.S. builder Safe Boats, for use in oil-rig defense duties and other maritime patrol–type operations.

In the Middle East nation of Oman, a 64-meter landing craft that was ordered in 2005 and build by Abu Dhabi Shipbuilding in the United Arab Emirates has now been delivered for service. The new landing craft is capable of carrying 50 troops or 46 tons of cargo. Design work continues on a new class of corvettes for Oman to be built by Vosper Thornycroft in the United Kingdom with deliveries estimated to begin in 2010. The new corvettes will likely be armed with an OTO-Melara gun, vertically launched Mica point defense surface-to-air missiles, and other weapons.

Libya hopes to modernize its fleet of Combatante II-class guided missile patrol craft
A. Vella

In September and again in November of 2006, news reports indicated that the Saudi Navy was studying an Aegis-equipped version of General Dynamics' Littoral Combat Ship design, as well as expressing interest in purchasing Type 45 destroyers from the United Kingdom.

By early 2007 all four MEKO A-200SAN frigates, *Amatola, Isandlwana, Spioenkop,* and *Mendi* had been delivered by Blohm + Voss and HDW for South African service and the class has proven successful enough that the option for a fifth unit was exercised in the summer of 2006. South Africa's submarine program continues as well with a third and final Type 209/1400 submarine expected to deliver late in 2007. Additionally, four Super Lynx 300 helicopters, ordered in 2003 for the South African Air Force, are expected for delivery in 2007, to be carried aboard their MEKO frigates.

The keel for the first Baynunah-class guided-missile patrol combatants has been laid down with five more of the new warships now on order for the United Arab Emirates. Current plans call for the 800-ton Baynunahs to be armed with Evolved Sea Sparrow and Exocet missiles, among other weapons. The first of the class is to enter service in 2008. Retired German mine-countermeasures vessels *Weiden* and *Frankenthal* were decommissioned and transferred to the United Arab Emirates in late June 2006. Both are Type 332 coastal minehunters and quite young by minehunting standards with many years of service life remaining. Since recommissioning into UAE service, *Weiden* has been renamed *Al Hasbah* and *Frankenthal* is now called *Al Murjan*.

The Americas

Argentina's Type 209/1200 submarine *Salta* has returned to service following a 2005 midlife upgrade, during which the boat received some much needed maintenance and a new battery. In Brazil, work continues, albeit slowly, on the new *Barroso* frigate, with plans calling for the first and likely only ship of the class to commission in December 2008. All five of the German Type 209/1400 Mod. 3–class submarines have now entered Brazilian service with the newest unit fully operational by early 2006.

Argentina's Type 209/1200 submarine *Salta* recently returned to service following a mid-life upgrade
A. Almendolara

In Canada, continuing budget problems have forced reexamination of upgrades to the *Halifax*-class frigates and have also delayed service reentry (until 2010) of the submarine *Chicoutimi,* which was damaged by a serious onboard fire in October 2004. Two of the four *Victoria*-class submarines are back at sea with a third to be fully operational by 2008. Needless to say, the Canadian submarine program has proven a disappointment, though the navy has worked to put these problems in the most positive light. Indeed the submarines are now expected to play increasingly important roles training and conducting special operations missions. Meanwhile, preliminary work continues on Canada's Joint Support Ship program with prime contractors for the project having been narrowed down to two shipbuilders prior to final selection by the Canadian government. Current plans call for the first of three Joint Support Ships to enter service by 2013, eventually replacing the aging *Protecteur*-class replenishment ships.

In Chile, two Scorpène-class submarines, *O'Higgins* and *Carrera,* have been delivered as has the first British Type 23 frigate, *Almirante Cochrane* (ex-HMS *Norfolk*). Two additional Type 23 frigates are expected to enter service by 2008, joining two retired Dutch *Jacob van Heemskerk* and *Karel Doorman*–class warships. Interestingly, the Chilean Navy has express interest in purchasing second-hand S-3 Viking maritime patrol aircraft from the United States. Being that these are very capable aircraft with much service life ahead of them, such an acquisition appears wise.

In Mexico, there is a substantial effort under way to expand the navy's role in countering piracy and terrorism and performing coastal-patrol duties. No doubt that new patrol ships like the 1,600-ton *Oaxaca* class and smaller Centerary and Interceptor classes can contribute greatly in this arena. Interestingly, the Mexican Navy is also looking to enhance its aviation capabilities and has been investigating the purchase of SU-27 fighters from Russian to join its recently acquired E-2C Hawkeye AWACS aircraft. Though no Russian fighter jets are in the offing for the small Caribbean nation of Trinidad and Tobago, the island nation has, in recent months, looked to purchase three offshore patrol vessels from the United Kingdom's VT shipbuilding group, though plans at this early stage remain preliminary.

Four 1,600-ton *Oaxaca*-class patrol ships recently entered service with the Mexican fleet Mexican Navy

The U.S. Navy has had a busy few years—to put it mildly. With more than 45% of its assets deployed and its fleet less than half the size it was twenty years ago, leaders have been forced to improvise, compromise, and economize.

Despite budget cuts, the navy's carrier program remains healthy and work continues on the newest and final *Nimitz*-class aircraft carrier, *George H. W. Bush*. Christened in October, the *Bush* will enter service in 2008. The new CVN-21 class of aircraft carriers, designed to increase sortie generation, reduce manpower requirements, and innovate engineering systems, is expected to begin construction in 2008. One of the nation's last remaining nonnuclear carriers, *John F. Kennedy,* was suffering from arrester gear corrosion and a host of other problems due to navy neglect and the carrier is now scheduled to decommission in late 2007.

With looming missile threats from North Korea and Iran, among others, there has been a dramatic increase in efforts to field naval missile-defense capabilities. Variants of the Standard SM-2 and SM-3 surface-to-air missiles performed reasonably well during recent testing and at least three *Ticonderoga*-class cruisers are currently armed to intercept ballistic missiles. Other efforts to modernize the entire cruiser fleet are ongoing, though all nonvertical launch system–equipped cruisers have been retired. The navy plans to order a new type of cruisers, the CG(X), beginning around 2011, though preliminary design work continues.

Today's fleet of *Arleigh Burke*–class destroyers provide a strong, multipurpose surface-warfare capability, and the newest of the class, *Gridley,* commissioned on 16 January 2007. The next generation of destroyers, named the *Zumwalt* class, will be armed with two 155-mm advanced gun systems and long-range cruise missiles, but price increases and an estimated cost of more than $3 billion per ship is cause for great concern among budget watchers and taxpayers.

The real push in recent years has been for the U.S. Navy's Littoral Combat Ship (LCS) program, but cost continues to rise here as well—by as much as 49%, according to some reports. Two prototype teams (one led by Lockheed Martin and one by General Dynamics) are in the process of building "Flight 0" prototypes of their LCS designs. The General Dynamics design, named the *Independence* class, includes a trimaran hull with a scalable design. It is lighter and wider but with a deeper draft than the Lockheed Martin design, named the *Freedom* class. As costs continue to rise, the navy has had to take drastic steps to keep costs in check, including a 90-day work stoppage on LCS-3 while cost matters are investigated.

The U.S. Navy's submarine community has recently accepted the reentry into service of the submarines *Ohio, Florida,* and *Michigan,* which have been reconfigured as guided cruise-missile submarines and are capable of taking part in a broad range of naval special operations duties. USS *Georgia* is to rejoin the fleet in 2007. *Virginia*-class attack submarines are also entering service as planned with the second of the class, *Texas,* delivered in September 2006. A funding contract was awarded for the ninth attack submarine late in the year. A number of older nuclear submarines were decommissioned in 2006, including the *Los Angeles*–class attack submarines *Salt Lake City* and *Honolulu* and the experimental submarine *Dolphin*.

The schedule for construction of amphibious ships for the navy remains busy. Seven *Wasp*-class amphibious assault ships are now in service with the eighth, *Makin Island,* scheduled for delivery in 2008. The number of *Tarawa*-class LHAs will decline as replacements, including the new LHA-6 class, are delivered. Six units of the *San Antonio*–class amphibious transport docks are under construction with the last of the class, *Somerset,* due to enter service in 2011.

If the budget crunch and wartime pace has been difficult for the navy, it has been even more problematic for the far smaller U.S. Coast Guard. Though increases in manpower have helped, the job of homeland security is enormous and the Coast Guard fleet is in dire need of replacement. The Deepwater program aims to help solve these problems, but apparent flaws in Deepwater cutter designs and the discovery of large quantities of money having gone unspent on the program raise red flags that will hopefully open the door to greater oversight for what is arguably the most important program in Coast Guard history.

Venezuela's bellicose leader, Hugo Chavez, continues to shake his fist in the direction of the United States and has been working diligently to cement ties and anti-American alliances with foreign nations generally considered hostile to the western world. As such, Venezuela's recent naval and military buildup has been seen as worrisome in Washington. Among the top items on Chavez's military shopping list were Spanish C-295 maritime-patrol aircraft which, due to U.S. technology transfer laws, have been blocked from transfer to the oil-rich nation. Israel and Sweden are among many other nations now banning arms exports to Venezuela, though Russia has offered several export versions of the Lada-class submarine, three of which Venezuela is expected to purchase in the near future.

It has indeed been a busy time for naval developments.

HOW TO USE THIS BOOK

This book provides a bi-annual "snapshot" of the world's maritime forces—their ships, aircraft, and armament. For each ship-class entry in the text, the first number between the diamond symbol and the class or ship name indicates the number of units in inventory as of 1 January 2007. Numbers following in parentheses indicate additional ships under construction and may be followed, after a plus sign, by additional numbers indicating further units planned or on option. When units within a class are retained in decommissioned reserve, a total is given on the class entry line, and the names of the ships or craft, where appropriate, are given in italics. Ships that are already completed but that were in overhaul or reconstruction as of press time are counted as part of the total inventory.

The ship-type designation system used in *Combat Fleets* is defined in detail in the Terms and Abbreviations section; the ship-type letter designations are found in brackets after combatant header–type sections within each fleet (as in "Destroyers [DD]") and after each class or single-ship entry in the Auxiliaries and Service Craft sections (as in "*Jones*-class large harbor tugs [YTB]").

Users are urged to consult the remarks sections for the various entries for additional information on construction programs, individual differences between units of a class, and further details of systems and capabilities. The remarks sections have been followed, where appropriate, by sections about deletions within the class, hull systems, aviation systems, combat systems, and other categories as appropriate. Unless otherwise specified, figures given in dollars ($) are in U.S. dollars.

A brief study of the Terms and Abbreviations section on the succeeding pages will help the user understand the condensed data format used in the book. Conversion tables between the English measurements system and the metric system are also given. One deviation, however, has been made from the use of the metric system for U.S.–owned ships, because many of the users from the United States are less familiar with the metric system. *Displacements for U.S.–owned ships have been retained in terms of long tons of 2,240 lbs.* For those seeking to make "exact" comparisons between a U.S. ship and a similar foreign vessel, convert the U.S. displacement figure to metric tons (1,000 kg) by multiplying it by 1.01605, or convert the metric displacement to English long tons by multiplying it by 0.98421.

Major naval weapons systems, sensors, and naval aircraft are described at the beginning of each country-of-origin entry, after any entries on numbers of personnel, base locations, fleet organization, naval aviation forces, marine or naval infantry organizations and strengths, and coastal defense resources. A comprehensive index of all ship names.

TERMS AND ABBREVIATIONS

Most surface ship characteristics are presented as in the following sample (♦ indicates the beginning of a class or individual ship entry):

FRIGATES [FF]

♦ 4 (+ 1 + 1) Álvaro de Bazán–class (Project F-100)
Bldr: Navantia (ex-Izar), Ferrol

	Laid down	L	In serv.
F 101 Álvaro de Bazán	14-6-99	27-10-00	19-9-02
F 102 Almirante Juan de Borbón (ex-*Roger de Lauria*)	27-10-00	28-2-02	3-12-03
F 103 Blas de Lezo	28-2-02	16-5-03	16-12-04
F 104 Méndez Nuñez	16-5-03	12-11-04	28-2-06
F 105 Roger de Lauria	2008	2009	2011

Almirante Juan de Borbón (F 102) Leo van Ginderen, 3-06

Blas de Lezo (F 103) Michael Winter, 6-05

Álvaro de Bazán (F 101) U.S. Navy, 7-05

D: 4,555 tons (5,802 fl) **S:** 28.5 kts (27 kts sustained)
Dim: 146.72 (133.20 pp) × 18.60 (17.50 wl) × 4.75 (4.84 at full load)
A: 8 RGM-84F Harpoon Block 1D SSM; 48-cell Mk 41 VLS syst. (32 Standard SM-2 Block IIIA and 64 RIM-162 Evolved Sea Sparrow SAM); 1 127-mm 54-cal. Mk 45 Mod. 2 DP; 1 12-barreled 20-mm Meroka-2B CIWS; 2 single 20-mm 90-cal. AA; 2 pair fixed 324-mm Mk 32 Mod. 9 ASW TT; 1 SH-60B Seahawk LAMPS III Block II ASW helicopter

Blas de Lezo (F 103) Leo van Ginderen, 6-05

Electronics:
Radar: 1 Thales Scout nav./surf. search; 1 Raytheon SPS-67(V)4 surf. search; 1 Lockheed Martin SPY-1D 3-D tracking, target-designation, and weapons control; 2 Raytheon SPG-62 target illuminators; 1 AESN RAN-30L/X Meroka f.c, 1/FABA Dorna gun f.c.
Sonar: ENOSA-Raytheon DE 1160LF (I) hull-mounted; EDO UQN-4 deep-water echo sounder; EDO Model 5400 underwater telephone; provision for active/passive towed linear hydrophone array
EW: Indra SLQ-380 Aldebarán intercept/jammer suite; CESELSA Elnath Mk 9500 comms intercept; . . . laser detection and countermeasure syst.; Mk 36 Mod. 2 SRBOC decoy RL syst. (4 6-round Mk 137 RL); SLQ-25A Enhanced Nixie acoustic torpedo decoy syst.
E/O: Thales SIRIUS optronic surveillance; FABA Dorna radar/optronic weapons f.c.s.
M: CODOG: 2 G.E. LM 2500 gas turbines (23,324 shp each), 2 Bazán-Caterpillar 3600-series low-r.p.m. diesels (6,000 shp each); 2 LIPS 4.65-m dia., 5-bladed CP props; 46,648 shp max.
Electric: 4,400 kw tot. (4 × 1,100 kw Bazán-MTU 12C396 diesel sets)
Range: 5,000/18 **Endurance:** 21 days
Crew: 35 officers, 215 enlisted (including 11 air unit; accomm. for 250, including 16 flag group)

Remarks: Were to have been constructed under a 27-1-94 cooperative venture with Germany and the Netherlands. Spain, however, withdrew from the radar and weapons control portions of the agreement on 6-6-95. Authority to construct four was granted by the Council of Ministers on 24-1-97, the contract was placed on 31-1-97, and fabrication of modules began during 11-97. Cost about $540 million each. Intended to serve for 30 years. The Standard SAM system provides AAW coverage out to 150 km. All are based at Rota. A fifth unit of the class was ordered during 6-05. A sixth unit is planned.
Hull systems: Have fin stabilizers. The ships are to be able to operate in 100-kt winds. A design growth margin of 450 tons was provided, and maximum permissible displacement will be 6,250 tons. The hull has four internal decks and is built of AH-36 high-tensile steel. The hangar can accommodate two SH-60-sized helicopters, but only one will be assigned to each ship; the flight deck will be 26.4 m long. Fireproof internal paneling is employed, and special efforts have been made to reduce radar, acoustic, and heat signatures. Are to have Sperry MarineWQN-2 doppler speed and motion logs.
Combat systems: The SPY-1D Aegis radar system has the Lockheed Martin Distributed Advanced Naval Combat System with much the same Aegis Baseline 5 Phase III system used on current-construction U.S. *Arleigh Burke*–class destroyers, but the Spanish version will have a federated data-distribution architecture, giving it some features of the later Aegis Baseline 6 Phase I on the first two ships and Baseline 7 Phase 1 on the latter two. F 105 is expected to have more advanced antiballistic missile capabilities than the earlier units. Hardware and software requirements are being defined by Fábrica de Artillería de Bazán (FABA) so as to integrate Spanish- and U.S.-origin equipment via a redundant local-area net. Hewlett-Packard 743 VME processors are being used. There are 14 SAINSEL CONAM2000 color command consoles and two integrated command display consoles. The ships have NATO Link 11 and Link 16 datalink. WSC-3 UHF SATCOM and a Spanish SHF SATCOM will be fitted.
Also incorporated in the combat system is FABA's DORNA optronic and radar naval fire-control system. The torpedo fire-control system will be the SAINSEL DLT 309. SAINSEL, CESELSA, and ENOSA are all part of the Indra Electronics Group. The U.S. UPX-29 fixed-array IFF interrogation system with Sanders OE-120/UPX electronically-steered interrogation antenna is installed, as is the Lucent UYS-2A(V) DEM E electronic and acoustic intercept signal processing system. Space is provided for later installation of a towed linear sonar array.
The point-defense RIM-7PTC Evolved Sea Sparrow Missiles will be carried in "quadpacks," four per Mk 41 launch cell, and Standard SM-2 Block IIIA missiles will be used for area air-defense. May later be equipped to carry U.S. BGM-109C Tomahawk land-attack missiles. The 127-mm guns are surplus U.S. Navy mountings from *Tarawa*-class LHAs upgraded to Mod. 2 by Izar's FABA armament division. Plans to install ABCAS ASW mortars have been canceled. The Aegis system will provide target cueing for the CIWS. The ships will have a full LAMPS-III ASW helicopter capability, with the SQQ-28 LAMPS-III electronics package and SRQ-4 datalink.

Number of units: The number of units in inventory as of January 2007 is given. Additional ships or craft under construction or on order are given in parentheses, with a second number in parentheses indicating additional units planned. Any alternative designations for the class are given in parentheses in bold, and the number of units in reserve may be indicated in a *non*-bolded parentheses after the class name entry. The standardized type designation for each class is given in brackets, either on the class line or at the end of the bolded type designation header when there are more than one class of combatants of the same type in service, as in "Destroyers [DD]."

Bldr: The name and location of the building yard(s) is given, often in abbreviated form (see abbreviations list below).

Dates: Dates are given in the sequence day-month-year or month-year. "In serv." is the commissioning date for warships or delivery date for noncommissioned units. Delivery dates for warships are frequently *not* the same as date of commissioning, which often comes considerably later, after training and certification. Where applicable, other dates may appear with the ship name and number entries, such as year of authorization for construction or dates for major modernizations, conversions, or decommissionings to reserve, as indicated. For some entries, a column may also be devoted to fleet or home port assignments.

D: Displacement. In most cases, standard displacement as defined by the Treaty of Washington (1922) is given. Where possible, this information is followed by the full-load displacement in parentheses; there are occasional instances of other displacements, such as trials, normal, or light ship (empty of all disposables). For submarines, two displacements are normally given: surfaced full load and submerged full load. When available, the standard surfaced displacement precedes the surfaced and submerged displacements.

S: Speed. Given in knots and taken as maximum unless specifically defined otherwise. In some cases, sustained or trials speeds are given. For submarines, surfaced speed precedes submerged speed.

Dim: Dimensions. Given as length overall × beam × draft (taken as maximum navigational unless otherwise defined). Other significant dimensions are given in parentheses, where warranted. Length between perpendiculars (vertical reference points normally coinciding with bow waterline and rudderpost in single-rudder ships or stern waterline in multiple-rudder ships) is given as "pp," and length at waterline (if different) as "wl."

A: Armament. Generally given in the following order: antiship missiles, surface-to-air missiles, major guns, antisurface torpedo systems, point-defense surface-to-air missiles, antiaircraft guns, antisubmarine rocket or missile systems, antisubmarine torpedo systems, depth charges, mines and minelaying systems, and aircraft. For ships with a significant aircraft-carrying mission, a separate header, "Air group," is used. For guns, the caliber of the barrel is given after the bore; caliber times bore equals the length of the barrel.

Electronics: Electronic equipment is presented in the following order: radars, sonar systems, TACAN (aircraft navigation beacon/control systems), electronic warfare (EW) systems and countermeasures, and electro-optical (E/O), where applicable. Within radars, "nav." indicates a navigational set and "f.c." indicates fire control. For sonars, nominal operating frequencies are given in kilohertz in parentheses or indicated by general category, e.g., "HF" for high-frequency (above 20 kHz), "MF" for medium frequency, "LF" for low frequency (7 kHz and below).

M: Machinery. The manufacturer's name and propulsion machinery model nomenclature, where known, are given, with multiple-drive systems headed by the accepted abbreviation, as in CODAG for COmbined Diesel And Gas turbine, CODOG for COmbined Diesel Or Gas turbine, and so forth. The number and type of propellers or other propulsive devices follows the first semicolon with "CP" indicating a controllable-pitch propeller. The maximum horsepower of the system is given after the second semicolon, often followed for diesel plants by the sustained rating of the plant in parentheses. Auxiliary propulsion systems such as bow and stern side-thrusters or low-speed auxiliary propulsors are listed after a dash. To obtain kilowatt power from brake horsepower (bhp), multiply by 0.7457.

Boilers: For steam turbine–powered ships only. Make and model are followed by operating pressure and temperature.

Electric: Electrical generating plant. Total output is given in kilowatts (kw) or in kilovolt-amperes (kVA). Where known, details of the components of the plant are given in parentheses.

Range: Given in nautical miles, with the speed at which the range is achievable following a slash. Multiple entries may be included, particularly for submarines.

Fuel: Given in metric tons or, for smaller units, liters or U.S. gallons as specified. Additional fuels may also be listed, such as aviation fuel or diesel fuel for auxiliary machinery or gasoline for embarked vehicles.

Endurance: The number of days for which the ship can operate unsupported, determined by the most critical disposable carried (food, fuel, water, etc.).

Crew: Either the normal total complement or broken down into officers, petty officers, and other enlisted personnel, as applicable. Additional personnel who can be carried follow a "+" sign, and total accommodations (if more than the standard complement) are given in parentheses.

Remarks: Programmatic, general design information, and significant operational information are given in the initial paragraph. For more important classes, the Remarks section may be subdivided into Hull systems (and Propulsion systems, if warranted), Aviation systems, and Combat systems. For classes where a large number of units have been either recently discarded or placed in reserve, there will also be a Status section. When a significant number of ships within a class have been stricken or transferred elsewhere, a Disposals section will be included; when an entire class has been deleted since the last edition, a separate Disposal Note will be placed in sequence where the class appeared in the previous edition. Separate Note paragraphs include data not appropriate for the class entries, such as preliminary information about new programs, and may appear anywhere in the text.

SHIP TYPE DESIGNATION SYSTEM

A unified ship-type designator system is applied to all ship classes, regardless of the local system employed by the navy being described; local designations, where employed, are provided in the ship-class header line, followed in brackets by the letter system detailed below, or the brackets appear at the end of the ship-type designation header for combatant classes. The system, which is not without its incongruities, is nonetheless the best available and is closely aligned with that employed by the U.S. Department of Defense and widely understood elsewhere. Note that the categorizations are both functional and by size of ship.

Ship descriptions are grouped together under classes when there is more than one (or prospects for more than one) unit of the design. The class of a ship does not change when it is transferred to or built for a country other than that which originated the design. Thus, a Russian-built *Kilo*-class submarine is a *Kilo* regardless of what the Chinese, Indian, Polish, Algerian, or other navies might locally call the class.

As modifications to the basic ship-type designators listed below, several suffixes and one prefix may be employed:

Prefix:

W For all ship types not subordinated to a navy, such as coast guards, customs services, border guards, or government-owned scientific ships.

Suffixes:

A For all ships or craft intended to operate with aerodynamic lift (wing-in-ground-effect craft) or pressurized air lift (surface-effect units, air-cushion vehicles). Two *exceptions* are SSA, for auxiliary submarine, and ATA, for auxiliary ocean tug.

G *For major surface combatants,* a "G" suffix means that the class is equipped with an area air-defense missile system with a maximum effective range of greater than 10 n.m. (which implies that the missiles provide an air-defense escort capability rather than merely self-defense). *For submarines and minor surface combatants,* the "G" suffix is used only when aerodynamic cruise missiles are the principal weapon system carried.

H Applied either for specialized aircraft-carrying ships capable of operating only vertical or short takeoff and landing fixed-wing aircraft or to other types of major combatants carrying three or more helicopters. An "H" suffix is *also* used to signify minor surface combatants that are equipped with hydrofoils.

N Used either to indicate that major ships have nuclear propulsion systems *or*, for service craft, that they are non-self-propelled.

T Employed to indicate that a specific type of ship has been equipped to perform additional duties as a training vessel (in AXT, for training ship, the "T" is a part of the basic designator). *Exceptions* are the designations AOT and AWT, where the "T" means "transport."

BASIC SHIP-TYPE DESIGNATORS

The designations for combatants (including mine warfare units and amphibious warfare units) are presented in the order in which ship types are presented in this book.

Aircraft Carriers:

CV Aircraft Carrier: Warships intended primarily to carry and operate combat aircraft (as distinguished from "L"-series amphibious warfare ships that carry aircraft primarily in support of amphibious warfare operations).

CVV Aircraft Carrier, V/STOL: As for CV, but not capable of operating fixed-wing, conventional takeoff and landing (CTOL) aircraft, i.e., not equipped with arrestor gear and therefore capable only of operating vertical- or short-takeoff or landing aircraft (V/STOL or VTOL).

Submarines:

SSB Ballistic-Missile Submarine: Submarines equipped primarily to launch strategic ballistic missiles from vertically mounted tubes.

SSG Cruise-Missile Attack Submarine: Submarines designed to launch aerodynamic cruise missiles from launchers other than the normal torpedo tubes. By U.S. Navy custom, the "G" has not been applied to submarines that are equipped with vertical cruise-missile launch tubes, although the *Ohio*-class cruise-missile submarines will be officially termed SSGN.

SS Attack Submarine: Submarines with a principal armament employing horizontal tubes to launch weapons such as torpedoes, mines, and cruise missiles; some SS or SSN may also have vertical tubes for cruise (but not, by definition, ballistic) missiles or mines.

SSC Coastal Submarine: Submarines of less than 500 tons submerged displacement intended primarily for limited endurance and/or coastal defense missions.

SSA Auxiliary Submarine: Submarines designed or adapted for noncombatant roles such as training, trials, or target duties.

SSM Midget Submarine: Combatant submarines of less than 150 tons submerged displacement.

Major Surface Combatants:

C Cruiser: Large surface combatants equipped with a major command, control, and communications capability in addition to major weapons systems. Cruisers having guns of greater than 130-mm and less than 180-mm bore are still referred to as CL, for Light Cruiser (only Peru now has such a ship in service). Cruisers now in service displace between 5,000 and 27,000 tons.

DD Destroyer: Major surface combatants not possessing the scope of command, control, and communications capabilities of a cruiser and generally intended to perform supporting roles in a group of combatants centered on cruiser or carrier forces. Some older destroyers of less than 4,000 tons displacement are still in service, while some of the largest units now exceed 10,000 tons displacement.

FF Frigate: Formerly applied to surface combatants with weapons systems tailored toward one specific role, such as antisubmarine warfare, but now generally applied to ships with lesser capabilities and of generally smaller size than a destroyer. The two categories are, indeed, beginning to blend, and there are frigates in service or planned ranging from 1,500 tons to over 6,000 tons full load displacement. For internal political reasons, some navies refer to ships as "frigates" when they are in fact destroyers, and a few navies refer to ships as "destroyers" that would more properly be termed frigates.

FFL Corvette: Surface combatants of less than 1,500 tons but more than 1,000 tons full load displacement—essentially, fourth-rate surface combatants. Note that the designation "corvette" as used here essentially refers to smaller frigates and does not correspond to the European concept of corvettes as any warship larger than a patrol craft but smaller than a frigate.

Minor Surface Combatants:

PS Large Patrol Ship: Ships intended for offshore patrol duties and generally characterized by slower speeds and lesser armament than major surface combatants, trading speed for seaworthiness and endurance. In size, they are normally greater than 1,000 tons full load displacement.

PG Patrol Combatant: Units of between 500 and 1,000 tons full load displacement intended for offshore operations and generally possessing speeds in excess of 25 knots. Most modern PGs are equipped with antiship missiles and are hence typed "PGG," a type often referred to as a "missile corvette."

PTG Guided-Missile Patrol Craft: Craft of less than 500 tons full load displacement equipped to launch antiship missiles. The designation is traditional and derives from the late 1950s when the first such craft were essentially torpedo boat designs with missiles instead of torpedoes.

PT Torpedo Boat: Any craft of up to 500 tons equipped primarily to launch antiship (vice antisubmarine) torpedoes—an almost extinct type.

PC Coastal Patrol Craft: Gun and antisubmarine warfare weapon–equipped craft between 100 and 500 tons, not equipped to carry antiship missiles.

PB Patrol Boat: Any craft of less than 100 tons equipped primarily to carry out patrol duties in relatively sheltered waters, harbors, or rivers.

PM River Monitor: Armored, low-freeboard craft of less than 500 tons full load displacement intended for riverine duties. There is no separate category for smaller, unarmored riverine patrol craft, which are grouped with other PB (Patrol Boat) classes.

Mine Warfare Ships and Craft:

MM Minelayer: Ships intended primarily to lay mines. They may also carry out tasks such as acting as flagships, mine-countermeasures support ships, or training vessels.

MCS Mine-Countermeasures Support Ship: Vessels intended to provide command, control, and communications and logistics support specifically tailored to mine warfare operations. Such ships are frequently essentially auxiliaries, and some are also capable of operating mine-countermeasures helicopters and/or of minelaying.

MHS Minehunting Ship: Mine warfare vessels of 500 tons or greater full load displacement equipped to locate mines by means of specialized sensors and then to destroy them. Minehunters also capable of towing sweep arrays remain typed as minehunters. Some are also equipped to lay mines.

MSF Fleet Minesweeper: Mine-countermeasures units of greater than 500 tons full load displacement equipped primarily to tow sweep arrays of all kinds and not equipped with specialized bottomed-mine location systems (but normally having some sort of moored-mine avoidance sonar sensor). They may also be equipped to perform patrol and antisubmarine duties and are frequently equipped to lay mines. In general, this is an obsolescent type, and the numbers of such ships are declining.

MHC Coastal Minehunter: As for MHS, but intended for operation in more sheltered waters and displacing less than 500 tons full load.

MSC Coastal Minesweeper: As for MSF, but intended for operations in more sheltered waters; the designation is normally applied to minesweepers of between 250 and 500 tons full load displacement.

MSI Inshore Minesweeper: As for MSC, but intended for sheltered water operations or for harbor or roadstead work; the designation is applied to minesweepers of between 100 and 250 tons full load displacement.

MSB Minesweeping Boat: Shallow water or riverine mine-countermeasures craft displacing less than 100 tons full load.

MSD Minesweeping Drone: Any mine-countermeasures craft primarily intended for remote-controlled operation.

MSS Specialized Minesweeper: Catch-all category for ships and craft equipped to perform either one specialized mine-countermeasures role (such as line-charge laying or magnetic pulse generation) or for craft intended primarily to support mine disposal divers.

Amphibious Warfare Ships and Craft:

LPH Amphibious Warfare Helicopter Carrier: Major ships intended primarily to operate helicopters to transport embarked troops; corresponds to U.S. Navy LPH, LHD, and LHA types. They may also carry vertical takeoff and landing fixed-wing aircraft embarked primarily for troop-support ground-attack duties.

LPD Amphibious Transport Dock: Major ships designed to carry and launch craft from a wet well deck at the stern. Distinguished from LSDs by carrying larger numbers of troops at the expense of vehicles and cargo.

LSD Dock Landing Ship: Another wet well–configured ship but with the cargo being predominantly vehicles.

LST Tank Landing Ship: Ships designed to beach and discharge cargo via a bow ramp system. Applied to ships of this configuration of greater than 2,000 tons full load displacement and capable of landing 400 or more metric tons of cargo.

LSM Medium Landing Ship: A smaller version of the LST, generally between 500 and 2,000 tons full load displacement and capable of delivering a cargo of less than 400 metric tons to a beach.

LPA Amphibious Transport: Ships primarily configured to carry assault troops who are delivered to the beach via embarked landing craft launched via davits or cranes.

LCFS Fire Support Landing Craft: Craft equipped with guns and/or rocket launchers for shore bombardment in support of amphibious assault troops.

LCU Utility Landing Craft: Larger, generally open-topped, bow ramp–equipped landing craft capable of transporting at least 100 metric tons of vehicles and personnel to a beach. LCUs are not generally large enough to make extended ocean voyages in a loaded condition, and most can be transported in the wet wells of larger landing ships.

LCM Medium Landing Craft: Beachable landing craft capable of transporting up to 100 tons of vehicle cargo and/or personnel and that can be transported to the scene of the amphibious assault aboard larger ships.

LCVP Vehicle/Personnel Landing Craft: Bow ramp–equipped, ship-transportable craft capable of carrying troops and small vehicles to a beach; cargo capacity limited to around 15 tons maximum.

LCP Personnel Landing Craft: Craft suitable only for transporting assault troops to a beach; if ramp-equipped, the ramp is suitable only for personnel, not vehicles.

LCW Special Warfare Support Craft: Small, high-speed, low-observable craft used to transport special warfare forces.

LSDV Swimmer Delivery Vehicle: Self-propelled submersibles intended to transport combat swimmers.

Auxiliaries:

ADG Deperming/Degaussing Ship: Seagoing ships intended to provide mobile deperming services and/or to transport and support degaussing ranges.

AE Ammunition Ship: Vessels intended to transport replenishment combat munitions for transfer at sea to combatant ships. U.S. Navy ammunition ships in service also carry cargo fuels.

AEM Missile Tender: Auxiliaries configured to transport ballistic missiles or large cruise missiles.

AF Stores Ship: Vessels intended primarily to transport refrigerated and dry provisions to combatants and to transfer their cargoes while under way. May also have smaller quantities of munitions, spares, and even replenishment fuels.

AFT Transport Stores Ship: As for AF, but without underway replenishment capability.

AG Miscellaneous Auxiliary: Any auxiliaries whose functions are not defined by one of the other auxiliary definitions.

AGE Experimental Auxiliary: Vessels configured to test weapons, sensors, communications systems, and so forth.

AGF Auxiliary Command Ship: Vessels employed as flagships but clearly not configured as combatants.

AGI Intelligence Collection Ship: Vessels configured for the collection of foreign intelligence, primarily electronic, but also including acoustic and electro-optical.

AGL Buoy Tender: Vessels intended to transport, lay, retrieve, and often repair navigational and mooring buoys. They usually also have a significant salvage capability.

AGM Missile Range Instrumentation Ship: Auxiliaries intended to collect data about domestic ballistic missile and cruise missile flight-paths and performance and, in some cases, also to act as communications relay vessels for space vehicles.

AGOR Oceanographic Research Ship: Auxiliaries intended to collect information on the physical and biological properties of the sea.

AGP Patrol Craft Tender: Ships specifically configured to provide logistic support, repairs, and often command facilities and munitions for minor combatant vessels.

AGS Hydrographic Survey Ship: Auxiliaries intended primarily to perform bottom surveys and to process data intended for the creation of navigational charts. They frequently also have a significant oceanographic research capability.

AH Hospital Ship: Auxiliaries intended for the care and transportation of wounded or otherwise incapacitated military or civilian personnel—and clearly identified as such. By international agreement, they must be painted white and carry prominent red crosses or red crescents viewable from above and each side and must not be armed (but Russian hospital ships double as transports, and Chinese hospital ships are armed).

AK Cargo Ship: Auxiliaries intended primarily to transport dry cargo in support of naval forces. They may carry a minor proportion of their cargo in the form of refrigerated provisions and/or ammunition. AKs are not normally configured for underway transfer of cargo.

AO Oiler: Auxiliaries intended to transport and transfer fuels to warships while under way, although they may have small quantities of ammunition, water, lube oil, provisions, etc., for transfer as well.

AOR Replenishment Oiler: Auxiliaries configured to transport liquid and dry cargoes to warships while under way. While the principal cargo is fuels and water, the ships have a significant fraction of their transferable cargo in the form of ammunition, dry and refrigerated provisions, and spare parts—essentially, one-stop underway replenishment platforms.

AOS Special Liquids Tanker: Auxiliaries intended to transport liquid cargoes other than ship propulsion fuels, lubricants, or water; generally applied to Russian Navy liquid nuclear waste transports and missile fuel transports.

AOT Transport Oiler: Tankers intended primarily for point-to-point transportation of liquid cargoes and not generally capable of being employed for underway replenishment.

AP Transport: Vessels intended for the point-to-point transport of personnel, distinguished from LPAs in that they are not intended to transport amphibious assault troops. They may also have a significant dry cargo and/or provisions transport capacity.

AR Repair Ship: Ships intended to provide repair and spare parts services to surface combatants. This subsumes the U.S. Navy categories of AR (Repair Ship) and AD (Destroyer Tender).

ARC Cable Ship: Auxiliaries intended to transport, lay, retrieve, and service undersea cables.

ARR Nuclear Propulsion Repair Ship: Auxiliaries having specialized facilities for the servicing of shipboard nuclear propulsion plants, including facilities to transport nuclear fuel rods. This designator applies only to several Russian Navy classes and does not include ships configured to carry liquid radiological wastes (see AOS).

ARS Salvage and Rescue Ship: Auxiliaries, usually of tug configuration, intended to support salvage, rescue, and firefighting operations.

AS Submarine Tender: Auxiliaries intended to provide logistic support and repair services to submarines.

ASR Submarine Rescue Ship: Auxiliaries intended for the rescue of personnel from sunken submarines. Most ASRs are also capable of performing general salvage and ocean towing duties.

ATA Ocean Tug: Auxiliaries configured primarily for oceangoing towing, but usually also capable of secondary rescue, salvage, and firefighting missions.
AW Water Tanker: Auxiliaries intended for the transport and underway transfer of water to other ships.
AWT Water Transport: As for AW, but without underway transfer capability.
AXT Training Ship: Auxiliaries equipped primarily for the training of cadets and/or enlisted personnel. Also applies to large sail training vessels in naval service.

Service Craft:

YAG Miscellaneous Service Craft: Service craft whose function is not covered by other definitions or that has several equally significant functions.
YAGE Experimental Service Craft: Small trials craft for trials-associated duties with weapons systems, sensors, and other naval systems.
YC Open Barge: Any open-topped, non-self-propelled dry cargo barges.
YD Floating Crane: Most are non-self-propelled, but by convention (and because self-propulsion systems for floating cranes are only for very local movements and positionings), craft without propulsion systems do not receive an "N" suffix.
YDG Deperming/Degaussing Platform: Nonseagoing craft intended to support deperming services or to support a degaussing range.
YDT Diving Tender: Service craft primarily equipped to support noncombatant divers. (Large, seagoing diving tenders are generally typed ARS, while ships and craft configured primarily to support mine disposal divers are typed MSS.)
YE Ammunition Lighter: Self-propelled, nonseagoing craft for local transport of munitions.
YF Covered Lighter: Self-propelled craft for local transport of dry cargo. (A YFN is a covered or deckhouse-equipped non-self-propelled barge.)
YFB Ferry: Self-propelled craft for local transport of vehicles as well as personnel (as distinguished from a YFL, which cannot transport vehicles).
YFDB Large Floating Dry Dock: Open-ended floating dry docks with a lift capacity of 20,000 metric tons or more.
YFDM Medium Floating Dry Dock: Open-ended floating dry docks with a lift capacity between 5,000 and 20,000 metric tons.
YFDL Small Floating Dry Dock: Open-ended floating dry docks with a lift capacity of less than 5,000 metric tons.
YFL Launch: Small, self-propelled craft for local transportation of personnel.
YFNB Large Covered Barge: Large, towable, non-self-propelled barges for the ocean transport of dry cargo.
YFND Dry Dock Companion Barge: Non-self-propelled barges equipped with machinery intended to support floating dry docks.
YFP Floating Power Barge: Non-self-propelled craft equipped with generators or alternators to supply electricity (a few YFPs do have self-propulsion for local movement). The designation is also applied to craft employed to charge submarine batteries.
YFR Refrigerated Lighter: Self-propelled craft for local transport of refrigerated (and, often, dry) provisions.
YFU Harbor Utility Lighter: Beachable, ramp-equipped, self-propelled craft for local logistic support duties.
YG Garbage Lighter: Self-propelled craft for the transport of garbage or for the treatment and disposal of human waste. Not good duty.
YGL Small Navigational Aids Tender: Self-propelled service craft intended to service navigational aids buoys and other navigational markers; they may or may not be equipped to lay, recover, and service navigational aids buoys.
YGS Survey Craft: Small self-propelled craft intended for the collection of bottom configuration data for the purpose of preparing navigational charts. They may either be independently operable or intended to be transported to the scene of operations aboard a larger vessel (usually an AGS).
YGT Target Service Craft: Surface ships or craft of any size intended to act as targets or as specialized drone target control craft. (Stationary floating or towed targets are typed YGTN.)
YH Ambulance Craft: Self-propelled local service craft intended for the transport of ill or injured personnel and, in some cases, to provide emergency medical services in remote, sheltered areas.
YM Dredge: Self-propelled or, by convention, non-self-propelled craft equipped to deepen channels, harbors, or inland waterways.
YNG Net Tender: Service ships or craft of any size intended to transport and/or service antisubmarine harbor defense nets and warning devices. They may also have a significant salvage capability due to heavy-lift facilities.
YO Fuel Lighter: Self-propelled craft for local transport of fuels. They are generally for harbor use, but may have a limited seagoing capability.
YPB Floating Barracks: Ships or craft intended primarily to provide stationary accommodations and support for personnel. If self-propelled, the capability is primarily for local movement.
YPT Torpedo Retriever: Self-propelled craft intended to recover expended exercise torpedoes and missiles (and, in some cases, exercise mines).
YR Floating Workshop: Non-self-propelled harbor craft equipped to perform repair and maintenance on other ships and craft.
YRC Cable tender: Self-propelled local service craft for laying, retrieving, and, often, servicing underwater cables.
YRD Auxiliary Repair Dock: Floating dry docks with one end enclosed in a ship-like bow intended to permit rapid towing (corresponds to U.S. Navy ARD).
YRG Tank Cleaning Craft: Service craft intended to clean shipboard fuel tanks and sewage tanks.
YRRN Nuclear Propulsion Repair Barge: Non-self-propelled harbor craft intended to support nuclear-powered ships and submarines.
YRS Salvage Craft: Service craft of a variety of configurations intended to support salvage operations; included are salvage pontoons and small self- propelled harbor salvage craft (but not diving tenders, which are YDT).
YSS Service Submersible: Small submersible craft employed for research, salvage, and/or personnel rescue.
YTB Large Harbor Tug: Tugs intended for harbor and coastal service and having a total horsepower of 1,200 bhp or more.
YTM Medium Harbor Tug: Tugs intended primarily for harbor service but capable of limited coastal operations and having a total horsepower between 400 and 1,200 bhp.
YTL Small Harbor Tug: Tugs intended primarily for harbor and dockyard service and having a total horsepower of up to 400 bhp.
YTR Fireboat: Self-propelled craft intended primarily for firefighting duties and not generally intended for towing.
YTS Sail Training Craft: Craft powered primarily by sails and intended to provide seamanship training.
YXT Training Craft: Smaller, self-propelled craft intended to provide seamanship, navigational, and maneuvering training and generally not intended for sustained seagoing operations.

ACRONYMS AND ABBREVIATIONS

A Armament
AA Antiaircraft
A&C Shipbuilding Yard (*Atelier & Chantier*)
AAW Anti-air Warfare
a.c. Alternating current
accomm. Accommodations
ADAWS Action Data Automation Weapon System (U.K.)
ADI Australian Defence Industries
AEW Airborne Early Warning
AIP Air-independent propulsion
ARM Antiradiation Missile
ARPA Automatic Radar Plotting Aid
ASM Antiship Missile
ASROC Antisubmarine Rocket (U.S.)
Ast. Nav. Shipyard (*Astilleros Navales*)
ASW Antisubmarine warfare
Auth. Authorized
avg. Average, normal
BAE British Aerospace
bbl Barrels
bhp Brake horsepower (diesel and gasoline engines)
Bldr Builder
Bros. Brothers
BW Boat Works
BY Boat Yard
CAAIS Computer-Assisted Action Information System (U.K.)
cal. Caliber (length of gun barrel divided by bore diameter)
Cant. Shipyard (*Cantieri*)
Ch. Shipyard (*Chantier*)
CIC Combat Information Center
CIWS Close-In Weapon System (U.S., but now widely used)
C.N. Naval shipyard (*Cantiere Navale, Chantier Naval*)
COD Carrier Onboard Delivery (U.S.)
COGAG/CODAD/COSAG/COGOG/CODOG Combined propulsion systems: CO = combined; D = diesel, G = gas turbine, S = steam; A = and, O = or—e.g., CODOG = combined diesel or gas turbine
Const. Constructed or construction
cont. Continuous
COOP Craft of Opportunity
COTS Commercial off-the-shelf
CP Controllable-pitch (propeller)
cyl. Cylinder
D Displacement
dc Direct current
d.c. Depth charge
DD Dry dock
del. Delivered
desig. Designation, designator
Det. Detachment
D/F Direction finding, direction finder
dia. Diameter
DICASS Directional command-activated sonobuoy system
DIFAR Directional low-frequency analysis and ranging
Dim Dimensions
DoD Department of Defense (U.S.)
DP Dual-purpose (gun, meaning for surface and antiaircraft firing)
DSRV Deep Submergence Rescue Vessel (U.S.)
dwt Deadweight tonnage
DY Dockyard
EADS European Aeronautic, Defence, and Space Co.: a joint venture (formed in 2000) of DaimlerChrysler and Thomson-CSF with BAE Systems, Matra BAe Dynamics, Aérospatiale-Matra, Alenia Marconi Systems, LFK (Lenkflugkörpersystem GmbH), DaimlerBenz Aerospace; other joint ventures include an agreement with Nortel, Ontario
ECCM Electronic counter-countermeasures
ECM Electronic countermeasures
EEZ Economic Exclusion Zone
ELINT Electronic intelligence
E.N. Shipyard (*Empresa Nacional*)
Eng. Engineering
E/O Electro-optical
ESM Electronic support measures (i.e., passive EW)
est. Estimated
Est. *Estalleiros*
EW Electronic Warfare
f.c. Fire-control
f.c.s. Fire-control system
fl Full load (displacement)
FLIR Forward-looking infrared
FM Frequency modulation
FRAM Fleet Rehabilitation and Modernization (U.S.)
freq. Frequency
ft. Foot, feet
fwd Forward
FY Fiscal Year

g.	Gravity
G.E.	General Electric Co. (U.S.)
gen.	Generator
GFCS	Gun fire-control system
GHz	Gigahertz
G.M.	General Motors Corp. (U.S.)
GPS	Global Positioning System
GRP	Glass-reinforced plastic (fiberglass)
grt	Gross registered tons (a measurement of volume, not weight)
GWS	Guided Weapon System (U.K.)
HF	High frequency
HFD/F	High-frequency direction-finder
H.M.	Her Majesty's (U.K.)
HMAS	Her Majesty's Australian Ship
HMDY	Her Majesty's Dockyard
HMS	Her Majesty's Ship (U.K.)
hp	Horsepower
hr	Hours
IADT	Integrated automatic detection and tracking
IFF	Identification, friend or foe
IHI	Ishikawajima-Harima Heavy Industries: formed in 1960 with the merger of Ishikawajima Heavy Industries, Ltd., and Harima Heavy Industries, Ltd.; naval shipbuilding efforts combined with Sumatomo Heavy Industries in 2000 to form Marine United, Inc.
ihp	Indicated horsepower (for reciprocating steam engines)
IOC	Initial operational capability
IR	Infrared
IRST	Infrared search-and-track
ISAR	Inverse synthetic aperture radar
kg	Kilograms
kHz	Kilohertz
Kon. Mij.	Royal Company (Netherlands)
kph	Kilometers per hour
kT	Kilotons
kts	Knots
kVA	Kilovolt-Amperes
kw	Kilowatts
L	Launched
LAMPS	Light Airborne Multipurpose System (U.S. helicopter)
LF	Low frequency
LOFAR	Low-frequency analysis and ranging
m	Meters
M	Machinery
MAD	Magnetic anomaly detection
MARAD	Maritime Administration (U.S.)
max.	Maximum
MCM	Mine countermeasures
MEKO	*Mehrzweck Kombination* (German Blohm + Voss containerized modular shipboard systems installation system)
MF	Medium frequency
MFD/F	Medium-frequency direction-finder
Mfr.	Manufacturer
mg	Machinegun
min	Minutes
min.	Minimum
MIRV	Multiple independent reentry vehicle
mm	Millimeters
Mod.	Modified, modification
M.O.D.	Ministry of Defence (Germany, U.K.)
MPA	Maritime patrol aircraft
ms	Milliseconds
MSC	Military Sealift Command (U.S.)
MTU	Motoren und Turbinen Union
Mw	Megawatts
NATO	North Atlantic Treaty Organization
nav.	Navigation, navigational
Nav.	Naval
navaid	Navigational aid
NBC	Nuclear, biological, and chemical
NDY	Naval Dockyard
n.m.	Nautical miles
nrt	Net registered tonnage
NSY	Naval Shipyard
NTDS	Naval Tactical Data System
NY	Navy Yard
o.a.	Overall
PDMS	Point-Defense Missile System (U.S.)
pdr.	Pounder (referring to nominal weight of shell)
pp	Between perpendiculars
Pty.	Proprietary
R&D	Research and development
RBOC	Rapid-Blooming Overboard Chaff (U.S.)
rds	Rounds
RDY	Royal Dockyard
Recce	reconnaissance
RIB	Rigid inflatable boat
RL	Rocket launcher
RM	Relative motion (radar plot)
Ro/Ro	Roll-on/roll-off
ROV	Remotely operated vehicle
rpm	Revolutions per minute
S	Speed
SAM	Surface-to-air missile
SAR	Search-and-rescue
SATCOM	Satellite communications
SB	Shipbuilding
sec	Seconds
serv.	Service
SFCN	Société Française de Constructions Navale
SHF	Super-high frequency
shp	Shaft horsepower (steam and gas-turbine engines)
SINS	Ships' Inertial Navigation System (U.S.)
SLAR	Side-looking airborne radar
SLBM	Submarine-Launched Ballistic Missile
SLEP	Service Life Extension Program
Sqn.	Squadron
SRBOC	Super Rapid-Blooming Offboard Chaff (U.S.)
SSB	Single-sideband
SSM	Surface-to-surface missile
SSTD	Surface Ship Torpedo Defense
std.	Standard
STIR	Separate Track and Illumination Radar (U.S. and Dutch)
sub.	Submerged
surf.	Surface, surfaced
SURTASS	Surface Towed Array Surveillance System (U.S.)
sust.	Sustained
SWATH	Small waterplane area, twin-hull
SY	Shipyard
syst.	System
TACAN	Tactical Air Navigation System
TACTASS	Tactical Towed Acoustic Sensor System (U.S.)
TAS	Target Acquisition System (U.S.)
TASS	Towed Acoustic Array System (U.S.)
3-D	Three-dimensional (i.e., height, distance, and bearing)
TM	True motion (radar plot)
tot.	Total
TT	Torpedo tubes/launchers
t.v.	Television
2-D	Two-dimensional (i.e., distance and bearing)
UAV	Unmanned aerial vehicle
UHF	Ultra-high frequency
UNREP	Underway replenishment
V	Volts
VDS	Variable-depth sonar
VHF	Very high frequency
VLS	Vertical-launch system
V/STOL	Vertical/short takeoff and landing
VTOL	Vertical takeoff and landing
WASS	Whitehead Alenia Sistemi Subacquei (formerly Whitehead Motofides)
WIG	Wing-in-ground-effect
Wks.	Works
wl	Waterline

CONVERSION TABLES

◆ **METERS (m.) to FEET (ft.)**
based on 1 inch = 25.4 millimeters

m	0	1	2	3	4	5	6	7	8
	ft.	ft.	ft.	ft.	ft.	ft.	ft.	ft.	ft.
—	—	3.28084	6.5617	9.8425	13.1234	16.4042	19.6850	22.9659	26.2467
10	32.8084	36.0892	39.3701	42.6509	45.9317	49.2126	52.493	55.774	59.005
20	65.617	68.898	72.178	75.459	78.740	82.021	85.302	88.583	91.863
30	98.425	101.706	104.987	108.268	111.549	114.829	118.110	121.391	124.672
40	131.234	134.514	137.795	141.076	144.357	147.638	150.919	154.199	157.480
50	164.042	167.323	170.604	173.884	177.165	180.446	183.727	187.008	190.289
60	196.850	200.131	203.412	206.693	209.974	213.255	216.535	219.816	223.097
70	229.659	232.940	236.220	239.501	242.782	246.063	249.344	252.625	255.905
80	262.467	265.748	269.029	272.310	275.590	278.871	282.152	285.433	288.714
90	295.276	298.556	301.837	305.118	308.399	311.680	314.961	318.241	321.522
100	328.084	331.365	334.646	337.926	341.207	344.488	347.769	351.050	354.331
10	360.892	364.173	367.454	370.735	374.016	377.296	380.577	383.858	387.139
20	393.701	396.982	400.262	403.543	406.824	410.105	413.386	416.667	419.947
30	426.509	429.790	433.071	436.352	439.632	442.913	446.194	449.475	452.756
40	459.317	462.598	465.879	469.160	472.441	475.722	479.002	482.283	485.564
50	492.126	495.407	498.688	501.97	505.25	508.53	511.81	515.09	518.37
60	524.93	528.22	531.50	534.78	538.06	541.34	544.62	547.90	551.18
70	557.74	561.02	564.30	567.59	570.87	574.15	577.43	580.71	583.99
80	590.55	593.83	597.11	600.39	603.67	606.96	610.24	613.52	616.80
90	623.36	626.64	629.92	633.20	636.48	639.76	643.04	646.33	649.61
200	656.17	659.45	662.73	666.01	669.29	672.57	675.85	679.13	682.41
10	688.98	692.26	695.54	698.82	702.10	705.38	708.66	711.94	715.22
20	721.78	725.07	728.35	731.63	734.91	738.19	741.47	744.75	748.03
30	754.59	757.87	761.15	764.44	767.72	771.00	774.28	777.56	780.84
40	747.40	790.68	793.96	797.24	800.52	803.81	807.09	810.37	813.65
50	820.21	823.49	826.77	830.05	833.33	836.61	839.89	843.18	846.46
60	853.02	856.30	859.58	862.86	866.14	869.42	872.70	875.98	879.26
70	885.83	889.11	892.39	895.67	898.95	902.23	905.51	908.79	912.07
80	918.63	921.92	925.20	928.48	931.76	935.04	938.32	941.60	944.88
90	951.44	954.72	958.00	961.29	964.57	967.85	971.13	974.41	977.69
300	984.25	987.53	990.81	994.09	997.38	1000.66	1003.94	1007.22	1010.50
10	1017.06	1020.34	1023.62	1026.90	1030.18	1033.46	1036.75	1040.03	1043.31
20	1049.87	1053.15	1056.43	1059.71	1062.99	1066.27	1069.55	1072.83	1076.12
30	1082.68	1085.96	1089.24	1092.52	1095.80	1099.08	1102.36	1105.64	1108.92
40	1115.49	1118.77	1122.05	1125.33	1128.61	1131.89	1135.17	1138.45	1141.73
50	1118.29	1151.57	1154.86	1158.14	1161.42	1164.70	1167.98	1171.26	1174.54

◆ **MILLIMETERS (mm.) to INCHES (in.)**
based on 1 inch = 25.4 millimeters

mm	0	1	2	3	4	5	6	7	8
	in.	in.	in.	in.	in.	in.	in.	in.	in.
—	—	0.03937	0.07874	0.11811	0.15748	0.19685	0.23622	0.27559	0.31496
10	0.39370	0.43307	0.47244	0.51181	0.55118	0.59055	0.62992	0.66929	0.70866
20	0.78740	0.82677	0.86614	0.90551	0.94488	0.98425	1.02362	1.06299	1.10236
30	1.18110	1.22047	1.25984	1.29921	1.33858	1.37795	1.41732	1.45669	1.49606
40	1.57480	1.61417	1.65354	1.69291	1.73228	1.77165	1.81102	1.85039	1.88976

◆ **MILLIMETERS (mm.) to INCHES (in.)**
based on 1 inch = 25.4 millimeters (*continued*)

mm	0	1	2	3	4	5	6	7	8
	in.	in.	in.	in.	in.	in.	in.	in.	in.
50	1.96850	2.00787	2.04724	2.08661	2.12598	2.16535	2.20472	2.24409	2.28346
60	2.36220	2.40157	2.44094	2.48031	2.51969	2.55906	2.59843	2.63780	2.67717
70	2.75591	2.79528	2.83465	2.87402	2.91339	2.95276	2.99213	3.03150	3.07087
80	3.14961	3.18898	3.22835	3.26772	3.30709	3.34646	3.38583	3.42520	3.46457
90	3.54331	3.58268	3.62205	3.66142	3.70079	3.74016	3.77953	3.81890	3.85827
100	3.93701								

CONVERSION FACTORS

Meter	Yard	Foot	Inch	Centimeter	Millimeter
1	1.093 61	3.280 84	39.370 1	100	1 000
0.914 4	1	3	36	91.44	914.4
0.304 8	0.333 333	1	12	30.48	304.8
0.254	0.027 777 8	0.083 333	1	2.54	25.4 j
0.01	0.010 936 1	0.032 808 4	0.393 701	1	10
0.001	0.001 093 61	0.003 280 84	0.039 370 4	0.1	1

Nautical mile		Statute mile		Meters
1	=	1.151 52	=	1 853.18

◆ Boiler working pressure

Kilogram per square centimeter (atmosphere)		*Pounds per square inch*
1	equivalent →	14.223 3
0.070 307	← equivalent	1

◆ Conversion for Fahrenheit and centigrade scales

1 degree centigrade = 1.8 degrees Fahrenheit
1 degree Fahrenheit = 5/9 degree centigrade
t°F = 5/9(t − 32)°C.
t°C = (1.8t + 32)°F.

◆ Weights

1 kilogram = 2.204 62 *pounds* (av)
1 *pound* = 0.453 592 *kilograms*
1 ton (metric) = 0.984 21 *ton*
1 *ton* = 1.016 05 *metric ton*

◆ Power

1 CV = 0.986 32 *horsepower* (HP) 0.735 88 kilowatt (Greenwich) (75 kgm s)
1 *horsepower* (HP) = 1.013 87 (CV) 0.746 08 kilowatt (Greenwich)

ALBANIA

Republic of Albania

ALBANIAN NAVAL DEFENSE FORCES

Personnel: About 2,000 total (400 officers), including about 300 Coast Guard troops

Bases: Naval headquarters is at Tirana. 1st Naval District Headquarters is at Durres and 2nd Naval District headquarters at Pasalimani, Vlore, with the 1st Naval Base at Shengjin and the 2nd at Sarande. Repair facilities at the Pasalimani base, destroyed during 1997, were upgraded with assistance from Turkey, which is also assisting in reestablishing the Albanian Naval Academy. Italy's Customs Service (*Guardia di Finanza*) maintains four patrol boats at Durres.

Note: Renamed from the Coastal Defense Command of the Albanian Army in 1996. All former Soviet equipment was transferred prior to 1961. The last operational Whiskey-class (Project 613) submarine, *Qemel* (022), was retired at the end of 1995.

TORPEDO BOATS [PT]

♦ 1 Chinese Shanghai-II class (Project 062)

P-115 (ex-P-123)

Shanghai-II-class P-123—with Italian Guardia Finanza escort
EPA/PA News, 2-97

D: 122.5 tons (134.8 fl) **S:** 28 kts **Dim:** 38.78 × 5.41 × 1.55 (props)
A: 2 twin 37-mm 63-cal. Type 74 AA; two twin 25-mm 80-cal. Type 81 AA; 2 single 533-mm TT
Electronics: Radar: 1 Type 351 (Pot Head) nav.
M: 2 Type L12-180 diesels (1,200-bhp each) and 2 Type L12-180Z (910-bhp each) diesels; 4 props; 4,220 bhp
Electric: 39 kw **Range:** 750/16.5 **Endurance:** 7 days **Crew:** 36 tot.

Remarks: Transferred from China in 1974–75. Torpedo tubes removed from Huchuan-class torpedo boats have been mounted at the stern, firing aft. P-115 defected to Italy during 3-97 but was returned at the end of the year. Five sisters are beyond repair.

♦ 5 Chinese Huchuan-class semi-hydrofoils

S-101 S-103 S-109
S-102 S-104

Huchuan-class S-209
French Navy, 12-93

D: 39 tons (45.8 fl) **S:** 50 kts **Dim:** 22.30 × 3.80 (6.26 over fenders) × 1.15
A: 2 single 533-mm TT; 2 twin 14.5-mm 93-cal. Type 81 mg
Electronics: Radar: 1 Zarnitsa (Skin Head) nav.
M: 3 L12-180 diesels; 3 props; 3,600 bhp **Electric:** 5.6 kw tot.
Range: 500/30 **Crew:** 11 tot.

Remarks: Transferred 1974–75. The units listed here went to Italy in 1997, along with S-406, which was considered beyond repair by 1998; S-101 and S-305 were returned on 5-11-97, and the others during 1998–99 after repairs in Italy. Pennant 902 defected 5-91 to Italy, where the crew requested asylum; the craft was returned in 10-91. At least six others had been cannibalized, and another dozen are beyond repair. Bow foils only; stern planes on surface. The foils have been removed from several of the boats.

Note: Twelve Soviet-supplied P-4-class (Project 123K) torpedo boats, built in the early 1950s, are in land storage and are unlikely to see further service. S-107 and S-108 were retired in 2004.

MINE WARFARE SHIPS

♦ 2 Soviet T-43-class ocean minesweepers [MSF]

M-222 (ex-M-111) M-223 (ex-M-112)

D: 535 tons (569 fl) **S:** 14 kts **Dim:** 58.0 × 8.75 × 2.5 (3.5 sonar)
A: 2 twin 37-mm 63-cal. V-11-M AA; 4 twin 12.7-mm 79-cal. mg; 2 BMB-1 d.c. mortars; 2 mine rails
Electronics:
Radar: 1 Decca . . . nav.; 1 Lin' (Ball End) surf. search
Sonar: Tamir-11 HF searchlight
M: 2 Type 9-D diesels; 2 CP props; 2,200 bhp **Electric:** 175 kw tot.
Range: 3,200/10; 4,400/8.3 **Fuel:** 68 tons **Crew:** 53 tot.

Remarks: One unit, numbered AS-342, defected to Brindisi, Italy, on 17-3-97 and interned; the ship was returned to Albania at the end of 1997. M-222 was refitted in 2002. M-223 may no longer be operational.

♦ 2 Soviet T-301-class (Project 255) coastal minesweepers [MSC]

M-225 (ex-M-113) M-227 (ex-M-114)

T-301-class M-225
French Navy, 7-99

D: 147.8 tons (164 fl) **S:** 12.5 kts **Dim:** 38.00 × 5.70 × 1.58
A: 1 45-mm Type 21-KM AA; 2 twin 12.7-mm 79-cal. mg; up to 18 mines
Electronics: Radar: 1 Decca . . . nav.—Sonar: Tamir-10 HF searchlight-type
M: 3 Type 3D-12 diesels; 3 props; 900 bhp (690 sust.)
Electric: 60 kw tot. (2 × 30-kw diesel-driven sets).
Range: 2,400/7.1 **Fuel:** 10.1 tons **Endurance:** 5 days **Crew:** 35 tot.

Remarks: May no longer be operational. Two others have been discarded, and two more have been cannibalized for spares. The hull shell plating has no compound curves. Mine countermeasures gear includes OPT bottom contact sweep, MT-3 contact sweep, PEMT-4 coil sweep, and two BAT-2 acoustic sweeps.

SERVICE CRAFT

♦ 1 Soviet Nyryat'-1-class (Project 522) diving tender [YDT]
(In serv. ca. 1960)

A-534

D: 105.4 tons (115 fl) **S:** 10 kts **Dim:** 28.50 × 5.50 × 1.70
A: none **Electronics:** Radar: 1 Mius (Spin Trough) nav.
M: 1 Type 6CSP 28/3C diesel; 1 prop; 450 bhp
Range: 900/9 **Endurance:** 10 days **Crew:** 22 tot.

Remarks: Can support hard-hat divers to 20-meter depths. May have been transferred to the Coast Guard in 2003.

♦ 2 Soviet PO-2 (Yaroslavets)-class workboats (Project 376) [YFL]
(In serv. late 1950s)

A 210 A 212

D: 32.2 tons (38.2 fl) **S:** 9-10 kts **Dim:** 21.00 × 3.90 × 1.40 (max.; 1.26 mean)
Electronics: Radar: May have 1 Mius (Spin Trough) nav.
M: 1 Type 3D-6S1 diesel; 1 prop; 150 bhp
Electric: 10 kw tot. (1 × 10 kw, DGPN-8/1500 diesel driving)
Range: 1,600/8 **Fuel:** 1.5 tons **Endurance:** 5 days **Crew:** 4–6 tot.

Remarks: Built in the former USSR. Can be operated safely in Force 8 winds and 2-m seas. Can break light ice and serve as a harbor tug.

♦ 1 ex-Italian LCT(3)-class repair tender [YR]
(In serv. 1943–44)

A 223 (ex-M.O.C. 1203, A 5333)

D: A 223: 579 tons (fl); A . . .: 711 tons (fl) **Dim:** 58.25 × 9.22 × 2.0
Electronics: Radar: 1/BX-732 nav.
M: 2 Paxman diesels; 2 props; 1,000 bhp **Crew:** 1–2 officers, 20–26 enlisted

Remarks: A 223 was transferred from Italy to Albania in 1999. Ex-M.O.C. 1204 was incorrectly reported as having been transferred to Albania during 2003, but was actually transferred to Tunisia. M.O.C. = *Moto Officina Costiera* (Coastal Repair Ship). Equipped for minor repairs to small craft. Bow door/vehicle ramps were welded closed.

Note: The customs service operates four Arcor 24–class inspection craft (2.1 tons, 35 kts, 7.7-m o.a.) delivered from France in 11-90; there are as many as 40 smaller craft in use on various lakes.

COAST GUARD (*ROJA BREGDETARE*)

PATROL BOATS [WPB]

♦ 3 ex-U.S. Sea Spectre PB Mk III class
Bldr: Peterson Bldrs., Sturgeon Bay, Wis. (In serv. 1976)

R 215 (ex-65PB753) R 217 (ex-65PB758)
R 216 (ex-65PB757)

D: 28 tons (36.7 fl) **S:** 30 kts (now less) **Dim:** 19.78 × 5.50 × 1.80 (props)
A: . . . **Electronics:** Radar: 1 or 2 Furuno . . . nav.
M: 3 G.M. 8V71 TI diesels; 3 props; 1,800 bhp
Range: 450/26; 2,000/. . . **Endurance:** 3 days **Crew:** 1 officer, 8 enlisted

Remarks: Originally planned for transfer in 2-97, but delayed until 27-2-99. Have trouble making maximum speed. Aluminum hull construction. Can accept a variety of weapons up to 40-mm bore on forward mounting position and have four other weapons locations, including one atop the pilothouse for a twin 12.7-mm mg.

♦ 2 U.S. 45-foot Patrol Craft, Coastal (PCC) class
Bldr: Peterson Bldrs., Sturgeon Bay, Wis. (In serv. 27-2-99)

R 117 R 118

D: 16.2 tons (17.7 fl) **S:** 35 kts (30 sust.) **Dim:** 13.86 × 3.96 × 0.86
A: small arms **Electronics:** Radar: 1 Raytheon 40X nav.
M: 2 MTU 8V183 TE92 diesels; 2 Hamilton 362 waterjets; 1,314 bhp
Range: 200/30 **Fuel:** 490 gal. **Crew:** 4 tot.

Remarks: Built mid-1990s as stock for now-canceled U.S. Special Defense Acquisition Fund; originally to have been donated to Albania in 2-97. Aluminum construction, trailerable. Intended for riverine and harbor patrol. Ten sisters serve in the Egyptian Coast Guard, where they are armed with one 12.7-mm and two 7.62-mm mg.

♦ 3 ex-Italian CP 231–class inshore patrol launches (Super Speranza) Bldr: Rodriguez, Messina (In serv. 1966–70)

R 124 (ex-CP 235) R 225 (ex-CP 234) R 226 (ex-CP 236)

R 124—at Valona Luciano Grazioli, 11-02

D: 14 tons (16 fl) **S:** 26 kts **Dim:** 13.40 × 4.80 × 1.30
Electronics: Radar: 1 . . . nav.
M: 2 AIFO 8281 SRM diesels; 2 props; 900 bhp
Range: 400/ . . . **Crew:** 7 tot.

Remarks: Transferred on 18-6-02, with R 124 based at Durazzo and the other two at Valona. Wooden construction. All have been re-engined. CP 236 was decommissioned from the Italian Coast Guard on 30-9-01 and stricken on 31-12-01; CP 235 was stricken on 31-5-01; CP 234 was decommissioned on 30-9-02 and stricken for transfer on 31-12-02.

♦ 1 ex-Italian CP 228–class inshore patrol launch
Bldr: Navaltecnica, Anzio (In serv. 1967)

R 123 (ex-CP 229)

D: 15.1 tons (fl) **S:** 22–24 kts **Dim:** 13.40 × 4.75 × 1.26
M: 2 AIFO 8281 SRM diesels; 2 props; 900 bhp **Range:** 400/20 **Crew:** 7 tot.

Remarks: CP 229 was decommissioned from the Italian Coast Guard on 30-9-01 and stricken on 31-12-01; transferred to Albania on 18-6-02. Wooden construction. Based at Durazzo.

♦ 7 ex-Italian CP 2010 class
Bldr: Motomar, Lavagna, Genoa, Italy (In serv. 1975)

R 224 (ex-CP 2010) and 6 others

D: 11 tons (fl) **S:** 14 kts **Dim:** 12.57 × 3.64 × 1.00
M: 2 diesels; 2 props; 420 bhp
Range: 400/ . . . **Crew:** 4 tot.

Remarks: R 224 was transferred from the Italian Coast Guard on 18-6-02 and is based at Valona for harbor patrol duties. Wooden construction, Keith Nelson pilot boat design.

♦ 1 ex-Italian CP 603 class (Seppietta class)
Bldr: Italcraft, Gaeta (L: 6-5-88)

R 122 (ex-CP 603)

D: 3.5 tons **S:** 16 kts **Dim:** 8.50 × 2.78 × 0.80
M: 2 VM HR 694 diesels; 1 prop; 248 bhp **Range:** 200/16 **Crew:** 2 tot.

Remarks: Former rescue launch CP 603 was decommissioned from the Italian Coast Guard on 30-9-01 and transferred to Albania on 18-6-02 for use as a patrol launch, based at Durazzo.

ALGERIA

Democratic and Popular Republic of Algeria

MARINE DE LA RÉPUBLIQUE ALGERIENNE

Personnel: About 7,500 total, with about 500 officers (includes 600 Naval Infantry). About 500 total serve in the Coast Guard.

Naval Aviation: The Algerian Air Force uses 3 Fokker F-27 (Maritime) Mk 400, 6 Beech 1900D Multi-Mission Surveillance Aircraft, and 2 Beech Super King Air 200T patrol aircraft for maritime surveillance, and 3 Kamov Ka-28 Helix helicopters for search and rescue duties. Algeria has an additional requirement for a dozen maritime surveillance aircraft.

Bases: 1st Naval Region: Algiers; 2nd Naval Region: Seas-el-Kebir; 3rd Naval Region: Jijel; Coast Guard: Annaba (with detachments in major ports).

Coastal Defense: There are four batteries of SS-C-3 Styx missiles, using twin-tube truck-mounted launchers; their operational status is uncertain.

ATTACK SUBMARINES [SS]

♦ 2 Soviet Kilo class (Project 677EM)
Bldr: United Admiralty SY, St. Petersburg (In serv. 1987, 1988)

012 Raïs Hadj M'barek 013 El Hadj Slimane

Raïs Hadj M'barek (012) U.S. Navy, 5-95

D: 2,325 tons surf./3,076 tons sub. **S:** 10 kts surf./17 kts sub.
Dim: 72.60 (70.0 wl) × 9.90 × 6.6
A: 6 bow 533-mm TT (18 torpedoes or 24 mines); 1 SA-N-5/8 SAM syst. (8 missiles)
Electronics:
Radar: 1 MRK-50E (Snoop Tray) search
Sonar: MGK-400 (Shark Gill) LF active/passive suite; passive hull array; MG-519 (Mouse Roar) HF active classification/mine avoidance
EW: Brick Pulp or Squid Head intercept; Quad Loop (6701E) D/F
M: 2 Type 2D-42 diesel generator sets (1,825 bhp/1,500 kw each), electric drive: 1 motor; 1/6-bladed prop; 5,900 shp—1 130-shp low-speed motor—2 low-speed maneuvering motors; 2 ducted props; 204 shp
Range: 6,000/7 surf.; 400/3 sub. **Fuel:** 172 tons **Endurance:** 45 days
Crew: 12 officers, 41 enlisted

Remarks: First unit left the Baltic on 15-9-87 for delivery, the second during 1-88; both returned to Russia for overhaul during 1993 with work on 012 completed 5-95 and on 013 early in 3-96.
Hull systems: Propulsion plant suspended for silencing. Hull has 32% reserve buoyancy at 2,350 m^3 surfaced displacement. At rest on the surface, the submarine trims down 0.4 m by the bow. Maximum diving depth is 300 m, normal depth 240 m, and periscope depth 17.5 m. Have anechoic hull coating. Two batteries, each with 120 cells, providing 9,700 kw/hr. Hull has six watertight compartments.
Combat systems: Combat system, designated Murena or MVU-110EM, can conduct two simultaneous attacks while tracking three other targets manually. Sonar suite supplemented by MG-519 active mine-avoidance set, MG-553 sound velocity meter, and MG-512 own-ship's cavitation detector. The manual SAM launch position is located in after portion of the sail. Weapons carried can include E53-777 wire-guided, E53-60 and E53-85 wake-homing, and E53-67 acoustic-homing torpedoes along with KMD-500, KMD-1000, KMD-II 500, KMD-II 1000, and UMD mines.

Note: Two Romeo-class submarines transferred from the USSR had become nonoperational by 1988. One of these remains in Algeria and is probably used as battery charging and pierside training hulk.

FRIGATES [FF]

Note: During 2006 unconfirmed reports indicated that Algeria may have purchased a 120-m frigate from China for use as a naval flagship. If correct, the frigate may be delivered in 2007–8.

FRIGATES [FF] *(continued)*

♦ **3 Soviet Koni class (Project 1159)**
Bldr: Krasniy Metallist Zavod, Zelenodol'sk

	Laid down	L	In serv.
901 Mourad Raïs (ex-SKR-482)	10-6-78	22-1-79	20-12-80
902 Raïs Kellich (ex-SKR-35)	11-6-80	30-4-81	24-3-82
903 Raïs Korfo	19-1-83	11-11-83	8-1-85

Mourad Raïs (901) Bernard Prézelin, 8-04

Raïs Korfo (903) Guy Shaeffer via Paolo Marsan, 8-04

D: 1,593 tons normal (1,670 fl) **S:** 27 kts (29.67 trials; 22 on diesels)
Dim: 95.51 × 12.55 × 4.12 (5.72 over sonar)
A: 1 Osa-M (SA-N-4) SAM syst. (20 9M-33/Gecko missiles); 2 twin 76.2-mm 59-cal. AK-276 DP; 2 twin 30-mm 65-cal. AK-230 AA; 2 12-round RBU-6000 ASW RL (120 RGB-60 rockets); 2 mine rails (up to 14 mines)—903 only: 2 twin 533-mm TT—901 and 902 only: 2 d.c. racks (12 BB-1 d.c. tot.)
Electronics:
Radar: 1 Don-2 nav.; 1 MR-302 Rubka (Strut Curve) (903: Pozitiv-ME1.2) air/surf. search; 1 MPZ-301 (Pop Group) missile f.c.—901, 902 only: 1 MR-105 Turel' (Hawk Screech) 76.2-mm gun f.c.; 1 (903: 2) MR-104 Rys (Drum Tilt) gun f.c.
Sonar: Titan/Vychegda suite (hull-mounted MF and HF f.c.)
EW: 901, 902: 2 Bizan-4B (Watch Dog-B) intercept (2-18 GHz); 1 Cross Loop-A D/F; 2 16-round RK-16 decoy RL—903: . . . intercept/jamming array; 4 6-round decoy RL syst. (VI × 4)
M: CODAG: 1 M-813 gas turbine (18,000 shp), 2 Type 68-B, 8,000-bhp diesels, 3 props; 35,000 hp
Range: 4,456/14.98 **Crew:** 130 tot.

Remarks: In-service dates reflect delivery dates. Were the 5th, 7th, and 10th units of the class built. All were overhauled in 1992–94 and given new generators. 903 was sent to Kronshtadt, Russia, for modernization overhaul in 5-97, and was to have been concluded in 8-98 but was not completed until 11-00.
Combat systems: Depth charge racks bolt to mine rails. During the ongoing modernizations, a Pozitiv-ME1.2 single-face, rotating planar array air-search radar is replacing the MR-302, a second MR-104 gun fire-control radar is replacing the MR-105 atop the bridge, and a new EW system (possibly of Chinese origin) is being installed. The modified ships are receiving longer-ranged Splav 90R ASW rockets for the RBU-6000 launchers.

GUIDED-MISSILE PATROL COMBATANTS [PGG]

♦ **3 C-58 design** Bldr: ONCN/CNE, Mers-el-Kébir

	L	In serv.
351 Djebel Chenoua	3-2-85	11-88
352 El Chihab	2-90	6-95
353 El Kirch		2005

El Kirch (353) Ralph Edwards, 7-05

El Chihab (352)—Note two paired C-802 antiship missile launchers at stern
Bernard Prézelin, 7-05

D: 496 tons (540 fl) **S:** 35 kts (31 sust.) **Dim:** 58.40 (54.00 pp) × 8.40 × . . .
A: 4 C-802 SSM; 1 76.2-mm 59-cal. AK-176 DP; 1 30-mm 54-cal. AK-306 AA
Electronics:
Radar: 1 Decca 1226 nav.; 1 . . . surf./air-search; 1 Type . . . gun f.c.
EW: . . . intercept; 2 Type . . . 6-round decoy RL
M: 3 MTU 20V538 TB92 diesels; 3 props; 14,990 bhp
Range: . . . / . . . **Crew:** 6 officers, 46 enlisted

Remarks: First two were ordered 7-83. Reportedly of Algerian design and construction. Difficulties in fitting out the prototype forced suspension of work on the other pair prior to launch. Post-2000, have been rearmed and given new electronics. *El Kirch* (translated as Shark) appears to have entered service early in 2005.
Combat systems: Were originally to have mounted an OTO Melara 76-mm Compact forward and a twin OTO Melara 40-mm AA mount aft, with an optronic director for the 76-mm gun and an optical director for the twin 40-mm. The radar, EW gear, and fire-control equipment are of Chinese origin. The antiship missile launchers are paired, facing forward, at the extreme stern. 351 has two additional decoy or grenade launchers on the 01 level, just abaft the mainmast.

♦ **3 Soviet Nanuchka-II class (Project 1234E)**
Bldr: Sudostroitel'noye Obyedineniye "Almaz," Petrovskiy SY, St. Petersburg

801 Raïs Hamidou (ex-*Zyb*)
802 Salah Raïs (ex-*Liven*)
803 Raïs Ali (ex-*Burun*)

Salah Raïs (802)—returning from modernization L. V. Pappens, 11-00

D: 560 tons (675 fl) **S:** 30 kts **Dim:** 59.3 × 12.6 × 2.4
A: 2 twin P-20 (SS-N-2C Styx) SSM (802: 4 quadruple launchers for Kh-35 Uran/SS-N-25 Switchblade SSM); 1 twin Osa-M (SA-N-4) SAM syst. (20 9M-33/Gecko missiles); 1 twin 57-mm 70-cal. AK-725 DP—802 only: 1 30-mm 54-cal. AK-306 gatling AA
Electronics:
Radar: 801, 803: 1 Mius nav.; 1 Rangout (Square Tie) surf. search/missile target desig., 1 MPZ-301 (Pop Group) SA-N-4 f.c.; 1 MR-103 (Muff Cob) gun f.c.—802: 1 DON-2 . . . nav.; 1 Pozitiv-ME1.2 surf./air search; 1 Garpun-E (Plank Shave) surf. search/missile target desig.; 1 MR-104 Rys' (Drum Tilt) gun f.c.
EW: 801, 803: 1 Bell Tap intercept; 1 Cross Loop MFD/F; 2 16-round RK-16 decoy RL—802: . . . intercept/jamming; 4 6-round decoy RL
M: 3 M517 diesels; 3 props; 30,000 bhp
Electric: 750 kw tot. (2 × 300-kw, 2 × 75-kw diesel sets)
Range: 900/30; 2,500/12 **Crew:** 10 officers, 50 enlisted

Remarks: 801 arrived in Algeria 4-7-80, 802 in 2-81, 803 in 5-82. They bore the listed ex-Russian names during construction phase. 802 was delivered to Kronshtadt in 5-97 for a modernization that was to have been concluded in 8-98 but was not completed until 11-00.

GUIDED-MISSILE PATROL COMBATANTS [PGG] *(continued)*

Combat systems: On 801 and 803, the Rangout surface target tracking radar antenna is mounted within the Band Stand radome atop the bridge. The SA-N-4 SAM system employs a ZIF-122 retractable launcher for the Gecko missiles. The AK-725 mount uses a ZIF-72 automatic, unmanned mounting. During the current modernizations, Kh-35-Uran antiship missiles are replacing P-20 missiles, the EW suite is being replaced by a suite possibly of Chinese origin, the MR-104 f.c. radar is replacing the original MR-103, and an AK-306 lightweight gatling AA gunmount is being added aft.

GUIDED-MISSILE PATROL CRAFT [PTG]

♦ 9 Soviet Osa-II class

644 645 646 647 648 649 650 651 652

Osa-II 650 French Navy, 1988

D: 184 tons (226 fl; 245 with emergency fuel) **S:** 40 kts **Dim:** 38.6 × 7.6 × 1.9
A: 4 single SS-N-2B Styx SSM launchers; 2 twin 30-mm 65-cal. AK-230 AA
Electronics: Radar: 1 Rangout (Square Tie) surf. search/missile target desig.; 1 MR-104 Rys' (Drum Tilt) gun f.c.
M: 3 M504B diesels; 3 props; 15,000 bhp **Electric:** 200 kw
Range: 500/34; 750/25 **Fuel:** 40 tons (normal)
Endurance: 5 days **Crew:** 28 tot.

Remarks: Transferred 1976–78, except for one in 12-80. A shortage of parts for the M-504 diesels, which require frequent overhauls, has kept them from being fully effective.

Disposal note: All Soviet Osa-I class (Project 205E) missile craft have been retired.

PATROL CRAFT [PC]

Note: There are plans to acquire six 40-m patrol craft powered by MTU diesels; two would be built abroad and the others in Algeria with foreign assistance. A reported contract for licensed construction of up to 25 Russian Mirazh-class (Project 1431.2) high-speed patrol craft may have been under discussion in 1998, but the project now appears dormant.

♦ 12 Brooke Marine 37.5-meter patrol boats

Bldr: 341–343: Brooke Marine, Lowestoft; others: ONCN/CNE, Mers el-Kébir

	In serv.		In serv.
341 El Yadekh	12-82	347 El Saher	1993
342 El Morakeb	12-6-83	348 El Moukadem	1993
343 El Kechef	5-84	349 El . . .	1993
344 El Moutarid	1985	356 El Kanass	. . .
345 El Rassed	10-11-85	357 El Mayher	2004–5
346 El Djari	10-11-86	358	2005

El Morakeb (342) Skyfotos, 1983

D: 166 tons (250 fl) **S:** 27 kts **Dim:** 37.50 (34.74 pp) × 6.86 × 1.78
A: 341, 342: 1 76-mm 62-cal. OTO Melara DP; 2 twin 14.5-mm 93-cal. 2M-7 mg—343–349: 2 twin 14.5-mm 93-cal. Type 81 AA
Electronics: Radar: 1 Decca 1226 nav.
M: 2 MTU 12V538 TB92 diesels; 2 props; 6,000 bhp
Range: 2,500/15 **Crew:** 3 officers, 24 enlisted

Remarks: Also known as the "Kebir" class. 347–349 ordered 1984; three more were sighted for the first time during 2004–5. Based at Algiers, Annaba, Oran, Ghazaouet, and Djidjeli. These craft have been reported as under Coast Guard subordination from time to time but appear to be naval manned. 341 and 342 were refitted by Vosper Thornycroft in the U.K. during 1990–91.
Combat systems: The 76-mm gun on the first two is controlled by a lead-computing optical director.

AMPHIBIOUS WARFARE SHIPS

♦ 2 tank landing ships [LST]

	Bldr	L	In serv.
472 Kalaat beni Hammed	Brooke Marine, Lowestoft	18-4-84	4-84
473 Kalaat beni Rached	Vosper Thornycroft, Woolston	15-5-84	10-84

Kalaat beni Rached (473) Bernard Prézelin, 7-05

D: 2,130 tons (fl) **S:** 16 kts **Dim:** 93.0 (80.00 pp) × 15.0 × 2.5
A: 1 twin 40-mm 70-cal. OTO Melara AA; 2 twin 25-mm 80-cal. 2M-3M AA
Electronics:
Radar: 1 Decca TM 1226 nav.; 1 Marconi S800 gun f.c.
EW: Racal Cutlass intercept; Racal Cygnus jammer; 2 Wallop Barricade decoy RL
M: 2 MTU 12V1163 TB92 diesels; 2 props; 6,000 bhp
Range: 3,000/12 **Endurance:** 28 days (10 with troops)
Crew: 81 tot. + 240 troops

Remarks: 472 was ordered 10-81; 473 was subcontracted to Vosper Thornycroft 18-10-82 and laid down on 20-12-82.
Hull systems: The vehicle deck is 75 m long by 7.4 m wide and is served by a 30-m by 7-m hatch. The bow ramp extends to 18 m and is 4–5 m wide, while the stern ramp measures 5 m by 4 m. The traveling crane has a 16-ton capacity. Minimum beaching gradient is 1:40. Can carry 650 tons of cargo, but beaching limit is 450. Helicopter deck aft. Pontoon sections can be stowed on deck forward.
Combat systems: A Matra Défense Naja optronic director fitted for the twin 40-mm mount.

♦ 1 Soviet Polnocny-B-class (Project 771) medium landing ship [LSM]

Bldr: Stocznia Polnocna, Gdansk, Poland (transferred 9-76)

471

Polnocny-B-class 471 1982

D: 558 tons light, 640 tons std. (884 fl) **S:** 18 kts
Dim: 75.00 (70.00 wl) × 9.00 (8.60 wl) × 1.20 fwd/2.40 aft (2.07 mean)
A: 1 or 2 twin 30-mm 65-cal. AK-230 AA; 2 18-round 140-mm WM-18 barrage RL (180 rockets)
Electronics: Radar: 1 Mius (Spin Trough) nav., 1 MR-104 Rys' (Drum Tilt) f.c.
M: 2 Type 40DM diesels; 2 props; 4,400 bhp **Range:** 700/18; 2,000/16
Crew: 5 officers, 32 enlisted + 60–180 troops

Remarks: Transferred newly built 9-76
Hull systems: Has a bow door only. The hull has a "beak" projecting forward below the waterline at the bow to aid in beaching. Cargo: 237 tons max., including six tanks or 180 troops and their equipment; 30 vehicle crew are carried with tank loadout. Vehicle deck is 44.3 m long by 5.3 m wide and 3.6 m high; hatches to upper deck are for loading and ventilation only, as the upper deck cannot support much weight.

AUXILIARIES

Note: There are plans to acquire a 3,000- to 4,000-ton training ship for naval and merchant marine use; in addition to a crew of 85, it would carry up to 120 cadets.

♦ **1 250-grt survey ship [AGS]**
Bldr: Matsukara Zosen, Hirao, Japan (L: 17-4-80)

A 673 El Idrissi

Remarks: Reportedly of 540 tons (fl), with a crew of six officers and 22 enlisted. Resembles a smaller edition of salvage ship 261, even to including an A-frame gantry at the stern (for oceanographic sampling gear) and carries two small survey launches in davits aft.

♦ **1 Chinese-built salvage ship [ARS]**

261 El Mourafik

D: approx. 600 tons (fl) **S:** . . . kts **Dim:** 59.0 × 8.4 × 2.1
A: 2 single 12.7-mm mg **Electronics:** Radar: 1 . . . nav.
M: 2 Type 9 D-8 diesels; 2 props; 2,200 bhp **Crew:** 60 tot.

Remarks: Was in Algeria by 9-90. Has a firefighting monitor on the mast platform. An A-frame gantry at stern may also be used to handle small mooring and navigational buoys, and the ship can carry containerized cargo on the main deck, aft.

SERVICE CRAFT

♦ **1 ex-Soviet Poluchat-1-class (Project 368T) torpedo retriever [YDT]** Bldr: Sosnovka Zavod

A 641

D: 84.7 tons (92.8 fl) **S:** 21.6 kts **Dim:** 29.60 × 6.10 (5.80 wl) × 1.56 (1.90 props)
Electronics: Radar: 1 Don-2 or Mius (Spin Trough) nav.
M: 2 M-50F-4 diesels; 2 props; 2,400 bhp **Range:** 250/21.6; 550/14
Crew: 1 officer, 2 warrant officers, 12 enlisted

Remarks: Transferred during early 1970s. Has Gira-KM gyrocompass and NEL-3 echo-sounder. The hull has seven watertight bulkheads. There is a stern torpedo recovery ramp.

Disposal note: Nyryat-1-class diving tender *Yaudezan* (VP 650) was no longer in service as of 2005.

♦ **1 coastal tug [YTB]** (In serv. 1989)

A 210 Kader

Dim: 29.6 × 6.6 × 2.8 **S:** 11
M: 2 ... diesels

Remarks: No additional data available. Also in service is tug *El Chadid* (A 211) and tugs *Mazafran* 1, 2, 3 and 4 (numbered Y 206 through Y 209)

♦ **1 floating dry dock [YFD]** Bldr: M.A.N., Germany (In serv. 1991)

Bejaia

COAST GUARD

PATROL CRAFT [WPC]

♦ **7 Chui-E class**

GC 251 El Mouderrib-I through GC 257 El Mouderrib-VII

El Mouderrib-I (GC 251) H&L Van Ginderen, 9-90

D: 363 tons (388 fl) **S:** 30.5 kts **Dim:** 58.77 × 7.20 × 2.20 (hull)
A: 1 twin 14.5-mm 93-cal. Type 81 AA
Electronics: Radar: 1 Type 756 nav. Sonar: Tamir 111
M: 3 Type 12VE 23015/2 diesels; 3 props; 6,600 bhp
Range: 2,000/14 **Crew:** 11 officers, 21 enlisted, 25 midshipmen

Remarks: Also known as the Huludao class. First three arrived in 3-90, two in 1-91, and final two in 7-91. Simplified version of Chinese Hainan-class antisubmarine patrol craft with enlarged superstructure and boats stowed on fantail. Have also been employed as midshipman training craft for the navy. An additional twin 14.5-mm mg mount can be mounted on a ring on the fantail. During midshipman cruises they have carried a single 14.5-mm mg atop the after portion of the deckhouse.

PATROL BOATS [WPB]

♦ **4 Chinese-built GC 231-class search-and-rescue craft** (In serv. 1990–91)

GC 231 El Mounkid I
GC 232 El Mounkid II
GC 233 El Mounkid III
GC 234 El Mounkid IV

Remarks: First three transferred 4-90, GC 234 in 1991. Given names in 1995. Resemble small tugs, but do not have towing equipment. Are about 25 m overall and probably can make about 12 kts maximum.

♦ **4 Type 20-GC class** Bldr: Baglietto, Italy (In serv. 8-76 to 12-76)

GC 325 El Hamil
GC 326 El Assad
GC 327 Markhad
GC 328 Etair

D: 44 tons (fl) **S:** 36 kts **Dim:** 20.4 × 5.2 × 1.7
A: 1 20-mm 90-cal. Oerlikon AA
M: 2 CRM 18DS diesels; 2 props; 2,700 bhp **Range:** 445/20 **Crew:** 11 tot.

Remarks: Given names in 1995. Six sisters have been discarded, and the status of the four possible survivors is unknown.

Note: The Algerian Customs Service possesses three 38.5-ton, P 1200-class patrol craft (*Bouzagza, Djurdjura,* and *Hodna*) and two 8-m, British-built P 802-class launches (*Aures* and *Hoggar*) delivered from the U.K. in 11-85; and up to a dozen 18-ton, 10-m *Djebel Antar*–class launches completed at Mers el-Kébir during 1982–83.

ANGOLA

People's Republic of Angola

MARINHA DI GUERRA

Personnel: About 2,400 tot.

Bases: Headquarters at Luanda, with smaller bases at Cabinda, Lobito, Namibe, and Soro

Naval Aviation: One Fokker F-27-200 Maritime and two EMB 111 Bandeirante maritime patrol aircraft. A Boeing 707 is on order from Israel, to be fitted out for surveillance missions.

Note: Portugal agreed in 11-00 to provide assistance with new patrol boats and spare engines and parts for existing craft; no details of the planned craft have been announced.

PATROL CRAFT [PC]

♦ **4 Mandume class** Bldr: E. N. Bazán, San Fernando, Spain

	L	In serv.		L	In. serv.
P 100 Mandume	11-9-92	28-1-93	P 104 Atlantico	2-93	4-93
P 102 Polar	11-9-92	28-1-93	P 106 Golfinho	2-93	4-93

D: 104.5 tons (fl) **S:** 27.5 kts (25 sust.) **Dim:** 29.13 (26.50 pp) × 5.93 × 1.44
A: 1 20-mm 90-cal. Oerlikon GAM-B01 AA; 2 single 12.7-mm mg
Electronics: Radar: 1 Decca . . . nav.
M: 2 Paxman Vega 12-SETCWN diesels; 2 props; 3,560 bhp
Electric: 140 kw tot. **Range:** 800/15 **Crew:** 1 officer, 10 enlisted

Remarks: Ordered 12-90 for fisheries patrol duties. First unit laid down 18-12-91. Steel hull, aluminum superstructure. Seven watertight compartments. Have hydraulic drive to permit low-speed operations, as well as Loran-C, Transit, and GPS receivers.

Polar (P 102) Izar (E. N. Bazán), 1-93

PATROL BOATS [PB]

♦ **3 Patrulheiro class** Bldr: C. N. Couach, Arcachon, France (In serv. 1993)

Patrulheiro Preservador Temerario

D: . . . tons (fl) **S:** 25 kts **Dim:** 19.30 × 5.55 × . . .
A: small arms **Electronics:** Radar: 1 Furuno 1830-24MN nav.
M: 2 Baudouin V12BTI diesels; 2 props; 1,680 bhp
Range: 1,000/18 **Crew:** . . . tot.

PATROL BOATS [PB] *(continued)*

Remarks: Intended for fisheries protection duties and operated for the Ministry of Fisheries. Composite GRP hull construction. Do not have pennant numbers.

Patrulheiro C. N. Couach, 1993

ANGUILLA

MARINE POLICE

Personnel: About 32 tot.

PATROL BOATS [WPB]

♦ **1 M160 class** Bldr: Halmatic, U.K. (In serv. 30-12-89)

DOLPHIN

D: 17.3 tons (fl) **S:** 27+ kts **Dim:** 15.40 (12.20 pp) × 3.86 × 1.15
A: 1 7.62-mm mg **Electronics:** Radar: 1 Decca 370BT nav.
M: 2 G.M. 6V92 TA diesels; 2 props; 1,100 bhp (770 sust.)
Range: 300/20 **Fuel:** 2,700 liters **Crew:** 6 tot.

Remarks: Provided by U.K. government. Has davits aft for inflatable inspection boat.

♦ **1 U.S. Boston Whaler 27-foot class**
Bldr: Boston Whaler, Rockland, Mass. (In serv. 1990)

LAPWING

D: 2.2 tons (fl) **S:** 32 kts **Dim:** 8.5 × 3.0 × 0.5
M: 2 Evinrude gasoline outboards; 450 bhp **Crew:** 2 tot.

Remarks: Employed for fisheries protection, police, and search-and-rescue duties. GRP construction; has pilothouse and can tow small boats. Not fitted with radar.

ANTIGUA-BARBUDA

COAST GUARD

ANTIGUA-BARBUDA DEFENCE FORCE

Personnel: 45 tot.

Base: Deepwater Harbor, St. John's

PATROL BOATS [WPB]

♦ **1 U.S. Dauntless class** Bldr: SeaArk, Monticello, Ark. (In serv. 1995)

P-02 PALMETTO

D: 12 tons (15 fl) **S:** 28 kts **Dim:** 12.19 (11.13 wl) × 3.86 × 0.69 (hull)
A: 2 single 12.7-mm mg; 2 single 7.62-mm mg
Electronics: Radar: 1 Raytheon R40X nav.
M: 2 Caterpillar 3208TA diesels; 2 props; 850 bhp (720 sust.)
Range: 200/30; 400/22 **Fuel:** 250 gal. **Crew:** 5 tot.

Remarks: Ordered 4-94. Aluminum construction. C. Raymond Hunt, "Deep-Vee" hull design.

♦ **1 U.S. 65-foot Commercial Cruiser class**
Bldr: Swiftships, Inc., Morgan City, La. (In serv. 30-4-84)

P-01 LIBERTA

D: 31.7 tons (36 fl) **S:** 22 kts **Dim:** 19.96 × 5.59 × 1.52
A: 1 12.7-mm M2 mg; 2 single 7.62-mm mg
Electronics: Radar: 1 Raytheon 1210 nav.
M: 2 G.M. Detroit Diesel 12V71 TI diesels; 2 props; 1,350 bhp (840 sust.)
Electric: 20 kw **Range:** 500/18 **Crew:** 9 tot.

Remarks: Aluminum construction. U.S. Grant-Aid donation; U.S. Coast Guard–trained.

Liberta (P 01) PH2 Pixier, USN, 1987

♦ **1 ex-U.S. Coast Guard 82-foot Point class**
Bldr: J. Martinac SB, Tacoma, Wash. (In serv. 26-4-67)

P-03 HERMITAGE (ex-*Point Steele,* WPB 82359)

D: 66 tons (fl) **S:** 23 kts **Dim:** 25.3 × 5.23 × 1.95
A: 2 single 12.7-mm M2 mg
Electronics: Radar: 1 Raytheon SPS-64(V)1 nav.
M: 2 Caterpillar 3412 diesels; 2 props; 1,480 bhp
Range: 490/23.7; 1,500/8 **Fuel:** 5.7 tons **Crew:** 1 officer, 7 enlisted

Remarks: Deactivated by U.S. Coast Guard on 9-7-98 and transferred 9-7-98 as a grant; recommissioned 4-9-98.
Hull systems: Hull built of mild steel. High-speed diesels controlled from the bridge. Well equipped for salvage and towing. Re-engined during the early 1990s.

SERVICE CRAFT

♦ **2 Boston Whaler 27-foot-class launches [WYFL]**
Bldr: Boston Whaler, Rockland, Mass. (In serv. 1988)

071 072

D: 2.2 tons (fl) **S:** 30 kts **Dim:** 8.2 × 3.0 × 0.5
A: small arms **M:** 2 Evinrude gasoline outboards: 400 bhp **Crew:** 2 tot.

Remarks: U.S. Grant-Aid. Foam-core, GRP hull construction.

Note: Also in service is an 8.23-m Hurricane RIB acquired in 1998.

ARGENTINA

Argentine Republic

ARMADA REPÚBLICA

Personnel: Approximately 17,500 (2,300 officers) plus 7,000 civilians and 2,500 in the Marine Corps.

Organization: The administrative head of the Armada is the Jefatura del Estado Mayor de la Armada, under whom are the Subjefatura del Estado Mayor de la Armada and the Secretaria General Naval. To the former is subordinated the Dirección de Inteligencia Naval, Dirección de Bienestar Naval, Dirección de Instrucción Naval, Dirreción de Material Naval, Servicio de Hidrografia Naval, Servicio de Communicaciones, Comando de Transito Maritimo, Servicio de Salvamento y Medio Ambiente, Servicio de Transportes Navals, and Comando de Operaciones Navales. Under the Comando de Operaciones Navales come the Comando de la Flota de Mar (with the 2º Division de Destructores, Division de Patrullado Marítimo, 2ª Division de Corbetas, Comando Naval Anfibio, and Base Naval Puerto Belgrano), the Comando de la Aviación Naval (for subordinate organizations, see the Naval Aviation section below), and

ARMADA REPÚBLICA *(continued)*

Comando de la Infatería de Marina (for subordinate organizations, see the Marines section below). Also subordinate to the Comando de Operaciones Navales are the Area Naval Atlantica (with the Division de Submarinos and Base Naval Mar del Plata), Area Naval Fluvial (with Base Naval Zárate), Fuerza Antartica Naval, Agrupación Lanchas Rapidas, and Base Naval Ushuaia.

Bases: Located at Zárate (Area Naval Fluvial), Mar del Plata, Puerto Belgrano, Caleta Paula, Ushuaia (*Almirante Berisso*), and Orcadas. The Naval Academy and training facilities are at Río Santiago, La Plata; submarine base at Mar del Plata; main naval base and dockyard facilities at Puerto Belgrano; and Riverine Flotilla base at Zárate. Domecq garcia submarine shipyard is in the process of being reactivated to assist with submarine overhaul operations and for possible assembly of a third TR-1700 submarine. A small patrol boat base was established in 1997 at Caleta Paula, Santa Cruz province. The Argentine Navy Engineering School was moved to Puerto Belgrano in 1998. Aviation bases are at Ezeiza (Buenos Aires), Puerto Belgrano (*Comandante Espora*), Trelew (*Almirante Zar*), Río Grande (*Almirante Hermes Quijada*), Punta Indio, and Ushuaia.

Naval Aviation: Fixed-wing aircraft include 11 Super Étendard fighter-bombers (most in storage), 5 S-2UP Turbo Tracker ASW aircraft (with 3 S-2G in storage), 8 MB-326GB attack/trainers, 1 Fokker F-28-3000M and 2 Fokker F-28-3132C transports, 6 P-3B Orion maritime patrol aircraft, 7 Beech Super King Air B200T reconnaissance/training/light transports, 1 Pilatus PC-6B/H2 Turbo Porter light transport, 10 Beech T-34C-1 trainers, and 1 Stearman PT-17 glider tug. Helicopters include 2 Agusta-Sikorsky ASH-3D (S-61) Sea King and 4 SH-3D (S-61D-4) Sea King ASW (with at least one equipped during 2000 to launch AM-39 Exocet missiles), 7 Bell UH-1H transports, 3 Aerospitale Alouette III, and 4 AS.355MN Fennec reconnaissance and missile targeting.

UH-1H helicopter—Attached to the 3rd Helicopter Squadron
Ignacio Almendolara, 5-04

Argentine Navy Beech Super King Air B200T Julio Montes, 2005

The S-2UP Tracker configuration from S-2G aircraft has Garrett TPE-331-15 AW turbines in place of the original reciprocating engines and other improvements to extend service life an additional 20 years.

Argentina also hopes to acquire 6–8 ex-USN SH-3-series Sea King helicopters.

Naval aviation assets are organized under the Comando de la Aviación Naval into Fuerza Aeronaval 6 (with the Escuadrilla de Transporte, Escuadrilla de Exploración, and Base Aeronaval *Almirante Zar*), Fuerza Aeronaval 2 (with the 2ª Escuadrilla de Caza y Ataque, 1ª and 2ª Escuadrilla de Helicopteros, Escuadrilla Antisubmarina, and Base Aeronaval *Comandante Espora* subordinated), and the Escuadra de Instrucción Aeronaval (with the Escuela de Aviación Naval, 1ª Escuadrilla de Caza y Ataque, and base Aeronaval Punta Indio subordinated). There are also small airfields at Río Grande and Ushuaia and a Central Maintenance Unit at Bahía Blanca.

Marines: The Fuerza de Apoyo de Infantería is composed of Batallón 1 and 2, Batallón Vehículos Anfibios, the Compañía de Communicaciones, and the Batallón de Artillería, and the Fuerza Nº 1 (with Batallóns 4 [reserve] and 5). Major bases are located at Río Gallegos and Baterias. The amphibious warfare support group is located at Puerto Belgrano. Batallón 3 is located in Zárate Naval base, specializing in riverine operations with 4 Boston Whaler Guardian 22-foot craft and several smaller boats. Small security detachments are maintained at Buenos Aires, Río Santiago, Punta Indio, Azul, Mar del Plata, *Comandante Espora* naval base, Zárate, Ezeiza, Trelew, Ushuaia, and Río Grande.

Note: Ship names are prefaced by A.R.A. (*Armada República Argentina*).

ATTACK SUBMARINES [SS]

♦ 2 TR-1700 class Bldr: Thyssen Nordseewerke, Emden

	Laid down	L	In serv.
S 41 SANTA CRUZ	6-12-80	28-9-82	14-12-84
S 42 SAN JUAN	18-3-82	20-6-83	18-11-85

Santa Cruz (S 41) Ignacio Amendolara, 7-04

D: 1,770 tons std., 2,150 tons surf./2,356 tons sub.
S: 15 kts surf./13 kts snorkel/25 kts max. sub. **Dim:** 65.50 × 7.30 × 6.50
A: 6 bow 533-mm TT (22 SST-4 Mod. 1 wire-guided torpedoes and/or mines)
Electronics:
Radar: 1 SMA MM/BPS-704 surf. search/nav.
Sonar: STN Atlas Elektronik CSU-83 suite with Thales DUUX-5 passive array
EW: Sea Sentry III intercept/radar warning
M: diesel-electric: 4/MTU 16V652 MB80 (1,680 bhp each), 4 alternator sets (1.1 Mw each); 1 6,600-kw motor; 1 prop; 8,970 shp (8,000 sust.)
Range: 14,000/8, 17,000/5 surf.; 20/25, 50/20, 110/15, 460/6 sub.
Fuel: 319 tons **Endurance:** 70 days
Crew: 8 officers, 21 enlisted + 12 spare or 30 commandos

Remarks: Ordered 30-11-77. Originally only the first unit was to have been built in Germany. Are the largest submarines built in Germany since World War I. Three sisters (of a planned four) were laid down at Argentina's Astilleros Domecq Garcia, but all work had ceased by the late 1980s: *Santa Fé* (S 43) was laid down 4-10-83 and *Santiago del Estero* (S 44) on 5-8-85, while some work was accomplished on the third unit. The remaining components were cannibalized for spares. Both have recently completed refits, S 42 at Puerto Belgrano and S 41 at Rio de Janeiro from 1-10-99 to 20-2-01.
Hull systems: Displacements also given as 2,116 tons surf./2,264 sub. Pressure hull 48.0 m long and 7.0 m in diameter. The Varta-made battery set has eight groups of 120 cells, 5,858-amp/10-hr, and weighs 500 tons. Range also given as 15,000/5 snorkel; 300/10, 70/20 sub. Have the ability to accept a U.S. Deep Sea Rescue Vehicle submersible and have a divers' lockout capability. Engineering equipment is mounted in double resilient mountings. Hull has 10% reserve buoyancy in surfaced condition. Maximum operating depth is 300 m.
Combat systems: Have Thales SINBADS (Submarine Integrated Battle and Data System) weapons control system and SAGEM plotting table. Torpedoes can be auto-reloaded in 50 seconds; swim-out launching is employed. Are equipped with an inertial navigation system, have Kollmorgen Model 76 search and attack periscopes.

♦ 1 German Type 209/1200 class

	Bldr	Laid down	L	In serv.
S 31 SALTA	Howaldtswerke, Kiel	3-4-70	9-11-72	7-3-74

Salta (S 31)—following 2005 modernization Alejandro Amendolara, 10-05

D: 1,000 tons std., 1,140 tons surf./1,248 sub.
S: 11.5 surf./12 kts snorkel/22 kts max. sub. **Dim:** 55.9 × 6.30 × 5.50
A: 8 bow 533-mm TT (14 SST-4 Mod. 1 wire-guided torpedoes)

ATTACK SUBMARINES [SS] *(continued)*

Electronics:
Radar: 1 Thales Calypso nav.
Sonar: STN Atlas Elektronik CSU-3 suite (including AN 526 active, AN 5039 passive, and AN 5041 active attack); Thales DUUX-2CN passive ranging array; Thales DUUG-1D acoustic intercept
EW: Thales DR-2000U intercept
M: 4 MTU 12V493 TY60, 600-bhp diesels, 4 425-kw generators, Siemens electric motor; 1 prop; 4,500 shp
Range: 6,000/8 snorkel; 230/8; 400/4 sub. **Fuel:** 63 tons **Endurance:** 40 days
Crew: 5 officers, 26 enlisted

Remarks: Built in four sections at Kiel and assembled at the Tandanor Shipyard, Buenos Aires. *Salta* was reported to be for sale in 1986 but entered Domecq Garcia SY 1988 for new engines and a new electronics suite; the submarine was relaunched during 10-94 and recommissioned in 3-95. Sister *San Luís* (S 32) was stricken in 1997. During 9-05, as part of a mid-life upgrade, S 31 underwent a general maintenance overhaul and received a new battery.
Hull systems: Has four 120-cell, 11,500 amp-hr, Varta batteries totaling 257 tons.
Combat systems: Fitted with the Thales M8 fire-control system.

DESTROYERS [DD]

♦ 4 MEKO 360 H2 class   Bldr: Blohm + Voss, Hamburg

	Laid down	L	In serv.
D 10 Almirante Brown	8-9-80	28-3-81	2-2-83
D 11 La Argentina	31-3-81	25-9-81	19-7-83
D 12 Heroína	24-8-81	17-2-82	7-11-83
D 13 Sarandi	9-3-82	31-8-82	27-4-84

Sarandi (D 13) U.S. Navy, 10-95

D: 2,900 tons (3,360 fl) **S:** 30.5 kts
Dim: 125.90 (119.00 pp) × 15.00 × 4.32 (5.80 sonar)
A: 8 MM 40 Exocet SSM; 1 8-cell Albatros SAM syst. (24 Aspide missiles); 1 127-mm 54-cal. OTO Melara DP; 4 twin 40-mm 70-cal. OTO Melara AA; 2 triple 324-mm ILAS-3 ASW TT (18 WASS A-244S torpedoes); 1 d.c. rack (9 d.c.); 1 AS.355MN Fennec or SH-3D Sea King helicopter
Electronics:
Radar: 1 Decca 1226 nav.; 1/Thales ZW-06 surf. search; 1 Thales DA-08A air/surf. search; 1 Thales WM-25 track-while-scan f.c.; 1 Thales STIR f.c.; 2 Thales LIROD f.c.
Sonar: STN Atlas Elektronik KAE 80, hull-mounted MF
EW: Racal Rapids intercept, Racal Scimitar jammer, 2 20-round OTO Melara SCLAR decoy RL; G1738 towed torpedo decoy
M: COGOG: 2 Rolls-Royce Olympus TM-3B gas turbines (25,800 shp each); 2 Rolls Royce Tyne RM-1C gas turbines (5,100 shp each) for cruise; 2 Escher-Wyss CP props; 51,600 shp max.
Electric: 2,600 kw (2 × 940-kw and 2 × 360-kw diesel sets)
Range: 4,500/18 **Crew:** 26 officers, 84 petty officers, 90 other enlisted

Remarks: Considered to be destroyers by Argentine Navy. Ordered 11-12-78 as a class of six; four were to be built in Argentina, but altered to four total when the MEKO 140-series frigate program was introduced. Similar to Nigeria's *Aradu*. D 13 is fleet flagship.
Combat systems: Have Thales SEWACO weapons data/control system. The Albatros SAM system has a 16-missile Aspide SAM rapid-reload magazine nearby. The two LIROD radar/optronic directors each control two 40-mm mounts. A total of 10,752 rds of ammunition can be carried. The sonar is a commercial version of the DSQS-21BZ. Can carry up to 10 ASW torpedoes for the helicopter, which is equipped to provide over-the-horizon targeting for the Exocet missiles.

FRIGATES [FF]

♦ 6 MEKO 140 A16 class   Bldr: AFNE, Río Santiago, Ensenada

	Laid down	L	In serv.
P 41 Espora	10-3-80	23-1-82	5-7-85
P 42 Rosales	7-1-81	4-3-83	14-11-86
P 43 Spiro	1-4-82	24-6-83	24-11-87
P 44 Parker	9-2-82	31-3-84	17-4-90
P 45 Robinson	6-6-83	15-2-85	28-8-00
P 46 Gomez Roca (ex-*Seaver*)	1-12-83	14-11-86	17-5-04

Spiro (P 43) Ignacio Amendolara, 6-05

D: 1,560 tons (1,790 fl) **S:** 27 kts **Dim:** 91.2 (86.4 pp) × 11.0 × 3.33 (hull)
A: 4 MM 38 Exocet SSM; 1 76-mm 62-cal. OTO Melara DP; 2 twin 40-mm 70-cal. OTO Melara AA; 2 single 12.7-mm mg; 2 triple 324-mm ILAS-3 ASW TT (WASS A-244S torpedoes); 1 AS.355MN Fennec helicopter
Electronics:
Radar: 1 Decca TM 1226 nav. (P 45 and 46 only: 1 Consilium Selesmar NavBat nav); 1 Thales DA-05/2 surf./air search; 1 Thales WM-28 track-while-scan f.c., 1 Thales LIROD f.c.
Sonar: 1 STN Atlas Elektronik AQS-1 hull-mounted MF
EW: Decca RDC-2ABC intercept; Decca RCM-2 jammer; 2 Dagaie decoy RL
M: 2 SEMT-Pielstick 16 PC2-5V400 diesels; 2 5-bladed props; 22,600 bhp
Electric: 1,410 kVA tot. (3 × 470 kVA diesel sets)
Range: 4,000/18 **Fuel:** 230 tons **Crew:** 11 officers, 46 petty officers, 36 enlisted

Remarks: Ordered 8-79. Blohm + Voss design. 44 flooded out 2-10-86, delaying completion. New hull numbers were assigned 1988 (originally were P 10–P 15). Fitting out of 45 and 46 suspended in 1992, briefly restarted in 7-94, and resumed on 18-7-97, providing improved automation, communication, and electronics systems. The entire class is based at Puerto Belgrano.
Hull systems: Have fin stabilizers. Carry 5 tons aviation fuel, 70 tons fresh water. A telescoping helicopter hangar is fitted on 44 through 46 only.
Combat systems: Have Thales DAISY combat data system (and P 45 also has an Argentinian designed command system). The LIROD radar/electro-optical system controls 40-mm mounts; a planned second set was not installed.

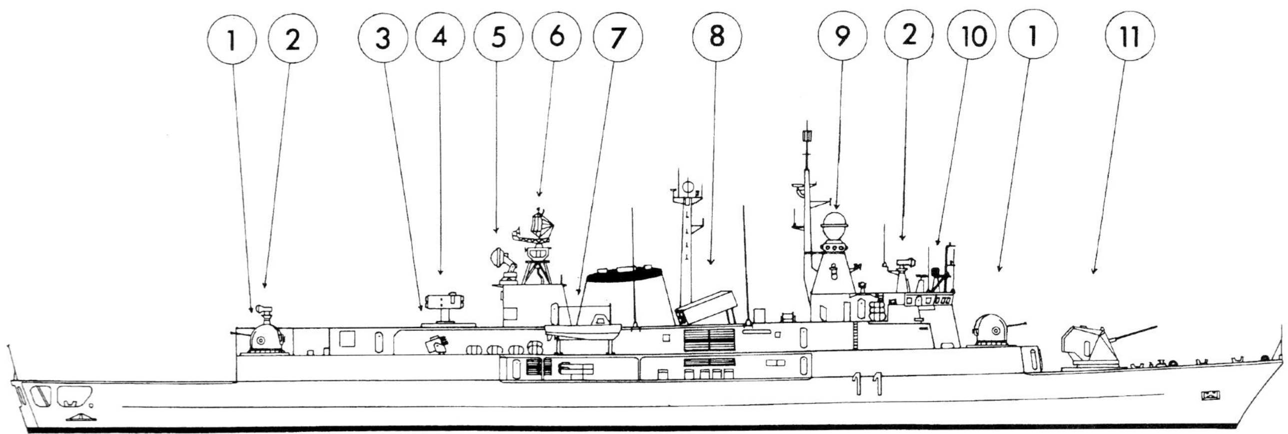

La Argentina (D 11) 1. Twin OTO Melara 40-mm AA 2. LIROD radar/optronic 40-mm gun director 3. SCLAR decoy launcher 4. Octuple launcher for Albatros SAM system 5. STIR radar missile director 6. DA-08A early warning radar antenna 7. ASW torpedo tubes 8. MM 40 Exocet antiship missiles 9. WM-25 track-while-scan radar director 10. ZW-06 surface-search radar 11. 127-mm 54-cal. OTO Melara gun
Drawing by Robert Dumas

CORVETTES [FFL]

♦ 0 (+ 5) PAM High Speed Patrol Ships

Bldr: Arsenal Naval de Río Santiago (In serv. 2008–13)

D: 1,800 tons **S:** 20 kts max **Dim:** 80 × 13 × . . .
A: 1 single 30-mm AA **M:** diesel-electric: 2 diesels
Range: 4,082/ . . . **Crew:** 42 total

Remarks: PAM = Patrullero de Alta Mar (High Seas Patrol Craft). Intended for maritime and fisheries patrol, interception, oceanographic survey, pollution control, and SAR duties. Current plans call for all five to be constructed in Argentina to a foreign design. Bids are expected by Blohm + Voss of Germany and Izar of Spain. Construction of first ships to begin in 2006. Additional units to be built one per year through 2010.
Hull systems: Diesel electric propulsion system. Electric-only drive capable of speeds of 8 knots. At speeds above 8 knots, the electric motors will function as generators. Will have a flight deck but no helicopter hangar.

♦ 3 French Type A-69 class

Bldr: DCN Lorient

	Laid down	L	In serv.
P 31 DRUMMOND (ex-*Transvaal,* F 102; ex-*Commandant l'Herminier,* F 791)	12-3-76	5-3-77	10-78
P 32 GUERRICO (ex-*Good Hope,* F 432; ex-*Lieutenant de Vaisseau le Henaff,* F 784)	11-10-76	13-9-77	10-78
P 33 GRANVILLE	1-12-78	28-6-80	22-6-81

Drummond (P 31) Ignacio Amendolara, 2-05

D: 1,170 tons (1,320 fl) **S:** 23.3 kts
Dim: 80.5 (76.0 pp) × 10.3 × 3.55 (5.25 sonar)
A: 4 MM 38 Exocet; 1 100-mm 55-cal. Mod. 1968 DP; 1 twin 40-mm 70-cal. OTO Melara AA; 2 single 20-mm 70-cal. Oerlikon AA; 2 single 12.7-mm Colt M2 mg; 2 triple 324-mm ILAS-3 ASW TT (WASS A-244S torpedoes)
Electronics:
Radar: 1 Consilium Selesmar NavBat nav.; 1 Thales DRBV 51A air/surf. search; 1 Thales DRBC-32E f.c.
Sonar: Thales Diodon hull-mounted MF
EW: Thales DR 2000 S3 intercept; Thales Alligator 51 jammer; 33 only: 2 Matra Défense Dagaie decoy RL; 31, 32: 2 18-round Corvus decoy RL
M: 2 SEMT-Pielstick 12 PC 2.2 V400 diesels; 2 CP props; 12,000 bhp
Electric: 840 kw tot. **Range:** 3,000/18; 4,500/16 **Endurance:** 15 days
Crew: 5 officers, 79 enlisted (accomm. for 95 tot.)

Remarks: Have fin stabilizers. The first two were originally ordered by South Africa, but delivery was embargoed, and they were purchased by Argentina on 25-9-78. The entire class is based at Mar del Plata.
Combat systems: Armament and some electronic gear differ from French Navy version; for example, the class is fitted with an Argentinian designed command system. There is a Matra Défense Panda Mk 2 optronic director for the 100-mm gun. All now have OTO Melara twin 40-mm AA controlled by a Naja Mk 2 optronic director. The DRBV 51A radar incorporates IFF interrogation.

PATROL SHIPS [PS]

♦ 1 former U.S. oilfield tug/supply vessel

Bldr: Quality SY, Houma, La. (In serv. 1981; acquired 15-11-87)

A 2 TENIENTE OLIVIERI (ex-*Marsea 10*)

D: 1,640 tons (fl) **S:** 14 kts **Dim:** 56.29 × 12.20 × 3.66
A: 2 single 12.7-mm mg **Electronics:** Radar: . . .
M: 2 G.M. EMD 16-645-E6 diesels; 2 props; 3,700 bhp (3,230 sust.)—300-shp bow-thruster
Electric: 198 kw tot. **Range:** 2,800/10 **Crew:** 4 officers, 11 enlisted

Remarks: Previous reports of the sale to a commercial U.S. owner proved erroneous. 293 grt/992 dwt. Purchased from the U.S. Maritime Administration 15-11-87 and delivered 5-88 as a "dispatch boat," i.e., a patrol vessel. Cargo capacity on 35.06 × 9.33-m open deck aft: 610 tons. As a commercial vessel, could carry 315 tons cargo fuel, 514 tons drilling water, 44 tons potable water, and 113 tons drilling mud; in Argentine service, carries 600 tons fuel or 800 tons water. Based at Puerto Belgrano and is used primarily as a supply vessel, carrying deck cargo and liquids to remote facilities.

♦ 3 U.S. Abnaki and Achomawi class

Bldr: A 1, A 3: Charleston SB & DD Co., Charleston, S.C.; A 6: United Engineering, Alameda, Calif.

	Laid down	Launch	In serv.
A 1 COMANDANTE GENERAL IRIGOYEN (ex-*Cahuilla,* ATF 152)	16-6-44	2-11-44	10-3-45
A 3 FRANCISCO DE GURRUCHAGA (ex-*Luiseno,* ATF 156)	7-11-44	17-3-45	16-6-45
A 6 SUBOFICIAL CASTILLO (ex-*Takelma,* ATF 113)	7-4-43	18-9-43	3-8-44

Suboficial Castillo (A 6) Ignacio Amendolara, 7-05

D: 1,291 tons (1,731 fl) **S:** 16 kts **Dim:** 62.48 (59.44 wl) × 11.73 × 5.20
A: 1 (A 1: 3) double 40-mm 60-cal. Bofors AA; 1 (A 6) single 40-mm 60-cal. Bofors
Electronics: Radar: 2 Sperry Marine VT-3400C nav./surf. Search; A-6: 1 Furuno nav.
M: 4 G.M. 12-278A (A 6: B.S. 539) diesels, electric drive; 1 prop; 3,000 shp
Electric: 400 kw tot. **Range:** 6,500/15; 15,000/8 **Fuel:** 363 tons **Crew:** 85 tot.

Remarks: Former fleet tugs. A 1 transferred 9-7-61 as an ocean tug; rerated a patrol ship in 1966. A 3 was purchased on 1-7-75. A 6 was transferred as a gift on 30-9-93 and was unarmed at time of transfer. All retain tug and salvage facilities. Received new radar suites, gyros, and digital chart plotters in 1995.

♦ 1 U.S. Sotoyomo class

Bldr: Levingston SB, Orange, Texas

	Laid down	L	In serv.
A 9 ALFEREZ SOBRAL (ex-*Salish,* ATA 187, ex-ATR 114)	29-8-44	29-9-44	7-12-44

Alferez Sobral (A 9) Ignacio Amendolara, 1996

D: 534 tons (835 fl) **S:** 13 kts **Dim:** 43.59 (41.00 pp) × 10.31 × 4.01
A: 1 single 40-mm 60-cal. Bofors AA; 2 single 20-mm 70-cal. Oerlikon AA
Electronics: Radar: 1 Racal Decca 1226 nav.
M: 2 G.M. 12-278A diesels, electric drive; 2 props; 1,500 shp
Electric: 120 kw **Range:** 16,500/18 **Fuel:** 171 tons **Crew:** 49 tot.

Remarks: Former auxiliary ocean tug transferred 10-2-72. Had been retired by the late 1980s, but was restored to service due to her economy of operation and the lack of other assets. The ship survived two Sea Skua missile hits amidships in 1982 during the Falklands/Malvinas War. The original bridge was replaced in 1982 and is now kept at the Naval Museum in Tigre, Buenos Aires.
Disposals: *Yamona* (A 6, ex-ATA 146) was stricken 1984 and *Saniviron* (A 8, ex-ATA 228) during 4-97. *Comodoro Somellera* (A 10, ex-*Catawba,* ATA 210, ex-ATR 137) was rammed and sunk by *Suboficial Castillo* (A 6) at Ushuaia during 8-98; salved but not repaired.

♦ 2 Murature class

Bldr: Arsenal Naval de Río Santiago

	Laid down	L	In serv.
P 20 MURATURE	30-3-40	28-7-43	12-4-45
P 21 KING	15-6-38	3-11-43	18-11-46

D: 913 tons (1,032 fl) **S:** 18 kts **Dim:** 77.0 × 8.8 × 2.3
A: 3 single 105-mm 45-cal. Bofors DP; 1 twin and 2 single 40-mm 60-cal. Bofors AA; 5 single 12.7-mm mg
Electronics: Radar: 1 Decca 1226 nav.; 1 Furuno . . . nav.
M: 2 Werkspoor 4-cycle diesels; 2 props; 2,500 bhp
Range: 9,000/12 **Fuel:** 90 tons **Crew:** 130 tot.

Remarks: Patrol boats of riveted construction. Since 1969, have been assigned to the Riverine Fleet and based at Zárate on the Paraná de las Palmas branch of the Río Paraná delta for training and patrol duties. Main guns are single-fire weapons manufactured prior to World War II.

PATROL SHIPS [PS] *(continued)*

King (P 21) Harmut Ehlers, 4-00

GUIDED-MISSILE BOATS [PTG]

♦ **2 TNC 45 class** Bldr: Friedrich Lürssen Werft, Vegesack, Germany

	L	In serv.		L	In serv.
P 85 Intrépida	2-12-73	3-8-74	P 86 Indómita	8-4-74	10-4-75

Intrépida (P 85) Argentine Navy, 1994

D: 240 tons (265 fl) **S:** 37.8 kts **Dim:** 44.9 (42.3 pp) × 7.4 × 2.28 (props)
A: P 85 only: 2 single MM 38 Exocet SSM launchers; both: 1 76-mm 62-cal. OTO Melara Compact DP; 2 (P 85: 1) single 40-mm 70-cal. Bofors L70 AA; 2 single 533-mm TT (SST-4 wire-guided torpedoes)
Electronics:
Radar: 1 Decca 1226 nav., 1 Thales WM-22 track-while-scan f.c.
EW: Decca Cutlass intercept
M: 4 MTU MD872 diesels; 4 props; 14,400 bhp **Electric:** 330 kw
Range: 640/36; 1,700/16 **Crew:** 5 officers, 37 enlisted

Remarks: Both were refitted 1995–96. P 85 was equipped with Exocet missiles in place of the amidships single 40-mm AA. P 86 remains in the original configuration. Both craft are normally based at Ushuaia. Have antirolling fin stabilizers.

PATROL BOATS [PB]

Note: Six new riverine patrol craft are sought for service on the Río Paraguay.

♦ **4 Israeli Dabur class**
Bldr: Israeli Aircraft Industries, Israel

	In serv.		In serv.
P 61 Baradero	2-8-79	P 63 Clorinda	23-4-79
P 62 Barranqueras	3-12-78	P 64 Concepción del Uruguay	13-4-79

D: 31 tons (39 fl) **S:** 19 kts **Dim:** 19.80 × 5.50 × 1.80
A: 2 single 20-mm 70-cal. Oerlikon AA; 2 twin 12.7-mm Colt M2 mg
Electronics: Radar: 1 Decca 101 nav.
M: 2 G.M. 12V71 TA diesels; 2 props; 1,200 bhp (840 sust.)
Range: 450/13 **Crew:** 8 tot.

Remarks: Operate from Ushuaia. Were originally capable of 23 kts. Aluminum construction.

Clorinda (P 63) Ignacio Amendolara, 1996

♦ **2 ex-U.S. Coast Guard 82-foot Point class**
Bldr: U.S. Coast Guard Yard, Curtis Bay, Md.

	In serv.
P 65 Punta Mogotes (ex-*Point Hobart,* WPB 82377)	13-7-70
P 66 Río Santiago (ex-*Point Carrew,* WPB 82374)	18-5-70

Río Santiago (P 66) Ignacio Amendolara, 2002

D: 64 tons (69 fl) **S:** 22.6 kts **Dim:** 25.3 × 5.23 × 1.95
A: 2 single 12.7-mm M2 mg
Electronics: Radar: 1 Raytheon SPS-64(V)1 nav.; 1 Furuno . . . nav.
M: 2 Caterpillar 3412 diesels; 2 props; 1,480 bhp
Range: 320/22.6; 1,200/8 **Fuel:** 5.7 tons **Crew:** 1 officer, 7 enlisted

Remarks: Stricken from U.S. Coast Guard and donated to Argentina; recommissioned on 12-8-00. Based at the Naval Academy, Río Santiago, Buenos Aires. Hull built of mild steel. High-speed diesels controlled from the bridge. A small Furuno navigational radar was added after transfer.

MINE WARFARE SHIPS

Note: The two remaining British Ton-class minehunters were decommissioned in February 2003, making this the first time in generations the Argentine Navy has been without mine warfare vessels.

AMPHIBIOUS WARFARE SHIPS AND CRAFT

♦ **2 ex-French Ouragan-class dock landing ships [LSD]**
(1 nonoperational) Bldr: DCN Brest

. . . (ex-Ouragan, L 9021) . . . (ex-Orage, L 9022)

D: 5,965 tons (8,500 fl; 15,000 flooded) **S:** 17.3 kts (L 9021: 15 kts)
Dim: 149.00 (144.50 pp) × 21.50 × 5.40 (8.70 flooded)
A: 2 2-round Simbad SAM syst. (. . . Mistral missiles); 2 single 40-mm 60-cal. Bofors (L 9022: 2 single 30-mm OTO Melara-Mauser) AA; 4 single 12.7-mm mg
Electronics:
Radar: 2 DRBN-34 nav.
E/O: L 9022 only: 2 DIBC-2A optronic weapons directors
M: L 9021: 2 SEMT-Pielstick 12 PC 2V 2 diesels; 2 CP props; 8,640 bhp; L 9022: 2 SEMT-Pielstick 12 PC 2.1 V400 diesels; 2 CP props; 9,400 bhp
Electric: 2,650 kw tot. **Range:** 9,000/15
Crew: 12 officers, 78 petty officers, 115 ratings + up to 470 troops

Remarks: Data reflect the class while still in French service. Transferred 3-06. One of the class will remain active while the other is to be used for cannibalized spare parts.

♦ **(1) Former British Sheffield class [LPA]**

	Bldr	Laid down	L	In serv.
B 52 (Ex-D1) Hercules	Vickers, Barrow	16-6-71	24-10-72	12-7-76

AMPHIBIOUS WARFARE SHIPS AND CRAFT *(continued)*

Hercules (B 52) Ignacio Amendolara, 2-03

D: 3,150 tons (4,100 fl) **S:** 28 kts **Dim:** 125.0 (119.5 pp) × 14.34 × 4.2 (hull)
A: 4 single Exocet MM 38 SSM launchers; 1 114-mm 55-cal. Mk 8 DP; 2 single 20-mm 70-cal. Oerlikon AA; 2 triple 324-mm ILAS-3 ASW TT (WASS A-224S torpedoes); 2 SH-3 Sea King helicopters
Electronics:
Radar: 1 Kelvin-Hughes Type 1006 nav.; 1 Marconi Type 965M early warning; 1 Marconi Type 992Q surf./air search; 1 Marconi Type 909 missile and gun f.c.
Sonar: Graseby Type 184M LF hull-mounted, Kelvin-Hughes Type 162M bottomed-target classification
EW: Decca RDL-2 intercept, Decca RCM-2 jammer, 2 Corvus 8-round decoy RL
M: COGOG: 2 Rolls-Royce Olympus TM 3B gas turbines (27,200 shp each); 2 Rolls-Royce Tyne RM 1A cruise gas turbines (4,100 shp each); 2 5-bladed CP props
Electric: 4,000 kw tot. **Range:** 4,000/18 **Crew:** 270 tot.

Remarks: Ordered 18-5-70. Underwent conversion to fast transport for Marine/Special Operations missions. Completed a refit in Chile 11-00 during which her hangar was enlarged to enable carrying 2 Sea King helicopters.
Combat systems: Has ADAWS-4 data system and NATO Link 10 datalink, refitted 1980 and again in 2000. The Sea Dart SAM system has been removed.

Disposal note: Former British Sheffield-class destroyer, *Santísima Trinidad* (D 2), long used for cannibalization, has been inactive since the 1980s and will be turned into a museum ship.

♦ 1 Costa Sur–class amphibious transport [LPA]
Bldr: Principe & Menghe SY, Maciel

	Laid down	L	In serv.
B 4 Bahía San Blas	11-4-77	29-4-78	27-11-78

Bahía San Blas (B 4) Ignacio Amendolara, 10-05

D: 7,640 tons (10,894 fl) **S:** 16.3 kts **Dim:** 119.9 × 17.5 × 7.49
A: none **Electronics:** Radar: . . . nav.
M: 2 AFNE-Sulzer 6ZL 40/48 diesels; 2 props; 6,400 bhp **Crew:** . . . tot.

Remarks: 4,600 grt/5,800 dwt. Was to have been retired in 1998 but was instead adapted to support naval infantry forces and to act as a fleet supply ship. Repainted gray and based at Puerto Belgrano. Deployed to Haiti in support of UN peacekeeping operations during 2004–5.
Hull systems: The forward crane was removed after 1998, and there are plans to put a helicopter flight deck over the forward hold. Remaining are one 5-ton, one 12.5-ton, and one 20-ton crane. Has a maximum cargo capacity of 9,856 m^3 (about 6,300 tons), including 210 m^3 refrigerated.

♦ 8 U.S. LCVP-class landing craft [LCVP]
EDVP 30–37

D: 13 tons (fl) **S:** 9 kts **Dim:** 10.90 × 3.21 × 1.04 (aft)
M: 1 G.M. Gray Marine 64 HN9 diesel; 225 bhp **Range:** 110/9

Remarks: Cargo: 36 troops or 3.5 tons. Five others were discarded post-1982.

Note: The Argentine Marine Corps operates 18 LVTP-7 amphibious armored troop carriers, one LVTC-7 amphibious command vehicle, and one LVTR-7 amphibious vehicle recovery vehicle, as well as one or more U.S. LARC-5 amphibious cargo lighters.

AUXILIARIES

♦ 3 ex-U.S. Coast Guard Red-class general-use ships [AG]
Bldr: U.S. Coast Guard Yard, Curtis Bay, Md.

	Laid down	L	In serv.
Q 61 Ciudad de Zárate (ex-*Red Cedar,* WLM 688)	1-7-69	1-8-70	18-12-70
Q 62 Ciudad de Rosario (ex-*Red Wood,* WLM 685)	1-7-63	4-4-64	4-8-64
Q 63 Punta Alta (ex-Q 12, ex-*Red Birch,* WLM 687)	6-7-64	19-2-65	7-6-65

Ciudad de Zárate (Q 61) Ignacio Amendolara, 7-00

D: 371 tons light (556 fl) **S:** 14 kts (12.8 sust.)
Dim: 47.85 (45.72 pp) × 10.05 (9.60 wl) × 1.99 **A:** none
Electronics: Radar: 1 Raytheon SPS-65(V)9 nav.; 1 Furuno 1831 nav.
M: 2 Caterpillar D398A diesels; 2 CP props; 1,800 bhp—150-shp bow thruster
Range: 2,248/12.8; 3,055/11.6 **Crew:** 4 officers, 27 enlisted (in U.S. service)

Remarks: Former U.S. Coast Guard medium navigational aids tenders. Officially rated as "Multipurpose Ships" in 12-00, when Q 63 was renumbered. Q 63 was transferred from the U.S. Coast Guard on 10-6-98. Q 61 and Q 62 were transferred by donation on 30-7-99, with the former recommissioning on 28-3-00 and the latter on 14-10-99 at Curtis Bay, Md. Can break light ice and can break 1-ft. ice at 3 kts continuously or 2-ft. ice by ramming. Have a 10-ton buoy-handling derrick. Q 63 is based at Bahía Blanca and the other two are based at Zárate on the Río Paraná as transports, training craft, and humanitarian-assistance vessels.

♦ 1 Antarctic support ship/icebreaker [AGB]
Bldr: Wärtsilä, Helsinki, Finland

	Laid down	L	In serv.
Q 5 Almirante Irizar	4-7-77	3-2-78	15-12-78

Almirante Irizar (Q 5) Ignacio Amendolara, 2002

D: 11,811 tons (14,899 fl) **S:** 17.2 kts **Dim:** 121.3 × 25.2 × 9.5
A: 2 single 12.7-mm mg
Electronics:
Radar: 2 Kelvin Hughes Nucleus 6000A (3-cm and 10-cm) nav.; 1 Raytheon RM-70 nav.; 1 Plessey AWS-2 air search
M: diesel-electric: 4 SEMT-Pielstick 8 PC 2.5 L/400 diesels; 4 4,000 kVA alternator sets, 2 Stromberg twin motors; 2 props; 16,200 shp
Electric: 2,640 kw tot. **Crew:** 123 ship's company + 100 scientists

Remarks: Ordered 17-12-75. Now used as an amphibious warfare transport for exercises. Was used as a hospital ship during the Falklands/Malvinas War. Began a 2-year refit during 9-02; post-overhaul navigation and communications improvements include a Satellite communication system and internet connectivity. Red hull, cream upperworks.
Hull systems: Canadian RASair bubbler system is fitted to keep ice from hull bottom. Has a 60-ton towing winch and two 16-ton cranes. Has 1,800-m^3 cargo capacity. Carries two hydrographic survey launches and two LCVP-type landing craft.
Armament: The two 40-mm AA guns have been replaced by 12.7-mm mg.

♦ 1 Puerto Deseado–class oceanographic survey ship [AGS]
Bldr: ASTARSA (Astilleros Argentinos Río de la Plata), San Fernando

	Laid down	L	In serv.
Q 20 Puerto Deseado	17-3-76	4-12-77	26-2-79

AUXILIARIES *(continued)*

Puerto Deseado (Q-20) Ignacio Amendolara 2-03

D: 2,133 tons (2,400 fl) **S:** 14 kts **Dim:** 76.81 (67.0 pp) × 15.8 × 3.5
Electronics: Radar: 2 Raytheon . . . nav.—Sonar: . . . HF mapping
M: 2 M.A.N. 9L20/27 diesels (1,206 bhp each), 2 ABB alternators, 2 electric motors; 1,600 shp—Berg electric auxiliary propulsor; 1 CP prop; 160 shp
Electric: 1,280 kVA tot. **Range:** 12,000/12
Crew: 81 tot. (accomm. for 12 officers, 53 enlisted, 20 scientists)

Remarks: Assigned to CONICET (Consejo Nacional de Investigaciónes Científicas y Técnicas) and used for hydrometeorological reporting and general oceanographic research work. Was readied for use as an auxiliary hospital ship during the Falklands/Malvinas War in 1982 and has been used in Antarctic survey and research work since 1996, with the hull painted orange.
Mission systems: Has four Hewlett-Packard 2108-A computers for data analysis/storage and seismic, gravimetric, and magnetometer equipment. GPS-equipped. Has geology laboratory.
Hull systems: Ice-reinforced hull. Re-engined in 1995, with electric slow-speed auxiliary propulsion added.

♦ 1 Comodoro Rivadavia-class hydrographic survey ship [AGS]
Bldr: Mestrina, Tigre

	L	In serv.
Q 11 COMODORO RIVADAVIA	29-11-73	6-12-74

Comodoro Rivadavia (Q 11) H&L Van Ginderen, 8-88

D: 655 tons (827 fl) **S:** 12 kts **Dim:** 52.2 × 8.8 × 2.6
Electronics: Radar: 2 Decca 1226 (3-cm and 10-cm) nav.
M: 2 Werkspoor Stork RHO-218K diesels; 1,160 bhp
Range: 6,000/12 **Crew:** 36 tot.

Remarks: Has a small helicopter platform. Is equipped with Kelvin Hughes MS 32 echo sounder, a Magnavox NAVSAT receiver, and Trimble differential GPS receiver. Carries a 5.6-ton Callegari semirigid inflatable launch with a Johnson 70-bhp outboard motor, GPS receiver, and Hidronav survey system. Also fitted with two 8-meter survey launches.

Disposal note: Of the two former merchant bulk carriers taken over from Astramar Compañía Argentina de Navegación S.A.C. and operated in revenue service, *Astra Federico* (B 8, ex-*Ciudad de San Fernando*) lost certification in 1999 and was stricken, and *Astra Valentina* (B 9, ex-*Ciudad de Tigre*) followed in 5-00. Collier *Río Gallegos* (B 6, ex-*Santa Cruz*) and cargo ship *Capitán Tulio Panigadi* were sold during 1999.

♦ 1 dry cargo ship [AK]
Bldr: . . . (In serv. 1973)

B . . . CAPITÁN TULIO PANIGADI

D: . . . tons **S:** 14 kts **Dim:** 150.00 × 17.20 × 6.60
M: 1 diesel; 1 prop; . . . bhp

Remarks: 6,794 dwt dry cargo ship acquired 2001 for revenue service. Has a naval crew.

♦ 1 ex-French Durance-class replenishment oiler [AOR]
Bldr: DCN Brest

	Laid down	L	In serv.
B 1 PATAGONIA (ex-*Durance,* A 629)	10-12-73	6-9-75	1-12-76

Patagonia (B 1) Ignacio Amendolara, 8-00

D: 7,600 tons (17,800 fl) **S:** 20 kts (19 sust.)
Dim: 157.20 (149.00 pp) × 21.20 × 8.65 (10.8 fl)
A: 2 single 40-mm 60-cal. Bofors AA
Electronics:
Radar: 2 Decca 1226 nav.
EW: Thales DR-2000 intercept, EADS Telegon HFD/F
M: 2 SEMT-Pielstick 16 PC 2.5 V400 diesels; 2 CP props; 20,760 bhp
Electric: 5,400 kw tot. **Range:** 9,000/15 **Fuel:** 750 tons
Crew: 8 officers, 62 petty officers, 89 other enlisted (in French service)

Remarks: Purchased and transferred 1999, and began a tow to Argentina late 7-99 for reactivation refit; renamed 31-8-99 and recommissioned 12-7-99. Four sisters remain in French Navy service, and a near-sister is operated by Australia.
Hull systems: Has two Canadian-designed dual solids/liquids underway-replenishment stations per side. Can supply two ships alongside and refuel one astern. Has hangar for one small helicopter and flight deck for larger helicopters. No longer carries fuel oil or separate diesel-fuel cargo. Cargo: 9,500 tons gas turbine fuel, 130 tons distilled water, 170 tons fresh provisions, 150 tons munitions, 50 tons spare parts.

♦ 1 former merchant tanker [AOT]
Bldr: ASTARSA (Astilleros Argentinos Río de la Plata), Tigre

	Laid down	L	In serv.
B 13 INGENIERO JULIO KRAUSE	28-10-78	2-2-80	1981

D: 8,346 tons (fl) **S:** 14.5 kts (14 sust.) **Dim:** 111.51 (103.99 pp) × 17.21 × 6.70
M: 1 AFNE-Sulzer 8ZL40/48, 8-cyl. diesel; 1 CP prop; 5,800 bhp
Electric: 1,134 kw tot. (3 × 378-kw diesel sets) **Crew:** 32 tot.

Remarks: 4,814 grt/6,000 dwt. Taken over 5-3-93 from Argentine state petroleum agency, Yacimientos Petrolíferos Fiscales, and operated in revenue service. Cargo: 7,500 m^3 in 15 tanks. Has been fitted for underway replenishment.

♦ 2 Costa Sur–class transports [AP]
Bldr: Principe & Menghe SY, Maciel Isl.

	Laid down	L	In serv.
B 3 CANAL BEAGLE	10-1-77	14-10-77	28-4-78
B 5 CABO DE HORNOS (ex-*Bahía Camarones*)	29-4-78	4-11-78	18-7-79

Canal Beagle (B 3) Ignacio Amendolara 12-96

D: 7,640 tons (10,894 fl) **S:** 16.3 kts **Dim:** 119.9 × 17.5 × 7.49
A: none **Electronics:** Radar: 2 . . . nav.
M: 2 AFNE-Sulzer 6ZL 40/48 diesels; 2 props; 6,400 bhp **Crew:** . . . tot.

Remarks: 4,600 grt/5,800 dwt. Used to supply remote stations and also carry passengers and cargo in commercial service. Sister *Bahía San Blas* (B 4) is now used as an amphibious warfare transport.

AUXILIARIES *(continued)*

Hull systems: Have a maximum cargo capacity of 9,856 m^3 (about 6,300 tons), including 210 m^3 refrigerated. B 5 has two 1.5-ton cranes, one 5-ton, one 20-ton, and one 40-ton, while B 3 has one of 5-ton, one of 12.5-ton, and one of 25-ton capacity.

♦ 2 auxiliary ocean tugs [ATA] Bldr: Ast. Vicente Forte, Buenos Aires

R 2 QUERANDI (In serv. 22-8-78) R 3 TEHUELCHE (In serv. 2-11-78)

D: 370 tons (fl) **S:** 12 kts **Dim:** 33.6 × 8.4 × 3.0
M: 2 M.A.N. 6V 23.5/33 diesels; 1,200 bhp
Range: 1,200/12 **Crew:** 30 tot.

♦ 1 sail-training vessel [AXT]

	Bldr	L	In serv.
Q 2 LIBERTAD	AFNE, Rio Santiago	30-5-56	1962

Libertad (Q 2) A. A. de Kruijf, 8-02

D: 3,165 tons (3,765 fl) **S:** 12.5 kts
Dim: 103.7 (94.25 hull; 79.9 pp) × 14.31 × 6.75 **Electronics:** 1 Decca nav.
A: 4 single 47-mm saluting cannon
M: 2 Sulzer diesels; 2 props; 2,400 bhp—sail area: 2,683.5 m^2 max.
Range: 12,000/8 **Crew:** 26 officers, 192 enlisted, 150 cadets.

Remarks: Foremast is 48.66 m high, mainmast 50 m, and mizzen 43.17 m. Have extensive medical and dental facilities. Began midlife overhaul in 2004 at Astillero Río Santiago. Expected to be completed during 2007, the modernization includes a new propulsion system and other improvements to extend service life through 2044. During 2004 midshipmen training took place aboard two MEKO 140 craft and during 2005 aboard the Chilean Navy's *Esmeralda.*

Note: The former sail-training ship *Presidente Sarmiento* (1898) and the sail corvette *Uruguay* (1874) are maintained by the navy in museum status at Buenos Aires.

SERVICE CRAFT

♦ 1 floating crane [YD]

♦ 2 miscellaneous floating dry docks [YFD]

Y 1 (ex-U.S. ARD 23) (In serv. 1944): 3,500-ton capacity; 149.0 × 24.7 × 7.3 (light)
Y 3: 750-ton capacity; 65.8 × 14

Disposal note: Floating dry dock Y 4 is no longer in service, while dry docks A and B are not naval-owned.

Floating dry dock Y 1 Ignacio Amendolara, 1997

♦ 1 flag officer launch [YFL]
Bldr: Cadenazzi SY, Tigre (In serv. 1979)

Q 73 ITATI II

Itati II (Q 73) Alejandro Amendolara, 7-98

D: 80 tons (fl) **S:** 15 kts **Dim:** 25.0 × 6.0 × 2.2
M: 2 . . . diesels; 2 props; . . . bhp
Remarks: Large cabin cruiser stationed at the Apostadero Naval San Fernando, Buenos Aires, for ceremonial duties.

♦ 1 coastal and riverine survey craft [YGS]
Bldr: AFNE, Río Santiago (In serv. 20-2-64)

Q 15 CORMORÁN

D: 82 tons (102 fl) **S:** 11 kts **Dim:** 25.3 × 5.0 × 1.8
Electronics: Radar: 1 Decca 101 (3 cm) nav.; 1 Raytheon R-21 (3 cm) nav.
M: 2 G.M. Detroit Diesel 6-71 diesels; 2 props; 440 bhp **Crew:** 21 tot.

Note: Also used for riverine survey duties are the small launches *Monte Blanco* and *Kualchink,* transferred from the Secretaría de Agricultura Ganadería in 1996 and 2004 respectively. Neither small craft carries a naval pennant number.

Disposal note: Coastal and riverine survey craft *Petrel* (Q 16) was stricken in 12-00.

♦ 3 Huarpe-class medium harbor tugs [YTM] Bldr: . . . , Argentina

R 4 MATACO (1971) R 7 ONA (1964) R 8 TOBA (1964)

Toba (R 8) Ignacio Amendolara, 7-05

SERVICE CRAFT *(continued)*

D: 208 tons (fl) **S:** 12 kts **Dim:** 30.3 × 8.4 × 3.2
M: 2 M.A.N./GEC diesel generators; 2 GEC electric motors; 1 prop; 830 bhp
Crew: 2 officers, 8 enlisted

Remarks: Acquired 1988 from another government agency. Sister *Huarpe* (R 1) was stricken during 1997.

♦ 6 U.S. YTL 422–class small harbor tugs [YTL]

Bldrs: R 5, 16, 18: Robt. Jacobs, City I., N.Y.; R 6, 19: H. C. Grebe Co.; R 10: Everett Pacific BY, Everett, Wash. (In serv. 1944–45)

R 5 Mocovi (ex-YTL 441)
R 6 Calchaqu (ex-YTL 445)
R 10 Chulupi (ex-YTL 426)
R 16 Capayan (ex-YTL 443)
R 18 Chiquillan (ex-YTL 444)
R 19 Morcoyan (ex-YTL 448)

Chulupi (R 10), left, and Chiquillan (R 18) Ignacio Amendolara, 8-05

D: 70 tons (80 fl) **S:** 10 kts **Dim:** 20.16 × 5.18 × 2.44
M: 1 Hoover-Owens-Rentschler diesel; 300 hp **Electric:** 40 kw tot.
Fuel: 7 tons **Crew:** 5 tot.

Remarks: R 16, 18, and 19 leased 3-65, others 3-69; all purchased outright 16-6-77. R 5 and R 6 based at Puerto Belgrano Naval Base, R 10 and R 18 at Mar del Plata Naval Base, and R 16 and R 19 at the Naval Academy, Río Santiago, Buenos Aires, the latter for cadet training.

♦ 4 small sail-training yachts [YTS]

Q 75 Fortuna II . . . 17 tons
Bldr: Tandanor, Buenos Aires (In serv. 04-09-76) **D:** 31.5 tons
Q 74 Fortuna . . . 31.5 tons
Bldr: Tandanor, Buenos Aires (In serv. 22-11-49) **D:** 17 tons
Q 76 Fortuna III . . .
Bldr: Arsenal Naval, Buenos Aires (In serv. 10-07-04)
Q . . . Tijuca . . . 32 tons (In serv. 1993)
Bldr: . . .

Q 76 Fortuna III Ignacio Amendolara, 2-05

Remarks: *Tijuca* was donated to the navy and is assigned to the Escuela de Nática.

♦ 1 fisheries training craft [YXT]

Bldr: Nishinippon-F.R. Shipbuilding, Japan (In serv. 15-1-85)

Q 51 Luisito

D: 22 tons light **S:** 9 kts (3 kts with net deployed) **Dim:** 19.0 × 4.1 × 2.0
M: . . .

Remarks: A small stern-haul trawler assigned to the navy but employed in training fisheries students.

Luisito (Q 51) Ignacio Amendolara, 1-96

PREFECTURA NAVAL ARGENTINA

Personnel: Approx. 13,240 tot.

Note: The Prefectura Naval, which traces its origins to 1756, was transferred from naval control to the Ministry of Defense in 10-84; the navy would like to obtain control over the organization, which does not seem likely to happen in the near future. Most personnel serve ashore in port security and control-of-shipping duties, and the organization is responsible for riverine and inshore security patrol out to the 12-mile limit, search and rescue, pilot services, firefighting and antipollution duties, and operation of the National Diving School. Ships and craft are painted white, with two unequal-width blue diagonal stripes on the hull sides with anchors superimposed on the larger stripe; name "Prefectura Naval" appears on the sides. Smaller service craft have black hulls.

Organization: Ten districts: Río Paraná, Upper Río Paraná and Río Paraguay, Lower Río Paraná, Upper Río Uruguay, Lower Río Uruguay, Delta, Río Plate, Argentine Sea, Southern Argentine Sea, and Lakes.

Maritime Aviation: 5 CASA C-212-200 Aviocar light transports (3 with Bendix RDS 32 radars for use as maritime patrol aircraft) and 2 AS.330 Super Puma, 2 AS 365 Dauphin, and 6 float-equipped Schweizer 300C helicopters.

AS 365 Dauphine 2 Ignacio Amendolara, 2-05

PATROL SHIPS [WPS]

♦ 5 Halcón class Bldr: E. N. Bazán, El Ferrol, Spain

	Laid down	L	In serv.
GC 24 Doctor Manuel Mantilla	16-2-81	29-6-81	20-12-82
GC 25 Azopardo	1-4-81	14-10-81	28-4-83
GC 26 Thompson	2-81	7-12-81	20-6-83
GC 27 Prefecto Pique	9-81	24-2-82	29-7-83
GC 28 Prefecto Derbes	11-81	16-6-82	20-11-83

D: 767 tons normal (900 fl) **S:** 21.5 kts **Dim:** 67.0 (63.0 pp) × 10.0 × 3.06
A: 1 40-mm 70-cal. AA OTO Melara-Bofors AA; 2 single 12.7-mm mg; 1 HB.350B Esquilo helicopter
Electronics: Radar: 1 Decca AC 1226 nav.; 1 Decca . . . nav.
M: 2 Bazán-MTU 16V956 TB91 diesels; 2 props; 9,000 hp (7,500 sust.)
Electric: 710 kw **Range:** 5,000/18 **Endurance:** 20 days
Crew: 10 officers; 24 enlisted, 4 cadets

Remarks: Ordered 3-79 to patrol 200-n.m. economic zone. Same class also built for Mexico. All are based at Buenos Aires except GC 26 at Mar del Plata.
Hull systems: For rescue duties, are fitted to carry one 6.1-m rigid rescue craft with an Evinrude outboard and a capacity of 12 personnel; there is a four-person sick bay. Equipped with Magnavox MS 1102 SATNAV receivers.
Combat systems: The 40-mm gun is locally controlled, and the ships can carry 144 rounds of 40-mm ammunition.

PATROL SHIPS [WPS] *(continued)*

Doctor Manuel Mantilla (GC 24) Alejandro Amendolara, 2000

♦ 1 former whale-catcher
Bldr: NV IJsselwerf, Rotterdam, the Netherlands (In serv. 4-57)

GC 13 Delfín (ex-R 1)

D: 900 tons (1,280 fl) **S:** 15 kts **Dim:** 56.88 (50.98 pp) × 9.35 × 4.34
A: 1 20-mm 70-cal. Oerlikon AA; 2 single 12.7-mm mg
Electronics: Radar: 2 . . . nav.
M: 2 M.A.N.-Deutz 10-cyl. diesels; 1 prop; 2,965 bhp (2,300 sust.)—bow-thruster
Electric: 360 kw tot. (2 × 120-kw, 2 × 60-kw diesel sets)
Range: 6,720/10 **Crew:** 27 tot.

Delfín (GC 13) Hartmut Ehlers, 1-98

Remarks: Purchased 1969 from Calpe Shipping Co., Gibraltar, and converted for patrol duties, commissioned 23-1-70.

PATROL CRAFT [WPC]

♦ 2 Lynch class
Bldr: AFNE, Río Santiago (In serv. 1964–67)

GC 21 Lynch GC 22 Toll

D: 100 tons (117 fl) **S:** 22 kts **Dim:** 27.44 × 5.80 × 1.85
A: provision for 1 20-mm 70-cal. Oerlikon AA
M: 2 Maybach diesels; 2 props; 2,700 hp
Range: 2,000/. . . **Crew:** 16 tot.

Remarks: Sister *Erezcano* (GC 23) stricken 1986. Designed after the U.S. Coast Guard Cape class.

PATROL BOATS [WPB]

♦ 1 Bazán 39–class fast launch
Bldr: E. N. Bazán, San Fernando (In serv. 1997)

GC 142 Surel

D: 14.5 tons (fl) **S:** 38 kts **Dim:** 11.90 × 3.00 × 0.70
A: 1 12.7-mm mg **Electronics:** Radar: 1 . . . nav.
M: 2 M.A.N. D2848 diesels; 2 Hamilton 362 waterjets; 1,360 bhp
Range: 300/25 **Crew:** 5 tot.

Surel (GC 142) Ignacio Amendolara 11-01

Remarks: Plans to acquire more of this class did not reach fruition. GRP construction.

♦ 10 Alucat 1050–class riverine patrol launches
Bldr: Damen, Gorinchem, the Netherlands (First 3: in serv. 8-94, others in 2-00)

GC 137 Cormoran
GC 138 Cisne
GC 139 Pejerrey
GC 143 Surubi
GC 144 Boga
GC 145 Sabalo
GC 146 Huala
GC 147 Pacu
GC 148 Manduruyu
GC 149 Corvina

D: 10.5 tons (15 fl) **S:** 18 kts **Dim:** 11.45 × 3.80 × 0.60
Electronics: Radar: 1 Furuno 12/24 nav.
M: 2 Volvo Penta 61 ALD diesels; 2 Hamilton 273 waterjets; 600 bhp
Range: 290/. . . **Crew:** 4 tot.

Alucat 1050-class GC 146 Hartmut Ehlers, 4-00

Remarks: An enlarged version of the Alucat 850 class; used for antismuggling patrol along the river border with Paraguay.

♦ 33 Alucat 850–class lake patrol launches
Bldr: Damen, Gorinchem, the Netherlands (In serv. 1995–2000)

CG 152 through CG 184

D: 9 tons (fl) **S:** 18 kts **Dim:** 9.20 × 3.25 × 0.60
Electronics: Radar: 1 Furuno 12/24 nav.
M: 2 Volvo Penta TAMD 41B diesels; 2 Hamilton 273 waterjets; 394 bhp
Range: 300/. . . **Crew:** 4 tot.

Alucat 850-class CG 156 (displaying old number) official Prefectura Naval photo

Remarks: Constructed in seven batches between 1994 and 2000.

♦ 18 Z-28 class
Bldr: Blohm + Voss, Hamburg (In serv. 9-79 to 1-80)

GC 64 Mar del Plata
GC 65 Martin Garcia
GC 66 Río Lujan
GC 67 Río Uruguay
GC 68 Río Paraguay
GC 69 Río Parana
GC 70 Río Plata
GC 71 La Plata
GC 72 Buenos Aires
GC 73 Cabo Corrientes
GC 74 Quequen
GC 75 Bahía Blanca
GC 76 Ingeniero White
GC 77 Golfo San Matias
GC 78 Madryn
GC 79 Río Deseado
GC 80 Ushuaia
GC 81 Canal de Beagle

D: 81 tons (fl) **S:** 22 kts **Dim:** 27.65 (26.0 pp) × 5.30 × 1.65
A: 1 20-mm 90-cal. Oerlikon GAM-B01 AA; 2 single 12.7-mm mg
Electronics: Radar: 1 Decca 1226 nav.
M: 2 MTU 8V331 TC92 diesels; 2 props; 2,100 bhp (1,770 sust.)
Electric: 90 kVA **Range:** 780/18; 1,200/12 **Crew:** 3 officers, 11 enlisted

PATROL BOATS [WPB] *(continued)*

Bahía Blanca (GC 75) Ignacio Amendolara, 2-05

Remarks: Ordered 24-11-78. Fin stabilizers fitted. During the Falklands/Malvinas War, *Río Iguazú* (GC 83) was lost, and *Islas Malvinas* (GC 82) was captured by British forces. Not all units carry the 20-mm gun.

♦ **34 GC 48 class**
Bldr: Cadenazzi SY, Tigre (except GC 88–114: Ast. Belen de Escobar)

GC 48–GC 61 (In serv. 1978–79)
GC 88–GC 95, GC 102–GC 114 (In serv. 1984–86)

GC 48–class GC 93 Ignacio Amendolara, 2-05

D: 13 tons (15 fl) **S:** 25 kts **Dim:** 12.54 × 3.57 × 1.10
A: 1 12.7-mm mg
M: 2 G.M. Detroit Diesel 6V71N diesels; 2 props; 514 bhp
Range: 400/20 **Crew:** 3 tot.

Remarks: Constructed in three batches. All are named except GC 102–114.

♦ **1 patrol boat** Bldr: Río Santiago Naval Base (In serv. 17-12-39)

GC 101 Dorado

D: 43 tons (fl) **S:** 12 kts **Dim:** 21.2 × 4.3 × 1.5
A: small arms **M:** 2 G.M. Gray Marine 6071-6A diesels; 2 props; 360 hp
Range: 1550/12 **Crew:** 1 officer, 6 enlisted

♦ **1 patrol boat** Bldr: Otholan, Tigre (1941)

GC 102 Anchoa (ex-LP 4)

D: 10 tons **Dim:** 14.0 × 4.0 × 2.1 **M:** 2 G.M. diesel; 360 kw **Crew:** 3/10 crew

♦ **1 patrol boat** Bldr: Otholan, Tigre (1944)

GC 106 Narval (ex-LP 106)

D: 26 tons **Dim:** 15.0 × 3.2 × 2.5 **M:** 2 Bedford diesels; 160 kw
Crew: 3/10 crew

♦ **1 patrol boat RIOMAR** Bldr: Baader, Tigre (1952)

GC 114

D: 26 tons **Dim:** 12.0 × 3.5 × 1.4 **M:** 1 G.M. diesel; 180 kw **Crew:** 3/10 crew

♦ **1 patrol boat** Bldr: Parodi, Tigre (1937)

GC 115 Talita II

D: 26 tons **Dim:** 19.0 × 4.5 × 2.3 **M:** 2 G.M. diesels; 360 kw **Crew:** 3/10 crew

♦ **1 patrol boat** Bldr: Otholan, Tigre (1960)

GC 117 Adhara II (ex-*Gloria;* ex-*Cormorán,* GC 35)

D: 26 tons **Dim:** 21.0 × 4.5 × 2.3 **M:** 2 G.M. diesels; 360 kw **Crew:** 3/10 crew

♦ **8 Stan Tender 2200 patrol boats**
Bldr: Damen, Gorinchem, the Netherlands

GC 122 Lago Mascardi (ex-SP 17)
GC 123 Lago Viedna (ex-SP 20)
GC 124 Lago San Martín (ex-SP 21)
GC 125 Lago Buenos Aires (ex-SP 22)
GC 129 Lago Colhue (ex-SP 16)
GC 130 Maria L. Pendo (ex-SP 18, ex-*Lago Argentino*)
GC 150 Lago Fagnano (ex-SP 23)
GC 151 Lago Nahuel Huapi (ex-SP 19)

D: 55 tons **Dim:** 23.5 × 5.3 × 2.9 **A:** small arms **M:** 2 G.M. 600 kw
Crew: 3/10

♦ **3 Stan Tender 1750 patrol boats**
Bldr: Damen, Gorinchem, the Netherlands

GC 118 Lago Alumine (ex-SP 14)
GC 119 Lago Traful (ex-SP 15)
GC 133 Lago Futalaufquen (ex-SP 30)

Lago Alumine (GC 118) Ignacio Amendolara, 11-02

D: 60 tons **Dim:** 16.5 × 4.7 × 2.5 **A:** small arms **M:** 2 G.M. 600 kw
Crew: 3/10

♦ **6 Cat 1100 patrol boats** Bldr: Damen, Gorinchem, the Netherlands

GC 120 Lago Lacar (ex-SP 24)
GC 126 Lago Musters (ex-SP 26)
GC 131 Lago Roca (ex-SP 28)
GC 132 Lago Puelo (ex-SP 29)
GC 141 Lago Quillen (ex-SP 27)
SP 25 Lago Catriel

Lago Puelo (GC 132) Alejandro Amendolara, 2000

♦ **3 Cat 1100 patrol boats** Bldr: Mestrina, Tigre, Argentina

GC 135 Lago Huechulafquen (ex-SP 33)
GC 136 Lago Hess (ex-*Lago Colhe Huapi;* ex-SP 34)
GC 140 Lago Yehuin (ex-SP 35)

♦ **6 21-ft. Hurricane rigid inflatable boats [WYFL]**
Bldr: American Zodiac

SR 2901 through SR 2906

Remarks: Entered service 2004–5. Can have either open cabin or enclosed pilothouse.

PATROL BOATS [WPB] *(continued)*

SR 9206 alongside sisters SR 9205 and SR 2904—with enclosed pilothouses
Ignacio Amendolara, 2005

AUXILIARIES

♦ **1 pilot station ship [WAG]**
Bldr: ASTARSA (Astilleros Argentinos Río de la Plata), San Fernando

DF 15 RECALADA (ex-*Río Limay*)

D: 10,070 tons (fl) **S:** 18 kts **Dim:** 147.61 (138.00 pp) × 20.20 × 8.25
M: 1 AFNE-GMT B750-7L reversing diesel; 1 prop; 10,500 bhp
Range: 14,000/18 **Fuel:** 1,197 tons **Crew:** 3 officers, 25 enlisted

Remarks: 9,059 grt. Acquired 9-91 to act as Río Plata pilot station ship and commissioned 24-12-91. Former general cargo ship, with forward cargo-handling gear removed and forward hatch reinforced as a helicopter platform. Has been given a 20-bed hospital facility. "Recalada" painted on hull sides.

♦ **1 salvage tug [WARS]**
Bldr: Sanym S.A., San Fernando (In serv. 21-10-77)

GC 47 TONINA

D: 103 tons (153 fl) **S:** 11 kts **Dim:** 25.5 × 5.3 × 2.1
A: 1 20-mm 70-cal. Oerlikon AA; 2 single 12.7-mm mg
Electronics: Radar: 1 Decca 1226 nav.
M: 2 G.M. Detroit Diesel 16V71N 162-2000 diesels; 2 props; 1,500 hp
Range: 2,800/10 **Crew:** 3 officers, 8 enlisted

Tonina (GC 47)—inboard Damen "PushyCat" tug Canal Emilio Mitre (SB 8)
Hartmut Ehlers, 1-98

Remarks: Used as training ship until 1986. Has divers' facilities including a decompression chamber.

SERVICE CRAFT

♦ **6 miscellaneous small tugboats [WYTL]**

SB 3 . . . SB 8 CANAL EMILIO MITRE SB 10 . . .
SB 4 . . . SB 9 CANAL COSTANERO SI 4 (ex-SB 5) P. DE BUENOS AIRES

Remarks: SB 8: 53 tons (fl); 10 kts; Damen "PushyCat 1500" design, built 1982.

♦ **1 fireboat [WYTR]** (In serv. 1960)

SI 1 RODOLFO D'AGOSTINI

D: 32 tons **Dim:** 30.0 × 7.6 × 2.2 **Crew:** 4/30 crew

♦ **1 sail-training yacht [WYTS]** (L: 12–68)

ESPERANZA

D: 32 tons **S:** 15 kts (6 under power) **Dim:** 19.0 × 4.3 × 2.7
M: 1 G.M. diesel; 90 bhp **Crew:** 6 crew + 6 cadets

Remarks: Also in use are sailing yacht *Adhara II* (ex-*Gloria*, ex-*Cormorán*, GC 36), of 30 tons, with one G.M. auxiliary diesel, capable of 10–15 kts; *Dr. Bernardo Houssay* (ex-*El Austral*), a 46-ton ketch built 1930 in Denmark and acquired in 1996; and cabin cruiser *Talita II*.

♦ **1 Dorado-class training craft [WYXT]**
Bldr: Río Santiago Naval Base (In serv. 1940)

GC 43 MANDUBI

D: 208 tons (270 fl) **S:** 11 kts **Dim:** 33.2 × 4.0 × 1.9
A: 2 single 12.7-mm mg
M: 2 M.A.N. G6V 23.5/33 diesels; 2 props; 880 bhp
Range: 800/14; 3,400/10 **Crew:** 12 crew + 20 trainees

Remarks: Two sisters were stricken 1985–86. Used as a training craft for cadets. Tug-type vessel.

Note: Also in use are over 400 smaller launches, RIBs, and service craft such as floating cranes.

AUSTRALIA

Commonwealth of Australia

Personnel: The permanent trained forces consist of 13,167 total plus 1,600 reservists. In addition civilian numbers are capped at 734. The private firm Defence Maritime Services employs civilian personnel to operate various service craft.

Note: The operation and maintenance of support craft such as torpedo retrievers, tugs, and range support services was contracted for 10 years in mid-1997 to Defence Maritime Services Pty, Ltd. (DMS), a joint venture company established by P&O Maritime Australia and Serco Defence Services. DMS also provides submarine trials and support services and maintenance and training on all motor- and sail-training craft.

Bases: Maritime Headquarters is at Sydney, along with Fleet Base East, HMAS *Waterhen* (mine countermeasures), HMAS *Watson* (training), and HMAS *Kuttabul* (administration). Fleet Base West is at HMAS *Stirling,* Cockburn Sound, Fremantle, Western Australia, with administration, submarine base, HMAS *Albatross* air station at Nowra, HMAS *Creswell* Naval College, Jervis Bay firing range, and maintenance facilities. Other facilities include HMAS *Coonawarra* communications facility and patrol boat base at Darwin, Northern Terr.; Headquarters Patrol Force at HMAS *Cairns,* Cairns, Queensland; HMAS *Cerberus* (training and small warship facilities) at Westernport, Victoria; *Harold E. Holt* communications station at North West Cape, Western Australia; HMAS *Harman* area administration and communications station, Canberra; and Naval Headquarters, Port Kembla, Tasmania. Noncommissioned establishments include the Jervis Bay range facility; the Naval Supply Center, Sydney; Naval Armaments Depots at Kingswood, New South Wales, and Somerton, Victoria; and Naval Armament and Equipment Depots at Garden Island, Western Australia, and Maribyrnong, Victoria. An ammunition storage facility opened in 2002 at Twofold Bay, New South Wales.

Naval Aviation: Commander, Australian Naval Aviation Forces was reestablished 1-3-96 at HMAS *Albatross,* Nowra, New South Wales. About 900 personnel serve in aviation billets.

Aircraft in service include 11 Kaman SH-2G(A) Super SeaSprite shipboard ASW/attack helicopters in HS-805 Sqn., 16 Sikorsky S-70B-2 Seahawk shipboard ASW helicopters in HS-816 Sqn. (U.S. Navy LAMPS-III-equivalent, with MEL Super Searcher radar in place of LN-66, GE T700-401C turboshaft engines, one 7.62-mm machinegun, two Mk 46 ASW torpedoes), seven Mk 50A Sea King helicopters in HS-817 Sqn. (an 8th unit, attached to HMAS Kanimbla, crashed on 2-4-05, with the loss of nine men, while conducting humanitarian operations at the village of Tuindrao, Indonesia. A Board of Inquiry was convened on 6-9-05 to investigate the crash) and 13 AS-350B Écureuil light utility helicopters in HC-723 Sqn.

Five (plus one lost) of the Sea King helicopters have been modified for utility service (ASW equipment deleted) and rehabilitated to serve through 2008. RAN Sea Kings are powered by two Rolls-Royce Gnome H1400-1 turbines of 1,650 shp each and can carry either 23 troops or 2,750 kg of stores; range is about 500 n.m. at 100 kts, and maximum speed 138 kts.

The 16 S-70B-2 Seahawk helicopters were modernized with new ESM and forward-looking infrared sensors with 1993–94 budget funds; at a later date it is hoped to add a lightweight dipping sonar and an antiship missile-launching capability. The Seahawk helicopters began receiving Boeing AAR-54(V) missile-warning systems and Raytheon AAQ-27 FLIR in 2-00; the same equipment will later be fitted to the SH-2G(A) helicopters. 12 NH-90 helicopters were ordered in 2004.

SH-2G(A) SeaSprite—with flotation bags deployed Kaman, 2001

AS.350B Écureuil RAN, 1999

S-70B-2 Seahawk Michael Nitz, 5-05

On 17-1-97 the Kaman SH-2G(A) Super SeaSprite was selected as the helicopter for employment with the *Anzac*-class frigates; the first was delivered during 2-01 and the last in 2-02. They have a Litton LN-100G integrated tactical avionics system, Rockwell Collins GEM III GPS, Telephonics APS-143B(V)3 radar (with inverse synthetic aperture capability for target identification), Raytheon AAQ-47 (3FOV) FLIR, Elisra LWS-20 laser warning and AES-210 ESM, Litton Link 11, Northrop Grumman AAR-54(V) passive missile approach warning system, and Tracor ALE-47 decoy dispensers, but no sonar equipment. The operational date for the SH-2G Super SeaSprite helicopters has been delayed to 2004, due to late delivery of the Litton mission control system. Other characteristics for the new SH-2G(A) Super SeaSprite helicopter include:

Rotor diameter: 13.51 m **Length:** 12.93 m folded/16.00 m over rotors
Weight: 6,441 kg (max. takeoff) **Speed:** 150 kts max.
Engines: 2 G.E. T700-GE-401 turboshafts (1,723 shp each)
Ceiling: 20,400 ft. (14,600 ft. hovering) **Range:** 546 n.m. **Endurance:** 5.3 hrs
Crew: 2 + up to 6 troops **Payload:** 2,296 kg
Weapons: 2 AGM-119B Penguin Mk 2 Mod. 7 ASM or 2 Mk 46 torpedoes or 2 Mk 11 d.c.

The remaining Bell 206B Kiowa utility helicopters were transferred to the Australian Army in 8-00, in return for additional AS.350B Écureuil helicopters. The two HS-748 fixed-wing EW training aircraft were retired on 22-6-00.

The RAAF operates 18 P-3C Orion maritime patrol aircraft equipped with AQS-901 receiver/processors for the Australian-developed Barra SSQ-801 sonobuoy and capable of carrying two AGM-84A or -84C Harpoon antiship missiles. Under a 1994 contract with E-Systems, Greenville, Texas, 18 P-3Cs are receiving Elta EL/M-2022A(V)3 radars, new EW intercept equipment, a new MAD sensor, GPS and SATCOM receivers, a new acoustic processor, anticorrosion treatment, and weight-saving measures during modernizations completed in 2001; the modernization is expected to permit the newly styled AP-3C Sea Sentinel aircraft to be operated until 2015. During 2004–5, 15 Star SAFIRE III Electro Optic Surveillance systems were purchased for use with the AP-3C fleet. Three ex-USN P-3B Orions perform training duties. Four Boeing 737 AEH aircraft have been purchased by the air force for delivery between 2007 and 2008.

Aerial surveillance of Australia's immensely long northern coastline is conducted by the Customs Service Coastwatch, using contractor-operated aircraft and with the assistance of RAAF Orions. National Jet Systems operates five de Havilland Canada Dash 8-202 MPA, five Reims F406 Caravan II, six Pilatus Britten-Norman BN2B-20 Islanders, and one Rockwell Shrike Commander for the Coastwatch, while Reef Helicopters operates a Bell LongRanger IV helicopter in the Torres Strait region. One each Dash 8-202 MPA and Reims F406 operate from Broome, Darwin, and Cairns, while the Islanders are based at Broome, Darwin, Horn Island, and Cairns (the latter with the Shrike Commander). The Dash 8-202 MPAs and F406s carry the Texas Instruments APS-134 digital radar, and the Dash 8-202 MPAs have an integrated tactical data system, a Westcam 16T optronics surveillance turret with Mitsubishi IRST, and low-light television sensors.

Coast Defense: A network of surveillance radars, termed the Jindalee Operational Radar Network (JORN) over-the-horizon system, supports air defense along the northern coast. Operational trials of the Surface-wave Extended Coastal Area Radar (SECAR; also known as Project Iluka) began in 2000; it will provide a surface- and low-altitude search adjunct to the JORN.

Future Programs: Under the 12-00 Defence Capabilities Plan, the navy is to receive through 2015: three DDGs (the first to enter service in 2013); replacements for one of the U.S. LSTs and *Tobruk;* replacement utility landing craft and two replacement underway replenishment oilers by 2009; upgrades to antiship missile defenses and improved antiship weaponry for the *Anzac*-class frigates; replacement patrol craft to enter service starting 2004–5; full updates to all six *Collins*-class submarines; a new submarine torpedo beginning in 2006; and a midlife update to the Seahawk helicopter fleet.

WEAPONS AND SYSTEMS

The Royal Australian Navy primarily uses U.S. equipment and systems. U.S. Mk 48 torpedoes and Sub-Harpoon missiles have been purchased for use by submarines, and Harpoons are also carried by *Perry*-class frigates and RAAF P-3C, F/A-18, and F-111 aircraft. In 2002 an additional 64 RGM-84L Harpoon missiles were requested by Australia for $90 million. During 2005, 175 SM-2 Standard missiles were requested by Australia for US $315 million.

Kongsberg Defence & Aerospace, Norway, received a five-year, $50.7 million contract in 1998 for Penguin air-to-surface antiship missiles; an additional $40 million was added during 1-99, with deliveries commencing 7-01 and ending by end-2003.

The Australian-manufactured Mulloka sonar is a high-frequency set tailored to local coastal water/sound propagation conditions. The Karriwarra towed passive sonar array entered service in 1985 for submarines. The Albatross sonar system (formerly ASSTASS—Australian Surface Ship Towed Array Surveillance System) is being developed by Thales for use on the modernized *Perry*-class FFGs. To be incorporated in the update to the *Perry*-class frigates is the indigenously developed Petrel navigational and mine-avoidance sonar, with a vertical linear, stabilized active hydrophone array, and a horizontal linear receiving array. In the fall of 2002 Australia became the first nation to receive ESSM Sea Sparrow missiles. In 1-03 HMAS *Warramunga* fired an ESSM, successfully engaging a towed test target.

The Nulka (formerly Winnin) countermeasures system with hovering chaff/IR decoy rockets uses the same Mk 137 6-round launcher as the U.S. Mk 36 SRBOC system, with the Nulka tubes replacing the chaff tubes. The production order was placed in 8-96.

The first Mini-Dyad reconfigurable permanent magnet influence sweep arrays were ordered in 1996; they employ a 6.4 × 0.53-m, hollow, two-section mild steel pipe with two reconfigurable strontium-ferrite inserts.

Two Australian Acoustic Generator (AAG) towed acoustic mine-countermeasures sets (with another 16 planned) were ordered on 5-6-01 for use with the Huon class and other RAN mine-countermeasures craft. Powered by a water turbine, the AAG is intended to complement the DYAD magnetic system, with both being components of the Australian Minesweeping and Surveillance System (AMASS). AAG is programmable to simulate different sizes and types of ship.

The BAe Systems Stonefish Mk III was selected in 5-00 to fulfill the Project Bay-awirri (Defence Project SEA 2045) requirement to provide the RAN with an offensive sea mining capability that will employ air- or submarine-launched standoff mines, with a later submarine-launched variant to include a mobile-mine payload.

Major ships are equipped with one of 47 TESS (Tactical Environmental Support System) sets acquired in the early 1990s to assist the commanding officer with decisions about which sensors to employ under given environmental conditions. TESS 2, configured to overcome "Y2K" hardware and software problems, entered service prior to the end of 1999, and an improved TESS 3 is in development.

About 100 MU 90 Impact lightweight ASW torpedoes were ordered from Eurotorp on 18-2-02 for shipboard, helicopter, and RAAF AP-3 Orion aircraft use. In 2003 Australia announced that it plans to acquire the Mk 48 Mod 7 ADCAP torpedo, to be developed through a collaborative program between the United States and Australia. The weapons are due to enter service in 2006. There is also ongoing cooperation on the Mk 48 Common Broadband Advanced Sonar System (CBASS) Heavyweight Torpedo for improved littoral operations.

The 37 ships with Magnavox MX1100 SATNAV systems have been updated to use the Global Positioning System.

ATTACK SUBMARINES [SS]

♦ 6 Collins class (Kockums Type 471)

Bldr: Australian Submarine Corp., Port Adelaide, South Australia

	Laid down	L	In serv.
SSG 73 Collins	14-2-90	28-8-93	27-7-96
SSG 74 Farncomb	1-3-91	15-12-95	31-1-98
SSG 75 Waller	19-3-92	14-3-97	10-7-99
SSG 76 Dechaineux	4-3-93	12-3-98	23-2-01
SSG 77 Sheean	17-2-94	1-5-99	23-2-01
SSG 78 Rankin	12-5-95	26-11-01	29-3-03

D: 2,450 tons light, 3,051 surf./3,353 tons sub.
S: 10.5 kts surf./snorkel and 21 kts sub. **Dim:** 77.42 × 7.80 × 7.00
A: 6 bow 533-mm TT (23 UGM-84C Harpoon SSM and Mk 48 Mod. 4 wire-guided torpedoes (Mk 48 will be replaced by the MU-90 wire-guided and passive/active homing torpedoes beginning in 2006)
Electronics:
Radar: GEC-Marconi Type 1007 surface search
Sonar: Thales Scylla bow and flank arrays; first two: Thales Karriwarra passive towed array; others: Thales Karriwarra or Thales Narama towed array
EW: ArgoSystems Phoenix AR-740-US intercept (Currently on SSG 76 and 77 only; will eventually be back fitted on the remainder)
M: diesel-electric: 3 Garden Island-Hedemora HV V18B/15Ub (VB 210) 18-cyl. diesel generator sets (6,000 bhp/4,425 kw tot.); 1 Jeumont-Schneider motor; 1 7-bladed (4.22 m dia.) prop; 7,200 shp—100-hp retractable hydraulic emergency propulsor
Range: 11,500/10 surf. (see remarks); 9,000/10 snorkel; 32.6/21 sub.; 480/4 sub.
Endurance: 70 days **Crew:** 6 officers, 36 enlisted

Dechaineux (SSG 76) Brian Morrison, 2004

ATTACK SUBMARINES [SS] *(continued)*

Rankin (SSG 78) CPOPH Mal Back, RAN 3-03

Sheean (SSG 77) RAN 2004

Dechaineux (SSG 76)—note tube protruding aft for dispensing the towed sonar array Brian Morrison, 2004

Remarks: Contract announced 18-5-87 for six, with option for two more (later dropped). Cost about $550 million (U.S.) each. The Australian Submarine Corp. was originally a consortium of Kockums, Hardie, Ltd., and the government-owned Australian Industrial Development Co. The bow and stern sections of first two were built at Malmö, Sweden, by Kockums. Initial surface trials for *Collins* began 31-10-94, and first dive was made 11-6-95. All are based at Fleet Base West, HMAS *Stirling*, south of Fremantle.

In 7-96, it was announced that plans for possible backfitting of units of the class with AIP had been dropped because of the excellent submerged endurance and low indiscretion rates experienced with the *Collins*.

None of the class was fully ready for operational deployments before 2000 because of software integration problems, though the first two were able to perform limited combat functions by 1998; the final software suite was not delivered until mid-1999 and required a one-year trial period in the *Collins*. The first two suffered a number of setbacks, including hydrodynamic flow problems that mask the passive sonar systems, cracked propellers, periscope vibration, engine and gearbox seal problems, and severe combat system software deficiencies. SSG 75 and SSG 76 began upgrading prior to delivery, with improvements to the sonar and the combat data- and fire-control systems, while noise signature was reduced and vibration problems with the periscopes and propellers were effectively eliminated. Cancellation of a proposed contract to upgrade the combat systems for the class in 5-01 will delay full operational capability for the class until around 2009. On 16-10-01 it was announced that all refits for the class will be performed by the Australian Submarine Corporation at Adelaide. In early 2003 *Dechaineux* is reported to have nearly sunk during a dive due to flooding from a broken hose. As a result, the entire fleet was called back to port and repaired.

Rolls Royce received a three-year contract (with two-year extension option) to provide assistance in the managing of the maintenance of the operational submarines of the class at the building yard and at Fleet Base West.

Hull systems: Said to be the quietest, most shock-resistant diesel-electric submarines in the world. Modular construction. Intended to meet a mission requirement of a 3,500 n.m. radius at 10 kts submerged, plus 47 days on station at 4 kts. Battery capacity gives 120 hours at 4 kts. Diving depth is stated as "in excess of 180 meters."

All after the first were to be completed with an anechoic tile hull coating; *Collins* was backfitted after comparative trials. Marconi SDG-1802 degaussing gear is fitted. The outer hull casing form has been altered to reduce flow noise; the prototype form was tested at sea in *Collins* in mid-1999, and *Dechaineux* and *Sheean* were similarly altered starting during 2000; all three have improved engine mountings to reduce vibration.

Combat systems: Have the Raytheon SCCS Mk 2 f.c.s., for which Version 2.0 software was delivered 12-99; to be replaced by the Raytheon CCS Mk 2 system between 2006 and 2010. The EW suite is also to be replaced. They have a receive-only interface with the Link-11 combat information system datalink. Periscopes from Pilkington Optronics include a CK 43 search and a CH 93 attack.

The sonar suite is derived from the Thales (Thomson-Sintra) Eledone and includes a bow-mounted cylindrical passive array, a 5-kHz active array at the forward edge of the sail, bow-mounted mine avoidance active and passive intercept arrays, flank arrays, two aft-mounted intercept arrays, and towed array (developmental models of the Australian Karriwarra, with 1,000-m array, 45 mm in diameter, in the first two, with the installation in the later four to be decided by a competion between Karriwarra, Thomson-Sintra's Narama, and the U.S. TB-23 thin-line array system. There are also 16 self-noise measurement hydrophones, 16 accelerometers, and an 8–11 kHz underwater telephone. The British Strachan & Henshaw submerged signal and decoy ejector system is installed.

U.S. Tomahawk strategic cruise missiles may be added later. In 2003 Australia announced that it plans to acquire the U.S./Australian developed Mk 48 Mod 7 ADCAP torpedo for service entry around 2006.

Note: The remotely operated submarine personnel rescue vehicle *Remora* was delivered 1996 on a 5-year lease from the Australian Submarine Corp. Built in Canada by Can-Dive Marine Services, Vancouver, the 16.5-ton craft can operate in up to 550 m of water. In 1998 the general-purpose ship *Seahorse Spirit* was assigned as tender. As part of the complex, two 36-seat recompression chamber modules are carried on the tender.

GUIDED MISSILE DESTROYERS [DDG]

♦ 0 (+ 3) Air Warfare Destroyers
Bldr: ASC, Australia

	Laid down	L	In serv.
D . . . Hobart	2007	. . .	2013
D . . . Brisbane	. . .	. . .	2014
D . . . Sydney	. . .	. . .	2016

Remarks: A replacement destroyer project, Sea 1400, is in the advanced stages of definition. The ships may be armed with U.S. Standard SM-2 and Evolved Sea Sparrow vertically launched SAMs, though the use of an existing foreign ship design adapted to Australian requirements and built in Australia is preferred. On 25-5-00, the Australian Ministry of Defence declined the offer of ships of the U.S. Kidd (DDG 993) class to fulfill this role (they were later sold to Taiwan). The U.S. naval architectural firm Gibbs & Cox offered a 5,900-ton, scaled-down, lesser-capability version of the Arleigh Burke class; the ships would carry SPY-1D Aegis, SM-2, Evolved Sea Sparrow, and RAM SAMs and RGM-84 Harpoon antiship missiles. Spain's Navantir (formerly Izar and E.N. Bazán) and its F-100 design, Germany's Blohm +Voss Type 124 (Sachsen-class) and BAE Systems, with a variant of the British Type 45 DDG were the other design tenders under consideration.

On 16-8-05 the Ministry of Defense selected the AEGIS equipped Gibbs & Cox Arleigh Burke–class variant as preferred designer for this project. ASC Shipbuilder Pty Ltd. has been selected as the shipyard for building the three ships and Raytheon, Australia was selected as the Combat Systems Engineer. Construction is to begin in 2007. The three ships will begin to enter service around 2013 with the second unit to follow in 2014 and the final unit in 2016.

Disposal note: The final U.S. Charles F. Adams–class guided missile destroyer in RAN service, *Brisbane* (DDG 41, ex-U.S. DDG 27), was retired on 19-10-01 (sunk for use as an artificial fishing reef off Stradbroke Island, Queensland, Australia on 31-7-05; the ship's entire bridge and operations room had been removed and are on display at the Australian War Memorial in Canberra). *Perth* (DDG 38, ex-U.S. DDG 25) was retired on 15-10-99 and *Hobart* (DDG 39, ex-U.S. DDG 26) on 12-5-00.

GUIDED MISSILE FRIGATES [FFG]

♦ 4 U.S. Oliver Hazard Perry class
Bldrs: First three: Todd Shipyards, Seattle; FFG 05, 06: AMECON, Melbourne

	Laid down	L	In serv.
FFG 03 Sydney (ex-FFG 35)	16-1-80	26-9-80	29-1-83
FFG 04 Darwin (ex-FFG 44)	2-7-81	26-3-82	21-7-84
FFG 05 Melbourne	12-7-85	5-5-89	15-2-92
FFG 06 Newcastle	21-7-89	21-2-92	11-12-93

D: 3,073 tons (3,962 fl) **S:** 29 kts
Dim: 138.80 (126.0 wl) × 13.72 × 4.52 (7.47 max.)

GUIDED MISSILE FRIGATES [FFG] *(continued)*

Newcastle (FFG 06) Chris Sattler, 3-05

Melbourne (FFG 05)—note that the Mk 15 Phalanx CIWS has been removed in this photograph Chris Sattler, 7-05

Sydney (FFG 03)—note Mk 41 VLS system fitted forward of Mk 13 missile launcher Chris Sattler, 2-05

Darwin (FFG 04) Brian Morrison, 11-04

A: 1 8-cell Mark 41, Mod. 5 VLS syst. (Standard SM-2 SAM and 32 Evolved Sea-Sparrow [ESSM] in quad packs); 1 Mk 13 Mod. 4 launcher (40 Standard SM-1A SAM and RGM-84L Harpoon missiles); 1 76-mm/62-cal.U.S. Mk 75 DP; 1 20-mm Mk 15 Phalanx CIWS; 2 single 12.7-mm M2 mg; 2 triple 324-mm Mk 32 ASW TT (Mk 46 Mod 5 torpedoes); 2 helicopters (see remarks)

Electronics:

Radar: 1 Cardion SPS-55 surf. search; 1 Raytheon SPS-49(V)1 air search; 1 Lockheed Martin Mk 92 mod. 12 track-while-scan gun/missile f.c.; 1 Lockheed Martin SPG-60 STIR missile/gun f.c.

Sonar: Raytheon SQS-56 (7.5 kHz) (FFG 05, 06: EMI/Honeywell Mulloka)—TACAN: URN-25

EW: Raytheon SLQ-32A(V)2 intercept; Elbit EA 2118 intercept (2–40 GHz); modified Mk 36 SRBOC decoy syst. (4 10-tubed modified Mk 137 RL, with Nulka capability); SLQ-25 Nixie towed torpedo decoy

E/O: Rademac 2500 surveillance and tracking; 2 Mk 24 target desig.

M: 2 G.E. LM-2500 gas turbines; 1 CP prop; 41,000 shp—2 350-shp drop-down electric propulsors

Electric: 3,000 kw tot. **Range:** 4,200/20; 5,000/18

Fuel: 587 tons (plus 64 tons helo fuel)

Crew: 15 officers, 172 enlisted (plus air group)

Remarks: First four ordered between 2-76 and 4-80. The two Australian-built ships were ordered 12-10-83. FFG 01, 02, and 04 have been transferred to Fleet Base West, HMAS Stirling, near Fremantle in the 1990s; the others are based at Fleet Base East, Sydney. A class-wide modernization program was contracted with ADI on 13-11-98, but under a contract finalized in 5-99 only the last four units are to be modernized. The vessels are to be modernized in the order of construction with the first unit taking 50 weeks and the remainder 38-40 weeks. HMAS Sydney began hers in 9-03 with completion late in 2005. The entire program is scheduled to complete in 2007 (for further comments see under "Modernization" below.)

The first two were originally due for retirement in 2008, and the next pair in 2012, but planned modernizations will delay the retirements to 2015 or later. A class-wide modernization program contracted for with ADI was to begin 9-03 and complete in 2007.

Hull systems: Two drop-down, diesel-electric-driven propellers are located forward beneath the hull for emergency propulsion and maneuvering. The selection of the Sikorsky S-70B2 helicopter for these ships required that the first three be lengthened 9 feet and have fin stabilization systems added at Garden Island Dockyard; the RAST helicopter downhaul and traversing system was also added. FFG 03 completed lengthening 1-89, FFG 01 in 8-89, and FFG 02 completed 1991. Have fin stabilizers and are equipped with the Prairie/Masker air bubbler system to reduce radiated machinery noise below the waterline.

Combat systems: The Australian-built units have Mulloka sonars in place of SQS-56. FFG 01 and FFG 02 had the two Mk 24 optical target designators atop the pilothouse and EW systems added after delivery. All carry WSC-3 UHF SATCOM sets. Israeli Elbit intercept equipment added 1989–90. The ships normally carry one S-70B-2 and one Écureuil helicopter, with the S-70B-2 Seahawk able to carry two Penguin Mk 2 Mod. 7 antiship missiles or two ASW torpedoes. Rademac 2500 electro-optical surveillance and tracking systems in place on all by 1998; they incorporate HK202 daylight television, Ranger-600 laser rangefinder, and LRTS thermal imager in one stabilized mounting. The 12.7-mm mg are located atop the pilothouse. All have been upgraded with Nulka decoy rocket launchers. FFG 06 was equipped with a prototype modular berthing compartment that can add six or twelve additional bunks, plus a head, to the normal 210 maximum; the module is accommodated in one of the two hangars when only one helicopter is aboard.

Modernization: Australian Defence Industries (ADI) has been selected to perform an extensive $636-million modernization on all six ships, but under a contract finalized in 5-99 only the last four units of the class are to be modernized. The work is to be completed at Garden Island, Sydney. Lockheed Martin and Gibbs & Cox of the U.S.A. are assisting. The Mk 92 f.c.s. has/will be upgraded to Mod. 12, and one 8-cell Mk 41 vertical missile launch group (32 Evolved Sea Sparrow SAM in Quad Packs) has/will be added forward of the Mk 13 missile launcher in place of the current helicopter replenishment spot. In the future, the class may receive the SM-2 SAM system. The Rafael-Elisra C-PEARL EW suite will replace the present SLQ-32 system (which was upgraded to SLQ-32A(V)2 in the late 1990s), and UYQ-70 displays and a Link 16 capability will be added. The SPS-49(V)2 radar is also to be upgraded to SPS-49A(V)1, and the sonar is to be replaced by the Thales TMS 4131, with Petrel 5424 mine-avoidance sonar beginning with HMAS *Sydney*. Also added will be an improved torpedo detection capability using the Sea Defender suite with an Albatross detection sonar and the current SLQ-25A decoy system has been added. Late in 2002 the Terma SKWS decoy launch control system was purchased for the ships.

Disposals: HMAS *Canberra* (FFG-02), an unmodernized unit, was stricken on 11-11-05. HMAS *Adelaide* (FFG-01), the other unit not modernized, was stricken in 2006. HMAS *Sydney* is scheduled to retire by 2015.

FRIGATES [FF]

♦ 8 Anzac (MEKO 200 ANZ) class

Bldr: Tenix Defence Systems (Transfield Shipbuilding), Williamstown, Victoria

	Laid down	L	In serv.
FFH 150 Anzac	5-11-93	16-9-94	18-5-96
FFH 151 Arunta (ex-*Arrerente*)	22-7-95	28-6-96	12-12-98
FFH 152 Warramunga (ex-*Warumungu*)	26-7-97	23-5-98	31-3-01
FFH 153 Stuart	25-7-98	17-4-99	17-8-02
FFH 154 Parramatta	24-4-99	17-6-00	4-10-03
FFH 155 Ballarat	4-8-00	25-5-02	26-6-04
FFH 156 Toowoomba	26-7-02	16-5-03	8-10-05
FFH 157 Perth	24-7-03	20-3-04	12-06

Ballarat (FFH 155) Chris Sattler, 7-04

FRIGATES [FF] *(continued)*

Anzac (FF 150) Michael Nitz, 5-05

Toowoomba (FFH 156) Chris Sattler, 9-05

Anzac (FF 150)—with Seahawk helicopter on the flightdeck Michael Nitz, 5-05

D: 3,300 tons (3,600 fl) **S:** 27 kts (20 kts on diesel)
Dim: 117.50 (109.50 pp) × 14.80 (13.80 wl) × 5.99 (4.37 hull)
A: 1 8-celled Mk 41 Mod. 5 VLS syst. (8 RIM-7P Sea Sparrow SAM); FF 152 and later: ESSM (see comments in Combat systems); Provisions for 2 quad RGM-84L Harpoon Block II ASM canister launchers (see Modernization comments); 1 127-mm 54-cal. Mk 45 Mod. 2 DP; provision for 1 20-mm Mk. 15 Phalanx CIWS; 4 single 12.7-mm mg; 2 triple 324-mm Mk 32 ASW TT (Mk 46 Mod. 5 torpedoes); 1 SH-2G(A) Super SeaSprite helicopter

Electronics:
Radar: 1 STN Atlas Elektronik 9600-M ARPA nav.; 1 Ericsson 150 HC Sea Giraffe target desig.; 1 Raytheon SPS-49(V)8 early warning; 1 CelsiusTech Ceros 200 f.c.
Sonar: Thales Spherion-B hull-mounted (7 kHz)
EW: Racal-Thorn Sceptre-A intercept (2–18 GHz); EADS PST 1720 comms intercept; Thales Telegon 10 Maigret HFD/F; Mk 36 Mod. 1 SRBOC decoy syst. (2 8-tubed Mk 137 RL with Sea Gnat Mk 214 and Nulka decoys); SLQ-25A Nixie towed torpedo decoy
M: CODOG: 2 MTU 12V1163 TB83 diesels (4,420 bhp each), 1 G.E. LM-2500-30 gas turbine (30,172 shp); 2 CP props
Electric: 2,480 kw (4 × 620-kw MTU 8V396 TE54 diesel sets)
Range: 900/27; 6,000/18 (1 diesel) **Fuel:** 423 tons
Crew: 22 officers, 41 petty officers, 100 other enlisted

Remarks: Contract awarded 14-8-89 to Australian Marine Engineering Consolidated, Ltd. (AMECON), with options for two or four more for New Zealand, which decided in 9-89 to order only two. AMECON was bought out in 1999 by the Transfield conglomerate, now known as Tenix. The design is based on the version of the MEKO 200 built in Germany for Portugal. The spelling for the name of the third unit was initially changed to *Warumungu* at the request of contemporary Aborigine tribal leaders but was restored in 1995 to commemorate earlier ships of the same name; an earlier decision to make a similar change for the second unit to *Arrerente* was rescinded 17-8-93. F 153–155 are based at Fleet Base West, HMAS *Stirling,* Western Australia. All others will operate from Fleet Base East, Sydney.

Hull systems: Were originally to have had two G.E. LM-2500 gas turbines and a maximum speed of 31.75 kts; however, the starboard turbine was eliminated to save money. Either diesel can drive either or both shafts. Electrical current is at 400 V/60 Hz from the four Siemens generators; there are two switchboards. Fin stabilizers are fitted. Endurance is considerably greater than in other countries' units of this class, due to enhanced fuel supply. Carry 29 m^3 dry provisions, 26 m^3 refrigerated provisions, and 54 tons fresh water. The first four were found to have bilge keel and hull plating cracking problems during surveys made in the fall of 2002. The hulls were strengthened in the vicinity of the cracking.

Combat systems: Have the CelsiusTech 9LV 453 Mk 3 combat data/fire-control system, with only one Ceros 200 director (although space for a second is present); the director has television and infrared tracking, as well as a J-band radar, a laser rangefinder, and t.v. and IR tracking. The full class is scheduled to receive Mk 3E variants from 2006 to 2010. FFH 157 will have the larger 9LV453 Mk 3E version, which uses the Saab CETRIS combat management system. Mk 3E can accommodate up to ten dual-screen work stations, while the earlier ships have seven dual-screen Type IIA combat system displays. The ships have NATO Link 11 data-sharing. The G-band Sea Giraffe radar employs a CelsiusTech 9G AXYZ antenna. The SPS-49(V)8 radar's antenna carries the antenna for the Cossor IFF interrogator. FFH 152 and 153 were completed with U.S. MILSATCOM equipment aboard, and the later ships of the class will probably also receive it.

The SAMs are controlled by a Raytheon Mk 73 Mod. 1 system; FFH 152 and later are equipped to employ the Evolved Sea Sparrow missile in "quad packs," which will quadruple the potential missile load. Weight and space for Mk 15 Phalanx CIWS are reserved.

The Spherion-B sonar has triple-rotation direct transmission to increase radiated sound level by 6 dB and incorporates a torpedo-warning feature. A lightweight version of the Indal RAST (Recovery Assist, Secure and Traverse) helicopter deck-handing system is incorporated. Have decoy rocket launchers, each with four tubes for Nulka decoys as well as six tubes for regular chaff rockets. Navigation equipment includes GPS receivers and two Sperry Mk 49 inertial navigational systems. The Albatross (formerly ASSTASS—Australian Surface Ship Towed Array Surveillance System) is to be added.

FFH 152 and later are capable of launching the ESSM Sea Sparrow missile. FFH 152 was the world's first active warship fitted with the ESSM and the first of her class to be fitted with two quad Harpoon launchers as part of the Advanced Harpoon Weapon Control System.

FFH 152 and 154 have the new faceted gunhouse for the 127-mm gun but retain the original 54-cal. barrel.

Modernization: A Warfighting Improvement Program (WIP) that was to have updated the entire class was canceled late in 1999, although a number of lesser improvements will still be carried out. A towed sonar array is to be installed. The Sceptre intercept system is to be upgraded to Centaur status and will provide warning and D/F on emitters operating from 500 MHz to 18 GHz.

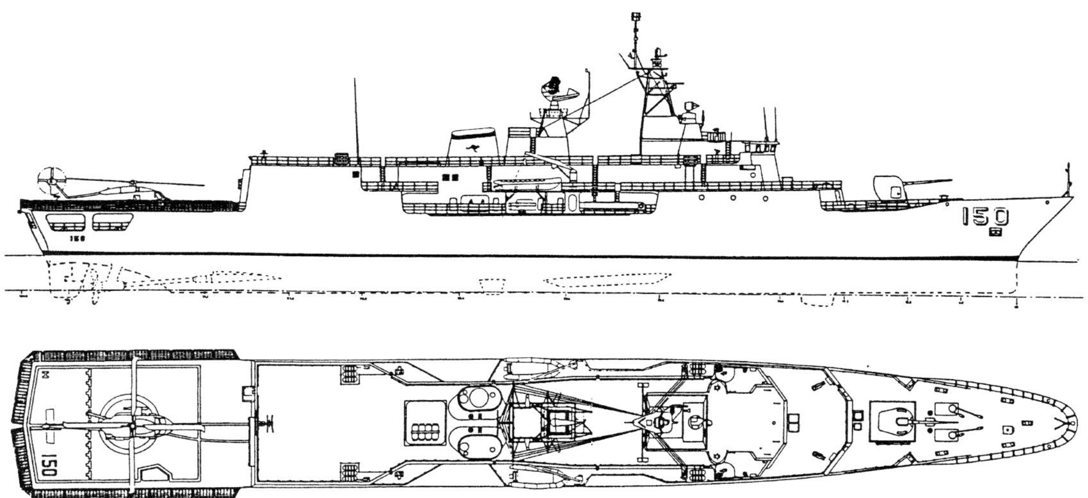

Anzac (FF 150) RAN

FRIGATES [FF] *(continued)*

During 11-02, an order was placed for 64 Boeing RGM-84L Harpoon Block II anti-ship missiles, some of which are to be installed on this class, another batch on the modernized FFGs, and the rest to be kept as spares. Each ship will receive two 4-cell launch container groups. The first installation completed in 2005; the ships are already equipped with a Harpoon Launch control system. During 2005–6, the ships are also to receive an improved torpedo decoy system, a mine-avoidance sonar. Between 2008 and 2012, all of the ships will be also upgraded with modernized command and control systems in addition to infrared search and track systems for improved ASMs detection.

PATROL CRAFT [PC]

♦ 8 (+ 3 + 2) Armidale-class Replacement Patrol Boat project

Bldr: Austal Ships, Henderson, Western Australia

	Laid down	L	In serv.
ACPB 83 Armidale	2004	21-1-05	24-6-05
ACPB 84 Larrakia		20-8-05	10-05
ACPB 85 Bathurst		8-10-05	1-06
ACPB 86 Albany			2-06
ACPB 87 Pirie			3-06
ACPB 88 Maitland			5-06
ACPB 89 Ararat			6-06
ACPB 90 Broome			9-06
ACPB 91 Bundaberg			10-06
ACPB 92 Wollongong			2-07
ACPB 93 Childers			2-07
ACPB 94 Launceston			5-07
ACPB 95 . . .			
ACPB 96 . . .			

Larrakia (ACPB 84)—during sea trials Austal, 10-05

D: 270 tons **S:** 25 kts. **Dim:** 56.8 × 10.0 × 9.68 (molded)
A: 1 25-mm/75-cal. Typhoon-G Mk 25 DP; 2 single 12.7-mm machine guns
Electronics: 1 BAE Systems . . . surface search
EW: PRISM III Intercept and D/F
M: 2 MTU 16V M70 diesels; 2 props; . . . bhp
Range: 3,300/. . . **Endurance:** 42 Days
Crew: 29 total + emergency room for up to 20 additional passengers

Remarks: This class (Project SEA 1444), a replacement program for the *Fremantle* class (Project SEA 1444), was instituted in 1998 upon cancellation of Offshore Patrol Combatant. A request for bids was issued 9-01. Potential builders were short-listed from nine to three in 7-00: ADI, Tenix Defence, and Austal Ships, the latter in conjunction with Defence Maritime Services. Austal was selected winner in 9-03. The craft are being delivered between 2005 and mid-2008. The cost, per unit, of the first 12 units is approx. US$21.2 million (Aus$28.0 million).

Two more units are to be ordered in the immediate future to boost counterterrorism sources in the Northwest Shelf oil and gas area. Upon completion they will likely be homeported at Dampier.
Combat systems: The stabilized 25-mm Rafael Typhoon-G gun system employs the Alliant Tech Systems M242 25-mm Bushmaster cannon; see data in U.S. section. With the exception of the first mount, all will be made by General Motors Defence Australia (GMDA) at Adelaide. There will be no helicopter operations capability.

♦ 12 Fremantle class

Bldr: North Queensland Engineers & Agents, Cairns (P 203: Brooke Marine, Lowestoft)

	L	In serv.	Based
FCPB 203 Fremantle	15-2-79	17-3-80	Cairns
FCPB 205 Townsville	16-5-81	18-7-81	Cairns
FCPB 206 Wollongong	17-10-81	28-11-81	Darwin
FCPB 207 Launceston	23-1-82	6-3-82	Darwin
FCPB 209 Ipswich	25-9-82	13-11-82	Cairns
FCPB 211 Bendigo	9-4-83	28-5-83	Cairns
FCPB 212 Gawler	9-7-83	27-8-83	Darwin
FCPB 213 Geraldton	22-10-83	10-12-83	Darwin
FCPB 214 Dubbo	21-1-84	10-3-84	Darwin
FCPB 215 Geelong	14-4-84	2-6-84	Darwin
FCPB 216 Gladstone	28-7-84	8-9-84	Cairns
FCPB 217 Bunbury	3-11-84	15-12-84	Darwin

Ipswich (FCPB 209) Chris Sattler, 5-05

Bendigo (FCBP 211) Brian Morrison, 4-05

D: 200 tons (220 fl) **S:** 30 kts **Dim:** 42.0 × 7.15 × 1.8
A: 1 40-mm 60-cal. Bofors AN-4 AA; 2 single 12.7-mm mg; 1 81-mm mortar
Electronics:
Radar: 1 Decca BridgeMaster-E ARPA surf. search
EW: AWA Type 133 PRISM intercept and D/F (2–18 GHz; not in FCPB 203, 204)
M: 2 MTU 16V538 TB91 diesels; 2 CP props; 7,200 bhp
Range: 1,450/30; 2,360/12; 4,800/8 **Crew:** 4 officers, 20 enlisted

Remarks: Ordered 9-77. Brooke Marine PCF-420 design. Five more were authorized but canceled in 1982. Were to have been retired in 2000–2003, but are now to be refurbished to delay start of retirements. FCPB 203, 204 and 217 were transferred to Darwin, arriving 20-11-01.
Hull systems: FCPB 203 and 208 were given visual signature-reduction paint schemes in 1997, with the former in pale blue and the latter employing toned-down pendant numbers. The centerline Dorman 12JTM cruising diesel has now been removed from all.
Combat systems: The 40-mm guns were modernized during the late 1980s by the Government Ordnance Factory to improve firing rate and elevation and train speeds. Carry a 4.7-m Zodiac RIB for inspection missions. The surface-search radars can track 40 targets simultaneously.
Disposals: HMAS *Cessnock* (FCPB-210) was stricken 6-05, followed by HMAS *Whyalla* (FCPB-208) in 9-05. More units will follow through 2008. HMAS *Warrnambool* (FCPB-204) was stricken 29-11-05.

PATROL BOATS [PB]

♦ 1 Southerly 65 class

Bldr: Geraldton Boat Builders, Geraldton, Western Australia (In serv. 21-5-96)

2003 Malu Baizam

Malu Baizam (2003) *The Navy*, 5-96

D: 85 tons (fl) **S:** 25 kts **Dim:** 19.95 (18.07 wl) × 5.64 × 1.46 (aft)
A: small arms **Electronics:** Radar: 1 JRC JMA-3610 nav.
M: 2 MTU 8V183 TE diesels; 2 props; 1,300 bhp **Electric:** 17 kw
Range: 650/21 **Fuel:** 5,000 liters **Crew:** 1 officer, 1 enlisted + 18 troops

PATROL BOATS [PB] *(continued)*

Remarks: Assigned to Thursday Island at the Torres Strait sea border with Indonesia. Name means "Ocean Shark" in two local languages. Commanding officer is a lieutenant commander, with a senior enlisted assistant, and the craft can transport three 6-man Army patrols and three 4.2-meter inflatable dinghies. Sister *Coral Snake* (AM 1353) is operated by the Australian Army, and near-sisters *Seal* (2001), *Shark* (2004), and *Dugong* are configured as diving tenders (see below).
Hull systems: Equipped with Furuno FCV-581 echo sounder, GP-80 GPS receiver, and FAP-330 autopilot. Has sleeping accommodations for seven.

MINE-COUNTERMEASURES SHIPS

♦ 6 Huon-class minehunters [MHC]

Bldr: Intermarine/Australian Defence Industries (ADI), Throsby Basin, Newcastle, New South Wales

	Laid down	L	In serv.
M 82 HUON	9-94	25-7-97	15-5-99
M 83 HAWKESBURY	12-9-95	24-4-98	12-2-00
M 84 NORMAN	16-9-96	3-5-99	26-8-00
M 85 GASCOYNE	13-9-97	11-3-00	2-6-01
M 86 DIAMANTINA	4-8-98	2-12-00	4-5-02
M 87 YARRA	12-6-99	19-1-02	1-3-03

Gascoyne (M 85) Chris Sattler, 6-05

Hawkesbury (M 83) Chris Sattler, 6-05

D: 720 tons (fl) **S:** 14 kts max; (sust.; 6 kts on thrusters)
Dim: 52.50 × 9.90 × 4.87 **A:** 1 30-mm/75-cal. MSI DS30B AA; 2 12.7-mm machine guns; 2 SUTEC Double Eagle mine disposal vehicles; Oropesa Mechanical sweep gear carried; Mini-Dyad reconfigurable permanent magnet influence sweep array carried; provision for towing AMASS Influence sweep gear
Electronics:
Radar: 1 Kelvin-Hughes Type 1007 nav.
Sonar: Thomson-Marconi Type 2093M variable-depth minehunting
EW: AWA Type 133 PRISM radar warning and D/F; 2 12-round Wallop Super Barricade decoy RL
E/O: Radamec 1500 surveillance
M: 1 Fincantieri GMT BL230-BN diesel; 1 CP prop; 1,985 bhp—3 retractable 120-hp Riva Calzoni azimuthal thrusters
Electric: 1,200 kw tot (3 × 350-kw Isotta-Fraschini ID 36SS diesel sets, 1 × 150-kw ID 36N emergency diesel set)
Range: 1,500/12 (with 30% fuel reserve) **Fuel:** 50+ tons
Endurance: 19 days **Crew:** 6 officers, 33 enlisted, up to 13 trainees

Remarks: Ordered 12-8-94. Design based on Italian Intermarine *Gaeta* class. All named for former RAN ships bearing the names of Australian rivers. The bare hull (with superstructure shell and masting) of M 82 was handed over in Italy on 16-7-95 and shipped via heavy lift vessel, arriving in Australia 1-9-95 for fitting out; the second and later units had their hulls erected in Australia.
Hull systems: Single-skin, monocoque foam-core GRP hull without ribs, frames, or stiffeners. Machinery on cradles suspended from bulkheads and overheads and non-integral fuel tanks to reduce acoustic transmissions. Two rudders are fitted. The shrouded azimuthal thrusters are mounted two aft and one centerline forward just abaft the variable-depth sonar housing. All but one main engine for the ships will be erected at ADI's Bendigo factory, while the generator sets are built in Italy.
Combat systems: Have the Thomson-Marconi Mullauna (modified Nautis-II M) combat data system with NATO Link 11 display capability and five display consoles. Carry two Bofors Underwater Systems Sutec Double Eagle remote-controlled minehunting submersibles, each with a searchlight, low-light television, and high-frequency sonar. Lightweight double Oropesa wire sweep gear is also carried, as is the Australian-developed Mini-Dyad reconfigurable permanent magnet influence sweep array. Eighteen ADI-built Australian Acoustic Generator water-turbine powered towed arrays were ordered for the class on 5-6-01. Have portable decompression chamber for divers. A Kelvin-Hughes GPS set is fitted. The 30-mm gun can fire at up to 600 rds/min.

Disposal note: Bay-class catamaran minehunters *Rushcutter* (M 80) and *Shoalwater* (M 81) were decommissioned on 14-8-01 and sold in 2002 for further service in the Persian Gulf region. As of press time, it remains unclear whether they will serve commercial or naval purposes.

Craft-of-Opportunity (COOP) Program Note: In addition to the Bay class, the RAN has a COOP (Craft-Of-Opportunity) program for employing fishing craft as auxiliary mine-countermeasures craft. To equip the craft, a number of 100 500 kHz U.S. Klein Type 590 side-scan sonars have been purchased, each equipped with a Klein 595 transceiver/graphic recorder. Four Meridian Ocean Systems QUILS-II (Q-route Underwater Identification and Location System) were ordered during 1990 for use on COOP vessels. Also employed are the Mini-Dyad, a 6.4 × 0.53-m, hollow, two-section mild steel pipe with two strontium-ferrite inserts for countering magnetic mines. The HMAS *Creswell* navigational training ship *Seahorse Horizon,* operated by Defence Maritime Services, can also be used as an auxiliary minesweeper.

♦ 2 large auxiliary minesweepers, MS(L) [MSA]

Bldr: Mipe Shipbuilding (Pte) Ltd., Singapore (In serv.: 1982)

Y 298 BANDICOOT (ex-*Greenville VII*)
Y 299 WALLAROO (ex-*Greenville V*)

Bandicoot (Y 298) Chris Sattler, 9-05

Wallaroo (Y 299) Chris Sattler, 1-05

D: 520 tons (fl) **S:** 11 kts **Dim:** 29.34 (26.83 pp) × 8.54 × 4.42
Electronics: Radar: 1 Furuno 7040D nav.
M: 2 Stork-Werkspoor diesels; 2 Kort-nozzle props; 2,160 bhp
Electric: 150 kw (2 × 75 kw; 2 G.M. 4-71 diesels)
Range: 6,300/11 **Endurance:** 24 days **Crew:** 12 tot.

Remarks: 242.37 grt. Acquired 3-8-90 and 8-8-90, respectively, from Maritime (Pte) Ltd., Singapore, for use as COOP minehunters and as tugs to handle visiting foreign warship at Sydney. Arrived Australia in 9-90 and completed conversion mid-1991. Originally had 30-ton bollard pull, but the towing capability was removed as part of the COOP conversion. Can tow the Mini-Dyad reconfigurable permanent magnet influence sweep array.

MINE-COUNTERMEASURES SHIPS *(continued)*

♦ 1 small auxiliary minesweeper, MS(S) [MSA]
Bldr: . . . (In serv. . . .)

1121 Bermagui (ex-*Nadgee* 2)

Bermagui (1121) John Mortimer, 12-97

D: 110 tons **S:** 10.5 kts **Dim:** 19.9 × . . . × . . .
Electronics:
Radar: 1 Furuno 7040D nav.
Sonar: Klein 590 towed side-scan HF
M: G.M. Detroit Diesel 12V71 diesel; 1 prop; 359 bhp **Crew:** 8 tot.

Remarks: Former tuna fishing boat purchased 1994. Can tow the Mini-Dyad reconfigurable permanent magnet influence sweep array.

♦ 1 small auxiliary minesweeper, MS(S) [MSA]
Bldr: Kali Slipway, Port Adelaide, Australia (In serv. 1974)

1185 Koraaga (ex-*Grozdana A.*)

Koraaga (1185) H&L Van Ginderen, 1-00

D: 119 tons (fl) **S:** 10.5 kts **Dim:** 21.9 × 6.4 × 3.0
Electronics:
Radar: 1 Furuno 7040D nav.
Sonar: Klein 590 towed side-scan HF
M: 1 Caterpillar D346 diesel; 1 prop; 470 bhp **Crew:** 9 tot.

Remarks: A former tuna boat purchased from Australian Fishing Enterprises and delivered to RAN 16-2-89. 119–120-grt wooden-hulled craft operated from HMAS *Waterhen,* Sydney, to develop tactics and doctrine for mine-countermeasures equipment. Equipped with GPS receiver and HFD/F. Can tow the Mini-Dyad reconfigurable permanent magnet influence sweep array.

Disposal note: Small auxiliary minesweeper *Brolga* (1102) was retired from service and sold to Marta Fishing Company during 2004.

♦ 3 mine-countermeasures drones [MSD]
Bldr: Hamil Haven Yacht (In serv. 1991–92)

MSD 02 MSD 03 MSD 04

D: . . . tons **S:** 45 kts (8 kts sweeping) **Dim:** 7.3 × 2.8 × 0.6
M: 2 Yamaha gasoline outboards; 300 bhp

Remarks: For use with the COOP craft. Can each tow a Mini-Dryad magnetized pipe at 8 kts for magnetic mine clearance. Are fitted with differential GPS receivers and the Sydelis Vega automated navigation system.

Minesweeping drone MSD 04 RAN, 1992

AMPHIBIOUS WARFARE SHIPS

♦ 0 (+ 2) Canberra-class amphibious assault ship (general purpose) [LHD]
Bldr:

	Laid down	L	In serv.
Canberra	. . .		2012
Adelaide	. . .		2014

D: 27,000+ tons (fl) **S:** 21.5 kts **Dim:** 231.00 × 32.00 × . . .
A: 4 . . .
Air group: up to 12 helicopters or 8 Harrier-II V/STOL attack fighters
M: 4 . . . diesels (8718 bhp each), 4 alternator sets; 2 electric azimuthal thrusters; . . . shp—bow-thruster
Electric: Main engines plus 1 × 650 kw emergency diesel-driven set
Range: 7,000/18; 9,000/15
Crew: 110 tot. + 1,000 troops and naval and amphibious staff

Remarks: The first stage of this project (Joint Project 2048, Phase 4B), designed to provide replacements for HMAS *Kanimbla* and HMAS *Manoora,* was approved by the Australian government on 11-8-05. The two ships will provide the Navy with a world-class capability to deploy land forces, participate in regional disaster relief operations, humanitarian aid, and peacekeeping operations well into the 21st century. The competing designs for this project are the Spanish Navantia design (27,000 tons) and the French Armaris Mistral ship (22,000 tons) with additional troop-carrying capacity. The modified Mistral design is the more mature of the designs, having undergone sea trials during 2005, though the Spanish design is not far behind. Requests for tender will be issued in the spring of 2006 with a construction contract expected in early 2007.
Hull systems: Will have an island superstructure offset to starboard on the full-length helicopter deck. The floodable stern well will accommodate four LCM(8)-sized landing craft or one LCAC. Will have extensive medical facilities, a stern docking well, and a helicopter deck with 6 landing/take-off spots. The ships will be able to transport up to 150 vehicles including M-1A1 Abrams tanks and armored vehicles.
Aviation features: Will have 185-m long flight deck with landing spots for four CH-47, six NH-90, or eight AB-212 helicopters. The hangar will accommodate twelve helicopters or eight Harrier V/STOL attack aircraft.

♦ 2 U.S. Newport-class auxiliary transports [LPA]
Bldr: National Steel SB, San Diego, Calif.

	Laid down	L	In serv.
L 51 Kanimbla (ex-*Saginaw,* LST 1\188)	24-12-69	7-2-70	23-1-71
L 52 Manoora (ex-*Fairfax County,* LST 1193)	28-3-70	19-12-70	16-10-71

Manoora (L 52) Chris Sattler, 5-05

AMPHIBIOUS WARFARE SHIPS *(continued)*

Kanimbla (L 51) Chris Sattler, 4-05

Manoora (L 52) Chris Sattler, 5-05

D: 4,975 tons light (8,534 fl) **S:** 20 kts **Dim:** 159.20 × 21.18 × 5.30 (aft; 1.80 fwd)
A: 6 single 12.7-mm mg; 4 UH-60 Blackhawk helicopters or 3 SH-3 Sea King helicopters; 1 20-mm Mk 15 Phalanx CIWS
Electronics: Radar: 1 Kelvin-Hughes Type 1007 nav.
EW: 1 Mk 36 SRBOC decoy system (2 8-tubed Mark 137 launchers)
M: 6 Alco 16-251 diesels; 2 CP props; 16,500 bhp—bow-thruster
Range: 14,250/14 **Fuel:** 1,750 tons + 250 tons aviation fuel
Crew: 12 officers, 168 enlisted + troops: 25 officers, 425 enlisted

Remarks: These two ships were originally built as two of the *Newport*-class landing ship tanks (LST). Decision to purchase them was made 15-12-93. Original official type designation was to have been THSS (Training and Helicopter Support Vessel), then LPH (Amphibious Warfare Helicopter Carrier), and finally as above in mid-1998. *Kanimbla* was transferred 24-8-94 and recommissioned on 29-8-94, arriving in Sidney 18-11-94. *Manoora* arrived in Sydney 19-9-94 with a mixed RAN and USN crew for decommissioning and transfer 27-9-94; formally commissioned 25-11-94. Two of a total of 20 built for the U.S. Navy. Conversion contract for both let to Forgacs Dockyard, Newcastle, New South Wales, 12-95; various problems, including extensive internal hull corrosion, delayed completion until mid-2000 for L 52 and 2-01 for L 51. L 51 carries a Phalanx CIWS. L 52 was refitted in 2004.
Hull systems: Can transport 2,000 tons cargo and/or vehicles on 810 m^2 of deck space. Aft is a stern door for loading and unloading vehicles. The tank deck has a 75-ton-capacity turntable at both ends. Modifications include deletion of the bow ramp and beaching capability; installation of bilge keels; erection of a hangar capable of accommodating four Australian Army S-70 Blackhawk or three RAN Sea King helicopters between the funnels (which required deleting the starboard landing craft davit); installation of a 70-ton crane forward to handle two LCM(8) landing craft and two Army LARC-5 wheeled amphibious vehicles; and reconverting two (of three originally installed) vehicle fuel tanks to provide tankage for 250 tons of aviation fuel for the helicopters, for which there are three landing spots (one forward, for use after the landing craft have been offloaded). Provision to carry four pontoon causeway sections was deleted. In L 51 only, medical facilities were enlarged to accommodate 90 patients. A classroom/briefing room was added to both, and accommodations for troops were improved. Evaporator capacity was increased to 300,000 liters/day. Future plans call for further conversion with command facilities, an elevator to permit stowing helicopters on the vehicle deck, and side vehicle-loading doors. Twelve Australian Army LARC-V amphibious resupply vehicles were refurbished for use with these ships during 1998–99.
Combat systems: Installation of Joint Task Force Headquarters (JTFHQ) on L 52 was completed during 5-01 and later in 2001 on L 51; the system occupies four compartments and provides the navy's most comprehensive afloat command, control, and communications facilities.

♦ 1 modified British Sir Bedivere–class heavy landing ship (LSH) [LST]

	Bldr	Laid down	L	In serv.
L 50 TOBRUK	Carrington Slipways, Tomago	7-2-79	1-3-80	23-4-81

D: 3,600 tons (5,800 fl) **S:** 17 kts **Dim:** 129.50 × 19.60 × 4.30
A: 2 single 12.7-mm mg; 2 SH-3 Sea King helicopters
Electronics:
Radar: 1 Decca RM 916 nav.; 1 Kelvin-Hughes Type 1006 nav.
EW: Racal Matilda radar intercept, Mk 36 SRBOC decoy syst. (2 6-round Mk 137 RL)
M: 2 Mirrlees-Blackstone KDMR8 diesels; 2 props; 9,600 bhp
Electric: 1,990 kw tot. (4 × 460-kw diesel alternator sets, 1 × 150-kw diesel emergency set; 450-V 60-Hz 3-phase a.c.)
Range: 8,000/15 **Crew:** 13 officers, 131 enlisted

Tobruk (L 50) Brian Morrison, 11-03

Tobruk (L 50) Chris Sattler, 2005

Remarks: Announced 8-76 as a replacement for the *Sydney,* a former light carrier converted for use as a troopship. Homeported at Fleet Base East, Sydney. Expected to serve until 2010 when it will be replaced by a 20,000 ton amphibious ship (Joint Project 2048, Phase 4A). Refitted in 2000.
Hull systems: Can carry up to two Sea King troop helicopters operating from platform amidships and aft, and can carry up to 520 troops, 18 Leopard tanks, and 40 Armored Personnel Carriers (APCs) or other military vehicles, for a total of 1,300 tons cargo. Two LCVPs are carried in davits aft. Can carry two LCM(8) landing craft as deck cargo. Two 4.5-ton cranes are mounted forward, and a 60-ton heavy-lift derrick is fitted before the bridge. The bow ramp is 14.6 m long and 3.93 m wide, while the stern ramp is 14.2 m long by 4.73 m wide. Can accommodate Australian Army NLE pontoon lighters *Caspor* (201) and *Pollux* (202) on the hull sides.
Combat systems: Two locally controlled single 40-mm 60-cal. AA guns were removed during the 2000 refit, but their platforms on the forecastle remain in place.

♦ 0 (+ 6) landing craft heavy (LCH) replacement program [LCU]
Bldr: ADI Ltd.

Remarks: Under the Joint Project 2048 Amphibious Watercraft program, several designs are being studied as a replacement class for the *Balikpapan* class. A monohull design of some 1,291 tons (full load) and 70 m in length would be powered by a single 4,000-bhp diesel engine and would carry a cargo of over 200 tons at a speed of over 17 kts. An alternative catamaran design would displace 1,241 tons full load, be 61.5 m long, and would be powered by two 4,000-bhp diesels driving waterjets. Both versions would accommodate 200 or more troops in modular 12-berth containers on the vehicle deck, would be beachable on a 1:50 slope, and would have a covered, drive-through vehicle cargo deck with bow/stern ramps and side access doors. A helicopter deck would be incorporated, and one 30-mm gun would be fitted. To be operated by the Australian Army.

♦ 6 Balikpapan-class landing craft heavy (LCH) [LCU]
Bldr: Walkers Ltd., Maryborough, Australia

	Laid down	L	In serv.
L 126 BALIKPAPAN	5-71	15-8-71	1971
L 127 BRUNEI	7-71	15-10-71	5-1-73
L 128 LABUAN	10-71	29-12-71	9-3-73
L 129 TARAKAN	12-71	16-3-71	15-6-73
L 130 WEWAK	3-72	18-5-72	10-8-74
L 133 BETANO	9-72	5-12-72	8-2-74

Wewak (L 130) Chris Sattler, 4-04

AMPHIBIOUS WARFARE SHIPS *(continued)*

D: 316 tons (503 fl) **S:** 9 kts **Dim:** 44.5 × 10.1 × 1.9
A: 2 single 7.62-mm mg **Electronics:** Radar: 1 Decca RM 916 nav.
M: 2 G.M. Detroit Diesel 6-71 diesels; 2 props; 675 bhp
Range: 3,000/10 (light); 1,300/9 with 175 tons cargo, 2,280/9 with 150 tons
Crew: 13 total

Remarks: Originally the class was to be army-subordinated, and L 126 was operated by the Army Water Transport Command until transferred to the RAN on 27-9-74. L 127 and L 133, used for many years as inshore survey craft, became diving training vessels at the Mine Warfare and Patrol Boat Base, HMAS Waterhen, Sydney, on 27-10-88 and 16-12-88, respectively. L 126 and L 129 were placed in storage ashore at Cairns in 1985, but L 129 and L 126 were reactivated in 1988 and 1990 respectively as naval reserve research and training vessel at Cairns. L 130, placed in storage in 1985, began reactivation in 6-99 for service at Darwin and recommissioned 4-00. L 128 transferred to Cairns on 10-9-93. A Life-Of Type Extension (LOTE) overhaul for five of the class was begun in 2000 at Tropical Reef SY, Queensland; all are now to operate through 2008, and the first to be completed, L 128, rejoined the fleet during 10-01, with the last refit, on L 127, completed 9-02.
Disposals: *Salamaua* (L 131) and *Buna* (L 132) transferred to Papua New Guinea in 1974.
Hull systems: Can carry three Leopard tanks; maximum cargo capacity is 180 tons. More powerful diesel alternator sets were substituted during the LOTE refits, and a reverse-osmosis desalinization plant was added, along with new air-conditioning and sewage-treatment equipment.

♦ 4 personnel and vehicle landing craft [LCVP]
Bldr: Geraldton Boat Builders, Geraldton, Western Australia (In serv. 1993)

160 T 4 1099 T 5 1102 T 6 1015 T 7

T 5 (1099)—being lowered from davits aboard *Tobruk* (L 50) RAN, 8-99

D: 5.5 tons light (11 fl) **S:** 21 kts (11 loaded)
Dim: 13.20 (11.37 wl) × 3.36 (3.20 wl) × 0.50 (loaded)
M: 2 Volvo Penta 42B Sterndrive diesels; 2 props; 335 bhp
Range: 110/11 (loaded) **Fuel:** 0.75 tons **Crew:** 3 tot. + 36 troops

Remarks: T 5 and T 6 are carried by *Tobruk* and T 7 by *Success.* T 4 is kept as an operational spare at HMAS *Cairns.* Aluminum construction. Capable of transporting 36 fully armed troops or one Land Rover with half-ton trailer or 4.5 tons cargo in the 8-m-long cargo hold. Are maintained by Defence Maritime Services (DMS).

AUXILIARIES

Note: Since 12-97, port service auxiliaries and all service craft have been operated under contract to Defence Maritime Services Pty, Ltd. (see separate Defence Maritime Services section).

♦ 2 Pacific-class hydrographic survey ships [AGS]
Bldr: North Queensland Engineers & Agents (NQEA), Cairns, Australia

	Laid down	L	In serv.
A 245 Leeuwin (ex-HS 01)	30-8-96	19-7-97	27-5-00
A 246 Melville (ex-HS 02)	9-5-97	23-6-98	27-5-00

Melville (A 246) Brian Morrison, 3-04

Leeuwin (A 245) Brian Morrison, 11-03

D: 2,550 tons (fl) **S:** 14 kts **Dim:** 71.10 (63.60 pp) × 15.20 × 4.37
A: 2 single 12.7-mm mg
Electronics:
Radar: 1 STN Atlas 9600 ARPA nav.
Sonar: C-Tech CMAS 36/39 hull-mounted HF mapping, Klein 2000 towed Lightweight sidescan sonar, STN-Atlas Elektronic . . . mapping, Simrad, STN Atlas Fansweep-20 multibeam echo-sounder
M: diesel-electric drive: 4 GEC-Ruston 6RK215 diesels, 4 GEC-Alsthom 6RK 215 diesel generator sets (800 kw each), 2 electric motors (1,000 kw each); 2 5-bladed props; 2,700 shp— Schottel bow thruster (6 kts)
Range: 8,000/12; 18,000/9 **Crew:** 8 officers, 52 enlisted

Remarks: Ordered 2-4-96. Based at Cairns, with three crews to rotate in operating each of the units some 300 days per year. In the fall of 2001, both began being used as patrol ships to counter illegal immigration and were painted gray in 1-02. Pennant numbers were changed from previous HS-01 and HS-02 during 2004.
Hull systems: Can carry three *Fantôme*-class survey launches (see data under [YGS]) each and accommodate a Bell 206 or AS.350B Écureuil helicopter (no hangar). Capable of surveying in waters 0 to 6,000 m deep and also able to perform oceanographic research. Ships' service power comes from 660-V transformers delivering power at 415 V/50 Hz. Have a dual-tank passive stabilization system. Navigational suite includes GPS receiver, collision-avoidance sonar, electromagnetic and doppler logs, two gyrocompasses, and an autopilot. As patrol ships, have been fitted to carry two 7.2-m RIB patrol and inspection launches.

Note: The above ships and the smaller *Paluma* class operate in support of the Australian Hydrographic Office, Wollongong, New South Wales. The agency operates a Fokker F-27 turboprop aircraft to support the Laser Airborne Depth Sounder; the system can measure depths to 50 m while the aircraft is flying at 500 m altitude and 145 kts and can survey about 50 km^2/hr. For the *Paluma*-class inshore survey craft, see under [YGS].

♦ 0 (+ 1) replacement underway replenishment ships [AOR]
Bldr: . . .

D: 18,000–20,000 tons (fl) **S:** 20 kts **Dim: . . .**
M: . . .

Remarks: A design decision is soon to be reached on the direct replacement for HMAS *Success* (AOR 304). The replacement vessel must be capable of carrying 10,000 tons of ship fuel, 1,300 to 1,500 tons of aviation fuel, and ammunition and provisions; in addition, requirements call for hangar and flight deck facilities capable of supporting two helicopters. A low-noise propulsion system is sought. Designs being examined are the Spanish/Dutch *Amsterdam* class and the German Type 702 (*Berlin*) class. Scheduled to enter service in 2015.

♦ 1 modified French Durance-class underway replenishment ship [AOR]

	Bldr	Laid down	L	In serv.
AO 304 Success	Cockatoo Dockyard, Sydney, Aust.	9-8-80	3-3-84	23-4-86

Success (AO 304) Chris Sattler, 4-05

D: 17,933 tons (fl) **S:** 20 kts **Dim:** 157.2 (149.0 pp) × 21.2 × 10.8
A: 2 single 40-mm/60-cal. Bofors AA; 2 20-mm Mk 15 Phalanx CIWS; 4 single 12.7-mm mg
Electronics:
Radar: 2 Kelvin-Hughes Type 1006 nav.;
EW: Racal Matilda radar intercept; Mk 36 SRBOC decoy syst. (2 6-tubed Mk 137 RL)

AUXILIARIES *(continued)*

M: 2 SEMT-Pielstick 16 PC 2.5 V400 diesels; 1 CP prop; 20,800 bhp
Electric: 5,440 kw tot. **Range:** 8,600/15 **Fuel:** 750 tons
Crew: 25 officers, 195 enlisted

Remarks: Ordered 9-79 from design prepared by DCN, France. A proposed second ship was not built. Homeported at Fleet Base East, Sydney. To retire by 2015.
Hull systems: Carries 8,770 tons distillate fuel, 975 tons aviation fuel, 250 tons munitions (including missiles and torpedoes), 183 tons provisions, 116 tons water, and 95 tons of spare parts. Carries one stores-handling landing craft in davits on the starboard side and is able to refuel three ships simultaneously.
Combat systems: Fitted with two Mk 15 Phalanx CIWS atop the hangar in 1997, at the expense of one 40-mm AA/60-cal. Bofors AA. The second 40-mm was removed shortly thereafter. Hangar modified 1991–92 to accept Sea King helicopter, but normally carries an Écureuil. Fitted summer 1996 with prototype Pilgrim C-band Asynchronous Transfer Mode satellite communications system under Project Takari; also has a smaller commercial SATCOM system.

Disposal note: Catamaran-hulled personnel transport *Jervis Bay* (AKR 45) was returned to her owner on 11-5-01 at the expiration of her two-year charter.

♦ 1 . . . 37,000-ton underway replenishment oiler [AO]
Bldr: Hyundai Mipo Dockyard Co., Ulsan, South Korea

	Completed
AO . . . Sirius (ex-M/T *Delos*)	1-6-04

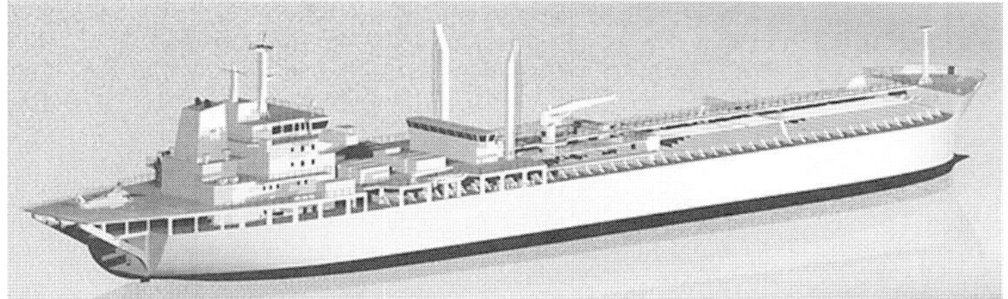

Artist's rendering of the new replenishment oiler *Serius,* a refurbished merchant tanker — Tenix, 2005

D: 37,000 tons (fl) **S:** 15.0 kts. **Dim:** 175.9 (168.0 pp) × 31.03 × 17.0
A: prob. provision for 2 20-mm Mk 15 Phalanx CIWS; 4 single 12.7-mm mg
Electronics:
Radar: 2 navigation
EW: prob. Racal Matilda radar warning
M: 1 Hyundai Heavy Industries Co. diesel; 11,640 hp; one prop—one bow-thruster
Range: . . . **Fuel:** . . . **Crew:** . . .

Remarks: 25,142 grt/37,432 dwt. One of a class of four merchant tankers. Launched in June 2004 and completed on 1-6-04. Purchased on 2-6-04 from Tsakos Energy Navigation Ltd., Athens, Greece, for US$50 million to replace HMAS *Westralia.* Delivered to the Australian Navy in July 2004. A contract for the design and modifications necessary to convert her to a naval vessel were issued late in 2004. Tenders for the actual conversion of the ship were issued in 2005. Expected to enter service during 2006–7.
Hull systems: The ship is a new double-hulled ship that meets all environmental conditions demanded by Australian treaty obligations.

♦ 1 British Appleleaf-class underway replenishment oiler [AO]
Bldr: Cammell Laird, Birkenhead, Scotland

	L	In serv.
AO 195 Westralia (ex-*Appleleaf,* ex-*Hudson Cavalier*)	24-7-75	11-79

Westralia (AO 195) — Brian Morrison, 2003

D: 40,870 tons (fl) **S:** 16.4 kts **Dim:** 170.69 (163.51 pp) × 25.94 × 11.56
A: 4 single 12.7-mm mg; provision for 2 20-mm Mk 15 Phalanx CIWS
Electronics:
Radar: 2 Kelvin-Hughes Type 1007 nav.
EW: Racal Matilda radar warning

Westralia (AO 195) — Brian Morrison, 2003

M: 2 Crossley-Pielstick 14 PC2V-400 diesels; 1 CP prop; 14,000 hp
Range: 7,260/15 **Fuel:** 2,498 tons **Crew:** 8 officers, 53 enlisted

Remarks: 20,440 grt/33,750 dwt. Leased 9-10-89 for five years; purchased 1994. Based at Fremantle. Refitted 12-78 to 11-79 for British Royal Fleet Auxiliary service: stack raised 3.5 m, dry cargo hold added forward, replenishment-at-sea working deck added amidships, and superstructure enlarged aft. Refitted 1993 and 1996 at Forgacs Engineering, Newcastle, when she was equipped to carry two Mk 15 Phalanx CIWS. Suffered an engine-room fire and explosion, 5-5-98; four killed, five injured. Repairs completed 11-99 by ADI Marine. To be replaced in 2006/early 2007 by *Sirius.*
Hull systems: Cargo: 22,000 tons diesel fuel, 3,800 tons JP-5. Has one fueling station per side, plus astern refueling position. Helicopter vertical replenishment (but not landing) platform and superstructure mounting for refrigerated provisions containers added in 1991. Another replenishment-at-sea winch was added in 1996 and internal cargo piping system was revised.

SERVICE CRAFT

Note: Most service craft are now operated by contractor Defence Maritime Services Pty, Ltd.; see separate Defence Maritime Services section. In addition to the RAN-operated craft below, floating dry dock FD 1002 remains in service at Garden Island.

♦ 4 Paluma-class survey motor launches (SML) [YGS]
Bldr: EGLO Eng., Port Adelaide, South Australia

	Laid down	L	In serv.
A 01 Paluma	21-3-88	6-2-89	27-2-89
A 02 Mermaid	19-7-88	24-11-89	4-12-89
A 03 Shepparton	21-9-88	5-12-89	24-1-90
A 04 Benalla	25-11-88	6-3-90	20-3-90

Benalla (A 04) — Navpic/James W. Goss, 11-92

D: 320 tons (fl) **S:** 12 kts (10 sust.) **Dim:** 36.6 (33.0 pp) × 13.7 × 1.90
Electronics:
Radar: 1 JRC JMA-3710-6 nav.
Sonar: ELAC LAZ 72 side-scan mapping HF, Skipper S113 hull-mounted scanning HF
M: 2 G.M. Detroit Diesel 12V-92T A diesels; 2 props; 1,290 bhp
Range: 1,800/10 **Fuel:** 41,000 liters **Endurance:** 14 days
Crew: 3 officers, 11 enlisted (accommodations for 18 tot.)

Remarks: Have Catamaran hulls and are employed as survey ships. Based at HMAS *Cairns* on northeast Queensland coast to conduct Great Barrier Reef surveys. Work in pairs. Have Racal HYDLAPS (Hydrographic Data Logging and Processing System). A 02 was used for trials with the Thomson-Marconi Sonar Pty Petrel 5424 obstacle/mine-avoidance sonar system. All were repainted naval gray during 2002.

SERVICE CRAFT *(continued)*

♦ 8 Fantôme-class survey motor boats [YGS]
Bldr: Pro Marine, Seaford, Victoria (In serv. 10-92 to 7-93)

(624) SMB 1005 Fantôme
(1112) SMB 1006 Meda
(1113) SMB 1007 Investigator
(1499) SMB 1008 Duyfken
(320) SMB 1009 Tom Thumb
(321) SMB 1010 John Gowland
(1114) SMB 1011 . . . . . .
(1115) SMB 1012 . . . . . .

Tom Thumb (SMB 1009/DMS 320) Chris Sattler, 8-05

D: 7.48 tons (fl) **S:** 28 kts **Dim:** 10.70 (10.20 wl) × 2.90 × 0.60
Electronics: Radar: 1 JRC JMA-2141 nav.
M: 2 Volvo Penta AQAD 41D/SP290 diesels; 2 outdrives; 400 bhp
Range: 720/20 **Fuel:** 1,320 l **Endurance:** 36 hrs at 20 kts
Crew: 1 officer, 3 enlisted

Remarks: Naval-operated, except for SMB 1009 and SMB 1010, which are stationed at the Hydrographic School, HMAS *Penguin,* and are managed and operated by Defense Maritime Services, which maintains all of them. The others are carried aboard the *Leeuwin* (A 245) and *Melville* (A 246).
Hull systems: Aluminum construction. Painted white, with orange top to pilothouse. Carry STN Atlas Elektronik Deso 22 echo sounder, Sercel NR 103 differential GPS, and magnetic compass and are equipped to carry portable side-scan mapping sonars.

♦ 1 Antarctic survey launch [YGS]
Bldr: Pro Marine, Seaford, Victoria (In serv. 1993)

(329) ASV 01 Wyatt Earp

Wyatt Earp (ASV 01/DMS 329)—with overall red paint scheme
Brian Morrison, 12-00

D: 5.77 tons (fl) **S:** 22.5 kts **Dim:** 9.20 (8.15 wl) × . . . × 0.53
Electronics: Radar: 1 JRC JMA-2141 nav.
M: 2 Volvo Penta AQAD 41D/SP290 diesels; 2 outdrives; 400 bhp
Range: 306/18 **Fuel:** 880 liters **Crew:** 4 tot.

Remarks: Similar to the *Fantôme* class but configured especially for Antarctic service. Based at Port Kembla, Tasmania. Aluminum construction. Has STN Atlas Elektronik Deso 22 echo sounder and differential GPS receiver.

♦ 1 sail training ship [YTS]
Bldr: Brooke Marine Yachts Ltd., Lowestoft, U.K. (Completed: 3-8-87)

Young Endeavour

D: 200 tons (239 fl) **S:** 14 kts (sail)/10 kts (diesel)
Dim: 44.00 (31.00 hull, 28.30 wl) × 7.80 × 4.00
Electronics: Radar: 1 . . . nav.

Young Endeavour Ralph Edwards, 10-01

M: 740.6 m^2 sail area; 2 auxiliary Perkins diesels; 2 prop; 334 bhp
Range: 1,500/7 (under power) **Crew:** 9 RAN officers, 24 trainees

Remarks: Gift of the U.K. government on Australia's 200th anniversary. Officially commissioned on 25-1-88. RAN supplies officer/instructors for youth trainees. Based at Fleet Base East, Sydney. No hull number assigned. Built to a Brigatine design. The ship's hull is steel with a composite plywood and teak laid deck.

♦ 1 reserve training craft [YXT]
Bldr: Stebercraft, Taree, New South Wales (In serv. 1984)

P 225 Argus

D: 8.8 tons **S:** 25 kts **Dim:** 10.4 × 3.4 × 1.0
A: none **Electronics:** Radar: 1 FCR 1411 nav.
M: 2 Volvo Penta TAMD 60C diesels; 2 props; 304 bhp
Range: 400/24 **Crew:** 3 tot.

Remarks: Acquired 8-6-90 from Federal Police for use as Cairns Port Division RANR Torres Strait Reserve Unit training and liaison craft at Thursday Island.

DEFENCE MARITIME SERVICES PTY, LTD.

Note: Since 12-97, port service auxiliaries and all service craft have been operated under a 10-year contract to Defence Maritime Services (DMS); all such ships and craft are being repainted with dark blue or black hulls and buff or gray-colored superstructures. The official start of the contract was on 1-7-98. DMS is contracted to provide tugs, target services, practice weapon recovery, range support, submarine trials and calibration support, and a wide range of training services. DMS is also responsible for acquisition and maintenance of all boats and outboard motors carried aboard RAN ships and in addition is responsible for over 120 mooring buoys, 18 floating fenders, and numerous buildings, vehicles, boat trailers, and other equipment. DMS has its own hull numbering system for smaller units, given here in parentheses, while the original RAN numbers are also still effective. Large units have neither RAN nor DMS numbers, and many craft have not yet received DMS numbers. The use of DMS numbers remains inconsistent, with some craft having an extra "0" before the actual number. Craft operating in the vicinity of Sydney seem also to have an *additional* small five-digit number on the sides of their pilothouses.

AUXILIARIES

♦ 2 general-purpose tenders [WAG]
Bldr: Marystown Ship Yard, Marystown, Newfoundland, Canada

	In serv.
Seahorse Spirit (ex-*British Viking,* ex-*Balder Hudson*)	1980
Seahorse Standard (ex-*British Magnus,* ex-*Balder Cabot*)	1981

Seahorse Standard ABPH Gavin Hainsworth, RAN 12-02

D: 3,967 tons (fl) **S:** 14 kts max. (7 kts on one engine)
Dim: 72.07 (66.60 pp) × 16.41 (16.01 wl) × 6.5
Electronics:
Radar: *Seahorse Spirit:* 1 Decca RM-916C nav.; 1 Furuno FP-2010 ARPA nav.; *Seahorse Standard:* 1 Kelvin Hughes Nucleus 6000A nav.; 1/Kelvin-Hughes Nucleus 5000R nav.
M: 2 Montreal Locomotive Works-Alco 12V251F V-12 diesels; 2 Liannen-Hjelset CP props; 5,480 bhp—CP thrusters: 2 fore and 2 aft
Electric: 3,855 kVA tot. (2 × 1,200-kVa shaft alternators, 3 × 485-kVa diesel-driven sets

DEFENCE MARITIME SERVICES AUXILIARIES *(continued)*

Range: 14,400/10 **Fuel:** 850 tons **Endurance:** 60 days
Crew: 8–11 tot. (accommodations for 64)

Remarks: 2,090 grt/2,170 dwt. Purchased 1998 by Defence Maritime Services from Dramgate Ltd., London, U.K. *Seahorse Spirit* replaced *Protector* (now *Seahorse Horizon*) as submarine trials support ship at Adelaide in 4-98, and *Seahorse Standard* was assigned to HMAS *Stirling,* Western Australia, on 2-12-98. They are capable of being used for submarine rescue, Naval Reserve training, refueling at sea (via stern hoses), exercise torpedo retrieval, target towing, and deck transport of small mine-countermeasures craft.
Hull systems: Former oilfield tug/supply vessels, with ice-strengthened hulls, dynamic positioning systems, pollution-control equipment, a capability to support hard-hat divers to 54-m depths, and centerline moonpools. Both can support the *Remora* submarine rescue suite. Have Furuno SATCOM and F-851-S echo sounder; they are GPS receiver-equipped. Have no helicopter deck, but do have 41 × 11.5-m clear deck area capable of vertical replenishment employment. Retain oilfield cargo tankage, including 1,180 m^3 drill water, 600 m^3 potable water, and 12,000 ft^3 cement tanks; can transfer fuel and water to other ships at 150 tons/hr.

♦ 1 navigational training ship [WAXT]
Bldr: Elder-Prince Marine Services, Fremantle (In serv. 1984)

SEAHORSE HORIZON (ex-*Protector,* ASR 241, ex-*Blue Nabilla,* ex-*Osprey*)

Seahorse Horizon Brian Morrison, 2-00

D: 390 tons light (670 fl) **S:** 11.5 kts (10.5 sust.)
Dim: 42.70 (40.75 wl; 38.99 pp) × 9.50 × 3.00 max.
Electronics:
Radar: 1 Kelvin-Hughes 1007 nav.; 1 Koden MD 3010 nav.
Sonar: 1 Klein side-scan; 1 Simrad Skipper obstacle-avoidance
M: 2 G.M. 12V-92A diesels; 2 CP props; 1,360 bhp—twin bow- and stern-thrusters
Electric: 700 kVA tot. (2 × 350-kVA diesel sets)
Range: 4,560/9.5 **Fuel:** 175 tons **Endurance:** 14 days
Crew: 1 officer, 5 unlicensed civilians or 9 RAN (accommodations for 31)

Remarks: 282 grt. Referred to as a "Sea Familiarization Vessel." Acquired 18-10-90 by the RAN from Victorian Division of the National Safety Council, which had used her as a pollution control ship. Commissioned 20-3-91 and based at Adelaide from 1-96 to support *Collins*-class submarine trials. Decommissioned 17-4-98 and transferred to Defence Maritime Services to serve as interim seagoing training ship for the HMAS *Creswell* Naval College, Jervis Bay. Renamed 1-7-98. When trainees are embarked, the ship is manned by a commander and eight other RAN personnel; the civilian crew operates the ship when she is used as a diving tender or auxiliary mine clearance craft.
Hull systems: Lengthened 8.00 m and a helicopter platform added in 1988 then removed in 1992. Has Magnavox and Trimble GPS receivers, Koden D/F, two echo sounders, and Inmarsat SATCOM. A six-man divers' recompression chamber is carried, and the ship can carry three 20-ft. standard freight containers on deck.

YARD AND SERVICE CRAFT

♦ 20 60-ton flat-top lighters [WYC]
Bldr: Cockatoo Island Dockyard, New South Wales (In serv. . . .)

(5) FTL 60101
(6) FTL 60102
(7) FTL 60103
(8) FTL 60104
(9) FTL 60105
(10) FTL 60107
(11) FTL 60108
(12) FTL 60109
(14) FTL 60110
(15) FTL 60115
(16) FTL 60116
(470) FTL 60117
(471) FTL 60118
(472) FTL 60119
(473) FTL 60120
(474) FTL 60121
(475) FTL 60111
FTL 60112
FTL 60113
FTL 60114

D: 35.6 tons light (96.5 fl) **Dim:** 18.56 × 7.94 × . . .

Remarks: 61-ton-capacity steel barges used to transport general stores and ammunition on deck and sullage in hull tanks. Are based at Sydney, Fremantle, and HMAS *Creswell.* 11, 12, and 471 are used as paint stages, 14 as an "amenities lighter," 16 as a ferry wharf, and 470 as a fleet landing. FTL 60112–14, at Fleet Base West, do not have DMS hull numbers.

♦ 3 Southerly 65-class diving tenders [WYDT]
Bldr: Geraldton Boat Builders, Geraldton, Western Australia

(462) 2001 SEAL (In serv. 6-93)
2004 SHARK (In serv. 8-93)
DUGONG (In serv. 3-99)

Dugong Chris Sattler, 5-05

D: 85 tons (fl) **S:** 26 kts **Dim:** 19.95 (18.07 wl) × 5.35 × 1.64 (aft)
Electronics: Radar: 1/JRC JMA-2144 (*Dugong:* Furuno Mk 2) nav.
M: 2 G.M. Detroit Diesel 12V92 TA diesels; 2 props; 1,314 bhp
Electric: 7.5 kw tot. (1 × 7.5 kw, Kubota D1402 diesel driving)
Range: 450/20 (*Dugong:* 550/20) **Fuel:** 5,000 liters (*Dugong:* 6,780 liters)
Crew: 2 tot. + up to 18 divers

Remarks: First two ordered in 1992 as diving support tenders, with 2001 based at HMAS Waterhen and 2002 at Fleet Base West, Fremantle. Sister *Porpoise* (2002) grounded in 1995 and was found to be beyond economical repair. A replacement, *Dugong,* was built in 1996. She is based at Sydney and has no DMS or RAN hull number. *Coral Snake* (AM 1353) is operated by the Australian Army, and near-sister *Malu Baizam* (2003) is configured as a patrol boat.
Hull systems: Are intended to support divers in waters up to 54 m deep. Also capable of employment as harbor patrol craft. Equipped with JRC JLU-121 GPS receiver, echo sounder, and Saura CP80 autopilot. Can maintain 3 kts minimum speed and 20 kts fully loaded in Sea State 2.

Note: Naval-manned landing craft *Brunei* (L 127) and *Betano* (L 133) are also employed as diving tenders, based at HMAS *Waterhen,* Sydney. Also available are an unknown number of aluminum Diving Demolition Boats built by Stessi Pty, Queensland. These can carry ten or more personnel or 1,200 tons of cargo at 8 kts and are used to transport personnel and explosives; they displace 304 kg and are 5.26 m overall by 2.25 m beam.

♦ 6 miscellaneous concrete ammunition lighters [WYE]

(429) CAL 10011
(430) CAL 10012
(431) CAL 10013
(432) CAL 10014
(440) CAL 209
(443) CAL 5012

Remarks: 429–432 are 100-ton capacity; 440 is 200-ton, and 443 is 50-ton. All are constructed of concrete, steel, and wood, and all are based at Spectacle Island ammunition magazine, Fleet Base East.

♦ 3 Wattle-class Crane Stores lighters [WYF]
Bldr: Cockatoo Dock Yard, Sydney

	In serv.
CSL 01 WATTLE	15-8-72
(457) CSL 02 BORONIA	25-9-72
(458) CSL 03 TELOPEA	31-10-72

Telopea (CSL 03/DMS 458) Ralph Edwards, 10-01

D: 147 tons (fl) **S:** 8 kts **Dim:** 24.22 × 10.00 (9.75 wl) × 1.66
M: 2 Caterpillar D333C diesels; 2 props; 600 bhp
Range: 320/8 **Endurance:** 24 hours **Crew:** 4 tot.

Remarks: Catamarans employed to transport ammunition and general stores and also for oil-spill containment duties. They can also tow lighters of up to 1,220 tons displacement. Have one 3-ton electric crane. Based on AWL 304 design, but with pilothouse aft. All three were due for disposal in 1997 but have been retained in service, CSL 02 and 03 at Sydney and CSL 01 (which has no DMS hull number) at Darwin.

DEFENCE MARITIME SERVICES YARD AND SERVICE CRAFT
(continued)

♦ **10 Steber 43 naval general-purpose workboats [WYFL]**
Bldr: Steber Craft, . . . (In serv. 1998)

NGPWB 01 Patonga
NGPWB 02
NGPWB 03
NGPWB 04 Sea Dragon
NGPWB 05
NGPWB 06
NGPWB 07
NGPWB 08
NGPWB 09 Sea Witch
NGPWB 10

Steber 43 general-purpose workboat Chris Sattler, 9-05

D: 13.7 tons (fl) **S:** 25 kts (see remarks) **Dim:** 13.20 × 4.70 × 1.34
M: 2 (07–10: 1) . . . diesels; 1 or 2 props; . . . bhp
Range: 150/15 **Crew:** 3 tot. + 22 passengers (as tenders: 3 crew + 15 divers)

Remarks: GRP-hulled general-purpose launches usable as diving tenders and for light towing and stores transport (cargo: 2.05 tons). NGPWB 01–06 have two engines and can achieve 25 kts; the others have one engine and can reach 20 kts. All but NGPWB 01, 02, 07, and 08 are to receive navigational radars and GPS receivers, and all have an echo sounder. NGPWB 01, 02, 07, and 08 are based at Sydney, NGPWB 03 at HMAS *Creswell,* NGPWB 04 and 09 at Fleet Base West, and NGPWB 06 at HMAS *Cerberus.* Only NGPWB 01 is assigned a DMS hull number, 1160. One of the class is named *Elouera.*

♦ **4 Noosacat 930 harbor personnel boats [WYFL]**
Bldr: Noosacat Australia, Noosaville, Queensland

0901 (In serv. 15-12-93)
0902 (In serv. 2-94)
(452) 0903 (In serv. 4-94)
(453) 0904 (In serv. 4-94)

Noosacat 930–class launch 0904 (DMS 453)
Brian Morrison/H&L Van Ginderen, 11-97

D: . . . tons **S:** 30 kts **Dim:** 9.30 (hull; 8.37 wl) × 3.495 (3.105 wl) × 0.70
Electronics: Radar: 0902 only: JRC JMA-2141 nav.
M: 2 Volvo Penta ADQ41DP diesels; 2 props; 400 bhp
Range: 240/20 **Crew:** 1 tot. + 20 passengers

Remarks: GRP-construction catamaran hull with 18 watertight compartments. Length given does not include protruding inboard/outboard propeller shafts. Can carry up to 1,900 kg payload or 21 persons plus 500 kg. 0903 and 0904 are based at Sydney, 0902 (RAN-operated) at HMAS *Creswell,* Jervis Bay, and 0901 at HMAS *Cerberus.* 0901 and 0902 do not have DMS hull numbers assigned.

♦ **1 Riviera-class VIP launch [WYFL]**
Bldr: . . . (In serv. 1993)

(148) 38103 Tresco II

D: . . . tons **S:** 17.5 kts **Dim:** 11.58 × 4.11 × 1.05
M: 2 inboard/outboard-drive diesels; . . . bhp **Fuel:** 455 liters
Crew: 3 + 20 passengers

Remarks: GRP-hulled admiral's barge, based at HMAS *Waterhen,* Sydney. RAN hull number is 38103.

♦ **1 admiral's barge [WYFL]**
Bldr: . . . (In serv. 2-93)

(1) AB 1201 Green Parrot

D: . . . tons **S:** 21 kts **Dim:** 12.70 (10.69 wl) × 3.90 × 0.93
M: 2 Perkins M 240 diesels; 2 props; 480 bhp—1 Perkins 102-4 auxiliary propulsion diesel; . . . bhp
Fuel: 600 liters **Crew:** 3 + 10 passengers

Remarks: Wooden-hulled craft with dark green hull and varnished wood topside. Based at HMAS *Waterhen,* Sydney, for ceremonial and VIP transportation duties.

♦ **4 Shark Cat 800 harbor personnel boats [WYFL]**
Bldr: Sharkcat, Noosaville, Queensland (In serv. 1980s)

(649) 0801 (652) 0802 (655) 0803 0805

Sharkcat 800–class launch 0802 (DMS 652) Chris Sattler, 5-05

D: . . . tons **S:** 30 kts **Dim:** 8.35 (7.50 wl) × 2.80 × 1.0 (motors down)
Electronics: Radar: 1 portable Furuno . . . nav.
M: 2 Mercury gasoline outboards; 500 bhp
Range: 290/24 **Crew:** 1 tot. + 11 passengers (23 in emergency)

Remarks: GRP construction catamarans used for general-purpose, target towing, and naval police duties; with portable radar fitted, are also used in range-clearance work. Based at Sydney, except for 0805 (with no DMS hull number) at HMAS *Creswell.*

♦ **12 naval work boats [WYFL]**
Bldr: North Queensland Engineers, Cairns (In serv. 1979–81)

(901) NWB 1230
(902) NWB 1260
(219) NWB 1281 Otter
(699) NWB 1282 Walrus
(220) NWB 1285 Grampus
(221) NWB 1286 Dolphin
(541) NWB 1287
(214) NWB 1288
(215) NWB 1289
(617) NWB 1290
(1140) NWB 1291
(222) NWB 1292 Turtle

Naval work boat—renumbered 1140, name unknown Chris Sattler, 5-05

D: 12.56 tons (fl) **S:** 12 kts **Dim:** 12.42 × 3.82 (3.66 wl) × 1.08
M: 2 G.M. Detroit Diesel 6V53 diesels; 2 Kort-nozzle props; 274 bhp
Range: 240/12 **Endurance:** 20 hours **Fuel:** 1,380 liters
Crew: 2 tot. + 10 passengers

Remarks: Some (including NWB 1288) are configured as diving tenders. Aluminum construction, poor maneuverability. Cargo capacity 2.5 tons in lieu of passengers. Have 3-ton bollard pull towing capacity. Seven Australian Army sisters sold 1993. Sister *Dugong* (NWBD 1287) was stricken by 3-99, and several others have been discarded since. NWB 1230 and 1260 are based at Fleet Base West, NWB 1289 at Cairns, NWB 1287 and 1291 at Darwin, and the others at Sydney. Have magnetic compass but no radar. One of the class appears to have been renumbered 1140.

DEFENCE MARITIME SERVICES YARD AND SERVICE CRAFT *(continued)*

♦ 1 Halvorsen-design workboat [WYFL]
Bldr: Lars Halvorsens Pty (In serv. 1945–46)

(379) AWB 4011

AWB 4011 (DMS 379) Brian Morrison/H&L Van Ginderen, 2-99

D: 9.25 tons (13 fl) **S:** 11 kts **Dim:** 12.20 × 4.00 × 1.48
M: 1 G.M. Gray Marine 64HN9 diesel; 1 prop; 165 bhp
Range: 150/11 **Fuel:** 470 liters **Crew:** 1 tot. + 30 passengers

Remarks: Wooden-hulled craft, based at Sydney to transport cargo and passengers. Open cockpit aft, low pilothouse. No radar fitted.

♦ 9 40-foot Mk 1 and 1963-design* workboats [WYFL]
Bldr: Phoenix Shipbuilding, Tasmania (In serv. ca. 1963)

(776) AWB 404	(422) AWB 424	AWB 1658
AWB 421	(390) AWB 436	AWB 4006*
AWB 423	(224) AWB 440	(428) AWB 4007*

AWB 436 (DMS 390) Phil Barling, RAN, 1-01

D: Mk 1: 9.11 tons (13.7 fl); 1963-design: 8.8 tons (13 fl)
S: Mk. 1: 9.6 kts; 1963-design: 9.9 kts **Dim:** 12.20 × 3.86 × 1.48
M: 1 G.M. Gray Marine 64HN9 diesel; 1 prop; 175 bhp
Range: Mk 1: 450/9.6; 1963-design: 145/9.9
Fuel: Mk 1: 1,410 l; 1963-design: 477 liters **Crew:** 1 + up to 44 passengers

Remarks: Wooden-hulled craft employed for local passenger service and stores transport. No radars fitted. AWB means "Australian Workboat."

♦ 1 AWB Mod. II workboat [WYFL]
Bldr: Williamstown Dockyard, Victoria (In serv. 1944–46)

(368) 4010

AWB 4010 (DMS 368) H&L Van Ginderen, 7-94

D: 9.11 tons (13.7 fl) **S:** 9.9 kts **Dim:** 12.20 × 3.86 × 1.48
M: 1 G.M. . . . diesel; 1 prop; 170 bhp
Range: 450/9.9 **Fuel:** 1,410 liters **Crew:** 1 + up to 44 passengers

Remarks: Based at Sydney. Can carry up to three tons of cargo in lieu of passengers, and can be employed for light towing. Wooden construction.

♦ 2 AWB short and long group cabin workboats [WYFL]
Bldr: Phoenix SB Co., Tasmania (In serv. 1944–46)

Amethyst (AWB 420) 4002

Amethyst (AWB 420) Chris Sattler, 9-05

D: 9 tons (13 fl) **S:** 9.9 kts **Dim:** 12.50 × 3.86 × 1.48
M: 1 G.M. 64HN9 diesel; 1 prop; 165 bhp
Range: 145/9.9 **Fuel:** 477 liters **Crew:** 1 + up to 44 passengers

Remarks: Wooden hull modernized with GRP pilothouse and passenger cabin. Can carry up to three tons cargo in lieu of passengers. Based at Sydney. AWB in RAN-class designation stands for "Australian Workboat." Does not have a DMS number. *Amethyst* (AWB 420), previously thought to have been retired, was sighted in service during 9-05. Sister *Onyx* (AWB 416) had been removed from service by 2001.

♦ 27 7.2-m rigid hulled inflatable boats [WYFL]
Bldr: Zodiac (Aust) Pty.

0701 through 0727

D: 1,958 kg (fl) **S:** 31+ kts **Dim:** 7.20 × 2.74 × 0.53
M: 1 inboard/outboard gasoline sterndrive; . . . bhp
Range: 75/15 **Fuel:** 200 liters **Crew:** 18 passengers (25 emergency)

Remarks: GRP hull, Hypalon inflatable collar. Based at various shore facilities and also carried by ships for transportation and training duties.

Note: Also widely used are Mks I–III 4.7-m Zodiac RHIBs, powered by 30–40 bhp gasoline outboard motors and capable of carrying 10–12 personnel or 1,100–1,300 kg of cargo. Open aluminum launches of the 5-m lightweight utility boat (LUB) types C and D are also widely used for training, diver support, inshore survey, and general utility work; type C is 6.50 × 2.50 × 0.40 m and is powered by a 175-bhp Johnson gasoline outboard, while type D is 5.125 × 1.90 × 0.40 m and is powered by a 40-bhp Johnson outboard; both types can achieve about 8 kts and can carry six or seven people. Other light aluminum launches are the 4.3-m and 12-ft. aluminum dinghy classes: 4.3/4.3 × 1.85/1.54 m and weighing 150 kg (4.3 m) or 66 kg (12 ft.) without their outboard motors.

Hydrographic survey launches [YGS] *Tom Thumb* (320, ex-SMB 1009) and *John Gowland* (321, ex-SMB 1010) are managed and operated by Defense Maritime Services but remain RAN property (see under [YGS]). They are employed at the Hydrographic School.

♦ 6 radio-controlled surface targets [WYGT]
Bldr: Hydrofield, Queensland (In serv. . . .)

RCST 06 through RCST 11

D: . . . tons **S:** 25 kts **Dim:** 6.40 × 2.46 × 1.10
M: 1 Evinrude Ocean Runner gasoline outboard; 150 bhp **Range:** 200/25

Remarks: Orange-colored radio-controlled GRP-construction trimaran launches used to tow surface and air targets. Can be operated from cockpit. Two are based at Fleet Base West, Fremantle, and the others at HMAS *Creswell.* They do not have DMS hull numbers assigned.

Note: Used as towed targets are an unknown number of 6.4-m × 4.4-m, 600-kg Mk 1 towed target sleds completed during 1980 at Garden Island Dockyard. Two are based at HMAS *Creswell* and a third is towed by the torpedo retriever *Trevally.*

♦ 4 water and fuel lighters [WYO]
Bldr: Williamstown DY, Victoria

	In serv.
(331) Wallaby (ex-WFL 8002)	3-2-83
(332) Wombat (ex-WFL 8003)	10-2-83
(333) Warrigal (ex-WFL 8001)	10-84
(334) Wyulda (ex-WFL 8004)	10-84

D: 265 tons light (1,210 fl) **S:** 7 kts light (6.3 loaded)
Dim: 39.25 (38.00 wl) × 11.00 (9.80 wl) × 4.80 max.
M: 2 G.E.C. diesels; 1 Harbormaster outdrive prop fwd, 1 aft; 564 bhp
Electric: 45 kVa tot. (1 G.M. diesel driving)
Range: 144/6 **Fuel:** 9.68 tons **Crew:** 4 tot.

DEFENCE MARITIME SERVICES YARD AND SERVICE CRAFT
(continued)

Wallaby (DMS 331) Chris Sattler, 1-05

Remarks: Used to transport and deliver diesel fuel and desalinated water and to remove and transport sullage and ballast liquids. Also employed for oil-spill containment. Cargo 56 tons diesel fuel, 100 tons feedwater, 100 tons distilled water, 110 tons waste, and 80 tons ballast. Have one 400-ton/hr and three 40-ton/hr cargo pumps and a 1,000-kg capacity deck crane. *Warrigal* is based at Darwin, *Wallaby* at Sydney, and *Wombat* at Fremantle. Are expected to remain in service until 2013.

♦ 3 torpedo-recovery craft [WYPT]
Bldr: Williamstown DY, Victoria (In serv. 1970–71)

446 Tuna (ex-TRV 801) 448 Tailor (ex-TRV 803)
447 Trevally (ex-TRV 802)

Trevally (447) Ralph Edwards, 10-01

D: 93 tons (fl) **S:** 13 kts (TRV 803: 12 kts)
Dim: 26.96 (26.82 wl) × 6.38 (6.10 wl) × 2.11
Electronics:
Radar: TRV 801: 1 Kodan MD-3220 Mk 2 nav.; TRV 802: 1 Tokimec nav.; TRV 803: 1 JRC JMA2144 nav.
M: 3 (TRV 803: 2) G.M. Detroit Diesel 6-71 diesels; 3 props; 684 (TRV 803: 456) bhp
Electric: 50 kVA tot. (2 × 25 kVa sets, G.M. 3-53 diesels driving)
Range: 420/12–13; 500/8 **Fuel:** 5.75 tons
Crew: 3 licensed officers, 3 nonrated (9–10 accommodations)

Remarks: 446 is based at HMAS *Creswell,* Jervis Bay, and is also used for target towing; 447 is at HMAS *Waterhen,* Sydney, and 448 at HMAS *Stirling,* Western Australia. All were due to be stricken during the late 1990s, but no replacements have been procured. 408 lacks the centerline diesel-propulsion engine. 447 is assigned a Mk 1 tow-target.

♦ 1 coastal tug [WYTB]
Bldr: Australian SB Industries, South Coogee, West Australia

	Laid down	L	In serv.
2601 Tammar	20-4-83	10-3-84	15-3-84

D: 267 tons (302.4 fl) **S:** 11.5 kts **Dim:** 27.00 (24.38 wl; 23.63 pp) × 8.86 × 3.58
Electronics: Radar: 1 JRC JMA-2144 nav.
M: 2 G.M. 16V149 TI diesels; 2 Kort-nozzle props; 2,560 bhp
Electric: 50 kVa tot. **Range:** 900/12; 1400/10 **Fuel:** 48 tons
Endurance: 2 days **Crew:** 4–6 tot. (accommodations for 10)

Remarks: Ordered 30-3-83 for use at HMAS *Stirling,* Fleet Base West, Western Australia, for towing, torpedo recovery, oil-spill containment, and target towing. 160 grt. Bollard pull 35 tons permits towing ships of up to 20,000 tons displacement. Has JRC JFV-60 echo sounder and GPS receiver. Has 68 tons ballast-water capacity. Does not have a DMS hull number assigned and may no longer wear RAN number 2601.

Tammar (2601) Ralph Edwards, 10-01

♦ 2 coastal tugs [WYTB]
Bldr: . . . Sibu, Malaysia

	Launched	In serv.
Seahorse Quenda	01-2003	28-2-03
Seahorse Chuditch	01-2003	28-2-03

Seahorse Quenda Chris Sattler, 2005

D: . . . **S:** 12 kts **Dim:** 23.5 × . . . × . . .
Electronics: . . .
M: . . .
Electric: . . .
Range: approx. 3,500 miles **Fuel:** . . . tons **Endurance:** . . . days **Crew:** 3

Remarks: Built for the Defence Maritime Services, bollard pull in excess of 16 tons; have secondary roles towing targets and participating in consort duties, equipment trials, etc. *Seahorse Quenda* is based at Fleet Base East and *Seahorse Chuditch* at Fleet Base West.

♦ 1 medium harbor tug [WYTM]
Bldr: Shoreline Eng., Portland, Victoria (L: 10-83)

1801 Quokka

Quokka (1801) ABPH Stuart Farrow, RAN, 7-98

DEFENCE MARITIME SERVICES YARD AND SERVICE CRAFT
(continued)

D: 110 tons (fl) **S:** 11.3 kts
Dim: 18.17 (17.15 wl; 16.84 pp) × 6.20 (5.91 wl) × 2.40
Electronics: Radar: 1 JRC JMA-2144 nav.
M: 2 G.M. 8V53 diesels; 2 Kort-nozzle props; 633 bhp
Electric: 52 kw tot. (2 × 26-kw Stamford gen. sets)
Range: 750/10.5 **Fuel:** 12.6 tons **Endurance:** 2 days **Crew:** 6 tot. (civilian)

Remarks: Reassigned to Darwin in 1998 for towing and target towing. Bollard pull: 11.3 tons. Has 13 m^3 ballast-water capacity. Fitted with GPS and JRC JFV-60 echo sounder. Formerly carried naval number 1801 and has not been assigned a DMS hull number.

♦ 3 Bronzewing-class harbor tugs [WYTL]
Bldr: Stannard Bros., Sydney (HTS 504: Perrin Eng., Brisbane)

	In serv.
(152) (HTS 501) Bronzewing	12-68
(153) (HTS 502) Currawong	1969
(154) (HTS 504) Mollymawk	1966

Bronzewing (DMS 152) Chris Sattler, 1-05

D: 34 tons (48.15 fl; HTS 504: 48.26 fl) **S:** 9.13 kts (HTS 504: 8 kts)
Dim: 15.50 (14.12 wl) × 4.88 (4.57 pp) × 2.06
M: 2 G.M. diesels; 2 props; 340 bhp
Range: 710/9.13 **Crew:** 3 tot. (civilian)

Remarks: HTS 503 given to Papua New Guinea in 1974. Were due for disposal during 1996 but remain in service. Have 5.08-ton bollard pull and can tow barges of up to 1,220 tons displacement. HTS 504 is 15.55 m overall (14.39 wl), draws 2.07 m, and has larger stacks, not raked forward as in the other two. Do not have radar or gyrocompass.

♦ 1 sail-training craft [WYTS]
Bldr: . . . . . ., Brisbane (In serv. 1982)

850576 Salthorse

D: 32.3 tons (fl) **S:** 8 kts (under power) **Dim:** 19.74 (15.24 wl) × 5.13 × 2.28
Electronics: Radar: 1 JRC JMA-2253 nav.
M: 1 Ford Lehman diesel; 1 prop; 120 bhp
Electric: 15 kVa tot. (1 × 8 kVA, Yanmar diesel-driven, 1 × 7 kVa emergency, Volvo Penta P7 1500 diesel driven)
Range: 1,400/6 (under power) **Fuel:** 600 gallons **Crew:** . . . tot.

Remarks: Ketch acquired in 1999 for officer training and recreation at HMAS *Creswell.* Steel hull with aluminum masts (17.5-m foremasthead). Has Furuno GP-30 GPS receiver. Designed by John Pugh.

♦ 5 Swarbrick III–class small training yachts [WYTS]
Bldr: Swarbrick Bros., Osbourne Park, West Australia (In serv. 1984)

STY 3807 Alexander of Cresswell
STY 3808 Friendship of Leeuwin
STY 3809 Lady Peryhyn of Nirimba
STY 3810 Charlotte of Cerberus
STY 3811 Scarborough of Cerberus

D: 4.35 tons (fl) **S:** . . . kts **Dim:** 11.10 (9.60 wl) × 3.20 × 1.975
M: 1 Yanmar 3 GMO diesel; 22 bhp **Crew:** 8 tot.

Remarks: GRP training yachts based at Sydney, Fremantle, HMAS *Cerberus,* and HMAS *Creswell.* STY stands for "Swarbrick Sail Training Yacht." Are planned to be replaced by new craft of about 14 m overall.

♦ 63 Tasar sail dinghies [WYTS] (In serv. 1970)
Series 1925–2546

D: 93 kg (rigged) **S:** . . . kts **Dim:** 4.57 × 1.75 × 0.62 **Crew:** 2 tot.

Remarks: GRP sloops used at Fremantle, HMAS *Creswell,* HMAS *Cerberus,* NSO Tasmania, etc., for training and recreation. Survivors of 70 built for the RAN; do not have DMS hull numbers. Mainsail is 8.36 m^2, jib 3.07 m^2.

♦ 1 ASI 315–class navigation and seamanship training craft [WYXT]
Bldr: Tenix SB WA, South Coogie, West Australia

Seahorse Mercator (L: 15-10-98; in serv. 26-11-98)

Seahorse Mercator Chris Sattler, 1-05

D: 165 tons (fl) **S:** 16 kts **Dim:** 31.50 (28.60 wl) × 8.21 × 2.60
Electronics: Radar: 1 Furuno FE 606 nav.; 1 Decca Bridgemaster ARPA nav.
M: 2 Caterpillar 3304 diesels; 2 props; 2,820 bhp (2,400 sust.)
Electric: 116 kw (2 × 50 kw; Caterpillar 3304 diesels; 1 × 16 kw)
Range: 2,880/8 **Fuel:** 27.9 tons **Endurance:** 15 days (7 days with 20 aboard)
Crew: 5 tot. + 3 instructors, 18 trainees

Remarks: Ordered early 1998. Twenty near-sisters operate as patrol boats in a number of Southwest Pacific–area island nations. Extensive navigational suite including Furuno NAVSAT receiver, echo sounder, and doppler log. Operated in the Sydney area since 12-98 by a Defence Maritime Services civilian contract crew, assigned to HMAS *Waterhen.* Has a secondary capability to act as a mine-countermeasures craft and is equipped with GPS and autopilot.

ROYAL AUSTRALIAN ARMY CORPS OF ENGINEERS

Personnel: Approx. 300

♦ 6 Amphibious Watercraft System (AWC) program [WLCM]
Bldr: ADI Ltd., Newcastle (in serv. 12-03 to 4-05)

D: 60 tons light (131 fl) **S:** 14 kts **Dim:** 25.00 × . . . × . . .
A: 2 single 12.7-mm mg
M: 2 diesels; 2 waterjets; . . . bhp **Crew:** up to 5 tot.

Australian Army Amphibious Watercraft System—two can be carried by each Newport class transport Brian Morrison, 7-04

Remarks: Ordered 17-7-02. To replace Army LCM(8) craft for use with *Kanimbla* (L 51) and *Manoora* (L 52). All assigned to 10 Force Support Battalion, Townsville, Queensland, with two carried aboard each *Newport*-class transport.
Hull systems: Aluminum construction. Can carry five 13-ton ASLAV light armored vehicles each, and bow and stern ramps are fitted. Movable by 70-ton cranes, have a combat load of 35 to 50 tons, and are beachable on gradients up to 1:50.

♦ 14 U.S. LCM(8)-class landing craft [WLCM]
Bldrs: AB 1050–1061: North Queensland Engineers, Cairns (In serv. 1967); others: Dillingham SY, Fremantle (In serv. 1972)

AB 1050 AB 1051 AB 1053 AB 1056 AB 1058–AB 1067

D: 34 tons light (116 fl) **S:** 11 kts (9 loaded)
Dim: 22.70 × 6.41 × 1.37 (mean; 1.30 fwd/1.68 aft loaded)
M: 4 G.M. 6V71 diesels; 2 props; 600 bhp **Range:** 290/10 **Crew:** 3 tot.

Remarks: AB 1050 is named *Coconut Queen* and AB 1053 *Sea Widow.* Based at Cairns and Fremantle, some in land storage. All to be retired by 2005.
Disposals: AB 1057 was transferred to Tonga in 1982; AB 1055 was stricken in 1984; and AB 1052 and AB 1054 were sold for civilian use in 1992.
Hull systems: Steel construction. AB 1050–1061 originally had range of 230 n.m. at 10 knots. Both variants have a 55-ton cargo capacity.

AB 1051—moored at the stern ramp of *Manoora* (L 52) RAN, 2000

ROYAL AUSTRALIAN ARMY CORPS OF ENGINEERS *(continued)*

♦ 1 Special Action Forces Craft Offshore Large [WLCP]
Bldr: Geraldton Boat Builders, Geraldton, Western Australia (In serv. 1994)

AM 1353 Coral Snake

D: 85 tons (fl) **S:** 28 kts **Dim:** 19.95 (18.07 wl) × 5.64 × 1.46 (aft)
Electronics: Radar: 1 JRC JMA-2144 nav.
M: 2 G.M. Detroit Diesel 12V92 TA diesels; 2 props; 1,800 bhp
Range: 350+/25 **Fuel:** 8,000 liters **Crew:** 3 tot.

Remarks: Sister to RAN's *Seal* class, but with an Effer hydraulic crane at the stern and a smaller cabin topped by a flying bridge. Used to support divers and for transport of stores and personnel. Based in Western Australia.

♦ 12 ex-U.S. Army LARC-V (Design 8005) amphibious wheeled lighters [WLCP] Bldr: . . ., U.S.A. (In serv. 1960s)

Four Australian Army LARC-V amphibious wheeled lighters in formation RAN, 2000

D: 8.9 tons light (13.4 fl) **S:** 8 kts loaded (55 km/hr on land)
Dim: 10.67 × 3.05 × 3.10 **M:** 1 . . . diesel; 1 prop; 300 bhp
Range: 70/8 (sea); 400 km/ . . . (land) **Crew:** 1–2 tot.

Remarks: Acquired 1964–65 and deactivated early 1990s. Reactivated for service with landing ships *Manoora* and *Kanimbla* between 6-98 and 2-99; the original Cummins diesels were replaced. Based at Townsville. Some 52 additional are maintained in reserve. Cargo: 4,536 kg.

♦ 18 Commando Operational Watercraft (COW) [WLCP]
Bldr: Western Boat Builders, . . . (In serv. 2002–3)

D: 2.2 tons (fl) **S:** 32 kts **Dim:** 7.65 × 2.70 × 0.35
M: 1 6-cyl. . . . diesel; 1 Hamilton 292 waterjet; 260 bhp
Range: 200/ . . . **Fuel:** 500 liters **Crew:** 2 tot. + 8 commandos

Remarks: RIB design, with trihedral, welded aluminum hull. Are rotary and fixed wing air-transportable. Can operate in Sea State 4 (seas up to 2.5 m high).

♦ 0 (+ 24) bridge erection propulsion boats [WLCP]
Bldr: ADI Ltd., Newcastle

D: . . . **S:** . . . **Dim:** . . .
M: 2 6BTA diesels; 2 swiveling waterjets; 450–630 bhp
Crew: 2 tot.

Remarks: A request for bids for a replacement class of bridge-erection boats was issued on 12-8-02; they would replace launches in service for some 30 years. The ADI design was short-listed on 11-12-02.

♦ 159 assault boats [WLCP]
Bldr: Australian Boat Mfgrs., Ltd., Perth (In serv. 1990–91)

D: 210 kg light (1,500 kg fl) **S:** 10 kts **Dim:** 5.0 × 2.0 × . . .
M: 1 outboard; 40 bhp **Cargo:** 1,200 kg or 12 troops

Remarks: Intended to replace earlier craft of this type. Aluminum construction; will float while loaded if flooded out.

♦ 2 NLE-class self-propelled pontoons [WYFL]

201 Caspor 202 Pollux

D: 32.6 tons light (127 loaded) **S:** 4–6 kts **Dim:** 25.60 × 7.46 × 1.25
M: 2 G.M. Detroit Diesel 4-71 diesels in Harbormaster portable outdrives; 224 bhp

Remarks: Composed of steel pontoon cubes 1.52 m square by 2.13 m high, which can be arranged either in 12 × 3 or 14 × 3.5 configuration; in former, can carry 75 tons cargo or 50 personnel, and in latter (used for stowage on sides of RAN landing ship *Tobruk*) 80 tons cargo or 50 personnel. NLE stands for "Naval Lighterage Equipment."

♦ 9 Shark Cat 880 Express–class launches [WYFL]
Bldr: Noosacat, Noosaville, Queensland (In serv. 1990–95)

AM 237 through AM 244 AM 428

D: . . . tons **S:** 40 kts (27 cruise) **Dim:** 9.40 (8.15 hull) × 2.82 × 0.63 (hull)
Electronics: Radar: 1 Furuno FR 1941 nav.
M: 2 Johnson gasoline outboards; 450 bhp
Fuel: 1,000 liters **Crew:** 2 tot. + 10 passengers

Remarks: GRP construction. Cargo capacity of 1.5 tons. Used for water safety patrol and local transport of personnel and stores. Each has an associated road trailer. These replace the 7-m Shark Cat–series launches acquired in 1980. Have Furuno FC 581 echo sounders, a Trimble GPS receiver, and three radio sets. Carry 110 liters of potable water.

♦ 5 9-meter rigid inflatable offshore safety launches [WYFL]

AM 227 AM 228 AM 229 AM 230 AM 231

Remarks: No data available.

AUSTRALIAN CUSTOMS NATIONAL MARINE UNIT

Note: Australian Customs craft are charged with Federal Police, quarantine, fisheries and wildlife protection, and other ancillary duties.

♦ 8 Roebuck Bay–class customs patrol boats [WPB]
Bldr: Austal Ships, Henderson, Western Australia

	In serv.		In serv.
ACV 01 Roebuck Bay	2-99	ACV 05 Corio Bay	2-00
ACV 02 Holdfast Bay	10-99	ACV 06 Storm Bay	8-00
ACV 03 Botany Bay	16-9-99	ACV 07 Dame Roma Mitchell	8-00
ACV 04 Hervey Bay	2-00	ACV 08 Arnhem Bay	8-00

Roebuck Bay (ACV 01) Chris Sattler, 7-05

D: 28 tons **S:** 21 kts **Dim:** 38.20 (32.10 wl) × 7.20 × 2.35
Electronics: Radar: 2 Kelvin-Hughes Nucleus 2 5000 ARPA nav.
M: 2 MTU 16V 2000 M70 diesels; 2 props; 2,800 bhp—bow-thruster
Range: 1,000/20 **Endurance:** 28 days **Crew:** 8 tot. + 8 passengers

Remarks: 30.2 dwt. Ordered 5-98 for $38 million (U.S.). Aluminum construction. One radar operates in X band, the other in S, and up to 50 contacts can be tracked simultaneously; an electronic chart system displays charts on the radar operating screens. Capable of towing craft of up to 150 tons displacement. Carry two 6-m inspection/landing launches, each with two 90-bhp Yamaha outboard motors and a range of 150 n.m. at 25 kts and equipped with SATCOM. Are capable of supporting scuba divers and can transport, land, and recover one ton of cargo and eight law-enforcement officers in addition to the crew. Have Austal Ocean Leveller ride control system and fin stabilizers. The design is offered for export in an armed version.

Note: Other craft operated by the Australian Customs Service include three Collector-class 6.99-m aluminum launches powered by Volvo Penta AQD40A stern drives (two based at Sydney and one at Brisbane); the Minister-class patrol craft *Charles Kingston,* 19.99 m long and powered by two MTY 396 V-8 diesels; the 22-m, aluminum-hulled *Delphinus,* powered by two MTY 183-series diesels; and the 24-m *Cheetah,* an aluminum-hulled catamaran powered by two MWM V-12 diesels.

AUSTRIA

Republic of Austria

AUSTRIAN ARMY DANUBE FLOTILLA

Personnel: 2 officers, 30 enlisted

Base: *Marinekaserne Teggethof* at Vienna/Kuchelau. All craft operate on the Danube River and its tributaries.

PATROL BOATS [WPB]

♦ 1 Niederösterreich class Bldr: Korneuberg Werft AG

	Laid down	L	In serv.
A 604 Niederösterreich	31-3-69	26-7-69	16-4-70

Niederösterreich (A 604) Erwin Sieche, 4-85

PATROL BOATS [WPB] *(continued)*

D: 73 tons (fl) **S:** 22 kts **Dim:** 29.67 × 5.41 × 1.10
A: 1 20-mm Oerlikon SPz Mk 66 AA; 1 12.7-mm M2 mg; 2 single 7.62-mm mg; 1 84-mm Carl Gustav PAR 66 mortar
M: 2 MWM V-16 diesels; 1,620 bhp
Range: 900/ . . . **Fuel:** 9.3 tons **Crew:** 1 officer, 8 enlisted

Remarks: Re-engined 1985. Original plans called for building 11 more.

♦ **1 Oberst Brecht class** Bldr: Korneuberg Werft AG

A 601 Oberst Brecht (In serv. 14-1-58)

D: 10 tons **S:** 14 kts **Dim:** 12.30 × 2.51 × 0.75
A: 1 12.7-mm M2 mg; 1 84-mm Carl Gustav PAR 66 mortar
M: 2 Graf & Stift 6-cyl. diesels; 290 bhp
Range: 160/10 **Crew:** 5 tot.

Remarks: A replacement to be ordered shortly.

SERVICE CRAFT

♦ **Several motorized pontoons [WYAG]**

D: 8.5 to 40 tons (fl) **Dim:** 19.0 × 1.70 (some 3.00) × 0.7

Note: For police duty, four aluminum patrol craft were ordered 1989 from Dieter Schulte Österreichse Schiffswerften AG, Autriche: 15.46 × 3.74 × 1.10; M: 2 Volvo Penta TMD.70c diesels; Schottel rudder props; 17.25 kts. The small patrol boat *Greif* (B 704), completed in 3-87 and 9.5-m long, is also police subordinated.

♦ **10 M-boot 80–class launches [WYFL]**
Bldr: Schottel Werft, Spay, Germany (In serv. 1984)

D: 4.7 tons (fl) **S:** 14 kts **Dim:** 7.5 × 2.5 × 0.6
M: 1 Klöckner-Humboldt-Deutz V-12 diesel; . . . bhp

Remarks: Push-boat/personnel launches.

AZERBAIJAN

Republic of Azerbaijan

Personnel: Approx. 1,750 tot.

Bases: All ships and craft are based at Baku.

Organization: The navy was formed on 27-7-92. There are patrol, gunboat, amphibious landing, and mine-countermeasures divisions. Russia provided guidance, operational control of craft, and maintenance from 1995 to 1999.

PATROL CRAFT [PC]

♦ **1 ex-Turkish AB 25 class**
Bldr: Istinye SY

Araz (ex-AB 34, P 134)

D: 150 tons (170 fl) **S:** 22 kts **Dim:** 40.24 × 6.40 × 1.65
A: 1 40-mm 60-cal. Mk 3 Bofors AA; 1 20-mm 70-cal. Oerlikon AA; 2 single 12.7-mm mg; 2 4-railed Mk 20 Mousetrap ASW RL; 4 single d.c. release racks
Electronics: Radar: 1 Decca TM 1226 nav.—Sonar: Plessey PMS-26 hull-mounted HF
M: 2 SACM-AGO V16CSHR diesels; 2 props; 4,800 bhp; 2 cruise diesels; 300 bhp
Crew: 3 officers, 28 enlisted

Remarks: Transferred 7-00. Fourteen others are assigned to the Marine Police. Built with French technical assistance. The cruise diesels are geared to the main shafts.

PATROL BOATS [PB]

♦ **1 ex-U.S. Coast Guard Point-class**
Bldr: Coast Guard Yard, Curtis Bay, Md.

S 201 (ex-*Point Brower,* WPB 82372)

S 201 George R. Schneider, 5-03

D: 64 tons (66 fl) **S:** 23.7 kts **Dim:** 25.3 × 5.23 × 1.95
A: 2 single 12.7-mm Colt M2 mg
Electronics: Radar: 1 Hughes-Furuno SPS-73 nav.
M: 2 Caterpillar 3412 diesels; 2 props; 1,480 bhp
Range: 490/23.7; 1,500/8 **Fuel:** 5.7 tons **Crew:** 1 officer, 7 enlisted

Remarks: Transferred 26-1-03. Hull built of mild steel. High-speed diesels controlled from the bridge. Well equipped for salvage and towing.

♦ **1 ex-Russian Zhuk (Gryf) class (Project 1400 or 1400M)**
Bldr: . . . . . . (In serv. 1971–86)

137 (ex-AK-55)

D: 35.9 tons (39.7 fl) **S:** 30 kts
Dim: 23.80 (21.70 wl) × 5.00 (3.80 wl) × 1.00 (hull; 1.90 max.)
A: 1 twin 14.5-mm 93-cal. 2M-7 AA *or* 1 twin 12.7-mm 60-cal. Utës-Ma mg
Electronics: Radar: 1 Lotsiya nav.
M: Project 1400M: 2 M-401 diesels; 2 props; 2,200 bhp; Project 1400: 2 M-50F4 diesels; 2 props; 2,400 bhp
Electric: 48 kw total (2 × 21-kw, 1 × 6-kw diesel sets)
Endurance: 5 days **Range:** 500/13.5 **Crew:** 1 officer, 9 enlisted

Remarks: Former Caspian Flotilla unit transferred circa 7-92.
Hull systems: Aluminum alloy hull. Range also reported as 700 n.m. at 28 kts, 1,100 n.m. at 15 kts.

MINE-COUNTERMEASURES SHIPS AND CRAFT

♦ **2 ex-Russian Yevgenya-class (Project 1258) inshore minesweepers [MSI]**
Bldr: Sudostroitel'noye Obyedineniye "Almaz" (Sredniy Neva), Kolpino (In serv. 1970–76)

237 (ex-RT-136) . . . (ex-RT-473)

D: 88.5 tons light, 94.5 normal (97.9 fl) **S:** 11 kts **Dim:** 26.13 × 5.90 × 1.40
A: 1 twin 14.5-mm 93-cal. 2M-7 or 25-mm 80-cal. 2M-3M AA; 1 7-round MRG-1 grenade launcher; 4 single d.c. racks (+ 8 d.c. emergency stowage)
Electronics: Radar: 1 Mius (Spin Trough) nav.—Sonar: MG-7 HF dipping
M: 2 Type 3D12 diesels; 2 props; 600 bhp—hydraulic slow-speed drive
Electric: 100 kw tot. (2 × 50-kw DG-50 diesel sets)
Range: 400/10 **Fuel:** 2.7 tons **Endurance:** 3 days
Crew: 1 officer, 9 enlisted (+ 2–3 clearance divers)

Remarks: Transferred 3-7-92. Referred to as "roadstead minesweepers" in Russian service.
Hull systems: Glass-reinforced plastic hull. Navigational equipment includes Girya-MA gyrocompass and NEL-7 echo sounder.
Combat systems: Employ a television minehunting system useful to 30-m depths that dispenses marker buoys to permit later disposal of mines by divers or explosive charges. The sonar is lowered via one of the stern davits. Carry GKT-1 mechanical, AT-2 acoustic, and SEMT-1 solenoid coil sweep gear. Have Khrom-KMN IFF system.

Disposal note: Sonya-class (Project 1258) coastal minesweepers BT-16, BT-103, and BT-155 transferred from the Russian Caspian Flotilla in 1992; are no longer in service.

AMPHIBIOUS WARFARE SHIPS AND CRAFT

♦ **1 ex-Russian Polnocny-B-class (Project 771A) medium landing ship [LSM]** Bldr: Stocznia Polnocna, Gdansk, Poland (In serv. 1967–70)

309 (ex-MDK-107)

D: 558 tons light, 640 tons std. (884 fl) **S:** 18 kts
Dim: 75.00 (70.00 wl) × 9.00 (8.60 wl) × 2.07 mean (1.20 fwd/2.40 aft)
A: 1 or 2 twin 30-mm 65-cal. AK-230 AA; 2 18-round 140-mm WM-18 barrage RL; 2 or 4 4-railed SA-N-8 SAM syst. (16 Strela-3M/Grail missiles)
Electronics: Radar: 1 Mius (Spin Trough), 1 MR-104 Rys' (Drum Tilt) f.c.
M: 2 Type 40DM diesels; 2 props; 4,400 bhp **Range:** 700/18; 2,000/16
Crew: 5 officers, 32 enlisted + 60 to 180 troops

Remarks: Stricken from the Russian Caspian Flotilla in 7-92 and transferred to Azerbaijan in 8-92.
Hull systems: Has a bow door only, and the hull has a "beak" projecting forward below the waterline at the bow to aid in beaching. Hatches to upper deck are for loading and ventilation only. Cargo: 237 tons max., including six tanks or 180 troops and their equipment; 30 vehicle crew are carried with tank loadout. Vehicle deck is 44.3 m long by 5.3 m wide and 3.6 m high.

♦ **2 ex-Russian Polnocny-A-class (Project 770) medium landing ships [LSM]**
Bldr: Stocznia Polnocna, Gdansk, Poland (In serv. 1962 to 1967)

291 (ex-MDK-36) 380 (ex-MDK-37)

D: 600 tons light (820 fl) **S:** 19 kts
Dim: 73.00 (70.00 wl) × 9.00 (8.60 wl) × 1.98 mean (1.13 fwd/2.33 aft)
A: 2 twin 30-mm 65-cal. AK-230 AA; 2 18-round 140-mm WM-18 barrage RL (180 rockets); 4 4-railed SA-N-5/8 SAM systems (32 Strela-3M/Grail or Gremlin missiles)
Electronics: Radar: 1 Mius (Spin Trough) nav., 1 MR-104 Rys' (Drum Tilt) f.c.
M: 2 Type 40DM diesels; 2 props; 4,400 bhp **Range:** 700/18; 1,800/16
Crew: 4 officers, 38 enlisted + 35 vehicle crew

Remarks: Stricken 3-7-92 from the Russian Caspian Flotilla and transferred to Azerbaijan.
Hull systems: Cargo capacity includes up to five heavy tanks for a total of about 180 tons. Vehicle deck is 42.3 m long by 5.3 m wide and 3.6 m high.

AMPHIBIOUS WARFARE SHIPS AND CRAFT *(continued)*

♦ 1 ex-Russian T-4-class (Project 1785) landing craft [LCM]

. . . (ex-D-603)

D: 35 tons light (93 fl) **S:** 10 kts (light) **Dim:** 19.9 × 5.6 × 1.4 max. aft
M: 2 Type 3D6 diesels; 2 props; 300 bhp **Range:** 1,500/10 **Crew:** 2 tot.

Remarks: Transferred at Baku, 3-7-92. Can accommodate up to 50 tons cargo. Now nearly 40 years old and may have been discarded.

AUXILIARIES

♦ 1 ex-Russian Emba-class (Project 1172) cable layer [ARC]

Bldr: Wärtsilä SY, Turku, Finland (In serv. 5-80)

. . . (ex-Emba)

D: 1,443 tons (2,145 fl) **S:** 11.8 kts **Dim:** 75.90 (68.50 pp) × 12.60 × 3.10
Electronics: Radar: 2 Mius (Spin Trough) nav.
M: diesel-electric: 2 Wärtsilä Vasa 6R22 diesels; 2 shrouded Schottel props; 1,360 shp—bow tunnel thruster
Range: 7,000/7 **Endurance:** 25 days **Crew:** 38 tot. (civilian)

Remarks: 1,910 grt. Cargo: 300 tons cable. Transferred to Azerbaijan after 1992; may be subordinate to an agency other than the navy. Intended for use in shallow coastal areas, rivers, and harbors. Has one 5-ton crane.

♦ 1 ex-Russian Luga-class (Project 888) cadet training ship [AXT]

Bldr: Stocznia Polnocna, Gdansk, Poland (In serv. 1977)

Oka

D: 1,474 tons (1,848 fl) **S:** 17 kts **Dim:** 71.40 × 11.60 × 4.17 (max.)
Electronics: Radar: 3 Don-2 nav.
M: 2 Cegielski-Sulzer 6TD48 diesels; 2 CP props; 3,600 bhp
Electric: 594 kw tot. **Range:** 7,500/11 **Endurance:** 30 days
Crew: 56 tot. + 8 instructors and 85 cadets

Remarks: *Oka* was based at the now-Azerbaijani port of Baku in the Caspian to support the Kirov Naval Academy and was transferred to Azeri control in early 1990s. Equipped for navigational training. Similar to Polish and East German units of the *Wodnik* class, but has a slightly larger superstructure, has its pilothouse one deck higher, and is not armed.

SERVICE CRAFT

♦ 1 ex-Russian Shelon' (TL-1127)-class (Project 1388) torpedo retriever [YPT]

Bldr: Sosnovka Zavod (In serv. 1978–84)

930 (ex-TL . . .)

D: 270 tons (fl) **S:** 30 kts **Dim:** 46.0 × 6.0 × 2.0
Electronics: Radar: 1 Kuban nav.—Sonar: Oka-1 helicopter dipping-type (HF)
M: 2 M-504 diesels; 2 props; 10,000 bhp
Range: 1,500/10 **Endurance:** 10 days **Crew:** 20 tot.

Remarks: Transferred to Azerbaijan during 1992; High-speed hull with a covered torpedo-recovery ramp aft. Can be armed with a twin 25-mm 80-cal. AA mount forward.

♦ 1 ex-Russian Petrushka-class (Project TS-39 or UK-3) training cutter [YXT]

Bldr: Stocznia Wisla, Gdansk, Poland (In serv. 1982– . . .)

385 (ex- . . .)

D: 212 tons light (236 fl) **S:** 10.5 kts **Dim:** 39.10 (36.00 pp) × 8.40 × 2.20
Electronics: Radar: 2 Mius (Spin Trough) nav.
M: 2 Wola H12, 1,000-rpm diesels; 2 props; 610 bhp
Electric: 180 kw tot. (2 × 90 kw; 2 Wola H6 diesels driving)
Range: 1,200/10.5 **Crew:** 13 tot. + 30 instructors and students

Remarks: Probably transferred summer 1992. Two classrooms and a navigational training facility on the bridge, and an MFD/F loop on a short mast aft. Is equipped with NBC warfare defense measures. Similar to the SK-620-class ambulance craft from the same builder. Has echo sounder, gyrocompass, MFD/F, and electromagnetic log. Two 23-person-capacity workboats are carried.

BORDER GUARD

PATROL CRAFT [WPC]

♦ 2 ex-Russian Stenka (Tarantul) class (Project 205P)

Bldrs: Sudostroitel'noye Obyedineniye "Almaz," Petrovskiy SY, St. Petersburg; Yaroslavl Zavod; etc. (In serv. 1967–90)

. . . (ex-AK-234) . . . (ex-AK-374)

D: 170 tons light; 211 std. (245 fl) **S:** 35 kts
Dim: 39.80 (37.50 wl) × 7.60 (5.90 wl) × 1.96
A: 2 twin 30-mm 65-cal. AK-230 AA; 4 fixed 402-mm OTA-40 TT (4 SET-40 ASW torpedoes); 2 d.c. racks (12 d.c.)
Electronics:
Radar: 1 Baklan (Pot Drum) or Peel Cone nav./surf. search, 1 MR-104 Rys' (Drum Tilt) gun f.c.
Sonar: Bronza hull-mounted HF (helicopter dipping-type)
EW: SPO-3 intercept
M: 3 M-504B or M-520 diesels; 3 props; 15,000 bhp
Range: 500/35; 800/20; 1,500/11.5 **Endurance:** 10 days
Crew: 4–5 officers, 26–27 enlisted

Remarks: Transferred 7-92. The dipping sonar is recessed into the port side of the transom stern, although, with no submarines in the Caspian Sea, it is unlikely that the sonar equipment or the torpedo tubes are maintained operational.

Note: Several other small launches are also in service.

BAHAMAS

Commonwealth of the Bahamas

ROYAL BAHAMAS DEFENCE FORCES

Personnel: Approx. 860 total.

Base: HMBS *Coral Harbour,* New Providence I.

Naval Aviation: One Cessna 404 and one Cessna 421C are used for maritime patrol and reconnaissance duties.

Note: Craft names are preceded by HMBS (Her Majesty's Bahamian Ship).

PATROL CRAFT [PC]

Note: Plans to purchase four 43-m "Nassau"-class patrol craft from Friede Goldman Halter were canceled in 2000.

♦ 2 Bahamas class

Bldr: Halter Marine Group—Moss Point Marine, Escatawpa, Miss.

P 60 Bahamas (In serv. 14-7-99) P 61 Nassau (In serv. 2000)

Nassau (P 61)—fitting out Leo Dirkx, 11-99

D: 375 tons (fl) **S:** 24 kts **Dim:** 60.62 × 8.90 × 2.60
A: 1 25-mm Mk 88 Bushmaster low-angle; 3 single 7.62-mm mg
Electronics: Radar: . . .
M: 3 Caterpillar 3508 DITA diesels; 3 props; 3,900 bhp
Range: 3,000+/14 **Endurance:** 21 days **Crew:** 62 tot. accomm.

Remarks: Ordered 14-3-97 for $13 million each. Steel hulls, with aluminum superstructures fabricated at Halter's Gulfport, Miss., facility. Design is a licensed, expanded version of the Vosper "Europatrol 250." Employed on counterdrug, search-and-rescue, EEZ patrol, and disaster-relief missions. Keel laid for first unit on 19-12-97. The 25-mm gun is in a Kollmorgen Mk 98 stabilized mounting.

♦ 3 Protector class

Bldr: Fairey Marine, Cowes, U.K. (In serv. 20-11-86)

P 03 Yellow Elder P 04 Port Nelson P 05 Samana

Samana (P 05) RN, 1996

D: 100 tons (fl) **S:** 30 kts (26 sust.) **Dim:** 33.00 (28.96 wl) × 6.73 × 1.95 (props)
A: 1 20-mm 70-cal. Oerlikon Mk 7A AA; 2 single 7.62-mm mg
Electronics: Radar: 1 Furuno FR-701 nav.
M: 3 G.M. Detroit Diesel 16V149 TIB diesels; 3 props; 5,400 bhp
Range: 300/24; 1,400/14 **Fuel:** 16 tons **Crew:** 2 officers, 18 enlisted

Remarks: Ordered 12-84. Steel construction. Have Racal MNS 2000 navigation system.

PATROL BOATS [PB]

♦ 2 40-foot Dauntless class

Bldr: SeaArk, Monticello, Ark. (In serv. 1-96)

P 42 P 43

PATROL BOATS [PB] *(continued)*

P 42 and P 43 Royal Bahamas Defence Forces, 1996

D: 11 tons (15 fl) **S:** 28 kts **Dim:** 12.19 (11.13 wl) × 3.86 × 0.69 (hull)
A: 2 single 12.7-mm mg; 2 single 7.62-mm mg
Electronics: Radar: 1 Raytheon R40X nav.
M: 2 Caterpillar 3208TA diesels; 2 props; 850 bhp (720 sust.)
Range: 200/30; 400/22 **Fuel:** 250 gal. **Crew:** 5 tot.

Remarks: U.S. Grant-Aid craft ordered 1995. Aluminum construction. C. Raymond Hunt, "Deep-Vee" hull design.

♦ **2 Wahoo-class launches**
Bldr: Boston Whaler, Edgewater, Fla. (In serv. 23-10-95)

P 112 P 113

D: 1.5 tons (fl) **S:** 35 kts **Dim:** 6.81 × 2.26 × 0.36
M: 2 Mariner gasoline outboards; 180 bhp
Range: 167/40; 750/ . . . **Fuel:** 243 liters **Crew:** 3 tot.

Remarks: Standard "Whaler" hullform with open cockpit amidships.

♦ **2 Impact-class launches**
Bldr: Boston Whaler, Edgewater, Fla. (In serv. 25-9-95)

P 110 P 111

Impact-class patrol launch Royal Bahamas Defence Forces, 1996

D: 1.5 tons (2.25 fl) **S:** 40 kts **Dim:** 6.81 × 2.26 × 0.36
M: 2 Mariner gasoline outboards; 180 bhp
Range: 167/40; 750/ . . . **Fuel:** 243 liters **Crew:** 3 tot.

Remarks: GRP hulls with semi-rigid inflatable gunwhale, fitted for rescue and towing.

♦ **1 Challenger-class launch**
Bldr: Boston Whaler, Edgewater, Florida (In serv. 9-95)

P 41

D: 8 tons (fl) **S:** 25 kts **Dim:** 8.23 × 17 × 0.3
A: 1 7.62-mm mg **Electronics:** Radar: none
M: 2 Evinrude gasoline outboards; 450 bhp **Crew:** 4 tot.

Remarks: GRP hull, fitted for rescue and towing.

♦ **1 Acklins class**
Bldr: Vosper Thornycroft (In serv. 10-12-77)

P 27 Inagua

D: 30 tons (37 fl) **S:** 19.5 kts **Dim:** 18.29 (17.07 pp) × 5.03 × 1.53
A: 2 single 7.62-mm mg **Electronics:** Radar: 1 Furuno . . . nav.
M: 2 Caterpillar 3408 TA diesels; 2 props; 950 bhp
Electric: 29 kVA tot. **Range:** 650/16 **Fuel:** 4 tons **Crew:** 11 tot.

Remarks: GRP construction, air-conditioned. First unit, *Acklins* (P 21), destroyed by fire in 1980. *San Salvador* (P 24) stricken 1982. *Eleuthera* (P 22), *Andros* (P 23), *Abaco* (P 25), and *Exuma* (P 26) were stricken during 1995, with P 23 preserved as a museum exhibit.

SERVICE CRAFT

♦ **1 support craft [YF]**

AO 1 Fort Montague (ex- . . .)

D: 90 tons (fl) **S:** 10 kts **Dim:** 28.6 × 7.0 × 1.8
A: 2 single 7.62-mm mg **Electronics:** Radar: 1 Decca . . . nav.
M: 2 G.M. Detroit Diesel 12-71 diesels; 2 props; 680 hp
Range: 3,000/10 **Crew:** 16 tot.

Remarks: Purchased 6-8-80. Fishing boat hull with long deckhouse.

Disposal note: Former U.S. Navy harbor utility craft *Fort Charlotte* (A 02, ex-YFU 97, ex-LCU 1611) was reportedly stricken during 1999.

BAHRAIN

State of Bahrain

DEFENSE FORCES

Personnel: Approx. 1,200 total

Base: Mina Sulman

Naval Aviation: Two AS.365F Dauphin helicopters and two Eurocopter Bo-105 helicopters, the latter with RDR 1500B radars.

GUIDED-MISSILE FRIGATES [FFG]

♦ **1 ex-U.S. Oliver Hazard Perry class**
Bldr: Bath Iron Works, Bath, Maine

	Laid down	L	In serv.
90 Sabha (ex-*Jack Williams,* FFG 24)	25-2-80	30-8-80	19-9-81

Sabha (90) Maritime Photographic, 2-99

D: 2,769 tons light (3,658 fl) **S:** 29 kts (30.6 trials)
Dim: 135.64 (125.9 wl) × 13.72 × 5.8 (6.7 max.)
A: 1 Mk 13 Mod. 4 launcher (4 Harpoon and 36 Standard SM-1 MR missiles); 1 76-mm 62-cal. Mk 75 DP; 1 20-mm Mk 15 Phalanx Block 1B gatling CIWS; 4 single 12.7-mm mg; 2 triple 324-mm Mk 32 Mod. 5 ASW TT; 1-2 AS.365F Dauphin helicopters
Electronics:
Radar: 1 Cardion SPS-55 surf. search; 1 Raytheon SPS-49(V)4 air-search; 1 Lockheed Martin Mk 92 Mod. 2 missile/gun f.c.; 1 Lockheed Martin STIR (SPG-60 Mod.) missile/gun f.c.
Sonar: Raytheon SQS-56 (7.5 kHz)
EW: Raytheon SLQ-32(V)2 passive; Mk 36 SRBOC decoy RL syst. (2 6-tubed Raytheon Mk 137 launchers); SLQ-25 Nixie towed acoustic torpedo decoy
TACAN: URN-25—E/O: 2 Mk 24 target designators
M: 2 G.E. LM-2500 gas turbines; 1 5.5-m dia. CP, 5-bladed prop; 41,000 shp (40,000 sust.)—2 350-shp drop-down electric propulsors
Electric: 3,000 kw tot.
Range: 4,200/20; 5,000/18 **Fuel:** 587 tons + 64 tons helicopter fuel
Crew: 21 officers, 195 enlisted (incl. aviation group)

Remarks: *Sabha* decommissioned from U.S. Navy and transferred under Grant-Aid program 13-9-96. Serves as fleet flagship.
Hull systems: Particularly well protected against splinter and fragmentation damage, with 19-mm aluminum-alloy armor over magazine spaces, 16-mm steel over the main engine-control room, and 19-mm Kevlar plastic armor over vital electronics and command spaces. Speed on one turbine alone is 25 kts; the auxiliary power system uses two retractable pods located well forward and can drive the ship at up to 6 kts. The two fin stabilizers extend 2.36 m. Equipped with the Prairie-Masker air bubbler system to reduce radiated machinery noise below the waterline.
Combat systems: The Mk 92 Mod. 2 fire-control system controls missile and 76-mm gunfire; it uses a STIR antenna amidships and a U.S.–built version of the Thales WM-28 radar forward and can track four separate targets. A Mk 13 weapons-direction system is fitted. The only ship-launched ASW weapons are the Mk 46 Mod. 5 torpedoes in the two triple torpedo tubes; a total of 24 torpedoes can be carried. Harpoon missiles are launched via the SWG-1 launch control system. WSC-3 SATCOM equipment was removed prior to transfer. No towed passive sonar array is fitted.

GUIDED-MISSILE PATROL COMBATANTS [PGG]

♦ **2 Type FPB 62-001**
Bldr: Friedrich Lürssen Werft, Vegesack, Germany

50 Al Manama (In serv. 3-2-88) 51 Al Muharraq (In serv. 3-2-88)

D: 632 tons (fl) **S:** 34.7 kts (32.25 sust.) **Dim:** 62.95 (59.90 pp) × 9.30 × 2.90
A: 4 MM 40 Exocet SSM; 1 76-mm 62-cal. OTO Melara Compact C Mod. 6 DP; 1 twin 40-mm OTO Melara 70-cal. L70B AA; 2 single 12.7-mm mg; 1 AS.365F Dauphin or Bo-105 helo

GUIDED-MISSILE PATROL COMBATANTS [PGG] *(continued)*

Al Manama (50) C. E. Castle, 2-99

Electronics:
Radar: 1 Decca 1226 nav.; 1 Ericsson Sea Giraffe 50HC surf./air-search; 1 CelsiusTech 9LV 200 f.c.
EW: Racal Cutlass B-1 intercept; Racal Cygnus jammer; Thales Telegon 8 HFD/F; 2 Matra Défense Dagaie decoy RL
E/O: 2 Matra Défense Panda Mk 2 optronic f.c.
M: 4 MTU 20V538 TB93 diesels; 4 props; 19,600 bhp
Electric: 408 kw (3 × 136 kw) **Range:** 4,000/16 **Fuel:** 120 tons
Crew: 7 officers, 18 petty officers, 18 ratings

Remarks: Ordered 2-84. Are well overdue for refit.
Combat systems: Have CelsiusTech 9LV-331 weapons-control system. Carry 900 rounds 76-mm, 4,400 rounds 40-mm ammunition. Two 20-mm AA have been replaced by machineguns. EW *system* is Racal 242, with SADIE processor. The raised helicopter platform incorporates an elevator to lower the helicopter to the hangar below.

GUIDED-MISSILE PATROL CRAFT [PTG]

♦ 4 TNC 45 class
Bldr: Friedrich Lürssen Werft, Vegesack, Germany

	In serv.		In serv.
20 Ahmed Al Fateh	5-2-84	22 Abdul Rahman al-Fadel	10-9-86
21 Al Jaberi	3-5-84	23 Al Taweelah	25-3-89

Al Taweelah (23) C. E. Castle, 2-99

D: 203 tons light (259 fl) **S:** 40.5 kts **Dim:** 44.9 (42.3 fl) × 7.3 × 2.05 (2.31 props)
A: 4 MM 40 Exocet SSM; 1 76-mm 62-cal. OTO Melara DP; 1 twin 40-mm 70-cal. OTO Melara AA; 2 single 12.7-mm M2 mg
Electronics:
Radar: 1 Decca 1226 nav.; 1 Ericsson Sea Giraffe 50 surf./air-search; 1 CelsiusTech 9 LV 223 f.c.s.
EW: Racal RDL-2 ABC (22, 23: Cutlass B-1) intercept; 1 Matra Défense Dagaie decoy RL—22, 23 only: Racal Cygnus jammers
E/O: Matra Défense Panda optical backup f.c.
M: 4 MTU 16V538 TB92 diesels; 4 props; 15,600 bhp (13,460 sust.)
Electric: 405 kVA **Range:** 500/38.5; 1,500/16 **Fuel:** 45 tons
Crew: 6 officers, 30 enlisted

Remarks: First pair ordered 1979, second pair 5-85. Similar to TNC 45–class units built for United Arab Emirates. One of the class was refitted by the builder in Germany during 2000, and bids to refit another locally were requested 2-99.
Combat systems: Carry 250 rounds 76-mm, 1,800 rounds 40-mm, 6,000 rounds 12.7-mm ammunition. Also carry a Bofors 57-mm rocket flare launcher.

PATROL CRAFT [PC]

♦ 2 FPB 38 class
Bldr: Friedrich Lürssen Werft, Vegesack, Germany

	L	In serv.		L	In serv.
10 Al Riffa	4-81	3-3-82	11 Hawar	7-81	3-3-82

D: 188 tons normal (205 fl) **S:** 34 kts **Dim:** 38.5 (36.0 pp) × 7.0 × 2.2 (props)
A: 1 twin 40-mm 70-cal. OTO Melara AA; 2 mine rails
Electronics:
Radar: 1 Decca 1226 nav.; 1 CelsiusTech 9GR 600 f.c.
EW: Racal RDL-2 intercept; 1 Wallop Barricade decoy RL
E/O: 1 Matra Défense Lynx optical gun f.c.
M: 2 MTU 16V538 TB92 diesels; 2 props; 9,000 bhp (6,810 sust.)
Electric: 130 kVA **Range:** 550/31.5; 1,100/16 **Crew:** 3 officers, 24 enlisted

Remarks: Ordered 1979. Carry two 3-pdr. saluting cannon. A Bofors 57-mm flare rocket/chaff launcher is fitted abaft the mast.

Hawar (11) Joe Straczek, 11-01

PATROL BOATS [PB]

♦ 2 U.S. 65-foot Commercial Cruiser class
Bldr: Swiftships, Morgan City, La.

30 Al Jarim (In serv. 9-2-82) 31 Al Jasrah (In serv. 26-2-82)

Al Jarim (30) Navpic-Holland, 4-96

D: 33 tons (fl) **S:** 30 kts **Dim:** 19.17 × 5.56 × 1.98
A: 1 20-mm 90-cal. Oerlikon GAM-B01 AA
Electronics: Radar: 1 Decca 110 nav.
M: 2 G.M. 12V71 TI diesels; 2 props; 1,200 bhp **Range:** 1,200/18

Remarks: Aluminum construction. Overdue for retirement.

MINISTRY OF THE INTERIOR COAST GUARD

Personnel: Approx. 260 total in seagoing component

Base: Al Hadd

PATROL BOATS [WPB]

♦ 4 M200 class
Bldr: Halmatic, Havant, U.K. (In serv. 1991–92)

Dera'a 2 Dera'a 6 Dera'a 7 Dera'a 8

Bahraini M200- (background) and M140-class patrol boats on trials Halmatic, 1992

D: 31.5 tons (fl) **S:** 25 kts **Dim:** 20.10 × 5.28 × 1.54
A: 2 single 7.62-mm mg **Electronics:** Radar: 1 Decca . . . nav.
M: 2 G.M. Detroit Diesel 12V71 TA diesels; 2 props; 820 bhp
Range: 500/20 **Fuel:** 6,800 liters **Crew:** 7 tot.

Remarks: Glass-reinforced plastic construction.

♦ 6 M140 class
Bldr: Halmatic, Havant, U.K. (In serv. 1991–92)

Saif 5 Saif 6 Saif 7 Saif 8 Saif 9 Saif 10

D: 17 tons (fl) **S:** 35 kts **Dim:** 14.40 × 3.86 × 1.15
A: 2 single 7.62-mm mg **Electronics:** Radar: 1 Decca . . . nav.
M: 2 G.M. Detroit Diesel 12V71 TA diesels; 2 props; 820 bhp
Electric: 17.6 kVA (1 G.M. diesel set)
Range: 440/20 **Fuel:** 3,400 liters **Crew:** 4 tot.

Remarks: Glass-reinforced plastic construction.

PATROL BOATS [WPB] *(continued)*

Bahraini M140 class Halmatic, 1992

♦ **1 30-meter Wasp class**
Bldr: Souter, Cowes, U.K. (In serv. 12-8-85)

AL YUSRAH

D: 90 tons (103 fl) **S:** 23.6 kts **Dim:** 30.0 (26.75 wl) × 6.40 × 1.60
A: 1 20-mm 90-cal. Oerlikon GAM-B01 AA; 2 single 7.62-mm mg
Electronics: Radar: 1 . . . nav.
M: 2 G.M. Detroit Diesel 16V149 TI diesels; 2 props; 3,100 bhp
Electric: 47 kVA **Range:** 500/22; 1,000/12 **Fuel:** 17 tons **Crew:** 16 tot.

Remarks: Enlarged version of standard 20-m Wasp, ordered 3-8-84 and laid down 15-11-84. GRP construction. Outfitted as a yacht; VIP lounge is built over the stern. Name also reported as *Al Muharraq.*

♦ **2 20-meter Wasp-class fiberglass-hulled**
Bldr: Souter, Cowes, U.K. (In serv. 1983)

DERA'A 4 DERA'A 5

D: 34 tons (36.3 fl) **S:** 21 kts **Dim:** 20.0 (16.0 wl) × 5.0 × 1.5
A: 2 single 7.62-mm mg **Electronics:** Radar: 1 Decca . . . nav.
M: 2 G.M. Detroit Diesel 12V71 TI diesels; 2 props; 1,200 bhp **Crew:** 8 tot.

♦ **4 Sword class**
Bldr: Fairey Marine, Cowes, U.K. (In serv. 1980)

SAIF 1 SAIF 2 SAIF 3 SAIF 4

D: 15.2 tons **S:** 28 kts **Dim:** 13.7 × 4.1 × 1.32
M: 2 G.M. Detroit Diesel 8V71 TI diesels; 2 props; 850 bhp
Range: 500/ . . . **Crew:** 6 tot.

Remarks: GRP construction. Are due for disposal. Carry small arms only.

Disposal note: Tracker-class patrol boats *Dera'a 1* and *Dera'a 3* had been retired by 1999.

SERVICE CRAFT

♦ **1 miscellaneous support/supply boat [WYF]**
Bldr: Halmatic, Havant, U.K. (In serv. 1992)

SAFRA 3

Safra 3 Halmatic, 1992

D: 165 tons (fl) **S:** 13 kts **Dim:** 25.91 × 5.87 × 1.57
A: None **Electronics:** Radar: 1 Decca . . . nav.
M: 2 G.M. Detroit Diesel 16V92 TA diesels; 2 props; 2,480 bhp
Electric: 74 kVA tot. (2 × 37-kVA diesel alternators)
Range: 700/13 **Crew:** 6 tot.

Remarks: GRP-construction hull, with aluminum superstructure. Can carry up to 15 tons of deck cargo and personnel.

♦ **1 logistic support landing craft [WYF]**
Bldr: Swiftships, Inc., Morgan City, La. (In serv. 21-10-82)

41 AJIRAH

Ajirah (41) Navpic-Holland, 4-96

D: 428 tons (fl) **S:** 12 kts **Dim:** 39.62 × 10.97 × 1.30
A: none **Electronics:** Radar: 1 Decca . . . nav.
M: 2 G.M. Detroit Diesel 16V71N diesels; 2 props; 1,800 bhp
Fuel: 20 tons **Range:** 1,500/10 **Crew:** 2 officers, 6 enlisted

Remarks: Aluminum construction. Cargo: vehicles, supplies, up to 100 tons cargo fuel and 88 tons water. Has a bow ramp and 15-ton crane. Turning radius 77 m. Two sisters are in Venezuelan service.

Disposal note: Loadmaster II-class landing craft *Sabha* (40) was stricken by 2005.

♦ **4 ex-U.S. Army LCU 1466–class utility landing craft [WYF]**
Bldr: General Ship & Eng. Wks. (In serv. 1976–78)

42 MASHTAN (ex-LCU . . .)
43 RUBODH (ex-LCU . . .)
44 SUWAD (ex-LCU . . .)
45 JARADAH (ex-LCU . . .)

Jaradah (45) Joe Straczek, 11-01

D: 180 tons light (347 fl) **S:** 8 kts **Dim:** 35.08 × 10.36 × 1.60 (max.)
A: 2 single 12.7-mm mg **Electronics:** Radar: 1 . . . nav.
M: 3 G.M. Gray Marine 64 YTL diesels; 3 props; 1,200 bhp
Range: 1,200/6 (700/7 loaded) **Fuel:** 11 tons **Crew:** 11 tot.

Remarks: Transferred during 1991 from surplus U.S. Army stocks. Cargo: 150 tons in 15.8 × 9.0-m open deck with ramps at both ends.

♦ **About 10 wooden motor dhows for logistics and patrol duties [WYFL]**

♦ **1 Tiger-class utility hovercraft [WYFLA]**
Bldr: AVL, Cowes, U.K. (In serv. 1995)

NIJOOD

D: 4.5 tons (fl) **S:** 35 kts **Dim:** 8.0 × 3.8 × 2.3 high
M: 1 AMC gasoline engine; 180 bhp

BANGLADESH

People's Republic of Bangladesh

Personnel: Approximately 9,000 tot. The navy hopes to establish a battalion of marines.

Bases: BNS *Issah Khan* naval base and BNS *Bhatiary* repair facilities at Chittagong; BNS *Patenga* naval academy; BNS *Haji Mohsin* naval base at Dhaka; BNS *Titumir* at Khulna; BNS *Shaheed Moazzem* facility at Kaptai; and BNS *Mongla* at Mongla seaport, Bagerhat (completed 4-02). The government-owned Khulna Shipbuilding & Engineering Works, Ltd., was taken over by the navy in 2-99. During 8-05, the turnover to the navy of the the Chittagong fish harbor was announced, to be used as an additional naval facility in the region.

Naval Aviation: Two or more helicopters are to be purchased for use with F 25, and long-range plans call for procurement of land-based maritime patrol aircraft.

Note: Naval ship names are preceded by BNS (Bangladesh Naval Ship).

SUBMARINES [SS]

Note: Bangladesh has announced a desire to purchase four submarines by 2012.

FRIGATES [FF]

Note: In addition to the units listed below, the navy was said by Ukrainian sources to be negotiating with the Ukrainian Research-Design Shipbuilding Center for an export version (to be built at Mikolayiv) of the Sapsan-2100-class multipurpose frigate; no contract has yet been reported, however. In 8-02 the Bangladeshi prime minister announced that the country would soon purchase two ex-Italian navy *Lupo*-class frigates, but the ships were instead sold to Peru.

♦ 1 DW2000H design
Bldr: Daewoo Shipbuilding and Marine Engineering Co., Okpo, South Korea

	Laid down	L	In serv.
F 25 . . . (ex-*Bangabandhu*)	. . .	. . .	30-5-01

F 25 (ex-Bangabandhu) Daewoo, 2001

D: 2,300 tons (fl) **S:** 25.3 kts **Dim:** 103.50 (98.00 pp) × 12.00 × 3.60
A: 4 Alenia Otomat Mk 2 Block IV SSM; 1 76-mm 62-cal. OTO Melara DP; 2 twin 40-mm 70-cal. OTOMelara Fast Forty AA; 2 single 12.7-mm mg; 2 triple 324-mm B515 ASW TT; 2 mine rails; 1 helicopter
Electronics:
Radar: Thales Variant surf. search; Thales DA-08 air search; Thales Lirod Mk 2 f.c.
Sonar: . . .
EW: Thales Cutlass 242 intercept and Scorpion jammer
E/O: Thales Mirador-FD surveillance/tracking/f.c.
M: 4 SEMT-Pielstick . . . diesels; 2 props; . . . bhp
Range: 4000/18 **Crew:** 186

Remarks: Ordered 11-9-97. Paid for with funds from $100-million Saudi Arabian grant. Arrived in Bangladesh 6-01. The ship was decommissioned on 14-2-02 for repairs, due to numerous defects in the machinery and combat systems. Now at the Chittagong Naval Base, she was expected to recommission under another name in the near future.
Combat systems: Has Thales TACTICOS combat command/data system. A helicopter deck and hangar are fitted, although the navy has no aircraft. Provision was made for later installation of a short-range SAM system, such as Sea Sparrow.

♦ 1 Chinese Jianghu-I class (Project 053H1)
Bldr: Hudong SY, Shanghai

	L	In serv.
F 18 Osman (ex-*Xiangtan*, 556)	1986	8-11-89

Osman (F 18) Hartmut Ehlers, 10-03

D: 1,568 tons (1,702 fl) **S:** 25.5 kts **Dim:** 103.2 × 10.2 × 3.05 (hull)
A: 4 Fei Long-1 SSM; 2 twin 100-mm 56-cal. DP; 4 twin 37-mm 62-cal. Type 74 AA; 2 5-round Type 81 ASW RL; 4 d.c. mortars; 2 d.c. racks
Electronics:
Radar: 1 Type 756 nav.; 1 MX-902 (Eye Shield) air-search; 1 Type 256 (Square Tie) missile target desig.
Sonar: Echo Type 5 MF hull-mounted
EW: RW-23-1 (Jug Pair) intercept
M: 2 SEMT-Pielstick 12 PA6 280 BTC diesels; 2 props; 16,000 bhp
Electric: 1,320 kw (3 × 400-kw, 1 × 120-kw diesel sets)
Range: 4,000/15; 1,750/25 **Endurance:** 15 days
Crew: 27 officers, 273 enlisted

Remarks: Transferred from Chinese navy inventory 9-89. Badly damaged forward in 8-91 collision with merchant vessel and repaired 1992–93. Planned transfer of a second unit in 1990 was canceled.
Combat systems: Has a Wok Won nonstabilized optical director for the 100-mm guns but no fire-control radar; the other weapons are improvements on Soviet-era systems. The antiship missiles are an improved copy of the original Soviet Styx (Termit) system. The depth charge racks are mounted belowdecks and discharge through transom doors. The antiaircraft guns are on-mount controlled, via ringsights.

♦ 1 ex-British Salisbury class (Type 61)
Bldr: Hawthorne Leslie, Hebburn-on-Tyne

	Laid down	L	In serv.
F 16 Umar Farooq (ex-*Llandaff*, F 61)	27-8-53	30-11-55	11-4-58

Umar Farooq (F 16) H&L Van Ginderen, 1999

D: 2,170 tons (2,408 fl) **S:** 24 kts **Dim:** 103.60 (100.58 pp) × 12.19 × 4.80
A: 1 twin 114-mm 45-cal. Mk 6 DP; 1 twin 40-mm 60-cal. Bofors Mk 5 AA; 1 3-round Mk 4 Squid ASW mortar
Electronics:
Radar: 2 . . . nav.; 1 Type 965 early warning; 1 Type 993 air/surf. search; 1 Type 277 height-finder; 1 Type 275 f.c.
Sonar: Type 174 HF search; Type 170B searchlight HF targeting
EW: UA-3 intercept, FH-4 HFD/F
M: 8 Admiralty 16VVS ASR 1 diesels; 2 props; 12,400 bhp
Range: 2,300/24; 7,500/16 **Crew:** 14 officers, 223 enlisted

Remarks: Transferred from U.K. on 10-12-76. As of 10-98 still retained all topside equipment aboard at transfer, making her a veritable museum of 1950s British naval technology. Had a major engineering plant failure in 1985; repaired. Has four additional 16VVS ASR 1 diesels driving generator sets. The 114-mm mount is controlled by a Mk 6 f.c.s., while the 40-mm mount is locally controlled. The Squid triple ASW mortar has been removed.

♦ 2 ex-British Leopard class (Type 41)

	Bldr	Laid down	L	In serv.
F 15 Abu Bakr (ex-*Lynx*, F 27)	John Brown, Clydebank	13-8-53	12-1-55	14-3-57
F 17 Ali Haider (ex-*Jaguar*, F 37)	Wm. Denny, Dumbarton	2-11-53	30-7-57	12-12-59

Ali Haider (F 17) Brian Morrison, 2-01

D: 2,300 tons (2,520 fl) **S:** 23 kts **Dim:** 103.63 (100.58 pp) × 12.19 × 4.8 (fl)
A: 2 twin 114-mm 45-cal. Mk 6 DP; 1 40-mm 60-cal. Mk 9 AA; 2 single 20-mm 70-cal. Oerlikon AA
Electronics:
Radar: 3 . . . nav./surf. search; 1 Type 965 early warning; 1 Type 993 air/surf. search; 1 Type 275 f.c.
EW: UA-4 intercept, FH-5 HFD/F
M: 8 Admiralty 16 VVS ASR 1 diesels; 2 CP props; 12,400 bhp
Range: 2,300/23; 7,500/16 **Crew:** 15 officers, 220 enlisted

Remarks: F 17 purchased 6-7-78; arrived Bangladesh 11-78 after overhaul. F 15 purchased 12-3-82, commissioned 19-3-82. F 15 is to continue in service as training ship, while F 17 was to be hulked on delivery of the new Korean-built frigate but remains in service. Have fin stabilizers. On a visit to Myanmar during 5-02, F 15 carried 16 officers, 25 cadets, and 252 enlisted personnel.
Combat systems: Squid ASW mortar and sonars removed while in Royal Navy service. One Mk 6 GFCS with Type 275 radar for 114-mm guns; 40-mm, local control only; in F 17, the 40-mm mount may be a 70-cal. Bofors mounting. The Type 993 radar is probably no longer operational. A fourth small navigational or surface-search radar set antenna appears to be mounted atop the foremast on the F 17.

PATROL SHIPS [PS]

♦ 5 ex-U.K. Island-class offshore patrol vessels
Bldr: Hall Russell, Aberdeen

	L	In serv.
P 713 Sangu (ex-*Lindisfarne,* P 300)	1-6-77	26-1-78
P 714 Turag (ex-*Guernsey,* P 297)	17-2-77	28-10-77
P 912 Kapatkhaya (ex-*Alderney,* P 278)	27-2-79	6-10-79
P 913 Karatoa (ex-*Shetland,* P 298)	22-11-76	14-7-77
P 914 Gomati (ex-*Anglesey,* P 277)	18-10-78	1-6-79

Sangu (P 713) Marion Wright, 3-04

Turag (P 714) Marion Wright, 3-04

D: 998 tons (1,280 fl) **S:** 16.5 kts **Dim:** 61.10 (51.97 pp) × 11.00 × 4.27
A: delivered unarmed
Electronics:
Radar: 1 Kelvin-Hughes Type 1006 nav.
Sonar: Simrad SU "Sidescan"
EW: Racal UAN (1) Orange Crop intercept
M: 2 Ruston 12 RK 3 CM diesels (750 rpm); 1 CP prop; 5,640 bhp (4,380 sust.)
Electric: 536 kw tot. (3 × 162-kw, 1 × 50-kw diesel alternator sets; 440 V a.c.)
Range: 11,000/12 **Fuel:** 310 tons **Crew:** 4 officers, 29 enlisted

Remarks: *Karatoa* was transferred on 29-7-02 and *Kapatkhaya* on 31-10-02. *Gomati* transferred in 7-03 and *Sangu* and *Turag* during 2004. Sister *Shaheed Ruhul Amin* (A 511, ex-*Jersey,* P 295) has operated as a training ship [AXT] since acquisition in 12-93; sister *Orkney* (P 299) was offered in 5-99 but was not acquired.
Hull systems: Have fin stabilizers and can maintain 12-15 kts in a Force 8 gale. Two Avon Searaider semi-rigid dinghies replaced the original Geminis for inspection purposes. Carry 28.6 tons detergent (a 6-hr supply) for oil-spill cleanup. Have additional accommodations for 25.
Combat systems: The Racal CANE DEA-1 action data system is installed. All armament was removed prior to transfer.

GUIDED-MISSILE PATROL CRAFT [PTG]

♦ 5 Chinese Huangfeng class (Project 021)
Bldr: Jiangnan SY, Shanghai

P 8125 Durdharsha, P 8126 Durdanta, P 712 Salem (ex-8127), P 8128 Durdanda, P 8131 Anirban

Durdharsha (P 8125) French Navy, 1996

D: 175 tons light, 186.5 normal (205 fl) **S:** 35 kts
Dim: 38.75 × 7.60 × 1.70 (mean)
A: 4 HY-1 SSM; 2 twin 30-mm 65-cal. Type 69 AA
Electronics: Radar: 1 Type 256 (Square Tie) surf. search/target desig.
M: 3 M-503A diesels; 3 props; 12,000 bhp **Electric:** 65 kw tot.
Range: 800/30 **Crew:** 5 officers, 60 enlisted
Remarks: Chinese copy of the Soviet Osa-I (Project 205) design. First four commissioned in Bangladesh fleet on 10-11-88. Two sank during the 4-91 cyclone but have been salvaged; two others were damaged but have been repaired. P 8131 was delivered 6-92 as a replacement but ended up as a force enhancement. Lack fire control radar director for the 30-mm guns (copies of the Russian AK-230 system), which are instead controlled by two remote ringsight directors. Reported crew size seems excessive.

♦ 5 Chinese Houku class (Project 024)

P 8111 Durbar, P 8112 Duranta, P 8113 Durvedya, P 8114 Durdam, P 8141 Uttal

D: 68 tons (79 fl) **S:** 37 kts **Dim:** 27.00 × 6.50 × 1.80 (1.3 hull)
A: 2 HY-1 SSM; 1 twin 25-mm 80-cal. Type 61 AA
Electronics:
Radar: 1 Type 256 (Square Tie) surf. search/target desig.
M: 4 M-50F-4 (Type L12V-180) diesels; 4 props; 4,800 bhp **Electric:** 65 kw tot.
Range: 400/30; 500/24 **Endurance:** 5 days **Crew:** 4 officers, 13 enlisted

Remarks: Steel construction. First two delivered 6-4-83, two others 10-11-83. P 8141 was delivered 8-92 as a replacement for one of the two badly damaged during the 4-91 cyclone. The gunmount is a copy of the Russian 2M-3M mounting.

TORPEDO BOATS [PT]

♦ 8 Chinese Huchuan class/P-4 class*

T 8221 TB 1*, T 8222 TB 2*, T 8223 TB 3*, T 8224 TB 4*, T 8235 TB 35, T 8236 TB 36, T 8237 TB 37, T 8238 TB 38

D: 39 tons (45.8 fl) **S:** 50 kts
Dim: 22.50 × 3.80 (6.26 over foils) × 1.15 (1.12 foilborne)
A: 2 twin 14.5-mm 79-cal. Type 81 AA; 2 fixed 533-mm TT
Electronics: Radar: 1 Type 753 nav.
M: 3 M-50F-4 (Type L12V-180) diesels; 3 props; 3,600 bhp **Electric:** 5.6 kw
Range: 500/30 **Crew:** 3 officers, 20 enlisted

Remarks: TB 1–4 are former Chinese Navy units commissioned on 1-3-88 into Bangladesh service. TB 35–38 were donated during 1992 by Pakistan to replace units sunk during the 1991 cyclone. Cruising speed is 32 kts. Foils mounted forward only, with a small auxiliary foil beneath the bow to aid in getting foilborne; the stern has no hydrofoils and planes on the surface. Only four may be operational.

PATROL CRAFT [PC]

♦ 1 Chinese Haizhui class
Bldr: Guijian SY (In serv. 9-4-96)

P 711 Barkat

D: 150 tons (170 fl) **S:** 29 kts **Dim:** 41.0 × 5.41 × 1.80
A: 2 twin 37-mm 63-cal. Type 76 AA; 2 twin 25-mm 80-cal. Type 81 AA
Electronics: Radar: 1 Anritsu 726 UA nav./surf. search
M: 4 Type L12-180Z diesels; 4 props; 4,800 bhp (4,400 bhp sust.)
Range: 750/16 **Crew:** 4 officers, 24 enlisted

Remarks: Donated as a replacement for discarded Shanghai-II-class units, of which this is an updated variant. Has fin stabilizers.

♦ 2 Meghna class
Bldr: Vosper Pty, Tanjong Rhu, Singapore

P 211 Meghna (L: 19-1-84) P 212 Jamuna (L: 19-3-84)

Jamuna (P 212)—outboard Meghna (P 211) Gilbert Gyssels, 1987

D: 410 (fl) **S:** 22 kts **Dim:** 46.50 (42.50 pp) × 7.50 × 2.00 (hull)
A: 1 57-mm 70-cal. Bofors SAK 57 Mk 1 AA; 1 40-mm 70-cal. Bofors AA; 2 single 7.62-mm mg

PATROL CRAFT [PC] *(continued)*

Electronics: Radar: 1 Decca TM 1229C nav.
M: 2 Paxman Valenta 12 CM diesels; 2 props; 6,000 bhp (5,460 sust.)
Electric: 218 kw tot. (2 × 109-kw diesel sets)
Range: 2,000/16 **Fuel:** 42 tons **Crew:** 3 officers, 45 enlisted

Remarks: Operated for the Ministry of Agriculture by the navy for 200-n.m. economic zone patrol and fisheries protection duties. Both damaged during the 4-91 typhoon but have been repaired. P 212 was badly damaged by fire on 24-9-02 while undergoing refit at Chittagong.
Combat systems: P 212 may have been rearmed with two twin 40-mm AA in place of the 57-mm gun. Both have an Alenia NA 18B optronic gun director.

♦ 1 Chinese Hainan-class submarine chaser

P 812 NIRBHOY (In serv. 1-12-85)

D: 375 tons normal (400 fl) **S:** 30.5 kts **Dim:** 58.77 × 7.20 × 2.20 (hull)
A: 2 twin 57-mm 70-cal. Type 66 AA; 2 twin 25-mm 80-cal. Type 61 AA; 4 5-round Type 81 ASW RL; 2 d.c. mortars; 2 d.c. racks; 2 mine rails
Electronics:
Radar: 1 Type 753 surf. search—Sonar: 1 Tamir-11 searchlight HF
M: 4 diesels; 4 props; 8,800 bhp **Range:** 2,000/14 **Crew:** 70 tot.

Remarks: Sister *Durjoy* (P 811) damaged beyond repair in 1995 and stricken. Both had been damaged during the 4-91 typhoon. All gunmounts are locally controlled.

♦ 7 Chinese Shanghai-II class

P 411 SHAHED DAULUT
P 412 SHAHEED FARID
P 413 SHAHEED MOHIBULLAH
P 414 SHAHEED AKHTARUDDIN
P 612 TAWFIQ
P 613 TAMJEED
P 614 TANVEER

D: 122 tons (135 fl) **S:** 28.5 kts **Dim:** 38.78 × 5.41 × 1.55 (max.)
A: 2 twin 37-mm 63-cal. Type 74 AA; 2 twin 25-mm 80-cal. Type 61 AA
Electronics: Radar: 1 Type 351 (Pot Head) nav.
M: 2 Type L12-180 diesels (1,200 bhp each), 2 Type L12-180Z diesels (910 bhp each); 4 props; 4,220 bhp
Electric: 39 kw tot. **Range:** 750/16.5 **Crew:** 36 tot.

Remarks: Delivered 5-82. *Tawheed* (P 611) of this class was assigned to the Coast Guard during 1995. The radar is a copy of the 1950s Soviet Reya set.

♦ 1 salvaged Pakistani patrol boat
Bldr: Brooke Marine, Lowestoft, U.K. (In serv. 20-5-65)

P 311 BISHKALI (ex-*Jessore*)

D: 115 tons (143 fl) **S:** 24 kts **Dim:** 32.62 (30.48 pp) × 6.10 × 1.55
A: 2 single 40-mm 70-cal. OTO Melara AA
Electronics: Radar: 1 Decca . . . nav.
M: 2 MTU 12V538 diesels; 2 props; 3,400 bhp **Crew:** 30 tot.

Remarks: Sunk in 1971 war of independence; salvaged and repaired at Khulna SY and recommissioned 23-11-78.

♦ 2 ex-Indian Ajay class
Bldr: Hooghly D & E, Calcutta (In serv. 1-62)

P 312 PADMA (ex-*Akshay,* P 3136) P 313 SURMA (ex-*Ajay,* P 3135)

D: 120 tons (151 fl) **S:** 18 kts **Dim:** 35.75 (33.52 pp) × 6.1 × 1.9
A: P 312: 2 quadruple 20-mm 90-cal M-75 AA—P 313: 1 40-mm 60-cal. Bofors Mk 3 AA; 1 quadruple 20-mm 90-cal. M-75 AA
Electronics: Radar: 1 Decca . . . nav.
M: 2 Paxman YHAXM diesels; 2 props; 1,000 bhp
Range: 500/12; 1,000/8 **Crew:** 3 officers, 32 enlisted

Remarks: Indian version of British Ford class, donated by India and commissioned 12-4-73 and 26-7-74, respectively. Rearmed in late 1980s with Yugoslav-made weapons; P 313 has a 40-mm gun aft in place of one quadruple 20-mm mount.

♦ 2 ex-Yugoslav Kraljevica class (In serv. 1956)

P 314 KARNIPHULI (ex-PBR 502) P 315 TISTA (ex-PBR 505)

Karniphuli (P 314) French Navy, 1996

D: 190 tons (202 fl) **S:** 18 kts **Dim:** 41.0 × 6.3 × 2.2
A: 2 single 40-mm 60-cal. Bofors Mk 3 AA; 4 single 20-mm Hispano AA; 2 U.S. Mk 6 d.c. mortars; 2 d.c. racks; 2 5-round 128-mm artillery RL
Electronics:
Radar: 1 Decca 1229 nav.—Sonar: QCU-2 hull-mounted searchlight HF
M: 2 M.A.N. W8V 30/38 diesels; 2 props; 3,300 bhp
Range: 1,000/12 **Crew:** 4 officers, 40 enlisted

Remarks: Transferred 6-6-75. P 314 was reduced to reserve in 1988 but was re-engined in 1995 and reactivated; P 315 re-engined in 1997–98. The sonar may no longer function.

PATROL BOATS [PB]

Note: Negotiations were ongoing in spring 1999 with Severnoye Design Bureau, St. Petersburg, Russia, for the design of high-speed patrol boats to be constructed in Bangladesh. During 6-00, two 9.50-m and six 5.40-m rigid inflatable patrol launches were ordered from Delta Power, Stockport, U.K.

♦ 4 Pabna-class riverine
Bldr: DEW Narayengonj, Dhaka

P 112 NOAKHALI (In serv. 7-72)
P 113 PATUAKHALI (In serv. 11-74)
P 114 RANGAMATI (In serv. 6-77)
P 115 BOGRA (In serv. 6-77)

D: 69.5 tons (fl) **S:** 10 kts **Dim:** 22.9 × 6.1 × 1.9
A: 1 40-mm 60-cal. Bofors Mk 3 AA
M: 2 Cummins diesels; 2 props
Range: 700/8 **Crew:** 3 officers, 30 enlisted

Remarks: Last two differ in configuration, gun forward. Form River Patrol Squadron 11, based at Mongla. No radar fitted. In 1995 Sister *Pabna* (P 111) was assigned to the Coast Guard.

MINE WARFARE SHIPS

♦ 1 Chinese T-43-class (Project 010) fleet minesweepers [MSF]
Bldr: Wuzhang SY or Guangzhou SY, China (In serv. 27-4-95)

M 91 SAGAR

Sagar (M 91) French Navy, 1996

D: 500 tons (590 fl) **S:** 14 kts **Dim:** 60.0 × 8.6 × 2.16
A: 2 twin 37-mm 63-cal. Type 74 AA; 2 twin 25-mm 80-cal. Type 61 AA; 2 twin 12.7-mm 93-cal. mg; 2 d.c. mortars; 2 mine rails (12–16 mines)
Electronics:
Radar: 1 Type 756 nav.—Sonar: C-Tech CMAS-36/39 HF mine avoidance
M: 2 Type 9D diesels; 2 props; 2,200 bhp **Electric:** 550 kw tot.
Range: 3,200/10 **Fuel:** 70 tons **Crew:** 12 officers, 58 enlisted

Remarks: Design originated in Russia in the late 1940s and has been built in China since the late 1950s. M 91, ordered 1993 as new custom build for Bangladesh, has acoustic and magnetic sweep gear in addition to MPT-1 and MPT-3 wire sweeps and paravanes. M 92–94 were to have been delivered one per year from 1996–98, but the order was apparently never consummated. The Canadian C-Tech mine-avoidance sonar was delivered fall 1997 as a replacement for the obsolete Tamir-11 set.

♦ 4 ex-U.K. River-class fleet minesweepers [MSF]
Bldr: Richards (Shipbuilders) Ltd., Great Yarmouth (M 95: Lowestoft), U.K.

	Laid down	L	In serv.
M 95 SHAPLA (ex-*Waveney,* M 2003)	21-2-83	8-9-83	29-9-84
M 96 SHAIKAT (ex-*Carron,* M 2004)	21-2-83	23-9-83	29-9-84
M 97 SHUROBI (ex-*Dovey,* M 2005)	3-3-83	1-12-83	30-3-84
M 98 SHAIBAL (ex-*Helford,* M 2006)	12-10-83	17-5-84	7-6-85

Shaibal (M 98) Ben Sullivan, 10-94

D: 630 tons (770 fl) **S:** 14 kts (15 on trials; 12 sust.)
Dim: 47.60 (42.00 pp) × 10.50 × 3.10 (3.75 max.)
A: 1 40-mm 60-cal. Bofors Mk 3 AA; 2 single 7.62-mm mg
Electronics:
Radar: 2 Decca TM 1226 nav.
Sonar: C-Tech CMAS-36/39 HF mine-avoidance (not in M 98)
M: 2 Ruston 6 RKCM diesels; 2 4-bladed CP props; 3,040 bhp

MINE WARFARE SHIPS *(continued)*

Electric: 460 kw tot. **Range:** 4,500/10 **Fuel:** 88 tons
Crew: 9 officers, 23 enlisted

Remarks: 638 grt. Decommissioned from Royal Navy 23-10-93, purchased 9-94, and delivered late 10-94. All four officially commissioned in Bangladesh service at Chittagong on 27-4-95. In 3-97 M 98 was equipped to serve as a survey vessel in support of the Franco-Bangladeshi Hydro Bangla Project, although a mine-countermeasures capability was retained; a second ship may be similarly reequipped. The others are primarily employed as offshore patrol vessels.
Hull systems: Steel hulls with a single-compartment damage standard. Navigation gear includes two Kelvin-Hughes MS 48 echo sounders, Decca QM 14(1) and Decca HiFix Mk 6 radio navaids, and a satellite navigation receiver.
Combat systems: Have mechanical minesweeping capability only, having been transferred with a full suite of paravanes, cutters, and depressors. Have the Racal Sytem 880 Integrated Minehunting System (QX3/1). The 40-mm gun is hand-operated.

AMPHIBIOUS WARFARE CRAFT

♦ 1 Danish-built former commercial landing craft [LCU]
Bldr: Danyard, Frederikshavn (In serv. 1988)

L 900 Shah Amanat

D: 366 tons (fl) **S:** 9.5 kts **Dim:** 47.0 × 10.4 × 2.4
A: . . . **Electronics:** Radar: . . .
M: 2 Caterpillar D343 diesels; 2 props; 720 bhp
Crew: 3 officers, 28 enlisted

Remarks: Acquired for naval service during 1990. A sister remains in commercial service. Resembles U.S. LCU 1466–class utility landing craft but has shorter vehicle cargo deck and longer poop with more extensive superstructure.

♦ 2 ex-U.S. Army LCU 1466 class [LCU]

L 901 Shah Poran (ex-*Cerro Gordo,* LCU 1512)
L 902 Shah Makhdum (ex-*Cadgel,* LCU 1566)

D: 180 tons light (347 fl) **S:** 8 kts **Dim:** 35.08 × 10.36 × 1.60 (max.)
A: 2 single 12.7-mm M2 mg
Electronics: Radar: 1 Canadian Marconi LN-66 nav.
M: 3 G.M. Gray Marine 64 YTL diesels; 3 props; 1,200 bhp
Range: 1,200/6 (700/7 loaded) **Fuel:** 11 tons **Crew:** 11 tot.

Remarks: Transferred during 1991 from surplus U.S. Army stock and commissioned 16-5-92 after refits. Cargo: 150 tons in 15.8 × 9.0-m open deck with ramps at both ends.

♦ 3 Chinese Yuchai-class (Project 068) landing craft [LCM]

A 584 LCT 101 A 585 LCT 102 A 587 LCT 104

Bangladeshi Navy Yuchai-class landing craft French Navy, 1996

D: 85 tons (fl) **S:** 11.5 kts **Dim:** 24.8 × 5.2 × 1.3
A: 2 twin 14.5-mm 93-cal. Type 81 AA **Electronics:** Radar: none
M: 2 Type 12V-150 diesels; 2 props; 600 bhp
Range: 450/11.5 **Crew:** 23 tot. (including vehicle crew)

Remarks: Two transferred 4-5-86, two 1-7-86. Two badly damaged during the 4-91 cyclone but later repaired. A 586 had been retired by 2005.

♦ 3 Bangladeshi-design landing craft [LCM]
Bldr: Khulna SY (LCVP 013: DEW Narayangong)

LCVP 011 LCVP 012 LCVP 013

D: 83 tons (fl) **S:** 12 kts (light) **Dim:** 21.3 × 5.2 × 1.5 **A:** none
M: 2 Cummins diesels; 2 props; 730 bhp **Crew:** 1 officer, 9 enlisted

♦ 4 ex-U.S. LCM(8)-class landing craft [LCM]

D: 34 tons light (121 fl) **S:** 12 kts (light) **Dim:** 22.43 × 6.40 × 1.40 (aft)
M: 4 G.M. Detroit Diesel 6-71 diesels; 2 props; 560 bhp **Range:** 150/12

Remarks: Transferred 4-91 during U.S. Navy disaster-relief efforts. Can carry 56 tons cargo or 150 troops. Aluminum construction.

AUXILIARIES

♦ 1 small underway-replenishment oiler [AO]
Bldr: . . . SY, Japan (In serv. 1983)

A 515 Khan Jahan Ali

D: 2,900 tons (fl) **S:** 12 kts **Dim:** 76.1 × 11.4 × 5.3
A: 2 single 20-mm 70-cal. Oerlikon AA **Electronics:** Radar: 1 . . . nav.
M: 1 6-cyl. diesel; 1 prop; 1,350 bhp **Crew:** 3 officers, 23 enlisted

Khan Jahan Ali (A 515) Gilbert Gyssels, 6-87

Remarks: 1,342 grt. Transferred 1983 from state-owned shipping line and equipped for underway refueling. Cargo: 1,500 tons.

♦ 1 Chinese Dinghai-class seagoing tug [ATA]
Bldr: Wuhu SY

A 721 Khadem

D: 1,472 tons (fl) **S:** 14 kts **Dim:** 60.22 × 11.60 × 4.44
A: 2 single 12.7-mm mg **Electronics:** Radar: 2 . . . nav.
M: 2 diesels; 2 props; 2,640 bhp
Range: 7,200/14 **Crew:** 7 officers, 49 enlisted

Remarks: 980.28 grt. Transferred new 6-5-84.

♦ 1 ex-U.K. Island-class training ship [AXT]
Bldr: Hall Russell, Aberdeen

	L	In serv.
A 511 Shaheed Ruhul Amin (ex-*Jersey,* P 295)	18-3-76	15-10-76

D: 998 tons (1,280 fl) **S:** 16.5 kts **Dim:** 61.10 (51.97 pp) × 11.00 × 4.27
A: 1 40-mm 60-cal. Bofors Mk 3 AA; 2 single 7.62-mm FN mg
Electronics: Radar: 1 Type 1006 nav.—Sonar: Simrad SU side-scan
M: 2 Ruston 12 RK 3 CM diesels (750 rpm); 1/CP prop; 4,380 bhp
Electric: 536 kw **Range:** 11,000/12 **Fuel:** 310 tons
Crew: 5 officers, 29 enlisted (in Royal Navy service)

Remarks: Former offshore patrol vessel decommissioned from Royal Navy 16-12-93 and purchased as a replacement for the former ship of the same name and number in the Bangladeshi Navy (the former Canadian coastal passenger-cargo vessel *Anticosti*); recommissioned 29-1-94. Five sisters purchased 2002–3 operate as offshore patrol ships.
Hull systems: Has fin stabilizers. Can maintain 12–15 kts in a Force 8 gale. Has Decca CANES-2 navaid. Avon Sea Raider semi-rigid dinghies replaced the original Geminis for inspection purposes. Can carry 28.6 tons detergent (a 6-hr supply) for oil-spill cleanup.

SERVICE CRAFT

♦ 1 self-propelled floating crane [YD]
Bldr: Khulna SY (In serv.: 18-5-88)

A 731 Balaban

D: . . . tons **S:** 9 kts **Lift capacity:** 70 tons **Dim:** . . . × . . . × . . .
M: . . . **Crew:** 2 officers, 27 enlisted

♦ 1 floating dry dock [YFDL]
Bldr: Tito SY, Trogir, Yugoslavia (In serv. 15-8-80)

A 701 Sundarban

Lift capacity: 3,500 tons **Dim:** 117.0 × 27.6 × 0.3 (loaded)

Remarks: Self-docking type with seven sectional pontoons. Measures 17.6 m between dock walls, which are 101.4 m long. A second, commercial floating dry dock (16,500 tons capacity, 182.9 m, delivered 1981) is also available.

♦ 5 5-meter aluminum workboats [YFL]
Bldr: . . ., U.S. (In serv. 1993)

♦ 3 7-meter aluminum workboats [YFL]
Bldr: . . ., U.S. (In serv. 1993)

Remarks: Both workboat classes provided as Grant-Aid for riverine search and rescue work.

♦ 1 general-purpose harbor tender [YFU]
Bldr: . . . (Acquired 1989)

A . . . Sanket

D: 80 tons (fl) **S:** 16 kts **Dim:** 29.4 × 6.1 × 1.8
A: 1 20-mm 70-cal. Oerlikon AA **Electronics:** Radar: 2 . . . nav.
M: 2 Deutz Sea 16M diesels; 2 props; 2,430 bhp
Range: 1,000/16 **Crew:** 1 officer, 23 enlisted

Remarks: Taken over from civilian service in 1989; sister *Shamikha* remains in civilian service. Has the appearance of a small patrol boat and does not wear a pennant number.

SERVICE CRAFT *(continued)*

♦ 1 coastal survey craft [YGS]

A 583 Agradoot (ex- . . .)

Remarks: Acquired 1996 from commercial service and refitted for commissioning in 1998. 45 m overall; no other data available.

♦ 1 coastal survey craft [YGS]

Bldr: . . . , Japan

A 513 Shahjalal (ex-*Gold 4*)

D: 600 tons (fl) **S:** 12 kts **Dim:** 40.2 × 9.1 × 2.5
A: 2 single 20-mm Oerlikon AA **M:** 1 16-cyl. diesel; . . . bhp
Range: 7,000/12 **Crew:** 3 officers, 52 enlisted

Remarks: Former Thai fishing boat confiscated and commissioned 15-1-87 for fisheries patrol duties, the "A"-series pennant number notwithstanding. Converted 1995–96 for use as a survey craft.

♦ 2 Chinese Yuchin-class (Project 069) inshore survey craft [YGS]

(In serv. 1983)

A 581 Darshak A 582 Talleshi

Talleshi (A 582) French Navy, 1996

D: 83 tons (fl) **S:** 11.5 kts **Dim:** 24.1 × 5.2 × 1.1
M: 2 Type 12V150 diesels; 2 props; 600 bhp
Range: 700/11.5 **Crew:** 1 officer, 25 enlisted

Remarks: Former medium landing craft (LCM).

♦ 1 harbor fueling lighter [YO]

A 516 Imam Gazzali

Remarks: Acquired 1996 from commercial service. 45 m overall; no other data available.

♦ 1 small repair ship [YR]

A 512 Shahayak

D: 477 tons (fl) **S:** 11.5 kts **Dim:** 44.7 × 8.0 × 2.0
A: 1 20-mm 70-cal. Oerlikon AA **Electronics:** Radar: 1 . . . nav.
M: 1 Cummins 12 VTS diesel; 1 prop; . . . bhp
Range: 3,800/11.5 **Crew:** 1 officer, 44 enlisted

Remarks: Former riverine passenger ship. Purchased, re-engined and refitted at Khulna Shipyard, and commissioned as a tender in 1978.

Note: Two new tugs, *Rupsha* and *Shibsa*, were ordered from Khulna Shipyard late in 1999 and entered service during 2005; they incorporate equipment and materials of South Korean origin and were built with Dutch assistance. No additional information is yet available.

♦ 1 large harbor tug [YTB]

Bldr: . . . SY, Dhaka (In serv. 1995)

A 722 Sebak

Remarks: No data available. Appears to be about 400 tons full load and is probably capable of seagoing towing. Has a firefighting water monitor.

COAST GUARD

Personnel: Approx. 20 officers, 250 enlisted

Bases: Headquarters and Eastern Section base at Chittagong and Western Section base at Khulna.

Note: Force structure planning called for ordering two 35-m, two 25-m, and two harbor patrol boats in 1996 and a 60-m patrol craft, two more 35-m patrol boats, and two more harbor patrol boats in 1997. Very little of this plan has been accomplished, however. An aircraft is sought for maritime patrol duties. Ships and craft are painted white with a broad red diagonal stripe, followed by narrow white and blue stripes, on the hull sides.

PATROL COMBATANTS [WPG]

♦ 1 HDP 600 class

Bldr: Hyundai SY, South Korea (In serv. 1997)

P 911 Madhumati

Madhumati (P 911) French Navy, 10-98

D: 635 tons (650 fl) **S:** 23.5 kts **Dim:** 60.80 × 8.00 × 2.70
A: 1 57-mm 70-cal. Bofors Mk 1 DP; 140-mm 70-cal. Bofors AA; 2 single 20-mm 70-cal. Oerlikon AA; 2 single 7.62-mm mg
Electronics:
Radar: 1 GEM SPN-753B nav.; Kelvin-Hughes Type 1007 nav./surf.-search
E/O: NA 18L optronic f.c. director
M: 2 SEMT-Pielstick 16 PA 4V200 diesels; 2 props; 9,600 bhp
Range: 6,000/15 **Crew:** 7 officers, 36 enlisted

Remarks: Ordered 7-95 as the first unit to be built for the new Coast Guard. Has Vosper Series 300 fin stablizers.

PATROL CRAFT [WPC]

♦ 1 PZ class

Bldr: Hong Leong–Lürssen, SY, Butterworth, Malaysia (In serv. 10-99)

P 201 Ruposhi Bangla

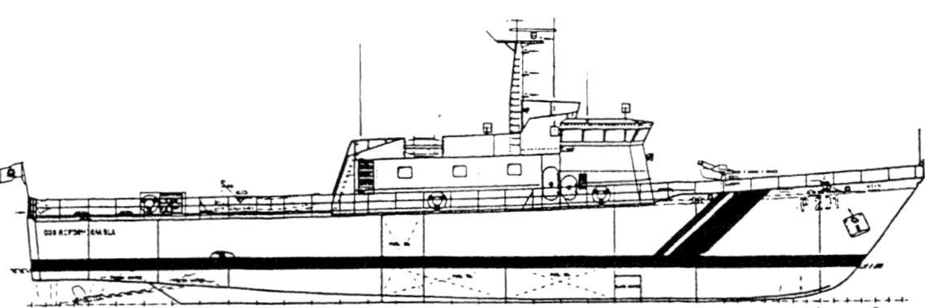

Ruposhi Bangla (P 201) Hong Leong–Lürssen, 1999

D: 195 tons (fl) **S:** 30 kts **Dim:** 38.50 (36.00 wl) × 7.00 × 1.75
A: 1 25-mm OTO Melara KBA AA; 2 single 7.62-mm Manroy mg
Electronics: Radar: 1 Furuno . . . nav.
M: 2 Paxman 12VP185 diesels; 2 props; 6,636 bhp
Electric: . . . kw tot. (3 Stamford generators, Perkins diesels driving)
Range: . . . / . . . **Fuel:** 41,000 liters **Crew:** 5 officers, 22 enlisted

Remarks: Updated version of the PZ design built for the Malaysian Marine Police in early 1980s. Steel hull, aluminum superstructure. Carries two RIB rescue launches.

♦ 1 Chinese Shanghai-II class

P 61 Tawheed (ex-P 611)

Tawheed (P 61) Bangladeshi Coast Guard, 12-95

D: 122 tons (135 fl) **S:** 28.5 kts **Dim:** 38.78 × 5.41 × 1.55 (max.)
A: 2 twin 37-mm 62-cal. Type 74 AA; 2 twin 25-mm 80-cal. Type 61 AA
Electronics: Radar: 1 Type 751 (Pot Head) surf. search
M: 2 M-50F-4 1,200-bhp and 2 910-bhp diesels; 4 props; 4,220 bhp
Electric: 39 kw **Range:** 750/16.5 **Crew:** 36 tot.

Remarks: Transferred from the navy in 1996. Originally delivered 5-82.

♦ 2 ex-South Korean Sea Dolphin PKM 201 class

Bldr: Korea Tacoma SY, Chinhae or Korea SB & Eng., Masan (In serv. 1970s–80s)

Dhansiri (ex-PKM 2 . . .) Chitra (ex-PKM 2 . . .)

D: 113 tons (144 fl) **S:** 32 kts **Dim:** 33.10 (31.25 wl) × 6.92 × 1.75 (2.45 props)
A: 1 40-mm 60-cal. Bofors Mk 3 AA; 1 twin 30-mm 75-cal. Emerlec EX-30 AA; 2 single 20-mm 70-cal. Oerlikon AA
Electronics: Radar: 1 Raytheon 1645 nav./surf. search
M: 2 MTU 16V538 TB90 diesels; 2 props; 10,800 bhp (9,000 sust.)
Electric: 100 kw tot. (2 × 50-kw diesel sets)
Range: 500/32; 1,000/20 **Fuel:** 15 tons **Crew:** 5 officers, 26 enlisted

Remarks: Donated 4-00 and departed Chinhae on a heavy-lift ship on 17-4-00 for delivery.

PATROL BOATS [WPB]

♦ **1 Pabna-class riverine**
Bldr: DEW Narayengonj, Dhaka (In serv. 6-72)

P . . . PABNA (ex-P 111)

D: 69.5 tons (fl) **S:** 10 kts **Dim:** 22.9 × 6.1 × 1.9
A: 1 20-mm 70-cal. Oerlikon AA **M:** 2 Cummins diesels; 2 props
Range: 700/8 **Crew:** 3 officers, 30 enlisted

Remarks: Assigned to the Coast Guard in 1995.

BARBADOS

BARBADOS DEFENCE FORCE COAST GUARD

Personnel: Approx. 11 officers, 85 enlisted

Base: HMBS *Willoughby Fort,* Bridgetown

Note: Ship names are prefixed HMBS (Her Majesty's Barbadian Ship).

PATROL CRAFT [WPC]

♦ **1 37.5-meter class**
Bldr: Brooke Marine, Lowestoft, U.K.

	L	In serv.
P 01 TRIDENT	14-4-81	11-81

D: 155.5 tons (190 fl) **S:** 29 kts **Dim:** 37.50 × 6.86 × 1.70
A: 2 single 12.7-mm mg
Electronics: Radar: 1 Decca TM 1226C nav.
M: 2 Paxman Valenta 12 RP 200 diesels; 2 props; 5,000 bhp
Range: 3,000/12 **Crew:** 28 tot.

Trident (P 01) Maritime Photographic, 11-93

Remarks: Refitted Bender SB & Repair, Mobile, Ala. 6-6-90 to 14-9-90; armament reduced from original one 40-mm 60-cal. Bofors AA and one 20-mm Rheinmetall AA. Refitted again in 1997–98 by Cable Marine. Near-sisters are in Algerian service.

PATROL BOATS [WPB]

♦ **2 U.S. 40-ft. Dauntless class**
Bldr: SeaArk, Monticello, Ark.

P 04 ENDEAVOUR (In serv. 4-97) P 05 EXCELLENCE (In serv. 4-99)

D: 15 tons (fl) **S:** 28 kts **Dim:** 12.19 (11.13 wl) × 3.86 × 0.69 (hull)
A: 2 single 12.7-mm mg; 2 single 7.62-mm mg
Electronics: Radar: 1 Raytheon R40X nav.
M: 2 Caterpillar 3208TA diesels; 2 props; 850 bhp (720 sust.)
Range: 200/30; 400/22 **Fuel:** 250 gallons **Crew:** 5 tot.

Remarks: P 04 ordered 10-96 for $396,000. Aluminum construction. C. Raymond Hunt, "Deep-Vee" hull design. Sisters operate in several Caribbean nation forces. One more is sought. P 05 has also been seen in police markings.

♦ **3 U.S. 22-foot Whaler class**
Bldr: Boston Whaler, Rockland, Mass./Edgewater, Fla.

P 08 (In serv. 1989) P 09 (In serv. 1989) P 10 (In serv. 1996)

D: 1.5 tons light (2.25 fl) **S:** 40 kts **Dim:** 6.81 × 2.26 × 0.36
A: 1 7.62-mm mg **Electronics:** Radar: 1 Raytheon R40X nav.
M: 2 Johnson OMC gasoline outboard engines; 360 bhp
Range: 167/40; 750/. . . **Fuel:** 243 liters **Crew:** 3 tot.

Remarks: GRP-hulled open launches. P 10, built in Florida, may differ in configuration.

Note: A 7.3-m Zodiac Hurricane RIB capable of 25 kts was delivered 7-95 for search-and-rescue duties.

BELARUS

BORDER GUARD

PATROL BOATS [WPB]

♦ **3 ex-Soviet Shmel' class (Project 1204)**
Bldr: Kamysh Burun Zavod, Kerch', or 61 Kommunara Zavod, Nikolayev (In serv. 1967–74)

D: 77.4 tons (fl) **S:** 24 kts **Dim:** 27.70 × 4.32 × 0.90 (2.00 moulded depth)
A: 1 76.2-mm, 48 cal. D-56TM low-angle gun (in a PT-76 tank turret); 1 twin 25-mm 80-cal. 2M-3M AA; 2 mine rails (up to 8 tot. mines)
Electronics: Radar: 1 Donets-2 nav.—Sonar: NEL-7 echo-sounder
M: 2 M-50F-4 diesels; 2 props; 2,400 bhp
Electric: 50 kw tot. (2 × 25-kw diesel sets)
Range: 240/20; 600/10 **Fuel:** 4.75 tons **Endurance:** 7 days
Crew: 1 officer, 2 warrant officers, 11 enlisted

Remarks: Transferred from Russia post-1991 and employed on the Dnieper River. One is former Russian Federal Border Guard unit PSKR-389.
Hull systems: Screws are mounted in tunnels to reduce draft. Armor includes 10 mm over the pilothouse and gun barbettes, 8 mm over the hull and internal bulkheads, and 5 mm over the deck and pilothouse. Have a Gradus-2 gyrocompass and NEL-7 echo sounder.
Combat systems: Some have also carried up to four 30-mm Plamya grenade launchers and four pintle-mounted 7.62-mm machineguns. One 7.62-mm machinegun is mounted coaxially with the 76-mm gun (with 40 rounds carried on-mount). Mine loads vary from four UDM-500 or two UDM-1000 to six KPM or eight YaM mines.

SERVICE CRAFT

♦ **5 Gepard-class hovercraft launches [WYFLH]**
Bldr: Svir SY, Nikelskoye, Russia

D: . . . **S:** 35 kts **Dim:** 7.20 × 3.80 × . . .
M: 1 ZMZ-53 gasoline engine; 1 airscrew prop; 120 bhp
Range: 108/35 **Crew:** 4 tot.

Remarks: Carry an operator and three inspection personnel for use on the Dnieper River. The third was delivered on 17-4-01.

BELGIUM

Kingdom of Belgium

KONINKLIJKE MARINE VAN BELGÏE

Personnel: 2,450 total (620 reservists). The Marine Infantry Division has been disbanded.

Bases: Zeebrugge, with some small units based at Ostend. There is a naval training facility at Sint-Kruis, Bruges. Mine warfare training is conducted at Ostend. The shore staff is housed at Evere, and the operational staff is collocated with that of the Royal Netherlands Navy at Den Helder.

Naval Aviation: Three Aérospatiale AS.316B Alouette-IIIB helicopters (soon to be upgraded with new communications and navigation systems) are based at Koksijde along with five Air Force Westland Sea King Mk 48 helicopters used for search-and-rescue duties. By 2007 the Navy hopes to purchase 8-10 NH-90 helicopters to replace the Navy's Sea King helicopters. Six are to be equipped for ASW (two being assigned to the ex-Netherlands frigates recently purchased) and four for transport duties.

Belgian Navy Alouette-IIIB Rob Cabo, 1-01

KONINKLIJE MARINE VAN BELGÏE *(continued)*

Marine Infantry: The 100 personnel of "DIVMAR" are assigned to guard duties at naval bases, security details, and ceremonial honor guard duty. One of the three Belgian Army Paracommando battalions has maritime-oriented duties.

Note: The Belgian naval staff was formally integrated with that of the Netherlands at Den Helder in 1996.

FRIGATES [FF]

♦ 0 (+ 2) Netherlands Karel Doorman class
Bldr: Schelde Shipbuilding, Vlissingen

	Laid down	L	In serv.
. . . (ex-Netherlands *Van Amstel,* F-831)	3-5-88	19-5-90	27-5-93
. . . (ex-Netherlands *Van Ness,* F-833)	10-1-90	16-5-92	24-6-94

Ex-Netherlands frigate Van Ness (F-833)—shown here while still in Dutch service Leo Van Ginderen, 6-05

D: 2,800 tons light (3,320 fl) **S:** 29 kts (21 kts on diesels)
Dim: 122.25 (114.40 pp) × 14.37 (13.10 wl) × 4.30 (6.05 sonar)
A: 4 RGM-84A/C Harpoon SSM; 16-cell Mk 48 Mod. 1 VLS (16 RIM-7M NATO Sea Sparrow SAM); 1 76-mm/62-cal. OTO/Melara DP; 1 30-mm Goalkeeper gatling CIWS; 2 single 20-mm/70-cal. Oerlikon Mk 10 AA; 4 fixed, paired 324-mm Mk 32 Mod. 9 ASW TT (Mk 46 Mod. 5 torpedoes); prob. 1 NH-90 ASW configured helicopter
Electronics:
Radar: 1 Decca 1690/9 nav.; 1 Thales Scout nav./surf.-search; 1 Thales SMART-S 3-D air-search; 1 Thales LW-08 early-warning; 2 Thales STIR-18 missile f.c.; 1 Thales Goalkeeper f.c. array
Sonar: PHS-36 (SQS-509) hull-mounted MF; last four also: provision for Thales Anaconda (DSBV-61A) towed array
EW: ArgoSystems APECS-II intercept and AR-740 jammer; Mk 36 SRBOC decoy syst. (2 6-round Raytheon Mk 137 RL), SLQ-25 Nixie towed acoustic torpedo decoy syst.
M: CODOG: 2 Stork-Wärtsilä 12 SWD 280 V-12 cruise diesels (4,225 bhp each); 2 Rolls-Royce Spey RM-1A or C gas turbines; 2 CP props; 48,252 shp max. (F 827: 37,530 shp max.)
Electric: 2,720 kw (4 × 650-kw diesel sets, Stork-Wärtsilä DRo 218K diesels driving; 1 × 120-kw diesel set)
Range: 5,000+/18 **Endurance:** 30 days
Crew: 16 officers, 138 enlisted (163 max. accomm.)
Remarks: Originally ordered on 10-4-86 for the Royal Netherlands Navy. Accommodations for female crew members are incorporated, plus bunks for 30 marines. Purchased by Belgium in 07-05 as replacements for the two remaining *Wielingen* (Type E-71) -class frigates. Following an overhaul by Royal Schelde, the two frigates will be officially handed over during 2007–8.

With the exception of the helicopter fit, characteristics are the same as in Dutch service. Combat systems and crew size will likely be altered upon entering Belgian service.
Hull systems: Have a computer-controlled rudder roll-stabilization system instead of fins. Carry three RIBs.
Combat systems: Have the Thales DAISY VII/SEWACO VII(B) data system with full LINK 10, 11, and 16 capability. The 76-mm gun fires a maximum of 100 rpm.

♦ 2 Wielingen class (Type E 71)

	Bldr	Laid down	L	In serv.
F 910 WIELINGEN	Boelwerf, Temse	5-3-74	30-3-76	20-1-78
F 911 WESTDIEP	Cockerill, Hoboken	2-9-74	8-12-75	20-1-78

Westdiep (F 911) Bernard Prézelin, 11-04

D: 1,940 tons (2,430 fl) **S:** 26 kts on gas turbine/18 on diesels
Dim: 106.38 (103.00 pp) × 12.30 × 3.90 (5.40 over sonar)
A: 4 MM 38 Exocet SSM; 1 8-round Mk 29 SAM launcher (AIM-7P NATO Sea Sparrow missiles); 1 100-mm 55-cal. Model 1968 DP; 6 single 12.7-mm mg; 1 6-round 375-mm Bofors ASW RL; 2 fixed, internal launching racks for L 5 Mod. 4 ASW torpedoes

Wielingen (F 910) Bernard Prézelin, 2003

Electronics:
Radar: 1 Kelvin-Hughes KH 1007 nav.; 1 Thales Scout surf. search; 1 Thales DA-05 air search; 1 Thales WM-25 f.c.
Sonar: Computing Devices Canada SQS-510 hull-mounted (7.0 kHz)
EW: ArgoSystems AR 900B intercept; Elcos-1 HFD/F; Mk 36 SRBOC decoy syst. (2 6-round Mk 137 RL); SLQ-25 Nixie torpedo decoy syst.
E/O: 2 SAGEM VIGY-105 EOMS optronic f.c. and surveillance
M: CODOG: 2 Cockerill CO-240V-12 diesels (3,000 bhp each); 1 Rolls-Royce Olympus TM-3B gas turbine (28,000 shp); 2 CP props
Electric: 2,000 kw (4 × 500-kw diesel sets) **Range:** 4,500/18; 6,000/16
Fuel: 280 tons **Crew:** 14 officers, 143 enlisted

Remarks: F 910 was reactivated in 1995 and refitted in 1997–98
Disposals: Sister *Westhinder* (F 913), newest of the class, decommissioned 1-7-93 and after several years as a spare parts hulk, was towed to Ghent for scrapping on 7-11-00. *Wandelaar* (F 912) was stricken in late 2004 as part of the "Strategic Plan 2000–2015" and sold to Bulgaria, which may also purchase F 910 and F 911. She was officially handed over on 21-10-05. Both are to be replaced during 2007-8 by two recently purchased Netherlands Karel Doorman–class frigates.
Hull systems: Have lost 2 kts from original 28-kt trial speeds after modifications. Have Vosper fin stabilizers. Can make 15 knots on one diesel. Ring-laser gyros and new internal and external communications systems are being fitted along with new diesel engines.
Combat systems: Have Thales SEWACO IV automatic tactical data system and Link 11 and Link 14 datalinks. Two SAGEM VIGY E/O sensors are provided (one atop the bridge and one abaft the stack), and optronic directors on platforms abreast the foremast can control the 100-mm gun, which has been upgraded to fire at 80 rds/min. Under a 6-95 contract, the Raytheon TM 1645/9X navigational radars were replaced with the Thales Scout, and the other radar systems were refurbished. The sonar has been upgraded from SQS-505A to SQS-510 standard with the addition of the AN/UYS-501 programmable signal processor and display system. Are to receive new data plotting tables.

MINE WARFARE SHIPS

♦ 1 mine-countermeasures support ship [MCS]

	Bldr	Laid down	L	In serv.
A 960 GODETIA	Boelwerf, Temse	15-2-65	7-12-65	23-5-66

Godetia (A 960) Leo Van Ginderen, 7-05

Godetia (A 960) Leo Van Ginderen, 7-05

MINE WARFARE SHIPS *(continued)*

D: 1,700 tons (2,500 fl) **S:** 18 kts **Dim:** 91.83 (87.85 pp) × 14.0 × 3.5
A: 6 single 12.7-mm mg
Electronics: Radar: 2 Decca 1229 nav.—EW: Telegon-6 HFD/F
M: 4 ACEC-M.A.N. diesels; 2 CP props; 5,400 bhp
Range: 2,250/15; 8,700/12 **Fuel:** 294 tons
Crew: 8 officers, 84 enlisted + 40 cadets

Remarks: Received major midlife overhaul 1981–82. Recently used for cadet training, with accommodations for 40 cadets. Scheduled for retirement in 2010 but may be extended to 2015 or beyond depending on replacement availability. Also employed as a Fisheries Protection vessel.
Hull systems: Can make 15 kts on one diesel. Has passive tank stabilization and protected closed-circuit ventilation. Can accommodate oceanographic research personnel and has space for laboratory. Minesweeping cables are stowed on reels on the helicopter deck, which was extended aft to continue to permit one Alouette-III to land (but the forward end of the helicopter deck has been used for replacement sweep cable drum stowage for many years).
Disposal: The mine-countermeasures support ship *Zinnia,* in reserve since 1993, was officially stricken in 2003.

♦ 6 Tripartite-class minehunters [MHC]
Bldr: Béliard Polyship, Ostend and Rupelmonde

	Laid down	L	In serv.
M 915 Aster	26-4-83	29-6-84	18-12-85
M 916 Bellis	9-2-83	22-2-85	18-9-86
M 917 Crocus	9-10-84	2-10-85	5-2-87
M 921 Lobelia	4-12-86	3-2-88	10-5-89
M 923 Narcis	25-2-88	20-6-89	27-9-90
M 924 Primula	10-11-88	8-7-90	18-5-91

Narcis (M 923) Derek Fox, 6-05

Crocus (M 917) Rob Cabo, 7-05

D: 511 tons (595 fl) **S:** 15 kts **Dim:** 51.6 (47.1 pp) × 8.96 × 2.49 (hull)
A: 1 20-mm 90-cal. GIAT F-2 AA (except M 922); 2 single 12.7-mm M2 mg; 2 PAP-104 remote-controlled mine locators; mechanical sweep gear
Electronics:
Radar: Decca 1229 nav.
Sonar: Thales DUBM-21B variable-depth minehunting (100 kHz)
EW: Thales DR-2000S intercept; Telegon-4 HFD/F
M: 1 Brons/Werkspoor A-RUB 215X 12 diesel; 1 CP prop; 1,900 bhp (1,200 rpm)—2 120-hp maneuvering props (active rudder)—bow-thruster
Electric: 880 kw **Range:** 3,000/12
Crew: 6 officers, 39 enlisted (accomm. for 49)

Remarks: Ordered 12-2-81. Hulls were launched at Ostend and fitted out by Béliard Mercantile at Rupelmonde, Antwerp. Between 2005 and 2008, six of the ships are undergoing a Capability Upkeep Program (CUP) to keep them in service until 2015–20; they may be fitted with additional equipment to permit their use as minesweepers.
Disposals: Sisters *Dianthus* (M 918), *Fuchsia* (M 919), and *Iris* (M 920) were decommissioned during 1993, reconditioned, and sold to France with deliveries taking place throughout 1997.
Hull systems: Glass-reinforced-plastic construction. Three Astazou-IV, 320-kw gas-turbine generators and one 140-kw diesel set. Have active-tank stabilization.
Combat systems: Have two PAP-104 remote-controlled mine locators, automatic pilot, automatic track-plotter, Toran and Sydelis radio navigation systems, and conventional wire sweep. Carry portable divers' decompression van aft on 01 deck just above forecastle break. Under a 10-12-01 contract with STN Atlas Elektronik, the sonar system is to be improved, the tactical data system improved or replaced, the PAP-104 submersibles upgraded or replaced, a drifting mine detection capability added, and onboard systems integrated to permit reducing crew size. The BENECUP (Belgian-Netherlands Capability Upgrade Program) modernization program is to employ the same systems that are being fitted to the modernized units of the class in Dutch service; M 921 will be first to be upgraded.

Disposal note: *Myosotis* (M 922) was decommissioned in 3-04, reportedly for use as a spare parts source.

AUXILIARIES

Note: A 19,000-ton "Command, Logistic Support and Transport Ship," to start construction between 2008 and 2015, is planned to replace the stricken mine-countermeasures support ship *Zinnia.* Approximate measurements will be: 125.0 m × 18.0 m × 4.0 m. The ship will have a top speed of 20 kts and be helicopter capable and able to transport the vehicles and equipment for an army battalion and will have the capability to support them ashore. It is anticipated that the ship will be a variation of the Dutch *Rotterdam*-class amphibious transport dock (LPD).

♦ 1 oceanographic research ship [AGOR]

	Bldr	Laid down	L	In serv.
A 962 Belgica	Boelwerf, Temse	17-10-83	6-1-84	5-7-84

Belgica (A 962) Leo Van Ginderen, 7-05

D: 835 tons (1,160 fl) **S:** 12 kts **Dim:** 50.90 (44.95 pp) × 10.00 × 4.40
Electronics: Radar: 1 Decca . . . nav.
M: 1 ABC 6M DZC-1000-150 diesel; 1 Kort-nozzle prop; 1,570 bhp—150-hp thrusters fore and aft
Electric: 640 kw **Range:** 20,000/12 **Fuel:** 158 tons
Crew: 15 naval + 11 scientists

Remarks: For use in North and Irish Seas for fisheries and hydrographic research and for fisheries patrol. Can carry two laboratory containers on deck. 150-hp thrusters fore and aft. Painted white with very bluff hull lines, bulbous bow. Received major refit in 1999.

♦ 1 ex-Swedish Kbv 171 miscellaneous auxiliary [AG]
Bldr: Karlskronavarvet, Karlskrona

	L	In serv.
A 963 Stern (ex-*Karlskrona* Kbv 171)	11-79	3-9-80

Stern (A 963) Frank Findler, 6-05

D: 375 tons (fl) **S:** 18.5 kts **Dim:** 49.90 (46.00 pp) × 8.52 × 2.40
Electronics: Radar: 2 Kelvin-Hughes 6000A nav.
M: 2 Hedemora V16A/15 diesels; 2 KaMeWa CP props; 4,480 bhp
Electric: 340 kVA tot. **Range:** 500/20; 3,000/12 **Crew:** 12 tot.

AUXILIARIES *(continued)*

Remarks: Former Swedish Coast Guard Class "A" cutter purchased 28-9-98 for use as a general-purpose tender, training craft, and fisheries patrol craft; commissioned in Belgian Navy on 13-10-98. Will also be used in mine-countermeasures system trials.
Hull systems: The GRP sandwich hull was lengthened by 6 m in 1981. Has helicopter platform, bow-thruster, a firefighting monitor, and Roll-Nix rudder roll-control system. The Simrad Subsea sonar was removed prior to transfer.

SERVICE CRAFT

♦ 1 public affairs launch, former river patrol craft [YFL]
Bldr: Theodor Hitzler, Regensburg, Germany

	Laid down	L	In serv.
P 902 Libération	12-3-54	29-7-54	4-8-54

Libération (P 902) Leo Van Ginderen, 7-05

D: 27.5 tons (30 fl) **S:** 19 kts **Dim:** 26.00 (24.10 pp) × 4.13 (3.90 wl) × 0.93
A: 2 single 12.7-mm M2 mg **Electronics:** Radar: 1 Decca 1214 nav.
M: 2 MWM diesels; 2 props; 480 bhp **Range:** 2300/10
Crew: 1 officer, 6 enlisted

Remarks: Survivor of an original class of eight. Based at Zeebrugge.

♦ 1 personnel launch/tug [YFL]
Bldr: Scheeps en Yachtwerf Akerboom, Lisse, the Netherlands (In serv. 1958)

A 997 Spin

Spin (A 997) Leo Van Ginderen, 7-05

D: 22.75 tons (32 fl) **S:** 8 kts **Dim:** 14.60 × 4.25 × 1.00
M: 1 diesel; 1 Voith-Schneider vertical cycloidal prop; 250 bhp
Crew: 1 chief petty officer, 3 nonrated

Remarks: Based at Ostend and used primarily as a personnel launch. Also in service is the small harbor launch RIB *Werl* (A 998).

♦ 1 small royal yacht [YFL]

A 982 Alpa (ex-*Trifoglio*)

Remarks: A 23-ton, GRP-hulled cabin cruiser employed by King Albert II. Built at Poole, Dorset, U.K., in 1995 and based at Zeebrugge.

♦ 1 Valcke-class coastal tug [YTB]
Bldr: H.H. Bodewes, Millengen a/d Ryn

	Laid down	L	In serv.
A 950 Valcke (ex-*Astroloog*, ex-*Steenbank*)	2-6-60	16-11-60	16-12-60

D: 420 tons (fl) **S:** 13 kts **Dim:** 30.08 × 7.55 × 3.10
Electronics: Radar: 1 Decca 1229 nav.
M: 2 Deutz BA8M 528, 4-cycle, single-acting 8-cyl. diesels, electric drive; 1 prop; 1,250 shp—1 30-shp bow-thruster
Fuel: 76 m^3 **Crew:** 3 chief petty officers, 6 enlisted

Remarks: 183 grt. Purchased 1980 from A. Smit. Based at Zeebrugge. Overhauled during 1995. Carries 18.1 m^3 fresh water. Was reported to have engineering problems as of late 1997, was back in operation in 1998, but by mid-2000 was again inactive. By 6-02 she was again listed active. Sister *Ekster* (A 998, ex-*Astronoom*, ex-*Schouwenbank*) was scrapped in 2000.

Valcke (A 950) Jasper Van Raemdonck, 2-04

♦ 1 medium coastal tug [YTM]
Bldr: C. N. & Atelier Const. de Hemiksem (In serv. 1971)

A 954 Zeemeeuw

Zeemeeuw (A 954) Van Ginderen, 7-05

D: 400 tons (fl) **S:** 9 kts **Dim:** 27.94 (26.60 pp) × 7.29 × 3.37
Electronics: Radar: 1 Decca 1229 nav.
M: 2 ABC 6-cyl. diesels; 2 props; 1,050 bhp
Electric: 96 kw tot. **Crew:** 2 chief petty officers, 4 enlisted

Remarks: 146 grt/24 nrt. Acquired from Administration de Marine, Ostende, Belgium on 27-11-81. Based at Zeebrugge and used on pollution-control duties.

♦ 1 ex-Dutch Westgat-class medium tug [YTM]
Bldr: Rijkswerf Willemsoord, Den Helder

	Laid down	L	In serv.
A 996 Albatros (ex-*Westgat*, A 872)	3-4-67	22-8-67	10-1-68

D: 206 tons (fl) **S:** 12 kts **Dim:** 27.18 × 6.97 × 2.34
Electronics: Radar: 1 Kelvin-Hughes 14/9 nav.
M: 1 Bolnes diesel; 1 prop; 720 bhp **Range:** 3,800/11 **Crew:** 12 tot.

Remarks: Retired from Royal Netherlands Navy 12-3-96 and sold to Belgium to replace the *Ekster* (A 998). Transferred 9-97 following a refit.

SERVICE CRAFT *(continued)*

Albatros (A 996) Bernard Prézelin, 6-05

♦ 2 Wesp-class medium harbor tugs [YTM]

	Bldr.	In serv.
A 952 WESP (ex-*Stadssleepboot 63*, ex-*Stadssleepboot 43*)	C. N. de Liège-Monsin	1959
A 955 MIER (ex-*Stadssleepboot 66*, ex-*Stadssleepboot 46*)	St. Pieter SY, Hemiksem	23-3-62

Mier (A 955) A. A. de Kruijf, 7-05

D: 195 tons **S:** 11.3 kts **Dim:** 26.23 × 7.50 × 3.25
Electronics: Radar: 1 . . . nav.
M: 2 ABC Type 6MDUS diesels; 2 Voith-Schneider 20E/125 vertical-cycloidal props; 1,000 bhp
Range: . . . / . . . **Crew:** 4 tot.

Remarks: Purchased from the Port of Antwerp on 7-12-98 for $800,000. Delivered 4-99 following refit. Names mean "Wasp" and "Ant," respectively. Have a 14-ton bollard pull and are capable of limited icebreaking.

Disposal note: *Bij*-class small tugs *Bij* (A 953) and *Krekel* (A 956) were laid up in 1999 and sold for scrap during 11-00.

♦ 1 sail-training craft [YTS]

	Bldr	Laid down	L	In serv.
A 958 ZENOBE GRAMME	Boelwerf, Temse	7-10-60	23-10-61	1962

D: 149 tons **S:** 9 kts under sail (8 under power)
Dim: 28.15 (23.10 wl; 31.50 over bowsprit) × 6.85 × 2.64
Electronics: Radar: 1 . . . nav.
M: 1 MWM 518A diesel; 232 bhp—240 m^2 max. sail area
Range: . . . / . . . **Fuel:** 9 tons **Crew:** 2 officers, 13 enlisted

Remarks: Fitted out as Bermudian ketch. Formerly also used for oceanographic research. Carries 22 tons lead and 4 tons bronze ballast. Main mast is 31.5 m high.

Note: Also in service at the *Zeilschool van de Marine* (Sailing School of the Navy) are a number of small sailing craft and rowboats.

Zenobe Gramme (A 958) Jaroslaw Cislak, 7-03

BELGIAN ARMY

♦ 1 Type 2000 TDX(M) assault hovercraft [LCPA]

Bldr: Griffon Hovercraft, Ltd., Salisbury Green, U.K. (In serv. 7-95)

A 999 BARBARA

Barbara (A 999) A. A. de Kruijf, 7-02

D: 3.7 tons light (5.6 fl) **S:** 35 kts (28 kph over land)
Dim: 11.00 (11.68 over skirt) × 4.56 (5.68 over skirt) × 2.75 high (4.30 over skirt)
A: 1 7.62-mm mg **Electronics:** Radar: 1 Raytheon . . . nav.
M: 1 Deutz BF8L-513 diesel driving 0.91-m dia. lift fan and 1.8-m dia. CP airscrew; 355 bhp (320 sust.)
Range: 200/35 **Fuel:** 385 liters **Crew:** 2 tot. + 16 troops

Remarks: Ordered 1995. Based at Lombardzijde as range safety craft, a unit of the 14th Antiaircraft Regiment. Aluminum hull structure, C-130 Hercules transportable. Payload is 16 troops or 2 tons of equipment. Maximum speed can be attained in Sea State 1, while 25 kts is maintainable in Sea State 3. The craft is able to travel over water, ice, and land. Has GPS receiver, HF and VHF radios. Cab top can be removed to permit carrying two one-ton NATO standard cargo pallets.

♦ 17 river-crossing boats [LCP]

Bldr: Meuse & Sambre, Beez (In serv. . . .)

D: 5.5 tons **S:** . . . **Dim:** . . . × . . . × . . .
M: 2 Deutz 6-cyl 190K turbocharged diesels; 2 props **Crew:** 3 tot.

BELGIAN ARMY *(continued)*

Remarks: Survivors of about 40. All are assigned to the 3rd Engineer Battalion, based at Jambes. The battalion also has some 66 floating bridge sections, for placement by crossing boats.

♦ 11 Zodiac Mk 6HD personnel landing craft [LCP]
Bldr: Zodiac Boats, U.K. (In serv. 1997–99)

D: 320 kg (without engines) **S:** 22–32 kts (depending on load)
Dim: 7.00 × 2.88 × . . . **M:** 2 Evinrude gasoline outboards; 140 bhp
Crew: 1–3 tot. + 15 fully equipped soldiers or 20 passengers

Remarks: RIBs for use by the paracommando brigade.

Belgian Army Zodiac Mk 6HD RIB H&L Van Ginderen, 7-00

Note: The Belgian Army also operates Zodiac AC 0348 and Zodiac AC 0338 RIBs. The AC 0348 is 4.25 m long by 1.75 m in beam, can carry 5–6 persons, and weighs 100 kg empty and 990 kg max. loaded; it is powered by a single 25-bhp outboard or ten paddles. The AC 0338 is 4.70 m long by 2.10 m beam, weighs 120 kg light and 1,910 kg max. loaded, and is also powered by a 25-bhp outboard; it can carry up to 10 persons.

Seventeen truck-transportable river crossing boats (of 40 constructed at the Meuse et Sambré yard, Beez) remain in use by the Third Engineer Battalion; displacing 5.5 tons, they are powered by two Deutz 6-cyl. 190K diesels and have a crew of three. Some 23 others are in storage at Haasdonk.

BELIZE

DEFENCE FORCE MARITIME WING

Personnel: Approx. 6 officers, 45 enlisted.

Base: Headquarters and principal base at Placencia, Belize City; small detachment at Hunting Cay

Aviation: 2 Pilatus-Britten-Norman BN-2B Defender light maritime patrol aircraft and 1 Slingsby T67M Firefly trainer are operated by the Defence Force Air Wing.

SERVICE CRAFT

♦ 2 launches [YFL] Bldr: Bradley's Boatyard, Belize (In serv. 1996)

OCEAN SENTINEL REEF SNIPER

Remarks: GRP construction, 10.67 m long and powered by two 200-bhp Yamaha gasoline outboards for 35-kt max. speeds.

♦ 2 Halmatic 22-ft. rigid inflatable launches [YFL]
Bldr: Halmatic, Hamble, U.K. (In serv. 1996)

STINGRAY COMMANDO BLUE MARLIN RANGER

Remarks: Powered by two 115-bhp Yamaha gasoline outboards for 35 kts max. speeds.

♦ 5 miscellaneous launches [YFL]

Remarks: Mexican and Colombian craft confiscated 1995–97. Powered by two Yamaha 200-bhp gasoline outboard motors each for 35-kt max. speeds.

Note: The Police Maritime Wing operates up to ten Boston Whaler Guardian–class foam-core, GRP-hulled launches in the P-1 series. Deliveries began in 1993. The craft are 3.86 tons (fl); can achieve 35 kts on 2 OMC gasoline outboards (200 bhp each); are 8.10 × 3.05 × 0.51 m; have a range of 250 n.m. at 30 kts; and carry a crew of three.

Disposal note: *Wasp*-class patrol boats *Dangriga* (PB 01) and *Toledo* (PB 02) appear to have been retired by 2005.

BENIN

People's Republic of Benin

Personnel: Approx. 30 officers, 180 enlisted

Base: Cotonou

Naval Aviation: 2 Dornier Do-128 and 1 DHC-6 Twin Otter light twin-engine transports

PATROL BOATS [PB]

♦ 2 Chinese 25-meter class (In serv. 1999)

P 798 MATELOT BRICE KPOMASSE P 799 LA SOTA

La Sota (P 799) Navpic-Holland, 1-01

D: 82 tons **S:** 14 kts **Dim:** 26.0 (25.0 pp) × 4.1 × 1.4
A: 2 twin 14.5-mm 93-cal. AA **Electronics:** Radar: 1 JRC . . . nav.
M: 2 MWM V-8 diesels; 2 props; 1,600 bhp **Range:** 900/11 **Crew:** 13 tot.

Remarks: Donated by China. They are equipped with JRC (Japan Radio Corporation) Navigator GPS receivers.

♦ 5 Boston Whaler patrol launches
Bldr: Boston Whaler, Edgewater, Florida (In serv. 1994)

P 14 P 15 P 201 P 204 P . . .

D: 1.5 tons (2 fl) **S:** 30 kts **Dim:** 6.81 × 2.26 × . . .
M: 2 gasoline outboards; 230 bhp **Crew:** 2 tot.

Remarks: "Unsinkable" GRP foam-core construction. P 201 (with a 75-bhp outboard motor) and P 204 (with a 110-bhp outboard) were acquired prior to 1994 and appear to be somewhat larger; they have an enclosed pilothouse near the stern. Two of the other three are painted white and are powered by a single outboard motor. Not all may be operable.

Disposal note: Patrol boat *Patriote* (P 17) was derelict and irreparable as of 1-01; the four Soviet-supplied Zhuk-class (Project 1400M) patrol boats—P 763, P 764, P 769, and P 779—have been sold for scrap.

BERMUDA

The Crown Colony of Bermuda

BERMUDIAN POLICE

Base: Hamilton

PATROL BOATS [WPB]

♦ 1 16-meter patrol boat
Bldr: Austal Ships, Henderson, Western Australia (In serv. 2006)

D: . . . **S:** 28 kts max. **Dim:** 16.0 × 4.87 × 1.25
M: 2 × Caterpillar C12 diesels **Range:** 400/20
Fuel: 27,000 liters **Crew:** 3–4

Remarks: Ordered 8-05. Police patrol boat for general patrols, search-and-rescue, and dive operations. Aluminum construction.

PATROL BOATS [WPB] *(continued)*

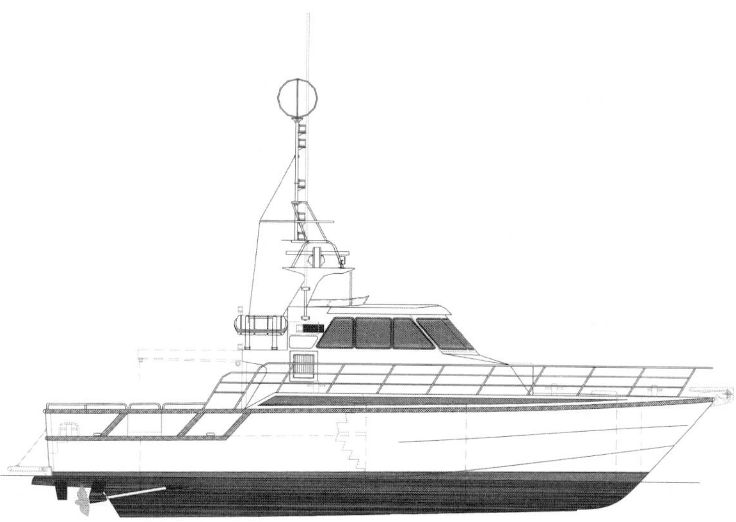

16-meter police patrol boat—design drawing Austal, 2005

SERVICE CRAFT

♦ 1 Design 3006 large harbor tugs [WYTB]
Bldr: . . . United States (In serv. mid-1950s)

Edward M. Stowe (ex-LT 2090)

D: 295 tons light (390 fl) **S:** 12.75 kts **Dim:** 32.61 × 8.08 × 3.71 (max.)
M: 1 G.E. EMD 12V-645-E7 diesel); 1 prop; 1,200 bhp
Electric: 80 kw **Range:** 3,323/12 light **Fuel:** 54 tons
Crew: 16 tot. (accomm. for 20)

Remarks: Transferred from the United States during 2004. Bollard pull of 31.5 tons; can pump 2,000 gallons of firefighting foam per minute. Underwent modernization during the 1990s.

♦ 1 search-and-rescue launch [WYFL]

Blue Heron

Remarks: A cabin cruiser donated by the U.S. Drug Enforcement Agency in 5-96; about 14 m overall, the craft carries a crew and is assigned to the Joint Marine Interdiction Team.

♦ 3 Boston Whaler patrol and rescue launches [WYFL]
Bldr: Boston Whaler, Rockland, Mass./Edgewater, Fla.

Heron I (In serv. 8-97) Heron II (In serv. 8-88) Heron III (In serv. 10-92)

D: 1.5 tons (2 fl) **S:** 30 kts **Dim:** 6.81 × 2.26 × . . .
M: 2 Yamaha gasoline outboards; 230 bhp **Crew:** 2 tot.

Remarks: "Unsinkable" GRP foam-core construction. *Heron II,* built at Edgewater, Fla., replaced an earlier craft with the same name and is 2.2 tons (fl) and 8.23 m overall.

♦ 2 Arctic-class rigid inflatable boats [WYFL]
Bldr: Osbourne, U.K. (Rescue I: Vosper-Halmatic, Havant)

Rescue I (In serv. 9-98) Rescue II (In serv. 5-88)

D: 1.45 tons (fl) **S:** 50 kts **Dim:** 7.32 × . . . × . . .
M: 2 Yamaha gasoline outboards; 230 bhp **Crew:** 3 tot.

Remarks: The original *Rescue I,* completed 9-86, was replaced by the present unit.

Note: The Bermuda Customs Service also operates patrol craft, including at least one Fairey Protector patrol boat.

BOLIVIA

Republic of Bolivia

Personnel: 3,500 total plus 1,700 marines

Organization and Bases:

- 1st Naval District Beni on the Río Bene and Río Mamoré, with bases at Loma Suarez and Puerto Villarroel
- 2nd Naval District Mamoré, with bases at Loma Suarez and Puerto Villarroel
- 3rd Naval District Madera on the Río Madre de Dios, with bases at Puerto Guayaramerin, Cachuela Esperanza, La Horquilla, and Ramón Dario Gutierrez
- 4th Naval District Titicaca, with base at San Pedro de Tequina on Lake Titicaca
- 5th Naval District Santa Cruz de la Sierra, with base at Puerto Quijarro on the Río Paraguay
- 6th Naval District Cobija on the Río Acre, with bases at Cobija, Madre dos Dios, and Santa Rosa del Abuna
- Area Naval No. 1 Cochabamba, with the Astilleros Naval Puerto Villarroel and the task of transporting petroleum products from Puerto Villarroel to Trinidad and Guayaramerin
- Area Naval No. 2 Santa Cruz, with logistic support duties
- Area Naval No. 3 Bermejo, with Base Brigadier Gen. Nestor Paz Galarza at Bermejo
- The Fuerza de Tarea "Diablos Azules" has five task groups to provide combat and logistical support in antidrug operations; its bases are located at Trinidad, Puerto Villarroel, Riberalta, Guayaramerin, and Copacabana (on Lake Titicaca). The Diablos Azules employ 33 Piranha launches, 42 Zodiac RIBs, and six support craft.

Naval Aviation: 1 Cessna 402C light transport. Six Air Force Helibras SA.315B Gavião helicopters are provided for assistance to the navy as needed.

Marines: Almirante Grau Battalion, based at Tiquina.

Note: Prefix to ship names is ARB (*Armada de República Bolivia*). The navy also operates a commercial riverine cargo company, Transnaval, with six cargo barges and six tow-barges.

PATROL BOATS [PB]

Note: 27 launches of 8-, 11-, and 17-m length were ordered from Rodman Polyships, Vigo, Spain, during 1998 and delivered together during 2-99; no data available. One 11-m unit is numbered BTL-601, and one of the 17-m launch is numbered M-343.

♦ 42 Pirana Mk II patrol launches
Bldr: Boston Whaler, Rockland, Mass./Edgewater, Fla. (In serv. 1992–99)

LP-01 through LP-42

Remarks: Foam-core GRP-hulled open launches provided by the U.S. for drug-enforcement duties. Characteristics similar to the other Bolivian Boston Whaler craft. All are assigned to the Diablos Azules special forces.

♦ 11 U.S. Whaler GRP-hulled
Bldr: Boston Whaler, Rockland, Mass.

D: 1.5 tons (2 fl) **S:** 40 kts **Dim:** 6.81 × 2.26 × . . .
A: 1 12.7-mm mg; small arms
M: 2 gasoline outboard motors; 360 bhp **Range:** 167/40; 750/ . . . **Crew:** 3 tot.

Remarks: U.S. Grant-Aid for use in drug interdiction. Four delivered late 1989, two in 12-90, and nine in 1991, from which only 11 remained in service as of 1997. Foam-core GRP hull construction.

♦ 4 13-meter class
Bldr: Guayaramerin Boatyard (L: 9-90)

PR-101 Presidente Paz Zamora (ex-PR 11)
PR-221 Capitán Palomeque (ex-PR 21)
PR-301 General Banzer (ex-PR 31)
PR-302 Antofagasta (ex-PR 32)

D: 8 tons **S:** 27 kts **Dim:** 13.0 × 3.2 × 0.5
A: 1 7.62-mm mg **M:** 2 diesels; 2 props; . . . bhp **Crew:** 4 tot.

Remarks: Wooden construction. Data apply to PR-21; the others, however, are similar. Used for river service in the 1st, 2nd, and 3rd Naval Districts.

♦ 6 Capitán Bretel class
Bldr: . . . , Bolivia (In serv. 1990s)

LP-410 Capitán Bretel
LP-411 Teniente Soliz
LP-412 T.F. Bocarezza
LP-413 Copacabana
LA-414 Guaqui
LP-415 Chaguaya

D: 5 tons **S:** 15 kts **Dim:** 12.9 × 3.9 × 1.0
A: 1 12.7-mm mg **Electronics:** Radar: 1 Raytheon 1900 nav.
M: 2 diesels; 2 props; . . . bhp **Crew:** 5 tot.

Remarks: Aluminum construction. Operate in the 4th Naval District. LA-414 is assigned to logistics support duties.

♦ 1 U.S.-built
Bldr: Hope/Progressive Shipbuilders, Houma, La. (In serv. 1985)

PR 501 Santa Cruz de la Sierra (ex-PR 51)

D: 46 tons (fl) **S:** 20 kts **Dim:** 20.4 × 5.8 × 1.2
A: 2 single 12.7-mm mg **Electronics:** Radar: 1 Furuno . . . nav.
M: 2 G.M. Detroit Diesel diesels; 2 props; . . . bhp
Range: 800/16 **Crew:** 10 tot.

Remarks: Aluminum-hulled unit used for patrol and logistics service on the Río Paraguay in the 5th Naval District.

SERVICE CRAFT

♦ 1 vehicle and personnel ferry [YFB]
Bldr: Astilleros Naval Puerto Villaroel (In serv. 22-7-98)

TB-01 Guayaramerin

Remarks: No data available.

♦ 2 Chinese-built personnel launches [YFL]
Bldr: . . . (In serv. 1996)

D: 7.4 tons **S:** 30 kts **Dim:** 11.50 × 2.38 × 0.45
M: 1 Type 12V150 diesel; 1 waterjet; 450 bhp **Crew:** 2 tot. + 7 passengers

SERVICE CRAFT *(continued)*

♦ 8 miscellaneous river transports [YFL]

Bldr: various, Bolivia (In serv. . . .)

M-101 Almirante Grau
M-103 Comandante Arandia
M-223 Libertador
M-224 Trinidad
M-225 J. Chavez Suarez
M-315 Ingeniero Palacios
M-341 Ingeniero Gumucho
M-501 Suarez Arana

Remarks: No data available. Wooden or iron construction. M-341 displaces 70 tons (fl), is 24 m overall by 6.5 m beam, has a range of 500 n.m. at 12 kts, and carries a crew of 11.

♦ 2 30-ton hydrographic survey launches [YGS]

LH-01 Pionera LH-03 Centauro

♦ 2 hospital launches [YH]

TNBH-401 Julian Apaza TNBH-01 Xavier Pinto Telleria

Remarks: TNBH-401, paid for by the U.S., was assembled on Lake Titicaca in the summer of 1972; displacing 150 tons, the craft is 27.4 m long by 8.53 m beam and is powered by two outboard motors. TNBH-01, which operates on the Río Mamoré, was commissioned on 23-10-97 as AH-02 and was built by Astilleros Naval Puerto Villarroel; no data available.

♦ 6 fuel lighters [YO]

BTP 01-06

Remarks: All of 40–45 tons with capacity of 250,000 liters. BTL-01 through BTL-04 were prefabricated in the U.S. and assembled at Astillero Naval Puerto Villarroel during 1976–77. BTP-05 was launched 29-11-91 by Astilleros Naval Puerto Villarroel, and the final unit was laid down by the same yard during 10-98.

♦ 7 small push-tugs [YTL]

Bldr: Astilleros Naval Puerto Villarroel

TNR-01 General Pando
TNR-02 Nicolas Suarez
TNR-03 Mariscal Cruz
TNR-04 Max Paredes
TNR-05 Capitán Olmos
TNR-06 V. A. H. Ugartche
TNR-07 Thames Crespo

Remarks: The first four were acquired in 1976–77. TNR-05 was converted from a Brazilian-built barge in 1987. TNR-07 was laid down in 10-98 by Ast. Naval Puerto Villarroel. They operate with the six fuel barges listed (see [YO]).

♦ 1 training craft (In serv. 24-4-04)

D: 80 tons (fl) **S:** 18 kts **Dim:** 36.0 × 9.20 × 1.2
A: . . . **M:** 2 diesels; 2 props; 1,300 bhp **Crew:** 11 + 50 trainees

Remarks: Catamaran-hulled craft built for service on Lake Titicaca and planned for completion late in 2001. Carries guns for training purposes.

BOTSWANA

PATROL BOATS [WPB]

♦ 2 U.S. Raider class

Bldr: Napco, Hopkins, Minn. (In serv. 1988)

D: 2.95 tons (fl) **S:** 40 kts **Dim:** 6.80 (6.40 wl) × 2.26 × 0.86
A: 2 single 12.7-mm mg **Electronics:** Radar: 1 Raytheon 1900 nav.
M: 2 gasoline outboard motors; 2 props; 310 bhp
Range: 167/40; 220/30; 750/ . . . **Crew:** 3 tot.

Remarks: Provided under FY 1988 Military Aid Program funds. Additional units have been requested. Use Boston Whaler GRP hulls molded in Rockland, Mass. Current status remains unknown.

Note: Several 18-ft. (5.49-m) airboats (airscrew propeller–driven, shallow-draft smallcraft) were purchased from the United States in 1991; the U.S. provided maintenance assistance in 1998–99.

BRAZIL

Federative Republic of Brazil

MARINHA DO BRASIL

Personnel: 32,850 total, plus 14,600 marines

Organization: Under the commander-in-chief (*comandante de marinha*) are the Base Naval do Rio, Centre de Apoio e Suporte Administrativo (CASOP), Força de Submarinos, Força de Superficie (Surface Force), and two operating forces. Subordinated to the Força de Superficie are the Centro de Adestramento da Esquadra; the destroyer, frigate, corvette, amphibious ship, and support squadrons; and naval auxiliary vessel U 27 (*Brasil*). Other than the main fleet organization, the Brazilian Navy is organized into six subsidiary Naval Districts, numbered and headquartered as follows:

- 1st Naval District, comprising the states of Espírito Santo and Rio de Janeiro, with the Grupamento Naval do Sudeste (GrupNSE) patrol force: P 44, P 45, R 22, R 23, and R 25.
- 2nd Naval District, comprising the state of Bahia, with the Minesweeping Force (ForMinVar): minesweepers M 15–20 and patrol ship V 19.
- 3rd Naval District, comprising the states of Pernambuco, Ceara, Paraíba, Alagoas, and Rio Grande do Norte, with the Grupamento Naval do Nordeste (GrupNNE): P 40, P 41, P 42, and R 24.
- 4th Naval District, comprising the states of Amazonas, Acre, Rondônia, Roraima, Pará, Maranhão, and Amapá, with the Amazon Flotilla (FlotAM): P 20, P 21, P 30–P 32, U 17 through U 19; and the Grupamento Naval do Norte (GrupNN).
- 5th Naval District, based at Estação Naval do Rio Grande and comprising the states of Paraná, Santa Catarina, and Rio Grande do Sul, with Grupamento Naval do Sul (GrupNS): P 46 and V 15
- 6th Naval District, comprising the states of Mato Grosso and Mato Grosso do Sul, with the Mato Grosso Flotilla (FlotMT): U 17, P 10, P 11, P 14, P 15, G 15, G 17, and G 19.
- 7th Naval District, Comando Naval de Brasília: no units assigned
- 8th Naval District, São Paulo: established 1997, units assigned not available.

Bases: Rio de Janeiro (Base Naval Almirante Castro e Silva submarine base, Base Naval do Rio de Janeiro main naval base, and Arsenal de Marinha do Rio de Janeiro naval shipyard); Bahia (Base Naval de Aratu naval base and repair facility); Natal (Base Naval de Natal); Pará (Base Naval de Val-de-Cães riverine base and repair facility); Rio Grande do Norte (Base Naval Almirante Ary Parreiras naval base and repair facility); Mato Grosso do Sul (Base Fluvial de Ladário naval base and repair facility); Amazonas (Estação Naval do Rio Negro naval riverine base and repair facility); and Rio Grande (Estação Naval do Rio Grande). See also marine and naval air sections below.

There are port captaincies at 1st Naval District at Espírito Santo and Rio de Janeiro; 2nd Naval District at Bahia; 3rd Naval district at Pernambuco, Ceará, Paraíba, Alagoas, and Rio Grande do Norte; 4th Naval District at Pará/Amapá; 5th Naval District at Santa Catarina, Rio Grande do Sul, and Paraná; 6th Naval District at Mato Grosso do Sul/Mato Grosso; and 8th Naval District, São Paulo.

Naval Aviation: Fixed wing aircraft: 18 AF-1 (A-4KU) and two AF-1A (TA-4KU) Skyhawk shipboard attack aircraft. Helicopters: five AS.332F (UH-14) Super Puma/Cougar (with AM 39 Exocet missiles), six Augusta-Sikorsky SH-3H (SH-3B) and seven SH-3D (SH-3A) Sea King (SH-3A are AM 39 Exocet-capable), 16 Bell Jet-Ranger III (IH-6B), eight Helibras AS.315B Gavião (Aérospatiale Lama), nine Westland Super Lynx HAS-21, 13 Westland Mk 21 (SAH-11) Lynx, 18 AS.350B Esquilo-I (UH-12), and 16 Helibras AS.355F2 Esquilo-II (UH-13).

The six ex-USN Sea Kings delivered in 5-96 are equipped with AQS-18(V) dipping sonars. All Lynx-series helicopters are equipped to launch Sea Skua antiship missiles.

Brazil purchased 20 A-4KU and three TA-4KU Skyhawk light attack fighters from Kuwait on 30-4-98, of which 18 AF-1 (A-4KU) and the three two-seat AF-1A have been returned to service, the rest being kept as spares. The aircraft are based at Base Aérea Naval de São Pedro da Aldeia as VF-1 (1st Esquadrão de Aviões de Interceptação e Ataque). The Skyhawks are armed with AIM-9H Sidewinder air-to-air missiles.

Naval aircraft are organized:

Base Aérea Naval de São Pedro da Aldeia (BAeNSPA), Rio de Janeiro except HU-5:

- VF-1: 1st Esquadrão de Aviões de Interceptação e Ataque, with AF-1 and AF-1A Skyhawk light attack aircraft
- HU-1: 1st Esquadrão de Helicópteros de Emprego Geral, with AS.355F2 Esquilo-II and AS.350BA Esquilo-I helicopters
- HU-2: 2nd Esquadrão de Helicópteros de Emprego Geral, with AS.332F1 Super Puma/Cougar helicopters
- HU-5: detachment based at Rio Grande, Rio Grande do Sul, with AS.350 (UH-12) Esquilo-I
- HA-1: 1st Esquadrão de Helicópteros de Esclarecimento e Ataque Anti-Submarino, with Mk 21 Lynx
- HS-1: 1st Esquadrão de Helicópteros Anti-Submarinos, with SH-3A/B Sea King
- HI-1: 1st Esquadrão de Helicópteros de Instrução: Bell 206B JetRanger III

Base Aérea de Manaus, Amazon region:

- HU-3: 3rd Esquadrão de Helicópteros de Emprego Geral: AS.350A Esquilo-I

Base Fluvial de Ladário, Matto Grosso do Sul:

- HU-4: 4th Esquadrão de Helicópteros de Emprego Geral: AS.350A Esquilo-I

The Brazilian Air Force makes available to the navy three Gates Learjet (R-35A) and 20 EMB 111 (P-95A/B) Bandeirante in a sea-surveillance version. The air force also operates two Piper/Embraer Seneca II, 15 Neiva T-25 Universal aircraft, and six AS.332F (UH-14) Super Puma helicopters for search-and-rescue purposes, and has ordered five EMB 120 Brasilia transports equipped with Ericsson Erieye phased array air early-warning radars. Also used occasionally in support of maritime surveillance is an R-35A Learjet with EW equipment. The Brazilian Air Force has received 12 surplus P-3A Orion maritime patrol aircraft from the U.S. and plans to activate the aircraft by 2008. Eight of the P-3 aircraft are to be upgraded to P-3BR standard by EADS CASA in Spain under the PX program.

Marines: Headquartered at Fort São José, Rio de Janeiro. The Fleet Marine Force, supported by a command and services company and the Special Operations Battalion, has the amphibious division at Base de Fuzileiros Navais da Ilha do Governador, with a command company, tank company, communications company, three infantry battalions, an artillery battalion, and an antiaircraft battery; also subordinated are the Comando de Reforço at Base de Fuzileiros Navais da Ilha das Flores, with a combat engineering battalion, logistic battalion, amphibious assault vehicles battalion, police company, and electronic warfare company. In addition to a Center of Repairs and Special Supplies, the marines are supported by the Admiral Sylvio de Camargo, Admiral Milciades Portela Alves, and Marambaia Island Instruction Centers. Security

MARINHA DO BRASIL *(continued)*

A-4 Skyhawk—conducting a "touch and go" landing aboard *São Paulo* (A 12)
U.S. Navy, 6-04

groups are stationed at each of the naval district headquarters. A 900-strong marine battalion was established at Manaus by the end of 2004.

A total of 26 U.S. AAV-7A1 amphibious armored, tracked personnel carriers are in service with the marines, 12 of them delivered new in 1-97 along with one AAVC-7A1 command vehicle and one AAVR-7A1 recovery vehicle. Air defense is provided by wheeled Bofors 40-mm 70-cal. AA mounts and Mistral heat-seeking missiles. The Marine Corps also operates the Bofors RBS-56 Bill antitank missile and in 1998 ordered 18 Royal Ordnance Factory 105-mm light artillery weapons, 14 CLANF amphibious vehicles, and 17 Steyr-Daimler-Puch SK-105 tank destroyers.

Coastal Defense: Coastal defense is the responsibility of the Brazilian Army, which took delivery of its first ASTROS II multiple-barreled rocket launcher in 5-98 for coast-defense use by the 8th Motorized Coastal Artillery Group, based at Rio de Janeiro.

Weapons and Sensors: Existing U.S. Mk 46 Mod. 2 ASW torpedoes are to be upgraded to Mod. 5, and additional Mk 46 Mod. 5 torpedoes are to be acquired. Bofors Tp 62 wire-guided torpedoes for submarines were ordered in 1998. In late 2005 the Brazilian government asked to buy 30 Mk 48 Mod 6 submarine-launched torpedoes from the United States. The deal, if concluded, would include support and test equipment, spare parts and personnel training with an estimated of cost U.S. $60 million.

Brazil's Consub manufactures the acoustic/magnetic MFC 01/100 modular mine, a 770-kg moored contact weapon with a 160-kg trotyl explosive charge that can be laid in depths from 10 to 100 m and is also available in a bottom-mine version with magnetic or acoustic-influence fusing.

A number of Danish Terma navigational radars were ordered 1991 to equip patrol and service craft.

IPqM developed the SICONTA (*Sistema de Controle Tático*) modular combat data system for employment on various new and refitted warships; using the TTI-2700 display terminal and Link YB, it can share data with other similarly equipped ships. The prototype went to sea in the now-retired destroyer *Mariz e Barros,* and the system is undergoing further development by the navy.

AIRCRAFT CARRIERS [CV]

♦ 1 ex-French Clemenceau class

Bldr: Ch. de l'Atlantique, St. Nazaire, France

	Laid down	L	In serv.
A 12 São Paulo (ex-*Foch,* R 99)	2-57	28-7-60	15-7-63

São Paulo (A 12)—with Skyhawk, Super Puma and Sea King aircraft on deck
U.S. Navy, 6-04

D: 30,884 tons (33,673 fl) **S:** 30 kts
Dim: 265.0 (238.0 pp) × 31.72 beam (51.20 flight deck) × 7.50 light draft (8.60 fl)
Air Group: 37 aircraft maximum; typical loadout includes: 14 AF-1 Skyhawk fighter-bombers, 2 SH-3A Sea King, 1 UH-13 Esquilo II, 1 IH-6B Jetranger, and 1 UH-14 Super Puma helicopters;
A: 2 8-round Albatros SAM syst. (Aspide 2000 missiles—to be fitted); 2 40-mm/70 cal. (SAK) AA (to be fitted); 5 12.7-mm machineguns
Electronics:
Radar: 1 Racal Decca 1226 nav.; 1 DRBV-23B air search; 1/DRBV-15 3-D air-search; 2 DRBI-10 height-finder; 2 AESN-Orion RTN-30X to be fitted in place of current DRBC-32C f.c.; 1 NRBA-51 air-control (all by Thales)
TACAN: U.S. SRN-6
EW: ARBR-16 intercept; ARBR-17 intercept; ARBB-33 jamming; 2 AMBL-2A Sagaie decoy RL
M: 2 sets Parsons geared turbines; 2 props; 126,000 shp
Boilers: 6 watertube; 45 kg/cm^2, 450° C
Electric: 14,000 kw tot.
Range: 4,800/24; 7,500/18 **Fuel:** 3,720 tons **Endurance:** 60 days
Crew: 1,030 total + 670 air group

Remarks: Purchased 8-00 for US $41 million (including cost of overhaul); transferred on 15-11-00 and departed 1-2-01 for arrival in Brazil on 16-2-01. Sister *Clemenceau,* retired on 1-10-97, was employed as a source of spares for the *São Paulo's* predelivery overhaul at Brest, which included removal of asbestos insulation and deletion of all armament. As *Foch,* underwent a 14-month refit in 1992–93, receiving new propulsion turbine rotors, refitted catapults certified for 6,000 further shots, a nose-gear catapult launch capability, and numerous habitability improvements. Further improvements were made during a 1995–97 refit, including increasing the size of the jet-blast deflectors and adding enlarged retractable "ski-jumps" to the forward ends of both catapults. Underwent minor refit during 2003, which included retubing of boilers and catapult refurbishments.
Hull systems: Armor protection includes the reinforced flight deck, armored bulkheads in engine room and magazines, and reinforced-steel bridge superstructure. The machinery spaces and boilers are enclosed in what amounts to an armored redoubt. Living spaces are air-conditioned. The island has three bridges: flag, navigation, and aviation.
Aviation systems: The flight deck is 257 m in length overall with an 8°, 165.5 × 29.5-m angled portion; the deck forward of the angled deck measures 93 × 28 m and the width of the deck abreast the island is 35 m. Hangar is 180 m long × 22 to 24 m wide × 7 m clear height. The two 16 × 11-m elevators, one forward on the main flight deck, one slightly abaft the island, are able to raise a 15-ton aircraft 8.50 m in 9 seconds. Two 50-m Mitchell-Brown type BS5 steam catapults are able to launch 15- to 20-ton aircraft at 110 knots; one is located forward, the other on the angled deck. Has French-made mirror landing equipment. Carries 1,800 m^3 of jet fuel and about 3,000 m^3 of aviation munitions. A small, retractable 1.5° ski-jump structure at the forward end of each catapult was added around 1994.

The air group listed is an estimate, based on the use of all flyable Skyhawk light fighter-bombers and the helicopter complement of the *Minas Gerais.* Additional aircraft, should they become available, could be accommodated.
Combat systems: All but the navigational radars are unique to this ship, which will likely complicate maintenance. Has the SENIT 2 combat data system, updated to SENIT 8.01 (OP3A) status with three display stations. Two Italian Albatros self-defense SAM systems, with Aspide missiles, were to be added during the 2002–4 refit.

Note: The ex-British *Colossus*-class aircraft carrier *Minas Gerais* (A 11, ex-HMS *Vengeance*) was formally decommissioned on 16-10-01. Sold to an Indian scrapping firm in late 2004, she was towed to Alang, India, for breaking up.

NUCLEAR-POWERED ATTACK SUBMARINES [SSN]

Note: The Brazilian Navy has had a program under way since 1979 to develop a nuclear-powered attack submarine and has already devoted well over $1 billion to the development of a nuclear propulsion reactor, without significant results; most of the funding was withdrawn in 1994. As many as four SSNs had been planned. The navy is said to be willing to sacrifice other more urgent programs in favor of continued work on the SSN.

ATTACK SUBMARINES [SS]

♦ 4 (+ 1) German Type 209/1400 Mod. 3 class

Bldrs: S 30: Howaldtswerke Deutsche Werft (HDW), Kiel; others: Arsenal de Marinha do Rio de Janeiro (AMRJ)

	Laid down	L	In serv.
S 30 Tupi	8-3-85	25-4-87	6-5-89
S 31 Tamoio	15-7-86	18-11-93	17-7-95
S 32 Timbira	15-9-87	5-1-96	15-12-96
S 33 Tapajó (ex-*Tapajós*)	8-92	11-6-98	12-99
S 34 Tikuná (ex-*Tamandare*)	12-98	9-3-05	13-12-05

D: 1,150 tons light, 1,453 tons surf./1,590 tons sub.
S: 11 kts surf./21.5 kts sub.
Dim: 61.20 × 6.20 (7.60 over stern planes) × 5.50
A: 8 bow 533-mm TT (16 Mk 24 Mod. 1 Tigerfish and/or Bofors Tp 62 wire-guided torpedoes)
Electronics:
Radar: 1 Thomson-CSF Calypso-III search/nav.
Sonar: STN Atlas-Elektronik CSU-83/1 suite (DBSQS-21 active; passive flank arrays)
EW: Thales DR-3000U intercept
M: 4 MTU 12V493 TY60, 600-bhp (S 34: MTU 12V396, 940-bhp) diesels 4 AEG 420-kw (S 34: 4 AEG . . . -kw) generators, electric drive; 1 prop; 5,000 shp
Range: 10,000/8 snorkel; 25/21.5, 50/16, 230/8, 400/4 sub.
Fuel: 116 tons **Endurance:** 50 days **Crew:** 33 tot.

Remarks: S 30 was ordered 8-82 and handed over by the builders on 20-8-88; after training in European waters, the submarine arrived on 27-6-89. Plans to construct two more were canceled in 1992, but a fourth Brazilian-built unit was restored to the program in 10-94. The names of S 33 and S 34 were changed in 1995 to standardize names to indicate an Indian who is a member of a particular tribe. Construction of S 34 has been delayed by funding problems. Work on the S 34 was halted between 2002 and 2004 due to a lack of funds.

S 34 is seen as an intermediate stage prior to the building of Brazil's first SSN. *Tikuná* will be 0.85-m longer in order to use a different electric motor and more powerful diesels; also different will be the sensor and communications suites. New torpedoes will be carried, and the submarine is to have reduced radiated noise, a lower indiscretion rate, a freshwater distilling system, the ISUS 83-13 weapons-control system, ONA self-noise measurement hydrophones, a nonpenetrating periscope-mounted electronic intercept system, interfacing between the inertial navigational system and a GPS receiver, higher-precision gyros, the ability to launch mines and guided missiles from the torpedo tubes, improved endurance, fittings to accept a submarine rescue submersible and the ability to put two persons at a time in the rescue lock-out chamber, a distress-warning system, increased air-conditioning plant output, and automatic depth control.

ATTACK SUBMARINES [SS] *(continued)*

Tamoio (S 31) Ralph Edwards, 5-00

Tupi (S 30)—alongside *Tamoio* (S 31) and retired *Tonelero* (S 21) Ralph Edwards, 5-00

Hull systems: Can make 25 knots submerged for a brief period. Diving depth: 250 m. Has a 480-cell battery. The bow pressure hull cap, with its integral torpedo tube foundations, is made in Germany, with the remainder of the structure being of Brazilian manufacture.
Combat systems: S 30 through S 33 have Ferranti KAFS A10 action data system, Kollmorgen Model 76 search and attack periscopes, and Sperry Mk 29 Mod. 2 Ship's Inertial Navigation System (SINS). Type 42 torpedoes began to supplant the Tigerfish in 2001. During late 2005, Brazil expressed interest in purchasing 30 MK 48 Mod 6 torpedoes to equip its submarine force.

Disposal note: *Oberon*-class submarine *Tonelero* (S 21), used for several years for underway training, sank alongside while at Rio de Janeiro on 25-12-00 during the latter stages of a minor overhaul; the submarine was raised on 4-1-01 but was found to be not worth repairing and was stricken on 21-6-01. Sister *Humaitá* (S 20) was retired on 8-4-96, and *Riachuelo* (S 22) was decommissioned and relegated to museum service on 12-11-97.

FRIGATES [FF]

♦ 0 (+ 1) Barroso class
Bldr: Arsenal de Marinha do Rio de Janeiro (AMRJ)

	Laid down	L	In serv.
V 34 Barroso	21-12-94	20-12-02	12-08

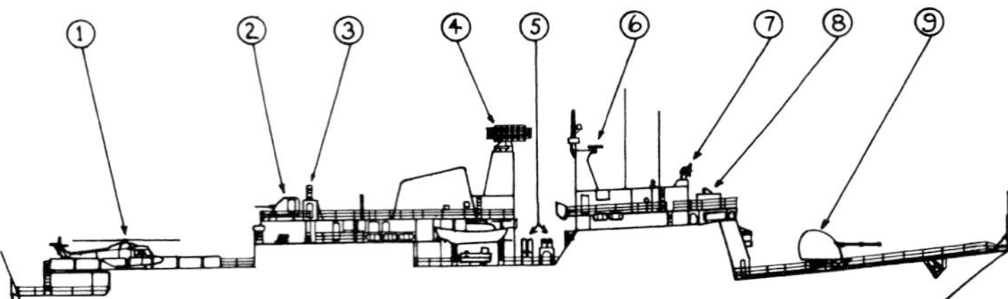

Barroso (V 34) 1. One Lynx helicopter 2. 40-mm AA 3. EOS-400 optronic director 4. RAN-20S surface/air-search radar 5. MM 40 Exocet antiship missiles 6. Decca navigational radar 7. Orion RTN-30X gun fire-control radar 8. OFD optical gun director 9. 114-mm Vickers Mk 8 gun Drawing by A. D. Baker III

Barroso (V 34)—builders model Julio Montes, 2005

D: 1,785 tons (2,350 fl) **S:** 27 kts
Dim: 100.66 (93.90 pp) × 11.40 × 3.96 (mean hull; 5.50 over sonar)
A: 4 MM 40 Exocet SSM; 1 114-mm 55-cal. Vickers Mk 8 DP; 1 40-mm 70-cal. Bofors Mk 3 AA; 2 triple 324-mm ASW TT (U.S. Mk 46 Mod 2 torpedoes); 2 Westland SAH-11A Lynx helicopters
Electronics:
Radar: 1 Decca TM 1226 nav.; 1 AESN RAN-20S air/surf. search; 2 Alenia-Elsag RTN-30X f.c.
Sonar: EDO 997 hull-mounted LF
EW: Elebra SLQ-2-IPQM active/passive syst.; 4 Elebra 12-tubed decoy RL
E/O: MSI Defense OFD (114-mm gun f.c.); Saab Dynamics EOS-400 (40-mm gun f.c.)
M: CODOG: 1 G.E. LM 2500 gas turbine (27,490 shp); 2 MTU 1163-series diesels (. . . bhp each); 2 CP props
Electric: 2,000 kw (4 Siemens 500-kw alternators)
Range: 4,000/15 **Crew:** 154

Remarks: Plans to construct a fifth, improved unit of the *Inhaúma* class were announced during 1992, but funding to order the V 34 was not made available until late in 1994. Three additional units were at one time planned, but work on V 34 itself has been progressing very slowly, due to funding problems. Work on the ship was scaled back dramatically between 2002 and 2004 due to lack of funds. Fitting out progress has been very slow.
Hull systems: The hull is 4.2 meters longer than that of the *Inhaúma* class to accommodate more powerful diesel engines (for 20.5 knots on diesels alone) and provide more useful internal volume. The extra length allows installation of improved crew accommodations, additional rake and freeboard to the bow, and a longer helicopter deck. Vosper Thornycroft Series 500 fin stabilizers will be fitted.
Combat systems: The ship will use, insofar as possible, the same systems that are being employed in the modernization of the *Niterói* class, including the Siconta-2 combat data and direction system. The sonar fit may differ from that listed. The 40-mm gun mounting is the same as that employed by the Bofors Trinity CIWS but lacks the integral radar.

♦ 4 Inhaúma class
Bldr: First two: Arssenal de Marinha do Rio de Janeiro (AMRJ); others: EMAQ-Verolme Estaleiros S.A., Angra dos Reis (now IVI-Indústria Verolme-Sihibras S.A.)

	Laid down	L	In serv.
V 30 Inhaúma	23-9-83	3-12-86	12-12-89
V 31 Jaceguai	15-10-84	8-6-87	2-4-91
V 32 Julio de Noronha	15-11-87	12-91	27-10-92
V 33 Frontin	15-12-87	6-2-92	11-3-94

Jaceguai (V 31)—Rio de Janeiro Ralph Edwards, 4-00

FRIGATES [FF] *(continued)*

Jaceguai (V 31) Ralph Edwards, 4-00

D: 1,670 tons light, 2,092 normal (2,350 fl) **S:** 26 kts
Dim: 95.77 (90.00 pp) × 11.40 × 3.70 mean hull (5.30 over sonar dome)
A: 4 MM 40 Exocet SSM; 1 114-mm 55-cal. Vickers Mk 8 DP; 2 single 40-mm 70-cal. Bofors L70 AA; 2 triple 324-mm ASW TT (U.S. Mk 46 Mod 2 torpedoes); 1 SAH-11 Lynx helicopter
Electronics:
Radar: 1 Decca TM 1226 nav.; 1 Siemens-Plessey AWS-4 air search; 1 Alenia Orion RTN-10X f.c.
Sonar: STN Atlas Elektronik DSQS-21C
EW: Racal Cutlass B-1 intercept; Racal Cygnus (V 30, 32: IPqM ET/SLQ-1/L) jammer; Telegon HFD/F; 2 6-round Plessey Shield decoy RL
E/O: Saab OES-400 optronic gun director
M: CODOG: 1 G.E. LM 2500 gas turbine, 27,490 shp; 2 MTU 16V956 TB91 diesels, 7,880 bhp; 2 CP props
Electric: 2,000 kw tot. (4 Siemens 500-kw diesel-driven alternators)
Range: 4,000/15 **Crew:** 20 officers, 115 enlisted (162 tot. accomm.)

Remarks: Originally were to have been a program of 12 smaller "corvettes." Four were authorized 11-81, with the first two ordered 15-2-82 and the others on 9-6-86, originally for delivery 1989, but greatly delayed by shipyard labor problems and bankruptcy. They form the 1st Corvette Squadron and are based at Rio de Janeiro.
Hull systems: Reported to suffer from topweight problems, which helped to delay the entry into full active service of the first two.
Combat systems: Have Ferranti CAAIS 450 (Computer-Assisted Action Information System) with Ferranti WSA-421 weapons-control system. The U.S. Mk 15 Phalanx CIWS was selected 1988 for installation on the stern but has not yet been ordered. V 30 has a unique IPqM ET/SDR-2 EW suite with a directional ET/SLQ-1 jammer (8–16 GHz) antenna in a radome atop the after mast.

♦ 3 ex-U.K. Broadsword (Type 22) class
Bldr: Yarrow (Shipbuilders) Ltd., Scotstoun, Glasgow

	Ordered	Laid down	L	In serv.
F 46 Greenhalgh (ex-*Broadsword,* F 88)	8-2-74	7-2-75	12-5-76	4-5-79
F 48 Bosisio (ex-*Brazen,* F 91)	21-10-77	18-8-78	4-5-80	2-7-82
F 49 Rademaker (ex-*Battle Axe,* F 89)	7-9-75	4-2-76	18-5-77	28-3-80

Bosisio (F 48) Ralph Edwards, 4-00

D: 3,900 tons (4,400 fl) **S:** 30 kts (18 cruise)
Dim: 131.20 (125.00 wl) × 14.80 × 4.30 (6.00 sonar)
A: 4 MM 40 Exocet SSM; 2 sextuple Sea Wolf GWS.25 SAM syst.; 2 single 40-mm 70-cal. Bofors L70 AA; 2 single 20-mm 90-cal. BMARC-Oerlikon GAM B 01 AA; 2 triple 324-mm STWS.2 ASW TT (Stingray torpedoes); 1 or 2 SAH-11 Lynx helicopters

Rademaker (F 49) U.S. Navy, 10-05

Electronics:
Radar: 1 Kelvin-Hughes Type 1006 nav.; 1 Marconi Type 967-968 surf./air-search; 2 Marconi Type 910 f.c.
Sonar: Ferranti-Thomson Type 2050 hull-mounted, Type 2008 underwater telephone
EW: UAA-1 intercept, 2 Type 670 jammer, 4 6-round DLB decoy RL; Type 182 towed torpedo decoy
M: COGOG; 2 Olympus TM-3B gas turbines, 27,300 shp each for high speed; 2 Tyne RM-1A, 4,100 shp each for cruising; 2 CP props; 54,600 shp max.
Electric: 4,000 kw (4 Paxman Ventura 12PA 200CZ diesel sets)
Range: 4,500/18 (on Tyne); 1,200/29 (on Olympus)
Crew: 17 officers, 222 enlisted + 65 additional accomm.

Remarks: Agreement to purchase signed 18-11-94, with transfers ensuing as the ships retired from the Royal Navy. Purchase price was $170 million for the four. They provide Brazil with its first modern shipboard air-defense system. F 46 transferred and recommissioned 30-6-95, arriving in Brazil on 24-10-95; F 47 and F 48 transferred and recommissioned on 30-8-96, arriving at Rio de Janeiro on 9-12-96; and F 49 transferred on 30-4-97. The ships are assigned to the 1st Naval Division's 2nd Frigate Squadron, based at Rio de Janeiro. While taking part in international exercises in 11-04, F 49 was accidently fired upon by Argentine frigate *Rosales,* suffering damage to her bridge, mast, and seawolf launcher.
Hull systems: Berthing and training facilities for 65 officer trainees per ship were added to all four by the end of 1992. Fin stabilizers and Prairie/Masker air bubbling radiated noise suppression systems are fitted.
Combat systems: F 46 was transferred with MM 38 Exocet missiles; plans to substitute MM 40 in the others prior to turnover did not reach fruition. Have the CAAIS combat data system. The 967-968 radar is a back-to-back array with track-while-scan features. F 49 has four 6-round Mk 137 chaff RL (Outfit DLD) in addition to standard Outfit DLC. Two Lynx helicopters can be carried, but only one would normally be aboard. Two single Bofors 40-mm mounts removed from the *Niterói* class during modernization have been fitted to all four on the upper deck forward of the hangar; the 20-mm guns have been placed on the upper deck abreast the gas turbine intakes.
Disposals: *Dodsworth* (F 47, ex-HMS *Brilliant,* F 90) was retired on 11-30-04 for use as a spare parts hulk.

♦ 6 Niterói (Vosper Thornycroft Mk 10) class
Bldrs: F 40–F 43: Vosper Thornycroft, Woolston; others: Arsenal de Marinha do Rio de Janeiro (AMRJ)

	Laid down	L	In serv.
F 40 Niterói	8-6-72	8-2-74	20-11-76
F 41 Defensora	14-12-72	27-3-75	5-3-77
F 42 Constituição	13-3-74	15-4-76	31-3-78
F 43 Liberal	2-5-75	7-2-77	18-11-78
F 44 Independência	11-6-72	2-9-74	3-9-79
F 45 União	11-6-72	14-3-75	12-9-80

União (F 45) Ralph Edwards, 4-00

D: 3,355 tons (3,707 fl) **S:** 30.5 kts
Dim: 129.24 (121.92 pp) × 13.52 × 4.20 (5.94 sonar)

FRIGATES [FF] *(continued)*

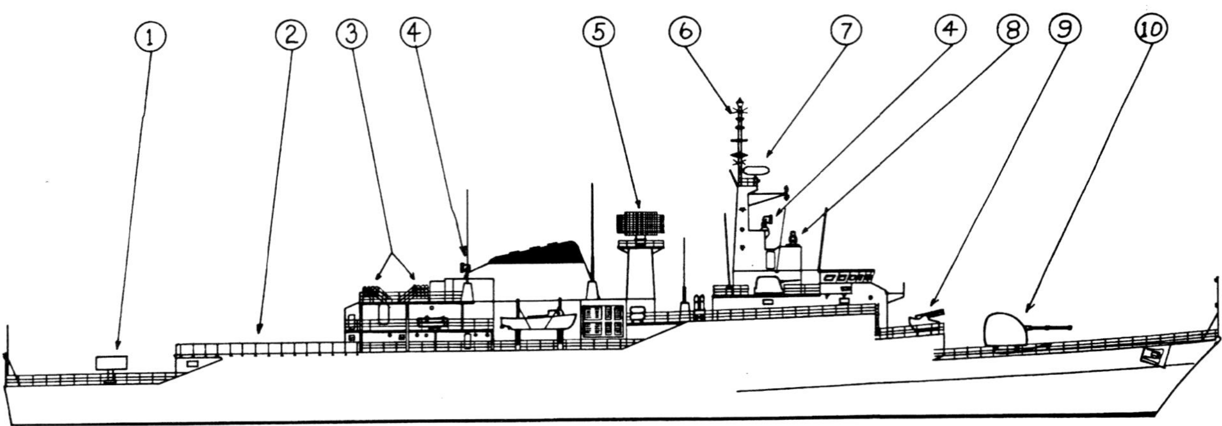

Liberal (F 43)—as modernized: 1. Albatros SAM launcher 2. Helicopter flight deck 3. Decoy rocket launchers 4. Orion RTN-30X weapon-control radars 5. RAN-20S surface/air-search radar 6. MAGE EW array 7. Surface-search radar 8. EOS-400 optronic gun director 9. Twin 375-mm ASW rocket launcher 10. 114-mm Mk 8 gun

Drawing by A. D. Baker III

Defensora (F 41) Ralph Edwards, 4-00

A: 4 MM 40 Exocet SSM (2 twin launchers); 1 octuple launcher for Albatros SAM syst. (Aspide missiles); 1 114-mm 55-cal. Vickers DP; 2 single 40-mm 70-cal Bofors Trinity AA; 1 2-round 375-mm Bofors SR-375A ASW RL; 2 triple 324-mm ASW TT (Honeywell Mk 46, Mod. 5 ASW torpedoes); 1 d.c. rack (5 charges); 1 SAH-11 Lynx helicopter

Electronics:

Radar: 1 Terma/Scanter MiP surf.-search; 1 Furuno FR-1942, Mk. 2 navigation; 1 AESN RAN-20S air/surf.-search; 2 AESN RTN-30X f.c.

Sonar: EDO 997F hull-mounted active search and attack, MF; EDO 700E variable depth sonar, active search-and-attack MF (F 41 and F 42 only)

EW: Elebra MAGE active/passive suite; Racal Cutlass B-1B Intercept (F 40 and F 41 only); Elebra/Brazilian Navy-developed ESM suite (remainder); Racal Cygnus or IPqM/Elebra ET/SLQ-2X jammer; 4 IPqM/Elebra MDLS octuple chaff launcher; FH-5 HFD/F

E/O: Saab-Combitech EOS-400/10B optronic surveillance/f.c.

M: CODOG: 2 Rolls-Royce Olympus TM-3B gas turbines, 28,000 shp each; 4 MTU 16V956 TB93 diesels, 3,940 bhp each; 2 Escher-Wyss CP props; 56,000 shp max.

Electric: 4,002.5 kw tot. (4 × 1,000-kw diesel sets, 1 × 2.5-kw emergency set)

Range: 1,300/29; 4,200/19 (4 diesels), 5,300/17.5 (2 diesels)

Fuel: 480 tons + 26 tons aviation fuel **Crew:** 22 officers, 187 enlisted

Remarks: Ordered 20-9-70. The Brazilian-built units experienced considerable delays during fitting out. All are being extensively modernized. Modernizations of F 41 and F 43 were completed by 2004 and the remaining units are expected to be upgraded by 2006. The class constitutes the 1st Frigate Squadron and is based at Rio de Janeiro.

Hull systems: Fitted with retractable fin stabilizers. An automated engineering plant monitoring system developed by the São Paulo Navy Technology Center (CTMSP), the Navy Research Institute (IPqM), and the Ship Design Center (CPN) was to be installed during the modernizations but is now being fitted independently, starting late in 2001. MTU 1163-series diesels are replacing the original 16V956 TB91 engines during the modernizations. Have tankage for 50 tons of fresh water, and the two desalination plants can each produce 32 tons per day.

Combat systems: Under a 3-95, $385-million contract with Alenia of Italy, the AWS-2 radars are being replaced with RAN-20S surveillance radars, the RTN-10X weapons-control radars with two RTN-30X, and the Sea Cat SAM systems by an Albatros SAM system with an octuple launcher for Aspide missiles on the fantail in all six ships. On 20-9-96 a contract was let to a consortium led by Elebra of Brazil with DCN France and three other Brazilian companies (Consub, Dolfin, and Holosys) to integrate Siconta-II, a variant of the French Navy SENIT 8 system, with the other combat systems; it replaces the original British CAAIS combat data system. Two Bofors 40-mm Mk 3 Trinity radar-directed guns are replacing the manually directed 40-mm mounts. In F 42 and F 43, the Albatros SAM launcher replaces the after 114-mm gunmount. A Saab Dynamics EOS-400 optronic fire-control system is being added atop the pilothouse. Racal Cutlass B-1B ESM is replacing RDL on F 40 and F 41, while an Elebra- and Brazilian Navy–developed ESM suited will be substituted on the others; all six will get an Elebra/Brazilian Navy–developed MAGE active jammer system and four 12-round decoy rocket launchers. The ASW rocket launcher system is being upgraded to SR-375A and now uses Brazilian-made projectiles. The ASW torpedo tubes and sonar systems will be retained (including the VDS sets in F 41 and F 42), with the 610E hull-mounted sets upgraded to Mod. 1.

♦ 1 U.S. Garcia class

Bldrs: D 27: Lockheed SB, Seattle

	Laid down	L	In serv.
D 27 Pará (ex-*Albert David,* FF 1050)	29-4-64	19-12-64	19-10-68

D: 2,624 tons (3,560 fl) **S:** 27 kts

Dim: 126.33 (121.90 wl) × 13.47 × 7.90 (over sonar)

A: 2 single 127-mm 38-cal. DP; 1 octuple Mk 112 ASROC ASW RL; 2 triple 324-mm Mk 32 ASW TT; 1 Esquilo-1 UH-12/13 helicopter

Electronics:

Radar: 1 LN-66 nav.; 1 SPS-10 surf. search; 1 Lockheed Martin SPS-40 air search, 1 Westinghouse Mk 35 f.c. (on Mk. 56 director)

Sonar: SQS-26 BX bow-mounted LF

EW: WLR-1 and WLR-3 intercept; ULQ-6 jammer; Mk 33 RBOC decoy syst. (2 6-round launchers); SLQ-25 Nixie towed torpedo decoy syst.

TACAN: SRN-15

M: 1 set G.E. geared steam turbines; 1 prop; 35,000 shp

Boilers: 2 Foster-Wheeler turbopressurized; 83.4 kg/cm, 510° C

Electric: 2,000 kw tot. **Range:** 4,000/20 **Fuel:** 600 tons

Crew: 18 officers, 268 enlisted

Remarks: May no longer be in service. During 2005 a cargo vessel, also named *Pará* (U 15) entered service with the Brazilian fleet, possibly indicating that D 27 has been retired.

Hull systems: Fin stabilizers and Prairie/Masker air bubbling radiated noise suppression systems are fitted. The boilers are vertical, have turbopressurized combustion, and are very difficult to maintain.

Combat systems: Both have the Mk 56 gun fire-control system for the 127-mm guns and the Mk 114 ASW fire-control system. D27 carried the SQR-15 TASS towed sonar array prior to transfer and retains the original small DASH drone helicopter hangar, which cannot accommodate Lynx helicopters. D 27 has a reload magazine with eight missiles for the ASROC system. The ASROC missiles, assuming any were transferred with the ships, are unlikely still to be viable.

Disposal note: *Paraíba* (D 28) (ex-USS *Davidson,* FF-1045) and *Paraná* (D 29) (ex-USS *Sample,* FF-1048) were decommissioned on 26-7-02. Both were sold for scrapping. *Paraiba* sank while under tow, enroute to Alang, India. *Pernambuco* (D 30) (ex-USS *Bradley,* FF-1041) was stricken on 11-3-04 due to budget constraints.

PATROL SHIPS [PS]

♦ 4 ex-U.K. River class

Bldr: Richards Shipbuilders, Lowestoft (P 61: Great Yarmouth), U.K.

	Laid down	L	In serv.
P 60 Bracuí (ex-*Jorge Leite,* H 45; ex-*Itchen,* M 2009)	26-3-84	16-11-84	12-10-85
P 61 Benevente (ex-*Melo Baptista,* ex-*Blackwater,* M 2008)	16-1-84	29-8-84	20-6-85
P 62 Bocaina (ex-*Andromeda,* ex-*Spey,* M 2013)	12-11-84	22-5-85	19-7-86
P 63 Babitonga (ex-*Arun,* M 2104)	4-2-85	20-8-85	29-8-86

PATROL SHIPS [PS] *(continued)*

Bocaina (P 62) Maritime Photographic, 8-98

D: 630 tons (720 fl) **S:** 14 kts (15 on trials; 12 sust.)
Dim: 47.60 (42.00 pp) × 10.50 × 3.10 (3.75 max.)
A: 1 40-mm/60-cal. Bofors Mk 3 AA; 2 single 12.7-mm mg
Electronics: Radar: 2 Decca TM 1226 nav.
M: 2 Ruston 6 RKCM diesels; 2 4-bladed CP props; 3,040 bhp
Electric: 460 kw tot. **Range:** 4,500/10 **Fuel:** 88 tons
Crew: 7 officers, 7 petty officers, 16 other enlisted

Remarks: 638 grt. Former minesweepers purchased 23-8-96 for transfer on retirement from Royal Navy, 4-98 to 9-98. Two were originally to be employed as navigational buoy tenders and training ships and the other two converted to serve as survey ships. P 60 was transferred on 8-4-98, P 61 and P 62 on 10-7-98, and P 63 on 18-9-98. Two Brazilian Navy sisters serve as hydrographic survey ships and a third as navigational buoy tender.
Hull systems: Have steel hulls built to commercial single-compartment damage standard. There have been upper-deck corrosion problems. Navigation gear includes two Kelvin-Hughes MS 48 echo sounders, Decca QM 14(1) and Decca HiFix Mk 6 radio navaids, and a NAVSAT receiver. Modifications in Brazil include installation of air-conditioning equipment.
Combat systems: Sweep gear removed prior to transfer. The 40-mm gun is locally controlled and is hand trained and elevated.

♦ **2 Imperial Marinheiro class**
Bldr: L. Smit, Kinderdijk, the Netherlands

	L	In serv.
V 15 Imperial Marinheiro	24-11-54	8-6-55
V 19 Caboclo	28-8-54	4-55

D: 911 tons (960 fl) **S:** 15 kts **Dim:** 55.72 × 9.55 × 3.6
A: 1 76.2-mm 50-cal. U.S. Mk 26 DP; 4 single 20-mm 70-cal. Oerlikon Mk 10 AA
Electronics: Radar: 1 Decca . . . nav.
M: 2 Sulzer diesels; 2 props; 2,160 bhp
Range: . . . / . . . **Fuel:** 135 tons **Crew:** 60 total

Remarks: Oceangoing tug design with 15-ton bollard pull towing capacity. Were intended to be convertible for minesweeping or minelaying. Officially designated "vedettes" and used on Amazon River system in district patrols and in support of the 200-mile economic exclusion zone.
Disposals: *Iparanga* (V 17) was stricken during 1983; *Iguatemi* (V 16) on 9-8-96; and *Mearim* (V 22) on 4-12-98. *Forte de Coimbra* (V 18) was stranded on Baixinha Reefs, off Natal, on 12-11-96 and subsequently stricken. *Bahiana* (V 21) was stricken on 5-3-02. *Purus* (V 23) was stricken in 2002 and transferred to Namibia in 6-03. *Solimoes* (V 24) was stricken in 2003 and became a museum ship. *Angostura* (V 20) was stricken in 2004 for disposal.

PATROL COMBATANTS [PG]

Note: Designs are in preparation for a new class of small river gunboats of between 150 and 250 tons displacement; each would carry two LAR (Lanchas Armadas Rapidas—Fast Attack Boats) and a marine rifle platoon.

♦ **2 Pedro Teixeira class**
Bldr: Arsenal de Marinha do Rio de Janeiro (AMRJ)

	L	In serv.
P 20 Pedro Teixeira	11-6-72	17-12-73
P 21 Raposo Tavares	11-6-72	17-12-73

Pedro Teixeira (P 20) Brazilian Navy

D: 690 tons (fl) **S:** 14 kts **Dim:** 63.56 × 9.71 × 1.70
A: 1 40-mm 70-cal. Bofors L70 AA; 4 single 12.7-mm mg; 2 single 81-mm mortar/12.7-mm mg combinations; 2 single 7.62-mm mg; 1 UH-12 Esquilo-I helicopter
Electronics: Radar: 2 Decca . . . nav.
M: 2 MEP-M.A.N. V6V16/18 TLS diesels; 2 props; 3,840 bhp
Range: 6,800/10 **Crew:** 6 officers, 52 enlisted + up to 80 troops

Remarks: Assigned to the Amazon Flotilla. Carry two armed LCVPs on fantail. Hull has a small bow bulb. Have accommodations for 20 troops below decks; 60 others can be accommodated for brief periods on the upper deck. Maximum speed going upstream is about 8 kts. Both ships are to be re-engined for continued service.

♦ **1 river monitor**
Bldr: Arsenal de Marinha, do Rio de Janeiro (AMRJ)

	Laid down	L	In serv.
U 17 Parnaíba	11-6-36	2-9-37	9-3-38

Parnaíba (U 17) Hartmut Ehlers, 5-00

D: 620 tons (720 fl) **S:** 12 kts **Dim:** 55.0 × 10.1 × 1.6
A: 1 76.2-mm 50-cal. U.S. Mk 22 DP; 2 single 40-mm 70-cal. Bofors AA; 6 single 20-mm 70-cal Oerlikon Mk 10 AA
Electronics: Radar: 1 Furuno 3600 nav.; 1 Decca . . . nav.
M: 2 . . . diesels; 2 props; . . . bhp
Range: 1,350/10 **Fuel:** 90 tons **Endurance:** 16 days **Crew:** 74 tot.

Remarks: Assigned to the Mato Grosso Flotilla and wears an auxiliary pennant number. Has some side and deck armor protection. The original reciprocating steam propulsion plant was replaced in refit from 1-98 to 6-5-99 at the *Ladário* Riverine Naval Base, and she is expected to continue operating for the foreseeable future. A helicopter platform has been added over the fantail. The 40-mm 70-cal. guns mounted aft were taken from *Niterói*-class frigates in refit, replacing two 20-mm mounts.

PATROL CRAFT [PC]

♦ **12 Graúna class**

	Bldr.	L	In serv
P 40 Grajau	Arsenal de Marinha do Rio de Janeiro (AMRJ)	21-5-93	1-12-93
P 41 Guaiba	Arsenal de Marinha do Rio de Janeiro (AMRJ)	10-12-93	12-9-94
P 42 Graúna	Estaleiros Mauá, Niterói	10-11-93	14-8-94
P 43 Goiana	Estaleiros Mauá, Niterói	26-1-94	26-2-97
P 44 Guajará	Peenewerft, Wolgast, Germany	24-10-94	28-4-95
P 45 Guaporé	Peenewerft, Wolgast, Germany	25-1-95	29-8-95
P 46 Gurupá	Peenewerft, Wolgast, Germany	11-5-95	8-12-95
P 47 Gurupi	Peenewerft, Wolgast, Germany	6-9-95	23-4-96
P 48 Guanabara	INACE, Fortaleza, Ceará	5-11-97	9-7-99
P 49 Guarujá	INACE, Fortaleza, Ceará	5-98	30-11-99
P 50 Guaratuba	Peenewerft, Wolgast, Germany	16-6-99	1-12-99
P 51 Gravataí	Peenewerft, Wolgast, Germany	26-8-99	17-2-00

Guaporé (P 45) H&L Van Ginderen, 1-00

D: 213 tons light, 242 tons normal (263 fl)
S: 24.3 kts (22 sust.) **Dim:** 46.50 (42.50 pp) × 7.50 × 2.30
A: 1 40-mm 70-cal. Bofors 40L/70350 AA; 2 single 20-mm 90-cal. Oerlikon GAM-B01 AA

PATROL CRAFT [PC] *(continued)*

Gurupá (P 46) Ralph Edwards, 5-00

Electronics: Radar: 1 Decca 1290A nav.
M: 2 MTU 16V396 TB94 diesels; 2 props; 6,688 bhp (5,560 sust.)
Electric: 300 kw tot. (2 × 100-kw diesel sets, 1 × 100-kw shaft generator)
Range: 2,200/12 **Endurance:** 18 days
Fuel: 23.25 tons **Crew:** 4 officers, 25 enlisted

Remarks: The first two were ordered late 1987 to a design by Vosper QAF, Singapore, with actual work beginning late in 1988. The second pair was ordered in 9-90 and the third pair in 11-93. The fourth pair was ordered mid-1994 and paid for from profits from the state Petrobras oil company. P 48 and P 49 were laid down at INACE (Industria Naval do Ceará, S.A.) on 22-4-96. P 50 and P 51 were built with a construction loan from the German government for $30 million each.

The original contract with Estaleiros Mauá for P 42 and P 43 was canceled 8-92 due to slow progress, and the craft ordered there were fitted out at the Arsenal de Marinha. The craft have been renumbered to reflect the delivery sequence; P 42 and P 43 were originally to have been P 40 and P 41.
Hull systems: The displacement has also been reported variously as 242 tons full load and as 197 tons light and 217 tons full load.
Combat systems: Have a ten-person capacity rigid inflatable inspection boat on the stern, handled by a telescoping electrohydraulic crane. The 40-mm gunmounts on the German-built units employ Mauser mountings.

♦ 3 Roraima class

Bldr: MacLaren Estaleiros e Serviços Marítimos, S.A., Niterói

	L	In serv.		L	In serv.
P 30 Roraima	9-11-72	21-2-75	P 32 Amapá	9-3-73	1-76
P 31 Rondônia	10-1-73	3-12-75			

Roraima (P 30) Brazilian Navy

D: 340 tons (365 fl) **S:** 14.5 kts **Dim:** 46.30 × 8.45 × 1.37
A: 1 40-mm 70-cal. Bofors AA; 2 single 20-mm/90-cal. Oerlikon GAM-B01 AA; 4 single 12.7-mm mg; 2 single 81-mm/12.7-mm mortar/mg combination mountings; 2 single 7.62-mm mg
Electronics: Radar: 2 . . . nav.
M: 2 MEP-M.A.N. V6V16/18 TL diesels; 2 props; 1,824 bhp
Range: 6,000/11 **Crew:** 9 officers, 31 enlisted

Remarks: River gunboats operating in the Amazon Flotilla. Carry a single armed LCVP on fantail, handled by crane. The 40-mm mount has an armored gunhouse. The U.S.-design mortar/machinegun mounts are carried at the aft ends of the 02-level deckhouse, with the single machineguns being atop the pilothouse and at the aft end of the 01-level deckhouse. Both ships are to be re-engined for continued service.

♦ 6 Piratini class

Bldr: Arsenal de Marinha do Rio de Janeiro (AMRJ)

	In serv.
P 10 Piratini (ex-PGM 109)	30-11-70
P 11 Pirajá (ex-PGM 110)	3-71
P 12 Pampeiro (ex-PGM 118)	6-71
P 13 Parati (ex-PGM 119)	7-71
P 14 Penedo (ex-PGM 120)	9-71
P 15 Poti (ex-PGM 121)	10-71

D: 146 tons (fl) **S:** 18.0 kts **Dim:** 28.95 × 5.8 × 1.55
A: 1 20-mm 70-cal. Oerlikon Mk 10 AA; 2 single 12.7-mm mg; 1 81-mm mortar
Electronics: Radar: 1 Decca RM 1070A nav.

Pirajá (P 11) Hartmut Ehlers, 5-00

M: 4 Cummins VT-12M diesels; 2 props; 1,100 bhp
Electric: 40 kw **Range:** 1,000/15; 1,700/12
Crew: 2 officers, 15 enlisted

Remarks: The design is based on that of the U.S. Coast Guard 95-foot Cape class, and the craft were funded by the United States. Formerly used for coastal patrol, but in 1996, P 11 and P 15 were attached to the Mato Grosso Flotilla, followed by the others. All are now based at Ledário. A 20-mm mount has replaced the 12.7-mm/81-mm mortar formerly carried forward, and the mortar was moved to the stern. Have GPS receivers.

PATROL BOATS [PB]

♦ Up to 16 AVINPA-21 class

Bldr: ETN (Empresa Técnica Nacional, S.A.), Belém (In serv. . . .)

D: 40 tons light, 44.50 standard (48 fl) **S:** 41.8 kts (38 sust.)
Dim: 22.80 (20.00 wl) × 5.50 × 1.17 (0.90 hull)
A: . . .
Electronics: Radar: 1 . . . nav.
M: 2 MTU 12V396 TB93 diesels; 2 props; 3,560 bhp (2,960 sust.)
Electric: 64 kVA tot. **Range:** 700/20 **Fuel:** 7,500 liters
Endurance: 4 days **Crew:** 9 tot.

Remarks: Ordered 3-98 for riverine and coastal patrol; total program cost: $14.7 million. GRP construction. Design, based on that of the C.N. Baglietto, Varazze, Italy, *Meattini* class, was selected 1-98. Craft of similar design were built for the Italian Customs Service between 1972 and 1985 as the *Meattini* class and also for Algeria and the United Arab Emirates. Four of this class were to be assigned to the new Núcleos Especiais de Polícia Marítima (NEPOMS). The status of this program is uncertain.

♦ 144 LAEP-series riverine training and patrol launches

Bldr: Estleiro Itajaí, S.A. and Estaleiro Wilson Sons, Guarujá (In serv. 1995–98)

D: . . . tons **S:** . . . kts **Dim:** 7.0, 8.0, 10.0, or 11.0 × . . . × . . .
A: small arms **M:** 1 Volvo Penta outdrive diesel; 1 prop; 230 bhp

LAEP 07 Julio Montes, 2005

Remarks: LAEP stands for *Lancha de Apoio ao Ensino e Patrulha* (Instruction Support and Patrol Launch). The original series of 5 LAEP-10 and 15 LAEP-7 launches were ordered from Estaleiro Wilson Sons, Guarujá, on 16-10-96. Are outboard-powered launches in 7-m (LAEP-7), 8-m (LAEP-8), 10-m (LAEP-10), or 11-m (LAEP-11) length for riverine patrol and public assistance training. Five of the LAEP-10 variant are assigned to the new Núcleos Especiais de Polícia Marítima (NEPOMS).

♦ 6 Tracker-20-class patrol craft

Bldr: Estaleiro do Sul, Porto Alegre (In serv. LP 01–04: 5-91; others: 5-95)

LP 01 through LP 06

D: 39 tons (45 fl) **S:** 25 kts **Dim:** 20.90 (19.3 pp) × 5.18 × 1.55
A: 2 single 12.7-mm M2 mg **Electronics:** Radar: 1 Decca RM 1070A nav.
M: 2 MTU 8V396 TB83 diesels; 2 props; 2,000 bhp
Electric: 40 kw (2 × 20 kw) **Range:** 450/15
Fuel: 4.66 tons **Endurance:** 5 days **Crew:** 2 officers, 6 enlisted

PATROL BOATS [PB] *(continued)*

LP 05 Hartmut Ehlers, 4-00

Remarks: Construction was licensed from Fairey Marine, Cowes, U.K., in 4-87. The builder is also known as "Ebin So." First unit delivered 22-2-90, but the class was not formally commissioned until all were completed. Have molded GRP hulls. All are assigned to the Port Captain service.

♦ **10 U.S. Swift Mk II patrol craft**
Bldr: R 61–64: Swiftships, Morgan City, La.; others: DM-Comercio, Importação e Manutenção de Productos Nauticos

R 61 through R 64 and R 71 through R 76

D: 22.5 tons (fl) **S:** 22 kts **Dim:** 15.66 × 4.55 × 1.1
A: 1 12.7-mm mg **Electronics:** Radar: 1 . . . nav.
M: 2 G.M. Detroit 12V71 TI diesels; 2 props; 850 bhp
Electric: 6 kw **Range:** 400/22 **Crew:** 6 tot.

Remarks: Employed by naval police and Port Captain service. Six were ordered 16-1-81 in Brazil. Four earlier units were built in the U.S. and were transferred in 1972–73. Port Captain–subordinated units bear names and hull numbers in the 5000 series.

MINE WARFARE SHIPS

♦ **6 German Schütze-class patrol minesweepers [MSC]**
Bldr: Abeking and Rasmussen, Lemwerder, Germany

	L	In serv.		L	In serv.
M 15 Aratú	27-5-70	5-5-71	M 18 Araçatuba	1971	13-12-72
M 16 Anhatomirim	4-11-70	30-11-71	M 19 Abrolhos	7-5-74	16-4-75
M 17 Atalaia	14-4-71	13-12-72	M 20 Albardão	9-74	21-7-75

Aratú (M 15) Brazilian Navy, 1996

D: 253 tons (280 fl) **S:** 24 kts **Dim:** 47.44 × 7.16 × 2.4
A: 1 40-mm 70-cal. Bofors AA **Electronics:** Radar: 1 . . . nav.
M: 4 Maybach diesels; 2 Escher-Wyss vertical cycloidal props; 4,500 bhp
Electric: 120 kw tot. plus 340-kw sweep generator
Range: 710/20 **Fuel:** 22 tons **Crew:** 32 total

Remarks: Four ordered 4-69, two 11-73. Fitted for magnetic, mechanical, and acoustic minesweeping. Wooden hulls.

AMPHIBIOUS WARFARE SHIPS

Note: Brazil plans to acquire two new amphibious ships, of an as yet undecided class, as eventual replacements for the ex-U.S. *Thomaston* class remaining in service.

♦ **2 U.S. Thomaston-class dock landing ships [LSD]**
Bldr: Ingalls Shipbuilders, Pascagoula, Miss.

	Laid down	L	In serv.
G 30 Ceará (ex-*Hermitage,* LSD 34)	11-4-55	12-6-56	14-12-58
G 31 Rio de Janeiro (ex-*Alamo,* LSD 33)	11-10-54	20-1-56	24-8-56

Rio de Janeiro (G 31) Hartmut Ehlers, 4-00

D: 6,880 tons light (12,150 fl) **S:** 22.5 kts **Dim:** 155.45 × 25.60 × 5.40 (5.80 max.)
A: 3 twin 76.2-mm 50-cal. Mk 33 DP
Electronics: Radar: 1 CRP-3100 nav.; 1 SPS-10 surf. search
M: 2 sets G.E. geared steam turbines; 2 props; 24,000 shp
Boilers: 2 Babcock & Wilcox, 40.8 kg/cm^2 pressure
Range: 5,300/22.5; 10,000/20; 13,000/10 **Fuel:** 1,390 tons
Crew: 20 officers, 325 enlisted + troops

Remarks: G 30 was acquired upon decommissioning from U.S. Navy on 2-10-89. G 31 was decommissioned from the U.S. Navy on 30-9-90 and recommissioned 18-1-91 in Brazilian service. Both had been on lease until permanently transferred on 24-1-01.
Hull systems: Can carry 3 LCU or 18 LCM(6) or 6 LCM(8) in 119.2 × 14.6-m well deck, with 975 m^2 of vehicle parking space forward of the docking well. Carry 2 LCVPs, 2 LCPLs in davits. Maximum cargo capacity: 7,400 tons. Have two 50-ton cranes and a helicopter deck.
Combat systems: Two Mk 56 and two Mk 63 radar gun director systems were removed in 1977, leaving the gunmounts with local control only. The obsolete SPS-6 air-search radar was deleted after transfer.

♦ **1 ex-U.S. Newport-class tank landing ship [LST]**
Bldr: National Steel Shipbuilding, San Diego, Calif.

	Laid down	L	In serv.
G 28 Mattoso Maia (ex-*Cayuga,* LST 1186)	28-9-68	12-7-69	8-8-70

Mattoso Maia (G 28) Ralph Edwards, 4-00

D: 4,975 tons light (8,576 fl) **S:** 22 kts (20 sust.)
Dim: 159.2 (171.3 over horns) × 21.18 × 5.3 (aft) × 1.80 (fwd)
A: 1 20-mm Mk 15 Phalanx gatling CIWS; 4 single 12.7-mm mg
Electronics:
Radar: 1 Raytheon SPS-64(V)9 nav.; 1 Raytheon SPS-10F surf. search
M: 6 Alco 16-251 diesels; 2 CP props; 16,500 bhp
Range: 14,250/14 **Fuel:** 1,750 tons
Crew: 257 tot. + 500 troops (+ 72 emergency accommodations)

Remarks: G 28 was transferred 26-8-94 on five-year lease with option to purchase, arriving 10-94 at Rio de Janeiro; permanently transferred 24-1-01.
Hull systems: Can transport 2,000 tons cargo or, for beaching, 500 tons of cargo on 1,765 m^2 of deck space. A side-thruster propeller forward helps when marrying to a causeway. There is a 34-m-long, 75-ton-capacity mobile aluminum ramp forward, which is linked to the tank deck by a second from the upper deck. Aft are a 242-m^2 helicopter platform and a stern door for loading and unloading vehicles. Four pontoon causeway sections can be carried on the hull sides. The tank deck, which has a 75-ton-capacity turntable at both ends, can carry 23 AAV-7A1 armored personnel carriers or 29 M 48 tanks or 41 2.5-ton trucks, while the upper deck can accept 29 2.5-ton trucks. Normally carries three LCVP and one LCP in davits. Has two 10-ton cranes. Carries 141,600 gallons vehicle fuel.
Combat systems: Two Mk 63 radar gun fire-control systems were removed during 1977–78 and the two twin 76.2-mm gunmounts in 1993–94. May still carry Canadian Marconi LN-66 navigational radar in lieu of SPS-64(V)9.

Disposal note: U.S. *DeSoto County*–class landing ship *Duque de Caxias* (G 26, ex-*Grant County,* LST 1174) was retired on 17-2-00.

Note: The three U.S. LCU 1610–class utility craft *Guarapari* (L 10), *Tambaú* (L 11), and *Camboriú* (L 12) were decommissioned during 1991 and reassigned to local naval districts as logistics support craft.

♦ **5 GED 801–class landing craft [LCM]**
Bldr: GED-801: Arsenal de Marinha do Rio de Janeiro (AMRJ); others: INACE, Fortaleza, Ceará (In serv. 9-12-94)

GED 801 through GED 805

D: 61 tons (130 fl) **S:** 12 kts (light) **Dim:** 21.65 × 6.58 × 1.10 aft (light)
M: 2 G.M. Detroit Diesel 12V71-series diesels; 2 props; 800 bhp (590 sust.)
Range: 190/12 (light) **Crew:** 5 tot.

Remarks: Design based on that of the U.S. LCM(8) class, for which plans were acquired in 1991. Brazilian type designation is EDVM. Completion date for first unit unknown; others all delivered 1994. Are assigned to the *Grupamento de Embarcações de Desembarque.* Cargo: 72 tons or 150 fully equipped troops in open tank deck, 56 m^2.

AMPHIBIOUS WARFARE SHIPS *(continued)*

GED 802—alongside sisters 801, 803, 804, and 805 Ralph Edwards, 5-00

♦ **3 LCM(6)-class landing craft [LCM]**
Bldr: . . . , Brazil

GED 301 through GED 303

D: 24 tons (56 fl) **S:** 10 kts **Dim:** 17.07 × 4.37 × 1.17 (aft)
M: 2 G.M. Detroit Diesel 6-71 diesels; 2 props; 330 bhp
Range: 130/10 **Crew:** 3 tot. + 80 troops for short distances

Remarks: Can carry 29 tons cargo.

♦ **30 EDVP-class landing craft [LCVP]**
Bldr: . . . , Japan (in serv. 1959–60) and . . . , Brazil (in serv. 1971)

EDVP 501 through EDVP 530

D: 13 tons (fl) **S:** 9 kts **Dim:** 10.90 × 3.21 × 1.04 (aft)
M: 1 Yanmar diesel; 1 prop; 180 bhp **Range:** 110/9 **Crew:** 3 tot. + 36 troops

Remarks: EDVP 501–521 are a wooden construction version of the standard U.S. Navy LCVP design; others, built in 1971 in Brazil, have GRP hulls and are powered by a 153-bhp Saab Scania diesel. Can carry 36 troops or 3.5 tons cargo in 5.24 × 2.29-m cargo space with 2.0-m-wide access through the bow ramp. Eight (armed with two single 12.7-mm mg each) are carried by Amazon Flotilla gunboats, and eight, supported by the tug/transport *Leverger,* are assigned to the Mato Grosso Flotilla.

♦ **28 U.S. AAV-7-series amphibious armored personnel carriers**
Bldr: United Defense LP, San Jose, Calif. (new units)

D: 18.25 tons light (23.64 loaded) **S:** 30 mph land/7 kts water
Dim: 7.9 × 3.3 × . . . (1.83 draft, loaded)
A: 1 12.7-mm M85 mg
M: 1 G.M. Detroit Diesel 8V53T diesel; 2 tracks/waterjets; 400 bhp
Range: 300 miles/25 mph (land) **Crew:** 2 + 25 troops

Remarks: Employed by the Brazilian Marine Corps. Originally typed the LVTP-7. First prototype for U.S. Marine Corps was completed in 1967, and the vehicle entered production in 1971. Weights apply to troop version; command and recovery variants weigh slightly less. Two updated AAVP-7-A1 troop carrier versions were purchased from the U.S. in 8-92, and 14 new units (12 AAV-7A1 troop carriers, one AAVC-7A1 command vehicle, and one AAVR-7A1 recovery vehicle) were ordered 1996 and delivered 1-97. Have aluminum armor to hulls: up to 44 mm on sides, 30 mm on top and bottom, and 35 mm across stern. The cargo compartment is 4.26 m long by 1.82 m wide and 1.68 m high.

AUXILIARIES

♦ **1 target service vessel, former oilfield supply tug [AG]**
Bldr: J. G. Hitzler, Lauemburg, Germany (L: 1968)

R 26 Trinidade (ex-*Nobistor*)

Trinidade (R 26)—with former pennant number Don S. Montgomery, USN, 10-90

D: 1,308 (fl) **S:** 12.5 kts **Dim:** 53.67 × 11.00 × 3.55
A: 2 single 12.7-mm mg **Electronics:** Radar: 1 Furuno 1830 nav.
M: 2 MWM diesels; 2 props; 2,740 bhp
Range: 8,700/12.5 **Endurance:** 37 days **Crew:** 2 officers, 20 enlisted

Remarks: 1,308 grt/499 dwt. Former Panamanian-registry oilfield supply tug seized during 1987 for smuggling and converted for naval use at Rio de Janeiro Naval Arsenal, commissioned 31-1-90. Equipped with NAVSAT receiver. Used for target towing and recovering aerial targets. Originally wore pennant number R 26, then U 16; changed again spring 2001.

♦ **1 ex-U.K. River-class navigational aids tender [AGL]**
Bldr: Richards, Great Yarmouth

	Laid down	L	In serv.
H 37 Garnier Sampaio (ex-*Helmsdale,* M 2010)	21-5-84	11-1-85	6-6-85

D: 630 tons (890 fl) **S:** 14 kts
Dim: 47.60 (42.00 pp) × 10.50 × 3.10 (3.75 max.) **A:** removed
Electronics: Radar: 2 Decca TM 1226C nav.
M: 2 Ruston 6 RKCM diesels; 2 4-bladed CP props; 3,040 bhp
Electric: 460 kw tot. **Range:** 4,500/10 **Fuel:** 88 tons
Crew: 7 officers, 7 petty officers, 16 other enlisted

Remarks: 638 grt. Former minesweeper, purchased 11-94 and transferred 2-95. Began conversion as a navigational buoy tender and training ship at the Arsenal de Marinha do Rio de Janeiro (AMRJ), with the work then completed at Estaleiro de Ilha, S.A. (EISA), Itajaí, early in 1997. Painted white, with orange stacks and mast.
Hull systems: Steel hull built to commercial standards, following the design of a North Sea oilfield supply vessel. Navigation gear includes two Kelvin-Hughes MS 48 echo sounders, Decca QM 14(1) and Decca HiFix Mk 6 radio navaids, and a NAVSAT receiver. Modifications in Brazil include installation of an A-frame gallows crane at the stern, a 10-ton buoy crane amidships, and air-conditioning equipment.

♦ **1 lighthouse and buoy tender [AGL]**
Bldr: Ebin S.A. Indústria Naval, Niterói

	L	In serv.
H 34 Almirante Graça Aranha	23-6-74	9-9-76

Almirante Graça Aranha (H 34) Julio Montes, 2005

Almirante Graça Aranha (H 34) Ralph Edwards, 5-00

D: 1,343 tons (2,390 fl) **S:** 13 kts **Dim:** 75.57 × 13.0 × 3.71
A: None **Electronics:** Radar: 2 Decca . . . nav.
M: Diesel; 1 CP prop; 2,000 bhp—1 bow-thruster
Crew: 13 officers, 82 enlisted (accomm.)

Remarks: Has a telescoping hangar for one Bell 206 JetRanger (UH-11) helicopter. Two LCVPs are carried as supply lighters. Has one electrohydraulic buoy-handling crane. Painted white, with red-orange stack and mast.

Disposal note: Icebreaker/research ship [AGL] *Barão de Teffé* (H 42) was stricken on 23-7-02.

♦ **1 icebreaker/research ship [AGOR]**
Bldr: G. Eides Sonner A/S, Hoylandsbygd, Norway (In serv. 22-01-81)

H 44 Ary Rongel (ex-*Polar Queen*)

AUXILIARIES *(continued)*

Ary Rongel (H 44)—with two Esquilo helicopters on deck aft Brazilian Navy, 1995

D: 3,670 tons (fl) **S:** 14.5 kts (12 sust.) **Dim:** 75.32 × 13.06 × 6.20 (max.)
A: None **Electronics:** Radar: 1 . . . nav.; 2 . . . nav.
M: 2 Krupp-MaK 6M453Ak diesels, 1 CP prop; 4,500 bhp—bow- and stern-thrusters
Electric: 1,720 kw tot (1 × 1,320-kw, 2 × 200-kw diesel sets)
Range: 19,500/14 **Fuel:** 790 tons **Endurance:** 60 days
Crew: 12 officers, 39 enlisted + 22 scientific party

Remarks: 1,982 grt. Former research and seal-survey ship purchased from Rieber Shipping A/S, Bergen, for $15.9 million in 3-94. Operated for the Brazilian Antarctic Program (PROANTAR) to support Brazil's *Comandante Ferraz* Antarctic station on King George Island in the South Shetland Archipelago. Hull painted red, superstructure white, masts and stack cream.
Hull systems: Has side loading doors, one 6-ton crane, one 25-ton derrick, and an A-frame gallows crane at the stern. Has 1,097 m^3 refrigerated cargo space, two holds (each with an 18.7-m-long by 5.0-m-wide hatch). Helicopter flight deck and open deck stowage for one Esquilo-I helicopter. Has Inmarsat SATCOM terminal.

Disposal note: *Almirante Camara* (H 41, ex-USNS *Sands,* TAGOR-6) was stricken by the Brazilian Navy in 2004.

♦ 2 ex-U.K. River-class survey ships [AGS]
Bldr: Richards Shipbuilders Ltd., Lowestoft

	Laid down	L	In serv.
H 35 Amorim do Valle (ex-*Humber,* M 2007)	21-10-83	17-5-84	7-6-85
H 36 Taurus (ex-*Jorge Leite,* ex-*Ribble,* M 2012)	17-9-84	7-5-86	28-6-86

Amorim do Valle (H 35) Brazilian Navy, 1996

D: 630 tons (890 fl) **S:** 14 kts (15 on trials; 12 sust.)
Dim: 47.60 (42.00 pp) × 10.50 × 3.10 (3.75 max.) **A:** removed
Electronics: Radar: 2 Decca TM 1226 nav.
M: 2 Ruston 6 RKCM diesels; 2 4-bladed CP props; 3,040 bhp
Electric: 460 kw tot. **Range:** 4,500/10 **Fuel:** 88 tons
Crew: 7 officers, 7 petty officers, 16 other enlisted

Remarks: 638 grt. Former minesweepers, purchased 11-94 and transferred 2-95. H 36 was originally converted as a navigational aids tender and was modified again in 2000 and renamed. Are painted white, with orange stacks and masts. Steel hull, built to commercial single-compartment damage standards.

♦ 1 oceanographic research ship [AGOR]
Bldr: Mjellem & Karlsen A/S, Bergen (In serv. 1984)

H 40 Antares (ex-*Lady Hamilton*)

D: 855 tons light (1,076 fl) **S:** 13.5 kts **Dim:** 55.0 × 10.3 × 4.3
Electronics: Radar: 2 Decca . . . nav.
M: 1 Burmeister & Wain Alpha diesel; 1 CP prop; 1,860 bhp—bow thruster
Range: 10,000/12 **Crew:** 11 officers, 38 enlisted

Remarks: Acquired from Racal Energy Resources and commissioned 6-6-88. Painted white with red-orange upperworks. Has small helicopter platform at stern.

Antares (H 40) Hartmut Ehlers, 4-00

♦ 1 Sirius class [AGS]
Bldr: Ishikawajima-Harima Heavy Industries, Tokyo

	Laid down	L	In serv.
H 21 Sirius	12-56	30-7-57	1-1-58

Sirius (H 21) H&L Van Ginderen, 5-95

D: 1,463 tons (1,900 fl) **S:** 15 kts **Dim:** 77.90 × 12.03 × 3.70
Electronics: Radar: 2 . . . nav.
M: 2 Sulzer 7T6-36 diesels; 2 CP props; 2,700 bhp
Range: 12,000/11 **Fuel:** 343 tons **Crew:** 102 tot. + 14 scientific party

Remarks: Carries 1 SAH-11 or Esquilo helicopter, 1 LCVP, and 3 small survey craft. Sister *Canopus* (H 22) was stricken on 7-1-97.

Disposal notes: Of the *Argus*-class survey ships, *Taurus* (H 33) was stricken on 26-2-96, *Orion* (H 32) on 1-2-01, and *Argus* (H 31) in 2005.

♦ 1 logistic support cargo ship [AK]
Bldr: Ishikawajima do Brasil, Rio de Janeiro (In serv. 1986)

G 40 Atlantico Sul (ex-*Lloyd Atlantico*)

D: Approx. 39,000 tons (fl) **S:** 19 kts **Dim:** 188.02 (178.01 pp) × 30.71 × 11.02
A: None **Electronics:** Radar: 1 . . . nav.
M: 1 Ishikawajima do Brasil-Sulzer 6RTA76 diesel; 1 prop; 16,560 bhp
Electric: 4,700 kw tot. (1 × 1,400-kw and 3 × 1,100-kw diesel sets)
Range: . . . / . . . **Crew:** . . .

Remarks: 22,201 grt/28,977 dwt. Former container ship purchased 2001 from Companhia de Navegação Lloyd Brasileiro (Lloydbras) for conversion by AMRJ for use as a logistics support vessel. Has four holds, equipped with fixed cell guides, and is of 1,210-TEU container capacity. Is equipped with two 35-ton and one 22-ton cranes and can provide power to up to 308 20-ft.-equivalent refrigerated cargo containers.

♦ 1 cargo ship [AK]
Bldr: Maclaren IC Estaleiros e Servicos S.A. Niteroi (yard No. 149), Brazil (In serv. 1982)

U 15 Para

D: 1,050 tons (fl) **S:** 9.8 kts **Dim:** 56.11 × 21.42 (molded) × 5.01
M: 2 Daihatsu type 6PSHTCM-22 diesels; 2 props; 1,050 shp
Electric: 292 kW (2 × 146 kW) **Range:** . . .
Crew: 66 tot. (7 officers, 59 enlisted) + 175 troops

Remarks: 695 grt/1,982 dwt. General passenger/cargo ship type purchased from Empresa de Navegacao de Amazonia S.A. (ENASA), Belem, Brazil, in 12-04. Commissioned into the Brazilian Navy on 19-01-05. Cargo capacity is 1,250 tons. Used for logistics support and carrying troops in Brazil's many rivers.

AUXILIARIES *(continued)*

♦ 1 replenishment oiler [AO]
Bldr: Ishikawajima do Brasil, Rio de Janeiro

	Laid down	L	In serv.
G 27 Marajó	13-12-66	31-1-68	22-10-68

Marajó (G 27) Hartmut Ehlers, 4-00

D: 16,000 tons (fl) **S:** 13.6 kts **Dim:** 137.10 (127.69 pp) × 19.22 × 7.35
A: None **Electronics:** Radar: 2 . . . nav.
M: 1 Sulzer GRD 68 diesel; 1 prop; 8,000 bhp
Electric: 1,200 kw tot. **Range:** 9,200/ . . . **Fuel:** 700 tons
Crew: 80 tot.

Remarks: 6,600 grt/11,119 dwt. Was to have been retired on completion of *Almirante Gastão Motta* but was refitted for further service; as of 2000 was planned for imminent retirement. Cargo capacity: 7,200 tons liquid. Has two liquid replenishment stations per side. Handicapped by low speed and unreliable engine.

♦ 1 replenishment oiler [AOR]
Bldr: Ishikawajima do Brasil, Rio de Janeiro

	Laid down	L	In serv.
G 23 Almirante Gastão Motta	11-12-89	1-6-90	26-11-91

Almirante Gastão Motta (G 23) French Navy, 4-97

D: 9,328 tons (fl) **S:** 20.5 kts **Dim:** 135.00 (128.00 pp) × 19.00 × 7.50
A: 2 single 12.7-mm mg **Electronics:** Radar: 2 Decca . . . nav.
M: 2 Wärtsilä Vasa 12V32 diesels; 1 CP prop; 11,700 bhp
Electric: 3,600 kw (2 × 900-kw shaft generators; 3 × 600-kw alternators, 3 Ishibras-Wärtsilä 4-R22 diesels driving)
Range: 10,000/15 **Fuel:** 600 tons
Crew: 13 officers, 108 enlisted + 12 spare berths

Remarks: 6,000 dwt. Ordered 15-12-87. Replaced the uncompleted conversion of the former Lloyd Brasileiro Steamship Co. tanker *Itatinga* (also to have been named *Almirante Gastão Motta,* G 29; sold 1987) as a replacement for *Marajó* (G 27), which was to have been stricken at the end of 1991 but remains in service.
Hull systems: Cargo fuel capacity: 5,000 tons; also carries 200 tons dry stores. Has a single replenishment station each side amidships and no astern refueling capability. No helicopter facilities.

♦ 1 Custódio de Mello–class transport [AP]
Bldr: Ishikawajima Jukogyo, Tokyo

	Laid down	L	In serv.
G 21 Ary Parreiras	12-55	24-8-56	29-12-56

D: 6,520 tons (7,433 fl) **S:** 15 kts **Dim:** 119.44 (110.34 pp) × 16.06 × 6.25
A: 2 single 76.2-mm 50-cal. U.S. Mk 26 DP; 2 single 20-mm 70-cal. Mk 10 Oerlikon AA
Electronics: Radar: 2 . . . nav.
M: 2 sets double-reduction geared steam turbines; 2 props; 4,800 shp
Boilers: 2 Foster-Wheeler 2-drum water-tube; 350° C **Fuel:** 861 tons
Crew: 127 tot. + up to 1,972 troops (497 normal)

Remarks: 4,874 grt/4,125 dwt. Is occasionally used in commercial service under the management of TRANSPOMAR (Comando da Força de Transporte da Marinha).
Hull systems: Has 425-m^3 refrigerated cargo space and can carry about 4,000 tons general cargo in three holds. Living spaces mechanically ventilated and partially air-conditioned. Has a helicopter platform aft.
Disposals: *Barroso Pereira* (G 16) was stricken on 3-4-95; *Soares Dutra* (G 22) on 26-6-01; and *Custódio de Mello* (G 20, ex-U 26) on 8-10-02.

♦ 1 submarine rescue and general salvage ship [ASR]
Bldr: Stord Vaerft A/S, Stord, Norway (In serv. 1979)

K 11 Felinto Perry (ex-*Holger Dane,* ex-*Wildrake*)

Felinto Perry (K 11) Hartmut Ehlers, 12-97

D: Approx 4,000 fl **S:** 14.5 kts **Dim:** 77.78 × 17.48 × 4.66
A: None **Electronics:** Radar: 2 Raytheon . . . nav.
M: 2 Bergen Mek. Verksteder KVGB 12 diesels (4,880 bhp tot.); 2 Bergen Mek. Verksteder KVGB 16 diesels (6,520 bhp tot.); 2 Daimler-Benz OM414 diesels (910 hp); 2 × 1,712-kw generators, electric drive; 2 CP props; 7,000 shp; 4 550-shp side-thrusters
Electric: 6,160 kw (2 × 2,280 kw, 2 × 300 kw) **Crew:** 9 officers, 56 enlisted

Remarks: 1,769 grt/496 dwt. Former North Sea oilfield rescue ship purchased 11-88 from Rederiet H. H. Faddersbjll A/S for use as a submarine rescue and general salvage ship as replacement for the U.S. *Penguin*-class submarine rescue ship *Gastão Moutinho* (K 10).
Hull systems: Very well equipped for salvage and firefighting duties. Has a 19.0-m octagonal helicopter deck mounted above the pilothouse. Equipped with centerline moonpool and capable of conducting saturation diving to 300 m. Has an 8-man pressurized divers' lifeboat. Working deck is 238 m^2. Has one 30-ton, one 7-ton, and two 3-ton electrohydraulic cranes. Equipped with Kongsberg AOP 503 Mk II dynamic positioning system and has 4-point mooring system. Three water and two foam fire monitors, with 200-m water/60-m foam range. Submarine rescue and salvage equipment is transported in a portable module.

♦ 3 Tritão-class oceangoing tugs [ATA]
Bldr: ESTANAVE, Manaus

	In serv.
R 21 Tritão (ex-*Sarandi*)	23-7-86
R 22 Tridente (ex-*Sambaiba*)	19-2-87
R 23 Triunfo (ex-*Sorocaba*)	8-10-87

Triunfo (R 23) Yvan Gomel via Paolo Marsan, 10-03

D: 1,680 fl **S:** 15 kts **Dim:** 55.4 × 11.61 × 3.35
A: 2 single 20-mm 70-cal. Mk 10 Oerlikon AA
Electronics: Radar: 2 . . . nav.
M: 2 Burmeister & Wain Alpha diesels; 2 props; 2,480 bhp—bow-thruster
Endurance: 45 days **Crew:** 49 tot.

Remarks: Begun as oilfield supply tugs for Petrobras but purchased 5-86 while still under construction. Intended for 200-n.m. economic zone patrol and SAR duties. Have bow-thrusters and are capable of 23.5-ton bollard pull for ocean towing.

♦ 2 Almirante Guilhem–class oceangoing tugs [ATA]
Bldr: Sumitomo Heavy Industries, Japan (Both L: 1976)

R 24 Almirante Guilhem (ex-*Superpesa 4*)
R 25 Almirante Guillobel (ex-*Superpesa 5*)

Almirante Guillobel (R 25) Julio Montes, 2005

AUXILIARIES *(continued)*

D: 2,400 tons (fl) **S:** 14 kts **Dim:** 63.15 × 13.40 × 4.50
A: 2 single 20-mm 70-cal. Mk 10 Oerlikon AA
Electronics: Radar: 2 Decca . . . nav.
M: 2 G.M. 20-645 ET diesels; 2 CP props; 7,200 bhp—525-shp bow-thruster
Electric: 550 kw **Fuel:** 670 tons **Crew:** 40 tot.

Remarks: Former oilfield supply tugs purchased 1980 from Superpesa Maritime Transport, Ltd., and commissioned 22-1-81. Have 84-ton bollard pull.

♦ 1 Stad Amsterdam–class sail training ship [AXT]
Bldr: Damen SY, Gorinchem, and Nista BV, Amsterdam, the Netherlands

	L	In serv.
U 20 Cisne Branco	4-8-99	12-99

Cisne Branco (U 20) Bernard Prezélin, 7-05

D: 1,038 tons (fl) **S:** 17 kts (under sail; 11 kts on engine)
Dim: 76.0 × 10.50 × 4.80 max. **A:** 2 47-mm saluting cannons
M: 1 Caterpillar 3508 DITA SCAC diesel; 1 prop; 1,060 bhp—2,195 m^2 max. sail area—300-kw bow-thruster
Electric: 506 kVA tot. (2 × 200-kVA, 1 × 106-kVA diesel sets)
Crew: 8 officers, 14 enlisted, 30 cadets

Remarks: Ordered 9-98 for completion by 1-1-00 to permit participating in a race from Lisbon to Rio de Janeiro to commemorate 500th anniversary of the discovery of Brazil. Three-masted, full-rigged ship with design based on late 19th-century Dutch ship *Amsterdam.* Hull has 6.45-m molded depth.

♦ 1 cadet training ship, modified Mk 10 frigate design [AXT]
Bldr: Arsenal de Marinha do Rio de Janeiro (AMRJ)

	Laid down	L	In serv.
U 27 Brasil	18-9-81	23-9-83	21-8-86

Brasil (U 27) Michael Nitz, 9-05

D: 3,729 fl **S:** 18 kts (15 sust.)
Dim: 131.25 × 13.52 × 4.21 (mean, fl)
A: 2 single 40-mm 70-cal. Bofors L70 AA; 4 single 3-pdr. saluting cannon
Electronics: Radar: 2 Decca . . . nav.
M: 2 Ishikawajima Brasil–Pielstick 6 PC. 2 L400 diesels; 2 props; 7,800 bhp
Range: 7,000/15 **Endurance:** 30 days
Crew: 28 officers, 190 enlisted + 204 cadets

Remarks: Uses hull of the Mk 10 frigate design, but has less powerful propulsion plant and far simpler weapons and electronics. Replaced transport *Custódio de Mello* (G 20, then U 26) for training cadets from naval and merchant marine academies.
Hull systems: Has a command center with three remote training command spaces, navigational training compartment for 40 trainees, and two other classrooms.
Combat systems: A planned 76-mm OTOMelara Compact mount forward was not installed, nor was the planned helicopter hangar, although the helicopter platform can accommodate one Sea King helicopter. There is a single remote optical director for the two 40-mm gunmounts. Has two commercial SATCOM systems.

YARD AND SERVICE CRAFT

Note: Small units without pennant numbers are assigned local dockyard numbers; craft attached to Rio de Janeiro have BNRJ-series numbers.

Disposal note: Fisheries research oceanographic vessel *Suboficial Olivera* (U 15) was no longer in service as of 2005.

♦ 1 lightship [YAG]
Bldr: Ebin S.A. Indústria Naval, Niterói (In serv. 31-4-91)

Risca do Zumbi

D: 150 tons (fl) **Dim:** 20.0 × 8.0 × 1.5

Remarks: Anchored 12 n.m. off Rio Grande do Norte. Powered by solar panels.

♦ 6 munitions lighters [YE]

	In serv.		In serv.
São Francisco dos Santos	1964	Miguel dos Santos	1968
Ubirajara dos Santos	1968	Aprendiz Lédio Conceição	1968
Operario Luis Leal	1968	U 30 Almirante Hess	27-10-83

D: 88.2 tons (fl) **S:** 13.5 kts **Dim:** 23.6 × 6.0 × 2.0 **M:** . . .

Remarks: Last three transport torpedoes; the others projectiles only. Only U 30 has a pennant number.

♦ 1 personnel and stores transport [YF]
Bldr: Empresa Brasileira de Construção (Ebrasa), Itajaí, Santa Catarina (L: 29-8-74)

Sargento Borges (ex-R 47)

D: 108.5 tons (fl) **S:** 10 kts **Dim:** 28.0 × 6.5 × 1.5
M: 2 diesels; 2 props; 480 bhp
Range: 400/10 **Crew:** 10 tot. + 106 passengers

Note: Also in service, with the Mato Grosso Flotilla, is the tug/transport *Leverger;* no data available.

♦ 4 Rio Pardo–class harbor passenger ferries [YFB]
Bldr: Inconav Niterói Shipbuilders (In serv. 1975–76)

BNRJ 06 Rio Pardo (ex-U 40)	BNRJ 09 Rio Chui (ex-R 42)
BNRJ 07 Rio Negro (ex-R 41)	BNRJ 08 Rio Oiapoque (ex-R 43)

Rio Chui (BNRJ 09)—with Rio Negro (BNRJ 07) in the background
Ralph Edwards, 5-00

D: 150 tons **S:** 14 kts **Dim:** 35.38 × 6.5 × 1.9
M: 2 diesels; 2 props; 1,096 bhp **Crew:** . . . tot. + 400 passengers

♦ 6 Rio Doce–class harbor ferries [YFB]
Bldr: G. deVries Leutsch, Amsterdam

	In serv.		In serv.
Rio Doce (ex-U 20)	12-5-54	Rio Real (ex-U 23)	1955
Rio das Contas (ex-U 21)	15-9-54	Rio Turvo (ex-U 24)	16-12-54
Rio Formoso (ex-U 22)	10-54	Rio Verde (ex-U 25)	12-8-54

D: 150 tons (200 fl) **S:** 14 kts **Dim:** 36.6 × 6.5 × 2.1
M: 2 Sulzer diesels; 2 props; 450 bhp
Range: 700/14 **Crew:** 10 tot. + 600 passengers

♦ 1 river transport [YFB]
Bldr: Estaleiro SNBP, Mato Grosso (In serv. 1982)

U 29 Piraim

D: 73.3 tons (91.5 fl) **S:** 7 kts **Dim:** 25.0 × 5.5 × 0.91
A: 4 single 7.62-mm mg **Electronics:** Radar: 1 Furuno 3600 nav.
M: 2 MWM diesels; 2 props; 400 bhp **Electric:** 60 kVA tot.
Range: 700/7 **Crew:** 2 officers, 13 enlisted, 2 civilian pilots

YARD AND SERVICE CRAFT *(continued)*

Piraim (U 29) Hartmut Ehlers, 5-00

Remarks: Assigned to the Mato Grosso Flotilla. Can transport two marine platoons.

♦ 1 river transport [YFB]
Bldr: Amsterdam Droogdok, the Netherlands (In serv. 1951)

G 15 Paraguassu (ex-*Garapuava*)

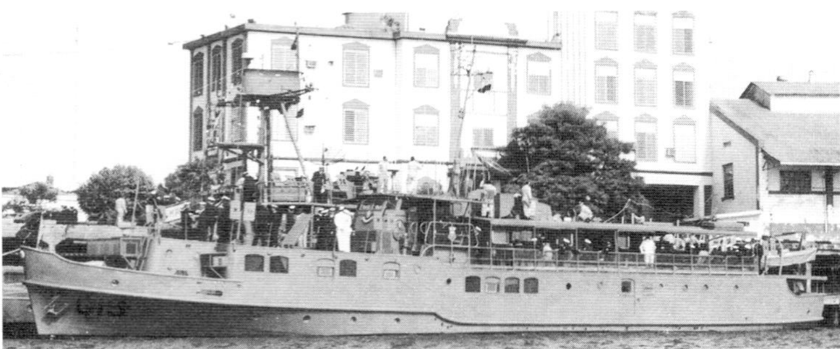
Paraguassu (G 15) Hartmut Ehlers, 5-00

D: 200 tons (285 fl) **S:** 12 kts **Dim:** 40.00 × 7.00 × 1.55
A: 6 single 7.62-mm mg **Electronics:** Radar: 1 Furuno 3600 nav.
M: 3 diesels; 1 prop; 1,500 bhp
Range: 2,000/10 **Crew:** 4 officers, 31 enlisted + 178 marines

Remarks: Former commercial river passenger vessel converted for troop use and commissioned on 20-6-72. Operates in the Mato Grosso Flotilla and is based at Ladário.

♦ 1 U.S. AFDL 34–class floating drydock [YFDL]
Bldr: V. P. Loftis (In serv. 10-44)

G 27 Cidade de Natal (ex-U.S. AFDL 39)

Lift capacity: 2,800 tons **Dim:** 118.6 × 25.6 × 2.84 (light)

Remarks: Loaned 10-11-66; purchased 28-12-77. Concrete construction. 17.7-m clear width inside, 105.2-m length on blocks.

♦ 1 U.S. AFDL 1–class small floating dry dock [YFDL]
Bldr: Chicago Bridge & Iron (In serv. 12-43)

G 26 Almirante Jeronimo Gonçalves (ex-*Goiaz,* ex-AFDL 4)

Lift capacity: 1,000 tons **Dim:** 60.96 × 19.51 × 1.04 (light)

Remarks: Loaned 10-11-66; purchased 28-7-77. Steel construction. 13.7-m clear width inside, 56.4-m length on blocks. Transferred from Belem to Rio Negro during 2002.

♦ 1 U.S. ARD 12–class floating drydock [YFDL]
Bldr: Pacific Bridge, Alameda, Calif. (In serv. 12-43)

G 25 Afonso Peña (ex-*Ceará,* ex-ARD 14)

Afonso Peña (G 25) Hartmut Ehlers, 4-00

Lift capacity: 3,500 tons **Dim:** 149.86 × 24.69 × 1.73 (light)

Remarks: Loaned 1963; purchased outright 28-12-77. Steel contruction, enclosed bow to improve towing characteristics. Dock area is 118.6 m on blocks by 18.0 m clear width. Transferred to Manaus during 2002.

Note: Also in use for submarines at the Arsenal de Marinha do Rio de Janeiro (AMRJ) is the floating dry dock *Almirante Schiek,* completed in 1995; no data available.

♦ 2 personnel launches [YFL]

Tenente Fabio Tenente Raul

D: 55 tons **S:** 10 kts **Dim:** 20.28 × 5.1 × 1.2 **M:** 1 diesel; 135 bhp
Cargo capacity: 22 tons **Range:** 350/10

Remarks: For service with the Mato Grosso Flotilla

Note: The Capitania Fluvial do Pantanal, Mato Grosso, has several small launches for which no data are available: one floating classroom (*Agencia Escola Flutante*), one NAJA-19 launch, one LPPN-1 launch, three craft of the LAE-7 type, and eight of the LPF-6 type. The Capitani Fluvial do Teite-Paraná operates the school launch (ex-passenger ferry) *Ahanguera* (18.30 × 6.50 × 1.50; 525 n.m./7 kts).

♦ 1 historic personnel ferry [YFL]
Bldr: Vickers, Barrow-in-Furness, U.K. (In serv. 1910)

Laurindo Pitta

D: 514 tons (fl) **S:** . . . **Dim:** 39.04 × 7.77 × 4.60
Electronics: Radar: 1/. . . nav.
M: 2 . . . diesels; 2 props; . . . bhp

Remarks: Former large harbor tug, now used as a ferry from the Naval Cultural Center at Rio de Janeiro to the museum ship exhibits at Ilha Fiscal. Although stricken some years ago, was restored to service in 2000, with the original reciprocating steam engines and boilers replaced by diesel engines.

♦ 3 U.S. LCU 1610–class harbor logistics transports [YFU]
Bldr: Arsenal de Marinha do Rio de Janeiro (AMRJ)

	L	In serv.
GED 10 Guarapari (ex-L 10)	16-6-77	27-3-78
GED 11 Tambaú (ex-L 11)	14-9-77	27-3-78
GED 12 Camboriú (ex-L 12)	. . .	1989

Guarapari (GED 10) Ralph Edwards, 5-00

D: 200 tons (396 fl) **S:** 11 kts **Dim:** 41.0 × 8.42 × 2.0
A: 3 single 12.7-mm mg. **Electronics:** Radar: 1. . . nav.
M: 2 G.M. Detroit Diesel 12V71 diesels; 2 props; 1,000 bhp
Range: 1,200/8 **Crew:** 6 tot. + 120 troops for short distances

Remarks: Former landing craft officially decommissioned 1991 and reassigned to local naval establishments as logistics support craft. Typed EDCG (*Embarcações de Desembarque de Carga Generales*). Uncompleted sister *Tramandai* (L 13) was scrapped in 1983. Can carry 143 tons cargo; cargo space: 30.5 × 5.5 m. Have bow and stern vehicle ramps.

♦ 10 Achernar-class navigational aids tenders [YGL]
Bldr: Wilson Sons S.A. and Comércio, Indústria e Agência de Navegação, Guarujá

	In serv.		In serv.
CPSP 02 Achernar	20-12-95	CPPR 05 Fomalhaut	2-12-96
SSN 224 Aldebaran	23-3-96	SSN 4204 Regulus	3-2-97
CPSF 03 Betelgeuse	5-6-96	SSN 506 Rigel	30-4-97
CPES 03 Capella	1-8-96	. . . Pollux	1998
SSN 4103 Denebola	30-9-96	. . . Vega	1998

D: 102.4 tons (130 fl) **S:** 10 kts **Dim:** 19.76 (18.00 pp) × 6.04 × 1.98 (max.)
M: 2 Cummins NT855M diesels; 2 props; 648 bhp
Electric: 90 kVA tot. (2 × 45 kVa; Lister-Blackstone diesels driving)
Range: . . . / . . . **Fuel:** 13.2 m^3 **Crew:** 6 tot.

YARD AND SERVICE CRAFT *(continued)*

Rigel (SSN 506) IJ Plokker, 4-98

Remarks: Are described as "buoy tender launches." Prefixes to the pennant numbers apparently refer to operating bases. Designed in the Netherlands. Have an Effer Model 14500-1S electrohydraulic buoy crane with 7.2-ton capacity at 1.9-m radius or 2.2 tons at 6.5 m.

♦ 4 Comandante Varella–class navigational aid tenders [YGL]
Bldr: São João de Nilo SY (H 18: Arsenal de Marinha do Rio de Janeiro/ AMRJ)

	In serv.
H 18 Comandante Varella	30-9-82
H 19 Tenente Castelho	. . .
H 20 Comandante Manhães	15-12-83
H 25 Tenente Boanerges	1985

Comandante Varella (H 18) IJ Plokker, 4-98

D: 300 tons light (440 fl) **S:** 12 kts **Dim:** 37.51 (34.5 pp) × 8.60 × 2.56
M: 2 8-cyl. diesels; 2 props; 1,300 bhp **Range:** 2,880/12 **Crew:** 22 tot.

Remarks: Can be reconfigured as minelayers.

Disposal note: *Mestre João dos Santos*–class navigational aids tenders *Mestre João dos Santos* (H 13) and *Castelhanos* (H 24) were stricken during 2000.

♦ 1 "130-ton" navigational aid tender [YGL]
Bldr: . . . . . . (In serv. 21-1-84)

H 26 Faroleiro Mario Seixas

D: 242 tons (fl) **S:** . . . kts **Dim:** 25.48 × 6.65 × 3.6
Electronics: Radar: 1 Furuno 1831 nav.
M: 2 Scandia DSI-14M03 diesels; 2 props; 708 hp
Range: . . . / . . . **Crew:** 17 tot.

Remarks: Modified fishing trawler. Built 1962, acq.navy 1979. Rebuilt as nav. aid tender. The similar "130-ton" series tenders *Faroleiro Areas* (H 27) and *Faroleiro Nascimento* (H 30) were stricken during 2000.

Note: Also in service, with the Mato Grosso Flotilla, are the river buoy tenders *Lufada* and *Piracema;* no data available.

♦ 6 Paraíbano-class survey craft [YGS]
Bldr: Bormann, Rio de Janeiro

	In serv.		In serv.
H 11 Paraíbano	10-68	H 15 Itacurussa	3-71
H 12 Rio Branco	10-68	H 16 Camocim	1971
H 14 Nogueira da Gama (ex-*Jaceguai*)	3-71	H 17 Caravelas	1971

D: 32 tons (50 fl) **S:** 11 kts **Dim:** 16.0 × 4.6 × 1.3
M: 2 G.M. 6-71 diesels; 2 props; 330 bhp
Range: 600/11 **Crew:** 2 officers, 9 enlisted

Remarks: Wooden construction. Operate primarily with the Amazon Flotilla, with H 17 assigned to the Mato Grosso Flotilla. All were officially decommissioned in 1991 but have been retained as district survey support craft.

♦ 1 Doutor Montenegro–class river hospital ship [YH]
Bldr: Estaleiro Conave, Manaus (In serv. 1997)

U 16 Doutor Montenegro

D: 400 tons (fl) **S:** 6 kts **Dim:** 42.00 × 11.00 × . . .
Electronics: Radar: 1 . . . nav.
M: 2 . . . diesels; 2 props; 600 bhp
Range: . . . / . . . **Crew:** 8 officers, 41 enlisted, 11 medical personnel

Remarks: Officially typed NASH (*Navio de Asstencia Hospitalar*). Completed for the State of Acre in 1997 and handed over to the navy on 19-5-01. The ship has a rectangular barge-like hull and has a flight deck for one UH-12 Esquilo-I helicopter. Serves in the Amazon Flotilla.

♦ 2 Oswaldo Cruz–class river hospital ships [YH]
Bldr: Arsenal de Marinha do Rio de Janerio (AMRJ)

	Laid down	L	In serv.
U 18 Oswaldo Cruz	1981	11-7-83	31-5-84
U 19 Carlos Chagas	1982	16-4-84	12-84

Carlos Chagas (U 19) Brazilian Navy, 1996

D: 500 tons (fl) **S:** 9 kts **Dim:** 47.18 (45.00 pp) × 8.45 × 1.75
Electronics: Radar: 1 Decca . . . nav.
M: 2 Volvo Penta diesels; 2 props; 714 bhp
Electric: 420 kVA (2 × 180-kVA, 1 × 60-kVA diesel sets)
Range: 4,000/9 **Fuel:** 77,450 liters
Crew: 25 tot. + 6 doctor/dentists, 15 other health personnel

Remarks: Officially typed NASH (*Navio de Asstencia Hospitalar*). Have two sick bays (6 total beds), an operating theater, two clinics, a dental laboratory, and X-ray facilities. Have tankage for 34,200 liters fresh water. Have a flight deck for one UH-12 Esquilo-I helicopter. Serve in Amazon Flotilla.

♦ 1 river oiler [YO]
Bldr: Papendrecht, the Netherlands (L: 16-3-38)

G 17 Potengi

D: 594 tons **S:** 10 kts **Dim:** 54.5 × 7.5 × 1.8
A: 2 single 7.62-mm mg **Electronics:** Radar: 1 Furuno 3600 nav.
M: 2 diesels; 2 props; 550 bhp **Range:** 600/8 **Crew:** 19 tot.

Potengi (G 17) Hartmut Ehlers, 5-00

Remarks: Assigned to the Mato Grosso Flotilla. In 1996, began conversion into a general-purpose riverine force support vessel at Ladário, completed 6-5-99 with tankage altered to carry diesel and aviation fuel and water and a deckhouse built over the cargo tank area. Cargo capacity: 450 tons.

♦ 1 torpedo recovery craft [YPT]
Bldr: INACE, Fortaleza (In serv. 2-12-83)

BACS 02 Almirante Hess (ex-U 30)

D: 91 tons (fl) **S:** 13 kts **Dim:** 23.6 × 6.0 × 2.0
Electronics: Radar: 1 Decca 110 nav.
M: 2 . . . diesels; 2 props; . . . bhp **Crew:** 14 tot.

YARD AND SERVICE CRAFT *(continued)*

Remarks: Decommissioned in 1991 but then transferred to service craft category. Has an electrohydraulic crane and a stern ramp for recovery and stowage of up to four torpedoes.

♦ 4 StanTug 2207 design large harbor tugs [YTB]
Bldr: Scheepswerf Damen B.V., Gorinchem, the Netherlands

BNRJ 16 Intrepido
BNRJ 17 Arrojado
BNRJ 18 Valente
BNRJ 19 Impavido

Valente (BNRJ 18) Ralph Edwards, 4-00

D: 200 tons (fl) **S:** 12.75 kts **Dim:** 22.65 (20.36 pp) × 7.25 × 2.81 max. aft
M: 2 Caterpillar 3508TA diesels; 2 Kort-nozzle props; 1,580 bhp

Remarks: 134 grt. 22.5 tons bollard pull. First two delivered 6-92, others in 9-92. "BNRJ" in the pennant number indicates assignment to the Rio de Janeiro naval base.

♦ 4 Comandante Marriog–class yard tugs [YTB]
Bldr: Turn-Ship Ltd., U.S.A. (In serv. 1981)

BNRJ 03 Comandante Marriog (ex-R 15)
BNRJ 04 Comandante Didier (ex-R 14)
BNRJ 05 Tenente Magalhaes (ex-R 17)
BNRJ 06 Cabo Schramm (ex-R 18)

Comandante Marriog (BNRJ 03) Hartmut Ehlers, 4-00

D: 115 tons (fl) **S:** 10 kts **Dim:** 19.8 × 7.0 × 2.0
M: 2 G.M. diesels; 2 props; 900 bhp **Crew:** 6 tot.

Remarks: "BNRJ" in the pennant number indicates assignment to the Rio de Janeiro naval base. Sisters *Audaz* (R 31) and *Guarani* (R 33) were stricken 1986.

♦ 2 Isaias de Noronha–class tugs [YTM] (In serv. 1972–74)

BNRJ 01 Tenente Lahmeyer . . . D.N.O.G.

Tenente Lahmeyer (BNRJ 01) Brazilian Navy, 1996

D: 100 tons (fl) **Dim:** 32.0 × . . . × . . . **M:** . . .

Remarks: Name "D.N.O.G." refers to the Brazilian naval contingent in Europe during World War I. "BNRJ" in the pennant number indicates assignment to the Rio de Janeiro naval base.

♦ 2 Itapura-class water tankers [YW]
Bldr: . . . (L: 1957)

Itapura (ex-R 42) Paulo Afonso (ex-R 43)

D: 485.3 tons **Dim:** 42.8 × 7.0 × 2.5 **M:** 1 diesel **Cargo:** 389 tons

♦ 3 miscellaneous small water tankers [YW]

Doutor Gondim (ex-R 38) Guairia (ex-R 40) Iguaçu (ex-R 41)

Remarks: *Doutor Gondim* is 485 tons (fl) and 42.8 × 7.0 × 2.5 m; capacity: 380 tons. No data available for the other two.

♦ 3 Rosca Fina–class training craft [YXT]
Bldr: CARBRASMAR, Rio de Janeiro (In serv. 1983–84)

CN 31 Rosca Fina (ex-U 31)
CIAW 09 Voga Picada (ex-U 32)
CIAW 10 Leva Arriba (ex-U 33)

D: 130 tons (fl) **S:** 11 kts **Dim:** 18.60 × 4.70 × 1.20
Electronics: Radar: 1 . . . nav.
M: 1 MWM diesel; 1 prop; 650 bhp
Range: 200/11 **Crew:** 5 tot. + 11 trainees

Remarks: Used for maneuvering training at the Centro de Instruçao Almirante Braz de Aguiar along with the captured ex-U.S.-registry fishing vessel *Night Hawk.*

♦ 3 Aspirante Nascimento–class training craft [YXT]
Bldr: Empresa Brasileira de Construção Naval, S.A. (Ebrasa), Itajaí, Santa Catarina (In serv. 1980–81)

U 10 Aspirante Nascimento
U 11 Guarda-Marinha Jansen
U 12 Guarda-Marinha Brito

D: 136 tons (fl) **S:** 10 kts **Dim:** 28.00 (25.00 pp) × 6.50 × 1.80
A: 1 12.7-mm mg **Electronics:** Radar: 1 Decca . . . nav.
M: 2 MWM D232V12 diesels; 2 props; 650 bhp
Range: 700/10 **Crew:** 2 officers, 10 enlisted + 24 midshipmen

Remarks: Used for navigation and seamanship training at the naval academy.

Guarda-Marinha Brito (U 12) Ralph Edwards, 4-00

♦ 6 Ajuri-class training craft [YXT]
Bldr: Estaleiros Rio Negro (ERIN), Manaus (In serv.: first two: 14-6-96, others in 1997)

U . . . Ajuri U . . . Mutirum . . . .

D: 28 tons (fl) **S:** 15 kts **Dim:** 17.40 × 7.20 × 0.92
M: 2 . . . diesels; 2 props; . . . bhp

Remarks: Intended to provide training to local populations along Amazon River network. Have a 15-student classroom deckhouse. First two ordered 1995 and four more on 7-8-96. Also in use for the same purpose is the *Gaiva* (ex-SSN 6 of the Serviçio de Sinalização Náutica); no data available.

Note: Also used for training at the naval academy are two sailboats of 23.2-m and 16.5-m overall length and two other racing yachts. Five small riverine training support launches were ordered from Estaleiros Rio Negro (ERIN), Manaus, on 7-8-96 to operate with the *Ajuri* class above. The 144 riverine patrol launches in the LAEP (*Lancha de Apoio ao Ensino e Patrulha*) series described under patrol boats are also used for training.

BRUNEI

State of Brunei Darussalem

ANGKATAN TENTERA LAUT DIRAJA BRUNEI

Personnel: 1,000 total

Base: Muara

ANGKATAN TENTERA LAUT DIRAJA BRUNEI *(continued)*

Naval Aviation: Three IPTN Indonesian-built CN-235 MPA light maritime patrol aircraft were to be ordered, but apparently the deal was never concluded and Brunei is still in the market for an MPA. A single CN-235, to be used as a transport and trainer, has been delivered.

Note: Ship names are prefixed KDB: *Kapal Diraja Brunei* (Ship of the Rajah of Brunei).

FRIGATES [FF]

♦ **3 (+) Nakhoda Ragam (F2000) class**
Bldr: BAE Systems, Scotstoun, Scotland

	Start	L	Completed
28 NAKHODA RAGAM	16-3-99	13-1-01	12-03
29 BENDAHARA SAKAM	15-11-99	23-6-01	5-04
30 JERAMBAK	5-4-01	22-6-02	12-04

Bendahara Sakam (29) Ben Sullivan, 4-04

D: 1,500 tons (1,940 fl) **S:** 30+ kts
Dim: 95.0 (89.9 wl) × 12.8 × 4.5 max. (3.6 hull)
A: 8 MM 40 Exocet Block 2 SSM; 1 Sea Wolf vertical missile launch SAM syst. (16 missiles); 1 76-mm 62-cal. OTO Melara SuperRapid DP; 2 single 30-mm 75-cal. DS-30 AA; 2 single 7.62-mm mg, 2 triple 324-mm Mk 32 ASW TT
Electronics:
Radar: 1 Thales Scout nav.; 1 BAe Systems AWS-9(3D) air search; 2 AMS 1802SW gun/missile f.c.
Sonar: Thales TMS 4130C1 hull-mounted (4–13 kHz)
EW: Racal Cutlass 242 intercept and Scorpion jammer Super Barricade decoy RL
E/O: Rademac 2500 surveillance and tracking
M: 4 M.A.N.-B&W Ruston Paxman 20RK270 diesels; 2 CP props; 40,504 bhp
Electric: . . . kw tot. (4 . . . diesel sets)
Range: 5,800/12 **Endurance:** 14 days
Crew: 8 officers, 54 enlisted + 24 passengers

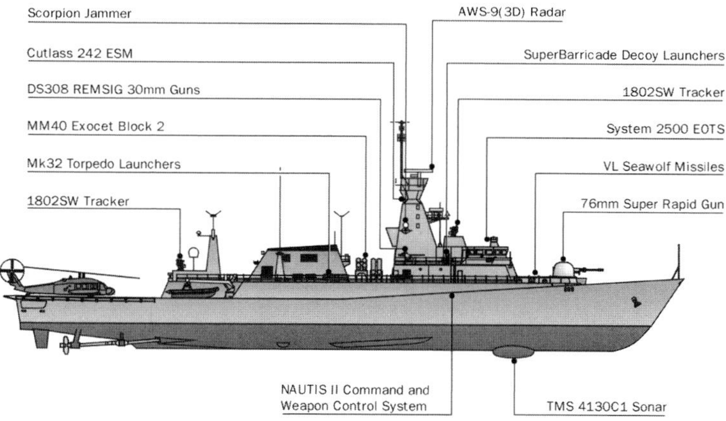

Nakhoda Ragam class BAE Systems

Remarks: Bids requested 28-4-95 with contract originally to have been let by 3-95; decision announced 12-95, but the actual contract was not signed until 14-1-98, due to delays in selecting the weapons system and weapons-control package. Design is a reduced version of the *Lekiu* class built for Malaysia. Were to cost about $323 million each. As of late 2005 Brunei had refused to accept the vessels for unspecified reasons. All three remained tied up in "red tape" at Scotland while the debate heads to International Court.
Hull: Have fin stabilizers. Are able to meet normal loads with one generator. Carry two Osborne Pacific 24 RIBs. The fantail is equipped as a helicopter landing pad, but there are no support facilities or hangar.
Combat systems: Have GEC-Marconi Nautis II command and weapons-control system with separate radar/E/O directors for 76-mm gun and two thermal imagers. Have eight tactical data display consoles. EW suite includes Racal Cutlass 242 intercept and Scorpion jammer; fitted with Wallop SuperBarricade decoy launchers. The sonar incorporates a torpedo-warning capability. The 3-D air-search radar is the same as the Type 996 used in Royal Navy ships.

GUIDED-MISSILE PATROL CRAFT [PTG]

♦ **3 Waspada class**
Bldr: Vosper Pty., Singapore

	L	In serv.
P 02 WASPADA	3-8-77	7-78
P 03 PEJUANG	3-78	1979
P 04 SETERIA	22-6-78	1979

Seteria (P 04) Brian Morrison, 5-98

D: 150 tons (206 fl) **S:** 30 kts **Dim:** 36.88 (33.53 pp) × 7.16 × 1.8
A: 2 MM 38 Exocet SSM; 1 twin 30-mm BMARC-Oerlikon GCM-B01 AA; 2 twin 7.62-mm mg
Electronics:
Radar: 1 Kelvin-Hughes Type 1007 nav. EW: Decca RDL-2 intercept
E/O: Rademac 2500 tracking and f.c.
M: 2 MTU 20V538 TB91 diesels; 2 props; 9,000 bhp (7,500 sust.)
Range: 1,200/14 **Fuel:** 16 tons **Crew:** 4 officers, 30 enlisted

Remarks: P 02 has enclosed upper bridge (open on other two) and facilities for training. Modernized early 1990s with new EW suite and twin mg, but a planned 2-m hull stretch was canceled. Can accommodate 7 officers and 37 enlisted. New radars and electro-optical equipment were added 1998, with four Kelvin-Hughes color tactical displays added to P 02 and three to the others. To be retained in service into 2012.

PATROL BOATS [PB]

♦ **3 Periwa class**
Bldr: Vosper Pty., Singapore

	L	In serv.
P 14 PERIWA	5-74	9-9-74
P 15 PEMBURU	30-1-75	17-6-75
P 16 PENYERANG	20-3-75	24-6-75

Penyerang (P 16) Navpic-Holland, 7-94

D: 30 tons (38.5 fl) **S:** 32 kts **Dim:** 21.7 × 6.1 × 1.2
A: 2 single 20-mm 85-cal. BMARC-Oerlikon GAM-B01 AA; 2 single 7.62-mm mg
Electronics: Radar: 1 Decca RM 1290 nav.
M: 2 MTU 12V331 TC81 diesels; 2,700 bhp
Range: 600/20; 1,000/16 **Crew:** 2 officers, 12 enlisted

Remarks: Wooden construction. One was reported inoperable as of 1996.

AMPHIBIOUS WARFARE CRAFT

♦ **2 Serasa-class landing craft [LCM]**
Bldr: Transfield Shipbuilding, Western Australia (L: 8-11-96)

L 33 SERASA L 34 TERABAN

D: 336 tons (fl) **S:** 12 kts **Dim:** 36.50 (32.95 hull; 30.00 wl) × 8.00 × 1.50
A: 2 20-mm 90-cal. Oerlikon GAM-B01 AA; 2 single 7.62-mm mg
Electronics: Radar: 1 Decca . . . nav.
M: 2 Caterpillar 3508 diesels; 2 props; 1,930 bhp
Range: 1,000/8 **Crew:** 3 officers, 9 enlisted

Remarks: Ordered 30-11-95 for delivery 8-96. Intended to carry deck cargo, vehicles, and liquid cargo (fuel and water in four tanks). There are two Caterpillar diesel-driven generator sets. Can transfer fuel, water, and stores to other craft at sea. In addition to a bow ramp, there are short loading ramps on both sides of the vehicle deck.

AMPHIBIOUS WARFARE CRAFT *(continued)*

Serasa (L 33) Brian Morrison/H&L Van Ginderen, 5-98

♦ **2 Loadmaster-class landing craft [LCM]**
Bldr: Cheverton, Cowes, U.K.

L 31 Damuan (In serv. 5-76) L 32 Puni (In serv. 2-77)

Puni (L 32) French Navy, 6-98

D: 64.3 tons (light) **S:** 8.5 kts **Dim:** 22.86 × 6.1 × 1.07
Electronics: Radar: 1 Decca RM 1216 nav.
M: 2 G.M. Detroit Diesel 6-71 diesels; 2 props; 348 bhp
Range: 300/8.5; 1,000/6 **Crew:** 8 tot.

Remarks: L 31: 19.8 m overall, 60 tons light. Both can carry 30 tons cargo.

♦ **17 small armed river craft for the Special Combat Squadron [LCP]**

D: 3–5 tons (fl) **S:** 24–30 kts **Dim:** 5.0 to 6.0 × . . . × . . .
A: 1 7.62-mm mg **M:** 1 gasoline outboard; 140 bhp

Remarks: Used by the Special Combat Squadron infantry. Four have been retired.

SERVICE CRAFT

♦ **1 support launch [YFL]**
Bldr: Cheverton, Cowes, U.K. (In serv. 1982)

Burong Nuri

D: 23 tons (fl) **S:** 12 kts **Dim:** 17.8 × 4.3 × 1.5
Electronics: Radar: 1 Decca 060 nav.
M: 2 G.M. Detroit Diesel 6-71 diesels, 2 props; 400 bhp **Crew:** 5 tot.

Remarks: Used as tug, target tug, diving tender, or for antipollution duties. GRP construction.

MARINE POLICE

PATROL BOATS [WPB]

♦ **3 Bendeharu class**
Bldr: P.T. Pal, Surabaya, Indonesia (In serv. 1991)

P 21 Bendeharu P 22 Maharajalela P 23 Kemaindera

D: 68 tons (fl) **S:** . . . kts **Dim:** 28.5 × 5.4 × 1.7
A: 1 12.7-mm mg **M:** 2 MTU diesels; 2 props; 2,260 bhp **Crew:** 16 tot.

♦ **7 14.5-meter class**
Bldr: Singapore SB & Eng. (In serv. 5-10-87 to 12-87)

PDB 11 PDB 13 PDB 15 PDB 68
PDB 12 PDB 14 PDB 63

D: 20 tons (fl) **S:** 30 kts **Dim:** 14.54 × 4.23 × 1.20 (props)
A: 1 7.62-mm mg **Electronics:** Radar: 1 . . . nav.
M: 2 M.A.N. D2840 diesels; 2 props; 1,270 bhp
Range: 310/22 **Fuel:** 2,600 litres **Crew:** 7 tot.

Remarks: Aluminum construction craft similar to Singapore Marine Police Force's PT 1 class. Ordered 28-10-86.

♦ **11 PDB 01 class**
Bldr: Singapore SB & Eng. (In serv. . . .)

PDB 01 through PDB 11

Remarks: No data available. Are about half the size of the 14.5-m class above and have the same navigational radar set.

♦ **2 FPB 512 class**
Bldr: Rotork Marine, U.K.

07 Behagia 10 Selamat

D: 8.8 tons (fl) **S:** 27 kts **Dim:** 12.7 × 3.2 × . . .
A: 3 single 7.62-mm mg **Electronics:** Radar: 1 Decca 060
M: 2 Ford Mermaid diesels; 2 Castoldi Type 06 waterjets; 430 bhp
Range: 100/12 **Crew:** 3 tot.

Remarks: GRP hulls, bow ramps. For patrol and transport duties.

Note: Also in service for riverine use are personnel launches *Aman* (01), *Damai* (02), *Sentosa* (04), and *Sejahtera* (06); no data available.

The Brunei Fisheries Department of the Ministry of Industry and Primary Resources ordered a 16-m, 30-kt fisheries patrol boat from Syarikat Cheoy Lee Shipyards late in 2002.

BULGARIA

Republic of Bulgaria

VOENNOMORSKI SILI

Personnel: 4,370 total plus 7,500 reservists

Bases: Headquarters, main naval base, training facilities, and air station at Varna; smaller naval bases at Atiya, Balchik, Burgas, and Sozopol and at Vidin on the Danube. Repair facilities at Flotski Arsenal, Varna. Higher Naval School Nikola Yonkov Vaptsarov at Varna.

Naval Aviation: Ten Mi-14PL Haze A land-based ASW helicopters are in inventory, but only 3 are flyable and several are now being refurbished. During 2005 six AS 565MB Panther helicopters were ordered for Bulgarian naval search-and-rescue duties.

Coastal Defense: Six twin-tubed SS-C-3 Styx self-propelled launch vehicles in missile battalion. Some 130-mm and 100-mm fixed coastal artillery positions may still be in use.

Weapons and Sensors: Bulgarian naval units employ weapons and sensors largely of Soviet/Russian origin, although a locally made navigational radar is used. Bulgaria offers for export the PDM-1B shallow-water, tilt-rod-fused mine, which has a 17-kg explosive charge and is intended for anti-invasion use in waters 1–2 m deep.

ATTACK SUBMARINES [SS]—BULGARIA

Note: Denmark has offered the Type 207 submarine ex-*Saelen* (S 323) to Bulgaria as a gift; transfer is likely to occur by 2007.

♦ **1 Soviet Romeo (Project 633) class**

84 Slava

D: 1,319 tons surf./1,712 tons sub. **S:** 15.2 kts surf./13 kts sub.
Dim: 76.60 × 6.70 × 4.95
A: 8/533-mm TT (6 fwd, 2 aft; 14 torpedoes or 24 mines)
Electronics:
Radar: 1/Snoop Plate surf. search—EW: Stop Light-B intercept
Sonar: MF active; passive array
M: 2 Type 37D diesels (2,200 bhp each), electric drive; 2 shrouded props; 3,000 shp—2/50-shp electric creep motors
Range: 7,000/5 snorkel **Endurance:** 45 days **Crew:** 60 tot.

Remarks: Survivor of four units transferred in 1971–72 was originally to have been retired in 1994 or 1995 and by 2000 had become inoperable, although the boat was sighted still in commission as of 7-02, with a second Romeo in hulk condition. Could dive to 300 m when new, but can now only operate to 50 m.

FRIGATES [FF]

♦ **1 ex-Belgian Wielingen class (Type E 71)**
Bldr: Boelwerf, Temse, Belgium (In serv. 27-10-78)

41 Druzki (ex-*Wandelaar,* F 912)

Druzki (41)—while still in Belgian service A. A. de Kruijf, 7-03

D: 1,940 tons (2,430 fl) **S:** 26 kts on gas turbine/18 on diesels
Dim: 106.38 (103.00 pp) × 12.30 × 3.90 (5.40 over sonar)
A: Able to carry 4 MM 38 Exocet SSM; 1 8-round Mk 29 SAM launcher (AIM-7P NATO Sea Sparrow missiles); 1 100-mm 55-cal. Model 1968 DP; 6 single 12.7-mm mg; 1 6-round 375-mm Bofors ASW RL; 2 fixed, internal launching racks for L 5 Mod. 4 ASW torpedoes
Electronics:
Radar: 1 Kelvin-Hughes KH 1007 nav.; 1 Thales Scout surf. search; 1 Thales DA-05 air search; 1 Thales WM-25 f.c.
Sonar: Computing Devices Canada SQS-510 hull-mounted (7.0 kHz)
EW: ArgoSystems AR 900B intercept; Elcos-1 HFD/F; Mk 36 SRBOC decoy syst. (2 6-round Mk 137 RL); SLQ-25 Nixie torpedo decoy syst.
E/O: 2 SAGEM VIGY-105 EOMS optronic f.c. and surveillance
M: CODOG: 2 Cockerill CO-240V-12 diesels (3,000 bhp each); 1 Rolls-Royce Olympus TM-3B gas turbine (28,000 shp); 2 CP props
Electric: 2,000 kw (4 × 500-kw diesel sets) **Range:** 4,500/18; 6,000/16
Fuel: 280 tons **Crew:**14 officers, 143 enlisted

Remarks: Specifications listed above reflect data while in Belgian Service. Modernized at Antwerp during 2000–2001. Sold by Belgium during 2004 for 30 million Euros. Transferred 21-10-05 likely without Exocet SSM missiles. The two remaining units will likely be transferred from Belgium in 2007–8.

♦ **1 Soviet Koni class (Project 1159T)**
Bldr: Krasniy Metalist Zavod, Zelenodol'sk

	Laid down	L	In serv.
11 Smeli (ex-Soviet *Del'fin*)	25-5-71	21-4-73	19-7-75

Smeli (11) Cem D. Yaylali, 6-04

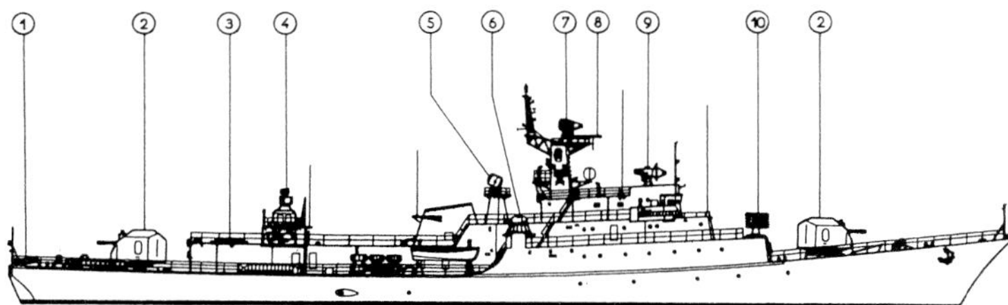

Smeli (11) 1. Depth-charge racks (atop mine rails) 2. Twin 76.2-mm AK-726 DP gunmounts 3. Twin-rail, retractable Osa-M (SA-N-4) SAM system 4. MPZ-301 (Pop Group) radar director for Osa-M system 5. MR-104 Rys' (Drum Tilt) radar director for 30-mm guns 6. Twin 30-mm AK-230 AA gunmounts port and starboard 7. MR-302 Rubka (Strut Curve) surface/air-search radar 8. Don-2 navigational radar 9. MR-105 Fut-B (Hawk Screech) radar director for 76.2-mm guns 10. Two 12-round RBU-6000 ASW rocket launchers Drawing by L. Gassier

D: 1,515 tons normal (1,670 fl) **S:** 27 kts (29.67 on trials; 22 on diesels alone)
Dim: 95.51 × 12.55 × 4.12 (5.72 sonar)
A: 1 twin-rail Osa-M (SA-N-4) SAM syst. (20 9M-33/Gecko missiles); 2 twin 76.2-mm 59-cal. AK-726 DP; 2 twin 30-mm 65-cal. AK-230 AA2 12-round RBU-6000 ASW RL (120 RGB-60 rockets); 2 d.c. racks (6 BB-1 d.c. each); up to 14 mines (in lieu of d.c.)
Electronics:
Radar: 1 Don-2 nav.; MR-302 Rubka (Strut Curve) air/surf. search; 1 MPZ-301 (Pop Group) missile f.c.; 1 Fut-B (Hawk Screech) 76.2-mm gun f.c.; 1 MR-104 Rys' (Drum Tilt) 30-mm gun f.c.
Sonar: MG-322T Vychegda MF hull-mounted
EW: 2 Bizan'-4B (Watch Dog) intercept (2–18 GHz); 1 MFD/F; 2 16-round PK-16 decoy RL
M: CODAG: 1 M-813 18,000-shp gas turbine, 2 Type 68B, 8,000-bhp diesels; 3 props; 34,000 hp
Range: 1,800/14 **Crew:** 96 tot.

Remarks: Transferred 11-2-91 and recommissioned 1-6-91 after having been used by the Soviet Navy in the Black Sea to train the foreign crews of export units. Had one refit in Russia since 1991. To decomission in the near future.

CORVETTES [FFL]

Note: In 11-02 the Chief, Bulgarian Navy Headquarters stated that there was a plan to acquire six corvettes under a newly approved National Shipbuilding Program, with the first ship to cost $138.12 million. Delivery dates remain uncertain.

PATROL SHIPS [PS]

Note: Requests for bids for the construction of two European Union–funded maritime patrol ships for the Bulgarian Navy were issued 4-02.

GUIDED-MISSILE PATROL COMBATANTS [PGG]

♦ **1 Soviet Tarantul-II class (Project 1141.1M)**
Bldr: Sudostroitel'noye Obyedineniye "Almaz," Petrovskiy SY, St. Petersburg

101 Mulnaya (ex-*Poltavskiy Komsomolets*)

Mulnaya (101) H&L Van Ginderen, 7-00

D: 385 tons light (455 fl) **S:** 43 kts
Dim: 56.10 (49.50 pp) × 10.20 (9.40 wl) × 2.14 hull (4.0 props)
A: 4 P-20/P-21 Termit (SS-N-2C Styx) SSM; 1 76.2-mm 59-cal. AK-176 DP; 1 4-round SA-N-8 SAM syst. (12 Igla-1 missiles); 2 single 30-mm 54-cal. AK-630 gatling AA
Electronics:
Radar: 1 Kivach-3 nav.; 1 Monolit (Band Stand) target detection and tracking; 1 MR-123 Vympel' (Bass Tilt) gun f.c.
EW: no intercept; 2 16-round PK-16 decoy RL
M: M-15E COGAG plant: 2 DMR-76 cruise gas turbines (4,000 shp each), 2 PR-77 boost gas turbines (12,000 shp each); 2 props; 32,000 shp
Electric: 500 kw tot. (2 × 200-kw, 1 × 100-kw diesel sets)
Range: 760/43; 1,400/13 **Fuel:** 50 tons **Endurance:** 10 days
Crew: 7 officers, 32 enlisted

Remarks: Transferred from Soviet Black Sea Fleet 6-90 to begin replacement of the obsolete Osa-I and Osa-II missile boats. Planned transfer of two more canceled.
Hull systems: The cruise gas turbines exhaust through a stack, while the high-speed turbines exhaust through the transom stern, adding their residual thrust to the propulsive power; all four are employed simultaneously via planetary gearing for maximum power.
Combat systems: A Light Bulb missile datalink antenna is installed at the masthead, while the Band Stand radome conceals a missile target acquisition and guidance radar that can also operate in the passive mode. Some 252 rounds of 76.2-mm and 6,000 rounds of 30-mm ammunition are carried. Has racks for three smoke floats or small depth charges mounted at the stern.

GUIDED-MISSILE PATROL CRAFT [PTG]

♦ **6 Soviet Osa I* and Osa-II class (Project 205*/205M)**

102 Uragon	104 Grum	112 Typfun*
103 Burya*	111 Svetkavitsa*	113 Smerch*

Uragon (102)—Osa-II H&L Van Ginderen, 8-99

D: 184 tons (226 fl) **S:** 40 kts **Dim:** 37.5 × 7.6 × 1.9 mean
A: 4 P-15M Termit (SS-N-2B Styx) SSM; 2 twin 30-mm 65-cal. AK-230 AA
Electronics: Radar: 1 Rangout (Square Tie) surf. search/missile target desig.; 1 MR-104 Rys' (Drum Tilt) gun f.c.
M: 3 M-504B diesels; 3 props; 15,000 bhp **Electric:** 200 kw tot.
Range: 500/34; 750/25 **Endurance:** 5 days **Crew:** 28 tot.

GUIDED-MISSILE PATROL CRAFT [PTG] *(continued)*

Remarks: Transferred in 1978, 1982, and 1984. Based at Sozopol and rarely go to sea. 111 and 113 are Osa-I (Project 205) versions with hooded missile launchers; they displace 171 tons light (209.5 fl) and could achieve 38.5 kts on 12,000 bhp from their M-503A2 diesels when new.

PATROL CRAFT [PC]

♦ 2 ex-Soviet Pauk-I class (Project 1241.2)

Bldr: Yaroslavl Zavod

13 Reshitelni (ex-MPK-146) 14 Bodri (ex-MPK-124)

Bodri (14) C. Devrim Yaylali 9-02

D: 425 tons (495 fl) **S:** 32 kts (28 sust.)
Dim: 58.5 (49.5 pp) × 10.2 (9.4 wl) × 2.14 hull (4.0 props)
A: 1 76.2-mm 59-cal. AK-176 DP; 1 4-round SA-N-8 SAM syst. (16 Igla-1 missiles); 1 30-mm 54-cal. AK-630 gatling AA; 2 5-tubed RBU-1200 ASW RL (30 RGB-12 rockets); 4 406-mm ASW TT; 2 d.c. racks (12 d.c.)
Electronics:
Radar: 1 Pechora nav.; 1 . . . (Peel Cone) nav./surf.-search; 1 MR-123 Vympel' (Bass Tilt) f.c.
Sonar: MGK-345 Bronza MF hull-mounted and dipping
EW: 2 . . . (Half Hat-B) intercept; 2 16-round PK-16 decoy RL
M: 2 M-517 diesels; 2 props; 20,800 bhp (16,180 bhp sust.)
Range: 2,000/20; 3,000/12 **Fuel:** 50 tons normal **Endurance:** 10 days
Crew: 7 officers, 32 enlisted

Remarks: Also known as the Molniya-2 class. Transferred 9-89 and 12-90 from the then-Soviet Black Sea Fleet. Based at Varna.
Hull systems: This class uses same hull as the Tarantul-class missile corvette but has ASW armament vice antiship missiles and an all-diesel propulsion plant vice the Tarantul's COGAG/CODAG system. The large housing for a dipping sonar system projects 2 m out from the stern. The large hull-mounted sonar dome is located approximately beneath the gun fire-control radar. The hull is constructed of mild steel, while the middle part of the deck plating, some internal bulkheads, and much of the superstructure are made of aluminum-magnesium alloy. Range on normal fuel load is 1,600 n.m. at 12 kts.
Combat systems: The combat data system is designated SU-580. There is a Kolonka-2 backup ringsight director for the single gatling AA gun; The MR-123 radar director can control both the 76.2-mm and 30-mm guns. Normal ammunition load is 152 rounds 76-mm (all ready-service, on-mount) and 2,000 rounds 30-mm. MGK-345 applies to both the hull-mounted and dipping sonars, and the dipping sonar transducer can be lowered to 200 m.

♦ 4 Soviet Poti class (Project 204A) (In reserve)

Bldr: Zelnodol'sk Zavod, Tatarstan, Russia

41 Letyashi (ex-K- . . .) 44 Khabri (ex-K-159)
42 Bditelni (ex-K- . . .) 46 Bezstrashni (ex-K- . . .)

Khabri (44) H&L Van Ginderen, 7-00

D: 428.5 tons (536.5 fl) **S:** 38 kts (32–34 sust.); 17.5 max. on diesels
Dim: 58.62 (55.63 wl) × 8.14 × 2.38 mean hull (3.11 over sonar)
A: 1 twin 57-mm 75-cal. AK-275 DP; 2 12-round RBU-6000 ASW RL (96 RGB-60 rockets); 4 406-mm OTA-40-204 fixed ASW TT
Electronics:
Radar: 1 Don-2 nav.; 1 MR-302 Rubka (Strut Curve) surf./air search; 1 MR-103 Bars (Muff Cob) f.c.
Sonar: MG-312 Titan-2 hull-mounted MF search and HF attack
EW: 2 Bizan'-4B (Watch Dog) intercept (2–18 GHz); 2 16-round PK-16 decoy RL
M: CODAG: 2 M-520T diesels (4,800 bhp each); 2 GTK-D2 gas turbines (15,000 shp each); 2 props mounted in venturi tunnels
Electric: 400 kw tot (2 × 200-kw DG-200 diesel sets)
Range: 500/37; 1,500/17.5; 2,650/13.75 **Fuel:** 108 tons **Endurance:** 7 days
Crew: 4–5 officers, 52–55 enlisted

Remarks: *Khabri* transferred 28-6-75, *Letyashi* in 1986, and the other two in 1990. Sisters *Strogiy* (42, ex-K-160) and *Naporisti* (43) were stricken at the end of 1993. The others are unlikely to remain in service much longer, as their weapon and sensor systems are obsolete and unsupportable. All four were in reserve at Attiya as of 7-02.
Hull systems: Gas turbines force air into tubes abaft the propellers in a kind of waterjet system. Hull has eight watertight bulkheads. The diesel engines have also been reported to be Type M-504A. With emergency fuel, range could be extended to 3,500 n.m. at 13.75 kts.
Combat systems: The MR-103 radar gun director is equipped with a television backup system. Have been updated with decoy rocket launchers and may still carry a WGS-2 Oka-M helicopter dipping sonar in addition to the hull-mounted sets. Navigation suite includes Kurs-4 gyrocompass, LG-4 log, ARP-50 HFD/F, NEL-5 echo sounder, AP-3 autoplot, and Al'batros automatic pilot. The ZIF-31B 57-mm gunmount has 1,100 rounds ready-service ammunition.

MINE WARFARE SHIPS

Note: Offered for export is a 200-ton, 36-m-long by 10-m-beam catamaran mine-countermeasures ship design to be armed with a 30-mm gun and a point-defense SAM system. The craft would be built of GRP, carry remote-controlled mine disposal submersibles, and be equipped with a computerized navigation and minehunting control system.

♦ 4 Soviet Sonya (Yakhont)-class (Project 1265) coastal minesweepers [MSC]

Bldr: Avangard Zavod, Petrozavodsk

61 Briz 62 Shkval 63 Priboy 64 Shtorm

Priboy (63) Boris Lemachko, 2002

D: 401–427 tons (430–460 fl) **S:** 14 kts
Dim: 48.80 (46.00 wl) × 10.20 (9.20 wl) × 2.40–2.50 mean hull (2.75–2.85 max.)
A: 1 twin 30-mm 65-cal. AK-230M AA; 1 twin 25-mm 80-cal. 2M-3M AA; 5 mines
Electronics:
Radar: 1 Mius (Spin Trough) nav.
Sonar: MG-89 Serna HF hull-mounted, MG-35 underwater telephone, NEL-MZB echo sounder
M: 2 DRA-210-A or DRA-210-B diesels; 2 3-bladed CP props; 2,200 or 2,000 bhp—2 low-speed thrusters
Electric: 350 kw tot. (3 × 100-kw, 1 × 50-kw diesel sets; 380 V 50 Hz a.c.)
Range: 1,700/10 **Fuel:** 27.1 tons **Endurance:** 15 days
Crew: 5–6 officers, 26–40 enlisted (45 tot. accomm.)

Remarks: Two transferred 1982, the others in 1985. Designed under Valeriy Ivanovich Nemudrov. Wooden construction with glass-reinforced plastic hull sheathing. Carry acoustic, loop and towed solenoidal magnetic, and net-sweep and mechanical sweep equipment and can lay linear mine disposal charges. The 25-mm mount is aimed by the on-mount operator, while the 30-mm mount is controlled by a Kolonka-1 ringsight director. Bollard pull: 10 tons at 9 kts.

♦ 4 Soviet Vanya-class (Project 257DME) coastal minesweepers [MSC]

Bldr: Avangard Zavod, Petrozavodsk

31 Iskar 32 Tsib'r 33 Dobrotich 34 Evstati Vinarov

Tsib'r (32) and Evstati Vinarov [34]—with sisters Alexandre Sheldon-Duplaix, 6-02

MINE WARFARE SHIPS *(continued)*

D: 220 tons light, 254 tons std. (270 fl) **S:** 14 kts
Dim: 39.9 (38.0 wl) × 7.5 × 1.8 hull (2.08 max.)
A: 1 twin 30-mm 65-cal. AK-230 AA; 8–12 mines
Electronics: Radar: 1 Donets-2 nav.—Sonar: MG-69 Lan' HF hull-mounted
M: 2 M-870 FTK diesels; 2 CP props; 2,400 bhp
Electric: 250 kw tot. (2 × 100-kw DG-100 diesel sets, 1 × 50-kw DGR-50 set)
Range: 1,500/10; 2,400/9 **Endurance:** 5 days **Crew:** 37 tot.

Remarks: Two transferred in 1970, two in 1971, and two in 1985; sisters (35) and *Kapitan 1 Rang Dimitri Paskadev* (36) deleted 1992. Wooden construction. The gunmount is controlled by a remote Kolonka-1 ringsight director. Updated version of standard Soviet Navy design with improved accommodations.

♦ **4 Soviet Yevgenya-class (Project 1258) inshore minesweepers [MSI]** Bldr: Sudostroitel'noye Obyedineniye "Almaz" (Sredniy Neva), Kolpino

65 66 67 68

D: 88.5 tons (91.5 fl) **S:** 11 kts **Dim:** 26.13 × 6.10 (5.90 wl) × 1.38
A: 1 twin 25-mm 80-cal. 2M-3M AA
Electronics: Radar: 1 Mius (Spin Trough) nav.—Sonar: MG-8 hull-mounted HF
M: 2 Type 3D12 diesels; 2 props; 600 bhp **Electric:** 100 kw tot.
Range: 300/10 **Fuel:** 2.7 tons **Endurance:** 3 days
Crew: 1 officer, 9 enlisted (+ 2–3 clearance divers)

Remarks: All transferred 1977. GRP construction. Employ a television minehunting system useful to 30-m depths that dispenses marker buoys to permit later disposal of mines.

♦ **6 Soviet Olya-class (Project 1259) harbor minesweepers [MSI] (In reserve)** Bldr: . . ., Bulgaria (In serv. 1988–96)

51 52 53 54 55 56

Bulgarian Olya 52 H&L Van Ginderen, 7-00

D: 62 tons (66 fl) **S:** 12 kts (10 sust.) **Dim:** 22.77 × 4.50 × 1.40
A: 1 twin 12.7-mm Utës-M mg; . . . mines
Electronics: Radar: 1 Chernomore MR 2512 nav.
M: 2 Type 3D-6N diesels; 2 props; 470 bhp
Electric: 100 kw tot. (2 × 50-kw DG-50 diesel sets)
Range: 400/8 **Crew:** 15 tot.

Remarks: Although not considered a successful design in Soviet service, the design was licensed to Bulgaria, which also offers it for export. GRP hull. Sweep gear includes AT-6 acoustic, SEMT-1 solenoid coil, and GKT-2 mechanical arrays. Not all are active.

AMPHIBIOUS WARFARE SHIPS

♦ **2 ex-Soviet Polnocny-A-class (Project 770) medium landing ships [LSM]** Bldr: Stocznia Polnocna, Gdansk, Poland

701 SIRIUS (ex–*Ivan Zagubanski*) 702 ANTARES (ex–*Anton Ivanov*)

Antares (702) Cem D. Yaylali, 4-05

D: 770 tons (fl) **S:** 19 kts **Dim:** 73.0 × 8.6 × 1.9 (aft)
A: 1 twin 30-mm 65-cal. AK-230 AA; 2 18-round 140-mm barrage RL
Electronics: Radar: 1 Mius (Spin Trough) nav.
M: 2 Type 40DM diesels; 2 props; 4,400 bhp
Range: 900/18; 1,500/14 **Crew:** 35 tot.

Remarks: Transferred 1986–87. Based at Atiya. Cargo: about 180 tons of vehicles. Plans to convert them to serve as minelayers have been canceled; normally used as logistics support transports but have been mostly inactive in recent years.

♦ **6 Soviet Vydra-class (Project 106K) utility landing craft [LCU]** Bldr: Kherson SY (In serv. 1966–70)

703 through 707 712

Vydra-class 705—although reportedly in reserve, appears to be in operating condition H&L Van Ginderen, 7-00

D: 308 tons (442 fl) **S:** 10.5 kts **Dim:** 54.5 × 7.7 × 2.4
A: 2 single . . . AA; . . . mines
Electronics: Radar: 1 Chernomore MR 2512 nav.
M: 2 Type 3D12 diesels; 2 props; 600 bhp
Range: 2,700/10 **Crew:** 1 officer, 4 enlisted

Remarks: Ten transferred from USSR in 1970, 14 others built under license in Bulgaria between 1974 and 1978. 708–711 were stricken in 1993. From time to time have been used in moving civilian cargo. Cargo: 260 tons maximum or 3 heavy tanks or 10 GAZ-66 trucks or 200 troops. Have been altered to serve as minelayers if needed. Two were donated to Georgia on 6-7-01. Based at Atiya.

AUXILIARIES

♦ **1 ex-Italian Proteo-class salvage ship/submersible tender [ARS]** Bldr: CNR, Ancona (In serv. 24-8-51)

A 224 . . . (ex-*Proteo,* A 5310, ex-*Perseo*)

A 224—while still in Italian service Luciano Grazioli, 6-02

D: 1,865 tons (2,147 fl) **S:** 16 kts **Dim:** 75.10 × 11.70 × 6.10
A: 2 single 20-mm 70-cal. Mk 10 Oerlikon AA
Electronics: Radar: 1 SMA SPN-748 nav.
M: 2 Fiat diesels; 1 prop; 4,800 bhp
Range: 7,500/13 **Crew:** 8 officers, 114 enlisted

Remarks: Transferred from Italy during 2004. Has a submersible decompression chamber, extensive divers' support equipment, and a four-point mooring capability. Refitted 1984–85 with a new stack and an electrohydraulic crane. Played a destroyer in the film *U-571,* complete with two twin dummy gunmounts.

♦ **1 Soviet Bereza-class (Type 130) deperming tender [ADG]** Bldr: Stocznia Polnocna, Gdansk, Poland

	Laid down	L	In serv.
206 KAPITAN 1 RANG DIMITRI DOBREV (ex-SR-548)	20-10-87	30-6-88	7-89

D: 1,850 tons light (2,051 fl) **S:** 13.8 kts **Dim:** 69.50 × 13.80 × 3.99
A: none **Electronics:** Radar: 1 Kivach nav.
M: 2 Zgoda-Sulzer 8AL25/30, 750-rpm diesels; 2 CP Kort-nozzle props; 2,940 bhp—bow-thruster
Electric: 2,200 kw total
Range: 1,000/13.8 **Crew:** 48 tot.

Remarks: Intended for degaussing surface ships and submarines, conducting magnetic field measurements of ships and vessels. Also used as naval cadet training ship. Eighteen others serve in the Russian Navy.
Hull systems: Can service two ships simultaneously. Has three laboratories, a machine shop, and a cable hold. Molded depth of hull is 5.60 m. A large crane is fitted aft to handle deperming cables.

AUXILIARIES *(continued)*

Kapitan 1 Rang Dimitri Dobrev (206) Alexandre Sheldon-Duplaix, 6-02

♦ **1 Soviet Moma-class (Project 861) survey ship/buoy tender [AGS]** Bldr: Stocznia Polnocna, Gdansk, Poland (In serv. 1977)

401 Admiral Branimir Ormanov

Admiral Branimir Ormanov (401) H&L Van Ginderen, 7-01

D: 1,260 tons (1,540 fl) **S:** 17 kts **Dim:** 73.3 × 10.8 × 3.8
A: none **Electronics:** Radar: 2 Don-2 nav.
M: 2 Zgoda-Sulzer 6TD48 diesels; 2 CP props; 3,600 bhp
Endurance: 35 days **Range:** 8,700/11 **Crew:** 5 officers, 32 enlisted

♦ **1 Mesar-class (Project 102) replenishment oiler [AOR]**
Bldr: Russe, Bulgaria (In serv. 1987)

302 Atiya

Atiya (302) H&L Van Ginderen, 7-00

D: 3,240 (fl) **S:** 20 kts **Dim:** 97.5 × 13.2 × 5.2
A: 2 twin 30-mm 65-cal. AK-230 AA **Electronics:** Radar: 2 Don-2 nav.
M: 2 diesels; 2 props; 12,000 bhp **Range:** 12,000/15 **Crew:** 32 tot.

Remarks: Sister *Dimitri A. Dimitrov* (202), completed in 1979, was stricken and offered for sale on 12-12-96. Cargo capacity: 1,593 tons liquid. Conducts over-the-stern underway refueling; also has dry stores cargo. Unusually fine hull lines for an oiler design. "Mesar" is NATO nickname. The guns are controlled by two Kolonka-1 ringsight directors.

♦ **1 East German Type-700 salvage tug-icebreaker [ATA]**
Bldr: V.E.B. Peenewerft, Wolgast (In serv. 20-3-64)

221 Jupiter

D: 700 tons (791 fl) **S:** 12.75 kts **Dim:** 44.71 (38.99 pp) × 10.72 × 3.91
A: None **Electronics:** Radar: . . .
M: 4 Johannisthal Type 12 KVD 21 diesels (550 bhp each), 4 generators, 2 electric motors; 2 props; 1,680 shp

Jupiter (221) H&L Van Ginderen, 7-00

Electric: 264 kw tot. (2 × 120-kw, 1 × 24-kw d.c. diesel sets)
Range: 3,000/12 **Crew:** 39 tot.

Remarks: 505 grt. Operated for the Varna Port Authority since the early 1990s, but remains under naval ownership and employs naval crew.

♦ **1 Dimitar Blagoev–class training ship [AXT]**
Bldr: Georgi Dimitrov SY, Varna (In serv. 1969)

421 Dimitar Blagoev

Dimitar Blagoev (421) Guy Schaeffer via Paolo Marsan, 6-04

D: Approx. 2,100 tons (fl) **S:** 14 kts **Dim:** 68.00 × 10.11 × 5.46
A: None **Electronics:** Radar: 2 . . . nav.
M: 2 Russkiy Dizel . . . diesels; 2 props; 1,200 bhp
Electric: 588 kw tot. (3 × 188-kw, 1 × 24-kw diesel sets) **Crew:** . . . tot.

Remarks: 1,129 grt. Former Nav. Mar. Bulgare passenger/cargo vessel acquired as a cadet training ship around 1997. The 191-m^3 cargo hold forward has two 2.2 × 2.8-m hatches, but the crane has been removed. Can accommodate 94 passengers. Sister *Georgi Kirkov* may still be in commercial service.

SERVICE CRAFT

♦ **2 Project 245 diving tenders [YDT]**

223 323

Project 245 diving tender 223 Siegfried Breyer Collection, 1994

D: 112 tons light (165 fl) **S:** 10 kts **Dim:** 27.9 × 5.2 × 2.2
M: 2 MCK 83-4 diesel generator sets, electric drive; 1 prop; 300 shp
Range: 400/10 **Crew:** 6 tot. + 7 divers

SERVICE CRAFT *(continued)*

Remarks: Can support divers to 60 m. Stern A-frame gantry supports divers' stage. Can mount a twin 12.7-mm machinegun.

♦ 2 miscellaneous flag officer yachts [YFL]

Bulgarian Navy flag officer yacht H&L Van Ginderen, 7-00

Remarks: Data not available; the larger of the pair may serve as the presidential yacht.

♦ 2 inshore survey craft [YGS] (In serv. 1986–88)

231 331

D: 114 tons (fl) **S:** 12 kts **Dim:** 26.7 × 5.8 × 1.5
Electronics: Radar: 1 Chernomore MR 2512 nav.
M: 2 Type 3D12 diesels; 2 props; 600 bhp **Range:** 600/10 **Crew:** 9 tot.

♦ 2 support tankers [YO]

Bldr: Burgas SY, Burgas (In serv. 203: 1994, 303: 2000)

203 303

Support tanker 303 H&L Van Ginderen, 7-00

D: 1,250 tons (fl) **S:** 12 kts **Dim:** 55.4 × 11.0 × 3.5
A: 1 twin 23-mm AA **Electronics:** Radar: 2 Chernomore MR 2512 nav.
M: 2 Sulzer 6AL-20/24 diesels; 2 props; 1,500 bhp
Range: 1,000/8 **Crew:** 23 tot.

Remarks: 203 was laid down in 1989, launched in 1993. Cargo: 650 tons. Has small crane to facilitate hose handling. Capable of coastal voyages.

♦ 2 fireboats [YTR]

224 321

Fireboat 224—wrapped in deperming cables H&L Van Ginderen, 7-00

D: 531 tons (fl) **S:** 13 kts **Dim:** 38.50 × 10.00 × 3.03
A: 1 4-round Fasta-M SAM launcher (Strela-2M missiles)
Electronics: Radar: 1 Chernomore MR 2512 nav.
M: 2 diesels; 2 props; 2,060 bhp **Range:** 600/10
Endurance: 4–5 days **Crew:** 14 (+ 4 spare berths)

Remarks: Not, as stated in earlier editions, a variant of the YGS survey craft design described above. Have three 500-m^3/hr water monitors, with a range of 70–80 m. Completed 1996.

♦ 1 Polish Type B79/II sail-training craft [YTS]

Bldr: Stocznia Komuny Paryskiej, Gdynia (In serv. 1984)

KALIAKRA

Kaliakra Cem D. Yaylali, 5-05

D: 381 tons (498 fl) **S:** 10.2 (under power)
Dim: 49.00 (42.70 hull; 36.00 pp) × 8.01 × 3.16
M: 1 Wola 68H12 diesel; 1 CP, 356 rpm, 1.5-m-dia. prop; 310 bhp—ketch-rigged (1,038 m^2 max./960 m^2 normal sail area)
Crew: 5 officers, 12 petty officers, 45 cadets
Remarks: 300 grt/100 dwt. A 3-masted barkentine used for naval and merchant marine officer cadet training. Has 63 total berths; can also be used for oceanographic research. Is also advertised for private vacation cruising.

Note: Also in service are small torpedo retriever 205, small tug 222, and about five small barracks barges for which no data are available.

BORDER POLICE

Note: The Border Police is subordinated to the Ministry of the Interior.

PATROL CRAFT [WPC]

♦ 3 FPB 21–class patrol craft

Bldr: Lürssen, Bardenfleth, Germany (In serv. 2003–5)

513 VARNA 514 BURGAS KABAPHA

Kabapha Michael Nitz, 9-05

D: 50 tons **S:** 30 kts **Dim:** 21.0 × 5.8 × 1.4
A: Small arms
Electronics: . . . nav.
M: 2 Deutz MWM TBD 616 diesels; 2,970 bhp; 2 shafts
Range: . . . **Fuel:** . . . **Crew:** . . .
Remarks: *Kabapha,* third and final unit of the class, entered service 10-05 and is based at Kavarna.

♦ 3 ex-German Sea Border Guard Neustadt class

Bldrs: Lürssen, Vegesack

	Laid down	L	In serv.
524 BALCHIK (ex-*Duderstadt,* BG 14)	21-2-69	3-6-69	1970
525 SOZOPOL (ex-*Rosenheim,* BG 18)	8-11-69	12-3-70	11-70
526 NESEBAR (ex-*Neustadt,* BG 11)	25-11-68	27-2-69	25-11-69

D: 191 tons (218 fl) **S:** 30 kts **Dim:** 38.50 (36.00 pp) × 7.00 × 2.15
A: . . .
Electronics: Radar: 1 AESN ARP 1645 nav.; 1 . . . nav.
M: 2 Maybach 16-cyl. diesels; 2 props; 7,200 bhp—cruise engine: 1 MWM cruise diesel; 1 prop; 685 bhp
Electric: 156 kw tot. **Range:** 450/27 **Fuel:** 15 tons **Crew:** 24 tot.

BORDER POLICE PATROL CRAFT [WPC] *(continued)*

Nesebar (526) Martin Mokrus, 5-04

Remarks: 525 transferred unarmed as a gift during 6-02. 524 and 526 followed in 2004. Original armament of two 40-mm 70-cal. Bofors L70 AA guns were removed in 1997.

♦ 1 Soviet Shershen class (Project 206)
Bldr: Zelenodol'sk or Yaroslavl SY

515 (ex-116)

D: 145 tons (170 fl) **S:** 45 kts **Dim:** 34.60 × 6.75 × . . .
A: 2 twin 30-mm 65-cal. AK-230 AA
Electronics:
Radar: 1 Baklan (Pot Drum) surf. search, 1 MR-104 Rys' (Drum Tilt) f.c.
M: 3 M-503A radial diesels; 3 props; 12,000 bhp
Electric: 56 kw tot (2 × 28-kw DG-28 diesel sets)
Range: 460/42; 600/35; 800/30 **Crew:** 20 tot.

Remarks: Survivor of six transferred new from the USSR in 1970; transferred to the Border Police without torpedo tubes. Sister 114 was still afloat at Sozopol in 8-00, but is in derelict condition and disarmed.

PATROL BOATS [WPB]

Note: Two 50-ton patrol boats were ordered from Friedrich Lürssen Werft, Germany, during 11-02; 75% of the cost is being borne by the European Union.

♦ 9 Soviet Zhuk class (Project 1400M)

511 512 513 521 522 523 531 532 533

D: 35.9 tons (39.7 fl) **S:** 30 kts
Dim: 23.80 (21.70 wl) × 5.00 (3.80 wl) × 1.00 (hull)
A: 2 twin 12.7-mm Utës-M mg **Electronics:** Radar: 1 Lotsiya nav.
M: 2 M-401B diesels; 2 props; 2,200 bhp
Electric: 48 kw total (2 × 21-kw, 1 × 6-kw diesel sets)
Range: 500/13.5 **Endurance:** 5 days **Crew:** 3 officers, 8 enlisted

Remarks: Transferred new in 1980–81.

♦ 2 U.S. 27-foot Vigilant class
Bldr: Boston Whaler, Rockland, Mass. (In serv. 4-93)

D: 1.5 tons light (2 tons fl) **S:** 40 kts **Dim:** 8.23 × 2.26 × . . .
A: 1 7.62-mm mg **M:** 2 Johnson outboard motors; 360 bhp
Range: 167/40; 750/ . . . **Crew:** 3 tot.

Remarks: GRP hulls. Transferred for use in enforcing the UN embargo against Serbia on the Danube. Have an enclosed pilothouse, navigational radar, and a pedestal mount for a 7.62-mm mg aft. A third unit was badly damaged 6-93 in a collision and discarded.

Note: There are also two British-built 25-kt RIBs with a range of 350 n.m., supplied for patrol duties on the Danube, and two locally built small patrol launches.

BURUNDI

NAVAL SECTION OF THE BURUNDIAN GENDARMARIE

Personnel: Approx. 100 total

Base: Bujumbura, Lake Tanganyika

PATROL BOATS [WPB]

♦ 1 Nicole class
Bldr: C.N. de Tanganyika, Bujambura

P 106 . . . (L: 6-91)

D: 7 tons (fl) **S:** 18 kts **Dim:** 11.6 × 2.6 × . . .
A: 1 12.7-mm mg; 1 7.62-mm mg
M: 2 Cummins 4 BT3-9M diesels; 2 props; 260 bhp
Electric: 16 kVA (2 shaft generators) **Crew:** 6 tot. + 12 passengers

Remarks: Has also been reported as having Caterpillar diesels totaling 750 bhp for a 25-kt maximum speed. Sister *Nicole* (P 105) was inoperative as of 11-96.

♦ 1 Chinese Yulin class
Bldr: . . ., China (In serv. 1964–68)

D: 9.8 tons (fl) **S:** 20 kts **Dim:** 13.0 × 2.9 × 1.1
A: 1 twin and 1 single 14.5-mm mg **Electronics:** Radar: 1 Furuno . . . nav.
M: 1 3D6 diesel; 1 prop; 150 bhp **Crew:** 4–6 tot.

Remarks: Survivor of four transferred in the 1960s. Has larger superstructure than standard units of the class and has been equipped with navigational radars. Name is either *Ruvubu* or *Cohoha*.

CAMBODIA

Democratic Kampuchea

MARINE ROYAL KHMER

Personnel: Approx. 2,800 total (including 1,500 naval infantry)

Bases: Headquarters at Phnom Penh. Operating facilities at Ream (near Sihanoukville) for seagoing craft and at Chroy Chang for riverine craft.

Organization: Nine Coastal Division naval infantry battalions and seven River Division battalions.

PATROL CRAFT [PC]

Note: During 9-05, China gifted six patrol boats to Cambodia for use combating crime and piracy in Cambodian waters. The handover took place at Sihanoukville. No additional data are yet available.

♦ 2 Soviet Stenka class (Project 205P)
Bldr: Sudostroitel'noye Obyedineniye "Almaz," Petrovskiy SY, St. Petersburg

1133 Mondolkiri 1134 Ratanakiri

D: 170 tons (210 fl) **S:** 24 kts **Dim:** 39.5 × 7.6 × 1.8
A: 2 single 40-mm 60-cal. Bofors AA; 1 twin 23-mm ZSU-23 AA; 1 4-round SAM syst. (14 Igla-1/SA-14 missiles)
Electronics: Radar: 1 . . . nav.
M: 3 Caterpillar . . . diesels; 3 props; . . . bhp
Range: . . . / . . . **Crew:** 5 officers, 20 enlisted

Remarks: Two delivered 10-85 and two 10-87, all without standard fit of four 400-mm ASW torpedo tubes and helicopter-type dipping sonar. Use Osa-I (Project 205) hull and propulsion. All four had manned missile launcher atop the pilothouse and were rehabilitated for further service by UN forces during 1992. 1133 and 1134 were refitted and re-engined at Hong Leong–Lürssen Shipyard, Malaysia, starting in 1994 and returning 10-2-96; they are no longer capable of speeds beyond about 24 kts but have been rearmed. Sisters 1101 and 1102 have been cannibalized.

Note: The two remaining Turya-class (Project 206) semi-hydrofoil gunboats are no longer in service, although their hulks remain afloat at Ream as floating barracks.

PATROL BOATS [PB]

♦ 2 Kaoh Chlam class
Bldr: Hong Leong–Lürssen, Butterworth, Malaysia (In serv. 20-1-97)

1105 Kaoh Chlam 1106 Kaoh Rung

D: 41 tons (44 fl) **S:** 35 kts **Dim:** 21.0 × 5.00 × . . .
A: 1 14.5-mm 93-cal. AA; 2 single 12.7-mm 79-cal. mg
M: 2 Deutz-MWM TBD 616 V 16 diesels; 2 props; 2,948 bhp
Electric: 40 kw tot. (2 × 20-kw Onan MDKAE diesel-driven sets)
Range: 560/35 **Fuel:** 5,600 liters **Crew:** 13 tot.

Remarks: Laid down 12-3-96. Funded by the Malaysian government. Designed by Fassmerwerft, Fassmer, Germany. Aluminum construction.

Disposal note: Soviet-supplied Zhuk-class (Project 199) patrol boats 41 and 42 had ceased to be operational by 2000. Also discarded have been the four Soviet Shmel'-class (Project 1204) river monitors 31 through 34.

♦ 2 U.S. PBR (patrol boat, riverine) Mk II
Bldr: Uniflite, Bellingham, Wash. (In serv. 1974)

D: 8.9 tons (fl) **S:** 24 kts **Dim:** 9.73 × 3.53 × 0.81
A: 1 14.5-mm mg; 1 6-round 120-mm rocket launcher
Electronics: Radar: 1 Raytheon 1900 (SPS-66) nav.
M: 2 G.M. Detroit Diesel 6V53N diesels; 2 Jacuzzi water jets; 430 bhp
Range: 150/23 **Crew:** 4 tot.

Remarks: Survivors of a group donated in 1974. Glass-reinforced plastic hull, plastic armor. Have been considerably modified from the original design as delivered.

AMPHIBIOUS WARFARE CRAFT

♦ 1 ex-U.S. LCM(8)-class medium landing craft

60

D: 34 tons light (121 fl) **S:** 12 kts **Dim:** 22.43 × 6.43 × 1.35 (fwd; 1.47 aft)
M: 4 G.M. Detroit Diesel 6-71 diesels; 2 props; 590 bhp **Range:** 190/12
Crew: 4–5 tot. enlisted

AMPHIBIOUS WARFARE CRAFT *(continued)*

Remarks: Probable Mk4 aluminum version that began building in 1967. Cargo: 60 tons or 150 troops for short distances in 12.8 × 4.3-m open well with 54.6 m^2 space. May have been donated during early 1990s UN intervention.

♦ 5 ex-U.S. LCM(6)-class medium landing craft [LCM]

63 64 65 68 69

D: 24 tons (64 fl) **S:** 10.2 kts **Dim:** 17.07 × 4.37 × 1.22 (fwd; 1.52 aft)
M: 2 Gray Marine 64HN9 (G.M. 6V71 on Mk 3) diesels; 2 props; 330 bhp
Range: 140/10 **Crew:** 4–5 tot.

Remarks: Designed during World War II and built during the 1950s; all converted for various riverine service duties. Another six survive as hulks and may be returned to service.

Disposal note: By 2000 the two Soviet-supplied T-4-class and four Kano-class (Project 1598) landing craft were no longer in service.

Note: Also available may be two small tugs, up to 20 Zodiac RIBs brought by UN peacekeeping forces, and about 170 wooden canoes, around ten of which have outboard motors. The 350-ton-capacity floating dry dock at Ream is no longer operational, but a marine railway capable of handling 500-ton craft was to have been completed in 1997, though no data has yet to appear.

CAMEROON

Republic of Cameroon

MARINE NATIONALE RÉPUBLIQUE

Personnel: About 1,300 total

Bases: Douala (headquarters), Limbe, and Kribi

Naval Aviation: Two Dornier Do-128-6 maritime patrol aircraft with MEL Marec radar

PATROL CRAFT [PC]

♦ 1 French P 48S class
Bldr: Société Française de Constructions Navales (SFCN),Villeneuve-la-Garenne

	Laid down	L	In serv.
P 104 Bakassi	12-81	22-10-82	8-10-83

D: 270 tons (308 fl) **S:** 26 kts **Dim:** 50.20 (47.00 pp) × 7.15 × 2.35
A: 2 single 40-mm 70-cal. Bofors AA
Electronics: Radar: 2 Furuno . . . nav.
M: 2 SACM 195V16 CZSHR diesels; 2 props; 6,400 bhp
Electric: 280 kw tot. **Range:** 2,000/16
Crew: 6 officers, 21 petty officers, 12 nonrated

Bakassi (P 104) Bernard Prézelin, 8-99

Remarks: Ordered 14-12-80; enlarged version of P 48 class. Was refitted at Lorient, France, from 1-99 to 8-99, when provision for launching 8 MM 40 Exocet SSM was deleted, a prominent exhaust stack was added amidships, the radars were replaced, and the EW system was deleted.
Combat systems: The Racal CANE 100 (Command and Navigation Equipment) is fitted. Two Matra Défense Naja optronic directors for the 40-mm AA are carried; they employ the RADOP ranging system, using data from the navigation radars.

♦ 1 French PR 48 class
Bldr: SFCN, Villeneuve-la-Garenne

	Laid down	L	In serv.
P 103 L'Audacieux	23-4-75	30-10-75	11-6-76

D: 250 tons (fl) **S:** 18 kts **Dim:** 47.50 (45.50 pp) × 7.10 × 2.25
A: 2 single 40-mm 60-cal. Bofors AA
Electronics: Radar: 1 Decca 1226 nav.
M: 2 SACM V12CZSHR diesels; 2 props; 4,200 bhp **Electric:** 100 kw tot.
Range: 2,000/15 **Fuel:** 90 tons **Crew:** 4 officers, 21 enlisted

Remarks: Ordered 9-74. Had been reported inoperable and hulked, but was put back into service after a refit in 1995; may again be inoperable, however.

PATROL BOATS [PB]

♦ 4 Rodman 46 class
Bldr: Rodman-Polyships, Vigo, Spain (In serv. 2000)

VS 201 Idabato VS 202 Isongo
VS 203 Mouanko VS 204 Campo

D: 18.5 tons (fl) **S:** 44 kts **Dim:** 14 × 3.80 × 0.80
A: 1 12.7-mm mg **Electronics:** Radar: 1 . . . nav.
M: 2 M.A.N. D2842 LXE diesels; 2 waterjets
Range: . . . **Crew:** . . .

Remarks: GRP construction.

♦ 2 Rodman 101 class
Bldr: Rodman-Polyships, Vigo, Spain

P 106 Akwafaye P 107 Jabanne

D: 46 tons (fl) **S:** 33 kts **Dim:** 30.00 (24.96 pp) × 6.51 (6.00 wl) × 1.50
A: 1 12.7-mm mg **Electronics:** Radar: 1 Furuno . . . nav.
M: 2 MTU 12V2000 diesels; 2 Hamilton HM-571 waterjets; 2,900 bhp (2,760 bhp sust.)
Electric: 42 kw (2 × 21-kw diesel sets) **Range:** 800/25 **Crew:** 9 tot.

Remarks: Sister ships are operated by Surinam.

♦ 6 38-ft. class
Bldr: Swiftships, Morgan City, La. (In serv. 1986–87)

PR 01 through PR 20 series

PR 02 on trials Swiftships, 1986

D: 11.7 tons (fl) **S:** 33 kts **Dim:** 11.58 × 3.81 × 1.00
A: 2 single 12.7-mm M2 mg; 2 single 7.62-mm mg
Electronics: Radar: 1 . . . nav.
M: 2 Stewart & Stevenson–G.M. 6V 92 MTA diesels; 2 props; 1,100 bhp
Range: 216/20 **Crew:** 4 tot.

Remarks: A contract for 30 of these craft (10 for the Gendarmerie) was signed 29-8-86, with all deliveries to be made by end-1987. For use on the Chad River, based at Doula. Aluminum construction. Hull of 1.90-m molded depth. The first 10 arrived in Cameroon 3-87, the second 10 in 9-87. By early 1997, most were no longer operational.

Disposal note: The three NAPCO Raider-class launches are no longer in service.

♦ 1 Motto class
Bldr: A.C.R.E., Libreville, Gabon (In serv. 12-11-73)

Quartier-Maître Alfred Motto

Quartier-Maître Alfred Motto French Navy, 11-97

D: 96 tons (fl) **S:** 15.5 kts **Dim:** 29.10 × 6.20 × 1.85 (props)
A: 2 single 12.7-mm M2 mg **Electronics:** Radar: 1 . . . nav.
M: 2 Baudouin diesels; 2 props; 1,290 bhp **Crew:** 2 officers, 15 enlisted

Remarks: Out of service by 1991, but was reactivated early in 1996 and in use in local patrol duties and troop transportation.

AMPHIBIOUS WARFARE CRAFT

♦ **2 small landing craft [LCM]** (In serv. 1973)

BETIKA (ex-*Bakassi*) BIBUNDI

D: 57 tons (fl) **S:** 9 kts **Dim:** 17.5 × 4.28 × 1.3
M: 2 Baudouin diesels; 490 bhp

Betika—note pilothouse raised above vehicle deck French Navy, 11-97

Remarks: First unit built by Tanguy Marine, France; the second by Carena, Abidjan, Ivory Coast, with French assistance. Refitted 1987.

SERVICE CRAFT

♦ **1 floating dry dock [YFDL]**
Bldr: Flenderwerft, Lübeck, Germany (In serv. 23-7-87)

BAMUSSO

Remarks: Government-owned, for repair of commercial and government vessels. Capacity: 10,000 tons.

♦ **2 10-ton harbor launches [YFL]**

BIMBIA SANAGA

♦ **1 buoy tender [YGL]**
Bldr: Cossens, Emden (In serv. 12-90)

NYONG

Nyong A. A. de Kruijf and Piet Sinke, 2-91

D: 218 grt **S:** 11.5 kts **Dim:** . . . (41.40 pp) × 11.50 × 3.00
M: 2 MWM TBD-440-6K diesels; 2 props; 2,200 bhp **Crew:** 15 tot.

GENDARMERIE

PATROL BOATS [WPB]

♦ **4 SM.360 class**
Bldr: Simonneau Marine, Fontenay-le-Comte, France (In serv. 3-91)

D: 7.5 tons (fl) **S:** 27 kts **Dim:** 11.10 (10.10 hull) × 3.50 × 0.80
A: 1 7.62-mm mg **Electronics:** Radar: 1 Furuno . . . nav.
M: 2 Volvo TAMD61 diesels; 2 props; 900 bhp (504 bhp sust.)
Range: 230/18 **Crew:** 1 officer, 5 enlisted

Remarks: Transferred from the navy 10-91. Aluminum construction.

♦ **Up to 10 38-foot class**
Bldr: Swiftships, Morgan City, La. (In serv. 3-88)

Remarks: For characteristics, see above under naval entry.

Note: Gendarmerie forces also operate up to six 9.1-m launches built by Société Africaine d'Étude de la Réalisation Industrielle (SAERI), Douala, in 1986–87 and several survivors from among the 12 Type 650 and Type 800 launches of 3.5 tons delivered 1977–82 by Chantiers Plascoa, Cannes, France. **Dim:** 8.50 × 3.00 × 0.72.

CANADA

MARITIME COMMAND

Personnel: Approx. 12,000 total active, plus 4,000 in the Naval Reserve (in 24 divisions)

Bases: Fleet headquarters at Ottawa, with bases at Esquimalt on the Pacific coast and Halifax on the Atlantic. At Nanoose Bay, Vancouver Island, is the Canadian Forces Maritime Experimental and Test Range, operated jointly with the U.S. Navy. Fleet Maintenance Facility *Cape Breton,* at Esquimalt, has had various facilities consolidated into two new buildings. A historic building was renovated to support submarine activities. The nearby fueling facility at Colwood was also renovated.

Organization: The unified military organization of Canada comprises four operational commands and two support groups under the Canadian Armed Forces. Operational commands include the Mobile Force (army), Air Command, Maritime Command, and Communications Command. These are supported by the Personnel Group and the Material Group. Canadian maritime aircraft are subordinated to the Air Command but under the operational control of the Maritime Command.

The Fleet is organized into Maritime Command Atlantic (MARLANT) and Maritime Command Pacific (MARPAC). Subordinate to MARLANT are Maritime Operations Groups (MAROPGRU) 1 and 3, while subordinate to MARPAC are MAROPGRU 2 and 4.

Under a 12-99 decision, naval readiness is to be reduced, maintaining only one Contingency Task Group (consisting of one DD, two FFs, one AOR, one SS, and six maritime patrol aircraft) available for deployment with a 30-day warning, one National Task Group (with similar composition) available within 60 days, and five additional *Halifax*-class frigates capable of deployment within 90 days. Ships of the first two groups will receive 120 days of sea-time annually, while the others will have only 80 days; other ships will be retained on 180-day deployment readiness and may have as little as 20 days at sea per year.

Maritime Aviation: 29 CH-124A/B/C Sea King (SAR/Utility) helicopters; 15 CH-149 Cormorant (a variant of the EH-101 Merlin design); 18 CP-140 Aurora maritime patrol aircraft; 3 CP-140A Arcturus for Arctic patrol and training; 3 CC-130E Hercules SAR aircraft/transports and 2 CC-144 Challenger utility/medical evacuation transports. Beginning in 2008, the aging Sea King helicopters will be replaced by 28 Sikorsky Superhawk helicopters (a militarized version of the H-92). Given the designation CH-148 Cyclone, the new aircraft will enter service at a rate of one per month.

The Aurora (a variant of the U.S. P-3 Orion airframe) has the Orion's A-NEW system, based on the miniaturized Univac ASQ-114 computer. There are 36 launching chutes for dropping active and passive sonobuoys and racks for 120 reserve sonobuoys. Other principal systems are 2ASN-84 inertial navigation computers; doppler radar; tactical recorder; flight-control director; tactical datalink system: FLIR (Forward-Looking Infrared); SLAR (Side-Looking Airborne Radar) antennas; detectors for lasers; and a low-light television pod. Beginning 7-97, the Aurora fleet began a modernization program incorporating upgrading the APS-116 radar to include a "spotlight" synthetic aperture capability, substitution of a 99-channel sonobuoy receiver, an acoustic processor and EW upgrade (including installation of ALR-76), installation of GPS, and updated communication gear; was completed in 2004, extending the fleet's life span through 2010, but two of the 18 are to be retired without modification.

CP-140 Aurora maritime patrol aircraft Bernard Prézelin, 6-04

CH-124-series Sea King ASW helicopter Martin Mokrus, 4-05

CH-149 Cormorant SAR helicopter, 442 Sq.
Canadian Forces Combat Camera, 9-04

MARITIME COMMAND *(continued)*

The CP-140A Arcturus has APS-134 radar, APN RAWS, ASW-502 autopilot, APN-510 doppler navigation radar, LN-33 inertial navigation system, and ASH-502 flight recorder—but no ASW equipment. A GPS receiver, ESM gear, and a 99-channel sonobuoy receiver/processor are to be added later; the aircraft are to be retired shortly.

The last CH-113 Labrador SAR helicopter was retired in 2004, after 41 years of active service. All of the CE-133 Silver Star and all but two EC-144C Challenger electronic support and training aircraft have been retired.

Maritime Aviation Squadron Organization:

8 Wing, CFB Trenton, Ont.	CH-149 Cormorant
9 Wing, CFB Gander, Nfld.	CH-149 Cormorant: 103 SAR Sq.
	CH-113A Labrador: 103 SAR Sq. (2 aircraft)
14 Wing, CFB Greenwood, N.S.	CP-140 Aurora: MP 404, MP 405, MP 415
	CC-130 Hercules: 413 Sq.
	CH-113A Labrador: 413 Sq. (2 aircraft)
	Challenger 600/601: 434 Sq.
12 Wing, CFB Halifax, N.S.	CH-124A/B Sea King: HS 423, HT 406
19 Wing, CFB Comox, B.C.	CP-140 Aurora: MP 407
	CH-113A Labrador: 1 aircraft
	CH-149 Cormorant: 442 Sq.
Victoria Municipal Airport, Esquimalt, B.C.	CH-124A/B Sea King: HS 443

WEAPONS AND SYSTEMS

A. MISSILES

Surface-to-air missiles: NATO Sea Sparrow RIM-7P is used from Mk 48 vertical launchers in the *Halifax* class; to be replaced by Evolved Sea Sparrow starting late in 2004.

Vertically launched Standard SM-2 MR Block II replaced Sea Sparrow in the *Iroquois* (Tribal) class; ten new SM-2 Block IIIA missiles were ordered in 3-98 and another 12 were requested on 25-6-02.

Surface-to-surface missiles: Canada has purchased the U.S. AGM-84C Harpoon missile for use by CP-140 Aurora aircraft and the RGM-84C for use by surface ships. In 1984 34 RGM-84D shipboard versions were ordered, and another 12 were ordered in 1998. Consideration is being given to procuring a limited number of AGM-84E Sea SLAM missiles for land-attack missions.

B. GUNS

76-mm 62-cal. OTO Melara Super Rapid: Single mount on the Iroquois class. See Italy section for data.

57-mm Bofors SAK Mk 2: Single mount on the *Halifax* class. See Swedish section for data.

40-mm Mk N1/1 Bofors AA on Mk 5c "Boffin" mounting: Standard 60-cal. gun on powered mount originally designed for twin 20-mm Oerlikon AA during World War II. Mounts formerly used for airfield defense in Europe. One mount each on *Kingston*-class reserve training ships.

20-mm U.S. Mk 15 Block 1 Phalanx CIWS: On *Iroquois*-class destroyers and *Halifax*-class frigates and *Protecteur*-class replenishment ships. All 21 mounts in service have been updated to Block 1B under a $29,850,000 contract with Raytheon signed on 1-5-02; first conversion kit delivered 9-02 and the last during 2005. See characteristics in U.S. section.

C. TORPEDOES

U.S. Mk 46 Mod. 5: ASW torpedoes aboard ships, Sea King helicopters, and maritime patrol aircraft. A total of 524 are available (374 new, delivered 1988–91, and 150 updated from Mod 1).

U.S. Mk 48 Mod. 4: On submarines. 48 ordered in 1985; 13 in 1988; 26 in 1989. *Upholder*-class submarines are being altered to employ Mk 48s.

D. ELECTRONICS

♦ Radars

DA-08: Thales surface/air search in *Iroquois* class.
LIROD-8: Thales X-band fire-control radar in *Iroquois* class.
LW-08: Thales long-range air search in *Iroquois* class.
SPG-501: Raytheon-made STIR 1.8 tracker/illuminator in *Iroquois* class.
SPG-503: Thales-made STIR 1.8 tracker/illuminator in *Halifax* class.
SPS-49(V)5: Raytheon 2-D air-search radar on *Halifax* class.
Sea Giraffe 150HC: Swedish Ericsson surface search on the *Halifax* class.
Type 1006: Kelvin-Hughes submarine general-purpose search radar.

Note: In 2000 Raytheon Systems Canada demonstrated the SWR-503, a shore-based HF surface-wave ocean surveillance sonar, intended for monitoring or detecting illegal drug and smuggling activities, piracy, illegal fishing, etc., to ranges greater than 200 n.m. from shore.

♦ Sonars

SQR-501 CANTASS: Towed passive linear hydrophone array for the *Halifax* class; uses "wet end" of U.S. AN/SQR-19A system with Canadian UYS-501 receiver/processor and UYQ-501 displays.
SQS-505: Hull-mounted and towed LF installed in the *Iroquois* class (SQA-502 hoist).
SQS-505 TASP with digital acoustic processing and SHINPADS display: Tested in an *Iroquois*-class ship from 1985 to 1988. Latest version, SQS-505(V)6, carried by *Halifax* class vice planned SQS-510. It operates at 7 kHz. *Protecteur*-class SQS-505(V)3 was removed in 1998.
SQS-510: Hull-mounted. MF set operating between 4.3 and 8.0 kHz, intended as successor to SQS-505.

♦ Sonobuoys

SSQ-522 active, SSQ-527 passive LOFAR, and SSQ-530 passive DIFAR sonobuoys are used by helicopters and fixed-wing aircraft.

♦ Countermeasures

SLQ-25: U.S. Aerojet Nixie towed acoustic homing torpedo decoy (to be upgraded to SLQ-25A solid-state variant in 17 ships by 2009)
SLQ-501: MEL CANEWS (Canadian Electronic Warfare System) intercept for frigates and destroyers
SLQ-502: GEC-Marconi Shield rocket decoy launcher on *Iroquois* and *Halifax* classes; AORs fitted with MK36 SRBOC, *Iroquois* class with Australian Nulka rocket decoy launch capability
SLQ-503: Lockheed RAMSES (Reprogrammable Advanced Multimode Shipboard ECM System) jammer for the *Halifax* class
SLQ-504: Racal Kestrel 242 intercept
SRD-501: HFD/F system on *Iroquois*-class destroyers
SRD-502: Southwest-made Telegon-4 HFD/F on *Halifax*-class frigates
SRN-504: Combat direction-finding system for missile targeting; similar to the U.S. SSQ-108 system

♦ Communications

Canadian Maritime Forces employs two civilian communications satellites, Anik-E1 and Anik-E2.

ATTACK SUBMARINES [SS]

♦ 4 ex-U.K. Upholder class

Bldrs: Chicoutimi: VSEL, Barrow-in-Furness; others: Cammell Laird, Birkenhead

	Laid down	L	In serv.
SS 876 VICTORIA (ex-*Unseen,* S 41)	12-8-87	14-11-89	20-7-91
SS 877 WINDSOR (ex-*Unicorn,* S 43)	13-3-90	16-4-92	25-6-93
SS 878 CORNER BROOK (ex-*Ursula,* S 42)	10-1-89	28-2-91	8-5-92
SS 879 CHICOUTIMI (ex-*Upholder,* S 40)	2-86	2-12-86	7-12-90

Windsor (SS 877) Alan Rowlands, Canadian DND, 10-01

Chicoutimi (SS 897)—awaiting rescue, following fire off the coast of Scotland
Canadian DND, 10-04

ATTACK SUBMARINES [SS] *(continued)*

Chicoutimi (SS 897)—aboard transport ship for voyage back to Canada
Canadian DND, 1-05

D: 1,870 tons std., 2,185 tons surf./2,400 tons sub.
S: 12 kts surf./20 kts sub. **Dim:** 70.26 (47.5 pressure hull) × 7.60 × 5.50
A: 6 bow 533-mm TT (18 tot. Alliant Mk. 48 Mod. 4 torpedoes)
Electronics:
Radar: 1 Kelvin-Hughes Type 1007 nav./surf. search
Sonar: Thales Type 2040 Argonaut bow active/passive; Type 2041 MicroPUFFS passive flank array; SUBTASS towed array; Type 2019 (PARIS) intercept
EW: Decca PORPOISE intercept; 2 SSE Mk 8 decoy tubes (Type 2066 Bandfish and Type 2071 decoys)
M: 2 Paxman Valenta 16 RPA 200SZ 16-cyl. diesel generators (2,035 bhp each); 2 G.E.C.-Alsthom 2,500-kw alternators, 1 GEC double-armature electric motor; 1 7-bladed prop; 5,400 shp
Range: 8,000/8 (snorkel); 54/20, 270/3 sub.
Fuel: 200 tons **Endurance:** 50 days **Crew:** 7 officers, 37 enlisted

Remarks: Leased for eight years for US $427 million total on 2-7-98, with another $98 million to be spent on improvements; at the end of the eight years, the quartet are to be purchased for a nominal £1. Delivery of the *Victoria* was to have come during 5-00, with the others to follow at six-month intervals, but piping weld problems delayed the work by about three months per boat, and the reactivations were performed for prime contractor BAe Systems by Cammell Laird at Birkenhead, with the work on SS 876 started on 4-7-00. All four required replacement of the diesel exhaust system valves. During 6-02, due to the unexpected costs involved in reactivating the submarines, plans to install an Air-Independent Propulsion (AIP) system in two of the class were deferred to around 2013.

SS 876 was handed over to Canada on 6-10-00 and recommissioned at Halifax on 2-12-00. SS 877 was handed over on 6-7-01 and arrived in Canada during 10-01. She was commissioned on 4-10-03, following Canadian Work Package modifications. SS 878 was handed over on 21-2-03 and recommissioned into Canadian service 29-6-03. SS 879 was handed over on 2-10-03. Part of the lease cost is being offset by not charging the U.K. for troop training facilities in Canada. Included in the acquisition were four shore-based trainer sets, initial crew training, and spare parts for two to three years of operations.

The four had been decommissioned from U.K. service on 6-4-94, 16-10-94, 6-94, and 29-4-94, respectively. They are expected to operate for about 30 years. Are superior in virtually every respect to the contemporary Russian Kilo series.

On 5-10-04, two days after her acceptance by the Canadian Navy, a major fire broke out in an electrical panel aboard HMCS *Chicoutimi.* The fire, which resulted from seawater entering the boat through open hatches in rough seas, caused one death and several serious injuries among the Canadian crew. The submarine lost power and was subsequently towed back to Faslane. Following temporary repairs, *Chicoutimi* was transported back to Halifax aboard a heavy lift ship, where repairs continued throughout 2005. As a result of this fire, all Canadian submarine operations were briefly halted while a new SubSafe program was implimented. HMCS *Victoria* was the first of the class returned to operational service on 20-5-05.

Hull systems: Able to snorkel at 19 kts and can remain submerged 90 hours at 3 knots. Operating depth: over 250 m. Have rubber anechoic hull coating. Are intended to operate 15,000 hrs (7 years) between overhauls. Need only 40–60 min./day battery charging at normal patrol speeds. Have 11% reserve buoyancy when surfaced. Two 240-cell lead-acid batteries, 6,080 amp-hr at one-hour rate, 8,800 amp-hr at five-hour rate. There is a five-person divers' lockout chamber in the sail. Single-hull design. The sail has a glass-reinforced plastic skin. A 200-kw air-independent auxiliary propulsion system may be added during mid-life refits around 2013. Have extremely small acoustic and magnetic signatures.

Combat systems: During reactivation, were fitted to launch U.S. Mk 48 torpedoes; the original weapons-control system is being replaced with a Singer Librascope Mk 1 Mod. 0 (BYG-501) fire-control system using a UYK-20 computer; these are being recycled from the *Oberon* class and a shore trainer. Originally had two Ferranti FM 1600E computers, Thorn E.M.I. 1553B data system, and inertial navigation system. Have a Pilkington Optronics CK 35 search periscope with EW array and a CH 85 attack scope with infrared capability. Type 2040 sonar is a version of the Thales Argonaut system; the cylindrical transducer array is at the bow, with intercept hydrophones arranged along the sides. The Guardian Star electronic intercept equipment is also being recycled from the *Oberon* class, and Canadian communications (including WSC-3 SATCOM gear) and cryptologic equipment is being substituted. The sonar system was to be updated during reactivation, including substitution of a Canadian-made SUBTASS towed array. Have two 102-mm SSE Mk 8 decoy and signal launch tubes. They will not be equipped to launch UGM-84 Harpoon missiles. Signals intelligence collection equipment is to be added. Plans were announced 8-01 for an air-defense/anti-smallcraft missile system to be installed during refits from 2009 to 2014. Minelaying capability removed in the U.K. prior to transfer.

GUIDED-MISSILE DESTROYERS [DDG]

Note: A replacement program for the *Iroquois* class, dubbed CADRE (Command and Control and Air-Defence Replacement) has been abandoned in favor of a Single Combat Class (SCC) to replace the *Iroquois* destroyers and *Halifax*-class frigates. The first units would be fitted as AAW ships and the remaining vessels as General Purpose Warships.

♦ 3 Iroquois (DDH 280) class

Bldrs: DDH 280: Marine Industries, Sorel; DDH 282, 283: Davie SB, Lauzon

	Laid down	L	In serv.
DDH 280 Iroquois	15-1-69	28-11-70	29-7-72
DDH 282 Athabaskan	1-6-69	27-11-70	30-11-72
DDH 283 Algonquin	1-9-69	23-4-71	30-9-73

Algonquin (DDH 283) U.S. Navy, 6-04

Iroquois (DDH 280)—following Sea King helicopter accident
Canadian DND, 2-03

Algonquin (DDH 283) U.S. Navy, 6-04

D: 4,450 tons (5,100 fl) **S:** 29 kts (27 sust.)
Dim: 128.84 (121.31 pp) × 15.24 × 4.69 (7.86 max.)
A: 1 Mk 41 VLS group (32 Standard SM-2 Block IIIA missiles); 1 76-mm/62-cal. OTO Melara SuperRapid DP; 1 20-mm U.S. Mk 15 Mod. 11 Block 1A Phalanx gatling CIWS; 2 triple 324-mm Mk 32 Mod. 5 ASW TT; 2 CH-124A Sea King helicopters

GUIDED-MISSILE DESTROYERS [DDG] *(continued)*

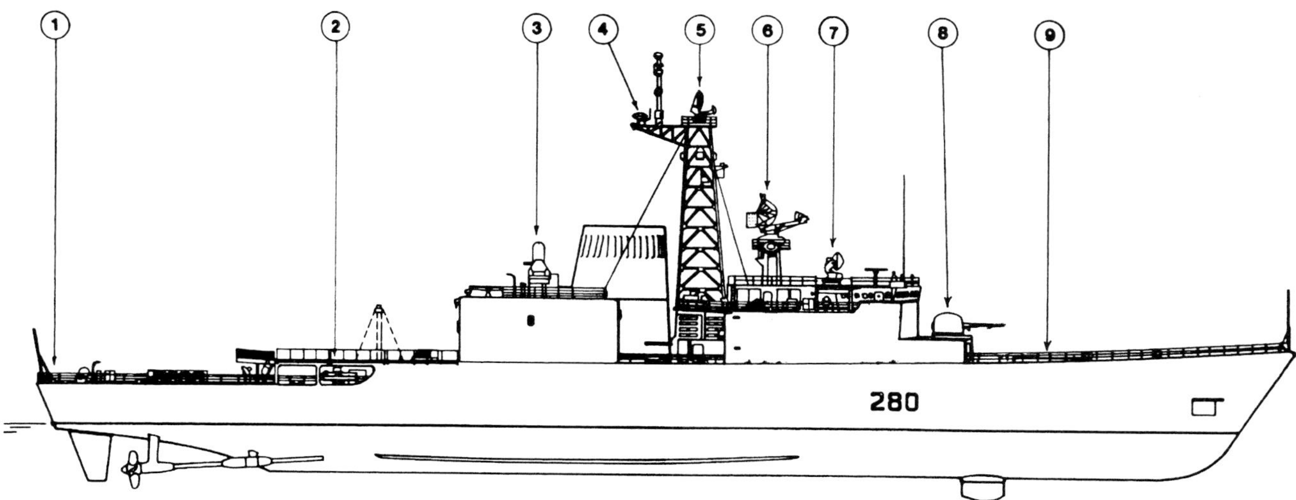

Iroquois (DDH 280) 1. VDS housing 2. Triple Mk 32 ASW TT 3. 20-mm Mk 15 Phalanx CIWS 4. URN-25 TACAN antenna 5. SPQ-501 air/surface-search radar 6. SPQ-502 early-warning radar 7. SPG-501 tracker/illuminators (side-by-side) 8. 76-mm 62-cal. OTOBreda SuperRapid DP gun 9. Mk 41 vertical launch cells for Standard SM-2 missiles
Drawing by A. D. Baker III

Electronics:
Radar: 2 Raytheon 1900 Pathfinder nav.; 1 Thales SPQ-501 (DA-08/2LS) surf./air search; 1 Thales SPQ-502 (LW-08) early warning; 2 Raytheon SPG-501 (STIR 1.8/OT-134) tracker/illuminators; 1 Gen. Dynamics Mk 90 Phalanx f.c.; 1 Thales LIROD-8 gun f.c.
Sonar: Westinghouse SQS-510(V)4 hull-mounted; Westinghouse SQS-505(V)5 VDS; C-Tech Spectra 3000 mine-avoidance
TACAN: URN-25
EW: Racal SLQ-503 (CANEWS) intercept; SRD-503 HFD/F; U.S. ULQ-6B jammer, 4 6-round Plessey Shield decoy RL (with Nulka decoy-launch capability); SLQ-25A Nixie towed acoustic torpedo decoy
E/O: Westcam 14 multi-spectral IR/laser/t.v.

M: COGOG: 2 Pratt & Whitney FT4A-2 boost gas turbines (23,747 shp each); 2 G.M. Allison 570KF cruise gas turbines (6,445 shp each); 2 five-bladed CP props; 47,494 shp max.
Electric: 3,750 kw tot. **Range:** 3,500/20; 4,500/15
Crew: 26 officers, 266 enlisted + air group: 9 officers, 21 enlisted (DDH 281: 75 tot. caretaker crew)

Remarks: These ships have been updated under a design prepared by Litton Systems Canada. DDH 283 began a TRUMP ("Tribal" Update and Modernization Program) conversion period 26-10-87 at MIL-Davie, Lauzon, Quebec, but the conversion was delayed by two fires and other problems, and the ship was not accepted until 11-10-91, with first missile firings not until 18-1-92; the ship returned to the West Coast 12-93. DDH 280 began conversion 25-10-88 at the same facility and was accepted 3-7-92. Work on DDH 282 began 10-91 and completed 4-6-94, with the ship re-entering full service in 5-95. A refit for DDH 283 was awarded to Victoria SY on 24-2-03 (to extend the ship's service for five years). The remaining three ships are scheduled to serve until 2010.

Hull systems: Modernization has increased the seaworthiness of the ships considerably, reducing the roll and limiting heel to 17° during turns. Limiting displacement is 5,220 tons. Have fin stabilizers. During modernization, a G.M. 1,000-kw diesel generator was fitted and accommodations and climate control were considerably improved. Water ballast compensation has been fitted for the fuel tanks.

Combat systems: The UYC-501 SHINPADS command-and-control system incorporates UYQ-504 and UYQ-507 computers and employs NATO Links 11 and 14 (Link 16 was to reported to have been added in 2000 and Link 22 is to be added around 2005–6). The U.S. Mk 41 VLS (Vertical Launch System) for 32 Standard SM-2(MR) Block III SAMs replaced the OTO Melara 127-mm gun forward, while an OTO Melara 76-mm DP gun was installed in the former Sea Sparrow magazine area. The Mk 15 CIWS was placed atop the hangar, and ASW torpedo stowage and handling was improved. The Standard missiles are controlled by two illuminator/trackers and the 76-mm gun by the LIROD-8 radar/electro-optical director atop the pilothouse. The planned SLQ-503 jammer was not installed and the obsolescent U.S. ULQ-6 was instead retained. The U.S. SLQ-25 Nixie torpedo decoy was added and is now being upgraded to SLQ-25A, and the U.S. WSN-5 inertial navigation system and SRR-1 SATCOMM are installed. All have the Bear Trap positive-control helicopter landing system. Have an onboard UYS-503(V) processor to analyze signals from helicopter-dropped sonobuoys. ASW systems in the modernized ships are basically unchanged, except for removal of the Limbo mortar and its depth-finding sonar.

Nulka decoy launchers were installed during 1999 immediately aft of the flight deck on the three active ships. DDH 280 and DDH 282 completed installation of an enhanced communications suite including a Matra Marconi SHF SATCOM system, an eight-transmitter Harris SRC-503 HF, three Harris narrowband transceivers, 10 UHF transceivers, two Have Quick II UHF SATCOM transceivers, Marconi VLF receivers, and a digital INMARSAT commercial SATCOM. Plans to upgrade the West Coast pair were canceled (although DDH 283 has received a Have Quick UHF SATCOM). UHF transceivers and VLF communications receivers were also added, while the commercial SATCOM system was upgraded to INMARSAT-B. All have WSC-4 and SSR-1 SATCOM. DDH 280 may retain a Koden MD 373 radar atop the hangar; in the others, the after Raytheon navigational set is located there for helicopter control.

Disposals: *Huron* (DDH 281) was laid up on 23-10-00 at Esquimalt, with a 75-man caretaker crew. Though maintained in 60–90–day activation reserve she was extensively cannibalized for spares and formally decommissioned on 31-3-05.

FRIGATES [FF]

♦ 12 Halifax class

Bldrs: A: St. John SB, N.B.; B: MIL Group Davie SY, Lauzon, Que. (sterns by MIL, Tracy)

	Bldr	Laid down	L	In serv.
FFH 330 Halifax	A	19-3-87	30-5-88	29-6-92
FFH 331 Vancouver	A	19-5-88	8-7-89	23-8-93
FFH 332 Ville de Québec	B	16-12-88	16-5-91	14-7-94
FFH 333 Toronto	A	22-4-89	15-6-91	29-7-93
FFH 334 Regina	B	6-10-89	25-11-91	30-9-94
FFH 335 Calgary	B	15-6-91	28-8-92	12-5-95
FFH 336 Montreal	A	9-2-91	28-2-92	21-7-94
FFH 337 Fredericton	A	25-4-92	26-6-93	10-9-94
FFH 338 Winnipeg	A	19-3-93	25-6-94	23-6-95
FFH 339 Charlottetown	A	17-12-93	1-10-94	9-9-95
FFH 340 St. John's	A	24-8-94	12-2-95	24-6-96
FFH 341 Ottawa	A	29-4-95	22-11-95	28-9-96

Toronto (FFH 333) U.S. Navy, 6-04

D: 3,922 tons light, 4,305 tons std. (4,761 fl)
S: 29.2 kts (27 sust.; 18 max. on diesel)
Dim: 135.5 (124.50 pp) × 16.40 (14.80 wl) × 4.94 mean hull (6.15 max.)
A: 8 RGM-84C/D Harpoon SSM; 2 Mk 48 Mod. 0 Sea Sparrow VLS SAM launch groups (16 RIM-7M missiles); 1 57-mm 70-cal. Bofors SAK-57 Mk 2 DP; 1 20-mm Mk 15 Phalanx Block 1B gatling CIWS; 4 single 12.7-mm mg; 2 paired, fixed 324-mm Mk 32 Mod. 9 ASW TT (24 Mk 46 Mod. 1 or Mod. 5 torpedoes); 1 CH-124A Sea King helicopter

FRIGATES [FF] *(continued)*

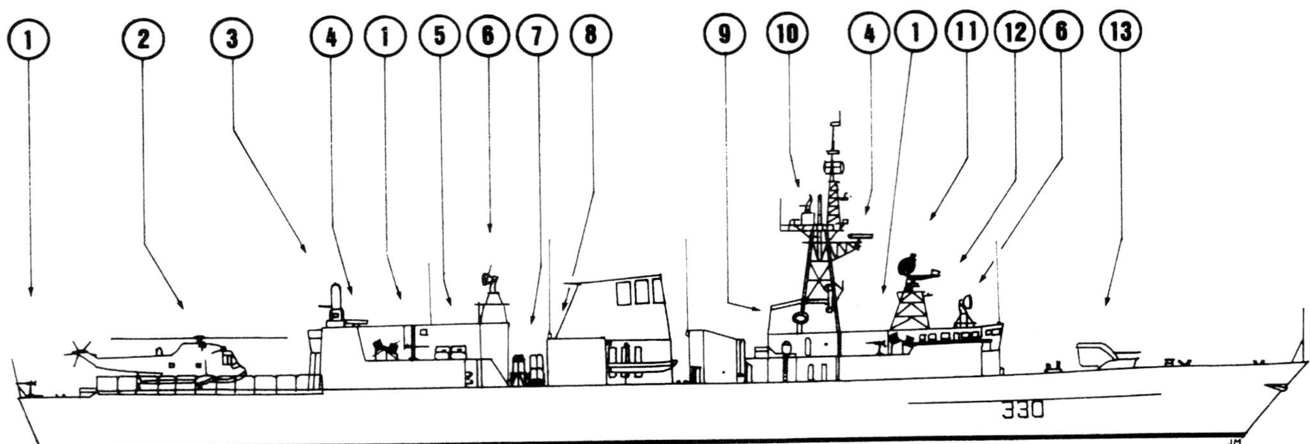

Halifax (FFH 330) 1. 12.7-mm machineguns 2. CH-124 Sea King helicopter 3. 20-mm Mk 15 Phalanx CIWS 4. navigational and helicopter-control radars 5. twin, fixed Mk 32 ASW TT in deckhouse at main deck level 6. SPG-503 tracker/illuminator radars 7. RGM-84 Harpoon SSM in quadruple launch canister groups 8. Mk 48 vertical launch cells for Sea Sparrow SAMs 9. OE-82 antennas for the U.S. WSC-3 UHF SATCOM system 10. Sea Giraffe 150HC search radar 11. SPS-49(V)5 air-search radar 12. Decoy RL on bridge wings 13. 57-mm SAK 57 DP gun — Drawing by Jean Moulin

Montreal (FFH 336) — Bernard Prézelin, 6-05

Halifax (FFH 330) — Martin Mokrus, 9-05

Electronics:

Radar: 2 Sperry Mk 340X (FFH 335, 337–341: Kelvin-Hughes Type 1007) nav.; 1 Ericsson Sea Giraffe 150HC air/surf. search; 1 Raytheon SPS-49(V)5 long-range air search; 2 Thales SPG-503 (VM-25 STIR 1.8) f.c.

Sonar: SQS-510(V) hull-mounted, variable depth; SQR-501 CANTASS passive towed array; WQC-501(V) underwater telephone; UYS-503 sonobuoy processor

EW: Racal SLQ-504 (CANEWS) intercept; Lockheed SLQ-503 (RAMSES) jammer; Southwest SRD-502 (Telegon 4) HFD/F; 4 six-round SLQ-502 (Marconi-GEC Shield-II) decoy RL; Aerojet SLQ-25QA Nixie towed acoustic torpedo decoy (FFH 338 also: SRD-504 combat D/F)

E/O: Westcam 14 multi-spectral IR/laser/t.v.—TACAN: URN-25

M: CODOG: 2 G.E. LM-2500-30 gas turbines (23,747 shp each at 3,600 rpm), 1 SEMT-Pielstick 20PA6-V280-BTC diesel (11,780 bhp max., 8,675 bhp sust.); 2 Escher-Wyss CP props; 47,494 shp

Electric: 3,400 kw tot. (4 MWM TBO-602 V-16K diesel generator sets)

Range: 4,500/15 on one gas turbine; 7,100/15 diesel **Fuel:** 550 tons

Crew: 22 officers, 202 enlisted (peacetime complement: 180 total)

Montreal (FFH 336)—note 57-mm SAK 57 DP gun on forecastle, SPG-503 tracker/illuminator radar atop the bridge, vertical SAM launchers abreast stack and Phalanx CIWS on starboard side of the hangar roof — Martin Mokrus, 6-05

FRIGATES [FF] *(continued)*

Remarks: First six ordered 29-7-83 from consortium of St. John Shipbuilding, Ltd., Paramax Electronics (later Unisys GSG Canada), and Sperry, with three subcontracted to Marine Industries (later MIL Group). Second flight of six ordered 18-12-87, all from St. John. FFH 330, 332, 333, 336, 337, 339, and 340 are assigned to MARLANT, the others to MARPAC.
Hull systems: Full-load displacement has grown by 496 tons since construction began; limiting displacement is 5,100 tons. The ships have a bubbler noise-reduction system. Do not have fin stabilizers. Measures have been taken to minimize the infrared signature, and the ships have NBC warfare-proof citadels. The engines are raft-mounted to reduce radiated noise, but they have been found to be noisier than expected. The Indal Bear Trap helicopter haul-down and deck transit system is installed. Fuel capacity has been increased from the original 479 tons. FFH 330, 332, and 333 experienced propulsion diesel cracking problems; until repairs were made by the manufacturer during 1995–96, the unrepaired ships were restricted to 13–15 kts on diesel power. FFH 336 has 12,500 synthetic rubber anechoic tiles on the hull on the exterior of the underwater hull in the vicinity of the machinery spaces to reduce radiated noise.
Combat systems: The Thales UYQ-501(V) SHINPADS (Shipboard Integrated Processing and Display System) data system with UYC-501(V) databus is fitted. Were originally to have had the newer SQS-510 hull-mounted sonar. The transducer for the SQS-505(V)6 set is mounted in a C5 retractable dome. SQR-501 CANTASS towed tactical passive hydrophone array system uses the "wet end" of the U.S. SQR-19A TACTASS. Have UYS-503(V) sonobuoy data processing system.

A planned additional 12 VLS Sea Sparrow reload SAMs will not now be carried; as a further money-saving move, the ships do not have the latest version of the Harpoon missile weapons-control system, being fitted instead with SWG-1(V) vice SWG-1A. Have the SHINCOM (Shipboard Integrated Communications) system and are fitted with two U.S. OE-82 antennas for the WSC-3 UHF SATCOM system. One of the two navigational radar antennas is mounted atop the helicopter hangar, to port, to assist in helicopter takeoffs and landings; they may later be reequipped with a Thales Scout covert continuous-wave radar set forward. All are planned to receive the SRD-504 Combat Direction Finding system, and the jamming system may be replaced.

Navigational equipment includes Sperry SQN-502/SRD-331 doppler speed log, two Sperry SSN-502 (Mk 49) inertial navigation systems, and Internav SRN-501 LORAN-C receiver. Hazeltine Mk 12 IFF equipment is installed.
Modernization: Four were planned to be backfitted with H.S.A. APAR 3-D search radar during post-2005 refits, funds permitting; installing the system would increase displacement by 105 tons, due to the need for ballasting. Are planned to receive Link 16 Cooperative Engagement Capability, and the EW suite is to be updated. The TIAPS (Towed Integrated Active-Passive Sonar) may be substituted for the CANTASS passive-only towed array. U.S. Evolved Sea Sparrow missiles began replacing the Current RIM-7P version during refits starting late 2004, but the Mk 48 launchers will not be modified to accept quad packs to permit quadrupling the missile load. SLQ-25 has been upgraded to SLQ-25A solid-state variant. Ongoing plans call for the replacement of Sea Sparrow missiles with the Evolved Sea Sparrow System (ESSM), upgrade of the towed sonar arrays, installation of new screws and anechoic tiles to reduce noise emission. HMCS *Montreal* was first to complete the upgrade.

PATROL SHIPS [PS]

♦ 12 Kingston-class Maritime Coastal Defense Vessels

Bldr: Halifax Shipyard Division, Ltd., St. John SB, Ltd., Group, Halifax, N.S.

	Laid down	L	In serv.
MM 700 Kingston	15-12-94	12-8-95	21-9-96
MM 701 Glace Bay	28-4-95	22-1-96	26-10-96
MM 702 Nanaimo	10-8-95	17-5-96	10-5-97
MM 703 Edmonton	7-12-95	16-8-96	21-6-97
MM 704 Shawinigan	28-3-96	15-11-96	14-6-97
MM 705 Whitehorse	25-7-96	24-2-97	17-4-98
MM 706 Yellowknife	4-11-96	5-6-97	18-4-98
MM 707 Goose Bay	22-2-97	4-9-97	26-7-98
MM 708 Moncton	31-5-97	5-12-97	12-7-98
MM 709 Saskatoon	5-9-97	30-3-98	5-12-98
MM 710 Brandon	5-12-97	10-7-98	5-6-99
MM 711 Summerside	28-3-98	26-9-98	18-7-99

Goose Bay (MM 707) Derek Fox, 3-05

D: 772 tons light (979 fl) **S:** 14 kts
Dim: 55.31 (49.00 pp) × 11.30 × 3.42
A: 1 40-mm 60-cal. Bofors Mk 1N/1 AA in Mk 5c Boffin mounting; 2 single 12.7-mm Browning M2 mg
Electronics:
Radar: 1 Kelvin-Hughes Nucleus 6000 X-band nav.; 1 Kelvin-Hughes Nucleus 6000 S-band surf. search
Sonar: 1 MacDonald Dettwiler Towfish towed passive array
EW: Shiploc intercept, VHFD/F

Shawinigan (MM 704)—beside *Goose Bay* (MM 707) at Portsmouth, UK
Ralph Edwards, 4-05

M: electric drive: 4 Wärtsilä-SACM UD232V12, 1,800-kw diesels driving 4 Jeumont ANR 53-50-4 alternator sets (715 kw each); 2 Jeumont DC CI 560L electric motors (1,150 kw each); 2 Lips FS-1000 Z-drive Kort-nozzle azimuthal props; 3,084 shp
Electric: 405 kw tot. (1 × 300-kw ship's service, 1 × 105-kw emergency)
Range: 5,000/8 **Endurance:** 18 days
Crew: 47 max. total

Remarks: Were originally to have been steel-hulled mine-countermeasures and training ships. Now primarily intended for offshore patrol duties and based at Halifax and Esquimalt, with four of the East Coast units to operate on the Great Lakes or in the Gulf of St. Lawrence from May to November each year. MM 700, 701, 707, 708, and 711 are assigned to Atlantic Coast, the others to the Pacific. The ships are to have a 25-year service life and have a 93-ton lifetime displacement growth margin. MM 701 collided with a U.S. fishing boat off Boston, Mass., on 27-1-98.
Hull systems: Built to commercial standards, but naval standards were applied to stability, maneuverability, and magazines. Were to be able to maintain 15 kts in State 2 sea, but can only achieve 14 kts under optimum conditions; they are not considered to be good seaboats. Accommodation arrangements permit adding female crewmembers. Trials with the first unit showed the ships to be top-heavy, and 9 tons of permanent ballast were added, and some equipment was relocated. All have degaussing coil arrays fitted, but only in the first three is there a control system. Planned bow-thrusters omitted. Have a large radar signature.
Combat systems: Thomson-CSF provided the combat system integration management. The 40-mm AA are refurbished World War II mountings returned from Europe where they were used by the Canadian Army for airfield defense. Using modular systems, are capable of route survey work in support of mine countermeasures and are able to carry a remote-controlled drone submersible for examining undersea objects. Two MacDonald Dettwiler modular minesweeping systems, four modular route survey systems, and one remotely controlled inspection submersible module have been procured, with the latter using the Trailblazer 25 ROV; the ROV module is based at Esquimalt, while two route survey modules are on each coast. Two mechanical minesweeping arrays are kept at Halifax for towing by units of this class. Leica Navigation MX300 GPS receivers and Knudsen 320 echo-sounders are installed in all.

MINE WARFARE SHIPS

Note: Mine-countermeasures trials and support ship *Anticosti* (MSA 110, ex-*Jean Tide,* ex-*Lady Jean*) and *Moresby* (MSA 112, ex-*Joyce Tide,* ex-*Lady Joyce*) were paid off on 8-3-00, with MSA 110 transferred to Crown Assets for disposal on 1-10-01. The twelve *Kingston*-class vessels described above have a rudimentary mine warfare capability, but the necessary equipment has not been acquired in quantity.

AMPHIBIOUS WARFARE SHIPS

Note: During early 2005, senior Canadian defense and military officials began investigating the purchase of new or used amphibious warfare vessels. The program, however, remains in its infancy.

AUXILIARIES

♦ 1 Quest-class oceanographic research ship [AGOR]

	Bldr	Laid down	L	In serv.
AGOR 172 Quest	Burrard DD, Vancouver	2-10-67	9-7-68	21-8-69

D: 2,203 tons (fl) **S:** 16 kts **Dim:** 77.20 (71.62 pp) × 12.80 × 4.60
Electronics: Radar: 2 Racal-Decca BridgeMaster nav.
M: 2 Fairbanks-Morse 38D8$^1/_8$-9 diesels, G.E. electric drive; 2 props; 2,950 shp—bow-thruster
Electric: 1,900 kw tot. (1 x 750 kw, 2 x 500 kw, 1 emergency 150 kw)
Range: 10,000/12 **Fuel:** 300 tons
Crew: 10 licensed officers, 14 unlicensed, 21 scientists

Remarks: In recent years has performed sonobouy research for the Defence Research Establishment, Atlantic (DREA), Special Projects Unit, operating from Halifax under the control of the Canadian Forces Auxiliary Vessel organization. Given midlife refit commencing fall 1996 at Maystown SY with Lockheed Martin Canada as prime contractor; acoustic signature reduced. In 2-99 began tests with the Towed Integrated Active-Passive Sonar (TIAPS) array.

AUXILIARIES *(continued)*

Quest (AGOR 172) Ralph Edwards, 3-05

Hull systems: Ice-reinforced hull construction. Has two electrohydraulic 5- and 9-ton cranes and a passive tank stabilization system. The small helicopter deck is now used for equipment stowage. Employs a Concurrent Model 6650 onboard data reduction and storage computer.

♦ 0 (+ 3) Joint Support Ships/new replenishment and transport vessels [AOR] (In serv. 2012–13)

Computer rendering of the Joint Support Ship Canadian DND, 2004

D: 28,000 tons (fl) **S:** 21 kts sustained **Dim:** 200.0 (195.00 pp) × 32.0 × 8.50
A: 2 20-mm Mk 15 Mod. 12 Phalanx CIWS; 4 medium helicopters
Electronics:
Radar: 1 nav.; 1 air/surface search
Sonar: hull-mounted mine avoidance set
EW: CANEWS intercept system, provision for towed homing torpedo decoy
M: 2 medium-speed diesels; 1 prop; 27,200 bhp—bow- and stern-thrusters
Range: 10,800/15
Crew: 165 tot. + 75 joint force staff + 300 max. troops

Remarks: The Joint Support Ship project is intended to replace the *Protecteur* class and the stricken *Provider,* with the additional capability to transport and support peacekeeping forces and their equipment. Start of construction of the first was moved forward from 2006 to 2004 in 6-00, but the number to be built was reduced from four. The budgeted cost is currently US$1.8 billion for all three. Will be new construction ships built in Canada. Currently scheduled to enter service between 2011 and 2013, though progess has been slow and dates can be expected to shift.

Alternatively, the government may lease commercial ships for the mission or may charter commercially built and owned ships built expressly for the mission.

Hull systems: Cargo capacity: approx. 8,000 tons fuel, 840 tons aviation fuel, 300 tons ammunition; combination of up to (120) 20-ft. containers and vehicles/equipment including 2,500 lane meters for roll-on/roll-off vehicle cargo on two decks, accessed via ramps at the stern and on either side forward. The troop and cargo capacity represents enough support for 90% of the Army's Vanguard Battle Group for 30 days. The area around the fuel tanks will have double bottoms. There are to be four replenishment-at-sea stations—fueling and heavy jackstay on both sides of each ship. Sealift cargo would be carried above the liquid cargo tankage. There would be a 25-ton capacity elevator from the helicopter hangar to both vehicle cargo decks; four helicopters could be carried. Self-propelled pontoon barges will be stowed on the ships' sides. Would have two helicopter landing positions for aircraft up to CH-47 Chinook size. Would be able to carry a modular hospital facility and 200 troops, or 300 troops and their equipment. 1998 configuration resembles RFA *Argus,* with superstructure forward, stack structure aft to starboard, and large open deck for helicopters or container cargo; the vehicle ramp would be on the starboard quarter and there would be a vehicle access door forward to starboard. Are to be able to navigate through 0.7-m ice.

♦ 2 Protecteur-class replenishment ships [AOR]

Bldr: St. John SB & DD, St. John, N.B.

	Laid down	L	In serv.
AOR 509 Protecteur	17-10-67	18-7-68	30-8-69
AOR 510 Preserver	17-10-67	29-5-69	30-7-70

D: 8,380 tons light (24,700 fl) **S:** 21 kts **Dim:** 172.0 (166.42 pp) × 23.16 × 9.15
A: 2 20-mm Mk 15 Mod. 0 Block 1 Phalanx CIWS; 6 single 12.7-mm mg; 3 CH-124A Sea King helicopters (normally 1 or 2 embarked)
Electronics:
Radar: 1 Decca TM 1629 nav.; 1 Decca TM 969 nav.
TACAN: URN-22A
EW: SLQ-504 (Racal Kestrel Type 242) intercept; Southwest SRD-502 (Telegon 4) HFD/F; 2 6-round Plessey Shield decoy RL; SLQ-25 Nixie towed torpedo decoy
M: 1 set Canadian G.E. geared turbines; 1 prop; 21,000 shp
Boilers: 2 Babcock & Wilcox watertube
Electric: 3,500 kw **Range:** 4,100/20; 7,500/11.5
Crew: 365 tot. (27 officers, 338 enlisted) + up to 57 passengers

Protecteur (AOR 509)—with HMCS *Algonquin* (DDH 283) and HMCS *St. John's* (FFH 340) alongside Canadian DND, 9-02

Preserver (AOR 510)—at Halifax Ralph Edwards, 3-05

Remarks: AOR 510 based at Halifax; AOR 509 at Esquimalt. AOR 509 was refitted at Victoria SY from 5-4-01 to 9-01. Refitted again in 2004 at Maclarens Shipyard. Expected to retire in 2010 but will likely be extended due to delays in the replacement program.

Hull systems: Cargo capacity: 14,590 tons total, with 12,000 tons distillate fuel, 600 tons diesel oil, 400 tons aviation fuel, 1,048 tons dry cargo, and 1,250 tons ammunition. Four replenishment-at-sea stations, one elevator abaft the navigation bridge, two 11-ton cranes on the afterdeck. Daily fresh-water distillation capacity is 80 tons. Can be used to carry military vehicles and troops for commando purposes. Carry four LCVPs.

Combat systems: Twin 76.2-mm gun mounts, formerly carried at the extreme bow, were removed in 1983. Two single 40-mm AA have been removed from AOR 509. The SLQ-25 is to be upgraded to SLQ-25A solid-state variant by 2009.

SERVICE CRAFT

Note: Most service craft are operated by the Canadian Forces Auxiliary Vessels (CFAV) organization, which is headed by the Queen's Harbor Master, a naval officer, at the bases at Esquimalt and Halifax; nearly all personnel are civilian employees. CFAV is also responsible for providing pilots and for pollution control.

♦ 24 miscellaneous barges [YC]

Based at Esquimalt: YC 50, YC 51, YC 52, YC 53, YC 54, YC 404, YC 406, YC 408, YC 414, YC 416, YC 418
Based at Halifax: YC 415, YC 417, YC 419, YC 451, YC 453, YC 455, YC 457, YC 459, YC 461, YC 467, YC 494, YC 600, YC 601

Remarks: YC 50–54 are steel-hulled open lighters; the other Esquimalt units are wooden-hulled, open lighters, with YC 418 used for storage. YC 415 is the flag-officer landing stage at Halifax; YC 417 through 461 and YC 467 are landing stages; YC 51 and 52 are water barges; YC 600 and YC 601 are cargo barges; YC 494 is operated for the Defence Research Establishment, Atlantic (DREA), in support of the *Quest* (AGOR 172).

♦ 2 floating cranes [YD]

YD 250 YD 253

Floating crane YD 250—at Esquimalt Canadian Forces, 1996

SERVICE CRAFT *(continued)*

Remarks: YD 250 based at Esquimalt, YD 253 at Halifax. Crews of five each. Non-self-propelled.

♦ 2 small deperming barges [YDGN]

YDG 2 YDG 3

Small deperming barge YDG 2 Ralph Edwards, 3-05

Remarks: YDG 2 based at Halifax, YDG 3 at Esquimalt. Are also used as fuel barges and have messing facilities for 35 personnel each.

♦ 4 small diving tenders [YDT]

Bldr: Celtic SY, . . . (In serv. 1997)

D: 22 tons (fl) **S:** 36 kts **Dim:** 11.90 × 3.80 × 0.70
Electronics: Radar: 1 . . . nav.
M: 2 Caterpillar 3126 TA diesels; 2 WMC 357 waterjets; 740 bhp
Range: 600/29 **Crew:** 3 + up to 14 divers

Remarks: Aluminum construction, two based on each coast. Have blunt, planing bows. Bollard pull of 2.9 tons for towing service.

Disposal note: Ammunition lighters [YE] YE 216 and YE 217 were stricken during 5-01.

♦ 2 Gemini-class personnel launches (1 in *reserve*) [YFL]

(In serv. 15-11-85)

YAG 650 GEMINI YAG 651 *PEGASUS*

Gemini (YAG 650) and Pegasus (YAG 651) Pradignac & Léo, 1991

D: . . . tons **S:** . . . kts **Dim:** 17.00 × 4.20 × 1.14

Remarks: YAG 650 based at Halifax and YAG 651 in reserve at Esquimalt.

♦ 2 YAG-12-class personnel launches [YFL]

Bldr: Charlottetown SY, P.E.I. (In serv. . . .)

YFB 316 YFB 318

D: 80.9 tons (85 fl) **S:** 9.5 kts (sust.) **Dim:** 22.86 × 5.08 × 1.73
Electronics: Radar: 1 Furuno . . . nav.
M: YFB 316: 2 Cummins . . . diesels, YFB 318: 2 G.M. 6-71 diesels; 2 props; 264 bhp
Range: 420/9.5 **Crew:** 4 tot.

Remarks: Known locally as the "Blue Boats" for their hull color. Both based at Esquimalt. Are nearing the ends of their useful lives and may be replaced by contract craft. Sisters YAG 306, 308, 312, 314, 317, 319, and 320 are employed as training craft at Esquimalt.

Personnel launch YFB 318 Ralph Edwards, 10-03

♦ 6 YFU 121–class sea trucks [YFL]

YFU 121 SEA TRUCK 1	YFU 124
YFU 122 SEA TRUCK 2	YFU 125
YFU 123 SEA TRUCK 3	YFU 126

YFU 125 Ralph Edwards, 3-05

Remarks: Aluminum-construction, beachable landing craft with enclosed pilothouse at the stern. YFU 121–123 are used to transport pilots, other personnel, and equipment at Esquimalt; the other two are based at Halifax. About 10 m overall. YFU 126 was sighted in service during 2005 and has apparently been constructed to a slightly different design than the other units of the class.

♦ 5 target craft [YGTN]

Remarks: No longer assigned pennant numbers; formerly numbered YTG 8 and YTG 12–YTG 15. Based at Esquimalt; non-self-propelled, yellow-painted punts about 5 m in length.

♦ 2 special liquids barges [YON]

YOM 252 YOM 402

Liquid barge YOM 252 Ralph Edwards, 10-03

Remarks: Based at Esquimalt. YOM 252 is a sullage lighter and also has maintenance facilities to repair local smallcraft. YOM 402 is used for pollution collection, treatment, and storage.

♦ 4 experimental and test range support vessels [YPT]

Bldr: West Coast Manly SY, Vancouver, B.C. (L: 10-11-90)

TSRV 611 SIKANNI	YDT 610 SECHELT
TSRV 613 STIKINE	YDT 612 SOOKE

D: 254.7 tons (290 fl) **S:** 12.5 kts **Dim:** 33.00 (30.25 pp) × 7.70 × 2.46
Electronics: Radar: 1 . . . nav.—Sonar: . . .
M: 2 Caterpillar 3412 diesels; 2 props; 1,342 bhp (1,080 bhp sust.)
Range: 1,000/12 **Crew:** 4–6 tot.

SERVICE CRAFT *(continued)*

Sooke (YDT 612) W. Michael Young, 3-01

Remarks: Ordered 9-88 and delivered 6-90 to 8-91 to serve the Maritime Experimental and Test Range at Nanoose Bay on Vancouver Island as torpedo retrievers, range safety craft, etc. YDT 610 and 612 were converted to act as diving tenders in 11-97, supporting divers to 80 m; they operate from Shearwater NS and Esquimalt respectively. TSRV 611 and 613 are active at Nanoose Bay with civilian crews.

♦ 3 YRG 60–class sludge removal barges [YRGN]

YRG 60 YRG 61 YRG 62

Sludge removal barge YRG 61 Ralph Edwards, 10-03

Remarks: YRG 61 is at Esquimalt, the others at Halifax. Equipped with the Wheeler System steam-cleaning method for cleaning fuel tanks and bilges; the tanks are then cleaned with detergents and vacuum-collected for storage in the craft's storage tanks. YRG 60 has a crew of five, YRG 62 is manned by YRG 60 crew supplemented by relief party when necessary. Can hold 50,000 gallons of recycled oil.

♦ 5 Glen-class large harbor tugs [YTB]

Bldrs: YTB 640, 641: Yarrow, Esquimalt; others: Georgetown SY, P.E.I.

	In serv.		In serv.
YTB 640 Glendyne	8-8-75	YTB 643 Glenbrook	16-12-76
YTB 641 Glendale	16-9-75	YTB 644 Glenside	20-5-77
YTB 642 Glenevis	9-8-76		

D: 255 tons (350 fl) **S:** 11.5 kts **Dim:** 28.2 × 8.5 × 3.8
Electronics: Radar: 2 Decca BridgeMaster E Series nav.
M: 2 Ruston AP-3 diesels; 2 Voith-Schneider vertical cycloidal props; 1,750 bhp
Fuel: 54 tons **Crew:** see Remarks

Remarks: Carry crew of three officers (two when on East Coast), three unlicensed in harbor service; five officers, four unlicensed on coastal service. Carry 20 tons fresh water and are equipped for firefighting. Rated at 18.3 tons bollard pull ahead, 15 tons astern, and 12 tons sideways. Likely to remain in service until 2015–20 time frame.

Glenbrook (YTB 643) Ralph Edwards, 3-05

♦ 1 medium harbor tug [YTM]

YTM 555 Tillicum (ex-*Island Defender*)

Tillicum (YTM 555) Ralph Edwards, 10-03

D: 140 tons **S:** . . . **Dim:** 15.24 × 6.4 × . . .
M: 15-ton bollard pull twin engine **Crew:** 3 tot.

Remarks: Based at Esquimalt.

♦ 5 new Ville-class harbor tugs [YTL]

Bldrs: YTL 590, 594: Vito Steel & Barge Co.; others: Georgetown SY, P.E.I. (In serv. 1974)

YTL 590 Lawrenceville
YTL 591 Parksville
YTL 592 Listerville
YTL 593 Merrickville
YTL 594 Granville (ex-*Marysville*)

Listerville (YTL 592) Ralph Edwards, 3-05

SERVICE CRAFT *(continued)*

D: 70 tons (fl) **S:** 9.8 kts (8.5 cruise) **Dim:** 14.20 (13.60 pp) × 4.50 × 1.93
M: 1 Caterpillar diesel; 365 bhp (593: G.M. diesel, 165 bhp) **Crew:** 3 tot.

Remarks: YTL 590 and 591 are based at Esquimalt, the others at Halifax. Are locally known as the Pup class. Bollard pull is 5.9 tons. Likely to remain in service until 2015–20 time frame. YTL 594 was renamed during 2004–5.

♦ 2 130-ton fireboats [YTR]
Bldr: Vancouver SY, B.C. (In serv. 1978)

YTR 561 Firebird   YTR 562 Firebrand

Firebird (YTR 561)—130-ton fireboat   Ralph Edwards, 3-05

D: 48 tons light (100 fl) **S:** 7.5 kts **Dim:** 23.20 × 6.25 × . . .
M: 1 Vivian diesel; Voith-Schneider vertical cycloidal prop; 240 bhp
Crew: 8 licensed officers, 4 unlicensed

Remarks: Based at Halifax and Esquimalt, respectively. Have two 5,700-liter/min firepumps.

♦ 1 sailing ketch for cadet training [YTS]
Bldr: George Lawley, Neponset, Mass. (In serv. 1921)

KC 480 Oriole (ex-*Oriole IV,* QW 3)

Oriole (KC 480)   Canadian Forces, 2000

D: 78.2 tons (92 fl) **S:** 14 kts (sail)/8 kts (power)
Dim: 31.09 (27.58 hull) × 5.69 × 3.04
Electronics: Radar: 1 Furuno . . . nav.
M: 1 G.M. Detroit Diesel 6V71 diesel; 1 prop; 230 hp—1,300 m^2 max. sail area
Endurance: 60 days **Crew:** 1 officer, 5 enlisted, 18 trainees

Remarks: Built for George H. Gooderham of Toronto and acquired in 1949 by the Navy League of Canada. Transferred to navy in 1952. Is Canada's smallest and oldest commissioned ship. Based at Esquimalt and used to train students from the Naval Officers' Training Center and the Canadian Forces Fleet School. Has Marconi rig, no power winches. Working sails total 570 m^2, plus a 650-m^2 spinnaker. The mainmast is 31.7 m high. Navigation equipment includes Raystar 920 GPS receiver with Gimbel transponder, Loran-C receiver, and Weatherfax receiver. Sailed with crew of 22 on 13-10-97 on 17,000-n.m. voyage to Australia, New Zealand, and other South Pacific ports, returning 13-5-98.

Note: Also in use for sail training are the 11.13-m class CS 36S GRP sloops *Tuna,* at the Fleet Training School, Halifax, and *Goldcrest,* at Esquimalt, both bought 5-85.

♦ 6 (+ 2) Orca-class training ships [YXT]
Bldr: Victoria Shipyards Co. Ltd., Canada (In serv. 2006–8)

D: . . . tons **S:** 20 kts (15 kts. cruising) **Dim:** 33.00 x . . . x 1.80
Electronics: Radar: 1 . . . nav.
M: 2 . . . diesels; 2 props; . . . bhp
Range: 750/15 **Crew:** . . .

Remarks: Intended to replace the YAG 300-class training units. A contract for six ships US$69.7 million was awarded on 8-11-05 with an option for two additional ships. The first ship is scheduled for delivery in mid-2006 and the sixth unit in 2008. Can provide secondary inshore patrol capability. All boats will be based at Esquimalt, British Colombia.

♦ 7 YAG 300–class training launches [YXT]
Bldr: Charlottetown SY, P.E.I. (In serv. 1950s)

YAG 306 YAG 308 YAG 312 YAG 314 YAG 317 YAG 319 YAG 320

D: 80.9 tons (85 fl) **S:** 9.5 kts (sust.) **Dim:** 22.86 × 5.08 × 1.73
Electronics: Radar: 1 Furuno . . . nav.
M: 2 Cummins . . . diesels; 2 props; 264 bhp **Range:** 427/9.5 **Crew:** 4 tot.

Remarks: Are employed as training craft at Esquimalt. Sisters YFB 316 and YFB 318 are used as personnel launches at Esquimalt. Are to be replaced by the Orca-class training ships by 2008.

Note: 6–8 vessels are planned as YAG replacements. The Treasury Board approved construction 6-03. Rough dimensions are 25 m and 100 tons displacement. To feature improved accommodations. To be replaced by the Orca class.

Disposal note: PB 196 and all 6 Ville-class tugs were stricken in 2003.

COAST GUARD

Note: The resources of the Department of Fisheries and Oceans and the Canadian Coast Guard were combined into one agency under the Ministry of Fisheries and Oceans on 1-4-95. Ships, craft, and aircraft were gradually repainted in Coast Guard colors, with red hull (with white diagonal stripe), white superstructure, and funnel with red maple leaf. Other than small arms, the ships are not armed, but those assigned to patrol duties assist the Royal Canadian Mounted Police in drug interdiction and other police functions when needed.

Personnel: 4,700 total (all civilian).

Organization: Headquarters at Ottawa, field offices for operating regions at Vancouver, B.C. (Pacific Region); Winnipeg, Man. (Central and Arctic Region); Quebec City, Que. (Laurentian Region); Dartmouth, N.S. (Maritimes Region); and St. John's, Nfld. (Newfoundland Region).

Aviation: The Canadian Coast Guard operates one DeHavilland Dash-8 and one DeHavilland DHC-6 twin-engined fixed-wing transports and 27 helicopters: one Sikorsky S-61N, four CH-146 Griffon/Bell 212, four Bell 206L and two Bell 206L-1 LongRanger, and 16 MBB BO-105CBS.

Note: Ships and craft are listed below in the order of the categories now assigned by the Canadian Coast Guard. Standard ship-type designations are given in brackets for each class. Ships and craft listed in the previous edition that are not listed below have either been retired or transferred to other Canadian government agencies. Those seeking more information about the ships and craft, including plans and additional photography, should consult the excellent Canadian Coast Guard website at www.ccg.gcc.gc.ca.

OFFSHORE MULTITASK PATROL VESSELS [WPS]

♦ 1 Sir Wilfred Grenfell class [WPS]
Bldr: Marystown SY, Marystown, Newfoundland

	Region	In serv.
Sir Wilfred Grenfell	Newfoundland	1987

Sir Wilfred Grenfell   Canadian Coast Guard

COAST GUARD OFFSHORE MULTITASK PATROL VESSELS [WPS] *(continued)*

D: 3,753 tons (fl) **S:** 16 kts **Dim:** 68.48 (59.59 pp) × 15.30 × 5.42
Electronics:
Radar: 1 Decca Bridgemaster II C252 (X-band) nav.; 1 Decca Bridgemaster II C253 (S-band) nav.
M: 2 Deutz 268-2SBV16M and 2 Deutz SBV9M diesels, geared drive; 2 CP props; 12,864 bhp—bow- and stern-thrusters
Electric: 3,120 kw tot. (2 × 1,120-kw shaft generators; 2 × 440-kw, G.M. 12V-92T diesels driving
Range: 11,000/11.5 **Fuel:** 879 m^3 **Endurance:** 35 days
Crew: 9 officers, 11 non-officers

Remarks: 2,404 grt/1,265 dwt. Converted firefighting and anchor-handling tug/supply ship. Ice-strengthened hull. Based at St. John's, Nfld.
Hull systems: Has six fire monitors, two Hurricane 740 fast rescue RIBs, one Zodiac RIB, and a lifeboat. Is equipped with a 70-ton electrohydraulic crane, two 2.6-ton cranes, and two 12-ton winches. Navigational equipment includes Trimble Navtrac and Northstar GPS sets, Taiyo TD-C338-HS MFD/F, OAR 320E VHFD/F, and Elac LAZ-72 echo sounder.

♦ 1 Leonard J. Cowley class [WPS]
Bldr: West Coast Manly SY, Vancouver

	Region	Laid down	L	In serv.
Leonard J. Cowley	Newfoundland	15-1-84	24-10-84	6-85

Leonard J. Cowley Canadian Coast Guard

D: 1,470 tons light (2,080 fl) **S:** 15 kts
Dim: 72.01 (61.45 pp) × 14.20 × 4.51 (4.90 max.)
Electronics: Radar: 2 Sperry 3400 (S-and X-band) nav.
M: 2 Nohab Polar F312A diesels; 1 Kort-nozzle CP prop; 4,242 bhp—bow-thruster
Electric: 1,350 kw tot. (3 × 450-kw diesel sets)
Range: 12,000/12 **Fuel:** 400 m^3 **Endurance:** 28 days
Crew: 7 officers, 12 non-officers

Remarks: 2,243 grt/592 dwt. Ordered 8-11-83. Built for Pacific Region but now operates from St. John's, Nfld. Variants of this design are in Irish Navy and Mauritius Coast Guard service. Two single 12.7-mm mg can be mounted.
Hull systems: Helo deck and telescoping hangar. Both radars have CAS II ARPA capability and are linked to a Sperry/TRAC IVB Qubit integrated navigational computer/recorder. Carries two Zodiac RIBs and two workboats. Navigational equipment includes Trimble Navtrac XL and Northstar GPS, Taiyo TD-C338-HS MFD/F, Taiyo TD-L1620 HFD/F, and Elac LAZ-2300 and LAZ-72 echo sounders.

♦ 2 Cape Roger class [WPS]

	Region	Bldr	In serv.
Cape Roger	Newfoundland	Ferguson, Pictou, N.S.	8-77
Cygnus	Maritimes	Marystown SY, Nfld.	5-82

Cape Roger—in former gray paint scheme Susan Lindberg, 7-92

D: 1,461 tons (fl) **S:** 17 kts **Dim:** 62.50 (57.00 pp) × 12.22 × 5.30
Electronics: Radar: Cape Roger: 1 Decca Bridgemaster II C252/6 (X-band) nav.; 1 Sperry Rascar 3400M (S-band) nav.—Cygnus: 1 Decca BT502 (X-band) nav.; 1 Decca Bridgemaster II (X-band) nav.; 1 Decca 2690 ARPA (S-band) nav.
M: 2 Wärtsilä-Nohab Polar F30.12V diesels; 2 CP props; 4,410 bhp—bow-thruster
Electric: 575 kw (2 × 250 kw, 1 × 75 kw)
Range: *Cape Roger:* 10,000/12—*Cygnus:* 10,800/13
Fuel: *Cape Roger:* 200 m^3—*Cygnus:* 401 m^3
Endurance: 31 days (*Cygnus:* 21)
Crew: 7 officers, 12 non-officers (*Cygnus:* 10)

Remarks: *Cape Roger:* 1,255 grt; *Cygnus:* 1,210 grt/1,442 dwt. Have two complete crews who alternate on 14-day patrols. Can be equipped with two 12.7-mm mg. *Cape Roger* (refitted in 1996) is based at St. John's, Nfld., and *Cygnus* at Dartmouth, N.S.
Hull systems: *Cape Roger* has a telescoping helicopter hangar; both have 132 m^2 helicopter flight decks. Both completed refits in 1997 and are to serve for another 20 or more years. *Cape Roger* carries two Zodiac RIBs and two workboats, while *Cygnus* has one Hurricane and one Avon Searider RIBs and one workboat. Navigational equipment on *Cape Roger* includes Trimble GPS, Furuno FD-177 MFD/F, Taiyo TD-1620 HFD/F, and JMC F-830 and JMC V-122 echo sounders; *Cygnus* has Northstar 8000 GPS, Taiyo TD L1620 VHFD/F, and Elac-Honeywell 1200, LAZ 5000, LAZ-51, and LAZ-72 echo sounders.

INTERMEDIATE MULTITASK (PATROL) CUTTERS [WPC/WPS]

♦ 1 Arrow Post class [WPC]
Bldr: Hike Metal Products, Wheatley, Ont.

	Region	In serv.
Arrow Post	Pacific	1994

Arrow Post Canadian Coast Guard

D: Approx. 300 tons **S:** 12 kts **Dim:** 28.97 × 8.80 × 3.35
Electronics: Radar: 1 Raytheon Rasterscan R81-6 (X-band) nav.; 1 Raytheon Rasterscan R82-9 (X-band) nav.
M: 1 Caterpillar 12-cyl. 3512 TA diesel; 1 CP prop: 1,280 bhp—bow-thruster
Electric: 184 kw tot. (3 × 92-kw diesel sets)
Range: 2,800/11 **Fuel:** 52.6 m^3 **Endurance:** 28 days
Crew: 3 officers, 3 non-officers

Remarks: 228 grt. Based at Prince Rupert, B.C.
Hull systems: Carries two 4-m Zodiac RIBs. Navigation equipment includes Northstar 941X and Taystar 9206 GPS, Raytheon 789 Loran, Taiyo TD-L1530 MFD/F, JMC DF550 VHFD/F, Wesmar SS265 side-scan sonar, and JRC JFF-10 and MV-105 echo sounders.

♦ 1 Gordon Reid class [WPS]
Bldr: Versatile Pacific SY, Vancouver, B.C.

	Region	In serv.
Gordon Reid	Pacific	7-91

Gordon Reid Canadian Coast Guard

COAST GUARD INTERMEDIATE MULTITASK (PATROL) CUTTERS [WPC/WPS] *(continued)*

D: Approx. 1,100 tons (fl) **S:** 17 kts **Dim:** 49.95 (46.00 wl) × 11.00 × 4.00
Electronics: Radar: 2 Decca Bridgemaster (X-band) nav.
M: 4 Deutz-MWM SBV-6M-628 diesels; 2 CP props; 4,800 bhp—bow-thruster
Electric: 830 kw tot. (3 × 250-kw, Mitsubishi 56B-PTR diesels driving; 1 × 80-kw emergency, Mitsubishi 6D144T diesel driving)
Range: 2,500/12 **Fuel:** 148.2 m^3 **Endurance:** 28 days
Crew: 6 officers, 8 non-officers (24 tot. accomm.)

Remarks: 879.61 grt. Formerly listed as Type 500 intermediate search-and-rescue cutters. They are based at Victoria, B.C.
Hull systems: Has two 650-ton/hr-capacity fire and salvage pumps and roll-stabilization tanks. A 7-m, 50-kt. Hurricane 733 RIB rescue craft is launched from a stern ramp, and a Zodiac Mk III RIB and Dunlop inflatable boats are also carried. Navigational equipment includes CSI MBX-1 GPS, Simrad-Taiyo C338HS MFD/F, OAR 320E VHFD/F, and Datarmarine 3000 echo sounder.

Disposal note: *John Jacobson* was sold during 2003.

♦ 1 Louisbourg class [WPC]
Bldr: Breton Industrial & Machinery, Port Hawkesbury, N.S.

	Region	In serv.
LOUISBOURG	Laurentian	1977

D: Approx. 370 tons (fl) **S:** 13.5 kts **Dim:** 37.80 × 8.20 × 2.60
Electronics: Radar: 2 Decca Bridgemaster 180 (X-band) nav.
M: 2 Caterpillar 16-cyl diesels; 2 props; 2,400 bhp
Electric: 280 kw tot. (2 × 140-kw diesel-driven sets)
Range: 3,840/10 **Fuel:** 56 m^3 **Endurance:** 16 days
Crew: 4 officers, 4 non-officers

Remarks: 295 grt. Based at Gaspé, Qué.
Hull systems: Carries one 6.4-m Zodiac 640 Mk 2 rescue RIB, launched and recovered from a stern ramp. Navigational equipment includes Trimble NT 200D and Furuno 500 GPS, Tiayo 70-L1550 VHFD/F, and two Raytheon V860 and one Elac LAZ-12 echo sounders.

♦ 1 Tanu class [WPS]
Bldr: Yarrow Ltd., Esquimalt, B.C.

	Region	In serv.
TANU	Pacific	7-9-68

Tanu—in former gray paint scheme H&L Van Ginderen, 11-94

D: 880 tons (925 fl) **S:** 13.5 kts **Dim:** 54.69 (50.17 pp) × 9.96 × 4.75
Electronics:
Radar: 1 Raytheon M34 ARPA (X-band) nav.; 1 JRC JMA825-9 (S-band) nav.
Sonar: Wesmar HD600E fish-finding (60 kHz); JRC-JFF-11 echo sounder; Furuno FCV-1000 echo sounder
M: 2 Fairbanks-Morse 38D8⅛-diesels; 1 CP prop; 2,624 bhp—125-shp Pleuger active-rudder stern-thruster
Electric: 500 kw tot. (3 × 150-kw, 1 × 50-kw diesel sets)
Range: 5,000/11 **Fuel:** 236 m^3 **Endurance:** 22 days
Crew: 6 officers, 10 non-officers

Remarks: 753.7 grt. Refitted and modernized during 1987 at Allied Shipyard, North Vancouver, B.C. Can mount two 12.7-mm mg. Based at Patricia Bay, B.C. Planned decommissioning in 2003, though unconfirmed.
Hull systems: Aluminum superstructure. Navigation equipment includes Sperry Mk 37 gyro and SRP-690 autopilot, Raystar 920 and Northstar 941X GPS sets, JRC-JNA 761 Loran-C receiver, Taiyo TD-C338HS MFD/F, and Taiyo TD-l1520 VHFD/F. Has VHF and HF comms but no SATCOMM. Hurricane 530 and 440 RIBs are carried, tended by a 2.2-ton crane.

♦ 1 E.P. le Québecois class [WPC]
Bldr: Les Chantier Maritime, Paspebiac, Qué.

	Region	In serv.
E.P. LE QUÉBECOIS	Laurentian	1968

D: Approx. 300 tons (fl) **S:** 11 kts **Dim:** 28.30 × 7.10 × 3.10
Electronics: Radar: 2 Furuno FR-2110 (X-band) nav.
M: 1 Caterpillar 3509-DITA diesel; 1 CP prop; 510 bhp—bow-thruster
Electric: 205 kw tot. (2 × 75-kw, 1 × 55-kw emergency sets)
Range: 2,800/10 **Fuel:** 35.6 m^3 **Endurance:** 9.5 days
Crew: 4 officers, 4 non-officers

Remarks: 186.38 grt. Refitted 1994. Based at Sept Îles, Qué.
Hull systems: Carries one 7-m Hurricane RIB, launched and recovered via a stern ramp. Navigational equipment includes Northstar 941X GPS, Furuno LC90 Loran, Taiyo VHFD/F, and Furuno FCV-582 echo sounder.

SMALL MULTITASK ICE-STRENGTHENED CUTTERS [WPC]

♦ 1 Harp class [WPC]
Bldr: Georgetown SY, Georgetown, P.E.I.

	Region	Laid down	L	In serv.
HARP	Newfoundland	15-12-85	20-9-86	12-12-86

Harp Canadian Coast Guard, 1988

D: 225 tons (fl) **S:** 11 kts **Dim:** 24.5 (21.50 pp) × 7.60 × 2.50
Electronics: Radar: 2 Decca Bridgemaster II C181/4 (X- and S-band) nav.
M: 2 Caterpillar 3408-BDITA diesels; 2 CP, Kort-nozzle props; 750 bhp
Electric: 80 kw (2 × 40-kw sets, Perkins 635A diesels driving)
Range: 500/9.5 **Fuel:** 34.6 m^3 **Crew:** 2 officers, 5 non-officers

Remarks: 179.2 grt. Ordered 26-4-85. Steel rescue ships to operate up to 100 n.m. from land. Have towing, firefighting, and medical evacuation capabilities. *Harp* is based at St. Anthony, Newfoundland.
Hull systems: The hulls are reinforced to operate in light ice. Carry a Zodiac rescue RIB. Navigational equipment includes Magnavox MS-200 and Trimble NT-200D GPS, Furuno LC-90 Loran, Furuno FD-177 MFD/F, OAR 320E VHFD/F, and Elac LAZ-50 echo sounder.
Disposals: *Hood* was retired in 2005 for disposal.

SMALL MULTITASK CUTTERS [WPB/WPC]

♦ 3 Lewis Reef class [WPB]
Bldrs: *Lewis Reef:* Rivtow Straits, Ltd., Vancouver, B.C.; others: Canoe Cove Mfgr., Ltd., Sidney, B.C. (In serv. 1988–90)

ESTEVAN REEF LEWIS REEF ROBSON REEF

Lewis Reef—in former gray paint scheme

COAST GUARD SMALL MULTITASK CUTTERS [WPB/WPC]
(continued)

D: . . . tons **S:** 11–11.5 kts **Dim:** 17.50 × 5.20 × 2.40
Electronics: Radar: 1 Furuno FR-1510 nav.
M: 1 Deutz BA6M816 diesel; 1 CP prop; 444 bhp **Electric:** 25 kw tot.
Range: 1,100/10 **Fuel:** 5.3 m^3 **Endurance:** 5 days
Crew: 2 officers, 1 non-officer

Remarks: 52 grt. Based at Patricia Bay, B.C.; Prince Rupert, B.C.; and Sidney, B.C., respectively. Navigational equipment includes Northstar 941 GPS, Simrad-Taiyo L1520 MFD/F, and Furuno RU-1000 echo sounder. Carry a Zodiac RIB.

♦ 1 Cumella class [WPC]
Bldr: A. F. Theriault & Son, Ltd., Meteghan River, N.S. (In serv. 1983)

CUMELLA

Cumella Canadian Coast Guard

D: Approx. 110 tons (fl) **S:** 15 kts **Dim:** 23.20 × 4.80 × 2.00
Electronics: Radar: 1 Furuno FR-8050D nav.; 1 Furuno FR-8100D nav.
M: 2 G.M. Detroit Diesel V-6 diesels; 2 props; 1,680 bhp **Electric:** 10 kw tot.
Range: 600/12 **Fuel:** 7.3 m^3 **Crew:** 2 officers, 2 non-officers

Remarks: 79.95 grt. Assigned to Maritimes Region and based at Grand Manaan, N.B. Carries a Hurricane rescue RIB. Navigational equipment includes Northstar 941X GPS, Simrad-Taiyo TD-L1620 VHFD/F, and Elac LAZ-2120 echo sounder.

♦ 4 Point Henry class [WPB]
Bldr: Breton Industry & Machinery, Point Hawkesbury, N.S.

	Region	In serv.		Region	In serv.
POINT HENRY	Pacific	1980	POINT RACE	Pacific	4-82
ÎLE ROUGE	Laurentian	1980	CAPE HURD	Central & Arctic	4-82

Point Henry H&L Van Ginderen, 7-94

D: 77 tons light (97 fl) **S:** 21–24 kts **Dim:** 21.30 × 5.50 × 1.70
Electronics: Radar: 2 nav. (see remarks)
M: 2 MTU 8V396 TC82 (*Point Henry:* Caterpillar 3412) diesels; 2 props; 1,740 bhp (*Point Henry:* 2,146 bhp)
Range: 500/18; 1,400/16 **Fuel:** 7 tons **Crew:** 2 officers, 3 non-officers

Remarks: 56.7 grt. Formerly typed as small search-and-rescue cutters (Type 400). *Point Henry* is based at Prince Rupert, B.C.; *Île Rouge* at Tadoussas, Que.; *Point Race* at Campbell River, B.C.; and *Cape Hurd* at Goodrich, Ont. Aluminum alloy construction. Radar installations vary.

♦ 4 Sooke Post class [WPB]
Bldr: Philbrooks Shipyard, Ltd., Sidney, B.C.

	In serv.		In serv.
SOOKE POST	1973	ATLIN POST	1975
KITIMAT II	1974	CHILCOE POST	1975

D: Approx. 70 tons (fl) **S:** 15 kts **Dim:** 19.80 × 5.20 × 1.50
Electronics: Radar: 1 Furuno FP-150D nav.; 1 Furuno FR-1011 nav.
M: 2 G.M. Detroit Diesel V-12 diesels; 2 props; 1,100 bhp
Electric: 30 kw tot. (2 × 15-kw sets) **Range:** 400/12 **Fuel:** 5.4 m^3
Endurance: 10 days **Crew:** 3 officers, 1 non-officer

Remarks: 57 grt. All are assigned to the Pacific Region, with *Sooke Post* and *Chilcoe Post* based at Port Hardy, B.C.; *Atlin Post* at Patricia Bay, B.C.; and *Kitimat II* at Prince Rupert, B.C. Carry a 4.4-m Hurricane RIB. Sister *Comox Post* was retired on 26-11-02.

♦ 1 Advent class [WPC]
Bldr: Alloy Manufacturing, Ltd., Lachine, Qué. (In serv. 1972)

ADVENT

D: Approx. 105 tons (fl) **S:** 16 kts **Dim:** 23.50 × 5.60 × 1.60
Electronics: Radar: 1 Sitex T-100 nav.; 1 Decca Bridgemaster C180/4 nav.
M: 2 G.M. Detroit Diesel 12V71 TI diesels; 2 props; 1,020 bhp
Electric: 60 kw tot. **Range:** 640/16 **Endurance:** 2 days
Crew: 2 officers, 2 non-officers

Remarks: 72 grt. Oilfield crewboat design. Assigned to Central and Arctic Region and based at Cobourg, Ont. Carries a Zodiac Mk 3 RIB and is equipped with an 8-m^2 hydrology laboratory. Navigational equipment includes an OAR 320E VHFD/F and Raytheon DC-2002 echo sounder.

INSHORE MULTITASK PATROL VESSELS [WPB]

♦ 11 miscellaneous inshore patrol launches [WPB]

	In serv.	GRT	Based
A. H. CHEVARIE	1978	10.8	Summerside, P.E.I.
AQUARIEL	1985	31	Havre Boucher, N.S.
ARCADIE	1990	18.3	Caraquet, N.B.
HOWE POINT	1989	11	Souris, P.E.I.
OTTER BAY	1992	21.3	Victoria, B.C.
TUCHO MARINER	1991	34.7	Hay River, N.W.T.
TUEBOR	1985	34.7	St. John, N.B.
VIGILANCE	1989	28.3	Digby, N.S.
W. FERGUSON	1990	18	Val Comeau, N.B.
6C-4828	1986	18	Neguac, N.B.
GELIGET	2003	. . .	Yarmouth, N.S.

Remarks: Most are of modified lobster-boat design, with a generally similar appearance. Overall lengths run from 12.8 m to 14.6 m, with the *Tucho Mariner* being the longest. They are used for general transportation and local patrol and rescue duties. All are powered by a single Caterpillar 3116 (275-bhp) or 3208 (340-bhp) diesel, and speeds range between 10 and 12.5 knots (*A. H. Chevarie:* 20 kts). One or two small navigational radars are fitted, and the crews are generally one officer and two non-officers. *Geliget,* most recent to enter service, was manufactured by ABCO Industries, Ltd. of Nova Scotia. Dimensions: 14.6 × 4.9 m. Powered by two Volvo D12 engines with 1300 hp total; can reach 30 kts using waterjets.

Disposal note: Patrol launch *North Bar* was no longer in service as of 2005.

HEAVY GULF ICEBREAKERS [WAGB]

♦ 1 former commercial icebreaking tug/supply ship [WAGB]
Bldr: Burrard Yarrows Corp., Vancouver Div., North Vancouver (In serv. 1983)

	Region	L	In serv.
TERRY FOX	Maritimes	1982	1983

D: Approx. 7,100 tons (fl) **S:** 16 kts
Dim: 88.02 (75.39 pp) × 17.94 (17.51 wl) × 8.30
Electronics: Radar: 1 Decca ARPA (X-band); 1 Decca Bridgemaster Conrad nav; 1 Furuno FCR-1411 Mk 2 nav.
M: 4 Stork Werkspoor 8TM410 diesels; 2 CP props; 23,202 bhp—stern CP propeller thruster and bow jet-thruster
Electric: 3,500 kw tot. (2 × 1,000-kw shaft generators, 2 × 750-kw Caterpillar V-12 diesel-driven sets)
Range: 19,200/15 **Fuel:** 1,919 m^3 **Endurance:** 58 days
Crew: 10 officers, 14 non-comm.

Remarks: 4,234 grt/2,113 dwt combination Arctic oilfield tug/supply and anchor-handling vessel with icebreaking hull, firefighting capability, and deck cargo capacity. Had been on charter since 8-91 from Gulf Canada Resources, Vancouver; was purchased 1-11-93 and formally commissioned 1-6-94. Named for a gallant Canadian athlete and cancer victim. Formerly classified as Type 1300. Based at Dartmouth, N.S.
Hull systems: Has a 231-m^2 helicopter deck and a 40-ton crane. The towing winch produces 220 tons bollard pull. Navigation equipment includes Magnavox MX-200 and Trimble Navtrac GPS, JMC 22215 MFD/F, Simrad-Taiyo VHFD/F, and 2 Elac LAZ 72 echo sounders. Carries two Zodiac RIBs and an aluminum workboat.

♦ 1 Louis S. St. Laurent class [WAGB]
Bldr: Canadian Vickers, Montreal, Que.

	Region	L	In serv.
LOUIS S. ST. LAURENT	Maritimes	3-6-66	8-69

D: 13,800 tons (fl) **S:** 20 kts **Dim:** 119.63 × 24.46 × 9.91
Electronics: Radar: 2 Sperry Rascar (X- and S-band); 1 Decca Bridgemaster (X-band)

COAST GUARD HEAVY GULF ICEBREAKERS [WAGB] *(continued)*

Louis S. St. Laurent H&L Van Ginderen, 9-99

M: 5 Krupp MaK 16M453C diesels (8,000 bhp each), 3 2,400-kw generator sets, 3 G.E. electric motors; 3 props; 27,000 shp
Electric: . . . kw (main generators + 2 Krupp MaK 6M282 diesel sets, 1,100 kw each)
Range: 23,000/16 **Fuel:** 4,800 m^3 **Endurance:** 205 days
Crew: 13 officers, 33 non-comm.

Remarks: 11,441 grt. Had serious fire 3-82 and again 30-12-85. In modernization 1987 to 9-92, had new bow installed, original geared turbine steam plant with four Babcock and Wilcox boilers replaced, a Wärtsilä bubbler underhull deicing system added, and the original hangar below the flight deck replaced by telescoping hangar on deck. Is based at Dartmouth, N.S.
Hull systems: Has accommodations for 216 persons total, Flume passive stabilization tanks, and a 25-ton-capacity pedestal crane and two 5-ton cranes. Carries an LCM-type landing craft. Scientific laboratories include three 45-m^2 wet labs, five 25-m^2 utility labs, and one 4-m^2 photo lab. Navigational equipment includes Magnavox MX-200 GPS, Taiyo 121 ATS MFD/F, OAR 320E VHFD/F, and LAZ-72 echo sounder.

MEDIUM GULF-RIVER ICEBREAKERS [WAGB]

♦ 1 Improved Radisson class [WAGB]

Bldr: Versatile Pacific, North Vancouver, B.C.

	Region	Laid down	L	In serv.
Henry Larsen	Newfoundland	15-8-85	3-1-87	1-7-88

D: 5,798 light, 6,172 tons normal (6,600 Great Lakes load, 8,290 fl)
S: 16.5 kts (13.5 cruise) **Dim:** 100.03 (87.95 pp) × 19.82 × 7.24
Electronics: Radar: 2 Decca Bridgemaster II (X- and S-band); 1 Decca Bridgemaster Conrad (aft)
M: 3 Wärtsilä Vasa 16V32 diesels (8,160 bhp each), 3 G.E. 5,000-kw generators, 2 electric motors; 2 props; 16,328 shp
Electric: 2,078 kw tot. (1 × 924-kw Wärtsilä 6L22, 1 × 804-kw Caterpillar 3512, and 1 × 350-kw Caterpillar 3508 diesel-driven sets)
Fuel: 1,900 tons; 20 tons for helo **Range:** 15,000/13.5
Man: 11 officers, 20 non-officers

Remarks: 6,166 grt/2,478 dwt (1,860 dwt Gt. Lakes, 2,490 dwt Arctic). Ordered 25-5-84. Design based on *Pierre Radisson* class, but with improved bow form. Is based at Dartmouth, N.S. Refitted 1998 to 3-99 by St. John's Dry Dock.
Hull systems: Has Wärtsilä bubbler underwater deicing system, with two 600-kw generators associated. Has a 100-ton cargo hold, 20 tons refrigerated cargo stowage, and an 8.5-ton crane. A 34 m^2 "special chart room" is fitted. Navigational equipment includes Magnavox MX 200 and Trimble Navtrac GPS, Sperry ADG autopilot, Taiyo 8121 ATS MFD/F, OAR 320E VHFD/F, an LAZ-72 (30 Hz) echo sounder, and a 50-Hz LAZ echo sounder.

♦ 3 Pierre Radisson class [WAGB]

Bldrs: *Pierre Radisson:* Burrard DD Co., Ltd., Vancouver, B.C. (*Des Groseilliers:* Port Weller DD Co., Ltd., Ont.)

	Region	L	In serv.
Pierre Radisson	Laurentian	3-6-77	6-78
Amundsen (ex-*Sir John Franklin*)	Newfoundland	10-3-78	3-79
Des Groseilliers	Laurentian	20-2-82	7-8-82

Des Groseilliers H&L Van Ginderen, 1-96

D: 6,400 tons (7,721 fl) **S:** 16.2 kts **Dim:** 98.25 (88.04 pp) × 19.84 × 7.43
Electronics: Radar: 1 Sperry 3400 Rascar (X-band); 1 Decca Bridgemaster Conrad
M: Diesel-electric: 6 Bombardier-Alco 16V251F diesels (17,580 bhp total); 6 G.E.C. alternators (11,100 kw); 2 G.E.C. motors; 2 props; 13,600 shp
Electric: 2,250 kw (main generators + 3 × 250-kw diesel sets)
Range: 15,000/13.5 **Fuel:** 2,215 m^3 **Endurance:** 120 days
Crew: 12 officers, 26 non-officers

Remarks: *Radisson:* 5,910 grt/2,820 dwt; 440 m^3 cargo capacity. *Des Groseilliers:* 5,910 grt. Used on St. Lawrence River and Great Lakes in winter, in Arctic in summer. *Amundsen* was badly damaged 20-6-96 but later returned to service; stricken in 2000 and recommissioned in 2003 as an oceanographic research ship (AGOR). She will continue to serve as a medium icebreaker during wintertime. *Amundsen* was renamed in 2003.
Hull systems: *Radisson* carries an Orpheus scientific minisub. Have a 500-m^3 cargo hold, two 8-ton cranes, and a telescoping hangar and flight deck for one BO-105 helicopter. Have passive-tank stabilization. Have a 22.4-ton bollard-pull towing winch. Navigational equipment includes Magnavox MX-200 GPS, Taiyo 7DV330 Mk 2 MFD/F, OAR 320E VHFD/F, and two LAZ-72 echo sounders.

LIGHT ICEBREAKER/MAJOR NAVAIDS TENDERS [WAGB]

♦ 6 Martha L. Black class [WAGB]

	Bldr	Laid down	L	In serv.
Martha L. Black	Versatile Pacific, Vancouver, B.C.	3-84	6-9-85	3-4-86
George R. Pearkes	Versatile Pacific, Victoria, B.C.	3-84	30-11-85	17-4-86
Ann Harvey	Halifax Ind., N.S.	1984	12-12-85	29-6-87
Sir William Alexander	Marine Industries, Tracy, Que.	24-2-86	23-10-86	13-2-87
Edward Cornwallis	Marine Industries, Tracy, Que.	5-7-84	22-2-86	14-8-86
Sir Wilfrid Laurier	Canadian SB, Collingwood, Ont.	14-5-85	6-12-85	15-11-86

George R. Pearkes H&L Van Ginderen, 4-94

D: Typical: 3,287 tons light (4,861 fl) **S:** 16.5 kts
Dim: 83.01 (75.01 pp) × 16.26 × 5.75–6.20
Electronics: Radar: 2 Decca Bridgemaster II (X- and S-band) nav.; 1 Decca Bridgemaster Conrad nav. (not in *Pearkes* or *Laurier*)
M: Diesel-electric: 3 Bombardier-Alco 16V-251F diesels (2,991 bhp each), 3 Can. G.E. generators (2,100 kw each), 2 Can. G.E. motors; 2 props; 7,100 shp—bow-thruster
Electric: 600 kw tot. (1 × 500-kw Caterpillar 3508TA, 1 × 100-kw Caterpillar 3306T diesel sets + power from main generator sets)
Range: 6,500/11 **Fuel:** 783.7 m^3 **Endurance:** 120 days
Crew: 10 or 12 officers, 15–16 non-officers

Remarks: *Martha L. Black:* 3,818 grt/1,688 dwt; *Pearkes:* 3,809 grt/1,689 dwt; *Harvey:* 3,853 grt/1,815 dwt; *Alexander:* 3,728 grt/1,660 dwt; *Cornwallis:* 3,728 grt/1,660 dwt; *Laurier:* 3,812 grt/1,647 dwt. Construction of the pair assigned to Marine Industries was delayed by a strike; both have lower superstructures and derricks on king posts, while on the others the derricks are stepped on the bridge face. *Cornwallis* was equipped to serve as a hydrographic survey ship during a 1997–98 refit. Are assigned and based as follows:

	Region	Based
Martha L. Black	Laurentian	Québec City, Que.
George R. Pearkes	Laurentian	Québec City, Que.
Ann Harvey	Newfoundland	St. John's, Nfld.
Sir William Alexander	Maritimes	Dartmouth, N.S.
Edward Cornwallis	Maritimes	Dartmouth, N.S.
Sir Wilfrid Laurier	Pacific	Victoria, B.C.

Hull systems: Dimensional and displacement data above refer to *Martha L. Black;* the others vary slightly. Carry 17.3 m^3 fuel for their one Bell 212 helicopter. Cargo capacity is 400 tons in forward hold, 50 tons aft. Carry 670 tons water ballast. Navigational equipment includes Magnavox MX-200 and Trimble Navtrack GPS, Taiyo 121 ATS MFD/F. PAR 320E VHFD/F, and two LAZ-72 echo sounders. One Zodiac Hurricane and one Zodiac RH 1 RIBs are carried.

COAST GUARD LIGHT ICEBREAKER/MAJOR NAVAIDS TENDERS [WAGB] *(continued)*

♦ 1 Griffon class [WAGB]
Bldr: Davie SB, Lauzon, Que.

	Region	In serv.
GRIFFON	Central & Arctic	12-70

Griffon H&L Van Ginderen, 7-98

D: 3,096 tons (fl) **S:** 13.0 kts **Dim:** 71.32 (65.23 pp) × 15.09 × 4.73
Electronics: Radar: 2 Decca Bridgemaster II (X- and S-band) nav.
M: 4 Fairbanks-Morse 38D8⅛-8 diesels (1,334 bhp each), 4 820-kw generators, 2 electric motors; 2 props; 4,000 shp
Electric: 826 kw tot. (3 × 212-kw Caterpillar D353TA; 1 × 190-kw Paxman diesel sets
Range: 5,500/11 **Fuel:** 368 m^3 **Endurance:** 90 days
Crew: 9 officers, 16 non-officers

Remarks: 2,212 grt/786 dwt. Major refit 1994–95 at Pascol Engineering, Thunder Bay, Ont., was intended to extend life to 2005. Based at Prescott, Ont.
Hull systems: Has a 970-m^3 cargo hold and one 15-ton buoy derrick. A 24-m^2 scientific laboratory is fitted. Has Flume passive tank stabilization. There is a 118-m^2 helicopter flight deck but no hangar. Navigational equipment includes Trimble Navtrack GPS, Taiyo 121 ATS MFD/F, OAR 320F VHFD/F, and LAZ-4401, Atlas 480, and Lowerance echo sounders.

♦ 1 J. E. Bernier class [WAGB]
Bldr: Davie SB, Lauzon, Que.

	Region	In serv.
J. E. BERNIER	Newfoundland	8-67

D: 3,150 tons (fl) **S:** 13 kts **Dim:** 70.70 (64.80 pp) × 15.09 × 5.20
Electronics: Radar: 1 Sperry Rascar 3400M nav.; 1 Sperry 127 nav.
M: 4 Fairbanks-Morse 38D8⅛-8 diesels, 4 865-kw generators, 2 electric motors; 2 props; 4,218 shp
Electric: 848 kw tot. (4 × 212-kw Paxman 12RPHZ diesel-driven sets)
Range: 4,000/11 **Fuel:** 512 m^3 **Crew:** 9 officers, 12 non-officers

Remarks: 2,457 grt/1,082 dwt. Refitted 5-89 to 7-90 and again 1992–93. Based at St. John's, Nfld.
Hull systems: Has telescoping helo hangar, 320-m^2 helicopter deck, and Flume passive stabilization tanks. There is a 10-ton buoy derrick and a 214-m^3 cargo hold. Two Zodiac RIBs and two workboats are carried. Navigational equipment includes Taiyo 121 ATS MFD/F, OAR 320E VHFD/F, and two LSZ 440 echo sounders.

Disposal note: Icebreaker *Sir Humphrey Gilbert* was retired late in 2001.

LIGHT ICEBREAKER/MEDIUM NAVAIDS TENDERS [WAGB]

♦ 2 Samuel Risley class [WAGB]

	Bldr	Region	In serv.
SAMUEL RISLEY	Vito Steel Boat & Barge, Vancouver, B.C.	Central & Arctic	6-85
EARL GREY	Pictou SY, Pictou, N.S.	Maritimes	30-5-86

Earl Grey Canadian Coast Guard

D: 2,260 tons light (2,935 fl) **S:** 12 kts **Dim:** 69.73 (59.01 pp) × 14.36 × 5.84
Electronics: Radar: 2 Decca Bridgemaster II (X- and S-band) nav.; 1 Decca Bridgemaster Conrad nav.
M: *Risley:* 4 Bombardier/Wärtsilä 12V22HE diesels; 2 Kort-nozzle CP props; 8,846 bhp—750-bhp bow-thruster—400-bhp stern-thruster; *Grey:* 4 Deutz SBV 9M628 diesels; 2 Kort-nozzle props; 8,718 bhp
Electric: *Risley:* 2,790 kw tot. (2 × 1,000-kw shaft generators; 2 × 395-kw, G.M. 16V71 diesels driving)—*Grey:* 2,232 kw tot. (2 × 800-kw shaft generators; 2 × 316-kw Caterpillar 3412DITA diesel-driven sets)
Range: *Risley:* 16,700/12; *Grey:* 18,000/11 **Fuel:** *Risley:* 692 m^3; *Grey:* 634 m^3
Endurance: 58 days **Crew:** 9 officers, 22 non-officers

Remarks: *Samuel Risley:* 1,967 grt/1,186 dwt; *Earl Grey:* 1,988 grt/1,159 dwt. Design based on offshore supply vessel technology. Are able to break 0.6-m ice. *Risley* is based at Parry Sound, Ont.; *Grey* at Charlottetown, P.E.I.
Hull systems: Buoy crane capacity is 15 tons at 8.0-m radius, 8.5 tons at 20-m. Two fire monitors produce 600 m^2/hr. to 75 m range. Have 90-ton bollard-pull towing winch. *Risley* has a 29.8-m^2 oceanographic laboratory.

ICE-STRENGTHENED MEDIUM NAVAIDS TENDERS [WAGL]

♦ 2 Provo Wallis class [WAGL]
Bldr: Marine Industries, Sorel, Que.

	Region	In serv.
PROVO WALLIS	Maritimes	10-69
BARTLETT	Pacific	12-69

Provo Wallis Ralph Edwards, 3-05

D: *Wallis:* . . . tons (fl); *Bartlett:* 1,722 tons (fl) **S:** 12.5 kts
Dim: *Wallis:* 63.78 × 13.09 × 3.66; *Bartlett:* 57.68 × 13.09 × 4.10
Electronics:
Radar: *Wallis:* Sperry Rascar 2500M (X-band) nav.; Sperry 3400M (S-band) nav.—*Bartlett:* 2 Decca Bridgemaster II (X- and S-band) nav.
M: 2 National Gas–Mirrlees-Blackstone KLSDM6 direct-drive diesels; 2 CP props; 2,100 bhp (1,760 sust.)—bow-thruster
Electric: *Wallis:* 995 kw tot. (3 × 270 kw, Iveco 8 281 SRM44 diesels driving; 1 × 185-kw, Paxman 8RPHZ emergency diesel set)—*Bartlett:* 1,056 kw tot. (3 × 352-kw, Paxman 8RPH diesels driving)
Range: 3,300/11 **Fuel:** *Wallis:* 240 m^3; *Bartlett:* 213 m^3
Endurance: 21 days **Crew:** 9 officers, 14 (*Wallis:* 15) non-officers

Remarks: *Provo Wallis:* 1,313 grt/515 dwt (prior to lengthening); *Bartlett:* 1,317 grt. *Bartlett* refitted 1987 with bow-thruster, flush between decks hatches to cargo hold, new winches, modifications to the navigation bridge, a new sewage system, and other improvements; refitted again 6-91 to 4-92. Transferred to Pacific in 1995, where she is based at Victoria, B.C.

Provo Wallis, lengthened during refit 5-89 to 5-90 at Marystown Shipyards, is 6 m longer, is based at St. John, N.B., and operates with alternating crews; also fitted with bow- and stern-thrusters, new generators, a modified Liebherr boom crane, and a Miranda davit to handle an RI 22–class fast rescue RIB.
Hull systems: Both have a 15-ton derrick tending the 507-m^3 cargo hold and carry one 9.1-m landing craft. Both have Magnavox MX-200 GPS, Taiyo 121 ATS MFD/F, and OAR 320E VHFD/F. *Wallis* has one and *Bartlett* two Elac LAZ-72 echo sounders.

♦ 1 Nahidik class [WAGL]
Bldr: Allied SB, North Vancouver, B.C.

	Region	In serv.
NAHIDIK	Central & Arctic	1974

D: 1,122 tons (fl) **S:** 13 kts **Dim:** 53.35 (52.89 pp) × 15.24 × 1.98
Electronics: Radar: 1 Decca Bridgemaster II nav.; 1 Sperry Mk 127 nav.
M: 2 G.M. Detroit Diesel-Allison 12-645-ES diesels; 2 props; 1,600 bhp
Electric: 200 kw tot. (2 × 100 kw Kato sets, G.M. diesels driving)
Range: 5,000/12 **Fuel:** 231 m^3
Crew: 6 officers, 6 non-officers, 11 passengers

COAST GUARD ICE-STRENGTHENED MEDIUM NAVAIDS TENDERS [WAGL] *(continued)*

Nahidik Canadian Coast Guard

Remarks: 856 grt/562 dwt. Based at Hay River, Northwest Territories, assigned to the Central and Arctic Region.
Hull systems: Has helicopter platform aft, twin side-by-side stacks, and a 328-m^3 cargo hold tended by a 10-ton crane. Navigational equipment includes a Magnavox MX-200 GPS, Taiyo TD-A121 MFD/F, OAR 320E VHFD/F, and Elac LAZ 72 and Furuno ED-222 echo-sounders. Is also equipped with three Furnuno FCV-667 Video Sounders linked to the display for the ED-222 set for survey purposes. Can carry portable Simrad Mesotech color-imaging Model 971 mapping sonar.

♦ 1 Tracy class [WAGL]
Bldr: Port Weller Dry Dock, Ltd., Port Weller, Ont.

	Region	In serv.
TRACY	Laurentian	17-4-68

Tracy H&L Van Ginderen, 7-93

D: 1,320 tons (fl) **S:** 13.5 kts **Dim:** 55.32 (50.30 pp) × 11.64 × 3.66
Electronics: Radar: 1 Sperry 340 (X-band) nav.; 1 Sperry 340CA (S-band) nav.
M: 2 Fairbanks-Morse 38D8$^1/_8$-8 diesels, 4 405-kw generators, 2 electric motors; 2 props; 2,500 shp—bow-thruster
Electric: 422 kw tot. (3 × 110-kw Paxman 6RPHZ diesel-driven sets; 1 × 92-kw Paxman 4RPHZ emergency diesel-driven set)
Range: 5,000/12 **Fuel:** 155.1 m^3 **Endurance:** 17 days
Crew: 8 officers, 13 non-officers

Remarks: 963 grt/419 dwt. Based at Sorel, Que.
Hull systems: Has a 10-ton buoy derrick and a 5-ton bollard-pull towing winch. Carries an 8-m self-propelled work barge and a smaller workboat. Navigational equipment includes a Magnavox MX-200 GPS, Taiyo TD-C338 Mk II MFD/F, OAR 320E VHFD/F, and ELAC 30-kHz and 50-kHz echo sounders.

♦ 1 Simcoe class [WAGL]
Bldr: Canadian Vickers, Montreal

	Region	In serv.
SIMCOE	Central & Arctic	1962

D: 1,392 tons (fl) **S:** 14 kts **Dim:** 54.62 (50.35 pp) × 11.64 × 3.83
Electronics: Radar: Decca Bridgemaster II (X- and S-band) nav.
M: 2 Paxman YLCZ 12-cyl. diesels (1,500 bhp each), 4 410-kw generators, 2 electric motors; 2 props; 2,000 shp
Electric: 650 kw tot. (2 × 270-kw Caterpillar 3406 diesel-driven; 1 × 110-kw Caterpillar 3304 diesel-driven emergency set)
Range: 5,000/10 **Fuel:** 156 m^3 **Endurance:** 21 days
Crew: 10 officers, 17 non-officers

Remarks: 961 grt/457 dwt. Based on Lake Ontario at Prescott, Ont.
Hull systems: The 532-m^3 buoy hold is tended by a 10-ton crane. Carries a Boston Whaler, a workboat, and a self-propelled work barge. Navigational equipment includes Magnavox MX-200 GPS, Marconi 2464A MFD/F, OAR 320E VHFD/F, and Elac LAZ 72 and STN-Atlas Elektronik 480 echo sounders.

Disposal note: Icebreaker *Simon Fraser* was stricken on 29-11-02.

Simcoe H&L Van Ginderen, 10-89

OFFSHORE RESEARCH AND SURVEY [WAGOR/WAGS]

♦ 1 John P. Tully–class survey ship [WAGS]
Bldr: Bel-Aire SY, Vancouver, B.C.

	Region	Laid down	L	In serv.
JOHN P. TULLY	Pacific	30-1-84	27-10-84	5-85

John P. Tully—in former paint scheme Fisheries & Oceans, 1988

D: 2,200 tons (fl) **S:** 14 kts **Dim:** 68.92 (61.68 pp) × 14.18 × 4.50
Electronics: Radar: 1 Sperry 2500M nav.; 1 Sperry 3400M nav.
M: 2 Deutz SBV-628 8-cyl. diesels; 1 CP prop; 3,126 bhp—bow and stern jet-pump thrusters
Electric: 1,880 kw tot. (4 × 470-kw diesel-driven sets)
Range: 12,000/10 **Fuel:** 483 m^3 **Endurance:** 50 days
Crew: 17 officers, 3 non-officers + up to 20 scientists/hydrographers

Remarks: 2,021 grt. Based at Patricia Bay, B.C.
Hull systems: A 190-m^2 helicopter deck is located forward. Four hydrographic sounding boats can be carried. There is a 5-ton crane. A 50-m^2 dry lab and a 6-m^2 wet oceanographic lab are fitted. Navigational equipment includes Trimble XL6PS GPS, Taiyo C338-RS MFD/F, Taiyo TD616 VHFD/F, and JEC JEV-216, Furuno FE-881, and Simrad EA-500 echo sounders.

Disposal note: Research vessel *Parizeau* is no longer in service and was offered for sale during 6-04.

♦ 1 Hudson class [WAGOR]
Bldr: Saint John SB & DD, Saint John, N.B. (In serv. 1963)

HUDSON

Hudson *Ships of the World,* 1998

D: Approx. 5,400 tons (fl) **S:** 17 kts **Dim:** 90.4 × 15.4 × 6.8
Electronics: Radar: 2 Decca Bridgemaster II (X- and S-band) nav.
M: 4 Alco 16-cyl diesels, 4 generators, 2 electric motors; 2 props; 8,636 shp
Electric: 1,222 kw tot. (2 × 611-kw, Caterpillar D358D diesel-driven sets)
Range: 23,100/10.5 **Fuel:** 1,268 m^3 **Endurance:** 105 days
Crew: 11 officers, 26 non-officers

Remarks: 3,740 grt. Modernized 1990 by builder. Assigned to the Maritimes Region and based at Dartmouth, N.S.

COAST GUARD OFFSHORE RESEARCH AND SURVEY [WAGOR/WAGS] *(continued)*

Hull systems: Laboratories include a 112-m² hydrographic, 20-m² oceanographic, 40-m² geological/chemical, and 18-m² general purpose labs. Has a 1,380-m² helicopter flight deck and 280-m² hangar. Has a 4.3-ton crane and a 200-m³ cargo hold. Navigational equipment includes a Magnavox MX-300 GPS terminal, TD-338H5 MFD/F, Taiyo VHFD/F, and Elac LAZ 440 echo sounder.

COASTAL/INSHORE RESEARCH AND SURVEY [WAGS/WYGS]

♦ 1 Matthew-class hydrographic survey ship [WAGS]
Bldr: Versatile Marine, Montreal (In serv. 1990)

MATTHEW

Matthew Canadian Coast Guard

D: Approx. 1,150 tons (fl) **S:** 12 kts **Dim:** 50.3 × 10.5 × 4.3
Electronics: Radar: 1 Decca Bridgemaster nav.; 1 Decca BT 502 nav.
M: 2 Caterpillar 3508 8-cyl diesels; 2 CP props; 1,810 bhp
Electric: 750 kw tot. (3 × 250-kw, Caterpillar 3406 diesels driving)
Range: 4,000/12 **Fuel:** 119 m³ **Endurance:** 20 days
Crew: 5 officers, 8 non-officers, 6 scientists/technicians

Remarks: 856.8 grt. Assigned to Maritimes Region and based at Dartmouth, N.S.
Hull systems: Has a 90-m² helicopter deck. Carries two hydrographic survey launches, one Zodiac 520 RIB, and two smaller inflatable boats. Has a 107-m² cartographic lab and a 13.5-m² hydrology lab. Navigational equipment includes a Magnavox MX-300 GPS terminal, Taiyo TD-338HS MFD/F, Taiyo ADDFTD-L1620 VHFD/F, and Elac LAZ-series echo sounder.

♦ 1 R. B. Young–class hydrographic survey ship [WYGS]
Bldr: Allied Shipbuilding, North Vancouver, B.C. (In serv. 1990)

R. B. YOUNG

D: Approx. 350 tons (fl) **S:** 11.6 kts **Dim:** 32.30 × 8.00 × 2.30
Electronics: Radar: 2 Raytheon R81 nav.
M: 2 Caterpillar 6-cyl diesels; 2 CP props; 1,052 bhp—bow-thruster
Electric: 190 kw tot. (2 × 95-kw, Caterpillar diesels driving)
Range: 5,000/10 **Fuel:** 51 m³ **Crew:** 4 officers, 3 non-officers, 3 scientists

Remarks: 299.96 grt. Assigned to Pacific Region and based at Patricia Bay, B.C.
Hull systems: Has a 17-m² wet laboratory. Navigational systems include a Simrad EM 1002 multibeam mapping sonar, Furuno FE 880 echo sounder, and Taiyo TA-L1520 MFD/F.

♦ 1 Louis M. Lauzier–class hydrographic survey ship [WYGS]
Bldr: Breton Industries, Ltd., Port Hawkesbury, N.S. (In serv. 1976)

LOUIS M. LAUZIER

D: Approx. 350 tons (fl) **S:** 12.5 kts **Dim:** 37.10 × 8.20 × 2.13
Electronics: Radar: 1 JRC JMA-627-6 (X-band) nav.; 1 Decca 6520/CAD (X-band) nav.
M: 2 Cummins K2300 diesels; 2 props; 1,600 bhp—bow-thruster
Electric: 280 kw tot. (2 × 140-kw diesel-driven sets)
Range: 1,800/12.5 **Fuel:** 53 m³ **Crew:** 3 officers, 7 non-officers

Remarks: 322.25 grt. Re-engined in 1986. Former fisheries protection ship. As of 2001 was on charter to the Memorial University of Newfoundland.
Hull systems: Navigational equipment includes Trimble Navtrac XL GPS, Taiyo TD-4550 VHFD/F, Elac LAZ-72 echo sounder, and Lowerance X-16 echo sounder.

♦ 1 Limnos-class hydrographic survey ship [WYGS]
Bldr: Port Weller Dry Docks, St. Catherines, Ont. (In serv. 1968)

LIMNOS

D: Approx. 650 tons (fl) **S:** 10 kts **Dim:** 44.81 × 9.75 × 2.60
Electronics: Radar: 1 Decca Bridgemaster ARPA (X-band) nav.; 1 Decca Bridgemaster (S-band) nav.
M: 2 Caterpillar 3412 diesels; 2 Harbormaster 360 azimuthal props; 1,006 bhp
Electric: 400 kw tot. (2 × 150 kw, 1 × 100 kw diesel-driven)
Range: 3,500/10 **Fuel:** 80 m³ **Crew:** 6 officers, 8 non-officers, 14 scientists

Remarks: 460 grt. Modernized in 1981. Assigned to Central and Arctic Region and based at Burlington, Ont.
Hull systems: Has 10-m² dry and 6-m² wet laboratories. A 15-ton crane is fitted. One Boston Whaler 5-m launch and an Ambar 550 workboat are carried. Navigational equipment includes an STN Atlas Elektronik DESO-10 mapping sonar, Lowerance and Elac echo sounders, and Taiyo VHFD/F.

♦ 1 Vector-class hydrographic survey ship [WYGS]
Bldr: Yarrows, Ltd., Esquimalt, B.C. (In serv. 1967)

VECTOR

D: Approx. 680 tons (fl) **S:** 12 kts **Dim:** 39.74 × 9.46 × 3.50
Electronics: Radar: 1 Decca 2090B nav.; 1 Raytheon M25 nav.
M: 1 Caterpillar 3208 diesel; 1 CP prop; 800 bhp
Electric: 740 kw tot. (2 × 370 kw, Caterpillar 3306 and 3406 diesels driving)
Range: 3,500/10 **Fuel:** 74 m³ **Endurance:** 20 days
Crew: 5 officers, 7 non-officers, 8 scientists

Remarks: 515 grt. Performs general oceanographic research as well as survey work. Was re-engined in 1995. Assigned to Pacific Region and based at Patricia Bay, B.C.
Hull systems: Has a 65-m² laboratory. Equipped with Simrad EA500 mapping sonar, Firimp FCV-251 and JRC RD-5000 echo sounders, Northstar 941X GPS, and Taiyo TL-Lq520 VHFD/F.

SMALL NAVAIDS TENDERS [WYGL]

♦ 1 Traverse class [WYGL]
Bldr: Metalcraft Marine, Kingston, Ont. (In serv. 1998)

TRAVERSE

D: . . . tons **S:** 9 kts **Dim:** 19.81 × 7.30 × 0.60
Electronics: Radar: 1 Furuno M1832 nav.
M: 2 Volvo Penta diesels; 2 props; 180 bhp
Electric: 30 kw tot. (1 × 30-kw diesel-driven set) **Range:** 800/8
Fuel: 2 m³ **Endurance:** 10 days **Crew:** 1 officer, 3 non-officers

Remarks: 70.66 grt. Aluminum-construction, unpainted catamaran. Assigned to the Central and Arctic Region and based at Kenora, Ont.
Hull systems: Has a 1.5-ton buoy crane and carries a 5.5-m aluminum workboat. Navigational equipment includes a GPS set and two FCV 561 echo sounders.

♦ 4 Partridge Island class [WYGL]
Bldr: Breton Industrial & Marine, Hawkesbury, N.S.

	Region	Laid down	L	In serv.
PARTRIDGE ISLAND	Maritime	1-11-84	2-7-85	31-10-85
ÎLE DES BARQUES	Laurentian	1-11-84	3-7-85	26-11-85
ÎLE SAINT-OURS	Laurentian	7-5-85	25-4-86	15-5-86
CARIBOU ISLE	Central & Arctic	7-5-85	7-5-86	16-6-86

Île Saint-Ours H&L Van Ginderen, 9-94

D: 133 tons (fl) **S:** 10 kts **Dim:** 23.00 (22.50 wl) × 6.00 × 1.35
Electronics: Radar: 1 Sperry Mk 1270 nav.
M: 2 G.M. 8V92 diesels; 2 props; 640 bhp **Electric:** 70 kw (2 gen.)
Range: 1,800/8 **Fuel:** 26,000 liters **Endurance:** 7–10 days **Crew:** 5 tot.

Remarks: First two ordered 23-7-84 and others on 23-11-84. *Partridge Island* is based at St. John, N.B.; *Île des Barques* and *Île Saint-Ours* at Sorel, Que.; and *Caribou Isle* at Sault Ste. Marie, Ont. Cargo capacity is 20 tons. Have a fire monitor with 2,500-liter/min capacity to 60-m range.

♦ 1 Tsekoa II class [WYGL]
Bldr: Allied Shipbuilders, Vancouver (In serv. 1984)

TSEKOA II

D: . . . tons **S:** 12 kts **Dim:** 26.70 × 7.25 × 2.00
Electronics: Radar: 1 Raytheon R 80 nav.; 1 Raytheon R 81 nav.
M: 2 G.M. Detroit Diesel 8V92 diesels; 2 props; 640 bhp
Range: . . . /11 **Fuel:** 13 m³ **Crew:** 3 officers, 4 non-officers

Remarks: 160.75 grt. Assigned to the Pacific Region and based at Victoria, B.C.
Hull systems: Has a 10-ton buoy crane and carries a Mk 5 Zodiac RIB.

COAST GUARD SMALL NAVAIDS TENDERS [WYGL] *(continued)*

Tsekoa II R. Brytan, 3-97

♦ 2 Cove Isle class [WYGL]
Bldr: Canadian Dredge & Dock, Kingston, Ont. (In serv. 1980)

COVE ISLE GULL ISLE

D: 116 tons (fl) **S:** 12 kts **Dim:** 20.00 × 6.00 × 1.70
Electronics: Radar: 1 Decca Bridgemaster IIC 181/4 nav.
M: 2 Cummins diesels; 2 props; 500 bhp
Electric: 80 kw tot. (2 × 40-kw diesel-driven sets)
Range: 2,500/11 **Fuel:** 20.5 tons **Endurance:** 14 days
Crew: 1 officer, 4 non-officers

Remarks: 92.05 grt. Both are assigned to the Central and Arctic Region, with *Cove Isle* based at Parry Sound, Ont., and *Gull Isle* at Amherstburg, Ont.
Hull systems: Have a 20-ton buoy crane and a 4-ton bollard-pull winch. Navigational equipment includes a Datamarine echo sounder and two Elac LAZ-series echo sounders.

♦ 1 Namao class [WYGL]
Bldr: Riverton Boatworks, Manitoba (In serv. 1975)

	Region	In serv.
NAMAO	Central & Arctic	1975

Namao Canadian Coast Guard, 1988

D: 386 tons (fl) **S:** 12 kts **Dim:** 33.62 × 8.53 × 2.13
Electronics: Radar: 1 Decca Bridgemaster IIC 181/4 nav.
M: 2 G.M. Detroit Diesel-Allison 12V149 diesels; 2 props; 1,350 bhp
Range: 3,000/11 **Fuel:** 34.5 m^3 **Crew:** 4 officers, 7 non-officers

Remarks: 327.91 grt. Assigned to the Central and Arctic Region and based at Selkirk, Man.; employed as buoy tender on Lake Winnipeg.
Hull systems: Has a 220-m^3 cargo hold. Navigational equipment includes a Furuno GP-70 Mk 2 GPS, OAR 320E VHFD/F, and Raytheon DE 719C echo sounder.

SPECIAL RIVER NAVAIDS TENDERS [WYGL]

♦ 1 Eckaloo class [WYGL]
Bldr: Vancouver SY, Ltd., North Vancouver, B.C.

	L	In serv.
ECKALOO	31-5-88	31-8-88

D: 534 tons (fl) **S:** 13 kts (11 sust.) **Dim:** 49.03 (48.01 pp) × 13.37 × 1.37
Electronics: Radar: 2 Decca Bridgemaster (X-band) nav.
M: 2 Caterpillar 3512TA diesels; 2 Kort-nozzle props; 2,116 bhp
Electric: 300 kw (3 × 100-kw Caterpillar 3306T diesels driving)
Range: 2,000/11 **Fuel:** 100 m^3 **Endurance:** 15 days
Crew: 4 officers, 6 non-officers + 12 passengers

Remarks: 661.13 grt. Refitted 1996 at NTCL Shipyard, Hay River. Is assigned to the Central and Arctic Region, based at Hay River, Northwest Territories.
Hull systems: Flat hull bottom; tunnel-mounted propellers. Has a 6-ton capacity (at 7.6-m radius) buoy crane. Can carry a portable Simrad Mesotech color-imaging Model 971 mapping sonar for survey duties. A 200-m^2 helicopter platform is fitted. Carries one 5.2-m Boston Whaler and one 4.3-m Zodiac RIB. Navigational equipment includes a Furuno GP-70 GPS, OPAR 320E VHFD/F, four Furuno FCV 667 echo sounders, and one Elac LAZ 72 echo sounder.

Eckaloo H&L Van Ginderen, 1994

♦ 1 Dumit class [WYGL]
Bldr: Allied SB, North Vancouver, B.C. (In serv. 7-79)

DUMIT

D: 628 tons (fl) **S:** 12 kts **Dim:** 50.91 (48.82 pp) × 12.58 × 1.64
M: 2 Caterpillar 12-cyl. diesels; 2 props; 2,250 bhp
Range: 9,000/10 **Fuel:** 175 tons **Crew:** 10 tot.

Remarks: 569 grt/85 dwt. Is based at Hay River, N.W.T., assigned to the Central and Arctic Region. Can carry a portable Simrad Mesotech color-imaging Model 971 mapping sonar for survey duties.

♦ 1 Tembah class [WYGL]
Bldr: Allied SB, Vancouver, B.C. (In serv. 10-63)

TEMBAH

Tembah Canadian Coast Guard

D: 181 tons (fl) **S:** 13 kts **Dim:** 39.37 (36.58 pp) × 8.06 × 0.91
M: 2 Cummins 12-cyl. diesels; 2 props; 680 bhp **Electric:** 85.5 kw tot.
Range: 1,000/11 **Fuel:** 21 tons **Crew:** 9 tot.

Remarks: 189 grt. Has one 5-ton crane, serving a 1.2 × 2.2-m hatch. Based at Hay River, N.W.T., and assigned to the Central and Arctic Region. Can carry a portable Simrad Mesotech color-imaging Model 971 mapping sonar for survey duties.

OFFSHORE/INSHORE FISHERIES RESEARCH [WAGOR]

♦ 2 Alfred Needler–class fisheries research ships [WAGOR]
Bldr: Ferguson, Pictou (In serv. 1982)

ALFRED NEEDLER WILFRED TEMPLEMAN

Alfred Needler Ralph Edwards, 3-05

D: Approx. 1,300 tons (fl) **S:** 15 kts **Dim:** 50.3 × 11.0 × 4.3
M: 1 Bombardier-Alco 16V-251F diesel; 1 prop; 3,138 bhp
Electric: 875 kw tot. (1 × 350-kw, 2 × 200-kw, 1 × 125-kw diesel sets)
Range: 9,300/15 **Fuel:** 209.5 tons **Crew:** . . .

Remarks: 925 grt stern-haul trawlers used for fisheries research. *Needler* based at Halifax, in Scotia/Fundy Region; *Templeman* based at St. John's, Nfld.

COAST GUARD OFFSHORE/INSHORE FISHERIES RESEARCH [WAGOR] *(continued)*

Note: Also in use for fisheries research are the *Calanus II* (1991, Laurentians Region, 160 grt); *Caligus; J. L. Hart* (1974, Maritimes, 93 grt); *Navicula* (1968, Maritimes, 106 grt); *Opilio* (1989, Maritimes, 74 grt); *Pandalus III* (1986, Maritimes, 13 grt); *Shamook* (1975, Newfoundland, 187 grt; 6 crew, 3 scientists); *Shark* (1971, Central and Arctic, 19 grt); *Teleost* (1996, Newfoundland District); and *W. E. Ricker* (ex-*Callistratus,* 1,040 grt, completed 12-78 and operating on the Pacific coast with a crew of 24 plus 12 scientists).

MULTITASK LIFEBOATS [WYH]

♦ 8 U.S. Coast Guard 44-foot Motor Lifeboat class [WYH]

	In serv.	Region
Bamfield	1964	Pacific
Port Hardy (ex-*Bull Harbor*)	1969	Pacific
Tofino	1970	Pacific
Tobermory (ex-CG 108)	1974	Central
Westfort (ex-*Thunder Bay,* ex-CG 109)	1974	Central
Shippegan (ex-CG 115)	1975	Maritimes
CG 141 (ex-*Cap-aux-Meules*)	1982	Maritimes
Souris	1985	Maritimes

A 44-ft. lifeboat in Canadian Coast Guard service Canadian Coast Guard

D: 17.9 tons (fl) **S:** 11.5 kts **Dim:** 13.45 × 3.86 × 1.20
Electronics: Radar: 1 Furuno FR-1510D or Raytheon 060 nav.
M: 2 Caterpillar 3208 diesels; 2 props; 360 bhp
Range: 150/10 **Fuel:** 1.2 tons **Crew:** 3–4 non-officers

Remarks: 11 grt. Are of self-righting, U.S. Coast Guard design. First unit was built at U.S. Coast Guard Yard, Curtis Bay, Md.; the others in Canada. Are based at ports whose names they bear, except for CG 141, which is maintained in standby at Mulgrave, N.S. Three others, *Cap Goélands,* CG 117, and CG 118, serve as training craft.
Disposals: *Burgeo* (CG 114), CG 116 (ex-*Clark's Harbour*), CG 117 (ex-*Sambro*), CG 118 (ex-*Louisbourg*), and CG 140 (ex-*Port Mouton*) have been retired.

MULTITASK HIGH-ENDURANCE LIFEBOATS [WYH]

♦ 10 Halmatic Arun 300B class [WYH]

Bldrs: *Bickerton:* Halmatic, Havant, U.K.; *Spindrift:* Georgetown SY, P.E.I.; *Spray* through *W. G. George:* Industries Raymond, Sept Îles, Que.; others: Hike Metal Products, Wheatly, Ont.

	In serv.		In serv.
Bickerton	8-89	W. G. George	9-95
Spindrift	10-93	Cap-aux-Meules	10-96
Spray	7-9-94	Clark's Harbour	9-96
W. Jackman	10-95	Sambro	1-97
Spume	7-10-94	Westport	5-97

Cap-aux-Meules H&L Van Ginderen, 8-96

D: 34 tons (fl) **S:** 20 kts **Dim:** 16.25 × 5.18 × 1.25
Electronics: Radar: 1 Furuno 1510 rasterscan or Decca Bridgemaster II nav.
M: 2 Caterpillar 3408BTA diesels; 2 props; 1,000 bhp
Range: 100/18; 150/16 **Endurance:** 1.5 days **Crew:** 2 officers, 2 non-officers

Remarks: 42 grt. Formerly typed as large search-and-rescue lifeboats (Type 310).
Hull systems: *Bickerton* has a Kevlar-construction hull; the rest were built of aluminum. Low freeboard aids in picking up survivors. Navigation equipment includes a GP-70 GPS, Furuno FD-177 MFD/F, OAR 320E VHFD/F, and Furuno FCV-561 echo sounder.

MULTITASK MEDIUM-ENDURANCE LIFEBOATS [WYH]

Note: A contract for 20 new lifeboats was given to Victoria Shipyards, Victoria, B.C., on 11-10-01.

♦ 25 (+ 6) U.S. Coast Guard 47-ft Motor Life Boat class [WYH]

Bldr: First 7: MIL Systems Engineering, Ottawa/Hike Metalcraft Marine Group, Kingston, Ont.; others: Victoria Shipyards, Victoria, B.C.

	In serv.		In serv.
Cape Sutil	12-98	Cape Spry	2004
Cape Calvert	8-99	Cape Ann	6-05
Cape St. James	11-99	Cape Edensaw	6-05
Cape Storm	1999	Cape Cockburn	9-05
Cape Lambton	2000	Cape Commodore	9-05
Thunder Cape	6-01	Cape Caution	9-05
Cape Mercy	12-01	Cape McKay	9-05
Cape De Rabast	2002	Cape Kuper	10-05
Cape Fox	2002	Cape Breton	2005
Cape Rozier	2002	Cape Chaillon	2005
Cape Norman	2003	Cape Discovery	2005
Cape Farewell	9-04	Cape Providence	2005
Cape Mudge	9-04		

Cape Ann Canadian Coast Guard, 2005

D: 18.15 tons (fl) **S:** 25 kts **Dim:** 14.61 (13.11 wl) × 4.27 × 1.37
Electronics: Radar: 1 Furuno 1942 nav.
M: 2 Caterpillar 3196 diesels; 2 props; 900 bhp **Electric:** 10 kw tot.
Range: 200/22 **Fuel:** 1,560 liters **Crew:** 1 officer, 3 non-officers

Remarks: Primary role considered to be search and rescue with secondary missions that include fisheries conservation, protection, and environmental response. First units ordered 1-4-97 to U.S. Textron Marine design; 20 more ordered 10-01 for delivery through 2006. The first Victoria-built unit was delivered on 31-1-03.
Hull systems: Aluminum construction, with deep-vee hullform. Can berth five survivors. Can maintain 20 kts in 2-ft. seas, tow craft displacing up to 150 tons, and survive an end-for-end pitch-pole and are capable of operating in 80-knot gales with 9-m swells and 6-m breaking seas. Navigation equipment includes Magnavox MX-400BR GPS, FMC 5500 VHFD/F, and Sitex CV 106 echo sounder.

♦ 1 CGR-100-class rigid inflatable rescue boat [WYH]

Bldr: Hurricane Rescue Craft, Vancouver (In serv. 1986)

CGR-100

D: 10.5 tons (fl) **S:** 34 kts **Dim:** 14.00 × 4.80 × 0.69
Electronics: Radar: 1 Furuno FR-1510D nav.
M: 2 Caterpillar 3176B diesels; 2 Hamilton 302 waterjets; 670 bhp
Range: 250/26 **Fuel:** 1.3 m^3 **Crew:** 1 officer, 2 non-officers

Remarks: 21.44 grt. World's largest rigid-hull inflatable craft when delivered. Modernized in 1997 by Hike Metal Products, Wheatley, Ont. Is assigned to the Central and Arctic Region, based at Port Weller, Ont.
Hull systems: Has deep-vee hullform with rigid inflatable collar. Navigational equipment includes a GP-70 Mk 2 GPS, OAR 320E VHFD/F, and Furuno FW-55 echo sounder.

MULTIHULLED SURVEY AND SOUNDING [WYGS]

♦ 1 Frederick G. Creed class [WYGS]

Bldr: Swath Ocean Systems, San Diego, Calif. (In serv. 1988)

Frederick G. Creed

COAST GUARD MULTIHULLED SURVEY AND SOUNDING [WYGS] *(continued)*

Frederick G. Creed Ralph Edwards, 3-05

D: . . . tons **S:** 21 kts **Dim:** 20.40 × 9.75 × 2.60
Electronics:
Radar: 1 Furuno 2110+ ARPA 23 nav.; 1 Furuno FR-8050D nav.
M: 2 G.M. Detroit Diesel 12V71 TA diesels; 2 props; 2,158 bhp
Electric: 66 kw tot. (2 × 33-kw, John Deere diesels driving)
Range: 1,500/16 **Fuel:** 15.8 m^3 **Endurance:** 3 days
Crew: 3 officers, 1 non-officer, 5 scientists

Remarks: 151.4 grt. SWATH (small waterplane twin hull) craft. Assigned to the Laurentian Region and based at Romouskie, Que. Has Simrad EM-1000 multibeam mapping sonar and a 13.5-m^2 dry laboratory.

♦ 1 F. C. G. Smith class
Bldr: Georgetown Shipyard, Georgetown, P.E.I. (In serv. 1985)

F. C. G. Smith

D: . . . tons **S:** 10 kts **Dim:** 34.80 × 14.00 × 2.10
Electronics: Radar: 2 Decca Bridgemaster II C252 ARPA nav.
M: 2 Baudouin diesels; 2 props; 800 bhp **Electric:** 270 kw tot.
Range: 15,000/10 **Fuel:** 38 m^3 **Endurance:** 7 days
Crew: 4 officers, 3 non-officers, 3 scientists

Remarks: 438.5 grt. catamaran. Assigned to the Laurentian Region and based at Québec City. Has a sweep boom sounding system with Navtronics multichannel echo-sounder system.

♦ 1 GC-03 class
Bldr: St. Catherine d/Alexandrie SY, Québec City, Que. (In serv. 1973)

GC-03

GC-03 H&L Van Ginderen, 4-93

D: . . . tons **S:** 10.5 kts **Dim:** 18.50 × 6.40 × 1.80
Electronics: Radar: 1 Sperry MIL 1040 nav.
M: 2 Caterpillar 3306 BTA diesels; 2 props; 584 bhp
Range: 400/9 **Fuel:** 1.4 m^3 **Crew:** 1 officer, 3 non-officers

Remarks: 56.64-grt catamaran. Assigned to Laurentian Region and based at Sorel, Que. Has a 12-m^2 hydrographic lab and is equipped with a sweep boom sounding system, along with Seatec and Navitrac echo sounders.

SMALL MULTITASK UTILITY CRAFT [WYFL]

Note: Two 10-m Zodiac aluminum-hulled RIBs were ordered from Zodiac Hurricane Technologies, Delta, B.C., on 1-2-02 for conservation and game protection duties at Prince Rupert and Queen Charlotte islands. A 10-m RIB was ordered from Canadian Custom RIB on 11-2-02 for delivery 3-03 to be based at Victoria, B.C., for search-and-rescue duties.

♦ 4 U.S. Coast Guard 41-ft. Utility Boat class [WYFL]
Bldrs: Matsumoto, Vancouver, B.C. (Sterne: Shore Boatbuilders, Richmond, B.C.)

	In serv.		In serv.
Mallard	28-2-86	Skua	14-3-86
Osprey	3-5-86	Sterne	1987

Osprey Rob Cabo, 8-04

D: 12.8 tons (15 fl) **S:** 26 kts **Dim:** 12.40 × 4.11 × 1.24
Electronics: Radar: Raytheon Rasterscan R-81 nav.
M: 2 Mitsubishi S6B MPTD diesels; 2 props; 640 bhp
Range: 312/26 **Crew:** 3 non-officers

Remarks: First three are assigned to the Pacific Region: *Mallard* at Powell River, B.C.; *Osprey* at Kitsilano, B.C., *Skua* at Ganges, B.C.; *Sterne* is assigned to the Laurentian Region and is based at Québec City. Some 207 sisters were built in the U.S.A. for the U.S. Coast Guard.

♦ 5 miscellaneous utility launches [WYFL]

	In serv.	grt	Based at
CG 119 (ex-*Grebe*)	1973	20	Prescott, Ont.
Bittern	1982	21	Amherstburg, Ont.
Manyberries	1969	. . .	Canoe Cove, B.C.
Sora	1982	21	Amherstburg, Ont.
Waubino	1972	. . .	Gimli, Man.

Remarks: All are assigned to the Central and Arctic Region, except *Manyberries*, to the Pacific Region. *Sora* and *Bittern* are sisters, 12.5 × 4.3 × 1.24 m, powered by two Cummins M903VT diesels producing 1,036 bhp for 26 kts. GC 119 is an unsinkable lifeboat, resembling a smaller version of the U.S. Coast Guard 44-ft. class and able to reach 18 kts on one 420-bhp diesel.

AIR-CUSHION VEHICLES [WYFLA]

♦ 1 AP.1-88/100S-class air-cushion vehicles [WYFLA]
Bldr: Hoverwork Ltd., Ryde, Isle of Wight, UK (rebuilt 2003/2004)

Penac (ex-*Liv Viking*)

D: 45,400 tons (fl) **S:** 45 kts **Dim:** 25.40 × 11.00 × . . .
Electronics: Radar: 1 . . . nav.
M: 2 MTU type 12V183 TB 32 diesels; 2 4-bladed; 820 bhp for propulsion; two Deutz BF12L 513FC diesels; 525 bhp for lift
Range: . . . / . . . **Fuel:** 5,682.5 liters **Crew:** 7 tot.

Remarks: Originally built in the 1980s by an unknown builder, *Penac* served previously as a commercial ferry between Denmark and Sweden, though she has been of commercial service since 1990. Purchased in late 2003 for search and rescue, fisheries enforcement, environmental, and aid to navigation duties. Entirely rebuilt in 2004 at Hoverwork to meet Canadian Coast Guard specifications. Placed in service with the Coast Guard on 4-8-04. Operates out Sea Island, British Columbia.

♦ 2 AP.1-88/400 class air-cushion vehicles [WYFLA]
Bldr: GKN Westland/Hike Metal Products, Wheatley, Ont.

Sipu Muin (In serv. 4-98) Siyay (In serv. 9-98)

D: 70 tons (fl) **S:** 48 kts (calm water; 45 loaded) **Dim:** 28.50 × 11.00 × . . .
Electronics: Radar: 1 Sperry 1040 nav.

COAST GUARD AIR-CUSHION VEHICLES [WYFLA] *(continued)*

Siyay Canadian Coast Guard

M: 4 Caterpillar 3412TTA diesels (990 bhp each; 2 for lift, 2 for propulsion); 2 Hoffman 4-bladed ducted airscrews; 1,960 bhp
Range: 540/45 **Fuel:** 11,000 liters **Crew:** 3 officers, 3 non-officers

Remarks: Ordered 5-96. GKN Westland is prime contractor, with structural work by Hike Metal Products. *Sipu Muin* ("Sea Bear") is assigned to the Laurentian Region and based at Trois-Rivières, Que.; *Siyay* is assigned to the Pacific Region and is based at Richmond, B.C.
Hull systems: Longer version of AP.1-88/200 design with 20-ton payload on a 13.1 × 4.6-m open deck for use in servicing and recovery of navigation buoys, search and rescue, light icebreaking, and oil-spill recovery operations. Have a 3.8-m wide bow ramp and can transport over 20 tons of cargo; a 0.5-ton capacity Palfinger crane is fitted. Lift engines are operated at 900 bhp each, propulsion engines at 1,020 bhp. A small hospital is to be fitted into the cabin on *Siyay,* and the deck can support a firefighting truck.

♦ 1 AP.1-99-class rigid sidewall air-cushion vehicle [WYFLA]
Bldr: Westland/British Hovercraft, Cowes, U.K. (In serv. 15-7-87)

WABAN-AKI

Waban-Aki H&L Van Ginderen, 5-93

D: 47.6 tons light **S:** 50 kts (35 cruise) **Dim:** 24.5 × 11.2 × . . .
Electronics: Radar: 1 Decca RM 914C nav.
M: 4 Deutz BF 12L 513CP diesels; 2 Hoffman airscrews; 6 lift fans; 2,400 bhp
Range: 600/35 **Crew:** 3 officers, 1 non-officer

Remarks: Ordered 26-2-86; laid down 23-7-86; launched 1-5-87. Name means "People of the Dawn," a reference to the Indians living in the region of Quebec. Assigned to the Laurentian Region and based at Trois-Rivières, Que. Cargo capacity: 12 tons.

Disposal note: SRN-6-class hovercraft CG 045 was retired during 2002 and has been offered as a museum exhibit.

COLLEGE TRAINING VESSELS [WYXT]

♦ 3 U.S. Coast Guard 44-foot lifeboat–class training craft [WYXT]
Bldrs: *Cap Goélands:* Hike Metal, Wheatley, Ont. (In serv. 1985); others: Eastern Equipment, Ltd., Montreal, Que. (In serv. 1975)

CAP GOÉLANDS CG 117 GC 118

Remarks: Data essentially as for the lifeboat-assigned units of the class. CG 117 and CG 118 are assigned to the Coast Guard College at Sydney, N.S., while *Cap Goélands* is assigned to the Laurentian Region and is based at Rivière-au-Renard, Que.

ROYAL CANADIAN MOUNTED POLICE

The RCMP's Transport Management Branch, Services and Supply Directorate, operates five craft over 17 m in length. The RCMP's Inland Water Transport Force has 377 boats smaller than 9.2 m long, ranging from car-top boats and canoes to rigid inflatables and larger inboard- and outboard-powered launches. The five large craft are:

Inkster (In serv. 27-6-96): 19.75 aluminum catamaran based at Prince Rupert, B.C. Has two M.A.N. D2840 LE401 V-10 diesels totaling 1,640 bhp for a speed of about 35 kts; a crew of four is carried.

Nadon, Higgitt, Lindsay, and *Simmonds:* 17.7-m catamarans with the same plan as *Inkster* and capable of 36 kts; *Simmonds* is based on the south coast of Newfoundland and the rest on the Pacific coast.

CAPE VERDE

Republic of Cape Verde

COAST GUARD

Personnel (2001): Approx. 100 total

Bases: Headquarters at Praia; repair facilities at Porto Grande on Isla de São Vicente.

Maritime Aviation: One EMB 110P1 Bandeirante and one Dornier Do-228-212 maritime surveillance aircraft (the latter was acquired in 2000).

PATROL CRAFT [WPC]

♦ 1 ex-German Kondor-I-class (Project 89.1)
Bldr: VEB Peenewerft, Wolgast

	Laid down	L	In serv.
P 521 VIGILANTE (ex-*Kühlungsborn,* BG 32, ex-GS-07, ex-G 445)	9-9-69	14-1-70	3-6-70

D: 327 tons (339 fl) **S:** 20 kts **Dim:** 52.00 × 7.12 × 2.40
A: None (as transferred)
Electronics: Radar: 1 Decca 360 nav.; 1 . . . surf.-search
M: 2 Type 40DM diesels; 2 CP Kort-nozzle props; 4,400 bhp (4,000 sust.)
Range: 1,900/15; 2,200/11 **Crew:** 12 tot.

Remarks: Former East German "High Seas Minesweeper" taken over by Germany in 1991 and assigned to the German Border Guard (*Bundesgrenzschutz-See*). Donated to the Cape Verde Islands after a 5-98 to 9-98 conversion to serve as a fisheries protection patrol craft at A&R Neptun Boat Service GmbH, Rostock; handed over on 25-9-98. A helicopter platform atop a deckhouse replaced the original mine-countermeasures winch and cable drum area aft; new communications gear radars were fitted. Two sisters have been transferred to Malta and five to Tunisia.

PATROL BOATS [WPB]

♦ 1 U.S. 51-Foot Mk 4 class
Bldr: Peterson Bldrs., Sturgeon Bay, Wisconsin (In serv. 19-8-93)

P 151 ESPADARTE

Espadarte (P 151)—on builder's trials Peterson Builders, 4-93

D: 24 tons (fl) **S:** 24 kts **Dim:** 15.54 × 4.47 × 1.30
A: 1 twin 12.7-mm M2 mg; 2 single 7.62-mm mg
Electronics: Radar: 1 Furuno . . . nav.
M: 2 G.M. Detroit Diesel 6V92 TA diesels; 2 props; 900 bhp (520 bhp sust.)
Electric: 15 kw tot. **Range:** 500/20 kts **Fuel:** 800 U.S. gallons **Crew:** 6 tot.

Remarks: Aluminum construction. Ordered 25-9-92, launched 8-4-93 and delivered in Cape Verde 11-93. Carries a 4.27-m rigid inflatable inspection craft (with 50 bhp outboard motor) on the stern. Sisters operate in the Senegalese Navy.

♦ 1 Soviet Zhuk class (Project 1400M)

D: 35.9 tons (39.7 fl) **S:** 30 kts
Dim: 23.80 (21.70 wl) × 5.00 (3.80 wl) × 1.00 (hull)
A: 2 twin 12.7-mm Utës-M mg **Electronics:** Radar: 1 Lotsiya nav.
M: 2 M-401B diesels; 2 props; 2,200 bhp
Electric: 48 kw total (2 × 21 kw, 1 × 6 kw diesel sets)
Range: 500/13.5 **Endurance:** 5 days **Crew:** 3 officers, 8 enlisted

Remarks: Survivor of three transferred in 1980; the other pair are providing spares.

CAYMAN ISLANDS

ROYAL CAYMAN ISLANDS POLICE

PATROL BOATS [WPB]

♦ **1 48-ft. Dauntless class**
Bldr: SeaArk, Monticello, Arkansas (In serv. 7-94)

CAYMAN PROTECTOR

D: 14 tons (fl) **S:** 26 kts **Dim:** 14.63 × 4.88 × 1.37 (props)
A: Small arms **Electronics:** Radar: 1 Raytheon R40X nav.
M: 2 Caterpillar 3208TA diesels; 2 props; 850 bhp (720 sust.)
Range: 400/22 **Fuel:** 250 gallons **Crew:** 5 tot.

Remarks: Aluminum construction. C. Raymond Hunt, "Deep-Vee" hull design.

Note: Also in use is a small outboard-powered launch. The Customs Service also has one or more launches.

Cayman Protector SeaArk, 1994

CHILE

Republic of Chile

ARMADA DE CHILE

Personnel: 19,398 total, including 3,500 marines, 1,600 coast guard, and 600 naval aviation.

Bases: Fleet Headquarters and Headquarters 1st Naval Zone at Valparaiso, which also has repair yard, naval air base, and principal training facilities; Headquarters 2nd Naval Zone at Talcahuano, which also has major repair facilities and the submarine base; Headquarters 3rd Naval Zone at Punta Arenas, which has repair facilities and an air base; and Headquarters 4th Naval Zone at Iquique. Smaller facilities are located at Puerto Montt and at Puerto Williams, which has an air station.

Naval Aviation: Officially known as *Aviacion Naval Chilena* (Chilean Naval Aviation Service). Fixed-wing aircraft include 2 P-3A Orion maritime surveillance aircraft, 6 UP-3 Orion transports, 3 Embraer 110C Bandeirante communications/VIP planes, 6 Embraer 111N, and maritime surveillance aircraft; 2 UP-3A and 4 Casa 212A Aviocar transports; 10 Pilatus PC-7 Turbo-Trainer light attack/trainers; and 10 Cessna O-2A Skymaster trainers. Helicopters include 7 Aerospatiale AS.332SC Cougar, 1 Aérospatiale AS.332B Super Puma, 8 Bell 47G/J utility helicopters, 7 MBB BO-105c light, 10 SA.319B Alouette III, and 6 Bell 206B JetRanger (designated SH-57 in Chilean service). All AS.532C Cougar and AS-332 Super Puma helicopters are collectively referred to as Cougars and are designated SH-32. The AS.332SCs are equipped with Thales HS-312 dipping sonars and AM-39 Exocet missiles.

Chilean UP-3B Orion Julio Montes, 2005

Chilean Navy AS.532SC Cougar helicopter Julio Montes, 4-02

Chilean Navy Bell 412 Julio Montes, 4-02

Chilean Navy BO-105 helicopter Julio Montes, 4-00

The Aviation Service is divided into two Naval Air Forces. They are organized as follows:

Naval Air Force One—based at Torquemada NAS/Vina del Mer
VP-1: Maritime reconnaissance: UP-3B Orion, P-111 Bandeirante, EMB C-95
VC-1: Transport and general purpose: CASA 212, EMB 111AN Bandeirante, and 8 O-2A Skymaster
HU-1: Utility helicopter: MBB BO.105C, Bell 206B
VT-1: Training: PC-7 (also light attack)

Naval Air Force Two—based at Ibanez AB/Chabunco/Punta Areanas
HA-1: Shipboard Attack: AS.532SC Cougar/AS.332 Super Puma (SH-32)
VP-1 (Detachment): Maritime reconnaissance: Embraer 110
VC-1 (Detachment): Transport and general purpose: Embraer 110, Bell 412—based at Los Condores AB/Iquique

Naval Infantry: 1st Marine Infantry Detachment *Patricio Lynch* at Iquique; 2nd Marine Infantry Detachment *Miller* at Viña del Mar; 3rd Marine Infantry Detachment *Sargento Aldea* at Talcahuano; and 4th Marine Infantry Detachment *Cochrane* at Punta Arenas. There are also the 51st Commando Group, at Valparaiso, a logistics battalion, and several engineering units. Artillery in use includes 18 155-mm Puteaux cannon made during World War I and a number of Korean-made 105-mm howitzers. Chile is seeking 30 LVTP-7 amphibious armored personnel carriers from the U.S.

Weapons and Systems: Most equipment is of Israeli, U.S., German, or British origin, but Chile has a growing military electronics industry and produces its own naval combat information systems. ASW torpedoes ordered from France in 1989 have not yet been delivered, due to lengthy delays in the MU-90 torpedo program. The Whitehead-Alenia Sistem Subacquei (WASS) Black Shark 533-mm torpedo was selected during 5-00 for use in new submarines.

ATTACK SUBMARINES [SS]

♦ **2 Scorpène class**
Bldr: DCN, Cherbourg, France, and Navantir, Cartagena , Spain

	Final assembly	Laid down	L	In serv.
22 O'HIGGINS	DCN, Cherbourg	18-11-99	1-11-03	9-9-05 (del.)
23 CARRERA	Navantir, Cartagena	11-00	2004	2006

ATTACK SUBMARINES [SS] *(continued)*

O' Higgins (22) Bernard Prézelin, 9-04

O'Higgins (22)—pierside at DCN Cherbourg DCN, 11-03

D: 1,650 tons surf./1,908 tons sub **S:** 12 kts surf./20+ kts sub.
Dim: 66.40 × 6.20 (8.00 over stern planes) × 5.8 (surf.)
A: 6 bow 533-mm TT (18 DCN-WASS Black Shark and STN Atlas Elektronik SUT 266 wire-guided torpedoes)
Electronics:
Radar: 1 Kelvin-Hughes Type 1007 nav./surf. search
Sonar: Thales SUBTICS suite, with TSM 2253 passive flank arrays
EW: Condor Systems AR-900 intercept
M: Diesel electric: 4 MTU 16V396 SE84 diesels (840 bhp each), Jeumont Schneider Magtronic axial-flux permanent magnet electric motor; 1 prop; 4,694 shp
Range: 6,500/8 (surf.); 550/4 (sub.) **Endurance:** 50 days
Crew: 6 officers, 25 enlisted

Remarks: Ordered 17-12-97 for $420 million total. DCN is performing about 60% of the construction work, including manufacturing the pressure hulls and outfitting the bow and amidships sections; Navantir is fitting out the stern sections, and each company will do final outfitting on one unit. Stern sections for *O'Higgins* left Cherbourg for Spain on 3-7-00 for outfitting, and the completed stern was returned to Cherbourg late in 2002. As built, these submarines do not employ an Air Independent Propulsion system.
Hull systems: Employ HLES 80 steel in the pressure hull, permitting operating depths to 300-m.. No air-independent propulsion system was ordered. Two sets of Hagen batteries totaling 360 cells are fitted. All machinery is "rafted" for sound isolation. Only nine personnel will be on watch under normal conditions. The lower rudder is shorter to allow for "bottoming." The casing and sail are fabricated from GRP.
Combat systems: The UDS International SUBTICS (Submarine Tactical Information and Command System) weapons-control system is similar to French Navy's SET (*Système d'Exploitation Tactique*) and will have six two-screen display consoles and a separate tactical display table. The Chilean SP100C datalink is fitted. The Thales Underwater Systems sonar suite includes an 800-Hz-range cylindrical bow transducer array, an active array, a 20-kHz-max. passive ranging array, 2.5–100 kHz acoustic intercept system, and passive flank arrays; no towed array is planned. A SAGEM SMS optronic search periscope and a SAGEM APS attack periscope will be fitted. A Litef integrated navigation system will be employed. Two of the torpedo tubes have pneumatic ram launching to allow for the launch of SM 39 antiship missiles (which have not been ordered); the other four tubes are of the swim-out variety.

♦ 2 IKL Type 209/1400
Bldr: Howaldtswerke, Kiel, Germany

	Laid down	L	In serv.
20 Thomson	1-11-80	28-2-82	31-8-84
21 Simpson	15-2-81	29-7-83	18-9-84

Thomson (20) H&L Van Ginderen, 2-00

D: 1,158 tons light; 1,285 tons surf./1,395 tons sub.
S: 11 kts surf./12 kts snorkel/ 21.5 kts sub.
Dim: 59.5 × 6.20 (7.60 over stern planes) × 5.50 (surf.)
A: 8 bow 533-mm TT (16 SUT Mod. 1 wire-guided torpedoes)
Electronics:
Radar: 1 Thales Calypso-II nav./surf. search
Sonar: STN-Atlas Elektronik CSU-3 suite
EW: Thales DR-2000U intercept
M: 4 MTU 12V493 AZ-80 diesels; 4 450-kw AEG generators; 1 Siemens electric motor; 1 7-bladed prop; 4,600 shp
Range: 400/4, 16/21.5 (sub.); 10,000/8 (snorkel) **Fuel:** 116 tons
Endurance: 50 days **Crew:** 5 officers, 26 enlisted

Remarks: Ordered 12-80. Used components from a canceled Iranian order. 21, damaged in collision 29-3-84 on trials, was completed 18-9-84. 20 was completed 7-5-84. On 21-6-04 plans were announced to upgrade the tactical and combat systems based on the SUBTICS command and control combat fire-control system. The first SUBTICS system will be installed during the spring of 2007 and the second in April 2008.
Hull systems: Have higher casing than earlier IKL-designed submarines. Sail and masting 0.5 m higher than on other ships of this class, to cope with heavy seas in Chilean operating areas.
Combat systems: The later sonar suite from the retired *Oberons* may be transferred to this pair. Have Carl Zeiss SERO 40 Stab (stabilized) optical periscope system, with AS 40 attack and BS 40 search scopes.

Note: The last Chilean Oberon-class submarine *O'Brien* was decommissioned 30-3-03.

DESTROYERS [DD]

♦ 1 ex-U.K. County class
Bldr: 11: Swan Hunter, Wallsend-on-Tyne; 12: Fairfield SB & Eng., Govan

	Laid down	L	In serv.
12 Almirante Cochrane (ex-*Antrim*)	20-1-66	19-10-67	14-7-70

D: 5,510 tons (6,270 fl) **S:** 30.5 kts (28 sust.)
Dim: 158.55 (153.9 pp) × 16.46 × 6.3
A: 4 MM 38 Exocet SSM; 2 8-cell Barak VLS SAM launch groups; 1 twin 114-mm 45-cal. Mk 6 DP; 2 single 20-mm 70-cal. Mk 4 Oerlikon AA; 2 triple 324-mm Mk 32 ASW TT (U.S. Mk 46 Mod. 5 torpedoes); 2 (11: 1) AS.332B Cougar helicopters (with SM-39 Exocet missiles)
Electronics:
Radar: 1 . . . nav.; 1 Type 965M early warning; 1 Marconi Type 992Q air search; 2 Elta EL/M-2228S AMDR Barak target desig.; 1 Plessey Type 903 gun f.c.
Sonar: Type 184 MF hull-mounted (7–9 kHz), Type 162 bottomed-target classification (15 kHz)
EW: UA-8/9 intercept; Type 667 jammers; FH-5 HFD/F; 4 18-round Wallop Barricade decoy RL
M: COSAG: 2 sets A.E.I. geared steam turbines (15,000 shp each) and 4 English Electric G6 gas turbines (7,500 shp each); 2 props; 60,000 shp
Boilers: 2 Babcock & Wilcox; 49.2 kg/cm^2, 510° C
Electric: 4,750 kw tot. (2 × 750-kw diesel sets, 2 turboalternators)
Range: 3,500/28 **Fuel:** 600 tons **Crew:** 36 officers, 434 enlisted

Almirante Cochrane (12) Maritime Photographic, 7-01

Remarks: *Cochrane* was purchased from the U.K. 22-6-84 and recommissioned 22-6-84. Has been converted to carry combat helicopters; Sea Slug missile facilities were deleted and replaced with a larger helicopter hangar and flight deck to handle two helicopters each at ASMAR, Talcahuano. Scheduled retire by 2007 when new Dutch warships arrived, at which time a new *Almirante Cochrane* (ex-HMS *Norfolk,* F 230) will be entering service.
Hull systems: Four pairs of fin stabilizers. Twin rudders. Each propeller is driven by one steam turbine for cruise, adding one or two gas turbines for boost. There are three steam turboalternators and three gas-turbine generators.
Aviations systems: During 1992–93 conversion the original hangar (which opened to port) was replaced by a twin hangar capable of holding two Cougar helicopters; the helicopter decks have been increased to 617 m^2 from the original 325 m^2; two 55-meter Indal Assist deck-traversing systems have been installed; and the new flight deck extends to the stern. In 11, there is only a single-place new hangar, and the flight deck does not extend to the stern. The Cougar helicopters are equipped with Thomson-Sintra HS-312 dipping sonar and can launch either U.S. Mk 46 Mod. 2 torpedoes or AM 39 Exocet missiles.
Combat systems: The original ADAWS-1 combat data system has been replaced by the Chilean-developed SISDEF SP-100 system; employing Ada computer "language," it has several fully autonomous multifunction tactical consoles linked by a local area network, can track radar 512 targets and 100 ESM bearings simultaneously, and was first installed in *Blanco Encalada* in 1993. SP-100 employs three vertical display consoles and two horizontal plot displays. Normally only two Exocet missiles are carried. Israeli Barak SAM system was installed in *Cochrane* during a refit completed in 5-94. The Israeli Elta AMDR (Automatic Missile Detection Radar) antenna is located on the foremast, and the system is said to have a 90% chance of detecting a 0.1-m^3 target at Mach 3 at up to 15 km range; the Barak radar directors are mounted atop the pilothouse and abaft the after stack.

DESTROYERS [DD] *(continued)*

Disposals: *Capitan Prat* (11, ex-HMS *Norfolk*) was stricken 12-05 and *Almirante Blanco Encalada* (15, ex-HMS *Fife*) was decommissioned on 12-12-03 for disposal. The unconverted *Almirante Latorre* (14, ex-HMS *Glamorgan*) was placed in reserve on 30-12-98 and serves as a spares source. *Almirante Williams*–class destroyer *Almirante Riveros* (D 18) was stricken on 1-01-95 and is employed as floating barracks hulks. Sister ship *Almirante Williams* (D-19) was stricken on 24-04-96 for disposal.

GUIDED MISSILE FRIGATES [FFG]

♦ 2 ex-Dutch Jacob Van Heemskerck class
Bldr: Schelde Shipbuilding, Vlissingen

	Laid down	L	In serv.
11 Almirante Latorre (ex-*Jacob Van Heemskerck,* F 812, ex-*Pieter Florisz*)	21-1-81	5-11-83	15-1-86
14 Comandante Prat (ex-*Witte De With,* F 813)	15-12-81	25-8-84	17-9-86

D: 3,000 tons (3,750 fl) **S:** 30 kts (20 kts on cruise engines)
Dim: 130.20 (121.8 pp) × 14.40 × 4.23 (6.0 props)
A: 8 RGM-84C Harpoon SSM; 1 single-rail Mk 13 Mod. 4 missile launcher (40 Standard SM-1 MR missiles); 1 8-round Mk 29 missile launcher (24 RIM-7M Sea Sparrow missiles); goalkeeper CIWS; 2 single 20-mm/70-cal. Oerlikon Mk 10 AA; 4 fixed, paired 324-mm Mk 32, Mod. 9 ASW TT (Mk 46 Mod. 5 torpedoes); 1 Cougar (SH-32) helicopter
Electronics:
Radar: 1 Thales Scout nav./surf. search; 1 Thales ZW-06 surf. search; 1 Thales SMART-S air search; 1 Thales LW-08 early warning; 1 Thales STIR-18 gun f.c.; 2 Thales STIR-24 missle f.c.; 1 Thales 1 Goalkeeper f.c. array
Sonar: PHS-36 (SQS-509) hull-mounted MF
EW: Thales Sphinx intercept; Thales Ramses active (with SRR03/100 jammer); Mk 36 SRBOC decoy syst. (2 6-round Raytheon Mk 137 RL); SLQ-25 Nixie acoustic torpedo decoy syst.
M: COGOG: 2 Rolls-Royce Olympus TM-3B gas turbines (25,800 shp each); 2 Rolls-Royce Tyne RM-1C cruise gas turbines (4,900 shp each); 2 Lips CP props; 51,600 shp max.
Electric: 3,000 kw tot. **Range:** 4,700/16 (on 1 Tyne turbine)
Crew: 23 officers, 174 enlisted plus 20 flag staff

Comandante Prat (14)—still with old hull number, shown here after decommissioning from the Netherlands and preparing for transfer to Chile Rob Cabo, 7-05

Remarks: Have the basic Dutch *Kortenaer* design with modifications to replace the helicopter facility with the U.S. Standard missile system. These vessels have been equipped to act as flagships. Originally scheduled for retirement from the Dutch Navy in 2010 and 2012, budget cuts enacted by the Dutch government during 2002 forced their early deactivation. Chile announced their purchase of these vessels (along with two *Karel Doorman*–class frigates) on 2-2-04. Newly renamed *Almirante Latorre* transferred to Chilean service during 12-05, to be followed in 2007 by *Capitan Prat.*

Combat systems: Have the SEWACO II data system and LINK 11 data-link capability. While still in Dutch service both were backfitted with the Thalespulse-Doppler S-band SMART-S 3-D radar in place of the DA-08 radar and Scout in place of Decca 1226 during 1995–96 refits; at the same time, the STIR-18 radar was modified to permit its use as a third fire-control channel for SM-1 missiles, U.S. OE-82 antennas were added for the WSC-3 UHF SATCOM system, a U.S. JMCIS (Joint Maritime Command Information System) terminal was added, and new software was substituted in the missile fire-control system. Two hand-served 20-mm AA have been added just abaft the bridge. The 30-mm Goalkeeper CIWS mount on each ship was removed prior to transfer.

FRIGATES [FF]

Note: Initial plans to build six MEKO A 200–class frigates (Project Tridente program) was rejected in favor of the 2004 purchase of two *Jacob Van Heemskerck*–class FFGs and two *Karel Doorman*–class FF from the Netherlands.

♦ 1 Boxer-class (Type 22 Batch 2) ASW
Bldrs: Swan Hunter (Shipbuilders) Ltd., Wallsend-on-Tyne

	Laid down	L	In serv.
19 Almirante Williams (ex-*Sheffield,* F 96)	29-3-84	26-3-86	26-7-88

D: 4,250 tons (4,850 fl) **S:** 30 kts (18 kts on cruise engines)
Dim: 148.10 (140.00 pp) × 14.75 × 4.30 hull (6.00 max.)
A: 4 MM40 Exocet SSM; 2 6-round Sea Wolf GWS.25 Mod. 3 SAM syst.; 1 76-mm 62-cal. OTO Melara Compact DP; 2 triple 324-mm STWS.2 ASW TT (III × 2); 1 or 2 AS.532SC Cougar helicopters
Electronics
Radar: 1 Kelvin-Hughes Type 1007 nav.; 1 BAe Systems Type 967M–968 surf./air search; 2 BAe Systems Type 911 missile f.c.
Sonar: BAe Systems Type 2016 (4.5–7.5 kHz)
EW: Racal UAA(2) intercept; SRD-19 LF-UHFD/F; SLR-16 countermeasures receiver; SLR-23 automated narrowband receiver; DLB decoy syst. (4 6-round Mk 137 RL); 2 DEC laser-dazzler; 4 DLF(2) floating decoy launchers; Type 182 towed torpedo decoy syst.
M: COGAG: 2 Rolls-Royce Spey SM.1A boost gas turbines (18,770 shp each) and 2 Rolls-Royce Tyne RM.1C cruise gas turbines (5,340 shp each); 2 CP props; 48,220 shp max.
Electric: 4,000 kw (4 × 1,000-kw Paxman Valenta 12PA 200CZ diesel-driven alternator sets)
Range: 7,000/18; 12,000/14 (one shaft) **Fuel:** 700 tons, + 80 tons aviation fuel
Crew: 19 officers, 246 enlisted (accomm. for 320 tot.)

Remarks: Ordered for Royal Navy on 14-12-82 and decommissioned on 14-11-02. Purchased for $15 million during 1-03, refitted in the U.K., and recommissioned into Chilean service 5-03. A $35 million modernization was to follow at ASMAR, Talcahuano, with the ship to enter service during 2005, though this was delayed into 2006.
Hull systems: Two auxiliary boilers and two 50-ton/day flash evaporators are installed. Water-displacement fuel tanks are used, and the class is said to have twice the range of the "Batch 1" *Broadsword* class. Has fin stabilization system and Agouti bubble sound-damping system. The hangar has been enlarged to accommodate Chilean Cougar helicopters.
Combat systems: The original CACS 1 combat data system was to be replaced by the Chilean SISDEF SP21K system; most radars have been retained, but may be replaced during a future update. The U.S. SSQ-108(V)2 Outboard combat direction-finding and intercept system was removed prior to transfer. The Type 275(2) jammers and the Type 2031Z towed linear passive hydrophone array have also been removed, with the winch room for the latter converted into a gymnasium. The current 76-mm gun will likely be replaced with a Vickers 114-mm Mark 8 gun prior to 2008.

♦ 1 (+ 1) ex-Dutch Karel Doorman class
Bldr: Schelde Shipbuilding, Vlissingen

	Laid down	L	In serv.
15 Almirante Blanco Encalada (ex-*Abraham Van Der Hulst,* F-832)	8-2-89	7-9-91	15-12-93
18 Almirante Riveros (ex-*Tjerk Hiddes,* F-830)	28-10-86	9-12-89	26-2-93

Admiral Blanco Encalada (15)—while still in Dutch service Brian Morrison, 11-02

D: 2,800 tons light (3,320 fl) **S:** 29 kts (21 kts on diesels)
Dim: 122.25 (114.40 pp) × 14.37 (13.10 wl) × 4.30 (6.05 sonar)
A: 4 RGM-84A/C Harpoon SSM; 16-cell Mk 48 Mod. 1 VLS (16 RIM-7M NATO Sea Sparrow SAM); 1 76-mm 62-cal. OTO Melara DP; 2 single 20-mm 70-cal. Oerlikon Mk 10 AA; 4 fixed, paired 324-mm Mk 32 Mod. 9 ASW TT (Mk 46 Mod. 5 torpedoes); 1 Cougar (SH-32) helicopter
Electronics:
Radar: 1 Decca 1690/9 nav.; 1 Thales Scout nav./surf. search; 1 Thales SMART-S 3-D air-search; 1 Thales LW-08 early-warning; 2 Thales STIR-18 missile f.c.; 1 Thales Goalkeeper f.c. array
Sonar: PHS-36 (SQS-509) hull-mounted MF
EW: ArgoSystems APECS-II intercept and AR-740 jammer; Mk 36 SRBOC decoy syst. (2 6-round Raytheon Mk 137 RL), SLQ-25 Nixie towed acoustic torpedo decoy syst.
M: CODOG: 2 Stork-Wärtsilä 12 SWD 280 V-12 cruise diesels (4,225 bhp each); 2 Rolls-Royce Spey RM-1C gas turbines; 2 CP props; 48,252 shp max.
Electric: 2,720 kw (4 × 650-kw diesel sets, Stork-Wärtsilä DRo 218K diesels driving; 1 × 120-kw diesel set)

FRIGATES [FF] *(continued)*

Range: 5,000+/18 **Endurance:** 30 days
Crew: 16 officers, 138 enlisted (163 max. accomm.)

Remarks: Originally known as the "M"-class. Ordered on 10-4-86 and 29-2-84 for the Royal Netherlands Navy. Accommodations for female crew members are incorporated, plus bunks for 30 marines. The purchase of these two ships was announced by the Chilean Defense Minister on 2-2-04. *Almirante Blanco Encalada* underwent a refit at Den Helder Naval Base in the Netherlands before transfer in 11-05. *Almirante Riveros* will undergo a similar refit before her 4-07 transfer.
Hull systems: Have a computer-controlled rudder roll-stabilization system instead of fins. Carry three RIBs. During predelivery refit, the helicopter hangar was enlarged and helicopter deck extended to accommodate Chilean Cougar (SH-32) helicopter operations.
Combat systems: Have the Thales DAISY VII/SEWACO VII(B) data system with full LINK 10, 11, and 16 capability. The 76-mm gun fires at up to 100 rpm. F 830 conducted trials with the class-standard IMCS (Integrated Monitoring and Control System) during 1992. Each is fitted with the Electrospace SHF SATCOM. The 30-mm Goalkeeper CIWS mount was removed prior to transfer.

♦ 0 (+ 3) ex-UK Duke (Type 23)-class general-purpose

Bldr: Marconi Marine-Yarrow (Shipbuilders), Ltd., Scoutstoun, Glasgow, U.K. (except *Almirante Carlos Condell:* Swan Hunter Shipbuilders, Ltd., Wallsend-on-Tyne, UK)

	Laid down	L	In serv.
. . . Almirante Cochrane (ex-HMS *Norfolk,* F 230)	14-12-85	10-7-87	1-6-90
. . . Almirante Lynch (ex-HMS *Grafton,* F 80)	13-5-93	5-11-94	29-5-97
. . . Almirante Carlos Condell (ex-HMS *Marlborough,* F 233)	22-10-87	21-1-89	14-6-91

D: 3,600 tons (4,300 fl) **S:** 28 kts (15 kts on electric drive)
Dim: 133.00 (123.00 pp) × 16.10 (15.00 wl) × 4.30 (5.50 max.)
A: 8 RGM-84C Harpoon (GWS.60) SSM; Sea Wolf GWS.26 vertical-launch SAM syst. (32 missiles); 1 114-mm 55-cal. Vickers Mk 8, Mod. 1 (except *Almirante Lynch:* Mk 8, Mod. 0); 4 fixed 324-mm Cray Marine DMTS 90 ASW TT; 1 Cougar (SH-32) helicopter
Electronics:
Radar: 1 Kelvin-Hughes Type 1007 nav.; 1 Decca Type 1008 nav.; 1 BAE Systems Type 996(2) 3-D surf./air-search; 2 BAE Systems Type 911(1) missile/gun f.c.
Sonar: Thales Type 2050NE bow-mounted (4.5-7.5 kHz); Dowty Type 2031(Z) towed linear passive array (not in last six)
EW: Racal UAF(1) Cutlass (except *Almirante Lynch:* UAT(1) intercept); DLB decoy syst. (4 6-round RL); 2 DEC laser dazzler; 2 DLF(2) Floating decoy dispensers; Type 182 or Type 2070 (SLQ-25A) towed torpedo decoy syst.
E/O: 1 GSA.8/GPEOD Sea Archer gun f.c. and surveillance
M: CODLAG (COmbined Diesel-eLectric and Gas turbine): 2 Rolls-Royce SM1A Spey gas turbines (18,770 shp each, 17,000 sust.) (except *Almirante Lynch:* 2 Rolls Royce SM1C Spey (26,150 shp each); all: 4 Paxman Valenta 12 RPA 200CZ diesel generator sets (5,200 kW tot.); 2 2,000-shp electric cruise motors; 2 props; 41,540 shp max. (except *Almirante Carlos Condell:* 52,300 shp max.)
Range: 7,800/17 **Fuel:** 800 tons **Electric:** 1,890 kw tot.
Crew: 17 officers, 168 enlisted

Remarks: Originally built for the British Royal Navy to serve as replacements for the *Leander*-class frigates. Were expected to serve only 18 years, without midlife modernization. Purchased from the Royal Navy 9-05 at a cost of US $350 million to include missiles, refitting, overhaul and training. Payable over 10 years *Almirante Cochrane* expected to transfer 9-06, *Almirante Lynch* in 4-07 and *Almirante Carlos Condell* in 1-08.
Hull systems: Flush-decked hull, with large helicopter hangar, helo haul-in system, and one set of fin stabilizers. The design grew considerably as a result of Falklands War "lessons learned." The propulsion system permits running the shaft-concentric electric propulsion motors with the power from any combination of the four 1,300-kw ship's service generators; power from both the gas turbines and the electric motors can be obtained; ship's service power is derived from two 945-kw converter sets, and there is also a 250-kw emergency alternator powered by a Perkins CV 250GTCA diesel. Have fixed-pitch props, with astern power available only by electric drive. The more powerful engines in *Almirante Carlos Condell* provide 1-2 knots additional speed. Superstructure external bulkheads are sloped about 7-deg. to reduce radar signature, and radar-absorbent coatings were applied while in British service.
Combat systems: All are equipped with two SCOT 1C antennas for the Skynet SATCOM system and also carry a commercial SATCOM terminal (with antenna mounted on the forward edge of the stack). There have been problems with the accuracy of the Type 996(2) radar, which also produces excess numbers of false tracks, and there have been software problems with the vertical-launch missile system.
While still in Royal Navy service the 114-mm guns (on all except *Almirante Lynch*) were updated by VSEL to Mod. 1 status, saving about 6 tons in weight and considerable volume below-decks. The GSA.8/GPEOD Sea Archer optronic/IR director is mounted on the mast for the 114-mm gun.
Almirante Carlos Condell is capable of operating the new Merlin HM.1. Her other modernizations include a PRISM deck-handling system, new glide-path indicator and gyro-stabilized horizon indicator, improved deck lighting, modular servicing systems in the hangar and a Ship Helicopter Operating Limits Instrumentation System (SHOLIS) on the bridge.

♦ 2 British Leander class

Bldr: Yarrow & Co., Scotstoun, Glasgow, Scotland

	Laid down	L	In serv.
06 Almirante Condell	5-6-71	12-6-72	21-12-73
07 Almirante Lynch	6-12-72	6-12-73	25-5-74

D: 2,500 tons (3,190 fl) **S:** 29 kts
Dim: 113.38 (109.73 pp) × 13.12 × 4.50 (5.49 props)

Almirante Lynch (07) U.S. Navy, 6-04

Almirante Condell (06) Alexandre Sheldon-Duplaix, 12-02

A: 4 MM 40 Exocet SSM; 1 twin 114-mm/45-cal. Mk VI DP; 1 20-mm Mk 15 Phalanx CIWS (FF 07 only); 2 twin 20-mm/70-cal. Mk 24 Oerlikon AA; 2 triple 324-mm ASW TT; 1 AS.332B Super Puma ASW helicopter
Electronics:
Radar: 1 Kelvin-Hughes Type 1006 nav.; 1 Marconi Type 966 early warning; 1 Marconi Type 992Q air/surf. search; 1 Plessey Type 903 gun f.c.; 1 Plessey Type 904 Sea Cat f.c.
Sonar: Type 177 (PF 08: Type 184M) hull-mounted MF; Type 170B HF attack; Type 162 bottomed-target classification
EW: Elta NS-9003A intercept; Elta NS-9005 jammer; 4 twin-rail Wallop Barricade decoy RL
M: 2 sets White-English Electric geared steam turbines; 2 props; 30,000 shp
Boilers: 2 Babcock & Wilcox; 38.7 kg/cm^2, 450° C
Electric: 2,500 kw tot. **Range:** 4,500/12 **Fuel:** 500 tons
Crew: 22 officers, 11 chief petty officers, 214 other enlisted

Remarks: 06 and 07 were ordered 14-1-70. 07 completed a modernization refit in the spring of 2002 during which she received improved armament, a new air-conditioning plant and habitability upgrades. Planned modifications to 06 were canceled on 7-9-05 due to the purchase of three U.K. Duke (Type 23) -class frigates as replacements for this class. *Almirante Lynch* (07) is expected to be decommissioned by 4-07 and *Almirante Condell* (06) will likely be retired by 1-08.

Combat systems: The combat data system has been replaced by the Chilean-developed SISDEF Imagen SP-100(06) system with several fully autonomous multifunction tactical consoles linked by a local area network. A British MRS 3 gun fire-control system is fitted for the 114-mm mount in 06; it has been replaced by the Chilean Maitèn system in 07. 06 and 07 originally had MM 38 Exocet missiles at the stern in lieu of the Limbo ASW mortar fitted in British ships; the missiles were exchanged for the later MM 40 and were relocated flanking the hangar in refits at the end of the 1980s, at which time the EW suites were updated with Israeli-supplied equipment. In addition, the hangars were raised and the helo pad lengthened, permitting them to operate AS.332B Super Puma helicopters. Plans to fit the Israeli Barak SAM system on 06 and 07 have been canceled.
During her 2000–2002 modernization, 07 had the Seacat SAM system replaced by a single Phalanx CIWS. The Seacat system aboard 06 is no longer operational. Plans to add two Sadral twin launchers for Mistral SAMs or the MBDA vertical-launch Mica SAM have been canceled. Are both expected to retire by 2008.
Disposals: *General Baquedano* (09, ex-HMS *Ariadne*), purchased and transferred 4-6-92, was not modernized and was placed in reserve on 30-12-98 for use as a spares source. *Ministro Zenteno* (PFG 08, ex-HMS *Achilles*) of this class was retired by 2006.

GUIDED-MISSILE PATROL CRAFT [PTG]

♦ 3 Israeli Reshev (Sa'ar IV) class

Bldr: Israeli SY, Haifa

	L	In serv.	Transferred
LM 30 Casma (ex-*Romach*)	1-74	3-74	8-11-79
LM 31 Chipana (ex-*Keshet*)	23-8-73	10-73	30-12-80
LM 34 Angamos (ex-*Reshev*)	19-2-73	4-73	1-6-97

D: 415 tons (450 fl) **S:** 32 kts **Dim:** 58.10 × 7.60 × 2.40
A: 4 Gabriel-II SSM; 2 single 76-mm/62-cal. OTO Melara DP; 2 single 20-mm/70-cal. Oerlikon AA (except LM-31: 4 20-mm); 2 12.7-mm M2 mg (LM 34 only)

GUIDED-MISSILE PATROL CRAFT [PTG] *(continued)*

Casma (LM 30) Chilean Navy, 1997

Electronics:
Radar: 1 Thales THD 1040 Neptune search; 1 Elta M-2221 (Orion RTN-10X) f.c.
EW: Elta MN-53 intercept; Elta Rattler jammer; Elta EA-2118 comms intercept; 4 ACDS decoy RL; 72 LCRL decoy RL
M: 4 MTU 16V396 series diesels; 4 props; 12,000 bhp (11,880 sust.)
Electric: 352 kw tot. (4 × 88 kw) **Range:** 1,500/30; 3,000/20; 5,000/15
Endurance: 10 days **Crew:** 8 officers, 44 enlisted

Remarks: LM 30 and LM 31 were acquired 8-11-79 and 30-12-79, respectively. The planned transfer of four additional units was canceled in 1984, but LM 33 and LM 34 were purchased on 1-6-97, commissioned on 29-7-97, and arrived in Chile at Iquique on 29-7-97; LM 30 was re-engined during 2000 at Talcahuano with MTU 16V396-series diesels, producing a total of 13,000 bhp and a 31-kt maximum speed; work on *Chipana* was completed in 2003.

Disposal note: *Papudo* (LM 33) was stricken for cannibalization in 1998. Former Israeli Sa'ar III-class guided missile patrol craft *Iquique* (LM 32; ex-*Hanit*) and *Covadonga* (LM 33; ex-*Hetz*) were retired on 1-2-00.

♦ 4 ex-German Type 148
Bldrs: CMN, Cherbourg (LM 37, 38: Friedrich Lürssen Werft, Vegesack)

	Laid down	L	In serv.
LM 36 Guardiamarina Riquelme (ex-*Wolf,* P 6149)	23-1-73	11-1-74	26-2-74
LM 37 Teniente Orella (ex-*Elster,* P 6154)	29-6-73	8-7-74	14-11-74
LM 38 Teniente Uribe (ex-*Kranich,* P 6160)	9-5-74	26-5-75	6-8-75
LM 39 Teniente Serrano (ex-*Tiger,* P 6141)	11-10-71	27-9-72	30-10-72

D: 234 tons (264 fl) **S:** 35.8 kts **Dim:** 47.0 (45.9 pp) × 7.1 × 2.66 (fl)
A: 4 MM 38 Exocet SSM; 1 76-mm 62-cal. OTOBreda DP; 1 40-mm 70-cal OTOBreda-Bofors AA; 8 mines in place of the 40-mm AA
Electronics:
Radar: 1 SMA 3RM 20 navigation; 1 Thales Triton-G air/surf. search; 1 Thales Castor-II f.c.
M: 4 MTU type 16V396 series 16-cyl. diesels; 4 props; 13,000 tot. bhp
Electric: 270 kw tot. **Range:** 570/30; 1,600/15 **Fuel:** 39 tons
Crew: 4 officers, 17 petty officers, 9 ratings

Almirante Uribe (LM 38) Maritime Photographic, 7-01

Remarks: LM 36 and LM 37 were transferred on decommissioning from German Navy on 27-8-97 to form a squadron to cover the 4th Naval Zone south of the Peruvian border. They arrived at Talcahuano 11-10-97. The other two were transferred 10-98 along with sisters *Luchs* (P 6143) and *Pelikan* (P 6153), which were to be used for cannibalization spares; the four departed Germany 22-9-98 aboard the dockship *Clipper Cheyenne,* but LM 38 and LM 39 were badly damaged during a storm in the Bay of Biscay; all four arrived at Talcahuano on 24-11-98. The craft were ordered for the German Navy 18-12-70, as CMN's type *Combattante II* A4L. Design by Friedrich Lürssen Werft, Vegesack. All hulls fitted out at Cherbourg by CMN.
Hull systems: Steel construction. All four of the class have been re-engined with MTU 16V396-series diesels producing 13,000 bhp total.
Combat systems: Thomson-CSF Vega fire-control system with Pollux radar; Triton is used for target designation. All have the PALIS (Passive-Active-Link) system for data sharing and can use NATO Link 11. OTO Melara-made Bofors 40-mm mountings with Mauser GRP-enclosed gunhouses have been fitted in place of the original open Bofors 40-mm L70 mountings aft. The German EW suite was removed prior to transfer.

PATROL COMBATANTS [PG]

♦ 6 Contramestre Micalvi–class (Project Taitão) multirole
Bldr: ASMAR, Talcahuano

	Laid down	L	In serv.
PSG 71 Contramestre Micalvi	2-1-92	27-9-92	27-1-93
PSG 72 Contramestre Ortiz	28-6-92	23-7-93	13-12-93
PSG 73 Aspirante Isaza	28-9-92	7-1-94	27-5-94
PSG 74 Aspirante Morel	28-12-92	21-4-94	5-7-94
PSH 77 Corneta Cabrales	. . .	4-4-96	29-6-96
PSG 78 Piloto Sibbald	. . .	5-6-96	29-8-96

D: 483 tons (518 fl) (PSH 77: 532 fl) **S:** 15 kts (PSH 77: 16.5 kts)
Dim: 42.50 (36.30 pp) × 8.50 × 2.90 (PSH 77: 4.02 draft)
A: 1 40-mm 60-cal. Bofors Mk. 3 AA; 2 single 20-mm 70-cal. Oerlikon AA (except PSH 77: 2 12.7-mm machineguns)
Electronics: Radar: 2 Decca . . . nav.
M: 2 Caterpillar 3512TA diesels; 2 props; 2,560 bhp (PSH 77, PSG 78: 2 diesels; 2 props; 3,600 bhp)
Electric: 210 kw tot. **Range:** 1,650/12 normal; 3,400/12 max.
Fuel: 43 m^3 + 70 m^3 in cargo hold **Endurance:** 30 days
Crew: 5 officers, 18 enlisted + 30 passengers

Contramestre Ortiz (PSG 72) Maritime Photographic, 7-01

Remarks: Designed with the assistance of NEVASABU, the Netherlands. Intended for offshore patrol duties, cargo and troop transportation, lighthouse and navigational buoy support, torpedo retrieval, and fisheries protection. May later be upgraded with the provision of a sonar, bow-thruster, fin stabilizers, and mine rails, but plans to add a mine-countermeasures capability have been canceled. PSG 75 and PSG 76 were built for potential foreign sales but were instead purchased 1996 for the *Dirección General del Territorio Marítimo y de la Marine.* In 4-99 PSG 77 was fitted to serve as a Patrol Boat for the hydrographic service (*Servicio Hidrográfico y Oceanográfico de la Armada de Chile,* SHOA) and is specifically equipped for these types of activities.
Hull systems: Have two generator sets, electrohydraulic crane on the fantail, and provision for stowing two 9-ton cargo containers on deck aft; have 70 m^3 stores or liquid fuel capacity (35 tons). Can carry 35 m^3 fresh water. Hull has a bulbous bow and eight watertight compartments. PSG 77 and PSG 78 have more powerful propulsion plants. PSG 77 has an STN Atlas Elektronik dual-frequency multibeam sounding sonar operating at 50 kHz to 1,500-m depths and at 200 kHz for depths to 300 m; also fitted is an STN Atlas Elektronik DESO-25 single-beam echo sounder, a Dynabase motion sensor, a forward-looking sonar, and an STN Atlas Elektronik Hydromap data acquisition, storage, and navigation workstation, while a survey launch carried by the ship has two DESO-17 echo sounders, Hydromap, and digital GPS.

AMPHIBIOUS WARFARE SHIPS

♦ 1 ex-U.S. Newport-class tank landing ship [LST]
Bldr: National Steel & Shipbuilding, San Diego, Calif.

	Laid down	L	In serv.
R 93 Valdivia (ex-*San Bernardino,* LST 1189)	12-7-69	28-3-70	27-3-71

D: 4,975 tons light (8,576 fl) **S:** 22 kts (20 sust.)
Dim: 159.2 (171.3 over horns) × 21.18 × 5.3 (aft; 1.80 fwd)
A: 1 20-mm Mark 15 CIWS gatling gun; 10 single 12.7-mm mg; 1 Cougar (SH-32) helicopter
Electronics: Radar: 1 Raytheon SPS-64(V)9 nav.; 1 Raytheon SPS-10F surf. search
M: 6 Alco 16-251 diesels; 2 CP props; 16,500 bhp
Range: 14,250/14 **Fuel:** 1,750 tons
Crew: 13 officers, 244 enlisted + troops: 20 officers, 294 enlisted + 72 emergency accom.

Valdivia (R 93) Alexandre Sheldon-Duplaix, 12-02

AMPHIBIOUS WARFARE SHIPS *(continued)*

Remarks: Decommissioned from U.S. Navy 30-9-95 and leased to Chile the same day. Purchased outright by Chile on 23-6-99. Plans to acquire a second unit have been shelved. Ran aground mid-1997 but has been repaired. The R 93's Phalanx CIWS was removed during 2001 and placed aboard the frigate *Lynch* (PF 07).
Hull systems: Can transport 2,000 tons cargo, or, for beaching, 500 tons of cargo on 1,765 m^2 of deck space. A side-thruster propeller forward helps when marrying to a causeway. There is a 34-m-long, 75-ton capacity mobile aluminum ramp forward, which is linked to the tank deck by a second from the upper deck. Aft is a 242-m^2 helicopter platform and a stern door for loading and unloading vehicles. The tank deck, which has a 75-ton-capacity turntable at both ends, can carry 23 armored personnel carriers or 29 M 48 tanks or 41 2.5-ton trucks, while the upper deck can accept 29 2.5-ton trucks. Formerly carried three LCVP and one LCP in Welin davits. Has two 10-ton cranes. Carries 141,600 gallons vehicle fuel.

Note: U.S. Navy sister *La Moure County* (LST 1194), which went hard aground on 12-9-00 in southern Chile, was stricken on 17-11-00 at Valparaiso and was cannibalized for spares before being sunk as a target.

♦ 2 French BATRAL-class landing ship/transports [LSM]
Bldr: ASMAR, Talcahuano

	L	In serv.		L	In serv.
R 92 Rancagua (ex-R 93)	26-3-82	1-7-83	R 95 Chacabuco	16-7-85	1-4-86

D: 770 tons (1,330 fl) **S:** 13 kts **Dim:** 79.40 (68.00 pp) × 13.16 × 3.50
A: 2 single 40-mm 60-cal. Bofors AA; 1 20-mm 70-cal. Oerlikon AA; 2 single 81-mm mortars
Electronics: Radar: 1/Decca 1229 nav.
M: 2 SEMT-Pielstick 12PA4 V185VG diesels; 2 props; 4,000 bhp
Electric: 360 kw
Range: 4,500/13 **Crew:** 49 ship's company + 180 troops.

Rancagua (R 92) Maritime Photographic, 7-01

Remarks: Constructed with French technical assistance. Sister *Maipo* (R 91) was placed in reserve in 1998 and stricken in 1999.
Hull systems: Cargo: 350 tons vehicles and/or dry cargo, 208 tons potable water or ballast. Bow ramp has 40-ton capacity. The helicopter platform can accommodate a Super Puma. Hull has eight watertight compartments and a double bottom.
Disposal note: Sister ship *Maipo* (R 91) was placed in reserve on 22-12-98 and stricken soon thereafter.

♦ 2 Elicura-class logistics landing ships/transports [LSM]

	Bldr	In serv.
R 90 Elicura (ex-AP 95)	ASMAR, Talcahuano	10-12-63
R 94 Orompello (ex-AP 94)	Dade DD Co., Miami, Fla.	15-9-64

D: 290 tons (750 fl) **S:** 11 kts **Dim:** 49.20 (46.00 pp) × 10.40 × 2.30
A: 2 single 20-mm 70-cal. Mk 10 Oerlikon AA
Electronics: Radar: 1 Raytheon 1500B Pathfinder nav.
M: 2 Cummins VT-17-700M diesels; 2 props; 1,006 bhp (900 sust.)
Electric: 120 kw tot. **Range:** 2,900/10.5 **Fuel:** 71 tons
Endurance: 15 days **Crew:** 19 tot. + 180 troops or 18 passengers

Orompello (R 94) Chilean Navy, 1997

Remarks: Two near-sisters are operated by a Chilean commercial firm. The guns are not always aboard. *Orompello* is assigned to the Third Naval Zone
Hull systems: Have bow ramp, one 10-ton-capacity cargo boom, one smaller forward. Cargo capacity: 380 tons. Can transport an infantry company of 180 troops if necessary and can carry tanks weighing up to 40 tons.

AUXILIARIES

♦ 1 ex-Canadian icebreaker/supply vessel [AGB]
Bldr: Vickers, Montreal (In serv. 10-69)

AP 46 Contre-Almirante Oscar Viel Toro (ex-*Norman McLeod Rogers*)

D: 6,320 tons (6,506 fl) **S:** 15.0 kts **Dim:** 90.10 (81.16 pp) × 19.13 × 6.10
A: 2 20-mm/70 cal. Oerlikon AA
Electronics: Radar: 2 Kelvin-Hughes 14/12 nav.
M: 4 Fairbanks Morse 38D-8⅛-12 diesels, 8 1,380-kw generator sets, 2 electric motors; 2 props; 12,000 shp—2 Westinghouse gas turbines, geared drive; 16,000 shp
Range: 12,000/12 **Fuel:** 1,095 tons **Crew:** 33 tot. (78 accom.)

Contre-Almirante Oscar Viel Toro (AP 46) Chilean Navy, 1995

Remarks: 4,299 grt/2,357 dwt. Commissioned into Chilean service on 14-1-95 and refitted at ASMAR, Talcahuano, to support the *Teniente Marsh* and *Teniente Carvajal* scientific bases in the Antarctic. Had been used by Canadian Coast Guard as a river icebreaker, supply ship, and navigational aids tender. Cargo: 900 tons. Can carry one helicopter and has a telescoping hangar. Re-engined during refit 7-11-83 to 14-9-84, with both a diesel-electric and an alternate gas turbine-propulsion system. Retains Canadian paint scheme with red hull and cream upperworks.

♦ 1 buoy tender and salvage ship [AGL]
Bldr: B. V. J. Pattje Scheepswerf, Waterhuizen, the Netherlands (In serv. 7-78)

63 Ingeniero George Slight Marshall (ex-*Vigilant*)

D: 1,210 tons **S:** 12.5 kts **Dim:** 52.96 (47.86 pp) × 11.16 × 3.52
A: 2 single 20-mm 70-cal. Oerlikon AA **Electronics:** Radar: 1 . . . nav.
M: 2 Ruston 6AP230 diesels; 2 props; 1,360 bhp—bow-thruster
Electric: 504 kw tot. (3 × 168-kw diesel sets)

Ingeniero George Slight Marshall (63)—with since-sold tug *Colo Colo* (ATF 69) H&L Van Ginderen, 1-99

Remarks: 817 grt/445 dwt. Purchased 1996 from the Mersey Docks and Harbour Co., which had employed her as a navigational buoy and salvage vessel in the River Mersey and Liverpool Bay area. Commissioned in Chilean service on 5-2-97. Named for the late-19th-century English founder of the Chilean lighthouse system. Has one 15-ton buoy-handling derrick. The ship is also equipped for firefighting and can lay and recover light communications cable over the bow.

♦ 1 ex-U.S. Robert D. Conrad–class research ship [AGOR]
Bldr: Marinette SB, Marinette, Wisc.

	L	In serv.
AGOR 60 Vidal Gormaz (ex-*Thomas Washington*, AGOR 10)	1-8-64	17-9-65

D: 1,096 tons light (1, 370 fl) **S:** 13.5 kts (10 sust.)
Dim: 63.51 (58.37 pp) × 11.89 × 4.66 hull

AUXILIARIES *(continued)*

A: 2 single 20-mm 70-cal. Oerlikon AA **Electronics:** Radar: 1 . . . nav.
M: 2 Fairbanks-Morse 38D8⅛-5 diesels (697 bhp each), electric drive; 1 prop; 1,000 shp—1 175 shp bow azimuth-thruster
Electric: 1,015 kw tot. (2 × 300-kw diesel-driven, 1 × 200-kw gas turbine–driven, 1 × 150-kw shaft-generator, 1 × 65-kw emergency)
Range: 8,200/11 **Fuel:** 211 tons **Endurance:** 32 days
Crew: 23 Chilean Navy + 22 scientific party

Vidal Gormaz (AGOR 60) Maritime Photographic, 7-01

Remarks: 1,151 grt/1,017 dwt. Transferred 28-9-92. Formerly assigned to the private Scripps Institute of Oceanography, La Jolla, Calif., by the U.S. Office of Naval Research. Electric bow-thruster/propulsor, which provides up to 4.5 kts. Carries the Sea Beam bottom contour-mapping sonar system and was modernized 1981–84 with new oceanographic winches and cables to work to 4,000–5,000-m depths. Has 21.5-m² wet lab and 137-m² dry laboratory.

♦ 1 replenishment oiler [AOR]
Bldr: Burmeister & Wain, Copenhagen

	L	In serv.
AO 53 ARAUCANO	21-6-66	5-1-67

D: 17,300 tons (23,630 fl) **S:** 17 kts **Dim:** 160.93 × 21.95 × 8.80
A: 2 twin 40-mm 60-cal. U.S. Mk.1 Mod. 2 AA
Electronics: Radar: 2 . . . nav.
M: 1 Burmeister & Wain 62 VT 2 BF 140, 9-cyl. diesel; 1 prop; 10,800 bhp
Range: 12,000/14.5 **Crew:** 13 officers, 117 enlisted

Araucano (AO 53) Alexandre Sheldon-Duplaix, 12-02

Remarks: Ordered 19-2-65. Can replenish two ships alongside under way simultaneously. Carries 21,126 m³ liquid and 1,444 m³ dry cargo. Has two U.S. Mk 51 lead-computing directors for the 40-mm AA mounts; the original U.K. Mk 5 twin mounts have been replaced with U.S. mountings, and the forward two pair have been removed. A large bow bulb and greatly enlarged anchor hawse fittings were added prior to 1998.

♦ 1 transport and disaster-relief ship [AP]
Bldr: ASMAR, Talcahuano

	Laid down	L	In serv.
AP 47 AQUILES	27-5-86	4-12-87	15-7-88

D: 2,767 tons light (4,550 fl) **S:** 18 kts (15 sust.)
Dim: 103.00 (97.00 pp) × 17.00 × 5.50 **A:** none
Electronics: Radar: 2 . . . nav.
M: 2 MaK 8M453B diesels; 1 CP prop; 7,200 bhp—bow-thruster
Electric: 1,375 kw (1 × 500 kw, 2 × 400 kw, 1 × 75 kw) **Fuel:** 460 tons
Crew: 15 officers, 68 enlisted + 250 passengers

Remarks: 1,800 dwt. Has two cargo holds totaling 2,900 m³ and one 20-ton electric crane. Can carry up to 890 tons ballast water and 470 tons potable water. The helicopter deck is large enough to accept a Super Puma. Has double-chine hullform with bulbous bow.

♦ 1 ex-Swedish Älvsborg-class submarine tender [AS]
Bldr: Karlskronavarvet, Karlskrona, Sweden

	Laid down	L	In serv.
42 ALMIRANTE JOSÉ TORIBIO MERINO CASTRO (ex-*Älvsborg,* A 234; ex-M 02)	16-11-68	11-11-69	10-4-71

D: 2,660 tons (fl) **S:** 16 kts **Dim:** 92.4 (83.3 pp) × 14.7 × 4.0
A: 3 single 40-mm 70-cal. Bofors SAK 40/48 AA
Electronics:
Radar: 1 Terma Scanter 009 nav.; 1 Raytheon . . . nav.; 1 Ericsson Sea Giraffe 50HC surf./air search; 1 CelsiusTech 9LV 200 f.c.
M: 2 Nohab-Polar 112VS, 12-cyl. diesels; 1 CP prop; 4,200 bhp—350-shp bow-thruster
Electric: 1,200 kw tot. **Crew:** 20 officers, 70 enlisted

Almirante José Toribio Merino Castro (42)—still in Swedish Navy camouflage scheme Leo Dirkx, 3-98

Remarks: Purchased 10-96 for use as a submarine tender and transferred 7-2-97. Built as a minelayer for the Swedish Navy, but had been used as a submarine tender in peacetime and with accommodations for 205 submarine crew members; was laid up in Sweden at the end of 1993 and redesignated a "general support ship." Has a helicopter deck. Sister *Visborg* (A 265) remains a minelayer in the Swedish Navy and *Almirante José Toribio Merino Castro* retains this capability.

♦ 2 Norwegian-built tug/supply vessels [ATA]
Bldr: Aukra Bruk A/S, Aukra, Norway (In serv. 1973–74)

ATF 66 GALVARINO (ex-*Maersk Traveller*)
ATF 67 LAUTARO (ex-*Navimer I,* ex-*Maersk Tender*)

Galvarino (ATF 66) Maritime Photographic, 7-01

D: 941 tons light (2,380 fl) **S:** 15 kts (14 sust.)
Dim: 58.32 (52.20 pp) × 12.63 × 3.97
A: ATF 66: 2 single 20-mm 70-cal. Oerlikon AA; ATF 67: 1 40-mm 60-cal. Bofors AA
Electronics: Radar: 1 Furuno FR 240 nav.; 1 Terma Pilot 7T-48 nav.
M: 2 Atlas-MAK 8M 553AK diesels; 2 CP props; 6,400 bhp (5,300 sust.)—bow-thruster
Electric: 533 kw tot. (1 × 240 kw, 1 × 160 kw, 1 × 133 kw)
Range: . . . / . . . **Fuel:** 132 tons **Crew:** 5 officers, 15 enlisted

Remarks: 499 grt/832 dwt. Former anchor-handling tug/supply vessels. ATF 66 was purchased 1987, left Europe 14-12-87, and was commissioned 26-1-88 in Chile for use as patrol and search-and-rescue ship and logistics transport in Chile's southern regions. ATF 67 was acquired 21-12-90 from Athene Transport Corp. Cargo capacity: 1,400 tons. Ice-strengthened hulls. 65-ton bollard pull, 100-ton towing winch. ATF 66 has a helicopter landing platform built above the fantail; ATF 67 does not.
Disposals: *Janequero* (ATF 65, ex-*Maersk Transporter*) was placed in reserve at the end of 1998 and stricken in 1999.

♦ 1 Dutch-built Smit Lloyd 40–class tug/supply vessel [ATA]
Bldr: Scheepswerf De Waal, Zaltbommel (In serv. 1972)

ATF 68 LEUCOTÓN (ex-*Lilen,* ex-*Smit Lloyd 44*)

D: 1,750 tons (fl) **S:** 13 kts **Dim:** 53.14 (49.31 pp) × 12.30 × 4.45
A: 1 single 40-mm 60-cal. Bofors AA
Electronics: Radar: 2 . . . nav. (X- and S-band)
M: 2 Burmeister & Wain Alpha 8430, 8-cyl. diesels; 2 CP props; 2,800 bhp—bow-thruster
Electric: 270 kw tot. (2 × 135-kw diesel sets)
Range: . . . / . . . **Fuel:** 259 tons **Crew:** 13 tot.

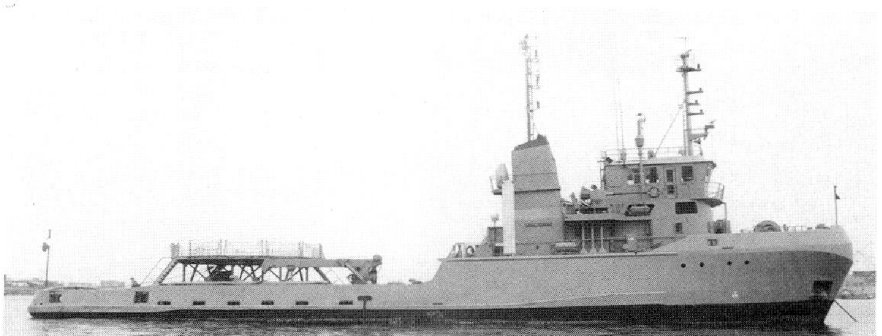

Leucotón (ATF 68)—with 40-mm guns between stacks and pilothouse Chilean Navy, 1997

Remarks: 743 grt. Former anchor-handling tug/supply vessel acquired 6-8-90, modified for naval service at Punta Arenas, and commissioned on 29-1-91.
Disposals: *Colo Colo* (ATF 69) was sold to Omega Shipping, Ltd., Panama, and renamed *Sea Guardian* in 1999; *Yelcho* was placed in reserve in 1998 and later sold to Omega Shipping as the *Independent.*

AUXILIARIES *(continued)*

◆ **1 sail-training ship [AXT]** Bldr: Izar, Cadiz, Spain

	L	In serv.
BE 43 Esmeralda (ex-*Don Juan de Austria*)	12-5-53	15-6-54

D: 3,420 tons (3,754 fl) **S:** 11 kts (under power)
Dim: 109.8 (94.1 pp) × 13.1 × 8.7
A: 2 single 47-mm saluting cannon **Electronics:** Radar: 1 . . . nav.
M: 1 Fiat diesel; 1,400 bhp—2,500 m^2 max. sail area
Range: 8,000/8 under power **Crew:** 271 ship's company + 80 midshipmen

Esmeralda (BE 43) Mitsuhiro Kadota, 10-03

Remarks: Four-masted schooner, originally ordered by Spain. Heavily damaged by fire on 18-8-47 in an explosion at the Spanish submarine base next to the shipyard. Sold to Chile on 23-10-52 for US$2,980,000. Similar to the Spanish *Juan Sebastian de Elcano.* Refitted in South Africa, 1977, and several times thereafter. She has been re-engined at least three times.

SERVICE CRAFT

◆ **1 historic relic, former monitor [YAG]**
Bldr: Laird, Scotland

	L	Completed
Huascar	7-10-1865	12-1865

D: 1,180 tons; 2,030 tons (fl) **S:** 12.3 kts **Dim:** 57.91 × 10.67 × 5.56
A: 1 twin 254-mm low-angle in turret; 2 single 40-pdr. cannon
M: 1 set reciprocating steam: 1 prop; 1,650 ihp **Boilers:** 4 fire-tube
Fuel: 300 tons (max.) **Crew:** 170

Huascar H&L Van Ginderen, 2-99

Remarks: Data above refer to ship as built. Although in exceptionally fine condition, is not operational. Captured in damaged condition from Peru, 8-10-1879. Employed for many years as a gunnery training ship and then converted as a museum and stationary harbor flagship at Talcahuano. Has 114-mm armor belt with 52-mm ends. Turret armor varies from 135 to 203 mm. Conning tower has 76-mm armor. Ship built of iron. Peru continues to claim ownership.

◆ **2 miscellaneous floating cranes [YD]**

Remarks: One is of 30 tons capacity and one of 180 tons capacity.

◆ **1 Pisagua-class support logistics landing craft [YF]**
Bldr: SIMAR, Santiago (In serv. 11-7-95)

YFP 116 Pisagua

D: 32 tons light (95 fl) **S:** 8 kts **Dim:** 22.23 × 6.00 × 1.60
M: 2 diesels; 2 props; 300 bhp
Range: 500/8 **Crew:** 6 tot.

Remarks: Design modeled after the U.S. LCM(8) class. Intended to provide logistics support to the Seamen's School at Quiriquina Island. Cargo: 50 tons. Has a bow ramp and a small crane to starboard amidships.

◆ **1 1,300-ton-capacity covered floating dry dock [YFDL]**
Bldr: ASMAR, Talcahuano (In serv. 2-4-98)

Contralmirante Arturo Young Ward

Remarks: Displaces 1,105 tons light. Has sliding roof panels to provide controlled environment.

◆ **1 1,200-ton-capacity floating dry dock [YFDL]**
Bldr: ASMAR, Talcahuano

	Laid down	L	In serv.
Ingeniero 3ro José Gutiérrez	5-9-90	27-9-91	27-9-91

Remarks: Length overall: 80 m. Displaces 1,050 tons empty.

◆ **1 800-ton-capacity floating dry dock [YFDL]**
Bldr: Mohlen & Seebeck, Göstmunde, Germany (In serv. 6-08)

Manterola

Remarks: Employed at ASMAR, Talcahuano, since 2-4-60; displaces 658 tons empty.

◆ **1 10,000-ton-capacity medium floating dry dock [YFDM]**
Bldr: ASMAR, Talcahuano (L: 8-10-83)

Valparaiso III

D: 4,150 tons (light)
Dim: 167.0 (151.2 on blocks) × 32.1 (26.1 interior width) × 3.95

Remarks: Built for shipyard rather than naval service, but available to the navy.

◆ **2 ex-U.S. ARD 24–class medium floating dry docks [YFDM]**
(In serv. 1944)

131 Ingeniero Mery (ex-ARD 25) 132 Mutilla (ex-ARD 32)

Capacity: 3,500 tons **Dim:** 149.86 × 24.69 × 1.73 (light)

Remarks: 131 leased 1973 and transferred to ASMAR in 10-88; 132 transferred to Chile on 15-12-60 and transferred to ASMAR on 28-2-63. Both are based at Talcahuano. Dock inside dimensions: 118.6 m on blocks, 18.0 m clear width, 6.3 m draft over blocks. Bow end closed and pointed. Displace 10,000 tons at full load condition.

◆ **1 ex-U.S. ARD 4–class medium floating dry dock [YFDM]**
Bldr: Pacific Bridge, Alameda, Calif. (In serv. 6-42)

133 Talcahuano (ex-*Waterford,* ARD 5)

Dim: 148.1 × 21.6 (14.9 clear width) × 1.6 (9.9 flooded max.)

Remarks: Capacity: 3,500 tons. Purchased 10-3-99; left for Chile under tow on 12-5-99 and recommissioned at Talcahuano on 30-8-99. Crew in U.S. service totaled 131.

◆ **1 admiral's barge (YFL)**
Bldr: ASMAR, Talcahuano (In serv. 1997)

Remarks: Laid down early 1996 as commander-in-chief's barge. No data available.

◆ **2 Meteoro-class personnel transports [YFL]**
Bldr: ASMAR, Talcahuano

	L	In serv.
YFP 110 Meteoro	29-1-68	3-6-68
YFP 112 Grumete Pérez Huemel	. . .	12-12-75

Meteoro (YFP 110) Chilean Navy, 1992

SERVICE CRAFT *(continued)*

D: 165 tons (205 fl) **S:** 8 kts **Dim:** 24.4 × 6.7 × 2.6
A: 1 20-mm 70-cal. Oerlikon AA
M: 1 Cummins diesel; 365 bhp **Range:** 2,600/9
Crew: . . . tot.

Remarks: Both attached to the Seamen's School, Isla Quiriquina, as harbor transports. Are of modified fishing trawler design, with the main-deck superstructure extended. Can carry 15 tons of cargo in addition to 210 (YFP 112: 290) passengers. YFP 112 has a 370-bhp diesel and can achieve 10 kts.

Disposal note: Sister *Sobenes* has been stricken. Coastal tanker *Guardian Brito* (AO 55) was placed in disposal reserve on 1-1-99.

♦ 1 large harbor tug [YTB]
Bldr: Southern Shipbuilders, Faversham, U.K. (In serv. 6-8-75)

YT 115 Gálvez

D: 216 tons (fl) **S:** 11.5 kts **Dim:** 25.5 × 7.3 × 2.8
M: 2 diesels; 1 prop; 1,000 bhp

Remarks: 112 grt. Painted white. Subordinated to ASMAR, Talcahuano.

♦ 1 sail-training craft [YTS]
Bldr: Naturoy Oy, Wilhelm Shauman AB, Pietarsaari, Finland (In serv. 25-1-78)

Blanca Estela

Remarks: 32-ton ocean-racing ketch, purchased new on 3-20-77.

CHILEAN COAST GUARD
GENERAL DIRECTORATE OF THE MARITIME TERRITORY
(*Dirrección General del Territorio Marítimo y de la Marine Mercante*)

Founded 1848 and now responsible for regulating the Chilean merchant marine and water sports, coastal and port patrol, and navigational aids maintenance. Also intended to organize the merchant marine as a potential naval reserve. In addition to the units listed below, there are also a large number of very small launches, rigid inflatable boats, etc. The coast guard operates several navy-manned MBB BO-105 helicopters acquired 1991. All personnel are seconded from the Chilean Navy.

Personnel: About 1,600 tot.

PATROL SHIPS [WPS]

♦ 0 (+ 2) 80-meter patrol ship
Bldr.: ASMAR, Talcahuano (In serv. 2007/2008)

LSG . . . LSG . . .

D: 1,850 (fl) S: 21+ kts **Dim:** 80.60 × 13.00 ×x 3.80
A: Pending
Electronics: Radar: 2 . . . nav.
M: 2 Wartsila 12V26 diesels; 2 Wartsila LIPS CP propeller; 10,943 bhp
Electric: 2 × 200 kW diesel sets
Range: 8,600/12 **Fuel:** 300 cu. m. **Crew:** 30 total crew + 30 passengers

Remarks: Specifically designed by FASSMER GmbH & Co. KG, Germany for Chile. First unit to be delivered in 2007 and commissioned in 2008 with the second unit expected to follow in 2009.
Hull systems: Fitted with a helicopter deck big enough to support 1 Cougar (SH-32) helicopter. Built of steel except for aluminum wheelhouse. Carries two RIBs and fitted with a 4-ton capacity crane for RIB handling. Makes use of signature reduction "stealth" design features.

PATROL CRAFT [WPC]

♦ 16 Danubio 1 class
Bldr: ASMAR, Valparaiso

	Delivered
LSG 1609 Aysen	12-07-99
LSG 1610 Corral	29-6-00
LSG 1611 Concepción	12-09-00
LSG 1612 Caldera	18-12-00
LSG 1613 San Antonio	18-12-00
LSG 1614 Antofagasta	18-04-01
LSG 1615 Arica	21-8-01
LSG 1616 Coquimbo	13-12-01
LSG 1617 Puerto Natales	13-12-01
LSG 1618 Valpataiso	16-05-02
LSG 1619 Punta Arenas	01-8-02
LSG 1620 Talcahuano	25-10-02
LSG 1621 Quintero	15-01-03
LSG 1622 Chiloe	10-03
LSG 1623 Puerto Montt	03-04
LSG 1624 Iquique	05-04

D: 125 tons (fl) **S:** 25 kts **Dim:** 33.10 (29.00 pp) × 6.60 × 1.90
A: 1 12.7-mm mg
Electronics: Radar: 1 Decca . . . nav.
M: 2 MTU 16V2000 M90 diesels; 2 props; 3,200 bhp
Electric: 104 kVA tot. (2 × 52-kVA diesel sets)
Range: 1,100 max. **Fuel:** 22 tons **Crew:** 2 officers, 8 enlisted

Coquimbo (LSG 1616) Werner Globke, 12-04

Remarks: Design locally derived from that of the 32-m *Protector* class. Ordered 4-99 to replace the *Pillan* class and patrol the Chilean coastal zones. LSG stands for Launcha de Servicio General, or Patrol Boats for General Service. May be expanded to include three more vessels. Can handle 18 total personnel in an emergency. Three additional units may be purchased at a later date.

♦ 2 32-meter UK Protector class
Bldr: ASMAR, Talcahuano, Chile (In serv. 24-6-89)

LSG 1603 Alacalufe LSG 1604 Hallef

D: 107 tons (fl) **S:** 20 kts (18 sust.) **Dim:** 32.70 (28.96 wl) × 6.70 × 2.10
A: 1 20-mm 70-cal. Oerlikon AA
Electronics: Radar: 1 Decca . . . nav.
M: 2 MTU diesels; 2 props; 2,600 bhp **Range:** 1,100/16 **Fuel:** 20 tons
Crew: 2 officers, 12 enlisted

Alacalufe (LSG 1603) Chilean Navy, 1997

Remarks: Although initially announced as being intended for the Customs Service when ordered in 1987 and labeled as "pilot boats" (LEP), they are now assigned to patrol and search-and-rescue duties in the Straits of Magellan area and are typed *Lanchas de Servicio General.*

♦ 2 Guacolda class
Bldr: E.N. Bazán, San Fernando, Spain

	In serv.
LSG 1605 Guacolda (ex-80)	30-7-65
LSG 1606 Fresia (ex-81)	9-12-65

D: 134 tons (fl) **S:** 28 kts **Dim:** 36.20 (34.00 wl) × 5.60 × 2.20
A: 1 40-mm 70-cal. Bofors AA; 2 single 12.7-mm mg
Electronics: Radar: 1 Decca . . . nav.
M: 2 Mercedes-Benz MB839Bb diesels; 2 props; 4,800 bhp
Electric: 90 kVA tot. **Range:** 1,500/15 **Crew:** 18 tot.

Remarks: Designed by Friedrich Lürssen Werft, Germany, and built under license. Were equipped as torpedo boats, with two 40-mm AA and four fixed British Mk IV torpedo tubes using old straight-running British Mk 8 Mod. 3 torpedoes until redesignated as *Lanchas de Servicio General* on 26-12-97 and transferred to the Chilean Coast Guard; the torpedo equipment and after 40-mm gun were removed and mechanical minesweeping gear was added on the stern.
Disposals: Sister ships *General Quidora* (LSG 1607) and *General Tegualda* (LPM 1608) were decommissioned and stricken for disposal during 2001 and 2002 respectively.

PATROL BOATS [WPB]

♦ 10 Israeli Dabur class
Bldr: Israeli Aircraft Industries, Be'er Sheva (In serv. 1973–77)

LPC 1814 Grumete Venanzio Díaz
LPC 1815 Grumete Luciano Bolados
LPC 1816 Grumete Santiago Salinas
LPC 1817 Grumete Blas Segundo Tellez
LPC 1818 Grumete Juan Bravo
LPC 1819 Grumete David Campos
LPC 1820 Grumete Samuel Machado
LPC 1821 Grumete Rudecindo Troncoso
LPC 1822 Grumete Domingo Johnson
LPC 1823 Grumete Manuel Hudson

COAST GUARD PATROL BOATS [WPB] *(continued)*

D: 29 tons (39 fl) **S:** 19 kts **Dim:** 19.8 × 5.8 × 0.8
A: 2 single 20-mm 70-cal. Oerlikon AA; 2 single 12.7-mm mg (see comments below)
Electronics: Radar: 1 Decca 916 nav.
M: 2 G.M. 12V71 TI diesels; 2 props; 960 bhp (840 bhp sust.)
Electric: 20 kw **Range:** 1,200/17 **Crew:** 2 officers, 8 enlisted

Grumete Manuel Hudson (LPC 1823) Maritime Photographic, 7-01

Remarks: LPC 1814 through LPC 1819 purchased used in 9-90 and commissioned in Chile 3-1-91, all for service in the 4th Naval Zone. LPC 1820 through LPC 1823 purchased in 1995, commissioned 16-3-95, and based at Iquique. Quarters air-conditioned and spacious. Aluminum construction. Carry a semi-rigid inflatable inspection boat aft. When new, could make 25 knots but are now operating at about five tons over designed displacement.
Combat systems: Carry two 20-mm mounts and two 12.7-mm machineguns (except LPC 1817 and 1819, which carry only two 12.7-mm machineguns and LPC 1818, which carries just one 12.7-mm machinegun).

Disposal note: Of the *Pillan* class, *Antuco* (LPC 1807) and *Choshuenco* (LPC 1809) were both decommissioned on 1-1-98, *Pillan* (LPC 1801) and *Troncador* (LPC 1802) in 1998, *Rano-Kau* (LPC 1803) on 30-7-99, *Corcovado* (LPC 1805) on 13-9-99, *Villarrica* (LPC 1804) on 30-8-00. *Llaina* (LPC 1806) was no longer in service as of 2000. *Osorono* (LPC 1808) was decommissioned on 15-12-99 and *Copahue* (LPC 1810) was decommissioned on 31-1-01.

SERVICE CRAFT

♦ 15 Rodman 800–class harbor launches [WYFL]
Bldr: Rodman Polyship S.A., Vigo, Spain (In serv. 1996)

PM 2031 through PM 2045

D: 9 tons (fl) **S:** 30 kts **Dim:** 8.9 × 3.0 × 0.80
A: 1 12.7-mm mg **Electronics:** Radar: 1 Raytheon . . . nav.
M: 2 Volvo Penta outdrive diesels; 300 bhp
Range: 150/25 **Crew:** 3 tot.

Rodman 800–class PM 2034 Maritime Photographic, 7-01

Remarks: GRP construction. Eighteen more may be ordered. Used for harbor patrol and search-and-rescue duties.

Note: Several earlier harbor patrol launches in the PM number series are also in service, including PM 2023.

Disposal note: Service launch *Petrohue* (LPM 1916) was decommissioned on 1-1-98 and stricken for disposal.

♦ 1 ASMAR 1160 rigid inflatable search-and-rescue craft [WYH]
Bldr: ASMAR, Valparaiso

LSR 1700 Tokerau (In serv. 14-2-92)

D: 7.8 tons light (10 fl) **S:** 25 kts (22 sust.)
Dim: 12.66 (11.73 hull, 10.78 wl) × 3.90 (3.30 hull) × 0.75
A: None **Electronics:** Radar: 1 Decca RD-80 nav.
M: 2 Volvo Penta TAMD-61A diesels; 2 Hamilton 291 waterjets; 612 bhp
Range: 310/20; 500/16 **Fuel:** 1,800 liters
Crew: 4 tot. + up to 32 survivors

Tokerau (LSR 1700) ASMAR, 8-91

Remarks: GRP hull has 60-cm-diameter inflatable surrounding bulwark. The craft are designed to self-right in case of capsizing in heavy seas. Extensive navigational suite includes Magellan NAV 1000 GPS receiver, Koden KS-5538 HFD/F, anemometer, echo sounder, and gyrocompass. Have diving, first-aid, and firefighting systems and carry a six-man life raft. A plan to procure eight more has not been carried out.
Disposals: Sister *Kimitahi* (LSR 1701) was stricken 30-12-00.

♦ 10 Maule-class search-and-rescue craft [WYH]
Bldr: ASENAV, Valdivia (In serv. 1982–83)

LPM 1901 Maule	LPM 1905 Isluga	LPM 1909 Cau-Cau
LPM 1902 Lauca	LPM 1906 Loa	LPM 1910 Pudeto
LPM 1903 Aconcagua	LPM 1907 Maullín	
LPM 1904 Rapel	LPM 1908 Copiapó	

D: 14 tons (fl) **S:** 18 kts **Dim:** 13.3 × 3.5 × 1.0
A: 1 12.7-mm mg **Electronics:** Radar: 1 Raytheon . . . nav.
M: 2 MTU 6V331 TC82 diesels; 2 props; 1,320 bhp (1,012 bhp sust.)

Copiapó (1908) Werner Globke, 12-04

Remarks: One unit of this class has reportedly been renamed *Robinson Crusoe*.

♦ 6 ex-U.S. Coast Guard 44-foot rescue launches [WYH]
Bldr: U.S.C.G. Yard, Curtis Bay, Md. (In serv. 31-3-61 to 8-5-73)

LSR 1703 Pelluhue	LSR 1706 Queitao
LSR 1704 Arauco	LSR 1707 Guaiteca
LSR 1705 Chacao	LSR 1708 Curaumilla

D: 14.9 tons light (17.7 fl) **S:** 13 kts (11.8 sust.)
Dim: 13.44 × 3.87 × 1.19 **Electronics:** Radar: 1 SPS-57 nav.
M: 2 G.M. Detroit Diesel 6V53 diesels; 2 props; 372 bhp
Range: 185/11.8; 200/11 **Fuel:** 1.2 tons **Crew:** 4 tot.

Remarks: Donated and transferred 3-02. "Unsinkable" design. Can carry up to 21 rescued personnel. LSR = Lancha de Salvamento y Rescate (Salvage and Rescue Launch). Are based at Constitución, Lebu, Maullín, Quellón, Melinka, and Valparaiso, respectively.

Note: There is also another Chilean agency charged with search-and-rescue duties. It operates a number of red or red-and-white-painted craft, including at least one U.K.-built *Arun*-class seagoing rescue launch.

CHILEAN ARMY

The Chilean Army operates a number of ASMAR-built, British FBM Marine-designed combat support boats:

D: . . . tons **S:** 24 kts **Dim:** 8.38 (6.98 wl) × 2.49 × 0.66 loaded
M: 2 diesels; 2 waterjets; 424 bhp **Fuel:** 170 liters

Remarks: Aluminum construction. Capable of operating in Force 5 gales. Used for river crossing and local support duties. Equipped to act as push-tugs.

CHINA

People's Republic of China

PEOPLE'S LIBERATION ARMY NAVY

Personnel: About 145,000, including about 7,000 naval infantry, 24,000 coast-defense artillery and missile troops, and 20,000 in naval aviation. Chinese People's Liberation Army troops are being cross-trained in amphibious operations. During 2002, U.S. DoD provided Congress with a higher figure of 290,000 total People's Liberation Army Navy (PLAN) uniformed personnel. Most transport auxiliaries and service craft are civilian-manned.

Bases: PLAN Headquarters is located in Beijing. The North Sea Fleet headquarters is at Qingdao, in Shandong Province, where all nuclear submarines assigned to the fleet are also homeported, with other major bases at Lüshun (surface combatants), and Huludao (conventional submarines) and smaller facilities at Jiaonan, Weihai, Chengshan, Yingkou, Qinhuangdao, Tianjin, Yantai, and Liugongdao.

Important shipbuilding facilities are located at Dalian and Huludao, which houses China's only nuclear submarine construction and support facilities.

The East Sea Fleet has its main headquarters at Ningbao, with other major bases at Zhoushan (surface combatants), Xiangshan (submarines), and Wusong (Shanghai). Smaller facilities are located at Lianyungang, Dinghai, Wenzhou, Ningde, Fuzhou, and Xiamen.

Important shipbuilding facilities are located in Shanghai at Jiangren Shipyard and Hudong-Zhonghua Shipyard (China's largest surface ship construction yards) and at the inland Wuhan, on the Yangzi River (diesel submarine construction facilities).

The South Sea Fleet, currently the largest and most modern of the three PLAN fleets, is headquartered at Zhanjiang, Guangdong, with other major bases at Yulin and Guangzhou and smaller facilities at Beihai, Shantou, Haikou, Mawei, and Hong Kong.

Paranaval Forces: In addition to the PLAN, several other agencies operate armed ships, including the Customs Service (*Hai Guan*), the Maritime Section of the Public Security Bureau (*Hai Gong*), and the Maritime Command of the Border Security Force (*Gong Bian*). There are also a fisheries inspection service and a coast guard.

Hong Kong: Although the former Royal Hong Kong Police Force and its Marine Region craft became Chinese government property as of 1-7-97, it continues to be subordinated to the semiautonomous Hong Kong government, as does the Hong Kong Government Flying Service (see separate listing for Hong Kong).

Naval Aviation: Under the operational control of the PLAN, the Naval Air Arm consists of a force of approx. 25,000 personnel and some 800 aircraft. Currently, the PLANAF comprises nine front-line aviation divisions, each with two or three aviation regiments, as well as a number of independent aviation regiments used in support roles. Major naval air stations are at Huludao, Shanhaiguan, Liangxiang, Laiyang, Jiaodong, Qingdao, Shanghai-Dachang, Luqiao, Leiyang, Haikou, Lingshui, and Sanya/Yulin International airport.

The Naval Air Arm's order of battle includes some 800 aircraft, includes the following (all figures are approx.):

Fixed-Wing:

200	Shenyang F-6 (J-6) interceptors (MiG-19 "Farmer" copy)
26	Xian F-7 (J-7) "Fishbed" interceptors (a modified copy of the MiG-21F)
48	Xian F-8D (J-8) "Finback" all-weather fighters (one naval J-8B fighter from the 8th Aviation Division rammed a U.S. Navy EP-3E Aries-II surveillance aircraft on 31-3-01 and crashed at sea)
20	Xian JH-7 Flying Leopard strike aircraft
30	J-11 (Russian Su-30MK2 "Flanker") attack aircraft
30	Nanchang Q-5 Fantan strike aircraft
50	B-5 (H-5) bombers (copy of the Soviet Il-28 "Beagle")
18	B-6 (H-6D) bombers (copy of the Tu-16 "Badger"—some equipped to carry two HY-4 antiship missiles [version B-6D] and others converted for aerial refueling)
4	Shaanxi Y-8 ASW maritime patrol aircraft (modified copy of An-12 "Cub"—equipped with Racal Skymaster radar)
3	Harbin Y-12 maritime surveillance aircraft, with Terma SLAR (the aircraft are assigned to the China Maritime Services, ostensibly for environmental and oil-spill surveillance)
4	PS-5 ASW aircraft
7	Harbin SH-5 amphibians used for reconnaissance (powered by four 3,150-hp turboprops for a cruising speed of 300 kts and a 2,850-n.m. range, 1,200-n.m. patrol radius at 45 tons max. takeoff weight, 10-ton payload [including 6 tons depth bombs]. Equipped with MAD boom, guns, and radar. First flight 3-4-76. Can operate 12 hours on four engines or 15 on two at 6,000-ft. altitude
3	HY-6D tanker aircraft (modified copy of Russian Tu-16 "Badger")
6	Russian AN-26 "Curl" transport aircraft
3	Cot Y-8 ASW transport aircraft (modified copy of An-12 "Cub")
4	Xi'an Y-7 transport aircraft
50	Shijiazhuang Y-5 transport aircraft
2	YAK-42 "Clobber" transport aircraft

Helicopters:

27	Super Frélon SA.321 (also built in China as the Z-8) heavy shipboard helicopters (two or three equipped with Thales HS 3125 dipping sonars)
4	Kamov Ka-28PL ASW Helix
4	Kamov Ka-28PS search-and-rescue helicopters (delivered in 1999–2000)
8	Eurocopter AS.565 "Dauphin" ASW helicopters (built in China as the Z-9)
8	Russian MI-8 "Hip" transport helicopter

Z-8 Super Frélon—note ASW torpedo on pylon *Ships of the World,* 1999

Z-9 Dauphin—note lack of stores pylons PLAN, 1998

The new Chinese Changhe Aircraft Industries Z-11 helicopter, a virtual copy of the Eurocopter AS.350B Écureuil, may be acquired in small numbers as a liaison helicopter.

About two dozen Su-30MKK land-based attack aircraft, armed with Kh-31A antiship missiles, were ordered on 27-1-03 for the PLAN, with an option for 22 more. These may replace a number of the fixed-wing aircraft and will likely be equipped with AS-20 Kayak antiship missiles, a variant of the Kh-35 shipboard weapon, as well as R-27-series (AA-10 Alamo) air-to-air missiles purchased from Ukraine. FH-7 fighter-bombers may be equipped with Zvezda-Strela Kh-31 (AS-17 Krypton) antiship missiles.

The Xian JH-7 Flying Leopard fighter-bomber began to enter naval service late in 1998. Export version known as FBC-1. Design appears patterned after the Anglo-French Jaguar and is about 30 years behind U.S. and European state of the art. About 72 aircraft are to be operated in three regiments.

Wingspan: 12.7 m **Length:** 22.325 m **Height:** 6.575 m
Weight: 28,475 kg max. takeoff
Speed: Mach 1.7 max. (625 kts at sea level)
Propulsion: 2 Rolls-Royce Spey 202 (WS-9) turbojets
Range: 1,969 n.m. ferry **Combat radius:** 889 n.m. **Fuel:** 10,050 kg max.
Combat load: 6.5 tons on six hard-points plus two wingtip AAM positions; weapons include C.802 antiship missiles

Naval Infantry: The current organization was established in 1980 as the 1st Brigade of Naval Infantry and is attached to the South Sea Fleet (a second brigade was established in the South Sea Fleet in 2001 at Zhanjiang). Each brigade has about 6,000 to 7,000 personnel and includes three mechanized infantry battalions, a fourth, nonmechanized infantry battalion, two tank battalions, a special operations force battalion, a missile battalion, an engineering chemical defense battalion, a communications/electronic warfare battalion and logistical support units. Though lacking in organic artillery assets, Naval Infantry employs T-59 tanks (Chinese version of the Russian T-54A), T-63A amphibious tanks (Russian PT-76 with 85-mm gun), Types 86 and 63/89 amphibious armored personnel carriers, 82-mm and 120-mm mortars, the Hunjian-73/HJ-8 antitank missile, 82-mm and 107-mm recoilless rifles, and 37-mm AA guns. Amphibious forces for the other fleets appear to be drawn from Chinese Army (PLA) units.

WEAPONS AND SENSORS

The ballistic missiles on the Xia-class SSBNs and nearly all other weapons on Chinese ships are of Chinese manufacture, with many being copies or derivatives of Soviet or European systems. Increasingly, however, Chinese weapons and sensors are of indigenous design and manufacture, although the technology employed remains decades behind that found in equivalent Western naval systems.

A. MISSILES

♦ Strategic Ballistic Missiles

Ju Lang-1 (JL-1/C-SS-N-3)—Became "operational" 7-88 after proof launch from the one Xia-class submarine, but there are conflicting reports on whether or not it has entered service. Single stage, solid fuel. *Ju Lang* means "Giant Voice." Approx. 250 kT warhead and CEP of 350 m.

Length: 10.0 m **Diameter:** 1.5 m
Weight: 14,000 kg **Range:** 2,700–3,600 km

Ju Lang-2 (JL-2/CSS-NX-4)—Successor to Ju Lang-1 (JL-2/CSS-N-3) in development. Essentially a navalized version of the land-based DF-31A, JL-2 is to have a maximum range of 8,000 km and carry either a single 250–650-kT or three 90-kT warheads. Three stages, solid propellant. First sea-based launch took place mid-1-01, from the modified Xia-class submarine.

WEAPONS AND SENSORS *(continued)*

♦ Strategic Cruise Missiles

Hong Niao-3 (HN-3): A turbofan-powered weapon in development for launch from 533-mm submarine torpedo tubes. Range to be 2,500 km. An evolved version of the HN-1, which was only produced in small numbers for land launch; HN-2, which reportedly flew in 1996 and had a range of 1,500 km, did not enter production. All three may have been intended to carry a warhead of about 300–400 kg weight, possibly with a nuclear yield of 90 kT. Data for HN-1:

Length: 6.4 m **Diameter:** 520 mm **Wingspan:** 3.0 m
Weight: approx. 1,400 kg **Speed:** subsonic **Range:** 600 km

♦ Antiship Cruise Missiles

C-101 Hai Ying-3 (HY-3/CSS-C-5 Sabbot): Coast-defense and air-launched weapon with a 400-kg high-explosive, armor-piercing warhead. Has two ramjet sustainers.

Length: 7.20 m **Diameter:** 0.76 m **Wingspan:** 1.20 m
Weight: 2,000 kg **Speed:** Mach 2.0 **Range:** 50 km **Altitude:** 300 m

C-201 Hai Ying-2 (HY-2/CSS-N-1): Improved version of the Russian P-15 Termit (NATO SS-N-2 Styx). Uses a jettisonable solid-rocket booster and a solid-fuel sustainer, vice the liquid fuel used with the HY-1. Guidance is by gyro autopilot, with radar terminal homing. Have a 513-kg high explosive warhead.

Length: 7.36 m **Wingspan:** 2.41 m **Weight:** 2,998 kg
Speed: Mach 0.9 **Range:** 70 km **Altitude:** 30–100 m

Other versions include the Hai Ying-2A with infrared, vice radar, terminal homing, and the Hai Ying-2G, which is radar altimeter–equipped, with 20-m cruise altitude, descending to 8 m during radar terminal homing. Also reported to have a coast-defense variant (C-201W) with a range of 45 km.

C-202 Hai Ying-4 (HY-4/CSS-C-2 Silkworm): Air-launched, carried two per B-6D (Badger) bomber. Turbojet engine, radar-homing.

Length: 7.36 m **Wingspan:** 2.41 m **Weight:** 2,000 kg
Speed: Mach 0.85 **Range:** 135 km **Altitude:** 70–200 m

C-301 (CSS-C-6 Sawhorse): Coast-defense and land-attack weapon with two ramjet sustainer engines, in development since 1996. To have 512-kg high-explosive, armor-piercing warhead. Employing inertial guidance with GPS course correction, the weapon will be powered by two ramjet sustainer engines and four solid-fuel boosters.

Length: 9.85 m **Diameter:** 0.76 m **Wingspan:** 1.20 m
Weight: 3,400 kg **Speed:** Mach 2.0 **Range:** 180 km
Altitude: 100–300 m cruise (terminal altitude of 7 to 50 m)

C-601 (CSA-1 Kraken): Air-launched, rocket-powered weapon with 510-kg warhead. Derived from Russian P-15 Termit.

Length: 7.38 m **Diameter:** 0.76 m **Weight:** 2,440 kg
Speed: Mach 0.9 **Range:** 25–100 km **Altitude:** 30–100 m

C-602: Canister launched long-range antiship missile, resembles the American Tomahawk cruise missile. For shipboard or coastal use. Unveiled 9-05. A possible high-altitude land attack mode may allow for longer ranges

Range: 50-280km **Speed:** Mach 0.7
Altitude: 30 m (target approach 8–10 m) **Warhead:** 300kg

C-611: Air-launched, turbojet variant of C-601 with same warhead and speed, 220-km range.

C-701: Developmental television-guided antiship missile for aircraft, helicopter, or surface-ship launch. For shipboard launch, employs four-unit, square-section canister launchers. Rocket-propelled. Offered for export by China National Precision Machinery Import and Export Corporation (CPMIEC).

Length: 2.507 m **Diameter:** 0.18 m **Wingspan:** . . . m **Weight:** 100 kg
Warhead: approx 30 kg **Speed:** Mach 0.8 **Range:** 15 km (air-launched)

C-801 Ying Ji-1 (YJ-1 "Hawk Attack"/CSS-N-4 Sardine): Wholly Chinese weapon, using a box launcher similar to that of Exocet MM 38. Land-based version is Fei Long-7. Air-launched and submerged-launch versions are Ying Ji-6 and Ying Ji-8 Mod. 3, respectively. Propelled by solid rocket, with two solid boosters. Has 165-kg high-explosive, armor-piercing warhead. Offered for export by China Precision Machinery Import & Export Corporation. C-801A version has folding wings and can fit in the same tube as that used by the C-802 turbojet-powered version.

Length: 5.814 m **Diameter:** 0.36 m **Wingspan:** 1.18 m **Weight:** 815 kg
Speed: Mach 0.9 **Range:** 45 km **Altitude:** 255 m

C-802 Ying Ji-2 (YJ-2/YJ-82/CSS-N-8 Saccade): French Microturbo turbojet-powered version of YJ-1/C-801. Has high-explosive, armor-piercing warhead. Has been exported to Iran. Also available in land-based coast-defense version. Employs active radar and incorporates ECCM features. Said to be based very closely on the French Exocet missile system.

Length: 6.392 m over booster (5.160 without) **Diameter:** 0.36 m
Wingspan: 1.18 m **Weight:** 715 kg (530 kg without booster)
Warhead: 165 kg **Speed:** Mach 0.9 **Range:** 15–120 km
Altitude: 20–30 m cruise, 5–7 terminal homing

C-803 Ying Ji-83 (YJ-83/CSS-N-9 . . .): In development by 2001, with several test launches in 2002 and an aircraft test-launch early in 2003. Said to have a range of 250 km when launched at altitude. Also intended for use from surface ships.

Fei Long-1 (FL-1/CSS-N-2 Safflower): Said to have entered service 1980 aboard Luda-class destroyers and various frigate classes, but there is considerable confusion as to whether it even exists. Rocket powered. Has 513-kg high-explosive, shaped-charge warhead. Radar- and infrared-homing versions said to be available.

Length: 6.42 m **Diameter:** 0.54 m **Wingspan:** 2.40 m
Weight: 2,000 kg **Speed:** Mach 0.9 **Altitude:** 30–100 m (8–15 m terminal)

Fei Long-2 (FL-2): Said to have entered service 1993 as a shipboard weapon. Liquid-fueled, rocket-powered, with 365-kg armor-piercing, high-explosive warhead. Radar homing. Some confusion exists on this missile, which has also been reported as the "Fei Long-7," weighing 1,800 kg and having a speed of Mach 1.4 and a cruise altitude of 50–100 m.

Length: 6.00 m **Diameter:** 0.54 m **Wingspan:** 1.705 m
Weight: 1,550 kg **Speed:** Mach 0.9 **Altitude:** 30–100 m (8–15 terminal)

Shui Ying-1 ("Sea Eagle-1"/CSS-N-1): A direct copy of the Soviet P-15 Termit (SS-N-2A Styx). Radar homing, with 400-kg high-explosive warhead. Rocket propelled.

Length: 5.80 m **Weight:** 2,300 kg **Range:** 40 km
Wingspan: 2.41 m **Speed:** Mach 0.85 **Altitude:** 100–300 m

Ying Ji-6 (YJ-6): Air-launched version of Ying Ji-1 (C-801). Identical in most respects to Ying Ji-1 except for range of 50 km when launched at altitude.

Ying Ji-8 Mod. 3 (YJ-8): Said to be a version of Ying Ji-1 (C-801) adapted for submerged launch from the torpedo tubes of the Song-class submarines. It may instead be a variant of the Ying Ji-2 (C-802) turbojet-powered version of the Ying Ji-1.

Note: Forty-eight Russian 3M-80 Moskit (NATO SS-N-22 Sunburn) supersonic, sea-skimming missiles were ordered in 7-98 for use with Russian-built *Sovremennyy*-class guided-missile destroyers. Deliveries began in 5-00.

♦ Surface-to-Air Missiles

Hong Qian-2J (HQ-2J): Two-stage coast-defense SAM. Range: 34 km.

Hong Qian-7 (HQ-7): Chinese name for an unauthorized copy of the French Crotale Modulaire short-range shipboard SAM system. HQ-7 is aboard Luhu-class destroyer 113, Luhai-class destroyer 167, and the Jiangwei-II-class frigates. Imported Crotale Modulaire systems are aboard Luda-class destroyer 109 and Luhu-class destroyer 112.

Hong Qian-9 (HQ-9): A naval variant of the land-based Chinese version of the Russian SA-10 (also known as S-300) missile system. Offered for export as the FT-2000. Has an approximate horizontal range of 100 km and altitude of 20 km. Said to employ a "cold launch" system, with the missile being ejected from the launcher prior to low-altitude rocket ignition.

Hong Qian-61 (HQ-61/CSA-N-1): Short-range SAM system that began development in the 1960s but was used only on the four frigates of the Jiangwei-I class. Cumbersome launcher with six cells for missiles with nonfolding fins; there are no reloads. Data below are from a Chinese source:

Length: 3.99 m **Diameter:** 0.286 m **Wingspan:** 1.66 m
Propulsion: Single-stage, solid-fuel rocket **Speed:** Mach 3.0
Range: 10 km max./3 km min. **Altitude:** 8 km
Guidance: Command, using radar tracker/illuminator, semiactive homing

FN-6: Shoulder-launched weapon introduced summer 2000 by China National Precision Machinery Import and Export Corporation. Can attack targets traveling up to 360 m/sec and is claimed to have a 70% kill probability.

Length: 1.495 m **Diameter:** 72 mm **Weight:** 16 kg with launcher
Range: 5 km max./0.5 km min. **Altitude:** 3,500 m max./15 m min.

Hong Nu 5 (HN-5): Land-based derivative of Soviet SA-7 **Weight:** 16 kg; range: 4 km.

Hong Nu 5A (HN-5A): Heat-seeking weapons offered with the Type 90 close-in defense system. Navy version of land-use PL-9.

Length: 2.90 m **Diameter:** 157 mm **Wingspan:** 856 mm
Weight: 115 kg **Warhead:** 35 kg **Speed:** Mach 2.1 kg
Range: 10 km max./1 km min. **Altitude:** 4,500 m max./50 m min.

KS-1: Medium-range coast-defense SAM with similar guidance to HQ-61/HQ-7.

Length: 5.6 m **Diameter:** 0.4 m **Speed:** 1,200 m/sec.
Range: 42 km max./7 km min. **Altitude:** 25 km max. (0.5 km min.)

LY-60N: Revealed 1995 as a point-defense system with a missile based closely on the Alenia Aspide. Range is 10 km against targets 30–12,000 m in altitude. Sold to Pakistan for use on three Type 21 frigates but not used by the PLAN.

QW-1 Vanguard: Shoulder-launched, two-stage weapon entering service in 1994 as successor to HN-5 series (which was a copy of the Russian SA-7 Grail), but with improved performance and a supercooled infrared seeker. Resembles Russian SA-18. Manned twin-round and eight-round naval launchers are offered, as is a variant of the Type 76 twin 37-mm AA mount with two missiles. Made by China National Precision Machinery Import and Export Corporation (CPMIEC).

Length: 1.532 m **Diameter:** . . . **Weight:** 16.5 kg **Warhead:** . . . kg
Range: 0.5 to 5.0 km **Altitude:** 30–4,000 m

Note: The Russian 9M-38M1 Smerch (NATO SA-N-7 Gadfly) surface-to-air is installed aboard the Russian-built *Sovremennyy*-class guided missile destroyers.

♦ Air-to-Air Missiles

PL-2: Warhead: 11 kg; range: 8 km; infrared-homing.

PL-5: Speed: Mach 4.5; range: 16 km; infrared-homing.

PL-7: Warhead: 12 kg; range: 14 km; infrared-homing.

PL-9: Weight: 120 kg; range: 16 km; infrared-homing. Speed: Mach 3.5

Note: Israeli-manufactured Python heat-seeking missiles arm PLAN F-8 interceptors. (Chinese designation is PL-8.)

B. SHIPBOARD CONVENTIONAL WEAPONS

♦ Guns

Note: The Russian twin AK-130 130-mm dual-purpose gun and AK-630 30-mm gatling guns are carried by *Sovremennyy*-class guided missile destroyers.

WEAPONS AND SENSORS *(continued)*

130-mm 58-cal. DP: Chinese version of the twin mounting used on the now discarded Kotlin-class destroyers of the Soviet Navy, but without cross-level stabilization.

Muzzle velocity: 900 m/sec. **Rate of fire:** 65 rds/min/mount
Arc of elevation: –15° to +85° **Range:** 28,000 m surface

100-mm 56-cal. DP single and twin: The standard single and twin 100-mm mounts used on Chinese ships employ the gun developed in the 1930s for the Soviet Navy. The single mounts are a direct copy of the Soviet BU-34. The twin ENG-2 mountings are manned and have loading from below decks. Both versions can be locally controlled.

Shell Weight: 13.5 kg **Muzzle velocity:** 850 m/sec.
Rate of fire: 15 rds/min/barrel **Arc of elevation:** –5° to +40°
Range: 16,000 m (10,000 m effective)

100-mm 55-cal. DP twin: For the Luhai- and Luhu-class destroyers and Jiangwei-II-class frigates, a new twin 100-mm automatic gunmount has been designed, probably employing operating concepts copied from one of the two French Creusot-Loire 100-mm Compact mounts purchased in the late 1980s. Estimated performance characteristics are:

Muzzle velocity: 870 m/sec. **Rate of fire:** 20, 45, or 90 rds/min/barrel
Arc of elevation: –15° to +80°
Range: 17,200 (12,000 max. effective; 6,000 m AA)

57-mm twin DP: Two types of twin, open, manned 57-mm 62-cal. mount are used: Type 66 and Type 76, the latter with fan-type ready-service feed. Neither is apparently considered very satisfactory.

37-mm Type 76A: Enclosed, automatic mount closely resembling the Italian OTO Melara Dardo mounting, from which it is said to have been copied. Has 1,600 rounds ready-service on mount. Carried by Luda-III- and Luhu-class destroyers, Jiangwei- and Jianghu-V-class frigates, and some recent missile boats. Offered for export as the Type H/PJ76A system. When sighted in 2-01, Yuting-class LST 909 displayed a variant of the mount adapted to accept an on-mount operator. Data for the gun include:

Muzzle velocity: 1,000 m/sec. **Rate-of-fire:** 760 rds/min./barrel
Range: 3,500 m effective/9,400 max.

37-mm Type 74 and Type 76: Type 74 twin 37-mm 63-cal. mounting, a copy of the Soviet V-11M manned mount with manual cross-level stabilization. Type 76 uses the same guns but substitutes auto-loading from trays and retains personnel on-mount for elevation and training. On at least one Jianghu, two point-defense SAM launchers are fitted to each mount. Type 76, in conjunction with two PL-8H point-defense SAMS, has been offered for export as the Type 715-I system. The basic Type 76 is mounted on most Jianghu-series frigates and on Yuting-class landing ships. Type 76 characteristics include:

Rate-of-fire: 360–380 rd/min/barrel
Range: 9,400 m max. **Altitude:** 7,200 m

30-mm Type 730: A CIWS under development that employs a multibarrel gatling gun and comounted search and tracking radars. Strongly resembles the Thales Goalkeeper in concept although there are numerous differences in detail.

30-mm Type . . . : A copy of the Russian six-barreled 30-mm AK-630MI gatling gun mounting that completed development in 1995 in cooperation with Russia's Tulamach Zavod. Said to use a Chinese-developed fire-control system 100% more accurate than the MR-123 Vympel (Bass Tilt) radar system used on Russian ships. The associated search radar set is designated SR-47B and the tracking radar TR-47, and there is an OFD-630 optronic backup director. Normally, the gunmounts are to be installed in pairs.

30-mm Type 69 twin: A copy of the Russian 30-mm 65-cal. AK-230.

25-mm Type 61: A copy of the standard Russian twin 25-mm 80-cal. 2M-3M mounting; no longer being manufactured, but many are still in use, and others have been recycled for further use aboard auxiliaries.

14.5-mm Type 81: A twin, side-by side 14.5-mm 79-cal. mounting developed in China and exported aboard small combatants as well as being employed domestically.

♦ Torpedoes

In addition to imported Italian WASS A-244 lightweight antisubmarine torpedoes and 15 TEST-71EM-NK and 53-65KE wake-homing Russian torpedoes (for use with the Kilo-class submarines), China has developed and put into production the following domestic designs:

Yu-1: 533-mm straight-running air-steam weapon that entered production in 1971.

Yu-2: A copy of the Russian 1950s-era RAT-52 rocket-propelled antisubmarine torpedo. Entered service in 1971.

Yu-3: 533-mm electric-powered acoustic homing torpedo for submarines entering service in 1984.

Yu-4A/4B: 533-mm submarine-launched antiship weapons; Yu-4A employs passive acoustic homing and was developed by the Dong Fen Factory, while Yu-4B, developed by Xi Bei University is passive/active. Both versions are said to be in production.

Current-production torpedoes also offered for export include:

ET-32: Heavyweight acoustic homing torpedo. Available in active and passive-only versions and also in active/passive variant. Has both impact and proximity fuzes. Exercise variant weights 1,203 kg. Employs silver-zinc batteries.

Diameter: 533 mm **Length:** 6.60 m **Weight:** 1,340 kg
Warhead: 190 kg HE **Speed:** 35 kts **Range:** 13 km
Depth: 6–250 m operating (up to 150 m launch depth)

ET-34: Wire-guided, electrically powered torpedo. Employs a combination of wire guidance and active or passive acoustic homing, with 5-m range proximity fuze. Powered by a zinc-silver battery driving two coaxial propellers. Exercise version has a range of 9–10 km at high speed.

Diameter: 533 mm **Length:** 6.60 m **Weight:** . . . kg
Warhead: . . . kg **Speed:** 25 or 36 kts
Range: 25 km at 25 kts, 15–16 km at 36 kts
Depth: 5–250 m

ET-36: Wire-guided, electrically powered torpedo. Employs a combination of wire guidance and active or passive homing, with a 5-m range proximity fuze. Exercise version has a range of 8 km at 40–42 kts.

Diameter: 533 mm **Length:** 6.60 m **Weight:** . . . kg
Warhead: . . . kg **Speed:** 28 or 40 to 42 kts
Range: 30 km at 28 kts, 18–20 km at 40–42 kts
Depth: 5–300 m

ET-52: Lightweight ASW torpedo for aircraft and surface launch. Probable copy of either the U.S. Mk 46 or Italian A-244.

Diameter: 324 mm **Length:** 2.60 m **Weight:** 235 kg
Warhead: 45 kg **Speed:** 42 kts **Range:** 10 km
Depth: 6 to 400 m

VA-111 Shkval: High-speed torpedoes were ordered from Kazakhstan in mid-1998, but they were reportedly delivered without a fire-control system and were not put to use.

♦ ASW Rockets

The five-tubed ASW rocket launcher used on most Chinese ASW-capable ships is referred to as the EDS-32 or Type 81; although the launcher outwardly resembles that of the Russian RBU-1200, the weapon has over twice the range (3,200 m maximum/55 m minimum) using the Type 62 rocket. The larger EDS-25A (Type 75), 12-tubed ASW rocket launcher on Luda-class destroyers fires the Type 81 rocket to 2,500-m maximum ranges. The Type 87 rocket launcher is an improved version of the Type 81 using a two-stage rocket to reach ranges of up to 5,000 m. Also used are copies of the Soviet BMB-1 and BMB-2 depth charge mortars.

Note: The "CY-1" antisubmarine missile, purported to be launched from the Luda-class destroyers is likely a journalistic creation. Russian RBU-1000 rocket launchers, primarily for defense against homing torpedoes but also employable against submarines, will be carried on Russian-built *Sovremennyy*-class guided-missile destroyers.

♦ Artillery Rockets

A new 122-mm, 40-tubed artillery rocket launcher has been tested; the rockets weigh 66.6 kg, and the warhead weight is 18.4 kg. Three of the launchers, carried by especially configured trucks, were carried aboard a merchant cargo ship to provide shore bombardment during a March 1996 naval demonstration opposite Taiwan, but the weapon has not since been publicized and doesn't appear to be on any PLAN ships.

♦ Mines

Older Chinese-designed mines reported in service include the L-1, -2, and -3 large, medium, and antenna-equipped moored mines; L-4 moored acoustic mine; L-4A and -4B with solid-state circuitry, which entered service in 1980 and 1985, respectively; C-1 acoustic bottom mine; C-2 solid-state electronics acoustic bottom mine; C-3 countermine-countermeasures mine for use in waters 6 to 100 m deep; C-4 lightweight, man-portable mine; C-5 man- or mule-portable pressure mine for riverine use; T-1 (or PRAM) rocket-propelled rising mine, which entered service in 1987; and T-2-1 remote-controlled mine. Current-production mines offered for export include the following:

EM-11: Multipurpose bottom mine, which comes in Type 500 and Type 1000 variants, deployable by aircraft or submarine. The Type 500 can be laid at 80-m minimum spacing and the Type 1000 at 50 m. Fuze type not specified, but probably includes combinations of acoustic, magnetic, and pressure. Target counter up to 20 targets. Some versions may be deployed in water up to 100 m deep. Data for Type 500 (Type 1000):

Length: 2.79 m (3.35 m) aircraft/1.98 (2.90) submarine
Diameter: 450 m (533) m **Weight:** 500 kg (1,000 kg)
Warhead: 300 kg (700 kg) **Depth:** 5–30 m (5–50 m)
Service life in water: 1 year

EM-12: Bottom mine, with any combination of acoustic, magnetic, and pressure fuzes; deployed via aircraft, surface ships, and submarines. Can be fitted with any combination of acoustic, magnetic, and pressure fuzes.

Length: 1.5 or 2.6 m **Diameter:** 533 mm **Weight:** 570 or 950 kg
Warhead: 320 or 700 kg **Depth:** 5–200 m
Service life in water: 2 years

An exercise version, which can be laid at depths up to 50 m, is also available; it weighs either 570 kg or 950 kg, depending on length (1.86 m or 2.96 m) employed.

EM-52: Rocket-propelled mine, which, when laid at its maximum depth, can deliver its warhead to an area of 3,400 m^3. Equipped with a 1- to 99-target counter.

Length: 3.70 m **Diameter:** 450 mm **Weight:** 620 kg
Warhead: 140 kg RS 211 **Range:** . . . km
Depth: 110 m max. **Service life in water:** 1 year

EM-55: Rocket-propelled rising anchored mine. Produced in 533-mm version for laying by submarines and 450-mm version for surface ship employment. Fuzing is magnetic, active or passive acoustic, or combinations thereof. Can be set to activate up to 480 hours after laying and to self-destruct up to 8,640 hours later.

Length: 3.54 m or 3.35 m **Weight:** 840 kg or 620 kg
Warhead: 130 kg **Depth:** 50–200 m
Service life in water: 1 year

EM-56: Self-propelled mine, submarine laid, has a combination LF acoustic and pressure fuze:

Length: 7.738 m **Diameter:** 533.4 mm **Weight:** 1,840 kg
Warhead: 380 kg TNT **Range:** 13 km+
Depth: 45 m max. **Service life in water:** 9 months

EM-57: Remote-controlled mine, for control by submarines, in two variants, Type 500 and Type 1000. Usable against surface ships and submarines, it employs either an acoustic/magnetic or magnetic-induction fuze and can be activated by the controlling submarine at ranges of up to 30 km. Data for Type 500 (Type 1000):

WEAPONS AND SENSORS *(continued)*

Length: 2.140 m (3.140 m) **Diameter:** 450 mm (533 mm)
Weight: 510 kg (1,010 kg) **Warhead:** 300 kg (700 kg) TNT
Depth: 6–100 m **Service life in water:** 6 months

EM-71: Multipurpose exercise ground mine, comes in three variants (Type 1000U, Type 500A, and Type 500S), and can be laid by aircraft, surface ships, or submarines. Can be equipped with LF acoustic/magnetic, magnetic alone, or magnetic/pressure fuze.

Length: 3.0, 2.865, or 1.52 m **Weight:** 700, 500, or . . . kg.

C. ELECTRONIC SYSTEMS

Chinese radars, formerly either made in the USSR or copied from Russian models, are increasingly of Chinese design and manufacture. French Thales (formerly Thomson-CSF) radars are used on the largest surface combatants, while British-made Litton-Decca RM 1290A/D ARPA navigational radars are widely employed on major combatants as navigational and surface-search sets. Japanese electronics systems, including Oki and Anritsu navigational radars, are also widely used. The major radar sets currently in use include:

Name:	*Origin:*	*Band:*	*Function:*
Ball End	USSR	E/F	Surface search (obsolescent)
Bean Sticks	China	S	Long-range air early warning, with 16 yagi antenna arrays
ESR-1	China	X?	Low-flier detection
Fin Curve	U.K.	I	Nav. (Decca 707 copy)
Fog Lamp	China	I	100-mm gun f.c. on Luda, Luhai classes; Chinese EFR-1
Hai Ying	France?	S	Long-range air search (God Eye)
LR-66	China	I	"Short-range Anti-Missile Radar System"
Pea Sticks	China	S	Long-range air early warning; 16 yagi transmitter arrays
Rice Field	China	G	3-D phased-array air search (Chinese "Sea Eagle")—in two versions
Skin Head	USSR	I	Surface search; few, if any, left
Type 341	China	I	Gun control (Rice Lamp)
Type 343	USSR	I	Gun f.c. (Sun Visor-B)
Type 347G	China	I	Gun f.c.
Type 351	USSR	X	Copy of Russian Reya (Pot Head)
Type 352/352C	USSR	. . .	Target detection and tracking (Square Tie)
Type 354	China	E/F	Surface search (Eye Shield)
Type 360	China	E/F	Successor to Eye Shield; also target desig. Made by Nanjing Marine Radar Institute, which calls it the Type 2405; has mechanically stabilized antenna
Type 30N6E?	China	I/J	AEGIS style phased radar (Tombstone), Developed by the Nanjing Research Institute of Electronic Technology
Type 363	China	S	Early warning, yagi array
Type 702	China	X	Gun f.c.
Type 726	Japan	X	Imported Anritsu sets, used on patrol craft
Type 756	China	S	Nav. (copy of Decca 1226 or 1229 set)
Type 765	China	E/F	Missile targeting on Houjian class; may be a variant of the Type 360

IFF systems have only come into general use since the early 1980s. Chinese sonars are of Soviet design derivation, with an active program under way to acquire modern Western systems. The BM/HZ-8610 intercept system is employed on some larger warships; covering 2–18GHz, it has 5-MHz frequency accuracy and 2.5° bearing accuracy. Also employed is the GT-1 chaff dispensing system, while U.S.-designed Mk 137 decoy rocket launchers (as used with the Mk 36 SRBOC system) are offered for use on export warships. Two Great Wall communications satellites were launched during 1984–85, but there is no indication that they are used by the PLAN, other than possibly by the new Luhu- and Luhai-class destroyers, which appear to have satellite communications antenna radomes, although the radomes may instead cover steerable jammer arrays.

CLASS NAMES AND PENNANTS

The class names used below are generally those assigned by Western intelligence services; the Chinese Navy uses a project number system for which few of the designations are known, and there is also an export project number system employed in foreign sales efforts. The Western nicknames are a mix of geographic, dynastic, and animal names, while others are mere nonsense words.

For combatants, three-digit hull numbers are assigned. Small combatants have a four-digit pennant number, the first number of which signifies area subordination. Until recently, auxiliaries had three-digit numbers preceded by a letter signifying function, but that system has now been superceded by one employing two or more Chinese ideographs describing the ship's fleet (first character: *Bei* for North Sea Fleet, *Dong* for East Sea Fleet, and *Nan* for South Sea Fleet) and function. In addition, the numerous ships subordinated to the various districts of the Maritime Border Defense Force have four-digit pennants preceded by a letter signifying the district; known prefixes include "S" for Shenyang, "N" for Nanjing (commonly seen in the Shanghai area), and "G" for Guangzhou.

Note: The Hudong and Zhonghua Shipyards at Shanghai were merged early in 2001 and now trade as the Hudong Zhonghua Shipbuilding Group.

AIRCRAFT CARRIERS [CV]

Note: Although rumors were rampant during mid-1992 that China was arranging to purchase the incomplete Russian Navy carrier *Varyag,* both China and Russia officially denied that the sale was to take place. The ship was finally purchased by a Chinese entrepreneur as an exhibit, but attempts to tow it to China in 6-00 were thwarted for over a year by Turkish refusal to permit the vessel to pass through the Bosphorus. The ship finally arrived in China during 2002 after a 627-day tow through the Mediterranean and around South Africa.

As of mid-2005, there is no indication that any carrier is under construction by or for China, however reports continue to surface that Chinese shipyard workers have been working on the derelict ex-Russian aircraft carrier *Varyag,* some argue with the intent to turn her into an operational asset of the Chinese fleet. Still others argue that no work has taken place aboard the ex-*Varyag* and that, if anything, the dilapidated carrier will be used for scrap or perhaps turned into an amusement park attraction.

NUCLEAR-POWERED BALLISTIC-MISSILE SUBMARINES [SSBN]

♦ 0 (+ 4) Jin class (Project 094)

Bldr: Huludao SY

	Laid down	L	In serv.
. . .	11-99	28-7-04	2008

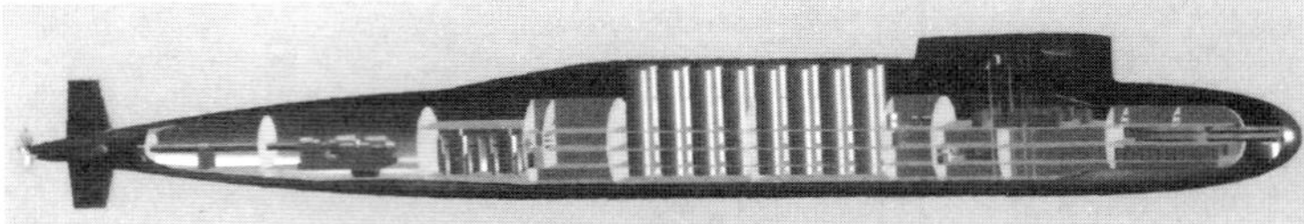

Project 094 SSBN—artist's speculation U.S. Navy, 1997

D: 8,000 tons surf/9,000 tons sub. **S:** . . . **Dim:** 125 × 11.0 × . . .
A: 16 Ju Lang-2; 6 533-mn TT
M: 2 . . . MW pressurized-water nuclear reactors, two steam turbines; 1 prop

Remarks: Construction of at least four nuclear-powered ballistic missile submarines of the Project 094 design reportedly commenced in 11-99 and sources indicate that by May 2004 the first unit was at Huludao in the early stages of fitting out. Due to ongoing nuclear reactor difficulties, the desire to successfully test fire the Ju Lang-2 (JL-2) SLBM and the need for lengthy sea trials required of a new class, she may not reach operational status until 2010. The class is expected to carry 16 of the 8,000-m JL-2 missiles, each of which carries a 400-kT warhead. Will reportedly receive Russian passive towed-array sonar equipment and a new Russian torpedo fire-control system. Ships are a dramatic improvement over the *Xia*-class (Project 092) with improved quieting and sensor systems and an improved propulsion system.

♦ 1 Xia class (Project 092)

Bldr: Huludao SY

	Laid down	L	In serv.
406	1971	30-4-81	10-88

Xia-class 406 *Ships of the World,* ca. 1988–89

D: 7,000 tons (sub.) **S:** 22 kts sub. **Dim:** 120.0 × 10.6 × 8.0
A: 12 Ju Lang-1 (CSS-N-3) strategic missiles; 6 bow 533-mm TT
Electronics:
Radar: 1 Snoop Tray surface search
Sonar: 1 Trout Creek bow-mounted, medium frequency active/passive search and attack; 1 French DUUX-5 low frequency passive ranging and intercept.
EW: Type 921-A radar warning receiver and direction finder
M: 1 58 megawatt pressurized-water nuclear reactor, two steam turbines; 1 prop; 14,400 shp
Endurance: 90 days **Crew:** 100 tot.

Remarks: The *Xia*-class submarine was launched from the same facility that builds the *Han*-class nuclear-powered attack submarine, 200 km northeast of Beijing in Liaoning province. The design is essentially that of the *Han,* lengthened to accommodate the missile tubes. At least two additional units were expected, but construction of further units was canceled around 1985 in favor of developing an all-new, larger design with longer-range missiles. The single *Xia* was based near Qingdao at a base equipped with a 12-story-high underground maintenance cavern. Underwent refit at Huladao Shipyard from 1995 through 2001 that included improving sensors and replacing the original JL-1 SLBM with the longer ranged JL-1A missile. This submarine has never sailed beyond Chinese home waters. Will probably be used for trials with the Ju Lang-2 missile. This submarine is expected to remain in service until at least 2011 and is currently attached to the 9th Submarine Fleet.
Hull systems: Pressure hull plating thickness is 40 mm. Maximum operating depth is 300 m. On-board machinery noise is said to be uncomfortably high.
Combat systems: The first Ju Lang-1 submerged launch took place from the Golf-class trials submarine on 12-10-82 to a range of 1,600 km. The missile is believed to have two solid-propulsion stages and to have a range of 1,700 km. The first *Xia* missile launch took place 7-88, and no further launches have been announced. EW suite may incorporate Thomson-CSF DR-2000U intercept set. Navigational aids include an inertial navigations system, stellar sight, receiver for U.S. Navstar navigational satellite data, and Omega receiver.

NUCLEAR-POWERED ATTACK SUBMARINES [SSN]

♦ 2 (+ 4–6) Chin class (Project 093)

Bldr: Huludao SY (In serv. 2006–21)

	Laid down	L	In serv.
. . .	1998	24-12-02	2006
. . .	. . .	Late-2003	2007
. . .	. . .	. . .	2011?
. . .	. . .	. . .	2014?
. . .	. . .	. . .	2017?

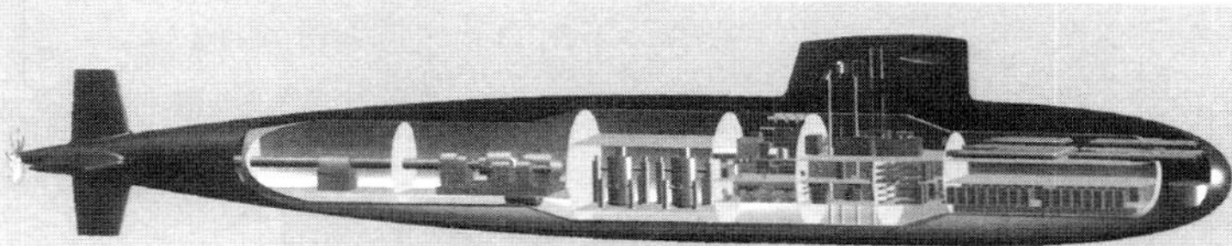

Project 093 SSN—artist's speculation U.S. Navy, 1997

D: 6,000 tons sub. **S:** 30 kts sub. **Dim:** 107.0 × 11.0 × 7.5
A: 6 533-mm TT fwd (. . . torpedoes, mines, antiship missiles)
M: 1 pressurized water reactor; geared electric drive; 1 prop; 20,000 shp
Crew: 100 tot.

Remarks: Similar in performance and design to the Russian *Victor-III*-class SSN's, this class is being built as replacements for the *Han* class. The first two units have reliably been reported to having been launched and currently undergoing sea trials. Initially it was reported that China had encountered a range of technical difficulties in developing this class, especially in the nuclear radiation and noise reduction areas, but Russian technical assistance appears to have helped solved these problems by 2000. Four to six of this type are expected to eventually enter service.
Hull systems: Double hull design. Anechoic tiles have been applied to each hull.
Combat systems: The Project 093 was said to be intended to launch antiship missiles as well as torpedoes from its torpedo tubes, with the cruise missile probably being a follow-on to the current C-801 and capable of being submerged-launched. All data above are speculative.

♦ 5 Han class (Project 091) (2 nonoperational in *reserve*)

Bldr: Huludao SY

	Laid down	L	In serv.
401 Chang Zheng-1	1967	26-12-70	1-8-74
402 Chang Zheng-2	1974	1977	1-80
403 Chang Zheng-3	1980	1983	21-9-84
404 Chang Zheng-4	1984	1987	12-88
405 Chang Zheng-5	1987	8-4-90	12-91

D: 4,500 tons sub. (403–405: 5,550 tons sub.) **S:** 25 kts sub. (12 surfaced)
Dim: 98.8 (403–405: 106.8) × 10.6 × 7.4
A: 6 bow 533-mm TT (18 SET-65E active/passive homing and Type 53-51 torpedoes or 36 mines carried; 403–405: Ying Ji-8 Mod. 3 (C-801) antiship missiles, Yu-3 ASW and Yu-4 antiship torpedoes)
Electronics:
Radar: 1 Snoop Tray nav.—EW: CEIEC Model 921-A intercept
Sonar: Trout Cheek active; Thomson-Marconi DUUX-5 passive hull array
M: 1 48-MW pressurized-water nuclear reactor, two steam turbines; 1 prop; 12,000 shp
Endurance: 60 days **Crew:** 75 tot.

Han-class 404—long-hulled variant U.S. Navy, 2-96

Han-class 402—short-hulled variant *Ships of the World,* 1990

Remarks: Sea trials for the first unit were protracted, and the two earliest units proved unreliable, being referred to by the Chinese Navy—at least initially—as "sharks without teeth." Technical problems include high internal radiation levels and an inability to fire missiles while submerged. One Western visitor referred to the *Han* as a "Whiskey with a reactor" in terms of the level of technology employed. The first two were refitted during the late 1980s to the mid-1990s but have apparently been nonoperational since 2000; refits of 403 and 404 were completed by 2000 and both units have returned to service. 405 completed refit during 2002. Names mean "Long March"–1 through 5. All assigned to the North Sea Fleet and based near Qingdao, but one active unit has been deployed to the South Sea Fleet and is based at a newly built sub base on Hainan Island. Recent reports indicate that 405 may no longer be operational.
Hull systems: Pressure hull plating thickness is 40 mm. Maximum operating depth is 300 m.
Combat systems: EW suite may incorporate the Thales DR-2000U intercept set. Reported to carry both straight-running and wire-guided torpedoes. Units 403 through 405 received inertial guidance systems during construction, which have been backfitted to the earlier pair. The Model 921-A EW system is said to be a copy of the Israeli Timnex 4CH(V)2 intercept system. Contrary to some reports, the longer units do not carry cruise missiles in tubes abaft the sail.

ATTACK SUBMARINES [SS]

♦ 2 (+ . . .) Yuan-class (Project 041)

Bldr: Wuhan Shipbuilding Industry Co., Wuhan, China

	Laid down	L	In serv.
330 . . .	. . .	31-5-04	2005
. . .	. . .	12-04	2006

D: 2,400 tons surf./3,000 tons sub. **S:** 23 kts. sub. (16 surfaces)
Dim: 72.0 × 8.4 × . . .
A: 6 bow 533-mm TT (approx. 18 Yu-3 ASW, Yu-4 antiship torpedoes carried and Ying Ji 83 antiship missiles); approx. 36 approx. mines in lieu of torpedoes)
Electronics:
Radar: 1 . . . surf.-search/nav.
Sonar: 1 . . . passive bow array; 1 . . . flank array
EW: . . . intercept
M: Diesel electric: 4 Shaanxi diesels, 2 generator sets; 1/7-bladed prop; 6,092 shp
Range: . . . / . . . **Crew:** 58

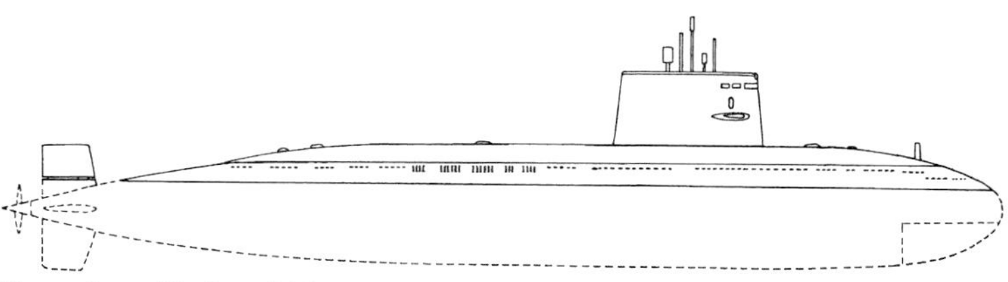

Yuan class (Project 041) *Ships of the World,* 2005

Yuan class (Project 041) *Ships of the World,* 2005

Remarks: Though the sail structure bears a strong resemblance to the older Song-class, the Yuan-class appears to have been heavily influenced by the Russian Kilo design, and is likely comparable in terms of technology and performance. Also referred to as the project 039A.
Hull systems: Double Hull Design with a diving depth of approx. 300m. Powerplant may be the same or similar to the MTU 16V396 SE 83/84 diesels carried in the Song class. Project 041 submarines may be fitted with an Air-Independent Propulsion system.

♦ 14 Song class (Project 039)

Bldr: Wuhan Shipbuilding Industry Co.., Wuhan, China; Jiangnan Shipyard, Shanghai, China (Yuan Zheng 14, 15, 16–19)

	L	In serv.
320 Yuan Zheng-20	25-5-94	6-99
321 Yuan Zheng-21	11-11-99	12-01
322 Yuan Zheng-22	28-6-00	12-01
323 Yuan Zheng-23	5-02	7-03
324 Yuan Zheng-24	28-11-02	12-03
325 Yuan Zheng-25	3-12-02	2004
314 Yuan Zheng-14	19-5-03	2004
315 Yuan Zheng-15	29-9-03	2004
316 Yuan Zheng-16	28-8-04	2005
317 Yuan Zheng-17	2-12-04	2005
326 Yuan Zheng-26	7-04	2005
327 Yuan Zheng-27	8-04	2005
328 Yuan Zheng-28	9-04	2006
329 Yuan Zheng-29		

ATTACK SUBMARINES [SS] *(continued)*

D: 1,700 tons surf./2,250 tons sub. **S:** 15 kts surf./22 kts sub.
Dim: 76.60 × 8.40 × 5.25
A: 6 bow 533-mm TT: Ying Ji-8 Mod. 3 (or YJ-82) antiship missiles, Yu-3 ASW and Yu-4 antiship torpedoes, and mines
Electronics:
Radar: 1 . . . nav./surf. search
Sonar: Thales TSM 2233 Eledone passive bow array; Thales TSM 2255 Fenelon or Chinese SQB-2 flank array
EW: CEIEC Model 921-A intercept
M: Diesel electric: 4 MTU 16V396 SE 83/84 diesels, 2 generator sets; 1 7-bladed prop; 6,092 shp
Range: 22/22 sub., 72/3 **Crew:** 10 officers, 50 enlisted

Two Song-class submarines *Ships of the World*

Yuan Zheng-24 (324) *Ships of the World,* 2003

Remarks: All data above are estimates. Initially referred to by Western agencies as the "Wuhan-C," but commonly referred to now as the *Yuan*-class by the Chinese Navy. The first unit is a Project 039, the second through six units as Project 039G and the 7th and later units as Project 039G1. During 11-05, three of the Project 039G1 units were fitting out at Wuhan Shipyard and two units (pennant no. 324 and 325) at Jiangnan Shipyard. The prototype *Song*-class design had serious design technical problems which became evident on sea trials, including unsatisfactory underwater performance and high noise levels. Major reedesign work led to the Project 039G units (with no stepped sail). All are based in the Eastern Fleet.
Hull systems: Diving depth: 300m. The sail on 320 is unusual in form, in that it is stepped, with the bow planes mounted on the lower, forward portion, which also houses a forward-looking hydrophone array. 321 and later boats have a normal, high sail.
Combat systems: A number of small hydrophones are mounted atop the bow. The submarine is capable of submerged-launching the "No. 8 Mod. 3" antiship missile (probably meaning the Ying Ji-8 Mod. 3), believed to be a submerged-launch variant of the C-801 antiship missile. Other reports indicate that the class is armed with the YJ-82 and fitted with an indigenous combat data system, capable of multiple target tracking.

♦ 10 Improved Kilo class (Russian Project 636)

Bldrs: 366–367: United Admiralty Shipyard, St. Petersburg; 368: Krasnoye Sormovo Zavod 199, Nizhniy Novgorod; others: see Remarks

	L	In serv.
366 Yuan Zhang 66 (ex-B-871)	24-4-97	6-1-98
367 Yuan Zhang 67 (ex-B-466)	17-6-98	2-12-98
368 (ex-B- . . .)	4-4-01	20-10-04
. . .	2002	5-05-05
. . .	2002	2005
. . .	2002	18-7-05
. . .	2002	2005
. . .	2003	2006
. . .	27-5-04	2006
. . .	19-8-04	2006

Project 636 Kilo-class 366—in repair at Shanghai, alongside a former U.S. Army repair barge H&L Van Ginderen, 5-00

Project 636 Kilo-class 367—en route China aboard lift-ship Super Servant 3 RAAF, 1-99

D: 2,325 tons (surf.)/4,000 tons (sub.) **S:** 10 kts (surf.)/17 kts (sub.)
Dim: 73.80 × 9.90 × 6.60 max. (6.20 mean hull amidships, surfaced)
A: 6 bow 533-mm TT (18 torpedoes combination of TEST 71 wire-guided active/passive homing or 53-65 wave-homing antisurface torpedoes or 24 mines); 1 shoulder-launched SAM position; 4th and later units: 3M-54E1 Klub-S antiship missiles
Electronics:
Radar: 1 MPK-50E (Snoop Tray) nav./surf. search
Sonar: MGK-400 (Shark Gill) LF active/passive suite; passive hull array; 1 MG-519 (Mouse Roar) active object avoidance; MT-553 sound velocity measurement; MG-512 self-cavitation measurement
EW: MPM-25EM intercept

ATTACK SUBMARINES [SS] *(continued)*

M: 2 Type 4-2AA-42M turbocharged diesel generator sets (1,500 kw each at 700 rpm), 1 electric motor; 1 7-bladed prop; 5,500 shp—1 MT-140 electric low-speed motor (183 shp)—2 MT-168 internal electric creep/maneuvering motors; 2 ducted props; 204 shp (for 3 kts)
Range: 7,500/7 (snorkel); 400/3 (sub.) **Endurance:** 45 days
Crew: 52 tot. (13 officers, 39 enlisted)

Remarks: An across-the-board improvement over the standard Project 877–series *Kilo* that has been offered for foreign sale since 1993. The first two were ordered in 7-94 and the third during 5-00 for around $100 million; begun in 1992 for the Soviet Navy. A contract for an additional eight boats was let on 3-6-02. The contract called for five to be built at Admiraleiskiye Verf, St. Petersburg; two at Amur Dockyard, Komsomol'sk-na-Amur; and one at Nizhniy Novgorod's Karsnoye Sormovo Zavod; the contract contained an option for another three to be built by Semashpredprityatiye, Severodvinsk. But after the contracts were signed, the two Amur Dockyard boats were reassigned to Sevmashpredprityatiye, which had not built a diesel submarine in over four decades. Most, if not all, are based at Xiangshan in the Eastern Fleet.
Hull systems: Offers improved sound quieting over the Project 877 series and a greater degree of automation. The electric propulsion motor is mounted on a flexible raft, and the maximum shaft rpm has been halved to 250 rpm. Maximum snorkeling speed is 8–10 kts. The bow has been reshaped to improve flow, and some auxiliary machinery has been moved aft from the bow compartment to reduce noise interference with the passive bow sonar array. More efficient models of the diesel generator sets have been added. The 7.2-m-diameter pressure hull has been lengthened to 53.0 m to accommodate the rafted main engines, allowing more tankage for additional diesel fuel. Pressure-hull thickness is 24–27 mm, except in some reinforced areas, where it is 30–35 mm thick. There are three 614-mm-diameter access hatches. The outer hull is coated with 0.8-m-square rubber anechoic tiles, attached with glue over special studs. Stern planes, rudder, and the bow planes mounted just forward of the sail are controlled by a Pirit-23 hydraulic system. The two maneuvering propellers are mounted in internal ducts just forward of the stern planes, with the shafts to the motors protruding directly aft through the after pressure bulkhead. Normal operating depth: 240 m; maximum operating depth: 300 m.
Periscope depth is 17.5 m; there are two attack periscopes with 1.5× and 6× magnification. There are two 120-cell Type 446 lead-acid batteries. Height from keel to the top of the 5-m high sail is 14.7 m.
Combat systems: Only the two outer torpedo tubes in the lower row can accommodate TEST-71EM-NK wire-guided torpedoes, while all tubes can launch Types 53-65KE, 53-56B, 53BA, and SET-53ME torpedoes; an automatic reload system permits reloading within two minutes. Torpedoes can be launched down to 240-m depths. Using 12 in the tubes and 12 in the racks, 24 Type AM-1 mines can be carried in lieu of some torpedoes; mines can be laid only to a depth of 50 m. The third unit is reportedly equipped to launch 3M-54E Klub-S supersonic antiship missiles.
The combat system is the digital MVU-110EM, with three computer/processors; five targets can be tracked simultaneously (two automatically). Radio communication gear fitted includes two P-654-MP transmitters, three P-680-1 HF/VHF receivers, 1 P-683-1 LF receiver, 1 P-625 UHF transceiver, and 1 P-608H portable set. The MPM-25EM intercept array incorporates the transponder for the Khrom-K IFF system.

♦ 2 Russian Kilo class (Russian Project 877EKM)
Bldr: Krasnoye Sormovo Zavod 199, Nizhniy Novgorod (In serv. 1995–96)

364 (ex-B-171) 365 (ex-B-177)

D: 2,325 tons surf./3,076 tons sub. **S:** 10 kts surf./17 kts sub.
Dim: 74.30 (70.00 wl) × 10.00 × 6.60
A: 6 bow 533-mm TT (18 torpedoes: Test 71MKE wire-guided active/passive homing or 53-65KE wave-homing antisurface torpedoes or 24 mines); 1 shoulder-launched SAM position (8 9K-32M Strela missiles)
Electronics:
Radar: 1 MRK-50E (Snoop Tray-2) nav./surf. search
Sonar: MGK-400 (Shark Gill) LF active/passive suite; passive hull array; MG-519 (Mouse Roar) HF active classification/mine avoidance
EW: MRP-25ZM (Brick Pulp) intercept; 6701E (Quad Loop) D/F
M: 2 Type 2D-42, 1,825-bhp diesel generator sets (1,825 bhp/1,500 kw each), electric drive: 1 motor; 1 6-bladed prop; 5,900 shp—1 130-shp low-speed motor—2 102-shp emergency propulsion motors
Range: 6,000/7 (surf.); 400/3 (sub.) **Endurance:** 45 days
Crew: 52 total (13 officers, 39 enlisted)

Project 877EKM Kilo-class 364 *Ships of the World,* 2000

Remarks: First unit departed Baltic as deck cargo on heavy lift ship *Sea Tern* in mid-12-94. The second unit was launched 31-3-95 and delivered 5-9-95 at St. Petersburg, then transported to China aboard a heavy-lift ship. Although it was announced during spring 1997 that they were to be refitted at Bol'shoy Kamen Shipyard on the Russian Primoriy Peninsula, the contract was not signed until 2-99; one was inoperable at Shanghai as of 8-98, in need of a new diesel generator set. Based at Xiangshan.
Hull systems: Propulsion plant is suspended raft-mounted for silencing. Hull has 32% reserve buoyancy at 2,350-m^3 surfaced displacement. At rest on the surface, the submarine trims down 0.4 m by the bow. Maximum diving depth is 300 m, normal depth 240 m, and periscope depth 17.5 m. Has anechoic hull coating. Two batteries, each with 120 cells, provide 9,700 kw/hr. Hull has six watertight compartments.
Combat systems: Combat system, designated Murena or MVU-110EM, can conduct two simultaneous attacks while tracking three other targets manually. The SAM launch position is located in after portion of the sail. Weapons carried on standard export version can include TypeTEST-71ME wire-guided, E53-60 and E53-85 wake-homing, and E53-67 acoustic homing torpedoes and the KMD-500, KMD-1000, KMD-II-500, KMD-II-1000, and UMD mines.

♦ 21 Ming class (Project 035)
Bldr: Wuhan SY (In serv. 1975–2003)

342	352	353	354	356	357	358
359	360	361	362	363	305	306
307	308	309	310	311	312	313

Ming class—lengthened Mod-II boat 2002–3

Ming-class 358 China Shipbuilding Trading Co., 1999

Ming-class 352 and 342—with *Romeo* 239 (to right) Stefan Karpinski, 6-02

D: 1,584 tons surf./2,113 tons sub. **S:** 15 kts surf./10 kts snorkel/18 kts sub.
Dim: 76.00 × 7.60 × 5.10
A: 8 533-mm TT (6 fwd, 2 aft; 16 torpedoes or 28 mines)
Electronics:
Radar: 1 Snoop Plate nav./surf. search
Sonar: Herkules active/passive, Feniks passive
EW: CEIEC Model 921-A or Thales DR-2000U intercept
M: diesel-electric: 2 Type 6E390ZC diesels (2,600 bhp each); 2 props; 3,500 shp—2 75-shp creep motors
Range: 8,000/8 (snorkel); 330/4 (sub.) **Endurance:** 60 days
Crew: 9 officers, 46 enlisted

Remarks: First two launched 1975, third in 1982; series construction recommenced around 1988. One of the first three built was lost after a fire. Based on *Romeo* design, but with different propulsion plant and fuller hullform. Numbers 342, 352–354, 356–359, and 362–363 are modified variants sometimes called "*Ming* Mod." Numbers 305–310 began delivery in 5-97 and sometimes known as the "*Ming* Mod-II." The construction program was thought to have terminated in 1996, but series production resumed, apparently running through completion of the final unit in 2003. Older boats are assigned to the Northern Fleet while the newer "*Ming* Mod-II" types have been assigned to the Southern Fleet.
Hull systems: Diving depth: 300 m. The *Ming* Mod-II type is 2.0 m longer than the earlier units. Noise levels have been reduced through the use of anechoic tiles and a redesign of the flooding ports.
Combat systems: There are no reload torpedoes for the two aft tubes. Later units have passive sonar arrays patterned after the French DUUX-5 (Thales TSM 2255 Fenelon) system, with three flank transducers per side mounted in the casing.
Disposals/accidents: On 16-4-03 the Chinese government reported that submarine number 361 suffered a severe "mechanical malfunction" during training activities, killing all 70 aboard. Later reports indicate that the crew died as a result of oxygen depletion caused by an onboard fire. She was later towed back to port. Her future operating status remains in doubt and has thus been removed from the in-service list above.

ATTACK SUBMARINES [SS] *(continued)*

On 26-5-05 another (unidentified) *Ming* boat suffered an onboard fire while operating submerged in the South China Sea. The damaged submarine was towed back to the Yulin Naval port on Hainan Island and her status remains uncertain.

♦ Up to 32 Soviet Romeo class (Project 033)
Bldrs: Wuhan SY, Guangzhou SY, Jiangnan SY, Huludao SY (In serv. 1960–84)

From among:

256–260	268–272	275–280	249–260	286–287
291–304	342–349	355		

D: 1,319 tons surf./1,712 tons sub. **S:** 15.2 kts surf./13 kts sub.
Dim: 76.60 × 6.70 × 4.95
A: 8 533-mm TT (6 fwd/2 aft; 14 torpedoes or 28 mines)
Electronics:
Radar: 1 Snoop Plate nav./surf. search
Sonar: Tamir-5L active; Feniks passive (see Remarks)
EW: CEIEC Model 92-A intercept
M: Diesel-electric: 2 Type 1Z38 diesels, 2,400 bhp each; 2 props; 2,700 shp—2 electric creep motors; 100 shp tot.
Endurance: 60 days **Range:** 14,000/9 surf.; 350/9 sub.
Crew: 8 officers, 43 enlisted

Romeo-class 272 H&L Van Ginderen, 3-95

Romeo-class 355 Stefan Karpinski, 6-02

Remarks: Generally similar to the Soviet version built in the late 1950s, but with numerous changes in equipment and detail. The first to be built entirely with Chinese-produced materials and equipment, named *New China No. 42,* was not completed until 22-6-69. Some 84 were built for the PLAN, plus four each for export to Egypt (1982–83) and North Korea (1973–75). One reserve unit was reported in the Chinese press to have been successfully reactivated during 1994, and one was lost in an accident in 1993–94. During 2001–2, a number of boats were reactivated from reserve, and the class has recently been operated more extensively than in the past.
Disposal note: All Romeos are expected to be withdrawn from service by 2010.
Hull systems: Maximum operating depth: 300 m. 224-cell battery: 6,600 amp-hr.
Combat systems: One unit (probably 250) has one of two Thales DUUX-5 passive sonar suites delivered in 1983, and the export version is offered with that gear plus an enlarged chin sonar dome. Hull 250 is also reported to have the Thales DR-2000U intercept suite.

AUXILIARY SUBMARINES [SSA]

♦ 1 Soviet Golf-class (Project 031) ballistic missile trials submarine
Bldr: Dalian SY

	Laid down	L	In serv.
200	1961	1964	1966

D: 2,500 surf./2,900 tons **S:** 14 kts sub. **Dim:** 99.00 × 8.50 × 6.50
A: 1 Ju Lang-2 ballistic missile; 10 533-mm TT (6 fwd, 4 aft)
Electronics:
Radar: 1 Snoop Tray nav./surf. search
Sonar: 1 Herkules or Tamir-5L high frequency active/passive search and attack
EW: . . . intercept
M: 3 Type 37D diesels, electric drive; 3 5-bladed props; 6,000 shp
Range: 9,000/5 **Crew:** 87 tot.

Remarks: Plans and components were furnished by the Soviet Union at a time when relations between the two countries were good. Originally equipped to launch three Russian R-11FM (Chinese designation Type 1060) missiles while surfaced only, but the missiles were never supplied. Altered from 1968 to 1972 with only two tubes for Ju Lang-1 missile submerged-launch trials, but did not launch first successful Chinese SLBM until 12-10-82. After many years with little use, was reconfigured to launch the second-generation Ju Lang-2 SLBM, with the first (and, to date, only) reported at-sea launch taking place in mid 1-01, apparently from the Xia; thus, the Golf may have been retired.

♦ 1 Deep Submergence Rescue Vehicle (DSRV)

D: 35 tons (fl) **S:** 4 kts **Dim:** 14.88 × 2.6 × 2.6
M: 2 silver zinc batteries, 1 prop, . . . bhp
Range: 40/2 **Crew:** 3 tot.

Remarks: 35-ton submersible(s) first appeared in 1986 and can dive to 600 m. Capable of rescuing up to 22 personnel from waters up to 200-m deep or can be used for underwater salvage work. Equipped with a sonar, t.v., and a manipulator arm. Capable of speeds up to 4 kts, and an endurance of 20 hours at 2 kts; has lock-out chamber; carries up to six swimmers. The large Dajaing-class submarine tenders serve as mother ships.

GUIDED MISSILE CRUISERS [CG]

Note: During 6-02, Ukraine offered the incomplete *Moskva*-class guided missile cruiser *Ukrayina* to China.

GUIDED-MISSILE DESTROYERS [DDG]

♦ 0 (+ 2) Luhai II class (Project 051C)
Bldr: Dalian SY, Dalian, China

	Laid down	L	In serv.
115 Shijiazhung	2003	28-12-04	2006
. . .			

D: 8,000–10,000 tons (fl) **S:** . . . kts **Dim:** 155.0 × 17.0 × 6.0
A: 6 8-round vertical launch SAM groups (48 SA-N-6 S-300F/Grumble missiles) in rotating launchers; 2 quad YJ-82 (C-802) SSM launchers; 1 100-mm/55 cal. DP; 2 30-mm Type 730 CIWS gatling guns; 2 triple 324-mm Yu-7 ASW torpedo tubes; mines
Electronics: 1 Top Plate 3-D air search
1 Type 364 (Seagull-C) air/surf. search
1 Russian Band Stand fire control (for SSM missile and main gun)
M: CODOG: 2 Mashproekt-Zorya DN-80 reversible gas turbines (36,300 shp each), 2 MTU 12V1163 TB83 diesels
Crew: . . . tot.

Remarks: As many as four of this class may be planned; hull design is nearly identical to the *Luhai* (Type 51B) class. No stealth or signature reduction features appear to have been included. Though not equipped with a hangar, a flight deck is fitted at the stern for a KA-28 Helix–sized helicopter. Two revolver-type vertical launch systems are located at the bow and the remaining four in the deckhouse in front of the helicopter deck.

♦ 2 (+ 2) Lu Yang II class (Project 052C)
Bldr: Jiangnan Shipyard, Shanghai, China

	Laid down	L	In serv.
170 Lanzhou	2002	29-4-03	17-7-04
171 Haikou	11-02	29-10-03	2005
172 . . .	. . .	. . .	2006
173 . . .	. . .	. . .	. . .

D: 6,500 tons (fl) **S:** 29 kts **Dim:** 154.0 × 17.0 × 6.0
A: 1 48-cell HQ-9 VLS SAM syst. (48 HQ-9 [Russian made S-300F/Grumble, SA-N-6] missiles); 2 quad YJ-83 (C-803) SSM missile launchers; 1 100-mm/55 cal. DP; 2 30-mm Type 730 CIWS gatling guns; 4 18-barrel multiple rocket launchers; 2 triple 324-mm ASW torpedo tubes; 2 Z-9 or Ka-28 Helix helicopters
Electronics: 1 30N6E (Tombstone) multifunction phased array radar system; 1 Type 517H-1 (Knife Rest) long range 2-D air search; 1 . . . surf. search; 1 . . . nav.; 1 Russian Band Stand fire-control SSM/100-mm gun f.c.; . . . radar tracker/illuminators 2 Type 341 (Rice Lamp) CIWS f.c.
M: Two Ukraine DA80/DN80 gas turbines (48,600 shp total); 2 Shaanxi diesels (8,840 bhp total); 2 props
Crew: 280 tot.

Lanzhou (170) *Ships of the World,* 2004–5

Lanzhou (170)—note layout of the VLS system *Ships of the World,* 2004–5

Haikou (171) *Ships of the World,* 2005

Remarks: Represents the first Chinese surface combatant with a true air defense capability. Based on the same hull as the Type 52B destroyers, this class is equipped with an AEGIS (SPY-1) style phased array radar capability and a VLS air defense system along with modern antiship missiles. Built almost entirely using indigenous technology.
Hull systems: There has been some shaping of the superstructure to reduce radar signature, bulwarks at the bows, and a single stack. Compared to the previous class, this class has a much taller bridge fitted with fixed phased-array radar antennas on four sides.
Combat systems: It is likely that this class employs a new, domestically developed command-and-control system. Helicopter deck is fitted on the stern with a hangar large enough to accommodate two medium-sized helicopters. The new 100-mm gunmount incorporates noticeable radar signature reduction features. The 30N6E phased array radar system, developed by the Nanjing Research Institute of Electronic Technology, can direct 12 missiles against 6 targets simultaneously.

GUIDED-MISSILE DESTROYERS [DDG] *(continued)*

♦ 2 Luyang I class (Project 052B)
Bldr: Jiangnan Shipyard, Shanghai, China

	Laid down	L	In serv.
168 GUANGZHOU	1999	25-5-02	15-7-04
169 WUHAN	2000	29-10-02	17-7-04

D: 6,500 tons (fl) **S:** 29 kts. **Dim:** 154.0 × 17.0 × 6.0
A: 2 single-rail launchers for SA-N-7 Shtil SAM system; 4 quad C-803 JY-83 SSM; 1 100-mm/75 cal. DP; 2 30-mm Type 730 gatling CIWS; 4 18-barrel multiple rocket launchers; 2 triple 324-mm ASW torpedo tubes; 1 Z-9 or Ka-28 helicopter
Electronics: Radar: 1 MR-760-series Fregat 3-D air-search radar; 4 Russian Front Dome fire control (for SA-N-7 SAM); 1 Russian Band Stand fire control (for SSM missile and 100-mm gun)
M: Two Ukraine DA80/DN80 gas turbines (48,600 shp total); 2 Shaanxi diesels (8,840 bhp total); 2 props
Crew: 280 tot.

Guangzhou (168) 2003

Remarks: A much-modified version of the Luhai design, with some shaping of the superstructure to reduce radar signature, bulwarks at the bows, and a single stack, this class is thought to be comparable to recently acquired Russian *Sovremenny*-class in terms of performance and capability. Number 168 was originally thought to have been named Yantai.
Hull systems: Fitted with a helicopter deck and hangar that can accommodate mid-sized ASW helicopter.
Combat systems: Carries what is believed to be an improved version of the combat suite carried by the Luhai-class (Project 52) destroyers with one SA-N-7 launcher located abaft the 100-mm gun and the second carried starboard, aft, next to the helicopter hangar.

♦ 4 ex-Russian Sovremennyy (Sarych) class (Project 956E and Project 956EM*)
Bldr: Severnaya Verf 190, St. Petersburg, Russia

	Laid down	L	In serv.
136 HANGZHOU (ex-*Yekaterinburg*, ex-*Vazhnyy*)	4-11-88	23-5-94	25-12-99
137 FUZHOU (ex-*Aleksandr Nevskiy*, ex-*Vdumchivyy*)	22-2-89	16-4-99	25-12-00
138 TAIZHOU*	27-6-02	27-4-04	12-05
139 . . . *	15-11-03	23-7-04	3-06

Taizhou (138) Bernard Prézelin, 1-06

Taizhou (138) Bernard Prézelin, 1-06

D: 6,600 tons light, 7,520 normal (8,440 fl) **S:** 33.4 kts (32.7 sust.)
Dim: 156.37 (145.00 wl) × 17.19 (16.30 wl) × 5.99 mean hull (7.85 max.)
A: 8 P-270 Moskit or P-100 Moskit-M (SS-N-22 Sunburn) SSM (3M-80E missiles; 2 4-round KT-190E fixed launchers); 136-137 only: 2 single-rail 9R-90 Uragan (SA-N-7 Gadfly) SAM syst. (MS-196 launchers, 48 9M-38 Buk-M1 or 9M-38M1 Smerch missiles); 138–139 only: Shtil-1 SAM system; 136–137 only: 2 twin 130-mm 54-cal. AK-130 DP (138–139 only: 1 twin 130-mm AK-130 DP); 136–137 only: 2 twin 30-mm 54-cal. AK-630M gatling CIWS; 138–139 only: 2 Kashtan CIWS systems (9M-311/SA-N-11 Grison missiles and 2 single 30-mm mounts per system; all units: 2 twin 533-mm DTA-53-956 TT (4 SET-65KE or 53-65KE torpedoes); 2 6-tubed RBU-1000 ASW RL (48 RGB-10 rockets); up to 40 mines; 1 Ka-28 Helix-ASW helicopter; 2 single 45-mm Type 21-KM saluting cannon
Electronics:
Radar: 3 MR-212/201/202/203 Vaygach-U (Palm Frond) nav./surf.search; 1 MR-760MA Fregat-M2-EM (Top Plate-B) 3-D air search; 6 OP-3 (Front Dome) SAM f.c.; 1 MR-184E Lev (Kite Screech-C) 130-mm gun f.c., 2 MR-123-02 Vympel (Bass Tilt) 30-mm gun f.c.; 1 Mineral-E surf. target tracking and designation
Sonar: 1 MG-335MS Platina-MS-E (Bull Horn) MF bow-mounted; MG-7 (Whale Tongue) HF f.c.
EW: 2 MP-405M Start-2 or MR 401 intercept syst. (MRP-11M/12M) (Bell Shroud); 2 Bell Squat intercept; 4 Foot Ball-B intercept; MR 407 jamming syst; 2 2-tubed PK-2M trainable decoy RL (ZIF-121 launchers; 200 rockets); 8 fixed 10-round PK-10 decoy RL (420 rockets)
E/O: 1 Squeeze Box multisensor; 1 Tall View periscope; 2 Watch Box bridge periscopes; 2 or 4 Spektr-F (Half Cup) laser warning
M: 2 sets GTZA-674 geared steam turbines; 2 4-bladed props; 100,000 shp (99,500 sust.)—2 drop-down azimuthal stern thrusters; 1 drop-down bow-thruster
Boilers: 4 turbopressurized Type KVG-3; 640 kg/cm^2, 500° C
Electric: 4,900 kw tot. (2 × 1,250-kw turboalternators; 4 × 600-kw diesel sets)

Fuzhou (137)—calling at Portsmouth, England, en route to China Maritime Photographic, 12-00

GUIDED-MISSILE DESTROYERS [DDG] *(continued)*

Range: 1,345/32.7; 3,920/18 (5,340/18.4 with overload fuel)
Fuel: 1,740 tons + 5 tons aviation fuel **Endurance:** 30 days
Crew: Accomm. for 38 officers, 330 enlisted

Remarks: A contract for $667 million for the pair was signed during 9-98. *Hang Zhou* was handed over to Chinese control on 24-2-99. *Fuzhou* was handed over on 25-11-00. These are the incomplete 18th and 19th units of the class initially ordered for the Russian Navy. The first was 65% complete when purchased and the other 35%. The ships are primarily intended for surface-warfare tasks, including antiship, shore-bombardment, and antiair defense; the minimal ASW capability is primarily for self-defense. Although this is by no means a state-of-the-art design (the ships were designed in the mid-1960s), they are superior to anything else in Chinese service. All are expected to remain based at Zhoushan Naval Base in the East Sea Fleet.

A preliminary contract, for $1.4 billion total, for two additional units to be built at Severnaya Verf, was signed on 30-12-01 with an option for two more; the initial pair to be delivered by the end of 2005. Work on the first unit began during 6-02 and during 8-02 on the second, but the effort was slowed by a 7-10-02 decision by the Baltiyskiy Shipyard not to manufacture components for Severnaya Verf.

Hull systems: The propulsion plant is essentially the same as that of the preceding Russian Kresta-I and Kresta-II classes and employs turbo-pressurized boilers. Fin stabilizers are fitted.

Combat systems: The first pair were begun as Project 956A ships to carry longer cruise-missile tubes to accept a probable extended-range Moskit missile and a naval version of the SA-17 Grizzly SAM, vice the SA-N-7 system's original 9K-37 Smerch missiles.

Forty-eight Moskit antiship missiles were ordered for these ships in 7-98, with the first 24 delivered 5-00. The ships have the large Band Stand (Monolit or Mineral) radome associated with surface-to-surface missile-targeting systems. There are also two small spherical Light Bulb radomes on the sides of the stack that are missile data link–associated.

The 130-mm guns are of a fully automatic, water-cooled model, capable of AA or surface fire; they are restricted to firing arcs of 40 degrees each side of the centerline. Each ship carries 2,000 rounds of 130-mm ammunition. The two newer units of the class carry only 1,000 rounds as they do not carry the after twin 130-mm gun. The AK-630 guns are restricted to firing arcs of −5 degrees across the centerline through 160 degrees for the forward mounts and 15 degrees off centerline forward through 170 degrees for the after mounts. Each ship carries 16,000 rounds of 30-mm ammunition. Squeeze Box is an optronic gunfire-control director combining a laser rangefinder, low-light-level television, and infrared devices. The second two have improved weapon systems and sensors, the AK-130 guns have been removed and updates include the Shtil-11 SAM system and a new longer-range variant of the SS-N-22. The SAM launchers in this class may be limited to launch angles within 30 degrees of the centerline, a significant handicap.

DESTROYERS [DD]

♦ 1 Luhai class (Project 051B)

Bldr: Dalian SY

	Laid down	L	In serv.
167 Shenzhen	5-96	16-10-97	1-99

D: 6,600 tons (fl) **S:** 29 kts **Dim:** 153.0 × 16.5 × 6.0
A: 16 C-802 Ying Ji-8-2 SSM; 1 8-round HQ-7 (16 missiles); 1 twin 100-mm 56-cal. DP; 4 twin 37-mm 63-cal. Type 76A AA; 2 triple 324-mm ILAS-3 ASW TT; 2 Z-9A or Ka-28 Helix-A helicopters
Electronics:
Radar: 2 Decca RM 1290A/D ARPA nav., 1 . . . surf.-air search, 1 Thales Sea Tiger (TSR-3004) air-search; 1 Sea Eagle (Rice Field) 3-D air search; 1 Type 363 early warning; 2 Type 347G 37-mm f.c.; 1 EFR-1 (Fog lamp) 100-mm f.c.; 1 . . . missile illuminator
Sonar: . . . bow-mounted LF
EW: 2 . . . intercept, . . . jammers; BM 8610 intercept/jammer array, 2 15-round decoy RL
E/O: 2 GDG-775 radar/t.v./laser/IR directors

Shenzhen (167)—note heavy (and vulnerable) battery of cruise missile launchers amidships U.S. Navy, 10-03

Shenzhen (167) U.S. Navy, 10-03

M: CODOG: 2 Mashproekt-Zorya GT25000 gas turbines (48,600 hp each), 2 Shaanxi diesels (8,840 bhp total); 72,600 shp max.; 2 props
Crew: 250 tot., 40 officers, 210 enlisted

Remarks: An enlarged version of the Luhu class. Sea trials commenced in 9-98, after what would have been a remarkably short fitting-out period by Chinese standards. 167 is assigned to the South Sea Fleet and is based at Zhanjiang. 167 underwent refit during 2004–5; improvements include the incorporation of signature reduction features in a new 100-mm gun mount.

Hull systems: The gas turbines in this ship were manufactured in Ukraine, but China signed a technology transfer contract with Zorya in 5-01 that is intended to result in production of the DA-80 (or DN-80) in China for future naval ships. The Chinese diesels are licensed copies of the MTU 12V1163 TB83 diesel.

Combat systems: ASW capabilities have been reduced from those of the Luhu class, as there is no VDS or towed array, and the ASW rocket launchers have been omitted. The space between the SAM launcher and the bridge superstructure is occupied by a belowdecks reload magazine; there is no provision for vertical launchers. The listed GDG-775 radar system listed may not be installed. A twin hangar and a French-designed Samahe harpoon-type recovery and dual deck traversing system are fitted for the helicopters.

♦ 2 Luhu class (Project 052)

	Bldr	Laid down	L	In serv.
112 Harbin	Qiuxin SY, Shanghai	24-5-90	6-91	2-2-93
113 Qingdao	Jiangnan SY, Shanghai	1991	10-93	3-96

Harbin (112) JMSDF, 7-99

D: 4,800 tons (5,700 fl) **S:** 31.5 kts (20 on diesel)
Dim: 148.0 (142.6 wl) × 16.0 (15.6 wl) × 7.5 (5.0 hull)
A: 113: 8 C-801A Ying Ji-1 (CSS-N-4 Sardine); 112 only: 16 C-803 Ying Ji 8-3 SSM; 1 8-round HQ-7 SAM syst. (16 missiles); 1 twin 100-mm 55-cal. DP; 4 twin 37-mm 63-cal. Type 76A AA; 2 triple 324-mm ILAS-3 ASW TT; 2 12-round Type 75 ASW RL; 2 Z-9A helicopters

Shenzhen (167) 1. Helicopter deck 2. Twin 37-mm Type 76A AA 3. Type 347G radar director for 37-mm AA 4. Type 363 early-warning radar 5. Sea Eagle 3-D air-search radar 6. 16 C-802 or C-801A SSM launch containers in four groups of four 7. Decoy launchers on platforms above the triple ASW torpedo tubes 8. Sea Tiger air-search radar 9. Navigational radar 10. Radar director for the 100-mm gunmount 11. Octuple launcher for the HQ-7 SAM system 12. Twin 100-mm 55-cal. DP gunmount
Drawing by A. D. Baker III

DESTROYERS [DD] *(continued)*

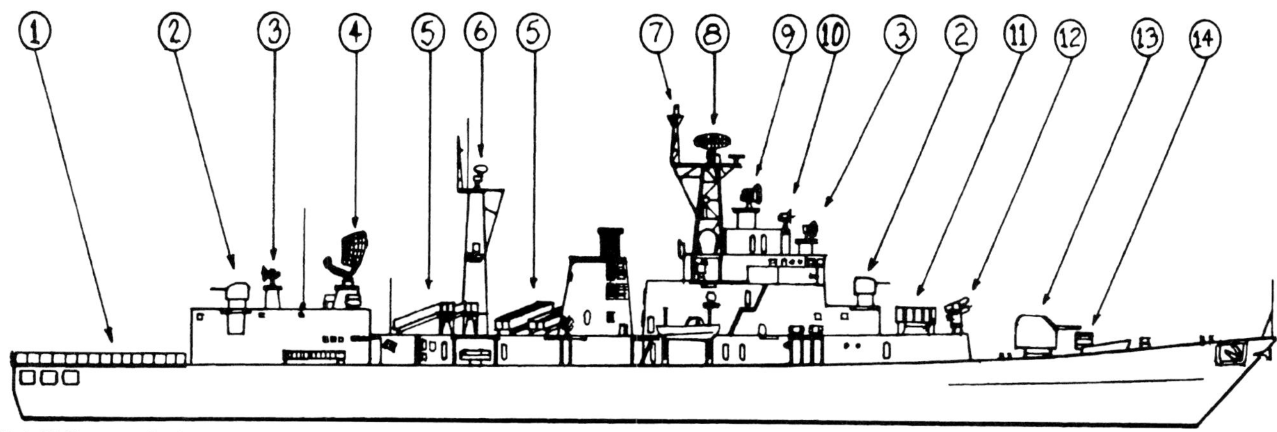

Qingdao (113) 1. Helicopter platform with French Samahe landing system 2. Twin 37-mm Type 76A AA 3. Type 347G radar f.c. directors for 37-mm AA 4. Hai Ying early-warning radar 5. 8 C-802 or C-801A SSM launch containers in four groups of two 6. ESR-1 sea-skimmer detection radar 7. EW intercept antenna array 8. Sea Tiger air-search radar 9. EFR-1 radar director for the 100-mm gunmount 10. Radar director for the HQ-7 SAM system 11. On-deck reload magazine for the HQ-7 SAM system 12. Octuple launcher for the HQ-7 SAM system 13. Twin 100-mm 55-cal. DP gunmount 14. 12-round Type 75 ASW rocket launchers Drawing by A. D. Baker III

Quingdao (113) Peruvian Navy, 8-02

Electronics:
Radar: 2 Decca RM 1290A/D ARPA nav.; 1 . . . surf./air search; 1 Thales Sea Tiger (TSR-3004) air search; 1 Hai Ying ("God Eye") early warning; 1 ESR-1 sea-skimmer detection; 2 Type 347G 37-mm f.c., 1 EFR-1 (Fog Lamp) 100-mm f.c.; 112 only: 1 Thales DRBC-32F (Castor-C) Crotale SAM target illuminator
Sonar: . . . LF bow-mounted; HF fire-control; ESS-1 MF VDS
EW: 2 . . . intercept; . . . jammers; BM 8610 intercept/jammer array, 2 15-round decoy RL
E/O: 2 GDG-775 radar/t.v./laser/IR directors
M: CODOG: 2 G.E. LM-2500 gas turbines (26,800 shp each), 2 MTU 12V1163 TB83 diesels (4,420 bhp each); 2 CP props; 53,600 shp max.
Range: 4,000/16 **Endurance:** 15 days **Crew:** 230 tot.

Remarks: China's first modern surface combatant design, though still equipped with weapon and sensor systems decades behind those aboard contemporary Western units.
Hull systems: Have an unusually high freeboard. Are air-conditioned and have a full NBC warfare protection system. Hull has two sets of nonretractable fin stabilizers. A twin hangar and a French-designed Samahe harpoon-type recovery and dual deck traversing system are fitted for the helicopters.
Combat systems: Have a combat information center (CIC) equipped with the Alenia IPN-10 combat data system and the Link-W data link. EW suite may employ a derivative of the Thales RAPIDS (Radar Passive Identification System) intercept and RAMSES (Reprogrammable Multimode Shipborne ECM System) jammers; the two radomes on the sides of the forward superstructure appear to conceal steerable jammers. Located at bridge level are two GDG-775 multifunction optronic directors; equipped with a ranging radar, a laser rangefinder, low-light t.v., and IR sensors, they are normally operated from the CIC. The twin 100-mm gunmount is of a new, fully enclosed, automatic design based on that of the single French mount on the Jianghu-IV-class frigate *Siping;* the gunhouse was altered to reduce radar reflectivity during the 2002–3 refit of 112. 112 also received C-803 (YJ-8-3) missiles in place of C-801 and had the French-made Crotale Modulaire SAM system replaced by the indigenous version, HQ-7. The 113 will probably receive a similar update. Reload surface-to-air missiles are contained in a box magazine immediately abaft the launcher.

♦ 1 Luda-III class (Project 051G)
Bldr: Dalian SY (166) and Donglang SY (165)

	Laid down	L	In serv.
165 Zhanjiang	. . .	. . .	10-91
166 Zhuhai	8-88	1991	1993

Zhuhai (166)—with temporary pennant number
Brian Morrison/H&L Van Ginderen, 8-95

Zhuhai (166) U.S. Navy, 5-94

D: 3,250 tons light, 3,670 std. (3,960 fl) **S:** 35 kts (32 sust.)
Dim: 132.00 (127.50 pp) × 12.80 × 4.39 (5.30 sonar)
A: 16 C-801 Ying Ji-1 (CSS-N-4 Sardine) SSM; 1 HQ-7 SAM syst.; 2 twin 100-mm DP; 4 twin 37-mm 63-cal. Type 76A AA; 2 12-tubed Type 75 ASW RL; 2 triple 324-mm ASW TT (WASS A-244 torpedoes); 2 mine rails (38 max. mines)
Electronics:
Radar: 1 Decca RM 1290A/D ARPA nav.; 1 ESR-1 sea-skimmer detection; 1 Sea Eagle (Rice Field) 3-D air search; 1 Type 363 long-range air early warning; 1 Type 343 (Sun Visor-B) 130-mm f.c.; 2 Type 347G AA gun f.c.
Sonar: . . . MF bow-mounted; ESS-1 MF VDS
EW: 2 . . . intercept, 2 RW-23-1 (Jug Pair-2) intercept; 2 . . . jammers; 2 15-round decoy RL
M: 2 sets geared steam turbines; 2 props; 72,000 shp (60,000 sust.)
Boilers: 4 **Range:** 1,100/32; 2,970/18; 5,000/14 **Endurance:** 10 days
Crew: 27 officers, 275 enlisted

Remarks: Improved version of Luda design incorporating bow-mounted sonar, VDS, C-801 antiship missiles, and Italian Alenia IPN-10 combat data system.
Combat systems: The EW suite may be a modified copy of the Thales DR-2000S intercept and the Alligator jammer systems, but the decoy rocket launchers are of Chinese design. The VDS appears to be a copy of the U.S. Raytheon DE 1160 or 1164 system. The long-range air early warning radar, mounted on a pedestal atop the after conning station between the mainmast and the after stack employs four yagi arrays. The antenna for the ESR-1 sea-skimmer detection radar is mounted atop the foremast, while the antenna for the Sea Eagle three-dimensional air-search radar is atop the mainmast. All of the search radar antennas are mechanically stabilized, indicating a lack of computer capability in Chinese radar design. The box launchers for the C-801 antiship missiles are fixed in bearing and elevation.

♦ 14 Luda I and II class (Project 051)
Bldrs: 105–110: Lüda (Dalian) SY;131–134: Donglang SY; 161–164: Guangzhou SY, Shanghai (In serv. 1972–91)

105 Jinan	110 Dalian	161 Changsha
106 Xian	131 Nanjing	162 Nanning
107 Yinchuan	132 Hefei	163 Nanchang
108 Xining	133 Chongqing	164 Guilian
109 Kaifeng	134 Zunyi	

Jinan (105)—the only Luda with helicopter facilities, added at the expense of the after twin 130-mm and 37-mm gunmounts *Ships of the World*

D: 3,250 tons light, 3,670 std. (3,960 fl) **S:** 35 kts (32 sust.)
Dim: 132.00 (127.50 pp) × 12.80 × 4.39 hull (5.30 sonar)

DESTROYERS [DD] *(continued)*

Luda-class Hefei (132) 1. 4 BMB-2 depth-charge mortars 2. Twin 130-mm 58-cal. DP gunmounts 3. Twin 37-mm 63-cal. Type 74 AA mounts 4. Type 341 Rice Lamp AA radar directors 5. Triple trainable launchers for C-201 SSMs 6. Bean Sticks early-warning radar 7. Type 352C Square Tie surface target detection and tracking radar 8. Type 354 Eye Shield air/surface-search radar 9. Wok Won optical director for 130-mm guns 10. Twin 25-mm 80-cal. Type 61 AA mounts 11. 12-round Type 75 ASW rocket launchers

Drawing by A. D. Baker III

Kaifeng (109) Stefan Karpinski, 6-02

Kaifeng (109) Stefan Karpinski, 6-02

A: 109, 110 only: 1 8-round HQ-7 SAM syst. (8 reloads); 109, 110 only: 16 C-801 Ying Ji-1 (CSS-N-4 Sardine) SSM—all others: 6 C-201 HY-2 (CSS-N-1) SSM—all: 2 twin 130-mm 58-cal. DP; 4 (109: 3) twin 37-mm 63-cal. Type 76A AA; 2 twin 25-mm 80-cal. Type 61 AA; 2 12-round Type 75 ASW RL; 4 single BMB-2 D.C. mortars; 2 d.c. racks; 2 mine rails (38 mines max.)

Electronics:

Radar: 1 Fin Curve or Decca RM 1290A/D ARPA nav.; 1 Type 354 (Eye Shield) short-range air search; 1 Bean Sticks or Pea Sticks (antenna variant) early warning; 1 Type 352C (Square Tie) antiship missile targeting; 1 Type 343 (Sun Visor-B) 130-mm gun f.c. (not on all); 2 Type 341 (Rice Lamp) AA gun f.c. (not on all); 108, 110 also: Sea Eagle (Rice Field) long-range 3-D air search; 109 also: 1 Thales Sea Tiger air search; Thales DRBC-32E Castor-IIJ SAM f.c.; 1 Type 347G 37-mm gun f.c.

Sonar: . . . MF hull-mounted

EW: 2 Jug Pair (RW-23-1) intercept; 109 only: 2 15-round decoy RL

M: 2 sets geared steam turbines; 2 props; 72,000 shp (60,000 sust.)

Boilers: 4 **Range:** 1,100/32; 2,970/18; 5,000/14 **Endurance:** 10 days

Crew: 27 officers, 275 enlisted (normally operate with 220 total)

Remarks: Also known as Project EF4. First unit, 105, completed 12-72 at Dalian. Design based on the unsuccessful Russian Project 41, *Tallin,* class. Completed in the following order: 105, 160 (lost), 106, 161, 107, 162, 131, 108, 132, 109, 163, 110, 133, 134, and 164. 106–110 are assigned to the Northern Fleet and homeported at Yuchi. 131–134 are assigned to the East Sea Fleet and homeported at Dalian and Pennants 161–164 are assigned to the Southern Fleet and homeported at Zhanjiang. One South Sea Fleet ship of this class (probably 160) was lost after an explosion 8-78 near Zhanjiang.

Combat systems: Equipment varies greatly from ship to ship, with only five (105, 108, 131, 161, and 162) having fire-control radar systems, even on the Soviet Wasp Head ("Wok Wan") 130-mm stabilized optical director for the 130-mm guns. All are now equipped for underway fueling. The ships are said to lack sufficient electrical generating capacity to operate all weapons and sensor systems simultaneously.

The twin 57-mm mounts originally carried on a few units are gradually being replaced with 37-mm guns during overhauls. Pea Sticks long-range air search is carried by 107, 131, 132, and 162; the remainder have Bean Sticks. 108, 110, and 132 had a larger variant of the Rice Screen (Sea Eagle) 3-D phased-array air-search radar atop the after mast and were intended to act as leaders; in 132 the Rice Screen was replaced by a commercial SATCOM antenna in 1999, possibly only temporarily, but 164 had had Sea Eagle added by that year. The Bean Sticks air early-warning radar's antenna has 32 yagi radiators, while that of the Pea Sticks has only 16. The 131 and 164 may have bow-mounted sonars. The triple missile launcher mounts rotate; on 109 the 4-round missile launchers are fixed.

Modifications: The class prototype, 105, completed a refit in 5-87 with a helicopter flight deck and hangar in place of the after twin 130-mm DP mount, after twin 37-mm AA, and the 4 d.c. mortars; she also has a new sonar, improved EW equipment, satellite navigation gear, and an Alenia IPN-10 combat data system; she had previously been employed as a trials ship for equipment to be used in this and later classes. A report that 110 has also been fitted with a flight deck and hangar has not been substantiated. The other ships do not have air-conditioning, NBC warfare protection systems, or a central combat command space (CIC). In 9-97, 132 had been fitted with the antenna for a commercial SATCOM system atop the mainmast and a Type 341 Rice Lamp AA fire-control radar on a platform aft.

109 has been backfitted with a Crotale NG octuple SAM launcher in place of the after 37-mm gunmount; a reload magazine is installed just forward of the launcher. To control the SAM system, a Thales DRBC-32F (Castor-IIJ) radar has been added. By 1999 109 had been further modified with four sets of quadruple, fixed-launch containers for antiship missiles, and enclosed, automatic Type 76A AA mounts had replaced the manned mounts. 110 carries two copies of the Italian ILAS-3 (B515) ASW torpedo tube mounting and probably has WASS A-244 torpedoes. 165 and one or two others may have EW suite consisting of Thales DR 2000S intercept, Thales Alligator jammer, and two Chinese-designed 15-round decoy rocket launchers.

GUIDED-MISSILE FRIGATES [FFG]

♦ 0 (+ 2) Jaingkai II class (Project 54A)

Bldr: Hudong Zhonghua Shipyard, Shanghai (first unit); Huangpu Shipyard, Guanzhou (second unit)

	Laid down	In serv.
. . .	2004	2007?
. . .	2005	2008?

D: 3,450 tons, 3,850 tons(fl) **S:** 30 kts **Dim:** 125.0 ×14.0 × 5.0

A: 1 48-cell HQ-9 VLS SAM syst. (48 HQ-9/Russian S-300F Grumble SA-N-6 missiles); 2 quad C-802 YJ-2 (CSS-N-8 Saccade) SSM missile launchers; 1 100-mm 55 cal. DP; 2 30-mm Type 730 CIWS gatling guns; 4 18-barrel multiple rocket launchers; 2 triple 324-mm Type B515 ASW torpedo tubes; 1 Ka-28 Helix or Z-9 helicopter

Electronics:

Radar: 1 Top Plate 3-D air search; 1 Type 363S (French DRBV-15 Sea Tiger) 2-D air/surf. search; 1 MR-36A surf. search; 2 Racal-Decca RM-1290 nav.; 1 Russian Band Stand fire control (SSM missile and main gun); 2 Type 347G (EFR-1—Rice Lamp) fire control (30-mm guns)

EW: 1 Type 922-1 radar warning intercept; 1 HZ100 shipborne electronic countermeasures [ECM] and electronic intelligence (ELINT) system; 2 15-round Type 946 100-mm decoy RL

M: Four French SEMT-Pielstick type diesels (21,000 bhp); two props

Crew: 180 tot.

Remarks: An improved variant of the Project 054 frigates, the Project 054A appears to have replaced the Ma'anshan class in the Chinese production schedule. Likely intended to replace the Jianghu-I and II-classes. Significant efforts have been dedicated to signature reduction techniques. Fitted with a VLS system between the bridge and the 100-mm gun, in the main deck.

♦ 2 Jiangkai class (Project 054)

Bldr: Hudong Zhonghua SY, Shanghai (525) and Huangpu SY, Guanzhou (526)

	Laid down	L	In serv.
525 Maanshan	2002	11-9-03	18-2-05
526 Wenzhou	2003	11-03	26-9-05

GUIDED-MISSILE FRIGATES [FFG] *(continued)*

D: 3,400 tons, 3,800 tons (fl) **S:** 30 kts **Dim:** 125.0 × 14.0 × 5.0
A: 1 8-round HQ-7A (FM-80) SAM system (16 missiles); 2 quad C-802 YJ-2 (CSS-N-8 Saccade) SSM missile launchers; 1 twin 100-mm/55 cal. ENG-2 DP; 4 30-mm/54 cal. (AK-630) gatling CIWS; 2 triple 324-mm ASW torpedo tubes; 1 Ka-28 or Z-9 helicopter
Electronics:
Radar: 1 Type 363S (French DRBV-15 Sea Tiger) 2-D air/surf. search; 1 MR-36A surf. search; 2 Racal-Decca RM-1290 nav.; 1 Type 345 (Castor IIJ) fire control (for the HQ-7A system); 1 MR-34 fire control (for the 100-mm gun); 2 Type 347G (EFR-1—Rice Lamp) fire control (for 30-mm guns)
EW: 1 Type 922-1 radar warning intercept; 1 HZ100 shipborne electronic countermeasures [ECM] and electronic intelligence (ELINT) system; 2 15-round Type 946 100-mm decoy RL
M: CODAD: Four French SEMT-Pielstick type 16PA6 STC diesels (21,000 bhp); two Shaanxi diesels; two props
Crew: 190 tot.

Maanshan (525) 2003

Maanshan (525)—under construction 2003

Remarks: Next-generation Chinese FFG design incorporating numerous signature reduction features. Both units are active in the East Sea Fleet. Only two frigates of this class are planned with follow-on units being built to the 054A design. The diesels are licensed built versions of the MTU Type 20V 956TB82 diesels.
Combat systems: Not equipped with a phased array radar or VLS system. The AK-630 mounts are fitted either side of the stack and atop the helicopter hangar. The HQ-7A launcher is located aft of the 100-mm gun and forward of the bridge on the main deck. Carries the indigenously built ZKJ-4B/6 combat data system. May be fitted with a newly developed SSM, dubbed Ying Ji-85 (C-805), if available.

FRIGATES [FF]

♦ 10 Jiangwei-II class (Project 53H3)

	Bldr	Laid down	L	In serv.
521 Jiaxing	Hudong SY, Shanghai	11-96	5-6-97	11-98
522 Lianyungang	Hudong SY, Shanghai	1-97	8-8-97	2-99
523 Sanming	Hudong SY, Shanghai	11-97	6-98	10-99
524 Putian	Hudong SY, Shanghai	12-97	12-98	12-99
564 Yichang	Huangpu SY, Guanzhou	12-97	10-98	12-99
565 Yulin	Huangpu SY, Guanzhou	5-98	4-99	3-00
566 Yuxi	Hudong SY, Shanghai	5-00	1-01	3-02
567 Xiangfan	Huangpu SY, Guanzhou	3-01	8-01	9-02
527 . . .	Hudong SY, Shanghai	. . .	9-04	2005
528 Mianyang	Huangpu SY, Guanzhou	. . .	30-5-04	2006

D: 1,913 tons (2,393 fl) **S:** 27.2 kts
Dim: 114.5 (108.0 wl) × 12.4 (12.2 wl) × 3.6 (hull)
A: 8 C-802 YJ-2 (CSS-N-8 Saccade) SSM; 1 8-round HQ-7 SAM system (16 missiles); 1 twin 100-mm 55-cal. ENG-2 DP; 4 twin 37-mm 63-cal. Type 76A AA; 2 6-round Type 87 ASW RL; 1 Z-9A helicopter
Electronics:
Radar: 1 Decca RM 1290A/D ARPA nav.; 1 Type 360 (SR-60) air/surf. search; 1 Type 363 early warning; 1 . . . SAM tracker/illuminator; 1 Type 343 (Sun Visor-B) 100-mm surface gun f.c.; 1 Type 341 (Rice Lamp) 37-mm AA f.c.
Sonar: S-07H bow-mounted MF
EW: NRJ-5 system: RWD-8 intercept; NJ81-3 jammer; 2 6-round PJ46 decoy RL
M: 4 Type 18E390VA diesels; 2 CP props; 23,674 bhp
Electric: 1,720 kw (4 × 400 kw, 1 × 120 kw) **Range:** 4,000/18
Crew: 170 tot.

Jiangwei-II–class Yichang (564) John Mortimer, 10-01

Remarks: First two may originally have been ordered for Pakistan. First unit ran trials late 1998 and was originally numbered 597 and possibly intended for Pakistan. 521 through 524 are assigned to the East Sea Fleet, the others to the South Seas Fleet.
Combat systems: Differ from *Jiangwei-I* class primarily in having far more effective SAM system; the after pair of 37-mm AA mounts are a deck higher, and the Type 343 (Sun Visor-B) gun f.c. radar antenna is mounted on a stabilized pedestal rather than a manned director. There may be an E/O surveillance and/or f.c. device atop the pilothouse, possibly a single GDG-775 multisensor director. ASW ordnance is limited to short-range rocket launchers. The manufacturer's designation for the Type 360 radar is Type 2405, and the combat system is designated the 7KJ-3C. There have been reports that the C-802 SSM missile armament fitted in some older units is being replaced by a multiple launch rocket system intended to support troops ashore.

Lianyungang (522) JMSDF, via *Ships of the World,* 4-00

FRIGATES [FF] *(continued)*

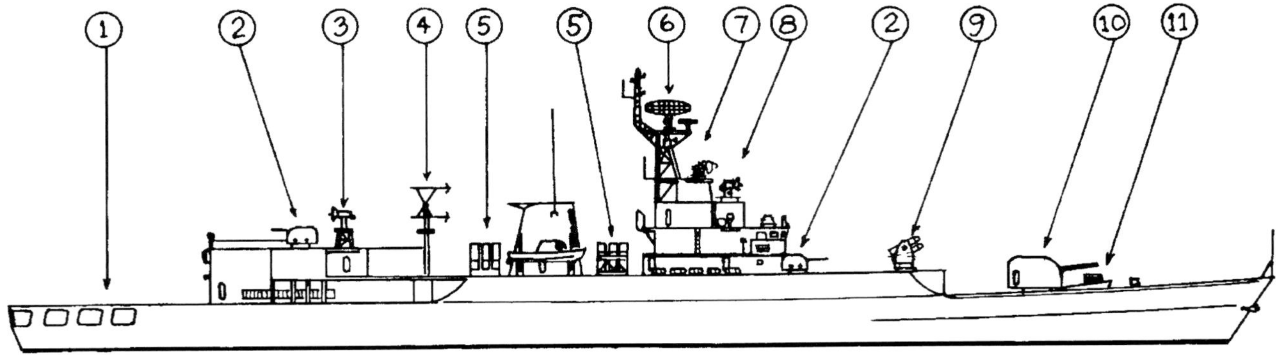

Jiangwei-II class 1. Helicopter flight deck 2. Twin 37-mm 63-cal. Type 76A automatic AA 3. Type 341 Rice Lamp gun fire-control radar 4. Type 363 early-warning radar 5. 6 C-802 Ying Ji-2 SSM in triple, fixed sets 6. Type 360 air/surface-search radar 7. Type 343 radar director for 100-mm gunmount 8. Radar illuminator/tracker for HQ-7 SAM system 9. Octuple launcher for HQ-7 SAM system 10. Twin 100-mm 55-cal. ENG-2 DP gunmount 11. 6-round Type 87 ASW rocket launchers — Drawing by A. D. Baker III

♦ 4 Jiangwei-I class (Project 055)

Bldr: Hudong SY, Shanghai

	Laid down	L	In serv.
539 Anqing	1988	7-91	12-91
540 Huainan	1989	12-91	12-92
541 Huaibei	1990	3-93	8-93
542 Tonqing	1991	9-93	10-94

D: 1,700 tons (2,180 fl) **S:** 27.2 kts
Dim: 114.5 (108 wl) × 12.4 (12.2 wl) × 3.5 (hull)
A: 6 C-802 Ying Ji-2 (CSS-N-8 Saccade) SSM; 1 6-round HQ-61 SAM syst. (no reloads); 1 twin 100-mm 56-cal. ENG-2 DP; 4 twin 37-mm 63-cal. Type 76A AA; 2 6-round Type 87 ASW RL; 1 Z-9A helicopter
Electronics:
Radar: 1 Decca RM 1290A/D ARPA nav.; 1 Type 360 (SR-60) air search; 1 Type 363 early warning; 1 Type 343 (Sun Visor-B) surf. gun f.c.; 2 Type 341 (Rice Shield) AA f.c.
Sonar: S-07H bow-mounted MF
EW: NRJ-5 system: RWD-8 intercept; NJ81-3 jammer; 2 6-round PJ46 decoy RL
M: 4 Type 18E390VA diesels; 2 CP props; 23,674 bhp
Electric: 1,720 kw (4 × 400 kw, 1 × 120 kw) **Range:** 4,000/18 **Crew:** 170 tot.

Huainan (540) — *Ships of the World,* 2000

Anqing (539) — *Ships of the World,* 2000

Remarks: 539 also been reported to be named *Tianshan.*
Combat systems: Have China's first computerized weapons data and control system, CCS-3, which incorporates a combat datalink. The unusual sextuple SAM launcher forward has no reload magazine; the large diameter of the tubes is necessitated by the 5.4-n.m. range missiles' having nonfolding fins. No provision seems to have been made for ASW torpedoes, depth charges, or mines; there is no torpedo decoy system. The Type 76A 37-mm AA mounts are of the new, enclosed version. The helicopter is intended for over-the-horizon targeting for the missiles, liaison, and search and rescue; it can carry ASW torpedoes but has no ASW sensors. There is a French-style harpoon-type helicopter haul-down system but no deck traversing arrangements. The complete EW suite is referred to as the NRJ-5 system and incorporates a 2–18 GHz intercept capability, 8–16 GHz noise jammer, and 7–16 GHz deception jammer.

♦ 6 Jianghu-V class

Bldr: Hudong SY, Shanghai (In serv. 1993–96)

558 Zigong	561 Shantou
559 Kangding	562 Jiangmen
560 Dongguan	563 Zhaoging

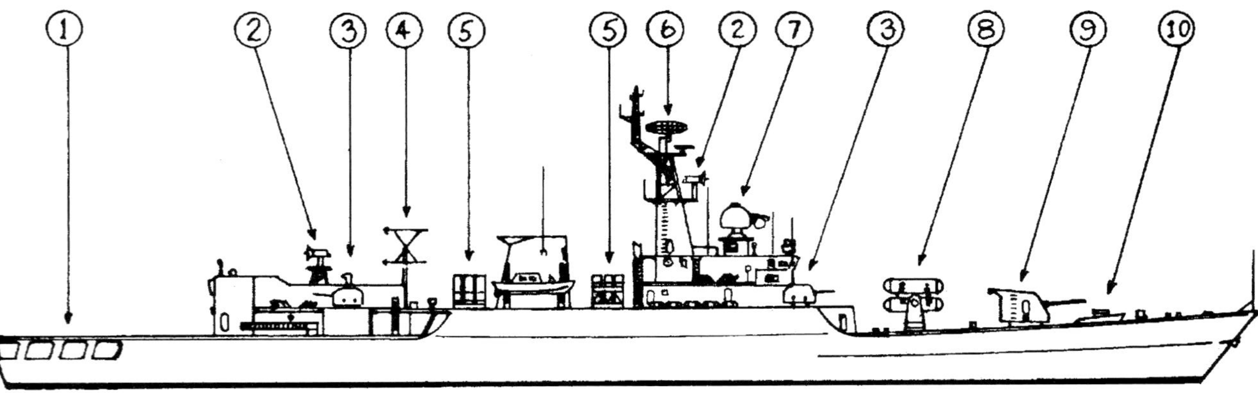

Jiangwei-I class 1. Helicopter flight deck 2. Type 341 Rice Shield AA fire-control radars 3. Twin 37-mm 63-cal. Type 76A automatic AA 4. Type 363 early-warning radar 5. 6 C-802 Ying Ji-2 SSM in triple, fixed sets 6. Type 360 air/surface-search radar 7. Wok Won gun director with Type 343 f.c. radar 8. Sextuple, nonreloading launcher for HQ-61 SAM system 9. Twin 100-mm 56-cal. ENG-2 DP gunmount 10. 6-round Type 87 ASW rocket launchers — Drawing by A. D. Baker III

FRIGATES [FF] *(continued)*

Zigong (558)—note enclosed "mack"-type stack, surmounted by the early-warning radar antenna — 92 Wing Det., RAAF, 2-95

Kangding (559) — 92 Wing Det., RAAF, 1-99

D: 1,425 tons (1,702 fl) **S:** 25.5 kts **Dim:** 103.2 × 10.2 × 3.05 (hull)
A: 4 C-201 Hai Ying-2 (CSS-N-1) SSM; 2 twin 100-mm 56-cal. DP; 4 twin 37-mm 63-cal. Type 76A AA; 2 5-round Type 75 ASW RL
Electronics:
Radar: 1 Decca RM 1290A/D ARPA nav.; 1 Type 360 surf./air search; 1 Type 363 early warning; 1 Type 343 (Sun Visor-B) 100-mm gun f.c.; 1 Type 341 (Rice Lamp) 37-mm gun f.c.
Sonar: EH-5A MF hull-mounted
EW: Elettronica Newton-Beta suite: 2 Type 211 (Jug Pair) intercept; Type 318 noise jammer; Type 521 deception jammer; 2 15-round decoy RL
M: 2 SEMT-Pielstick 12 PA6 280 BTC diesels; 2 props; 16,000 bhp (14,400 sust.)
Electric: 1,320 kw (3 × 400 kw, 1 × 120 kw)
Range: 3,000/18; 1,750/25 **Endurance:** 10 days **Crew:** 195 tot.

Remarks: A simplified version of the Jianghu-II put back into production after the first four Jiangwei-class frigates, probably as an inexpensive way to maintain order of battle. They are visually distinguishable by the unique stack, which has the long-range air-search radar antenna mounted on its forward edge. The final unit was completed during 2-96. All in this class are assigned to the South Seas Fleet.
Combat systems: The ASW suite, including the rocket launchers, sonar, and 2KJ-5 display console, is designated SJD-5. The EW suite employs Type 923 omnidirectional antennas for the Type 521 deception jammer, and Type 981 omnidirectional and Type 929 directional antennas, all mounted on the mast and superstructure sides; the equipment is of Italian design, license-built in China. The 100-mm guns are controlled by the Wok Wan director atop the pilothouse (with integral Type 343 Sun Visor radar), while the Rice Lamp radar aft provides range inputs to the 37-mm guns, which are arranged to cover one quadrant for each mount. The 100-mm guns have a rate of fire of 25 rds/min and a range of 16 km and employ a French-designed autoloader. The 37-mm mounts are automatic. There is a Matra Défense Naja manned optronic backup director for the 37-mm mounts, located between the after pair of 37-mm mounts. The surface/air-search radar evidently also performs target detection and designation for the antiship missiles, as there is no Type 352C (Square Tie) radar fitted; it probably can also function (like Type 352C) in the passive mode. The missile launcher mounts rotate.

♦ 1 Jianghu-IV class (Project 053HT(H))
Bldr: Hudong SY, Shanghai

	L	In serv.
544 Siping	9-85	11-86

D: 1,600 tons (1,820 fl) **S:** 25.5 kts **Dim:** 103.2 × 10.2 × 3.05 (hull)
A: 2 C-201 Hai Ying-2 (CSS-N-1) SSM; 1 100-mm 55-cal. Creusot-Loire Compact DP; 4 twin 37-mm 63-cal. Type 76 AA; 2 triple 324-mm ILAS-3 ASW TT (WASS A-244S torpedoes); 2 5-tubed Type 81 ASW RL; 1 Z-9A helicopter
Electronics:
Radar: 1 Decca RM 1290A/D ARPA nav.; 1 Type 354 (Eye Shield) air search; 1 ESR-1 sea-skimmer detection; 1 Type 347G (Rice Lamp) gun f.c.
Sonar: Type EH-5 HF hull-mounted
EW: 2 RW-23-1 (Jug Pair) intercept; U.S. Mk 33 RBOC decoy syst. (2 6-round RL)

Siping (544) — Stefan Karpinski, 6-02

Siping (544) — Stefan Karpinski, 6-02

M: 2 SEMT-Pielstick 12 PA6 280 BTC diesels; 2 props; 16,000 bhp (14,400 sust.)
Electric: 1,320 kw (3 × 400 kw, 1 × 120 kw) **Range:** 4,000/15; 1,750/25
Endurance: 15 days **Crew:** 25 officers, 160 enlisted

Remarks: The first Chinese combatant to incorporate a helicopter facility and Western ASW torpedoes. Adding the helicopter to the Jianghu design cost the after medium-caliber gunmount and twin SSM positions.
Combat systems: The 100-mm gun, which can fire at 90 rds/min, is controlled by a Rice Lamp (Type 341) radar director, added in 2002 atop the helicopter hangar. ESR-1 replaced the original Type 352C (Square Tie) antiship missile targeting radar on the foremast in the mid-1990s and may also be able to provide surface target range and bearing data.

♦ 3 Jianghu-III class (Project 053HT)
Bldr: Hudong SY, Shanghai

535 Huangshi (In serv. 14-12-86)
536 Wuhu (In serv. 1987)
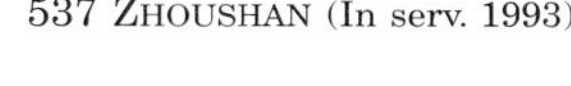
537 Zhoushan (In serv. 1993)

Zhoushan (537) — Stefan Karpinski, 6-02

Zhoushan (537) — Stefan Karpinski, 6-02

D: 1,655 tons std., 1,800 tons normal (1,960 fl) **S:** 28 kts
Dim: 103.20 × 10.83 × 3.10 (hull)
A: 8 C-801 YJ-1 (CSS-N-4 Sardine) SSM; 2 twin 100-mm 56-cal. ENG-2 DP; 4 twin 37-mm 63-cal. Type 76 AA: 2 5-round Type 81 ASW RL; 2 BMB-2 d.c. mortars
Electronics:
Radar: 1 Decca RM 1290A/D ARPA nav.; 1 Type 354 (Eye Shield) air search; 1 Type 352C (Square Tie) missile targeting; 1 Type 341 (Rice Lamp) f.c.; 1 Type 343 (Sun Visor) f.c.; 537 also: 1 Type 363 long-range air search
Sonar: Type EH-5 bow-mounted MF
EW: Elettronica Newton-Beta suite; Type 211 intercept; Type 318 noise jammer; Type 521 deception jammer; 2 . . .-round decoy RL

FRIGATES [FF] *(continued)*

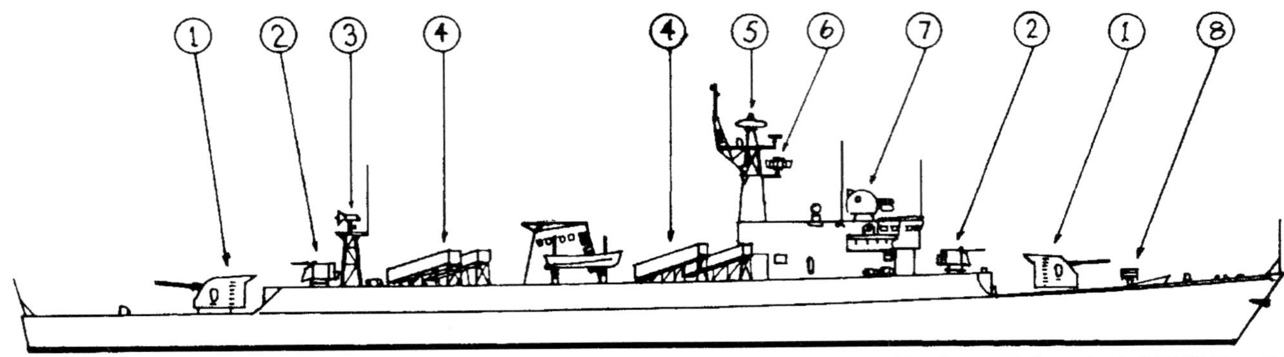

Jianghu-III class 1. Twin 100-mm 56-cal. ENG-2 DP gunmounts 2. Twin 37-mm 63-cal. Type 76 AA 3. Type 341 Rice Lamp AA f.c. radar 4. 8 C-801 Ying Ji-1 SSM in eight fixed canister launchers 5. Type 354 Eye Shield air/surface-search radar 6. Type 352C Square Tie surface target detection and tracking radar 7. Wok Won director with Type 343 f.c. radar 8. 5-round Type 81 ASW rocket launchers
Drawing by A. D. Baker III

M: 2 SEMT-Pielstick 12 PA6 280 BTC diesels; 2 props; 16,000 bhp (14,400 sust.)
Electric: 1,720 kw (4 × 400 kw, 1 × 120 kw)
Range: 3,000/18; 1,750/25 **Endurance:** 10 days **Crew:** 168 tot.

Remarks: An improved version of the Jianghu-I/II series, on the same hull and propulsion plant, but with a full shelter deck amidships supporting four pairs of SSM launchers. All three units are based in the East Sea Fleet at Dinghai.
Hull systems: Equipped with fin stabilizers. The export versions had a more powerful propulsion plant.
Combat systems: Have a Wok Won (a copy of the Russian Wasp Head) optical director forward (with Type 343 radar) for surface gunfire and a Type 341 (Rice Lamp) radar director aft for AA. The 100-mm mounts are auto-loading. The EW intercept system is reportedly based on the Italian Elettronica Newton system. In 537, the anti-ship missile tubes are paired symmetrically, whereas in the other two they are staggered; this may indicate that 537 can carry a later missile, possibly the C-802 Jing Yi-2 (CSS-N-8 Saccade).

Huayin (513) Antonio Scrimali, 7-02

♦ 21 Jianghu-I and -II* class (Projects 053, 053H)

Bldrs: Jianghu-I: Jiangnan SY, Shanghai; Jianghu-II: Hudong SY, Shanghai (In serv. 1975–93)

509 Changde	516 Jiujiang*	545 Linfen*
510 Shaoxing	517 Nanping	551 Maoming
511 Nantong	518 Ji'an	552 Yibin
512 Wuxi	519 Changzhi	553 Shaoguan*
513 Huayin	533 Ningbo*	554 Anshun
514 Zhenjiang	534 Jinhua*	555 Zhaotong
515 Xiamen	543 Dandong*	557 Jishou*

D: 1,425 tons (1,702 fl) **S:** 25.5 kts **Dim:** 103.2 × 10.2 × 3.05 (hull)
A: Jianghu-I: 4 C-201 Hai Ying-2 (CSS-N-1) SSM; 2 single 100-mm 56-cal. DP; 6 twin 37-mm 63-cal. Type 74 or 76 AA; 2 or 4 5-round Type 81 ASW RL; 4 BMB-2 d.c. mortars; 2 d.c. racks; 2 mine rails—Jianghu-II: 4 C-201 Hai Ying-2 (CSS-N-1) SSM; 2 twin 100-mm 56-cal. ENG-2 DP; 4 twin 37-mm 63-cal. Type 74 or 76 AA; 2 5-round Type 81 ASW RL; 4 BMB-2 d.c. mortars; 2 d.c. racks; 2 mine rails
Electronics:
Radar: 1 Type 756 nav.; Decca RM 1290A/D ARPA nav.; 1 Type 354 (Eye Shield) surf./air search; 1 Type 352C (Square Tie) antiship missile targeting—Jianghu-II also: 1 Type 343 (Sun Visor-B) 100-mm surface f.c.; 1 Type 341 (Rice Lamp) AA f.c.—543, possibly others: 1 Type 363 long-range air search
Sonar: EH-5 MF hull-mounted
EW: none or 2 RW-23-1 (Jug Pair) intercept; some: U.S. Mk 36 SRBOC decoy syst. (2 6-round Mk 137 RL)

Jiujiang (516) JMSDF, via *Ships of the World*, 5-99

M: 2 SEMT-Pielstick 12 PA6 280 BTC diesels; 2 props; 16,000 bhp (14,400 sust.)
Electric: 1,320 kw (3 × 400 kw, 1 × 120 kw)
Range: 3,000/18; 1,750/25 **Endurance:** 10 days **Crew:** 195 tot.

Remarks: Have also been referred to as Project EF3H or the Changsha class. First ship, 515, launched 28-6-75 and was commissioned 28-12-75, and construction on the class continuing into 1993. Units with square stacks were built by Jiangnan SY; the others have rounded stacks. Two sisters with twin 57-mm vice 100-mm guns were built for Egypt and delivered in 1984–85, and sister *Xiangtan* (556) was transferred to Bangladesh in 1990. *Kaifeng* (520) was reported stricken during 1993. Numbers 509–519, 551 and 552 are assigned to the East Sea Fleet. Numbers 533, 534, 543 and 553–555 and 557 are assigned to the South Sea Fleet.

Jianghu-I-class Wuxi (512) 1. BMB-2 depth-charge mortars 2. Single 100-mm 56-cal. DP gunmounts 3. Twin 37-mm 63-cal. Type 74 AA 4. Twin trainable launcher for SSM 5. Type 354 Eye Shield air/surface-search radar 6. Navigational radar 7. Type 352C Square Tie surface target detection and tracking 8. Optical rangefinder for 100-mm guns 9. 5-round Type 81 ASW rocket launchers
Drawing by A. D. Baker III

FRIGATES [FF] *(continued)*

Combat systems: Ships with twin 100-mm ENG-2 mounts (533, 534, 543, 545, 553, 557) are referred to as Jianghu-II; they omitted two twin 37-mm AA and are the only units with a Wok Won director for the 100-mm guns. In the Jianghu-I group, 100-mm gunfire control is by a simple stereoscopic rangefinder. The twin 100-mm ENG-2 mounts are auto-loading. 509 through 519 have the manually fed Type 74 37-mm AA mount; later units have Type 76 with auto-feed. On at least one unit of the class, the 37-mm mounts each have two co-mounted launchers for QW-1 or HN-5 point-defense SAMs. Only units 515 and 516 have four ASW rocket launchers. The antiship missiles are carried in two twin, fixed-elevation, trainable launchers.

GUIDED-MISSILE PATROL CRAFT [PTG]

♦ 4 (+ . . .) C-14-class fast attack catamarans

Bldr: 2208 and 2211: Qiuxin Shipyard, Shanghai; 2209: Huangpu Shipyard, Shanghai; 2210: Lushun Shipyard

	L	In serv.
2208	4-04	2005
2209	2004	2005
2210	2005	2005
2211	2005	2005

Fast attack catamaran (2211) *Ships of the World,* 2005

Fast attack catamaran (2211) *Ships of the World,* 2005

Fast attack catamaran (2208) *Ships of the World,* 2005

D: 250 tons (fl) **S:** Approx. 45 kts **Dim:** Approx. 43 × 12 × 2
A: 4 SSM missiles (type unknown); 1 30-mm/60 cal. (AK-630) gatling CIWS
Electronics:
Radar: 1 Type 362 (ESR-1) surf. search; 1 nav.; 1 missile targeting; 1 gun fire-control system
EW: Intercept/jammer
M: 2 diesels; 2 waterjet propulsors; 6,865 bhp
Range: . . . / . . . **Crew:** Approx. 12

Remarks: Data above are estimates only. Have catamaran hull, apparently based on a civil design from AMD Marine Consulting, Australia and militarized by Guangzhou Sea Bus International. Intended for mass production, which likely began during 2005, to replace many of the Navy's aging small combatants. Includes numerous signature reduction and stealth features. Wave piercing hull is likely of aluminum alloy construction.

♦ 7 Houjian class (Project 520T)

Bldr: Huangpu SY, Shanghai

	L	In serv.
770 Yangjiang	1-91	7-91
771 Shunde	7-94	2-95
772 Nanhai	2-95	4-95
773 Panyu	5-95	7-95
774 . . .	9-98	2-99
775 . . .	4-99	11-99
776 . . .	2000	2001

D: 542 tons (normal) **S:** 33.6 kts (32 sust.) **Dim:** 65.39 × 8.40 × 2.38
A: 770–775: 6 C-801 YJ-1 (CSS-N-4 Sardine) SSM; 1 twin 37-mm 63-cal. Type 76A AA; 2 twin 30-mm 65-cal. Type 69 AA—776: 6 C-801 YJ-1 (CSS-N-4 Sardine) SSM; 1 76.2-mm 59-cal. AK-176 DP; 1 30-mm 54-cal. AK-630 gatling AA
Electronics:
Radar: 1 Decca RM 1290A/D ARPA nav.; 1 Type 765 missile targeting; 1 Type 347G gun f.c. (776: 1 MR-123-02 Vympel gun f.c.)
EW: Type 900-series intercept/jammer
M: 3 SEMT-Pielstick 12PA6V 280MPC diesels; 3 props; 17,280 bhp (15,840 sust.)
Range: 1,800/18; 2,200/. . . **Crew:** 47 tot.

Yangjiang (770) China Shipbuilding Trading Co., 1999

Shunde (771) China Shipbuilding Trading Co., 1996

Remarks: 770–773 were based at Hong Kong as of 7-97. Design offered for export, as Type EM3D(H), with OTO Melara 76-mm Compact in place of the twin 37-mm mount, optronic gun directors, and decoy rocket launchers. Production for PLAN had been thought to have ended in 1998, but 774 was photographed during 2000, modified with Russian guns and gun fire-control equipment.
Combat systems: First six have Type 88C weapons control system. There is an unmanned electro-optical director for the 30-mm AA, and a radar director with separate optronic director for the enclosed-model 37-mm AA. The missiles are mounted one-over-two. The seventh unit, 776, has an imported Russian 76.2-mm gunmount and radar fire-control system, either for trials or as the start of a new construction series with more formidable defensive armament. Recent photographs have shown all six SSM canister positions occupied.

♦ 22 (. . .) Houxin class (Type 343M or 037-II)

Bldr: Qiuxin SY, Shanghai (In serv. 6-91–2004)

651–656 751–760 764–769

Houxin-class 759 JMSDF, via *Ships of the World,* 5-99

D: 478 tons (fl) **S:** 32 kts **Dim:** 62.00 × 7.20 × 2.24 (mean hull)
A: 4 C-801 YJ-1 (CSS-N-4 Sardine) SSM; 2 twin 37-mm 63-cal. Type 76A AA; 2 twin 14.5-mm 93-cal. Type 61 AA

GUIDED-MISSILE PATROL CRAFT [PTG] *(continued)*

Electronics:
Radar: 1 Anritsu Type 723 nav.; 1 Type 352C (Square Tie) missile targeting; 1 Type 341 (Rice Lamp) gun f.c.
EW: . . .
M: 4 diesels; 4 props; 13,200 bhp **Range:** 750/18; 2,000/14 **Crew:** . . . tot.

Remarks: Design based on that of the Haizhui-class subchaser/patrol boat. First unit was ordered 23-12-87 and laid down 1989. Pennant numbers have been changed in some. Design is a simpler, less-expensive variant of the Houjian class. Production may have stopped in favor of the new 2208 class.

♦ 8 Huangfeng class (Project 021)
Bldr: Jiangnan SY, Shanghai (In serv. 1960–75)

2304, 3114, 6107, 6119, 6120, 6122, 6123, 6124

Huangfeng-class 6119—with 25-mm guns and no f.c. radar
JMSDF, via *Ships of the World,* 5-99

Huangfeng-class 3114—with 30-mm gunmounts and spherical radome covering a presumed gun fire-control radar *Ships of the World*

D: 167 tons light, 186.5 normal (205 fl) **S:** 35 kts
Dim: 38.75 × 7.60 × 1.70 mean hull (2.99 over props)
A: 4 C-201 HY-2 (CSS-N-1) SSM; 2 twin 25-mm 80-cal. Type 81 or 30-mm 65-cal. Type 69 (Russian AK-230) AA
Electronics:
Radar: 1 Type 352 (Square Tie) surf. search/target desig.; some: 1 Type . . . (Round Ball) gun f.c.
M: 3 M-503A (42-160) diesels; 3 props; 12,000 bhp
Electric: 65 kw tot. **Range:** 800/30 **Crew:** 28 tot.

Remarks: Around 104 were built for the PLAN, but nearly all have been discarded or transferred to foreign clients. The design is a copy of the Russian Project 205E Osa but with simplified systems.
Hull systems: Soviet-design M-503A multirow radial diesels are difficult to maintain and offer only about 600 hours between overhauls; it is unlikely that the Chinese-made version is more reliable. Have hull portholes, not found on the Russian-built versions.
Combat systems: Most Chinese-built units had two twin 25-mm AA until early 1980s, when increasing numbers with a Chinese-built version of the Soviet AK-230, 30-mm AA began to appear; more recently, several have had a "Round Ball" radome installed aft for a probable f.c. radar for the 30-mm AA. The 1980s also saw the introduction of IFF equipment.

♦ About 30 Houku (Project EM1A or Project 24) class
[25 in reserve] Bldr: Wuhu Shipyard (In serv. circa 1955–69)

Houku-class 1103—and two sisters Poly Technologies, 1986

D: 69 tons, 79.2 tons (fl) **S:** 37.5 kts
Dim: 27.0 × 6.50 (6.30 wl) × 1.8
A: 2 twin SY-1 (Russian SS-N-2C Styx) SSM launchers; 2 twin 25-mm/80-cal. (Type 61) AA
Electronics: Radar: 1 Type 352 (Square Tie) surf. search/missile target desig.
M: 4 Type L-12V-180 diesels; 4 props; 4,800 bhp **Electric:** 65 kW tot.
Endurance: 5 days **Range:** 400/30 **Crew:** 17 tot., 2 officers, 15 enlisted

Remarks: Also referred to as the "Hegu" class, this is a Chinese built steel-hull copy of the Russian Komar class PTG. Some 30 of the 200+ units remain in Chinese service, though 25 are laid up ashore, and likely in poor condition. Fourteen were stricken in 2003.

TORPEDO BOATS [PT]

♦ 5 Huchuan-class (Project 025 and 026) semi-hydrofoils
Bldr: Hudong SY, Shanghai (In serv. 1966–80)

D: 39 tons (45.8 fl) **S:** 50 kts **Dim:** 22.50 × 3.80 (6.26 over foils) × 1.146
A: 2 fixed 533-mm TT; 2 twin 14.5-mm 93-cal. Type 81 mg
Electronics: Radar: 1 Type 756 nav.
M: 3 M-50F-4 diesels; 3 props; 3,600 bhp **Electric:** 5.6 kw
Range: 500/30 **Crew:** 11 tot.

Huchuan-class 1247—Project 026 variant, with gunmount forward
Ships of the World

Remarks: Survivors of 120 built; all remaining units are in the North Sea Fleet and used primarily for training purposes. Not all units have the foils fitted forward. No foils were fitted aft, as the stern planes on the sea surface, but there are auxiliary foils forward to assist in getting the boat "on foil." In the Project 025, both gunmounts are aft, but in later-construction Project 026 units, one mount is forward. Project 025 units had Skin Head radar, while Project 026 ships have a Type 756 slotted-waveguide radar antenna.

PATROL CRAFT [PC]

♦ 35 (+ . . .) Haiqing class (Project 037-I)
Bldr: Qiuxin SY, Shanghai (In serv. 1992–97)

611–614, 631–635, 710–717, 743–744, 761–764, 786–797

Haiqing-class 634 *Ships of the World,* 2001

D: 478 tons (fl) **S:** 28 kts **Dim:** 62.80 × 7.20 × 2.40
A: 2 twin 37-mm 63-cal. Type 76 AA; 2 twin 14.5-mm 93-cal. Type 81 AA; 2 6-tubed Type 87 ASW RL
Electronics: Radar: 1 Anritsu Type 723 nav.—Sonar: HF hull-mounted
M: 4 Type PR 230ZC diesels; 4 props; 4,000 bhp
Range: 1,300/15 **Crew:** 71 tot.

Remarks: Appears to be a replacement for the Hainan class and is said to be building at the rate of about three per year; two other yards are said to have entered the program. One has been exported to Sri Lanka. Units are now operating in all three fleets.

♦ 2 Haijiu class
Bldr: . . . (In serv. 1987–approx. 1995)

693 697

D: 450 tons (fl) **S:** 28 kts **Dim:** 62.0 × 7.20 × 2.24 (hull)
A: 1 twin 57-mm 62-cal. Type 66 AA (693: 2 twin 57-mm AA); 2 twin 30-mm 65-cal. Type 69 (AK-230) AA; 4 6-round Type 87 ASW RL; 2 BMB-2 d.c. mortars; 2 d.c. racks; 2 mine rails
Electronics:
Radar: 1 Type 351 (Pot Head) surf. search; 1 Round Ball gun f.c.
Sonar: HF hull-mounted; Thomson-Marconi SS 12 VDS
M: 4 diesels; 4 props; 8,800 bhp **Range:** 750/18 **Crew:** 70 tot.

Remarks: A lengthened version of the Hainan class, with somewhat newer AA weapons. Have an optical f.c. director. 697 has French Thomson-Marconi SS 12 variable-depth sonar in lieu of aft twin 57-mm mount of the earlier units. Range can be extended to 1,800 n.m. by using void tankage. Sister 694 reported scrapped in 1995 and 688 by 1997.

TORPEDO BOATS [PT] *(continued)*

♦ 94 Hainan class (Project 037) (In serv. 1964–96)

From among: 275–285, 290, 302, 305, 609, 610, 618–622, 626–629, 636–687, 689–692, 695–699, 701, 707, 723–733, 740–742, and others

D: 395 tons (430 fl) **S:** 30.5 kts (28 sust.) **Dim:** 58.77 × 7.20 × 2.24 (hull)
A: 2 twin 57-mm 62-cal. Type 66 AA; 2 twin 25-mm Type 61M AA; 4 5-round Type 81 ASW RL; 2 BMB-2 d.c. mortars; 2 d.c. racks; 2 mine rails
Electronics:
Radar: 1 Type 351 (Pot Head) surf. search
Sonar: Tamir-11 hull-mounted searchlight HF
M: 4 diesels; 4 props; 8,800 bhp **Range:** 750/18; 1,800/14 **Crew:** 78 tot.

Hainan-class 680 JMSDF, via *Ships of the World,* 5-99

Remarks: The first unit was laid down in 8-62, launched in 12-63, and ran trials in 3-64. Early units (which are beginning to be retired) had two single 76.2-mm DP U.S. Mk 26 vice the 57-mm AA and had Skin Head radars. Two were transferred to Pakistan in 1976 and two more in 1980. Eight were delivered to Egypt 1983–85; eight to Bangladesh 1982–85; six to North Korea in 1975–78; and 12 to Myanmar in 1991–94. Class production has ceased and units are gradually being replaced by the Haiqing (Type 037-1) class.

♦ 18 Haizhui class (Project 062/062-1)
Bldr: Guijian SY (In serv. 1992–98)

1203, 1204, 1208, 1239, 1240, 2327, 2328, 2329, 4339, 4340–4348

D: 150 tons (170 fl) **S:** 29 kts **Dim:** 41.0 × 5.41 × 1.80
A: 1 twin 37-mm 63-cal. Type 76 AA; 1 twin 25-mm 80-cal. Type 81 AA; 2 twin 14.5-mm 93-cal. AA
Electronics: Radar: 1 Anritsu 726 UA or Decca RM 2090 ARPA nav./surf. search
M: 4 Type L12-180Z diesels; 4 props; 4,800 bhp (4,400 bhp sust.)
Range: 750/16 **Crew:** 4 officers, 24 enlisted

Haizhui-class 4340 Chris Delgoffe/H&L Van Ginderen, 5-00

Haizhui-class 4339 Chris Delgoffe/H&L Van Ginderen, 5-00

Remarks: Lengthened successor to the Shanghai-II design. Being built in small numbers for domestic use and also for export, with seven delivered to Sri Lanka through 1998 and two more ordered in 1999. Differ from the Shanghai-II in having four more powerful diesel engines and in having power-operated 37-mm AA mounts. Some or all probably have fin stabilizers.

♦ Up to 40 Shanghai-II class (Project 062) (In serv. 1962–88)

D: 122.5 tons (134.8 fl) **S:** 28.5 kts
Dim: 38.78 × 5.41 × 1.49 (hull; 1.554 full load)
A: 2 twin 37-mm 63-cal. Type 74 AA; 2 twin 25-mm 80-cal. Type 61M AA; 4 d.c. in tilt racks—some also: 2 5-round Type 81 ASW RL
Electronics:
Radar: 1 Type 756 nav.
Sonar: HF searchlight-type on some
M: 2 M-50F-4, 1,200-bhp, and 2 Type 12D6, 910-bhp diesels; 4 props; 4,200 bhp
Electric: 39 kw tot. **Range:** 750/16.5 **Endurance:** 7 days **Crew:** 36 tot.

Shanghai-II 3314—with two Type 81 ASW rocket launchers forward 1988

Remarks: No longer being constructed, and numbers are declining through transfers abroad and attrition; well over 300 were built. At least 72 others have been transferred to foreign navies, and Romania also built the design. Very unsophisticated and sparsely equipped. The Type 12D6 diesels are used during cruising, with the high-speed M-50F-4 diesels for maximum speeds. Type 756 navigational radars have replaced the earlier Pot Head (or Skin Head on earliest units), and a number were noted during the mid-1980s with two EDS-32 (Type 81) ASW rocket launchers added forward; presumably a sonar had been installed as well.

PATROL BOATS [PB]

Note: The number of PLAN patrol boats is unknown but is far exceeded by craft assigned to the various paranaval organizations such as the Customs Service, Marine Police, Border Security groups, and Border Defense organization. One naval class for which some data are available is described below.

♦ 4 25-meter class (In serv. 1960s–90s)

7360 and three others

25-meter patrol boat J 1301 H&L Van Ginderen, 3-95

D: 82 tons **S:** 14 kts **Dim:** 25.0 × 4.1 × 1.4
A: 2 twin 14.5-mm 93-cal. Type 81 AA
Electronics: Radar: 1 Type 756 or Fin Curve (or none)
M: 2 3D6 diesels; 2 props; 900 bhp **Range:** 900/11 **Crew:** 12

Remarks: Also employed by other agencies. Have also been exported to Albania and Benin, the latter with MWM diesels and Japanese radar.

MINE WARFARE SHIPS

♦ 1 Bulieijian-class minelayer [MM] (In serv. 1988)

814 Wolei

D: 3,100 tons (fl) **S:** 18 kts **Dim:** 93.8 × 14.4 × 4.0
A: 4 twin 37-mm 63-cal. Model 76 AA; approx. 300 mines
Electronics: Radar: . . .
M: 4 . . . diesels; 2 props; 6,400 bhp
Range: 6,000/14 **Crew:** approx. 200 tot.

Remarks: Also known as *Wolei* class. Can also be employed as mine-countermeasures support ship (MCS).

♦ 1 (+ . . .) Type 821 minesweeper
Bldr: Qiuxin Shipyard, Shanghai, China (In serv. 2005–)

804 Huoqiu

Huoqiu (804) photo via Jaroslaw Malinowski, 2005

MINE WARFARE SHIPS *(continued)*

D: 575 tons (fl) **S:** 16 kts **Dim:** 55.0 × 9.3 × 6.0
A: 1 twin 37-mm/63-cal. (Type 76) AA
Electronics: Radar: 1 . . . nav.
M: 2 diesels
Range: . . . / . . . **Crew:** . . . tot.

Remarks: Launched 4-04, likely of GRP construction. At least a dozen units are expected to enter service.

♦ 40 Soviet T-43-class (Project 010) fleet minesweepers [MSF]
(28 in reserve) Bldrs: Wuchang SY, Guangzhou SY
(In serv. 1956–70s, mid-1980s- . . .)

364–366, 377–379, 386–389, 396–397, 398–399, 801–803, 807–809, 821–823, 829–832, 853–854, 863, 994–996, etc.

T-43-class minesweeper 831 Werner Globke Collection, 8-02

D: 500 tons (590 fl) **S:** 14 kts **Dim:** 60.0 × 8.6 × 2.16
A: 2 twin 37-mm 63-cal. Type 74 AA; 2 twin 25-mm Type 61 AA; 2 twin 12.7-mm mg; 2 BMB-2 d.c. mortars; 2 mine rails (12–16 mines)
Electronics:
Radar: 1 Ball End surf. search or Type 756 nav.
Sonar: Tamir-11 hull-mounted searchlight HF
M: 2 Type 9D diesels; 2 props; 2,200 bhp
Electric: 550 kw tot. **Range:** 3,200/10 **Fuel:** 70 tons
Crew: 10 officers, 60 enlisted

Remarks: Around four 58-meter, 570-ton units were transferred from the USSR in the 1950s; the majority, however, are long-hulled ships and were built in China. Production began again in the mid-1980s at Guangzhou, and one new unit was delivered to Bangladesh during 1995. Several others were built or converted as surveying ships, civilian research ships, and submarine rescue ships.
Combat systems: At least three of the active units were fitted with a 65-mm 52-cal. gun mount, instead of a twin 37-mm, for use as a patrol ship. Have acoustic and magnetic sweep gear in addition to MPT-1 and MPT-3 wire sweeps and paravanes. Lightweight side-by-side 12.7-mm mg mounts are replacing the original over-and-under mountings. A few still retain the obsolescent Russian Ball End navigational radar.

♦ 4 (+ . . .) Wosao-class coastal minesweepers [MSC]
Bldr: Wusung SY, Shanghai (In serv. 1988– . . .)

800–803

Wosao-class minesweeper 4422 Chris Delgoffe/H&L Van Ginderen, 5-00

D: 310 tons (fl) **S:** 15.5 kts **Dim:** 44.79 × 6.20 × 2.27
A: 2 twin 25-mm 80-cal. Type 61 AA; 2 mine rails
Electronics: Radar: 1 Type 756 nav.—Sonar: probably none
M: 2 Type 12-180 diesels; 2 props; 2,000 bhp
Range: 500/. . . **Crew:** 3 officers, 14 enlisted

Remarks: Pennant numbers changed during 2002, previous numbers were 4422, 4423, 4425, plus one unknown. Ex-4422 is equipped only to sweep moored mechanical mines. Ex-4423, with a modified bridge incorporating bridge wings, was first sighted during 1997, and two more had been completed by early 2003. All known units are based at Shanghai. Steel-hulled. The design is offered for export with explosive sweep, magnetic, and acoustic sweep gear. Employs boom-mounted side-looking sonar equipment for mine location and safe route mapping.

♦ 46 Futi-class (Project 312) drone minesweepers [MSD]
(42 in reserve) (In serv. 1984– . . .)

D: 46.95 tons (fl) **S:** 11.5 kts **Dim:** 20.94 × 4.20 (3.90 wl) × 1.30
M: 1 Type 12-150C diesel; 1 CP prop; 300 hp
Range: 150/11.5 **Crew:** 3 tot. (for ferrying)

Remarks: Normally operated by radio control to a range of 3 n.m., but can be manned. All but four were reportedly in land storage by 1993; officially stated not to be good seaboats. Electric propulsion for sweeping at 1–5 kts. Diesel generator amidships powers integral electromagnet for magnetic sweeping and a noisemaker for actuating acoustic mines. All equipment shock-mounted. Laser precision navigation system. Class has been exported to Thailand and Pakistan.

AMPHIBIOUS WARFARE SHIPS

♦ 0 (+ 1 + . . .) Project 071 amphibious transport dock (LPD)
Bldr: Dalian SY

D: 12,300 std. (17,600 fl) **S:** . . . **Dim:** . . . × . . . × . . .
A: HQ-7A SAM system; 4 twin 37-mm AA; . . . 7.62-mm mg; . . . helicopter
Electronics: Radar: . . .
M: 2 SEMT-Pielstick diesels
Range: . . . / . . . **Crew:** . . .

Remarks: Data listed above remain speculative. Laid down in 2004, reports indicate this to be a newly designed amphibious transport dock under construction in covered slipways at Dalian Shipyard. The LPD has a helicopter deck and is also capable of docking air cushion landing craft. No additional data are yet available.

♦ 10 (+ . . .) Yuting II–class (Project 072 IIA) landing ship tank LST]
Bldr: 911, 912, and 996: Dalian SY; 913, 993, and 995: Zhonghua SY; 992, 994, and 997: Wuchang SY (In serv. 2003–)

911 912 913 918 992–997

Yuting II–class 913 *Ships of the World,* 2004

Yuting II–class 911—alongside sister *Ships of the World,* 2004

D: 3,430 tons (normal) **S:** 18 kts **Dim:** Approx. 130.0 × 16.0 × 3.0
A: 3 twin 37-mm/63 cal. (Type 76A) AA ; 2 40-round 122-mm (Type 81H) multiple rocket launchers (some units only); 1 Z-8 or 2 Z-9 helicopters
Electronics: Radar: 1 surf. search; 1 Type 756 nav.; 1 JPT-4G fire-control system (for 37-mm guns)
M: Probably 2 SEMT-Pielstick 12 PA6V-280MPC diesels; 2 props; 9,600 bhp
Range: 3,000/14 **Crew:** 120 tot.

Remarks: Above data are approximate. This is an updated version of the Yuting class that began construction in 2002. As many as 17 more of this class may be built.
Hull systems: Able to transport approx. 300 Marines and 12 tanks or 800 tons of cargo. The superstructure can be sealed for NBC operations. Fitted with floodable docking well, the class is compatible with the Type 724 air cushion landing craft. A helicopter deck, but no hangar, is fitted on the stern above the docking well. Each ship carries at least two LCVPs.

♦ 11 (+ . . .) Yuting-class landing ships (Project 72-II) [LST]
Bldr: Zhonghua SY, Shanghai (In serv. 1991 to 1-97, 2000–2001)

908 909 910 934 935 Xuefengshan
936 937 Qingchengshan 938 939 940 991

Yuting-class 908—this unit has Type 76A enclosed, automatic 37-mm AA mounts, but they are modified to accept an on-mount operator
JMSDF, via *Ships of the World,* 2-01

Yuting-class 910—also with Type 76A gunmounts
Chris Delgoffe/H&L Van Ginderen, 5-00

AMPHIBIOUS WARFARE SHIPS *(continued)*

D: 3,430 tons (normal) **S:** 18 kts **Dim:** 119.50 × 16.40 × 2.80
A: 3 twin 37-mm 63-cal. Type 76 or Type 76A AA
Electronics: Radar: 2 Type 756 nav.
M: 2 SEMT-Pielstick 12 PA6 280MPC diesels; 2 props; 9,490 bhp
Range: 3,000/14 **Crew:** 104 tot.

Remarks: Updated version of the Yukan class, distinguishable principally by the provision of a helicopter platform aft and a lighter defensive armament. The stack is higher, and the tripod mainmast is more massive than on the Yukan class. Cargo capacity is 250 marines and ten tanks or 500 tons of cargo. The cargo deck area is 810 m^2. Fitted with floodable docking well, the class is compatible with the Type 724 air cushion landing craft. A helicopter deck, but no hangar, is fitted on the stern above the docking well. Each ship carries at least two LCVP's. 934–938 and 991 were the first batch of the class constructed.

♦ **7 Yukan-class (Project 072) landing ships [LST]**
Bldr: Zhonghua SY, Shanghai (In serv. 1978–80)

927 ZIJINSHAN 928 929 930 931 932 933

Yukan-class 928 JMSDF, via *Ships of the World,* 2-01

Yukan class—with stern ramp open Antonio Scrimali, 7-02

D: 3,110 tons (fl) **S:** 18 kts **Dim:** 119.50 × 15.60 × 2.82
A: 4 twin 57-mm 62-cal. Type 66 AA; 4 twin 25-mm 80-cal. Type 61 AA
Electronics: Radar: 2 Type 756 nav.
M: 2 SEMT-Pielstick 12 PA6 V280 diesels; 2 props; 9,600 bhp
Range: 3,000/14 **Crew:** 109 tot.

Remarks: Built to replace aging World War II–era U.S. LSTs, these ships are larger and considerably faster than their predecessors. Carry two U.S.-design LCVPs. At least one has a twin 57-mm DP gunmount forward and only two twin 37-mm AA. The bow ramp is 17.2 m long by 4.8 m wide and can support a 50-ton vehicle; the stern ramp can support a 20-ton vehicle. Beaching load is 500 tons. Two modified units of this design were built as Yantai-class fleet supply ships. Construction was terminated after 7 units due to the introduction of the more capable Yuting (Project/Type 072-II) class. All are assigned to the South Seas Fleet.

♦ **10 (+ . . .) Yunshu-class (Project . . .) medium landing craft [LSM]** Bldrs: Hudong-Zhonghua Shipyard Shanghai (3 units); Qindao Naval Dockyard (2 units); Lushun Shipyard (3 units) and Wuhu Shipyard (2 units) (In serv. 2004– . . .)

944–950

D: 1,460 tons, 1,850 tons (fl) **S:** 17 kts **Dim:** 87.00 × 12.60 × 2.25
A: 2 twin 57-mm/62 cal. (Type 61) AA
M: 2 diesels; 2 props **Range:** 1500/14 **Crew:** 70 tot.

Remarks: Modified Yudeng class LSM. Series production in several shipyards indicates this may become a large class. First unit was launched in June 2003.

♦ **1 Yudeng-class medium landing ship (Project/Type 073-III) [LSM]** Bldr: Zhonghua SY, Shanghai (In serv. 8-94)

990

D: 1,460 tons normal (1,850 tons fl) **S:** 17 kts **Dim:** 87.00 × 12.60 × 2.25
A: 2 twin 37-mm 63-cal. Model 74 AA **Electronics:** Radar: 1 Type 756 nav.
M: 2 SEMT-Pielstick 6PA6L-280 diesels; 2 props; 4,740 bhp
Range: 1,500/14 **Crew:** 74 tot.

Remarks: Launched 3-91. Only one unit built. Appears to be more vehicle cargo vessel than combatant. Has an electrohydraulic, telescoping cargo crane amidships. Resembles a reduced version of the Yukan-class LST. Cargo capacity is 250 tons, with cargo decks totaling 440 m^2. A bow door and ramp are fitted. Assigned to the South Sea Fleet.

Disposal note: The remaining eight units of the Yudao-class (Project 073) had all been stricken by 4-05.

Yudeng-class 990 China Shipbuilding Trading Co.

♦ **13 (+ . . .) Yuhai-class utility landing craft [LCU]**
Bldr: Wuhu SY and . . . SY (In serv. 1995– . . .)

6562 7593 7579 7595 and nine other units

Yuhai-class N 1122—of the Nanjing Maritime Border Defense Force
Chris Delgoffe/H&L Van Ginderen, 5-90

D: 799 tons (fl) **S:** 14 kts **Dim:** 58.4 × 10.4 × 2.7
A: 1 twin 25-mm 80-cal. Type 61 AA **Electronics:** Radar: 1 Type 756 nav.
M: 2 M.A.N. 8L 20/27 diesels; 2 props; 4,900 bhp
Range: 1,000/12 **Crew:** 56 tot.

Remarks: Most may be other than naval subordinated. Essentially an enlarged LCU and appears to have been designed with commercial or logistic support duties rather than military service in mind. Bow ramp only. Cargo capacity is two tanks and 250 troops or up to 150 tons of miscellaneous cargo. Two have been built for Sri Lanka, and construction may be continuing. Three units are assigned to the North Sea Fleet, four to the East Sea Fleet and six to the South Sea fleet.

♦ **31 Yuling-class (Project 079) utility landing craft [LCU]**
(In serv. 1971–83) Bldr: 1st 27 units: Guangzhou Shipyard, Guangzhou, China (1972–1976); 28 through 31: Xiamen Shipyard, China (1972–82)

957–964 966–988 and 10 others

D: 730 tons; 833.4 tons (fl) **S:** 14 kts **Dim:** 53.0 × 10.00 × 2.36
A: 2 twin 25-mm 80-cal. Type 61 AA; 2 40-round 122-mm Type 81H multiple rocket launchers
Electronics: Radar: 1 Type 756 nav.
M: 2 6300Zc diesels (1,200 bhp total and two type 12V135Ca-1 diesels) (480 total bhp); 2 props; . . . bhp
Range: 1,000/15 **Endurance:** 15 days **Crew:** 36 tot.

Remarks: All 31 ships of this class are assigned to the South Sea Fleet. Cargo capacity is 200 tons (5 main battle tanks or 4 trucks plus four towed 85-mm cannon guns). Newest four units of the class possess a blunt bow incorporating a beaching ramp.

♦ **9 (+ . . .) Yubei-class (Project . . .) utility landing craft [LCU]**
Bldr: 3232: Shanghai Shipyard International; 3128–3129, . . .: Qingdao Naval Dockyard; 3316, 3318, . . . : Dinghai Naval Dockyard; 3315: Zhanjiang Shipyard North (In serv. 2004– . . .)

3128–3129, 3315–3316, 3318, and 3232–3235

D: 1,200 tons (fl) **S:** . . . kts **Dim:** 64.00 × 11.00 × 2.70
A: 2 twin ... gun mounts
M: 2 diesels; 2 props; . . . bhp **Range:** . . . / . . . **Crew:** . . . tot.

Remarks: Hull number 3232 was class prototype. Cargo capacity is believed to be 10 tanks or 150 troops. Additional units are anticipated.

♦ **235 Yunnan-class (Project 067) landing craft [LCM]**
(200 in reserve) Bldr: Huangzhou SY (In serv. 1968– . . .)

D: 133.2 tons (fl) **S:** 10.5 kts **Dim:** 27.50 (24.07 pp) × 5.40 × 1.40s
A: 1 or 2 twin 14.5-mm 93-cal. Type 82 mg
M: 2 diesels; 2 props; 600 bhp **Range:** 500/10 **Crew:** 6 tot.

Remarks: Production believed to have ceased in 1992 after approx. 280 units were built. Not all the active craft are used in the amphibious role. It is believed that 12 of the active craft are based in the South Sea Fleet and the remainder in the East Sea Fleet. Cargo capacity is one main battle tank or two light vehicles or 46 tons of cargo. Cargo deck measures 15.0 × 4.0 m.

AMPHIBIOUS WARFARE SHIPS *(continued)*

Yunnan-class N 3003 J. Pierre via Paolo Marsan, 6-04

♦ 14 Type 271 class mechanized landing craft [LCM]
Bldr: . . . , Shanghai, China (In serv. 1968–late 1980s)

481, 3703, 6562, 7559, N-1122–1123, N-2011–2012, N-3001 and 5 others

D: 85 tons (fl) **S:** 11.5 kts **Dim:** 24.80 × 5.20 × 1.30
A: 2 twin 25-mm 80 cal. Type 62 AA mounts or 2 twin 14.5-mm/93-cal. Type 82 machineguns
M: 2 6300 diesel; 2 props; 600 bhp
Range: 450/11.5 **Crew:** 12 tot.

Remarks: Survivors of a class of approximately 300 built over a twenty-year period. Units with an "N" before their pennant number are assigned to the Nanjing Maritime Border Defense Force and are used in secondary roles. Can carry 100 tons of cargo.

♦ 40 Yuqin-class (Project 069) landing craft [LCM] (31 laid up)
(In serv. 1962–72)

454, 2350, 3221, 4507–4508, and 35 others

D: 85 tons (fl) **S:** 11.5 kts **Dim:** 24.80 × 5.20 × 1.30
A: 2 twin 14.5-mm/93-cal. (Type 82) machineguns
M: 2 Type 12V 150C diesels; 2 props; 600 bhp
Range: 450/11.5 **Crew:** 12 tot.

Yuqin-class N 2332—of the Nanjing Maritime Border Defense Force H&L Van Ginderen, 3-95

Remarks: Built domestically. Intended primarily for personnel transport. All are assigned to the South Sea Fleet. Two transferred to Bangladesh in 1984 as survey craft. Can carry up to 150 troops over short distances.

♦ 30+ Yuchai-class (Project 068) landing craft [LCM]
Bldr: Kailing SY, Zhoushan

Yuchai-class Y 761 Ross Gillett, 9-84

D: 85 tons (fl) **S:** 11.5 kts **Dim:** 24.8 × 5.2 × 1.3
A: 2 twin 14.5-mm 93-cal. mg
M: 2 Type 12V-150 diesels; 2 props; 600 bhp
Range: 450/11.5 **Crew:** 23 tot. (including vehicle crews)

Remarks: Number in Chinese service unknown; two each built for Bangladesh (in early 1980s) and Tanzania (in 1995). First observed in late 1960s. Based on the Russian T-4 class LCM. The tank deck measures 9.5 m × 3.9 m and can carry 50 tons of cargo.

♦ 4 Qiongsha-class troop transports [AP]
Bldr: Guangzhou SY (In serv. 1980– . . .)

830 831 832 836

Qiongsha-class transport 832 U.S. Navy, 5-83

D: 2,150 tons (fl) **S:** 16.2 kts **Dim:** 86.0 (76.0 pp) × 13.4 × 3.9
A: 4 twin 14.5-mm 93-cal. Type 82 AA
Electronics: Radar: 2 Fin Curve nav.
M: 3 8NVD48A-2U diesels; 3 props; 3,960 bhp
Electric: 575 kw tot. **Fuel:** 195 tons **Crew:** 59 tot. + 400 troops

Remarks: Built for South Sea Fleet service. Carry about 400 troops. Cargo holds fore and aft, each tended by two 1-ton derricks, can accommodate 350 tons. Carry four merchant marine–type lifeboats in Welin davits vice landing craft. Near-sisters *Nankang* (833) and one other are configured as hospital ships. Pennant numbers are now plain, without a letter or character prefix.

♦ 0 (+ 8) Russian Pomornik (Zubr)–class (Russian Project 1232.2) air-cushion utility landing craft [LCUA]
Bldr: Sudostroitel'noye Obyedineniye "Almaz," Dekabristov Verf, St. Petersburg, Russia

D: 340 tons light, 415 normal (550 fl) **S:** 63 kts (55 sust.)
Dim: 57.3 (56.2 hull) × 25.6 (22.0 hull) × 21.9 high
Electronics:
Radar: 1 . . . nav.; 1 MR-123-2 Vympel gun-fire control
E/O: 1 . . . surveillance/fire control
M: 5 NK-12MV (M-70) gas turbines (12,100 shp each; 2 to power lift fans); 3 ducted CP airscrew propellers; 4 NO-10 lift fans; 36,300 shp for propulsion
Electric: 200 kw tot. (2 × 100 kw GTG-110 gas turbine sets)
Range: 300/55 (with 130-ton payload); 1,000/55 light **Fuel:** 56 tons
Endurance: 5 days (1 day with full troop complement)
Crew: 4 officers, 27 enlisted + 360 troops

Remarks: Armament fit unknown. Above data reflect Greek units of the Pomornik (Zubr) class currently in service. Officially typed as "fast transport vessels." Negotiations for the purchase of eight units began during 3-02 and concluded in 12-04. There have been significant reliability problems with the class while in Russian service.
Hull systems: The dimensions above include flexible skirt. All hull systems are intended to have a 16-year service life. Constructed in part using flammable light alloys. The vehicle deck can hold up to three main battle tanks or 8–10 armored personnel carriers or 360 troops and 130 tons of combat cargo. Have small bow and stern ramps.
Propulsion systems: Three of the gas-turbine engines are mounted on pylons and drive airscrew propellers; they are equipped with exhaust thrust diverters to enhance mobility. The lift-fan gas turbines drive four blowers to maintain skirt pressure and are mounted near the stern in the wing compartments and exhaust through the stern.

♦ Up to 30 Payi-class air-cushion personnel landing craft [LCPA]
Bldr: . . . China (In serv. 1996– . . .)

8536 8537 and others

Payi-class air-cushion personnel landing craft 8538—with a Yuting-class LST in background *Ships of the World,* 2000

D: 6.4 tons **S:** 40 kts **Dim:** 12.40 × 4.70 × 3.70
A: None **Electronics:** Radar: none
M: 2 diesel-engines; 2 ducted airscrew props; . . . bhp
Crew: 2 + 8–10 troops

Remarks: As few as 13 may be in service. Swiveling puff ports forward and rudder abaft the propellers are used for control. Yuting-II-class LSTs can carry two each in their well deck. All active units are based in the South Sea Fleet. Cargo capacity: 15 tons.

AMPHIBIOUS WARFARE SHIPS *(continued)*

Disposal note: Type 722-II air-cushion landing craft (LCAC), number 452 was scrapped in 2001 as was the last Dagu-A (Type 772-II) Class LCAC.

AUXILIARIES

There is no authoritative, comprehensive information on the PLAN's logistic support fleet, but China has designated and built large numbers of auxiliary vessels, running the spectrum of logistics support, repair, hydrographic survey, and research types, including a great many tugs and small oilers. Known types and classes are listed below.

♦ 6 Yanbai-class degaussing/deperming tenders [ADG] (In serv. . . .)

203 735 736 745 HAIZU 746 DONGQIN 863

Yanbai-class degaussing tender Shuguang 203 French Navy, 11-97

D: 746 tons (fl) **S:** 16.5 kts **Dim:** 65.00 × 9.00 × 2.60
A: 1 twin 37-mm 63-cal. AA Type 74 AA
Electronics: Radar: 1 Type 756 or Fin Curve nav.
M: diesel-electric drive: 2 Type 12VE 230ZC diesels, 2 Type ZDH-99/57 motors; 2 props; 2,200 bhp
Range: 800/16.5 **Crew:** Approx. 60 tot.

Remarks: Resemble enlarged T-43-class minesweepers. Main engine generator sets used to provide current for deperming ships and submarines of up to 7,000 tons displacement. Two twin 25-mm gunmounts have been removed.

♦ 3 Yantai-class ammunition ships [AE]
Bldr: Zhongua SY, Shanghai (In serv. 1992)

938 800 801

D: 3,330 tons (fl) **S:** 18 kts **Dim:** 115.00 × 15.60 × 3.00
A: 1 twin 37-mm 63-cal. AA **Electronics:** Radar: 1 Type 756 nav.
M: 2 SEMT-Pielstick 12 PA6 V280 diesels; 2 props; 9,600 bhp
Range: 3,000/14 **Crew:** 100 tot.

Remarks: Based on the Yukan tank landing ship design, these converted cargo vessels have a shorter forecastle, blunter bow-form, no bow door, and cargo-handling cranes fore and aft, tending two holds forward of the bridge superstructure and one aft. Both are assigned to the South Sea Fleet. The original pennant numbers, 800 and 801, were changed to amphibious warfare ship–series numbers during 2001, when photos showed 938 transferring torpedoes to a Ming-class submarine and a cruise-missile canister (atop its lattice support foundations) to a guided-missile frigate—both events at sea, dead-in-the-water and employing a large electrohydraulic crane installed between the two hatches forward.

♦ 2 Dayun-class fleet supply vessels [AF]
Bldr: Hudong SY, Shanghai (In serv. 1992)

883 (ex-*Nanyun* 951) 884 (ex-*Nanyun* 952)

Dayun-class Nanyun 884 92 Wing Det., RAAF, 2-95

D: 10,975 tons **S:** 20 kts **Dim:** 156.2 × 20.6 × 6.8
A: 2 twin 37-mm 63-cal. Type 76A AA; 2 twin 25-mm 80-cal. Type 61 AA
Electronics: Radar: 2 Type 756 nav.
M: 2 Xin Zhong–M.A.N. K9Z60/105E diesels; 2 props; 9,000 bhp **Crew:** . . .

Remarks: Appear to be an adaptation of the Dajiang-class submarine tender to serve as fleet supply vessels and personnel transports but have lower freeboard. Carry four small landing craft. Two small electric cranes forward serve probable refrigerated holds. Have helicopter platform but no hangar.

♦ 1 Yanbing-class intelligence collection ship [AGI]
Bldr: . . . (In serv. late 1970s)

HAIDIAO 723 (ex-*Haidiao* 525, ex-*Haibing* 723)

Yanbing-class icebreaker Haidiao 723—traversing the Tsugaru Strait on an intelligence-collection mission JMSDF, via *Ships of the World,* 5-00

D: Approx. 5,000 tons (fl) **S:** 16 kts **Dim:** 94.5 × 17.1 × 5.9
A: 4 twin 37-mm 63-cal. Type 74 AA
Electronics: 1 Fin Curve nav., 1 Type 756 nav.
M: 2 or 4 diesels; 2 props; . . . bhp **Crew:** approx. 100 tot.

Remarks: Former icebreaker equipped for intelligence collection duties. An enlarged variant of the Yanha class with two radomes on the centerline forward of the bridge. Can also be used for ocean towing or icebreaking

♦ 3 Yanha-class intelligence collection ship [AGI]
Bldr: Qiuxin SY, Shanghai

HAIBING 519 (In serv. 1989?) HAIBING 722 (L: 1972)
HAIBING 721 (L: 26-12-69)

D: 3,200 tons **S:** 16 kts **Dim:** 84.0 × 15.0 × 5.0
A: 4 twin 37-mm 62-cal. Type 74 AA; 4 twin 25-mm 80-cal. Type 61 AA
Electronics: Radar: 2 Fin Curve nav.
M: 2 diesels, electric drive; 2 props; 5,200 bhp **Crew:** 90 tot.

Remarks: Differ in details of superstructure. Primary duty is intelligence collection. Can break 1.2-m ice, can also be used as ocean tugs. Resemble a slightly smaller version of Haidiao 723 above, with one less level of superstructure above the bridge and no after mast. Haibing 519 has a small tripod mast aft not found on the others. All three are assigned to the North Sea Fleet.

♦ 1 Wuhu-B-class trials ship [AGE]
Bldr: Wuhu SY (In serv. 8-97)

891 (ex-*Shiyan* 970; ex-909)

891—with old pennant number *Ships of the World,* 1999

D: 6,000 tons (fl) **S:** 20 kts **Dim:** 130.0 × 17.5 × 7.00 **A:** None
Electronics:
Radar: 1 or 2 . . . nav., 1 Type 354 (Eye Shield) air search
Sonar: . . .
EW: . . .
M: 2 diesels; 2 props; . . . bhp
Range: . . . / . . . **Crew:** 80 tot.

Remarks: 4,630 grt. Pennant number changed 2002. Has a large helicopter deck but no hangar. Thus far, most of the antenna positions have remained empty. Dimensional data, displacement, and speed were reported in a Chinese publication. Operational compartments are enlarged to permit seating trainees. Has also been referred to as an intelligence collection ship, and the previous "Shiyan" prefix to the hull number meant "experimental."

♦ 1 Yanxi-class weapons trials support ship [AGE]
Bldr: . . . SY, Shanghai (In serv. 1970)

HSUN 701

D: 1,200 tons (fl) **S:** 16 kts **Dim:** 60.0 × 11.0 × 3.5
A: 1 twin 37-mm 63-cal. Type 74 AA; 2 twin 14.5-mm 93-cal. AA
Electronics: Radar: 1 Fin Curve nav.
M: 2 Type 8300Z diesels; 2 props; 2,200 bhp **Range:** 4,500/11

Remarks: Apparently intended to support antiship cruise missile trials or, possibly, to act as a drone target launch and recovery ship.

♦ 1 Xingfengshan-class intelligence collection ship [AGI]
Bldr: Guangzhou Shipyard, Guangzhou, China (In serv. 1988)

XINGFENGSHAN 856

AUXILIARIES *(continued)*

D: 5.500 tons (fl) **S:** 16 kts **Dim:** 115.00 × 15.00 × 4.30
A: 2 twin 37-mm/63-cal. Type 74 AA; 2 twin 14.5-mm/93-cal. Type 81 mg
Electronics: Radar: 1 . . . nav.
M: 2 diesels; 2 props; . . . bhp **Range:** . . . / . . .
Crew: . . .

Remarks: Based on the Dalang-class design.

♦ 1 Dadie-class intelligence collection ship [AGI]
Bldr: Wuhan SY, Wuchang (In serv. 1987)

Beidiao 900 (ex-841)

D: 2,550 tons (fl) **S:** 17 kts **Dim:** 94.0 × 11.3 × 4.0
A: 2 twin 14.5-mm 93-cal. Type 81 AA
Electronics:
Radar: 2 Type 756 or Decca RM 1290A/D ARPA nav.
EW: see Remarks
M: 2 diesels; 2 props; . . . bhp **Crew:** 170 tot., 18 officers, 152 enlisted

Dadie-class Beidiao 900—with old pennant number *Ships of the World*

Remarks: Subordinated to North Sea Fleet. Has been deployed as far as the Japanese coast. Has bow centerline anchor and a sharply raked bow, and therefore may be equipped with a bow-mounted sonar array. Intercept arrays are mounted on the lattice masts and atop the pilothouse. Has one machinegun mount on the forecastle, two side by side on the stern.

♦ 7 or more Yannan-class navigational buoy tenders [AGL]
Bldr: Zhonghua SY, Shanghai (In serv. late 1970s)

124	463	Beibiao 983	B-25
Dongce 263	Beibiao 982	B-22	

Yannan-class Beibiao 982 U.S. Navy, 7-94

D: 1,550 tons (fl) **S:** 14 kts (sust.) **Dim:** 71.40 (63.00 pp) × 10.50 × 3.60
A: 2 twin 37-mm 62-cal. Type 74 AA; 2 twin 14.5-mm 93-cal. Type 81 AA
Electronics: Radar: 1 Fin Curve nav.
M: 2 Type 8300Z diesels; 2 props; 2,200 bhp

Remarks: Design built for both military and civil use. Buoy tender version of the Youdian-class small cable ship.

♦ 1 . . . -class missile-range instrumentation ship [AGM]
Bldr: Qiuxin SY, Shanghai (completed 1999)

851 Dongdiao (ex-232, ex-970, ex-909)

Missile-range instrumentation ship Dongdiao 851 PLAN, 2003

D: Approx 4,600 tons (fl) **S:** 17 kts **Dim:** 121.0 × 15.8 × 4.8
A: 1 twin 37-mm 63-cal. Type 74 AA; 2 twin 25-mm 80-cal. Type 61 AA
Electronics:
Radar: 3 . . . nav., 2 . . . missile-tracking/telemetry
EW: . . . intercept
M: 2 SEMT-Pielstick 6PC2-5L diesels; 2 props; 7,200 bhp (14,400 sust.)
Range: 5,000/15 **Crew:** . . . tot.

Remarks: Has tracking radars atop pilothouse, after lattice mast and a large telemetry dish on a pedestal amidships, and a theodolite tracking camera in a dome forward of the bridge. Helicopter deck and hangar fitted. Electrohydraulic weapons-recovery cranes fitted at forward end of helicopter deck. Has a commercial Marisat SATCOM antenna. Characteristics data above are based on the Daxin-class cadet training ship *Zhenghe* (81), to which this ship is similar. Equipment aboard would also make the ship suitable for intelligence collection duties.

♦ 3 Yuanwang 1–class space event support ships [AGM]
Bldr: Hudong SY, Shanghai (First two in serv. 1980, third 4-95)

Yuanwang 1 Yuanwang 2 Yuanwang 3

Yuanwang 3—note large superstructure block forward of the helicopter deck *Ships of the World*

Yuanwang 2 Yvan Gomel via Paolo Marsan, 10-04

D: 17,100 tons (21,000 fl) **S:** 20 kts **Dim:** 190.0 × 22.6 × 7.5
A: None **Electronics:** See Remarks
M: 1 Dalian-Sulzer 8LRB66 diesel; 1 prop; 17,400 bhp
Range: 18,000/20 **Endurance:** 100 days
Crew: 470, including technicians

Remarks: *Yuanwang* means "Long Look." First two, initially observed during 5-80 Chinese ICBM tests in the central Pacific, were refitted 1986–87 and again in 1991–92. Have been subordinated to China's satellite launch and tracking control department and are officially known as "Space Event Ships."
Hull systems: Among the 54 research-associated antennas are one large parabolic tracking antenna, two log-periodic HF ("fish-spine") antennas, several precision theodolite optical tracking stations, and two smaller missile-tracking radars, as well as positions for later installation of equipment. Large helicopter deck but no hangar. Have a bow-thruster and retractable fin stabilizers. Navigational equipment includes SINS (Ship's Inertial Navigation System) and NAVSAT receiver. Equipped with satellite communications gear; both were refitted 1990 with improved communications and data-handling gear.
Yuanwang 3 differs from the earlier pair in having a larger superstructure block just forward of the helicopter deck and the funnel mounted farther forward; the ship also has a single mast aft supporting a large, trainable HF antenna, and at least three small SATCOM antennas are fitted, along with three large, trainable SATCOM dish antennas.

♦ 1 Xiangyanghong 10–class space event support ship [AGM]
Bldr: Jiagnan SY, Shanghai (In serv. 1980)

Yuanwang 4 (ex-*Xiangyanghong 10*)

Yuanwang 4 RAN, 12-02

D: 10,975 tons **S:** 20 kts **Dim:** 156.2 × 20.6 × 6.8
M: 2 Xin Zhong–M.A.N. K9Z60/105E diesels; 2 props; . . . bhp
Crew: 200 total

AUXILIARIES *(continued)*

Remarks: Converted during 4-month refit to a "seaborne monitor and control section of China's monitor and control system for satellite launches" from a high-seas oceanographic research and survey ship at Chengxi Shipyard, China Shipbuilding Industrial Group, Nanjing, and reentered service 18-7-99.
Hull systems: Uses same hull and propulsion as the Dajiang-class submarine tenders, but has twin, side-by-side funnels; the crane forward is smaller, and the king posts abaft the stacks and the heavy foremast support large log-periodic HF antennas. Has hangar space for two Z-8 Super Frelon helicopters. Retractable fin stabilizers are fitted.

♦ 1 Xiangyanghong 01–class intelligence collection ship [AGI]
Bldr: Hudong Shipyard, Shanghai (In serv. 1979)

XIANGYANGHONG 09

D: 1,153 tons **S:** 20 kts **Dim:** 112.00 × 15.20 × 5.00
Electronics: Radar: 2 Fin Curve nav. **M:** 2 diesels; 2 props; . . . bhp
Crew: 150 tot.

♦ 2 Kan Yang–class coastal survey ships [AGS]
Bldr: Zhonghua Shipyard, Shanghai, China (In serv. 1975)

NANCE 426 NANCE 428

Kan Yang–class Nance 428 OS2 John Bouvia, USN, 11-90

D: Approx. 600 tons (fl) **S:** Approx. 14 kts **Dim:** Approx. 50.0 × 8.0 × . . .
A: 1 twin 25-mm 80-cal. Type 61 AA **Electronics:** Radar: 1 . . . nav.
M: 2 . . . diesels; 2 props; . . . bhp

Remarks: Small survey craft operating in South Sea Fleet. *Nance* means "survey, fathom, or measure."

Disposal note: Survey ship *Nance* 420 of the Ganzhou class was stricken in 2004 for disposal. The five survey ships of the Yanlai class (*Dong Biao* 200, *Dong Baio* 226, *Dong Baio* 943, *Nance* 426, and *Nance* 427) were stricken between 1995 and 2005 for disposal.

♦ 3 Modified T-43 class hydrographic survey ships [AGS]
Bldr: Zhuijiang Shipyard, China (In serv. late 1960s)

SHUGUANG 01 (ex-993) SHUGUANG 03 (ex-995)
SHUGUANG 02 (ex-994)

Shuguang 02—with old pennant number Boris Lemachko Collection

D: 500 tons, 590 tons (fl) **S:** 14 kts **Dim:** 60.00 × 8.60 × 2.16
Electronics: Radar: 1 Fin Curve nav.
M: 2 Type 9D-8 diesels; 2 props; 2,200 bhp
Range: 3,200/10 **Fuel:** 70 tons **Crew:** 70 tot.

Remarks: Modified T-43-class minesweeper design. Extended after deckhouse, no minesweeping equipment. This class may have been retired from service.

♦ 2 Qiongsha-class hospital ships [AH]
Bldr: Guangzhou SY (In serv. 1980– . . .)

833 NANKANG . . .

Qiongsha-class hospital ship Nankang (833) *Ships of the World,* 1993

D: 2,150 tons (fl) **S:** 16.2 kts **Dim:** 86.0 (76.0 pp) × 13.4 × 3.9
A: 4 twin 14.5-mm 93-cal. Type 82 AA
Electronics: Radar: 2 Fin Curve nav.
M: 3 8NVD48A-2U diesels; 3 props; 3,960 bhp
Electric: 575 kw tot. **Fuel:** 195 tons **Crew:** 59 tot.

Remarks: Built for South Sea Fleet service. Similar to troop transport version but are configured as hospital ships; white-painted and bearing International Red Cross markings, they nonetheless retain the standard armament suite. Pennant numbers are now plain, without a letter or character prefix.

♦ 7 or more Hongqi 081–class cargo ships [AK]
Bldr: . . . (In serv. 1970s)

433 443 528 755 756 771 836

Hongqi 081–class cargo ship 528 Stefan Karpinski, 6-02

D: 1,950 tons (fl) **S:** 14 kts **Dim:** 62.0 (58.0 wl) × 12.0 × 4.5
A: 2 twin 25-mm 80-cal. Type 61 AA **Electronics:** Radar: 1 Type 756 nav.
M: 1 diesel; 1 prop; 1,200 bhp **Range:** 2,500/11 **Crew:** 30 tot.

Remarks: 875 grt/1,100 dwt. Used to support offshore island garrisons and appear to be able to carry some passengers. Sisters in commercial service.

♦ 2 Romanian Galati-class cargo ships [AK]
Bldr: Santieral SY, Galati (In serv. early 1970s)

HAIYUN 318 HAIJIU 600

D: 5,200 tons (fl) **S:** 12.5 kts **Dim:** 100.60 (93.70 pp) × 13.92 × 6.60
A: . . .
Electronics: Radar: 2 . . . nav.
M: 1 Sulzer 5TAD56 diesel; 1 prop; . . . bhp **Electric:** 345 kw
Range: 5,000/12.5 **Fuel:** 250 tons **Crew:** 50 tot.

Remarks: Cargo capacity 3,750 tons.

♦ 7 Danlin-class cargo ships [AK] (In serv. 1960–62)

HAILENG 531 HAILENG 592 HAIYUN 794 HAIYUN 975
HAILENG 591 HAILENG 594 HAIYUN 972

Danlin-class cargo ship Haiyun 794 7-89

D: 1,290 tons (fl) **S:** 14 kts **Dim:** 60.5 × 9.0 × 4.0
A: 1 twin 37-mm 63-cal. Type 74 AA; 2 twin 14.5-mm 93-cal. AA
Electronics: Radar: 1 Fin Curve or Type 756 nav.
M: 1 Type 6DRN 30/50 diesel; 1 prop; 750 bhp **Crew:** 35 tot.

Remarks: *Haiyun* series in East Sea Fleet; *Haileng* series in South Sea Fleet. Three holds, served by two electrohydraulic cranes; cargo about 750 dwt, including refrigerated stores. Others are in civilian service.

AUXILIARIES *(continued)*

♦ . . . trawler-type coastal cargo ships [AK]

Trawler-type coastal cargo ship N 1121—of the Nanjing Maritime Border Defense Force Ross Gillett, 9-84

Remarks: There were a number of units of this design (including N 1121 and N 3215), most of which seem to have been subordinated to the Maritime Border Defense Force districts; of about 450 tons (fl) displacement, they have a single cargo hold amidships, are equipped with a Type 756 navigational radar, and are armed with two twin side-by-side 14.5-mm mg mounts. Maximum speed is about 9 kts on a single 300-bhp Type 12-150C diesel.

♦ 2 Fuchi-class replenishment oilers [AO]

Bldr: Qiandaohu: Hudong-Zhonghua Shipyard, Shanghai, China
Weishanhu: Huangpu Shipyard, Guangzhou, China

	L	In serv.
886 Qiandaohu	7-03	30-4-05
887 Weishanhu	6-03	2005

Qiandaohu (886) *Ships of the World*

Weishanhu (887) *Ships of the World*

D: 22,000 tons (fl) **S:** 20 kts (19 sust.) **Dim:** 178.50 × 24.80 × 8.70
A: 1 helicopter
Electronics: Radar: 1 Decca 1290 nav.; Type 341 Rice Lamp radar f.c. director
M: 2 SEMT-Pielstick 16PC2 6V400 diesels; 2 KaMeWa CP props; 24,000 bhp
Range: 10,000/15 **Crew:** 19 officers, 138 enlisted + 26 passengers

Remarks: Observed under construction during 2003. Much-modified, flush-decked version of the Fuqing class; layout resembles a French *Durance*-class ship. Sister ship is in service with Thailand. *Qiandahou* is assigned to the East Sea Fleet.
Hull systems: Both have two liquid transfer stations each side and one sliding-stay solid transfer station per side. Can also refuel over the stern. Has hangar for one helicopter to provide vertical replenishment of solid stores, two refueling stations on either beam. Carries 11,400 tons cargo, including 7,900 tons diesel fuel, 2,500 tons aviation fuel, 250 tons fresh water, 70 tons lube oil, and 680 tons dry cargo, ammunition, and stores.
Combat systems: May be fitted with the Type 354 (Eye Shield) search and target designation radar. Fitted for, though not armed with, 4 twin 37-mm/63-cal. (Type 74) AA.

♦ 2 Fuqing-class replenishment oilers [AO]

Bldr: Dalian SY (In serv. 1980–82)

881 Hongzhu (ex-*Taicang*, ex-*Beiyu* 575)
882 Fencang (ex-*Dongyun* 615)

Fuqing-class oiler Fencang (882) *Ships of the World*

D: 14,600 tons (21,740 fl) **S:** 18.6 kts **Dim:** 168.20 (157.00 pp) × 21.80 × 9.40
A: 881: 4 twin 37-mm 63-cal. Type 74 or 76A AA; 882: 2 twin 14.5-mm 93-cal. mg
Electronics: Radar: 2 Fin Curve nav.
M: 1 Dalian-Sulzer 8RLB 66 diesel; 1 prop; 17,400 bhp (15,000 sust.)
Electric: 2,480 kw **Range:** 18,000/14.6 **Crew:** 26 officers, 120 enlisted

Remarks: A sister, *Nasr* (A 47), was delivered to Pakistan in 1988, and in 1989, the third PLAN ship of the class, *Hongcang* (X 950), was placed in merchant service and renamed *Hailang*. *Taikang* was armed during 1994 and *Fencang* in 2000. The original pennant numbers were changed during 2002.
Hull systems: Have two liquid replenishment stations per side, with constant-tension solid transfer stations each side just forward of the stack. Helicopter deck, but no hangar. Have four small electric cranes for stores handling. Carry 11,000 tons fuel oil, 1,000 tons diesel fuel, 200 tons feedwater, 200 tons potable water, and 50 tons lube oil.

♦ 1 Russian Komandarm Fedko–class replenishment ship [AOR]

Bldr: Kherson Shipyard, Kherson, Russia (In serv. 2-6-96)

Qinghai-Hu (AO 885) (ex-Chinese *Nancang, Nanyun* 953; ex-Russian *Vladimir Peregudov*)

Qinghai-Hu (AO 885) *Ships of the World*

D: Approx. 37,000 tons (fl) **S:** 16.4 kts (15.48 sust.)
Dim: 188.90 (165.00 pp) × 25.33 × 10.41 (12.0 max.)
A: Provision for 3 twin 30-mm 65-cal. AA **Electronics:** Radar: . . .
M: 1 Bryansk-Burmeister & Wain 6DKRN74/160-3 diesel; 1 prop; 10,600 bhp
Electric: 2,000 kw tot., (3 × 500-kw, 5 × 100-kw diesel sets)
Range: 12,000/15.48 **Fuel:** 1,606 tons heavy oil, 305+ tons diesel
Endurance: 45 days **Crew:** . . .

Remarks: Laid down 1-89 for the Soviet Navy as a replenishment oiler, with design modified from that of a standard 27,400-dwt product oiler class. Capable of refueling three warships simultaneously. Purchased 1992 by China for a reported $10 million and delivered nearly complete in spring 1993 to Dalian SY for fitting out. Handed over to the PLAN on 8-5-96. Assigned to the South Sea Fleet.
Hull systems: Is equipped with six cranes, four fuel-replenishment stations and two solid-transfer stations; can also refuel over the stern. A sponson has been added across the transom stern to support a helicopter deck, and there is a small hangar. Superstructure enlarged, with deckhouse added forward of bridge area and working deck built over cargo tank area. Additional generators added. Cargo: 23,000 tons fuel, water, and solid stores. Merchant version has ten cargo tanks totaling 31,398 m^3, but several tanks have been converted to dry cargo stowage or engineering and berthing spaces in this ship.
Combat systems: Has provision for three twin 30-mm/65 cal. AA mounts, controlled from cupola-mounted lead-computing optical directors.

♦ 3 Jinyou-class transport oilers [AOT]

Bldr: Kanashashi SY, Japan (In serv. 1989–90)

Dongyun 622 Dongyun 625 Dongyun 675

Jinyou-class Dongyun 625 James W. Goss/NAVPIC, 6-95

D: 2,500 tons light (4,800 fl) **S:** 15 kts **Dim:** 99.0 × 31.8 × 5.7
A: None **Electronics:** Radar: 2 Type 756 nav.
M: 1 SEMT-Pielstick 8PC2.2L diesel; 1 prop; 3,000 bhp
Range: 4,000/9 **Cargo:** 25,000 bbl liquid **Crew:** 40 tot.

AUXILIARIES *(continued)*

♦ 2 Shengli-class transport oilers [AOT]
Bldr: Hudong SY, Shanghai (In serv. 1981– . . .)

Dongyun 620 Dongyun 621

Shengli-class Dongyun 620 Antonio Scrimali, 2002

D: 4,940 tons (fl) **S:** 14 kts **Dim:** 101.0 (92.0 pp) × 13.8 × 5.5
A: 1 twin 37-mm 63-cal. Type 74 AA; 2 twin 25-mm 80-cal. Type 61 AA
Electronics: Radar: 2 Type 756 nav.
M: 1 Type 6 ESDZ 43 diesel; 1 prop; 2,600 bhp **Range:** 2,400/14

Remarks: 3,318.5 dwt. Cargo: 3,002 tons fuel oil (4,240 m^3).

Disposal note: *Dongyun* 632 was no longer in service by 2004.

♦ 14 Fulin-class transport oilers [AOT]
Bldr: Hudong SY, Shanghai (In serv. 1972– . . .)

Dongyun 583, Dongyun 606, Dongyun 607, Dongyun 609, Dongyun 623, Dongyun 626, Dongyun 628, Dongyun 629, Dongyun 633, Dongyun 923, Nanyun 923, Nanyun 924, Nanyun 940, N 1104

Fulin-class Dongyun 589—since retired Stefan Karpinski, 6-02

D: 2,200 tons (fl) **S:** 10 kts **Dim:** 66.0 × 10.0 × 4.0
A: 2 twin 25-mm 80-cal. Type 61 AA
Electronics: Radar: 1 Fin Curve nav.
M: 1 diesel; 1 prop; 600 bhp **Range:** 1,500/8 **Crew:** 30 tot.

Remarks: Part of a series of more than 20, the others of which went into merchant service. Several reported to have a single underway replenishment rig. At least one (N 1104) is subordinated to the Nanjing Maritime Border Defense Force. Resemble an enlarged Fuzhou.

Disposal note: *Dongyun* 560, 563, 582, 589, 620, 630, 632, *Nanyun* 922 were stricken between 2003 and 2005.

♦ 20 Fuzhou-class transport oilers [AOT]
Bldr: Hudong SY, Shanghai (In serv. 1964–70)

Dongyun 570, Dongyun 573, Dongyun 580, Dongyun 581, Dongyun 608, Dongyun 903, Nanyun 904, Nanyun 906, Nanyun 907, Nanyun 909, Nanyun 910, Nanyun 912, Nanyun 920, Nanyun 926, Nanyun 927, Nanyun 930, Nanyun 935, Nanyun 941, Nanyun 1101, Nanyun 1104

Fuzhou-class Dongyun 573—with 570 in background Stefan Karpinski, 6-02

D: 1,200 tons (fl) **S:** 10–12 kts **Dim:** 60.0 (55.0 pp) × 9.0 × 3.5
A: 2 twin 25-mm 80-cal. Type 61 AA; 2 twin 14.5-mm 93-cal. Type 82 AA
Electronics: Radar: 1 Fin Curve or Type 756 nav.
M: 1 diesel; 1 prop; 600 bhp **Crew:** 30 tot.

Remarks: Cargo: 600 tons. Five also built in a water-tanker version. Some of the oilers (including N 1101) are subordinated to the Nanjing Maritime Border Defense Force. Some are not armed. Dongyun units are in the East Sea Fleet, Nanyun units in the South Sea Fleet; others may serve the North Sea Fleet.

Disposal notes: *Dongyun* 582, 606, 629, and *Nanyun* 945 were stricken between 2003 and 2005.

♦ 5 Leizhou-class transport oilers [AOT]
Bldr: . . . (In serv. early 1960s)

D: 900 tons **S:** 10–12 kts **Dim:** 53.0 (48.0 pp) × 9.8 × 3.0
A: 2 twin 37-mm 62-cal. Type 74 AA; 2 single 14.5-mm 93-cal. AA
M: 1 diesel; 1 prop; 600 bhp **Crew:** 30 tot.

Remarks: Four also built in a water-tanker version, and another was built as a cargo ship (Y 737) with a single king post and two cargo holds amidships. Others are in civilian service.

♦ 3 Youzhong-class cable ships [ARC]
Bldr: Zhonghua SY, Shanghai (In serv. 1982– . . .)

G 2693 N 2304 N 2404

D: 750 tons (fl) **S:** 14.5 kts **Dim:** 59.0 × 10.50 × 2.8
A: 2 twin 14.5-mm 93-cal. Type 82 AA
Electronics: Radar: 1 Fin Curve nav.
M: 2 Type 8300Z diesels; 2 props; 2,200 hp

Remarks: Smaller version of Youdian class, with shallower draft and only 50 m^3 of cable stowage (600 tons). All three are assigned to Maritime Border Defense Forces.

♦ 6 or more Youdian-class cable ships [ARC]
Bldr: Zhonghua SY, Shanghai (In serv. late 1970s)

Nanlan 233, Nanlan 234, Beilan 764, Beilan 765, Donglan 873, Donglan 874

Youdian-class Donglan 874 Navpic-Holland, 5-98

D: 1,550 tons (fl) **S:** 14 kts (sust.) **Dim:** 71.40 (63.00 pp) × 10.50 × 3.60
A: 2 twin 37-mm 62-cal. Type 74 AA; 2 or 4 twin 14.5-mm 93-cal. Type 82 AA
Electronics: Radar: 1 Fin Curve nav.
M: 2 Type 8300Z diesels; 2 props; 2,200 bhp

Remarks: Design built for both military and civil use. Cable tank has 187-m^3 capacity; ship can lay cable up to 100-mm thick. The buoy-tender version of the design is referred to as the Yannan class.

♦ 1 Daozha-class salvage ship [ARS]
Bldr: Zhonghua SY, Shanghai (In serv. 1993)

Daozha . . .

D: 4,000 tons (fl) **S:** 18 kts **Dim:** 84.0 × 12.6 × 5.4
A: . . . **Electronics:** Radar: . . .
M: 2 diesels; 2 props; 8,600 bhp **Range:** . . . / . . . **Crew:** 125 tot.

Remarks: Large tug-type vessel with twin, side-by-side funnels amidships and extended forecastle with crane at aft end. Fitted for ocean towing. Assigned to the South Sea Fleet.

♦ 1 Kansha-class salvage ship [ARS]
Bldr: Zhonghua SY, Shanghai (In serv. 7-81)

Hailao . . .

D: 1,400 tons (fl) **S:** 13.5 kts **Dim:** 69.9 × 10.5 × 3.6
A: . . . **Electronics:** Radar: . . .
M: 2 Type 8300ZC diesels; 2 props; 2,200 bhp **Range:** 2,400/13.5

Remarks: Carries French-supplied SM-358-S salvage submersible, 7 m overall, with 300-m working depth. Has one 5-ton crane forward and a 2-ton crane aft. Operates in East Sea Fleet.

Disposal note: Yanting-class salvage ships *Hailao* 456, *Hailao* 520, and *Hailao* 523, along with Dinghai-class salvage ships *Hailao* 446, *Hailao* 447, and *Hailao* 511 were stricken for disposal between 1995 and 2000.

♦ 4 Tuzhong-class salvage tugs [ARS]
Bldr: Zhonghua SY, Shanghai (In serv. late 1970s)

T 154 T 710 T 830 T 890

Tuzhong-class T 710 *Ships of the World*

AUXILIARIES *(continued)*

D: 3,600 tons (fl) **S:** 18.5 kts **Dim:** 84.90 (77.00 pp) × 14.00 × 5.50
A: None **Electronics:** Radar: 1 Fin Curve nav. (see Remarks)
M: 2 Type 9 ESDZ 43/82B diesels; 2 CP props; 9,000 bhp
Range: 18,000/ . . . **Crew:** Approx 60 tot.

Remarks: Powerful salvage tugs equipped for fire fighting and emergency repairs. Have high-capacity pumps and a 35-ton-capacity towing winch. T 710 has a Type 352 (Square Tie) cruise-missile fire-control radar on foremast, possibly for weapons trials purposes. There is provision to install at least two twin 37-mm AA mounts.

♦ 3 Dajiang-class submarine tenders [AS]
Bldr: Hudong SY, Shanghai (In serv. 1976–80)

861 CHANGXINGDAO (ex-121)
862 CHONGMINGDAO (ex-302)
863 YONGXINGDAO (ex-506, R 327, J 506)

Chongmingdao (862)—note deep submergence rescue vehicle (DSRV) forward of the bridge *Ships of the World*

D: 10,087 tons (fl) **S:** 20 kts **Dim:** 156.2 × 20.6 × 6.8 **A:** None
Electronics: Radar: 2 Fin Curve; 1 Type 354 (Eye Shield) air/surf. search
M: 2 Xin Zhong–M.A.N. K9Z60/105E diesels; 2 props; . . . bhp

Remarks: Also capable of employment as general salvage vessels. Carry two Z-8 Super Frelon helicopters in a double hangar. 861 differs in not having the deep anchor recesses at the stern (evidently intended to permit a four-point moor). The huge crane forward tends two trainable cradles just forward of the bridge; the cradles are semicircular in section and support salvage-and-rescue submersibles.

The ships share the hull and propulsion of the space support ship *Yuanwang 4* (formerly the research ship *Xiangyanghong 10*) and probably also have fin stabilizers. 506 was transferred to the Academy of Sciences in 1983 and renumbered R 327; a large log-periodic HF communications antenna was added. By 1989, the ship had been returned to naval service and is based at Yulin in the South Sea Fleet.

♦ 2 Dalang-II-class submarine support ships [AS]
Bldr: Wuhu SY

428 (L: 6-96) 911 (In serv. 1986)

Dalang-II-class 911 French Navy, 11-97

D: 3,700 tons (4,200 fl) **S:** 16 kts **Dim:** 115.0 × 14.6 × 4.3
A: 2 twin 37-mm 63-cal. Type 74 AA; 2 twin 25-mm 80-cal. Type 61 AA
Electronics: Radar: 1 Type 756 nav.
M: 2 diesels; 2 props; 4,000 bhp
Range: 8.000/14 **Crew:** approx 200 tot.

Remarks: Primarily intended for general salvage and towing duties in support of submarines. Other than an electrohydraulic crane aft, they have few outward attributes of a repair or resupply tender and are probably intended to provide in-port berthing and command facilities.

♦ 2 Dalang-I-class submarine rescue ships [ASR]
Bldr: Guangzhou SY

332 (ex-122) (In serv. 1986) 503 (In serv. 11-75)

D: 3,500 tons (4,000 fl) **S:** 16 kts **Dim:** 111.9 × 14.6 × 4.3
A: 4 twin 37-mm 63-cal. Type 74 AA; 2 twin 14.5-mm 93-cal. Type 82 AA
Electronics: Radar: 1 Fin Curve nav.
M: 2 diesels; 2 props; 4,000 bhp
Range: 8.000/14 **Crew:** approx 180 tot.

Remarks: Primarily intended for general salvage and towing duties in support of submarines. Have nothing in common with the Dalang-II class above, and 332 differs from 503 in having a larger, more elaborate superstructure and a rectangular stack; she also carries a submersible decompression chamber in an A-frame gantry to port.

Dalang-I-class 332 Werner Globke Collection, 8-02

♦ 1 Dazhi-class submarine tender [AS]
Bldr: Hudong SY, Shanghai (In serv. 1965)

920

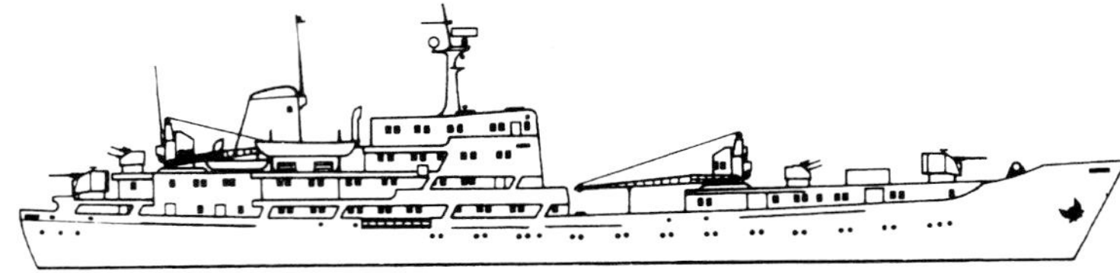

Dazhi-class 920

D: 5,800 tons (fl) **S:** 14 kts **Dim:** 106.7 × 15.3 × 6.1
A: 2 twin 37-mm 63-cal. Type 74 AA; 4 twin 25-mm 80-cal. Type 61 AA
Electronics: Radar: 1 Type 756 nav.
M: 1 diesel; 1 prop; . . . bhp

Remarks: The only PLAN submarine tender equipped on the Soviet scheme with spare torpedoes, a battery charging station, and command-and-control facilities and for light repair duties; the others are primarily intended for submarine rescue and salvage. Assigned to East Sea Fleet. Intended to provide services primarily in-port. Has not been photographed since the mid-1990s.

♦ 1 Hudong-class submarine rescue ship [ASR]
Bldr: Hudong SY, Shanghai (In serv. 1969)

HAIJIU 512 (ex-J 301)

Hudong-class Haijiu 512 Ross Gillett, 9-84

D: 5,000 tons (fl) **S:** 15 kts **Dim:** 95.0 × 17.0 × 4.5
A: 3 twin 37-mm 63-cal. Type 74 AA; 2 twin 14.5-mm 93-cal. Type 82 AA
Electronics: Radar: 1 Fin Curve nav.
M: 1 diesel; 1 prop; 3,600 bhp **Range:** 5,000/12
Crew: 225

Remarks: Has large gantry over stern for lowering a submarine rescue chamber, and is equipped with stern-quarter anchors to permit a 4-point moor.

♦ 2 Dazhou-class submarine rescue ships [ASR]
Bldr: Hudong SY, Shanghai (In serv. 1976–77)

HAIJOU 502 HAIJOU 504

D: 1,100 tons (fl) **S:** 18 kts **Dim:** 79.0 × 9.5 × 2.6
A: 1 twin 37-mm 63-cal. Type 74 AA; 2 twin 14.5-mm 93-cal. Type 82 AA
Electronics: Radar: 1 Fin Curve nav.
M: 2 diesels; 2 props; . . . bhp **Crew:** Approx. 130 tot.

Remarks: Both assigned to South Sea Fleet, where they have also been employed in intelligence gathering. Flush-decked, low-freeboard ships resembling hydrographic survey ships and having no obvious submarine rescue equipment visible.

♦ 11 Hujiu-class seagoing tugs [ATA]
Bldr: . . . (In serv. 1980s)

147 155 622 711 717 837 842 843 867
875 877

AUXILIARIES *(continued)*

Hujiu-class tug 877 Antonio Scrimali, 7-02

D: 750 tons (fl) **S:** 13.5 kts **Dim:** 49.0 (44.5 pp) × 9.5 × 3.7
A: None **Electronics:** Radar: 1 Type 756 nav.; 1 Fin Curve nav.
M: 2 LVP 24 diesels; 2 CP props; 1,800 bhp
Electric: 336 kVA **Range:** 2,200/13.5; 1,100/9 (towing) **Fuel:** 135 tons
Crew: 56

♦ 3 Dinghai-class seagoing tugs [ATA]
Bldr: Wuhu SY (In serv. late 1970s)

717 842 843

D: 1,472 tons (fl) **S:** 14 kts **Dim:** 60.22 × 11.60 × 4.44
A: none **Electronics:** Radar: 1 Type 756 nav.
M: 2 diesels; 2 props; 2,460 hp **Range:** 7,200/14
Crew: 53

Remarks: 980.28 grt.; 25-ton-capacity towing winch. Equipped for fire fighting. One sister transferred to Bangladesh Navy, 5-84. Class also built for civil use.

♦ 17 Soviet Gromovoy-class seagoing tugs [ATA]
Bldr: Guangzhou Shipyard, Guangzhou, China, and Wuhu Shipyard, Wuhu, China (In serv. 1958–62)

149 166 680 684 802 811 814 822 827
156 167 683 716 809 813 817 824

Gromovoy-class 802—in refit 7-89

D: 795 tons (890 fl) **S:** 11 kts **Dim:** 45.7 (41.5 pp) × 9.45 × 4.6
A: 2 twin 12.7-mm or 14.5-mm mg/AA
Electronics: Radar: 1 Fin Curve, Type 756, or Oki X-NE-12 nav.
M: 2 diesels; 2 props; 1,200 bhp
Range: 7,000/7 **Fuel:** 175 tons **Crew:** 30 tot.

Remarks: Soviet commercial tug design, built under license. 149–167 operate in North Sea Fleet, 680–716 in the South Sea Fleet, and the others in the East Sea Fleet.

♦ 17 Soviet Roslavl-class seagoing tugs [ATA] (In serv. 1964–65)

153 159 161–164 518 604 613 646
707 852–854 862–863 867

Roslavl-class 854 Chris Delgoffe/H&L Van Ginderen, 5-00

D: 750 tons (fl) **S:** 11 kts **Dim:** 44.5 × 9.5 × 3.5
A: 2 twin 14.5-mm 93-cal. Type 82 AA **Electronics:** Radar: 1 . . . nav.
M: 2 diesels, electric drive; 2 props; 1,200 bhp
Range: 6,000/11 **Fuel:** 90 tons **Crew:** 28 tot.

Remarks: One was transferred from the USSR; the others were built circa 1964–65 in China. Some sources indicate that as many as 20 may be in naval service.

♦ 8 Fuzhou-class water tankers [AWT]
Bldr: Hudong SY, Shanghai (In serv. 1964–70)

From among 570, 573, 580, 581, 608, 903, 904, 906, 908, 938, and others

Fuzhou-class water tanker Nanshui 938 Giorgio Arra, 1996

D: 1,200 tons (fl) **S:** 10–12 kts **Dim:** 60.0 (55.0 pp) × 9.0 × 3.5
A: 2 twin 25-mm 80-cal. Type 61 AA; 2 twin 14.5-mm 93-cal. Type 82 AA
Electronics: Radar: 1 Fin Curve or Type 756 nav.
M: 1 diesel; 1 prop; 600 bhp **Crew:** 30 tot.

Remarks: Also used by the PLAN in a transport oiler version. Lack raised cargo expansion tank top amidships. Cargo: approx. 600 tons. Some East Sea Fleet (Hai-prefix) units are not armed.

♦ 4 Leizhou-class water tankers [AWT]
Bldr: . . . (In serv. early 1960s)

HAISHUI 412 HAISHUI 555 HAISHUI 558 HAISHUI 645

Leizhou-class water tanker Haishui 645—without armament
Chris Delgoffe/H&L Van Ginderen, 5-00

D: 900 tons **S:** 10–12 kts **Dim:** 53.0 (48.0 pp) × 9.8 × 3.0
A: 2 twin 37-mm 62-cal. Type 74 AA; 2 single 14.5-mm 93-cal. AA
M: 1 diesel; 1 prop; 600 bhp **Crew:** 30 tot.

Remarks: Five sisters serve as fuel tankers and can be distinguished by their raised cargo expansion trunks down the centerline of the welldeck. East Sea Fleet unit *Haishui 645* had been disarmed by 1997, and the others may have been also. Names and pennant numbers may have changed.

♦ 1 Shichang-class aviation training ship [AXT]
Bldr: Qiuxin SY, Shanghai (In serv. 28-12-96)

82 SHICHANG

Sichang (82)—with flight deck configured for personnel berthing modules
RAN, 5-98

D: 9,500 tons (fl) **S:** 17.5 kts **Dim:** 125.0 × 19.0 × 10.6
A: none **Electronics:** Radar: 2 Decca . . . nav.
M: 2 diesels; 2 props; . . . bhp
Range: 8,000/17 **Crew:** 200 tot. as navigational training ship

Remarks: Officially described as a training ship and as a "national defense mobilization ship," *Shichang* was originally to have been converted from the roll-on/roll-off vehicle cargo ship *Hua Yuan Kou.* The ship is equipped with a helicopter flight deck running most of her length. A modular helicopter hangar and control space can be erected on the forward portion of the flight deck, which can also be used for the transport of up to 300 standard 20-ft. cargo containers. Space is provided for the transport of a large number of personnel, and provision was made for a 30-person staff hospital with full surgical and x-ray facilities; up to 100 medical trainees can be accommodated. There are two navigational plotting spaces, capable of holding up to 60 trainees.

AUXILIARIES *(continued)*

♦ 1 Daxin-class naval cadet training ship [AXT]

	Bldr	L	In serv.
81 ZHENGHE	Qiuxin SY, Shanghai	12-7-86	27-4-87

Zhenghe (81) U.S. Navy, 1994

D: 4,500 tons (5,448 fl) **S:** 20 kts (17 sust.) **Dim:** 132.07 × 16.40 × 5.30
A: 2 twin 57-mm 62-cal. Type 66 AA; 2 twin 30-mm Type 69 (AK-230) AA; 2 5-round Type 81 ASW RL
Electronics:
Radar: 2 Type 756 nav.; 1 Type 354 (Eye Shield) air search; 1 Round Ball f.c.
Sonar: EH-5 hull-mounted HF searchlight-type
M: 2 SEMT-Pielstick 6PC2-5L diesels; 2 props; 7,800 bhp
Range: 5,000/15; 10,000/. . .
Crew: 190 ship's company, 30 instructors, 180 cadets

Remarks: As completed, bore pennant V 856. Resembles a frigate. Helicopter deck aft. Officially stated to employ British navigation and radar systems. Subordinated to the naval academy; has made voyages to Hawaii (1989) and the Indian Ocean. Named for the admiral who led exploratory voyages in the Indian Ocean between 1405 and 1453.

YARD AND SERVICE CRAFT

The number of PLAN service craft is not even approximately known. In service are a vast number of service types, such as yard oilers, tugs, barges, floating dry docks, dredges, personnel launches, and the like. No details are available.

NON-NAVAL PATROL BOATS AND CRAFT

Note: Most patrol craft and boats in Chinese waters are not assigned to the PLAN but are rather subordinated to local Maritime Border Defense Forces, the Customs Service, the China Maritime Safety Administration, the Ministry of Fisheries, and various police forces. They number in the thousands, and very little information has become available about any of them. A few classes for which data have been published are described and/or illustrated below.

The China Maritime Safety Administration operates ships, craft, and helicopters characteristically painted white and bearing a broad diagonal red stripe followed by three narrow stripes on each side of the hull. The organization is headquartered in Beijing. Coastal district commands are located from north to south at Shandong, Hebei, Tianjin, Heilongjiang, Liaoning, Yantai, Lianyungang, Shanghai, Zehjiang, Fujian, Xiamen, Shantou, Shenzhen, Guangdong, Zhanjiang, Hainan, and Guangxi; inland district headquarters are located at Jiangsuy and Changjiang.

OFFSHORE PATROL SHIPS [WPS]

♦ 20–24 Qui-M . . . class
Bldrs: . . . SY, Qingdao; . . . SY, Shanghai; and . . . SY, Huangpu (In serv. 2000–2001)

D: . . . tons **S:** . . . kts **Dim:** 80.4 × . . . × . . .
A: 1 twin 37-mm 63-cal. Type 76 AA
M: 4 Deutz 620-series, 16-cyl diesels; 2 props; 12,000 bhp

Remarks: Wear the insignia of and are subordinated to the Customs Service, but are reported to be naval manned. Intended to increase the Chinese presence around the numerous islands in the South China Sea. Have Zahnradfabrik BW 755 gearboxes and Centa hydraulic engine couplings. Are fitted with a stern ramp to permit launch and recovery of the two fast inspection launches that are carried.

PATROL CRAFT [WPC]

♦ . . . Wuting class (Project 206 and Project 611)
Bldrs: Wuxi SY and Huangpu SY (In serv. 1987– . . .)

Wuting-class Project 611 patrol craft H 3101 French Navy, 11-97

D: 162 tons normal (180 fl) **S:** 17 kts (Type 611: 28.5 kts)
Dim: 43.80 × 6.50 × 1.65 (mean)
A: 1 or 2 twin 14.5-mm 93-cal. Type 82 AA (see Remarks)
Electronics: Radar: . . .
M: 2 Deutz-MWM TBD-234 (Project 611: MTU 12V396 TB94) diesels; 2 props; 2,448 bhp (Project 611: 4,400 bhp)
Range: 1,000/15 (Project 611: 600/16) **Endurance:** 5 days **Crew:** 24 tot.

Remarks: First Project 611 units were ordered in 12-89. Built in large numbers. Also referred to as the Huludao class. Design offered for export also. Some have a twin 25-mm mount forward and two twin 14.5-mm mounts aft; others are unarmed.

♦ 7 Project P-58A–class miscellaneous command ships [WAGF]
Bldr: Huangpu SY, Guangzhou (In serv. 1990–98)

HAI GUAN 901–HAI GUAN 907

Type P-58A customs patrol craft Hai Guan 901

D: 400 tons (fl) **S:** 28 kts **Dim:** 58.00 × 7.60 × 2.20
A: 1 twin 37-mm 63-cal. Type 74 AA; 2 twin 14.5-mm 93-cal. AA
Electronics: Radar: 1 or 2 . . . nav.
M: 4 MTU 16V396 TB93 diesels; 4 props; . . . bhp
Range: 1,000/16; 1,500/12 **Endurance:** 7 days **Crew:** . . . tot.

Remarks: Serve as Customs Force flagships in South China area. Variations of this design have been delivered to Pakistan and Algeria. The hullform is the same as that of the Hainan-class ASW patrol craft.

♦ 20 or more Huxin class
Bldr: . . . (In serv. 1980s)

GONGBIAN 62 GONGBIAN 178 GONGBIAN 233 and others

D: 165 tons (fl) **S:** 13 kts **Dim:** 28.0 × 4.2 × 1.6
A: 2 twin 14.5-mm 93-cal. Type 82 AA
Electronics: 1 . . . nav.
M: 2 diesels; 2 props; 2,200 bhp **Range:** 400/10 **Crew:** 26 tot.

Remarks: Modified Huangpu design. *Gongbian* 178 is fitted as a command vessel with an enlarged superstructure. Subordinated to the Border Security Force Maritime Command.

PATROL BOATS [WPB]

♦ 2 Swedish SRC 90E class
Bldr: Storebro Bruks AB, Storebro (In serv. 1998)

D: 6.5 tons (8.5 fl) **S:** 40 kts (37 loaded) **Dim:** 111.88 (10.80 wl) × 2.90 × 0.79
A: . . . **Electronics:** Radar: 1 . . . nav.
M: 2 Saab Scania DSI-14 diesel; 1 FF-Jet FF-410 waterjet; 560 bhp (at 3,800 rpm; 340 bhp sustained)
Range: . . . / . . . **Fuel:** 600 liters **Crew:** 2 tot.

Remarks: Purchased 1998 for the "Chinese Coast Guard." Patrol boat version of Swedish ambulance craft; capable of carrying 1 ton of cargo in addition to 10 troops or 4–5 stretcher cases. Hulls constructed of carbon-fiber reinforced vinyl ester.

♦ 42 . . . -class patrol craft (WPB)
Bldr: . . ., Shanghai, China (In serv. 1992)

HAI GUAN 801–HAI GUAN 842

D: 98 tons (fl) **S:** 32 kts **Dim:** 31.00 × 4.70 × 1.70
A: 2 twin 14.5-mm/93-cal. Type 82 mg
Electronics: 2 Racal-Decca 1290 ARPA surf. search/nav.
M: 2 diesels; 2 props; 2,200 bhp **Range:** 400/10 **Crew:** 26 tot.

Remarks: Building at a rate of about six a year before the program stopped in 1999, though construction of additional units remains a possibility.

COLOMBIA

Republic of Colombia

ARMADA DE REPÚBLICA

Personnel: Approx. 22,000 total, including 14,000 marines, 100 naval aviation, and 200 coast guard plus 4,800 in the naval reserve.

Bases: Headquarters at Bogotá. Principal bases are located at Cartagena (ARC *Bolivar*) on the Atlantic coast, and Bahía Málaga (ARC *Bahía Málaga*) on the Pacific coast, and Leticia on the Río Meta; smaller riverine bases are located at Puerto Leguízamo on the Río Putumayo and at Puerto Orocué and Puerto Carreño. There is a coast guard base for the San Andrés Archipelago Command at San Andrés Island and a small station at Providencia. Enlisted training is conducted at Barranquilla (ARC *Barranquilla*); warrant officer training at Barranquilla; and officer training at the naval academy at Cartagena de Indias. A new naval base may be built at El Portete near the Venezuelan border.

ARMADA DE REPÚBLICA *(continued)*

Organization: The chain of command runs from the Commander General of the Navy, to the Second Commander of the Navy, under whom are the Chief of Naval Operations, Chief of Logistic Operations, Chief of Material, Chief of Human Development, and Commandant of Marines. Under the Chief of Naval Operations are the Atlantic Naval Force, the Pacific Naval Force, Southern Naval Force (at Leguízamo Naval Base on the Río Putamayo), Riverine Naval Force (at Barrancabermeja on the Río Magdalena), and Coast Guard Corps. The actual bases and stations are subordinated to the Chief of Logistic Operations. Under the Chief, Atlantic Naval Force (headquartered at *Bolívar* naval base, Cartagena), are subordinated the Surface and Submarine Flotillas, 1st Marine Brigade, Atlantic Air Naval Group, and Atlantic Coast Guard Group. Under the Chief, Pacific Naval Force (headquartered at *Bahía Málaga* Naval Base) are the 2nd Marine Brigade, Pacific Air Naval Group, and Pacific Coast Guard Group.

Naval Aviation: Fixed-wing aircraft include two Aero Commander, two Piper PA-28 Cherokee, three to five Piper PA-31 Turbo Navajo, one Short 330, and two Cessna Stationair liaison transports; helicopters include at least one Eurocopter AS.550S-2, two or more MBB BO-105CB helicopters, and one Bell 206.

Marine Corps: Headquartered at Bogotá. Organized into three brigades:

- 1st Marine Brigade under command of the Atlantic Naval Force, with the 1st, 3rd, and 5th Marine Battalions, Special Forces Battalion, 31st and 33rd Counterinsurgency Battalions, 1st Naval Military Police Battalion, 1st Training Battalion, 1st Combat Service Support Battalion, and 1st Marine Training Center.
- 2nd Marine Brigade (headquartered at Buenaventura) under command of the Pacific Naval Force, with the 2nd and 6th Battalions, 30th Counterinsurgency Battalion, 2nd Naval Military Police Battalion, and 2nd Marine Training Center.
- River Brigade (organized 8-99, with 4,000 personnel; headquartered at Puerto Leguízamo on the Río Putamayo but under the command of the Marine Headquarters, Bogotá) with the 50th, 60th, 70th, 80th, and 90th Marine River Battalions.

The 8th Independent Battalion provides security services at the Navy and Marine Corps Headquarters, Bogotá.

Note: Ship names are preceded by ARC (*Armada República de Colombia*).

ATTACK SUBMARINES [SS]

♦ 2 German Type 209/1200 class
Bldr: Howaldtswerke, Kiel

	L	In serv.
SS 28 Pijao	10-4-74	17-4-75
SS 29 Tayrona	16-7-74	18-7-75

Pijao (SS 28)—with *Tayrona* (SS 29) on the opposite side of the pier
Hartmut Ehlers, 6-95

D: 1,000 tons (std.)/1,180 (surf.)/1,285 (sub.)
S: 11.5 kts (surf.)/22 kts (sub.; 1 hr.) **Dim:** 56.10 × 6.20 × 5.50 (surf.)
A: 8 bow 533-mm TT (14 tot. SST Mod. 0 wire-guided torpedoes)
Electronics:
Radar: 1 Thomson-CSF Calypso II nav./surf. search
Sonar: STN Atlas Elektronik CSU-3-2 suite with PRS-3-4 passive-ranging; Thomson-Marconi AUUD-1C acoustic intercept
EW: Thales DR-2000U intercept
M: 4 MTU 12V493 TY60 diesels, 600 bhp each; 4 A.E.G. 405-kw generators; 1 Siemens motor, 5,000 shp (3,670 kw)
Range: 8,000/8 (snorkel), 11,300/4 (snorkel), 460/4 (sub.)
Fuel: 85 tons **Endurance:** 30 days **Crew:** 7 officers, 24 enlisted

Remarks: Ordered 1971. Both refitted beginning 11-90 in Germany at Howaldtswerke (HDW) facility at Gaarden, with SS 28 completing 5-91 and SS 29 in 8-91.
Hull systems: The four 120-cell batteries weigh a total of 257 tons and produce 11,500 amp/hr. Maximum operating depth: 250 m.
Combat systems: The H.S.A. M8 Mod. 24 combat data system is carried, with Mk 8 Mod. 24 torpedo f.c.s. Have Type AS C18 attack periscope, Type BS 19 search periscope.

MIDGET SUBMARINES [SSM]

♦ 2 Italian S.X. 506 midgets
Bldr: COS.M.O.S, Livorno, Italy (1972–74)

SS 20 Intrépido SS 21 Indomable

D: 58 tons (surf.)/70 tons (sub.) **S:** 8.5 kts (surf.)/7 kts (sub.)
Dim: 23.0 × 2.0 × 4.0
M: 1 diesel generator set, electric drive; 1 prop; 300 shp
Range: 1,200/7 (surf.); 60/7 (sub.) **Crew:** 5 tot. + 8 frogmen

Remarks: Sisters *Roncador* (SS 23) and *Quitasueño* (SS 24) were out of service by the mid-1980s. Cargo capacity: 2,050 kg of explosives; 8 fully equipped combat swimmers; 2 submarine vehicles (for the swimmers) supported by a fixed system on lower part of the hull, one on each side. Used mostly for training, due to short range and meager performance. They are served by the special floating dry dock/tender *Mayor Jaime Arias* (DF 170).

Indomable (SS 21) Hartmut Ehlers, 10-90

FRIGATES [FF]

♦ 4 FS 1500 class
Bldr: Howaldtswerke, Kiel, Germany

	Laid down	L	In serv.
FM 51 Almirante Padilla	3-81	8-1-82	31-10-83
FM 52 Caldas	6-81	14-6-82	14-2-84
FM 53 Antioquia	22-6-81	28-8-82	30-4-84
FM 54 Independiente	22-6-81	21-1-83	27-7-84

Almirante Padilla (FM 51)—during UNITAS Chris Cavas, 3-02

Almirante Padilla (FM 51) U.S. Navy, 8-04

D: 1,600 tons (1,850 fl) **S:** 27 kts **Dim:** 95.3 (90.0 pp) × 11.3 × 3.5 (hull)
A: 8 MM 40 Exocet SSM; 1 76-mm 62-cal. OTO Melara DP; 1 twin 40-mm 70-cal. OTO Melara AA; 2 triple 324-mm Mk 32 ASW TT; 1 MBB BO-105CB or AS.550S-2 liaison helicopter
Electronics:
Radar: 1 . . . nav.; 1 Thales Sea Tiger air search; 1 Thales Castor-IIB f.c.
Sonar: STN Atlas Elektronik ASO 4-5 hull-mounted
EW: Argo Phoenix AC-672 intercept; Thales SUSIE analyzer; Phillips/EMI Scimitar deception jammer; Telegon HFD/F; 2 Matra Défense Dagaie decoy RL
M: 4 MTU 20V1163 TB82 diesels; 2 CP props; 23,000 bhp (21,000 sust.)
Electric: 2,120 kw **Range:** 5,000/14 **Fuel:** 200 tons **Crew:** 92 tot.

Remarks: Ordered 1980. Formerly numbered CM as *Corbetas Misileras* (missile corvettes) but were retyped FM *Fragatas Misileras Ligeras* in 1999. FR 51 and FM 52 were refitted at Kiel during 1992–97 and the other two at Cartegena Navy Yard, with work on FM 53 having begun during 7-98.
Hull systems: Have fin stabilizers. Engines were a new model not previously installed in a ship. Were to be re-engined beginning in 1994, but funds were not available. All four have had the helicopter deck extended to permit operating Bell 212 and Bell 412P helicopters.
Combat systems: Have the Thales TAVITAC combat direction system, with Thales Vega II f.c.s. for the 76-mm gun, and 2 Matra Défense Canopus optronic directors. The Israeli Barak SAM system has long been planned for installation forward of the bridge and abreast the hangar but has not yet been purchased. Normally carry only four MM 40 Exocet missiles.

PATROL SHIPS [PS]

Disposals: *Pedro de Heredia* (RM 72) and *Sebastian De Belalcazar* (RM 73), former *Cherokee*-class fleet tugs operating as patrol ships were no longer in service as of 2004. Near-sister, *Abnaki*-class *Rodrigo de Bastedas* (RM 74; ex-*Hidatsa,* ATF 102), was stricken during 1999, and *Bahía Solano* (RM 76; ex-*Jacarilla,* ATF 104) was retired in 1987.

PATROL CRAFT [PC]

Note: The Colombian Navy hopes eventually to operate eight Riverine Combat Elements from seven Advanced Riverine Bases. The groups will be comprised of a total of eight 10.7- to 12.4-m command craft, 24 22-ft. Boston Whaler Piranha patrol craft, and eight ex-U.S. Army utility landing craft acting as logistic support craft and mother ships. Additional patrol craft and patrol boats are assigned to the Coast Guard.

♦ 1 Sargento 2° Julio Correa Hernández–class armored tug/river patrol craft [PC] Bldr: . . . (In serv. . . .)

604 Sargento 2° Julio Correa Hernández

Sargento 2º Julio Correa Hernández (604)
Columbian Navy via Carlos Hernandez, 7-97

D: 120 tons (fl) **S:** . . . kts **Dim:** 32.0 × 8.0 × . . .
A: 6 single 12.7-mm mg **Electronics:** Radar: 1 . . . nav.
M: 2 . . . diesels; 2 props; . . . bhp
Range: . . . / . . . **Endurance:** 45 days **Crew:** 15 tot. + 45 passengers

Remarks: Completed 11-month conversion 8-97 to serve as command ship for *Piranha*-class patrol launches of the *Flotilla Fluvial de Oriente* on the Meta and Orinoco rivers. Hull and superstructure are covered over 80% of their area with bulletproof plate. Former commercial riverine tugs.

♦ 2 Río Hacha–class large river patrol craft [PC]
Bldr: Union Industrial de Barranquilla, Barranquilla (In serv. 1956)

CF 135 Río Hacha CF 137 Arauca

Arauca (CF 137)—with old number

D: 170 tons (184 fl) **S:** 13 kts **Dim:** 47.25 × 8.23 × 1.0
A: 2 single 76.2-mm 50-cal. Mk 26 DP; 4 single 20-mm AA
M: 2 Caterpillar diesels; 2 props; 800 bhp **Range:** 1,000/12
Crew: 27–43 tot.

Remarks: Sister *Leticia* disarmed and equipped as a hospital boat. Not fitted with radar. The Mk 26 gun mountings use Mk 22 guns, which are locally controlled by ringsights. Operate on the Río Putumayo.

Note: Also in service is the river patrol craft *Sargento Manuel A. Moyar* (602), on which no additional data are available.

PATROL BOATS [PB]

♦ 9 U.S. 40-foot river patrol boats
Bldr: Bender SB & Repair, Mobile, Alabama (In serv. 10-93)

LR 181 Tenerife	LR 184 Orocué	LR 187 Monclart
LR 182 Tarapacá	LR 185 Calamar	LR 188 Caucaya
LR 183 Mompox	LR 186 Magangué	LR 189 Mitú

40-ft. river patrol boat Bender, 10-93

D: 21 tons (fl) **S:** 29 kts **Dim:** 12.40 × 2.89 × 0.61
A: 1 twin and 1 single 12.7-mm M2 mg; 2 single 7.62-mm mg; 1 40-mm Mk 19 grenade launcher
Electronics: Radar: 1 Raytheon 1900 nav.
M: 2 Caterpillar 3208TA diesels; 2 Rolla surface-piercing props; 850 bhp
Range: 500/15 **Fuel:** 1.9 tons (2,217 liters) **Crew:** 5 tot. + 12 troops

Remarks: Intended to conduct antidrug trade patrol on Colombian rivers. Aluminum construction. Can be transorted in a C-130 transport. Have GPS receiver, VHF AM and FM radios, HF radio. The propellers are mounted within tunnels.

♦ 11 U.S. PBR Mk II–class patrol craft
Bldr: Uniflite, Bellingham, Wash. (In serv. 1968–71)

LR 176 Río Magdalena	LR 191 Río Caqueta
LR 177 II Río Cauca	LR 192 Río Orinoco
LR 178 Río Atrato	LR 193 Río Orteguaza
LR 179 Río Sinu	LR 194 Río Vichada
LR 180 Río San Jorge	LR 195 Río Guaviare
LR 190 Rio Putumayo	

Río San Jorge (LR 180) Hartmut Ehlers, 11-90

D: 8.9 tons (fl) **S:** 30 kts (24 sust.) **Dim:** 9.73 × 3.53 × 0.81
A: 1 twin 12.7-mm mg; 1 7.62-mm mg; 1 60-mm mortar
Electronics: Radar: 1 Raytheon 1900 nav.
M: 2 G.M. 6V53T diesels; 2 Jacuzzi waterjets; 550 bhp (296 sust.)
Range: 150/22 **Crew:** 6 tot.

Remarks: Glass-reinforced plastic construction, plastic armor. First five transferred 11-89, others in 1993. First five (listed above) were ex-U.S. Navy hulls 31RP6886, 31RP7121, 31RP7128, 31RP7129, and 31RP7130, while the others were new.

♦ 59 (+ up to 78) U.S. 22-foot Piranha class
Bldr: Boston Whaler, Rockland, Mass., and Edgewater, Fla. (In serv. 1990–2000)

Dim: 1.5 tons light (2 fl) **S:** 35 kts **Dim:** 6.81 × 2.26 × . . .
A: 2 single 12.7-mm mg **Electronics:** Radar: 1 SPS-66 nav.
M: 2 outboard motors; 250 bhp **Range:** 167/40 **Crew:** 3–4 tot.

Remarks: Glass-reinforced plastic construction, for riverine patrol use. First five were transferred 1990. Three additional units were ordered in 12-91, and another 51 ordered in 3-93 were delivered 10-93. An additional 78 units may be somewhat larger, as they are intended to transport 12 troops each.

♦ 10 Diligente-series river patrol launches
Bldr: Ast. Naval, Cartegena (In serv. 1952–54)

LR 121 Diligente	LR 126 Humberto Cortés
LR 122 Juan Lucio	LR 127 Calibio
LR 123 Alfonso Vargas	LR 128 Carlos Galindo
LR 124 Fritz Hagale	LR 129 Valerosa
LR 125 Vengadora	LR 130 Luchadora

D: 33 tons (fl) **S:** 13 kts **Dim:** 23.2 × 3.7 × 0.8
A: 1 or 2 single 20-mm 70-cal. Oerlikon AA; 0 or 4 single 81-mm mortars
M: 2 G.M. Detroit Diesel 4-71 diesels; 2 props; 280 bhp
Crew: 10 tot.

Remarks: Reactivated from storage during mid-1990s to combat drug trade. Units with two 20-mm guns have no mortars. Not all are identical. Do not have radars.

AMPHIBIOUS WARFARE CRAFT

♦ 7 ex-U.S. Army LCU 1466–class utility landing craft [LCU]
(In serv. 1954)

TM 246 Morrosquillo (ex-LCU 1516)
TM 248 Bahía Honda (ex-LCU 1543)
TM 249 Bahía Potrete (ex-LCU 1583)
TM 251 Bahía Solano (ex-LCU . . .)
TM 252 Bahía Cupica (ex-LCU . . .)
TM 253 Bahía Utria (ex-LCU . . .)
TM 254 Bahía Málaga (ex-LCU . . .)

Morrosquillo (TM 246) Colombian Navy, 1999

D: 180 tons light (347 fl) **S:** 8 kts **Dim:** 35.08 × 10.36 × 1.60 (aft)
A: 2 single 12.7-mm mg **Electronics:** Radar: 1 Raytheon . . . nav.
M: 3 Gray Marine 64 YTL diesels; 3 props; 675 bhp **Electric:** 40 kw
Range: 1,200/6 (700/7 loaded) **Fuel:** 11 tons **Crew:** 11 tot.

Remarks: First four transferred from U.S. Army reserve stocks in 10-90 and made operational in 1-92. The others were transferred during 1992. Cargo: 150 tons or 300 troops on 15.8 × 9.0-m deck with 4.3-m-wide bow ramp. Used as troop transports and tenders to patrol craft on the river system.

♦ 2 Ocho de Octubre–class ramped personnel landing craft [LCP]
Bldr: Swiftships, Inc., Morgan City, La. (In serv. 1992)

. . . Ocho de Octubre . . . Veintisiete de Octubre

D: 6 tons **S:** . . . kts **Dim:** 13.6 × . . . × . . .
A: 1 12.7-mm mg; 2 single 7.62-mm mg
M: 2 . . . diesels: 2 props **Crew:** 4 tot. + 8 marines

Remarks: GRP construction. Are reportedly similar to the Sea Truck–type launches described below.

Note: Former U.S. LCM(8) landing craft *B. Sapzurro* (240) is assigned to the coast guard.

♦ 2 Sea Truck–type landing craft [LCVP]
Bldr: Rotork, U.K. (In serv. 1989–90)

PM 107 Jamie Rook PM 108 Manuela Saenz

D: 9 tons (fl) **S:** 25 kts **Dim:** 12.7 × 3.2 × 0.7
A: 1 12.7-mm mg; 2 single 7.62-mm mg
Electronics: Radar: 1 . . . nav.
M: 2 Caterpillar diesels: 2 props; 240 bhp

Remarks: Based at Cartagena and used for local patrol and logistics support duties. GRP construction. Have small bow ramp and can carry light vehicles. Cargo capacity: 4 tons.

♦ 4 ex-U.S. LCVP landing craft [LCVP]

3602 Altair 3603 Castor 3604 Pollux 3605 Vega

D: 13 tons (fl) **S:** 9 kts **Dim:** 10.90 × 3.21 × 1.04 (aft)
M: 1 Gray Marine 64HN9 diesel; 225 bhp **Range:** 110/9

Remarks: Transferred late in 1993. Built late 1960s. Glass-reinforced plastic hulls. Can carry 36 troops or 3.5 tons cargo. Cargo deck is 5.24 × 2.29 m, with 2.00-m-wide access through the bow ramp.

AUXILIARIES

♦ 2 Malpelo-class oceanographic research ships [AGOR]
Bldr: Martin Jansen Werft, Leer, Germany (In serv. 24-7-81)

BO 155 Providencia BO 156 Malpelo

Providencia (BO 155) Colombian Navy, 1999

D: 1,090 tons (fl) **S:** 13 kts **Dim:** 50.3 (44.0 pp) × 10.0 × 4.0
M: 2 M.A.N. 6-cyl. diesels; 1 Kort-nozzle prop; 1,570 bhp **Range:** 16,000/11.5
Crew: 5 officers, 16 enlisted, 6 scientists

Remarks: 830 grt. Operated for DIMAR (*Dirección General Maritima Portuario*), BO 155 for geophysical research, BO 156 for fisheries. White painted. Naval manned. Bow-thruster, flapped Becker rudder. Prime contractor: Ferrostaal, Kiel.

♦ 2 ex-German Type 701A patrol boat tenders [AGP]
Bldr: Flensburger Werft, Flensburg, Germany

	Laid down	L	In serv.
BL 161 Cartagena de Indias (ex-*Lüneburg*, A 1411)	8-7-64	3-5-65	31-1-66
BL 162 Buenaventura (ex-*Nienburg*, A 1416)	16-11-65	28-7-66	1-8-68

Cartagena de Indias (BL 161) V. Lemonos via Boris Lemachko, 5-03

D: 1,896 tons (3,483 fl) **S:** 17 kts **Dim:** 104.15 (98.00 pp) × 13.22 × 4.29
A: 2 twin 40-mm 70-cal. Bofors AA
Electronics: Radar: 1 Kelvin-Hughes 14/9 nav.
M: 2 Maybach MD 874 diesels; 2 CP props; 5,600 bhp
Electric: 1,935 kw tot. **Range:** 3,000/17; 3,200/14 **Crew:** 71–82 tot.

Remarks: BL 161, decommissioned from German Navy 2-6-94, and the ship was purchased 27-6-97 for recommissioning 2-11-97 after refit at HDW, Kiel. BL 162 was decommissioned from the German Navy on 26-3-98 and transferred the same date. Departed Germany for Colombia on 29-5-98. They are used as offshore command and logistics support ships for patrol craft.
Hull systems: Configured to carry more than 1,100 tons of cargo, including 640 tons fuel, 205 tons ammunition, 100 tons spare parts (10,000 separate items), and 131 tons fresh water, plus 267 m^3 refrigerated stores. Equipped with fin stabilizers, one 3-ton and two 2-ton cranes. Small helicopter deck.
Combat systems: Lead-computing optical directors are furnished for the 40-mm mounts.

♦ 1 hydrographic survey ship [AGS]
Bldr: Lindigoverken, Lindigo, Sweden (L: 28-5-54)

31 Gorgona (ex-BO 154)

D: 560 tons (574 fl) **S:** 13 kts **Dim:** 41.15 × 9.00 × 2.83
A: 2 single 12.7-mm mg **Electronics:** Radar: 1 . . . nav.
M: 2 Nohab diesels; 2 props; 900 bhp **Crew:** 45 tot.

Remarks: Former lighthouse tender, laid up early 1980s but began reactivation late 1990 for further service as a survey ship, completing during 1992. May have been re-engined.

♦ 1 ex-U.S. hydrographic survey ship [AGS]
Bldr: Niagara SB, Buffalo, N.Y. (In serv. 11-11-43)

BO 153 Quindio (ex-U.S. YFR 433)

D: 380 tons (600 fl) **Dim:** 40.4 × 9.10 × 2.5
M: 2 Union diesels; 2 props; 600 bhp **Crew:** 2 officers, 15 enlisted

Remarks: Former refrigerated stores lighter leased 7-64; purchased 31-3-78. Used on coastal survey duties.

♦ 1 sail training ship [AXT]
Bldr: Celaya, Bilbao, Spain (In serv. 7-9-68)

Gloria

Gloria Michael Nitz, 8-05

AUXILIARIES *(continued)*

D: 1,150 tons (1,300 fl) **S:** 10.5 kts (power) **Dim:** 76.00 (64.7 wl) × 10.6 × 6.6
M: 1 diesel; 530 bhp—1,400 m^2 max. sail area (bark-rigged)
Endurance: 60 days **Crew:** 10 officers, 41 enlisted, 88 cadets

SERVICE CRAFT

♦ 4 (+ 8) Nodriza-class riverine support lighters [YF]
Bldr: Cartagena Naval SY

	Laid down	L	In serv.
146 Clo Wilson Londoño	9-97	6-98	3-00
607 Senen Alberto Araujo (ex-147)	9-97	9-98	19-4-00
148	. . .	. . .	2002
149 . . .	. . .	. . .	2003

CLO Wilson Londoño (146)—at launch 6-98

D: 260 tons **S:** 9 kts **Dim:** 38.4 × 9.5 × 2.8
A: 8 single 12.7-mm mg **Electronics:** Radar: 1 . . . nav.
M: 2 diesels; 2 props; 880 bhp **Crew:** 18 + 82 troops

Remarks: First two launched 9-98. Intended to provide afloat logistic support to riverine forces. As many as 40 total may be built, with four in the first batch and another eight programmed. Have 80-mm armor to the hull sides below the waterline. Medical facilities are fitted. The "2.8-m" figure in the dimensions may have referred to molded depth rather than draft. A helicopter deck is fitted. Third unit of the series may be named *Tony Pastrana Contreras*. *CLO Wilson Londoño*'s name and hull number may have been changed to *Guillermo Londono Vargas* (608).

♦ 1 floating dry dock/midget submarine tender [YFDL]

DF 170 Mayor Jaime Arias

Mayor Jaime Arias (DF 170) Hartmut Ehlers, 6-95

D: 700 tons (fl) **Dim:** 42.7 × 13 × . . . **Capacity:** 165 tons

Remarks: Employed primarily as the mother ship for Colombia's two midget submarines.

Note: On loan to the Compañía Colombiana de Astilleros Limitada (CONASTIL) are the former Colombian Navy service craft *Capitán Rodriguez Zamora* (ex-U.S. Navy floating dry dock ARD 28); *Victor Cabillos* (ex-U.S. dry dock service craft YFND 16), and *Mantilla* (ex-U.S. floating repair shop YR 66).

♦ 1 ex-U.S. LCPL Mk 11–class personnel launch [YFL]
Bldr: Miami Beach Yacht Co., Miami Beach, Fl. (In serv. 1966)

. . . (ex-36PL6465)

D: 9.75 tons light (13 fl) **S:** 19 kts **Dim:** 10.98 (9.26 pp) × 3.97 × 1.13
Electronics: Radar: 1 SPS-59 (Canadian Marconi LN-66) nav.
M: 1 G.M. 8V71 TI diesel; 350–425 bhp **Range:** 150/19
Fuel: 630 liters **Crew:** 3 tot. + 17 passengers

Remarks: Donated to Colombia in 1993, having been stricken from the USN in 1990. Glass-reinforced plastic construction.

♦ 1 admiral's yacht [YFL]

Contralmirante Bell Salter

Remarks: No characteristic data available. Based at Cartagena.

♦ 1 Cienaga de Mallorquin–class buoy tender [YGL]
Bldr: UNIAL, Barranquilla (In serv. 9-5-97)

BB 34 Cienaga de Mallorquin

D: 162 tons (fl) **S:** . . . kts **Dim:** 21.00 × 7.0 × 1.20
M: 2 G.M. Detroit Diesel 6-71N diesels; 348 bhp
Remarks: Has a 6.5-ton-capacity navigational aids buoy crane. Based at Barranquilla.

Note: Other buoy tenders in service include *Capitan Binney* (BB 32), *Abadia Mendez* (BB 33), and *Isla Palma* (BB 35), commissioned 11-00 and built by AST. Naval ARC Bolivar, Cartagena. No additional data available.

♦ 2 riverine hospital craft [YH]
Bldr: Cartagena Naval DY (In serv. 1956)

131 Socorro (ex-BD 33, ex-*Alberto Gomez*, TF 53)
132 Teniente Hernando Gutierrez (ex-BD 35, TF 52)

Socorro (BD 131)—with old number Colombian Navy, 1999

D: 70 tons **S:** 9 kts **Dim:** 25.00 × 5.50 × 0.75
A: 2 single 12.7-mm mg **M:** 2 G.M. diesels; 2 props; 270 bhp
Range: 650/9 **Crew:** 12 tot. + medical staff

Remarks: Originally built as riverine transports for 56 troops; now used as mobile surgeries.

♦ 1 Río Hacha–class riverine hospital ship [YH]
Bldr: Union Industrial de Barranquilla, Barranquilla (In serv. 1956)

BD 136 Leticia

D: 170 tons (184 fl) **S:** 13 kts **Dim:** 47.25 × 8.23 × 1.00
A: 2 single 12.7-mm mg **M:** 2 Caterpillar diesels; 2 props; 800 bhp
Range: 1,000/12 **Crew:** 39 tot. + 6 medical staff

Remarks: Former river gunboat. Sister to the two *Río Hacha*–class river gunboats. Has six-bed ward, surgery facilities, etc.

♦ 1 ex-U.S. small harbor tug [YTL]
Bldr: Henry C. Grebe (In serv. 2-9-43)

RM 73 Teniente Ricardo Sorzano (ex-YTL 231)

D: 70 tons (80 fl) **S:** 9 kts **Dim:** 20.2 × 5.2 × 1.5
M: 1 Cooper-Bessemer diesel; 240 bhp
Electric: 15 kw **Fuel:** 7 tons **Crew:** 10 tot.

Remarks: Loaned 1963; purchased 31-3-78. On semi-permanent loan to Compañía Columbiana de Astilleros Limitada (CONASTIL) dockyard, Cartagena, but also available to support naval operations.

♦ 2 river tug/transports [YTL]
Bldr: Servicio Naviero Armada República de Colombia, Puerto Leguízamo

603 Igaraparaña (ex-RR 92) (In serv. 6-85)
605 Mana Casias (ex-RR 95) (In serv. 6-86)

D: 104 grt **S:** 7 kts **Dim:** 31.2 × 7.2 × 0.9
M: 2 G.M. 4-71 diesels; 2 props; 230 bhp
Range: 1,600/7 **Crew:** 1 officer, 6 enlisted

♦ 5 Capitán Castro–class riverine tugs [YTL]

RR 81 Capitán Castro
RR 84 Capitán Alvaro Ruis
RR 86 Capitán Rigoberto Giraldo
RR 87 Teniente Vladimir Valeck
RR 88 Teniente Luis Bernal

D: 50 tons **S:** 9 kts **Dim:** 19.20 × 4.25 × 0.75
M: 2 G.M. 4-71 diesels; 260 bhp

Remarks: Sister *Cándido Leguízamo* (RR 82) stricken 1987.

♦ 10 miscellaneous service craft

NF 141 Filogonio Hichamón
RM 76 Josué Avarez
RM 93 Segiri
RM . . . Calima
RR 96 Inrida
RR . . . Mitu
TM 44 Tolú
TM . . . Teniente de Navio Alejandro Bal Domero Salgado
TM . . . Teniente Primo Alcala
. . . Teniente Luis Guillermo Alcala (ex-*Joanna*)

SERVICE CRAFT *(continued)*

Remarks: Characteristics unknown; placed in service 1981 to help combat drug traffic in the Caribbean. Many are captured former drug runners. Craft with RR- and RM-series pendants are small tugs; TM 44 is used as a diving tender and others in similar support roles.

COAST GUARD

Note: The Colombian Coast Guard is subordinated to—and operated by—the Colombian Navy.

PATROL SHIPS [WPS]

♦ 1 ex-U.S. Coast Guard Reliance class (210-ft. class)
Bldr: U.S. Coast Guard Yard, Curtis Bay, Md.

	Laid down	L	In serv.
44 VALLE DE CAUCA (ex-*Durable,* WMEC 628)	1-7-66	29-4-67	8-12-68

D: 879 tons (1,050 fl) **S:** 18 kts **Dim:** 64.16 (60.96 pp) × 10.36 × 3.25
A: 2 single 12.7-mm M2 mg; 1 helicopter
Electronics: Radar: 2 Hughes-Furuno SPS-73 nav.
M: 2 Alco 16V-251B diesels; 2 CP props; 5,000 bhp
Electric: 500 kw tot. **Range:** 2,700/18; 6,100/14 **Endurance:** 30 days
Crew: . . . tot. (accomm.: 12 officers, 72 enlisted)

Remarks: Decommissioned from U.S. Coast Guard on 20-9-01. Designed to operate up to 500 miles off the coast.
Hull systems: During modernization, received a new stack, enlarged superstructure, and greater firefighting capability; topweight was reduced, but the helicopter deck was reduced in area. The crews were enlarged to 86 total, provisions capacities were enlarged, and engine exhausts were rearranged; displacements rose from 930 to 1,050+ tons. High superstructure permits 360° visibility. Can tow a 10,000-ton ship. Is equipped with 6.86-m Zodiac Hurricane 630 rigid inflatable boat with a Volvo Penta outdrive diesel engine; the craft has a GPS receiver and an echo sounder and can carry 11 personnel. One 25-ft. Mk V Motor Surf Boat is also carried. Is fitted with an electronic Integrated Navigation System employing electronic charts.

PATROL CRAFT [WPC]

♦ 2 Juan Nepomuceno Eslava class
Bldr: Bender SB & Repair Co., Mobile, Ala.

	In serv.
GC 113 JOSÉ MARIA GARCIA DE TOLEDO	15-6-94
GC 114 JUAN NEPOMUCENO ESLAVA	25-5-94

José Maria Garcia de Toledo (GC 113) Gary Davies, 6-01

D: 131 tons (fl) **S:** 30+ kts **Dim:** 35.36 × 7.62 × 2.10
A: 1 25-mm 87-cal. Mk 38 Bushmaster low-angle; 2 single 12.7-mm M2 mg
Electronics: Radar: 1 Raytheon. . . nav.
M: 2 MTU . . . diesels; 2 props; . . . bhp
Range: 2,000/ . . . **Crew:** 5 officers, 20 enlisted

Remarks: Used for drug detection and enforcement, search and rescue, and fisheries patrol. Have modern command and control, data processing, and equipment monitoring capabilities. Have reached 32 kts in light conditions.

♦ 1 ex-Spanish Cormorán class
Bldr: E.N. Bazán, Ferrol (In serv. 28-12-89)

PO 41 ESPARTANA (ex-GC 41, ex-*Cormorán,* P 41)

Espartana (PO 41) Colombian Navy, 8-96

D: 300 tons (374 fl) **S:** 33 kts **Dim:** 55.60 × 7.59 × 1.97 (hull)
A: 1 40-mm 70-cal. Bofors AA; 1 20-mm 70-cal. Oerlikon AA
Electronics: 1 Raytheon 1620/6 nav.
M: 3 Bazán-MTU MA 16V956 TB91 diesels; 3 props; 13,500 bhp
Range: 2,000/15 **Crew:** 5 officers, 27 enlisted

Remarks: Purchased 5-3-95. Refitted at Cadiz prior to delivery. Based at San Andrés Island. Has an Alcor-C optronic director for the 40-mm gun. Launched 10-85 on speculation but was not purchased by any foreign fleet, and the ship was accepted for Spanish Navy service in 1989. Was decommissioned from the Spanish Navy in early 1994 and returned to the builder after only four years' service. A second hull was built but not completed.

♦ 2 U.S. 110-foot Commercial Cruiser class
Bldr: Swiftships, Inc., Morgan City, La.

GC 103 JOSÉ MARIA PALAS (In serv. 10-89)
GC 104 MEDARDO MONZON (In serv. 4-90)

José Maria Palas (GC 103) V. Lemonos via Boris Lemachko, 4-03

D: 100 tons (fl) **S:** 25 kts (22 cruise) **Dim:** 33.53 × 7.62 × 2.13
A: 1 40-mm 60-cal. Mk. 3 AA; 2 single 12.7-mm mg
Electronics: Radar: 1 . . . nav.
M: 4 G.M. 12V71 TI diesels; 4 props; 2,400 bhp
Range: 1,800/15 **Fuel:** 31,608 liters **Crew:** 3 officers, 16 enlisted

Remarks: Procured via the U.S. Foreign Military Sales program. Aluminum construction. The 40-mm gun is mounted on the fantail.

♦ 2 U.S. 105-foot Commercial Cruiser class
Bldr: Swiftships Inc., Berwick, La. (In serv. 2-83)

GC 102 C. N. RAFAEL DEL CASTILLO Y RADA
CG 115 JAIME CARDENAS GOMEZ (ex-AN 21, ex-*Olaya Herrera*)

D: 103 tons (fl) **S:** 25 kts **Dim:** 31.5 × 6.6 × 2.1
A: 1 40-mm 60-cal. U.S. Mk 3 AA; 2 single 12.7-mm mg
M: 2 MTU 12V331 TC92 diesels; 2 props; 7,000 bhp
Electric: 113 kw **Range:** 1,600/25; 2,400/15 **Crew:** 3 officers, 16 enlisted

Remarks: Sister *Carlos Alban* (AN 22) serves in the Customs Service. Aluminum construction. Had been out of service between 1986 and 1992. The 40-mm gun is mounted on the fantail.

♦ 2 ex-Spanish Lazaga class
Bldr: E.N. Bázan, La Carraca, Cadiz, Spain

	L	In serv.
PO 42 CAPITÁN PABLO JOSÉ DE PORTO (ex-PM 116; ex-*Recalde,* P 06)	16-10-75	15-12-77
PO 43 C.T.C.I.M. JORGE ENRIQUE MARQUEZ DURAN (ex-PM-117; ex-*Cadarso,* P 03)	8-1-75	10-7-76

C.T.C.I.M. Jorge Enrique Marquez Duran (PO 43)
Maritime Photographic, 6-01

D: 275 tons (397 fl) **S:** 29.7 kts **Dim:** 57.40 (54.40 pp) × 7.60 × 2.70
A: 1 40-mm 70-cal. Bofors AA; 1 20-mm 90-cal. Oerlikon GAM-B01 AA; 2 single 12.7-mm M2 mg
Electronics: Radar: 1 Raytheon 1620/6 nav.; 1 . . . surf. search
M: 2 MTU MA-16V956 TB91 diesels; 2 props; 7,780 bhp
Electric: 405 kVA tot. **Range:** 2,260/27; 4,200/17 **Fuel:** 112 tons
Crew: 4 officers, 35 enlisted

Remarks: Purchased 6-97; refitted at E.N. Bazán, San Fernando, Spain, and handed over on 9-9-98. Both had been decommissioned 30-6-93 from Spanish naval service and placed in reserve. During refits prior to transfer were rearmed, new radars were provided, and accommodations for a small number of marines were added; a 76-mm gun and its associated track-while-scan radar set were removed.

PATROL CRAFT [WPC] *(continued)*

♦ 2 U.S. Asheville class

	Bldr	Laid down	L	In serv.
GC 111 Albuquerque (ex-*Welch*, PG 93)	Peterson SB, Sturgeon Bay, Wisc.	8-8-67	25-7-68	8-9-69
GC 112 Quitasueño (ex-*Tacoma*, PG 92)	Tacoma Boat, Tacoma, Wash.	24-7-67	13-4-68	14-7-69

Quitasueño (GC 112) Hartmut Ehlers, 6-95

D: 225 tons (245 fl) **S:** 40 kts (16 cruising) **Dim:** 50.14 (46.94 wl) × 7.28 × 2.9
A: 1 76.2-mm 50-cal. Mk 34 DP; GC 112 only: 1 40-mm 70-cal. Bofors L 70 AA; both: provision for 2 twin 12.7-mm mg
Electronics: Radar: 1 Canadian Marconi LN-66 nav.; 1 Raytheon 1900 nav.
M: CODOG: 1 G.E. 7LM-1500-PE 102 gas turbine; 13,300 shp (12,500 sust.); 2 Cummins VT 12-875M diesels, 1,650 bhp (1,450 sust.); 2 CP props
Electric: 100 kw **Range:** 325/35; 1,700/16 **Fuel:** 50 tons **Crew:** 25 tot.

Remarks: Leased 16-5-83, towed to Jonathan Corp., Norfolk, Va., for reactivation for use on antidrug patrol. GC 112 is based at San Andrés Island. Offer of two more not taken up due to difficulty of maintaining engineering plants on this pair, which are generally inoperative. The Mk. 63 g.f.c.s., with SPG-50 f.c. radar, has been removed, leaving the 76.2-mm gun with local control capability only. The U.S. Mk 3 40-mm gun formerly mounted on the fantail of GC 111 has been removed to allow for the space to be configured as a small helicopter deck; the gun on the fantail of GC 112 is now of a later Bofors model. Transferred to the coast guard in 1992.

PATROL BOATS [WPB]

♦ 21 261-B class

Bldr: . . . Columbia (1st two units: Mako Marine, Miami, Fla.) (In serv. 1992–93)

Antares	Capricornio	Acuario	Piscis	Aries
Tauro	Geminis	Deneb	Rigel	Leo
Aldebaran	Spica	Denebola	Libra	Escorpion
Alpheraz	Bellatrix	Canopus	Procyon	Tulcan
Capella				

D: 5 tons **S:** 35 kts **Dim:** 7.92 × 2.59 × 0.94
A: 1 12.7-mm M2 mg; 2 single 7.62-mm M-60 mg
Electronics: Radar: 1 Raytheon R40X nav.
M: 2 Evinrude gasoline outboards; 350 bhp
Range: . . . / . . . **Crew:** 3 tot.

Remarks: GRP hulled. Can be carried aboard a C-130 Hercules.

♦ 2 U.S. Sea Spectre PB Mk III class

Bldr: Peterson Bldrs., Sturgeon Bay, Wis. (In serv. 1975–79)

GC 105 Jaime Gomez Castro GC 106 Juan Nepomuceno Peña

Jaime Gomez Castro (GC 105) Hartmut Ehlers, 11-90

D: 28 tons (36.7 fl) **S:** 30 kts (now less) **Dim:** 19.78 × 5.50 × 1.80 (props)
A: 2 single 12.7-mm mg; 2 single 7.62-mm mg; 1 40-mm Mk 19 grenade launcher
Electronics: Radar: 1 . . . nav.
M: 3 G.M. 8V71 TI diesels; 3 props; 1,800 bhp **Electric:** 30 kw tot.
Range: 450/26; 2,000/. . . **Endurance:** 3 days **Crew:** 1 officer, 8 men

Remarks: Transferred to Colombia 1990. Aluminum construction. The 40-mm weapon is in a special stabilized Mk 3 Mod. 9 mounting with a removable reload magazine. Not as heavily armed as when in U.S. Navy service.

♦ 4 ex-U.S. Coast Guard 82-foot Point class

Bldrs: Coast Guard Yard, Curtis Bay, Md. (GC 144: J. Martinac SB, Tacoma, Wash.)

	In serv.
GC 141 Cabo Corrientes (ex-*Point Warde*, WPB 82368)	14-8-67
GC 142 Cabo Manglares (ex-*Point Wells*, WPB 82343)	20-11-63
GC 143 Cabo Tiburón (ex-*Point Estero*, WPB 82344)	11-12-66
GC 144 Cabo de la Vela (ex-*Point Sal*, WPB 82352)	5-12-66

Cabo Manglares (CG 142) V. Lemonos via Boris Lemachko, 5-03

D: 64 tons (66–69 fl) **S:** 23.7 kts (see Remarks) **Dim:** 25.3 × 5.23 × 1.95
A: 2 single 12.7-mm M2 mg (I × 2)
Electronics: Radar: 1 Raytheon SPS-64(V)1 nav.
M: 2 Caterpillar 3412 diesels; 2 props; 1,480 bhp
Range: 490/23.7; 1,500/8 **Fuel:** 5.7 tons **Crew:** 1 officer, 7 enlisted

Remarks: Transferred by donation 29-6-00, 13-10-00, 8-2-01, and 24-5-01, respectively, upon retirement from U.S. Coast Guard. Hull built of mild steel. High-speed diesels controlled from the bridge. Well equipped for salvage and towing and in excellent condition, despite age. Considered to be heavy rollers.

Note: In addition to the craft above, a 10-m, GRP-hulled launch numbered GC 61 is assigned to patrol duties at Barranquilla; built by Industrias Profibra, Barranquilla, no other information available.

SERVICE CRAFT

♦ 1 ex-U.S. LCM(8)-class landing craft [LCM]

GC 240 B. Sapzurro

D: 34 tons light (121 fl) **S:** 9 kts **Dim:** 22.43 × 6.43 × 1.35 fwd./1.47 aft
M: 4 G.M. Detroit Diesel 6-71 or 2 12V-71 diesels; 2 props; 590 bhp
Range: 190/9 (loaded) **Crew:** 4–5 tot. enlisted

Remarks: Transferred late in 1993. Cargo: 60 tons or 150 troops for short distances in 12.8 × 4.3-m open well with 54.6-m^2 space.

Note: The Colombian Customs Service, the DIAN (*Dirección de Impuestos y Aduanas Nacionales*), has an antidrug role but is hampered by a lack of suitable craft to perform the function. Its craft no longer carry weapons larger than small arms. Craft in service include the patrol craft *Carlos Alban* (AN 22) and the launch *Felix J. Lievano.*

COMOROS

Federal Islamic Republic of the Comoros

Base: Moroni

FISHERIES PATROL BOATS [WPB]

♦ 2 Japanese Yamayuri class

Bldr: Ishihara DY, Takasago (In serv. 10-81)

Kasthala Ntringhui

D: 27 tons (40.3 fl) **S:** 20.7 kts **Dim:** 18.0 × 4.3 × 0.82 (1.1 prop)
A: 2 single 12.7-mm mg **Electronics:** Radar: 1 . . . nav.
M: 2 Nissan Type RD 10TA 06 diesels; 2 props; 900 bhp **Crew:** 6 tot.

Remarks: Identical to craft built for the Japanese Maritime Safety Agency. Employed in fisheries protection.

Note: Also in service with the civil police is a small launch named *Barracuda.*

CONGO

Democratic Republic of the Congo

Personnel: Approx. 1,000 total

Bases: Banana, Boma, Kalemie (Lake Tanganyika), and Matadi

Note: The name of the country was changed from Zaire on 17-5-97 by the winning forces in the civil war that deposed the dictator Mobutu.

PATROL CRAFT [PC]

♦ **1 Chinese Shanghai-II class**

106 . . .

D: 122.5 tons (134.8 fl) **S:** 28.5 kts **Dim:** 38.78 × 5.41 × 1.49 (1.554 max.)
A: 2 twin 37-mm 63-cal. Type 74 AA; 2 twin 25-mm 60-cal. Type 81 AA
Electronics: Radar: 1 Type 351 Pot Head nav.
M: 2 Type L12-180 (1,200-bhp each) and 2 Type L12-180Z (910-bhp each) diesels; 4 props; 4,200 bhp
Electric: 39 kw tot. **Range:** 750/16.5 **Endurance:** 7 days **Crew:** 36 tot.

Remarks: Two operable units delivered 2-87, but the *Ubangi* (103) sank 23-11-00 at Boma. Four earlier units delivered 1976–78 are beyond repair. Intended for coastal patrol duties at the mouth of the Congo River, operating from Boma.

Note: All craft formerly operated on Lake Tanganyika had ceased operations by mid-1997. There may be a number of additional small riverine patrol and logistics support craft.

CONGO

Republic of the Congo

Personnel: 800 total, including up to 600 marines

Base: Pointe-Noire, Brazzaville, and Mossaka

Note: The naval forces are divided into a coastal navy and a river navy. Most or all of the craft listed below are in poor condition, and none at all may be operable.

COASTAL NAVY

PATROL CRAFT [PC]

♦ **3 Spanish Piraña class**
Bldr: E. N. Bazán, Cádiz

	In serv.
P 601 Marien Ngouabi (ex-*L'Intrépide*)	10-11-82
P 602 Les Trois Glorieuses (ex-*Le Vaillant*)	1-83
P 603 Les Maloango (ex-*Le Terrible*)	3-83

Les Maloango (P 603) French Navy, 12-90

D: 125 tons (138 fl) **S:** 34 (29 sust.) **Dim:** 32.70 (30.60 pp) × 6.15 × 1.55
A: 1 40-mm 70-cal. OTO Melara AA; 1 20-mm Oerlikon GAM B01 AA; 2 single 12.7-mm Browning M2 mg
Electronics: Radar: 1 Raytheon RM 1220/6X8 nav.
M: 2 MTU 12V538 TB92 diesels; 2 props; 6,120 bhp (5,110 sust.)
Electric: 210 kw **Range:** 1,000/17 **Crew:** 3 officers, 16 enlisted

Remarks: Ordered 1980. Renamed on delivery; arrived in Congo 1-6-83. Overhauled at builders in 1985. Quickly became near-inoperable, with their current status remaining uncertain. Had a Matra Défense Panda optronic director for the 40-mm gun.

RIVER NAVY

PATROL BOATS [PB]

♦ **2 Arcor-43-class GRP-hulled**
Bldr: Arcor, . . ., France (In serv. 1982)

Andre Matsoua Maître Christian Malongga Mokoko

D: 12 tons (fl) **S:** 25 kts **Dim:** 13.00 (11.60 pp) × 4.0 × 1.5
A: 1 7.62-mm mg **M:** 2 diesels; 2 props; 450 bhp

♦ **2 ARCOR-38-class GRP-hulled** Bldr: ARCOR, France (In serv. 1982)

Enseigne de Vaisseau Yamba Lamass

D: 7.5 tons (fl) **S:** 28 kts **Dim:** 11.40 (9.90 pp) × 3.60 × 1.10
A: 1 7.62-mm mg **M:** 2 diesels; 2 props; 250 bhp

♦ **Up to 10 locally built outboard-powered craft**

Remarks: No data available.

COOK ISLANDS

Note: The Cook Islands is an independent republic but is under the protection of New Zealand. Craft name is preceded by CIPPB (Cook Islands Pacific Patrol Boat).

PATROL BOAT [PB]

♦ **1 Australian ASI 315 class** Bldr: Australian SB Ind. (WA), South Coogie

	Laid down	L	In serv.
Te Kukupa	5-6-88	27-1-89	1-9-89

Te Kukupa H&L Van Ginderen, 6-95

D: 165 tons (fl) **S:** 20 kt (sust.) **Dim:** 31.50 (28.60 wl) × 8.10 × 2.12
A: Small arms
Electronics:
Radar: 1 Furuno 1011 nav.
EW: Furuno 120 MF–HFD/F; Furuno 525 VHFD/F
M: 2 Caterpillar 3516 diesels; 2 props; 2,820 bhp (2,400 sust.)
Electric: 116 kw (2 × 50 kw, 1 × 16 kw) **Range:** 2,500/12 **Fuel:** 27.9 tons
Endurance: 8–10 days **Crew:** 3 officers, 14 enlisted

Remarks: A unit of the Australian "Pacific Patrol Boat" foreign aid program. Extremely well equipped with navaids: SATNAV receiver, doppler log, etc. Carries a 5-m Stressl aluminum boarding boat with a 40-hp outboard.

COSTA RICA

Republic of Costa Rica

COAST GUARD

(Servicio Nacional Guardacostas)

Personnel: 300 total

Bases: Golfito, Puntarenas, and Puerto Limón

Maritime Aviation: The Air Section of the Civil Guard has four Cessna 206 and two Cessna O-2A fixed-wing aircraft and two Hughes 500E helicopters.

COAST GUARD *(continued)*

Note: A supply of U.S. 20-mm 70-caliber 20-mm single gunmounts has been acquired, should the larger units below need heavier armaments. Most of the larger craft listed below are in poor condition and will have to be discarded shortly. The name of the organization has been changed from the Guardia Civil Sección Maritimo, and the new pennant number system indicates the length in feet, followed by a dash and the number of the actual craft.

PATROL CRAFT [WPC]

♦ 1 U.S. 105-foot Commercial Cruiser class

Bldr: Swiftships, Morgan City, La. (In serv. 2-78)

SNGC 105-1 Isla del Coco (ex-SP 1055)

Isla del Coco (SNGC 105-1) Swiftships, 4-85

D: 118 tons (fl) **S:** 33 kts (30 sust.) **Dim:** 31.73 × 7.1 × 2.16
A: 1 12.7-mm M2HB mg; 2 twin 7.62-mm mg; 1 60-mm mortar
Electronics: Radar: 1 Furuno . . . nav.
M: 3 MTU 12V331 TC92 diesels; 3 props; 10,500 bhp
Range: 1,200/18 **Fuel:** 21 tons **Electric:** 80 kw (2 × 40 kw)
Crew: 3 officers, 11 enlisted

Remarks: Refitted 1984 to 3-85 by builders. Aluminum construction. Overhauled in 2001.

PATROL BOATS [WPB]

♦ 3 ex-U.S. Coast Guard Point class

Bldr: U.S. Coast Guard Yard, Curtis Bay, Md.

	In serv.
SNGC 82-2 Santamaria (ex-*Point Camden,* WPB 82373)	4-5-70
SNGC 82-3 Juan Rafael Mora (ex-*Point Chico,* WPB 82339)	29-10-62
SNGC 82-4 Pancho Carrasco (ex-*Point Bridge,* WPB 82338)	. . .

Santamaria (SNGC 82-2) Costa Rican C.G., 2-00

D: 64 tons (69 fl) **S:** 23.7 kts **Dim:** 25.3 × 5.23 × 1.95
A: 2 12.7-mm M2HB mg **Electronics:** Radar: 1 SPS-73 nav.
M: 2 Caterpillar 3412 diesels; 2 props; 1,480 bhp
Range: 490/23.7; 1,500/8 **Fuel:** 5.7 tons **Crew:** 1 officer, 7 enlisted

Remarks: SNGC 82-2 was transferred on 15-12-99 and SNGC 82-3 on 22-6-01; both are in excellent condition. SNGC 82-4 was transferred by sale on 28-9-01. Sister *Colonel Alfonso Monje* (SNGC 82-1, ex-SP 821; ex-*Point Hope,* WPB 82302), transferred in 5-91 and stricken by 5-01.

♦ 1 ex-U.S. Coast Guard Cape class

Bldr: Coast Guard Yard, Curtis Bay, Md.

	In serv.	Transferred
SNGC 95-1 Astronauta Franklin Chang (ex-SP 951; ex-*Cape Henlopen,* WPB 95328)	5-12-58	28-9-89

D: 90 tons (fl) **S:** 20 kts **Dim:** 28.96 × 6.10 × 1.55
A: 2 single 12.7-mm M2HB mg
Electronics: Radar: 1 Raytheon SPS-64(V)1 nav.
M: 2 G.M. 16V149 TI diesels; 2 props; 2,470 bhp
Electric: 60 kw **Range:** 550/20; 1,900/11.5 **Endurance:** 5 days
Crew: 1 officer, 13 enlisted

♦ 1 U.S. 36-foot aluminum patrol launch

Bldr: Swiftships, Morgan City, La. (Both in serv. 3-86)

SNGC 36-1 Puerto Quepos (ex-*Telamanca,* SP 361)

Puerto Quepos (SNGC 36-1) Costa Rican C.G., 2-00

D: 9 tons (10.7 fl) **S:** 24 kts **Dim:** 10.97 × 3.05 × 0.80
A: 1 12.7-mm M2HB mg; 1 60-mm mortar
Electronics: Radar: 1 Raytheon 1900 nav.
M: 2 G.M. DD8240 MT diesels; 2 props; 500 bhp
Range: 248/18 **Crew:** 1 officer, 3 enlisted

Remarks: Sister *Cariara* (SP 362) had been discarded by 5-01.

♦ 2 U.S. 65-foot Commercial Cruiser class

Bldr: Swiftships, Morgan City, La. (In serv. 1978)

SNGC 65-3 Cabo Blanco (ex-SP 658)
SNGC 65-4 Isla Burica (ex-SP 654)

Cabo Blanco (SNCG 65-3)—painted white with blue and red stripes A. A. de Kruijf, 11-03

D: 24.9 tons (35 fl) **S:** 23 kts (19 sust.) **Dim:** 19.77 (17.90 wl) × 5.56 × 1.98
A: 1 12.7-mm M2HB mg; 2 twin 7.62-mm mg; 1 60-mm mortar
Electronics: Radar: 1 Furuno . . . nav.
M: 2 MTU 8V331 diesels; 2 props; 1,400 bhp
Electric: 20 kw **Range:** 1,300/18 **Fuel:** 4.8 tons **Crew:** 2 officers, 7 enlisted

Remarks: Aluminum construction. Refitted by builder in 1985–86 but are again in poor condition. Sister *Cabo Velas* (SP 656) was derelict by mid-1995, and *Punta Uvita* (SP 654) was out of service by 1998.

SERVICE CRAFT

♦ 1 U.S. 42-foot aluminum hospital launch [YH]

Bldr: Swiftships, Morgan City, La. (In serv. 9-86)

SNGC 42-1 Primera Dama (ex-*Donna Margarita,* SP 421; ex-*Puntarenas*)

D: 11 tons (16.2 fl) **S:** 34 kts **Dim:** 12.80 × 4.26 × 0.90
M: 2 G.M. 8V92 TI diesels; 2 props; 700 bhp
Range: 300/30; 450/18 **Crew:** 1 officer, 3 enlisted

Remarks: Former patrol craft employed as a hospital launch.

Note: Also in use are six U.S.-funded, locally manufactured Apex RIB launches (each powered by two Honda outboard motors) and one locally built 12.2-m GRP launch.

CROATIA

HRVATSKA RATNA MORNARIČA

Personnel: Approx. 1,800 active duty, including two companies of marines; plus 8,300 naval reservists

Bases: Headquarters at Lora-Split, with facilities at Šibenik, Split, Pula, and Ploče and minor facilities at Lastovo and Vis. The River Patrol flotillas are based at Sisak on the Sava and Osijek on the Drava.

Naval Infantry: Nine companies, deployed to Brač, Dubrovnik, Jelsa, Korčula, Lošinj, Pelješac, Pula, Šibenik, and Zadar.

Coastal Defense: At least two batteries of coastal defense missiles, each with two Tatra 815 trucks and each truck equipped with four RBS-15 antiship missiles, are in service with the Croatian Navy. There are also 16 radar-directed coastal artillery batteries.

Organization: The Croatian Navy was created 12-9-91. All ships are incorporated in the Fleet, which has the 1st Brigade (missile patrol combatants, fast minelayer), the Patrol Ship Division, the Landing Ship Section, the Submarine Section, the Minesweeper Section, the Training Ship Section, and the Auxiliary Section.

Maritime Aviation: The Croatian Air Force operates three CASA/Tusas Aerospace Industries CN-235 maritime patrol aircraft with two more on order. In addition, Mi-24 attack helicopters have been used to drop antisubmarine torpedoes in coordination with naval surface craft.

Note: Ship names are prefaced by HRM (*Hrvatska Ratna Mornariča*). Those photographs in this section attributed to the Croatian magazine *HVG* are courtesy of Dr. Zvonimir Freivogel.

MIDGET SUBMARINES [SSM]

Note: A 120-ton midget submarine with four 533-mm torpedo tubes and the ability to transport four swimmer delivery vehicles is said to be in the planning stages. See also the Amphibious Warfare section.

♦ **1 Modified Una (M-100D) class (Type C-11)**
Bldr: RH-ALAN-Brodosplit, Split, Croatia (P 01 in serv. 5-85/17-9-96)

P 01 VELEBIT (ex-*Soca,* P 914)

Velebit (P 01) Dario Vuljanic via Zvonimir Freivogel, 2002

D: 88 tons (surf.)/99 tons (sub.) **S:** 8.0 kts (surf.)/11.0 kts (sub.)
Dim: 20.92 × 2.70 × 4.42 molded depth
A: 6 500-kg mines or 4 R1 swimmer-delivery vehicles, externally carried
Electronics: Radar: . . . —Sonar: STN-Atlas Elektronik PP-10 active and PSU-1-2 passive
M: 1 diesel-driven (140-bhp) generator, two 20-kw Koncar electric motors; 1 5-bladed prop; 54 shp
Range: 135/3 (sub.); 500/8 (snorkel) **Endurance:** 7 days
Crew: 4 crew + 6 swimmers

Remarks: Captured 1991 during the breakup of Yugoslavia. The building yard at Split added a section to the Type M-100D hull incorporating a diesel generator set. The modified submarine was relaunched in 9-93. No second unit is foreseen for the immediate future. In need of a new battery, she remained laid up as of late 2005.
Hull systems: The original displacement was 76 tons surfaced/88 submerged, and the original length was 18.8 m overall. Working depth is 105 m, with test depth at 120 m and estimated collapse depth of 182 m. Theoretically capable of remaining submerged for 96 hours. Originally had no radar, but a small portable navigational set may have been added. Fitted with GPS. Has two 128-cell, 1,450 amp-hr (5-hour rate) batteries.

GUIDED-MISSILE PATROL CRAFT [PTG]

♦ **2 (+ 2) Kralj Petar Krešimir IV class (Type R-03)**
Bldr: Kraljevica SY

	L	In serv.
RTOP 11 KRALJ PETAR KREŠIMIR IV (ex-*Sergei Masera,* RTOP 501)	21-3-92	7-92
RTOP 12 KRALJ DMITAR ZVONIMIR (ex-*Milan Spasic*)	30-3-01	12-01

Kralj Petar Krešimir IV (RTOP 11) Dario Vuljanic via Zvonimir Freivogel, 2002

Kralj Dmitar Zvonimir (RTOP 12) Dario Vuljanic via Zvonimir Freivogel, 2002

D: 350 tons (385 fl) **S:** 36 kts (32.5 sust.)
Dim: 53.63 (RTOP 12: 55.10) × 8.54 × 2.00
A: 4 RBS-15 SSM; 1 57-mm 70-cal. Bofors SAK 57 Mk 1 DP; RTOP 11 only: 1 30-mm 54-cal. AK-630 gatling AA; both: 2 single 12.7-mm mg; 4 AIM-70 or 6 SAG-1 mines
Electronics:
Radar: RTOP 11: 1 Decca RM 1290A nav.; 1 CelsiusTech 9LV 249 Mk 2 search/f.c. suite—RTOP 12: 1 Decca BT 502 nav.
EW: RTOP 11 only: 2 18-round Wallop Barricade decoy RL
M: 3 Soviet M-504B-2 diesels; 3 props; 14,550 bhp
Electric: 420 kw (3 × 140-kw diesel sets)
Range: 1,700/20 (RTOP 12: 1,700/18) **Endurance:** 10 days
Crew: 5 officers, 12 noncommissioned officers, 16 enlisted

Remarks: The first unit was captured incomplete and finished by Croatia. Construction of the second employs some components left behind in 1991 but is largely new material; funding problems have slowed construction, and the craft was launched without armament and without some superstructure elements. Two additional units are tentatively planned, with the names *Kralj Tomislav, Nikola Subic Zrinski,* or *Ban Josip Jelacic* to be used.
Hull systems: Hull has eleven watertight compartments, a round bilge-form, and no fin stabilizers. The ships have a CBR protection system, Collins and Harris communications gear, a Furuno Loran-C receiver, a DB-14B echo sounder, and a Thales doppler log.
Combat systems: The missiles were originally delivered for coast defense use and were adapted for shipboard launching. The missile containers can be stacked two high to double the load-out. There is a Russian Kolonka-2 ringsight director for the 30-mm gatling gun on the RTOP 11. Both could carry eight RBS-15 missiles, but the available missiles have been divided between the pair.

♦ **1 Rade Končar class (Type 240 or R-02)**
Bldr: Tito SY, Kraljevica

	L	In serv.
RTOP 21 ŠIBENIK (ex-*Vlado Četovič,* RT 402)	28-8-77	3-78

GUIDED-MISSILE PATROL CRAFT [PTG] *(continued)*

Šibenik (RTOP 21)—with only two missiles aboard Dario Vuljanic, *HVG,* 2000

D: 242 tons (271 fl) **S:** 39 kts (37 sust.) **Dim:** 45.00 × 8.00 × 1.80 (2.50 props)
A: 4 RBS-15 SSM; 1 57-mm 70-cal. Bofors SAK 57 Mk 1 DP; 1 30-mm 54-cal. AK-630 gatling AA
Electronics:
Radar: 1 Decca 1226 nav.; 1 CelsiusTech 9LV 202 Mk 2 target detection/f.c. suite
EW: 2 18-round Wallop Barricade decoy RL
M: CODAG: 2 Rolls-Royce Proteus gas turbines (4,500 shp each); 2 MTU 20V538 TB92 diesels (3,600 bhp each); 4 CP props; 16,200 hp max.
Electric: 300 kVA tot. **Range:** 880/23; 1,650/15 **Endurance:** 7 days
Crew: 5 officers, 10 petty officers, 15 enlisted

Remarks: Of Yugoslav design, using Swedish fire control and guns and Soviet missiles. Steel hull, aluminum superstructure. Has CBR warfare protection. In RTOP 21 the after 57-mm mount was removed and replaced with a Soviet-supplied 30-mm gatling gun on a cylindrical magazine pedestal to improve antimissile defenses. The gatling gun is controlled only by a Kolonka-2 ringsight director mounted in a cupola just abaft the mast.

PATROL CRAFT [PC]

♦ **4 Mirna class (Type 140)**
Bldr: Kraljevica SY (In serv. 1982–84)

PB 61 "Novi Grad" (ex-*Koprivnik* or *Biokovo,* PČ 171)
PB 62 Šolta (ex-*Mukos,* PČ 176)
PB 63 "Vrlika" (ex-*Cer,* PČ 180)
PB 64 Hrvatska Kostajnica (ex-*Kozolo,* PČ 181)

Šolta (PB 62) Dario Vuljanic, via Zvonimir Freivogel, 2002

D: 125.3 tons (142.3 fl) **S:** 29 kts
Dim: 32.00 (29.25 pp) × 6.68 × 1.76 (2.41 max.)
A: 1 40-mm 70-cal. Bofors L70 AA; 1 quadruple 20-mm 90-cal. M75 AA; 1 4-round Fasta-4M SAM syst. (12 Igla missiles); 8 Type MDB-MT3 d.c.
Electronics: Radar: 1 Decca 1216C nav.—Sonar: Simrad SQS-5Q3D/SF hull-mounted HF
M: 2 SEMT-Pielstick 12 PA4 200GDS diesels; 2 props; 6,000 bhp—electric motors for low speeds (6 kts)
Range: 400/20 **Fuel:** 16.2 tons **Crew:** 2 officers, 19 enlisted

Remarks: Ordered 1979. PB 61 and 62 were captured badly damaged but have been repaired. All four may be transferred to the new coast guard. The names *Novi Grad* and *Vrlika,* attributed to PB 61 and PB 63, are unofficial.
Hull systems: Endurance at 20 kts can be increased to 530 n.m. in emergencies. Peacetime endurance is four days; wartime: eight days.
Combat systems: A quadruple-rack launcher for SA-7 Grail/Igla infrared point-defense missiles has been added abaft the mast. Two quadruple illumination/chaff launchers are now mounted aft. The Croatian units of the class have a quadruple 20-mm gunmount aft, while Federal Yugoslav units have a single mount.

PATROL BOATS [PB]

♦ **1 M 301–class riverine**
Bldr: Macvanska, Mitroviča (In serv. 1952)

PB 91 (ex-*Slavonač,* RLM 307)

PB 91 Siegfried Breyer Collection, 1993

D: 38 tons (fl) **S:** 12 kts **Dim:** 19.4 × 4.4 × 1.4
A: 1 40-mm 60-cal. Bofors AA; 2 single 12.7-mm mg
Electronics: Radar: 1 . . . nav.
M: 2 . . . diesels; 2 props; 300 bhp **Crew:** 9 tot.

Remarks: Based at Sisak, on the Sava River, with PB 92 (see below) and PB 93, for which no data are available.

♦ **1 PB 92 class**
Bldr: Breki, Domagoj (In serv. 1950s)

PB 92

PB 92 Siegfried Breyer Collection, 1993

D: 46 tons (fl) **S:** 12 kts **Dim:** 20.5 × 4.5 × 1.4
A: 1 40-mm 60-cal. Bofors AA 1 quadruple and 1 single 12.7-mm mg
M: 2 diesels; 2 props; 300 bhp **Range:** 400/12 **Crew:** 10 tot.

Remarks: Based at Sisak, on the Sava River.

Note: Based at Osijek on the Danube River are patrol launches *Breki, Vukovar '91, Domagoj, Tomislav, Okic, Tina,* and an unnamed small launch; no data available, except that *Tina* is armed with a triple 20-mm AA mount forward, while the smaller *Vukovar '91* has a 40-mm Bofors mount.

MINE WARFARE SHIPS AND CRAFT

♦ **1 (+ . . .) MPMB-class coastal minesweeper [MSC]**
Bldr: RH-ALAN d.o.o., Vela Luka SY, Korčula, (L: . . .)

. . .

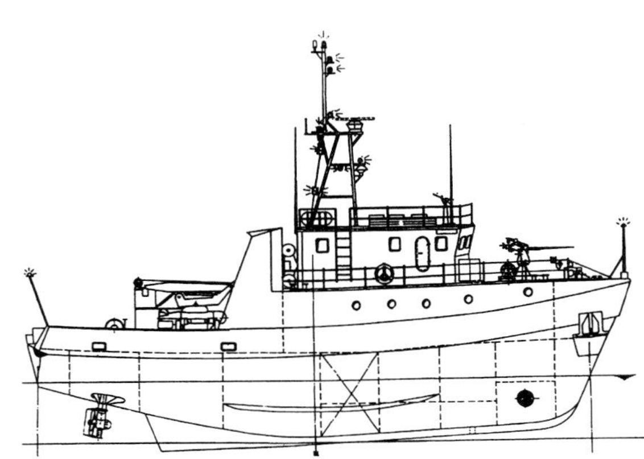

MPMB coastal minesweeper RH-ALAN, 1996

D: 173 tons (fl) **S:** 11 kts **Dim:** 25.70 × 6.80 × 2.64
A: 1 20-mm 90-cal. M71 AA; mines
Electronics:
Radar: 1 Kelvin-Hughes 5000 ARPA nav.
Sonar: Reson mine avoidance, Klein 2000 side-scan route survey
M: 2 MTU 8V183 TE62 diesels; 2 Holland Roerpropeler azimuthal props; 990 bhp—1 bow-thruster; 190 shp
Endurance: . . . / . . . **Crew:** 14 tot.

MINE WARFARE SHIPS AND CRAFT *(continued)*

Remarks: The prototype began construction in 1996, but the program has been much delayed by the lack of funding; the craft was supposed to have been in service by 31-7-97 but remains in land storage at the building yard. Has a glass-reinforced plastic hull, with form derived from that of a fishing craft. Would carry one each ECA PAP 105 remote-controlled mine countermeasures and Super Sea Rover submersibles and would be equipped with an MDL-3 wire mechanical sweep array.

Disposal note: The ex-Soviet *Osa-I*–class (Project 205) patrol craft converted to fast minelayer, *Dubrovnik* (PBM 41), appears to have been withdrawn from service.

AMPHIBIOUS WARFARE SHIPS AND CRAFT

♦ 2 Silba-class tank landing craft/minelayers [LSM]

	Bldr	L	In serv.
DBM 81 Cetina (ex-*Rab,* DBM 242)	Brodosplit, Split	18-7-92	19-2-93
DBV 82 Krka	Brodosplit, Split	17-9-94	9-3-95

Cetina (DBM 81) Dario Vuljanic via Zvonimir Freivogel

D: 750 tons normal (880 fl) **S:** 13 kts (12 sust.)
Dim: 49.70 (43.90 pp) × 10.20 × 2.60 max.
A: DBV 82 only: 1 40-mm 70-cal. Bofors L70 AA; DBM 81 only: 2 twin 30-mm 65-cal. AK-230 AA; 1 quadruple 20-mm 90-cal. M-75 AA; both: 1 4-round MTU-4 SAM launcher (. . . Strela-2M missiles); 2 mine rails (94 SAG-1 mines)
Electronics: Radar: 1 Decca 1290A nav.
M: 2 Burmeister & Wain Alpha 10V23L-VO diesels; 2 CP props; 3,100 bhp
Range: 1,200/12
Crew: 3 officers, 6 senior petty officers, 24 enlisted + up to 300 troops

Remarks: DBM stands for "landing ship, minelayer," while DBV indicates use as a water tanker. The first ship of the class was completed in 1990 and is in Federal Yugoslav Navy hands.
Hull systems: Have bow and stern ramps, with continuous covered vehicle deck also used for portable minerails. Cargo capacity: 460 tons or six tanks totaling 264 tons or up to seven armored personnel carriers; in DBV 82, ballast tankage is presumably employed to transport fresh water to offshore island garrisons.
Combat systems: Have two 128-mm illumination rocket launchers. On DBM 81, the 30-mm gunmounts are mounted port and starboard, just abaft the bridge, while the 20-mm mount is located near the stern. On DBV 82, the single gunmount is located forward.

♦ 1 DTM 211–class landing craft/minelayer [LCU]
Bldr: Yugoslavia (In serv. 1950s)

DTM 219 "Jastreb" (ex-DTM 217)

"Jastreb" (DTM 219) Dario Vuljanic, *HVG,* 2000

D: 240 tons (410 fl) **S:** 10.3 kts **Dim:** 49.80 × 8.60 (6.55 wl) × 1.66 (2.10 max.)
A: 1 triple 20-mm M-75 AA; 2 mine rails (98 SAG-1 mines)
M: 3 Torpedo B.539RM/22 diesels; 3 props; 768 bhp
Range: 500/9.3 **Crew:** 27 tot.

Remarks: DTM = *Desantni Tenkonosac/Minopolagac.* Near-duplicate of the World War II–German MFP-D class. Equipped with 1-m-wide hull sponsons, extending beam to 8.6 m and providing space for two mine rails with a total capacity of up to 100 small mines. Bow ramp. Can carry 140 tons of vehicles or 200 troops. Was re-engined in 1973. The similar *Slavyy* (DSM 110), initially put into service for the Croatian Navy, had been retired by 5-97. The name "*Jastreb*" is unofficial and may no longer be carried.

♦ 1 ex-German Siebel Ferry–class utility landing craft [LCU]
Bldr: . . . (In serv. 1943–44)

DSM 110 (ex-DST 105)

DSM 110 Dario Vuljanic, *HVG,* 1998

D: 129 tons (167 fl) **S:** 9 kts **Dim:** 25.84 × 14.05 × 1.09
A: 2 single 20-mm 90-cal. M-71 AA; 2 mine rails
Electronics: Radar: 1 . . . nav.
M: 2 Mercedes-Benz truck diesels; 2 props; 400 bhp
Range: . . . / . . . **Crew:** 2 officers, 18 enlisted

Remarks: Catamaran with twin pontoon-type hulls. Refitted and re-engined at Pula in 1956. Sister PDS 713 is configured as a dredge.

♦ 2 DJČ 621–class (Type 22) landing craft [LCVP]
Bldr: Gleben SY, Vela Luka, Korčula (In serv. 1976–77)

DJČ 106 (ex-DJČ 624)

Lupac

DJČ 106—with DJČ 613- and DJČ 601–class units Dario Vuljanic, *HVG,* 2000

D: 48 tons (. . . fl) **S:** 30 kts **Dim:** 22.30 × 4.84 × 1.07 (1.58 props)
A: 1 20-mm 90-cal. M-71 AA; 1 30-mm BP-30 grenade launcher
Electronics: Radar: 1 Decca 101 nav.
M: 2 MTU . . . diesels; 2 waterjets; 1,740 bhp
Range: 320/22 **Crew:** 8 tot. + 40 troops

Remarks: DJČ = *Desantni Jurisni Čamac.* Of the units of the DJČ 621–class landing craft captured, three were assigned as civilian fireboats and one (ex-DJČ 622) is used by a police agency; of the two employed by the navy, DJČ 105 (ex-DJČ 623) was discarded in 1996 and DJČ 106 (ex-DJČ 624) was stricken in 1997 but restored to service in 1998. GRP construction hull with bow ramp. Can carry 15 tons of vehicles in 32-m^2 cargo area.

♦ 2 DJČ 613–class (Type 21) landing craft [LCVP]
Bldr: Gleben SY, Vela Luka, Korčula (In serv. 1976–77)

DJČ 104 (ex-DJČ 615) DJČ 107 (ex-DJČ 613)

DJČ 104 Dario Vuljanic, *HVG,* 1997

AMPHIBIOUS WARFARE SHIPS AND CRAFT *(continued)*

D: 32 tons (38 fl) **S:** 23.5 kts **Dim:** 21.30 × 4.84 × 1.07 (1.58 props)
A: 1 20-mm M-71 AA—2 30-mm BP-30 grenade launchers
Electronics: Radar: 1 Decca 101 nav.
M: 1 MTU 12V331 TC81 diesel; 1 prop; 1,450 bhp
Range: 320/22 **Crew:** 6 tot. + 40 troops

Remarks: DJČ = *Desantni Jurisni Čamac.* Glass-reinforced plastic construction with bow ramp. Can carry vehicles totaling six tons in the 32-m^2 cargo area. Two others of the four captured were badly damaged and were not repaired.

♦ 3 DJČ 601–class (Type 11) personnel landing craft [LCVP]
Bldr: Gleben SY, Vela Luka, Korčula, (In serv. 1987)

DJČ 101 (ex-DJČ 602) DJČ 103 (ex-DJČ 612)
DJČ 102 (ex-DJČ 603)

DJČ 102 Dario Vuljanic, *HVG,* 1996

D: 32 tons (38 fl) **S:** 23 kts **Dim:** 21.30 × 4.84 × 1.07 (1.58 props)
A: 1 20-mm M-71 AA—1 30-mm BP-30 grenade launcher
Electronics: Radar: 1 Decca 101 nav.
M: 1 MTU 12V331 diesel; 1 prop; 1,250 bhp
Range: 320/22 **Crew:** 6 tot. + 40 troops

Remarks: GRP construction. Bow ramp. Can carry vehicles totaling six tons in 32-m^2 cargo area.

Note: Also in service is fast personnel landing craft BDČ . . . (ex-BDČ 82), said to be of British origin; no data available.

♦ 2 Mala-class (Type R2) swimmer delivery vehicles [LSDV]
Bldr: Brodosplit, Split, Croatia

Mala-class swimmer delivery vehicle Split Shipyard BSO

D: 1.4 tons **S:** 4.4 kts **Dim:** 4.90 × 1.22 × 1.32 (1.70 fins) **A:** 2 50-kg mines
M: 1 electric motor; 1 prop; 6 hp **Range:** 18/4.4; 23/3.7 **Crew:** 2 tot.

Remarks: Diving depth: 60 m. Free-flooding personnel space enclosed within clear-plastic dome. Sweden has acquired one, and six were sold to Libya; the USSR may also have received examples. Croatia is said to have captured two of the four Yugoslav units of this class; one of the pair is described as being of Type R2M, indicating some modification.

Note: Also available are two R1 "chariot"-type swimmer delivery vehicles with a length of 3.72 m, a beam of 1.05 m, and a surfaced draft of 0.80 m; the craft have a range of 6 n.m. at 3 kts on their 1-kw electric motors and can dive to 60 m. Three personnel can be carried astride the craft.

AUXILIARIES

♦ 1 submarine rescue and salvage ship [ASR]
Bldr: Tito SY, Belgrade (In serv. 10-9-76)

PT 73 Faust Vrančič (ex-*Spasilac,* PS 12)

D: 1,590 tons (fl) **S:** 13.4 kts **Dim:** 55.50 × 12.00 × 3.84 (4.34 max.)
A: provision for 2 quadruple M-75 and 2 single M-71 20-mm AA
Electronics: Radar: 1 . . . nav.
M: 2 diesels; 2 Kort-nozzle props; 4,340 bhp
Electric: 540 kVA **Range:** 4,000/13.4 **Crew:** 53 tot. (72 accomm.)

Remarks: Resembles an oilfield supply vessel; low freeboard aft. Sister *Aka* was in the Iraqi Navy, and one Yugoslav Navy unit was sold to Libya (ex-*Zlatica*). Equipped for underwater cutting and welding, towing, salvage lifting, fire fighting, and other salvage tasks. Can carry up to 250 tons deck cargo, transferring 490 tons cargo fuel, 48 tons cargo water, and 5 tons lube oil. Can support divers to 300 m with a three-section decompression chamber. Also has capability to support a small rescue submersible. Has a bow-thruster and can lay a four-point moor. Conducted a port visit to Venice during 10-05.

Faust Vrančič (PT 73) H&L Van Ginderen, 2-97

♦ 1 Soviet Moma-class cadet training ship [AXT]
Bldr: Stocznia Polnocna, Gdansk, Poland (In serv. 1971)

PT 72 Andrija Mohorovičič (ex-PS 72, ex-PH 72, ex-PH 33)

Andrija Mohorovičič (PT 72) Dario Vuljanic, *HVG,* 1999

D: 1,260 tons (1,540 fl) **S:** 17 kts **Dim:** 73.3 × 10.8 × 3.8
Electronics: Radar: 1 Don-2 nav.
M: 2 Zgoda-Sulzer 6TD48 diesels; 2 CP props; 3,600 bhp
Range: 8,700/11 **Crew:** 4 officers, 33 enlisted

Remarks: Transferred from the USSR in 1972. Carries one survey launch. Five-ton crane for navigational buoy handling. Four laboratories totaling 35 m^2 deck space. Formerly used for oceanographic research, hydrographic surveys, and buoy tending, but now employed mostly for training for the Croatian Naval Academy.

SERVICE CRAFT

♦ 1 diving tender [YDT]
Bldr: Macvanska Mitroviča (In serv. 1952)

BRM 83 Zirje

D: 38 tons (46 fl) **S:** 12 kts **Dim:** 20.50 (19.4 pp) × 4.50 × 1.42
A: 1 40-mm 60-cal. Bofors AA; 1 quadruple 12.7-mm mg
Electronics: Radar: 1 Decca 101 nav.
M: 2 diesels; 2 props; 304 bhp **Range:** 400/12 **Crew:** 9 tot.

Remarks: Same basic design as Federal Yugoslav Navy BRM 82-87–series transports. Sister BRM 82 became the police patrol craft *Zečevo.*

Note: Also in service are the former Federal Yugoslav Navy diving tenders BRM 53 and BRM 51; no data available.

♦ 1 PT 71–class cargo lighter [YF]
Bldr: Split SY, Croatia (In serv. 1956)

PT 71 Medusa

Medusa (PT 71) Dario Vuljanic via Zvonimir Freivogel, 2002

SERVICE CRAFT *(continued)*

D: 310 tons (428 fl) **S:** 7 kts **Dim:** 43.1 × 7.2 × 4.85
M: 1 Burmeister & Wain diesel; 1 prop; 300 bhp

Remarks: PT = *Pomocni Transporter.*

♦ 1 yacht [YFL]

JADRANKA (ex-*Smile*)

Jadranka Dario Vuljanic, *HVG,* 2000

Remarks: No data available.

Disposal note: Yacht *UČKA* (ex-*Podgorika*) was damaged in a fire during 2001 and was not repaired.

♦ 5 BMT 1–class personnel and cargo launches [YFL]

BMT 1 KAKANJ (ex-BM 64)
BMT 2 KRASNIČA
BMT 3 . . .
BMT 4 . . .
BMT 5 . . .

D: 38 tons (46 fl) **S:** 12 kts **Dim:** 20.50 (19.4 pp) × 4.50 × 1.42
A: 1 20-mm 90-cal. M71 AA
Electronics: Radar 1 . . . nav.
M: 2 diesels; 2 props; 304 bhp **Range:** 400/12 **Crew:** 10 tot.

Remarks: Wooden-hulled design, similar to diving tender listed above. *Kakanj* is ex-Yugoslav, while *Krasniča* was launched 1-2-96. Five are likely to remain in service.

♦ 1 ex-German Siebel Ferry–class dredge [YM]

Bldr: . . . (In serv. 1943–44)

PDS 713 (ex-DSM 105, ex-DST 105, ex- . . .)

D: 129 tons (167 fl) **S:** 9 kts **Dim:** 25.84 × 14.05 × 1.09
Electronics: Radar: 1 . . . nav.
M: 2 Mercedes-Benz truck diesels; 2 props; 400 bhp
Range: . . . / . . . **Crew:** . . . tot.

Remarks: Catamaran with twin pontoon-type hulls, built as a landing craft. One of two Croatian survivors of ten originally in Yugoslav service. Refitted and re-engined at Pula in 1956. Sister DSM 110 (see above) remains configured as a landing craft.

♦ 2 LR 67–class harbor tugs [YTM]

Bldr: Split SY, Croatia (In serv. 1960s)

LR 71 LR 73

LR 73 Boris Lemachko Collection, 12-02

D: 550 tons (fl) **S:** 11 kts **Dim:** 32.0 × 8.0 × . . .
M: 2 diesels; 1 prop; . . . bhp

Remarks: LR = *Lučki Remorker* (Harbor Tug). Sisters LR 72 and LR 77 remain in Federal Yugoslav Navy hands.

♦ 2 small riverine tugs [YTL]

R 301 BIZON R 303

Remarks: Based at Sisak, on the Save River; no data available.

♦ 1 sail-training craft [YTS]

KRALJIČA JELENA (ex-*ACI No. 1*)

Remarks: No data available.

Disposal note: M 117–class training craft and former minesweeper *Lastovo* (LM 117) was sold for commercial use.

1ST CROATIAN GUARDS CORPS

Note: The 1st Croatian Guards is a triservice presidential guard and operates a small number of craft based at Pula and in the Brioni Islands.

♦ 3 Galeb-class (Type 15) riverine and lake patrol craft [WPB]

CISTA VELIKA DUBRAVIČE KRASNIČA

D: 19.5 tons (fl) **S:** 16 kts **Dim:** 16.87 × 3.90 × 0.65 (0.70 props)
A: 1 20-mm M-71 AA: 1 quadruple 14.5-mm 93-cal. mg
Electronics: Radar: 1 Decca 110 nav.
M: 2 diesels; 2 props; 330 bhp **Range:** 160/12 **Crew:** 6 tot.

Remarks: Steel hull, glass-reinforced plastic superstructures. Four sisters delivered to the Sudan, 5-89, and a number of others remain in Federal Yugoslav service. These three came under Croatian control and were commissioned during 8-92; they were subsequently transferred to the 1st Croatian Guards Corps.

♦ 1 BMT 1–class patrol boat [WPB]

ZEČEVO (ex-BRM 82)

Zečevo Dario Vuljanic, *HVG,* 2000

D: 38 tons (46 fl) **S:** 12 kts **Dim:** 20.50 (19.4 pp) × 4.50 × 1.42
A: 1 20-mm 90-cal. M-71 AA
Electronics: Radar 1 . . . nav.
M: 2 diesels; 2 props; 304 bhp **Range:** 400/12 **Crew:** 10 tot.

Remarks: Same basic design as the naval diving tender BRM 83 and the BMT 1–class personnel launches listed above. Wooden hull.

Note: A number of other small patrol craft are in 1st Croatian Guards Corps service, including *Zalac* (M2), armed with one 20-mm AA.

COAST GUARD AND POLICE

Note: Croation Coast Guard craft are painted white and have a broad blue and narrow red diagonal stripe on the hull sides forward. Units carry the inscription "Kapetanija" on the hull sides. Vessels known to be in service include small craft 1 ST, 2 SB, and two larger vessels, *Draga* and *Vid.*

Several other craft, including six small patrol boats numbered P 111 through P 116, patrol vessels *Marino* (P-2), *Sveti Mihovil* (P-101) and a number of RHIB craft, are also in service with the federal Maritime Police force.

Coast Guard patrol vessel Vid Martin Mokrus, 7-04

COAST GUARD AND POLICE *(continued)*

Police patrol boat Marino (P-2) Martin Makrus, 7-04

CUBA

Republic of Cuba

MARINA DE GUERRA REVOLUCIONARIA

Personnel: Approx. 3,000 total, including at least 550 naval infantry.

Naval Aviation: The 4 Kamov Ka-28 Helix-A and up to 14 Mil Mi-14PL Haze-A ASW helicopters likely remain in service, though they appear minimally operational at best.

Bases: The navy is organized into three districts, headquartered at Cabañas, Cienfuegos, and Holguín. Principal bases are at Cabañas, Canasi, Cienfuegos, Havana (where most repair work is accomplished), Mariel, Punta Ballenatos, and Varadero. The Naval Infantry Regiment is housed at Granma.

Coastal Defense: In addition to Russian P-20/21 Termit (SS-C-3 Styx-C) truck-mounted antiship missiles delivered in the 1980s, the Cuban Navy has adapted shipboard Styx missiles for land launch, using the indigenously developed Bandera-VI mobile launcher.

Disposal Note: Of the three Soviet-provided *Koni*-class (Project 1159) frigates, the *Mariel* (350, ex-SKR 28; in serv. 24-9-81) remained intact into 1999 when it was announced that she would be restored to service, but instead the ship remains derelict; the second unit (356, name not known; delivered 8-2-84) was sold to the Cayman Islands in 8-96 and renamed *Captain Keith Tibbetts* for use as a sunken attraction for scuba divers at Cayman Brac; and the *Monkada* (353, ex-SKR-451; in service 10-4-88) was sunk for the same purpose off the Cuban coast on 16-7-98.

PATROL COMBATANTS [PG]

♦ **1 Soviet Modified Pauk class (Project 1241PE)**
Bldr: Volodarskiy SY, Rybinsk (In serv. 22-5-90)

321

Modified Pauk 321—with 25-mm gunmounts added abreast the sonar housing at the stern French Navy, 12-98

D: 425 tons (495 fl, 554 max.) **S:** 32 kts (28 sust.)
Dim: 58.5 (49.5 pp) × 10.40 (9.40 wl) × 2.14 hull (4.0 props)
A: 1 76.2-mm 59-cal. AK-176 DP; 1 Fasta-4M SAM syst. (16 9M-313 Igla-1 missiles); 130-mm 54-cal. AK-630 gatling AA: 2 twin 25-mm 80-cal. 2M-3M AA; 2 5-round RBU-1200 ASW RL (30 RGB-12 rockets); 4 fixed 533-mm TT (2 SET-65E and 2 53-65KE torpedoes); 2 d.c. racks (12 d.c.)
Electronics:
Radar: 1 Mius (Spin Trough) nav.; 1 Positiv-E (Cross Dome) air/surf. search, 1 MR-123E Vympel AME (Bass Tilt) f.c.
Sonar: MGK-345 MF hull-mounted and MF dipping
EW: 2 16-round PK-16 decoy RL
M: 2 M-521-TM5 diesels; 2 props; 17,330 bhp
Range: 2,000/20; 2,600/14; 3,000/12 **Fuel:** 50 tons **Endurance:** 10 days
Crew: 7 officers, 32 enlisted

Remarks: Delivered under tow. Three additional units were to have been transferred, but the collapse of the USSR and the crumbling Cuban economy forced cancellation. Differs from standard Russian Navy version in having a larger pilothouse, incorporating a Positiv radar, and using 533-mm torpedo tubes (which are able to carry antiship as well as ASW torpedoes) vice 400-mm ASW TT. Four virtually identical units were built for India, one was retained by the Russian Navy, and two others were never delivered by the builder. The Cuban unit was nonoperational by 1997 but was refitted and reactivated during 1999.
Hull systems: The large housing for a dipping sonar system projects 1.5 m out from the stern. The large hull-mounted sonar dome is located approximately beneath the gun fire-control radar. The hull is constructed of mild steel, while the middle part of the deck plating, some internal bulkheads, and much of the superstructure are made of aluminum-magnesium alloy. Range with normal fuel allowance is only 1,600 n.m. at 12 kts.
Combat systems: The combat data system is designated SU-580E. There is a Kolonka-2 backup ringsight director for the single gatling AA gun; the MR-123 radar director can control both the 76.2-mm and 30-mm guns. Normal ammunition load is 152 rounds 76-mm (all ready-service, on-mount) and 2,000 rounds 30-mm. MGK-345 applies to both the hull-mounted and dipping sonars, and the dipping sonar transducer can be lowered to 200 m. In 1999, twin 25-mm AA mounts were added flanking the VDS housing at the stern.

PATROL CRAFT [PC]

♦ **6 Soviet Osa-II class (Project 205EM)**

261 262 267 268 271 274

Cuban Navy Osa-II U.S. Navy, 8-84

D: 184 tons (226 normal fl; 245 overload) **S:** 40 kts (35 sust.)
Dim: 38.6 (37.5 wl) × 7.6 (6.3 wl) × 2.0 hull (3.1 props)
A: 2 twin 30-mm 65-cal. AK-230 AA; 1 shoulder-launcher for Strela or Igla-1 heat-seeking missiles
Electronics: Radar: 1 Rangout (Square Tie) surf. search; 1 MR-104 Rys' (Drum Tilt) gun f.c.
M: 3 M-504 or M-504B diesels; 3 props; 15,000 bhp **Electric:** 400 kw tot.
Range: 500/34; 750/25 **Endurance:** 5 days **Crew:** 4 officers, 24 enlisted

Remarks: Transferred: two in 1977, three in 1978, two in 1979, two in 11-81, two in 1-82, two in 2-82. Seven have been discarded. As of 1997, the missiles had been removed from all and transferred to shore-based launchers; the shipboard launchers have been retained aboard, however. The remaining craft are rarely operated.

MINE WARFARE CRAFT

♦ **2 Soviet Sonya-class (Project 1265) coastal minesweepers [MSC]** Bldr: . . . Russia (In serv. 1985)

570 578

D: 401 tons (430 fl) **S:** 14 kts
Dim: 48.80 (46.00 wl) × 10.20 (9.20 wl) × 2.40 mean hull (2.75 max.)
A: 1 twin 30-mm AA; 1 twin 25-mm 80-cal. AA; mines
Electronics:
Radar: 1 . . . nav.
Sonar: MG-69 /79 hull-mounted
M: 2 . . . diesels;
Range: 3,000/10 **Fuel:** 27.1 tons **Crew:** 45 total accomm.

Remarks: Transferred from the Soviet Union in 1985, along with two sisters that have since been stricken.

♦ **4 Soviet Yevgenya-class (Project 1258) inshore minesweepers**
Bldr: Sredniy Neva SY, Kolpino

D: 88.5 tons light, 94.5 normal (97.9 fl) **S:** 11 kts
Dim: 26.13 (24.20 wl) × 5.90 (5.10 wl) × 1.38
A: 1 twin 25-mm 80-cal. 2M-3M AA; 1 7-round MRG-1 grenade launcher; 4 d.c. in individual tilt racks (+ 8 emergency stowage)
Electronics:
Radar: 1 Mius (Spin Trough) or Kivach nav.
Sonar: MG-7 HF dipping

MINE WARFARE CRAFT *(continued)*

M: 2 Type 3D12 diesels; 2 props; 600 bhp—hydraulic slow-speed drive
Electric: 100 kw tot. (2 × 50-kw diesel sets)
Range: 400/10 **Fuel:** 2.7 tons **Endurance:** 3 days
Crew: 1 officer, 9 enlisted (+ 2–3 clearance divers)

Remarks: Two transferred 11-77, one in 9-78, two in 11-79, two in 12-80, two in 12-81, one in 10-82, and two in 11-84; two others, delivered 9-84, were further transferred to Nicaragua. At least eight have been stricken. Equipped to search for mines in depths of up to 30 m using towed television camera, marker buoys, and standard wire cable gear. Glass-reinforced plastic construction.

AUXILIARIES

♦ **1 Spanish-built navigational buoy tender [AGL]**
Bldr: Maritime del Musel, Gijon (In serv. 1979)

H 102 Taino

D: 1,100 tons **S:** 12 kts **Dim:** 53.0 (42.0 pp) × 10.4 × 3.5
M: 2 diesels; 2 props; 1,550 bhp **Electric:** 360 kw **Crew:** . . . tot.

Remarks: 669 grt/572 dwt. Primarily a buoy tender but can also be used for hydrographic surveys.

♦ **1 Soviet Biya-class hydrographic survey ship [AGS]**
Bldr: Stocznia Polnocna, Gdansk, Poland (In serv. 1972–76)

H 103 Guama (ex-GS 186)

D: 750 tons (fl) **S:** 13 kts **Dim:** 55.0 × 9.2 × 2.6
Electronics: Radar: 1 Don-2 nav.
M: 2 diesels; 2 CP props; 1,200 bhp
Range: 4,700/11 **Fuel:** 90 tons **Endurance:** 15 days **Crew:** 25 tot.

Remarks: Transferred 11-80. Carries one survey launch and has one 5-ton crane. Also useful as a navigational buoy tender. Operated for the Institute of Hydrography.

♦ **1 hydrographic survey vessel, converted trawler [AGS]**
Bldr: Ast. Talleres de Celaya, Bilbao, Spain (In serv. 1968)

H 101 Siboney

D: 600 tons (fl) **S:** 11.4 kts **Dim:** 40.2 × 8.3 × 2.6
M: 2 Stork-Werkspoor RHD-216K diesels; 1 prop; 910 bhp
Electric: 160 kw **Crew:** . . . tot.

♦ **1 Soviet Pelym-class (Project 1799) training ship [AXT]**

40 (ex-SR-77)

Cuban Pelym-class 40 2-82

D: 1,050 tons (1,200 fl) **S:** 13.5 kts **Dim:** 64.06 × 11.71 × 3.51
Electronics: Radar: 1 Don-2 nav.
M: 1 diesels; 1 prop; 1,536 bhp
Range: 1,000/13.5 **Crew:** 40 tot.

Remarks: Arrived in Cuba 2-82 under tow. As delivered, was equipped to deploy, operate, and recover deperming cable array, but by 1999 she was employed as fleet training ship, with deperming gear deleted.

SERVICE CRAFT

♦ **3 Lamda-class survey craft [YGS]** (In serv. 1960s)

H 76 H 77 H 78

D: 150 tons (fl) **S:** 10 kts **Dim:** 29.0 × 6.0 × 2.1 **M:** 1 diesel; 1 prop; 250 bhp

Remarks: Converted, wooden-hulled fishing boats.

♦ **3 Soviet Prometey-class large harbor tugs [YTB]**

D: 319 tons (fl) **S:** 12 kts **Dim:** 29.8 (28.2 pp) × 8.30 × 3.20
A: 3 single 12.7-mm 79-cal. mg
Electronics: Radar: 1 Mius (Spin Trough) nav.
M: 2 Type 6D30/50.4 diesels; 2 CP props; 1,200 bhp
Electric: 50 kw (2 × 25 kw) **Crew:** 8 tot.

Remarks: Two transferred 1967, one in 1972. Bollard pull: 14 tons.

MINISTRY OF THE INTERIOR BORDER GUARD
(Tropas de Guardia Frontera)

PATROL CRAFT [WPC]

♦ **3 Soviet Stenka class (Project 205P)**

D: 170 tons (210 fl) **S:** 36 kts **Dim:** 39.50 × 7.0 × 1.80
A: 2 twin 30-mm 65-cal. AK-230 AA
Electronics:
Radar: 1 Baklan (Pot Drum) surf. search; 1 MR-104 Rys' (Drum Tilt) gun f.c.
EW: 2 16-round PK-16 decoy RL
M: 3 M-504 diesels; 3 props; 15,000 bhp
Range: 500/35; 800/20 **Crew:** 5 officers, 27 enlisted

Remarks: Two transferred in 2-85, two in 9-85. Do not have the four fixed 400-mm ASW TT and stern-mounted dipping sonar found on standard version and have no antisubmarine capability. One other had ceased to operate by 2000.

PATROL BOATS [WPB]

♦ **18 Soviet Zhuk-class (Project 1400) patrol craft**

Cuban Border Guard Zhuk 532 U.S. Coast Guard, 1992

D: 35.9 tons (39.7 fl) **S:** 30 kts
Dim: 23.80 (21.70 wl) × 5.00 (3.80 wl) × 1.00 (hull)
A: 1 twin 12.7-mm 60-cal. Utës-M mg **Electronics:** Radar: 1 Lotsiya nav.
M: 2 M-401B diesels; 2 props; 2,400 bhp
Electric: 48 kw total (2 × 21-kw, 1 × 6-kw diesel sets)
Range: 500/13.5 **Endurance:** 5 days **Crew:** 3 officers, 14 enlisted

Remarks: Transferred between 12-71 and 9-89. At least 17 others have been passed onward to Nicaragua or stricken. Have enclosed, side-by-side machinegun mountings.

CYPRUS

Republic of Cyprus

Personnel: Approx. 350 total, including 250 maritime police personnel

Base: Limassol. A new base at Paphos began construction fall 1998, allegedly for use by visiting Greek warships.

Maritime Aviation: All naval air elements belong to the Cyprus Air Force. Three Agusta-Bell 47G helicopters are assigned coastal patrol duties, as is one Pilatus-Britten-Norman BN-2A Maritime Defender coastal reconnaissance aircraft.

Coast Defense: At least 24 truck-mounted MM 40 Exocet Block 2 antiship missiles were acquired from France during 1994 for the National Guard; each truck carries two missiles.

NAVAL COMMAND OF THE NATIONAL GUARD

PATROL BOATS [PB]

Note: Two 27-m patrol boats were to be ordered from Italy late in 2002, and are to be armed with a 35-mm gun and mine rails. Two sisters are already in service with the Maritime Police.

♦ **1 Type 32L**
Bldr: C.N. de l'Esterel, Cannes (In serv. 24-5-83)

P 01 Salamis

D: 98 tons (fl) **S:** 32 kts (30 sust.) **Dim:** 32.1 × 6.45 × 1.9
A: 2 2-round Simbad SAM syst. (Mistral missiles); 1 40-mm 70-cal. OTOBreda-Bofors AA; 1 20-mm 90-cal. Rheinmetall AA
Electronics: Radar: 1 Decca 1226 nav.
M: 2 SACM 195 CZSHRY 12 diesels; 2 props; 4,680 bhp
Range: 1,500/15 **Crew:** 22 tot.

PATROL BOATS [PB] *(continued)*

Salamis (P 01) Dieter Wolf, 1-02

Remarks: Wooden construction. Manned launchers for the point-defense SAM system were aboard by 5-00, mounted atop the superstructure abaft the mast.

♦ 1 ex-Greek Dilos class
Bldr: Hellenic SY, Skaramanga (In serv. 1979)

P 02 Kyrinia (ex-*Knossos,* P 269)

D: 75 tons (86 fl) **S:** 27 kts **Dim:** 29.00 (27.00 wl) × 5.00 × 1.62
A: 2 single 20-mm 70-cal. Oerlikon Mk 10 AA
Electronics: Radar: 1 Decca 1226C nav.
M: 2 MTU 12V331 TC81 diesels; 2 props; 2,720 bhp
Range: 1,600/25 **Crew:** 15 tot.

Remarks: Donated 3-00. Designed by Abeking & Rasmussen, Germany. Round-bilge, steel-construction hull. Sisters operate in the Georgian Coast Guard and in the Greek Coast Guard and Customs services.

♦ 2 Rodman 55 class
Bldr: Rodman-Polyships, Vigo, Spain (In serv. 2002)

Panagos Agathos

D: 15.7 tons (fl) **S:** 40 kts **Dim:** 16.5 × 3.8 × 0.7 **A:** 2 7.62-mm mg
Electronics: Radar: 1 Ericsson . . . nav.
M: 2 Bazán-M.A.N. D2848 LXE diesels; 2 Hamilton waterjets; 1,360 bhp
Range: 500/25 **Crew:** 7 tot.

MARITIME POLICE

PATROL BOATS [WPB]

♦ 2 Italian Corrubia-class patrol boats
Bldr: . . ., Italy (In serv. 2004–5)

PV 23 Thexas PV 24 . . .

D: 75 tons (83.3 fl) **S:** 43 kts **Dim:** 26.80 × 7.60 × 1.20
A: 2 single 7.62-mm mg
Electronics: Radar: 1 . . . nav.
M: 2 . . . diesels **Range:** 700/35 **Crew:** 5 tot.

Thexas (PV 23) Pierre Joly via Paolo Marsan, 3-05

Remarks: Based on the design operated by the Italian Customs Service. Ordered late 2002. Two additional units have been ordered for naval service.

♦ 1 Israeli Shaldag class
Bldr: Israel Shipyards, Haifa (In serv. 2-98)

PV 22 Odysseus

Odysseus (PV 22)—operated by the Cypriot Maritime Police Pierre Joly via Paolo Marsan, 3-05

D: 40 tons (56 fl) **S:** 46 kts **Dim:** 24.80 × 6.00 × 1.15
A: 1 20-mm 90-cal. Oerlikon AA; 2 single 12.7-mm mg
Electronics: Radar: 1 Furuno FR 8250 nav.
M: 2 MTU 12V396 TE 94 diesels; 2 waterjets; 3,260 bhp
Electric: 50 kw tot. (2 × 25-kw, 440 V a.c. diesel sets)
Range: 890/45; 990/33 **Endurance:** 2–3 days **Crew:** 15 tot.

Remarks: Acquired late in 1997. Deep-vee, aluminum-construction hull. Five watertight compartments. Air-conditioned.

♦ 2 Yugoslav FAC-23 class
Bldr: Brodotehnika, Belgrade (In serv. 21-11-91)

PV 20 Poseidon PV 21 Evagoras

Evagoras (PV 21) Pierre Joly via Paolo Marsan, 3-05

D: 57 tons (fl) **S:** 42 kts **Dim:** 24.60 (20.60 pp) × 5.70 × 1.05
A: 1 20-mm 90-cal. Rheinmetall AA; 2 single 7.62-mm mg; 1 ISBRS unguided rocket launcher
Electronics: Radar: 1 Decca 1226 nav.
M: 2 diesels; 2 KaMeWa waterjets; 4,270 bhp **Range:** 400/40; 600/20
Endurance: 5 days **Crew:** 9 tot.

Remarks: Aluminum construction. One seems to have borne the temporary name *Sergey Krtanovic.*

♦ 1 Plascoa 18-meter class
Bldr: C.N. de l'Esterel, Cannes (In serv. 1982)

PL 2 Kimon

D: 28 tons (fl) **S:** 26 kts **Dim:** 17.2 × 5.2 × 1.3
A: 1 12.7-mm mg **Electronics:** Radar: 1 Decca 1226 nav.
M: 2 MTU diesels; 2 props; . . . bhp **Crew:** 8 tot.

Remarks: GRP construction. Another unit of this class was discarded in 1991.

♦ 5 ex-East German SAB 12 launches

PL 11 Dionysos (ex-GS 12, ex-G 55)
PL 12 Kourion (ex-GS 27, ex-G 55)
PL 13 Ilarion (ex-GS 25, ex-G 52)
PL 14 Karpasia (ex-GS 10, ex-G 50)
PL 15 Akamas (ex-GS 28, ex-G 57)

D: 14 tons (fl) **S:** 16 kts **Dim:** 12.6 × 4.0 × 1.1
A: Small arms **Electronics:** Radar: 1 Decca . . . nav.
M: 2 Volvo Penta TAMD-series diesels; 2 props; 540 bhp **Crew:** 5 tot.

Remarks: Transferred 12-92 from Germany.

MARITIME POLICE PATROL BOATS [WPB] *(continued)*

Dionysos (PL 11)—with unidentified sister in the background
Pierre Joly via Paolo Marsan, 3-05

NORTH CYPRUS

Turkish Republic of Northern Cyprus

Note: The independence of North Cyprus is not recognized by the United Nations. Defense forces are Turkish controlled and largely Turkish manned.

PATROL BOATS [PB]

♦ **1 Turkish-built**
Bldr: Profilo Holding Proteksan SY, Tuzla, Istanbul (L: 23-9-88)

74 Ras Denktas

D: 10 tons (fl) **S:** 28 kts **Dim:** 11.9 × 3.5 × . . .
A: 1 12.7-mm mg **Electronics:** Radar: 1 Raytheon . . . nav. **Crew:** 6 tot.
M: 2 Volvo Aquamatic diesels; 2 props; 400 bhp **Range:** 250/ . . .

Note: Also in service is *Caner Gönyeli* (P 145), a 14.6-m, 700-bhp patrol craft built at Taskizak Shipyard, Turkey.

DENMARK

Kingdom of Denmark

DET KONGELIGE DANSKE SØVÆRN

Personnel: 3,800 total, plus 7,300 Naval Reservists and 4,500 Naval Home Guard.

Bases: Frederikshavn and Korsør in Denmark, Grønnedal in Greenland

Maritime Aviation Assets: Denmark's Naval and Army air arms were merged with the Air Force in 1973. Maritime assets include eight Mk 90B Lynx helicopters (refurbished from Mk 80A/90 configuration). Helicopter upgrades include Gem 42 engines, Sea Spray 3000 radar, FLIR, and the capability to launch Sea Spray antiship missiles. Designated S-134, S-142, S-170, S-175, S-181, S-191, S-249, and S-256, these helicopters are attached to SHT (Sovaemets Helicopter Tjeneste) Squadron and based at Karup Air Base for use in ship/shore-based ASW and fishery protection duties. The SHT squadron is expected to be renamed Esk-728 once all OH-6A Cayuse helicopters are withdrawn from service in the near future.

The Danish Air Force has 3 Bombardier Challenger CL-604 for maritime patrol aircraft (the last one being delivered in 2006). Eight Sikorsky S-61A-1 Sea King helicopters in Esk-772 Squadron, at Karup Air Base. Vandal Air Base was closed on 23-7-03. Under a contract dated 7-12-01 delivery of the first of 14 Agusta-Westland EH.101 helicopters began in 2004. They will replace the eight Sea King helicopters.

Coastal Defense: Two mobile Harpoon coast defense batteries each consist of two trucks with four missiles each and a third command center vehicle. The batteries employ RGM-84A missiles removed from the stricken frigates of the *Peder Skram* class. The fortress of Stevns at the Baltic approaches to the Great Belt is equipped with 150-mm artillery and 40-mm AA guns, and there are also six coastal radar stations.

Danish Mk 90B Lynx—painted royal blue, aboard *Esberne Snare* (L 17)
Leo Van Ginderen, 6-05

Weapons and Sensors: Most equipment is of European origin, except for the U.S. Sea Sparrow and Harpoon missile systems. The Harpoon inventory was upgraded from Block IC to Block II under a 3-99 contract with Boeing, with the first updated missiles delivered 26-4-02. Some 3,000 SM.2G sea mines were delivered 1990–93. NATO Link 11 datalink is employed by major surface units, and Denmark is participating in the Link 22 development program. Eurotorp MU90 ASW torpedoes were ordered 1-99 for use on the *Flyvefisken* class. The Danish firm Terma A/S provides navigational and surface-search radars. Chemring Chimera dual-mode seduction rounds were ordered early in 2000 for use with Terma's 130-mm Soft-Kill Weapon System decoy launchers.

Note: Ship names are prefaced by HDMS (His Danish Majesty's Ship).

ATTACK SUBMARINES [SS]

Note: Scandanavia's Viking submarine program, of which Denmark was a key partner along with Sweden and Norway, was abandoned during 2004.

Disposals: *Kronborg* (S 325), originally built for the Royal Swedish Navy as *Nacken,* was decommissioned on 27-10-04 and returned to Sweden where she resumed her original Swedish name. Her current status in the Swedish Navy is unclear.

The Danish Navy's submarine arm was formally decommissioned on 25-11-05 at a ceremony at Fredrikshavn Naval Base. Of the three ex-Norwegian *Kobben* class in the Danish Navy at the time, *Tumleren* (S 322) was decommissioned on 17-8-04, *Springeren* (S 324) on 25-11-04, and *Sælen* (S 323) on 21-12-04. *Tumleren* and *Springeren* were sold for scrapping and *Tumleren* was transferred to the Royal Danish Naval Museum for refurbishing as a museum ship.

FRIGATES [FF]

♦ **0 (+ 3) Flexible Patrol Ship class**
Bldr: . . . Odense, Denmark (In serv. 2011–12)

D: 4,000 tons (6,200 tons fl) **S:** 26 kts **Dim:** 137.0 × 19.5 × 6.3
A: 8 RGM-84C Block II Harpoon SSM; 4 8-round Mk 41 VLS SAM missile launcher (24 Evolved Sea Sparrow and 8 SM-2 MR Block II missiles); 1 35-mm Millennium gun; 176-mm 162-cal. OTO Melara Compact DP; 1 EH-101 helicopter
Electronics:
Radar: 3-D surveillance/fire control; 1 air/surf. search; 1 navigation
Sonar: hull-mounted and towed passive array
EW: 2 Terma DLS Mk II DL-12T 12-round decoy RL
M: 4 MTU 20V800 M70 diesels; 2 CP props; 21,460 bhp
Range: 9,000/15 **Endurance:** 28 days
Crew: 100 total

Remarks: Intended to replace the *Niels Juel* class. If current plans are carried out, the first should enter service in 2011, the second is expected to be ordered in 2008 and the third in 2009. At least two more may be ordered post-2012. Intended for fisheries and EEZ patrol; incorporate signature-reduction features.
Combat systems: The C-Flex combat system will be incorporated and will be able to employ Links 11, 16, and (when available) 22; the ships will have the Infocom ICS 2000 communications system, including SATCOM, HF, UHF, and VHF radio. Will carry antitorpedo and antimissile decoys. There will be six modular weapons installation stations and a hold large enough to accommodate six 20-ft equivalent (TEU) mission modules. One 35-mm gun is to be carried forward of the bridge and a second aft atop the hangar roof.

CORVETTES [FFL]

♦ **3 Niels Juel (Type KV 72) class**
Bldr: Ålborg Værft, Ålborg, Denmark

	Laid down	L	In serv.
F 354 Niels Juel	20-10-76	17-2-78	26-8-80
F 355 Olfert Fischer	6-12-78	15-1-80	16-10-81
F 356 Peter Tordenskiold	3-12-79	30-4-80	2-4-82

Peter Tordenskiold (F 356) Frank Findler, 6-05

CORVETTES [FFL] *(continued)*

Niels Juel (F 354) Martin Mokrus, 4-05

D: 1,100 tons (1,320 fl) **S:** 26 kts (20 on diesel)
Dim: 84.00 (80.00 pp) × 10.30 × 4.80
A: 8 RGM-84C Block II Harpoon SSM (2 quad launchers); 2 6-round Sea Sparrow Mk 48, mod 3 VLS Sea Sparrow SAM missile launcher (12 Sea Sparrow RIM-7P missiles); 2 4-round short-range Stinger SAM launchers; 1 76-mm/62 cal. OTO Melara Compact DP; 2 20-mm Oerlikon-AA; 7 12.7-mm machineguns; 1 Mk 3 d.c. rack
Electronics:
Radar: 2 Terma Scanter Mil 009 nav.; 1 EADS TRS-3D air search; 1 CelsiusTech 9GR 600 surf. search; 1 CelsiusTech 9 LV 200 gun f.c. (with Type 771 low-light t.v. tracker); 1 General Dynamics Mk 95 missile f.c. syst. (2 directors)
Sonar: Plessey PMS-26 hull-mounted MF (10 kHz)
EW: Racal Cutlass B-1 intercept; Telegon HFD/F; 4 6-round SEA GNAT/SBROC Mk. 36 illumination/chaff launchers
M: CODOG: 1 G.E. LM-2500 gas turbine (25,700 shp), 1 MTU 20V956 TB82 diesel (4,800 bhp); 2 CP props
Electric: 1,500 kw (3 × 500-kw diesel sets) **Range:** 800/28; 2,500/18
Fuel: 130 tons **Crew:** 91 tot. (18 officers, 73 enlisted)

Remarks: Ordered 5-12-75. F 356 underwent midlife overhaul 15-5-96 to 5-98; F 354 completed in April 1999 and F 355 completed in 12-01. All three are homeported in Korsoer, Seeland Island.
Combat systems: During midlife refits, the DataSAAB CEPLO data system was replaced by the Terma-CelsiusTech SF-300 system, a variant of the 9LV Mk 3 system with NATO Link 11 datalink; the octuple Mk 29 Sea Sparrow launcher on the fantail was replaced by two sets of six round Mk 48 Mod. 3 vertical Sea Sparrow SAM launchers with the later RIM-7P missile (two modules are normally carried); and the EADS TRS-3D surveillance and weapons-control radar replaced the original Plessey AWS-5. Two cranes have been mounted at the after corners of the forecastle to handle reload missiles and boats. The ships are expected to serve until 2010 or later and are to be given a NATO Maritime Command-and-Control Information System (MCCIS) and UHF/SHF SATCOM capabilities.

PATROL SHIPS [PS]

Note: There are a total of seven crews for the four fisheries patrol vessels described below; the crews are rotated to the ships while on station off Greenland and the Faeroe Islands.

♦ 4 Thetis class (Stanflex 2000)
Bldr: Svendborg Skibsværft, Svendborg, Denmark

	Laid down	L	In serv.
F 357 Thetis	10-10-88	14-7-89	1-7-91
F 358 Triton	27-6-89	16-3-90	2-12-91
F 359 Vædderen	19-3-90	21-12-90	9-6-92
F 360 Hvidbjørnen	2-1-91	11-10-91	30-11-92

Thetis (F 357) Frank Findler, 6-04

Hvidbjørnen (F 360) Jaroslaw Cislak, 6-02

D: 2,600 tons (3,500 fl) **S:** 21.5 kts **Dim:** 112.50 × 14.40 × 6.00
A: 4 quad Stinger SAM missile launcher; 1 76-mm 62-cal. OTO Melara Compact DP; 2 37-mm saluting guns; 4 12.7-mm machineguns; 1 d.c. launcher; 1 Westland Lynx Mk. 80/91 helicopter
Electronics:
Radar: 1 Plessey AWS-6 air search; 1 Furuno FR-1505 DA surf. search; 2 Terma Scanter Mil 009 nav.; 1 CelsiusTech 9 LV 200 gun f.c.
Sonar: 1 C-Tech CTS-36 hull-mounted; 1 Thales Salmon HF variable depth sonar (except F 357: none—see remarks)
EW: Racal Cutlass B-1 intercept; Racal Scorpion jammer; 2 12-round Terma DL-12T decoy RL using Chemring Chimera decoys (F 357 and F 360 only)
M: 3 M.A.N.-Burmeister & Wain type 12V 28/32 diesels; 13,000 total bhp; 1 KaMeWa controllable pitch propeller—1 884-hp bow-thruster
Electric: 1,500 kw (3 x 500-kw diesel sets) **Range:** 8,500 nm at 15.5 kts.
Fuel: 130 tons **Crew:** 12 officers, 49 enlisted + 12 passengers

Remarks: Ordered 10-87. Intended primarily for fisheries patrol. *Thetis* was equipped during spring 1991 at Århus Shipyard with a towed array with six pneumatic seismic survey "guns" for use in oil exploration along the eastern coast of Greenland under charter to the Nunaoil consortium; employed on oil survey duties July through October 1991. All four are based at Frederikshavn and are assigned to the 1st Squadron, with F 357 in Division 11 and the others in Division 12.
F 360 has been adapted as interim flagship for the Danish Task Group intervention force, with upper deck cleared of gear to make room for a communications van and a command-and-control center. The ship has been given NATO Link 11, and extra accommodations are fitted. A permanent flagship capability was added to F 357 during 2002.
Hull systems: Engines are on resilient mountings to reduce radiated noise. Have ice-reinforced hulls. The single rudder is of the Becker flapped type. Retractable fin stabilizers and liquid antiroll tanks are fitted. The 28 × 14-m helicopter deck can accommodate heavy helicopters such as the Sea King; the hangar can accommodate a Lynx. All deck gear is mounted below the forecastle on the first platform and one deck below the helicopter platform.
Combat systems: Have the CelsiusTech 9LV 200 Mk 3 weapons-direction system for 76-mm gun, with t.v. tracker/director and four multifunction operator consoles. The Stinger launchers were added 2003–4.
Disposal note: The patrol frigate *Beskyterren* (F 340) was decommissioned on 21-11-00 without replacement and donated to Estonia on 22-11-00.

GUIDED-MISSILE PATROL CRAFT [PTG]

♦ 14 Flyvefisken-class (Stanflex 300) multifunctional
Bldr: Aalborg Værft, Aalborg

	Laid down	L	In serv.
P 550 Flyvefisken*	15-8-85	26-4-86	19-12-89
P 551 Hajen*/**	2-88	6-12-88	19-7-90
P 552 Havkatten**	8-88	30-5-89	1-11-90
P 553 Laxen**	18-5-89	17-10-89	22-3-91
P 554 Makrelen**	13-10-89	7-3-90	1-10-91
P 555 Støren**	5-2-90	14-12-90	24-4-92
P 556 Sværdfisken*	. . .	1-91	1-2-93
P 557 Glenten***	1-91	8-92	29-4-93
P 558 Gribben****	. . .	10-92	1-7-93
P 559 Lommen*****	. . .	. . .	21-1-94
P 560 Ravnen***	. . .	. . .	17-10-94
P 561 Skaden***	. . .	. . .	10-4-95
P 562 Viben***	. . .	. . .	15-1-96
P 563 Søløven****	. . .	6-6-95	28-5-96

Note: The status and configuration of this class is as follows:
* Laid up pending decommissioning in 2008
** Configured for mine warfare
*** Configured as a small combatant
**** Configured as an intelligence collection ship (AGI)
***** Configured as an AGI, but presently being used as a test ship. To decommission in FY 2007.

Viben (P 562)—in small combatant configuration carrying Harpoon missile canisters Frank Findler, 9-04

GUIDED-MISSILE PATROL CRAFT [PTG] *(continued)*

Støren (P 555)—in mine-countermeasures configuration Leo Van Ginderen, 10-05

D: 320 tons (450 fl) **S:** 35 kts (20 diesel)
Dim: 54.00 (50.00 pp) × 9.00 × 2.50 max. hull
A: 1 76-mm/62-cal. OTO/Melara Super Rapid DP (all versions) plus gunboat/mine-countermeasures versions: 2 single 12.7-mm mg.
Guided-missile boat: 2 twin or two quad RGM-84C Harpoon SSM and 1 6-round Sea Sparrow SAM Mark 48, mod. 0 VLS launcher or 2 6-round Sea Sparrow SAM Mark 48, mod. 0 VLS launcher (Sea Sparrow RIM-7P missiles)
Minelayer: 1 6-round Sea Sparrow SAM Mark 48, mod. 0 VLS launcher or 2 6-round Sea Sparrow SAM Mark 48, mod. 0 VLS launcher (both Sea Sparrow RIM-7P missiles) and 60 mines
ASW version: 1 variable depth sonar; 2 twin 323-mm ASW torpedo launchers (Eurotorp MU-90 torpedoes)
Electronics:
Radar: 1 Terma Scanter Mil 009 nav. or 1 Furuno FR-1505 DA surf. search, 1 Plessey AWS-6 (P 557 and later: EADS TRS-3D/16; P 560: none) air search; Terma-CelsiusTech 9LV 200 f.c. (see Remarks)
Sonar: C-Tech CTS-36 hull-mounted HF (36 kHz); Thales Salmon (TSM 2640) MF towed array (19 kHz)
EW: Racal Mermaid intercept (0.6–40 GHz); 2 6-round Terma DL-6T decoy RL (Chemring Chimera decoys)
E/O: Thales Albatross surveillance and f.c.
M: CODAG: 1 G.E.-Fiat LM-500 gas turbine (5,680 shp) centerline, 2 MTU 16V396 TB94 diesels (3,480 bhp each), 1 G.M. Detroit Diesel 12V71 diesel (500 bhp) to windmill centerline prop and to power slow-speed hydraulic drive system; 3 props (CP outboard)—bow-thruster
Electric: 600 kw (3 × 200 kw; GM 6-71 diesels driving) **Range:** 2,400/18
Crew: 4 officers, 13 enlisted as patrol boat; 4 officers, 15 enlisted as missile boat (29 tot. accom.)

Remarks: P 550 through P 556 were ordered 27-7-85 to a Karlskrona design. A second group of six was ordered during 6-90, originally without the gas turbines, guns, and other equipment. The final units were ordered under the 1993–94 budget. P 550 began trials on 27-10-87. One unit is normally equipped for intelligence collection duties. All had their electronics and communications systems updated between 2002 and 2006.

The boats are intended to be convertible to perform antiship, ASW, and patrol duties, as well as being configurable as minesweepers, fast minelayers, survey ships, oceanographic research ships, buoy tenders, fishery protection ships, and other semi-combatant and auxiliary missions.

Hull systems: The hull for P 550 was fabricated in Sweden by Karlskrona. Foam-core glass-reinforced plastic hull construction; due to weight-saving measures, the eighth and later boats displace about 15 tons less. The boats employ passive tank stabilization at low speeds, when they are powered by hydraulic drive for noise suppression; at high speeds, rudder roll control is employed, and there are trim tabs fitted at the stern. The outboard, diesel-driven props are controllable pitch; the centerline screw is windmilled by the auxiliary diesels when the gas turbine is not operating, in order to reduce drag. All machinery is controlled from the bridge. Kevlar armor panels are incorporated. Navigation systems include Decca precision radio navaid receiver and GPS receiver, and Sperry/Anschütz gyros.

Combat systems: Employ a Terma-CelsiusTech Flexfire 9LV Mk 3 weapons control system; the associated 9LV 200 fire-control radar is mounted on the port side, atop the pilothouse. Most have the U.S. WSC-3 UHF communications system, and NATO Link 11 is being added to all.

Starting with one ship in 2003, the Terma-Systematic C-Flex combat data/weapons control system is to replace the original equipment; five more are to follow in 2004–5. To outfit the class, the following portable modules were procured: 16 76-mm guns, 16 cranes, 16 minelaying sets, 16 air-defense sets, 12 antiship missile and fire-control sets, 12 torpedo tube sets, 5 mine clearance sets, and 16 electronic warfare sets; later it is hoped to add 6 ASW modules. Seven sonar sets and three towed linear hydrophone arrays were ordered for use on the ships. In mid-1992 the Bofors Underwater Systems Double Eagle remotely operated vehicle was selected as the minehunting disposal vehicle for the class, and six ship-sets were acquired (12 ROVs).

The modular mine-countermeasures sets each consist of two Danyard-built, remote-controlled minehunting drones (each towing a Thales TSM 2054 side-scan sonar), with the IBIS 43 minehunting system and Thales 2061 tactical mine-countermeasures data system. The second minehunting set was delivered 12-91, six more were delivered 1994–95, and approval for three more was given on 29-5-96. The first drone, MRF 1, was completed 3-91. MRF 1 and MRF 2 operate with P 552. See the Mine Warfare Ships section for description. P 562 and P 563 are more or less permanently outfitted for mine-countermeasures duties.

Four modular Sea Sparrow SAM systems were ordered from Raytheon in 11-93 for installation in these boats, with an option for ten more sets. There are three Mk 48 Mod. 3 launchers per module, and each ship-set includes an autonomous fire-control radar system. Eurotorp MU-90 ASW acoustic homing torpedoes were ordered 1-99 for use on this class. When wire-guided torpedoes are carried, a section of the bulwark on the fantail is removed to permit the single tubes to train out for launching.

Disposal note: All *Willemoes*-class missile/torpedo boats in service were retired by 2002. This includes *Rodsteen* (P 546), *Sehested* (P 547), *Bille* (P 540), *Bredal* (P 541), *Hammer* (P 542), *Huitfeldt* (P 543), *Krieger* (P 544), *Suenson* (P 548), and *Willemoes* (P 549). P 548, P 544, and P 542 were scrapped at Grenaa in 2002.

PATROL CRAFT [PC]

Note: The following units are used on fisheries protection duties and carry pennant numbers in the service craft series. The craft would be used in midshipman training and hydrographic survey duties in peacetime in addition to their fisheries protection duties; in wartime, combat system modules would be added.

♦ 3 (+ 7) 125-ton Minor Standard Craft Mk 1 class
Bldr: Danish Yacht A/S, Skagen, Denmark (In serv. 2006–8)

	L	In serv.		L	In serv.
A 541 . . .	10-12-05	27-1-06	A 544 . . .		
A 542 . . .		3-06	A 545 . . .		
A 543 . . .			A 546 . . .		

D: 98 tons (fl) **S:** 12 kts **Dim:** 28.90 × 6.40 × 1.80
A: none
Electronics: Radar: 1 Terma 20T48 nav.; 1 Skanter Mil 009 nav.; 1 Furuno FR-1505 DA surf. search
M: 2 Scania type DC 16 diesels; 1,000 bhp—bow-thruster
Range: 600/10 **Crew:** 3 + 10 passengers

Remarks: Design based on that of the four MRD-STOR-class drone minesweepers. Contract awarded for the class on 8-9-04 with an option for six more to be based at Korsoer, Seeland Island. A 541 and A 543 will operate as survey ships, while A 542 and A 544 will be used to train cadets. A 545 and A 546 will be used for mine countermeasures.
Hull systems: Will have space for one Standard Flex container.

♦ 0 (+ 6) 175-ton Minor Standard Craft Mk 2 class
Bldr: Faaborg Vaeft A/S, Denmark

	Laid down	L	Completed	In serv.
Y . . .	27-10-05	27-3-06	31-1-07	4-07
Y. . .	21-10-05	29-8-06	6-6-07	9-07
Y . . .	15-6-06	29-11-06	28-9-07	12-07
Y . . .	7-9-06	27-3-07	18-1-08	4-08
Y . . .	6-12-06	30-7-07	30-4-08	7-08
Y . . .	9-3-07	19-10-07	30-4-08	7-08

D: Approx. 180 tons (fl) **S:** 18 kts **Dim:** 43.0 × 8.2 × 2.0
A: 2 12.7-mm machineguns
Electronics: Radar: 1 Furuno type nav.
M: 2 MTU type 16V396 TB 94 diesels; 2,816 bhp; one waterjet
Crew: 9 crew + 6 passengers

Remarks: Ordered 12-04. Glass-fiber reinforced plastic (GRP) construction. Built as replacements for the *Barso* class. Can be reconfigured within several hours for a number of different missions including fisheries protection, patrol, and search and rescue.

♦ 3 Agdlek class Bldr: Svendborg Værft, Svendborg

Y 386 Agdlek (In serv. 12-3-74) Y 388 Tulugaq (In serv. 26-6-79)
Y 387 Agpa (In serv. 14-5-74)

Agdlek (Y 386) Danish Navy, 1994

D: 330 tons (fl) **S:** 12 kts **Dim:** 31.2 (except Y-388: 31.6) × 7.7 × 3.3
A: 2 12.7-mm machineguns
Electronics: Radar: 1 Terma 20T48 nav.; 1 Skanter Mil 009 nav.; 1 Furuno FR-1505 DA surf. search
M: 1 Burmeister & Wain Alpha AO8-26 VO diesel; 800 bhp
Range: 3,525/10.9 **Crew:** 15 tot.

PATROL CRAFT [PC] *(continued)*

Remarks: Are assigned to Division 19, 1st Squadron, based at Frederikshavn for fisheries patrol service in Greenland waters. Can carry two survey launches. Y 388 has only one navigational radar (but is equipped with Inmarsat), is 0.3 m longer, displaces 330 tons (fl), and can make 14 kts. All have a Telegon HFD/F set. No longer carry 20-mm AA but probably have one or more 7.62-mm mg aboard.

♦ 9 Barsø class
Bldr: Svendborg Værft, Svendborg, Denmark

	In serv.		In serv.
Y 300 Barsø	20-5-69	Y 305 Vejrø	30-9-69
Y 301 Drejø	18-6-69	Y 306 Farø	6-2-73
Y 302 Romsø	4-7-69	Y 307 Læsø	28-3-73
Y 303 Samsø	31-7-69	Y 308 Romø	22-6-73
Y 304 Thurø	30-8-69		

Romsø (Y 302) Harmut Ehlers, 7-01

Læsø (Y 307)—converted as a diving tender Danish Navy, 1998

D: 155 tons (fl) (except Y 307: 223.2 tons) **S:** 11 kts **Dim:** 25.5 × 6.0 × 2.8
A: 1 12.7-mm mg (none in Y 307)
Electronics: Radar: 1 Furuno FR-1505 DA nav.
M: 1 Burmeister & Wain Alpha diesel; 1 prop; 385 bhp
Crew: 4 officers, 16 enlisted

Remarks: Y 307, with decompression chamber forward, is disarmed and is used as a diving tender; the forecastle extends directly aft to the bridge area, and there is a large constant-tension towed acoustic array–handling rig on the fantail. All have a Telegon HFD/F set.
Hull systems: Built with steel hull and aluminum superstructure. The last three units of the class, Y 306/308, are identical with the previous units except for having an extended closed bridge.
Combat systems: Original armament of two single 20-mm Oerlikon AA mounts on the bridge deck was been replaced by 12.7-mm machineguns in 2004.

PATROL BOATS [PB]

♦ 6 Swedish SRC 90E–class landing craft personnel
Bldr: Storebro Bruks AB, Storebro, Sweden

LCP 1 (In serv. 2003)	LCP 4 (In serv. 2004)
LCP 2 (In serv. 2003)	LCP 5 (In serv. 2005)
LCP 3 (In serv. 2004)	LCP 6 (In serv. 2005)

D: 6.5 tons (8.5 fl) **S:** 40 kts (37 loaded) **Dim:** 11.88 (10.80 wl) × 2.90 × 0.79
A: 1 shoulder fired Stinger SAM missile launcher; 1 12.7-mm machine gun
M: 1 Saab Scania DSI-14 diesel; 1 KaMeWa 410 waterjet; 625 bhp
Range: 200/ . . . **Fuel:** 600 liters **Crew:** 3 max. tot.

Remarks: Ordered 2003, for use aboard the *Absalon* (L 16)-class *SF 3000* Flexible Support Ships. Used for transportation of personnel and cargo, survey of harbor entrance routes and harbors, rescue missions, military surveillance tasks, insertion of soldiers and transportation of wounded personnel. Load capacity in excess of 2,000 kg, can carry up to 10 seated passengers or 4 stretchers. Equipped with a front ramp for embarkation/debarkation of troops and/or cargo.

LCP 1 Martin Mokrus, 4-05

♦ 2 VTS 2–class guardships
Bldr: Mulder & Rijke, the Netherlands (In serv. 1997–98)

VTS 3 VTS 4

D: 34 tons (fl) **S:** 33 kts **Dim:** 17.0 × 4.9 × . . .
A: 1 7.62-mm mg
Electronics: Radar: 1 Furuno M-1831 nav.; 1 Furuno FR-1505 Mk 2 nav./surf. search
M: 2 MWM TBD 616 V12 diesels; 2 waterjets; 979 bhp
Range: 300/30 **Crew:** 3 tot.

Remarks: Used as patrol and chase boats in the Danish Belt and Straits areas. Are typical Dutch police boats, equipped with reinforced hull sides to permit coming alongside. Also equipped for rescue duties.

♦ 1 patrol boat, converted trawler
Bldr: Nipper, Skagen, Denmark (In serv. 1941)

Lunden (ex-*Sofus Nipper*)

D: 42 tons (fl) **S:** 8 kts **Dim:** 18.0 × 5.2 × 2.3
A: 1 7.62-mm machinegun
Electronics: Radar: 1 NWS-3 nav.
M: 1 Hundested Marine Engine diesel; 170 bhp
Range: 300/30 **Crew:** 4 tot.

Remarks: Incorrectly reported as retired in previous editions, but seen active during 4-05. Used as a patrol and chase boat in the Danish Belt and Straits areas. Named *Lunden* in 1974. Previously carried pennant numbers P 13 and Y 343. Wooden hull construction.

Note: The Home Guard (*Marine Hjemmeværnets*) is responsible for coastal waters surveillance, harbor traffic control, naval installations guard duties, and search-and-rescue operations. The paramilitary organization has about 4,400 personnel and operates the following craft in the MHV series:

♦ 6 Eno (MHV 900) class
Bldr. Søby Motorfabrik & Staalskibsværft, Æro

	In serv.		In serv.
MHV 901 Eno	18-10-04	MHV 904 Lyo	30-9-05
MHV 902 Mano	8-5-04	MHV 905 . . .	2006
MHV 903 Hjorto	29-1-05	MHV 906 . . .	2006

D: 87 tons **S:** 13 kts **Dim:** 27.2 × 5.6 × 2.5
A: 2 7.62-mm machineguns
Electronics: Radar: 1 Furuno FR-1505 DA nav.
M: 2 Scania diesel; 1 prop; 500 bhp
Range: 1,800/11 **Crew:** 12 tot.

Remarks: This class is an improved version of the *Aldebaran* (MHV 800) class. It is approx. 3.5 meters longer and 10 tons heavier. The ships are intended for patrol, search-and-rescue, and environmental protection duties.

♦ 18 Aldebaran (MHV 800) class
Bldr: Søby Motorfabrik & Staalskibsværft, Æro

	In serv.		In serv.
MHV 801 Aldebaran	5-92	MHV 810 Luna	30-5-96
MHV 802 Carina	9-92	MHV 811 Apollo	30-11-96
MHV 803 Aries	30-3-93	MHV 812 Hercules	30-5-97
MHV 804 Andromeda	28-2-94	MHV 813 Baunen	17-12-97
MHV 805 Gemini	6-94	MHV 814 Budstikken	9-98
MHV 806 Dubhe	30-11-94	MHV 815 Kureren	30-5-99
MHV 807 Jupiter	30-11-94	MHV 816 Patrioten	25-2-00
MHV 808 Lyra	30-5-95	MHV 817 Partisan	11-00
MHV 809 Antares	30-11-95	MHV 818 Sabotøren	10-01

D: 80 tons (83 fl) **S:** 12 kts **Dim:** 23.70 (20.26 pp) × 5.60 × 2.20
A: 2 single 7.62-mm machine guns
Electronics: Radar: 1 Furuno FR-1505 DA nav./surf. search
M: 2 Saab-Scania DSI-14 diesels; 2 props; 900 bhp
Range: 990/11 **Fuel:** 7,800 liters **Endurance:** 3 days
Crew: 12 total

Remarks: Intended as replacements for numerous Home Guard patrol craft. First three were ordered 5-91, second increment in 7-92, and third in 9-93. The last six were contracted for in 2-97. Under the 1993–94 budget, only an additional four were funded, and the program progressed at a slower pace than first envisioned. A total of 25 units were originally planned. Built using steel construction, the ships are intended for patrol, search-and-rescue, and environmental protection duties
Combat systems: Provisions for carrying 1 20-mm 70-cal. Oerlikon AA gun.

Disposal note: Of the six units of the MHV 20 class, *Budstikken* (MHV 21) was retired during 1999, *Kureren* (MHV 22) and *Patrioten* (MHV 24) in 2000, and *Partisan* (MHV 23) and *Sabatøren* (MHV 25) in 2001, with *Baunen* (MHV 20), the last unit in the class, stricken by 2003.

PATROL BOATS [PB] *(continued)*

Gemini (MHV 805) Michael Nitz, 5-05

Sabotøren (MHV 818) Michael Nitz, 5-05

♦ 6 MHV 90–class patrol boats

Bldr: Sakskobing Maskinfabrik og Skibsvaerft, Denmark (MHV 94–95: Svendborg Skibsværft, Svendborg, Denmark)

	In serv.		In serv.
MHV 90 BOPA	1973	MHV 93 HVIDSTEN	6-75
MHV 91 BRIGADEN	3-74	MHV 94 RINGEN	20-12-74
MHV 92 HOLGER DANSKE	3-75	MHV 95 SPEDITØREN	20-12-74

Holger Danske (MHV 92) Frank Findler, 7-04

D: 85 tons (130 fl) **S:** 10.5 kts **Dim:** 19.75 × 5.70 × 2.50
A: 2 single 7.62-mm machineguns
Electronics: Radar: 1 Furuno FR-1505 DA nav.
M: 1 Burmeister & Wain Alpha type VO diesel; 1 shaft; 400 bhp
Crew: 12 total

Remarks: First Danish Home Guard cutters to be built of steel. Initially commissioned only with pennant numbers. Names assigned in 1988. The ships are intended for patrolling at sea, search and rescue, and environmental protection. The original 20-mm mount has been removed.

Brigaden (MHV 91) Frank Findler, 6-05

♦ 3 MHV 70–class patrol boat

Bldr: Royal Dockyard, Copenhagen (In serv. 1958)

MHV 70 SATURN MHV 71 SCORPIUS MHV 72 SIRIUS

Scorpius (MHV 71) Ralph Edwards, 9-98

D: 78 tons (130 fl) **S:** 10 kts **Dim:** 20.1 × 5.1 × 2.5
A: 2 single 7.62-mm mg **Electronics:** Radar: 1 Raytheon 1290S nav.
M: 1 diesel; 200 bhp **Crew:** 6 tot.

Remarks: Wooden hull construction. Assigned to the Danish Home Guard.

♦ 4 MHV 80–class patrol boats

	Bldr.	In serv.
MHV 80 FÆNØ (ex-MHV 69, ex-MS 6)	Ejvinds	22-10-41
MHV 81 ASKØ (ex-Y 386, ex-M 560, ex-MS 2)	Holbæk	1-8-41
MHV 84 BAAGØ (ex-Y 387, ex-M 561, ex-MS 3)	Korsør	9-8-41
MHV 85 HJORTØ (ex-Y 389, ex-M 564, ex-MS 7)	Korsør	24-9-41

Baagø (MHV 84) Guy Schaeffer, via Paolo Marsan, 6-00

D: 74 tons (80 fl) **S:** 11 kts **Dim:** 24.38 × 4.56 × 1.5
A: 2 single 7.62-mm mg **Electronics:** Radar: 1 Raytheon RM 1290S nav.
M: 1 Burmeister & Wain Alpha type diesel; 1 prop; 250 bhp **Crew:** 11 tot.

Remarks: Have wooden hulls. Originally built as inshore minesweepers (MSI). *Fænø* was transferred to the Danish Home Guard service on 10-2-60 and converted to a patrol boat (all minesweeping gear removed).
Disposals: *Manø* (MHV 83) was retired in 1999 and *Enø* (MHV 82) and *Lyø* (MHV 86) in 2000.

Note: Two firefighting tugs were ordered in late 2001 for the Danish Coast Guard (*Sovaernet;* n.f.i.) from Hvide Sande Skibs-og. Baadebyggeri A/S. Delivered in 2002, they measure 16.00 meters long with a 6.5-m beam and are powered by a single 550 BHP MTU diesel.

MINE WARFARE SHIPS

Disposal note: By the end of 2004, the Danish navy had decommissioned all six dedicated minelayers. Of the four *Falster* class, *Falster* (N 80) and *Saelland* (N 83) were decommissioned on 1-1-00 and scrapped the following year. *Fyen* (N 81) was decommissioned 10-03, followed by *Moen* (N 82) on 22-10-04. Of the *Lindormen* class, *Lindormen* (N 43) and *Losser* (N 44) both decommissioned on 22-10-04 for disposal.

♦ 4 MRD-STOR-class drone minesweepers [MSD]

Bldr: Danyard, Ålborg (In serv. 1998–99)

	In serv.		In serv.
MSF 1	8-98	MSF 3	1-99
MSF 2	1998	MSF 4	1-99

MSF 3 Frank Findler, 6-05

MSF 3—note side-scan sonar "fish" beneath A-frame crane at stern
Leo Van Ginderen, 10-05

D: 102 tons (125 fl) **S:** 12 kts (11 sust.)
Dim: 26.50 (24.15 wl; 23.90 pp) × 7.00 × 2.20
Electronics: Radar: 1 Raytheon 40 nav.—Sonar: Thales STS 2054 towed side-scan HF
M: 2 Saab Scania DSI 14.74.M diesels; 2 Schottel SPJ.82T azimuthal waterjets; 960 bhp—bow-thruster
Range: 420/10 **Crew:** 3 tot. (for transits; accomm. for 11 tot.)

Remarks: The prototype Surface Auxiliary Vessel (SAV), SF 100, was delivered in 1-96 to a somewhat smaller design, and the four production versions were ordered during 1-97. GRP construction. Can be operated by crews as inshore minehunter/ minesweepers or by remote control in pairs by *Flyvefisken*-class multipurpose craft.
Combat systems: Employ the IN-SNEC sonar and television datalink and INFOCOM low-rate craft command datalink. Use containerized mine countermeasures equipment. Can be used to deploy Sutec Double Eagle mine location and disposal ROVs or to stream sweep gear, including the Australian Dyad magnetic sweep. Have a 7-kN bollard pull at 8.5 kts. U.S. Anteon A/N37U-1 deep mechanical sweep arrays were ordered for these craft on 29-4-02.

♦ 6 MRF 1-class drone minesweepers [MSD]

Bldr: Danyard, Ålborg (In serv. 1991–96)

MRD 1 (In serv. 3-91)	MRD 3 (In serv. 10-95)	MRD 5 (In serv. 10-96)
MRD 2 (In serv. 12-91)	MRD 4 (In serv. 11-95)	MRD 6 (In serv. 10-96)

D: 32 tons (38 fl) **S:** 12 kts **Dim:** 18.20 (16.90 wl) × 4.75 × 1.20
Electronics: Radar: 1 Furuno . . . nav.—Sonar: Thales TSM 2054 towed side-scan
M: 2 G.M. Detroit Diesel . . . diesels; 2 Schottel Type 80 pump jets; 350 bhp
Crew: 4 tot. (debarked during operations)

Remarks: Units 3 through 6 were ordered 7-94. Intended to operate two per each *Flyvefisken*-class multipurpose combatant.
Hull systems: Glass-reinforced foam-core plastic hull construction. MRD 2 and later have smaller stacks.

MRD 2 A. A. de Kruijf, 8-99

Combat systems: Australian ADI Mini-Dyad reconfigurable permanent magnet influence sweep arrays were ordered in 1996 for use with these craft; they employ a 6.4 × 0.53-m, hollow, two-section mild steel pipe with two reconfigurable strontium-ferrite inserts. U.S. Anteon A/N37U-1 deep mechanical sweep arrays were ordered for these craft on 29-4-02.

AUXILIARIES

♦ 2 SF 3000 flexible support ships [AG]

Bldr: Odense Staalskibsvaerft A/S, Odense

	Laid down	L	In serv.
L 16 Absalon	28-11-03	25-2-04	19-10-04
L 17 Esbern Snare	2004	21-6-04	18-4-05

Esbern Snare (L 17) Leo Van Ginderen, 6-05

Esbern Snare (L 17)—with Lynx helicopter on the flight deck
Chris Sattler, 7-05

Absalon (L 16) Ralph Edwards, 2-05

D: 4,500 tons light (6,300 fl) **S:** 23 kts **Dim:** 137.6 × 19.5 × 6.3
A: 16 RGM-84C Block II Harpoon SSM; 1 Mk 48 Mod. 3 VLS cells (. . . Sea Sparrow ESSM SAM); 1 127-mm/62 cal. United Defense Mk 45 Mod. 4 DP; 2 12.7-mm machineguns; 2 35-mm Millennium CIWS; two triple MTU-90 ASW torpedoes; 1 or 2 EH-101-sized helicopters
Electronics:
Radar: 1 Thales SMART-S 3-D Air Search; 1 Celsius Tech Ceros 200 F.C.; 1 Therma Scanter Nav.
Sonar: . . .
EW: . . . intercept; 2 Terma DLS Mk II DL-12T 12-round decoy RL

AUXILIARIES *(continued)*

M: 2 MTU 20V800 M70 diesels; 2 CP props; 21,993 bhp—one bow thruster
Range: 9,000/15 **Endurance:** 28 days
Crew: 100 tot. + 75 command staff + 25 aviation crew

Remarks: Approved 6-99 for ordering under the 2000–2003 Procurement Plan. The contract was awarded to Maersk's Odense Staalskibsværft during 10-01. Intended as multipurpose units for peacetime expeditionary support operations, using six to eight portable functional modules installed amidships to carry either a 20-strong task group commander and staff, a 50-strong maritime component commander and staff, or a 70-strong combined joint task force commander and staff. A 22 ISO-standard module hospital facility can also be fitted. Missions foreseen include ASW (with VDS module and torpedo tubes), mine countermeasures, and humanitarian aid. Though intended primarily for support duties, they are sometimes referred to as frigates due to their heavy armament. Both are based at Frederikshavn.
Hull systems: Have side and stern ramps to handle up to 46 vehicles and 250 lane-meters of parking. To carry one 10- to 12-ton or two 5-ton helicopters and two SRC-90E assault landing craft. An 84-m-long by 10.5-m-wide by 4.5-m-high section aft is equipped to take various operational modules and/or vehicles up to tank weight; there will be a stern vehicle ramp. A total of 1,700 tons of cargo can be carried.
Combat systems: The Terma C-Flex combat system will be incorporated and will be able to employ Links 11, 16, and (when available) 22. The ships will employ the ES 3701 Tactical Radar Electronic Support Measures (ESM) and Surveillance System and the Infocom ICS 2000 communications system, including SATCOM, HF, UHF, and VHF radio. Will carry antitorpedo and antimissile decoys. The 127-mm guns for the first two ships were ordered on 22-10-02, and the U.S. EX-171 Extended-Range Guided Munition is to be procured later for the guns.

♦ 2 Gunnar Thorson–class pollution control ships [AG]
Bldr: Ørskov Staalskibværft, Frederikshavn

A 560 Gunnar Thorson (Del. 8-5-81)
A 561 Gunnar Seidenfaden (Del. 2-7-81)

Gunnar Thorson (A 560) — Martin Mokrus, 4-05

D: 672 tons (750 fl) **S:** 14.5 kts **Dim:** 55.61 (49.10 pp) × 12.40 × 3.87
M: 2 Burmeister & Wain Alpha 8V23L-VO diesels; 2 CP props; 2,320 bhp—bow-thruster
Electric: 564 kw tot. (2 × 208 kw, 1 × 148 kw diesel sets)

Remarks: Pennant numbers not normally worn. 869 grt/684 dwt. Transferred from the Ministry of the Environment in early 1996. Modified anchor-handling offshore supply tug design. Have firefighting equipment. One 7-ton crane was added in 1988 to allow them to act as navigational buoy tenders. *Thorson,* based at Copenhagen, is also equipped to act as a salvage vessel. *Seidenfaden* is based at Korsør. Both have civilian crews. Have orange-painted hulls, cream superstructure with broad and narrow red-orange diagonal stripe on sides.

♦ 1 royal yacht [AG]
Bldr: Royal Dockyard, Copenhagen

	Laid down	L	In serv.
A 540 Dannebrog	2-1-31	10-10-31	20-5-32

D: 1,130 tons (fl) **S:** 14 kts **Dim:** 74.9 × 10.4 × 3.7
A: Removed
Electronics: Radar: 1 Skanter Mil 009 nav.
M: 2 Burmeister & Wain Alpha 6 T23L-KVO diesels; 2 CP props; 1,600 bhp; Bowthruster
Electric: 676 kw tot.
Crew: 58 total plus 27 from the royal household and 14 passengers

Remarks: Re-engined, new electrical generating plant installed, winter 1980–81; bow-thruster fitted during 1988–89 overhaul. Does not wear pennant number. Equipped with SATCOM transceiver in 1992.

Note: Danish icebreakers were transferred to the Ministry of Defense in early 1996 from the Ministry of Industry. During summer months, the Danish Navy at Frederikshavn maintains them. All remain civilian manned. They have black-painted hulls, cream superstructures.

Dannebrog (A 540) — Anthony Vella, 8-04

♦ 1 Thorbjørn-class icebreaker [AGB]
Bldr: Svendborg Skibsværft, Svendborg (L: 6-80)

A 553 Thorbjørn

Thorbjørn (A 553) — A. A. de Kruijf 10-02

D: 2,250 tons (fl) **S:** 16.5 kts **Dim:** 65.11 (57.92 pp) × 15.35 × 4.92
M: 4 Burmeister & Wain Alpha 16U28L-VO diesels; 2 props; 6,360 bhp
Electric: 840 kw tot. (3 × 280-kw diesel sets)
Range: 21,800/16 **Fuel:** 855 tons **Crew:** 22 tot.

Remarks: 1,547 grt/2,345 dwt. Used for hydrographic surveys when not needed for icebreaking, and can also act as a tug. Geared drive vice electric. Assigned to Division 15, 1st Naval Squadron, and based at Frederikshavn. Can carry six small survey launches on the aft deck.

♦ 2 Danbjørn-class icebreakers [AGB]
Bldr: Lindø Værft, Odense

A 551 Danbjørn (In serv. 1965) A 552 Isbjørn (In serv. 1966)

Isbjørn (A 552) — Ralph Edwards, 9-98

D: 3,685 tons (fl) **S:** 14 kts **Dim:** 77.15 (67.98 pp) × 17.33 × 6.50
M: 6 Holeby-Burmeister & Wain 12-26MTBH-40V diesels (1,750 bhp each), 6 1,370-kw generators, 8 electric motors (870 shp each forward), 1,750 shp each aft); 4 props (2 forward); 5,240 shp
Electric: 1,312 kw tot (4 × 328 kw) **Range:** 11,480/16.5
Fuel: 580 tons **Crew:** 34 tot.

Remarks: 3,023 grt. Assigned to Division 15, 1st Naval Squadron, and based at Frederikshavn. Transferred from the Ministry of Environment in 1996.

Disposal note: The icebreaker *Elbjørn* (A 550) was stricken in 2003.

♦ 2 Tor Anglia–class vehicle cargo ships [AKR]
Bldr: Tor Anglia: Lindenau, Keil; Tor Futura: Visentini, Donada

Tor Anglia (Completed 1989) Tor Futura (Completed 1996)

AUXILIARIES *(continued)*

D: 17,492 grt (*Tor Futura:* 18,469 grt) **S:** 15 kts
Dim: 171.94 (*Tor Futura:* 183.1) × 21.7 × 6.9
M: 2 sets Krupp-MAK type 9M551AK diesels; 4 KaMeWa controllable pitch propellers
Range: . . . / . . . **Crew:** 12 tot.

Remarks: *Tor Anglia* was chartered 5-03 and *Tor Futura* 9-04 for use as part of Denmark's contribution to the NATO Response Force need for maritime heavy lift capacity. No pennant number is assigned and they retain their commercial names and paint scheme.

SERVICE CRAFT

♦ 2 Sea Truck–design pollution control craft [YAG]

	Bldr	In serv.
A 562 Mette Miljø	Nykobing Mors Vaerft A/S, Denmark	22-2-80
A 563 Marie Miljø	Nykobing Mors Vaerft A/S, Denmark	22-2-80

Mette Miljø (A 562) Guy Schaeffer, via Paolo Marsan, 6-00

D: 157 tons **S:** 10 kts **Dim:** 29.8 × 8.0 × 1.6
M: 2 Grena GF 24 diesels; 2 props; 660 bhp **Crew:** 8 tot. (civilian)

Remarks: Transferred from the Ministry of the Environment early in 1996. Have orange hulls, cream superstructures.

♦ 2 Miljø 101–class pollution control boats [YAG]
Bldr: Eljvinds, Svendborg

Y 340 Miljø 101 (In serv. 1-11-77) Y 341 Miljø 102 (In serv. 1-12-77)

Miljø 102 (Y 341) Ralph Edwards, 9-98

D: 16 tons **S:** 15 kts **Dim:** 16.2 × 4.2 × 2.2
M: 1 MWM TBD232 V12 diesel; 1 prop; 454 bhp
Range: 350/8 **Crew:** 3 tot. (naval crew)

Remarks: Transferred from the Ministry of the Environment early in 1996. Glass-reinforced plastic construction. Carry spill containment gear.

♦ 1 Kugsag-class support craft [YAG]
Bldr: Selfa Bat Trondheim A/S Norway

Y 309 Kugsag (In serv. 28-5-03)

D: . . . tons **S:** Approx. 25 kts. **Dim:** 10.66 × 3.64 × . . .
M: 1 Volvo-Penta . . . diesel engine; 1 prop; 310 bhp—1 bow-thruster
Range: . . . **Crew:** 3 tot.

Disposal note: The mine transport MSA 4 was stricken in 2003.

♦ 1 Y 378–class fast launch [YFL]

Y 379

Remarks: Small, GRP-hulled cabin cruisers, based at Korsør. No data available. Sister Y 378 was stricken in 2004.

Y 379 Ralph Edwards, 9-98

♦ 6 921-class harbor personnel launches [YFL]

921 through 926

921-class launch 925 Guy Schaeffer, via Paolo Marsan, 6-00

Remarks: GRP personnel launches employed for local transportation at Danish naval bases; no data available.

♦ 6 SKA 11–class inshore survey launches [YGS]
Bldr: Jeros Marine A/S, Rantsausminde

	In serv.		In serv.		In serv.
SKA 11	15-4-81	SKA 13	26-6-82	SKA 15	1984
SKA 12	5-5-81	SKA 14	25-3-82	SKA 16	12-14-85

SKA 16 Dieter Wolf, 6-04

D: 52 tons (fl) **S:** 13 kts **Dim:** 19.96 (19.20 pp) × 5.20 × 2.10
Electronics: Radar: 1 Skanter Mil 009 nav.
M: 1 G.M. 16V-71N diesel; 1 prop; 540 bhp **Electric:** 15 kw tot.
Fuel: 10,000 liters **Crew:** 1 officer, 5 enlisted

Remarks: GRP construction. Have an EMRI ACU autopilot and a Navitronic Seadig 201 survey system with HDH-1 data-handler and a Hewlett-Packard 9825 computer. Designed to operate in Greenland waters.

Disposal note: U.S. YO 65–class fuel lighters *Rimfaxe* (A 568, ex-YO 226) and *Skinfaxe* (A 569, ex-YO 229) were sold on 31-1-01 to a Nigerian operator who has renamed them the *Chinky Star* and *Betty Nelo,* respectively.

♦ 1 torpedo transport/retriever [YPT]
Bldr: Åbenrå Skibsværft, Åbenrå (In serv. 18-7-86)

A 559 Sleipner

D: 450 tons (fl) **S:** 11 kts **Dim:** 36.50 (34.00 pp) × 7.60 × 2.70
Electronics: Radar: 1 Terma Skanter Mil 009 nav.
M: 1 Callesen 427 EOT diesel; 1 prop; 575 bhp **Crew:** 6 tot.

Remarks: Replaced earlier former coastal freighter of the same name. Cargo capacity: 150 tons. Black hull, yellow superstructure.

SERVICE CRAFT *(continued)*

Sleipner (A 559)—with LCP 4 in background Martin Mokrus, 4-05

♦ 3 small torpedo retrievers [YPT]
Bldr: Eivinds Plasticjolle & Bødeverft, Svendborg

TO 8 Hugin (In serv. 7-4-96) TO 9 Munin (In serv. 4-5-76)
TO 10 Mimer (In serv. 1978)

D: 23 tons (fl) **S:** 15 kts **Dim:** 16.15 × 4.15 × 1.25
Electronics: Radar: 1 Terma Scanter Mil 009 nav.
M: 1 MWM diesel; 1 prop; 450 bhp **Crew:** 4 tot.

Remarks: Are similar in appearance to pollution control craft *Miljø 101* and *Miljø 102* and employ the same GRP-construction hull.

♦ 2 medium harbor tugs [YTM]
Bldr: Hvide Sande Skibsvaerft & Baadebyggeri, Denmark

Y 344 Arvak (In serv. 18-11-02) Y 345 Alsin (In serv. 18-11-02)

Arvak (Y 344) Martin Mokrus, 4-05

D: 79 tons (fl) **S:** . . . kts **Dim:** 16.00 × 6.56 × 2.80
Electronics: Radar: 1 . . . nav.
M: 1 MTU . . . diesel; 1 prop; 737 bhp—1 Hundested 103 bhp bow-thruster
Range: Approx. 1,000/10 **Crew:** 3 + 12 passengers

Remarks: Ordered 3-02 for $2.4 million for use at Frederikshaven Naval Base as tugs, personnel launches, and stores carriers. Equipped with a crane capable of handling any one of the Standard Flex container configurations.

♦ 2 20-grt dockyard tugs [YTL]
Bldr: Assens Skibsværft (In serv. 1983)

Balder (In serv. 15-9-83) Hermod (In serv. 15-11-83)

D: 319 tons **S:** 8.7 kts **Dim:** 11.85 × 4.00 × 1.65
M: 1 G.M. 6-71 series diesel; 1 prop; 300 bhp **Crew:** 3 total

Remarks: Assigned to the Naval Base at Kørsør.

♦ 2 small sail-training yawls [YTS]
Bldr: Molich, Hundested (In serv. 1960–61)

Y 101 Svanen Y 102 Thyra

D: 32 tons (fl) **S:** 7.5 kts (power) **Dim:** 19.2 × 4.8 × 2.4
M: 1 Volvo Penta diesel; 1 prop; 72 bhp **Sail area:** 500 m^2 max.

Remarks: Assigned to the Naval Academy as training platforms.

Thyra (Y 102)—at left, with Svanen (Y 101) alongslide Michael Nitz, 8-05

♦ 1 Y 375–class training boat [YXT]
Bldr: Botved (In serv. 1974)

Y 376

Y 376 A. A. de Kruijf, 8-99

D: 12 tons (fl) **S:** 26 kts **Dim:** 13.3 × 4.5 × 1.1
A: 1 7.62-mm mg **Electronics:** Radar: 1 NWS-3 nav.
M: 2 diesels; 2 props; 680 hp

Remarks: Officially typed as a "*Bevogtningsbåd.*" Has facilities for combat swimmers. Near-sister Y 375 burned and sank 27-5-95 off the island of Læsø.

Note: The ships and craft of the Ministry of Fisheries (*Den Danske Stat-Fiskerministeriet*) are described and illustrated in the 1998–99 and earlier editions. Among those vessels in service are fisheries patrol craft *Havørnen;* fisheries research ship *Dana;* fisheries research craft *Jens Væver* and *Leda;* salvage, rescue, and firefighting tug *Veskysten; Nordjylland*-class search-and-rescue ships *Nordjylland* and *Nordsøen;* and inspection launch *Viben* (a former Swedish Coast Guard Kbv 236–class launch).

Two firefighting tugs were ordered in late 2001 for the Danish Coast Guard (*Sovaernet;* n.f.i.) from Hvide Sande Skibs-og. Baadebyggeri A/S. Delivered in 2002, they are 16-m o.a. by 6.5-m beam and are powered by a single 550-bhp MTU diesel.

DJIBOUTI

Republic of Djibouti

Personnel: 200 total

Base: Djibouti (also used as a base by the French Navy's Indian Ocean Squadron)

PATROL BOATS [PB]

Note: Patrol boats worth $2 million total were to be provided by the U.S. during 2003.

♦ 2 HPSB class
Bldr: Assab, Eritrea (In service 11-01)

P 16 Hassan Gouled Aptidon P 17 . . .

PATROL BOATS [PB] *(continued)*

Hassan Gouled Aptidon (P 16) Bernard Prézelin Collection, 2002

D: 26 tons (36 fl) **S:** 35 kts **Dim:** 17.05 × 5.20 × 1.60
A: 1 twin 14.5-mm 93-cal. mg
Electronics: Radar: 1 . . . nav.
M: 2 MTU 12V183 TE92 diesels; 2 props; 1,000 bhp
Range: 630/30 **Crew:** 8 tot.

Remarks: HSPB = High-Speed Patrol Boat. The design is of Australian origin.

♦ **7 9-meter launches**
Bldr: Gulf Craft, Dubai (In serv. 1989–90)

Remarks: Transferred from Iraq. Carry one machinegun and are powered by two 150-bhp diesels. GRP construction. No other data available.

♦ **1 Moussa Ali class**
Bldr: Plascoa, Cannes, France (In serv. 16-2-86)

P 11 Mont Arreh

D: 30 tons (35 fl) **S:** 24.5 kts **Dim:** 23.30 × 5.50 × 1.50
A: 1 20-mm 90-cal. GIAT AA; 1 12.7-mm Browning mg
Electronics: Radar: 1 Decca 36 MN nav.
M: 2 SACM-Wärtsilä V12-520 M25 diesels; 2 props; 1,700 bhp
Range: 750/12; 460/15 **Crew:** 15 tot.

Remarks: GRP construction. Ordered 10-84 as a gift from France, where the craft was last refitted in 1988. Sister *Moussa Ali* (P 10) was stricken during 2001.

♦ **1 Iraqi Sawari-21 class**

P 13

P 13 French Navy, 11-95

D: Approx. 20 tons (fl) **S:** 27 kts **Dim:** 21.0 × . . . × . . .
A: 1 triple 14.5-mm 93-cal. mg
M: 2 diesels; 2 props; . . . bhp

Remarks: Transferred 1989–90. No other data available.

Disposal note: Sister P 12 was stricken during 2002. P 15, the Boghammar hydroplane launch acquired in 1996 from Ethiopia, was stricken during 2002, along with Iraqi-built *Sawari*-series launches P 05, P 06, and P 07.

AMPHIBIOUS WARFARE CRAFT

♦ **1 ex-French LCM(8)-class landing craft [LCM]**
Bldr: CMN, Cherbourg, France

. . . (ex-CTM 14)

Ex-CTM 14 Dieter Wolf, 5-02

D: 56 tons light (150 fl) **S:** 9.5 kts **Dim:** 23.80 × 6.35 × 1.25
A: 2 single 12.7-mm mg **Electronics:** Radar: 1 . . . nav.
M: 2 Poyaud-Wärtsilä UD18 V8M1 diesels; 2 props; 450 bhp
Range: 380/8 **Fuel:** 3.4 tons **Crew:** 6 tot.

Remarks: CTM-14 transferred in 1999 from the French Navy. Cargo capacity: 90 tons. The machineguns are usually not mounted.

DOMINICA

COAST GUARD

Personnel: About 30 total

Base: Roseau

PATROL BOATS [WPB]

♦ **1 U.S. 40-foot Dauntless class**
Bldr: SeaArk, Monticello, Ark. (In serv. 1995)

D 05 Ukale

Ukale (D 05) SeaArk, 11-95

D: 11 tons (15 fl) **S:** 28 kts **Dim:** 12.19 (11.13 wl) × 3.86 × 0.69 (hull)
A: 1 7.62-mm mg **Electronics:** Radar: 1 Raytheon R40X nav.
M: 2 Caterpillar 3208TA diesels; 2 props; 850 bhp (720 sust.)
Range: 200/30; 400/22 **Fuel:** 250 gallons **Crew:** 5 tot.

Remarks: Ordered 4-94. Aluminum construction. C. Raymond Hunt, "Deep-Vee" hull design.

♦ **1 U.S. 65-foot Commercial Cruiser class**
Bldr: Swiftships, Morgan City, La. (In serv. 2-5-84)

D-4 Melville

Melville (D-4) Maritime Photographic, 11-93

D: 34 tons (fl) **S:** 23 kts **Dim:** 19.96 × 5.58 × 1.52
A: Small arms **Electronics:** Radar: 1 Raytheon 1210 nav.
M: 2 G.M. 12V71 TI diesels; 2 props; 1,350 bhp
Electric: 20 kw **Range:** 500/18 **Crew:** 6 tot.

Remarks: One of three sisters presented to Caribbean island republics by the U.S. government, the others going to Antigua-Barbuda and St. Lucia. Aluminum construction. Blue hull, white upperworks.

SERVICE CRAFT

♦ 2 U.S. Boston Whaler utility launches [WYFL]
Bldr: Boston Whaler, Rockland, Mass. (In serv. 1988)

OBSERVER   VIGILANCE

Observer Maritime Photographic, 11-93

D: 2.4 tons (fl) **S:** 28 kts **Dim:** 8.2 × 2.6 × 0.3
M: 1 Evinrude V6 gasoline outboard; 225 bhp **Crew:** 3 tot.

Remarks: Glass-reinforced, foam-core construction. Employed for patrol and SAR duties and is capable of towing small craft.

Note: Also in use is the similar-sized, U.S.-supplied *Rescuer,* a RIB acquired in 1994 and powered by two Johnson gasoline outboards, crewed by two, and equipped with a Raytheon navigational radar.

DOMINICAN REPUBLIC

MARINA DE GUERRA

Personnel: Approx. 4,000 officers and enlisted (including marines)

Note: Bases are located at Santo Domingo (the headquarters, *27 de Febrero*), Las Calderas, Haina, and Puerto Plata. Many of the older ships and craft described below are in only marginal operating condition.

Maritime Aviation: The Dominican Republic Air Force operates four Cessna T-41D light training aircraft and two Aérospatiale AS.316B Alouette-III helicopters on coastal patrol and search-and-rescue duties.

PATROL SHIPS [PS]

♦ 2 ex-U.S. Cohoes-class former net tenders

	Bldr	L	In serv.
P 208 SEPARACIÓN (ex-*Passaconaway,* AN 86)	Marine Iron & Railway, Duluth, Minn.	30-6-44	27-4-45
P 209 CALDERAS (ex-*Passaic,* AN 87)	Leatham D. Smith, Sturgeon Bay, Wisc.	29-6-44	6-3-45

D: 650 tons (785 fl) **S:** 12.3 kts **Dim:** 51.36 (44.5 pp) × 10.31 × 3.3
A: P 208: 2 single 76.2-mm 50-cal. U.S. Mk 26 DP—both: 3 single 20-mm 70-cal. Mk 10 Oerlikon Mk 10 AA
Electronics: Radar: 1 Raytheon SPS-64(V)6 nav./surf. search
M: diesel-electric: 2 Busch-Sulzer BS-539 diesels, 1 motor; 1 prop; 1,200 shp
Electric: 120 kw tot. **Fuel:** 88 tons **Crew:** 5 officers, 59 enlisted

Remarks: Reactivated from the U.S. Maritime Commission's reserve fleet, where they had been laid up since 1963, and transferred 9-76. Despite low speed and general unsuitability, they are employed as patrol ships, tugs, general-support ships, navigational aids tenders, and hydrographic survey ships. P 208 had the net tender "horns" at the bow removed and a new, curved stem added; she also received a second 76.2-mm gun on the forecastle and new radars. P 209 is used primarily as a survey ship and has a deckhouse in place of the 76.2-mm gun. Sister *Cambiaso* (P 207; ex-*Etlah,* AN 79) had been hulked by 12-94.

Separación (P 208) Alexandre Sheldon-Duplaix, 9-99

♦ 1 ex-U.S. Admirable class
Bldr: Associated SB, Seattle, Wash.

	Laid down	L	In serv.
C 454 PRESTOL BOTELLO (ex-*Separación;* ex-*Skirmish,* MSF 303/AM 303)	8-4-43	16-8-43	30-6-44

D: 600 tons (903 fl) **S:** 15 kts **Dim:** 54.24 × 10.06 × 4.4
A: 1 76.2-mm Mk 26 DP; 2 single 40-mm 60-cal. Mk 3 Bofors AA; 4 single 20-mm 70-cal. Mk 10 Oerlikon AA
Electronics: Radar: 1 Raytheon SPS-64(V)9 nav.
M: 2 Cooper-Bessemer GSB-8 diesels; 2 props; 1,710 bhp
Electric: 240 kw **Range:** 5,600/9 **Fuel:** 260 tons
Crew: 8 officers, 82 enlisted

Remarks: Former minesweeper transferred 13-1-65. Renamed 1976 and pennant number changed from BM to C (*Cañonero*—gunboat) during 1995 refit. All weapons are locally controlled. Sister *Tortuguero* (C 455; ex-*Signet,* MSF 302/AM 302) was stricken and hulked in 1997.

♦ 2 ex-U.S. Coast Guard Balsam class
Bldr: Marine Iron & SB, Duluth, Minn.

	Laid down	L	In serv.
C 456 ALMIRANTE JUAN ALEJANDRO ACOSTA (ex-*Citrus,* WMEC 300, ex-WLB 300, ex-WAGL 300)	29-4-42	15-8-42	30-5-43
C 457 ALMIRANTE DIDIEZ BURGOS (ex-*Buttonwood,* WLB 306)	5-10-42	30-11-42	24-9-43

Almirante Didiez Burgos (C 457) Alexandre Sheldon-Duplaix, 8-02

D: C 456: 694 tons light; 935 tons std. (1,025 fl)—C 457: 697 tons light (1,038 fl)
S: 13 kts **Dim:** 54.86 (51.81 pp) × 11.28 × 4.24
A: C 456: 1 102-mm 45-cal. DP; 2 single 20-mm 70-cal. Oerlikon AA; 4 single 7.62-mm M60 mg—C 457: 2 single 20-mm 70-cal. Oerlikon Mk 10 AA

PATROL SHIPS [PS] *(continued)*

Electronics: Radar: 2 Raytheon SPS-64(V)1 nav.
M: C 456: 2 Cooper-Bessemer 8-cyl. diesel generator sets, 2 electric motors; 1 prop; 1,000 shp—C 457: 2 G.E. EMD 8-645E6A diesel generator sets, 2 electric motors; 1 prop; 1,200 bhp—bow-thruster
Electric: 400 kw tot. (C 457: 3 G.M. 6-71 and 1 8V71 diesels driving)
Range: C 456: 7,600/12.9—C 457: 5,500/10 **Crew:** 8 officers, 42 enlisted

Remarks: C 456 was transferred 29-9-95 from U.S. Coast Guard (from which she had been decommissioned on 1-9-94) as Grant-Aid. C 457 was transferred on 28-6-01 on retirement and had remained configured as a buoy tender; the ship had been given a major modernization and re-engined from 3-91 to 3-93. They were built as icebreaking navigational buoy tenders and have 20-mm waterline ice protection plating. During 1943, C 456 sank a German submarine off Miami, Fla. Carry a RIB inspection dinghy. C 456 was given a heavier armament during 2002, including an old British 102-mm mount on the forecastle.

PATROL CRAFT [PC]

♦ 1 ex-U.S. PGM 71 class
Bldr: Peterson SB, Sturgeon Bay, Wisc.

GC 102 Betelgeuse (ex-PGM 77)

Betelgeuse (GC 102)—alongside Enriquillo (RM 22) Alexandre Sheldon-Duplaix, 2000

D: 130 tons (145.5 fl) **S:** 16 kts **Dim:** 30.8 (30.2 pp) × 6.4 × 1.85
A: 1 20-mm 70-cal. Oerlikon AA; 2 single 12.7-mm mg
Electronics: Radar: 1 . . . nav.
M: 2 Caterpillar D-348TA diesels; 2 props; 1,450 bhp
Range: 1,000/12 **Crew:** 3 officers, 17 enlisted

Remarks: Transferred 14-1-66. One of many gunboats of this class transferred to smaller navies by the United States. Re-engined and armament reduced in 1980.

PATROL BOATS [PB]

♦ 3 110-foot Commercial Cruiser class
Bldr: Swiftships, Morgan City, La.

GC 107 Colón (ex-*Canopus*) (In serv. 6-84) GC 109 Orion (In serv. 8-84)
GC 112 Altair (In serv. 2003)

Colón (GC 107) Alexandre Sheldon-Duplaix, 9-99

D: 93.5 tons (fl) **S:** 23 kts (20 sust.) **Dim:** 33.53 × 7.32 × 1.83
A: 1 40-mm 60-cal. Bofors Mk 3 AA; 2 single 12.7-mm mg
Electronics: Radar: 1 . . . nav.
M: 3 G.M. 12V92 TI diesels; 3 props; 2,700 bhp
Range: 1,500/12 **Crew:** 3 officers, 16 enlisted

Remarks: Aluminum construction. The 40-mm gun is mounted aft. GC 107 was renamed in 1992. CG 112 may be of a different design and likely has a slightly modified armament fit.

♦ 3 ex-U.S. Coast Guard 82-foot Point class
Bldr: Coast Guard Yard, Curtis Bay, Md. (GC 103: J. Martinac SB, Tacoma, Wash.)

	In serv.
GC 101 Aries (ex-*Point Martin,* WPB 82379)	20-8-70
GC 105 Antares (ex-*Point Batan,* WPB 82340)	21-11-62
GC 110 Sirius (ex-*Point Spencer,* WPB 82349)	25-10-66

Aries (GC 101) Alexandre Sheldon-Duplaix, 9-99

D: 64 tons (66–69 fl) **S:** 23.7 kts (see Remarks) **Dim:** 25.3 × 5.23 × 1.95
A: 2 single 12.7-mm M2 mg
Electronics: Radar: 1 Raytheon SPS-64(V)1 nav.
M: 2 Caterpillar 3412 diesels; 2 props; 1,480 bhp
Range: 490/23.7; 1,500/8 **Fuel:** 5.7 tons **Crew:** 1 officer, 7 enlisted

Remarks: GC 101 was transferred on 22-9-99. Hull built of mild steel. High-speed diesels controlled from the bridge. Are well equipped for salvage and towing, but are considered to be heavy rollers.

♦ 4 U.S. 85-foot Commercial Cruiser class
Bldr: Sewart Seacraft, Berwick, La.

	In serv.
GC 103 Procion (ex-U.S. 85NS671)	1967
GC 104 Aldebarán (ex-U.S. 85NS721)	1972
GC 106 Bellatrix (ex-U.S. 85NS673)	1967
GC 108 Capella (ex-U.S. 85NS683)	1968

Capella (GC 108) Alexandre Sheldon-Duplaix, 8-02

D: 60 tons (fl) **S:** 21.7 kts **Dim:** 25.9 × 5.7 × 2.1
A: 3 single 12.7-mm mg **Electronics:** Radar: 1 . . . nav.
M: 2 G.M. 16V71N diesels; 2 props; 1,400 bhp **Range:** 800/20
Crew: 5 officers, 14 enlisted

Remarks: All but CG 108 were overhauled and "rebuilt" by Swiftships boatyard in Morgan City, La., during 2003.

♦ 2 miscellaneous small patrol launches

GC 110 Luperon (In serv. 1988) GC 111 Alto Velo

Remarks: No data available. GC 110 is reported to be a cabin cruiser about 18 m overall.

AUXILIARIES

♦ 1 U.S. Sotoyomo-class auxiliary ocean tug [ATA]

	Bldr	Laid down	L	In serv.
RM 22 Enriquillo (ex-*Stallion,* ATA 193)	Levingston SB, Orange, Tex.	26-10-44	24-11-44	1-2-45

D: 534 tons (860 fl) **S:** 13 kts **Dim:** 43.59 × 10.31 × 3.96
A: 1 76.2-mm 50-cal. U.S. Mk 26 DP; 2 single 20-mm 70-cal. Mk 10 Oerlikon AA
Electronics: Radar: 1 Raytheon 1500B nav.; 1 . . . nav.
M: 2 G.M. 12-278A diesels, electric drive; 1 prop; 1,500 shp
Electric: 120 kw **Range:** 8,000/8 **Fuel:** 160 tons **Crew:** 45 tot.

Remarks: Leased from the U.S. on 30-10-80 and donated outright on 10-6-97. Sister *Caonabo* (RM 18; ex-*Sagamore,* ATA 208), was returned to U.S. control in 1993 for scrapping.

AUXILIARIES *(continued)*

Enriquillo (RM 22) Alexandre Sheldon-Duplaix, 8-02

SERVICE CRAFT

♦ 1 ex-U.S. floating crane [YD]

GRUA FLOTANTE (ex-YD 86)

Grua Flotante Alexandre Sheldon-Duplaix, 1-94

D: 1,407 tons (1,560 fl) **Lift capacity:** 90 ton **Dim:** 42,67 × 21.3 × . . .

Remarks: Leased from the U.S. 1-71 and donated outright on 10-6-97. Has 90-ton lift capacity.

♦ 1 ex-U.S. Navy floating dry dock [YFDL]

Bldr: Chicago Bridge & Iron (In serv. 1943)

DF-1 (ex-*Endeavor,* AFDL 1)

Lift capacity: 1,000 tons **Dim:** 60.96 × 19.51 × 1.07 (light)

Remarks: Leased from U.S. on 8-3-86 and donated outright on 10-6-97. Length on blocks: 56.39 m; clear width: 13.75 m; draft over blocks: 4.42 m; max. draft: 8.23 m.

♦ 2 miscellaneous harbor launches [YFL]

BA 1 COJINOA BA 14 BEATA

Remarks: No data available.

♦ 2 ex-U.S. Coast Guard White-class (133-foot) navaids tenders [YGL]

Bldr: 1: Erie Concrete & Steel Supply, Erie, Pa.; 2: Niagara Shipbuilding, Buffalo, N.Y.

	Laid down	L	In serv.
BA-1 TORTUGUERO (ex-*White Pine,* WLM 547, ex-YC 548)	12-6-43	28-8-43	11-7-44
BA-2 CAPOTILLO (ex-*White Sumac,* WLM 540, ex-YF 416)	31-8-42	14-6-43	6-11-43

D: 435 tons (600 fl) **S:** 9.8 kts **Dim:** 40.49 × 9.14 × 2.67
A: None **Electronics:** Radar: 1 Raytheon SPS-64(V) nav.
M: 2 diesels; 2 props; 600 bhp **Electric:** 90 kw tot.
Range: 2,100/9.8; 4,500/5.1 **Fuel:** 40 tons **Crew:** 24 tot.

Tortuguero (BA-1) Alexandre Sheldon-Duplaix, 9-99

Remarks: BA-1 was donated on decommissioning from the U.S. Coast Guard on 29-6-99 and BA-2 on 2-8-02. Both had been transferred to the U.S. Coast Guard from the U.S. Navy on 3-8-48. Have one 10-ton buoy-handling derrick.

♦ 3 self-propelled dredges [YM]

Two Dominican Republic Navy dredges Alexandre Sheldon-Duplaix, 9-99

Remarks: Three self-propelled dredges are in service; name are *Pureto Plata, San Pedro Ia,* and *Quisqueya.* There may be a similar number of non-self-propelled dredges in service as well. No additional data available.

♦ 1 U.S. YO 153–class small oiler [YO]

Bldr: Ira S. Bushey, Brooklyn, N.Y.

	Laid down	L	In serv.
BT 5 CAPITÁN BEOTEGUI (ex-U.S. YO 215)	23-4-45	30-8-45	17-12-45

Capitán Beotegui (BT 5) Alexandre Sheldon-Duplaix, 6-97

D: 370 tons (1,076 fl) **S:** 8 kts **Dim:** 47.63 × 9.32 × 3.66
A: 2 single 20-mm 70-cal. Mk 10 Oerlikon AA **Electronics:** Radar: none
M: 1 Union diesel; 1 prop; 525 bhp **Electric:** 39 kw tot. **Crew:** 23 tot.

Remarks: Loaned by U.S. during 4-64 and donated outright on 10-6-97. Cargo: 6,071 barrels fuel (660 tons). Sister *Capitán W. Arvelo* (BT 4) sank at sea during 2-89.

Note: The fuel barge *Mencia* (BC 1) has also been reported in service. No data available.

♦ 2 Hercules-class harbor tugs [YTM]

Bldr: Ast. Navales Dominicanos (In serv. 1960)

RP 12 HERCULES RP 13 GUACANAGARIX

D: 200 tons (fl) **S:** . . . kts **Dim:** 21.4 × 4.8 × 2.7
M: 1 Caterpillar diesel; 1 prop; 500 bhp **Crew:** 8 tot.

SERVICE CRAFT *(continued)*

♦ **1 ex-U.S. Navy medium harbor tug [YTM]**
Bldr: . . . (In serv. 1944)

RM 17 Magua (ex- . . .)

Magua (RM 17) Alexandre Sheldon-Duplaix, 9-99

Remarks: Transferred during late 1990s. Rebuilt with new pilothouse above original structure and fitted with a broader stack.

♦ **1 harbor tug, former LCM(6)-class landing craft [YTM]**

RDM 303 Ocoa

D: 50 tons (fl) **S:** 9 kts **Dim:** 17.1 × 4.3 × 1.2
M: 2 G.M. Detroit Diesel 6-71 diesels; 2 props; 450 bhp
Range: 130/9 **Crew:** 5 tot.

Remarks: Modified for use as a tug about 1976. Retains bow ramp.

♦ **1 U.S. YTL 422–class small tug [YTL]**
Bldr: Robt. Jacob, City Isl., N.Y. (In serv. 25-7-45)

RP 16 Bohechio (ex-*Mercedes,* ex-YTL 600)

D: 70 tons (80 fl) **S:** 10 kts **Dim:** 20.1 × 5.5 × 2.4
M: 1 Hoover-Owens-Rentschler diesel; 1 prop; 375 bhp **Fuel:** 7 tons
Crew: 6 tot.

Remarks: Leased from U.S. during 1-71 and donated outright on 10-6-97.

Note: Also in service is the small harbor tug *Puerto Hermoso* (RP 14); no data available.

♦ **1 sail-training craft for naval academy [YTS]** (In serv. 1979)

BA 7 Nube del Mar (ex-*Catuan*)

D: 40 tons (fl) **S:** 12 kts **Dim:** 12.8 × 3.6 × . . .
M: 1 Volvo Penta 21A diesel; 1 prop; 75 bhp

EAST TIMOR

Personnel: 36 total

Base: Hera

PATROL BOATS [PB]

♦ **2 ex-Portuguese Albatroz class**
Bldr: Arsenal do Alfeite, Lisbon, Portugal (In serv. 1974–76)

Ataúro (ex-*Acor*) Oécusse (ex-*Albatroz*)

D: 45 tons (fl) **S:** 20 kts **Dim:** 23.6 (21.88 pp) × 5.25 × 1.6
A: 1 20-mm 70-cal Oerlikon AA; 2 single 12.7-mm mg
Electronics: Radar: 1 Decca 316P nav.
M: 2 Cummins diesels; 2 props; 1,100 bhp
Range: 450/18; 2,500/12 **Crew:** 1 officer, 7 enlisted

Remarks: Transferred to East Timor on 12-1-02. Steel construction. The Portuguese Navy provided training and technical assistance with the boats until 20-5-02, when East Timor became officially independent from Indonesia.

ECUADOR

Republic of Ecuador

ARMADA DE GUERRA

Personnel: About 5,500 total, including about 1,700 marines and 250 naval aviation personnel.

Bases: Principal naval bases are located at Guayaquil, Jaramijó, Salinas, and San Lorenzo. Naval infantry are based at Guayaquil, Oriente, and in the Galápagos Islands, where there is also a small naval facility. The naval academy is located at Salinas and the Naval War College at Guayaquil, the principal naval facility and fleet headquarters. The facilities at Jaramijó were expanded in 1998–99.

Naval Aviation: Two Bell 230T and seven Bell 206B JetRanger helicopters; two CASA CN-235, one Beech Super King Air 200T, four Cessna 337, one Cessna 320E, one Cessna Citation light transports; and four T-35 Pillánt are used for training. Contrary to previous reports, no Bell 412EP Sentinel helicopters have been delivered.

Note: Pennant numbers on Ecuadorian ships are changed every few years. Ship names are prefaced with BAE (*Buque de Armada de Ecuador*).

ATTACK SUBMARINES [SS]

♦ **2 German Type 209/1300**
Bldr: Howaldtswerke, Kiel

	Laid down	L	In serv.
S 101 Shyri	5-8-74	6-10-76	6-11-77
S 102 Huancavilca	20-1-75	15-3-77	16-3-78

Shyri (S 101)—with Coast Guard patrol boat *Río Puyango* (LG-41) in background *Ships of the World,* 2000

D: 1,100 tons light; 1,265 tons surf./1,395 tons sub.
S: 11 kts surf./21.4 kts sub. (1 hr.) **Dim:** 59.50 × 6.30 × 5.50
A: 8 bow 533-mm TT (14 SST Mod. 0 wire-guided torpedoes)
Electronics:
Radar: 1 Thales Calypso nav./surf. search
Sonar: STN Atlas Elektronik CSU-3 suite: A526 passive; CSU AN407 A9 active; Thales DUUX-2 passive-ranging hull array
EW: Thales DR-2000U intercept
M: 4 MTU 12V493 TY60 diesels; 4 Siemens 405-kw generators, electric drive: 1 Siemens motor; 1 prop; 5,000 shp (4,600 shp sust.)
Range: 8,400/8, 11,200/4 snorkel; 25/20, 445/4 sub.
Fuel: 87 tons normal/106 max. **Endurance:** 45 days
Crew: 5 officers, 28 enlisted

Remarks: Ordered 3-74. S 101 refitted at her builders in 1983, S 102 in 1984; both underwent local refit 1993–94 but were in need of further work by 1999, when S 101 began a refit at ASMAR, Valparaiso, Chile. The 257-ton battery installation includes four sets of 120 cells and is rated at 11,500 amp.-hr. Have Thales M8 Mod. 24 torpedo f.c.s. Both are based at Guayaquil, where S 101 suffered a serious fire on 2-2-03, leaving one dead.

FRIGATES [FF]

♦ **2 British "Exocet Leander" Batch 2B conversions**

	Bldr	Laid down	L	In serv.
FM-01 Presidente Eloy Alfaro (ex-*Penelope,* F 127; ex-*Coventry*)	Vickers-Armstrong Barrow-in-Furness	14-3-61	17-8-62	31-10-63
FM-02 Moran Valverde (ex-*Danae,* F 47)	HM Dockyard, Devonport	16-12-64	31-10-65	7-9-67

D: 2,650 tons (3,200 fl) **S:** 28 kts
Dim: 113.38 (109.73 pp) × 12.50 × 4.80 (6.20 props)
A: 4 MM 38 Exocet SSM; 3 2-round Simbad SAM syst. (36 Mistral missiles); 2 single 40-mm 60-cal. Mk 9 AA; 2 triple 324-mm ILAS-3 ASW TT (WASS A-244S torpedoes); 1 helicopter
Electronics:
Radar: 1 Type 1006 nav.; 1 Type 994 air/surf. search; 1 Type 965 early warning
Sonar: Type 184P (7.5 kHz) hull-mounted; Type 162M (50 Hz) HF classification; Type 185 underwater telephone
EW: UA-8/9 passive; Type 668 or 669 jammer; FH-12 HFD/F; 2 6-round DLD decoy RL (Raytheon Mk 137 launchers)

FRIGATES [FF] *(continued)*

Moran Valverde (FM-02) Ecuadorian Navy, 1996

Presidente Eloy Alfaro (FM-01) Ecuadorian Navy, 1996

M: 2 sets White-English Electric geared steam turbines; 2 props; 30,000 shp
Boilers: 2 Babcock & Wilcox 3-drum; 38.7 kg/cm^2, 450° C
Electric: 1,900 kw tot. **Range:** approx. 4,000/12 **Fuel:** 460 tons
Crew: 20 officers, 228 enlisted (in U.K. service)

Remarks: FM-01 paid off from Royal Navy service 31-3-91, was sold with FM-02 to Ecuador 25-4-91, and recommissioned on 25-5-91. FM-02 transferred at the end of 7-91 on completion of Royal Navy service. Both ships have been badly in need of overhauls and rearming, but a contract for refits appears to have been signed with ASMAR of Chile.
Hull systems: Have twin rudders and one pair of fin stabilizers, set well aft of amidships.
Combat systems: When transferred, had CAAIS combat data system, but the Chilean SISDEF 100 system is to be substituted during forthcoming refits. French Simbad point-defense SAM system launchers have been added, one atop the pilothouse and two abreast atop the hangar. The former two Sea Cat SAM system launchers and their associated Type 904 radar directors have been removed. Were transferred without MM 38 antiship missiles, which were procured later. The torpedo tubes, mounted on the main deck just abaft the helicopter hangar, were taken from units of the *Wadi M'ragh* class. The 40-mm guns are power operated and entirely locally controlled. A commercial SATCOM system has been added. In FM-01, the EW intercept system has been replaced by Israeli-made gear.

GUIDED-MISSILE PATROL COMBATANTS [PGG]

♦ **6 Italian modified Wadi M'ragh class** (2 in *reserve*)

	Bldr	Laid down	L	In serv.
CM-11 Esmeraldas	CNR, Muggiano	27-9-79	5-10-80	7-8-82
CM-12 Manabí	CNR, Ancona	1-2-80	5-2-81	21-6-83
CM-13 Los Ríos	CNR, Muggiano	1-9-79	28-2-81	1-10-83
CM-14 El Oro	CNR, Ancona	1-3-80	5-2-81	10-12-83
CM-15 *Galapagos*	CNR, Muggiano	20-10-80	5-7-81	26-5-84
CM-16 *Loja*	CNR, Ancona	6-2-81	27-2-82	26-5-84

Manabí (CM-12)—with Bell 206B JetRanger on deck Peruvian Navy, 2000

D: 620 tons (700 fl) **S:** 37 kts **Dim:** 62.3 (57.8 pp) × 9.3 × 2.8
A: 6 MM 40 Exocet SSM; 1 4-round Albatros SAM system (Aspide missiles, no reloads); 1 76-mm 62-cal. OTO Melara DP; 1 twin 40-mm 70-cal. OTO Melara AA; 4 units only: 2 triple 324-mm ILAS-3 ASW TT (WASS A-244S torpedoes); 1 Bell 206B helicopter

El Oro (CM-14)—during exercise PANAMAX 2005 U.S. Navy, 8-05

Electronics:
Radar: 1 Decca TM 1226 nav.; 1 AESN RAN-10S air/surf. search; 1 AESN Orion 10X f.c.; 1 AESN Orion 20X f.c.
Sonar: Thales Diodon hull-mounted (11–13 kHz)
EW: Elettronica ELT-318 Newton Gamma intercept; Telegon HFD/F, 1 20-round 105-mm OTO Melara SCLAR decoy RL
M: 4 MTU 20V956 TB92 diesels; 4 props; 24,400 bhp (20,400 sust.)
Electric: 750 kw **Range:** 1,200/31; 4,000/18 **Fuel:** 126 tons **Crew:** 51 tot.

Remarks: Ordered 1978 from CNR del Tirreno. More powerful engines than earlier Libyan units of class. Were to be modernized with updated electronics and a combat-information datalink capability, but funds are not available, and all are in need of refits.
Combat systems: Selenia IPN-10 data system, with NA 21 Mod. 0 radar f.c.s. and two CO3 directors for guns and SAM system. Have a helicopter platform, but no hangar.

GUIDED-MISSILE PATROL CRAFT [PTG]

♦ **3 FPB 45 class** (1 in *reserve*)
Bldr: Friedrich Lürssen Werft, Vegesack, Germany

	L	In serv.
LM-21 *Quito*	20-11-75	13-7-76
LM-22 Guayaquil	5-4-76	22-12-77
LM-24 Cuenca	12-76	17-7-77

Quito (LM-21) Ecuadorian Navy, 1996

D: 250 tons (265 fl) **S:** 35 kts **Dim:** 45.0 × 7.0 × 2.4
A: 4 MM 38 Exocet SSM; 1 76-mm 62-cal. OTO Melara DP; 1 twin 35-mm 90-cal. Oerlikon AA
Electronics:
Radar: 1 Decca TM 1226 nav.; 1 Thales Triton air/surf. search; 1 Thales Pollux f.c.
EW: Thales DR-2000S intercept
M: 4 MTU 16V396 diesels; 4 props; 13,600 bhp **Electric:** 330 kw tot.
Range: 600/30 **Fuel:** 39 tons **Crew:** 34 tot.

Remarks: Were re-engined 1994–95, but LM-21 was in reserve by 2000. Carry 250 rounds of 76-mm and 1,100 rounds of 35-mm ammunition. Have the Thales Vega gun fire-control system.

AMPHIBIOUS WARFARE SHIPS AND CRAFT

♦ **1 ex-U.S. LST 542–class tank landing ship [LST]**
Bldr: Chicago Bridge & Iron

	Laid down	L	In serv.
TR-61 Hualcopo (ex-*Summit County*, LST 1146)	15-2-45	23-5-45	1-6-45

D: 1,650 tons (4,080 fl) **S:** 11.6 kts **Dim:** 100.04 × 15.24 × 4.3
A: 2 twin 40-mm 60-cal. Bofors Mk 1 Mod. 2 AA; 4 single 40-mm 60-cal. Bofors Mk 3 AA; 2 single 20-mm 70-cal. Oerlikon AA (I × 2)
Electronics: Radar: 1 . . . nav.
M: 2 G.M. 12-567A diesels; 2 props; 1,700 bhp **Electric:** 300 kw tot.
Range: 7,200/10 **Crew:** 119 ship's company + 147 troops

Remarks: Bought 14-2-77. Used as transport. Has ice-reinforced waterline, an asset of limited value in tropical waters. In poor condition after a serious fire in 7-98 and may not be operational. Cargo capacity is about 600 tons.

AMPHIBIOUS WARFARE SHIPS AND CRAFT *(continued)*

♦ **10 river personnel launches [LCP]**
Bldr: ASTINAVE, Guayaquil

D: . . . tons **S:** 20 kts **Dim:** 6.70 × . . . × . . .
A: 1 7.62-mm mg **M:** 2 gasoline outboards; 200 bhp
Crew: 2 + 21 troops

Remarks: Ordered 1991. Kevlar construction. Same class operated by coast guard and army.

AUXILIARIES

♦ **1 oceanographic research ship [AGOR]**
Bldr: Ishikawajima Harima, Tokyo (In serv. 21-10-81)

BI-91 ORION (ex-*Dometer*)

Orion (BI-91)—red hull, white superstructure Ecuadorian Navy

D: Approx. 1,500 tons (fl) **S:** 12.5 kts **Dim:** 70.19 (64.22 pp) × 10.72 × 3.60
Electronics: Radar: 2 Decca 1226 nav.
M: 3 G.M. Detroit Diesel–Allison 16V92 TA diesels (960 bhp each), 3 600-kw generator sets, 2 electric motors, reverse-reduction gearing; 2 props; 900 shp
Electric: 700 kw tot. **Range:** 6,000/12
Crew: 6 officers, 25 enlisted, 19 scientists

Remarks: 1,105 grt/461 dwt. *Dometer* was delivery name, changed to *Orion* on arrival for commissioning. Equipped to conduct physical and biological oceanography, geophysical research, and hydrographic surveys for the *Instituto Oceanográfico de la Armada del Ecuador.* Also does weather reporting. Earlier bore pennants HI-91 and HI-92.

♦ **1 ex-British Kinterbury-class supply ship [AK]**
Bldr: Cleland SB, Wallsend-on-Tyne (In serv. 20-9-77)

TR-62 CALICUCHIMA (ex-*Throsk,* A 379)

Calicuchima (TR-62)—as *Throsk* (A 379) James W. Goss/Navpic, 6-91

D: 2,193 tons (fl) **S:** 14 kts **Dim:** 70.57 (64.31 pp) × 11.90 × 4.57
A: None **Electronics:** Radar: 1 Type 1006 nav.
M: 2 Mirrlees-Blackstone diesels; 1 prop; 3,000 bhp
Range: 1,500/14; 5,000/10 **Crew:** 8 officers, 16 enlisted

Remarks: 1,150 dwt. Former Royal Corps of Transport ammunition transport; purchased 11-91 and departed for Ecuador 2-92, commissioning 24-3-92. Can carry 760 tons cargo in the two holds, which total 750 m^3, plus 25 tons on deck. Has two cranes.

♦ **1 coastal transport tanker [AOT]**
Bldr: ASTINAVE, Guayaquil (In serv. 1985)

TR-65 TAURUS (ex-T-66)

D: Approx 1,800 tons (fl) **S:** 11 kts **Dim:** 53.1 × 11.0 × 4.4
A: . . .
M: 2 G.M. Detroit Diesel 6-71 diesels; 1 prop; 750 bhp **Crew:** 20 tot.

Remarks: 1,110 grt/1,175 dwt. Transferred to naval service in 1987.

♦ **1 ex-U.S. Abnaki-class fleet tug [ATA]**
Bldr: Charleston SB & DD, Charleston, S.C.

	Laid down	L	In serv.
RA-70 CHIMBORAZO (ex-*Chowanoc,* ATF 100)	24-4-43	20-8-43	21-2-44

Chimborazo (RA-70) Ecuadorian Navy

D: 1,235 tons (1,675 fl) **S:** 16.5 kts **Dim:** 62.48 (59.44 wl) × 11.73 × 4.67
A: 2 single 12.7-mm mg
Electronics: Radar: 1 Decca 916 nav.
M: 4 Busch-Sulzer BS-539 diesels, electric drive; 1 prop; 3,000 shp
Electric: 400 kw tot. **Range:** 16,000/8; 7,000/15 **Fuel:** 376 tons
Crew: 85 tot.

Remarks: Purchased 1-10-77 from U.S. Has earlier borne pennants R-710, R-71, and R-105. Near-sister *Cayambe* (RA-71) was in the coast guard.

♦ **1 sail-training ship [AXT]**
Bldr: Ast. Celaya, Bilbao, Spain

	L	In serv.
BE-51 GUAYAS	23-9-76	23-7-77

Guayas (BE-51)—pennant number is not displayed A. D. Baker III, 6-00

D: 934 grt **S:** 10.5 kts **Dim:** 76.2 × 10.6 × 4.2
M: 1 G.M. 12V149T diesel; 1 prop; 700 bhp
Crew: 50 tot. × 80 cadets (180 accomm.)

Remarks: 934 grt/234 dwt. Steel-hulled barque.

SERVICE CRAFT

♦ **1 inshore oceanographic research craft [YAG]**
Bldr: Halter Marine, New Orleans (In serv. 1975)

LH-94 RIGEL (ex-LH-92)

D: 50 tons **S:** 10 kts **Dim:** 19.7 × 5.2 × 1.1
M: 2 diesels; . . . bhp **Crew:** 2 officers, 8 enlisted

♦ **3 ex-U.S. ARD 12–class auxiliary repair docks [YFDL]**
Bldr: Pacific Bridge, Alameda, Calif. (In serv. 1944–45)

DF-81 AMAZONAS (ex-ARD 17)
DF-82 NAPO (ex-ARD 24)
DF-83 . . . (ex-*Alamagordo,* ARDM 2; ex-ARD 26)

Capacity: 3,500 tons **Dim:** 149.9 × 24.7 × 1.7 (light)

Remarks: DF-81 transferred 7-1-61, DF-82 in 1988, and DF-83 (which had been converted to service nuclear-powered attack submarines) on 18-12-00. Pointed bow. Length over blocks: 118.6 m; 18.0 m clear width. *Amazonas* earlier bore pennant DF-121.

Disposal note: U.S. YR 24–class repair barge *Putamayo* (BT-84, ex-YR 34) was stricken during 1999.

♦ **5 Tungurahua-class medium harbor tugs [YTM]**
Bldr: . . . (In serv. 1950s–1960s)

RB-74 ANTIZANA (ex-R-723)
RB-75 SIRIUS (ex-R-724)
RB-76 ALTAR (ex-R-725)
RB-77 TUNGURAHUA (ex-R-722)
RB-78 QUILOTOA (ex-R-726)

SERVICE CRAFT *(continued)*

D: 490 grt **S:** 8 kts **Dim:** 30.6 × . . . × 2.5
M: . . . diesels; 1 prop; . . . bhp

♦ **1 medium harbor tug [YTM]** (In serv. 1952)

RB-72 SANGAY (ex-*Losa*)

D: 295 tons (390 fl) **S:** 12 kts **Dim:** 32.6 × 7.9 × 4.25
M: 1 Fairbanks-Morse diesel; 1 prop; . . . bhp

Remarks: Bought 1964. Renamed 1966. Earlier bore pennants R-720, R-102, and R-53.

♦ **1 former U.S. Army medium harbor tug [YTM]**
Bldr: Equitable Bldg., New Orleans (In serv. 1945)

RB-73 COTOPAXI (ex-*R. T. Ellis*)

D: 150 tons **S:** 9 kts **Dim:** 25.0 × 6.62 × 2.9
M: 1 diesel; 1 prop; 650 bhp

Remarks: Bought 1947. Earlier bore pennants R-721, R-103, and R-52.

♦ **1 ex-British Water-class water lighter [YW]**
Bldr: Drypool, Hull (In serv. 1968)

TR-64 QUISQUIS (ex-*Waterside,* Y 20)

D: 344 tons (fl) **S:** 11 kts **Dim:** 40.02 (37.50 pp) × 7.50 × 2.44
Electronics: Radar: 1 Decca . . . nav.
M: 1 Lister-Blackstone ERS-8MGR diesel; 1 prop; 600 bhp
Electric: 155 kw tot. **Range:** 1,500/11 **Crew:** 8 tot.

Remarks: 285 grt. Purchased 11-91 and delivered 2-92. Cargo: 150 tons.

♦ **1 ex-U.S. water lighter [YW]**
Bldr: Leatham D. Smith, Sturgeon Bay, Wisc. (In serv. 17-9-45)

TR-63 ATALHUAPA (ex-YW 131)

D: 440 tons (1,390 fl) **S:** 7 kts **Dim:** 53.1 × 9.8 × 4.6
M: 1 G.M. 8-278 diesel; 1 prop; 640 bhp **Fuel:** 25 tons **Crew:** 20 tot.

Remarks: Transferred 2-5-63; purchased 1-12-77. Stricken 1988 but restored to service in 1990. Despite small size and minimal freeboard, has been used to deliver water to the Galápagos Islands. Cargo: 930 tons water. Has earlier borne pennants T-63, T-62, T-33, T-41, and A-01.

COAST GUARD

Personnel: 270 total

Note: "LG" in pennant number system stands for *Lancha de Guarda (de Costa).*

Disposal note: U.S. *Abnaki*-class patrol ship, former seagoing tug *Cayambe* (RA-71; ex-*Los Ríos;* ex-*Cusabo,* ATF 155) was stricken during 1999.

PATROL CRAFT [WPC]

♦ **1 (+ 2) Vigilante-class patrol craft**
Bldr: Babcock Marine and Astilleros De Murueta

. . . (In serv. 2006)
. . . (In serv. 2007)
. . . (In serv. 2007)

Vigilante-class patrol craft Babcock Marine, 2004

D: 300 tons **S:** 35 kts **Dim:** 45.0 × 9.8 × 2.5
A: . . .
Electronics: Radar: 1 . . . nav.; ...
M: 2 MTU 16V4000 M90 diesels; 1 MTU 12V 4000 M90 diesel for cruise/loiter; 3 fixed pitch props
Range: 3,000/12 **Crew:** 27

Remarks: Contract awarded 3-04. Steel hull monohull design derived from the *Protector* class. Launched during 2005. Carries a 5.2m launch for boarding duties. Used for coastal and offshore patrol duties. Modified for tropical operations in up to 104° Fahrenheit/40° Centigrade and 90% humidity.

♦ **2 Manta class**
Bldr: Friedrich Lürssen Werft, Vegesack, Germany

LG 37 9 DE OCTUBRE (ex-*Manta,* LM-25) (In serv. 11-6-71)
LG 38 27 DE OCTUBRE (ex-*Nueva Rocafuerte,* LM-27, ex-*Tena*) (In serv. 23-6-71)

9 de Octubre (LG 37) Ecuadorian Navy, 1996

D: 119 tons (134 fl) **S:** 35 kts **Dim:** 36.2 × 5.8 × 1.7
A: 1 twin 30-mm 75-cal. Emerlec AA; small arms
Electronics: Radar: 1 . . . nav.; 1 Thales Pollux f.c.—EW: Thales DR-2000S intercept
M: 3 Mercedes-Benz diesels; 3 props; 9,000 bhp
Range: 700/30; 1,500/15 **Fuel:** 21 tons **Crew:** 19 tot.

Remarks: Transferred to the Coast Guard during 2001. Similar to the Chilean *Guacolda* class, but faster. New guns added 1979; Gabriel missiles (in four single, fixed launch canisters) and Thales Vega fire-control system (without Triton search radar) replaced two single 533-mm TT 1980–81. The missiles are no longer carried and have likely passed their shelf-life expiration dates. Replacements for the craft were being sought as long ago as 1987. Sister *Tulcan* (LM-26) was lost in collision with a commercial tug during 9-98.

♦ **2 Espada class**
Bldr: Trinity-Moss Point Marine, Escatawpa, Miss.

LG-33 5 DE AGOSTO (In serv. 5-91) LG-34 27 DE FEBRERO (In serv. 11-91)

5 de Agosto (LG-33)—on trials Halter Marine, 5-91

D: 120 tons (fl) **S:** 27 kts **Dim:** 34.14 (31.62 pp) × 6.86 × 2.14 max.
A: 1 40-mm 60-cal. Bofors Mk 3 AA; 2 single 12.7-mm M2 mg
Electronics: Radar: 1 Decca TM 1226 nav.
M: 2 G.M Detroit Diesel 16V149 MTI diesels outboard (1,280 bhp each); 1 G.M. Detroit Diesel 16V92 TAB cruise diesel centerline (860 bhp); 3 props; 3,420 bhp
Range: 1,500/13 **Crew:** 5 officers, 14 enlisted

Remarks: Built under U.S. Foreign Military Sales program for Galápagos Islands service. Carry a 10-person rigid inflatable inspection boat.

♦ **1 U.S. PGM 71 class**
Bldr: Peterson Bldrs, Sturgeon Bay, Wisc. (In serv. 30-11-65)

LG-31 25 DE JULIO (ex-*Quito*)

D: 130 tons (147 fl) **S:** 17 kts **Dim:** 30.81 (30.20 pp) × 6.45 × 2.3
A: 1 40-mm 60-cal. Bofors Mk 3 AA; 2 twin 20-m 70-cal. Oerlikon Mk 24 AA; 2 single 12.7-mm mg
Electronics: Radar: 1 Raytheon 1500B Pathfinder nav.
M: 4 MTU diesels; 2 props; 3,520 bhp **Electric:** 30 kw tot.
Range: 1,000/12 **Fuel:** 16 tons **Crew:** 15 tot.

PATROL CRAFT [WPC] *(continued)*

Remarks: Built as U.S. PGM 75 as foreign aid. Transferred from Ecuadorian Navy to Coast Guard in 1980 and discarded 1983. Refitted and re-engined 1988–89 for further service. Earlier bore pennants LGC-31 and LC-71. Sister *24 de Mayo* (LG-32, ex-*Guayaquil,* ex-LC 71, ex-LGC-32, ex-LC 72, ex-U.S. PGM 76) lost in collision with merchant ship *Dole Ecuador* on 29-8-95.

PATROL BOATS [WPB]

♦ 2 U.S. 45-foot PCR class
Bldr: Swiftships, Morgan City, La. (In serv. 9-92)

LG-47 Rio Esmeraldas LG-48 Rio Santiago

U.S. 45-foot PCR patrol boat Skeets Photo/Swiftships, 7-92

D: 17 tons (fl) **S:** 28 kts **Dim:** 13.72 × 3.58 × 0.51 (at rest)
A: 2 single 12.7-mm M-2HB mg; 2 single 7.62-mm M-60D mg
Electronics: Radar: 1 Raytheon 40X nav.
M: 2 G.M. Detroit Diesel 6V92TA diesels; 2 Hamilton 362 waterjets; 900 bhp
Range: 650/22 **Fuel:** 1,045 gallons **Endurance:** 5 days
Crew: 4 tot. + 8 troops

Remarks: Act as command-and-control craft for groups of smaller riverine patrol craft. PCR = Patrol Craft, Riverine. Left New Orleans as deck cargo 14-9-92.
Hull systems: Aluminum construction with Kevlar armor over crew positions. Made 32 knots on trials. Can make 28 knots at 105% combat load at 100° F and can operate in Sea State 2 conditions. Can be transported on trailers.
Combat systems: The 12.7-mm mg are mounted in tubs that can also accommodate twin 12.7-mm mg or 40-mm Mk 19 grenade launchers. Communications equipment includes VHF transceiver with direction finder, HF/SSB transceiver, and two UHF hand-held radios. Navigation equipment includes magnetic compass, depth sounder, and a handheld GPS receiver.

♦ 6 Río Puyango class
Bldrs: First two: Halter Marine, New Orleans; others: ASTINAVE, Guayaquil

	In serv.		In serv.
LG-41 Río Puyango	6-86	LG-44 Río Chone	11-3-88
LG-42 Río Mateje	6-86	LG-45 Río Daule	17-6-88
LG-43 Río Zarumilla	11-3-88	LG-46 Río Babhoyo	17-6-88

D: 17 tons (fl) **S:** 26 kts **Dim:** 13.41 (12.39 pp) × 4.12 × 0.76
A: 1 12.7-mm M-2HB mg; 1 7.62-mm M-60D mg
Electronics: Radar: 1 Furuno 2400 nav.
M: 2 G.M. 8V71 TI diesels; 2 props; 850 bhp **Electric:** 12 kw
Range: 500/18 **Fuel:** 1.6 tons **Crew:** 1 officer, 4 enlisted

Remarks: First two were purchased for service in the Galápagos Islands. The other four were built in Ecuador from U.S.-supplied kits. Have a 250-gal./min. fire monitor to starboard and two firepumps to port. Aluminum construction. Used for drug interdiction.

♦ 6 river patrol craft Bldr: ASTINAVE, Guayaquil (In serv. 1991)

D: . . . tons **S:** 20 kts **Dim:** 6.70 × . . . × . . .
A: 1 7.62-mm mg **M:** 2 gasoline outboards; 200 bhp
Crew: 2 + 21 troops

Remarks: Ordered 1991. Kevlar plastic construction. Additional units may be ordered later. Same class operated by naval infantry and army.

♦ 1 ex-U.S. Coast Guard 82-foot Point class
Bldr: J. Martinac SB, Tacoma, Wash. (In serv. 25-8-67)

LG-32 24 de Mayo (ex-*Point Richmond,* WPB 82370)

D: 64 tons (69 fl) **S:** 23.7 kts (see Remarks) **Dim:** 25.3 × 5.23 × 1.95
A: 2 single 12.7-mm mg **Electronics:** Radar: 1 Raytheon SPS-64(V)1 nav.
M: 2 Caterpillar 3412 diesels; 2 props; 1,480 bhp
Range: 490/23.7; 1,500/8 **Fuel:** 5.7 tons **Crew:** 1 officer, 7 enlisted

Remarks: Purchased 22-8-97 to replace another unit of the same name. Hull of mild steel. High-speed diesels controlled from the bridge.

ECUADORIAN ARMY

PATROL BOATS [WPB]

♦ 10 riverine craft Bldr: ASTINAVE, Guayaquil

D: . . . tons **S:** 20 kts **Dim:** 6.70 × . . . × . . .
A: 1 7.62-mm mg **M:** 2 gasoline outboards; 200 bhp
Crew: 2 + 21 troops

Remarks: Ordered 1991. Kevlar plastic construction. Same class operated by the coast guard and naval infantry.

EGYPT

Arab Republic of Egypt

EGYPTIAN NAVY

Personnel: Approx. 18,500 total including 2,000 in coast guard, plus 14,000 reserves.

Bases: Naval facilities are located at Aboukir, Alexandria, Hurghada, Mers Matrouh, Port Said, Safaqa, Suez, and Hurghada.

Maritime Aviation: Maritime aviation assets include 10 SH-2G(E) shipboard ASW helicopters. The air force operates five Westland Sea King Mk 47 helicopters and 12 AS.12 wire-guided missile-equipped Aerospatiale AS.342L Gazelle helicopters in support of the navy. The air force also has two Beech 1900C light coastal-surveillance aircraft with Litton radar and Singer S-3075 ESM. The 10 SH-2G(E) helicopters were delivered 1997–98 after conversion by Kaman Helicopters from SH-2F configuration at a cost of $380 million; they received G.E. T700-401 engines and Allied Signal/Bendix AQS-18(V) dipping sonars. Egyptian Air Force E-2C Hawkeye aerial surveillance and tracking aircraft had their APS-138 radars changed to APS-145 during 2000, permitting overland surveillance. Two Schiebel Camcopter 5.1 UAV helicopters were delivered in 2003 for use from Egyptian Navy frigates; the aircraft have an endurance of six hours and carry a color video camera.

SH-2G(E) Super SeaSprite Robert F. Dorr, 1998

Coast Defenses: The navy is responsible for coastal defenses. Fifty coastal defense, truck-mounted versions of the Italian Otomat missile were purchased in 1983 for use by three trucks, each able to carry two missiles. They were updated to Mk 2 standard in 2005. There are two naval-controlled artillery brigades, equipped with Russian-made 100-mm, 130-mm, and 152-mm guns. Five U.S. TPS-59(V)2 coastal surveillance radars were upgraded to (V)3E and given a capability to detect and track theater ballistic missiles in 2000, and six SPS-48E 3-D early-warning radars were ordered on 29-6-01 for land-based use.

Weapons and Sensors: Egypt bought 32 U.S. Harpoon missiles and 46 Mk 46 ASW torpedoes during 1994 in support of its acquisition of *Knox*-class frigates. Another 42 Harpoons were purchased during 1998 and 53 Harpoon, Block II (RGM-84L) missiles were ordered in 11-02. In 9-97, 84 Mk 46 Mod. 5 ASW torpedoes were purchased from Alliant Techsystems in the U.S. The 50 BAE Systems Sting Ray Mod. 0 lightweight ASW torpedoes completed refurbishment and upgrade to Mod. 1, with improved software, late in 2002 to extend their service lives to 2013.

Otomat missiles are being updated to the Otomat Mk 2 configuration (Teseo) employed by the Italian Navy under a 12-00 contract to Alenia Marconi Systems; the work was completed during 2005. Four Raytheon 20-mm Phalanx CIWS (three Block 0, one Block 1B) were ordered during 6-01 for installation on unspecified ships.

Note: Ship names are preceded by ENS (Egyptian Navy Ship).

ATTACK SUBMARINES [SS]

Note: The planned acquisition of 2 Moray 1400-class submarines was abandoned in 2002 due to budget constraints. Surplus Type 206A submarines have been offered as an alternative solution by Germany, which began discussions with Egypt in 12-04.

♦ 4 Chinese-built Romeo class (Project 033)
Bldr: Jiagnan Shipyard, Shanghai (In serv. 1983–84)

849 852 855 858

Modernized Romeo-class 855 H&L Van Ginderen, 10-96

ATTACK SUBMARINES [SS] *(continued)*

Modernized Romeo-class 855—outboard sister 858
Chris Delgoffe/H&L Van Ginderen, 3-00

D: 1,320 tons (surf.)/1,712 tons (sub.) **S:** 15.2 kts (surf.)/13 kts (sub.)
Dim: 77.60 × 6.70 × 4.95
A: 6 bow and 2 stern 533-mm TT (14 UGM-84C Harpoon SSM and NT-37F torpedoes or up to 28 mines)
Electronics:
Radar: 1 Snoop Plate nav./surf. search
Sonar: STN Atlas Elektronik CSU-3-4 active/passive suite, with PSU-2/83 passive array and STU-3 sonar training set
EW: ArgoSystems Phoenix AR-700-S5 intercept
M: 2 Type 37D diesels (2,000 bhp each), 2 generators, 2 motors; 2 props; 2,700 shp—2 50-shp creep motors
Range: 350/4 sub.; 14,000/9 surf.; 7,000/5 snorkel
Endurance: 60 days **Crew:** 8 officers, 43 enlisted

Remarks: Two units, launched in 1980, were delivered from China on 28-3-83; the second Chinese-built pair was delivered 3-1-84 and commissioned 21-5-84. Six Soviet-built units were transferred earlier, five in 1966, one in 1969; all have been stricken.
Hull systems: Have 224 battery cells, producing 6,000 amp-hr. Normal maximum operating depth is 270 m (300 max.). Displacements and dimensions above reflect premodernization figures; the submarines may be a bit longer due to the enlarged chin sonar dome, and the displacement figures have probably risen considerably, reducing reserve buoyancy. Based in Alexandria, though current operational status remains uncertain.
Modernization: Loral Sonar Systems Corp., began modernizing the quartet in 4-92. They received new 54-ton-capacity air-conditioning systems; new power distribution systems with two new 7-kVA, 60-Hz, 120-volt a.c. motor generator sets; U.S. Alliant NT-37F wire-guided torpedoes and Sub-Harpoon missile launch capability (while retaining the ability to launch existing stocks of Chinese-supplied straight-running torpedoes); a Loral Librascope ENFCS (Egyptian Navy fire-control system) with two multifunction displays; a Librascope-assembled Atlas Elektronik sonar suite (with a greatly enlarged chin sonar dome and topside sonar dome); Kollmorgen Model 76 periscopes and Model 86 optronic telescoping masts; Boeing ArgoSystems AR-700-S5 EW equipment (with the array mast also accommodating GPS, D/F, and UHF communications antennas); an inertial navigation system; and a towed buoyant radio communications cable system (with the cable drum housed in the extended lower forward portion of the sail). Also installed were a Link Y datalink system to permit over-the-horizon targeting and encrypted communications equipment. The first unit completed modernization early in 1994 and the last during 1996. Kollmorgen optronic surveillance systems were ordered for the boats in 1-00, with deliveries completed by 1-02. Sperry Mk 39 Mk 3A ring-laser gyros were ordered for all four during 12-02 and have been installed.

GUIDED-MISSILE FRIGATES [FFG]

♦ 4 ex-U.S. Oliver Hazard Perry class

	Bldr	Laid down	L	In serv.
901 SHARM EL-SHEIKH (ex-*Fahrion,* FFG 22)	Todd, Seattle	1-12-78	24-8-79	16-1-82
906 TOUSHKA (ex-*Lewis B. Puller,* FFG 23)	Todd, San Pedro	23-5-79	15-3-80	17-4-82
911 MUBARAK (ex-*Copeland,* FFG 25)	Todd, San Pedro	24-10-79	26-7-80	7-8-82
916 TABA (ex-*Gallery,* FFG 26)	Bath Iron Works	17-5-80	20-12-80	5-12-81

Toushka (906) William C. Clarke, 1-99

Mubarak (911) Cem D. Yaylali, 5-99

Sharm el-Sheikh (901) Chris Delgoffe/H&L Van Ginderen, 3-00

D: 2,948 tons light (3,881 fl) **S:** 29 kts (30.6 trials)
Dim: 135.64 (125.9 wl) × 13.72 × 5.8 (7.62 max.)
A: 1 single-rail Mk 13 Mod. 4 launcher (4 RGM-84C Harpoon and 36 Standard SM-1 MR missiles); 1 76-mm 62-cal. Mk 75 DP; 1 20-mm Mk 15 Phalanx gatling CIWS; 4 single 12.7-mm mg; 2 triple 324-mm Mk 32 Mod. 5 ASW TT; 1 or 2 SH-2G(E) Super SeaSprite ASW helicopters
Electronics:
Radar: 1 Furuno type nav.; 1 Cardion SPS-55 surf. search.; 1 Raytheon SPS-49(V)4 air-search; 1 Lockheed Martin Mk 92 Mod. 2 missile/gun f.c.; 1 Lockheed Martin STIR (SPG-60 Mod.) missile/gun f.c.; 1 Raytheon Mk 90 Phalanx f.c. (on mount); 1 JRC type helo control
Sonar: Raytheon SQS-56 (7.5 kHz) hull-mounted, active search and attack, MF
TACAN: URN-25
EW: Raytheon SLQ-32A(V)2 passive (SLQ-32(V) 2 in 901); Mk 36 SRBOC decoy RL syst. (2 6-round Mk 137 launchers); SLQ-25 Nixie towed acoustic torpedo decoy
M: 2 G.E. LM-2500 gas turbines; 1 5.5-m-dia., CP, 5-bladed prop; 41,000 shp (40,000 sust.)—2 350-shp drop-down electric propulsors
Electric: 3,000 kw tot.
Range: 4,200/20; 5,000/18 **Fuel:** 587 tons + 64 tons helicopter fuel
Crew: 17 officers, 195 enlisted (217 max. accomm.)

Remarks: 911 was transferred under the U.S. Grant-Aid program on 18-9-96. 916 was transferred by sale ($106 million, including 35 Standard missiles, 12 Mk 46 Mod. 5 torpedoes, and gun ammunition) on 25-9-96 and was given a three-month refit in the U.S. prior to departure. 911 and 916 were formally dedicated in Egypt on 13-7-97. 901 was decommissioned from the USN on 3-3-98 and transferred 31-3-98 as Grant-Aid, and 906 followed on 18-9-98, also as Grant-Aid, but underwent refit in the U.S. prior to departing for Egypt, arriving 12-98.
Hull systems: Particularly well protected against splinter and fragmentation damage, with 19-mm aluminum-alloy armor over magazine spaces, 16-mm steel over the main engine-control room, and 19-mm Kevlar plastic armor over vital electronics and command spaces. Speed on one turbine alone is 25 knots; the auxiliary power system uses two retractable pods located well forward and can drive the ships at up to 6 kts. Two nonretractable fin stabilizers are fitted. Are equipped with the Prairie/Masker air bubbler system to reduce radiated machinery noise below the waterline.
Combat systems: The Mk 92 Mod. 4 fire-control system controls missile and 76-mm gunfire; it uses a STIR (modified SPG-60) antenna amidships and a U.S.-built version of the Thales WM-28 radar forward and can track four separate targets. The Mk 75 gun is a license-built version of the OTO Melara Compact. A Mk 13 weapons-direction system is fitted. There are two Mk 24 optical missile and gun target designators mounted in tubs atop the pilothouse. Up to 24 Mk 46 Mod. 5 torpedoes can be carried. Harpoon missiles are launched from the Mk 13 launcher. Were not transferred with towed sonar arrays. All received a navigational radar prior to transfer, and a JRC navigational radar has been added atop the hangar for helicopter control.

FRIGATES [FF]

♦ 2 Chinese Jianghu-I class
Bldr: Hudong SY, Shanghai

951 NAJIM AL-ZAFIR (In serv. 27-10-84) 956 EL NASSER (In serv. 16-4-85)

D: 1,586 tons (1,702 fl) **S:** 25.5 kts **Dim:** 103.20 × 10.20 × 3.05 (hull)
A: 2 twin, trainable launchers for C-201 SSM; 2 twin 57-mm 70-cal. Type 76 DP; 6 twin 37-mm 63-cal. Type 74 AA; 4 5-round Type 81 ASW RL; 4 BMB-2 d.c. mortars; 2 internal d.c. racks; 2 mine rails, 60 mines max.
Electronics:
Radar: 1 Decca RM 1290A nav.; 1 Type 756 nav.; 1 Type 354 (MX-902 Eye Shield) air/surf. search; 1 Type 352C (Square Head) missile target desig.
Sonar: E-5 hull-mounted HF searchlight
EW: Elettronica Newton-Beta suite (Type 211 intercept; Type 318 noise jammer; Type 521 deception jammer); Litton Triton intercept

FRIGATES [FF] *(continued)*

Najim al-Zafir (951) French Navy, 11-95

El Nasser (956) Chris Delgoffe/H&L Van Ginderen, 3-00

M: 2 SEMT-Pielstick 12 PA 6 280BTC diesels; 2 props; 14,400 bhp
Electric: 1,320 kw tot. **Range:** 1,750/25; 4,000/15
Endurance: 15 days **Crew:** 195 tot.

Remarks: Ordered 1982. Planned future modernization efforts include removal of the after armament and superstructure and installation of a helicopter hangar and flight deck. Both ships are based at Hurdhada.
Combat systems: Differ from Chinese Navy units in having twin 57-mm guns vice single or twin 100-mm mounts fore and aft, and in having an enclosed housing for the optical rangefinder atop the bridge. There is no radar fire-control equipment for the eight gun mounts, all of which are locally controlled via on-mount sights. Elettronica EW equipment and second navigational radar have been added after delivery. Equipped with U.S. Litton Triton radar threat warning receivers during 1994.

♦ 2 Spanish Descubierta class
Bldr: E.N. Bazán, Cartagena

	Laid down	L	In serv.
F 941 Abuqir (ex-*Centinela*)	31-10-78	6-10-79	21-5-84
F 946 El Suez (ex-*Serviola*)	28-2-79	20-12-79	27-10-84

El Suez (F 946) Stefan Karpinski, 2-03

D: 1,363 tons (1,575 fl) **S:** 26 kts **Dim:** 88.88 (85.80 pp) × 10.40 × 3.70
A: 8 RGM-84C Harpoon SSM; 1 8-round Mk 29 SAM launcher (24 RIM-7M NATO Sea Sparrow missiles); 1 76-mm 62-cal. OTO Melara Compact DP; 2 single 40-mm 70-cal. Bofors AA; 1 2-round 375-mm Bofors ASW RL; 2 triple 324-mm Mk 32 ASW TT (Stingray torpedoes)
Electronics:
Radar: 1 Thales ZW-06/Z nav./surf. search; 1 Thales DA-05/2 air/surf. search; 1 Thales WM-25 f.c.
Sonar: Raytheon DE 1167LF and hull-mounted VDS (7.5 kHz)
EW: Elettronica Beta intercept/jammer suite; Telegon HFD/F
M: 4 Bazán-MTU16V956 TB91 diesels; 2 CP props; 18,000 bhp
Electric: 1,810 kw tot. **Range:** 6,000/18 **Fuel:** 250 tons
Crew: 10 officers, 106 enlisted (146 accom.)

Remarks: Originally ordered 25-5-76 for the Spanish Navy, but sold to Egypt 1982, while building. F 946 completed 28-2-84 and F 941 on 6-9-84.
Hull systems: Have fin stabilizers, plus U.S. Prairie/Masker bubbler system to reduce sound radiation below the waterline.
Combat systems: Have Thales Nederland SEWACO weapons-control system. Carry 600 rounds of 76-mm ammunition. The U.S. supplied the Harpoon missiles in 1984; the ships normally carry fewer than the maximum weapons load. Have separate IFF interrogation antenna on after mast below and to starboard of the DA-05/2 antenna.

♦ 2 ex-U.S. Knox class
Bldr: Avondale SY, Avondale, La.

	Laid down	L	In serv.
961 Damiyat (ex-*Jesse L. Brown,* FFT 1089, FF 1089)	8-4-71	18-3-72	17-2-73
966 Rasheed (ex-*Moinester,* FFT 1097, FF 1097)	25-8-72	12-7-73	2-11-74

Damiyat (961) Chris Delgoffe/H&L Van Ginderen, 3-00

Rasheed (966) Chris Delgoffe/H&L Van Ginderen, 3-00

D: 3,130 tons light (4,260 fl) **S:** 27+ kts
Dim: 134.00 (126.49 wl) × 14.33 × 4.77 (7.83 over sonar)
A: 8 RGM-84C Harpoon SSM (see Remarks); 1 127-mm 54-cal. Mk 42 DP; 1 20-mm Phalanx Mk 15 CIWS; 1 8-cell Mk 112 ASROC ASW RL; 2 pair 324-mm Mk 32 Mod. 9 fixed ASW TT; 1 SH-2G(E) Super SeaSprite LAMPS-I ASW helicopter
Electronics:
Radar: 1 Raytheon SPS-64(V)9 nav.; 1 Norden SPS-67 surf search; 1 Lockheed SPS-40D air search; 1 Western Electric SPG-53F gun f.c.; 1 General Dynamics Mk 90 Phalanx f.c.
Sonar: EDO-G.E. SQS-26CX bow-mounted LF; SQR-18A(V)1 TACTASS towed array
TACAN: SRN-15A
EW: 961: Raytheon SLQ-32(V)2 intercept; 966: Raytheon SLQ-32(V)1 intercept; both: Mk 36 SRBOC decoy syst. (2 6-round Mk 137 RL); 961: SLQ-25 Nixie, 966: T-Mk 6 Fanfare towed acoustic torpedo decoy
M: 1 set Westinghouse geared steam turbines; 1 prop; 35,000 shp
Boilers: 2 Combustion Engineering V2m, M-Type; 84 kg/cm^2, 510° C
Electric: 3,000 kw tot. (3 × 750-kw turbogenerators, 1 × 750-kw diesel set)
Range: 4,300/20 **Fuel:** 750 tons max.
Crew: 17 officers, 261 enlisted

Remarks: Two units transferred on lease, 961 on 27-7-94 and 966 on 28-6-94; purchased outright on 25-3-98.
Hull systems: Bow bulwarks and a spray strake have been added forward to reduce deck wetness, a problem in this class; the addition added 9.1 tons and extended the overall length from the original 133.59 m. Have a TEAM (SM-5) computer system for the continual monitoring of the ship's electronic equipment. Antirolling fin stabilizers fitted in all. Prairie/Masker bubbler system fitted to hulls and propellers to reduce radiated noise. Both units have had serious boiler problems while in Egyptian service and engineering refits are planned when funds become available.
Combat systems: A 20-mm Mk 15 Phalanx CIWS gatling AA system was added after 1982. The ASW torpedo tubes are fixed, in the forward end of the hangar superstructure, aimed outboard at an angle of 45°. Have Mk 114 ASW fire-control system. The ASROC system has an automatic reloading magazine beneath the bridge; no ASW missiles were transferred and the launcher may be removed and replaced with two quadruple canister launchers for Harpoon missiles. Some 4,000 rounds 127-mm and 40,000 rounds 20-mm ammunition were transferred for use with these ships.

FRIGATES [FF] *(continued)*

Carry an Mk 68 gunfire-control system with SPG-53D or -53F radar. The ASW TDS (Tactical Data System) is installed, and they also have a form of "mini-NTDS" called FFISTS (Frigate Integrated Shipboard Tactical System) that employs off-the-shelf desktop computers. Also have SQR-17 sonar data-link processors. May receive an Elettronica EW suite in place of SLQ-32. The towed array system employs the hoist gear and fish of the inactivated SQS-35 VDS to tow the linear passive hydrophone array. Two SLQ-25A digital Nixie towed decoy systems were procured for these ships but have not been installed.

GUIDED-MISSILE PATROL CRAFT [PTG]

Note: The purchase of four Ambassador-III design guided missile patrol craft, announced in 2001, has been canceled. During 11-05 three missile patrol craft of a new design were ordered from VT Halter-marine for delivery beginning 2007. Total cost of the program is expected to be $565 million.

♦ 6 Chinese Houku class (2 in *reserve*)

Bldr: . . . (In serv. 27-10-84)

609 611 613 615 *617* *619*

Houku-class 609 French Navy, 1999

D: 68 tons light, 73.88 normal (79.19 fl) **S:** 37 kts
Dim: 27.0 × 6.50 × 1.80 (1.295 hull)
A: 2 HY-2 SSM; 1 twin 23-mm 60-cal. AA
Electronics:
Radar: 1 Type 352C (Square Tie) search/target desig.
EW: Litton Triton radar intercept
M: 4 M-50F-4 (Type L-12V-180) diesels; 4 props; 4,800 bhp
Electric: 65 kw tot. **Range:** 500/24 **Endurance:** 5 days
Crew: 2 officers, 15 enlisted

Remarks: Delivered 9-84 and commissioned together the following month. Steel construction. Former hull numbers 401–406. The Type 352C radar can also be employed as a passive radar intercept and direction-finding device. The gunmount is a standard Soviet 2M-3M mounting with Egyptian-made guns substituted for the original 25-mm weapons. Equipped with U.S. Litton Triton radar threat warning receivers during 1994.

♦ 6 Ramadan class (2 in *reserve*)

Bldr: Vosper Thornycroft, Portchester, U.K.

	Laid down	L	In serv.
670 *Ramadan*	22-9-78	6-9-79	20-7-81
672 Khyber	23-2-79	31-1-80	15-9-81
674 *El Kadesseya*	23-4-79	19-2-80	6-4-82
676 El Yarmouk	15-5-79	12-6-80	18-5-82
678 Badr	29-9-79	17-6-81	17-6-82
680 Hettein	29-2-80	25-11-80	28-10-82

El Kadesseya (674)—laid up at Alexandria Bernard Prézelin collection, 2002

D: 262 tons (312 fl) **S:** 35 kts **Dim:** 52.0 (48.0 pp) × 7.6 × 2.0 (hull)
A: 4 Otomat Mk I SSM; 1 76-mm 62-cal. OTO Melara Compact DP; 1 twin 40-mm 70-cal. OTO Melara AA
Electronics:
Radar: All Marconi: 1 S 810 nav.; 1 S 820 air/surf. search; 2 ST 802 f.c.
EW: Racal Cutlass-E intercept; Racal Cygnus jammer; Telegon HFD/F; Protean decoy syst. (4 36-round RL)
M: 4 MTU 20V538 TB91 diesels; 4 props; 16,000 bhp **Electric:** 420 kw tot.
Range: 2,000/15 **Fuel:** 43 tons **Crew:** 4 officers, 27 enlisted

Remarks: Ordered 4-9-77. First pair arrived Egypt 13-11-81, second pair 23-7-82, and third pair in 12-82. 674 was reported to be laid up in 2000 as was *Ramadan* by 2005.

Combat systems: Have Marconi Sapphire fire-control system with two ST 802 radar/t.v. directors and two Lawrence Scott optical directors. Ferranti CAAIS automated data system. Reportedly, Soviet shoulder-launched SA-7 Grail surface-to-air missiles are carried. All six are to have their communications systems upgraded by Alenia Marconi Systems under a 3-00 contract. Two had their radars upgraded under a 1998 contract with Alenia Marconi Systems, and a contract for the other four was let in 3-01, with the work to be completed in 53 months. Alenia-Marconi won a contract in 4-00 to update command and control systems on this class, with the work completed by mid-2003; the Nautis-3 system will replace the CAAIS equipment, but much of the same software will be retained.

♦ 6 October class (2 in *reserve*)

Bldr: Alexandria Naval Dockyard (In serv. 1980–81)

781 783 *785* 787 789 *791*

6 October class H&L Van Ginderen, 7-80

D: 71 tons (82 fl) **S:** 40 kts **Dim:** 25.3 × 6.0 × 1.8
A: 2 Otomat Mk I SSM; 2 twin 30-mm 75-cal. Oerlikon A32 AA
Electronics:
Radar: 1 Alenia-Marconi S 810 nav./surf. search; 1 Alenia-Marconi ST 802 f.c.
EW: Litton Triton radar intercept; 2 6-round MEL Protean Decoy RL
M: 4 CRM 18V-12D/55 YE diesels; 4 props; 5,400 bhp
Range: 400/30 **Crew:** 20 tot.

Remarks: Wooden hulls, built at Alexandria DY, Egypt, 1969–75. Fitted out by Vosper Thornycroft at Portchester, Portsmouth, England, 1979–81, with Italian-French missiles and British guns; diesels are Italian. Basic design is that of the former Soviet Komar class. 791 was lost overboard during delivery 16-12-80, salvaged, returned to U.K. 30-6-81, and completed repairs 13-8-82. Use Marconi Sapphire radar/t.v. fire-control system. Equipped with U.S. Litton Triton radar threat warning receivers during 1994. 781 and 783 were not retired in 1999, as erroneously reported in earlier editions.

♦ 5 ex-German Type 148

Bldrs: A: Lürssen, Vegesack; B: CMN, Cherbourg

	Bldr	Laid down	L	In serv.
601 23 July (ex-*Alk*)	B	9-4-74	15-11-74	7-1-75
602 6 October (ex-*Fuchs*)	A	10-3-72	21-5-73	17-10-73
603 21 October (ex-*Löwe*)	A	10-7-72	10-9-73	9-1-74
604 18 June (ex-*Dommel*)	A	13-12-73	30-10-74	12-2-75
605 25 April (ex-*Weihe*)	B	2-7-74	13-2-75	3-4-75

21 October (603) Michael Nitz, 2003

6 October (602) Frank Behling, 4-03

GUIDED-MISSILE PATROL CRAFT [PTG] *(continued)*

D: 234 tons (264 fl) **S:** 35.8 kts **Dim:** 47.0 (45.90 pp) × 7.10 × 2.66 (fl)
A: 4 MM 38 Exocet; 1 76-mm 62-cal. OTO Melara DP; 1 40-mm 70-cal. OTO Melara-Bofors AA
Electronics:
Radar: 1 SMA 3RM 20 nav.; 1 Thales Triton-G air/surf. search; 1 Thales Castor-II f.c.
EW: Racal Octopus suite (Cutlass intercept, Scorpion jammer); 2 6-round Buck-Wegmann Hot Dog/Silver Dog decoy RL, Wolke chaff dispenser
M: 4 MTU 16V538 TB90 (MD 872) diesels; 4 props; 14,000 bhp (at 1,515 rpm; 12,000 bhp sust.)
Electric: 270 kw tot. (3 × 90-kw diesel sets) **Range:** 570/30; 1,600/15
Fuel: 39 tons **Crew:** 4 officers, 17 petty officers, 9 ratings

Remarks: Transfer agreement was reached on 11-01. All hulls were fitted out at Cherbourg prior to transfer. 601 was retired on 13-5-02 and departed German waters on 20-7-02; the others were retired in 12-02 and transferred to Egypt in 3-03, without refit or upgrade and without training or support from Germany.
Combat systems: Have the Thales Vega fire-control system with Pollux radar; Triton is used for target designation. OTO Melara-made Bofors 40-mm mountings with Mauser GRP enclosed gunhouses have been fitted in place of the original open Bofors 40-mm L70 mountings aft.

♦ 5 ex-Soviet Osa-I class (Project 205E) (2 in *reserve*)

633 *637* *639* 641 643

Osa-I-class 641 H&L Van Ginderen, 6-97

D: 171 tons (209.5 fl) **S:** 38.5 kts
Dim: 38.6 (37.5 wl) × 7.6 (6.3 wl) × 1.8 hull (2.9 props)
A: 4 P-20/21 Termit (SS-N-2C Styx) SSM; 1 SA-7 Grail SAM launch position; 2 twin 30-mm 65-cal. AK-230 AA; 2 single 12.7-mm mg
Electronics:
Radar: 1 Rangout (Square Tie) surf. search/target-desig., 1 MR-104 Rys' (Drum Tilt) gun f.c.
EW: Litton Triton radar intercept
M: 3 M-503A2 diesels; 3 props; 12,000 bhp **Electric:** 200 kw tot.
Range: 500/34; 750/25 **Endurance:** 5 days **Crew:** 4 officers, 24 enlisted

Remarks: Survivors of 13 transferred 1966–68. All carry shoulder-launched SA-7 Grail (SA-N-5) SAMs, launched from a tub amidships. Three (635, 637, and 639) were inoperable by end-1989, but 637 was restored to service in 1991 and 633 and 639 were again operational by 1993; by 1998, 639 was again out of service. During 1994 the class was re-engined and equipped with Litton Triton radar intercept systems.

PATROL CRAFT [PC]

♦ 8 Chinese Hainan class (4 in reserve)

	In serv.		In serv.
430 Al Nour	23-10-83	442 Al Qatar	21-5-84
433 Al Hadi	23-10-83	445 Al Saddam	6-84
436 Al Hakim	21-5-84	448 Al Salam	6-84
439 Al Wakil	21-5-84	451 Al Rafia	6-84

Four Egyptian Navy Hainan-class patrol craft
Chris Delgoffe/H&L Van Ginderen, 3-00

D: 375 tons normal (392 fl) **S:** 30.5 kts **Dim:** 58.77 × 7.20 × 2.20 (hull)
A: 2 twin 57-mm 70-cal. Type 76 DP; 2 twin 23-mm 60-cal. AA; 4 5-round Type 81 ASW RL; 2 BMB-2 d.c. mortars; 2 d.c. racks; 2 mine rails, 12 mines max.
Electronics:
Radar: 1 Type 351 (Pot Head) surf. search; 1 Decca nav.
Sonar: Tamir-11 (MG-11) hull-mounted searchlight-type (25–31 kHz)
EW: none
M: 4 Type 9D-8 diesels; 4 props; 8,800 bhp **Range:** 2,000/14 **Crew:** 70 tot.

Remarks: First pair arrived 10-83, next three in 2-84, and final trio in 6-84. Reportedly, the original 25-mm AA guns were replaced with Egyptian-made 23-mm weapons on the same 2M-3M mountings. May now carry a commercial navigational radar in addition to the undereffective Type 351 surface search. It is not known which four units are in reserve.

♦ 4 Chinese Shanghai-II class

793 795 797 799

D: 122.5 tons normal (134.8 fl) **S:** 28.5 kts **Dim:** 38.78 × 5.41 × 1.55
A: 2 twin 37-mm 63-cal. Type 74 AA; 2 twin 23-mm 60-cal. AA
Electronics: Radar: 1 Type 351 (Pot Head) surf. search
M: 2 Type L-12V-180 diesels (1,200 bhp each), 2 Type L12-180SZ diesels (910 bhp each); 4 props; 4,220 bhp
Electric: 39 kw **Range:** 750/16.5 **Endurance:** 7 days **Crew:** 36 tot.

Remarks: Transferred 1984 with transfer numbers E 601–604. Do not have depth charges, as on Chinese Navy examples. The original 25-mm guns have reportedly been exchanged for Egyptian-made 23-mm weapons on the same 2M-3M mountings. 799 is based at Harghada and the other three at Suez. 795 was refitted in 1998.

♦ 5 Soviet Shershen class

753 755 757 759 761

D: 145 tons (170 fl) **S:** 45 kts **Dim:** 34.60 × 6.75 × 1.5
A: 2 twin 30-mm 65-cal. AK-230 AA; 1 SA-7 Grail shoulder-launched SAM position
Electronics:
Radar: 1 Baklan (Pot Drum) surf. search; 1 MR-104 Rys' (Drum Tilt) f.c.
EW: Thales DR-875 radar warning.
M: 3 M-503A diesels; 3 props; 12,000 bhp (8,025 sust.)
Electric: 84 kw tot. (3 × 28-kw diesel sets)
Range: 460/42; 800/30 **Fuel:** 30 tons **Crew:** 22 tot.

Remarks: Survivors of seven transferred 1967–68. Four were armed with two 20-tubed 122-mm artillery rocket launchers instead of torpedoes; the launchers have subsequently been removed, as have the torpedo tubes.

MINE WARFARE SHIPS

♦ 0 (+ 2) ex-U.S. Osprey-class coastal minehunters [MHC]

Bldrs: Intermarine U.S.A., Savannah, Ga.

	Begun	L	In serv.
. . . (ex-USS *Cardinal*, MHC 60)	1-2-94	9-3-96	8-10-97
. . . (ex-USS *Raven*, MHC 61)	15-11-94	8-9-96	5-9-98

D: ex-MHC 60: 828 tons light; 950 max. tons (fl)
ex-MHC 61: 817 tons light; 960 max. tons (fl)
S: 12 kts **Dim:** 57.25 (53.10 pp) × 11.60 × 3.35 max.
A: 2 single 12.7-mm M2 mg
Electronics:
Radar: 1 Raytheon AN/SPS-64(V)9 nav.
Sonar: 1 Raytheon AN/SQQ-32 variable-depth minehunting
M: 2 Isotta-Fraschini ID 36 SS 8V-AM diesels; 2 Voith-Schneider vertical cycloidal props; 1,600 bhp—2 180-shp hydraulic motors for quiet running—1 180-shp bow-thruster
Electric: 900 kW (3 × 300 kW, Isotta-Fraschini ID SS 6V-AM diesels driving)
Range: 2,500/12 **Endurance:** 5 days **Crew:** 51 tot. 5 officers, 46 enlisted

Remarks: Transferred during 2006–7. Monocoque foam-core GRP hull construction, with the design based on that of the Italian Navy *Lerici*-class. Have the SSQ-109 Ship/Machinery Control System and two 400 Hz motor-generator sets. Later units have additional space for provisions and stores.
Combat systems: Employ the Alliant SLQ-48(V)2 Mine Neutralization System remote-controlled submersible. Have Paramax SYQ-13 tactical navigation/command and control equipment, which integrates machinery and ship control, the minehunting sonar, the mine-neutralization system, inputs from the surface search radar, the precision navigation systems, and various environmental sensors. Other navigation equipment includes WRN-6 GPS terminal and Decca URN-30 Hyperfix radio navaid.
The ships have an Indal 3-drum winch capable of carrying 1,524 m of sweep cable on the main drum and 595 meters each on the other drums to stream and tow the SLQ-53 array.

♦ 4 Soviet Yurka-class (Project 266E) fleet minesweepers [MSF]

530 Giza 533 Aswan 536 Qena 539 Sohag

Sohag (539)—alongside a sister Chris Delgoffe/H&L Van Ginderen, 3-00

D: 400 tons light, 540 tons (fl) **S:** 16 kts **Dim:** 52.10 × 9.60 × 2.65
A: 2 twin 30-mm 65-cal. AK-230 AA; 2 mine rails (10 tot. mines)

MINE WARFARE SHIPS *(continued)*

Electronics:
Radar: 1 Don-2 nav.
Sonar: Tamir-11 (MG-11) hull-mounted searchlight (25–30 kHz)
M: 2 M-503B-3E diesels; 2 CP props; 5,000 bhp
Electric: 500 kw tot. (2 × 200-kw, 1 × 100-kw diesel sets)
Range: 600/16; 1,500/12 **Endurance:** 7 days **Crew:** 50 tot.

Remarks: Delivered new 1969. Plans to modernize with new MTU diesels, towed side-scan sonar, and remotely operated minehunting vehicles have been set aside, though at least one unit of the class has been sighted carrying an unknown Remotely Operated Vehicle. 536 was refitted during 2000.
Hull systems: Low magnetic signature, aluminum-steel alloy hull, with low magnetic signature machinery. Automatic-controlled degaussing equipment, with local coils around massive equipment. Special measures to reduce acoustic signature. Maximum sweep speed with arrays deployed is 14 kts.
Combat systems: Are intended to sweep mines in 25- to 150-m depths. Did not have the standard MR-104 Rys' (Drum Tilt) radar fire-control system. The sonar transducer is mounted in a large dome that can be hoisted within the hull.

♦ 4 Soviet T-43-class (Project 254K) fleet minesweepers [MSF]
(1 in *reserve*) (In serv. 1956–59)

507 Daqahliya 513 *Sinai*
510 Bahariya 516 Assiout

Assiout (516) M. Ottini, 3-98

D: 535 tons (569 fl) **S:** 14 kts **Dim:** 59.10 × 8.75 × 2.50
A: 2 twin 37-mm 63-cal. V-47M AA; 4 twin 12.7-mm mg; 2 BMB-1 d.c. mortars; 2 mine rails (20 tot. mines)
Electronics:
Radar: 1 Don-2 nav.
Sonar: 1 Stag Ear hull-mounted, active search and attack, HF
EW: 2 Watch Dog-A intercept (2–18 GHz)
M: 2 Type 9D diesels; 2 CP props; 2,200 bhp **Electric:** 550 kw tot.
Range: 1,500/14; 4,400/8.3 **Fuel:** 68 tons **Endurance:** 7 days
Crew: 5 officers, 48 enlisted

Remarks: Survivor of a group delivered in the early 1970s; all were of the early 1950s–built "short hull" version. Plans to modernize them with new engines, Gayrobot Pluto remote-controlled submersibles, and towed side-scan sonars have been abandoned. These ships are not equipped to deal with modern bottom mines. 507 and 510 were in refit as of 2000.

Disposal note: *Gharbiya* (501) and *Sharikya* (504) of this class had been decommissioned by 2002 and are currently being utilized for spare parts.

♦ 3 U.S. coastal minehunters [MHC]
Bldr: Swiftships, Morgan City, La.

	L	Del.	In serv.
542 Dat Assawari (ex-CMH 1)	4-10-93	25-4-94	13-7-97
545 Navarin (ex-CMH 2)	13-11-93	20-6-94	13-7-97
548 Burullus (ex-CMH 3)	4-12-93	30-7-94	13-7-97

Burullus (548) Bernard Prézelin collection, 2002

D: 175 tons (203 fl) **S:** 12.4 kts **Dim:** 33.53 (31.91 wl) × 8.23 (7.62 wl) × 2.24
A: 2 single 12.7-mm Browning M2 mg (I × 2)
Electronics:
Radar: 1 Sperry Rastar nav.
Sonar: Thales-Thoray TSM 2022 hull-mounted HF
M: 2 MTU 12V183 TE61 DB51L diesels; 2 Schottel SRP.300E Z-drives; 1,034 bhp—1 White Gill 300-shp thruster (4 kts)
Electric: 170 kw tot. (2 × 85-kw, 380/220-V a.c., 50-Hz sets)
Range: 2,000/10 **Fuel:** 26,500 liters **Crew:** 5 officers, 20 enlisted

Remarks: Ordered 12-90. GRP construction hull; design based on a successful fishing boat class by the same builder. Originally to have been a class of six. Also for use as route survey craft in peacetime. Delivered to Egyptian waters, two in 11-95 and one in 2-96.
Hull systems: Completed at considerably over the designed displacement, 188 tons. Electrical power at 380 and 220 V a.c., 50 Hz, and 24 V d.c.
Combat systems: Capable of mine neutralization in waters up to 100 m deep. Have Paramax integrated mine-countermeasures control system, a simplified version of the U.S. Navy's SYS-12 system. Navigational aids include GPS, Loran-C receiver, HF radio navaid, dynamic positioning system, doppler speed log, bathythermograph, gyrocompass. Sonars by Thoray, Lexington, Mass., a joint venture of the U.S. Raytheon and French Thomson-Sintra (now Thales) companies. Carry two Westinghouse-made Gayrobot Marine Pluto mine neutralization vehicles. Have a portable decompression chamber for mine clearance divers.

♦ 2 U.S. mine-route survey craft [MSA]
Bldr: Swiftships, Inc., Morgan City, La. (In serv. 1-10-94)

610 Safaga (ex-RSV 1) 613 Abu el-Ghoson (ex-RSV 2)

Safaga (610) Chris Delgoffe/H&L Van Ginderen, 3-00

D: 155.2 tons (165 fl) **S:** 12.4 kts **Dim:** 27.43 × 7.54 × 2.27
A: 1 12.7-mm Browning M2 mg
Electronics: Radar: 1 Furuno FR-2020 nav.—Sonar: EG&G side-scan VHF
M: 2 MTU 12V183 TE61 diesels; 2 props; 900 bhp—60-shp bow-thruster
Electric: 100 kw tot. (2 × 50-kw, 380/220-V a.c., 50-Hz sets)
Range: 1,500/10 **Fuel:** 22,710 liters **Crew:** 2 officers, 14 enlisted

Remarks: Ordered 11-90. GRP construction. Intended to survey harbor and coastal navigational channels during peacetime to chart bottom obstructions. Also equipped to stream Edo-Western 606A-602 shallow and 606A-604 deep tow-body side-scan sonars.

Note: Former U.S. Naval Reserve COOP-conversion route-survey craft ex-YP 663 and ex-YP 665 were transferred to Egypt in 1988, departing the U.S. as deck cargo on 20-12-88 for use as interim route-survey craft; they have likely been retired.

AMPHIBIOUS WARFARE SHIPS

♦ 3 Soviet Polnocny-A-class (Project 770) medium landing ships [LSM]
Bldr: Stocznia Polnocna, Gdansk, Poland

301 303 305

Polnocny-A-class 305—with sterns of two Vydra-class landing craft obscuring the stern at the right Chris Delgoffe/H&L Van Ginderen, 3-00

D: 704 tons std., 751 tons normal (770 tons fl) **S:** 18.5 kts
Dim: 73.00 (70.00 pp) × 8.62 × 0.90 fwd./1.85 aft

AMPHIBIOUS WARFARE SHIPS *(continued)*

A: 1 twin 30-mm 65-cal. AK-230 AA; 2 18-round 140-mm artillery RL (180 rockets)
Electronics: Radar: 1 Decca . . . nav.; 1 MR-104 Rys' (Drum Tilt) gun f.c.
M: 2 Kolomna Type 40DM diesels; 2 props; 4,000 bhp
Range: 900/18; 1,500/14 **Endurance:** 5 days **Crew:** 4 officers, 38 enlisted

Remarks: Transferred 1974. Cargo capacity is 350 tons or six main battle tanks and 180 troops.

♦ 9 ex-Soviet Vydra-class (Project 106K) utility landing craft [LCU] Bldr: Kherson SY, Russia (In serv. 1967–69)

330 332 334 336 338 340 342 344 346

Vydra-class 344—with single 40-mm AA guns
Chris Delgoffe/H&L Van Ginderen, 6-00

D: 425 tons standard; 600 tons (fl) **S:** 10.5 kts **Dim:** 54.5 × 7.7 × 2.4
A: 2 single 40-mm 60-cal. Bofors Mk 3 AA; or 2 twin 37-mm 63-cal. AA
Electronics: Radar: 1 Decca . . . nav.
M: 2 Type 3D12 diesels; 2 props; 600 bhp
Range: 1,500/10 **Crew:** 20, plus 100 troops

Remarks: Built new for Egypt. Some (including 332 and 338) have twin 37-mm 63-cal. Soviet VM-47 AA vice 40-mm; guns removed altogether in others, as have been the BM-21, 122-mm artillery rocket launchers mounted in several units of the class during the 1970s. Cargo: 260 tons.

♦ 6 U.S. Seafox-class swimmer delivery craft
Bldr: Uniflite, Bellingham, Wash. (In serv. 1982–83)

21 23 25 27 28 30

D: 11.3 tons (fl) **S:** 30 kts **Dim:** 11.0 × 3.0 × 0.84
A: 2 single 12.7-mm Browning M2 mg; 2 single 7.62-mm M-60 mg
Electronics: Radar: 1 Canadian Marconi LN-66 nav.
M: 2 G.M. Detroit Diesel 6V92 TA diesels; 2 props; 900 bhp **Crew:** 3 tot.

Remarks: Survivors of 10 originally acquired. Ordered 1982. Glass-reinforced plastic construction. Based at Aboukir. 25 and 28 were undergoing refit during 2006.

AUXILIARIES

♦ 1 ex-German Type 760 ammunition ship [AE]
Bldr: Orenstein & Koppel, Lübeck

	Laid down	L	In serv.
231 HALAIB (ex-*Odenwald,* A 1436)	3-11-65	5-5-66	23-3-67

Halaib (231)—ex-German ammunition ship Frank Findler, 4-03

D: 3,460 tons (4,014 fl) **S:** 17 kts **Dim:** 105.27 × 14.02 × 3.70 (4.50 max.)
A: Removed **Electronics:** Radar: 1 Kelvin-Hughes 14/9 nav.
M: 2 Maybach MD 874 diesels; 2 CP props; 5,600 bhp—bow-thruster
Electric: 1,285 kw tot. **Range:** 3,500/17 **Crew:** 31 tot.

Remarks: Was to have been stricken on 19-12-01 from the German Navy but was extended in service until 2-03 and was finally transferred to Egypt 4-4-03. Cargo: 1,080 tons. Two 3-ton electric cranes are fitted, as well as three lighter-capacity cargo booms. Originally had two twin 40-mm and two lead-computing directors, which have been removed.

Halaib (231) Frank Findler, 4-03

♦ 1 presidential yacht [AG]
Bldr: Samuda, Poplar, U.K. (In serv. 1865)

EL HORRIA (ex-*Mahroussa*)

El Horria Chris Delgoffe/H&L Van Ginderen, 3-00

D: 4,561 tons (fl) **S:** 16 kts **Dim:** 145.64 (128.02 wl, 121.92 pp) × 13.03 × 5.26
M: 3 sets geared steam turbines; 3 props; 5,500 bhp
Boilers: 5 Inglis watertube **Fuel:** 346 tons **Crew:** 160 tot.

Remarks: Had been retired by the mid-1980s, but was reactivated in 1992. Available for training, presidential yacht, and barracks duties. Iron hull construction. One of the world's oldest active naval ships. Had been converted to steam turbine propulsion at Glasgow in 1905.

♦ 1 ex-German Type 701E replenishment ship [AOR]
Bldr: Flensburger Werft

	Laid down	L	In serv.
230 SHALATEIN (ex-*Glücksburg,* A 1414)	18-8-65	3-5-66	9-7-68

Shalatein (230)—ex-German replenishment ship Frank Findler, 4-03

Shalatein (230) Frank Findler, 4-03

D: 3,680 tons (fl) **S:** 17 kts **Dim:** 118.30 × 13.22 × 4.29
A: 2 twin 40-mm 70-cal. Bofors AA

AUXILIARIES *(continued)*

Electronics:
Radar: 1 Kelvin-Hughes 14/9 nav.—EW: Thales DR 2000S intercept
M: 2 MTU type MD 16V538 TB 90 diesels; 2 CP props; 5,600 bhp; 1 Bow thruster
Electric: 1,935 kw tot. **Range:** 3,000/17; 3,200/14 **Crew:** 71 tot.

Remarks: Was decommissioned on 19-12-01 but kept in service until 2-02, pending transfer to Egypt in early 2003. Converted 1981–84 to support Type 122 frigates and is equipped with helicopter facilities to permit vertical replenishment, space for nine spare Harpoon missiles, repair facilities for Mk 88 Lynx helicopters, and new articulated cranes. Equipped with fin stabilizers. The original twin Bofors L70 mount aft was fully operational in 1996 and had a Bofors lead-computing director aboard in a state of preservation. The forward mount was removed between 1993 and 1995. Cargo capacity is 1,100 tons which includes 640 tons of fuel, which can be trans. from stations on either beam forward, 200 tons of ammunition and 100 tons of spare parts.

♦ 1 El Hurreya–class troop transport [AP]
Bldr: Alexandria Shipyard, Egypt

	Laid down	L	In serv.
. . . El Hurreya	2002	27-01-04	2006

D: 6,000 tons (fl) **S:** . . . kts **Dim:** . . . × . . . × . . .
A: . . .
Electronics: Radar: 1 . . . nav.
M: 2 diesels; 2 props; . . . bhp
Range: 8,600/ . . . **Crew:** 71 tot., 9 officers, 62 enlisted

Remarks: 9,800 grt ships for which a project management contract with MPC Marine, Germany, was signed during 4-02; will carry troops and vehicles. An option was included for a second unit, but not taken up.

♦ 2 . . . class oceangoing tugs [ATA]
Bldr: . . . (In serv. 2000)

113 . . . 115 . . .

Oceangoing tug 113 Guigné via A. D. Baker III, 1-02

Remarks: Two former commercial oilfield tug-supply vessels were operating from Alexandria as of 2002, probably in place of retired Okhtenskiy-class tugs. Larger than the Okhtenskiys and are equipped for firefighting and for handling divers over the starboard side.

♦ 5 Soviet Okhtenskiy-class oceangoing tugs [ATA]
Bldr: Petrozavod SY, St. Petersburg, Russia

103 Al Maks	107 Antar	111 Al Iskandarani
105 Al Agami	109 Al Dikhila	

Al Dikhila (109) Stefan Karpinski, 2-03

D: 663 tons light (926 fl) **S:** 13.3 kts **Dim:** 47.3 (43.0 pp) × 10.3 × 5.5
Electronics:
Radar: 1–2 Don-2 or Mius (Spin Trough) nav.
M: diesel-electric: 2 Type D5D50 diesels; 1 prop; 1,500 shp **Electric:** 340 kw
Range: 6,000/13; 7,800/7 **Fuel:** 197 tons **Crew:** 38 tot.

Remarks: Two transferred complete in 1966. The remaining units were built in Egypt at Alexandria Naval Dockyard from components built at St. Petersburg. Bollard pull: 27 tons initial, 17 sustained. *Kalir* (113) had retired by 2003.

Disposal note: Former British Z-class destroyer *El Fateh* (921; ex-*Zenith*, ex-*Wessex*) and former British *Black Swan*–class patrol ship *Tariq* (931; ex-*Maleh Farouk*, ex-*Whimbrel*), both employed in recent years as stationary training platforms [AXT], have been retired. In 2003, the British Historic Warship Preservation Society agreed to purchase *Tariq* for use as a memorial and museum.

SERVICE CRAFT

♦ 1 Soviet Nyryat'-I-class diving tender [YDT]

146

D: 92 tons (116.1 fl) **S:** 11 kts **Dim:** 28.58 × 5.20 × 1.70
Electronics: Radar: 1 Mius (Spin Trough) nav.
M: 1 Type 6CSP 28/3C diesel; 1 prop; 450 bhp
Range: 1,500/10 **Crew:** 15 tot.

Remarks: Transferred 1964. One sister stricken 1991. The charthouse/laboratory is 6 m^2, and there are two 1.5-ton derricks.

♦ 9 Soviet Toplivo-2-class coastal-transport tankers [YO]
Bldr: Alexandria SY, Egypt (In serv. 1972–77)

210 Ayeda 4	213 Al Nil	216 Ayeda 3
211 Maryut	214 Akdu	218 El Burullus
212 Al Furat	215 Atbarah	222 ...

Toplivo-2-class diving tender Stefan Karpinski, 2-03

D: 466 tons (1,180 fl) **S:** 10 kts **Dim:** 54.26 (49.40 pp) × 9.40 × 3.40 max.
Electronics: Radar: 1 Mius (Spin Trough) nav.
M: 1 Russkiy Dizel 6 DR 30/50-5-2 diesel; 1 prop; 600 bhp
Electric: 250 kw **Range:** 1,500/10 **Fuel:** 19 tons **Crew:** 16 tot.

Remarks: 308 grt/508 dwt. Part of a series of 26 ordered in Egypt for the USSR prior to that country's expulsion. Cargo: 606 m^3 (500 tons diesel oil); some are used as water tankers. Other names reported (not correlated to hull numbers) are *Dina, El Porat,* and *Karun.* Sister *Al Mazilla* (217) was reported stricken in 1997. In 2002, one of the class was seen with the pennant number 222.

♦ 1 Soviet Poluchat-I-class torpedo retriever [YPT]

937

D: 84.7 tons (92.8 fl) **S:** 21.6 kts **Dim:** 29.60 × 5.98 × 1.56 (hull)
A: Removed
Electronics: Radar: 1 Mius (Spin Trough) nav.
M: 2 M-50F-4 diesels; 2 props; 1,700 bhp **Electric:** 14 kw tot.
Range: 250/21.6; 550/14; 900/10 **Crew:** 3 officers, 12 enlisted

Note: Completed in 1970. One sister had been stricken by 2003.

♦ 1 naval academy navigational training ship [YXT]

El Kousser (ex-*El Emir Fawzia*)

Remarks: No data available other than that she is said to be of 1,000 tons displacement.

♦ 1 Soviet Sekstan-class training tender [YXT]
Bldr: Laivateolissus SY, Turku, Finland (In serv. 1953–57)

160

D: 280 tons (400 fl) **S:** 9 kts **Dim:** 40.6 × 9.3 × 4.3
Electronics: Radar: 1 Don-2 or Mius (Spin Trough) nav.
M: 1 diesel; 1 prop; 400 bhp
Range: 8,000/9 **Endurance:** 37 days **Crew:** 24 tot. + cadets

Remarks: Wooden construction former degaussing tender, built in mid-1950s. Now used as a training craft at the naval academy.

♦ 1 500-ton naval academy training yacht [YXT]

Intisar (ex-*Fakir el Bihar*)

Remarks: Former yacht, attached to the naval academy.

Note: Several naval tugs operate at the Alexandria base, including two surplus U.S. *Natick*-class large harbor tugs that were acquired in 1989.

SERVICE CRAFT *(continued)*

Intisar Chris Delgoffe/H&L Van Ginderen, 3-00

COAST GUARD

Note: The coast guard is a branch of the naval service in Egypt. Its personnel are included in the total listed above. During 2-02, Lockheed Martin was given a contract to develop a fully integrated maritime safety system for the Gulf of Suez area, with 6 patrol boats and three motor lifeboats to be delivered by 2007.

PATROL CRAFT [WPC]

♦ **3 Type 83 class**
Bldr: Osman Shipyard, Ismalia, Egypt (In serv. 1996–97)

46, 47, and 54

D: 85 tons (fl) **S:** 24 kts **Dim:** 25.5 × 6.5 × 1.7
A: 1 twin 23-mm 60-cal. AA; 1 20-mm 90-cal. GAM-B01 Oerlikon AA
Electronics: Radar: 1 Furuno . . . nav.
M: 2 diesels; 2 props; . . . bhp **Crew:** 12 tot.

Remarks: First two reported in service 13-7-97; may be locally built version of the following class.

Disposal note: Type 83–class sisters 48–53 are no longer in service.

♦ **9 U.S. Commercial Cruiser design**
Bldrs: 35–37: Swiftships, Morgan City, La.; others: Osman Ahmed Osman & Co., Ismailia, Egypt. (In serv.: 35–37: 15-1-85; 38: 9-9-85; 39: 24-10-85; 40: 24-11-85; others: 1986)

35 36 37 38 39 40 41 42 43

Commercial Cruiser 37 French Navy, 4-99

D: 102 tons (fl) **S:** 27 kts **Dim:** 28.30 × 5.66 × 1.60
A: 1 twin 23-mm 60-cal. AA; 1 14.5-mm 90-cal. 2M-8 AA
Electronics: Radar: 1 Furuno . . . nav.
M: 2 MTU 12V331 TC92 diesels; 2 props; 2,660 bhp
Range: 1,000/12 **Fuel:** 11.7 tons **Crew:** 2 officers, 12 enlisted

Remarks: Ordered 11-83. First three built in U.S.; remainder assembled in Egypt from U.S.-supplied components. Steel construction. Original armament of one 20-mm and one 12.7-mm guns has been replaced by surplus Soviet-made weapons, with 23-mm guns replacing the original 25-mm 80-cal. guns.

♦ **15 Timsah-II class**
Bldr: Timsah SY, Ismailia (In serv. 1988–89)

07 TIMSAH 7 through 021 TIMSAH 21

D: 99 tons (106 fl) **S:** 27 kts (24 sust.) **Dim:** 28.35 × 5.66 × 1.50
A: 2 single 20-mm 90-cal. Oerlikon GAM-B01 AA
Electronics: Radar: . . .

Timsah-II class—number 19 Ben Queun via Paolo Marsan, 4-05

M: 2 MTU 12V331 TC92 diesels; 2 props; 2,660 bhp
Range: 600/ . . . **Fuel:** 10 tons **Crew:** 13 tot.

Remarks: Revised version of original *Timsah* class, with different engines and waterline exhausts vice stack. Ordered 1-85.

♦ **5 Timsah class**
Bldr: Timsah SY, Alexandria (In serv. 1981–84)

01 02 04 05 06

D: 100 tons (fl) **S:** 25 kts **Dim:** 29.0 × 5.2 × 1.48
A: 1 single 20-mm 90-cal. Oerlikon GAM-B01 AA
Electronics: Radar: 1 Decca nav.
M: 2 MTU 8V331 diesels; 2 props; 2,960 bhp
Range: 600/. . . **Fuel:** 10 tons **Crew:** 13 tot.

Remarks: First unit laid down 1-1-80, launched 11-81, delivered 12-81. Sister *Timsah 3* (03) lost 1993.

PATROL BOATS [WPB]

♦ **3 47-foot Motor Life Boat class [WPB]**
Bldr: Textron Marine and Land Systems, New Orleans, La. (In serv. 2004)

D: 17.9 tons (fl) **S:** 25 kts (20 sust.) **Dim:** 14.61 × 4.27 × 1.40 (0.80 hull)
Electronics: Radar: 1 Raytheon R41X AN/SPS-69 nav.
M: 2 G.M. Detroit Diesel 6V92 TA diesels; 2 props; 840 bhp
Range: 220/25; 208/10 **Fuel:** 1,560 liters **Crew:** 4 tot. plus 5 survivors

Remarks: Ordered 26-8-02 under a subcontract from Lockheed Martin for Gulf of Suez search-and-rescue service. The U.S. and Canadian Coast Guards have well over 100 in service
Hull systems: Aluminum construction, with deep-vee, self-righting hull form. Trials in heavy seas were highly successful; can maintain 20 kts in 2-ft. seas and tow craft displacing up to 150 tons. Capable of operating in 80-kt gales with 9-m swells and 6-m breaking seas.

♦ **3 48-foot Patrol Craft Coastal (PCC) class**
Bldr: Peterson Bldrs., Sturgeon Bay, Wisc. (In serv. 1996)

80 81 82

D: 20 tons (fl) **S:** 32 kts **Dim:** 14.77 × 3.96 × 0.86
A: 2 single 12.7-mm M2 mg
Electronics: Radar: 1 Raytheon . . . nav.
M: 2 MTU 8V183 TE92 diesels; 2 Hamilton 362 waterjets; 1,314 bhp
Range: 300/30 **Crew:** 4 tot.

Remarks: Aluminum construction. Used primarily as pilot boats.

♦ **9 45-foot Patrol Craft Coastal (PCC) class**
Bldr: Peterson Bldrs., Sturgeon Bay, Wisc. (In serv. 6-95)

71 through 79

Peterson 45-ft. patrol boats Peterson Builders, 1995

PATROL BOATS [WPB] *(continued)*

D: 18 tons (17.7 fl) **S:** 34 kts **Dim:** 13.86 × 3.96 × 0.86
A: 2 single 12.7-mm M2 mg
Electronics: Radar: 1 Raytheon 40X nav.
M: 2 MTU 8V183 TE92 diesels; 2 Hamilton 362 waterjets; 1,314 bhp
Range: 200/30 **Fuel:** 490 gallons **Crew:** 4 tot.

Remarks: Aluminum construction. Standard U.S. Navy export design. Can be transported on trailers. Sisters serve the Albanian Navy.

♦ 5 modified Soviet P-6 class (Project 183)

701 Thar — 713 Nisr — . . . Al Bahr
703 Nur — 719 Nimr

D: 56 tons (66.5 fl) **S:** 45 kts **Dim:** 25.90 × 6.24 × 1.24 hull (1.70 props)
A: 2 twin 23-mm 60-cal. AA **Electronics:** Radar: 1 Decca 1226 nav.
M: 4 M-50F-4 diesels; 4 props; 4,800 bhp **Electric:** 100 kw tot.
Range: 600/33; 1,000/14 **Fuel:** 7.2 tons **Crew:** 16 tot.

Remarks: Survivors of some 20 torpedo boats transferred during the early 1960s. Wooden construction. All had been laid up by 1985, but these five were reported back in service as of 1991. They may, in fact, have new hulls built at the Alexandria Naval Dockyard, and the engines may be Italian CRM 12D/SS diesels vice the original equipment listed here. The former twin 25-mm 2M-3M gunmounts have been adapted for Egyptian-made guns. No longer carry a BM-21 122-mm artillery rocket launcher aft.

♦ 6 small patrol craft
Bldr: Swiftships, Inc., Morgan City, La. (In serv. 2006–7)

D: . . . tons **S:** 40 kts **Dim:** 25 × . . . × . . .
A: 2 7.62-mm machineguns
M: 1 diesel; one prop; . . . bhp **Crew:** 12 tot.

Remarks: Ordered in 9-04 as part of the Gulf of Suez Maritime Safety Improvement Project.

♦ 6 MV70 class, GRP-hulled
Bldr: Crestitalia, Ameglia (La Spezia), Italy (In serv. 1981–82)

D: 33 tons (41.5 fl) **S:** 35 kts **Dim:** 21.0 × 5.2 × 0.9
A: 1 twin 30-mm 75-cal. Oerlikon A32; 1 20-mm 70 cal. Oerlikon AA; 2 single 12.7-mm mg
M: 2 MTU 12V331 TC92 diesels; 2 props; 2,800 bhp **Range:** 500/32

♦ 29 DC-35 class
Bldr: Dawncraft, Wroxham, U.K. (In serv. 1977)

DC-35 class — Maritime Photographic, 2-97

D: 4 tons (fl) **S:** 25 kts **Dim:** 10.7 × 3.5 × 0.8
M: 2 Perkins T6-354 diesels; 2 props; 390 bhp **Crew:** 4 tot.

Remarks: GRP construction. For harbor police duties. One lost 9-94.

Note: Also reported to be in service are the harbor tugs *Ajmi* and *Jihad,* delivered in 1988 and small harbor tugs *Khafra, Khoufou, Krier,* and *Ramse* delivered in 1982 by Damen, Gorinchem, the Netherlands.

CUSTOMS SERVICE

PATROL BOATS [WPB]

♦ 12 U.S. Sea Spectre PB Mk III class
Bldr: Peterson Builders, Sturgeon Bay, Wisc. (In serv. 1980–81)

D: 28 tons (36.7 fl) **S:** 30 kts **Dim:** 19.78 × 5.50 × 1.80 (props)
A: 2 single 12.7-mm mg **Electronics:** Radar: 1 Raytheon … nav.
M: 3 G.M. Detroit Diesel 8V71 TI diesels; 3 props; 1,800 bhp
Range: 450/26 **Endurance:** 3 days
Crew: 1 officer, 8 noncommissioned

EL SALVADOR
Republic of El Salvador

FUERZA NAVAL DE EL SALVADOR

Personnel: About 700 total, including 90 naval infantry.

Bases: Acajutla, La Libertad, La Unión, and El Triunfo

Maritime Aviation: The Salvadorean Air Force uses Cessna O-2 and Douglas C-47 fixed-wing aircraft for coastal surveillance and also has a flight of UH-1H helicopters that support the *Fuerza Naval.* The maritime support aircraft are operated from El Tamarindo near La Unión and at the Comalapa Air Force Base.

Note: The pennant number prefixes were changed during 5-01, with PM indicating *Patrulla Maritima,* PC for *Patrullera Costera,* PF for *Patrullera Fluvial,* PFR for *Patrulla Fluvial Rapida,* and BD for *Buque de Desembarco.*

PATROL SHIP [PS]

♦ 1 ex-U.S. Coast Guard Balsam class
Bldr: Zenith Dredge Co., Duluth, Minn.

	Laid down	L	In serv.
BL-01 Gral. Manuel José Arcé (ex-*Madrona,* WLB 302)	6-7-42	11-11-42	30-5-43

Gral. Manuel José Arcé — Julio Montes, 7-02

D: 697 tons light (1,038 fl) **S:** 12.8–13 kts **Dim:** 54.9 (51.8 pp) × 11.3 × 4.0
A: 2 single 12.7-mm M2 mg
Electronics: Radar: 1 Hughes-Furuno SPS-73 nav.
M: 2 diesels, electric drive; 1 prop; 1,200 shp
Range: 4,600/12: 14,000/7.4
Electric: 400 kw tot. **Crew:** 6 officers, 47 enlisted

Remarks: Was transferred on 4-12-02, having been decommissioned from the U.S. Coast Guard the same date. Acts as flagship of the navy and is used as an offshore patrol vessel. Sturdy construction, many years' service remaining despite advanced age. Former navigational aids tender, equipped with a 20-ton buoy-handling derrick and equipped with a large cargo hold. A second unit of the class, to be used as a base ship for small patrol boats, is sought.

PATROL CRAFT [PC]

Note: A contract for the construction of two 32-m *Protector*-class patrol craft by ASMAR, Valparaiso, Chile, was canceled during 2001.

♦ 3 aluminum-hulled
Bldr: Camcraft, Crown Point, La.

PM-6 (In serv. 24-10-75) — PM-7 (In serv. 3-12-75) — PM-8 (In serv. 11-75)

PATROL CRAFT [PC] *(continued)*

PM-7—on land for maintenance Julio Montes, 9-00

D: 100 tons (fl) **S:** 25 kts **Dim:** 30.5 × 6.4 × 1.5
A: GC-6 only: 1 twin 12.7-mm mg—GC-7, GC-8: 2 single 12.7-mm M2HB mg—all: 1 81-mm mortar
Electronics: Radar: 1 Furuno . . .
M: 3 G.M. 12V71 TI diesels; 3 props; 1,200 bhp **Range:** 780/24
Crew: 15 tot.

Remarks: Rebuilt 1985–86 by Lantana Boatyard, Lantana, Fla.; deckhouse extended 6 m, new radar, new radios. When purchased, had operated for several years as commercial oilfield crewboats in the Gulf of Mexico.

PATROL BOATS [PB]

Note: Two 12.19-m (40-ft.) patrol boats were acquired during early 2001; no data available.

♦ **1 U.S. 77-foot Commercial Cruiser class**
Bldr: Swiftships, Morgan City, La. (In serv. 6-5-85)

PM-11

PM-11 COPREFA. via Julio Montes, 12-94

D: 48 tons (fl) **S:** 26 kts **Dim:** 23.47 × 6.10 × 1.52
A: 1 twin 12.7-mm mg; 2 single 12.7-mm mg; 1 81-mm mortar
Electronics: Radar: 1 Furuno . . . nav.
M: 3 G.M. 12V71 TI diesels; 3 props; 1,800 bhp
Range: 600/18 **Fuel:** 7,600 liters **Crew:** 10 tot.

Remarks: Aluminum construction.

♦ **1 U.S. 65-foot Commercial Cruiser class**
Bldr: Swiftships, Morgan City, La. (In serv. 14-6-84)

PM-10

D: 36 tons (fl) **S:** 23 kts **Dim:** 19.96 × 5.59 × 1.52
A: 2 single 12.7-mm M2HB mg; 1 81-mm mortar
Electronics: Radar: 1 Furuno . . . nav.
M: 2 G.M. 12V71 TI diesels; 2 props; 1,350 bhp (1,200 sust.)
Electric: 20 kw tot. **Range:** 500/18 **Crew:** 6 tot.

Remarks: Aluminum construction. Out of service by 1989, but has been repaired and reactivated.

PM-10 Julio Montes, 10-93

♦ **1 ex-U.S. Coast Guard 82-foot Point class**
Bldr: J. Martinac SB, Tacoma, Wash. (In serv. 17-3-67)

PM-12 (ex-*Point Stuart,* WPB 82358)

PM-12 V. Lemonos via Boris Lemachko, 10-03

D: 64 tons (66 fl) **S:** 23.7 kts **Dim:** 25.3 × 5.23 × 1.95
A: 1 twin 12.7-mm M2 mg
Electronics: Radar: 1 Hughes-Furuno SPS-73 nav.
M: 2 Caterpillar 3412 diesels; 2 props; 1,480 bhp
Range: 490/23.7; 1,500/8 **Fuel:** 5.7 tons **Crew:** 1 officer, 7 enlisted

Remarks: Transferred by grant on 26-4-01. Hull built of mild steel. High-speed diesels controlled from the bridge. Has a 4.27-m Avon Searider rigid-inflatable boat powered by a 40-bhp outboard engine.

Disposal note: The two Mercougar coastal interceptor boats had been discarded by 5-01.

♦ **9 Protector class**
Bldr: SeaArk, Monticello, Ark. (In serv. 1988–89)

PC-0301 through PC-0310 series

D: 8.9 tons (fl) **S:** 28 kts **Dim:** 12.40 (11.13 wl) × 3.04 × 0.53 (hull)
A: 2 single 12.7-mm mg; 2 single 7.62-mm mg; 6 M-16 rifles
Electronics: Radar: 1 Furuno 2400 nav.
M: 2 Caterpillar 3208TA diesels; 2 props; 690 bhp
Range: 575/20 **Fuel:** 1,993 liters **Crew:** 6 tot.

Remarks: Formerly operated by the naval infantry. Aluminum construction. Two had been discarded by 1998, but one of those had been restored to service by 2001.

PATROL BOATS [PB] *(continued)*

Protector-class unit Julio Montes, 2002

♦ **5 Piranha-class riverine**
Bldr: Lantana Boatyard, Lantana, Fla. (In serv. 2-87)

From among: PF-01 through PF-06

Three Piranha-class patrol boats—LOF-022 at right Julio Montes, 2-96

D: 9 tons (fl) **S:** 26 kts (22 sust.) **Dim:** 12.19 × 3.05 × 0.53
A: 2 single 12.7-mm mg; 2 single 7.62-mm mg; 1 60-mm mortar
Electronics: Radar: 1 Furuno 3600 nav.
M: 2 Caterpillar 3208 TA diesels; 2 props; 630 bhp
Endurance: 5 days **Crew:** 5 tot.

Remarks: Aluminum construction with Kevlar plastic armor. Lengthened version of eight-unit class built for Honduras, 1986. Operated by the marines. Two had been discarded by 1998.

Note: During 1998 two prototype riverine patrol boats were completed using modified drop tanks from C-123K Provider transport aircraft; armed with one 7.62-mm M-60D and two single 5.56-mm M-249 light machineguns, the camouflage-painted, trailer-transportable craft are powered by a single Mercury outboard engine and have a crew of three. One craft uses only the drop tanks for flotation, while the other has a central, wooden hull in addition. Also in use at the end of 2001 was a single Delta RIB, donated by Taiwan.

AMPHIBIOUS CRAFT

♦ **3 U.S. LCM(8)-class landing craft [LCM]**

BD-02 BD-04 BD-05

BD-05 Julio Montes, 11-04

D: 34 tons light (121 fl) **S:** 12 kts **Dim:** 22.43 × 6.40 × 1.40 (aft)
A: 2 single 12.7-mm mg **Electronics:** Radar: 1 Furuno 2400 nav.
M: 4 G.M. 6-71 diesels; 2 props; 590 bhp
Range: 150/12 **Cargo:** 58 tons or 120 troops **Crew:** 6 tot.

Remarks: Two transferred in 1987 (of which LD-03 was lost) and two in 1996 (recommissioned 7-6-96).

♦ **10 airboat shallow-draft personnel launches [WLCP]**

PFR 01 through PFR 10

Remarks: Rectangular, aluminum-hulled craft powered by a single gasoline engine driving a five-bladed airscrew. Have seating for operator and eight troops.

Note: For use by army special forces personnel, four small outboard-powered Zodiac RIBs have been acquired; the navy uses another four.

SERVICE CRAFT

♦ **4 ex-U.S. Coast Guard 44-foot motor life boat–class lifeboats [WYH]** Bldr: U.S.C.G. Yard, Curtis Bay, Md. (In serv. 31-3-61 to 8-5-73)

PRM-01 PRM-02 PRM-03 PRM-04

PRM-04—in front of an LCM(8)-class landing craft Julio Montes, 11-04

D: 14.9 tons light (17.7 fl) **S:** 13 kts (11.8 sust.) **Dim:** 13.44 × 3.87 × 1.19
Electronics: Radar: 1 JRC . . . nav.
M: 2 G.M. Detroit Diesel 6V53 diesels; 2 props; 372 bhp
Range: 185/11.8; 200/11 **Fuel:** 1.2 tons **Crew:** 4 tot.

Remarks: Transferred 2001. "Unsinkable" design. Can carry up to 21 rescued personnel.

MINISTRY OF PUBLIC SECURITY
POLICE MARITIME UNIT

Note: Established 28-3-99, with training for personnel commenced 11-98 by the navy. Craft are tasked with customs and security patrols along the Jaltepeque and Costa del Sol, La Paz Province, and will later be extended.

♦ **10 Rodman 800–class harbor launches [WPB]**
Bldr: Rodman Polyship S.A., Vigo, Spain (In serv. 1999)

L-01-01 through L-01-10

Rodman patrol launch L-01-10 Julio Montes, 2000

D: 9 tons (fl) **S:** 30 kts **Dim:** 8.9 × 3.0 × 0.80
A: small arms **Electronics:** Radar: 1 Raytheon . . . nav.
M: 2 Volvo Penta outdrive diesels; 300 bhp
Range: 150/25 **Crew:** 3 tot.

Remarks: Cost $100,000 each. Armament consists only of crew's Galil semiautomatic rifles. GRP construction. Class also used by the Chilean Coast Guard.

EQUATORIAL GUINEA

Republic of Equatorial Guinea

Personnel: Approx. 120 total

Note: Craft are based at Malabo on the island of Bioko and at Bata on the mainland at Río Muni.

PATROL BOATS [PB]

♦ **1 68-foot U.S.-built** (nonoperational)
Bldr: Lantana Boatyard, Lantana, Fla.

	Laid down	L	In serv.
037 *Isla de Bioko*	3-87	3-88	5-88

D: 33 tons (fl) **S:** 24 kts (28 trials) **Dim:** 20.73 × 5.50 × 1.50
A: 1 12.7-mm M2 mg; 2 single 7.62-mm mg
Electronics: Radar: 1 Furuno 3600 nav.
M: 2 G.M. Detroit Diesel 8V92 TI diesels; 2 props; 1,170 bhp
Range: 800/15 **Crew:** 2 officers, 10 enlisted

Remarks: Aluminum construction; delivered unpainted. Paid for by U.S. Grant-Aid program. A planned, larger ship from the same builder was not funded.

♦ **2 ex-Russian Zhuk (Gryf) class (Project 1400A or 1400M)**
Bldr: Morye Zavod, Feodosiya

039 Miguel Ela Edjodjomo
041 Hipolito Micha

D: 35.9 tons (39.7 fl) **S:** 30 kts
Dim: 23.80 (21.70 wl) × 5.00 (3.80 wl) × 1.00 (hull; 1.90 max.)
A: 1 twin 12.7-mm 60-cal. Utës-Ma mg
Electronics: Radar: 1 Lotsiya nav.
M: Project 1400M: 2 M-401 diesels; 2 props; 2,200 bhp; Project 1400A: 2 M-50F4 diesels; 2 props; 2,400 bhp
Electric: 48 kw total (2 × 21 kw, 1 × 6 kw diesel sets)
Endurance: 5 days **Range:** 500/13.5 **Crew:** 1 officer, 9 enlisted

Remarks: Transferred from the Ukraine during 2000. Units of this class were built between 1971 and 1994. Aluminum alloy hull; capable of operating in up to Sea State 4 or 5. Range also reported as 700 n.m. at 28 knots, 1,100 n.m. at 15 kts.

♦ **2 ex-Ukraine Kalkan class (Project 50030)**
Bldr: Morye Feodosiya Production Association

043 Gaspar Obiang Esono
045 Ferdando Nuara Engonda

D: 7 tons (fl) **S:** 30 kts **Dim:** 10.6 × 3.3 × 0.6
A: Small arms **Electronics:** Radar: none
M: 1 Type 457K diesel; 1 waterjet; 496 bhp (442 bhp sust.)
Range: 254/ . . . **Crew:** 2 + 6 passengers

Remarks: Built during the late 1990s and transferred from Ukraine during 2001, Aluminum hulls with GRP superstructures.

♦ **1 ex-Nigerian P/20 class** (nonoperational)
Bldr: Van Mill Marine Service, Hardinxveld-Giessendam, the Netherlands (In serv. 17-1-86)

Riowele (ex-P 220)

D: 45 tons (fl) **S:** 32.5 kts **Dim:** 20.26 (18.00 wl) × 5.30 × 1.75
A: 1 20-mm 90-cal. Rheinmetall AA; 2 single 7.62-mm mg
Electronics: Radar: 1 Decca . . . nav.
M: 2 MTU 6V331 TC82 diesels; 2 props; 2,250 bhp
Range: 950/25; 1,200/11 **Crew:** 2 officers, 10 enlisted

Remarks: Transferred as a gift from Nigeria 27-6-86. GRP construction.

ERITREA

Republic of Eritrea

Personnel: Approx. 1,400 total

Base: Massawa on mainland and Dahlak Islands, with access to Djibouti for repairs

PATROL CRAFT [PC]

♦ **3 U.S. 104-foot Commercial Cruiser class**
Bldr: Swiftships, Morgan City, La. (In serv. 4-77)

P-201 P-203 P-204

D: 118 tons (fl) **S:** 32 kts **Dim:** 31.73 × 7.10 × 2.16
A: 2 twin 23-mm ZSU-23 AA; 2 single 12.7-mm mg
Electronics: Radar: 1 Decca RM 916 nav.
M: 2 MTU MB 16V538 TB90 diesels; 2 props; 7,000 bhp
Range: 1,000/18 **Crew:** 21 tot.

Remarks: Purchased 1996 from among former Ethiopian Navy units at Djibouti. Retained original pennant numbers. P-201 is armed with two twin Emerlec EX-30, 30-mm AA. Aluminum construction.

PATROL BOATS [PB]

♦ **5 (+ ?) . . . class 17-meter patrol boats**
Bldr: Harena Boat Yard, Assab, Ethiopia (In serv. 2000–2001)

P-084 P-085 P-086 P-087 P-088

D: 35.5 tons **S:** 35 kts **Dim:** 17.1 × 5.2 × 1.6
A: 1 twin 23-mm ZSU-23 AA; 2 single 12.7-mm mg
Electronics: Radar: 1 . . . nav.
M: 2 MTU . . . diesels; 2 props
Range: 680/30 **Crew:** 8

Remarks: Additional units are planned.

♦ **6 Israeli Super Dvora class**
Bldr: RAMTA-Israeli Aircraft Industries, Be'er Sheva (In serv. 1994)

P-111 P-112 P-113 P-114 P-115 P-116

D: 48 tons (54 fl) **S:** 36–46 kts **Dim:** 22.40 × 5.49 × 1.00
A: 2 single 20-mm 70-cal. Oerlikon AA; 2 single 12.7-mm mg
Electronics: Radar: 1 Raytheon . . . nav.
M: 3 G.M. Detroit Diesel 16V92 TA diesels; 3 Arneson surface-piercing props; 2,070 bhp
Electric: 30 kw **Range:** 700/14 **Crew:** 1 officer, 8 enlisted

Remarks: Transferred in pairs 12-93, 3-94, and 6-94. Aluminum construction. All based at Massawa.

♦ **15–20 small launches**

Remarks: Small, 4.5- to 6.0-m, GRP-hulled craft with twin 75-bhp outboard motor propulsion and 12.7- or 14.5-mm machineguns and small artillery rocket launchers for armament. No further data available.

AMPHIBIOUS WARFARE CRAFT

♦ **1 Chamo-class utility landing craft [LCU]**
Bldr: Schichau Seebeckwerft A.G., Bremerhaven, Germany (In serv. 12-88)

Denden (ex-*Chamo*)

D: Approx. 750 tons (fl) **S:** 10 kts **Dim:** 60.20 (55.40 pp) × 12.02 × 1.44
A: . . . **Electronics:** Radar: 1 . . . nav.
M: 2 MTU 6V396 TC62 diesels; 2 props; 1,332 bhp
Electric: 304 kw tot. (2 × 152-kw sets, MTU diesels driving)
Range: . . . / . . . **Crew:** . . . tot.

Remarks: 995 grt/352 dwt. Former Ethiopian Shipping Lines commercial landing ship taken over for Eritrean commercial service and in 1998 taken over for the navy. A sister was destroyed during the early 1990s revolution. Has a bow door and 4.5-m-long by 4.3-m-wide vehicle ramp. Can transport up to 24 standard 20-ft. cargo containers on deck.

♦ **2 Soviet T-4-class (Project 1785) landing craft [LCM]**

LST-63 LST-64

D: 35 tons light (93 fl) **S:** 10 kts (light) **Dim:** 20.4 × 5.4 × 1.2 max. aft
M: 2 Type 3D6 diesels; 2 props; 300 bhp
Range: 300/8 **Endurance:** 2 days **Crew:** 2–3 tot.

Remarks: Survivors of four transferred to Ethiopia. Can accommodate up to 50 tons cargo on the 9.5 × 3.9-m vehicle deck. Based at Massawa.

ESTONIA

ESTONIAN NAVY

(Eesti Merevägi)

Personnel: 331 total (including 123 conscripts)

Bases: Principal base at Tallinn, with small base at Paldiski

Maritime Aviation: The Estonian Air Force received Robinson R44 helicopters in 2002 from the U.S. for search and observation duties; the air force's three Mi-2 helicopters no longer appear flyable.

Note: A joint Baltic Squadron ("Baltron") was formed with Latvia and Lithuania during 1997.

PATROL SHIPS [PS]

♦ **1 ex-Danish Modified Hvidbjørnen class**
Bldr: Ålborg Værft, Ålborg, Denmark

	Laid down	L	In serv.
A 230 Admiral Pitka (ex-*Beskytteren,* F 340)	15-12-74	27-5-75	27-2-76

PATROL SHIPS [PS] *(continued)*

Admiral Pitka (A 230) Michael Winter, 6-05

Admiral Pitka (A 230) Michael Winter, 6-05

D: 1,640 tons (1,970 fl) **S:** 18 kts **Dim:** 74.70 (69.00 pp) × 12.16 × 4.50
A: 1 76.2-mm 50-cal. U.S. Mk 22 DP; 1 . . . helicopter
Electronics:
Radar: 1 Skanter Mil 009 nav.; 1 . . . nav.
EW: Racal Cutlass B-1 intercept; Telegon HFD/F; 2 6-round decoy RL
M: 4 Burmeister & Wain Alpha V23-LU diesels; 1 CP prop; 7,440 bhp
Electric: 1,140 kw tot. (1 × 452-kw shaft alternator, 2 × 344-kw diesel alternator sets)
Range: 6,000/13 (one engine) **Crew:** 10 officers, 46 enlisted

Remarks: Donated by Denmark in 6-00 and recommissioned 21-11-00 after a refit. Ice-reinforced hull with Flume-type passive roll stabilization. Has helicopter hangar and deck, but no helicopter was transferred with the ship. The obsolete 76.2-mm gun is largely for ceremonial use. The Plessey PMS-26 sonar and AWS-6 air-search radar were removed prior to transfer, although the radome for the latter remains aboard. The EW equipment listed may have been deleted.

PATROL CRAFT [PC]

♦ 2 ex-Finnish Rihtniemi class
Bldr: Rauma-Repola, Rauma (In serv. 21-2-57)

P 421 Suurop (ex-*Rymattyla,* 52) P 422 Ristna (ex-*Rihtniemi,* 51)

Suurop (P 421) Hartmut Ehlers, 6-03

D: 115 tons (135 fl) **S:** 18 kts **Dim:** 34.0 × 5.7 × 1.8
A: 2 twin 23-mm 60-cal. Sako AA; 2 RBU-1200 ASW RL
Electronics: Radar: 1 Decca 1226 nav.
M: 2 Mercedes-Benz diesels; 2 CP props; 2,500 bhp **Crew:** 20 tot.

Remarks: Transferred at the end of 1999 after retirement. Former convertible minesweeper/gunboats, modernized and lengthened 1977–81. Sonar removed after transfer.

Disposal note: Former East German modified Kondor-I-class patrol craft *Sulev* (M 412, ex-*Komet,* D 42) had been discarded by 9-00.

PATROL BOATS [PB]

Disposal note: Last remaining Zhuk class, *Grief* (P 401), was donated to the Estonian Maritime Museum in 2002.

MINE-COUNTERMEASURES SHIPS AND CRAFT

Note: Estonia began discussions with the U.K. in 1-06 for the possible acquisition of several surplus *Sundown*-class minehunters.

♦ 2 ex-German Type 331B minehunters [MHC]
Bldr: Burmester, Bremen

	L	In serv.
M 311 Wambola (ex-*Cuxhaven,* M 1078)	11-3-58	11-3-59
M 312 Sulev (ex-*Lindau,* M 1072)	16-2-57	24-4-58

Sulev (M 312) **Derek Fox, 6-04**

Wambola (M 311) **Michael Nitz, 7-05**

D: 388 tons (402 fl) **S:** 16.5 kts
Dim: 47.45 × 8.5 × 2.8 (3.68 with sonar extended)
A: 1 40-mm 70-cal. Bofors AA; 2 single 12.7-mm mg
Electronics: Radar: 1 Raytheon SPS-64(V) nav.
Sonar: EFS DSQS-11A
EW: 2 6-round Hot Dog decoy RL
M: 2 MTU 16V538 TB90 diesels; 2 CP props; 5,000 bhp
Electric: 220 kw tot. **Range:** 1,400/16; 3,950/9
Crew: 5 officers, 29 enlisted + 6 divers

Remarks: M 311 donated after planned retirement from German Navy 8-2-00; recommissioned at Tallinn on 29-9-00 with M 312, which was transferred at Tallinn after striking from the German Navy on 27-9-00 and recommissioned on 9-10-00. Converted to minehunters 1975–79 from Klasse 320, *Lindau*-class, wooden-hulled minesweepers. Sister *Göttingen* (M 1070), donated 1-01 for use as cannibalization spares, was lost on 2001, while under tow, en route to Tallinn.
Hull systems: Wooden construction, with nonmagnetic engines. Minehunting speed is 6 kts, on two 50-kw electric motors.
Combat systems: Six divers and two French PAP-104 remote-controlled minehunting devices are carried. Have no mechanical sweep gear. A Bofors lead-computing optical director on the bridge controls the 40-mm gun. The machineguns are carried atop the after superstructure.

♦ 3 ex-German Klasse 394 inshore minesweepers [MSI]
Bldr: Krögerwerft, Rendsburg

	L	In serv.
M 414 Kalev (ex-*Minerva,* M 2663)	25-8-66	16-6-67
M 415 Olev (ex-*Diana,* M 2664)	13-12-66	21-9-67
M 416 Vaindlo (ex-*Undine,* M 2662)	16-5-66	20-3-67

D: 238 tons (246 fl) **S:** 14.3 kts **Dim:** 38.01 × 8.03 × 2.10
A: 1 40-mm 70-cal. Bofors AA
Electronics: Radar: 1 STN-Atlas Elektronik TRS-N
M: 2 Mercedes-Benz MB 820 Db diesels; 2 props; 2,000 bhp
Electric: 554 kw tot. **Range:** 648/14; 1,770/7 **Fuel:** 30 tons
Crew: 2 officers, 23 enlisted (in German service)

Remarks: M 414 and M 415 were transferred 19-6-97 and 8-8-97, respectively, after reactivation refits and training period at Olpenitz, Germany. Had been stricken from German service on 16-2-95. Both had engine overhauls at Wilhelmshaven prior to transfer. M 416 was retired from the German Navy on 1-7-02, transferred on 8-10-02, and recommissioned into Estonian service 4-2-03. Sister *Loreley* (M 2665) was transferred during 3-03 for use as a spares source, and the former German Navy research service craft *Holnis* was towed to Estonia during 2-01 for the same purpose. Wooden construction. Have a 260-kw sweep current generator. Atop the pilothouse is a Bofors lead-computing director for the 40-mm gun.

MINE-COUNTERMEASURES SHIPS AND CRAFT *(continued)*

Vaindlo (M 416) Dieter Wolf, 6-05

SERVICE CRAFT

◆ **1 ex-Danish Mågen class [YAG]**
Bldr: Helsinger Værft (In serv. 5-60)

A 431 Ahti (ex-*Mallemukken,* Y 385)

Ahti (A 431) Hartmut Ehlers, 6-03

D: 175 tons (190 fl) **S:** 10 kts **Dim:** 27.00 × 7.20 × 2.75
A: 2 single 12.7-mm mg
Electronics: Radar: 1 Terma 20T48 nav.; 1 Terma Scanter Mil 009 nav.
M: 1 Burmeister & Wain Alpha diesel; 1 prop; 350 bhp **Crew:** 14 tot.

Remarks: Transferred as a gift 19-3-94; had been stricken from Danish Navy in 1992 after 33 years' service in Greenland and Færoes area service. Arrived in Estonia 29-3-94 and recommissioned same day. The 25-mm gunmount has been removed from the forecastle, along with the two single 20-mm mounts carried in Danish service. Machineguns are fitted aft of the bridge. Served as fleet flagship and operational headquarters until 1997. Also used for route surveillance.

Disposal note: Ex-Russian general-purpose craft *Laine* (A 432) is no longer in service as of 2003.

◆ **1 Kalev-class minelaying submarine relic [YAG]**
Bldr: Vickers-Armstrong, Barrow-in-Furness (L: 7-7-36)

Lembit

D: 600 tons surf./820 tons sub. **S:** 13.5 kts surf./8.5 kts sub.
Dim: 58.00 × 7.30 × 3.30
A: 4 bow 533-mm TT (8 torpedoes); 10 minelaying tubes (20 total mines)
Electronics: Radar: . . .
M: 2 Vickers diesels (600 bhp each), 2 generator sets, 2 electric motors (450 shp each); 2 props; 1,200 bhp surf./900 shp sub.
Range: 2,000/10 (surfaced) **Crew:** 38 tot.

Remarks: Returned to Estonia at Tallinn in 1979 for use as a memorial; the ship had been taken over 13-8-40 when Estonia was overrun by Russia and had apparently been used in trials through the 1970s. Although officially commissioned as a unit of the new Estonian Fleet in 8-92, she is not operable and is in fact a memorial at Tallinn. The mines were carried two per tube in inclined tubes in the saddle tanks flanking the pressure hull. Was originally equipped with one 45-mm AA and one 20-mm AA. Sister *Kalev* lost 11-41.

Disposal note: Ex-Danish launch *Mardus* (A 433, ex-*Rylen*) was stricken during 2000.

MARITIME BORDER GUARD
(Eesti Piirivalve)

A small coastal patrol force was established under the Ministry of Internal Affairs on 22-4-92 when the first of four Kbv 236–class 16.2-m patrol craft donated by Sweden was delivered to the Estonian Maritime Border Guard. In wartime, it would come under the Commander-in-Chief of Defense Forces.

Personnel: Approx. 300 total

Maritime Aviation: The *Piirivalve Lennusalk* (Border Guard Aviation Group) operates two ex-*Luftwaffe* Let 410UVP light transports and 1 Schweizer 300C and two ex-*Luftwaffe* Mi-8S/TB HipSAR helicopters, all based at Tallinn International Airport. One Mi-8S/TB and a former East German commercial Mi-8T are in storage at Pärnu awaiting funding to equip them for SAR duties.

Note: In addition to the ships and craft listed below, *Triin* (PVL 200, ex-*Bester*) and *Reet* (PVL 201, Ex-EVA 003), both 88 tons, 34 m, 8–9 kts, entered service during 5-01, built at Sretensk, Russia, during 1974 and 1984 respectively. A unit named *Oisko* was added early in 1999; no data available.

Maritime Border Guard Patrol Ship Reet (PVL 201) Hartmut Ehlers, 6-03

During 10-01, EADS Business Unit Systems & Defence Electronics received a contract to install a network of 20 X-band coastal surveillance radars for the border guard; these are being tied to four regional operational centers and one national center at Tallinn.

PATROL COMBATANTS [WPG]

◆ **1 Finnish Silmä class**
Bldr: Laivateollisuus Oy, Turku

	Laid down	L	In serv.
PVL 107 Kõu (ex-*Silmä*)	30-8-62	23-3-63	19-8-63

Kõu (PVL 107) H&L Van Ginderen, 6-00

D: 530 tons **S:** 15 kts **Dim:** 48.3 × 8.3 × 4.3
A: 1 twin 25-mm 80-cal. 2M-3M AA
Electronics: Radar: 3 . . . nav.—Sonar: Simrad SS 105 (14 kHz)
M: 1 Werkspoor diesel; 1 prop; 1,800 bhp **Crew:** 22 tot.

Remarks: Transfer announced 1-12-94, the ship was transferred 1-95 and recommissioned during 4-95. Equipped for firefighting, towing, and salvage. A firefighting monitor is located at the extreme bow. An electrohydraulic crane handles two RIB inspection launches.

PATROL CRAFT [WPC]

◆ **1 Vapper class**
Bldr: Baltic Ship Repair, Tallinn (Commissioned 1-6-00)

PVL 111 Vapper

D: 118 tons (fl) **S:** 27 kts **Dim:** 31.40 (27.80 pp) × 6.00 × 1.66
A: 1 twin 25-mm 80-cal. 2M-3M AA
Electronics: Radar: 1 . . . nav.
M: 2 Deutz TBD620-V12 diesels; 2 props; 4,080 bhp
Electric: 88 kw tot. (2 × 44-kw diesel alternator sets)
Range: . . . / . . . **Fuel:** 13 tons **Crew:** . . . tot.

PATROL CRAFT [WPC] *(continued)*

♦ **1 ex-Norwegian Storm class**
Bldr: Bergens Mekaniske Verksted, Bergen (L: 24-5-66)

PVL 105 TORM (ex-*Arg*, P 968)

D: 105 tons (125 fl) **S:** 37 kts **Dim:** 36.53 × 6.3 × 1.55
A: 1 twin 25-mm 80-cal. 2M-3M AA; 1 twin 14.5-mm 93-cal. mg
Electronics: Radar: 1 Decca TM 1226 nav.
M: 2 Maybach MB 872A (MTU 16V538 TB90) diesels; 2 props; 7,200 bhp
Range: 550/36 **Crew:** . . . tot.

Remarks: Stricken from Norwegian Navy during 1993. PVL 105 was rehabilitated during 1994 and transferred 16-12-94 with armament systems deleted. Sisters were also donated to Latvia and Lithuania.

♦ **1 ex-Finnish Viima class**
Bldr: Laivateollisuus Oy, Turku

	L	In serv.
PVL 106 MARU (ex-*Viima*)	20-7-64	12-10-64

Maru (PVL 106) Findler & Winter, 6-96

D: 135 tons **S:** 23 kts **Dim:** 35.7 × 6.6 × 2.0
A: 1 twin 25-mm 80-cal. 2M-3M AA; 1 7.62-mm mg
Electronics: Radar: 1 . . . nav.
M: 3 Maybach diesels; 3 CP props; 4,050 bhp **Crew:** 12 tot.

Remarks: A variant of the Finnish Navy's *Ruissalo* class. Transfer announced 1-12-94, with the craft arriving in Estonia during 1-95 and recommissioned 4-95. Radar has unusual double slotted waveguide configuration.

AIR-CUSHION PATROL BOATS [WPBH]

♦ **1 2000-TDX(M) class**
Bldr: Griffon Hovercraft, Salisbury Green, Southampton, U.K. (In serv. 10-99)

PVL . . .

D: 6.75 tons (fl) **S:** 35 kts **Dim:** 11.04 × 4.60 × 0.52
A: provision for 1 7.62-mm mg **Electronics:** Radar: 1 Furuno . . . nav.
M: 1 Deutz BF8L-513 diesel driving lift fan and 1 CP airscrew; 320 bhp
Range: 300/25 (loaded) **Fuel:** 284 liters **Crew:** 3 tot.

Remarks: Can carry 2,200 kg cargo in lieu of troops. GRP construction hull.

PATROL BOATS [WPB]

♦ **1 Pikker class**
Bldr: Baltic Ship Repair, Tallinn (L: 22-12-95; in serv. 4-96)

PVL 103 PIKKER

Pikker (PVL 103) Hartmut Ehlers, 6-03

D: 88 tons (fl) **S:** 24 kts **Dim:** 30.0 × 5.8 × 1.5
A: 1 twin 14.5-mm 93-cal. AA; 2 single 7.62-mm mg
Electronics: Radar; 1 . . . nav.
M: 2 Type 12YH 18/20 diesels; 2 props; 2,700 bhp **Crew:** 6 tot.

Remarks: Was to have been first of a class of ten, but the others were canceled due to financial constraints. Capable of search-and-rescue, firefighting, towing, pollution control, and light icebreaking duties in ice up to 30 cm thick. Carries one rigid inflatable rescue and inspection dinghy.

♦ **2 ex-Finnish Koskelo class**
Bldr: Valmet, Helsinki (In serv. 1955–60)

PVL 101 (ex-*Kuikka*) PVL 102 (ex-*Kaakuri*)

PVL 101 Hartmut Ehlers, 6-03

D: 75 tons (97 fl) **S:** 23 kts **Dim:** 29.42 × 5.02 × 1.5
A: 1 12.7-mm mg **Electronics:** Radar: 2 . . . nav.
M: Mercedes-Benz diesels; 2 props; 2,700 bhp **Crew:** 11 tot.

Remarks: Modernized and re-engined 1970–74 by Laivateollisuus, Turku. Sisters *Koskelo, Kuovi,* and *Kiisla* were stricken from the Finnish Coast Guard in 1986–87, *Kurki* in 1990. Transferred to Estonia 16-11-92. PVL 100 retired 2003; remaining units were reported inactive ashore as of 9-03.

AMPHIBIOUS WARFARE CRAFT

♦ **1 Russian Serna-class fast medium landing craft [WLCM]**
Bldr: Volga Zavod, Nizhniy Novgorod (In serv. 10-94)

PVL 104 TIIR

Tiir (PVL 104) Stefan Marx, 1997

D: 53 tons light (105 fl) **S:** 30 kts **Dim:** 25.65 × 5.85 × 1.52 (1.30 at speed)
A: . . . **Electronics:** Radar: 1 Liman nav.
M: 2 Zvezda M-503A-3 diesels; 2 shrouded props; 3,300 bhp
Electric: 32 kw tot (2 × 16-kw DGR-16/1,500 diesel sets)
Range: 100/30 loaded; 600/30 half-load **Crew:** 4 tot.

Remarks: Private venture design by the R. Alekseyev Central Hydrofoil Design Bureau. Four prototypes were built, two of which were sold to a commercial operator in the United Arab Emirates in 1994 and the other delivered to the Russian Baltic Fleet. The design is on offer for export for naval and civilian customers. "Serna" is the builder's project name.
Hull systems: Said to have a useful load of 45–50 tons on a 13 × 4 × 2.5-m cargo deck that extends about 2 m beneath the pilothouse. A portable canopy and seats for 100 personnel can be installed. The semi-planing hull incorporates an air cavity to provide underhull lubrication. Aluminum-magnesium alloy construction. Articulating bow ramp. Range with half load of 600 n.m. can be achieved by using reserve void tanks to carry fuel.

AUXILIARIES

♦ **1 ex-U.S. Coast Guard Balsam-class navigational buoy tender [WAGL]** Bldr: Duluth Iron & SB Co., Duluth, Minn.

	Laid down	L	In serv.
PVL 109 VALVAS (ex-*Bittersweet,* WLB 389)	16-9-43	11-11-43	11-5-44

D: 697 tons light (1,038 fl) **S:** 13 kts **Dim:** 54.9 (51.8 pp) × 11.3 × 4.0
A: 1 twin 25-mm 80-cal. 2M-3M AA; 2 single 12.7-mm M2 mg
Electronics: Radar: 1 Raytheon SPS-64(V)1 nav.
M: 2 diesels, electric drive; 1 prop; 1,200 shp
Electric: 400 kw tot. **Range:** 4,600/12; 14,000/7.4
Fuel: varies **Crew:** 6 officers, 47 enlisted (in USCG service)

AUXILIARIES *(continued)*

Valvas (PVL 109) Stefan Marx, 1998

Remarks: PVL 109 was retired from U.S. Coast Guard 18-8-97 and donated to Estonia; transferred 5-9-97. Acts as the flagship for the coast guard. Sturdy construction; still has many years' service remaining despite advanced age.
Hull systems: Hull is of icebreaker form and can break light ice. Has a 20-ton buoy derrick.

SERVICE CRAFT

♦ 1 Ex-Swedish Class A pollution-control depot ship [WYAG]
Bldr: . . . (In serv. 1960)

PVL 202 Kati (ex-Kbv 003 *Rivöfjord,* ex-*Rangoon*)

Kati (PVL 202) Hartmut Ehlers, 6-03

D: 477 tons (fl) **S:** 11 kts **Dim:** 40.0 × 6.46 × 3.52
M: . . .

Remarks: Transferred from Sweden; entered Estonian service 5-02. While in Swedish service, she was lengthened 6.0 m and given a bow bulb in 1987 by Dockstavarvet AB. Has salvage diver support capabilities.

Disposal note: Russian Nyryat 2–class diving tender PVK 019 was scrapped 3-00.

♦ 2 FF Jet Combi Patrol 10–class launches [WYFL]
Bldr: FF Marine, Finland (In serv. 1994)

PVK 012 PVK 016

D: . . . tons **S:** . . . kts **Dim:** 10.00 × 2.75 × 0.60
M: 1 Cummins 6CTA8.3-M2 diesel; 1 KaMeWa FF 310 waterjet; 400 bhp
Crew: 6 tot.

Remarks: A gift from Finland for use on Lake Peipus in smuggling prevention and fisheries patrol. Transferred 8-94 and 11-94. The foredeck can accept 1,000 kg of cargo.

♦ 3 ex-Swedish Kbv 236–class launches [WYFL] (In serv. 1961–72)

PVK 001 (ex-Kbv 257) PVK 002 (ex-Kbv 259) PVK 003 (ex-Kbv 246)

D: 17 tons **S:** 22 kts **Dim:** 16.2 × 3.7 × 1.4
A: small arms **Electronics:** Radar: 1 . . . nav.
M: 2 Volvo Penta TAMD 120A diesels; 2 props; 700 bhp **Crew:** 5 tot.

Remarks: PVK001 transferred from the Swedish Coast Guard 4-4-92, the others on 20-10-93; recommissioned 10-4-92, 1-94, and 6-12-93, respectively. Aluminum construction.

PVK 003 Hartmut Ehlers, 9-96

♦ 1 Slavyanka-class (Project 20150) harbor utility craft [YFU]
Bldr: . . ., Libau, Latvia

PVL 110

Utility landing craft PVL 110 Hartmut Ehlers, 6-03

D: 36 tons light (78.2 fl) **S:** 8 kts **Dim:** 18 × 5.81 × 1.6
M: 2 diesel; 2 prop; 470 bhp **Crew:** 2 tot.

Remarks: Data above derived from similar Russian designs. Unnamed landing craft; completed in 1992 and acquired 11-97.

♦ 1 ex-Finnish training craft [WYXT]
Bldr: Valmet, Turku

PVL 108 Linda (ex-*Kemiö,* 93; ex-*Valvoja II*)

Linda (PVL 108) Hartmut Ehlers, 6-03

D: 340 tons (fl) **S:** 11 kts **Dim:** 36.70 × 9.40 × 3.20
A: . . . **Electronics:** Radar: 1 . . . nav.
M: 1 Burmeister & Wain Alpha diesel; 1 prop; 480 bhp
Electric: 5 kw **Fuel:** 38.5 tons **Crew:** 10 tot.

Remarks: 406 grt. Transferred 12-92. Former buoy tender, acquired by Finnish Navy from Board of Navigation in 1983 and refitted for naval service as a command ship by Hollming, Rauma. Based at Riga and also used as training ship by the Marine Education Seamanship School, Tallinn. 25-mm AA gun removed during 2003.

Note: Other PVK-series harbor patrol craft of over 12-m length include PVK 006–008 and 013, all ex-Finnish 13.7-ton icebreaking launches; PVK 017 (ex-EVA 203), a small passenger-carrying tender; and PVK 018 (ex-EVA 204), a 22-kt launch donated by

SERVICE CRAFT *(continued)*

Finland in 1993. PVK 019 is a diving tender (see below). Also in use are the following launches of under 12-m length: PVK 004, built in 1987 and donated by the U.S., commissioned 1-12-93; PVK 010, completed at Baltic Ship Repairers, Tallinn, 1997, 15-m, can break 25 cm of ice; PVK 011, completed 1-99; PVK 020, completed 1982 in Sweden and transferred 5-95; PVK 021, completed 1988 in Finland and transferred 9-94; and PVK 022 and PVK 023, transferred from Finland 11-96. PVK 025 (Ex-Swedish Kbv 275) was transferred in 1-97.

Note: Ships and craft operated by Estonia's Shipping and Navigation Authority (*Eesti Veeteede Amet*) include the ex-Finnish icebreaker *Tarmo,* ex-Finnish *Seili*-class navigational aids tender EVA 316 (ex-*Lonna*); ex-Russian Kamenka-class survey and navigational aids tender EVA 308 (ex-*Vern'er,* GS-108); ex-Russian Samara-class survey and navigational aids tender EVA 307 (ex-*Zenit*); ex-Russian BGK-380-class inshore survey craft EVA 309 (ex-BGK-117) and EVA 310 (ex-BGK-630); ex-Russian PO-2 (Yaroslavets)-class survey launch EVA 311 (ex-BGK-931); and ex-Russian T-4-class landing craft EVA 314. Characteristics data and illustrations for these units can be found in the 1998–99 and earlier editions.

Ex-Finnish *Karhu*-class icebreaker *Karu* (ex-*Kapten Tchubakov,* ex-*Kapitan Chubakov,* ex-*Karhu*), acquired by Russia in 1987, was transferred to Estonia in 1990 and operated by the Tallinn Port Authority; the ship was placed up for sale on 12-3-02. Russian Navy Baltic Fleet *Emba*-class cable tender *Nepryada* was purchased from Russia in 1997 and may be operated either by the Shipping and Navigation Board or another government agency.

FÆROE ISLANDS

Note: The Færoe Islands are a semiautonomous territory of Denmark.

COAST GUARD AND FISHERY PROTECTION SERVICE

(Færøar Landsstyri)

Personnel: Approx. 65 total

Base: Tórshavn, Strømø Island

PATROL SHIPS [WPS]

♦ **1 Brimil-class fisheries patrol ship**
Bldr: Myklebust Mek Verksted AS, Gursken, Norway (In serv. 2000)

BRIMIL

D: Approx. 1,900 tons (fl) **S:** . . . kts **D:** 63.60 (55.75 pp) × 12.60 × 4.30
M: 1 Ulstein-Normo KVMB12 diesel (. . . bhp), 1 Ulstein-Normo KRMB6 cruise diesel (. . . bhp); 1 CP prop; . . . bhp
Range: . . . / . . . **Crew:** . . .

Remarks: 1,500 grt. The hull was fabricated by Kleven Verft AS, Ulsteinvik, and then fitted out by Myklebust. The main engine is installed to port, the "daughter" engine to starboard; only one can be geared to the propeller at one time.

♦ **1 fisheries protection ship and rescue tug**
Bldr: Solvær Værft, Norway (In serv. 1976)

TJALDRID

D: 650 tons (fl) **S:** 15 kts **Dim:** 44.51 (38.49 pp) × 10.11 × 4.02
A: Provision for 1 20-mm 70-cal Oerlikon Mk 10 AA
Electronics: Rada: 4 . . . nav.
M: 2 MWM 6-cyl. diesels; 1 prop; 2,400 bhp—bow-thruster
Electric: 234 kw tot. (3 × 78-kw diesel sets)
Range: 5,300/14.5 **Fuel:** 122 tons **Crew:** 18 tot. + 4 divers

Remarks: 437 grt/125 nrt. Acquired 1987. Equipped for firefighting, salvage, and ocean towing. The 57-mm single-fire gun formerly carried has been replaced by provision for a single 20-mm 70-cal. Oerlikon gun. Of the four radars carried, one is a large Raytheon S-band set suitable for surface-search work; an HFD/F set is installed. To support salvage divers, a portable decompression chamber can be carried.

FALKLAND ISLANDS

Note: The Falkland Islands are a colony of the United Kingdom. The Royal Navy is responsible for physical security in the waters around the Falklands and the other United Kingdom territories in the South Atlantic. HMS *Clyde,* a new 1800-ton offshore patrol vessel designed for Falkland Islands service, will take up patrol duties upon commissioning in 2007. The ships listed below provide fisheries surveillance within the declared exclusion zone surrounding the Falkland Islands.

Maritime aviation: In addition to RAF assets stationed in the Falklands, the local government has acquired a Dornier Do-228–200 maritime surveillance aircraft with Sperry Primus radar and two Pilatus-Britten-Norman Defender twin-engined surveillance aircraft.

FISHERIES PATROL SHIPS [WPS]

♦ **1 Polish Project B675-1**
Bldr: Stocznia imeni Komuny Paryskiej, Gdynia, Poland (In serv. 12-7-94)

DORADA

D: Approx. 3,300 tons (fl) **S:** 16 kts (14.8 sust.)
Dim: 76.60 (69.00 pp) × 14.60 × 5.25
A: Small arms **Electronics:** Radar: 2 Furuno 2120 nav.
M: 1 Cegielski-Sulzer 12ATV25H diesel; 1 CP prop; 2,366 bhp—1 Cegielski-Sulzer 6ATV25H cruise diesel; 1,183 bhp—bow-thruster
Electric: 2,100 kw tot. (. . . diesel sets; 400 V, 50 Hz)
Range: 14,000/12 **Fuel:** 440 m^3 heavy oil; 50 m^3 diesel **Endurance:** 45 days
Crew: 26 tot., including 11 scientific staff and cadets

Remarks: 2,360 grt/1,185 dwt. Laid down 1991 as a stern-haul trawler and fish-processing ship for a British owner who defaulted. Operated briefly for a New Zealand company but placed under arrest for debts on 13-2-96. Conversion to fisheries patrol ship begun 20-8-97 at Lyttelton, New Zealand, for Byron Marine, Ltd. Carries two rigid-inflatable inspection launches aft. Has two auxiliary boilers. Medical and berthing facilities upgraded, new deck machinery installed, and oceanographic gear-handling equipment added. Conversion completed 12-12-97, and the ship departed for the Falklands the next day.

♦ **1 former stern-haul fish processing trawler**
Bldr: Charles D. Holmes & Co., Ltd., Beverley, Hull, U.K. (In serv. 1-73)

CRISCILLA (ex-*Lady Hammond,* ex-*Hammond Innes*)

Criscilla H&L Van Ginderen, 1998

D: Approx. 1,400 tons (fl) **S:** 15 kts **Dim:** 53.62 (50.91 pp) × 11.31 × . . .
Electronics: Radar: 1 Koden MD 3120 nav.; 1 Furuno 2110 ARPA nav.
M: 1 Stork-Werkspoor 6TM410 6-cyl, 4-stroke diesel; 1 prop; 2,500 bhp
Electric: 488 kw tot. (2 × 244-kw diesel sets; 440 V, 50 Hz a.c.)
Range: . . . / . . . **Crew:** 15 tot.

Remarks: 924 grt/437 dwt. Chartered 1998 through 5-00 from Marbella Ltd.; charter has been extended. Has red hull, white superstructure, with "Fisheries Patrol" painted prominently amidships on the hull sides. Carries one Avon Searaider rigid inflatable inspection boat. Has MFD/F, echo sounder, SATCOM terminal, and GPS.

FIJI

Republic of Fiji

Personnel: Approx. 330 total

Note: The navy is subordinate to the Minister of Home Affairs. All units are based at Walu Bay, Suva. Training is conducted at RFNS *Captain Stanley Brown,* Togalevu. Ship names are preceded by RFNS (Republic of Fiji Naval Ship). Regular economic exclusion zone patrols were ended 1-98 due to financial constraints.

Naval aviation: The Fiji Air Wing was dissolved in 5-95. The French Navy provides occasional maritime surveillance flights by Falcon 200 aircraft stationed at New Caledonia.

PATROL CRAFT [PC]

♦ **3 ASI 315 class**
Bldr: Transfield ASI, Pty, Ltd., South Coogie, W.A., Australia

201 KULA (In serv. 28-5-94)
202 KIKAU (In serv. 27-5-95)
203 KIRO (In serv. 14-10-95)

PATROL CRAFT [PC] *(continued)*

Kiro (203) Brian Morrison, 9-98

D: 148 tons (162 fl) **S:** 26 + kts
Dim: 32.60 (31.50 hull, 28.60 wl) × 8.20 × 1.60 (hull)
A: 1 20-mm 70-cal. Oerlikon Mk 10 AA; 2 single 7.62-mm mg
Electronics: Radar: 1 Furuno. . . nav.
M: 2 Caterpillar 3516 Phase II diesels; 2 props; 2,820 bhp (2,400 sust.)—1 Caterpillar 3412 TA cruise diesel; 1 Hamilton 521 waterjet; 775 bhp
Electric: 186 kVA (2 Caterpillar 3306T diesel sets)
Range: 600/18; 2,500/12 **Fuel:** 28 tons **Endurance:** 8–10 days
Crew: 4 officers, 15 enlisted

Remarks: With the change in Fiji's government, the order placed on 3-10-85 for four Australian "Pacific Forum" ASI 315–class patrol boats was canceled, and the boats were earmarked for Tonga and other Pacific island nations. The program was reinstated during 7-92, but for only three boats, at least initially; the order was placed in 12-92. Name for 203 was originally to have been *Ruve*. Are of the improved, lighter-weight version built for Hong Kong and Kuwait and are the only units of the class to carry weapons heavier than a 12.7-mm mg. Carry a 5-m aluminum boarding boat. Has an extensive navigational suite.

PATROL BOATS [PB]

♦ 2 former oilfield support craft
Bldr: Beaux's Baycraft, La. (In serv. 1979–80)

101 Levuka (ex-*Maranatha*) 102 Lautoka (ex-*Rapture*)

D: 97 tons (fl) **S:** 27 kts **Dim:** 33.80 × 7.40 × 1.50
A: 1 12.7-mm mg **Electronics:** Radar: 2 Decca. . . nav.
M: 4 G.M. Detroit Diesel 12V71 TI diesels; 4 props; 2,156 bhp **Crew:** . . .

Remarks: Aluminum craft purchased 9-87 and commissioned 22-10-87 and 28-10-87, respectively. Correlation of former names to Fijian names uncertain.

♦ 4 ex-Israeli Dabur class
Bldr: Israeli Aircraft Industries, Be'er Sheva (In serv. 1973–77)

301 Vai 302 Ogo 303 Saku 304 Saqa

Ogo (302) H&L Van Ginderen, 1-96

D: 25 tons (35 fl) **S:** 19 kts **Dim:** 19.8 × 5.8 × 0.8
A: 2 single 20-mm 70-cal. Oerlikon AA; 2 single 7.62-mm mg
Electronics: Radar: 1 Decca Super 101 Mk 3 nav.
M: 2 G.M. Detroit Diesel 12V71 TI diesels; 2 props; 960 bhp
Electric: 20 kw tot. **Range:** 1,200/17 **Crew:** 2 officers, 7 enlisted

Remarks: Former Israeli Navy units acquired and commissioned 22-11-91. Were considered surplus and may be offered to other Fiji government agencies as launches. Aluminum construction. Could make 25 kts when new, and range may have been reduced to 450 n.m. at 13 kts. 301 has only one 20-mm AA.

Note: The small yacht [YFL] *Cagi Donu* is operated by the navy for the prime minister.

FINLAND

Republic of Finland

SUOMEN MERIVOIMAT

Personnel: 5,000 total including Coastal Artillery. There are also large numbers of reservists.

Organization and Bases: In 8-98, the fleet was combined into a single rapid-reaction force, with the Finnish Army Coastal Artillery and Coastal Infantry forces integrated within the navy. Major organizational commands are now the Gulf of Finland Naval Command, at Uppinniemi; the Archipelago Sea Naval Command, at Pansio; the Kotka Coastal Command; and the Uusimaa Jaeger Brigade, at Tammisaari.

Maritime Aviation: The navy has no aircraft of its own. The separate Frontier Guard (q.v.) operates a number of helicopters and fixed-wing aircraft. The air force operates one Fokker 27 Mk 400 M twin-engine maritime surveillance aircraft and the army operates seven Mil Mi-8 Hip helicopters for SAR and utility duties.

Coast Defense: The two Coastal Artillery regiments operate Swedish RBS-15 antiship missiles mounted four per vehicle on Sisu trucks, 155-mm and 130-mm fixed artillery, and 100-mm fixed and mobile artillery.

WEAPONS AND SYSTEMS

The minelayer *Pohjanmaa* has a single-barrel automatic Bofors 120-mm gun with the following characteristics:

Length: 46 calibers **Weight without munitions:** 28.5 tons
Projectile weight: 35 kg **Muzzle velocity:** 800 m/sec
Max. rate of fire: 80 rounds/min **Arc of elevation:** –10° to +80°
Training speed: 40°/sec **Elevation speed:** 30°/sec
Max. effective range for surface fire: 12,000 m

The other major weapons employed are Swedish RBS-15 antiship missiles, Bofors 40-mm L70 AA guns, and 23-mm 60-cal. Finnish-made Sako AA twin mountings.

The Finnyards SONAC PTA towed sonar, a 78-m passive array with 24 hydrophones designed to be towed at 3–12 kts on a 600-m cable, can be installed on *Rauma*-class missile boats.

Combatant ships are being treated with an application of HPA-1 (High-Performance Absorber) radar signature reduction coating, a sandwich of GRP and various doped resins that significantly reduces radar signal returns in the 5–18 GHz range.

Note: Of the two *Turunmaa*-class patrol combatants, the *Turunmaa* (03) was retired in 1999, and the *Karjala* (04) during 2001.

GUIDED-MISSILE PATROL CRAFT [PTG]

♦ 4 Hamina (Rauma 2000) class
Bldr: Aker Finnyards, Rauma

	Laid down	L	Delivered
80 Hamina	8-97	5-98	24-8-98
81 Tornio	2001	2002	13-5-03
82 Hanko	2004	2005	10-05
83 Pori	2005	2005	6-06

Hamina (80)—with old pennant number Finnish Navy, 1998

Hamina (80)—note 57-mm Bofors mount forward Ralph Edwards, 6-03

GUIDED-MISSILE PATROL CRAFT [PTG] *(continued)*

D: 235 tons (268 fl) **S:** 32 kts **Dim:** 50.80 (44.30 pp) × 8.30 × 2.00
A: 4 RBS-15SF SSM; 1 57-mm 70-cal. Bofors SAK-57 Mk 3 DP; 1 8-cell Denel Umkhonto VLS SAM syst; 2 single 12.7-mm mg; provision for 4 9-round Saab Elma LLS. 920 ASW RL
Electronics:
Radar: 1 EADS TRS-3D air search; 1 Thales Scout nav./surf. search; 1 CelsiusTech Ceros 200 f.c.
Sonar: provision for Finnyards SONAC-PTA towed array
EW: . . . intercept, 2 32-round Wallop Barricade decoy RL
M: 2 MTU 16V538 TB93 diesels; 2 KaMeWa 90SII waterjets; 8,000 bhp
Electric: 386 kw tot. (2 × 193-kw Saab Scania 11DGSJGM diesel-driven sets; 220 V a.c.)
Range: 500/30 **Fuel:** . . . tons **Crew:** 5 officers, 14 enlisted

Remarks: Hamina was ordered on 26-1-97 for $21.6 million. A third and fourth unit were ordered in 2003, following decommissioning of the prototype hovercraft *Tuuli* (10).
Hull systems: Aluminum hull structure with six watertight compartments; superstructure construction is made of composite materials rather than aluminum. Have extensive signature reduction measures. The engineering plant is on resilient mountings to reduce the acoustic signature, and the engine exhaust is ducted through seawater spray to reduce the infrared signature. The craft have a full NBC warfare protective system.
Combat systems: 80 has the Danish INFOCOM ICS-2000 integrated communications suite, but no combat data system was aboard in 2001, when EADS received the combat system development contract. A Saab Dynamics EOS-400 optronic gun director controls the 40-mm mount, which is in a special low-radar-reflectivity gunhouse. As completed, had no ASW equipment. A Thales-Nederland Tacticos combat management system was leased for trials in 74 from 1-00 to 8-00 and then removed. The Lacroix ATOS (Anti-Threat Optronic System) rocket-powered decoy system is to be installed in 2002; it uses two 16-round launchers firing 80-mm rockets. Updated with the Thales-Instrumentointi Shipbourne Integrated Electronic Warfare System (SIEWS) under a 3-02 contract.
South African Denel-Kentron Omkhonto-IR point defense VLS SAM systems were ordered for the class on 18-10-12. The new missiles, which began delivery in 2006, replace the older Sako SAM/Mistral missile systems.

♦ 4 Rauma (Helsinki-II) class
Bldr: Finnyards, Rauma

	In serv.		In serv.
70 Rauma	18-10-90	72 Porvoo	27-4-92
71 Raahe	20-8-91	73 Naantali	23-6-92

Rauma (70)—with VDS aft and only two missile canisters installed
Jaroslaw Cislak, 6-99

Porvoo (72) H&L Van Ginderen, 6-97

D: 215 tons (248 fl) **S:** 30+ kts **Dim:** 48.00 (41.00 pp) × 8.00 × 0.87
A: Up to 6 RBS-15SF SSM; 1 40-mm 70-cal. Bofors L70-600E AA; 1 6-round Sako SAM launcher (. . . Mistral missiles); 2 single 12.7-mm mg; 2 9-round Saab Elma LLS.920 ASW RL; mines
Electronics:
Radar: 1 Raytheon . . . ARPA nav.; 1 9GA208 surf. search; 1 9LV 225 f.c.
Sonar: Simrad SS 304 hull-mounted HF; provision for Finnyards SONAC-PTA towed array (see Remarks)
EW: MEL Matilda-E (9EW 300) intercept, 1 32-round Wallop Barricade decoy RL; EADS COLDS laser countermeasure
M: 2 MTU 16V538 TB93 diesels; 2 Riva Calzone IRC 115 waterjets; 8,000 bhp
Electric: 386 kw (2 × 193 kw; 2 Saab Scania DS11 diesel driving)
Crew: 5 officers, 14 enlisted

Remarks: Construction approved 2-87, with the first laid down fall 1987. Shorter and shallower in draft than *Helsinki* class. Name of first unit was originally to have been *Luokka.*
Combat systems: Have CelsiusTech 9LV Mk 3 weapons-control system with two multifunction operator consoles and two navigational radar consoles, 9LV200 Mk 3 optronic fire-control system and 9EW 300 EW system. The surface-to-air missile launcher is a Finnish-designed converted 23-mm 60-cal. AA gunmount equipped with infrared and t.v. cameras for fire control; two 23-mm guns are interchangeable with the missile mountings. Two portable ship-sets of the Finnyards SONAC-PTA (Passive Towed Array) sonar have been acquired for this class; it can be installed in about 24 hrs at the expense of the after two RBS-15 missile canisters. The COLDS (Common Opto-electronic Laser Detection System) detects laser missile seekers and directs an equivalent pulse-repetition-frequency laser beam of its own against a safe spot on the ocean to spoof the missile. Are to be updated with the Thales- Instrumentointi Shipbourne Integrated Electronic Warfare System (SIEWS) under a 3-02 contract.

♦ 4 Helsinki (PB 80) class
Bldr: Wärtsilä, Helsinki

	Laid down	L	In serv.
60 Helsinki	3-9-80	5-11-80	1-9-81
61 Turku	1-1-84	1985	1-6-85
62 Oulu	. . .	. . .	1-10-85
63 Kotka	. . .	. . .	16-6-86

Kotka (63) Leo Van Ginderen, 6-05

D: 250 tons (280 fl) **S:** 30 kts **Dim:** 45.00 × 8.90 × 3.00 (props)
A: 3 or 4 RBS-15SF SSM; 1 57-mm 70-cal. Bofors SAK 1 DP; 2 twin 23-mm 60-cal. Sako AA; 2 d.c. racks (3 d.c. each); mines
Electronics:
Radar: 1 Raytheon . . . ARPA nav., 1 9GA 208 surf. search, 1 9L V 225 f.c.
Sonar: Simrad SS 304 hull-mounted HF, Finnyards SONAC-PTA towed array
EW: Thales DR-2000U intercept; 2 32-round Wallop Barricade decoy RL
M: 3 MTU 16V538 TB92 diesels; 3 props; 12,000 bhp
Range: . . . / . . . **Crew:** 30 tot.

Remarks: Prototype ordered 5-10-78. Three additional ordered 13-1-83. Further construction deferred in favor of the *Rauma* class above. Aluminum hull.
Combat systems: The DataSaab EOS-400 optronic f.c.s. mounted atop pilothouse to control the 57-mm gun on 61–63, which had a revised pilothouse shape; 60 was later brought up to same standard. The 23-mm mounts are controlled by Galileo lead-computing directors mounted on the after corners of the bridge deck. Minelaying missions require dismounting the depth charge racks and RBS-15SF missiles, of which up to eight can be carried if required (paired atop one another). The towed-array sonar hoist and reel system replaces the after starboard missile rack position, and the craft are now normally seen with three missiles and the sonar.

PATROL AIR-CUSHION CRAFT [PBA]

Note: Prototype NB 432-class (T2000) patrol surface effect craft *Tuuli* (10) was decommissioned in 2003 after less than a year in service due to cost and other concerns. Instead, the Finnish Navy plans to buy two additional *Rauma 2000*–class guided-missile patrol craft (see above).

PATROL CRAFT [PC]

Disposal note: The last two remaining *Rihtniemi*-class patrol craft in Finish service, *Raisio* (54) and *Röytta* (55), were apparently retired during 2004–5, after more than 45 years of service.

MINE WARFARE SHIPS AND CRAFT

Note: In addition to the ships and craft listed in this section as having minelaying capabilities, most other classes of Finnish combatants, auxiliaries, and service craft are also equipped for minelaying.

♦ 3 . . . -class minesweepers [MSC]
Bldr: . . ., Finland

D: Approx. 400 tons (fl) **S:** . . . **Dim:** 45 × . . . × . . .

Remarks: Approximately 400 tons displacement and 45 meters long. Expected to enter service between 2008 and 2012. No additional data available.

♦ 2 Hämeenmaa-class minelayers [MM]
Bldr: Finnyards, Rauma

	Laid down	L	In serv.
02 Hämeenmaa	2-4-91	11-11-91	15-4-92
05 Uusimaa	12-11-91	6-92	2-12-92

MINE WARFARE SHIPS AND CRAFT *(continued)*

Hämeenmaa (02) Ralph Edwards, 6-03

Uusimaa (05) Ralph Edwards, 6-03

D: 1,000 tons (1,330 fl) **S:** 20 kts **Dim:** 77.00 (69.60 pp) × 11.60 × 3.00
A: 2 single 40-mm 70-cal. Bofors AA; 1 6-round Sako SAM launcher (. . . Mistral missiles); 2 twin 23-mm 60-cal. Sako AA; 2 5-round RBU-1200 ASW RL (60 RGB-12 rockets); 2 d.c. racks (6 d.c. each); 4 mine rails (100–150 mines; 200 m rail-length total)
Electronics:
Radar: 3 Selesmar . . . ARPA nav.
Sonar: Simrad SS 304 hull-mounted HF
EW: MEL Matilda intercept; 2 12-round Wallop Super Barricade decoy RL
M: 2 Wärtsilä-Vasa 16V22MD diesels; 2 CP props; 6,400 bhp—250-shp bow-thruster
Crew: 45 tot. (accommodations for 100)

Remarks: Authorized 9-88 and originally ordered 7-89 from Wärtsilä Shipyard, Helsinki, for delivery 1991; reordered 29-12-89 after Wärtsilä's bankruptcy. Have bow and stern ramps to permit use as logistics transports as well as minelayers, and also have side loading ports. Have four mine rails exiting stern. Built to Ice Class IA standards and able to break 40-cm ice continuously; the bow is cut away sharply above the waterline to facilitate ice navigation. Have Rademac System 2400 optronic director atop the pilothouse for the 40-mm guns. Two Galileo lead-computing directors are mounted fore and aft for the 23-mm weapons.

♦ 1 minelayer/training ship [MM]
Bldr: Wärtsilä, Helsinki

	Laid down	L	In serv.
01 Pohjanmaa	4-5-78	28-8-78	8-6-79

Pohjanmaa (01) Chris Sattler, 7-05

D: 1,100 tons (1,476 fl) **S:** 19 kts **Dim:** 78.30 × 11.60 × 3.20
A: 1 57-mm 70-cal. Bofors SAK 1 DP; 2 single 40-mm 70-cal. Bofors L70 AA; 2 twin 23-mm 60-cal. AA; 2 single 12.7-mm mg; 2 5-round RBU-1200 ASW RL; 2 d.c. racks (6 d.c. each); 120 mines
Electronics:
Radar: 2 Raytheon . . . ARPA nav.; 1 Thales Scout surf. search; 1 Thales DA-05 air search; 1 CelsiusTech 9GA 208 search; 1 CelsiusTech 9LV100 f.c.
Sonar: 2 hull-mounted HF sets (one for bottomed target classification)
EW: ArgoSystems . . . intercept, 2 18-round Wallop Barricade decoy RL
M: 2 Wärtsilä-Vasa 16V22 diesels; 2 CP props; 5,800 bhp—bow-thruster
Electric: 1,070 kw tot.
Range: 3,500/17 **Crew:** 80 ship's company plus 70 cadets

Remarks: Modernized in 1997–98.
Combat systems: Has CelsiusTech 9LV200 gun fire-control system. Two twin 23-mm AA forward were replaced by two single 12.7-mm mg during 1992. The original Bofors 120-mm DP gunmount was replaced in 1998. The training facilities are fitted in portable containers mounted on the two internal mine rails and are easily removable if the ship is required for combat.

♦ 3 Pansio-class coastal minelayer/antipollution ships [MM]
Bldr: Olkiluoto SY, Telakka

475 Pyhäranta (In serv. 26-4-92)
777 Porkkala (In serv. 29-10-92)
876 Pansio (ex-576) (In serv. 25-9-91)

Pansio (876) IJ Plokker, 2-00

D: 450 tons (fl) **S:** 10 kts **Dim:** 44.00 (39.20 wl) × 10.00 × 2.00
A: 1 twin 23-mm 60-cal. Sako AA; 12.7-mm mg; 50 mines (100 m rail-length tot.)
Electronics: Radar: 1 Raytheon . . . ARPA nav.
M: 2 MTU 12V 183 TE62 diesels; 2 props; 1,500 bhp—bow-thruster
Crew: 12 tot.

Remarks: Ordered 5-90 for delivery 1991–92 as combination coastal minelayers, antipollution ships, landing craft, and vehicle/cargo carriers to supply Coastal Artillery facilities. Have bow and stern ramps as well as side-loading ports. Have 100-m total mine rails on vehicle deck, which can also accommodate 4 × 40-ft. standard cargo containers or two large cargo trucks. Have a 15-ton electrohydraulic knuckle crane to port forward and a 1.2-ton crane aft. Capable of light icebreaking. Employ the Polaris ProMare minefield planning system.

♦ 4 Soviet Osa-II-class (Project 205ME) fast minelayers [MM]

11 Tuima 12 Tuisku 14 Tuuli 15 Tyrsky

Tuima (11) H&L Van Ginderen, 4-94

D: 184 tons (226 normal fl, 245 overload) **S:** 40 kts (35 sust.)
Dim: 38.6 (37.5 wl) × 7.6 (6.3 wl) × 2.0 hull (3.1 props)
A: 2 twin 30-mm 65-cal. AK-230 AA; 2 mine rails (. . . mines)
Electronics: Radar: 1 Raytheon . . . ARPA nav.
M: 3 M-504B diesels; 3 props; 15,000 bhp **Electric:** 400 kw tot.
Range: 500/34; 750/25 **Endurance:** 5 days **Crew:** 4 officers, 24 enlisted

Remarks: Transferred 1974. 11 converted to fast minelayer 1992–93 by deleting missile installation and adding rails on deck for mines, and 14 followed in 1994. 12 and 15 had the missile systems removed at the end of 1995 and were converted for minelaying during 1996. The craft were also re-engined, and the missile targeting and gun fire-control radars were removed. A rigid inflatable rubber inspection dinghy is now carried atop the superstructure aft, handled by a telescoping electrohydraulic crane on the fantail. The mine rails extend from the gunmount on the forecastle to the stern.

♦ 2 minelaying barges [MM]
Bldr: Lehtinen, Rauma (In serv. 1987)

721 821

D: 130 tons (fl) **Dim:** 15.0 × 7.0 × 1.5 **A:** . . . mines

Remarks: Non-self-propelled craft intended primarily to transport mines but also capable of being used to lay mines.

♦ 6 Kuha-class inshore minesweepers [MSI]
Bldr: Laivateollisuus, Turku

	In serv.		In serv.		In serv.
21 Kuha 21	28-6-74	23 Kuha 23	7-3-75	25 Kuha 25	17-6-75
22 Kuha 22	10-1-74	24 Kuha 24	7-3-75	26 Kuha 26	13-11-75

Kuha 21 (21)—as modified Finnish Navy, 1998

D: 125 tons (fl) **S:** 12 kts **Dim:** 31.60 × 6.90 × 2.00
A: 1 twin 23-mm 60-cal. Sako AA; 1 12.7-mm mg
Electronics: Radar: 1 Decca . . . nav.—Sonar: Patria Finavitec SONAC HF minehunting

MINE WARFARE SHIPS AND CRAFT *(continued)*

M: 2 Cummins NT-380M diesels; 2 outboard-drive props; 660 bhp
Crew: 2 officers, 12 enlisted

Remarks: Glass-reinforced plastic hulls. Plans for eight additional units canceled. Modernized and lengthened by Tyovenne Shipyard, Uusikaupunki, completing 22-12-97, 26-6-98, 30-9-98, 13-11-98, 12-12-99, and 30-5-00, respectively.
Hull systems: Engines, flexibly mounted, drive rudder/propellers through hydrostatic transmissions. Were originally 90 tons (fl), 26.6 m overall.
Combat systems: Can tow Type F-82 electrode sweep, and also have provisions for mechanical and acoustic mine sweeping. One unit has been equipped for trials with the Finnish Elesco Family of Integrated Minesweeping Systems (FIMS) sweep array with MRK-960 three-electrode magnetic sweep and MKR-400 pipe-type noncontrollable noisemaker; the data processing system is Elesco's SSCP, with differential GPS.

♦ 7 Kiiski-class inshore minesweepers [MSI]
Bldr: Fiskar's Turun, Turku

	Laid down	L	In serv.
521 Kiiski 1	. . .	. . .	1983
522 Kiiski 2	20-1-83	21-10-83	4-11-83
523 Kiiski 3	14-2-83	10-11-83	28-11-83
524 Kiiski 4	5-4-83	28-11-83	12-12-83
525 Kiiski 5	16-5-83	2-5-84	24-5-85
526 Kiiski 6	29-8-83	9-5-84	24-5-85
527 Kiiski 7	12-9-83	10-5-84	24-5-85

Kiiski 5 (525)—alongside sister *Kiiski 6* (526) Ralph Edwards, 6-03

D: 17.7 tons (20 fl) **S:** 10.7 kts **Dim:** 15.18 (13.00 pp) × 4.10 × 1.20
A: None **Electronics:** Radar: 1. . . nav.
M: 2 Valmet 611 CSMP diesels; 2 Hamilton Model 1341 waterjets; 340 bhp
Range: 250/10 **Crew:** 4 tot.

Remarks: Were to have been operated by crews or under remote control by *Kuha*-class inshore minesweepers, but are now operated in manned mode only. Glass-reinforced plastic construction. Tow a Type F-82 electrode sweep to counter magnetic mines and can also counter acoustic mines.

AMPHIBIOUS WARFARE CRAFT

♦ 3 Kampela-class utility landing craft [LCU]
Bldr: Enso-Gutzeit, Savonlinna (557: Finnmekano, Teija)

371 Kampela 1 (In serv. 29-7-76)
376 Kampela 2 (In serv. 21-10-76)
557 Kampela 3 (In serv. 23-10-79)

Kampela 2 (376) 7-96

D: 90 tons (260 fl) **S:** 9 kts **Dim:** 32.5 × 8.0 × 1.5
A: 2 single 12.7-mm mg; 20 mines
Electronics: Radar: 1 Decca 1226 nav.; 1 Decca . . . nav.
M: 2 Saab Scania diesels; 2 props; 460 bhp **Crew:** 10 tot.

Remarks: *Kampela 1* is operated for Coastal Artillery logistics support service. The twin 23-mm mounts formerly fitted on the bridge wings have been replaced by single 12.7-mm machineguns.

♦ 2 Kala-class utility landing craft [LCU]
Bldr: Rauma-Repola, Rauma (In serv. 1956–59)

Kala 4 Kala 6

Kala 6 Alexandre Sheldon-Duplaix, 7-88

D: 60 tons (200 fl) **S:** 9 kts **Dim:** 27.0 × 8.0 × 1.8
A: 2 single 12.7-mm mg; 34 mines
Electronics: Radar: 1 Decca 1226 nav.
M: 2 Valmet diesels; 2 props; 360 bhp **Crew:** 10 tot.

Remarks: Sisters *Kala 2* and *Kala 5* were stricken in 1992, *Kala 3* in 1993 and *Kala 1* in 2002.

♦ 2 Lohi-class personnel transports [LCP]
Bldr: Savonlinna SY (In serv. 7-9-84)

351 Lohi (ex-251) 452 Lohm

D: 28 tons (38 fl) **S:** 24 kts **Dim:** 20.50 × 5.90 × 1.00
A: 1 twin 23-mm 60-cal. Sako AA; 1 12.7-mm mg
Electronics: Radar: 1 Decca 1226 nav.
M: 2 Wizeman–Mercedes-Benz diesels; 2 KaMeWa waterjets; 1,100 bhp
Range: 240/24 **Crew:** 4 tot.

Remarks: Have a near-vertical bow door and ramp for landing personnel embarked. Ordered 17-1-83 and laid down 8-83 and 9-83. Aluminum construction. Used as VIP transports, patrol craft, hospital launches, etc. Guns not always mounted. Operated for the Coastal Artillery service.

♦ 16 Uisko 600–class landing craft [LCP]
Bldr: Marine Alutech Oy, Teijo, Finland (In serv. 2001–3)

U 601 through U 616

D: 13 tons **S:** 37 kts **Dim:** 13.9 × 3.7 × 0.7
A: 1 12.7-mm mg
M: 2 Caterpillar . . . diesels; 2 . . . waterjets
Crew: 3 tot. + 20 troops

Remarks: Aluminum construction. Improved versions of Meriusko class.

♦ 36 Meriusko-class assault boats [LCP]
Bldr: Alumina Varvet, Kokkola

U 200 series U 300 series U 400 series

Meriusko-class U 405 Ralph Edwards, 6-03

D: 8.5 tons (10.2 fl) **S:** 36 kts (30 loaded) **Dim:** 11.3 × 3.5 × 0.6
M: 2 Volvo TAMD70E diesels; 2 Hamilton 291 waterjets; 600 bhp—*or* 1 MTU V8 diesel; 1 waterjet
Crew: 3 tot. + 25 troops

Remarks: Small bow ramp. U 203 and one other have cable-handling equipment to enable them to act as boom defense boats. Design by Wico-Boat Oy (now Finnspeed) and known commercially as the "Sea-Wico" class. First 11, completed 1983–86, originally had a low pilothouse and no radar but now have a full-height structure and radar; later units have a larger pilothouse.

♦ 2 Vietivisko-class assault boats [LCP]
Bldr: Alumina Varvet, Kokkola (In serv. 1983)

U 201 U 202

AMPHIBIOUS WARFARE CRAFT *(continued)*

D: 10.72 tons (fl) **S:** 25 kts **Dim:** 11.3 × 3.5 × 0.6
M: 2 Volvo TAMD70E diesels; 2 props; 600 bhp

Remarks: Similar to Meriusko class.

AUXILIARIES

♦ 1 Halli-class pollution cleanup ship and vehicle transport [AG]

	Bldr	Laid down	L	In serv.
899 HALLI	Hollming, Rauma	18-3-86	25-6-86	1-87

Halli (899) Ralph Edwards, 6-03

D: 1,600 tons (fl) **S:** 11.3 kts **Dim:** 60.50 × 12.40 × 3.0
Electronics: Radar: 3 different . . . nav.
M: 2 Wärtsilä-Vasa 6R22 diesels; 2 Aquamaster azimuthal props; 2,650 bhp
Range: 3,000/11.3 **Crew:** 13 tot.

Remarks: 1,400 grt/1,200 dwt. Operated for the Ministry of the Environment by the Ministry of Navigation under navy control with a civilian crew. Enlarged version of *Hylje*. Employs MacGregor-Navire MacLORI pollution collection system; sweeps 30-m path at 1.5 kts. Has 360-m^3 waste-collection tank. Can also be used as a landing ship and logistic support vessel; has 11-m bow ramp for 48-ton vehicles.

♦ 1 Hylje-class pollution cleanup and vehicle transport ship [AG]
Bldr: Laivateollisuus, Turku (In serv. 3-6-81)

799 HYLJE

D: 1,436 (fl) **S:** 7 kts **Dim:** 49.90 × 12.50 × 3.00
Electronics: Radar: 2 Raytheon . . . nav.
M: 2 Saab-Scania DSI-14 diesels; 2 Jastram RP03 retractable, steerable props; 590 bhp
Electric: 690 kVA tot. (2 × 300-kVA Stamford, 1 × 90-kw Stamford diesel sets)
Range: . . . / . . . **Fuel:** 55 m^3 **Crew:** 7 tot. (accom. for 14)

Remarks: Operated for the Ministry of the Environment by the Ministry of Transportation under navy control with civilian crew. Can carry 100 tons of deck cargo on the flush open deck forward, and there is a bow ramp with 42 tons capacity. A 6-ton crane is fitted. Storage tanks can hold 550 m^3 of recovered seawater/oil slurry and 860 m^3 recovered or cargo oil. One 10-m and one 13-m oil-skimming boat carried, and there is a 120 m^3/hr foam monitor. Can be operated in light ice.

♦ 1 intelligence collector [AGI]
Bldr: Valmet, Turku (In serv. 1963)

99 KUSTAANMIEKKA (ex-*Valvoja III*)

Kustaanmiekka (99) H&L Van Ginderen, 4-94

D: 340 tons (fl) **S:** 11 kts **Dim:** 36.70 × 9.40 × 3.20
A: Provision for 2 single 12.7-mm mg **Electronics:** Radar: 1. . . nav.
M: 1 Burmeister & Wain Alpha diesel; 1 prop; 480 bhp
Fuel: 38.5 tons **Crew:** 10 tot.

Remarks: 406 grt. Former buoy tender, acquired from Board of Navigation in 1989 and refitted for naval service by Hollming, Rauma. As of late 1993, had been converted into an intelligence collector, with large dielectric radome aft and intercept antennas on foremast. Sister *Kemiö* (93) was transferred to Estonia in 12-92.

Disposal note: Salvage ship *Parainen* (420; ex-*Pellinki*, ex-*Meteor*) was sold for commercial purposes during 2001.

SERVICE CRAFT

♦ 1 trials craft [YAGE] Bldr: Reposaaron Konepaja, Pori

	Laid down	L	In serv.
826 ISKU	11-68	4-12-69	1970

Isku (826) Finnish Navy, 1990

D: 180 tons (fl) **S:** 18 kts **Dim:** 33.35 × 8.70 × 1.80
A: . . . mines **Electronics:** Radar: 1 Raytheon . . . ARPA nav.
M: 4 Soviet M-50-F4 diesels; 4 props; 4,800 bhp **Crew:** 25 tot.

Remarks: "Seasled" planing hull with rectangular planform. Built as a guided-missile patrol boat and armed with four Soviet P-15 Termit (SS-N-2A Styx) missiles and a twin 30-mm AK-230 AA mount. Never made designed speed and was relegated to trials duties. In 1989–90 was lengthened 7 m by Uusikaupunki Shipyard, with the deckhouse lengthened, mine rails added, and an articulated crane added near the bow.

♦ 1 modified Valas-class diving tender [YDT]
Bldr: Hollming Oy, Rauma (In serv. 10-80)

98 MERSU

D: 300 tons (fl) **S:** 12 kts **Dim:** 30.65 × 8.1 × 3.4
A: 1 twin 23-mm 60-cal. Sako AA; 1 12.7-mm mg; 28 small mines
Electronics: Radar: 1 Decca . . . nav.
M: 1 Wärtsilä-Vasa 22 diesel; 1 prop; 1,450 bhp
Crew: 1 officer, 6 enlisted + 20 divers

Remarks: Can also be used to transport 300 personnel. Appearance generally as the *Valas* class.

♦ 4 Valas-class general-service tenders [YF]
Bldr: Hollming Oy, Rauma (In serv. 1979–81)

897 VALAS (ex-97) 121 VAHAKARI 222 VAARLEHTI 323 VÄNÖ

Valas (897) Ralph Edwards, 6-03

D: 100 tons (275 fl) **S:** 12 kts **Dim:** 30.65 × 7.85 × 3.40
A: 1 twin 23-mm 60-cal. Sako AA; 1 12.7-mm mg; 28 small mines
Electronics: Radar: 1 Decca . . . nav.
M: 1 Wärtsilä Vasa 22 diesel; 1 prop; 1,300 bhp **Crew:** 11 tot.

Remarks: Ordered in 1978. Can break .4-m ice. Carry 35 tons of cargo or 150 passengers. Stern ramp for vehicle loading or minelaying. 121, 222, and 323 are operated by the Coastal Artillery service.

♦ 1 presidential yacht [YFL] Bldr: Uusikaupunki SY (In serv. 5-84)

KULTARANTA VII

D: 15 tons (fl) **S:** 25 kts **Dim:** 12.5 × 4.0 × 1.4
M: 2 diesels; 2 props; 700 bhp

Remarks: Described as a "communications ship" and used as a presidential yacht in summer and for search and rescue and medical transport in winter.

SERVICE CRAFT *(continued)*

Kultaranta VII Ralph Edwards, 6-03

♦ **4 Hila-class personnel and stores transports [YFL]**
Bldr: Kotkan Telakka (In serv. 1991–94)

237 Hila 238 Harun 339 Hästö 430 Högsåra

Hästö (339) Hartmut Ehlers, 9-96

D: 50 tons (fl) **S:** 12 kts **Dim:** 15.00 × 4.00 × 1.80
Electronics: Radar: 1 . . . nav.
M: 2 Volvo Penta TAMD-61E diesels; 2 props; 416 bhp **Crew:** 4 tot.

Remarks: Ordered 8-90. Used by the Coastal Artillery service as personnel and stores carriers. Have ice-strengthened steel hulls, with 339 having greater sheer to the bow area.

♦ **7 Vihuri-class personnel transport and command launches [YFL]** Bldr: Waterman, Turku (In serv. 1991–93)

511 Jymy 531 Syöksy 992 Träskö 994 Alskär
521 Raju 541 Vinha 993 Torsö

Jymy (511) Ralph Edwards, 6-03

D: 13 tons (14.5 fl) **S:** 35 kts (30 sust.) **Dim:** 13.65 × 4.00 × 0.60
M: 2 MTU diesels; 2 FF waterjets; 772 bhp **Crew:** 6 tot.

Remarks: 521, 531, and 541 are configured as command launches used by the navy, while the others are configured as ambulance/personnel launches under Coastal Artillery control. GRP construction. Class prototype *Vihuri* was lost to fire in late 1991 and *Jymy* was built as a replacement.

♦ **2 Askeri-class personnel transport and command launches [YFL]** Bldr: Kotkan Telakka (In serv. 1991–92)

91 Viiri 241 Askeri

Viiri (91) Hartmut Ehlers, 9-96

D: 20 tons (25 fl) **S:** 22 kts **Dim:** 16.0 × 4.4 × 1.4
Electronics: Radar: 1 Raytheon 1900 Pathfinder nav., 1 . . . nav.
M: 2 Volvo Penta TAMD-series diesels; 2 props; 1,100 bhp **Crew:** 6 tot.

Remarks: 241 is used by the Coastal Artillery service. GRP construction.

♦ **10 L 100–class personnel transports [YFL]**
Bldr: Finnspeed Boats Oy (In serv. 1991–92)

L 100 through L 109

L 108 H&L Van Ginderen, 7-00

D: 13 tons (fl) **S:** 13 kts **Dim:** 13.00 × 4.00 × 0.60
Electronics: Radar: 1 Raytheon 1900 Pathfinder nav.
M: 1 Volvo TAMD 71 diesel; 380 bhp

Remarks: Glass-reinforced plastic construction craft intended for interisland transport and conscript boat-handling training duties. Seven were delivered in 1991, the others in 1992. Finnspeed is the successor to Wico-Boat Oy and is owned by Hollming Shipyard.

♦ **6 Hauki-class personnel transports [YFL]**
Bldr: First three: Linnan Telakka, Turku; others: Valmet Oy, Kolka (In serv. 1978–80)

133 Havouri 235 Hirsala 431 Hakuni
232 Hauki 334 Hankoniemi 436 Houtskär

D: 46 tons (fl) **S:** 10 kts **Dim:** 14.4 × 4.6 × 2.2
Electronics: Radar: 1 Raytheon 1900 Pathfinder nav.
M: 2 Valmet 611 CSM diesels; 1 prop; 586 bhp **Crew:** 2 tot.

Remarks: Cargo: 40 personnel or 6 tons of supplies. Can break .2-m ice. Operated for the Coast Artillery service.

SERVICE CRAFT *(continued)*

Havouri (133) Ralph Edwards, 6-03

♦ 1 Pikkala-class personnel transport [YFL]
Bldr: Crichton-Vulkan SY, Turku (In serv. 1946)

96 PIKKALA (ex-*Delta,* ex-*Fenno*)

Pikkala (96) Ralph Edwards, 6-03

D: 66 tons (fl) **S:** 10 kts **Dim:** 23.0 × 4.4 × 2.0
Electronics: Radar: 1 Raytheon 1900 Pathfinder nav.
M: 1 Valmet diesel; 1 prop; 180 bhp **Crew:** 5 tot.

Remarks: Built as a commercial interisland personnel ferry. Acquired for navy 28-10-67 and given current name. Refitted 1977 and again in 1988. Initially used for training but now employed as a personnel transport and public affairs craft for both the Ministry of Defense and the navy. Oldest unit in the Finnish Navy.

♦ 1 fuel and water lighter [YO]

PA 3 (In serv. 1979)

D: 540 tons (fl) **S:** 2 kts (normally towed) **Dim:** . . . × . . . × . . .

♦ 1 cable tender [YRC]
Bldr: Rauma-Repola, Rauma (L: 15-12-65)

92 PUTSAARI

D: 430 tons (fl) **S:** 10 kts **Dim:** 45.5 × 8.9 × 2.3
M: 1 Wärtsilä diesel; 1 prop; 450 bhp—bow-thruster **Crew:** 20 tot.

Remarks: Refitted 1987 by Wärtsilä. Has two 10-ton cable winches and bow cable-laying sheaves. Capable of operating in light ice.

♦ 2 harbor tugs [YTM]
Bldr: Teijon Telakka (In serv. 12-85)

731 HAUKIPÄÄ 831 KALLANPÄÄ

Kallanpää (831) H&L Van Ginderen, 9-93

D: 38 grt **S:** 9 kts **Dim:** 14.0 × 5.0 × 2.3
M: 2 diesels; 2 vertical cycloidal props; 360 bhp **Crew:** 2 tot.

♦ 1 Tiira-class training launch [YXT]
Bldr: Valmet-Laivateollisuus, Turku

	Laid down	L	In serv.
56 KAJAVA	25-11-85	25-3-86	28-8-86

D: 65 tons (fl) **S:** 25+ kts **Dim:** 26.80 (24.20 pp) × 5.50 × 1.40 (1.85 props)
A: Provision for 1 or 2 twin 23-mm 60-cal. Sako AA
Electronics: Radar: 1 . . . nav.—Sonar: Simrad SS-242 hull-mounted
M: 2 MTU 8V396 TB82 diesels; 2 props; 2,286 bhp
Electric: 62 kVA tot. **Fuel:** 8 tons **Crew:** 2 officers, 6 enlisted

Remarks: Transferred 1999 from the Frontier Guard. Development of *Lokki* design, with hard-chine vice round-bilged hull form. Aluminum construction. Sister *Kihu* was donated to Lithuania late in 1997, and *Tiira* had been discarded by 2000.

♦ 1 Lokki-class training launch [YXT]
Bldr: Valmet-Laivateollisuus, Turku (In serv. 27-11-81)

57 LOKKI

D: 53 tons (60 fl) **S:** 25 kts **Dim:** 26.80 × 5.20 × 1.40 (1.85 props)
A: Provision for 1 twin 23-mm 60-cal. Sako AA
Electronics: Radar: 1 . . . nav.
M: MTU 8V396 TB83 diesels; 2 props; 2,040 bhp
Electric: 62 kVA tot. **Crew:** 2 officers, 6 enlisted

Remarks: Transferred 1999 from the Frontier Guard. Aluminum construction. Ordered 17-5-80.

♦ 1 training craft, former patrol craft prototype [YXT]
Bldr: Fiskar's Turan, Veneveistamo SY/Laivateollisuus

30 HURJA

D: 54 tons (60 fl) **S:** 42 kts **Dim:** 21.7 × 5.0 × 2.0
A: Removed **Electronics:** Radar: 1 . . . nav.
M: 3 diesels; waterjets; 3,800 bhp **Crew:** 10 tot.

Remarks: Glass-reinforced plastic prototype hull delivered 1-7-80 to Laivateollisuus for fitting out. The gun mount was aft. This class was intended to replace at least seven of the *Nuoli* class during the 1980s, but no further orders materialized and *Hurja* is now employed in naval reserve training.

Note: Used at the naval academy for basic training are the launches 681, 683, and 685; no data available.

FRONTIER GUARD
MINISTRY OF THE INTERIOR

Personnel: Approx. 650 total

Note: All ships now have dark green hulls with a red-white-red diagonal stripe. Upperworks are gray.

Aviation: Fixed-wing aircraft include 2 Dornier Do-228-212 maritime patrol aircraft with GEC-Marconi Seaspray 2000 maritime surveillance radars. Helicopters include 4 Agusta-Bell AB-412EP Griffin maritime surveillance helicopters, 3 Aérospatiale AS. 332L1 Super Pumawith French dipping sonars for ASW work, and 4 Agusta-Bell AB-206B JetRanger utility helicopters.

PATROL SHIPS [WPS]

♦ 1 Merikarhu class
Bldr: Finnyards, Rauma (In serv. 28-10-94)

MERIKARHU

Merikarhu IJ Plokker, 9-99

D: 1,100 tons (fl) **S:** 15+ kts **Dim:** 57.80 (52.12 pp) × 11.00 × 4.60
A: Provision for 1 twin 23-mm 60-cal. Sako AA
Electronics: Radar: 1 Decca . . . nav.; 1 Selesmar . . . surf. search
M: 2 Wärtsilä 8R22/26 diesels; 1 CP prop; 3,640 bhp
Electric: 1,050 kVA (shaft generator, plus 2 × 270-kw diesel sets)
Crew: 30 tot.

Remarks: Ordered late spring 1993 as an offshore-patrol and environmental-cleanup vessel. An improved version of the *Tursas* class. Has 30-ton bollard-pull towing capacity.

PATROL COMBATANTS [WPG]

♦ 2 Tursas class

Bldr: Rauma-Repola Oy, Uusikaupunki

	Laid down	L	In serv.
TURSAS	4-9-85	31-1-86	6-6-86
UISKO	4-4-86	19-6-86	27-1-87

Tursas 5-94

D: 750 tons (fl) **S:** 15.5 kts **Dim:** 49.00 (43.80 pp) × 10.40 × 4.00
A: 1 twin 23-mm 60-cal. Sako AA
Electronics: Radar: 2 . . . nav.—Sonar: Simrad SS 105 (14 kHz)
M: 2 Wärtsilä-Vasa 8-R22 diesels; 2 props; 3,200 bhp
Electric: 1,070 kw (1 × 750 kw, 2 × 160 kw) **Fuel:** 73 tons **Crew:** 32 tot.

Remarks: First unit ordered 12-12-84, second on 20-3-86. Ice-strengthened hulls; equipped for towing and salvage duties. A sister was ordered for Sweden in 1989.

♦ 1 improved Valpas class

Bldr: Laivateollisuus Oy, Turku (In serv. 15-12-77)

TURVA

Turva H&L Van Ginderen, 1993

D: 550 tons (fl) **S:** 16 kts **Dim:** 48.5 × 8.6 × 3.9
A: Provision for 1 twin 23-mm 60-cal. Sako AA
Electronics: Radar: 2 . . . nav.; Sonar: Simrad SS 105 (14 kHz)
M: 2 Wärtsilä diesels; 1 prop; 2,000 bhp **Crew:** 22 tot.

Remarks: Ordered 24-6-75. An improved *Valpas;* similar in appearance.

Disposal note: *Valpas,* the sole unit of the *Valpas* class, was transferred to Latvia in 12-02.

PATROL CRAFT [WPC]

♦ 2 (+ 1) Telkkä class

Bldr: Workboat Työvene, Uusikaupunki

	In serv.		In serv.
TELKKÄ	7-99	TIIRA	27-5-04
TAVI	2002		

Tavi Jaroslaw Cislak, 5-03

D: 400 tons (fl) **S:** 22 (*Telkkä:* 20.5) kts **Dim:** 49.20 × 7.50 × 3.70 max.
A: 1 twin 23-mm 60-cal. Sako AA **Electronics:** Radar: . . .
M: *Telkkä:* 2 Cummins-Wärtsilä 16V170 diesels; 2 CP props; 5,580 bhp (sustained); others: 2 Wärtsilä 12V200 diesels; 2 CP props; 6,700 bhp
Electric: 375 kVA tot. (2 × 170-kVA, 1 × 35-kVA Valmet diesel sets)
Fuel: 55,000 liters **Crew:** 8 tot. + 12 passengers

Remarks: Second and third units were ordered 8-12-00.
Hull systems: Steel hull with aluminum superstructure. Has integrated navigation and environmental monitoring system, digital chart system, autopilot, dynamic positioning system, two gyrocompasses, echo sounder, radio D/F, GPS receiver, and infrared surveillance camera. Oil-spill recovery equipment includes deployable spill-containment booms and a 50-m^3-capacity rubber storage barge. A firefighting monitor with a range of 100 m is fitted, and a rigid-inflatable rescue boat is stowed on a launch-and-recover ramp at the stern.

♦ 2 Kiisla class

Bldr: Hollming Oy, Rauma

	Laid down	L	In serv.
50 KIISLA	12-2-86	18-9-86	25-5-87
KURKI	3-8-89	. . .	11-90

Kiisla (50) Ralph Edwards, 6-03

D: 250 tons (270 fl) **S:** 25 kts **Dim:** 48.30 (41.80 pp) × 8.80 × 2.20
A: 1 twin 23-mm 60-cal. Sako AA
Electronics: Radar: 2 . . . nav.; Sonar: Simrad SS 304 hull-mounted and VDS
M: 2 MTU 16V538 TB93 diesels; 2 KaMeWa 90S62 waterjets; 4,500 bhp
Electric: 264 kw tot. **Fuel:** 53 tons **Crew:** 22 tot.

Remarks: *Kiisla* ordered 21-11-84; three more on 22-11-88, of which two were later canceled. Aluminum construction. Can also act as minesweepers, minelayers, or ASW escorts; in the latter mode, can carry two 5-round Soviet RBU-1200 RL. Equipped for fire fighting and carry a 5.7-m rigid inflatable inspection boat. Have Rademac 2100 E/C electro-optical surveillance device atop pilothouse.

PATROL BOATS [WPB]

♦ 2 (+ . . .) 10.5-m rigid inflatable rescue boats

Bldr: Delta Power Services, . . . , U.K. (In serv. 12-00)

D: 4.6 tons (fl) **S:** 50 + kts **Dim:** 10.5 × . . . × . . .
Electronics: 1 . . . nav.
M: 2 Yamaha gasoline outboards; 500 bhp **Crew:** 3 tot.

Remarks: Ordered 6-00. Have GRP foam-sandwich hulls with 600-mm-dia. rigid inflatable collar. Have color radar, electronic charts. Intended for patrol, rescue, and smuggler interception. Delta is said to have earlier delivered other, smaller search-and-rescue RHIBs.

♦ 2 (+ . . .) RIB C-3500-class rigid inflatable rescue boats

Bldr: Boomeranger Boats Oy, Loviisa

D: 4.5 tons (fl) **S:** 50 kts (47 sust.) **Dim:** 10.2 × 3.5 × . . .
Electronics: Radar: 1 . . . nav.
M: 2 Mariner gasoline outboards; 500 bhp **Crew:** 3 tot. + 2 passengers

Remarks: First unit delivered 5-96, second early in 1998. Aluminum structure with inflatable rubber buoyancy collar. Have an enclosed pilothouse.

♦ 10 (+ ?) RV-90 class

Bldr: Uudenkaupungin Telakka, Uusikaupunki (In serv. 3-92 to 1996)

RV-150 . . .	RV-154 . . .	RV-157 . . .	RV-160 . . .
RV-151 . . .	RV-155 . . .	RV-158 . . .	
RV-152 . . .	RV-156 . . .	RV-159 . . .	

D: 23.7 tons (25 fl) **S:** 12 kts **Dim:** 15.00 (12.83 pp) × 4.00 × 1.80
Electronics: Radar: 1 . . . nav. **M:** 1 Caterpillar 3408 diesel; 1 prop; 476 bhp

Remarks: Icebreaking tug-type hulls. Intended to replace the older RV-series patrol launches listed below. Additional units may be constructed at a later date.

♦ 7 RV-37 class

Bldr: Hollming Oy, Rauma (In serv. 1978–85)

RV-37 RV-38 RV-39 RV-40 RV-41 RV-142 RV-243

D: 20 tons (fl) **S:** 12 kts **Dim:** 14.3 × 3.6 × 1.6
Electronics: Radar: 1 . . . nav. **M:** 1 Mercedes-Benz diesel; 300 bhp

♦ 14 PV-11-class patrol launches

Bldr: Fiskar's Turun, Turku (In serv. 9-84)

PV-11, -12, -104, -108, -205, -209, -210–212, -306, -307 + 4 others

D: 10 tons **S:** 29 kts **Dim:** 10.0 × . . . × . . .
M: 2 Volvo Penta diesels; 2 waterjets; . . . bhp **Crew:** 2 tot.

FRONTIER GUARD PATROL BOATS [WPB] *(continued)*

Note: Also in use for patrol and search-and-rescue duties by the Frontier Guard are 27 older patrol craft: 9 RV-9 series (1959–60) of 12 tons; 11 RV-10 series (1961–63) of 18 tons; and 7 RV-30 series (1973–74) of 19 tons. All can make 10 kts.

♦ 5 rigid inflatable boats
Bldr: Avon Boats, U.K. (In serv. 1993)

D: . . . **S:** 50 kts **Dim:** 8.4 × . . . × . . .
M: 2 outboard engines; 450 bhp **Crew:** 4 tot.

Remarks: Ordered 3-93 for use in search-and-rescue duties and as antismuggling inspection boats.

AIR-CUSHION PATROL CRAFT [WPBA]

♦ 3 2000-TDX(M)-class air cushion vehicles
Bldr: Griffon Hovercraft, Salisbury Green, Southampton, U.K. (In serv. 1-12-94 to 1999)

D: 6.8 tons (fl) **S:** 50 kts (33 loaded) **Dim:** 11.0 × 4.60 × . . .
A: Provision for 1 7.62-mm mg **Electronics:** Radar: 1 . . . nav.
M: 1 Deutz BF8L513 diesel; 1 shrouded CP airscrew; 320 bhp
Range: 300/25 loaded **Crew:** 2 tot. + 16 troops

Remarks: Can carry 2,200-kg cargo in lieu of troops. First two delivered 1-12-94, third on 27-5-95. GRP construction hull.

♦ 4 SAH-2200-class air cushion vehicles
Bldr: Slingsby Amphibious Hovercraft Co., U.K. (In serv. 9-92)

D: 5.5 tons (fl) **S:** 50 kts **Dim:** 10.60 × 4.20 × . . .
A: Provision for 1 7.62-mm mg **Electronics:** Radar: 1 Raytheon R41 nav.
M: 1 Cummins 6CTA-8.3M1 diesel; 1 shrouded CP airscrew; 300 bhp
Range: 500/50 **Fuel:** 510 liters **Crew:** 2 tot. + 12 troops

Remarks: Can carry 1,200-kg cargo in lieu of troops. Three more ordered in 1998 and delivered by 2002.

Note: The icebreakers and other ships and craft operated by the Board of Navigation (*Merenkulkuhallitus*), the cable ship operated by the Central Board of Post and Telegraphy (*Suomen Posti-ja Lennatinhallitus & Post-och Telegrafstyrelsen*), and the survey ships operated by the Ministry of Trade and Industry are described and illustrated in the 1998–99 and earlier editions.

FRANCE
French Republic

FRENCH NAVY

Personnel: 46,195 total, including 6,443 naval aviation and 2,050 marine personnel plus 6,000 naval reservists. 10,265 civilians are also employed.

Organization and Bases: Fleet command is concentrated at the Interforces Operations Center in Paris. The First Maritime Region is headquartered at Brest and the Second at Toulon. The Naval Action Force (*Force d'Action Navale*), based at Toulon, includes the aircraft carrier, four amphibious warfare ships, three logistics support ships, and nine destroyers and frigates, including *Cassard* and *Jean Bart*. At Brest are based the *Force Oceanique Stratégique,* with the ballistic missile and attack submarines, and the Anti-Submarine Action Group, with destroyers, A-69-class corvettes, and two logistics support ships. Also based at Brest is the Mine Warfare Force, although four minehunters are normally based at Toulon. Small naval bases are located overseas at Fort-de-France, Martinique; Degrad des Cannes, French Guiana; St.-Denis, La Réunion; Nouméa, New Caledonia; and Papeete, Tahiti. Major naval shipyards are located at Brest (major warships), Toulon (major warships), and Cherbourg (submarines, patrol craft). Aviation facilities are located as listed in the naval aviation section below.

Naval Aviation: Principal aircraft totals include 48 Super Étendard (in service) and 12 Rafale-M fighters (60 are planned); 3 E-2C Hawkeye surveillance; 28 Atlantique 2, 5 Gardian, and 4 Falcon 50 maritime patrol; and 9 Super Frelon, 28 Lynx helicopters, and 15 Panther helicopters. 27 NH-90 helicopters were ordered with deliveries beginning in 2005. Details may be found in the aviation section following the aircraft carrier entries.

Gendarmarie: The French Navy provides patrol boats to the maritime forces of the Gendarmarie Maritime, with about 1,200 total personnel. The Gendarmarie Maritime is subordinate directly to the Ministry of Defense and is headquartered at Paris. Its personnel wear standard French Navy uniforms. Within France, craft and personnel are organized into four groups, based at Toulon, Rochefort, Lorient, Brest, and Cherbourg. Overseas afloat forces are assigned at Pointe-à-Pitre, Guadaloupe; Dakar, Senegal; Cayenne, French Guiana; Papeete, Tahiti; Djibouti; Port des Galets, La Réunion; and Nouméa, New Caledonia.

The Gendarmarie Nationale is a separate organization with about 2,700 officers and 77,000 noncommissioned officers, as well as some 1,300 civilian employees. The organization has several hundred river and seagoing craft plus 29 Écureuil and 11 Alouette-III helicopters.

Special Forces: Maritime troop assets comprise the French Army's Grupement des Fusiliers-Marins Commandos, with 3,500 personnel, and an amphibious combat swimmer company from the French Foreign Legion.

WEAPONS AND SYSTEMS

Note: France's major military electronics firm, Thomson-CSF, changed its corporate name to Thales on 18-12-00. The missile design, development, and manufacturing efforts of France's Aérospatiale Matra and the UK's BAe Systems (including its subsidiary Alenia Marconi Systems) were combined early in 3-01 as MBDA, which stands for Matra BAe Dynamics, Alenia Marconi Systems, and Aérospatiale Matra.

Thales and government-owned ship design and construction entity DCN (Direction des Constructions Navales) established a joint company, Armaris, on 1-9-02 to act as a marketer for their export warship and combat systems products.

A. MISSILES

♦ Strategic ballistic missiles

M 45: Weights and dimensions essentially the same as the retired M 4. Uses the TN-75 reentry vehicle to a range of 5,000 km, although one was officially reported to have traveled 6,000 km on 4-3-86. Operational in late 1996 aboard *Le Triomphant* and in 2001 on *L'Inflexible.* Made by Aérospatiale-Matra.

Total height: 11.05 m **Diameter:** 1.93m **Launch:** Powder charge
Launch weight: 36 tons (first stage: 20 tons; second stage: 8 tons; third stage: 1.5 tons)
Thrust: First stage: 70 tons; second stage: 30 tons; third stage: 7 tons
Duration of thrust: First stage: 65 sec; second stage: 75 sec; third stage: 45 sec
Max. range: 5,000 km **Payload:** 6 × 150 kt warheads

M 51: A new weapon being developed by the EADS Launch Vehicles and G2P (*Groupement pour la Propulsion a Pudre*) (SNECMA and SNPE) consortium for the "second generation" ballistic-missile submarines and expected to enter service in 2010 aboard *Le Terrible* (S 619). Originally to have carried 10–12 TN-75 independently targeted warheads (MIRV), the missile will now carry four, and it will employ the third stage of the M 45 missile. M 51 is being backfitted into earlier units of the *Le Triomphant* class.

Total height: 12 m **Diameter:** 2.30 m **Weight:** 56 tons **Range:** 8,000 km

♦ Surface-to-air missiles

SAAM (*Système d'Autodéfense AntiMissile*): Was intended to become operational in 2001 aboard the carrier *Charles de Gaulle,* although it will now be delayed. It will be vertically launched from eight-missile Sylver modular cell groups. Guidance will be supported by the Thales Arabel (*Antenne Radar à Balayage Electronique*) I/J-band missile detection radar, which has a range of 100 km. The SAMP/T version is intended for land-based use. The two-stage Aster-15 missile, which will be highly maneuverable, will have the following characteristics:

Length: 4.20 m **Diameter:** 0.18 m **Wingspan:** 0.36 m
Weight: 298 kg **Warhead:** 15 kg **Maneuverability:** 15 g
Speed: 1,000 m/sec (Mach 2.5) **Range:** 2–20 km

The first 12 operational Aster-15 missiles were ordered during 1995 and 20 more in 1996; under the 1997 budget, 40 were ordered.

A 30-km range version, Aster-30, is also in development in a system known as SAMP/N (*Sol-Air Moyenne Portée/Naval*) to replace the SM-1 MR missile as part of the NATO project FSAF (*Famille de Systèmes Surface-Air Futurs*), which is also known as the LAMS (Local Area Missile System). It was to be installed on the *Forbin*-class frigates to enter service around 2006. Development is shared by France's Aérospatiale (25%), Thales (25%), and MBDA (50%), with the United Kingdom, Germany, and Spain also involved. The system will incorporate the French Arabel and Astral (Air Surveillance and Targeting Radar, L-band) radars in French service. Manufacturer: Aérospatiale. The following characteristics have been announced:

Length: 4.80 m **Diameter:** 0.18 m **Weight:** 450 kg
Warhead: 15 kg **Speed:** Mach 3.5 **Range:** 3 to 70 km
Altitude: 60 to 20,000 m

Note: The Masurca area-defense SAM system is no longer supported as of 2000. Only a single launcher remains aboard an active ship, the destroyer *Duquesne* (D 603).

Standard SM-1 MR: A one-stage U.S.-designed and -manufactured solid-fuel missile.

Length: 4.60 m **Diameter:** .41 m **Weight:** 590 kg
Max. range: 50,000 m **Interception altitude:** 60–80,000 ft.
Guidance: Semiactive homing, proximity fuze.

The system consists of the Mk 13 launcher with a vertical stowage-loader containing 40 missiles, various computers, DRBJ-11B height-finding radar, and 2 SPG 51C tracking radars. The two *Cassard* AAW-type destroyers carry SM-1 MR.

Crotale/Crotale EDIR: A French Air Force missile adapted for naval use. Electronics are by Thales and the missile by Matra. Characteristics for the R440N missile are:

Length: 2.930 m **Diameter:** 0.156 m **Wingspan:** 0.54 m with fins extended
Weight: 85.1 kg **Warhead:** 14 kg **Launcher:** Octuple
Speed: Mach 2.4 **Range:** 13,000 m **Interception altitude:** 150–12,000 ft
Guidance: Beam riding; detonation by infrared fuze incorporated in the missile

Installed on the F 67 and *Cassard* destroyer classes, four Saudi Arabian frigates, and two Chinese combatants (China has copied the system, with the pirated version known as HQ-61). In French ships, it is used with DRBV-51C radar and has Thales Ku-band tracking radar.

Crotale has been updated to enable it to handle Mach 2.0 targets at altitudes down to 4 m. The missiles, named Crotale EDIR (*Écartometrie Différentielle Infra Rouge*), have been equipped with a new proximity fuze and an infrared tracker has been fitted to the launcher/director; range was increased from 8,000 m to 13,000 m.

Crotale Modulaire: A lightweight system, Crotale modulaire employs an octuple launcher and any of a number of control systems. It has been purchased by Oman and the United Arab Emirates.

Crotale NG: A further improvement of the basic missile, designated Crotale NG ("New Generation"), uses a VT-1 hypervelocity, Mach 3.5, missile and is carried by *La Fayette*–class frigates. The VT-1 missile has a 14-kg warhead and employs computer-controlled command guidance, using simultaneous inputs from the shipboard system's J-band radar, t.v., and infrared trackers. One source indicates that only about 200 have been manufactured during the 1980s and 1990s.

Thales teamed with the Russian Fakel design bureau to develop a vertical-launch version of the VT-1 missile, using a cold-launch gas generator ejection system; it was to be available for production by 2001–2, but the program seems to have halted.

WEAPONS AND SYSTEMS *(continued)*

VL Mica: A modification of the current air-to-air Mica. Altitude of 10 km and range of 10–12 km, with eight-cell vertical launch groups firing at as little as 2-sec intervals. Guidance is by infrared and active radar seekers, using thrust-vector control. Also offered for land use. Manufacturer: Matra-BAE Dynamics.

SADRAL (*Système d'Autodéfense Rapprochée Anti-aérienne Léger*): A point-defense, 6-round, short-range system employing the Mistral IR-homing missile with laser-backup proximity and impact fuzing. Manufacturer: Matra. Characteristics for the missile itself are:

Length: 1.80 m **Diameter:** 0.90 m **Weight:** 24 kg
Warhead: 3 kg (1,500 tungsten balls) **Speed:** Mach 2.5
Range: Less than 500 to around 6,000 m **Min. altitude:** 3 m

SIMBAD (*Système Intégré de Mistral Bimunition pour l'Autodéfense*): A lightweight, twin-launcher system for Mistral. In the French Navy, it is aboard the destroyers *Primauguet, La Motte-Picquet,* and *Latouche-Tréville;* the *Floréal*-class patrol ships; dock landing ships; and the *Durance*-class replenishment vessels.

♦ Surface-to-surface missiles

Note: The ANF (*Anti-Navir Futur*) antiship missile program was terminated 12-99.

SCALP Naval: A surface ship- and submarine-launched variant of SCALP-EG proposed for use as a strategic weapon for use on the *Barracuda*-class SSN and the new *Frégates d'Action Navale* class (from which it would be vertically launched from the Sylver VLS system). The missile is propelled by a Microturbo TR160-30 turbojet and employs a combination of inertial guidance, GPS, and terrain reference for navigation, with an autonomous target recognition system using a BAE Systems/Detexis infrared sensor. SCALP is planned to enter service in 2011, with initial production to commence during 2006 and a total of 250 to be procured; it will be capable of torpedo tube and vertical launch. Manufacturer: MBDA.

Length: . . . **Diameter:** . . . **Wingspan:** . . .
Weight: 1,300 kg **Warhead weight:** . . .
Speed: Mach 0.9 **Range:** More than 600 km

SCALP-EG: Some 500 of the 300-km-ranged *Système de Crioisière Conventionnel Autonome à Longue Protée Précis–Emploi Général Purpose* missiles were ordered 1-98 for the French Air Force and Navy for $745 million for delivery beginning in 2003. The weapon is a variant of the Storm Shadow ASM produced by the same company for the U.K. and uses a video datalink to assist in targeting. Manufacturer: Matra-BAE Dynamics.

MM 15: A surface-launched variant of the AS 15 air-launched missile. Not used by the French Navy. Manufacturer: Aérospatiale.

MM 40 Exocet: An improved version of the MM 38 and the AM 39, the MM 40 is an over-the-horizon missile whose range is adapted to radar performance and which is able to use fire-control data relayed by an outside source. It employs a cylindrical GRP launcher, which, because it is lighter and has fewer fittings than the rectangular metal launcher used by the MM 38, potentially increases firepower by allowing more missiles to be carried. To employ fully the range of the missile, helicopters or aircraft must provide over-the-horizon targeting. The missile initially uses inertial guidance, switching to radar terminal homing at a preset distance from the target (usually 12–15 km), and the seeker incorporates a number of electronic counter-countermeasure (ECCM) features. It can cruise at preset altitudes between 3 and 15 m and employs a solid-fuel rocket engine. The current Exocet Block 2 features evasive maneuvering, an improved seeker, ECCM, and improved sea-skimming capability.
MM 40 is employed by a number of countries worldwide. France plans to acquire only 30 new missiles between 2001 and 2011. Manufacturer: MBDA.

Length: 5.80 m **Diameter:** 0.35 m **Wingspan:** 1.135 m
Weight: 850 (Block 2: 855) kg **Warhead weight:** 165 kg
Speed: Mach 1.0 **Range:** 65 km

MBDA was given permission to start development of an "Extended-Range" MM 40 Block 3 Exocet in 10-02. The missile will employ a turbojet sustainer engine and will have a range of 180 km and a new jam-resistant J-band seeker. The missile will be compatible with current launcher and launch-control systems and will employ GPS-designated targeting and variable approach azimuth flight profiles.

SM 39 Exocet: A submarine torpedo-tube-launched version of the Exocet concept, SM 39 began in 1981 aboard the *Narval*-class submarine *Requin.* Employs either 550-mm or 533-mm launch capsules, each with four solid-fuel launch motors. After broaching the surface, the missile rises to 50 m and then descends to cruising altitude. The system became operational in 1985. Manufacturer: MBDA.

Length: 4.69 m (5.80 in capsule) **Diameter:** 0.35 m **Wingspan:** 1.135 m
Weight: 652 kg (1,350 with capsule) **Warhead weight:** 165 kg
Speed: Mach 1.0 **Range:** 50 km

MM 38 Exocet: A fire-and-forget homing missile with solid-fuel propulsion. The fire-control solution requires a fix on the target provided by the surface radar of the firing ship and uses the necessary equipment for launching the missile and determining the correct range and height bearing of the target. A total of 1,260 were built for over a dozen navies, some of which have retired the system. Remaining stocks are reaching the end of their shelf lives, with some nations now ordering replacement propellant sections, which should keep those missiles in use until 2011–21. The French Navy plans to refuel and upgrade about 50 MM 38s.
The missile is launched at a slight elevation (about 15°). After the boost phase, it reaches its flight altitude of between 3 and 15 m. A radar altimeter maintains altitude. During the first part of the flight, the missile is automatically guided by an inertial system that has received the azimuth of the target. When within about 12–15 km from the target, automatic homing radar begins to seek the target, picks it up, and directs the missile. Great effort has been made to protect the missile from countermeasures during this phase. A "Super ADAC" seeker, with improved antijamming features, is offered for backfit to earlier missiles. Detonation takes place upon impact or by pseudo-proximity (time-to-target estimation) fuze, according to interception conditions, size of the target ship, and the condition of the sea. Manufacturer: MBDA.

Length: 5.20 m **Diameter:** 0.35 m **Wingspan:** 1.00 m
Weight: 735 kg **Warhead weight:** 165 kg
Speed: Mach 1.0 **Range:** 42 km

♦ Air-to-ground missiles

ASMP-A (*Air-Surface à Moyenne Portée-Ameliore*): Development contract issued to EADS-Aérospatiale-Matra in 10-00, with deployment to take place in 2007 to replace the current ASMP; will have a range of up to 500 km.

ASMP (*Air-Surface à Moyenne Portée*): Entered service in 1990–91 on Super Étendard fighter-bombers. ASMP has a 300-kT nuclear warhead, uses inertial guidance, has a radar altimeter, and is very resistant to countermeasures. Range is dependent on the altitude and speed of the launch aircraft. ASMP can achieve Mach 3.0 at launch at high altitudes. Became operational 1-5-86 on the French Air Force Mirage IV and during 7-88 on the Mirage 2000N. Manufacturer: Aérospatiale.

Length: 5.38 m **Diameter:** 0.35 m **Wingspan:** 0.956 m
Weight: 840 kg **Speed:** Mach 2.4 **Range:** 100–300 km

AM 39 Exocet: The air-to-sea version of the MM 38, operational since 1978 and currently employed by Atlantique Mk 2 and Super Étendard aircraft. After being launched, it has the same flight characteristics as the MM 38. Range is dependent on the altitude and speed of the launch aircraft. Manufacturer: Aérospatiale.

Length: 4.633 m **Diameter:** 0.348 m **Wingspan:** 1.004 m
Weight: 670 kg **Warhead weight:** 165 kg
Speed: Mach 1.0 **Range:** 50–70 km

AS 30: Radio command or laser-designated (AS 30L) weapon for firing from a maneuvering aircraft at middle, low, or very low altitude. Used by the Super Étendard. Range dependent on speed and altitude of launch aircraft. The laser-guided version entered service 1996 for use on modernized Super Étendard aircraft and is 3.65 m long and weighs 540 kg. The most recent order was for 20 under the 1997 budget. Manufacturer: Aérospatiale.

Length: 3.785 m **Diameter:** 0.342 m
Wingspan: 1.000 m **Weight:** 528 kg
Range: Maximum 9,000 to 12,000 m; minimum 1,500 m

AS 20: Training missile for the AS 30. Radio command guidance. Range dependent on launch aircraft speed and altitude. Manufacturer: Aérospatiale.

Length: 2.60 m **Diameter:** 0.25 m **Wingspan:** 0.80 m
Weight: 140 kg **Range:** 4,000–8,000 m

AS 15TT: For use by light helicopters. Developed under the Saudi Arabian "Sawari" program. Uses Thales Agrion radar for target determination and tracking. Export weapon; not employed by the French Navy. First production deliveries 3-85. Manufacturer: Aérospatiale.

Length: 2.16 m **Weight:** 96 kg
Warhead weight: 30 kg **Speed:** 280 m/sec **Range:** 15+ km

AS 12: A wire-guided system with optical aim. Used by WG-13 Lynx helicopter and has been exported to several countries. Manufacturer: Aérospatiale.

Length: 1.870 m **Diameter:** 0.210 m
Wingspan: 0.650 m **Weight:** 75 kg
Range: Max. 7,500–8,000 m; min. 1,500 m

♦ Air-to-air missiles

Météor: Under joint development for France, the U.K., Italy, Spain, and Sweden. Planned to enter service in 2011.

Length: 3.65 m **Weight:** 185 kg
Speed: Mach 4 **Range:** 100 km

R 550 Magic: The Magic 2 version is now in service for Super Étendard fighters. Manufacturer: Matra.

Length: 2.75 m **Diameter:** 0.157 m **Weight:** 89 kg
Wingspan: 0.660 m **Warhead:** 11.5 kg
Range: 300–8,000 m **Guidance:** Infrared-homing

Mica: Active radar or infrared homing being developed as the successor to Magic for use on the Rafale-M fighter. MICA=*Missile d'Interception, de Combat, et d'Autodéfense.* Program is a fusion of Matra's in-house effort and the Italian Selenia Aspide Mk 2. Uses command-inertial guidance with active terminal homing. Some 250 are to be delivered to the navy during the 2003–8 National Defence Program. A land-based, 8-round launch system is in use, and a variant for submerged launch by submarines is in development. Manufacturer: Matra.

Length: 3.10 m **Diameter:** 0.16 m
Weight: 100 kg **Warhead weight:** 12 kg
Speed: Mach 4 **Range:** 50–60 km

B. GUNS

Note: GIAT is studying the development of a 155-mm naval mounting with a weight of 34 tons.

100-mm Compact: Single-barrel automatic, for export only. Weighing 13.5 tons, it carries 12 rounds ready to fire on the mount and 12 in an auxiliary ready magazine. Standard installations have a 42-round magazine, while those for Malaysia had 90-round magazines. Firing rates of 20, 45, or 90 rds/min can be selected. Maximum surface range is 15 km, while practical range against air targets is 6 km. Proximity-fuzed, prefragmented; high explosive; and illuminant rounds are available. Also used by Saudi Arabia and China. Manufacturer: USINOR/Creusot-Loire.

Length of barrel: 55 calibers **Mount weight:** 17.3 tons
Muzzle-velocity: 870 m/sec **Rate of fire:** 20, 45, or 90 rds/min, or single fire
Arc of elevation: –15 to +80°
Max. training speed: 50°/sec **Max. elevation speed:** 33°/sec
Range: 17,200 m **Max. effective range for surface fire:** 12,000 m
Max. effective range for antiaircraft fire: 6,000 m

100-mm Models 1953, 1964, and 1968: Single-barrel automatic, for use against aircraft, surface vessels, or land targets. Model 1968 is a lighter version of model 1953; model 1964 is virtually identical to model 1953. The ammunition is the same for all three. Models 1953 and 1964 require two operators on-mount, while model 1968 can operate in full automatic. Characteristics of model 1968:

WEAPONS AND SYSTEMS *(continued)*

Length of barrel: 55 calibers **Mount weight:** 22 tons
Max. rate of fire: 78 rds/min **Arc of elevation:** –15° to +80°
Max. training speed: 40°/sec **Max. elevation speed:** 25°/sec
Range: 17,000 m at 40° elevation
Max. effective range for surface fire: 15,000 m
Max. effective range for antiaircraft fire: 8,000 m

Models 1953 and 1964 use an analog fire-control system with electromechanical and electronic equipment for the fire-control solution. The director can be operated in optical and radar modes. Used in *Jeanne d'Arc* and the *Suffren* class.

Model 1968 uses a digital fire-control system, with central units and memory disks or magnetic tape for data storage. Light radar gun director. Optical direction equipment can be added. Used in the *Tourville* class. The first four units of the *Georges Leygues* class and the A 69–class frigates employ a hybrid system of digital and analog computers. In *Primauguet* and later *Georges Leygues*–class frigates, the *Cassard* class, and the *Suffren* class, multiple sensors effect control.

Under the CADAM (*CADence de tir AMéliorée*) program, the rate of fire of all three versions was increased from the original 60 rds/min to 78 rds/min. A variant with a new 42-round ready-service stowage rack will permit firing 62 rounds before reloading is required from the magazine below.

40-mm L/60: French-made, Bofors-design general-purpose weapon used aboard patrol ship *Albatros,* P 400–class gunboats, and a few amphibious warfare and auxiliary classes in single mountings.

Length of barrel: 60 calibers **Weight:** 2 tons
Muzzle velocity: 853 m/sec
Rate of fire: 130 rds/min **Range:** 3,600 m max. practical

30-mm OTO Melara-Mauser Model F "Single 30": Selected 1994 as light weapon for future surface combatants. Uses U.S. Bushmaster-II gun with GAU-8-type ammunition including TP, HEI, HEI-SD, API, and APDS projectiles. Muzzle velocity is 1,000 m/sec, and firing rate is 800 rds/min. Are controlled either by the VIGY optronic system, manned remote directors located nearby, or, in an emergency, by a single operator on-mount.

20-mm CN MIT-20F2: A general-purpose weapon on a DCAN-designed mounting, used aboard P 400–class gunboats, mine-countermeasures ships, and a number of amphibious warfare classes. Generally known as the "F2." Has two 300-round ready-service magazines attached. Manufacturer: GIAT.

Length: 2.60 m overall **Weight:** 322 kg empty
Muzzle velocity: . . . **Rate of fire:** 650–720 rds/min
Arc of elevation: –15° to + 65°

20-mm 70-cal. Oerlikon: Employs 60-round ammunition canisters. Being phased out.

Length: 2.20 m overall **Weight:** 480 kg empty
Muzzle velocity: . . . **Rate of fire:** 450 rds/min
Arc of elevation: –15° to +90°

12.7-mm machinegun:

Range: 1,200 m **Rate of fire:** 500 rpm

C. TORPEDOES

Note: A = for surface-ship use, B = submarine use, C = aircraft use

	Use	Length in m	Weight in kg	Diameter in mm	Range in km	Speed in kts	Depth in m
F 17 Mod. 1	B	—	1,300	533	—	35	—
F 17 Mod. 2	B	5.38	1,300	533	18	40	600
F 21	B	. . .	533	50	50	. . .	. . .
L 4	C	3.03	525	533	6	300	
L 5 Mod. 1	B	—	1,000	533	—	35	—
L 5 Mod. 3	B	—	1,300	533	7.7	35	—
L 5 Mod. 4	A	4.40	935	533	7.0	35	500
Mk 46	C	2.59	232	323.7	11	—	—
MU-90	B, C	2.96	285	323.7	10	29–50	1,000

Note: The French Thomson-Marconi Murène and Italian Whitehead Alenia Systemi Subacquei (WASS) A-290 torpedo programs were combined into one effort in 1991 as the MU-90 Impact under a consortium called Eurotorp. Some 300 are expected to be produced for the French Navy and another 300 for Italy; MU-90 is usable in waters as little as 25 m deep. Impact uses a 50-kg warhead, travels at either 29 or 50 kts, and can operate between 25-m and 1,000-m depths. It employs a silver oxide–aluminum battery and has a pumpjet propulsor. A hard-kill, antitorpedo version, MU-90HK, has been developed with deliveries beginning in 2003.

The E 15 Mod 2 export torpedo employs L 3, E 14, and Z 16 torpedoes updated with AH 8 homing heads and silver-zinc batteries and offers 2,000-m detection range, 300-m depth capability, 31-kt speed, and a range of 12 km with a 300-kg warhead. DCN St.-Tropez and STN Atlas Elektronik are offering to develop for export a wake-homing version of the F 17 torpedo. A wake-homing sensor is offered with export versions of the F 17 Mod. 2 torpedo.

The F 21 is being developed jointly by DCN and WASS as the BlackShark/IF21 and is being offered for export. The French Navy plans to use it to replace the F 17 heavyweight series

D. MINES

FG 18 and FG 29: For use by submarines. Weight: 1,000 kg, with 600-kg explosives.

FG 26: For use by surface ships.

E. RADARS

♦ Navigational radars

DRBN-32: French Navy designator for Decca 1226 navigational radar.
DRBN-34/34A: French Navy designator for the Decca 1229–series navigational radars (Decca 2090 in the *La Fayette* class).
Decca 20V90: An ARPA-equipped successor to DRBN-32, with 48 ordered 4-99 from Decca; used earlier in the *La Fayette* class (DRBN number not yet known; the radar is also known as the BridgeMaster E).
Type 1007: British Kelvin-Hughes set being fitted in some destroyers during refits.

♦ Air-search radars

DRBV-21A: On *Floréal*-class frigates and the *Foudre.* Frequency-agile surveillance radar using the solid-state transmitter of the DRBV-26C and the antenna of the DRBV-22A. Range: over 100 km. L-band. Thales Mars TRS 3015 is the commercial version.
DRBV-22D: *Jeanne d'Arc* only. L-band.
DRBV-26A: S-band. Mounted in the *Tourville* class, first four *Georges Leygues* class. Range: 280 km. Commercial name: Thales Jupiter.
DRBV-26C: Upgraded DRBV-26 A with solid-state transmitter. Range: 360 km. Carried by *Cassard* class.
DRBV-26D: Further development of DRBV-26 for the *Charles de Gaulle* and for future antiaircraft combatants. Thales commercial Jupiter-I using Thales Nederland LW-08 antenna.

♦ Height-finding/three-dimensional radars

DRBI-23: Mounted in the *Duquesne;* monopulse.
DRBJ-11B: S-band, pulse-coded radar for the *Cassard*-class guided-missile destroyers and the carrier *Charles de Gaulle.* Range: 300 km.
S 1850M: Intended for the *Forbin*-class frigates; replaces the Thales TRS 3505 ASTRAL (Air Surveillance and Targeting Radar, L-band) (which was to have been designated DRBV-27) and is derived from the Thales SMART-L. Range: 400 km.
Herakles: 3-D, E/F (S)-band multifunction set in development by Thales as a primary air- and surface-surveillance and f.c system. A navalized version of the Master-A land system. Rotates 360°/sec. while performing electronic scanning in elevation and azimuth. Range to 200 km and capable of tracking 200 targets.

♦ Surface and low-altitude air-search radars

DRBV-15A: S-band, pulse-doppler design, with pulse-compression and frequency agility. In *Primauguet, La Motte-Picquet,* and *Latouche-Tréville.* Range: 110 km.
DRBV-15C: Improved DRBV 15 with stabilized antenna. Range: 100 km against an aircraft and 50 km against a missile. Is aboard the missile range instrumentation ship *Monge, La Fayette*–class frigates, and the carrier *Charles de Gaulle.* Commercial name: Sea Tiger Mk 2.
DRBV-51A: Mounted on A 69–class corvettes and the *Jeanne d'Arc.*
DRBV-51B: Mounted on the *Tourville* class.
DRBV-51C: Mounted on the initial four *Georges Leygues* class.

♦ Fire-control radars

ARABEL: *Antenne Radar à Balayage Électronique.* SDC X-band multifunction radar associated with SAAM. Used on the carrier *Charles de Gaulle*
CTM: Used for the f.c. system on the *La Fayette*–class frigates.
EMPAR: Multifunction, three-dimensional set for the SAM system on the *Forbin*-class destroyers.
DRBC-32A: For the 100-mm guns on the *Jeanne d'Arc.* X-band.
DRBC-32D: Mounted on the *Tourville* class. X-band.
DRBC-32E: Mounted on the A 69–class corvettes and the first four *Georges Leygues*–class destroyers. X-band.
DRBC-33A: Monopulse, frequency-agile. On *Cassard* and *Suffren* classes and the final three *Georges Leygues*–class destroyers.
DRBR-51: Tracking radar for the Masurca on *Duquesne.* C-band (5-cm) tracker, 7-cm command signal.
SPG-51C: U.S. tracker/illuminator for the Standard system on the *Cassard* class.

F. ELECTRO-OPTICS

DIBC-2A: Optronic director for small-caliber guns. Commercial name is VIGY 105.
DIBV-1A: Vampir infrared detection and surveillance system by Thales; used aboard destroyer *Cassard* and the *Charles de Gaulle.*
DIBV-2A: Lightweight version of DIBV 1A for destroyers.
MSTIS: Surveillance and f.c. system for the *Forbin*-class frigates.
NAJIR: 100-mm gun control on the *Floréal*-class patrol ships.

G. SONARS

♦ Surface ship sonars

	Type	Frequency	Comments
DSBV-61	Towed	VLF	Passive linear array system
DSBV-62C	Towed	VLF	Passive linear array system
DSBX-1	Towed	LF	SLASM variable-depth set
DUBA-25	Hull	8/9/10 kHz	TSM 2400; see Remarks
DUBM-21B	Hull	100/420 kHz	TSM 2021; on Tripartite minehunters
DUBM-21D	Hull	100/420 kHz	Digital DUBM-21B; on *Sagittaire*
DUBM-40A	Towed	745 kHz	For small craft
DUBM-41	Towed	500 kHz	Side-scan minehunting; on *Glycine* class
DUBM-42	Towed	500 kHz	Multibeam DUBM-41 with DUBM-60 forward-looking sonar
DUBM-43A	Handheld	VHF	U.S. Klein side-scan for mine clearance divers
DUBV-23	Bow	4.9–5.4 kHz	See Remarks
DUBV-24	Hull	5 kHz center	Average range: 6,000 m; on *Jeanne d'Arc*
DUBV-24C	Hull	5 kHz center	See Remarks
DUBV-43	Towed	5 kHz center	See Remarks
DUPM-1	Handheld	50–90 kHz	For divers

Remarks: DUBV-23 and DUBV-43 are used simultaneously and, under normal sound-propagation conditions, achieve ranges of 10,000 m (20,000 under ideal conditions); they are carried on *Tourville* and the three early units of the *Georges Leygues* class. The four later units of the *Georges Leygues* class carry DUBV-43C VDS, which operates at depths of up to 700 m. *Primauguet, La Motte-Picquet,* and *Latouche-Tréville* have a sonar suite comprising the DUBV-43C VDS, the DUBV-24C hull-mounted sonar (in place of DUBV-23), and the DSBV-61 towed array (with a range of over 150 km).

WEAPONS AND SYSTEMS *(continued)*

The DUBA-25 is installed on the A-69 escorts and the destroyer *Cassard* (her sister *Jean Bart* has the DUBV-24C). The DSBV-62C towed array, intended for the *Tourville* class and the frigate *Dupleix*, has a 3-km-long towing cable.

The DSBX-1 SLASM (*Système de Lutte Anti-Sous-Marine*), a variable-depth towed active array, is aboard destroyers *Tourville* and *De Grasse;* it employs two 1-kHz transmitters and a receiver array in a 10-ton towed body and can be operated down to 600-m depths. Thales (formerly Thomson-Marconi) is now embarked with BAE Systems in developing a new very low frequency active sonar (the ATBF, *Actif Très Basse Fréquence*) and ATAS (Active Towed Array Sonar).

The DUBM-41B can be towed at 10 kts and covers a 400-m swath, compared to the 4-kt/50-m capability of the DUBM-41. Thales is offering the Versatile Underwater System (VERSUS) as an upgrade to current DUBM-21 and TSM 2022 minehunting sonar arrays. VERSUS would include a propelled variable-depth sonar with the TSM 2022 transducer and a towed TSM 2054 side-scan sonar, along with new signal-processing capabilities to allow identification of mines to 200-m depths.

♦ Submarine sonars

French listening devices, active-passive sonars, and underwater telephone equipment include:

DMUX-20: Sonar suite designation for the *Améthyste* class.
DSUV-22: Hydrophone array on the *Améthyste* class. Part of the commercial Eledone array from Thales. Also known as Scylla or TSM 2040.
DSUV-23: Passive hydrophone array on ballistic-missile submarines.
DSUV-61B: Towed passive array for ballistic-missile submarines.
DSUV-62C: Towed passive array for the *Améthyste* class.
DSUX-21: Multifunction system for *L'Inflexible* and *L'Indomptable.*
DUUA-2B: Active set on the modernized *Améthyste* class, with a 10° beam searchlight set operating at 8 kHz. Has a 2.5–15-Hz passive narrowband and broadband adjunct.
DUUG-2: Sonar intercept in the *Améthyste* class.
DUUG-6: Velox M5; stand-alone sonar intercept system.
DUUV-23: Panoramic passive array on ballistic-missile submarines.
DUUX-5: Fenelon passive hull array. Can track three targets simultaneously, covers 2–15 kHz, and has three hydrophone arrays on each side of the submarine.

♦ Helicopter sonars

	Frequency	Remarks
DUAV-4	21/22.5/24 kHz	WG-13 Lynx; 150 m max depth
FLASH	. . .	NH-90 helicopter; range: 23 km

♦ Sonobuoys

DSTA-3E	9/10/11 kHz	16-channel active, 20 or 100 m deep
DSTV-4L/M (TSM 8010)	10 Hz–20 kHz	31-channel passive, 20 or 100 m deep (300 m option in DSTV 4M)
DSTV-7 (TSM 8030)	5 Hz–20 kHz	99-channel passive LOFAR (TSM 8030)
TSM 8040	6.5/7.5/9.5 kHz	Commercial DICASS active
TSM 8050A/B	6.0/6.71/7.5/8.4/ 9.4/10.5 kHz	Commercial 12-channel active; A: 20 or 150 m; B: 20 or 450 m deep
TSM 8060	. . .	Passive DIFAR; commercial

H. COMBAT INFORMATION SYSTEMS

SENIT (*Système d'Exploitation Naval des Informations Tactique*): This system serves four principal purposes:

- It establishes the combat situation from the manual collection of information derived from detection equipment on board and from the automatic or manual collection of information from external sources.
- It disseminates the above data to the ship and to other vessels by automatic means (Links 11 and 14).
- It assists in decision making and transmits to the target-designation console all the information it requires.

The several versions of the SENIT are similar in general concept but differ in construction and programming in order to ensure fulfillment of the various missions assigned to each type of ship:

SENIT 3: Two Type 1230 computers; in the *Tourville* class.
SENIT 4: One Iris N 55 computer, seven display consoles; in *Georges Leygues* class.
SENIT 5: Original TAVITAC commercial system from Thales.
SENIT 6: Seven Type 15M 125X computers and 13 consoles; in *Cassard* class.
SENIT 7: Thales TAVITAC 2000, with two Type MLX 32 computers and five color video display consoles; in the *La Fayette* class. Also known as SACEIT (*Système Automatisé de Commandement et d'Exploitation des Informations Tactiques*).
SENIT 8: Derived from SENIT 6 for the *Charles de Gaulle.* Also known as SISC (*Système d'Intégration du Système de Combat*). Has 25 consoles, eight 32-bit computers. Able to maintain 2,000 contacts.
SENIT 8.01: Reduced version of SENIT 8 installed in *Georges Leygues*–class DDs. Also referred to as the OP3A enhanced self-defense combat system, it interfaces with the *existing* SENIT systems. Employs six operators. Intended to detect "leakers" at up to 10 km range and respond in less than three seconds.

AIDCOMER (*AIDe de COmmandement à la MER*): Decision-making system intended to provide artificial intelligence assistance in situation assessment, decision making, and resource management of ships and aircraft within a task force, as well as to act with the land-based SYCOM NG command-and-control system. AIDCOMER interfaces with the SENIT data systems and with the Syracuse SATCOM system and contains an extensive threat database.

OPSMER or SEAO (*Système Embarqué d'Aide aux Opérations*): A simplified version of AIDCOMER intended for destroyers and the *Forbin*-class frigates. A version will also be carried aboard ballistic-missile and nuclear-powered attack submarines. The *Foudre*-class landing ships and the command ship–oiler *Var* have specialized versions as well.

ALTESSE (*ALerte et TÉnue de Situation de SurfacE*): Decison aid system by Thales to be carried by *La Fayette*–class frigates to improve ESM system performance and to provide an overview of the local surface situation. Installed in *Tourville* in 1995.

DLT D3: All submarines use the *Direction de Lancement Torpilles,* DLT D3. There are three identical data displays for current and historical target data, and the system can be used to launch torpedoes and missiles.

I. COUNTERMEASURES

♦ Intercept systems

For surface ships: ARBR/ARBA-10C/D, ARBR-16 (Thales DR 2000 Mk 1), ARBR-17 (Thales DR-4000S, C–G band), and ARBR-21 (Thales DR 3000). Also ARBG-1A SAIGON (*Système Automatisé d'Interception et de GONiométrie*) for interception of VHF through UHF communications. The ARBG-2 Énigme is aboard *Charles de Gaulle.*

For submarines: ARUR-10B/C, ARUR-11 (with DALIA analyzer), ARUR-12 (with DALIA analyzer), and ARUX-1.

For aircraft: ARAR-13 (with DALIA analyzer) for Atlantique Mk 2 aircraft.

♦ Jammers

ARBB-32: For surface ships; work against reception antennas and jammers. Manufacturer: Électronique Serge Dassault.

ARBB-33: Dassault's Salamandre integrated EW suite.

♦ Countermeasures launchers

Dagaie (AMBL-1B): *Dispositif d'Autodéfense pour la Guerre Anti-missiles Infra-rouge et Électro-magnétique.* Made by Matra Défense. Launches both IR and chaff-type decoys, relying on input from SENIT systems. The launcher holds 10 "suitcases," each with 33 projectiles with four charges in the antiradar version or 34 projectiles in the infrared version. Improved version known as AMBL-1C (Dagaie Mk 2). In development is a version to launch up to six Spartacus antitorpedo decoys. Weight: 500 kg. Range: 750 m.

Sagaie (AMBL-2A): *Système d'Autodéfense pour la Guerre Anti-missiles Infra-rouge et Électro-magnétique.* Made by Matra Défense. Launches decoy rockets for confusion, seduction, or distraction. The launcher is trainable and holds ten containers launching infrared or radar-jamming rockets 170 mm in diameter and weighing 45 kg. An antitorpedo round is being developed, either the Euroslat SLAT or the Whitehead Alenia (WASS) A-200 LCAW, of which 10–12 would be carried on the launcher. Range: 3,000 m. Launcher weight: 1,600 kg.

Note: In development is the 12-round New Generation Decoy System (NGDS).

♦ Torpedo countermeasures

SLAT: *Système de Lutte Anti-Torpilles.* A directional towed array detector to be used in conjunction with the Spartacus active decoy, which is to be launched by Sagaie; in development. Also known as Salto, the system will employ the Alto 42-element towed, linear acoustic intercept array to detect torpedoes and the Contralto countermeasure system. A prototype system went to sea at the end of 1994. Joint development contract with French government and Euroslat (a consortium of DCN, Thales, and Whitehead Alenia Sistemi Subacquei/WASS) was signed in 1-01.

SLQ-25 Nixie: U.S.-made towed acoustic torpedo decoy in surface combatants.

SPDT-1A: Torpedo detector in development by Crozet-Safare.

NUCLEAR-POWERED AIRCRAFT CARRIER [CVN]

♦ 1 Charles de Gaulle class

Bldr: DCN, Brest

	Laid down	L	Del.	In serv.
R 91 CHARLES DE GAULLE (ex-*Richelieu*)	14-4-89	14-5-94	28-9-00	18-5-01

Charles de Gaulle (R 91) Michael Nitz, 7-05

D: 37,085 tons (40,600 fl) **S:** 25.2 kts (23.5 kts sust.; see Remarks)
Dim: 261.50 (238.00 pp) × 64.36 (31.50 wl) × 8.70 (9.50 max.)
Air Group: 10 Rafale-M interceptors; 16–20 Super Étendard strike fighters; 2–3 E-2C Hawkeye surveillance and air-control aircraft; 2 Super Frelon heavy transport helicopters; 3 Panthir/Dauphin SAR and liaison helicopters
A: 2 16-round Sylver A 43 vertical-launch SAAM system (32 Aster-15 missiles); 2 6-round Sadral point-defense SAM syst. (Mistral missiles); 8 20-mm Giat (20F2) guns, 4 single 12.7-mm mg
Electronics:
Radar: 1 DRBV-26D early warning; 1 DRBJ-11B height-finder; 1 DRBV-15C air/surf. search; 2 DRBN-34 (Decca 1229) nav.; 1 Arabel SAAM target designation
EW: ARBR-21 radar intercept; ARBG-2 Maigret comms intercept; 2 ARBB-33 jammers, 4 6-round AMBL-2A Sagaie decoy RL; SLAT torpedo decoy syst.
E/O: DIBV-2A surveillance; 2 DIBC-2A panoramic electro-optical f.c.

NUCLEAR-POWERED AIRCRAFT CARRIER [CVN] *(continued)*

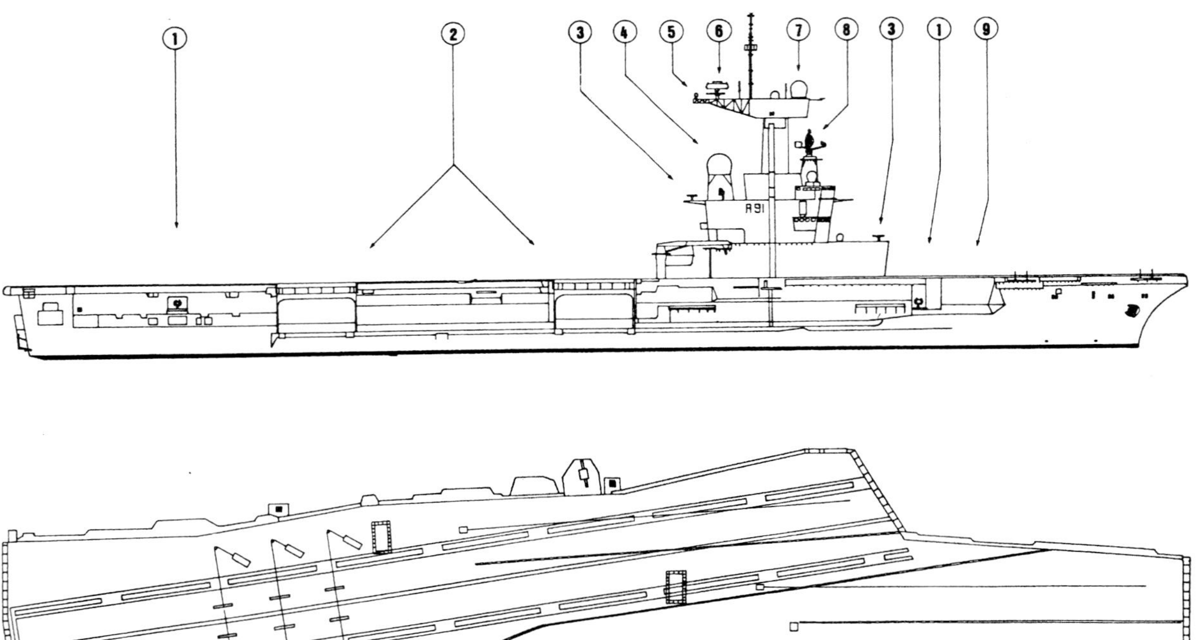

Charles de Gaulle (R 91) 1. Sagaie decoy launcher 2. Aircraft elevators 3. DRBN-34 navigational and air-control radars 4. DRBJ-11B height-finding radar 5. DIBV-1 infrared sensor 6. DRBV-15C air- and surface-search radar 7. Arabel missile target-designation and -illumination radar 8. DRBV-26D early-warning radar 9. SAAM missile launch group
Drawing by Jean Moulin from *Flottes de Combat*

Charles de Gaulle (R 91)—with Super Étendards on the flight deck
Martin Mokrus, 6-04

Charles de Gaulle (R 91) Martin Mokrus, 6-04

Charles de Gaulle (R 91) M. Wright, 6-04

M: 2 150-Mw K15 pressurized-water reactor plants; double-reduction geared steam turbines; 2 5-bladed props; 83,000 shp
Electric: 21,400 kw tot. (4 × 4,000-kw turboalternators; 4 × 1,100-kw diesel sets; 4 × 250-kw turboalternators)
Endurance: 45 days
Crew: 1,950 total (177 officers, 890 petty officers, 833 nonrated, including 550 tot. in the air group; can also carry up to 800 troops)

Remarks: Ordered 4-2-86. Work began 24-11-87, and the ship was to have been launched 1-5-92; in 6-89, it was announced that the original 1996 date of operation would be delayed two years, and significant further delays continued. The hull was briefly afloat on 20-12-92 to reposition it within the graving dock for the addition of the angled deck. Was christened 7-5-94 but not floated out until 14-5-94. Dockside propulsion trials commenced 26-5-98. Sea trials were to commence 1-7-98 but were delayed to 27-1-99 by problems with the propulsion system and had to be halted due to an electrical generation capacity problem; sea trials recommenced on 18-3-99. Ownership of the ship was passed to the French Navy on 1-2-97.

A $80 million post-shakedown yard period starting in fall 1999 was provided for extending the angled deck, improving reactor safety, replacing corroded piping, curing rudder vibration, and improving power supply to the reactor water cooling circulation pumps; the work was extended, however, delaying commissioning. Post-repair trials began 19-5-00. Other changes made were the removal of the yardarms and the provision of a crew gangway position low at the stern. During precommissioning cruise to the West Indies in 11-00, lost a propeller blade and had to return to Toulon for repairs, which were not fully completed until 10-01.

Construction consideration of a second unit was canceled in 2004 in favor of a conventionally powered alternative.

Hull systems: The SATRAP (*Système Automatique de Tranquillisation et de Pilotage*) system controls seakeeping behavior to permit air operations in sea states up to 5 or 6; it incorporates two groups of twelve lead stabilization weights totaling 500 tons that are moved athwartships on rails to reduce roll to 0.5°. Four pairs of fin stabilizers and a rudder roll stabilization system are also installed. The low-mounted hull sponsons are designed to provide additional righting moment when they are immersed at approximately 7° roll. Pressurized and filtered air is employed by the NBC-protection citadel. Special attention has been paid toward reducing the ship's signature by shaping the hull and island to reduce the radar return, sound-isolating engineering systems, and installing a comprehensive degaussing system. In addition to being able to embark up to 800 troops, the ship can accept a modular hospital installation with 50 beds and two operating rooms.

Propulsion systems: The plant is located in five compartments. The reactors, which are identical to those in the ballistic-missile submarines of the *Le Triomphant* class, also supply steam for the turboalternators and the catapults and are contained within protective structures. Each main turboalternator propulsion set incorporates a high-pressure and a low-pressure turbine driving a single shaft through double-reduction gearing. Electrical power is available in 3-phase, 440 V, 60 Hz; 1- and 3-phase 440 V, 400 Hz; 115 V, 60 Hz for lighting; and 28 V emergency lighting. The ship, however, lacks adequate propulsion power for aviation activities and was restricted to 25 kts after 1-01 due to temporary use of mismatched spare propellers from *Clemenceau* and *Foch* until six new, tailored units were fabricated. The temporary port propeller caused vibration problems and the temporary screws limited maximum speed to only 25.2 kts, but new propellers have now been installed.

Aviation systems: As initially operational in 2001, the ship was to carry four Rafale-M and 29 Super Étendard fighters, two E-2C Hawkeye surveillance aircraft, and two

NUCLEAR-POWERED AIRCRAFT CARRIER [CVN] *(continued)*

Super Frelon and two Dauphin helicopters. Ultimately, the ship is intended to carry 32 Rafale fighters, three E-2C Hawkeye surveillance aircraft, and four helicopters. The flight deck is 261.5 m long, with a 195-m, 8.3° angled-deck portion. The angled deck was belatedly found to be 4.4 m too short for safe operation of the E-2C aircraft in all weather and was extended during 1999. Maximum flight deck width is 64.36 m for an area of over 12,300 m^2. There are two 75-m U.S. Type C13 F steam catapults, each capable of launching aircraft of up to 25 metric tons weight, with one on the angled deck and the other on the port side of the bow, an arrangement that emphasizes deck parking arrangements over an ability to launch and land simultaneously. Three arrestor wires are fitted. There are two 21 × 12-m, 36-ton deck-edge elevators, both to starboard amidships, and two ammunition elevators. The nuclear propulsion arrangement requires the island to be mounted much farther forward than is standard practice, ahead of both elevators. The 138-m-long by 29-m-broad (4,600 m^2) by 6.1-m-high hangar is lower than on the *Clemenceau* class, but considerably larger in area and better protected; it can accommodate 23 fixed-wing aircraft and two helicopters at one time. Aviation fuel capacity is normally 3,600 m^3, with provision for up to 5,000 m^3 if necessary. The munitions magazines can accommodate 2,100 tons. The ship has the Matra Défense DALAS (*Dispositif d'aide à l'Appontage au LASer*) deck approach and landing laser system.
Combat systems: The SENIT 8 combat data and control system uses eight Hewlett-Packard PA-VME RISC processors and 24 HP 9000 series 700 UNIX workstations, of which 15 are dual-screen system operator consoles; it is able to track 100 targets and attack 10 simultaneously through the Arabel radar. SENIT 8 incorporates the SYTEX (*Système de Transmissions Extérieures*) communications control with Thales SDG (*Système de Grand Diffusion*) integrated-services digital communications system with high-speed fiberoptic voice and data transmission network; SCEB (*Système de Contrôle des Emissions du Bâtiment*); the AIDCOMER command decision support system; and the GESVOL aviation coordination system, which tracks pilot and aircraft assignments, launches data such as aircraft weight and speed, and weather and monitors airborne aircraft and flight plans. GESVOL employs Hewlett-Packard Vectra computers, Sun Microsystems displays, and an Ethernet data movement system. The ship has NATO Link 11, Link 14, and Link 16 data links. An inertial navigation system is carried. The Aster-15 missile system will not be available for installation until 2005. Sylver is an acronym for *SYstème de Launcement VERtical.* The planned eight single 20-mm guns were not installed and have been replaced, at least temporarily, by four 12.7-mm mg.

AIRCRAFT CARRIER [CV]

♦ 0 (+ 1) PA 2 class

Bldr: Chantiers de l'Atlantique, Saint Nazaire, France

	Laid down	L	In serv.
. . .	2008	. . .	2015

D: 66,000 tons (fl) **S:** 27 kts. **Dim:** 284.0 (275.0 pp) × 79.0 × 12.0
Air Group: Total aircraft: Approx. 58 aircraft: 48 U.S. Lockheed-Martin Joint Strike Fighters (F-35) or Dassault Rafale-M strike fighter (or a mix), 3–4 U.S. Hawkeye (E-2C) AEW aircraft, 6 Augusta-Westland EH-101 ASW/support helicopters
A: PAAMS SAM Syst. (Aster-15 missiles)
Electronics:
Radar: 1 . . . 3-D air-search; 1 . . . air search; 2 . . . height-finder; 1 . . . nav
TACAN: . . .
EW: . . .
M: 4 . . . gas turbines
Electric: . . .
Range: 10,000 /15 **Endurance:** 45 days
Crew: 900 total + 1,770 air group

Remarks: Due to the high cost of nuclear propulsion, the decision was made 2-04 to build a conventionally powered carrier rather than a second nuclear-powered variant. The ship will have a longer flight deck than the cramped *Charles de Gaulle,* though a slightly less powerful onboard defensive armament. A large degree of compatibility is expected between these ships and the new British *Queen Elizabeth*–class carriers, particularly in relation to the superstructure.
The French parliament authorized the carrier on 15-3-03 and a construction contract is expected in late 2006 or early 2007. Officials hope to have the new carrier operational before the beginning of *Charles de Gaulle*'s first refueling and comprehensive overhaul, scheduled to begin in 2015. Fitting out will take place at DCN, Brest. When commissioned she will be based at Toulon.
Hull systems: There will be a high level of automation built into the ship's systems. The ship will be propelled by Integrated Full Electric Propulsion (IFEP) driven by four gas turbines. Aviation systems are expected to include two 90.0-m long C-13 steam catapults and arrestor gear.

Disposal note: The carrier *Foch* (R 99) was purchased 8-00 by Brazil for US$41.0 million ($10.5 million for the ship; $29.5 million for the cost of an overhaul). She was decommissioned and stricken on 15-11-00 and transferred to Brazil the same date. Sister *Clemenceau* (R 98) was retired on 1-10-97 and was used as a source of spares for the *Foch* until being sold for scrap.

HELICOPTER CARRIERS [CH]

♦ 1 helicopter carrier and cadet training ship

Bldr: Brest Arsenal

	Laid down	L	In serv.
R 97 Jeanne d'Arc (ex-*La Résolute*)	7-7-60	30-9-61	30-6-64

Jeanne d'Arc (R 97) Bernard Prézelin, 6-04

D: 10,575 tons (13,270 fl) **S:** 27 kts (26.5 sustained)
Dim: 181.38 (175.00 pp/172.00 wl) × 24.00 (22.00 wl) × 7.30 (aft max.)
Air Group: Up to 8 helicopters (Super Frelon, Dauphin, Lynx, etc.)
A: 6 MM 38 Exocet SSM; 2 single 100-mm 55-cal. Model 1953 DP; 4 single 12.7-mm mg
Electronics:
Radar: 2 DRBN-34 nav.; 1 DRBV-22D air search; 1DRBV-51 surf./air search, 3 DRBC-32A f.c.
Sonar: DUBV-24C hull-mounted (5 kHz)
TACAN: NRPB-20 (U.S. SRN-6)
EW: Removed (see Remarks)

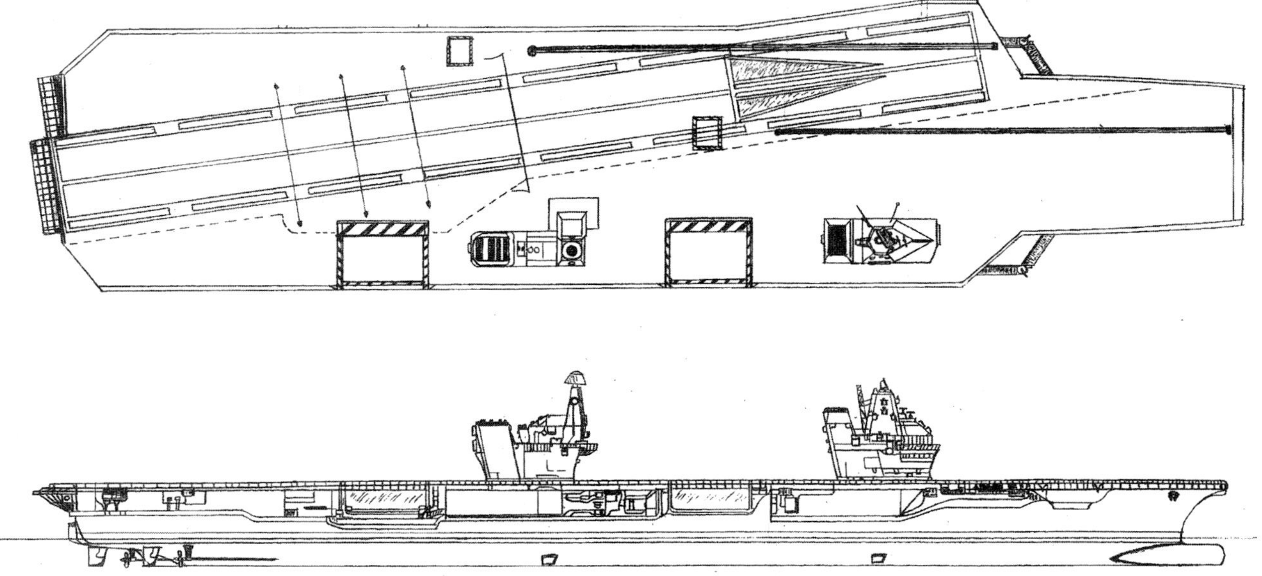

HELICOPTER CARRIERS [CH] *(continued)*

Jeanne d'Arc (R 97) Bernard Prézelin, 11-04

Jeanne d'Arc (R 97) SeaPhoto, 2-99

M: 2 sets Rateau-Bretagne geared steam turbines; 2 props; 40,000 shp
Boilers: 4 asymmetric, multitube; 45 kg/cm^2, 450° C
Electric: 4,400 kw tot.
Range: 3,000/26.5; 3,750/25; 5,500/20; 6,800/16 **Fuel:** 1,360 tons
Crew: 46 officers, 473 enlisted, 158 cadets

Remarks: Replaced the former cruiser *Jeanne d'Arc* as a training ship for officer cadets. In wartime, she was intended to be used for ASW missions, amphibious assault, or as a troop transport. The number of Super Frelon heavy helicopters can be quickly augmented by simple structural changes. The ship was expected to serve until 2003 and then be replaced by a modified unit of the *Foudre* class, but in 1998, expected service was extended through at least 2006–7.
Hull systems: In addition to the navigation bridge, the forward superstructure contains a helicopter-control bridge, a modular-type information-and-operations center, and a combined control center for amphibious operations. The engineering spaces are divided into two compartments, each with two boilers and a turbine, separated by a bulkhead. Can carry two LCVP-type landing craft in place of the large launches in the Welin davits.
Aviation systems: The 62 × 21-m flight deck aft of the island structure permits the simultaneous takeoff of three helicopters, while two machines can be stationed forward of the takeoff area and two others astern, one on each side of the 12-ton capacity elevator at the after end of the flight deck. The hangar deck can, if some of the living quarters used by midshipmen are removed, accommodate eight helicopters. At the after end of the hangar deck there are machine shops for maintenance and repair, including helicopter electronic equipment and an area for inspection; the compartments for handling weapons and ammunition (torpedoes, missiles, etc.) are there also. During her 1998–99 world cruise, the ship carried three Dauphin, one Alouette-III, and two French Army Cougar helicopters.
Combat systems: Two additional 100-mm guns mounted aft were removed during 10-00 to reduce personnel requirements. The DRBI-10 height-finding radar was removed in 1983–84 and the DRBV-50 surface/air-search radar has since been replaced by a DRBV-51 set. The EW suite (ARBR-16 intercept, ARBX-10 radar intercept, and two 8-round AMBL-2A Syllex decoy launchers) had been removed by 10-00.

NAVAL AVIATION

Organization: Authority over naval aviation has been assigned since 19-6-98 to a single rear admiral: ALAVIA. Combatant squadrons have two-digit numbers followed by *F* (for *Flotille*), while support squadron numbers are followed by *S*.

Bases: Landivisiau (shipboard fighters); Lann-Bihoué and Nîmes-Garons (maritime patrol); Lanvéoc-Poulmic and Hyères (helicopters); and Cuers-Pierrefeu (repair/rework). The base at St.-Mandrier was closed during 2002.

OPERATIONAL FLOTILLAS:

Formation	Base	Type	Mission
4F	Lann-Bihoué	3 E-2C Hawkeye	Aerial surveillance
10S	Hyères	1 Super Étendard	Training
		1 Lynx	Training
		1 Alouette III	Training
11F	Landivisiau	14 Super-Étendard (Rafale in 2007)	Attack
12F	Landivisiau	10 Rafale-M F1	Interception
17F	Landiviau	14 Super-Étendard (Rafale in 2008)	Attack
21F	Nîmes-Garons	8 Atlantique	Maritime patrol
22S	Lanvéoc-Poulmic	14 Alouette III	Training
23F	Lann-Bihoué	8 Atlantique	Maritime patrol
24F	Lann-Bihoué	4 Falcon 50M	Maritime surveillance
		4 Xingu	Training and liaison
25F	Faa'a (Tahiti) and Tontouta (New Caledonia)	4 Gardian	Maritime surveillance
28F	Nîmes-Garons	10 Nord 262E	Maritime surveillance
		4 Xingu	Training and liaison
31F	Hyères	9 Lynx WG-13	Shipboard ASW and attack
32F	Lanvéoc-Poulmic	7 Super Frelon	Transport and rescue
34F	Lanvéoc-Poulmic	9 Lynx WG-13	Shipboard ASW and attack
35F	Hyères	6 Dauphin	Rescue and liaison
		3 Dauphin	Rescue and liaison
		5 Alouette III	Rescue and liaison
36F	Hyères	12 Panther	Shipboard ASW and attack
50S	Lanvéoc-Poulmic	6 MS 880 Rallye	Training
		7 Cap 10B	Training
57S	Landivisiau	5 Falcon 10 Mer	Training and transportation

PRINCIPAL COMBAT AIRCRAFT

A. SHIPBOARD FIXED-WING AIRCRAFT

♦ **Rafale-Marine interceptor/attack**
Manufacturer: Dassault

Rafale-M—single-seat interceptor Bernard Prézelin, 7-02

Wingspan: 10.86 m **Length:** 15.27 m **Height:** 5.00 m
Weight: 14,000 kg (19,000 kg max.) **Speed:** Mach 2.0
Propulsion: 2 SNECMA M88-2 E2 or E4 turbojets (7,500 kg thrust each)

PRINCIPAL COMBAT AIRCRAFT *(continued)*

Max. ceiling: 50,000 ft **Range:** 1,000 n.m.
Weapons: 4 missiles, 1 30-mm cannon; MM 40, ASMP, or AS 30 missiles, bombs and/or rockets in attack mode
Avionics: RBE-2 radar, Spectre EW suite, Link 16.

Remarks: Plan to acquire 86 cut to 60 in 2-96. First naval prototype flew 11-91, and the first production prototype aircraft was delivered 9-96. Have jump-strut nose gear to assist takeoff. The empty weight of the naval interceptor version is 760 kg more than that of the land version. Considerable use of composite material was made.

The first ten operational aircraft were ordered in 5-97. Seven more were ordered on 14-1-99 and eight more on 26-12-01; the first of these is to deliver in 2008 and the last in 2012. The first two operational aircraft were delivered on 4-12-00, with 10 more in service by 2002 with 12F, formed at Landivisiau in 6-01. During 9-04 the decision was made to purchase only single-seat-model Rafaels for naval service with two seat models going instead to the Air Force.

The first 12 are of the F1 version, equipped only as interceptors, with Mica radar-guided and Magic-2 IR-seeking missiles (but without the capability to carry the ASMP stand-off weapon, automatic terrain-following capability, the Spectre defensive subsystem, a helmet-mounted sight, or voice-commanded controls); all were to be updated to F1.1 configuration with Link 16 capability and IR-seeking Mica missiles by the end of 2002. The F2 ground-attack variant will have the ability to carry SCALP and AASM missiles and bombs, while the F3 will be capable of launching the ASMP missile for nuclear strikes.

SNECMA is developing the M88-3C engine with 9,000-kg thrust for introduction into French aircraft, including the Rafale, around 2010 and is doing research on an M88-3D version with thrust vectoring. The M88-2 E4 began replacing the E2 version on existing aircraft during 2002–4; it provides a 3–4% improvement in fuel economy.

♦ Super-Étendard fighter-bomber   Manufacturer: Dassault

Wingspan: 9.60 m **Length:** 14.50 m **Height:** 3.85 m
Weight: 11,900 kg **Speed:** Mach 1.0 at 11,000 m; Mach 0.97 at low altitude
Propulsion: 1 SNECMA 8 K 50 turbojet, 5,000-kg thrust
Max. ceiling: 35,000 ft
Range: 750 n.m. (1 hr 45 min or, with external fuel, 2 hr 15 min)
Weapons: 2 30-mm cannon, bombs, rockets, or 1 AM 39 Exocet or ASMP or 2 AS 30L laser-guided missiles

Super Étendard—aboard *Charles de Gaulle* (R 91)   Martin Mokrus, 6-04

Remarks: Have been modified to carry the ANT 52 nuclear bomb. During 1990–97, 50 Super Étendard received the Anémone radar, Thales Sherloc radar warning receiver and Barracuda jammer EW equipment, podded Alkan Type 5081 chaff and flare dispensers, head-up display, and a SAGEM UAT 90 computer in place of the UAT 10 and other improvements. The aircraft are to be phased out of service between 2004 and 2010. Aircraft destined for service aboard *Charles de Gaulle* are equipped to carry AS 30L laser-guided ground-attack missiles. Six aircraft have been modified to perform photoreconnaissance duties.

Note: Two Grumman E-2C Hawkeye radar surveillance aircraft were ordered 5-95 for $561.8 million, and the third was ordered on 28-3-01. All had been delivered by 9-03. The E-2Cs have APS-145 radar, ALR-73 intercept, four-color displays, JTIDS (Link 16) and Link 11 datalink, Loral high-speed processors, and Allison T56A-147 turboshaft engines; they carry crews of five. The first was delivered on 28-4-98 and the second during 6-98, with the first arriving in France on 18-12-98 and the second during 3-99. An option exists for a fourth E-2C. Additional data for the E-2C can be found in the U.S.A. section.

French Navy E-2C Hawkeye—with wings folded for easy storage
Bernard Prézelin, 6-04

B. LAND-BASED MARITIME RECONNAISSANCE

♦ Atlantique Mk 2   Manufacturer: Dassault-Bréguet

Wingspan: 37.30 m **Length:** 32.62 m **Height:** 10.80 m
Weight: 46,200 kg (25,000 kg light) **Speed:** 320 kts

Atlantique Mk 2   Bernard Prézelin, 6-04

Propulsion: 2 Rolls-Royce Tyne 21 turboprops (6,000 shp each)
Max. ceiling: 30,000 ft. **Range:** 4,300 n.m. (18 hrs.)
Weapons: 2 AM 39 Exocet missiles or 8 ASW torpedoes, depth charges, sonobuoys, etc. (3,000 kg total)
Avionics: Iguane radar, MAD Mk 3, FLIR system, Tango FLIR camera, DSAX 1 sonobuoy processor, ARAR 13 EW gear

Remarks: The original plan was to acquire 42 at the rate of three per year, but in 1992, the force goal was reduced to 28 and in 1996 it was reduced to 22. The first operational aircraft entered service 7-89. The final unit of 28 ordered was delivered on 21-11-97, and six are being rotated through storage and overhaul to maintain 22 operational. To be backfitted with Thomson-Marconi SADANG sonobuoy processing system.

A single Mk 3 prototype has been converted by the manufacturer in hopes of garnering export sales; the aircraft features six-bladed Dowty carbon-composite propellers, is powered by two Allison–Rolls-Royce AE2100H gas turbines, has a new combat control system with eight operator positions, and is equipped with a modern "glass" cockpit.

♦ Falcon 50M SAR and surveillance   Manufacturer: Dassault-Bréguet

French Navy Falcon 50   Bernard Prézelin, 6-04

Wingspan: 18.86 m **Length:** 18.52 m **Height:** 6.97 m
Weight: 18,500 kg max. **Speed:** 370 kts **Max. ceiling:** 45,000 ft.
Propulsion: 3 Garrett TFE 731-3-1C turbojets (1.6-ton thrust each)
Range: 2,700 n.m. (6-hr 30-min endurance)

Remarks: Four Falcon 50 SURMAR (SURveillance MARitime) jet transports were ordered in 1995 (with an option for a fifth); configured for search-and-rescue duties with Thales/EADS OM 100 Ocean Master search radar and Chlio FLIR and carrying eight 25-person life rafts, the first was delivered 11-98, the third in 3-01, and the fourth in 3-02.

♦ Gardian SAR and surveillance   Manufacturer: Aérospatiale

Gardian   French Navy

Wingspan: 16.30 m **Length:** 17.15 m **Height:** 5.32 m
Weight: 15,200 kg (10,500 kg empty) **Speed:** Mach 0.86

PRINCIPAL COMBAT AIRCRAFT *(continued)*

Propulsion: 2 Garrett ATF 3-6 turbojets **Max. ceiling:** 42,000 ft
Range: 2,200 n.m. (5 hr 30 min) **Weapons:** none

Remarks: Version of the Falcon 200 transport, with Varan radar. Ventral trap door to permit launching rescue equipment.

♦ Nord 262E maritime surveillance and training
Manufacturer: Nord

Nord 262 Bernard Prézelin, 6-04

Wingspan: 21.90 m **Length:** 19.28 m **Height:** 6.27
Weight: 10,600 kg max. **Speed:** 214 kts **Max. ceiling:** 22,500 ft
Propulsion: 2 Turbomeca Bastan V1 turboprops (1,080 shp each)
Range: 800 n.m. (4 hr 30 min.)

Remarks: Carry a crew of six and are fitted with the ORB-32 sea surveillance radar.

♦ EMB 121 Xingu training and liaison
Manufacturer: EMBRAER, Brazil

Xingu Bernard Prézelin, 3-03

Wingspan: 14.45 m **Length:** 12.25 m **Height:** 4.74 m
Weight: 5,670 kg max (3,830 kg empty) **Speed:** 230 kts
Propulsion: 2 Pratt & Whitney PT6 A28 turboprops (680 shp each) or PT6 A 35 turboprops (750 shp each)
Max. ceiling: 22,500 ft **Range:** 930 n.m. (4 hr 30 min)

Remarks: Carry a crew of two and up to seven passengers.

C. HELICOPTERS

♦ NH-90 antisubmarine
Manufacturer: Aérospatiale-MBB-AgustaWestland

NH-90 Bernard Prézelin, 7-02

Rotor diameter: 16.00 m **Length:** 19.50 m (13.14 folded)
Height: 5.20 m
Weight: 10,600 kg max. **Speed:** 157 kts (132 cruise)
Propulsion: 2 Rolls-Royce or Turbomeca 322-01/02 turboshafts, 2,120 shp
Max. ceiling: 20,000 ft **Endurance:** 4 hr 45 min
Weapons: MU-90 torpedoes, AM 39 missiles (total: 2,000 kg max.)

Remarks: Cooperative European venture. Prototype rolled out 29-9-95. Will eventually replace the Super Frelon and the WG 13 Lynx in the French Navy. Plan to acquire 60 reduced to 27 in 5-96, with 14 equipped for ASW and 13 for the transport and SAR role. Composite materials employed in construction. In ASW configuration would carry pilot, copilot, and two equipment operators. Will have Thales FLASH dipping sonar and a MAD sensor. Italian versions will have G.E.-FiatAvio T700/T6E1 turboshaft engines.

♦ Super Frelon heavy transport
Manufacturer: Aérospatiale

Rotor diameter: 18.90 m **Length:** 23.00 m **Height:** 6.70 m
Weight: 13,000 kg **Speed:** 145 kts
Propulsion: 3 Turbomeca III C3 turboshafts (1,500 shp each)
Max. ceiling: 10,000 ft **Range:** 420 n.m. (3 hr 30 min)
Weapons: None

Super Frelon Bernard Prézelin, 6-04

Remarks: No longer equipped for ASW or ship-attack role. Despite age, are to be kept in service until 2005 to 2008. Have ORB-42 radar. Can carry 27 passengers or three tons of cargo.

♦ Lynx (WG 13) antisubmarine/antiship
Manufacturer: AgustaWestland-Aérospatiale

Lynx Martin Mokrus, 4-05

Rotor diameter: 12.80 m **Length:** 15.2 m **Height:** 3.60 m
Weight: 4,150 kg **Speed:** 150 kts
Propulsion: 2 Rolls-Royce BS 360 turboshafts (900 shp each)
Max. ceiling: 12,000 ft **Endurance:** 2 hr 30 min, part in transit, part hovering
Weapons: Mk 46 torpedoes, AS 12 wire-guided missiles

Remarks: Have ORB 31 radar, DUAV-4 dipping sonar. Capable of localization, classification, and attack of submarine and surface targets.

♦ Panther (AS.365MF) SAR and transport
Manufacturer: Aérospatiale

Panther Michael Winter, 6-05

Rotor diameter: 13.29 m. **Length:** 11.41 m **Height:** 4.00 m
Weight: 4,250 kg max. **Speed:** 175 kts max.; 155 max. cruise; 135 cruise
Propulsion: 2 Turbomeca Arreil 1 MN turboshafts (770 shp each)
Max. ceiling: 12,000 ft **Radius:** 400 n.m. (4 hr 45 min) **Fuel:** 1,100 liters

Remarks: Fifteen Aérospatiale-Matra AS.565MB Panther helicopters (a derivative of the AS.365N2 Dauphin 2) were delivered 1993–98 and assigned to 35F at Lanvéoc-Poulmic to replace Alouette-IIIs. Each can carry up to 12 passengers. Have ORB-32 radar, doppler radar altimeter, and Nadir Mk II navigational computer. The Panthers supplement the six similar AS.365N2 Dauphin ordered 1988–89. Flight duration is four hours.

♦ SA.319 Alouette-III liaison and training
Manufacturer: Aérospatiale

Radar-equipped Alouette-III Bernard Prézelin, 4-04

Rotor diameter: 11.02 m **Length:** 12.84 m **Height:** 3.00 m
Weight: 2,200 kg (1,104 kg light) **Speed:** 110 kts
Propulsion: 1 Turbomeca Astazou turboshaft (870 shp)
Max. ceiling: 10,000 ft. **Range:** 325 n.m. (2 hr 30 min)

Remarks: A few are of the earlier SA.316 version.

NUCLEAR-POWERED BALLISTIC-MISSILE SUBMARINES [SSBN]

Note: To augment security, names and pennant numbers ceased to be displayed on 1-1-83.

♦ 3 (+ 1) Le Triomphant class
Bldr: DCN, Cherbourg

	Laid down	L	In serv.
S 616 LE TRIOMPHANT	9-6-89	26-3-94	21-3-97
S 617 LE TÉMÉRAIRE	18-12-93	21-1-98	23-12-99
S 618 LE VIGILANT	1997	19-9-03	29-11-04
S 619 LE TERRIBLE	24-10-00	2008	2010 (del.)

Le Téméraire (S 617) Bernard Prézelin, 4-04

Le Téméraire (S 617) Bernard Prézelin, 4-04

Le Vigilant (S 618) Bernard Prézelin, 4-04

D: 12,640 tons surf./14,335 tons sub. **S:** 25 kts sub. (12 kts surf.)
Dim: 138.00 × 12.50 (17.0 over planes) × 10.65
A: 16 M 45 (S 619: M 51) SLBM; 4 bow 533-mm TT (18 SM 39 antiship missiles and F 17 Mod. 2 torpedoes)
Electronics:
Radar: 1 DRUA-33 nav./search
Sonar: DMUX-80 suite: DUUV-23 panoramic passive array; DSUV-61B towed linear array; DUUX-5 acoustic intercept
EW: ARUR-13 (Thales DR-4000U and DR-3000U) intercept suite
M: 1 Type K15, 150-Mw pressurized-water reactor; 1 pump-jet prop; 41,500 shp—diesel-electric emergency propulsion: 2 SEMT-Pielstick 8 PA4 V200 diesel generator sets (1,225 bhp/900 kw each); 5,000 n.m. range
Crew: 2 crews in rotation: 15 officers, 96 enlisted each

Remarks: A "new generation," first announced 1981. Announced during 9-92 that the class will be curtailed at four vice the planned five. Work on S 616 was ordered slowed late in 9-91 for financial reasons; she was rolled out of the production hall on 13-7-93. S 618 was ordered 27-5-93. Are expected to last 25 years each, with refits and recorings at seven-year intervals. Problems with pressure-hull welds delayed sea trials for S 616 until 15-4-94. Production of S 618 was slowed under the FY 95 budget. It had been hoped to order the fourth in FY 97, but the planned order was delayed to 28-7-00. First operational patrol for S 616 began 3-97. S 616 underwent overhaul from 2002 to 2004. S 618, ten months late being launched, underwent sea trials during 2003–4.
Hull systems: Use NLES 100, high-elasticity steel for pressure hull and a potential 500-m diving depth. Careful attention to radiated noise reduction, including an elaborate "rafted" (isolated) propulsion plant and a pump-jet propulsor. Sail-mounted bow planes and vertical surfaces at ends of stern planes. More highly automated than their predecessors, hence the smaller crews.
Combat systems: The first three have (or will have) the M 45 missile with TN-75 warheads. The replacement M 51 missile will not be available until 2010. Have Syracuse II SATCOM capability, SEAO/OPSMER combat decision-making system, and a precision navigation system. S 619 will have the DCN SYCOBS (*Système de Combat pour Barracuda et SSBN*) combat system. A Sagem OMS optronic mast is fitted; gyrostabilized, it carries television, infrared and X-band radar sensors, SFIM L-series search periscope, and MRA-2 star-tracking navigational periscope.

♦ 1 Le Redoutable class
Bldr: DCN, Cherbourg

	Laid down	L	In serv.
S 615 L'INFLEXIBLE	27-3-80	23-6-82	1-4-85

L'Inflexible (S 615) Bernard Prézelin, 2-04

D: 8,087 tons surf./9,000 (S 615: 8,094) tons sub. **S:** 20+ kts sub.
Dim: 128.70 × 10.60 × 10.00
A: 16 M45 SLBM; 4 bow 550-mm TT (18 SM 39 Exocet antiship missiles and/or L 5 Mod. 3 and F 17 Mod. 2 torpedoes)
Electronics:
Radar: 1 DRUA-33 nav./search
Sonar: DMUX-21 suite: DUUV-23 panoramic passive array; DUUX-5 acoustic intercept; DSUV999-61B towed passive array
EW: ARUR-12 (Thales DR-4000U and DR-2000U) intercept suite
M: 1 pressurized-water reactor, 2 steam turbines with 1 set turbo-reduction gears; 1 prop; 16,000 shp—2 SEMT-Pielstick 8 PA4 V185 alternator sets (450 kw each) for battery charging (5,000 n.m. range)
Crew: 2 crews in rotation, each of 15 officers and 120 enlisted

Remarks: Six of this class were originally built. S 615 was ordered 9-78, and equipped from the outset with the M 4 missile, re-equipped with the M 45 missile in 2001. First patrol began 25-5-85, took advantage of many technological advances in propulsion, sonar systems, navigation systems, etc. Based at Île Longue, Brest. Expected to remain in service through 2008, but may be extended in service if completion of S 619 is delayed. Maximum operating depth: 300 meters. Have the SEAO/OPSMER combat decision-aid system and Pivair SPS-S optronic periscopes.
Disposals: *Le Redoutable* (S 611), unmodified, completed her last patrol early in 1991 and, after trials employment, was stricken 12-91 for eventual use as a museum exhibit; work began 23-3-93 to remove her reactor compartment. *Le Terrible* (S 612) was stricken on 1-7-96, *Le Foudroyant* (S 610) on 30-4-98, *Le Tonnant* (S 614) during 9-99, and *L'Indomptable* (S 613) on 14-5-05.

NUCLEAR-POWERED ATTACK SUBMARINES [SSN]

♦ 0 (+ 6) Barracuda class
Bldr: DCN, Cherbourg

	Laid down	L	Trials	In serv.
S . . .	2006	. . .	2011	2014
S . . .	2007	. . .	2013	2016
S . . .	2009	. . .	2015	2018
S . . .	2011	. . .	2017	2020
S . . .	2013	. . .	2019	2022
S . . .	2015	. . .	2021	2024

D: 4,600 tons surf./5,300 tons sub. **S:** 14 kts. surf./25+ kts sub. **Dim:** 97.0 × 8.8 × 7.3
A: 4 bow 533-mm TT (18 tot. Scalp Naval land-attack missiles, Scalp-Naval antiship missiles, Black Shark wire-guided torpedoes, and/or mines)
Electronics:
Radar: . . . nav./surf. search
Sonar: . . .
EW: . . .

NUCLEAR-POWERED ATTACK SUBMARINES [SSN] *(continued)*

M: 1 Type K15, 150-Mw pressurized-water reactor; 1 pumpjet prop; 41,500 shp—diesel-electric emergency propulsion: 2 SEMT-Pielstick 8 PA4 V200 diesel generator sets (1,225 bhp/900 kw each); 5,000 n.m. range
Endurance: 70 days **Crew:** Two crews of 60 tot. (8 officers plus 52 enlisted)

Remarks: Successor to the *Sous-Marins d'Attaque Futurs* (SMAF) program. Feasibility studies began on 5-10-98, with the first submarine to have been ordered in 2001 but that was delayed to 2006, a second unit will likely be ordered in 2008, a third in 2009, and fourth in 2010. The class will be deeper-diving than the *Améthyste* class and will be equipped with improved combat systems and improved sound quieting. Will be entirely a French design and will be faster than current French SSNs. The six are to be in service to 2050 through 2062. Were originally to have cost about $950 million each, but the Finance Ministry demanded a reduction to about $675 million each in 1-00—an unattainable goal if performance is not to suffer severely. The first was originally to have been delivered in 2010, but two years were lost in programming delays.
Hull systems: Maximum operating depth is to be 400 m. The reactor design will be based on that of the K15 pressurized water reactor; will use electric propulsion for cruising speeds and geared turbines for maximum speeds.
Combat systems: Will have the DCN SYCOBS (*Système de Combat pour Barracuda et SSBN*) combat system. Thales Underwater Systems will provide the sonar suite, which will include bow, wide-angle aperture flank, and thin-line towed passive arrays.

♦ 6 Améthyste class (Type SNA 72)
Bldr: DCN, Cherbourg

	Laid down	L	In serv.
S 601 Rubis (ex-*Provence*)	11-12-76	7-7-79	23-2-83
S 602 Saphir (ex-*Bretagne*)	1-9-79	1-9-81	6-7-84
S 603 Casabianca (ex-*Bourgogne*)	9-81	22-12-84	21-4-87
S 604 Émeraude	10-82	12-4-86	15-9-88
S 605 Améthyste	31-10-83	14-5-88	3-3-92
S 606 Perle	22-3-87	22-9-90	7-7-93

Casabianca (S 603) Bernard Prézelin, 4-05

Émeraude (S 604) Bernard Prézelin, 3-04

D: 2,280 tons std., 2,410 tons surf./2,680 tons sub.
S: 26.5 kts sub. (23.5 kts sustained sub.)
Dim: 73.60 × 7.60 × 6.45
A: 4 bow 533-mm TT (14 F 17 Mod. 2 torpedoes and SM 39 missiles, or up to 32 FG 29 mines)
Electronics:
Radar: 1 DRUA-33 nav./search
Sonar: DMUX-20 suite; DSUV-22 multifunction passive array; DUUA-2B active (8 kHz); DUUX-5 acoustic intercept, TUUM underwater telephone; DSUV-62C towed passive array; DUUG-2 sonar intercept
EW: ARUR-13 (Thales DR-4000U and DR-2000U) intercept suite
M: 1 CAS-48 48-Mw pressurized-water reactor; two 3,950-kw turboalternator sets; 1 electric motor; 1 prop; 9,500 shp—1 electric motor driven by batteries powered by 1 SEMT-Pielstick 8 PA4 V185 diesel generator set (480 kw)
Electric: 1,700 kw (2 × 850-kw alternators) **Endurance:** 60 days
Crew: 10 officers, 52 petty officers, 8 other enlisted (2 crews each)

Remarks: *Améthyste* is both the name of the fifth unit and an acronym for *Amélioration Tactique Transmission Écoute* (reduced radiated noise transmission). S 602 was brought up to *Améthyste* standard 10-89 to 5-91; S 601 from 9-92 to 7-93; S 603 during 1993–94; and S 604 from 5-94 to 12-95. During late 2002 the operational availability rate for the class was reported to be only 38.8%.
Names for the first three were changed in 11-80. *Rubis*'s reactor became operational early 2-81 and trials started 6-81. S 605 and S 606 were ordered on 17-10-84 and *Turquoise* (S 607) on 24-4-90. Late in 9-91, it was announced that the eighth unit, *Diamant* (S 608), would not be built and that work on S 607 would not start until 1993. In 6-92, S 607 was canceled outright, but by 9-92 it had been decided to offer the incomplete submarine as a diesel-powered unit for export; no customer was found, however. S 604 experienced a leak in the secondary steam loop on 30-3-94, resulting in the death of the commanding officer and nine other personnel. S 602 experienced excessive radioactivity in the primary reactor loop in 9-00 and was withdrawn from service for six months to undergo an unscheduled recoring. All six are based at Toulon. S 601 is planned to retire in 2012 and the last in 2022.
Hull systems: The pressure hull is constructed of HLES 80, 100,000-psi steel. The superstructure and external bow form are built of GRP. Diving depth is over 300 m. The ships have two SAGEM Minicin inertial navigation systems and two data-buses. Endurance on battery power is about 15 hours. The bow was reconfigured to a more streamlined shape and lengthened by 1.5 m in the four modernized units. The reactor uses natural water circulation cooling at speeds below 6 kts; the entire engineering plant is considerably noisier than on U.S.- and British-built nuclear submarines.
Combat systems: All have the TITAC automated combat data system and NATO Link 14. Are receiving the SEAO/OPSMER combat decision aid system. The number of reload weapons has been reduced to provide additional berthing. Have Pivair SPS-S optical search periscopes and SFIM K-series search periscope.

Disposal note: Of the *Agosta*-class diesel-electric attack submarines, *Agosta* (S 620) was decommissioned 28-10-97 and placed in special reserve to await disposal; *Bévéziers* (S 621) followed on 6-2-98; *La Praya* (S 622) was retired on 30-6-00; and *Ouessant* (S 623) was decommissioned 1-7-01 but was reactivated and recommissioned during 2005 to serve as a training boat for Malaysian crews during construction of two Scorpène-class submarines for Malaysia. S 623 may eventually transfer to Malaysia once the Scorpène program is completed.

GUIDED-MISSILE DESTROYERS [DDG]

♦ 0 (+ 2) Forbin class (Project Horizon)
Bldr: DCN, Lorient

	Laid down	L	In serv.
D 620 Forbin	16-1-04	10-3-05	1-08
D 621 Chevalier Paul	2005	12-7-06	12-08

Forbin (D 620) Bernard Prézelin, 7-06

Chevalier Paul (D 621)—under construction Bernard Prézelin, 7-06

D: 5,600 tons standard/6,635 tons (fl) **S:** 29 kts
Dim: 152.87 × 20.30 (17.60 wl) × 5.40 (mean hull)
A: 8 MM 40 Mod. 2 Exocet SSM; 6 8-cell Sylver A50 SAM launch groups (32 tot. Aster-30 and 16 Aster-15 missiles); 2 6-round Sadral SAM syst. (Mistral missiles); 2 single 76-mm 62-cal. OTO Melara Super Rapid DP; 2 single 20-mm 90-cal. GIAT F2 Type A AA; 2 fixed ASW torpedo launchers (MU-90 Impact torpedoes); 1 NH-90 helicopter (AM 39 Exocet missiles and/or MU-90 Impact torpedoes)
Electronics:
Radar: 2 GEM SPN-753 nav.; 1 EMPAR target designation/tracking; 1 AMS/Thales S 1850 missile target designation/f.c.; 1 AMS NA-25XP gun f.c.
Sonar: Thales-WASS TMS 4110CL hull-mounted LF
EW: . . . intercept, 2 12-round Matra Défense NGDS decoy syst.; SLAT torpedo countermeasure syst.
E/O: DIBV-1A Vampir IR detection and tracking; 1 Sagem VIGY-20 tracker

GUIDED-MISSILE DESTROYERS [DDG] *(continued)*

M: CODAG: 2 Fiat-G.E. LM 2500 gas turbines (31,280 shp each), 2 SEMT- Pielstick 12 PA6B STC diesels, geared drive (5,800 bhp each); 2 props; 62,560 shp max.—bow-thruster
Electric: . . . kw tot. (4 × . . . kw; Isotta Fraschini VL 1716 T2 ME diesels driving)
Range: 7,000/18; 3,500/25 **Endurance:** 45 days
Crew: 174 tot., 26 officers, 148 enlisted (plus 32 staff/passengers as required)

Note: Agreement was made with the U.K. and Italy to design a ship acceptable to all three navies in a venture initially announced 12-3-91. An international joint-venture corporation, Horizon Ltd., was established 21-2-95 to build at least the initial units of the class for the three partner countries by the three then-prime contractors, GEC-Marconi, DCN International, and Orissonte SpA. The U.K. pulled out of the platform portion of the program on 21-4-99 but remains committed to the SAM program. On 16-9-99, it was decided that France and Italy would go ahead with a joint program, and an order for two ships was finally placed on 26-10-00. First steel was cut for the D 620 on 8-4-02. A third ship was authorized in 9-02 but then plans for the third and a fourth unit were scrapped in 9-05, likely in favor of new FREMM warships.
Hull systems: Will have two sets of fin stabilizers. Numerous radar, heat, and acoustic signature reduction measures are to be incorporated.
Combat systems: The combat data system will probably be a variant of SENIT 8. The ships will have an integrated communications system and will be NATO Improved Link 11–, Link 14–, and Link 16–compatible; they are to have Syracuse SHF and, possibly, EHF SATCOM systems, as well as Inmarsat UHF SATCOM. The helicopter will be used for ASW and for attacking surface ships with missiles and will be launchable and landable in up to Sea State 6. The torpedoes will be ejected through shutters in the hull sides beneath the helicopter pad.

♦ 2 Cassard class (Type C 70)

	Bldr	Laid down	L	In serv.
D 614 CASSARD	DCN, Lorient	3-9-82	6-2-85	29-7-88
D 615 JEAN BART	DCN, Lorient	12-3-86	19-3-88	1-9-91

Cassard (D 614) Jim Saunderson, 2004

D: 4,560 tons (5,060 fl) **S:** 29.6 kts
Dim: 139.00 (129.00 pp) × 15.00 (14.00 wl) × 6.70 (4.40 hull)

Jean Bart (D 615) Michael Winter, 6-05

A: 8 MM 40 SSM; 1 Mk 13 SAM launcher (40 Standard SM-1 MR missiles); 2 6-round Sadral SAM syst. (39 tot. Mistral missiles); 1 100-mm 55-cal. Model 1968 DP; 2 single 20-mm 70-cal. Oerlikon AA; 4 single 12.7-mm mg; 2 fixed KD-59E torpedo catapults (10 L 5 Mod. 4 ASW torpedoes); 1 AS.365MF Panther liaison helicopter
Electronics:
Radar: 2 DRBN-34A (Decca RM 1229) nav./helicopter control; 1 DRBJ-11B 3-D air search; 1 DRBV-26C early warning; 2 Raytheon SPG-51C missile illumination; 1 DRBC-33A gun f.c.
Sonar: DUBA-25A (D 615: DUBA-24C) hull-mounted; TUUM-2D underwater telephone; NUBS-8A echo sounder—D 615 *also:* U/RDT-1A torpedo detection system
EW: ARBR-17 intercept; ARBB-33 Salamandre jammer; ARBG-1A Saigon comms VHFD/F; Telegon-10 HFD/F; 2 330- to 340-round AMBL-1C (Matra Défense Dagaie 2) decoy RL; 2 6-round AMBL-2A (Matra Défense Sagaie) countermeasures RL; SLQ-25 Nixie towed acoustic torpedo decoy syst.
E/O: DIBV-1A Vampir surveillance, DIBC-1A (Piranha III) IR/t.v./laser weapons director
TACAN: U.S. SRN-6
M: 4 SEMT-Pielstick 18 PA 6V 280 BTC diesels; 2 5-bladed props; 42,300 bhp
Electric: 3,400 kw (4 × 850-kw Jeumont-Schneider alternators, 4 AGO 195-V12-CSHR diesels driving)
Range: 4,800/24; 8,000/17 **Fuel:** 600 tons **Endurance:** 30 days
Crew: 244 total (222 enlisted)

Remarks: Typed as *Frégates Lance-Missiles* (FLM). 1977–82 program; D 614 was authorized under the 1978 budget and D 615 under the 1979 budget. A third and fourth were authorized in 1983 but were canceled 27-2-84. Are to be retired 2012–14. Both are based at Toulon.
Hull systems: There are 16 watertight bulkheads to the hull, the sides of which were strengthened to reduce cracking during 2002 through the addition of a doubling plate near the upper deck. Aluminum superstructure. Fin stabilizers are fitted. Have an NBC warfare protection citadel system. The main engines are rated at 10,800 bhp each at 1,050 rpm. A SAMAHE 210 (*Système d'Aide à la Manutention des Hélicoptères Embarqués*) deck traversing system is fitted for the helicopter. Have two "Mini SINS" inertial navigation aids. During 2002 D 614 was fitted with hull-strengthening strakes at the upper deck level, adding 1 m to the beam; the modifications added 120 tons of structural steel and required adding 210 tons of permanent ballast. They measure 46 m from waterline to top of the mast.

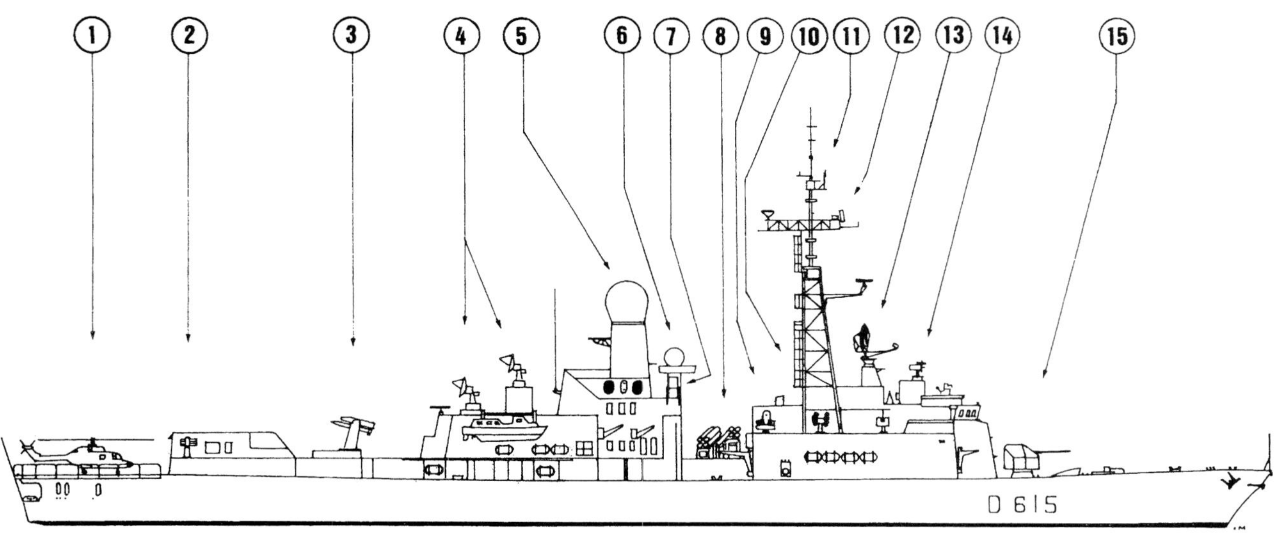

Jean Bart (D 615) 1. Helicopter platform 2. Sadral SAM system (port and starboard) 3. Mk 13 launcher for Standard SM-1 SAM system 4. SPG-51C tracker-illuminator radars for the Standard SAM system 5. DRBJ-11B 3-D air-search radar 6. Syracuse SATCOM antenna radomes (port and starboard) 7. ARBB-33 ECM antennas 8. MM 40 Exocet anti-ship missiles (four missiles per set) 9. Dagaie decoy launcher 10. Sagaie decoy launcher 11. ARBR-17 ESM antennas 12. DIBV-1A Vampir IR surveillance syst. 13. DRBV-26C early-warning radar 14. DRBC-33 100-mm gun f.c. radar 15. 100-mm Model 1968 DP gun Drawing by Jean Moulin from *Flottes de Combat*

GUIDED-MISSILE DESTROYERS [DDG] *(continued)*

Combat systems: Have the SENIT 6 digital data system, with Link 11 and 14 data-link capability. The DRBC-33 radar fire-control director has a Piranha III optronic attachment and is backed up by a Najir III DMaB optronic t.v./laser director. Also installed are two Matra Défense Type 88-DD00-ZA optronic target designators. The Mk 13 SAM launchers and missile fire-control systems were taken from the retired destroyers *Kersaint* and *Bouvet.* Both were at one time planned to receive the SAMP/N SAM system with Aster-30 missiles in place of Standard SM-1 MR. The Model 1968 CADEM gun has a 78-rd/min firing capability. The helicopter can be used to provide over-the-horizon targeting for the antiship missiles.

The intended DRBJ-11B radar in D 614 was initially replaced by DRBV-15 because of developmental problems; she was brought up to the same standard as D 615 in 1992. The EW sensor arrays are integrated by the NEWSY system, with a dedicated computer. Thales SPIN jam-resistant HF radios are fitted, as is the Syracuse SATCOM. The space beneath the helicopter deck was intended to accommodate a DSBV-61 towed linear passive hydrophone array system.

Note: Of the two *Suffren*-class guided-missile destroyers, the *Suffren* (D 602) was placed in disposal reserve on 2-4-01, and the Masurca SAM system on the *Duquesne* (D 603) is no longer operational; the class is now listed below under [DD].

♦ 1 Suffren class

	Bldr	Laid down	L	In serv.
D 603 DUQUESNE	DCN, Brest	1-2-65	11-2-66	1-4-70

Duquesne (D 603) A. A. de Kruijf, 5-05

Duquesne (D 603) A. A. de Kruijf, 5-05

D: 5,335 tons (6,780 fl) **S:** 34 kts
Dim: 157.60 (148.00 pp) × 15.54 × 7.25 (max.)
A: 4 MM 38 Exocet SSM; 2 single 100-mm 55-cal. Model 1964 DP; 1 twin Mascura SAM launcher (48 missiles carried); 4 single 20-mm 70-cal. Oerlikon AA; 4 single 12.7-mm mg; 2 fixed KD-59E torpedo catapults (10 L 5 Mod. 4 ASW torpedoes); 2 100-mm 55-cal. Model 1964 DP
Electronics:
Radar: 1 DRBN-32 nav.; 1 DRBV-15A air/surf. search; 1 DRBI-23 3-D air search; 2 DRBR-51 SAM f.c.; 1 DRBC-33A gun f.c.
Sonar: DUBV-23 hull-mounted; DUBV-43 VDS
TACAN: NRBP-2A (U.S. URN-20)
EW: ARBR-17 intercept; ARBB-33 Salamandre jammer; Telegon-4 HFD/F; 2 6-round AMBL-2A Sagaie decoy RL; SLQ-25 Nixie towed torpedo decoy
E/O: DIBC-1A (Pirhana III) optronic weapons director
M: 2 sets Rateau double-reduction geared steam turbines; 2 props; 72,500 shp
Boilers: 4 multitube, automatic-control; 45 kg/cm^2, 450° C
Electric: 3,440 kw (2 × 1,000-kw turbogenerators, 3 × 480-kw diesel alternators)
Range: 2,000/30; 2,400/29; 5,100/18
Crew: 24 officers, 209 petty officers, 113 ratings

Remarks: Typed as *Frégates Lance-Missiles* (FLM). Built under the 1960–65 plan. Sister *Suffren* (D 602) was placed in disposal reserve on 2-4-01, several years ahead of schedule. The Masurca SAM system remains operational, despite reports that it was deactivated during 2000. D 603 is not scheduled for retirement until 2008. Based at Toulon.

Hull systems: Three pairs of nonretractable fin stabilizers provide excellent seaworthiness. Living and operating spaces are air-conditioned. Has an NBC warfare protection citadel.
Combat systems: In a refit ending during 1991, the DRBC-33 fire-control radar with Piranha III optronic (t.v., laser, infrared) attachment was substituted for DRBC-32, the ARBR-17 and ARBB-33 EW equipments were substituted for earlier equipment, the *Amélie* microcomputer-assisted data system was added, the Masurca SAM system was updated, the SENIT 1 combat data system was updated to SENIT 2, the DRBI-23 radar received a transistorized transmitter and receiver, and the DUBV-43 variable-depth sonar was modernized. The 100-mm guns fire at up to 78 rds/min. Has two SAGEM DMA optronic target designation sights. The Malafon ASW missile system was removed in 1998. Syracuse SATCOM equipment is fitted.

DESTROYERS [DD]

♦ 7 Georges Leygues class (Type F 70)
Bldr: DCN, Brest

	Laid down	L	In serv.
D 640 GEORGES LEYGUES	16-9-74	17-12-76	10-12-79
D 641 DUPLEIX	17-10-75	2-12-78	16-6-81
D 642 MONTCALM	5-12-75	31-5-80	28-5-82
D 643 JEAN DE VIENNE	26-10-79	17-11-81	25-5-84
D 644 PRIMAUGUET	19-11-81	17-3-84	5-11-86
D 645 LA MOTTE-PICQUET	9-2-82	6-2-85	18-2-88
D 646 LATOUCHE-TRÉVILLE	31-5-85	19-3-88	16-7-90

La Motte-Picquet (D 645) Bernard Prézelin, 4-05

Georges Leygues (D 640) Bernard Prézelin, 9-05

Latouche-Tréville (D 646) Bernard Prézelin, 9-05

D: D 640: 3,880 tons (4,830 fl); D 641–643: 3,831 tons (4,500 fl); D 644–646: 4,010 tons (4.910 fl)
S: 30 kts (gas turbines), 21 kts (diesels)
Dim: 139.00 (129.00 pp) × 15.00 (14.00 wl) × 5.60 (hull; 5.90–5.96 props)
A: D 640: 4 MM 38 Exocet; 1 8-round Crotale EDIR SAM system (26 missiles); 2 2-round Simbad SAM syst.; 1 100-mm 55-cal. Model 1968 CADAM DP; 2 single 20-mm 70-cal. Oerlikon Mk 10 Mod. 23 AA; 2 single 12.7-mm mg; 2 fixed KD-59E torpedo catapults (10 L 5 Mod. 4 ASW torpedoes); 2 WG-13 Lynx helicopters.

DESTROYERS [DD] *(continued)*

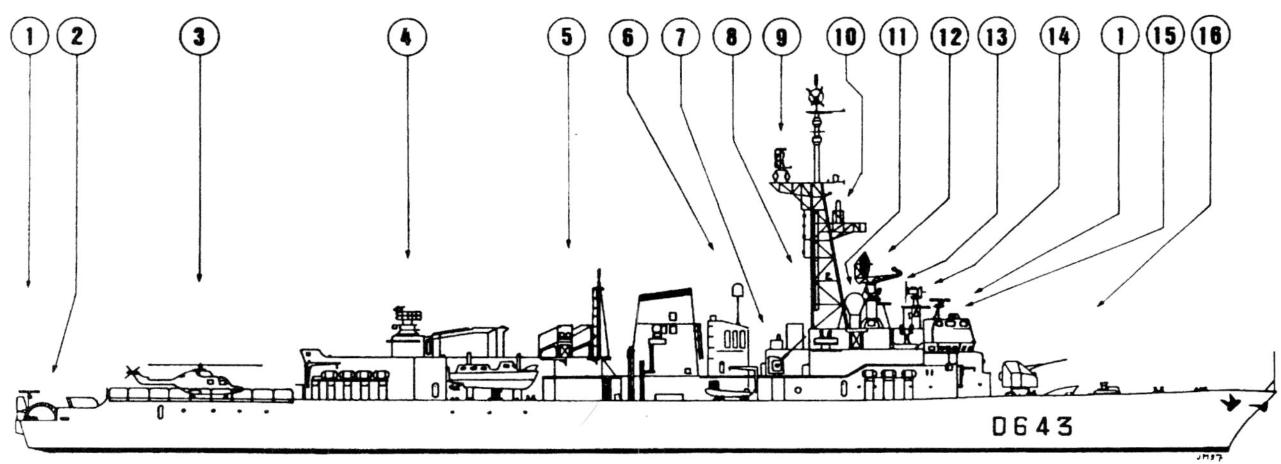

Jean de Vienne (D 643) 1. DRBN-32 radar for helicopter landing control 2. DUBV-43C VDS 3. Lynx helicopter 4. Crotale SAM launcher (abaft reload magazine) 5. MM 40 Exocet antiship missile launchers (now two twin sets per side on D 643 only) 6. Inmarsat SATCOM antenna radome 7. 30-mm AA 8. Dagaie decoy launcher 9. DRBC-51C air-search and targeting radar 10. DIBC-2A IR surveillance sensor and f.c. director 11. Syracuse SATCOM antenna radomes 12. DRBV-26 early-warning radar 13. ARBB-36 ECM antennas 14. DRBC-32E gun f.c. radar 15. Sadral SAM syst. 16. 100-mm Model 1968 DP gun. This drawing in general applies to D 641–643.

Drawing by Jean Moulin from *Flottes de Combat*

D 641–646: 4 MM 40 Exocet SSM; 1 8-round Crotale EDIR SAM system (26 missiles); D 641–643 *only:* 2 6-round Sadral SAM syst. (39 Mistral missiles); D 645 *only:* 2 2-round Simbad SAM syst. (. . . Mistral missiles); *all:* 1 100-mm 55-cal. Model 1968 CADAM DP; D 641–643: 2 single 30-mm 70-cal. OTO Melara-Mauser AA; *others:* 2 single 20-mm 70-cal. Oerlikon Mk 10 Mod. 23 AA; *all:* 2 single 12.7-mm mg; 2 fixed KD-59E torpedo catapults (10 L-5 Mod.4 ASW torpedoes); 1–2 WG-13 Lynx helicopters

Electronics:

Radar: D 640, 641, 643: 2 DRBN-34 nav.; 1 DRBV-26A early warning; 1 DRBV-51C (D 640: DRBV-51D; D 641: DRBV-15A) surf./air search; 1 DRBC-32D gun f.c.; D 642, 644–646: 2 DRBN-34 or Kelvin-Hughes Type 1007 nav.; 1 DRBV-15A surf./air search; 1 DRBC-33A gun f.c.

Sonar: D 640–643: DUBV-23 hull-mounted; DUBV-43B (D 643: DUBV-43C) VDS; D 641 *also:* DSBV-62C towed array; D 644–646: DUBV-24C hull-mounted; DUBV-43C VDS; DSBV-61A towed array

EW: D 640, 641, 643: ARBR-16 (DR 2000S) intercept; ARBB-36A jammer; ARBR-11B D/F; ARBX-10 radar intercept; Telegon-4 HFD/F; 2 33- or 34-round AMBL-1C (Dagaie Mk 2) decoy RL; 2 twin Replica floating radar decoys; SLQ-25A Nixie towed acoustic torpedo decoy; D 642, 644–646: ARBR-17 (DR 4000) intercept; ARBB-32B jammer; 2 33- or 34-round AMBL-1C (Dagaie Mk 2) decoy RL; 2 twin Replica floating radar decoys; SLQ-25 Nixie towed torpedo decoy (D 644, 645 *also:* ARBG-1A SAIGON HF/VHF communications monitoring syst.)

E/O: D 640, 641, 643, 645: DIBV-2A Vampir IR surveillance; D 640–643: 2 DIBC-2A f.c.; D 645, 646: Piranha III t.v./IR f.c. for 100-mm gun

M: CODOG: 2 Rolls-Royce Olympus TM3B gas turbines (26,000 shp each); 2 SEMT-Pielstick 16 PA 6 CV 280 diesels (5,360 bhp each); 2 CP 4-bladed props; 52,000 shp max. (gas turbine; 46,000 shp sust.; 10,720 bhp on diesels)

Electric: 3,400 kw (4 × 850-kw diesel alternator sets)

Range: 1,000/30; 10,000/15 (diesels) **Fuel:** 600 tons distillate

Crew: D 643 and other OP3A modernization ships: 22 officers, 145 petty officers, 77 nonrated; D 640: 15 officers, 90 petty officers, 111 nonrated; D 645: 20 officers, 120 petty officers, 95 nonrated

Remarks: D 645 and D 646 were built at Brest and fitted out at Lorient Dockyard. The final three had a modified sensor suite and the pilothouse placed one deck higher. D 644 and 646 are based at Brest; D 641, 642, 643, and 645 are based at Toulon as part of the *Force d'Action Navale* (FAN); D 640 is based at Toulon, became companion ship to the cadet training ship *Jeanne d'Arc* in 7-99, and was to be retired during 2000 but will now operate until 2008. The others are now planned to be retained until 2009 to 2017—at which point they will have been in service for 30 years—without significant modernization.

Hull systems: Denny Brown 21.5-m^2 automatic fin stabilizers are fitted, and the propellers have air venting to reduce cavitation noise. Have an NBC warfare protective citadel, and the navigation bridge is equipped with two optical periscopes. Accommodations for female crewmembers are incorporated in all. An Arcor 670 launch is carried to port, a 9-m, 250-bhp VD 9 launch to starboard, and two Zodiac RIBs are stowed on deck. The 21-m-long by 12.20-m-wide helicopter deck has a SPHEX (*Système Pousseur pour Hélicoptère Embarqué Expérimental*) Compact-II landing system with harpoon-type landing grid and two deck-traversing rails to move the helicopters in and out of the spacious hangar, which is 13.5 m long, 11.4 m wide, and 4.3 m high. All had their hulls reinforced during 2002–3 due to hull cracking, which was particularly severe on D 640 and D 643; the modifications added 120 tons of structural steel and required adding 210 tons of permanent ballast. D 644 began poststrengthening sea trials on 2-10-02. D 641 and D 642 have completed the hull strengthening, work on D 642 is under way, and work on D 645 is under way.

Propulsion systems: Main propulsion and auxiliary equipment is divided among four compartments, from forward to aft: forward auxiliary room, turbine room, diesel room with the reduction gears, and after auxiliary room. Full speed on the gas turbines can be reached in three minutes from a standing start. On diesel power and with the DUBV-43 sonar in the water, maximum speed is 19 knots. The propulsion control system transfers power automatically from the diesels to the gas turbines. Centralized control of the propulsion machinery from the bridge greatly reduces the engineering staff required (3 officers, 23 petty officers, 24 ratings).

Combat systems: Have SENIT 4 data system with eight multifunction display stations; are equipped for NATO Link 11 and Link 14; and have Syracuse II SHF and commercial INMARSAT SATCOM equipment. All have the "Minicin" inertial navigation system. The helicopters can be used for ASW with Mk 46 Mod. 5 torpedoes or Mk 54 depth bombs or for antiship duties with AS 12 missiles. In D 643, there are four twin racks for MM 40 missiles, while in the other MM 40 ships there are two quadruple racks. Normally, only four missiles are carried.

Under the OP3A (*Opération d'Amélioration de l'Autodéfense Anti-missiles*) program, all but D 640 were to be equipped with Mistral infrared-homing missiles with either sextuple Sadral or twin Simbad launchers, two 30-mm OTO Melara-Mauser mounts in place of the 20-mm mounts, two DIBC-2A (SAGEM VIGY 105) optronic directors, a DIBV-2A Vampir infrared surveillance and tracking system, and the ARBB-36A jamming system. The control position for the new weapons systems, installed first in D 643 in 1996, is located in a new deckhouse atop the bridge superstructure and is used to provide own-ship defense within a 10-km radius. OP3A provides very rapid reaction time as well as continuous monitoring of the ship's vicinity by a variety of optical, infrared, and radar sensors; a total of 16 video displays are provided for the various operators, with the unified system being known as SENIT 8.01 (or SARA) and interfaces with the principal SENIT 4 system. The deckhouse is surmounted by a faceted conical cockpit structure for the close-defense systems control petty officer, who has windows to see outside and is surrounded by the control displays. D 641 completed similar modifications in 4-99, and D 642 received the equipment during 1999–2000. The 30-mm guns can be controlled from the OP3A station by means of the Vigy 105 E/O system; from small manned directors placed one deck above the guns; or, in emergency, by an on-mount operator. Six ready-service reload Mistral missiles can be stowed near each Sadral launcher. D 644–646 are to be equipped to carry two Simbad modular twin, manned launchers for the Mistral missile rather than the more expensive Sadral. The 12.7-mm mg are mounted near the Crotale SAM launcher. D 641–643 have the SEAO/OPSMER combat decision aid system.

The VDS employs a 10-ton "fish" and has been modified to operate at depths down to 700 m; it is normally operated concurrently with the bow-mounted sonar. D 644 and D 645 have the SAIGON (*Système Automatisé d'Interception et de Goniométries de Émissions*) VHF/UHF communications intercept system. During refits, the ARBB-32 jammer is to be replaced by ARBB-36 (Dassault Salamandre). D 642, D 644, and D 646 have a new antenna for the DRBV-15 radar. During 2002 D 641 received the DRBV 15 radar from *Suffren* (D 602) in place of her DRBV-51 set.

♦ 2 Tourville class (Type F 67, ex-C 67A)

Bldr: DCN Lorient

	Laid down	L	In serv.
D 610 Tourville	16-3-70	13-5-72	21-6-74
D 612 De Grasse	14-6-72	30-11-74	1-10-77

Tourville (D 610) Edward McDonnell, 2005

D: 4,650 tons (6,100 fl) **S:** 30 kts

Dim: 152.75 (142.0 pp) × 15.80 (15.30 wl) × 5.70 hull (6.60 props)

A: 6 MM 38 Exocet SSM; 1 8-round Crotale EDIR SAM syst. (24 tot. missiles); 2 single 100-mm 55-cal. Model 1968 DP; 2 single 20-mm 70-cal. Mk 10 Mod. 23 Oerlikon AA; 4 single 12.7-mm mg; 2 fixed KD-59E torpedo catapults (10 L 5 Mod. 4 ASW torpedoes); 1–2 WG-13 Lynx ASW helicopters

DESTROYERS [DD] *(continued)*

De Grasse (D 612) Martin Mokrus, 4-05

Electronics:
Radar: 2 DRBN-34 nav.; 1 DRBV-26A early warning; 1 DRBV-51B air/surf. search; 1DRBC-32D f.c.; 1 DRBC-32 f.c.
Sonar: DUBV-23 hull-mounted; DSBX-1 SLASM bistatic active VDS with SYVA torpedo-warning adjunct
EW: ARBR-16 intercept; ARBB-32 jammer; 2 8-round Syllex decoy RL; SLQ-25 Nixie towed acoustic torpedo decoy syst.
E/O: DIBV-1A Vampir IR surveillance
M: 2 sets Rateau double-reduction geared steam turbines; 2 props; 54,400 shp
Boilers: 4 asymmetric, multitube, automatic-control; 45 kg/cm^2, 450° C
Electric: 4,440 kw (2 × 1,500-kw turbogenerators, 3 × 480-kw diesel alternators)
Range: 1,900/30; 4,500/18 **Crew:** 24 officers, 178 petty officers, 96 ratings

Remarks: Unmodernized sister *Duguay-Trouin* (D 611), refitted 2-93 to 1-94 and equipped as a flagship, was retired on 13-7-99. D 610 is to be retired in 2008 and D 612 during 2009. Both are based at Brest.
Hull systems: All three had a heavy stiffening strake added after completion at the upper deck level amidships to prevent hull cracking. Fin stabilizers and an NBC warfare protective citadel are fitted. During her Crotale installation refit, D 610 had her boilers converted to burn distillate fuel, which had been burned by the others from the outset. During 1990s modernizations, provisions storage areas were improved, and the former Malafon ASW missile magazine was converted to accommodations and office spaces. The 264-m^2 helicopter deck measures 22 m long by 12 m wide, while the hangar is 13.60 m long, 11.4 m wide, and 4.80 m high. The top of the mast is 43.20 m above the waterline.
Combat systems: The SENIT 4 data system is fitted. *Tourville* was equipped with the Crotale antiaircraft missile system during 1980, and *De Grasse* in 1981. In preparation for Crotale, the third 100-mm gun mount atop the helicopter hangar on *Tourville* and *Duguay-Trouin* was removed; *De Grasse* never carried it. The Crotale EDIR missile system was substituted in 1990. Carry AS 12 wire-guided missiles as well as Mk 46 Mod. 5 torpedoes and depth charges for the helicopters.

During refit from 2-94 to 9-95, D 610 received the prototype DSBX-1 SLASM (*Système de Lutte ASM*) towed low-frequency active sonar array installation and provision for the Milas antisubmarine missile system in place of Malafon; ARBB-33 jammers were added; the Thales Altesse decision aid was added; and Syracuse-II replaced the Syracuse-I SATCOM system. Planned replacement of the obsolescent Syllex countermeasures launchers by two Sagaie launchers has not occurred. *De Grasse* received the same modifications during 9-95 to 8-96 refit. Both have the SEAO/OPSMER combat decision aid system.

FRIGATES [FF]

♦ 0 (+ 8 + 9) FREMM Program Bldr: DCN, Lorient (In serv. 2011–14)

	Laid down	L	In serv.
. . .	2006	2009	2011

D: 4,500 tons (5,600 fl) **S:** 27 kts **Dim:** 140.00 × 19.40 × 4.20
A: 16 Scalp Naval SSM and 32 Aster-15 and Aster-30 SAMs (in 48 Sylver A70 VLS cells); 1 76-mm OTO/Melara Compact DP; 4 fixed ASW torpedo launchers (MU-90 Impact torpedoes); 1 NH-90 helicopter
Electronics:
Radar: . . .
Sonar: DSBX 1 SLASM bistatic active VDS with SYVA torpedo-warning adjunct
M: 2 Fiat-G.E. LM 2500 gas turbines
Range: 7,000/18 **Crew:** 108 (tot. accommodations for 120)

Remarks: FREMM = Frégates Européennes Multi-Mission intended to replace the *Tourville-* and *Georges Leygues*–class destroyers, this program was launched during 10-04. Two versions are planned to be built on the same hull, propulsion system, and combat data system: eight in the ASW-oriented FASM (*Frégate d'Action Anti-SousMarin*) configuration and nine in the land-attack

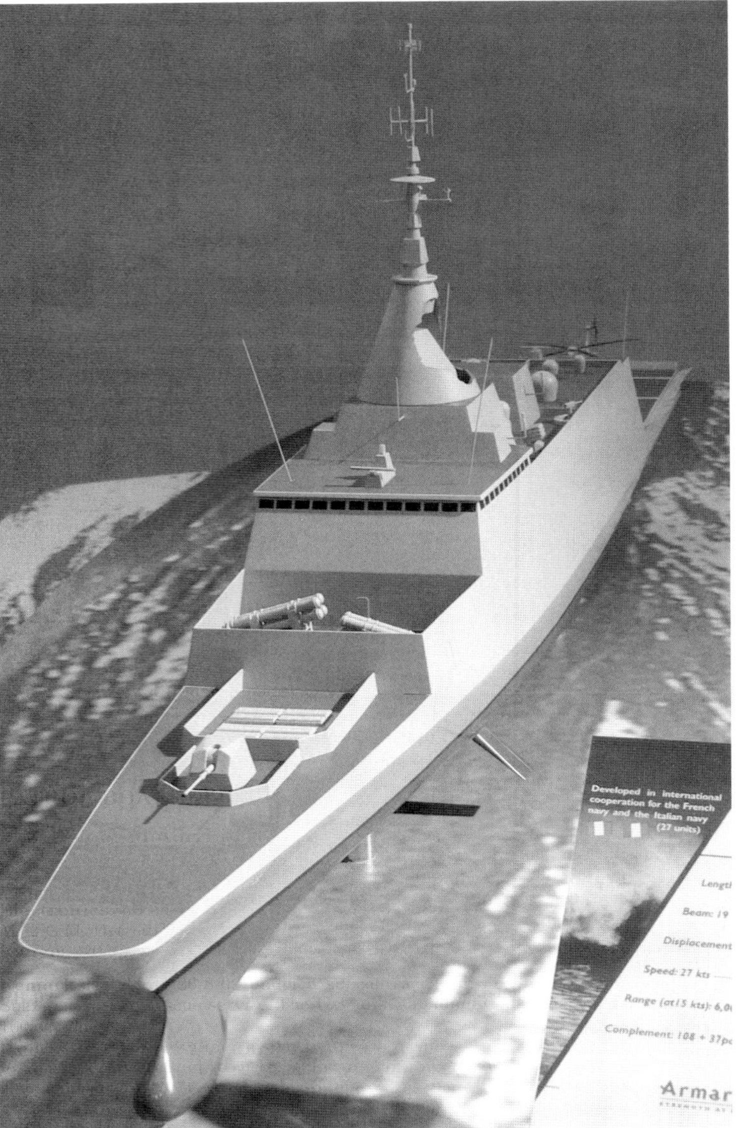

FREMM—builders model Hans Karr, 5-05

cruise missile–configured FAVT (*Frégate d'Action Vers la Terre*) version, with the ASW versions to be built first. Are intended to serve for 30 years each. Under an 8-11-02 agreement, the design and construction of ships of this class will be conducted in cooperation with Italy. The first eight were ordered on 16-11-05 under the FY 03–08 program. Are to receive D (Destroyer) series pennant numbers.
Combat systems: Both versions will be able to launch land-attack missiles, but only the FAVT will have independent targeting facilities, while the FASM will have a more elaborate sonar suite. The cruise missile envisioned for the land-attack version is to be a vertically launched variant of the SCALP-EG, with a new airframe married to the current guidance system. Both versions will also have vertically launched Aster 15 SAMs for self defense.

♦ 5 La Fayette class Bldr: DCN, Lorient

	Laid down	L	In serv.
F 710 La Fayette	15-12-90	13-6-92	22-3-96
F 711 Surcouf	6-7-92	3-7-93	7-2-97
F 712 Courbet	15-9-93	12-3-94	1-4-97
F 713 Aconit (ex-*Jauréguiberry*)	5-8-96	8-7-97	3-6-99
F 714 Guépratte	1-10-98	3-3-99	29-10-01

Surcouf (F 711) Bernard Prézelin, 2-04

FRIGATES [FF] *(continued)*

Guépratte (F 714) Bernard Prézelin, 1-04

Courbet (F 712) Bernard Prézelin, 1-04

D: 3,200 tons std. (3,600 fl) **S:** 25 kts
Dim: 124.20 (115.00 pp) × 15.40 (13.60 wl) × 4.10 hull (4.80 max.)
A: 8 MM 40 Exocet Block 2 SSM; 1 8-round Crotale CN2 SAM syst.; (24 VT-1 missiles); 1 100-mm 55-cal. Model 1968 CADAM DP; 2 single 20-mm 90-cal. GIAT F2 AA; 2 single 12.7-mm mg; 1 AS.565MA Panther helicopter
Electronics:
Radar: 2 DRBN-34 (Decca 20V90) nav.; 1 DRBV-15C 3-D surf./air search; 1 Castor IIJ f.c., 1 CTM Crotale f.c.
Sonar: None
EW: ARBR-21 intercept; ARBB-33 Salamandre jammer; F 710–712: ARBG-1A SAIGON VLF-UHF/DF; F 713, 714: ARBG-2 Maigret; 2 33- or 34-round AMBL-1C Dagaie Mk 2 decoy RL; SLQ-25 Nixie towed acoustic torpedo decoy syst.
E/O: SAGEM TDS 90 target designation sight
M: 4 SEMT-Pielstick 12 PA 6V280 STC, 1,050-rpm, sequentially turbocharged diesels; 2 5-bladed CP props; 21,000 bhp (23,200 bhp overload)—bow-thruster
Electric: 2,250 kw (3 × 750-kw diesel sets: 440 and 115 V, 60 and 400 Hz)
Range: 7,000/15; 9,000/12 **Fuel:** 350 tons usable + 80 m^3 aviation fuel
Endurance: 50 days
Crew: 15 officers, 85 petty officers, 53 ratings (+ 25 commandos)

Remarks: Although typed as frigates, they are intended for overseas possessions patrol and a role in the protection of Europe in a crisis and have no ASW sensors or weapons; their effectiveness is further hindered by their low maximum speed. The first three were ordered on 14-3-88 and the second three on 23-9-92; construction of the sixth unit, *Ronarc'h* (F 715), was canceled during 5-96. Six similar ships with heavier armament were built for Taiwan, and three are under construction for Saudi Arabia. F 710 was brought up to the same equipment standard as the second and third units during a 2-98 to 6-98 refit. The first three are based at Toulon as part of the *Naval Action Force (FAN)*.
Hull systems: A particular effort has been made to reduce the ships' signatures; the diesel propulsion engines are mounted in pairs on isolation platforms, and the superstructure, masts, and forecastle are covered with radar-reflectant GRP-resin compound. Much of the superstructure is built of a sandwich of GRP and balsawood layers. Vertical hull and superstructure surfaces are slanted at plus or minus 10° to control radar reflectivity. The ships are also fitted with degaussing equipment, extensive NBC warfare protection, and all but F 714 have the Prairie/Masker hull and propeller air bubbling system to reduce acoustic radiation. Special armor is provided for the magazines and operations spaces. All chocks, bollards, and boat recesses are covered to reduce radar reflectivity. Boats are stowed in superstructure recesses that are covered with retractable screens to reduce radar reflection; near the waterline on both beams is a door providing access to the boats once launched.

The ships employ modified deep-vee hull form, fin stabilizers, and rudder-controlled roll reduction to improve seaworthiness. There are two rudders, and the hull form incorporates twin skegs aft. Hull has 11 watertight compartments. A stern compartment holds 5-m semi-rigid boats for use by embarked commando forces; the boats are placed in the sea and recovered via a traveling crane on the inside of the stern door. The SAMAHE (*Système d'Aide à la Manutention des Hélicoptères Embarqués*) deck transit system is installed for helicopter movement on the 30 × 15-m flight deck, and there is a 1.8-m-diameter grid for the Harpoon positive landing system; the ships are able to launch and recover 10-ton helicopters in sea states up to 5 to 6. Can carry up to 60 tons fresh water (and evaporators can produce up to 36 tons per day) and 80 m^3 of aviation fuel (sufficient for 150 flying hours). F 714 has special facilities to accommodate female crewmembers.
Combat systems: The SENIT 7 (Thales TAVITAC 2000) combat data system with five VISTA display terminals and the Syracuse II SATCOM system are carried, along with the AIDCOMER decision-making assist system. The ships are equipped with NATO Link 11 and Link 14 capability. The ALTESSE (*Alerte et Ténue de Situation de Surface*) warning and surface-situation data display system is being installed to provide an artificial intelligence boost to the ESM system and will provide direction finding of a signal within 500 msec with an accuracy better than 0.5°.

The design permits the future addition or substitution of later weapon systems, including two 8-cell Sylver vertical launch installations for Aster-5 missiles between the 100-mm gun and the bridge area, the associated Arabel radar, and the SLAT antitorpedo system. Some 600 rounds of 100-mm ammunition can be carried. One of the two Decca radars is mounted aft for helicopter control; both have ARPA consoles on the bridge and in CIC. The Castor-IIJ gunfire-control radar can provide a second missile-guidance channel. A digital internal communications system is fitted. F 710 has been used for trials with sextuple launchers for the Contralto rocket-propelled torpedo decoy system. Are planned to be backfitted with the OP3A/SENIT 8.01 self-defense combat control system, including improved EW arrays. F 713 and F 714 have a later-model communications intercept system, the German ARBG-2 Maigret system.

◆ 6 Floréal-class surveillance ships
Bldr: Chantiers de l'Atlantique, St. Nazaire

	Laid down	L	In serv.
F 730 Floréal	2-4-90	6-10-90	27-5-92
F 731 Prairial	11-9-90	16-3-91	20-5-92
F 732 Nivôse	16-1-91	11-8-91	15-10-92
F 733 Ventôse	28-6-91	14-3-92	20-4-93
F 734 Vendémiaire	17-1-92	23-8-92	20-10-93
F 735 Germinal	17-8-92	14-3-93	17-5-94

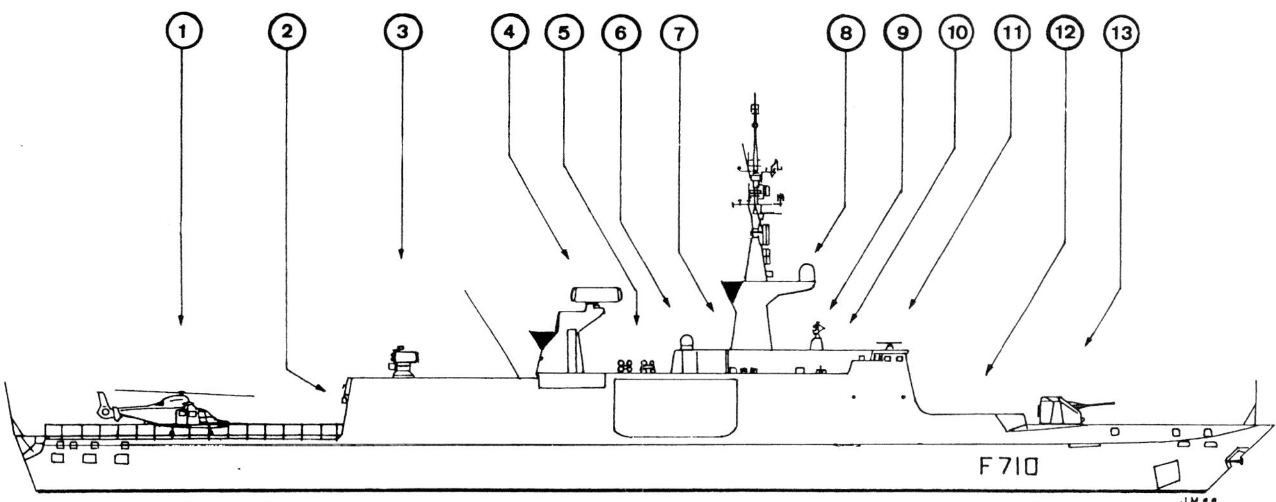

La Fayette (F 710) 1. Panther helicopter 2. Helicopter hangar 3. Crotale SAM launcher 4. DRBV-15C search and targeting radar 5. MM 40 Exocet missiles 6. Inmarsat SATCOM antenna radome 7. Dagaie decoy launcher 8. Syracuse II SHF SATCOM antenna radome 9. Castor-IIJ gun f.c. radar 10. 20-mm F2 AA on bridge wings 11. Decca 20V90 navigational radar 12. Space and volume reserved for later backfitting of the SAAM missile system 13. 100-mm Model 1968 DP gun

Drawing by Jean Moulin from *Flottes de Combat*

FRIGATES [FF] *(continued)*

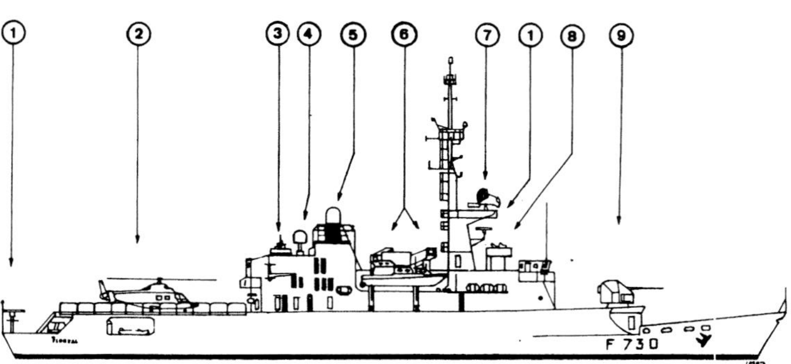

Floréal (F 730) 1. DRBN-34A navigational and helicopter approach control radars 2. Panther helicopter 3. 20-mm F2 AA 4. Inmarsat SATCOM antenna radome 5. Syracuse II SHF SATCOM antenna radome 6. MM 38 Exocet missile launchers 7. DRBV-21A air-search radar 8. Najir optronic gun f.c. radar 9. 100-mm Model 1968 DP gun
Drawing by Jean Moulin from *Flottes de Combat*

Vendémiaire (F 734) Chris Sattler, 5-05

Germinal (F 735) Bernard Prézelin, 9-04

D: 2,600 tons (2,950 fl) **S:** 20 kts **Dim:** 93.50 (85.20 pp) × 14.00 × 4.40
A: 2 MM 38 Exocet SSM; 1 100-mm 55-cal. Model 1968 CADAM DP; 2 single 20-mm 90-cal. GIAT F2 AA; 1 AS.565MA Panther or AS.319 Alouette-III helicopter (see Remarks); F 735 *also:* 1 2-round Simbad SAM syst. (. . ., Mistral missiles)
Electronics:
Radar: 2 DRBN-34A (Decca RM 1229) nav.; 1 DRBV-21A surf./air search
Sonar: None
EW: F 730, 733 *only:* ARBG-1A Saigon VHF–UHFD/F; F 735 *only:* ARBR-16 intercept
M: 4 SEMT-Pielstick 6PA6 L280 BTC diesels; 2 CP props; 8,800 bhp—250 kw bow-thruster
Electric: 1,770 kw tot. (3 × 590-kw sets, 3 Baudouin 12 P15 2SR diesels driving)
Range: 10,000/15 **Fuel:** 390 tons **Endurance:** 50 days
Crew: 12 officers, 49 petty officers, 22 ratings + 13 aviation party

Remarks: Intended for operations in low-risk areas for ocean surveillance, economic exclusion zone patrol, fisheries protection, and maritime policing duties. The first two were ordered 20-1-89, the next two on 9-1-90, and the final pair during 2-91. Military equipment was added at the Lorient Arsenal after delivery by the builder. Two sisters were ordered for Morocco in 10-98. The ships are expected to serve for 30 years each.
Hull systems: Constructed to Veritas commercial standards. Design emphasis was on seaworthiness, with helicopter operations possible up to Sea State 5. Equipped with fin stabilizers. The helicopter hangar can accept the AS.332F Super Puma and will be able to accommodate the NH-90; were initially assigned Alouette-III helicopters. Helicopter deck is 23 × 14 m. Have accommodations for 24 commandos.
Combat systems: There is no SENIT combat data system. A Matra Défense Najir optronic director controls the 100-mm gun. Provision is made for later installation of ARBR-17 (Thales DR-2000) intercept equipment and two Dagaie decoy rocket launchers. Two Simbad twin launchers for Mistral point-defense SAMs can be installed on the 20-mm gun foundations normally carried. Antennas for the Syracuse II SATCOM system have been installed in F 730 and F 733, while the others are fitted with an Inmarsat terminal.

CORVETTES [FFL]

♦ 9 D'Estienne d'Orves class (Type A-69)

Bldr: Lorient Arsenal

	Laid down	L	In serv.
F 789 Lieutenant de Vaisseau le Hénaff	11-13-77	16-9-78	13-2-80
F 790 Lieutenant de Vaisseau Lavallée	11-11-77	29-5-79	16-8-80
F 791 Commandant L'Herminier	7-5-79	7-3-81	19-1-86
F 792 Premier-Maître L'Her	15-12-78	28-6-80	15-12-81
F 793 Commandant Blaison	15-11-79	7-3-81	28-4-82
F 794 Enseigne de Vaisseau Jacoubet	11-4-79	26-9-81	23-10-82
F 795 Commandant Ducuing	1-10-80	26-9-81	17-3-83
F 796 Commandant Birot	23-3-81	22-5-82	14-3-84
F 797 Commandant Bouan (ex-*Commandant Levasseur*)	12-10-81	23-4-83	11-5-84

Commandant L'Herminier (F 791) Leo Van Ginderen, 7-05

Premier-Maître l'Her (F 792) Jim Sanderson, 2005

Lieutenant de Vaisseau Lavallée (F 790) Bernard Prézelin, 5-05

D: 1,100 tons (1,300 fl); F 791: 1,181 tons (1,296 fl)
S: 23.3 kts **Dim:** 80.00 (76.00 pp) × 10.30 × 3.00–3.20 (5.30–5.50 sonar)
A: F 792–797: 4 MM 40 Exocet SSM; F 789 through F 791: 2 MM 38 Exocet SSM; *all:* 1 100-mm 55-cal. Model 1968 CADAM DP; F 792–797 *only:* 1 2-round Simbad SAM syst (. . . Mistral missiles); *all:* 2 single 20-mm 70-cal. Mk 10 Mod. 23 Oerlikon AA; 2 or 4 single 12.7-mm mg; F 791 *only:* 1 6-round 375-mm Model 1972 F1 ASW rocket launcher; *all:* 4 fixed ASW TT (L 5 torpedoes; no reloads)

CORVETTES [FFL] *(continued)*

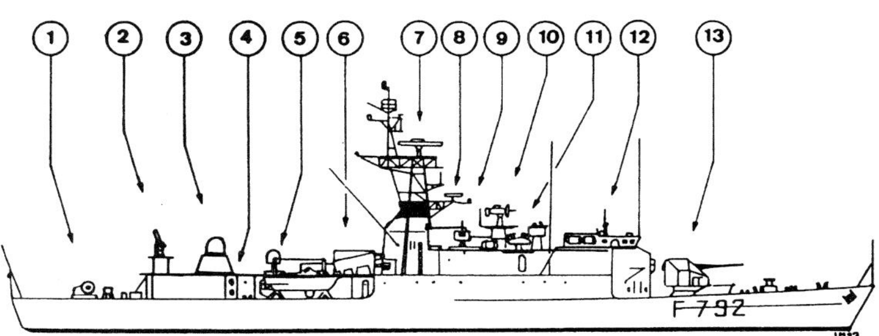

Premier-Maître l'Her (F 792) 1. SLQ-25 Nixie towed acoustic torpedo decoy and handling gear 2. Simbad SAM launcher 3. Syracuse II SHF SATCOM antenna radome 4. Fixed ASW torpedo tubes in deckhouse 5. Inmarsat commercial SATCOM antenna radome 6. MM 40 Exocet antiship missile launchers 7. DRBV-51A air/surface-search radar 8. DRBN-32 navigational radar 9. 20-mm AA 10. DRBC-32E gun f.c. radar 11. Dagaie decoy launcher 12. 12.7-mm mg 13. 100-mm Model 1968 DP
Drawing by Jean Moulin from *Flottes de Combat*

Electronics:
Radar: 1 Decca 1126 or DRBN-34 or Type 1007 nav.; 1 DRBV-51A surf./air search; 1 DRBC 32E f.c.
Sonar: DUBA-25 hull-mounted MF
EW: ARBR-16 intercept; 2 33- or 34-round AMBL-1A Dagaie Mk 1 decoy RL; SLQ-25 Nixie towed acoustic torpedo decoy syst.
M: 2 SEMT-Pielstick 12 PC 2 V400 diesels; 2 CP props; 12,000 bhp
Electric: 840 kw (2 × 320-kw, 1 × 200-kw diesel-driven sets)
Range: 4,500/15 **Endurance:** 15–20 days
Crew: 7 officers, 63 petty officers, 20 ratings; F 791–797: 9 commandos also

Remarks: Very economical and seaworthy ships designed for coastal antisubmarine warfare, but available for scouting missions, training, and showing the flag. Although originally intended to accommodate a commando of one officer and 17 troops, they were not carried in practice until F 793 was modified to accommodate nine special forces personnel during 1993 (F 791–797 now all have this feature). F 794 through F 797 are based at Toulon and the others at Brest. The remaining units are to be retired between 2009 and 2016.
Hull systems: Have fin stabilizers; F 797 has a "dynamic" stabilization system. Stacks and masts were modified from the *Jean Moulin* (F 785) onward; the heightened stack was backfitted in earlier units. F 791 has 2 SEMT-Pielstick 12 PA6 BTC diesels totaling 14,400 hp, with infrared signature suppression features; protracted trials delayed her commissioning.
Combat systems: The control system for the 100-mm gun consists of a DRBC-32E monopulse, X-band radar, and a semi-analog, semi-digital computer; there is also a Matra Défense Naja optical director. From 1986 on, all units of the class were refitted with a new 100-mm gun, U.S. SLQ-25 Nixie torpedo decoy, upgraded sonar, Dagaie launchers, L 5 ASW torpedo capability, and waste processing system. Twin-launcher Simbad point-defense missile system trials were conducted with F 792 in 1989; another ship tested the Crotale Modulaire launcher in place of the 100-mm gun in 1987–88. In F 793 the ASW rocket launcher was replaced by an antenna for the Syracuse II SATCOM system in a refit completed 19-5-93; F 792, F 794, F 795, and F 796 have been similarly fitted, and ASW rocket launchers had been removed from all but F 791 by 11-97. Toulon-based units have had a platform added aft atop the torpedo room deckhouse to accommodate the Simbad launcher, which had been installed in F 792 and F 797 by mid-1997. Most carry an Inmarsat terminal, with the antenna radome mounted amidships.
Disposals: *Détroyat* (F 784) was retired on 25-7-97 and *Jean Moulin* (F 785) on 14-5-99, *Commandant de Pimodan* (F 787), *Drogou* (F 783), *Quartier-Maitre Anquetil* (F 786), *D'Estienne d'Orves* (F 781), *Amyot d'Inville* (F 782), and *Second-Maître le Bihan* (F 788) were decomissioned and transferred to Turkey during 2001–2.

PATROL SHIPS [PS]

♦ 1 La Pérouse–class patrol ship
Bldr: DCN, Lorient

	Laid down	L	In serv.
P 675 Arago (ex-A 795)	26-6-89	6-9-90	9-7-91

Arago (P 675) Bernard Prézelin, 2-05

D: 850 tons light, 970 tons std. (1,100 fl) **S:** 15 kts
Dim: 59.00 (53.00 pp) × 10.90 × 3.63 **A:** 2 single 12.7-mm mg
Electronics: Radar: 1 DRBN-32 nav.; 1 Furuno . . . nav.—Sonar: see Remarks
M: 2 SACM-Wärtsilä UD30-V12-M6 diesels; 2 CP props; 2,500 bhp—160-shp bow-thruster
Electric: 620 kw tot. **Range:** 6,000/12
Crew: 3 officers, 14 petty officers, 13 nonrated

Arago (P 675) Bernard Prézelin, 7-04

Remarks: Ordered 22-1-86. Returned from Papeete during 5-02 and employed since 10-02 as a public-service patrol ship in home waters, based at Toulon; three sisters continue to operate as survey vessels (see under [AGS]).
Mission systems: Has a Thales-Marconi CSFTSM 5425 Lennermor multifunction wreck identification/echo sounder and can carry two 9-m KL Industrie d'Auray launches. Other navigation/hydrographic equipment includes Trident, Syledis, TORAN, RANA, and Navstar receivers, Atlas DESO 20 100-kHz and 66/210-kHz echo sounders (also on the two survey launches), a Raytheon 12-kHz echo sounder, Sippican bathythermograph, Barringer magnetometer, and Edgerton side-looking sonar.

♦ 1 fisheries patrol ship
Bldr: C.N. Le Trait, Le Havre (In serv. 1967)

P 681 Albatros (ex-*Névé*)

Albatros (P 681) Arjun Sarup, 1-05

D: 1,940 tons (2,800 fl) **S:** 15 kts **Dim:** 85.00 (75.00 pp) × 13.50 × 6.00
A: 1 40-mm 60-cal. Bofors AA; 2 single 12.7-mm mg
Electronics: Radar: 2 DRBN-34 nav.—EW: 2 ARBR-16 intercept
M: 2 SACM-Wärtsilä UD33V12 S4 diesel generator sets (1,120 kw each), 2 electric motors; 1 prop; 2,310 shp—2 250-shp electric cruise motors
Electric: 750 kw (2 × 375-kw diesel sets) **Range:** 14,700/14, 25,000/9
Crew: 6 officers, 23 petty officers, 19 ratings + 15 passengers

Remarks: Former stern-haul trawler purchased 4-83 from Société Navale Caenaise for use in Antarctic-area fisheries-patrol duties, off Kerguelen, Île Crozet, St. Paul, and Amsterdam Islands. Commissioned in French naval service 23-3-84. Re-engined at Lorient during 7-90 to 3-91 refit. Scheduled to remain in service until 2015. Based at La Réunion.
Hull systems: Has six-bed hospital, 200-ton cargo capacity, and helicopter vertical replenishment area aft, but no landing platform. Carries one launch and one small landing craft. Has an Inmarsat SATCOM terminal.
Combat systems: Received new EW equipment during 2002 refit in France.

PATROL CRAFT [PC]

♦ 3 Flamant (OPV 54) class

	Bldr.	Laid down	L	In serv.
P 676 Flamant	CMN, Cherbourg	3-94	24-4-95	18-12-97
P 677 Cormoran	Leroux & Lotz, Lorient	25-5-94	15-5-95	29-10-97
P 678 Pluvier	CMN, Cherbourg	1995	2-12-96	18-12-97

D: 314 tons (390 fl) **S:** 23 kts (22 sust.)
Dim: 54.00 (48.50 pp) × 9.80 × 2.60 (2.90 props)
A: 2 single 12.7-mm mg
Electronics: Radar: 1 Decca 250 nav.; 1 Decca 20V90 ARPA nav.

PATROL CRAFT [PC] *(continued)*

Pluvier (P 678) Frank Findler, 5-05

Flamant (P 676) Bernard Prézelin, 10-04

M: 2 Deutz-MWM TBD 620 V16 diesels (3,000 bhp each), 2 Deutz-MWM TBD 234 V12 diesels (980 bhp each); 2 CP props; 7,960 bhp tot.
Electric: 370 kw tot. (2 × 150-kw sets, Deutz-MWM TBD 234 diesels driving, 1 × 70-kw diesel set)
Range: 1,400/23; 4,500/12; 14,000/7.5 **Fuel:** 55 tons
Endurance: 21 days **Crew:** 4 officers, 10 petty officers, 6 ratings

Remarks: Typed PSP (*Patrouilleurs de Service Public*). Three units were ordered during 1992, but construction was delayed by closing of original contract yard and the transfer of part of the contract to CMN, which also acquired the design rights; another hull was completed by Leroux et Lotz (LNI), Lorient, for Mauritania, and four larger versions were built for Morocco. Two more, to have been ordered spring 1995 for the French Navy, were canceled. P 676 and 677 are based at Cherbourg, and P 678 at Brest. The class underwent minor hull modifications during 2004.
Hull systems: Commercial design employing deep-vee hullform capable of operating at speed in Sea State 4. Have a stern embarkation ramp for a 7-m Hurricane rigid inflatable, waterjet-propelled inspection boat capable of 30 kts. Can also carry up to 22 passengers. A 400 m^3/hr firefighting monitor is installed, and there are two 7-m^3-capacity spill recovery holding tanks. Any combination of engines can be used to drive the shafts.
Combat systems: All have been fitted with two additional navigational radars, with the antennas mounted on the pilothouse roof. An Inmarsat-M SATCOM terminal is also fitted.

♦ 1 Grèbe class

	Bldr	L	In serv.
P 679 Grèbe	SFCN, Villeneuve La Garenne	16-11-89	8-90

Grèbe (P 679) Bernard Prézelin, 3-04

D: 300 tons (410 fl) **S:** 18 kts **Dim:** 52.00 (44.50 pp) × 9.80 × 2.30 (2.75 props)
A: 2 single 12.7-mm mg
Electronics: Radar: 1 Decca 2690 ARPA nav.; 1 Koden . . . nav.

Grèbe (P 679) Bernard Prézelin, 6-04

M: 2 SACM-Wärtsilä UD33V12 RVR diesels; 2 CP props; 4,800 bhp—2 90-kw electric auxiliary propulsion motors; 250 shp (7.5 kts)
Electric: 370 kw tot. (2 × 150 kw, 1 × 70 kw)
Range: 1,400/23; 4,500/12; 14,000/7.5 (electric power) **Fuel:** 55 tons
Endurance: 21 days **Crew:** 4 officers, 9 petty officers, 6 ratings

Remarks: Ordered 13-7-88 and began trials 13-9-89. Based at Brest and is used primarily as a fisheries protection craft. Commercial Espadon 50 design employing deep-vee hullform capable of operating at speed in a State 4 sea. Has a stern embarkation ramp for an EDL 700, 7-m waterjet-propelled RIB inspection boat capable of 30 kts. A 400-m^3/hr firefighting monitor is installed, and there are two 7-m^3-capacity spill-recovery holding tanks. An Inmarsat-M SATCOM terminal is fitted.

♦ 1 Jonathan-class fisheries protection craft
Bldr: SOCARENAM, Boulogne (In serv. 1990)

P 740 Fulmar (ex-*Jonathan*)

D: 550 tons (680 fl) **S:** 12 kts **Dim:** 40.00 × 8.50 × 4.70
A: 1 12.7-mm mg **Electronics:** Radar: 2 Furuno . . . nav.
M: 1 Stork-Wärtsilä diesel; 1 prop; 1,200 bhp—bow-thruster
Range: 3,500/12 **Endurance:** 30 days **Crew:** 1 officer, 8 enlisted

Remarks: Former 200-grt side-haul fishing cutter purchased 10-96 from Meas Christian, Dunkerque, for use by the Gendarmarie Maritime at St.-Pierre and Miquelon as a local patrol craft. Was converted for naval service from 10-96 to 6-97 by LNI SY and DCN Lorient and commissioned during 2-99. Has an Inmarsat-M SATCOM terminal.

♦ 10 P 400 (Super PATRA) class
Bldr: CMN, Cherbourg

	Laid down	L	In serv.	Op. Area/base
P 682 L'Audacieuse	11-4-83	21-3-84	10-9-86	Fr. Guiana
P 683 La Boudeuse	15-6-83	21-5-84	25-7-86	La Réunion
P 684 La Capricieuse	12-9-83	31-10-84	26-9-86	Fr. Guiana
P 685 La Fougeuse	25-11-83	17-12-84	19-2-87	Martinque
P 686 La Glorieuse	21-2-84	25-1-85	25-3-87	Nouméa
P 687 La Gracieuse	26-4-84	26-3-85	17-7-87	Brest
P 688 La Moqueuse	4-10-84	8-4-86	25-3-87	Nouméa
P 689 La Railleuse	27-12-84	2-9-86	16-5-87	Tahiti
P 690 La Rieuse	14-3-85	17-10-86	13-6-87	La Réunion
P 691 La Tapageuse	13-8-85	16-2-87	24-2-88	Tahiti

La Moqueuse (P 688) A.A. de Kruijf, 6-04

D: 373 tons (480 fl) **S:** 23 kts **Dim:** 54.50 (50.00 pp) × 8.00 (7.70 wl) × 2.54
A: 1 40-mm 60-cal. AA; 1 20-mm 90-cal. GIAT F2 AA; 2 single 7.62-mm mg
Electronics: Radar: 1 DRBN-32 (Decca 1226) nav.
M: 2 SEMT-Pielstick 16 PA 4V200 VGDS diesels; 2 props; 8,000 bhp
Electric: 360 kw tot. (3 × 120-kw diesel sets)
Range: 4,200/15 **Fuel:** 73 tons **Endurance:** 15 days
Crew: 4 officers, 14 petty officers, 11 nonrated + 20 passengers

Remarks: First six ordered 5-82, remainder on 6-3-84. Are expected to serve for 25 years each. P 682 transferred to Brest from Cherbourg during 9-01.
Hull systems: Propulsion problems with P 682 greatly delayed entire program, and the ships are well beyond their 422-ton designed displacement. P 682, P 683, and P 685 were fitted with two exhaust stacks abaft the bridge during 1990 to replace unsuccessful underwater exhaust system; the others completed the modification by end 1995. Have two 35-m^3 cargo holds. All ten units of the class completed a six-month overhaul during 2006.
Combat systems: Carry 840 rds. 40-mm and 2,100 rds. 20-mm ammunition; deck reinforced for possible addition of two Exocet missiles and a fire-control radar.

PATROL CRAFT [PC] *(continued)*

♦ 1 Sterne class
Bldr: A & C de la Perriere, Lorient

	Laid down	L	In serv.
P 680 Sterne (ex-PM 41)	18-5-79	31-10-79	18-7-80

Sterne (P 680) Bernard Prézelin, 11-04

D: 250 tons (380 fl) **S:** 19 kts **Dim:** 49.00 (43.60 pp) × 7.50 × 2.80 hull (3.30 max.)
A: 2 single 12.7-mm mg
Electronics: Radar: 1 Furuno . . . nav.; 1 Decca 2690 ARPA nav.
M: 2 SACM V12 CZSHR diesels; 2 props; 4,200 bhp
Electric: 240 kw tot. (2 × 120 kw)
Range: 1,500/19; 4,900/12 **Endurance:** 15 days
Crew: 3 officers, 10 petty officers, 6 nonrated

Remarks: Constructed to merchant marine specifications for fisheries patrol duties within the 200-n.m. economic zone, including rescue services. Based at Brest. Equipped with an infirmary. Passive tank stabilization system. Can patrol at speeds up to 6.5 kts on an electrohydraulic drive system connected to the starboard propeller. Two RIB inspection dinghies are carried. An Inmarsat-M SATCOM terminal has been added. To be retired in 2010.

♦ 2 Trident ("PATRA") class

	Bldr	L	In serv.	Based at
P 671 Glaive	Auroux, Arcachon	25-8-76	2-4-77	Cherbourg
P 672 Épée	CNM, Cherbourg	31-3-76	9-10-76	Lorient

Épée (P 672) Bernard Prézelin, 11-04

D: 120 tons (150 fl) **S:** 26 kts **Dim:** 40.70 (38.5 wl) × 5.90 × 1.60
A: 1 40-mm 60-cal. AA; 2 single 7.62-mm mg
Electronics: Radar: 1 Decca 1226 nav.
M: 2 AGO 195V12 CZSHR diesels; 2 CP props; 5,000 bhp (4,400 sust.)
Electric: 120 kw **Range:** 750/20; 1,500/15; 1,750/10
Crew: 2 officers, 15 enlisted

Remarks: Transferred to Gendarmerie Maritime control in 1986–87. Only four were built of original 30 planned. Two sisters were also built for the Ivory Coast, and another, initially commissioned as *Rapiere* (P 674) in the French Navy, was sold to Mauritania in 1982. Were to have been retired during 2001–2 but have been extended to 2005–6 until they can be replaced by two new *Géranium*-class patrol boats.
Disposals: *Trident* (P 670) was stricken summer 1996, *Pertuisane* (P 673) early in 1997.
Combat systems: Carry 500 rounds of 40-mm and 2,000 rounds of 12.7-mm ammunition. Six SS 12 wire-guided missile launchers atop the superstructure have been replaced by two 7.62-mm mg.

PATROL BOATS [PB]

♦ 19 (+ 5) Elorn class
Bldr: CNB-Bénéteau, L'Herbaudière, Noirmoutier (In serv. 2003–9)

	In serv.
P 601 Elorn	20-6-03
P 602 Verdon	17-7-03
P 603 Adour	10-10-03
P 604 Scarpe	31-10-03
P 605 Vertonne	15-1-04
P 606 Dumbéa	15-10-04
P 607 Yser	26-2-04
P 608 Argens	4-6-04
P 609 Hérault	24-2-05
P 610 Gravona	22-4-05
P 611 Odet	25-4-05
P 612 Maury	12-5-05
P 613 Charente	19-7-05
P 614 Tech	10-05
P 615 Penfeld	2005
P 616 Trieux	2006
P 617 Vésubie	2006
P 618 Escaut	2006
P 619 Huveaune	2006
P 620 Sèvre	2007
P 621 Aber Wrach	2007
P 622 Esteron	2007
P 623 Mahury	2008
P 624 Organbo	2008

Vertonne (P 605) Bernard Prézelin, 7-04

Verdon (P 602) Bernard Prézelin, 8-04

D: 40 tons (fl) **S:** 25 kts **Dim:** 20.00 (17.25 pp) × 5.39 × 1.45
A: 1 7.62-mm mg **Electronics:** Radar: 1 Furuno . . . nav.
M: 2 MAN V12 diesels; 2 props; 2,000 bhp
Range: 400/ . . . **Crew:** 8 tot.

Remarks: Typed VCSM-*Vedette Cotière de Serveillance Maritime*. First batch of 11 ordered 5-12-01, second batch ordered in 2003. Being constructed in cooperation with Raidco Marine, Lorient, and are intended to serve for 20 years. All are to be assigned to the Gendarmerie Marine. Are named for French rivers. Have a stern ramp to launch and recover a 4.70-m inspection and rescue RIB. Have one firefighting water monitor. Lead unit based at Concarneau.

♦ 2 Jonquille-class vedettes
Bldr: Guy Couach–Plascoa, Bordeaux

	Laid down	L	In serv.	Based at
P 721 Jonquille	21-11-95	4-7-96	19-11-96	Papeete
P 723 Jasmin	1996	13-1-97	10-97	Port-des-Galets

Jonquille (P 721) Bernard Prézelin, 7-97

PATROL BOATS [PB] *(continued)*

D: 82 tons (98 fl) **S:** 30 kts (28 sust.) **Dim:** 32.00 (29.00 wl) × 6.50 × 1.10
A: 1 12.7-mm mg; 1 7.62-mm mg
Electronics: Radar: 1 Decca BridgeMaster II CH180/6 nav.
M: 2 MWM-Deutz TRD 616 V16 diesels; 2 props outboard; 2,882 bhp—1 MWM-Deutz TRD 616 V12 diesel; 1 Hamilton 422 waterjet centerline; 1,082 bhp
Electric: 90 kw tot. (2 × 45-kw Onan diesel sets, 380 V a.c.)
Range: 1,200/15 **Endurance:** 10 days **Crew:** 12 tot.

Remarks: Builder's Plascoa-32 design. Have GRP hulls and GRP sandwich superstructures capable of withstanding 9-mm bullets. Are fitted with Sercel NR 58 GPS receivers and a JMC V-108A echo sounder. Differ from *Géranium* class in having a different hullform and superstructure configuration; the hull is not pierced with portholes. Carry one RIB inspection boat. Are expected to serve for 25 years. Operated by the Gendarmerie Nationale.

♦ 2 Géranium-class vedettes
Bldr: DCN, Lorient

	L	In serv.	Based at
P 720 Géranium	27-6-96	31-10-96	Cherbourg (*Gendarmerie Maritime*)
P 722 Violette	1996	2-97	Pointe-à-Pitre, Guadaloupe

Géranium (P 720) M. Wright, 9-03

D: 73 tons light, 80 std. (100 fl) **S:** 30 kts (28 sust.)
Dim: 32.15 (30.50 pp) × 6.10 × 1.80
A: 1 12.7-mm mg; 1 7.62-mm mg
Electronics: Radar: 1 Decca Bridgemaster II CH180/6 nav.
M: 2 MWM-Deutz TRD 616 V16 diesels; 2 props outboard; 2,882 bhp—1 MWM-Deutz TRD 616 V12 diesel; 1 Hamilton 422 waterjet centerline; 1,082 bhp
Electric: 90 kw tot. (2 × 45-kw Onan diesel sets, 380 V a.c.)
Range: 1,200/15 **Endurance:** 10 days **Crew:** 14 tot.

Remarks: An expanded version of the 24-m P 60 class below. P 720 made 30.5 kts on trials. Have GRP hulls and GRP sandwich superstructures capable of withstanding 9-mm bullets. Are fitted with Sercel NR 58 GPS receivers and a JMC V-108A echo sounder. Two sisters are in *Affaires Maritime* police service.

♦ 1 P 60 class
Bldr: DCN, Lorient

	L	In serv.	Based at
P 776 Sténia	2-93	1-3-93	Pariacabo, French Guiana

D: 52 tons (60 fl) **S:** 28 kts **Dim:** 24.90 × 6.10 × 1.70 (max.)
A: 1 12.7-mm mg **Electronics:** Radar: 1 DRBN-32 nav.
M: 3 . . . diesels; 2 props, 1 waterjet; 2,520 bhp
Range: 700/22 **Crew:** 2 crews of 4 tot. each

Remarks: Operated by the Gendarmerie Maritime. Carries a RIB inspection craft handled by hydraulic crane to port. Hull forefoot is raked sharply forward. Considered to be unsuccessful craft; Sister *Stellis* (P 775) was returned to France in 2001 with engineering defects and was stricken on 1-2-03.

♦ 5 Type V 14
Bldrs: Stento, Balaruc-les-Bains; DCN, Lorient (P 791: Sibiril, Grantec)

	In serv.	Based
P 755 Miri (ex-Y 755)	28-10-92	. . .
P 761 Mimosa	20-3-87	Ajaccio
P 778 Réséda	1-10-87	Adour
P 789 Mélia	27-3-87	Toulon
P 791 Hortensia	1-8-90	Brest

D: 16 tons (20 fl) **S:** 20 kts **Dim:** 14.60 (13.20 wl) × 4.60 × 1.90 (1.20 hull)
A: 1 12.7-mm mg; 1 7.62-mm mg
Electronics: Radar: 1 Decca 060 or Furnuo . . . nav.
M: 2 Baudouin 12 F 11S diesels; 2 props; 800 bhp
Range: 360/18 **Crew:** 7 tot.

Remarks: GRP hulls. Designed by DCN Cherbourg. Carry a rigid inflatable inspection dinghy on davits at the stern. The names became official in 1993. Sisters serve as service launches and as fireboats (see below). Sister *Vétiver* (P 790) was transferred to the local government at Mayotte, La Réunion, in 1997 but returned to French Navy service during 2002 as a service craft

Disposal note: Volte 43–class patrol launch *Oeillet* (P 772) was stricken during 7-03 and sister *Camélia* (P 774) during 9-03. P 760 was no longer in service as of 2006.

Réséda (P 778)—note hull stripe added in 2003 Bernard Prézelin, 2-04

♦ 8 Arcor 34 police launches
Bldr: Arcor (In serv. 1985–96)

	Based at		Based at
P 703 Lilas	Dunkerque	P 711 Gentiane	. . .
P 704 Bégonia	Rochefort	P 713 Capitaine Moulié	. . .
P 707 MDLC Robert	St.-Malo	P 716 MDLC Jacques	Nice
P 709 MDLC Richard	. . .	P 717 Lavande	. . .

MDLC Robert (P 707) Bernard Prézelin, 7-04

D: 7 tons (fl) **S:** 25 kts **Dim:** 10.32 × 3.74 × 1.03
A: 1 7.62-mm mg **Electronics:** Radar: 1 Furuno . . . or Raytheon . . . nav.
M: 2 Volvo Penta TAMD-61 diesels; 2 props; 500 bhp **Crew:** 4 tot.

Remarks: Originally intended for the Gendarmerie Nationale but were transferred to the Gendarmerie Maritime during 1993–96. GRP construction. Are painted white. There are some differences in superstructure configuration.
Disposals: *Bellis* (P 715), *Nymphéa* (P 706), and *Général Delfosse* (P 710) were retired during 2003. P 705, P 708, P 712, and P 714 were retired during 2004.

MINE WARFARE SHIPS

♦ 0 (+ 1) converted mine-countermeasures support ship [MCS]
Bldr: Dubigeon, Nantes

	Laid down	L	In serv.
L 9077 Bougainville	28-1-86	3-10-86	25-2-88

Bougainville (L 9077)—prior to conversion as mine-countermeasures support ship Bernard Prézelin, 3-04

D: 3,600 tons light (5,200 fl)
S: 15 kts (14.6 sust.) **Dim:** 112.78 (105.00 pp) × 17.00 × 4.34
A: 2 single 12.7-mm mg
Electronics: Radar: 2 DRBN-32 nav.—EW: ARBG 2 comms intercept suite
M: SACM-Wärtsilä 195 V12 RVR (UD33V12 M5) diesels; 2 CP props; 4,800 bhp—1/400-hp side-thruster
Electric: 1,600 kw tot. (2 × 480-kw, 2 × 320-kw diesel-driven sets)
Range: 6,000/12 **Fuel:** . . . tons **Endurance:** 45 days
Crew: 6 officers, 17 petty officers, 29 ratings + 30 technicians

MINE WARFARE SHIPS *(continued)*

Bougainville (L 9077)—prior to MCS conversion Bernard Prézelin, 6-05

Remarks: Began conversion from AGI to a mine-countermeasures support ship (MCS) in 2006 as a replacement for *Loire* (A 615). Conversion is expected to complete by 2008. Her configuration and characteristics as an MCS are not yet known. Replaced in the surveillance role by A 759. Former BTMS (*Bâtiment de Transport Moyen et de Soutien*), built for the Directorate of Nuclear Experimentation for use between Papeete and the Muraroa Test Center. Ordered 22-11-84; completed after launch by Ch. de l'Atlantique, St.-Nazaire, when building yard closed. Converted 12-98 to 7-99 to serve as an electronic intelligence collection vessel in place of the *Berry* (A 644).
Hull systems: Miniature LSD design with still-functional 78.00 × 11.48 (10.2 clear)-m docking well for landing craft or 40 20-ft containers. Maximum cargo weight in the docking well: 1,200 tons. Draft aft 9.20 m when flooded, providing 3.15 m clear over deck. 37-ton crane with 12-m reach mounted aft to starboard. Six-m ramp to starboard can accommodate 53 tons. Has 70 m^3 helicopter fuel, and the helicopter deck can accommodate two medium helicopters. Can also act as a repair and stores ship. Ship's boats include an LCVP and a launch.

♦ 1 Rhin-class mine countermeasures support ship [MCS]
Bldr: Lorient Arsenal

	Laid down	L	In serv.
A 615 Loire	9-7-65	1-10-66	10-10-67

Loire (A 615) Bernard Prézelin, 4-04

Loire (A 615) Bernard Prézelin, 4-04

D: 2,050 tons (2,445 fl) **S:** 16.5 kts **Dim:** 101.05 (92.05 pp) × 13.10 × 4.25
A: 3 single 40-mm 60-cal. AA; 3 single 12.7-mm mg
Electronics: Radar: 3 DRBN-32 nav.
M: 2 SEMT-Pielstick 12 PA 4 V 185 diesels; 1 prop; 3,600 bhp
Electric: 920 kw tot. **Range:** 13,000/13
Crew: 11 officers, 100 petty officers, 40 ratings

Remarks: A 615 is specifically equipped to support mine-countermeasures ships, while retired sisters *Rhône* (A 622) and *Rhin* (A 621) were general repair and electronics repair ships. A 615 is to be retired in 2008.
Hull systems: A 615 has a divers' decompression chamber. It has a helicopter platform, but only A 615 has a hangar (for one Alouette-III). There are about 700 m^2 of workshop space and 1,700 m^3 of storeroom space. It has one 5-ton (at 12 m) crane and have Inmarsat SATCOM terminals.
Disposals: *Rhône* (A 622) was stricken 17-3-97 and is used as a breakwater at Lorient; *Rhin* (A 621) was stricken on 12-12-02.

Note: Upon completion of intelligence collection duties, the former landing ship *Bougainville* (L 9077) began a 2006 conversion to serve as a mine-countermeasures support ship to replace *Loire* (A 615) by 2008. A new class of mine-countermeasures ships is to be ordered around 2010.

♦ 13 Tripartite-class coastal minehunters [MHC]
Bldr: DCN, Lorient (M 651–653: Béliard, Ostend and Antwerp, Belgium)

	Laid down	L	In serv.
M 641 Éridan	20-12-77	2-2-79	16-4-84
M 642 Cassiopée	26-3-79	28-9-81	5-5-84
M 643 Andromède	6-3-80	22-5-82	19-10-84
M 644 Pégase	22-10-80	24-4-83	30-5-85
M 645 Orion	17-8-81	6-2-85	14-1-86
M 646 Croix du Sud	22-4-82	6-2-85	14-11-86
M 647 Aigle	2-12-82	8-3-86	1-7-87
M 648 Lyre	14-10-83	15-11-86	16-12-87
M 649 Persée	20-10-84	9-3-88	4-11-88
M 650 Sagittaire	1-2-93	14-1-95	2-4-96
M 651 Verseau (ex-*Iris*, M 920)	23-5-86	19-6-87	3-10-88
M 652 Céphée (ex-*Fuchsia*, M 919)	31-10-85	27-11-86	20-3-88
M 653 Capricorne (ex-*Dianthus*, M 918)	4-4-85	16-4-86	18-8-87

Croix du Sud (M 646) Frank Findler, 5-05

Andromède (M 643) Bernard Prézelin, 4-05

Lyre (M 648) Bernard Prézelin, 7-05

D: 535 tons (605 fl) **S:** 15 kts on main engine, 7 kts while hunting
Dim: 51.50 (47.10 pp) × 8.90 × 2.49 hull (3.50 max.)
A: 1 20-mm 90-cal. GIAT F2 AA; 2 single 12.7-mm mg; M 647 and M 649 *also:* 2 single 7.5-mm mg
Electronics:
Radar: 1 DRBN-34A nav.
Sonar: DUBM-21B hull-mounted HF minehunting (M 650: DUBM-21D; M 643: Thales TUS 2022 Mk 3); M 643: PVDS UAV (see Remarks)
M: 1 Werkspoor-Wärtsilä A RUB 215V12 diesel; 1 CP prop, 1,900 bhp—2 ACEC electric maneuvering props, 120 shp each—bow-thruster
Electric: 910 kw tot. (3 × 250-kw gas turbine-driven, 1 × 160-kw diesel-driven)
Range: 3,000/12 **Crew:** 5 officers, 32 petty officers, 12 ratings + 6 EOD personnel

MINE WARFARE SHIPS *(continued)*

Remarks: France, Belgium, and the Netherlands cooperated in building these ships for the requirements of the three countries, and others were built for Indonesia. The original *Sagittaire* (M 650) was transferred to Pakistan 24-9-92 and was replaced with a new-construction unit; two other hulls were built for Pakistan. M 651–653 were purchased from Belgium during 1996; M 651 was transferred 28-3-97, M 652 on 29-5-97, and M 653 on 28-8-97. M 645, 648, and 649, are based at Toulon, the others at Brest.
Hull systems: Hull built of glass-reinforced polyester plastic. Have an NBC warfare protective citadel.
Combat systems: Have the EVEC-20 automatic plotting table, Decca HiFix and Sydeldis and Toran radio precision navigation equipment, and two PAP-104 remote-controlled minehunting submersibles. No longer carry a six-man portable decompression chamber module at the aft end of the forecastle deck, having replaced it with a lightweight, helicopter-transportable chamber. Have one OD-3 mechanical drag sweep and in 1985 began to receive the AP-4 acoustic sweep capability. M 650 has the digital DUBM-21D sonar, with hybrid circuitry, Mustang computer, higher-definition displays, built-in test equipment, and integration into the tactical system.
Modernization: Under a 2-99 contract, all are being updated with the Thales TUS 2022 Mk 3 sonar and a Propelled Variable-Depth Sonar (PVDS) based on the Bofors Double Eagle remotely operated submersible vehicle (10 units, to be shared among the 13 ships). A new mine warfare command-and-control system was substituted, while the PAP 104 submersibles were updated, differential GPS receivers added, and a new autopilot fitted. All units completed modernization between 2001 and 2005 at a rate of four per year with M 649 being the final unit.

♦ 4 Vulcain-class mine-countermeasures divers' tenders [MSA]

	Bldr	Laid down	L	In serv.
M 611 VULCAIN	La Perriere, Lorient	15-5-85	17-1-86	11-10-86
A 613 ACHÉRON	CMN, Cherbourg	5-2-86	19-11-86	17-6-87
M 614 STYX	CMN, Cherbourg	20-5-86	3-3-87	22-7-87
M 622 PLUTON	La Perriere, Lorient	11-10-85	13-5-86	12-12-86

Styx (M 614) Bernard Prézelin, 5-04

Pluton (M 622) Guy Schaeffer via Paolo Marsan, 1-04

D: 409 tons (490 fl) **S:** 13.7 kts **Dim:** 41.60 (36.96 pp) × 7.50 × 3.20
A: 1 (M 622: 2 single) 12.7-mm mg **Electronics:** Radar: 1 DRBN-32 nav.
M: 2 SACM-MGO V16 ASHR diesels; 2 Kort-nozzle CP props; 2,200 bhp—75-shp bow-thruster
Electric: 176 kw tot. **Range:** 2,850/13.5; 7,400/9 **Fuel:** 92 m^3
Crew: 1 officer, 8 petty officers, 6 ratings + 12 divers and 2 medical personnel

Remarks: Typed BBPD (*Bâtiment de Plongeurs Démineurs*). Derived from the *Chamois*-class local support-tender design and are used as mine-clearance diver-support tenders, except A 613, which is training ship for the diving school. M 611 and M 622 were ordered on 11-10-84, the other pair on 7-85 under subcontract. Can support 12 divers. Hydraulic crane on fantail can lift 5 tons at 6-m radius, 3.5 tons at 10 m. The Sydelis automatic route recording system is fitted. There is a two-man decompression chamber. M 622 has a cap to the exhaust stack.

♦ 3 modified Glycine-class mine route survey craft [MSA]
Bldr: SOCARENAM, Boulogne-sur-Mer

	Laid down	L	In serv.
M 770 ANTARÈS	10-92	30-8-93	15-12-93
M 771 ALTAÏR	1993	11-93	30-7-94
M 772 ALDÉBARAN	15-11-93	2-94	15-3-95

Antarès (M 770) Bernard Prézelin, 5-04

D: 295 tons (340 fl) **S:** 10 kts **Dim:** 28.30 (24.50 pp) × 7.70 × 3.80
A: 1 12.7-mm mg
Electronics: Radar: 1 DRBN-34A nav.—Sonar: DUBM-41B towed side-scan
M: 1 Baudouin 12B 152 S5 diesel; 1 CP prop; 800 bhp—bow-thruster
Electric: 175 kVA tot. (115 kVA from shaft generator, 660 kVA from 1 Deutz D 226 B6 diesel set)
Range: 3,600/10 **Fuel:** 50 m^3
Crew: 24 total

Remarks: Typed BINRS (*Bâtiment d'Instruction à la Navigation et de Remorquage de Sonar*) in the dual role of training craft and tow vessel for a DUBM-41B minehunting side-scan sonar. Can search waters up to 80 m deep. Can also tow mechanical minesweeping array and are intended for wreck reconnaissance, search-and-rescue, and economic exclusion zone patrol. Carry Oropesa float aft to support the towed sonar. Equipped with Syledis route-recording system, autopilot, and GPS receiver, and has two 4.5-ton cranes at the stern to handle minehunting systems. A replacement for the towed sonar is being studied. Two half-sisters are typed BIN (*Bâtiment d' Instruction à la Navigation*) [YXT] and are used for maneuvering training. All three are based at Brest.

Note: The mine countermeasures systems trials ship [AGE] *Thétis* (A 785) and nine units of the *Coralline*-class diving tenders [YDT] can serve as mine route clearance charting units; see entries below.

AMPHIBIOUS WARFARE SHIPS AND CRAFT

♦ 2 Mistral-class helicopter-carrying landing ships [LH]
Bldr: DCN, Brest, and Alstom, St.-Nazaire

	Laid down	L	In serv.
L 9013 MISTRAL	10-7-03	11-04	27-2-06
L 9014 TONNERRE	5-5-04	2005	12-06

Tonnerre (L 9014) Bernard Prézelin, 7-05

Mistral (L 9013) Bernard Prézelin, 7-05

D: 16,500 tons (21,500 fl) **S:** 19 kts
Dim: 210.0 (199.00 wl) × 32.00 (28.00 wl) × 6.20
Air group: 20 French Army Cougar or French Navy NH-90 helicopters
A: 2 6-round Simbad SAM syst. (. . . Mistral missiles); 2 30-mm Breda-Mauser F2 AA; 4 single 12.7-mm mg
Electronics:
Radar: 2 . . . nav., 1 MRR 3-D surf./air search; 2 BridgeMaster 250E helicopter control
EW: 1 ARBR-21 radar interceptor; 1 bsm ½ jammer
M: 4 Wärtsilä 16V32 diesel generator sets (4,850 kw each), electric drive; 2 Mermaid podded azimuthal thruster props; 19,040 shp—bow-thruster
Range: 11,000/15; 6,000/18 **Endurance:** 30 days
Crew: 160 tot. + 450 troops (900 for short voyages)

Remarks: Ordered on 22-12-00 to replace *Ouragan* and *Orage*. Originally typed NTCD (*Noveaux Transports de Chalands de Débarquement*) and to have been near sisters to the *Foudre* class, they are now known as BPC (*Bâtiment de Projection et de Commandement*). Cost about $236 million each and are to serve for 30 years.

AMPHIBIOUS WARFARE SHIPS AND CRAFT *(continued)*

Mistral (L 9013) Bernard Prézelin, 3-05

Bow sections and accommodations modules were built by Alstom at St.-Nazaire, with the remainder of the hulls and fitting out accomplished at DCN Brest. L 9013 is to eventually replace the training ship *Jeanne d'Arc;* she is specially configured to carry cadets and displays of French military equipment but will remain available for amphibious warfare duties. Work on both began during 7-02. A similar ship may be built for Belgium. Both based at Brest.
Aviation systems: Have a 1,800-m^2 helicopter hangar with a capacity of 16 NH-90 helicopters, two elevators to starboard aft, a 1,000-m^3 operations direction space, and a 750-m^2 hospital with two operating rooms and 69 beds. They have a bow-to-stern flight deck totaling 5,000 m^2 and equipped with six deck landing spots for aircraft up to CH-53E Super Stallion and MV-22B Osprey size. There are 2,650 meters of vehicle parking space, enabling the carriage of 54.5-ton Leclerc heavy tanks, and side-loading vehicle ramps. An 885.5 m^2 (57.5 m long × 15.4 m broad × 8.2 m high) stern docking well can accommodate one CDIC or four LCM(8)-sized landing craft or two U.S. Navy LCAC air-cushion landing craft. A 17-ton capacity crane is fitted. There is an NBC protection citadel for the crew, and fin stabilizers are fitted.
Combat systems: Will have Syracuse-III SHF, U.S. Fleetsatcom, RITA, and Inmarsat-M SATCOM systems. The SENIT 8 combat system will be fitted.

♦ 2 Foudre-class (TCD 90) dock landing ships [LSD]
Bldr: DCN, Brest

	Laid down	L	In serv.
L 9011 FOUDRE	26-3-86	19-11-88	7-12-90
L 9012 SCIROCO	9-5-95	14-12-96	21-12-98

Sciroco (L 9012)—with helicopters visible on deck Bernard Prézelin, 9-03

Foudre (L 9011) Bernard Prézelin, 9-05

D: L 9011: 8,190 tons light/9,300 tons std. (11,880 fl; 17,200 flooded). L 9012: 8,230 tons light (12,013 fl; 17,205 flooded)
S: 21 kts **Dim:** 168.00 (160.00 pp) × 23.50 (22.00 wl) × 5.60 (9.10 flooded)
A: 3 (L 9012: 2) 2-round Simbad SAM syst (. . . Mistral missiles); 3 single 30-mm OTO Melara-Mauser AA; 4 single 12.7-mm mg; 4 Army AS.332 Super Puma helicopters
Electronics:
Radar: 1 Decca 2459 nav./surf. search; 2 DRBN-34A (Decca RM 1229) nav.; 1 DRBV-21A surf./air search
EW: ARBB-36 jammer, SLQ-25 Nixie towed acoustic torpedo decoy syst.
E/O: 2 DIBC-2A weapons control
M: 2 SEMT-Pielstick 16 PC2.5 V400 diesels; 2 CP props; 20,760 bhp—940-shp bow-thruster

Sciroco (L 9012) Bernard Prézelin, 9-03

Electric: 4,250 kw (5 × 850-kw diesel sets)
Range: 11,000/15 **Fuel:** . . . **Endurance:** 30 days
Crew: 224 tot. (19 officers, 205 enlisted) + 470 tot. troops

Remarks: TCD = *Transport de Chalands de Débarquement.* L 9011 was ordered 5-11-84 and conducted trials 19-11-89. L 9012 was ordered on 11-4-94. Two others were deferred and have since been recast as the *Mistral* class. They are intended to carry one mechanized regiment plus 1,880 tons of combat vehicles and cargo for the Rapid Action Force; are also able to act as logistics support ships. L 9011 has been brought up to the same standard of weapons and sensor equipage as the later L 9012. Both are based at Toulon.
Hull systems: Have an NBC warfare protective citadel. Docking well 122.0 × 14.30 (1,740 m^2) × 7.70 m (high) for two CDIC (EDIC replacement), one large tug, ten CTM landing craft, or one patrol boat; the forward third can be separated by a cofferdam and kept dry for vehicle stowage. Vehicle cargo area of 1,360 m^2 can be extended by using dock floor; a 56-ton elevator (13.5 × 8 m) connects dock floor and cargo decks. To flood down for loading and unloading embarked craft, with up to 3 m of water over the sill, has 7000-m^3 ballast capacity and can ballast down fully in 30 minutes and deballast in 45. Side-loading doors. Carries two LCVP-type landing craft. A passive roll stabilization system was installed in L 9011 during 1993–94. Can carry a total of 150 metric tons of cargo fuel. Medical spaces total 600 m^2. Typical combat load would include 10 LCK, 6 AMX-30 tanks, 15 AMX-10 combat vehicles, 8 infantry fighting vehicles, 22 jeeps, 29 5.5-ton trucks, 29 half-ton trucks, a tow truck, and a grid-laying vehicle. *Sciroco* can accommodate 54.5-ton Leclerc heavy tanks. There are two rudders.
Aviation systems: Helicopter deck is 47.0 × 23.0 m (1,080 m^2) with two spots equipped with SAMAHE hold-down systems. The hangar can accommodate up to 4 Super Puma helicopters. The 30.0 × 15.0-m, portable, single-spot helicopter and vehicle stowage platform at the stern breaks down into five 25-ton floatable sections that can be lifted off by the 37-ton capacity vehicle and boat crane. Can carry 184,000 liters JP-5 fuel for the helicopters.
Combat systems: Both now have the SENIT 8.01 (OP3A) combat system, with Link 11 reception. They have extensive command/communications facilities, including Syracuse and Inmarsat SATCOM systems. L 9011 will later receive the French Army Rodéo air control radar, with antenna on a platform on the after side of the lattice mast; she received the DRBV-21A (Thales Mars) air-search radar during her 1997 refit, which also saw the single 40-mm and two single 20-mm AA replaced with the new enclosed 30-mm gunmount. One DRBN-34A radar is mounted aft to assist in helicopter flight control. During spring 2002, L 9011 received a third Simbad launch system atop the bridge.

Disposal note: The two *Ouragan*-class LSDs were decomissioned for transfer abroad. *Orage* (L 9022) was stricken in 4-05 and *Ouragan* (L 9021) in 2006, both for transfer to Argentina.

♦ 4 Champlain-class medium landing ships [LSM]
Bldrs: 9031: DCN Brest; others: At. Français de L'Ouest, Grand-Quevilly

	Laid down	L	In serv.
L 9031 FRANCIS GARNIER	1973	17-11-73	21-6-74
L 9032 DUMONT D'URVILLE	15-12-80	27-11-81	5-2-83
L 9033 JACQUES CARTIER	10-81	28-4-82	23-9-83
L 9034 LA GRANDIÈRE	27-8-84	11-12-85	20-1-87

La Grandière (L 9034)—high superstructure version Arjun Sarup, 6-05

D: 9031: 770 tons (1,330 fl); L 9032–9034: 820 tons (1,385 fl)
S: 16 kts (13 cruising) **Dim:** 80.00 (68.00 pp) × 13.00 × 3.00 (2.50 hull)
A: L 9031: 2 single 40-mm 60-cal. AA; 2 single 81-mm mortars; 2 single 12.7-mm mg—others: 2 single 20-mm 90-cal. GIAT F2 AA; 2 single 81-mm mortars; 2 single 12.7-mm mg

AMPHIBIOUS WARFARE SHIPS AND CRAFT *(continued)*

Francis Garnier (L 9031) Anthony Vella, 2-04

Electronics: Radar: 1 DRBN-32 nav.
M: 2 SACM-Wärtsilä UD 33 V12 M4 (195 V12 CSHR) diesels; 2 CP props; 3,600 bhp
Electric: 360 kw tot. **Range:** 3,500/13
Crew: 4 officers, 25 petty officers, 23 ratings

Remarks: A sister ship was built for Gabon. Morocco has three, the Ivory Coast one, and Chile has built three. L 9034, built on speculation, was acquired for French Navy. L 9031 is based at French Guiana, L 9032 at Papeete, L 9033 at New Caledonia, and L 9034 at Toulon. L 9030 decomissioned 8-04, L 9031 to retire 2008 followed by the remaining units by 2011.
Hull systems: Cargo (9031): 350 tons. Living quarters for a landing team (5 officers, 15 noncommissioned officers, 118 troops) and its 12 vehicles, including Guépard armored personnel carriers. L 9032 through L 9034 are able to transport 180 troops; they have a 40-ton-capacity bow ramp, improved accommodations, and carry one LCVP and one LCP landing craft. Their superstructure is one deck higher, and they can carry a 330-ton vehicle cargo for beaching and 208 tons of potable water. All have a helicopter deck aft; that on the L 9034 is longer than on the others.

Note: New EDA (*Engins de Débarquement Amphibies*) are being designed to replace the current CDIC/EDIC craft for use with the new *Mistral*-class helicopters.

♦ 2 CDIC utility landing craft [LCU]
Bldr: SFCN, Villeneuve-la-Garenne

	L	In serv.
L 9061 Rapière	25-2-88	28-7-88
L 9062 Hallebarde	3-11-88	17-2-89

Rapière (L 9061) Bernard Prézelin, 4-05

D: 369 tons light (750 fl) **S:** 10.96 kts
Dim: 59.40 (55.45 pp) × 11.90 × 1.10 (1.76 aft)
A: 2 single 20-mm 90-cal. GIAT F2 AA
Electronics: Radar: 1 DRBN 32 Racal-Decca 1226 nav.
M: 2 SACM UD30V12 M1 diesels; 2 props; 1,080 bhp
Electric: 156 kw tot. **Range:** 2,880/8 **Fuel:** 20 tons
Endurance: 15 days **Crew:** 6 petty officers, 12 nonrated

Remarks: CDIC = *Chalands de Débarquement d'Infanterie et de Chars* (landing ships for infantry and tanks). Based at Toulon. Named in 1997. Although intended for service with ships of the *Foudre* class, these ships have sufficient navigational equipment and accommodations to permit a coastal voyage of several days' duration. Plans to construct three more were canceled. Are to be retired in 2008 and 2009. Cargo capacity: 336 tons in the 40.0 × 10.4-m cargo deck, which has a 4.5-m-wide ramp at the bow. The mast folds to permit entry into the landing ship's docking well.

♦ 2 EDIC 700 utility landing craft [LCU]
Bldr: SFCN, Villeneuve-la-Garenne

	L	In serv.
L 9051 Sabre	3-3-87	13-6-87
L 9052 Dague	10-9-87	19-12-87

Sabre (L 9051) Bernard Prézelin, 7-05

D: 282 tons light (726 fl) **S:** 12 kts
Dim: 59.40 (55.85 pp) × 11.90 × 1.40 hull (1.70 max.)
A: Fitted for 1 20-mm 90-cal. GIAT F2 AA; 2 single 12.7-mm mg
Electronics: Radar: 1 DRBN-32 nav.
M: 2 SACM-Wärtsilä UD30V12 MB diesels; 2 props; 1,400 bhp
Electric: 156 kw tot. **Range:** 1,000/10 **Fuel:** 20 tons
Crew: 1 officer, 7 petty officers, 9 ratings

Remarks: Financed by the French nuclear testing center (DIRCEN). L 9051 is based at Papeete, L 9052 at Djibouti. Cargo capacity: 340 tons in 28.5 × 8-m cargo deck with bow ramp. An identical sister was built for Senegal and two others for Lebanon. The armament is not usually installed. Are to be retired in 2007.

♦ 1 utility transport/ferry [LCU]
Bldr: Ch. Serra, La Seyne (In serv. 4-10-87)

L 9090 Gapeau

Gapeau (L 9090) Rob Cabo, 9-03

D: 563 tons light (1,089 fl) **S:** 11 kts **Dim:** 66.23 × 12.54 × 2.14 max.
A: None
Electronics: Radar: 1 Decca RM 914 nav.; 1 Furuno FRS 1000 nav.
M: 2 Baudouin 12P15 25R diesels; 2 props; 1,360 bhp
Electric: 270 kw tot. **Range:** 1,920/10
Crew: 7 petty officers, 1 nonrated + 30 passengers

Remarks: Designed to serve as support craft for the *Centre d'Essais de la Méditerranée* missile range, Île de Levant. Cargo capacity: 460 tons on drive-through deck with bow and stern ramps. Due to more extensive superstructure (which spans the vehicle deck to increase its useful length), the ship cannot be transported aboard the large landing ships. To be retired in 2007.

♦ 15 U.S.-design LCM (8)–class landing craft [LCM]
Bldr: CMN, Cherbourg (three by C.N. Auroux, Arcachon)

CTM 17	CTM 22 Kien An	CTM 27 Indochine
CTM 18	CTM 23 Song Can	CTM 28 Tonkin
CTM 19 Do Ha	CTM 24	CTM 29 Nui Dho
CTM 20 Néké Grav	CTM 25	CTM 30 Khoan Bo
CTM 21 Guéréo	CTM 26	CTM 31 Phu Doan

Guéréo (CTM 21) Bernard Prézelin, 4-05

D: 56 tons light (150 fl) **S:** 9.5 kts **Dim:** 23.80 × 6.35 × 1.25
A: 2 single 12.7-mm mg
Electronics: Radar: 1 portable Koden or Furuno . . . nav.
M: 2 Poyaud-Wärtsilä 18 V8 M1 diesels; 2 props; 450 bhp **Range:** 380/8
Fuel: 3.4 tons **Endurance:** 48 hours at half power **Crew:** 4 tot.

Remarks: CTM = *Chalands de Transport de Matériel.* Completed in 1982–92. Cargo capacity: 90 tons. The machineguns are usually not mounted. The French Army Transport Corps has six other units of the class, based at La Pallice. CTM 17 and 18 are based at Lorient, CTM 19–23 and 27–31 at Toulon, CTM 24 and 25 at Djibouti, and CTM 26 at Dakar. Navy sisters CTM 2, 5, 9, 10, and 12 through 16 were stricken in 1999; CTM 15 and CTM 16 were transferred to the Ivory Coast in 3-99, CTM 14 to Djibouti in 1999, CTM 5 to Senegal in 5-99, and CTM 2 to Morocco in 5-99.

AMPHIBIOUS WARFARE SHIPS AND CRAFT *(continued)*

♦ 20 + LCVP
Bldr: . . . (In serv. . . .)

D: 13 tons (fl) **S:** 8 kts **Dim:** 10.90 × 3.21 × 1.09 (aft)
M: 1 diesel; 225 bhp **Range:** 110/8

Remarks: GRP construction, based on standard U.S. design. Can carry 36 troops or 3.5 tons cargo in 5.2 × 2.3-m cargo well. At least 20 are in service, aboard various landing ships and auxiliaries.

AUXILIARIES

♦ 1 Type RR 2000 multipurpose support ship [AG]

	Bldr	Laid down	L	In serv.
A 633 Taape	Ch. de la Perriere, Lorient	22-10-82	14-4-83	30-6-83

Taape (A 633) Bernard Prézelin, 5-04

D: 383 tons (505 fl) **S:** 14.2 kts **Dim:** 41.02 (38.50 pp) × 7.5 × 3.18
A: None
Electronics: Radar: 1 DRBN-32 nav.
M: 2 SACM-Wärtsilä UD 30 V 16 M3 (MGO V16 ASHR) diesels; 2 CP Kort-nozzle props; 2,800 bhp
Range: 6,000/12 **Crew:** 2 officers, 7 petty officers, 2 nonrated + 6 passengers

Remarks: Ordered 11-10-82. Construction financed by the nuclear test center, DIRCEN. A variation of the FISH (Feronia International Shipping)-class oilfield tug/supply vessel design, which was also used in the *Chamois*-class tenders. Transported in the landing ship *Orage* in 4-84 to Muraroa for duty in the Pacific; she was based at Papeete until spring 1998, when she returned to Toulon. Was due for disposal in 2005 but has been extended to 2013.
Hull systems: 24.8-ton bollard pull. Can carry 100 tons of cargo on the long, open afterdeck.

♦ 3 Chamois-class multipurpose support ships [AG]
Bldr: Ch. de la Perriere, Lorient

	Laid down	L	In serv.
A 768 Élan	16-3-77	28-7-77	7-4-78
A 774 Chevreuil	15-9-76	8-5-77	7-10-77
A 775 Gazelle	30-12-76	7-6-77	13-1-78

Chevreuil (A 774) Bernard Prézelin, 8-04

D: 305 tons light (505 fl) **S:** 14.5 kts **Dim:** 41.50 (36.96 pp) × 7.50 × 3.18
A: 2 single 12.7-mm mg
Electronics: 1 . . . nav.
M: 2 SACM-Wärtsilä UD30V16 M3 (MGO V16 AFHR) diesels; 2 CP Kort-nozzle props; 2,800 bhp
Range: 7,200/12 **Fuel:** 92 m^3 **Crew:** 2 officers, 16 petty officers, 2 nonrated

Remarks: A 774 is employed mostly to carry cargo, while A 768 is used primarily as a water tanker. All can also be used for coastal towing and cleaning up oil spills, as transports for 28 passengers, as minelayers, or as torpedo retrievers. A 774 and A 775 due to retire in 2007 and A 768 in 2008.
Disposals: *Chamois* (A 767) was stricken 1-9-95 and transferred to Madagascar in 5-96. *Isard* (A 776) was retired during 2005.
Hull systems: Have two rudders and an 80-hp bow-thruster. The stern winch has a 28-ton bollard pull. A portable 50-ton gallows crane for mooring buoy handling can be shipped at the stern. All can carry 100 tons dry cargo on deck or 125 tons fuel and 40 tons water (or 65 tons fuel and 125 tons water).

♦ 1 chartered submersible support ship [AG]
Bldr: Aukra Bruk A/S, Aukra, Norway (In serv. 1975)

Aquitaine Explorer (ex-*Abeille Supporter,* ex-*Seaway Hawk,* ex-*Seaway Devon*)

Aquitaine Explorer—painted white, with blue bulwarks at the bow
Bernard Prézelin, 1-05

D: 2,500 tons (fl) **S:** 14 kts **Dim:** 63.58 (55.00 pp) × 13.42 × 5.75
Electronics: Radar: 2 . . . nav.
M: 2 Atlas-MaK 12M453AK diesels; 2 CP props; 8,000 bhp—bow-thruster
Electric: 500 kw tot. (1 × 300 kw, 2 × 100 kw)
Range: 7,900/14 **Fuel:** 530 tons
Crew: 11 ship's company + 27 passengers (including 6 divers)

Remarks: 1,189 grt/1,330 dwt. Oilfield tug/supply vessel chartered by *Délégation Général pour l'Armement* (*Direction des Missiles et de l'Espace*) for support of the Landes missile range from Société Abeille International until 7-00, when management was switched to ABC Maritime and the name changed; the ship is owned by Société Boulonnaise de Remorquage, Lorient. Based at Bayonne.
Hull systems: Painted yellow and white. Hull reinforced for operation in light ice. Has a 30-ton A-frame gantry at the stern, one 10-ton electrohydraulic crane, and one 4-ton crane. Divers' facilities include two decompression chambers and a diving bell. Has dynamic positioning system, Sydelis radio navigation system, and passive hull stabilization. Equipped with 100-ton bollard pull winch aft. As of 2003 was operating with the submersible *Abyssub 5000:* **D:** 1.7 tons; **Speed:** 2.4 kts; **Dim:** 2.10 × 1.20 × 1.70; **Diving depth:** 5,000 m.

♦ 1 mine-countermeasures experimental ship [AGE]
Bldr: DCN, Lorient

	Laid down	L	In serv.
A 785 Thétis (ex-*Néreide*)	8-3-86	15-11-86	9-11-88

Thétis (A 785) Bernard Prézelin, 7-05

D: 900 tons (1,050 fl) **S:** 15 kts **Dim:** 59.00 (53.00 pp) × 10.90 × 3.80
A: 2 single 12.7-mm mg; mines
Electronics:
Radar: 1 Decca . . . nav.
Sonar: DUBM-42 Lagadmor towed array; TSM 2022 Mk 3 (PVDS) towed array
M: 2 SACM-Wärtsilä UD30V12-M6 diesels; 2 CP props; 2,500 bhp—2 electric motors for low speeds; 120 shp—200-hp bow-thruster
Electric: 875 kw tot. (4 diesel-driven alternators) **Range:** 6,000/12
Crew: 2 officers, 36 enlisted + 10 technicians

Remarks: Typed BEGM (*Bâtiment d'Expérimentation de la Guerre des Mines*) and operates for the Groupe d'Études Sous-Marines de l'Atlantique (GESMA) under the direction of the Direction Générale des Armements (DGA), primarily as a mine-countermeasures trials ship. Ordered 11-10-84. A planned second unit never built. Uses same hull and machinery as the *La Pérouse*–class hydrographic survey ships. Performs trials with the DUBM-42 Lagadmor towed minehunting sonar (for which a winch with 700 m of cable is provided), new remotely operated mine-disposal vehicle, and the AD-4 acoustic sweep. In late 1994, conducted trials with the Thales PVDS (Propelled Variable-Depth Sonar) using a Bofors-Sutec Double Eagle ROV equipped with Thales' TSM 2022 Mk 3 high-frequency (165 kHz and 400 kHz) sonar and low light-level television; the device can operate at 5 kts at up to 600 m ahead of the control ship and at depths to 200 m, and it weighs 400 kg. Normally carries three Double Eagle ROVs and is also conducting trials with the Redermor variable-depth minehunting sonar (with a 300-m depth capability, a range of 1,000 m, a length of 5 m, and a weight of 3 tons, powered by four 7.5 kw electric motors).

AUXILIARIES *(continued)*

♦ 1 environmental monitoring ship [AG]
Bldr: DCN Brest

	Laid down	L	In serv.
P 764 D'Entrecasteaux (ex-A 757)	7-69	30-5-70	8-10-70

D'Entrecasteaux (P 764) Frank Findler, 6-05

D'Entrecasteaux (P 764) Bernard Prézelin, 1-05

D: 1,630 tons light/2,058 tons std. (2,450 fl) **S:** 15 kts
Dim: 95.65 (89.00 pp) × 13.00 × 4.20 (5.50 props)
A: None **Electronics:** Radar: 2 DRBN-32 nav.
M: 2 SACM-Wärtsilä UD33V12 diesels, electric drive; 2 CP props; 2,720 shp—2 retractable Schottel propellers, 1 fwd, 1 aft
Range: 12,000/12; 17,000/10 **Crew:** 55 tot.

Remarks: Built for oceanographic research and hydrographic duties and was to have been retired during 2003 but was retyped a "BSE" on 1-8-03 and now operates as a training ship and environmental monitoring and cleanup ship. Based at Brest.
Hull systems: Has a dynamic mooring/maneuvering system permitting station-keeping in 5,000-m depths. Can take soundings and surveys to a depth of 5,000 m. Helicopter platform and hangar for an Alouette-III. Electrohydraulic oceanographic equipment cranes, one landing craft, three hydrographic launches, hull-mounted scanning sonar. Three echo sounders (one stabilized). Has Trident, Sydelis, Toran, Transit and Global Positioning System navigation equipment, plus *Hydrac* and *Hydrai* automatic data systems.

♦ 1 chartered oilfield tug/supply ship for sonar research [AGE]
Bldr: Halter Marine, New Orleans, La (In serv. 1980)

Langevin (ex-*Martin Fish,* ex-*Percy Navigator*)

Langevin—blue lower hull, white above Bernard Prézelin, 8-04

D: Approx. 2,700 tons (fl) **S:** 12 kts **Dim:** 67.67 (65.84 pp) × 13.42 × 4.88
Electronics: Radar: 2 . . . nav.
M: 3 G.M. EMD 16V149 TI diesel generator sets, 2 electric motors; 2 props; 3,600 shp
Range: . . . **Crew:** . . .

Remarks: 1,600 grt. Former oil field tug/supply vessel chartered 5-90 from Compagnie Nationale de Navigation for use by the *Direction des Constructions Navales* (DCN), *Sous-Direction Études de la DCN de Toulon* for a variety of purposes connected with the new-generation nuclear-powered ballistic missile submarine program. In 9-95 began trials with the ATBF-2 low-frequency active towed surface-ship sonar array system. Has an Inmarsat-M SATCOM terminal.

Disposal note: The shipboard weapons trials ship *Île d'Oléron* (A 610) was retired 30-3-02.

♦ 1 intelligence collection ship [AGI]
Bldr: Royal Niester Sanders, Groningen, the Netherlands

	Laid down	L	In serv.
A 759 Dupuy de Lôme	1-12-02	27-3-04	3-06

Dupuy De Lôme (A 759)—painted white Guy Schaeffer via Paolo Marsan, 5-05

Dupuy De Lôme—note absence of two white center radomes
Guy Schaeffer via Paolo Marsan, 3-05

D: 3,200 tons (fl) **S:** 16 kts (cruise) **Dim:** 101.8 x 15.8 x 4.9
A: 2 2-round Simbad SAM syst. (. . . Mistral missiles)—2 single 20-mm 90-cal. GIAT F2 AA
Electronics:
Radar: . . .
EW: SIGINT, COMINT, and ELINT arrays
M: 2 MaK 9M25 diesels; 2 props; 8,130 bhp
Range: 3,400/16 **Endurance:** 30 days
Crew: 32 ship's company + 78 technicians

Remarks: Ordered 14-1-02, from prime contractor Thales Naval France, Thales Communications responsible for electronics installations, Thales Systèmes Aéroportés responsible for the ELINT system, and Compagnie Nationale de Navigation's Compagnie Maritime Nantaise providing the ship platform, whose hull was subcontracted to a Dutch yard. Replaced the *Bougainville* (L 9077) and to operate 350 days per year for 25 years, the ship is to be able to proceed at 16 kts in Sea State 3 and 10 kts in Sea State 6. Under the contract, Thales and Compagnie National de Transport will be responsible for maintenance and operational support for the ship for five years. Fin stabilizers will be fitted, and the ship will be painted white.
Combat systems: Will have a helicopter deck but no hangar. The MINREM (*Moyens Interarmées de Renseignements Électromagnétiques*) data collection system will be installed, employing the modular system ordered in 2002 for use on the L 9077.

♦ 2 Alcyon-class chartered moorings tenders [AGL]
Bldr: At. et Ch. de la Manche, Dieppe

Alcyon (ex-*Bahram*) (In serv. 1981) Ailette (ex-*Cyrus*) (In serv. 1982)

AUXILIARIES *(continued)*

Alcyon—sea-green hull, white upperworks Bernard Prézelin, 2-04

D: Approx. 1,900 tons (fl) **S:** 13.5 kts **Dim:** 53.01 (51.01 pp) × 13.01 × 4.50
Electronics: Radar: 2 . . . nav.
M: 2 Bergens-Normo KVMB-12 diesels; 2 CP props; 5,200 bhp—bow-thruster
Crew: 7 tot.

Remarks: 487 grt/1,000 dwt. Typed BSHM (*Bâtiments de Soutien de Haute Mer*). Oilfield tug/supply vessels chartered 1988 from Compagnie des Moyens de Surface Adaptes a l'Exploitation des Oceans (SURF) for service at Brest as moorings tenders and pollution control ships.
Hull systems: The 30-ton portal crane at the stern has been replaced by a buoy-handling crane on the afterdeck. Have two firefighting water monitors. Are also equipped for antipollution duties and have a 500-m^3-capacity holding tank. Hulls painted green, superstructures white. Bollard pull: 60 tons initial.

♦ 1 missile-range tracking ship [AGM]

	Bldr	Laid down	L	In serv.
A 601 Monge	Ch. de l'Atlantique, St.-Nazaire	26-3-90	6-10-90	4-11-92

Monge (A 601) Bernard Prézelin, 2-04

D: 17,760 tons (21,040 fl) **S:** 15.8 kts **Dim:** 225.60 (203.40 pp) × 24.84 × 7.66
A: 2 single 20-mm 90-cal. GIAT F2 AA; 2 single 12.7-mm mg; 2 Super Frelon helicopters
Electronics:
Radar: 2 DRBN-34A nav.; 1 DRBV-15C air search; 1 Gascogne tracking; 2 Armor tracking; 1 Savoie tracking; 1 Stratus (L-band) tracking (1 transmission antenna, 1 tracking)
TACAN: NRPB-3A
M: 2 SEMT-Pielstick 8PC 2.5 L400 diesels; 1 CP prop; 9,000 bhp—1,340-shp bow-thruster
Electric: 7,560 kw (6 × 1,200-kw, 1 × 360-kw diesel sets)
Range: 15,000/15 **Endurance:** 60 days
Crew: 10 officers, 116 enlisted + 100 scientific staff (about 25 civilian); accommodations for 292 tot.

Remarks: Accepted from builder 6-3-91 for trials. Tracking equipment began installation 3-6-91, with operational trials beginning 5-92. Painted white. Intended to remain in service for 30 years. Employed as tracking and telemetry support ship for strategic ballistic missile trials.
Hull systems: Computer-controlled passive tank stabilization system to reduce roll to 9° maximum at Sea State 6. The hangar can accommodate two Super Frelon helicopters. Carries 160 tons aviation fuel.
Mission systems: The Thales TAVITAC 2000 command system is installed. The Syracuse I, Syracuse II, and Marisat SATCOM systems are fitted, along with Navstar NAVSAT receivers. Extensive tracking equipment is installed, as on her predecessor, including LIDAR (LIght Detection And Ranging) green-laser upper atmospheric analysis equipment. There are also 14 telemetry antennas.

♦ 1 Pourquoi Pas?–class oceanographic research ship [AGOR]
Bldr: Alstom, St. Nazaire

	Laid down	L	In serv.
Pourquoi Pas?	1-04	14-10-04	3-05

Pourquoi Pas? Bernard Prézelin, 9-05

Pourquoi Pas? Bernard Prézelin, 5-05

D: 6,500 tons (fl) **S:** 14.5 kts **Dim:** 107.6 × 20.0 × 6.9
Electronics: Radar: 1 Furuno type nav.
M: Diesel-electric: 4 diesel alternator sets (1,440 kw each); 2 props; 4,350 shp; 3 bow-thrusters; 1 stern thruster
Range: 8,100/10 **Endurance:** 60 days **Crew:** 30 tot. + 60 science party

Remarks: Ordered 24-12-02. Will be used 45% of the year (150 days) by the French Navy and the rest by the government research agency IFREMER (*Institute Français de Recherches pour l'Exploitation de la Mer*). Will carry the research submersibles *Nautilus* and *Victor 6000* and two 8-m survey launches built by KL Industrie, Auray. The stern working area is 25 × 20 m and is served by a 22-ton portal crane at the stern. Space has been reserved for installation of a helicopter deck. Does not carry a pennant number.

Note: IFREMER also operates three other oceanographic research ships: *L'Atlante* (1990; **Dim:** 84.60 × 15.87 × 5.05); *Thalassa* (1995; **Dim:** 74.00 × 14.90 × 6.00); and *Le Suroit* (1975; **Dim:** 56.34 × 10.98 × 3.96); and also operates coastal survey ships *L'Europe* (1993; **Dim:** 29.60 × 10.60 × 3.45), *Gwen Drez* (1975; **Dim:** 24.49 × 7.40 × 3.14), and *Thalia* (1978; **Dim:** 24.52 × 7.40 × 2.55).

♦ 1 Beautemps-Beaupré-class hydrographic survey ship [AGS]
Bldr: Alstom, St. Nazaire

	Laid down	L	In serv.
A 758 Beautemps-Beaupré	17-7-01	26-4-02	13-12-03

Beautemps-Beaupré (A 758) Bernard Prézelin, 8-04

D: 2,125 tons (3,300 fl) **S:** 14 kts (12.5 sust.)
Dim: 80.60 (72.10 pp) × 14.90 × 6.90 max.
A: 2 12.7-mm mg
Electronics: Radar: 2 Kongsberg . . . ARPA nav. Sonar: see remarks
M: Diesel-electric: 4 diesels, 4 Mitsubishi alternator sets, 1 motor, 1 prop; 3,000 shp—590-shp tunnel bow-thruster, two 295-shp azimuthal stern thrusters
Range: 8,100/10 **Endurance:** 45 days **Crew:** 25 tot. + 25 survey party

Remarks: Ordered 7-3-01. Capable both of ocean survey and oceanographic research duties and replaces the stricken survey ship *L'Espérance* and the AGOR *D'Entrecasteaux.* Designed to merchant marine standards and is similar to the IFREMER research ship *Thalassa.* Was delivered on 11-2-03.

Equipped with three laboratories and four preparation spaces. Has Simrad EM 120 multipath, deep-ocean mapping and EM 1002 vertical echo sounders, as well as a towed side-scan mapping sonar. Carries current measurement gear, gravimeter, accelerometer, bathymetric gear, and a magnetometer. Is equipped with a 10-ton gallows crane at the stern and a 5-ton side gallows crane. Carries two 8-m hydrographic launches built by KL Industrie, Auray.

AUXILIARIES *(continued)*

♦ 3 La Pérouse–class hydrographic survey ships [AGS]

Bldr: DCN, Lorient

	Laid down	L	In serv.
A 791 La Pérouse	11-6-85	15-11-86	20-4-88
A 792 Borda	2-9-85	15-11-86	16-6-88
A 793 La Place	1-9-87	9-11-88	5-10-89

La Place (A 793) Derek Fox, 9-05

La Pérouse (A 791) Bernard Prézelin, 1-05

D: 850 tons light, 970 tons std. (1,100 fl) **S:** 15 kts
Dim: 59.00 (53.00 pp) × 10.90 × 3.63 **A:** 2 single 7.62-mm mg
Electronics:
Radar: 1 DRBN-32 nav.; 1 Furuno . . . nav.
Sonar: See Remarks
M: 2 SACM-Wärtsilä UD30V12 M6 diesels; 2 CP props; 2,500 bhp—160-shp bow-thruster
Electric: 620 kw tot. **Range:** 6,000/12
Crew: 3 officers, 10 petty officers, 17 nonrated + 15 survey party

Remarks: First two ordered 24-7-84 and the third on 22-1-86. Painted white and operated for the *Service Hydrographique et Océanographique de la Marine* (SHOM). A 793 is based at New Caledonia, and the others at Brest. Sister *Arago* (A 675) is now employed as a Public Service patrol ship in home waters.
Mission systems: All but A 791 can carry two 8-m hydrographic survey launches and are equipped with the Hydrac and Hydrai survey data systems. A 791 is equipped with a DUBM-21C minehunting sonar for trials, wreck identification, and channel certification. The other three have the Thales-Marconi CSFTSM 5425 Lennermor multifunction wreck identification/echo sounder and carry two 9-m KL Industrie d'Auray survey launches each. Other navigation/hydrographic equipment includes Trident, Syledis, Toran, RANA, and Navstar receivers, Atlas DESO-20 100-kHz and 66/210-kHz echo sounders (also on the two survey launches), a Raytheon 12-kHz echo sounder, Sippican bathythermograph, Barringer magnetometer, and Edgerton side-looking sonar. All carry one scientific and two data-reduction computers.

Note: Six hydrographic survey launches (*Albatros, Cormoran, Goéland, Guillemot, Macareux, Pélican,* and *Phaéton*) were constructed for this class by KL Industrie, Auray; new davits for the launches were installed on A 792 and A 793 at Fassmer Verft, Germany, during 2003; the launches are 7.85 m long by 2.72-m beam and 0.50-m draft, displacing 5 tons full load and being capable of 12 kts on the power from one 235-bhp Volvo 41TD diesel.

♦ 4 Durance-class replenishment oilers [AOR]

Bldr: DCN, Brest (A 631: CNIM, La Seyne)

	Laid down	L	In serv.
A 607 Meuse	2-6-77	2-12-78	2-8-80
A 608 Var	8-5-79	9-5-81	29-1-83
A 630 Marne	4-8-82	6-2-85	16-1-87
A 631 Somme	3-5-85	3-10-87	7-3-90

D: A 607: 7,600 tons (17,800 fl); others: 7,800 tons (17,900 fl)
S: 20 kts (19 sust.) **Dim:** 157.20 (149.00 pp) × 21.20 × 8.65 (10.80 max.)
A: 3 2-round Simbad SAM syst. (. . . Mistral missiles); 1 40-mm 60-cal. AA; 2 single 20-mm 70-cal. Mk 10 Mod. 23 Oerlikon AA; 2 single 12.7-mm mg; 1 Alouette-III or Lynx helicopter
Electronics:
Radar: 2 DRBN-34A nav.
EW: Thales DR-2000 intercept; Telegon HFD/F; SLQ-25 Nixie towed torpedo decoy syst.
M: 2 SEMT-Pielstick 16 PC2.5 V400 diesels; 2 CP props; 20,760 bhp
Electric: 5,400 kw tot. **Range:** 9,000/15 **Fuel:** 750 tons
Crew: 10 officers, 62 petty officers, 91 ratings (all but A 607: 45 command staff also)

Var (A 608) Bernard Prézelin, 11-04

Meuse (A 607) Bernard Prézelin, 6-05

Remarks: A 631 was ordered 3-84 from CNM, La Seyne, on speculation and purchased 10-87 for the French Navy; the ship is identical to A 608 and A 630. A near-sister was built in Australia for the RAN, and two smaller variants were built for Saudi Arabia. Sister *Durance* (A 629) was placed in reserve in 7-97 and transferred to Argentina on 12-7-99. All are based at Toulon.
Hull systems: Have one SYTAR (*Système de Tensionnement Automatique poir Ravitaillement à la Mer*) dual solid and two liquid underway replenishment stations per side and are also equipped to refuel over the stern under way. Cargo: *Meuse:* 5,090 tons fuel oil, 4,014 tons diesel, 1,140 tons JP-5, 250 tons distilled water, 180 tons provisions, 122 tons munitions, and 45 tons spare parts. *Var* and *Marne:* 5,090 tons fuel oil, 3,310 tons diesel, 1,090 tons JP-5, 260 tons distilled water, 170 tons ammunition, 180 tons provisions, 15 tons spares. *Somme:* 9,250 tons fuel oil, 250 tons water, 190 tons provisions, 45 tons spares. The helicopter deck is large enough to accept Super Frelon helicopters.
Combat systems: In A 607 the 40-mm AA is aft; in the others it is forward. May receive two Dagaie Mk 2 countermeasures rocket launchers, and are planned to receive a reduced version of the OP3A self-defense combat control system. *Var, Marne,* and *Somme* are equipped as flagships for a major area commander and can accommodate 257 persons, including 45 command staffers; their forward superstructure blocks are extended aft by 8 m to provide increased accommodations, and the two beam-mounted stores cranes immediately abaft the bridge are replaced by a single, centerline crane; the Syracuse I SATCOM system and the SEAO/OPSMER computerized combat decision aid system are fitted. Most are equipped with Inmarsat terminals. All but A 607 carry two LCVP landing craft. A 607 received a third Simbad launch system during the spring of 2002.

♦ 1 Jules Verne–class multipurpose repair ship [AR]

Bldr: DCN, Brest

	Laid down	L	In serv.
A 620 Jules Verne (ex-*Achéron*)	1969	30-5-70	1-6-76

Jules Verne (A 620) Bernard Prézelin, 8-04

Jules Verne (A 620) Bernard Prézelin, 3-04

AUXILIARIES *(continued)*

D: 7,815 tons (10,250 fl) **S:** 18 kts **Dim:** 151.00 (138.00 pp) × 21.56 × 6.50
A: 2 single 40-mm 60-cal. AA; 4 single 12.7-mm mg
Electronics: Radar: 1 DRBN-32 nav.; 1 Decca BridgeMaster II nav.
M: 2 SEMT-Pielstick 12 PC V400 diesels; 1 prop; 12,000 bhp
Electric: 3,800 kw tot. **Range:** 9,500/18
Crew: 16 officers, 150 petty officers, 116 ratings + 130 passengers

Remarks: Six years after being launched as an ammunition ship, the uncompleted *Jules Verne* completed conversion to a multi-purpose repair ship to provide support to a force of from three to six surface warships. Completed six-month overhaul in France 29-6-95 and another in 12-97. In collision with oiler *Var* (A 608) during 5-98. Based at Toulon. Was to be retired in 2007 but has been extended until 2012.
Hull systems: Has significant capabilities for regular maintenance and battle-damage repair. The 13 workshops include mechanical, engine, electrical, sheet-metal, and electronics. Also carries torpedoes and ammunition. Has four 12-ton cranes and a 16-bed medical facility with a decompression chamber. Has a 300-m^2 hangar for two helicopters and a 500-m^2 flight deck.

♦ 1 Ulstein UT 710–class salvage and rescue tug [ARS]
Bldr: Aker-Brevik Construction A/S, Norway (In serv. 12-12-03)

ARGONAUTE (ex-*Island Patriot*)

Argonaute—black hull, with white upperworks Bernard Prézelin, 3-05

D: 2,371 tons std., 4,420 tons (fl) **S:** 15.5 kts **Dim:** 68.9 × 15.6 × 5.9
Electronics: Radar: 1 ... nav.
M: 2 Rolls-Royce Bergen BRM-9 diesels; 2 props; 10,800 bhp
Range: 18,000/10 **Crew:** 9 tot.

Remarks: Chartered in 1-04 to complement *Alcyon, Ailette,* and *Carangue*. Based at Brest.

♦ 1 Mérou-class chartered salvage and rescue tug [ARS]
Bldr: Scheepswerf Waterhuizen B.V. J. Pattje, Groningen (In serv. 1982)

MÉROU (ex-*King Fish*)

Mérou—painted gray, with white pilothouse Bernard Prézelin, 11-04

D: Approx. 2,500 tons (fl) **S:** 14.2 kts **Dim:** 59.52 (51.82 pp) × 15.02 × 5.00
Electronics: Radar: 2 . . . nav.
M: 4 Wichmann AXAG diesels; 2 CP props. 7,992 bhp—500-shp bow- and stern-thrusters
Range: 6,300/12 **Fuel:** 244 tons **Endurance:** 50 days
Crew: 4 officers, 5 unlicensed (accomm. for 8 officers, 18 unlicensed mariners, and 12 passengers)

Remarks: 1,471 grt/1,477 dwt. Leased from FISH (Feronia International Shipping) in 1987 and based at Toulon; purchased 1998 by Compagnie Chambon and charter renewable at two-year intervals.
Hull systems: Bollard pull: 100 tons initial, up to 250 tons under way. One 1,200 m^3/hr firepump; two water cannon with 120-m range. Equipped for pollution cleanup duties. Ice-strengthened hull. Has extensive pollution cleanup equipment.

♦ 1 Carangue-class chartered salvage and rescue tug [ARS]
Bldr: Samsung SB Co., Ltd., Koje, South Korea (In serv. 1980)

CARANGUE (ex-*Pilot Fish,* ex-*Maersk Handler,* ex-*Smit Lloyd* 119, ex-*Atlas Tasman*)

Carangue Guy Schaeffer via Paolo Marsan, 12-04

D: 1,300 tons (1,940 fl) **S:** 16 kts **Dim:** 64.42 (56.42 pp) × 13.81 × 5.09
Electronics: Radar: 2 . . . nav.
M: 2 Bofors-Nohab Polar F2116V-D diesels; 2 CP props; 7,040 bhp—725-shp bow-thruster
Electric: 725 kw tot. (3 × 200-kw, 1 × 125-kw diesel sets)
Range: 21,000/10 **Crew:** 4 officers, 4 unlicensed + 12 passengers

Remarks: 1,179 grt/2,100 dwt. Oilfield deck-cargo and anchor-handling tug chartered 1995 from FISH (Feronia International Shipping) for towing and antipollution duties in the Mediterranean and is based at Toulon. Purchased 1998 by Compagnie Chambon and charter extended since. Bollard pull: 90 tons initial, 150 sustained. Has two 600 m^3/hr firepumps serving two water cannon with 90-m range. Has extensive pollution cleanup equipment.

♦ 2 chartered Abeille Bourbon–class salvage tugs [ARS]
Bldr: Ulstein Hatlo A/S, Ulsteinvik, Norway (In serv. 2005)

ABEILLE BOURBON ABEILLE LIBERTE

Remarks: Replacements for two previous chartered salvage tugs, *Abeille Flandre* and *Abeille Languedoc*. Entered service mid-2005. 200-ton bollard pull. *A. Bourbon* is based at Brest, *A. Liberte* at Cherbourg.

Note: Under an agreement signed on 19-3-90 by the French Navy, the Ministry of Maritime Affairs, and the Dunkerque Society of Towing and Salvage, the commercial salvage tugs *Robuste, Puissant,* and *Hardi* (all 2,600 bhp, 40-ton bollard pull), based at Dunkerque, are maintained at the call of the Maritime prefect of Cherbourg to ensure the safety of navigation in the Calais area. They have green hulls and white superstructures.

♦ 2 Type RR 4000–class seagoing tugs [ATA]
Bldr: Breheret, Couëron, Nantes

	L	In serv.
A 634 RARI	16-4-84	5-2-85
A 635 REVI	15-5-84	6-2-85

Rari (A 634) Bernard Prézelin, 6-02

D: 1,057 tons light (1,557 fl) **S:** 14.5 kts **Dim:** 51.00 (49.50 wl) × 12.60 × 4.10
A: None **Electronics:** Radar: 1 DRBN-34 nav.
M: 2 SACM-Wärtsilä UD33V12 M6 (AGO 195 V12 RVR) diesels; 2 CP props; 4,000 bhp—2 2.5-ton side-thrusters
Electric: 600 kw (2 × 300 kw) **Range:** 6,000/12 **Fuel:** 300 tons
Crew: 2 officers, 17 petty officers, 7 ratings + 18 passengers

Remarks: Built for DIRCEN, the French Pacific nuclear testing center. A 634 transferred to Brest in 1998, and A 635 remains based at Papeete.
Hull systems: Bollard pull: 47 tons. Have a 14-ton quadrantial gantry at the extreme stern and two water cannons for fire fighting. Can carry fuel cargo in ballast tanks or 400 tons of cargo on the open deck aft. Are to be retired in 2015.

AUXILIARIES *(continued)*

♦ 2 Tenace-class seagoing tugs [ATA]

	Bldr	L	In serv.
A 664 Malabar	Oelkers, Hamburg	16-4-75	3-2-76
A 669 Tenace	Oelkers, Hamburg	12-71	15-11-73

Malabar (A 664) Bernard Prézelin, 9-05

D: 970 tons (1,440 fl) **S:** 13.5 kts **Dim:** 51.0 × 11.5 × 5.7
Electronics: 1 DRBN-32 (Decca 1226) nav.; 1 Decca 060 nav.
M: 2 MaK 9-cyl. diesels; 1 Kort-nozzle CP prop; 4,600 bhp
Electric: 502 kw (2 × 227-kw, 1 × 48-kw diesel-driven sets)
Range: 9,500/13 **Fuel:** 500 tons
Crew: 2 officers, 15 petty officers, 13 ratings (accomm. for 42 tot.)

Remarks: Both are based at Brest. Sister *Centaure* (A 674) was stricken in 12-98 and sold to Turkey, transferring 16-3-99; A 669 is to be retired during 2007 and A 664 during 2011.
Hull systems: Pumps include one of 350 m³/hr (serving two fire monitors with a range of 60 m) and one of 120 m³/hr, plus numerous smaller salvage and firefighting pumps. Carry two RIBs each. Have Inmarsat SATCOM terminals. Living quarters air-conditioned. Bollard pull: 60 tons.

SERVICE CRAFT

♦ 2 Phaéton-class submarine towed-array tenders [YAG]
Bldr: Chaudronnerie Industrielle de Bretagne (CIB), Brest

Y 656 Phaéton (L: 7-94) Y 657 Machaon (L: 18-5-94)

Machaon (Y 657) Bernard Prézelin, 7-04

D: 69 tons (fl) **S:** 8.5 kts **Dim:** 19.20 (16.50 wl) × 6.82 (6.50 hull) × 1.20
Electronics: Radar: 1 Decca 181-4 nav.
M: 2 SACM UD18V8 M1 diesel; 1 Schottel SPJ 57 waterjets; 326 bhp—1 Hydro Armor Type 800 bow-thruster (660 kg thrust)
Range: . . . / . . . **Crew:** 4 tot.

Remarks: Intended to tow, install, and recover submarine-towed linear passive hydrophone arrays. Y 656 is based at Toulon, Y 657 at Brest. Hull has pronounced bow bulb, with upswept bottom aft between sidewalls creating a combined monohull/catamaran hullform. Aluminum construction. Have a large cable reel amidships and carry a Zodiac RIB.

♦ 1 modified Glycine-class ASW trials tender [YAGE]
Bldr: J. Chauvet, Paimbœuf (L: 7-86)

L'Aventurière II

D: 250 tons (295 fl) **S:** 10 kts **Dim:** 28.30 (24.50 pp) × 7.86 × 3.75
Electronics: Radar: 1 Furuno . . . nav.—Sonar: . . .
M: 1 Poyaund diesel; 1 CP prop; 650 bhp—150-shp bow-thruster
Range: 3,600/10 **Fuel:** 49 m³ **Crew:** . . . tot.

Remarks: 270 grt. No hull number. Used by GESMA (*Group d'Etudes Sous-Marines de l'Atlantique*) at Brest in mine warfare research. Civilian crewed and is technically owned by DCN rather than the French Navy, hence the lack of a pennant number.

L'Aventurière II Bernard Prézelin, 5-04

♦ 1 sonar trials support tender [YAGE]
Bldr: IMC, Tonnay-Charente (In serv. 1983)

BR 69478301 Dora

Dora (BR 69478301) Bernard Prézelin, 2-04

D: . . . tons **S:** 7.5 kts **Dim:** 41.10 (38.00 pp) × 10.72 × 2.93
Electronics: Radar: 2 . . . nav.—Sonar: . . .
M: 2 MWM TBD 234V8 diesels; 2 props; 740 bhp—bow-thruster

Remarks: Used at Brest by DCN (*Direction des Constructions Navales*) for acoustic trials. Has a large crane forward to handle arrays and a cable reel and winch aft for towed systems. Has a blunt bow-form. Civilian operated and technically not part of the Navy. DCN craft have serial numbers, often preceded by two letters indicating the name of their base or the letters DCN.

♦ 1 trials support diving tender [YAGE]
Bldr: . . . (In serv. . . .)

Mérou

Mérou Bernard Prézelin, 4-03

D: 120 tons **S:** . . . kts **Dim:** 30.00 × 5.00 × 1.20
M: 2 diesels; 2 props; . . . bhp

Note: Used by DCN and DGA (*Direction Generale des Armements*) at Toulon for underwater system trials. DCN operates a large number of miscellaneous launches at Brest and other naval bases.

♦ 1 catamaran weapons trials tender [YAGE]
Bldr: SFCN, Villeneuve-la-Garenne (In serv. 1975)

DCN 72 49453 Pégase

D: 120 tons (fl) **S:** . . . kts **Dim:** 25.00 × 8.00 × 2.20
A: 1 550-mm TT **Electronics:** Radar: . . .
M: 2 diesels; 2 props; 880 bhp **Crew:** 4 tot.

Remarks: Civilian operated and based at the ECAN, St.-Tropez, torpedo trials center. Is assisted by the small GRP-hulled launch *Heraclea* (DCN 72 49443).

SERVICE CRAFT *(continued)*

Pégase (DCN 72 49453) Bernard Prézelin, 2-04

♦ 1 ASW weapons support tender [YAGE]
Bldr: DCN, Toulon (In serv. 15-7-76)

A 743 Denti

Denti (A 743) Guy Schaeffer via Paolo Marsan, 6-05

D: 170 tons (fl) **S:** 12 kts **Dim:** 34.70 (30.00 pp) × 6.60 × 2.27
Electronics: Radar: 1 Decca 1226 nav.; 1 Furuno . . . nav.
M: 2 Baudoouin DNP8 diesels; 2 props; 960 bhp **Electric:** 130 kw tot.
Range: 800/12 **Crew:** 4 tot. + 15 trials technicians

Remarks: Employed by DCN at Toulon in support of weapons trials. Essentially a recovery craft with an overhead rail gantry crane aft. Can carry divers. Painted white. Was to have been retired during 2001 but has been extended in service to 2005.

♦ 5 miscellaneous self-propelled floating cranes [YD]

GFA 1 (In serv. 10-2-64)
GFA 2 Girafe (In serv. 10-2-64)
GFA 3 (In serv. 16-2-63)
GFA 4 Lama (In serv. 27-7-67)
GFA 6 Alpaga (In serv. 12-12-86)

Crane GFA 3—with tug *Sicié* (A 680) H&L Van Ginderen, 10-99

Remarks: Are quite similar but have differing lift capacities of 7.5 to 15 tons maximum. GFA (*Grue Flottante Automotrice*) *Alpaga* (completed 1984 to a different design) and *Girafe* are based at Brest, the others at Toulon. Construction of a new floating crane by DCN Lorient is planned.

Disposal note: Degaussing tender *Station de Démagnétisation No. 3* (Y 732) was retired during 2003.

♦ 1 Alize-class diving tender (YDT)
Bldr: SOCARENAM, Boulogne, France

	Laid down	In serv.
A 760 Alize	01-04	12-05

D: 1,000 tons std., 1,500 tons (fl) **S:** 14 kts **Dim:** 60.0 × 13.0 × 4.0
Electronics: Radar: 1 DRBN-38A (Racal-Decca BridgeMaster 250E) nav.
A: 2 12.7-mm mg
M: 2 diesels; 2 props; 2,800 bhp—1 bow-thruster
Electric: 3 × 150 kW diesel-generators
Range: 7,500/12 **Endurance:** 8 days
Crew: 17 tot., 3 officers, 14 enlisted + 30 passengers

Remarks: Replaced the *Chamois*-class unit *Isard* (A 776). Based at Toulon.

♦ 10 Coralline class diving tenders [YDT]
Bldr: DCN, Lorient

	In serv.		In serv.
A 790 Coralline	5-10-90	Y 794 Magnolia	16-1-96
Y 790 Dionée	9-8-90	Y 795 Ajonc	20-3-96
Y 791 Myosotis	27-8-91	Y 796 Genet	27-7-95
Y 792 Gardénia	17-12-92	Y 797 Giroflée	23-6-96
Y 793 Liseron	16-9-92	Y 798 Acanthe	11-4-96

Gardénia (Y 792) Bernard Prézelin, 7-05

D: 35 tons light (49 fl) **S:** 13 kts **Dim:** 21.70 × 4.90 × 1.60
Electronics: Radar: 1 Furuno . . . nav.—Sonar: Klein . . . towed side-scan
M: 2 diesels; 2 props; 530 bhp **Crew:** 4 tot. (A 790: 7 tot.)

Remarks: A 790 was completed 2-90 as radiological monitoring craft at Cherbourg. Y 790 is currently used as a radiological measurement craft, and Y 791 assigned as training craft at the École de Plongée, while Y 792 and Y 798 serve as training craft for mine-disposal frogmen at Toulon. The others are employed as diving support craft and general-purpose diving tenders at Toulon, Cherbourg, and Brest. All but A 790 carry a two-person decompression chamber and have received Klein towed side-scan sonars for object location and identification (and can therefore act as minefield route clearance craft); they can carry a RIB atop the after superstructure. GRP construction.

♦ 1 combat swimmer diving tender [YDT]

	Bldr	L	In serv.
A 722 Poséidon	SICCNAV, St.-Malo	5-12-74	14-1-77

Poséidon (A 722) Guy Schaeffer via Paolo Marsan, 9-02

D: 200 tons (239 fl) **S:** 13 kts **Dim:** 40.50 (38.50 pp) × 7.20 × 2.20
Electronics: Radar: 1 DRBN-32 (Decca 1226) nav.
M: 1 SACM-Wärtsilä UD30V12 M3 diesel; 1 prop; 820 bhp
Endurance: 8 days **Crew:** 1 officer, 9 petty officers + 23 trainees

Remarks: Used for training combat frogmen. Refitted 1994 and equipped with a large hydraulic crane on the fantail. Based at Toulon. Is scheduled to be retired during 2010.

Note: Small harbor motor launches *Pastenauge* and *Stenella* are used as diving tenders at Brest as are *Girelle* and *Camarétoise* at Cherbourg.

♦ 12 Thomery-class motor lighters [YF]
Bldr: CIB, Brest (In serv. 1987–89)

CHA 27 through 38

D: 20 tons (50 fl) **S:** 7 kts **Dim:** 15.2 × 4.4 × 1.6
M: 1 Poyaud-Wärtsilä UD18L6 M4 diesel; 300 bhp

Remarks: Carry stores and personnel in harbor and roadstead service. Early units (CHA 1–26) were converted LCM(3) landing craft; later units were built for the purpose but use bow ramps recycled from stricken landing craft. CHA 27–34 were completed in 1988, 35–38 in 1989.
Disposals: CHA 8, 14, 17, and 19 were retired during 1994–95, and CHA 23 (*Telgruc*), CHA 24 (*Tévennec*), and CHA 25 (*Lambézellec*) in 2002.

SERVICE CRAFT *(continued)*

CHA 32 Bernard Prézelin, 7-05

♦ 5 Ariel-class coastal personnel transports [YFB]
Bldr: Y 613, 662: SFCN, Villeneuve-la-Garenne; others: DCN, Brest

	L		L
Y 613 Faune	8-9-71	Y 701 Ondine	4-10-79
Y 662 Dryade	10-12-72	Y 702 Naiade	4-10-79
Y 700 Néréide	17-2-77		

Naiade (Y 702) Bernard Prézelin, 8-04

D: 195 tons (225 fl) **S:** 15 kts **Dim:** 40.50 × 7.45 × 3.30
Electronics: Radar: 1 DRBN-32 nav.
M: 2 SACM-Wärtsilä UD30V12 M3 diesels; 2 props; 1,730 bhp
Range: 940/14 **Crew:** 9 tot. + 400 passengers (250 seated)

Remarks: Based at Brest, except Y 702 at Toulon. No replacement program has been announced.
Disposals: *Ariel* (Y 604) was stricken during 1999, *Korrigan* (Y 661) during 2001, and *Alphée* (Y 696) and *Elfe* (Y 741) during 2003. Y 613 and Y 662 are to retire in 2005, Y 700 and Y 701 in 2007, and Y 702 in 2010.

♦ 1 Merlin-class coastal personnel transport [YFB] (In reserve)
Bldr: C.N. Franco-Belges (L: 14-6-73)

Y 671 Morgane

Morgane (Y 671) Guy Schaeffer via Paolo Marsan, 8-04

D: 133 tons (170 fl) **S:** 11 kts **Dim:** 31.50 × 7.06 × 2.40
M: 2 Poyaud-Wärtsilä UD6150 M1 diesels; 2 props; 960 bhp **Crew:** . . . tot.

Remarks: In reserve at Toulon and planned for disposal during 2004. No radar. Carries up to 400 passengers. Sisters *Merlin* (Y 735) and *Mélusine* (Y 736) were stricken in 1998. Y 671 is scheduled for retirement in 2004.

♦ 1 floating dry dock [YFDL] (In serv. 1975)

Remarks: Capacity: 3,500 tons. Based at Papeete.

♦ 2 Gouandour-class personnel launches [YFL]
Bldr: DCN, Lorient

Y 766 Rostellec (L: 3-01) Y 767 Gouandour (L: 7-00)

D: 25 tons **S:** . . . kts **Dim:** 16.50 × 4.65 × . . .
M: 2 . . . diesels; 2 props; . . . bhp

Remarks: GRP hull. Can carry 45 passengers. Y 766 is based at Lorient.

Rostellec (Y 766) Bernard Prézelin, 4-04

♦ 1 Surf-class service launch [YFL]
Bldr: . . . (In serv. 1990)

Y 789 Haari

D: 9 tons (fl) **S:** 25 kts **Dim:** 13.00 × 4.00 × 0.70
M: 2 diesels; 2 waterjets; . . . bhp **Crew:** 3 tot.

Remarks: GRP-hulled craft with rigid inflatable fenders on hull sides, built for the Muraroa nuclear test range. Sisters *Mamanu* (Y 752) and *Burao* (Y 788) were transferred to Morocco during 10-99.

Note: In service at Papeete is the catamaran service launch *Vaimiti* (Y 757); no data available.

♦ 13 Type V 14 service launches [YFL]
Bldrs: A: Sibiril, Carantec; B: Stento, Balaruc-les-Bains

	Bldr	In serv.		Bldr	In serv.
Y 754 Taina	A	22-2-91	Y 779	B	17-3-88
Y 762 Étoile de Mer	A	29-8-91	Y 780	A	6-93
Y 763 Dharuba	A	17-12-90	Y 781	B	25-6-88
P 764	A	19-4-88	Y 786 Aute	A	18-6-91
Y 765 Avel Mor	A	15-2-92	Y 787 Tiaré	B	20-3-87
Y 776	B	8-1-88	P 790 Vétiver	B	7-5-87
Y 777 Palingrin	B	1-4-88			

Palingrin (Y 777) Bernard Prézelin, 2-04

Y 781—pilot boat variant Guy Schaeffer via Paolo Marsan, 12-03

D: 16 tons (20 fl) **S:** 20 kts **Dim:** 14.60 (13.20 pp) × 4.60 × 1.90
A: Y 763, P 790 *only:* 1 12.7-mm mg
Electronics: Radar: 1 Decca 060 , Raytheon . . ., or Furuno . . . nav.
M: 2 Baudouin 12 F 11S diesels; 2 props; 800 bhp
Range: 360/18 **Crew:** 4 tot.

SERVICE CRAFT *(continued)*

Remarks: GRP hulls. Can carry a RIB inspection dinghy on davits at the stern. Y 763, P 764, and P 790 are classed as *Vedettes de Servitude Citière* (VSC); Y 779, Y 780, and Y 781 as *Vedettes de Pilotage* (VP); Y 754, Y 786, and Y 787 as *Vedettes de Servitude et de Transport de Personnel* (VSTP); Y 762 and Y 765 as *Vedettes de Servitude et de Transport d'Autorités* (VSTA); and Y 776 and Y 777 as *Vedettes de Surveillance Radiologique* (VSR). The last two have modified superstructures with the pilothouse farther forward. Y 786–787 are based at Mururoa and Papeete and have extended passenger cabins. Y 780 and Y 781 have two 500-bhp diesels and can make 23 kts. Seven near-sisters serve as patrol boats, and three others are equipped as fireboats. Pilot boat *Miri* (Y 755) was reclassified as a patrol launch and renumbered P 755 in 2002. P 790 was transferred to the local government at Mayotte in 1997 but returned to French Navy control in 2002.

♦ 2 weapons-range safety patrol boats [YFL]
Bldrs: C.N. de L'Estérel, Cannes

	L	In serv.
A 712 Athos	20-11-79	22-11-79
A 713 Aramis	9-9-80	22-9-80

Athos (A 712) Bernard Prézelin, 1-05

D: 80 tons (108 fl) **S:** 28 kts **Dim:** 32.10 × 6.50 × 1.90 (2.10 max.)
A: 1 12.7-mm mg **Electronics:** Radar: 1 Decca . . . or Furuno nav.
M: 2 SACM-Wärtsilä Type 195 V12 diesels; 2 props; 4,640 bhp
Electric: 80 kw tot. **Range:** 1,200/15
Crew: 1 officer, 12 enlisted (including 6 divers)

Remarks: Typed *Vedettes de Surveillance des Sites* (VSS). Based at Bayonne for use at the Landes Test Center, both as range safety craft and for weapons recovery duties. Wooden hulls. The 20-mm AA was replaced by a machinegun during 2002. To be retired in 2010.

Note: Numerous other small launches [YFL] are used for harbor service to transport stores and personnel and to support divers. DP 23 through DP 25 are based at Brest, along with EN 1 and EN 2, which are assigned to the Poulmic Naval School.

♦ 1 small mooring-buoy tender [YGL]
Bldr: IMC, Rochefort-sur-Mer

	L	In serv.
Y 692 Telenn Mor	4-4-85	16-1-86

Telenn Mor (Y 692) Bernard Prézelin, 2-04

D: 518 tons (fl) **S:** 8 kts **Dim:** 41.40 (37.00 pp) × 9.10 × 1.88
Electronics: Radar: 1 . . . nav.
M: 2 diesels; 2 Saver thrusters; 900 bhp **Electric:** 350 kw tot. **Crew:** 10 tot.

Remarks: Based at Brest. Has fixed lift-horns at the bow and a heavy electrohydraulic crane amidships. Can also be used for salvage work. Due for replacement in 2016.

Disposal note: Mooring-buoy tender *Calmar* (Y 698) was retired during 2003.

♦ 1 remote-controlled target craft [YGT]
Bldr: DCN, Lorient (L: 9-7-01)

Ness Thor

D: 135 tons **S:** 10 kts **Dim:** 39.0 × 6,50 × . . .
M: 2 diesels, electric drive; 2 azimuthal props; 560 bhp

Remarks: Employed by the Centre d'Essais de la Méditerranée at the Île du Levant range.

♦ 1 La Prudente–class mooring-buoy tender [YNG]
Bldr: A&C La Rochelle-Pallice (In serv. 3-3-69)

Y 750 La Persévérante

La Persévérante (Y 750) Guy Schaeffer via Paolo Marsan, 6-05

D: 446 tons (626 fl) **S:** 10 kts **Dim:** 43.50 (42.00 pp) × 10.00 × 2.80
Electronics: Radar: 1 Decca RM-914 nav.
M: 2 Baudouin . . . diesels, electric drive; 1 prop; 620 shp
Electric: 440 kw **Range:** 4,000/10 **Crew:** 6 tot.

Remarks: Employed as a mooring-buoy tender at Toulon. Lifting is performed via a pivoting gantry mounted at the bow. Was to have been retired during 2001 but has been extended until 2008 at Toulon with a much-reduced crew (earlier carried 1 officer, 8 petty officers, and 21 nonrated men). Sister *La Prudente* (Y 749) was stricken during 2001, and *La Fidèle* (Y 751) sank on 30-4-97 after an explosion.

Disposal note: Single-unit mooring-buoy tender *Tupa* (Y 667) was stricken during 2000.

♦ . . . liquid cargo lighters [YON/YSR/YW]

Lighters CIE 27 (Water), CIEM 36 and 35 (Sludge) Christian Peron via Paolo Marsan, 10-01

Remarks: Nos. 5 and 6 in Tahiti, No. 2 at Brest, Nos. 1 and 11 at Toulon, No. 12 at Lorient, others at the CEP (*Centre d'Expérimentation Pacifique*). Eleven are configured as fuel lighters (CIC), eight as sludge barges (CIEM 30–37), two are 400-ton pollution storage barges (CIEP 1 and 2), and six as water lighters (CIE). Some are not self-propelled.

♦ 2 Esterel-class coastal tugs [YTB]
Bldr: SOCARENAM, Boulogne

	Laid down	L	In serv.
A 641 Esterel (ex-Y 601)	15-4-01	16-11-01	27-3-02
A 642 Luberon (ex-Y 602)	19-11-01	26-4-02	4-7-02

Esterel (A 641) Bernard Prézelin, 8-04

D: 510 tons (670 fl) **S:** 10 kts **Dim:** 36.30 (33.00 wl) × 11.45 × 5.00
Electronics: Radar: 1 Furuno . . . nav.
M: 2 ABC 8DZ1000.179 diesels, electric drive; 2 Voith-Schneider vertical cycloidal props; 5,120 shp
Electric: 465 kw tot. **Range:** 1,500/10 **Crew:** 8 tot.

Remarks: Ordered 15-12-00. Intended to support the carrier *Charles de Gaulle* at Toulon. Have 50-ton initial bollard pull. The hull has five watertight compartments. Have a single firefighting water monitor forward and are equipped with Inmarsat Mini-M SATCOM. Were renumbered during 2003.

SERVICE CRAFT *(continued)*

♦ 16 Type RPC 12 large harbor tugs [YTB]
Bldrs: A: LNI (Ch. La Perriere/Leroux & Lotz), Lorient;
B: SOCARENAM, Boulogne

	Bldr:	In serv.	Based
Coastal service:			
A 675 Fréhel	A	23-5-89	Cherbourg
A 676 Saire	A	6-10-89	Cherbourg
A 677 Armen	A	6-12-91	Brest
A 678 La Houssaye	A	30-10-92	Lorient
A 679 Kéréon (ex-*Sicié*)	A	5-12-92	Brest
A 680 Sicié	A	6-10-94	Toulon
A 681 Taunoa	B	9-3-96	Toulon
A 682 Rascas	B	22-11-03	Cherbourg
Harbor service:			
Y 638 Lardier	B	12-4-95	Toulon
Y 639 Giens	B	2-12-94	Toulon
Y 640 Mengam	B	6-10-94	Toulon
Y 641 Balaguier	B	8-7-95	Toulon
Y 642 Taillat	B	18-10-95	Toulon
Y 643 Nividic	B	13-12-96	Brest
Y 647 Le Four	B	13-3-98	Brest
Y 649 Port-Cros	B	21-6-97	Brest

Nividic (Y 643)—note water cannon forward of bridge Bernard Prézelin, 7-05

D: 220 tons (259 fl) **S:** 11 kts (10 sust.) **Dim:** 25.00 (23.50 pp) × 8.40 × 2.20
Electronics: Radar: 1 Decca . . . nav.
M: 2 SACM-Wärtsilä UD30V12 M3 diesels; 2 Voith-Schneider 18 GII/115 vertical cycloidal props: 1,360 bhp
Electric: 195 kw (3 × 65-kw diesel alternator sets)
Range: 800/10 **Fuel:** 32 m^3 **Crew:** A-pennants: 8 tot.—Y-pennants: 5 tot.

Remarks: General type is RPC = *Remorqueur Portuaire et Cotier.* Units with "A"-pennants are classed as coastal tugs (*remorqueurs cîtiers*) and units with "Y"-pennants are dockyard tugs (*remorqueuer de rade ci-après*). The French Navy has requested funds to begin building seven additional units.
Hull systems: Equipped with firefighting water cannon that can spray 3,400 liters/min and a 4,000-liter emulsion tank. Have a 12-ton bollard pull hydraulic towing winch with 140 m of cable.

♦ 3 Maito-class large harbor tugs [YTB]
Bldr: SFCN, Villeneuve-la-Garenne

	Laid down	L	In serv.
A 636 Maito	24-6-83	6-1-84	27-2-84
A 637 Maroa	30-8-83	20-1-84	30-3-84
A 638 Manini	15-11-84	19-4-85	12-9-85

Maito (A 636) Bernard Prézelin, 5-03

D: 228 tons light (280 fl) **S:** 11 kts **Dim:** 27.60 (24.50 wl) × 8.90 × 3.50
Electronics: Radar: 1 Decca RM 914 nav.
M: 2 SACM-Wärtsilä UD30L6 M6 diesels; 2 Voith-Schneider vertical cycloidal props; 1,280 bhp
Range: 1,200/11 **Crew:** 6 tot. + 4 passengers

Remarks: Built for service at Muraroa for DIRCEN. A 636, based at Brest since 1998, was transferred to Fort-de-France in 10-03. The other two remain at Papeete. Bollard pull: 12 tons. Have a firefighting water cannon. Are fully seagoing.

♦ 3 Bélier-class large harbor tugs [YTB]
Bldr: DCN, Cherbourg

	L	In serv.
A 695 Bélier	4-12-79	25-7-80
A 696 Buffle	18-1-80	19-7-80
A 697 Bison	20-11-80	16-4-81

Bison (A 697) Bernard Prézelin, 1-04

D: 356 tons light (500 fl) **S:** 11 kts **Dim:** 31.78 (29.00 pp) × 9.24 × 4.30
Electronics: Radar: 1 Decca RM 914C nav.
M: 2 SACM-Wärtsilä UD33V12 M4 diesels, electric drive; 2 Voith-Schneider vertical cycloidal props; 2,600 bhp
Electric: 160 kw tot. **Crew:** 1 officer, 7 petty officers, 4 nonrated

Remarks: Bollard pull: 25 tons. Have one firefighting monitor atop pilothouse. All based at Toulon. Were intended to last 30 years in service.

♦ 1 Actif-group large harbor tug [YTB]

	Bldr	In serv.
A 693 Acharné	C.N. La Perrière, Lorient	5-7-74

Acharné (A 693) Guy Schaeffer via Paolo Marsan, 6-03

D: 226 tons light (288 fl) **S:** 11.8 kts **Dim:** 28.3 (25.3 pp) × 7.9 × 4.3
Electronics: Radar: 1 Decca 914C nav.
M: 1 SACM-Wärtsilä UD30V16 M3 diesel; 1,100 bhp **Range:** 4,100/11
Crew: 12 tot.

Remarks: Bollard pull: 17 tons. Was to have been retired in 2003 but has been extended to 2010.
Disposals: *Hercule* (A 667), *Robuste* (A 685), and *Valeureux* (A 688) were stricken in 1993; *Courageux* in 1980; *Actif* (A 686) in 7-95; *Laborieux* (A 687) in 1998; and *L'Utile* (A 672), *Lutteur* (A 673), and *Efficace* (A 694) in 1999. *Le Fort* (A 671) and *Travailleur* (A 692) were retired during 2002.

♦ 4 RP-10-class medium-harbor tugs [YTM]
Bldr.: SOCARENAM, Boulogne, France (In serv. 5-10-05)

Y 770 Morse	Y 772 Loutre
Y 771 Otarie	Y 773 Phoque

SERVICE CRAFT *(continued)*

Phoque (Y 773) Bernard Prézelin, 6-05

D: 83.2 tons std., 96.7 tons (fl) **S:** 11 kts **Dim:** 15.55 × 6.40 × 2.10
Electronics: Radar: 1 DRBN-39A (Furuno M1832) nav.
M: 2 Baudoin 6R123SR diesels, 2 prop., 850 bhp **Range:** 4,100/11
Crew: 4 tot.

Remarks: Bollard pull: 10 tons. *Morse* replaced *Papayer* (Y 740) at Cherbourg. The three others are based at Toulon.

♦ 4 PSS 10–class push-tugs for ballistic-missile submarines [YTM]

Bldr: Lorient-Naval Industries, Lorient (In serv. 7-93)

102 103 104 105

Push-tug 102 Bernard Prézelin, 7-04

D: 44 tons light **S:** 6 kts **Dim:** 17.00 (15.9 pp) × 6.4 × 2.4
M: 2 Poyaud-Wärtsilä UD25L6 M4 diesels; 2 cycloidal props; 456 bhp (440 sust.)
Crew: 2 tot.

Remarks: Were to have been completed in 1989 by La Perriere, Lorient; contract taken over by new operators of the building facility. Have a hydraulically powered quadrantial push-fender at the bow.

Disposal note: The four earlier push-tugs for ballistic-missile submarine support—P 1, P 2, P 3 (*Monde*), and P 4 (*Oursin*)—were reportedly stricken during 2002–3, though reports indicate that P 1 and P 2 may still be operational.

♦ 29 P 4–class port-service push-tugs [YTM]

Bldr: La Perriere, Lorient, and DCN, Lorient (In serv. 1976–97)

2 3 4 6 13 through 24 26 through 38

Push-tug 22 Bernard Prézelin, 5-04

D: 24 tons (fl) **S:** 9.2 kts **Dim:** 11.50 (11.25 wl) × 4.30 × 1.45
M: 2 Poyaud-Wärtsilä UD18V8 M1 (2–6: UD6PZ M1) diesels; 2 props; 456 bhp (440 bhp sust.)
Range: 191/9.1, 560/8 **Fuel:** 1.7 tons **Crew:** 3 tot.

Remarks: For dockyard use. Primarily for pushing, but have 4.1-ton bollard pull (hence the “P 4–class” designation). No names or NATO pennant numbers assigned, and the “P” prefix to the side number has been dropped. 2 through 18 were completed 1976–83, the others in 1989–97. P 25 was stricken 15-5-96 after colliding with *Rari* (A 634). Sister 11 was transferred to the Ivory Coast in 9-99. Four others were retired during 2002–3.

Disposal note: The final remaining Acajou-class medium harbour tug, *Papayer* (Y 740), was decomissioned in 2005, as were Bonite-class tugs *Bonite* (Y 630) and *Rouget* (Y 634).

♦ 1 Aigrette-class small harbor tugs [YTL]

Y 636 Martinet (In serv. 6-72)

Mésange (Y 621)—since retired Guy Schaeffer via Paolo Marsan, 3-04

D: 56 tons (64 fl) **S:** 9 kts **Dim:** 18.40 × 5.70 × 2.50
M: 1 Poyaud-Wärtsilä UD8150 M1 diesel; 1 prop; 250 bhp
Range: 1,700/9 **Crew:** 4 tot.

Remarks: Built during early 1960s. Have two-letter contractions of names, “MS” and “MA,” on bows instead of official pennant numbers. Bollard pull capacity: 3.5 tons. Y 621 in expected to retire in 2007.
Disposals: *Ibis* (Y 658) is on loan to Senegal. *Cigogne* (Y 625), *Cygne* (Y 632), *Alouette* (720), *Sarcelle* (Y 724), and *Vanneau* (Y 722) were stricken in 1993; *Moineau* (Y 673), *Pinson* (Y 691), *Passereau* (Y 687), and *Toucan* (Y 726) in 1994; *Bengali* (Y 611), *Engoulevent* (Y 723), *Fauvette* (Y 687), *Goéland* (Y 648), *Macreuse* (Y 727), *Marabout* (Y 725), *Martin-Pecheur* (Y 675), and *Pivert* (Y 694) during 1996–97; *Ara* (Y 730) in 1998; and *Colibri* (Y 628), *Gélinotte* (Y 748), *Grand-duc* (Y 728), *Loriot* (Y 747), and *Merle* (Y 670) during 1999. *Mouette* (Y 617) and *Eider* (Y 729) were retired during 2002–3 and *Mesange* (Y-621) in 2005.

♦ 3 Type V 14 small fireboats [YTR]

Bldr: Alain Sibiril, Carentec

Y 783 Elorn (In serv. 12-4-94)
Y 784 La Loude (In serv. 25-2-94)
Y 785 La Divette (In serv. 24-11-93)

La Loude (Y 784)—painted red Guy Schaeffer via Paolo Marsan, 9-05

D: 14 tons light (23.5 fl) **S:** 17 kts **Dim:** 14.60 (13.20 pp) × 4.60 × 1.90
Electronics: Radar: 1 Raytheon . . . nav.
M: 2 Baudouin V6T diesels; 2 props; 750 bhp **Crew:** 6 tot.

Remarks: Have two fire monitors, each with a 150-m^3/hr pump and a range of 120 m. Same GRP hull and basic superstructure as Type V 14 patrol boats and service launches. Are painted all red. Three more are planned to be built to replace the *Cascade* class.

♦ 2 Cascade-class fireboats [YTR]

Bldr: SFCN, Villeneuve-la-Garenne

Y 745 Aiguière (In serv. 29-10-69) Y 746 Embrun (In serv. 4-4-69)

SERVICE CRAFT *(continued)*

Embrun (Y 746)—note water cannon forward and atop the bridge
Bernard Prézelin, 7-05

D: 81 tons (fl) **S:** 11 kts **Dim:** 23.8 × 5.3 × 1.7
M: 1 Poyaud-Wärtsilä UD6PZ M1 diesel; 1 prop; 400 bhp **Crew:** 7 tot.

Remarks: Have two fire monitors atop the pilothouse, one atop the foremast, and one on a folding mast aft. Painted red with white superstructure. Planned to strike in 2006.
Disposals: *Geyser* (Y 646) was stricken in 1993, *Gave* (Y 645) and *Oued* (Y 684) in 1994, *Cascade* (Y 618) in 1996; *Aiguière* (Y 745) was to have been retired during 2001 but has remained in use.

♦ 2 auxiliary sail-training barkentines [YTS]
Bldr: Chantiers de Normandie, Fécamp

A 649 Étoile (L: 7-7-32)
A 650 Belle Poule (L: 8-2-32)

Belle Poule (A 650) Bernard Prézelin, 2-05

D: 227 tons (275 fl) **S:** 9 kts under power
Dim: 40.45 (37.50 hull, 32.25 pp) × 7.40 × 3.65
Electronics: Radar: 1 Furuno . . . nav.
M: 1 Baudouin diesel; 300 bhp—450 m^2 max. sail area
Crew: 1 officer, 11 petty officers, 8 ratings + 20 cadets

Remarks: Assigned to the naval academy. Oregon pine hull construction. The tallest mast is 32.50 m high. A 650 given major refit 11-93 to 16-5-94; received new 300-bhp diesel, increased powered speed to 9 kts; A 649 similarly refitted.

♦ 1 sail-training yawl [YTS]
Bldr: Fidèle, Marseilles (L: 1932)

A 653 La Grande Hermine (ex-*LaRoute Est Belle,* ex-*Ménestrel*)

D: 7 tons (13 fl) **S:** 7 kts (sail) **Dim:** 14.00 (12.78 wl) × 4.10 × 2.00
Electronics: Radar: 1 Koden . . . nav.
M: 1 MWM D 225A diesel; 1 prop; 55 bhp; 142 m^2 max. sail area
Crew: 7 tot.

Remarks: Purchased in 1964 for the reserve officers' school and now used by the Centre d'Instruction Naval at Brest. Wooden construction.

La Grande Hermine (A 653) Bernard Prézelin, 6-05

♦ 1 sail-training ketch [YTS]
Bldr: Florimond-Guignardeau, Sables-d'Olonne (L: 18-3-27)

A 652 Mutin

Mutin (A 652) Ralph Edwards, 6-02

D: 42 tons (57 fl) **S:** 11 kts (sail) **Dim:** 33.00 (21.00 wl) × 6.35 × 3.40 (1.50 fwd)
Electronics: Radar: 1 Furuno . . . nav.
M: 1 Baudouin 6-cyl. diesel; 1 prop; 112 bhp—312 m^2 max. sail area.
Electric: 10 kw tot. **Range:** 585/6 (diesel) **Crew:** 12 tot. crew + 13 trainees

Remarks: Assigned to the annex of the seamanship school. Mainmast is 21 m tall.

SERVICE CRAFT *(continued)*

♦ 2 Glycine-class navigational training craft [YXT]
Bldr: SOCARENAM, Boulogne-sur-Mer

	Laid down	L	In serv.
A 770 Glycine	8-91	1992	11-4-92
A 771 Eglantine	11-91	1992	9-9-92

Glycine (A 770) Bernard Prézelin, 5-05

D: 250 tons (295 fl) **S:** 10 kts **Dim:** 28.30 (24.50 pp) × 7.70 × 3.75
A: None **Electronics:** Radar: 1 Furuno . . . nav.
M: 1 Baudouin 12B152 S5 diesel; 1 CP prop; 800 bhp—150-shp bow-thruster
Electric: 175 kVA tot (115-kVA shaft generator, 1 × 60-kVA Deutz D 226 B6 diesel set)
Range: 3,600/10 **Fuel:** 49 m^3 **Crew:** 10 ship's company + 16 cadets

Remarks: 270 grt. Trawler-hulled craft built to replace *Engageante* (A 772) and *Vigilante* (A 773), which were stricken during 1992. Typed BIN (*Bâtiment d' Instruction à la Navigation*). Carry a single Zodiac RIB. Three near-sisters listed under mine warfare ships are styled BINRS (*Bâtiment d'Instruction à la Navigation et de Remorquage de Sonar*) in the dual role of training craft and to tow a DUBM-41B minehunting side-scan sonar; another serves as the DCN ASW systems trials craft *L'Aventurière II.*

♦ 8 Léopard-class navigational training craft [YXT]

	Bldr	Laid down	L	In serv.
A 748 Léopard	SICNAV, St.-Malo	6-4-81	4-6-81	4-12-82
A 749 Panthère	SICNAV, St.-Malo	9-6-81	3-9-81	4-12-82
A 750 Jaguar	SICNAV, St.-Malo	27-9-81	29-10-81	18-12-82
A 751 Lynx	La Perriere, Lorient	23-7-81	27-2-82	18-12-82
A 752 Guépard	SICNAV, St.-Malo	11-10-82	1-12-82	1-7-83
A 753 Chacal	SFCN, Villeneuve-la-Garenne	11-10-82	11-2-83	10-9-83
A 754 Tigre	La Perriere, Lorient	16-4-82	8-10-82	1-7-83
A 755 Lion	La Perriere, Lorient	21-2-82	13-12-82	10-9-83

Tigre (A 754) Bernard Prézelin, 2-05

D: 335 tons (460 fl) **S:** 15 kts **Dim:** 43.00 (40.15 pp) × 8.30 × 3.21
A: 2 single 12.7-mm M2 mg
Electronics: Radar: 1 DRBN-32 (Decca 1226) or Decca . . . nav.
M: 2 SACM-Wärtsilä UD30V16 M3 (75 V16 ASHR) diesels; 2 props; 2,200 bhp
Electric: 160 kw tot. **Range:** 4,100/12
Crew: 1 officer, 10 petty officers, 4 ratings + 2 officer instructors, 2 petty officer instructors, 18 trainees

Remarks: First four authorized 1980, second group 1981. Also for use as antipollution patrol vessels if required. Were intended to serve for 25–30 years each. The original 20-mm Oerlikon AA guns were replaced by machineguns during 2003.

♦ 2 training tenders [YXT]
Bldr: Ch. Bayonne (In serv. 1971)

Y 706 Chimère Y 711 Farfadet

D: 100 tons **S:** 11 kts **Dim:** 30.50 × 5.25 × 1.75
Electronics: Radar: 1 DRBN-34A nav. **M:** 1 diesel; 200 bhp

Remarks: Used by the training facility at Poulmic for training in basic seamanship. Were due for disposal in 2000 but have been extended to 2010.

Chimère (Y 706) Bernard Prézelin, 2-04

FRENCH ARMY

The Armée de Terre 519th Régiment du Train operates several small units and landing craft at La Rochelle.

PATROL BOATS [WPB]

♦ 1 Cassiopée class
Bldr: Arcor (In serv. . . .)

D 300098 Cassiopée

Cassiopée (D 300098) Bernard Prézelin, 9-03

D: . . . tons **S:** 24 kts **Dim:** 14.0 × 3.90 × . . .
A: small arms **Electronics:** Radar: 1 Raytheon . . . nav.
M: 2 . . . diesels; 2 props; 560 bhp

♦ 1 Type E 400052
Bldr: PechAlu, Hennebont (In serv. 8-94)

E 400052 Andromède

Andromède (E 400052) Bernard Prézelin, 6-02

D: . . . tons **S:** 23 kts **Dim:** 14.50 (13.00 pp) × 5.10 × 1.35
M: 2 diesels; 2 CP props; 710 bhp **Crew:** 12 tot.

Remarks: Used to train army divers; based at La Pallice.

AMPHIBIOUS WARFARE CRAFT

♦ 6 U.S. LCM(8)-class landing craft [WLCM]
Bldr: CMN, Cherbourg (In serv. . . .)

CTM 12 through 17

D: 56 tons (150 fl) **S:** 9.5 kts **Dim:** 23.80 × 6.35 × 1.17
M: 2 Poyaud-Wärtsilä UD18V8 M1 diesels; 2 props; 450 bhp
Range: 380/8 **Crew:** 4 tot.

Remarks: Essentially identical to the French Navy version, but have an enclosed conning station atop the pilothouse. Operated by the French Army Transport Corps and based at La Pallice.

AMPHIBIOUS WARFARE CRAFT *(continued)*

CTM 14—alongside sisters, note conning station atop pilothouse
Bernard Prézelin, 9-03

Note: In use by the French Army at Abidjan, Sierre Leone, is the locally built landing craft *Camou,* completed in 1998; no data available.

♦ 14 U.S. Army LARC XV–class amphibious landing craft [WLCP]

LARC XV-57 through LARC XV-68 LARC XV-70 LARC XV-71

D: 20.8 tons light (35.7 fl) **S:** 8.25 kts water/29.5 mph land
Dim: 13.72 × 4.42 × 4.75 (high, on land) **M:** 2 diesels; 1 prop; 600 bhp
Range: 45/8.25 water, 300/29.5 mph land **Crew:** 2 tot.

Remarks: U.S. Army Design 8004 craft transferred during late 1950s. Four-tired vehicles, each with 15-ton payload, unloading ramp. LARC XV-58 is named *Aflou* and -64 *Fort Boyard.*

AFFAIRES MARITIMES
MARITIME POLICE

Administered by the Ministry of Equipment and Transport for the enforcement of maritime laws and regulations. The patrol-series craft are divided into two categories: the flotilla of six 28-m to 46-m craft categorized as *Vedettes Régionales de Surveillance* that are employed to cover the 200-n.m. economic exclusion zone, and the 19 craft for littoral service (*Vedettes de Surveillance Rapprochée*). Also in use are a large number of launches ranging from 7 m to 17 m in length. Except for the officers (who serve on land and are commissioned) the personnel are civilians. Patrol craft and boat hull numbers begin with PM (*Police Maritime*). Also operated by the Affaires Marines in conjunction with the Gens de Mer (DAMGM) are a number of navigational aids tenders that also perform pollution-control duties. All units are painted gray, with blue hull sides aft and diagonal blue-white-red stripes separating the gray and blue regions of the hull sides. Navigational aids tenders carry the words "Phares & Balises" one the sides of the superstructure and have all-gray hulls with the usual stripes, except for the new *Armorique,* which has the stern area painted blue, as on patrol units.

PATROL CRAFT [WPC]

♦ 1 Themis class
Bldr: CMN, Cherbourg (In serv. 7-04)

PM 41 Themis

Themis (PM 41) Paolo Marsan, 11-04

D: 409 tons **S:** 21 kts **Dim:** 52.50 × 9.00 × 2.27
A: 1 12.7-mm mg **Electronics:** Radar: . . .
M: 2 16 MTU 4000 M70 diesels; 2 props; 6,310 bhp
Range: 3,000/12 **Crew:** 15 tot. + 4 passengers

Remarks: Ordered 27-11-02. Employs the same hull form as the French Navy's P 400 patrol craft. Has fin stabilizers and carries two 6-m RIB inspection launches, each powered by a 130-bhp gasoline outboard. Replaced the *Tourne-Pierre* (PM 28) at Cherbourg. A second may be built for Mediterranean service.

PATROL BOATS [WPB]

Regional Surveillance Craft: (*Vedettes Régionales de Surveillance*)

♦ 1 DCN 32-meter class
Bldr: DCN, Lorient (In serv. 25-8-95)

PM 32 Armoise (Based at St.-Nazaire)

Armoise (PM 32) Paolo Marsan, 6-05

D: 73 tons (91 fl) **S:** 23 kts **Dim:** 31.15 (30.50 wl) × 6.100 × 1.80
A: 1 7.5-mm mg
Electronics: Radar: 1 Decca C180/6 nav.; 1 Raytheon R20XX nav.
M: 2 MWM-Deutz TBD234V15 diesels; 2 props; 3,000 bhp—1 MWM-Deutz TBD234V16 diesel; 1 waterjet; 680 bhp
Electric: 70 kw tot. **Range:** 1,200/16 **Crew:** 9 tot.

Remarks: GRP hull. A sister to the Gendarmerie Maritime patrol boats *Géranium* (P 720) and *Violette* (P 722).

♦ 1 Origan class
Bldr: DCN, Lorient (In serv. 5-7-93)

PM 31 Origan (Based at Boulogne)

Origan (PM 31) Paolo Marsan, 10-04

D: 70 tons (84 fl) **S:** 22 kts **Dim:** 28.00 × 5.50 × 1.60 (1.20 hull)
A: 1 7.5-mm mg
Electronics: Radar: 1 Decca . . . nav.; 1 Furuno . . . nav.
M: 2 MWM-Deutz . . . diesels; 2 props; 2,100 bhp—1 MWM-Deutz TBD234V16 diesel; 1 waterjet; 680 bhp
Range: 1,200/16 **Endurance:** 80 hours **Crew:** 9 tot.

♦ 1 Iris class
Bldr: C.N. de l'Esterel, Cannes (L: 21-12-88)

PM 40 Iris (ex-P 696) (Based at Lorient)

Iris (PM 40)—with SATCOM antenna radome Paolo Marsan, 9-03

MARITIME POLICE PATROL BOATS [WPB] *(continued)*

D: 210 tons (230 fl) **S:** 23 kts **Dim:** 45.80 × 8.50 × 2.25
A: 1 12.7-mm mg **Electronics:** Radar: 2 Furuno . . . nav.
M: 2 MTU 16V396 TB83 diesels; 2 props; 4,000 bhp
Electric: 300 kw tot. **Range:** 3,000/13 **Crew:** 15 tot.

Remarks: Built for Thales (then Thomson-CSF) as a sales demonstrator for weapons systems. Operated by the French Navy from 1990 to 1993, when she was placed in reserve. Acquired by the *Affaires Maritimes* in 1996. Has had medical facilities and two RIB inspection launches added. Has Vosper fin stabilizers. Propulsion plant is highly automated.

♦ 1 Gabian class Bldr: C.N. de l'Esterel, Cannes (In serv. 1986)

PM 30 Gabian (Based at La Rochelle)

Gabian (PM 30) Guy Schaeffer via Paolo Marsan, 7-03

D: 76 tons (fl) **S:** 23 kts **Dim:** 32.10 × 6.46 × 3.03 (molded depth)
A: 1 12.7-mm mg **Electronics:** Radar: 1 . . . nav.
M: 2 Baudouin diesels; 2 props; 900 bhp
Range: 1,280/15 **Endurance:** 100 hours **Crew:** 8 tot.

Disposal note: The *A.E.C. Ancelle*–class patrol boat *Patron Louis Renet* (PM 26) was retired during 2002 and *Tourne-Pierre*–class patrol boat *Tourne-Pierre* (PM 28) was retired in 2004.

♦ 1 Mauve class Bldr: C.N. de L'Estérel, Cannes (In serv. 1984)

PM 29 Mauve (Based at Bayonne)

Mauve (PM 29) Guy Schaeffer via Paolo Marsan, 9-04

D: 65 tons (fl) **S:** 26 kts **Dim:** 30.50 × 5.70 × 2.78 molded depth
A: 1 12.7-mm mg; 1 7.5-mm mg **Electronics:** Radar: 1 . . . nav.
M: 2 MWM-Deutz diesels; 2 props; 2,120 bhp
Range: 900/15.5 **Endurance:** 61 hours **Crew:** 9 tot.

Remarks: Re-engined in 1990. Sister to the Customs Service's *Avel Gwalarn* (DF 41) and *Suroît* (DF 42).

♦ 1 Osiris class

Osiris (ex-*Lince*)

D: . . . **S:** . . . **Dim:** 53 × 11 × . . .
M: . . . diesels; props; . . . bhp
Range: . . . / . . . **Crew:** 10 tot.

Remarks: Former Mauritian flagged vessel seized in 1-03, converted and entered service with Affaires Maritimes in 12-03.

Inshore Surveillance Craft (*Vedettes de Surveillance Rapprochée*):

♦ 4 FPB 50 Mk 2 class
Bldr: Océa, Les Sables d'Olonne

	In serv.	Based at
PM 100 Calisto	27-4-01	Ajaccio
PM 101 Deimos	27-4-01	Sète
PM 102 Telesto	18-5-01	Nice
PM 103 Phobos	18-5-01	Martigues (near Marseilles)

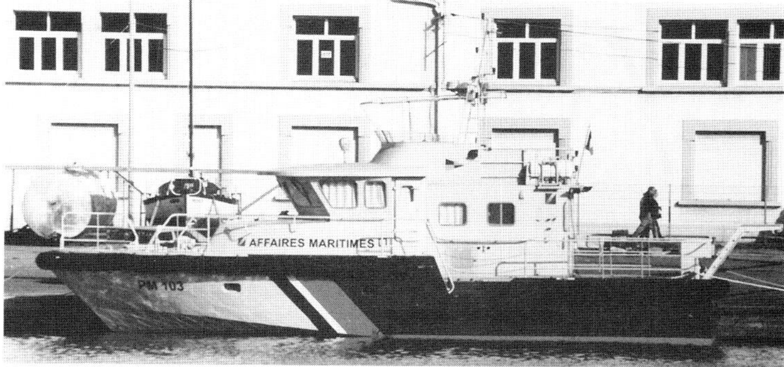

Phobos (PM 103) Bernard Prézelin, 3-05

D: 22 tons (fl) **S:** 25 kts **Dim:** 16.15 × 4.81 × 1.20
A: Small arms **Electronics:** Radar: 1 Furuno M1832 nav.
M: 2 M.A.N. 2866LE403 diesels; 2 props; 500 bhp
Range: 300/23 **Crew:** 4 tot.

Remarks: Ordered 6-99; were originally to have been six.

♦ 1 Arcor 56 class
Bldr: CNA, la Teste (In serv. 1991)

PM 64 Cap d'Ailly

Cap d'Ailly (PM 64) Bernard Prézelin, 6-04

D: 25 tons (fl) **S:** . . . kts **Dim:** 17.00 × 4.85 × . . .
A: Small arms **Electronics:** Radar: 1 Furuno . . . nav.
M: 2 Baudouin diesels; 2 props; 1,400 bhp **Crew:** 4 tot.

Remarks: Based at Dieppe.

♦ 1 Eider class
Bldr: Polymer, Tregunc (In serv. 1988)

PM 63 Eider (Based at Bayonne)

Eider (PM 63) Bernard Prézelin, 7-01

D: 28 tons **S:** 20 kts **Dim:** 16.80 × 4.50 × 2.10 molded depth
A: none **Electronics:** Radar: 1 Furuno . . . nav.
M: 2 M.A.N. diesels; 2 props; 1,250 bhp **Crew:** . . .

MARITIME POLICE PATROL BOATS [WPB] *(continued)*

♦ **1 Pétrel class** Bldr: C.N. de l'Esterel, Cannes (In serv. 1985)

PM 61 Pétrel (Based at Douarnenez)

Pétrel (PM 61) Bernard Prézelin, 7-02

D: 26 tons (fl) **S:** 25 kts **Dim:** 17.10 × 4.58 × 2.24 molded depth
A: Small arms **Electronics:** Radar; 2 Furuno . . . nav.
M: 2 Poyaud diesels; 2 props; 450 bhp **Endurance:** 30 hours **Crew:** . . .

Disposal note: Arcor 43–class *Valériane* (PM 54) was retired during 2001.

Inshore Surveillance Craft (*Vedettes de Surveillance Littoral*):

♦ **5 Pointe du Hoc class** (In serv. 1994)

PM 290 Pointe du Hoc
PM 291 L'Arundel
PM 292 An Alre
PM 294 Île Dumet
PM 295 La Varde

Île Dumet (PM 294) Guy Schaeffer via Paolo Marsan, 5-04

D: 10 tons (fl) **S:** 27 kts **Dim:** 11.80 × . . . × . . .
M: 2 diesels, 2 props; 460 bhp

♦ **12 miscellaneous units:**

PM 269 Mor Braz (ex-*La Cauchoise*), PM 271 Auzance,
PM 273 Lou Labech (1981–82): 8.0 m o.a.; 140 bhp
PM 279 Sarriette (1988): 10.90 m o.a.; 500 bhp, 26 kts
PM 281 Pertuisane (1988): 8 tons, 10.60 m o.a., 460 bhp, 25 kts
PM 283 Girondine (1988): 9.15 m o.a.; 440 bhp; 17 kts
PM 284 Cap D'Azur (ex-*Cap de Nice*) (1990): 10.30 m o.a.; 500 bhp; 26 kts
PM 285 Syndic Victor Salez (1990): 8.15 m o.a.; 250 bhp; 18 kts
PM 286 An Oriant (1991): 8.00 m o.a.; 140 bhp, 20 kts
PM 287 Men Goe (1991): 7.00 m o.a.; 85 bhp, 18 kts
PM 288 Catalane (1992): 11.40 m o.a.; 500 bhp, 26 kts
PM 293 Colibri (1994): 12 tons, 11.98 m o.a.; 750 bhp, 27 kts

Syndic Victor Salez (P 285) Bernard Prézelin, 7-05

Remarks: In addition to the above launches, there are a number of units between 5.0 and 7.0 m overall. The *Korrigan* (PM 270) was stricken during 2002.

SMALL NAVIGATIONAL AIDS TENDERS [WYGL]

♦ **2 (+ 1) Armorique class**
Bldr: SOCARENAM, Boulogne

Armorique (In serv. 9-10-02) Hauts de France (In serv. 3-03)

Armorique Bernard Prézelin, 7-04

D: 530 grt **S:** 13 kts **Dim:** 47.50 × 10.00 × 3.30
M: Diesel-electric: 2 Caterpillar 3508B-driven alternator sets; 2 Voith-Schneider vertical cycloidal propellers; 1,280 shp—300-shp bow-thruster
Range: . . . / . . . **Crew:** 10 tot.

Remarks: The hull was built by Alstom Leroux Naval at St.-Malo. *Hauts de France* is 44.5 m overall. Have a 12-ton capacity buoy crane serving the 180-m^2 working area aft. *Armorique* is based at Brest and *Hauts de France* at Dunkerque; a third sister is to be ordered to replace the *André Blondel* at Verdon.

♦ **1 Chef de Caux class**
Bldr: Ocea, Les Sables d'Olonne (In serv. 2-02)

Chef de Caux

D: . . . tons **S:** 12.5 kts **Dim:** 30.10 × 8.20 × 2.00
M: 2 Baudouin 6M 262NRT diesels; 2 Voith-Schneider vertical cycloidal props: 900 bhp
Crew: 7 tot.

Remarks: Based at Le Havre. Has one 4-ton electrohydraulic crane at the stern.

♦ **1 Provence class**
Bldr: CRNP, Paimboeuf (In serv. 1-90)

Provence

Provence Guy Schaeffer via Paolo Marsan, 3-05

D: 326 tons (375 fl) **S:** 12.5 kts **Dim:** 38.00 (35.50 pp) × 9.00 × 2.50
M: Diesel-electric: 2 Caterpillar 3508 diesel-driven alternator sets; 2 Voith-Schneider vertical cycloidal props; 900 shp—282-shp bow-thruster
Range: 1,000/10 **Crew:** . . .

Remarks: Based at Marseilles. Has a 24-ton portal crane at the stern and also a 2-ton crane.

♦ **2 Le Kahouanne class**
Bldr: Ocea, Les Sables d'Olonne (In serv. 2001, 2002)

Le Kahouanne Louis Henin

D: . . . tons **S:** 12 kts **Dim:** 28.75 × 7.70 × 1.30
M: 2 Baudouin 6M 26SR diesels; 2 props; 900 bhp

Remarks: *Le Kahouanne* is based at Point-a-Pitre, Guadaloupe, West Indies, and is slightly shorter (27.30 m overall) and has two Baudouin 6R 124SR diesels producing 800 bhp tot. *Louis Henin* is based at Nouméa, New Caledonia, and is also used for hydrographic survey work.

♦ **1 Îles Sanguinaires class**
Bldr: De Rovere, La Seyne-sur-mer (In serv. 1977)

Îles Sanguinaires (ex-*Jengu*)

MARITIME POLICE SMALL NAVIGATIONAL AIDS TENDERS [WYGL] *(continued)*

D: . . . tons **S:** 11 kts **Dim:** 24.90 × 6.75 × 2.50
M: 1 G.M. 12V71 TI diesel; 1 prop; 400 bhp

Remarks: Based at Ajaccio.

♦ 1 L'Esquillade class
Bldr: De Rovere, Lay Seyne-sur-mer (In serv. 1977)

L'ESQUILLADE

D: . . . tons **S:** 16 kts **Dim:** 19.00 × 6.00 × 1.15
M: 2 Baudouin 6R 120SR diesels; 2 props; 600 bhp—bow-thruster

Remarks: Based at Toulon. Has one 8-ton capacity electrohydraulic crane aft.

Note: The 27-ton, 17-meter tender *Charles Cornic* entered service in 2004. Also used for navigational aids tender duties are the *Charles Babin* (1949) at Saint-Nazaire, *André Blondel* (1933) at Verdon, *Roi Gradlon* (1948) at Lorient, and launches *Amfard* (based at Le Havre), *Traversaine* (based at Saint-Malo), and *Saint-Clair 7* (based at Sète). Most are in need of replacement.

CUSTOMS SERVICE

(Douanes)

Note: The French Customs Service (*Douanes*), under the Ministry of the Budget, operates patrol craft with hull numbers beginning with "DF" (*Douanes Française*). Aircraft in service include: 2 Cessna 404 twin-engine light transports, 12 Riems Aviation 406 light aircraft (3 equipped for oil-spill detection), and 6 AS.335 F2 Écureuil helicopters. Patrol boats and craft are painted gray and, since 2002, have had narrow diagonal stripes of blue and white and a broad red diagonal painted on the hull sides. Some 650 personnel are assigned. Principal patrol craft and boats include:

- 1 *Arafenua* class: *Arafenua* (DF 48): 105 tons, 25 kts; based at Papeete.
- 8 *Haize Hegoa* class: *Alizé* (DF 31), *Vent d'Aval* (DF 37), *Haize Hegoa* (DF 43), *Mervent* (DF 44), *Vent d'Autan* (DF 45), *Avel Sterenn* (DF 46), *Lissero* (DF 47), and . . .: 75 tons, 28 kts; 2 *Avel Gwalarn* class: *Avel Gwalarn* (DF 41) and *Suroît* (DF 42): 67 tons, 28 kts
- 1 *Vent d'Amont* class: *Vent d'Amont* (DF 40): 71 tons, 25 kts
- 2 *Mistral* class: *Mistral* (DF 38) and *Aquilon* (DF 39): 45 tons, 30 kts
- 3 *Cers* class: *Tramontana* (DF 17), *Umarinu* (DF 18), and *Cers* (DF 19): 34 tons, 27.5 kts
- 3 *Rafale* class: *Sua Louiga* (DF 24), *Marinda* (DF 30), and *Rafale* (DF 49): 41 tons, 34 kts
- 1 *Gregau* class: *Gregau* (DF 16): 41 tons, 28 kts
- 7 *Noirot* class: *Nordet* (DF 14), *Norues* (DF 15), *Karina* (DF 20), *Macari* (DF 21), *Lagarde* (DF 25), *Orsuro* (DF 28), and *Muntese* (DF 29): 35 tons, 28 kts
- 2 *Libecciu* class: *Libecciu* (DF 26) and *Levant* (DF 27): 30 tons, 28 kts
- 4 *Aigly* class: *Liane* (DF 50), *Yser* (DF 51), *Aigly* (DF 56), and *Touloubre* (DF 57): 13.5 tons, 27 kts
- 1 *Louisiane* class: *Louisiane* (DF 2): 24 tons, used for training
- 1 training launch: *Pingouin:* 6.8 m

In addition, there were 23 *vedettes de surveillance rapprochée* (VSR) between 8 and 13.5 m overall length and 5 *vedettes portuaire* (VSP) of less than 8-m length overall.

Note: The *Gendarmerie Nationale* operated patrol launches G 9501 (17 m, 22 kts) and G 7501 (13.3 m, 20 kts) on the Rhine and the 15.8-m diver-training launch *Antibes* (G 9602) at Antibes. Other, smaller patrol launches in service are numbered G 7005, G 7906, G 8602, G 8905 (*Athelia*), G 8909, G 9002, G 9958, G 9959, G 9963, G 9964, G 9965, G 9966, G 9976, and G 9977.

GABON

Gabonese Republic

MARINE GABONAISE

Personnel: Approx. 500 total

Bases: Port-Gentil and Mayumba

Maritime aviation: One Embraer EMB 111 Bandeirante maritime patrol aircraft is operated by the air force.

PATROL CRAFT [PC]

♦ 2 French Super PATRA class
Bldr: CMN, Cherbourg

	Laid down	L	In serv.
P 07 GÉNÉRAL D'ARMÉE BA OUMAR	2-7-86	18-12-87	6-8-88
P 08 COLONEL DJOUÉ DABANY	5-89	29-3-90	24-10-90

D: 371.5 tons (446 fl) **S:** 24.5 kts
Dim: 54.60 (50.0 pp) × 8.00 (7.70 wl) × 2.54 (2.08 hull)
A: P 07: 1 57-mm 70-cal. Bofors SAK 57 Mk 2 DP; 1 20-mm GIAT F2 AA—P 08: 2 single 20-mm 90-cal. GIAT F2 AA
Electronics: 1 Decca 1226C nav.
M: 2 SACM-Wärtsilä UD33V16 M7 diesels; 2 CP props; 8,000 bhp
Electric: 360 kw
Range: 4,400/14.5 **Fuel:** 73 tons **Endurance:** 15 days
Crew: 4 officers, 28 enlisted + 23 passengers or 20 troops

Général d'Armeé Ba Oumar (P 07)—note twin stacks and 57-mm gun forward
French Navy, 7-92

Remarks: P 07 ordered 11-84, P 08 during 2-89.
Combat systems: For search-and-rescue use, carry inflatable launch and can accommodate 23 rescued personnel. Have two contraband storerooms. P 07 has a Matra Défense Naja optronic gun director for the 57-mm gun. Armament reduced on P 08 to save money; delivery of the unit was delayed by re-engining. P 07 had twin stacks installed during a 1991–92 refit in France, as in the French Navy versions of the class.

Disposal note: The wooden-hulled patrol craft *Général Nazaire Boulingui* (P 10) was reported stricken in 1999.

AMPHIBIOUS WARFARE SHIPS AND CRAFT

♦ 1 Champlain-class troop transport [LPA]
Bldr: Atelier Français de l'Ouest, Grand Quevilly, Rouen, France

	Laid down	L	In serv.
L 05 PRÉSIDENT EL HADJ OMAR BONGO	7-3-83	16-4-84	3-11-84

Président el Hadj Omar Bongo (L 05) French Navy, 1999

D: 820 tons (1,386 fl) **S:** 16 kts **Dim:** 80.00 (68.0 pp) × 13.00 × 2.50
A: 1 40-mm 70-cal. Bofors AA; 2 single 20-mm 90-cal. GIAT F2 AA; 1 7.62-mm mg
Electronics: Radar: 1 Decca 1226 nav.
M: 2 SACM 195V12 diesels; 2 CP props; 3,600 bhp
Electric: 360 kw tot. **Range:** 4,500/13 **Crew:** 47 tot. + 138 troops

Remarks: Purchase announced 28-2-84. By tradition, the largest ship of the Gabonese Navy bears the name of the nation's "president for life." Refitted 1996–97 at Cape Town, South Africa, by Denel, during which time the bow doors were welded closed, eliminating the beaching capability.
Hull systems: Cargo capacity: 340 tons stores and 208 tons potable water. Cargo is handled by a large electro-hydraulic crane just forward of the bridge. Has a helicopter platform aft. Carries one Tanguy Marine 10-m SeaTruck-type landing craft and one 12-m Tanguy Marine personnel launch.

♦ 1 utility landing craft [LCU]
Bldr: DCAN, Dakar (In serv. 11-5-76)

MANGA

D: 152 tons (fl) **S:** 9 kts **Dim:** 24.0 × 6.4 × 1.3
A: 2 single 12.7-mm mg **Electronics:** Radar: Decca 101 nav.
M: 2 Poyaud V8-520 diesels; 2 props; 480 bhp
Range: 600/5 **Crew:** 10 tot.

Remarks: Equipped with bow door and ramp. Refitted 1997–98 at LNI, Lorient, France.

Note: In 1989, the gendarmerie received a 10-unit afloat patrol launch flotilla built by Simonneau, Fontenay, France. Included were one 11.8-m and two 8.10-m patrol craft, each powered by a Volvo Penta TAMD-608 inboard/outboard diesel of 235 bhp, and seven 6.8-m personnel landing craft powered by one 110-bhp Volvo Penta AQAD-30/DP diesel each. Some are likely to have ceased to function.

THE GAMBIA

Republic of the Gambia

Personnel: Approx. 70 total

Base: Banjul

Note: In 1986, the maritime element of the Gambian armed forces officially changed its name from the "Marine Unit of the Gambian National Army" to the *Gambian Navy*.

PATROL BOATS [PB]

♦ **2 . . . class patrol boats**
Bldr: . . . (In serv. 1999)

PT01 Fatimah
PT02 Sulayman Junkung

D: 25 tons **S:** 40 kts **Dim:** 16.10 × 4.40 × 1.60
A: Small arms
Electronics: . . .
M: 1 . . . diesel

Remarks: No additional data available.

♦ **1 U.S. 51-ft. class**
Bldr: Peterson Bldrs., Sturgeon Bay, Wis. (In serv. 1-94)

P 14 Bolongkantaa

D: 24 tons (fl) **S:** 24 kts **Dim:** 15.54 × 4.47 × 1.30
A: Fitted for 1 twin 12.7-mm mg; 2 single 7.62-mm mg
Electronics: Radar: 1 Raytheon R41X nav.
M: 2 G.M. Detroit Diesel 6V92A diesels; 2 props; 900 bhp
Electric: 15 kw tot. **Range:** 500/20 kts **Fuel:** 800 U.S. gallons
Crew: 6 tot.

Remarks: Ordered late in 1993 and paid for by U.S. Aluminum construction. Carries a 4.27-m RIB inspection craft (with 50-bhp outboard motor) on the stern. Contract included training in operation and maintenance. Sisters were given to Cape Verde, Senegal, and Guinea-Bissau. Has not been seen with armament aboard.

GEORGIA

Republic of Georgia

GEORGIAN NAVY

Personnel: Approx. 1,350 tot.

Bases: Main facility at Poti, with naval academy and minor patrol boat base at Batumi

Note: The Romanian government transferred one "corvette" to Georgia in 2000 and also provided naval uniforms; the actual type and class of ship or craft transferred, however, is not available.

HYDROFOIL GUIDED-MISSILE PATROL BOATS [PTGH]

♦ **1 Combattante II class**
Bldr: CMN, Cherbourg

	Completed
303 Dioscuria (ex-*Ipopliarchos Batsis,* P 15)	1971

D: 234 tons (255 fl) **S:** 36.5 kts **Dim:** 47.0 (44.0 pp) × 7.1 × 2.5 (fl)
A: 2 twin 35-mm 90-cal. Oerlikon GDM-A AA; 2 fixed, aft-launching 533-mm TT (SST-4 wire-guided torpedoes)
Electronics:
Radar: 1 Decca 1226 nav.; 1 Thales Triton air/surf. search; 1 Thales Castor f.c.
EW: Thales DR-2000S intercept
M: 4 MTU MD 872 diesels; 4 props; 12,000 bhp
Range: 850/25; 2,000/15 **Fuel:** 39 tons **Crew:** 4 officers, 36 enlisted

Remarks: Transferred from Greece in 2004. Steel hull, light steel alloy superstructure. Have the Thales Vega weapon-control system. Were transferred without exocet missiles.

♦ **1 ex-Ukrainian Matka (Vikhr')-class semi-hydrofoil (Project 206MR)** Bldr: Sudostroitel'noye Obyedineniye "Almaz" (Sredniy Neva) Kolpino, Russia (In serv. 1979–81)

P 302 Tbilisi (ex-*Konotop,* U 150; ex-R-15)

Tbilisi (P 302) Hartmut Ehlers, 10-02

D: 233 tons (258 fl, 268 max.) **S:** 42 kts
Dim: 38.60 (37.50 wl) × 12.5 (7.6 hull; 5.9 wl)) × 2.10 (hull; 3.26 foils)
A: 2 P-15M Termit (SS-N-2C Styx) SSM; 1 76.2-mm 59-cal. AK-176M DP; 1 30-mm 54-cal. AK-630 gatling AA; . . . SA-14/16 shoulder-launched SAM
Electronics:
Radar: 1 Cheese Cake nav.; 1 Garpun (Plank Shave) target detection/tracking; 1 MR-123 Vympel-AM (Bass Tilt) gun f.c.
EW: no intercept equipment; 2 16-tubed PK-16 decoy RL
M: 3 M-520TM5 diesels; 3 props; 14,400 bhp
Electric: 300 kw tot. (1 × 100-kw DGF2A-100/1500 and 1 × 200-kw DRGA-2A-200/1500 diesel sets; 380 V, 50-Hz a.c.)
Range: 600/35; 1,200/22–24; 1,800/11–12 **Fuel:** 38 tons (max. overload)
Endurance: 8 days **Crew:** 25–28 tot.

Remarks: P 302 was transferred from Russian Black Sea Fleet to Ukraine on 12-8-97 in poor condition; donated to Georgia late in 1999.
Hull systems: Steel hull with aluminum/magnesium alloy superstructure. The stern planes on the surface while the bow is supported by the hydrofoils at high speeds. Both the foils and the transom stern flap are remotely controlled via a Baza 02065 gyro system to improve the ride.
Combat systems: Positions for EW intercept antennas remain empty. Can employ weapons in Sea State 6. Carries 152 rds 76.2-mm and 2,000 rds 30-mm ammunition. Has SPO-3 radiation-warning equipment and the R-784 automated radio system. Missiles may not have been transferred with the craft.

PATROL CRAFT [PC]

♦ **1 ex-Russian Stenka (Tarantul) class (Project 205P)**
Bldr: Sudostroitel'noye Obyedineniye "Almaz," Petrovskiy SY, St. Petersburg (In serv. 1967–90)

P 301 Batumi (ex-PSKR 648)

D: 170 tons light; 211 std. (245 fl) **S:** 35 kts
Dim: 39.80 (37.50 wl) × 7.60 (5.90 wl) × 1.96
A: 2 single 37-mm 63-cal. Type 70K (Model 1939) AA
Electronics:
Radar: 1 Baklan (Pot Drum) or Reyd (Peel Cone) nav./surf. search; 1 MR-104 Rys' (Drum Tilt) gun f.c.
EW: SPO-3 intercept
M: 3 M-504 or M-520 diesels; 3 props; 15,000 bhp
Range: 500/35; 800/20; 1,500/12 **Endurance:** 10 days
Crew: 4–5 officers, 26–27 enlisted

Remarks: Transferred in 1999 from Russia. The original twin 30-mm AK-230 gunmounts have been replaced with old 37-mm manually operated guns, and the ASW torpedo tubes were removed, along with the sonar system. Was laid up at Balaklava, Ukraine, as of 10-02, possibly discarded.

♦ **1 ex-Turkish AB 25 class**
Bldr: Taskizak SY (In serv. 21-2-69)

P 202 Kutaisi (ex-AB 30, P 130, ex-P 1230)

Kutaisi (P 202) Hartmut Ehlers, 10-02

D: 150 tons (170 fl) **S:** 22 kts **Dim:** 40.24 × 6.4 × 1.65
A: 1 40-mm 60-cal. Mk 3 Bofors AA; 1 twin 23mm ZU-23-2 87-cal AA; 2 single 12.7-mm mg
Electronics:
Radar: 1 Decca . . . nav.
Sonar: Plessey PMS-26 hull-mounted MF
M: 2 SACM-AGO V16CSHR diesels; 2 props; 4,800 bhp—2 cruise diesels; 300 bhp
Crew: 3 officers, 28 enlisted

Remarks: Transferred as a gift from Turkey on 5-12-98. Cruise diesels are geared to the main shafts. May be assigned to the coast guard rather than the navy. ASW equipment has been removed.

PATROL BOATS [PB]

♦ **2 ex-Greek Dilos class**
Bldr: Hellenic SY, Skaramanga (In serv. 1977–78)

P 201 Iveriya (ex-*Lindos,* P 269) P 203 Mestria (ex-*Dilos,* P 267)

D: 75 tons (86 fl) **S:** 27 kts **Dim:** 29.00 (27.00 wl) × 5.00 × 1.62
A: 2 twin 23-mm 87-cal. ZU-23-2 AA **Electronics:** Radar: 1 . . . nav.
M: 2 MTU 12V331 TC81 diesels; 2 props; 2,720 bhp
Range: 1,600/25 **Crew:** 15 tot.

Remarks: P 201 was transferred by donation during 1-98 and P 203 during 9-99. Designed by Abeking & Rasmussen, West Germany, for air/sea rescue. Round-bilge steel-construction hull.

PATROL BOATS [PB] *(continued)*

Iveriya (P 201) Hartmut Ehlers, 10-02

♦ **3 Aist-class launches (Project 1398)**
Bldr: Sretenskiy Zavod, Kokuy (In serv. 1975–86)

10 12 14

Aist-class launch number 10—on land next to number 12
Hartmut Ehlers, 10-02

D: 3.55 tons (5.8 fl) **S:** 20 kts **Dim:** 9.50 × 2.60 × 0.50
A: 1 7.62-mm mg **Electronics:** Radar: none
M: 1 3D-20 diesel; 1 waterjet; 235 bhp **Fuel:** 0.37 tons **Crew:** . . . tot.

Remarks: Rail-transportable launches originally designed for employment on the Amur-Ussuri River system in the Soviet Far East. 10 and 12 were in storage at Poti as of 10-02; 14 is employed as a survey launch.

♦ **1 ex-Russian Project 360**
Bldr: Sudostroitel'noye Obyedineniye "Almaz," Petrovskiy SY, St. Petersburg (In serv. 1961–64)

101 Tskaltubo (ex-*Merkuriy*)

Tskaltubo (101) Hartmut Ehlers, 10-02

D: 137 tons (150 fl) **S:** 35.6 kts **Dim:** 37.15 × 7.50 × 2.41
A: 1 37-mm 63-cal. Type 70-K (Model 1939) AA
Electronics: Radar: 1. . . nav.
M: 2 M-503-series diesels; 2 props; 6,600 bhp
Range: 460/26 **Endurance:** 5 days **Crew:** 13 tot.

Remarks: Former Black Sea Fleet flag officer yacht transferred to Georgia during 1997 for use as a patrol boat. The manually operated gun is on the stern.

♦ **1 ex-Russian Poluchat-I (TL-1)-class (Project 368T)**
Bldr: Sosnovka Zavod (In serv. 1960–77)

P 102 Akhmeta (ex-TL . . .)

Poluchat-I-class patrol boat P 102—with a Stenka-class patrol craft in background
Hartmut Ehlers, 8-00

D: 84.7 tons (92.8 fl) **S:** 21.6 kts **Dim:** 29.60 × 6.10 (5.80 wl) × 1.56 (1.90 props)
A: 1 single 37-mm 63-cal. Type 70-K (Model 1939) AA; 1 17-tubed 140-mm BM-14-17 PU artillery rocket launcher
Electronics: Radar: 1 Don-2 or Mius (Spin Trough) nav.
M: 2 M-50F-4 diesels; 2 props; 2,400 bhp **Range:** 250/21.6; 550/14
Crew: 1 officer, 2 warrant officers, 12 enlisted

Remarks: Former torpedo retriever. Bought in 1997 from commercial sources in the Ukraine. Has Gira-KM gyrocompass, NEL-3 echo sounder. The hull has seven watertight bulkheads. Underwent refit at Balaklava from 2-00 through 11-02.

♦ **1 ex-Russian Admiralets-class workboat (Project 371U)**
Bldr: . . . (In serv. 1956– . . .)

04 Gali II

Gali II (04)—on land for repairs Hartmut Ehlers, 10-02

D: 9.41 tons (fl) **S:** 13.5 kts **Dim:** 12.61 × 3.23 × 1.10
M: 1 3D-6 diesel; 1 prop; 150 bhp **Range:** 140/13 **Crew:** 2 tot.

Remarks: A sister named *Gali I* was out of service and in poor condition as of 2002. Normally employed for harbor patrol and personnel transport. Undergoing refit at Poti.

Note: Also in service for patrol duties is the small armed fishing craft *Gantiadi* (016); fitted with 1 twin 23-mm AA and 2 12.7-mm mg.

AMPHIBIOUS WARFARE CRAFT

♦ **2 ex-Bulgarian Vydra-class (Project 106K) utility landing craft [LCU]** Bldr: Burgas SY, Bulgaria (In serv. 1974–75)

001 Guria (ex-DK-608) 002 Atia

Atia (002)—with sister *Guria* (001) in the background Hartmut Ehlers, 10-02

AMPHIBIOUS WARFARE CRAFT *(continued)*

D: 308 tons (442 fl) **S:** 10.5 kts **Dim:** 54.5 × 7.7 × 2.4
A: 2 twin 23-mm 87-cal. ZU-23-2 AA
Electronics: Radar: 1 Chernomore MR 2512 nav.
M: 2 Type 3D12 diesels; 2 props; 600 bhp
Range: 2,700/10 **Crew:** 1 officer, 4 enlisted

Remarks: Transferred, along with a load of uniforms and military equipment and 33 vehicles, on 16-7-01. Cargo: 260 tons maximum or 3 heavy tanks or 10 GAZ-66 trucks or 200 troops.

♦ **2 ex-Russian Ondatra (Akula)-class (Project 1176) landing craft [LCM]** (In serv. 1979–91)

01 MDK-01 (ex-D-237) 02 MDK-02 (ex- . . .)

MDK-02 (02) Hartmut Ehlers, 10-02

D: 90 tons normal (107.3 fl) **S:** 11.5 kts **Dim:** 24.50 × 6.00 × 1.55
A: 2 12.7-mm mg **Electronics:** Radar: 1 Mius (Spin Trough) nav. (portable)
M: 2 Type 3D12 diesels; 2 props; 600 bhp **Range:** 330/10; 500/5
Endurance: 2 days **Crew:** 5 tot. (enlisted)

Remarks: Typed DKA—*Desantnyy Kater* (Landing Craft). Cargo well is 13.7 × 3.9 m and can accommodate one 40-ton tank or up to 50 tons of general cargo; some 20 troops/vehicle crew can be carried. Left behind by the Soviet Black Sea Fleet and commissioned into Georgian Navy service 2-93. MDK-01 has been inactive since 2002.

SERVICE CRAFT

♦ **1 Flamingo (Tanya)-class (Project 1415) survey craft [YGS]**
Bldr: . . .

DHK 82 (ex-BGK-1628)

DHK-82 Hartmut Ehlers, 10-02

D: 42 tons (54 fl) **S:** 11 kts **Dim:** 21.20 × 3.93 × 1.40
Electronics: Radar: 1 Lotsiya nav. (not always fitted)
M: 1 Type 3D-12A or 3D-12L diesel; 1 prop; 300 bhp
Electric: 12 kw tot. (DGR 1A-16/1500 generator)
Range: 200/11 **Endurance:** 5 days **Crew:** 4 tot. + 27 passengers

Remarks: Civilian manned and based at Batumi.

♦ **1 ex-Russian GPB-480-class inshore-survey craft (Projects 1896, 1896U) [YGS]** Bldr: Vympel Zavod, Rybinsk (In serv. 1955–60s)

81 DHK-81 (ex-BGK-176)

DHK-81 (81) Hartmut Ehlers, 10-02

D: 92 tons (116.1 fl) **S:** 12.5 kts (11.8 sust.) **Dim:** 28.58 × 5.20 × 1.70
Electronics: 1 SNN-7 nav.
M: 1 Type 6CSP 28/3C diesel; 1 prop; 450 bhp (300 sust.)
Range: 1,500/10 **Endurance:** 10 days **Crew:** 14–15 tot.

Remarks: Also referred to as the GS-204 class and by NATO as the Nyryat-1 class. Carries the words "Hydrographic Service" in English on the sides of the hull. Civilian manned and based at Poti as of 9-03.
Hull systems: The charthouse/laboratory is 6 m^2, and there are two 1.5-ton derricks. Employs a dual side-looking mapping sonar system using transducers mounted on swinging-arm davits amidships. Displacement has grown with age and may be as much as 98 tons light, 126 full load.

Note: Project 727M shipboard survey launch MHK-83 (ex-MGK-1424) was out of service as of 2002.

GEORGIAN BORDER DEPARTMENT COAST GUARD

Bases: Poti and Batumi

Note: Craft have white hulls and carry the words "Coast Guard" in English on their sides.

PATROL CRAFT [WPC]

♦ **1 ex-Russian Stenka (Tarantul) class (Project 205P)**
Bldr: Sudostroitel'noye Obyedineniye "Almaz," Petrovskiy SY, St. Petersburg (In serv. 1967–90)

P 21 Giorgi Toreli (ex-*Anastasia,* ex-PSKR-629)

Giorgi Toreli (P 21) Hartmut Ehlers, 10-02

D: 170 tons light; 211 std. (245 fl) **S:** 35 kts
Dim: 39.80 (37.50 wl) × 7.60 (5.90 wl) × 1.96
A: 2 single 37-mm 63-cal. Type 70K (Model 1939) AA
Electronics:
Radar: 1 Baklan (Pot Drum) or Reyd (Peel Cone) nav./surf. search; 1 MR-104 Rys' (Drum Tilt) gun f.c.
EW: SPO-3 intercept
M: 3 M-504 or M-520 diesels; 3 props; 15,000 bhp
Range: 500/35; 800/20; 1,500/12 **Endurance:** 10 days
Crew: 4–5 officers, 26–27 enlisted

Remarks: Transferred in 1999. The original twin 30-mm AK-230 gunmounts have been replaced with old 37-mm manually operated guns, and the ASW torpedo tubes were removed, along with the sonar system.

♦ **1 ex-German Klasse 331B former minehunter**
Bldr: Burmester, Bremen

	L	In serv.
P 22 Ayety (ex-*Minden,* M 1085)	9-6-59	22-1-60

Ayety (P 22) Hartmut Ehlers, 10-02

D: 388 tons (402 fl) **S:** 16.5 kts **Dim:** 47.45 × 8.5 × 2.8
A: 1 40-mm 70-cal. Bofors AA; 2 single 12.7-mm mg
Electronics: Radar: 1 Raytheon SPS-64(V)5 nav.
M: 2 MTU 16V538 TB90 diesels; 2 CP props; 5,000 bhp—2 50-shp electric cruise motors (6 kts)
Electric: 220 kw tot. **Range:** 1,400/16; 3,950/9 **Crew:** 5 officers, 29 enlisted

COAST GUARD PATROL CRAFT [WPC] *(continued)*

Remarks: *Ayety* was donated by Germany and transferred disarmed on 22-10-98; delivered to Georgia aboard heavy lift ship *Condock V,* arriving 16-11-98 at Poti. Had been decommissioned on 4-12-97. Converted 1975–79 to a minehunter from a Klasse 320, *Lindau*-class, wooden-hulled minesweeper. Painted white prior to transfer and has diagonal "Coast Guard" striping on the hull sides forward. Planned transfer of two more did not take place. Based at Poti.
Hull systems: Wooden construction, with nonmagnetic engines.
Combat systems: The 40-mm gun is controlled by a lead-computing optical director on the bridge. The DSQS-11A minehunting sonar was removed prior to transfer and no towed sweep gear was retained, although the sweep winch remains in place.

PATROL BOATS [WPB]

♦ 2 U.S. 40-foot Dauntless class
Bldr: SeaArk, Monticello, Ark.

P 106 (ex-P 208) (In serv. 2-98)   P 209 (In serv. 3-99)

P 209 Hartmut Ehlers, 10-02

D: 15 tons (fl) **S:** 28 kts **Dim:** 12.19 (11.13 wl) × 3.86 × 0.69 (hull)
A: 2 single 12.7-mm mg; 2 single 7.62-mm mg
Electronics: Radar: 1 Raytheon R40X nav.
M: 2 Caterpillar 3208TA diesels; 2 props; 850 bhp (720 sust.)
Range: 200/30; 400/22 **Fuel:** 250 gallons **Crew:** 5 tot.

Remarks: Paid for by U.S. Defense Special Weapons Threat Reduction Program. C. Raymond Hunt, "Deep-Vee" hull design. Sisters operate in several Caribbean nation forces. P 106 is based at Batumi, P 209 at Poti.

♦ 8 Zhuk (Gryf) class (Project 1400M)
Bldr: P 103: Batumi Ship Repair Yard (In serv. 1997–98)

P 102   P 103   P 104   P 203   P 204   P 205
P 206 (ex-Navy AK-103)   P 207 (ex-Navy AK-104)

Zhuk-class P 203—alongside sisters P 204 and P 205 Hartmut Ehlers, 10-02

D: 35.9 tons (39.7 fl) **S:** 30 kts
Dim: 23.80 (21.70 wl) × 5.00 (3.80 wl) × 1.00 (hull; 1.90 max.)
A: P 203: 1 twin 12.7-mm 60-cal. Utës-Ma mg—all: fitted for 1 twin 23mm ZU-23-2 87-cal AA
Electronics: Radar: 1 Lotsiya nav.
M: 2 M-401 diesels; 2 props; 2,200 bhp
Electric: 48 kw total (2 × 21-kw, 1 × 6-kw diesel sets)
Range: 500/13.5 **Endurance:** 5 days **Crew:** 1 officer, 9 enlisted

Remarks: P 104 was donated by Ukraine in 3-97. First three are based at Batumi, the others at Poti. As of 10-02, P 205 was under refit and P 206 and P 207, though inactive, remain in service.

♦ 4 Aist-class (Project 1398) launches
Bldr: Sretenskiy Zavod, Kokuy (In serv. 1975–86)

P 212   P 702   P 704   P . . .

D: 3.55 tons (5.8 fl) **S:** 20 kts **Dim:** 9.50 × 2.60 × 0.50
A: 1 7.62-mm mg **Electronics:** Radar: none
M: 1 3D-20 diesel; 1 waterjet; 235 bhp **Fuel:** 0.37 tons **Crew:** . . . tot.

P 212 Hartmut Ehlers, 10-02

Remarks: Rail-transportable launches originally designed for employment on the Amur-Ussuri River system in the Soviet Far East. First three are based at Poti, the other at Batumi.

Disposal note: Remaining two units of ex-Turkish SG 40 class were retired during 2001.

♦ 2 ex-U.S. Coast Guard 82-foot Point class
Bldr: Coast Guard Yard, Curtis Bay, Md. (In serv. 8-8-62)

	In serv.
P 210 Tsotne Dadiani (ex-*Point Countess,* WPB 82335)	8-8-62
P 211 General Mazniashvili (ex-*Point Baker,* WPB 82342)	30-10-63

General Mazniashvili (P 211) Hartmut Ehlers, 10-02

D: 64 tons (66 fl) **S:** 23.7 kts **Dim:** 25.3 × 5.23 × 1.95
A: 2 single 12.7-mm Colt M2 mg
Electronics: Radar: 1 Hughes-Furuno SPS-73 nav.
M: 2 Caterpillar 3412 diesels; 2 props; 1,480 bhp
Range: 490/23.7; 1,500/8 **Fuel:** 5.7 tons **Crew:** 1 officer, 7 enlisted

Remarks: P 210 was transferred by donation during 6-00 and P 211 was transferred on 12-2-02. Hull built of mild steel. High-speed diesels controlled from the bridge. Well equipped for salvage and towing. Both are based at Poti.

Note: Also said to be in service are a patrol launch named *Tornado* (P 105) and a small launch numbered P 101, both based at Batumi. A small patrol craft named *Niko Nikoladse* reportedly entered service in 2003.

AMPHIBIOUS WARFARE CRAFT

♦ 2 ex-U.K. Rigid Raider assault boats Mk 3 [WLCP]
Bldr: RTK Marine, Poole, Dorset (In serv. 1996–98)

D: 2.2 tons light **S:** 40 kts (36 loaded) **Dim:** 7.58 × 2.75 × . . .
M: 1 Yamaha gasoline outboard; 220 bhp **Crew:** 2 + 8 commandos

Remarks: Transferred at Poti on 11-1-99.

AUXILIARIES

♦ 1 ex-Ukrainian tug
Bldr: Chrichton-Vulcan A.B., Turku, 1956)

56 Poti (ex-*Zorro*)

Remarks: Acquired in 1999; from commercial firm; out of service by 10-02 but will be repaired. Painted with coast guard stripe. No data available.

GERMANY

Federal Republic of Germany

DEUTSCHE MARINE

Personnel: 24,650 total (including 5,090 officers and 11,400 NCOs) active duty naval personnel in uniform.

Bases: Fleet headquarters is at Glücksburg, with Flag Officer, Naval Command, at Rostock. North Sea bases are located at Borkum, Emden, and Wilhelmshaven. Baltic bases are at Kiel, Eckernförde, Olpenitz, and Warnemünde. Naval training is conducted at Brake, Bremerhaven, Glückstadt, List/Sylt, and Plön. Naval repair facilities (arsenals) are located at Kiel and Wilhelmshaven. All submarines are now based at Kiel, frigates are based at Wilhelmshaven, missile boats at Warnemünde, and all mine-countermeasures units at Olpenitz. The bases at Neustadt and Grossenbrode were closed during 2000.

Naval Aviation: Name changed to *Marineflieger Flotilla* on 1-4-94. About 4,000 personnel serve in the *Marineflieger.* Aircraft include 8 P-3C Orion maritime patrol aircraft purchased from the Netherlands in 2005 (which are expected to replace some of the 13 Bréguet Atlantic Mk 1 maritime patrol aircraft, four of which have been modified for EW duties, now in service), 21 Sea King Mk 43 SAR helicopters, 15 Westland/Bréguet Lynx Mk 88 and 7 Super Lynx Mk 88A shipboard ASW helicopters, 4 Dornier Do-228-212 light transports (2 for VIP transport, 2 for pollution control surveillance), and 4 AIA Westwind target tugs (contractor-operated). Thirty-eight NH-90 helicopters are on order to begin replacing the Sea Kings in 2007–8.

German Navy Atlantic Mk 1 Michael Nitz, 3-05

P-3C Orion—pictured just prior to transfer from the Netherlands Michael Nitz, 3-05

German Navy Super Lynx Mk 88A—note chin-mounted radar Frank Findler, 3-04

German Navy Dornier Do-228-212 Frank Findler, 9-02

German Navy Sea King Mk 43—in SAR configuration Frank Findler, 6-05

Organization:

- Naval Air Group MFG 3 at Nordholz: two squadrons of Atlantics, one of Lynx helicopters, plus two Dornier Do-228-212 for pollution-control duties.
- Naval Air Group MFG 5 at Kiel-Holtenau: 1 squadron Sea Kings and 2 Dornier Do-228-212 transports. Sea King detachments for SAR duties are maintained at Borkkum, Sylt, and Helgoland.

As a result of budget cuts, all German Navy Tornado attack aircraft were retired by 2005 and the associated Naval Air Group MFG 2 (Marine Flieger Geschwader) at Eggebek was disestablished. The Atlantic Mk 1 maritime patrol aircraft have been refurbished to remain in service until 2010, at which time they will be over four decades old; new avionics and communications suites are being fitted, and a forward-looking FLIR is being added.

Twenty Sea Kings have been upgraded to permit carrying four Sea Skua antiship missiles, a Sea Spray Mk 3 search radar, electronic intercept gear, chaff, Link 11 computer data system, ALR-68 radar warning system, and the Bendix AQS-18 dipping sonar.

The Lynx Mk 88 ASW helicopters employ the DAQS-18 dipping sonar. The seven Super Lynx Series 100 (RN HAS.8 equivalent) were ordered in 10-96, with the first completed 15-7-99, and the earlier Lynx units are being upgraded to Mk 88A status to extend service to 2012; all are being equipped to launch Sea Skua antiship missiles and will have Marconi Seaspray 3000 radars and a FLIR system.

WEAPONS AND SYSTEMS

A. MISSILES

♦ Surface-to-air missiles

Standard SM-2 Block III: On board the Type 124 guided-missile destroyers (see U.S. section for characteristics).

RIM-116A RAM (Rolling Airframe Missile): Developed as a close-in defense weapon in cooperation with General Dynamics in the United States. The system will carry 21 missiles per launcher. By 1995 some 2,000 missiles had been ordered from RAMSYS GmbH, along with 52 Mk 49 launchers.

♦ Surface-to-surface missiles

MM 38 Exocet: On board Type 123 frigates and Type 143A and 143 guided-missile patrol boats (see French section for characteristics).

Harpoon (RGM-84A/C): Carried by the Type 124 and 122 frigates (see U.S. section for characteristics).

Polyphem: Manufacturer: EADS-LFK (*Lenkflugkörpersysteme*). Development was begun by TRIFOM: Aérospatiale Matra (France), EADS (formerly DaimlerChrysler Aerospace) (Germany), and Consorzio Italmissile (Italy), with Northrop Grumman affiliation in the U.S. Intended for submerged launch from submarines against surface targets and against low-flying aircraft or helicopters. Intended for use in the antiship role by Germany and the land warfare role by Italy and France.

Note: In 7-03 Germany withdrew from the program, likely bringing to an end the naval variant of the missile. The Swedish Saab Bofors RBS-15 Mk 3 has been selected as the eventual replacement for the MM 38 Exocet antiship missiles and is to be installed first on the new Type 130 corvettes (see data in the Swedish section).

♦ Air-to-surface missiles

Kormoran and U.S. HARM: Carried by Tornado aircraft. Some 262 Kormoran-I missiles were remanufactured to Kormoran-II configuration between 1992 and 1998 by Messerschmidt-Bölkow-Blohm (MBB). The original 165-kg warhead was enlarged to 220 kg and has 21 fragments vice 16, a phased-array radar seeker has been substituted, post-boost coast-glide cruise is employed to increase range, and logistic support and reliability were to be improved.

B. GUNS

76-mm OTO Melara Compact: On frigates and Type 143 and 143A guided-missile patrol boats. All mounts have been upgraded by OTO Melara to have a 120 rd/min. firing rate.

40-mm 70-cal. Bofors: In single or twin mounts on many types of ships. Replaced by open OTO Melara mountings in combatants. Bofors Trinity elevating masses and 100-round ready-service magazines were ordered 1986 to update existing 40-mm mounts.

27-mm Mauser MLG 27 (MN 27 GS): Up to 90 remotely controlled mounts are being procured to replace existing 40-mm and 20-mm mounts. Developed from the 45-cal. BK 27 aircraft gun, it fires a frangible subcaliber round with a 1.75-kg projectile; 90

WEAPONS AND SYSTEMS *(continued)*

rounds are carried on-mount. The associated E/O fire-control system, developed by STN Atlas Elektronik, includes day and night vision sensors and provides automatic target tracking.

Mount weight: 850 kg **Projectile weight:** 225 g
Muzzle velocity: 1,150 m/sec **Rate of fire:** 1,700 rds/min
Arc of elevation: –15° to +60° **Range:** 4,000 m surf./2,500 m air

20-mm 90-cal. RH 202 AA: Rheinmetall guns in single mountings

C. ASW WEAPONS

TORPEDOES

U.S. Mk 46 Mod. 5 ASW: On frigates, Atlantic Mk I ASW patrol aircraft, and Lynx helicopters

DM-1 Seeschlange: Wire-guided on submarines; anti–surface ship version for Type 143 missile boats is SST-4, and export ASW version is the SUT (see descriptions below). Data for DM-1:

Diameter: 533 mm **Weight:** 1,370 kg **Warhead:** 275 kg
Speed: 18 or 34 kts **Range:** 20,000 m

DM-2A1 Seeal: Wire-guided for Class 206 submarines:

Diameter: 533 mm **Warhead:** 100 kg **Speed:** 33 kts **Range:** 10,000 m

DM-2A3 Seehecht: Wire-guided. Used on submarines. Export version is known as Seehake. In early 1996, STN Atlas Elektronik received an order for 20 new DM-2A3 torpedoes plus kits to upgrade 20 DM-2A1 to DM-2A3. DM-2A4 version for the Class 212 submarines will be deeper diving and will have a new 275-kw stepless permanent-magnet DC motor propulsion system driving counter-rotating propellers. The DM-2A5 variant, with internal fiber-optic command-and-control conduits, is to enter service in 2005. STN Atlas received an order for 73 Improved DM-2A4 torpedoes with delivery in 2003. DM-2A3 data include:

Diameter: 533 mm **Length:** 6.60 m **Weight:** 1,370 kg
Warhead: 260 kg **Speed:** 35 kts **Range:** 20,000 m

The following torpedoes have been sold for export:

SST-4: a wire-guided, antisurface weapon in either Mod. 0 version with impact fuzing or Mod. 1 with proximity fuze.

Diameter: 533 mm **Length:** 6.08 m **Weight:** 1,414 kg **Warhead:** 260 kg
Speed: 34 kts max. **Range:** 11,000 m/34 kts; 20,000 m/28 kts; 36,000 m/23 kts

SUT (Surface/Underwater Target): Dual-purpose wire-guided weapon derived from the German Navy's Seeschlange and Seeal. Some 439 have been exported. SUT Mod. 2 has a computerized acoustic data processor to transmit target data to the launching ship.

Diameter: 533 mm **Length:** 6.39 m **Weight:** 1,414 kg **Warhead:** 260 kg
Speed: 34 kts max. **Range:** 12,000 m/34 kts; 28,000 m/23 kts

MU-90 Impact: An initial contract for $281 million was placed with Eurotorp (a consortium of Whitehead Alenia Sistemi Subacquie, DCN, and Thales) and STN Atlas Elektronik early in 1998 with Eurotorp for 285 antisubmarine homing torpedoes. See French section for system details.

D. MINES

DM-11: Spherical moored contact or remote detonated. Entered service 1968.

Diameter: 830 mm **Weight:** 550 kg **Mooring depth:** 300 m max.

DM-41: Seabed mine with mechanical, acoustic, magnetic, or pressure fuzing or remote-controlled detonation. Deployed from surface ships, aircraft, or portable mine-belts on Class 206A submarines.

Length: 2.40 m **Diameter:** 534 mm **Weight:** 771 kg (535 kg explosives)

DM-51: Seabed anti-invasion mine. Entered service late 1980s. Has active acoustic sensor or can be remote-control detonated.

Diameter: 710 mm **Height:** 300 mm **Weight:** 110 kg

DM-61: Joint German-Danish weapons also known as "Seabed Mine 80." Bottom mine with acoustic, magnetic, and pressure fuzing (or a combination of the three) uses an onboard microprocessor. Built by STN Atlas Elektronik; 3,000 were delivered 1990–93.

Length: 2.00 m **Diameter:** 600 mm **Weight:** 730 kg

Note: Also in service is a small anti-invasion, beach-protection mine. The "Seemine G3" is also under development.

E. ELECTRONICS

Thales Nederland and the multinational EADS established ET Marinesysteme GmbH on 19-4-01 to maintain existing Thales Nederland (formerly H.S.A. or Signaal) combat systems on German and Dutch naval units, develop the combat system for the German Type 130 corvette program, continue development of the APAR radar, and cooperate on development of a joint Maritime Tactical Ballistic Missile Defense system.

The German Navy uses Thales Nederland radars and radars developed by EADS (originally Daimler Aerospace SA/DASA; later DaimlerChrysler Aerospace).

Sonars are of German origin, built by STN Atlas Elektronik (formerly Krupp Atlas). These include the DSQS-21BZ (ASO-80), DSQS-23BZ (ASO-90), and ELAC 1BV on surface ships, and the DBQS-21D (CSU-83), WSN AN 410A, GHG AN 5039A1, and SRSM1H for submarines. The DSQS-21-series sonars were updated in 1996–97 to provide a capability to detect mines. In development for surface ships are the EFS/Thales (Thomson-Marconi) LFTASS (Low-Frequency Active Towed Array Sonar System) and a new hull-mounted set. The STN Atlas COTASS (Compact Towed Array Sonar System) began trials in 11-00 on the research ship *Planet* for use in a torpedo-detection system; COTASS employs an active towed array about 200 m abaft the ship and the passive receiving array 500 m abaft the active array.

STN Atlas is developing the MTW (Mini-Torpedo Welcome), an antitorpedo homing device launched from surface ships by rocket and employing an underwater rocket motor while homing on the target torpedo.

The STN Atlas Elektronik Modular Sensor Platform (MSR) was ordered in 1998, with 66 delivered by 2003 for use on ships. The two-axis stabilized mount carries a thermal imager, a daylight t.v. camera, and a laser rangefinder, and the system is to be used for passive surveillance, tracking, and weapons control.

EADS's LFK division manufactures the COLDS (Common Opto-electronic Laser Detection System), which detects a laser missile seeker and directs a laser beam of equivalent pulse-repetition frequency against a safe spot on the ocean surface to spoof the missile.

The Buck Neue Technologien DM39 Bullfighter IR/radar decoy was selected early in 2000 to replace earlier 130-mm decoy rounds launched by the Mk 36 SRBOC system in the Type 122 and Type 124 frigates.

The widely used FL1800S EW system intercepts from 0.5 to 18 GHz and can jam from 7.5 to 17 GHz. The Stage II version employs a SADIE parallel processor covering nine bands.

The STN Atlas Elektronik Seefuchs mine-countermeasures system uses the Seefuchs I mine identification vehicle (which rides a sonar beam to the vicinity of a contact and then uses its own sonar and t.v. camera to inspect the object) and the Seefuchs-C expendable mine disposal vehicle. The disposal drone is 1.3 m long and weighs 40 kg; it costs about $50,000—well in excess of the cost of many bottom mines.

ATTACK SUBMARINES [SS]

♦ 4 (+ 2) Type 212A

Bldr: ARGE U 212 Consortium (HDW, Kiel, and Thyssen Nordseewerke, Emden)

	Bldr	Start	L	In serv.
S 181 U 31	HDW, Kiel	1-7-98	20-3-02	19-10-05
S 182 U 32	Thyssen, Emden	11-7-00	11-03	19-10-05
S 183 U 33	HDW, Kiel	30-4-01	8-04	30-1-06
S 184 U 34	Thyssen, Emden	12-01	5-05	29-9-06

U 31 (S 181) Michael Nitz, 2-05

U 32 (S 182) Michael Nitz, 10-05

U 33 (S 183)—while under construction Martin Mokrus, 3-05

ATTACK SUBMARINES [SS] *(continued)*

U 31 (S 181)—on trials Michael Nitz, 2-05

D: 1,370 tons light; 1,460 tons surf./1,840 tons sub.
S: 12 kts surf./20 kts sub.; 8 kts on fuel cells
Dim: 57.15 (55.90 pp) × 7.00 × 7.00
A: 6 bow 533-mm TT (DM-2A4 wire-guided torpedoes)—provision for minelaying belt (24 tot. mines)
Electronics:
Radar: Kelvin-Hughes Type 1007 nav./search
Sonar: CSU-90 suite with EFS DBQS-40FTC MF active/passive, FAS 3-1 flank array, PRS 3-15 passive ranging, AN 5039A1 intercept, EFS/Allied Signal FMS-52 (MOA 3070) active mine-avoidance (30 and 70 kHz), EFS DSQS-21DG bow MF active, and TAS-3 towed LF linear passive hydrophone array
EW: EADS FL-1800U intercept; HDW-WASS C303/S Circe torpedo decoy system (40 tubes)
M: Diesel-electric, with 9 Siemens Polymer Electrolytic Membrane fuel cells (34 kw each) for air-independent cruising, 1 MTU 8V183 SE83 diesel generator set (1,040 kw), 1 Siemens Permasyn motor; 1 7-bladed prop; 2,400 shp
Range: 8,000/8 surf.; 420/8 sub. **Crew:** 5 officers, 22 enlisted

Remarks: Program development began 1988. To cost around $406 million each and the entire program eventually to cost around $2.7 billion if two planned additional groups of four are funded. The contract for detailed design and construction was signed with German Submarine Consortium (Howaldtswerke, Thyssen Nordseewerke, Ferrostaal AG, and Thyssen Rheinstahl Technik GmbH) on 6-4-94 but did not take effect until the German FY 95 budget was approved. Italy is building two sisters, with an option to build two more. All four initial German units are to be assigned to Submarine Squadron 1. U 31 began sea trials 4-03. Two additional boats may be built for delivery in 2010.
Hull systems: Use a nonmagnetic Type 1.3964 austenitic steel pressure hull, 6.80 m in diameter forward, tapering via a conical section to 5.75 m abaft the control room; i.e., the boats are single-hulled forward and double-hulled aft. There are two accommodation decks forward. The engineering plant is suspended in a raft for sound reduction, with individual equipment also using soundproof mountings. The air-independent propulsion (AIP) system will employ a solid-polymer, metal-hydride fuel-cell system. The ship control system is by DataSAAB. Will use Hawker sodium-sulfide batteries. Hydrazine gas generators will be used to blow ballast tanks for emergency surfacing. There are no separate watertight compartments within the pressure hull in order to improve silencing.
Combat systems: The MSI-90U Mk 2 combat system is an improved version of the Norsk Forsvarsteknolgi A/S, Norway, MSI-90U, used previously in Norway's *Ula* class; it can track 25 targets and control eight torpedoes simultaneously and employs Sun Microsystems lightweight work stations.

The sonar suite incorporates six passive ranging transducers, flank arrays, a 0.3- to 12-kHz bow array, mine-avoidance set, echo sounder, 12–24 self-noise sensors, and a towed passive linear array (10–1,200 Hz), the first of its type in a German submarine and capable of providing frequency resolution to 0.01 Hz. The mine-avoidance sonar will operate at 30 kHz for detection and 70 kHz for classification.

The torpedo tubes will use the water-ram ejection method, using two water rams; the torpedo tube arrangement is assymetrical, with two rows of three tubes, four of which are to port of the centerline.

Communications equipment includes HF, VHF, UHF, and VLF radios and Inmarsat-C and UHF SATCOM sets. Navigation equipment includes a Litef PL-41 Mk 4 inertial navigation system, electromagnetic log, and echo sounder. The EW system antenna will be mounted on the Carl Zeiss SERO 40 periscope system; an optical rangefinder and GPS antenna will be collocated on the BS 40 search periscope and optical and laser rangefinders on the AS 40 attack periscope; only the search periscope penetrates the pressure hull. The FL-1800U EW system will cover 2–18 GHz and will employ a pressurized USK800/4 antenna with a second integrated GPS antenna.

♦ 9 Type 206A

Bldrs: (A): Howaldtswerke-Deutsche Werft, Kiel; (B): Rheinstahl Nordseewerke (NSWE), Emden—Modernized by: (C): Howaldtswerke; (D): Nordseewerke

	Bldr/Mod.	Laid down	L	In serv.
S 194 U 15	A/D	1-6-70	15-6-72	17-7-74
S 195 U 16	B/C	1-11-70	29-8-72	9-11-73
S 196 U 17	A/C	1-10-70	10-10-72	28-11-73
S 197 U 18	B/C	1-4-71	31-10-72	19-12-73
S 172 U 23	B/D	5-3-72	5-5-73	2-5-75
S 173 U 24	B/D	20-3-72	26-6-73	16-10-74
S 174 U 25	A/C	1-7-71	23-5-73	14-5-74
S 175 U 26	B/D	14-7-72	20-11-73	13-3-75
S 179 U 30	B/D	5-12-72	4-4-74	13-3-75

U 17 (S 196) Frank Findler, 2-05

U 15 (S 194) Leo Van Ginderen, 6-05

U 25 (S 174) Michael Nitz, 6-05

D: 450 tons surf./520 tons sub. **S:** 10 surf./17 kts sub. (5 snorkel)
Dim: 48.60 × 4.70 × 4.30 (surf.)
A: 8 bow 533-mm TT (8 DM-2A3 Seehecht torpedoes or 16 mines); 24 mines in external mine belt container
Electronics:
Radar: 1 Kelvin-Hughes 1625x 6/U nav./search
Sonar: STN Atlas Elektronik DBQS-21D integrated suite, with passive and active bow arrays, flank array, DUUX 2 intercept array, etc.
EW: Thales DR-2000U intercept; Thorn-EMI SARIE-2 analyzer
M: 2 MTU 12V493 AZ80 GA diesels (600 bhp each), 2/405-kw generators, 1 electric motor; 1 prop; 2,300 shp (1,800 shp sust.)
Range: 4,500/5 snorkel; 200/5 sub. **Fuel:** 23.5 tons
Crew: 4 officers, 18 enlisted

Remarks: *U 13* to *U 24* were authorized in 1969, *U 25* to *U 30* in 2-70. Modernization from Type 206 to Type 206A began with *U 29* at HDW on 9-6-87 and on *U 23* at Thyssen on 18-7-87; the final unit, *U 26,* was completed in 2-92.
Hull systems: Pressure hulls are constructed of high-tensile-strength austenitic (nonmagnetic) steel. Three Hawker (ex-*Varta*) batteries, 92 cells each, weigh 98 tons total. Have Anschütz Nautoplot automatic plot, Rockwell WRN-6(V) SATNAV receiver, Aeronautical & General Instruments AGILOG electromagnetic log, and Anschütz Std 6S and Litef PL 41 Mk 3 compasses.
Combat systems: Have the STN Atlas Elektronik SLW-83 (CSU 83) weapons control system with four ISUS display terminals, DBQS-21D active/passive sonars, provision for a towed passive hydrophone array, new periscopes, extensively overhauled propulsion plants, GPS receivers, and accommodations improvements. The sonar suite can resolve frequencies to 0.1 Hz. SARIE-2 (Selective Automatic Radar Identification

ATTACK SUBMARINES [SS] *(continued)*

Equipment) is fitted as stand-alone equipment with manual input to the combat system. One unit has conducted trials with an STN Atlas Elektronik acoustic passive target classification system. Carl Zeiss ASC 17 optical attack and NavS search periscopes are fitted.
Disposals: *U 27* (S 176) was stricken 13-6-96 for scrapping (sold for scrap 5-00), and *U 20* (S 199) was retired on 26-9-96. *U 13* and *U 14* were retired 18-9-97 and 25-9-97, respectively. *U 19* was stricken on 30-4-98 and *U 21* on 11-6-98. On 1-9-98 Indonesia deferred acquisition of *U 19–21,* and ex-*U 13* and *U 14* remained in Germany under the Indonesian flag until handed back in 11-98 to the German Navy for scrapping during 1999–2001. *U 20* and *U 13* were scrapped at Emden and Kiel, respectively, during 2000. *U 28* retired during 2004, and *U 22* and *U 29* during 2006.
The last remaining Type 205B submarine, *U 11* (S 190) was decomissioned during 6-05. She had served as an auxiliary submarine since 1992.

MIDGET SUBMARINES [SSM]

♦ 1 Orca class
Bldr: EFS (In serv. . . .)

Orca-class midget submarine STN Atlas Elektronik

D: 28 tons sub. **S:** 5+ kts sub. **Dim:** 12.0 × 2.0 × . . .
M: Battery, 1 electric motor; 1 prop; . . . shp
Range: 150/5 **Crew:** . . . tot.

Remarks: Built some years ago, but existence only disclosed 10-96. Dry diver delivery submersible for special operations, with single operator. Equipped with forward-looking sonar, t.v. cameras, downward-looking doppler sonar, an underwater telephone, and echo sounders. Navigational equipment includes a GPS receiver, and there is a telescopic mast-mounted t.v. camera for surface observation. No diesel generator set, but the battery provides an endurance of up to 96 hours. Can be deployed from shore, surface ships, or a submarine.

GUIDED-MISSILE DESTROYERS [DDG]

Note: The last remaining destroyer, the former U.S. *Charles F. Adams*–class (Type 103B) *Lütjens* (D 185, ex-DDG 28), was retired on 18-12-03 and sunk as a target by the U.S. Navy in 2005.

GUIDED-MISSILE FRIGATES [FFG]

♦ 3 Sachsen class (Type 124)

	Bldr	Started	L	Del.	In serv.
F 219 Sachsen	Blohm + Voss, Hamburg	1-2-99	20-1-01	29-11-02	4-11-04
F 220 Hamburg	HDW, Kiel	1-9-00	16-8-02	24-9-04	13-12-04
F 221 Hessen	Thyssen, Emden	14-9-01	26-7-03	7-12-04	15-12-05

Sachsen (F 219) Michael Winter, 6-05

D: 5,690 tons (fl) **S:** 29 kts (18 kts on diesels alone)
Dim: 143.00 (132.15 wl) × 17.44 (16.68 wl) × 5.00 hull (7.00 over sonar)
A: 8 RGM-84F Harpoon SSM; 32-cell Mk 41 Mod. 10 VLS syst. (24 Standard SM-2 Block IIIA and 32 Evolved Sea Sparrow SAM); 2 21-round Mk 49 RAM point-defense SAM launchers (RIM-116A missiles); 1 76-mm 62-cal. OTO Melara SuperRapid DP; 2 single 27-mm Rheinmetall-Mauser MLG 27 (MN 27 GS) AA; 2 triple 324-mm ASW TT (MU-90 torpedoes); 2 Super Lynx helicopters (NH-90 later)

Hamburg (F 220) Michael Nitz, 5-05

Hessen (F 221) Frank Findler, 2-05

Electronics:
Radar: 2 STN Atlas 9600M ARPA nav./surf. search; 1 Thales Triton-G surf. search; 1 ET Marinesysteme APAR 3-D phased array target designation and tracking; 1 Thales SMART-L early warning
Sonar: DSQS-24BZ (STN Atlas Elektronik ASO-90) hull-mounted (6–9 kHz); provision for STN Atlas Elektronik TASS 6-3 (LFTASS) active towed array
TACAN: URN-25
EW: EADS FL-1800 Stage II ELOKA intercept; . . . active; EADS Maigret comms intercept; Mk 36 SRBOC decoy syst. (6 6-round Mk 137 launchers, DM39 Bullfighter 130-mm decoys); . . . torpedo decoy
E/O: SMP 500 surveillance; provision for Thales Sirius IRSCAN
M: CODAG: 1 G.E. 7 LM-2500 PF/MLG gas turbine (31,500 shp), 2 MTU 20V1163 TB93 diesels (10,050 bhp each at 1,350 rpm); 2 5-bladed Escher-Wyss CP props; 51,600 hp max.
Electric: 4,000 kw tot. (4 × 1,000-kw diesel generator sets; 400 V and 115 V, 60 Hz a.c.)
Range: 4,000+/18 **Endurance:** 21 days
Crew: 38 officers, 64 senior petty officers, 140 ratings + staff: 3 officers, 4 senior petty officers, 6 ratings

Remarks: Approval for construction given 13-6-96 for three, with an option for a fourth (to have been named *Thüringen* and very unlikely to be built). The building yards formed the ARGE-124 consortium under the leadership of Blohm + Voss. F 219 will serve as combat systems trials ship for the class. First steel was cut for assembly of F 219 on 27-2-98. All are assigned to the 1st Frigate Squadron based at Wilhelmshaven.
Hull systems: Designed to have as much commonality as possible with the Type 123 but have enhanced signature-reduction features. Are of all-steel construction and employ the MEKO modular equipment installation concept. Some 270 tons of growth margin are built into the design. Accommodations for a task group commander and staff are fitted, and provision is made for female crewmembers. Have rudder roll-rate stabilization system, using the single rudder. Turning radius is about 570 m, and the ships will be able to operate helicopters of up to 15 tons weight in Sea State 6.
The unusual propulsion plant employs a cross-connected gearbox, and the entire engineering plant has an integrated monitoring system. The gas turbine engine is installed within a special MTU-designed sound-quieting module. Will have the same three box-girder hull strength feature as Type 123 and will have seven main watertight compartments. There will be a library, physical fitness room, and four mess compartments; the sickbay will have five berths. The helicopter deck will be equipped with an MBB–Forder & Hebesysteme HHS deck-traversing and handling system.
Combat systems: The combat data system is based on the Thales SEWACO-FD architecture; there will be 17 display consoles, one databus with 11 interface units, a mass memory system, two large-screen displays, two data recording modules, a closed t.v. system, 11 bus interface units, a Cosmos console, and two OP-SW-CDS workstations. There will be two optical target designation sights on the bridge wings. Will have NATO Link 11 and Link 16 combat data-sharing links, with provision for later installation of Link 22. Mk XII Mod. 4 IFF will be provided.
May later carry LCAW lightweight antisubmarine weapons. The Standard SM-2 Block IVA missile may be substituted in part later to provide defense against theater ballistic missile attack.
The SMART-L radar will be able to maintain up to 1,000 tracks, while APAR can maintain 200 tracks and provide guidance illumination for over 30 tracks (the combat system allows for 16 air targets to be attacked at once, along with two surface and two subsurface contacts). The orientation of the four phased-array faces of the APAR radar was changed late in 1997 to fore and aft, port and starboard, rather than at 45° off the centerline as originally intended. Initial sea trials with the APAR radar were carried out aboard the F 219. The Rhode & Schwarz integrated communications suite includes UHF/SHF SATCOM, an integrated message-handling and control system (IMUS), and cryptographic equipment. Navigational equipment includes two NAVSAT terminals, two inertial navigational systems (MINS), and a weather satellite receiver.
During 1-03, F 220 was used for a one-day dockside installation trial with the Krauss-Maffei Wegmann and Rheinmetall MONARC (Modular Naval Artillery Concept) turret from a 155-mm 52-cal. PzH2000 howitzer and a modular recoil effect limitation system; the gun has a range of 40 km and a rate of fire of 10 rds/min.

FRIGATES [FF]

♦ 0 (+ 4) F 125–class frigates (Type 125)

	Bldr	Started	L	In serv.
F- . . .	. . .	. . .	. . .	2011
F- . . .	. . .	. . .	. . .	. . .
F- . . .	. . .	. . .	. . .	. . .
F- . . .	. . .	. . .	. . .	. . .

D: 5,500 tons (fl) **S:** 27 kts (20 kts on diesels)
Dim: 139.0 × 18.0 × 5.00 hull (7.00 over sonar)
A: 8 AGM-84 series Harpoon or Swedish RBS 15 (Mark 3) SSM; 2 21-round RAM (Mark 49) point-defense SAM (RIM-116A missiles); 1 155-mm DP; 1 navalized 12-round MLRS (with reloads); 2 single 27-mm Rheinmetall-Mauser MLG 27 (MN 27 GS)AA; 5 12.7-mm mg; 2 NH-90 helicopters
Electronics:
Radar: . . . phased-array; 2 . . . nav.
Sonar: . . .
EW: . . . intercept; . . . jamming; . . . laser warning system; 4 decoy rocket launchers
M: CODLAG: 1 gas turbine (26,820 shp); 2 electric motors; 4 diesel generators; 2 CP props; 1 bow-thruster
Electric: . . .
Range: 4,000/ . . . **Endurance:** 21 days
Crew: 110 (plus up to 50 commandos)

Remarks: Intended to replace some of the Type 122 (*Bremen*-class) multipurpose frigates beginning around 2010. Data listed above are expected to change as preliminary requirements are still under development. Originally eight ships of this class were to be built, but financial constraints in Germany reduced the program to four units. The ships are planned to have "autonomous internal zones" divided by flexible watertight blast and fragmentation-resistant bulkheads. Current requirements indicate that the vessels are to remain operational 5,000+ hours per year with the capability to operate away from homeports up to two years at a time.
Combat systems: The ships will also carry remote operating vehicles.

♦ 4 Brandenburg class (Type 123)

	Bldr	Laid down	L	In serv.
F 215 Brandenburg	Blohm + Voss, Hamburg	11-2-92	28-8-92	14-10-94
F 216 Schleswig-Holstein	Howaldtswerke, Kiel	1-7-93	3-6-94	24-11-95
F 217 Bayern	Thyssen, Emden	16-12-93	30-6-94	15-6-96
F 218 Mecklenburg-Vorpommern	Bremer Vulkan, Bremen	23-11-93	8-7-95	6-12-96

Mecklenburg-Vorpommern (F 218) Michael Nitz, 8-05

D: 3,600 tons (4,490 fl) **S:** 29+ kt on gas turbines, 18 kts on diesels
Dim: 138.85 (126.90 pp) × 16.70 (15.74 wl) × 4.35 (6.30 over sonar)
A: 4 MM 38 Exocet SSM; 1 Mk 41 Mod. 4 vertical-launch SAM syst. (16 RIM-7M Sea Sparrow missiles); 2 21-round Mk 49 RAM point-defense SAM syst. (RIM-116A missiles); 1 76-mm 62-cal. OTO Melara SuperRapid DP; 2 single 20-mm 90-cal. Rheinmetall Rh-202 AA; 2 paired, fixed 324-mm Mk 32 ASW TT; 1–2 Super Lynx helicopters
Electronics:
Radar: 2 Raytheon Raypath nav.; 1 Thales LW-08 air search; 1 Thales SMART-S air/surf. search and targeting; 2 Thales STIR-18 f.c.
Sonar: STN Atlas Elektronik DSQS-23BZ (ASO-90) hull-mounted (6–9 kHz); provision for TASS 6-3 (LFTASS) towed array
EW: EADS FL-1800S Stage II intercept; 2 18-round OTO Melara SCLAR decoy RL; F 216 and F 217 also: EADS Maigret comms intercept system (1–1,000 MHz)
M: CODOG: 2 G.E. 7 LM-2500 9A-ML gas turbines (25,840 shp each), 2 MTU 20V956 TB92 diesels (5,535 bhp each); 2 5-bladed Escher-Wyss CP props; 51,680 shp max.
Electric: 3,000 kw tot. (4 × 750-kw van Kaick sets, MWM TBD-602-V16K diesels driving; 400 V and 115 V, 60 Hz a.c.)
Range: 4,000+/18 **Endurance:** 21 days
Crew: 26 officers, 193 enlisted (including 22 air department) + 11 command staff

Remarks: Ordered 28-6-89 from a consortium lead by Blohm + Voss with Nordseewerke (NSWE) and Howaldtswerke. Comprise the 6th Frigate Squadron, based at Wilhelmshaven. Command and control and combat systems aboard all four units will be modernized under a 9-05 contract with Thales.
Hull systems: Employ Blohm + Voss MEKO modular outfitting concepts, with extremely strong hull structure having six double-walled bulkheads, two internal 1.2-m-sq. box girders at the outer edge of the upper deck over 80% of the hull length, and a centerline 1.5 × 0.6-m box girder for strength. There are 12 major watertight compartments and four damage-control zones, each with its own zone-control station. Two diesel-driven and ten electric firepumps are fitted. Steel superstructure. Fin stabilizers fitted. Extensive signature reduction measures, with radar cross section only 10% that of the preceding Type 122. Have 230-ton displacement growth margin.
Combat systems: Have the STN Atlas Elektronik SATIR-III F-123 combat data system, using U.S. AN/UYK-43 computers, 14 STN Atlas Elektronik BM 802-52 multifunction consoles, Ada programming language, and distributed data concepts; are NATO Link 11 datalink-compatible. Have Norden TMS (Track Management System) radar track data fusion system. The SMART (Signal Multibeam Acquisition Radar for Targeting) radar surmounts the foremast. SCOT-3 SHF SATCOM terminals were ordered for these ships during 6-97. The antisubmarine system is the EFS ASO-90, using Mk 264 torpedo control panels cannibalized from *Hamburg*-class destroyers; the torpedo tubes are fixed and launch through the hull sides at a 45° angle from the centerline from positions on the main deck abreast the funnels. Are receiving the STN Atlas Elektronik–Zeis Eltro WBA (*Wärmebildanlage*) MSP 500 stabilized thermal-imaging sensor. Ophelios thermal imagers, a t.v. camera, and a laser rangefinder for the 20-mm mounts were installed beginning in 1999.

The vertical-launch SAM module forward is arranged so that the number of launch cells can be doubled at a later date. The 76-mm gun can also be controlled by the target designation sights mounted on the bridge wings. A Thales Vespa transponder system is used for helicopter control. The hull-mounted sonar had a mine-detection capability added during 1996–97. The STN Atlas Elektronik TASS 6-3 towed passive linear hydrophone array (15 Hz–1.2 kHz, with 2,400-kHz broadband) was to be backfitted around 1997 but has not yet been procured. A joint French-German Low Frequency Active Sonar System operating at 2–3 kHz is planned to be backfitted. Have the Honeywell-ELAC UT 2000 underwater telephone.

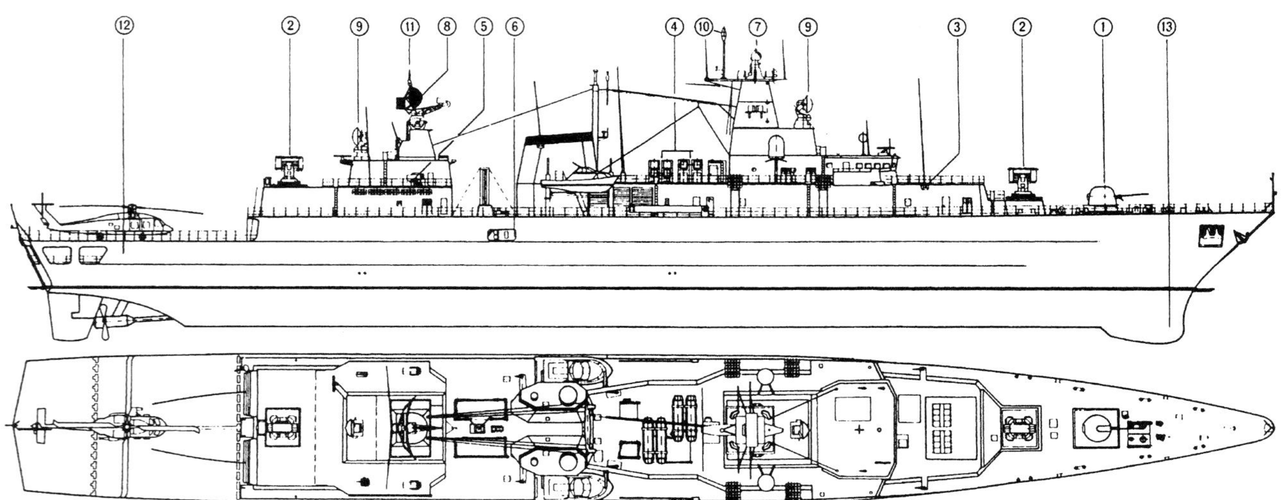

Brandenburg (F 215) 1. 76-mm OTOBreda DP gun 2. RAM missile launchers 3. Mk 41 Mod. 4 Vertical-launch system for Sea Sparrow missiles 4. MM 38 Exocet antiship missile launch canisters 5. SCLAR decoy launcher 6. Mk 32 Mod. 9 fixed ASW TT 7. SMART-S search radar 8. LW-08 early-warning radar 9. STIR radar missile tracker/illuminators 10. FL-1800S Stage II EW antenna suite 11. Type 1990 IFF interrogator antenna atop LW-08 antenna 12. Provision for future towed sonar array 13. DSQS-23BZ bow sonar
Drawing by Blohm + Voss

FRIGATES [FF] *(continued)*

Brandenburg (F 215) A. A. de Kruijf, 7-05

Bayern (F 217) Martin Mokrus, 9-05

♦ 8 Bremen class (Type 122A)

	Bldr	Laid down	L	In serv.
F 207 Bremen	Bremer-Vulkan	9-7-79	27-9-79	7-5-82
F 208 Niedersachsen	AG Weser, Bremen	9-11-79	9-6-80	15-10-82
F 209 Rheinland-Pfalz	Blohm + Voss, Hamburg	25-9-79	3-9-80	9-5-83
F 210 Emden	Nordseewerke, Emden	23-6-80	17-12-80	7-10-83
F 211 Köln	Blohm + Voss, Hamburg	16-6-80	29-5-81	19-10-84
F 212 Karlsruhe	Howaldtswerke, Kiel	10-3-81	8-1-82	19-4-84
F 213 Augsburg	Bremer-Vulkan	4-4-87	17-9-87	3-10-89
F 214 Lübeck	Thyssen, Emden	1-6-87	15-10-87	19-3-90

Bremen (F 207) Frank Findler, 4-05

Karlsruhe (F 212) Frank Findler, 3-05

Emden (F 210) Bernard Prézelin, 2-05

D: 2,950 tons (3,800 fl) **S:** 30 kts
Dim: 130.00 (121.80 wl) × 14.40 × 4.26 (6.00 sonar)
A: 8 RGM-84C Harpoon SSM; 1 8-round Mk 29 launcher for NATO Sea Sparrow SAM system (24 RIM-7M missiles); 2 21-round Mk 49 RAM SAM launchers (RIM-116A missiles); 1 76-mm 62-cal. OTO Melara DP; 2 single 20-mm 90-cal. Rheinmetall Rh-202 AA; 2 twin fixed 324-mm Mk 32 Mod. 9 ASW TT (Mk 46 Mod. 5 torpedoes); 2 Lynx Mk 88 helicopters
Electronics:
Radar: 1 S.M.A. 3RM 20 nav.; 1 Thales DA-08 (F 208, 210, 211, 212: EADS TRS-3D/32 3-D) air search; 1 Thales WM-25 track-while-scan f.c.; 1 Thales STIR-18 missile f.c.
Sonar: STN Atlas Elektronik DSQS-21BX (BO) bow-mounted LF
EW: EADS FL 1800S Stage II intercept array (7.5–17 GHz); Mk 36 SRBOC decoy syst. (4 6-round Mk 137 launchers, DM39 Bullfighter 130-mm decoys); SLQ-25 Nixie torpedo decoy
E/O: F 207, F 210: STN Atlas Elektronik–Zeiss Eltro WBA tracker
M: CODOG: 2 G.E.-Fiat LM-2500 GT (51,000 shp); 2 MTU 20V956 TB92 diesels (11,070 bhp); 2 5-bladed Escher-Wyss CP props
Electric: 3,000 kw (4 × 750-kw diesel sets) **Range:** 5,700/17 **Fuel:** 610 tons
Crew: 21 officers, 160 enlisted (plus 6-officer/12-enlisted air complement)

Remarks: First six ordered 7-77, last two 12-85. Bremer-Vulkan performed the weapons and electronics outfitting and integration. Comprise the 2nd and 4th Frigate Squadrons, based at Wilhelmshaven.

FRIGATES [FF] *(continued)*

Hull systems: Fin stabilizers are fitted. Have the U.S. Prairie/Masker bubbler system to reduce radiated noise and have a citadel NBC protection system. F 212 has a revised engine air intake system. During refits from 1992 to 1997, enhanced signature reduction measures were incorporated.
Combat systems: Have the SATIR tactical data system (with Unisys UYK-7 computers). Are Link 11-compatible. The Norden TMS (Track Management System) radar track data fusion system was fitted during late 1990s refits. The helicopters are equipped with DAQS-13D dipping sonar and Mk 46 Mod. 5 torpedoes. A Thales Vesta helicopter transponder and the Beartrap haul-down and deck control system are installed. Carry 16 torpedoes for helicopters, 8 for the tubes. Three sets U.K. SCOT 1A SHF SATCOM gear have been acquired for use aboard deployed units of this class.

The ships were designated Type 122A on completion of refits from 1992 to 1999, during which two Mk 49 RAM launchers were installed atop the hangars, the WM 25 fire-control systems were updated, the UYK-7 computers were replaced by UYK-43s, and the EW suite was upgraded to FL1800S Stage II status with Racal SADIE processors and EADS high-resolution color displays. A concurrent effort was to have been made to replace the DA-08 search radar with the EADS TRS-3D/32 (C-band), but as of late 2002, only four ships had been modified. The hull-mounted sonar had a mine-detection capability added during 1996–97. F 210 is equipped with the prototype STN Atlas Elektronik–Zeiss Eltro WBA (*Wärmebildanlage*) MSP 500 stabilized thermal-imaging sensor, which is to be backfitted in all; the system can control the 76-mm gun. Ophelios thermal imagers, a t.v. camera, and a laser rangefinder were added for the 20-mm mounts beginning in 1999. Command and control and combat systems are to be modernized aboard all units under a 9-05 contract with Thales.

CORVETTES [FFL]

♦ 0 (+ 5) Braunschweig class (Type 130)

	Bldr	Laid down	L	In serv.
F 260 Braunschweig	Blohm + Voss, Hamburg	3-12-04	2006	5-07
F 261 Magdeburg	Lürssen, Vegesack	19-5-05	2006	2007
F 262 Erfurt	Nordseewerke, Emden	22-9-05	2007	2008
F 263 Oldenburg	Blohm + Voss, Hamburg	17-10-05	2008	2008
F 264 Ludwigshafen	Lürssen, Vegesack	2006	2008	11-08

Magdeburg (F 261)—at launching Michael Nitz, 9-06

Magdeburg (F 261)—at launching Michael Nitz, 9-06

D: 1,690 tons (fl) **S:** 26+ kts **Dim:** 88.75 (82.80 pp) × 13.23 × 3.2
A: 4 Saab Bofors RBS-15 Mk 3 SSM; 2 21-round Mk 49 RAM SAM launcher (RIM-116 Block 1B missiles); 1 76-mm 62-cal. OTO Melara DP; 2 single 27-mm Mauser MLG 27 AA; 4 portable mine rails (. . . mines); 2 . . . drone reconnaissance helicopters
Electronics:
Radar: 2 Raytheon-STN Atlas Pathfinder/ST Mk 2 ARPA nav.; EADS TRS-3D/16 surf./air search; 2 Thales Mirador radar-E/O directors
Sonar: . . . hull-mounted; STN Atlas Elektronik COTASS active/passive towed array
EW: EADS SPS-N/KJS-5000 intercept, KJS-N-5000 jammer, 2 Buck MASS decoy RL; EADS COLDS laser countermeasure
E/O: 2 STN Atlas Elektronik Mirador MSP 500 stabilized E/O gun directors
M: 2 . . . diesels; 2 CP props; 19,850 b/shp
Electric: 2,200 kw tot. (4 × 550 kw, diesel-driven sets)
Range: 4,000+/15 **Endurance:** 21 days
Crew: 11 officers, 16 senior petty officers, 38 other enlisted (76 accomm.)

Remarks: A new class of up to 15 guided missile–carrying corvettes, named for German cities, was planned to replace the Type 143, 143A, and 148 missile boats. The program was cut to five in 11-00. The team of Blohm + Voss, Friedrich Lürssen Werft, and Nordseewerke (NSWE) (with EADS Deutschland and Thales as systems integrators) was selected on 17-7-00, but the building contract was not signed until 13-12-01; the ships are to cost about $186 million each. The design is based closely on Blohm + Voss's MEKO A100 design, but the MEKO modular weapons and sensor installation system will not be employed. All are planned to be based at Warnemünde.
Hull systems: The propulsion system will probably employ two diesel engines with a waterline exhaust system to reduce IR signature. Accommodations will be provided for a flag officer and 25 staff in addition to the normal crew; personnel will be accommodated in two-, four-, or six-berth staterooms. The hull and superstructure are configured to reduce the radar cross-section to less than that of a Type 143 PTG. Will be able to maintain 15 kts Sea State 5 and Beaufort Force 12 wind; on one engine, the ship will be able to maintain 20 kts. The flight deck aft will be 24 m long by 12.6 m wide and will be able to accommodate a 12-ton helicopter. The design allows for a growth of 110 tons displacement. A bulbous forefoot is fitted to the bow. Automatic rudder roll stabilization is provided.
Combat systems: The combat system will be based on the Thales Sigma Splice (SEWACO-FD) and will incorporate Links 11 and 16 and seven multifunction display consoles, four workstations, and two combat system databuses. The communications suite will include UHF SATCOM with provision for later installation of SHF SATCOM; Inmarsat B and M commercial SATCOM will also be provided, along with a German Army communications set.

The flight deck aft is to be able to accommodate a Lynx or NH-90 helicopter, but there will be no hangar other than a small one for the two drone surveillance helicopters that were to have entered service in 2006 but have been delayed. In theory, the drones will serve as the class's principal sensor, operating in a radius of up to 100 km from the ship. The 76-mm guns are to be recycled from stricken PTGs. A torpedo defense system is to be added starting in 2008; it will employ adjuncts to the sonar array and a launcher mounted in place of the after RAM launcher, which will be moved to a higher location.

GUIDED-MISSILE PATROL CRAFT [PTG]

♦ 10 Type 143A

Bldrs: A: Lürssen, Vegesack; B: Kröger, Rendsburg

	Bldr	Laid down	L	In serv.
P 6121 Gepard (S 71)	A	11-7-79	25-9-81	15-12-82
P 6122 Puma (S 72)	A	17-12-79	8-2-82	15-2-83
P 6123 Hermelin (S 73)	B	1-2-80	8-12-81	28-4-83
P 6124 Nerz (S 74)	A	24-7-80	18-8-82	14-7-83
P 6125 Zobel (S 75)	B	3-7-80	30-6-82	29-9-83
P 6126 Frettchen (S 76)	A	22-12-80	26-1-83	16-12-83
P 6127 Dachs (S 77)	B	9-3-80	14-12-82	22-3-84
P 6128 Ozelot (S 78)	A	25-6-81	7-6-83	25-5-84
P 6129 Wiesel (S 79)	A	5-10-80	8-8-83	12-7-84
P 6130 Hyäne (S 80)	A	7-12-81	5-10-83	13-11-84

Puma (P 6122) Michael Nitz, 3-05

D: 300 tons (390.6 fl) **S:** 36 kts (32 fl)
Dim: 57.6 (54.4 pp) × 7.76 × 2.99 (2.56 hull)
A: 4 MM 38 Exocet SSM; 1 21-round Mk 49 RAM point-defense SAM syst.; (RIM-116A missiles); 1 76-mm 62-cal. OTO Melara DP; 2 single 12.7-mm mg; 2 mine rails
Electronics:
Radar: 1 SMA 3RM 20 nav.; 1 Thales WM-27 track-while-scan f.c.
EW: EADS FL-1800S Stage II intercept; 2 6-round Buck-Wegmann Hot Dog/ Silver Dog decoy RL; Wolke chaff dispenser

GUIDED-MISSILE PATROL CRAFT [PTG] *(continued)*

Hyäne (P 6130) Michael Nitz, 5-05

Zobel (P 6125) Bernard Prézelin, 3-05

M: 4 MTU 16V956 TB91 diesels; 4 props; 16,000 bhp (at 1,515 rpm)
Electric: 540 kw tot. **Range:** 600/30; 2,600/16 **Fuel:** 116 tons
Crew: 4 officers, 18 petty officers, 12 ratings

Remarks: Ordered 1978 from AEG-Telefunken, with shipbuilders listed above as subcontractors. Design is a repeat of Type 143 with RAM point-defense SAM system in place of the Type 143's after 76-mm gun and mine rails in place of the wire-guided torpedoes. Were originally to have been retired by 2007, but in 1999 they began refits to extend their lives by 10 years. The first five constitute the 7th Fast Attack Craft Squadron and the remainder the 2nd Fast Attack Squadron; both squadrons are based at Warnemünde. Will eventually be replaced by the Type 130 corvettes.
Hull systems: Wood-planked hull on steel frame. Round-bilge hull form.
Combat systems: Type 143A missile patrol boats carry the AGIS fire-control system combined with Thales WM-27M radar. AGIS has two computers, one for fire control and the other for real-time threat-processing. WM 27 has two antennas within its dome, one for search and one for tracking. An automatic datalink permits AGIS to share information with other units of the Type 143/143A units and with major surface combatants. The combat data systems were updated starting in 1999 by a consortium led by Thales.

The craft lack the after optical gun director found on Type 143. Chaff is dispensed from a vertical pipe attached to the after side of the tripod mast. Mk 49 RAM launchers were added on sterns during refits 1993–97. In 2000 P 6123 was the first to complete an EW suite update with Racal SADIE processors and high-resolution color displays by EADS. P 6128 conducted successful trials with the STN Atlas Elektronik MSP 500 stabilized E/O director for the 76-mm gun during 9-00; the director will be mounted on the 76-mm gunhouses of the rest of the class.

Disposal note: All of the 20 missile craft of Type 148 have been retired by 2003.

All ten Type 143–class guided missile patrol craft have been retired from service by 2005. P 6113, P 1115, P 6116 and P 6118–P 6120 were transferred to Tunisia during 2005–6.

MINE WARFARE SHIPS

♦ 10 Type 332 coastal minehunters [MHC]

Bldrs: A: Abeking & Rasmussen, Lemwerder; B: Lürssenwerft, Vegesack; C: Krögerwerft, Rendsburg

	Bldr	Laid down	L	In serv.
M 1058 Fulda	A	12-95	29-9-97	16-6-98
M 1060 Weiden	A	1-3-90	14-5-92	30-3-93
M 1061 Rottweil	C	17-4-90	12-3-92	7-7-93
M 1062 Sulzbach-Rosenberg	B	1-9-92	27-4-95	23-1-96
M 1063 Bad Bevensen	B	19-11-90	21-1-93	9-12-93
M 1064 Grömitz	C	2-4-91	22-4-93	23-8-94
M 1065 Dillingen	A	15-1-92	26-5-94	25-4-95
M 1067 Bad Rappenau	A	20-2-91	3-6-93	19-4-94
M 1068 Datteln	C	11-11-91	27-1-94	8-12-94
M 1069 Homburg	B	17-2-92	21-4-94	15-8-95

D: 590 tons (650 fl) **S:** 18 kts **Dim:** 54.40 (51.00 pp) × 9.20 × 2.60 (3.3 props)
A: 1 40-mm 70-cal. Bofors AA; 2 Stinger/Fliegerfaust point-defense SAM positions; up to 60 mines
Electronics:
Radar: 1 Raytheon SPS-64(V) nav.
Sonar: STN Atlas Elektronik DSQS-11M minehunting
EW: Thales DR 2000 intercept; 2 6-round Buck-Wegmann Hot Dog/Silver Dog decoy RL
M: 2 MTU 16V396 TB84 diesels; 2 Voith-Schneider vertical cycloidal props; 6,140 bhp—low-speed drive

Homburg (M 1069) Michael Nitz, 8-05

Bad Bevensen (M 1063) Leo Van Ginderen, 6-05

Electric: 690 kw tot. (3 × 230 kw; 3 MWM 6-cyl. diesels driving)
Range: . . . / . . .
Crew: 5 officers, 6 chief petty officers, 13 petty officers, 6 ratings

Remarks: First ten ordered 26-2-88 from prime contractor Messerschmidt-Bölkow-Blohm. Two more were added to the 1996 budget and ordered 8-95; the hulls for both were fitted out by Krögerwerft. The design is a minehunter version of Type 343 with slightly different hullform, minehunting sonar, and low-speed drive. Constitute the 1st Mine Countermeasures Squadron, based at Olpenitz. *Frankenthall* (M 1066) and *Weilheim* (1059) were sold to the United Arab Emirates in 2006. Five of the class will reportedly enter reserve status to save money.
Hull systems: Shock mountings are provided for virtually every piece of equipment and for all crew seats. Navigation systems are, surprisingly, not extensive.
Combat systems: Have the STN Atlas Elektronik MWS 80-4 minehunting system with SATAM command system. Carry two Pinguin B3 remote-controlled mine location/destruction submersibles and four mine-clearance divers. The Pinguin weighs 1.35 tons, is 3.5 m long, travels at up to 8 kts, and has an STN Atlas Elektronik AIS 11 high-frequency sonar. Haux Spacestar three-man decompression chambers for mine disposal divers are carried. The 40-mm gun is in a standard Bofors mounting but has the Trinity autoloading feature. The Stinger SAM-launching positions are in armored tubs on the upper deck amidships.

Five of the class are to receive a new minehunting system: MA 2000 (*Minenabwehr Ausrüstung* 2000) uses two 99-ton Seepferd drones, each towing an underwater sensor vehicle with side-scan, mine-avoidance, and buried-mine detector sonars; the ships will also carry an EFS Expendable Mine Disposal System. M 1060 conducted trials with the STN Atlas Elektronik-Zeiss Eltro WBA (*Wärmebildanlage*) stabilized thermal sensor system, which can be used to control the gun.

♦ 5 Type 333 coastal minhunter conversions [MHC]

Bldrs: A: Abeking & Rasmussen, Lemwerder; B: Krögerwerft, Rendsburg

	Bldr	Laid down	L	In serv.
M 1091 Kulmbach	A	14-9-87	15-6-89	24-4-90
M 1095 Überherrn	A	15-12-86	30-8-88	19-9-89
M 1096 Passau	A	1-7-88	1-3-90	18-12-90
M 1097 Laboe	B	2-3-87	13-9-88	7-12-89
M 1099 Herten	B	16-6-88	22-12-89	26-2-91

D: 620 tons (fl) **S:** 18 kts **Dim:** 54.40 (51.00 pp) × 9.20 × 2.50 (3.20 props)
A: 2 single 40-mm 70-cal. OTO Melara-Bofors AA; 2 Stinger/Fliegerfaust point-defense SAM positions; up to 60 mines
Electronics:
Radar: 1 Raytheon SPS-64 nav.; 1 WM-20/2 track-while-scan f.c.
Sonar: STN Atlas Elektronik DSQS-11M hull-mounted retractable HF
EW: Thales DR 2000 intercept; 2 6-round Buck-Wegmann Hot Dog/Silver Dog decoy RL
M: 2 MTU 16V396 TB84-DB51L diesels; 2 Escher-Wyss CP props; 6,080 bhp
Electric: 1,050 kw (3 MWM TBD 601 65 diesels, 639 bhp each, driving)
Range: . . . / . . . **Crew:** 4 officers, 20 petty officers, 13 ratings

Remarks: Ordered from prime contractor Messerschmidt-Bölkow-Blohm (MBB) on 10-1-85 as Type 343 minesweepers. Under a 1-98 contract with STN Atlas Elektronik, these five have been modified as Type 333 minehunters by Peenewerft, Wolgast. M 1091 was the first completed, on 24-9-99, with M 1097 following in 3-00. Are based at Olpenitz.

MINE WARFARE SHIPS *(continued)*

Herten (M 1099) Michael Nitz, 5-05

Kulmbach (M 1091) Martin Mokrus, 2-04

Hull systems: Constructed using antimagnetic steel left over from the Type 206 submarine program.
Combat systems: The SM 343 conversions have the DSQS-11M hull-mounted variable-depth minehunting sonar, remotely operated minehunting submersibles (either PAP 104 Mk 5 or Pinguin B3, eventually to be supplanted by Seefuchs I identification and Seefuchs-C expendable mine disposal drones); support systems for mine disposal divers (including a three-man decompression chamber), and modifications to the propulsion plant and rudders to permit low-speed operations.

They have PALIS and Link 11 data link, a SARIE signal analyzer for the EW system, and a NAVSTAR SATNAV receiver. The WM-20 radar systems come from stricken *Zobel*-class torpedo boats. The 40-mm Bofors guns are in OTO Melara mountings and have enclosed GRP gunhouses made by Mauser.

♦ 5 Type 352 drone mine-countermeasures craft control ships [MSA]
Bldrs: A: Lürssen Werft, Vegesack; B: Krögerwerft, Rendsburg

	Bldr	Laid down	L	In serv.
M 1090 Pegnitz	A	6-7-87	13-3-89	9-3-90
M 1092 Hameln	A	18-6-86	15-3-88	29-6-89
M 1093 Auerbach/Opf	A	3-1-89	18-6-90	7-5-91
M 1094 Ensdorf	A	15-3-88	8-12-89	25-9-90
M 1098 Siegburg	B	13-10-87	14-4-89	17-7-90

Auerbach/Opf (M 1093) Frank Findler, 10-04

D: 620 tons (fl) **S:** 18 kts **Dim:** 54.40 (51.00 pp) × 9.20 × 2.50 (3.20 props)
A: 2/40-mm 70-cal. OTO Melara-Bofors AA—2 Stinger/Fliegerfaust point-defense SAM positions—up to 60 mines

Pegnitz (M 1090) Leo Van Ginderen, 7-05

Electronics:
Radar: 1 Raytheon SPS-64 nav., 1 H.S.A. WM-20/2 track-while-scan f.c.
Sonar: STN Atlas Elektronik DSQS-11M hull-mounted retractable HF
EW: Thales DR-2000 intercept, 2 6-round Buck-Wegmann Hot Dog/Silver Dog decoy RL
M: 2 MTU 16V396 TB84-DB51L diesels; 2 Escher-Wyss CP props; 6,080 bhp
Electric: 1,050 kw (3 MWM TBD 601 65 diesels, 639 bhp each, driving)
Range: . . . / . . . **Crew:** 4 officers, 20 petty officers, 13 ratings

Remarks: Ordered from prime contractor Messerschmidt-Bölkow-Blohm (MBB) on 10-1-85 as Type 343 minesweepers. Under a 12-97 contract with STN Atlas Elektronik, have been converted as HL 352 (*Hohlstab Lenkboot*) drone control vessels, with M 1093 the first to complete, in 11-99, and all finished by end 2001. M 1092 and M 1094 were converted by Lürssenwerft, the others by Abeking & Rasmussen. All are based at Olpenitz.
Hull systems: Constructed using antimagnetic steel left over from the Type 206 submarine program.
Combat systems: As converted with a new control system developed jointly with the Netherlands, they now can control three of the existing Seehund drones each; also carried are a mine-avoidance sonar and remotely controlled submersibles for use in clearing moored mines. In the latter part of the 2000 decade, the MA 2000 program will result in another modernization that will employ the planned Seepferd drone, which will deploy a towed mine location sonar and sophisticated hull-mounted sonars, with all sensors integrated via computer. Seepferd is expected to displace 99 tons and to be 26 m overall. Also under development are Seewolf expendable bottomed-mine disposal drone and the smaller Seefuchs expendable disposal drone.

They have PALIS and Link 11 datalink, a SARIE signal analyzer for the EW system, and a NAVSTAR SATNAV receiver. The WM 20-radar systems come from stricken *Zobel*-class torpedo boats. The 40-mm Bofors guns are in OTO Melara mountings and have enclosed GRP gunhouses made by Mauser.

Disposal note: Of the *Lindau*-class minehunters, Type 331A variants *Flensburg* (M 1084) and *Fulda* (M 1086) were stricken 6-91 and 26-3-92, respectively, with M 1084 transferred to the city of Duisburg as *Jugendschiff Ruhrort* on 7-4-95. Of the Type 331B variants, *Weilheim* (M 1077) was stricken 15-6-95; *Wetzlar* (M 1075) on 30-6-95 (sold for scrap 1-7-96); *Tübingen* (M 1074) on 26-6-97 (sold for private use in Italy); *Göttingen* (M 1070) on 11-9-97 (transferred to Estonia for cannibalization spares 2-01, lost en route); *Minden* (M 1085) on 4-12-97 (transferred to Georgia on 22-10-98); *Völklingen* (M 1087) on 23-3-99 (transferred to Latvia on 24-3-99); *Koblenz* (M 1071) on 4-12-99 (transferred to Lithuania on the same date); and *Cuxhaven* (M 1078) on 15-1-00 (transferred to Estonia 9-00); *Lindau* (M 1072) on 27-9-00 (transferred to Estonia on 9-10-00); and *Marburg* (M 1080) on 25-5-00 and transferred to Lithuania on 16-11-00.

Of the six Type 351 drone control ships, *Ulm* (M 1083) was retired 21-9-99, *Paderborn* (M 1076) on 30-6-00, and *Schleswig* (M 1073), *Düren* (M 1079), *Konstanz* (M 1081), and *Wolfsburg* (M 1082) on 29-9-00; all six were transferred to South Africa on 15-1-01 and departed on 25-0-01 as deck cargo.

♦ 1 prototype SWATH drone
Bldr: Abeking & Rasmussen (In serv. 2004)

Explorer

Explorer—prototype SWATH vessel Frank Findler, 4-05

D: 135 tons (fl) **S:** 18 kts **Dim:** 25.2 × 13.0 × 2.7
Electronics:
Radar: 1 . . . nav.
Sonar: 1 . . . STN Atlas towed array

MINE WARFARE SHIPS *(continued)*

M: 2 MTU 12V2,000 M-70 diesels; 2 waterjets
Electric: 1,580 kw
Range: . . . / . . . **Crew:** . . .

Remarks: Order approved by Parliament summer 2002, with a consortium of Abeking & Rasmussen, EADS, Friedrich Lürssen Werft, and STN Atlas Elektronik to participate. SWATH (Small Waterplane Area, Twin-Hull) hull design based on Abeking & Rasmussen's 25-m pilot boats of 1999. Construction began in 2003. The vessel is officially leased to the German Navy for trials.

♦ 18 Type HL 351 Troika drones [MSD]
Bldr: MAK, Kiel

	In serv.		In serv.
Seehund 1	1-8-80	Seehund 10	11-11-81
Seehund 2	1-8-80	Seehund 11	11-11-81
Seehund 3	1-8-80	Seehund 12	11-11-81
Seehund 4	17-7-81	Seehund 13	1-9-82
Seehund 5	17-7-81	Seehund 14	1-9-82
Seehund 6	17-7-81	Seehund 15	1-9-82
Seehund 7	17-9-81	Seehund 16	13-5-82
Seehund 8	17-9-81	Seehund 17	13-5-82
Seehund 9	17-9-81	Seehund 18	13-5-82

Seehund 7 Michael Nitz, 5-05

D: 91 tons (96.5 fl) **S:** 9.4 kts **Dim:** 24.92 × 4.46 × 1.8
M: 1 MWM TRHS 518A diesel; Schottel prop; 445 hp
Electric: 208 kw **Range:** 520/8.8 **Crew:** 3 tot. (for transit)

Remarks: Ordered 1977 to operate three-apiece with the Type 351 control ships. Beginning 1999, were converted to work with the Type 352–conversion control ships.
Combat systems: Essentially remote-controlled, self-propelled magnetic minesweeping solenoids with all machinery highly shock-protected. Also able to stream two sets Type SDG-21 Oropesa mechanical minesweeping gear.

Disposal note: The remaining Type 394A inshore minesweepers, *Frauenlob* (M 2658) and *Gefion* (M 2660), were decommissioned together on 27-3-02, and *Loreley* (M 2665) was decommissioned on 27-6-02 and transferred to Estonia during 2003 as a spare parts source. *Nixe* (M 2655) was sold to the city of Hamburg on 8-4-94. *Nautilus* (M 2659) was stricken 28-4-94 after incurring damage and was sold for scrap 1-7-96. *Minerva* (M 2663) and *Diana* (M 2664) were stricken 16-2-95 and were transferred to Estonia in 1997. *Atlantis* (M 2666) and *Acheron* (M 2667) were stricken 20-3-95 (with the former donated 23-4-00 as a museum ship at Dresden and the latter sold for scrap on 1-7-96). *Medusa* (M 2661) was stricken on 14-6-01 and *Undine* (M 2662) on 28-6-01, with the latter transferred to Estonia on 12-11-02.

Note: The hulk of Type 394 minesweeper *Gazelle* is stationed at the Naval Technical School, Parow, with the last remaining *Schütze*-class minesweeper, the *Widder,* for use in familiarization, seamanship, and damage control training; both remain armed and fully equipped but do not carry pennant numbers and do not get under way.

♦ 1 Type 340 mine countermeasures diver support ship [MSA]

	Bldr	L	In serv.
M 1052 Mühlhausen (ex-*Walther von Ledebur,* A 1410; ex-Y 841)	Burmester, Bremen	30-6-66	21-12-67

Mühlhausen (M 1052) Martin Mokrus, 8-05

D: 775 tons (825 fl) **S:** 19 kts **Dim:** 63.20 × 10.60 × 3.00
A: None **Electronics:** Radar: 1 Kelvin-Hughes 14/9 nav.
M: 2 Maybach 16-cyl. diesels; 2 props; 5,200 bhp
Electric: 1,620 kw tot. **Crew:** . . . tot.

Remarks: Employed in mine warfare research until decommissioning 24-3-94. Reactivated 3-3-95 and converted to serve as replacement for *Stier* (M 1050) and recommissioned under new name on 6-4-95. As research ship, was equipped with mechanical, acoustic, and magnetic mine-countermeasures gear. Has two 600-kw sweep current generators. Refitted and updated 1997 at Peenewerft, with new diver support equipment. Wooden construction. Based at Eckernförde.

AMPHIBIOUS WARFARE SHIPS AND CRAFT

Note: Plans to construct two amphibious warfare dock landing ships [LPD] similar to the Netherlands' *Rotterdam* (L 800) were announced 11-00 but were canceled as a result of budget cuts.

♦ 2 Type 520 utility landing craft [LCU]
Bldr: Howaldtswerke, Hamburg

	In serv.
L 762 Lachs	17-2-66
L 765 Schlei	17-5-66

Schlei (L 765) Michael Winter, 6-05

D: 166 tons (403 fl) **S:** 11 kts **Dim:** 40.04 (36.7 pp) × 8.8 × 1.6 (2.1 max.)
A: Provision for 2 single 20-mm Rheinmetall Rh 202 AA; mines
Electronics: Radar: 1 Kelvin-Hughes 14/9 nav.
M: 2 MWM 12-cyl. diesels; 2 props; 1,200 bhp
Electric: 130 kVA **Range:** 1,200/11 **Crew:** 17 tot.

Remarks: Design based on the American LCU 1646 class. Cargo: 237 tons max.; 141.6 normal. Both are attached to the Mine Warfare Command and are maintained at Olpenitz as part of the 3rd Minesweeping Squadron. Armament has been removed.
Disposals: Sisters *Renke* (L 798) and *Salm* (L 799) transferred to Greece 16-11-89; *Barbe* (L 790), *Delphin* (L 791), and *Dorsch* (L 792) were stricken 26-9-91 and transferred to Greece; *Karpfen* (L 761) was stricken on 30-1-92, *Rochen* (L 764) on 14-2-92 (and transferred to Greece 20-10-92), *Stör* (L 766) on 16-9-92, *Tümmler* (L 767) on 16-9-92, *Wels* (L 768) on 11-12-92, *Butt* (L 786) on 4-12-92, *Brasse* (L 789) on 16-4-92, *Felchen* (L 793) and *Forelle* (L 794) on 1-11-91 (and transferred to Greece), *Inger* (L 795) on 30-9-92, *Makrele* (L 796) on 8-11-91, and *Muräne* (L 797) on 14-2-92 (transferred to Greece on 20-10-92). L 761, 766, 767, and 789 were sold for scrap on 17-7-96; L 768, 786, and 795 were sold for scrap 19-7-95. *Flunder* (L 760) was stricken on 16-5-01 and *Plötze* (L 763) on 7-9-01. *Zander* (769) was stricken 2-02.

♦ 2 Type 521 landing craft [LCM]
Bldr: Rheinwerft, Walsum (In serv. 1966–67)

LCM 14 Sardelle LCM 25 Muschel (ex-L 784)

Sardelle (LCM 14) Frank Findler, 7-04

D: 116 tons (168 fl) **S:** 10.6 kts **Dim:** 23.56 × 6.40 × 1.46
Electronics: Radar: 1 . . . nav.
M: 2 MWM 8-cyl. diesels; 2 props; 684 bhp
Electric: 28 kw tot. **Range:** 690/10; 1,430/7 **Crew:** 7 tot.

Remarks: Design based on U.S. LCM(8). Cargo: 60 tons or 50 troops. LCM 23 was reactivated on 14-6-95 and converted for use as an oilspill skimmer craft at Warnemünde. Two are now assigned to Kiel, one at Wilhelmshaven, and one at Parow. Reverted to original LCM-series numbers in mid-1990s.
Disposals: Sisters LCM 1–11 were transferred to Greece and shipped on 25-4-91. Most of the other units of the class have been converted to serve as pollution clearance craft and transferred to various local governments. LCM 14 is expected to retire by 2007.

AUXILIARIES

♦ 1 Type 760 ammunition ships [AE]

Bldr: Orenstein & Koppel, Lübeck

	Laid down	L	In serv.
A 1435 WESTERWALD	3-11-65	25-2-66	11-2-67

Westerwald (A 1435) Martin Mokrus, 9-03

D: 3,460 tons (4,014 fl) **S:** 17 kts **Dim:** 105.27 × 14.02 × 3.70 (4.50 max.)
A: Removed
Electronics: Radar: 1 Kelvin-Hughes 14/9 nav.
M: 2 Maybach MD 874 diesels; 2 CP props; 5,600 bhp—bow-thruster
Electric: 1,285 kw tot. **Range:** 3,500/17 **Crew:** 31 tot. (civilian)

Remarks: Similar to Type 701 replenishment tenders, but carries only ammunition. Cargo: 1,080 tons. Two 3-ton electric cranes are fitted, as well as three lighter-capacity cargo booms. Homeported at Wilhelmshaven.

Disposal note: Sister *Odenwald* (A 1436) was extended in service until 2-02 and transferred to Egypt during 8-02.

♦ 3 Type 423 intelligence collection ships [AGI]

Bldr: Flensburger Schiffbaugesellschaft, Flensburg

	Laid down	L	In serv.
A 50 ALSTER	14-3-88	3-11-88	5-10-89
A 52 OSTE	21-11-86	15-5-87	30-6-88
A 53 OKER	15-12-86	24-9-87	24-11-88

Oste (A 52) Leo Van Ginderen, 6-05

D: 2,375 tons (3,200 fl) **S:** 20 kts **Dim:** 83.50 (75.70 pp) × 14.60 × 4.18
A: Provision for 2 single 27-mm Mauser MLG 27 AA
Electronics:
Radar: 1 . . . nav; 1 . . . surf. search; 1 . . . ranging and tracking
Sonar: STN Atlas Elektronik AISYS passive array
EW: 300 MHz–40 GHz intercept suite; EADS COLDS laser countermeasure
M: 2 Deutz-MWM SBV 16M 628 diesels; 2 fixed-pitch, 6-bladed props; 8,800 bhp—2 380-shp electric motors for low speed, quiet operations (2 MWM-KHD 604 V12 diesel generator sets)
Electric: . . . kw tot. (3 Deutz MWM 6-cyl., 280-bhp diesels driving)
Range: 5,000/18 **Crew:** 42 ship's company + 38 technicians

Remarks: A 52 and A 53 were ordered 3-7-85 as replacements for ships of the same name; A 50 was ordered on 15-12-86. Also carry electro-optical surveillance equipment. Built to commercial standards. All three are based at Kiel. The COLDS (Common Opto-electronic Laser Detection System) detects laser missile seekers and projects an equivalent pulse-repetition-frequency beam at a safe spot on the ocean surface to spoof the missile. During refits beginning in 1999, were said to have received gun armament, replenishment-at-sea facilities, and improved accommodations, but the guns have yet to be installed.

♦ 1 Type 751 oceanographic research ship [AGOR]

Bldr: Nordseewerke (NSWE), Emden

	Laid down	L	Del.	In serv.
A 1437 PLANET	26-04-02	12-8-03	6-04	2004

Planet (A 1437) Michael Nitz, 5-05

D: 3,500 tons (fl) **S:** 15 kts (sust.) **Dim:** 73.00 × 27.20 (25.00 deck) × 6.80
A: 1 fixed, submerged 533-mm TT
Electronics: Radar: 2 . . . nav.—Sonar: . . .
M: Diesel-electric drive: 4 . . . diesels, 5,400 kw tot. generator capacity, 2 Jeumont-Framatome axial-flux permanent magnet motors; 2 shrouded props; 6,000 shp—2 bow- and 2 stern-thrusters
Range: 5,000/15 **Endurance:** 30 days
Crew: 25 + 20 trials personnel or scientists

Remarks: The *Wehrforschungs und Erpropungsschiff* (WFES) trials vessel was ordered on 7-12-00. Assisted with trials of the DM-2A4 torpedo and Type 212 submarines during 2004–6.
Hull systems: Employs a SWATH (Small Waterplane Area, Twin-Hull) catamaran configuration. A containerized fuel cell supplies emergency and in-port electrical requirements. A stern radial gallows equipment crane is installed, as is a twin-drum towing winch. Up to five portable laboratory/equipment vans can be accommodated. The trials torpedo tube is installed in the lower, starboard hull pontoon. A full suite of oceanographic equipment, including precision cranes, can be carried, and the ship is equipped for trials with new sonar systems.

Disposal note: Type 750 oceanographic research ship *Planet* (A 1452, ex-Y 843) was retired 12-03.

♦ 2 Type 704 replenishment oilers [AO]

Bldr: Krögerwerft, Rendsburg

	L	In serv.
A 1442 SPESSART (ex-*Okapi*)	13-2-75	23-9-77
A 1443 RHÖN (ex-*Okene*)	23-8-74	5-9-77

Spessart (A 1442) Bernard Prézelin, 4-05

Rhön (A 1443) Martin Mokrus, 9-05

AUXILIARIES *(continued)*

D: 14,260 tons (fl) **S:** 16.3 kts **Dim:** 130.15 × 19.33 × 8.20
A: 2 Stinger/Fliegerfaust point-defense SAM positions
Electronics: Radar: 1 . . . nav.
M: 1 MAK 12-cyl. diesel; CP prop; 8,000 bhp
Electric: 2,000 kw tot. **Range:** 7,400/16 **Crew:** 42 tot. (civilian)

Remarks: 6,103 grt/10,800 dwt. Purchased from Bulk Acid Carriers, Monrovia, Liberia, in 1976 and converted as replenishment oilers, A 1442 at Bremerhaven Naval Arsenal and A 1443 by Krögerwerft. Fitted with one underway-replenishment station per side. Cargo: 9,500 m^3 distillate fuel, 1,650 m^3 fuel oil, 400 m^3 water. Hull has a pronounced bulbous bow. Protected shoulder-launch SAM positions were added during the mid-1990s.

♦ 2 Type 703 small replenishment oilers [AO]
Bldr: Lindenauwerft, Kiel

	Laid down	L	In serv.
A 1425 Ammersee	28-3-66	9-7-66	2-3-67
A 1426 Tegernsee	21-4-66	22-10-66	23-3-67

Ammersee (A 1425) Martin Mokrus, 8-04

D: 2,191 tons (fl) **S:** 12.5 kts **Dim:** 71.94 × 11.22 × 4.40
Electronics: Radar: 2 . . . nav.
M: 2 MWM 12-cyl. diesels; 1 KaMeWa CP prop; 1,200 bhp
Electric: 635 kw tot. **Range:** 3,250/12 **Crew:** 21 tot. (civilian)

Remarks: Cargo capacity: 1,130 m^3 fuel, 60 m^3 water. The one alongside-refueling station can work to either beam. The ships are frequently used to accompany deploying Type 143A missile boats.

Disposal note: A 1427 was retired during 2003. Sister *Walchensee* (A 1424) was stricken on 19-12-01.

♦ 2 (+ 1) Type 702 (KSV 90) replenishment ships [AOR]
Bldr: Flensburger Schiffbau-Gesellschaft (FSG) & Lürssen-Krögerwerft

	Laid down	L	In serv.
A 1411 Berlin	4-1-99	30-4-99	11-4-01
A 1412 Frankfurt/Main	28-8-00	5-1-01	27-5-02
A 1413 . . .			2009

Frankfurt/Main (A 1412) Frank Findler, 6-05

Frankfurt/Main (A 1412) A. A. de Kruijf, 4-05

D: 10,115 tons light (20,243 fl) **S:** 20 kts
Dim: 173.70 (162.00 pp) × 24.00 × 7.40
A: 4 single 20-mm 90-cal. Rheinmetall Rh 202 AA; provision for 2 Stinger/Fliegerfaust point-defense SAM positions
Electronics: Radar: 3 . . . nav.—Sonar: . . . mine avoidance
M: 2 M.A.N.-B&W 12V32/40 diesels; 2 5-bladed props; 14,154 bhp—bow-thruster
Electric: . . . kw tot. (4 × . . . kw, Deutz-MWM . . . diesels driving)
Range: . . . / . . . **Endurance:** 45 days
Crew: 60 ship's crew + 50 medical staff + 30 helicopter group + 140 troops (233 tot. accomm.)

Remarks: 18,640 grt. Typed *Einsatzgruppe Versorgungsshiffen* (Deployment Group Support Ships). In early 1994, the program was cut from four to one, and approval to build the first was granted 10-96. A 1412 was restored in the 1996 budget, and construction was authorized in 6-98. Plans to request the third and fourth again after 2010 have been dropped. FSG built the hulls, with Lürssen providing electrical system outfitting and Krögerwerft the superstrutures, final outfitting, and trials services. Commissioning was delayed by software problems. A 1411 was not considered ready for deployment until 4-02. A 1412 began sea trials on 19-2-02. A 1411 is based at Wilhelmshaven, and A 1412 is based at Kiel. A third unit is planned and a fourth may also be ordered.
Hull systems: Carry 9,000 m^3 (7,600 tons) diesel fuel, 600 m^3 (490 tons) aviation fuel, 1,100 m^3 potable water, 50 m^3 boiler feed water, 60 m^3 lube oil, 100 tons spare parts, 230 tons provisions, and 195 tons ammunition. One sliding-stay replenishment station per side and two electrohydraulic container and cargo cranes are fitted; they are also able to refuel over the stern. Have a helicopter deck and hangar to accommodate two Sea Kings or NH 90s and are fitted with the MBB-Forder & Hebesysteme HHS deck traversing and handling system. Employ double-hull construction, and there is a pronounced bow bulb.

They can embark a modular Operations Rescue Center (*Marine-Einsatzettungs system/MERZ*), supplied by Dornier GmbH; it consists of 26 20-ft. cargo containers equipped to provide emergency surgery, intensive care, internal medicine, and dental capabilities for up to 50 patients. Maximum container stowage is 84 20-ft. container-equivalents.
Combat systems: Will be able to carry antennas for portable SCOT-1A SHF SATCOM set, on either side of the funnel, and will normally have a commercial Marisat system aboard. The guns are mounted on the four corners of the first level of the aft superstructure block. Two planned Stinger/Fliegerfaust point-defense SAM positions were omitted. One X-band radar is mounted aft for helicopter landing/takeoff operations.

Disposal note: Type 701C missile boat and submarine supply ship *Meersburg* (A 1418) and Type 701E frigate supply ship *Freiburg* (A 1413) have both retired by 2005.

♦ 6 Type 404 multipurpose tenders [AR]
Bldrs: A: Bremer Vulkan, Bremen; B: Neue Flensburger Schiffsbau, Flensburg; C: Flenderwerke/Krögerwerft, Vegesack

	Bldr	Laid down	L	In serv.	Current function
A 511 Elbe	A	11-5-92	24-6-92	28-1-93	PTG tender
A 512 Mosel	A	29-12-92	22-4-93	22-7-93	minecraft tender
A 513 Rhein	B	7-10-92	11-3-93	22-9-93	minecraft tender
A 514 Werra	B	11-11-92	17-6-93	9-12-93	minecraft tender
A 515 Main	C	3-8-92	15-6-93	23-6-94	PTG tender
A 516 Donau	C	25-6-93	24-3-94	22-11-94	PTG tender

Donau (A 516) Martin Mokrus, 5-05

Elbe (A 511) Bernard Prézelin, 3-05

D: 3,590 tons (fl) **S:** 15 kts (11 kts cruise)
Dim: 100.58 (87.00 pp) × 15.40 × 4.10

AUXILIARIES *(continued)*

A: 2 single 20-mm 90-cal. Rheinmetall Rh-202 AA; 2 Stinger-Fliegerfaust shoulder-launched SAM positions
Electronics: Radar: 1 . . . nav.
M: 1 Deutz-MWM SBV 12M 628 diesel; 1 prop; 3,360 bhp—47-kN bow-thruster
Electric: 1,200 kw tot. **Range:** 2,000/11 **Endurance:** 30 days
Crew: 4 officers, 36 enlisted + 12 squadron staff, 38 technicians

Remarks: Ordered 10-90. Built to commercial standards. A 516 began lengthening by 24 meters to increase storage capacity to serve the 2nd *Schnellbootgeschwader* starting 1-6-01, while one of the others may be converted to serve as a submarine tender.
Hull systems: Can carry up to 24 standard-sized 20-ft, 7.5-ton containers for supplies and repair shops, 450 tons of cargo fuel, 11 m^3 of lube oil, 150 m^3 of fresh water, 27 tons of provisions, and 129 tons of ammunition. There are alongside underway refueling stations on either beam and two more for over-the-stern refueling. There is a helicopter platform aft with refueling facilities but no hangar. They have one 12.5-ton (at 15 m; 3-ton at 21-m reach) electrohydraulic crane. The hull has 13 watertight compartments, with watertight cargo passage doors between the five cargo holds, which are equipped with 1,250-kg- and 800-kg-capacity bridge cranes. The engines have also been listed as being of model 510BL6. A Becker flapped rudder of 7.24 m^2 area is fitted to improve harbor maneuvering. The distilling plant can produce 10 m^3 of potable water per day.
Combat systems: As an interim defensive armament, two 20-mm AA mounts have been added on the forecastle at its after end; the SAM positions are located atop the pilothouse.

♦ 5 Baltrum-class (Type 722 and 754*) seagoing tugs [ATA]
Bldr: Schichau, Bremerhaven

	Laid down	L	In serv.
A 1439 Baltrum (ex-Y 1661, ex-A 1454)*	29-6-66	2-6-67	8-10-68
A 1440 Juist (ex-Y 1644, ex-A 1456)*	23-9-67	15-8-68	1-10-71
A 1441 Langeoog (ex-Y 1665, ex-A 1453)*	12-7-66	2-5-67	14-8-68
A 1451 Wangerooge	1-10-65	4-7-66	9-4-68
A 1452 Spiekeroog	20-11-65	26-9-66	14-8-68

Langeoog (A 1441) Martin Mokrus, 3-04

Spiekeroog (A 1452) Frank Findler, 5-05

D: 854 tons (1,025 fl) **S:** 13.6 kts **Dim:** 51.78 × 12.11 × 4.20
A: Removed **Electronics:** Radar: 1 Kelvin-Hughes 14/9 nav.
M: 4 MWM TRHS 518 V16-31 AE 16-cyl. diesel generator sets (700 kw each), electric drive; 2 Kort-nozzele shrouded props; 2,400 shp
Electric: 540 kw **Range:** 5,000/10
Crew: 31 tot. (civilian in A 1439, A 1440)

Remarks: A 1439 through A 1441 were converted 1977–78 as Type 754 training support tugs with accommodations for up to 33 additional personnel, with A 1439 and A 1440 employed as diving training ships based at Neustadt and carrying recompression chambers. The other three are configured as Type 722 salvage and rescue tugs; A 1451 is used at Cuxhaven in support of aircrew survival training and A 1452 acts as a submarine safety vessel. Bollard pull: 33 tons. Single 40-mm gun was removed in 1993. All are fitted for fire fighting.
Disposals: Sister *Norderney* (A 1455) was transferred to Uruguay in 2002.

♦ 1 Helgoland-class (Type 720) salvage tug [ATA]
Bldr: Schichau, Bremerhaven

	Laid down	L	In serv.
A 1458 Fehmarn	23-4-65	25-11-65	1-2-67

Fehmarn (A 1458) Hartmut Ehlers, 5-03

D: 1,304 tons (1,558 fl) **S:** 16.6 kts **Dim:** 67.91 × 12.74 × 4.20
A: Removed
Electronics: Radar: 1 Kelvin-Hughes 14/9 nav., 1 Decca . . . nav.
M: 4 MWM 12 RS 18/22-21 AE 1 diesel generator sets (700 kw each), electric drive; 2 props; 3,300 shp
Electric: 1,065 kw tot. **Range:** 6,400/16 **Crew:** 34 tot.

Remarks: Serves as a safety tender to the submarine training establishment. Sister *Helgoland* (A 1457) was transferred to Uruguay 21-9-98. A 1458 is equipped to serve as mine planter, if required. Has a high-frequency sonar for salvage work and is equipped for fire fighting. Ice-strengthened hull permits use as a harbor icebreaker. A twin Bofors-OTO Melara 40-mm 70-cal. AA mount can be mounted on the forecastle. Bollard pull: 35 tons.

♦ 1 Eisvogel-class (Type 721) icebreaking tug [ATA]
Bldr: Hitzler, Lauenburg

	Laid down	L	In serv.
A 1401 Eisvogel	10-3-59	28-4-60	11-3-61

Eisvogel (A 1401) Leo Van Ginderen, 6-05

D: 496 tons (641 fl) **S:** 13 kts **Dim:** 37.80 × 9.73 × 4.60
Electronics: Radar: 2 . . . nav.
M: 2 Maybach 12-cyl. diesels; 2 KaMeWa CP props; 2,400 bhp
Electric: 180 kw **Range:** 2,000/12 **Crew:** 16 tot. (civilian)

Remarks: Completed refit 10-91 at Warnowwerft, Warnemünde, in former East Germany. Sister *Eisbär* (A 1402) was stricken on 30-10-97 and operates as the commercial *Cardinal D.* Has a 20-ton bollard pull capability. Is based at Kiel and is expected to operate until 2012. Provision is made to install a 40-mm Bofors AA aft.

♦ 1 Type 441 sail training ship [AXT]

	Bldr	Laid down	L	In serv.
A 60 Gorch Fock	Blohm + Voss, Hamburg	24-2-58	23-8-58	17-12-58

AUXILIARIES *(continued)*

Gorch Fock (A 60) Frank Findler, 6-04

D: 1,819 tons (2,005 fl) **S:** 12 kts (15 kts under sail)
Dim: 89.32 (81.44 hull, 70.20 pp) × 12.02 × 5.25
Electronics: Radar: 2 . . . nav.
M: 1 Deutz-MWM SBV 6 M 628 diesel; 1 KaMeWa CP prop; 1,660 bhp—1,904 m^2 max. sail area
Electric: 450 kw tot. (3 × 150 kw; 3 Deutz-MWM 6-234 250 bhp diesels driving)
Range: 1,100/10 **Crew:** 10 officers, 56 enlisted, 140 cadets

Remarks: Has made 296 n.m. progress in one day. Major refit 1985. Re-engined by Motorenwerke Bremerhaven during refit 21-1-91 to 24-5-91. Has Marisat commercial SATCOM and an extensive navigation aids suite. Carries 350 tons permanent ballast.

YARD AND SERVICE CRAFT

♦ 2 Type 738 pollution-control ships [YAG]
Bldr: C. Lühring, Brake

	Laid down	L	In serv.
Y 1643 Bottsand	14-11-83	22-9-84	26-10-84
Y 1644 Eversand	. . .	. . .	11-6-88

Bottsand (Y 1643) Leo Van Ginderen, 6-05

D: Approx. 1,100 tons (fl) **S:** 10 kts **Dim:** 46.30 × 12.00 × 3.10
Electronics: Radar: 1 . . . nav.
M: 2 Deutz BA 12M 816 diesels, 2 rudder-props, 1,600 bhp—2 omnidirectional bow-thrusters; 400 bhp
Crew: 3 officers, 3 unlicensed (civilian)

Remarks: 500 grt/650 dwt. Y 1643 was built for the Niedersachsen Ministry for the Environment, but was loaned to the German Navy on 24-1-85. Y 1643 is based at Warnemünde and Y 1644 at Wilhelmshaven.
Hull systems: Twin hulls, hinged near the stern to open scissors-fashion to 65°, leaving a 42-m-wide V-shaped opening to collect oil spills at the rate of approx. 140 m^3/hr, at a speed of 1 kt. When folded, can also be used as coastal tankers and bunkerage craft. Six cargo/spill tanks total 790 m^3.

♦ 3 Type 748 multipurpose trials craft [YAGE]

	Bldr	Laid down	L	In serv.
Y 860 Schwedeneck	Nobiskrug, Rendsburg	20-5-86	14-10-86	20-10-87
Y 861 Kronsort	Elsflether Werft, Elsfleth	6-10-86	9-5-87	2-12-87
Y 862 Helmsand	Krögerwerft, Rendsburg	18-3-87	31-7-87	11-2-88

Helmsand (Y 862) Frank Findler, 7-04

D: 1,018 tons (fl) **S:** 14.5 kts **Dim:** 56.50 (50.00 pp) × 10.80 × 3.65
Electronics: Radar: 2 Raytheon . . . nav.
M: 3 MTU 6V396 TB93 (700 bhp each) diesels, electric drive, 2 750-kw AEG alternators; 1 prop; 1,490 shp—side-thrusters fore and aft
Range: 2,400/12 **Crew:** 13 civilians + 10 technicians

Remarks: 850 grt. Ordered 14-12-85 with Lürssen as prime contractor, subcontracted to yards above. Y 862 was used for trials with the Mauser 27-mm guns and associated f.c.s.
Hull systems: Have space for four modular trials equipment containers, two on fantail, two amidships. Scientific equipment crane at stern. Y 860 is fitted with a Siemens three-phase Permasyn propulsion motor as prototype for the installation in the Type 212 submarines. All three have NAVSTAR GPS.

♦ 3 Type 745 small multipurpose trials tenders [YAGE]

	Bldr	Laid down	L	In serv.
Y 863 Stollergrund	Krögerwerft, Rendsburg	26-5-88	1-9-88	31-5-89
Y 864 Mittelgrund	Elsflether Werft	26-5-88	26-4-89	21-9-89
Y 866 Breitgrund	Elsflether Werft	10-1-89	2-10-89	14-2-90

Stollergrund (Y 863) Martin Mokrus, 8-05

D: 400 tons (456 fl) **S:** 12.5 kts **Dim:** 38.55 (34.60 wl; 32.12 pp) × 9.20 × 3.10
Electronics: Radar: 2. . . nav.
M: 1 KHD-SBV 6M 628 diesel; 1 prop; 1,210 bhp
Electric: 372 kw (2 MWM D234V8 diesels driving)
Range: 900/12 **Fuel:** 18 tons **Endurance:** 5 days
Crew: 6 civilian + 6 technicians

Remarks: Built under subcontract from Lürssen. Nine were originally programmed. Two more were planned for delivery post-1995, but budget constraints forced cancellation. All are based at Eckernförde Armed Forces Technical Center except Y 867, at Wilhelmshaven.
Hull systems: A torpedo recovery ramp is located to starboard through the transom stern, and a divers' stage to port. Space for two trials equipment vans on stern. Have a Becker flap rudder to improve low-speed maneuvering.
Disposals: *Bant* (Y 867) and *Kalkgrund* (Y 865) were transferred to Israel in 1-06.

♦ 1 Type 741 trials tender [YAGE]
Bldr: Schürenstedt, Bardenfleth

	Laid down	L	In serv.
A 1409 Wilhelm Pullwer (ex-Y 838, ex-SP 2)	4-10-65	16-8-66	22-12-67

D: 132 tons (160 fl) **S:** 12.5 kts **Dim:** 31.54 × 7.50 × 2.20
Electronics: Radar: 1 . . . nav.
M: 2 Mercedes-Benz 8 cyl. diesels; 2 Voith-Schneider cycloidal props; 792 hp
Electric: 120 kw **Crew:** 17 civilian + trials personnel

Remarks: Used in experimental trials. Wooden hull. Built as a net tender. Sister SP 1 (A 1408, ex-Y 837) was stricken 31-10-94 after having been damaged in a grounding.

YARD AND SERVICE CRAFT *(continued)*

Wilhelm Pullwer (A 1409) Findler & Winter, 3-99

♦ **2 Type 711 self-propelled floating cranes [YD]**
Bldr: Rheinwerft, Walsum

Y 875 HIEV (In serv. 2-10-62) Y 876 GRIEP (In serv. 15-5-63)

Griep (Y 876) Frank Findler, 4-05

D: 1,830 tons (1,875 fl) **S:** 6 kts **Dim:** 52.9 × 22.0 × 2.1
M: 3 MWM 600-bhp diesels, electric drive; 3 vertical cycloidal props; 1,425 bhp
Electric: 358 kVA tot. **Crew:** 12 tot. (civilians)

Remarks: Electric crane capacity: 100 tons.

Disposal note: All *Wolkan*-class (Type 945) diving tenders have been retired by 2006. *Poseidon* was scrapped in 1998, *Düker* by 2005, and *Bums* during 2006.

♦ **1 East German Warnow-class (Project 1344) diving tender [YDT]** Bldr: Yachtswerft, Berlin (In serv. 1974)

A 41

A 41 H&L Van Ginderen, 11-98

D: 25.5 tons (fl) **S:** 8 kts **Dim:** 15.25 × 3.97 × 0.92
M: 1 Type 6VD 14.5/12-1 diesel; 1 prop; 140 bhp (100 sust.) **Crew:** 3 tot.

Remarks: Former small harbor tug used as a diving tender at Warnemünde.
Disposals: All eleven in the class had been discarded by the *Volksmarine* during 7-90. A 17, originally activated for further service in 1991, had been stricken by end 1992. Six others were not taken over. Two taken over by the German Navy for service at Peenemünde, A 15 and A 16, were discarded early in 1995.

♦ **2 Type 712 small floating dry docks [YFDL]**
Bldr: Krupp, Rheinhausen

HEBEWERK A (In serv. 13-1-61) HEBEWERK 2 (In serv. 15-3-61)

D: 1,000 tons **Dim:** 66.01 × 21.10 × . . .

Remarks: Serviced by four Type 713 *Hebeponton* (lifting pontoons): 500 tons, 56 m by 14.8 m. *Hebewerk 2* is based at Wilhelmshaven and *Hebewerk A* at Kiel.

Disposal note: *Schwimmdock B* (Y 879) was stricken on 31-12-00.

♦ **1 Type 715 small floating dry dock [YFDL]**
Bldr: Flenderwerke, Lübeck (In serv. 8-9-67)

Y . . . DRUCKDOCK C (*"Dock C"*)

"Dock C" (Druckdock) Leo Van Ginderen, 6-05

D: . . . tons **Dim:** 93.0 × 26.5 × 3.6

Remarks: Contains a large pressure vessel used to test submarine pressure hulls. Based at Kiel.

Disposal note: Type 715 medium floating dry dock *Schwimmdock* 3 (Y 842) was retired in 2003.

♦ **5 Type 905 range safety and rescue craft [YFL]**
Bldr: Friedrich Lürssen Werft, Bremen-Vegesack

	Laid down	L	In serv.
Y 835 TODENDORF	11-92	5-10-93	25-11-93
Y 836 PUTLOS	3-93	25-1-94	24-2-94
Y 837 BAUMHOLDER	7-93	24-2-94	30-3-94
Y 838 BERGEN	9-93	14-4-94	22-6-94
Y 839 MUNSTER	10-93	13-6-94	10-8-94

Baumholder (Y 837) Frank Findler, 6-05

D: 100 tons (fl) **S:** 18 kts **Dim:** 28.7 × 6.5 × 1.4
M: 2 Klöckner-Humboldt-Deutz TBD 234 diesels; 2 props; 2,054 bhp
Range: . . . / . . . **Crew:** 6 tot. (accomm. for 15)

Remarks: Are operated as gunnery range safety craft on behalf of the German Army. A plastic fabric–covered temporary structure can be erected over the stern.

♦ **2 Type 945 personnel launches [YFL]**
Bldr: Hans Boost, Trier (In serv. 30-8-92)

Y 1678 MA 1 Y 1685 ASCHAU

D: . . . tons (fl) **S:** . . . kts **Dim:** 16.2 × 4.5 × . . . (2.0 molded depth)
Electronics: Radar: 1 Hagenuk MD 505 Rasterscan nav.
M: 1 M.A.N. D 2866 TE diesel; 1 4-bladed prop; 300 bhp (at 2,100 rpm)
Crew: 2 tot. + up to 50 passengers

Remarks: Ordered 27-8-90. Y 1678 assigned to Wilhelmshaven, and Y 1685 to Eckernförde. Capable of operating in light ice conditions and of operating up to 5 n.m. offshore.

YARD AND SERVICE CRAFT *(continued)*

MA 1 (Y 1678) Findler & Winter, 6-00

♦ **1 support launch [YFL]**
Bldr: Motorenwerk, Bremerhaven (In serv. . . .)

Y 1686 AK 2

AK 2 (Y 1686) Stefan Karpinski, 7-05

D: 46 tons **S:** 10 kts **Dim:** 19.80 × 4.40 × 1.20
Electronics: Radar: 1 . . . nav. **M:** 1 M.A.N. diesel; 280 bhp

♦ **4 Type 946 utility trials launches [YFL]**
Bldr: Hans Boost, Trier

	In serv.		In serv.
Y 1671 AK 1	3-85	Y 1677 MA 3	7-85
Y 1676 MA 2	5-85	Y 1687 Borby	9-85

MA 3 (Y 1677) Frank Findler, 4-05

D: 25 tons (fl) **S:** . . . **Dim:** 12.00 × 3.90 × 1.90
M: 1 M.A.N. D2540 MTE diesel; 1 prop; 366 bhp **Crew:** . . .

Remarks: "MA" in alphanumeric name means the craft is assigned to the Wilhelmshaven Arsenal, and "AK" craft are assigned to the Kiel Arsenal. Are equipped with a bow fender for use as push tugs. AK 3 was no longer in service as of 2005.

♦ **2 Type 740 utility launches [YFL]**
Bldr: . . . (In serv. . . .)

Y 1683 AK 6 MT-Boot

AK 6 (Y 1683) Frank Findler, 6-05

D: 18.5 tons (fl) **S:** 18.5 kts **Dim:** 15.50 (14.40 wl) × 3.14 × 1.37
Electronics: Radar: 1 . . . nav.
M: 2 Klöckner-Humboldt-Deutz 6-cyl. diesels; 2 Schottel vertical cycloidal props; 500 bhp

Remarks: Used as general-purpose launches. "AK" craft are assigned to the Kiel Arsenal. *MT-Boot,* with a flush fantail area and a small crane aft, is also attached to Eckernförde but does not bear an official pennant number.
Disposals: AK 5 (Y 1673) and *Peter Bachmann* (Y 1684) were stricken 26-1-93 and 4-3-94, respectively, while ST 1, ST 2, and AM 1 served as navigational training craft and were transferred to the Border Guard on 3-5-78. Y 1674 was retired in 2005 and Y 1675 during 2006.

♦ **1 Type 743 support launch [YFL]**
Bldr: Fritz Staack, Lübeck (In serv. 1980)

Y 1679 AM 7

D: 27 tons (fl) **S:** 10 kts **Dim:** 16.30 × 4.38 × 1.06
Electronics: Radar: 1 . . . nav. **M:** 1 MWM diesel; 1 prop; 180 bhp

Remarks: Glass-reinforced plastic construction. Assigned to Eckernförde. Similar in appearance to the Type 740 launches but has a higher pilothouse. Was to have been retired during 2005, but remained in service into 2006.

♦ **19 Type 934 personnel launches [YFL]**

V 3–21

V 13 Frank Findler, 6-05

D: . . . tons (fl) **S:** 11 kts **Dim:** 14.5 × . . . × . . .
M: 2 6-cyl. M.A.N. diesels; 2 props; . . . bhp

♦ **3 ex-East German MB-14-class (Project 407) launches [YFL]**
Bldr: Yachtswerft, Berlin (In serv. 1976–81)

B 33 B 34 B 83

D: 18 tons (24 fl) **S:** . . . kts **Dim:** 14.55 (13.13 wl) × 3.97 × 1.05
M: 1 Type 6VD15.4/12-1 diesel; 1 prop; 140 bhp **Crew:** 2 tot.

Remarks: B 33 and B 34 are at the Technical Training Establishment, Parrow; B 83 is at Warnemünde.

YARD AND SERVICE CRAFT *(continued)*

B 34 Frank Findler, 6-04

♦ **1 Type 718 battery-charging craft [YFP]**
Bldrs: Jadewerft, Wilhelmshaven

LP 3 (In serv. 16-9-74)

LP 3 H&L Van Ginderen, 6-00

D: 267 tons **S:** 8 kts **Dim:** 27.6 × 7.5 × 1.8 **Crew:** 6 tot.
M: 1 MTU diesel; 250 bhp **Electric:** 960 kw (LP 3: 1,110 kw)

Remarks: Has two 405-kw generators and two 150-kw generators for charging submarine batteries. LP 3 differs in appearance from retired sisters in having the pilot house flush with the forward edge of the superstructure.

Disposal note: Sisters LP 1 and LP 2 were both retired by 2005.

♦ **14 Type 737 fuel barges [YON]** (In serv. 1986–87)

ÖLSCHUTE 1 through ÖLSCHUTE 12, 19 and 20

Ölschute 11—red below the main deck, black above Winter & Findler, 6-97.

D: . . . **Dim:** 20.00 × . . . × . . . **Cargo:** 150 tons

Remarks: Several newer fuel barges are also in service.

♦ **2 miscellaneous ex-East German fuel barges [YON]**

ex-C 41 (550 tons capacity) ex-C 65 (250 tons capacity)

♦ **1 Type 730D accommodations barge [YPB]**
Bldr: J. I. Sietas, Hamburg (In serv. 12-89)

Y 811 KNURRHAHN

Knurrhahn (Y 811) Frank Findler, 4-05

D: 1,424 tons (fl) **Dim:** 48.0 × 14.0 × 1.8 **Crew:** 230 berths

Remarks: Refitted 1998 at Elsflether Werft.

♦ **2 Vogtland-class barracks barges (Type 650) [YPB]**
Bldr: Peenewerft, Wolgast (In serv. 1984)

Y 891 ALTMARK (ex-H 11) Y 895 WISCHE (ex-*Harz,* H 31)

Altmark (Y 891) Frank Findler, 9-04

D: 2,393 tons (fl) **Dim:** 89.41 × 13.22 × 2.36
Electric: 4,800 kw tot (4 × 1,200-kw diesel sets) **Fuel:** 500 tons
Crew: Accomm. for 230 in 2-, 4-, and 6-person staterooms

Remarks: NATO Ohre class. Built as Project 162 to replace East Germany's non-self-propelled *Jugend*-class barracks/base ships and officially described as *Wohn-und-Kampfschiff.* Are stationed at Wilhelmshaven.
Disposals: Sister *Havilland* (Y 892, ex-H 51) was sold 22-5-93 and *Börde* (Y 894, ex-H 72) by 1995. *Vogtland* (Y 890, ex-H 71) and *Uckermark* (Y 893, ex-H 91) were stricken in April 2002. Y 895 was refitted early 1999 at Elsflether Werft.
Hull systems: Equipped with one 8-ton Type 2Hy SWK8 electrohydraulic crane. Are equipped with a cinema, gymnasium, sauna, "club," and bakery. Mess can seat 84 at one sitting. Original propulsion engines and bow-thruster have been removed and armament deleted.

♦ **1 Type 430 torpedo recovery craft [YPT]**
Bldr: Burmester, Bremen, and Schweers, Bardenfleth (L: 28-2-66)

Y 855 TF 5

TF 5 (Y 855) A. A. de Kruijf, 6-05

D: 56 tons (63.5 fl) **S:** 17 kts **Dim:** 25.22 × 5.40 × 1.60
Electronics: Radar: 1. . . nav.
M: 1 MWM 12-cyl. diesel; 1 prop; 1,000 bhp **Crew:** 6 tot.

Remarks: Wooden construction. Have a recovery ramp at the stern.
Disposals: TF 107 (Y 873) and TF 108 (Y 874) were stricken late 1989 and TF 4 (Y 854) and TF 106 (Y 872) were stricken in 1990, all for transfer to Greece. TF 101 was stricken 16-6-89, TF 2 on 15-10-92. TF 6 (Y 856) was retired during 2002. TF 3 (Y 853) was stricken 28-2-94 and TF 1 (Y 851) on 24-5-95 (and sold to the Netherlands in 1998).

♦ **2 ex–East German Project 414 (Type 660) harbor tugs [YTB]**
Bldr: Yachtwerft/Volkswerft, Stralsund

	In serv.
Y 1656 WUSTROW (ex-*Zander,* A 45)	25-5-89
Y 1658 DRANSKE (ex-*Kormoran,* A 68)	12-12-89

D: 286 tons (320 fl) **S:** 10.5 kts **Dim:** 30.87 (29.30 pp) × 8.77 × 2.50
Electronics: Radar: 1 . . . nav.
M: 1 SKL 6VD26/20 AL-1 diesel; 1 Kort-nozzle prop; 1,200 bhp (720 sust.)
Electric: 150 kw tot. **Range:** 1,800/10 **Crew:** 13 tot.

Remarks: 140 grt. Three units were completed of a planned six to replace earlier *Volksmarine* tugs. Designed to carry 23-mm gunmounts abreast the stack amidships. Fitted with one water monitor for fire fighting. Sister *Koos* (Y 1651) stricken 28-9-95 and sold to Turkey 7-10-96. The other two were scheduled to strike by 31-12-98 but have remained in service.

YARD AND SERVICE CRAFT *(continued)*

Dranske (Y 1658) Martin Mokrus, 4-04

♦ 6 Type 725 large harbor tugs [YTB]

Bldr: Y 812–Y 815: Husemer Schiffswerft; Y 816–Y 819: Orenstein & Koppel, Lübeck

	Laid down	L	In serv.
Y 812 Lütje Horn	30-8-89	. . .	9-90
Y 814 Knechtsand	22-9-89	. . .	10-90
Y 815 Scharhörn	13-10-89	. . .	16-11-90
Y 816 Vogelsand	1-4-86	30-1-87	14-4-87
Y 817 Nordstrand	1-4-86	24-10-86	20-1-87
Y 819 Langeness	1-4-86	28-11-86	15-5-87

Scharhörn (Y 815) Frank Findler, 2-05

D: 445 tons (fl) **S:** 12 kts **Dim:** 30.25 (28.00 pp) × 9.10 × 2.55
Electronics: Radar: 1 . . . nav.
M: 2 Deutz SBV 6M 628 diesels; 2 Voith-Schneider Model 24 G-11/165 vertical cycloidal props; 2,230 hp
Range: . . . **Crew:** 10 tot. (civilians)

Remarks: 212 grt. Bollard pull: 23 tons. Class originally intended to replace *all* older harbor tugs, with eventual total of 15 planned. Launched via crane. Second trio ordered 5-89. Plan to build six more during mid-1990s canceled due to availability of the new, East German–built Type 660 tugs and the decline in the size of the navy.

Disposal note: All remaining *Heppens*-class (Class 724) medium harbor tugs have been retired. *Neuende* (Y 1680) was withdrawn from service in 7-04. *Ellerbek* (Y 1682) was stricken 22-4-94 and transferred to Greece on 16-3-95. *Heppens* (Y 1681) was stricken 18-12-98 and also sold to Greece.

♦ 1 Type 368 training ketch [YTS] (In serv. 1942–44)

Y 834 Nordwind (ex-W 43)

D: 100 tons (110 fl) **S:** 11 kts **Dim:** 27.00 (24.00 hull, 21.48 pp) × 6.39 × 2.94
Electronics: Radar: 1 Kelvin-Hughes 14/9 nav.
M: 1 Demag 5-cyl. diesel; 1 prop; 137 bhp—195 m^2 max. sail area
Range: 1,200/7 **Crew:** 10 tot.

Remarks: Wooden-hulled former patrol fishing cutter taken over by U.S. Navy 1945; acquired 1-7-56 by German Navy. Wooden hull. Operated for the Mürwik Naval School.

Note: There are also 70 smaller sail-training craft, all bearing names. Included are 26 Type 914, 5 m long; 10 Type 913, 7.64 m long; 25 Type 910 (most 10.46 m o.a.); 6 Type 911; and 1 Type 912.

Nordwind (Y 834)—white-painted, with brown bulwarks and masting Frank Findler, 6-05

Disposal note: The last Type 705 water lighter, FW 5 (A 1405), was stricken on 14-12-00. Sister FW 2 was transferred to Turkey in 1975 and FW 3 to Greece in 1976. FW 4 (A 1404) was stricken 12-4-91 and transferred to Turkey same date; FW 6 (A 1406) was stricken 7-90 and transferred to Greece 5-3-91. FW 1 (A 1403) stricken 21-1-94.

ARMY RIVER ENGINEERS

Organized into four companies located at four cities on the Rhine at Krefeld, Koblenz, Neuwied, and Wiesbaden. Each company has nine landing craft, three patrol craft, and a tug. Craft based at Krefeld are numbered 80101–31, those at Koblenz 30111–31, those at Neuwied 85011–31, and those at Wiesbaden 85111–31. All craft are painted forest green.

PATROL BOATS [WPB]

♦ 12 25-meter class

Bldr: Hitzler, Regensburg (In serv. 1953–54)

Army 25-meter patrol boat H&L Van Ginderen, 1985

D: 27 tons (fl) **S:** 20.5 kts **Dim:** 25.0 × 3.8 × 1.0
A: 2 single 12.7-mm mg (I × 2) **Electronics:** Radar: 1 . . . nav.
M: 2 MWM RHS 418A diesels; 2 props; 440 bhp **Crew:** 7 tot.

Remarks: Sister craft are operated by Belgium and Federal Yugoslavia. The guns are normally not mounted.

AMPHIBIOUS WARFARE CRAFT

♦ 14 Mannheim 59–class landing craft [WLCM]

Bldr: Schiffs und Motorenwerke AG, Mannheim (In serv. 1959–60)

D: 89 tons (200 fl) **S:** 9 kts **Dim:** 27.4 × 7.2 × 1.2
A: 4 single 7.62-mm mg **Electronics:** Radar: 1 . . . nav.
M: 2 MWM RHS 518A diesels; 2 props; 432 bhp **Crew:** 9 tot.

Remarks: Cargo: 70 tons normal, 90 max. Five served in the German Navy until 4-65. Bow ramp, shallow tank deck. One was transferred to Tonga during 1989, and eight were put up for sale in 8-91.

AMPHIBIOUS WARFARE CRAFT *(continued)*

Mannheim 59–class landing craft F-85032 H&L Van Ginderen, 9-97

♦ 12 Bodan-class landing craft [WLCM]
Bldr: . . .

Bodan-class landing craft F-85031 H&L Van Ginderen, 9-97

D: 150 tons (fl) **S:** 6 kts **Dim:** 30.0 × 5.8 × . . .
A: 1 20-mm 70-cal. Oerlikon AA **Electronics:** Radar: 1 . . . nav.
M: 4 MWM diesels; 4 Schottel vertical cycloidal props; 596 bhp

Remarks: Each consists of 12 pontoon sections, with a folding ramp at either end and a small raised pilothouse module to starboard. Cargo capacity: 90 tons.

♦ 16 MB 3–class river-crossing craft [WLCP]
Bldr: Schottel (In serv. 1988–91)

MB 3–class river-crossing craft H&L Van Ginderen, 6-00

D: 0.39 tons light (4.7 tons fl) **S:** 8.5 kts loaded/16 kts light
Dim: 7.00 (6.45 pp) × 3.24 × 0.45 loaded
M: 2 diesels; 2 Schottel pumpjets; 356 bhp **Crew:** 2 + 10 passengers

Note: The German Army also operates 144 sisters, including some in the MB 3.2 bridge erection boat configuration.

SERVICE CRAFT

♦ 4 river tugs [WYTM]
Bldr: . . .

D: . . . **S:** 11 kts **Dim:** 28.0 × 5.9 × 1.2
A: 2 single 7.62-mm mg **Electronics:** Radar: 1 . . . nav.
M: 2 KHD SBF 12M716 diesels; 2 props; 760 bhp **Crew:** 7 tot.

Remarks: Have a small tub forward for one 12.7-mm mg. Had previously been numbered T-80001, T-80101, T-85001, and T-85101.

River tug T-821 H&L Van Ginderen, 4-95

COAST GUARD

A loosely organized German Coast Guard was formed on 1-7-94 and employs the ships and craft of the Border Guard, Customs Service, various police organizations, the Ministry of Fisheries, and the Shipping Administration. These organizations retain responsibility for the operation and maintenance of their own vessels and craft.

FEDERAL POLICE MINISTRY OF THE INTERIOR
(Bundespolizei)

Personnel: Approx. 550 tot.

Bases: Headquarters at Neustadt. Operating bases at Cuxhaven, Frankfurt/Oder, Karnin, Sassnitz, Stralsund, and Warnemünde. Organized into three flotillas, headquartered at Neustadt, Cuxhaven, and Warnemünde.

Maritime Aviation: In service as of 1-00 were 13 Eurocopter EC 155 (AS.365N4 Dauphin), 9 EC 135, 13 Bell UH-1D, 8 Bell 212, and 17 BO-105CBS-5EL "Super Five" helicopters; several AS.330 Puma helicopters and a few AS.318C Alouettes are also used. Helicopters are based at Bonn/Hangelar.

Note: Called the *Bundesgrenzschutz See* (Sea Border Patrol) until 1-7-05. Pennant number prefixes have changed from "BG" (Bundesgrenzschutz) to "BP" (Bundespolizei), reflecting their expanded mission. Craft have blue hulls with white superstructures. Seagoing units now carry the word *Küstenwache* (Coast Guard) on their hull sides and have the *Küstenwache* black, red, and yellow diagonal strip on each side of the hull. All 40-mm guns were removed during 1996–97.

PATROL SHIPS [WPS]

♦ 3 Bad Bramstedt class (Type 66)
Bldr: Yantar Verf, Kaliningrad, Russia, and Abeking & Rasmussen, Lemwerder

	In serv.
BP 24 Bad Bramstedt (ex-BG 24)	8-11-02
BP 25 Bayreuth (ex-BG 25)	2-5-03
BP 26 Eschwege (ex-BG 26)	18-12-03

Bayreuth (BP 25) Michael Nitz, 9-05

D: 800 tons (fl) **S:** 21.5 kts **Dim:** 65.90 × 10.60 × 3.20
A: 2 single 7.62-mm mg **Electronics:** Radar: 2 . . . nav.
M: 1 MTU 16V1163 TB37L diesel, electric drive: 1 Siemens AM 400 M4F electric motor; 1 prop; 6,974 bhp—1 1,073-shp electric motor for cruising—bow and stern Schottel side-thrusters
Electric: 1,119 kw tot. (2 × 498-kw, 1 × 123-kw emergency diesel sets)
Range: 6,500/12 **Fuel:** 115 tons **Endurance:** 30 days
Crew: 14 tot. (accomm. for 24)

Remarks: Ordered 21-7-00. Have a helicopter deck capable of accepting an NH-90 helicopter. Aluminum-alloy superstructure. All three are dual-assigned to the Coast Guard (*Küstenwache*) and will be used for EEZ and pollution-control and maritime safety and security duties. The hulls were built in Russia. They carry a 30-kt RIB. Up to ten sisters are being built for the Russian Federal Border Guard as the *Sprut* class.

♦ 1 seagoing patrol ship
Bldr: Elsflether Werft, Elsfleth

	Laid down	L	In serv.
BP 21 Bredstedt (ex-BG 21)	3-3-88	18-12-88	24-5-89

D: 673 tons (770 fl) **S:** 25 kts (12 cruise) **Dim:** 65.40 (57.25 pp) × 9.20 × 2.92
A: 2 single 7.62-mm mg
Electronics: Radar: 1 Decca AC 2960BT nav.; 1 Decca . . . nav.
M: 1 MTU 20V 1163 TB 93 diesel; 1 prop; 10,880 bhp (8,323 sust.)—A.E.G. diesel-electric cruise set; 500 shp (12 kts)—bow-thruster
Electric: 788 kw (2 × 344 kw, MTU 12V 183 diesels driving; 1 × 100 kw)
Range: 2,450/20; 7,000/10 **Crew:** 18 tot. + 4 spare berths

FEDERAL POLICE PATROL SHIPS [WPS] *(continued)*

Bredstedt (BP 21) Dieter Wolf, 7-05

Remarks: 673 grt. Ordered 21-11-87. Trials began 20-5-89. Helicopter platform aft. Has a stern ramp–launched Avon Searaider inspection/rescue launch, and a second RIB is carried to port amidships. Two firefighting water monitors are fitted. A single 40-mm AA was removed in 1996. Refitted 2002 and given a new pilothouse and a 30-kt RIB inspection boat; transferred to Baltic service spring 2003.

PATROL CRAFT [WPC]

♦ 2 ex-East German Sassnitz class (Type 620)
Bldr: VEB Peenewerft, Wolgast

	Laid down	L	In serv.
BP 22 Neustrelitz (ex-*Sassnitz,* P 6165, ex-591, ex-BG 22)	. . .	1988	31-7-90
BP 23 Bad Düben (ex-*Binz,* ex-593, ex-BG 23)	3-5-89	26-2-90	15-5-96

Neustrelitz (BP 22)—still wearing old "BG" pennant number prefix Frank Findler, 7-03

Bad Düben (BP 23)—with old pennant number prefix "BG" Martin Mokrus, 9-04

D: 317 tons light (396 fl) **S:** 26 kts
Dim: 48.90 (45.00 pp) × 8.65 (7.45 wl) × 2.28 max.
A: 2 single 7.62-mm mg
Electronics: Radar: 1 Decca AC 2690 BT nav.; 1 Decca . . . nav.
M: 2 MTU 12V595 TE90 diesels; 2 props; 8,812 bhp
Electric: 334 kw (1 × 110-kw, 2 × 112-kw diesel sets)
Range: 2,400/20 **Endurance:** 5 days
Crew: 16 tot. (accomm. for 22)

Remarks: The first of nine laid down out of a planned dozen for the East German *Volksmarine* and up to 38 others for the USSR and Poland; as prototype was given project number 151.0. When first seen by NATO, was given temporary code "Bal-Com-10." BG 22 was equipped with eight tubes for the Soviet SS-N-25 antiship missile for trials purposes, but they had been removed by the summer of 1990; the craft was decommissioned on 12-7-91 and transferred to the Border Guard by 10-91, along with sisters *Sellin* (BG 24, ex-592) and *Binz* (ex-593), which had never been operated by the German Navy. Three others were acquired by Poland on 3-10-90 and completed there. The unconverted *Sellin* was sold in 1999.

Under an order placed 12-5-92, *Sassnitz* was re-engined by her builder; the original plant incorporated three Type M 520 multirow radial diesels of 5,400 bhp each, driving three shafts for a top speed of 37 knots. The original armament of one 76.2-mm AK-176 DP gun, one 30-mm AK-630 gatling gun, and one SA-N-5 SAM system was removed, and the TSR-333 and Drum Tilt radars were replaced by modern surface surveillance radars. The superstructure was extended aft, and the pilothouse deckhouse enlarged. A lead-computing director served a 40-mm gun, which was removed in 1997. *Binz* was given a similar reconstruction 1995–96.

Disposal note: All *Neustadt*-class patrol craft have been decomissioned. *Uelzen* (BG 13) was transferred to Mauritania in 2-90. BG 12 and BG 17 were stricken in 2002 and BG 15 during 2003. *Rosenheim* (BG 18) was stricken in 1999; *Neustadt* (BG 11) and *Duderstadt* (BG 14) were retired in 2004, all three have been transferred to Bulgaria. *Alsfeld* (BG 16) was retired in 2005 for transfer to Romania.

PATROL BOATS [WPB]

♦ 2 Europa 1 class
Bldr: Schless-Werft, Wessel (In serv. 1975)

Europa 1 Europa 2

Europa 2 Dieter Wolf, 4-98

D: 10 tons **S:** 22.7 kts **Dim:** 14.50 × 3.80 × 0.95
Electronics: Radar: 1 Kelvin-Hughes 18/12R nav.
M: 1 M.A.N. D 2556/MXE diesel; 1 prop; 240 bhp

♦ 4 BG 41–class riverine
Bldr: Hain, Barmstadt (In serv. 1994)

BP 41 Küstrin/Kiez (ex-BG 41)
BP 42 Schwedt (ex-BG 42)
BP 43 Frankfurt/Oder (ex-BG 43)
BP 44 Aurith (ex-BG 44)

D: 7.3 tons (fl) **S:** 32 kts **Dim:** 10.20 × 3.20 × 1.00
Electronics: Radar: 1 . . . nav.
M: 2 Volva Penta TAMD 42 WJ462 diesels; 2 Hamilton 211 waterjets; 462 bhp
Range: 2000/25 **Crew:** 3

Remarks: For service in the Oder River system.

♦ 3 former East German Bremse (GB 23) class
Bldr: VEB Yachtswerft, Berlin (In serv. 1971–72)

BP 62 Uckermark (ex-GS 23, ex-G 34, ex-BG 62)
BP 64 Börde (ex-GS 50, ex-G 35, ex-BG 64)
BP 63 Altmark (ex-GS 21, ex-G 21, ex-BG 63)

Börde (BP 64) Dieter Wolf, 8-05

FEDERAL POLICE PATROL BOATS [WPB] *(continued)*

D: 25 tons light (48 fl) **S:** 17 kts **Dim:** 22.59 (20.97 wl) × 4.70 × 1.60
A: 2 7.62-mm mg **Electronics:** Radar: 1 Furuno FR 80310 nav.
M: 1 Motorenwerke Rosslau Type 6VD 18/15 AL 1 diesel; 1 prop; 510 bhp
Range: 300/12 **Fuel:** 485 liters **Crew:** 6 tot.

Remarks: Formerly used by the East German Border Guard for patrol on rivers and inland waterways. Five sisters were transferred to Tunisia, two to Jordan, and two to Malta in 1992. *Prignitz* (BG 61, ex-GS 31, ex-G 20) was retired on 16-11-00. BG 62 and BG 64 are based at Warnemünde, BG 63 at Sassnitz.

♦ 4 former East German MB 12 class
Bldr: VEB Yachtswerft, Berlin

BP 51 Vogtland (ex-GS 17, ex-G 53, ex-BG 51)
BP 52 Rhön (ex-GS 26, ex-G 52, ex-BP 52)
BP 53 Spreewald (ex-GS 16, ex-G 51, ex-BG 53)
BP 54 Oderbruch (ex- . . . , ex- . . . , ex-BG 54)

BP 51 Dieter Wolf, 8-05

D: 14 tons **S:** 16 kts **Dim:** 12.6 × 4.0 × 1.1
A: . . . **Electronics:** Radar: 1 . . . nav.
M: 2 . . . diesels;

Remarks: Previously reported as retired, all four remain in service. BP 54 is built to a slightly modified design.

Disposal note: Small tug *Rettin* (BG 5) was reported stricken during 1999. Training launches BG 6 and BG 7 were sold in 1996.

FISHERIES PROTECTION SHIPS
MINISTRY OF FOOD AND AGRICULTURE

Note: The fisheries protection ships are part of the new German Coast Guard formed in 1994 and have black hulls with *Küstenwache* on the sides in place of the original *Fischereischutz* (Fisheries Protection); superstructures are gray, masts are yellow, and shipboard boats are orange, while the Coast Guard (*Küstenwache*) black, red, and yellow diagonal strip is painted on each side of the hull.

PATROL SHIPS [WPS]

♦ 1 (+ 1) Seeadler class
Bldr: Peenewerft, Wolgast

Seeadler (In serv. 6-00) Frithjof (In serv. . . .)

Seeadler Wolfgang Kramer, 6-04

D: . . . tons **S:** 19 kts (20 on trials) **Dim:** 72.40 (67.20 pp) × 12.50 × 5.00
Electronics: Radar: 2 . . . ARPA X-band; 1. . . ARPA S-band
M: 2 MTU 16V 595 TE 70L diesel generator sets; 2 CP props; 10,200 bhp—2 electric low-speed motors; 2,000 shp—5.2-ton thrust bow-thruster
Electric: 2,381 kw tot. (2 × 1,030-kw sets, 2 MTU 12V396 TE diesels driving; 1 × 321-kw emergency set, MTU 12V183-series diesel driving)
Range: . . . / . . . **Fuel:** 400 m^3 **Crew:** 19 tot. (accomm. for 27)

Remarks: 1,774 grt/515 dwt. First unit ordered 3-98 to replace the old *Warnemünde;* the second ship is planned. *Seeadler* is based at Rostock, and *Frithjof* will be based at Cuxhaven.
Hull systems: Both the main diesel engines and the electric cruise engines drive the same two propellers through gearboxes, and both systems can be used simultaneously. Has two Becker flapped rudders to aid maneuverability and is fitted with fin stabilizers. Two RIB inspection boats are carried. There is a helicopter deck, but no hangar. Carries 125 m^3 ballast water, 40 m^3 fresh water, and 5 m^3 lube oil. Has an automated data collection system and meteorological equipment.

♦ 1 Seefalke class
Bldr: Orenstein & Koppel, Lübeck (In serv. 4-8-81)

Seefalke

D: 2,386 tons (fl) **S:** 20.5 kts **Dim:** 82.91 (76.21 pp) × 13.11 × 4.72
M: 2 MWM TBD 510-8 diesels; 2 CP props; 8,000 bhp
Electric: 1,000 kw tot. (2 × 500-kw diesel sets)
Range: 9,700/17 **Fuel:** 345.5 tons **Crew:** 29 tot.

Remarks: 1,786 grt/468 dwt. Equipped to operate in East Greenland Sea, with fin stabilizers, elaborate navigation equipment, helicopter platform, bow-thruster, seven-bed infirmary.

♦ 1 Meerkatze class
Bldr: Lürssen, Vegesack (In serv. 1976)

Meerkatze

Meerkatze Frank Findler, 5-05

D: 2,386 tons (fl) **S:** 15.5 kts **Dim:** 77.02 (66.71 pp) × 11.79 × 5.14
M: 4 MWM TBD602 V16K diesels (934 bhp each), electric drive; 2 props; 1,564 shp
Crew: 30 ship's company + 15 passengers/scientists

Remarks: 1,751 grt.

♦ 1 Frithjof class
Bldr: Schlichting, Travemünde (In serv. 1967)

Emsstrom (ex-*Frithjof*)

D: 2,140 tons (fl) **S:** 15 kts **Dim:** 76.76 (66.71 pp) × 11.79 × 5.14
M: 3 MWM 16-cyl., diesels (1,281 bhp each), 4 × 740-kw generators, 2 motors; 2 props; 2,800 shp—1 active propeller aft, bow-thruster forward
Electric: 668 kw tot. (1 × 420-kw, 1 × 195-kw, 1 × 53-kw diesel sets)
Range: 13,000/15 **Fuel:** 550 tons **Crew:** 35 tot.

Remarks: 1,716 grt. Homeported at Cuxhaven. Ice-strengthened hull. Renamed 1998.

Note: The Ministry of Food and Agriculture also operates fisheries patrol launches *Narwhal* (1998: 60 tons, 21 kts) and *Goldbutt* (1997: 59 tons, 23 kts) for service in home waters, research ships *Walther Herwig III* and *Solea,* and the research launch *Greif.* German government–owned research and survey ships and the various vessels of the Water and Navigation Board Maritime Police (*Schiffahrtspolizei*) are described in the 1998–99 and earlier editions; most of these ships are also assigned to the coast guard. The green and white-painted customs service (*Zoll*) craft and large numbers of boats and launches operated by local marine police organizations are illustrated in the 1998–99 and earlier editions of this book; many customs service units are also part of the coast guard.

GHANA

Republic of Ghana

Personnel: Approx. 1,000 total

Bases: Headquarters at Burma Camp, Accra. The Western Naval Command is located at Sekondi and the Eastern Naval Command at Tema.

Naval Aviation: Ghana's Air Force operates 2 Alouette-III helicopters; may also be used in the maritime support role.

PATROL SHIPS [PS]

♦ 2 ex-U.S. Coast Guard Balsam class
Bldr: Marine Iron SB Co. (P30: Duluth Iron & SB Co.)

	Laid down	L	In serv.
P 30 Anzone (ex-*Woodrush,* WLB 407)	4-2-44	28-4-44	22-9-44
P 31 Bonsu (ex-*Sweetbrier,* WLB 401)	3-11-43	30-12-43	26-7-44

PATROL SHIPS [PS] *(continued)*

Anzone (P 30) U.S. Air Force, 10-05

D: 697 tons light (1,038 fl) **S:** 12.8–13 kts **Dim:** 54.9 (51.8 pp) × 11.3 × 4.0
A: 2 single 12.7-mm mg **Electronics:** Radar: 1 Hughes-Furuno SPS-73 nav.
M: 2 diesels, electric drive; 1 prop; 1,200 shp **Electric:** 400 kw tot.
Range: P 30: 8,000/12; 23,500/7.5; P 31: 10,500/13; 31,000/7.5
Crew: 6 officers, 47 enlisted (in USCG service)

Remarks: Very sturdy vessels with a number of years' service remaining despite their advanced age. Ex-WLB 407 and ex-WLB 401 were decommissioned from the U.S. Coast Guard and transferred in 2001. Both are now used as patrol ships and as transport and supply ships for peacekeeping forces.
Hull systems: Have a 20-ton derrick and icebreaking hulls. Both have exceptionally long endurance.

PATROL CRAFT [PC]

♦ 2 Modified FBP 57 class
Bldr: Friedrich Lürssen Werft, Vegesack, Germany

	Laid down	L	In serv.
P 28 Achimota	1978	14-3-79	27-3-81
P 29 Yogaga	1978	14-3-79	27-3-81

Achimota (P 28) U.S. Air Force, 10-05

D: 380 tons (410 fl) **S:** 30 kts **Dim:** 58.10 × 7.62 × 2.83
A: 1 76-mm 62-cal. OTO Melara DP; 1 40-mm 70-cal. OTO Melara–Bofors AA
Electronics:
Radar: 1 Decca TM 1226C nav.; 1 Thales Canopus-B surf. search
E/O: Thales Nederland LIOD optronic gun director
M: 3 MTU 16V538 TB91 diesels; 3 props; 10,800 bhp (9,210 sust.)
Crew: 5 officers, 50 enlisted

Remarks: Used for fisheries patrol and search-and-rescue duties. Carry a rubber dinghy for air/sea rescue and inspection purposes. A planned refit for P 29 in 1998–99 was canceled for lack of funds. Ammunition supply includes 250 rounds 76-mm and 750 rounds 40-mm.

♦ 2 Modified FPB 45 class
Bldr: Friedrich Lürssen Werft, Vegesack, Germany

	Laid down	L	In serv.
P 26 Dzata	16-1-78	19-9-79	4-12-79
P 27 Sebo	1-78	19-9-79	2-5-80

Sebo (P 27) French Navy, 1996

D: 212 tons (252 fl) **S:** 30 kts **Dim:** 44.90 (42.25 wl) × 7.00 × 2.50 (props)
A: 2 single 40-mm 70-cal. OTO Melara–Bofors AA
Electronics: Radar: 1 Decca TM 1226 nav.
M: 2 MTU 16V538 TB91 diesels; 2 props; 7,200 bhp (6,140 sust.)
Electric: 408 kVA tot. **Range:** 1,100/25; 2,000/15 **Crew:** 5 officers, 40 enlisted

Remarks: Used for fisheries patrol and search-and-rescue duties. A planned refit for P 26 in 1998–99 was canceled for lack of funds. Have 57-mm illumination flare RL on sides of both 40-mm mounts.

GREECE

Hellenic Republic

NAVY

Personnel: 19,000 (including 9,800 conscripts) plus 24,000 reservists

Bases and Organization: Salamis and Suda Bay for ships, Marathon for aircraft. The fleet is divided into three naval districts: Aegean, Ionian, and Northern Greece. The naval firing range at the island of Giaros was closed during 2-02.

Naval Aviation: Eight Sikorsky S-70B-6 Aegean Hawk helicopters are in service for use on the MEKO200 frigates; equipment includes the AQS-18(V)3 dipping sonar, APS-143 radar, and ALR-66(V)2 EW suite, equipped with the Norwegian Penguin Mk 2 Mod. 7 antiship missile. Two more S-70B-6 were ordered in 5-00, and all ten are being fitted with FLIR. Also in use are ten Agusta-Bell AB-212 shipboard helicopters (two configured for EW work) and two AS.319 Alouette-III helicopters for training. Five AS.365 Dauphin 2 helicopters were ordered in 2003 to perform day and night surveillance missions for the Harbor Police of the Merchant Navy Ministry; all had been delivered by 2005.

Greek Navy S-70B-6 Aegean Hawk Edward McDonnell, 2003

Hellenic Air Force 353 Squadron, at Elefsis, operates six Greek Navy–owned, ex-U.S. Navy P-3B Orion maritime patrol aircraft acquired in 1995 on a three-year, cost-free lease after $63 million in refurbishment; the aircraft were further updated by Hellenic Aerospace Industry, with the first completed early in 2001. Four Hellenic Air Force Embraer 145SA AEW and maritime patrol aircraft are to be equipped with Ericsson Erieye AEW and surveillance radars; a Saab 340 with the same equipment was loaned during 1999 for familiarization. Mirage 2000EG fighters of 331 Geraki and 332 Aegeas Squadrons at Tanagra are equipped to launch two AM 39 Exocet antiship missiles each, and four Super Puma helicopters were delivered in 2000 for SAR work. Two Bombardier 415 amphibians were delivered during 2004 for SAR, maritime surveillance, illegal immigration patrol, and environmental monitoring duties. Two additional aircraft may be ordered.

Weapons and Sensors: Nearly all equipment is of Western European or U.S. manufacture. Additional Penguin Mk 2 Mod. 7 antiship missiles were ordered 9-96 for use with S-70B-06 helicopters, and 20 RGM-84C Harpoon missiles were ordered late in 1997. Two Crotale NG SAM systems were ordered from Thales in 10-98; the intended platform was not announced, but they were probably intended for naval base defense.

Coast Defenses: Three land-based MM 40 Exocet missile batteries were delivered during 1993 for use on various Aegean islands as coast-defense weapons.

Note: Ship names are prefixed by HS (Hellenic Ship). Germany's Howaldtswerke Deutsche Werft (itself 71% owned by Bank One, Chicago) formally took over ownership and operation of naval shipbuilding and repair yard Hellenic Shipyard on 23-6-02 for only $43 million.

ATTACK SUBMARINES [SS]

♦ 1 (+ 3) Type 214

	Bldr	Start	L	In serv.
S 120 Papanikolis	Howaldtswerke, Kiel	30-3-01	22-4-04	12-05
S 121 Pipinos	Hellenic SY, Skaramanga	15-10-02	1-10-05	2008
S 122 Matrozos	Hellenic SY, Skaramanga	30-3-03	11-06	2009
S 123 Katsonis	Hellenic SY, Skaramanga	30-3-04	2007	6-10

D: 1,700 tons surf./1,950 tons sub.
S: 10.5 kts surf./ 21.5 kts sub. (2–6 kts sub. on fuel cells) **Dim:** 65.30 × 6.30 × 6.6
A: 8 bow 533-mm TT (16 tot. wire-guided torpedoes and UGM-84C Harpoon missiles)
Electronics:
Radar: . . .
Sonar: Cylindrical MF bow passive array; LF through MF passive flank array; towed LF linear passive array; passive ranging array; active range and bearing array
EW: Elbit Timnex 2 intercept, Sonartech Atlas torpedo-detection and tracking syst.

ATTACK SUBMARINES [SS] *(continued)*

M: 2 MTU 16V 396–series diesel generator sets (1,000+ kw each), 1 Siemens Permasyn motor; 1 prop; . . . shp—2 120-kw Siemens PEM fuel-cell auxiliary propulsion units
Range: 12,000/ . . . surf.; 2,400/4 on fuel cells **Endurance:** 50 days
Crew: 27 tot. (accomm. for 35)

Papanikolis (S 120) Hans Karr, 2-05

Papanikolis (S 120)—during trials Michael Nitz, 2-05

Remarks: Under Project Neptune II, an agreement to order from the HDW–Ferrostaal AG consortium was announced 9-10-98, the program was approved by the Greek government in 7-99, and the contract for three for $1.26 billion was signed on 31-3-00, with an option for a fourth, which was taken up on 3-6-02 for an additional $654 million; as part of the contract, two German Navy missile craft are being given to Greece. Design is an expanded version of the German-Italian Type 212 design with double the diesel generator capacity. Work on the first of the Greek-assembled units started on 15-1-02. HDW acquired control of Hellenic Shipyards early in 2002. Maximum diving depth of 400m.
Hull systems: Inner and outer hull of austenitic steel. Battery set to develop 600–900 V. To have 10% reserve buoyancy. Will have the Siemens Nautos engineering systems automation system.
Combat systems: Will employ the STN Atlas Elektronik ISUS 90 system, with BAE's Link 11 datalink equipment. Sonar array to include cylindrical MF passive array forward, MF/LF passive flank system (with three arrays per side), towed LF passive array, an active ranging set, and a bow-mounted active mine-avoidance set. An optronic, non-hull-penetrating periscope and a standard, penetrating optical attack periscope will be fitted. Four of the eight weapons tubes will have expulsion systems to enable launching Harpoon missiles; the other tubes are of the swim-out launch variety.

♦ 4 Type 209/1200
Bldr: Howaldtswerke, Kiel

	Laid down	L	In serv.
S 116 Poseidon	15-4-76	21-3-78	22-3-79
S 117 Amfritití	16-9-76	14-6-78	14-8-79
S 118 Okeanos	1-10-76	16-11-78	15-11-79
S 119 Pontos	15-1-77	22-3-79	29-4-80

Poseidon (S 116) Bernard Prézelin, 4-05

D: 1,185 tons surf./1,285 tons sub. **S:** 11.5 kts surf./22 kts sub.
Dim: 56.10 × 6.20 × 5.90
A: 8 bow 533-mm TT (14 AEG SUT Mod. 0 wire-guided torpedoes)
Electronics:
Radar: Thales Calypso-II nav./search
Sonar: STN Atlas Elektronik CSU-3-4 suite: AN 526 passive, AN 406 A9 active, Thales DUUX-2 passive ranging
EW: Thales DR-2000U intercept
M: Diesel-electric propulsion; 4 MTU 12V493 TY60 diesels (550 bhp each), each linked to an AEG generator of 420 kw; 1 Siemens motor; 1 prop; 5,000 shp
Range: 11,300/4 snorkel; 28/20, 466/4 sub. **Fuel:** 85 tons
Endurance: 50 days **Crew:** 6 officers, 25 enlisted

Remarks: Essentially a lengthened variant of the Type 209/1100 with added fuel. A contract with HDW and Ferrostaal to upgrade at least three of the four at Hellenic Shipyards to the same standard as the upgraded Type 209/1100 units was signed on 3-6-02; in addition, the boats are to be lengthened through the insertion of a air-independent propulsion section of the same type being installed in the Type 214s. Work on S 117 was underway by 2005 with work to complete on three of the class by 2012. The modernizations cost $1.1 B (US) and will extend service life through 2020.
Hull systems: Diving depth: 250 m. The three modified boats will have two 120-kw Siemens PEM fuel-cell auxiliary propulsion units.
Combat systems: Have Thales SINBADS M8/42 weapons control with Mk 8 torpedo f.c.s. The EW system may have been replaced by the Boeing ArgoSystems AR-740.

♦ 4 Type 209/1100
Bldr: Howaldtswerke, Kiel

	Laid down	L	In serv.
S 110 Glavkos	1-9-68	15-9-70	5-11-71
S 111 Nereus	15-1-69	7-6-71	10-2-72
S 112 Triton	1-6-69	19-10-71	23-11-72
S 113 Proteus	1-10-69	1-2-72	23-11-72

Nereus (S 111) Guy Schaeffer, via Paolo Marsan, 6-00

D: 990 tons (light); 1,100 tons surf./1,207 tons sub.
S: 11.5 kts surf./22 kts sub. **Dim:** 54.10 × 6.20 × 5.90
A: 8 bow 533-mm TT (10 AEG SUT Mod. 0 wire-guided torpedoes and 4 UGM-84C Harpoon missiles)
Electronics:
Radar: Thales Calypso-II nav./search
Sonar: STN Atlas Elektronik CSU-83-90 suite with DBSQS-21 active set, flank arrays and DUUX-2 passive-ranging
EW: ArgoSystems AR-700-S5 intercept
M: Diesel-electric: 4 MTU 12V493 TY60 diesels (550 bhp each), each linked to an AEG generator of 420 kw; 1 Siemens motor; 1 prop; 5,000 shp
Range: 8,600/4 snorkel; 25/20, 230/8, 400/4 sub. **Fuel:** 49 tons
Endurance: 50 days **Crew:** 7 officers, 29 enlisted

Remarks: Have been updated to the same standard as the German Type 206A class under a contract placed 5-5-89 in Germany. S 112 upgrade completed in 7-93 at HDW, Kiel; S 110 in 12-95 at Salamis, and S 111 during 11-97 at Salamis. Work began at Salamis on S 113 in 12-97 for completion in 1999.
Hull systems: Single-hull design with two ballast tanks. Diving depth: 250 m. All have battery arrangement with four groups of 120 cells producing 11,500 amp-hr. Have two periscopes.
Combat systems: During their updates, they received Sub-Harpoon launch capability with the new HDW torpedo-tube launch system, new electronics, STN Atlas Elektronik CSU-83-90-series sonar suite, Unisys Kanaris fire-control system, Magnavox GPS receiver, Omega SATNAV receiver; crews grew by five. The combat system integrates a Unisys UYK-44 with the original torpedo fire-control system and can control the launch of Harpoon missiles as well as four SUT Mod. 0 wire-guided torpedoes simultaneously. One source reports that the new EW system is the Racal Sealion system rather than the listed ArgoSystems AR-700-S5.

GUIDED-MISSILE DESTROYERS [DDG]

Disposal note: The last two remaining ex-U.S. Navy *Charles F. Adams*–class destroyers, *Kimon* (D 218) and *Nearchos* (D 219) were retired from service in 2004. Sister *Themistokles* (D 221) was stricken on 18-2-02, and *Formion* (D 220) was retired on 29-7-02.

GUIDED-MISSILE FRIGATES [FFG]

♦ 0 (+ 2) new construction

Remarks: One guided-missile frigate, with an option for a second, was intended to be ordered during 2001, although funding problems have delayed the order well into 2006. The finalist designs include the Dutch *De Zeven Provinciën* and the Blohm + Voss Type 124 (*Sachsen*) classes.

FRIGATES [FF]

♦ 4 MEKO 200 Mk 3 class

	Bldr	Laid down	L	In serv.
F 452 Hydra	Blohm + Voss, Hamburg	17-12-90	25-6-91	12-11-92
F 453 Spetsai	Hellenic SY, Skaramanga	11-8-92	9-12-93	24-10-96
F 454 Psara	Hellenic SY, Skaramanga	12-12-93	20-12-94	30-4-98
F 455 Salamis	Hellenic SY, Skaramanga	20-12-94	15-3-96	16-12-98

FRIGATES [FF] *(continued)*

Hydra (F 452) Michael Winter, 6-05

Salamis (455) Cem D. Yaylali, 5-05

Hydra (F 452) Leo Van Ginderen. 7-05

D: 2,710 tons (3,200 fl) **S:** 31.75 kts (21 on diesel)
Dim: 117.50 (109.50 pp) × 14.80 (13.80 wl) × 6.00 (4.12 hull)
A: 8 RGM-84C Harpoon SSM; Mk 48 Mod. 2 VLS (16 RIM-7M NATO Sea Sparrow SAM); 1 127-mm 54-cal. Mk 45 DP; 2 20-mm Mk 15 gatling CIWS; 2 triple 324-mm Mk 32 ASW TT (Mk 46 Mod. 5 torpedoes); 1 Sikorsky S-70B-6 Seahawk helicopter (with Penguin Mk 2 Mod. 7 missiles and Mk. 46 Mod. 2 torpedoes)
Electronics:
Radar: 1 Decca 2690BT ARPA nav.; 1 Thales MW-08 3-D air search; 1 Thales DA-08 early warning; 2 Thales STIR-18 f.c.
Sonar: Raytheon DE 1160 (SQS-56) hull-mounted (7.5 kHz) with integrated VDS (12 kHz); WQC-2A underwater telephone; UQN-4A echo sounder
EW: ArgoSystems AR-700 intercept; ArgoSystems APECS-II jammer; EADS Telegon-10 HFD/F; Mk 36 Mod. 2 SRBOC decoy syst. (4 6-round Mk 137 RL); SLQ-25 Nixie torpedo decoy syst.
E/O: SAR-8 infrared surveillance
M: CODOG: 2 MTU 20V956 TB82 diesels (5,200 bhp each), 2 G.E. LM-2500-30 gas turbines (30,328 shp each); 2 CP props
Electric: 2,480 kw (4 × 620-kw diesel sets)
Range: 900/31.75; 4,100/18 (diesel) **Fuel:** 300 tons
Crew: 22 officers, 151 enlisted + 16 staff

Remarks: Basic order to Blohm + Voss 10-2-89, with subcontract for Greek-built trio placed 16-5-89. The Greek-assembled trio were far behind schedule due to financial difficulties at the builders; to speed the program, portions of F 453 were prefabricated in Germany. Armament and electronics were in large part financed by U.S. arms credits, although most equipment is European.
Hull systems: The design is basically similar to the version of the MEKO 200 built for Portugal, and Turkey has similar ships. Have fin stabilizers.
Combat systems: The Thales STACOS Mod. 2 combat data system is installed. Have NATO Link 11 and 14 datalinks, Thales Vesta helicopter transponder, Mk 73 Mod. 1 SAM control system, and SWG-1A(V) Harpoon missile launch system. The sonar system employs a single processor for both the hull sonar and VDS, which uses the towed array from Raytheon's DE 1167 system; Raytheon refers to the entire suite as the DE 1160 HM/VDS.

♦ **10 ex-Dutch Kortenaer class**
Bldr: Royal Schelde, Vlissingen

	Laid down	L	In serv.
F 450 Elli (ex-*Pieter Florisz,* F 812)	2-7-77	15-12-79	10-10-81
F 451 Limnos (ex-*Witte de With,* F 813)	13-6-78	27-10-79	18-9-82
F 459 Adrias (ex-*Callenburgh,* F 808)	30-6-75	12-3-77	26-7-79
F 460 Aegeon (ex-*Banckert,* F 810)	25-2-76	13-7-78	29-10-80
F 461 Navarinon (ex-*Van Kinsbergen,* F 809)	2-9-76	16-4-77	24-4-80
F 462 Kontouriotis (ex-*Kortenaer,* F 807)	8-4-75	18-12-76	26-10-78
F 463 Bouboulina (ex-*Pieter Florisz,* F 826; ex-*Willem Van Der Zaan*)	15-1-80	8-5-82	1-10-83
F 464 Kanaris (ex-*Jan Van Brakel,* F 825)	16-11-79	16-5-81	14-4-83
F 465 Themistokles (ex-*Philips Van Almonde,* F 823)	1-10-77	11-8-79	2-12-81
F 466 Nikiforos Fokas (ex-*Bloys Van Treslong,* F 824)	27-4-78	15-11-80	5-11-82

Aegeon (F 460) Bernard Prézelin, 8-05

Bouboulina (F 463) Anthony Vella, 10-04

Themistokles (F 465) Bernard Prézelin, 2-05

D: 3,000 tons (3,786 fl) **S:** 30 kts **Dim:** 130.2 (121.8 pp) × 14.4 × 4.4 (6.0 props)
A: F 450, 451: 8 RGM-84A/C Harpoon SSM; 1 8-round Mk 29 SAM syst. (24 RIM-7M Sea Sparrow missiles); 2 single 76-mm 62-cal. OTO Melara DP; 2 Mk 15 Phalanx gatling CIWS; 4 fixed 324-mm Mk 32 ASW TT; 2 AB-212 ASW helicopters—F 459–466: 8 RGM-84A/C Harpoon SSM; 1 8-round Mk 29 SAM syst. (24 RIM-7M Sea Sparrow missiles); 1 76-mm 62-cal. OTO Melara DP; 1 20-mm Mk 15 Phalanx gatling CIWS; 2 single 20-mm 70-cal. Oerlikon Mk 10 AA; 4 fixed 324-mm Mk 32 ASW TT; 2 AB-212 ASW helicopters
Electronics:
Radar: 1 Thales ZW-06 surf. search; 1 Thales LW-08 early warning; 1 Thales WM-25 track-while-scan f.c.; 1 Thales STIR-18 f.c.
Sonar: Canadian Westinghouse SQS-505 hull-mounted (7 kHz)
EW: F 450, 451: Elettronica Sphinx intercept syst.; Elettronica Ramses jammer—others: Elettronica ELT/715 intercept—all: Mk 36 SRBOC decoy syst. (4 6-round Mk 137 launchers); SLQ-25 Nixie towed torpedo decoy syst.
M: COGOG: 2 Rolls-Royce Tyne RM-1C cruise gas turbines (4,900 shp each); 2 Rolls-Royce Olympus TM-3B gas turbines (25,800 shp each); 2 LIPS CP props; 51,600 shp max.
Electric: 3,000 kw (4 × 750-kw SEMT-Pielstick PA4 diesel generator sets)
Range: 4,700/16 (on one Tyne turbine) **Crew:** 17 officers, 159 enlisted

Remarks: F 450 was transferred to Greece on 26-6-81, having been ordered 7-81, along with F 451. Both were taken from production originally intended for the Dutch Navy in order to speed delivery. Plans to build a third ship in Greece were canceled. F 459, F 460, and F 461 were bought from the Netherlands Navy and transferred on 14-5-93, 30-3-94, and 1-3-95, respectively, and all were formally recommissioned

FRIGATES [FF] *(continued)*

in Greek service on 30-6-95. F 462 was purchased 3-6-97, reactivated, and delivered 15-12-97. F 463 was decommissioned from the Netherlands Navy on 24-1-01 and was purchased by Greece on 7-6-01 for transfer on 1-12-01; the ship was recommissioned at Salamis on 4-4-02. F 464 was retired from the Dutch Navy on 12-10-01, was purchased on 27-3-02, and was transferred on 29-11-02 after a refit. F 465 was purchased on 22-10-02 and commissioned 24-10-03, after an extensive overhaul, and F 466 was purchased upon retirement from the Netherlands Navy.
Hull systems: Have Denny-Brown fin stabilizers. The helicopter hangar was lengthened 2.2 m on the first two to accept Italian-built helicopters vice the Lynx used by Dutch Navy. It has not been lengthened on the former Dutch Navy ships.
Combat systems: Have the Thales SEWACO II combat data system and NATO Link 10 and Link 11 datalink capability. One U.S. Mk 15 CIWS 20-mm gatling AA was to have been added in place of the after 76-mm gun for close-in defense in the original pair, but instead, in 1991, the 76-mm weapon was retained, *two* Mk 15 CIWS were added port and starboard forward of the hangar (in place of the Corvus decoy rocket launchers), the number of Harpoon missiles was doubled over the original installation, and U.S. Hycor Mk 137 decoy rocket launchers were added on the forward superstructure. The ex-Dutch Navy ships had their Harpoon missiles and Goalkeeper CIWS removed prior to transfer, a single Phalanx CIWS was added atop their hangar, and additional Harpoon missiles were procured from the United States. The pair purchased in 2001 had no CIWS when transferred. Normally, only one helicopter is carried. At time of transfer, F 464 also had no CIWS or Harpoon missiles.
Modernization: Six of the class are to receive mid-life modernizations under a 3-03 contract with Hellenic Shipyards, Skaramanga, Greece. F 462 was the first unit modernized. Upgrades include a TACTICOS combat systems, new radar and a 32-missile launching system for the ESSM version of Sea Sparrow. Four Phalanx Block IA CIWS were ordered for the two latest transfers on 19-12-02. Non-upgraded units are to be retired after 2015.

Disposal note: Of the former U.S. Navy *Knox*-class frigates, *Makedonia* (F 458; ex-*Vreeland,* FF 1068) was stricken during 12-98 but remains afloat; *Thraki* (F 457; ex-*Trippe,* FF 1075) was stricken on 29-7-02 and sunk as a target on 18-6-03.

PATROL COMBATANTS [PG]

♦ 6 Pyrpolitis-class
Bldr: Hellenic SY, Skaramanga

	Laid down	L	In serv.
P 57 Pyrpolitis	1-91	16-9-92	4-5-93
P 61 Polemistis	16-9-92	21-6-93	16-4-94
P 266 Mahitis	2001	4-6-02	29-10-03
P 267 Nikiforos	2001	13-12-02	4-04
P 268 Aititos	2002	2003	5-8-04
P 269 Krateos	2002	2004	11-04

Mahitis (P 266) Dieter Wolf, 6-04

Polemistis (P 61) Martin Mokrus, 5-04

D: 555 tons (fl) **S:** 24.7 kts (at 450 tons; 23.8 kts sust.)
Dim: 56.50 (51.53 wl) × 10.00 (9.50 wl) × 2.50 max.
A: 1 76-mm 62-cal. OTO Melara Compact DP; 1 40-mm 70-cal. Bofors AA; 2 single 20-mm 90-cal. Rheinmetall AA; portable mine rails (36 U.S. Mk 6, 16 U.S. Mk 55, or 18 German Mk 18 mines)
Electronics:
Radar: P 57, P 61: 1 Decca 1690 nav.; 1 Thales Triton air/surf.search; 1 Alenia RTN-10X f.c.—P 266–269: Decca Bridgemaster-E ARPA nav.; Thales Scout surf. search; Thales Variant air-search; Thales LIROD Mk 2 f.c.
EW: P 266–269 only: Thales DR 3000 SLW intercept
E/O: P 266–269 only: Thales Mirador surveillance
M: 2 Wärtsilä-Nohab 16V25 diesels; 2 props; 10,000 bhp
Electric: 690 kVA tot. (3 × 230-kVA diesel sets)
Range: 900/23.8; 2,200/15 **Fuel:** 104 tons **Endurance:** 10 days
Crew: 36 tot. + 25 troops

Remarks: Revised version of the modified Osprey design below; the design is also known as the "Hellenic 56" or *Pyrpolitis* class. Two units (with an unexercised option for a third) were ordered 19-2-89, and the first unit was reported laid down in 1-91. P 61 began trials during 2-93. An option exists for an additional two units of the class.
Hull systems: Other sources indicate only 50 tons of fuel carried. Can carry 40 tons of fresh water. There are two RIB inspection boats aboard, handled by a 1.3-ton-capacity crane. The ships have a steel hull with aluminum alloy superstructure.
Combat systems: The 76-mm gun is controlled by an Alenia NA 21 weapons-control system (RTN-10X radar). Two pairs of Harpoon SSM launchers can be accommodated but have not been installed. The single 40-mm gun aft is to be replaced by a twin Melara 40-mm mount when funds permit. P 266–269 have the Thales TACTICOS combat data system and NATO Link 11; they may have a twin 30-mm EVO-OTO Melara 30-mm AA mount aft in place of the twin 40-mm mount of the earlier pair.

♦ 2 modified Osprey 55 series
Bldr: Hellenic SY, Skaramanga

	Laid down	L	In serv.
P 18 Armatolos	8-5-89	19-12-89	9-3-90
P 19 Navhamos	9-11-89	16-5-90	15-7-90

Armatolos (P 18) Dieter Wolf, 10-97

D: 515 tons (fl) **S:** 24.7 kts (at 415 tons)
Dim: 54.75 (50.83 pp) × 10.50 (8.08 wl) × 2.55 (hull)
A: 1 76-mm 62-cal. OTO Melara Compact DP; 2 single 20-mm 90-cal. Rheinmetall AA; 2 portable mine rails
Electronics:
Radar: 1 Decca 1226 nav.; 1 Thales Triton air/surf. search; 1 Alenia RTN-10X f.c.
EW: Thales DR-2000S intercept, 2 . . . decoy RL
M: 2 MTU 1163 TB 93 diesels; 2 props, 9,870 bhp
Electric: 480 kw (2 × 240 kw, 2 MTU 12V183 AA51 diesels driving)
Range: 500/22 **Crew:** 36 ship's company + 25 troops

Remarks: Design licensed from Frederickshavn Værft, Denmark. First two ordered 3-88, with plans to construct up to ten, but further units were canceled in favor of the P 100 class. Formally commissioned 30-6-95. Similar ships are operated by Morocco and Senegal, and the original shorter-hulled version is operated by Mauritania and Myanmar. Have a stern ramp and internal stowage for a rigid-inflatable inspection/SAR launch at the stern.
Combat systems: Were originally planned to carry four Harpoon missiles amidships, an OTO Melara twin 40-mm AA mount aft, the Plessey AWS-6 air/surface search radar, and a Thales WM-25 track-while-scan weapons fire-control system, with an associated LIROD director. The 76-mm guns and associated Alenia NA 20 weapons-control system (with RTN-10X) radar were recycled from decommissioned *Gearing*-class destroyers and new search radars were added in 1995.

♦ 3 ex-German Thetis class (Type 420)
Bldr: Roland Werft, Bremen

	Laid down	L	In serv.
P 62 Niki (ex-*Thetis,* P 6052)	19-6-59	22-3-60	1-7-61
P 63 Doxa (ex-*Najade,* P 6054)	22-3-60	6-12-60	12-5-62
P 64 Elevtheria (ex-*Triton,* P 6055)	15-8-60	5-8-61	10-11-62

Karteria (P 65)—since stricken Stefan Karpinski, 10-02

D: 575 tons light (732 fl) **S:** 19.5 kts **Dim:** 69.78 (65.5 pp) × 8.20 × 2.65 (hull)
A: 1 twin 40-mm 70-cal. OTO Melara–Bofors AA; 2 single 12.7-mm mg; 2 triple 324-mm Mk 32 ASW TT (Mk 46 Mod. 5 torpedoes); 2 Mk 9 d.c. racks (6 Mk 9 d.c. each)

PATROL COMBATANTS [PG] *(continued)*

Electronics:
Radar: 2 Decca . . . nav.
Sonar: STN Atlas Elektronik ELAC 1BV hull-mounted HF
EW: Thales DR-2000S intercept with Thorn-EMI SARIE analyzer; 4 6-round Buck-Wegmann Hot Dog decoy RL; T Mk 6 Fanfare towed torpedo decoy syst.
M: 2 M.A.N. V8V 24/30 diesels; 2 props; 6,800 bhp **Electric:** 540 kw tot.
Range: 2,760/15 **Fuel:** 78 tons **Crew:** 5 officers, 43 enlisted

Remarks: Former torpedo-recovery boats, designed for operations in the Baltic. The first two were transferred to Greece and recommissioned on 6-9-91; the second pair were transferred on 7-9-92 and formally commissioned into Greek service on 30-4-93. The class underwent renovation in Greece, with new air-conditioning, refurbished accommodations, addition of two more generator sets, and improved firefighting capability. All are attached to the destroyer command but are to be retired in the near future.
Hull systems: *Doxa* had the forward superstructure extended toward the bow to accommodate a small medical facility. Original speeds have dropped considerably; when new, they could make 23.5 kts.
Combat systems: Have the Thales Mk 9 torpedo f.c.s. and a Bofors optical lead-computing gun director. The original German armament was replaced and triple, trainable ASW TT have replaced the original four fixed 533-mm TT.
Disposal note: *Agon* (P 66) was decomissioned 17-12-04 and *Karteria* (P 65) had retired from service by 2005.

GUIDED-MISSILE PATROL CRAFT [PTG]

♦ 4 (+ 1) Super Vita class
Bldr: Elefsis Shipyard and Industrial Enterprises

	L	In serv.
P 67 Ipopliarchos Roussen	12-11-02	11-04
P 68 Ipopliarchos DanIolos	8-7-03	6-05
P 69 Ipopliarchos Kristalidis	5-4-04	11-05
P 70 Ipopliarchos Grigoropoulos	. . .	2006
P 71 Antiplarchos Ritsos	. . .	2007

Vosper Super Vita design for Greece Vosper Thornycroft, 1999

D: 570 tons (fl) **S:** 34.2 kts **Dim:** 61.90 × 9.50 × . . .
A: 4 MM 40 Exocet Mk 2 SSM; 1 21-round Mk 49 Mod. 1 RAM SAM syst. (RIM-116A Block 1 missiles); 1 76-mm 62-cal. OTO Melara SuperRapid DP; 1 twin 30-mm EVO-OTO Melara AA; 2 fixed, aft-firing 533-mm TT (. . . wire-guided torpedoes); 2 mine rails
Electronics:
Radar: 1 Decca BridgeMaster-E ARPA nav.; 1 Thales Scout Mk 2 surf. search; 1 Thales MW-08 air search, 1 Thales Sting f.c.
EW: Thales DR 3000SLW active/passive suite; ALEX 130 decoy syst.
E/O: Thales Mirador-FD surveillance, tracking, and gun f.c.
M: 4 MTU 16V595-series diesels; 4 props; . . . bhp
Electric: 750 kw tot. (3 × 250 kw, MTU GR183 TE52 diesels driving)
Range: 1800/12. **Endurance:** 7 days **Crew:** 45 tot.

Remarks: The 21-9-99 contract included an order for three and an option to build four more (later reduced to two) in Greece. The initial trio cost about $324 million, with the contract including the transfer of two U.K. *Hunt*-class minehunters.
Hull systems: Steel hull with aluminum superstructure. One pair Vosper nonretractable fin stabilizers. Will carry a RIB, handled by an electrohydraulic crane.
Combat systems: Employ the Thales TACTICOS combat data system. There will be two displays for the BridgeMaster-E navigational radar. The Sperry Mk 39 Mod. 3A ring-laser gyro will be fitted. The antiship missile system was ordered on 31-8-00 and included 27 missiles with an option for 24 more.

♦ 9 Combattante IIIN class
Bldr: P 20–23: CMN, Cherbourg; others: Hellenic SY, Skaramanga

	L	In serv.
P 20 Antipliarchos Lascos	6-7-76	2-4-77
P 21 Antipliarchos Blessas	10-11-76	19-7-77
P 22 Antipliarchos Troupakis	6-1-77	8-11-77
P 23 Antipliarchos Mykonios	5-5-77	10-2-78
P 24 Simaiforos Kavalouthis	10-11-79	14-7-80
P 26 Ipopliarchos Deyiannis	14-7-80	12-80
P 27 Simaiforos Xenos	8-9-80	31-3-81
P 28 Simaiforos Simitzopoulos	12-10-80	6-82
P 29 Simaiforos Starakis	1981	12-10-81

Antipliarchos Troupakis (P 22)—with Exocet missiles H&L Van Ginderen, 9-98

Simaiforos Xenos (P 27)—with Penguin missiles H&L Van Ginderen, 7-00

D: P 20–23: 385 tons (447 fl)—P 24–29: 396 tons (fl) **S:** 36.5 (P 24–29: 32.6) kts
Dim: 56.65 (53.00 pp) × 8.00 × 2.70 (props; 2.04 hull)
A: P 20–23: 4 MM 38 Exocet SSM; 2 single 76-mm 62-cal. OTO Melara DP; 2 twin 30-mm 75-cal. Emerlec AA; 2 fixed, aft-launching 533-mm TT (2 SST-4 wire-guided torpedoes)—P 24–29: 6 Penguin Mk 2 SSM; 2 single 76-mm 62-cal. OTO Melara Compact DP (I × 2); 2 twin 30-mm 75-cal. Emerlec AA; 2 fixed, aft-launching 533-mm TT (2 SST-4 wire-guided torpedoes)
Electronics:
Radar: 1 Decca 1226 nav.; 1 Thales Triton surf./air search; 1 Thales Castor f.c.
EW: Thales DR-2000S intercept
E/O: 2 Matra Défense Panda optronic directors for the 30-mm guns
M: P 20–23: 4 MTU 20V538 TB92 diesels; 4 props; 20,800 bhp (18,000 sust.)—P 24–29: 4 MTU 20V538 TB91 diesels; 4 props; 15,000 bhp (13,400 sust.)
Electric: 450 kw (3 × 150-kw diesel-driven sets; 440 V, 60 Hz)
Range: 800/32.5; 2,000/15 **Crew:** 7 officers, 36 enlisted

Remarks: First four ordered 22-5-75. Second group, built in Greece, and with less expensive weapon, sensor, and propulsion systems, ordered 22-12-76. Sister *Antipliarchos Kostakos* (P 25) was rammed and sunk by Greek ferry *Samena* on 4-11-96, with a loss of four lives. P20–P23 are to be modernized at Elefsis shipyard under a 2003 contract. P 24 and P 26 may follow in the future.
Hull systems: Have excellent habitability; accommodations and operations spaces are air-conditioned.
Combat systems: Each 76-mm gun has 350 rounds, with 80 in ready service; the mounts have been updated to fire at 100 rds/min. The Emerlec 30-mm mounts are furnished with 3,200 rounds and fire at 700 rds/barrel/min. P 20–23 have a Thales Vega weapon-control system; the later ships have Vega II. The Penguin missiles in P 24–29 were to be refurbished to remain in service until 2015 under a 2-98 contract with Kongsberg.
Disposals: Combattante II–class guided missile patrol craft *Ipopliarchos Arliotis* (P 14) decommissioned during 2003. Remaining sisters *Ipopliarchos Anninos* (P 15), *Ipopliarchos Konidis* (P 16), and *Ipopliarchos Batsis* (P 17) were decomissioned in 2005 with P 15 transferring to Georgia.

♦ 6 ex-German Type 148
Bldrs: CMN, Cherbourg (P 51: Lürssen, Vegesack)

	Laid down	L	In serv.
P 72 Simaiforos Votsis (ex-P 51; *ex-Storch,* P 6152)	12-3-73	25-3-74	17-7-74
P 73 Antipliarchos Pezopoulos (ex-P 30; *ex-Iltis,* P 6142)	2-2-72	12-12-72	8-1-73
P 74 Plotarhis Vlakavas (ex-*Marder,* P 6144)	15-4-72	5-5-73	14-7-73
P 75 Plotarhis Maridhakis (ex-*Häher,* P 6151)	5-4-73	26-4-74	12-6-74
P 76 Plotarhis Tournas (ex-*Leopard,* P 6145)	29-11-72	20-9-73	13-11-73
P 77 Plotarhis Sakipis (ex-*Jaguar,* P 6147)	13-9-72	3-7-73	21-8-73

GUIDED-MISSILE PATROL CRAFT [PTG] *(continued)*

Plotarhis Maridhakis (P 75)—awaiting transfer, with *Plotarhis Vlakavas* (P 74), both still in German colors and with German pennant numbers
Hartmut Ehlers, 7-94

D: 234 tons (264 fl) **S:** 35.8 kts **Dim:** 47.0 (45.9 pp) × 7.1 × 2.66 (fl)
A: P 74, P 75: 8 RGM-84A Harpoon SSM—others: 4 MM 38 Exocet SSM—all: 1 76-mm 62-cal. OTO Melara DP; 1 40-mm 70-cal. Bofors AA; 8 mines in place of the 40-mm AA
Electronics:
Radar: 1 SMA 3RM 20 nav.; 1 Thales Triton-G air/surf. search; 1 Thales Castor-II f.c.
EW: Thales DR-2000 intercept; 2 6-round Buck-Wegmann Hot Dog decoy RL; Wolke chaff dispenser
M: 4 MTU MD 872 16-cyl. diesels; 4 props; 14,000 bhp (at 1,515 rpm; 12,000 sust.)
Electric: 270 kw tot. **Range:** 570/30; 1,600/15 **Fuel:** 39 tons
Crew: 5 officers, 37 enlisted

Remarks: Ordered 18-12-70, as CMN's Combattante II A4L type. Design by Friedrich Lürssen Werft, Vegesack. Fitted out at Cherbourg. P 72 and P 73 were transferred from Germany late in the summer of 1992 after having been stricken 15-10-92 and 16-11-92, respectively; after refits, the pair left Germany for Greece on 1-2-94. The second pair left Germany 16-3-95 as deck cargo after having been stricken 25-4-94 and 24-6-94, respectively. All four were formally recommissioned on 30-5-95. P 76 and P 77 arrived in Greece on 23-10-00, having been stricken from German service on 15-9-00; a contract to modernize and refit the pair was let to Ifestos Hellas SY in late 2002, with work completing in 2005. Steel construction.
Combat systems: Harpoon missiles, controlled by the SWG-1(V)32 launch system, were substituted on P 74 and P 75 after delivery to Greece.

♦ 2 Kelefstis Stamou class
Bldr: C.N. de l'Esterel, Cannes

P 286 Diopos Antoniou (In serv. 28-7-75)
P 287 Kelefstis Stamou (In serv. 4-12-75)

Kelefstis Stamou (P 287) Cem D. Yaylali

D: 80 tons (115 fl) **S:** 30 kts **Dim:** 32.0 × 5.8 × 1.5
A: 4 Aérospatiale SS 12 wire-guided SSM; 1 20-mm 90-cal. Rheinmetall AA; 2 single 12.7-mm mg
Electronics: Radar: 1 Decca 1226 nav.
M: 2 MTU 12V331 TC81 diesels; 2 props; 2,700 bhp
Range: 1,500/15 **Crew:** 17 tot.

Remarks: Wooden-hulled craft ordered by Cyprus but acquired by Greece. Pennant numbers were P 28 and P 29 until 1980.

TORPEDO BOATS [PT]

Disposal note: Following service during the 2004 Olympic Games, all four Norwegian *Nasty*-class torpedo patrol boats were retired from service. The last two ex-German Jaguar (Type 141) class torpedo boats *Kyklon* (P 53) and *Tyfon* (P 56) were retired in 2006.

♦ 2 U.S. Asheville class
Bldr: Peterson Bldrs., Sturgeon Bay, Wis.

	In serv.
P 229 Tolm (ex-*Green Bay,* PG 101)	5-12-69
P 230 Ormi (ex-*Beacon,* PG 99)	21-11-69

Ormi (P 230) H&L Van Ginderen, 8-99

D: 225 tons (240 fl) **S:** 16 kts **Dim:** 50.14 (46.94 pp) × 7.28 × 2.90
A: 1 76.2-mm 50-cal. Mk 34 DP; 1 40-mm 70-cal. Bofors L70 AA; 2 single 12.7-mm mg
Electronics: Radar: 1 Decca . . . nav.; 1 Sperry SPS-53 nav.; 1 Western Electric SPG-50 gun f.c.
M: 2 Cummins 875V12 diesels; 2 props; 1,450 bhp
Range: 325/35; 1,700/16 **Fuel:** 50 tons **Crew:** 3 officers, 21 enlisted

Remarks: Transferred 22-11-89, having been in reserve since 4-77. Commissioned 6-90 after overhauls in Greece. Have Mk 63 f.c.s for 76.2-mm gun, with the associated SPG-50 radar mounted on the gunhouse and the director atop the pilothouse. The original manually operated U.S. 40-mm 60-cal. Mk 3 AA aft has been replaced by a more modern Bofors mount in both. The original G.E. LM-1500 gas turbine, which could propel the craft to 40-kt speeds, was removed prior to transfer. Expected to decommission in the near future.

MINE WARFARE SHIPS AND CRAFT

Note: Two new minelayers are planned. Modified U.S. LSM 1–class minelayer *Aktion* (N 04; ex-MMC 6, ex-LSM 301) was stricken on 23-10-00 and sister *Amvrakia* (N 05; ex-MMC 7, ex-LSM 303) was stricken during 8-02.

♦ 2 Osprey class coastal minehunters [MHS]
Bldrs: Intermarine U.S.A., Savannah, Ga.; and Avondale Marine, Gulfport, Miss.

D: 825 tons light (950 tons fl) **S:** 12 kts
Dim: 57.25 (53.10 pp) × 10.95 × 3.35 max. **A:** 2 single 12.7-mm M2 mg
Electronics:
Radar: 1 Raytheon SPS-64(V)9 nav.
Sonar: Raytheon SQQ-32 variable-depth minehunting
M: 2 Isotta-Fraschini ID 36 SS 8V-AM diesels; 2 Voith-Schneider vertical cycloidal props; 1,600 bhp—2 180-shp hydraulic motors for quiet running—1 180-shp bow-thruster
Electric: 900 kw (3 × 300 kw, Isotta-Fraschini ID SS 6V-AM diesels driving)
Range: 2,500/12 **Endurance** 5 days **Crew:** 5 officers, 46 enlisted

Remarks: Two are authorized for transfer 5-05. Expected to enter service during 2006–7.
Hull systems: Monocoque foam-core GRP hull construction, with the design based on that of the Italian Navy *Lerici*-class. Have the SSQ-109 Ship/ Machinery Control System and two 400 Hz motor-generator sets. Later units have additional space for provisions and stores. Have berthing space for 15 female crewmembers.
Combat systems: Employ the Alliant SLQ-48(V)2 Mine Neutralization System remote-controlled submersible. Have Paramax SYQ-13 tactical navigation/command and control equipment, which integrates machinery and ship control, the minehunting sonar, the mine neutralization system, inputs from the surface search radar, the precision navigation systems, and various environmental sensors. Other navigation equipment includes WRN-6 GPS terminal and Decca URN-30 Hyperfix radio navaid.
The ships have an Indal 3-drum winch capable of carrying 1,524 m of sweep cable on the main drum and 595 m each on the other drums to stream and tow the SLQ-53 array.

♦ 2 ex-U.K. Hunt-class minehunters
Bldr: Vosper Thornycroft, Woolston

	Laid down	L	In serv.
M 62 Evropi (ex-*Bicester,* M 36)	2-1-85	4-6-85	14-2-86
M 63 Kallisto (ex-*Berkeley,* M 40)	9-9-85	3-12-86	14-1-88

Kallisto (M 63) Jim Sanderson, 3-01

MINE WARFARE SHIPS AND CRAFT *(continued)*

D: 625 tons (725 fl) **S:** 17 kts (15 sust.; 8 on hydraulic drive)
Dim: 60.00 (56.60 pp) × 9.85 × 2.20 (hull; 3.40 max.)
A: 1 30-mm 75-cal. DES-30B AA; 2 single 7.62-mm mg
Electronics:
Radar: 1 Kelvin-Hughes Type 1007 nav.
Sonar: Thales Type 193M Mod. 1 variable-depth minehunting (100/300 kHz), with Mills Cross Type 2059 submersible-tracking set incorporated
M: 2 Ruston-Paxman Deltic 9-59K diesels (1,600 rpm); 2 props; 1,900 bhp (1,770 sust.); slow-speed hydraulic drive for hunting (8 kts)—bow-thruster
Electric: 1,185 kw (3 200-kw Foden FD 12 Mk 7 diesel alternators for ship's service plus one 525-kw Deltic 9-55B diesel alternator for magnetic minesweeping and 1 60-kw emergency set)
Range: 1,500/12 **Crew:** 5 officers, 40 enlisted (in U.K. service)

Remarks: Equipped for both hunting and sweeping mines. M 62 was stricken from the Royal Navy on 1-7-00 and M 63 on 28-2-01; they were transferred to Greece on 31-7-00 and 28-2-01 as part of the arrangement to produce British-designed missile craft in Greece.
Hull systems: Glass-reinforced plastic hull. One Deltic 9-59B diesel (645 bhp) drives the 525-kw sweep current alternator *or* four Dowty hydraulic pumps can be used to power the props during minehunting; the Deltic 9-59B engine also provides power for the bow-thruster and the sweep winch. Have the Ferranti-Thomson VIMOS (Vibration Monitoring System), which reduces radiated noise by 3–10 dB.
Combat systems: Are equipped with CAAIS DBA-4 (64 contact-tracking) data system and Decca Mk 21 HiFix navigation system. Carry six or seven divers and two French PAP 104 Mk 3 remote-controlled mine location submersibles. Have Sperry Osborn TA 6 acoustic, M. Mk 11 magnetic loop and M. Mk 8 Orepesa wire sweeping gear as well. EW equipment was not transferred with the ships.

♦ 2 ex-Italian U.S. Adjutant-class minehunters [MHC]
Bldr: Henry C. V. Grebe & Co., Kingston, N.Y.

	In serv.
M 60 Erato (ex-*Castagno,* M 5504, ex-MSC 74)	7-8-55
M 61 Eyiki (ex-*Gelso,* M 5509, ex-MSC 75)	8-3-54

Erato (M 60) Luciano Grazioli, 6-99

D: 354.5 tons (405 fl) **S:** 11.4 kts **Dim:** 43.92 (42.1 pp) × 8.23 × 2.68
A: 1 twin 20-mm 70-cal. Mk 24 Oerlikon AA
Electronics: Radar: 1 SMA SPN-703 nav.—Sonar: FIAR SQQ-14(IT) HF VDS
M: 2 G.M. 8-268A diesels; 2 props; 880 bhp—1 Voith-Schneider vertical cycloidal propulsor for minehunting; 310 shp
Range: 2,500/10 **Fuel:** 40 tons **Crew:** 3 officers, 38 enlisted

Remarks: Built for Italy under the U.S. Military Aid Program and transferred to Greece on 10-10-95 after retirement from Italian service. Converted from minesweepers in 1983–84 by substituting the SQQ-14 sonar for the original UQS-1 and providing facilities for mine clearance divers and remote-controlled minehunting submersibles. Have wooden hulls and nonmagnetic fittings. M 61 is scheduled to retire in 2006–7.
Combat systems: Sonar upgraded to SQQ-14(IT) with solid-state electronics. Employ the Pluto remote-controlled submersible, capable of 4.5-kt speeds; the divers aboard use CAM-T destruction charges.

♦ 7 U.S. MSC 294–class coastal minesweepers [MSC]
Bldr: Peterson Bldrs, Sturgeon Bay, Wis.

	In serv.
M 211 Alkyon (ex-MSC 314)	3-12-68
M 213 Klio (ex-*Argo,* ex-MSC 317)	7-8-68
M 214 Avra (ex-MSC 318)	3-10-68
M 240 Pleias (ex-MSC 319)	22-6-67
M 241 Kichli (ex-MSC 308)	14-7-64
M 242 Kissa (ex-MSC 309)	1-9-64
M 248 Aedon (ex-MSC 310)	13-10-64

D: 300 tons (394 fl) **S:** 13 kts **Dim:** 44.32 × 8.29 × 2.55
A: 1 twin 20-mm 70-cal. Mk 24 Oerlikon AA
Electronics: Radar: 1 Decca. . . nav.—Sonar: UQS-1D HF
M: 2 Waukesha L-1616 diesels; 2 props; 1,200 bhp
Range: 2,500/10 **Fuel:** 40 tons **Crew:** 4 officers, 27 enlisted

Kissa (M 242) Bernard Prézelin, 7-04

Klio (M 213) Cem D. Yaylali, 6-04

Remarks: Built for Greece under the Military Aid Program; transferred on completion. Are planned to be re-engined, and a new sonar may be procured.
Disposals: *Aigli* (M 246, ex-MSC 299) was stricken during 1996. *Doris* (A 475, ex-M 245, ex-MSC 298) was employed as a hydrographic survey ship until stricken in 1995. *Dafni* (M 247, ex-MSC 307) was decomissioned on 17-12-04 along with Greece's last remaining *Adjutant*-class coastal minesweeper *Thalia* (M 210, ex-MSC 170).

♦ 4 ex-U.S. 50-foot-class minesweeping boats [MSB]

D: 21 tons (fl) **S:** 8 kts **Dim:** 15.20 × 4.01 × 1.31
M: 1 Navy DB diesel; 60 bhp **Range:** 150/8 **Crew:** 6 tot.

Remarks: Wooden-hulled former personnel launches loaned in 1972 and purchased during 1981. Intended for harbor use. Are around 50 years old.

AMPHIBIOUS WARFARE SHIPS

Disposal note: Ex-U.S. *Cabildo*-class dock landing ship *Nafkratoussa* (L 153; ex-*Fort Mandan,* LSD 21) was stricken on 29-2-00.

♦ 5 (+ 1) Jason-class tank landing ships [LST]
Bldr: Elefsis SY

	Laid down	L	In serv.
L 173 Chios	18-4-87	16-12-88	30-5-96
L 174 Samos	9-87	6-4-89	20-5-94
L 175 Ikaria	9-5-88	11-98	6-10-99
L 176 Lesbos	6-4-89	5-7-90	2-99
L 177 Rodos	20-11-89	6-10-99	5-00
L 178 . . .	. . .	. . .	. . .

Chios (L 173) A Couiline, via Bernard Prézelin, 10-02

D: 4,400 tons std. (4,916 fl) **S:** 16 kts
Dim: 115.90 (106.00 pp) × 15.30 × 3.44 (mean)
A: 1 76-mm 62-cal. OTO Melara DP; 2 single 40-mm 70-cal. Bofors AA; 2 single 20-mm 90-cal. Rheinmetall Rh 202 AA

AMPHIBIOUS WARFARE SHIPS *(continued)*

Samos (L 174) Guy Schaeffer via Paolo Marsan, 9-03

Electronics:
Radar: 1 Furuno . . . nav.; 1 Kelvin-Hughes Type 1007 nav.; 1 Thales TRS 3030 Triton V air/surf. search; 1 Thales Castor gun f.c.
EW: . . . radar warning; Mk 36 Mod. 1 SRBOC decoy syst. (2 6-round Mk 137 RL)
M: 2 Wärtsilä Nohab 16V25 diesels; 2 props; 10,600 bhp (9,200 sust.)
Range: . . . / . . .
Crew: 108 ship's company + 245–310 troops (1,200 in emergency)

Remarks: Ordered 15-5-86 as replacements for the U.S. LST 1/511 class. The program was considerably delayed by the builder's financial troubles, with the last ship originally scheduled to complete 9-90. A sixth ship was added to the program in 2000, but has not yet materialized.
Hull systems: Have a raised helicopter deck aft capable of supporting one Agusta-Bell AB-212B helicopter. Two LCVP landing craft and two lifeboats are carried. The bow ramp is capable of supporting 55-ton vehicles; there is also a stern loading ramp and a ramp from the upper deck amidships to the tank deck. Cargo: 250 tons (up to 20 heavy tanks, or 17 amphibious armored personnel carriers, or 15 trucks and 60 tons of ammunition).
Combat systems: Have two Matra Défense Panda Mk 2 optical gun directors. The 20-mm AA listed do not appear to have been mounted on L 174.

Disposal note: Of the two U.S. *Terrebone Parrish*–class tank landing ships, the *Kos* (L 116; ex-*Whitfield County,* LST 1169) was retired on 27-7-01 and the *Oinoussai* (L 104; ex-*Terrell County,* LST 1157) during 2003. U.S. LST 1–class tank landing ship *Lesbos* (L 172; ex-*Boone County,* LST 389) and LST 511–class *Ikaria* (L 154; ex-*Potter County,* LST 1086) were stricken during 1999; *Rodos* (L 157; ex-*Bowman County,* LST 391) in 1997; *Kriti* (L 171; ex-*Page County,* LST 1076) on 31-12-99. *Syros* (L 144, ex-LST 325), stricken 1-11-99, was donated to a U.S. museum organization and returned to U.S. waters during 12-00.
Of the former U.S. LSM 1–class landing ships, *Ipopliarchos Tornas* (L 162, ex-LSM 102) was stricken during 1990; *Ipopliarchos Grigoropoulis* (L 161, ex-LSM 45) and *Ipopliarchos Daniolos* (L 163, ex-LSM 227) were stricken during 1993, with L 161 going to the U.S. as a museum ship; and *Ipopliarchos Krystallidis* (L 165, ex-LSM 541) was stricken on 15-5-00. *Ipopliarchos Rousen* (L 164, ex-LSM 399) was stricken during 2003.

♦ 5 Russian Pomornik (Zubr)-class (Project 1232.2) air-cushion vehicle landing craft [LCUA]
Bldrs: Sudostroitel'noye Obyedineniye "Almaz," Dekabristov Verf, St. Petersburg, Russia; L 181: Morye Verf, Feodosiya, Ukraine

	L	In Greek serv.
L 180 Kefallinia (ex-MDK-50)	16-1-94	22-1-01
L 181 Ithaki (ex-*Ivan Bohun,* U 421)	9-12-00	7-2-01
L 182 Kerkyra	25-6-04	4-1-05
L 183 Zakynthos (ex-MDK- . . .)	28-5-01	2006
L 184 . . .	. . .	2006–7

Ithaki (L 181)—as Ukraine Navy *Horlivka* (U 423), with sister *Kramator'sk* (U 422) at the left Boris Lemachko, 2000

D: 340 tons light, 415 normal (550 fl) **S:** 63 kts (55 sust.)
Dim: 57.3 (56.2 hull) × 25.6 (22.0 hull) × 21.9 (high)
A: 2 or 4 4-round Igla-1M (SA-N-8) SAM syst. (32 9M-36 Strela-3/Gremlin missiles); 2 single 30-mm 54-cal. AK-630M gatling AA; 2 22-round 140-mm MS-227 Ogon' retractable artillery RL (132 rockets); up to 80 mines in lieu of vehicle cargo, using portable rails
Electronics:
Radar: 1 SRN-207 Ekran nav.; 1 MR-123-2 Vympel gun f.c.
E/O: 1 . . . surveillance/f.c.; 1 periscope
M: 5 NK-12MV (M-70) gas turbines (12,100 shp each/10,000 shp sust.; 2 to power lift fans); 3 ducted CP airscrew propellers, 4 NO-10 lift fans; 36,300 shp for propulsion L 184: . . . diesels
Electric: 200 kw tot. (2 × 100-kw GTG-110 gas turbine sets)
Range: 300/55 with 130-ton payload; 1,000/55 light **Fuel:** 56 tons
Endurance: 5 days (1 day with full troop complement)
Crew: 4 officers, 27 enlisted + 140–360 troops

Remarks: Officially typed "Fast Transport Vessels." Two were tentatively ordered from Russia in 6-99 and two more from Ukraine on 8-9-99. The final contracts were signed on 24-1-00 to provide one refurbished, 1993-vintage Russian Baltic Fleet unit; one "new" unit (one of the two incomplete units available as of 1994) delivered from the Almaz yard (for $101 million combined); and two "new" craft (actually refurbished former Russian Black Sea Fleet units transferred to Ukraine in 1996) from Ukraine's Ukrspetsexport for $100 million. The first Russian-provided unit, L 180, was originally completed in 1993 and was relaunched on 27-10-00, arriving in Salamis on 18-1-01. The second Russian unit, L 183, was relaunched on 28-5-01 for 7-01 delivery. The Ukrainian-furnished units were refurbished at Feodosiya during 2000–2001; L 181 was launched on 9-12-00. An option for four more from Russia for $51 million each was to be signed by 24-1-01, but is still pending. A second ex-Ukrainian unit was rejected on delivery due to numerous hull cracks and was scrapped at Feodosiya during 2002; a replacement was ordered from Russia for $63.9 million during 10-02 and laid down on 24-1-03. Maintenance of the craft is under contract to Hellenic Aerospace Industry (HAI). In Russian service, there have been significant reliability problems with the class. Are the "fast transport ships" for the Greek "rapid reaction force." L 180 was damaged in collision with merchant vessel *Viking Land* during 4-02 and is undergoing extensive repair work.
Hull systems: The dimensions above include the flexible skirt. The hull, intended to have a 16-year service life, is a complex structure constructed in part with flammable light alloys. The vehicle deck can hold up to eight M 113 armored personnel transport vehicles or three Leopard 1A5 heavy tanks plus a detachment of infantry—or up to 140 troops and 130 tons of combat cargo. Have small bow and stern ramps.
Propulsion systems: Three of the gas-turbine engines are mounted on pylons and drive airscrew propellers; they are equipped with exhaust thrust diverters to enhance mobility. The lift-fan gas turbines drive four blowers to maintain skirt pressure and are mounted near the stern in the wing compartments and exhaust through the stern. The engines for all four craft were made in Ukraine. L 184 will be fitted with diesels instead of gas turbines for increased reliability.
Combat systems: The navigational radar is mounted within a lozenge-shaped radome. The retractable artillery rocket launchers are located near the bow in the hull wing-walls and are reloaded below decks; the rockets have a range of 4.5–10 km and are launched via a DVU-3 control system. The Greek ships have two navigational radars, SATNAV receivers, a receiver for the Decca coastal radio navaid system, MFD/F, and a night-vision system.

♦ 6 German Type 520 utility landing craft [LCU]
Bldr: Howaldtswerke, Hamburg

	In serv.
L 167 Ios (ex-*Barbe,* L 790)	26-11-65
L 168 Sikinos (ex-*Dorsch,* L 792)	17-3-66
L 169 Irakleia (ex-*Forelle,* L 794)	20-4-66
L 170 Folegandros (ex-*Delfin,* L 791)	25-11-65
L 178 Naxos (ex-*Renke,* L 798)	2-9-66
L 179 Paros (ex-*Salm,* L 799)	23-9-66

D: 166 tons (403 fl) **S:** 11 kts **Dim:** 40.04 (36.70 pp) × 8.80 × 1.60 (2.10 max.)
A: 2 single 20-mm 90-cal. Rheinmetall AA
Electronics: Radar: 1 Kelvin-Hughes 14/9 nav.

Ios (L 167) H&L Van Ginderen, 9-97

M: 2 MWM 2-cyl. diesels; 2 props; 1,200 bhp
Electric: 130 kVA tot. **Range:** 1,200/11 **Crew:** 17 tot.

Remarks: Design based on U.S. LCU 1626 class. L 178 and L 179 were transferred on 16-11-89, L 167–L 170 on 31-1-92. Two others, ex-*Rochen* (L 764) and ex-*Mürane* (L 797), were transferred 20-10-92 as cannibalization spares. Cargo: 237 tons max.; 141.6 tons normal. Ramps fore and aft.

♦ 2 ex-British LCT(4)-class utility landing craft [LCU]
Bldrs: . . . , U.K. (In serv. 1945)

L 185 Kythera (ex-LCT 1198) L 189 Milos (ex-LCT 1300)

AMPHIBIOUS WARFARE SHIPS *(continued)*

D: 280 tons light (640 fl) **S:** 9.5 kts **Dim:** 57.07 × 11.79 × 1.30 (aft)
A: 2 20-mm 70-cal. Oerlikon AA **M:** 2 Paxman diesels; 2 props; 1,000 bhp
Range: 500/9.5; 3,100/7 **Crew:** 12 tot.

Remarks: Transferred 1946; survivors of a group of 12. Cargo: 350 tons.

♦ 11 ex-German Type 521 landing craft [LCM]
Bldr: Rheinwerft, Walsum (In serv. 1965–67)

ABM 20 (ex-*Seetaucher,* LCM 1)
ABM 21 (ex-*Seenadel,* LCM 2)
ABM 22 (ex-*Seedrache,* LCM 3)
ABM 23 (ex-*Seespinne,* LCM 4)
ABM 24 (ex-*Seeotter,* LCM 5)
ABM 25 (ex-*Seezunge,* LCM 6)
ABM 26 (ex-*Seelilie,* LCM 7)
ABM 27 (ex-*Seefeder,* LCM 8)
ABM 28 (ex-*Seerose,* LCM 9)
ABM 29 (ex-*Seenelke,* LCM 10)
ABM 30 (ex-*Huchen,* LCM 11)

ABM 21 H&L Van Ginderen, 9-94

D: 116 tons (168 fl) **S:** 10.6 kts max. **Dim:** 23.56 × 6.40 × 1.46
A: None **Electronics:** Radar: 1 . . . nav.
M: 2 MWM 8-cyl. diesels; 2 props; 684 bhp
Range: 690/10; 1,430/7 **Crew:** 7 tot. + 50–60 troops

Remarks: ABM 29 was transferred 5-3-91, the others on 25-4-91. Design based on U.S. LCM(8) class. ABM 29 has a 2-ton cargo boom and a 20-kw generator and can act as an armament stores tender (can carry up to 18 torpedoes); the others can carry up to 60 tons of cargo. As of late 1994, were showing OA 21 pennant number series. By 1998, some or all may have been given names and L-series pennants, with the name *Serifos* (L 195) reported.

♦ 12 LCVP 36–class landing craft [LCVP]
Bldr: Motomarine SA, Athens (In serv. . . .)

D: 13 tons (fl) **S:** 8 kts **Dim:** 10.90 × 3.21 × 1.04 (aft)
M: 1 . . . diesel; 200 bhp

Remarks: Ordered late 1999 as part of the contract for the three Type 214 submarines. Were to be of GRP construction.

♦ 7 LCVP-type landing craft [LCVP]
Bldr: Viking Marine, Piraeus (In serv. 1-80)

D: 13 tons (fl) **S:** 8 kts **Dim:** 10.90 × 3.21 × 1.04 (aft)
M: 1 G.M. 6-71 diesel; 200 bhp

♦ Up to 32 ex-U.S. LCVP-type landing craft [LCVP]

D: 13 tons (fl) **S:** 9 kts **Dim:** 10.90 × 3.21 × 1.04 (aft)
M: 1 Gray Marine 64HN9 diesel; 225 bhp **Range:** 110/9

Remarks: Carried by LSTs. Cargo: 36 troops or 3.5 tons. Ten were transferred in 11-56, 4 in 7-58, 10 in 1-62, 4 in 6-64, 3 in 10-69, and the remainder in 3-71; two were returned to the U.S. with the LST *Syros* during 12-00. Are being replaced by new-construction units for the *Jason*-class tank landing ships.

♦ 3 M-10C-class air-cushion landing craft [LCPA]
Bldr: ABS Hovercraft, U.K. (1 in service 26-6-98, 2 others in 2000)

D: 26 tons (fl) **S:** 50 kts (light; 35 loaded) **Dim:** 20.6 × 8.80 × 0.35 (at rest)
A: 1 12.7-mm mg **Electronics:** Radar: 1 . . . nav.
M: 2 Deutz BF12L513C diesels; 2 lift fans, 2 airscrew props; 1,050 bhp
Range: 600/30 **Fuel:** 4,600 liters **Crew:** 1 officer, 2 enlisted

Remarks: Several were said to be planned for acquisition as of 2-00.
Hull systems: Capable of carrying one tracked vehicle, or 50 seated troops, or one 20-ft. cargo container, or 20 stretcher cases. The hull is constructed of GRP carbon fiber and vinyl laminate, with a GRP/foam sandwich deck and Kevlar-reinforced superstructure. Can clear 1-m obstacles and can operate in 2.5-m seas.

♦ 1 UWC-7-class special forces craft [LCP]
Bldr: Fabio Buzz Design sri, Brianza, Italy (In serv. 20-4-01)

UWC-7

D: . . . tons **S:** 60+ kts **Dim:** 12.80 × . . . × . . .
A: 1 12.7-mm mg; 1 40-mm Mk 19 grenade launcher
Electronics: Radar: 1 . . . nav.
M: 2 . . . diesels; 2 props; 1,500 bhp
Range: 350–400/ . . . **Crew:** 4 + 12 commandos

Remarks: A high-speed, GRP-hulled racing RIB design, donated by private citizen Theodore Angelopoulos to the Greek Navy's Underwater Demolition Unit (*Monas Yporvryhion Katastrofon*), based at Skaramanga. Reportedly worth $917,000. The Underwater Demolition Unit also operates at least one planing-hulled swimmer delivery craft of about the same size.

♦ 2 E. Panagopoulos I–class ordnance disposal launches [LCP]
Bldr: Hellenic SY, Skaramanga (In serv. 1980–81)

P 70 E. Panagopoulos II P 96 E. Panagopoulos III

D: 35 tons (fl) **S:** 38 kts **Dim:** 23.00 (21.00 wl) × 5.00 × 0.97
A: 1 12.7-mm mg **Electronics:** Radar: 1 Decca . . . nav.
M: 2 MTU 12V331 TC92 diesels; 2 props; 3,060 bhp **Crew:** 6 tot.

Remarks: Aluminum alloy hull with hard-chine form. Sister *E. Panagopoulos I* (P 61) was stricken 1991. Both were stricken during 1993 but brought back into service around 1996 as explosive ordnance divers' launches.

AUXILIARIES

♦ 1 ex-German ammunition ship [AE]
Bldr: Dubigeon, Nantes, France

	Laid down	L	In serv.
A 415 Evros (ex-German *Schwarzwald,* A 1400; ex-French *Amalthée*)	30-6-55	31-1-56	7-6-56

D: 2,395 tons (fl) **S:** 15 kts **Dim:** 80.18 × 11.99 × 4.65
A: 2 twin 40-mm 70-cal. Bofors AA
M: 1 Sulzer 6-SD-60 diesel; 3,000 bhp **Electric:** 500 kw
Range: 4,500/15 **Crew:** 32 tot.

Remarks: 1,667 grt. Former cargo ship purchased 2-60 by the German Navy and converted for naval use, commissioning 11-10-61. Transferred to Greece 2-6-76.

Disposal note: Ex-Germany intelligence collection ship *Hermis* (A 373, ex-*Oker*, ex-*Hoheweg*) was retired in 2003.

♦ 1 ex-U.S. AN 103–class netlayer and mooring-buoy tender [AGL]
Bldr: Krögerwerft, Rendsburg (In serv. 4-60)

A 307 Thetis (ex-U.S. AN 103)

Thetis (A 307) D. Dervissis, 7-79

D: 560 tons (975 fl) **S:** 12.8 kts **Dim:** 48.50 (51.70 over horns) × 10.60 × 3.70
A: 1 40-mm 60-cal. Mk 3 Bofors AA; 3 single 20-mm 70-cal. Mk 10 Oerlikon AA
Electronics: Radar: 1 Decca 707 nav.
M: 1 M.A.N. G7V 40/60 diesel; 1 prop; 1,470 bhp
Range: 6,500/10.2 **Fuel:** 134 tons **Crew:** 5 officers, 45 enlisted

Remarks: Launched 1959. Transferred 4-60. Can carry 1,600 rounds of 40-mm and 25,200 rounds of 20-mm ammunition. Fitted with bow lift horns and a large winch forward and aft. A sister serves in the Turkish Navy.

♦ 2 Ikaravoyiannos Theophilopoulos–class lighthouse tenders [AGL]
Bldr: Anastassiadis Tsortanidis, Perama

A 479 Ikaravoyiannos Theophilopoulos (In serv. 2-1-76)
A 481 St. Lykoudis (In serv. 17-3-76)

D: 1,350 tons (1,450 fl) **S:** 15 kts **Dim:** 63.24 (56.50 pp) × 11.6 × 4.0
A: None **Electronics:** Radar: 2 Decca . . . nav.
M: 1 MWM TBD-500-8UD diesel; 2,400 bhp **Crew:** 40 tot.

Remarks: Near-sisters to hydrographic survey ship *Naftilos* (A 478). Have a helicopter platform aft.

Ikaravoyiannos Theophilopoulos (A 479) H&L Van Ginderen, 10-93

AUXILIARIES *(continued)*

♦ 1 Pytheas-class hydrographic survey ship [AGS]
Bldr: Anastassiadis Tsortanidis, Perama

	L	In serv.
A 474 Pytheas	19-9-83	12-83

D: 670 tons (840 fl) **S:** 15 kts **Dim:** 50.00 (44.91 pp) × 9.60 × 4.22
M: 2 G.M. Detroit Diesel 12V92 TA diesels; 2 props; 1,800 bhp (1,020 sust.)
Crew: 8 officers, 50 enlisted

Remarks: Programmed 1979, ordered 5-82. Carries two survey launches. A near-sister, *Aegeon,* was completed in 1985 for the civilian National Maritime Research Center.

♦ 1 Naftilos-class hydrographic survey ship [AGS]
Bldr: Anastassiadis Tsortanidis, Perama

	L	In serv.
A 478 Naftilos	19-11-75	3-4-76

Naftilos (A 478) H&L Van Ginderen, 9-99

D: 1,380 tons (1,480 fl) **S:** 15 kts **Dim:** 63.1 (56.5 pp) × 11.6 × 4.0
M: 2 Burmeister & Wain SS28LH diesels; 2 props; 2,640 bhp
Crew: 8 officers, 66 enlisted

Remarks: Near-sisters *St. Lykoudis* (A 481) and *Ikaravoyiannos Theophilopoulos* (A 479) are configured as lighthouse tenders. Can carry two survey launches. The helicopter deck has been replaced by two oceanographic equipment-handling gallows cranes.

♦ 2 ex-German Type 701C replenishment oilers [AO]
Bldr: A 464: Flensburger Schiffswerft, Flensburg; A 470: Blohm + Voss, Hamburg

	Laid down	L	In serv.
A 464 Axios (ex-*Coburg,* A 1412)	9-4-65	15-12-65	9-7-68
A 470 Aliakmon (ex-*Saarburg,* A 1415)	1-3-66	15-7-66	30-7-68

D: 3,709 tons (fl) **S:** 17 kts **Dim:** 114.90 (108.00 pp) × 13.20 × 4.20
A: 2 twin 40-mm 70-cal. Bofors AA **Electronics:** Radar: 1 . . . nav.
M: 2 Maybach MD 872 diesels; 2 CP props; 5,600 bhp—bow-thruster
Electric: 1,935 kw **Range:** 3,000/17; 3,200/14 **Crew:** 82 tot.

Aliakmon (A 470) A. A. de Kruijf, 8-02

Remarks: A 464 transferred and recommissioned 30-9-91. A 470 was transferred on 19-10-94 and was formally recommissioned in Greek service on 30-6-95. A 464 completed conversion to increase cargo fuel stowage from 640 tons to 1,400 tons at Skaramanga Shipyard in 9-00, and A 470 was under conversion during 2001. Spaces formerly devoted to carrying spare parts and 205 tons of ammunition were converted to fuel tanks, while 131 tons fresh water and 267 m^2 refrigerated stores can still be accommodated. Have fin stabilization system and one 3-ton and two 2-ton electric cranes. There are two lead-computing optical directors for the 40-mm guns.

Disposal note: Ex-U.S. *Patapsco*-class oilers *Arethousa* (A 377, ex-*Natchaug* AOG 54) and *Ariadni* (A 414, ex-*Tombigbee,* AOG 11) serving since World War II were no longer in service as of 2005.

♦ 1 Italian Etna-class replenishment oiler [AOR]
Bldr: Elefsis SY

	Laid down	L	In serv.
A 374 Prometeus	2000	19-2-02	8-7-03

Prometeus (A 374) Bernard Prézelin, 8-05

Prometeus (A 374) Bernard Prézelin, 8-05

D: 6,700 tons (13,400 fl) **S:** 21 kts **Dim:** 146.50 (137.00 pp) × 21.00 × 7.25
A: 2 single 40-m 70-cal. Bofors AA; 1 20-mm Mk 15 Phalanx Block IA CIWS; 2 single 20-mm AA
Electronics: Radar: . . .
M: 2 G.M.T.-Sulzer 12 ZAV 40S diesels; 2 props; 22,400 bhp—1,000-kw bow-thruster
Range: 7,600/18 **Crew:** 160 tot. (243 accomm.)

Remarks: Construction approved 7-99. Built with assistance from Italy's Fincantieri at a cost of $128 million.
Hull systems: Can carry 4,700 tons gas turbine/diesel fuel, 1,200 tons aviation fuel, 160 tons fresh water, 2,100 m^3 (about 280 tons) ammunition, 30,000 fresh rations, 30,000 dry-food rations, 20 tons spare parts, and 20 tons lubricant, and has space on deck for 12 cargo containers. Two replenishment stations on each beam. The Phalanx CIWS was not ordered for the ship until 12-02.

♦ 2 Zeus-class coastal tankers [AOT]
Bldr: Hellenic SY, Skaramanga

A 375 Zeus (In serv. 21-2-89) A 376 Orion (In serv. 5-5-89)

D: Approx. 2,100 tons (fl) **S:** 10.9 kts **Dim:** 67.02 (60.35 pp) × 10.00 × 4.20
A: None **Electronics:** Radar: 1 . . . nav.
M: 1 MWM–Burmeister & Wain 12V 20/27 diesel; 1 prop; 1,600 bhp
Crew: 28 (accomm.)

Remarks: 866 grt/1,240 dwt. Ordered 9-86. Cargo: 960 m^3 diesel or fuel oil, 102 m^3 JP-5, 115 m^3 fresh water, 146 m^3 potable water. Freeboard when loaded is only 0.45 m. Improved version of the *Ouranos* class, with a hose-handling crane on the platform forward. Sister *Stymfalia* (A 469) is configured as a water tanker [AWT].

Zeus (A 375) Stefan Karpinski, 4-02

AUXILIARIES *(continued)*

♦ 2 Ouranos-class coastal tankers [AOT]
Bldr: Kynossoura SY, Piraeus

	In serv.		In serv.
A 416 Ouranos	29-1-77	A 417 Hyperion	27-2-77

D: 2,100 tons (fl) **S:** 12 kts **Dim:** 67.70 (60.40 pp) × 10.00 × 4.70
A: 2 single 20-mm 70-cal. Mk 10 Oerlikon AA
Electronics: Radar: 1 . . . nav.
M: 1 M.A.N.–Burmeister & Wain 12V20 diesel; 1 prop; 1,750 bhp
Crew: 28 tot.

Remarks: Cargo: 1,323 m^3.

♦ 1 ex-U.K. Bustler-class salvage tug [ARS]
Bldr: Henry Robb, Leith, Scotland

	Laid down	L	In serv.
A 408 Atlas (ex-*Nisos Zakynthos*, ex-HMS *Mediator*)	18-10-43	21-6-44	8-11-44

Atlas (A 408) Dieter Wolf, 7-03

D: 1,118 tons (1,630 fl) **S:** 16 kts **Dim:** 62.48 (59.4 pp) × 12.32 × 5.18
M: 2 Atlas diesels; 2 props; 3,200 bhp **Range:** 3,400/11
Fuel: 340 tons **Crew:** 42 tot.

Remarks: Purchased from the Royal Navy in 1965 by a private owner. Acquired 1-8-79 by the Greek Navy and commissioned during 12-79.

♦ 1 Zeus-class water tanker [AWT]
Bldr: Hellenic SY, Skaramanga (In serv. 1990+)

A 469 Stymfalia

D: Approx. 2,100 tons (fl) **S:** 10.9 kts **Dim:** 67.02 (60.35 pp) × 10.00 × 4.20
A: None **Electronics:** Radar: 1 . . . nav.
M: 1 MWM–Burmeister & Wain 12V 20/27 diesel; 1 prop; 1,600 bhp
Crew: 28 (accomm.)

Remarks: 866 grt/1,240 dwt. Ordered 9-86. Begun and launched by Khalkis SY, but completed by Hellenic SY. Cargo: approx. 1,300 m^3 liquid. Two sisters, *Zeus* (A 375) and *Orion* (A 376), are configured as fuel transports [AOT]; see above.

♦ 1 training ship [AXT]
Bldr: Anastassiadis Tsortanidis, Perama

	Laid down	L	In serv.
A 74 Aris	10-76	4-10-78	1-81

Aris (A 74) Guy Schaeffer via Paolo Marsan, 9-03

D: 2,400 tons (2,630 fl) **S:** 17.8 kts **Dim:** 100.00 (95.00 pp) × 11.00 × 4.50
A: 1 76.2-mm 50-cal. U.S. Mk 26 DP; 2 single 40-mm 70-cal. Bofors AA; 4 single 20-mm 90-cal. Rheinmetall AA; 1 light helicopter
Electronics: Radar: 2 Decca TM 1226C nav.
M: 2 MAK diesels; 2 props; 10,000 bhp
Crew: 21 officers, 94 enlisted + 359 cadets

Remarks: Can serve as a hospital ship or transport in wartime. Completion delayed by payment dispute. During a 1986 refit, the ship received a new command center, and the helicopter facility was reactivated. Marisat was added in 1988. There are two lead-computing optical directors for the 40-mm guns. The 76.2-mm gun is probably now intended more as a saluting battery than a practical weapon.

SERVICE CRAFT

♦ 1 Italian Pisa-class armored cruiser historic relic [YAG]
Bldr: Orlando & Co., Livorno, Italy

	L	In serv.
Averoff (ex-*Georges Averoff*)	12-3-10	5-11

D: 9,958 tons (normal) **S:** 22.5 kts (as designed)
Dim: 140.8 (129.8 pp) × 21.0 × 7.5
A: Nonfunctional: 2 twin 234-mm 45-cal. low-angle; 4 twin 190-mm 45-cal. low-angle; 8 single 76.2-mm low-angle; 4 76.2-mm AA; 6 single 37-mm AA
M: 2 sets vertical triple expansion steam; 2 props; 19,000 ihp
Boilers: 22 Belleville water-tube, low-pressure **Range:** 7,125/10
Fuel: 600 tons coal, 1,500 tons oil **Crew:** 670 tot. (when operational)

Remarks: Stricken in 1946. Maintained afloat in excellent condition by the Greek Navy as a memorial at Piraeus. All data above refer to the ship when operational. Armor included 203-mm belt, tapering to 83-mm at ends; 50-mm deck; 203-mm on the turrets; and 178-mm on the conning tower.

♦ 5 miscellaneous floating cranes [YD]

♦ 2 Pandora-class personnel ferries [YFB]
Bldr: Perama SY

A 419 Pandora (In serv. 26-10-73) A 420 Pandrosos (In serv. 1-12-73)

Pandrosos (A 420) Martin Mokrus, 5-04

D: 350 tons (390 fl) **S:** 11 kts **Dim:** 46.80 × 8.30 × 1.90
Electronics: Radar: 1 Decca 1226 nav.
M: 2 diesels; 2 props; . . . bhp

Remarks: Can carry up to 500 personnel for short periods. No passenger berthing is fitted.

♦ 1 floating dry dock [YFDM]
Bldr: Elefsis SY (L: 2-5-88; In serv. 9-5-88)

Naval Drydock No. 7

Remarks: 6,000-ton capacity, 145.0 m o.a. Technical assistance in construction came from Götaverken, Arendal, Sweden.

♦ 1 floating dry dock [YFDM]
Bldr: M.A.N., Blexen, Germany (In serv. 1968)

Naval Drydock No. . . .

Remarks: 5,000-ton lift capacity. 140.0 m o.a. by 24.0 m between fenders by 7.40 clear draft over blocks. Based at Salamis.

Note: Floating dry docks 1, 3, and 6 were based at Souda Bay, but one was stricken in 1996; no information available on current status.

♦ 1 wooden trireme rowing galley [YFL]
Bldr: . . . (In serv. 1987)

Olympias

D: Approx. 120 tons (fl) **S:** 9–12 kts **Dim:** 37.0 × 5.2 × 1.5
M: 170 oars in three rows; auxiliary square sail
Crew: 10 officers, 170 galley "slaves"

Remarks: Built for historic research and to commemorate the Greek naval tradition. As rowers are volunteers, whips are unnecessary. Oregon pine construction. Refitted 1992. Was on display ashore at Port Faliron as of 2000.

Note: Small harbor launches BB 32 and BB 35 are employed at the Salamis Naval Base, and there may be others of the class.

♦ 1 Strabon-class inshore survey craft [YGS]
Bldr: Emanuil-Maliris SY, Perama

	L	In serv.
A 476 Strabon	9-88	27-2-89

D: 252 tons (fl) **S:** 12.5 kts **Dim:** 32.70 × 6.10 × 2.50
M: 1 M.A.N. D2842LE diesel; 1 prop; 1,200 bhp **Crew:** 2 officers, 18 enlisted

SERVICE CRAFT *(continued)*

Strabon (A 476) H&L Van Ginderen, 10-94

♦ 5 liquid-cargo barges [YON/YWN] Bldr: Elefsis SY (In serv. 1988)

D: Approx. 400 tons (fl) **Dim:** 27.1 × 7.2 × 1.5

Remarks: Cargo: 300 tons. Four for fuel oil, the other for water.

♦ 4 ex-German Type 430 torpedo retrievers [YPT]
Bldr: Schweers, Bardenfleth

	L
A 460 Evrotas (ex-TF 106, Y 872)	10-6-66
A 461 Arachthos (ex-TF 108, Y 874)	22-9-65
A 462 Strymon (ex-TF 107, Y 873)	13-9-65
A 463 Nestos (ex-TF 4, Y 854)	21-10-65

D: 56 tons (63.5 fl) **S:** 17 kts **Dim:** 25.22 × 5.40 × 1.60
Electronics: Radar: 1 . . . nav.
M: 1 MWM 12-cyl. diesel; 1 prop; 1,000 bhp **Crew:** 6 tot.

Remarks: A 460 transferred 5-3-91, A 461 on 12-4-90, A 462 on 16-11-89, and A 463 on 28-9-90. All have wooden hulls and a stern torpedo recovery ramp.

♦ 2 Kiklops-class coastal tugs [YTB]
Bldr: Hellenic SY, Skaramanga (In serv. 1989)

A 422 Kadmos A 435 Kekrops

Kadmos (A 422) Stefan Karpinski, 4-02

D: . . . tons **S:** . . . kts **Dim:** . . . × . . . × . . .
M: . . .

Remarks: Ordered 1-86. No data available.

♦ 3 Heraklis-class coastal tugs [YTB]
Bldr: Anastassiadis Tsortanidis, Perama

A 423 Heraklis (In serv. 6-4-78) A 425 Odisseus (In serv. 28-6-78)
A 424 Jason (In serv. 6-3-78)

Jason (A 424) Werner Schiefer, 11-98

D: 345 tons **S:** 12 kts **Dim:** 30.0 × 7.9 × 3.4 **M:** 1 MWM diesel; 1,200 bhp

♦ 2 Atromitos-class harbor tugs [YTB] (In serv. 20-6-68)

A 410 Atromitos A 411 Adamastos

D: 310 tons **S:** 10 kts **Dim:** 30.0 × 7.9 × 3.0
M: 1 diesel; 1 prop; 1,260 bhp

♦ 1 ex-U.S. Army Design 3006–class large harbor tug [YTB]
(In serv. 1954–55)

A 432 Gigas (ex-LT 1941)

Gigas (A 432) Stefan Karpinski, 4-02

D: 295 tons (390 fl) **S:** 12.75 kts **Dim:** 32.61 × 8.08 × 3.71
M: 1 Fairbanks-Morse 38D8⅛ diesel; 1 prop; 1,200 bhp **Electric:** 80 kw
Range: 3,300/12 **Fuel:** 54 tons **Crew:** 16 tot.

Remarks: Transferred 26-11-61. Bollard pull: 12 tons.

♦ 3 ex-U.S. YTM 764–class large harbor tug [YTB]
Bldr: Luders Marine Construction, Stamford, Conn. (A 412 in serv. 11-5-45)

A 409 Achilleus (ex- . . .)
A 412 Aias (ex-U.S. *Ankachak,* YTM 767, ex-YTB 501)
A 429 Perseus (ex- . . .)

Perseus (A 429) Werner Schiefer, 11-98

D: 260 tons (350 fl) **S:** 11 kts **Dim:** 30.48 × 7.62 × 2.92
M: 2 Enterprise diesels; 1 prop; 1,270 bhp **Crew:** 8 tot.

Remarks: A 409 transferred 7-47; previous identity unknown. A 412 transferred 1972.

♦ 2 ex-German Heppens-class medium harbor tugs [YTM]
Bldr: Schichau, Bremerhaven

	Laid down	L	In serv.
A 439 Atreus (ex-*Ellerbek,* Y 1682)	29-12-70	2-6-71	26-11-71
A 441 Theseus (ex-*Heppens,* Y 1681)	19-3-71	15-9-71	17-12-71

D: 232 tons (319 fl) **S:** 12 kts **Dim:** 26.51 × 7.42 × 2.81
Electronics: Radar: 1 . . . nav.
M: 1 MWM 8-cyl. diesel; 800 bhp **Electric:** 120 kw tot. **Crew:** 6 tot.

Remarks: A 439 transferred to Greece 3-95. A 441 was stricken from German Navy on 18-12-98 and sold to Greece in 3-99. *Neuende* remains in German service, though previously reported as being sold to Greece in 1999.

♦ 1 ex-U.S. YTM 518–class medium harbor tug [YTM]
Bldr: Gibbs Gas Engine Co., Jacksonville, Fla. (In serv. 2-1-45)

A 428 Nestor (ex-U.S. *Wahpeton,* YTM 527)

D: 260 tons (310 fl) **S:** 11 kts **Dim:** 30.8 × 8.5 × 3.3
M: 2 G.M. diesels; 1 prop; 820 bhp **Crew:** 8 tot.

Remarks: Transferred 22-11-89.

SERVICE CRAFT *(continued)*

Nestor (A 428) Werner Schiefer, 11-98

♦ 1 ex-U.S. YTM 174–class medium harbor tug [YTM]
Bldr: Gulfport Boiler Works, Port Arthur, Texas (In serv. 12-3-42)

A 427 Danaos (ex-U.S. *Dekanisora,* YTM 252, ex-YT 252, ex-BYT 4)

D: 210 tons (320 fl) **S:** 12 kts **Dim:** 31.1 × 7.6 × 3.0
M: 2 G.M. diesels; 1 prop; 820 bhp **Crew:** 8 tot.

Remarks: Transferred 22-11-89.

♦ 4 ex-German Lütje Horn–class small harbor tugs [YTL]

	L
A 413 Pilefs (ex-*Lütje Horn,* Y 812)	9-5-58
A 436 Minos (ex-*Mellum,* Y 813)	23-10-58
A 437 Pelias (ex-*Knechtsand,* Y 814)	3-12-58
A 438 Ægeus (ex-*Schärhorn,* Y 815)	9-5-58

Minos (A 436) Stefan Karpinski, 4-02

D: 52.2 tons (57.5 fl) **S:** 10 kts **Dim:** 15.2 × 5.06 × 2.2
M: 2 Deutz 8-cyl. diesels; 2 Voith-Schneider cycloidal props; 340 bhp
Range: 550/9 **Crew:** 4 tot.

Remarks: A 413 stricken from German Navy 18-12-89 and transferred 5-3-91, A 436 stricken 20-12-90 and transferred 25-4-91, A 437 stricken 18-10-90 and transferred 5-3-91, and A 438 stricken 2-8-90 and transferred 5-3-91. Sister *Trischen* (Y 818) was stricken on 20-12-90 and transferred on 25-4-91 but was used for cannibalization spares.

♦ 3 miscellaneous sail training craft [YTS]

A 233 Maistros A 234 Sorokos A 359 Ostria

Remarks: A 233 and A 234 are 14.8 m long and displace 12 tons; A 359 is smaller.

♦ 3 Doirani-class water lighters [YW]

A 434 Prespa (ex-*Doirani*) (In serv. 10-10-72)
A 467 Doirani (In serv. 1972)
A 468 Kalliroe (In serv. 26-10-72)

D: 850 tons (fl) **S:** 13 kts **Dim:** 54.77 × 7.95 × 3.87
Electronics: Radar: 1 Decca . . . nav.
M: 1 MWM 6-cyl. diesel; 1,300 bhp

Kalliroe (A 468) H&L Van Ginderen, 4-96

Remarks: A 467 is 58.88 m o.a., 4.02 m draft; 765 dwt. A 434 is 600 dwt. A 468 is 671 dwt and has a 1,005-bhp MWM diesel. A 434 was taken over from another government agency during 1979. Have a very low freeboard when fully loaded.

♦ 2 ex-German FW 1–class water lighters [YW]
Bldrs: A 433: Jadewerft, Wilhelmshaven; A 466: Renke, Hamburg

	Laid down	L	In serv.
A 433 Kerkini (ex-FW 3)	14-6-63	15-10-63	11-5-64
A 466 Trichonis (ex-FW 6)	4-11-63	25-2-64	19-6-64

Kerkini (A 433) H&L Van Ginderen, 12-84

D: 598 tons (624 fl) **S:** 9.5 kts **Dim:** 44.03 (41.10 pp) × 7.80 × 2.63
Electronics: Radar: 1 Kelvin-Hughes 14/9 nav.
M: 1 MWM 12-cyl. diesel; 1 prop; 230 bhp **Electric:** 83 kw
Range: 2,150/9 **Crew:** 12 tot.

Remarks: A 433 transferred 22-4-76, A 466 on 5-3-91. Cargo: 350 m^3.

GREEK ARMY

AMPHIBIOUS WARFARE CRAFT

♦ 4 (+ 26) Ultra-Fast Strike Catamarans (UFASC) [LCP]
Bldr: EBO Hellenic Arms Industry (In serv. first 4: 1994)

D: . . . tons **S:** 45+ kts **Dim:** 7.0 × . . . × . . .
A: 1 12.7-mm mg; 2 70-mm RL
M: 1 gasoline outboard; 150 or 200 bhp
Range: 250/36 **Endurance:** 7.5 hr **Crew:** 3 tot.

Remarks: Intended to replace 30 L-19-class fast launches used by Greek special forces in the Aegean Sea islands. GRP hull construction; production version was to be 9.0 m o.a., but there has been no report of a contract. Have a small commercial navigational radar.

MINISTRY OF THE MERCHANT MARINE
HELLENIC COAST GUARD
(*Limenikon Soma*)

Personnel: 5,879 tot. (1,098 officers, 2,015 subofficials, 2,277 port guard personnel, and 489 cadets)

Bases: Headquarters at Piraeus, with facilities at Corfu, Chalcis, Elefsis, Heraklion, Igoumenitsa, Kavala, Mytilene, Patra, Rafina, Rhodes, Thessalonica, and Volos. Small patrol boats are also based at a great many Greek mainland and island ports.

Maritime Aviation: Three Reims Aviation F 406 Surpolmar AC-21, 2 Cessna 172RG Cutlass, and 2 SOCATA TB20 Trinidad light aircraft operate from the Greek Air Force base at Dekelia for coastal patrol. Four Eurocopter AS.332C1 Super Puma helicopters are used for SAR duties; they have Bendix 1500B search radars, Thales CLIO FLIR, a Spectrolab searchlight, and various rescue and medical gear; the first two were delivered on 21-12-99 and the second pair during 3-00. The F 406 aircraft are fitted with FLIR, an underside 360° surveillance radar, and a side-looking radar mounted within the tail cone.

Note: Ships are painted dark gray and bear a blue-white-blue diagonal hull stripe with crossed anchor icon and "Coast Guard" or "Hellenic Coast Guard" in Greek and English on the hull sides.

PATROL CRAFT [WPC]

♦ 3 modified Sa'ar IV class
Bldr: Israel SY, Haifa (LS 060 and 070) and Hellenic SY, Greece (LS 080)

	Laid down	L	In serv.
LS-060 . . .	2003	. . .	23-12-03
LS-070 Fourniogo	2003	. . .	2-04
LS-080 Agios Eystratios	2003	. . .	4-04

Agios Eystratios (LS-080) Cem D. Yaylali, 7-04

Agios Eystratios (LS-080) Martin Mokrus, 5-04

D: 415 tons (450 fl) **S:** 32 kts **Dim:** 58.10 × 7.62 × 2.40
A: 1 30-mm AA; 1 20-mm AA; 2 single 12.7-mm mg
Electronics: Radar: 2 . . . nav.
M: 4 MTU 16V396 TB94 diesels; 4 props; 15,000 bhp
Range: 1,650/18 **Crew:** 30 total

Remarks: Purchased from Israel to assist with coastal security operations during the 2004 Olympic Games. No SSM missiles are carried.

♦ 1 Vosper Euro Patrol 250 Mk 1 class
Bldr: McTay Marine, UK (In serv. 11-94)

LS-050

LS-050 Martin Mokrus, 5-04

D: 245 tons **S:** 38.5 kts **Dim:** 47.30 × 7.50 × 2.50
A: . . . mg **Electronics:** Radar: 1 Racal-Decca nav.
M: 3 GEC/Paxman-Valenta 16-cm diesels; 3 props; 13,338 bhp
Range: 2,000/16 **Crew:** 21 tot.

Remarks: Built for the Customs Service and transferred to the Coast Guard during 2002.

PATROL BOATS [WPB]

♦ 3 CB-90NEX class
Bldr: Dockstavarvet, Docksta, Sweden (In serv. 6-7-98)

LS-134 LS-135 LS-136

LS-135 H&L Van Ginderen, 9-98

D: 13.2 tons light (18 fl) **S:** 46 kts **Dim:** 16.10 (13.00 wl) × 3.80 × 0.80
A: . . .
Electronics: Radar: 1 Furuno FAR-2815 ARPA nav.
M: 2 Volvo TAMD 163P diesels; 2 KaMeWa PF 450 waterjets; 1,540 bhp
Range: 160/20 **Fuel:** 1.5 tons **Crew:** 4 tot. + 10 passengers

Remarks: Ordered 12-97 and delivered 6-98. GRP construction. Design based on builder's *Enforcer* patrol boat demonstrator variant of an assault landing craft design. GRP construction. Capable of being beached. Cockpit has armor protection.

♦ 4 Dilos class
Bldr: Hellenic SY, Skaramanga (In serv. 1977–88)

LS-010 LS-020 LS-030 LS-040

LS-030 H&L Van Ginderen, 1-99

D: 75 tons (86 fl) **S:** 27 kts **Dim:** 29.00 (27.00 wl) × 5.00 × 1.62
A: 2 single 20-mm Oerlikon AA **Electronics:** Radar: 1 . . . nav.
M: 2 MTU 12V331 TC81 diesels; 2 props; 2,720 bhp
Range: 1,600/25 **Crew:** 15 tot.

Remarks: Designed by Abeking & Rasmussen, Germany. Used for air/sea rescue. Three each also built for navy and customs service. Round-bilge steel-construction hull.

♦ 34 Sunquestor 53–class inshore patrol boats
Bldr: Motomarine, Glifadha, Athens (In serv. 1994–96)

LS-115 through LS-123 LS-125 through LS-149

LS-119—first series Paolo Marsan, 4-05

COAST GUARD PATROL BOATS [WPB] *(continued)*

LS-138—second series, with high pilothouse farther forward Dieter Wolf, 7-03

D: 23.5 tons (fl) **S:** 34 kts (trials)
Dim: 16.26 (13.41 pp) × 4.68 × 0.76 (1.38 max.)
A: 1 12.7-mm mg; 1 7.62-mm mg **Electronics:** Radar: 1 . . . nav.
M: 2 M.A.N. D2840-LXE diesels; 2 props; 1,640 bhp
Range: 500/25 **Fuel:** 3,650 liters **Crew:** 5 tot.

Remarks: Ordered 1993. Employ GRP hulls molded by Colvic Craft, Colchester, U.K., using standard Sunquestor 53 yacht hulls. Can carry one spare crewmember if required. First two delivered early 1994 and last four of the initial batch in 5-94. LS 124 was lost through fire in 2-96. The second-series craft have a revised superstructure with a higher pilothouse.

♦ 16 LS-51-class inshore patrol boats
Bldr: Olympic Marine, Lavrio

LS-51, LS-52, LS-101, LS-155, LS-156, LS-157, LS-252, and others

LS-252—of the LS-51 class H&L Van Ginderen, 8-93

D: 13 tons (fl) **S:** 23 kts **Dim:** 13.2 × 3.5 × 1.0
A: 1 7.62-mm mg **Electronics:** Radar: 1 Decca . . . nav.
M: 2 diesels; 2 props; 600 bhp **Range:** 400/18 **Crew:** 4 tot.

Remarks: U.K. Keith Nelson GRP hull design. Very similar to the OL 44 class below.

♦ 13 OL 44 class
Bldr: Olympic Marine, Lavrio

LS-55, LS-65, LS-84, LS-88, LS-97, LS-106, LS-107, LS-110, LS-112, LS-114, and others

D: 13.8 tons (fl) **S:** 23 kts **Dim:** 13.50 (12.10 wl) × 4.35 × 0.61
A: 1 7.62-mm mg **Electronics:** Radar: 1 Decca . . . nav.
M: 2 diesels; 2 props; 600 bhp **Crew:** 4–6 tot.

Remarks: Keith Nelson–design hulls, GRP construction.

Note: There are an additional 86 small patrol boats, including 20 of 8.2-m, 17 of 7.9-m, and 26 of 5.8-m length for which characteristics are unavailable.

LS-106—of the OL 44 class NAVPIC-Holland, 5-01

SERVICE CRAFT

♦ 4 LS-413-class pollution-control vessels [WYAG]
Bldr: Astilleros Gondan, Castropol, Spain (In serv. 1993–94)

LS-413 LS-414 LS-415 LS-423

Pollution-control craft LS-415 and a sister Dieter Wolf, 7-94

D: 198 tons (230 fl) **S:** 15 kts **Dim:** 29.00 × 6.20 × 2.50
Electronics: Radar: 1 Furuno . . . nav.
M: 2 Caterpillar 3512 DITA diesels; 2 props; 2,560 bhp (sust.)
Range: 500/13 **Crew:** 12 tot.

Remarks: 198 grt. Have a rounded-down stern with roller to aid in setting pollution-control booms. LS-423 is referred to by the name *Alpha.*

♦ 11 miscellaneous antipollution craft [WYAG]

LS-66, LS-69, LS-70, LS-101, LS-401, LS-410, and others

Pollution control craft LS-401 Martin Mokrus, 5-04

Remarks: No data available.

♦ 38 8.23-meter class [WYFL]
Bldr: . . .

Remarks: Outdrive-powered GRP craft. Also in service for patrol/SAR duties are 26 5.7-m U.S. Chris Craft launches [WYFL] and 18 semi-rigid inflatable boats [WYFL] (the latter used by the 48-man Underwater Mission Squad).

LS 347—a modern, high-speed GRP-hulled craft with a rigid inflatable collar around the sides of the hull and a Raytheon radar; no additional data available NAVPIC-Holland, 5-01

♦ 10 18-meter Arun-class lifeboats [WYH]
Bldr: Motomarine, Athens (In serv. 1997–98)

LS-511 LS-515 LS-520 and others

D: 34 tons (fl) **S:** 18 kts **Dim:** 18.00 × 5.34 × 1.50
Electronics: Radar: 1 . . . nav.
M: 2 Caterpillar 3408BTA diesels; 2 props; 1,000 bhp **Crew:** 5 tot.

COAST GUARD SERVICE CRAFT *(continued)*

Arun-class lifeboat LS-520—black hull, orange superstructure
Martin Mokrus, 2005

Remarks: 34 grt. GRP hull molded by Halmatic, Northam, U.K. An enlarged version of a standard lifeboat used by the U.K., Canada, and Iran, among others. Have Furuno Loran C90 radio navaid, Anschutz gyrocompass, and integrated communication system on bridge. Low freeboard aids in picking up survivors. Hulls painted black, with orange superstructure.

Note: The Greek Coast Guard is also responsible for maintaining fireboats [WYTR] at major ports, including PS-6, PS-11, and two others at Piraeus. Also in service are more than two dozen outboard-powered RIB launches [WYFL] and numerous additional patrol craft including LS-015, LS-601 and others.

Fireboat PS-6—painted all red A. A. de Kruijf, 6-03

Note: The Greek Customs Service also operates about 20 boats in its Anti-Smuggling Flotilla, including one 240-ton Vosper Europatrol 250 Mk 1 patrol craft (A./L. 50) with provision for a 40-mm gun, three *Dilos*-class patrol boats (A./L. 16–18, sisters to units in the navy and coast guard), and 10 50-ton OL 76–class patrol boats.

GREENLAND

Note: Greenland has an independent domestic policy but is under the protectorship of Denmark for foreign affairs and defense matters.

GREENLAND POLICE

♦ 4 Sisak-class patrol craft [WPC]

Bldr: Torshavnar Skipasmidja, Skala (In serv. 1999–2001)

SISAK I SISAK II SISAK III SISAK IV

D: . . . tons **S:** 13 kts **Dim:** 24.15 (21.50 pp) × 6.30 × 2.30
A: Small arms **Electronics:** Radar: . . .
M: 2 Caterpillar 3508TA diesels; 2 props; 800 bhp
Range: . . . / . . . **Crew:** . . . tot.

Remarks: 139 grt. First three ordered 5-97, fourth in 1999. Modified fishing boats for police and fisheries protection duties.

GRENADA

COAST GUARD

Personnel: About 60 total, under the Commissioner of Police

Bases: Headquarters is at Prickly Bay, with small facilities at Grenville, Hillsborough, and the capital, St. George's.

PATROL BOATS [WPB]

♦ 1 U.S. Dauntless class

Bldr: SeaArk, Monticello, Ark. (In serv. 8-9-95)

PB 02 LEVERA

Levera (PB 02) SeaArk, 9-95

D: 11 tons (fl) **S:** 28 kts **Dim:** 12.19 (11.13 wl) × 3.86 × 0.69 (hull)
A: 2 single 12.7-mm mg; 2 single 7.62-mm mg
Electronics: Radar: 1 Raytheon R40X nav.
M: 2 Caterpillar 3208TA diesels; 2 props; 850 bhp (720 sust.)
Range: 200/30; 400/22 **Fuel:** 250 gallons **Crew:** 5 tot.

Remarks: Ordered 4-94 by U.S. Government; donated as foreign aid. Aluminum construction. C. Raymond Hunt, "Deep-Vee" hull design.

♦ 1 U.S. 106-foot Guardian class

Bldr: Lantana Boatyard, Lantana, Fla. (In serv. 21-11-84)

PB 01 TYRREL BAY

D: 94 tons (fl) **S:** 24 kts **Dim:** 32.31 × 6.25 × 2.13 (props)
A: 2 single 12.7-mm mg; 2 single 7.62-mm mg
Electronics: Radar: 1 Furuno 1411 Mk II nav.
M: 3 G.M. Detroit Diesel 12V71 TI diesels; 3 props; 2,250 bhp
Electric: 100 kw **Fuel:** 21 tons **Crew:** 4 officers, 12 enlisted

Remarks: Laid down 1-84 to U.S. Government order. Aluminum construction. Has a Magnavox MX4102 NAVSAT receiver. Was overhauled in fall 1995 at St. Croix.

Tyrrel Bay (PB 01) Lantana, 11-84

PATROL BOATS [WPB] *(continued)*

♦ 2 U.S. Boston Whaler series
Bldr: Boston Whaler, Rockland, Mass. (In serv. 1988–89)

D: 1.3 tons (fl) **S:** 40 kts **Dim:** 6.81 × 2.26 × 0.40
A: 1 12.7-mm mg **M:** 2 gasoline outboards; 240 bhp
Range: 167/40 **Crew:** 4 tot.

Remarks: Foam-core, "unsinkable" construction.

Note: Also in use are a RIB donated by the United States during 1994 and a locally built, outboard-powered wooden launch.

GUATEMALA

Republic of Guatemala

Personnel: About 1,250 total (including 130 officers and 650 marines)

Bases: Santo Tomás de Castilla on the Atlantic coast and Puerto Quetzal on the Pacific coast

Organization: Two fleets: Base Naval del Atlántico (BANATLAN) at Santo Tomás de Castilla, and Base Naval del Pacifico (BANAPAC) at Puerto Quetzal; subordinate to BANAPAC is the Sipacate Naval Detachment with the Centro de Adiestramento de Infanteria de Marina (Marine Training Center). Craft over 20 m long carry GC-series pennants, while smaller units carry P-series pennants. The two marine infantry battalions are based at Puerto Barrios on the Atlantic coast and at Puerto Quetzal; each consists of two rifle companies and one police company.

Note: Acquisition plans call for procuring three additional 32-m patrol boats and one 19.8-m patrol boat, funds permitting. All of the patrol craft and patrol boats of 65-ft. length and larger listed below were cycled through refit at Network Shipyard, Inc., Pierre Part, La., between 4-93 and 11-96. All units received new engines, had their accommodations renovated, and had new galley equipment, new pumps and generator sets, Furuno radars and communications suites (including single sideband radios), Raytheon GPS receivers, Data Marine echo sounders, and Danforth compasses installed. New engine controls and firefighting systems were fitted, and the repair yard provided training in all the new systems.

PATROL CRAFT [PC]

♦ 1 U.S. Broadsword class
Bldr: Halter Marine, Chalmette, La. (In serv. 4-8-76)

GC-1051 Kukulkan

Kukulkan (GC-1051) Julio Montes, 12-04

D: 90.5 tons light (110 fl) **S:** 25+ kts **Dim:** 32.0 (29.4 wl) × 6.3 × 1.9 (props)
A: 2 single 20-mm 90-cal. Oerlikon GAM-B01 AA; 2 single 12.7-mm M2HB mg
Electronics: Radar: 1 Furuno . . . nav.
M: 4 G.M. Detroit Diesel 8V92TA diesels; 2,600 bhp
Electric: 70 kw tot. (2 × 35-kw Perkins diesel sets)
Range: 1,150/20 **Fuel:** 16 tons **Crew:** 5 officers, 15 enlisted

Remarks: Aluminum construction. The original two G.M. 16V149-series engines were replaced, reducing speed from 32 kts. Based at Puerto Quetzal. Named for Mayan wind god.

PATROL BOATS [PB]

Note: The United States was to supply one boat and three helicopters for drug trade interdiction during 4-00 under Operation Maya-Jaguar; no information is available as to whether the equipment has been delivered.

♦ 1 U.S. Dauntless class
Bldr: SeaArk, Monticello, Ark. (In serv. 3-97)

P . . . Iximche

D: 11 tons (fl) **S:** 28 kts **Dim:** 12.19 (11.13 wl) × 3.86 × 0.69 (hull)
A: 1 7.62-mm mg **Electronics:** Radar: 1 Raytheon R40X nav.
M: 2 Caterpillar 3208TA diesels; 2 props; 850 bhp (720 sust.)
Range: 200/30; 400/22 **Fuel:** 250 gallons **Crew:** 5 tot.

Remarks: Donated by the U.S. Government as foreign aid. Aluminum construction. C. Raymond Hunt, "Deep-Vee" hull design.

♦ 2 U.S. 85-foot Commercial Cruiser class
Bldr: Sewart Seacraft, Berwick, La.

	In serv.
GC-851 Utatlan (ex-U.S. 85NS672)	5-67
GC-852 Subteniente Osorio Saravia (ex-U.S. 85NS722)	11-72

Subteniente Osorio Saravia (GC-852) José Turcios, via Julio Montes, 1-03

D: 43.5 tons (54 fl) **S:** 22 kts **Dim:** 25.9 × 5.8 × 2.2 (props)
A: 2 single 20-mm 90-cal. Oerlikon GAM-B01 AA; 2 single 12.7-mm M2HB mg
Electronics: Radar: 1 Furuno . . . nav.
M: 3 G.M. Detroit Diesel 8V92TA diesels; 3 props; 1,950 bhp
Electric: 70 kw tot. (2 × 35-kw Perkins diesel sets)
Range: 780/15 **Fuel:** 8 tons **Crew:** 7 officers, 10 enlisted

Remarks: Aluminum construction. Both refitted 1995–96 (see description in note at beginning of section) and rearmed after return to Guatemala. GC-851 is based Santo Tomás de Castilla, GC-852 at Puerto Quetzal.

♦ 6 U.S. Cutlass class
Bldr: Halter Marine, New Orleans

	In serv.		In serv.
GC-651 Tecunuman	26-11-71	GC-654 Tzacol	8-76
GC-652 Kaibil Balan	8-2-72	GC-655 Bitol	8-76
GC-653 Azumanche	8-2-72	BH-656 Gucumatz (ex-GC-H-656, ex-GC-656)	8-81

Azumanche (GC 653) Julio Montes, 12-04

Gucumatz (BH-656) José Turcios, via Julio Montes, 3-01

PATROL BOATS [PB] *(continued)*

D: 34 tons (45 fl) **S:** 25 kts Dim: 19.7 × 5.2 × 0.9
A: *All but* BH-656: 2 single 20-mm 90-cal. Oerlikon GAM-B01 AA; 2 single 12.7-mm M2HB mg—BH-656: 3 single 12.7-mm M2HB mg
Electronics: Radar: 1 Furuno . . . nav.
M: 2 G.M. Detroit Diesel 8V92TA diesels; 2 props; 1,300 bhp replaced by 3 . . . diesels
Electric: 70 kw tot. (2 × 35-kw Perkins diesel sets)
Range: 400/15 **Crew:** 2 officers, 8 enlisted

Remarks: Aluminum construction. GC-651, GC-654, and GC-655 are based at Santo Tomás de Castilla, the others at Puerto Quetzal. BH-656 is used as a survey craft; painted white and with a blue-bordered diagonal red stripe on the hull side, she is based in the Pacific and was rearmed for patrol duties during 1995. All were refitted 1993–95 as per note at beginning of section, with their original two 12-cylinder G.M. diesels replaced by three engines and more powerful generators substituted to handle the increased electrical load. At the same time, the pilothouse was enlarged.

♦ 3 or more Inmensa-class launches
Bldr: . . ., Guatemala (In serv. mid-1990s)

Kocapave . . . . . .

D: 1.7 tons (fl) **S:** . . . kts **Dim:** 7.60 × 1.9 × . . .
A: 1 7.62-mm mg **M:** 1 Evinrude gasoline outboard; 150 bhp

Remarks: Locally built, GRP-hulled craft distinguished by considerable sheer to the open hull and a proportionately thick sheer strake.

♦ 8 U.S. 27-foot Vigilant class
Bldr: Boston Whaler, Rockland, Mass. (In serv. 1993–96)

GC-271 Tohil — GC-275 . . .
GC-272 . . . — GC-276 . . .
GC-273 Tepeu — GC-277 . . .
GC-274 . . . — GC-278 . . .

Tepeu (GC-273) Julio Montes, 2-96

D: 2 tons (4.5 fl) **S:** 35 kts **Dim:** 8.23 × 3.00 × 0.50
A: 1 7.62-mm mg **Electronics:** Radar: 1 Furuno . . . nav.
M: 2 Evinrude gasoline outboards; 300 bhp **Crew:** 4 tot.

Remarks: Ordered under U.S. aid. Have an enclosed pilothouse and GPS receiver. Four are based on each coast for use by the marines. GC 277 and GC 278 may be nonoperational.

♦ 16 river patrol craft
Bldr: Trabejos Baros SY, Guatemala (In serv. 1979)

12 wooden-hulled:

Alioth	Kochab	Procyon	Spica
Deneb	Mirfa	Schedar	Stella Maris
Dubhe	Pollux	Sirius	Vega

4 aluminum-hulled:

Escuintla — Lago Atitlán — Mazatenango — Retalhuleu

D: 8 tons (wooden-hulled) **S:** 19 or 28 kts **Dim:** 9.14 × 3.66 × 0.61
A: 2 single 7.62-mm mg
M: 1 diesel; 1 prop; 150 or 300 bhp **Range:** 400–500 n.m.

Remarks: Wooden-hulled group has 150-bhp diesels and can make 19 kts; the aluminum-hulled craft have 300-bhp engines and can reach 28 kts. Operated by the marines.

♦ 4 captured fishing craft

Mavro-I — Mero — Pampano — Sardina

Remarks: Captured while engaged in smuggling and used for local patrol. No data available. Two are based on the Pacific coast.

AMPHIBIOUS WARFARE CRAFT

♦ 2 U.S. Machete-class personnel landing craft [LCP]
Bldr: Halter Marine, New Orleans (In serv. 4-8-76)

D-361 Picuda — D-362 Barracuda

D: 6 tons **S:** 36 kts **Dim:** 11.0 × 4.0 × 0.76
M: 2 G.M. 6V53 PI diesels; 2 waterjets; 540 bhp
Crew: 2 tot. + 20 troops

Remarks: Square bows, aluminum construction. Operated by the Marine Infantry Training Center on the Pacific coast.

SERVICE CRAFT

♦ 1 vehicle and passenger ferry [YFB]

T-691 15 de Enero

15 de Enero (T-691) H&L Van Ginderen, 1-96

Remarks: A 21-m craft based at Santo Tomás de Castilla.

♦ 2 miscellaneous sail training craft [YTS]

Margarita — Ostuncalco

Remarks: Based at Santo Tomás de Castilla with the training yacht *Mendieta*.

♦ 1 training craft [YXT]

Mendieta

Remarks: A former yacht, based at Santo Tomás de Castilla.

GUERNSEY

Note: Guernsey, in the Channel Islands, is a semiautonomous territory of the United Kingdom.

FISHERIES PATROL BOATS [WPB]

♦ 1 Stan Patrol 1850 patrol boat
Bldr: Damen SY, Gorinchem, the Netherlands (In serv. 1998)

Leopardess

Leopardess *Workboat,* 1998

D: . . . tons **S:** 23.5 kts **Dim:** 18.50 × . . . × . . .
Electronics: Radar: 1 . . . nav.
M: 2 Volvo Penta TAMD 122P turbocharged diesels; 2 props, 1,140 bhp
Range: . . . / . . . **Crew:** up to 6 tot.

Remarks: Aluminum construction. Carries an outboard-powered 5.4-m rigid inflatable rescue launch. Based at St. Peter Port. Painted gray.

GUINEA

Republic of Guinea

Personnel: About 400 total

Bases: Conakry and Kakanda

PATROL BOATS [PB]

♦ **1 Stan Launch 43–class fisheries inspection launch**
Bldr: Damen Shipyard, Gorinchem, the Netherlands (In serv. 2-99)

MATAKANG

D: . . . tons **S:** 8.1 kts **Dim:** 12.65 × 3.65 × 1.35
Electronics: Radar: 1 Furuno. . . nav.
M: 1 Caterpillar 3304 T/B diesel; 1 prop; 140 bhp

Remarks: Carries a rigid inflatable inspection dinghy and has a Furuno GPS terminal and echo sounder. Pennant number may be LP 43.

Disposal note: U.S.-built patrol boat *Vigilante* (P-300) has been inoperable since before 2000 and is unlikely to see further service.

♦ **1 U.S. 77-foot class**
Bldr: Swiftships, Morgan City, LA (In serv. 18-12-86)

P-328 INTRÉPIDE

D: 39.8 tons (47.6 fl) **S:** 24 kts **Dim:** 23.47 × 6.10 × 1.52
A: 2/12.7-mm mg; 2/7.62-mm mg
Electronics: Radar: 2 Raytheon nav.
M: 3 G.M. 12V71 Ti diesels; 3 props; 2,385 bhp
Range: 1,800/15 **Crew:** 10 tot.

Remarks: Had been nonoperational since 2000, but was returned to service in 2004.

GUINEA-BISSAU

Republic of Guinea-Bissau

Personnel: About 350 total

Base: Bissau

Naval Aviation: One Cessna 337 for coastal surveillance

PATROL BOATS [PB]

Note: One R 800–class, 8.7-m, 28-kt, GRP-construction patrol launch was purchased from Rodman Polyships, Vigo, Spain, in 1999; its pennant number is LP-43. No further details are available.

♦ **2 Cacine class**
Bldr: CONAFI, Vila Real de San António, Portugal (In serv. 9-3-94)

LF-01 CACINE LF-02 CACHEU

D: 55 tons (fl) **S:** 28 kts **Dim:** 20.40 (19.94 pp; 18.50 wl) × 5.80 × 1.00
A: Small arms **Electronics:** Radar: 1 Furuno FR 2010 nav.
M: 3 MTU 12V183 TE92 diesels; 3 Hamilton MH 521 waterjets; 3,000 bhp
Crew: 1 officer, 8 enlisted

Remarks: LF = *Lanchas Rápidas de Fiscalização* (Fast Customs Launches). Ordered 14-1-91 for the Ministry of Fisheries; a planned third was canceled. Both were fitted out at the Alfeite Arsenal, Lisbon. Paid for by the Republic of China (Taiwan). Glass-reinforced plastic hull with aluminum deck and superstructure. Intended to perform fisheries protection and customs enforcement duties.

Cacheu (LF-02) Ars. do Alfeite, 3-94

♦ **1 U.S. 51-foot Mk 4 class**
Bldr: Peterson Bldrs, Sturgeon Bay, Wis. (In serv. 22-10-93)

LF-03 ILHA DE CAIO

D: 24 tons (fl) **S:** 24 kts **Dim:** 15.54 × 4.47 × 1.30
A: 1 twin 12.7-mm M2 mg; 2 single 7.62-mm mg
Electronics: Radar: 1 Furuno FR 2010 nav.
M: 2 G.M. Detroit Diesel 6V92 TA diesels; 2 props; 900 bhp (520 sust.)
Electric: 15 kw tot. **Range:** 500/20 **Fuel:** 800 gallons **Crew:** 6 tot.

Remarks: Ordered 25-9-92. Aluminum construction. Contract included training in operation and maintenance. Carries a 4.27-m RIB with a 50-bhp outboard motor. Is identical to the unit of the class illustrated under Cape Verde.

SERVICE CRAFT

♦ **1 1,600-ton-capacity floating dry dock**

Remarks: Delivered 10-90 from the United States.

Note: The customs service operates one Netherlands-built, 33-ton patrol boat, the *Naga,* completed in 1981.

GUYANA

Cooperative Republic of Guyana

DEFENSE FORCES SEA DIVISION

Personnel: About 100 total, with 170 reserves

Bases: Georgetown and Benab

Maritime Aviation: China agreed early in 2001 to supply a Y-12 light transport for maritime surveillance duties, though it has yet to be delivered.

PATROL BOATS [PB]

♦ **4 ex-U.S. Coast Guard 44-foot patrol boats**

BARRACUDA (ex-. . .) HYMANA (ex-. . .)
PIRA (ex-. . .) TIRAPUKA (ex-. . .)

D: 18 tons (fl) **S:** 12 kts **Dim:** 13.46 × 3.85 × 1.0
M: 2 Detroit 6V53 diesels; 2 props; 370 bhp
Range: 150/12 **Crew:** 3 tot.

Remarks: Transferred from the U.S. Coast Guard in 2003. Built in the U.S.A.

PATROL SHIPS [PS]

♦ **1 ex-U.K. River class**
Bldr: Richards (Shipbuilders), Ltd., Great Yarmouth

	Laid down	L	In serv.
1026 ESSEQUIBO (ex-*Orwell*, M 2011)	4-6-84	7-2-85	27-3-85

Essequibo (1026) Derek Fox, 7-01

D: 630 tons (770 fl) **S:** 14 kts (15 on trials; 12 sust.)
Dim: 47.60 (42.00 pp) × 10.50 × 3.10 (3.75 max.)
A: Small arms
Electronics: Radar: 1 Decca TM 1226 nav.
M: 2 Ruston 6 RKCM diesels; 2 4-bladed CP props; 3,040 bhp
Electric: 460 kw tot. **Range:** 4,500/10 **Fuel:** 88 tons
Crew: 7 officers, 23 enlisted in RN service

Remarks: 638 grt. Retired from Royal Navy service on 13-7-00, was sold to Guyana during 4-01, and recommissioned on 22-6-01; the ship departed U.K. waters on 6-8-01. Sisters serve in the Bangladesh and Brazilian navies.
Hull systems: Steel hull built to commercial standards, following the design of a North Sea oilfield supply vessel. Single-compartment damage standard. Navigation gear includes two Kelvin-Hughes MS 48 echo sounders.
Combat systems: All sweep gear has been removed. Had been disarmed and used as a cadet training ship prior to retirement.

PATROL SHIPS [PS] *(continued)*

Disposal note: Boston Whaler *Houri* (DFS 1018) and former fishing boat *Waitipu* (DFS 1008) had been discarded by 8-00.

HAITI

Republic of Haiti

COAST GUARD

Personnel: About 40 total

Bases: Headquarters at Port au Prince, with secondary facilities at Les Cayes and Port de Paix.

PATROL BOATS [WPB]

♦ 4 U.S. 25-foot Guardian class
Bldr: Boston Whaler, Edgewater, Fla. (In serv. 6-96)

D: 2.2 tons (fl) **S:** 28 kts **Dim:** 7.6 × 2.4 × 0.2
A: Small arms **M:** 1 gasoline outboard; 225 bhp **Crew:** 2–3 tot.

Remarks: Delivered 30-5-96 to mid-June 1996 as U.S. grant aid. Were refitted at Miami, Fla., during 1999. Have foam-core, "unsinkable" GRP sandwich hulls.

Note: As a result of domestic turmoil, the status of Haiti's Coast Guard remains uncertain.

HONDURAS

Republic of Honduras

FUERZA NAVAL REPÚBLICA

Personnel: About 1,400 total, including 830 marines

Bases: Amapala, La Ceiba, Puerto Castilla, Puerto Cortés, and Puerto Trujillo

Naval Aviation: Two Lake Seawolf amphibians delivered 1987

PATROL CRAFT [PC]

♦ 3 U.S. 105-foot class Bldr: Swiftships, Morgan City, La.

FNH 101 GUAYMURAS (In serv. 4-77)
FNH 102 HONDURAS (In serv. 3-80)
FNH 103 HIBURES (In serv. 3-80)

Guaymuras (FNH 101) Edward B. McDonnell, 2004

D: 103 tons (111 fl) **S:** 24 kts **Dim:** 32.00 × 7.20 × 3.1 (props)
A: 1 twin 20-mm 90-cal. Hispano-Suiza HS-404 AA in IAI TCM-20 mount; 1 20-mm 70-cal. U.S. Mk 68 AA; 2 single 12.7-mm mg; 2 single 5.6-mm MAG-58 mg
Electronics: Radar: 1 . . . nav.
M: 2 MTU diesels; 2 props; 7,000 bhp **Electric:** 80 kw tot.
Range: 1,200/18 **Fuel:** 21 tons **Crew:** 3 officers, 14 enlisted

Remarks: Aluminum construction. Originally bore pennants FNH 1051–1053, changed in 1993.

PATROL BOATS [PB]

♦ 4 ex-U.S. Coast Guard 44-foot patrol boats

. . . (ex-. . .) . . . (ex-. . .) . . . (ex-. . .) . . . (ex-. . .)

D: 18 tons (fl) **S:** 12 kts **Dim:** 13.46 × 3.85 × 1.0
M: 2 Detroit 6V53 diesels; 2 props; 370 bhp
Range: 150/12 **Crew:** 3 tot.

Remarks: Transferred from the U.S. Coast Guard in 2003. Built in the U.S.A.

♦ 2 U.S. 106-foot Guardian class Bldr: Lantana Boatyard, Lantana, Fla.

FNH 104 TEGUCIGALPA (ex-FNH 107) (In serv. 1983)
FNH 105 COPAN (ex-FNH 106) (In serv. 6-86)

Copan (FNH 105)—with old pennant number; gatling gun shown inset
General Electric, via Julio Montes 1993

D: 94 tons (fl) **S:** 35 kts **Dim:** 32.31 × 6.25 × 2.13 (props)
A: 1 20-mm G.E. M 197 Sea Vulcan-20 gatling gun; 1 20-mm 70-cal. U.S. Mk 68 AA; 2 single 12.7-mm Browning M2HB mg
Electronics: Radar: 1 Furuno . . . nav.
M: 3 G.M. Detroit Diesel 16V92 TI diesels; 3 props; 3,900 bhp
Electric: 100 kw **Range:** 1,500/18 **Fuel:** 21 tons
Crew: 4 officers, 12 enlisted

Remarks: Aluminum construction. Have Magnavox MX 4102 NAVSAT receiver and two echo sounders. A Kollmorgen HSV-20NCS optronic control system is fitted for the gatling gun. A third unit, to have been named *Comayguela,* was canceled and became Jamaica's *Paul Bogle.*

♦ 5 U.S. 65-foot Commercial Cruiser class
Bldr: Swiftships, Morgan City, La.

	In serv.
FNH 651 NACAOME (ex-*Aguan,* ex-*Gral*)	12-73
FNH 652 GOASCORAN (ex-*Gral. J. T. Cabanas*)	1-74
FNH 653 PETULA	1980
FNH 654 ULUA	1980
FNH 655 CHULUTECA	1980

D: 33 tons (36 fl) **S:** 28 or 36 kts **Dim:** 19.9 (17.4 wl) × 5.6 × 1.6 (props)
A: 2 single 20-mm 70-cal. U.S. Mk 68 AA; 2 single 12.7-mm M2HB mg; 1 combination 81-mm mortar and 12.7-mm M2HB mg
Electronics: Radar: 1 Decca . . . nav.
M: 2 G.M. 12V71 TI or MTU diesels; 2 props; 1,300 or 1,590 bhp
Electric: 20 kw **Range:** 2,000/22 **Fuel:** 5 tons
Crew: 2 officers, 7 enlisted

Remarks: First pair was originally ordered for Haiti, delivered to Honduras for use as customs launches in 1977, and later transferred to the navy. The others, ordered 1979, have more powerful diesels. Aluminum construction.

♦ 1 or more high-speed chase boats
Bldr: . . . (In serv. 1996– . . .)

FNH 3701

FNH 3701—on travel trailer Julio Montes, 1996

PATROL BOATS [PB] *(continued)*

D: Approx. 8 tons (fl) **S:** . . . kts **Dim:** 11.27 × . . . × . . .
A: 2 single 12.7-mm M2HB mg **Electronics:** Radar: 1 Furuno 3600 nav.
M: 2 . . . diesels; 2 props; . . . bhp **Crew:** 5 tot.

Remarks: Origins uncertain. GRP construction.

♦ **3 Piranha-class river patrol craft**
Bldr: Lantana Boatyard, Lantana, Fla. (In serv. 3-2-86)

D: 8.16 tons (fl) **S:** 26 kts (22 sust.) **Dim:** 11.00 (10.06 wl) × 3.05 × 0.53
A: 2 single 12.7-mm mg; 2 single 7.62-mm mg
Electronics: Radar: 1 Furuno 3600 nav.—EW: VHF D/F
M: 2 Caterpillar 3208 TA diesels; 2 props; 630 bhp
Endurance: 5 days **Crew:** 5 tot.

Remarks: Aluminum construction, with Kevlar armor. Five others have been discarded; these last three may no longer be operational.

♦ **15 Taiwanese ARP-2001-class riverine patrol launches**
Bldr: . . ., Taiwan (In serv. 29-5-96)

D: 2 tons (fl) **S:** . . . kts **Dim:** 4.60 × . . . × . . .
A: 1 7.62-mm mg
M: 1 Mercury gasoline outboard; 115 bhp **Crew:** 4 tot.

Remarks: Open launches, delivered as a gift. Aluminum construction. Sisters are used by the Taiwanese Marine Corps. Three are based at Amapala, four at Puerto Castilla, two at Puerto Cortés, and the others at Tegucigalpa.

♦ **8 U.S. 25-foot Outrage-class inshore patrol launches**
Bldr: Boston Whaler, Rockland, Mass. (In serv. 1982–90)

D: 2.2 tons **S:** 35 kts **Dim:** 7.62 × 2.40 × 0.40
A: 1 12.7-mm mg; 1 7.62-mm mg **Electronics:** Radar: 1 Furuno 3600 nav.
M: 2 Evinrude gasoline outboard engines; 2 props; 300 bhp
Range: 200/35 **Crew:** 4 tot.

Remarks: Foam-core GRP construction. Radar not always fitted. Four others have been discarded.

AMPHIBIOUS WARFARE CRAFT

♦ **1 utility landing craft [LCU]**
Bldr: Lantana Boatyard, Lantana, Fla.

	Laid down	L	In serv.
FNH 1491 PUNTA CAXINAS	11-86	. . .	5-88

Punta Caxinas (FNH 1491) Lantana, 5-88

D: 419 tons light (625 fl) **S:** 14.5 kts **Dim:** 45.42 × . . . × . . . (loaded)
A: None **Electronics:** Radar: 1 Furuno 3600 nav.
M: 3 Caterpillar 3416 diesels; 3 props; 2,025 bhp
Range: 3,500/12 **Crew:** 3 officers, 15 enlisted

Remarks: Cargo can include 100 tons of vehicles or cargo on deck, or four standard 20-ft cargo containers and 50,000 gallons of fuel. Has Magnavox NAVSAT receiver.

♦ **2 U.S. LCM(8)-class landing craft [LCM]**
FNH 7401 WARUNTA FNH 7402 TANSIN

D: 56 tons (116 fl) **S:** 12 kts **Dim:** 22.43 × 6.40 × 1.40 (aft)
A: 2 single 12.7-mm mg **Electronics:** Radar: 1 . . . nav.
M: 4 G.M. 6-71 diesels; 2 props; 620 bhp **Range:** 140/9
Crew: 3–4 tot. + 150 troops for brief periods

Remarks: Transferred 1987. Cargo: 54 tons in 13.4 × 4.4-m cargo well. *Caratasca* (FNH 7403) has been nonoperational since at least 2003.

AUXILIARIES

♦ **1 ex-U.S. Coast Guard Hollyhock-class buoy tender [AGL]**
Bldr: Moore Dry Dock Co., Oakland, Calif.

	Laid down	L	In serv.
FNH 252 YOJOA (ex-*Walnut*, WLM 252, ex-WAGL 252)	5-12-38	22-3-39	27-6-39

D: 825 tons (986 fl) **S:** 12 kts **Dim:** 53.4 × 10.4 × 3.7
M: 2 diesels; 2 props; 1,350 bhp **Range:** 6,500/12; 10,000/7.5
Crew: 4 officers, 36 enlisted

Remarks: Transferred 1-7-82 for navigational aids support duties. Has one 20-ton buoy derrick. The original reciprocating steam propulsion plant was replaced in 1958. Refitted 1989 at Tracor Marine, Ft. Lauderdale, Fla.

SERVICE CRAFT

♦ **6 miscellaneous ex-fishing boats for logistics support [YFU]**

FN 7501 JULIANA	FN 7503 CARMEN	FN 7505 YOSURO
FN 7502 SAN RAFAEL	FN 7504 MAIRY	FN 7506 JOSE GREGORI

HONG KONG

HONG KONG POLICE FORCE MARINE REGION

Personnel: About 2,600 total

Bases: Headquarters at Tsim Sha Tsui, Kowloon, with “Sea Division” bases at Aberdeen, Ma Liu Shui, Sai Wan Ho, Tai Lam Chung, and Tui Min Hoi.

Maritime Aviation: The Government Flying Service (GFS; name changed from Royal Hong Kong Auxiliary Air Force on 1-4-93) operates maritime patrol–configured BAe Jetstream 41 aircraft for coastal patrol, three AS.332 L2 Super Puma helicopters for rescue work, and two Slingsby T-67M Firefly light aircraft for training. Five EC-155 B1 helicopters were to replace all Sikorsky helicopters in 2002; however, some of the two Sikorsky S-70A-27, five Sikorsky S-76A+, and three Sikorsky S-76C helicopters may remain in service for rescue work. The GFS operates from Chek Lap Kok airport. The Chinese military has based 10 Z-9A Haitun (AS.365 Dauphin) helicopters at Sek Kong airfield since 1-7-97.

Note: Although Hong Kong came under Chinese control at midnight on 30-6-97, the former Royal Hong Kong Police Force and its Marine Region craft continue to be subordinated to the Hong Kong government, which still retains a degree of autonomy. Mounted machineguns are no longer carried.

PATROL CRAFT [WPC]

♦ **6 Keka class**
Bldr: Australian Submarine Corp, Adelaide, and Cheoy Lee SY, Hong Kong (In serv. 5-01 through 5-02)

D: 120 tons (fl) **S:** 25 kts (sust.) **Dim:** 31.00 (28.00 pp) × 6.50 × 1.80
A: Small arms
Electronics: Radar: 1 Litton-Sperry SM5000 nav.
M: 2 MTU 16V2000 N90 SR diesels; 2 props; 3,600 bhp—1 waterjet cruise/loiter thruster; . . . shp
Electric: 160 kw (2 × 80-kw diesel sets)
Range: 1,300/15 **Fuel:** 20,000 liters **Endurance:** 7 days
Crew: 3 officers, 26 enlisted

Remarks: Similar to craft built for Thai Navy, but with a loiter propulsion system added. Aluminum construction. No additional information available.

♦ **2 Sea Panther–class command boats**
Bldr: Hong Kong SY, Kowloon

	Laid down	L	Del.	In serv.
PL 3 SEA PANTHER	17-6-86	17-4-87	27-7-87	1-2-88
PL 4 SEA HORSE	17-6-86	14-7-87	28-9-87	1-2-88

Sea Horse (PL 4) Giorgio Arra, 10-96

PATROL CRAFT [WPC] *(continued)*

D: 420 tons (450 fl) **S:** 14 kts **Dim:** 40.0 × 8.5 × . . . (3.2 molded depth)
A: Fitted for 2 single 12.7-mm mg
Electronics: Radar: 1 Decca C342 ARPA nav.; 1 Decca C348 ARPA nav.
M: 2 Caterpillar 3512 diesels; 2 props; 2,350 bhp **Range:** 1,300/14
Crew: 27–33 tot. + two platoons of police for short periods

Remarks: The original Racal CANE 100 data logging and navigational plot system was replaced by ARPA equipment when the Decca radio navaid system ceased functioning in the Hong Kong area.

♦ 6 ASI-315 Pacific Forum class
Bldr: Transfield ASI Pty, Ltd., South Coogee, Western Australia

	In serv.		In serv.
PL 51 Protector	18-10-92	PL 54 Preserver	7-4-93
PL 52 Guardian	18-1-93	PL 55 Rescuer	17-5-93
PL 53 Defender	4-3-93	PL 56 Detector	23-6-93

Detector (PL 56) Giorgio Arra, 6-96

D: 148 tons (170 fl) **S:** 26+ kts (24 sust.)
Dim: 32.60 (31.50 hull; 28.60 wl) × 8.20 × 1.60 (hull)
A: Equipped for 1 12.7-mm Browning mg; 2 single 7.62-mm mg
Electronics: Radar: 1 Decca . . . nav.
M: 2 Caterpillar 3516 TA Phase II diesels; 2 props; 5,640 bhp (4,400 sust.)—1 Caterpillar 3412 TA cruise diesel; 1 Hamilton 521 waterjet; 775 bhp
Electric: 186 kVA (2 Caterpillar 3306T diesel sets) **Range:** 600/18
Fuel: 21,000 liters **Endurance:** 8–10 days **Crew:** 19 tot.

Remarks: Ordered 8-91. Modified standard Australian foreign-aid patrol boat design, with less draft and fuel and a third engine added centerline for cruising. Carry a 5-m RIB boarding boat. Can carry a divisional commander and staff. Have a GEC V3901 stabilized optronic device for surveillance and data recording. Near-sisters serve the Kuwaiti Coast Guard.

PATROL BOATS [WPB]

Note: Two 30-m and the first two of a planned 10 21-m patrol boats were ordered in 1999 from Lung Teh SY, Kowloon; no data yet available.

♦ 6 PL 40 class
Bldr: Cheoy Lee SY, Kowloon (In serv. 2-00 to 7-00)

PL 40 through PL 45

D: 15 tons (fl) **S:** 35 kts **Dim:** 13.07 × 3.96 × 0.70
A: Small arms **Electronics:** Radar: 1 Decca BridgeMaster E180 nav.
M: 2 Deutz-M.A.N. D 2842 LE 403 diesels; 2 Hamilton waterjets; 720 bhp
Crew: 4 tot.

Remarks: Ordered spring 1999. U.S. Peterson Builders design.

♦ 5 Sea Stalker 1500 class
Bldr: Damen, Gorinchem, the Netherlands (In serv. 1999–2000)

PL 85 through PL 89

PL 88 A.A. de Kruijf, 6-99

D: Approx. 30 tons **S:** 60+ kts (42 sust.) **Dim:** 14.77 × 2.71 × 1.18 (aft)
A: Fitted for 2 single 7.62-mm mg
Electronics: Radar: 1 . . . nav. (X-band)
M: 3 Mercruiser Bulldog HP500 V-8 outdrive gasoline engines; 3 surface-piercing Bravo-1 props; 1,500 bhp
Range: . . . / . . . **Fuel:** 1.1 m^3 **Crew:** 5 tot. + 3–4 "specialists"

Remarks: Ordered 6-98. Aluminum construction. Designed in U.K. by Cougartek. Crew and passengers ride in shock-mounted seats. Made 62 kts on trials. Last unit delivered 10-99.

♦ 14 Damen Mk 3 design
Bldr: Chung Wah SB & Eng., Kowloon

	Laid down	L	In serv.
PL 70 King Lai	28-2-84	14-7-84	29-10-84
PL 71 King Yee	28-2-84	17-7-84	29-11-84
PL 72 King Lim	28-2-84	29-7-84	17-12-84
PL 73 King Hau	15-3-84	2-11-84	31-1-85
PL 74 King Dai	15-3-84	8-11-84	28-2-85
PL 75 King Chung	15-3-84	12-11-84	1-4-85
PL 76 King Shun	17-8-84	26-1-85	17-5-85
PL 77 King Tak	25-8-84	4-2-85	10-6-85
PL 78 King Chi	17-8-84	1-2-85	2-7-85
PL 79 King Tai	1-12-84	29-4-85	19-8-85
PL 80 King Kwan	1-12-84	4-5-85	18-9-85
PL 82 King Yan	8-3-85	19-8-85	4-11-85
PL 83 King Yung	8-3-85	30-8-85	25-11-85
PL 84 King Kan	8-3-85	2-9-85	18-12-85

King Hau (PL 73) Douglas A. Cromby, 11-96

D: 85 tons (97 fl) **S:** 25 kts **Dim:** 26.50 (24.27 pp) × 5.80 × 1.80
A: Fitted for 1 7.62-mm mg
Electronics: Radar: 1 Decca RM 1290 nav.
M: 2 MTU 12V396 TC83 diesels; 2 props; 2,966 bhp—1 M.A.N. MB OM-424A V-12 cruise diesel; 1 waterjet; 465 bhp
Range: 600/14; 1,400/8 **Crew:** 17 tot.

Remarks: PL 70–78 ordered 10-83; PL 79–84 ordered 1-12-84. Damen's Stan Patrol 2600/Chung Wah's Mk 3 design, a modified version of the Damen Mk 1 design. Can make up to 7 kts on the centerline waterjet. Carry an Avon Searaider semi-rigid inspection boat. Sister *King Mei* (PL 81) was stricken 1985 after damage. Three near-sisters were built for the Hong Kong Customs Service.

♦ 8 Damen Mk 1 design
Bldr: Chung Wah SB & Eng., Kowloon

	In serv.		In serv.
PL 60	29-2-80	PL 65	2-9-80
PL 61	29-2-80	PL 66	8-9-80
PL 63	1980	PL 67	1980
PL 64	1980	PL 68	1-81

PL 66 H&L Van Ginderen, 8-94

D: 86 tons (normal) **S:** 23 kts **Dim:** 26.2 × 5.9 × 1.80
A: Removed **Electronics:** Radar: 1 Decca 150 nav.
M: 2 MTU 12V396 TC82 diesels (1,300 bhp each), 1 M.A.N. D2566 cruise diesel (195 bhp); 3 props (Schottel on centerline); 2,600 bhp
Range: 1,400/8 **Crew:** 1 officer, 13 constables

PATROL BOATS [WPB] *(continued)*

Remarks: PL 60 was laid down during 9-79 to a Dutch design. The cruise engine provides 7- to 8-kt max. speeds. The 12.7-mm mg has been removed.
Disposals: Damen Mk 2 variants PL 57, PL 58, and PL 59 were discarded in 1999. Mk 1 PL 62 was transferred to the customs service in 1995.

♦ **7 Petrel-class harbor patrol craft**
Bldr: Chung Wah SB & Eng. Co. (In serv. 1986–87)

PL 11 Petrel — PL 14 Tern — PL 16 Puffin
PL 12 Auk — PL 15 Skua — PL 17 Gannet
PL 13 Gull

Skua (PL 15) Chris Sattler, 7-05

D: 36 tons **S:** 12 kts **Dim:** 16.0 × 4.6 × 1.5
A: Small arms **Electronics:** Radar: 1 Decca . . . nav.
M: 2 Cummins NTA 855M diesels; 2 waterjets; 700 bhp **Crew:** 7 tot.

Remarks: Are equipped with one water monitor for firefighting.

♦ **3 40-foot patrol launches**
Bldr: Cheoy Lee SY, Hong Kong

PL 6 Jetstream (In serv. 17-4-86) — PL 8 Tidestream (In serv. 12-6-86)
PL 7 Swiftstream (In serv. 25-5-86)

D: 24 tons (fl) **S:** 18 kts **Dim:** 16.4 × 4.5 × 0.85
A: Small arms **Electronics:** Radar: 1 Decca . . . nav.
M: 2 MTU diesels; 2 Hamilton 421 waterjets; 455 bhp
Range: 300/15 **Crew:** 8 tot.

Remarks: GRP construction. Replaced a trio by the same builder with the same names. Employed for patrol of the Deep Bay area.

SERVICE CRAFT

♦ **7 Challenger-class launches [WYFL]**
Bldr: Boston Whaler, Edgewater, Fla. (In serv. 1996)

PL 51 through PL 57

D: 1.86 tons light **S:** 25 kts **Dim:** 7.62 × 1.80 × 0.38
M: 2 Evinrude gasoline outboards; 450 bhp **Crew:** 2 tot. + 10 passengers

Remarks: GRP foam-core hull, fitted for rescue and towing. Also suitable for harbor patrol.

♦ **4 PL 46–class catamaran personnel launches [WYFL]**
Bldr: Sea Spray Boats, Fremantle, Western Australia (In serv. 1992)

PL 46 — PL 47 — PL 48 — PL 49

PL 47 Chris Sattler, 7-05

D: . . . tons (fl) **S:** 30 kts **Dim:** 11.4 × 4.2 × 1.3
M: 2 Caterpillar 3208TA diesels; 2 props; 550 bhp **Crew:** 4 tot.

Remarks: GRP construction. First unit delivered 6-92 to replace earlier personnel launches. Can carry 16 constables or 6 VIPs.

♦ **11 PL 22–class catamaran personnel launches [WYFL]**
Bldr: Sea Spray Boats, Fremantle, Western Australia (In serv. 1992–93)

PL 22 through PL 32

D: 5 tons (fl) **S:** 35 kts **Dim:** 9.90 × 4.20 × 1.20
Electronics: Radar: 1 Koden MD 3400 nav.
M: 2 Caterpillar 3208TA diesels; 2 props; 710 bhp
Range: . . . / . . . **Fuel:** 2 tons **Crew:** 4 tot.

Remarks: Aluminum construction. Prototype completed 6-92, four others during 1992, and the remainder in 1993. Can maintain 25 kts in Sea State 4.

Note: All of the rigid inflatable boats listed below are organized into the Small Boat Unit and are referred to as "High Speed Interceptors." The 7-m *Typhoon*-class rigid inflatables PV 30 through PV 37 were discarded during 1999.

♦ **3 9.5-meter Typhoon RIB launches [WYFL]**
Bldr: Task Force Boats, U.K.

PV 10 — PV 11 — PV 12

Remarks: Capable of 50 kts; powered by two V-8, 270-bhp outboard motors.

♦ **4 Tempest RIB launches [WYFL]**
Bldr: Task Force Boats, U.K.

PV 14 — PV 15 — PV 16 — PV 17

♦ **9 Stillinger RIB launches [WYFL]**
Bldr: Stillinger, U.K.

PV 90 through PV 98

Note: The Hong Kong Customs Service operates four Damen 26-m patrol boats similar in appearance and characteristics to sisters in police service: *Sea Glory* (6), *Sea Guardian* (7), *Sea Leader* (8), and PL 62 (transferred from the police in 1995). Two 32.15-m patrol boats were delivered by Wang Tak SY, Kowloon, during 7-00; these have a speed of 25 kts derived from two MTU 16V1200 diesels.
The Environmental Protection Department operates several craft, including the pollution clean-up vessel *Dr. Catherine Lam,* and the Marine Department operates boats equipped to handle navigational buoys and markers.

ICELAND

Republic of Iceland

COAST GUARD

(*Landhelgisgæslan*)

Personnel: Approx. 130 total

Base: Reykjavik

Maritime Aviation: One Fokker F-27 Mk 200 Friendship patrol aircraft and 1 AS.365N Dauphin II, 1 AS.332L-1 Super Puma, and 1 AS.350B Écureuil helicopters.

Note: Icelandic Coast Guard vessels have red, white, and blue diagonal stripes on either side of their dark gray-painted hulls, and the word *Landhelgisgæslan* (Coast Guard) is painted on both sides amidships.

FISHERIES-PROTECTION SHIPS [WPS]

♦ **2 Ægir class**

	Bldr	L	In serv.
Ægir	Ålborg SY, Denmark	1967	1968
Týr	Dannebrog Vaerft, Århus, Denmark	10-10-74	15-3-78

Tyr—outboard the *Ægir*, with *Baldur* alongside Werner Globke, 7-99

D: 1,150 tons (1,500 fl) **S:** 20 kts **Dim:** 69.84 (62.18 pp) × 10.02 × 5.02
A: 1 40-mm 60-cal. Bofors Mk 3 AA
Electronics:
Radar: 1 Sperry Rasterscan nav.; 1 Plessey AWS-6 air search
Sonar: *Týr* only: Sirad hull-mounted HF
M: 2 M.A.N. R8V 40/54 diesels; 2 KaMeWa CP props; 8,600 bhp
Electric: 630 kVa **Range:** 10,000/19 **Crew:** 22 tot.

Remarks: Although built ten years apart, these two ships are nearly identical. *Tyr* is 70.90 m o.a. The original single-fire 6-pdr (57-mm) guns, made in 1896, were replaced in 1989–90, and an articulating boat crane was placed at the starboard forward end of the helicopter platform to handle rigid inflatable launches. The radar fit was enhanced in 1994, and the flight deck was extended and the hull beneath it plated up in 1997. Have a 20-ton bollard-pull towing winch and passive antirolling tanks.

FISHERIES-PROTECTION SHIPS [WPS] *(continued)*

♦ 1 Odinn class

	Bldr.	Laid down	L	In serv.
Odinn	Ålborg SY, Denmark	1-59	9-59	1-60

Odinn Werner Globke, 7-99

D: 1,000 tons (fl) **S:** 18 kts **Dim:** 63.63 (56.61 pp) × 10.0 × 4.8
A: 1 40-mm 60-cal. Bofors Mk 3 AA
Electronics: Radar: 2 Sperry Rasterscan nav.
M: 2 Burmeister & Wain diesels; 2 props; 5,050 bhp
Range: 10,000/18 **Crew:** 22 tot.

Remarks: Rebuilt in 1975 by Århus Flydedock, Denmark, with hangar, helicopter deck, and passive antirolling tanks. An articulated crane was added to starboard at the forward end of the helicopter deck in 1989 to handle RIB inspection and rescue craft. The original single-fire 6-pdr (57-mm) gun was replaced in 1990.

SERVICE CRAFT

♦ 1 inshore survey craft [WYGS]

Bldr: Vélsmidja Seydhisfjördhur H/H, Seydhisfjörda (In serv. 8-5-91)

Baldur

Baldur—alongside the *Týr* Werner Globke, 7-99

D: 54 tons (fl) **S:** 12 kts **Dim:** 20.0 × 5.2 × 1.7
Electronics: Radar: 1 Furuno . . . nav.
M: 2 Caterpillar 3406TA diesels; 2 props; 640 bhp **Crew:** 5 tot.

Note: The 2,100-grt civilian agency oceanographic research ship *Arni Fridriksson* was delivered during 5-00 by ASMAR, Talcahuano, Chile, for the Icelandic Marine Research Institute. The ship is 70 m o.a. by 13.8 m in beam, and the single-screw diesel-electric propulsion plant produces about 4,000 shp for 16-kt speeds.

INDIA

Republic of India

INDIAN NAVY

Personnel: About 55,000 tot. (7,500 officers), including 1,200 Marine Commando force (MARCOS) and 7,000-strong Naval Air Arm, plus 45,000 civilians.

Note: In 1996, a number of Indian cities were officially renamed to reflect local linguistic and cultural customs. The major locations of naval interest are Mumbai, Chennai, Kochi, and Kanoor. The new names are employed in the listings below.

Bases: Headquarters is at INS *India,* New Delhi. Western Command Headquarters is at Mumbai and includes submarine base INS *Varabahu* and missile boat base INS *Agnibahu;* there is also a small naval facility at Okha near the Pakistani border. Eastern Command Headquarters is at Vishakhapatnam ("Vizag") and includes the submarine base INS *Virbahu;* also subordinate to Eastern Command are small naval facilities at Chennai, Calcutta, Port Blair (INS *Jarawa*) in the Andaman Islands, and Camorta in the Nicobar Islands and the naval VLF submarine communications facility at Vijayaraghavapuram. Southern Command Headquarters is at Kochi and includes the research and development station INS *Dronacharya.* The Naval Academy, now at Goa, is planned to move to INS *Jawarhalal Nehru* at Ezhimala in 2005. The College of Naval Warfare is at Karanja; the Marine Engineering School is at INS *Shivaji;* enlisted new-entry training is carried out at INS *Chilka,* Vishakhapatnam; and the logistics school is at INS *Hamla,* Mumbai. The Marine Gas Turbine Overhaul Center, INS *Eksila,* near Vishakhapatnam, was commissioned on 27-8-00.

Approval was given 24-11-94 for a seven-year, $433-million program to build a new major fleet base, INS *Sea Bird,* at Karwar, to begin replacement of Mumbai; completion of the entire facility is expected to take 30 years. Chenna Muttam harbor, near Cape Comorin on the southern tip of India, is to be developed as a naval base to protect the nearby Koodankulam nuclear-power project.

Naval air stations are at INS *Garuda,* Wellington Island, Kochi; INS *Hansa,* Goa; INS *Sea Bird,* Karwar; INS *Utkrosh,* Port Blair; INS *Rajali,* Arakkonam; Chennai; Mumbai; Vishwanath; Uchipuli, Tamil Nadu; Ramanathuram; Ramnad; and Bangalore. Naval aviation headquarters are located at Goa.

Naval Aviation: Shipboard aircraft include 17 Sea Harrier FRS.51 V/STOL fighters equipped with Magic air-to-air missiles (14 of these aircraft received substantial avionics and weapon systems upgrades, including the capability to fire the Raphael Derby air-to-air missile, from 2006–7); five Sea Harrier T Mk. 60 dual sea trainers; 42 Sea King helicopters (15 Mark 42/42A types delivered 14-10-70 to 23-11-79, six Mark 42C type transports delivered from 25-9-88, and 21 Mark 42B type, equipped with Sea Eagle antiship missiles and Sintra-Alcatel MS-12 dipping sonar, delivered from 17-5-85). 11 Helix-A (Ka-28) ASW helicopters (export versions of the KA-27PL model; three configured as trainers) are in use as are nine Helix-B (Ka-31) AEW helicopters. Ka-28 Helix (Ka-28) helicopters were reportedly refurbished at Sevastopol' from 10-00 to 2-01, but this remains unconfirmed. At least two Dhruv indigenous-built liaison helicopters and approximately 50 Chetak (Alouette-III, SA.319) light ASW/liaison helicopters remain in service.

For land-based maritime surveillance, five IL-38 May (IL-38), eight Tu-142MKE Bear F Mod. 3, six BN-42B/T Maritime Defender, and 24 Do-228 fixed-wing aircraft are in use. Training and logistics-support aircraft include eight HPT-32 propeller-driven Deepak and 12 HAL Kiran Mk I, IA, and II jet trainers, and 10 HAL HS.748M transports. Two Harrier T.4 trainers were delivered on 16-9-02. Two IL-38 May collided in flight near Goa on 1-10-02, with the loss of 12 aircrew. Russia donated two surplus IL-38 aircraft to replace the aircraft lost in the midair collision. Discussions continue with the U.S. for the purchase of six to eight Orion (P-3C) maritime patrol aircraft with two leased in the first half of 2006.

A contract to purchase 16 carrier-based Fulcrum (MiG-29K/KUB) aircraft was signed on 20-1-04 for $740 million. Of the 16, 12 will be single-seat "K" variants and four will be dual-seat "KUB" variant trainers. The contract also includes an option to buy up to 30 more aircraft by 2015. The first aircraft are due for delivery in 2007.

A total of 40 naval variants of the HAL Dhruv (formerly the Advanced Light Helicopter—ALH) are planned to replace the Chetaks for liaison, transport, search-and-rescue, and, later, ASW duties; the initial production order for 12, placed early in 1997, included two for the navy and two for the coast guard. Deliveries of the aircraft to the navy began on 30-3-02.

Plans to acquire six more Tu-142MKE aircraft by 2002 did not reach fruition and all are planned for retirement in 2010. With upgrades, the IL-38s are expected to remain in service through 2020. Four Tu-22M3 Backfire bombers were to be transferred from Russia in 2001 under a 5-10-00 agreement, but a final contract was never signed.

Of 24 Dornier Do-228 coastal surveillance aircraft, six are to be fitted with Elisra EW and Elta 2022 surveillance radars. The BN-42B/T Maritime Defender coastal patrol aircraft are being refurbished and re-engined with Allison 150 B17C turboprops (320 shp each).

Plans to order additional Sea Harriers were abandoned in favor of participation in the development of the Indian Light Combat Aircraft, which may enter Indian Navy service from shore bases around 2015. Some $125 million was allocated in 6-99 to update the existing FRS.51 Sea Harriers, which are increasingly obsolescent, but the update program was later canceled (although a new plan to update fourteen of the aircraft with Elta 2032 radars was announced in 4-01).

Data include:

Weight: 2,352 kg (5,000 kg max.) **Speed:** 156 kts
Engines: 2 Turbomeca TM 333-2B turbines (2,000 shp)
Range: 216 n.m. with 700 kg payload **Fuel:** 2,850 liters

Indian Navy Sea Harrier FRS.51 formation British Aerospace

INDIAN NAVY *(continued)*

Indian Navy Do-228 Mritunjoy Mazumdar, 2-01

Indian Navy Tu-142 Bear-F Brian Morrison, 2-01

Indian Navy Chetak Ralph Edwards, 10-02

Indian Navy Sea King Mk 42 Michael Winter, 6-05

Indian Air Force 6 Sqn. ("Dragons") operates 7 SEPECAT/HAL Jaguar-IM fighter-bombers dedicated to the maritime strike role and armed with two BAe Sea Eagle antiship missiles each.

Naval aircraft squadron home base assignments are as follows:

Squadron Designation	*Type of Aircraft Assigned*	*Naval Air Station Base*
INAS 300	Sea Harrier Mark 51, T Mark 60	INS Hansa
INAS 310	Dornier Do-228-101	INS Hansa
INAS 312	Tupolev 142M Bear-F	INS Rajali
INAS 315	Ilyushin-38 May	INS Hansa
INAS 318	Dornier Do-228-101 & HAL Chetak	INS Utkrosh
INAS 321	HAL Chetak	INS Kunjali-II
INAS 330	Sea King Mark 42	INS Kunjali-II
INAS 333	Ka-28 Helix	INS Dega
INAS 336	Sea King Mark 42, Mark 42A	INS Garuda,
INAS 339	Ka-28 (Ka-28 and Ka-31)	INS Kunjali-II
INAS 550	BN-2B/T Islander, HPT-32 Deepak and Dornier Do-228-101	INS Garuda
INAS 551	HJT-16 Kiran (Mark II)	INS Hansa
INAS 552	Sea Harrier (T Mark 60) trainer	INS Hansa
INAS 561	HAL Chetak & Hughes 300	INS Rajali

Indian Navy KA-31 Helix-B AEW helicopter Chris Sattler, 7-06

Indian Navy KA-28 Helix-A Arjun Sarup, 8-02

During 2006 the 1st Indian Navy UAV squadron became operational. Three UAV squadrons consisting of Israeli-built Heron and Searcher-II UAVs are planned during the next decade.

Weapons and Sensors: A mixture of Western (primarily British and Dutch) and Soviet weapons and sensors are used, with Western designs built in India under license, principally by Bharat Electronics. Hindustan Aeronautics Ltd. (HAL) is developing an air-to-ground missile for air force and navy use; it will have a range of 100 km at Mach 0.85 at 30,000-foot altitude and will have a 35-kg payload. Also under development by HAL is the Koral surface-launched antiship missile. Due to delays and unsuccessful tests, the 9-km-ranged Trishul SAM, based on the Russian SA-8, has been canceled.

Sixteen Zvezda Kh-35 Uran antiship missiles were delivered from Russia in 1997 for use with the *Delhi,* and 50 additional missiles were ordered in 1998. British Sea Eagle antiship missiles, in use with Indian Air Force Jaguar fighter-bombers, may be replaced with an air-launched version of the Russian Kh-35 Uran (AS-20 Kayak); integration problems caused cancellation of plans to integrate Sea Eagle with IL-38 and Tu-142MKE land-based patrol aircraft. Thirty Russian 3M-54E Klub subsonic antiship/land-attack missiles were procured during 2000 at a cost of $2.5 million each for use from submarines and surface combatants; India is said to be dissatisfied with their range performance during two launches in 5-02.

The supersonic Bramhos (alternate designation PJ-10), a reworked version of Russian 3M-55 Oniks (NATO's SS-NX-26 Yakhont) antiship missile, began development during 2000 for launch by surface ships and aircraft as an antiship and strategic land-attack weapon; the weapon is said to have a potential range of 300 km and to carry a 200-kg warhead; a nuclear-warhead version is being designed, and the missile may also be altered for submarine launch. Maximum range is achieved using a cruising altitude of 14,000 m, but in low-altitude cruise mode, range is reduced to about 120 km. The target can be altered until the missile is within 20 km of the original target. A reportedly successful test was carried out on 12-6-01 at Chandipur Missile Test Range; on 12-2-03, a successful launch was made from INS *Rajput* (D 51). Initial production deliveries were under way by 2005. Data include:

Length: 8.0 m **Weight:** 3000 kg
Warhead: 200 kg **Speed:** Mach 2.8
Altitude: wavetop **Range:** 160 km

By 2002, a submarine-launched missile named Sagarika ("Oceanic"), which has been under development since 1991, had been abandoned in favor of a navalized version of the Agni-2 medium-range ballistic missile. A nuclear payload is in development.

The Dhanush production variant of the Prithvi missile is being developed for launch by surface ships; the weapon will initially have a range of 250 km and a 500-kg payload, but a 350-km version is also planned. Minimum range of the land-based variant has been reported as 40 km (25 miles). Initial 11-00 at-sea firing was unsuccessful.

A decision was made in 1996 to procure the Israeli Barak vertical-launch, point-defense SAM system, and a single set was ordered for the carrier *Viraat* in 1997 (with installation completed 5-01); six more sets were ordered on 6-2-01. In light of Trishul SAM problems and eventual cancellation, the navy may purchase additional units.

INDIAN NAVY *(continued)*

Bharat Electronics has developed a navalized mounting for the Russian 30-mm automatic 2A42 cannon used on Indian Army BMP-2 infantry fighting vehicles; the "Medak" mount also incorporates a coaxial 7.62-mm mg and can be locally or remotely controlled. The mounting is intended eventually to replace 40-mm single Bofors guns in coast guard ships and craft and possibly in the Indian Navy's *Sukanya*-class patrol ships; it is also aboard the replenishment ship *Aditya*.

Some eight Dvigitel TEST-71EM-NK wire-guided torpedoes were purchased for use with the 10th Project 877 *Kilo*-class submarine. The Naval Scientific Laboratory, Vishakhapatnam, is developing the Shyena "Advanced Experimental Torpedo." The Maindeka dolphin-transported limpet mine is also in development.

Bharat Electronics develops and manufactures radar, sonar, and EW systems based on European-developed prototypes under license. Early in 1993, a license agreement was signed with Hollandse Signaal-Apparaaten (now Thales Nederland) to manufacture H.S.A.-developed radars and other electronic equipment to replace Soviet-made gear on Indian naval ships during the 1990s. Equipment that has entered service during the 1990s includes

Name	*Prototype*	*Function*
Aparna	Garpun-E	X(I)-band antiship missile targeting
Rashmi (PIN-524)	HSA ZW-06	X(I)-band navigation/surf. search
RAWL-02 (PLN-517)	HSA LW-02	L(D)-band air early warning
RAWS-03 (PFN-513)	HSA DA-05	L(D)-band air/surf. search

Bharat's APSOH digital sonar can employ both hull-mounted and VDS transducer arrays and features automated detection classification, as well as tracking and adaptive signal processing. An Indian-developed submarine sonar suite designated Panchendriya began testing at sea in 1997 on *Foxtrot*-class *Karanj* (S 21); it appears still in trials status, with no production yet programmed. The Ahalya helicopter dipping sonar is also being tested.

AIRCRAFT CARRIERS [CV]

♦ 0 (+ 1 + 1) Vikrant-class Air-Defense Ship

Bldr: Cochin Shipyard, Ltd, Kochi

	Laid down	L	In serv.
VIKRANT	7-05	2009	2012
. . .	. . .	. . .	2018

Vikrant-class Air-Defense Ship *Ships of the World,* 2000

D: 40,000 tons (fl) **S:** 28 kts **Dim:** Approx. 252.3.0 × 58.0 × 8.4
Air group: 12 Light Combat Aircraft (LCA) and/or MiG-29K fighters; 10 Sea King, 8 Advanced Light Helicopter (ALH), 2 Ka-31 Helix AEW helicopters
A: 2 Barak VLS SAM systems; 4 76-mm OTO/Melara Super Rapid DP
Electronics: 1 Russian Top-Plate 3D air search radar; 1 Russian . . . 3-D air search radar; 1 . . . nav.
M: 4 HAL-G.E. LM-2500 gas turbines; 2 props; 108,000 shp
Range: 7,500/18 **Crew:** 1,420 + air group

Remarks: Approved by the finance and defense ministries by 3-99, the ADS was given Cabinet Committee on Security approval in 6-99 to allocate roughly $750 million for construction of a ship whose genesis began in the mid-1980s; the projected cost has more than doubled since 1993. Will have a small air group for its size and is to employ a 14-deg. ski-jump bow for takeoffs and arrestor wires for landing (STOBAR: Short Take-Off But Arrested Landing). The design is said to be based on one for a somewhat larger ship prepared by France's DCN under a 21-12-88 contract. The building facility for the ship was completed on 23-1-03. In 2003 the Indian government expressed a desire to build three of these vessels. The building facility for the ship was completed on 23-1-03. A contract for construction of the first unit was awarded to Cochin in 3-05. A second unit of the class is expected. In 2003 the Indian government expressed a desire to build three of these vessels, but budgetary limitations may dictate otherwise.
Combat systems: To have antimissile SAM system, an E/O backup weapons-control system, ASW torpedoes, and a sonar set.

♦ 1 Ex-Russian Modified Kiev class (Project 11434)

Bldr: Chernomorskiy (Nosenko) SY 444, Nikolayev

	Laid down	L	In serv.
VIKRAMADITYA (ex-*Admiral Gorshkov*, ex-*Admiral Flota Sovetskogo Soyuza Gorshkov*, ex-*Baku*)	26-12-78	31-3-82	20-12-87

Proposed appearance of the Vikramaditya after conversion to aircraft carrier Nevelskoye Design Bureau, 1999

D: 33,000 tons light, 40,000 tons std. (44,570 fl) **S:** 29 kts
Dim: 283 × 53.0 (32.7 wl) × 10.2 (mean hull)
Air Group: 21 MiG-29K fighter-bombers, 15 Helix ASW and aerial surveillance helicopters
A: 6 CADS-N-1 (Kortik/Kashtan) SAM/gun systems (fitted with the capability of firing SA-N-11 Kortik (SA-19) missiles)
Electronics:
Radar: 1 . . . 3-D air-search; 2 . . . air/surf. search; 3 . . . nav.; 2 . . . automatic aircraft landing aid
EW: Bharat intercept and jammers; 2 twin trainable PK-2 decoy RL
TACAN: . . .
M: 4 sets GTZA 674 geared steam turbines; 4 props (4-bladed); 200,000 shp
Boilers: 8, turbopressurized KWG4, 64 kg/cm^2
Electric: 15,000 kw tot. (6 × 1,500-kw turboalternators, 4 × 1,500-kw diesel sets)
Range: 4,050/29; 7,000/18; 8,000/16.3; 13,500/10
Fuel: 7,000 tons + 1,500 tons aviation fuel **Endurance:** 30 days
Crew: 1,220 total crew + air group + 50 flag staff

Remarks: Some data above refer to the ship when in Russian Navy service. Negotiations to sell the *Admiral Gorshkov* to India began in 1994, and India signed a "letter of interest" on 21-12-98 to acquire the ship for free and modernize her with Russian equipment at Severodvinsk, where she arrived under tow on 13-7-99. A contract for the transfer of the ship to India was signed 4-10-00, and the vessel was transferred on 20-1-04 for delivery in the 2008 time frame. Conversion is taking place at the Sevmash Enterprise shipyards in Severodvinsk, Russia, with final outfitting done at Cochin Shipyard in India. A 14.3-deg. bow ski-jump is planned across the bow.

Has not been to sea under own power since 1996, she suffered a major fire while laid up during 1993 and a steam line break and subsequent 18-hour fire at Rosta Shipyard, Murmansk, on 2-2-94. Modifications are said to be expected to cost $800 million, while some $616 million is to be expended on MiG-29K aircraft and $207 million on Ka-31 helicopters for the ship.
Hull systems: Has a deeper draft than the preceding *Kiev* class and also trims down by the stern. The boilers produce up to 98 tons of steam per hour. Fin stabilizers are fitted.
Aviation systems: The bow would be altered to become a 14.3-deg. takeoff ski jump for conventional fighter aircraft, and no catapults would be fitted. There would be two takeoff positions, each with a jet-blast deflector and aircraft detents. The ship was originally intended to carry 14 Yak-41M Freehand and eight Yak-38 Forger VTOL fighters and 16 Ka-27-series helicopters. The angled portion of the flight deck is 195 × 20.7 m. Adding wire-type arrestor gear would probably reduce capacity of the 130-m-long by 22.5-m-wide by 6.6-m-high hangar. Two inboard aircraft elevators (19 × 10 m and 19 × 5 m) and three weapons elevators to the flight deck were fitted but may have to be moved and enlarged under the new configuration.

V/STOL AIRCRAFT CARRIERS [CVV]

♦ 1 U.K. Hermes class

Bldr: Vickers-Armstrong, Barrow-in-Furness

	Laid down	L	In serv.
R 22 VIRAAT (ex-*Hermes*)	21-6-44	16-2-53	18-11-59

Viraat (R 22)—with 6 Sea Harrier fighters, 3 Sea King and 2 Chetak helicopters visible on deck during exercise *Malabar '05* U.S. Navy, 9-05

D: 23,900 tons (28,700 fl) **S:** 28 kts
Dim: 226.85 (198.12 pp) × 48.78 (27.43 wl) × 8.80
Air Group: 10–12 Sea Harrier Mk 51 fighters; 3 Sea King Mk 42B ASW helicopters; 3 Sea King Mk 42C logistics helicopters; 4 Ka-28 Helix ASW helicopters; 2 Chetak liaison helicopters; 3 KA-31 Helix-B AEW helicopters
A: 1 Barak SAM VLS group (8 missiles); 2 single 40-mm 60-cal. Bofors Mk 3 AA; 2 twin 30-mm 65-cal. AK-230M AA
Electronics:
Radar: 2 Bharat Rashmi nav.; 1 Bharat RAWL early warning; 1 Bharat RAWS-J air/surf. search; 1 Elta EL/M-2221 GM STGR missile f.c.
Sonar: Graseby Type 184M hull-mounted (8–9 kHz) (probably inactivated)
TACAN: FT13-S/M
EW: Elettronica-Bharat RAWS/PFN-513 Ajanta intercept; 2 8-tubed Corvus decoy RL

V/STOL AIRCRAFT CARRIERS [CVV] *(continued)*

Viraat (R 22) Brian Morrison, 2-01

M: 2 sets Parsons geared steam turbines; 2 props; 76,000 shp
Boilers: 4 Admiralty 3-drum **Electric:** 9,000 kw tot.
Range: 6,500/14 **Fuel:** 4,200 tons, plus 320 tons aviation fuel
Crew: 143 officers, 1,207 enlisted (plus air group) + 750 troops

Remarks: Purchased 24-4-86, having been paid off 12-4-84 from the Royal Navy and stricken on 1-7-85. Turned over to Indian control 14-11-86 during reactivation and minor modernization overhaul, and recommissioned on 12-5-87 at Devonport. Formally commissioned in India 15-2-89. The name means "Mighty." Had been converted from a standard carrier to a helicopter commando carrier 1971–73 and converted again 1976–77 as an ASW helicopter carrier. Suffered severe engine-room flooding 10-9-93 when a main seawater induction valve failed in port during repairs. Was to have begun a final two-year major refit at Mumbai in 1997, but the start was delayed until 7-99, curtailed to 14–18 months, and limited to a $50-million expenditure; the work was completed during 2001, and the ship is now planned for retirement in 2010.
Hull systems: Has 25- to 50-mm armor over magazines and machinery spaces, and flight deck is approx. 20 mm thick. During reactivation, NBC warfare protection was improved.
Aviation systems: Modified during British service 5-80 to 9-5-81 to operate Sea Harrier V/STOL attack fighters, receiving a 230-ton, 45.7-m-long × 13.7-m-wide × 4.9-m-high 12-deg. "ski-jump" takeoff ramp. Retained commando transport capability for 750 troops and continues to carry four LCVP landing craft aft. Has two aircraft elevators. The Sea King Mk 42B ASW helicopters are equipped to launch Sea Eagle antiship missiles. There are two aircraft elevators, one to port on the angled deck and one aft on the centerline.
Combat systems: Has British CAAIS computerized combat data system. At time of transfer, had Deck Approach Projector System (DAPS), Horizon Approach Path Indicator (HAPI), the CTL all-weather approach system landing aids, new Decca Type 1006 navigational radars, and an Italian TACAN system (replacing the U.K. system removed in 4-82) added. New EW equipment was added in India. Carries up to 80 ASW torpedoes for the helicopters. Two 40-mm AA have been added, one at the forward end of the flight deck to starboard of the ski jump and the other just forward of the island. A Bharat-made radar has replaced the Type 994 surface/air-search set. The two Sea Cat GWS.22 point-defense missile launchers had been removed by 1995 and were replaced with Russian twin 30-mm gunmounts removed from stricken ships; these are controlled by simple ringsight directors.
Modernization: The 1999–2000 refit incorporated a new long-range radar, an improved communications suite, a new shipboard damage-control alarm system, fire curtains in the hangar space, and faster aircraft elevator operation. One 8-cell, vertically launched Israeli Barak SAM system was ordered for the ship in 1997 with installation completed by 2004. Two Russian Kashtan CIWS may be purchased later.

NUCLEAR-POWERED CRUISE MISSILE SUBMARINES [SSGN]

♦ 0 (+ 5) Advanced Technology Vessel (ATV) class
Bldr: Mazagon DY, Mumbai (In serv. 2009+)

D: 5,500 tons surf./7,000 tons sub. **S:** 30 kts sub. **Dim:** 100.0 × 15.0 × 9.0
A: 6 533mm TT; 16 SLCMs and torpedoes
M: 1 pressurized water reactors; steam turbines; 1 prop; . . . shp
Crew: Approx. 75

Remarks: Originally thought to have been an SSBN, it now appears more likely to be armed with cruise missiles than ballistic missiles. Data above are preliminary estimates. A total of five may be planned. Related research has been ongoing in India since 1974 toward the construction of an indigenously designed and constructed nuclear-powered submarine. In 4-96, it was reported that the program was experiencing severe delays and cost overruns and might be canceled. In 6-96, it was reported that initial trials in 11-95 and 12-95 with a prototype reactor for the submarine at Kalpakkam atomic power plant had been entirely unsuccessful. The reactor, under design since 1985 at the Bhaba Atomic Research Center, Mumbai, was said to weigh 600 tons. Russia is said to have been providing design and engineering assistance for the program since 1989. The pressure hulls for later units are to be assembled by Mazagon Dock from eight prefabricated sections manufactured by Larsen & Toubru.

A submersible test barge intended to launch trials missiles intended for the class was launched during 2001. Diving depth = 300 m.

NUCLEAR-POWERED ATTACK SUBMARINES [SSN]

Note: Negotiations with Russia for the purchase of two Project 971 Bars-class (NATO Akula-I) nuclear-powered attack submarines, reported under way since 3-99, continue in earnest. As of late 2006, signs point to a 10-year "lease with the option to buy" deal. During late 2005, 300 Indian naval personnel reportedly arrived in Russia to begin training for future service aboard Akula submarines.

ATTACK SUBMARINES [SS]

Note: Long-range Indian Navy plans approved early in 2000 call for the construction of 24 submarines in India by 2030; 12 of these would be of Russian design and 12 of European design.

♦ 0 (+ 6) Scorpène class (Project 75)
Bldr: Mazagon DY, Mumbai (In serv. 2012–18)

	Laid down	L	In serv.
S 48	2004	. . .	2012
S 49	. . .	. . .	. . .
S 50	. . .	. . .	. . .
S 51	. . .	. . .	. . .
S 52	. . .	. . .	. . .
S 53	. . .	. . .	2018

D: 1,564 tons surf./1,700 tons sub. **S:** 12 kts surf./20+ kts sub.
Dim: 66.40 × 6.20 × 5.4 (surf.)
A: 6 bow 533-mm TT (12 Black Shark wire-guided torpedoes and 6 SM 39 Exocet antiship missiles)
Electronics:
Radar: 1 Kelvin-Hughes Type 1007 nav./surf.-search
Sonar: Thales SUBTICS suite, with TSM 2253 passive flank arrays
EW: Condor Systems AR-900 intercept; WASS C303 anti-torpedo system
M: Diesel electric: 4 MTU 16V396 SE84 diesels (840 bhp each) Jeumont axial-flux permanent magnet electric motor; 1 prop; 4,694 shp
Range: 6,500/8 (surf.); 550/4 (sub.) **Endurance:** 50 days
Crew: 6 officers, 25 enlisted

Remarks: With negotiations ongoing since 2001, a contract was signed 6-10-05 for six Scorpène-class boats expected to cost $4.6 billion. All six subs will be built at Mazagon Dockyard with significant on-sight assistance from DCN and Navantia. All six are to be fitted with AIP propulsion.
Hull systems: Employ HLES-80 steel in the pressure hull, permitting diving depths in excess of 320 m. A 360-cell battery is employed. All machinery is "rafted" for sound isolation. Only nine personnel will be on watch under normal conditions. Some or all may have an MESMA air-independent auxiliary propulsion (AIP) system, which would lengthen the hull and increase displacements from the figures given above.
Combat systems: The UDS International SUBTICS (Submarine Tactical Information and Command System) weapons control system would be similar to the French Navy's SET (*Système d'Exploitation Tactique*) and would have six two-screen display consoles. The sonar suite would include a cylindrical bow transducer array, an active array, a passive ranging array, an acoustic intercept system, and passive flank arrays.

♦ 4 German Type 209/1500

	Bldr	Laid down	L	In serv.
S 44 Shishumar	Howaldtswerke, Kiel	1-5-82	13-12-84	28-9-86
S 45 Shankush	Howaldtswerke, Kiel	1-9-82	11-5-84	20-11-86
S 46 Shalki	Mazagon DY, Mumbai	5-6-84	30-9-89	7-2-92
S 47 Shankul	Mazagon DY, Mumbai	3-9-89	21-3-92	28-5-94

ATTACK SUBMARINES [SS] *(continued)*

Shankul (S 47) Brian Morrison, 2-01

Shishumar (S 44) John Mortimer, 2-01

D: 1,450 tons std.; 1,660 tons surf./1,850 tons sub. **S:** 13 kts surf./22.5 kts sub.
Dim: 64.40 × 6.50 × 6.20
A: 8 bow 533-mm TT (14 AEG SUT Mod. 1 wire-guided torpedoes); mines (see Remarks)
Electronics:
Radar: Kelvin-Hughes Type 1007 nav./surf. search
Sonar: STN Atlas Elektronik CSU-83 search and attack suite, Thomson-Marconi DUUX-5 passive ranging and intercept
EW: Argo Phoenix-II AR-700 intercept, C 303 acoustic decoys
M: 4 MTU 16V493 TY60 (or AZ 80) diesels (800 bhp each), 4 430-kw generators, 2 Siemens motors; 1 7-bladed prop; 6,100 shp (4,600 sust.)
Range: 13,000/10, 18,000/4.5 surf.; 8,200/8 snorkel; 30/20, 400/4.5, 524/4 sub.
Fuel: 157 tons **Endurance:** 50 days **Crew:** 8 officers, 28 enlisted

Remarks: The order for these four, signed 11-12-81, included a later-dropped option to build two additional units in India. The Indian-built pair were delivered several years late and cost more than twice as much as the pair built in Germany. India has reportedly been negotiating with Howaldtswerke, with a view toward modifying the two newer units to launch the Russian Klub missile and possibly refitting the earlier four with the same missile; the rescue sphere system would have to be removed to provide sufficient magazine space in the torpedo room. S 44 began a refit at Mazagon Dockyard in 1999, and the other three reportedly completed midlife refits by 2005. All based at Mumbai, in the 10th Submarine Squadron.
Hull systems: Maximum operating depth: 260 m. A Gäbler spherical escape chamber is installed forward of the sail to provide emergency exit from within the two-compartment pressure hull. The four 132-cell Hawker (ex-Varta) batteries in the German-built pair weigh 280 tons; the Indian-built units have license-built British Chloride Industrial Batteries, Ltd., batteries and the later MTU 12V493 AZ 80 diesel variant.
Combat systems: Have Singer-Librascope SFCS Mk 1 weapons-control system and Kollmorgen Model 76 search and attack periscopes. Strap-on minelaying pods were purchased for these ships; each can hold 24 mines. The first two Indian-built units received Thales ASM DUUX-5 Fenelon sonars, which were to be backfitted to the German-built pair during short refits commencing in 1995; also to be upgraded were the original CSU-3/4 sonar suites on the first pair. Also installed in S 46 and S 47 are French Nereides towed buoyant VLF communications antenna cables. Six ship-sets of the Thales ASM TSM 2272 Eledone active/passive sonar suite were ordered for delivery 1997–99 and were probably intended for installation on the proposed fifth and sixth ships and backfitting on the first four during midlife refits.

♦ 10 Soviet Kilo class (Project 877EKM)

Bldr: United Admiralty SY 199, St. Petersburg (S 63: Nizhniy Novgorod Zavod)

	Laid down	L	Del.	In serv.
S 55 Sindhugosh (ex-B-888)	29-5-83	29-6-85	25-11-85	30-4-86
S 56 Sindhuvaj (ex-B-898)	1-4-86	27-7-86	25-11-86	12-6-87
S 57 Sindhuraj (ex-B- . . .)	. . .	. . .	. . .	20-10-87
S 58 Sindhuvir (ex-B-860)	15-5-87	13-9-87	25-12-87	26-8-88
S 59 Sindhuratna (ex-B- . . .)	. . .	. . .	. . .	22-12-88
S 60 Sindhukesari (ex-B-804)	20-4-88	16-8-88	29-10-88	16-2-89
S 61 Sindhukirti (ex-B-468)	5-4-89	26-8-89	30-10-89	4-1-90
S 62 Sindhuvijay (ex-B 597)	6-4-90	27-7-90	27-10-90	8-3-91
S 63 Sindhurakshak (ex-B-477)	. . .	26-6-97	20-11-97	24-12-97
S 65 Sindhushastra (ex-B-470)	. . .	14-10-99	17-5-00	19-7-00

Sindhushastra (S 65)—the 10th Indian Navy Kilo Brian Morrison, 2-01

Sindhurakshak (S 63) Brian Morrison, 2-01

D: 2,325 tons surf./3,076 tons sub. **S:** 10 kts surf./17 kts sub.
Dim: 74.3 (70.0 wl) × 10.0 × 6.6
A: 6 bow 533-mm TT (18 Type E53-777 wire-guided, E53-60 and E53-85 wake-homing, and E53-67 acoustic homing torpedoes or 24 mines—S 55, 57–60, 62 also: 3M-54E1 Klub-S antiship missiles); 8 9M-32M Strela-M shoulder-launched SAMs
Electronics:
Radar: 1 MRK-50 Albatros (Snoop Tray-2) nav./search
Sonar: MGK-400 Rubikon (Shark Gill) LF active/passive suite with passive hull array; MG-519 Arfa (Mouse Roar) HF active classification/mine avoidance; MG-553 sound-velocity measuring; MG-512 cavitation detection; and MG-53 sonar intercept
EW: Brick Pulp or Squid Head intercept; 6701E (Quad Loop) D/F
M: Electric drive: 2 Type 4-2DL42M diesel generator sets (1,825 bhp; 1,500 kw at 700 rpm), 1 motor; 1 6-bladed prop; 5,900 shp—1 130-shp low-speed motor—2 low-speed maneuvering motors; 2 ducted props; 204 shp (3 kts)
Range: 6,000/7 snorkel; 400/3 sub. **Fuel:** 172 tons
Endurance: 45 days **Crew:** 12 officers, 41 enlisted

Remarks: Based at Vishakhapatnam and Mumbai. S 63 arrived in India on 5-3-98; she and S 65 (pennant number S 64 was not used) were built from surplus components originally assembled for Russian Navy production. S 58 was overhauled at Zvezdochka Machine-Building Enterprise, Yagriy Island, Severodvinsk, Russia, for $80 million, beginning in 6-97 and completing 29-7-99; she recommissioned in India on 31-10-99. S 57 and S 60 arrived at Admiralteyskiy Verf, St. Petersburg, in 4-99, with S 60 completed during 8-01 and S 57 on 2-11-01, several months late. S 59 was delivered to Severodvinsk for a $70-million overhaul during 5-00, with work completed on 12-9-02. A contract to refit S 55 at Severodvinsk was signed on 10-6-02; work began that year and was completed late in 2005. *Sindhuvijay*'s (S 62) overhaul began at Zvezdochare in 6-05.

Units based at Vishakhapatnam are assigned to the 11th Submarine Squadron and those based at Mumbai to the 12th. The Indian Navy is said to consider these to be inferior in most respects to the German-designed Type 209/1500 class. According to press reports in 2003, half of the Kilos in Indian service may be nonoperational due to maintenance problems and dry-dock delays.
Hull systems: Have two Indian-made battery sets, each with 120 cells, providing 9,700 kwh. Hull has six watertight compartments. Propulsion plant suspended for silencing. Hull has 32% reserve buoyancy. When at rest on the surface, the submarine trims down 0.4 m by the bow. Maximum diving depth is 300 m, normal depth 240 m, and periscope depth 17.5 m. Have a rubber anechoic hull coating, which must be wetted down every 30 min when the submarines are on the surface. Said to be improved in quieting over the basic Project 877 version, with improvements suggested by the Indian Navy. S 65 is said to have further improved noise-reduction features and an updated propulsion plant.
Combat systems: Have MVU-110EM Murena combat data system, which can conduct two simultaneous attacks while tracking three other targets manually. The sonar suite is considered superior to that of the Type 209/1500 class by the Indian Navy. Only two of the torpedo tubes can launch wire-guided weapons and missiles. The shoulder-launched SAM launch position is located in the after portion of the sail. Units overhauled in Russia are receiving the capability to launch Russian Novator 3M-54E Klub-S antiship and 91RE1 ASW cruise missiles from the torpedo tubes; the Indian Navy claims a land-attack capability for the Klub-S, of which four per ship will be carried. Units with the missile capability receive the 3P-14PE fire-control system, and all 10 are eventually to be missile-capable. S 65 is said to have later sonar systems than the others and is probably the unit equipped to launch the eight TEST-71EM-NK wire-guided torpedoes purchased from Russia.

♦ 2 Soviet Foxtrot class (Projects 641M and 641K)

Bldr: Admiralteiskiye Verfi 194, St. Petersburg

	Laid down	L	In serv.
S 40 Vela (ex-B-456)	28-9-71	28-1-72	31-8-73
S 42 Vagli (ex-B-464)	1-2-73	19-4-73	10-8-74

D: 1,957 tons surf. (2,203 tons max.)/2,484 tons sub.
S: 15.5 kts surf./10 kts snorkel (max.); 18 kts sub. (max., electric)
Dim: 91.30 (89.70 wl) × 7.50 × 6.06 (surf.)

ATTACK SUBMARINES [SS] *(continued)*

Karanj (S 21)—While still in active service; with three sonar domes atop the casing for the Panchendriya passive-ranging sonar system Brian Morrison, 2-01

A: 6 bow and 4 stern 533-mm TT (22 Type 53-56WA and SET-53M torpedoes or 32 Type AMD-1000 or MDT mines and 6 torpedoes)
Electronics:
Radar: 1 RKL-101 Flag nav./search
Sonar: MG-10M Gerkules HF active; MG-200 Arktika MF passive; MG-15 Tuloma underwater telephone; MG-13 Svyet-M sonar intercept
EW: 1 MRP-25 Nakat-M (Stop Light) intercept; Type 6701E Iva (Quad Loop) HFD/F
M: 3 Type 2D-42M diesels (1,825 bhp each), 3 electric motors (1 × 2,700-shp PG-102, 2 × 1,350-shp PG-101); 3 5- or 6-bladed props; 5,400 shp (sub.)—1 140-shp PG-104 electric low-speed motor on center shaft
Range: 20,000/8 surf.; 11,500/8 snorkel; 36/18, 380/2 sub.
Fuel: 360 tons **Endurance:** 70 days **Crew:** 8 officers, 67 enlisted

Remarks: All were new on delivery. S 40 collided with the destroyer *Rana* during 1990 leaving 17 dead. Refitting of *Vela* was completed 11-05 by Hindustan Shipyard. Work included installation of new primary and auxiliary machinery completing and hull maintenance. *Vela* is part of the 8th submarine squadron and homeported at Vishakapatnam, while *Vagli* sails from Mumbai.
Hull systems: Battery set has 448 cells. Can dive in as little as 45 seconds and have 527 tons reserve buoyancy in surfaced condition. The pressure hull has seven watertight compartments. Operating depth is 240 m normal, 280 maximum. Have an SPChM-FU-90 air-conditioning system.
Combat systems: The after torpedo tubes in these submarines may no longer be used. Have the Leningrad-641 torpedo fire-control system. The MG-200 passive sonar has a range of about 18 km and the MG-10M active set a range of about 3.5 km.

Disposals: *Kandheri* (S 22) was retired on 18-10-89, *Kalvari* (S 23) during 1996, *Vagsheer* (S 43) in 1998, and *Kursura* (S 20) in 2001 (now a museum exhibit). *Vagir* (S 41) was placed in reserve in 1999 and was stricken during 2001. *Karanj* (S 21) decommissioned 1-8-03.

Note: For operation by special forces personnel, the Indian Navy purchased 11 CE-2F/X100 two-man chariot submersibles from COS.M.O.S., Italy, in 1990. The craft displace 2,100 kg, are 7 m long, and have a range of 25 n.m.

GUIDED-MISSILE DESTROYERS [DDG]

♦ 0 (+ 3) Bangalore class (Project 15A)
Bldr: Mazagon Dock, Ltd., Mumbai

	Laid down	L	In serv.
D 63 Bangalore	26-9-03	2005	2008
D 64 . . .	2004	2006	2009
D 65 . . .	2005	2007	2010

D: 5,500 tons (6,900 fl) **S:** 28 kts **Dim:** 163.00 × 17.60 × 6.40
A: 16 . . . vertical SSM launchers (16 Brahmos missiles); 2 Shtil (SA-N-7) vertical SAM launchers. 1 100-mm 59-cal. A-190E DP; . . . CIWS; 1 quintuple 533-mm PTA-53 TT (Gidropribor SET-65E ASW torpedoes); 2 12-round RBU-6000 ASW RL; 2 helicopters
Electronics:
Radar: 1 MR-760MA Fregat-M2EM (Top Plate) 3-D air search; 23p-87 (Hot Flash) CIWS f.c.
Sonar: MGK-345 Bronza bow-mounted LF
EW: 1 Bharat-RAWL-2 early warning
M: COGAG M36E plant; 4 Mashproekt-Zorya DT-59 reversible gas turbines (64,000 shp total); 2 CP props
Electric: . . . kw tot. (4 × . . . -kw turbogenerators, 1 × . . . -kw diesel set)
Range: 5,000/. . . **Crew:** 40 officers, 320 enlisted

Remarks: Funding for three was requested in 8-98 as Project 15A; they are to have improved electronics of western design origin and incorporate stealth design features. Construction was delayed pending a redesign to incorporate both antiship and land-attack missiles variants of the Brahmos missile.

Builder's model of the Bangalore-class (Project 15A) guided missile destroyer Hans Karr, 5-05

♦ 3 Delhi class (Project 15)
Bldr: Mazagon Dock, Ltd., Mumbai

	Laid down	L	In serv.
D 60 Mysore	2-2-91	4-6-93	2-6-99
D 61 Delhi	14-11-87	1-2-91	15-11-97
D 62 Mumbai (ex-*Bombay*)	14-12-92	20-3-95	22-1-01

Delhi (D 61) Arjun Sarup, 6-05

Mumbai (D 62) Camil Busquets i Vilanova, 2005

D: 5,500 tons (6,900 fl) **S:** 28 kts **Dim:** 163.00 × 17.60 × 6.40
A: 16 Kh-35 Uran (SS-N-25 Switchblade) SSM (3M-24E missiles); 2 ZR-90 Shtil (SA-N-7) SAM syst. (2 single-rail MS-196 launchers; 48 Altair 9M-38M13 Buk-M3 missiles); 1 100-mm 59-cal. AK-100 DP; 2 single 30-mm 54-cal. AK-630M gatling AA; 8 Barak VL SAM cells; 1 quintuple 533-mm PTA-53 TT (Gidropribor SET-65E ASW torpedoes); 2 12-round RBU-6000 ASW RL; 2 Sea King Mk 42B helicopters (Sea Eagle antiship missiles and/or WASS A-244S torpedoes)

GUIDED-MISSILE DESTROYERS [DDG] *(continued)*

Mumbai (D 62)—with Sea King helicopter on the flight deck
A. A. de Kruijf, 7-05

Electronics:
Radar: 3 MR-212/201 Vaygach-U (Palm Frond) nav./surf. search; 1 Bharat RALW-02 early warning; 1 Salyut MR-755M2 Fregat-M2 (Half Plate) surf./air search; 1 Bharat Apurna (Garpun-Bal/Plank Shave) antiship missile target-desig.; 6 OP-3 (Front Dome) missile f.c.; 1 MR-145 Lev (Kite Screech) 100-mm gun f.c.; 2 MR-123 Vympel (Bass Tilt) 30-mm gun f.c.; . . . Elta EL/M 2221 missile illuminator.
Sonar: Bharat HUMVAD syst.: APSOH LF hull-mounted and VDS
EW: Elettronica-Bharat Ajanta intercept suite; Elettronica TQN-2 jammer; 2 2-round PK-2 decoy RL (200 rockets)
M: CODOG M-36N plant: 2 Mashproekt-Zorya DN-50 reversible gas turbines (27,000 shp max./23,100 shp sust. each), 2 Bergen Mek.Verk.–Garden Reach KVM-18 diesels (4,960 bhp each); 2 CP props; 54,000 shp (see Remarks)
Electric: . . . kw tot. (4 × . . . -kw turbogenerators, 1 × . . . -kw diesel set)
Range: 5,000/18 **Crew:** 40 officers, 320 enlisted

Remarks: First unit ordered 3-86 and cost $583.5 million. The third was renamed early in 2000.
Hull systems: The gas turbine installation has also been described as employing two M-36 "plants" that incorporate DT-59 turbines. Hull lines said to have been derived from the Kashin class. Have nonretracting fin stabilizers. D 61 reached 32 kts on 64,000 shp and 13 kts astern on trials. Helicopter landing aid and deck traversing equipment is installed. An NBC water washdown system is installed, and the ships are divided internally into six independent citadels with independent power and communications systems. *Mysore* has enhanced air-conditioning capability to prevent overheating of electronic components. All are equipped to serve as flagships.
Combat systems: Soviet and European weapons and European-designed/Indian-improved-and-manufactured electronics are being employed. Between 2003–2006 two Barak VL systems and their associated Elta radar illuminators were fitted in the class in place of two AK-630M gun mounts that were removed. The Bharat-built Shikari combat data system is said to be a variant of the AESN IPN-10 system and can track 12 targets and engage six simultaneously, while the Ajanta EW suite is based on the Elettronica INS-3 system. A Russian Purga ASW weapons-control system is fitted. The RALW-02 radar is a license-built Thales LW-02. Variable-depth sonars are handled by Indal-GRSE Model 15-750 deck-handling equipment. The hull-mounted component of the sonar system has also been reported to be Bharat Electronics's license-built Thales TSM 2633 Spherion. The 100-mm gun has 320 ready-service projectiles but no reloads; 12,000 rounds of 30-mm ammunition can be carried (8,000 ready service). The D 60 is said to incorporate improved electronics and the D 62 an improved sonar suite. The Russian SAM system is known as the Kashmir in Indian service. The launch system for the antiship missiles is the Russian 3R60UE system.

♦ 5 Soviet Kashin class (Project 61ME)
Bldr: 61 Kommunara Zavod 445, Nikolayev

	L	In serv.
D 51 RAJPUT (ex-*Nadezhnyy*)	9-77	30-9-80
D 52 RANA (ex-*Gubitel'nyy*)	10-78	28-6-82
D 53 RANJIT (ex-*Lovkiy*)	6-79	24-11-83
D 54 RANVIR (ex-*Tolkovoy*)	3-83	28-8-86
D 55 RANVIJAY (ex-*Tverdyy*)	2-86	15-1-88

Ranjit (D 53) Arjun Sarup, 7-03

Ranvijay (D 55) Arjun Sarup, 8-02

D: 4,050 tons (4,870 fl) **S:** 30 kts
Dim: 146.20 (134.50 wl) × 15.80 (14.00 wl) × 4.87 (hull)
A: D 51: 4 BrahMos antiship missiles—D 52–54: 4 P-20 Termit (SS-N-2C Styx) SSM—D 55: 16 Kh-35 Uran SSM (4-round KT-184 launchers; 3M-24E missiles)—all: 2 2-rail SA-N-1 Volna-P SAM syst. (32 B-601 Goa missiles); 1 twin 76.2-mm 59-cal. AK-726 DP; 4 twin 30-mm AK-230 65-cal. (D 54, 55: 4 single 30-mm 54-cal. AK-630 gatling) AA; 1 5-tube 533-mm PTA-53-61 TT; 2 12-round RBU-6000 ASW RL (192 RGB-60 rockets); 1 Ka-25 Hormone-A (D 54, 55: Ka-28 Helix-A) ASW helicopter
Electronics:
Radar: 2 Volga (Don Kay) nav.; 1 MP-310U Angara-M (Head Net-C) surf./air search; 1 MP-500 Kliver (Big Net) early warning; 2 Yatagan (Peel Group) SAM f.c.; 1 MR-105 Turel' (Owl Screech) 76.2-mm gun f.c.; 2 MR-104 Rys' (Drum Tilt) 30-mm AA f.c. (D 54, 55: MR-123 Vympel [Bass Tilt] f.c.)
Sonar: MG-335 Platina hull-mounted MF; hull-mounted HF attack; MF VDS
EW: D 51–54: 2 Nakhat-M (Watch Dog) intercept (2–18 GHz)—D 55: Ajanta intercept—all: 2 Krab-11 (Top Hat A) jammers; 2 Krab-12 (Top Hat-B) jammers; 4 16-round PK-16 decoy RL
M: COGAG M-3 plant: 4 Type M-8E gas turbines, 2 props (300 rpm max.); 96,000 shp (72,000 sust.)
Electric: 2,400 kw tot. (4 × 600-kw gas turbine sets)
Range: 900/32; 4,000/18 **Fuel:** 940 tons **Crew:** 37 officers, 350 enlisted

Remarks: New-construction Project 61E units, not conversions from former Soviet Navy units. Received Russian names for identification purposes during construction, meaning, respectively: "reliable," "destructive," "adroit," "steadfast," and "intelligent." D 51 and D 52 are based at Vishakapatnam, the others at Mumbai. D 55 was in modernization refit at Mumbai Naval Dockyard as of 2-01.
Hull systems: Fin stabilizers are fitted. The main propulsion plant is derated from that of sisters in Russian service but is less effective in tropical conditions. D 54 and D 55 have the helicopter platforms at the stern about 1 m higher to accommodate the additional height of the Helix helicopter.

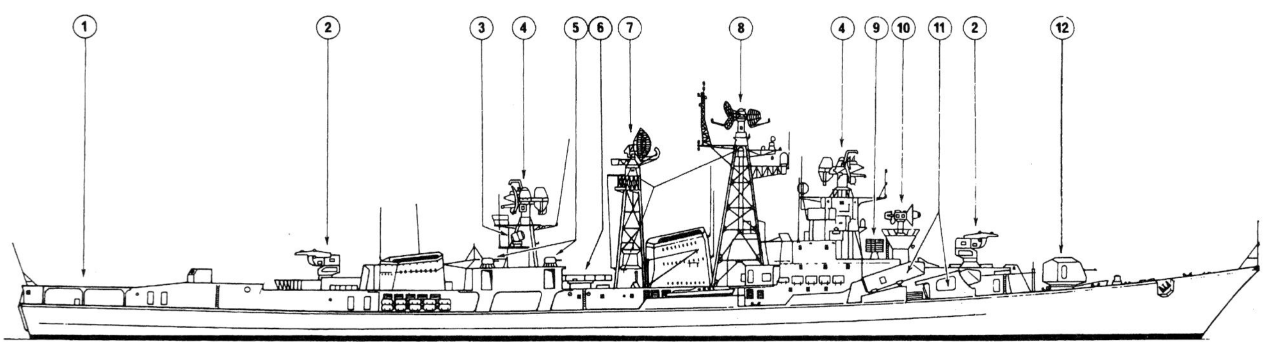

Rajput (D 51) 1. Helicopter deck atop VDS housing 2. Twin launcher for Volna-P (SA-N-1) SAM syst. 3. MR-104 Rys' (Drum Tilt) 30-mm radar gun directors 4. Yatagan (Peel Group) SAM control radars 5. Twin 30-mm AK-230 AA 6. Quintuple 533-mm TT mount 7. MR-500 Kliver (Big Net) early-warning radar 8. MP-310U Angara-M (Head Net-C) surf./air-search radar 9. RBU-6000 ASW RL (two abreast) 10. MR-105 Turel' (Owl Screech) fire-control radar for the 76.2-mm gunmount 11. P-20/21 Termit (SS-N-2C Styx) SSM launch tubes 12. Twin 76.2-mm DP gunmount
Drawing by Robert Dumas, *Flottes de Combat*

GUIDED-MISSILE DESTROYERS [DDG] *(continued)*

Combat systems: In contrast to Soviet Navy "Modified Kashins," the SS-N-2C missiles on Indian units were mounted forward and fire forward, while the after twin 76.2-mm gun mount was omitted in favor of a hangar below the main deck level in the location occupied by an aft 76.2-mm magazine in Soviet units; it is accessed via an inclined elevator. Carry 1,200 rounds for the 76.2-mm ZIF-67 gunmount. The MR-104 f.c. radars have been upgraded by DRDL in India and can detect targets operating at up to 900 kts. All are being refitted with the Ajanta EW system in place of Russian equipment. D 55 received 16 Kh-35 Uran antiship missiles in place of the SS-N-2C launchers during 2001, and D 54 is to follow. There may also be plans to replace the SA-N-1 SAM system with Barak, although one report indicates that the Russian system is being upgraded with digital fire control and an optical backup control system. D 51 was used for the initial at-sea proof launching of the new Brahmos missile on 12-2-03, with two pair of tube launchers having replaced the KT-138 launchers for P-20 Styx missiles forward.

FRIGATES [FF]

♦ 1 (+ 2 + 9) Shivalik class (Project 17)
Bldr: Mazagon Dockyard, Mumbai

	Laid down	L	In serv.
F . . . SHIVALIK	11-7-01	18-4-03	30-6-06
F . . . SAHYADRI	2002	4-6-04	2007
F . . . SATPURA	17-3-03	27-5-05	2008

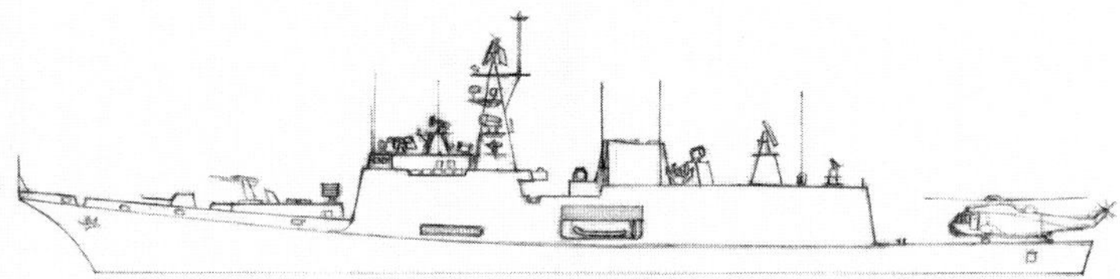

Project 17 class Drawing by Mritunjoy Mazumdar, 2003

Shivalik—at launching photo via Mritunjoy Mazumdar, 7-03

D: 4,600 tons (5,000+ fl) **S:** 32 kts **Dim:** 143.0 × 16.9 × 4.5
A: 8 3S-14NE vertical SSM launchers (8 3M-54E Klub-N or Brahmos missiles); 1 ZR-90 Shtil/Uragan (SA-N-7) SAM sys. (MS-196 launcher, 24 9M-38M13 Smerch missiles); 1 76-mm 62-cal. OTO Melara SuperRapid DP; 2 Kashtan CIWS (8 missiles on-mount; 64 9M-311/SA-N-11 Grison missiles; 2 30-mm gatling AA per mount also); 2 4-round Fasta-series SAM syst. (Igla-2M missiles); 2 pair fixed 533-mm fixed DTA-53 TT (SET-65E ASW and 53-65KE antiship torpedoes); 1 12-round RBU-6000 ASW RL (60 Splav 90R rockets); 2 helicopters (Ka-31 and/or Ka-28 Helix or Sea King Mk 42B and/or Dhruv helicopters)
Electronics:
Radar: 1 Decca BridgeMaster-E ARPA nav.; 2 MR-212/201-1 nav./surf. search; 1 MR-760MA Fregat-M2EM (Top Plate) 3-D air search; 1 Bharat RAWL-2 early warning; 2 Oerlikon-Contraves-Bharat Shikari (TMX-Ka) 76-mm gun f.c.; 4 OP-3 (Front Dome) SAM f.c.; 2 3P-87 (Hot Flash) on-mount CIWS f.c.; 1 Bharat Apurna (Garpun-E/Plank Shave) missile surf. target desig.
Sonar: Bharat-Thales HUS 001 (TSM 2630 Spherion) bow-mounted MF
EW: . . .
M: CODOG: 2 G.E.-HAL LM-2500 IEC gas turbines, 2 Kirloskar-Pielstick 16PA6 STC diesels (6,700 bhp each); 2 LIPS CP props; 63,400 shp max.
Electric: 3,200 kw tot. (4 × 800-kw Wärtsilä-Cummins GTA 50 G3 diesel sets)
Range: . . . / . . . **Crew:** 25 officers, 225 enlisted

Remarks: Named for mountain ranges. During 5-99, approval was given to begin construction of the first of three Project 17 "stealth" frigates of Indian design. Total cost for the program is to be $562.5 million. The construction schedule appears optimistic, given past Indian naval shipbuilding performance. Work on fabricating modules for the first unit began on 18-12-00. Severnoye Design Bureau, Russia, and DCN, France, reportedly are providing design and technical assistance, with the basic configuration being that of a much-enlarged version of the Talwar class below. Early plans call for as many as 12 units in several different batches, with the final ship entering service around 2027.
Hull systems: The first diesel engine for this class was made by SEMT-Pielstick in France; the others are being built at Nishak by Kirloskar Oil Engines, Ltd., on license. The Canadian Davis Engineering Infra-Red Suppression System has been used to reduce exhaust temperatures. The gas turbines will employ an Integrated Engine Control (IEC) system.
Combat systems: The SAM system is referred to as the Kashmir system in India, and its f.c. system will be able to engage six targets at once. The Shikari f.c. radar is based on the Contraves TMX. May be fitted with the Indian-Russian Brahmos ASM and perhaps the French Aster-15 SAM, though the armament fits are still in the early stages.

♦ 3 (+ 3) Talwar class (Russian Project 11356)
Bldr: Baltiyskiy Zavod, St. Petersburg, Russia

	Laid down	L	In serv.
F 40 TALWAR (ex-*Dozornyy*, ex-*Kashmir*)	10-3-99	12-5-00	18-6-03
F 43 TRISHUL (ex-*Udarnyy*, ex-*Arunchal Pradesh*)	24-9-99	24-11-00	25-6-03
F 44 TABAR (ex-*Toofan*, ex-*Sikkim*)	26-5-00	25-5-01	31-7-04

Trishul (F 43) Arjun Sarup, 6-05

Tabar (F 44) Frank Findler, 5-04

Trishul (F 43)—note the Helix helicopter visible on the flight deck
Arjun Sarup, 6-05

Talwar (F 40) Ralph Edwards, 7-03

FRIGATES [FF] *(continued)*

D: 3,300 tons normal (3,780 fl) **S:** 32 kts (30 sust.)
Dim: 125.3 (116.9 pp) × 15.2 (13.2 wl) × 4.9 (hull; 7.3 over sonar dome)
A: 8 3S-14NE vertical SSM launchers (8 3M-54TE Klub-N missiles); 1 ZR-90 Shtil/Uragan (SA-N-7) SAM system (single-rail MS-196 launcher, 24 9M-38M13 Smerch missiles); 1 100-mm 59-cal. A-190E DP; 2 Kashtan CIWS (8 missiles on-mount; 64 9M-311/SA-N-11 Grison missiles; 2 30-mm gatling AA per mount also); 2 4-round Fasta-series SAM launchers (Igla-1E missiles); 2 pair fixed 533-mm DTA-53 TT (SET-65E ASW and 53-65KE antiship torpedoes); 1 12-round RBU-6000 ASW RL (60 Splav 90R rockets); 1 Ka-31 or Ka-28 Helix or ALH helicopter
Electronics:
Radar: 1 Kelvin-Hughes Nucleus-2 6000A nav.; 2 MR-212/201-1 nav./surf. search; 1 MR-760MA Fregat-M2EM (Top Plate) 3-D air search; 1 MR-352 Pozitiv-E (Cross Dome) CIWS target desig.; 1 MR-221 100-mm f.c.; 4 OP-3 (Front Dome) SAM f.c.; 2 3P-87 (Hot Flash) on-mount CIWS f.c.; 1 Garpun-E (Plank Shave) missile surface target desig.
Sonar: Zvezda M-1 suite: MGK-345 Bronza bow-mounted LF and SSN-137 (Steer Hide) LF VDS (see remarks)
EW: ASOR intercept/jammer suite; 8 10-round PK-10 Smelyy decoy syst. (KT-216 RL)
M: COGAG M-7 plant: 2 DS-71 cruise gas turbines (9,000 shp each), 2 DT-59 boost gas turbines (19,500 shp each); 2 5-bladed props; 55,284 shp max.
Electric: 3,200 kw tot. (4 × 800-kw Wärtsilä-Cummins GTA 50 G3 diesel sets)
Range: 700/30; 3,900/20; 4,500/18 **Fuel:** 800 tons **Endurance:** 30 days
Crew: 200 tot.

Remarks: Government approval for construction for the first three was given in 5-98, and a contract was signed on 17-11-97; the Russian yard was said to be behind schedule due to misappropriation of two-thirds of the $64-million advance payment by India. The keel-laying dates above refer to the placing of the first hull section on the construction ways; at that time, about a third of the hull modules for the first ship had been completed. Plans to build three more of the class in India were approved in 6-99, but none have been ordered. The Indian designation is Project 17A. Program cost reported at $931.5 million. The first was only about 30% complete at launch. The names mean "Shield," "Trident," and "Axe," respectively. The Russian name *Dozornyy* was applied to the *Talwar* through sea trials for administrative purposes. Delivery of the *Talwar* was delayed further because of hull cracking below the waterline, both on builder's trials and again during owner's sea trials. All three are to be assigned to the Western Naval Command. Throughout 2003 problems with the Shitil missile system integration caused additional delays, though the first vessel was turned over to the Indian Navy in 6-03. India reportedly imposed $40 million in fines on Russia for the long delivery delay. Plans to build three additional units were approved in 6-99 and construction negotiations with Russia began 12-05. All three existing ships are assigned to the Western Naval Command.
Hull systems: Hull and propulsion system similar to the 1960s-vintage Krivak, with forecastle extended further aft. Entirely new superstructure, shaped to reduce the radar return. The Indian Navy describes the design as having "partial stealth" capabilities. Maximum propeller rpm is 300. Overall length also reported as 124.8 m and full load displacement as 3,620 tons.
Combat systems: The combat data and control system, known as Trebovaniye-M, can track 250 targets simultaneously. The 3M-54E supersonic antiship missiles employ vertical launchers and are to have a range of up to 300 km; Indian officials have stated that the missiles will also have a land-attack role. The 100-mm gun has 350 ready-service rounds, while each Kashtan CIWS system has 32 missiles and 3,000 rounds of 30-mm ammunition. The bow-mounted sonar has a range of 2–6 km and the reported VDS a range of 8 km, although at least the *Talwar* apparently has no provision for a VDS installation. The hull-mounted sonar has also been referred to as the "Humsa," and the VDS as the "SSSN-113." The 100-mm gun fires at up to 80 rds/min and is controlled by the 5P-10E Puma control system.

♦ 3 Improved Godavari class (Project 16A)
Bldr: Garden Reach SB & Eng., Calcutta

	Laid down	L	In serv.
F 31 Bramaputra	1989	29-1-94	14-4-00
F 32 Betwa	22-8-94	26-2-98	7-7-04
F 37 Beas	26-2-98	2002	11-7-05

Bramaputra (F 31) Hans Karr, 11-03

Bramaputra (F 31) Mritunjoy Mazumdar, 2-01

D: 3,850 tons (4,450 fl) **S:** 27 kts **Dim:** 126.4 (123.6 pp) × 14.5 × 4.6 (hull)
A: 16 Kh-35 Uran SSM (4 4-round KT-184 launchers; 3M-24E missiles); 1 8-round Barak vertical-launch point-defense SAM syst.; 1 76-mm 62-cal. OTO Melara SuperRapid DP; 4 single 30-mm 54-cal. AK-630 gatling AA; 2 triple 324-mm ILAS-3 ASW TT (WAAS A-244S or NST-58 torpedoes); 1 Sea King Mk 42B ASW helicopter; 1 Chetak or ALH liaison helicopter
Electronics:
Radar: 1 Decca Bridgemaster-E nav.; 1 Bharat Rashmi (ZW-06) surf. search; 1 Bharat RAWS-03 surf./air search; 1 Bharat RAWL-02 early warning; 1 Bharat Aparna surf. targeting; 3 Oerlikon-Contraves-Bharat Shikari (TMX-Ka) f.c.
Sonar: Bharat-Thales HUS 001 (TSM 2630 Spherion) bow-mounted MF; provision for Thales towed passive array
TACAN: Bharat FT13-S/M
EW: Bharat INDRA or Ajanta Mk IIC suite, 4 24-round Wallop/Grintek Ultrabarricade decoy RL; Graseby G 738 towed torpedo decoy
E/O: 1 OFC-3 gun f.c.
M: 2 sets Bhopal Eng. Y160 geared steam turbines; 2 5-bladed props; 31,000 shp
Boilers: 2 Babcock & Wilcox, 3-drum; 38.7 kg/cm^2, 450° C
Electric: . . . kw tot. (2 × 750-kw turbogenerators, 3 × . . . -kw diesel sets)
Range: 4,500/12; 3,500/18
Crew: 40 officers, 313 enlisted (incl. 13 aviation)

Remarks: Design is very similar to the previous *Godavari* class but with updated weapon and sensor suites. The difficulty in obtaining equipment ordered in Russia prior to the 1991 revolution delayed completion, and F 31 was commissioned without a SAM system. Named for rivers.
Hull systems: The propulsion system duplicates that of the *Godavari* class. The design is nonstealthy, with high, vertical hull sides, much topside clutter, and numerous corner reflectors. Have one pair of nonretractable fin stabilizers.
Combat systems: Employ a Bharat Electronics–developed variant of the Contraves IPN-10 (SADOC-1) combat direction system, with 10 linked Barco MPRD 9651 display/control consoles, linked by an FMC Unicom databus. Rashmi is an indigenously made version of the Thales ZW-06 radar, while RAWL-02 is an updated version of the Thales LW-02, and RAWS-03 is a version of the Thales DA-05. The Aparna target detection and tracking radar, a licensed-production version of the Russian Garpun-E (Plank Shave), operates in the X-band and is dedicated solely to the antiship missile fire-control system. An infrared search-and-track sensor is to be fitted later. A JRC commercial Inmarsat SATCOM terminal is fitted.
Two 8-cell Barak point-defense missile systems for each ship were ordered on 6-2-01. The OTO Melara 76-mm 62-cal. gun employs South African projectiles with Naschem and Fuchs anti–sea skimmer fuzes. The nomenclature for the sonar set has also been given as the HUMVAD.

♦ 3 Godavari class (Type 16)
Bldr: Mazagon Docks, Mumbai

	Laid down	L	In serv.
F 20 Godavari	2-6-78	15-5-80	10-12-83
F 21 Gomati	1981	20-3-84	16-4-88
F 22 Ganga	1980	15-11-81	1-1-86

Ganga (F 22)—the protruding sponsons supporting the antiship missile launchers readily distinguish this class from the later Bramaputra class
Mritunjoy Mazumdar, 2-01

Ganga (F 22) Kapil Chandni via Mritunjoy Mazumdar 12-02

D: 3,700 tons (4,300 fl) **S:** 29 kts **Dim:** 125.6 (123.6 pp) × 14.4 × 4.05 (hull)
A: 4 P-20/21 Termit (SS-N-2C Styx) SSM—F 22 only: 3 8-round Barak vertical-launch point-defense SAM syst.—F 20, 21 only: 1 2-rail Osa-ME (SA-N-4) SAM syst. (20 9M-33M Gecko missiles)—all: 1 twin 57-mm 70-cal. AK-257 DP; 4 twin 30-mm 65-cal. AK-230 AA; 2 triple 324-mm ILAS-3 ASW TT (WASS A-244S or NST-58 torpedoes); 1 Sea King Mk 42B ASW helicopter; 1 Chetak helicopter

FRIGATES [FF] *(continued)*

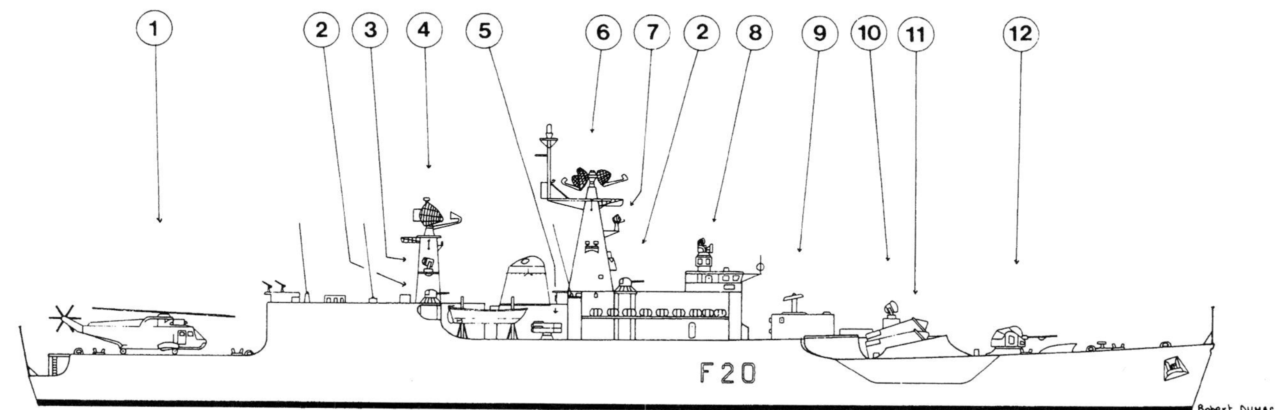

Godavari (F 20) 1. Sea King Mk 42 helicopter 2. Twin 30-mm AK-230 AA 3. MR-104 Rys' (Drum Tilt) 30-mm gun radar directors 4. Bharat RALW-02 early-warning radar 5. Triple ILAS-3 ASW TT 6. MR-310U Angara-M (Head Net-C) surf./air-search radar 7. ZW-06A nav./surf. search radar 8. MPZ-310 (Pop Group) SAM fire-control radar 9. ZIF-122 launcher for the Osa-ME (SA-N-4) SAM system 10. MR-103 Bars (Muff Cob) radar/electro-optical director for the 57-mm gunmount 11. P-20/21 Termit (SS-N-2C Styx) SSM 12. Twin 57-mm AK-257 DP gunmount
Drawing by Robert Dumas, *Flottes de Combat*

Electronics:
Radar: 2 Thales-Bharat ZW-06A surf. search; 1 MR-310U Angara-M (Head Net-C) air/surf. search; 1 Bharat RALW-02 early warning; 1 MPZ-310 (Pop Group) SAM f.c.; 1 MR-103 Bars (Muff Cob) 57-mm gun f.c.; 2 MR-104 Rys' (Drum Tilt) 30-mm gun f.c—F 22 also: Elta STAR air-search/target desig.; Elta EL/M 2221 missile illuminator
Sonar: Bharat-Thales TSM-2630 Spherion hull-mounted MF—F 20: Canadian Westinghouse SQS-505
TACAN: Bharat FT13-S/M
EW: Bharat Ajanta intercept; 4 24-round Wallop/Grintek Ultrabarricade decoy RL; Graseby G 738 towed torpedo decoy
M: 2 sets Bhopal Eng. geared steam turbines; 2 5-bladed props; 31,000 shp
Boilers: 2 Babcock & Wilcox, 3-drum; 38.7 kg/cm^2, 450° C
Electric: 3,000 kw tot. (2 × 750-kw turbogenerators, 3 × 500-kw diesel sets)
Range: 4,500/12 **Fuel:** 438 tons
Crew: 51 officers, 262 enlisted (362 accomm.)

Remarks: Design derived from the *Leander* class, with the same propulsion plant but considerably larger hull. Electronics and weapons systems a very diverse selection of Western European–designed/Indian-built and Russian systems. Are named for rivers.
Hull systems: Steel superstructure. Two pairs Vosper nonretractable fin stabilizers. The hangar is sized for two Sea Kings, but only one (often with a Chetak light helo) is normally carried for stability reasons. A helicopter landing and traversing system is fitted. Carry 91 tons fresh water.
Combat systems: The Selenia IPN-10 combat data system is employed. Bharat's RALW-02 radar uses the same antenna as the Thales DA-08. There are two backup manual directors for the twin AK-230 30-mm AA guns and two for the AK-57 57-mm mount. Probably also carry Igla-2M shoulder-launched heat-seeking point-defense SAMs.

Dunagiri (F 36)—note the small telescoping helicopter hangar and the pit abaft the flight deck for the Limbo mortar Ralph Edwards, 2-01

♦ 4 U.K. Leander class

Bldr: Mazagon Docks, Mumbai

	Laid down	L	In serv.
F 35 Udaygiri	14-9-70	24-10-72	18-2-76
F 36 Dunagiri	1-73	9-3-74	5-5-77
F 41 Taragiri	10-75	25-10-76	16-5-80
F 42 Vindhyagiri	5-11-76	12-11-77	8-7-81

Himgiri (F 34)—since stricken Brian Morrison, 2-01

D: F 35–36: 2,682 tons (2,962 fl)—F 41, 42: 2,970 tons (3,250 tons fl)
S: 30 kts **Dim:** 113.38 × 13.1 × 4.27 (F 41, 42: 5.50 max.)
A: 1 twin 114-mm 45-cal. Vickers Mk 6 DP; 2 twin 30-mm 65-cal. AK-230 AA—F 35–36: 1 3-round Limbo Mk 10 ASW mortar; 1 Chetak helicopter—F 41 and 42: 1 2-round 375-mm Bofors ASW RL; 2 triple 324-mm ILAS-3 ASW TT; 1 Sea King helicopter
Electronics:
Radar: 1 Decca 1226 nav.; 1 Thales ZW-06 surf. search; 1 Bhara RALW-02 early warning; 1 Thales M 44 gun f.c.
Sonar: F 35: APSOH hull mounted—F 36: Can. Westinghouse SQS-505 MF hull-mounted—F 35–36: Can. Westinghouse SQS-502 target depth–determining (for Limbo)—F 41, 42: Thales Diodon hull-mounted MF

Vindhyagiri (F 42)—the Bofors ASW rocket launcher is mounted at the forecastle break, just forward of the twin 114-mm gunmount John Mortimer, 2-01

TACAN: F 41 and 42 only: Bharat FT13-S/M
EW: Bharat Ajanta-P intercept; Racal Cutlass jammer; Telegon-4 HFD/F; Graseby G 738 towed torpedo decoy syst.
M: 2 sets Bhopal Eng. geared steam turbines; 2 5-bladed props; 30,000 shp
Boilers: 2 Babcock & Wilcox, 3-drum; 38.7 kg/cm^2, 450° C
Electric: 2,500 kw tot.
Range: approx. 4,500/12 **Fuel:** 382 tons **Crew:** 40 officers, 370 enlisted

Remarks: The first two built were very similar to British versions of the *Leander* class, but later units were progressively improved, using Thales-designed radars and an ever-greater proportion of Indian-built components. Are very crowded, due to unusually large crews. F 41 experienced severe fire damage in 1994 that took several years to repair. F 36 suffered a dockyard fire on 10-11-99. Although reported stricken in 1997, F 35 was officially stated to be in service and underwent a refit at Mumbai during 2001 to the same configuration as F 36. The similar *Krishna* (F 46, ex-British *Andromeda*), purchased in 5-94, is used strictly for training and is described under [AXT].
Combat systems: F 41 and F 42 have very large telescoping hangars and carry their twin Bofors ASW RLs on the forecastle; their hangars can accommodate a Sea King Mk 42 ASW helicopter, and their flight decks incorporate Canadian Bear Trap haul-down gear. F 41 and F 42 also have openings in the hull sides beneath the helicopter deck at the stern. F 36 has been refitted with smaller telescoping helicopter hangars, and F 36 has had her variable-depth sonar removed. The former two Sea Cat SAM launchers have been replaced in the entire class by two twin AK-230 gunmounts salvaged from discarded Osa-series missile boats. The ships probably also carry Igla-2M shoulder-launched heat-seeking point-defense SAMs.
Disposals: *Nilgiri* (F 33) was stricken on 31-5-96 and *Himgiri* (F 34) on 6-5-05.

CORVETTES [FFL]

♦ 0 (+ 4 + ?) . . . (Project 28)

Bldr.: Garden Reach Shipbuilding and Engineering, Calcutta

D: 1,800 tons light, 2,400 tons (fl) **S:** 22 kts **Dim:** 103 × 12.4 × 3.5
A: 1 76.2-mm/62 cal. OTO Melara, 2 12-round RBU-6000 ASW RL, 2 triple 324-mm ILAS-3 ASW TT; 1 Helix (Ka-28PL) ASW or 1 HAL Dhruv helicopter
Electronics: Radar: . . .
M: CODAG: 2 . . . gas turbines, 2 diesels; 2 CP props
Range: 7,500/ . . . **Endurance:** 15 days **Crew:** 120

Remarks: Proposed class, still in the preliminary design phase. Intended to perform offshore patrol, 200-n.m. economic zone patrol, fisheries protection, search-and-rescue duties and also to be employable as survey ships. Would have a helicopter facility and be capable of operating aircraft in up to Sea State 4 and remaining effective in up to Sea State 7. May eventually be armed with SSM and SAM missile systems. Could enter service post-2009.

♦ 8 Khukri class (Project 25/25A*)

	Bldr	Laid down	L	In serv.
P 44 Kirpan	Garden Reach SB, Calcutta	15-11-85	16-8-88	12-1-91
P 46 Khutar	Mazagon DY, Mumbai	13-9-86	15-4-89	7-6-90
P 47 Khanjar	Garden Reach SB, Calcutta	15-11-85	16-8-88	22-10-91
P 49 Khukri	Mazagon DY, Mumbai	27-9-85	3-12-86	23-8-89
P 61 Kora*	Garden Reach SB, Calcutta	10-1-90	23-9-92	10-8-98
P 62 Kirch*	Garden Reach SB, Calcutta**	1992	1996	22-1-01
P 63 Kulish*	Garden Reach SB, Calcutta	31-1-92	18-8-97	20-8-01
P 64 Kharmuk*	Garden Reach SB, Calcutta	27-8-97	6-4-00	2002

** Fitted out by Mazagon DY

Kora (P 61) Hartmut Ehlers, 9-03

Kirpan (P 44)—Project 25 version, with four antiship missiles Ralph Edwards, 2-01

D: 1,350 tons (fl; P 61 and later: 1,400 fl) **S:** 28 kts (25 sust.)
Dim: 91.11 × 10.45 × 2.50 (hull; 4.45 max.)
A: First four: 4 P 20/21 Termit (SS-N-2C) Styx SSM—P 61 and 62: 16 Kh-35 Uran-E (SS-N-25 Switchblade) SSM (4 4-round KT-184 launchers; 3M-24EM6 missiles)—all: 1 76.2-mm 59-cal. AK-176M (P 62 and later: 76-mm 62-cal. OTO Melara SuperRapid) DP; 2 single 30-mm 54-cal. AK-630 gatling AA; 2 SA-N-5 shoulder-launched SAM positions (Igla-2M missiles)
Electronics:
Radar: 1 Bharat 1245 (P 62: Bharat Rani) nav.; 1 MR-352 Pozitiv-E (Cross Dome) air search; 1 Bharat Aparna antiship missile target desig.; 1 MR-123 Vympel (Bass Tilt) gun f.c. (P 62 and later: 1 Oerlikon-Contraves-Bharat Shikari (TMX-Ka) gun f.c.)
Sonar: none
EW: all: Bharat Ajanta-P Mk II intercept—first four: 2 or 4 16-round PK-16 decoy RL—P 61 and later: 4 10-round PK-10 decoy RL—all: NPOL towed torpedo decoy
E/O: 1 Oventus infrared surveillance and tracking
M: 2 Kirloskar-SEMT-Pielstick 18 PA6 V280 diesels; 2 CP props; 14,400 bhp (10,600 sust.)
Electric: 1,400 kw tot. (4 × 350-kw, 415-V, 50-Hz, diesel-driven sets)
Range: 4,000/16 **Fuel:** 140 m^3 **Crew:** 9 officers, 70 enlisted

Remarks: Intended to replace the Petya class. First two ordered 12-83, next pair in 1985; units five through eight were ordered 4-90 as Project 25A and were originally to have incorporated gas turbines in the propulsion system and a Soviet-supplied Osa-M SAM system. Four more were at one time planned. Construction of these fairly simple ships has taken a great deal of time. P 61 carried a crew of 14 officers and 120 enlisted during a Persian Gulf cruise in 3-99. Based at Mumbai and Vishakhapatnam.
Hull systems: The diesels in the first four were made in France. Have nonretracting fin stabilizers and are fully air-conditioned. P 61 and later displace 50 additional tons and are 91.16 m overall.
Combat systems: Have no ASW capability. The Alenia IPN-10 combat data system (license-built as the Vympal system by Bharat in unit two onward) is fitted. All have a Magnavox MX 1102-NV NAVSAT receiver and an STN Atlas Elektronik echo sounder. Pozitiv-E air-search radar, in a radome (NATO Cross Dome) at the masthead, is a Russian set with a 70–75 n.m. range and was derived from the target designation component of the Cross Sword radar control system for the Soviet SA-N-9 SAM system. No helicopter hangars are fitted. P 61 and later have helicopter landing systems designed by SOFMA of France, carry four decoy rocket launchers, and have the Ajanta-P Mk II EW system. In P 62 and later, the Russian 76.2-mm gun has been replaced by an OTO Melara 76-mm 62-cal. SuperRapid DP mount with a European-designed f.c. radar and control system. In P 61 and later, the Kh-35 antiship missiles can be launched at 1-sec. intervals. *Kulish* and *Kharmuk* are to have only eight antiship missiles to save on topweight.

Note: The last remaining Soviet Petya-III-class corvettes, *Anjadip* (P 73) and *Amini* (P 75), were decommissioned in 2003 and 2006, respectfully.

PATROL SHIPS [PS]

♦ 6 Sukanya class

	Bldr	Laid down	L	In serv.
P 50 Sukanya	Korea-Tacoma, Masan	. . .	1989	31-8-89
P 51 Subhadra	Korea-Tacoma, Masan	. . .	1989	25-1-90
P 52 Suvarna	Korea-Tacoma, Masan	. . .	22-8-90	4-4-91
P 53 Savitri	Hindustan SY, Vishakhapatnam	6-88	23-5-89	27-11-90
P 55 Sharda	Hindustan SY, Vishakhapatnam	9-88	22-8-90	27-10-91
P 56 Sujata	Hindustan SY, Vishakhapatnam	11-88	25-10-91	3-11-93

Sharda (P 55) Arjun Sarup, 4-05

Suvarna (P 52) Arjun Sarup, 8-03

D: 1,650 tons (1,890 fl) **S:** 21.7 kts **Dim:** 101.95 (96.00 pp) × 11.50 × 3.40
A: P 55: 2 25-mm 80-cal. AA mounts—all: 1 40-mm 60-cal. Bofors Mk 3 AA; . . . Igla-2M shoulder-launched SAMs; 4 single 12.7-mm mg; 1 Chetak helicopter (P 1: Dhanush ballistic missiles; no helicopter)
Electronics:
Radar: 1 Bharat 1245 nav.; 1 Decca 2459 surf. search
TACAN: P 51 only: Bharat FT13-S/M
EW: P 51 only: Bharat Ajanta-P Mk II intercept
M: 2 Kirloskar-SEMT-Pielstick 16 PA6 V280 diesels; 2 props; 12,800 bhp
Range: 7,000/15 **Fuel:** 300 tons + 40 tons aviation fuel **Endurance:** 60 days
Crew: 10 officers, 60 enlisted (accomm. for 16 officers, 141 enlisted)

Remarks: Construction funded by the Oil and Natural Gas Commission. First three ordered from South Korea 3-87, and the others, built with Korean assistance, in 8-87. Three more were ordered for the Indian Coast Guard in 1990. Intended for offshore patrol vessel duties for the protection of oil platforms and the Indian economic exclusion zone. P 51 acts as trials ship for the Dhanush ballistic-missile system and has had the helicopter deck strengthened and converted into a missile launch pad. Two missiles can be housed in the helicopter hangar.
Hull systems: Have helicopter beacon, fin stabilizers, firefighting water monitor on hangar roof, pollution-control equipment, a towing capability, and Inmarsat SATCOM. Carry 60 tons fresh water and 9 tons lube oil and are fitted with freshwater generators.
Combat systems: The 40-mm gun is a simple Mk 3 powered mounting with local control only. A dual 30-mm 2A42 AA/12.7-mm Medak AA mount may be substituted. Carry a rigid inflatable inspection dinghy to starboard. In 2003 P 55 was seen fitted with two 25-mm 80-cal. AA mounts atop the pilothouse; other units are likely to receive this new fit as well. P 51 was altered during 1999 at Mumbai to act as trials

PATROL SHIPS [PS] *(continued)*

ship for a navalized version of the Dhanush ballistic missile; the entire class may be refitted to launch the missile, with vertical launchers in place of the helicopter flight deck. P 51 conducted the first launch at sea on 11-4-00 at the Balasore Test Range, Orissa. The missiles were stored in the helicopter hangar and moved to a stabilized platform set into the helicopter deck for erection and launching. P 51 is also equipped with EW gear, SATCOM, and a new navigational radar. Sister P 54 was transferred to Sri Lanka in 2000.

Disposal note: All Nanuchka-II-class guided missile patrol combatants have been retired. *Hosdurg* (K 73, ex-*Uragan*) was stricken in 6-99, *Vijaydurg* (K 71, ex-*Priliv*) in 2002 and *Sindhudurg* (K 72, ex-*Priboy*) in 2004.

GUIDED-MISSILE PATROL CRAFT [PTG]

♦ 2 (+ 2) Tarantul-IV class (Project 12418)

	Bldr	L	In serv.
K 91 Pralaya	Mazagon Goa SY, Goa	14-12-00	18-12-02
K 92 Prabal	Mazagon Dock, Mumbai	28-9-00	11-4-02

D: 445 tons (500 fl) **S:** 40 kts (35 sust.)
Dim: 56.9 × 13.00 (max.; 8.75 wl) × 2.65 (hull; 4.51 props)
A: 16 Kh-35 Uran-E (SS-N-25 Switchblade) SSM (4 4-round KT-184 launchers; 3M-24EM6 missiles); 1 76-mm 62-cal. OTO Melara SuperRapid DP; 1 4-round Strela-3 (SA-N-8) SAM syst. (12 Igla-2M missiles); 2 single 30-mm 54-cal. AK-630M gatling AA; 2 single 7.62-mm mg
Electronics:
Radar: 1 BEL Rani nav.; 1 Pozitiv-E (Cross Dome) air search; 1 Bharat Aparna (Garpun-BalE) surf. target detection/desig.; 1 Bharat Lynx gun f.c.
EW: . . . . intercept, 2 . . . decoy RL
M: M-15E COGAG plant: 2 DMR-76 cruise gas turbines (4,000 shp each), 2 PR-77 boost gas turbines (12,000 shp each); 2 props; 32,000 shp
Electric: 500 kw tot. (2 × 200-kw, 1 × 100-kw diesel sets; 415 V, 50 Hz a.c.)
Range: 760/43; 1,650/12 **Fuel:** 122,634 liters **Endurance:** 10 days
Crew: 44 total

Remarks: An improvement over an export version of the Tarantul design offered by Russia in 1993. *Prabal* was laid down on 30-8-98.
Hull systems: Maximum speed listed is achievable in 15-deg. C air temperature; 35 kts is said to be achievable under tropical conditions. Indian press sources claim that the craft are powered by one G.E. LM-2500 gas turbine rated at 23,500 shp and two MTU 12V538 TB92 diesels rated at 5,110 bhp each, in a CODOG installation providing a 36-kt maximum speed; range is said to be 2,000/20 on diesels or 400/36 on the gas turbine. Two additional units are under construction.
Combat systems: The Aparna (a license-built version of the Russian Garpun radar) radar system can track 15 targets simultaneously, in either active or passive mode. The navigational radar was manufactured locally by BEL as the "Rani."

♦ 10 Tarantul-I class (Project 1241RE)

	Bldr	L	In serv.
K 40 Veer	Volodarskiy SY, Rybinsk	10-86	12-5-87
K 41 Nirbhik	Volodarskiy SY, Rybinsk	10-87	3-2-88
K 42 Nipat	Volodarskiy SY, Rybinsk	11-88	15-1-89
K 43 Nishank	Volodarskiy SY, Rybinsk	6-89	12-9-89
K 44 Nirghat	Volodarskiy SY, Rybinsk	3-90	4-6-90
K 45 Vibhuti	Mazagon Dock, Mumbai	26-4-90	3-6-91
K 46 Vipul	Mazagon Dock, Mumbai	3-1-91	16-3-92
K 47 Vinash	Mazagon Goa SY, Goa	24-1-92	20-11-93
K 48 Vidyut	Mazagon Goa SY, Goa	12-12-92	16-1-95
K 83 Nashak	Mazagon Dock, Mumbai	12-11-93	29-12-94

Vipul (K 46) Alexandre Sheldon-Duplaix, 10-02

Nirbhik (K 41)—with boost gas turbine exhaust doors open in the transom stern Brian Morrison, 2-01

Pralaya (K 91)—note all sixteen Kh-35 missile tubes installed photo via Mritunjoy Mazumdar, 2002

GUIDED-MISSILE PATROL CRAFT [PTG] *(continued)*

D: 385 tons light (455 normal, 477 full load) **S:** 43 kts
Dim: 56.92 (49.50 pp) × 10.55 (9.40 wl) × 2.14 (hull; 4.0 props)
A: 4 P-20/21 Termit (SS-N-2C Styx) SSM; 1 76.2-mm 59-cal. AK-176 DP; 1 4-round SA-N-8 SAM syst. (12 Igla-2M missiles); 2 single 30-mm 54-cal. AK-630 gatling AA; 4 single 7.62-mm mg
Electronics:
Radar: 1 Kivach-3 or Decca BridgeMaster-E nav.; 1 Bharat Aparna or Garpun-E (Plank Shave) surface targeting; 1 MR-123 Vympel (Bass Tilt) gun f.c.
EW: K 40–44, 46: Ajanta Mk II intercept—all: 2 16-round PK-16 decoy RL
M: M-15E COGAG plant: 2 DMR-76 cruise gas turbines (4,000 shp each), 2 PR-77 boost gas turbines (12,000 shp each); 2 props; 32,000 shp
Electric: 500 kw tot. (2 × 200-kw, 1 × 100-kw diesel sets; 415 V, 50 Hz a.c.)
Range: 760/43; 1,400/13 **Fuel:** 122,634 liters **Endurance:** 10 days
Crew: 5 officers, 52 enlisted

Remarks: First five ordered 1984 for delivery 1986–89 from the USSR. Six to be built by Mazagon Dockyard at Mumbai were ordered 1-87, followed by orders for a reported nine to be built at Mazagon's Goa facility and three or more at Garden Reach Shipbuilding, Calcutta. Some sources indicate that as many as 35 were planned, but only 11 appear to have been built. All are assigned to the 22nd Missile Vessel Squadron. Sister *Prahak* (K 98) sank following a collision with a civilian vessel on 2-4-06.
Hull systems: Stainless-steel-alloy, seven-watertight-compartment hull with aluminum alloy superstructure, decks, and internal bulkheads. Very strongly constructed and rugged. Have difficulty maneuvering below 10 kts. Beginning with the units to be delivered in 1993, it had been intended to power the craft with one HAL-G.E. LM-2500 gas turbine (28,000 shp) and two Kirloskar-MTU 12V538 TB92 diesels (3,000 bhp max., 2,555 bhp sust.), driving two shafts in a CODOG arrangement, but all craft to date have had the standard, Russian-supplied propulsion system.
Combat systems: Weapons system employs analog computers and has many backup features. Normally carry two infrared-homing and two radar-homing missiles. The Garpun-E (NATO Plank Shave) radar set (license produced by Bharat as the Aparna for later units) can also serve as a passive radar intercept receiver. Carry 252 ready-service 76.2-mm rounds and another 150 in reserve. The 7.62-mm mg are mounted at the base of the mast, two per side.

Disposal notes: All remaining units of the Russian *Osa*-II (Project 205ME) -class guided missile patrol craft, had been decommissioned and stricken by 2005. Their missiles had long since been removed.

PATROL CRAFT [PC]

♦ 4 Soviet Pauk-II class (Project 1241PE)
Bldr: Volodarskiy SY, Rybinsk

	In serv.		In serv.
P 33 Abhay	3-89	P 35 Akshay	1-91
P 34 Ajay	24-1-90	P 36 Agray	2-91

Ajay (P 34) Brian Morrison, 2-01

Abhay (P 33)—note the dipping sonar compartment extending over the stern Brian Morrison, 2-01

D: 425 tons (495 fl) **S:** 32 kts (28 sust.)
Dim: 58.5 (49.5 pp) × 10.2 (9.4 wl) × 2.14 (hull; 4.0 props)
A: 1 76.2-mm 59-cal. AK-176 DP; 1 4-round Fasta-M (SA-N-8) SAM syst. (16 Igla-2M missiles); 1 30-mm 54-cal. AK-630 gatling AA; 2 5-round RBU-1200 ASW RL (30 RGB-12 rockets); 4 single 533-mm TT (2 SET-65E ASW and 2 53-65KE antiship torpedoes); 2 d.c. racks (6 d.c. each)
Electronics:
Radar: 1 Pechora nav.; 1 MR-352 Pozitiv-E (Cross Dome) surf./air search; 1 MR-123E Vympel-AME (Bass Tilt) gun f.c.
Sonar: MGK-345 Bronza hull-mounted MF and MF dipping syst.
EW: 2 16-round PK-16 decoy RL
M: 2 Type M-521-TM5 diesels; 3 props; 17,330 bhp
Range: 2,000/20; 3,000/12 **Fuel:** 50 tons **Endurance:** 10 days
Crew: 7 officers, 32 enlisted

Remarks: The Indian units of the class (and the unit built for Cuba) differ from the standard Russian version in having larger torpedo tubes, the pilothouse set farther forward on the superstructure, and Cross Dome radar substituted for the MR-302 Rubka (Strut Curve). All are assigned to the 23rd Patrol Vessel Squadron and are based at Mumbai. On 6-2-04, *Agray* suffered significant damage during what unconfirmed reports indicate was an explosion of an onboard torpedo. The ship has since been repaired.
Hull systems: The large housing for the dipping sonar system projects 1.5 m out from the stern. The large hull-mounted sonar dome is located approximately beneath the gunfire-control radar. The hull is constructed of mild steel, while the middle part of the deck plating, some internal bulkheads, and much of the superstructure are made of aluminum-magnesium alloy. Have propulsion diesels customized for tropical weather.
Combat systems: The combat data system is designated SU-580E. There is a Kolonka-2 backup ringsight director for the single gatling AA gun; the MR-123E radar director can control both the 76.2-mm and 30-mm guns. Normal ammunition load is 152 rounds 76.2-mm (all ready-service, on-mount) and 2,000 rounds 30-mm. The torpedo tubes must be trained out several degrees to launch. MGK-345 applies to both the hull-mounted and dipping sonars, and the dipping sonar transducer can be lowered to 200 m.

♦ 7 Modified SDB Mk 3 class
Bldr: Garden Reach SB & Eng., Calcutta

	L	In serv.
T 61 Trinkat	6-99	28-9-00
T 62 Tillangchang	10-11-99	4-01
T 63 Tarasa	5-5-00	24-8-01
T 65 Bangaram	11-12-04	11-05
T 66 Bitra	14-12-04	11-05
T 67 Bati Malv	29-6-05	2-06
T 68 Baratang	6-8-05	2-06

D: 260 tons (fl) **S:** 35 kts **Dim:** 46.0 × 7.5 × 3.9
A: 2 single 30-mm Medak AA
Electronics: Radar: 1 Bharat 1245 nav.
M: 3 MTU 16V 396 TB94 diesels; 2 props; 10,500 bhp
Range: 1,500/ . . . **Crew:** 35 tot.

Remarks: An enlarged version of the four built in the 1980s. Intended for coastal patrol, smuggling interdiction, fisheries protection, and policing duties.

Disposals: *Tarmugli* (T 64) was sold to the Republic of Seychelles on 23-2-05. SBD Mk 2 Class patrol craft T 54 and T 55 had been retired by 2005.

♦ 3 SDB Mk 3 class
Bldr: Mazagon Dock, Goa (In serv. 1984–85)

T 58 T 59 T 60 Rajkamal

D: 167 tons (210 fl) **S:** 30 kts **Dim:** 37.80 (32.20 pp) × 7.50 × 1.85
A: 2 single 40-mm 60-cal. Bofors Mk 3 AA
Electronics: Radar: 1 Bharat 1245 nav.
M: 2 MTU 16V 538 TB92 diesels; 2 props; 6,820 bhp **Crew:** 32 tot.

Remarks: Intended as an improved version of the SDB Mk 2 with better hullform and less rake to propeller shafts. Probably also have a centerline cruise engine. Speed also reported as 28 kts for Goa-built units. May have depth charge racks stored ashore.
Disposals: *Ajay* (T 56) was transferred to Mauritius in 1993, and T 57 was stricken during 1998.

PATROL BOATS [PB]

♦ 8 (+ 12) Israeli Super Dvora Mk II class
Bldr: T-80–T-82: Ramta, Israel; others: Vasco SY, Panaji, Goa

	In serv.		In serv.
T-80	24-6-98	T-84	19-4-04
T-81	6-6-99	T-85	16-2-05
T-82	9-10-03	T-86	2005
T-83	27-11-03	T-87	2006

Indian Navy Super Dvora Brian Morrison, 2-01

D: 48 tons (54 fl) **S:** 46 kts **Dim:** 22.40 × 5.49 × 1.00
A: 1 20-mm/90-cal. Oerlikon AA; 2 12.7-mm machine guns

PATROL BOATS [PB] *(continued)*

Electronics: Radar: 1 Koden. . . nav.; 1 Elop MSIS optronic syst. f.c.
M: 2 MTU 12V396 TE94 diesels; 2 Arneson surface-piercing, articulating props; 4,570 bhp
Electric: 30 kw tot. **Range:** 700/14 **Crew:** 2 officers, 8 enlisted

Remarks: Referred to as XFAC (eXtra Fast Attack Craft) by the Indian Navy. Do not wear their pennant numbers. A license for indigenous construction was signed on 24-9-96, with the first Indian-built unit to complete in 9-97 and additional units at three-month intervals, although the program ran far behind schedule, with the Israeli prototype not commissioned until 7-98. Cost about $8.5 million each. As many as 20 may be built, with some going to the coast guard. Sisters in Israeli, Sri Lankan, and Slovenian navies. Are fitted with an Elop optronic low-light-level surveillance and weapons direction device.

MINE WARFARE SHIPS

♦ 0 (+ 8) new-construction coastal minehunters [MHC]
Bldr: Goa SY

Remarks: Construction of a license-built version of a modern Western European GRP-construction, twin-screw minehunter is planned, if funding permits. The Tripartite, Karlskrona *Landsort,* Vosper Thornycroft *Sandown,* and Intermarine *Lerici* designs have been considered. No contracts have yet been let for the program, which is estimated to cost $1.0 billion. As planned, the first unit would enter service in 2010 and the last unit in 2020.

♦ 12 Soviet Natya-class (Project 266ME) fleet minesweepers [MSF]
Bldr: Sudostroitel'noye Obyedineniye "Almaz" (Sredniy Neva), Kolpino, Russia

	In serv.		In serv.
M 61 Pondicherry	2-2-78	M 67 Karwar	14-7-86
M 62 Porbandar	19-12-78	M 68 Cannanore	17-12-87
M 63 Bedi	27-4-79	M 69 Cuddalore	29-10-87
M 64 Bhavnagar	27-4-79	M 70 Kakinada	23-12-86
M 65 Alleppy	10-6-80	M 71 Kozhikode	19-12-88
M 66 Ratnagiri	10-6-80	M 72 Konkan	8-10-88

Alleppy (M 65) Brian Morrison, 2-01

Porbandar (M 62) Brian Morrison, 2-01

D: 750 tons std., 804 tons normal (873 fl) **S:** 17.6 kts (16 sust.)
Dim: 61.00 (57.60 wl) × 10.20 × 2.98 (hull)
A: 2 twin 30-mm 65-cal. AK-230 AA; 2 twin 25-mm 80-cal. 2M-3 AA—M 67 and later: 2 4-round SA-N-8 SAM syst. (18 Igla-2M missiles)—all: 2 5-round RBU-1200 ASW RL (60 RGB-12 projectiles); 2 mine rails (8 mines max.)
Electronics:
Radar: 1 Don-2 nav.; 1 MR-104 Rys' (Drum Tilt) gun f.c.
Sonar: MG-89 HF hull-mounted (49 kHz)
M: 2 M-503B-3E diesels; 2 CP props; 5,000 bhp
Electric: 600 kw tot. (3 × 200-kw DGR-200/1500 diesel sets)
Range: 1,800/16; 3,000/12; 5,200/10 **Fuel:** 87 tons **Endurance:** 10–15 days
Crew: 10 officers, 89 enlisted

Remarks: Second group of six, ordered 1982, were delivered out of pennant number sequence. Can be used as ASW escorts. One reportedly has been modified to act as an intelligence collector. Units assigned to the Western Fleet are in the 19th Mine Countermeasures Squadron; those assigned to the Eastern Fleet are in the 21st. Are expected to decomission at a rate of two per year beginning in 2008.
Hull systems: Differ from the units in the Russian Navy in that they do not have a ramp at the stern. The stem is cut back sharply below the waterline. Low-magnetic-signature, aluminum-steel-alloy hull construction. Have DGR-450/1500P diesel-driven degaussing system. Have enhanced air-conditioning capacity over their Russian Navy sisters and also have about 100 kw more generator capacity. The main engines are a derated version of the diesels that power Russian high-speed small combatants and have a low operating time between overhauls. Carry 45 tons water but do not have distilling equipment. Navigational equipment includes a GKU-2 gyrocompass, NEL-MZB echo sounder, Rumb MFD/F, Pirs-1M receiver for Decca radio navaid, and AP-4 automatic position plot. Khmel-1 infrared position-keeping and signaling equipment is carried.
Combat systems: The RBU-1200 ASW rocket launchers are primarily used for detonating mines. Sweep gear includes GKT-2 mechanical, AT-2 acoustic, and TEM-3 magnetic arrays, handled by two articulated KBG-5-TMI jib cranes fitted at the stern. The sonar incorporates a downward-looking, high-frequency, bottomed-mine-detection component with a range of 350–400 m. Some 2,149 rounds are carried for each 30-mm gunmount.

♦ 2 Soviet Yevgenya-class (Project 1258E) inshore minesweepers [MSI]
Bldr: Sudostroitel'noye Obyedineniye "Almaz" (Sredniy Neva), Kolpino, Russia (In serv.: M 83: 15-5-83; M 86: 3-2-84)

M 83 Mahe M 86 Malpe

D: 88.5 tons (91.5 fl) **S:** 12 kts **Dim:** 26.13 × 5.90 × 1.38
A: 1 twin 25-mm 80-cal. 2M-3M AA
Electronics:
Radar: 1 Mius (Spin Trough) nav.
Sonar: MG-7 HF hull-mounted HF mine location
M: 2 Type 3D12 diesels; 2 props; 600 bhp
Range: 300/10 **Fuel:** 2.7 tons **Endurance:** 3 days
Crew: 1 officer, 9 enlisted (+ 2–3 clearance divers)

Remarks: Glass-reinforced plastic construction. A plan to build additional units under license in India was dropped. Equipped for shallow-water minehunting to depths of 30 m with a towed television and marker-buoy dispenser. Both are based at Kochi as the 18th Mine Countermeasures Squadron.
Disposals: Sister *Magdala* (M 88) was reportedly stricken by 2001 while sisters *Malvan* (M 84), *Mangalore* (M 85), and *Mulki* (M 87) had all been retired by 2004.

AMPHIBIOUS WARFARE SHIPS

♦ 1 (+ 2) Shardul-class tank landing ships [LST]

	Bldr	L	In serv.
L . . . Shardul	Garden Reach SB, Calcutta	3-4-04	6-06
L . . . Kesari	Garden Reach SB, Calcutta	8-6-05	2007
L . . . Airavat	Garden Reach SB, Calcutta	27-3-06	2008

D: 5,655 tons (fl) **S:** 15.8 kts **Dim:** 124.50 (120.00 pp) × 17.50 × 3.50
A: 4 single 40-mm/60-cal. Bofors (Mark 3) AA; . . . Igla-2M shoulder-launched SAMs; 2 18-round 122-mm (WM-18) barrage RL
Electronics: Radar: 1. . . nav.—EW: Bharat Ajanta intercept
M: 2 Kirloskar-SEMT-Pielstick 12PA6 STC diesels; 2 props; 5,726 bhp
Range: . . . / . . . **Fuel:** . . . tons **Crew:** 136 tot., 16 officers, 120 enlisted

Remarks: Improved versions of the Magar-class; ordered 12-12-01. Carry four Sea Truck–type LCVP in separate davits amidships. Aft helicopter hangar can house a single Sea King or Dhruv helicopter and the hangar deck is capable of operating two aircraft. Fitted with a vehicle ramp forward from the upper deck to the tank deck. Cargo capacity is 11 main battle tanks or 500 troops.

♦ 2 Magar-class tank landing ships [LST]

	Bldr	L	In serv.
L 20 Magar	Garden Reach SB, Calcutta	7-11-84	15-7-87
L 23 Gharial	Hindustan SY, Vishakhapatnam	2-4-91	14-2-97

Magar (L 20)—with a Sea King helicopter on the flight deck aft
Brian Morrison, 2-01

Magar (L 20)—note the helicopter hangar within the superstructure and the twin, side-by-side stacks Brian Morrison, 2-01

AMPHIBIOUS WARFARE SHIPS *(continued)*

D: 3,200 tons (5,655 fl) **S:** 15 kts **Dim:** 124.80 (120.00 pp) × 17.50 × 3.50
A: 4 single 40-mm 60-cal. Bofors Mk 3 AA; . . . Igla-2M shoulder-launched SAMs; 2 18-round 122-mm barrage RL
Electronics: Radar: 1. . . nav.—EW: Bharat Ajanta intercept
M: 2 SEMT-Pielstick 8 PC2 V400 Mk 3 diesels; 2 props; 8,560 bhp (7,900 sust.)
Electric: 1,560 kw tot. (2 × 500-kw, 2 × 250-kw, 2 × 50-kw, 1 × 60-kw diesel sets)
Range: 3,000/14 **Fuel:** 420 tons **Crew:** 16 officers, 120 enlisted

Remarks: Based on the British Sir Lancelot design. L 23, fitted out at Garden Reach SB, has a crew totaling 143 and is assigned to the Eastern Fleet; she ran aground on 11-12-99 with minor damage. L 20 is assigned to the Western Fleet.
Hull systems: Carry four Sea Truck–type LCVPs in separate davits amidships. Helicopter deck and hangar aft for Sea King Mk 42C transport. There is a vehicle ramp forward from the upper deck to the tank deck. Both are now able to carry 15 Indian Arjun heavy tanks. No stern door/ramp. Can beach on 1:40 gradient.

♦ 5 Polnocny-C (Project 773I) and -D (Project 773IM*)-class medium landing ships [LSM]
Bldr: Stocznia Marynarki Wojennej, Gdynia, Poland

	L		L
L 17 Sharabh	4-9-75	L 21 Guldar*	4-6-85
L 18 Cheetah*	19-10-83	L 22 Kumbhir*	3-5-86
L 19 Mahish*	25-6-84		

Mahish (L 19)—Project 773IM unit with raised helicopter deck
Brian Morrison, 2-01

D: 1,192 tons normal (1,305 max. fl) **S:** 16.3 kts
Dim: 81.30 (76.00 pp) × 9.30 (8.61 wl) × 1.22 (fwd; 2.30 aft, loaded)
A: 2 twin 30-mm 65-cal. AK-230 AA; 2 18-round 140.4-mm WM-18 barrage RL (180 rds tot.)
Electronics: Radar: 1 Don-2 (L 18–21: Kivach) nav.; 1MR-104 Rys' (Drum Tilt) gun f.c.
M: 2 Type 40DM diesels; 2 props; 4,400 bhp
Electric: 360 kVA tot. (4 × 90-kVA diesel sets)
Range: 975/13 **Crew:** 11 officers, 107 enlisted + 84 troops

Remarks: All constructed for India. L 16 and L 17 were delivered in 1976, L 18 in 12-84, L 19 in 7-85, L 21 in 11-86, and L 22 in 2-86. First two (Polnocny-C/Project 773I) did not have a helicopter platform as on the Polnocny-D variant (Project 773IM). Cargo: 350 tons and up to 140 troops. The upper deck is primarily a shelter for the tank deck and cannot support heavy vehicles; there is no ramp to the tank deck, the hatch forward being intended for ventilation and for access during loading vehicles aboard by crane.
Hull systems: The survivors are to be re-engined with Kirloskar-Pielstick diesels.
Disposals: Project 773I units *Ghorpad* (L 14) and *Khesari* (L 15), in reserve since 1993, were reportedly stricken during 2001 and 1999, respectively. *Shardul* (L 16) was retired by 2005.

♦ 6 Vasco da Gama–class (LCU Mk II/Mk III) utility landing craft [LCU]
Bldrs: L 34, 35: Hoogly Dockyard, Calcutta; L 36–40: Goa SY

	L	In serv.		L	In serv.
L 34 Vasco da Gama	29-11-77	28-1-80	L 37 . . .	22-7-85	1986
L 35 . . .	16-3-80	17-12-83	L 38 Midhur	2-86	1987
L 36 . . .	13-1-79	1-12-80	L 39 Mangala	2-86	25-3-87

L 37—with after deckhouse to full width of the hull and hull bulwarks amidships
92 Wing Det. A, RAAF, 2-99

D: 500 tons (fl) **S:** 11.5 kts light; 9 kts loaded
Dim: 57.50 (53.20 pp) × 8.20 × 1.57 (aft)
A: 2 single 40-mm 60-cal. Bofors Mk 3 AA
Electronics: Radar: 1 Decca TM-1229 nav.
M: 3 Kirloskar-M.A.N. W8V 17.5/22 AMAL diesels; 3 Kort-nozzle props; 1,686 bhp
Range: 1,000/8 **Crew:** . . . tot. (207 max. personnel)

Remarks: Goa SY was a subsidiary of Mazagon Docks, Mumbai. The minelaying capability attributed to this class is not evident in photography. Many of the landing craft remain unnamed.
Hull systems: Total complement, including embarked troops, is said to be 287, with a cargo capacity of 250 tons (space for two PT-76 amphibious light tanks or two BMP-1 armored personnel carriers). L 35 has the pilothouse set further aft, after deckhouse not flush with sides of hull, and a smaller stack, and lacks bulwarks amidships (there is an inboard bulwark along the sides of the vehicle deck).
Disposals: L 31 was stricken by 2001, L 32 and 33 retired in 2002.

AUXILIARIES

♦ 1 Modified Sandhayak-class research ship [AGOR]
Bldr: Garden Reach SB & Eng., Calcutta

	L	In serv.
A 74 Sagardhwani	5-91	30-7-94

Sagardhwani (A 74) Brian Morrison, 2-01

D: 1,339 tons (2,050 fl) **S:** 16 kts **Dim:** 85.06 (78.80 pp) × 12.80 × 3.67
A: None
Electronics: Radar: 1 Decca TM-1629 nav., 1 . . . meteorological
M: 2 GRSE-M.A.N. G8V 30/45 ATL diesels; 2 props; 3,920 bhp—1 Pleuger 200-bhp active rudder (5 kts)
Electric: 1,700 kw tot. (2 × 500-kw, 2 × 350-kw diesel sets)
Range: 6,000/16; 14,000/10 **Fuel:** 231 tons
Crew: 10 officers, 70 enlisted + 16 scientists

Remarks: 1,949 grt. Hull and propulsion plant are the same as the *Sandhayak*-class survey ships, but A 74 has been configured as a research ship for the Naval Physical and Oceanographic Laboratory, Kochi. Officially referred to as the Marine Acoustic Research Ship (MARS).
Hull systems: There are a total of eight laboratories to permit conducting acoustic, geological, meteorological, chemical, and physical oceanography. The superstructure is set nearer the stern than that on her half-sisters, with the deck forward of the pilothouse cleared as a helicopter pad (for a Chetak) and a 10-ton quadrantial gallows-type equipment crane carried at the stern; most of the laboratories are acoustically isolated from the ship's structure. First ship in Indian Navy with accommodations for female personnel. Carries 116 tons fresh water.

Note: The modern and elaborately equipped research ships operated by the National Oceanographic Institute are non-naval. They include *Sagar Kanya, Sagar Sampada, Samudra Manthan, Samudra Sarveshak, Samudra Nidhi,* and *Samudra Sandhari.* The small inshore research craft *Gaveshani* and a sister launched in 1976 are also civilian.

♦ 8 Sandhayak-class hydrographic survey ships [AGS]
Bldr: Garden Reach SB & Eng., Calcutta (*Darshak, Sarvekshak:* Goa SY, Goa)

	L	In serv.
J 14 Nirupak	10-7-81	14-8-85
J 15 Investigator	8-8-87	11-1-90
J 16 Jumuna	4-9-89	31-8-91
J 17 Sutlej	1-12-91	19-2-93
J 18 Sandhayak	6-4-77	26-2-81
J 19 Nirdeshak	16-11-78	4-10-83
J 21 Darshak	28-4-98	28-4-01
J 22 Sarvekshak	11-99	14-1-02

Sutlej (J 17) Brian Morrison, 2-01

D: 1,329 tons (1,929 fl) **S:** 16.75 kts **Dim:** 85.77 (78.80 pp) × 12.80 × 3.34
A: 1 40-mm 60-cal. Bofors Mk 3 AA; 1 Chetak helicopter
Electronics: Radar: 1 Decca TM-1629 nav.
M: 1 GRSE-M.A.N. G8V 30/45 ATL diesel; 1 prop; 3,860 bhp—1 Pleuger 200-bhp active rudder (5 kts)—J 21 and *Sarvekshak:* 2 diesels; 2 props; 4,646 bhp
Electric: 1,006 kw tot. (5 × 200-kw, 1 × 6-kw diesel sets)
Range: 14,000/14 **Fuel:** 248 tons
Crew: 14 officers, 134 enlisted + 30 survey party

AUXILIARIES *(continued)*

Nirdeshak (J 19) Brian Morrison, 2-01

Remarks: 2,050 grt/535 dwt. Carry traditional white hull and superstructure. The Goa-built pair were laid down in 5-96 and 8-96, respectively, and may have a secondary mission as hospital ships. Another hull of this type, *Sagardhwani* (A 74), is configured for oceanographic research (see [AGOR]).
Hull systems: Have a telescoping helicopter hangar, and at least the two newest have harpoon landing grid systems. Carry four inshore survey launches with Hydrodist position-fixing system. Equipment includes three precision depth-finders, Decca Navigator, Decca HiFix, taut-wire measuring gear, and a gravimeter. Carry 163 tons potable water and 5 tons aviation fuel. Have Telegon-4 HFD/F. J 21 and *Sarvekshak* are said to draw 3.43 m and have a 6.5-ton crane to handle the survey craft; they also carry a 6.75-m Pacific 22 RIB in a gravity davit.

♦ 1 hospital ship [AH]
Bldr: Hindustan SY, Calcutta (L: 28-8-81)

Lakshadweep

D: 865 tons (fl) **S:** 12 kts **Dim:** 52.0 (46.8 pp) × 9.5 × 3.0
M: 2 diesels; 2 props; 900 bhp
Crew: 19 ship's company + 15 medical staff, 90 hospital berths

Remarks: Laid down 2-81.

♦ 1 Deepak-class replenishment oiler [AO]
Bldr: Bremer Vulkan Schiffbau, Bremen-Vegesack, Germany (In serv. 21-2-76)

A 57 Shakti

Shakti (A 57) NAVPIC-Holland, 1-98

D: 6,785 tons (22,000 fl) **S:** 20 kts **Dim:** 168.43 (157.50 pp) × 23.0 × 9.14
A: 4 single 40-mm 60-cal. Bofors Mk 3 AA; 24 Igla-2M shoulder-launched SAMs
Electronics:
Radar: 2 Decca 1226 nav.
EW: Bharat Ajanta intercept, EADS Telegon-4 HFD/F
M: 1 set Type BV/BBC geared steam turbines; 1 prop; 16,500 shp
Boilers: 2 Babcock & Wilcox **Range:** 5,500/18.5
Crew: 16 officers, 179 enlisted

Remarks: 12,690 grt/15,800 dwt. Refitted 2001 at the Mumbai Naval Dockyard. Sister *Deepak* (A 50) was stricken 30-4-96.
Hull systems: Two liquid-replenishment stations per side, with British-style jackstay rigs, plus over-the-stern fueling. Telescoping hangar and flight deck for one Chetak helicopter. Carries 12,624 tons fuel oil, 1,280 tons diesel fuel, 1,495 tons aviation fuel, 812 tons fresh water, and some dry cargo. Has a degaussing system.

♦ 1 Rajabagan Palan–class replenishment oiler [AOR]
Bldr: Garden Reach SB & Eng., Calcutta

	Laid down	L	In serv.
A 59 Aditya (ex-*Rajabagan Palan*)	1986	15-11-93	3-4-00

Aditya (A 59) Brian Morrison, 2-01

D: 24,612 tons (fl) **S:** 20 kts **Dim:** 172.00 × 23.00 × 9.14
A: 3 single 30-mm 2A42/7.62-mm Medak dual AA; 24 Igla-2M shoulder-launched SAMs; 1 Chetak or Sea King Mk 42B helicopter
Electronics: Radar: . . .

Aditya (A 59) John Mortimer, 2-01

M: 2 ECR-M.A.N./Burmeister & Wain 16V 40/45 diesels; 1 prop; 23,936 bhp—bow-thruster
Electric: 4,500 kw tot. (2 × 1,500-kw shaft generators, 3 × 500-kw diesel sets)
Range: 10,000/16
Crew: 16 officers, 140 enlisted + 6 aircrew (197 tot. accomm.)

Remarks: 16,211 dwt. Ordered 7-87 and was to have been in service by 1997. A second unit was planned, but there have been no reports of progress and the unit may have been canceled. Design is a modified version of the *Deepak* class, with a repair capability added and the navigating bridge superstructure block moved forward. Commissioning was delayed by propulsion problems. Attached to the Eastern Fleet and based at Vishakhapatnam. Had completed 189 underway replenishments though 2-01.
Hull systems: Cargo: 14,200 m^3 (12,000 tons) diesel and aviation fuel, 2,250 m^3 fresh water, and 2,170 m^3 (5,000 tons) ammunition, provisions, and spares. Can carry six standard cargo containers on deck. Has Canadian Hepburn replenishment equipment, with one fueling station and one solid-stores transfer station per side. A 20-ton cargo crane is fitted. The hangar can accommodate a Sea King helicopter. Is fully air-conditioned and has a repair workshop to assist other ships.
Combat systems: The locally operated Medak gunmounts are adapted from a turret designed for use on armored personnel carriers, where the turret has both a 30-mm cannon and a 7.62-mm machinegun; the machinegun has not been noted in available photos, however.

♦ 1 Russian Komandarm Fedko–class replenishment ship [AOR]
Bldr: Admiralty Shipyard 194, St. Petersburg, Russia

	L	In serv.
A 58 Jyoti	8-12-95	19-7-96

Jyoti (A 58) Brian Morrison, 2-01

Jyoti (A 58) John Mortimer, 2-01

D: 39,900 tons (fl) **S:** 16.4 kts (15.25 sust., loaded)
Dim: 178.24 (165.00 pp) × 25.33 × 10.41 (loaded)
A: 24 Igla-2M shoulder-launched SAMs
Electronics: Radar: . . .
M: 1 Bryansk-Burmeister & Wain 6DKRN60/195 diesel; 1 prop; 10,948 bhp
Range: 12,000/15 **Fuel:** 1,606 tons heavy oil, 305 tons diesel
Crew: 16 officers, 30 senior enlisted, 46 junior enlisted (as delivered)

Remarks: 21,142 grt. Begun as a 21,053-grt/28,400-dwt commercial tanker and converted prior to delivery as an underway replenishment oiler. Basic Russian project number is 15966. Is the largest ship in the Indian Navy. The name means "Light." A near-sister was commissioned in China in 6-96, and two merchant sisters were completed for various owners, *Indra* (ex-*Pulkovo*) and *Belania* (ex-*Pavlovsk*). Collided with unknown vessel in the Malacca Strait on 16-11-98, suffering significant hull damage.

AUXILIARIES *(continued)*

Hull systems: Liquid cargo: 31,398 m^3 in ten tanks (25,040 tons). Has ice-strengthened hull of double-hull construction, with external deck stiffeners. There are two refueling stations per side, and the ship can also refuel over the stern. Cargo pumps include four steam turbine–driven 750-m^3/hr pumps. Carries 192 tons potable water and 60 tons feedwater for the auxiliary boiler.
Combat systems: Delivered unarmed and is still without fixed defensive systems. In 2000, it was announced that she might be equipped with a point-defense SAM system.

Note: Also in service is the transport tanker *Ambika* (A 54), used to carry "high sulpher diesel fuel" and built by Hindustan Shipyard. Launched on 12-10-94 and commissioned 22-1-95, she is assigned to the Eastern Naval Command and based at Vishakhapatnam. No additional data are available.

♦ 2 Nicobar-class (Project B561) transports [AP]

	Bldr	In serv.
Nicobar	Stocznia Szczecinska im. A. Warskiego, Szczecin, Poland	5-6-91
Andamans	Stocznia Szczecinska im. A. Warskiego, Szczecin, Poland	5-99

Nicobar 92 Wing Det. A, RAAF, 1999

D: Approx. 20,000 tons (fl) **S:** 16 kts **Dim:** 157.00 (144.00 pp) × 21.00 × 6.71
A: None **Electronics:** Radar: 2 . . . nav.
M: 2 Cegielski-Burmeister & Wain 6L35MC 6-cyl. diesels; 2 props; 7,088 bhp—1 CP bow-thruster
Electric: 1,080 kw tot. (5 × 216-kw diesel sets; 400 V, 50 Hz a.c.)
Range: 8,450/15.5 **Fuel:** 751 tons heavy oil, 151 tons diesel
Crew: . . . tot.

Remarks: 14,195 grt/4,963 dwt. Requisitioned 3-99 from the Shipping Corporation of India, Mumbai (which operated the *Nicobar* for the Government of India Andaman and Nicobar Islands Administration), for military logistics support to the Andaman and Nicobar islands. Data here apply specifically to *Nicobar; Andamans* may differ.
Hull systems: Are passenger/cargo vessels with two holds forward and a large helicopter platform aft. As commercial vessels, had accommodations for 63 cabin, 300 berth, and 900 deck passengers. Can carry 39 standard 20-ft. cargo containers. Have NAVSAT and commercial SATCOM gear.

♦ 1 Soviet Ugra-class (Project 1886E) submarine tender [AS]
Bldr: Chernomorskiy Zavod, Nikolayev (In serv. 28-12-68)

A 54 Amba

D: 6,780 tons (7,980 fl) **S:** 20 kts **Dim:** 144.8 × 18.1 × 5.8
A: 2 twin 76.2-mm 59-cal. AK-276 DP
Electronics:
Radar: 1 Don-2 nav.; 1Fut-N (Slim Net) surf./air search; 2 Fut-B (Hawk Screech) f.c.
Sonar: MG-10 hull-mounted searchlight HF
M: 4 Type 2D-42 diesels (1,900 bhp each), electric drive; 2 props; 6,000 shp
Range: 6,500/17; 11,500/9 **Fuel:** 820 tons **Crew:** 18 officers, 202 enlisted

Remarks: Helicopter platform. Quarters for 750 men. Two 6-ton cranes, one 10-ton crane. Based at Mumbai; rarely goes to sea.

♦ 1 submarine rescue, salvage, and diving support ship [ASR]
Bldr: Mazagon DY, Mumbai

	Laid down	L	In serv.
A 15 Nireekshak	8-82	1-84	8-6-89 (Indian Navy)

D: 3,600 tons (fl) **S:** 12 kts **Dim:** 70.50 × 17.50 × 5.00
A: None **Electronics:** Radar: 2 . . . nav.
M: 2 Bergens Mek. Verk. KRM-8 diesels; 2 CP props; 5,015 bhp—2 bow-thrusters; 910 shp—2 stern-thrusters; 910 bhp
Electric: 2,340 kw tot. (1 × 1,140-kw shaft alternator, 4 × 300-kw diesel alternator sets; 415 V, 3-phase a.c.)
Range: . . . **Crew:** 15 officers, 48 enlisted

Remarks: 2,160 grt. Chartered 8-6-89 for three years, with option for purchase, to replace Russian T-58-class submarine rescue ship *Nistar* (A 55) until two since-canceled new units were available. Had been built as a commercial oilfield support ship and is capable of a variety of salvage and rescue missions.
Hull systems: Can support 12 divers at up to 300 m. Has two six-man decompression chambers and one three-man diving bell. Equipped with Kongsberg ADP 503 Mk II dynamic positioning system, a four-point mooring system, one 10-ton crane, and a passive-tank stabilization system. Carries the submarine rescue chamber formerly aboard the *Nistar;* it can rescue personnel down to 200 m. Navigational suite includes echo sounder, autopilot, gyrocompass, D/F, and Decca Navigator radio navaid.

♦ 1 Gaj-class oceangoing tugs [ATA]
Bldr: Hindustan Shipyard Ltd., Calcutta

A . . . Gaj (In serv. 20-10-02)

D: 560 tons (fl) **S:** 12 kts **Dim:** 34.00 × 10.00 × 2.75
M: 2 Wartsila type diesels; 2 Voith-Schneider CP props; 1,421 bhp
Range: . . . / . . . **Fuel:** . . . **Crew:** 23 tot., 1 officer, 22 enlisted

Remarks: Fitted for diving and salvage work. Has a 360-deg. rudder propulsion system for enhanced maneuverability. Not to be confused with the older tug *Gaj* (A 51) stricken in 1996.

♦ 1 Modified Gaj–class oceangoing tugs [ATA]
Bldr: Garden Reach SB & Eng., Calcutta

A 53 Matanga (In serv. 1983)

Matanga (A 53) Arjun Sarup, 4-03

D: 1,600 (fl) **S:** 15 kts **Dim:** 67.80 × 12.30 × 4.00
A: 1 40-mm 60-cal. Bofors Mk 3 AA
M: 2 GRSE-M.A.N. G7V diesels; 2 CP props; 3,920 bhp
Range: 8,000/12 **Fuel:** 242 tons **Crew:** 8 officers, 70 enlisted

Remarks: 1,313 grt/460.6 dwt. Fitted for diving and salvage work. Have 40-ton bollard pull. Half-sister *Gaj* (A 51) was stricken in 1996. A 53 was launched 29-10-83 and carries a diver's decompression chamber and other salvage equipment.

♦ 1 Tir-class cadet training ship [AXT] Bldr: Mazagon DY, Mumbai

	L	In serv.
A 86 Tir	15-4-83	21-2-86

Tir (A 86) Brian Morrison, 2-01

Tir (A 86) Brian Morrison, 2-01

D: 2,400 tons (3,200 fl) **S:** 18 kts **Dim:** 105.85 × 13.20 × 4.8
A: 1 twin 40-mm 60-cal. Mk 5 Bofors AA
Electronics:
Radar: 1 Bharat-Decca TM-1229 nav.; 1 Bharat-Decca 1245 nav.; 1 . . . nav.
EW: Racal Cutlass intercept
M: 2 Kirloskar-SEMT-Pielstick 18 PA6 V280 BTC diesels; 2 props; 6,970 bhp

AUXILIARIES *(continued)*

Electric: 1,000 kw tot. (4 × 250-kw diesel alternator sets; 415 V, 50 Hz. a.c.)
Range: 6,000/12 **Fuel:** 285 m^3
Crew: 25 officers, 204 enlisted + 10 instructors, 120 cadets

Remarks: Ordered 1981; was to have been completed during 3-84, but was delayed by labor and management problems. Second ship ordered 5-86 from same builder but subsequently canceled. The name means "Arrow." Is assigned to the 1st Training Squadron and is based at Kochi.
Hull systems: Helicopter deck, but no hangar. Has Telegon-4 HFD/F, Decca collision-avoidance system, NAVSAT, echo sounder, doppler log, plotting table, and four saluting cannon. Boats include two motorboats, four GRP dinghies, two RIBs, one motor whaleboat, and one sail-equipped whaleboat. Has 135-m^3 fresh water capacity and can generate 75 tons per day.

♦ 1 ex-U.K. Leander-class training frigate [AXT]
Bldr: HM Dockyard, Portsmouth

	Laid down	L	In serv.
F 46 KRISHNA (ex-*Andromeda*, F 57)	25-5-66	24-5-67	2-12-68

Krishna (F 46) Ben Sullivan, 8-95

D: 2,680 tons (3,140 fl) **S:** 25 kts
Dim: 113.38 (109.73 pp) × 13.12 × 4.60 (5.60 props)
A: 3 single 40-mm 60-cal. Bofors Mk 3 AA; 1 Chetak helicopter
Electronics:
Radar: 1 Kelvin-Hughes Type 1006 nav.; 1 Type 967-968 surf./air search
Sonar: Removed
EW: UAA-1 intercept; 2 Type 670 jammers; Type 182 towed acoustic torpedo decoy
M: 2 sets White–English Electric geared steam turbines; 2 5-bladed props; 30,000 shp
Boilers: 2 Babcock & Wilcox 3-drum; 38.7 kg/cm^2, 450° C
Electric: 2,500 kw tot. **Range:** approx. 4,500/12 **Fuel:** 500 tons
Crew: 19 officers, 241 enlisted (in RN service)

Remarks: Purchased 5-94 for a nominal price, having been decommissioned 7-4-93 and placed in 180-day recall reserve 4-6-93. Underwent 12-week reactivation overhaul at Devonport, running trials 31-7-95 and departing for India at the end of 8-95. Is employed purely as a training ship. While in British service, underwent conversion from a late-construction "Broad-beamed Leander" to incorporate Sea Wolf SAM system, antiship missiles, and improved ASW capability. Four sisters were discarded by the Royal Navy. Assigned to the Southern Naval Command, 1st Training Squadron, and based at Kochi.
Hull systems: Speed reduced about 2 kts from original due to weight growth. Has fin stabilizers.
Combat systems: During reactivation for Indian Navy service, the Sea Wolf system, two sets of triple ASW torpedo tubes, and four 20-mm single AA mounts were deleted, as were the Type 910 SAM control radar, the decoy rocket launchers, and the sonar suite. Hand-operated 40-mm AA mounts have been placed on the former Sea Wolf platform forward and on either beam amidships.

SERVICE CRAFT

Note: The majority of Indian Navy service craft do not carry pennant numbers, making it difficult to distinguish them from commercial craft in some instances. Hulls are normally painted black, with upperworks either white or yellow ("buff"). The following entries are not exhaustive but represent only those units for which either photography or some data are available.

♦ 3 diving tenders [YDT] Bldr: Cleback SY (In serv. 1979, 2-84, 8-84)

D: 36 tons (fl) **S:** 12 kts **Dim:** 14.89 (13.37 pp) × 4.40 × 1.21
M: 2 Premier Auto-Meadows diesels; 2 props; 130 bhp **Fuel:** 2 tons

♦ 3 Madhur-class personnel ferries [YFB]
Bldr: Goa SY, Goa (In serv. . . .)

MADHUR MANJULA MODAK

Madhur—black hull, white superstructure Brian Morrison, 2-01

D: Approx. 175 tons (fl) **S:** 11 kts **Dim:** 28.10 (25.15 pp) × 7.62 × 1.47
M: 2 diesels; 2 props; 604 bhp **Crew:** 6 tot. + 156 seated passengers

Remarks: The three listed units are based at Mumbai; there may be additional units in service. Also in use at Mumbai is the slightly larger *Nancy;* no data available.

Nancy Brian Morrison, 2-01

♦ 1 medium floating dry dock [YFDM]
Bldr: . . . , Japan (In serv. 1983)

FDN-1

Floating dry dock FDN-1 NAVPIC-Holland, 5-98

D: 7,345 tons light
Dim: 188.70 (176.40 over pontoon) × 41.03 (40.00 beam walls) × 3.80 (empty)

Remarks: Based at Port Blair in the Andaman Islands since 1987. Refitted 1998 by Hindustan DY, Vishakhapatnam. Has 12 anchors. Sank 7-11-02 in 20 m of water but was to be refloated and repaired.

♦ . . . personnel launches [YFL]
Bldr: Goa SY, Goa (In serv. . . .)

D: . . . tons **S:** 19 kts **Dim:** 17.80 (17.00 pp) × 5.00 × 1.40
M: 2 Kirloskar-Cummins diesels; 2 props; 1,000 bhp **Crew:** 4 tot.

Remarks: General-purpose utility launch design. No radar.

♦ . . . mooring buoy tenders [YGL]
Bldr: Goa SY, Goa (In serv. . . .)

D: . . . tons **S:** 10 kts **Dim:** 32.00 (30.00 pp) × 9.60 × 2.30
M: 2 diesels; 2 props; 992 bhp **Crew:** 20 tot.

Remarks: Single mooring buoy-handling crane on forecastle. No hold, but have working deck forward of bridge superstructure.

♦ 3 inshore survey craft [YGS]
Bldr: Goa SY (In serv. 1984–85)

J 34 MITHUN J 35 MEEN J 36 MESH

D: 185 tons (210 fl) **S:** 12.5 kts **Dim:** 37.50 (35.20 pp) × 7.50 × 1.85
A: 1 40-mm 60-cal. Bofors Mk 3 AA (not normally aboard)
Electronics: Radar: 1 Decca TM-1629 nav.
M: 2 diesels; 2 props; 1,124 bhp **Range:** 1,500/12.5
Crew: 4 officers, 24 enlisted

Remarks: J 34 launched 28-5-83 and J 35 on 10-8-83. Steel-hulled. Have the same hulls as SDB Mk 2 patrol-boat class, but with a less-powerful propulsion plant. Painted white except for large black area amidships on hull sides to mask exhaust staining. Carry a derrick-served inshore survey launch on the fantail, to port.
Disposals: Sister *Makar* (J 33) was retired in 2005.

♦ 1 coastal tanker [YO]
Bldr: Goa SY (In serv. 1990)

PUSHKAR

Pushkar—black hull, yellow upperworks Brian Morrison, 2-01

SERVICE CRAFT *(continued)*

D: 1,245 tons (fl) **S:** 12 kts **Dim:** 60.12 (56.10 pp) × 9.80 × 3.00
M: 2 Kirloskar-M.A.N. diesels; 2 props; 2,600 bhp
Electric: 200 kVA tot. (2 × 100-kVA diesel sets)
Range: 1,500/12 **Endurance:** 12 days **Crew:** 22 tot.

Remarks: Has six cargo tanks and can transport 400 tons of high-speed diesel fuel, 100 tons aviation fuel, and 100 tons water.

♦ 1 coastal tanker [YO]
Bldr: Central Inland Water Transport Corp., Rajabagan SY, Mumbai (In serv. 5-86)

PALAN

D: Approx. 1,200 tons (fl) **S:** 12 kts **Dim:** 57.94 (54.39 pp) × 9.10 × 3.10
M: 2 Kirloskar M.A.N. diesels; 1 prop; 1,440 bhp

Remarks: 624 grt/715 dwt.

♦ 2 Poshak-class fuel lighters [YO]
Bldr: Rajabagan SY, Mumbai

POSHAK (In serv. 4-82) PURAN (In serv. 1988)

D: 650 tons **S:** 8 kts **Dim:** 36.3 × 7.6 × 2.4
M: 1 M.A.N. diesel; 255 bhp **Cargo:** 200 tons

♦ 2 Purak-class fuel lighters [YO]
Bldr: Rajabagan SY, Mumbai

PURAK (In serv. 3-6-77) PRADHAYAK (In serv. 2-78)

D: 960 tons (fl) **S:** 9 kts **Dim:** 49.7 × 8.1 × 3.0
M: 1 diesel; 1 prop; 560 bhp **Cargo:** 376 tons

Note: Also in service, at Mumbai, is the small fuel lighter *Varida;* no data available.

♦ 1 torpedo trials and retrieval craft [YPT]
Bldr: P.S. & Co., Mumbai (In serv. 8-9-83)

A 71 ASTRAVAHINI

Remarks: No details available.

♦ 2 torpedo retrievers [YPT] Bldr: Goa SY

A 72 . . . (In serv. 16-9-82) A . . . (L: 5-11-80)

D: 110 tons (fl) **S:** 11 kts **Dim:** 28.50 (24.80 pp) × 6.10 × 1.40
M: 2 Kirloskar-M.A.N. 12-cyl. diesels; 2 props; 720 bhp **Crew:** 13 tot.

Remarks: Can stow two full-sized torpedoes on deck and two on recovery ramp.

♦ 5 Bhim-class large harbor tugs [YTB]
Bldr: Tebma Shipyard, Chennai

A . . . BHIM (In serv. 8-3-04) A . . . (In serv. 2004)
A . . . Bal shil (In serv. 23-8-04) A . . . Ajral (In serv. 17-12-04)
A . . . (In serv. 2004)

D: . . . tons (fl) **S:** 12 kts **Dim:** 28.5 × 9.5 × 2.8
M: 2 Cummins KTA38M2 diesels; 2 props; 1,200 bhp (sustained)
Range: . . . / . . . **Fuel:** . . . **Crew:** 13 tot.

Remarks: 25-ton bollard pull and a 360-deg. rudder propulsion system for enhanced maneuverability. *Bhim* and *Ajral* are assigned to the Eastern Naval Command and based at Vishakhapatnam. *Balshil* is assigned to the Southern Command and based at Kochi.

♦ 3 Madan Singh–class large harbor tugs [YTB]
Bldr: Tebma SY, Chennai (In serv. 1999)

MADAN SINGH TARAFDAR SHAMBHU SINGH

Tarafdar—black hull, white superstructure Brian Morrison, 2-01

D: . . . tons **S:** . . . kts **Dim:** . . . × . . . × . . .
M: 1 Wärtsilä 8L20 diesel; 1 prop; . . . bhp

♦ 4 Bajarang-class large harbor tugs [YTB]
Bldr: Mazagon Goa SY (In serv. 1991)

BAJARANG BALRAM . . . . . .

Balram—black hull, yellow superstructure Brian Morrison, 2-01

D: Approx. 400 tons (fl) **S:** 12 kts **Dim:** 29.70 (29.00 pp) × 9.70 × 4.30
M: 2 Kirloskar-SEMT-Pielstick 8PA4 V200 diesels; 2 Voith-Schneider vertical cycloidal props; 3,200 bhp
Crew: 12 tot.

Remarks: 216 grt. Have 30-ton bollard pull. Fitted with three monitors for fire fighting. *Bajarang* and *Balram* are based at Mumbai. *Anand,* formerly listed with this class, is a smaller tug of earlier design; no data available.

♦ 1 coastal tug [YTB]
Bldr: Garden Reach S.B. & Eng., Calcutta (In serv. 7-82)

RAJAJI

D: 428 tons **S:** 12.5 kts **Dim:** 30.5 × 9.5 × 3.8
M: 2 Garden Reach–M.A.N. diesels; 2 Kort-nozzle props; 2,120 bhp

♦ 4 miscellaneous large harbor tugs [YTB]
Bldr: Mazagon Dock, Mumbai (In serv. 1973–74) and Goa SY (In serv. . . .)

ANAND ARJUN ATHAK BALBIR

Balbir Ralph Edwards, 2-01

D: . . . tons **S:** 11 kts **Dim:** 29.25 (25.00 pp) × 8.50 × 2.60
M: 2 diesels; 2 Kort-nozzle props; 2,228 bhp **Crew:** 12 tot.

Remarks: Not a uniform class; there are at least two different appearance groups. Data above are believed to apply to the *Athak,* which has a lower superstructure, with the pilothouse only a half-deck above the main deck.

♦ 1 sail training craft [YTS]
Bldr: Goa SY, Vasco da Gama

	Laid down	L	In serv.
TARANGINI	20-6-95	11-12-95	11-11-97

D: 420 tons (fl) **S:** . . . kts **Dim:** 54.0 (42.8 pp) × 8.5 × 4.5
M: 2 Kirloskar-Cummins diesels; 2 props; 640 bhp—1,035-m^2 max. sail area
Range: 2,000/ . . . (on diesels)
Crew: 6 officers, 30 enlisted + 45 cadets

Remarks: Bark-rigged craft ordered late 1993. Designed by Three Quays Marine Services, and similar to British sail training ship *Lord Nelson.* Has three masts, square rigged on the fore and main. Carries 85 tons of ballast. Assigned to the Southern Naval Command, 1st Training Squadron, and based at Kochi. During 2003–4, *Tarangini* circumnavigated the globe, visiting 36 ports in 17 countries, a voyage repeated during 2006.

SERVICE CRAFT *(continued)*

Tarangini Michael Nitz, 8-05

♦ 1 sail-training craft [YTS]
Bldr: Alcock-Ashdown, Bhavnagar (In serv. 20-4-81)

VARUNA

D: 130 tons (fl) **Dim:** 30.5 × . . . × . . .

Remarks: Two-masted brig for training 26 Sea Cadets. Assigned to the Southern Naval Command, 1st Training Squadron, and based at Kochi.

♦ 2 water lighters [YW]
Bldr: Ambuda: Rajabagan SY, Mumbai; Kochi: Mazagon DY, Mumbai

AMBUDA KOCHI

D: 200 tons **S:** 9 kts **Dim:** 32.0 × . . . × 2.4
M: 1 diesel; 1 prop; . . . bhp

Remarks: *Ambuda* was laid down on 18-1-77; a planned third unit was not built.

COAST GUARD

The Indian Coast Guard was established 1-2-77 to ensure surveillance of India's 200-n.m. economic zone. Now commanded by an Indian Navy vice admiral, it consisted initially of ships and craft transferred from the Indian Navy. The Indian Customs Service was merged with the coast guard in April 1982. Although operationally subordinate to the Ministry of Defense, the coast guard is funded by the Department of Revenue. The name "Coast Guard" is written in large black letters on the sides of ship hulls, which are painted white and have diagonal coast guard–style stripes.

Personnel: Approximately 700 officers, 3,800 enlisted, 750 civilians

Bases: Headquarters at New Delhi, with regional headquarters at Mumbai, Chennai, and Port Blair (Andaman Islands). District headquarters at Mumbai, Campbell Bay, Kochi, Diglipur, Haldia, New Mangalore, Paradip, Porbandar, and Vishakhapatnam. Stations are maintained also at Mandapam, Okha, Tuticorin, and Vadinar.

Coast Guard Aviation: 17 Chetak helicopters are in service and more than half of the 36 Do-228 on order have been delivered. The first HAL Dhruv Advanced Light Helicopters for the coast guard were delivered 2-02 with 40 total planned. Coast guard squadrons in service include:

- No. 700 Sqn. at Calcutta: 6 Do-228
- No. 744 Sqn. at Chennai: 6 Do-228
- No. 745 Sqn. at Port Blair: 6 Do-228 (with 1 Chetak on detachment)
- No. 750 Sqn. at Daman: 6 Do-228, 2 Chetak (from 800 Sqn.)
- No. 800 Sqn. at Goa: 3 Chetak
- No. 841 Sqn. at Mumbai: 4 Chetak
- No. 848 Sqn. at Madras: 5 Chetak

PATROL SHIPS [WPS]

♦ 1 (+ . . .) Zalaria class
Bldrs: Goa SY, Goa

	In serv.
ZALARIA	2006
. . .	. . .
. . .	. . .
. . .	. . .

D: 1,930 tons (2,250 fl) **S:** 24 kts **Dim:** 105.00 × 12.4 × 3.50
A: 1 76-mm 62-cal. OTO Melara SuperRapid DP; 2 single 7.62-mm mg; 1 Chetak helicopter
Electronics: Radar: 1 . . . nav.; 1 Decca 2459 surf. search
M: 2 Kirloskar-SEMT-Pielstick . . . diesels; 2 props; . . . bhp
Electric: . . . **Range:** 6,000/15 **Fuel:** . . .
Crew: 126 total

Remarks: New class of patrol craft authorized in 1999. Construction began on the first unit in 2004. Additional units may be planned, though little information is yet available.

Note: Three 3,300-ton UT 517-class pollution control ships were ordered from AGB Surat in 2004 with deliveries expected to take place during 2007–8.

♦ 4 Samar class
Bldrs: Hindustan SY, Vishakapatnam

	Laid down	L	In serv.
42 SAMAR	1990	26-8-92	14-2-96
43 SANGRAM	1992	18-3-95	29-3-97
44 SARANG	1993	8-3-97	5-99
45 SAGAR	. . .	14-12-01	3-11-03

Samar (42) Brian Morrison, 2-01

Sangram (43) Mitsuhiro Kadota, 5-01

Sarang (44) Brian Morrison, 5-01

D: 1,765 tons (2,005 fl) **S:** 22 kts **Dim:** 101.95 (96.00 pp) × 11.50 × 3.50
A: 1 76-mm 62-cal. OTO Melara SuperRapid DP; 2 single 7.62-mm mg; 1 Chetak helicopter
Electronics:
Radar: 1 Bharat 1245 nav.; 1 Decca 2459 surf. search
TACAN: Bharat FT13-S/M
E/O: 1 Bharat-Radamec System 2400 optronic f.c. and surveillance
M: 2 Kirloskar-SEMT-Pielstick 16 PA6 V280 diesels; 2 props; 12,800 bhp
Electric: . . . **Range:** 7,000/15 **Fuel:** . . .
Crew: 12 officers, 112 enlisted (accomm. for 145 tot.)

Remarks: Ordered 4-90; are half-sisters to seven *Sukanya*-class units in the Indian Navy. A total of twelve was originally planned, then cut to six, and now terminated at three. Intended for offshore patrol vessel duties for the protection of oil platforms and the Indian economic exclusion zone. *Sangram* means "Struggle" in Hindi.
Hull systems: Differ from the Indian Navy *Sukanya* class in having heavier gun armament, having twin funnels flanking the helicopter hangar (which can accommodate a Sea King), lacking the deckhouse forward of the bridge, and having the helicopter deck terminate well short of the stern. Have fin stabilizers, firefighting water monitor, towing capability, and Inmarsat satellite communications. Additional accommodations are provided for passengers.
Combat systems: The 76-mm guns in the first two proved too expensive to maintain and operate and more powerful than is needed in the ships' essentially policing role, but plans to replace the 76-mm gun in the third unit were not carried out. The ships have a Bharat-made Radamec 2400 optronic director for the 76-mm gun.

♦ 9 Vikram class
Bldr: Mazagon DY, Mumbai (last two: Goa)

	L	In serv.		L	In serv.
33 VIKRAM	26-9-81	20-12-83	38 VIVEK	5-11-87	19-8-89
34 VIJAYA	. . .	12-4-85	39 VIGRAHA	12-88	12-4-90
35 VEERA	30-6-84	3-5-86	40 VARAD	2-9-89	19-7-90
36 VARUNA	1-2-86	27-2-88	41 VARAHA	. . .	11-3-92
37 VAJRA	31-1-87	22-12-88			

COAST GUARD PATROL SHIPS [WPS] *(continued)*

Varuna (36)—with 30-mm gun forward D. Billig via Werner Globke 3-04

Vijaya (34)—with 40-mm gun forward Ralph Edwards, 2-01

D: 1,064 tons (1,224 fl) **S:** 22 kts
Dim: 74.10 (69.00 pp) × 11.40 × 3.20 (3.68 props)
A: 1 40-mm 60-cal. Bofors Mk 3 or 30-mm 2A4Z/7.62-mm Medak AA (see remarks); 2 single 7.62-mm mg; 1 Chetak helicopter
Electronics: Radar: 1 Bharat-Decca 1226 nav.; 1 Bharat-Decca 1230 nav.
M: 2 SEMT-Pielstick 16 PA6 V280 diesels; 2 CP props; 12,800 bhp
Electric: 560 kw tot. (2 × 200-kw, 1 × 160-kw diesel alternators; 415 V, 3-phase a.c.)
Range: 4,000/16; 8,500/11 **Fuel:** 180 tons **Crew:** 11 officers, 85 enlisted

Remarks: First three ordered 1979; second three ordered 1983. *Varuna* has training facilities on the fantail in lieu of the antipollution equipment. Design not fully satisfactory; cannot operate helicopter in heavy weather due to rolling.
Hull systems: Have nonretractable fin stabilizers. Equipped with two 250-m^3/hr pumps and two firefighting monitors. Have a 4.5-ton crane, are air-conditioned, and carry diving and pollution-control equipment. Have hangar for Chetak helicopter and carry two RIB inspection craft and a GRP launch.
Combat systems: Carry one Matra Défense Lynx optronic gun director for the 40-mm gun, which is being replaced during refits by a dual 30-mm 2A42/7.62-mm Medak AA mounting, derived from the turret fitted to BMP-2 armored personnel carriers.

PATROL CRAFT [WPC]

♦ 3 Sarojini Naidu class Bldr: Mazagon Goa SY, Vasco da Gama

	In serv.
229 Sarojini Naidu	11-11-02
230 Durgabai Deshmukh	3-03
231 Kasturba Gandhi	2006

D: 235 tons (260 fl) **S:** 35 kts **Dim:** 48.14 (43.50 wl) × 7.50 × 2.00 (mean hull)
A: 1 30-mm 2A42 and 7.62-mm Medak AA; 2 single 7.62-mm mg
Electronics: Radar: 1 Bharat-Decca 1245/6X nav.
M: 3 MTU 16V4000 M90 diesels; 3 KaMeWa Type 71SI waterjets; 10,944 bhp
Electric: 160 kw (2 × 80 kw, diesel driven)
Range: 1,500/. . . **Endurance:** 7 days **Crew:** 35 tot.

Remarks: First craft assigned to the Coast Guard Western Region and based at Mangalore. Can operate in Sea State 6 and is intended to work in shallow coastal waters. Communications suite is sufficient to permit the craft to act as wartime coastal escorts and communications links. Capable of performing antismuggling, fisheries protection, and search-and-rescue duties. Improved versions of the Jija Bai Mod 1 class patrol craft.

♦ 7 Jija Bai Mod 1 class
Bldrs: Garden Reach SB & Eng., Calcutta (224, 225: Goa SY, Vasco da Gama)

	In serv.		In serv.
221 Priyadarshini	25-5-92	226 Kanak Lata Barua	27-3-97
223 Annie Beseant	7-7-91	227 Bhikaji Cama	24-9-97
224 Kamla Devi	20-5-92	228 Sucheta Kripalani	16-3-98
225 Amrit Kaur	20-3-93		

D: 215 tons light (306 fl) **S:** 24 kts (23 sust.)
Dim: 46.00 (43.50 wl) × 7.50 × 1.85 (2.09 props)
A: 1 40-mm 60-cal. Bofors Mk 3 AA 2 single 7.62-mm mg—224, 225: 1 30-mm 2A42 and 7.62-mm Medak AA; 2 single 7.62-mm mg
Electronics: Radar: 1 Bharat-Decca 1245/6X or Decca 1226 nav.
M: 2 MTU 12V538 TB82 diesels; 2 4-bladed props; 5,940 bhp (4,025 sust.)
Electric: 240 kw tot (3 × 80-kw, 415-V, 50-Hz diesel sets)
Range: 2,400/12 **Fuel:** 10 tons **Crew:** 5 officers, 29 enlisted

Remarks: A further refinement of the *Tara Bai* design, with greater beam. Sister *Razya Sultana* (222) foundered in bad weather 9-11-95 off Paradeep. In early 1998, 225 acted as trials platform for the Medak dual 30-mm/12.7-mm naval mounting, which is being backfitted in the other units. A modified version of this design has been offered for export; equipped with waterjet engines and two Medak gunmounts, it would have a maximum speed of 35 kts.

Amrit Kaur (225)—with the new 30-mm Medak gunmount forward John Mortimer, 2-01

♦ 6 Tara Bai class
Bldrs: 71, 72: Singapore SB & Eng., Ltd; others: Garden Reach SB & Eng., Ltd., Calcutta

	L	In serv.		L	In serv.
71 Tara Bai	4-87	20-5-87	74 Akka Devi	. . .	9-8-89
72 Ahalya Bai	5-87	9-9-87	75 Naiki Devi	. . .	19-3-90
73 Lakshmi Bai	. . .	20-3-89	76 Ganga Devi	. . .	19-11-90

Tara Bai (71) French Navy, 1996

D: 173 tons normal (195 fl) **S:** 26 kts
Dim: 44.90 (42.30 wl) × 7.00 × 1.89 (2.59 props)
A: 1 40-mm 60-cal. Bofors Mk 3 AA; 2 single 7.62-mm mg
Electronics: Radar: 1 Decca 1226 nav.
M: 2 MTU 12V538 TB82 diesels; 2 props; 5,940 bhp
Electric: 260 kw (2 × 100 kw, 1 × 60 kw) **Range:** 2,400/12
Fuel: 30 tons **Endurance:** 7 days **Crew:** 5 officers, 27 enlisted + 2 spare

Remarks: First two ordered 6-86, with license to build the other four in India. Are air-conditioned and have a five-ton bollard-pull towing hook and a rigid inflatable boat. Carry ten tons fresh water, with a three-ton/day distiller. Have HF/DF, an echo sounder, and an autopilot. Intended for SAR, fisheries patrol, sovereignty patrol, etc. Hull design based on standard Lürssen 45-m hull; steel construction. The new dual 30-mm/7.62-mm Medak naval mounting is to be backfitted to this class.

♦ 7 Jija Bai class
Bldr: Garden Reach SB & Eng., Calcutta (64: Sumidagawa SY, Tokyo)

	In serv.		In serv.
64 Jija Bai	22-2-84	68 Habbahkhatun	27-4-85
65 Chand Bai	22-2-84	69 Ramadevi	3-8-85
66 Kittur Chinnama	21-5-83	70 Avvayar	19-10-85
67 Rani Jindan	21-10-83		

Jija Bai (64) Sumidagawa, 1983

D: 181 tons light (273 fl) **S:** 25 kts (sust.)
Dim: 44.02 (41.10 pp) × 7.40 × 1.50 (hull)
A: 1 40-mm 60-cal. Bofors Mk 3 AA; 2 single 7.62-mm mg
Electronics: Radar: 1 Decca 1226 nav.

COAST GUARD PATROL CRAFT [WPC] *(continued)*

M: 2 MTU 12V538 TB82 diesels; 2 props; 5,940 bhp (4,030 sust.)
Range: 2,375/14 **Crew:** 7 officers, 27 enlisted

Remarks: Same basic design as Philippine Coast Guard's *Bessang Pass* class; also known as Type 956. Plan to build eight more dropped in favor of the *Tara Bai* class. The new dual 30-mm/12.7-mm Medak naval mounting is to be backfitted to this class.

♦ 2 SDB Mk 2 class
Bldr: Garden Reach, Calcutta (In serv. 1984–85)

RAJKIRAN RAJKAMAL

D: 210 fl **S:** 30 kts **Dim:** 37.80 × 7.50 × 1.85
A: 2 single 40-mm 60-cal. Bofors Mk 3 AA
Electronics: Radar: 1 Bharat 1245 nav.
M: 2 MTU 16V 538 TB92 diesels; 2 props; 6,820 bhp
Range: 1400/14 **Crew:** 28 tot.

Remarks: Previously reported as retired, both are apparently still in service.
Disposals: Sisters *Rajhans* (56), *Rajshree* (60) and *Rajatarang* (57) were all decomissioned by 1998.

AIR-CUSHION PATROL BOATS [WPBH]

♦ 6 8000TDX class
Bldrs: H 181, 182: Griffon Hovercraft, Woolston, U.K.; others: Garden Reach SB & Eng., Calcutta (In serv. 7-00 to 3-02)

H 181 through H 186

D: 27 tons (fl) **S:** 42 kts **Dim:** 21.15 (19.85 hull) × 11.30 (8.70 hull) × . . .
A: 1 12.7-mm mg **Electronics:** Radar: 1 . . . nav.
M: 2 MTU 12V183 TB32 diesels; 2 ducted CP airscrew props; 1,600 bhp
Range: 365/42 **Fuel:** 2,000 liters **Crew:** 4 tot + 80 troops

Remarks: Aluminum construction. The two British-built units were shipped on 3-7-00. Maximum hover height: 1.25 m. Can make 50 kts in light condition and can carry an 8-ton payload. Indian-built units H 183 and H 184 were delivered on 2-1-01 and 18-12-01, respectively.

PATROL BOATS [WPB]

♦ 2 (+ . . .) offshore patrol boats
Bldr: Agarwal Business Group, Surat (In serv. 2001–. . .)

D: . . . tons **S:** 32 kts **Dim:** . . . × . . . × . . .
M: 2 diesels; 2 KaMeWa waterjets; . . . bhp

Remarks: First unit launched 10-00 for delivery in 2001; second delivered 2-02. Aluminum construction. No other data available. Appear to be a commercial fast yacht design. Have hatches for two gunners with handheld weapons.

♦ 9 (+ 6) P-2000 Interceptor Boats
Bldr: Anderson Marine Pty, Kadras/Goa SY (In serv. 1993– . . .)

	In serv.		In serv.		In serv.
C 131	16-11-93	C 134	20-5-95	C 137	4-9-96
C 132	16-11-93	C 135	25-3-95	C 138	4-9-96
C 133	20-5-95	C 136	25-3-95	C 140	1998

C 134 (C 34) Brian Morrison, 2-01

D: 49 tons (fl) **S:** 40 kts **Dim:** 20.80 (18.00 pp) × 5.80 × 1.00
A: 1 7.62-mm mg
Electronics: Radar: 1 Furuno. . . I-band nav.
M: 2 Deutz-MWM TBD 234 V12 diesels outboard (823 bhp each), 1 Deutz-MWM TBD 234 V8 550-bhp loiter diesel centerline; 3 Hamilton 402–series waterjets; 2,200 bhp
Range: 600/15 **Crew:** 4 officers, 6 enlisted

Remarks: Initial 10 ordered 9-90, with an option for six more. Built in cooperation with Seaking Industries, with design services from Amgram, Ltd., Sussex, U.K. GRP hulls laid up by Anderson Marine employ molds originally built by Watercraft, Shoreham, U.K., for the Royal Navy *Archer* class. Are based at Goa and Kochi. Although the official pennant numbers are as given above, they wear only the last two digits. Sister C 139 was leased to Mauritius during 2001. Were originally to have had a 20-mm Oerlikon AA forward, but a remotely controlled 7.62-mm machinegun has been substituted.

♦ 6 South Korean Swallow 65 design
Bldr: Swallow Craft, Pusan (In serv. 1980–82)

C 01 C 02 C 04 C 05 C 06 C 63

D: 32 tons (35 fl) **S:** 20 kts **Dim:** 20.0 × 4.8 × 1.3
A: 1 7.62-mm mg **Electronics:** Radar: 1 . . .nav.
M: 2 G.M. Detroit Diesel 12V71 TA diesels; 2 props; 840 bhp
Range: 400/20 **Crew:** 8 tot.

Remarks: C 01–C 06 were placed in service 24-7-80; C 62 (stricken 2000) and C 63 were taken over from India Oil Corp. on 22-5-82. C 03 was stricken around 1996.

♦ 5 12.5-meter class
Bldr: Mandovani Marine . . . (In serv. 1980s)

D: 10 tons (fl) **S:** 18 kts **Dim:** 12.5 × . . . × . . .
M: 2 Cummins diesels; 2 Hamilton waterjets; 550 bhp

Remarks: GRP construction, deep-vee hullform.

Note: Fisheries Protection Craft *Kallyani, Kayerii, Karuna, Keishna,* and *Kalpaka,* delivered 10-96 by Cochin Shipyard, belong to another Indian government agency; no data available other than that they are 16.20 × 4.50 × 2.50 and are powered by two MWM diesel engines. The border security force also operates a small number of 17-m patrol boats for riverine border patrol and harbor antismuggling duties. The customs service operates fast patrol launches and also station craft in each major port.

INDONESIA

INDONESIAN NAVY

(Tentara Nasional)

Personnel: 45,000, including 15,000 marines and 1,000 naval aviation personnel. Plans were announced during 2-00 to expand the marine force to 22,800 and the navy to 52,500, but funding has not yet been provided.

Bases and Organization: The Tentara Nasional is organized into four operational commands: the Western, Eastern, Central, and Northern. The Eastern Command is headquartered at Surabaya, the Western Command at Teluk Ratai on Sumatra. There are also the Training Command, Military Sea Communications Command, and Military Sealift Command. Principal naval bases are at Tanjung Priok near Jakarta; Ujung, near Surabaya (the principal dockyard); Sabang, We Island; Medan, Sumatra; Ujung Pandang, Celebes; Balikpapan, East Borneo; Biak Island, north of New Guinea; Tanjung Pinang, Bintan Island, near Singapore; Manado, Celebes; Teluk Ratai, Sumatra; Banjarmasin, Borneo; and Manokwari, New Guinea. During 10-03, the Indonesian Navy announced plans to merge its western and eastern fleets, though no time frame has yet been set. In 1-04 plans were announced to establish a new eastern region base in Ambon.

Marine Commando Corps: Reorganized 27-3-01 into the 1st Marine Corps Group (Pasukan Korps Marinir 1), based at Surabaya with 6,500 personnel, and the Independent Marine Corps Brigade, based at Jakarta with about 3,500 personnel. A second Marine Corps Group, based at Piabung, at Teluk Ratai, Sumatra was established in 2004. Ultimately, the Marine Commando Corps hopes to have 22,800 uniformed personnel. Negotiations with Russia to purchase 17 BTR-80A armored personnel carriers remain deadlocked, but 32 BMP-2 infantry fighting vehicles were delivered during 2001, with another 32 planned.

Naval Aviation: Organized into the *Skwadron UdaraI* 200 with 10 M-28B Bryza maritime surveillance aircraft (ordered in 2005 for 2006 delivery), four DC-100 Lark Commander, two F-33A Bonanza, one TB-9 Tampico, and one PA-38 Tomahawk light transports; *Skwadron Udara* 400 with three EC-120EB Colibri, three NBO-105CB, three Wasp HAS.1, three NAS-332F Super Puma, and four or more NB-412S helicopters; *Skwadron Udara* 600 with eight NC-212M-200 Aerocar and two DHC-5D Buffalo transports; and *Skwadron Udara* 800 with 20 GAF N-22B Nomad, three GAF N-22SL Searchmaster, and six or more GAF N-24A Nomad light transport/surveillance aircraft. All squadrons are based at Lanudal Juanda, Surabaya, with headquarters at Dinas Penerbangan Angkatan Laut, Dinerbal.

The three Indonesian Aerospace (ex-Nuritanio)–built NAS-332F Super Puma helicopters are fitted with AS 39 Exocet antiship missiles, Omega ORB-22 radar, Thales HS-12 dipping sonar, and ASW torpedoes. Three Indonesian Aerospace CN235-220 maritime patrol aircraft with Thales Airborne Maritime Situation Control Systems (AMASCOS) were ordered during 6-01, with another six planned. Four new Mil Mi-171 helicopters were ordered during 2000. However, orders for additional Mi-171 and Mi-2 helicopters were canceled in 2002 due to funding shortages. Twelve helicopters are to be procured from Spain, according to a 12-02 official statement.

The Air Force has three Boeing 737-200 Surveiller long-range maritime patrol aircraft (first delivered 6-83) with Slammer side-looking radar; also used for maritime patrol are three C-130H-MP and six Nuritanio-CASA CN-235. Fourteen Hawk 100 and 10 Hawk 200 light fighters are used for training and maritime strike duties.

Weapons: In 1-05 Indonesia announced that it was beginning development of a domestically built antiship missile to arm locally constucted warships. Expected to cost $2.75 million, the program is called "Rudal Nasional," and testing is expected to begin in 2007.

Note: The names of Indonesian ships are preceded by the designation KRI (*Kapalperang Republik Indonesia,* or Ship of the Republic of Indonesia). As of 5-00 only about 20% of the seagoing ships were fully operational, due to the difficulty in obtaining spare parts and, in the case of the former East German units, problems with operating their machinery in tropical conditions. On 2-7-02 the commander in chief of the navy stated that the condition of the fleet was such that none of the principal ships and craft were capable of carrying out their combat tasks. Additional reports during 2003 suggested that only 30 ships were operational. In 9-03 the Indonesian province of Riau announced plans to independently purchase a 35-m KAL 35 patrol boat for U.S. $2.6 million to be used for combatting smuggling and other local threats. Soon afterwards other provinces announced similar purchases.

ATTACK SUBMARINES [SS] (nonoperational)

♦ 2 German Type 209/1300

Bldr: Howaldtswerke, Kiel

	Laid down	L	In serv.
401 Cakra	25-11-77	10-9-80	18-3-81
402 Nanggala (ex-*Candrasa*)	14-3-78	10-9-80	6-7-81

Cakra (401) NAVPIC-Holland, 6-93

Nanggala (402) Brian Morrison, 8-95

D: 1,100 tons std.; 1,265 tons surf./1,395 tons sub.
S: 11 kts surf./21.5 kts sub. **Dim:** 59.50 × 6.30 × 5.50
A: 8 bow 533-mm TT (14 AEG SUT Mod. 0 wire-guided torpedoes)
Electronics:
Radar: 1 Thales Calypso-II nav/search
Sonar: Atlas Elektronik CSU-3-2 suite: AN 526 passive, 407 A9 passive; Thales DUUX-2 intercept
EW: Thales DR-2000U intercept
M: 4 MTU 12V493 AZ80 GA31L diesel generator sets (600 bhp each), 1 Siemens electric motor; 1 prop; 5,000 shp (4,600 sust.)
Range: 8,200/11, 1,200/4 snorkel; 16/21.5, 25/20, 230/8, 400/4 sub.
Fuel: 87 tons (108 emergency) **Endurance:** 50 days
Crew: 6 officers, 28 enlisted

Remarks: Ordered 2-4-77 from consortium headed by Ferrostaal, Essen. Both received thorough refits by the builder, *Cakra* completing in 1987 and *Nanggala* in 9-89. 401 was refitted again from 6-93 to 6-96 in Indonesia with new batteries and an improved combat data system, and 402 began a similar refit in 10-97. Both, however, are now out of service awaiting repairs. During 1-04 it was announced that South Korea's Daewoo Corporation would be modernizing one of these boats, though further details, including which vessel is to be upgraded, remain unavailable.
Hull systems: Maximum operating depth: 250 m. Have four Hagen 120-cell batteries, producing 11,500 amp-hr and weighing 257 tons.
Combat systems: Have the Thales SINBADS weapons control. Equipped with Kollmorgen Model 76 attack periscope and a search periscope.

FRIGATES [FF]

♦ 6 ex-Netherlands Van Speijk class

Bldrs: 351, 352, 356: Nederlandse Dok en Scheepsbouw Mij, Amsterdam; others: Koninklijke Maatschappij de Schelde, Vlissingen

	Laid down	L	In serv.
351 Ahmad Yani (ex-*Tjerk Hiddes*, F 804)	1-6-64	17-12-65	16-8-67
352 Slamet Riyadi (ex-*Van Speijk*, F 802)	1-10-63	5-3-65	14-2-67
353 Yos Sudarso (ex-*Van Galen*, F 803)	25-7-63	19-6-65	1-3-67
354 Oswald Sihaan (ex-*Van Nes*, F 805)	25-7-63	23-6-66	9-8-67
355 Abdul Halim Perdanakasuma (ex-*Evertsen,* F 815)	6-7-65	18-6-66	21-12-67
356 Karel Satsuitubun (ex-*Isaac Sweers,* F 814)	6-5-65	10-3-67	15-5-68

D: 2,305 tons (2,940 fl) **S:** 28.5 kts (see Remarks)
Dim: 113.42 (109.75 pp) × 12.51 × 4.57
A: 4 RGM-84A Harpoon SSM (see Remarks); 2 4-round Sea Cat SAM syst. or 2 2-round Simbad SAM syst. (Mistral missiles); 1 76-mm 62-cal. OTO Melara DP; 4 single 12.7-mm mg; 2 triple 324-mm Mk 32 ASW TT (U.S. Mk 46 Mod. 2 torpedoes); 1 HAS.1 Wasp helicopter

Karel Satsuitubun (356) RAN, 10-04

Yos Sudarso (353) Brian Morrison, 8-95

Electronics:
Radar: 1 Decca TM 1229C nav.; 1 Thales DA-05/2 surf./air search; 1 Thales LW-03 early warning; 0 or 2 Thales M-44 f.c. (for Sea Cat; removed from ships with Simbad systems), 1 Thales M-45 gun f.c.
Sonar: 1 Thales PHS-32 hull-mounted MF
EW: British UA-8 and UA-9 intercept; FH-12 HFD/F (355, 356: UA-13 VHFD/F instead); 2 8-round Corvus decoy RL
E/O: 353, 354, 356: 1 Thales LIOD Mk 2 f.c.
M: 2 sets Werkspoor–English Electric double-reduction geared steam turbines; 2 props; 30,000 shp
Boilers: 2 Babcock & Wilcox; 38.7 kg/cm^2, 450° C
Electric: 1,900 kw **Range:** 4,500/12 **Crew:** 180 tot.

Remarks: 351 decommissioned 6-1-86 from Dutch Navy, 352 on 13-9-86; they were transferred to Indonesia on 13-10-86 and 1-11-86 respectively. 353 and 354 decommissioned 2-87 for transfer 2-11-87 and 11-88 respectively. 355 transferred 1-11-89 and 356 on 1-11-90. Design based on British *Leander* class, but with a broader enclosed bridge and two Sea Cat SAM systems, each with a radar director.
Hull systems: New infrared suppression stack caps were added during the early 1980s. Have fin stabilizers. They are now unable to make their intended speeds and are otherwise in poor material condition.
Combat systems: Major modifications were begun in 1977 while still in Dutch service; the twin Mk 6, 114-mm DP gunmount was replaced by the OTO Melara Compact 76-mm weapon, the Limbo ASW mortar was deleted and two triple ASW TT were added, the hangar was enlarged, and new sonars, radars, and the SEWACO-II data system were added. Modernizations took place: 351: 15-12-78 to 1-6-81; 352: 24-12-76 to 3-1-78; 353: 15-7-77 to 30-11-79; and 354: 31-3-78 to 1-8-80. Provision was made for carrying up to eight Harpoon SSM, but only four have been carried in practice; the U.S. SWG-1A launch control system is employed. The U.S. SQR-18A towed passive sonar array was removed from 355 and 356 before transfer, but they retain the associated small deckhouse at the extreme stern. During 1996–97, the 353, 354, and 356 were equipped with LIOD Mk 2 optronic gun directors, and the SEWACO-II combat direction system was updated; all were supposed to have their obsolete Sea Cat SAM systems removed and replaced with two manned Simbad launchers for Mistral heat-seeking SAMs.
Disposal note: The three former British Tribal-class frigates *Martha Khristina Tiyahahu* (331; ex-*Zulu,* F 124), *Wilhelmus Zakarias Yohannes* (332; ex-*Gurkha,* F 122), and *Hasanuddin* (333; ex-*Tartar,* F 133) were stricken during 2000.

♦ 2 ex-U.S. Claud Jones class

Bldrs: 341: Avondale Marine, Westwego, La.; 342: American SB, Toledo, Ohio

	L	In serv.
341 Samadikun (ex-*John R. Perry*, DE 1034)	29-7-58	5-5-59
342 Martadinata (ex-*Charles Berry*, DE 1035)	17-3-59	25-11-60

D: 1,720 tons (1,970 fl) **S:** 22 kts
Dim: 95.10 (91.75 wl) × 11.84 × 3.70 (hull; 5.54 sonar)
A: 341, 342: 1 76.2-mm 50-cal. Mk 34 DP; 1 twin 37-mm 63-cal. AA; 1 twin 25-mm 80-cal. 2M-3M AA; 2 single 12.7-mm mg; 2 triple 324-mm Mk 32 ASW TT (U.S. Mk 44 torpedoes); 2 Mk 6 d.c. mortars; 1 Mk 9 d.c. rack (18 total d.c.)—343, 344: 2 single 76.2-mm 50-cal. Mk 34 DP; 2 single 12.7-mm mg; 2 triple 324-mm Mk 32 ASW TT
Electronics:
Radar: 1 Decca 1226 nav.; 1 SPS-10 surf. search; 1 SPS-6E air search; 1 SPG-52 gun f.c.
Sonar: 341: EDO 786—342: SQS-45(V)
EW: WLR-1 intercept (not in 341)
M: 4 Fairbanks-Morse 38ND8⅛ diesels; 1 prop; 9,240 bhp (7,000 bhp sust.)
Electric: 600 kw tot. **Range:** 3,590/22; 10,300/9 **Fuel:** 296 tons
Crew: 12 officers, 159 enlisted

FRIGATES [FF] *(continued)*

Samadikun (341) Chris Delgoffe/H&L Van Ginderen, 5-00

Remarks: 341 was transferred on 20-2-73, 342 on 31-1-74. Both were refitted 1979–82 at Subic Bay Naval Station, the Philippines. Expected to retired in the near future. Both remaining units are easy to maintain and inexpensive to operate, although their weapons systems and sensors are obsolete.
Combat systems: Have Mk 70 Mod. 2 gunfire-control system for the 76.2-mm mounts and the Mk 105 ASW fire-control system. 341 and 342 have a twin Soviet 37-mm AA mount in place of one 76.2-mm on fantail and a twin 25-mm at the forecastle break, abaft the stack. Navigational radar added 1980–81. 341 has no EW equipment but does have additional ASW ordnance. The Hedgehog ASW spigot mortars have been removed.
Disposals: *Mongsidi* (343, ex-*Claud Jones,* DE 1033) and *Ngurah Rai* (344, ex-*McMorris*, DE 1036) were both retired by 2005.

TRAINING FRIGATES [FFT]

♦ 1 Hajar Dewantara class
Bldr: Uljanic SY, Split, Yugoslavia (Croatia)

	Laid down	L	In serv.
364 Hajar Dewantara	11-5-79	11-10-80	20-8-81

Hajar Dewantara (364) Vic Jeffery, 5-94

Hajar Dewantara (364) 92 Wing Det. A, RAAF, 1-94

D: 1,850 tons (fl) **S:** 27 kts **Dim:** 96.70 (92.00 wl) × 11.20 × 3.55
A: 4 MM 38 Exocet SSM; 1 57-mm 70-cal. Bofors SAK 57 Mk 1 DP; 2 single 20-mm 90-cal. Rheinmetall AA; 2 fixed ASW TT (2 AEG SUT wire-guided torpedoes); mines; 1 NBO-105 liaison helicopter
Electronics:
Radar: 1 Decca 1229 nav.; 1 Thales WM-28 track-while-scan f.c.
Sonar: Thales PHS-32 hull-mounted MF
EW: Thales SUSIE-I intercept
M: CODOG: 1 Rolls-Royce Olympus TM-3B gas turbine (27,250 shp); 2 MTU 16V956 TP91 diesels (7,000 bhp); 2 CP props
Range: 1,150/27 (gas turbine); 4,000/20 (diesels) **Fuel:** 338 tons
Crew: 11 officers, 80 enlisted + 14 instructors, 100 students

Remarks: Ordered 14-3-78 to same basic design as the ship laid down in 1977 for Iraq. A second unit, reportedly ordered 7-83, did not materialize. Can also be used as a troop transport.
Hull systems: Fin stabilizers. Carries 114 tons water ballast, 50 tons potable water, 7 tons helicopter fuel, and two LCVP-type landing craft. Gas turbine rated at 22,300 hp max. in tropics.
Combat systems: Has Thales SEWACO GM 101-41 computerized data system. Carries 1,000 rounds 57-mm and 3,120 rounds 20-mm ammunition. The torpedo tubes are located at the stern, under the helicopter deck; they launch their wire-guided weapons directly aft. Two rails for launching 128-mm rocket flares are mounted on either side of the 57-mm gunmount.

CORVETTES [FFL]

♦ 0 (+ 2 + 2) Diponegoro class
Bldr: Schelde Shipbuilding, Vlissingen (1st two); . . . Indonesia (2nd two)

	Laid down	L	In serv.
365 Diponegoro	2004	16-9-06	2007
366 Hasanuddin	2005	16-9-06	2007
. . .	2006		2008
. . .	2006		2008

Diponegoro (365) A.A. de Kruijf, 9-06

Diponegoro (365) A.A. de Kruijf, 9-06

D: 1,700 tons (fl) **S:** 28 kts **Dim:** 90 × 13 × . . .
A: 4 MM 40 Exocet SSM; 2 2-round Simbad SAM launchers (Mistral missiles); 1 76-mm 62-cal. OTO Melara DP; 2 single 20-mm 90-cal. Rheinmetall AA;
Electronics:
Radar: . . . nav.; 1 Thales MW-08 3-D air search; . . . Thales LIROD f.c.
Sonar: Thales Kingklip hull-mounted MF active/passive
EW: . . .
M: 2 . . . diesels; 2 CP props
Range: 4,000/ . . . **Fuel:** . . .
Crew: 80 total

Remarks: New construction units intended for patrol duties in and around Indonesian waters and the Malaccan Straits. Duties include antipiracy, counter-smuggling and fisheries patrol. The second two units were authorized in 5-05. Will be fitted with the TACTICOS combat management system, and a helicopter landing deck, but no hangar.

♦ 3 Fatahilah class
Bldr: Wilton-Fijenoord, Schiedam, the Netherlands

	Laid down	L	In serv.
361 Fatahilah	31-1-77	22-12-77	16-7-79
362 Malahayati	28-7-77	19-6-78	21-3-80
363 Nala	27-1-78	11-1-79	11-8-80

D: 1,160 tons (1,450 fl) **S:** 30 kts (21 on diesels) **Dim:** 83.85 × 11.10 × 3.30
A: 361, 362: 4 MM 38 Exocet SSM; 2 2-round Simbad SAM launchers (Mistral missiles); 1 120-mm 46-cal. Bofors DP; 1 40-mm 70-cal. Bofors L70 AA; 2 single 20-mm 90-cal. Rheinmetall AA; 1 2-round 375-mm Bofors SR-375A ASW RL; 2 triple 324-mm Mk 32 ASW TT (U.S. Mk 44 torpedoes)—363: 4 MM 38 Exocet SSM; 2 2-round Simbad SAM launcher (Mistral missiles); 1 120-mm 46-cal. Bofors L46 DP; 2 single 40-mm 70-cal. Bofors L70 AA; 2 single 20-mm 90-cal. Rheinmetall AA; 1 NBO-105 liaison helicopter
Electronics:
Radar: 1 Decca . . . nav.; 1 Decca AC 1229 nav.; 1 Thales DA-05/2 surf./air search; 1 Thales WM-28 track-while-scan gun f.c.
Sonar: Thales PHS-32 hull-mounted MF
EW: Thales SUSIE-I intercept; 2 8-round Corvus decoy RL
E/O: 1 Thales LIROD t.v./laser/IR backup gun director

CORVETTES [FFL] *(continued)*

Fatahilah (361)—no hangar RAN, 10-04

Nala (363)—with helicopter hangar Chris Delgoffe/H&L Van Ginderen, 5-00

M: CODOG: 1 Rolls-Royce Olympus TM-3B gas turbine (22,360 shp, tropical); 2 MTU 16V956 TB81 diesels (8,000 bhp); 2 CP props
Electric: 1,350 kw **Range:** 4,250/16 (diesels)
Crew: 11 officers, 71 enlisted

Remarks: Ordered 8-75. Are the most effective Indonesian major surface combatants.
Hull systems: Have an NBC warfare citadel. Living spaces are air-conditioned. Have nonretractable fin stabilizers.
Combat systems: *Nala* has a helicopter deck that folds around the helicopter to form a hangar, two single 40-mm AA instead of one, and *no* ASW torpedo tubes. All have the Thales DAISY computerized combat data system. Ammunition supply: 400 rounds 120-mm, 3,000 rounds 40-mm, 12 ASW torpedoes, 54 Nelli and Erica ASW rockets, 50 rounds chaff. The Simbad twin, manned SAM launchers were ordered for these ships in 1996 and installed during 1997.

PATROL COMBATANTS [PG]

♦ **16 Parchim-I class (Type 133.1)** (10 nonoperational)
Bldr: VEB Peenewerft, Wolgast, East Germany

	Laid down	L	In serv.
371 Kapitan Patimura (ex-*Prenzlau*, 231)	15-9-80	26-6-81	11-5-83
372 Untung Suropati (ex-*Ribnitz-Damgarten,* 233)	1-4-81	1982	29-10-83
373 Nuku (ex-*Waren*, 224)	9-6-80	27-3-81	23-11-82
374 Lambung Mangkurat (ex-*Angermünde,* 214)	. . .	. . .	26-7-85
375 Tjut Nya Dhien (ex-*Lübz*, P 6169, ex-221)	2-10-79	11-6-80	12-2-82
376 Sultan Thaha Syaifuddin (ex-*Bad Doberan,* 222)	15-12-79	30-9-80	30-6-82
377 Sutanto (ex-*Wismar*, P 6170, ex-241)	2-10-78	6-7-79	9-7-81
378 Sutedi Senoputra (ex-*Parchim*, 242)	9-1-79	9-10-79	9-4-81
379 Wiratno (ex-*Perleberg*, 243)	2-4-79	15-1-80	19-9-81
380 Memet Sastrawiria (ex-*Bützow*, 244)	2-7-79	12-3-80	30-12-81
381 Tjiptadi (ex-*Bergen*, 213)	. . .	. . .	1-2-85
382 Hasan Basry (ex-*Güstrow*, 223)	3-3-80	31-12-80	10-11-82
383 Iman Bonjol (ex-*Teterow*, P 6168, ex-234)	1-7-81	27-3-82	27-1-84
384 Pati Unus (ex-*Ludwigslust*, 232)	15-12-80	1-10-81	4-7-83
385 Teuku Umar (ex-*Grevesmühlen*, 212)	. . .	3-9-82	21-9-84
386 Silas Papare (ex-*Cut Meutia*, ex-*Gädebusch,* P 6167, ex-211)	1981	1982	31-8-84

Sutanto (377) 92 Wing Det. A, 5-95

D: 792 tons light; 873 tons normal (908 fl) **S:** 24.3 kts
Dim: 75.20 (69.00 pp) × 9.78 (8.95 wl) × 2.65 (hull; 4.40 sonar)
A: 1 twin 57-mm 70-cal. AK-257 DP; 1 twin 30-mm 65-cal. AK-230 AA; 2 4-round SA-N-5 Fasta-series SAM sys.; 4 fixed 406-mm ASW TT; 2 12-round RBU-6000 ASW RL; 2 d.c. racks (6 d.c. each)

Sutedi Senoputra (378) Leo Dirkx, 10-98

PATROL COMBATANTS [PG] *(continued)*

Electronics:
Radar: 1 TSR-333 nav.; 1 MR-302 Rubka (Strut Curve) air/surf. search; 1 MR-123 Vympel (Muff Cob) f.c.
Sonar: MG-332T hull-mounted MF; HF dipping sonar
EW: 2 Baklan-B (Watch Dog) intercept (2–18 GHz); 2 16-round PK-16 decoy RL
M: 3 Type M-504A-3, 56-cyl. diesels; 3 props; 14,250 bhp
Electric: 900 kw tot. (1 × 500-kw, 2 × 200-kw diesel sets)
Range: 1,200/20; 2,200/14 **Endurance:** 10 days
Crew: 9 officers, 71 enlisted (normally operated with 59 tot.)

Remarks: Transfer announced 7-92 and approved by German Bundestag 2-9-92. 371 and 372 arrived 22-11-93 in Indonesia, where they were subjected to further, more extensive modifications, including conversion of voids into additional fuel tankage. Four served briefly in the German Navy, hence the "P"-series former pennants. Twelve near-sisters operate in the Russian Navy. 371 and 372 were recommissioned on 23-9-93, 373 on 15-12-93, 374 on 12-7-94, 375 and 376 on 25-2-94, 377 on 10-3-95, 378 and 379 on 19-9-94, 380 on 2-6-95, 381 and 382 on 10-5-96, 383 on 26-4-94, 384 on 21-7-95, and 385 and 386 on 12-7-96—all while still in Germany. Two of the class were to have been activated during the 1-4-00 to 30-3-01 fiscal year. Their weapon and sensor systems are increasingly unsupportable and their engineering plants unsuitable for tropical climates. A mid-2001 report stated that none of the ships was operational and that a contract had been signed with Germany's Deutz to re-engine six of them at P.T. PAL SY, Surabaya. A 2003 report stated that six had completed re-engining by 2001 under a 1996 contract with a Ukrainian company and that six were in service as of 12-02.
Hull systems: The centerline shaft has a controllable-pitch propeller; the other two propellers are fixed pitch. Have fin stabilizers, but reportedly suffer from poor stability due to excessive topweight.
Combat systems: In an exception to German export policy toward former East German naval units, they retained their original armament and sensors on transfer to Indonesia. The helicopter-type dipping sonar deploys through a door on the starboard side of the main deck superstructure; next to it is another door with a second dipping device, possibly a bathythermograph. The d.c. racks exit through doors in stern.

GUIDED-MISSILE PATROL CRAFT [PTG]

♦ 4 PSK Mk 5 class
Bldr: Korea-Tacoma SY, Masan, South Korea

	In serv.		In serv.
621 Mandau	20-7-79	623 Badek	2-80
622 Rencong	20-7-79	624 Keris	2-80

Badek (623) Brian Morrison, 8-95

Mandau (621)—with only two MM 38 Exocet missiles aboard Brian Morrison, 8-95

D: 250 tons (290 fl) **S:** 41 kts **Dim:** 53.58 × 8.00 × 1.63 (hull)
A: 4 MM 38 Exocet SSM: 1 57-mm 70-cal. Bofors SAK 57 Mk 1 DP; 1 40-mm 70-cal. Bofors AA; 2 single 20-mm 90-cal. Rheinmetall AA
Electronics:
Radar: 1 Decca AC 1229 nav.; 1 Thales WM-28 f.c.
EW: Thales DR2000S Mk 1 intercept
M: CODOG: 1 G.E.-Fiat LM-2500 gas turbine (25,000 shp); 2 MTU 12V331 TC81 diesels (1,120 bhp each); 2 CP props
Electric: 400 kw tot. **Range:** 2,500/17 **Crew:** 7 officers, 36 enlisted

Remarks: First unit laid down 5-77. Modification of U.S. *Asheville*-class design. A planned second group of four was not ordered. Have an Alenia NA-18 optronic backup gun director. 623 and 624 have electronic intercept gear. Indonesia has not contracted with Aérospatiale to have the Exocet missiles overhauled, and they may no longer be effective.

PATROL CRAFT [PC]

♦ 1 ex-Singaporean diving tender
Bldr: Singapore Technologies Marine, Jurong, Singapore

	L	In serv.
. . . Cucuk (ex-Jupiter, A 102)	3-4-90	1-6-90

D: 170 tons (fl) **S:** 14.25 kts **Dim:** 35.70 (33.50 wl) × 7.10 × 2.30 (props)
A: 1 20-mm Oerlikon GAM B-01 AA; 2 single 12.7-mm mg
Electronics: Radar: 1 Decca 1226 nav.
M: 2 Deutz-MWM TBD 234 V12 diesels; 2 props; 1,360 bhp—azimuth thruster
Electric: 345 kw tot. (3 × 115-kw diesel-driven sets)
Range: 200/14.5; 288/4 on steerable thruster
Crew: 5 officers, 28 enlisted + divers

Remarks: Decommissioned from the Singapore Navy during 9-01 and transferred on 21-3-02 for use as a patrol craft. Sophisticated multipurpose craft originally capable of performing mine-clearance route survey work, acting as a diving tender, or assisting in salvage operations. Carries a towed side-scan high-resolution sonar and has an underwater data logging system and precision navigation equipment. To assist divers, has a two-man decompression chamber and two high-pressure compressors. Carries a ten-man rigid inflatable dinghy with a 60-bhp engine, handled by a 1.5-ton crane. Designed with German assistance.

♦ 4 Lürssen PB 57 Variant V
Bldr: P.T. PAL SY, Surabaya

803 Todak (In serv. 5-00)
804 Hiu (In serv. 9-00)
805 Layang (In serv. 11-7-02)
806 Lemadang (In serv. 8-04)

Todak (803) Hartmut Ehlers, 10-03

D: 447 tons (fl) **S:** 27 kts **Dim:** 58.10 (54.40 wl) × 7.62 × 2.85 (props)
A: 1 57-mm 70-cal. Bofors SAK 2 DP; 1 40-mm 70-cal. Bofors SAK 40 AA; 2 single 20-mm 90-cal. Rheinmetall AA
Electronics:
Radar: 1 Kelvin-Hughes Type 1007 nav.; 1 Thales Scout Variant surf. search; 1 Thales LIROD Mk 2 76-mm gun f.c.
EW: Thales DR-3000S1 intercept; EADS Telegon-8 HFD/F; 1 330- or 340-round Matra Défense Dagaie decoy RL
E/O: 1 Thales LIOD Mk 2 IR/t.v./laser 40-mm gun director
M: 2 MTU 16V956 TB92 diesels; 2 props; 8,850 bhp
Electric: 324 kw (3 × 108 kw) **Range:** 2,200/27; 6,100/15
Fuel: 110 tons **Endurance:** 15 days **Crew:** 9 officers, 44 enlisted

Remarks: Four ordered 6-93 for delivery 1997–98, later changed to having sea trials for first unit take place in 1998. Made 29 kts on trials.
Combat systems: Have the Thales TACTICOS combat system with two multifunction operator consoles and one tactical plotting table. In addition to the two gun directors, there is a manned target designation sight near the stern.

♦ 2 Lürssen PB 57 Variant IV
Bldr: P.T. PAL SY, Surabaya

801 Pandrong (In serv. 1990) 802 Sura (In serv. 1991)

Padrong (801) Brian Morrison, 11-99

D: 428 tons (fl) **S:** 27.25 kts **Dim:** 58.10 (54.40 wl) × 7.62 × 2.75 (props)
A: 1 57-mm 70-cal. Bofors SAK 2 DP; 1 40-mm 70-cal. Bofors SAK 40 AA; 2 single 20-mm 90-cal. Rheinmetall AA

PATROL CRAFT [PC] *(continued)*

Electronics:
Radar: 1 Decca 2459 nav./surf. search
EW: Thales DR-2000S3 intercept; EADS Telegon-8 HFD/F; 1 330- or 340-round Matra Défense Dagaie decoy RL
E/O: 1 Thales LIOD Mk 2 IR/t.v./laser gun director
M: 2 MTU 16V956 TB92 diesels; 2 props; 8,260 bhp
Electric: 324 kw (3 × 108 kw) **Range:** 2,200/27; 6,100/15
Fuel: 110 tons **Endurance:** 15 days **Crew:** 9 officers, 44 enlisted

Remarks: Similar to the Variant II group but lack sonar and torpedo tubes and have only one search radar. The LIOD optronic director was moved to the mainmast platform.

♦ 2 Lürssen PB 57 Variant II ASW craft
Bldrs: Lürssen, Vegesack, and P.T. PAL SY, Surabaya

	L	In serv.
651 Singa	1-10-86	8-88
653 Ajak	. . .	4-4-89

Singa (651) Hans Karr, 5-99

Singa (651)—torpedo tubes at stern draped in canvas
92 Wing Det. A, RAAF, 8-95

D: 423 tons (fl) **S:** 27.25 kts **Dim:** 58.10 (54.40 wl) × 7.62 × 2.73 (prop)
A: 1 57-mm 70-cal. Bofors SAK 2 DP; 1 40-mm 70-cal. Bofors SAK 40 AA; 2 single 20-mm 90-cal. Rheinmetall AA (I × 2); 2 fixed 533-mm TT (aft-launching, 2 reloads; AEG SUT wire-guided torpedoes)
Electronics:
Radar: 1 Decca 1226 nav.; 1 Thales WM-22 track-while-scan f.c.
Sonar: Thales PHS-32 hull-mounted MF
EW: Thales DR-2000S3 intercept; EADS Telegon-8 HFD/F; 1 330- or 340-round Matra Défense Dagaie Mk 2 decoy RL
E/O: Thales LIOD 73 IR/t.v./laser 57-mm gun f.c.
M: 2 MTU 16V956 TB92 diesels; 2 props; 8,260 bhp
Electric: 324 kw (3 × 108 kw) **Range:** 2,200/27; 6,100/15
Fuel: 110 tons **Endurance:** 15 days
Crew: 9 officers, 44 enlisted

Remarks: Optimized for ASW. 651 was shipped from Germany 7-84 with addition of bow, stern, and armament in Indonesia.
Disposals: Sisters *Andau* (650) and *Tongkak* (652) were no longer in service as of 2005.

♦ 4 Lürssen PB 57 Variant I search-and-rescue craft
Bldrs: Friedrich Lürssen, Vegesack, and P.T. PAL SY, Surabaya

	In serv.		In serv.
811 Kakap	29-6-88	813 Tongkol	26-2-89
812 Kerapu	5-4-89	814 Barakuda (ex-*Bervang*)	5-4-89

D: 356 tons (half load; 425 fl) **S:** 30.5 kts (28.1 sust.)
Dim: 58.10 (54.40 wl) × 7.62 × 2.73 (prop)
A: 1 40-mm 70-cal. Bofors SAK 40 AA; single 7.62-mm mg—813 only: 2 single 14.5-mm 93-cal. mg
Electronics:
Radar: 1 Decca 2459 nav.—814 also: 1 Decca . . . nav.
EW: Thales DR-2000S intercept
M: 2 MTU 16V956 TB92 diesels; 2 props; 8,260 bhp
Electric: 270 kVA (2 × 135 kVA, 450 V, 60 Hz)
Range: 2,200/28; 6,100/15 **Endurance:** 15 days
Crew: 9 officers, 40 enlisted + 8 spare berths

Remarks: Ordered 1982, with midbody sections for first two shipped from Germany. Manned and operated by the Indonesian Navy for the customs service, which paid for them. Intended for search-and-rescue and inspection duties. 814 was converted in 1995 to act as presidential yacht.

Tongkol (813) Brian Morrison, 2-01

Barakuda (814)—note bulwarks around reviewing stand atop pilothouse and the rescue launches carried on the stern Brian Morrison, 8-95

Combat systems: Have a 13 × 7.1-m flight deck to accommodate one NBO-105. Carry 1,000 rounds of 40-mm ammunition. Two water cannon with 294-m^3/hr capacity and 70-m range are fitted. Two rescue launches are stowed aft. 814 has a reviewing platform/open bridge atop the pilothouse; 812 is similarly equipped but lacks the extra navigational/surface-search radar added to 814. As of 2-01, two small rescue launches on 813 had been replaced by a single RIB, handled by a new boat crane, and two 14.5-mm mg had been added at the extreme stern.
Disposal note: Indonesian-designed patrol craft *Waigeo* (861) was no longer in service as of 2005.

♦ 8 Australian Attack class
Bldrs: 847, 848, 859, 862: Walkers, Ltd.; others: Evans Deakin, Ltd.

	Laid down	L	In serv.
847 Sibarau (ex-*Bandolier*)	7-68	2-10-68	14-12-68
848 Suliman (ex-*Archer*)	7-67	2-12-67	15-5-68
857 Sigalu (ex-*Barricade*)	12-67	29-6-68	26-10-68
858 Silea (ex-*Acute*)	4-67	29-8-67	26-4-68
859 Siribua (ex-*Bombard*)	4-68	6-7-68	5-11-68
862 Siada (ex-*Barbette*)	11-67	10-4-68	16-8-68
863 Sikuda (ex-*Attack*)	9-66	8-4-67	17-11-67
864 Sigurot (ex-*Assail*)	. . .	18-11-67	12-7-68

D: 146 tons (fl) **S:** 21 kts **Dim:** 32.76 (30.48 pp) × 6.2 × 1.9
A: 1 40-mm 60-cal. Bofors AA: 1 7.62-mm mg
Electronics: Radar: 1 Decca RM 916 nav.
M: 2 Davey-Paxman Ventura 16 YJCM diesels; 3,460 bhp
Range: 1,220/13 **Fuel:** 20 tons **Crew:** 3 officers, 19 enlisted

Remarks: Light-alloys superstructure. Air-conditioned. 847 transferred 16-11-73, 848 in 1974, 857 on 22-4-82, 858 on 6-5-83, 859 later in 1983, 862 on 2-2-85, 863 on 24-5-85, and 864 on 30-1-86.

PATROL CRAFT [PC] *(continued)*

Suliman (848) H&L Van Ginderen, 4-99

PATROL BOATS [PB]

♦ **16 Class 35/Class 36* patrol boats**
Bldrs: Pondok Dayung Naval Repair and Maintenance, Jakarta; Fasharkan Mentigi Naval DY; Fasharkan Manokwari Naval DY; Fasharkan Makassar Naval SY (In serv. 2004–5)

807 Boa	815 Sanca*	819 Tedong Naga	870 Taliwangsa*
808 Welang	816 Warakas	867 Kobra*	Plus 3 more
809 Suluh Pari	817 Panana	868 Anakonda*	
810 Katon	818 Kalakae	869 Potola*	

Kobra (867) Indonesian Navy, 2004

D: 90 tons **S:** 33.3 kts (Class 36: 31 kts) **Dim:** 35.00 × 7.0 × 1.3
A: 1 20-mm . . . AA; 1 12.7-mm mg (Class 36: 2 12.7-mm mg)
Electronics: Radar: 1 . . . nav.
M: 3 M.A.N. D2842 LE 410 diesels (Class 36: 3 caterpillar 3412E diesels); 3 props; . . . bhp
Range: . . . /17 **Crew:** 20 tot.

Remarks: All built locally. Class 35 boats carry a single RIB. Class 36 boats are fitted with different Caterpillar diesels for a top speed of 31 kts; endurance of five days. Armament varies within the classes. Some units carry a 20 mm Hispano-Suiza cannon or a heavy machinegun in pedestal mount on the foredeck and one or two Russian machineguns on the after deck. Others have been reported carrying a single 25-mm gun and twin 12.7-mm mg.

♦ **18 Kal Kangean class** Bldr: P. T. Kabrick Kapal (In serv. 1987–90)

1101 through 1118

D: 44.7 tons (fl) **S:** 18 kts **Dim:** 24.5 × 4.3 × 1.0
A: 1 twin 25-mm 80-cal. 2M-3M AA; 1 twin 14.5-mm 93-cal. 2M-7 AA
Electronics: Radar: 1 . . . nav.
M: 2 diesels; 2 props; . . . bhp **Range:** . . . / . . . **Crew:** . . . tot.

Remarks: Ordered 1984. Make use of surplus Soviet gunmounts removed from discarded Indonesian Navy ships and craft. Very low freeboard limits seaworthiness. Names include *Kal Kangean* (1101), *Kal Lau, Kal Sapudi,* and *Kal Lawu.*

♦ **7 . . . -class fast patrol boats**
Bldr: P.T. Mahalaya Utama (In serv. 1992–97)

1119 through 1125

D: 45 tons **S:** 34 kts **Dim:** 12.6 × . . . × . . .
A: . . .
Electronics: Radar: 1 . . . nav.
M: 2 Volvo Penta . . . diesels; 2 . . . waterjets; 2 props; . . . bhp

Remarks: High-speed patrol boats; armament fit is unknown.

MINE-COUNTERMEASURES SHIPS

♦ **2 Tripartite-class coastal minehunters [MHC]**
Bldr: Van der Giessen de Noord, Alblasserdam, the Netherlands

	Laid down	L	In serv.
711 Pulau Rengat (ex-*Willemstad*)	29-3-85	23-7-87	26-3-88
712 Pulau Rupat (ex-*Vlardingen*)	22-7-85	27-8-87	26-3-88

D: 510 tons (568 fl) **S:** 15.5 kts
Dim: 51.50 (47.10 pp) × 8.90 × 2.47 (2.62 max.)
A: 2 single 20-mm 90-cal. Rheinmetall AA
Electronics:
Radar: 1 Decca AC 1229 nav.
Sonar: Thales TSM 2022 hull-mounted HF minehunting
M: 2 MTU 12V396 TCDb51 diesels; 2 CP props; 1,900 bhp—2 75-hp bow-thrusters; 2 120-hp Schottel active rudders (7 kts)

Pulau Rupat (712) Brian Morrison, 8-95

Pulau Rupat (712)—note the second 20-mm AA aft where European navy units normally carry a diver's decompression chamber Brian Morrison, 8-95

Electric: 910 kw tot. (3 × 250 kw, 1 × 160 kw)
Range: 3,500/10; 3,000/12 **Endurance:** 15 days **Crew:** 46 tot.

Remarks: Ordered 29-3-85 and 30-8-85; taken from Royal Netherlands Navy production. Both left for Indonesia 18-8-88. Planned construction of up to ten more in Indonesia did not materialize.
Hull systems: Glass-reinforced plastic construction.
Combat systems: The minehunting system is the Thales IBIS V. Carry two PAP-104 Mk 5 remote-controlled minehunting/destruction submersibles. Have TSM 2060 plot and TMV 628 Trident III radio location system. Sweep equipment includes Fiskars F-82 magnetic sweep tail, SA Marine AS203 acoustic gear, and OD-3 mechanical sweep; there are two sweep-gear cranes. The guns are located on the forecastle and abaft the superstructure.

♦ **9 ex-German Kondor-II-class patrol minesweepers [MSC]**
(6 in reserve) Bldr: VEB Peenewerft, Wolgast

	L	In serv.
721 Pulau Rote (ex-*Grossenhai*, ex-*Wolgast*, V 811)	13-4-70	1-6-71
722 Pulau Raas (ex-*Hettstedt*, 353)	10-4-73	9-8-73
723 Pulau Romang (ex-*Pritzwalk*, 325)	30-7-71	22-12-71
724 Pulau Rimau (ex-*Bitterfeld*, M 2672, ex-332)	30-12-71	26-6-72
725 Pulau Rondo (ex-*Zerbst*, 335)	29-3-72	7-8-72
726 Pulau Rusa (ex-*Oranienburg*, 341)	7-6-72	30-9-72
727 Pulau Rangsang (ex-*Jüterbog*, 342)	30-6-72	1-11-72
728 Pulau Raibu (ex-*Sömmerda*, M 2670, ex-311)	30-11-72	7-4-73
729 Pulau Rempang (ex-*Grimma*, 336)	5-7-73	19-11-73

Pulau Rimau (724) Martijn Westers via A.A. de Kruijf, 7-06

D: 414 tons (479 fl) **S:** 18 kts **Dim:** 56.52 × 7.78 × 2.46
A: 2 twin 25-mm 80-cal. 2M-3M AA; 1 14.5-mm AA; 2 mine rails
Electronics: Radar: 1 TSR-333 nav.—Sonar: MG-11 Tamir-11 HF (24.5–30 kHz)
M: 2 Type 40DM diesels; 2 CP Kort-nozzle props; 4,400 bhp
Electric: 625 kw (5 × 125-kw diesel sets)
Range: 2,000/15 **Endurance:** 10 days **Crew:** 6 officers, 24 enlisted

MINE-COUNTERMEASURES SHIPS *(continued)*

Remarks: Transfer announced 7-92, and all were delivered together via heavy-lift ship to Surabaya for refit and reactivation on 22-10-93. Former Volksmarine units, with two having later served briefly in the German Navy. 726 and 727 were formally recommissioned on 2-2-95, and 725 is also active, but the others may be in too poor condition to reactivate.
Combat systems: Original armament retained. Most of the sweep gear was transferred with the ships, but they were to be employed primarily as patrol boats. Are being fitted with Australian Dyad towed magnetic mine countermeasures devices, with 725 as trials ship. The forward twin 25-mm AA mount has been replaced by a single 14.5-mm gun mounted on the superstructure forward of the pilothouse in the active units.

Disposal note: The last remaining T-43-class minesweeper *Palau Rani* (701) was no longer in service as of 2005. Five of the class were transferred from Russia during 1962–64; three were retired during the early 1980s. Sister *Pulao Ratawo* (702), in collision with merchant ship *Iris* on 17-5-00, was beached at Madura Island, Tanjung Priok, and will not be repaired. They had been used primarily for patrol duties.

AMPHIBIOUS WARFARE SHIPS

♦ 1 (+ 4) Tanjung Dalpele–class Amphibious Transport Dock [LPD]
Bldr: Dae Sun SB & Eng., Pusan, South Korea ; P.T. Pal, Surabaya, Indonesia (last two units)

	L	In serv.
972 Tanjung Dalpele	19-5-03	2004
. . .	. . .	2007
. . .	. . .	2007
. . .	. . .	2008

Tanjung Dalpele (972) photo via Mritunjoy Mazumdar, 2004

D: 11,394 tons (13,000 tons fl) **S:** 16 kts **Dim:** 109.2 × 22.0 × 4.9
A: 1 57 mm Mk 2 AA;1 twin 40-mm AA
Electronics: Radar: 1 . . . nav.
M: 1 M.A.N.-Burmeister & Wain Alpha 8L28/32A diesel; 1 prop; 2,665 bhp
Electric: . . . **Range:** 8600/12
Crew: 14 officers, 106 enlisted

Remarks: The first unit of this class was ordered for delivery to Indonesia during 2004.
Hull systems: Ordered in 2000 for $50 million, 972 is known officially as a hospital ship but serves primarily as command and flagship for the Indonesian fleet. In early 2005 Indonesia announced plans to spend $150 million on three follow-on vessels of the class, the first to be built at Dae Sun shipyard and the remaining two built domestically at P.T. Pal shipyard in Surabaya. Can carry two 23m LCUs.

♦ 6 Teluk Semangka–class tank landing ships [LST]
Bldr: Korea-Tacoma SY, Masan, South Korea

	In serv.		In serv.
512 Teluk Semangka	20-1-81	515 Teluk Sampit	6-81
513 Teluk Penyu	20-1-81	516 Teluk Banten	5-82
514 Teluk Mandar	7-81	517 Teluk Ende	2-9-82

Teluk Penyu (513)—standard unit, without helicopter hangar Brian Morrison, 8-95

D: 1,800 tons (3,770 fl) **S:** 15 kts **Dim:** 100.0 × 15.4 × 4.2 (3.0 mean)
A: 3 (516, 517: 2) single 40-mm 70-cal. Bofors AA; 2 single 20-mm 90-cal. Rheinmetall AA; 2 single 12.7-mm M2 mg
Electronics: Radar: 1 JRC . . . nav.; 1 Raytheon . . . surf. search

Teluk Ende (517)—command unit, with large helicopter hangar and raised helicopter deck Brian Morrison, 8-95

M: 2 diesels; 2 props; 6,860 bhp (5,600 sust.) **Electric:** 750 kw tot.
Range: 7,500/13 **Crew:** 13 officers, 104 enlisted + 202 troops

Remarks: First four ordered 6-79. 516 and 517, modified as command ships and fitted with helicopter hangars, were ordered in 6-81. 517 has been equipped to act as a hospital ship but remains armed.
Hull systems: Cargo: 690 tons (17 main battle tanks); max. beaching load: 1,800 tons. Carry four LCVP-type landing craft. There is a 50-ton-capacity turntable in the tank deck and an elevator to the upper deck. 516 and 517 have a large hangar incorporated into the superstructure, the helicopter deck raised one level, the forward helicopter positions deleted, the landing craft davits moved forward of the superstructure, and increased command facilities to act as flagships; they each can carry three Super Puma helicopters.
Combat systems: The 40-mm mounts in 516 and 517, both on the forecastle, are open topped to save weight; their associated Bofors lead-computing director was not installed, although a raised mounting position remains in place between the guns, but both gunmounts have 128-mm rocket flare launchers on either side of the shielding.

♦ 1 ex-U.S. LST 542–class tank landing ship [LST]
Bldrs: American Bridge, Ambridge, Pa.

	Laid down	L	In serv.
511 Teluk Bone (ex-*Iredell County*, LST 839)	25-9-44	12-11-44	6-12-44

Teluk Bone (511) Brian Morrison, 8-95

D: 1,650 tons light (4,080 fl) **S:** 11.6 kts **Dim:** 99.98 × 15.24 × 4.29
A: 4 single 40-mm 60-cal. Mk 3 Bofors AA; 2 twin 37-mm 63-cal. AA
Electronics: Radar: 2 . . . nav.
M: 2 G.M. 12-567A diesels; 2 props; 1,800 bhp
Electric: 300 kw tot. **Range:** 6,000/9 (loaded) **Fuel:** 590 tons
Crew: 119 ship's company + 264 troops

Remarks: Transferred in 7-70 under the U.S. Military Assistance Program. Can carry 2,100 tons of cargo. Sisters *Teluk Bajer* and *Teluk Tomani* are in the Military Sealift Command, as is the Japanese-built near-sister *Teluk Amboina.* Will probably be discarded soon.
Disposals: *Teluk Langsa* (501, ex-LST 1128), *Teluk Kau* (504, ex-LST 652), *Tekluk Ratai* (509, ex-*Teluk Sindoro;* ex-M/V *Inagua Shipper;* ex-*Presque Isle,* APB 44, ex-LST(M) 678), and *Teluk Saleh* (510; ex-*Clarke County,* LST 601) were placed in reserve in 1995–96 and are used as storage hulks.

♦ 12 ex-German Frosch-I-class (Type 108) medium landing ships [LSM]
Bldr: VEB Peenewerft, Wolgast

	Laid down	L	In serv.
531 Teluk Gelimanuk (ex-*Hoyerswerda,* 611)	25-11-74	1-7-75	12-11-76
532 Teluk Celukan Bawang (ex-*Hagenow,* 632, ex-612)	7-3-75	19-12-75	1-12-76
533 Teluk Cendrawasih (ex-*Frankfurt/Oder,* 613)	10-6-75	2-1-76	2-2-77
534 Teluk Berau (ex-*Eberswalde-Finow,* 634, ex-614)	10-9-75	15-7-76	28-5-77
535 Teluk Peleng (ex-*Lübben,* 632, ex-631)	11-12-75	2-10-76	15-3-78
536 Teluk Sibolga (ex-*Schwerin,* 612, ex-632)	17-3-76	18-1-77	19-10-77
537 Teluk Manado (ex-*Neubrandenburg,* 633)	21-8-76	6-4-77	28-12-77

AMPHIBIOUS WARFARE SHIPS *(continued)*

	Laid down	L	In serv.
538 TELUK HADING (ex-*Cottbus,* 614, ex-634)	22-11-76	16-6-77	26-5-78
539 TELUK PARIGI (ex-*Anklam,* 635)	21-2-77	22-9-77	14-7-78
540 TELUK LAMPUNG (ex-*Schwedt,* 636)	5-5-77	27-12-77	7-9-79
541 TELUK JAKARTA (ex-*Eisenhüttenstadt,* 615)	18-8-77	8-3-78	4-1-79
542 TELUK SANGKULIRANG (ex-*Grimmen,* 616)	2-11-77	30-5-78	15-6-79

Teluk Cendrawasih (533) Leo Dirkx, 10-98

Teluk Sangkulirang (542)—note mine-rail round-downs flanking the stern Brian Morrison, 8-95

D: 1,744 tons normal (1,900 fl) **S:** 19 kts (18 sust.)
Dim: 90.70 × 11.12 × 2.80 (mean; 3.40 max.)
A: 1 twin and 1 single 37-mm 63-cal. AA—536 also: 2 twin 25-mm 80-cal. 2M-3M AA; 2 mine rails (40 mines max.)
Electronics:
Radar: 1 TSR-333 nav.; 1 MR-302 Rubka (Strut Curve) surf./air search
EW: 533, 534 only: 2 16-round PK-16 decoy RL
M: 2 Type 61B 16-cyl. diesels; 2 CP props; 12,000 bhp
Range: 2,450/14 **Crew:** 42 tot.

Remarks: Purchase announced 7-92. Used to supply outlying naval and military facilities. 535 was the first to arrive in Indonesia, 22-11-93. 540 was damaged by heavy seas in the Bay of Biscay during her delivery voyage. 531 was recommissioned for Indonesian service on 12-7-94, 532 on 25-2-94, 533 on 9-12-94, 534 on 10-3-95, 535 on 23-9-93, 536 on 15-12-93, 537 on 2-6-95, 538 on 12-7-94, 539 on 21-7-95, 540 on 26-4-94, 541 on 19-9-94, and 542 on 9-12-94—all while still in Germany.
Hull systems: Cargo capacity 400–600 tons or 12 light tanks and a company of troops. Complex bow door/ramp mechanism; no stern ramp. The vehicle deck totals 425 m^2 and is 4.2 m high. During reactivation, air-conditioning was improved and a sick bay was added.
Combat systems: The original gun armament of two twin 57-mm 70-cal. AK-257 DP, their associated radar director, and two twin 30-mm 65-cal. AK-230 AA was removed from all prior to delivery. Also removed were two 40-tubed artillery rocket launchers, where fitted, and two PK-16 decoy rocket launchers. A twin V-11-M mount has replaced the forward 57-mm mount and a single 37-mm AA has replaced the after 57-mm gun, while 25-mm gunmounts have replaced the 30-mm mounts abreast the stack on 536 and possibly others; all gunmounts were recycled from stricken Soviet-built units formerly in Indonesian service.

♦ 2 Frosch-II-class (Type 109) amphibious support ships [LSM]
Bldr: VEB Peenewerft, Wolgast

	Laid down	L	In serv.
543 TELUK SIREBON (ex-*Nordperd,* E 171, ex-E 35)	26-1-78	30-8-78	3-10-79
544 TELUK SABANG (ex-*Südperd,* E 172, ex-E 36)	16-4-78	30-10-78	26-2-80

D: 1,530 tons normal **S:** 16 kts **Dim:** 90.70 × 11.12 × 3.40 (max.)
A: 1 twin and 1 single 37-mm 63-cal. AA; 2 mine rails (40 mines max.)

Teluk Sirebon (543) Chris Delgoffe/H&L Van Ginderen, 5-00

Teluk Sabang (544)—at start of delivery voyage to Indonesia, prior to installation of armament; note the large crane forward Hartmut Ehlers, 4-95

Electronics:
Radar: 1 TSR-333 nav.; 1 MR-302 Rubka (Strut Curve) surf./air search
EW: 2 16-round PK-16 decoy RL
M: 2 Type 61B 16-cyl. diesels; 2 CP props; 12,000 bhp **Crew:** 35 tot.

Remarks: Purchase announced 7-92. Both were recommissioned 25-4-95 after reactivation at Neustadt and arrived in Indonesia during 6-95. Are numbered as landing ships in Indonesian service.
Hull systems: Were typed as "High Seas Supply Ships" (*Hochseeversorger*) in Volksmarine service and have a 650-ton deadweight cargo capacity. Differed from Frosch-I class in having an 8-ton Type 2Hy SWK8 crane amidships and two cargo hatches, and in having 25-mm (mounted starboard forward to cover the beach) in place of 30-mm AA. The bow ramp was retained to permit a beaching capability, and they presumably can be used as assault landing ships if needed. During reactivation, the air-conditioning was improved, and a sick bay was added.
Combat systems: Two 16-tubed PK-16 chaff rocket launchers were added 1986, just forward of bridge. Gun armament of two twin 57-mm 70-cal. AK-257 DP and two twin 30-mm 65-cal. AK-230 AA were removed prior to delivery. Old Soviet weapons from storage were added after arrival in Indonesia.

♦ 20 U.S. LCM(6)-class landing craft [LCM]
Bldr: . . . SY, Taiwan (In serv. 1988)

D: 24 tons (57.5 fl) **S:** 13 kts (light) **Dim:** 17.07 × 4.37 × 1.14
M: 2 G.M. Detroit Diesel 6V71 diesels; 2 props; 450 bhp
Range: 130/9 (loaded) **Crew:** 5 tot. + 80 troops

Remarks: GRP construction. Cargo: 30 tons. Cargo well 11.9 × 3.7 m.

♦ Approx. 24 LCVP Mk 7 class [LCVP]

D: 13 tons (fl) **S:** 9 kts **Dim:** 10.90 × 3.21 × 1.04 (aft)
M: 1 Gray Marine 64HN9 diesel; 225 bhp **Range:** 110/9

Indonesian Navy LCVP—GRP-construction unit from LST *Teluk Penyu* (513) H&L Van Ginderen, 8-95

Remarks: Eighteen Korean-built units, delivered in 1981–82 with new LSTs, have GRP hulls. The others are survivors from among those delivered on World War II–era U.S.-built LSTs. Can carry 36 troops or 3.5 tons cargo. Cargo deck is 5.24 × 2.29 m, with 2.00-m-wide access through the bow ramp.

♦ 6 Sekoci-class personnel landing craft [LCP]
Bldr: Fasharkan Mentigi Naval DY (In serv. 5-94)

D: . . . tons (fl) **S:** 35 kts **Dim:** 28.0 × . . . × . . .
M: 2 . . . diesels; 2 props; . . . bhp **Crew:** . . . tot. + 30 troops

Remarks: GRP construction. Have a bow ramp for disembarking troops and light vehicles.

AUXILIARIES

♦ 1 command ship [AGF]
Bldr: Ishikawajima Harima, Tokyo, Japan (L: 13-6-61)

561 Multatuli

Multatuli (561) Brian Morrison, 8-95

D: 3,220 tons (6,741 fl) **S:** 18.5 kts **Dim:** 111.35 (103.0 pp) × 16.0 × 6.98
A: 2 twin and 2 single 37-mm 63-cal. AA; 2 twin 14.5-mm 93-cal. 2M-7 AA
Electronics: Radar: 1 . . . nav.
M: 1 Burmeister & Wain diesel; 5,500 bhp
Range: 6,000/16 **Fuel:** 1,400 tons **Crew:** 134 tot.

Remarks: Built as a submarine-support ship; converted as a fleet command ship in the late 1960s. Acts as fleet flagship for the Eastern Command. Has a helicopter platform aft. Equipped with British Marconi ICS-3 integrated communications suite. Can supply fuel and stores to ships in company. Construction of two similar ships of about 10,000 tons, to carry fuel, troops, and hospital facilities, is planned as a long-term goal.

♦ 1 Baruna Jaya VIII–class research ship [AGOR]
Bldr: CMN, Cherbourg, France (In serv. 1998)

KAL-IV-06 Baruna Jaya VIII

Baruna Jaya VIII (KAL-IV-06) A. A. de Kruijf, 9-98

D: 1,350 tons (fl) **S:** 13 kts **Dim:** 66.5 × 12.0 × 4.5
A: None
Electronics: Radar: 1 Furuno . . . X-band nav.; 1 . . . S-band nav.
M: 2 Pielstick 5PA5 L255 diesels; 1 CP prop; 2,990 bhp—200-shp bow-thruster—150-shp active rudder
Range: 7,500/12 **Crew:** 11 officers, 30 enlisted + 23 scientific staff

Remarks: Was to have been ordered 2-11-95, but the contract was delayed until early 1998. Employed for oil exploration work in eastern Indonesian waters. Equipped with a Marisat commercial SATCOM terminal.

♦ 4 Baruna Jaya I–class research ships [AGOR]
Bldr: CMN, Cherbourg, France

	In serv.
KAL-IV-02 Baruna Jaya I	15-9-89
KAL-IV-03 Baruna Jaya II	12-89
KAL-IV-04 Baruna Jaya III	4-90
KAL-IV-05 Baruna Jaya IV	2-11-95

D: 1,180 tons (1,350 fl) **S:** 14 kts **Dim:** 60.03 (55.28 pp) × 11.61 × 5.31
A: None
M: 2 Niigata-Pielstick 5 PA5 L255 diesels; 1 CP prop; 2,990 bhp—200-shp bow-thruster—150-shp active rudder
Electric: 1,856 kVA (3 628-kVA Leroy Somer shaft generators; 1 400-kVA Caterpillar 3406 diesel-driven; 1 200-kVA harbor diesel generator)
Range: 7,500/12 **Fuel:** 352 m^3
Crew: 8 officers, 29 enlisted + 26 scientific staff

Remarks: 300 grt/450 dwt. First three originally ordered from C.N. la Manche, Dieppe, 2-85. *Baruna Jaya IV,* ordered 1993, is 1,425 tons (fl) and is specially equipped for fisheries research. Operated by the Indonesian Navy Hydrographic Office for the "owners," the Agency for the Assessment and Application of Technology. Carry a small landing craft and one or more inshore survey launches and have a large A-frame gantry crane across the stern. *Baruna Jaya I* has a Marisat SATCOM radome added forward of the pilothouse, atop a lattice mast. *Baruna Jaya III* is available for commercial charter.

Baruna Jaya II (KAL-IV-03)—with two survey launches aboard
Brian Morrison, 8-95

Baruna Jaya I (KAL-IV-02)—with lattice mast forward to support a SATCOM antenna Chris Sattler/H&L Van Ginderen, 1-97

Baruna Jaya III is on long-term charter to Thales Geosystems (formerly Racal Survey) for cable-route survey operations and completed a refit at Pan United, Singapore, in 9-00, receiving a dual Simrad EM12D double-swath deep-ocean survey echo sounder, Elac BottomChart Mk II high-resolution medium- and shallow-depth bathymetric system, and Simrad EA500 dual-frequency deepwater single-beam echo sounder; the ship is also fitted with Thomson Marconi Posidonia 6000 hydroacoustic positioning system, deep-tow GeoChirp II side-scan sonar and bottom profiler, a 16-transducer hull-mounted sub-bottom profiler, a cesium magnetometer, a gravity piston-corer, a vibro-corer, and a computerized data recording system.

Note: Also in service is *Baruna Jaya VII,* a slightly smaller ship of unknown origin.

♦ 1 hydrometeorological and oceanographic ship [AGOR]
Bldr: Sasebo Heavy Industries, Japan (In serv. 12-1-63)

933 Jalanidhi

Jalanidhi (933) H&L Van Ginderen, 3-99

D: 740 tons (985 fl) **S:** 12.7 kts **Dim:** 53.9 (48.5 pp) × 9.5 × 4.3
Electronics: Radar: 1 Nikkon Denko . . . nav.; 1 Furuno . . . nav.
M: 1 M.A.N. G6V 30/42 diesel; 1 prop; 1,000 bhp
Electric: 261 kw tot. **Range:** 7,200/10.5 **Fuel:** 165 tons
Crew: 13 officers, 74 enlisted + 26 technicians/scientists

Remarks: Has a weather-balloon facility aft and a stern ramp for net hauls.

AUXILIARIES *(continued)*

♦ 1 Burudjulasad-class hydrographic survey ship [AGS]

	Bldr	L	In serv.
931 Burudjulasad	Schlichtingwerft, Travemünde	8-65	1967

Burudjulasad (931) H&L Van Ginderen, 4-99

D: 1,815 tons (2,165 fl) **S:** 19 kts **Dim:** 82.00 (78.00 pp) × 11.40 × 3.50
A: Provision for 1 twin 37-mm 63-cal. AA; 2 twin 12.7-mm mg
Electronics: Radar: 1 Decca TM 262 nav. (probably replaced)
M: 4 M.A.N. V6V 22/30 diesels; 2 CP props; 6,400 bhp
Electric: 1,008 kw **Range:** 14,500/15.7 **Fuel:** 600 tons
Crew: 15 officers, 93 enlisted + 28 technicians

Remarks: Can carry one light helicopter and is equipped to perform oceanographic and hydrometeorological research as well as hydrographic surveys. Carries one LCVP landing craft and three hydrographic launches. Refitted in U.K. 3-86 to 10-86. An armament of one twin 37-mm AA and two twin 12.7-mm mg was added circa 1991, with the twin 37-mm mount installed just forward of the bridge and the machineguns placed in the tubs abaft the boats, but these had been removed by 1999.

♦ 1 U.K. Hecla-class hydrographic survey ship [AGS]
Bldr: Yarrow & Co., Blythswood, Scotland

	Laid down	L	In serv.
932 Dewa Kembar (ex-*Hydra*, A 144)	14-5-64	14-7-65	5-5-66

Dewa Kembar (932) Chris Sattler/H&L Van Ginderen, 11-97

D: 1,915 tons (2,733 fl) **S:** 14 kts **Dim:** 79.25 (71.63 pp) × 14.94 × 4.00
A: 2 single 12.7-mm mg
Electronics: Radar: 2 Decca 1226 nav.—Sonar: British Type 2034 side-scan
M: Diesel-electric: 3 Paxman 12YJCZ Ventura diesels (1,190 bhp each), 3 G.E.C.-A.E.I. 610-kw generators, electric motor; 1 prop; 2,000 shp—bow-thruster
Electric: 820 kw tot. (2 × 300-kw diesel-driven sets; 1 × 200-kw and 1 × 20-kw diesel emergency sets)
Range: 12,000/11; 20,000/9 **Fuel:** 450 tons **Crew:** 14 officers, 109 enlisted

Remarks: Purchased 18-4-86; refitted by Vosper Thornycroft, Southampton, 24-4-86 to 16-7-86. Recommissioned 10-9-86 and left for Indonesia 1-10-86. Retains Marisat satellite communications gear. Carries two survey launches.
Hull systems: Has a passive-tank stabilization system. Main propulsion generators operate at 510 V. Has hangar and platform for a light helicopter.

♦ 1 ex-U.K. Rover-class replenishment oiler [AO]
Bldr: Swan Hunter, Hebburn-on-Tyne

	L	In serv.
903 Arun (ex-*Green Rover*, A 268)	19-12-68	15-8-69

D: 4,700 tons light (11,522 fl) **S:** 19.25 kts (17 sust.) **Dim:** 140.5 × 19.2 × 7.3
A: 2 single 40-mm 60-cal. Bofors AA; 2 single 20-mm 70-cal. Oerlikon AA

Arun (903) RAN, 10-04

Electronics: Radar: 1 Kelvin-Hughes Type 1006 nav.; 2 . . . nav.
M: 2 SEMT-Pielstick 16 PA4 diesels; 1 CP prop; 15,300 bhp
Electric: 2,720 kw **Range:** 14,000/15 **Fuel:** 965 tons
Crew: 16 officers, 31 enlisted

Remarks: 7,510 grt/6,822 dwt. Purchased 1-92 and sailed to Indonesia 9-92 after refit at Swan Hunter, Wallsend. Has 13 cargo tanks totaling 8,155 m^3 and one 387-m^3 dry cargo/provisions hold. Cargo capacity includes 7,460 m^3 for fuel, 325 m^3 for water, and 70 m^3 for lube oil; 600 m^3 aviation fuel or gasoline can be carried in lieu of ship fuel. The helicopter deck aft can handle up to a Sea King–sized aircraft, but there is no hangar. Re-engined 1973–74. Armament was added late in 1996.

♦ 1 Sorong-class replenishment oiler [AO]
Bldr: Trogir SY, Yugoslavia (In serv. 4-65)

911 Sorong

Sorong (911) Brian Morrison, 8-95

D: Approx. 8,700 tons (fl) **S:** 15 kts **Dim:** 112.17 × 15.4 × 6.6
A: 4 12.7-mm mg (II × 2) **Electronics:** Radar: 1 . . . nav.
M: 1 diesel; 1 prop; . . . bhp **Crew:** 110 tot.

Remarks: 4,090 grt/5,100 dwt.. Cargo: 3,000 tons fuel/300 tons water. Can conduct underway alongside replenishments using hoses from jackstay rigs at amidships king-post stations port and starboard; can also refuel over the stern.

♦ 1 small transport oiler [AOT]
Bldr: . . . (In serv. . . .)

906 Sungai Jerong

Remarks: Has been in service since at least 1996 and appears to have been built in Russia or another former Warsaw Pact country during 1960s. Is armed with one 37-mm 63-cal. AA gun. No other data available.

Disposal note: Ex-U.S. *Achelous*-class repair ship *Jaja Widjaja* (921, ex-*Askari*, ARL 30, ex-LST 1131) was retired by 2005. The hulk of the Russian Don-class (Project 310) submarine tender *Ratulangi* is still afloat and was displayed at the 8-95 naval review at Jakarta, but the ship is nonoperational.

♦ 1 Soputan-class salvage tug [ARS]
Bldr: Dae Sun SB & Eng., Pusan, South Korea (In serv. 27-9-96)

923 Soputan

D: Approx. 2,100 tons (fl) **S:** 13.5 kts **Dim:** 66.20 × 11.93 × 4.51
A: . . . **Electronics:** Radar: 2 Decca . . . nav.
M: 4 Pielstick–Sang Yong . . . 8-cyl. diesels, electric drive; 1 prop; 12,240 shp—bow-thruster
Range: . . . / . . . **Crew:** 42 tot.

Remarks: 1,279 grt/1,470 dwt. Very large and capable firefighting and salvage tugs with unusual two-deck forecastle design. 923 delivered 7-95 but not commissioned for over a year thereafter. Has a 120-ton bollard pull capacity.

Disposal note: Ex-U.S. *Cherokee*-class fleet tug *Rakata* (922, ex-*Menominee*, ATF 73) had been retired by 2005.

AUXILIARIES *(continued)*

Soputan (923) Brian Morrison, 8-95

Soputan (923) Brian Morrison, 8-95

◆ **1 sail-training barkentine [AXT]**
Bldr: H. C. Stülcken & Sohn, Hamburg (L: 21-1-52; in serv. 9-7-53)

DEWARUCI

Dewaruci Bernard Prézelin, 8-05

D: 847 tons (fl) **S:** 9 kts **Dim:** 58.30 (41.50 pp) × 9.5 × 4.23
M: 1 M.A.N. diesel; 575 bhp—max. sail area: 1,091 m^2
Crew: 110 ship's company + 78 cadets

Remarks: Steel construction. Has been very active in the past several years.

SERVICE CRAFT

◆ **1 Lampo Batang–class medium harbor tug [YTM]**
Bldr: Ishikawajima Harima, Tokyo (L: 4-61)

934 LAMPO BATANG

D: 250 tons **S:** 11 kts **Dim:** 28.1 × 7.6 × 2.6
M: 2 M.A.N. diesels; 2 props; 600 bhp
Range: 1,000/11 **Fuel:** 18 tons **Crew:** 13 tot.

◆ **2 Tambora-class medium harbor tugs [YTM]**
Bldr: Ishikawajima Harima, Tokyo (both L: 6-61)

935 TAMBORA 936 BROMO

D: 250 tons (fl) **S:** 10.5 kts **Dim:** 24.1 × 6.6 × 3.0
M: 2 M.A.N. diesels; 2 props; 600 bhp
Range: 690/10.5 **Fuel:** 9 tons **Crew:** 15 tot.

Remarks: 935 is on loan to the Indonesian Army.

◆ **1 sail-training schooner [YTS]**
Bldr: Hendrik Oosterbroek, Tauranga, New Zealand (L: 7-91)

ARUNG SAMUDERA (ex-*Adventurer*)

Arung Samudera H&L Van Ginderen, 1-98

D: 280 tons (fl) **S:** 10 kts (under power) **Dim:** 39.00 (31.60 wl) × 6.50 × 2.60
Electronics: Radar: 1 Furuno . . . X-band nav.
M: 2 Ford 2725E diesels; 2 props; 292 bhp—max. sail area: 433.8 m^2
Crew: 20 tot.

Remarks: 96 grt. Taken over and commissioned on 9-1-96.

Note: Also in use for training at the Naval Academy is the smaller, noncommissioned sailing craft *Phinbi Nusantara;* no data available. There are probably numerous other small tugs, launches, fuel lighters, and so forth, in service, but no information is available about their numbers or characteristics.

MILITARY SEALIFT COMMAND
(*Kolinlamil*)

The Military Sealift Command was formed in 1978 to coordinate the Indonesian Navy's logistic support for its far-flung bases and outposts in the Indonesian Archipelago. Some of the units have been taken over from the Indonesian Army and others from the navy.

AMPHIBIOUS LOGISTICS TRANSPORTS

◆ **1 Teluk Amboina–class tank landing ship [LST]**
Bldr: Sasebo Heavy Industries, Japan (L: 17-3-61)

503 TELUK AMBOINA

Teluk Amboina (503) Brian Morrison, 8-95

MILITARY SEALIFT COMMAND AMPHIBIOUS LOGISTICS TRANSPORTS *(continued)*

D: 4,145 tons (fl) **S:** 13 kts **Dim:** 99.90 (95.41 pp) × 15.24 × 4.60
A: 6 single 37-mm 63-cal. Soviet V-47M AA (I × 6)
M: 2 M.A.N. V6V 22.30 diesels; 2 props; 3,200 bhp (2,850 sust.)
Electric: 135 kw **Range:** 4,000/13 **Fuel:** 1,200 tons
Crew: 88 ship's company + 212 passengers

Remarks: Built as war reparations. Near-duplicate of U.S. LST 542 design. Cargo: 2,100 tons max.; can carry 654 tons cargo water. Has a 30-ton crane and davits for four LCVPs.

Note: Two former U.S. Navy LST 542–class tank landing ships transferred to the Military Sealift Command for cattle and cargo transport service, the *Teluk Bajer* (502, ex-LST 616) and the *Teluk Tomini* (508, ex-M/V *Inagua Crest;* ex-M/V *Brunei;* ex-*Polk County,* LST 356), were placed in reserve in 1995–96 and are unlikely to see further service.

♦ 3 Kupang-class utility landing craft [LCU]
Bldr: Surabaya DY

582 Kupang (In serv. 3-11-78) 584 Nusantara (In serv. 1980)
583 Dili (In serv. 27-2-79)

D: 400 tons (fl) **S:** 11 kts **Dim:** 42.9 (36.27 pp) × 9.14 × 1.80
M: 4 diesels; 2 props; 1,200 bhp **Range:** 700/11 **Crew:** 17 tot.

Remarks: Design based on U.S. LCU 1610 class. Cargo: 200 tons.

♦ 1 Amurang-class landing craft [LCU]
Bldr: Korneuberg SY, Austria (In serv. 1968)

580 Dore

D: 182 tons (255 fl) **S:** 8 kts **Dim:** 38.30 (36.00 pp) × 10.00 × 1.30
M: 2 diesels; 2 props; 420 bhp **Range:** 600/8 **Crew:** 14 tot.

Remarks: 200 grt. Sister *Banten* and one other are in merchant service. Naval unit *Amurang* (581) was lost at sea during 9-92.

AUXILIARIES

Note: During 10-03, it was reported that the Japanese Malacca Strait Council (MSC) had handed over the buoy tender *Jadayat* in an effort to improve navigational safety in the Straits of Malacca. The vessel is said to be based at Kianj Port on Bintan Island.

♦ 2 . . . -class pollution control ships [AG]
Bldr: Damen, Gorinchem, the Netherlands, and . . . Indonesia (In serv. 2003–5)

. . . . . .

D: . . . **S:** 17 kts **Dim:** 61.8 × 9.7 × 3.2
A: . . . **Electronics:** Radar: 1 . . . nav.
M: 2 MTU . . . diesels; 2 CP props; . . . bhp
Range: 3000/17 **Crew:** 51

Remarks: Used for pollution-control and search-and-rescue duties. Built in sections by Damen with construction completed by local shipyards. May serve in the Sea Communications Agency rather than the Navy.

♦ 2 Hungarian Tisza-class cargo ships [AK]
Bldr: Angyalfold SY, Budapest (In serv. 1963–64)

959 Teluk Mentawi 960 Karamaja

Karamaja (960) Piet Sinke, 6-93

D: 2,000 tons (fl) **S:** 12 kts **Dim:** 74.5 (67.4 pp) × 11.3 × 4.6
A: 2 twin 14.5-mm 93-cal. 2M-7 AA **Electronics:** Radar: 1 . . . nav.
M: 1 Lang 8-cyl. diesel; 1,000 bhp **Electric:** 746 kw
Range: 4,200/10.7 **Fuel:** 98 tons **Crew:** 26 tot.

Remarks: 1,296 grt/1,280 dwt. Taken over from the army in 1978. Cargo: 1,100 tons. Sisters *Telaud* (951), *Nusatelu* (952), *Natuna* (953), and *Karamundsa* (957) had been stricken by 1991.

♦ 1 Biscaya-class cargo ship (AK)
Bldr: . . . (In serv. 1950s)

952 Nusu Telu

Remarks: A small coastal cargo vessel dating from the late 1950s and armed with one twin 12.7-mm mg mount forward. Is about half the size of the *Tisza* class above. No other data available.

Nusu Telu (952) Brian Morrison, 8-95

♦ 1 small transport tanker [AOT]
Bldr: . . ., Japan (In serv. 1969)

902 Sambu (ex-*Taiyo Maru No. 3*)

Sambu (902) Brian Morrison, 8-95

D: 2,800 tons (fl) **S:** 11 kts **Dim:** 70.4 × 11.4 × 5.8
A: 2 twin and 2 single 12.7-mm mg **Electronics:** Radar: 3 . . . nav.
M: 1 diesel; 1 prop; . . . bhp **Crew:** . . . tot.

Remarks: Purchased 1978.

♦ 1 small transport tanker [AOT]
Bldr: . . . SY, Japan (In serv. 1965)

901 Balikpapan (ex-*Komado V*)

Balikpapan (901)—alongside survey ship *Dewa Kembar* (932)
Chris Delgoffe/H&L Van Ginderen, 5-00

D: . . . **S:** 11 kts **Dim:** 69.6 × 9.6 × 4.9
Electronics: Radar: 1 . . . nav.
M: 1 diesel; 1 prop; 1,300 bhp **Crew:** 26 tot.

Remarks: 1,780-dwt commercial tanker purchased 1977.

Disposal note: Former passenger/cargo ship *Tanjung Oisina* (972, ex-*Tjut Njak Dhien,* ex-*Prinses Irene*) was aground and partially stripped at Jakarta as of 11-00.

SERVICE CRAFT

♦ . . . coastal cargo lighter(s) [YF]
Bldr: Fasharkan DY, Manokwari, Irian Jaya

D: . . . **S:** 8 kts **Dim:** 31.1 × 6.26 × 1.80 **M:** Diesels

Remarks: 200 dwt. First unit delivered 7-3-82. Others may have been built.

INDONESIAN ARMY (ADRI)
(*Jawatan Angkutan Darat Militer*)

SERVICE CRAFT

♦ 3 ADRI XLI–class logistics landing craft [WYF]
Bldr: P.T. Kodja i, Tanjung Priok (In serv. 1982)

ADRI XLI ADRI XLII ADRI XLIII

D: Approx. 480 tons (fl) **S:** . . . kts **Dim:** 32.80 (28.50 pp) × 8.54 × 2.65
M: 2 G.M. Detroit Diesel 12V71-series diesels; 2 props; 680 bhp

Remarks: 171 grt.

♦ 5 ADRI XXXIII–class logistics landing craft [WYF]
Bldr: P.T. Kodja i and P.T. Adiguna Shipyards, Tanjung Priok (In serv. 1979–81)

ADRI XXXIII ADRI XXXV ADRI XXXVII
ADRI XXXIV ADRI XXXVI

D: Approx. 300 tons (fl) **S:** . . . kts **Dim:** 32.01 (28.25 pp) × 8.50 × 1.35
M: 2 G.M. Detroit Diesel 8V71N diesels; 2 props; 460 bhp
Electric: 70 kw tot. **Crew:** . . . tot.

Remarks: 169 grt/150 dwt. Have bow ramp and can be beached.

♦ 1 ADRI XXXII–class logistics landing craft [WYF]
Bldr: P.T. Ippa Gaya Baru, Tanjung Priok (In serv. 1979)

ADRI XXXII

ADRI XXXII H&L Van Ginderen, 8-95

D: Approx. 490 tons (fl) **S:** . . . kts **Dim:** 37.01 × 10.71 × 1.65
M: 2 G.M. Detroit Diesel 12V71TI diesels; 2 props; 1,050 bhp

Remarks: 390 grt/300 dwt. Deck cargo only.

♦ 1 ADRI XL–class general cargo lighter [WYF]
Bldr: . . . . SY, Indonesia (In serv. 1981)

ADRI XL

D: Approx. 520 tons (fl) **S:** 12 kts **Dim:** 44.73 (40.01 pp) × 7.60 × 2.65
M: 2 G.M. Detroit Diesel 16V71N diesels; 2 props; 910 bhp

Remarks: 320 grt/300 dwt.

♦ 2 ADRI XXXVIII–class general cargo lighters [WYF]
Bldr: P.T. Adiguna SY, Tanjung Priok (In serv. 1981)

ADRI XXXVIII ADRI XXXIX

D: Approx. 145 tons (fl) **S:** . . . kts **Dim:** 26.14 (23.09 pp) × 6.80 × 1.46
M: 2 Baudouin 12F11SR 12-cyl. diesels; 2 props; 468 bhp

Remarks: 125 grt/100 dwt.

♦ 4 ADRI XVI–class general cargo lighters [WYF]
Bldr: Wroclawska Stocznia Rzeczna, Wroclaw, Poland (In serv. 1963–64)

ADRI XVI ADRI XVII ADRI XVIII ADRI XIX

D: Approx. 700 tons (fl) **S:** 7 kts **Dim:** 53.52 (49.99 pp) × 8.26 × 2.59
M: 2 Karl Liebknecht S.K.L. 12-cyl diesels; 2 props; 600 bhp
Electric: 25 kw tot.

Remarks: 443 grt/549 dwt. Two holds. Two 3-ton derricks.

♦ 1 ADRI III–class general cargo lighter [WYF]
Bldr: Vereenigde Prauwen Verer, Tanjung Priok (In serv. 1954)

D: . . . tons **S:** . . . kts **Dim:** 34.45 (32.01 pp) × 5.49 × . . .
M: 1 Werkspoor diesel; 234 bhp

Remarks: 157 grt/152 dwt.

Note: The Indonesian Air Force logistics fleet has been sold or stricken.

SEA COMMUNICATIONS AGENCY

The Sea Communications Agency was established in 1978 to patrol Indonesia's 200-n.m. economic zone and to maintain navigational aids. Its full name is the Indonesian Directorate General of Sea Communication/Department of Transport, Communications, and Tourism. Patrol boats are now painted with blue hull (with white and red diagonal stripes) and white superstructure.

Note: Two 62-meter Dutch-built Damen 6210 patrol craft (one named *Tribula*) and 2 530-ton patrol ships named *Arda Dedali* and *Alugara* entered service between 2004 and 2006, though they may in fact serve with a newly formed Indonesian Coast Guard. The four craft are white with one wide orange and one thin blue stripe pointed on the sides.

PATROL CRAFT [WPC]

♦ 4 Golok class
Bldr: Schlichtingwerft, Harmsdorf, Germany

	In serv.		In serv.
PAT 206 GOLOK	12-3-82	PAT 208 PEDANG	12-5-82
PAT 207 PANAN	12-3-82	PAT 209 KAPAK	12-5-82

Kapak (PAT 209) Chris Sattler/H&L Van Ginderen, 11-98

D: 200 tons (fl) **S:** 28 kts **Dim:** 37.50 × 7.00 × 2.00
A: 1 20-mm AA
M: 2 MTU 16V652 TB61 diesels; 2 props; 4,200 bhp
Range: 1,500/18 **Crew:** 18 tot.

Remarks: Intended for search-and-rescue duties. 120-m^3/hr firepump and water monitor, rescue launch, eight-man sick bay. Hulls built by Deutsche Industrie Werke, Berlin.

♦ 5 Kujang class
Bldr: SFCN, Villeneuve-la-Garenne, France

	Laid down	L	In serv.
PAT 201 KUJANG	5-80	17-10-80	19-8-81
PAT 202 PARANG	7-80	18-11-80	19-8-81
PAT 203 CELURIT	9-80	20-3-81	1981
PAT 204 CUNDRIK	7-9-80	10-11-80	1981
PAT 205 BELATI	2-81	21-5-81	10-81

Cundrik (PAT 204) Chris Sattler/H&L Van Ginderen, 11-98

D: 126 tons (162 fl) **S:** 28 kts **Dim:** 38.32 (35.46 pp) × 6.00 × 1.78 (2.60 props)
A: 1 12.7-mm mg **Electronics:** Radar: 1 . . . nav.
M: 2 S.A.C.M. AGO V12 195 CZ SHR T5; 2 props; 4,400 bhp
Range: 1,500/18 **Crew:** 18 tot.

Remarks: Equipped for search-and-rescue duties.

PATROL BOATS [WPB]

♦ 6 PAT 01 class
Bldr: Tanjung Priok SY (In serv. 1978–79)

PAT 01 PAT 02 PAT 03 PAT 04 PAT 05 PAT 06

D: 12 tons (fl) **S:** 14 kts **Dim:** 12.15 × 4.25 × 1.0
A: 1 7.62-mm mg **M:** 1 Renault diesel; 260 bhp

Note: In addition to patrol boats, the Sea Communications Agency operates a large number of commercial passenger vessels in interisland service and is also responsible for undersea communications cable laying and maintenance and for navigational aids and dredging. In service are:

- 1 or more *Fudi*-class vehicle and passenger ships: *Fudi* (In serv. 2000)
- 9 14,610- to 14,800-grt *Dobensolo*-class passenger ships: *Dobensolo, Diremai, Bukit, Siguntang, Lambelu, Sinabung, Kelud, Doro Londa,* and *Nggapulu* (In serv. 1993–2002)

SEA COMMUNICATIONS AGENCY PATROL BOATS [WPB] *(continued)*

- 4 6,041-grt *Leuser*-class passenger ships: *Binaiya, Kukit Raya, Bukit Siguntang Mahameru,* and *Tilongkabila* (In serv. 1994–95)
- 5 5,685- to 6,041-grt *Lawit*-class passenger ships: *Lawit, Tatamailu, Awu, Telimutu,* and *Sirimau* (In serv. 1986–92)
- 5 13,861- to 13,954-grt *Kerinci*-class passenger ships: *Kerinci, Kambuna, Rinjani, Umsini,* and *Tidar* (In serv. 1983–88)
- 2 569-grt *Karakata*-class navigational aids tenders: *Karakata* and *Kumba* (In serv. 1976)
- 2 1,705-grt *Majang*-class navigational aids and lighthouse supply ships: *Majang* and *Mizan* (In serv. 1963)
- 1 1,250-dwt *Biduk*-class cable tender and navigational aids tender: *Biduk* (In serv. 1952)
- 4 miscellaneous dredges: *Batang Anai, Irian,* and 2 others

Note: The Customs Agency operates more than 100 patrol boats, all armed with one or more 12.7-mm mg:

- 5 BC 10001 class (In serv. 1999–2000): BC 10001, 10002, 20001–20003
- 10 BC 1601 class (In serv. 11-98 to 6-99): BC 1601–1610
- 4 12.6-m class (In serv. 1995): . . .
- 41 FBP 28 class (In serv. 1981–96): BC 4001–4006, 5001–5006, 6001–6005, 7001–7005, 8001–8005, 9001–9005, and nine others
- 7 BC 2001 class (In serv. 1980–81): BC 2001–2007
- 7 BC 3001 class (In serv. 1979–81): BC 3001–3007
- 3 BC 1001 class (In serv. 1975): BC 1001–1003
- up to 40 BC 401 class (In serv. 1960–62): BC 501–504, 601–604, 701–704, 801–804, and 901–904

Remarks: The first two BC 10001 class were built by Friedrich Lürssen Werft, Germany, and delivered 11-5-99 and 11-99; the others were built by P.T. Pal, Surabaya, Indonesia, and delivered 9-99 to 6-02. Data include:

D: 85 tons (fl) **S:** 40 kts **Dim:** 28.2 × 6.6 × 1.4
A: 2 single 7.62-mm mg **Electronics:** Radar: 1 Furuno FR8731 nav.
M: 2 MTU 16V396 TE94 diesels; 2 props; 2,996 bhp
Range: 1,100/30 **Crew:** 3 officers, 8 enlisted

The BC 1601 class was built entirely by Lürssen. Capable of 50 kts and employing a wave-piercing hullform, the 11-ton craft are powered by two 300-bhp MTU diesels, have a crew of one officer and four enlisted, and are armed with a 7.62-mm machinegun. Dimensions: 16.0 × 2.8 × 1.0 m.

Note: The National Police organization operates 57 or more patrol craft and boats, many armed with one to three single 20-mm Oerlikon AA. These are described and illustrated in previous editions and include:

- 9 DKN 908 class (In serv. 1961–64): DKN 908–916
- 10 DKN 504 class (In serv. 1963–64)
- 6 *Carpenteria* class (In serv. 1976–77): KAL-II.201 through KAL-II.206
- 32 "Chase Boats" (In serv. 1982–86)

The National Police ordered two 660-grt patrol ships from Astlleros Gondan SA, Spain, late in 2002; the ships will be 61 m overall by 9 m beam and will have a single 9,000-bhp MTU diesel propulsion engine.

Seven Jasa-class "inspection/navigation craft"—the *Antares, Altair, Adhara, Arcturus, Aldebaran, Mokmer,* and *Marapa*—are stationed at the ports of Sabang, Sibolga, Belawan, Tanjung Pinang, Jayapura, Banjarmasin, and Samarinda. Built by Jasa Marina Indah SY, they were delivered two in 1999, three on 31-1-00, and two on 29-2-00. No data are available other than that they are of 550 grt.

IRAN

Islamic Republic of Iran

IRANIAN NAVY

Personnel: Approximately 18,000 total Navy and 2,600 Marines. This does not include the Pasdaran Revolutionary Guard Corps Navy, which is listed separately.

Bases: Fleet headquarters and principal dockyard at Bandar Abbas, with lesser facilities in the Persian Gulf at Kharg Island and Khorramshahr, on the Arabian Sea at Chah Bahar, and on the Caspian Coast at Bandar Anzali, where the Fourth Naval Zone (with headquarters at Noushehr) operates some 50 patrol boats. Russian shipyards are to assist Iran in developing a submarine repair facility.

Maritime Aviation: Believed to be available for service are six ASH-3D Sea King, six AB-212, up to 10 Bell 206 JetRanger, and two RH-53D helicopters. Fixed-wing assets remaining include three P-3F Orion long-range maritime patrol aircraft, four Fokker F-27-400M Friendship transports, and four Falcon 20 transports. The Iranian Air Force also employs 20 ex-Russian Mi-8AMT(Sh)/Mi-171 helicopters (delivered from 4-00, with up to 30 more planned to be acquired), several Lockheed C-130H-MP long-range maritime reconnaissance aircraft, and five Dornier Do-228 light maritime reconnaissance aircraft.

Iranian Navy P-3F Orion Canadian DND, 3-04

Iranian Navy ASH-3D Sea King French Navy, 1998

Weapons: Guns and torpedoes are of Russian, U.S., Italian, Swedish, and British origin. Only a dozen U.S. Harpoon missiles were supplied, and all had been expended by 1988. Chinese C-802 turbojet-powered antiship missiles are being acquired for use on Houdong-class missile boats and are being backfitted onto the Combattante-IIB-class missile boats and the Vosper Mk 5 corvettes. Also claimed to be in production is a locally made version of the C-802, the "Tondar," which is said to have an improved guidance and datalink system. The missile was apparently used by Hezbollah militants to attack and damage an Israeli corvette during 7-06. An air-launched version of the C-802, the Fajr-e Darya, was tested during 2000. A variety of Russian, locally designed, and Chinese-supplied mines are available, including the Chinese rocket-propelled MC-52 rising mine. U.S.-supplied Standard SM-1 and Italian Sea Killer antiship missiles are no longer operational on ships.

During 3-00 Iran announced that it had developed an improved version of the U.S. Standard SM-1 (RIM-66) missile with digitized electronics and a semiactive command guidance system. The missile was said to be installed on La Combattante–class guided-missile craft.

Coastal Defense: Several hundred Chinese-supplied HY-4 (CSS-C-2 Silkworm) and C-801 (FL-7, known as the Karus in Iran and CSS-C-3 Seersucker to NATO) antiship missiles are employed at coastal positions, and there have been attempts to launch them from a naval auxiliary vessel as well. C-802 Tondar missiles have also been adapted for land launch. Reports of the acquisition of Russian 3M-80 Moskit (NATO SS-N-22 Sunburn) missiles for shore-based use appear to be untrue.

ATTACK SUBMARINES [SS]

♦ **3 Russian Kilo class (Project 877EKM)**
Bldr: United Admiralty Shipyard, St. Petersburg, Russia

	Laid down	L	Delivered	In serv.
901 TAREGH (ex-B-175)	5-4-91	24-9-91	25-12-91	21-11-92
902 NUH (ex-B-224)	30-4-92	16-10-92	31-12-92	7-8-93
903 YUNES (ex-B-219)	. . .	1993	25-11-96	26-1-97

Yunes (903) French Navy, 12-96

Nuh (902) 5-93

D: 2,325 tons surf./3,076 tons sub. **S:** 10 kts surf./17 kts sub.
Dim: 72.60 (70.0 wl) × 9.90 × 6.6
A: 6 bow 533-mm TT (18 Type 53-77 wire-guided, E53-60 and E53-85 wake-homing, and E53-67 acoustic homing torpedoes, or 24 mines)—1 Fasta-4 SAM shoulder-launched syst. (8 Strela missiles)
Electronics:
Radar: 1 MRK-50E Tobol (Snoop Tray-2) search
Sonar: MGK-400 (Shark Gill) LF active/passive suite; passive hull array; MG-519 (Mouse Roar) HF active classification/mine avoidance; MG-519 active mine-avoidance; MG-553 sound velocity meter; MG-512 own-ship's cavitation detection
EW: Brick Pulp or Squid Head intercept; 6701E (Quad Loop) D/F
M: 2 Type 2D-42 diesel generator sets (1,825 bhp/1,500 kw each), electric drive: 1 motor; 1 6-bladed prop; 5,900 shp—1 130-shp low-speed motor—2 low-speed maneuvering motors; 2 ducted props; 204 shp

ATTACK SUBMARINES [SS] *(continued)*

Range: 6,000/7 surf.; 400/3 sub. **Fuel:** 172 tons **Endurance:** 45 days
Crew: 12 officers, 41 enlisted

Remarks: Ordered under Russian B-series hull numbers. First unit (whose name means "Morning Star") left Baltic under Russian flag 26-9-92 and arrived in Iranian waters around 10-11-92. Second unit (whose name is Farsi for "Noah") departed the Baltic in mid-6-93 and arrived at the end of 7-93. The option for the third, whose name means "Jonah," was taken up during 10-92, but delivery of the completed unit was delayed by well over a year due to payment problems; the ship began her delivery voyage on 25-11-96 and arrived 19-1-97. All three are based at Bandar Abbas. Due to battery cooling problems, poor training, and inadequate maintenance, two were said to be nonoperational as of 4-01, although all three were officially stated to have participated in an exercise during 6-01. During 7-05, Iran was said to be negotiating with Russia for modernization of all three units at a cost of between $80-90 million.
Hull systems: Two batteries, each with 120 cells, providing 9,700 kwh, have proven unsatisfactory, lacking adequate cooling and hence increasing discharge rate and reducing lifespan. Propulsion plant suspended for silencing. Hull has six watertight compartments with 32% reserve buoyancy at 2,350 m^3 surfaced displacement. At rest on the surface, they trim down 0.4 m by the bow. Maximum diving depth is 300 m, normal depth 240 m, and periscope depth 17.5 m. Have anechoic hull coating.
Combat systems: Have MVU-110EM Murena combat data system, which can conduct two simultaneous attacks while tracking three other targets manually. The shoulder-launched SAM position is located in the after portion of the sail. Iran is seeking 3M-53E Novator Alfa supersonic, submerged-launch antiship missiles for these submarines.

Note: The two or three North Korean and 1980s-vintage, indigenously designed midget submarines [SSM] are believed to have been discarded. Other Iranian submersible projects are listed under the entry for the Swimmer Delivery Vehicle [LSDV].

FRIGATES [FF]

Note: During 10-01 Iran began negotiations with Russia's Severnaya Verf for the possible purchase of one or more Project 20382 frigates at $150 million each; Project 20382 would be an export variant of the newly ordered Russian Navy Project 20380.

♦ 3 Saam (Vosper Mk 5) class

	Bldr	Laid down	L	In serv.
71 Alvand (ex-*Saam*)	Vosper Thornycroft	22-5-67	25-7-68	20-5-71
72 Alborz (ex-*Zaal*)	Vickers, Newcastle	3-3-68	25-7-68	1-3-71
73 Sabalan (ex-*Rastam*)	Vickers, Barrow	10-12-67	4-3-69	28-2-72

Alvand (71) Mritunjoy Mazumdar, 2-01

Alvand (71)—note two triple ASW TT and four antiship missile launchers on the fantail, along with the twin 35-mm AA gunmount (the director for which appears to be missing from its mounting just abaft the stack) Brian Morrison, 2-01

D: 1,250 tons (1,540 fl) **S:** 39 kts (17.5 on diesels)
Dim: 94.5 (88.4 pp) × 11.07 × 3.25
A: 4 C-802 SSM; 1 114-mm 55-cal. Vickers Mk 8 DP; 1 twin 35-mm 90-cal. Oerlikon AA; 3 single 20-mm 90-cal. Oerlikon GAM-B01 AA; 2 single 12.7-mm mg; 2 single 81-mm mortar; 1 3-round Limbo Mk 10 ASW mortar—71 and possibly others: 2 triple 324-mm ASW TT
Electronics:
Radar: 1 Decca 1226 nav.; 1 Plessey AWS-1 air search; 2 Oerlikon-Contraves Sea Hunter RTN-10X fire control; 1 Type 352C missile target-detection and tracking
Sonar: Graseby Type 174 hull-mounted search (7–9 kHz); Type 170 hull-mounted attack (15 kHz)
EW: Decca RDL-2AC intercept; FH-5 HFD/F
M: CODOG: 2 Rolls-Royce Olympus TM-3A gas turbines; 2 Paxman 16-cyl. Ventura diesels for cruising; 2 CP props; 46,000 shp (turbines), 3,800 bhp (diesels)

Alborz (72) French Navy, 1997

Range: 5,000/15 **Fuel:** 150 tons (250 with overload) **Crew:** 135 tot.

Remarks: Ordered 25-8-66. All renamed 1985. Sister *Sahand* (ex-*Faramarz*), hit by three Harpoon missiles and cluster bombs, was lost to U.S. forces 19-4-88. *Sabalan*, severely damaged the same date, was declared repaired by the Iranian Navy during 1989; although operational, the ship appears to have severe speed restrictions. All three were active during a 6-01 exercise.
Hull systems: Air-conditioned. Retractable fin stabilizers. Aluminum superstructure.
Combat systems: Vickers Mk 8 automatic guns replaced the originally fitted semiautomatic Mk 6 during refits in the 1970s. Twin 23-mm 87-cal. ZU-23-2 Soviet AA mounts replaced the original Sea Cat SAM launcher and were in turn later replaced by single 20-mm mounts. The original quintuple-mount, trainable Sea Killer antiship missile system aft was replaced by fixed racks for Chinese-supplied C-802 missiles during 1996–98, and the associated target detection and tracking radar (which can also operate in the passive mode) has been stepped on a new lattice mast integrated into the forward edge of the original pylon mainmast. As of 2-01, 71 had two sets of triple ASW torpedo tubes added aft, abreast the Limbo mortar well; the origin of the tubes and the type of torpedoes they may carry are unknown.

CORVETTES [FFL]

♦ 1 (+ 2) Zolfaqar class

	Laid down	L	In serv.
376 Mouj	1997	. . .	2006
. . .	. . .	. . .	. . .
. . .	. . .	. . .	. . .

D: 1,400 tons (light or standard) **S:** 30 kts **Dim:** 88.0 × . . . × . . .
A: 4 C-802 SSM; 1 76-mm OTO-Melara compact Dp; . . . ASW RL
Electronics: . . .
M: . . .
Range: . . . **Crew:** . . .

Note: Iranian dubbed "destroyer" class to be capable of 30-kt speeds was said to be under design for construction in Iran as of 9-96; in late 9-00, the first unit was said to be ready for launch. However, in early 2003, it was reported that *Mouj* wouldn't be launched until sometime after 3-03. The class is said to accommodate a missile-armed helicopter and to be capable of antisubmarine, antiship, and antiaircraft missions. The initial ship was planned to be completed in 2001 and the third in 2003. The "hull" is said to be of 70% Iranian manufacture and the "missile launcher" 90%, indicating a large foreign input.

PATROL SHIPS [PS]

♦ 2 U.S. PF 103 class Bldr: Levingston SB, Orange, Texas

	Laid down	L	In serv.
81 Bayandor (ex-PF 103)	20-8-62	7-7-63	18-5-64
82 Naghdi (ex-PF 104)	12-9-62	10-10-63	22-7-64

Bayandor (81) 1990

Naghdi (82) H&L Van Ginderen, 7-94

PATROL SHIPS [PS] *(continued)*

D: 900 tons (1,135 fl) **S:** 20 kts **Dim:** 83.82 × 10.06 × 3.05 (4.27 sonar)
A: 2 single 76.2-mm 50-cal. Mk. 34 DP; 1 twin 40-mm 60-cal. Bofors Mk 1 Mod 2 AA; 2 single 20-mm 90-cal. Oerlikon GAM-B01 AA; 2 single 12.7-mm M2 mg
Electronics:
Radar: 1 Decca 1226 nav.; 1 Raytheon 1650 nav.; 1 SPS-6C air search
Sonar: SQS-17A hull-mounted HF search (probably removed)
M: 2 Fairbanks-Morse 38D8$^1/_8$ × 10 diesels; 2 props; 5,600 bhp
Electric: 600 kw tot. (2 × 300 kw; 2 Fairbanks-Morse 38F5$^1/_4$ × 6 diesels driving)
Range: 2,400/18; 3,000/15 **Fuel:** 110 tons **Crew:** 133 tot.

Remarks: Built and transferred under the Military Aid Program. Sisters *Milanian* (83, ex-PF 105) and *Kahnamuie* (84, ex-PF 106) reported lost to Iraqi forces by 1982–83. 82 was refitted and re-engined during 1988. Due to removal of ASW systems and gunfire-control equipment, they are now of limited utility. 81 collided with the U.S. guided-missile cruiser *Gettysburg* (CG 64) on 13-10-96 with little damage incurred.
Combat systems: Twin Soviet 23-mm 87-cal. ZU-23-2 AA were added forward of the bridge in place of the single Hedgehog ASW spigot mortar during the 1980s; the mount was in turn replaced with a single 20-mm AA. Had Mk 63 GFCS for 76.2-mm guns (radar on forward gun mount) and a Mk 51 Mod. 2 GFCS with lead-computing optical director for 40-mm mount. By 1990, the depth charge equipment had been removed from both and replaced by a single 20-mm at the extreme stern, while the Mk 34 fire-control radar associated with the original Mk 63 control system had been removed from the forward 76.2-mm gunmount.

GUIDED-MISSILE PATROL CRAFT [PTG]

Note: During 4-01 Iran was reported to be negotiating with Russia for the purchase of an unknown number of Project 12421 (Tarantul-III) guided-missile patrol craft, to be armed with 3M-80E Moskit (SS-N-22 Sunburn) antiship missiles.

♦ 1 (+ 1) or more Chinese . . . class
Bldr: . . . Bandar Addas

Sina-1

D: 350 tons **S:** . . . **Dim:** 28.00 × . . . × . .
A: Up to 8 C-701 antiship missiles; 1 . . . AA
Electronics: 1 ... nav.
M: . . . diesels; 2 props; . . .

Remarks: Catamaran design described as “frigates” in Iran. First deliveries were expected during early 2002, but the first indigenously built unit was reportedly launched in 3-03. May be assigned to the Pasdaran forces rather than the navy proper. The Chinese C-701, a new export missile, is said to have a range of 12 n.m.

♦ 10 Combattante-IIB class
Bldr: CMN, Cherbourg

	L	In serv.		L	In serv.
P 221 Kaman	8-1-76	6-77	P 228 Gorz	28-12-77	15-9-78
P 222 Zoubin	14-4-76	6-77	P 229 Gardouneh	23-2-78	23-10-78
P 223 Khadang	15-7-76	15-3-78	P 230 Khanjar	27-4-78	1-8-81
P 226 Falakhon	2-6-77	31-3-78	P 231 Neyzeh	5-7-78	1-8-81
P 227 Shamshir	12-9-77	31-3-78	P 232 Tabarzin	15-9-78	1-8-81

Shamshir (P 227)—with four C-802 antiship missiles U.S. Navy, 7-96

D: 249 tons (275 fl) **S:** 36 kts **Dim:** 47.0 × 7.1 × 1.9
A: 4 C-802 SSM; 1 76-mm 62-cal. OTO Melara DP; 1 40-mm 70-cal. Bofors AA
Electronics:
Radar: 1 Decca 1226 nav.; 1 Thales WM-28 track-while-scan f.c.
EW: Thales TMV-433 suite (DR-2000 receiver, Alligator 5-A jammer, DALIA analyzer)
M: 4 MTU 16V538 TB91 diesels; 4 props; 14,400 bhp
Electric: 350 kw **Range:** 700/33.7 **Fuel:** 41 tons **Crew:** 31 tot.

Remarks: Contracted 19-2-74 and 14-10-74. The last three were embargoed at Cherbourg 4-79 and released 22-6-81. P 232 was captured off Spain 13-8-80 by anti-Khomeini forces but abandoned later at Toulon. *Peykan* (P 224) was lost to Iraqi forces 11-80, and *Joshan* (P 225) was sunk by U.S. forces on 19-4-88.
Combat systems: P 231 and P 232 had no Harpoon tubes on delivery, and all Harpoon missiles delivered by the U.S. are believed to have been expended by 1988. They were given a C-802 missile launch capability during 1996–98. Iran claimed in 3-00 that these craft carry an updated version of the U.S. Standard SM-1 surface-to-air missile, which seems highly unlikely.

PATROL CRAFT [PC]

♦ 3 U.S. PGM 71 class
Bldr: Peterson Builders, Inc., Sturgeon Bay, Wis. (In serv. 1967–70)

211 Parvin (ex-PGM 103) 213 Nahid (ex-PGM 122)
212 Bahram (ex-PGM 112)

D: 102 tons light (142 fl) **S:** 17 kts **Dim:** 30.81 × 6.45 × 2.3
A: 1 40-mm 60-cal. Mk 3 AA; 1 20-mm 90-cal. Oerlikon GAM-B01 AA; 2 single 12.7-mm Colt M2 mg
Electronics: Radar: 1 . . . nav.
M: 8 General Motors 6-71 diesels; 2 props; 2,120 bhp
Electric: 30 kw tot. **Range:** 1,000/17 **Fuel:** 16 tons **Crew:** 30 tot.

Remarks: Thought to have been sunk during the Iran-Iraq War, but have been sighted still in service. ASW equipment originally fitted (SQS-17 hull-mounted sonar, Mousetrap ASW rocket launchers, and depth charges) has been removed, and the original radar may have been replaced. All three U.S. Coast Guard *Cape*-class patrol craft *Kayvan* (201), *Azadi* (202), and *Mehran* (203) appear to have been retired from service by 2005. They had been in continuous service since the 1950s.

PATROL BOATS [PB]

♦ 9 U.S. Mk III class
Bldr: Marinette Marine, Marinette, Wis. (In serv. 1975–76)

D: 28 tons (36.7 fl) **S:** 24 kts **Dim:** 19.78 × 5.50 × 1.80 (props)
A: 1 20-mm 90-cal. Oerlikon GAM-B01 AA; 1 twin and 2 single 12.7-mm mg
Electronics: Radar: 1 LN-66 nav.
M: 3 G.M. 8V71 TI diesels; 3 props; 1,800 bhp
Range: 450/26; 2,000/ . . . **Endurance:** 3 days **Crew:** 9 tot.

Remarks: Survivors of 20 originally delivered; remainder lost in Iran-Iraq War or worn out and scrapped. Aluminum construction, with pilothouse offset to starboard side. A 20-mm Oerlikon AA mounting has replaced the 12.7-mm machinegun formerly carried forward. Based at Bushehr and Bandar Abbas.

♦ 6 or more U.S. 50-foot class
Bldr: Peterson Bldrs., Sturgeon Bay, Wis. (In serv. 1975–78)

D: 20.1 tons (22.9 fl) **S:** 28 kts **Dim:** 15.24 × 4.80 × 1.9
A: 2 single 12.7-mm mg **Electronics:** Radar: 1 Raytheon SPS-66 nav.
M: 2 G.M. Detroit Diesel 8V71 TI diesels; 3 props; 850 bhp (460 sust.)
Range: 750/26 **Crew:** 6 tot.

Remarks: Sixty-one were ordered in 1976. Nineteen were delivered complete from the U.S., and the others were shipped as kits for assembly in Iran by Arvandan Maritime Corp., Abadan, where they were still being assembled into the 1980s. Placed under naval control in 1990. Many were lost during the Iran-Iraq War, and a number of the kits were apparently never completed. The survivors are said to operate in the Caspian Sea. Aluminum construction. Some have been equipped with British Tiger Cat surface-to-air missiles to be employed in a surface-to-surface mode.

♦ Up to 6 U.S. Enforcer class
Bldr: Bertram Yacht, Miami (In serv. 1972)

D: 4.7 tons (fl) **S:** 28 kts **Dim:** 9.5 × 3.4 × 0.9
A: 1 12.7-mm mg **Electronics:** Radar: 1 Apelco AD7-7 nav.
M: 2 G.M. 6V53 diesels; 2 props; 360 bhp **Range:** 146/16 **Crew:** 4 tot.

Remarks: Survivors of 36 delivered. GRP hull construction.

MINE WARFARE SHIPS

Note: Of the four U.S. *Falcon*-class coastal minesweepers transferred in the late 1950s, *Shahrokh* (301), long operational in the Caspian Sea as a training craft, had been discarded by 1995 but was refitted as a training craft and renamed *Hemzeh; Simorgh* (302) was lost to Iraqi action in 1980–81; *Karkas* (303) was lost in the Iran-Iraq War; and *Shabaz* (304) was lost in a fire in 1975.

♦ 1 U.S. Cape-class inshore minesweeper [MSI]

	Bldr	In serv.
312 Riazi (ex-MSI 14)	Tacoma Boat, Tacoma, Wash.	15-10-64

D: 203 tons (239 fl) **S:** 12.5 kts **Dim:** 34.06 × 7.14 × 2.40
A: 1 12.7-mm mg **Electronics:** Radar: 1 Decca 303 nav.
M: 4 G.M. Detroit Diesel 6-71 diesels; 2 props; 960 bhp
Electric: 120 kw **Range:** 1,000/9 **Fuel:** 20 tons
Crew: 5 officers, 16 enlisted

Remarks: Wooden construction. Built for Iran under the Military Aid Program. Thought lost with sister *Harachi* (311; ex-*Kahnamuie,* ex-MSI 13) during the Iran-Iraq War, but is apparently still in service—although probably not fully effective in her intended role. Appearance as for sisters in Turkish Navy.

AMPHIBIOUS WARFARE SHIPS AND CRAFT

♦ 2 (+ . . .) “dock landing ships” [LST]
Bldr: Construction Jihad, Nuh-e Nabi SY, Bandar Abbas

102 Chavoush (L: 30-9-95) 103 Chalak (L: 6-96)

D: Approx. 1,400 tons (fl) **S:** . . . kts **Dim:** 62.0 × 19.0 × . . .
A: . . .
M: . . . diesels; 2 props; . . . bhp

Remarks: 1,151 grt. Said to have an 800-ton cargo capacity and a docking well. Proportions indicate a barge-like design unlikely to have much utility as assault ships; molded depth of hull is 6.5 m. Despite official description as “dock landing ships,” they are probably not equipped to ballast down to launch amphibious craft and vehicles.

AMPHIBIOUS WARFARE SHIPS AND CRAFT *(continued)*

♦ 4 Hengam-class tank landing ships [LST]
Bldr: Yarrow & Co., Scotstoun

	L	In serv.		L	In serv.
511 HENGAM	27-9-73	12-8-74	513 LAVAN	12-6-78	16-1-85
512 LARAK	7-5-74	12-11-74	514 TONB	6-12-79	11-7-85

Tonb (514) 2-91

Tonb (514) 2-91

D: 2,940 tons (fl) **S:** 14.5 kts **Dim:** 92.96 (86.87 wl) × 14.94 × 3.00 (max.)
A: 4 twin 23-mm 87-cal. ZU-23-2 AA; 1 40-round 122-mm BM-21 RL; 2 single 12.7-mm mg; 2 4-round Fasta-M SAM syst. (Igla-1 missiles)
Electronics: Radar: 1 Decca TM 1229 nav.—TACAN: URN-25
M: 511, 512: 4 Paxman Ventura 12 YJCM diesels; 2 CP props; 5,600 bhp—513, 514: 4 MTU 12V562 TB61 diesels; 2 CP props; 5,800 bhp
Electric: 1,280 kw tot. **Range:** 3,500/12 **Fuel:** 295 tons
Crew: 75 ship's company + 168 troops

Remarks: Were used to transport small combatant craft during the Iran-Iraq War. 513 and 514, laid up since completion, were released by the British government 5-10-84, on the premise that they would be used as hospital ships. Negotiations continued into 1985 for the construction of two more, originally ordered 7-77, for which considerable material had been accumulated.
Hull systems: Flight deck for one Sea King–sized helicopter aft. Cargo capacity of 600 tons on 39.6 × 8.8 × 4-m (high) vehicle deck, with 15-m-long bow ramp. Can also carry up to 300 tons liquid cargo in lieu of some vehicle stowage. Can stow 12 Russian T-55 tanks. Upper deck forward has a 10-ton crane to handle two Uniflote cargo lighters (LCVP) and 12 Z-boat rubber personnel landing craft. Intended for logistics support (when 10 20-ton or 30 10-ton containers would be carried) or for amphibious assault.
Combat systems: 513 has an additional Decca 1216 nav. radar. First two had British SSR 1520 IFF gear.

♦ 2 Arya Sahand–class tank landing ships [LST]
Bldr: Teraoka SY, Japan (In serv. 1978)

IRAN ASR (ex-*Arya Akian*) IRAN GHADR (ex-*Arya Dokht*)

D: 614 tons light (2,274 fl) **S:** 11 kts **Dim:** 53.65 (48.01 pp) × 10.81 × 3.00
A: 2 single 12.7-mm mg; mines
Electronics: Radar: 1 . . . nav.
M: 2 diesels; 2 props; 2,200 bhp **Crew:** 30 tot.

Remarks: 984 grt/1,660 dwt. Blunt-bowed, commercial landing craft taken over by the Iranian Navy at the outset of the Iran-Iraq War. Have a bow ramp, single hatch with sliding cover, and one 10-ton cargo boom. Mines are deck-stowed atop the hatch cover and launched over the side. Sister *Iran Ajr* (ex-*Arya Rakhsh*) captured 21-9-87 by U.S. forces while laying mines in international waters and scuttled 26-9-87. Sisters *Iran Bahr* (ex-*Arya Sahand*) and *Iran Badr* (ex-*Arya Boum*) were lost during 1980.

Iran Ajr—just prior to scuttling, with a U.S. Navy LCM(8) landing craft alongside U.S. Navy, 9-87

♦ 3 (+ . . .) MIG-S-3700-class utility landing craft [LCU]
Bldr: Construction Jihad, Nuh-e Nabi SY, Bandar Abbas

101 FOQUE (L: 17-6-88) 103 . . . (L: 27-9-95)
102 . . . (L: 27-9-95)

D: 276 tons (fl) **S:** 10 kts **Dim:** 36.60 × 8.00 × 1.50
A: . . . **Electronics:** Radar: . . .
M: 2 MWM TBD 234 V8 diesels; 2 props; 490 hp
Range: 400/10 **Crew:** 10 tot.

Remarks: Shipyard also known as the Martyr Darvishi Marine Co. Cargo: 150 tons on deck plus 57 tons potable water and 79 tons cargo fuel in tanks. Hull has extremely low freeboard at tank deck, with no sidewall protection, rendering these ships of little use outside harbors and sheltered waters.

Note: Said to be in service is a single 50-m landing craft with a beam of 10.4 m. The craft resembles the MIG-S-3700 class.

♦ 1 (+ . . .) Iranian-designed air-cushion personnel landing craft [LCPA]
Bldr: . . . (In serv. 1-00)

D: . . . **S:** 43 kts loaded **Dim:** . . . × . . . × . . .
M: . . .
Range: 324/43 **Crew:** . . . tot. + 26 troops

Remarks: Prototype completed by 1-00 for the Ministry of Defense, with the intent to mass-produce the design.

♦ 4 BH.7 Wellington Mk 4– and Mk 5A–class air-cushion landing craft [LCPA]
Bldr: British Hovercraft, Cowes, U.K. (In serv. 1970–75)

D: 50–55 tons (fl) **S:** 65 kts **Dim:** 23.9 × 13.8 × 10.36 (high)
A: 2 single 12.7-mm mg **Electronics:** Radar: 1 Decca 914 nav.
M: 1 Rolls-Royce Proteus 15M549 gas turbine; 1 6.4-m-dia. prop; 4,250 shp
Electric: 110 kVA **Range:** 400/56 **Fuel:** 9 tons

Remarks: Four of the original six were of the logistics-support version, with a 14-ton payload. Two were of the Mk 4 version with recesses for two SSM, which were never mounted. The Mk 4 uses the Gnome 15M541 engine of 4,750 hp and can carry 60 troops in side compartments as well as assault vehicles on its 56-m cargo deck. Speed in both versions is reduced to 35 kts in a 1.4-m sea. Overhauled at builder's, with new engines, skirts, and so forth, two in 2-84 and two more in 1985. Two others, plus eight SR-N6 Winchester-class hovercraft, are inoperable or have been scrapped.

♦ 10 . . . meter swimmer delivery vehicles [LSDV]
Bldr: . . ., North Korea (In serv. 2003)

Remarks: Unconfirmed reports indicate that 10 midget submarines were delivered to Iran from North Korea in mid-2003. No additional information is available.

♦ 1 15-meter swimmer delivery vehicle [LSDV]
Bldr: Isafahan University-. . ., Bandar Abbas (In serv. 29-8-00)

AL SABIHA–15

D: . . . tons **S:** . . . kts **Dim:** 15.0 × . . . × . . .
A: Demolition charges, small arms
M: 1 electric motor; 50 shp
Crew: 2 tot. + 3 swimmers

Remarks: In 7-96 an Iranian newspaper claimed that Isfahan Technical University, under project "Underwater Oasis," had constructed the hull for the first of a new generation of midget submarines. The craft later underwent some 250 hours of sea trials and is said to be able to operate anywhere in the Persian Gulf.

AUXILIARIES

♦ 7 Delvar-class support ships [AE/AK/AW]
Bldr: Karachi SY & Eng. Wks., Pakistan (In serv. 1978–82)

CHARAK CHIROO DAYER DELVAR DILIM SIRJAN SOURU

D: Approx. 1,300 tons (fl) **S:** 9–11 kts **Dim:** 63.45 (58.48 pp) × 11.00 × 3.03
A: 1 twin 23-mm 87-cal. ZU-23-2 AA
Electronics: Radar: 1 Decca 1226 nav.
M: 2 M.A.N. G6V-23.5/33 ATL diesels; 2 props; 1,560 bhp **Crew:** 20 tot.

AUXILIARIES *(continued)*

Delvar-class support ship Piet Sinke, 2-87

Remarks: 900 grt. *Delvar* and *Sirjan* are configured as ammunition lighters; *Dayer* and *Dilim* (with rounded sterns and one crane vice two) are water tankers; the others are coastal cargo lighters. Designed and built with British assistance. All can be used to plant mines.

♦ 12 Hendijan-class general-purpose tenders [AG]

Bldr: Damen, Hardinxveld, the Netherlands (last four: Martyr Darvishi Marine Industries, Bandar Abbas)

	In serv.		In serv.		In serv.
Bakhtaran	1985	Konarak	11-88	Bahregan	1991
Koramshahr	1985	Genavah	9-88	Mogan	11-92
Hendijan	1987	Sirik	4-89	Rostam	1995
Kalat	1987	Gaveter	1990	Nayband	4-99

Bahregan U.S. Navy, 2-96

D: 446.5 (fl) **S:** 21 kts (Nayband: 27 kts) **Dim:** 47 (44.57wl) × 8.55 × 2.86
A: 1 20-mm 90-cal. Oerlikon GAM-B01 AA
Electronics: Radar: Decca 2070A nav.
M: 2 MWM TBD604V12 (*Nayband:* Mitsubishi S16U-MPTK) diesels; 2 props; 6,100 (*Nayband:* 6,560) bhp
Electric: 180 kw tot. (2 × 90-kw diesel sets)
Range: 1000/ . . . **Crew:** 15 tot. + 90–100 troops

Remarks: 439–445 grt/337 dwt. Iranian class designation is MIG-S-4700-SC. Used to transport cargo and personnel over short distances and also as patrol craft; were referred to as "destroyers" in reports of a 6-01 exercise. Cargo: 40 tons on deck, 12 below, plus 40 tons potable water. *Bahregan* was originally named *Geno.* One unit of this class reported launched on 30-9-95, probably *Rostam.* Well into the 1990s, Daman Shipyard continued to provide prefabricated modules from which the units are assembled in Iran. *Nayband,* launched on 8-12-92 as the first of a new series, has more-powerful engines and two 52-kw diesel generator sets.

♦ 1 Bushehr-A-class navigational buoy tender [AGL]

D: Approx. 3,000 tons (fl) **S:** . . . kts **Dim:** 67.0 × 14.0 × 6.0
A: None
M: 1 diesel; 1 prop; . . . bhp

Remarks: Has a large crane at the break of the forecastle and a second, smaller crane before the bridge, both tending a large buoy hold. No other data available. May belong to a ports and harbor authority rather than the navy.

♦ 1 large replenishment oiler [AOR]

	Bldr	Laid down	L	In serv.
431 Kharg	Swan Hunter, Wallsend-on-Tyne	1-76	3-2-77	25-4-80

Kharg (431) French Navy, 1997

D: 33,014 tons (fl) **S:** 21.5 kts **Dim:** 207.15 (195.00 pp) × 25.50 × 9.14
A: 1 76-mm 62-cal. OTO Melara Compact DP; 6 twin 23-mm 87-cal. ZU-23-2 AA
Electronics: Radar: 2 Decca 1229 nav.—TACAN: URN-20
M: 1 set Westinghouse geared steam turbines; 1 prop; 26,870 shp
Boilers: 2 Babcock & Wilcox 2-drum **Electric:** 7,000 kw **Crew:** 248 tot.

Remarks: Ordered 10-74. 21,100 grt/20,000 dwt. Carries fuel and ammunition and acts as the flagship of the Iranian Navy. Design is greatly modified version of the Royal Navy's *Olwen* class. Ran initial trials 11-78, but delays in fitting out made delivery before the revolution impossible; remained at builder's until released 5-10-84. Delivered without armament. Has Inmarsat SATCOM equipment. Can accommodate three Sea King–sized helicopters. Completed refit 16-10-93.

♦ 2 Bandar Abbas–class small replenishment oilers [AOR]

Bldr: C. Lühring, Brake, Germany

421 Bandar Abbas (L: 14-8-73) 422 Booshehr (L: 22-3-74)

Booshehr (422)—with telescoping hangar extended LSPH K. Degener, RAN, 12-90

D: 4,673 tons (fl) **S:** 20 kts **Dim:** 108.0 × 16.6 × 4.5
A: 1 twin 23-mm 80-cal. AA; 2 single 20-mm Oerlikon GAM B01 AA; 2 SA-7 Grail shoulder-launched SAM positions
Electronics: Radar: 1 Decca 1226 nav.; 1 Decca 1229 nav.
M: 2 M.A.N. R6V 52/56 diesels; 2 props; 12,000 bhp
Range: 3,500/16 **Crew:** 60 tot.

Remarks: 3,186 grt/3,250 dwt. Telescoping helicopter hangar. Carry fuel, food, ammunition, and spare parts. Armed after delivery. Used for patrol duties 1984 on, due to a shortage of operable combatants. 421 suffered an explosion at Bandar Abbas 26-12-98, with five killed, ten injured. Both participated in a major 6-01 exercise.

♦ 1 ex-U.S. Amphion-class repair ship [AR]

Bldr: Tampa SB, Fla.

	Laid down	L	In serv.
441 Chah Bahar (ex-Amphion, AR 13)	20-9-44	15-5-45	30-1-46

D: 8,670 tons light (14,450 fl) **S:** 16 kts **Dim:** 150.0 × 21.4 × 8.4
A: Removed **M:** 1 set geared steam turbines; 1 prop; 8,500 shp
Boilers: 2 Foster-Wheeler "D"; 30.6 kg/cm^2, 382° C **Electric:** 3,600 kw
Range: 13,950/11.5 **Fuel:** 1,850 tons **Crew:** accomm. for 921

Remarks: Transferred on loan in 10-71 and purchased 1-3-77. Employed as stationary repair facility at Bandar Abbas and no longer mobile.

♦ 2 water tankers [AW]

Bldr: Mazagon Dock, Mumbai, India

411 Kangan (L: 4-78) 412 Taheri (L: 17-9-78)

Kangan (411) U.S. Navy

D: 12,000 tons (fl) **S:** 12 kts **Dim:** 147.95 (140.00 pp) × 21.50 × 5.00
A: 1 twin 23-mm 87-cal. ZU-23-2 AA; 2 single 12.7-mm mg
Electronics: Radar: 1 Decca 1229 nav.
M: 1 M.A.N. 7L52/55A diesel; 7,385 bhp **Crew:** 20 tot.

Remarks: 9,430 dwt. Intended to supply Persian Gulf islands. Liquid cargo: 9,000 m^3. Also used in patrol duties from 1984 on. Have a helicopter landing pad amidships and carry two hose-handling boats in davits forward.

Disposal note: The former imperial yacht *Hamzeh* (ex-*Chah Sevar*) was apparently out of service by 1998, as her name was transferred to the former minesweeper *Sharokh,* which was reactivated that year as cadet training ship in the Caspian Sea.

♦ 1 ex-U.S. Falcon-class training ship [AXT]

Bldr: Peterson Builders, Sturgeon Bay, Wis. (L: 1958)

301 Hamzeh (ex-155, ex-*Sharokh,* ex-MSC 276)

D: 320 tons (378 fl) **S:** 12.5 kts **Dim:** 43.00 (41.50 wl) × 7.95 × 2.55
A: . . . **Electronics:** Radar: 1 . . . nav.
M: 2 G.M. electromotive Div. 8-268A diesels; 2 props; 890 bhp
Range: 2,500/10 **Fuel:** 27 tons **Crew:** . . .

Remarks: Said to operate as a diving tender. Wooden, nonmagnetic construction.

SERVICE CRAFT

♦ 1 large floating dry dock [YFDB]
Bldr: M.A.N.-G.H.H., Nordenham/Blexen, Germany (L: 22-11-85)

DOLPHIN

D: 28,000 tons lift **Dim:** 240.00 × 52.50 × . . .

Remarks: Docking well 230.00 m over keel blocks, 41.00 m free width, 8.50 m floodable over blocks.

♦ 1 ex-U.S. floating dry dock [YFDL]
Bldr: Pacific Bridge, Alameda, Calif. (In serv. 7-44)

400 (ex-*Arco,* ARD 29)

D: 3,500 tons lift **Dim:** 149.8 × 25.6 × 1.7 (light)

Remarks: Transferred 1-3-77.

♦ 1 garbage disposal lighter [YG]
Bldr: Karachi SY & Eng. Wks. (In serv. ca. 1985)

1712

Remarks: No further data available. Has a 120-m^3 hopper amidships, a trash compactor, and a conveyer bucket system to eject garbage over the stern. Has two diesel propulsion engines.

♦ 1 inshore survey craft, former yacht [YGS]
Bldr: Malahide SY, Dublin, Ireland

ABNEGAR (ex-*Glimmer*)

D: 85 tons (fl) **S:** . . . kts **Dim:** 20.7 × . . . × . . .
M: 1 Kelvin T8 diesel; 240 bhp

Remarks: Acquired 1974.

♦ 3 coastal fuel lighters [YO]
Bldr: Scheepswerf Ravestein, Deest, the Netherlands (In serv. 1983)

IRAN PARAK IRAN SHALAK IRAN YOUSHAT

D: Approx. 800 (fl) **S:** 6 kts **Dim:** 40.01 (38.82 pp) × 10.01 × 2.6
M: 2 G.M. 6-71 diesels; 2 props; 730 bhp **Electric:** 12 kw **Fuel:** 5 tons

Remarks: 400 grt/540 dwt. Originally purchased for commercial purposes.

♦ 2 Ksew-class fuel lighters [YO]
Bldr: Karachi SY & Eng. Wks. (In serv. 1981)

1703 1704

D: . . . **S:** 8 kts **Dim:** 30.51 × 9.30 × 1.83
M: 2 M.A.N. diesels; 2 props; 326 bhp

Remarks: 195 grt/200 dwt.

♦ 5 StanTug 2400/2600–class large harbor tugs [YTB]

	Bldr	L	In serv.
HAMOON	Deltawerf, Sliedrecht, Neth.	. . .	4-84
HIRMAND	Damen, Hardinxveld, Neth.	1-8-84	1984
MENAB	Damen, Hardinxveld, Neth.	. . .	1985
HARI-RUD	Damen, Hardinxveld, Neth.	. . .	1985
SEFID-RUD	Damen, Hardinxveld, Neth.	. . .	1985

D: 300 tons (fl) **S:** 12 kts **Dim:** 25.63 (23.53 pp) × 6.81 × 3.19
M: 2 MTU GV396 TC62 diesels; 2 props; 1,200 bhp

Remarks: First two are 24.0 m long. Last three are of 122 grt and are 25.63 m long. They may be employable as minelayers.

♦ 2 ex-German large harbor tugs [YTB]
Bldr: Oelkers, Germany (In serv. 1962–63)

1 (ex-*Karl*) 2 (ex-*Ise*)

D: 320 tons **S:** 11.5 kts **Dim:** 26.6 × 7.2 × 3.6 **M:** . . .

Remarks: 134 grt. Acquired on 17-6-74. Have fire monitor on platform abaft mast.

♦ 2 StanTug 2200-class small harbor tugs [YTL]
Bldr: B.V. Scheepswerf K. Damen, Hardinxveld-Giessendam, Netherlands (In serv. 1985)

ARAS ATRAK

D: 91 grt **S:** 12 kts **Dim:** 22.00 × 7.12 × 2.65 **M:** 2 MTU diesels; . . . bhp

♦ 2 water barges [YWN]
Bldr: Karachi SY & Eng. Wks. (In serv. 1977–78)

1701 1702

D: Approx. 2,100 tons (fl) **Dim:** 65.0 × 13.0 × 2.6

Remarks: 1,410 grt.

♦ 10 Qa'em-series training craft [YXT]
Bldr: Iranian Defense Marine Industries

D: 65 tons (fl) **S:** . . . kts **Dim:** 18.75 × 5.75 × . . .
M: . . . diesels; . . . props; . . . bhp

Remarks: *Qa'em 3* and *Qa'em 5,* launched at a Caspian Sea port on 30-9-96, were said to be the seventh and eighth of the class, and two more were completed around 5-00. Hull molded depth is 2.17 m. No further details available. Are also referred to as the *Kilas-e-Qasem* class.

Disposal note: Persian Gulf training craft and former imperial yacht *Kish* was reported to have been stricken by 2000.

Note: Karachi Shipyard and Engineering Works, Pakistan, delivered seven other yard and service craft between 1977 and 7-81. All were designed in Great Britain. A variety of craft were built, all initially numbered 1701 through 1718. Types included a self-propelled dredge (1711) [YM], a pontoon barge (1710) [YFN], and a 31-m diving tender (1705) [YDT] very similar in appearance to the *Ksew*-class fuel lighters.

PASDARAN REVOLUTIONARY GUARD CORPS NAVY

Note: This organization, with about 20,000 mostly nonseagoing personnel (including 5,000 Revolutionary Guard Marines), is administered separately from the Iranian Navy. In recent years, cooperation between the two forces is said to have improved, but the Revolutionary Guard Corps Navy's goals remain ideologically oriented and its leadership erratic.

GUIDED-MISSILE PATROL CRAFT [WPTG]

♦ 6 (+ 4) Chinacat-class catamaran
Bldr: China Shipbuilding Trading Co.

. . . (In serv. 2002)

Chinacat catamaran Alexandre Sheldon-Duplaix, 2001

D: 19 **S:** Up to 50 kts **Dim:** 23.0 × 4.0 ×1.0
A: 4 C-701 SSM; 1 23-mm AA
Electronics: Radar: 1 . . . search
M: 2 . . . diesels
Range: . . . **Crew:** 10

Remarks: A new unit of the Chinacat catamaran guided-missile boat design offered for export by China. As many as 10 of the craft, which carry up to four small antiship missiles and a light gun, may be acquired. Powered by two diesels, the 23-m prototype craft is claimed to have a speed of up to 50 kts and is fitted with a small search radar and an E/O gun/missile director.

♦ 10 Chinese Houdong class (In serv. 1995–96)

P 313-1 FATH
P 313-2 NASR
P 313-3 SAF
P 323-4 RA'D
P 313-5 FAJR
P 313-6 SHAMS
P 313-7 ME'RAJ
P 313-8 FALAQ
P 313-9 HADID
P 313-10 QADR

Houdong-class P 313-5—first series, with original pennant number French Navy, 9-94

D: 118 tons (135 fl) **S:** 37 kts (34 kts sust.)
Dim: 34.10 × 6.70 × 1.8 (1.295 mean hull)
A: 4 C-802 SSM; 1 twin 30-mm 65-cal. Model 69 AA; 1 twin 23-mm 87-cal. ZSU-23-2 AA
Electronics:
Radar: 2 Type RM 1070A nav.; 1 Type 341 (Rice Lamp) gun f.c.
EW: Last five: . . . intercept
M: 2 MTU 16V396 TB94 diesels; 2 props; 6,220 bhp
Electric: 65 kw **Range:** 500/24; 1,050/18
Endurance: 5 days **Crew:** 2 officers, 14 enlisted

REVOLUTIONARY GUARD GUIDED-MISSILE PATROL CRAFT [WPTG] *(continued)*

Houdong-class P 313-7 and a sister—second series, en route to Iran as deck cargo, with original pennant number U.S. Navy, 3-96

Remarks: Referred to locally as the Thondor class and were originally numbered 301 through 310. Reportedly were ordered in 1991 or 1992. First five delivered 9-94; second five, with added EW gear, were delivered in 3-96. P 313-3 was noted in 10-97 with a twin 23-mm mount installed abaft the lattice mast, and the others have probably been similarly equipped.

PATROL BOATS [WPB]

♦ 6 MIG-S-2600-PB class
Bldr: Joolaee Iran Marine Industries (In serv. . . .)

D: 80 tons (85 fl) **S:** 35 kts **Dim:** 26.20 × 6.20 × 1.40 (hull)
A: 1 12-round 107-mm artillery RL; 1 twin 14.5-mm 79-cal. AA
M: 4 MWM TBD-234-V16 diesels; 4 props; 4,000 bhp **Crew:** 10 tot.

Remarks: Also known as the Zafar class. Offered for export sale, and at least one prototype was built for Pasdaran Revolutionary Guard service. Design appears to be based on the North Korean Chaho class (of which three were transferred 4-87 and since discarded).

♦ 10 (+ . . .) MIG-G-1900 class
Bldr: Iran Marine Industries (In serv. 1992– . . .)

MIG-G-1900 series U.S. Navy

D: 28 tons (30 fl) **S:** 36 kts **Dim:** 19.45 × 4.20 × 0.90
A: 1 twin 23-mm 87-cal. ZSU-23-2 AA
Electronics: Radar: 1 . . . nav.
M: 2 MWM TBD 234-V12 diesels; 2 props; 1,646 bhp **Crew:** 8 tot.

Remarks: Hullform based closely on the U.S. Mk III patrol boat, but built with German-supplied diesel engines and with the pilothouse on the centerline.

♦ 50 MIG-G-1800-TRB class
Bldr: Iran Marine Industries (In serv. . . .)

MIG-G-1800-TRB class U.S. Navy

D: 54 tons (60 fl) **S:** 18 kts **Dim:** 18.67 × 5.76 × 1.05
A: 1 twin 23-mm 87-cal. ZSU-23-2 AA
Electronics: Radar: 1 . . . nav.
M: 2 MWM TBD 234-V12 diesels; 2 props; 1,646 bhp **Crew:** 10 tot.

Remarks: Intended primarily for customs service and police duties. Has a large deckhouse extending over nearly the entire length of the hull and appears unsuitable for open-water operations.

♦ . . . MIG-G-1200-SC class
Bldr: Iran Marine Industries (In serv. . . .)

D: 8 tons (fl) **S:** 23 kts **Dim:** 12.40 × 3.00 × 0.56
A: 1 14.5-mm 93-cal. mg; small arms
M: 2 gasoline outboards; 400 bhp **Crew:** 15 tot.

♦ . . . MIG-G-0900-CPB class
Bldr: Iran Marine Industries (In serv. . . .)

D: 5 tons (fl) **S:** 30 kts **Dim:** 9.20 × 2.82 × 0.40
A: Small arms **M:** 2 gasoline outboards; 400 bhp **Crew:** 3 tot.

♦ . . . MIG-G-0790-PB class
Bldr: Iran Marine Industries (In serv. . . .)

D: 2.55 tons (fl) **S:** 40 kts **Dim:** 7.95 × 2.41 × 0.55
A: Small arms **M:** 2 gasoline outboards; 400 bhp **Crew:** 2 tot.

♦ . . . MIG-G-0700-PB class
Bldr: Iran Marine Industries (In serv. . . .)

D: 1.7 tons (fl) **S:** 35 kts **Dim:** 7.00 × 2.50 × 0.35
A: Small arms **M:** 1 gasoline outboard; 150 bhp **Crew:** 2 tot.

Remarks: Open launch with forward area decked over.

♦ . . . MIG-G-0500-PL class
Bldr: Iran Marine Industries (In serv. . . .)

D: 1.1 tons (fl) **S:** 40 kts **Dim:** 5.00 × 2.15 × 0.30
A: Small arms **M:** 1 gasoline outboard; 115 bhp **Crew:** 2 tot.

Remarks: GRP construction, open hull.

Note: Other indigenous classes offered for export include the smaller MIG-G-0600-CN3, MIG-G-0610-GP, MIG-G-0500-PL (a 5-m Boston Whaler copy), MIG-G-0800-GP1 (an 8-m Whaler copy), MIG-G-0800-GP2 (same design, with a cabin and powered by two outboards), and MIG-G-1200-PS (a personnel launch with a cabin over nearly the entire length).

♦ Up to 32 "Boghammar Boat" special forces craft
Bldr: Boghammar Marin, Stockholm, Sweden (In serv. 1986– . . .)

"Boghammar Boat" P 120—with rocket launcher on bow and machinegun aft French Navy, 1998

D: 6.4 tons (fl) **S:** 45 kts **Dim:** 12.80 × 2.66 × 0.90
A: 2 single 12.7-mm mg or 23-mm 87-cal. ZU-23-2 AA; 1 106-mm recoilless rifle and/or RPG-7 antitank RL or 12-round 107-mm RL
Electronics: Radar: 1 Decca 170 nav. or none
M: 2 Volvo Penta TAMD-71A diesels; 2 props; 716 bhp
Range: 500/38 **Crew:** 5–6 tot.

Remarks: Known locally as the Toragh class. Ordered 1984, ostensibly for customs service duties; 37 had been delivered by 7-87 for use by Revolutionary Guards in attacks on undefended merchant ships, and ultimately as many as 51 may have been received. U.S. forces destroyed five during 1987–88, of which one was salvaged and taken to the U.S. for use as a training target. Three Iranian units were returned to Sweden in 1992 for refit. Two versions delivered: Model RL-118 and Model RL-130-4A.
Hull systems: Have aluminum-construction, stepped-hydroplane hullform. Were reported being re-engined with Seatek diesels in 1991.
Combat systems: A variety of armaments have been observed, with weapons fitted from whatever was available and according to missions foreseen.

♦ 35 or more GRP launches
Bldr: Boston Whaler, Rockland, Mass.

D: 1.3 tons (fl) **S:** 40 kts **Dim:** 6.7 × 2.3 × 0.4 (prop)
A: 1 12.7-mm mg and/or 1 12-round 107-mm RL
M: 2 gasoline outboard motors; 240 shp

Remarks: Some imported, some built locally in Iran. Used for harassing attacks on unarmed merchant vessels during Iran-Iraq War.

Note: Also in use by the Revolutionary Guards are 7.5-m Damen, Gorinchem-built assault boats, a few wooden dhows of around 23 m o.a. for mine laying, European-manufactured semi-rigid inflatable craft, and Iranian-built copies of the British Watercraft 800–series open workboat, the latter capable of 40-kt speeds.

AMPHIBIOUS LANDING CRAFT

Note: The Pasdaran Revolutionary Guards troops are also transported aboard naval *Hengam*-class landing ships, and there are several commercial landing craft that can also be pressed into service.

♦ 3 Iran Hormuz 24–class medium landing ships [WLSM]
Bldr: . . ., Inchon, South Korea (In serv. 1985–86)

24 Farsi 25 Sardasht 26 Sab Sahel

REVOLUTIONARY GUARD AMPHIBIOUS LANDING CRAFT
(continued)

D: . . . tons **S:** 12 kts **Dim:** 73.1 × 14.2 × 2.5
A: . . . **Electronics:** Radar: . . .
M: 2 Daihatsu 6DLM-22 diesels; 2 props; 2,400 bhp
Crew: 30 tot. + 110 passengers or 140 troops

Remarks: 2,014 grt. Although operated ostensibly in commercial service, these craft are said to support Pasdaran operations. Are beachable and have a bow vehicle ramp. Can accommodate nine medium tanks.

♦ 3 Hejaz-class (MIG-S-5000) medium landing ships [WLSM]
Bldr: Ravenstein SY, Netherlands (In serv. 1984–85)

21 Hejaz 22 Karabala 23 Amir

D: 1,280 tons (fl) **S:** 9 kts **Dim:** 65.0 × 12.0 × 1.5
A: . . . **Electronics:** Radar: . . .
M: 2 M.A.N. V12V-12.5/14 or MWM TBD 604 V12 diesels; 2 props; 1,460 bhp
Crew: 12 tot.

Remarks: 21 and 22 definitely work for the Pasdaran, while 23 probably does. Ramped landing craft with 600-ton cargo capacity. The design is also built at Bandar Abbas as the MIG-S-5000 class, for commercial use.

♦ 8 or more Type 412 Sea Truck landing craft [LCVP]
Bldr: Rotork, U.K.

D: 9 tons (fl) **S:** 28 kts **Dim:** 12.7 × 3.2 × 0.9
A: 2 or 4 single 7.62-mm mg
M: 2 Volvo Penta diesels; 2 props; 240 bhp

Remarks: GRP construction. Can carry up to 30 troops or a small vehicle. Also offered for export in a locally built version as the MIG-G-1200-SC class. Four have been stricken.

Note: Locally built, GRP-hulled smallcraft are also used to transport special forces personnel; a typical design is known as the Yavar class and is some 7.2 × 2.5 × 1.0 m in dimension and can achieve 25 kts.

♦ 2 (+ . . .) special forces landing craft [LCP]
Bldr: Boghammar Marin, Stockholm, Sweden (In serv. 1992, 1996)

Boghammar special forces landing craft—fitting out for Iran
Maritime Photographic, 8-92

D: 9 tons (fl) **S:** 54 kts **Dim:** 15.30 × 3.65 × 1.00
A: . . . **M:** 2 MWM 234V12 diesels; 2 props; . . . bhp
Range: . . . / . . . **Crew:** 3 tot. + 20 troops

Remarks: Enlarged version of standard "Boghammar Boat" with stepped hydroplane hull and a small ramp for troops worked into the stem of the hull. Second unit ordered 8-95.

IRAQ

THE IRAQI COASTAL DEFENSE

The new Iraqi Coastal Defense Force officially began training in January 2004, during which time 214 volunteers began attending a three-month boot camp. Technical and follow-on training of the force began on 21-4-04. The ICDF began coastal patrol operations on 1 October 2004 and currently consists of approximately 700 personnel. The missions of the ICDF include antismuggling, harbor and coastline defense, search-and-rescue operations, and various other operations inside a 12-mile international water boundary. In addition to the vessels listed below, a number of small boats of varying types are also in service.

Note: Six Italian Coast Guard class 200 patrol boats, including CP 267, CP 268 and four sisters will reportedly be transferred to Iraq during 2007. Additionally, twenty-five new construction patrol boats, four 15-m gun boats and two offshore patrol vessels are expected to begin entering service in 2008. No builder has yet been announced for these projects.

CORVETTES [FFL]

♦ 2 Assad class
Bldr: Fincantieri, Muggiano

	Laid down	L	Completed
F 210 Mussa Ben Nussair	15-01-82	22-10-82	17-9-86
F 212 Tariq Ibn Ziad	20-05-82	08-07-83	29-10-86

Mussa Ben Nussair (F 210)—moored alongside sister *Tariq Ibn Ziad* (F 212) at La Spezia Italy. Guy Schaeffer via Paolo Marsan, 10-03

D: 685 tons fl **S:** 37 kts **Dim:** 204.4 × 30.5 × 8
A: 1 76-mm OTO Melara DP, Provisions for Albatros SAM and Teseo Mk 2 SSMs, 1 small helicopter
Electronics:
Radar: 1/SMA SPN-703 nav., 1/AESN SPQ-712 (RAN-12L/X) surf. search, 1 . . . air search, 2/AESN SPG-73 (RTN-10X) f.c.
Sonar: ASO hull mounted
EW: AESN SLQ-747 (INS-3M) integrated suite—2/OTO Melara SCLAR decoy launch syst., SLQ-25 Nixie towed acoustic torpedo decoy
M: 4 MTU 20V956 TB92 diesels; 4 props; 20,120 hp (16,560 sust.)
Range: 4,000/18 **Crew:** 51, not including aircrew

Remarks: These two corvettes, previously held under embargo in Italy, were reportedly refurbished and handed over to the new Iraqi government by 2006. Iraqi crew training for the two vessels began in 2005. The data, as listed above, refer to the vessels' original configuration.

PATROL CRAFT [PC]

Note: In addition to the craft listed here, six new Iraqi-built patrol craft entered service during 2005–6. No additional information on the class is yet available.

♦ 5 27-meter class
Bldr: . . . , China (In serv. 2004)

P 101 through P 105

Iraqi Coastal Defense Force (ICDF) Patrol Craft P 102 U.S. Navy 4-04

P 102 U.S. Navy 2004

Remarks: These 27-m craft are the first vessels to make up the new Iraqi Coastal Defense Force. Based at Umm Qasr, the craft were originally to have arrived in 2002 under the oil-for-food program, but were not allowed to enter the country due to their military capabilities. The boats sat idle for two years in dry-docked at Jebel Ali, United Arab Emirates, before they sailed for Iraq during 4-04.

AUXILIARIES

Note: Custody of the Italian *Stromboli*-class replenishment oiler *Agnadeen* (A 102) (completed in 1984 and sequestered at Alexandria, Egypt, since 1986) was awarded to the builder, Fincantieri, in 8-96, but custody of the ship may eventually be reassigned to the Iraqi Coastal Defense Force. The 7,359-grt seagoing presidential yacht *Al Mansur* was heavily damaged by a coalition airstrike on 25-3-03 during Operation Iraqi Freedom.

IRELAND

Irish Republic

IRISH NAVAL SERVICE

(*An Seirbhis Chabhlaigh*)

Personnel: 1,100 total, plus approximately 300 reservists.

Base: Administrative and operational headquarters at Haulbowline Island, Cork. Naval Reserve companies at Dublin, Cork, Limerick, and Waterford.

Naval Aviation: The Irish Air Force operates two AS.365 Dauphin II helicopters for the navy and three others for land service. Two CASA CN-235-100MPA maritime patrol aircraft were delivered 12-94 for maritime surveillance duties. Two Sikorsky S-61N helicopters have been chartered since 1991 and continue to provide search-and-rescue services from Shannon Airport. The Coast Guard charters an additional S-61 for SAR operations from Waterford airport.

Note: Ship names are preceded by L.É. (*Long Éirennach*), meaning "Irish Ship."

PATROL SHIPS [PS]

Note: A new 1,000-ton class of patrol boats is planned to replace the *Emer*-class boats now in service. The class is still in the preliminary design phase, but three ships are expected to be built for service entry around 2008.

♦ 2 Roísín class

Bldr: Appledore Shipbuilders, U.K.

	L	In serv.
P 51 Roísín	13-9-99	15-12-99
P 52 Niamh	10-2-01	18-9-01

Niamh (P 52) Michael Winter, 6-05

Niamh (P 52) Michael Nitz, 6-05

D: 1,400 tons (1,579 fl) **S:** 22 kts
Dim: 78.84 (73.00 pp) × 14.00 × 3.50 (mean; 3.90 max.)
A: 1 76-mm 62-cal. OTO Melara SuperRapid DP; 2 single 12.7-mm mg; 4 single 7.62-mm mg
Electronics:
Radar: 1 Kelvin-Hughes I-band search; 1 Kelvin-Hughes F-band search
E/O: 1 Radamec 1500/2400 tracking and surveillance (laser rangefinder, t.v., and IR imager)
M: 2 Wärtsilä 16V26 diesels; 2 Lips CP props; 13,600 bhp—460-shp Brunvol electric azimuthal bow-thruster
Electric: 1,400 kw tot. (3 × 400 kw, Caterpillar 3412T diesels driving, 1 × 200 kw, Caterpillar 3306 diesel driving; all 380 V, 50 Hz)
Range: 6,000/15 **Fuel:** 251 tons **Endurance:** 21 days
Crew: 22 tot. (accomm. for 51)

Remarks: P 51 was ordered 16-12-97, originally to replace *Deirdre* (P 20). The design is a variant of the *Vigilant* design built in Chile for the Mauritius Coast Guard. Designed by Polar Associates, Canada. Construction costs 65% funded by the European Union. Cost $34 million, not including the 76-mm gun. P 52 was ordered on 6-4-00; her commissioning was delayed several months by gearbox problems found during trials, and she was delivered on 19-7-01.
Hull systems: Deep-vee hullform with twin rudders and signature-reduction superstructure shape to reduce head-on radar signature. Two firefighting monitors, with a single 600-m^3/hr firepump. Have Brown Brothers retractable fin stabilizers and a four-berth sick bay. Can carry several 20-ft. standard freight containers to support overseas-deployed Irish peacekeeping forces. Have a Kelvin-Hughes Integrated Bridge System (IBS) and a Litton-Decca ISIS-1500 engineering monitoring and control system. Two Delta 6.70-m rigid inflatable inspection launches, each powered by a 70-bhp outboard engine, are carried, as is one Avon 5.4-m RIB.

♦ 1 P 31 class

Bldr: Verolme Dockyard, Cork

	Laid down	L	In serv.
P 31 Eithne	15-12-82	19-12-83	7-12-84

Eithne (P 31) A. A. de Kruijf, 7-05

Eithne (P 31) A. A. de Kruijf, 7-05

D: 1,760 tons (1,915 fl) **S:** 19 kts **Dim:** 81.00 × 12.00 × 4.30
A: 1 57-mm 70-cal. Bofors SAK 57/70 Mk 1 DP; 2 single 20-mm 90-cal. Rheinmetall AA; 2 single 7.62-mm mg; 1 AS.365 Dauphin II helicopter
Electronics:
Radar: 1 Decca TM 1229C nav.; 1 Decca AC 1629C nav.; 1 Thales DA-05/4 surf./air search
Sonar: Plessey PMS-26L hull-mounted (10 kHz)
TACAN: MEL RRB transponder
E/O: Thales LIOD t.v./laser/IR f.c. and surveillance
M: 2 Ruston Paxman 12RKCM diesels; 2 CP props; 7,200 bhp (6,640 sust.)
Electric: 1,300 kVA tot. (3 × 400 kw, 1 × 100 kw) **Range:** 7,000/15
Fuel: 290 tons **Crew:** 9 officers, 76 enlisted

Remarks: Serves as flagship of the Irish Naval Service. P 31 ordered 23-4-82. Construction of a second unit deferred, in part because yard closed in 1983. Refitted 1998–99.
Hull systems: Denny-Brown retractable fin stabilizers are installed. Has considerable firefighting capability, with three firefighting water monitors, and can be replenished under way at sea. Boats include a 7.3-m crew boat, 5.5-m inspection boat, and Avon Searaider semi-rigid inflatable boats with 90-hp outboard motors. Has a harpoon landing system for the helicopter. The Kelvin-Hughes Integrated Bridge System (IBS) was installed in 1999.
Combat systems: Has two Thales t.v./optical target designators for the 57-mm gun. Carries two Wallop 57-mm flare RL.

PATROL SHIPS [PS] *(continued)*

♦ 3 Emer class
Bldr: Verolme Dockyard, Cork

	L	In serv.		L	In serv.
P 21 Emer	1977	16-1-78	P 23 Aisling	3-10-79	21-5-80
P 22 Aoife	12-4-79	29-11-79			

Aisling (P 23) Bernard Prezélin, 5-05

Aisling (P 23) Bernard Prezélin, 5-05

D: 1,003 tons (fl) **S:** 18.5 kts **Dim:** 65.20 (58.50 pp) × 10.40 × 4.36
A: 1 40-mm 60-cal. Mk 7 Bofors AA; 2 single 20-mm 90-cal. Oerlikon GAM B01 AA; 2 single 7.62-mm mg
Electronics:
Radar: 1 Kelvin-Hughes Mk IV nav.; 1 Kelvin Hughes Mk VI surf. search
Sonar: Simrad SU side-scan hull-mounted (34 kHz)
E/O: Rademac 1500 surveillance and gun f.c.
M: 2 SEMT-Pielstick 6 PA6 L280 diesels; 1 CP prop; 4,800 bhp
Range: 4,500/18; 6,750/12 **Fuel:** 170 tons **Crew:** 5 officers, 41 enlisted

Remarks: Developed version of the *Deirdre* with raised forecastle instead of bow bulwarks, to improve sea keeping. P 21 was extensively refitted during 1995.
Hull systems: Have advanced navigational aids and fin stabilizers. P 22 and P 23 have a 225-kw bow-thruster, a computerized plotting table, and a new-pattern KaMeWa controllable-pitch propeller. Only P 23 has evaporators. All have three Pamou-Markon alternators.
Combat systems: The 40-mm gun is locally controlled. New 20-mm AA and a Marisat SATCOM terminal were added in 1989, and all are now fitted with a SATNAV receiver and receivers for the Decca Mk 53 Navigator radio navaid system. All were given a new radar suite during mid-1990s refits.

Disposal note: Patrol ship *Deirdre* (P 20) was retired on 14-6-01 and was sold commercially for conversion into a cruise ship.

PATROL COMBATANTS [PG]

♦ 2 ex-U.K. Peacock class
Bldr: Hall Russell, Aberdeen

	Laid down	L	In serv.
P 41 Orla (ex-*Swift*, P 243)	23-9-83	11-9-84	3-5-85
P 42 Ciara (ex-*Swallow*, P 242)	24-4-83	30-3-84	16-11-84

D: 662 tons (712 fl) **S:** 28 kts (25 sust.) **Dim:** 62.60 (60.00 pp) × 10.00 × 2.72
A: 1 76-mm 62-cal. OTO Melara Compact DP; 2 single 12.7-mm mg; 2 single 7.62-mm mg
Electronics: Radar: 1 Kelvin Hughes 500A nav.; 1 Kelvin-Hughes Mk IV nav.
M: 2 APE-Crossley-SEMT-Pielstick 18 PA6 V280 diesels; 2 3-bladed props; 14,188 bhp—1 Schottel S103 drop-down, shrouded prop; 181 shp
Electric: 755 kw tot. **Range:** 2,500/17 **Fuel:** 44 tons
Crew: 6 officers, 33 enlisted (incl. boarding party)

Ciara (P 42) Julio Montes, 8-03

Remarks: Former patrol boats at Hong Kong, purchased 8-10-88 and commissioned 21-11-88 in Irish service. Three sisters were sold to the Philippines.
Hull systems: Have two rudders. Were bad rollers until deeper bilge keels were fitted. Carry two Avon Searaider 5.4-m-o.a., 30-kt, 10-man semi-rigid rubber inspection dinghies.
Combat systems: The 76-mm gun is controlled by a BAE Systems GSA.7 Sea Archer optronic director. Two 12.7-mm mg were added in 1989. Two 50-mm rocket flare launchers are fitted. A Marisat SATCOM terminal is carried. The present radar suite was fitted in 1993, along with a Nucleus 6000A command data system.

SERVICE CRAFT

♦ 4 naval service launches [YFL]
Barbara Heck Colleen II Freya Niamh

Freya Chris Hockaday, 7-96

Remarks: *Colleen II,* built in 1972, is the commanding officer's launch, Cork. The other three are miscellaneous, newer, 12-m craft operated by the naval reserve as Port and Territorial Waters Patrol Vessels. Last vessel has same name as P 52.

♦ 3 miscellaneous sail-training craft [YTS]
Bldr: Dufour, France

Creidne Nancy Bet Tailte

Remarks: First two are Bermuda ketches, 15.8 m and 14.6 m long, respectively, operated by the naval reserve (*An Slua Muiri*). *Tailte* is 10.7 m long and is operated by the regular navy.

Note: Also in use for training are five 5.5-m sail/oar boats.

DEPARTMENT OF DEFENCE—SERVICE CRAFT

SERVICE CRAFT

♦ 1 passenger launch [WYFL]
Bldr: Zwolle, the Netherlands (In serv. 1962)

David F

David F Chris Hockaday, 7-96

DEPARTMENT OF DEFENCE—SERVICE CRAFT *(continued)*

D: Approx. 100 tons (fl) **S:** 9.5 kts **Dim:** 23.0 × 6.4 × . . .
M: 1 Gardner diesel; 1 prop; 230 bhp

Remarks: 69 grt. On charter 1970 to 1-89, then taken over outright.

♦ **1 small passenger launch [WYFL]**
Bldr: Arklow Eng. Co., Arklow, Ireland (In serv. 1981)

FIACH DUBH (ex-*White Point*)

D: . . . tons (fl) **S:** 8 kts **Dim:** 13.31 × . . . × . . .
M: 1 Gardner diesel; 180 bhp

Remarks: Taken over 11-45. Can carry up to 51 passengers.

♦ **1 small passenger launch [WYFL]**
Bldr: . . . , Den Oever, the Netherlands (In serv. 1971)

FAINLEOG (ex-*Greta*)

D: . . . tons **S:** 14.5 kts **Dim:** 14.21 × . . . × . . .
M: 1 Saab Scania V8 diesel; 410 bhp

Remarks: 15 grt. Taken over 11-82. Carries up to 50 passengers.

♦ **1 small tug [WYTL]**
Bldr: Arklow Eng. Co., Arklow, Ireland (In serv. 1979)

SEABHAC (ex-*Raffeen*)

D: . . . tons (fl) **S:** 8 kts **Dim:** 10.87 × . . . × . . .
M: 1 Gardner diesel; 180 bhp

Remarks: 9 grt. Taken over 1982.

Note: The 120-ton sail-training craft *Asgard II* is the Irish National Youth Training Vessel; she is, on occasion, used by the Irish Defence Forces but does not belong to the Department of Defence.

The Commissioner of Irish Lights lighthouse tender *Granuaile* was replaced early in 2000 by a 2,625-grt ship of the same name built by Damen, Gorinchem, the Netherlands.

The Irish Marine Emergency Service was renamed the Irish Coast Guard early in 2000; it has responsibility for search-and-rescue, pollution-control efforts, and other emergency services and operates six small craft. The establishment of a new Irish Sea Safety Agency at the end of 2001 was approved during 8-01; the organization absorbs the existing Marine Survey Office and may eventually also incorporate the new coast guard.

Note: The survey and marine research ship *Celtic Expolorer*, in service since 2003, is operated from Galway by the Marine Institute as a national marine research asset. Built in the Netherlands, the *Celtic Explorer* is 65.5 meters long and carries a crew of 31 personnel, including 17–19 scientists.

ISRAEL

State of Israel

ISRAELI NAVY

(Heyl Yam)

Personnel: Active: about 5,500 total (including 2,500 conscripts). Plus about 3,500 reserve personnel.

Bases: Ashdod, Eilat, and Haifa. Major repairs are conducted at Haifa.

Maritime Aviation: One S.365G Dolpheen (the prototype U.S. Coast Guard HH-65A Dolphin) and six AS.565SA Atelef (Bat) helicopters are operated by Israeli Air Force squadron Tayeset 193 for shipboard service. Tayeset 195 operates three Navy-owned IAI Westwind 1124N Shahaf maritime reconnaissance aircraft (equipped with APS-504(V)2 search radar and able to launch two Gabriel antiship missiles) and has 25 Bell 212 helicopters for coastal surveillance and SAR; the Shahafs, though still in service, are to be retired from service now that the five Beech 200T King Air maritime patrol craft, ordered in 2001, have been delivered.

Note: Ship and craft names/numbers are preceded by INS (Israeli Naval Ship).

WEAPONS AND SYSTEMS

The Israeli Navy primarily uses foreign weapons, such as 76-mm OT Melara Compact, OTO Melara 40-mm, and Oerlikon guns. Israeli industry has perfected the Gabriel antiship and Barak antimissile SAM missile systems:

Gabriel-I: A 560-kg, solid-propellant, surface-to-surface missile. After being fired, it climbs to about 100 m, then, at 7,500 m from the launcher, descends slowly to an altitude of 20 m. Optical or radar guidance is provided in azimuth, and a radio altimeter determines altitude. At a distance of 1,200 m from the target, the missile descends to 3 m, under either radio command or semiactive homing. The explosive charge is a 75-kg conventional warhead. Obsolescent, it may have been retired.

Gabriel-II: A development of Gabriel-I that carries a television camera and a transceiver for azimuth and altitude commands. The television is energized when the missile has attained a certain height and sends to the firing ship a picture of the areas that cannot be picked up by shipboard radar. The operator then can send any necessary corrections during the middle and final phases of the missile's flight, and thus find a target that cannot be seen either by the naked eye or on radar. The range of the Gabriel-II is about 40 km.

Barak: A surface-to-air point-defense system, originally developed for use with an elevatable/trainable eight-cell box launcher, now uses eight-cell vertical launch groups. It entered service in 1996 and is also used by Chile and Singapore. Characteristics include

Length: 2.175 m **Diameter:** 170 mm **Wingspan:** 685 mm
Weight: 97.9 kg **Warhead:** 22 kg (tungsten pellets)
Speed: Mach 1.6 **Range:** 10 km engagement **Guidance:** Semiactive homing

Barak's system weight with 32 rounds requires 1.3 m of deck space plus 2 m^3 of below-decks volume. The intended fire-control system employs the AMDR (Advanced Missile Detection Radar), an S-band, pulse-doppler set capable of tracking 250 Mach 0.3–3.0 targets.

The U.S. RGM-84 Harpoon was first acquired in 1978 and is used on guided-missile patrol ships and craft, in Block 1B and 1C versions; 16 additional missiles were purchased in 1998. Israel is alleged by the U.S. Department of Defense to have modified its Harpoons for improved range and performance and may intend to produce its own modified Harpoons for export; also reported is the fitting of a datalink to the missiles, which permits the launching ship or a surveillance helicopter to designate targets using the missile's radar seeker data.

Fourteen U.S. Vulcan/Phalanx 20-mm close-in weapon systems were delivered for use in various units of the Sa'ar classes. Also in use are U.S.-supplied Redeye handheld, IR-homing missiles.

Most radar, weapons control, combat data, communications, and electronics warfare systems are now made in Israel, based primarily on European and U.S. models. In development since 1991 have been the Rafael ATC-1 towed torpedo decoy and Scutter expendable torpedo decoy, the latter a 1-m-long by 10-cm-diameter device weighing 7.8 kg and having an endurance of 10 minutes to a depth of 300 m.

ATTACK SUBMARINES [SS]

♦ **3 (+ 2) Dolphin (IKL Type 800) class**
Bldrs: HDW, Kiel, and Thyssen Nordseewerke, Emden (see remarks)

	Laid down	L	In serv.
DOLPHIN	1-4-92	15-4-96	27-7-99 (del. 29-3-99)
LEVIATHAN	10-92	27-5-97	29-6-99 (del.)
TEKUMA	7-94	9-7-98	22-10-00 (del. 25-7-00)
. . .	. . .	. . .	2009
. . .	. . .	. . .	2010

Dolphin H&L Van Ginderen, 6-99

Tekuma Winter & Findler, 6-00

D: 1,565 tons surf./1,720 tons sub. **S:** 11 kts snorkel/20 kts sub.
Dim: 57.30 × 7.60 × 6.20 (13.90 high, masts retracted)
A: 4 650-mm and 6 533-mm bow swim-out TT (16 DM-2A3 Seehake wire-guided torpedoes, UGM-84C Harpoon antiship and Triton antihelicopter missiles)
Electronics:
Radar: 1 . . . search
EW: Timnex 4CH(V)2 intercept (2–18 GHz)
Sonar: STN Atlas Elektronik CSU-90-1 suite, with DBSQS-21D active, AN 5039A1 passive, PRS-3-15 passive ranging, and FAS-3-1 passive flank arrays
M: Diesel-electric: 3 MTU 16V493 AZ80 diesels (800 bhp each), 3 diesel generator sets (313 kw each), 2 Siemens motors; 1 7-bladed prop; 5,000 shp (2,850 sust.)
Range: 8,000/8, 14,000/4 snorkel; 25/20, 420/8 sub.
Endurance: 60 days **Crew:** 6 officers, 24 enlisted

ATTACK SUBMARINES [SS] *(continued)*

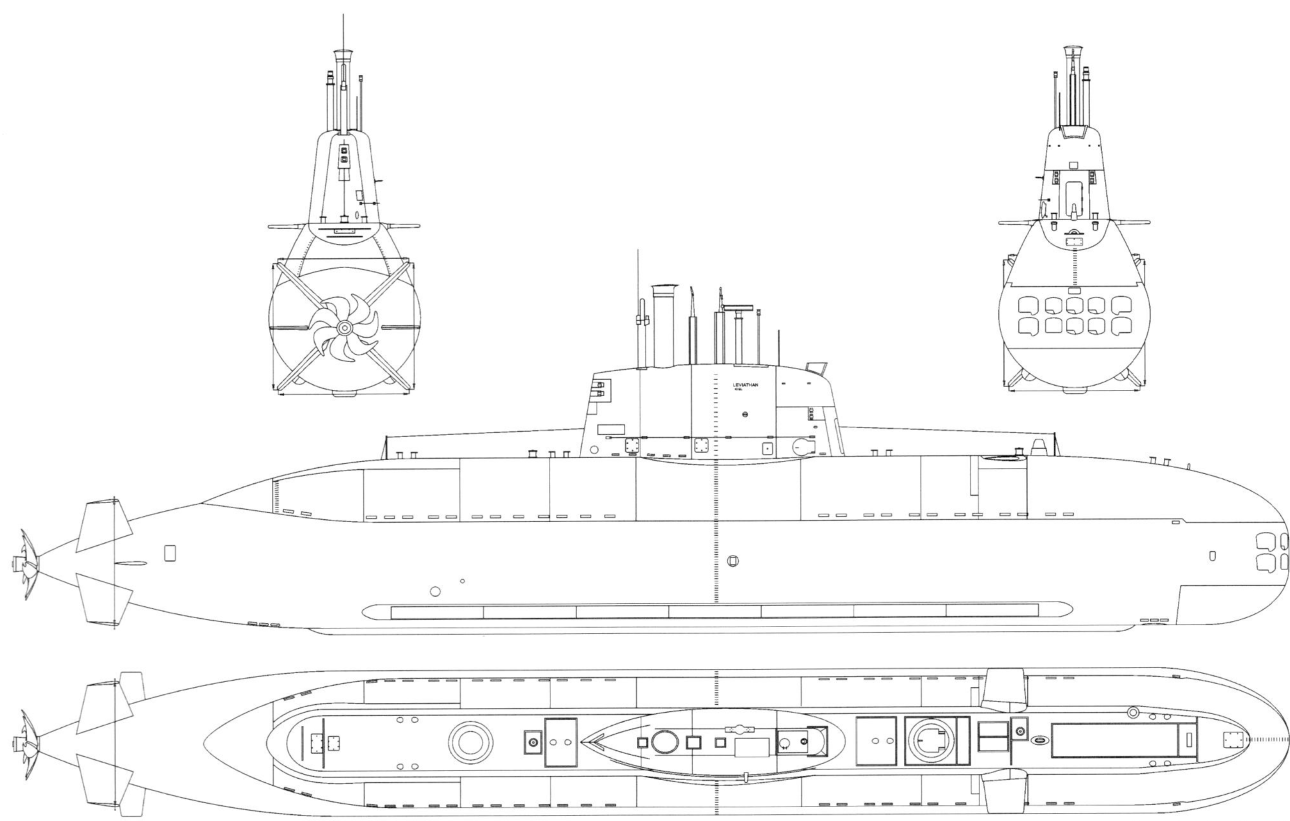

Leviathan Drawing by Tomek Grotnik, 2003

Remarks: Authorized 3-88, initially to replace the relatively recent IKL 500 submarines. Permission to build two vice the originally planned three was finally given in 8-89, but the project was canceled in 11-90. Originally, the ships were to be assembled at Ingalls Shipyard, Pascagoula, Miss., using sections prefabricated by HDW in Germany. In 1-91 the project was revived when the German government offered to finance fully the construction of two in Germany, using a German combat system vice the originally planned U.S. systems. The third submarine was reinstated in 2-95, with Israel and Germany sharing the $300 million cost equally; the name was originally reported as *Dakar*. Work on first unit began at Kiel on 15-2-92; Thyssen at Emden performed fitting out work. The submarines are painted a blue-green shade said to render them less visible in Mediterranean waters. Based at Haifa.

In 2005, Israel announced plans to purchase two additional units built in Germany at a cost of approximately $1.2 billion with $^1/_3$ of the cost paid by Germany. The new submarines will be built to a slightly modified design and will be able to remain submerged for longer periods of time, indicating that they will be fitted with an AIP system.

Hull systems: Operating depth 350 m; collapse depth 700 m. Have 10% reserve buoyancy and two 216-cell batteries. Turning circle 200 m in diameter at 15 kts submerged. The diesel engines have also been said to be of the 16V396 SE84 6BSL model, of 1,400 bhp each. An external keel some 80 cm wide and a reinforced lower bow allow for bottoming.

Combat systems: Have the STN Atlas Elektronik ISUS 90-1 combat data system. Equipped with swimmer lockout facilities in the sail and boat stowage for eight special forces personnel. Have Kollmorgen Model 76 search and attack periscopes. The torpedo tube arrangement is said to be very cramped, as additional tubes were fitted into the original design. The torpedo tubes are arranged in two horizontal rows, with the larger-diameter 650-mm tubes outboard; at least one 650-mm tube can be used for swimmer exit and ingress. The wire-guided torpedoes are an export version of the German Navy's DM-2A3, assembled by Lockheed Martin Tactical Systems Co. in cooperation with STN Atlas Elektronik; they are launched from the 650-mm tubes by means of liners. The EADS Triton fiber-optic-guided antihelicopter missile is being developed for these submarines; based on the technology of the Polyphem missile, it will have a 15-km range and can also be used against helicopters, surface craft, and coastal targets.

Disposal note: The three German-built IKL 500–class submarines *Gal* (72), *Tanin* (74), and *Rahav* (76) were retired during 1999 and offered for foreign sale. Media reports, however, indicate that two of the three are being modernized and may be returned to Israeli naval service. A reported sale to Ecuador early in 1999 fell through, and Poland declined to purchase them in 3-01. Thailand decided against purchasing two of the class during 7-02.

CORVETTES [FFL]

♦ 0 (+ 5) Sa'ar V+ class

Bldr: Northrop Grumman Litton Ship Systems, Pascagoula, Miss.

Remarks: Negotiations were under way during 2001 between Israel and Northrop Grumman for a class of up to five improved versions of the Sa'ar V class to replace the *Nirit* class around 2010. Current plans call for a displacement up to 3,000 tons and an armament fit of 16 Israeli Advanced Naval Attack missiles (ASAM) and 16 advanced Barak surface-to-air missiles, with the former to have a 200-km range against land and seaborne targets, a loiter capability, a datalink to the launch platform and/or a targeting aircraft or helicopter, and a dual radar and infrared seeker. The program would be paid for with part of the annual U.S. military aid fund.

♦ 3 Lahav (Sa'ar V) class

Bldr: Northrop Grumman Litton Ship Systems (formerly Ingalls SB), Pascagoula, Miss.

	Laid down	L	In serv.
501 Eilat	24-2-92	9-2-93	24-5-94
502 Lahav	25-9-92	20-8-93	23-9-94
503 Hanit	5-4-93	4-3-94	7-2-95

Sa'ar V class Israeli Navy

D: 1,075 tons (1,275 fl) **S:** 33+ kts (20 on diesels)
Dim: 85.64 (76.60 wl) × 11.88 (10.39 wl) × 3.17 (hull)
A: 8 RGM-84C Harpoon SSM; 8 8-round Barak vertical-launch SAM groups (64 missiles); 1 20-mm Mk 15 Phalanx CIWS; 2 single 20-mm 70-cal Oerlikon AA; 4 single 7.62-mm mg; 2 triple 324-mm Mk 32 ASW TT (U.S. Mk 46 Mod. 5 torpedoes); 1 AS.565SA Atelef helicopter (with rockets, etc.) (see Remarks)
Electronics:
Radar: 1 Cardion SPS-55 surf. search; 1 Elta EL/M-2228S 3-D variant air search; 2 Elta EL/M-2221 GM STGR f.c.; 1 Mk 90 Phalanx f.c.
Sonar: EDO Type 796 Mod. 1 hull-mounted (6–8 kHz); provision for Rafael Coris-TAS towed passive array (10–1,600 Hz)
EW: Elisra NS-9003A intercept (2–18 GHz); Tadiran NATACS MMI COMINT and D/F (20–500 MHz); 2 Rafael RAN-1010 jammers; Elbit DESEAVER decoy syst. (3 72-tube RL, 2 24-tube smoke RL); SLQ-25 Nixie towed acoustic torpedo decoy syst.
E/O: 2 El-Op MSIS multisensor, stabilized weapon directors

CORVETTES [FFL] *(continued)*

Lahav (502)—on builder's trials; note two groups of four eight-cell vertical launchers for Barak missiles, four forward of the bridge and four abaft the stack
Ingalls SB, 1994

M: CODOG: 1 G.E. LM-2500 gas turbine (30,000 shp), 2 MTU 12V1163 TB82 diesels (3,000 bhp each); 2 KaMeWa CP props; 30,000 shp max.
Electric: 1,880 kw (4 × 470-kw Siemens-MTU diesel sets)
Range: 3,500/17 **Endurance:** 20 days **Crew:** 62 tot. (including air group)

Remarks: Were originally to have been a class of eight, then four. Three (with option for fourth not taken up) were ordered on 8-2-89. Formal christening for *Eilat* occurred on 19-3-93, and the ship was delivered to Israel 12-93 for final fitting out, with an initial projected fully operational date of mid-1996 that slipped to late 1997/early 1998; the other two experienced similar delays. Cost around $260 million each. Can be used as a task force command ship. On 14-7-06, *Hanit* (503) was struck and damaged by an Iranian C802 SSM fired from Lebanon by Hezbollah militants. She has since been repaired.
Hull systems: Design emphasizes radar, noise, and heat signature suppression. Have 11 watertight compartments and Prairie-Masker bubbler underwater noise radiation suppression system.
Combat systems: The AIO III combat system by Elta has Elta EL/S-9000 computers (based on the Motorola 68020 microprocessor) and 17 display consoles. An OTO Melara 76-mm dual-purpose gun can be substituted for the Phalanx mount but to date has not been. The EL/M-2228S radar functions as an automatic missile detection system. Were intended eventually to carry three Elta EL/M-2221-GM missile fire-control radars, two flanking the foremast and one aft. The Ku-band search radar in the Phalanx CIWS can be used to provide target designation services for the Barak missiles. Have the ICS-2 integrated communications suite. The planned eight single launcher containers for Gabriel-II antiship missiles were not installed due to top-weight problems, and the planned G.E. 25-mm gatling guns have yet to replace the old Oerlikon 20-mm interim mountings.

GUIDED-MISSILE PATROL CRAFT [PTG]

♦ 8 Nirit class

Bldr: Israel Shipyards, Ltd., Haifa

	Laid down	L	In serv.	Conversion completed
KIDON	. . .	7-74	9-74	7-2-94
YAFO	. . .	2-75	4-75	1-7-98
NITZAHON	. . .	10-7-78	9-78	1995
ROMAT	. . .	1981	10-81	2000
KESHET	. . .	10-82	1982	2001
HETZ (ex-*Nirit*)	1984	10-90	3-91	—
SUFA	. . .	9-5-02	2003	—
HEREV	. . .	9-5-02	2003	—

Hetz Israeli Navy, via Norman Polmar, 1995

D: 488 tons (fl) **S:** 32 kts (30 sust.)
Dim: 61.70 (58.21 wl) × 7.62 (7.09 wl) × 2.76

Kidon—with heavy davits aft and an extensive masthead D/F array
C. E. Castle, 4-99

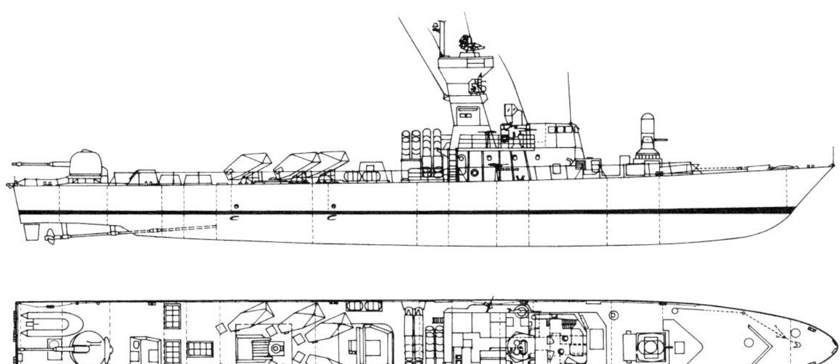

Nirit class Israel SY

A: 2 or 4 RGM-84C Harpoon SSM; 6 Gabriel-II SSM; 4 8-round Barak point-defense SAM vertical-launch groups; 1 76-mm OTO Melara Compact DP; 1 20-mm Mk 15 Phalanx CIWS; 2 single 20-mm 70-cal. Oerlikon AA; 4 single 12.7-mm mg—*Herev* only: 8 RGM-84C Harpoon SSM; 1 20-mm Mk 15 Phalanx CIWS; 1 25-mm 75-cal. Typhoon DP; 2 single 20-mm 70-cal. Oerlikon AA; 4 single 12.7-mm mg
Electronics:
Radar: 1 Elta EL/M-2218-S AMDR K-band surf./air search; 1 or 2 Elta EL/M-2221 GM STGR f.c. (see Remarks)
EW: Elta . . . intercept; 1 45-tube trainable decoy RL; 8 smoke RL; 2 24-tube decoy RL
E/O: 1 El-Op MSIS
M: 4 MTU 16V538 TB93 diesels; 4 props; 16,376 bhp (at 1,700 rpm)
Electric: . . . kw tot. (4 × 440-V, 60-Hz diesel sets)
Range: 3,000/17 **Fuel:** 116 tons **Crew:** 50 tot.

Remarks: *Hetz* was begun as a third unit of the *Romat* class but left incomplete as an economy measure; work began again in 1989 to complete her as the seagoing trials ship for the Barak antimissile system and advanced electronics intended for the *Eilat* class and for backfit into earlier missile combatants. The decision to update *Romat* and *Keshet* was made during 8-98.
Hull systems: Have a round-bilge, semi-displacement mild-steel construction hull with more-powerful diesel engines than earlier ships of the series. The converted ships were lengthened during modernization.
Combat systems: The four Barak vertical-launch groups are recessed into the after deck. The radar directors (essentially an Israeli-made version of the Alenia Orion RTN-10X) are mounted on platforms abreast the tower mast. The starboard director antenna is of open-mesh configuration, while at least on *Hetz* the portside antenna has a solid reflector dish. There is an optronic director for the Gabriel-II antiship missiles and an integrated weapons fire-control system. *Kidon* (and probably the others) can be fitted with heavy, paired davits on either beam aft; *Kidon* also has an extensive masthead D/F array. *Herev* as "completed" was equipped with dual davits for RIB combat swimmer craft; the craft lacked gun and missile f.c. radars and probably does not have Barak missile facilities.

Disposal note: *Aliyah* (Sa'ar 4.5) -class corvettes *Aliyah* and *Geoula* were decomissioned and transferred to Mexico in 7-04.

♦ 1 Reshev (Sa'ar IV) class

Bldr: Israel SY, Haifa

	L	In serv.
ATZMAUT	3-12-78	2-79

D: 415 tons (450 fl) **S:** 32 kts **Dim:** 58.10 × 7.62 × 2.40
A: 4 RGM-84C Harpoon SSM; 6 or 8 Gabriel-II SSM; 1 76-mm 62-cal. OTO Melara Compact DP; 1 20-mm Mk 15 Phalanx CIWS; 2 single 20-mm 70-cal. Oerlikon AA; 4 single 12.7-mm mg

GUIDED-MISSILE PATROL CRAFT [PTG] *(continued)*

Reshev class—rigged as a missile boat French Navy, 1983

Reshev class—rigged for ASW Israeli Navy

Electronics:
Radar: 1 Thales TH-D 1040 Neptune surf./air search; 1 Alenia Orion RTN-10X f.c.
EW: Elisra NS 9003/5 intercept/jammer suite; NATACS comms intercept; Elisra NS 9010 D/F; 0 or 1 45-tube trainable decoy RL; 4 or 6 24-tube fixed decoy RL; 4 single smoke RL
M: 4 MTU 16V956 TB91 diesels; 4 props; 14,000 bhp (10,680 sust.)
Range: 1,650/30; 4,000/17.5 **Crew:** 45 tot.

Remarks: Three of this design were built in Israel for South Africa, and six others were built there under license at Durban. *Atzmaut* is the only Israeli Navy Sa'ar IV not to have been lengthened and modernized.
Hull systems: Quarters are air-conditioned.
Combat systems: Original missile armament was seven fixed Gabriel launchers. The 76-mm gun has been specially adapted for shore bombardment. The elaborate ECM/ESM system was designed by the Italian firm Elettronica and manufactured in Israel. Has the Elbit Automatic Countermeasures Dispensing System (ACDS). Can be rigged for ASW, with a portable dipping sonar at the stern in place of the 76-mm mount and one triple 324-mm Mk 32 ASW TT on the port side; the missile complement is reduced to four Gabriel and two Harpoon missiles in that circumstance.
Disposals: Sisters *Keshet* and *Romach* were transferred to Chile 1979–80; *Reshev* and *Tarshish* were transferred in 11-96 (departing Israel on 1-6-97). *Komemiyut* and *Moledet* were transferred to Sri Lanka on 9-12-00.

PATROL BOATS [PB]

♦ 6 (+ 5) Super Dvora Mk III class
Bldr: IAI-Ramta, Be'er Sheva (In serv. 2004–6)

830 831 832 . . . .

Super Dvora Mk III–class 830 IAI, 11-04

D: 57 tons (65 fl) **S:** 45 kts **Dim:** 25.00 × 5.65 × . . .
A: 1 20-mm Rafael Typhoon gatling AA; 1 20-mm 90-cal. Oerlikon; 1 or more 40-mm Mk 19 grenade launchers
Electronics: Radar: 1 . . . nav.
M: 3 MTU 12V396 TE94 diesels; 3 Arneson ASD 16 outdrive semi-submerged props; 4,175 bhp
Electric: 30 kw **Range:** 700/14 **Crew:** 1 officer, 8 enlisted

Remarks: Six were ordered on 15-1-02, with an option for five more. First of the class, 830, entered service 11-11-04. Aluminum construction, with basic design evolved from that of earlier craft in the Dvora/Dabur series. Accommodations are to be superior to those in the earlier boats, and speeds are considerably increased.

♦ Tzir'a-class defender (25-foot) response boats
Bldr: Safe Boats, Port Orchard, Wash. (In serv. 2005)

231 . . . .

D: . . . tons **S:** 40+ kts **Dim:** 7.62 × 2.59 × . . .
A: 1 7.62-mm mg
Electronics: 1 Raytheon Raymarine . . . nav.
M: 2 Honda BF225 4-stroke gasoline outboards; 450 bhp **Range:** 175/35
Fuel: 125 gals. **Crew:** Up to 10 tot.

Remarks: Ordered 9-05 for a total cost of $700,000. Form the basis of a new port security unit operating from Ashkelon. Can operate efficiently in shallow 60-cm water, 30-mph winds, and 6-foot seas. Additional units may be purchased in the future. Used primarily for counter-terrorism.

♦ 2 (+ 3) Shaldag Mk II class
Bldr: Israel Shipyards, Haifa (In serv. 2003-04)

. . . . . .

Shaldag Mk II class Israel Shipyards

D: 40 tons (56 fl) **S:** 46 kts **Dim:** 24.37 (20.07 pp) × 6.00 × 1.15 (1.26 max.)
A: 1 20-mm Rafael Typhoon gatling AA; 1 20-mm 90-cal. Oerlikon; 2–4 single 7.62-mm mg; 2 40-mm Mk 19 grenade launchers
Electronics: Radar: 1 Furuno FR 8250 nav.
M: 2 MTU 12V396 TE94 diesels; 2 waterjets; 4,570 (3,260 sust.) bhp
Electric: 70 kw tot. (2 × 35-kw, 380-V a.c. diesel sets)
Range: 850/16 **Endurance:** 2–3 days **Crew:** 15 tot.

Remarks: Ordered 13-1-02. Although this design has been widely exported, it had not hitherto been ordered for the Israeli Navy. *Shaldag* means "Kingfisher" in Hebrew. Aluminum construction.

♦ 1 Alligator-class semi-submersible
Bldr: K-10 Corp., U.S. (In serv. 6-98)

D: 23.4 tons (fl) **S:** 30 kts (8 semi-sub.) **Dim:** 19.81 × 3.96 × . . .
A: . . .
Electronics: Radar: 1 . . . nav.
M: 2 . . . diesels; 2 props; . . . bhp
Range: . . . / . . . **Crew:** . . .

Remarks: Intended to ballast down to barely awash for clandestine operations at low speeds; all topside masts and antennas can be retracted or folded. Hull and superstructure configured to be low-observable. Has a five-ton payload. Tested by U.S. Navy prior to delivery.

♦ 3 T 2212 class
Bldr: T-Craft International, Cape Town, South Africa (In serv. 11-97)

D: 23 tons (45 fl) **S:** 41 kts (37 sust.) **Dim:** 22.00 × 7.00 × 0.90
A: 1 20-mm Oerlikon AA **Electronics:** Radar: 1 . . . nav.
M: 2 MTU 12V183 TE92 diesels; 2 waterjets; 2,000 bhp
Range: 525/30 **Crew:** 4 tot. + 15 passengers

Remarks: Purchased new in 11-98. This design had not proved successful in South African Navy service.
Hull systems: Unusual catamaran hullform with hydrofoils between the hulls. GRP construction. Have accommodations for 16 but can be operated with as few as four personnel. Carry a 3.4-m rigid inflatable rescue boat aft.

PATROL BOATS [PB] *(continued)*

♦ 13 Super Dvora Mk I and Mk II classes
Bldr: RAMTA–Israeli Aircraft Industries (IAI), Be'er Sheva (In serv. 1-89 to 1994)

Mk I: 811 through 819 Mk II: 820 through 823

Super Dvora Mk II–class 823 French Navy, 1996

D: 48 tons (54 fl) **S:** 36–38 kts **Dim:** 22.40 × 5.49 × 1.00
A: 2 single 20-mm 70-cal. Oerlikon AA; 2 single 12.7-mm mg; provision for Hellfire SSM and/or 1 84-mm Carl Gustav mortar
Electronics: Radar: 1 Raytheon . . . nav.
M: Mk I: 2 MTU 12V396 TB93 diesels; 2 Arneson outdrive semi-submerged props; 3,260 bhp—Mk II: 3 MTU 12V396 TE94 diesels; 3 Arneson ASD 16 outdrive semi-submerged props; 4,175 bhp
Electric: 30 kw **Range:** 700/14 **Crew:** 1 officer, 8 enlisted

Remarks: Improved version of basic Dvora design. Of six Mk I units ordered 3-87, the first was delivered 1-89 and the rest in 1989–90. The Mk II version was delivered during 1993–94. A planned Mk III version with three engines was not built. As of 4-01 IAI was negotiating to have the design built in the U.S. so that it could be purchased for foreign navies under the U.S. Foreign Military Sales program. A longer version of the basic design is in development for the Israeli Navy, and the builder is also working on a 17-m version to be known as "Wasp."
Exports: Six Mk I and four Mk II have been delivered to Sri Lanka, four Mk I to Eritrea, two Mk II to Slovenia, and two Mk II to India. License granted 1996 for indigenous construction of this class at Goa, India.
Hull systems: Aluminum construction.
Combat systems: Can be armed with depth charges, ASW torpedoes, or 130-mm barrage rocket launchers and can be fitted with an Elop optronic low-light-level surveillance and weapons direction device. Trials were conducted on 815 in 1997 with the General Dynamics Typhoon triple 12.7-mm mg mount forward. U.S.-supplied 25-mm Bushmaster guns may replace one or both 20-mm mountings.

♦ Up to 12 Dabur class
Bldr: Israeli Aircraft Industries, Be'er Sheva (In serv. 1973–77)

Dabur-class 854 ANBw/FAFIO, 8-97

D: 25 tons (35 fl) **S:** 25 kts (22 cruise) **Dim:** 19.8 × 5.8 × 0.8
A: 2 single 20-mm 70-cal. Oerlikon AA; 2 single 12.7-mm mg
Electronics:
Radar: 1 Decca 926 nav.
E/O: El-Op low-light t.v. surveillance and weapons desig.
M: 2 G.M. Detroit Diesel 12V71 TI diesels; 2 props; 960 bhp
Electric: 20 kw tot. **Range:** 1,200/17 **Crew:** 1 officer, 5 enlisted

Remarks: First ten (now retired) were built in U.S. by Sewart Seacraft. Five were given to Christian forces in Lebanon in 1976 (later returned), six were sold to Chile in 1991 and four more in 1995, four were sold to Argentina, four were transferred to Fiji in 11-91, and four were sold to Nicaragua in 1978. A dozen of the remaining Israeli Navy units were reportedly for sale as of 8-98, but at least one was still in active service in 4-99; the exact number still in service (if any) is not available. Pennant numbers are in the 850s, when worn.
Hull systems: Aluminum construction. Air-conditioned quarters. Small enough for transport by truck.

AMPHIBIOUS WARFARE SHIPS AND CRAFT

Note: Plans to constuct a 13,000-ton amphibious assault ship capable of carrying 600 troops, vehicles, and aircraft, were canceled in 2005 due to cost constraints.

AUXILIARIES

♦ 2 ex-German Type 745 small multipurpose trials tenders [YAGE]

	Bldr	Laid down	L	In serv.
BAT YAM (ex-*Kalkgrund,* Y 865)	Krögerwerft, Rendsburg	7-9-88	2-2-89	8-11-89
BAT GALIM (ex-*Bant,* Y 867)	Krögerwerft, Rendsburg	. . .	13-7-89	16-5-90

Bat Galim Michael Nitz, 12-05

D: 400 tons (456 fl) **S:** 12.5 kts **Dim:** 38.55 (34.60 wl; 32.12 pp) × 9.20 × 3.10
Electronics: Radar: 2 . . . nav.
M: 1 KHD-SBV 6M 628 diesel; 1 prop; 1,210 bhp
Electric: 372 kw (2 MWM D234V8 diesels driving)
Range: 1,000/12 **Fuel:** 18 tons **Endurance:** 5 days
Crew: 6 civilian + 6 technicians

Remarks: Decomissioned in Germany 11-04 and transferred to Israel 12-05. Based at Haifa. Have a torpedo recovery ramp located to starboard through the transom stern, a divers' stage to port and space for two trials equipment vans on the stern. Have a becker flap rudder to improve low-speed maneuvering.

♦ 2 miscellaneous patrol craft tenders [AGP]

NAHARYA (ex- . . .) NIR (ex-*Ma'oz*)

Remarks: *Nir* is a 3,000-ton oilfield-supply vessel used as an alongside missile-boat tender at Haifa; the ship was built for oilfield supply work in 1976 by Todd Shipyards, Seattle, Wash. *Naharya* (origins unknown) is used for a similar purpose at Eilat. Both are essentially immobile.

♦ 1 cargo ship [AK]
Bldr: Barreras, Vigo, Spain (In serv. . . .)

KARINE A

D: Approx. 5,000 tons (fl) **S:** 12 kts **Dim:** 97.36 (88.50 pp) × 14.01 × 6.23
M: 1 Deutz RBV12M-350 diesel; 1 prop; 4,020 bhp
Electric: 640 kw tot. (2 × 240-kw, 1 × 160-kw diesel sets)
Range: 11,115/12 **Fuel:** 390 tons heavy oil; 151 tons diesel **Crew:** . . . tot.

Remarks: 2,876-grt small cargo ship captured from Palestinian terrorist group using it to carry munitions and weapons to the Gaza Strip area. Assigned to the Israeli Navy on 22-4-02.

♦ 1 training ship [AXT]
Bldr: Kasado DY, Japan (In serv. 1979)

QESHET (ex- . . .)

D: . . . **S:** . . . **Dim:** 115.0 × . . . × . . .
M: . . . diesels; . . . props; . . . bhp

Remarks: Former 2,800-grt/4,634-dwt passenger/cargo vessel equipped as a training ship for the navy and merchant marine; replaced the *Nogah* in 1991. May also have been involved in Barak missile trials.

Note: The National Police also employ several 8.3-ton (fl) *Snaparit*-class patrol launches on the Sea of Galilee and the Israeli Army employs several 54-ton (light) river-crossing craft capable of transporting 130-ton loads.

ITALY

Italian Republic

ITALIAN NAVY

(*Marina Militare*)

Personnel: 33,100 total including 2,200 naval aviation and 2,000 marines. There were also about 21,000 reservists.

Bases: The principal bases are at La Spezia (2nd Frigate Squadron, Mine Countermeasures Command, Naval Special Forces Group) and Taranto (1st Frigate Squadron, Submarine Command, High Seas Command and a deployable command unit). The carrier *Giuseppe Garibaldi* and all auxiliaries are also based at Taranto. Other bases are located at Augusta (Coastal Patrol Force, corvettes, and offshore patrol vessels) and Brindisi (Landing Force Command with amphibious ships). Minor regional facilities remain at Cagliari, La Maddalena, Cagliari, and Venice.

Marines: The San Marco Battalion (*Battaglione San Marco*) has been expanded with a second rifle company and grew to regiment size in 1998; a helicopter support group with eight SH-3D Sea King troop carrier and seven AB-212 fire-support helicopters is attached. For use by seaborne assault troops, there are 24 LVTP-7 amphibious armored personnel carriers and one LVTC-7 amphibious armored command post.

Naval Aviation: About 1,600 personnel are involved in Italian naval aviation. The Marinavia operates 16 AV-8B+ and two two-seat TAV-8B Harrier shipboard fighters and the following helicopters: 24 SH-3D Sea King, 42 AB-212, and 22 EH.101. All 18 Harriers are assigned to GRUPAER and are based ashore at Grottaglie, near Taranto. The two SH-3D squadrons are based at Luni (1st Squadron) and Catania (3rd Squadron). The 2nd, 4th, and 5th (AB-212) Squadrons are based at Luni, Taranto, and Catania, respectively.

Three fixed-wing Piaggio P-180 aircraft are in use and fitted with an FLIR turret for liaison and surface surveillance duties. An AgustaWestland A.109 Hirundo helicopter was acquired during 2001 for use as a VIP transport.

To replace the AB-212s, which were built under license from Bell Helicopter by AgustaWestland, Italy has ordered 56 NH-90 helicopters (46 in ASW/antisurface configuration and 10 in the utility assault role; see France entry for description) powered by G.E.-FiatAvio T700/T6E1 turbines. The NH-90s are being delivered between 2006 and 2011.

Four more Harriers are sought as attrition replacements, and the Harrier is expected to serve in the Italian Navy until around 2020. 24 short takeoff and landing variants of the F-35 Joint Strike Fighter are expected to be purchased for delivery between 2011 and 2015. During the 1990s, 266 AIM-120 AMRAAM and 42 AGM-65 Maverick missiles were ordered for use with the Harriers, which are also equipped to drop Mk 81, 82, and 83 free-fall bombs, Mk 20 Rockeye bomblet-carriers, and unguided LAU rocket pods. All Italian Harriers, including the two-seat trainers, are powered by the 23,800-lb.-thrust Rolls-Royce Pegasus F 402 RR-408 engine, and the single-seaters have APG-65 radars and 25-mm guns.

The air force conducts fixed-wing maritime ASW patrol, using 16 navy-crewed Bréguet Atlantic Mk 1 aircraft ordered in 1968 and delivered by 1973; four more are in reserve. The Atlantics are based at Catania (No. 86 Squadron) and will remain in service for several more years, retiring through attrition. As a stopgap measure, four ATR-42MP have been ordered and are being fitted with SV-2022 radar and a turret-mounted FLIR and ALR-733 ESM system to serve until the arrival of six to eight MMA future maritime patrol aircraft for delivery around 2015. Italian Air Force Tornado strike fighters carry the Kormoran I missile for antiship missions (see Germany entry for aircraft and missile data). Fifteen AgustaWestland-built variants of the U.S. Coast Guard Sikorsky HH-3F Pelican helicopter are used by the air force for search-and-rescue service. The Italian Coast Guard (*Guardia Costiera*) and Customs Service (*Guardia di Finanza Servizio Navale*) have their own air forces, which are listed in the sections devoted to them.

Italian Navy AV-8B+ Harrier — Maurizio Brescia, 6-04

♦ EH.101 Series 100

Rotor diameter: 18.59 m **Length:** 22.81 m (15.75 folded)
Weight: 14,600 kg max. **Speed:** 150 kts cruise (167 max.)
Engines: 3 G.E. T700/T6A turboshaft, 2,040 shp each
Endurance: 5 hr **Crew:** 4 tot.
Armament: 4 MU-90 ASW torpedoes or 2 Marte Mk 2 ASM; 1/12.7-mm mg
Sensors: APS-784 radar, Helras Mk 2 dipping sonar, ALR-735 EW, GaliFlir FLIR, ELT/156X(V2) radar warning, RALM/1 laser warning

Remarks: Built by AgustaWestland at Vergiate. 22 had been ordered by 2-06, broken down as follows: 10 antisubmarine/antisurface (with Eliradar HEW-784 surface-search and target-tracking radar), four AEW and eight assault transport (fitted with a cargo hook, GaliFlir FLIR turret, an APS-705B radar, a 12.7-mm mg turret, and stub wings for rocket launchers). All versions will have FLIR and countermeasures systems.

Italian Navy EH.101 — Italian Navy

♦ SH-3D Sea King

Rotor diameter: 18.90 m **Length:** 22.16 m **Weight:** 9,300 kg max.
Speed: 118 kts cruise (144 max.) **Engines:** 2 1,400-shp turboshaft
Endurance: 4 hr 50 min **Crew:** 3 tot.
Armament: 2 Mk 46 torpedoes, depth charges, or 2 Marte Mk 2 ASM

Italian Navy SH-3D Sea King — Maurizio Brescia, 6-04

♦ AB-212

Rotor diameter: 14.60 m **Length:** 17.40 m **Height:** 4.40 m
Weight: 5,086 kg max. **Speed:** 100 kts cruise (130 max.)
Engine: 1 1,290-shp turboshaft **Ceiling:** 5,000 ft.
Endurance: 4 hr 15 min **Crew:** 3 tot.
Armament: 2 Mk 46 torpedoes, depth charges, or 2 AS-12 missiles
Sensors: AQS-13B dipping sonar

Italian Navy AB-212—aboard *Alpino* (A 5384) — Bernard Prézelin, 10-00

WEAPONS AND SYSTEMS

A. MISSILES

♦ Surface-to-air missiles

Standard SM-2 Block IIIA: Italy requested 50 Raytheon Standard SM-2 Block IIIA missiles for $135 million in 7-00. These are to replace existing SM-1 missiles and will require modifications to Italian ships to permit their use. See U.S. section for characteristics.

Standard SM-1 ER and SM-1 MR: See U.S. section for characteristics.

Aspide: Manufacturer: Alenia–OTO Sistemi Missilistici SpA. Aspide is, in effect, the Italian version of the U.S. Sea Sparrow. The system employs an octuple, 7-ton Albatros launcher built by OTO Melara and is controlled by the NA-30 radar fire-control system. Elevation: +5 deg. to +65 deg. A quadruple launcher has been produced for use on export corvettes. The Aspide 2000, now in development, is to have a 30–40% increase in dynamic performance, plus guidance and ECCM enhancements; it is intended either as an interim replacement until the joint Aster-15 is available or as a fallback should the French missile not be procured.

Length: 3.673 m **Diameter:** 0.204 m **Wingspan:** 0.644 m
Weight: 217 kg at launch **Range:** 10,000 m
Altitude: 15 m min.; 5,000 m max. **Guidance:** Semiactive homing

WEAPONS AND SYSTEMS *(continued)*

♦ Surface-to-surface missiles

Ulysses: Manufacturer: Alenia–OTO Sistemi Missilistici SpA. Formerly known as Teseo Mk 3. This conceptual design is to form the basis for a new weapon, which will incorporate reduced-signature ("stealth") features, a dual-mode infrared and radar seeker system, in-flight retargeting, infrared target identification gear, advanced counter-countermeasures features, and an advanced overland and overwater navigation system. It will have a range of 180 km and a 210-kg warhead, as well as improved target detection and discrimination. An air-launched variant is planned as well, but no information is available as to when it might enter service, and the weapon exists in conceptual form only.

Otomat Mk 2 ("Teseo Mk 2"): Manufacturer: Alenia–OTO Sistemi Missilistici SpA. Differs from the original 60-km-range Otomat Mk 1 in having an Italian (SMA) single-axis active radar homing head (8–16 GHz) instead of a French seeker and in employing folding wings; the Italian Navy's Teseo variant employs a datalink from a targeting helicopter to determine initial course to target. The original fixed-wing Otomat Mk 1/Teseo Mk 1 is also still in use by the Italian Navy. Alenia has offered to provide a new radar seeker, a new mission computer, an inertial midcourse guidance system with GPS receiver, terminal maneuvering, and trajectory height and impact-point selection. Saudi Arabia was the sole purchaser of the ERATO (Extended-Range Automatic Targeting Otomat) version.

A Mk 4 variant was available by 2005 that incorporates repackaged avionics to reduce volume, increased fuel capacity, a new radar signal processor, and a GPS receiver to permit use against land targets. Data for the Otomat Mk 2 include:

Length: 4.460 m **Diameter:** 0.460 m (1.060 with boosters)
Wingspan: 1.19 m **Weight:** 780 kg **Warhead weight:** 210 kg (65 kg Hertol)
Propulsion: Turbomeca TR 281 Arbizon-III turbojet (400 kg thrust)
Speed: 300 m/sec (Mach 0.9) **Range:** 5.5 km min.; 185 km max.
Guidance: Autopilot, active radar homing

♦ Air-to-surface missiles

Marte Mk 2: Made by Alenia–OTO Sistemi Missilistici SpA for use by Sea King helicopters. Guidance is by gyro autopilot and radar altimeter over midcourse, with active pseudo-monopulse radar homing, using the same seeker as the Otomat. Fuzing is influence and impact. The airframe is basically that of the now-retired Sistel Sea Killer surface-launched antiship missile, itself based on the U.S. Sea Sparrow airframe.

Length: 4.84 m (with 1.09-m booster) **Diameter:** 31.6 cm
Wingspan: 98.7 cm (cruciform) **Weight:** 340 kg **Warhead weight:** 70 kg
Speed: Mach 0.8 **Range:** more than 20 km

Alenia began developing a Marte Mk 2/S variant in 1998 for use with the EH.101 and NH-90 helicopters. Integration of this smaller and lighter variant, which employs a J-band active radar seeker, is complete for the EH.101 and ongoing for the NH-90.

Length: 3.80 m **Weight:** 320 kg **Warhead weight:** 70 kg
Speed: Mach 0.8 **Range:** 25+ km

Note: The French S.N.I.A.S. AS-12 wire-guided antiship missile has been adopted for use by AB-212 helicopters. The Harrier fighter-bombers use U.S. AGM-65 Maverick air-to-ground missiles.

♦ Air-to-air missiles

The U.S. AIM-120B AMRAAM is used by the Harrier fighter-bombers; 266 were ordered during the 1990s.

B. GUNS

127-mm OTO Melara Compact: The mount weighs 37.5 tons, employs a single-barreled automatic gun, and has a fiberglass shield. The gun has a muzzle brake; it can automatically fire 66 rounds, thanks to three loading drums, each with 22 rounds. Two hoists serve two loading trays with rounds coming from the magazine at the rate of 12 per minute, and a drum may be loaded even while the gun is firing. An automatic selection system allows a choice of ammunition (antiaircraft, surface target, pyrotechnics, or chaff for cluttering radar). The mount has been purchased by Argentina, Canada, Japan, the Netherlands (refurbished Canadian mounts), Nigeria, Peru, South Korea, and Venezuela.

Length: 54 calibers **Muzzle velocity:** 807 m/sec
Rate of fire: 43 rds/min (automatic setting) **Arc of elevation:** –15° to +83°
Max. effective range for surface fire: 15,000 m
Max. effective range for antiaircraft fire: 7,000 m

A lightweight, 22-ton 127/54LW version with reduced elevation (–15° through +70°) and a much smaller gunhouse began tests at sea on the *Bersagliere* in 10-00 and, after a three-year trials period, is to be retained on the ship. An extended-range munition with a range of 70 km is to be developed, and a 62-cal. barrel may be developed. The 127/54LW has a 40-rpm firing rate and a faceted, radar reflection reduction gunhouse.

76-mm OTO Melara Compact: Single-barreled, light antiaircraft automatic fire; entirely remote control with muzzle brake and cooling system. Used worldwide. Development is continuing on a course-corrected shell for this weapon, using a shipboard datalink to the projectile. Has 80 ready-service rounds in the drum. The current SuperRapid version of the weapon weighs 7.5 tons and fires at 1, 10, or 120 rds/min, with 85 rounds on-mount. The weapon is now offered with a faceted gunhouse to reduce radar signature.

Length: 62 calibers **Mount weight:** 7.35 tons
Muzzle velocity: 925 m/sec **Rate of fire:** 85 rds/min
Max. effective range for surface fire: 8,000 m
Max. effective range for antiaircraft fire: 4,000–5,000 m

76-mm OTO Melara: Single-barreled, automatic, for air, surface, and land targets; obsolescent and now found only on several Italian Navy auxiliaries.

Length: 62 calibers **Muzzle velocity:** 850 m/sec
Rate of fire: 60 rds/min
Max. effective range for surface fire: 8,000 m
Max. effective range for antiaircraft fire: 4,000–5,000 m

40-mm OTO Melara/Bofors Compact twin:

Length: 70 calibers **Projectile weight:** 0.96 kg
Muzzle velocity: 1,000 m/sec **Rate of fire:** 300 rds/min/barrel
Number of ready-service rounds: 444 or 736 (depending on installation)
Max. effective range for antiaircraft fire: 3,500–4,000 m
Fire control: Dardo system (Alenia RTN-20X radar)
Fuzing: Impact or proximity

30-mm 80-cal. OTO Melara/Mauser: Employed by the Guardia di Finanza and available for export. Available in enclosed twin and single mountings. Gas operated; can be fired at 800 rds/min in short bursts and 1–300 rds/min in rapid-fire mode.

Muzzle velocity: 1,040 m/sec **Rate of fire:** 800 rds/min
Arc of elevation: –13° to +85°
Max. effective range: 1,500 m surface/3,000 m air

25-mm 87-cal. Oerlikon–OTO Melara KBA: A new lightweight mount being procured to replace the venerable 20-mm Oerlikon mountings employed for close-defense, mine-disposal, and policing functions. Open, crew-served mounting.

C. TORPEDOES

U.S. Mk 46 Mod. 5 and Italian Whitehead Alenia Sistemi Subacquei (WASS, formerly Whitehead Motofides) A-244 small ASW torpedoes are used on ships (using the triple B-515 tube mount, similar to the U.S. Mk 32 Mod. 5 ASW torpedo tube set) and helicopters. They are to be replaced over the next decade by the Eurotorp MU-90 Impact light ASW torpedo.

The WASS A-290 lightweight ASW torpedo project, begun in 1981, was merged with the French Murène program in 1990 and is now known as MU-90 Impact. Its lithium battery produces 50-kt speeds. Delivery of the 2.85-m-long weapon began in 2001; it is for use with aircraft, surface ships, and the Milas missile. Italy plans to order 300, with an option for 100 more. The Franco-Italian production consortium is known as Eurotorp.

The WASS A-184 wire-guided torpedo is a 533-mm weapon with a range of more than 15,000 m. Length: 6.0 m; weight: 1,245 kg. A variant with terminal wake-homing in lieu of active acoustic terminal homing is also in service. The Mod. 3 variant, which entered service in 1996, employs the new TOSO active/passive acoustic seeker.

Trials began in 1998 on an upgraded version of the A-184 (A-184 Mod. 3) known as Black Shark for use with Italian Type 212A submarines and also on the foreign market in *Scorpène*-class submarines; it has a new ASTRA (Advanced Sonar Transmitting and Receiving Architecture), multibeam acoustic seeker, five-sensor acoustic wake-homing system, siver-zinc batteries, fiber-optic guidance link, new brushless motor, and quieter contrarotating 13-blade and 10-blade propellers; series production began in 2005, and the weapon is offered jointly for export by DCN, France, and WASS. Maximum speed is in excess of 50 kts and maximum range 50 km, using a silver oxide–aluminum battery.

WASS is also developing the A-200-series mini-torpedo, a 123.8-mm-diameter, 914.4-mm-long weapon weighing only 12.5 kg. The A-200/A, for the Italian Navy, would be air-dropped from conventional 127-mm sonobuoy dispensers, while the A-200/N would add a booster rocket for surface launch to 8-km ranges; a sextuple launcher would be used. The A-200 employs a d.c. electric motor, has 17-kt speed, and is intended to provide evidence that an actual submarine has been attacked; it employs a shaped-charge warhead. The A-202, also in development, would weigh some 16 kg, is to have an active/passive acoustic seeker, and would be used by combat swimmers, who would launch it from "Medusa" portable launchers; it is also to be launchable from tubes in midget submarines.

D. ANTISUBMARINE WEAPONS

Milas (*Missile de Lutte Anti-Sousmarine*): Under development by OTO Melara and France's Matra Défense using the Otomat propulsion section. Initial trials were conducted during 1989. At-sea firings began in 1993. Initial operational service, delayed since 1996, was reached in 2002. The French Navy abandoned the program in 1998.

Length: 6.0 m **Diameter:** 0.46 m **Wingspan:** 1.06 m
Weight: 800 kg (1,800 in launcher)
Speed: 1,080 kph **Range:** 5–55 km **Altitude:** 200 m (cruise)

Depth charges: WASS began developing the MS 500 depth charge in 1990; the weapon has a 100-kg CBX destructive charge and a lethal radius of 50 m.

E. MINES

The following Italian-made mines are available for domestic and export use:

- MR-80: Mod. A weighs 1,035 kg (with 856-kg explosive), Mod. B 790 kg (with 611-kg explosive), and Mod. C 630 kg (with 451-kg explosive). All versions can be used to 300-m depths.
- Manta: 240-kg (170-kg explosive) bottom influence mine; usable to 100-m depths
- Seppia: 870-kg (200-kg explosive) mine usable in waters up to 300 m in depth
- MAS/22: 22-kg (17-kg explosive), beach-defense, bottom contact mine
- MAL/17: 22-kg (17-kg explosive), beach-defense, moored contact mine
- TAR 6: 1,104-kg (175-kg explosive), submarine-laid, moored contact mine
- VS-SM-600: 780-kg (600-kg explosive) bottom influence mine

F. RADARS

The Italian Navy has used a number of American search and missile-control radars (SPS-12, SPS-52, SPG-51, SPG-55, etc.) but now primarily uses systems developed in Italy by Gem, Elettronica, SMA, and the Selenia-Elsag division of Alenia (known by the initials AESN until Alenia's absorption of the British Marconi corporation resulted in yet another change of acronym to AMS—Alenia Marconi Systems). The designation system employed by the Italian armed forces is like that used in the United States except that the prefix letters before the slash (omitted in the ship listings that follow) are "MM" (*Marina Militare*) vice "AN."

WEAPONS AND SYSTEMS *(continued)*

Type	*Band*	*Remarks*
MM/BPS-704	I/S (X)	SMA 3 RM 20 adapted for submarines
MM/BX-732	I	Gem nav. set widely employed on smaller ships
MM/SPG-70	I/J (X)	AMS gun and missile f.c. (RTN-10X Orion for Argo syst.)
MM/SPG-74	I/J (X)	AMS 40-mm gun f.c. (RTN-20X Dardo)
MM/SPG-75	I/J (X)	AMS missile f.c. (RTN-30X for Albatros syst.)
MM/SPN-703	I	SMA nav. radar; also known as 3 RM 28B
MM/SPN-704	I	SMA nav. radar, 3 RM 20 for submarines
MM/SPN-720	I	Landing-aid radar; a variant of SPS-702
MM/SPN-728	X	SMA nav./helicopter-control; dual antenna
MM/SPN-748	X	Gem Elettronica nav.
MM/SPN-749(V)	I (X)	Gem Elettronica nav. set on *Garibaldi;* 2 antennas (9345–9405 MHz)
MM/SPN-751	I (X)	Commercial nav. set, used in auxiliaries
MM/SPN-753(V)	I	Gem Elettronica nav. set; introduced in 1989
MM/SPQ-2A/D	I/J (X)	SMA nav./surf./air-search set; obsolescent
MM/SPS-702	I	SMA frequency-agile, sea-skimmer detector; modern version of SPQ-2
MM/SPS-768	D (S)	AMS 3-D air search; also known as RAN-3L
MM/SPS-774	E/J (S/X)	AMS air/surf. surveillance; also known as RAN-10S; entered service in 1980
MM/SPY-790	G	AMS EMPAR 3-D frequency-agile phased array surf./air search

G. SONARS

Type	*Function*	*Frequency*	*Manufacturer*
DE 1160B	Hull	MF	AMS-Raytheon
DE 1164	Hull or VDS	MF	AMS-Raytheon
SQS-23G	Hull	MF	Sangamo-G.E. (U.S.)
SQQ-14	Minehunting	HF	Unisys (U.S.)
SQQ-14IT	Minehunting	HF	FIAR

Note: Submarines use a variety of sonar equipment produced by AMS; see individual ship classes for details.

H. TACTICAL INFORMATION SYSTEM

The Italian Navy has developed the SADOC system, which is compatible with British, American NTDS, and French SENIT combat data systems through NATO Link 11.

I. COUNTERMEASURES

A wide variety of intercept arrays, many with stabilized cylindrical radome antennas, are in use. The Lambda intercept system employs the SLQ-D and SLR-4 intercept arrays, combined with a superheterodyne receiver; the similar Newton has a simpler receiver. Elettronica's Nettuno integrated ECM/ESM system employs four stabilized radome-mounted antennas.

The OTO Melara SCLAR chaff rocket-launching system is used on frigates and larger ships; it has 20 tubes for 105-mm rockets in a trainable, elevatable launcher. The SCLAR-H rapid response system is capable of launching 102- to 150-mm-diameter projectiles. A number of British Wallop Barricade chaff rocket launchers were ordered 1984 (as the Type 207/E system), and the French Matra Défense Sagaie decoy launcher is used on the *Luigi Durand de la Penne*–class guided-missile destroyers.

The WASS C303 Effector decoy system for submarines employs two 21-tube launcher arrays mounted in the sail.

Note: Diesel engine manufacturer Grandi Motori Trieste (GMT) was purchased by Wärtsilä NSD Corp. in 3-99 and is now trading as Wärtsilä NSD Italia SpA, abbreviated to Wärtsilä NSD below. Fincantieri and Howaldtswerke Deutsche Werft (HDW) of Germany announced a joint venture to design, produce, and market naval and merchant ships on 8-5-01.

During 2003, Italian industrial group Finmeccanica and shipbuilding firm Fincantieri negotiated an agreement to establish a Genoa-based joint warship design agency for the Italian Navy, with Fincantieri holding a 51% share.

V/STOL AIRCRAFT CARRIERS [CVV]

♦ 0 (+ 1) Cavour class

Bldr: Fincantieri, Muggiano, La Spezia

	Laid down	L	In serv.
C 552 Cavour	6-01	20-7-04	2007

Cavour—just after launching Maurizio Brescia, 2004

Cavour—following launch Maurizio Brescia, 2004

D: 22,130 tons std. (26,500 fl) **S:** 28+ kts (16 on one engine)
Dim: 234.40 (215.60 pp) × 39.00 (flightdeck; 29.50 wl) × 7.40 (mean hull; 8.70 max.)
Air group: 8 AV-8B+ Harrier or 12 EH.101 helicopters or a mix
A: 4 8-cell Sylver vertical-launch missile groups (132 Aster-15 SAM); 2 single 76-mm 62-cal. OTO Melara Super Compact DP; 3 single 25-mm 87-cal. Oerlikon–OTO Melara KBA AA; 4 fixed 324-mm ASW TT (MU-90 Impact torpedoes)
Electronics:
Radar: 2 SMA SPN-753 nav.; 1 AMS SPS-791 RASS surf. search; 1 AMS RAN-40S early warning; 1 AMS SPY-790 EMPAR target desig./tracking; 2 AMS SPG-76 (RTN-30X/I) gun f.c.; 1 SPN-41 CCA
Sonar: . . . bow-mounted MF and HF mine-avoidance
EW: Passive intercept and active; 2 20-round SCLAR-H decoy launchers; 2 SLAT torpedo decoy launchers; towed acoustic torpedo decoy syst.
E/O: . . . IR surveillance

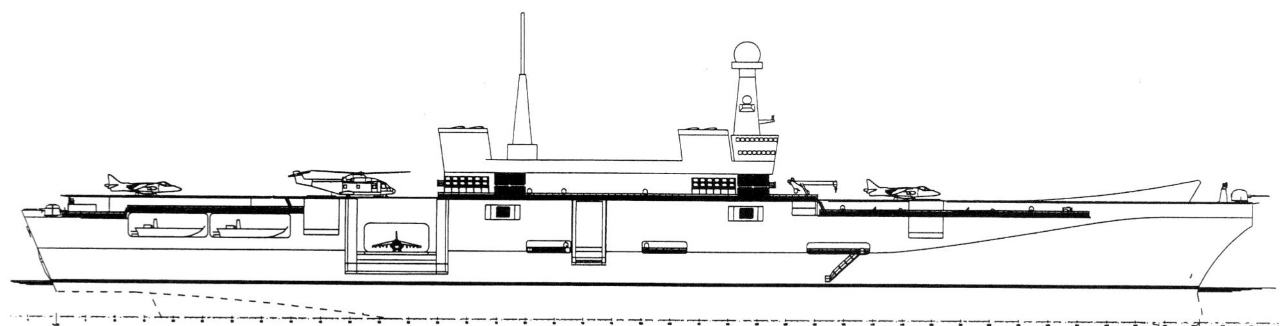

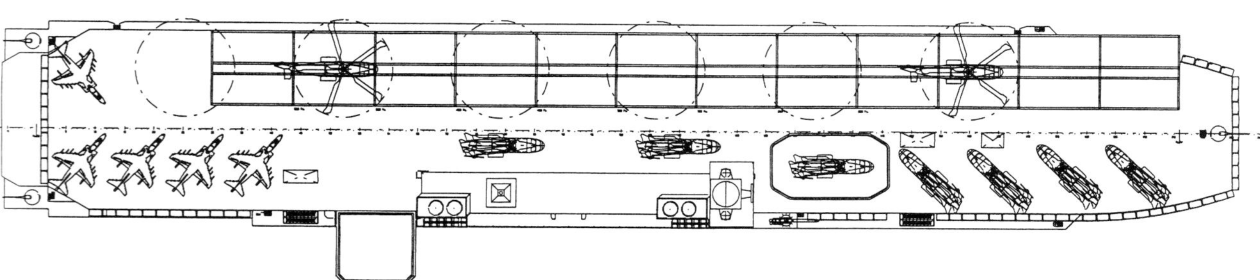

Cavour—preliminary design drawing Italian Navy, 2000

V/STOL AIRCRAFT CARRIERS [CVV] *(continued)*

M: CODLOG: 4 G.E.-FiatAvio LM-2500 gas turbines; 2 5-bladed CP props; 118,000 shp sust.—diesel-electric cruise from shaft generators (9 kts)—bow and stern tunnel thrusters
Electric: 13,200 kw tot. (6 × 2,200-kw Wärtsilä 1V200 diesel sets; 660 V, 50 Hz)
Range: 7,000/16
Crew: 486 tot. ship's company + 145 flag staff + 211 air group + 360 troops (450 in emergency)

Remarks: Initial design funding was provided in the 1996 budget; construction approved 2-98, with provisional order placed 22-11-00. Initially referred to as the UMPA (*Unita Maggiore Per Operazione Anfibe*) but officially conceded to be an aircraft carrier late in 1998 and is now called the NUM = *Nuova Unità Maggiore* (New Major Unit). Will be the largest warship built in Italy since World War II. The vessel was previously known unofficially as the *Andrea Doria*. Will be a multirole ship employable as an amphibious warfare asset, vehicle ferry, disaster-relief ship, strike carrier, or sea-control ship. To cost about $854 million, exclusive of the missile system and air group. Fabrication began 6-01, and the ship ran trials in 2006.
Hull systems: Is to be able to maintain over 29 kts on 85% full power. A planned 25 × 14-m docking well at the stern for four LCM(6)-size landing craft or two LCM(8) or one U.S. LCAC had been deleted by 2000. Will be able to carry 12 60-ton Ariete tanks or 100 light trucks. There will be two 60-ton-capacity vehicle loading ramps, one aft and one to starboard. Two pairs of fin stabilizers and two rudders will be fitted. The shaft generators can be used to power two electric motors to provide cruise and loitering speeds of up to 9 kts. Primary electrical current will be 660-V, 50-Hz a.c., stepped down to 440 V, 380 V, and 115 V by eight converters, as needed. Will have a hospital with three operating rooms and complete X-ray, CAT scan, dental, and laboratory services. Six 70-ton/day reverse-osmosis desalinators will be installed.
Aviation systems: The 5,900-m^2 flight deck is to be 232.6 m long by 34.5 m wide and will have a 12-deg. ski-jump takeoff ramp to port. There will be six deck spots for EH.101 or NH-90 helicopters. The 2,500-m^2 vehicle garage/hangar is to be 134.2 m long, 21.0 m wide, and 6.0 m high (with an 11-m-high area for maintenance); it will hold 12 EH.101 helicopters or eight AV-8B or U.S. Joint Strike Fighter (JSF) aircraft and can also be used to accommodate vehicles. The normal air group will be five Harriers and nine EH.101 helicopters, but the elevators and hangar are sized to accommodate the JSF. There will be two 30-ton elevators, one outboard aft to starboard and one just forward of the island, with the after elevator doubling as a vehicle ramp for operations alongside a pier.
Combat systems: The combat system contract went to the AMS consortium on 1-10-02; AMS (Elettronica, Fincantieri, Marconi Mobile, Galileo Avoinica, and OTO) will provide the radar, IR, IFF, radar landing system, command and control system, integrated telecommunications and electronic warfare systems, and short-range weapons system. Will have SHF and UHF SATCOM terminals and will be NATO JTIDS datalink compatible. The listed 76-mm guns and their two radar directors may not be installed initially, and the MF sonar and torpedo tubes may be eliminated in favor of a navigation aid and mine-avoidance sonar.

♦ 1 Giuseppe Garibaldi class
Bldr: Italcantieri, Monfalcone

	Laid down	L	In serv.
C 551 Giuseppe Garibaldi	26-3-81	4-6-83	30-9-85

Giuseppe Garibaldi (C 551)—during exercise Majestic Eagle U.S. Navy, 7-04

D: 10,100 tons (13,850 fl) **S:** 29.5 kts
Dim: 180.20 (173.80 wl; 162.80 pp) × 30.40 (23.80 wl) × 6.70 (8.20 over sonar)
Air group: 16 SH-3D Sea King helicopters, or 10 AV-8B+ Harrier and 1 Sea King
A: 2 8-round Albatros SAM syst. (48 Aspide missiles); 3 twin 40-mm 70-cal. OTO Melara Dardo AA; 2 triple 324-mm B-515 ASW TT (U.S. Mk 46 Mod. 5 torpedoes)
Electronics:
Radar: 1 SMA SPN-749(V)2 nav. (2 antennas); 1 SMA SPN-702 surf. search; 1 SPS-768 (RAN-3L) air early warning; 1 AMS SPS-774 (RAN-10S) air search; 1 Hughes SPS-52C 3-D air search; 3 AMS SPG-74 (RTN-20X) gun f.c.; 3 AMS SPG-75 (RTN-30X) missile f.c.; 1 AMS SPN-728(V)1 CCA; SATCOM
Sonar: WASS DMSS-2000
TACAN: SRN-15A; Type 718 beacon
EW: Elettronica SLQ-732 Nettuno integrated receiver/jammer syst.; SwRI Seagle D/F with AS-505 antenna; 2 2-round SCLAR-D 105-mm decoy RL; SLQ-25 Nixie towed torpedo decoy syst.
M: 4 G.E.-Fiat LM-2500 gas turbines; 2 5-bladed props; 80,000 shp
Electric: 9,360 kw tot. (6 Wärtsilä NSD B230-12M diesel alternator sets)
Range: 7,000/20 **Crew:** 550 ship's company + 230 air group + 45 flag staff

Remarks: Ordered 20-2-78. Ship type: *Incrociatore Porta-Aeromobili.* Serves as fleet flagship. The addition of Harrier V/STOL fighters permits the ship to act in air-defense and strike roles as well as her initial mission of ASW. Underwent refit and modernization during 2003; C4I upgrades included new SATCOM system and addition of an optronic tracker system as well as improved flag and command facilities resulting in the loss of one helicopter parking space in the hangar. Planned to be retired in 2016.

Giuseppe Garibaldi (C 551) U.S. Navy, 7-04

Giuseppe Garibaldi (C 551)—with French aircraft carrier *Charles de Gaulle* (R 91) in the background U.S. Navy, 7-04

Hull systems: Steel superstructure. To permit helicopter operations in heavy weather, much attention was given to stability, and the ship has two pairs of fin stabilizers. The bow has a small "ski-jump sheer," which is of assistance in Harrier launchings. There are five decks: the flight deck; the hangar deck, which is also the main deck; and two decks and a platform deck below the hangar deck. Thirteen watertight bulkheads divide the ship into 14 sections, and the interior can be sealed against NBC warfare. The propulsion train employs Tosi reverse/reduction gearing rather than controllable-pitch propellers. No longer carries personnel transport launches MEN 215 and MEN 216.
Aviation systems: The flight deck is 173.8 m long. There are two elevators, one forward of and one abaft the island. There are six flight-deck spaces for flight operations. The 110 × 15 × 6-m hangar can accommodate 12 Sea Kings, or 10 Sea Harriers and one Sea King. A Marconi Deck Approach Projector Sight (DAPS) landing aid was added during 1994.
Combat systems: Has the IPN-20 (SADOC-2) computerized data system with 13 consoles and is capable of handling 200 threat tracks simultaneously. Has Marisat HF SATCOM gear and can employ NATO Links 11, 14, and 16. The Teseo surface-to-surface missiles have been removed and replaced by a SATCOM system and radome during 2003. The AMS SPY-790 EMPAR radar is planned to replace the SPS-774 system. During 2003, the original sonar system was replaced by the DMSS-2000 and the SPN-728 radar was replaced by an optronic tracker.

ATTACK SUBMARINES [SS]

Note: Italian submarines ceased carrying their pennant numbers on the sides of their sails in 1995.

♦ 2 (+ 2) German Type 212A
Bldr: Fincantieri, Muggiano

	Laid down	L	In serv.
S 526 Salvatore Todaro	3-7-99	6-11-03	29-3-05 (del.)
S 527 Sciré	7-00	12-04	6-06

Salvatore Todaro (S 526) Italian Navy, 9-05

D: 1,360 tons std., 1,450 tons surf./1,840 tons sub.
S: 12 kts surf./20 kts sub. (6–8 on fuel cells)
Dim: 55.15 (55.90 pp) × 7.00 (6.80 pressure hull) × 7.00

ATTACK SUBMARINES [SS] *(continued)*

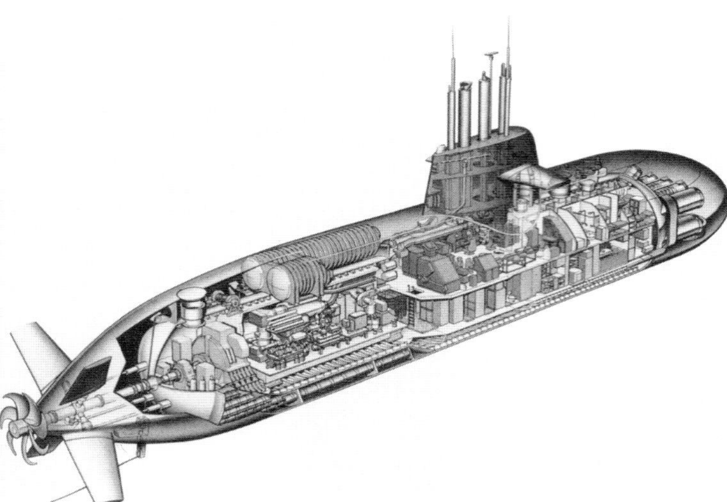

Type 212A HDW, 2000

A: 6 bow 533-mm TT fwd (12 WASS A-184 Mod. 3 Black Shark wire-guided torpedoes); provision for minelaying belt (24 tot. mines)
Electronics:
Radar: Kelvin Hughes Type 1007 search
Sonar: STN Atlas Elektronik DBQS-40FTC (CSU-90) suite: FAS 3-1 flank array; PRS 3-15 passive ranging; AN 5039A1 intercept; STN Atlas Elektronik/AlliedSignal FMS-52 (MOA 3070) mine-avoidance active (30 and 70 kHz); Atlas DSQS-21DG bow MF active; TAS-3 towed linear passive hydrophone array
EW: EADS FL-1800U intercept; HDW-WASS C303/S Circe torpedo decoy syst. (40 tubes)
M: Diesel-electric, with 9 Siemens Polymer Electrolytic Membrane fuel cells (34 kw each) for air-independent cruising, 1 MTU 8V183 SE83 diesel generator set (1,040 kw), 1 Siemens Permasyn motor; 1 prop; 4,184 shp
Range: 8,000/8 surf.; 420/8 sub. **Crew:** 9 officers, 16 enlisted (plus 13 extra accomm.)

Remarks: Being built under a late-1995 cooperative agreement between Italy and Germany; program development began in Germany in 1988. Formally ordered during 3-98 for $1.38 billion. Subassembly work on the first unit commenced during 5-99.
Hull systems: Will use a nonmagnetic Type 1.3964 austenitic steel pressure hull, 7.0 m in diameter forward, tapering via a conical section to 5.75 m abaft the control room; i.e., the boats are single-hulled forward and double-hulled aft. There will be two accommodations decks forward. The engineering plant is suspended in a raft for sound reduction, with individual engines also using soundproof mountings. The air-independent propulsion (AIP) system will employ an advanced Howaldtswerke solid-polymer, metal-hydride fuel cell system. Will have hydrazine gas generators to blow tanks for emergency surfacing. An Italian-developed ship control system will be employed. Normal maximum operating depth will be more than 200 m.
Combat systems: The combat system is to be an improved version of the Norsk Forsvarsteknolgi A/S MSI-90U, used previously in Norway's *Ula* class; it will employ the AMS MAGICS display consoles and a dual-redundant databus. The EW system antenna will be mounted on the Carl Zeiss SERO 14 surveillance periscope with an optical rangefinder, EW, and GPS antennas. The SERO 15 attack periscope will be equipped with optical and laser rangefinders. The FL-1800U electronic intercept system will cover 2–18 GHz and will employ a pressurized USK800/4 antenna with an integrated GPS antenna. Will have a LITEF PL-41 Mk 4 inertial navigation system.
The sonar suite incorporates six passive ranging transducers, flank arrays, a 0.3- to 12-kHz bow array, a mine avoidance set, an echo sounder, two self-noise sensors, and a towed passive linear array (10–1,200 Hz). The mine avoidance sonar will operate at 30 kHz for detection and 70 kHz for classification.
The torpedo tubes will use the water-ram ejection method, using two water rams. The torpedo tube arrangement is asymetrical, with two rows of three tubes, placing four tubes to port of the centerline.

♦ 2 Primo Longobardo class
Bldr: Italcantieri, Monfalcone

	Laid down	L	In serv.
S 524 Primo Longobardo	19-12-91	20-6-92	14-12-93
S 525 Gianfranco Gazzana Priaroggia	12-11-92	26-6-93	12-4-95

Gianfranco Gazzana Priaroggia (S 525) Carlo Martinelli, 2-99

D: 1,653 tons surf./1,862 tons sub. **S:** 11 kts surf./19 kts sub.
Dim: 66.35 (65.70 pp) × 6.83 × 6.00
A: 6 bow 533-mm TT (12 WASS A-184 Mod. 3 wire-guided torpedoes)
Electronics:
Radar: 1 SMA BPS-704 nav.
Sonar: S 524: AMS IPD-70/S active (200 Hz–7.5 kHz)/passive; AMS MD 100S passive ranging flank array; Velox M5 sonar intercept—S 525: STN Atlas Elektronik ISUS 90-20 integrated suite
EW: Elettronica BLD-727 Thetis intercept
M: Diesel-electric: 3 Wärtsilä NSD A210-16NM diesel alternator sets (895 kw each), 1 ABB electric motor; 1 7-bladed prop; 4,270 shp (3,000 sust.)
Range: 11,000/11 surf.; 5,100/5 snorkel; 240/4.5 sub. **Fuel:** . . . tons
Endurance: 45 days **Crew:** 7 officers, 43 enlisted

Remarks: Ordered 28-7-88. The design is a further development of the two preceding classes, employing improved hydrodynamic form. S 525 underwent a modernization refit at Muggiano from 10-99 through 2001; the refit of S 524 followed that of *Salvatore Pelosi* (S 522).
Hull systems: The pressure hull has a single watertight bulkhead, and the boats carry more fuel than their predecessors. Maximum operating depth is 300 m, with 600-m crush depth. The casing above the pressure hull is higher than on the two preceding classes, and the sail is larger. Have SEPA 8518 autopilot ship controls. During modernizations, are receiving anechoic hull coatings and Litton Mk 39 Mod. 3C and Mk 39 Mod. 3A ring-laser gyros.
Combat systems: As completed, had the SMA SACTIS BSN-716 combat system with NATO Link 11 receiving capability; combat systems in both were updated during modernization refits with a German STN Atlas Elektronik ISUS 90-20 integrated sonar and combat data system suite under a 1998 contract with Fincantieri. The new German sonar system has a bow-conformal passive hydrophone array, an active/ passive cylindrical bow array, and a passive ranging array; the new weapons system permits the control of four wire-guided torpedoes simultaneously. Navigation systems include Litton PL-41 inertial, Ferranti autopilot, Transit satellite navigation receiver, and Omega radio navigation receiver. Have U.S. Kollmorgen periscopes: S76 Model 322 attack with laser rangefinder and ESM array, and S76 Model 323 search with radar rangefinder and ESM antennas. Underwater telephone operates at 15 kHz. Can employ U.S. UGM-84 Sub-Harpoon antiship missiles, but none have been procured.

♦ 2 Salvatore Pelosi class
Bldr: Fincantieri, Monfalcone

	Laid down	L	In serv.
S 522 Salvatore Pelosi	23-7-86	29-11-86	14-7-88
S 523 Giuliano Prini	30-7-87	12-12-87	11-11-89

Giuliano Prini (S 523) Leo Van Ginderen, 6-05

Giuliano Prini (S 523) A. A. de Kruijf, 6-05

D: 1,476 tons surf./1,662 tons sub.
S: 11 kts surf./12 kts snorkel/19 kts sub. **Dim:** 64.36 × 6.83 × 5.66
A: 6 bow 533-mm TT (12 WASS A-184 wire-guided torpedoes)
Electronics:
Radar: 1 SMA BPS-704 nav.
Sonar: AMS IPD-70/S active (200 Hz–7.5 kHz)/passive; AMS MD 100S passive ranging flank array; Velox M5 sonar intercept
EW: Elettronica BLD-727 intercept
M: 3 Wärtsilä NSD A210-16NM diesel generator sets (895 kw each), 1 twin Marelli 3,140-kw motor (2,400 kw sust.); 1 7-bladed prop; 4,270 shp max. (at 233 rpm)
Range: 6,150/11 surf.; 2,500/12 snorkel; 250/4 sub. **Fuel:** 144 tons
Endurance: 45 days **Crew:** 7 officers, 43 enlisted

Remarks: Ordered 7-3-83. An improved version of the *Nazario Sauro* class, with 0.5 m length added amidships and one watertight bulkhead added to the pressure hull. Updated with a German STN Atlas Elektronik ISUS 90-20 integrated sonar and combat data system suite under a 1998 contract with Fincantieri; incorporate improved silencing features and improved ship-control systems following their respective refits (S 522 at Muggiano and S 523 at the Taranto Naval Shipyard).
Hull systems: Do not have a "crash-dive" ballast tank as in the *Sauro* class. Pressure hull is fabricated of U.S. HY-80 steel. Maximum operating depth is 300 m; collapse depth 600 m. Have two 148-cell batteries with 6,500 amp/hr. During modernization, are having SEPA 8518 autopilots and Litton Mk 39 Mod. 3A and Mk 39 Mod. 3C gyros added, and the hulls are having a revised upper casing and anechoic coatings fitted.

ATTACK SUBMARINES [SS] *(continued)*

Combat systems: Prior to modernization, had an SMA BSN-716(V)2 SACTIS combat data-weapons control system with NATO Link 11 receive-only capability. The new German sonar system has a bow-conformal passive hydrophone array, an active/passive cylindrical bow array, and a passive ranging array; it will permit the control of four wire-guided torpedoes simultaneously. Have one each Kollmorgen S76 Model 322 and 323 periscopes (one with laser rangefinder, one with ranging radar, both with ESM antennas). Have 15-kHz active ranging/underwater telephone transducers at the bow. Navigation systems include Litton PL-41 inertial, Ferranti autopilot, Transit satellite navigation receiver, and Omega radio navigation receiver. Have the capability to launch U.S. Sub-Harpoon SSMs, but missiles have not been acquired.
Disposal note: *Nazario Sauro*–class submarines *Carlo Fecia Di Cossato* (S 519) and *Leonardo Da Vinci* (S 520) were decommissioned early in 2004.

GUIDED-MISSILE DESTROYERS [DDG]

♦ 0 (+ 2) Project Horizon program
Bldr: Fincantieri, Riva Trigoso

	Laid down	L	In serv.
D 570 Andrea Doria (ex-*Carlo Bergamini*)	19-7-02	14-10-05	2007
D 571 Caio Duilio	2003	2006	2009

D: 5,800 tons (6,700 fl) **S:** 29 kts
Dim: 150.60 (141.80 wl) × 20.40 (18.10 wl) × 5.40 (mean hull)
A: 8 Teseo Mk 2 SSM; 6 8-cell Sylver A50 SAM launch groups (32 Aster-30 and 16 Aster-15 missiles); 2 single 76-mm 62-cal. OTO Melara SuperRapid DP; 2 single 25-mm 87-cal. Oerlikon–OTO Melara KBA AA; 4 ASW torpedo launchers (MU-90 Impact torpedoes); 1 EH.101 helicopter
Electronics:
Radar: 1 Gem SPN-753 ARPA nav.; 1 AMS SPS-791 RASS surf. search; 1 . . . helicopter flight control; 1 AMS SPY-790 EMPAR target desig./tracking; 1 AMS RAN-40S (S1850M) early warning; 3 AMS SPG-76 (RTN-30X/I) gun f.c.
Sonar: Thales-WASS TMS 4110CL hull-mounted LF
EW: Elettronica JANEWS intercept; 2 OTO Melara SCLAR-H 20-round decoy RL; SLAT torpedo countermeasures syst.
E/O: SAGEM Vampir IR detection and tracking
M: CODAG: 2 G.E.-Fiat LM-2500 gas turbines (27,500 shp each), 2 SEMT-Pielstick 12 PA6B STC diesels, geared drive; 2 props; 62,560 shp max.—bow-thruster
Electric: . . . kw tot. (4 × . . . kw; Isotta-Fraschini VL 1716 T2 ME diesels driving)
Range: 7,000/18; 3,500/25 **Endurance:** 45 days
Crew: 190 tot. (accomm. for 222)

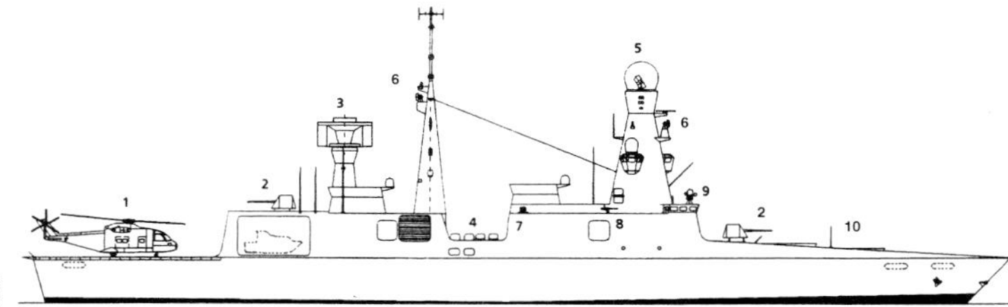

Horizon-class 1. EH.101 Merlin helicopter 2. 76-mm OTO Melara SuperRapid DP gun 3. RAN-40S early-warning radar 4. Eight Teseo Mk 2 antiship missiles 5. SPY-790 EMPAR target designation/tracking/illumination radar 6. SPG-76 76-mm gun f.c. 7. Decoy RL 8. 25-mm AA 9. SPS-791 RASS surface-search radar 10. Sylver A50 vertical-launch missile cell groups — Drawing by Maurizio Brescia

Italian Navy Project Horizon configuration—artist's rendering
Italian Navy, 2000

Remarks: Are the result of a 12-3-91 agreement made with France and the U.K. to design a ship acceptable to all three navies. An international joint-venture corporation, Horizon Ltd., was established 21-2-95 to build at least the initial units of the class for the three partner countries by the three prime contractors, GEC-Marconi, DCN International, and Orizzonte SpA. Italy originally planned to buy six ships, then four, to replace the *Audace*-class destroyers and the two already-stricken *Andrea Doria–class* cruisers. The program was reduced to two during 12-93 because of the expense incurred in the purchase of the ex-Iraqi *Lupo*-class frigates. The British pullout from the program on 21-4-99 put the program in temporary limbo, but France and Italy agreed 7-9-99 to continue and the first two were ordered on 26-11-00. The two deleted units may later be restored, with the first to complete in 2013 and the second in 2016, both equipped for ballistic-missile-defense duties. France is building two similar ships as the *Forbin* class.

Hull systems: Plans to incorporate a state-of-the-art, integrated propulsion/electrical generation plant have been dropped.
Combat systems: The combat data system is being developed by Alenia and Datamat. The ships are to have an integrated communications system and will be compatible with NATO Improved Link 11, Link 14, and Link 16. They were to have SHF and possibly EHF SATCOM systems. The helicopter is to be used for ASW and for attacking surface ships with missiles. The 76-mm mounts will be installed two abreast forward and one centerline atop the helicopter hangar to act as the point-defense system.

Disposal note: *Vittorio Veneto*–class training cruiser, *Vittorio Veneto* (C 550), in reserve for many years, is being turned into a floating museum.

♦ 2 Luigi Durand de la Penne class
Bldr: Fincantieri, Riva Trigoso (fitted out at Muggiano)

	Laid down	L	Del.	In serv.
D 560 Luigi Durand de la Penne (ex-*Animoso*)	26-7-86	29-10-89	18-3-93	11-12-93
D 561 Francesco Mimbelli (ex-*Ardimentoso*)	3-12-89	13-4-91	19-10-93	11-12-93

Luigi Durand de la Penne (D 560) — Michael Winter, 6-04

Luigi Durand de la Penne (D 560) — Ralph Edwards, 5-04

Francesco Mimbelli (D 561)—with AB-212 helicopter on the flight deck
Anthony Vella, 5-05

D: 4,500 tons (5,400 fl) **S:** 31.5 kts (21 on diesels)
Dim: 147.70 (135.60 pp) × 16.10 (15.00 wl) × 5.10 (hull; 6.80 over sonar; 7.10 over props)

GUIDED-MISSILE DESTROYERS [DDG] *(continued)*

A: 8 Teseo Mk 1 and Mk 2 SSM; 1 U.S. Mk 13 Mod. 4 SAM launch syst. (40 Standard SM-1 MR missiles); 1 8-round Albatros point-defense SAM syst. (16 Aspide missiles); 1 127-mm 54-cal. OTO Melara DP; 3 single 76-mm 62-cal. OTO Melara SuperRapid DP; 2 triple 324-mm B-515 ASW TT; 2 AB-212 helicopters
Electronics:
Radar: 1 Gem SPN-748 nav.; 1 SMA SPN-753 nav.; 1 SMA SPS-702 surf. search; 1 AMS SPS- . . . (RAN-21S) surf./air search; 1 AMS SPS- . . . (RAN-40S) early warning; 1 Hughes SPS-52C 3-D air search; 2 Raytheon SPG-51D SAM f.c.; 4 AMS SPG-76 (RTN-30X) missile and gun f.c.
Sonar: AMS-Raytheon DE 1164LF hull-mounted (3.5 kHz); AMS-Raytheon DE 1167LF integrated VDS (7.5 kHz)
TACAN: SRN-15A
EW: Elettronica SLQ-732 Nettuno integrated intercept; Elettronica SLC 705 jammers; Rohde & Schwarz . . . COMINT intercept; 2 6-round Matra Défense Sagaie decoy RL; SLQ-25 Nixie towed acoustic torpedo decoy syst.
M: CODOG: 2 G.E.-Fiat LM-2500 gas turbines (27,500 shp each); 2 Wärtsilä NSD BL230-20DVM diesels (6,300 bhp each); 2 5-bladed CP props
Electric: . . . **Range:** 7,000/18 (diesel) **Fuel:** . . .
Crew: 32 officers, 345 enlisted (accomm. for 35 officers, 365 enlisted)

Remarks: Ordered 9-3-86. Names changed 10-6-92 to honor World War II heroes. A planned two additional units were abandoned in favor of Italian participation in the Anglo-French Horizon program. D 561 was upgraded in 2005 and D 560 will follow in 2007; upgrades included replacement of the SPS-768 and SPS-774 radars (with RAN-40L and RAN-21S systems respectively), installation of a new IRST and a new combat data system.
Hull systems: Steel superstructure, with Mirex (Kevlar-derivative) armor. Two sets of fin stabilizers are fitted. Have a twin helicopter hangar, 18.5 m long. The flight deck is 24.0 × 13.0 m and is equipped with the Italian Navy's first haul-down and deck-transit system; it can accept Sea King and EH.101 helicopters. Have U.S. Prairie/Masker air-blowing, noise-masking system and flexibly mounted auxiliary engineering systems to reduce emitted noise below the waterline.
Combat systems: Have the SADOC-2 (IPN-20) combat data/weapons control system, with 10 operator consoles, two CDG-3032 mainframe computers, and NDC-160 processors. Four NA-30 weapons-control systems handle the Albatros SAM system and the four guns; the U.S. Mk 74 control system is fitted for the Standard missiles. Standard SM-2 Block IIIA missiles may be substituted for the aging SM-1 missiles. The U.S. Norden Systems SYS-1(V)2 sensor data fusion system is installed. The 127-mm guns come from the "B" positions of the modernized *Audace* and *Ardito*. The 76-mm SuperRapid guns are intended to perform as a close-in defense against sea-skimming missiles. Milas antisubmarine missiles will be substituted for some of the Teseo antiship missiles when Milas becomes operational after 2002 (but only 12 Milas are to be procured for the two ships). The Alenia Marconi SPY-790 EMPAR radar is planned to replace the SPS-774 system.
Disposal note: *Audace*-class destroyers *Ardito* (D 550) and *Audace* (D 551) were retired in 2005.

GUIDED-MISSILE FRIGATES [FFG]

♦ 0 (+ 6 + 4) FREMM program
Bldr: Fincantieri, . . . (In serv. 2008–17)

	Laid down	L	In serv.
F . . . Carlo Bergamini	. . .	. . .	2008
F . . .	. . .	. . .	2009
F . . .	. . .	. . .	2010
F . . .	. . .	. . .	2011
F . . .	. . .	. . .	2012
F . . .	. . .	. . .	2013
F . . .	. . .	. . .	2014
F . . .	. . .	. . .	2015
F . . .	. . .	. . .	2016
F . . .	. . .	. . .	2017

D: 5,400 tons (fl) **S:** 27 kts sust. **Dim:** 140.0 × 19.4 × 4.2
A: 16 Aster 15/30 SAM; Teseo VLS SSM; 1 127-mm 54-cal. OTO Melara LW DP; 2 single 76-mm 62-cal. OTO Melara DP; 2 single 20-mm 85-cal. AA; 2 triple 324-mm ASW TT (MU-90 Impact torpedoes); 2 NH-90 helicopters—ASW variants also: 8 Milas ASW missiles
Electronics:
Radar: 1 Gem . . . ARPA nav.; 1 AMS SPS-791 RASS surf. search; 1 . . . helicopter flight control; 1 AMS SPY-790 EMPAR target desig./tracking; 3 AMS SPG-76 (RTN-30X/I) gun f.c.
Sonar: . . . hull-mounted—ASW variants only: . . . VDS
EW: . . . intercept; provision for SLAT torpedo decoy syst.
M: . . ., electric drive; 2 props; . . . shp
Range: 6,000/18 **Endurance:** 45 days **Crew:** 160 tot.

Remarks: FREMM = *Fregate Multi-Missione*. Approval was given by the Italian parliament on 9-4-02 for a Franco-Italian frigate program to construct ten FNG (Frigate, New Generation) general-purpose guided-missile frigates to replace the *Maestrale* and *Lupo* classes, possibly employing elements of the Horizon design but emphasizing an ASW capability. As of late 2005, total cost for all ten of Italy's frigates was estimated to be 4.5 billion Euros. Six are to be built in general-purpose and land-attack configuration and the four others will be optimized for ASW. Under an 8-11-02 agreement, the design and construction of ships of this class will be conducted in cooperation with France. A final decision on selection of the propulsion system is expected by 2007.

FREMM—builders model Hans Karr, 5-05

FRIGATES [FF]

♦ 4 Artigliere class
Bldr: Fincantieri, Ancona (F 585: Fincantieri, Riva Trigoso)

	Laid down	L	Completed	Del.	In serv.
F 582 Artigliere (ex-*Hitteen,* F 14)	31-3-82	27-7-83	3-85	28-10-94	5-7-96
F 583 Aviere (ex-*Thi Qar,* F 15)	9-82	19-12-84	1985	4-1-95	5-7-96
F 584 Bersagliere (ex-*Al Yarmouk,* F 17)	12-3-84	20-6-85	4-87	20-3-96	5-7-96
F 585 Granatiere (ex-*Al Qadissiya,* F 16)	15-4-83	31-3-84	1986	8-11-95	5-7-96

Aviere (F 583) Guy Schaeffer via Paolo Marsan, 4-05

Bersagliere (F 584)—with 127-mm OTO Melara 127/54LW gunmount forward for trials Steve Zaloga, 3-01

FRIGATES [FF] *(continued)*

Granatiere (F 585) Maurizio Brescia, 2001

D: 2,213 tons (2,525 fl) **S:** 35 kts (20.5 diesel)
Dim: 113.2 (106.0 pp) × 11.98 × 3.84
A: 8 Teseo Mk 1 and Mk 2 SSM; 1 8-round Albatros SAM syst. (Aspide missiles; no reloads); 1 127-mm 54-cal. OTO Melara DP; 2 twin 40-mm 70-cal. OTO Melara Dardo AA; 2 single 20-mm 70-cal. Mk 10 Oerlikon AA; 1 AB-212 helicopter
Electronics:
Radar: 1 SMA SPN-703 nav.; 1 AMS SPQ-712 (RAN-12L/X) surf. search; 1 AMS SPS-774 (RAN-10S) air search; 1 AMS SPG-73 (RTN-10X) f.c.; 2 AMS SPG-74 (RTN-20X) f.c.
Sonar: Removed
EW: AMS SLQ-747 (INS-3M) integrated suite; 2 20-round SCLAR decoy RL; SLQ-25 Nixie towed acoustic torpedo decoy syst.
M: CODOG: 2 G.E.-Fiat LM-2500 gas turbines (25,000 shp each); 2 Wärtsilä NSD A230-20M diesels (3,900 bhp each); 2 CP props
Electric: 3,120 kw tot. (4 × 780-kw Wärtsilä NSD diesel-driven sets)
Range: 900/35 on gas turbines; 3,450/20.5, 5,300/16 on diesels
Crew: 17 officers, 170 enlisted

Remarks: Ordered by Iraq during 2-81. The Italian Council of Ministers decided in 1-92 to incorporate them into the Italian Navy as "Fleet Patrol Ships" (*Pattugliatori*), with the ASW systems removed; funding of $375 million to purchase and refit the ships was finally provided by the Italian Senate on 16-7-93. All were commissioned 8-7-96 at La Spezia and are now based at Taranto.
Hull systems: Fin stabilizers are fitted. The hangar, as completed for Italian service, is telescoping.
Combat systems: Have the AMS IPN-10 Mini-SADOC combat data system with NATO Link 11 capability; there are two weapons-designation plotting tables and four display consoles. The NA-21 control system is fitted for the Albatros SAM system. The 127-mm gun and SAM were originally controlled by two Elsag Mk 10 Mod. 0 systems with NA-10 radar directors, and the 40-mm fire control was provided by two Dardo systems. The original German Atlas ASO-4-2-V hull-mounted sonar and two sets of ASW torpedo tubes were removed during conversion. During 10-00, F 584 received the low-observable OTO Melara 127-mm 54-cal. lightweight gunmount for trials through 2003; the gun is to be retained aboard the ship.

♦ 8 Maestrale class
Bldr: CNR, Riva Trigoso (F 571: CNR, Muggiano)

	Laid down	L	In serv.
F 570 Maestrale	8-3-78	2-2-81	7-3-82
F 571 Grecale	21-3-79	12-9-81	5-2-83
F 572 Libeccio	1-8-79	7-9-81	5-2-83
F 573 Scirocco	26-2-80	17-4-82	20-9-83
F 574 Aliseo	26-2-80	29-10-82	20-9-83
F 575 Euro	15-4-81	25-3-83	7-4-84
F 576 Espero	1-8-82	19-11-83	4-5-85
F 577 Zeffiro	15-3-83	19-5-84	4-5-85

D: 2,700 tons light (3,060 normal; 3,200 fl) **S:** 33 kts (21 max. on diesels)
Dim: 122.73 (116.40 pp) × 12.88 × 4.20 (hull; 5.95 max.)
A: 4 Teseo Mk 1 and Mk 2 SSM; 1 8-round Albatros SAM syst. (24 Aspide missiles); 1 127-mm 54-cal. OTO Melara DP; 2 twin 40-mm 70-cal. OTO Melara Dardo AA; 2 fixed 533-mm ASW TT (WASS A-184 wire-guided torpedoes); 2 triple 324-mm Mk 32 Mod. 9 ASW TT (U.S. Mk 46 Mod. 5 torpedoes); 2 AB-212 ASW helicopters

Scirocco (F 573) Bernard Prézelin, 4-05

Aliseo (F 574) Guy Schaeffer via Paolo Marsan, 1-04

Scirocco (F 573) Cem D. Yaylali, 5-05

Libeccio (F 572)—with USS *Nimitz* (CVN 68) in the background
U.S. Navy, 7-05

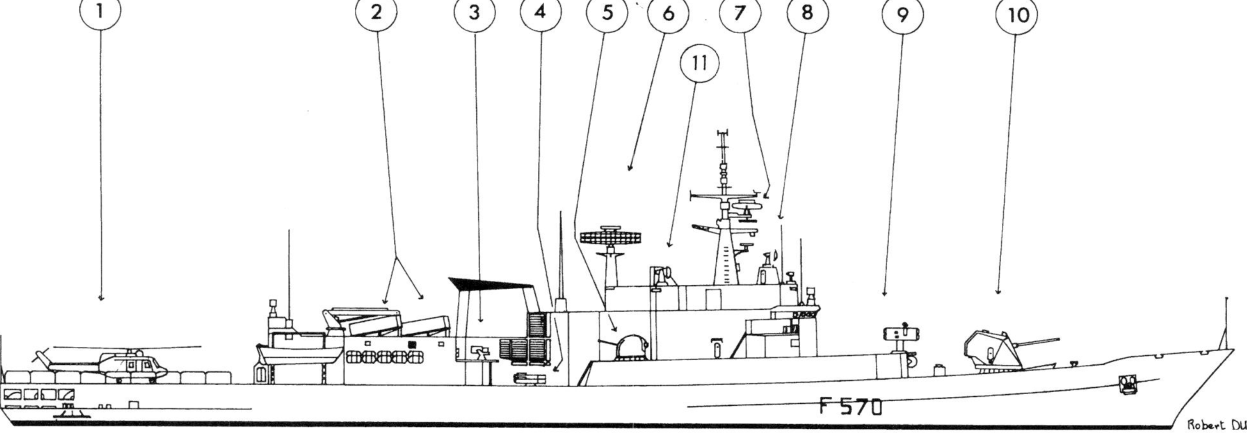

Maestrale (F 570) 1. AB-212 helicopter 2. Teseo Mk 2 antiship missile canisters 3. SCLAR decoy RL 4. triple 324-mm ASW TT 5. twin 40-mm Dardo AA 6. SPS-774 surface/air-search radar 7. SPS-702 surface-search radar 8. SPG-75 f.c. radar for 127-mm gun 9. Albatros launcher for Aspide SAMs 10. 127-mm OTO Melara DP gun 11. SPG-74 f.c. radars for 40-mm Dardo gunmounts
Drawing by Robert Dumas, from *Flottes de Combat*

FRIGATES [FF] *(continued)*

Electronics:
Radar: 1 SMA SPN-703 nav.; 1 SMA SPS-702 surf. search; 1 AMS SPS-774 (RAN-10S) surf./air search; 1 AMS SPG-75 (RTN-30X for NA-30A f.c.s.); 2 AMS SPG-74 (RTN-20X for Dardo f.c.s.)
Sonar: Raytheon DE 1164 hull-mounted MF; Raytheon DE 1164 VDS
EW: Elettronica SLR-4 Newton intercept with CO-NEWS comms intercept; 2 SLQ-D jammers; 2 20-round SCLAR (F 571: 2 Matra Défense Dagaie) decoy RL; SLQ-25 Nixie towed torpedo decoy syst.
M: CODOG: 2 G.E.-Fiat LM-2500 gas turbines (25,000 shp each); 2 Wärtsilä NSD B230-20DVM diesels (5,073 bhp each); 2 CP props
Electric: 3,120 kw tot. (4 × 780-kw diesel-driven sets)
Range: 1,500/30; 3,800/22; 6,000/15 **Endurance:** 90 days
Crew: 24 officers, 208 enlisted

Remarks: F 570–F 575 were ordered during 12-76, and F 576 and F 577 during 10-80. The design is an enlarged version of the *Lupo,* with better seaworthiness and hangar space for two helicopters at the expense of four antiship missiles and about 2.5 kts maximum speed. F 573 and F 577 began a 22-month upgrade in 2005 while F 572 and F 576 began theirs during 2006. Once modernization is complete, all four are to remain in service until at least 2015. F 570, F 571, F 574, and F 575 will not undergo modernization. F 570 is due to retire in 2011, F 571 and 574 in 2013, and F 575 in 2014.
Hull systems: Helicopter deck is 12 × 27 m. Have fin stabilizers and the U.S. Prairie/Masker air-bubbler noise-suppression system.
Combat systems: Have the SADOC-2 (IPN-20) computerized data system. There is a Galileo OG-30 optronic backup director to the NA-30A gun f.c.s. and two MM 59 optical backup directors for the 40-mm guns. The DE 1164 sonar is a VDS version of DE 1160 and operates on the same frequencies; the two sonar systems employ identical transducers, and an HF adjunct sonar has been fitted in the hull dome to detect moored mines. 2005–6 upgrades to F 572, 573, 576, and 577 include replacement of the SPS-774 and SPN-703 radars with more modern RAN-21S and SPN-753 radars and installation of an IRST.

Disposal note: The last of four remaining *Lupo*-class frigates, *Orsa* (F 567), was retired from service during 2003 and sold to Peru.

CORVETTES [FFL]

♦ 8 Minerva class
Bldr: Fincantieri, Muggiano and Riva Trigoso

	Yard	Laid down	L	In serv.
F 551 Minerva	Riva Trigoso	11-3-85	25-3-86	10-6-87
F 552 Urania	Riva Trigoso	11-3-85	21-6-86	10-6-87
F 553 Danaide	Muggiano	26-5-85	18-10-86	13-2-88
F 554 Sfinge	Muggiano	26-5-85	16-5-87	13-2-88
F 555 Driade	Riva Trigoso	18-3-88	12-3-89	7-9-91
F 556 Chimera	Muggiano	21-12-88	4-7-90	15-1-91
F 557 Fenice	Riva Trigoso	6-9-88	4-12-90	11-9-91
F 558 Sibilla	Riva Trigoso	16-10-89	15-2-90	16-5-91

Sibilla (F 558) Luciano Grazioli, 11-05

Driade (F 555) Luciano Grazioli, 6-04

Sibilla (F 558) Luciano Grazioli, 10-05

Fenice (F 557) Luciani Grazioli, 2-04

D: 1,029 tons (1,285 fl) **S:** 25 kts (24 sust.)
Dim: 86.60 (80.00 pp) × 10.50 × 3.16 (hull; 4.80 max.)
A: 1 76-mm 62-cal. OTO Melara SuperRapid DP—F 555–558: 1 8-round Albatros SAM syst. (8 Aspide missiles); 2 triple 324-mm B-515 ASW TT (U.S. Mk 46 Mod. 5 torpedoes)
Electronics:
Radar: 1 SMA SPN-728(V)2 nav.; 1 AMS SPS-774 (RAN-10S) surf./air search; 1 AMS SPG-76 (RTN-30X) for SAM and Dardo-E f.c.s.
Sonar: 1 Raytheon-Elsag DE 1167 hull-mounted (7.5–12 kHz)
EW: AMS SLQ-747 (INS-3) intercept/jammer suite; 2 Type 207/E (Wallop Barricade) decoy RL; SLQ-25 Nixie towed torpedo decoy syst.
E/O: 1 Elsag NA-18L Pegaso gun director
M: 2 Wärtsilä NSD BM230-20DVM diesels; 2 CP props; 11,000 bhp
Electric: 2,080 kw tot. (4 Isotta-Fraschini ID36.55 S12V diesels driving)
Range: 3,500/18 **Crew:** 7 officers, 106 enlisted

Remarks: First four authorized in 11-82; second four ordered in 1-87. Intended for surveillance, coastal escort, fisheries protection, training, and search-and-rescue duties. F 556 was delivered 15-1-91, F 557 on 11-9-90, and F 558 in 4-91; a year of trials and work-up ensued before commissioning. The first four are based at Augusta, Sicily.
Hull systems: Have fin stabilizers. The stacks have been raised and deflectors added since completion to reduce turbulence.
Combat systems: Have the AMS SADOC-2 combat data system with NATO Link 11 capability; there are two computers and three display consoles. The Dardo-E radar f.c.s. controls the SAM system or the gun, which also can be controlled by the NA-18L optronic director. Spherical radomes for Elmer Omega Transit SP 1090 satellite navigation system antennas were added during 1988. All now have the solid-dish OA-7104 antennna for the SPS-774 radar. The Albatros launcher and two triple torpedo tubes were removed from F 551–554 in 2002.

PATROL SHIPS [PS]

♦ 2 NUPA Program
Bldr: Fincantieri, Riva Trigoso

	Laid down	L	Del.
P 409 Sirio	. . .	11-5-02	30-5-03
P 410 Orione	. . .	27-7-02	1-8-03

Sirio (P 409) Maurizio Brescia, 3-05

D: 1,280 tons light (1,580 fl) **S:** 22 kts (21.8 on 80% power)
Dim: 88.40 (80.00 pp) × 12.20 × 3.43 (hull)
A: Provision for 1 76-mm 62-cal. OTO Melara SuperRapid DP; fitted with 2 single 25-mm 87-cal. Oerlikon–OTO Melara KBA AA; 1 AB-212 or NH-90 helicopter
Electronics:
Radar: 1 . . . ARPA nav.; 1 Alenia RASS surf. search; provision for 1 AMS SPG-76 (RTN-25X) f.c.
Sonar: None
EW: Elettronica . . . intercept
E/O: . . . optronic surveillance and f.c.

PATROL SHIPS [PS] *(continued)*

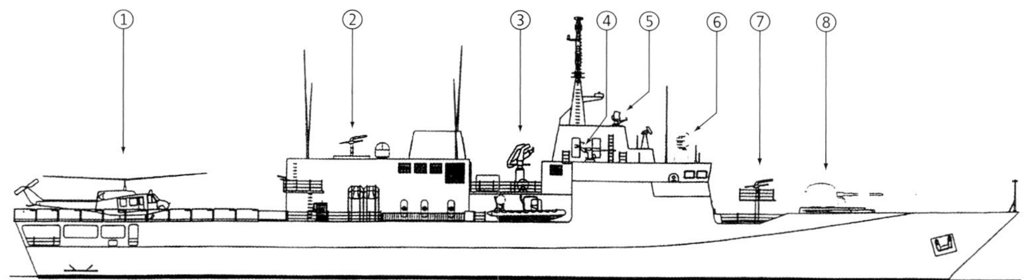

Sirio (P 409) 1. AB-212 helicopter 2. Firefighting monitor atop hangar 3. Articulating boat crane 4. 25-mm OTO Melara AA 5. Surface-search radar 6. Location for SPG-76 f.c. radar 7. Firefighting monitor 8. Location for 76-mm OTO Melara DP gun Drawing by Maurizio Brescia

M: 2 Wärtsilä NSD W12 V26XN diesels; 2 CP props; 11,588 bhp—bow-thruster
Electric: 2,250 kVA tot. (3 × 750-kVA; 3 Isotta-Fraschini 1708 T2ME diesels [600 kw each] driving; 390 V, 50 Hz)
Range: 3,300/17; 6,000/12 **Endurance:** 15 days
Crew: 6 officers, 48 enlisted (accomm. for 10 officers, 60 enlisted)

Remarks: NUPA = *Nuove Unità per il Pattugliamento d'Altura* (New High Seas Patrol Ships). A further, simplified version of the NUMC design, intended for fisheries and antismuggling patrol. Ordered 30-8-00 for $70 million each. Plans for a third were canceled. The ships were built with funds from the Transport and Navigation Ministry.
Hull systems: The hull and superstructure are shaped to reduce radar reflection. The boat pockets recessed into the superstructure amidships are covered by Faraday-shield mesh to eliminate radar returns, and exhaust cooling is fitted. Have a composite materials superstructure. The helicopter hangar is telescoping. Fin stabilizers and Flume-type passive-tank stabilization are fitted. The hull lacks the bulbous bow form given to the NUMC ships. Limiting displacement will be 1,890 tons (3.84-m mean hull draft). Equipped with twin 300-ton/hr firefighting water monitors and a 25-ton/hr oil-spill recovery pumping system.
Combat systems: Equipped only for patrol and policing duties, with no significant air defense and no ASW capabilities; IFF and NATO Link 11 equipment, however, will be fitted. There is provision to mount a 76-mm gun forward, but it is not fitted.

Comandante Constantino Borsini (P 491) Luciano Grazioli, 2-05

Comandante Cigala Fulgosi (P 490) Martin Mokrus, 6-04

♦ 4 NUMC Program

Bldr: Fincantieri, Riva Trigoso (fitted out at Fincantieri, Muggiano)

	Laid down	L	Del.	In serv.
P 490 Comandante Cigala Fulgosi	25-6-99	7-10-00	2-02	10-02
P 491 Comandante Constantino Borsini	21-7-99	17-2-01	6-02	2003
P 492 Comandante Ener Bettica	9-3-00	25-6-01	2-03	2003
P 493 Comandante Adriano Foscari	23-10-00	24-11-01	6-03	2004

Comandante Cigala Foscari (P 493) Luciano Grazioli, 10-05

Comandante Constantino Borsini (P 491) Luciano Grazioli, 2-05

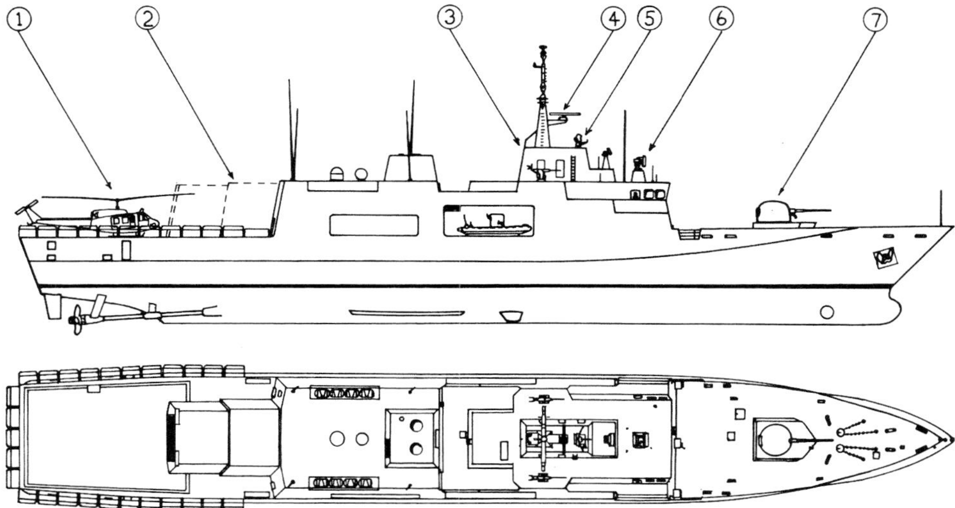

Comandante Cigala Fulgosi (P 490) 1. AB-212 helicopter 2. Telescoping hangar 3. 25-mm OTO Melara AA 4. Navigational radar 5. RASS surface-search radar 6. SPG-76 f.c. radar for 76-mm gun 7. 76-mm OTO Melara DP gun Drawing by A. D. Baker III

PATROL SHIPS [PS] *(continued)*

D: 1,520 tons (fl) **S:** 25+ kts **Dim:** 88.40 (80.00 pp) × 12.20 × . . .
A: 1 76-mm 62-cal. OTO Melara SuperRapid DP; 2 single 25-mm 87-cal. Oerlikon–OTO Melara KBA AA; 1 AB-212 or NH-90 helicopter
Electronics:
Radar: 1 Alenia RASS surf. search; 1 AMS SPG-76 (RTN-30X/I) f.c.
Sonar: None
EW: Elettronica . . . intercept, 2 20-round OTO Melara SCLAR-H decoy RL
E/O: . . . optronic surveillance and f.c.
M: 2 Wärtsilä NSD 18V 26XN diesels; 2 CP props; 17,370 bhp—bow-thruster
Electric: 2,700 kw tot. (3 × 900 kw, Isotta-Fraschini 1712 T2ME diesels driving; 380 V/50 Hz and 440 V/60 Hz)
Range: 3,500/14 **Endurance:** 10 days
Crew: 59 tot. (accomm. for 70)

Remarks: NUMC = *Nuove Unità Minori Combattenti* (New Minor Combatant Unit). The four were provisionally ordered 12-98 for $104 million each. Contract confirmed 4-99. Are used for economic exclusion zone patrol.
Hull systems: The hull and superstructure are shaped to reduce radar reflection. The boat pockets recessed into the superstruture amidships will be covered by Faraday-shield mesh to eliminate radar returns, and exhaust cooling will be fitted. The helicopter hangar is telescoping. Fin stabilizers are fitted, and the underwater portion of the hull has a pronounced bulbous bow form. P 493 employs a GRP superstructure, lower mast, and helicopter hangar delivered 1-01 by Intermarine; incorporating layers of Kevlar and GRP ballistic protection around the bridge and carbon fiber to shield against electromagnetic interference, the new structure weighs 60% less than the steel structures in the earlier three.
Combat systems: Have an AMS command system with NA-25 gun control, and they have an Elmer integrated internal/external communications suite. There are no significant air defense and no ASW capabilities.

♦ 4 Cassiopea class
Bldr: Fincantieri, Muggiano

	Laid down	L	In serv.
P 401 Cassiopea	16-3-87	19-7-88	21-10-89
P 402 Libra	16-3-87	27-7-88	23-3-91
P 403 Spica	5-9-88	27-5-89	23-3-91
P 404 Vega	30-6-89	24-2-90	8-5-92

Vega (P 404) Luciano Grazioli, 11-05

Vega (P 404)—with AB-212 helicopter on the flight deck Anthony Vella 6-04

Vega (P 404) Luciano Grazioli, 10-05

D: 1,126 tons (1,491 fl) **S:** 21 kts (20 continuous)
Dim: 79.80 (71.50 pp) × 11.80 (11.40 wl) × 3.60 (hull)
A: 1 76-mm 62-cal. OTO Melara DP; 2 single 20-mm 70-cal. Mk 10 Oerlikon AA; 1 AB-412 helicopter
Electronics:
Radar: 1 SMA SPN-748(V)2 nav.; 1 AMS SPS-702(V)2 surf. search; 1 AMS SPG-70 (RTN-10X) f.c.
EW: . . . intercept and D/F gear
M: 2 Wärtsilä NSD BL230-16 diesels; 2 CP props; 8,800 bhp max. (7,490 sust.)
Electric: 1,620 kw (3 × 500-kw Isotta-Fraschini 1D36.55 SS6V gen. sets; 1 × 120-kw emergency set)
Range: 3,300/17 **Fuel:** 165 tons **Endurance:** 35 days
Crew: 6 officers, 54 enlisted (accomm. for 10 officers, 70 enlisted)

Remarks: Operated on fisheries patrol, antipollution, and search-and-rescue duties. Construction authorized 31-12-82, funded by the Ministry of the Merchant Marine; ordered 12-86. There were originally to have been eight; the projected fifth unit, to have been named *Orione,* and a planned sixth were canceled in 1991.
Hull systems: Have pollution analysis, oil disposal, cargo transport, light repair, firefighting, and towing capabilities and can accommodate rescued personnel. Have passive tank stabilization, and fin stabilizers are fitted. A 500-m^3 tank is aboard to hold polluted water. Have a 22.0 × 8.0-m helicopter deck and a telescoping hangar. Hull has 8.50-m molded depth.
Combat systems: The old-model 76-mm guns and fire-control systems were taken from scrapped *Carlo Bergamini*–class frigates. The guns may later be replaced by the new Oerlikon–OTO Melara 25-mm mounting.

Disposal note: *Albatros*-class patrol ships *Alcione* (F 544, ex-U.S. PC 1620) and *Airone* (F 545, ex-U.S. PC 1621) were stricken on 1-2-02. Converted ex-U.S. *Agile*-class patrol ships *Storione* (P 5431) and *Squalo* (P 5433) were retired from service in 2001.

PATROL CRAFT [PC]

♦ 4 Esploratore class
Bldr: Co.I.Nav.Al., Cadimare, La Spezia

	L	Del.	In serv.
P 405 Esploratore	4-11-96	26-6-97	7-11-98
P 406 Sentinella	13-11-97	4-98	24-4-99
P 407 Vedetta	11-1-97	10-98	9-4-00
P 408 Staffetta	10-99	12-1-01	1-02

Vedetta (P 407) G. Ghilione, via A. A. de Kruijf, 9-00

Sentinella (P 406) Maurizio Brescia, 3-99

D: 164.5 tons light (230.5 fl) **S:** 22 kts (20 sust.)
Dim: 37.16 (34.70 pp) × 7.50 (7.06 wl) × 1.90 (hull; 2.30 max.)
A: 1 20-mm 70-cal. Mk 10 Oerlikon AA; 2 single 7.62-mm mg
Electronics:
Radar: 2 SMA SPS-753B/C nav./surf. search
E/O: AMS Medusa surveillance and tracking
M: 2 Isotta-Fraschini M1712 T2 diesels; 2 CP props; 3,810 bhp
Electric: 500 kw tot. (2 × 250-kw Marelli M7B-250 gen., VMDS9 diesels driving)
Range: 1,200/20 **Crew:** 2 officers, 13 enlisted

Remarks: First three (with an option for a fourth) were approved in 1996 budget to replace the converted U.S. *Adjutant*-class minesweepers used in U.N. patrol service in the Red Sea; P 408 was ordered during 2-98. Based at Brindisi. The names mean "Scout," "Sentry," "Despatch Rider," and "Lookout," respectively. Originally ordered in 12-93 from C.N. Ortona, which went out of business; the new builder was formed as a temporary consortium of small yacht-building companies. The 20-mm gun may later be replaced by a new Oerlikon–OTO Melara 25-mm 87-cal. mount.
Disposal note: Of the two remaining U.S. *Adjutant*-class patrol craft, former minesweeper *Bambú* (P 495, ex-M 5521; ex-U.S. MSC 214) was retired during 2000 and *Palma* (P 498, ex-M 5525; ex-U.S. MSC 238) in 1-03.

MINE WARFARE SHIPS

Note: A requirement has been identified to acquire four new Intermarine designed 1000-ton GRP minehunters. If funding is approved, construction may begin around 2007–8 with service entry dates between 2013 and 2019.

♦ 8 Gaeta-class minehunter/minesweepers [MHC]

Bldr: Intermarine, Sarzana

	Laid down	L	In serv.
M 5554 Gaeta	5-8-88	28-7-90	9-10-93
M 5555 Termoli	5-12-88	15-12-90	28-5-93
M 5556 Alghero	5-4-89	4-5-91	28-5-93
M 5557 Numana	5-8-89	26-10-91	11-6-94
M 5558 Crotone	5-12-89	11-4-92	11-6-94
M 5559 Viareggio	. . .	3-10-92	26-10-96
M 5560 Chioggia	. . .	9-4-94	1997 (del. 5-5-96)
M 5561 Rimini	. . .	17-9-94	1998 (del. 19-10-96)

Viareggio (M 5559) Bernard Prézelin, 4-05

Gaeta (M 5554) Bernard Prézelin, 9-04

Rimini (M 5561) Guy Schaeffer via Paolo Marsan, 4-05

D: 665 tons (697 fl) **S:** 14.3 kts **Dim:** 52.45 (46.50 pp) × 9.87 × 2.95
A: 1 20-mm 70-cal. Mk 10 Oerlikon AA
Electronics:
Radar: 1 SMA MM/SPN-728 nav.
Sonar: FIAR SQQ-14 (IT) minehunting HF, with U.K. Type 2048 (Plessey Speedscan) side-scan mapping
M: 1 Wärtsilä NSD BL230-BN diesel; 1 prop; 1,985 bhp (3 retractable 120-hp Riva Calzoni thrusters for 6-kt hunting speed)
Electric: 900 kw (3 × 250-kw ID 36SS diesel sets; 1 × 150-kw ID 36N diesel set)
Range: 1,500/14; 2,500/12 **Fuel:** 49 tons **Endurance:** 12 days
Crew: 4 officers, 43 enlisted (including 7 mine-disposal divers)

Remarks: Names were announced in 1980, but the first six ships were not ordered until 30-4-88. Two additional units were ordered in 1992 but canceled in 7-92 as an economy measure; M 5560 and M 5561 were then reordered during 1993 to ensure continuity of work at the yard. Are essentially a lengthened version of the *Lerici* design. Six very similar sisters were ordered by the Royal Australian Navy, and the U.S. Navy's *Osprey* class is an enlarged variant.
Hull systems: As for the *Lerici* class, but have a new minehunting auxiliary thruster system and an additional main generator set. Carry a Galeazzi two-man decompression chamber and are fitted with passive tank stabilization (by using stabilization tanks to carry fuel, the range can be extended by 1,500 n.m. at 12 kts).
Combat systems: Have the SSN-714 MACTIS command and control system. Carry one MIN Mk-2 remote-controlled mine disposal submersibles and Oropesa Mk 4 mechanical sweep gear. The minehunting sonar is an Italian-built version of the SQQ-14 (with digital processor) with the addition of the Plessey Speedscan (Type 2048) side-scan route-mapping sonar to the towed transducer array to provide a mine-route clearance capability. Have a Motorola MHS-1C NAVSAT receiver.

Disposal note: *Alpino*-class mine-countermeasures support ship, *Alpino* (A 5384), was retired during 2-05.

♦ 4 Lerici-class minehunter/minesweepers [MHC]

Bldr: Intermarine, Sarzana

	L	In serv.		L	In serv.
M 5550 Lerici	3-9-82	4-5-85	M 5552 Milazzo	4-1-85	14-12-85
M 5551 Sapri	5-4-84	14-12-85	M 5553 Vieste	18-4-85	14-12-85

Vieste (M 5553) Bernard Prézelin, 2-04

D: 488 tons (520 fl) **S:** 15 kts **Dim:** 49.98 (45.50 pp) × 9.56 × 2.70
A: 1 20-mm 70-cal. Mk 10 Oerlikon AA
Electronics:
Radar: 1 SMA SPN-703 nav.
Sonar: FIAR SQQ-14/IT minehunting HF, with U.K. Type 2048 (Plessey Speedscan) side-scan mapping
M: 1 Wärtsilä NSD B230-8M diesel; 1 prop; 1,840 bhp—2 retractable auxiliary thrusters; 470 hp for 7 kts
Electric: 650 kw (2 × 250-kw ID 36SS diesel sets; 1 × 150-kw diesel set)
Range: 1,500/14; 2,500/12 **Fuel:** 49 tons **Endurance:** 15 days
Crew: 4 officers, 43 enlisted (including 6–7 mine-clearance divers)

Remarks: Ordered 4-78. Delivery of the first two ships was delayed by the presence of a bridge blocking the seaward exit from the yard. Sisters were built for Nigeria and Malaysia. All four are to receive new navigational track maintenance and navigational systems.
Hull systems: Glass-reinforced, shock-resistant plastic construction throughout. Hull material is 140 mm thick. While minehunting, speed is 7 kts, using the two drop-down, shrouded thrusters. Range at 12 kts can be extended to 4,000 n.m. by using the passive roll stabilization tanks to carry fuel.
Combat systems: Have the SSN-714 command and control system and Motorola MHS-1A navigation system. The original U.S. SQQ-14 high-frequency minehunting sonar with a retractable transducer has been upgraded to the digital, Italian-made, repackaged SQQ-14/IT, which incorporates the Plessey Speedscan (Type 2048) side-scan sonar for route survey work at up to 12 kts. Carry 6–7 divers, who use CAM mine-destructor charges. One Pluto remote-controlled submersible is carried by each ship, along with Oropesa Mk 4 mechanical sweep gear.

AMPHIBIOUS WARFARE SHIPS AND CRAFT

Note: Initial planning is under way for a new LHD class to displace on the order of 20,000 tons full load. The design would have a crew of 750 total with the capability to accommodate command staff plus troops, AV-8B and F-35 aircraft.

♦ 1 modified San Giorgio–class dock landing ship [LPD]

Bldr: Fincantieri, Riva Trigoso

	Laid down	L	Del.	In serv.
L 9894 San Giusto	7-4-92	2-12-93	14-4-94	11-6-94

San Giusto (L 9894) Maurizio Brescia, 1-04

San Giusto (L 9894) Maurizio Brescia, 8-04

AMPHIBIOUS WARFARE SHIPS AND CRAFT *(continued)*

San Giusto (L 9894) Maurizio Brescia, 1-04

D: 5,600 tons (7,950 fl) **S:** 20 kts
Dim: 137.00 (118.00 pp) × 25.00 (20.50 hull) × 6.00
A: 1 76-mm 62-cal. OTO Melara Compact DP; 2 twin 20-mm 70-cal. Mk 24 Oerlikon AA; 3 CH-47 Chinook or 3 SH-3D Sea King or 5 AB-212 helicopters
Electronics:
Radar: 1 DMS SPN-753 nav.; 1 SMA SPS-702 surf. search; 1 AMS SPG-70 (RTN-10X) f.c.
EW: AMS SLR-730 intercept; AMS SLQ-747 jammer
M: 2 Fincantieri-DMD A.420.12 diesels; 2 CP props; 16,800 bhp—1,000-shp bow-thruster
Electric: 3,330 kw (4 × 770 kw, 1 × 250 kw) **Range:** 4,500/20; 7,500/16
Crew: 16 officers, 182 enlisted + 204 cadets and 62 instructors, or 349 troops (33 officers, 316 enlisted)

Remarks: Modified version of the *San Giorgio* class, intended to act as training ship for the naval academy at Livorno in peacetime. Authorized during 11-90 and ordered during 3-91. Based at Brindisi. To receive midlife modernization around 2007.
Hull systems: Has a broader island superstructure than the earlier *San Giorgio* class, and the boats are stowed on a sponson to port to restore flight deck area, providing a taxiway between the landing area at the stern and a smaller one to port at the bow. Up to six medium-sized helicopters can be accommodated on deck. There is no bow vehicle ramp, but the side doors and ramps are larger than on the earlier units. Is able to carry 34 combat vehicles totaling up to 1,200 tons below decks, and additional light vehicles can be carried on the flight deck. About 85 tons (80 m^3) of combat stores and 30 tons (80 m^3) of provisions can be accommodated. Landing craft include three 63-ton MTM-series medium landing craft in the 20.5 × 7.0-m stern docking well and three 14-ton MTP-series personnel landing craft in davits to port, plus one 9-ton motor launch.
Combat systems: Has IPN-20/SADOC-2 combat control system with two multifunction and four single-function operator consoles. Is equipped to send and receive NATO Link 11. The 76-mm gun is not of the newest (SuperRapid) model, but it has been upgraded to fire at up to 85 rpm.

♦ 2 San Giorgio–class dock landing ships [LPD]
Bldr: Fincantieri, Riva Trigoso

	Laid down	L	In serv.
L 9892 San Giorgio	26-5-85	25-2-87	13-2-88
L 9893 San Marco	26-3-85	21-10-87	6-5-89

San Marco (L 9893) Guy Schaeffer via Paolo Marsan, 4-05

D: 5,000 tons light, 6,687 tons std. (7,665 fl; 8,400 flooded down) **S:** 21 kts (sust.)
Dim: 133.30 (118.00 pp) × 20.50 × 5.25 (6.50 flooded down aft)
A: 2 single 20-mm 70-cal. Mk 10 Oerlikon AA; 2 single 12.7-mm mg; 3 CH-47 Chinook or 3 SH-3D Sea King or 5 AB-212 helicopters
Electronics: Radar: 1 SMA SPN-748 nav.; 1 SMA SPS-702 surf./air search
M: 2 Wärtsilä NSD A420-12, 12-cyl., 4-stroke diesels; 2 CP props; 16,800 bhp—1,000-bhp bow-thruster
Electric: 3,330 kw (4 × 770 kw, 1 × 250 kw) **Range:** 4,500/20; 7,500/16
Crew: 17 officers, 146 enlisted + 345 troops

Remarks: L 9892, initially requested in 1980, was approved in 1983 and ordered 5-3-84. L 9893, ordered 26-3-85 with funds from the Ministry of Civil Protection, is configured for disaster-relief service and has more extensive medical facilities. Both were fitted out at Muggiano and are based at Brindisi. Both are being modernized.

San Giorgio (L 9892) Guy Schaeffer via Paolo Marsan, 9-03

San Marco (L 9893) Bernard Prézelin, 4-05

Hull systems: In 1999–2000 with L 9892 and in 2001 with L 9893, the flight deck space was enlarged during refits at Taranto through the deletion of the 76-mm gun, extension of the flight deck to the bow, and the adding of a 5-m-wide sponson to port, providing spots fore and aft for EH.101 helicopters and two spots on the sponson for smaller helicopters. The bow doors were sealed, the two 13.0-m LCVPs resited below the sponson, the flight deck fitted for night operations, and aircraft support facilities enhanced. They continue to carry three 18.5-m LCMs, launched via a 20.5 × 7.0-m stern docking well equipped with a 40-ton traveling bridge crane. The helicopters are stowed on deck, not in the 100 × 20.5-m vehicle hangar below, which can hold 30 or more armored personnel carriers. The flight deck is served by a 13.5 × 3.5-m, 30-ton elevator and a 16-ton crane. There is stowage for 99 m^3 of refrigerated and 300 m^3 of dry stores and 60 tons of aviation fuel. Evaporators producing 90 tons water per day are fitted. Have passive tank stabilization.
Combat systems: The old-model 76-mm gun and its associated AMS Argo NA-10 f.c.s. were removed during the modernizations.

♦ 9 MTM 217–class vehicle landing craft [LCM]
Bldrs: MEN 217–222: MEN Fincantieri, Muggiano, La Spezia (in serv. 9-10-87 to 8-3-88); others: C.N. Balsamo (in serv. 1993)

MEN 217 through MEN 222 MEN 227 MEN 228 MEN 551

MEN 220 A. Guigné, 6-02

AMPHIBIOUS WARFARE SHIPS AND CRAFT *(continued)*

D: 62 tons (64.6 fl) **S:** 9 kts **Dim:** 18.50 × 5.10 × 0.90
M: 2 Fiat-AIFO 8280 diesels; 2 props; 560 bhp (400 sust.)
Range: 300/9 **Crew:** 3 crew + 80 troops

Remarks: GRP construction, with design based strongly on that of the U.S. LCM(6) class. First three were built for *San Giorgio,* next three for *San Marco.* Three more were ordered during 3-91 for *San Giusto.* Cargo capacity: 30 tons. The hull numbering designation has been changed from MTM (*Mototrasporti Medi*) to MEN, and the craft no longer carry the formerly assigned NATO "L"-series pennants.

Disposal note: All remaining LCM(6)-class vehicle landing craft, in service since World War II, were retired by 2005.

♦ 17 MTP 96–class vehicle and personnel landing craft [LCVP]

Bldrs: MDN 94, 95: Tecnomatic, Ancona (In serv. 1985); MDN 96–101: Tecnomatic, Bari (In serv. 1987–88); others: Tecnoplast, Venice (In serv. 1991–94)

MDN 94 through MDN 101 — MDN 108 — MDN 109 — MDN 114 through MDN 120

MDN 116 Dieter Wolf, 7-02

D: 14.3 tons (fl) **S:** 26 kts **Dim:** 13.70 × 3.80 × 0.70
M: 2 Fiat-AIOF 836J-SRM diesels; 2 props or waterjets; 700 bhp
Range: 180/24 **Crew:** 3 tot. + 45 troops

Remarks: GRP personnel launches for use with the *San Giorgio* class. Assigned NATO "L"-series pennants are no longer carried, and the craft have been renumbered from the original MTP (*Mototrasporti Personale*) series to MDN. The last three built had waterjets, and the propellers are being replaced by waterjets in the earlier units. Have a small bow ramp and can transport light vehicles. Cargo: 45 troops or 4.5 tons.

Note: For use by the San Marco Battalion seaborne assault troops, there are 24 LVTP-7 armored personnel carriers and 1 LVTC-7 armored command post, all tracked amphibious craft transferred from the United States. Personnel transports MEN 215 and MEN 216, built to be carried by the carrier *Giuseppe Garibaldi* for amphibious assault missions, are now used as personnel ferries and are described in the Service Craft section under [YFL]. The *Mario Marino*–class combat swimmer support craft are listed as diving tenders [YDT] under Service Craft.

AUXILIARIES

♦ 1 Alpino-class weapons systems trials ship [AGE]

Bldr: C.N. del Tirreno, Riva Trigoso

	Laid down	L	In serv.
F 581 Carabiniere (ex-*Climene*)	9-1-65	30-9-67	28-4-68

Carabiniere (F 581) Guy Schaeffer via Paolo Marsan, 4-03

D: 2,000 tons (2,689 fl) **S:** 28 kts **Dim:** 113.3 (106.4 pp) × 13.3 × 3.80 (hull)
A: 8 Sylver A43 VLS cells (8 Aster-15 missiles); 1 76-mm 62-cal. OTO Melara DP; 2 triple 324-mm ILAS-3 ASW TT
Electronics:
Radar: 1 SMA SPN-748 nav.; 1 AMS SPS-702(V)3 surf. search; 1 R.C.A. SPS-12 air search; 2 AMS SPG-70 (RTN-10X Argo systems) gun f.c.; 1 AMS SPY-790 EMPAR target desig./tracking
Sonar: Raytheon DE 1164 MF
EW: AMS SLQ-747 integrated intercept/jammer suite
M: CODAG: 4 Tosi OTV-320 diesels (4,200 bhp each); 2 Tosi-Metrovik G6 gas turbines (7,700 shp each); 2 props
Electric: 2,400 kw tot. **Range:** 4,200/17 **Fuel:** 275 tons
Crew: 13 officers, 150 enlisted

Remarks: Former frigate refitted to act as weapons trials ship in place of *Quarto* (A 5314); reclassified as an auxiliary 1-1-93. Completed a 15-month overhaul and modification in 10-00 to serve as system validation platform for Italian Navy use of the Aster-15 SAM system, with trials commencing 9-01. A further 10-month overhaul was completed by late 2003, with testing beginning shortly thereafter of the French/Italian PAAMS (Principal Anti-Air Missile System) configuration.
Hull systems: Fin stabilizers. Cruises at 22 kts on diesels. The gas turbine engines may have been removed or inactivated.
Combat systems: Received a bow-mounted sonar, improved combat data system, and EW equipment during a refit that ended 7-85. The fish for the DE 1164 VDS is no longer carried, although the hoist gear, winch, and cable reel were overhauled during 2000 and remain installed at the stern. Conducted initial sea trials with the AMS EMPAR (European Multifunction Phased-Array Radar) from 7-95 to 4-96; the associated AMS SADOC-3 combat system began installation during 12-94. Conducted the first Milas AS missile at-sea launch during 5-95; the canister launcher (now removed) was identical to that employed for the Teseo Mk 2 antiship missile and was mounted forward of the bridge superstructure, firing to starboard.

♦ 1 modified Alliance-class intelligence collector [AGI]

Bldr: Fincantieri, Muggiano

	Laid down	L	Del.
A 5340 Elettra	20-1-01	24-8-02	2-4-03

Elettra (A 5340) Antonio Scrimali via L. Grazioli, 2003

D: 2,466 tons (3,180 fl) **S:** 17 kts (16.5 sust.)
Dim: 93.50 (82.00 pp) × 15.50 × 5.10
A: 2 single 25-mm 87-cal. OTO Melara KBA AA; 2 single 12.7-mm mg
Electronics:
Radar: 2 Qubit–Kelvin-Hughes Nucleus 6000 nav. (X- and S-band)
Sonar: . . .
M: 2 Wärtsilä NSD B230-12M diesels, AEG CC 3127 generators (2,785-kVA output each); electric drive: 2 AEG 1,500-kw permanent magnet motors; 2 props; 4,000 shp—bow-thruster
Electric: Approx. 3,145 kw tot. (2 × 770-kVA diesel sets; 1 × 1,605-kw Kongsberg gas-turbine set)
Range: 8,000/12 **Crew:** 12 officers, 76 enlisted (accomm. for 14 officers, 80 enlisted)

Remarks: Program title: NUPS (*Nuovo Unità di Supporto Polivalente,* or New Multipurpose Support Unit). Ordered 10-12-99 for $67.28 million. Based on the design of the NATO acoustic research ship *Alliance* and the Taiwanese research ship *Ta Kuan.* Can carry some 27 different electronic and acoustic intelligence collection systems in order to collect communications, electronics, acoustic, and imagery intelligence. Also fitted will be oceanographic and hydrographic research equipment. Construction was slower than planned. To be operated in the Black Sea, Red Sea, Indian Ocean, Arabian Gulf, and Persian Gulf. Has updated C4 systems to enable use as a Maritime Component Commander flagship.
Hull systems: Has Flume-type passive tank stabilization. A helicopter deck is fitted aft, but no hangar. The ship will carry a remotely operated reconnaissance submersible.

♦ 5 Ponza-class navigational aids tenders [AGL]

Bldr: C.N. Mario Morini, Ancona

	Laid down	L	In serv.
A 5364 Ponza (MTF 1304)	25-3-87	24-9-88	20-12-88
A 5366 Levanzo (MTF 1305)	25-3-87	22-6-89	6-9-89
A 5367 Tavolara (MTF 1306)	25-3-87	28-11-88	28-2-89
A 5368 Palmaria (MTF 1307)	25-3-87	25-2-89	19-5-89
A 5383 Procida (MTF 1308)	14-9-89	23-6-90	14-11-90

D: 402 tons light (608 fl) **S:** 14.8 kts **Dim:** 56.72 (50.00 pp) × 10.00 × 2.40
A: Provision for 2 single 7.62-mm mg
Electronics: Radar: 1 SMA SPN-732 nav.
M: 2 Isotta-Fraschini ID36 SS8V diesels; 2 CP Kort-nozzle props; 1,800 bhp (1,690 sust.)—1 120-shp bow-thruster
Electric: 464 kw tot. (2 × 232 kw) **Range:** 1,500/14; 2,800/10
Crew: 2 officers, 32 enlisted

Remarks: MTF = *Mototrasporti Fari.* Employed as lighthouse supply and navigational buoy tenders. First four ordered 23-9-86. A variation of the design used for the MTC 1011–class coastal transports. Have one 15-ton-capacity electrohydraulic crane aft and one 1.5-ton crane forward. A 20-mm 70-cal. Mk 10 Oerlikon AA gun can be mounted atop the pilothouse.

AUXILIARIES *(continued)*

Procida (A 5383) Luciano Grazioli, 6-04

♦ 2 Aretusa-class coastal survey ships [AGS]
Bldr: Intermarine, Sarzana

	Laid down	L	In serv.
A 5304 Aretusa	1998	8-5-00	1-02
A 5305 Galatea	. . .	7-6-00	1-02

Galatea (A 5305) Luciano Grazioli, 4-04

Aretusa (A 5304)—Note catamaran hull Luciano Grazioli, 7-03

D: 390 tons (fl) **S:** 13 kts **Dim:** 39.21 (36.0 pp) × 12.60 × 3.60
A: 1 20-mm 70-cal. Mk 10 Oerlikon AA
Electronics:
Radar: 2 Gem SPN-753(V)B nav.
Sonar: Kongsberg MS 992 side-scan; Kongsberg EA 500 mapping echo sounder; Kongsberg EM 300 multibeam mapping sonar
M: 2 Isotta-Fraschini V1708 T2ME diesels, 2 Marelli M7R 400 MA generators, 2 ABB/AMA 400 Ma6 electric motors; 2 Schottel double-prop azimuthal thrusters; . . . shp—2 ABB electric bow-thrusters
Range: 1,700/13 **Crew:** 4 officers, 20 enlisted + 4 passengers (31 tot. accomm.)

Remarks: Were to be 300-ton units ordered 2-90 from Intermarine, Sarzana, as replacements for *Mirto* (A 5306) and *Pioppo* (A 5307), but were deferred for financial reasons and later redesigned. Finally ordered from Intermarine in 10-97. Both are based at La Spezia and operate for the Istituto Idrografico della Marina, Genoa.
Hull systems: Are of catamaran configuration, with GRP hulls having a bulbous bow configuration. They can operate at speeds below 3 kts for up to 8 hrs without overheating the plant. Two 5,000-m-depth echo sounders, one 5,000-m-depth multibeam mapping sonar, one 600-m-depth side-scan echo sounder, medium- and short-range radionavigation systems, one bottom-sampling device (1,500 m depth), a differential GPS receiver, a bottom profiler, and a data-recording system. The main deck between the hulls is 34.8 m long, and the hulls have a beam of 3.6 m each. A 7.6-m, echo sounder–equipped, dual-waterjet-propelled survey launch is carried in davits to starboard, and there is a gallows crane to handle survey equipment aft.

♦ 1 Ammiraglio Magnaghi–class hydrographic survey ship [AGS]
Bldr: C.N. del Tirreno, Riva Trigoso

	Laid down	L	In serv.
A 5303 Ammiraglio Magnaghi	13-6-73	11-9-74	2-5-75

Ammiraglio Magnaghi (A 5303) Antionio Scrimali, 4-02

D: 1,550 tons (1,700 fl) **S:** 17 kts **Dim:** 82.70 (76.80 pp) × 13.70 × 3.60
A: Provision for 1 40-mm 70-cal. OTO Melara–Bofors AA
Electronics: Radar: 1 SMA SPN-703 nav.
M: 2 Wärtsilä NSD B306-SS diesels; 1 CP prop; 3,000 bhp—1 electric auxiliary propulsion engine; 240 shp (4 kts)—bow-thruster
Range: 4,200/16; 5,500/12 **Crew:** 15 officers, 120 enlisted + 15 scientists

Remarks: Built under the 1972 construction program. Equipped for survey and oceanographic studies and for search-and-rescue duties. Based at Genoa and assigned to the Istituto Idrografico della Marina.
Hull systems: Has Flume-type passive tank stabilization. Chemistry, physical oceanography, photo, and hydrology labs, computerized data loggers, and an underwater t.v. capability are fitted. Has a helicopter pad aft. Received the Qubit TRAC V/CHART 100 integrated hydrographic data acquisition system during a major overhaul in 1990–91 that also saw modifications to the stack. Can accommodate four small hydrographic survey launches, but normally only two are aboard.

Disposal note: U.S. *Adjutant*-class hydrographic survey ships *Mirto* (A 5306, ex-M 5539) and *Pioppo* (A 5307, ex-M 5515, ex-MSC 135) were retired during 2002.

♦ 6 Gorgona-class coastal cargo ships [AK]
Bldr: C.N. Mario Morini, Ancona

	L	In serv.
A 5347 Gorgona (MTC 1011)	12-7-86	23-12-86
A 5348 Tremiti (MTC 1012)	13-9-86	2-3-87
A 5349 Caprera (MTC 1013)	8-11-86	10-4-87
A 5351 Pantelleria (MTC 1014)	31-1-87	26-5-87
A 5352 Lipari (MTC 1015)	7-5-87	10-7-87
A 5353 Capri (MTC 1016)	18-6-87	16-9-87

Lipari (A 5352) Luciano Grazioli, 4-05

AUXILIARIES *(continued)*

Caprera (A 5349) Luciano Grazioli, 6-04

D: 631 (fl) **S:** 14+ kts **Dim:** 56.72 × 10.00 × 2.50
A: 2 single 7.62-mm mg; portable mine rails
Electronics: Radar: 1 SMA SPN-732 nav.
M: 2 CRM 12D/SS diesels; 2 props; 1,520 bhp
Electric: 484 kw (2 × 192 kw, 1 × 100 kw)
Range: 1,500/14 **Crew:** 4 officers, 28 enlisted

Remarks: MTC = *Mototrasporti Costieri.* Replaced World War II–era MTCs of the MZ class. A 5347 is based at La Spezia, A 5348 at Ancona, A 5349 and A 5351 at La Maddalena, and the last two at the Naval Academy in Livorno. A 20-mm 70-cal. Mk 10 Oerlikon AA gun can be mounted atop the pilothouse.
Hull systems: Have two electrohydraulic cranes. Are intended to carry palletized cargo on their open decks and fuel and water below decks. Have an articulating vehicle ramp at the stern to load and unload vehicle cargo while Med-moored.

♦ 1 Etna-class replenishment oiler [AOR]
Bldr: Fincantieri, Riva Trigoso

	Laid down	L	In serv. (del.)
A 5326 Etna	4-7-96	12-7-97	29-7-98 (del.)

Etna (A 5326) Luciano Grazioli, 11-05

D: 6,700 tons (13,400 fl) **S:** 21 kts **Dim:** 146.50 (137.00 pp) × 21.00 × 7.25
A: Provision for 1 76-mm 62-cal. OTO Melara Compact DP; 2 single 25-mm 87-cal. Oerlikon–OTO Melara KBA AA; 1 EH.101 or 1 SH-3D Sea King or 2 AB-212 helicopters
Electronics:
Radar: 2 SPN-748 nav.; 1 SPQ-702 surf. search; provision for 1 AMS SPG-75 (RTN-30X) f.c.
M: 2 Wärtsilä-Sulzer 12 ZAV 40S diesels; 2 props; 22,400 bhp—1,000-kw bow-thruster
Range: 7,600/18 **Crew:** 160 tot. (accomm. for 243)

Remarks: Intended to accompany *Giuseppe Garibaldi.* Program was frozen in 2-90 but revived and approved in 1993. Was to have been laid down 3-94, but construction was delayed more than a year for lack of adequate funding. Construction contract signed 3-1-95. A sister was ordered for the Greek Navy in 7-99 for construction under license in Greece.
Hull systems: Can carry 5,400 tons gas turbine/diesel fuel, 1,200 tons aviation fuel, 160 tons fresh water, 2,100 m^3 (about 280 tons) ammunition, 30,000 fresh rations, 30,000 dry-food rations, 20 tons spare parts, and 20 tons lubricant and has space on deck for 12 cargo containers. Two replenishment stations on each beam.
Combat systems: Planned gun armament is not yet aboard; the one quadruple 25-mm gatling CIWS originally planned is to be replaced with the 25-mm guns if and when she is armed. Has two different commercial SATCOM terminals.

♦ 2 Stromboli-class replenishment oilers [AOR]
Bldr: C.N. del Tirreno, Riva Trigoso

	Laid down	L	In serv.
A 5327 Stromboli	1-10-73	20-2-75	31-10-75
A 5329 Vesuvio	1-7-74	4-6-77	18-11-78

Stromboli (A 5327)—with AB-212 helicopter visible on deck
Stefan Karpinski, 2003

D: 4,200 tons (8,706 fl) **S:** 19.5 kts
Dim: 129.00 (118.5 pp) × 18.00 × 6.50 (3.17 light)
A: 1 76-mm 62-cal. OTO Melara DP; 2 single 20-mm 70-cal. Mk 10 Oerlikon AA

Stromboli (A 5327) Stefan Karpinski, 2003

Electronics:
Radar: 1 SMA SPN-703 nav.; 1 SMA SPQ-2 surf. search; 1 AMS SPG-70 (RTN-10X) f.c.
M: 2 Wärtsilä NSD C428-SS diesels: 1 LIPS 4-bladed CP prop; 11,200 bhp (9,600 sust.)
Electric: 2,350 kw **Range:** 10,000/16 **Crew:** 10 officers, 114 enlisted

Remarks: Were to be retired 2005–8, but no replacement program has been announced. Sister *Agnadeen,* completed and handed over to Iraq, has been sequestered at Alexandria, Egypt, since 1986; in 8-96, custody of the vessel was awarded to the shipbuilder, Fincantieri, and the ship may be sold for use or scrap.
Hull systems: Cargo: 1,370 tons fuel oil, 2,830 tons diesel, 480 tons aviation fuel, and 200 tons miscellaneous (torpedoes, missiles, projectiles, spare parts). Capable of serving one unit on each beam using constant-tension fueling rigs, each capable of delivering 650 m^3/hr of fuel oil and 480 m^3/hr of diesel fuel or aviation fuel. Can also refuel over the stern at the rate of 430 m^3/hr. There are also constant-tension cargo transfer rigs on either side, each capable of transferring 1.8-ton loads, as well as two stations for lighter loads. The ships can also replenish via helicopters, although they do not have hangars. Twenty repair-party personnel can also be accommodated, and the ships can carry up to 250 passengers.
Combat systems: Have an NA-10 Argo f.c.s. for the old-model 76-mm gun.

♦ 1 Anteo-class salvage ship/submersible tender [ARS]

	Bldr	Laid down	L	In serv.
A 5309 Anteo	C.N. OTO Melara, Mestre	1977	11-11-78	31-7-80

Anteo (A 5309) Luciano Grazioli, 9-96

D: 2,857 tons (3,120 fl) **S:** 18.3 kts **Dim:** 98.40 (93.00 pp) × 15.80 × 5.20
A: 1 twin 20-mm 70-cal. Mk 24 Oerlikon AA; provision for 1 AB-212 helicopter
Electronics: Radar: 1 SMA SPN-748 nav.; 1 SMA SPN-751 nav.
M: 3 Wärtsilä NSD A230-12V diesels (4,050 bhp each), electric drive (2 motors); 1 prop; 5,600 shp (5,360 sust.)—500-shp bow-thruster
Range: 4,000/14 **Fuel:** 270 tons **Crew:** 12 officers, 125 enlisted

Remarks: Ordered in 1977. Based at La Spezia.
Hull systems: Carries USN-style submarine rescue equipment, including a McCann rescue bell capable of operating at up to 150 m depth and two decompression chambers. A Type MSM-1/S, 22-ton salvage submersible named *Usel* is also carried; 9.0 × 2.5 × 2.7 m in size and displacing 24 tons, the *Usel* can submerge to 600 m and has a 120-hr autonomous endurance with a 4-kt max. speed. Also carried is a Gaymarine Pluto remote-controlled underwater vehicle. During 2000, the ship was equipped with the SRV300 rescue submersible. The ship supports saturation diving to 350 m and has a 27-ton bollard pull towing capacity at 10 kts. There is a telescoping helicopter hangar. A Flume-type passive stabilization tank system is fitted.

Disposal note: *Proteo*-class salvage ship/submersible tender *Proteo* (A 5310) was retired from service in 2004 and sold to Bulgaria.

AUXILIARIES *(continued)*

♦ 6 Ciclope-class seagoing tugs [ATA]

Bldr: C.N. Ferrari, La Spezia

	L	In serv.		L	In serv.
A 5319 Ciclope	20-2-85	11-9-85	A 5328 Gigante	. . .	18-7-86
A 5324 Titano	2-3-85	7-12-85	A 5330 Saturno	29-7-87	5-4-88
A 5325 Polifemo	15-6-85	21-4-86	A 5365 Tenace	31-8-87	9-7-88

Tenace (A 5365) Douglas A. Cromby, 2003

D: 600 tons (658 fl) **S:** 14.5 kts **Dim:** 38.95 (32.30 pp) × 9.85 × 3.32
A: None **Electronics:** Radar: 1 SMA SPN-748 nav.
M: 2 Wärtsilä NSD BL230-6L diesels; 1 CP prop; 3,264 bhp
Electric: 500 kw (2 × 200 kw, 1 × 100 kw) **Range:** 3,000/14.5 **Crew:** 12 tot.

Remarks: Enlarged and improved version of the *Atlante* class. Last two ordered 29-5-86. Bollard pull: 45 tons initial, 36 tons sustained at 8.3 kts. Have two 130-m^3/hr water cannon and a 23-ton-capacity foam tank.

♦ 2 Atlante-class seagoing tugs (1 in *reserve*) [ATA]

Bldr: C.N. Visitini, Donada (Both in serv. 14-8-75)

A 5317 *Atlante* A 5318 Prometeo

Prometeo (A 5318) Luciano Grazioli, 8-04

D: 478 tons light (750 fl) **S:** 13.5 kts **Dim:** 38.9 × 9.6 × 3.70
A: None **Electronics:** Radar: 1 SMA SPN-748 nav.
M: 1 Tosi QT 320/8SS diesel; 1 CP prop; 2,670 bhp (3,000 max.)
Range: 4,000/12 **Crew:** 25 tot.

Remarks: *Atlante* was placed in reserve on 10-10-04.

♦ 2 modified Simeto-class water transport tankers [AWT]

Bldr: C.N. De Poli, Pellestrina

A 5376 Ticino (In serv. 12-3-94) A 5377 Tirso (In serv. 10-6-94)

Tirso (A 5377) Luciano Grazioli, 5-02

D: 663 tons light (1,983 fl) **S:** 13 kts **Dim:** 69.82 (63.60 pp) × 10.06 × 3.90
A: 2 single 7.62-mm mg **Electronics:** Radar: 2 SMA SPN-753B(V) nav.
M: 2 Wärtsilä NSD B230-6 diesels; 1 prop; 2,400 bhp—125-shp bow-thruster
Electric: 420 kw tot. (3 × 140-kw diesel sets)
Range: 1,800/12 **Crew:** 3 officers, 33 enlisted

Remarks: Ordered 5-92. Very similar to the *Simeto.* Molded depth: 4.85 m. Cargo: 1,200 tons fresh water. A 5376 operates from La Spezia and A 5377 serves the area around Sicily. Have a position abaft the stack for a 20-mm 70-cal. Mk 10 Oerlikon AA gun.

Disposal note: Water tanker *Simeto* (A 5375) was retired 17-7-02 and transferred to Tunisia. *Piave* (A 5354), the last *Piave*-class water transport tanker, was decommissioned on 1-11-03.

♦ 1 Basento-class water transport tanker (in reserve) [AWT]

Bldr: INMA, La Spezia (In serv. 19-7-71)

A 5356 Basento

D: 1,930 tons (fl) **S:** 12.5 kts **Dim:** 68.65 × 10.07 × 3.90
A: Removed **Electronics:** Radar: 1 SMA SPN-703 nav.
M: 2 Fiat LA-230 diesels; 1 prop; 1,730 hp
Range: 1,650/12.5 **Crew:** 3 officers, 21 enlisted

Remarks: Cargo: 1,200 tons. Can carry two single 20-mm AA. Can make 13.1 kts in light condition. Placed in reserve 1-10-04.
Disposals: *Bradano* (A 5357) was stricken on 1-12-01 and *Brenta* (A 5358) on 1-2-02.

♦ 1 full-rigged sail training ship [AXT]

Bldr: Nav. Mec. Castellammare

	Laid down	L	In serv.
A 5312 Amerigo Vespucci	12-5-30	22-2-31	15-5-31

Amerigo Vespucci (A 5312) Rob Cabo, 8-05

D: 3,545 tons (4,146 fl) **S:** 10 kts (under power)
Dim: 101.00 (over bowsprit; 82.38 hull; 70.72 pp) × 15.56 × 6.7
A: Removed **Electronics:** Radar: 2 SMA SPN-748 nav.
M: 2 Tosi E6 diesels, electric drive: 2 Marelli motors; 1 prop; 1,900 shp—2,100 m^2 max. sail area
Range: 5,450/6.5 **Crew:** 13 officers, 228 enlisted, 150 cadets

Remarks: Steel construction, including masts. Refitted 1984. Employed for the annual naval academy training cruises. No longer carries armament of four single 40-mm 60-cal. Bofors and one 20-mm 70-cal. Oerlikon AA, but is equipped with four 76-mm saluting cannon.

♦ 1 sail-training barkentine [AXT]

Bldr: Chantiers Dubigeon, Nantes, France (In serv. 1934)

A 5311 Palinuro (ex-*Cdt. Louis Richard*)

Palinuro (A 5311) Guy Schaeffer via Paolo Marsan, 7-04

AUXILIARIES *(continued)*

D: 1,042 tons (1,341 fl) **S:** 10 kts (7.5 under sail)
Dim: 68.9 (59.0 pp) × 10.1 × 4.8 **Electronics:** Radar: 1 SPN-748 nav.
M: 1 M.A.N. G8V23.5/33 diesel; 450 bhp—1,152 m² max. sail area
Range: 5,385/7.5 under power **Crew:** 4 officers, 44 enlisted

Remarks: Former French cod-fishing craft bought in 1951, refitted and recommissioned 16-7-55. Steel hull. Carries two 76-mm saluting cannon.

SERVICE CRAFT

Disposal note: Ex-British LCT(3)-class miscellaneous service craft A 5331 (M.O.C. 1201), in service since World War II, was retired in 2003. M.O.C. 1203 (A 5333) was decommissioned on 1-3-98 and transferred to Albania in 1999. M.O.C. 1205 (A 5335) was retired on 30-9-98, and M.O.C. 1202 (A 5332) on 31-3-99. M.O.C. 1204 (A 5334) was decommissioned in 2003 and donated to Tunisia.

♦ 1 underwater systems trials craft [YAGE]
Bldr: C.N. Picchiotti, Viareggio

	L	Del.	In serv.
A 5320 Vincenzo Martellotta	28-5-88	2-3-89	22-12-90

D: 340 tons (fl) **S:** 17.5 kts **Dim:** 44.50 × 7.90 × 2.30
A: 1 533-mm fixed TT; 1 triple 324-mm B-515 ASW TT
Electronics: Radar: 1 . . . nav.—Sonar: . . .
M: 2 Isotta-Fraschini ID36 N12V diesels; 2 CP props; 3,500 bhp—1 . . . drop-down outdrive aft for low-speed operations—bow-thruster
Range: 700/15 **Crew:** 1 officer, 8 enlisted + 8 technicians

Remarks: Revised version of the *Raffaele Rossetti* (A 5315), intended for ASW torpedo trials, the laying and recovery of acoustic buoys, and trials with remotely controlled underwater vehicles. Has a bulbous bow, unlike A 5315, and can lay a three-dimensional torpedo-tracking hydrophone array. Operated from La Spezia with A 5315 by the Commission for War Materials Experiments.

♦ 1 underwater systems trials craft [YAGE]
Bldr: C.N. Picchiotti, Viareggio

	L	In serv.
A 5315 Raffaele Rossetti	21-7-86	20-12-86

Raffaele Rossetti (A 5315) Carlo Martinelli, 3-99

D: 282 tons (320 fl) **S:** 14.5 kts **Dim:** 44.60 (40.00 pp) × 7.90 × 2.10
A: 2 533-mm TT (1 submerged, *Sauro*-type; 1 surface, *Maestrale*-type, for A-184-series wire-guided torpedoes); 1 triple 324-mm B-515 ASW TT
Electronics: Radar: 1 . . . nav.—Sonar: . . .
M: 2 Isotta-Fraschini ID36 N12V diesels; 2 CP props; 3,500 bhp
Electric: . . . kw (2 gen.) **Range:** 12,000/12
Crew: 1 officer, 8 enlisted + 8 technicians

Remarks: Ordered 3-84 for torpedo, sonar, and electronic warfare equipment trials. Has a 96-cell battery for electric, low-speed, silent propulsion. Operated from La Spezia with A 5320 by the Commission for War Materials Experiments.

♦ 1 Aragosta-class weapons trials craft [YAGE]
Bldr: C.N. Apuana, Marina di Currara (In serv. 1957)

A 5305 Murena (ex-*Scampo,* M 5466)

Murena (A 5305) Carlo Martinelli, 2-94

D: 130 tons (188 fl) **S:** 13.5 kts **Dim:** 32.35 × 6.47 × 2.14
A: 1 triple 324-mm B-515 ASW TT **Electronics:** Radar: 1 BX-732 nav.
M: 2 Fiat-MTU MB 820D diesels; 2 props; 1,000 bhp **Electric:** 340 kw
Range: 2,000/9 **Fuel:** 15 tons **Crew:** 4 officers, 12 enlisted

Remarks: Former inshore minesweeper, with a new superstructure and enclosed bridge. Formerly carried a fixed 533-mm torpedo tube at the stern, which has been fitted with a recovery ramp. The triple ASW TT mount is carried to port, just abaft the superstructure, while to starboard is an articulating hydraulic recovery crane.

♦ . . . floating cranes [YD]

Remarks: Sisters GA 1011, 1012, 1013, 1016, and 1017 are just five of a number of non-self-propelled floating cranes in service; no data available. GA 60 is a smaller floating crane employed at Taranto.

Floating crane GA 1016 Paolo Marsan, 8-03

♦ 1 degaussing tender [YDG]
Bldr: Intermarine-Crestitalia, Ameglia, La Spezia (In serv. 1989)

JDG 10

D: 135 tons (fl) **S:** 2–4 kts **Dim:** 25.20 × 8.00 × 0.95
M: 2 outboard engines; 110 bhp **Crew:** . . .

Remarks: Barge-like hull with tapered ends. Outboard engines are mounted within vertical wells through the hull.

♦ 2 Mario Marino–class swimmer support craft [YDT]
Bldr: Intermarine-Crestitalia, Ameglia, La Spezia

	Laid down	L	In serv.
Y 498 Mario Marino (ex-MEN 213)	8-9-83	1984	23-10-84
Y 499 Alcide Pedretti (ex-MEN 214)	8-9-83	1984	21-12-84

Alcide Pedretti (Y 499) Carlo Martinelli, 11-98

D: 69.5 tons light (96.6 fl) **S:** 28 kts **Dim:** 22.85 × 6.90 × 1.06 (1.50 max.)
Electronics: Radar: 2 . . . nav.
M: 2 Isotta-Fraschini ID36 SS12V diesels; 2 props; 3,040 bhp
Range: Y 498: 236/28; 264/23.2—Y 499: 450/23.5
Crew: 1 officer, 7 enlisted + . . . swimmers

Remarks: Typed MAS (*Motoscafi Appoggio Subacquei*). Built for Raggruppamento Incursori assault swimmers (COMSUBIN), based at La Spezia. GRP construction. Y 499 has a recessed stern for diver recovery and a divers' stage and decompression chamber fitted. One near-sister was built for the United Arab Emirates.

♦ 1 Cheradi-class personnel ferry [YFB] (In serv. 1993)

Cheradi

Cheradi Luciano Grazioli, 5-01

SERVICE CRAFT *(continued)*

Remarks: Replaced the ferry *Tarantola* at Taranto Naval Base. No characteristics data available.

♦ 7 GO 51–series medium floating dry docks [YFDM]
Bldr: C.N. Ferrari, La Spezia

GO 51 through GO 57

GO 51–series floating dry dock GO 53 Carlo Martinelli, 5-91

Capacity: 6,000 tons
Dim: 150.2 × 29.6 (21.6 internal) × 1.50 (light; 14.95 max.)

Remarks: GO 52, completed in 1979, may be to a somewhat different design; the others were completed 10-2-90 to 1996. GO 53 was laid down 30-1-89 and launched 10-2-90 for use at Augusta, Sicily. A new floating dry dock of about 6,000 tons capacity was completed by Metalcast, La Spezia, in 1998.

♦ 13 miscellaneous small dry docks [YFDL/YFDM]

	In serv.	Capacity (tons)		In serv.	Capacity (tons)
GO 1	1942	1,000	GO 18B	1920	600
GO 5	1893	100	GO 20	1935	1,600
GO 8	1904	3,800	GO 22	1935	1,000
GO 10	1900	2,000	GO 23	1935	1,000
GO 11	1911	2,700	GO 51	1971	2,000
GO 17	1917	500	GO 58	1995	2,000
GO 18A	1920	800			

Floating dry dock GO 17 Luciano Grazioli, 3-04

♦ 5 or more Azteca-class personnel launches [YFL]
Bldr: Crestitalia, Ameglia, La Spezia (In serv. . . .)

MCN 1574 MCN 1579 MCN 1614
MCN 1578 MCN 1583

D: 5 tons **S:** 24 kts **Dim:** 9.00 × 3.16 × 0.80
M: 2 AIFO CP3M diesels; 2 props; 320 bhp
Range: 240/18 **Crew:** 4 tot.

Remarks: MCN 1574 and MCN 1579 are of the same design as the Coast Guard CP 1001 class; MCN 1578 and MCN 1614 are of a later model with a larger cabin and pilothouse.

♦ 1 MEN 215–class personnel launch [YFL]
Bldr: Intermarine-Crestitalia, Ameglia, La Spezia (In serv. 1986)

MEN 216

D: 82 tons (fl) **S:** 28 kts (23 sust.) **Dim:** 27.28 × 6.98 × 1.10
Electronics: Radar: 1 SMA SPN-732 nav.
M: 2 Isotta-Fraschini ID36 SS12V diesels; 2 props; 3,200 bhp
Electric: 50 kVA (2 × 25-kVA gen.) **Range:** 250/14
Crew: 4 tot. + 250 passengers

Remarks: Built to be carried by the carrier *Giuseppe Garibaldi* as a commando transport and for search-and-rescue, disaster relief, and other transport duties. GRP construction. Now used as personnel ferry at the La Spezia naval base. Sister MEN 215 was retired 17-7-02.

MEN 216 Carlo Martinelli, 6-86

♦ 37 or more miscellaneous personnel launches [YFL]

MBN 1128, 1143, 1154, 1159, 1206
MCN 1594, 1602, 1605, 1611, 1617, 1618, 1619, 1623, 1631, 1633, 1643, 1644, 1647, 1649, 1651, 1661, 1662
MDN 90, 91, 102, 103, 107, 110, 111, 113, 119, 121, 173
MEN 1011, 1653, 1657, 1671

MCN 1594 Luciano Grazioli, 1-03

GRP-hulled utility launch MBN 1154—MBN 1143 and MBN 1159 are sisters
Luciano Grazioli, 6-99

Remarks: No data available. Miscellaneous personnel and utility launches.

♦ 4 seagoing fuel lighters [YO]
Bldr: Cantieri Ferrari, La Spezia

	L	In serv.
A 5370 MCC 1101	26-10-85	26-8-86
A 5371 MCC 1102	16-11-85	6-12-86
A 5372 MCC 1103	3-2-86	18-5-87
A 5373 MCC 1104	14-11-87	20-5-88

MCC 1103 (A 5372)—with a small deckhouse projecting on the tank deck at the forward end of the poop Carlo Martinelli, 7-95

D: 863 tons (fl) **S:** 13 kts **Dim:** 47.30 × 10.00 × 3.30
Electronics: Radar: 1 SMA SPN-732 nav.
M: 2 Isotta-Fraschini ID36 SS6V diesels; 2 props; 1,320 bhp
Range: 1,500/12 **Crew:** 2 officers, 9 enlisted

Remarks: Cargo: 550 tons. MMC = *Motocisterne Combustibili* (fuel lighter).

SERVICE CRAFT *(continued)*

♦ 4 GGS 1010–class harbor fuel lighters [YO]

Bldr: C.N. De Poli, Pellestrina, Venice

GRS/G 1010 GRS/G 1011 GRS/G 1012 GRS/J 1013

GRS/J 1013 Luciano Grazioli, 6-94

D: Approx. 700 tons (fl) **S:** 11 kts
Dim: 39.10 (37.50 pp) × 8.50 × 3.10 (4.00 molded depth)
M: 2 AIFO 8281 SRM 08 diesels; 2 props; 544 bhp **Crew:** 12 tot.

Remarks: 508 dwt. Five ordered 30-6-88, sixth on 15-9-89. Cargo: 500 m^3. GRS/G-designated units carry fuel, while GRS/J 1013 carries JP-5 aircraft fuel. Three sisters serve as water tankers (GGS 1012, 1014, and 1017).

Note: Also in use are an unknown number of non-self-propelled fuel barges [YON] in the GRS-series.

♦ 1 MEN 212–class torpedo retriever [YPT]

Bldr: Intermarine-Crestitalia, Ameglia, La Spezia (In serv. 10-83)

MEN 212

Torpedo retriever MEN 212—at top, with smaller retrievers MCN 1595 and MCN 1625 in foreground H&L Van Ginderen, 8-00

D: 32 tons (fl) **S:** 23 kts **Dim:** 17.65 × 5.10 × 1.00
M: 2 diesels; 2 props; 1,380 bhp **Range:** 250/20 **Crew:** 4 tot.

Remarks: Can stow three recovered torpedoes. Glass-reinforced plastic construction.

♦ 4 small torpedo retrievers [YPT]

Bldr: Intermarine-Crestitalia, La Spezia (In serv. 1980s)

MCN 1595 MCN 1603 MCN 1622 MCN 1625

Remarks: No characteristics available. Have a stern ramp for weapon recovery. GRP construction. A sister, *Whitehead I,* is operated by the torpedo manufacturer Whitehead Alenia Sistemi Subacquei (WASS). There is also an even smaller weapons recovery launch, MCN 1590, which operates from La Spezia.

♦ 9 Porto-class large harbor tugs [YTB]

Bldrs: first six: C.N. De Poli, Pellestrina; others: C.N. Giacalone, Mazzara del Vallo, Trapani

	L	In serv.
Y 413 Porto Fossone	. . .	24-9-90
Y 416 Porto Torres	3-9-90	16-1-91
Y 417 Porto Corsini	2-11-90	4-3-91
Y 421 Porto Empedocle	4-12-85	19-3-86
Y 422 Porto Pisano	22-10-85	20-8-86
Y 423 Porto Conte	21-11-85	28-9-86
Y 425 Porto Ferraio	21-7-85	3-4-86
Y 426 Porto Venere	13-5-85	12-2-86
Y 428 Porto Salvo	13-9-85	4-7-86

Porto Empedocle (Y 421) Luciano Grazioli, 1-04

D: 412 tons (fl) **S:** 11.5 kts **Dim:** 32.36 (28.00 pp) × 8.50 × 3.32
Electronics: Radar: 1 BX-732 nav.
M: 1 Wärtsilä NSD B230-8M diesel; 1 CP prop; 1,600 bhp
Electric: 200 kw (2 × 100 kw)
Range: 1,800/11.5 **Fuel:** 46 tons **Crew:** 13 tot.

Remarks: First six ordered 2-6-83. The other three were originally ordered from Ferbex, Naples, on 29-10-87, reordered 18-5-88 from Giacalone after Ferbex closed, and laid down 18-5-88. Bollard pull: 25 tons (15 tons at 5 kts). Two water cannon and two 130-m^3/hr pumps. The final three have two 200-kw generator sets. All have an ELAC LAZ-50 echo sounder.

Disposal note: *Porto d'Ischia*–class medium harbor tugs *Porto d'Ischia* (Y 436) and *Riva Trigoso* (Y 443) were retired 17-7-02.

♦ 9 RP 125–class small harbor tugs [YTL]

Bldrs: (A) C.N. Vittoria, Adria; (B) C.N. Ferrari, La Spezia; (C) CINET, Molfetta

	Bldr	In serv.		Bldr	In serv.
Y 478 RP 125	A	1983	Y 484 RP 131	B	28-8-84
Y 479 RP 126	A	24-9-83	Y 485 RP 132	C	7-7-84
Y 481 RP 128	B	4-84	Y 486 RP 133	C	3-11-84
Y 482 RP 129	B	5-6-84	Y 487 RP 134	B	1985
Y 483 RP 130	B	10-8-84			

RP 125 (Y 478) Luciano Grazioli, 2004

D: 78 tons (120 fl) **S:** 9.5 kts **Dim:** 19.85 (17.00 pp) × 5.20 × 2.10
M: 1 Fiat-AIFO 828-SM diesel; 1 prop; 368 bhp **Electric:** 28 kw
Range: 400/9.5 **Crew:** 3 tot.

Remarks: 76 grt. First six ordered 18-8-83. One 120-m^3/hr water cannon. Sister RP 127 (Y 480) was transferred to Tunisia early in 2003.

♦ 10 RP 113–class small harbor tugs [YTL]

Bldr: C.N. Visitini, Donada

	In serv.		In serv.
Y 463 RP 113	1978	Y 471 RP 120	1980
Y 464 RP 114	1980	Y 472 RP 121	1980
Y 465 RP 115	1980	Y 473 RP 122	1980
Y 466 RP 116	1980	Y 474 RP 123	1980
Y 470 RP 119	1980	Y 475 RP 124	1981

Remarks: Characteristics similar to RP 101 class, but with a larger superstructure. Details differ. RP 117 (Y 467) and RP 118 (Y 468) deleted, date not available. All normally have a crew of three.

SERVICE CRAFT *(continued)*

RP 115 (Y 465) Luciano Grazioli, 2-05

♦ 12 RP 101–class small harbor tugs [YTL]
Bldr: C.N. Visitini-Loreo, Donada (In serv. 1972–75)

Y 403 RP 101	Y 408 RP 105	Y 456 RP 109
Y 404 RP 102	Y 410 RP 106	Y 458 RP 110
Y 406 RP 103	Y 413 RP 107	Y 460 RP 111
Y 407 RP 104	Y 452 RP 108	Y 462 RP 112

RP 109 (Y 456) Paolo Marsan, 7-02

D: 36 tons (75 fl) **S:** 12 kts **Dim:** 18.8 × 4.5 × 1.9 **M:** 1 diesel; 270 bhp

♦ 3 VF 681–class fireboats [YTR] Bldr: C.N. De Poli, Pellestrina

VF 681 (In serv. 7-89)
VF 682 (In serv. 18-11-89)
VF 683 Enrico Squarcina (In serv. . . .)

Enrico Squarcina (VF 683) H&L Van Ginderen, 10-98

Remarks: First two serve at Venice. Have red hulls with white superstructures. Two fire monitors are fitted atop the stack structure and a third on the bow. No data available.

♦ 4 VF 444–class fireboats [YTR] Bldr: . . . (In serv. . . .)

VF 441 Massimo Inzan VF 442 VF 443 VF 444

VF 444 H&L Van Ginderen, 10-96

Remarks: No data available.

♦ 4 or more MEN 223–class fireboats [YTR]

MEN 223 MEN 224 MEN 233 MEN 234

MEN 233 Luciano Grazioli, 2-98

Remarks: Smaller version of the VF 681 class. Have an articulating boom-mounted fire monitor aft and another fire monitor on the foredeck. No data available.

Note: Other fireboats in service include the large VF 543 and the tiny VF 51.

♦ 2 sail-training ketches [YTS] Bldr: . . .

A . . . Aquarius (In serv. 6-94) A 5323 Orsa Maggiore (In serv. 30-1-94)

Orsa Maggiore (A 5323) Luciano Grazioli, 2-05

Remarks: Both of 70 tons; no other data available. A 5323 was assigned to the naval academy at Livorno on 30-12-94 and has made several world cruises.

♦ 1 Meattini-class presidential yacht [YTS]
Bldr: Italcraft, Gaeta (In serv, 1971–72)

Argo (Ex-MEN 209)

Argo—former tender now used as a presidential yacht Luciano Grazioli, 4-93

SERVICE CRAFT *(continued)*

D: 65 tons (fl) **S:** 34 kts **Dim:** 22.0 × 5.0 × 1.5
A: None **Electronics:** Radar: 1 Furuno . . . nav.
M: 2 CRM 18D-S2 diesels; 2 props; 2,500 bhp
Range: 560/21 **Fuel:** 5.8 tons **Crew:** 7 tot.

Remarks: Used as a presidential yacht. Superstructure is painted blue and white. Same hull and propulsion as the customs service's *Meattini* class, but has enlarged superstructure. Has a commercial SATCOM terminal. Previously employed as a service craft and tender.

♦ 1 RORC-class cruising yacht [YTS]
Bldr: Sangermani, Chiavari (In serv. 7-10-65)

A 5313 Stella Polare

Stella Polare (A 5313) Bernard Prézelin, 8-02

D: 41 tons (47 fl) **S:** . . . **Dim:** 20.9 × 4.7 × 2.9
M: 1 Mercedes-Benz diesel; 1 prop; 96 bhp—197 m^2 max. sail area
Crew: 2 officers, 14 cadets

Remarks: Based at the naval academy, Livorno.

♦ 1 sail-training yawl [YTS]
Bldr: Sparkman & Stevens, U.S.A. (In serv. 1963)

A 5322 Capricia

D: 49.9 tons net **S:** . . . kts **Dim:** 22.54 × 5.05 × . . .
M: 1 G.M. Detroit Diesel diesel; 160 bhp—254 m^2 max. sail area

Remarks: Donated by Italian Senator Agnelli and commissioned 1-94 for use at the La Spezia sailing club when the yard building the *Cristoforo Colombo II* went bankrupt.

♦ 1 sail-training yawl [YTS]
Bldr: Costaguta, Genoa (In serv. 5-1-61)

A 5316 Corsaro II

D: 41 tons **S:** . . . kts **Dim:** 20.9 × 4.7
Electronics: Radar: 1 Decca 060
M: 1 auxiliary engine; 96 bhp—205 m^2 max. sail area
Crew: 2 officers, 14 cadets

Remarks: Based at naval academy, Livorno. Very similar to *Stella Polare* (A 5313).

♦ 1 sail-training yawl [YTS]
Bldr: C.N. Baglietto, Varazze (In serv. 16-10-48)

A 5302 Caroly

D: 50.9 tons (60 fl) **S:** 9 kts (6.5 power) **Dim:** 26.60 (23.75 pp) × 4.80 × 3.10
M: 1 G.M. Detroit Diesel diesel; 100 bhp—210 m^2 max. sail area
Fuel: 1,390 liters **Crew:** 13 officers, 3 enlisted

Remarks: Donated to navy 25-4-83.

Note: There are also a number of smaller sail-training craft in use by the Sezioni Veliche, the local branch of Marivela, the Italian Navy's sporting organization, including the sloop *Scorpione* and boats named *Aquilante, Barracuda, Calypso, Gabbiano, Galatea, Gemini, Grifone Bianco, Murena, Pellicano, Penelope, Quadrante, Sestante, Ussaro,* and *Zeffiro.*

♦ 3 GGS 1010–class small water lighters [YW]
Bldr: C.N. De Poli, Pellestrina, Venice (In serv. 2-90 to 2-91)

GGS 1013 GGS 1014 GGS 1017

GGS 1015—since stricken Luciano Grazioli, 5-01

D: Approx. 700 tons (fl) **S:** 11 kts **Dim:** 39.10 (37.50 pp) × 8.50 × 3.10
M: 2 AIFO 8281 SRM 08 diesels; 2 props; 544 bhp **Crew:** 12 tot.

Remarks: 508 dwt. Cargo: 500 m^3. Four sisters serve as fuel tankers. Have a lower superstructure than the fuel-carrier version and a 4.00-m molded depth.

♦ 1 small water lighter [YW]
Bldr: . . . (In serv. . . .)

A 5359 Bormida (Ex-GGS 1011)

D: 471 tons (fl) **S:** 7 kts **Dim:** 40.2 × 7.2 × 2.2
M: 2 . . . diesels; 1 prop; 130 bhp **Crew:** 6 tot.

Remarks: Former yard fuel lighter, converted to water tanker in 1974. Cargo capacity: 260 tons. Used only in local service.

♦ 5 GGS 172–class water barges [YWN]

GGS 172 GGS 173 GGS 175 GGS 178 XI

Remarks: All of about 500 tons capacity. Also in use are five water barges in the GGS 502–507 series.

♦ 4 TIRMA Project navigational training craft [YXT]
Bldr: . . .

D: 120–140 tons (fl) **S:** . . . kts **Dim:** 33.00 × . . . × . . .
Electronics: Radar: . . .
M: 2 diesels; 2 props; . . . bhp

Remarks: Were to be ordered in 2000 for delivery starting in 2001 to replace the *Aragosta* class at the naval academy; as of 2003, however, no contract had been announced. Will have composite construction hulls and very extensive navigational aids and communications suites, but no armament.

♦ 3 Aragosta-class training craft [YXT]

	Bldr	L	In serv.
A 5379 Astice (ex-M 5452)	CRDA, Monfalcone	16-1-57	19-7-57
A 5380 Mitilo (ex-M 5459)	Picchiotti, Viareggio	1-6-57	11-7-57
A 5382 Porpora (ex-M 5464)	Costaguta, Voltri	1-6-57	10-7-57

SERVICE CRAFT *(continued)*

Porpora (A 5382) Antonio Scrimali via L. Grazioli, 2003

D: 120 tons (178 fl) **S:** 13.5 kts **Dim:** 32.35 × 6.47 × 2.14
A: None **Electronics:** Radar: 1 BX-732 nav.
M: 2 Fiat-MTU MB 820D diesels; 2 props; 1,000 bhp **Electric:** 340 kw
Range: 2,000/9 **Fuel:** 15 tons **Crew:** 2 officers, 13 enlisted

Remarks: Former inshore minesweepers of a design based on the British "Ham"-class design. Originally 20 in the class. Built with U.S. Military Assistance Program funds. Wooden construction. The single 20-mm AA forward has been removed. A 5382 was reclassified 1984–85 for use as an administrative tender and navigational training craft at the naval academy. *Murena* (A 5305) still serves as a torpedo trials and retriever craft [YAGE].
Disposals: *Aragosta* (A 5378, ex-M 5450) and *Polipo* (A 5381, ex-M 5463) were stricken 17-7-02 and transferred to Tunisia.

Note: There are a large number of harbor service craft, launches, and so forth with hull numbers in the G, GAA, GAS, GD, GGS, GHIF, GT, GTM, MCN, MDN, MEN, and VS series. Open barges [YC] GD 325–328, 18.0 × 5.97 m, were laid down 1989 by C.N. Vernaglione, Taranto (GD 328 by C.N. Balsamo, Brindisi). GHIF 261, 20.00 × 5.00 m, was laid down 10-8-89 by Vernaglione, Taranto. G 14, a sullage barge, was delivered 5-90 by C.N. Solimano, Savona.

COAST GUARD
(*Guardia Costiera*)

The Guardia Costiera was created as a branch of the Port Captain Corps (*Comando Generale delle Capitanerie di Porto*) of the Italian Navy on 8-6-89 and operates under the control of the Ministry of Transport and Navigation in peacetime and the navy in wartime; it has police, fisheries protection, oil-spill recovery, and SAR duties. The Guardia Costiera is the Italian agency responsible for rescue at sea under the Hamburg International Convention of 27-8-49.

Personnel: Approx. 8,457 tot. (1,185 officers). Two teams of frogmen, one based at Naples and one at San Benedetto del Tronto.

Organization: Coast guard headquarters are at Rome, and there are 13 Maritime Districts and 13 Maritime Area Operations Commands; additionally, there are 48 harbor offices, 44 maritime district offices, 140 local maritime offices, three fixed-wing air bases, one helicopter base, two Loran-C stations, one SARSAT station, and six antipollution operations centers.

Aviation: Two ATR-42-420MP and 14 Piaggio P-166DL3/SEM fixed-wing aircraft for surveillance duties and 12 AB-412EP helicopters. The three Gruppi Aerei are based at Sarzana/Luni, Catania/Fontanarossa, and Pescara.

Guardia Costiera Piaggio P-166DL3/SEM Luciano Grazioli, 10-04

Armament: Guardia Costiera ships and craft are normally unarmed, but a 25-mm OTO Melara KBA is mounted on the *Saettia,* a 20-mm cannon can be installed on the CP 409, CP 405, and CP 401 classes, and 7.62-mm machineguns can be installed on CP 200– and CP 300–series boats. Smaller boats can carry submachineguns and Franchi SPAS 15 riot guns.

Note: All units now have white hulls and lower superstructures. All have a broad red diagonal hull stripe, with narrow white and green trailing diagonals; within the red stripe is a black anchor in a white circle. The words "*Guardia Costiera*" have replaced "*Capitanerie*" on the hull sides. Hull numbers are in red. Decks are dark green or light gray.

Guardia Costiera AgustaWestland-Bell AB-412EP Piet Sinke, 8-05

PATROL CRAFT [WPC]

◆ 5 Michele Fiorillo class
Bldr: Fincantieri, Muggiano

	In serv.		In serv.
CP 902 Ubaldo Diciotti	20-7-02	CP 905 Alfredo Peluso	3-7-03
CP 903 Luigi Dattilo	30-11-02	CP 906 Oreste Corsi	8-1-04
CP 904 Michele Fiorillo	1-03		

Ubaldo Diciotti (CP 902) Luciano Grazioli, 9-04

Oreste Corsi (CP 906) Luciano Grazioli, 5-05

Luigi Dattilo (CP 903)—sailing alongside two sisters Luciano Grazioli, 9-04

D: 340 tons light (427 fl) **S:** 32 kts (29 sust.)
Dim: 52.85 (47.20 pp) × 8.10 × . . .
A: 1 25-mm OTO Melara KBA AA (1 12.7-mm mg initially)
Electronics: Radar: 2 Gem SPN-753XS(V)2 nav. (X- and S-band)
M: 4 Isotta-Fraschini V1716 T2MSD diesels; 4 CP props; 12,660 bhp (at 2,030 rpm)—bow-thruster
Electric: 624 kw tot. (3 × 208 kw, Isotta Fraschini L1306 T2ME diesels driving)
Range: . . . / . . . **Crew:** 3 officers, 27 enlisted

Remarks: Three ordered 14-9-00, with an option for a fourth and fifth later taken up. Revised version of the *Saettia* as modified for Guardia Costiera work; will have flush deck, cleared aft for helicopter hovering access. Nonretractable fin stabilizers are fitted. Will carry an Achille M-4 remotely operated surveillance submersible with a 300-m operating depth. The names for CP 902 and CP 903 were switched during 2-02. CP 902 was launched on 8-4-02, CP 904 on 30-11-02, and CP 906 in 9-03.

COAST GUARD PATROL CRAFT [WPC] *(continued)*

♦ 1 Saettia class
Bldr: Fincantieri, Muggiano

	Laid down	L	In serv.
CP 901 Saettia	6-84	12-84	12-85

Saettia (CP 901) Luciano Grazioli, 5-05

D: 322 tons light (392 normal; 427 fl) **S:** 40 kts (37.5 sust.)
Dim: 51.70 (47.20 pp) × 8.10 × 2.15
A: 1 25-mm OTO Melara KBA AA
Electronics: Radar: 2 Gem SPN-753SX(V)2 nav.
M: 4 MTU 16V538 TB93 diesels; 4 props; 17,600 bhp (16,560 sust.)
Electric: 450 kw tot. (3 × 150-kw Isotta-Fraschini ID38 SS6V diesel sets)
Range: 1,800/18 **Endurance:** 12 days **Crew:** 29 tot.

Remarks: Built as a demonstrator for Fincantieri's DA-360T-design guided-missile patrol craft and never acquired by the Italian or any foreign navy despite attempts to sell her. Laid up since the early 1990s, she was acquired by the coast guard and modified by the builder, delivered on 20-7-99. The original armament of one 76-mm OTO Melara Compact gun, a twin 40-mm 70-cal. Dardo AA mount, and four Otomat SSMs has been removed, along with the associated fire-control radars. A modified mast was fitted during 2000 and the gun during 2001. Based at Messina.

♦ 1 CP 409–class high-endurance patrol and rescue craft
Bldr: CNR, Ancona (In serv. 1992)

CP 409 Giulio Ingianni

Giulio Ingianni (CP 409) Luciano Grazioli, 4-04

D: 196 tons normal (205 fl) **S:** 21 kts **Dim:** 34.60 × 7.15 × 2.20
A: Provision for 1 20-mm 70-cal. Oerlikon AA
Electronics: Radar: 1 Decca 20V90 ARPA nav.; 1 Decca 2050/6 nav.
M: 2 Isotta-Fraschini ID36 SS16V.200 diesels; 2 KaMeWa CP props; 2,910 bhp
Range: 1,000/18 **Crew:** 13 tot.

Remarks: Ordered in 1991. Steel hull with light alloy superstructure. Carries a U.S.-made Boston Whaler Outrage-19 5.8-m launch powered by two 60-bhp Yamaha outboards. Has an electrohydraulic telescoping crane to assist in recovery, a firefighting water monitor on the mast platform, and a stern wedge to improve speed and fuel economy. Equipped with Vosper fin stabilizers. Has a Racal Decca GPS receiver, a Taiyo TL 900A Loran-C receiver, and MF, VHF, and UHF D/F receivers.

♦ 4 CP 405–class high-endurance patrol and rescue craft
Bldr: Bacino di Carenaggio SpA, Trapani (In serv. 1991–92)

CP 405 Francesco Mazzinghi	CP 407 Michele Lolini
CP 406 Antonio Scialoia	CP 408 Mario Grabar

Mario Grabar (CP 408) Luciano Grazioli, 9-04

Michele Lolini (CP 407) Luciano Grazioli, 9-04

D: 136 tons (fl) **S:** 24 kts **Dim:** 29.50 × 6.70 × 1.83
Electronics: Radar: 1 Decca . . . ARPA nav.
M: 2 Isotta-Fraschini ID36 SS8V diesels; 2 props; 6,500 bhp
Range: 1,000/ . . . **Crew:** 16 tot. + 50 rescuees

Remarks: Steel hull with light alloy superstructure. No "daughter boat" rescue craft. Have two water cannon for fire fighting. CP 408 launched 31-3-90, CP 406 the following month. Have GPS and Loran-C receivers, plus HF, VHF, and UHF D/F equipment. CP 405 and CP 406 were modernized and re-engined during 1998–99, CP 407 during 1999–2000, and CP 408 during 2001, all with new superstructures and electronics and two new engines in place of the original four CRM 12D/SS diesels totaling 5,500 bhp.

♦ 4 CP 401–class high-endurance patrol and rescue craft
Bldr: CNR, Ancona (In serv. 1987–91)

CP 401 Oreste Cavallari	CP 403 Walter Fachin
CP 402 Renato Pennetti	CP 404 Gaetano Magliano

Gaetano Magliano (CP 404) Luciano Grazioli, 12-00

D: 100 tons (fl) **S:** 22 kts **Dim:** 28.60 × 6.20 × 2.00
Electronics: Radar: 1 Decca . . . ARPA nav.; 1 . . . nav.
M: 4 Isotta-Fraschini ID36 SS8V diesels; 2 props; 3,520 bhp
Range: 1,000/ . . . **Crew:** 11 tot. + 50 rescuees

Remarks: Carry a 3.8-ton, 8.00 × 2.40 × 0.70-m "daughter boat" for rescue work on ramp aft. Can be equipped to carry one 20-mm AA and two 7.62-mm mg. All are named for former members of the Port Captain Corps of the Italian Navy who died or were wounded during World War II or were lost at sea. CP 403 delivered 1-9-90. Have fin stabilizers. Carry Loran-C and GPS receivers and HF and VHF D/F gear.

PATROL BOATS [WPB]

♦ 30 Class 200 patrol boats
Bldr: C.N. Rodriquez SpA, Messina

	In serv.		In serv.		In serv.
CP 265	21-2-01	CP 275	2002	CP 285	2003
CP 266	22-6-01	CP 276	2002	CP 286	2003
CP 267	22-6-01	CP 277	2002	CP 287	16-12-04
CP 268	18-10-01	CP 278	2002	CP 288	8-4-05
CP 269	2001	CP 279	2002	CP 289	13-4-05
CP 270	. . .	CP 280	16-12-02	CP 290	2005
CP 271	. . .	CP 281	16-12-02	CP 291	5-8-05
CP 272	. . .	CP 282	16-12-02	CP 292	4-8-05
CP 273	. . .	CP 283	. . .	CP 293	2005
CP 274	. . .	CP 284	12-2-04	CP 294	2005

D: 42.3 tons light (53.2 max. fl) **S:** 34 kts **Dim:** 25.00 (22.00 wl) × 5.76 × 0.92
Electronics: Radar: 1 Gem SPN-753X nav.
M: 3 Isotta-Fraschini V1312 T2 diesels; 2 props + centerline waterjet; 3,600 bhp (2,958 sust.)
Electric: 88 kw tot. (2 × 44-kw diesel sets)
Range: 630/31; 690/28; 730/25; 900/18 **Fuel:** 12.6 m^3 **Crew:** . . . tot.

COAST GUARD PATROL BOATS [WPB] *(continued)*

CP 289 Luciano Grazioli, 3-05

CP 279 Luciano Grazioli, 9-04

Remarks: Twenty-five were ordered in late 1999 for delivery within 30 months; option for five additional included in contract. Aluminum construction. Carry a 4.5-m rigid inflatable inspection launch with a 45-bhp gasoline outboard motor. Have SOLIS-SART satellite beacon system, D/F loop, and GPS. CP 267, CP 268 and four sisters will reportedly be transferred to Iraq during 2007.

♦ 4 CP 261–class GRP-construction patrol launches
Bldr: Intermarine, La Spezia (In serv. 1-00)

CP 261 CP 262 CP 263 CP 264

D: 30 tons **S:** 30 kts **Dim:** 16.4 × 4.5 × 1.0
M: 2 M.A.N. D22482 LE 4012 diesels; 2 props; 2,000 bhp
Range: 300/ . . . **Crew:** 5 tot.

♦ 3 CP 256–class inshore patrol launches
Bldr: Italcraft, Gaeta (In serv. 1985–89)

CP 256 CP 257 CP 258

CP 256 Guy Schaeffer via Paolo Marsan, 10-03

D: 20.75 tons (23.7 fl) **S:** 33 kts **Dim:** 16.00 × 5.25 (4.98 wl) × 0.98
Electronics: Radar: 1 . . . nav.
M: 2 CRM 12D/S-2 diesels; 2 Riva-Calzoni IRC 43 DC waterjets; 1,700 bhp
Range: 350/24 **Fuel:** 3,500 liters **Crew:** 7 tot.

Remarks: GRP hull. Have Loran-C receivers and an echo sounder.

♦ 4 CP 254–class inshore patrol launches
Bldr: Tecnomarine, Viareggio (In serv. 1984–89)

CP 254 CP 255 CP 259 CP 260

CP 254 Luciano Grazioli, 6-05

D: 21 tons (22.5 fl) **S:** 31 kts **Dim:** 15.10 × 5.25 × 0.98
Electronics: Radar: 1 . . . nav.
M: 2 Isotta-Fraschini ID36 SS6V diesels; 2 Riva-Calzoni IRC-43-DL waterjets; 1,520 hp
Range: 320/24 **Crew:** 7 tot.

Remarks: GRP hull. Have Loran-C receivers and an echo sounder.

♦ 8 CP 246/247–class Canav-design inshore patrol launches
Bldrs: CP 246: Navaltecnica, Anzio; others: Canados Navale, Ostia Lido, Rome

CP 246 (In serv. 1977) CP 247 through CP 253 (In serv. 1980–81)

CP 248 Luciano Grazioli, 9-02

D: 22 tons (fl) **S:** 27–30 kts **Dim:** 15.00 × 4.85 × 1.60
A: Small arms **Electronics:** Radar: 1 . . . nav.
M: 2 Isotta-Fraschini ID36 SS6V diesels; 2 props; 1,380 bhp
Range: 350/ . . . **Crew:** 7 tot.

Remarks: CP 246 is considered to be a separate class, and the others are essentially of an improved version. Wooden hulls. All have VHF and HF/SSB D/F gear.

Disposal note: The remaining CP 239–class inshore patrol launches are no longer in service. CP 242 was decommissioned on 30-9-02 and stricken on 31-12-02; CP 239, 243, 244, and 245 were decommissioned in 2004.

♦ 2 CP 231 (Super Speranza)–class inshore patrol launches
Bldr: Rodriguez, Messina (In serv. 1966–70)

CP 237 CP 238

CP 238 Luciano Grazioli, 8-00

COAST GUARD PATROL BOATS [WPB] *(continued)*

D: 14 tons (16 fl) **S:** 26 kts **Dim:** 13.40 × 4.80 × 1.30
Electronics: Radar: 1 . . . nav.
M: 2 AIFO 8281 SRM diesels; 2 props; 900 bhp
Range: 400/ . . . **Crew:** 7 tot.

Remarks: Wooden construction. Both have been re-engined.
Disposals: CP 231 and CP 236 were decommissioned on 30-9-01 and stricken on 31-12-01. CP 235 was stricken on 31-5-01. CP 234 was decommissioned during 2002. CP 234, CP 235, and CP 236 were transferred to Albania on 18-6-02. CP 233 was decommissioned in late 2003.

Disposal note: The last CP 228–class inshore patrol launch (CP 230) was decommissioned in the fourth quarter of 2002 while sister CP 229 was decommissioned in 2001 and transferred to Albania on 18-6-02.

AUXILIARIES

♦ 1 U.S. Cherokee-class oceanographic research ship [WAGOR]
Bldr: Charleston Shipbuilding and Dry Dock, Charleston, S.C.

	Laid down	L	In serv.
CP 451 Bannock (ex-ATF 81)	3-8-42	7-1-43	28-6-43

Bannock (CP 451) Luciano Grazioli, 8-00

D: 1,278 tons (1,675 fl) **S:** 16 kts
Dim: 62.57 (59.59 pp) × 11.73 (11.97 over fenders) × 4.10
Electronics: Radar: 1 AMS . . . nav.; 1 Koden . . . nav.
M: 4 G.M. Electromotive Div. 12-278 diesels, 2 × 1,800-kw M1B 315 MC alternators, 1 VM 1316 TI MH 14 electric motor; 1 prop; 3,000 shp—150-shp bow-thruster
Electric: 300 kw tot. (3 × 100-kw d.c. diesel sets)
Range: 12,000/10 **Fuel:** 300 tons **Endurance:** 60 days **Crew:** 25 tot.

Remarks: 1,277 grt/866 dwt. Former U.S. Navy fleet tug transferred to Italy on loan in 10-62 for the CNR–Navi Armemento Oceanographiche by Fratelli Cosulich SpA, Genoa, and converted 1963–64 by O.A.R.N., Genoa, to serve as a research ship in the Mediterranean. Acquired 12-92 for the Guardia Costiera and now operated in support of the University of Tor Vergata. Retains her original U.S. Navy name, for an Indian tribe in southern Idaho.
Hull systems: Has one 2-ton derrick. Has Koden KS 5150 and Lodestar 2460 D/F receivers, JRC Inmarsat tranceiver and Navstar 602S NAVSAT receiver, Koden LR 770 Loran-C receiver, and Decca 10350 automatic plot.

SERVICE CRAFT

♦ 1 ex-Italian Navy oceanographic research craft [WYAG]
Bldr: Navalmeccanico Senigallia (In serv. 1975)

CP 452 Barbara (ex-P 492)

Barbara (CP 452) H&L Van Ginderen, 2-00

D: 180 tons (190 fl) **S:** 9 kts **Dim:** 30.50 × 6.30 × 2.40
Electronics: 1 Gem BX-732 nav.
M: 2 Fiat-AIFO 828 SRM diesels; 2 props; 600 bhp
Range: 2,000/9 **Crew:** 8 tot.

Remarks: Purchased in 1975 by the Italian Navy for use in oceanographic research and in support of missile tests, but used from 1986 to 1996 as a range patrol craft at Sardinia. Transferred to the Guardia Costiera early in 1998 and operated as a training, oceanographic research craft in cooperation with the University of Cagliari. Has a 7.5-ton electrohydraulic crane at the stern.

Disposal note: The 20-ton research craft CP 453, loaned to the coast guard for ecological research in 1999, was handed over to the receiver when the craft's sponsor, the Polo Tecnologico Mercantile Marittimo, went bankrupt.

♦ 3 miscellaneous pollution-control craft [WYAG]

CP 09 CP 12 CP 18

CP 09 A. A. de Kruijf, 6-04

Remarks: No data available. CP 18 is largest of the three and CP 12 is a catamaran with debris collection gear between the hulls.
Disposals: CP 3 was retired in 1995 and CP 13 in 1998. CP 7, CP 8, CP 16, and CP 19 were decommissioned on 28-2-01 and stricken on 31-5-01.

♦ 26 "2000 44-foot"–class Keith Nelson–design harbor launches [WYFL]
Bldr: CP 2084–2103: Tencara, Venice; CP 2104–2109: . . . , Le Spezia

	In serv.		In serv.
CP 2084	10-8-01	CP 2097	2002
CP 2085	10-8-01	CP 2098	2002
CP 2086	11-10-01	CP 2099	2003
CP 2087	11-10-01	CP 2100	2003
CP 2088	2002	CP 2101	2003
CP 2089	2002	CP 2102	27-2-03
CP 2090	2002	CP 2103	23-3-03
CP 2091	2002	CP 2104	15-3-05
CP 2092	2002	CP 2105	15-3-05
CP 2093	2002	CP 2106	15-3-05
CP 2094	2002	CP 2107	28-4-05
CP 2095	2002	CP 2108	21-7-03
CP 2096	2002	CP 2109	12-8-05

CP 2088 Luciano Grazioli, 8-04

D: 11.7 tons normal (14.23 fl) **S:** 23.4 kts (20 sust.) **Dim:** 13.50 × 3.96 × 1.30
M: 2 IVECO AIFO 8460 RM 50 diesels; 2 props; 750 bhp
Range: 444/20 **Crew:** 4 tot.

Remarks: Will replace earlier Keith Nelson harbor launches. Hulls are molded in GRP by Halmatic division of Vosper Thornycroft in the U.K. The upper hull and interior design is derived from that of CP 2024.

♦ 56+ Keith Nelson–design harbor launches [WYFL]

	Bldr	In serv.
CP 2025	Keith Nelson, Viareggio	1975–76
CP 2035	Motomar, Lavagna	1975–76
CP 2036–2045	Keith Nelson, Viareggio	1976–78
CP 2046–2048	Motomar, Palermo	1978
CP 2049–2065	Balsamo, Brindisi	1978–79
CP 2066–2068	C.N. La Spezia	1980
CP 2069–2077	Balsamo, Brindisi	1980–83
CP 2078–2083	Mericraft, Baia, Naples	1985
CP 2084–2087	. . .	2001
CP 2201–2205	Motomar, Palermo	1986

COAST GUARD SERVICE CRAFT *(continued)*

CP 2038 Bernard Prézelin, 4-05

CP 2063 Guy Schaeffer via Paolo Marsan, 12-03

D: 11–15 tons **S:** 14–22 kts **Dim** (typical): 12.57 × 3.64 × 1.10
M: 2 AIFO V85, V85M, or 828M, Cummins V504M or VT8-370M, Isotta-Fraschini ID32 SS6L, ID32 SS6LM, or 6L diesels; 2 props; 420–800 bhp
Range: 400/ . . . **Crew:** 4 tot.

Remarks: A relatively homogenous group of GRP-hulled craft based on a British pilot-boat design, with numerous variations in superstructure and propulsion plants. CP 2025, 2032–2048 and 2201–2205 carry Pirelli self-inflating Type CP 65 rescue rafts in stern recesses. All have VHF (FM) D/F, a Loran-C receiver, and an echo sounder. CP 2084–2087 were completed, two on 10-8-01 and two on 11-10-01.
Disposals: CP 2016 was retired in 1997 and CP 2022 on 31-3-01. CP 2001, 2003–2006, 2008–2010, 2013, 2015, 2018, and 2019 were decommissioned 30-9-01 and stricken 31-12-01, with CP 2010 transferred to Albania on 18-6-02. CP 2007, 2011, 2020, 2023, and 2034 were decommissioned in 2002. CP 2002, 2012, 2014, 2017, 2021, and 2026–2033 were decommissioned on 30-9-03 and stricken on 31-12-03. CP 2024 has been retired from service by 2005.

♦ 10 CP 6001–class harbor launches [WYFL]
Bldr: Benetti/Azimut, Viareggio

CP 6013, CP 6014 (In serv. 14-11-88) CP 6015–6022 (In serv. 1988)

CP 6017 Paolo Marsan, 8-03

D: 3.72 tons **S:** 22–24 kts **Dim:** 8.00 × 2.50 × 0.50
Electronics: Radar: 1 . . . nav.
M: 2 VM 4R692-H9 diesels; 2 Castoldi 06 waterjets; 180 bhp
Range: 180/22 **Crew:** 3 crew + 4 passengers

Remarks: GRP, "unsinkable"-construction craft for use in shallow waters.
Disposals: CP 6003–6006, 6008, 6009, and 6012 were decommissioned 30-9-01 and stricken 31-12-01; CP 6002, 6007, and 6010 were decommissioned 30-9-02 and stricken 31-12-02; and CP 6011 was decommissioned 30-9-03.

♦ 8 CP 524–class harbor launches [WYFL]
Bldr: C.N. Vittoria, Rovigo (In serv. 29-11-99 to 5-12-00)

From among CP 524–CP 539

D: 6.5 tons (7.5 fl) **S:** 34 kts **Dim:** 9.73 × 3.50 × 0.70
M: 2 Isotta-Fraschini L1306 T2 diesels; 2 Castoldi 06 waterjets; 870 bhp
Range: 250/34 **Crew:** 3 tot.

Remarks: Eight remain in service from the numbers listed above.

♦ 49 CP 512–class GRP-hulled harbor launches [WYFL]

	Bldr.	In serv.
CP 512–CP 523	C.N. del Golfo, Gaeta	1-11-97 to 2-7-98
CP 540–CP 564	Cantiere Tencara, Porto Marghera	6-4-01-2003
CP 565–CP 576	C.N. Stanisci	2004

CP 553 Piet Sinke, 8-05

CP 515 Luciano Grazioli, 4-05

D: 6.5 tons (7.5 fl) **S:** 34 kts **Dim:** 9.73 × 3.50 × 0.70
M: 2 Isotta-Fraschini ID32 SS62M diesels; 2 props; 600 bhp
Range: 250/34 **Crew:** 3 tot.

Remarks: Same design as CP 506 class except for having propellers instead of waterjets; there are minor differences between the boats built by the different builders. The CP 565 group was ordered during 2001.

♦ 6 CP 506–class GPR-hulled harbor launches [WYFL]
Bldr: C.N. del Golfo, Gaeta (In serv. 1990)

CP 506 through CP 511

D: 6.5 tons (7.5 fl) **S:** 34 kts **Dim:** 9.73 × 3.50 × 0.70
M: 2 Isotta-Fraschini ID32 SS62M diesels; 2 Castoldi 06 waterjets; 600 bhp
Range: 250/34 **Crew:** 3 tot.

Disposal note: Harbor launch CP 501 was retired 31-3-01. CP 502–class harbor launches CP 502 and CP 503 were retired 30-9-01 and stricken 31-12-01. CP 504–class harbor launches CP 504 and CP 505 were decommissioned during 2002. All six harbor launches of the CP 1001 class (CP 1001 through CP 1006) were decommissioned 30-9-01 and stricken 31-12-01.

COAST GUARD SERVICE CRAFT *(continued)*

CP 511 H&L Van Ginderen, 9-91

♦ 30 CP 5001-series fast launches [WYFL]

	Bldr	In serv.
CP 5002, 5008	Vasnautica, Milan	1969–71
CP 5013, 5014, 5016–5020, 5029, 5032, 5038–5041, 5043	Marine Union, Milan	1973–79
CP 5034, 5035, 5037, 5045, 5050	Motomar, Milan	1973–79
CP 5053, 5054	Marine Union, Milan	1971
CP 5056, 5057	Motomar, Milan	1973
CP 5059–5060	Misc.	1988, 1990
CP 5062–5064	Misc.	1988–90

	Speed	Dim	Horsepower
CP 5002, 5008	24 kts	5.30 × 2.13 × 0.30	80–100 bhp
CP 5013 group	28–30 kts	6.50 × 2.20 × 0.30	130–140 bhp
CP 5034 group	22 kts	5.20 × 2.18 × 0.30	75–85 bhp + 20 bhp aux.

CP 5041 A. A. de Kruijf, 6-04

Remarks: All GRP construction. Powered by two Mercury or Yamaha gasoline outboard motors. Normal crew is two. All but CP 5038–5040 and CP 5054 carry two Pirelli CP 25 self-inflating rescue rafts. CP 5005, 5006, 5021, 5052, and 5058 are exhibited on land as gate guards at various stations.

♦ 7 shallow-draft launches [WYFL]

CP 115 (Vio, 1969): 9.00 × 2.20 × 0.70; 25 kts; 1 AIFO diesel, 145 bhp
CP 117–119 (1974): 7.17 × 2.28; 20 kts; 95 bhp
CP 121 (Oscar, 1985): 9.20 × 2.34 × 0.70; 21 kts; 1 AIFO diesel, 132 bhp
CP 122 (De Poli, 1991): 21.52 × 3.75 × 1.25; 25 kts; 1 AIFO diesel, 220 bhp
CP 123 (Cucchini, 1992): 9.15 × 2.29 × 0.30; 25 kts; 1 AIFO diesel, 180 bhp

CP 122—steel construction, all others built of wood Luciano Grazioli, 5-04

Remarks: All of the above craft operate on the Venice lagoon. All are built of wood except CP 122, which is of steel construction.

♦ 8 CP 151-class shallow-draft launches [WYFL]

CP 151 through CP 158

Remarks: Waterjet propelled, built by Motomar Palermo.

♦ Approximately 150 miscellaneous small boats [WYFL]

From among GC 002/B–GC 211/B; GC A01–GC A08, GC 221 and others

GC 123/B—a typical Guardia Costiera RIB, powered by a single Mercury outboard Luciano Grazioli, 11-03

Remarks: Semi-rigid inflatable boats, including craft for the Gruppo Subacqueo frogman group. Several different designs with very similar characteristics. GC 210 and 211 entered service in 2002. GC 221, a Boston Whaler boat, entered service in 2003. GC A01 through GC A08 are model 910 Zodiac Hurricanes built in Canada and purchased in 2005.

♦ 3 CP 455-class ambulance boats [WYH]

Bldr: C.N. del Golfo, Gaeta (In serv. 1999)

CP 454 CP 455 CP 456

D: 19.4 tons (fl) **S:** 26 kts **Dim:** 16.40 × 4.55 × 1.20
M: 2 Isotta-Fraschini 1306L T2 diesels; 2 props; . . . bhp
Range: 400/ . . . **Crew:** . . .

Remarks: Equipped with a centerline stern gangway to facilitate moving patients from craft at sea and onto a pier.

♦ 4 CP 314-class medium-endurance rescue boats [WYH]

Bldr: C.N. Baglietto, Varezze (CP 318: Rodriquez, Messina)

CP 314 (L: 20-2-88) CP 317 (In serv. 1991)
CP 316 (In serv. . . .) CP 318 (In serv. 5-91)

CP 318 Luciano Grazioli, 3-97

D: 43.1 tons (45 fl) **S:** 20 kts **Dim:** 18.05 (17.96 wl) × 5.75 × 1.20
Electronics: Radar: 1 . . . nav.
M: 2 Deutz . . . diesels; 2 props; 1,700 bhp **Range:** 400/16
Crew: 7 tot. + 20 rescuees

Remarks: Sister CP 315 burned out and was scrapped. GRP construction with low amidships freeboard to facilitate rescues. Have fin stabilizers. Self-righting design. A total of 18 was planned at one time. Have a Loran-C receiver and HF and VHF D/F gear. All have been re-engined.

♦ 1 Vosper Thornycroft medium-endurance rescue boat [WYH]

Bldr: Keith Nelson Italia, Viareggio (In serv. 1977)

CP 313 Dante Novarro

D: 57 tons (fl) **S:** 21 kts **Dim:** 22.85 × 6.10 × 1.75
Electronics: Radar: 1 . . . nav.
M: 2 Isotta-Fraschini ID36 SS diesels; 2 props; 2,760 bhp
Range: 1,000/18 **Crew:** 11 tot.

Remarks: GRP hull. Has a Loran-C receiver and HF and VHF D/F gear.

COAST GUARD SERVICE CRAFT *(continued)*

Dante Novarro (CP 313) Luciano Grazioli, 2-90

Disposal note: The sole CP 307–class rescue lifeboat, *Michelle Fiorillo* (CP 307), was stricken 1-4-01. U.S. Coast Guard 44-ft. rescue lifeboat CP 304 was stricken 1-4-01, and CP 303 was decommissioned 30-9-01, stricken 31-12-01, and transferred to Albania 18-6-02. The remaining CP 301–class, wooden-hulled lifeboats of the Ogni Tempo series have been stricken, except for CP 301, on exhibit at Citavecchia. CP 312–class seagoing rescue lifeboat *Bruno Gregoretti* (CP 312) was retired during 2003.

♦ 6 CP 829 (Giubileo)–class inshore rescue lifeboats [WYH]

Bldr: C.N. Vittoria, Rovigo (In serv. 13-1-00 to 24-3-00)

CP 829 through CP 831 CP 836 through CP 838

CP 830 Paolo Marsan, 12-04

D: 12 tons normal (13 fl) **S:** 30 kts **Dim:** 12.73 × 4.30 × 0.90
Electronics: Radar: 1 . . . nav.
M: 2 Isotta-Fraschini L1306 T2MS DHSCV diesels; 2 KaMeWa FF310 waterjets; 1,086 bhp
Range: 160/16 **Crew:** 3 tot.

Remarks: Ordered in 2000. Intended to rescue passengers from commercial aircraft crashes at sea. Aluminum construction. Have eight 65-person encapsulated life rafts in quick-release racks on either side aft and a low fantail to assist in bringing survivors aboard. Loran-C receiver, autopilot, doppler log, echo sounder, and VHF (AM and FM) and HF/SSB D/F gear are fitted.

♦ 42 CP 825–class inshore rescue lifeboats [WYH]

Bldr. C.N. Vittoria, Rovigo (In serv. 23-11-99 through 2002)

CP 825 through CP 828 CP 839 through CP 862
CP 832 through CP 835 CP 872 through CP 881

CP 876 Bernard Prézelin, 4-05

D: 12 tons **S:** 30 kts **Dim:** 12.73 × 4.30 × 0.80
Electronics: Radar: 1 . . . nav.
M: 2 Isotta-Fraschini L130 T2MLL diesels; 2 KaMeWa FF 310 waterjets; 1,072 bhp
Range: 160/16 **Crew:** 3 tot.

Remarks: A faster version of the CP 814 class. CP 852 was commissioned on 16-3-01, CP 856 and CP 857 4-5-01, with the rest to be completed during 2001–2. CP 839 and later differ in having a rescue platform at the stern and in not carrying encapsulated life rafts.

♦ 11 CP 814–class inshore rescue lifeboats [WYH]

Bldr: C.N. Vittoria, Rovigo (In serv. 1-6-96 through 1-8-97)

CP 814 through CP 824

CP 818—with amidships rescue areas and rigid inflatable collar around the hull
Jasper Van Raemdonck, 6-99

D: 12.5 tons normal (13.5 fl) **S:** 32 kts (16 sust.) **Dim:** 11.85 × 4.10 × 0.80
Electronics: Radar: 1 . . . nav.
M: 2 Cummins 6 CTA 8.3 M2 Diamond diesels; 2 KaMeWa FF310 waterjets; 840 bhp
Range: 160/16 **Crew:** 3 tot.

Remarks: Builder's FRB 38 design. First two were delivered in 5-96, CP 819 in 9-96. Aluminum-hulled, self-righting design with rigid inflated rubber fender. Have a Loran-C receiver, autopilot, doppler log, echo sounder, and VHF (AM and FM) and HF/SSB D/F gear.

♦ 9 CP 863–class rigid inflatable inshore rescue craft [WYH]

Bldr: Codecasa Due SpA, Viareggio (In serv. 2001)

CP 863 CP 865 CP 867 CP 869 CP 871
CP 864 CP 866 CP 868 CP 870

CP 864 Piet Sinke, 7-05

D: 9.3 tons (normal) **S:** 30.5 kts **Dim:** 10.60 × 4.10 × 0.76
Electronics: 1 Seatrack SC 1204 nav.
M: 2 Volvo Penta TAMD 71B diesels; 2 Hamilton 291 waterjets; 748 bhp
Range: 180/30 **Crew:** 3 tot.

Remarks: Improved version of the CP 807 class, with an aluminum, self-righting hull and rubber inflated outer fender section. Carry two inflatable rafts, each with 64-person capacity.

♦ 7 CP 807–class rigid inflatable inshore rescue craft [WYH]

Bldr: Codecasa Due SpA, Viareggio (In serv. 1996)

CP 807 CP 809 CP 811 CP 813
CP 808 CP 810 CP 812

D: 9.3 tons (normal) **S:** 30.5 kts **Dim:** 10.60 × 4.10 × 0.76
Electronics: 1 Seatrack SC 1204 nav.
M: 2 Volvo Penta TAMD 71B diesels; 2 Hamilton 291 waterjets; 748 bhp
Range: 180/30 **Crew:** 3 tot.

COAST GUARD SERVICE CRAFT *(continued)*

Remarks: Improved version of the CP 801 class, with an aluminum, self-righting hull and rubber inflated outer fender section. Carry two inflatable rafts each with 64-person capacity.

♦ 3 CP 804–class rigid inflatable inshore rescue craft [WYH]

Bldr: Codecasa Due SpA, Viareggio (In serv. fall 1992–spring 1993)

CP 804 CP 805 CP 806

CP 806 Guy Schaeffer via Paolo Marsan, 12-03

D: 9.1 tons (normal) **S:** 30.6 kts **Dim:** 10.60 × 4.10 × 0.74
Electronics: 1 Seatrack SC 1204/RD nav.
M: 2 Volvo Penta TAMD 71B diesels; 2 Hamilton 291 waterjets; 748 bhp
Range: 180/30 **Crew:** 3 tot.

Remarks: Variant of the CP 801 design, with an enclosed pilothouse. Have an aluminum, self-righting hull and rubber outer section. Carry two inflatable rafts, each with 64-person capacity. Electronic equipment includes an Intermark intercoastal navigation system, Garmin 100 GPS receiver, and King DL 8008 log.

♦ 3 CP 801–class rigid inflatable inshore rescue craft [WYH]

CP 801 CP 802 CP 803

CP 801 MARICOGECAP, Rome, 1995

D: 9.1 tons (normal) **S:** 30.6 kts (29 sust.) **Dim:** 10.60 × 4.10 × 0.74
Electronics: 1 Seatrack SC 1204/RD nav.
M: 2 Volvo Penta TAMD 71B diesels; 2 Hamilton 291 waterjets; 748 bhp
Range: 180/29 **Fuel:** 970 liters **Crew:** 6 tot. + up to 40 rescued personnel

Remarks: The Dutch Damen Valentijn class, built under license. Have an aluminum, self-righting hull with an inflatable rubber outer section. Can be launched and recovered over a beach. Equipped with Garmin 100 GPS receivers, the Intermark coastal navigation system, an autopilot, a Loran-C receiver, a Furuno FE 4300 echo sounder, and a VHFD/F. Carry two inflatable rafts, each with 64-person capacity.

♦ 9 CP 701–class rigid inflatable inshore rescue craft [WYH]

Bldr: Novamarine Due, Olbia (In serv. 1992–93)

CP 701 through CP 709

D: 6 tons (fl) **S:** 30 kts **Dim:** 9.60 × 3.15 × 0.55
Electronics: Radar: 1 Seatrack SC 1004/RD nav.
M: 2 AIFO 8061 SRM diesels; 2 Castoldi TD 238 waterjets; 600 bhp
Range: 280/ . . . **Crew:** 3 tot. + 40 rescued personnel

Remarks: GRP hull construction with inflated rubber skirt. Equipment includes a Furuno FD 527 D/F, Furuno FE 4300 echo sounder, Garmin 100 GPS receiver, Loran receiver, and autopilot. Contract to construct sisters CP 710–712 was canceled.

CP 701 MARICOGECAP, Rome, 1995

♦ 2 CP 603–class (Seppietta-class) inshore rescue craft [WYH]

Bldr: Italcraft, Gaeta (L: 6-5-88)

CP 604 CP 605

D: 3.5 tons **S:** 16 kts **Dim:** 8.50 × 2.78 × 0.80
M: 2 VM HR 694 diesels; 1 prop; 248 bhp **Range:** 200/16 **Crew:** 2 tot.

Remarks: Sister CP 603 was decommissioned in 2001 and transferred to Albania during 2002.

Disposal note: Seppietta-class inshore rescue craft CP 601 and CP 602 were decommissioned on 30-9-01 and stricken on 31-12-01.

ITALIAN ARMY

The Italian Army's Amphibious Troop Command and Amphibious Batallion were disbanded in 2001 and all vessels were turned over for commercial use. The craft remain available via contract service and were deployed to Iraq during 2003–4.

ITALIAN AIR FORCE

Note: The Italian Air Force operates a total of nine air-sea rescue boats: AMMA 901–903, AMMA 1021, AMMA 1050, AMMA 1053, AMMA 1054, AMMA 1056, and AMMA 1058. No characteristics data are available. Also in use is the launch AMMC 715.

Italian Air Force launch AMMA 901 Gildas Tual via Paolo Marsan, 5-04

CUSTOMS SERVICE

(*Guardia di Finanza, Servizio Navale*)

The Comando Generale of the Guardia di Finanza is organized into 16 administrative areas, 20 operational sectors, and 28 squadrons. In addition to craft in Italian ports, others operate on rivers and lakes.

Personnel: 5,400 tot.

Aviation: 3 ATR-42-400MP and 12 Piaggio P-166DL3/SEM maritime patrol aircraft; 1 AgustaWestland A-109C, 1 AgustaWestland A-109IFR, 19 AugustaWestland A-109AII, 18 AgustaWestland-Bell AB-412, and 53 Nardi-Hughes NH-500 helicopters are in service.

The two ATR-42-400MP transports, configured as maritime patrol aircraft with a Texas Instruments SV-2022 search radar in a pod, an infrared/television turret, and GPS receivers, were ordered in 1996; the first was delivered late in 12-96 and the second 10-3-97, but they did not enter service until 1999, based at Pratica di Mare and operated by the Gruppo Esplorazione Marittima.

CUSTOMS SERVICE PATROL CRAFT [WPC]

♦ 10 (+ 2) Bigliani VI series patrol craft
Bldr: Intermarine, Sarzana, La Spezia (~2000–2009)

	In serv.
G.116 Laganà	. . .
G.117 Sanna	. . .
G.118 Inzucchi	. . .
G.119 Vitali	. . .
G.120 Calabrese	. . .
G.121 Urso	. . .
G.122 La Spina	8-05
G.123 Salone	2006
G.124 Cavatorto	2006
G.125 Fusco	2007
G.126 . . .	. . .
G.127 . . .	. . .

Remarks: Composite construction. 27.0-m long, Top speed of 40 kts. No additional data available.

♦ 3 Bigliani V series Patrol Craft
Bldr: Intermarine, Sarzana, La Spezia

	In serv.
G.3 Di Bartolo	2003
G.4 Avallone	2004
G.5 Oltramonti	2005

Oltramonti (G.5) Luciano Grazioli, 2-05

D: 114.6 tons (fl) **S:** 35+ kts **Dim:** 35.50 (31.39 pp) × 7.55 × 2.10 max.
A: 1 30-mm 80-cal. Melara-Mauser AA; 2 single 7.62-mm MG 42/59 mg
Electronics:
Radar: 1 Gem GEMANT 2V3 ARPA nav.; 1 Gem SC-1210C/G/L nav.
E/O: 1 Alenia-Elsag Medusa Mk. 3 gun f.c.
M: 2 MTU 16V396 TB94 diesels; 2 props; 6,964 bhp (5,920 sust.)
Electric: 192.5 kw tot. (2 × 90-kw, 1 × 12.5-kw diesel sets)
Range: 900/20 **Crew:** 14 tot. + 3 instructors, 18 trainees

Remarks: 230 grt. Enlarged versions of the Bigliani-III series of patrol boats with longer superstructure. GRP hull construction. Used for coastal patrol, drug interdiction, and illegal immigration control. Sisters *Mazzei* (G.1) and *Vaccaro* (G.2) are used as training craft. (See WYXT, below.)

♦ 1 (+ 3) Improved Antonio Zara class
Bldr: Fincantieri, Muggiano

	Laid down	L	In serv.
P.03 Giovanni Denaro	14-11-96	4-11-97	1998

Giovanni Denaro (P. 03) Fincantieri, 1996

D: 340 tons (fl) **S:** 34.5 kts **Dim:** 51.00 (47.25 pp) × 7.50 × 2.00
A: 1 30-mm 80-cal. OTO Melara–Mauser AA; 2 single 7.62-mm mg
Electronics:
Radar: 2 Gem GEMANT 2V3 nav.
E/O: AMS Mk 3A Medusa gun director; 2 CSDA-10 desig. sights
M: 4 MTU 16V396 TB94 diesels; 2 props; 12,848 bhp
Electric: 402 kw tot. (2 × 176-kw, 1 × 50-kw diesel sets)
Range: 3,800/15 **Endurance:** 10 days
Crew: 2 officers, 10 petty officers, 20 finanzieri

Remarks: 380 grt. P.03 ordered 10-95. Originally reported planned to be named *Medaglia d'Oro.* Design based on the *Antonio Zara,* but with a more powerful propulsion plant. Has fin stabilizers, improved accommodations, and the Alenia Gem CTI-10 navigational data recording system. Three more craft of this class are planned.

♦ 2 Antonio Zara class
Bldr: Fincantieri, Muggiano

	Laid down	L	In serv.
P.01 Antonio Zara	. . .	22-4-89	23-2-90
P.02 Vizzari	31-5-88	25-11-89	4-90

Antonio Zara (P.01) Luciano Grazioli, 9-97

D: 316.5 tons (fl) **S:** 27 kts **Dim:** 51.00 (47.25 pp) × 7.50 × 1.90
A: 1 twin 30-mm 80-cal. OTO Melara–Mauser AA; 2 single 7.62-mm mg
Electronics:
Radar: 1 SPN-748 nav.; 1 SPN-751 nav.
E/O: AMS-Elsag Pegaso-F gun f.c.s. with two CSDA-10 target desig.
M: 2 Wärtsilä NSD BL230-12 diesels; 2 props; 7,270 bhp (6,610 sust.)
Range: 2,700/15 **Crew:** 2 officers, 10 petty officers, 20 finanzieri

Remarks: Design based on builder's *Ratcharit* class for Thailand, but with a less powerful propulsion plant and lighter armament. Has the Alenia IPN-10 combat data system.

PATROL BOATS [WPB]

Note: Beween 2004 and 2005, Intermarine shipyards in La Sperzia delivered fourteen "2000-class," 45 knot, 13.2-meter, patrol boats for the Guardia di Finanza. Twelve 54 knot, 12-meter "V.600-class" fast interceptor boats were also under construction during 2006 for the Guardia di Finanza. A total of 33 V.600 class units are expected in service by 2008.

Classes typed as Vedette d'Altura (seagoing patrol boat):

♦ 26 Corrubia class
Bldrs: G.90–G.100: C.N. del Golfo, Gaeta (In serv.: first two: 1990–91; others: 1996–97); G.101–G.103: Crestitalia SpA, La Spezia (In serv. 1996–97); G.104–G.115: Intermarine, Sarzana, La Spezia (In serv. 1997–99)

G.90 Corrubia	G.99 Garzone	G.108 Conversano
G.91 Giudice	G.100 Lippi	G.109 Inzerilli
G.92 Alberti	G.101 Lombardi	G.110 Letizia
G.93 Angelini	G.102 Miccoli	G.111 Mazzarella
G.94 Cappelletti	G.103 Trezza	G.112 Nioi
G.95 Ciorlieri	G.104 Apruzzi	G.113 Partipilo
G.96 D'Amato	G.105 Ballali	G.114 Puleo
G.97 Fais	G.106 Bovienzo	G.115 Zannotti
G.98 Feliciani	G.107 Carreca	

Fais (G.97) Luciano Grazioli, 12-03

D: G.90, G.91: 75 tons (83.3 fl)—others: 92 tons (fl) **S:** 43 kts
Dim: 26.80 × 7.60 × 1.20 (G.90, G.91: 26.17 × 7.40 × 1.06)
A: G.90–103: 1 30-mm 80-cal. OTO Melara–Mauser AA; 2 single 7.62-mm mg—G.104–115: 1 20-mm 90-cal. Astra AA; 2 single 7.62-mm MG 42/59 mg
Electronics:
Radar: G.90–91: 1 Gem GEMANT 2V1 nav.; 1 Gem SC-1410 nav.—others: 1 Gem GEMANT 2V3 ARPA nav.; 1 Gem SC-1210C/G/L nav.
E/O: Alenia-Elsag Medusa Mk 3 (G.90, G.91: Mk 2) gun f.c.
M: G.90, G.91: 2 Isotta-Fraschini ID36 SS16V diesels; 2 props; 6,400 bhp—others: 2 MTU 16V396 TB 94 diesels; 2 props; 7,684 bhp (6,964 sust.)
Range: 700/35 **Crew:** 1 officer, 4 petty officers, 8 finanzieri

Remarks: First two were essentially prototypes and are referred to as the Corrubia-I series; G.92 through G.103 (the Corrubia-II series) have longer, broader hulls, and the final units (the Corrubia-III series) have a different armament.
Hull systems: GRP construction. All have a Loran-C receiver, Magnavox MX 1402 NAVSAT receiver, and Furuno FE 881 echo sounder.

CUSTOMS SERVICE PATROL BOATS [WPB] *(continued)*

♦ 12 Bigliani (CNL 39) class

Bldrs: G.78, G.79, G.88, G.89: Intermarine, Sarzana, La Spezia (In serv. 1997–99); others: Crestitalia, Ameglia, La Spezia (In serv.: G.80, G.81: 10-10-87; G.82–G.87: 1991–92)

G.78 Ottonelli	G.82 Galiano	G.86 Buonocore
G.79 Barletta	G.83 Macchi	G.87 Squitieri
G.80 Bigliani	G.84 Smalto	G.88 La Malfa
G.81 Cavaglia	G.85 Fortuna	G.89 Rosati

Bigliani (G.80) Bernard Prézelin, 5-05

D: 73 tons (84.7 fl) **S:** 43 (G.80, G.81: 45) kts
Dim: 27.00 (G.80, G.81: 26.40) × 6.95 × 1.20 (G.80, G.81: 1.06)
A: 1 30-mm 80-cal. OTO Melara–Mauser AA; 2 single 7.62-mm mg
Electronics:
Radar: G.78, G.79, G.88, G.89: 1 Gem GEMANT 2V3 ARPA nav.; 1 Gem SC-1210/C/G/L nav.—G.80, G.81: 1 Gem SPN-749 ARPA nav.; 1 Gem BX-3072A nav.—G.82–G.87: 1 Gem GEMANT 2V1 ARPA nav., 1 Gem SC-1410 nav.
E/O: 1 Alenia Medusa Mk 3 (G.80, G.81: Mk 1) gun. f.c.
M: 2 MTU 16V396 TB94 diesels; 2 props; 7,680 bhp (6,964 sust.)
Range: 700/25; 1,200/18.5 **Crew:** 1 officer, 3 petty officers, 8 finanzieri

Remarks: The prototype pair, G.80 and G.81, are referred to as the Bigliani-I series. G.82–G.87 (the Bigliani-II series) are longer and have a revised superstructure and mast configuration, while G.78, G.79, G.88, and G.89 (the Bigilani-III series) have later electronics. Other than G.80 and G.81, the craft were not completed in pennant number sequence. Two lengthened sisters with larger superstructures were built as training craft; see under [YXT]. The original *Bigliani* and *Cavaglia* were ordered from C.N. Liguri, Riva Trigoso, and were to displace 210 tons each; the completed craft were rejected for service and smaller replacements of a new design were ordered in 1984 from Intermarine.

♦ 29 Meattini class

Bldrs: Baglietto, Varazze; Picchiotti, Viareggio; Italcraft, Gaeta; Navaltecnica, Messina; Cantiere di Pisa; Cantiere di Lavagna; Cantiere di Chiavari (In serv. 1972–78)

From among:

G.11 Amici	G.30 Cicalese	G.50 D'Agostino
G.13 R.D. 26	G.31 Di Sessa	G.51 Fiore
G.14 Gori	G.32 Coppola	G.52 Nuziale
G.15 Ramaci	G.33 Rizzi	G.53 Tavano
G.16 Denaro	G.35 Baccile	G.54 De Alexandris
G.18 Arcioni	G.36 Cavatorto	G.55 Stefannini
G.19 Steri	G.37 Fusco	G.56 Tridenti
G.20 Cotugno	G.38 De Turris	G.57 Fazio
G.21 Manoni	G.39 Chiaramida	G.58 Atzei
G.22 Giannotti	G.40 Cav. D'Oro	G.59 Cicale
G.23 Carrubba	G.41 Bianca	G.60 Fidone
G.24 Uglielmi	G.42 Nuvoletta	G.62 Tavormina
G.25 Salone	G.43 Preite	G.63 Colombina
G.27 Russo	G.46 Silanos	G.64 Darida
G.28 Zara	G.47 Ignesti	G.65 Pizzighella
G.29 Rando	G.48 Barreca	G.66 Sciuto
	G.49 Ciraulo	

Ciraulo (G.49) Luciano Grazioli, 6-05

D: 40 tons (fl) **S:** 35.4 kts **Dim:** 20.10 × 5.20 × 0.90 (hull)
A: 1 12.7-mm mg **Electronics:** Radar: 1 Gem SC-1210 nav.
M: 2 CRM 18D/S2 diesels; 2 props; 2,500 bhp
Electric: 48 kw (2 × 24 kw) **Range:** 560/21 **Fuel:** 5.8 tons
Crew: 4 petty officers, 7 finanzieri

Remarks: GRP construction. Were planned to have been retired by the end of 2000, but 29 remain in service.
Combat systems: The original armament of one 20-mm 70-cal. Mk 10 Oerlikon and two single 7.62-mm mg has been reduced.
Disposal note: *Meattini* (G.10), *Bambace* (G.17), *Esposito* (G.26), *D'Aleo* (G.34), *Mazzeo* (G.44), and *Sguazzini* (G.61) were stricken during 1996–97. *Di Bartolo* (G.12) had retired by 2005 as has Gabriele-class wooden-hulled patrol boats *Gabriele* (G.70) and *Grasso* (G.71).

Craft typed as Vedette Veloci (fast patrol boat):

Note: The initial "V" in the hull number for all of the Guardia di Finanza patrol launches stands for "*Vedetta.*" In addition to the boats listed below, V.607 and V.1692, for which no information is available, are also in service.

Fast patrol boat V.1692 Martin Mokrus, 5-05

♦ 11 V.6001-class interceptor craft

Bldr: Intermarine, Sarzana, La Spezia

V.6001 (In serv. 1998) through V.6011 (In serv. . . .)

D: 12 tons (fl) **S:** 70 kts **Dim:** 16.40 × 2.90 × 0.70
A: . . . **Electronics:** Radar: 1 Pathfinder 24-NM nav.
M: 3 Seatek 6-4V-10D diesels; 3 Rolla surface-piercing props; 1,500 bhp (sust.)
Range: 374/45 **Crew:** 4 tot.

Remarks: Advanced composite Kevlar and GRP laminate hull construction. Have a single rudder set well abaft the hull. Navigational aids include a Trimble Navtrac GPS receiver.

♦ 1 V.6000-class interceptor craft

Bldr: F. Buzzi Design, . . . (In serv. 1994)

V.6000

D: 7.8 tons light (10 fl) **S:** 64 kts **Dim:** 14.20 × 2.74 × 0.80
A: . . . **Electronics:** Radar: 1 Gem SC-1005-RDN nav.
M: 3 Seatek 6-4V-9L diesels; 3 Rolla surface-piercing props; 1,740 bhp
Range: 360/45 **Crew:** 4 tot.

Remarks: Plans to build nine more were canceled in favor of the V.6001 class.

♦ 1 V.6100-class prototype interceptor craft

Bldr: Bruno Abbate, Naples (In serv. 1994)

V.6100

D: 7.6 tons light (8.8 fl) **S:** 60+ kts **Dim:** 13.41 × 2.74 × 0.55 (0.80 over props)
A: . . . **Electronics:** Radar: 1 Gem SC-1005-RDN nav.
M: 2 Seatek 6-4V-9L diesels; 2 Rolla surface-piercing props; 1,160 bhp
Range: 360/45 **Crew:** 4 tot.

Remarks: Advanced composite laminate hull construction. Has a single rudder set well abaft the hull. Navigational aids include a Trimble Navtrac GPS receiver.

♦ 20 V.5001-class patrol launches

Bldr: C.N. Moschini, Fano (In serv. 1995–2000)

V.5001 through V.5020

V.5001 Carlo Martinelli, 10-98

CUSTOMS SERVICE PATROL BOATS [WPB] *(continued)*

D: 20.04 tons (27.1 fl) **S:** 52 kts (45 sust.) **Dim:** 16.50 × 4.60 × 1.20
A: 1 7.62-mm mg **Electronics:** Radar: 1 Gem SC-1210C/G/L nav.
M: 2 MTU 8V396 TE94 diesels; 2 waterjets; 3,000 bhp **Electric:** 3.5 kw
Range: 150/35 **Crew:** 2 petty officers, 2 finanzieri

Remarks: GRP construction. Builder's Super-Drago design. First unit laid down 3-10-88, second on 2-3-89; were initially rejected after trials failed to produce the required 50 kts and the craft were overweight. The final four are of a modified design.

♦ 2 prototype patrol launches
Bldr: Intermarine, Sarzana, La Spezia

V.5000 (In serv. 1992) V.5100 (In serv. 1988)

D: 20.04 tons (27.3 fl) **S:** 52 kts (45 sust.) **Dim:** 16.50 × 4.60 × 1.20
A: 1 7.62-mm mg **Electronics:** Radar: 1 Gem BX-132 nav.
M: 2 Isotta-Fraschini ID36 SS8V diesels; 2 waterjets; 2,200 bhp (1,950 sust.)
Electric: 3.5 kw tot. **Range:** 420/35 **Crew:** 2 petty officers, 3 finanzieri

♦ 8 V.4000-class patrol launches
Bldr: Italcraft, Venice; Cantieri della Spezia; and Technomarine (In serv. 1981–83)

V.4000 V.4002 V.4005 V.4010
V.4001 V.4004 V.4007 V.4011

V.4010 Guardia di Finanza, 1994

D: 6.9 tons (fl) **S:** 47.7 kts **Dim:** 13.1 × 3.0 × 0.7
A: Small arms **Electronics:** Radar: 1 Gem BX-132 nav.
M: 2 Isotta-Fraschini ID32 SS61 diesels; 2 props; 720 bhp
Range: 275/35 **Fuel:** 0.7 tons **Crew:** 4 tot.

Remarks: Survivors of a class of 15. Wooden construction.

Craft typed as Vedette (patrol boat):

♦ 34 V.5800-class patrol launches
Bldr: Mericraft, Motomar, Balsamo; and S. Prospero (In serv. 1979–85)

V.5800 through V.5833

V.5819 Paolo Marsan, 7-04

D: 15.6 tons (fl) **S:** 26 kts **Dim:** 12.6 × 3.6 × 1.2
A: 1 7.62-mm mg **Electronics:** Radar: 1 Furuno . . . nav.
M: 2 Fiat-AIFO 828 SRM diesels; 2 props; 1,000 bhp (880 sust.)
Range: 645/19 **Fuel:** 0.4 ton **Crew:** 5 tot.

Remarks: GRP construction. Keith Nelson–designed hulls. Near-sisters are in the coast guard and the Carabinieri fleets. All are essentially identical, unlike the coast guard series.

♦ 80 V.5500-class patrol launches
Bldr: Intermarine-Crestitalia, Ameglia, La Spezia (In serv. 1979–81)

From among V.5500 through V.5581

D: 7.8 tons (fl) **S:** 33.8 kts **Dim:** 12.00 × 3.80 × 0.60
A: Small arms **Electronics:** Radar: 1 Gem BX-732 nav.
M: 2 AIFO 8361 SRM diesels; 2 Castoldi 06 waterjets; 480 bhp
Range: 230/14.9 **Fuel:** 0.6 tons **Crew:** 5 tot.

V.5543 Guy Schaeffer via Paolo Marsan, 12-03

Remarks: GRP construction. V.5512 was lost in an accident, and one other has been retired. Sisters operate in the Portuguese Navy.

♦ 5 V.5901-class patrol launches
Bldr: Motomar, Lavagna (In serv.: V.5901–V.5904: 1977; V.5581: 1998)

V.5901 V.5902 V.5903 V.5904 V.5581

D: 10.5 tons (fl) **S:** 23 kts **Dim:** 12.3 × 3.3 × 1.0
M: 1 Fiat-AIFO CP3-SM diesel; 380 bhp
Range: 630/20 **Fuel:** 1.6 tons **Crew:** 3 tot.

♦ 2 V.5300-class patrol launches
Bldr: Motomar, Lavagna (In serv. 1979–82)

V.5301 V.5302

D: 5.1 tons (fl) **S:** 36 kts **Dim:** 8.3 × 2.8 × 0.5
M: 1 AIFO 8361-SM diesel; 1 prop; 480 bhp
Range: 154/36 **Fuel:** 0.5 ton **Crew:** 3 tot.

Remarks: GRP construction. Sister V.5300 has been retired.

Craft typed Vedette Litiranee, Portuali, e per Acque Interne (V.A.I.):

♦ 5 V.A.I.500-class launches

V.A.I.500 through V.A.I.504

Remarks: No data available; completed 1985–93.

♦ 6 V.A.I.400-class launches
Bldr: Cantieri Oscar and Cantieri Cucchini, Venice (In serv. 1985–93)

V.A.I.400 through V.A.I.405

V.A.I.401 Luciano Grazioli, 6-99

D: . . . tons **S:** 21–25 kts **Dim:** 9.20 × 2.34 × 0.70
M: 1 AIFO diesel; 1 prop; 132 or 185 bhp

Remarks: Employed at Venice. Wooden construction. Coast guard sisters also serve at Venice.

♦ 85 V.A.I.200-class launches
Bldrs: First unit: Mericraft, Baia, Naples; others: Cantieri Fiat de Napoli (In serv. 1986–89)

V.A.I.200 through V.A.I.270 V.A.I.272 through V.A.I.285

D: 4 tons (fl) **S:** 35 kts **Dim:** 8.10 (6.58 pp) × 2.48 × 0.65
M: 2 G.M. 6-92HT-9 diesels; 2 Castoldi Model 06 waterjets; 296 bhp
Range: . . . / . . . **Crew:** 3 tot.

Remarks: GRP construction. For harbor, river, and lake service. Sister V.A.I.271 was rammed and sunk on 17-8-98 by chemical tanker *Chemsea* at Ravenna. A craft numbered V.A.I. 301 is also in service, though no data are available.

CUSTOMS SERVICE PATROL BOATS [WPB] *(continued)*

V.A.I.216 Piet Sinke, 7-05

AUXILIARIES

♦ **1 training ship [WAXT]**
Bldr: C.N. Lucchese, Venice (In serv. 1971)

Giorgio Cini

Giorgio Cini Luciano Grazioli, 4-05

D: 770 tons (fl) **S:** 14 kts **Dim:** 54.00 × 10.20 × 2.9
A: 1 12.7-mm mg
Electronics: Radar: 1 Gem GEMANT 2V1-RS nav.; 1 Gem SC-1210C/G/L nav.; 1 . . . nav.
M: 1 Fiat B306-SS diesel; 1 prop; 1,500 bhp
Range: 800/14 **Fuel:** 65 tons **Crew:** 1 officer, 29 petty officers + 60 students

Remarks: Former merchant marine training ship, acquired in 1981; operational in 1984 after a refit. Carries a wide variety of navigation aids and communications equipment for training purposes.

SERVICE CRAFT

♦ **1 hydrofoil personnel launch [WYFLH]**
Bldr: C.N. del Golfo, Gaeta (In serv. 1999)

V. . . Di Amato

D: . . . tons **S:** 30 kts **Dim:** 24.00 × 7.40 (hull) × 1.20 (foilborne)
M: 2 MTU 16V396 TB 94 diesels; 2 props; 5,760 bhp

Remarks: 130 grt. Former commercial hydrofoil ferry, purchased in 1999 for transportation, SAR, and patrol duties. GRP hull.

♦ **2 Bigliani V-class training craft [WYXT]**
Bldr: Intermarine, Sarzana, La Spezia

	Laid down	L	In serv.
G.1 Mazzei	22-4-96	16-5-97	24-4-98
G.2 Vaccaro	23-9-96	1-9-97	29-4-98

D: 114.6 tons (fl) **S:** 35+ kts **Dim:** 35.50 (31.39 pp) × 7.55 × 2.10 (max.)
A: 1 30-mm 80-cal. OTO Melara–Mauser AA; 2 single 7.62-mm MG 42/59 mg
Electronics:
Radar: 1 Gem GEMANT 2V3 ARPA nav.; 1 Gem SC-1210C/G/L nav.
E/O: 1 Alenia-Elsag Medusa Mk. 3 gun f.c.

Mazzei (G.1) Carlo Martinelli, 10-98

M: 2 MTU 16V396 TB94 diesels; 2 props; 6,964 bhp (5,920 sust.)
Electric: 192.5 kw tot. (2 × 90-kw, 1 × 12.5-kw diesel sets)
Range: 900/20 **Crew:** 14 tot. + 3 instructors, 18 trainees

Remarks: 230 grt. Enlarged versions of the Bigliani-III series of patrol boats with a longer superstructure. Can be used for patrol duties if required. GRP hull construction.

♦ **1 105-foot Commercial Cruiser–class training craft [WYXT]**
Bldr: Sewart Swiftships, Berwick, La. (In serv. 1980)

Genna (ex-G.72, ex-*Gandora,* ex-*Pandora*)

Genna Luciano Grazioli, 7-02

D: 120 tons (fl) **S:** 35 kts **Dim:** 32.20 × 7.20 × 3.10
A: 1 12.7-mm mg
Electronics: Radar: 1 Furuno 865-3424 nav.; Furuno 711 nav.
M: 3 MTU 12V331 TC92 diesels; 3 props; 2,940 bhp **Electric:** 30 kw tot.
Range: 1,380/30 **Crew:** 13 tot.

Remarks: Former Guardia Costiera patrol boat transferred to the Guardia di Finanza in 1984 and used in recent years for training.

Note: Also in service are nine small sailboats for recreation and training and about 100 RIB service launches.

CARABINIERI
(*Commando Generale dell'Arma dei Carabinieri*)

Note: The Carabinieri's seagoing force (*Comando Generale dell'Arma dei Carabinieri Servizio Navale*) was established in 1969 for patrol out to the 3-n.m. limit, along with search-and-rescue, research, and police duties. The Carabinieri was made Italy's fourth official armed service during 4-00 and reports directly to the Minister of Defense; including ground and aviation personnel, some 111,000 personnel are in uniform. Carabinieri aviation assets include 12 Vulcan Air (ex-Partenavia) P.68 Observer maritime surveillance aircraft.

Carabinieri launch 703—black hull with red trim strip and white superstructure
Martin Mokrus, 9-02

By 2010, a total of 59 total craft, built by Cantieri Navali del Goldo shipyards, are expected to replace all but the 700 and 800 series now in service. Craft in service as of 2006 include:

- 20 800-series launches, plus 7 on order
- 1 S 001 launch (in serv. 5-98): 18 tons, 13.50 × 4.40 × 1.10; 20 kts
- 2 (plus two on order) 700-series launches: 16 tons, 12.8 × . . . × . . . ; 25 kts

CARABINIERI *(continued)*

Carabinieri launch 804 Bernard Prézelin, 4-05

- 17 600-series Keith Nelson launches (Carabinieri 601–616, Carabinieri 623; in serv. 1984–85): 11–12 tons, 12.54 × 3,61 × . . .; 20–21 kts
- 30 N 500–series launches (N 501–528, N 621, N 622; in serv. 1985): 5.8 tons, 10.00 × 3.40; 22 kts
- 3 S 500–series launches for combat swimmer support (S 501–503; in serv. . . .): 7 tons, 10.0 × 3.40; 22 kts
- 23 500-series launches: 2.6 tons, 6.46 × 2.37; 20 kts
- 54 400-series launches: 1.4 tons, 5.50 × 2.10; 25 kts
- 17 or more 300-series launches in the Venice lagoon area: 4 tons, 9.20 × 2.30 × 0.7; 25 kts
- 15 or more 200-series launches
- 21 or more miscellaneous personnel and inspection launches in the 100 series

Note: The National Police (*Polizia di Stato*) also operates a sizable force of patrol boats and launches, with more than 100 currently in operation. There are approximately 630 personnel in the organization. Craft include PS 212, PS 287–288, PS 358, PS 361–363, PS 385, PS 399–401, PS 409–439, PS 441, PS 445–460, PS 466, PS 468–499, and PS 500–507. PS 544–554 and PS 661–662 make up the Squalo class. The largest craft are about 12 m long and displace about 9 tons (fl). The Polizia also operates eight P-68 Observer aircraft, the first of which was delivered on 11-11-99.

Polizia launch PS 553 A. A. de Kruijf, 6-04

The Prison Police (*Polizia Penitenziaria*) operates at least nine small patrol boats numbered in the V-1 series.

IVORY COAST

Republic of Côte d'Ivoire

MARINE IVOIRIENNE

Personnel: Approx. 950 total (75 officers, 875 enlisted), including 80 naval infantry.

Base: Principal base and repair facilities at Abidjan, with minor facilities at San Pédro, Sassandra, and Tabou.

PATROL CRAFT [PC]

♦ 1 French Patra class

Bldr: Auroux, Arcachon

	Laid down	L	In serv.
L'Ardent	15-4-77	21-7-78	6-10-78

L'Ardent French Navy, 12-96

D: 125 tons (148 fl) **S:** 26.3 kts **Dim:** 40.70 (38.50 pp) × 5.90 × 1.55
A: 1 40-mm 70-cal. Bofors AA; 1 20-mm 70-cal. Oerlikon Mk 10 AA; 2 single 7.62-mm mg
Electronics: Radar: 1 Decca 1226 nav.
M: 2 AGO 195 V12CZ SHR diesels; 2 CP props; 5,000 bhp (4,400 sust.)
Electric: 120 kw **Range:** 750/20; 1,750/10 **Endurance:** 5 days
Crew: 2 officers, 17 enlisted

Remarks: Ordered 1-77. *L'Ardent* is in very poor condition but still capable of getting under way.

Disposal note: French-built P-48-class patrol craft *Le Valeureux,* in poor condition for many years, was stricken during 2000; sister *Le Vigilant* had been hulked by 1995 and *Le Intrépide* was nonoperational by 1999, though remains afloat, pierside, in very poor condition.

AMPHIBIOUS WARFARE SHIPS AND CRAFT

Disposal note: Since 2000, navy-owned BATRAL-E-class medium landing ship *Éléphant* has been operated by a private firm on commercial charter.

♦ 1 Yuqin-class (Project 069) landing craft [LCM]

Bldr: . . . , China

Atchan

D: 58 tons light (110 fl) **S:** 11.5 (9 loaded) kts
Dim: 24.1 × 5.2 × 1.1 **M:** 1 twin 14.5-mm 93-cal. AA
M: 2 diesels; 2 Type 12V50 props; 600 bhp

Remarks: Entered service during 2003–4.

♦ 2 ex-French LCM(8)-class landing craft [LCM]

Bldr: CMN, Cherbourg

Aby (ex-CTM 15) Tiaghi (ex-CTM 16)

Aby—while in French Navy service Guy Schaeffer, via Paolo Marsan, 8-96

D: 56 tons light (150 fl) **S:** 9.5 kts **Dim:** 23.80 × 6.35 × 1.25
A: 2 single 12.7-mm mg **Electronics:** Radar: 1 . . . nav.
M: 2 Poyaud 520 V8 diesels; 2 props; 480 bhp **Range:** 380/8
Fuel: 3.4 tons **Endurance:** 48 hr (at half power) **Crew:** 6 tot.

Remarks: Transferred 3-99. Cargo capacity: 90 tons.

♦ 3 Type 412 fast assault boats [LCP]

Bldr: Rotork, U.K. (In serv. 1979–80)

D: 5.2 tons (8.9 fl) **S:** 21 kts **Dim:** 12.65 × 3.20 × 0.90
M: 2 Volvo AQAD-40A outdrive diesels; 2 props; 240 bhp

Remarks: GRP construction with small bow ramp. Can carry 30 troops. Two were originally assigned to civilian tasks but were later taken over for the navy.

SERVICE CRAFT

♦ 2 ex-French Surf-class launches [YFL]

Bldr: Allais, Dieppe (In serv. 1989)

. . . (ex-*Burao,* Y 788) . . . (ex-*Mamanu,* Y 752)

Ex-Burao (Y 788)—just prior to transfer Bernard Prézelin, 8-99

SERVICE CRAFT *(continued)*

D: 9 tons (fl) **S:** 25 kts **Dim:** 13.0 × 4.0 × 0.7
Electronics: Radar: 1 . . . nav.
M: 2 diesels; 2 waterjets; . . . bhp **Crew:** 3 tot.

Remarks: Transferred 10-99. Originally built for use at the Muraroa nuclear test station. Have a GRP hull with an inflated rubber fender around the upper strake.

♦ 2 ex-French Acajou-class medium harbor tugs [YTM]

. . . (ex-*Marronnier,* Y 738)   . . . (ex-*Merisier,* Y 669)

D: 105 tons **S:** 11 kts **Dim:** 21.0 (18.4 pp) × 6.9 × 3.2
M: 1 diesel; 1 prop; 700 bhp

Remarks: Transferred 10-99. Built during the 1960s. Bollard-pull capacity: 10 tons.

♦ 1 ex-French P.1-class push-tug [YTM]
Bldr: La Perriere, Lorient

. . . (ex-11, ex-P.11)

D: 24 tons (fl) **S:** 9.2 kts **Dim:** 11.50 (11.25 wl) × 4.30 × 1.45
M: 2 Poyaud-Wärtsilä UD 18 V8 M1 diesels; 2 props; 456 bhp (440 sust.)
Range: 191/9.1, 560/8 **Fuel:** 1.7 tons **Crew:** 2 tot.

Remarks: Transferred in 9-99 for dockyard use. Primarily for pushing, but has a 4.1-ton bollard pull.

Note: The Gendarmerie operates the 15-ton launch *Le Barracuda* (in serv. 1974; 18 kts), an Arcor-30 launch (in serv. 1985; 20 kts), and two Arcor-31 launches (in serv. 1982; 5 tons), condition unknown.

JAMAICA

DEFENCE FORCE COAST GUARD

Personnel: 250 total (190 active plus 60 reservists)

Bases: Port Royal (HMJS *Cagway*), Coast Guard Station *Discovery Bay,* and a small facility at Middle Cay in the Pedro Cays

Maritime Aviation: The Jamaica Defence Force has three Bell 412EP Griffon and four Eurocopter AS.355N Ecureuil 2 helicopters for SAR duties and employs one Cessna 21-M, one Pilatus-Britten-Norman BN-2A, and one Beech 100 King Air fixed-wing aircraft on coastal patrol and liaison duties. Aircraft operate from Kingston's Norman Manley International Airport, Kingston, and Up Park Camp.

PATROL CRAFT [WPC]

♦ 3 Stan Patrol 4207 class
Bldr: Damen, Gorinchen (In serv. 2005–6)

	Delivered
421 CORNWALL	18-9-05
422 MIDDLESEX	11-05
423 SURREY	6-06

Cornwall (421) A. A de Kruijf, 2005

D: 205 tons **S:** 25 kts **Dim:** 41.8 × 6.8 × 2.5
A: Small arms **Electronics:** Radar: 1 JRC nav.
M: 2 Caterpillar 3516 DITA diesels; 5,600 bhp
Range: 1,800/12 **Fuel:** . . . gallons **Crew:** 14 crew (+ 4 passengers)

Remarks: Offshore patrol vessels; ordered 2005 with delivery completed by 2006.

PATROL BOATS [WPB]

♦ 3 44-foot class
Bldr: Silver Ships, Inc., Theodore, Ala. (In serv. 2002)

CG 131   CG 132   GC 133

44-ft. patrol boat—armed with 7.62-mm mg Silver Ships, 2003

D: 11.5 tons (fl) **S:** 40 kts **Dim:** 13.41 × 3.15 × 0.91
A: Small arms **M:** 1 Caterpillar 3196 diesel; 1 waterjet; 1,140 bhp
Electric: 6.5 kw
Range: 378/35 **Fuel:** 560 gallons **Crew:** 6 tot.

Remarks: Aluminum construction. Cruise at 35 kts. Armed with a single 7.62-mm mg.

♦ 1 Guardian class
Bldr: Lantana Boatyard, Lantana, Fla. (In serv. 26-9-85)

P 8 PAUL BOGLE (ex-*Comayguela*)

Paul Bogle (P 8) Lantana, 9-85

D: 93 tons (fl) **S:** 33 kts **Dim:** 32.31 × 6.25 × 1.24 (2.13 props)
A: 2 single 12.7-mm M2 mg **Electronics:** Radar: 1 Furuno 2400 nav.
M: 3 MTU 8V396 TB92 diesels; 3 props; 3,600 bhp
Electric: 100 kw (2 G.M. 4-71 diesels driving) **Endurance:** 7 days
Crew: 4 officers, 16 enlisted

Remarks: Begun and launched for Honduras, then purchased by Jamaica. Was originally to have been renamed *Cape George.* Aluminum construction. Sisters serve in Grenada and Honduras. A 12.7-mm machinegun has replaced the 20-mm AA added during the mid-1980s. Refitted in U.S. during 11-97.

♦ 1 Fort Charles class
Bldr: Teledyne Sewart, Berwick, La. (In serv. 1974)

P 7 FORT CHARLES

Fort Charles (P 7) H&L Van Ginderen, 11-95

D: 130 tons (fl) **S:** 32 kts **Dim:** 34.5 × 5.7 × 2.1
A: 2 single 12.7-mm M2 mg **Electronics:** Radar: 1 Sperry 4016 nav.
M: 2 MTU 16V538 TB90 diesels; 2 props; 6,000 bhp
Range: 1,200/18 **Crew:** 4 officers, 16 enlisted

Remarks: Can carry 24 soldiers or serve as an 18-bed floating infirmary. When refitted by Atlantic Marine at Jacksonville, Fla., in 1980–81, the craft's hull was lengthened by 3 m forward. Refitted again in 1998.

♦ 2 ex-U.S. Coast Guard 82-foot Point class
Bldrs: CG 251: J. Martinac SB, Tacoma, Wash.; CG 252: Coast Guard Yard, Curtis Bay, Md.

	In serv.
CG 251 SAVANNAH POINT (ex-*Point Nowell,* WPB 82363)	1-6-67
CG 252 BELMONT POINT (ex-*Point Barnes,* WPB 82371)	21-4-70

PATROL BOATS [WPB] *(continued)*

D: 64 tons (66 fl) **S:** 23.7 kts **Dim:** 25.3 × 5.23 × 1.95
A: 2 single 12.7-mm M2 mg
Electronics: Radar: 1 Hughes-Furuno SPS-73 nav.
M: 2 Caterpillar 3412 diesels; 2 props; 1,480 bhp
Range: 490/23.7; 1,500/8 **Fuel:** 5.7 tons **Crew:** 10 tot.

Remarks: CG 251 transferred by donation on 19-10-99, CG 252 on 12-1-00. Hull built of mild steel. Are well equipped for salvage and towing.

♦ 3 Avanu class
Bldr: Offshore Marine Performance, Miami, Fla. (In serv. 20-4-92)

CG 101 CG 102 CG 103

D: 3 tons (fl) **S:** 48 kts **Dim:** 9.96 × 2.49 × 0.51
A: 1 7.62-mm mg **Electronics:** Radar: 1 Raytheon R40X nav.
M: 2 Johnson OMC gasoline outboard motors; 450 bhp **Crew:** 3 tot.

Remarks: Cigarette boat–design, GRP-construction planing hulls. Used for counter-narcotics patrol and interception.

♦ 4 Dauntless class
Bldr: SeaArk, Monticello, Ark.

	In serv.
CG 121	10-9-92
CG 122	10-11-92
CG 123	12-92
CG 124	5-94

CG 121 SeaArk, 9-92

D: 15 tons (fl) **S:** 28 kts **Dim:** 12.19 (11.13 wl) × 3.86 × 0.69 (hull)
A: 2 single 12.7-mm mg; 2 single 7.62-mm mg
Electronics: Radar: 1 Raytheon R40X nav.
M: 2 Caterpillar 3208TA diesels; 2 props; 850 bhp (720 sust.)
Range: 200/30; 400/22 **Fuel:** 250 gallons **Crew:** 5 tot.

Remarks: Aluminum construction. First unit ordered 6-91 under U.S. FY 89 Foreign Military Sales program; second unit authorized 10-91 under FY 90 program. Two more were subsequently ordered under U.S. aid programs. C. Raymond Hunt, "Deep-Vee" hull design.

♦ 2 U.S. Guardian-27 class
Bldr: Boston Whaler, Rockland, Mass. (In serv. 7-92)

CG 091 CG 092

D: 2.25 tons (3.75 fl) **S:** 36 kts **Dim:** 8.10 × 3.05 × 0.50
A: 1 7.62-mm mg **Electronics:** Radar: 1 Raytheon R40X nav.
M: 2 Johnson OMC gasoline outboard engines; 400 bhp
Range: 167/40; 750/ . . . **Fuel:** 243 liters **Crew:** 3 tot.

Remarks: "Unsinkable," rigid foam-core GRP construction. Unlike the Guardian-22 class, have a small enclosed pilothouse amidships.

♦ 6 U.S. Guardian-22 class
Bldr: Boston Whaler, Rockland, Mass. (In serv. 1990)

CG 051 CG 052 CG 053 CG 054 CG 055 CG 056

D: 1.5 tons light (2.25 fl) **S:** 40 kts **Dim:** 6.81 × 2.26 × 0.36
A: 1 7.62-mm mg **Electronics:** Radar: 1 Raytheon R40X nav.
M: 2 Johnson OMC gasoline outboard engines; 360 bhp
Range: 167/40; 750/ . . . **Fuel:** 243 liters **Crew:** 3 tot.

Note: Also used by the coast guard is a 12-m sail-training craft. The Kingston Constabulary operates a 12-m Bertram patrol craft acquired in 1984 and a 19.8-m search-and-rescue boat purchased from Swiftships, Morgan City, La., in 1986.

JAPAN

MARITIME SELF-DEFENSE FORCE
(Kaijo Jieitai)

Personnel: 44,400 total, including 9,800 naval aviation personnel.

Organization: Under a 1998 reorganization, the principal units of the Japan Maritime Self-Defense Force (JMSDF) are assigned to the Escort Fleet and Submarine Fleet (both headquartered at Yokosuka); two Minesweeping Flotillas (at Kure and Yokosuka); five District Fleets (at Yokosuka, Kure, Sasebo, Maizuru, and Ominato) composed of older destroyers, frigates, missile craft, amphibious warfare units, and mine countermeasures units; and the Training Fleet.

Bases: Principal ship bases are at Yokosuka, Sasebo, and Kure, with other bases at Maizuru, Hanshin, and Ominato.

Naval Aviation: About 9,800 personnel are assigned. The JMSDF has approximately 330 operational aircraft, including 190 fixed-wing aircraft and 140 helicopters. Fixed-wing aircraft include 86 P-3C Orion maritime patrol, 13 US-1A SAR seaplanes, four YS-11M/M-A and five YS-11T-A transports, five EP-3D EW aircraft, three U-36A EW training/target service aircraft, one UP-3C, one UP-3D, one UC-90 photo-mapping and five LC-90 EW/utility aircraft, 22 TC-90 light transports, and four KM-2 and 38 T-5 trainers. Helicopters include 21 HSS-2B Sea King and 79 SH-60J Seahawk ASW, 10 MH-53E mine-countermeasures, 14 UH-60J and four S-61A SAR, and four OH-6J, six OH-6D, and one Bell 47G2A utility/trainers. Several Japanese Air Self-Defense Force (JASDF) C-130H transports are equipped to perform aerial sea minelaying.

Fixed-wing fleet naval air bases include 1st Fleet Air Wing, Kameya; 2nd Fleet Air Wing, Hachinohe; 4th Fleet Air Wing, Atsugi; and 5th Fleet Air Wing, Naha, Okinawa. Helicopter fleet naval air bases include 21st Fleet Air Wing, Tateyama; 22nd Fleet Air Wing, Omura; and 31st Fleet Air Wing, Iwakuni. A new fleet air wing helicopter base was opened at Maizuru on 22-3-01. The Air Training Command has bases at Shimofusa, Tokushima, Usuki, and Kanoya.

One P-3C has been converted to UP-3E surveillance aircraft (with SLAR, GPS, SATCOM, and improved cameras). The last P-3C was delivered in 8-97; of 101 built, 98 were built under license by Kawasaki and the original three were built by Lockheed Martin. Other P-3Cs are being converted to EP-3D electronic warfare configuration, with the seventh unit (a conversion) approved in the FY 01 budget.

Ultimately, it is planned to procure 100 SH-60J helicopters to complete replacement of the SH-3 Sea Kings, while a total of 18 UH-60Js will replace the S-61As for search-and-rescue duties. The SH-60J fleet is to be upgraded to SH-60J-kai in a two-stage program; the one FY 97 SH-60J was delivered in 1999 as the upgrade prototype, with the FY 98 example similarly equipped. The modifications will improve performance and allow the aircraft to perform maritime surveillance and law enforcement missions. Upgrades include a composite main rotor hub and blades, and active sonar linked to a new onboard tactical data system, an inverse synthetic aperture radar (ISAR), FLIR, upgraded EW support gear, decoy launchers, a laser-based landing aid, and the capability to launch ASM-1 antiship missiles. The Lockheed Martin AGM-114M Hellfire-II antiship missile is being procured at the rate of 6–10 rounds per year for use from SH-60J helicopters.

An initial order for 14 EH-101 medium-lift helicopters was placed during 2003 with deliveries beginning during 2006. Up to 80 Kawasaki-assembled EH-101s may eventually be purchased. Shin-Meiwa is converting one US-1A SAR seaplane to US-1A-kai configuration, with Allison AE2500 turboprops, new avionics, and a pressurized hull, as a prototype for a proposed US-X successor; the US-X would weigh about 50 metric tons and would have a 5,180-km range (compared to 4,225 for the current US-1A), and a 25,000-ft. ceiling (10,000 ft. for the US-1A).

The JASDF operates 14 Raytheon Corporate Jets U-125A search-and-rescue aircraft, with an eventual total of 27 planned through 2005. The U-125A is a variant of the Hawker HS-125-800 corporate jet transport. The aircraft are configured with observation windows, FLIR, dinghy launcher, and marker-buoy launchers.

P-3C Orion Mitsuhiro Kadota, 12-03

EP-3 Orion electronic warfare aircraft—note the two radomes atop the fuselage and one beneath *Ships of the World,* 1996

MARITIME SELF-DEFENSE FORCE *(continued)*

UP-3C surveillance aircraft Mitsuhiro Kadota, 12-03

US-1A search-and-rescue amphibian Mitsuhiro Kadota, 2004

U-36A target simulation and towing aircraft Mitsuhiro Kadota, 10-05

YS-11T-A transport Mitsuhiro Kadota, 9-03

TC-90 light transport and training variant Takatoshi Okano, 9-02

T-5 trainer *Ships of the World*

MH-53E mine-countermeasures helicopter Mitsuhiro Kadota, 10-05

SH-60J ASW helicopter Takatoshi Okano, 6-04

OH-6 utility helicopter Mitsuhiro Kadota, 2004

HSS-2B land-based ASW and utility helicopter Mitsuhiro Kadota, 2004

WEAPONS AND SYSTEMS

Until the 1970s, most weapons and detection gear were of American design, built under license in Japan. Subsequently, ships have been equipped with Japanese-designed, long-range, pulse-compression air-search radars and with the 76-mm and 127-mm OTO Melara guns. U.S. Vulcan/Phalanx 20-mm CIWS (Close-In Weapon System) and Harpoon antiship missiles were procured in quantity, with the latter now slowly being supplanted by the Mitsubishi SSM-1 family of antiship missiles.

The U.S. Standard SM-1 MR and SM-2 and Sea Sparrow RIM-7F surface-to-air missiles are in use, with the latter supplemented by the RIM-7M for use in vertical launchers. During the 1990s, some 116 Harpoon and 222 Standard SM-1, SM-2, and SM-2 Block III/IIIB missiles were ordered from the United States. Sixteen SM-2 Block IIA missiles were requested during 6-02.

In 1994, 27 vertical-launch ASROC missiles for the newest destroyers and frigates were purchased from the United States, and procurement has continued, with Japan having bought over 400 to date; an indigenous version, the Improved VL Antisubmarine Rocket, is being developed by Mitsubishi Heavy Industries and the Defense Agency Technical Research and Development Institute.

Mitsubishi has a license to build the U.S. Mk 46 Mod. 5 NEARTIP ASW torpedo, while the indigenously designed Type 89 (formerly GRX-2, a U.S. Mk 48 ADCAP equivalent) high-speed homing torpedo for submarine service and the Type 73 (formerly GRX-4) short-range ASW torpedo for aircraft have been developed for use from P-3 aircraft, helicopters, and surface ships; the Type 73 is equivalent to the U.S. Mk 50 and entered service during the mid-1990s.

A Japanese-developed pintle mounting for the three-barreled G.E. (now Lockheed Martin) Sea Vulcan 20P 20-mm M197 gatling gun is used aboard JMSDF mine countermeasures craft and by a great many Japan Coast Guard ships and craft as the JM-61-MB; it uses the same basic mount as did the twin 20-mm 70-cal. Mk 24 Oerlikon AA gun and has 300 rounds ready-service on mount. An enclosed, fully automatic version with a separate electro-optical director is used by PG 01–class guided-missile hydrofoils and by several new coast guard ships and craft. In both versions, the gun has a rate of fire of 750–1,500 rds/min, a maximum range of 6,000 yards, and a muzzle velocity of 1,287 m/sec.

Mitsubishi and Kawasaki are cooperating on a Sparrow AAM replacement that will also replace Sea Sparrow; antiship radiation-homing (ARM) and beach-defense missiles are also in development.

Japan employs the 1955-vintage, four-tubed Bofors Erika 375-mm ASW rocket launcher system, which is referred to as the Type 71 for the year of its introduction into the JMSDF; it can launch 250-kg rockets to a range of 1,635 m.

SSM-1 (Type 88): The original air-launched ASM-1 (Type 80) entered service in 1982 with the air force. SSM-1 (Type 88) entered service in the late 1980s as a coast-defense weapon, with 54 trucks equipped with the missiles, which employ two solid booster rockets at takeoff. The shipboard version, SSM-1B (Type 90), entered service in 1992 (with 384 ultimately manufactured). All three versions are powered by a Mitsubishi TJM-2 turbojet and employ active radar homing. ASM-2 (Type 93) uses IR homing and entered service in 1994. A longer-range antiship missile designated SSM-2 began development in 1988 but does not yet appear to have entered production. Data for the SSM-1B include:

Length: 5.08 m **Diameter:** 35 cm **Wingspan:** 1.2 m
Weight: 661 kg **Warhead:** 225 kg **Speed:** Mach 0.9 **Range:** 150 km

♦ Naval radars

Name	*Band*	*Remarks*
FCS-1	X (I/J)	Mitsubishi Electric; also known as Type 72
FCS-2-12E	. . .	Mitsubishi Electric; radome-enclosed for guns and Sea Sparrow SAM; also known as Type 79 (Type 72 in earlier analog version)
FCS-2-21A	. . .	Mitsubishi Electric; open radar mount for gun control; 8–20 GHz
FCS-3	. . .	Phased-array, 360°-scanning "Mini-Aegis" weapons control system now in development
OPN-11	X (I)	Koden navigational set
OPS-9	X (I/J)	Furuno navigational set; slotted-waveguide antenna
OPS-11C	X (G/H)	Melco air/surface search; Japanese design, bedspring antenna
OPS-12	D	NEC 3-D phased-array with planar antenna
OPS-14	L	Melco air search; OPS-14B has MTI (Moving-Target Indication); OPS-14C has further improvements; 1,250–1,350 MHz
OPS-15	D	Furuno surface search; based on U.S. SPS-10
OPS-16	X	JRC (Japan Radio Corporation) surface search
OPS-17	X	JRC surface search
OPS-18	C	JRC surface search/navigational
OPS-19	I	JRC navigational set; slotted-waveguide antenna
OPS-24	. . .	Furuno planar-array successor to OPS-14 series
OPS-28/28B	X (G/H)	JRC navigational set; slotted-waveguide antenna
OPS-29	X	Koden navigational set
SPG-51C	X	U.S. Raytheon radar for Standard SAM
SPG-62	X	U.S. Raytheon Mk. 99 illuminator for Aegis system
SPS-52C	(E/F)	U.S. Hughes 3-D for SAM-equipped ships
SPY-1D	S	U.S. G.E. phased planar array 3-D radar for Aegis system
ZPS-4	X (I)	JRC navigational/surface search for submarines; antenna in radome
ZPS-6	X (I)	JRC navigational/surface search for submarines; slotted-waveguide antenna

♦ Sonars

Name	*Freq.*	*Remarks*
OQS-3, -3A	LF	NEC or Hitachi license-built version of U.S. SQS-23; bow- or hull-mounted
OQS-4	LF	NEC-developed improvement on SQS-23/OQS-3
OQS-8	MF	Raytheon-Hitachi equivalent to U.S. DE 1167/SQS-56
OQS-101	LF	NEC equivalent to U.S. SQS-53; bow-mounted dome
OQS-102	LF	NEC equivalent to U.S. SQS-53C
RQS-1	HF	Handheld mine-detection sonar for divers
SQQ-32	HF	Raytheon variable-depth minehunting set on *Yaeyama* class
SQS-23B	LF	U.S. Sangamo-built equipment
SQS-35(J)	MF	U.S. EDO-built VDS in last five *Chikugo*-class frigates
SQS-36D/J	MF	NEC license-built version of U.S. system
ZQQ-4	. . .	Oki bow array for *Yuushio* class
ZQQ-5, -5B	. . .	Hughes-Oki bow array for *Harushio* class; system also incorporates clip-on ZQR-1 array
ZQR-1	LF	Clip-on towed linear array; equivalent to U.S. BGR-15
ZQS-2, -2B	HF	License-built version of Plessey Type 193M minehunting sonar; ZQS-2B is a version of the later Type 2093
ZQS-3	HF	Hitachi/NEC; updated version of ZQS-2B

Note: Ishikawajima Heavy Industries (IHI) and Sumitomo Heavy Industries consolidated their naval shipbuilding activities in 2000, forming Marine United, Inc., which laid down its first naval ship, a destroyer, at the former IHI yard in Yokohama early in 2001. Kawasaki Shipbuilding Corp. was spun off from Kawasaki Heavy Industries. A planned merger of IHI and Kawasaki Heavy Industries' shipbuilding efforts fell through in 10-01. Hitachi Zosen and NKK agreed to consolidate their shipbuilding efforts into a single company during 2-00, with the new organization, Universal Shipbuilding Corp., established during 2002.

ATTACK SUBMARINES [SS]

♦ (0 + 3 . . .) Improved Oyashio class

	Budget	Bldr	Laid down	L	In serv.
SS 601 . . .	2004	Mitsubishi, Kobe	3-05	2007	2009
SS 602 . . .	2005	Kawasaki, Kobe	2006	2008	2010
SS 603 . . .	2006	Mitsubishi, Kobe	2007	2009	2011

D: 2,900 tons std. surf./4,280 tons sub. **S:** 13 kts surf./20 kts sub.
Dim: 84.10 × 9.10 × 8.50
A: 6 bow 533-mm Type HU-603B TT (20 Type 89 torpedoes and UGM-84C Harpoon missiles)
Electronics:
Radar: 1 JRC ZPS-6 nav./surf. search
Sonar: . . . suite; . . . towed passive array
EW: . . .
M: 2 . . . diesels; 2 . . . electric motors—2 Sterling Air Independent Propulsion generators; 1 prop
Crew: 65 total

Remarks: Improved version of the *Oyashio* class now in the early stages of design. The first unit is not planned for delivery until 2009 at the earliest.

♦ 9 (+ 1) Oyashio class

	Budget	Bldr	Laid down	L	In serv.
SS 590 Oyashio	1993	Kawasaki, Kobe	26-1-94	15-10-96	16-3-98
SS 591 Michishio	1994	Mitsubishi, Kobe	16-2-95	18-9-97	10-3-99
SS 592 Uzushio	1995	Kawasaki, Kobe	6-3-96	26-11-98	9-3-00
SS 593 Makishio	1996	Mitsubishi, Kobe	26-3-97	22-9-99	29-3-01
SS 594 Isoshio	1997	Kawasaki, Kobe	9-3-98	27-11-00	14-3-02
SS 595 Narushio	1998	Mitsubishi, Kobe	2-4-99	4-10-01	4-3-03
SS 596 Kuroshio	1999	Kawasaki, Kobe	27-3-00	23-10-02	9-3-04
SS 597 Takashio	2000	Mitsubishi, Kobe	30-1-01	9-03	3-05
SS 598 Yaeshio	2001	Kawasaki, Kobe	14-1-02	10-04	9-3-06
SS 599 Setoshio	2002	Mitsubishi, Kobe	2003	10-05	3-07
SS 600 . . .	2003	Kawasaki, Kobe	23-2-04	10-06	3-08

Yaeshio (SS 598)—following launch Takatoshi Okano, 11-04

Uzushio (SS 592) Takatoshi Okano, 4-04

D: 2,750 tons std. surf./3,600 tons sub. **S:** 12 kts surf./20 kts sub.
Dim: 81.70 × 10.30 (8.90 wl) × 7.40
A: 6 bow 533-mm Type HU-603B TT (20 Type 89 torpedoes and UGM-84C Harpoon missiles)
Electronics:
Radar: 1 JRC ZPS-6 nav./surf. search
Sonar: Hughes-Oki ZQQ-6 suite; ZQR-1 towed passive array
EW: ZLA-7 intercept suite
M: 2 Kawasaki 12V-25/25S diesels (1,700 bhp each), 2 1,850-kw alternators, 2 tandem Fuji or Toshiba electric motors; 1 prop; 7,750 shp
Crew: 10 officers, 59 enlisted

ATTACK SUBMARINES [SS] *(continued)*

Remarks: An entirely new design, with SS 590 approved under the 1993 budget. SS 592, budgeted to cost $534 million, has increased-strength hull steel, as does SS 593. SS 590 and SS 592 constitute the 2nd Submarine Squadron, 2nd Submarine Flotilla, Yokosuka; SS 591 and SS 593 are in the 1st Submarine Squadron, 1st Submarine Flotilla, Kure.

Oyashio (SS 590) *Ships of the World,* 3-99

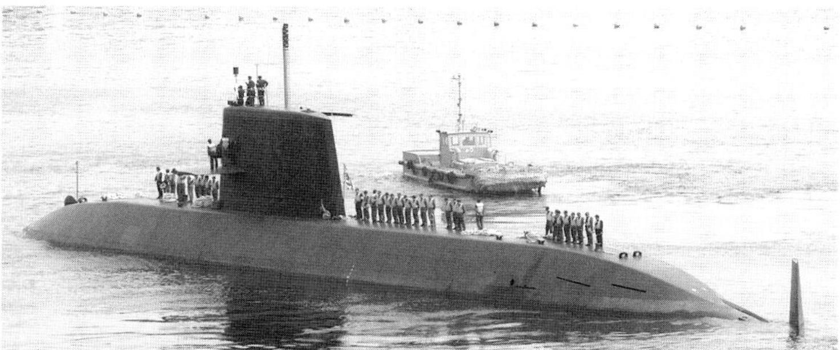

Oyashio (SS 590) Mitsuhiro Kadota, 5-03

Hull systems: The casing above the pressure hull is much higher than in previous Japanese designs and is tapered downward at the bow to accommodate the bow-mounted torpedo tubes and chin sonar array; the sail is of a new, tapered configuration. The outer hull has an anechoic coating on the sides, but not on the bottom.
Combat systems: Combat system designation is ZYQ-3. The towed hydrophone array is housed at the aft end of the casing. There are two conformal flank passive hydrophone arrays, the upper running nearly the full length of the submarine and the lower, shorter one running from just forward of the sail to roughly amidships.

♦ 6 Harushio class

	Budget	Bldr	Laid down	L	In serv.
SS 583 Harushio	1986	Mitsubishi, Kobe	21-4-87	26-7-89	30-1-90
SS 584 Natsushio	1987	Kawasaki, Kobe	8-4-88	20-3-90	20-3-91
SS 585 Hayashio	1988	Mitsubishi, Kobe	9-12-88	17-1-91	25-3-92
SS 586 Arashio	1989	Kawasaki, Kobe	8-1-90	17-3-92	17-3-93
SS 587 Wakashio	1990	Mitsubishi, Kobe	12-12-90	22-1-93	1-3-94
SS 588 Fuyushio	1991	Kawasaki, Kobe	12-12-91	16-2-94	7-3-95

Fuyushio (SS 588) Takatoshi Okano, 6-04

D: 2,450 tons std. surf./2,750 tons sub. **S:** 12 kts surf./20 kts sub.
Dim: 77.40 × 10.50 × 7.70
A: 6 amidships 533-mm Type HU-603B TT (20 Type 89 torpedoes and UGM-84C Harpoon missiles)
Electronics:
Radar: 1 JRC ZPS-6 nav./surf. search
Sonar: Hughes-Oki ZQQ-5B passive suite; . . . active; ZQR-1 (U.S. BQR-15) TASS towed passive array
EW: ZLA-7 intercept suite

Harushio (SS 583) Takatoshi Okano, 7-04

Hayashio (SS 585) Takatoshi Okano, 6-04

M: 2 Mitsubishi-M.A.N. V8/V24-30 MATL diesels (1,700 bhp each), 2 1,850-kw alternators, 2 tandem Toshiba electric motors; 1 prop; 7,220 shp
Crew: 10 officers, 65 enlisted

Remarks: An improved *Yuushio* design, incorporating provision for Sub-Harpoon missiles, a towed passive sonar array and passive flank arrays, a new EW suite, additional dc power, additional noise-reduction features (including anechoic coating), and a VLF radio receiver with towed wire antenna. SS 583 and SS 584 are assigned to the 5th Submarine Squadron, 1st Submarine Flotilla, Kure; SS 585, SS 586, and SS 588 to the 3rd Submarine Squadron, 1st Submarine Flotilla, Kure; SS 587 to the 6th Submarine Squadron, 2nd Submarine Flotilla, Yokosuka. Sister *Asashio* (SS 589), reclassified as training ship TSS 3601 on 9-3-00, had seen only three years' frontline service, mostly on trials duties.
Hull systems: Pressure hull is built of NS 110 steel (110 kg/mm^2 yield). Employ two Yuasa 480-cell battery sets.

♦ 2 Yuushio (Type S 122) class

	Bldr	Laid down	L	In serv.
SS 581 Yukishio	Mitsubishi, Kobe	11-4-85	23-1-87	11-3-88
SS 582 Sachishio	Kawasaki, Kobe	11-4-86	17-2-88	24-3-89

Takeshio (SS 580)—since retired Ralph Edwards, 10-02

D: 2,250 tons surf./2,500 tons sub.
S: 12 kts surf./13 kts snorkel (max.)/20 kts sub **Dim:** 76.20 × 9.90 × 7.40
A: 6 amidships 533-mm Type HU-603 TT (20 Type 72, Type 80, and Type 89 torpedoes and UGM-84C Harpoon SSM)
Electronics:
Radar: 1 JRC ZPS-6 nav./surf. search
Sonar: Hughes-Oki ZQQ-5B passive suite; SQS-36J active; ZQR-1 (U.S. BQR-15) TASS towed passive array
EW: ZLA-6 intercept suite
M: 2 Mitsubishi-M.A.N. V8/V24-30 MATL diesels (1,700 bhp each), 2 Kawasaki alternator sets (2,840 kw tot.), 2 tandem Fuji electric motors; 1 prop; 7,220 shp
Crew: 10 officers, 65 enlisted

Remarks: Assigned to the 4th Submarine Squadron, 2nd Submarine Flotilla, Yokosuka.
Hull systems: Double-hull design. Use two 480-cell Nihon-Denchi batteries. Both have the U.S. Masker bubbler acoustic noise-reduction system. Have pressure hulls of NS 80 (80 kg/mm^2 yield) and a 450-m maximum depth.
Combat systems: Have a ZYQ-1 computer/sonar data display system. Have a towed VLF communications antenna.
Disposals: Sister *Yuushio* (SS 573) became training submarine ATSS 8006 on 1-8-96 and has since been retired; *Mochishio* (SS 574) became ATSS 8007 on 1-8-97; *Setoshio* (SS 575) became ATSS 8008 on 10-3-99, was renumbered TSS 3602 during 3-00, and was retired 30-3-01; *Okishio* (SS 576) was redesignated training submarine TSS 3603 on 29-3-01; *Hamashio* (SS 578) is currently operating as a training submarine and has been renumbered TSS 3604. *Nadashio* (SS 577) was stricken on 5-6-01. *Akishio* (SS 579), and *Takeshio* (SS 580) retired from service by 2005. The remaning two units of the class will retire by 2008.

AUXILIARY SUBMARINES [SSA]

Note: The designation ATSS for submarines relegated to training duties was changed to TSS during 3-00.

♦ 1 Harushio class
Bldr: Mitsubishi, Kobe

	Laid down	L	In serv.
TSS 3601 Asashio (ex-SS 589)	15-4-83	21-1-85	5-3-86

Asashio (TSS 3601) Chris Delgoffe/H&L Van Ginderen, 5-00

D: 2,900 tons std. surf./3,200 tons sub. **S:** 12 kts surf./20 kts sub.
Dim: 87.00 × 10.50 × 7.70
A: 6 amidships 533-mm Type HU-603B TT (6 Type 89 torpedoes and UGM-84C Harpoon missiles)
Electronics:
Radar: 1 JRC ZPS-6 nav./surf. search
Sonar: Hughes-Oki ZQQ-5B passive suite; . . . active; ZQR-1 towed passive array
EW: ZLA-7 intercept suite
M: 2 Kawasaki 12V-25/25S diesels (1,700 bhp each), 2 2,840-kw generator sets, 2 1,850-kw alternator sets, 2 tandem Fuji electric motors; 1 prop; 7,220 shp—2 88-kw Sterling V4-275R Mk-II air-independent propulsion units
Crew: 10 officers, 62 enlisted + . . . trainees

Remarks: Reclassified as a training ship 9-3-00 after only three years front-line service. As compared to earlier units of the class, was fitted with new, more highly automated engineering control systems and an anechoic hull coating; the boat conducted an additional year of fitting out and trials time between launch and commissioning. Recommissioned 30-11-00 after AIP conversion. Is assigned with TSS 3604 to the 1st Submarine Training Squadron, 2nd Submarine Flotilla, Yokosuka.
Hull systems: Pressure hull built of NS 110 steel (110 kg/mm^2 yield). Employs two Yuasa 480-cell battery sets. Has a non-hull-penetrating optronic search periscope. Hull lengthened by 9.6 m and surfaced displacement increased by 400 tons when Sterling engine module added.

♦ 1 Yuushio class Bldr: Kawasaki, Kobe

	Laid down	L	In serv.
TSS 3604 Hamashio (ex-SS 578)	17-4-80	5-3-82	1-3-83

D: 2,200 tons surf./2,450 tons sub.
S: 12 kts surf./13 kts snorkel (max.)/20 kts sub. **Dim:** 76.20 × 9.90 × 7.40
A: 6 amidships 533-mm Type HU-603 TT (6 Type 72, Type 80, and Type 89 torpedoes and UGM-84C Harpoon SSM)
Electronics:
Radar: 1 JRC ZPS-6 nav./surf. search
Sonar: Hughes-Oki ZQQ-5B passive; SQS-36J active; ZQR-1 (U.S. BQR-15) TASS towed passive array
EW: ZLA-6 intercept suite
M: 2 Mitsubishi-M.A.N. V8/V24-30 MATL diesels (1,700 bhp each), 2 Kawasaki alternator sets (2,840 kw tot.), 2 tandem Fuji electric motors; 1 prop; 7,220 shp
Crew: 10 officers, 65 enlisted + . . . trainees

Remarks: Redesignated as training submarine in 2003 and assigned to the 1st Submarine Training Squadron, 2nd Submarine Flotilla, Yokosuka.
Hull systems: Double-hull design. Uses two 480-cell Nihon-Denchi batteries. Has the U.S. Masker bubbler acoustic noise-reduction system. The pressure hull was fabricated of NS 80 (80 kg/mm^2 yield) steel, and the boat has a 450-m maximum operating depth.
Combat systems: Has a ZYQ-1 computer/sonar data display system and a towed VLF communications antenna.
Disposals: *Setoshio* (TSS 3602, ex-ATSS 8008, ex-SS 575) was retired 30-3-01. *Okishio* (TSS 3603, ex-SS 576) was retired by 2004.

HELICOPTER-CARRYING DESTROYERS [DDH]

♦ 0 (+ 4) 13,500-ton class

	Bldr	Laid down	L	In serv.
DDH 145 . . .	Marine United, Yokohama	. . .	. . .	2009
DDH 146	. . .	. . .	. . .	2011
DDH 147	. . .	. . .	. . .	. . .
DDH 148	. . .	. . .	. . .	. . .

D: 13,500 tons standard (18,000 fl) **S:** 30 kts **Dim:** 195.00 × 32.00 × 7.00
Air group: 3 SH-60J ASW helicopters; 1 MH-53E mine-countermeasures helicopter
A: Mk 41 VLS (64 cells; RIM-7M Sea Sparrow and Vertical-Launch ASROC missiles); 2 20-mm Mk 15 Mod. 12 Block 1 Phalanx CIWS; 2 triple 324-mm Type 68 ASW TT (Type 73 or Mk 46 Mod. 5 torpedoes)

DDH 145—computer rendering showing full flight deck and superstructure confined to the starboard side *Ships of the World,* 2005

DDH 145—computer rendering *Ships of the World,* 2005

Electronics:
Radar: 1 OPS-20 nav.; 1 JRC OPS-28D air/surf. search; 1 Melco OPS-24 air search; 1 FCS-3 missile and gun f.c.
Sonar: . . . bow-mounted; . . . TASS
EW: . . .
M: 4 IHI-G.E. LM-2500 gas turbines; 2 CP props; approx. 120,000 shp
Range: 6,000/20 **Crew:** 345 tot.

Remarks: Intended to replace the *Shirane* and *Haruna* classes, with first unit requested under the FY 04 budget. The initial design had a flight deck space fore and aft, with superstructure amidships incorporating a hangar and with the stack uptakes offset to starboard, but the latest version resembles European small aircraft carriers, with the exception of not having a ski-jump bow. Two aircraft elevators and two sets of fin stabilizers will be fitted.

♦ 2 Shirane class

	Bldr	Laid down	L	In serv.
DDH 143 Shirane	IHI, Tokyo	25-2-77	18-9-78	17-3-80
DDH 144 Kurama	IHI, Tokyo	17-2-78	20-9-79	27-3-81

Kurama (DDH 144) Takatoshi Okano, 9-04

D: 5,200 tons (6,800 fl) **S:** 32 kts **Dim:** 158.8 × 17.5 × 5.3 (hull)
A: 2 single 127-mm 54-cal. U.S. Mk 42 Mod. 7 DP; 1 8-round Mk 29 SAM launcher (24 RIM-7F Sea Sparrow missiles); 2 20-mm Mk 15 Phalanx CIWS; 1 8-round Mk 112 ASROC ASW RL (16 missiles); 2 triple 324-mm Type 68 ASW TT (Type 73 or Mk 46 Mod. 5 torpedoes); 3 SH-60J ASW helicopters
Electronics:
Radar: 1 Koden OPN-11 nav.; 1 NEC OPS-12 3-D air search; 1 JRC OPS-28 surf./air search; 1 Thales WM-25 Sea Sparrow f.c.; 2 FCS-1A gun f.c.; 1 . . . helo control; 2 Mk 90 Phalanx f.c.
Sonar: NEC OQS-101 bow-mounted LF; EDO-NEC SQS-35(J) MF VDS; EDO-NEC SQR-18A TACTASS towed passive array
TACAN: ORN-6 (U.S. URN-25)
EW: Melco NOLQ-1 intercept; Fujitsu OLR-9B jammer; Mk 36 SRBOC decoy syst. (4 6-round Raytheon Mk 137 RL); SLQ-25 acoustic torpedo decoy syst.
M: 2 sets G.E.-Ishikawajima geared steam turbines; 2 props; 70,000 shp
Boilers: 2 (60 kg/cm^2, 480° C) **Crew:** 360 tot.

HELICOPTER-CARRYING DESTROYERS [DDH] *(continued)*

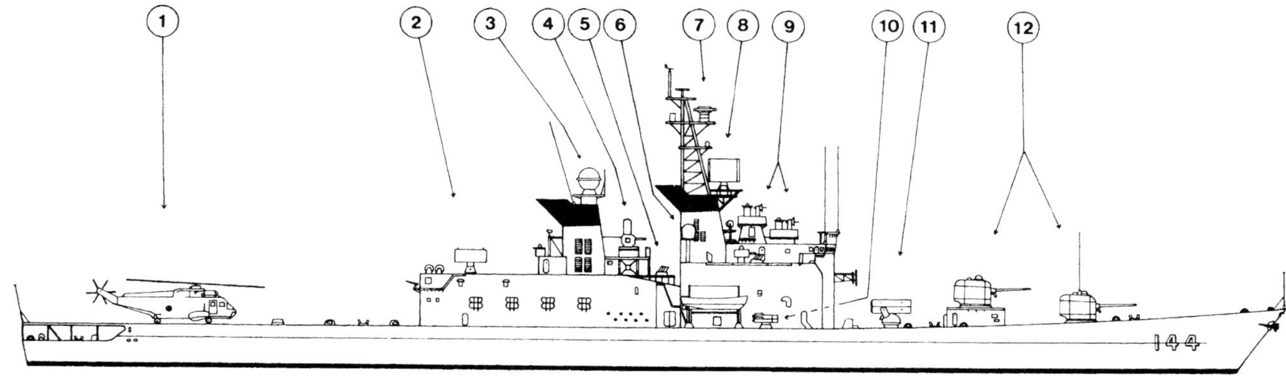

Kurama (DDH 144) 1. HSS-2B ASW helicopter (now carries SH-60J) 2. Mk 29 launcher for Sea Sparrow RIM-7 missiles 3. WM-25 track-while-scan fire-control radar 4. Mk 15 Phalanx CIWS 5. Mk 137 decoy launchers 6. Superbird SHF SATCOM antenna radomes 7. OPS-28 surface-search radar 8. OPS-12 3-D air-search radar 9. FCS-1A fire-control radars 10. Type 68 triple ASW TT 11. Mk 112 ASROC ASW missile launcher 12. 127-mm 54-cal. Mk 42 DP guns   Drawing by Robert Dumas, from *Flottes de Combat*

Kurama (DDH 144)   Mitsuhiro Kadota, 9-04

Remarks: Modified *Haruna* class. Each ship can carry a rear admiral and 20 staff; DDH 143 is flagship of the 1st Escort Flotilla, based at Yokosuka; DDH 144 is flagship of the 2nd Escort Flotilla, Sasebo. DDH 144 became the first Japanese warship to visit Russia in 71 years during a 7-96 call at Vladivostok.
Hull systems: Have two pair Vosper Thornycroft fin stabilizers fitted, and the Canadian Beartrap helicopter haul-down and deck traversing system is installed for the helicopters. Have U.S. Prairie and Masker bubble-generating systems to reduce radiated noise. There are two stacks, slightly staggered off centerline, compared to one on the *Haruna* class.

Shirane (DDH 143)   Mitsuhiro Kadota, 10-02

Combat systems: Both have a TDPS (Target Data Processing System) with a U.S. UYK-20 computer and OYQ-6 Tactical Data Processing System. Can employ NATO Link 11 and Link 14 data transmission systems. A U.S. Mk 114 fire-control system is employed for ASROC and torpedo launching. The helicopter landing-control radar is mounted to port of the after stack. The Japanese-developed Superbird SHF SATCOM system is fitted.

♦ 2 Haruna class

	Bldr	Laid down	L	In serv.
DDH 141 Haruna	Mitsubishi, Nagasaki	19-3-70	1-2-72	22-3-73
DDH 142 Hiei	IHI, Tokyo	8-3-72	13-8-73	27-12-74

Hiei (DDH 142)   Mitsuhiro Kadota, 6-04

HELICOPTER-CARRYING DESTROYERS [DDH] *(continued)*

Hiei (DDH 142) Mitsuhiro Kadota, 6-04

Haruna (DDH 141) Takatoshi Okano, 8-04

D: 4,950 tons (6,550 fl) **S:** 31 kts **Dim:** 153.0 × 17.5 × 5.3 (hull)
A: 2 single 127-mm 54-cal. U.S. Mk 42 Mod. 7 DP; 1 8-round Mk 29 SAM launcher (16 RIM-7F Sea Sparrow missiles); 2 20-mm Mk 15 Phalanx CIWS; 1 8-round Mk 112 ASROC launcher (16 missiles); 2 triple 324-mm Type 68 ASW TT (Type 73 or Mk 46 Mod. 5 ASW torpedoes); 3 SH-60J ASW helicopters
Electronics:
Radar: 1 Koden OPN-11 nav.; 1 JRC OPS-28 surf./air search; 1 Melco OPS-11C air search; 1 FCS-2-12E Sea Sparrow missile f.c.; 2 FCS-1A gun f.c.; 2 Mk 90 Phalanx f.c.
Sonar: Sangamo-Mitsubishi OQS-3 bow-mounted LF
TACAN: U.S. URN-25 (ORN-6)
EW: Melco NOLQ-1-3 intercept; Fujitsu OLR-9 jammer; OPN-7B D/F; OPN-11B D/F; Mk 36 SRBOC decoy syst. (4 6-round Raytheon Mk 137 RL); SLQ-25 towed acoustic torpedo decoy syst.

M: 2 sets G.E.-Ishikawajima geared steam turbines; 2 props; 70,000 shp
Boilers: 2 (60 kg/cm^2, 480° C) **Crew:** 36 officers, 304 enlisted

Remarks: DDH 141 was given a midlife modernization from 1986 to 1988; DDH 142 followed from 31-8-87 to 16-11-88. DDH 141 is flagship for the 3rd Escort Flotilla, Maizuru, and DDH 142 is flagship for the 4th Escort Flotilla at Kure. Are planned to be retired in 2008 and 2009.
Hull systems: The single combined mast/stack ("mack") is off centerline to port. Have two pair Vosper Thornycroft fin stabilizers. A Canadian Beartrap helicopter haul-down and traversal system is installed in the flight deck.
Combat systems: During modernizations, the superstructures were enlarged to accommodate additional electronics, a Sea Sparrow launcher was added atop the hangar and an FCS-2-12 director abaft the mack, two Mk 15 Phalanx CIWS were placed atop the superstructure, the aft FCS-1A was moved to atop the bridge, and new EW gear was added (including the Mk 36 decoy RL system). The OYQ-6 Combat Direction System (using the U.S. UYK-20A computer) was installed, replacing OYQ-3. Although provision was made for its mounting, a planned VDS was not installed, and antiship missile launchers were not added. The Japanese-developed Superbird SHF SATCOM system is carried.

GUIDED-MISSILE DESTROYERS [DDG]

♦ 0 (+ 2) Improved Kongo class

	Bldr	Laid down	L	In serv.
DDG 177 Atago	Mitsubishi, Nagasaki	2004	24-8-05	4-07
DDG 178 Ashigara	Mitsubishi, Nagasaki	6-4-05	30-8-06	2008

Atago (DDG 177)—the first Improved Kongo-class destroyer *Ships of the World,* 2005

Atago (DDG 177) *Ships of the World,* 2005

D: 7,700 tons light (10,000 fl) **S:** 30 kts **Dim:** 165.0 × 21.0 × 6.1
A: 8 RGM-84C Harpoon SSM; Mk 41 VLS syst. (96 tot. cells: 32 fwd, 64 atop hangar; SM-2 Block III, SM-3, and ESSM Sea Sparrow SAMs, Vertical-Launch ASROC ASW missiles); 1 127-mm 54-cal. OTO Melara DP; 2 20-mm Mk 15 Mod. 12 Block IB Phalanx CIWS; 2 triple 324-mm Type 68 ASW TT (Type 73 or Mk 46 Mod. 5 torpedoes); 2 SH-60J or EH.101 helicopters

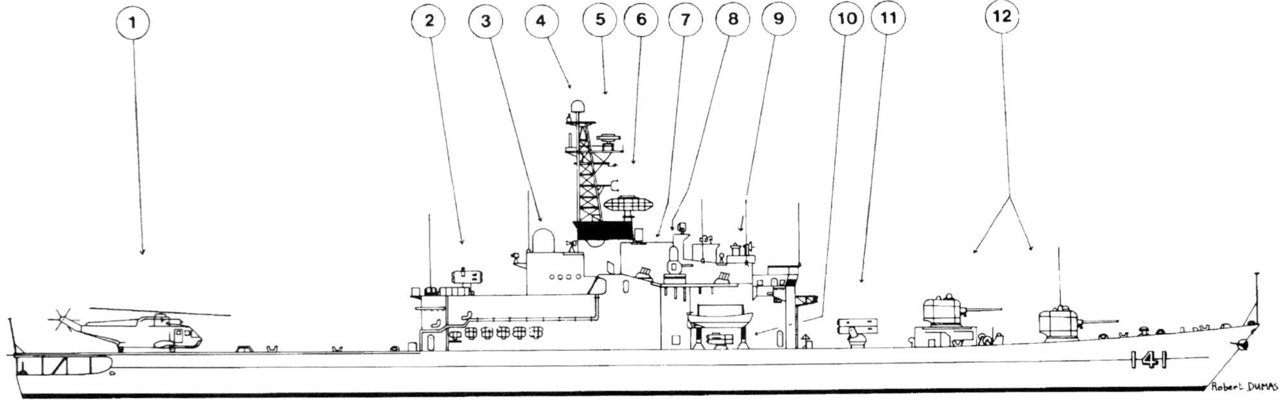

Haruna (DDH 141) 1. HSS-2B ASW helicopter (SH-60J now carried) 2. Mk 29 launcher for Sea Sparrow RIM-7 missiles 3. FCS-2-12E radar SAM director 4. ORN-6 TACAN 5. OPS-28 surface-search radar 6. OPS-11C surface/air-search radar 7. Mk 137 decoy launchers 8. Mk 15 Phalanx CIWS 9. FCS-1A radar director for 127-mm guns 10. Type 68 triple ASW TT 11. Mk 112 ASROC ASW missile launcher 12. 127-mm 54-cal. Mk 42 guns Drawing by Robert Dumas, from *Flottes de Combat*

GUIDED-MISSILE DESTROYERS [DDG] *(continued)*

Electronics:
Radar: 1 . . . nav.; 1 Lockheed Martin SPY-1D(V) Aegis 3-D; 3 Raytheon SPG-62 missile target illumination; 1 FCS-2-23 gun f.c., 2 General Dynamics Mk 90 Phalanx f.c.
Sonar: U.S. SQQ-89(V)15R suite: NEC OQS-102 bow-mounted LF; Oki OQR-2 (SQR-19A(V)) TASS
TACAN: ORN- . . .
EW: NOLQ-2 intercept; NOLQ-2 D/F; OLT-3 jammer; Mk 36 SRBOC decoy syst. (4 6-tubed Raytheon Mk 137 RL); SLQ-25A(V) Nixie acoustic torpedo decoy syst.
E/O: . . . surveillance and tracking
M: 4 IHI-G.E. LM-2500 gas turbines; 2 CP props; approx. 100,000 shp
Crew: 300 total

Remarks: A fifth Aegis destroyer was added to the 2001–5 procurement plan in 2-98 and a sixth on 7-1-00 to improve strategic ballistic-missile defense capabilities; the ships are costing $1.13 billion each. The design is essentially an enlargement of the *Kongo* so as to incorporate twin helicopter hangars on either side of the after missile launch group. DDG 177 is to be home-ported at Sasebo.
Combat systems: Are to have the U.S. Mk 7 Mod. 6(V) Aegis weapon system with CEC (Cooperative Engagement Capability), UPX-29(V) IFF interrogation system, Mk 34 gun weapon-control system, and SQQ-121 Computer-Aided Dead-Reckoning Tracker. They are to be capable of employment as theater ballistic-missile defense ships, using the U.S. Standard SM-2 Block III and SM-3 missiles. Will make considerable use of COTS (Commercial off-the-Shelf) computer and display equipment.

♦ 4 Kongo class

	Bldr	Laid down	L	In serv.
DDG 173 Kongo	Mitsubishi, Nagasaki	8-5-90	26-9-91	25-3-93
DDG 174 Kirishima	Mitsubishi, Nagasaki	7-4-92	19-8-93	16-3-95
DDG 175 Myoko	Mitsubishi, Nagasaki	8-4-93	5-10-94	14-3-96
DDG 176 Chokai	IHI, Tokyo	29-5-95	27-8-96	20-3-98

Chokai (DDG 176) Takatoshi Okano, 7-04

Kongo (DDG 173) Takatoshi Okano, 4-04

D: 7,250 tons light (9,485 fl) **S:** 30 kts
Dim: 161.00 (150.50 pp) × 21.00 (20.00 wl) × 6.20 (hull)
A: 8 RGM-84C Harpoon SSM; Mk 41 VLS (90 Standard SM-2 MR Block III SAM and Vertical-Launch ASROC ASW missiles); 1 127-mm 62-cal. Mk 45 Mod. 4 DP; 2 20-mm Mk 15 Mod. 12 Block I Phalanx CIWS; 2 single 12.7-mm mg; 2 triple 324-mm Type 68 ASW TT (Type 73 or Mk 46 Mod. 5 torpedoes)

Kongo (DDG 173) Takatoshi Okano, 12-02

Electronics:
Radar: 1 JRC OPS-20 nav.; 1 JRC OPS-28D surf./air search; 1 Lockheed Martin SPY-1D Aegis 3-D; 3 Raytheon SPG-62 (Mk 99) illuminators; 1 FCS-2-21 gun f.c.; General Dynamics Mk 90 Phalanx f.c.
Sonar: NEC OQS-102 bow-mounted LF; Oki OQR-2 (SQR-19A(V)) TASS
TACAN: ORN- . . .
EW: NOLQ-2 intercept; NOLQ-2 D/F; OLT-3 jammer; Mk 36 SRBOC decoy syst. (4 6-round Raytheon Mk 137 RL); SLQ-25 Nixie acoustic torpedo decoy syst.
M: 4 IHI-G.E. LM-2500 gas turbines; 2 CP props; approx. 100,000 shp
Electric: 6,000 kw tot. **Range:** 4,500/20 **Fuel:** 1,000 tons **Crew:** 310 tot.

Remarks: The design is an enlarged version of the U.S. *Arleigh Burke* class, adding a backup surface/air-search radar, using a faster-firing 127-mm gun with a dedicated fire-control system, and incorporating a more elaborate EW system with active jamming. First unit ordered 24-6-88. Great expense caused a considerable resistance to the program, delaying its start by two years. During 1995, their cost was reported as about $1.48 billion (U.S.) each. The ships are intended to assist in the aerial defense of Japan, as well as acting as AAW escorts for task forces. DDG 173 is assigned to the 62nd Escort Squadron, 2nd Escort Flotilla, Sasebo; DDG 174 to the 61st Escort Squadron, 1st Escort Flotilla, Yokosuka; DDG 175 to the 63rd Escort Squadron, 3rd Escort Flotilla, Maizuru; and DDG 176 to the 64th Escort Squadron, 4th Escort Flotilla, Kure.
Hull systems: Are equipped with the U.S. Prairie and Masker bubbler noise-radiation suppression systems and have infrared exhaust signature provisions. Do not have fin stabilizers, relying on broad, fixed bilge keels and hullform for roll reduction. The deck abaft after VLS missile installation is intended for use as a helicopter platform, but there is no hangar or deck-handling gear; twin stabilized horizon indicators are carried on the after superstructure to aid landings.
Combat systems: The combat data system is designated OYQ-8. Have U.S. NATO Link 11 and Link 14 capability; DDG 176 had Link 16 on completion, and it has been backfitted in the others. The VLS cells hold 61 missiles aft, 29 forward. The SPG-62 radar illuminators support three Mk 99 Mod. 1 missile fire-control direction systems, and the underwater battery fire-control system is the U.S. Mk 116 Mod. 7. Have the U.S.-made WSN-5 inertial navigation system and U.S. WSC-3 UHF SATCOM with two OE-82C antennas; also installed is the Japanese-developed Superbird SHF SATCOM system, with antennas flanking the bridge. The IFF transponder is the U.S. UPX-29; interrogation is via the SPY-1D radar. The OQS-102 sonar is equivalent to the U.S. SQS-53C. The 12.7-mm mg and night-vision equipment were added to detect and deter infiltration craft. The class will likely be upgraded to the theater ballistic-missile defense role. Class was fitted with the 127-mm 62-cal. Mk 45 Mod. 4 DP by 2005. Under a 7-06 contract Lockheed-Martin will begin upgrading the class for BMD rules with DDG 173 to be the first unit upgraded by 2007.

♦ 2 Hatakaze class

	Bldr	Laid down	L	In serv.
DDG 171 Hatakaze	Mitsubishi, Nagasaki	20-5-83	9-11-84	27-3-86
DDG 172 Shimakaze	Mitsubishi, Nagasaki	30-1-85	30-1-87	23-3-88

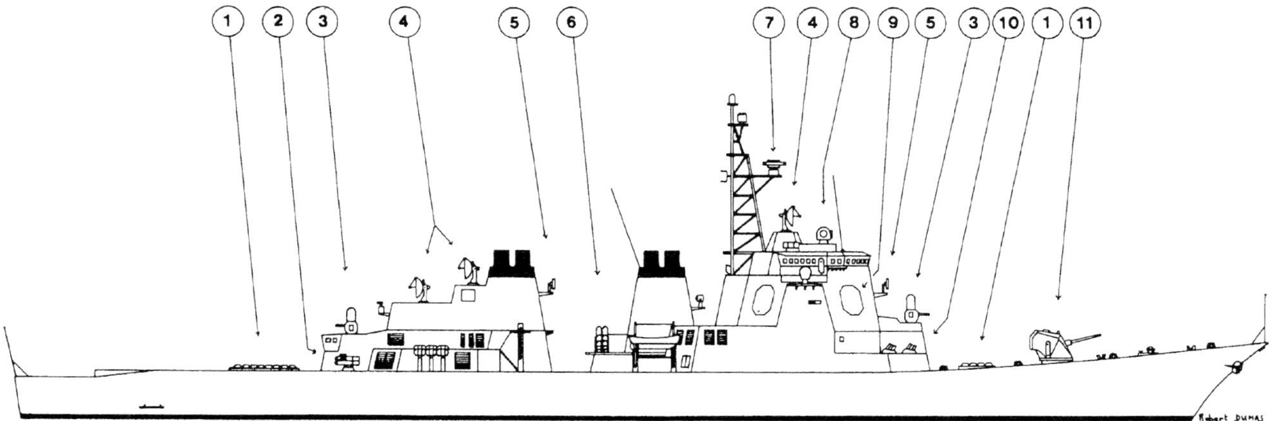

Kongo (DDG 173) 1. Mk 41 vertical launch system launcher-cell groups 2. Type 68 triple ASW TT 3. Mk 15 CIWS 4. SPG-62 radar target illuminators 5. OE-82 SATCOM antennas for the WSC-3 UHF SATCOM system 6. Harpoon antiship missiles (two groups of four) 7. OPS-28D surface/air-search radar 8. FCS-2-21 radar gun director 9. SPY-1D Aegis radar antenna array 10. Mk 137 decoy launchers 11. 127-mm 54-cal. OTOBreda DP gun Drawing by Robert Dumas, from *Flottes de Combat*

GUIDED-MISSILE DESTROYERS [DDG] *(continued)*

Shimakaze (DDG 172) Takatoshi Okano, 4-04

Hatakaze (DDG 171) Takatoshi Okano, 4-04

Shimakaze (DDG 172) Takatoshi Okano, 8-02

D: 4,650 tons (5,600 fl) **S:** 32 kts (30 sust.) **Dim:** 150.0 × 16.4 × 4.80 (hull)
A: 1 single-rail Mk 13 Mod. 4 missile launch syst. (40 Standard SM-1 MR missiles); 8 RGM-84C Harpoon SSM; 2 single 127-mm 54-cal. Mk 42 Mod. 7 DP; 2 20-mm Mk 15 Phalanx CIWS; 2 single 12.7-mm mg; 1 8-round Mk 112 ASROC ASW RL; 2 triple 324-mm Type 68 ASW TT (Type 73 or Mk 46 Mod. 5 ASW torpedoes)

Electronics:
Radar: 1 JRC OPS-28B surf./air search; 1 Melco OPS-11C air search; 1 Hughes SPS-52C 3-D air search; 2 Raytheon SPG-51C SAM f.c.; 2 FCS-2-21C gun f.c.; 2 Raytheon Mk 90 Phalanx f.c.
Sonar: NEC OQS-4 Mod. 1 bow-mounted MF
TACAN: NEC ORN-6
EW: Melco NOLQ-1-3 intercept/jammer syst.; OLR-9B intercept; Mk 36 Mod. 2 SRBOC decoy syst. (4 6-round Raytheon Mk 137 RL); SLQ-25 Nixie towed acoustic torpedo decoy syst.
M: COGAG: 2 Rolls-Royce Spey SM-1A cruise gas turbines (13,325 shp each) and 2 Olympus TM-3D boost gas turbines (24,700 shp each); 2 CP props; 74,100 shp
Range: . . . / . . . **Crew:** 260 tot.

Remarks: DDG 171 is assigned to the 61st Destroyer Division, 1st Escort Flotilla, Yokosuka; DDG 172 to the 63rd Escort Squadron, 3rd Escort Flotilla, Maizuru.
Combat systems: Have the U.S. Mk 74 Mod. 13 missile fire-control system (with two SPG-51C radar tracker/illuminators) for the Standard missile system. Have Link 11 and Link 14 datalinks, the OYQ-4 Mod. 1 combat data system, the NYPX-2 IFF system, and the WSC-3 UHF SATCOM with two OE-82C antennas; also installed is the Japanese-developed Superbird SHF SATCOM system, with antennas flanking the bridge. There is a landing pad for a helicopter but no hangar. Have been equipped with 12.7-mm mg and night-vision equipment to detect and deter infiltration craft.

♦ 3 Tachikaze class

	Bldr	Laid down	L	In serv.
DDG 168 TACHIKAZE	Mitsubishi, Nagasaki	19-6-73	12-12-74	26-3-76
DDG 169 ASAKAZE	Mitsubishi, Nagasaki	27-5-76	15-10-77	27-3-79
DDG 170 SAWAKAZE	Mitsubishi, Nagasaki	14-9-79	4-6-81	30-3-83

Tachikaze (DDG 168) Mitsuhiro Kadota, 7-05

D: 3,850 tons (4,800 fl) **S:** 32 kts **Dim:** 143.0 × 14.3 × 4.7 (hull)
A: 1 Mk 13 Mod. 4 missile launch syst. (40 Standard SM-1 MR SAM/RGM-84C Harpoon SSM); 2 (DDG 168: 1) single 127-mm 54-cal. Mk 42 Mod. 7 DP; 2 20-mm Mk 15 Phalanx CIWS; 2 single 12.7-mm mg; 1 8-round Mk 112 ASROC ASW RL; 2 triple 324-mm Type 68 ASW TT (Type 73 or Mk 46 Mod. 5 torpedoes)
Electronics:
Radar: 1 JRC OPS-17 (DDG 170: OPS-28) surf./air search; 1 Melco OPS-11B air search; 1 Hughes SPS-52C 3-D air search; 2 Raytheon SPG-51C SAM f.c.; 1 FCS-1A (DDG 170: FCS-2) gun f.c.; 2 General Dynamics Mk 90 Phalanx f.c.
Sonar: NEC OQS-3 (DDG 170: OQS-4) bow-mounted MF
EW: NEC NOLQ-1 (DDG 168: NOLR-6) intercept; Fujitsu OLT-3 jammer; Mk 36 Mod. 2 SRBOC decoy syst. (4 6-round Raytheon Mk 137 RL); SLQ-25 Nixie towed acoustic torpedo decoy syst.
M: 2 sets Mitsubishi geared steam turbines; 2 props; 70,000 shp
Boilers: 2 (60 kg/cm^2, 480° C) **Crew:** 250 (DDG 168: 277) tot.

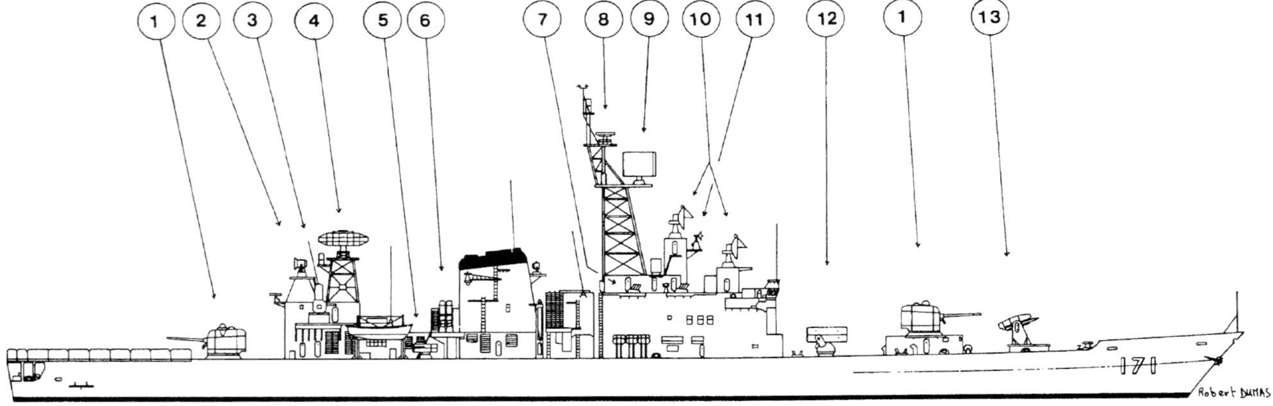

Hatakaze (DDG 171) 1. 127-mm 54-cal. Mk 42 DP guns 2. FCS-2-21C radar directors for the 127-mm guns 3. Mk 15 Phalanx CIWS 4. OPS-11C surface/air-search radar 5. Type 68 triple ASW TT 6. Harpoon SSM (two groups of four) 7. Mk 137 decoy launchers 8. OPS-28B surface/air-search radar 9. SPS-52C 3-D air-search radar 10. SPG-51C radar illuminators for Standard SM-1 MR SAMs 11. Telemetry antenna (since removed) 12. Mk 112 ASROC ASW rocket launcher 13. Mk 13 Mod. 4 launcher for Standard SM-1 MR SAMs
Drawing by Robert Dumas, from *Flottes de Combat*

GUIDED-MISSILE DESTROYERS [DDG] *(continued)*

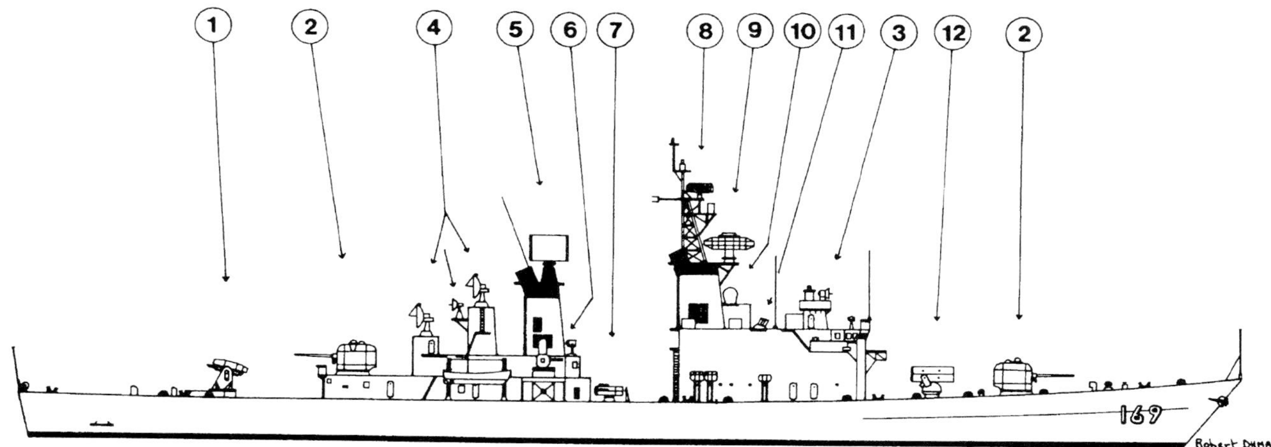

Asakaze (DDG 169) 1. Mk 13 Mod. 4 launcher for Standard SM-1 MR SAMs 2. 127-mm 54-cal. Mk 42 DP guns 3. FCS-1A radar director for 127-mm guns 4. SPG-51C radar illuminator for Standard SM-1 MR SAMs 5. SPS-52C 3-D air-search radar 6. Mk 15 Phalanx CIWS 7. Type 68 triple ASW TT 8. OPS-17 surface-search radar 9. OPS-11B surface/air-search radar 10. OLT-3 EW jammer antenna array 11. Mk 137 decoy launchers 12. Mk 112 ASROC ASW missile launcher

Drawing by Robert Dumas, from *Flottes de Combat*

Tachikaze (DDG 168)—an accommodations deckhouse is carried in place of the after 127-mm gunmount fitted aboard sister ships Mitsuhiro Kadota, 7-05

Remarks: DDG 168 became flagship of the Fleet Escort Force in 1998 and is based at Yokosuka. DDG 169 assigned to the 64th Escort Squadron, 4th Escort Flotilla, Kure; and DDG 170 to the 62nd Escort Squadron, 2nd Escort Flotilla, Sasebo.
Hull systems: The propulsion plant is identical to that of the *Haruna* class.
Combat systems: Have OYQ-4 Mod. 1 combat data system and are Link 14 datalink compatible. The missile-control system is Mk 74 Mod. 13 and uses the two SPG-51C radar tracker/illuminators. Have the U.S. Mk 114 ASW weapons-control system. The ASROC launcher has a reload magazine below the bridge. The after 127-mm mount was replaced by a deckhouse in DDG 168 in 1998 to increase accommodations. The WSC-3 UHF SATCOM system, with two OE-82C antennas, is fitted; also installed is the Japanese-developed Superbird SHF SATCOM system, with antennas flanking the bridge. Have been equipped with two 12.7-mm mg and night-vision equipment to detect and deter infiltration craft.

DESTROYERS [DD]

♦ 5 Takanami (4,600-ton) class

	Bldr	Laid down	L	In serv.
DD 110 Takanami	Sumitomo, Yokosuka	25-4-00	26-7-01	12-3-03
DD 111 Onami	Mitsubishi, Nagasaki	17-5-00	20-9-01	13-3-03
DD 112 Makinami	Marine United, Yokohama	13-7-01	8-03	18-3-04
DD 113 Sazanami	Mitsubishi, Nagasaki	14-4-02	29-8-03	16-2-05
DD 114 Suzunami	Marine United, Yokohama	24-9-03	26-8-04	16-2-06

D: 4,650 tons (approx. 5,350 fl) **S:** 32 kts (30 sust.)
Dim: 151.0 × 17.4 × 5.3 (mean hull)
A: 8 SSM-1B SSM; Mk 41 VLS launch syst. (16 ESSM Sea Sparrow SAM and Vertical-Launch ASROC ASW missiles); 1 127-mm 54-cal. OTO Melara DP; 2 20-mm Mk 15 Phalanx gatling CIWS; 2 triple 324-mm HOS-302 ASW TT (Type 73 or Mk 46 Mod. 5 torpedoes); 1 SH-60J ASW helicopter

Takanami (DD 110) Mitsuhiro Kadota, 8-05

Onami (DD 111) Mitsuhiro Kadota, 8-05

Electronics:
Radar: 1 JRC OPS-20 nav.; 1 JRC OPS-28D surf./air search; 1 Melco OPS-24 air search; 2 FCS-2-21 gun/SAM f.c.; 2 General Dynamics Mk 90 Phalanx f.c.
Sonar: OQS-5 bow-mounted MF; OQR-2 TASS towed passive array
TACAN: ORN-6 (U.S. URN-25)
EW: NOLQ-3 intercept/active syst.; OPN-7B and OPN-11 comms intercept; OLT-3 and OLT-5 jammers; Mk 36 SRBOC decoy syst. (4 6-round Raytheon Mk 137 RL); SLQ-25 Nixie towed acoustic torpedo decoy syst.

DESTROYERS [DD] *(continued)*

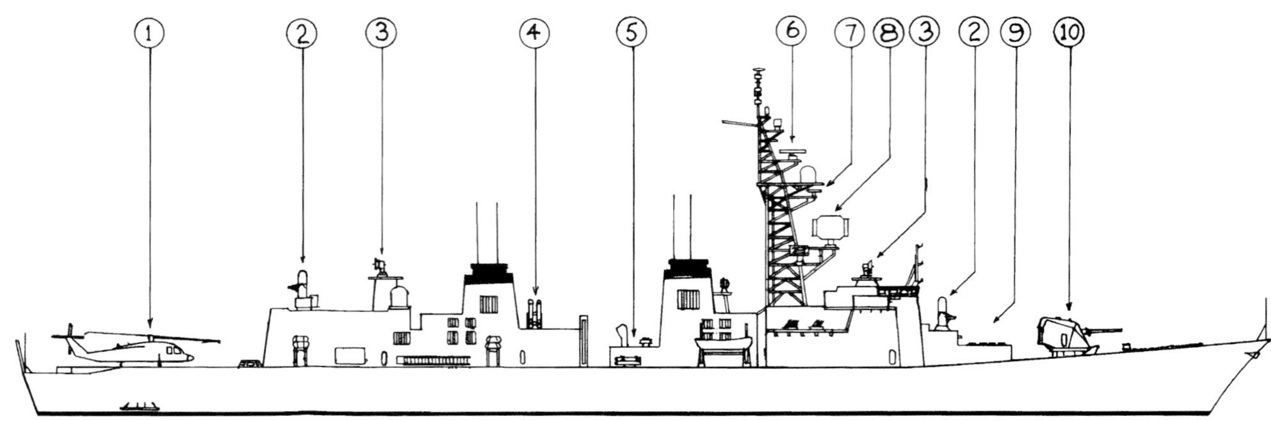

Takanami (DD 110) 1. SH-60J ASW helicopter 2. Mk 15 Phalanx CIWS atop helicopter hangar 3. FCS-2-21 missile and gun radar directors 4. SSM-1B antiship missiles (two groups of four) 5. HOS-302 triple ASW TT 6. OPS-28D surface-search radar 7. OPS-20 navigational radar 8. OPS-24 3-D air-search radar 9. Mk 41 vertical-launch system (32 cells) 10. 127-mm 54-cal. OTOBreda DP gun — Drawing by A. D. Baker III

Onami (DD 111) — Mitsuhiro Kadota, 8-05

Takanami (DD 110) — Mitsuhiro Kadota, 7-05

M: COGAG: 2 Kawasaki–Rolls-Royce Spey SM-1C cruise gas turbines (13,500 shp each), 2 G.E.-IHI LM-2500 boost gas turbines (16,500 shp each); 2 CP props; 60,000 shp max.
Range: . . . / . . . **Crew:** 170 tot.

Remarks: Funding approved for first two under FY 98 and the third under FY 99; DD 113 was approved under FY 01, DD 114 under FY 02. Improved version of the *Murasame* class.
Hull systems: Propulsion plant duplicates that of the preceding *Murasame* class, with a consequent slight loss in maximum speed.
Combat systems: Fitted with OYQ-9 combat data system and equipped with Link 11 datalink capability. Taking advantage of the larger hull, the ships mount a larger gun than the *Murasame* class, while they have a Mk 41 vertical missile launch group with twice as many cells but no Mk 48 launch system cells; this will permit greater versatility in loadouts in the future. Will have Superbird SHF SATCOM capability but not WSC-3 UHF SATCOM facilities. The U.S. SQQ-28 helicopter-deployed sonobuoy datalink is to be fitted. May have two 12.7- or 20-mm guns and night-vision equipment to detect and deter infiltration craft.

♦ 9 Murasame class

	Bldr	Laid down	L	In serv.
DD 101 Murasame	IHI, Tokyo	18-8-93	23-8-94	12-3-96
DD 102 Harusame	Mitsui, Tamano	11-8-94	16-10-95	24-3-97
DD 103 Yudachi	Sumitomo, Uraga	18-3-96	19-8-97	4-3-99
DD 104 Kirisame	Mitsubishi, Nagasaki	3-4-96	21-8-97	18-3-99
DD 105 Inazuma	Mitsubishi, Nagasaki	8-5-97	9-9-98	15-3-00
DD 106 Samidare	IHI, Tokyo	11-9-97	24-9-98	21-3-00
DD 107 Ikazuchi	Hitachi, Maizuru	25-2-97	24-6-99	14-3-01
DD 108 Akebono	IHI, Tokyo	29-10-99	25-9-00	19-3-02
DD 109 Ariake	Mitsubishi, Nagasaki	18-5-99	16-10-00	6-3-02

Murasame (DD 101) — Bernard Prézelin, 7-05

Inazuma (DD 105) — Takatoshi Okano, 4-04

D: 4,400 tons (approx. 5,100 fl) **S:** 33 kts (30 sust.)
Dim: 151.00 (145.00 wl) × 17.40 (15.70 wl) × 5.20
A: 8 SSM-1B SSM; Mk 48 VLS missile launch syst. (16 RIM-7M Sea Sparrow SAM); 1 Mk 41 VLS launch group (16 Vertical-Launch ASROC ASW missiles); 1 76-mm 62-cal. OTO Melara Compact DP; 2 20-mm Mk 15 Mod. 1 Block I Phalanx CIWS; 2 triple 324-mm HOS-302 ASW TT (Type 73 or Mk 46 Mod. 5 torpedoes); 1 SH-60J ASW helicopter

DESTROYERS [DD] *(continued)*

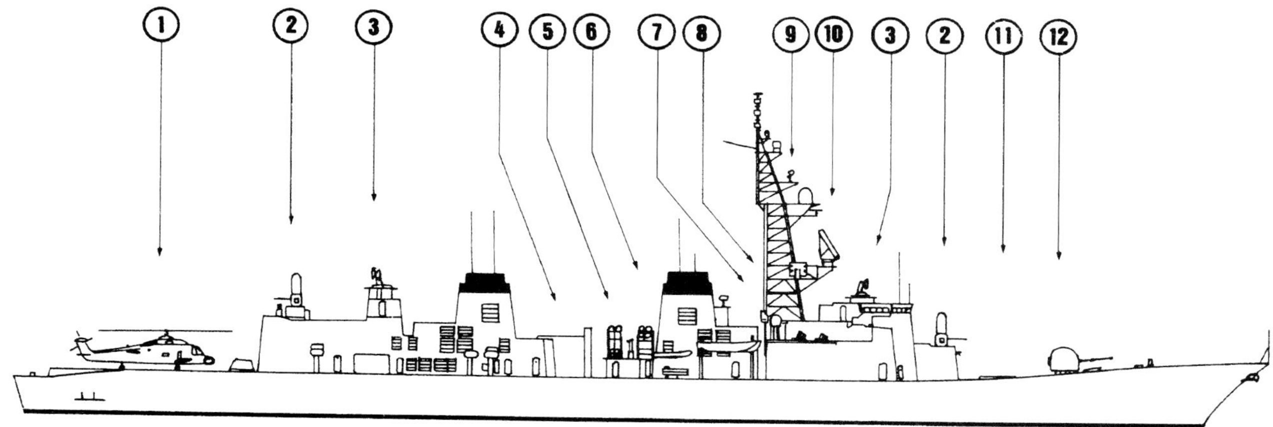

Murasame (DD 101) 1. SH-60J ASW helicopter 2. Mk 15 Phalanx CIWS atop helicopter hangar 3. FCS-2-21 gun and Sea Sparrow SAM radar directors 4. Mk 48 vertical-launch system for Sea Sparrow SAMs 5. SSM-1B antiship missiles (two groups of four) 6. HOS-302 triple ASW TT 7. Superbird SHF SATCOM antenna radomes 8. NOLQ-3 EW antenna array 9. OPS-28D surface/air-search radar 10. OPS-24 3-D air-search radar 11. Mk 41 vertical-launch system cell group for ASROC ASW missiles 12. 76-mm 62-cal. OTOBreda DP gun

Drawing by Jean Moulin, from *Flottes de Combat*

Yudachi (DD 103) Takatoshi Okano, 9-04

Electronics:
Radar: 1 JRC OPS-20 nav.; 1 JRC OPS-28D surf./air search; 1 Melco OPS-24 air search; 2 FCS-2-21 gun/SAM f.c.; 2 General Dynamics Mk 90 Phalanx f.c.
Sonar: Mitsubishi OQS-5 bow-mounted MF; OQR-2 TASS towed passive array
TACAN: ORN-6 (U.S. URN-25)
EW: NOLQ-3 intercept/active syst.; OPN-7B and OPN-11 comms intercept; OLT-3 and OLT-5 jammers; Mk 36 SRBOC decoy syst. (4 6-round Raytheon Mk 137 RL); SLQ-25 Nixie towed acoustic torpedo decoy syst.

M: COGAG: 2 Kawasaki–Rolls-Royce SM-1C Spey cruise gas turbines (13,500 shp each), 2 G.E.-IHI LM-2500 boost gas turbines (16,500 shp each); 2 CP props; 60,000 shp max.

Electric: . . . kw tot. **Range:** 4,500/18 **Crew:** 170 tot.

Remarks: First unit authorized under FY 91 budget and second under FY 92. Two were approved under FY 94, another pair under FY 95, and DD 107 under FY 96. DD 108 and DD 109 were approved under the FY 97 budget. DD 101 and DD 102 are assigned to 1st Escort Squadron, 1st Escort Flotilla, Yokosuka; DD 103 and DD 104 to the 6th Escort Squadron, 2nd Escort Flotilla, Sasebo; and DD 105 and DD 106 to the 4th Escort Squadron, 4th Escort Flotilla, Kure. DD 108 was the final ship constructed by IHI (Ishikawajima-Harima Heavy Industries), Tokyo.

Hull systems: Both the Rolls-Royce and G.E. gas turbines are considerably downrated from their normal maximum power. Although the plant could in theory generate a total of 106,500 shp, and any turbine or combination of turbines can be connected to either shaft, the maximum output is limited to 60,000 shp. Berthing for the crew is two high, and there is a small gymnasium.

Combat systems: Have the OYQ-7 Mod. 9 or, in later units: OYQ-9 combat data system and are equipped with Link 11. There are two VLS groups, a Mk 41 system group with 16 cells forward for Vertical-Launch ASROC missiles (and, later, Standard SM-2 SAMs), and a shorter Mk 48 group amidships with 16 cells for Sea Sparrow SAMs. SM-2 missiles will eventually be able to be launched from a *Murasame*-class unit and then controlled by an Aegis-equipped *Kongo,* as in the U.S. CEC Cooperative Engagement system. Planned adoption of the RIM-7P Evolved Sea Sparrow (ESSM) SAM will quadruple the total SAM capacity. Have Superbird SHF SATCOM capability but no WSC-3 UHF SATCOM facilities. The U.S. SQQ-28 helicopter-deployed sonobuoy datalink is fitted. Are being equipped with two 12.7- or 20-mm guns and night-vision equipment to detect and deter infiltration craft.

♦ 6 Asagiri class

	Bldr	Laid down	L	In serv.
DD 153 Yuugiri	Sumitomo, Uraga	25-2-86	21-9-87	28-2-89
DD 154 Amagiri	IHI, Tokyo	3-3-86	9-9-87	17-3-89
DD 155 Hamagiri	Hitachi, Maizuru	20-1-87	4-6-88	31-1-90
DD 156 Setogiri	Sumitomo, Uraga	9-3-87	12-9-88	14-2-90
DD 157 Sawagiri	Mitsubishi, Nagasaki	14-1-87	25-11-88	6-3-90
DD 158 Umigiri	IHI, Tokyo	31-10-88	9-11-89	12-3-91

Yuugiri (DD 153) Frank Findler, 7-05

Umigiri (DD 158) Takatoshi Okano, 2-04

Sawagiri (DD 157) Douglas A. Cromby, 2-03

D: 3,500 tons (4,300 fl) **S:** 30 kts **Dim:** 136.50 × 14.60 × 4.50 (mean hull)

A: 8 RGM-84C Harpoon SSM; 1 8-round Mk 29 missile launcher (18 RIM-7F Sea Sparrow missiles); 1 76-mm 62-cal. OTO Melara Compact DP; 2 20-mm Mk 15 Phalanx CIWS; 1 8-round Mk 112 ASROC ASW RL (. . . reloads); 2 triple 324-mm Type 68 ASW TT (Type 73 or Mk 46 Mod. 5 torpedoes); 1 SH-60J ASW helicopter

DESTROYERS [DD] *(continued)*

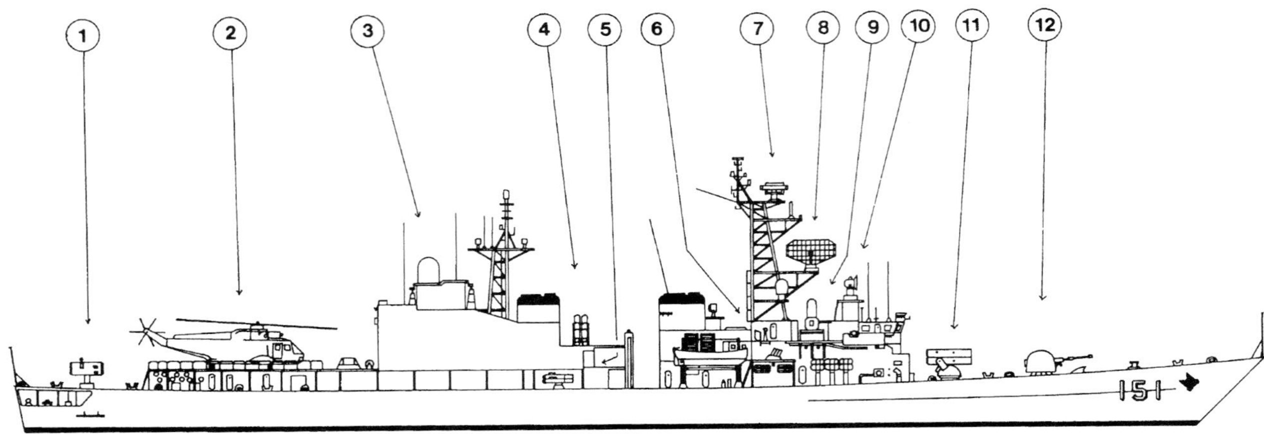

Asagiri (DD 151) 1. Mk 29 launcher for Sea Sparrow SAMs 2. HSS-2B ASW helicopter (now replaced by SH-60J) 3. FCS-2-12E radar director for Sea Sparrow SAMs 4. Harpoon antiship missiles (two groups of four) 5. Type 68 triple ASW TT 6. Mk 137 decoy launchers 7. OPS-28C surface/air-search radar 8. OPS-14C air-search radar (OPS-24 on later ships of the class) 9. Mk 15 Phalanx CIWS (port and starboard) 10. FCS-2-21A 76-mm radar director 11. Mk 112 ASROC ASW missile launcher 12. 76-mm 62-cal. OTOBreda DP gun Drawing by Robert Dumas, from *Flottes de Combat*

Yuugiri (DD 153) Bernard Prézelin, 7-05

Electronics:
Radar: 1 JRC OPS-20 nav.; 1 JRC OPS-28C or -28D surf./air search; 1 Melco OPS-14C (DD 155–158: OPS-24) air search; 1 FCS-2-21A gun f.c.; 1 FCS-2-12E SAM f.c.; 2 General Dynamics Mk 90 Phalanx f.c.
Sonar: Mitsubishi OQS-4A bow-mounted MF; EDO-NEC OQR-1 (U.S. SQR-18A(V) TASS) towed passive array
TACAN: ORN-6 (U.S. URN-25)
EW: NEC NOLR-6C intercept; NOLR-9C D/F; Fujitsu OLT-3 D/F; Mk 36 SRBOC decoy syst. (2 6-round Raytheon Mk 137 RL); SLQ-25 Nixie acoustic torpedo decoy syst.

M: COGAG: 4 Kawasaki–Rolls-Royce Spey SM-1A gas turbines; 2 CP props; 53,900 shp
Electric: . . . **Range:** . . . **Fuel:** . . . **Crew:** 220 tot.

Remarks: An improved *Hatsuyuki* design. DD 151 was ordered 29-3-84, DD 152–154 on 23-3-85, DD 155–157 in 3-86, and DD 158 in 3-87. DD 158 was the only ship authorized of two requested under FY 86. DD 157 is assigned to the 2nd Escort Squadron, 2nd Escort Flotilla, Sasebo; DD 153, 155, and 156 to the 7th Escort Squadron, 3rd Escort Flotilla, Maizuru; and DD 154 and 158 to the 5th Escort Squadron, 1st Escort Flotilla, Yokosuka.
Hull systems: Have fin stabilizers and a Beartrap/RAST-type helicopter landing and deck-traversing system. In the other ships, the mast is raised and retained on the centerline, while the after stacks are offset slightly to port. The U.S. Prairie/Masker bubble underwater noise suppression system is fitted.
Combat systems: Have the OYQ-6 combat data and command system, employing the U.S.-built UYK-20A computer and the Japanese OJ-194B digital display indicator. The OPS-24 D-Band air-search radar mounted in the last four employs hundreds of miniature transmitters arrayed on its planar face. A radome on a foremast platform houses the antenna for the U.S. SQQ-28 datalink system for the SH-60J ASW helicopter. DD 158 was first to complete with a towed tactical passive sonar array, backfitted in the rest. Have the Superbird SHF SATCOM system. NOLR-8 intercept equipment may be fitted in later units. Have been equipped with two 12.7- or 20-mm guns and night-vision equipment to detect and deter infiltration craft.
Disposals: *Yamagiri* (DD 152) and *Asagiri* (DD 151) are assigned as training ships and have been renumbered TV 3515 and TV 3516 respectively. They are listed under the *training ships* [AXT] heading.

♦ 11 Hatsuyuki class

	Bldr	Laid down	L	In serv.
DD 122 Hatsuyuki	Sumitomo, Uraga	14-3-79	7-11-80	23-3-82
DD 123 Shirayuki	Hitachi, Maizuru	3-12-79	4-8-81	8-2-83
DD 124 Mineyuki	Mitsubishi, Nagasaki	7-5-81	17-10-82	26-1-84
DD 125 Sawayuki	IHI, Tokyo	22-4-81	21-6-82	15-2-84
DD 126 Hamayuki	Mitsui, Tamano	4-2-81	27-5-82	18-11-83
DD 127 Isoyuki	IHI, Tokyo	20-4-82	19-9-83	23-1-85
DD 128 Haruyuki	Sumitomo, Uraga	11-3-82	6-9-83	14-3-85
DD 129 Yamayuki	Hitachi, Maizuru	25-2-83	10-7-84	3-12-85
DD 130 Matsuyuki	IHI, Tokyo	7-4-83	25-10-84	19-3-86
DD 131 Setoyuki	Mitsui, Tamano	26-1-84	3-7-85	31-1-87
DD 132 Asayuki	Sumitomo, Uraga	22-12-83	16-10-85	20-2-87

Haruyuki (DD 128) Takatoshi Okano, 7-04

Mineyuki (DD 124) Takatoshi Okano, 5-04

D: DD 122–128: 2,950 tons (3,700 fl)—DD 129–132: 3,050 tons (3,800 fl)
S: 30 kts **Dim:** 131.70 (126.00 wl) × 13.70 × 4.10 (DD 129–132: 4.30 hull)
A: 4 or 8 RGM-84C Harpoon SSM; 1 8-round Mk 29 missile launcher (18 RIM-7F Sea Sparrow missiles); 1 76-mm 62-cal. OTO Melara Compact DP; 2 20-mm Mk 15 Phalanx gatling CIWS; 1 8-round Mk 112 ASROC ASW RL (16 missiles); 2 triple 324-mm Type 68 ASW TT (Mk 73 or Mk 46 Mod. 5 torpedoes); 1 SH-60J ASW helicopter
Electronics:
Radar: 1 JRC OPS-18-1 surf. search; 1 Melco OPS-14B air search; 1 FCS-2-21 gun f.c.; 1 FCS-2-12A SAM f.c.; 2 General Dynamics Mk 90 Phalanx f.c.
Sonar: NEC OQS-4A hull-mounted MF; EDO-NEC OQR-1 towed passive array
TACAN: U.S. URN-25 (ORN-6)
EW: NEC NOLQ-6C intercept—DD 131–132 only: OLR-9B D/F—all: Fujitsu OLT-3 jammer; Mk 36 SRBOC decoy syst. (2 6-round Raytheon Mk 137 RL)
M: COGOG: 2 Kawasaki–Rolls-Royce Olympus TM-3B gas turbines (25,000 shp each), 2 Tyne RM-1C gas turbines (5,000 shp each); 2 CP props; 50,000 shp (45,000 normal max.)
Range: . . . / . . . **Fuel:** . . . **Crew:** 17–19 officers, 144–153 enlisted

DESTROYERS [DD] *(continued)*

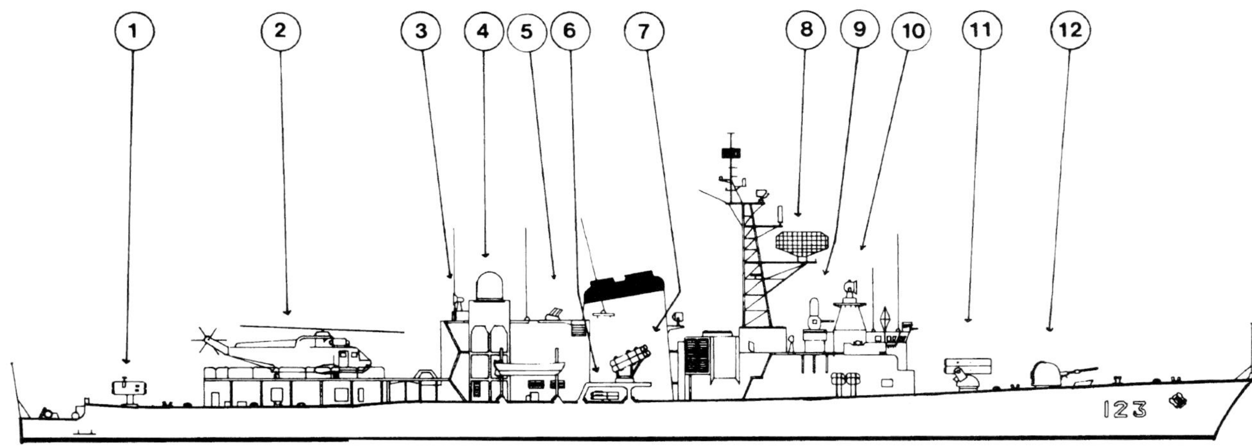

Shirayuki (DD 123) 1. Mk 29 launcher for Sea Sparrow SAMs 2. HSS-2B ASW helicopter (now replaced by SH-60J) 3. Helicopter hangar 4. FCS-2-12A radar director for Sea Sparrow SAMs 5. Mk 137 decoy launchers 6. Type 68 triple ASW TT 7. Harpoon SSM (two groups of two or four) 8. OPS-14B air-search radar 9. Mk 15 Phalanx CIWS (port and starboard) 10. FCS-2-21 radar director for 76-mm gun 11. Mk 112 ASROC ASW missile launcher 12. 76-mm 62-cal. OTOBreda DP gun

Drawing by Robert Dumas, from *Flottes de Combat*

Hamayuki (DD 126) Takatoshi Okano, 7-04

Remarks: DD 122, 123, and 125 are assigned to the 21st Escort Squadron, Yokosuka District Fleet; DD 124 and 126 to the 3rd Escort Squadron, 3rd Escort Flotilla, Maizuru; DD 129, 130, and 131 to the 8th Escort Squadron, 4th Escort Flotilla, Kure; and DD 127, 128, and 132 to the 23rd Escort Squadron, Sasebo District Fleet. Sister *Shimayuki* (DD 133) was redesignated TV 3513 on 18-3-99 and is employed as a training ship.

Hull systems: The Olympus engines are rated at 22,500 shp for cruise, 25,000 shp max., while the Tyne cruise engines are rated at 4,620 shp cruise/5,000 shp max. and can provide speeds up to 19.5 kts. Helicopter deck has the Canadian Beartrap traversing/landing system. Have fin stabilizers. Stack incorporates passive infrared cooling features and a water-spray system. DD 129 and later have steel vice aluminum superstructures. Most of the class easily made 32 kts on trials.

Combat systems: First seven have OYQ-5 TDPS (Tactical Data Processing System) with a U.S. UYK-20 computer; later units have OYQ-6. Have Link 14 data relay receiver only. Received OQR-1 (U.S. SQR-18) TACTASS towed passive linear arrays after completion, with DD 130 receiving hers under an FY 90 refit. DD 122 and DD 123 initially lacked the Mk 15 Phalanx CIWS, which was added in the mid-1990s. DD 131 and DD 132 have later EW equipment. All have NYPX-2 IFF systems and Superbird SHF SATCOM equipment. Are being equipped with two 12.7- or 20-mm guns and night-vision equipment to detect and deter infiltration craft. Increasingly, only four Harpoon missiles are being carried, rather than the full complement of eight.

Disposal note: *Kikizuki* (DD 165), last of the *Takatsuki* class, was decommissioned in 2003. *Yamagumo*-class destroyer *Yugumo* (DDK 121) was retired during 2005. Sisters *Yamagumo* (DDK 113) and *Makigumo* (DDK 114) were reclassified as training ships on 20-6-91 and later stricken; *Asagumo* (DDK 115) became auxiliary ASU 7018 on 18-10-93 and was later stricken; *Akigumo* (DD 120; ex-DDK 120) was reclassified as a cadet training ship on 13-6-00.

FRIGATES [FF]

♦ 6 Abukuma class

	Bldr	Laid down	L	In serv.
DE 229 Abukuma	Mitsui, Tamano	17-3-88	21-12-88	12-12-89
DE 230 Jintsu	Hitachi, Kanegawa	14-4-88	31-1-89	2-2-90
DE 231 Oyodo	Mitsui, Tamano	8-3-89	19-12-89	23-1-91
DE 232 Sendai	Sumitomo, Uraga	14-4-89	26-1-90	15-3-91
DE 233 Chikuma	Hitachi, Maizuro	14-2-91	22-1-92	24-2-93
DE 234 Tone	Sumitomo, Uraga	8-2-91	6-12-91	8-2-93

Jintsu (DE 230) Takatoshi Okano, 7-04

Jintsu (DE 230) Takatoshi Okano, 8-02

D: 2,050 tons (approx. 2,550 fl) **S:** 27 kts **Dim:** 109.0 × 13.4 × 3.8 (hull)
A: 4 RGM-84C Harpoon SSM; 1 76-mm 62-cal. OTO Melara Compact DP; 1 20-mm Mk 15 Phalanx CIWS; 1 8-round Mk 112 ASROC ASW RL; 2 triple 324-mm Type 68 ASW TT (Mk 73 or Mk 46 Mod. 5 torpedoes)
Electronics:
Radar: 1 JRC OPS-28 surf./air search; 1 Melco OPS-14C air search; 1 FCS-2-21A gun f.c.; 1 General Dynamics Mk 90 Phalanx f.c.
Sonar: OQS-8 bow-mounted MF
EW: NEC NOLQ-6C intercept; Fujitsu OLT-3 jammer; Mk 36 SRBOC decoy syst. (2 6-round Raytheon Mk 137 RL)
M: CODOG: 2 Kawasaki–Rolls-Royce Spey SM-1C gas turbines (13,500 shp each), 2 Mitsubishi S12U MTK S200 diesels (5,000 bhp each max.; 3,000 sust.); 2 CP props; 27,000 shp max.
Range: . . . / . . . **Crew:** 115 tot.

Remarks: First pair authorized under the FY 86 budget, second pair under FY 87, and third pair under FY 89. One more requested for FY 90 was rejected, and no more frigates are planned. First two were ordered 26-3-87, second two 26-2-88, and last two 24-1-89. The design has considerable improvements in sensors and firepower over the austere *Yubari* and *Ishikari* designs. DE 229 and 230 are assigned to the 31st Escort Squadron, Maizuru District Fleet, the others to the 26th Escort Squadron, Sasebo District Fleet, except for DE 233, transferred to the 25th Escort Squadron, Ominato District Fleet, 13-6-00.

Hull systems: Hull molded depth is 7.80 m. Have a helicopter VERTREP station aft, but no landing area.

FRIGATES [FF] *(continued)*

Combat systems: Have the OYQ-1 automated combat data system. The RAM (RIM-116A) point-defense SAM is planned to be added, although Japan has yet to order the system from the U.S. or Germany. Also planned to be added later is the U.S. SQR-19A towed tactical sonar system (TASS). The hull-mounted sonar is essentially the same as the U.S. Raytheon DE 1167. Have been fitted with Skybird SHF SATCOM equipment. Carry only four Harpoon missiles, possibly to reduce topweight. No torpedo decoy system is fitted.

♦ 2 Yubari class

	Bldr	Laid down	L	In serv.
DE 227 Yubari	Sumitomo, Uraga	9-2-81	22-2-82	18-3-83
DE 228 Yubetsu	Hitachi, Maizuru	14-1-82	25-1-83	14-2-84

Yubari (DE 227)—with four Harpoon missiles aboard *Ships of the World,* 2000

Yubetsu (DE 228)—with six Harpoon missiles aboard *Ships of the World,* 2000

D: 1,470 tons (1,760 fl) **S:** 25 kts **Dim:** 91.0 × 10.8 × 3.6 (hull)
A: 6 or 8 RGM-84C Harpoon SSM; 1 76-mm 62-cal. OTO Melara DP; 1 4-round 375-mm Type 71 (Bofors Erika) ASW RL; 2 triple 324-mm Type 68 ASW TT (Type 73 or Mk 46 Mod. 5 torpedoes)
Electronics:
Radar: 1 Fujitsu OPS-19B nav.; 1 JRC OPS-28C surf./air search; 1 FCS-2-21 gun f.c.
Sonar: OQS-4 hull-mounted MF
EW: NEC NOLQ-6C intercept; Fujitsu OLT-3 jammer; Mk 36 SRBOC decoy syst. (2 6-round Raytheon Mk 137 decoy RL)
M: CODOG: 1 Kawasaki–Rolls-Royce Olympus TM-3B gas turbine (28,390 shp); 1 Mitsubishi 6DRV 35/44 diesel (5,000 bhp max.); 2 CP props
Range: . . . / . . . **Crew:** 98 tot.

Remarks: An enlarged version of the *Ishikari* class, presumably because the earlier ship was too cramped for the mission requirements. DE 227 was ordered under the FY 79 budget, DE 228 under FY 80. A third was requested for FY 82 but was not authorized. Both are assigned to the 27th Escort Squadron, Ominato District Fleet, with DE 226.
Combat systems: Have the OYQ-5 combat data system. Did not receive the planned Mk 15 Phalanx CIWS or a torpedo decoy system. The number of Harpoon missiles carried has been reduced to six in recent years.

♦ 1 Ishikari class

	Bldr	Laid down	L	In serv.
DE 226 Ishikari	Mitsui, Tamano	17-5-79	18-3-80	30-3-81

D: 1,200 tons (1,450 fl) **S:** 25 kts **Dim:** 84.5 × 10.0 × 3.5 (mean hull)
A: 4 RGM-84C Harpoon SSM; 1 76-mm 62-cal. OTO Melara DP; 1 4-round 375-mm Type 71 (Bofors Erika) ASW RL; 2 triple 324-mm Type 68 ASW TT (Type 73 and Mk 46 Mod. 5 torpedoes)
Electronics:
Radar: 1 Fujitsu OPS-19B nav.; 1 JRC OPS-28 surf./air search; 1 FCS-2-21 gun f.c.
Sonar: OQS-4 hull-mounted MF
EW: NEC NOLQ-6C intercept; Fujitsu OLT-3 jammer; Mk 36 SRBOC decoy syst. (2 6-round Raytheon Mk 137 RL)

Ishikari (DE 226)—with four Harpoon missiles aboard *Ships of the World,* 2000

M: CODOG: 1 Kawasaki–Rolls-Royce Olympus TM-3B gas turbine (28,390 shp), 1 Mitsubishi 6DRV 35/44 diesel (5,000 bhp max.); 2 CP props
Range: . . . / . . . **Crew:** 90 tot.

Remarks: Ordered under FY 77 program. Smaller, more lightly armed, faster, and with fewer sensors than the preceding *Chikugo* class. Is assigned to the 27th Escort Squadron, Ominato District Fleet.
Hull systems: Aluminum superstructure. A highly automated ship with a very small crew for her size. Either the gas turbine or the single diesel will drive both propellers. Can make 19 kts max. on diesel.
Combat systems: The Combat Information Center (CIC) is below the waterline and is equipped with the OYQ-5 combat data system. Normally carries only four Harpoon SSM but four more could be fitted if required.

Disposal note: Of the frigates of the *Chikugo* class, *Chikugo* (DE 215) was stricken 15-4-96, *Ayase* (DE 216) on 1-8-96, *Mikuma* (DE 217) on 8-7-97, *Iwase* (DE 219) on 16-10-98; *Tokachi* (DE 218) on 15-4-98, *Chitose* (DE 220) on 13-4-99, *Niyodo* (DE 221) on 24-6-99, *Teshio* (DE 222) on 27-6-00, *Yoshino* (DE 223) on 15-5-01, and *Kumano* (DE 224) on 18-5-01. *Noshiro* (DE 225) was retired during 3-03.

HYDROFOIL GUIDED-MISSILE PATROL BOATS [PTGH]

♦ 3 modified Italian Sparviero class

Bldr: Sumitomo, Uraga

	Laid down	L	In serv.
PG 821 PG 01	25-3-91	17-7-92	22-3-93
PG 822 PG 02	25-3-91	17-7-92	22-3-93
PG 823 PG 03	8-3-93	15-6-94	13-3-95

PG 01 (PG 821)—riding on foils Takatoshi Okano, 7-04

D: 50 tons (63 fl) **S:** 50 kts (in calm sea; 46 sust.)
Dim: 22.95 (24.56 foils retracted) × 7.01 (12.06 max. over foils) × 1.87 (1.45 over foils at speed, 4.37 at rest)
A: 4 SSM-1B SSM; 1 20-mm JM-61-MB Sea Vulcan gatling AA

HYDROFOIL GUIDED-MISSILE PATROL BOATS [PTGH]
(continued)

PG 02 (PG 822) Takatoshi Okano, 7-04

Electronics:
Radar: 1 JRC OPS-28-2 surf. search
EW: . . . intercept; Mk 36 SRBOC decoy syst. (2 6-round Raytheon Mk 137 RL)
M: 1 G.E. LM-500 gas turbine; 1 waterjet; 5,200 shp (4,000 sust.)
Range: 400/45 **Crew:** 11 tot.

Remarks: First two were approved under FY 90, but the third unit, approved under FY 91, was deferred to help pay the cost of Japanese participation in the aftermath of the Persian Gulf War and was requested again under the FY 92 budget. A fourth unit, requested under FY 95, was turned down. The license to construct this modified version of the Italian Navy's *Sparviero* class (itself a modified version of the U.S. Navy's *Tucumcari,* PGH 1) was not granted until 3-91. All three are assigned to the Ominato District Fleet as the 1st Missile Boat Squadron, based at Amarushi.
Hull systems: The titanium hydrofoils are retractable, the bow unit swinging forward through an arc and the after pair pivoting outboard through an arc.
Combat systems: The gatling gun employs a simple pintle mounting and is of the same type as is employed on JMSDF mine-countermeasures ships and JCG patrol ships and craft. Have Link 11 datalink.

GUIDED-MISSILE PATROL BOATS [PTG]

♦ 8 Hayabusa class (200-ton PG)
Bldr: Mitsubishi, Shimonoseki

	Laid down	L	In serv.
PG 824 Hayabusa	9-11-00	13-6-01	25-3-02
PG 825 Wakataka	9-11-00	13-9-01	11-3-02
PG 826 Otaka	2-10-01	13-5-02	24-3-03
PG 827 Kumataka	2-10-01	2-8-02	24-3-03
PG 828 Umitaka	4-10-02	21-5-03	24-3-04
PG 829 Shirataka	4-10-02	8-8-03	24-3-04
PG 830 . . .	10-03	2005	2006
PG 831 . . .	10-04	2005	2006

Wakataka (PG 285) Takatoshi Okano, 7-04

D: 200 tons (. . . fl) **S:** 46 kts **Dim:** 50.1 × 8.40 × 1.7
A: 4 SSM-1B SSM; 1 76-mm 62-cal. OTO Melara SuperRapid DP; 2 single 12.7-mm mg
Electronics:
Radar: 1 JRC OPS-18 nav.; 1 JRC OPS-18-2 surf. search; 1 FCS-2-31C gun f.c.
EW: NOLR-9B intercept; Mk 36 SRBOC decoy syst. (2 6-round Raytheon Mk 137 RL)
E/O: OAX-2 surveillance and tracking syst.
M: 3 G.E. LM-500-GO7 gas turbines; 3 waterjets; 16,200 shp
Range: . . . / . . . **Crew:** 21 tot.

Remarks: New design, substituted for further hydrofoil construction. More than three times the displacement of the PG 01 series. First two were approved under the FY 99 budget, second pair under FY 00, and third pair under FY 01. As many as 10 are planned. Engines ordered 5-00. Carry a 6.3-m RIB for boarding and inspection duties. The ships reportedly cost around 9 billion yen to build.

Hayabusa (PG 824) Takatoshi Okano, 7-04

Umitaka (PG 828) Takatoshi Okano, 8-04

Combat systems: The OYQ-8 combat data system is fitted. Have a SATCOM system with two antennas. The 76-mm gun has a faceted gunhouse to reduce radar reflectivity.

MINE WARFARE SHIPS

♦ 2 Uraga-class mine-countermeasures support ship/minelayers [MCS]

	Bldr.	Laid down	L	In serv.
MST 463 Uraga	Hitachi Zosen, Maizuru	19-5-95	22-5-96	19-3-97
MST 464 Bungo	Mitsui, Tamano	31-8-95	24-4-97	23-3-98

Bungo (MST 464) Takatoshi Okano, 4-04

D: 5,650 tons (8,400 fl) **S:** 22 kts **Dim:** 141.0 (136.0 pp) × 22.0 × 5.4
A: MST 464 only: 1 76-mm 62-cal. OTO Melara DP—both: 230 large mines
Electronics:
Radar: 1 JRC OPS-18 nav.; 1 Melco OPS-14B air search—MST 464 only: 1 FCS-2-21A gun f.c.
M: 2 Mitsui 12V42M-A diesels; 2 props; 19,800 bhp—bow-thruster
Range: 4,600/20 **Crew:** 129 tot. + 32 mine warfare staff

Remarks: First unit approved under the FY 94 budget and second under FY 95. MST 463 is flagship for the Escort Fleet Minesweeper Flotilla, Yokosuka. MST 464 is based at Kure.
Hull systems: Hull has bulbous forefoot. Have a hangar and flight deck for one CH-53E mine-countermeasures helicopter. There is a stern door centerline, served by an articulating ramp to permit the service and resupply of craft being supported.
Combat systems: Flanking the stern door on either side on two deck levels are doors covering mine rails. MST 463 is fitted to receive a radar director and gun, but neither has been installed as yet.

Note: The former 1st and 2nd Fleet Minesweeper Flotillas have been combined into a single Fleet Minesweeper Flotilla.

MINE WARFARE SHIPS *(continued)*

Uraga (MST 463) —note the central door/ramp in the transom for deploying sweep gear to mine-countermeasures craft and the four flush doors flanking it on two levels for the minelaying rails Ralph Edwards, 10-02

♦ 3 Yaeyama-class deep-sea mine-countermeasures ships [MHS]

	Bldr	Laid down	L	In serv.
MSO 301 Yaeyama	Hitachi, Kanagawa	30-8-90	29-8-91	16-3-93
MSO 302 Tsushima	Nippon Kokan, Tsurumi	20-7-90	11-9-91	23-3-93
MSO 303 Hachijo	Nippon Kokan, Tsurumi	17-5-91	15-12-92	24-3-94

Tsushima (MSO 302) Mitsuhiro Kadota, 10-02

Hachijo (MSO 303) Mitsuhiro Kadota, 10-02

D: 1,000 tons (1,150 fl) **S:** 14 kts **Dim:** 67.0 × 11.8 × 3.1
A: 1 20-mm JM-61-MB Sea Vulcan gatling AA
Electronics:
Radar: 1 Fujitsu OPS-19 nav.
Sonar: ZQS-3 (Raytheon SQQ-32) minehunting HF VDS; Klein AQS-14 towed side-scan
M: 2 Mitsubishi 6NMU-series diesels; 2 CP props; 2,400 bhp—bow-thruster
Crew: 60 tot.

Remarks: First two units were authorized by the FY 89 budget, with two per year thereafter planned to a total of six, but only one was authorized under FY 90. Three more were planned during FY 1992–95 period, but further procurement has been canceled. Constitute the Escort Fleet's 51st Minesweeping Division, Yokosuka.
Hull systems: Wooden-hulled construction, with glass-reinforced plastic sheathing.
Combat systems: Equipped to deploy the Type S-7 autonomous minehunting vehicle and Type S-8 deep-sea mine disposal system, the latter a version of the U.S. Honeywell SLQ-48 remote-controlled submersible vehicle. Also carry Type S-2 noisemakers. Equipped with the Marisat commercial satellite communications system as well as sophisticated navigational equipment.

♦ 0 (+ 4) . . . -class minehunter/minesweepers [MHC]

	Bldr.	Laid down	L	In serv.
MSC 693 . . .	Hitachi, Kanagawa	17-5-05	9-06	2008
MSC 694 . . .	. . .	. . .	. . .	. . .
MSC 695 . . .	. . .	. . .	. . .	. . .
MSC 696 . . .	. . .	. . .	. . .	. . .

D: 570 tons **S:** 14.5
Dim: 57.00 × 9.80 × 3.00
A: 1 20-mm JM-61-MB Sea Vulcan gatling AA
Electronics: Radar: 1 . . . nav.—Sonar: . . . minehunting HF VDS
M: 2 Mitsubishi diesels; 2 CP props; . . . bhp—bow-thruster
Electric: . . . **Range:** 2,500/10 **Crew:** 45 total

Remarks: First four authorized 2005–6. Additional units may be planned.

♦ 11 (+ 1) Sugashima-class minehunter/minesweepers [MHC]

	Bldr.	Laid down	L	In serv.
MSC 681 Sugashima	Nippon Kokan, Tsurumi	8-5-96	25-8-97	16-3-99
MSC 682 Notojima	Hitachi, Kanagawa	8-5-96	3-9-97	16-3-99
MSC 683 Tsunoshima	Hitachi, Kanagawa	7-8-97	22-10-98	13-3-00
MSC 684 Naoshima	Nippon Kokan, Tsurumi	17-4-98	7-10-99	16-3-01
MSC 685 Toyoshima	Hitachi, Kanagawa	25-4-99	13-9-00	4-3-02
MSC 686 Ukushima	Nippon Kokan, Tsurumi	17-5-00	17-9-01	18-3-03
MSC 687 Izushima	Hitachi, Kanagawa	27-4-00	31-10-01	18-3-03
MSC 688 Aishima	Nippon Kokan, Tsurumi	17-4-01	8-10-02	16-2-04
MSC 689 Aoshima	Hitachi, Kanagawa	15-4-02	9-03	19-2-05
MSC 690 Miyajima	Nippon Kokan, Tsurumi	28-5-02	10-03	19-2-05
MSC 691 Shishijima	Nippon Kokan, Tsurumi	25-5-03	10-04	2006
MSC 692 Kuroshima	Hitachi, Kanagawa	15-5-04	31-8-05	2007

Toyoshima (MSC 685) Takatoshi Okano, 7-04

Sugashima (MSC 681) Mitsuhiro Kadota, 7-05

D: 510 tons (620 fl) **S:** 15.5 kts (14 sust.)
Dim: 58.00 (54.00 pp) × 9.50 (9.40 wl) × 2.50 (3.00 max.)
A: 1 20-mm JM-61-MB Sea Vulcan gatling AA
Electronics: Radar: 1 OPS-39B nav.—Sonar: Hitachi ZQS-4 minehunting HF VDS
M: 2 Mitsubishi 8NMU-TAI diesels; 2 CP props; 1,800 bhp—2 175-shp electric cruise motors (on main shafts)—bow-thruster
Electric: . . . **Range:** 2,500/10 **Crew:** 5 officers, 32 enlisted (45 accomm.)

Remarks: First two units approved under the FY 95 budget, MSC 683 under FY 96, MSC 684 under FY 97, MSC 685 under FY 98, MSC 686 and 687 under FY 99, MSC 688 under FY 00, and MSC 689 and 690 under FY 01. A total of 12 is planned. These are the first Japanese mine-countermeasures units with fully computerized combat systems. MSC 681, 682, and 683 are assigned to the 3rd Minesweeper Division, Yokosuka; MSC 684 is assigned to the Escort Fleet, 2nd Minesweeping Division, Sasebo.
Hull systems: Wooden construction. Forecastle is extended aft to provide shelter for remotely operated minehunting submersibles. Have twin funnels athwartships.
Combat systems: Use an NEC-built variant of the GEC-Marconi Nautis-IIM tactical data system, with three operator consoles, a chart table, and a plotter. The sonar is a license-built Thomson-Marconi Type 2093M, and the hoist gear is within the forward part of the superstructure. Carry two French PAP 105 Mk 5 remote-controlled minehunting submersibles. Sweep equipment includes an Australian Dyad magnetic and acoustic array and Oropesa Type 6 wire sweep gear. Have WRN-7 GPS receiver and Decca Hyperfix precision radio navigation aids.

♦ 9 Uwajima-class minehunter/minesweepers [MHC]

	Bldr	Laid down	L	In serv.
MSC 672 Uwajima	Nippon Kokan, Tsurumi	18-5-89	23-5-90	19-12-90
MSC 673 Ieshima	Hitachi, Kanagawa	12-5-89	12-6-90	19-12-90
MSC 674 Tsukishima	Hitachi, Kanagawa	27-5-91	23-7-92	17-3-93
MSC 675 Maejima	Hitachi, Kanagawa	1-6-92	10-6-93	15-12-93
MSC 676 Kumejima	Nippon Kokan, Tsurumi	17-2-93	9-11-93	12-12-94
MSC 677 Makishima	Hitachi, Kanagawa	12-5-93	26-5-94	12-12-94
MSC 678 Tobishima	Nippon Kokan, Tsurumi	22-6-93	31-8-94	10-3-95
MSC 679 Yugeshima	Hitachi, Kanagawa	10-4-94	24-5-96	11-12-96
MSC 680 Nagashima	Nippon Kokan, Tsurumi	14-4-94	30-5-96	25-12-96

MINE WARFARE SHIPS *(continued)*

Tobishima (MSC 678) Takatoshi Okano, 4-04

Nagashima (MSC 680) Takatoshi Okano, 6-04

D: 490 tons (590 fl) **S:** 14 kts **Dim:** 57.7 × 9.40 × 2.90
A: 1 20-mm JM-61-MB Sea Vulcan gatling AA
Electronics: Radar: 1 OPS-18B nav.—Sonar: Hitachi ZQS-3 minehunting HF VDS
M: 2 Mitsubishi 6NMU-TAI diesels; 2 CP props; 1,440 bhp
Electric: 1 × 1,450-kw dc; 2 × 160-kw a.c. **Range:** 2,400/10 **Crew:** 45 tot.

Remarks: A revised version of the *Hatsushima* class, lengthened primarily to permit two-high vice three-high bunking for enlisted personnel. Were to have been of GRP construction but are built of wood. MSC 672 is assigned to the Maizuru District Fleet; MSC 673, 675, and 677 to the Sasebo District Fleet; MSC 674 and 676 to the 42nd Minesweeping Division, Kure District Fleet; and MSC 678, 679, and 680 to the Escort Fleet, 1st Minesweeping Division, Kure.
Combat systems: Carry S-2 towed noisemakers and S-4 (with ZQS-2B sonar) and S-7 Mod.1 (with ZQS-3 sonar) autonomous minehunting vehicles.

♦ 5 Hatsushima-class minehunter/minesweepers [MHC]

	Bldr	Laid down	L	In serv.
MSC 666 Ogishima	Hitachi, Kanagawa	16-5-86	10-6-87	19-12-87
MSC 668 Yurishima	Nippon Kokan, Tsurumi	14-5-87	13-5-88	15-12-88
MSC 669 Hikoshima	Hitachi, Kanagawa	12-5-87	2-6-88	15-12-88
MSC 670 Awashima	Hitachi, Kanagawa	12-5-88	6-6-89	13-12-89
MSC 671 Sakushima	Nippon Kokan, Tsurumi	17-5-88	6-6-89	13-12-89

Ogishima (MSC 666) Ralph Edwards, 10-02

D: 440 tons (536 fl) **S:** 14 kts **Dim:** 55.00 (52.00 pp) × 9.40 × 2.40
A: 1 20-mm JM-61-MB Sea Vulcan gatling AA
Electronics:
Radar: 1 Fujitsu OPS-9 or OPS-18B nav.
Sonar: NEC-Hitachi ZQS-2B hull-mounted minehunting HF

M: 2 Mitsubishi YV12ZC-18/20 diesels; 2 CP props; 1,440 bhp
Electric: MSC 666–671: 1,770 kw tot. (1 × 1,450-kw gas turbine sweep gen., 2 × 160-kw ship's service diesel set)
Range: 2,400/10 **Crew:** 45 tot.

Remarks: An expansion of the preceding *Takami* design. MCL 724 and MCL 725 are designated as drone command ships and are assigned to the Escort Fleet, 4th Minesweeping Division, based at Sasebo; MSC 669 is assigned to the Sasebo District Fleet, 46th Minesweeper Division; and MSC 668, 670, and 671 are assigned to the Yokosuka District Fleet, 41st Minesweeping Division.

Awashima (MSC 670) Takatoshi Okano, 11-02

Hull systems: MSC 666 has Mitsubishi 6NMU-TAI diesels.
Combat systems: The sweep tail generates 4,300 amps. Carry Type S-2 towed noisemakers and Type S-4 autonomous minehunting vehicles with ZQS-2B sonars; these carry and lay their own disposal charges.
Disposals: Sister *Hatsushima* (MSC 649) was redesignated YAS 98 on 10-3-95. *Ninoshima* (MSC 650) and *Miyajima* (MSC 651) were redesignated YAS on 1-3-96. Later units were to be retired at two per year through 3-01, with no further units planned to be redesignated YAS. *Enoshima* (MSC 652) was stricken 5-12-96, *Ukishima* (MSC 653) on 12-3-97, *Oshima* (MSC 654) on 23-3-98, *Narushima* (MSC 657) on 25-6-99, *Chichijima* (MSC 658) on 13-3-00, *Torishima* (MSC 659) on 1-12-00, *Takashima* (MSC 661) on 4-6-01, and *Newajima* (MSC 662) and *Etajima* (MSC 663) on 29-5-02. *Niijima* (MSC 655) was reclassified as mine-countermeasures support ship MCL 722 on 23-3-98 and *Yakushima* (MSC 656) as MCL 723 on 13-5-99. *Hahajima* (MSC 660) was redesignated as a drone-control ship (MCL 724) on 4-3-02. *Moroshima* (MSC 667) was stricken by 2005.

♦ 2 Hatsushima-class mine countermeasures drone control ships [MSA]

	Bldr	L	In serv.
MCL 724 Kamishima (ex-MSC 664)	Nippon Kokan, Tsurumi	10-5-85	20-6-86
MCL 725 Himeshima (ex-MSC 665)	Hitachi, Kanagawa	16-5-85	10-6-86

Yakushima (MCL 723)—since retired, with SAM-class drones alongside under tow
Takatoshi Okano, 2-02

Yakushima (MCL 723)—since retired Takatoshi Okano, 7-99

MINE WARFARE SHIPS *(continued)*

D: 440 tons (536 fl) **S:** 14 kts **Dim:** 55.00 (52.00 pp) × 9.40 × 2.40
A: 1 20-mm JM-61-MB Sea Vulcan gatling AA
Electronics:
Radar: 1 Fujitsu OPS-9 nav.
Sonar: NEC-Hitachi ZQS-2B hull-mounted minhunting HF
M: 2 Mitsubishi YV122C-15/22 diesels; 2 CP props; 1,440 bhp
Electric: 1,690 kw tot. (2 × 725-kw diesel sweep gen., 3 × 80-kw ship's service diesel sets)
Range: 2,400/10 **Crew:** 28 tot.

Remarks: Wooden construction, former coastal minehunter/minesweepers. Reclassified by 2002 to act as control ships for the Swedish-built SAM-series drone mine-countermeasures craft. Have retained mechanical, acoustic, and magnetic sweep gear. Are assigned to the 101st Minesweeper Division, Kure.

Disposal note: Sister *Niijima* (MCL 722, ex-MSC 655) was stricken on 4-3-02 and *Yakushima* (MCL 723, ex-MSC 656) was retired by 2005.

♦ 6 SAM-01-class radio-controlled mine-countermeasures craft [MSD]
Bldr: Karlskronavarvet, Karlskrona, Sweden (In serv. 1998–99)

NAME 1 SAM-01	NAME 3 SAM-03	NAME 5 SAM-05
NAME 2 SAM-02	NAME 4 SAM-04	NAME 6 SAM-06

SAM-03 (NAME 3)—note row of eight danbuoy swept-lane markers across the stern JMSDF, 2000

D: 15 tons (20 fl) **S:** 8 kts **Dim:** 18.0 × 6.10 × 0.70 (1.60 prop)
M: 1 Volvo-Penta TAMD 70D diesel; 1 Schottel shrouded prop; 210 bhp
Range: 330/7

Remarks: Two were delivered to Japan in 2-98, with two further ordered in 4-98 and delivered 10-2-99, and two more delivered late in 1999. Are controlled two-each by MCL 723 and MCL 724, based at Kure. The catamarans also automatically lay eight swept-channel danbuoy markers. SAM = Self-propelled Acoustic and Magnetic. Sisters operate in the Swedish Navy.

Note: Former mine-countermeasures craft redesignated as YAS are used as diving tenders, including mine disposal diving; see under Service Craft section.

AMPHIBIOUS WARFARE SHIPS

♦ 3 (+ 1) Osumi-class dock landing ships [LSD]

	Bldr	Laid down	L	In serv.
LST 4001 Osumi	Mitsui, Tamano	7-12-95	18-11-96	11-3-98
LST 4002 Shimokita	Mitsui, Tamano	30-11-99	29-11-00	12-3-02
LST 4003 Kunisaki	Hitachi, Kanagawa	7-9-00	13-12-01	26-2-03
LST 4004 . . .	. . .	. . .	. . .	. . .

D: 8,900 tons light (approx. 13,000 fl) **S:** 22 kts
Dim: 178.0 (170.0 wl) × 25.8 × 6.00
A: 2 20-mm Mk 15 Phalanx CIWS
Electronics:
Radar: 1 JRC OPS-20 nav.; 1 JRC OPS-28 surf. search; 1 Melco OPS-14C air search; 2 General Dynamics Mk 90 Phalanx f.c.
M: 2 Mitsui–SEMT-Pielstick 16V42M-A diesels; 2 props; 26,000 bhp
Electric: 17,000 kw tot. (4 × 4,000-kw, 1 × 1,000-kw diesel sets)
Range: . . . / . . . **Crew:** 135 tot. + 330 troops (1,000 for brief periods)

Remarks: LST 4001 was ordered during 9-93. LST 4002 was authorized under the FY 98 budget and LST 4003 under FY 99. LST 4001 is based at Kure.

Osumi (LST 4001) Takatoshi Okano, 7-04

Shimokita (LST 4002) Takatoshi Okano, 7-04

Osumi (LST 4001) Takatoshi Okano, 7-04

Osumi (LST 4001)—note that the breadth of the island structure virtually prohibits use of the upper deck for fixed-wing flight operations Mitsuhiro Kadota, 9-00

Hull systems: Offical "standard" displacement appears to be several thousand tons below the actual figure. Although given an LST-type designation, the design is in reality a dock landing ship configured to accept two U.S. LCAC 1–class air-cushion vehicle landing craft in a 60- to 70-m-long docking well; there is no bow door, and the ship is not intended to beach. Although the upper deck is a relatively unobstructed 130 m long, only the after portion is used as a helicopter landing position (for two CH-47 Chinook-size aircraft). The remainder of the deck is used for vehicle cargo

AMPHIBIOUS WARFARE SHIPS *(continued)*

stowage. There are two vehicle elevators rising to the flight deck, one forward on the centerline and one to starboard abaft the island superstructure, but neither is large enough to accommodate a helicopter. The elevators serve a 50 × 15-m vehicle cargo deck, which also has side ramps port and starboard; abreast the side ramps on the centerline is a vehicle turntable. Cargo capacity is 1,400 tons, including up to 14 Type 90 heavy tanks. In an emergency, up to 1,000 passengers can be accommodated. The superstructure is shaped to reduce radar reflection, and its width, in combination with the breadth of the island structure, precludes using the flight deck for fixed-wing aircraft operations. Carries two nonbeachable personnel launches.
Combat systems: A previously planned 76-mm gun will not be installed.

♦ 0 (+ 3) planned new vehicle landing ships [LST]
Bldr: . . .

D: Approx. 1,900 tons std. **S:** . . . kts **Dim:** . . . × . . . × . . .
A: None **Electronics:** Radar: 1 . . . nav.
M: 2 . . . diesels; 2 CP props; . . . bhp
Range: . . . / . . . **Crew:** . . .

Remarks: Program was announced in 12-00 after it was belatedly discovered that the large *Osumi*-class "LSTs" cannot be used effectively in emergency assistance missions to offshore Japanese islands. The new ships will be beachable and will have a bow ramp. The first was requested under the FY 02 budget, and the three ships are to be attached to the Yokosuka and Ominato districts. Will not be armed, but provision will be made for installing a gunmount and a radar director, if required.

Disposal note: *Miura*-class landing ship *Satsuma* (LST 4513) was retired from service by 2005. *Atsumi*-class landing ship *Nemuro* (LST 4103) was retired on 17-6-05. Sister *Atsumi* (LST 4101) was retired on 13-2-98 and *Motobu* (LST 4102) on 12-4-99.

♦ 2 Yura-class utility landing craft [LCU]
Bldr: Sasebo Heavy Industries

	Laid down	L	In serv.
LSU 4171 YURA	23-4-80	10-8-80	27-3-81
LSU 4172 NOTO	23-4-80	1-11-80	27-3-81

Noto (LSU 4172) Takatoshi Okano, 6-04

D: 500 tons (590 fl) **S:** 12 kts **Dim:** 58.0 × 9.5 × 1.7 (aft)
A: 1 20-mm JM 61-MB gatling AA **Electronics:** Radar: 1 OPS-. . . nav.
M: 2 Fuji 6L 27.5X diesels; 2 CP props; 3,000 bhp
Range: . . . / . . . **Crew:** 32 tot. ship's company + 70 troops

Remarks: Both were in the 1979–80 budget; request for a third in the FY 81 budget was denied. Have bow doors and ramp and an open cargo deck. LSU 4171 is assigned to the Kure District Fleet and LSU 4172 to the Maizuru District Fleet.

♦ 2 LC 01–class utility landing craft [LCU]
Bldr: Sasebo Naval Dockyard

	Laid down	L	In serv.
LCU 2001 LC 01	11-5-87	1-10-87	17-3-88
LCU 2002 LC 02	15-5-91	1-10-91	11-3-92

D: 420 tons **S:** 12 kts **Dim:** 52.0 × 8.7 × 1.6
A: 1 20-mm JM-61-MB Sea Vulcan gatling AA
Electronics: Radar: 1 OPS- . . . nav.
M: 2 Mitsubishi 6SU-MTK diesels; 2 props; 3,000 bhp **Crew:** 28 tot.

Remarks: First unit approved under the FY 86 budget and ordered 24-3-87; the second was approved under FY 90. Have bluff bow/ramp and an open cargo deck. LCU 2001 is assigned to the Sasebo District Fleet and LCU 2002 to the Yokosuka District Fleet.

LC 02 (LCU 2002) Mitsuhiro Kadota, 12-02

♦ 8 U.S. LCAC 1–class air-cushion landing craft
Bldr: Textron Marine and Land Systems, New Orleans

	In serv.		In serv.		In serv.
LA-01	11-97	L-04	2-02	L-07	2003
LA-02	2-98	L-05	2002	L-08	2004
LA-03	11-01	L-06	2002		

LA-03 Takatoshi Okano, 7-04

LA-04 Takatoshi Okano, 6-04

D: 93 tons light (166.6 fl; 181.6 overload) **S:** 54 kts (40 when loaded)
Dim: 26.80 (24.69 hull) × 14.33 (13.31 hull) × 0.87 (at rest)
A: None **Electronics:** Radar: 1 . . . nav.
M: 4 Avco TF40B gas turbines (2 for lift); 2 3.58-m-dia. shrouded airscrews, 4 centrifugal, 1.60-m-dia.lift fans; 15,820 shp
Electric: 120 kw tot. (2 × 60-kw Turbomach T-62 APU)
Range: 223/48 (light); 200/40 (loaded) **Fuel:** 6.2 tons (7,132 gallons)
Crew: 5 tot. + 25 troops

Remarks: Decision to order in 11-93 for use on new *Osumi*-class LSTs. First unit funded under the FY 93 budget and the second under FY 95; the third and fourth were requested under FY 99, and two more were approved under FY 00 and ordered 22-5-01. Two more are planned for the fourth *Osumi*.
Hull systems: Cargo capacity: 60 tons normal/75 tons overload. Bow ramp is 8.8 m wide, stern ramp 4.6 m. The deck has 168 m^2 of parking area and is 204 m long by 8.3 m wide. Are difficult to tow if broken down and are vulnerable to defensive fire. Operator, engineer, navigator, and nine troops travel in starboard side compartments; deck hand, assistant engineer, load master, and 16 troops travel in port compartments. Cannot carry troops on deck, limiting their utility. Navigational equipment includes a GPS receiver. Are able to transport one Japanese Type 90 main battle tank or four Type 89 armored fighting vehicles.

♦ 4 U.S.-design LCM(6)-class landing craft

Japanese version of the LCM(6) Takatoshi Okano, 6-99

D: 24 tons (56 fl) **S:** 10 kts **Dim:** 17.07 × 4.37 × 1.17 (aft)
M: 2 Yanmar diesels; 2 props; 450 bhp **Range:** 130/9
Crew: 3 tot. + 80 troops for short distances

Remarks: Unnumbered units carried aboard the *Miura*-class LSTs. Built in Japan. Able to carry about 34 tons of vehicles or cargo. Others have been built as service craft with YF-series numbers (see under Service Craft section).

AMPHIBIOUS WARFARE SHIPS *(continued)*

♦ 6 U.S.-design LCVP-class landing craft

Japanese version of the LCVP Takatoshi Okano, 6-99

D: 13 tons (fl) **S:** 8 kts **Dim:** 10.90 × 3.21 × 1.04 (aft)
M: 1 Yanmar diesel; 1 prop; 180 bhp **Crew:** 3 tot.

Remarks: Japanese-built, GRP hulls. Unnumbered units carried by the older LSTs. Several others are also in service, employed as service craft and carrying YF-series hull numbers.

AUXILIARIES

♦ 1 Tenryu-class target service ship [AG]

Bldr: Sumitomo, Uraga

	Laid down	L	In serv.
ATS 4203 Tenryu	19-6-98	14-4-99	13-3-00

Tenryu (ATS 4203) Ralph Edwards, 10-02

D: 2,400 tons (approx. 3,500 fl) **S:** 22 kts **Dim:** 106.0 × 16.5 × 4.0 (mean hull)
A: 1 76-mm 62-cal. OTO Melara DP
Electronics:
Radar: 1 JRC OPS-18 surf. search; 1 Melco OPS-14B air search; 1 TMCATS target control (see remarks); 1 FCS-2-21A f.c.
Sonar: . . .
TACAN: URN-25
M: 4 Fuji 8L 27.5SX diesels; 2 props; 12,800 bhp—bow-thruster **Crew:** 150 tot.

Remarks: Requested under the FY 97 budget as a replacement for *Azuma* (ATS 4201). Design was originally to have been a 4,700-ton greatly enlarged *Kurobe* (ATS 4202) with a large hangar and flight deck for drones, helicopters, and VTOL aircraft (if acquired). The program was reduced to a much smaller, 2,400-ton, improved version of *Kurobe* for budgetary reasons, and the new ship is not capable of operating VTOL aircraft. Based at Kure.
Mission systems: Has the same Target Multi-Control and Tracking System (TMCATS) radar as does the *Kurobe*. Carries, launches, controls, recovers, and services U.S. Ryan BQM-34J Firebee high-speed and Northrop MQM-74C Chukar supersonic target drones. Also used for air-controlling U-36A manned target-tow aircraft.

Tenryu (ATS 4203) Takatoshi Okano, 10-02

♦ 1 Kurobe-class target service ship [AG]

	Bldr	Laid down	L	In serv.
ATS 4202 Kurobe	Nippon Kokan, Tsurumi	31-7-87	23-5-88	23-3-89

Kurobe (ATS 4202) Takatoshi Okano, 10-00

D: 2,270 tons (approx. 3,200 fl) **S:** 20 kts **Dim:** 101.0 × 16.5 × 4.0
A: 1 76-mm 62-cal. OTO Melara Compact DP
Electronics:
Radar: 1 JRC OPS-18 surf. search; 1 Melco OPS-14B air search; 1 TMCATS target control (see remarks); 1 FCS-2-21A f.c.
M: 4 Fuji 8L 27.5SX diesels; 2 props; 9,160 bhp
Range: . . . / . . . **Crew:** 17 officers, 126 enlisted

Remarks: Approved under the FY 86 budget as a supplement to *Azuma* (ATS 4201). Based at Kure.
Mission systems: Carries, launches, controls, recovers, and services U.S. Ryan BQM-34J Firebee high-speed and Northrop MQM-74C Chukar supersonic target drones. Also used for air-controlling U-36A manned target-tow aircraft. Has the TMCATS (Target Multi-Control and Tracking System) phased-array radar, with four planar arrays mounted on the faces of the tower mast; the system tracks targets and weapons and records the track data for analysis, employing TELES (Telemetry Measuring System). The large open deck and hangar aft are primarily for target drone operations, but helicopters can be accommodated.

♦ 3 (+ 2 + 2) Hiuchi-class multimission support ships [AG]

Bldr: Nippon Kokan, Tsurumi

	Laid down	L	In serv.
AMS 4301 Hiuchi	18-1-01	4-9-01	27-3-02
AMS 4302 Suo	19-9-02	25-4-03	16-3-04
AMS 4303 Amakusa	3-12-02	6-8-03	16-3-04
AMS 4304 . . .	. . .	. . .	. . .
AMS 4305 . . .	. . .	. . .	. . .

Suo (AMS 4302) Mitsuhiro Kadota, 3-04

Amakusa (AMS 4303) Mitsuhiro Kadota, 3-04

D: 980 tons (approx. 1,500 fl) **S:** 15 kts **Dim:** 65.0 × 12.0 × 3.5
Electronics: . . .
M: 2 diesels; 2 props; 5,000 bhp **Crew:** 40 tot.

AUXILIARIES *(continued)*

Remarks: First unit approved under FY 99 budget, second and third under FY 01. A fourth and fifth unit of the class are planned. Used for training, target-drone launching, diver support, safety patrol, firefighting, ocean towing, and supply duties. Are intended to replace the ASU 81 class. A total of seven are currently planned.

Disposal note: Of the ASU 81–class target-support craft, ASU 81 (ex-YAS 101) was stricken on 27-10-97, ASU 82 (ex-YAS 102) on 14-8-98, ASU 83 (ex-YAS 103) on 15-6-01, ASU 84 (ex-YAS 104) on 14-9-01, and ASU 85 (ex-YAS 105) on 30-10-02.

♦ 1 Hayase-class miscellaneous auxiliary [AG]

Bldr: Ishikawajima-Harima Heavy Industries, Tokyo

	Laid down	L	In serv.
ASU 7020 Hayase (ex-MST 462)	16-9-70	21-6-71	6-11-71

Hayase (ASU 7020) Takatoshi Okano, 7-99

D: 2,000 tons (3,050 fl) **S:** 18 kts **Dim:** 99.0 × 13.0 × 3.8
A: 1 twin 76.2-mm 50-cal. Mk 34 DP; 2 single 20-mm JM-61-MB Sea Vulcan gatling AA; 2 triple 324-mm Type 68 ASW TT (Mk 73 or Mk 46 Mod. 5 torpedoes); 116 mines
Electronics:
Radar: 1 JRC OPS-16C nav./surf. search; 1 Melco OPS-14 air search; 1 Western Electric Mk 34 f.c.
Sonar: U.S. SQS-11A hull-mounted MF; 1 ZQS-1B hull-mounted HF
M: 4 Kawasaki-M.A.N. V6V 22/30 ATL diesels; 2 props; 6,400 bhp
Range: 7,500/14 **Crew:** 180 tot.

Remarks: Former mine-countermeasures support ship and minelayer, reclassified 20-3-98 and now assigned to the 1st Submarine Flotilla, Kure, as a general support vessel.
Combat systems: Fantail cleared as a platform for helicopters. Has five mine rails exiting through the transom stern. Equipped with the U.S. Mk 63 gun f.c.s. for the 76.2-mm mounting.

♦ 1 400-ton-class yacht [AG]

Bldr: Hitachi, Kanagawa

	Laid down	L	In serv.
ASY 91 Hashidate	10-10-98	26-7-99	30-11-99

Hashidate (ASY 91) Takatoshi Okano, 2-04

D: 400 tons (approx. 560 fl) **S:** 20 kts **Dim:** 62.0 × 9.4 × 2.0
Electronics: Radar: 1 . . . nav.
M: 2 . . . diesels; 2 props; 5,500 bhp
Range: . . . / . . . **Crew:** 29 tot. + 60 passengers

Remarks: Requested under FY 97 budget as a replacement for *Hiyodori* (ASY 92, ex-PC 320) as the JMSDF C-in-C's ceremonial yacht. Has facilities to act in disaster relief service. Hull painted gray, superstructure white. Based at Yokosuka.

♦ 1 Shirase-class icebreaker [AGB]

	Bldr	Laid down	L	In serv.
AGB 5002 Shirase	Nippon Kokan, Tsurumi	5-3-81	11-12-81	12-12-83

D: 11,660 tons (18,900 fl) **S:** 19 kts **Dim:** 134.0 × 28.0 × 9.2
Electronics:
Radar: 1 OPS-22 nav.; 1 Melco OPS-18 surf. search; 1 . . . weather
TACAN: ORN-6 (U.S. URN-25)

Shirase (AGB 5002)—with red-orange hull and stack and cream-colored superstructure Chris Sattler, 3-05

Shirase (AGB 5002) Mitsuhiro Kadota, 4-03

M: 6 M.A.N.-Mitsui 12V42M diesels, electric drive; 3 props; 30,000 bhp
Range: 25,000/15 **Crew:** 37 officers, 137 enlisted + 60 passengers

Remarks: Built under the 1979–80 budget to replace *Fuji* (AGB 5001). Is the only ship in the JMSDF named for a person: Lt. Nobu Shirase, who led the first Japanese Antarctic expedition in 1912. Plans for completing a 22,000-ton, *nuclear*-powered replacement for *Shirase* have yet to be formalized. AGB 5002 is assigned to the Yokosuka District Fleet.
Hull systems: Cargo capacity: 1,000 tons. Has a hangar and flight deck for two S-61A and one OH-6D helicopters. Has a large radome-covered weather radar atop the hangar. Is also equipped to conduct oceanographic research. Has been equipped with a Navi-Sailor 2400 ECDIS electronic chart display system.

♦ 1 experimental weapons systems trials ship [AGE]

	Bldr	Laid down	L	In serv.
ASE 6102 Asuka	Sumitomo, Uraga	21-4-93	21-6-94	22-3-95

Asuka (ASE 6102) *Ships of the World,* 2000

D: 4,200 tons (4,900 fl) **S:** 27 kts **Dim:** 151.0 × 18.0 × 5.0 (mean hull)
A: Provision for 1 8-cell U.S. Mk 41 vertical missile launch group syst.; 1 SH-60J ASW helicopter
Electronics:
Radar: 1 Fujitsu OPS-19 nav.; 1 Melco OPS-14B air search; 1 Mitsubishi FCS-3 SAM f.c.
Sonar: . . . bow-mounted LF; flank-mounted active/passive array; towed array
EW: . . . intercept
M: COGLAG: 1 IHI-G.E. LM-250 gas turbine, 2 Rolls-Royce SM1C Spey gas turbines; 2 CP props; 43,000 shp max. (electric drive below 21 kts)
Range: . . . / . . . **Crew:** 71 ship's company + 100 technicians

Remarks: Requested under the FY 92 budget as an ASW sensor and weapons systems trials ship. Assigned to the 5th Research Center, Kurihama.
Hull systems: Propulsion plant is bridge controlled and drives the propellers at low rpm to reduce radiated noise. The hull has special vibration-damping structures in the vicinity of the very large sonar array, which occupies a 40-m-long sonar dome extending beneath the ship's keel as far aft as the tower mainmast. An air-bubbler system is also installed. Has provision for female crewmembers. Fin stabilizers and a helicopter haul-down and traversing system are fitted. The hangar can accommodate an SH-60J ASW helicopter.

AUXILIARIES *(continued)*

Combat systems: Conducts trials with surface warfare systems including the FCS-3 radar weapons-control system, which can track 10 targets simultaneously and employs four planar arrays to cover 360°; the XAAM-4 vertically launched SAM; the Canadian Davis "Dres Ball" infrared stack emission suppression system; the ASO self-propelled ASW target; the S-10 underwater navigation system; the K-RX2 ASW mine; composite armor; and radar-absorbent coatings. Has also conducted trials with infrared surveillance equipment and torpedo countermeasures systems. Provision was made for the installation of an 8-cell Mk 41 vertical missile launch system forward, but it has not yet been fitted.

♦ 1 Kurihama-class underwater weapons trials ship [AGE]

	Bldr	Laid down	L	In serv.
ASE 6101 Kurihama	Sasebo Heavy Industries	23-3-79	20-9-79	8-4-80

Kurihama (ASE 6101) Mitsuhiro Kadota, 9-04

D: 959 tons (approx. 1,400 fl) **S:** 15 kts **Dim:** 68.0 × 11.6 × 3.3
A: Various **Electronics:** Radar: 1 Fujitsu OPS-9B nav.
M: 2 Fuji 6S 30B diesels; 2 CP props; 2,600 bhp—2 200-shp electric auxiliary propulsors—retractable bow-thruster
Crew: 42 ship's company + 13 technicians

Remarks: In FY 79 budget. Operated for the Technical Research and Development Institute by the 5th Research Center, Kurihama.
Hull systems: Has Flume-type passive stabilization tanks and gas turbine–powered generators in the superstructure. Can be rigged for silent operation.
Combat systems: Has been used in trials with the S-8 deep minesweeping system, G-RX4 ASW torpedo, a torpedo countermeasures system, a mine-countermeasures computer, noise simulators, an antisubmarine sonar, a data-recording buoy, sonobuoy arrays, mines, a low-frequency sonar, an expendable radio jammer decoy, a towed surface array radio receiver, and the K-RX2 ASW mine. Has gun test facilities on the fantail and a torpedo elevator to port. Is equipped with acoustic target tracking equipment.

♦ 2 ocean surveillance ships [AGI]

	Bldr	Laid down	L	In serv.
AOS 5201 Hibiki	Mitsui, Tamano	28-11-89	27-7-90	30-1-91
AOS 5202 Harima	Mitsui, Tamano	26-12-90	11-9-91	10-3-92

Hibiki (AOS 5201) Takatoshi Okano, 9-04

D: 3,715 tons **S:** 11 kts **Dim:** 71.50 (67.00 pp) × 29.90 × 7.50
Electronics:
Radar: 1 JRC OPS-18 nav.; 1 Fujitsu OPS-19 nav.
Sonar: NQQ-2 SURTASS
M: Diesel-electric: 4 Mitsubishi S6U MPTK 1,200-bhp diesels, 4 800-kw alternators, 2 motors; 2 props; 3,200 shp
Range: 3,800/10 **Fuel:** 640 tons **Crew:** 40 tot.

Remarks: First unit approved under the FY 89 budget, second under FY 90. A total of five was originally planned. AOS 5201 became fully operational around 3-92 at the completion of installation, trials, and check-out of the SURTASS (Surveillance Towed-Array Sonar System) towed linear passive acoustic array and the satellite data-relay gear in the U.S.A. Both are based at Kure.
Mission systems: Are a Japanese equivalent of the U.S. T-AGOS 19 class, employing U.S.-supplied towed linear surveillance passive hydrophone array and WSC-6 satellite data relay (with the analysis center located near Yokosuka). Have SWATH (Small Waterplane Area, Twin Hull) configuration. The SURTASS employs a 2,600-m-long array with an 1,800-m-long towing cable.

Harima (AOS 5202) Takatoshi Okano, 5-01

♦ 1 Nichinan-class hydrographic survey ship [AGS]

	Bldr	Laid down	L	In serv.
AGS 5105 Nichinan	Mitsubishi, Shimonoseki	7-8-97	11-6-98	24-3-99

Nichinan (AGS 5105)—note the large cable sheaves at the bow *Ships of the World*, 2000

D: 3,300 tons (4,100 fl) **S:** 20 kts (18 sust.) **Dim:** 111.0 × 17.0 × 4.5 (mean hull)
Electronics:
Radar: . . .
Sonar: SeaBeam 2112 multibeam mapping (HF)
M: 3 diesel generator sets, electric drive: 2 motors; 2 CP props; 8,660 shp (5,800 sust.)—twin bow- and stern-thrusters
Range: 15,000/14 **Crew:** 90 tot.

Remarks: Requested under FY 96 budget to replace *Akashi* (AGS 5101) as a combination cable repair and hydrographic survey ship. Based at Kurihama, operated by the JMSDF's Ocean Management Group.
Mission systems: Carries a 5-ton, 2.9-m-long cable repair remotely operated submersible; a deployable environmental measurement buoy; a WQM-1B acoustic measurement buoy; AICM-2F ocean current measurement equipment; a magnetic cable location system; bottom core samplers; and four cranes. Equipped with a large articulating crane aft, to port; a quadrantial oceanographic equipment gantry at the stern; and cable sheaves at the bow.

♦ 2 Futami-class hydrographic survey ships [AGS]

	Bldr	Laid down	L	In serv.
AGS 5102 Futami	Mitsubishi, Shimonoseki	20-1-78	9-8-78	27-2-79
AGS 5104 Wakasa	Hitachi, Maizuru	21-8-84	25-5-85	25-2-86

Wakasa (AGS 5104) Takatoshi Okano, 7-04

D: 2,050 tons (3,175 fl) **S:** 16 kts **Dim:** 96.80 (90.00 pp) × 15.00 × 4.50
A: None **Electronics:** Radar: 1 JRC OPS-18 nav.
M: AGS 5102: 2 Kawasaki-M.A.N. V8V 22/30 ATL diesels; 2 CP props; 4,400 bhp—AGS 5104: 2 Fuji 6LS 27-5XF diesels; 2 CP props; 4,580 bhp—both: bow-thruster
Electric: 1,800 kw tot. **Fuel:** 556 tons **Crew:** 105 tot.

AUXILIARIES *(continued)*

Remarks: Configured for both hydrographic surveying and cable laying. Have three diesel and one gas-turbine generator sets. Carry one RCV-225 remote-controlled unmanned submersible. AGS 5104, ordered 29-3-84 under the FY 83 budget, has a taller stack and differs somewhat in equipage. Both are based at Kurihama, operated by the JMSDF's Ocean Management Group.

♦ 1 Suma-class hydrograpic survey ship [AGS]

Bldr: Hitachi Heavy Industries, Maizuru

	Laid down	L	In serv.
AGS 5103 SUMA	24-9-80	1-9-81	30-3-82

Suma (AGS 5103) Takatoshi Okano, 6-00

D: 1,180 tons **S:** 15 kts **Dim:** 72.0 × 12.8 × 3.4
A: None **Electronics:** Radar: 1 OPS- . . . nav.
M: 2 Fuji 6 LS 27.5X diesels; 2 CP props; 3,000 bhp—bow-thruster
Crew: 65 tot.

Remarks: Built under the 1979–80 budget. Carries one 7.9-m boat and one 11-m inshore survey launch. Flume-type passive tank stabilization is fitted. Operated by the JMSDF's Ocean Management Group and based at Kurihama.

♦ 2 (+ 1) Masyu-class replenishment oilers [AOR]

	Bldr	Laid down	L	In serv.
AOE 425 MASYU	Mitsui, Tamano	21-1-02	5-2-03	15-3-04
AOE 426 OUMI	Universal, Maizuru	2-03	2-04	3-3-05
AOE 427 . . .	. . .	2005	2006	2007

Masyu (AOE 425) Takatoshi Okano, 7-04

Masyu (AOE 425) Takatoshi Okano, 7-04

D: 13,500 tons (25,000 fl) **S:** 24 kts **Dim:** 221 × . . . × . . .
A: 2 20-mm Mk 15 Phalanx CIWS **Electronics:** Radar: . . .
M: COGAG: 2 Kawasaki–Rolls-Royce Spey . . . gas turbines; 2 CP props; . . . bhp
Range: 9,500/20 **Crew:** 145

Remarks: The first was approved under the FY 00 budget to replace the *Sagami* (AOE 421). The second will enhance the current replenishment force along with a third unit ordered in 2003. Were the largest naval ships built in Japan since World War II. Carries one helicopter.

♦ 3 Towada-class replenishment oilers [AOR]

	Bldr	Laid down	L	In serv.
AOE 422 TOWADA	Hitachi, Maizuru	17-4-85	25-3-86	24-3-87
AOE 423 TOKIWA	IHI, Tokyo	12-5-88	23-3-89	12-3-90
AOE 424 HAMANA	Mitsui, Tamano	8-7-88	18-5-89	29-3-90

Hamana (AOE 424) Mitsuhiro Kadota, 7-04

Towada (AOE 422) Mitsuhiro Kadota, 9-00

D: 8,300 tons (15,850 fl) **S:** 22 kts
Dim: 167.00 (160.00 pp) × 22.0 × 8.40 (15.90 molded depth) **A:** None
Electronics:
Radar: 1 JRC OPS-18-1 nav.
EW: . . . intercept; Mk 36 SRBOC decoy syst. (4 6-round Mk 137 RL)
M: 2 Mitsui 16V42M-A diesels; 2 props; 26,400 bhp
Electric: 3,200 kw (4 × 800-kw diesel sets)
Range: 10,500/20 **Fuel:** 1,659 tons **Crew:** 140 tot.

Remarks: All-purpose liquid, solid stores, and ammunition ships, with two liquid and one solid transfer stations per side. Cargo: 5,700 tons total. Helicopter deck aft for vertical replenishment. No provision for armament. All are assigned directly to the Escort Fleet, AOE 422 based at Kure, AOE 423 at Yokosuka, and AOE 424 at Maizuru.

Disposal note: *Sagami*-class replenishment oiler *Sagami* (AOE 421) was stricken by 2005.

♦ 1 Muroto-class cable layer [ARC]

	Bldr	Laid down	L	In serv.
ARC 482 MUROTO	Mitsubishi, Shimonoseki	28-11-78	25-7-79	27-3-80

Muroto (ARC 482) *Ships of the World,* 2000

D: 4,544 tons std. **S:** 17 kts **Dim:** 131.0 × 17.4 × 5.7
A: None **Electronics:** Radar: 1 Fujitsu OPS-9 nav.
M: 2 Mitsubishi MTU V8V 22/30 diesels; 2 CP props; 4,400 bhp—bow-thruster
Crew: 122 tot.

Remarks: Able to lay cable over bow or stern at 2–6 kts. Similar to the commercial *Kuroshio Maru.* Also has extensive facilities for oceanographic research. Has two commercial SATCOM terminals. Based at Kure.

AUXILIARIES *(continued)*

♦ 1 Chihaya-class submarine rescue ship [ASR]

	Bldr	Laid down	L	In serv.
ASR 403 Chihaya	Mitsui, Tamano	13-10-97	8-10-98	23-3-00

Chihaya (ASR 403) Takatoshi Okano, 3-00

D: 5,400 tons (6,200 fl) **S:** 20 kts **Dim:** 127.5 × 20.0 × 5.1
Electronics: Radar: 2 . . . nav.
M: 2 Mitsui 12V42M-A diesels; 2 CP props; 19,700 bhp—2 bow- and 2 stern-thrusters
Range: 6,000/13 **Crew:** 125 tot.

Remarks: Requested under the FY 96 budget. An enlarged version of *Chiyoda* (AS 405) with similar rescue submersible handling system amidships. Serves as flagship for the 1st Submarine Flotilla at Kure. Has Superbird SHF SATCOM terminal.
Hull systems: Carries a 40-ton, 12.4-m deep-submergence rescue vehicle (DSRV) and a small remotely operated work submersible. The DSRV mates directly to large decompression chambers and is lowered and recovered through a centerline moonpool. A computerized Rescue Information Center is fitted. Is able to support saturation divers to 415-m depths. Has a raised platform at the stern for helicopters up to MH-53E size.

♦ 1 Chiyoda-class submarine rescue ship [ASR]

	Bldr	Laid down	L	In serv.
AS 405 Chiyoda (ex-ASR 405)	Mitsui, Tamano	19-1-83	7-12-83	27-3-85

Chiyoda (ASR 405)—note DSRV carried amidships Mitsuhiro Kadota, 7-05

Chiyoda (ASR 405) Mitsuhiro Kadota, 10-02

D: 3,690 tons (4,450 fl) **S:** 17 kts (16 sust.)
Dim: 112.5 (106.0 pp) × 17.6 (18.0 max.) × 4.8
A: None **Electronics:** Radar: 1 JRC OPS-16 surf. search
M: 2 Mitsui 8LV42M diesels; 2 CP props; 11,500 bhp—bow- and stern-thrusters
Crew: 120 tot.

Remarks: Acts as flagship for the 2nd Submarine Flotilla, Yokosuka. Is equipped with commercial HF and Superbird SHF SATCOM equipment. The DSRV is deployed over the side, using hoist equipment similar to that of the U.S. Navy's ex-*Pigeon* (ASR 21) class. There is also a deep-diving rescue bell. The helicopter platform can accommodate an HSS-2 Sea King.

DSRV Note: Carries a deep-submergence rescue vehicle (DSRV) launched 15-10-84 by Kawasaki, Kobe; its characteristics include:

D: 40 tons **S:** 4 kts **Dim:** 12.4 × 3.2 × 4.3 (high)
M: electric motors; 40 hp **Crew:** 12 passengers

Disposal note: Submarine rescue ship *Fushimi* (ASR 402) was retired 24-3-00.

♦ 1 Kashima-class cadet training ship [AXT]

	Bldr	Laid down	L	In serv.
TV 3508 Kashima	Hitachi, Kanegawa	20-4-93	23-2-94	26-1-95

Kashima (TV 3508) Frank Findler, 7-05

D: 4,050 tons **S:** 25 kts **Dim:** 143.0 × 18.0 × 4.6
A: 1 76-mm 62-cal. OTO Melara Compact DP; 2 triple 324-mm Type 68 ASW TT (Type 73 and Mk 46 Mod. 5 torpedoes); 4 saluting cannon
Electronics:
Radar: 1 Fujitsu OPS-19 nav.; 1 Melco OPS-14C surf. search; 1 FCS-2-22 f.c.
Sonar: . . .
EW: probable NORL-6 intercept
M: CODOG: 2 . . . diesels (. . . bhp each), 2 Kawasaki–Rolls-Royce Spey SM1C gas turbines (26,150 shp each); 2 CP props; 52,300 shp max.
Range: . . . / . . . **Crew:** 370 (incl. cadets)

Remarks: Authorized under FY 91 budget, but construction was deferred as part payment for Japan's contribution to the Persian Gulf War; requested again under FY 92 and approved. Has a modest wartime potential as a command ship. Is flagship of the Training Fleet, based at Kure.
Hull systems: Has accommodations for both male and female cadets, all berthed in two-person staterooms. The large open deck aft acts as a ceremonial, assembly, and exercise area but is also able to accept helicopters.

♦ 2 Asagiri-class training ships [AXT]

	Bldr	Laid down	L	In serv.
TV 3515 Yamagiri (ex-DD 152)	Mitsui, Tamano	5-2-86	8-10-87	25-1-89
TV 3516 Asagiri (ex-DD 151)	IHI, Tokyo	13-2-85	19-9-86	17-3-88

Yamagiri (TV 3515)—prior to service as a training ship Mitsuhiro Kadota, 10-02

D: 3,500 tons (4,300 fl) **S:** 30 kts **Dim:** 136.50 × 14.60 × 4.50 (mean hull)
A: 8 RGM-84C Harpoon SSM; 1 8-round Mk 29 missile launcher (18 RIM-7F Sea Sparrow missiles); 1 76-mm 62-cal. OTO Melara Compact DP; 2 20-mm Mk 15 Phalanx CIWS; 1 8-round Mk 112 ASROC ASW RL (. . . reloads); 2 triple 324-mm Type 68 ASW TT (Type 73 or Mk 46 Mod. 5 torpedoes); 1 SH-60J ASW helicopter

AUXILIARIES *(continued)*

Electronics:
Radar: 1 JRC OPS-20 nav.; 1 JRC OPS-28C or -28D surf./air search; 1 Melco OPS-14C air search; 1 FCS-2-21A gun f.c.; 1 FCS-2-12E SAM f.c.; 2 General Dynamics Mk 90 Phalanx f.c.
Sonar: Mitsubishi OQS-4A bow-mounted MF; EDO-NEC OQR-1 (U.S. SQR-18A(V) TASS) towed passive array
TACAN: ORN-6 (U.S. URN-25)
EW: NEC NOLR-6C intercept; NOLR-9C D/F; Fujitsu OLT-3 D/F; Mk 36 SRBOC decoy syst. (2 6-round Raytheon Mk 137 RL); SLQ-25 Nixie acoustic torpedo decoy syst.
M: COGAG: 4 Kawasaki–Rolls-Royce Spey SM-1A gas turbines; 2 CP props; 53,900 shp
Electric: . . . **Range:** . . . **Fuel:** . . . **Crew:** 220 tot.

Remarks: Were assigned as a training ships during 2004–5, respectively. Sisters are listed above as destroyers [DD]

♦ 1 Hatsuyuki-class training ship [AXT]
Bldr: Mitsubishi, Nagasaki

	Laid down	L	In serv.
TV 3513 Shimayuki (ex-DD 133)	8-5-84	29-1-86	31-3-87

Shimayuki (TV 3513) Takatoshi Okano, 9-04

D: 3,050 tons (3,800 fl) **S:** 30 kts
Dim: 131.70 (126.00 wl) × 13.70 × 4.30 (mean hull)
A: 8 RGM-84C Harpoon SSM; 1 8-round Mk 29 missile launcher (18 Sea Sparrow missiles); 1 76-mm 62-cal. OTO Melara Compact DP; 2 20-mm Mk 15 Phalanx CIWS; 1 8-round Mk 112 ASROC ASW RL (16 missiles); 2 triple 324-mm Type 68 ASW TT (Type 73 and Mk 46 Mod. 5 torpedoes); 1 SH-60J ASW helicopter
Electronics:
Radar: 1 JRC OPS-18-1 surf. search; 1 Melco OPS-14B air search; 1 FCS-2-21 gun f.c.; 1 GFCS-2-12 SAM f.c.; 2 General Dynamics Mk 90 Phalanx f.c.
Sonar: NEC OQS-4A hull-mounted MF; OQR-1 towed passive array
TACAN: U.S. URN-25 (ORN-6)
EW: NEC NOLQ-6C intercept; OLR-9B D/F; Fujitsu OLT-3 jammer; Mk 36 SRBOC decoy syst. (2 6-round Raytheon Mk 137 RL)
M: COGOG: 2 Kawasaki–Rolls-Royce Olympus TM-3B gas turbines (25,000 shp each), 2 Tyne RM-1C gas turbines (5,000 shp each); 2 CP props; 45,000 shp (50,000 max.)
Range: . . . / . . . **Fuel:** . . . **Crew:** 19 officers, 153 enlisted

Remarks: The newest unit of the *Hatsuyuki* class was redesignated TV 3513 on 18-3-99 and is employed as a cadet training ship, assigned to the 1st Training Squadron, Kure.
Hull systems: The Olympus engines are rated at 22,500 shp for cruise, 25,000 shp max., while the Tyne cruise engines are rated at 4,620-shp cruise/5,000 shp max. and provide speeds up to 19.5 kts. Helicopter deck has the Canadian Beartrap traversing/landing system. Has fin stabilizers and a steel superstructure. Stack incorporates passive infrared cooling features and a water-spray system.
Combat systems: Has OYQ-6 TDPS (Tactical Data Processing System) with Link 14 data relay receiver only. Received OQR-1 (U.S. SQR-18) TACTASS towed passive linear array after completion. Has NYPX-2 IFF systems and Superbird SHF SATCOM equipment.
Disposal note: *Yagamumo*-class training ship *Akigumo* (TV 3514, ex-DD 120, ex-DDK 120) was retired from service in 2003 following a serious engine room fire at Kure on 2-2-03.

SERVICE CRAFT

Note: Japanese Navy service ships and craft employ a two- or three-letter designator system to define their functions. Self-propelled units have two-digit hull numbers following the letter designator (as in "YO 01"). Non-self-propelled craft with the same functions have three-digit numbers starting with "1" (as in "YO 102"); craft converted from another function had three-digit hull numbers starting with "2," but there are some anomalies.

♦ 1 catamaran "sweeper boat" [YAG]
Bldr: . . . (In serv. 30-3-79)

YS 01

D: 80 tons **S:** 9 kts **Dim:** 22.0 × 7.80 × 1.40
M: 2 diesels; 2 props; 460 bhp **Crew:** 6 tot.

Remarks: Debris clearance craft, stationed at Iwakuni Air Station seaplane base; used to clear floating debris in seaplane landing lanes and as a marker-buoy tender.

Disposal note: All remaining YV 01–class seaplane buoy tenders have been withdrawn from service as of 2003. A 60-ton replacement YV was requested under the FY 99 budget but was not authorized.

♦ 1 YAL 01–class mine trials and service craft [YAGE]
Bldr: . . . (In serv. 22-3-76)

YAL 01

YAL 01 Takatoshi Okano, 7-97

D: 240 tons (265 fl) **S:** 12 kts **Dim:** 37.00 × 8.00 × 1.90
A: mine rails **M:** 2 Type 64 H 19-E-4A diesels; 2 props; 800 bhp **Crew:** 16 tot.

♦ 1 YL 119–class barge (non-self-propelled) [YCN]
Bldr: . . . (In serv. 20-3-71)

YL 119

YL 119—non-self-propelled barge Ralph Edwards, 10-02

D: 200 dwt **Dim:** 34.00 × 13.00 × 1.00

♦ 3 YL 116–class barges (non-self-propelled) [YCN]
YL 116 (In serv. 21-12-63) YL 117 (In serv. 25-2-64) YL 118 (In serv. 31-3-66)

D: 100 dwt **Dim:** 21.50 × 8.40 × 1.00

♦ 1 YL 114–class barge (non-self-propelled) [YCN]
YL 115 (In serv. 12-3-63)

D: 80 dwt **Dim:** 18.40 × 7.40 × 0.90

Remarks: Sister YL 114 was stricken 5-9-95.

♦ 1 YC 09–class self-propelled floating crane [YD]
YC 09 (In serv. 25-2-74)

YC 09 Mitsuhiro Kadota, 10-04

D: 260 tons **S:** 6 kts **Dim:** 26.0 × 14.0 × 0.9 **M:** 2 diesels; 2 props; 280 bhp

♦ 3 YC 06–class self-propelled floating cranes [YD]
YC 06 (In serv. 31-3-69) YC 07 (In serv. 28-2-70) YC 08 (In serv. 29-3-72)

D: 150 tons **S:** 5 kts **Dim:** 24.0 × 10.0 × 0.8 **M:** 2 diesels; 2 props; 240 bhp

Disposal note: YC 05–class floating crane YC 05 was stricken 20-6-00.

SERVICE CRAFT *(continued)*

♦ 6 YDT 01–class diving tenders [YDT]
Bldrs: First two: Yokohama Yacht; others: Maekata SY, Sasebo

	Laid down	L	In serv.
YDT 01	14-6-99	17-12-99	24-3-00
YDT 02	14-6-99	22-12-99	24-3-00
YDT 03	13-7-00	18-10-00	21-3-01
YDT 04	20-4-01	26-7-01	18-12-01
YDT 05	15-4-02	7-02	3-03
YDT 06	15-4-02	10-02	3-03

YDT 04 Takatoshi Okano, 2-02

D: 309 tons light; 380 tons normal (440 fl) **S:** 15 kts **Dim:** 46.0 × 8.6 × 2.2
A: None **Electronics:** Radar: 1 . . . nav.
M: 2 6NSDL diesels; 2 props; 1,500 bhp
Electric: 240 kw tot. (2 × 120-kw diesel sets)
Range: . . . / . . . **Crew:** 15 tot. + 15 explosive ordnance disposal divers

Remarks: First two requested under the FY 97 budget to begin replacement of YAS-redesignated former minesweepers as mine clearance diver and general-purpose diving tenders and as exercise torpedo and missile recovery ships. The initial request was disapproved, but the first two units were approved under the FY 98 budget; YDT 03 was approved under FY 99, YDT 04 under FY 00, and YDT 05 and YDT 06 under FY 01.
Hull systems: Have diving team accommodations amidships. A large electrohydraulic crane for boat and weapons recovery is mounted aft at the forecastle break. Two 4.2-m RIBs are carried for swimmer support. Have a submersible divers' stage at the stern, to port.

Disposal note: *Hatsushima*-class mine clearance divers' support ship *Hatsushima* (YAS 98, ex-MSC 649) was stricken on 13-7-01; sisters *Ninoshima* (YAS 01, ex-MSC 650) and *Miyajima* (YAS 02, ex-MSC 651) were stricken on 23-5-02. The last *Takami*-class mine clearance divers' support craft, the *Okitsu* (YAS 96, ex-MSC 646), was stricken 21-3-00.

♦ 7 YL 09–class landing craft lighters [YF]
Bldr: Ishihara DY, Takasago

	Laid down	L	In serv.
YL 09	24-11-79	3-3-80	28-3-80
YL 10	. . .	17-12-82	28-2-83
YL 11	21-12-87	14-3-88	25-3-88
YL 12	8-12-92	29-1-93	15-3-93
YL 13	4-3-94	29-8-94	26-9-94
YL 14	10-3-95	7-95	28-7-95
YL 15	23-4-98	7-9-98	30-9-98

YL 13 Ralph Edwards, 10-02

D: 50 tons light (120.5 fl) **S:** 9–10 kts **Dim:** 27.00 × 7.00 × 1.04
M: 2 Isuzu E 120 T-MF6 RE diesels; 2 props; 560 bhp **Crew:** 5 tot.

Remarks: Officially typed "Cargo Craft." 50 dwt. Resemble a U.S. LCM(8) landing craft and have a bow ramp and two 2-ton stores cranes. YL 13–15 have UM6 SD1 TCC diesels.

Disposal note: YL 08–class cargo lighter YL 08 was stricken 21-3-00.

♦ 12 YF 2121–class landing craft cargo lighters [YF]
Bldr: Ishihara Dockyard, Takasago

	In serv.		In serv.		In serv.
YF 2121	1989	YF 2128	31-3-92	YF 2138	13-3-96
YF 2124	26-2-90	YF 2129	21-3-92	YF 2150	3-03
YF 2125	20-3-90	YF 2132	31-3-93	YF 2151	3-03
YF 2127	27-3-92	YF 2135	30-3-95	YF 2152	2004

YF 2150 Takatoshi Okano, 4-04

D: 33 tons (56 fl) **S:** 10 kts **Dim:** 17.00 × 4.30 × 0.70
M: 2 Isuzu E120-MF6R diesels; 2 props; 480 bhp **Range:** 130/9 **Crew:** 4 tot.

Remarks: Officially designated as "Communications Boats." Design based on the U.S. LCM(6) landing craft. Employed as local transports for stores and personnel. Cargo: 30 tons or up to 80 personnel. YF 2138 has UM6 SD1 TCA diesels.

♦ 1 YF 2137–class 30-ton GRP personnel launch [YFL]
Bldr: . . . (In serv. 27-9-95)

YF 2137

YF 2137 Takatoshi Okano, 3-01

D: 38.2 tons **S:** 26.5 kts **Dim:** 22.5 × 5.1 × 0.9
Electronics: Radar: 1 . . . nav.
M: 2 MTU 12V183 TE92 diesels; 2 props; 1,820 bhp **Crew:** 2 tot.

Remarks: Approved under FY 94, laid down 9-5-95, and launched 13-9-95. Can carry 92 personnel. GRP construction.

♦ 4 YF 2131–class GRP personnel launches [YFL]
Bldr: Ishihara Dockyard, Takasago

YF 2131 (In serv. 31-3-92) YF 2136 (In serv. 30-3-95)
YF 2133 (In serv. 15-3-93) YF 2140 (In serv. 22-3-96)

YF 2136 *Ships of the World*, 3-95

D: 5.3–5.5 tons (fl) **S:** 15 kts **Dim:** 11.0 × 3.2 × 0.5–0.6
M: 1 UM6 BG1 TCB diesel; 1 prop; 210 bhp **Crew:** 2 tot.

SERVICE CRAFT *(continued)*

Remarks: First two have less powerful engines and can only achieve 15 kts; they also have a continuous upper deck line. GRP construction with heavy rubber fenders. Can carry 15 passengers.

♦ 1 YF 2126–class GRP personnel launch [YFL]

Bldr: Shinju Zosen (In serv. 30-3-94)

YF 2134

YF 2134 *Ships of the World,* 3-94

D: 12 tons **S:** 18 kts **Dim:** 15.0 × 4.2 × 0.7
M: 2 Type UM6 BD1 diesels; 2 props; 520 bhp
Crew: 3 tot. + 40 passengers

Remarks: Requested under FY 93 budget. GRP construction officers' barge.

♦ 3 YF 2123–class personnel launches [YFL]

Bldr: Ishihara Dockyard, Takasago

YF 2123 (In serv. 30-1-87) YF 2130 (In serv. 31-3-92)
YF 2126 (In serv. 28-3-91)

D: 14.3 tons **S:** 10 kts **Dim:** 15.0 × 4.2 × 1.6
M: 2 Type UM6 BD1 diesels; 2 props; 480 bhp

Remarks: YF 2130 was in FY 91 budget; laid down 5-12-91 and launched 3-3-92. An updated version of the single-unit YF 2020 class.

♦ 5 YF 1029–class GRP-hulled personnel launches [YFL]

Bldr: Ishihara Dockyard, Takasago

YF 1029 (In serv. 1982) YF 1032 (In serv. 27-3-98)
YF 1030 (In serv. 1982) YF 1033 (In serv. 21-3-00)
YF 1031 (In serv. 25-3-88)

YF 1031 Ralph Edwards, 10-02

D: 11 tons (13.5 fl) **S:** 18 kts **Dim:** 13.50 (12.40 pp) × 3.80 × 0.70
M: 2 Isuzu 6BDITC-MRD diesels; 2 props; 360 bhp
Crew: 2 tot. + 20 passengers

Remarks: YF 1033 has Mitsubishi UM6 BG1 TCC diesels.

♦ 7 U.S. LCVP-class service launches [YFL]

YF 2072 YF 2073 YF 2080 YF 2084 YF 2085 YF 2086 YF 2087

D: 8 tons (13 fl) **S:** 9 kts **Dim:** 10.5 × 3.2 × 0.6
M: 1 Yanmar 6CH-DTE diesel; 1 prop; 180 bhp **Crew:** 3 tot.

Remarks: GRP-hulled versions of the standard U.S. Navy LCVP design, with bow ramp. Can carry up to 40 personnel.
Disposals: YF 2069 was stricken 16-2-94, YF 2074 on 30-3-94, YF 2078 on 29-9-95, YF 2079 on 2-11-95, YF 2081 on 30-10-95, and YF 2083 on 18-1-96.

♦ 11 YF 2088–class personnel launches [YFL]

Bldr: Ishihara Dockyard, Takasago

YF 2117 through YF 2119 YF 2139 YF 2143 through YF 2149

YF 2118 Takatoshi Okano, 7-04

D: 5.9 tons (5.9 fl) **S:** 10–11 kts **Dim:** 11.0 × 3.2 × 0.6
M: 1 UM6 BG1 TCA diesel; 1 prop; 135 bhp **Crew:** 2 tot.

Remarks: GRP construction. YF 2139, completed 8-3-96, and higher-numbered units are repeats of the earlier units, most of which were built in the late 1980s. YF 2143, YF 2144, and YF 2145 were delivered 25-3-98, while YF 2146 and YF 2147 were ordered during 1988 and completed 19-3-99. YF 2148 and YF 2149 were delivered 21-3-00 and are powered by UM6 BG1 TCX diesels.
Disposals: YF 2088 and YF 2090 were stricken 25-3-98, YF 2089 on 7-1-99, YF 2092 on 19-3-99, YF 2093 on 31-3-99, YF 2095 on 29-3-99, YF 2094 on 6-3-00, YF 2111 through YF 2113 on 28-1-00, YF 2114 on 17-3-00, YF 2115 on 21-3-00, and YF 2116 on 21-9-93.

♦ 2 YF 1022–class personnel launches [YFL]

Bldr: . . . (In serv. 1980)

YF 1027 YF 1028

D: 9 tons (11 fl) **S:** 14 kts **Dim:** 13.00 × 3.80 × 0.60
M: 2 Type E 120 T-MF6RE diesels; 2 props; 280 bhp
Crew: . . . + 73 passengers

Remarks: Sister YF 1022 was stricken on 27-9-95, YF 1024 and YF 1025 on 31-3-98, and YF 1026 on 5-11-99.

♦ 4 miscellaneous service launches [YFL]

	Tons (light)	Dim	S (kts)	bhp
YF 2075	22.0	17.0 × 3.7 × 0.7	10	400
YF 2076, YF 2077	0.8	7.0 × 2.2 × 0.3	8	22
YF 2120	12.6	15.0 × 3.6 × 0.7	10	230

Remarks: YF 2075 is essentially a U.S. LCM(6) landing craft adapted as a utility craft. YF 2120 is a wooden-hulled craft resembling a tugboat, but with open personnel seating fore and aft.

♦ 3 miscellaneous dockyard service craft [YFL]

YD 03 (In serv. 1978): 1.7 tons, 7.60 × 1.90
YD 04 (In serv. 25-12-79): 0.5 tons
YD 05 (In serv. 21-3-00): 1.6 tons, 7.1 × 1.8

YD 03—on trailer Ralph Edwards, 10-02

Remarks: YD 05, a GRP-hulled open launch propelled by a 25-bhp Yamaha outboard, was approved under the FY 99 budget. The 0.8-ton YD 01 was stricken 3-12-99 and the identical YD 02 on 6-3-00.

♦ 9 YO 29–class fuel lighters [YO]

Bldr: Maehata Iron Works, Sasebo

	Laid down	L	In serv.
YO 29	2-7-91	25-9-91	28-11-91
YO 30	9-91	25-11-91	24-1-92
YO 31	11-91	22-1-92	19-3-92
YO 33	26-4-93	8-93	21-9-93
YO 34	17-2-95	19-5-95	28-7-95
YO 35	17-2-95	28-7-95	20-9-95
YO 36	14-5-97	10-7-97	7-10-97
YO 37	6-10-97	18-12-97	6-3-98
YO 38	15-5-98	28-7-98	30-9-98

SERVICE CRAFT *(continued)*

YO 35 Ralph Edwards, 10-02

D: 490 tons (750 fl) **S:** 10 kts **Dim:** 46.4 × 7.8 × 2.2
M: 2 Isuzu UM6 SD1 T diesels; 2 props; 460 bhp **Crew:** 10 tot.

Remarks: Cargo: 340 m^3 liquid, plus a small hold aft for dry cargo. YO 34 and YO 35 have 6MA-series diesels of 250 bhp each.

♦ 2 YO 28–class fuel lighters [YO]
Bldr: Maehata Iron Works, Sasebo

YO 28 (In serv. 27-7-90) YO 32 (In serv. 16-10-92)

YO 28 Mitsuhiro Kadota, 4-99

D: 270 tons **S:** 9 kts **Dim:** 27.7 × 6.8 × 2.6
M: 2 Isuzu UM6 SD1 T diesels; 2 props; 360 bhp

♦ 7 YO 21–class fuel lighters [YO]

	Bldr	Laid down	L	In serv.
YO 21	Yoshiura SB	. . .	15-3-80	31-3-80
YO 22	Yoshiura SB	11-11-80	26-2-81	28-2-81
YO 23	Yoshiura SB	26-11-82	12-3-83	31-3-83
YO 24	Yoshiura SB	4-11-83	20-1-84	29-2-84
YO 25	Naikai, Innoshima	14-11-87	15-7-88	20-9-88
YO 26	Sagami, Yakosuka	18-4-87	28-7-88	26-9-88
YO 27	Sumidigawa, Tokyo	. . .	2-6-89	18-7-89

YO 23 *Ships of the World,* 1995

D: 490 tons (694 fl) **S:** 9–10 kts **Dim:** 45.5 × 7.8 × 2.9
M: 2 Yanmar 6 MA diesels; 2 props; 460 bhp **Crew:** 10 tot.

Remarks: YO 25 and 26, with 520-m^3 cargo capacity, were authorized under the FY 87 budget; YO 27, under FY 88, was ordered 6-12-88 and carries 630 m^3 of cargo.

♦ 1 YO 14–class fuel lighter [YO]
Bldr: . . . (In serv. 31-3-76)

YO 14

D: 490 dwt **S:** 9 kts **Dim:** 45.0 × 7.8 × 2.9 **M:** 2 diesels; 2 props; 460 bhp

♦ 2 YO 10–class fuel lighters [YO]
Bldr: . . .

YO 12 (In serv. 21-3-67) YO 13 (In serv. 31-3-67)

D: 290 dwt **S:** 9 kts **Dim:** 36.5 × 6.8 × 2.6 **M:** 2 diesels; 2 props; 360 bhp

Remarks: Sisters YO 10 and YO 11 were stricken during 1998.

YO 13 Takatoshi Okano, 3-96

♦ 5 YG 07–class jet engine fuel craft [YO]
Bldr: IHI, Tokyo; YG 205: Maehata Iron Works

	In serv.		In serv.
YG 201 (ex-YG 07)	30-3-73	YG 204	2-7-89
YG 202 (ex-YO 20, ex-YG 08)	29-3-77	YG 205	16-7-90
YG 203	20-9-88		

YG 204 *Ships of the World,* 1995

D: 270 dwt **S:** 9 kts **Dim:** 36.0 × 6.80 × 2.80
M: 1 Shinko-Zaki Ogaki S617-S1CM diesel; 1 prop; 360 bhp **Crew:** 5 tot.

Remarks: YG 08 was reclassified YO 20 in 1979, then again reclassified YG 202 in 1981. YG 203 and YG 204 are 37.7 m o.a. YG 205 was ordered 13-12-89 under the FY 90 budget and launched 21-5-90; she has UM6 SD1 T diesels and two shafts.

♦ 1 YB 01–class oil sludge removal lighter [YSR]

YB 01 (L: 31-3-75)

D: 176.7 tons **S:** 9 kts **Dim:** 27.5 × 5.2 × 1.9
M: 1 diesel; 230 bhp **Cargo:** 100 tons

♦ 4 YB 101–class oil sludge removal barges (non-self-propelled) [YSRN]
Bldr: . . . (In serv. 1975–76)

YB 101 YB 102 YB 103 YB 104

YB 102 *Ships of the World*

D: 100 dwt **Dim:** 17.0 × 5.2 × 2.0

♦ 20 YT 58–class large harbor tugs [YTB]
Bldr: Yokohama Yacht (YT 89, 90: Ishikawajima Ship & Chemical, Tokyo)

	L	In serv.		L	In serv.
YT 58	. . .	31-10-78	YT 72	25-4-90	27-7-90
YT 63	. . .	27-9-82	YT 73	13-5-91	31-7-91
YT 64	. . .	30-9-83	YT 74	7-91	9-91
YT 65	. . .	20-9-84	YT 78	24-5-94	28-7-94
YT 66	. . .	20-9-85	YT 79	22-7-94	29-9-94
YT 67	7-6-86	4-9-86	YT 81	6-96	7-96
YT 68	9-6-87	9-9-87	YT 84	21-8-98	20-10-98
YT 69	15-6-87	16-9-87	YT 86	10-12-99	21-3-00
YT 70	14-6-88	2-9-88	YT 89	22-12-00	16-3-01
YT 71	19-5-89	28-7-89	YT 90	26-12-00	16-3-01

D: 262 tons **S:** 11 kts **Dim:** 28.40 × 8.60 × 2.50
Electronics: Radar: 1 . . . nav. **Crew:** 10 tot.
M: 2 Niigata 6L25BX diesels; 2 pivoting Kort-nozzle props; 1,800 bhp

Remarks: The design has evolved over its 24-year construction history, with improved equipment in the later units. Have one or two firefighting water cannon. YT 70 was rated at 1,600 bhp. YT 89 and YT 90 were laid down 11-5-00.

SERVICE CRAFT *(continued)*

YT 73 Takatoshi Okano, 7-02

♦ 4 YT 53–class large harbor tugs [YTB]

	In serv.		In serv.
YT 53	1974	YT 56	13-7-76
YT 55	22-8-75	YT 57	22-8-77

YT 53 Brian Morrison, 10-02

D: 195 tons (200 fl) **S:** 11 kts **Dim:** 25.70 × 7.00 × 2.30
M: 2 Kubota M6D20BUCS diesels; 1 prop; 1,500 bhp **Crew:** 10 tot.

♦ 10 YT 75–class harbor pusher tugs [YTM]
Bldr: Yokohama Yacht (YT 87, 88: Nagasaki Zosen)

	Laid down	L	In serv.
YT 75	13-5-92	27-8-92	29-9-92
YT 76	10-3-93	23-7-93	30-7-93
YT 77	10-3-93	8-93	16-9-93
YT 80	14-4-95	10-95	29-11-95
YT 82	9-96	12-96	3-97
YT 83	23-6-97	26-1-98	2-3-98
YT 85	28-8-98	2-12-98	5-3-99
YT 87	14-5-99	24-1-00	15-3-00
YT 88	14-5-99	30-8-99	5-10-99
YT 91	24-4-02	1-03	3-03

YT 75 Mitsuhiro Kadota, 9-04

D: 50 tons (75 fl) **S:** 8 kts **Dim:** 17.0 × 4.8 × 1.20
M: 2 Type UM6 SD1 TCB diesels; 2 props; 500 bhp **Crew:** 4 tot.

Remarks: YT 91 was approved under the FY 01 budget.

♦ 3 YT 60–class harbor pusher tugs [YTL]
Bldr: Yokohama Yacht

YT 60 (In serv. 31-3-80) YT 61 (In serv. 26-3-80) YT 62 (In serv. 16-3-81)

YT 61 *Ships of the World,* 1995

D: 30 tons (37 fl) **S:** 8.6 kts **Dim:** 15.50 × 4.20 × 1.50 (0.97 hull)
M: 2 Isuzu E 120-MF64A diesels; 2 cycloidal props; 380 bhp

♦ 3 YT 34–class harbor pusher tugs [YTL]

YT 51 (In serv. 28-2-72) YT 54 (In serv. 24-3-75) YT 59 (In serv. 16-1-79)

YT 59 Ralph Edwards, 10-02

D: 28 tons (30 fl) **S:** 9 kts **Dim:** 14.50 × 4.00 × 1.00
M: 2 diesels; 2 props; 320 bhp **Crew:** 3 tot.

Remarks: YT 59 displaces 30 tons std. Sisters YT 27 and 33 were stricken during 1979, YT 32 during 1981, YT 34 on 8-7-91, YT 39 on 26-3-93, YT 38 on 30-3-94, YT 36 on 29-11-95, YT 42 on 2-3-98, YT 43 on 2-10-98, YT 47 on 5-10-99, and YT 49 on 16-3-01.

♦ 2 YR 01–class fireboats [YTR]
Bldr: Ishikawajima-Harima Heavy Industries

	Laid down	L	In serv.
YR 01	28-8-00	18-1-01	16-3-01
YR 02	23-8-01	6-11-01	20-3-02

YR 01 Takatoshi Okano, 9-02

D: 60 tons **S:** 19 kts **Dim:** 25.0 × 5.5 × 1.1
Electronics: Radar: 1 . . . nav.
M: 2 UM6 WG1 TCG diesels; 2 props; 1,500 bhp **Crew:** 10 tot.

Remarks: YR 01 was approved for construction under the FY 99 budget and YR 02 under FY 00. Have a UM6 RB1 TCG diesel to power the pump supporting the three water monitors forward and are fitted with a crane aft.

SERVICE CRAFT *(continued)*

♦ 11 "Y"-group sailboats [YTS]

Y 7021 through Y 7031

Remarks: Y 7021 and Y 7022 were delivered on 26-2-85, Y 7025 and Y 7026 on 30-10-92; and Y 7029–Y 7031 on 24-3-95. Y 7014 and Y 7015 were stricken 30-10-92, Y 7016 and Y 7017 on 25-3-94, and Y 7018–Y 7020 on 24-3-95. All are attached to the Etajima Naval Academy. Small GRP-hulled sloops; no other data available.

♦ 8 YW 17–class water lighters [YW]

Bldr: Maehata Iron Works, Sasebo (YW 17: Shikoku Dockyard)

	L	In serv.		L	In serv.
YW 17	19-7-88	27-9-88	YW 21	1-97	3-97
YW 18	9-5-89	28-7-89	YW 22	15-12-97	4-3-98
YW 19	30-9-92	29-12-92	YW 23	16-7-99	21-3-00
YW 20	30-5-94	20-9-94	YW 24	9-99	23-3-00

YW 23—in light condition *Ships of the World,* 3-01

D: Approx. 450 tons (fl) **S:** 10 kts **Dim:** 37.7 × 6.8 × 2.8
M: 2 UM6 SD1 T diesels; 2 props; 360 bhp **Crew:** 5 tot.

Remarks: 310 dwt. Water lighters are required because many JMSDF warships lack the means to make potable water, relying on onboard tankage only.

Disposal note: YW 12–class water lighters YW 15 and YW 16 were stricken 21-3-00.

♦ 1 YTE 13–class training tender [YXT]

Bldr: . . .

	Laid down	L	In serv.
YTE 13	19-7-01	7-12-01	20-3-02

YTE 13 Takatoshi Okano, 3-02

D: 170 tons **S:** 16 kts **Dim:** 35.3 × 7.4 × 1.7
Electronics: Radar: 1 . . . nav.
M: 2 12LAK-ST2 diesels; 2 props; 2,200 bhp
Crew: 4 officers, 10 enlisted, 25 cadets

Remarks: Approved under the FY 00 budget to replace YTE 11 at Etajima Naval Academy; for use teaching officer cadets ship handling and navigation.

Disposal note: *Tokiwa*-class training tender YTE 12 (ex-*Tokiwa*) was retired from service by 2005 and YTE 11–class training craft YTE 11 was stricken on 20-3-02.

♦ 9 "B"-series miscellaneous training craft [YXT]

B 4006: 8 tons; 13.00 × 3.20 × 0.50; 14 kts (In serv. 16-3-76)
B 4007, 4011: 1 ton; 5.00 × 2.10 × 0.40; 22 kts (Both in serv. 26-1-76)
B 4014–4016: 8 tons; 13.00 × 3.20 × 0.50; 14 kts (In serv. 1978–80)
B 4017: 16 tons; 17.4 × 3.9 × 1.5; 10 kts (In serv. 28-3-85)
B 4021, 4022: . . . (In serv. 22-3-96)

Remarks: GRP hulled. B 4016 is capable of 18 kts. B 4006 is basically the same as B 4014–B 4016. B 4017 has a GRP hull with pilothouse offset to port; 180 bhp. B 4008 was stricken 22-3-96 and B 4012 and 4013 on 22-3-96.

♦ 64 "C"-class rowing boats [YXT]

C 5158–C 5221 series

D: 1.5 tons **Dim:** 9.0 × 2.5 × . . .

Remarks: C 5204–C 5208 were delivered 20-3-98, C 5209–C 5212 in 3-99, C 5213–C 5218 on 21-3-00, and C 5219–C 5221 on 22-3-02. The total number is maintained through a regular retirement of four or more per year and replacement by new units, with all now being of a uniform design. Are stationed at the Etajima Naval Academy or at other training facilities.

C 5206 Takatoshi Okano, 5-01

Disposals: Recent retirements include C 5148–C 5152 on 22-3-00, C 5156 on 14-3-01, and C 5153 on 51-3-01. C 5154–C 5157 were stricken on 22-3-02.

♦ 41 "T"-class punts [YXT]

T 6077 T 6081 through T 6120

T 6115 Takatoshi Okano, 3-01

D: 0.5 tons **Dim:** 6.0 × 1.6 × . . .
M: 1 Tohhatsu or Yamaha outboard; . . . bhp

Remarks: Molded GRP construction. The wooden-hulled T 6077 may also still be in service. T 6110–T 6113 were delivered 22-3-96, T 6118–T 6120 on 20-3-98. T 6067–T 6069 were stricken 24-3-95; T 6070, T6071, T 6074, and T 6076 on 22-3-96; and T 6078–T 6080 on 20-3-98. Are stationed at the Etajima Naval Academy or at other training facilities.

JAPAN COAST GUARD

The name of the organization was changed to the Japan Coast Guard on 1-4-00. The preceding Maritime Safety Agency (MSA), which was organized in 1948, underwent a massive expansion in the 1970s, which by 1982 made it one of the world's largest and best-equipped coast guards. It is directed by the Department of Transportation. Although most of its ships are armed, they are not considered part of the navy and fly only the national colors (a red disk on a white background), not the ensign flown by naval ships. Most ships and craft are now painted white, with the stylized Coast Guard "S" in blue on the hull sides; a few patrol craft and service craft are still painted gray. Most units have green-painted decks. The words "Japan Coast Guard" are being painted on the hull or superstructure sides.

Personnel: 12,260 total (Including approximately 2,650 officers)

Organization: The Coast Guard is organized into 11 districts, 65 offices, 25 detachments, 52 stations, 14 air stations, 11 district communications centers, and a traffic advisory service; there are also 4 hydrographic observatories and 132 aids-to-navigation offices.

Aviation: The Japan Coast Guard operates 33 fixed-wing aircraft including two Gulfstream Vair/sea surveillance aircraft, four Saab 340B (two of which were delivered in late 2006), two Dassault-Breguet Falcon 900 long-range search-and-rescue aircraft; 10 Beech 350, two Beech B200T Super King Air, and seven Beech 200T Super King Air search-and-rescue aircraft; five YS-11A transports; and one Cessna U206G light transport/utility aircraft and 46 helicopters (4 Aérospatiale AS.332L1 Super Puma, four Sikorsky S-76C, eight Bell 412, 26 Kawasaki-Bell 212, and four Bell 206B). All fixed-wing aircraft bear names; as examples, the two Saab 340B aircraft (MA 951 and MA 952) are named *Hamataka No. 1* and *Hamataka No. 2,* the two Falcon 900 aircraft (LAJ 570 and LAJ 571) are named *Ootaka No. 1* and *Ootaka No. 2,* Super Puma MH 686 is named the *Umitaka,* and Beech 350 MA 867 is named *Toki.*

Falcon 900 long-range SAR aircraft Mitsuhiro Kadota, 2004

JAPAN COAST GUARD *(continued)*

Japan Coast Guard Gulfstream V — Mitsuhiro Kadota, 5-05

Saab 340B long-range SAR aircraft MA 952 — Takatoshi Okano, 5-04

Beech 200T SAR aircraft MA 819 — *Ships of the World*

Beech 350 SAR aircraft MA 863A — Takatoshi Okano, 5-04

YS-11A transport LA 782 — Takatoshi Okano, 5-04

AS.332L1 Super Puma MH 686 — Takatoshi Okano, 5-03

Sikorsky S-76C MH 905 — Takatoshi Okano, 5-04

Kawasaki-Bell 212 MH 607 — Takatoshi Okano, 5-04

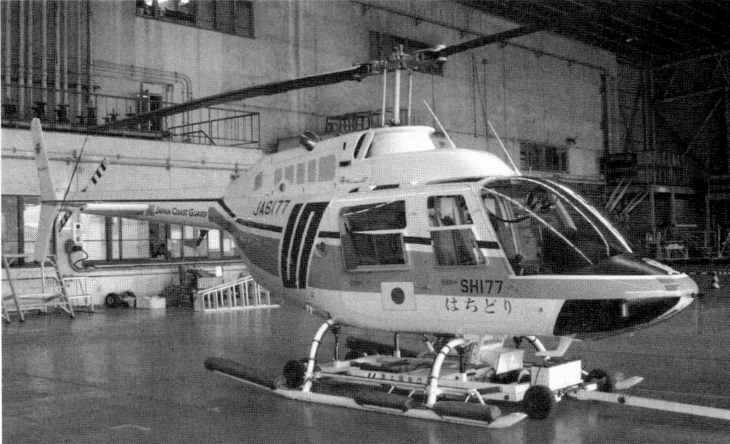

Bell 206 SH 177 — Mitsuhiro Kadota, 5-03

Air stations are located as follows: 1st Region Headquarters at Otaru on Hokkaido, with subsidiary air stations at Chitose, Hakodate, and Kushiro; 2nd Region Headquarters at Shiogama, Miyaga Prefecture, with subsidiary air stations at Miyaga and Sendai; 3rd Region Headquarters at Yokohama, with a subsidiary air station at Haneda Airport near Tokyo; 4th Region Headquarters at Nagoya, Aichi Prefecture, with a subsidiary air station at Ise; 5th Region Headquarters at Kobe, with a subsidiary air station at Yao, Osaka Prefecture; 6th Region Headquarters at Ujina, Hiroshima Prefecture; 7th Region Headquarters at Moji-ka, Kita-Kyushu, Fukuoka Prefecture, with a subsidiary air station at Fukuoka; 8th Region Headquarters at Maizuru, Kyoto Prefecture, with a subsidiary air station at Miho, Shimane Prefecture; 10th Region Headquarters at Kagoshima; and 11th Region Headquarters at Naha on Okinawa, with subsidiary air stations at Ishigaki Island and Yaeyama.

Note: The organization and designations of the ships and craft below are a compromise between the Japan Coast Guard system, which is based as much on mission as on size, and the system adopted for this book as a whole, which is based on size and capabilities. Thus, some of the classes below will not meet the strict requirements of the standard *Combat Fleets* designation system, but it was felt that keeping classes with the same Japanese type designator together should take precedence. The letter designations used by the Coast Guard include:

JAPAN COAST GUARD *(continued)*

- PL—Patrol vessel, Large
- PM—Patrol vessel, Medium
- PS—Patrol vessel, Small
- PC—Patrol Craft
- CL—Craft, Large
- LS—Lighthouse service vessel, Small
- MA—Medium (fixed-wing) Aircraft
- MH—Medium Helicopter

PATROL SHIPS [WPS]

♦ 1 Shikishima-class high-endurance helicopter-carrying cutter

Bldr: IHI, Tokyo

	Laid down	L	In serv.
PLH 31 SHIKISHIMA	4-28-90	27-6-91	8-4-92

Shikishima (PLH 31) Mitsuhiro Kadota, 5-05

Shikishima (PLH 31) Mitsuhiro Kadota, 5-05

D: 6,500 tons light; 7,175 tons std. (9,350 fl) **S:** 25 kts
Dim: 150.0 × 16.5 × 7.00
A: 2 twin 35-mm 90-cal. Oerlikon AA; 2 single 20-mm JM-61-MB Sea Vulcan gatling AA; 2 single 12.7-mm M2 mg; 2 Aérospatiale AS.332L1 Super Puma helicopters
Electronics: Radar: 1 JMS 1596 nav.; 1 JMA 8303 surf. search; 1 JMA 3000 helo control; 1 Melco OPS-14C surf./air search
M: 2 IHI–SEMT-Pielstick 16 PC2.5 V400 diesels; 2 CP props; 20,800 bhp—bow-thruster
Range: 20,000/18 **Crew:** 110 tot. + 30 aircrew

Remarks: Intended to act as escort for a ship to carry plutonium from Europe to Japan for use in nuclear electric-power generation stations, but, after a single such voyage in 8-93 escorting the chartered plutonium transport *Akatsuki Maru* (ex-*Pacific Crane*), has been used as a general patrol ship assigned to the Yokohama Maritime Safety Department.
Combat systems: The enclosed 20-mm gatling gunmounts are the same as those used on the JMSDF's PG 01–class missile hydrofoils. There are two optronic directors for the twin 35-mm mountings. The planned ORN-6 TACAN was not fitted. Is equipped with two water cannon for fire fighting and harassment control. Has SHF and commercial UHF SATCOM gear.

♦ 2 Mizuho-class high-endurance helicopter-carrying cutters

	Bldr	Laid down	L	In serv.
PLH 21 MIZUHO	Mitsubishi, Shimonoseki	27-8-84	5-6-85	19-3-86
PLH 22 YASHIMA	Nippon Kokan, Tsurumi	3-8-87	20-1-88	1-12-88

D: 4,960 tons light; 5,317 tons fl. **S:** 23.3 kts
Dim: 130.00 (123.00 wl) × 15.50 × 5.25
A: 1 35-mm 90-cal. Oerlikon AA; 1 20-mm JM-61-MB Sea Vulcan gatling AA; 2 Kawasaki-Bell 212 helicopters
Electronics: Radar: 2 JMA 3000 nav.; 1 JMA 8303 nav.
M: 2 IHI–SEMT-Pielstick 14 PC2.5 V400 (PLH 22: 12 PC2 V) diesels; 2 CP props; 18,200 bhp—bow-thruster
Electric: 1,875 kVA (3 diesel sets) **Range:** 8,500/22 **Crew:** 130 tot.

Yashima (PLH 22) Mitsuhiro Kadota, 5-03

Mizuho (PLH 21)—with helicopter on the flight deck Mitsuhiro Kadota, 5-03

Remarks: Intended to operate 200 n.m. to sea or farther, if necessary. Are the first Japan Coast Guard class to carry two helicopters. Have a flight deck–traversing system and two pairs of fin stabilizers. An SHF SATCOM system was added to PLH 21 in 1989, and both have Marisat commercial SATCOM. PLH 21 is based at Nagoya.

♦ 2 Ryukyu-class high-endurance helicopter-carrying cutters

	Bldr	Laid down	L	In serv.
PLH 09 RYUKYU	Mitsui, Tamano	24-6-98	10-9-99	31-3-00
PLH 10 DAISEN	Nippon Kokan, Tsurumi	8-3-99	27-4-01	3-10-01

Daisen (PLH 10) Mitsuhiro Kadota, 5-03

COAST GUARD PATROL SHIPS [WPS] *(continued)*

D: 3,100 tons (3,900 fl) **S:** 22 kts **Dim:** 105.00 (100.00 wl) × 15.00 × 4.85
A: 1 35-mm 90-cal.; 1 20-mm JM-61-MB Sea Vulcan gatling AA; 1 Kawasaki-Bell 212 helicopter
Electronics: Radar: 1 . . . nav.; 1 . . . surf. search; 1 . . . helo control
M: 2 diesels; 2 CP props; 16,000 bhp—bow-thruster
Range: 5,700/18 **Crew:** . . .

Remarks: Intended to operate 100 n.m. or more to sea. Design is a modernized version of the preceding *Tsugaru* class, with somewhat finer hull lines and a bulbous forefoot to the bow. Have a Marisat UHF SATCOM installation. The 20-mm gun is in a new, remotely operated, automatic mounting. PLH 09 is based at Naha, Okinawa, and patrols the Nansei Islands area.

♦ 7 Tsugaru-class high-endurance helicopter-carrying cutters

	Bldr	Laid down	L	In serv.
PLH 02 TSUGARU	IHI, Tokyo	18-4-78	6-12-78	17-4-79
PLH 03 OOSUMI	Mitsui, Tamano	1-9-78	1-6-79	18-10-79
PLH 04 HAYATO (ex-*Uraga*)	Hitachi, Maizuru	14-3-79	12-10-79	5-3-80
PLH 05 ZAO	Mitsubishi, Nagasaki	23-10-80	29-10-81	19-3-82
PLH 06 CHIKUZEN	Kawasaki, Kobe	20-4-82	18-3-83	28-9-83
PLH 07 SETTSU	Sumitomo, Uraga	5-4-83	21-4-84	27-9-84
PLH 08 ECHIGO	Mitsui, Tamano	29-3-88	4-7-89	28-2-90

Echigo (PLH 08) Takatoshi Okano, 5-04

Zao (PLH 05) Mitsuhiro Kadota, 5-03

D: 3,221 tons light; 3,730 tons std. (4,037 fl) **S:** 21.5 kts
Dim: 105.40 (100.00 wl) × 14.60 × 4.85
A: PLH 02, 03: 1 40-mm 60-cal. Bofors AA—others: 1 35-mm 90-cal. Oerlikon AA—PLH 02, 05–07: 1 20-mm 70-cal. Oerlikon AA—all: 1 Kawasaki-Bell 212 helicopter
Electronics: Radar: 1 JMA 1596 nav.; 1 JMA 1576 surf. search; 1 . . . helo control
M: 2 SEMT-Pielstick 12 PC2.5 V400 diesels; 2 CP props; 15,600 bhp (13,260 bhp sust.)—bow-thruster
Electric: 1,160 kw tot. (2 × 520 kw, 1 × 120 kw) **Range:** 5,700/18
Fuel: 864 tons **Crew:** 21 officers, 7 warrant officers, 28 enlisted + 15 spare

Remarks: Intended to operate 100 n.m. or more to sea. Redesignated from PL in 1985–86. Have two pair of fin stabilizers and Flume-type passive stabilization tanks in the superstructure. The engines were manufactured by different builders. Have a Marisat UHF SATCOM installation.

♦ 1 Soya-class high-endurance helicopter-carrying cutter

	Bldr	Laid down	L	In serv.
PLH 01 SOYA	Nippon Kokan, Tsurumi	12-9-77	3-7-78	22-11-78

D: 3,139 tons light; 3,562 tons std. (4,089 fl) **S:** 21 kts **Dim:** 98.6 × 15.6 × 5.2
A: 1 40-mm 60-cal. Bofors AA; 1 20-mm 70-cal. Oerlikon AA; 1 Kawasaki-Bell 212 helicopter
Electronics: Radar: 4 . . . nav. (1 aft for helo control)
M: 2 Nippon Kokan–Pielstick 12 PC2.5 V400 diesels; 2 CP props; 16,000 bhp (13,260 hp sust.)
Electric: 1,160 kw tot. (2 × 520 kw, 1 × 120 kw)
Range: 5,700/18 **Fuel:** 650 tons **Crew:** 71 tot.

Remarks: Built under the 1977 program. Has an icebreaking bow and operates in the north. Passive tank stabilization only, no bow-thruster. Has a rounded stern, vice the squared one on the *Tsugaru* class. Redesignated PLH from PL on 13-12-85. The armament is not normally fitted.

Soya (PLH 01) Mitsuhiro Kadota, 5-03

♦ 2 (+ 1) 1,800-ton class cutter
Bldr: Mitsubishi, Shimonoseki (In serv 2006-)

	L	In serv.
PL 51 HIDA	21-10-05	4-06
PL 52 AKAISHI	2005	2006
PL 53 . . .	2006	2007

Hida (PL 51) *Ships of the World,* 2005

Hida (PL 51) *Ships of the World,* 2005

D: 1,800 tons std. **S:** 30 **Dim:** 95.0 × 13.0 × 6.0
A: 1 40-mm AA; 1 20-mm gatling AA Electronics: 1 . . . nav.
M: . . . diesels; . . . waterjets;

Remarks: PL 51 began sea trials late in 2005. Long flush deck aft serves as a helicopter platform, though the class does not have a hangar.

♦ 1 Izu-class (3,500-ton) disaster-relief cutter

	Bldr	Laid down	L	In serv.
PL 31 IZU	Nippon Kokan, Tsurumi	22-3-96	7-2-97	25-9-97

D: 3,680 tons (fl) **S:** 20 kts **Dim:** 110.40 × 15.00 × 3.60
A: 1 20-mm JM-61-MB Sea Vulcan gatling AA
Electronics: Radar: 1 JMA . . . nav.; 1 JMA . . . surf. search
M: 2 . . . diesels; 2 CP props; 12,000 bhp—bow-thruster **Crew:** . . . tot.

Remarks: PL 31, approved under the FY 95 budget, replaced an earlier unit with the same name and number. Has a large helicopter platform aft but no hangar. Equipped with a bow-thruster and with passive stabilization tanks. Has extensive medical facilities and is intended to serve in disaster relief roles. Based at Yokohama.

COAST GUARD PATROL SHIPS [WPS] *(continued)*

Izu (PL 31) Mitsuhiro Kadota, 5-03

♦ 4 Hakata-class (1,000-ton) high-endurance cutters

	Bldr	Laid down	L	In serv.
PL 05 Hakata	IHI, Tokyo	22-10-97	7-6-98	26-11-98
PL 06 Dejima	Mitsui, Tamano	1-9-98	28-6-99	29-10-99
PL 07 Satsuma	Kawasaki, Kobe	4-9-98	3-6-99	29-10-99
PL 08 Motobu	Mitsui, Tamano	8-9-99	9-6-00	31-10-00

Hakata (PL 05) Mitsuhiro Kadota, 5-03

D: 1,365 tons light; 1,930 tons std. (2,055 fl) **S:** 20 kts **Dim:** 93.5 × 11.5 × 4.0
A: 1 35-mm 90-cal Oerlikon AA; 1 20-mm JM-61-MB Sea Vulcan gatling AA; 1 12.7-mm mg
Electronics: Radar: 2 . . . nav.
M: 2 Fuji S540B diesels; 2 CP props; 7,000 bhp—2 bow-thrusters
Range: 4,400/19 **Crew:** . . . tot.

Remarks: Design evolved from the *Ojika* design. PL 08 is based at Naha, Okinawa, and operates in the waters off the Senkaku Islands, primarily as a fisheries patrol ship.

♦ 3 Ojika-class (1,000-ton) high-endurance cutters

	Bldr	Laid down	L	In serv.
PL 02 Erimo (ex-*Ojika*)	Mitsui, Tamano	28-9-90	23-4-91	3-10-91
PL 03 Kudaka	Hakodate DY	9-9-93	10-5-94	25-10-94
PL 04 Yahiko (ex-*Satsuma*)	Sumitomo, Uraga	21-9-94	29-5-95	26-10-95

Yahiko (PL 04) Takatoshi Okano, 7-02

D: 1,268 tons light, 1,883 tons std. (2,006 fl) **S:** 20 kts
Dim: 91.40 (87.00 pp) × 11.00 × 3.50
A: 1 20-mm JM-61-MB Sea Vulcan gatling AA
Electronics: Radar: 1 . . . nav.; 1 . . . surf. search
M: 2 Fuji S540B diesels; 2 CP props; 7,000 bhp—2 bow-thrusters
Range: 4,400/19 **Crew:** 38 tot.

Remarks: PL 02 ordered 11-89. PL 04 was renamed in 1999 and PL 02 on 31-10-00. PL 03 was contracted to Hitachi, which subcontracted her to Hakodate Dockyard.
Hull systems: PL 03 and PL 04 are 1,250 tons standard/1,880 tons full load and incorporate a cargo hold beneath the helicopter pad that is tended by a telescoping crane. All four have a computerized rescue data system, special display room, helicopter platform, and fin stabilization. There is a stern dock for an "unsinkable" rescue craft. Have 30-ton bollard pull towing capacity. Equipped with SHF and commercial UHF SATCOM systems.

♦ 1 Nojima-class (1,000-ton) high-endurance cutter

	Bldr	Laid down	L	In serv.
PL 01 Oki (ex-*Nojima*)	IHI, Tokyo	16-8-88	30-5-89	21-9-89

Oki (PL 01) Mitsuhiro Kadota, 5-01

D: 820 tons light; 993 tons std. (1,500 fl) **S:** 20 kts (19 sust.)
Dim: 85.00 × 10.50 × 3.50 **A:** 1 20-mm JM-61-MB Sea Vulcan gatling AA
Electronics:
Radar: 1 . . . nav.; 1 . . . surf. search
Sonar: side-looking wreck-location HF
M: 2 Fuji S8540B diesels; 2 CP props; 7,000 bhp
Electric: 450 kVA tot. (3 × 150-kVA diesel-driven sets)
Range: 4,400/19 **Crew:** 39 tot.

Remarks: 850 grt. Authorized under the 1986 budget. Sharp sheer to bow improves seakeeping while keeping amidships freeboard low. Unusual in having a raised helicopter deck over the fantail and a second bridge above and abaft the main pilothouse. Fin stabilizers are fitted. Has a Marisat commercial UHF SATCOM system. A rescue diving crew is assigned to the ship. Renamed during 1999. Based at Sakai and operates in the Sea of Japan.

♦ 26 Shiretoko-class high-endurance cutters

	Bldr	L	In serv.
PL 101 Shiretoko	Mitsui, Tamano	13-7-78	8-11-78
PL 102 Esan	Sumitomo, Oshima	8-78	16-11-78
PL 103 Wakasa	Kawasaki, Kobe	8-78	29-11-78
PL 104 Shimanto (ex-*Yahiko*)	Mitsubishi, Shimonoseki	8-78	16-11-78
PL 106 Rishiri	Shikoku DY	27-3-79	12-9-79
PL 107 Matsushima	Tohoku DY	11-4-79	14-9-79
PL 108 Iwaki	Naikai, Innoshima	28-3-79	10-8-79
PL 109 Shikine	Usuki SY, Usuki	27-4-79	20-9-79
PL 110 Suruga	Kurushima DY, Onishi	20-4-79	28-9-79
PL 111 Rebun	Narasaki SY, Muroran	6-79	21-11-79
PL 112 Chokai	Nipponkai Heavy Ind., Toyama	6-79	30-11-79
PL 113 Nojima (ex-*Ashizuri*)	Sanoyasu DY, Oshima	6-79	31-10-79
PL 114 Tosa (ex-*Oki*)	Tsuneishi SY, Numakuma	6-79	16-11-79
PL 115 Noto	Miho SY, Shimuzu	7-79	30-11-79
PL 117 Iwami (ex-*Kurikoma*, ex-*Kudaka*, ex-*Daisetsu*)	Hakodate DY	22-8-79	31-1-80
PL 118 Shimokita	Ishikawajima, Tokyo	9-79	12-3-80
PL 119 Suzuka	Kanasashi SY, Toyohashi	4-10-79	7-3-80
PL 120 Kunisaki	Koyo DY, Mihara	8-10-79	29-2-80
PL 121 Amagi (ex-*Genkai*)	Oshima SY, Oshima	9-79	31-1-80
PL 122 Goto	Onomichi SY, Onomichi	10-79	29-2-80
PL 123 Koshiki	Kasado DY, Kasado	9-79	25-1-80
PL 124 Hateruma	Osaka DY	11-79	12-3-80
PL 125 Katori	Tohoku DY, Shiogama	5-80	17-10-80
PL 126 Kunigami	Kanda SY, Kawashiri	28-3-80	21-10-80
PL 127 Etomo	Naikai, Innoshima	30-9-81	17-3-82
PL 128 Yonakuni (ex-*Amigi*, ex-*Mashu*)	Shikoku DY, Kochi, Takamatsu	14-10-81	12-3-82

D: 965.3–974 tons std. (1,350–1,360 fl) **S:** 20 kts
Dim: 77.8 (73.6 pp) × 9.6 × 3.42
A: PL 101–117, 119–121, 123: 1 40-mm 60-cal. Bofors AA—PL 118, 122, 124–128: 1 35-mm 90-cal. Oerlikon AA—PL 101–102, 104: 1 20-mm 70-cal. Oerlikon AA—PL 103: 1 20-mm JM-61-MB Sea Vulcan gatling AA
Electronics: Radar: 1 JMA 1596 nav.; 1 JMA 1576 surf. search
M: 2 Niigata 8MA 40 or Fuji 8 S40B diesels; 2 CP props; 7,000 bhp
Electric: 625 kVA tot. **Range:** 4,406/17 **Fuel:** 191 tons **Crew:** 41 tot.

Remarks: Building program helped small shipyards to stay in business. Intended to patrol the 200-n.m. economic zone. PL 120 had a serious fire 15-2-82. Name of PL 117 changed 1-4-88 and again on 1-8-94. PL 116 was decommissioned in 2005.

COAST GUARD PATROL SHIPS [WPS] *(continued)*

Kunisaki (PL 120) Takatoshi Okano, 5-04

Nojima (PL 113) Mitsuhiro Kadota, 5-03

Hull systems: PL 101, 103, 107, 108, 110–113, 117, 121, 122, 124, and 127 have Fuji 8S40B diesels. Carry 153 tons of water. Fuel capacities and endurances vary. Have Flume-type passive tank stabilization, with tanks in superstructure. Range greater for some: PL 127 has a range of 5,200 n.m. at 17 kts.
Combat systems: On PL 103, the 20-mm gatling gun has been mounted on a tall pedestal on the foredeck.
Disposals: *Motobu* (PL 105), renamed *Ojika* on 1-10-00, received serious damage in a collison with fishing boat *Zentoku Maru No. 3* on 6-10-00 and was stricken on 20-10-00. *Daio*-class high-endurance cutter *Muroto* (PL 16) had been retired by 2005.

♦ 1 Miura-class (3,000-ton) high-endurance training cutter [WPST]

	Bldr	Laid down	L	In serv.
PL 22 Miura	IHI, Tokyo	12-3-97	11-3-98	28-10-98

Miura (PL 22) Takatoshi Okano, 9-04

D: 3,167 tons **S:** 18 kts **Dim:** 115.0 × 14.0 × . . .
A: 1 20-mm JM-61-MB Sea Vulcan gatling AA **Electronics:** Radar: 3 . . . nav.
M: 2 . . . diesels; 2 CP props; 8,000 bhp—bow-thruster
Range: 8,000/18 **Crew:** 40 officers, 110 enlisted

Remarks: PL 22 is employed primarily for Japan Coast Guard School enlisted training duties. Externally PL 22 is very similar to the *Kojima* (PL 21). Has a large helicopter deck but no hangar and is equipped with Flume-type water tank stabilization system. Hull has 7.3-m molded depth. Has both SHF and UHF SATCOM systems.

♦ 1 Kojima-class (3,000-ton) training cutter [WPST]

	Bldr	Laid down	L	In serv.
PL 21 Kojima	Hitachi, Maizuru	7-11-91	10-9-92	11-3-93

Kojima (PL 21) George R. Schneider, 5-03

D: 2,650 tons light; 2,950 tons std. (3,136 fl) **S:** 18 kts
Dim: 115.00 × 14.00 × 3.53
A: 1 35-mm 90-cal. Oerlikon AA; 1 20-mm JM-61-MB Sea Vulcan gatling AA; 1 12.7-mm mg
Electronics: Radar: 2 JMA 1596 nav.
M: 2 . . . diesels; 2 CP props; 7,886 bhp—bow-thruster
Range: 7,000/15 **Crew:** 118 tot.

Remarks: Authorized under FY 90 budget. Used as a coast guard officer cadet training ship at Kure Academy. Officially of the "3,000-ton" class. Has both SHF and UHF SATCOM systems. The after deck serves as a helicopter platform and ceremonial/exercise space; there is no hangar. Flume-type water-tank stabilization is fitted.

PATROL COMBATANTS [WPG]

♦ 3 (+ 1) 770-ton class cutter

	Bldr	Laid down	L	In serv.
PL 41 Aso	Mitsubishi, Shimonoseki	18-12-03	28-10-04	15-3-05
PL 42 Dewa	Universal Kokan, Tsurumi	5-4-04	9-5-05	4-06
PL 43 Hakusan	Universal Kokan, Tsurumi	5-4-04	5-10-05	4-06

Aso (PL 41) Mitsuhiro Kadota, 5-05

D: 770 tons std. **S:** 30 kts **Dim:** 79.0 × 10.0 × 6.0
A: 1 30-mm AA **Electronics:** 1 . . . nav
M: . . . diesels; 2 waterjets; . . .

Remarks: First unit was ordered on 17-3-02. More than twice the displacement of the *Tokara*-class combatants.

♦ 3 Tokara class

	Bldr	Laid down	L	In serv.
PM 21 Tokara	Hitachi, Kanegawa	15-3-02	4-12-02	12-3-03
PM 22 Fukue	Mitsubishi, Shimonoseki	15-3-02	10-12-02	2003
PM 23 Oirase	Mitsui, Tamano	16-3-02	. . .	2004

Oirase (PM 23) Takatoshi Okano, 5-04

D: 335 tons std. **S:** 30+ kts **Dim:** 56.0 × 8.5 × 4.4
A: 1 20-mm JM-61-MB Sea Vulcan gatling AA
Electronics: Radar: 1 . . . nav.
M: 3 diesels; 3 waterjets; 15,000 bhp

Remarks: First two were ordered under FY 01 budget; third was in FY 02 budget. Only the two outboard waterjets have "bucket"-type rudders.

COAST GUARD PATROL COMBATANTS [WPG] *(continued)*

♦ 1 Teshio-class (500-ton) medium-endurance icebreaking cutter

	Bldr	Laid down	L	In serv.
PM 15 TESHIO	Nippon Kokan, Tsurumi	7-10-94	20-4-95	19-10-95

D: 563 tons (883 fl) **S:** 14.5 kts **Dim:** 54.90 × 10.60 (10.20 wl) × 3.30
A: 1 20-mm JM-61-MB Sea Vulcan gatling AA **Electronics:** Radar: 2 . . . nav.
M: 2 . . . . . . diesels; 2 Kort-nozzle props; 3,600 bhp—bow-thruster
Crew: 35 tot.

Remarks: Approved under FY 93 budget. Icebreaking hull with 5.0-m molded depth; able to break 75-cm ice by ramming and 55-cm ice at 3 kts continuous. Hullform is unusual for an icebreaking hull in that it has a hard chine amidships and single-curvature hullform over most of the middle portion of the hull. A television surveillance camera is fitted atop the pilothouse.

♦ 4 Amami-class (350-ton) medium-endurance cutters

	Bldr	Laid down	L	In serv.
PM 95 AMAMI	Hitachi, Maizuru	22-10-91	22-6-92	28-9-92
PM 96 KURAKAMI (ex-*Matsuura*)	Mitsubishi, Shimonoseki	9-9-94	31-5-95	24-11-95
PM 97 KUNASHIRI	Mitsubishi, Nagasaki	30-9-97	26-5-98	26-8-98
PM 98 MINABE	Mitsubishi, Nagasaki	30-9-97	26-5-98	26-8-98

Minabe (PM 98) Takatoshi Okano, 7-04

D: 230 tons (249 fl) **S:** 25 kts (20 sust.) **Dim:** 56.00 × 7.50 × 1.50
A: 1 20-mm JM-61-MB Sea Vulcan gatling AA
Electronics: Radar: 2 . . . nav.
M: 2 Fuji 8S40B diesels; 2 props; 8,120 bhp (7,000 sust.) **Crew:** 33 tot.

Remarks: Carry a 5.5-m rigid inflatable rescue boat on an internal ramp at the stern. The gunmounts on PM 97 and PM 98 are on raised bandstands. PM 96 was renamed on 3-4-00.

♦ 14 Teshio-class (500-ton) medium-endurance cutters

	Bldr	L	In serv.
PM 01 NATSUI (ex-*Teshio*)	Shikoku DY, Kochi	30-5-80	30-9-80
PM 02 KITAKAMI (ex-*Oirase*)	Naikai, Taguma, Innoshima	15-5-80	29-8-80
PM 03 ECHIZEN	Usuki Iron Wks., Usuki	2-6-80	30-9-80
PM 04 TOKACHI	Narazaki, Muroran	21-11-80	24-3-81
PM 05 HITACHI	Tohoku SY, Shiogama	15-11-80	19-3-81
PM 06 OKITSU	Usuki Iron Wks., Usuki	5-12-80	17-3-81
PM 07 ISAZU	Naikai, Taguma, Innoshima	29-10-81	18-2-82
PM 08 CHITOSE	Shikoku DY, Kochi	7-7-81	17-11-82
PM 09 KUWANO	Naikai, Taguma, Innoshima	8-81	10-3-83
PM 10 SORACHI	Tohoku SY, Shiogama	27-4-84	27-9-84
PM 11 YUBARI	Usuki Iron Wks., Usuki	20-8-85	28-11-85
PM 12 MOTOURA	Shikoku DY, Takamatsu	7-8-86	21-11-86
PM 13 KANO	Naikai, Taguma, Innoshima	7-8-86	13-11-86
PM 14 SENDAI	Shikoku DY, Takamatsu	21-1-88	1-6-88

Natsui (PM 01) Mitsuhiro Kadota, 10-04

D: 540–562 tons (670–692 fl) **S:** 18.0–18.6 kts
Dim: 67.80 (63.00 pp) × 7.90 × 2.65
A: 1 20-mm JM-61-MB Sea Vulcan gatling AA **Electronics:** Radar: 2 JMA 159B nav.
M: 2 Fuji 6S32F or Arataka 6 M31EX diesels; 2 CP props; 3,000 bhp
Electric: 240 kVA tot. **Range:** 3,500/16 **Endurance:** 15 days **Crew:** 33 tot.

Remarks: 540 grt. PM 07 is also used for training and has a lengthened after deckhouse. PM 12 has Niigata 6M31 diesels, a range of 3,900 n.m. at 16 kts, and a full load displacement of 692 tons. PM 01 was renamed during 11-95 and PM 02 during 2-04.

♦ 2 Takatori-class (350-ton) medium-endurance cutters

	Bldr	L	In serv.
PM 89 TAKATORI	Naikai, Taguma, Innoshima	8-12-77	24-3-78
PM 94 KUMANO	Naikai, Taguma, Innoshima	2-11-78	23-2-79

Takatori (PM 89) Takatoshi Okano, 5-04

D: 469 tons normal (634 fl) **S:** 15.7 kts **Dim:** 45.70 (44.25 pp) × 9.20 × 3.88
A: None **Electronics:** Radar: 1 JMA 1596 nav.; 1 JMA 1576 surf. search
M: 2 Niigata 6M31EX diesels; 1 CP prop; 3,000 bhp
Electric: 200 kVA **Range:** 750/15 **Crew:** 34 tot.

Remarks: 469 grt. Rescue-tug types, equipped for firefighting, salvage, and pollution-control duties. Two firefighting water cannon (3,000 liters/min each) are fitted. Carry an 8-m rescue boat and a 4.6-m speedboat and can lay an oil-spill containment boom.

♦ 17 Bihoro-class (350-ton) medium-endurance cutters

	Bldr	In serv.
PM 73 BIHORO	Tohoku SY, Shiogama	28-2-74
PM 74 KUMA	Usuki Iron Wks., Usuki	28-2-74
PM 78 ISHIKARI	Tohoku SY, Shiogama	13-3-76
PM 79 ABAKUMA	Tohoku SY, Shiogama	30-1-76
PM 80 ISUZU	Naikai SY, Taguma	10-3-76
PM 81 KIKUCHI	Usuki Iron Wks., Usuki	6-2-76
PM 82 KUZURYU	Usuki Iron Wks., Usuki	18-3-76
PM 83 HOROBETSU	Tohoku SY, Shiogama	21-1-77
PM 84 SHIRAKAMI	Tohoku SY, Shiogama	3-3-77
PM 85 MATSUURA (ex-*Sagami*)	Naikai SY, Taguma	30-11-76
PM 86 TONE	Usuki Iron Wks., Usuki	30-11-76
PM 87 MISASA (ex-*Yoshino*)	Usuki Iron Wks., Usuki	28-1-77
PM 88 KUROBE	Shikoku DY, Kochi	15-2-77
PM 90 CHIKUGO	Naikai, Taguma	27-1-78
PM 91 YAMAKUNI	Usuki Iron Wks., Usuki	26-1-78
PM 92 KATSURA	Shikoku DY, Kochi	15-2-77
PM 93 OYODO	Tohoku SY, Shiogama	23-2-78

Karashima (PM 76)—since stricken Takatoshi Okano, 9-00

D: 495 tons light; 636 tons normal (657 fl) **S:** 18 kts **Dim:** 63.35 × 7.80 × 2.53
A: 1 12.7-mm mg

COAST GUARD PATROL COMBATANTS [WPG] *(continued)*

Electronics: Radar: 1 JMA 1596 nav.; 2 JMA-159B or 1 JMA 1576 nav./surf. search
M: 2 Niigata 6M31EX diesels; 2 CP props; 3,000 bhp
Electric: 200 kVA tot. (2 × 100-kVA diesel sets)
Range: 3,260/16 **Crew:** 34 tot.

Remarks: PM 85 was renamed on 3-4-00, and PM 87 on 18-5-00. The 20-mm JM-61-MB Sea Vulcan gatling guns have been replaced by a shielded 12.7-mm mg.

Disposals: Sisters *Fuji* (PM 75), *Kabashima* (PM 76), and *Okishiri* (PM-77, ex-*Sado*) were stricken by 2005. *Kunashiri*-class medium-endurance cutters *Miyake* (PM 70) and *Yaeyama* (PM 72) were retired by 2004. Sisters *Kunashiri* (PM 65) and *Minabe* (PM 66) were stricken on 31-7-98, *Sarobetsu* (PM 67) on 24-1-01, and *Awaji* (PM 71) on 22-2-01. *Kamishima* (PM 68) was retired during 3-03. The last *Yahagi*-class (350-ton) medium-endurance cutter, the *Misasa* (PM 69, ex-*Okinawa*), was stricken 18-5-00.

PATROL CRAFT [WPC]

Note: Two "High-Speed Special Patrol Ships" were under construction by Mitsubishi and Hitachi Zosen during 3-02; the craft are to be powered by two Niigata Engineering V20FX 16-cylinder high-speed diesels of 5,365 bhp each. On 28-8-02, the Japan Coast Guard announced that it was seeking funds under the FY 03 budget to start a four-year construction program for 11 additional such craft. A total of seven new high-speed patrol craft were being sought, with one to have a 40-kt speed.

♦ 6 Tsurugi-class (180-ton) "High-Speed Special Patrol Ships"
Bldr: Hitachi Zosen, Kanegawa

	Bldr	Laid down	L	In serv.
PS 201 Tsurugi	Hitachi, Kanagawa	15-3-00	9-11-00	15-2-01
PS 202 Hotaka	Sumitomo, Shimonoseki	11-5-00	14-12-00	16-3-01
PS 203 Norikura	Mitsui, Tamano	23-5-00	14-12-00	16-3-01
PS 204 Kaimon	Mitsui, Tamano	24-6-03	12-03	4-04
PS 205 Asama	Mitsui, Tamano	24-6-03	3-12-03	4-04
PS 206 Houo	Mitsui, Tamano	26-2-04	9-12-04	27-1-05

Hotaka (PS 202) Takatoshi Okano, 5-04

D: 220 tons (fl) **S:** 40 kts **Dim:** 50.0 × 8.0 × . . .
A: 1 20-mm JM-61-MB Sea Vulcan gatling AA **Electronics:** Radar: 1 . . . nav
M: 3 . . . diesels; 3 waterjets; 15,000 bhp

Remarks: Acquired to permit pursuit of North Korean incursion craft on the Sea of Japan coast. Based at Niigata, Maizuru, and Kanazawa, respectively. Are named for mountains. Have IR search and E/O surveillance systems and carry a large rigid inflatable inspection boat. Second batch (PS 204–PS 206) was constructed between 2003 and 2005.

♦ 12 Mihashi-class (180-ton) short-endurance cutters

	Bldr	Laid down	L	In serv.
PS 01 Shinzan (ex-*Akiyoshi*, ex-*Mihashi*)	Mitsubishi, Shimonoseki	16-12-87	18-6-88	9-9-88
PS 02 Saroma	Hitachi, Kanagawa	12-12-88	28-6-89	28-11-89
PS 03 Inasa	Mitsubishi, Shimonoseki	18-5-89	20-10-89	31-1-90
PS 04 Kirishima	Hitachi, Kanagawa	10-5-89	18-1-90	22-3-91
PS 05 Kamui	Mitsubishi, Shimonoseki	12-4-93	15-11-93	31-1-94
PS 06 Banna (ex-*Bizan*)	Hitachi, Kanagawa	6-4-93	15-11-93	31-1-94
PS 07 Ashitaki	Mitsui, Tamano	9-12-93	24-6-94	30-9-94
PS 08 Kariba (ex-*Kurama*)	Mitsubishi, Shimonoseki	21-9-94	25-5-95	29-8-95
PS 09 Arase	Hitachi, Kanagawa	9-4-96	4-10-96	29-1-97
PS 10 Sanbe	Mitsubishi, Shimonoseki	9-4-96	22-10-96	29-1-97
PS 11 Mizuki	Mitsui, Tamano	16-3-99	28-4-00	9-6-00
PS 12 Koya	Universal Kokan, Tsurumi	24-3-03	11-03	3-04

Koya (PS 12) Takatoshi Okano, 7-04

D: 182 tons normal (197 fl) **S:** 35 kts **Dim:** 46.0 × 7.5 × 1.7
A: 1 12.7-mm mg (PS 03, 11: 1 20-mm JM-61-MB Sea Vulcan gatling AA)
Electronics: Radar: 1 Furuno . . . nav.
M: 2 Mitsubishi S16U-MTK (SEMT-Pielstick 16 PA4 V200 VGA) diesels (3,200 bhp each), 1 Mitsubishi S8U-MTK (SEMT-Pielstick 12 PA4 V200 VGA) diesel (2,500 bhp); 2 props, 1 waterjet
Range: 650/34 **Crew:** 15 tot.

Remarks: An expansion of the preceding *Shizuki* class, incorporating a centerline waterjet propulsor. First four are 43.0 m o.a. and displace 180 tons light, 200 tons fl; the later units are referred to as the *Banna* class (formerly *Bizan* class) and carry a crew of 13. The name for PS 01 was changed on 28-1-97 and again on 24-1-01. PS 12 was authorized for the FY 02 budget.
Mission systems: During 2000, PS 03 had the 12.7-mm mg replaced by an automatic 20-mm gatling gun with an optronic director atop the pilothouse; PS 11 was completed with the same armament and has thick rubbing fenders on the hull sides in the bow area.

♦ 2 Takatsuki-class (130-ton) short-endurance cutters

	Bldr.	Laid down	L	In serv.
PS 108 Takatsuki	Sumidigawa, Tokyo	. . .	. . .	23-3-92
PS 109 Nobaru	Hitachi, Kanagawa	8-9-92	27-1-93	22-3-93

Takatsuki (PS 108) Mitsuhiro Kadota, 5-01

D: 114 tons (180 fl) **S:** 35 kts **Dim:** 35.0 × 6.70 × 1.20
A: 1 12.7-mm mg **Electronics:** Radar: 1 . . . nav.
M: 2 MTU 16V396 TB 94 diesels; 2 KaMeWa 71 waterjets; 5,300 bhp
Crew: 10 tot.

Remarks: An improved version of the *Akagi* class incorporating outdrive surface-piercing propulsors. Have infrared surveillance and low-light t.v. cameras atop the pilothouse. PS 108 is based at Uwajima and performs SAR and fisheries protection duties.

♦ 7 Akagi-class (130-ton) short-endurance cutters

	Bldr	Laid down	L	In serv.
PS 101 Akagi	Sumidigawa, Tokyo	31-7-79	5-12-79	26-3-80
PS 102 Tsukuba	Sumidigawa, Tokyo	7-7-81	29-10-81	24-2-82
PS 103 Kongo	Ishihara DY, Takasago	1-8-86	17-12-86	16-3-87
PS 104 Katsuragai	Yokohama Yacht	14-10-87	21-1-88	24-3-88
PS 105 Bizan (ex-*Hiromine*)	Ishihara DY, Takasago	. . .	8-1-88	24-3-88
PS 106 Shizuki	Sumidigawa, Tokyo	26-10-87	21-12-87	24-3-88
PS 107 Takashio	Sumidigawa, Tokyo	28-10-87	23-12-87	24-3-88

Kongo (PS 103) Takatoshi Okano, 7-04

D: 105 tons light; 134 tons normal (189 fl) **S:** 26.5 kts
Dim: 35.0 (33.0 wl) × 6.3 × 1.3
A: 1 12.7-mm mg **Electronics:** Radar: 1 . . . nav.
M: 2 Fuji-Pielstick 16 PA4 V185 VG diesels; 2 props; 4,800 bhp
Electric: 40 kVA tot. **Range:** 570/20 **Crew:** 12 tot.

COAST GUARD PATROL CRAFT [WPC] *(continued)*

Remarks: Carry a 25-man rubber rescue dinghy. The machinegun can be interchanged with a firefighting water cannon. PS 104 and PS 105 are optimized for service on Japan's Inland Sea and have longer superstructures and an enlarged pilothouse. First five have glass-reinforced plastic hulls and four-day endurance; PS 106 and PS 107 have a 4.0-m-molded-depth aluminum alloy hull of deep-vee form and are powered by two Ikegai-MTU 16V652 TB 81 diesels: 4,400 bhp for 27 kts; they have two 60-kVA generators. PS 105 was renamed in 2004.

♦ 4 (+ 4) Yodo-class firefighting craft

Bldr: Kurodagama, Tokyo

	L	In serv.
PC 51 Yodo	2-10-01	20-3-02
PC 52 Kotobiki	23-10-02	27-3-03
PC 53 Nachi	29-1-03	27-3-03
PC 54 Nunobiki	4-12-02	27-3-03

Yodo (PC 51)—with telescoping fire monitor raised Takatoshi Okano, 5-04

Nunobiki (PC 54)—with telescoping fire monitors retracted Mitsuhiro Kadota, 4-03

D: 128 tons light (190 fl) **S:** 25 kts **Dim:** 37.0 × 6.7 × 1.5
A: None **Electronics:** Radar: 1 . . . nav.
M: 2 diesels; 2 props; 6,500 bhp

Remarks: Principally intended for fire fighting and are equipped with firefighting monitors on the bow, atop the pilothouse, and atop the two side-by-side combination mast/stacks. PC 52–54 were authorized under the FY 02 budget. A total of eight are planned.

♦ 3 Kagayuki-class (32-meter) coastal patrol craft

Bldr: Mitsubishi, Shimonoseki

	Laid down	L	In serv.
PC 105 Hamayuki (ex-Kagayuki)	16-3-99	28-9-99	24-12-99
PC 106 Murakumo	. . .	3-5-02	19-8-02
PC 107 Izunami	. . .	24-12-02	18-3-03

D: 100 tons (. . . fl) **S:** 36 kts **Dim:** 32.0 × 6.50 × 3.3
A: 1 12.7-mm mg **Electronics:** Radar: 1 . . . nav.
M: 2 . . . diesels; 2 waterjets; 5,200 bhp **Crew:** 30 tot.

Remarks: PC 105 was approved under the FY 99 budget. Completed with rubbing fenders on the hull sides forward, but they had been removed by 4-00. The name was changed on 22-2-01. The second and third units were authorized under the FY 02 budget.

Izunami (PC 107) Takatoshi Okano, 5-04

♦ 1 Matsunami-class (35-meter) coastal patrol craft

Bldr: Mitsubishi, Shimonoseki (In serv. 22-2-95)

PC 01 Matsunami

Matsunami (PC 01) Mitsuhiro Kadota, 5-03

D: 165 tons (204 fl) **S:** 28.3 kts (25 sust.) **Dim:** 38.00 (35.50 wl) × 8.0 × . . .
A: None **Electronics:** Radar: 1 . . . nav.
M: 2 . . . diesels; 2 waterjets; 5,300 bhp **Range:** 7,000/14 **Crew:** 30 tot.

Remarks: Yacht-like unit with three-level superstructure. Built under the FY 93 program, PC 01 is configured as an oceanographic research craft for the emperor. Internal fittings are luxurious, and the craft is, in effect, the imperial yacht.

♦ 4 Asogiri-class (30-meter) coastal patrol craft

	Bldr	Laid down	L	In serv.
PC 101 Asogiri	Yokohama Yacht	12-5-94	7-10-94	19-12-94
PC 102 Murozuki	Ishihara DY	21-9-94	6-6-95	27-7-95
PC 103 Wakagumo	Sumidigawa, Tokyo	12-3-96	1996	17-7-96
PC 104 Naozuki	Sumidigawa, Tokyo	. . .	14-10-96	23-1-97

Murozuki (PC 102) Mitsuhiro Kadota, 2002

COAST GUARD PATROL CRAFT [WPC] *(continued)*

D: 101 tons normal **S:** 30 kts **Dim:** 33.00 × 6.30 × 2.00
A: 1 12.7-mm M2 mg **Electronics:** Radar: 1 . . . nav.
M: 2 diesels; 2 props; 5,200 bhp **Crew:** . . .

Remarks: Have an infrared/t.v. optronic surveillance system. The machinegun is not normally mounted. Are painted with gray hull sides and white superstructures.

♦ 15 Hayanami-class (35-meter) coastal patrol craft

	Bldr	Laid down	L	In serv.
PC 11 Hayanami	Sumidigawa, Tokyo	9-9-92	7-1-93	25-3-93
PC 12 Setogiri (ex-*Shikinami*)	Sumidigawa, Tokyo	21-7-93	13-10-93	24-3-94
PC 13 Mizunami	Ishihara DY, Takasago	30-7-93	27-12-93	24-3-94
PC 14 Ionami	Sumidigawa, Tokyo	9-12-93	11-4-94	30-6-94
PC 15 Kurinami	Sumidigawa, Tokyo	10-3-94	3-10-94	30-1-95
PC 16 Hamanami	Sumidigawa, Tokyo	29-8-95	19-1-96	28-3-96
PC 17 Shinonome	Sumidigawa, Tokyo	29-8-95	27-11-95	29-2-96
PC 18 Haruname	Ishihara DY, Takasago	4-9-95	31-1-96	28-3-96
PC 19 Kiyozuki	Ishihara DY, Takasago	4-9-95	7-11-95	23-2-96
PC 20 Ayanami	Yokohama Yacht	13-9-95	19-12-95	28-3-96
PC 21 Tokinami	Yokohama Yacht	13-9-95	22-12-95	28-3-96
PC 22 Hamagumo	Sumidigawa, Tokyo	2-12-98	16-4-99	27-8-99
PC 23 Awanami	Sumidigawa, Tokyo	2-12-98	14-5-99	27-8-99
PC 24 Uranami	Sumidigawa, Tokyo	10-3-99	3-10-99	24-1-00
PC 25 Shikinami	Sumidigawa, Tokyo	7-4-00	4-8-00	24-10-00

Shikinami (PC 25)—later version, with firefighting mast Takatoshi Okano, 7-04

Hamanami (PC 16)—early group, without firefighting mast Ralph Edwards, 10-02

D: 113 tons normal **S:** 25 kts **Dim:** 35.00 × 6.30 × 1.20
A: None **Electronics:** Radar: 1 . . . nav.
M: 2 . . . diesels; 2 props; 4,000 bhp
Range: . . . / . . . **Crew:** 13 tot.

Remarks: Two firefighting water cannon are mounted abreast on the foredeck, and there is no fitting for a machinegun mount. All have infrared and low light-level t.v. surveillance sensors atop the pilothouse. PC 22 and later have a tall telescoping mast supporting a firefighting water monitor, a second monitor atop the pilothouse, and a maximum speed of 24 kts. The name for PC 12 was changed on 10-10-00. Are painted white.

♦ 20 Murakomo-class (30-meter) coastal patrol craft

	Bldr	In serv.
PC 202 Kitagumo	Hitachi, Kanagawa	17-3-78
PC 203 Yukigumo	Hitachi, Kanagawa	27-9-78
PC 205 Hayagumo	Mitsubishi, Shimonoseki	30-1-79
PC 206 Akigumo	Hitachi, Kanagawa	28-2-79
PC 207 Yaegumo	Mitsubishi, Shimonoseki	16-3-79
PC 208 Natsugumo	Hitachi, Kanagawa	22-3-79
PC 210 Kawagiri	Hitachi, Kanagawa	27-7-79
PC 211 Bizan (ex-*Teruzuki*)	Maizuru Heavy Ind.	26-6-79
PC 212 Natsuzuki	Maizuru Heavy Ind.	26-7-79
PC 213 Miyazuki	Hitachi, Kanagawa	13-3-80
PC 214 Nijigumo	Mitsubishi, Shimonoseki	29-1-81
PC 215 Tatsugumo	Mitsubishi, Shimonoseki	19-3-81
PC 216 Iseyuki (ex-*Hamayuki*)	Hitachi, Kanagawa	27-2-81
PC 217 Isonami	Mitsubishi, Shimonoseki	19-3-81
PC 218 Nagozuki	Hitachi, Kanagawa	29-1-81
PC 219 Yaezuki	Hitachi, Kanagawa	19-3-81
PC 220 Yamayuki	Hitachi, Kanagawa	16-2-82
PC 221 Komayuki	Mitsubishi, Shimonoseki	10-2-82
PC 222 Asagiri	Mitsubishi, Shimonoseki	17-2-82
PC 223 Umigiri	Hitachi, Kanagawa	23-2-83

Kawagiri (PC 210) Mitsuhiro Kadota, 2004

D: 88 tons light; 125 tons normal (149 fl) **S:** 31 kts
Dim: 31.0 (28.5 pp) × 6.3 × 1.17
A: 1 12.7-mm M2 mg **Electronics:** Radar: 1 . . . nav.
M: 2 Ikegai MTU 16V652 TB81 diesels; 2 props; 4,800 bhp (4,400 sust.)
Electric: 40 kVA tot. **Range:** 350/28 **Crew:** 10 tot.

Remarks: The name for PC 216 was changed on 22-2-01 and that of PC 211 during 1999. Hull sides are painted gray and superstructures white. Have a firefighting monitor on the foredeck, to port.

Disposals: Sister *Murakomo* (PC 201) was retired on 3-8-02, *Asagumo* (PC 204) on 12-2-05, and *Yamagiri* (PC 209) on 2-3-03.

♦ 2 Natsugiri-class (23-meter) coastal patrol craft

Bldr: Ishihara Dockyard (In serv. 29-1-90)

PC 86 Natsugiri PC 87 Suganami

Natsugiri (PC 86) Takatoshi Okano, 5-04

D: 55 tons (68 fl) **S:** 27.5 kts **Dim:** 27.0 × 5.6 × 1.2
A: None **Electronics:** Radar: 1 . . . nav.
M: 2 . . . diesels; 2 props; 3,000 bhp **Electric:** 40 kVA tot. (2 × 20 kVA)
Range: 200/ . . . **Crew:** 9 tot.

Remarks: Put in the FY 88 budget for service in the Yokosuka area as a result of the poor performance of earlier 23-m-series patrol craft during the rescue efforts after the collision of the submarine *Nadashio* (SS 577) with a fishing boat. Have longer hulls and greater propeller tip clearance to reduce pitching. Are painted white.

COAST GUARD PATROL CRAFT [WPC] *(continued)*

♦ 3 Shimagiri-class (23-meter) coastal patrol craft

Bldr: Mitsubishi, Shimonoseki

	In serv.		In serv.
PC 83 SHIMAGIRI	7-2-84	PC 85 HAYAGIRI	22-2-85
PC 84 OKINAMI (ex-*Setogiri*)	22-3-85		

Okinami (PC 84) Takatoshi Okano, 2-02

D: 40 tons (50 fl) **S:** 30 kts **Dim:** 23.00 × 5.30 × 1.12
A: PC 85 only: 1 20-mm 70-cal. Oerlikon AA
Electronics: Radar: 1 FRA 10 Mk 2 nav.
M: 3 Mitsubishi 12V175RTC diesels; 3 props; 3,000 bhp **Electric:** 40 kVA
Range: 250/21.5 **Crew:** 10 tot.

♦ 9 Akizuki-class (23-meter) coastal patrol craft

Bldr: Mitsubishi, Shimonoseki

	In serv.		In serv.
PC 72 URAYUKI	31-5-75	PC 79 SHIMANAMI	23-12-77
PC 75 HATAGUMO	21-2-76	PC 80 YUZUKI	22-3-79
PC 76 MAKIGUMO	21-2-76	PC 81 TAMANAMI (ex-*Hanayuki*)	27-3-81
PC 77 HAMAZUKI	29-11-76	PC 82 AWAGIRI	27-12-82
PC 78 ISOZUKI	18-3-77		

Urayuki (PC 72) Ralph Edwards, 10-02

D: 77 tons light; 110 tons normal (123.7 fl) **S:** 22.1 kts
Dim: 26.00 × 6.30 × 1.12
A: None **Electronics:** Radar: 1 FRA 10 Mk 2 nav.
M: 3 Mitsubishi 12 DM 20 MTK diesels; 3 props; 3,000 bhp
Electric: 40 kVA **Range:** 290/21.5 **Crew:** 10 tot.

Remarks: All are of aluminum hull construction and have a folding rescue platform at the waterline on the starboard side.

Disposal note: Of units of the *Shikinami* (23-meter) class, *Shikinami* (PC 54) was stricken 7-3-94; *Isenami* (PC 57) on 13-6-94; *Tomonami* (PC 55) on 2-12-94; *Takanami* (PC 58) on 13-1-95; *Wakanami* (PC 56) in 1-95; *Kiyozuki* (PC 62) on 8-2-96; *Mochizuki* (PC 60), *Haruzuki* (PC 61), and *Urazuki* (PC 63) on 11-3-96; *Wakagumo* (PC 71) on 28-6-96; *Mutsuki* (PC 59) early in 1997; *Tamanami* (PC 67) and *Minegumo* (PC 68) on 12-8-99; *Kiyonami* (PC 69) on 8-12-99; *Uranami* (PC 66) on 7-1-00; *Okinami* (PC 70) on 9-10-00; and *Asoyuki* (PC 74) during 2002. Sister *Shinonome* (PC 65) was stricken in 1996, *Akizuki* (PC 64) on 11-3-96, and *Iseyuki* (PC 73) on 22-2-01.

PATROL BOATS [WPB]

♦ 124 Suzukaze-class (20-meter) inshore patrol boats

	Bldr	Laid down	L	In serv.
CL 11 SUZUKAZE	Sumidigawa, Tokyo	...	...	20-2-92
CL 12 ASAKAZE	Ishihara Dockyard	...	...	9-3-92
CL 13 SUGIKAZE	Yokohama Yacht	...	...	28-2-92
CL 14 FUJIKAZE	Shinki Zosen, Osaka	...	...	24-3-92
CL 15 MIYAKAZE	Wakamatsu Zosen	...	...	25-3-92
CL 16 HIBAKAZE	Kiso Zosen	...	...	19-3-92
CL 17 SATAKAZE	Nagasaki Zosen	...	...	25-3-92
CL 18 TOMAKAZE	Sumidigawa, Tokyo	6-8-92	26-11-92	22-1-93
CL 19 YURIKAZE	Sumidigawa, Tokyo	6-8-92	25-12-92	8-2-93
CL 20 FUSAKAZE	Yokohama Yacht	18-8-92	7-1-93	24-2-93
CL 21 UMEKAZE	Shinki Zosen, Osaka	18-8-92	17-2-93	25-3-93
CL 22 SHIGIKAZE	Ishihara DY, Takasago	19-8-92	30-11-92	22-1-93
CL 23 UZUKAZE	Ishihara DY, Takasago	19-8-92	12-1-93	16-2-93
CL 24 AKIKAZE	Nagasaki Zosen	18-9-92	27-1-93	26-2-93
CL 25 KUREKAZE	Kiso Zosen	3-9-92	27-1-93	26-2-93
CL 26 MOJIKAZE	Wakamatsu Zosen	30-9-92	4-2-93	22-3-93
CL 27 SODEKAZE	Yokohama Yacht	7-1-93	26-2-93	31-3-93
CL 28 KINUKAZE	Nagasaki Zosen	7-1-93	26-2-93	29-3-93
CL 29 MAYAKAZE	Ishihara DY, Takasago	7-1-93	2-3-93	29-3-93
CL 30 SETOKAZE	Nagasaki Zosen	7-1-93	26-2-93	29-3-93
CL 31 MAKIKAZE	Sumidigawa, Tokyo	2-2-93	24-5-93	28-6-93
CL 32 HIMEKAZE	Ishihara DY, Takasago	2-2-93	28-5-93	29-6-93
CL 33 KUGAKAZE	Kiso Zosen	19-1-93	3-6-93	28-6-93
CL 34 KAMIKAZE	Ishihara DY, Takasago	8-7-93	12-93	24-1-94
CL 35 UMIKAZE	Yokohama Yacht	8-7-93	12-93	27-1-94
CL 36 KIRIKAZE	Yokohama Yacht	8-7-93	12-93	4-2-94
CL 37 HAKAZE	Shinki Zosen, Osaka	9-7-93	12-93	14-2-94
CL 38 SHACHIKAZE	Shinki Zosen, Osaka	9-7-93	12-93	25-1-94
CL 39 ISEKAZE	Wakamatsu Zosen	14-7-93	12-93	24-3-94
CL 40 NIJIKAZE (ex-*Komakaze*)	Nagasaki Zosen	21-7-93	12-93	27-1-94
CL 41 KISHIKAZE	Nagasaki Zosen	21-7-93	12-93	4-2-94
CL 42 KIKUKAZE	Ishihara DY, Takasago	9-9-93	10-2-94	24-3-94
CL 43 OTOKAZE	Yokohama Yacht	9-9-93	23-2-94	29-3-94
CL 44 HIROKAZE	Nagasaki Zosen	3-9-93	16-2-94	29-3-94
CL 45 ASHIKAZE	Kiso Zosen	28-9-93	28-2-94	29-3-94
CL 46 TOYOKAZE	Sumidigawa, Tokyo	27-7-93	13-1-94	24-3-94
CL 47 SATSUKAZE	Nagasaki Zosen	21-7-93	12-10-94	4-2-94
CL 48 SHIOKAZE	Yokohama Yacht	8-2-94	9-6-94	14-7-94
CL 49 AWAKAZE	Yokohama Yacht	8-2-94	9-6-94	14-7-94
CL 50 HAMAKAZE	Sumidigawa, Tokyo	10-2-94	9-6-94	28-7-94
CL 51 MIOKAZE	Shinki Zosen, Osaka	1-2-94	30-5-94	22-7-94
CL 52 TOMOKAZE	Kiso Zosen	2-2-94	24-6-94	26-7-94
CL 53 KIBIKAZE	Sumidigawa, Tokyo	10-2-94	21-6-94	28-7-94
CL 54 NACHIKAZE	Ishihara DY, Takasago	25-1-94	30-6-94	29-7-94
CL 55 MITSUKAZE	Ishihara DY, Takasago	25-1-94	23-6-94	29-7-94
CL 56 HATAKAZE	Wakamatsu Zosen	7-2-94	15-6-94	29-7-94
CL 57 SEKIKAZE	Nagasaki Zosen	8-2-94	15-6-94	29-7-94
CL 58 TERUKAZE	Kiso Zosen	2-6-94	1-12-94	27-1-95
CL 59 SHIMAKAZE	Wakamatsu Zosen	30-5-94	12-12-94	31-1-95
CL 60 SASAKAZE	Yokohama Yacht	30-5-94	1-12-94	31-1-95
CL 61 KIIKAZE	Ishihara DY, Takasago	12-5-94	8-12-94	26-1-95
CL 62 IKIKAZE	Shinki Zosen, Osaka	13-5-94	1-11-94	27-1-95
CL 63 MINEKAZE	Sumidigawa, Tokyo	10-5-94	28-11-94	27-1-95
CL 64 TORIKAZE	Sumidigawa, Tokyo	10-5-94	31-10-94	26-1-95
CL 65 AMAKAZE	Nagasaki Zosen	31-5-94	30-11-94	30-1-95
CL 66 AOKAZE	Nagasaki Zosen	31-5-94	16-11-94	30-1-95
CL 67 KUNIKAZE (ex-*Ogikaze*)	Ishihara DY, Takasago	12-5-94	30-11-94	31-1-95
CL 68 TACHIKAZE	Yokohama Yacht	30-5-94	1-11-94	31-1-95
CL 69 DEIGO	Ishihara DY, Takasago	28-2-95	19-9-95	28-9-95
CL 70 YUNA	Sumidigawa, Tokyo	28-2-95	22-9-95	1-11-95
CL 71 ADAN	Nagasaki Zosen	1-3-95	9-95	13-11-95
CL 72 KIJIKAZE	Kiso Zosen	...	15-2-96	28-3-96
CL 73 HATSUKAZE	Nagasaki Zosen	1-8-95	...	29-2-96
CL 74 YURAKAZE	Nagasaki Zosen	1-8-95	10-1-96	19-3-96
CL 75 HINOKAZE (ex-*Yanakaze*)	Shinki Zosen, Osaka	1-8-95	...	22-3-96
CL 76 TOSATSUBAKI (ex-*Washikaze*)	Kiso Zosen	29-8-95	...	22-3-96
CL 77 MUTSUKAZE	Sumidigawa, Tokyo	29-8-95	6-2-96	28-3-96
CL 78 TONEKAZE	Nagasaki Zosen	22-12-95	27-2-96	29-3-96
CL 79 SHIZUKAZE	Wakamatsu, Kitakyushu	18-12-95	31-1-96	28-3-96
CL 80 KOMAKAZE	Shinki Zosen, Osaka	19-12-95	22-2-96	28-3-96
CL 81 YUKIKAZE	Yokohama Yacht	25-1-96	23-4-96	30-7-96
CL 82 NAKAKAZE	Yokohama Yacht	25-1-96	26-4-96	30-7-96
CL 83 KAWAKAZE	Kiso Zosen	21-12-95	19-3-96	19-6-96
CL 84 KIYOKAZE	Ishihara DY, Takasago	11-1-96	26-4-96	30-7-96
CL 85 HIKOKAZE	Sumidigawa, Tokyo	21-1-96	19-3-96	28-6-96
CL 86 OSAKAZE	Wakamatsu, Kitakyushu	18-12-95	22-3-96	19-6-96
CL 87 WAKAKAZE	Shinki Zosen, Osaka	12-1-96	26-4-96	31-7-96
CL 88 IKEKAZE	Yokohama Yacht	25-12-95	22-3-96	28-6-96
CL 89 NOMOKAZE	Nagasaki Zosen	22-12-95	25-3-96	28-6-96
CL 90 YUMIKAZE	Shinki Zosen, Osaka	19-12-95	29-3-96	28-6-96
CL 91 KUMAKAZE	Yokohama Yacht	25-12-95	19-3-96	28-6-96
CL 92 HARUKAZE	Ishihara DY, Takasago	...	2-8-96	1-11-96
CL 93 HOSHIKAZE	Ishihara DY, Takasago	...	...	18-11-96
CL 94 OITSUKAZE	Kiso Zosen	12-3-97	2-9-97	25-11-97
CL 95 KOCHIKAZE	Ishihara DY, Takasago	12-3-97	5-9-97	25-11-97
CL 96 HAMANASU	Sumidigawa, Tokyo	18-3-97	17-9-97	18-12-97
CL 97 AKASHIA	Sumidigawa, Tokyo	18-3-97	17-9-97	18-12-97
CL 98 TOSAMIZUKI	Shinki Zosen, Osaka	13-3-97	17-9-97	18-12-97
CL 99 OKIKAZE	Yokohama Yacht	12-3-97	29-9-97	18-12-97

COAST GUARD PATROL BOATS [WPB] *(continued)*

CL 100 Sachikaze	Wakamatsu, Kitakyushu	18-3-97	11-9-97	18-12-97
CL 101 Ogikaze	Yokohama Yacht	12-3-97	29-9-97	18-12-97
CL 102 Natsuzaze	Nagasaki Zosen	12-3-97	25-9-97	18-12-97
CL 103 Sawakaze	Sumidigawa, Tokyo	16-12-98	16-2-99	31-3-99
CL 104 Benibana	Sumidigawa, Tokyo	16-12-98	22-2-99	31-3-99
CL 105 Yamazakura	Yokohama Yacht	16-12-98	26-2-99	30-3-99
CL 106 Kaido	Yokohama Yacht	16-12-98	26-2-99	30-3-99
CL 107 Sazanka	Yokohama Yacht	16-12-98	26-2-99	30-3-99
CL 108 Aoi	Wakamatsu, Kitakyushu	16-12-98	10-2-98	31-1-99
CL 109 Suisen	Sumidigawa, Tokyo	16-12-98	24-2-99	31-3-99
CL 110 Yaezakura	Kiso Zosen	16-12-98	23-2-99	30-3-99
CL 111 Yanakaze	Ishihara DY, Takasago	16-12-98	25-2-99	30-3-99
CL 112 Yukitsubaki	Sumidigawa, Tokyo	16-12-98	8-2-99	31-3-99
CL 113 Washikaze	Ishihara DY, Takasago	16-12-98	4-3-99	30-3-99
CL 114 Nogekaze	Ishihara DY, Takasago	27-10-99	15-2-00	9-3-00
CL 115 Imakaze	Nagasaki Zosen	11-12-00	28-2-01	30-3-01
CL 116 Komakusa	Shinki Zosen, Osaka	18-12-00	3-3-01	30-3-01
CL 117 Shiragiku	Ishihara DY, Takasago	20-12-00	26-2-01	30-3-01
CL 118 Katsukaze	Yokohama Yacht	27-12-00	23-2-01	29-3-01
CL 119 Satsuke	Wakamatsu, Kitakyushu	20-12-00	2-3-01	30-3-01
CL 120 Yaguruma	Sumidigawa, Tokyo	15-1-02	1-2-02	29-3-02
CL 121 Murokaze	Sumidigawa, Tokyo	17-12-01	27-2-02	29-3-02
CL 122 Fuyo	Sumidigawa, Tokyo	17-12-01	1-3-02	29-3-02
CL 123 Tsubaki	Sumidigawa, Tokyo	15-12-01	28-2-01	29-3-02
CL 124 Higokaze	Ishihara DY, Takasago	17-12-01	27-2-02	29-3-02
CL 125 Shirahagi	Ishihara DY, Takasago	15-1-01	8-2-02	29-3-02
CL 126 Ashibi	Ishihara DY, Takasago	17-12-01	27-2-02	29-3-02
CL 127 Suiren	Ishihara DY, Takasago	17-12-01	5-3-02	29-3-02
CL 128 Kobai	Yokohama Yacht	27-12-01	27-2-02	29-3-02
CL 129 Yamayuri	Shinki Zosen, Osaka	15-1-02	15-2-02	29-3-02
CL 130 Kurikaze	Nagasaki Zosen	15-1-02	22-2-02	29-3-02
CL 131 Sorakaze	Kiso Zosen	25-12-01	25-2-02	29-3-02
CL 132 Murakaze	Wakamatsu, Kitakyushu	27-12-01	28-2-02	29-3-02
CL 133 Aikaze	Wakamatsu, Kitakyushu	27-12-01	28-2-02	29-3-02
CL 134 Ayame	. . .	2002	2002	16-12-02

Ashibi (CL 126) Takatoshi Okano, 7-04

Imakaze (CL 115) Mitsuhiro Kadota, 2004

D: 19 tons (23 fl) **S:** 30 kts **Dim:** 20.00 × 4.30 × 1.00
A: 1 12.7-mm mg or none **Electronics:** Radar: 1 . . . nav.
M: 2 M.A.N. D-2842LYE diesels; 2 props; 1,820 bhp
Range: 160/30 **Crew:** 5 tot.

Remarks: Replacements for *Chiyokaze* class. Gun is interchangeable with a firefighting water cannon; usually they carry neither. Had white superstructures and gray hulls without the stylized blue "S" as completed, but CL 65 was repainted all white (with the "S") in 9-00, and CL 119 was completed that way. Some, including CL 53 and CL 59, have been fitted with fendering at the bows. CL 120 and later have 2,040 total bhp, a beam of 4.5 m, and a displacement of 26 tons.

♦ **4 Isokaze-class (15-meter) inshore patrol boats**
Bldr: Yokohama Yacht

CL 01 Isokaze (In serv. 23-3-89)
CL 02 Hayakaze (In serv. 23-3-89)
CL 03 Nadakaze (In serv. 15-3-91)
CL 04 Kotokaze (In serv. 15-3-91)

Isokaze (CL 01) Mitsuhiro Kadota, 5-03

D: 18–19 tons (22.8–23.0 fl) **S:** 20 (CL 03, 04: 29) kts **Dim:** 18.00 × 4.30 × . . .
A: None **Electronics:** Radar: 1 . . . nav.
M: CL 01, 02: 2 Nissan RD10-TA06 diesels; 2 props; 900 bhp—CL 03, 04: 2 . . . diesels; 2 props; 1,400 bhp
Range: 180/19 (CL 03, 04: 150/29) **Crew:** 5 tot. (CL 03, 04: 6 tot.)

Remarks: Revised *Yamayuri* design, with higher superstructure and finer hull lines. CL 01 and 02 laid down 20-9-88 and launched 7-2-89; CL 03 and 04, laid down 17-9-90 and launched 8-2-91. Second pair is considered a separate class, displacing more and having more-powerful engines.

♦ **42 Yamayuri-class (15-meter) inshore patrol boats**
Bldrs: A: Ishihara DY, Takasago; B: Sumidigawa, Tokyo; C: Yokohama Yacht; D: Shinki SY, Osaka; E: Nobutaka SY; F: Shigi SY, Sakai

	Bldr	In serv.		Bldr	In serv.
CL 206 Miyagiku (ex-*Hamanasu*)	B	29-9-79	CL 244 Hamayuu	A	29-1-82
CL 207 Suzuran	B	31-7-79	CL 245 Sasayuri	B	25-1-83
CL 208 Isogiku	B	12-9-79	CL 246 Kosumosu	A	17-2-83
CL 209 Isegiko	B	31-8-79	CL 247 Takagiku (ex-*Shiogiku*)	B	29-11-82
CL 211 Ajisai	C	26-9-79	CL 248 Yamahagi	C	29-11-82
CL 213 Hazakura	C	29-8-79	CL 249 Mokuren	D	25-1-83
CL 214 Hinagiku	A	9-7-79	CL 250 Isofuji	A	7-3-83
CL 215 Hamagiku	C	19-9-79	CL 251 Tamatsubaki	B	26-1-84
CL 226 Tsutsuji	B	22-2-80	CL 252 Yodoki	D	22-11-83
CL 228 Satozakura	A	26-2-80	CL 253 Iozakura	A	25-11-83
CL 231 Ezogiku	C	18-11-80	CL 254 Himetsubaki	A	18-1-84
CL 232 Hayagiku (ex-*Akashio*)	B	18-11-80	CL 255 Tokikusa	B	24-2-84
			CL 256 Mutsugiku	B	15-11-84
CL 233 Kozakura	C	18-11-80	CL 257 Terugiko	F	19-12-84
CL 234 Shirame	A	28-11-80	CL 258 Mayazakura	A	20-12-84
CL 235 Sarubia	A	28-11-80	CL 259 Yamagiko	C	22-1-85
CL 237 Hatsugiku	A	29-1-81	CL 260 Tobiume	A	24-1-85
CL 238 Hamayura	A	29-1-80	CL 261 Kotozakura	B	28-2-85
CL 239 Airisu	C	18-2-82	CL 262 Minogiku	A	14-2-85
CL 240 Yamabuki	B	17-12-81	CL 263 Kuroyuri	C	15-11-84
CL 241 Shirayuri	E	1-2-82	CL 264 Chiyogiku	F	8-3-88
CL 242 Karatachi	A	17-12-81			

Mayazakura (CL 258) Takatoshi Okano, 6-04

D: 27 tons light; 35.7 tons normal (40.3 fl) **S:** 20 kts
Dim: 18.00 (16.60 wl) × 4.30 × 0.82 (1.10 props)
A: Small arms **Electronics:** Radar: 1 . . . nav.
M: 2 RD10T AO6 diesels; 2 props; 900 bhp
Range: 180/19 **Crew:** 6 tot.

COAST GUARD PATROL BOATS [WPB] *(continued)*

Remarks: Have three water cannon for fire fighting. CL 250 and CL 252–CL 263 have waterjets vice propellers and can make 21.9 kts; their engines are type S6A-MTK (450 bhp each), and the craft are externally distinguishable by having their pilothouses set closer to amidships and by the protective frame over the waterjet effluxes at the stern. The final unit, CL 264, reverted to the original propulsion plant. CL 240 also has a modified pilothouse.

Disposals: *Sazanka* (CL 218) and *Yaezakura* (CL 221) were stricken on 16-3-99; *Aoi* (CL 219), *Suisen* (CL 220), *Benibana* (CL 224), and *Yukisubaki* (CL 229) on 17-3-99; *Yamayuri* (CL 201) on 25-2-00; *Muratsubaki* (CL 225) on 15-3-01; and *Tachibana* (CL 202), *Komakusa* (CL 203), *Shiragiku* (CL 204), and *Satsuki* (CL 230) on 16-3-01. *Yaguruma* (CL 205), *Himawari* (CL 212), *Fuyume* (CL 216), *Tsubaki* (CL 217), *Akebi* (CL 222), *Shirahagi* (CL 223), *Ashibi* (CL 227), *Suiren* (CL 236), and *Kobai* (CL 243) were stricken on 15-3-02. *Ayame* (CL 210) was retired in 2003.

♦ 2 Hayate-class (12-meter) guard boats
Bldr: Yokohama Yacht (In serv. 21-12-87)

GS 01 Hayate GS 02 Inazuma

Hayate (GS 01)—with fenders added at the bow *Ships of the World,* 7-94

D: 7.9 tons (8.2 fl) **S:** 30 kts **Dim:** 12.20 (11.90 pp) × 3.20 × 1.5
M: 2 . . . diesels; 2 props; 580 bhp **Range:** 195/28 **Crew:** 8 tot.

Remarks: Ordered 9-6-87. Hull molded depth: 1.5 m. Officially typed "Guard Boats, Small" and used at Kansai International Harbor until 1996, when they were transferred to the Osaka Special Security Base. Aluminum hulls.

Note: The coast guard ordered 30 6-m Avon Searider rigid inflatable launches during spring 2000 for use in patrolling waters off Okinawa during an economic summit; the craft are powered by two 90-bhp Yamaha gasoline outboard engines.

AUXILIARIES

♦ 1 Tsushima-class navigational aids tender [WAG]

	Bldr	Laid down	L	In serv.
LL 01 Tsushima	Mitsui, Tamano	10-6-76	7-4-77	9-9-77

Tsushima (LL 01) Mitsuhiro Kadota, 2004

D: 1,718 tons light (2,055 fl) **S:** 16 kts (17.6 trials)
Dim: 75.00 (70.00 wl) × 12.50 × 4.15 **Electronics:** Radar: 2 . . . nav.
M: 1 Fuji-Sulzer 8S 40C diesel; 1 CP prop; 4,200 bhp—bow-thruster
Electric: 900 kVA tot. **Range:** 12,000/15 **Fuel:** 477 tons **Crew:** 54 tot.

Remarks: Intended for use as a lighthouse supply ship and also has equipment to test the luminosity of lighthouses and other navigational lights and to test the accuracy of radio navaids; is not equipped to lay or recover navigational aid buoys. Has Flume-type passive stabilization tanks in after part of superstructure. Intelsat SATCOM was added in 1988 and SHF SATCOM capability by 1992. Based at Tsushima.

♦ 3 Hokuto-class navigational buoy tenders [WAGL]

	Bldr	Laid down	L	In serv.
LL 11 Hokuto	Sasebo DY	19-10-78	20-3-79	29-6-79
LL 12 Kaio	Sasebo DY	17-7-79	20-10-79	11-3-80
LL 13 Ginga	Kawasaki, Kobe	13-6-79	16-11-79	18-3-80

Ginga (LL 13) Takatoshi Okano, 9-04

D: 620 tons light (839 fl) **S:** 13.8 kts **Dim:** 55.00 (51.00 wl) × 10.60 × 2.65
M: 2 Asakasa MH23 (LL 11: Hanshin 6L 24SH) diesels; 2 props; 1,400 bhp
Electric: 300 kVA tot. **Range:** 3,460/13 **Fuel:** 62 tons
Crew: 9 officers, 20 enlisted + 2 technicians

Remarks: Intended to recover, service, and redeploy heavy navigational buoys.

♦ 1 Shoyo-class survey ship [WAGS]

	Bldr	Laid down	L	In serv.
HL 01 Shoyo	Mitsui, Tamano	4-10-96	23-6-97	20-3-98

Shoyo (HL 01) Mitsuhiro Kadota, 5-03

D: 3,128 tons (fl) **S:** 17 kts (16.5 sust.) **Dim:** 98.00 × 15.20 × 3.60
M: . . . diesels, electric drive; 2 CP props; 5,600 shp
Range: 12,000/16.5 **Crew:** 37 tot.

Remarks: Replaced the former *Shoyo* (HL 01). Name can also be rendered *Shouyou.* Carries a 10-m survey boat equipped with a Reson Seabat 9001S mapping sonar. Principal mapping sonar is the U.S.-made Sea Beam 2112, 12-kHz system. Carries 6-ton, 10-m Manbo-II-class inshore survey launches capable of maintaining 10 kts. Has Flume-type passive tank stabilization system. No helicopter facilities.

♦ 2 Meiyo-class survey ships [WAGS]

	Bldr	Laid down	L	In serv.
HL 03 Meiyo	Kawasaki, Kobe	24-7-89	29-6-90	24-10-90
HL 05 Kaiyo	Mitsubishi, Shimonoseki	7-7-92	26-4-93	7-10-93

Kaiyo (HL 05) Takatoshi Okano, 5-04

D: 550 tons light; 621 tons normal (1,035 fl) **S:** 15 kts **Dim:** 60.00 × 10.5 × 3.0
Electronics: Radar: 2 . . . nav.
M: 2 Daihatsu 6 DLM-24S(L) diesels; 2 CP props; 2,200 bhp—bow-thruster

COAST GUARD AUXILIARIES *(continued)*

Kaiyo (HL 05) Mitsuhiro Kadota, 5-03

Electric: 480 kw tot. (2 × 160-kw shaft gen., 2 × 80-kw diesel sets)
Range: 5,000/14.5 **Crew:** 38 tot.

Remarks: 1,096 grt. Carry the same survey equipment as the larger *Takuyo* (HL 02), plus the 11,000-m-depth, 12-kHz U.S.-made Sea Beam 2112 mapping sonar. Navigation equipment includes Loran-C, GPS, and doppler log. Carry a 16-m survey launch. to port. Have Flume-type, superstructure-mounted passive roll-damping and also pitch-damping tanks. The engines are on sound-damping mountings.

♦ 1 Tenyo-class survey ship [WAGS]

	Bldr	Laid down	L	In serv.
HL 04 Tenyo	Sumitomo, Uraga	11-4-86	5-8-86	27-11-86

Tenyo (HL 04) *Ships of the World,* 1995

D: 435 tons light (770 fl) **S:** 14.2 kts **Dim:** 56.0 × 9.8 × 2.9
Electronics: Radar: 2 JMA 1596 nav.
M: 2 Akasaka MH23 diesels; 2 CP props; 1,300 bhp
Electric: 320 kVA (2 × 160-kVA diesel sets) **Range:** 5,400/12
Crew: 38 tot. (18 officers, 25 enlisted accomm.)

Remarks: 430 grt. Carries one 10-m survey boat. Has superstructure-mounted passive tank stabilization. Survey equipment includes the 11,000-m-depth-capable, 12-kHz Sea Beam mapping sonar. Homeported at Tokyo.

♦ 1 Takuyo-class (2,600-ton) survey ship [WAGS]

	Bldr	Laid down	L	In serv.
HL 02 Takuyo	Nippon Kokan, Tsurumi	14-4-82	24-3-83	31-8-83

Takuyo (HL 02) Brian Morrison, 10-02

D: 2,481 tons light; 2,979 tons normal (3,370 fl) **S:** 18.2 kts
Dim: 96.00 (90.00 wl) × 14.20 × 4.51 (mean; 4.91 max. over sonar)
Electronics: Radar: 2 . . . nav.
M: 2 Fuji 6S40B diesels; 2 CP props; 5,200 bhp—bow-thruster
Electric: 965 kVA tot. **Range:** 12,800/16.9 **Endurance:** 50 days
Crew: 24 officers, 36 enlisted + 22 survey party

Remarks: 2,481 grt. Has U.S.-made Sea Beam 210 12-kHz, side-looking, contour-mapping sonars, plus precision echo sounders, and so forth. Carries two survey launches. Has superstructure-mounted Flume-type passive tank stabilization. Navigational equipment includes Magnavox MX 702 SATNAV receiver and Loran-C. Homeported at Tokyo.

SERVICE CRAFT

♦ 1 Katsuran-class radiation monitoring craft [WYAG]
Bldr: Ishihara Dockyard, Takasago (In serv. 18-12-97)

MS 03 Katsuran

Katsuran (MS 03) *Ships of the World,* 12-97

D: 26 tons (fl) **S:** 25 kts **Dim:** 19.6 × 4.5 × 2.3 (molded depth)
M: 2 diesels; 2 props; 1,800 bhp **Range:** . . . / . . . **Crew:** . . . tot.

♦ 1 Saikai-class radiation monitoring craft [WYAG]
Bldr: Ishihara Dockyard, Takasago (In serv. 4-2-94)

MS 02 Saikai

Saikai (MS 02) Takatoshi Okano, 8-02

D: 24 tons (fl) **S:** 15 kts **Dim:** 18.1 × 4.3 × 1.3
M: 2 diesels; 2 props; 1,000 bhp **Range:** 170/ . . . **Crew:** 8 tot.

♦ 1 Kinagusa-class catamaran radiation monitoring craft [WYAG]
Bldr: Ishihara Dockyard, Takasago (In serv. 31-1-92)

MS 01 Kinagusa

Kinagusa (MS 01) Mitsuhiro Kadota, 10-02

D: 39 tons (fl) **S:** 15 kts **Dim:** 18.0 × 9.0 × 1.3
M: 2 diesels; 2 props; 1,000 bhp **Range:** 170/ . . . **Crew:** 8 tot.

♦ 11 Polar Star–class oil-spill surveillance craft [WYAG]
Bldr: Yanmar, Gamagori

	In serv.		In serv.
SS 36 Polar Star	28-3-96	SS 42 Pollux	12-3-96
SS 37 Subaru	28-3-96	SS 43 Aries	12-3-96
SS 38 Lyra	12-3-96	SS 44 Triton	22-3-96
SS 39 Aquarius	22-3-96	SS 45 Pulsar	12-3-96
SS 40 Scorpio	22-3-96	SS 46 Haimuru	12-3-96
SS 41 Libra	12-3-96		

D: 4.7 tons **S:** 30 kts **Dim:** 8.0 × 3.0 × 1.0
Electronics: Radar: 1 Furuno . . . nav.
M: 2 inboard/outboard diesels; . . . bhp **Crew:** 2–3 tot.

Remarks: Commercial cabin cruiser–type craft of about 6 m length. GRP construction. Have a Furuno navigational radar.

COAST GUARD SERVICE CRAFT *(continued)*

Triton (SS 44) Takatoshi Okano, 4-02

♦ 2 Lynx-class oil-spill surveillance craft [WYAG]
Bldr: Yanmar, Gamagori (In serv. 25-3-99)

SS 65 Lynx SS 66 Taurus

Taurus (SS 66) *Ships of the World,* 3-99

D: 5 tons **S:** 50 kts **Dim:** 12.00 × 2.80 × 1.0
Electronics: Radar: 1 Furuno . . . nav.
M: 2 inboard/outboard diesels; 2 props; 700 bhp

Remarks: GRP construction.

♦ 22 New Orion–class oil-spill surveillance craft [WYAG]
Bldr: Yanmar, Gamagori

	In serv.		In serv.
SS 51 Orion	25-3-93	SS 61 Sirius	21-3-97
SS 52 Pegasus	25-3-93	SS 62 Antares	21-3-97
SS 53 Neptune	23-3-94	SS 63 Vega	20-3-98
SS 54 Jupiter	24-3-94	SS 64 Spica	26-3-99
SS 55 Venus	24-3-94	SS 67 Leo	24-3-99
SS 56 Cassiopeia	22-3-95	SS 68 Deneb	30-3-01
SS 57 Phoenix	22-3-95	SS 69 Southern Cross	29-3-02
SS 58 Carina	24-3-95	SS 70 Perseus	2002
SS 59 Capella	18-3-96	SS 71 Centaurus	2002
SS 60 Serpens	12-3-96	SS 72 Hercules	2002
SS 73 Andromeda	2004	SS 74 Aldebaran	2005

Capella (SS 59) Mitsuhiro Kadota, 12-02

D: 4.9 tons (5 fl) **S:** 40 kts **Dim:** 10.0 × 2.6 × . . .
Electronics: Radar: 1 Furuno . . . nav.
M: 2 Volvo KD 42 diesels; 2 props; 460 bhp **Crew:** 2 tot.

Remarks: First two authorized in the FY 92 budget, laid down 25-11-92, and launched 11-3-93. SS 64 was ordered in 1998 to replace SS 12. GRP construction. The names are rendered in English above, as they appear most frequently in that form in Japan Coast Guard publications.

Disposal note: *Southern Cross*–class oil-spill boat *Southern Cross* (SS 35) was stricken on 29-3-02.

♦ 3 Old Orion–class oil-spill surveillance craft [WYAG]
Bldr: Yanmar, Arai (In serv. 1974–79)

SS 30 Comet SS 32 Betelgeuse SS 34 Pleiades

Andromeda (SS 25)—since retired Takatoshi Okano, 7-99

D: 4.8 tons (fl) **S:** 21 kts **Dim:** 6.00 × 2.40 × . . .
M: 1 Yanmar AQ 200 inboard/outboard diesel; 1 prop; 280 bhp
Range: 76/21 **Crew:** 6 tot.

Remarks: GRP construction. Survivors of a class of 32. Recent retirements include *Leo* on 24-3-00, *Deneb* on 30-3-01, and *Polaris* (SS 18) on 29-3-02. SS 23 through SS 25 and SS 27 and SS 33 were retired by 2006. No radar fitted.

♦ 1 23-meter-class navigational aids tender [WYGL]
Bldr: Sumidigawa, Uraga (In serv. 16-3-01)

LM 208 Koun

Koun (LM 208) Takatoshi Okano, 7-04

D: 47 tons normal (50 fl) **S:** 17 kts **Dim:** . . . × . . . × . . .
Electronics: Radar: 1 . . . nav.
M: 2 . . . diesels; 2 props; 1,820 bhp **Crew:** 11 tot.

Remarks: White-painted on completion.

♦ 8 Hakuun-series (24-meter) navigational aids tenders [WYGL]
Bldr: Sumidigawa, Tokyo

LM 114 Tokuun (In serv. 6-3-96)
LM 201 Shoun (In serv. 26-3-86)
LM 202 Seiun (In serv. 6-9-88)
LM 203 Sekiun (In serv. 12-3-91)
LM 204 Houn (In serv. 22-2-91)
LM 205 Reiun (In serv. 28-2-92)
LM 206 Genun (In serv. 19-3-96)
LM 207 Ayabane (In serv. 9-3-00)

D: 57.6 tons light; 62.7 tons normal (75 tons fl) **S:** 14.5 kts
Dim: 24.00 (23.00 pp) × 6.00 × 1.00
Electronics: Radar: 1 FRA-10 Mk III nav.
M: 2 G.M. 12V71 TI diesels; 2 props; 1,080 bhp (980 sust.)
Electric: 30 kVA **Range:** 420/13 **Fuel:** 2 tons **Crew:** 10 tot.

Remarks: LM 201 and LM 202 replaced 23-m craft of the same names. LM 202, built under the FY 88 budget, was laid down 6-9-88 and launched 7-12-88. LM 206 was laid down 12-9-95 to an improved design with enlarged pilothouse. LM 207 was laid down 2-9-99. Class name-ship *Hakuun* (LM 106) was stricken 30-3-01. *Toun* (LM 107) was stricken on 12-3-02.

Disposal note: Single-unit navigational aids tender *Ayabane* (LM 112) was stricken on 24-2-00.

COAST GUARD SERVICE CRAFT *(continued)*

Ayabane (LM 207) *Ships of the World,* 3-00

♦ 1 Zuiun-class (270-ton) navigational aids tender [WYGL]

	Bldr	Laid down	L	In serv.
LM 101 Zuiun	Usuki Iron Wks., Usuki	19-1-83	27-4-83	27-7-83

Zuiun (LM 101) *Ships of the World,* 1996

D: 370 tons normal (398 fl) **S:** 15.1 kts **Dim:** 44.50 (41.40 pp) × 7.50 × 2.23
Electronics: Radar: 1 JMZ 1596 nav.; 1 JMA 159B surf. search
M: 2 Mitsubishi-Akasaka MH 23-series diesels; 2 CP props; 1,300 bhp
Electric: 120 kw tot. **Range:** 1,440/14.5 **Fuel:** 34 m^3 **Crew:** 20 tot.

Remarks: Lighthouse service vessel, not equipped to lay or recover navigational aids. Cargo: 85 tons. One diesel is model MH23F, the other MH23. A second unit was requested under the FY 85 budget but not approved.

Disposal note: *Miyojo*-class navigational buoy tender *Miyojo* (LM 11) had been retired by 2005.

♦ 1 17-ton inshore navigational aids tender [WYGL]

Bldr: . . . (In serv. 2003)

LS 201

D: 17 tons std. **S:** 20 kts **Dim:** 15.0 × 4.2 × . . .
M: 2 diesels; 2 props; 880 bhp

Remarks: Prototype for a new class to replace the existing *Shoko* class.

♦ 5 Nahahikari-class inshore navigational aids tenders [WYGL]

Bldr: Nagasaki Zosen

LS 222 Shimahikari (In serv. 17-12-01)
LS 223 Maihikari (In serv. 12-3-02)
LS 233 Nahahikari (In serv. 13-3-00)
LS 234 Michihikari (In serv. 22-3-01)
LS 235 Nijihikari (In serv. 26-3-02)

Maihikari (LS 223) Takatoshi Okano, 9-02

D: 27 tons (29 fl) **S:** 25 kts **Dim:** 20.0 × 4.8 × 1.1
Electronics: Radar: 1 . . . nav.
M: 2 M.A.N. D-2842LYE diesels; 2 props; 1,800 bhp
Range: 160/25 **Crew:** 11 tot.

Remarks: Intended to replace the *Hatsuhikari* class and are an improved version of the *Himehikari* class.

♦ 2 Himehikari-class inshore navigational aids tenders [WYGL]

Bldr: Nagasaki Zosen (In serv. 23-3-99)

LS 231 Himehikari LS 232 Matsuhikari

Himehikari (LS 231) Takatoshi Okano, 9-00

D: 23 tons (27 fl) **S:** 29 kts (25 sust.) **Dim:** 20.0 × 4.5 × 1.1
Electronics: Radar: 1 . . . nav.
M: 2 M.A.N. D-2842LYE diesels; 2 props; 1,820 bhp
Range: 160/29 **Crew:** . . . tot.

Remarks: Essentially the same design and appearance as the *Suzukaze*-class (CL) small patrol boats, with fenders added on the sides aft and a small boat carried to starboard aft on davits. Construction was approved under the FY 99 budget. Have a firefighting monitor (water cannon) on the bow.

♦ 9 Hatsuhikari-class inshore navigational aids tenders [WYGL]

Bldr: Yokohama Yacht (LS 216: Sumidigawa, Tokyo; LS 217 221: Ishihara DY, Takasago)

	In serv.		In serv.
LS 212 Wakahikari	5-3-82	LS 218 Setohikari	31-1-89
LS 213 Miyohikari	18-3-83	LS 219 Tohikari	28-2-90
LS 214 Urahikari	27-1-84	LS 220 Takahikari	31-1-90
LS 216 Fusahikari	18-2-88	LS 221 Sekihikari	31-1-90
LS 217 Haruhikari	6-1-89		

Miyohikari (LS 213) Takatoshi Okano, 4-04

D: 20 tons light; 25 tons normal (35.2 fl) **S:** 16.3 kts (15 sust.)
Dim: 17.20 × 4.30 × 0.80
M: 2 Isuzu E-120T-MF6R diesels; 2 props; 560 bhp
Range: 230/14.5 **Endurance:** 2 days **Crew:** 8 tot.

Remarks: Are officially the "17-meter" class. Pilothouse configurations vary.
Disposals: *Hatsuhikari* (LS 204) was stricken 10-3-99, *Matsuhikari* (LS 206) on 5-3-99, *Nahahikari* (LS 205) on 25-2-00, and *Michihikari* (LS 207) on 8-3-01. *Kamihikari* (LS 209) was stricken on 22-2-02 and *Shimahikari* (LS 210) on 15-2-02. *Nishihikari* (LS 208) and *Akihikari* (LS 211) had been stricken by 2005.

♦ 8 Shoko-class inshore navigational aids tenders [WYGL]

Bldr: Ishikawajima, Tokyo (Yokosuka; LS 194, 195: Ishihara DY, Takasago)

	In serv.		In serv.
LS 188 Taiko	24-1-85	LS 192 Suiko	30-1-87
LS 189 Choko	20-12-85	LS 193 Saiko	2-2-87
LS 190 Miyoko	24-12-85	LS 194 Aiko	24-11-87
LS 191 Kyoko	21-1-86	LS 195 Hakuko	24-11-87

COAST GUARD SERVICE CRAFT *(continued)*

Toko (LS 186)—since stricken *Ships of the World*

D: 9.4 tons light (14 fl) **S:** 15 kts **Dim:** 12.00 × 3.20 × 0.60
M: 1 diesel; 1 prop; 210 bhp **Range:** 120/13.5 **Crew:** 6 tot.

Remarks: GRP construction. Are officially the "12-meter" class. *Shoko* (LS 185) was stricken 31-3-01, *Toko* (LS 186) on 31-3-02. *Keiko* (LS 181) and *Getsuko* (LS 187) had been stricken by 2005.

♦ 3 Reiko No. 1–class navigational aids tenders [WYGL]
Bldr: . . .

LS 168 Reiko No. 1 (In serv. 2-12-86)
LS 169 Reiko No. 2 (In serv. 30-11-87)
LS 170 Reiko No. 3 (In serv. 30-11-87)

Reiko No. 2 (LS 169) *Ships of the World,* 1996

D: 4.5 tons (4.9 fl) **S:** 15 kts **Dim:** 9.9 × 2.5 × 1.1
M: 1 diesel; 1 prop; 115 bhp **Range:** 130/13 **Crew:** 8 tot.

Remarks: GRP construction. Are officially of the "10-meter" class.

♦ 5 Zuiko No. 1–class navigational aids tenders [WYGL]
Bldr: . . .

	Laid down	L	In serv.
LS 161 Zuiko No. 1	20-9-85	20-11-85	5-12-85
LS 164 Zuiko No. 2	29-9-85	26-11-85	12-12-85
LS 165 Zuiko No. 3	8-10-85	2-12-85	18-12-85
LS 166 Zuiko No. 4	16-10-85	19-12-85	17-1-86
LS 167 Zuiko No. 5	24-10-85	9-1-86	24-1-86

Zuiko No. 2 (LS 164) *Ships of the World,* 1996

D: 4.5 tons (4.9 fl) **S:** 14 kts **Dim:** 9.9 × 2.8 × 1.6
M: 1 diesel; 1 prop; 115 bhp **Range:** 130/13 **Crew:** 8 tot.

Remarks: GRP construction. Are officially a "10-meter" class.

♦ 2 Kaiko No. 1–class navigational aids tenders [WYGL]
Bldr: Nippon Hikoki, Yokosuka

LS 149 Kaiko No. 5 (In serv. 1982)
LS 155 Kaiko No. 7 (In serv. 12-1-84)

Kaiko No. 9 (LS 158)—since stricken *Ships of the World*

D: 5.0 tons (5.2 fl) **S:** 13 kts **Dim:** 9.00 × 2.25 × . . .
M: 2 Nissan FD606 diesels; 1 prop; 230 bhp **Range:** 130/12.5 **Crew:** 6 tot.

Remarks: GRP construction. Are officially a "10-meter" class. *Kaiko No. 1* (LS 144), *Kaiko No. 2* (LS 145), and *Kaiko No. 3* (LS 146) were stricken 31-3-01. *Kaiko No. 4* (LS 148) was stricken 31-3-02. *Kaiko No. 6* (LS 154), *Kaiko No. 8* (LS 157), *Kaiko No. 9* (LS 158), and *Kaiko No 10.* (LS 160) had been stricken by 2005.

♦ 1 (+ . . .) Jinbei-class inshore survey boat [YGS]
Bldr: Nippon Kokan, Tsurumi

	Laid down	L	In serv.
HS 11 Jinbei	24-5-01	20-9-01	21-1-02

D: 5.0 tons **S:** 9 kts **Dim:** 10.0 × 2.8 × 1.4
Electronics: Radar: . . .
M: 1 . . . diesel; 1 prop; 120 bhp

Remarks: GRP construction. Additional units may be planned.

♦ 7 Hamashio-class (20-meter) inshore survey boats [WYGS]
Bldrs: HS 21–23: Yokohama Yacht; HS 24–27: Ishihara DY, Takasago

	In serv.		In serv.
HS 21 Hamashio	25-3-91	HS 25 Iseshio	10-3-99
HS 22 Isoshio	25-3-93	HS 26 Hayashio	10-3-99
HS 23 Uzushio	20-12-95	HS 27 Kurushima	16-4-03
HS 24 Okishio	4-3-99		

Uzushio (HS 23) Takatoshi Okano, 7-04

D: 27 tons light (42 fl) **S:** 15 kts **Dim:** 20.30 × 4.50 × 1.00
M: 2 diesels; 2 props; 900 bhp—1 cruise diesel; 1 prop; 115 bhp
Range: 200/ . . . **Crew:** 10 tot.

Remarks: Superstructures vary: HS 21–23 have a high pilothouse; HS 24–27 have deckhouse/pilothouse all at one level. HS 27 was launched on 11-12-02.

♦ 1 Akashi-class (15-meter) inshore survey boat [WYGS]
Bldr: . . . (In serv. 1977)

HS 35 Kurushima

D: 21 tons normal (26.8 fl) **S:** 10.2 kts **Dim:** 15.0 × 4.0 × 0.84
M: 1 Nissan-MTU UD626 diesel; 180 bhp **Range:** 630/9.7 **Crew:** 7 tot.

Remarks: GRP hull. Sister *Akashi* (HS 31) was stricken 4-12-95 and *Hayatomo* (HS 33) and *Kurihama* (HS 34) on 22-2-99.

♦ 5 Shirasagi-class oil-spill recovery craft [WYSR]
Bldrs: Various (In serv. 1977–79)

OR 01 Shirasagi, OR 02 Shiratori, OR 03 Mizunagi, OR 04 Chidori, OR 05 Isoshigi

COAST GUARD SERVICE CRAFT *(continued)*

Chidori (OR 04) *Ships of the World*

D: 78.5 tons light; 100 tons normal (153 fl) **S:** 6.8 kts **Dim:** 22.0 × 6.4 × 0.9
M: 2 UD 626 diesels; waterjet drive; 390 bhp **Range:** 160/6 **Crew:** 7 tot.

♦ 3 Uraga-class oil-spill skimmer craft [WYSR]
Bldr: Lockheed, U.S.A.

OS 01 Tsurumi (ex-*Uraga*) (In serv. 31-3-75)
OS 02 Bisan (In serv. 31-3-75)
OS 03 Naruto (In serv. 25-2-76)

Bisan (OS 02) *Ships of the World*

D: 9 tons (11 fl) **S:** 6 kts **Dim:** 8.26 × 5.00 × 0.70
M: 1 HR-6 diesel; 2 props; 90 bhp **Range:** 90/4.5 **Crew:** 4 tot.

Remarks: Can be broken down into sections for truck transport. Catamaran hulls, with oil-spill and debris sweeping gear between. All OR/OS/OX-series cleanup craft are painted bright red-orange.

♦ 18 M 101–class oil-spill extender barges [WYSRN]
Bldrs: Various (In serv. 1974–76)

OX 01 M 101 through OX 06 M 106
OX 08 M 108 through OX 19 M 119

M 108 (OX 08) Ralph Edwards, 10-01

D: 48 tons (93 fl) **Dim:** 22.00 × 7.20 × 0.45

♦ 1 New Hiryu–class large fireboat [WYTR]
Bldr: Nippon Kokan (NKK), Tsurumi

	Laid down	L	In serv.
FL 01 Hiryu	18-3-97	5-9-97	24-12-97

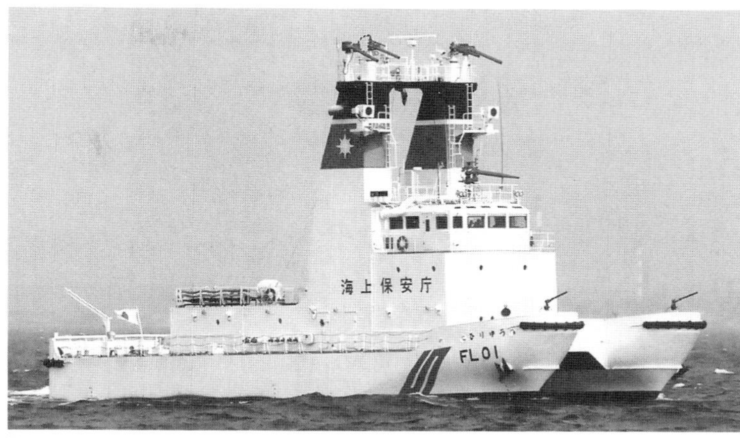

Hiryu (FL 01)—with telescoping fire monitor masts retracted
Takatoshi Okano, 5-04

D: 280 tons normal (322 fl) **S:** 14.0 kts **Dim:** 35.10 × 12.20 × . . .
M: 2 diesels; 2 azimuthal CP props; 4,000 bhp **Crew:** 14 tot.

Remarks: Replacement design for the original *Hiryu* (FL 01) class, with the first authorized under the FY 96 budget. To date, however, no further units have been ordered.
Hull systems: Catamaran hulls. Has four 5,000-liter/min fire monitors atop the tower mast (two of them on telescoping masts), one 20,000-liter/min monitor atop the pilothouse, and a 1,000-liter/min monitor at the bow of each hull. FL 01 is stationed at Yokohama.

Note: Most JCG patrol ships, boats, and craft are also fitted for firefighting.

♦ 4 Old Hiryu–class large fireboats [WYTR]
Bldr: Nippon Kokan, Yokohama (FL 05: Yokohama Yacht)

	In serv.		In serv.
FL 02 Shoryu	4-3-70	FL 04 Kairyu	18-3-77
FL 03 Nanryu	4-3-71	FL 05 Suiryu	24-3-78

Nanryu (FL 03)—with telescoping fire monitor mast raised and all monitors spraying
Takatoshi Okano, 7-04

D: 200.3 tons normal (216 fl) **S:** 13.7 kts **Dim:** 27.50 × 10.40 × 2.1
M: 2 Ikegai-MTU MB820Db diesels; 2 props; 2,200 bhp
Electric: 70 kVA tot. **Range:** 300/13 **Crew:** 14 tot.

Remarks: Catamaran hulls. Intended for fighting supertanker fires. Have a 14.5-m^3 tank for firefighting chemicals, one 45-m-range chemical sprayer, and seven 60-m-range water cannon. One fire monitor is atop a telescoping mast. Class name-ship *Hiryu* (FL 01) was stricken during 12-97.

♦ 4 Ninobiki-class medium fireboats [WYTR]
Bldrs: FM 02, 06, 08, 10: Sumidigawa, Tokyo; others: Yokohama Yacht

	In serv.		In serv.
FM 04 Shiraito	25-2-75	FM 09 Ryusei	24-3-80
FM 08 Minoo	27-1-78	FM 10 Kyotaki	25-3-81

COAST GUARD SERVICE CRAFT *(continued)*

Ryusei (FM 09) *Ships of the World*

D: 89 tons normal (99 fl) **S:** 13.4 kts **Dim:** 23.00 × 6.00 × 1.55
M: 1 Ikegai MTU MB820Db and 2 Nissan UDV 816 diesels; 3 props; 1,600 bhp
Electric: 40 kVA **Range:** 180/13.4 **Crew:** 12 tot.

Remarks: Have four firepumps: one of 6,000 liters/min, two of 3,000 liters/min, and one of 2,000 liters/min. Have two 750-liter and one 5,000-liter foam tanks. Sister *Otowa* (FM 03) was retired 12-8-99, *Ninobiki* (FM 01) on 31-10-00, and *Yodo* (FM 02) on 13-3-02. *Kotobiki* (FM 05), *Nachi* (FM 06) and *Kegon* (FM 07) had been stricken by 2005.

♦ **2 C I–class training craft [WYXT]**
Bldr: Yanmar, Arai

C I (In serv. 26-3-99) C II (In serv. 24-3-00)

C II—red-orange hull, white upperworks *Ships of the World,* 3-00

D: 1.5 tons **S:** 27 kts **Dim:** 5.40 × 2.10 × 0.5
M: 1 Yanmar inboard/outboard diesel; 1 prop; 96 bhp **Crew:** 4 tot.

Remarks: Open-cockpit, GRP-hulled runabouts; replaced craft with same names. Have a red-orange hull and white superstructure.

♦ **1 A-class training craft [WYXT]**
Bldr: . . . (In serv. 26-3-96)

Aoba

Aoba *Ships of the World,* 3-96

D: 15 tons (19 fl) **S:** 22 kts **Dim:** 16.0 × 4.1 × 2.0
M: 1 diesel; 380 bhp **Crew:** 3 instructors, 12 students
Range: 243/15.5

Remarks: Replaced a similar craft of the same name. GRP-construction cabin cruiser.

JERSEY

Note: Jersey, in the Channel Islands, is a semiautonomous territory of the United Kingdom.

PATROL BOATS [WPB]

♦ **1 Norman le Brocq class**
Bldr: Souter, Cowes, U.K. (In serv. 1998)

Norman le Brocq

D: 17 tons (fl) **S:** 24 kts **Dim:** 15.00 × . . . × . . .
A: Small arms **Electronics:** Radar: 1 . . . nav.
M: 2 Saab Scania DSI-11 diesels; 2 props; 1,000 bhp
Range: . . . / . . . **Crew:** 3 tot.

Remarks: Ordered 20-11-97. GRP construction. Has one Avon Searider rigid inflatable inspection dinghy mounted on a ramp at the stern. Used for local police and fisheries protection duties.

JORDAN

Hashemite Kingdom of Jordan

Personnel: Approximately 500 total

Base: Aqaba

Note: The Coastal Guard was restyled the Royal Jordanian Naval Force in 1991. The United States delivered two 40-ft. and one 65-ft. patrol boats from surplus stocks on 14-12-96 and the U.S. Coast Guard three "cutters" in 1999.

PATROL CRAFT [PC]

♦ **3 Hawk-class patrol boats**
Bldr: Vosper Thornycroft, Portchester (In serv. 10-91)

101 Al Hussein 102 Al Hussan 103 Abdullah

Al Hussein (101) ANBw/FAFIO, 8-97

D: 95 tons light (124 fl) **S:** 32.5 kts **Dim:** 30.45 (26.55 pp) × 6.87 × 1.50 (hull)
A: 1 twin 30-mm 75-cal. Oerlikon–Royal Ordnance GCM-A03-2 AA; 1 20-mm 90-cal. Oerlikon GAM-B01 AA; 2 single 7.62-mm mg
Electronics:
Radar: 1 Kelvin-Hughes Type 1007 nav.
EW: 2 Wallop Stockade decoy RL
M: 2 MTU 16V396 TB94 diesels; 2 props; 5,800 bhp—2 Volvo TAMD 71A cruise diesels; . . . bhp
Range: 750/15 **Fuel:** 18 tons **Crew:** 3 officers, 13 enlisted

Remarks: Ordered 3-88. 101 was launched during 12-88 and ran trials 17-5-89; 102 completed in 12-89 and 103 during 6-90. All were commissioned after delivery together as deck cargo in 9-91. GRP construction. Have a Rademac 2000 optronic director for the 30-mm mount.

PATROL BOATS [PB]

♦ **1 ex-U.S. Navy 65-foot Air/Sea Rescue Boat**

201 (ex-65AR682)

D: 27.6 tons (31.5 fl) **S:** 24 kts **Dim:** 19.80 × 5.25 × 1.14
A: 2 7.62-mm mg **Electronics:** Radar: 1 SPS- . . . nav.
M: 2 G.M. Detroit Diesel 12V71T diesels; 2 props; 1,170 bhp
Electric: 10 kw tot. (1 × 10-kw Onan Model 10 MDZB-3R set)
Range: 250/24 **Fuel:** 3,028 liters **Crew:** 6 tot.

PATROL BOATS [PB] *(continued)*

Remarks: Donated late 1996. Aluminum construction craft similar to U.S. Navy 65-ft. torpedo retriever design. Can accommodate eight litter patients but is probably to be used as a patrol boat. Had previously been employed at Subic Bay, the Philippines, by the U.S. Navy.

♦ **4 U.S. Bertram 38-foot class**
Bldr: Bertram Yacht, Miami (In serv. 1974)

FAYSAL HAN HASAYU MUHAMMED

U.S. Bertram 38-ft. patrol launch ANBw/FAFIO, 8-97

D: 8 tons **S:** 25 kts **Dim:** 11.6 × 4.0 × 0.5
A: 1 12.7-mm mg; 2 single 7.62-mm mg
Electronics: Radar: 1 Decca . . . nav.
M: 2 G.M. Detroit Diesel 8V71S diesels; 2 props; 600 bhp
Range: 240/20 **Crew:** 8 tot.

Remarks: GRP construction. Since delivery, have had a flying bridge built on above the original cockpit.

SERVICE CRAFT

♦ **2 ex-U.S. Navy 40-foot personnel boat Mk 4 launches [YFL]**
Bldr: . . . (In serv. 1991)

. . . (ex-40PE9002) . . . (ex-40PE9003)

D: 7.9 tons light (11.6 fl) **S:** 15.9 kts **Dim:** 12.26 × 3.68 × 0.86
M: 1 G.M. Detroit Diesel 6-71 diesel; 1 prop; 280 bhp
Range: 120/12 **Crew:** 3 tot.

Remarks: Donated in late 1996. GRP-hulled craft formerly carried by aircraft carriers. Can carry 40 passengers but are employed primarily in patrol duties.

♦ **3 U.K. Sea Truck utility launches [YFL]**
Bldr: Rotork, U.K. (In serv. 9-91)

AL FAISAL AL HASHIM AL HAMZA

Al Hashim Royal Jordanian Navy, 1996

D: 9 tons (fl) **S:** 28 kts **Dim:** 12.7 × 3.2 × 0.9
A: 1 12.7-mm mg; 1 7.62-mm mg **Electronics:** Radar: 1 Decca . . . nav.
M: 2 Perkins diesels; 2 props; 240 bhp **Crew:** 2 + 30 troops

Remarks: Delivered with the *Hawk*-class patrol boats. For use on the Dead Sea. Truck transportable. Have a bow ramp and are beachable.

Note: The 15-m pilot boat/patrol craft *Husni* at Aqaba, delivered in 1988 by Trinity Marine's Equitable Shipyard, New Orleans, is not under naval control.

KAZAKHSTAN

Personnel: About 300 total

Bases: Headquarters at Aktau (formerly Shevchenko) and minor facilities at Bautino on the Caspian Sea and at Atyrau on the Aral Sea

Naval Aviation: Three Mil Mi-8 and 6 Mi-2 helicopters. The air force operates twelve former Soviet Su-24s, which are used for attack and surveillance.

Note: The armed forces of Kazakhstan were founded during 5-92. The naval flotilla of the border guard was formally dedicated on 17-8-96 at Aktau. An "Advanced Naval School of the Defense Ministry of the Republic of Kazakhstan" was established on 9-8-01 at Aktau with 180 trainees and 44 instructors.

PATROL CRAFT [PC]

♦ **3 ex-South Korean Sea Dolphin class (PKM 200 series)**
Bldrs: Korea-Tacoma SY, Chinhae, and Korea SB & Eng., Masan (In serv. 1970s–80s)

D: 113 tons (143 fl) **S:** 38 kts **Dim:** 33.10 (31.25 wl) × 6.92 × 1.75 (2.45 props)
A: 1 40-mm 60-cal. Bofors Mk 3 AA; 1 twin 30-mm 90-cal. Emerlec AA; 2 single 20-mm 70-cal. Oerlikon Mk 10 AA; 2 single 7.62-mm M2 mg
Electronics: Radar: 1 Raytheon 1645 nav./surf. search
M: 2 MTU 16V538 TB90 diesels; 2 props; 10,800 bhp (9,000 sust.)
Electric: 100 kw tot. (2 × 50-kw diesel sets)
Range: 500/32; 1,000/20 **Fuel:** 15 tons **Crew:** 5 officers, 26 enlisted

Remarks: Transfer announced 4-05. AN/APX-72 Identification Friend-or-Foe (IFF) transponder system was removed prior to transfer in compliance with U.S. export rules. Designed for 38 kts; can now make only 32 kts continuous.

♦ **2 ex-Turkish AB 25 class**
Bldrs: Haliç SY, Turkey (In serv. 1969)

. . . (ex-AB 32) . . . (ex-AB 26)

D: 150 tons (170 fl) **S:** 22 kts **Dim:** 40.24 × 6.40 × 1.65
A: 1 40-mm 60-cal. Mk 3 Bofors AA; 1 20-mm 70-cal. Oerlikon AA; 2 single 12.7-mm mg
Electronics: Radar: 1 Decca TM 1226 nav.
M: 2 SACM-AGO V16CSHR diesels; 2 props; 4,800 bhp—2 cruise diesels; 300 bhp
Crew: 3 officers, 28 enlisted

Remarks: Ex-AB 36 was transferred on 3-7-99 and ex-AB 26 during 2001, both from the Turkish Navy. The cruise diesels are geared to the main shafts.

PATROL BOATS [PB]

♦ **1 Type 22180 patrol boat**

	Bldr	Laid down	L	In serv.
. . .	Zenit Zavod, Ural'sk	. . .	. . .	7-06

Remarks: Delivered 7-06. 200 tons displacement; no additional data available.

♦ **1 Russian Zhuk class (Project 1400M)**

	Bldr	Laid down	L	In serv.
BERKUT	Zenit Zavod, Ural'sk	1996	22-5-98	15-7-98

D: 35.9 tons (39.7 fl) **S:** 30 kts
Dim: 23.80 (21.70 wl) × 5.00 (3.80 wl) × 1.00 (hull)
A: 1 twin 14.5-mm 93-cal. 2M-7 AA **Electronics:** Radar: 1 Lotsiya nav.
M: 2 M-401B diesels; 2 props; 2,200 bhp
Electric: 48 kw total (2 × 21-kw, 1 × 6-kw diesel sets)
Range: 500/13.5 **Endurance:** 5 days **Crew:** 1 officer, 9 enlisted

Remarks: Two others were to be transferred 2-96 from the Russian Caspian Flotilla but were apparently not put into service. *Berkut* means "Golden Eagle."

♦ **1 U.S. 42-foot Dauntless class**
Bldr: SeaArk, Monticello, Ark. (In serv. 17-8-96)

106 ABAY

Abay (106) SeaArk, 11-95

PATROL BOATS [PB] *(continued)*

D: 11 tons (12.7 fl) **S:** 35 kts **Dim:** 12.80 × 4.27 × 1.32 (max.)
A: 1 12.7-mm mg; 2 single 7.62-mm mg
Electronics: Radar: 1 Furuno . . . nav.
M: 2 G.M. Detroit Diesel 8V92 TA diesels; 2 props; 1,270 bhp
Electric: 12 kw tot. **Range:** 200/30; 400/22 **Fuel:** 250 gallons **Crew:** 4 tot.

Remarks: Transferred as aid by the U.S. Defense Nuclear Agency and delivered 11-95. Aluminum construction. C. Raymond Hunt, "Deep-Vee" hull design. Is equipped with GPS receiver, VHF radio, air-conditioning, and a siren.

♦ **2 Saygak class (Project 1408M)**
Bldr: Zenit Zavod, Ural'sk (In serv. 1995)

D: 13 tons (fl) **S:** 38 kts (35 sust.) **Dim:** 14.05 × 3.50 × 0.65
A: 1 7.62-mm mg **Electronics:** Radar: 1 . . . nav.
M: 1 Type M-401B (12CHSN18/20) diesel; 1 waterjet; 1,000 bhp
Electric: 8 kw (1 Type DGK8/1500 diesel driving; 27 V)
Range: 135/35 **Fuel:** 1.15 tons **Crew:** 2 tot. + 4–8 police personnel

Remarks: Locally built version of a class designed for Russian use on the Amur-Ussuri River system in the Far East. Rail transportable, the craft are intended for use in coastal waters in seas up to Sea State 3. Aluminum alloy construction. Three additional 14-ton units may have been delivered during 2004–5.

♦ **5 U.S. 27-foot Vigilant class**
Bldr: Boston Whaler, Edgewater, Fla. (In serv. 17-8-96)

Kazakhstani Vigilant Boston Whaler, 1995

D: 2.27 tons light (4.0 fl) **S:** 34 kts **Dim:** 8.10 × 3.05 × 0.48
A: 1 12.7-mm mg; 2 single 7.62-mm mg
Electronics: Radar: 1 Furuno . . . nav.
M: 2 Johnson gasoline outboards; 350 bhp
Range: . . . / . . . **Fuel:** 648 liters **Crew:** 4 tot.

Remarks: Presented as aid under a U.S. Defense Nuclear Agency contract. Delivered 11-95. GRP foam-core construction.

Disposal note: The four ex-German KW 15–class patrol boats transferred in 1995 after refits were out of service as of 2000.

SERVICE CRAFT

♦ **1 former fishing trawler [YFU]**

TYULEN II

Remarks: Acquired in 1997. Measures 39 m o.a. and is powered by one 578-bhp diesel for 10 kts. Used for logistics support and fisheries inspection duties. No other information available.

Note: Some 20 "small hydrographic launches" were also said to be in service.

KENYA

Republic of Kenya

Personnel: 1,620 total, including 120 marines

Bases: Mombasa and Magogoni. The navy also operates nine coastal radar stations.

GUIDED-MISSILE PATROL CRAFT [PTG]

♦ **2 Province class**
Bldr: Vosper Thornycroft, Portchester, U.K.

	Laid down	L	In serv.
P 3126 NYAYO	11-84	20-8-86	23-7-87
P 3127 UMOJA	11-84	5-3-87	7-9-87

D: 311 tons light (363 fl) **S:** 40 kts **Dim:** 56.7 (52.0 pp) × 8.2 × 2.1
A: 4 Otomat Mk II SSM; 1 76-mm 62-cal. OTO Melara Compact DP; 1 twin 30-mm 90-cal. BMARC-Oerlikon GCM-A02 AA; 2 single 20-mm 90-cal. BMARC-Oerlikon GAM-B01 AA
Electronics:
Radar: 1 Decca AC 1226 nav.; 1 Plessey AWS-4 surf./air search; 1 Thales LIROD-423 radar/optronic f.c.
EW: Racal Cutlass-E intercept; Racal Cygnus jammer; 2 18-round Wallop Barricade decoy RL

Nyayo (P 3126) Ralph Edwards, 2-01

M: 4 Paxman Valenta 18 RP 200 CM diesels; 4 props; 17,900 bhp (15,000 sust.)—2 electric cruise outdrives; 160 bhp
Electric: 420 kw tot. **Range:** 2,000/15 **Fuel:** 45.5 tons **Crew:** 40 tot.

Remarks: Ordered 9-84. Generally similar to craft built for Oman and Egypt. Use the Ferranti WSA.423 combat data/fire-control system. Carry a semi-rigid inspection boat on the stern. Both departed the U.K. for Kenya on 29-3-88. They constitute Squadron 86.

Disposal note: Brooke Marine 32-meter-class guided-missile patrol craft *Madaraka* (P 3121) and Brooke Marine 37.5-m guided-missile patrol craft *Mamba* (P 3100) were retired during 2000.

PATROL CRAFT [PC]

♦ **2 Shupavu class**
Bldr: Construnaves-CNE, Gondan, Spain

	Laid down	L	In serv.
P 3131 SHUPAVU (ex-P 6129)	. . .	. . .	1998
P 3130 SHUJAA (ex-P 6130)	. . .	. . .	1998

Shujaa (P 3130) Brian Morrison, 2-01

D: 480 tons (fl) **S:** 22 kts **Dim:** 58.0 × 8.2 × 2.8
A: 1 76-mm 62-cal. OTO Melara SuperRapid DP; 1 25-mm 90-cal. Oerlikon AA
Electronics: Radar: 1 Furuno . . . nav.; 1 Furuno . . . surf. search
M: . . . diesels; 2 props; . . . bhp
Range: . . . / . . . **Crew:** 24 tot.

Remarks: Ordered 3-97. Intended for offshore patrol duties. Are equipped with two rigid inflatable inspection launches and a handling crane. Were delivered without armament early in 1998. An electro-optical director for the 76-mm gun is fitted above the pilothouse, and a similar director for the 25-mm gun is located just forward of it. Both were renumbered early in 2005.

PATROL BOATS [PB]

♦ **5 ex-Spanish P 101 class**
Bldr: ARESA, Arenys del Mar, Barcelona (In serv. 1978–82)

P 943 P 944 P 945 P 946 P 947

D: 16.9 tons (21.7 fl) **S:** 26 kts **Dim:** 15.90 (13.70 pp) × 4.36 × 1.33
A: 1 12.7-mm mg **Electronics:** Radar: 1 Decca 110 nav.
M: 2 Baudouin-Interdiesel DNP-8 MIR diesels; 2 props; 768 bhp
Electric: 12 kVA tot. **Range:** 430/18 **Fuel:** 2.2 tons
Crew: 2 officers, 4–5 enlisted

Remarks: Former Spanish Navy units purchased in 1995. GRP construction. May be assigned to the customs service rather than the navy.

AMPHIBIOUS WARFARE SHIPS

♦ **2 Galana-class medium landing ships [LSM]**
Bldr: Construnaves-CNE, Gondan, Spain (In serv. 2-94)

L 38 GALANA L 39 TANA

D: 1,400 tons (fl) **S:** 12.5 kts (12.9 on trials) **Dim:** 63.5 × 13.3 × 2.4
A: None **Electronics:** Radar: 1 Decca . . . nav.
M: 2 MTU-Izar . . . diesels; 2 props; 2,700 bhp—bow-thruster
Range: . . . / . . . **Crew:** 30 tot.

AMPHIBIOUS WARFARE SHIPS *(continued)*

Tana (L 39) A. Guigné, 2002

Remarks: Ordered by Galway, Ltd., for commercial service but taken over by the navy prior to completion. Have a 4-m-wide bow ramp capable of supporting 70-ton loads and also have a portside vehicle loading ramp.

SERVICE CRAFT

♦ **1 large harbor tug [YTB]**
Bldr: James Lamont, Port Glasgow, U.K.

NGAMIA (In serv. 1969)

D: . . . **S:** 14 kts **Dim:** 35.3 × 9.3 × 3.9 **M:** Diesels; 1 prop; 1,200 bhp

Remarks: 298 grt. Transferred to the Kenyan Navy from the Mombasa Port Authority in 1-83.

Disposal note: Vosper 110-ft. training craft and former patrol craft *Simba* (P 3110) was stricken during 2000.

Note: The customs service operates 12 12-m German-built patrol boats delivered 1989–90; the Netherlands-built, 55-ton pilot boat *Kiongozi* (in serv. 1983); 17-m workboats *M'Chunguzi* and *M'Linzi;* and an 18-m, a 14-m, and two 12-m launches, the 12-m launches for service on Lake Victoria.

KIRIBATI

Note: Ship names are preceded by RKS (Republic of Kiribati Ship).

PATROL CRAFT [PC]

♦ **1 ASI 315 class**
Bldr: Transfield ASI Pty, Ltd., South Coogee, Western Australia (In serv. 22-1-94)

301 TEANOAI

Teanoai (301) LSPH Shaun Hibbit, 1-94

D: 165 tons (fl) **S:** 21 kts (20 sust.) **Dim:** 31.50 (28.60 wl) × 8.10 × 2.12 (1.80 hull)
A: Provision for 1 12.7-mm mg
Electronics: Radar: 1 Furuno 1011 (I/J-band) nav.
M: 2 Caterpillar 3516 diesels; 2 props; 2,820 bhp (2,400 sust.)
Electric: 116 kw (2 × 50-kw Caterpillar 3304 diesels; 1 × 16 kw)
Range: 2,500/12 **Fuel:** 27.9 tons **Endurance:** 8–10 days
Crew: 3 officers, 14 enlisted

Remarks: Ordered in late 1992. An Australian foreign aid program "Pacific Patrol Boat," with numerous sisters in a number of Southwest Pacific–area island nation forces. In refit 2001 in Australia and expected to serve until 2024. Carries a 5-m aluminum boarding boat and has an extensive navigational suite, including Furuno FSN-70 NAVSAT receiver, 525 HFD/F, 120 MF–HFD/F, FE-881 echo sounder, and DS-70 doppler log. The 12.7-mm machinegun is not normally mounted.

KOREA, NORTH

Democratic People's Republic of Korea

Personnel: Approximately 46,000, plus 65,000 reserves

Bases: The fleet is divided between the Yellow Sea and Sea of Japan, and units do not transfer between them. The East Coast Fleet is headquartered at Toejo Dong, with major bases at Najin and Wonsan and submarines based at Chaho; minor facilities exist at Kimchaek, Ksong-up, Muchon-up, Namer-ri, Pando, Sanjin-dong, Songjon, and Yohori. The much smaller West Coast Fleet is headquartered at Nampo, with submarines based at Pipa Got and minor facilities at Chodo, Pupo-ri, Sagon-ri, Sohae-ri, Sunwi-do, Tasa-ri, and Yogampo-ri.

Naval Aviation: There is no naval aviation per se, but the air force operates the obsolescent Il-28 Beagle bomber (approximately 80 total aircraft), which can perform torpedo attacks, plus approximately 20 obsolescent Su-7 Fitters and approximately 150 even older MiG-19 Farmers that are configured for ground attack. There are also a number of Su-25 Frogfoot ground-attack aircraft.

Coastal Defense: There are about a dozen coastal-defense antiship missile battalions employing fixed and mobile SS-C-2 and HY-2 Styx-type weapons. Artillery in 130-mm and smaller sizes is also emplaced around the coast, and there are a number of coastal radar stations. North Korea has been attempting to develop its own antiship cruise missile, but the degree of success is not known.

Note: Data for North Korea are only marginally reliable, due to secrecy of the North Korean government and the reluctance of the South Korean and other governments to release information. Most weapons and sensors are 1940s to 1950s equipment of Soviet or Chinese origin, except for imported Japanese commercial navigational radars. Nearly all naval ship and craft construction has now halted, and the entire fleet, while still numerous, is essentially obsolescent. In the past several years, most of the older patrol craft have been retired.
There is also reported to be a "Maritime Coastal Security Police" with several patrol boats and up to 100 small patrol launches.

ATTACK SUBMARINES [SS]

♦ **20 Soviet (Chinese version) Romeo class (Project 033)**
Bldr: See remarks (In serv. 1973–95)

D: 1,319 tons surf./1,712 tons sub. **S:** 15.2 kts surf./13 kts sub.
Dim: 76.60 × 6.70 × 4.95
A: 8 (6 fwd/2 aft) 533-mm TT (14 torpedoes or 28 mines)
Electronics:
Radar: 1 Snoop Plate nav./surf. search
Sonar: Tamir-5L active, MG-10 Feniks passive
EW: MRP-11-14-series (Stop Light) intercept (1–18 GHz)
M: Diesel-electric: 2 Type 37D diesels (2,000 bhp each); 2 props; 2,700 shp—2 electric creep motors: 100 shp
Range: 14,000/9 surf.; 350/9 sub.
Endurance: 60 days **Crew:** 8 officers, 43 enlisted

Remarks: Aging Russian design, as modified by China. Four are of Chinese construction (with Type IZ38 diesels of 2,400 bhp each), two transferred in 1973 and two in 1974; they operate on the west coast. By 10-02, two were no longer in service. The others are based on the east coast and were built at Mayang Do in North Korea, completing between 1976 and 1995. One additional unit was lost off the east coast 20-2-85. Diving depth: 300 m (270 normal). 224-cell battery: 6,600 amp-hr.

Disposal note: Four Russian Whiskey-class (Project 613) submarines transferred during the 1960s, while possibly still afloat, are no longer operational; they may, however, be being used as stationary training devices or battery-charging stations.

COASTAL SUBMARINES [SSC]

♦ **6 Sang-o class**
Bldr: Bong Dao Bo SY, Singpo (In serv. 1991–97)

Sang-o-class special forces variant *Ships of the World,* 1996

D: 295 tons surf./325 tons sub. **S:** 7 kts surf./8 kts sub.
Dim: 34.0–35.5 × 3.8 × 3.2
A: Armed version: 4 bow 533-mm TT (no reloads)—transport version: 16 mines in external racks

COASTAL SUBMARINES [SSC] *(continued)*

Electronics:
Radar: 1 Furuno . . . nav.
Sonar: Probable passive array only
M: 1 diesel generator set (probable 300 bhp); 1 shrouded prop; 200 shp
Range: 2,700/8 snorkel
Crew: 11 tot. + 15 special forces or 19 tot. in torpedo-armed version

Remarks: The type is sized somewhere between the midget submarines and the Romeo and Whiskey classes and, from the functional designation, the craft are apparently intended primarily for antiship, coastal defense duties and also for offensive minelaying and special forces insertion. Two or more from the total are unarmed variants equipped to carry special forces personnel. The name means "Shark" and was applied by U.S. intelligence agencies, not North Korea. Said to have been built at about two per year, but production had apparently stopped by 1999. Two, in poor condition, were sold to Vietnam in 1996, and another 16 have been discarded or are in unmaintained reserve.

The special forces transport version unit captured off the South Korean east coast on 17-9-96 was of crude design and manufacture and was specially configured for operation in support of North Korea's Reconnaissance Bureau of the Ministry of the People's Armed Forces, which has two other submarines of the same class under its control based at Toejo Dong; the stranded craft had what appeared to be 16 mine or external cargo canister-carrying fixtures, eight per side, above the waterline but did not have any torpedo tubes.

MIDGET SUBMARINES [SSM]

♦ 36 Yugo class (most in reserve)
Bldr: Yukdaeso-ri SY (In serv. 1965–late 1980s)

Yugo-class special forces variant Associated Press, 8-98

Yugo-class special forces variant Associated Press, 8-98

D: 76 tons surf./90 tons sub. **S:** 10 kts surf./4 kts sub.
Dim: 20.0–22.0 × 2.0 × 1.6
A: Some: 2 bow 533-mm TT (no reloads)
M: 1 MTU diesel, electric drive; 1 7-bladed prop; 160 shp—1 5-bladed freewheeling auxiliary prop for noise reduction
Range: 550/10 surf.; 50/4 sub. **Crew:** 2 + 6–7 special forces personnel

Remarks: Western nickname derives from the probably erroneous belief that Yugoslavia provided some design and technical support input to this extremely primitive design. Primarily intended for the insertion of saboteurs and other special forces personnel and operated for (and possibly by) the Reconnaissance Bureau of the Ministry of the People's Armed Forces rather than the navy proper. As many as 50 may have been built. The oldest units have reached the ends of their useful lives, and nine or more have been discarded. One unarmed unit was caught in a fishing net off the northeast coast of South Korea on 22-8-98 and after the murder/suicide of the nine-man crew was brought into a South Korean port; the craft was not equipped with a sonar system and had no torpedo tubes. The casing and sail are made of GRP. There are 10 watertight compartments to the pressure hull. Small arms and antitank rockets are carried for the saboteur swimmers, as is a rubber boat.

FRIGATES [FF]

♦ 1 Soho class
Bldr: Najin SY (In serv. 5-82)

823

D: 1,600 tons (1,845 fl) **S:** 25 kts **Dim:** 73.8 × 15.5 × 3.8 (hull)
A: 4 P-15 Termit (SS-N-2A Styx) SSM; 1 100-mm 56-cal. B-34 DP; 2 twin 37-mm 63-cal. AA; 2 twin 30-mm 65-cal. AK-230 AA; 2 twin 25-mm 80-cal. 2M-3M AA; 2 5-round RBU-1200 ASW RL
Electronics:
Radar: 1 . . . nav.; 1 Rangout (Square Tie) missile target desig.; 1 MR-104 Rys' (Drum Tilt) gun f.c.
Sonar: MG-10 hull-mounted HF searchlight
M: 2 or 4 diesels; 2 props; approx. 16,000 bhp **Crew:** 190 tot.

Remarks: Reportedly launched in 1980. Catamaran hull. Has a helicopter platform aft. Design was evidently not a success.

CORVETTES [FFL]

♦ 1 Najin class Bldr: Najin SY

631 (In serv. 1975)

Najin-class corvette 531—since stricken JMSDF, 5-93

D: 1,200 tons (1,500 fl) **S:** 25 kts **Dim:** 100.0 × 10.0 × 2.7
A: 2 P-15 Termit (SS-N-2A Styx) SSM; 2 single 100-mm 56-cal. B-34 DP; 2 twin 57-mm 70-cal. AA; 2 twin 30-mm 65-cal. AK-230 AA; 4 twin 25-mm 80-cal. 2M-3 AA; 2 d.c. racks; up to 30 mines
Electronics:
Radar: 1 . . . nav.; 1 Type 351 (Pot Head) surf. search; 1 Fut-B (Slim Net) air search; 1 Rangout (Square Tie) surf. search/missile target acquisition; 1 MR-104 Rys' (Drum Tilt) gun f.c.
Sonar: Probable hull-mounted HF search (Russian Tamir-11 equivalent)
EW: . . . intercept array, 6 3-round decoy RL
M: 2 diesels; 2 props; 15,000 bhp **Range:** 4,000/14 **Crew:** 180 tot.

Remarks: Very primitive design, crude in finish and appearance and not related in origin to any Chinese or Russian design. The trainable twin Termit missile launcher mount replaced a triple 533-mm torpedo tube mount in the early 1980s. The trainable launcher was subsequently replaced by fixed Styx launchers evidently removed from an Osa-class missile boat during the later 1980s; the launchers are oriented directly forward, and the slightest failure during launch would spell disaster. Also added since completion are two AK-230 twin 30-mm AA mountings located centerline abaft each stack, while four twin 14.5-mm AA, two depth-charge mortars, and four RBU-1200 ASW RL have been deleted.

Disposals: Sister 531 was out of service by 10-02.

GUIDED-MISSILE PATROL CRAFT [PTG]

♦ 7 Soju class
Bldr: North Korea (In serv. 1981–93)

D: Approx. 220 tons (fl) **S:** 34 kts **Dim:** 43.0 × 7.5 × 1.8
A: 4 P-15 Termit (SS-N-2A Styx) SSM; 2 twin 30-mm 65-cal. AK-230 AA
Electronics: Radar: 1 Rangout (Square Tie) surf. search/missile target acquisition; 1 MR-104 Rys' (Drum Tilt) gun f.c.
M: 3 Type M-503A diesels; 3 props; 12,000 bhp
Range: . . . / . . . **Crew:** 30–40 tot.

Remarks: North Korean version of the Russian Osa-I. The last two of some 15 to 17 built were delivered during 1993, but by 10-02 only seven remained in use.

♦ 5 Sohung class
Bldr: North Korea (In serv. 1980–81)

D: 80 tons (fl) **S:** 40 kts **Dim:** 26.8 × 6.2 × 1.5
A: 2 P-15 Termit (SS-N-2A Styx) SSM; 1 twin 25-mm 80-cal. 2M-3M AA
Electronics: Radar: 1 Rangout (Square Tie) surf. search/missile target acquisition
M: 4 M-50F-4 diesels; 4 props; 4,800 bhp **Crew:** 19–20 tot.

Remarks: Steel-hulled version of the Soviet Komar class, of which North Korea operated as many as 10 until around 1990. Considering the small number of Sohungs built, the design may not have been successful. One had been stricken by 10-02.

Disposal note: The four ex-Chinese Huangfeng-class guided-missile patrol boats had been discarded by 10-02 as had eight older Soviet-donated Osa-I-class missile boats.

TORPEDO BOATS [PT]

♦ 63 Sin Hung class
Bldr: North Korea (In serv. 1970s)

D: 25 tons (fl) **S:** 40 kts **Dim:** 19.8 × 3.4 × 1.7
A: 2 twin 14.5-mm 93-cal. 2M-7 AA; 2 fixed 450-mm TT

TORPEDO BOATS [PT] *(continued)*

Electronics: Radar: 1 Zarnitsa (Skin Head) or Type 351 (Pot Head) surf. search
M: 2 M-50-F-series diesels; 2 props; 2,400 bhp **Crew:** 15–20 tot.

Remarks: A small number were transferred to foreign clients. Some 21 built during 1981–85 are reported to have had hydrofoils fitted forward as in the Chinese Huchuan class and are referred to as the Sin Hung-Mod. class. A few may have 533-mm torpedo tubes vice 450-mm. More than 50 have been retired or discarded, as the craft were very lightly constructed.

Disposal note: All remaining Soviet-donated P 6–class (Project 183) torpedo boats had been discarded by 10-02.

PATROL CRAFT [PC]

♦ 2 Chongju class
Bldr: . . . (In serv. 1998– . . .)

Remarks: 38-m "stealth" patrol boats with faceted hull and superstructure. Said to be in service as of late 1998, to be capable of 50 kts, to have a crew of 30, and to be armed with 57-mm and 37-mm gunmounts. No other data are available, but the units are unlikely to have modern low-detectable features.

♦ 2 Taechong I and 4 Taechong II class
Bldr: Najin SY (In serv. 1975–95)

D: 385 tons (410 fl) **S:** 30 kts **Dim:** 59.8 × 7.2 × 2.0
A: 1 100-mm 56-cal. B-34 DP; 1 twin 57-mm 70-cal. Type 66 AA; 1 twin 25-mm 80-cal. Type 61M; 2 twin 14.5-mm 93-cal. AA; 2 5-round RBU-1200 ASW RL; 2 d.c. racks; . . . mines
Electronics:
Radar: 1 Type 351 (Pot Head) surf. search
Sonar: Tamir-11 HF (24.5–30 kHz)
M: 4 Soviet Type 40D diesels; 4 props; 8,800 bhp **Range:** 2,000/12
Crew: 75–80 tot.

Remarks: Design strongly resembles the Chinese Hainan class but has a lower superstructure and less freeboard to the hull. The first two have characteristics as above; later units (Taechong II, sometimes referred to as the Mayang class) are 60.8 m o.a. and displace about 420 tons full load but are otherwise similarly equipped. One Taechong I was badly damaged by South Korean Navy gunfire on 15-6-99 in the Yellow Sea. By 10-02, a number of others had been discarded.

Disposal note: All six Chinese Hainan-class and all 14 Chinese Shanghai II–class patrol craft had been discarded by 10-02.

♦ 2 Sariwon class
Bldr: North Korea (In serv. 1965)

D: 450 tons (490 fl) **S:** 21 kts **Dim:** 62.1 × 7.3 × 2.4
A: 2 twin 57-mm 70-cal. AA; 4 quadruple 14.5-mm 93-cal. AA
Electronics:
Radar: 1 Don-2 nav.; 1 Type 351 (Pot Head) surf. search
EW: No intercept; 4 6-round decoy RL
M: 2 diesels; 2 props; 3,000 bhp **Range:** 2,700/18 **Crew:** 65–70 tot.

Remarks: Data are approximate only. Possible current pennant numbers: 725, 726, 727, 728. One reportedly serves as flagship of the Maritime Coastal Security Police fleet, and a third unit has been stricken. Have been rearmed with Chinese-made 57-mm mounts fore and aft and 14.5-mm machinegun mounts; all ASW ordnance appears to have been removed. Similar to the *Tral*-class unit but have a more angular and higher bridge superstructure. May have mine rails.

♦ 4 Soviet S.O. 1 class (Project 215) (In serv. 1957–68)

D: 190 tons (215 fl) **S:** 28 kts **Dim:** 42.0 × 6.1 × 1.9
A: 1 85-mm 52-cal. DP; 2 single 37-mm 63-cal. AA; 2 twin 14.5-mm 93-cal. 2M-7 AA
Electronics: Radar: 1 Don-2 nav. or 1 Type 351 (Pot Head) surf. search
M: 3 Type 40D diesels; 3 props; 7,500 bhp **Range:** 1,100/13 **Crew:** 30–40 tot.

Remarks: Six were transferred from the USSR in antisubmarine configuration during 1957–61; the remainder were built in North Korea for patrol purposes and were all in service by 1968. A dozen had been discarded by 10-02. Design was considered cramped by the Soviets, and the craft are bad rollers and very noisy. These are the last operated by any navy.

Disposal note: The remaining *Tral*-class patrol craft (former minesweeper), 671, had been discarded by 10-02.

PATROL BOATS [PB]

♦ 18 Sinpo class (In serv. 1970s–80s)

D: 60 tons (70 fl) **S:** 43 kts **Dim:** 25.40 × 6.24 × 1.35
A: 2 single 37-mm 63-cal. AA; 4 d.c. in tilt racks
Electronics: Radar: 1 Zarnitsa (Skin Head) or Type 351 (Pot Head) surf. search
M: 4 M-50F-4 diesels; 4 props; 4,800 bhp **Range:** 600/30, 900/14
Crew: 15–20 tot.

Remarks: Built on a steel version of the P-6 torpedo boat hull. Some may also have one or two twin 25-mm 2M-3M AA mounts, making them badly overloaded and unsteady gun platforms.

♦ 14 Chong Jin class
Bldr: North Korea (In serv. 1975– . . .)

D: 82 tons (fl) **S:** 40 kts **Dim:** 27.7 × 6.4 × 1.8
A: 1 85-mm 52-cal. tank gun; 2 twin 14.5-mm 93-cal. 2M-7 AA
Electronics: Radar: 1 . . . nav. or Zarnitsa (Skin Head) or Type 351 (Pot Head) surf. search
M: 4 Soviet M-50-series diesels; 4 props; 4,800 bhp
Range: 325/19 **Crew:** 24 tot.

Remarks: A variant of the Chaho class, differing primarily in armament. One was sunk by South Korean naval forces on the west coast on 14-6-99. By 10-02 37 others had been discarded.

♦ 18 Chaho class
Bldr: North Korea (In serv. 1974–late 1970s)

D: 82 tons (fl) **S:** 40 kts **Dim:** 27.7 × 6.4 × 1.8
A: 2 twin 14.5-mm 93-cal. 2M-7 AA; 1 40-round 122-mm BM-21 artillery RL (40 reloads)
Electronics: Radar: 1. . . nav. or Zarnitsa (Skin Head) or Type 351 (Pot Head) surf. search
M: 4 Soviet M-50-series diesels; 4 props; 4,800 bhp
Range: 325/19 **Crew:** 24 tot.

Remarks: Based on the P-6 torpedo boat design, but with a steel hull. Three transferred to Iran in 4-87 had a twin 23-mm AA mount aft and no gunmount forward; some or all of the North Korean examples may now be similarly armed. The rockets are primarily intended to be expended at surface ship targets, although they may have a secondary shore bombardment function. By 10-02 34 others had been discarded.

♦ 10 or more TB-11PA class
Bldr: . . ., North Korea (In serv. 1980s)

D: 8 tons (fl) **S:** 35 kts **Dim:** 11.2 × 2.7 × 1.0
A: 1 14.5-mm 93-cal. mg **Electronics:** Radar: 1 Type 24 nav.
M: 2 DOHC diesels; 2 props; 520 bhp **Range:** 200/15 **Crew:** 4 tot.

Remarks: GRP hull-construction. Used for harbor patrol by the Maritime Coastal Security Police. There is also a larger version known as the "TB 40A," of which six or more may be in service. The "Type 24" radar is probably a Japanese commercial import.

♦ . . . infiltration craft
Bldr: . . ., North Korea

D: 5 tons (fl) **S:** 35 kts **Dim:** 9.3 × 2.5 × 1.0
A: 1 14.5-mm 93-cal. mg **Electronics:** Radar: 1 Furuno 701 nav.
M: 1 8-cyl. OHC diesel; 260 bhp **Crew:** 2 tot. + 4–6 infiltrators

Remarks: Above characteristics are typical of the large number of craft built over the last 30 years to infiltrate saboteurs into South Korea. Most have had wooden hulls and are distinguished by a very low freeboard to avoid being detected.

MINE-COUNTERMEASURES CRAFT

♦ 18 Yukto I– and 1 Yukto II–class minesweeping boats [MSB]
Bldr: . . ., North Korea

D: 60 tons (fl) **S:** 12 kts **Dim:** 24.0 × 4.0 × . . .
A: 1 twin 14.5-mm 93-cal. 2M-7 AA; 4 mines
M: 2 diesels; 2 props; 300 bhp **Crew:** 16–20 tot.

Remarks: Characteristics are estimated. Built during the 1980s as replacements for the 1950s-supplied Soviet KM-4 class. The surviving Yukto II class is reportedly 21.0 m o.a. All are of wooden construction and are capable only of sweeping moored mechanical mines.

AMPHIBIOUS CRAFT

♦ 4 Hantae-class utility landing craft [LCU] (In serv. 1980s)

D: 350 tons (fl) **S:** 12 kts **Dim:** 48.0 × 6.5 × 2.0
A: 4 twin 25-mm 80-cal. 2M-3M AA
M: 2 diesels; 2 props; 4,350 bhp **Range:** 2,000/12 **Crew:** 40 tot.

Remarks: All data estimated. Can transport three tanks and up to 350 unsheltered troops for short distances. Six others had been discarded by 10-02.

♦ 4 Hanchon-class medium landing craft [LCM]
Bldr: North Korea

D: 145 tons (fl) **S:** 10 kts **Dim:** 35.7 × 7.9 × 1.2
A: 1 twin 14.5-mm 93-cal. AA
Electronics: Radar: 1 Zarnitsa (Skin Head) surf. search
M: 2 Soviet 3D12 diesels; 600 bhp **Range:** 600/6 **Crew:** 16 tot.

Remarks: Data are estimated. Believed capable of carrying two tanks or 200 troops for short distances. Five others have been retired.

Disposal note: All 18 Hangnam-class vehicle landing craft [LCM] had been discarded by 10-02.

♦ 7 U.S. Hand Grenade–series fast infiltration launches [LCP]
Bldr: Fountain Powerboat Industries, Inc., Beaufort County, N.C. (In serv. 1993)

Remarks: Ordered between 11-92 and 3-93 were three 11.6-m, one 14.3-m, and three 14.6-m high-speed boats allegedly for racing purposes but actually for saboteur infiltration. All are said to be capable of speeds greater than 100 kts and are powered by diesel engines producing 2,000 bhp (although they are said to require intensive maintenance and to have engines that easily self-destruct). The craft are radar-equipped and probably carry small arms. The total cost was $1.71 million. The American agent who purchased the craft was belatedly indicted in 11-98 under the Trading with the Enemy Act, but by then the craft had been delivered.

♦ 60 Nampo-class assault landing craft [LCP]
Bldr: North Korea

D: 82 tons (fl) **S:** 40 kts **Dim:** 27.7 × 6.1 × 1.8
A: 2 twin 14.5-mm 93-cal. AA
Electronics: Radar: 1 Zarnitsa (Skin Head) or Type 351 (Pot Head) surf. search
M: 4 M-50F-4 diesels; 4 props; 4,800 bhp **Range:** 325/19 **Crew:** 19 tot.

AMPHIBIOUS CRAFT *(continued)*

Nampo-class personnel landing craft—configured as a patrol boat with Najin-class corvette in the background Siegfried Breyer Collection

Remarks: Some were exported as patrol boats with the bow door welded up, and some may be in a similar status in North Korea. The steel hull is essentially that of the Chaho/Sin Hung series, using the forward compartment to accommodate about 30 troops but no vehicles. Troops debark via a narrow gangway over the bow. After a sustained voyage with the craft planing, the troops would probably be in no condition to conduct combat operations. By 10-02 35 other units of the class had been discarded.

♦ **40 Kong Bang–series surface-effect personnel landing craft [LCPA]** Bldr: North Korea (In serv. mid-1980s to 1992)

Remarks: Probably based on an imported British Hovercraft SRN-6 prototype. Aside from the 25-m Mod. 1 prototype, there are about 55 twin-engine, 21-m Mod. 2 and 79 single-engine, 18-m Mod. 3. Each variant can probably transport not more than one squad of fully equipped troops, and ranges (assuming they are meant to return) are probably not more than 120–150 n.m. in loaded condition, at around 40–45 kts. By 10-02, 95 others of the class had been discarded.

♦ **. . . saboteur infiltration submersibles [LSDV]**

D: 10 tons sub. **S:** 40–50 kts surf./4–6 kts sub. **Dim:** 12.8 × . . . × . . .
M: 3 gasoline outdrive engines; 3 props
Range: . . . / . . . **Crew:** 4 crew + 2–5 swimmers

Remarks: Can fully submerge to a depth of about 3 m. Based on the east coast at Impo-ri. A craft of this type was sunk by gunfire on 18-12-98, the four-man crew having committed suicide. May be of GRP construction. Like the Cluster Osprey class, this design is launched by a 50- to 100-ton mother ship disguised as a fishing boat.

♦ **8 or more Cluster Osprey–class semi-submersible saboteur infiltration launches [LSDV]**
Bldr: . . . SY, Wonsan (In serv. 1985– . . .)

Cluster Osprey semi-submersible—artist's impression *Ships of the World,* 3-99

D: 5 tons **S:** 50 kts (surf.) **Dim:** 9.3 × 2.50 × . . .
M: 3 gasoline outdrive engines; 3 props **Crew:** 6 tot.

Remarks: Intended for saboteur delivery to South Korea, traveling surfaced until near the insertion point and then ballasting down to run in awash.

Note: Also said to be in use for sabotage and infiltration missions are several two-man submersibles capable of diving to 5–8 m depth.

AUXILIARIES

♦ **1 Kowan-class submarine rescue ship [ASR]**
Bldr: Najin SY (In serv. late 1980s)

5992

Kowan-class submarine rescue ship 5992 Boris Lemachko Collection

D: Approx. 2,100 tons (fl) **S:** 12–14 kts **Dim:** 84.0 × 14.3 × 3.9
A: 6 twin 14.5-mm 93-cal. 2M-7 AA
Electronics: Radar: 1 . . . nav.
M: 4 diesels; 2 props; 8,000 bhp **Crew:** 160 tot.

Remarks: Catamaran hull, presumably intended to straddle a sunken submarine, although there is no sign of heavy lift gear or even a rescue bell.

Note: There are said to be eight oceangoing cargo ships adapted for use as midget submarine mother ships [AS], with names reported to be *Choong Seong-Ho No. 1, Choong Seong-Ho No. 2, Choong Seong-Ho No. 3, Dong Hae-Ho, Geon Ae Gook-Ho, Hae Gum Gang-Ho, Song Rim-Ho,* and *Soo Gun-Ho;* no data available. Converted fishing craft are believed by South Korea to be used as intelligence collection vessels [AGI].

SERVICE CRAFT

Remarks: There are undoubtedly a large number of small service craft for use as stores carriers, personnel ferries, and so forth, but no data are available. The civilian hydrographic service operates four coastal survey craft.

KOREA, SOUTH

Republic of Korea

SOUTH KOREAN NAVY

Personnel: About 63,000 total, including 28,000 marines

Bases: Fleet headquarters is at Chinhae. First Fleet Headquarters is at Donghae, with lesser facilities at Kojin, Kisamun, Pohang, Chukpyon, and Kuryonpo. Second Fleet Headquarters is at Pyongtaek, with lesser facilities at Daechung Do, Ochong Do, Ijak Do, and Yong Pyong Do. Third Fleet Headquarters is at Chinhae, near Pusan, with repair and submarine facilities at Chinhae, repair facilities at Pusan and Ulsan, and lesser facilities at Kadok Do, Yokchi Do, Komun Do, Hansan Do, Cheja Do, Cheju Do, Mokpo, and Geoje Do. Air bases are at Chinhae and Pohang. A new surface combatant base is to be constructed south of Pusan at Namsu to replace Chinhae as headquarters of the Third Fleet.

Naval Aviation: Fixed wing: eight P-3C Update III Orion (with AGM-84C Harpoon SSM) and eight S-2C/E Tracker maritime patrol aircraft, and five Reims-Cessna F-406 Caravan II target-services aircraft. Helicopters: 17 AgustaWestland Super Lynx Mk 99 and 13 Super Lynx Mk 100 helicopters for shipboard service, six AS.316B and AS.319B Alouette-III helicopters assigned to the marine corps, 10 UH-60 Blackhawk and 10 UH-1 Huey utility helicopters, and two OH-58 Kiowa training helicopters. ROK Air Force F-16 fighters are equipped to launch U.S.-supplied AGM-84C Harpoon antiship missiles, of which 36 were ordered during 1995. The radars in the P-3C Orion aircraft have been upgraded from APS-134(V)6 to APS-137(V)6, adding an inverse synthetic aperture (ISAR) capability for tracking and identifying targets. Permission was requested of the U.S. Congress during 8-02 for the sale of nine excess P-3B Orion airframes, along with new engines and updated avionics.

South Korean Super Lynx Mk 100—aboard destroyer Kwanggaeto-Daewang (DD 971) Mitsuhiro Kadota, 2-01

Coastal Defense: Three batteries of shore-based RGM-84 Harpoon antiship missiles were ordered early in 1987. There are radar surveillance sites at frequent intervals along the coast.

Weapons and Sensors: Most systems still in use are of U.S. or European origin, although Korean electronics firms such as GoldStar and Samsung are manufacturing European electronics under license. GoldStar is developing the White Shark heavyweight wire-guided submarine torpedo based on the U.S. Alliant NT-37 series, and the lightweight Blue Shark ASW torpedo is also under development. White Shark uses the battery and propulsion system from the German SUT. Blue Shark is to have an ROK-designed acoustic seeker and a 60-km fiber-optic cable connection to the launching ship. It will search passively at 18 kts, closes targets at 35 kts, and has a final run-in speed of 53 kts. The standard ASW torpedo is the U.S. Mk 46 Mod. 1 or Mod. 2, although a few earlier KT-44 (a license-built U.S. Mk 44 of 1960s vintage) may still be available.

SOUTH KOREAN NAVY *(continued)*

South Korean Navy Blackhawk helicopter U.S. Navy, 8-03

On 19-7-00, 110 Standard SM-2 Block IIIA missiles and related equipment were requested from the U.S., at a cost of $159 million.

South Korean destroyers and patrol craft employ a locally built gatling AA mount using the G.E. M197 three-barreled 20-mm Vulcan gun. Daewoo Shipyard developed and manufactures the Nobong, a twin powered mounting for Bofors 40-mm 60-cal. AA guns; the mount incorporates an enclosed local control station.

An antiship missile similar to the U.S. Harpoon but with a range of 200 km is in development; it was planned to enter service in 2003 but is facing delays. Shipboard Super Lynx helicopters are equipped with Sea Skua antiship missiles, of which up to four can be carried.

The Marine Corps acquired 28 U.S. SMAW (Shoulder-launched Multipurpose Assault Weapon) launchers in 10-98, with plans to acquire 200 more later; the Mk 153 Mod. 1 launcher can fire either Mk 6 Mod. 0 HEAA (High-Explosive Anti-Armor) or HEDP (High-Explosive Dual-Purpose) rockets to a range of 500 m.

Note: Pennant numbers are subject to change at unspecified intervals. The numerals 0 and 4 are considered unlucky and are not used.

ATTACK SUBMARINES [SS]

♦ 0 (+ 3) German Type 214/1700

Bldr: Hyundai Shipyard, Ulsan

	Laid down	L	In serv.
S . . .	. . .	. . .	2007
S . . .	. . .	. . .	2008
S . . .	. . .	. . .	2009

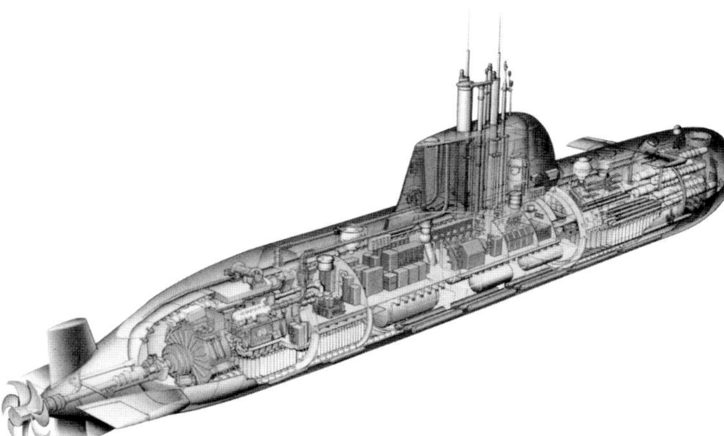

Type 214 submarine HDW, 2000

D: 1,700 tons surf./1,860 tons sub.
S: 10.5 kts surf./21.0 kts sub. (2–6 kts sub. on fuel cells)
Dim: 65.00 × 6.30 × 6.6
A: 8 bow 533-mm TT (16 tot. wire-guided torpedoes and UGM-84C Harpoon missiles)
Electronics:
Radar: 1 . . . nav./surf. search
Sonar: cylindrical MF bow passive array, LF through MF passive flank array; towed LF linear passive array; passive ranging array; active range and bearing array
EW: . . . intercept; Sonartech Atlas torpedo-detection and tracking syst.
M: 2 MTU 16V 396–series diesel generator sets (1,000+ kw each), 1 Siemens Permasyn motor; . . . shp—2 × 120-kw Siemens PEM fuel-cell auxiliary propulsion units
Range: 12,000/. . . surf.; 8,000/8 snorkel; 2,400/4 sub. on fuel cells; 420/8 on battery
Endurance: 50 days **Crew:** 27 tot. (accomm. for 35)

Remarks: The design was selected 3-11-00. The submarines will be built in South Korea with the technical assistance of Howaldtswerke, which will also assist South Korean designers in preparing a follow-on 3,000-ton submarine design. The German government approved the delivery of the necessary $590 million worth of production equipment on 6-5-01. There were originally to have been six second-generation submarines ordered. The Type 214 is an expanded version of the German-Italian Type 212 design; three others have been ordered for the Greek Navy.
Hull systems: Inner and outer hulls are of austenitic steel. The submarines are to have 10% reserve buoyancy. Maximum diving depth is 400 meters. Battery set to develop 600–900 V. Are to have the hydrogen peroxide Siemens Polymer Electrolite Membrane (PEM) fuel-cell air- independent auxiliary propulsion system.
Combat systems: May employ the STN Atlas Elektronik ISUS 90 combat data system. The sonar array is to include cylindrical MF passive array forward, an MF/LF passive flank system (with three arrays per side), a towed LF passive array, an active ranging set, and a bow-mounted active mine-avoidance set. A Zeiss SERO 400 optronic, non-hull-penetrating periscope and Zeiss OMS 100 mast will be used. Four of the eight weapons tubes will have expulsion systems to enable launching antiship missiles; the others will be of the swim-out variety.

Note: A Russian offer of two to six Kilo-class (Project 636) submarines, made during 5-98, was formally declined late during 10-00.

♦ 9 German Type 209/1200

Bldr: Daewoo SY, Okpo (SS 061: Howaldtswerke, Kiel)

	L	In serv.
SS 61 Jang Bogo	18-6-92	2-6-93
SS 62 Lee Chun	12-10-92	30-4-94
SS 63 Choi Museon	7-8-93	27-2-95
SS 65 Park Wi	21-5-94	3-2-96
SS 66 Lee Jongmu	17-5-95	29-8-96
SS 67 Jeong Un	5-5-96	3-98 (del. 29-8-97)
SS 68 Lee Sunsin	21-5-98	2-00 (del. 31-1-00)
SS 69 Na Daeyong	6-99	11-00
SS 71 Lee Eokgi	26-5-00	30-11-01 (del.)

Jang Bogo (SS 061) U.S. Navy, 7-04

Choi Museon (SS 063) U.S. Navy, 10-00

Park Wi (SS 065) Brian Morrison, 6-00

D: 1,100 tons surf./1,285 tons sub. **S:** 11 kts surf./22 kts sub.
Dim: 56.10 × 6.20 (7.60 over stern planes) × 5.50 (surf.)
A: 8 bow 533-mm TT (14 STN Atlas Elektronik SUT Mod. 2 torpedoes or 28 mines)
Electronics:
Radar: 1 . . . multimode
Sonar: STN Atlas Elektronik CSU-83 suite
EW: G.T.E. Ferret intercept (1–40 GHz); ArgoSystems AR-700 intercept

ATTACK SUBMARINES [SS] *(continued)*

M: 4 MTU 12V493 AZ 80 diesels (800 bhp each), 4 Siemens 405-kw generator sets, 1 electric motor; 1 prop; 5,000 shp
Range: 7,500/8 surf.; 11,300/4 snorkel; 28/20, 230/8, 466/4 sub. **Fuel:** 85 tons
Endurance: 50 days **Crew:** 8 officers, 27 enlisted (39 accomm.)

Remarks: SS 61 was built in Germany and handed over 15-10-92, while the next two were assembled in South Korea using components shipped from Germany. Phase II units were assembled in Korea, with a steadily increasing proportion of all-Korean materials and components, but some critical structures and all sensor and machinery equipment continued to be imported. The first three were ordered during 2-88, to standard IKL design; a second group of three was ordered during 1991. The third increment was ordered by 5-95, but a planned fourth trio was dropped. SS 61 left Kiel 16-4-93 aboard the dock ship *Dock Express 11.* Average cost said to be $186 million. SS 63 was named for Admiral Choi Museon, who defeated 500 Japanese ships in 1326.

Consideration is being given to adding an AIP (Air-Independent Propulsion) module and the ability to launch UGM-84C Harpoon antiship missiles during future refits.
Hull systems: Are reportedly the quietest-yet Type 209 submarines, due to the use of advanced sound-damping rafting of the machinery. Maximum diving depth is 320 m, with a 250-m working depth. Have four 120-cell, 11,500-amp-hr batteries weighing a total of 257 tons.
Combat systems: Equipped with the STN Atlas Elektronik ISUS 83 (Integrated Sensor Underwater System) combat data system, with four display consoles. Have the Ferranti FMS-15 acoustic processor for a towed passive linear hydrophone system and also the Ferranti AP2000 autopilot. Reported to have an ArgoSystems intercept system with a Deutsche Aerospace USK 800/1 periscope-mounted antenna. Only 96 SUT torpedoes were ordered, the intention being to switch to an indigenous weapon made by South Korea's GoldStar. SS 68 and later were to employ nonpenetrating optronic sensor masts. SS 69 and SS 71 are equipped to launch UGM-84 Harpoon antiship missiles, but no missiles have been ordered.

MIDGET SUBMARINES [SSM]

♦ 6 or more Italian-designed S.X. 756 class
Bldrs: First unit: COS.M.O.S., Livorno; others: Korea Tacoma SY, Masan (In serv. 1988–92)

D: 78 tons surf./83 tons sub. **S:** 8.5 kts surf./6 kts sub. **Dim:** 25.20 × 2.02 × . . .
A: 2 533-mm torpedoes in drop gear or 6–8 mines or 40 limpet mines
M: Diesel-electric: 1 diesel generator set; 1 prop; . . . shp—bow-thruster
Range: 1,600/7 surf.; 60/4.5 sub. **Endurance:** 20 days
Crew: 6 tot. + 8 commandos

Remarks: The design was originated by COS.M.O.S. and was built under license or possibly from prefabricated kits. Can operate at up to 100-m depth. Have one fixed and one telescoping periscope. A passive sonar transducer array surrounds the small sail.

♦ 3 KSS-1 (Dolgorae) class
Bldr: Hyundai SY, Ulsan

	In. serv
SSM 51	1-3-85
SSM 52	8-11-90
SSM 53	10-12-91

D: 150 tons surf./175 tons sub. **S:** 6 kts surf./9 kts sub. **Dim:** . . . × . . . × . . .
A: 2 bow 533-mm TT (no reloads)
Electronics: Sonar: STN Atlas Elektronik active set and passive array
M: 1 diesel generator set; 1 prop; . . . shp
Crew: 6 tot. + 8 combat swimmers

Remarks: Reportedly the first was delivered in 1983, the others in 1988. May not be assigned to the ROKN proper. Photos show a broad hull, a bulbous bow sonar installation, and a small sail incorporating a folding snorkel mast. There is a single periscope. Are supported by the tender *Dadohae* (ASL 50).

GUIDED-MISSILE DESTROYERS [DDG]

♦ 0 (+ 3) KDX-III class
Bldr: Hyundai Heavy Industries, Ulsan (In serv. 2008–12)

	L	In serv.
. . .	2006	12-08
. . .	2008	2010
. . .	2010	2012

KDX-III class—computer rendering Hyundai Heavy Industries, 2005

D: 7,000 tons (10,000 fl) **S:** 30+ kts **Dim:** 165.0 × 22.0 × 10.5
A: 16 RGM-84C Block II Harpoon SSM; 2 Mk 41 vertical-launch groups (128-total Standard SM-2 MR Block III SAM, VLA ASROC and ESSM missiles); 1 21-round RAM Mk 31 Mod. 1 point-defense SAM syst.; 1 127-mm 62-cal. U.S. Mk 45 Mod. 4 DP; 1 30-mm Goalkeeper CIWS; 2 triple 324-mm Mk 32 ASW TT (Blue Shark or Mk 46 Mod. 2 torpedoes); 2 Super Lynx Mk 99 ASW helicopters
Electronics:
Radar: 1 AIL SPS-67(V)3 surf. search; 1 Lockheed Martin SPY-1D 3-D search/weapons control; 3 Raytheon SPG-62 target illumination; 1 Thales SMART-L early warning; 1 Thales Goalkeeper f.c.
Sonar: . . .
EW: . . . intercept/jamming; Mk 36 SRBOC decoy syst. (4 6-round Raytheon Mk 137 RL); Daewoo towed torpedo decoy syst.
M: COGAG: 4 G.E. LM-2500 gas turbines (32,480 shp each)
Electric: 9,000 kw tot.
Range: 4,500/20 **Crew:** 350 tot.

Note: Under a 25-7-02 decision, the three KDX-III guided-missile destroyers will be equipped with the Lockheed-Martin SPY-1-series Aegis principal radar/combat system, which will cost $950 million for the three. The first is to enter service in 2008, the second in 2010, and the third commissioned in 2012. Another three may be built later. Hyundai started detailed design during 2001.

DESTROYERS [DD]

♦ 4 (+ 2) KDX-II class
Bldr: Daewoo Shipbuilding, Okpo and Hyundai SY, Ulsan*

	L	In serv.
975 Choong Moo Gong Lee Soon Shin	20-5-02	2003
976 Moonmu Daewang*	11-4-03	30-9-04
977 Dae Jo Young	12-11-03	6-05
978 Wang Geong*	3-5-05	2006
979 Gang Gam Chan	16-3-06	2007
980 Chae Yaon	2007	2008

Choong Moo Gong Lee Soon Shin (DD 975) Michael Winter, 6-05

Choong Moo Gong Lee Soon Shin (DD 975) Michael Nitz, 7-05

Choong Moo Gong Lee Soon Shin (DD 975) Michael Nitz, 7-05

D: 4,200 tons (5,000 fl) **S:** 30+ kts **Dim:** 149.5 × 17.4 × 4.3 (hull)
A: 8 RGM-84C Harpoon SSM; 4 8-cell Mk 41 vertical launch modules (32 Standard SM-2 MR Block IIIA missiles and Vertical-Launch ASROC ASW missiles); 1 21-round RAM Mk 31 Mod. 1 point-defense SAM syst.; 1 127-mm 62-cal. U.S. Mk 45 Mod. 4 DP; 1 30-mm Goalkeeper CIWS; 2 single 20-mm M61A1 Vulcan gatling AA; 2 triple 324-mm Mk 32 ASW TT (Blue Shark or Mk 46 Mod. 2 torpedoes); 2 Super Lynx Mk 99 ASW helicopters

DESTROYERS [DD] *(continued)*

Electronics:
Radar: 1 . . . nav.; 1 Thales-GoldStar MW-08 surf./air search; 1 Raytheon SPS-49(V)5 air search; 2 Thales-GoldStar STIR 2.4 f.c.; 2 Raytheon OT-134 missile target illuminators; 1 Thales Goalkeeper f.c.
Sonar: STN Atlas Elektronik DSQS-21 hull-mounted LF; Daewoo . . . towed linear passive array
EW: . . . intercept/jamming; Mk 36 SRBOC decoy syst. (4 6-round Raytheon Mk 137 RL); Daewoo towed torpedo decoy syst.
M: CODOG: 2 G.E. LM-2500 gas turbines (32,480 shp each), 2 MTU 20V956 TB92 diesels (5,140 bhp each); 2 Bird-Johnson CP props; 64,960 shp max.
Electric: 3,200 kw tot. (4 × 800-kw diesel sets)
Range: 4,500/18 **Crew:** 320 tot.

Remarks: Follow-on to KDX-I design, with improved armament. Cost approximately $385 million each. *Moonmu Daewang* is sometimes referred to as *Moomnu the Great* in English translations.
Hull systems: Are the first ROKN combatant ships with accommodations for female crew.
Combat systems: Has BAE Systems–Samsung KDCOM combat data system with 10 display consoles, Thales databus, and U.S. WDS Mk 14 weapon-direction system. The Link 11–equivalent Korean Naval Tactical Datalink System (KNTDS) is also carried.

♦ 3 Kwanggaeto-Daewang (KDX-I) class
Bldr: Daewoo Shipbuilding, Okpo

	Laid down	L	In serv.
DD 971 Kwanggaeto-Daewang	10-95	28-10-96	27-7-98
DD 972 Ulchimundok	. . .	15-10-97	1-9-99
DD 973 Yang Manchun	1997	10-98	6-00

Yang Manchun (DD 973) Mitsuhiro Kadota, 2004

Kwanggaeto-Daewang (DD 971) Mitsuhiro Kadota, 2004

D: 3,181 tons light (3,855 fl) **S:** 33 kts (18 on diesels)
Dim: 135.4 × 14.2 × 4.3 (hull)
A: 8 RGM-84C Harpoon SSM; 1 Mk 48 Mod. 2 vertical missile launch syst. group (16 Sea Sparrow RIM-7M SAM); 1 127-mm 54-cal. OTO Melara DP; 2 30-mm Goalkeeper gatling CIWS; 2 triple 324-mm ASW TT; 2 Super Lynx helicopters (Sea Skua ASM and Mk 46 Mod. 2 ASW torpedoes)
Electronics:
Radar: 1 ISC-Cardion SPS-55M surf. search; 1 Thales MW-08 surveillance; 1 Raytheon SPS-49(V)5 air search; 2 Thales STIR 1.8 f.c.; 2 Thales Goalkeeper f.c. sets
Sonar: STN Atlas Elektronik DSQS-21BZ hull-mounted; provision for Thales towed linear passive hydrophone array
EW: ArgoSystems APECS-II/AR-700 intercept/jammer suite; 2 330- to 340-round Matra Défense Dagaie Mk 2 decoy RL syst.; SLQ-25 Nixie towed acoustic torpedo decoy syst.
M: CODOG: 2 G.E. LM-2500 gas turbines (29,500 shp each), 2 MTU 20V956 TB92 diesels (5,140 bhp each); 2 Bird-Johnson CP props; 59,000 shp max.
Electric: 3,200 kw tot. (4 × 800-kw diesel sets)
Range: 4,500/18 **Crew:** 15 officers, 170 enlisted (286 tot. accomm.)

Remarks: Totals as high as 17–20 had originally been planned, but only three were built. The first unit is named for the 19th monarch of the Koguryo Dynasty, who ruled from 391 to 413 A.D. over most of what is now North Korea.

Kwanggaeto-Daewang (DD 971) Mitsuhiro Kadota, 2004

Hull systems: Have a constant-pressure sealed NBC warfare protective citadel.
Combat systems: The BAE Systems–Thales SSCS Mk 7 system (similar to that in the British Type 23 frigate class), with two Thales multifunction weapons-control consoles and eight fiber optic–linked operator consoles, is fitted; more than 100 distributed microprocessors are employed. Have Warner UPX-27 IFF interrogation for the Mk 10 IFF system. The listed passive towed-array sonar system may be added later but was not aboard as of 1999.

♦ 2 ex-U.S. Gearing FRAM I class
Bldr: Consolidated Steel, Orange, Texas (DD 922: Federal SB, Newark, N.J.)

	Laid down	L	In serv.
DD 921 Kwangju (ex-*Richard E. Kraus*, DD 849)	31-7-45	2-3-46	23-5-46
DD 922 Kangwon (ex-*William R. Rush*, DD 714)	19-10-44	8-7-45	21-9-45

Kwangju (DD 921)—with retired *Daejeon* (DD 919) and *Cheju* (APD 822) alongside *Ships of the World*, 10-98

D: 2,425 tons (3,500 fl) **S:** 30 kts
Dim: 119.03 (116.74 wl) × 12.52 × 4.45 (6.4 sonar)
A: 8 RGM-84C Harpoon SSM; 2 twin 127-mm 38-cal. Mk 30 DP; 1 twin 40-mm 60-cal. Nobong AA; 2 single 20-mm G.E. Vulcan gatling AA; 2 triple 324-mm Mk 32 ASW TT; 1 Mk. 9 d.c. rack (12 Mk 9 d.c.); 1 Super Lynx Mk 99 ASW helicopter
Electronics:
Radar: 1 Raytheon SPS-10 surf. search; 1 Thales DA-08 air search; 1 Western Electric Mk 25 f.c.
Sonar: Raytheon DE 1191 hull-mounted (5–7 kHz)
TACAN: SRN-15
EW: WLR-1 intercept; 2 decoy RL; T Mk 6 Fanfare acoustic torpedo decoy
M: 2 sets General Electric geared steam turbines; 2 props; 60,000 shp
Boilers: 4 Babcock & Wilcox; 39.8 kg/cm^2, 454° C **Electric:** 1,200 kw tot.
Range: 975/32; 2,400/25; 4,800/15 **Fuel:** 640 tons **Crew:** 274 tot.

Remarks: DD 921 was purchased 25-2-77 and DD 922 on 1-7-78. DD 921 is based at Inchon, and DD 922 at Donghae.
Combat systems: Have one director for the Mk 37 f.c.s. for the 127-mm guns and a Mk 51 Mod. 2 lead-computing director for the 40-mm mount. The U.S. Mk 1 Mod. 2 40-mm AA mount added forward between the ASW torpedo tubes was replaced with a powered Nobong mounting. Korean-designed mountings for the Vulcan gatling guns are located amidships on the Harpoon ships. Harpoon missiles were added amidships during 1979. The obsolete U.S. Mk 29 radars were replaced by DA-08 during the mid-1990s.
Disposals: *Kyonggi* (DD 923, ex-*Newman K. Perry,* DD 883) was stricken in 1998. *Jeonju* (DD 925, ex-*Rogers,* DD 876) was stricken during 2000 and is now a memorial at Tonghae. *Daejeon* (DD 919, ex-*New*, DD 818) was retired from service by 2005. Ex-Gearing FRAM II–class *Chungbuk* (DD 915) was no longer in service as of 2000.

FRIGATES [FF]

♦ 9 Ulsan (HDF 2000) class

	Bldr	L	In serv.
FF 951 Ulsan	Hyundai SY, Ulsan	8-4-80	1-1-81
FF 952 Seoul	Korea SB, Pusan	24-4-84	30-6-85
FF 953 Chungnam	Hanjin Industrial SB, Masan	26-10-84	1-6-86
FF 955 Masan	Daewoo SB & Heavy Mach., Okpo	26-10-84	20-7-85
FF 956 Keongbuk	Korea SB, Pusan	15-1-86	30-5-86
FF 957 Jeonnam	Hyundai SY, Ulsan	19-4-88	17-6-89
FF 958 Cheju	Daewoo SB & Heavy Mach., Okpo	3-5-88	1-1-90
FF 959 Pusan	Daewoo SB & Heavy Mach., Okpo	20-3-92	1-1-93
FF 961 Cheongju	Hyundai SY, Ulsan	18-2-92	1-6-93

FRIGATES [FF] *(continued)*

Cheju (FF 958) Mitsuhiro Kadota, 2004

Chungnam (FF 953) Takatoshi Okano, 9-02

Cheju (FF 958) Mitsuhiro Kadota, 2004

D: 1,600 tons (1,940 normal, 2,180 fl) **S:** 35+ kts (18 on diesels)
Dim: 105.00 (98.00 pp) × 12.00 × 3.50
A: 8 RGM-84C Harpoon SSM; 2 single 76-mm 62-cal. OTO Melara Compact DP—FF 951–955: 4 twin 30-mm 75-cal. Emerlec EX-30 AA—FF 956–961: 3 twin 40-mm 70-cal. OTO Melara Compact AA—all: 2 triple 324-mm Mk 32 ASW TT; 2 Mk 9 d.c. racks (6 d.c. each)
Electronics:
Radar: FF 951–956: Thales ZW-06 surf. search; 1 Thales DA-05 air search; 1 Thales WM-25 track-while-scan f.c—FF 957–961: 1 SPS-10 surf. search; 1 Samsung-Marconi 1810 surf./air search; 1 Thales DA-05 air search; 1 Samsung-Marconi ST-1802 f.c.
Sonar: Raytheon DE 1167 hull-mounted MF
TACAN: SRN-15
EW: GoldStar ULQ-11K intercept; Mk 36 SRBOC decoy syst. (4 6-round Mk 137 RL); SLQ-25 Nixie towed acoustic torpedo decoy syst.
M: CODOG: 2 G.E. LM-2500 gas turbines (27,200 shp each), 2 MTU 12V956 TB82 diesels (3,600 bhp each); 2 CP props; 54,400 shp each
Electric: 1,600 kw tot. (4 × 400-kw diesel sets)
Range: 900/35; 4,000/18 **Crew:** 16 officers, 134 enlisted

Remarks: First South Korean design of a major combatant. FF 953's builder was originally named the Korea-Tacoma Shipbuilding Corp. FF 951 and 953 are based at Chinhae; 952, 957, 958, and 961 at Inchon; and 955, 956, and 959 at Donghae.
Hull systems: Have stern-wedge hullform to improve fuel efficiency and maximum speed. Steel hull and aluminum superstructure.
Combat systems: Have two Thales LIOD optronic standby gun directors in the first five units. FF 955–958 employ three twin OTO Melara 40-mm AA in lieu of the four 30-mm mounts on the first three ships; in addition, FF 957 and later have a radar fire-control system for the after two 40-mm mounts, which are mounted a deck higher than in the other ships. All received a Litton Data Systems computerized combat data/control system, beginning in 1992. The PHS-32 sonars in the first six units had been replaced by the DE 1167 system by 1999.

CORVETTES [FFL]

♦ 24 Pohang (KCX) class

	Bldr.	In serv.	Based at
PCC 756 Pohang	Korea SB & Eng., Pusan	18-12-84	Donghae
PCC 757 Kunsan	Hanjin Industrial SB, Masan	18-12-84	Donghae
PCC 758 Keongju	Hyundai SY, Ulsan	1986	Donghae
PCC 759 Mokpo	Daewoo SB & Hvy. Mach., Okpo	1988	Donghae
PCC 761 Kimchon	Korea SB & Eng., Pusan	5-85	Donghae
PCC 762 Chung Ju	Korea Tacoma, Masan	5-85	Donghae
PCC 763 Jinju	Hyundai SY, Ulsan	1986	Donghae
PCC 765 Yeosu	Daewoo SB & Hvy. Mach., Okpo	1986	. . .
PCC 766 Chinhae	Korea SB & Eng., Pusan	2-89	Inchon
PCC 767 Sunchon	Hanjin Industrial SB, Masan	6-89	Inchon
PCC 768 Yeeree	Hyundai SY, Ulsan	1989	Donghae
PCC 769 Wonju	Daewoo SB & Hvy. Mach., Okpo	8-89	Donghae
PCC 771 Andong	Hanjin Industrial SB, Masan	11-89	Donghae
PCC 772 Cheonan	Korea SB & Eng., Pusan	11-89	Inchon
PCC 773 Seongnam	Daewoo SB & Hvy. Mach., Okpo	5-89	Inchon
PCC 775 Bucheon	Hyundai SY, Ulsan	4-89	Inchon
PCC 776 Jecheon	Hanjin Industrial SB, Masan	5-89	Inchon
PCC 777 Daecheon	Korea SB & Eng., Pusan	4-89	Inchon
PCC 778 Sokcho	Hanjin Industrial SB, Masan	2-90	Inchon
PCC 779 Yeongju	Hyundai SY, Ulsan	3-90	Inchon
PCC 781 Namwon	Daewoo SB & Hvy. Mach., Okpo	4-90	Pusan
PCC 782 Kwangmyeong	Korea SB & Eng., Pusan	7-90	Pusan
PCC 783 Sinheung	Hanjin Industrial SB, Masan	3-93	Chinhae
PCC 785 Gongju	Daewoo SB & Hvy. Mach., Okpo	28-2-94	Chinhae

Mokpo (PCC 759)—early unit with two MM 38 Exocet missile canisters aft and twin 30-mm AA mounts forward and on fantail John Mortimer, 10-98

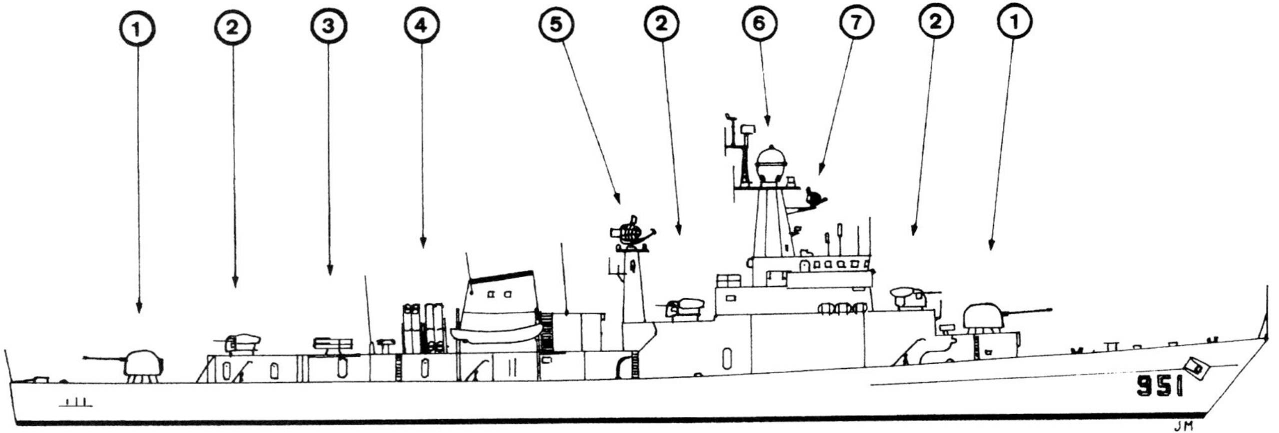

Ulsan (FF 951) 1. 76-mm OTO Melara Compact DP gun 2. 30-mm twin Emerlec AA 3. Triple 324-mm ASW TT 4. Harpoon SSM launch canisters 5. DA-05 surface/air-search radar 6. WM-25 track-while-scan fire-control radar 7. ZW-06 surface-search radar Drawing by Jean Moulin, from *Flottes de Combat*

CORVETTES [FFL] *(continued)*

D: 950 tons (1,220 fl) **S:** 31 kts (15 on diesels)
Dim: 88.30 (83.47 wl) × 10.00 (9.80 wl) × 3.00 (hull)
A: PCC 756–759: 2 MM 38 Exocet SSM; 1 76-mm 62-cal. OTO Melara Compact DP; 2 twin 30-mm 75-cal. Emerlec AA; 2 triple 324-mm Mk 32 ASW TT; 2 Mk 9 d.c. racks (6 Mk 9 d.c. each)—PCC 761 and later: 2 single 76-mm 62-cal. OTO Melara Compact DP; 2 twin 40-mm 70-cal. OTO Melara Compact AA; 2 triple 324-mm Mk 32 ASW TT; 2 Mk 9 d.c. racks (6 Mk 9 d.c. each)

Chinhae (PCC 766)—with Marconi search and fire-control radars
John Mortimer, 10-98

Jinju (PCC 763)—with two single 76-mm mounts and two twin 40-mm mounts, but no antiship missiles
John Mortimer, 10-98

Electronics:
Radar: PCC 756–765:1 Raytheon SPS-64(V) nav.; 1 Thales WM-28 track-while-scan f.c.—PCC 766 and later: 1 Raytheon SPS-64(V) nav.; 1 Marconi ST 1802 surf./air search; 1 Marconi S 1810 f.c.
Sonar: Thales PHS-32 hull-mounted MF
EW: GoldStar ULQ-12K intercept/jammer—PCC 756–759: Mk 36 SRBOC decoy syst. (2 6-round Raytheon Mk 137 RL)—761 and later: 4 9-round Protean decoy RL
M: CODOG: 1 G.E. LM-2500 gas turbine (27,200 or 27,800 shp), 2 MTU 12V956 TB82 diesels (3,130 bhp each); 2 CP props
Electric: 800 or 1,200 kw tot. **Range:** 800/31 (turbine); 4,000/15 (diesel)
Crew: 10 officers, 85 enlisted

Remarks: The weapons and electronics suites evolved over the course of construction of this series. The original name for Hanjin Industrial Shipbuilding Corp. was Korea-Tacoma Shipbuilding Corp.
Hull systems: The first four have a gas turbine rated at 27,200 shp; later units, one rated at 27,800 shp. PCC 766 and later units may have substituted two SEMT-Pielstick 12 PA6 V280 diesels (4,800 bhp each) for the 2 MTU 12V956 TB82 diesels listed. Daewoo advertised only two 400-kw diesel generators on its version, but the other ships may have three.
Combat systems: The first four have the Thales SEWACO ZK combat data system; the others have the Ferranti WSA 423. Only the first four have antiship missiles; they also have a manned twin 30-mm AA mount on the fantail in place of the after 76-mm mount. Units through PCC 765 are equipped with one Thales LIROD optronic director for the 76-mm guns, with the 30-mm weapons being essentially locally controlled. PCC 766 and later have two twin OTO Melara 40-mm AA and no SSM, mount the Marconi 1810 radar at the masthead, and have two Rademac 2400 optronic directors for their 40-mm guns. All carry Motorola MX 1105 NAVSAT.

♦ 4 Donghae (HDC 800) class

	Bldr	In serv.
PCC 751 Donghae	Korea SB & Eng, Pusan	8-82
PCC 752 Suwon	Hanjin Industrial SB, Masan	10-83
PCC 753 Kangreung	Hyundai SY, Ulsan	30-11-83
PCC 755 Anyang	Daewoo SB & Heavy Machinery, Okpo	12-83

D: 800 tons (1,076 fl) **S:** 31 kts
Dim: 78.50 × 10,00 (9.60 wl) × 2.60 (mean hull)
A: 1 76-mm 62-cal. OTO Melara Compact DP; 1 twin 40-mm 60-cal. Bofors AA (U.S. Mk 1 Mod. 2 mount); 2 twin 30-mm 75-cal. Emerlec AA; 2 triple 324-mm Mk 32 ASW TT; 2 Mk 9 d.c. racks (6 Mk 9 d.c. each)
Electronics:
Radar: 1 Raytheon SPS-64(V) nav.; 1 Thales WM-28 track-while-scan f.c.
Sonar: EDO 786 hull-mounted MF
EW: . . . intercept; Mk 34 RBOC II decoy syst. (2 6-round Mk 135 RL)

Anyang (PCC 755) H&L Van Ginderen, 1-00

Donghae (PCC 751) 9-90

M: CODOG: 1 G.E. LM-2500 gas turbine (27,800 shp), 2 MTU 12V956 TB82 diesels (3,120 bhp each); 2 CP props
Range: 800/31; 4,000/15 **Endurance:** 21 days **Crew:** 10 officers, 85 enlisted

Remarks: A more heavily armed version of a similar class built for the South Korean Coast Guard. Distinguished from the *Pohang* class by narrower superstructure, lattice mast, and less distance between mast and stack. All four are based at Chinhae. The ROKN considers these ships to be a part of the KCX class although their characteristics differ in several significant respects.
Combat systems: There is a Thales LIOD optronic director for the 76-mm gun. The 40-mm twin AA is of World War II design and is controlled by an electro-optical director or U.S. Mk 51 gun f.c.s.

GUIDED-MISSILE PATROL BOATS [PTG]

♦ 1 (+ 32) PKM-X Project (new construction)
Bldr: Kangnam, Pusan (In serv. 2003–7)

D: 350 tons (fl) **S:** . . . **Dim:** 56.0 × . . . × . . .
A: 8 RGM-84C Block II Harpoon SSM; 1 76-mm 62-cal. OTO Melara Compact DP; 2 single 40-mm 60-cal. Nobong AA
Electronics:
Radar: 1 Thales MW-08 3-D air search; 1 CelsiusTech Ceros 200 f.c.
Sonar: Simrad SP70 omnidirectional hull-mounted HF
EW: . . . intercept; GoldStar Sonata active jammer
M: CODOG: 2 G.E. LM-500 gas turbines (5,680 shp each), 2 MTU . . . diesels; 2 . . . waterjets

Remarks: The first unit, apparently a prototype, was in service by 2006. A total of 32 are expected to enter service by 2007. The craft are to replace the Chamsuri (Sea Dolphin) patrol craft. Earlier plans to install an OTO Melara 76-mm gun were changed to the employment of Bofors 40-mm guns in locally made powered mountings because the radar f.c. system for the 76-mm gun was thought likely to interfere with control of the short-range Sea Skua missiles. The missiles will be in two twin mountings. The craft will have inferior armament to their North Korean potential adversaries but will have superior fire-control and communications systems.

Disposal note: All eight Paekku (PSMM-5) -class guided missile patrol boats PGM 581, 582, 583, 585, 586, 587, 589, and 591 were retired from service in 2005.

♦ 81 Chamsuri-class (Sea Dolphin) series
Bldr: Hanjin Industrial SB, Chinhae, and Korea SB & Eng., Masan (In serv. 1970s–1980s)

From among . . .

PKM 201 series:

PKM 215	PKM 236	PKM 256	PKM 266	PKM 282	PKM 295
PKM 216	PKM 237	PKM 257	PKM 267	PKM 283	PKM 296
PKM 221	PKM 238	PKM 258	PKM 268	PKM 285	PKM 298
PKM 222	PKM 239	PKM 259	PKM 269	PKM 288	PKM 299
PKM 223	PKM 251	PKM 261	PKM 273	PKM 291	
PKM 227	PKM 252	PKM 262	PKM 276	PKM 292	
PKM 228	PKM 253	PKM 263	PKM 279	PKM 293	
PKM 233	PKM 255	PKM 265	PKM 281	PKM 294	

PKM 301 series:

PKM 311	PKM 321	PKM 329	PKM 339	PKM 359	PKM 368
PKM 312	PKM 322	PKM 331	PKM 351	PKM 361	PKM 369
PKM 313	PKM 323	PKM 333	PKM 352	PKM 362	PKM 371
PKM 316	PKM 325	PKM 335	PKM 353	PKM 363	PKM 372
PKM 317	PKM 326	PKM 336	PKM 355	PKM 365	PKM 373
PKM 318	PKM 327	PKM 337	PKM 356	PKM 366	PKM 375
PKM 319	PKM 328	PKM 338	PKM 358	PKM 367	

D: 113 tons light (156 fl) **S:** 34 kts **Dim:** 33.10 (31.25 wl) × 6.92 × 1.75 (2.45 props)
A: Early PKM 201 series: 1 40-mm 60-cal. Bofors Mk 3; 1 twin 30-mm 75-cal. Emerlec EX-30; 2 single 20-mm 70-cal. Mk 10 Oerlikon AA—late PKM 201 series: 1 twin 30-mm 75-cal. Emerlec EX-30 AA; 1 or 2 single 20-mm Vulcan gatling AA; 2 single 12.7-mm mg—PKM 301 series: 1 40-mm 60-cal. Bofors AA; 2 single 20-mm Vulcan gatling AA; 2 single 12.7-mm M2 mg

GUIDED-MISSILE PATROL BOATS [PTG] *(continued)*

PKM 301-series PKM 372—with enclosed 40-mm AA forward, two enclosed 20-mm gatling guns aft Lt. Cdr. Liza Stephenson, RAN, 10-98

PKM 201-series PKM 282—with twin 30-mm AA mount forward H&L Van Ginderen, 5-97

Electronics: Radar: 1 Raytheon 1645 nav./surf. search
M: 2 MTU 16V538 TB90 diesels; 2 props; 10,800 bhp (9,000 sust.)
Electric: 100 kw tot. (2 × 50-kw diesel sets)
Range: 500/32; 1,000/20 **Fuel:** 15 tons **Crew:** 5 officers, 26 enlisted

Remarks: Built in two series. To be replaced by a new class with heavier armament and better fire-control system.
Hull systems: Designed for 38 kts; can make 32 kts continuous. Daewoo offered the design for export as the DW 150P, or Dangpo, class at 150 tons full load, 37 m o.a., with a top speed of 37 kts and a range of 600 n.m. at 20 kts.
Combat systems: Later units, with 301-series hull numbers, have an enclosed, manned 40-mm mount on the forecastle and enclosed gatling gun mountings atop the superstructure and often also on the fantail; the 40-mm mounts use Mauser GRP enclosures. Most 201-series units have an Emerlec manned, power-operated twin 30-mm mount on the forecastle, and a few older units have an open 40-mm mount on the fantail.
Disposals: Three units were transferred to Kazakhstan in 2006 and five to the Philippines on 15-6-95. Another five were stricken the same year; two of the latter were donated to Bangladesh during 4-00;. PK 357 was sunk during an attack by a North Korean gunboat on 29-6-02; raised on 21-8-02, the craft was found too badly damaged to be returned to service.

MINE WARFARE SHIPS

♦ 1 Wonsan-class minelayer [MM] Bldr: Hyundai SY, Ulsan

	Laid down	L	In serv.
MLS 560 Wonsan	12-94	9-96	9-97

Wonsan (MLS 560) Mitsuhiro Kadota, 2004

D: 3,300 tons (fl) **S:** 22 kts **Dim:** 103.75 (98.00 pp) × 15.20 × 4.15
A: 1 76-mm 62-cal. OTO Melara Compact DP; 2 twin 40-mm 70-cal. OTO Melara Fast Forty AA; 2 triple 324-mm Mk 32 ASW TT; up to 300 mines
Electronics:
Radar: 1 Raytheon SPS-64(V) nav.; 1 Samsung-Marconi 1810 surf./air search; 1 Thales DA-05 air search; 2 Samsung-Marconi ST-1802 f.c.
Sonar: . . . bow-mounted MF
EW: . . . intercept; Mk 36 SRBOC decoy syst. (2 6-round Raytheon Mk 137 RL)
M: 4 SEMT-Pielstick 12 PA6–series diesels; 2 props; 17,200 bhp
Range: 4,500/15 **Crew:** 160 tot.

Remarks: First unit ordered 10-94, with an option for two more that was not taken up. In addition to minelaying, is able to act as a minehunter and also as a training ship and ASW escort. Has a helicopter landing platform aft for aircraft up to CH-53E size, an extensive EW suite, and optronic backup directors for guns. Carries an LCVP landing craft to port.

♦ 2 (+ 5 + 3) Yangyang-class minehunters [MHC]
Bldr: Kangnam SB, Pusan

	L	In serv.
MHC 571 Yangyang	2-99	2000
MHC 572 Ong Jin	2002	. . .
MHC 573 . . .	. . .	. . .
MHC 575 . . .	. . .	. . .
MHC 576 . . .	. . .	. . .
MHC 577 . . .	. . .	. . .
MHC 578 . . .	. . .	. . .

D: 500 tons (730 fl) **S:** 15 kts **Dim:** 59.4 × 10.5 × 56
A: 1 20-mm Vulcan gatling AA; 2 single 7.62-mm mg
Electronics:
Radar: 1 . . . nav.
Sonar: Raytheon SQQ-32 variable-depth HF minehunting
M: 2 MTU . . . diesels; 2 props; . . . bhp
Range: 3,000/12 **Crew:** 61 tot.

Remarks: Combination minehunters/minesweepers to replace the remaining U.S.-built mine-countermeasures craft. Design began in 1992. Have an Alliant SLQ-48 remotely operated minehunting and disposal submersible. Engine control systems for the second and third units were ordered from CAE, Canada, on 3-8-01.

♦ 6 SK 5000–class minehunters [MHC]
Bldr: Swallowcraft, Kangnam SB, Pusan

	In serv.		In serv.
MHC 561 Kangkyeong	12-86	MHC 565 Kimpo	4-93
MHC 562 Kangjin	5-91	MHC 566 Kochang	10-93
MHC 563 Koryeong	11-91	MHC 567 Kumwha	4-9-4

Kangjin (MHC 562) John Mortimer, 10-98

Kangjin (MHC 562) H&L Van Ginderen, 1-00

D: 470 tons (520 fl) **S:** 15 kts **Dim:** 50.0 × 9.6 (8.31 wl) × 2.6
A: 1 20-mm 70-cal. Oerlikon Mk 10 AA; 2 single 7.62-mm mg
Electronics:
Radar: 1 Raytheon SPS-64(V)-series nav.
Sonar: Thales Type 193M Mod. 1 hull-mounted (see remarks)
M: 2 MTU . . . diesels; 2 Voith-Schneider vertical cycloidal props; 1,600 bhp—bow-thruster
Range: 2,500/12 **Crew:** 5 officers, 39 enlisted + 4 mine-disposal divers

Remarks: Design based on Italian *Lerici* design, but not built under license from the *Lerici* builder, Intermarine. Second and third ordered in 1987, final three in 1989.
Hull systems: Single-skin, glass-reinforced plastic construction.
Combat systems: Carry two Gaymarine Pluto Plus mine-disposal vehicles and are equipped with Racal-Decca MAINS plotting gear. Sonar transducer body incorporates Type 2048 Speedscan forward-looking component; the sixth and last Type 193M set was delivered during 11-92; later units carry the Type 193M Mod. 3 or the Type 2093.

♦ 5 ex-U.S. MSC 289–class coastal minesweepers
Bldr: Peterson Bldrs, Sturgeon Bay, Wis.

	In serv.
MSC 555 Namyang (ex-MSC 295)	8-63
MSC 556 Hadong (ex-MSC 296)	11-63
MSC 557 Samkok (ex-MSC 316)	7-68
MSC 558 Yeongdong (ex-MSC 320)	2-10-75
MSC 559 Okcheon (ex-MSC 321)	2-10-75

MINE WARFARE SHIPS *(continued)*

Samkok (MSC 557)—with original pennant number U.S. Navy, 4-68

D: 315 tons (380 fl) **S:** 14 kts **Dim:** 44.32 × 8.29 × 2.7
A: 1 twin 20-mm 70-cal. Oerlikon Mk 24 AA; 3 single 12.7-mm mg
Electronics:
Radar: 1 Decca. . . nav.
Sonar: UQS-1 or Thales 2022 hull-mounted HF
M: 4 G.M. 6-71 diesels; 2 props; 1,020 bhp **Electric:** 1,260 kw tot.
Range: 2,500/14 **Fuel:** 33 tons **Crew:** 40 tot.

Remarks: Wooden construction. Built under the U.S. Military Aid Program. Have a gas-turbine sweep generator and a lower superstructure than on the MSC 268 class. MSC 556–559 may have been reequipped with Thales 2022 minehunting sonars.

♦ 3 U.S. MSC 268–class coastal minesweepers
Bldr: Harbor Boat Building, Terminal Island, Calif.

	In serv.
MSC 551 Kumsan (ex-MSC 284)	6-59
MSC 552 Koheung (ex-MSC 285)	8-59
MSC 553 Kumkok (ex-MSC 286)	10-59

D: 320 tons (370 fl) **S:** 14 kts **Dim:** 43.0 (41.5 pp) × 7.95 × 2.55
A: 1 twin 20-mm 70-cal. Oerlikon Mk 24 AA; 3 single 12.7-mm mg
Electronics: Radar: 1 Decca 45 nav.—Sonar: UQS-1 hull-mounted HF
M: 2 G.M. Electromotive Div. 8-268A diesels; 2 props; 1,200 bhp
Range: 2,500/16 **Fuel:** 40 tons **Crew:** 40 tot.

Remarks: Built under the U.S. Military Aid Program. Wooden construction.

AMPHIBIOUS WARFARE SHIPS

♦ 0 (+ 2) LPX-class amphibious warfare helicopter carriers [LH]
Bldr: Hanjin Heavy Industries and Construction, Masan

	Laid down	L	In serv.
6111 Dokdo	28-10-02	8-7-05	30-6-07
6112 Marado	2006	2008	2010

Dokdo (6111)—at launching *Ships of the World/Platoon* Magazine, 7-05

Dokdo (6111)—at launching *Ships of the World/Platoon* Magazine, 7-05

D: 18,860 tons (fl) **S:** 22 kts **Dim:** 200.0 × 32.0 × 6.5
Air Group: 10 EH-101 Merlin helicopters
A: 2 21-round Mk 31 SAM launchers (RIM-116A RAM missiles); 2 30-mm Goalkeeper CIWS
Electronics: Radar: 1 Thales MW-08 3-D air search; 1 Thales SMART-L early warning
M: 4 Doosan Heavy Industries (DHICO) license-assembled SEMT-Pielstick diesels; 2 props; 32,000 bhp
Range: 10,000/12 **Crew:** 448 tot. + 720 troops

Note: Plans to lay down a 10,000-ton "LPX" dock landing ship in 2002 for delivery in 2005 were announced on 17-1-00. The construction contract for the first was announced on 17-9-02, with the ships to cost $266.2 million. Will have a docking well at the stern, capable of carrying two LCAC-type surface-effect landing craft, and will have one helicopter elevator to port. Vehicle capacity will include 10 heavy tanks.

♦ 4 (+ 5) HDL 4000–class landing ships [LST]
Bldr: Hanjin Industrial SB, Masan

	L	In serv.
LST 681 Kojoonbong	9-92	24-3-94
LST 682 Birobong	12-96	1-12-97
LST 683 Hyangrobong	10-98	8-99
LST 685 Seonginbong	2-99	11-99

Kojoonbong (LST 681) U.S. Navy, 3-04

Seonginbong (LST 685)—offloading a South Korean Type 88 tank during exercises U.S. Navy, 3-04

D: 4,278 tons (fl) **S:** 16 kts **Dim:** 106.90 × 15.40 × 3.00
A: 1 twin 40-mm 60-cal. Nobong (LST 683, 685: 40-mm 70-cal. OTO Melara Fast Forty) AA; 2 single 20-mm Vulcan gatling AA
Electronics:
Radar: 1 Raytheon SPS-64(V)9 nav.; 1 Raytheon SPS-64(V)6 nav.
TACAN: SRN-15A
E/O: AESN NA-18 optronic gun f.c.
M: 2 SEMT-Pielstick 16 PA6 V280 diesels; 2 props; 12,800 bhp
Electric: 750 kw tot. **Range:** 7,500/13; 10,000/12
Crew: 14 officers, 106 enlisted

Remarks: First two ordered 6-90 to begin replacement of the LST 1 and LST 542 classes. A total of nine is planned, but no further construction contracts have been announced. One unit of this class was ordered for delivery to Indonesia during 2003.
Hull systems: Have a helicopter deck aft and resemble LSTs built in South Korea for Venezuela and Indonesia, except that they have a drive-through tank deck and stern ramp. Are able to carry up to 1,800 tons of cargo (690 maximum beaching load) and about 200 troops; up to 17 main battle tanks can be accommodated. The articulating bow ramp extends to 14.5 m and is 4.5 m wide; the articulating stern ramp extends to 10.9 m and is 4.9 m wide. A 6.1-m-diameter turntable is fitted at the forward end of the tank deck, and there is a 9 × 4-m elevator to the upper deck.

♦ 5 ex-U.S. LST 1*– and U.S. LST 542–class landing ships [LST]

	Bldr	L	In serv.
LST 671 Unbong (ex-LST 1010)	Bethlehem, Fore River	29-3-44	25-4-44
LST 675 Gaebong (ex-LST 288)*	American Bridge, Pa.	7-11-43	20-12-43
LST 676 Weebong (ex-*Johnson County,* LST 849)	American Bridge, Pa.	30-12-43	16-1-44
LST 677 Suyeong (ex-*Kane County,* LST 853)	Chicago Bridge, Seneca, Ill.	17-11-44	11-12-44
LST 678 Bukhan (ex-*Lynn County,* LST 900)	Dravo, Pittsburgh	9-12-44	28-12-44

D: 1,653 tons (4,080 fl) **S:** 10 kts **Dim:** 99.98 (96.32 wl) × 15.24 × 4.29
A: 2 twin 40-mm 60-cal. Bofors Mk 1 Mod. 2 AA; 4 single 40-mm 60-cal. Bofors Mk 3 AA; 2 single 20-mm 70-cal. Oerlikon Mk 10 AA
Electronics: Radar: 2 . . . nav.
M: 2 G.M. Electromotive Div. 12-567A or 12-278A diesels; 2 props; 1,800 bhp
Electric: 300 kw tot. **Range:** 15,000/9 **Fuel:** 569 tons **Crew:** 70 tot.

Remarks: Transferred 1955–58; all purchased outright 15-11-74.
Disposals: *Tukbong* (LST 672, ex-LST 227) was stricken during 1989 after grounding; *Bibong* (LST 673; ex-*Berkshire County,* LST 218) had been stricken by 2-99; and *Hwasan* (LST 679; ex-*Pender County,* LST 1080) was stricken during 2000 and serves as a memorial in Chung Chong Province.

AMPHIBIOUS WARFARE SHIPS *(continued)*

Hull systems: The LST 1 class had an elevator from the upper deck to the tank deck, but all now have ramps. Can carry a maximum of 1,230 tons of cargo (815 tons for beaching), plus up to 350 troops.

♦ 2 ex-U.S. LSM 1–class medium landing ships [LSM]
Bldr: Brown SB, Houston, Texas

	Laid down	L	In serv.
LSM 657 Wolmi (ex-LSM 57)	30-6-44	21-7-44	17-8-44
LSM 658 Kirin (ex-LSM 19)	24-4-44	14-5-44	14-6-44

D: 520 tons (1,095 fl) **S:** 13 kts **Dim:** 62.0 × 10.52 × 2.53
A: 1 twin 40-mm 60-cal. Bofors Mk 1 Mod. 2 AA; 4 single 20-mm 70-cal. Oerlikon Mk 10 AA
Electronics: Radar: 1 . . . nav.
M: 2 Fairbanks-Morse 38D8Q × 10 diesels; 2 props; 2,880 bhp
Electric: 240 kw tot. **Range:** 5,000/7 **Fuel:** 160 tons **Crew:** 75 tot.

Remarks: Transferred in 1956. Cargo: 350 tons (165 for beaching), plus 48 troops.
Disposals: *Taecho* (LSM 651, ex-U.S. LSM 546) and *Tyoto* (LSM 652, ex-U.S. LSM 268) were stricken during 1982; *Gadeok* (LSM 653, ex-U.S. LSM 462) during 1995; and *Pungto* (LSM 650, ex-U.S. LSM 54), which was capable of laying mines, *Keomun* (LSM 655, ex-U.S. LSM 30), *Pian* (LSM 656, ex-U.S. LSM 96), *Nungra* (LSM 659, ex-U.S. LSM 84), *Sinmi* (LSM 661, ex-U.S. LSM 316), and *Ulreung* (LSM 662, ex-U.S. LSM 17) during 1998.
U.S. *Crosley*-class former high-speed transport *Cheju* (APD 822; ex-828; ex-*William M Hobby,* APD 95, ex-DE 236) was stricken from service in 2002 and sunk as a target in 2003.

♦ 9 Mulkae-class utility landing craft [LCU]
Bldr: Hanjin Industrial SB, Masan

	In serv.		In serv.		In serv.
LCU 72	1979	LCU 76	1980	LCU 79	30-9-97
LCU 73	1979	LCU 77	1981	LCU 81	31-10-97
LCU 75	1980	LCU 78	1981	LCU 82	31-11-97

D: 220 tons (415 fl) **S:** 12 kts **Dim:** 41.07 × 9.07 × 2.08
A: 2 single 20-mm 70-cal. Oerlikon Mk 10 AA **Electronics:** Radar: 1 . . . nav.
M: 4 G.M. 6-71 diesels; 2 Kort-nozzle props; 1,200 bhp
Range: 560/11 **Crew:** 2 officers, 12 enlisted

Remarks: Copies of the U.S. LCU 1610 design with a higher pilothouse; built with imported equipment. *Mulkae* means "Fur Seal." Cargo capacity: 143 tons. Cargo deck 30.5 × 5.5 m.

♦ 1 Modified U.S. LCAC 1–class air-cushion landing craft [LCUA]
Bldr: . . . (In serv. 1997)

LSF 611 Solgae

D: Approx. 80 tons light (182 max. fl) **S:** 54 kts (40 when loaded)
Dim: 26.8 (24.7 hull) × 14.3 (13.1 hull) × 0.9 (at rest)
A: 2 single 12.7-mm mg **Electronics:** Radar: 1 . . . nav.
M: 4 Avco TF40B gas turbines (2 for lift); 2 3.58-m-dia. shrouded airscrews, 4 centrifugal 1.60-m-dia. lift fans; 15,820 shp
Electric: 120 kw tot. (2 × 60-kw Turbomach T-62 gas turbine APU)
Range: 223/48 (light); 300/35 (loaded) **Fuel:** 6.2 tons (7,132 gallons)
Crew: 5 tot. + 25 troops

Remarks: Design based closely on the U.S. Navy version, but with a slightly modified pilothouse arrangement.
Hull systems: Uses the same propulsion plant as the USN LCAC 1 class. Cargo capacity: 60 tons normal. Bow and stern ramps are fitted. Operator, engineer, navigator, and nine troops travel in starboard side compartments, and deck hand, assistant engineer, load master, and vehicle crew travel in portside compartments.

♦ 3 ex-Russian Tsaplya-class (Project 1206.1 Murena) air-cushion vehicle landing craft [WLCMA]
Bldrs: Yuzhnaya Tochka SY, Feodosiya, and Ussuri SY, Khabarovsk (In serv. 2005–6)

D: 104 tons (149 fl); 80 tons light; 135 tons normal
S: 55 kts empty (50 with 24-ton load)
Dim: 31.60 (over skirt) × 12.90 (14.80 over skirt) × 1.6 (at rest)
A: 2 single 30-mm 54-cal. AK-306 gatling AA; 1 shoulder-launched SAM position (. . . Igla-M missiles); 1 twin 12.7-mm Utës-M mg; 2 40-mm BP-30 Plamya grenade launchers (1,800 grenades); 10–24 mines in lieu of vehicles
Electronics: Radar: 1 SRN-207 Ekran (Curl Stone-B) nav.
M: 2 PR-77 gas turbines; 2 3.5-m-dia. airscrew props; 8,000 shp—2 2.2-m-dia. axial lift fans (powered by main engines)
Range: 500/50; 200/55 with 24-ton payload **Endurance:** 1–3 days
Crew: 3 officers, 8 enlisted + 80–130 troops

Remarks: During 5-02, Russia offered to transfer one Murena-class (Project 1206.1; NATO Tsaplya-class) air-cushion landing craft in part payment for loan debts; the offer was accepted during 8-02 and approved on 13-12-02, and the craft came from among the eight Russian Federal Border Guard units operating on the Amur-Ussuri River network. The initial craft was found acceptable and two additional units were delivered during 2006.
Hull systems: Cargo: 24 tons under normal conditions, but up to 40–42 tons with a 10-kt speed reduction: one amphibious tank plus 80 troops, or 25 tons of stores and 160 soldiers, or 225 soldiers. Other cargo: one T-72M or T-80 tank or two PT-76 amphibious tanks or three BTR-70 armored personnel carriers. The bow ramp is 5.5 m long by 5.0 m wide. The cargo deck has about 130 m^2 useful space. Light alloy hull with rubberized fabric skirt. Can maintain 50 kts in Sea State 2 or 30 kts in Sea State 3. Gas turbine plant also reported as two MT-70R installations; the engines drive an integrated lift/propulsion plant with one axial lift fan and one airscrew propeller on either side. Can cross 1-m obstacles or ditches up to 4–5 m wide. The detachable, rubberized cloth flexible skirts are cylindrical in section.

Combat systems: The gatling guns are controlled by SP-521 Rakurs (Kolonka-2) ringsight directors on platforms abaft the pilothouse. The grenade launchers flank the bow ramp. May also carry "AGS-17" rockets. Carries 1,000 rounds 30-mm and 1,000 rounds 12.7-mm ammunition.

Note: The ROKN also has at least one air-cushion personnel landing craft resembling a British Hovercraft design; no data available.

♦ 10 ex-U.S. Army LCM(8)-class landing craft [LCM]

D: 58.8 tons light (116 fl) **S:** 9.2 kts (loaded)
Dim: 22.40 × 6.42 × 1.40 (mean) **M:** 2 G.M. 6-71 diesels; 2 props; 600 bhp
Range: 150/9.2 (loaded) **Fuel:** 2.4 tons **Crew:** 2–4 tot.

Remarks: Transferred 9-78. Data apply to final 96 built—the Mod. 1—delivered late 1960s–1972. Earlier Army LCM(8) Mod. 0 were rated at 57.8 tons light/111.4 full load. Mod. 1 carries up to 57.4 tons cargo, Mod. 0: 53.5 tons. Can also carry troops for short distances.

Note: South Korea also builds glass-reinforced plastic-hulled versions of the U.S. LCVP landing craft. A small troop-carrying prototype air-cushion landing craft has been completed, and as many as 30 may be built. For use by the ROK Marines, there are 24 LVTP-7A and 53 LVTP-7 troop-carrying, one LVTC-7A1 and five LVTC-7 command, and three LVTR-7 recovery armored tracked amphibious landing vehicles. Current plans call for acquiring 57 improved AAV-7A and upgrading the current fleet.
The ROK Army has 192 aluminum-construction British FBM Marine–designed river bridging craft in service, with 56 delivered 1995–96 by Hanjin Industrial Shipbuilding, Masan. Characteristics include:

D: . . . tons **S:** 24 kts **Dim:** 8.38 (6.98 wl) × 2.49 × 0.66 (loaded)
M: 2 diesels; 2 waterjets; 424 bhp **Fuel:** 170 liters

AUXILIARIES

♦ 3 Cheonji-class replenishment oilers [AOR]
Bldr: Hyundai SY, Ulsan

	L	In serv.
AOE 57 Cheonji	29-12-90	1-92
AOE 58 Daecheong	1-97	31-3-98
AOE 59 Hwacheon	7-97	31-8-98

Hwacheon (AOE 59) Mitsuhiro Kadota, 2004

Cheonji (AOE 57) Frank Findler, 6-05

Cheonji (AOE 57) Michael Winter, 6-05

D: 9,000 tons (fl) **S:** 20 kts **Dim:** 133.0 (122.5 pp) × 17.8 × 6.5
A: 2 twin 40-mm 70-cal. OTO Melara Fast Forty (AOE 57: 2 twin 30-mm 75-cal. Emerlec) AA; 2 single 20-mm Vulcan gatling AA

AUXILIARIES *(continued)*

Electronics: Radar: 2 . . . nav.
M: AOE 57: 2 SEMT-Pielstick 16 PA6 V280 diesels; 2 CP props; 15,600 bhp (see remarks)
Electric: 725 kw tot. **Range:** 4,500/15 **Crew:** . . . tot.

Remarks: First unit ordered in 6-90, second two in 5-95. Builder's HDA 8000 design, a reduced version of the *Endeavour* built for New Zealand. A near-sister was ordered for Venezuela in 7-99.
Hull systems: Cargo: 4,200 tons fuels, 450 tons stores. Two replenishment stations on each beam, one for liquids and one for solid cargo transfer; also able to refuel over the stern. Helicopter platform and hangar aft. AOE 58 and AOE 59 have newer-model diesels than those in AOE 57.
Combat systems: AOE 58 and AOE 59 have enclosed twin 40-mm AA mounts fore and aft, with remote directors.

♦ 2 ex-U.S. Edenton-class salvage-and-rescue ships [ARS]
Bldr: Brooke Marine, Lowestoft, U.K.

	Laid down	L	In serv.
ARS 27 Pyongtaek (ex-*Beaufort*, ATS 2)	19-2-68	20-12-68	22-1-72
ARS 28 Kwangyang (ex-*Brunswick*, ATS 3)	5-6-68	14-11-69	19-12-72

Pyongtaek (ARS 27)—when still in U.S. Navy service Piet Sinke, 3-91

D: 2,650 tons (3,200 fl) **S:** 16 kts **Dim:** 88.0 (80.5 pp) × 15.25 × 4.6
A: 2 single 12.7-mm mg
Electronics: Radar: 1 Sperry SPS-53 nav.; 1 Raytheon SPS-64(V)9 nav.
M: 4 Paxman 12 YLCM 900-rpm diesels; 2 Escher-Wyss CP props; 6,000 bhp
Electric: 1,200 kw tot. **Range:** 10,000/13 **Crew:** 7 officers, 110 enlisted

Remarks: Both were decommissioned to reserve from the U.S. Navy on 8-3-96, sold to South Korea 29-8-96, delivered 7-2-97, and commissioned in the ROKN 20-2-97.
Hull systems: Can tow ships up to 50,000-ton size. Have 272-ton dead lift over the bow. There is a 20-ton crane aft and a 10-ton boom forward. Can conduct dives to 260 m. Powerful pumps and complete firefighting equipment. Equipped with a bow-thruster.

♦ 1 midget-submarine tender [AS]

ASL 50 Dadohae

Remarks: No data available. Is used to support (and possibly to deploy) the midget submarines of the S.X.756 and KSS-1 classes.

♦ 1 submarine rescue ship [ASR]
Bldr: Daewoo SB & Heavy Machinery, Okpo

	Laid down	L	In serv.
ARS 21 Chonghaejin	12-94	17-10-95	3-97

Chonghaejin (ARS 21) Hartmut Ehlers, 9-03

D: 4,330 tons (fl) **S:** 18.5 kts (15 sust.) **Dim:** 102.8 × 16.4 × 4.6
A: 6 single 12.7-mm M2 mg
Electronics: Radar: 1 . . . nav.—Sonar: hull-mounted HF—TACAN: . . .
M: 4 M.A.N. 16V 28/32 diesels (2,950 bhp each), electric drive: 2 motors; 2 CP props; 5,440 shp—3 bow-thrusters, 2 stern-thrusters
Electric: 5,600 kw tot. (2 × 2,000-kw shaft generators, 4 × 400-kw diesel sets)
Range: 9,500/15 **Crew:** 130 tot. (accomm.)

Remarks: Offered for export by Daewoo as its DW 4000R, or Koje, class. One unit of this design was also ordered in 1992 to support the new ROKN submarine force.
Hull systems: Carries a deep-submergence (300-m) submarine rescue vehicle, handled by an A-frame crane at the stern. Extensive diving systems furnished; has a nine-man rescue diving bell and a large decompression chamber. Has dynamic positioning system and four-point mooring system. The rudders are of the "flapped" type to enhance low-speed maneuverability. Has a helicopter platform and two electrohydraulic, telescoping cranes. Able to provide battery charging, provisions, fuel, oxygen, and water services to submarines. Carries two LCVP-type workboats.

SERVICE CRAFT

♦ 1 weapons systems trials craft [YAGE]
Bldr: Hyundai SY, Ulsan (In serv. 4-93)

AGS 11 Seonjin

D: 310 tons (fl) **S:** 21 kts **Dim:** 34.5 × 15.0 × 3.5
A: None **Electronics:** Radar: 1 . . . nav.
M: 2 MTU 16V396 TE diesels; 2 props; 2,680 bhp
Range: 600/16 **Crew:** 5 tot. + 20 technicians

Remarks: Ordered 6-91 for the Defense Development Agency and is civilian operated. Has an aluminum-alloy hull with a SWATH twin-hullform. Used for trials with towed linear passive hydrophone sensors, navigational systems, and an indigenous torpedo development program. Has stern A-frame for torpedo recovery.

Disposal note: Ex-U.S. 174-foot-class harbor tanker YO 6 (ex-YO 179) was retired from service by 2006.

Note: There are also nine or more harbor tugs, including OI 51, OI 52, OI 53 and OI 55, YTL 13 (ex-USN YTL 550), YTL 22 (ex-Army ST 2097), YTL 23 (ex-Army ST 2099), YTL 25 (ex-Army ST 2106), YTL 26 (ex-Army ST 2065), YTL 30 (ex-Army ST 2101), and YTL 38 (ex-Army ST . . .). A number of other yard and service craft are also in use.

MARITIME POLICE

The former Republic of Korea Coast Guard has been combined with the Maritime Police. There are about 4,000 personnel, most in shore billets. Patrol ships and craft are painted with blue hulls and white superstructures, while the large seagoing salvage ships are painted all white; the word "Police" is lettered in Korean and English on the side of the superstructure or, on the larger vessels, on the hull sides, and there is a green stack stripe with the Maritime Police seal centered on it; rescue ships additionally have a red-yellow-blue diagonal stripe set on the hull side, with a larger shield superimposed.

Aviation: In use are an unknown number of Kamov Ka-27 Helix-series rescue and firefighting helicopters. Bombardier, Canada, delivered a single Challenger 604 maritime surveillance aircraft following a 16-6-99 order; additional units may later be ordered.

PATROL SHIPS [WPS]

♦ 2 (+ 1) 1,650-ton class
Bldr: Daewoo SB, Okpo (L: 22-1-99)

PC 1006 Seomjinkang PC 1008 . . .

Seomjinkang (PC 1006) *Ships of the World,* 7-00

D: 1,650 tons (fl) **S:** 21 kts **Dim:** 84.0 × 10.4 × 3.6
A: 1 20-mm Vulcan gatling AA—4 single 12.7-mm mg
Electronics: Radar: 1. . . nav.; 1 Kelvin-Hughes . . . surf. search
M: 2 Wärtsilä-Nohab 16V25 diesels; 2 props; 10,000 bhp
Range: 4,500/18 **Crew:** 7 officers, 50 enlisted

Remarks: Ordered in 1997. Intended for seagoing patrol, salvage, and rescue duties.

♦ 1 HDC 1150 class
Bldr: Korea SB & Eng., Pusan (In serv. 12-85)

PC 1005 Hankang

D: 980 tons (1,150 fl) **S:** 31 kts **Dim:** 87.84 × 10.0 × 2.36
A: 1 76-mm 62-cal. OTO Melara Compact DP; 1 40-mm 60-cal. Bofors Mk 3 AA; 2 single 20-mm Vulcan gatling AA
Electronics: Radar: 1 Raytheon SPS-64(V) nav.; 1 Thales WM-28 f.c.
M: CODOG: 1 G.E. LM-2500 gas turbine (27,800 shp); 2 MTU 12V956 TB 82 diesels (6,260 bhp each); 2 CP props
Range: 4,000/15 **Endurance:** 21 days **Crew:** 11 officers, 61 enlisted

Remarks: A lower-powered and more lightly armed version of the *Pohang*-class frigates built for the navy. Has the Rademac System 2400 optronic director and a visual backup to supplement the Thales WM-28 detection/tracking radar.

MARITIME POLICE PATROL SHIPS [WPS] *(continued)*

Hankang (PC 1005) *Ships of the World,* 1997

♦ 3 HDP 1000 class

Bldr: Hanjin Industrial SB, Pusan (PC 1002: Hyundai SY, Ulsan)

	In serv.
PC 1001 Mazingga	29-11-81
PC 1002 . . .	31-8-82
PC 1003 . . .	31-8-83

Mazingga (PC 1001) Korea SB & Eng., 1981

D: 1,200 tons (1,450 fl) **S:** 21.5 kts **Dim:** 81.50 × 9.80 × 3.15
A: 1 40-mm 60-cal. Bofors Mk 3 AA; 2 twin 20-mm 70-cal. Oerlikon Mk 24 AA
Electronics: Radar: 2 . . . nav.
M: 2 Niigata SEMT-Pielstick 12 PA6 280 diesels; 2 props; 9,600 bhp
Range: 7,000/18 **Crew:** 11 officers, 58 enlisted

Remarks: Ordered 7-11-80. PC 1001 acts as maritime police flagship. Have passive tank stabilization system. Engines were built in Japan under license.

♦ 6 Sea Whale class

	Bldr	In serv.
PC 501	Hanjin Industrial SB, Chinhae	25-12-78
PC 502	Hanjin Industrial SB, Chinhae	1979
PC 503	Hanjin Industrial SB, Chinhae	5-5-79
PC 505	Korea SB & Eng., Pusan	31-5-80
PC 506	Hyundai SY, Ulsan	28-9-81
PC 507	Hanjin Industrial SB, Chinhae	31-7-82

Sea Whale–class PC 503 Official photo, 7-94

D: 410 tons (500 fl) **S:** 24 kts **Dim:** 60.80 × 8.00 × 2.29
A: 1 40-mm 60-cal. Bofors Mk 3 AA; 2 single 20-mm 70-cal. Oerlikon AA; 2 single 7.62-mm mg
Electronics: Radar: 2 . . . nav.
M: 2 Niigata-Pielstick 12 PA6 V280 diesels; 2 props; 9,600 bhp
Range: 1,500/25; 2,400/20 **Crew:** 11 officers, 28 enlisted

Remarks: Intended for rescue and inspection duties. Flume-type passive tank roll stabilization is on one unit, with an AA gun in the same position on the others. PC 503 has two 5,440-bhp Wärtsilä-Nohab diesels.

PATROL CRAFT [WPC]

♦ 5 32.2-meter class

Bldr: Hyundai SY, Ulsan (In serv. 1997)

PC 105 PC 113 PC 118 PC 121 PC 125

D: 110 tons (fl) **S:** 25 kts **Dim:** 32.2 × 6.0 × 1.4
A: 1 20-mm 70-cal. Oerlikon Mk 10 AA; 2 single 12.7-mm mg
Electronics: 1 Furuno nav.
M: 2 . . . diesels; 2 props; . . . bhp **Crew:** 19 tot.

♦ 6 430-ton class

Bldr: Hyundai SY, Ulsan (PC 301: Daewoo SY, Okpo)

	In serv.		In serv.
PC 300	10-4-94	PC 303	20-12-91
PC 301	20-4-90	PC 402	12-91
PC 302	15-12-90	PC 403	1993

430-ton-class PC 301 H&L Van Ginderen, 8-00

D: 300 tons light (430 fl) **S:** 19 kts **Dim:** 55.50 (53.70 pp) × 7.40 × 2.48
A: 1 or 2 single 20-mm Vulcan gatling AA; 4 single 12.7-mm M2 mg
Electronics: Radar: 1 or 2 . . . nav.
M: 2 MTU 16V396 TB83 diesels; 2 props; 4,392 bhp
Range: 2,100/15 **Crew:** 4 officers, 35 enlisted

Remarks: Equipped for search-and-rescue service and for towing. Previously listed as two different classes, but photography shows them to be virtually identical.

♦ 4 Bukhansan class

Bldrs: Hyundai SY, Ulsan, and Daewoo SB & Heavy Machinery, Okpo (In serv. 1989–90)

PC 278 PC 279 PC 281 PC 282

Bukhansan-class PC 278 Hyundai, 1989

D: 350 tons (380 fl) **S:** 28+ kts **Dim:** 53.10 (47.8 pp) × 7.10 × 2.40
A: 1 twin 40-mm 70-cal. OTO Melara Fast Forty AA; 2 single 12.7-mm mg
Electronics: Radar: 1 . . . nav. **M:** 2 MTU diesels; 2 props; 8,300 bhp
Electric: 260 kw tot. (2 × 130-kw diesel sets)
Range: 2,500/15 **Crew:** 3 officers, 32 enlisted

Remarks: A development of the Sea Wolf/Sea Shark series; Daewoo referred to the design as the DW 300P or Salsu class. PC 278 may bear the name *Bukhansan* and PC 279 the name *Cheolmasan.* Have an optronic director for the 40-mm mount, as well as a target-designation sight. PC 278 is armed with a twin Melara 40-mm Compact gunmount forward; the others appear to have Rheinmetall single Bofors 40-mm weapons.

♦ 1 PC 277 class

Bldr: Hanjin Industrial SB, Chinhae (In serv. 10-12-86)

PC 277

D: 250 tons **S:** 28 kts **Dim:** 47.75 × 7.10 × 2.35
A: 1 40-mm 60-cal. Bofors Mk 3 AA; 1 20-mm Vulcan gatling AA; 2 single 12.7-mm mg
Electronics: Radar: 1 . . . nav.
M: 2 MTU 20V538 TB91 diesels; 2 props; 9,000 bhp
Range: 2,400/25 **Crew:** 3 officers, 32 enlisted

♦ 22 Sea Shark/Sea Wolf class

Bldrs: Hyundai SY, Ulsan; Daehau SB; and Hanjin Industrial SB, Masan (In serv. 1979–82)

D: 250 tons (280 fl) **S:** 28 kts **Dim:** 47.75 × 7.10 × 2.12 (2.50 over props)
A: 2 twin or 1 twin and 2 single 20-mm 70-cal. Oerlikon AA; 2 single 12.7-mm mg
Electronics: Radar: 1 . . . nav.
M: 2 MTU 16V538-series diesels; 2 props; 7,320 bhp
Range: 1,600/20; 3,300/15 **Crew:** 5 officers, 24 enlisted

Remarks: Some have a raised platform aft, and there are numerous small differences, depending on when built and by whom. Units from Hyundai are known as the Sea Shark class, those from Hanjin as the Sea Wolf. Range is also given as 2,000 n.m. at 17 kts. Pennant numbers appear to have been changed to the 100 series; as completed, they ran from PC 251 through PC 277.

MARITIME POLICE PATROL CRAFT [WPC] *(continued)*

Sea Shark/Sea Wolf–class PC 127—with raised pilothouse and what is probably a 20-mm Oerlikon AA mount forward H&L Van Ginderen, 8-00

PATROL BOATS [WPB]

♦ 3 18.7-meter class
Bldr: Kangan SY & Miwon SY (In serv. 1992–93)

D: 28 tons (fl) **S:** 35 kts **Dim:** 18.70 × 4.40 × 0.90
A: 1 12.7-mm mg **Electronics:** Radar: 1 . . . nav.
M: 2 MTU 12V183 TE92 diesels; 2 Hamilton waterjets; 2,000 bhp
Electric: 48 kw tot. **Range:** 250/28 **Crew:** 7 tot.

♦ . . . Swallow class
Bldr: Korea SB & Eng., Pusan (In serv. 1980s)

Swallow-class P 387 H&L Van Ginderen, 3-99

D: 32 tons (fl) **S:** 25 kts **Dim:** 20.0 × 4.7 × 1.3
A: 1 12.7-mm mg; 1 7.62-mm mg
M: 2 G.M. 12V71 TI diesels; 2 props; 1,060 bhp
Range: 500/20 **Crew:** 8 tot.

Remarks: Glass-reinforced plastic construction.

♦ 18 Sea Gull class
Bldr: Korea SB & Eng., Pusan (in serv. early 1970s)

D: 80 tons **S:** 30 kts **Dim:** 24.0 × 5.5 × 2.0
A: 1 or 2 single 20-mm 70-cal. Oerlikon AA
M: 2 MTU diesels; 2 props; 3,920 bhp **Range:** 950/20 **Crew:** 18 tot.

AUXILIARIES

♦ 1 Sambongho-class ocean salvage tender [WARS]
Bldr: Hyundai, Ulsan

	Laid down	L	In serv.
5001 Sambongho	. . .	. . .	2001

Sambongho (5001) *Seawaves* Magazine, 2005

D: 5,000 fl **S:** 21 kts **Dim:** . . . × . . . × . . .
A: 1 twin 20-mm Vulcan gatling AA
Electronics: Radar: 2 . . . nav.
M: . . .

Remarks: Enlarged version of the *Taepyeongyang II*–class tenders. Equipped with a helicopter deck and painted white, with "Police" prominently visible on the hull sides.

♦ 1 Taepyeongyang II–class ocean salvage tender [WARS]
Bldr: Hyundai, Ulsan

	Laid down	L	In serv.
3002 Taepyeongyang II	. . .	. . .	11-98

Taepyeongyang II (3002) *Ships of the World,* 7-00

D: 3,900 tons (5,000 fl) **S:** 18 kts **Dim:** 110.50 × 15.40 × . . .
A: 1 20-mm Vulcan gatling AA; 6 single 12.7-mm mg
Electronics: Radar: 2 . . . nav.
M: 4 Sangyong–Burmeister & Wain 16V 28/32 diesels; 2 CP props; 11,800 bhp—bow- and stern-thrusters
Electric: 1,950 kw total (2 × 800 kw; 1 × 350 kw)
Range: 8,500/15 **Fuel:** 825 m^3 **Crew:** 120 tot.

Remarks: Has firefighting, towing, oil-spill containment, and salvage equipment. Equipped with a helicopter deck. Hull sides are heavily reinforced with rubbing strakes. Painted white, with "Police" prominently visible on the hull sides.

♦ 1 Taepyeongyang I–class ocean salvage tender [WARS]
Bldr: Hyundai, Ulsan

	Laid down	L	In serv.
3001 Taepyeongyang I	2-91	10-91	18-2-93

Taepyeongyang I (3001) *Ships of the World,* 7-00

D: 3,200 tons (4,300 fl) **S:** 21 kts **Dim:** 104.70 × 15.00 × 5.20
A: 1 20-mm Vulcan gatling AA; 6 single 12.7-mm mg
Electronics: Radar: 2 . . . nav.
M: 4 Sangyong–Burmeister & Wain 16V 28/32 diesels; 2 CP props; 11,800 bhp—3 bow- and 2 stern-thrusters
Electric: 1,950 kw tot. (2 × 800 kw; 1 × 350 kw)
Range: 8,500/15 **Fuel:** 825 m^3 **Crew:** 121 tot.

Remarks: 4,300 grt. Has firefighting, towing, oil-spill containment, and salvage equipment. Equipped with a helicopter deck. Bow is equipped with sheaves for cable laying and repair. Can lay and recover a four-point moor for salvage purposes. Hull sides are heavily reinforced with rubbing strakes. Painted white, with "Police" prominently visible on the hull sides.

♦ 1 salvage ship [WARS]
Bldr: Hyundai, Ulsan (In serv. 11-88)

1503 Jaemin III

Jaemin III (1503) H&L Van Ginderen, 8-00

MARITIME POLICE AUXILIARIES *(continued)*

D: 3,900 tons (4,200 fl) **S:** 18 kts **Dim:** 110.5 × 15.4 × 4.9
A: 2 single 20-mm Vulcan gatling AA; 6 single 12.7-mm mg
Electronics: Radar: 2 . . . nav./surf. search
M: 2 . . . diesels; 2 props; . . . bhp
Range: . . . / . . . **Crew:** 120 tot.

Remarks: Ordered in 1996. Has a large helicopter deck aft but no hangar. Intended for ocean patrol and salvage duties.

♦ 1 salvage ship [WARS]

	Bldr	L	In serv.
1502 Jaemin II	Hyundai SY, Ulsan	15-7-95	4-96

Jaemin II (1502) *Ships of the World,* 7-00

D: 2,500 tons (fl) **S:** 20 kts **Dim:** 88.0 × 14.50 × 4.60
A: 1 20-mm Vulcan gatling AA **Electronics:** Radar: 2 . . . nav.
M: 2 MTU . . . diesels; 2 KaMeWa CP props; 12,662 bhp—bow- and stern-thrusters
Range: 4,500/15 **Crew:** 81 tot.

Remarks: Ordered 12-93. An enlarged version of *Jaemin I* (1501); distinguishable by twin side-by-side stacks. Painted white, with red-white-blue diagonal stripe on hull side, which also bears the legend "Police." Is equipped for firefighting, towing, ocean patrol, rescue, and salvage duties.

♦ 1 salvage ship [WARS]
Bldr: Daewoo, Okpo (In serv. 28-12-92)

1501 Jaemin I

Jaemin I (1501) Daewoo, 12-92

D: 2,072 tons (fl) **S:** 18 kts **Dim:** 77.58 × 13.50 × 4.20
A: 1 20-mm Vulcan gatling AA **Electronics:** Radar: 2 . . . nav.
M: 2 MTU 16V1163 TB62 diesels; 2 CP props; 8,000 bhp
Range: 4,500/12 **Crew:** 72 tot.

Remarks: Modeled after the U.S. *Bolster* class but is much larger. Has telescoping hydraulic cranes fore and aft. Can lay and recover a four-point mooring. Carries two LCVP-type workboats. Equipped for ocean towing. Hull sides are heavily reinforced with rubbing strakes.

SERVICE CRAFT

♦ 3 pollution-control craft [WYAG]
Bldr: Wuri SB Industries

	In serv.
. . .	10-92
. . .	30-10-92
. . .	9-93

D: 220 tons (fl) **S:** 12 kts **Dim:** 31.10 × 8.50 × 1.54
Electronics: Radar: . . .
M: 2 Cummins KTA 19M diesels; 1 prop; 1,000 bhp **Electric:** 144 kw tot.
Range: 700/10 **Fuel:** 26 m^3 **Crew:** 11 tot.

♦ 1 16-ton bollard-pull tug [WYTB]
Bldr: Wuri SB Industries (In serv. 5-93)

D: 320 tons (fl) **S:** 11.5 kts **Dim:** 27.50 × 7.60 × 2.40
M: 2 Cummins VTA 28M diesels; 2 Aquamaster azimuth drives; 1,450 bhp
Electric: 236 kw tot. **Range:** 500/10.5 **Fuel:** 27 m^3 **Crew:** 6 tot.

Note: The customs service also operates an unknown number of patrol boats, including the 50-ton vessels *Incheon* (304) and *Jeonnam* (305), launched during 2005. Also in service are three 47-ton craft numbered 805, 820 and 825, armed with a single 20-mm Oerlikon gun and twin 12.7-mm machineguns.

KUWAIT

State of Kuwait

KUWAITI NAVY

Personnel: Approx. 2,000 total, including 500 in the Coast Guard

Bases: Ras al Qalayah

Naval Aviation: The air force has four AS.332F Super Puma helicopters that can be armed with AM 39 Exocet antiship missiles, and its 39 F/A-18 Hornet fighters are eventually to be able to conduct maritime strikes. Plans for the acquisition of antiship missile–armed helicopters for the navy appear to have come to naught.

GUIDED-MISSILE PATROL BOATS [PTG]

♦ 8 P37 BRL class
Bldr: CMN, Cherbourg

	Laid down	L	In serv.
P 3711 Um Almaradim	11-94	27-2-97	31-7-98
P 3713 Ouha	2-95	29-5-97	31-7-98
P 3715 Failaka	5-95	29-8-97	19-12-98
P 3717 Maskan	8-95	6-1-98	19-12-98
P 3719 Al Ahmadi	11-95	2-4-98	1-7-99
P 3721 Al Fahaheel	2-96	16-6-98	1-7-99
P 3723 Al Yarmook	5-96	3-3-99	7-6-00
P 3725 Garoh	8-96	4-6-99	7-6-00

Um Almaradim (P 3711)—note the canister launchers for four Sea Skua missiles at the stern Edward B. McDonnell, 7-04

Garoh (P 3725) Edward B. McDonnell, 7-04

D: 225 tons (247 fl) **S:** 38 kts (30 sust.)
Dim: 42.00 (37.50 pp) × 8.50 (8.20 waterline) × 1.98 (hull; 2.80 max.)
A: 4 Sea Skua SSM; 1 40-mm 70-cal. OTO Melara Fast Forty AA; 1 20-mm 90-cal. GIAT Type 15A AA; 2 single 12.7-mm M2HB mg
Electronics:
Radar: 1 Racal-Decca 20V90 nav.; Thales-Matra MRR (TRS-5204) 3-D air search; 1 Marconi Avionics Seaspray 3000 missile target-acquisition and tracking
EW: Thales DR-3000S1 Compact intercept (1–18 GHz); . . . IR detection syst.; provision for 1 330- to 340-round Matra Défense Dagaie Mk 2 decoy RL
E/O: Matra Défense Najir Mk 2 gun f.c. and surveillance

GUIDED-MISSILE PATROL BOATS [PTG] *(continued)*

M: 2 MTU 16V538 TB93 diesels; 2 KaMeWa waterjets; 8,000 bhp
Electric: 420 kw tot. **Range:** 1,350/14; 1,700/12 **Fuel:** 30 tons
Endurance: 7 days **Crew:** 5 officers, 19 enlisted

Remarks: Referred to locally as the *Garoh* class. Ordered 27-3-95. P 3711 began sea trials in 4-97. Each unit was to have two complete crews. The first four craft arrived in Kuwaiti waters on 15-8-99, and the second quartet departed France on 17-8-00 for arrival in 11-00. The class took considerably longer to build and deliver than had been planned.
Hull systems: Steel hull, aluminum superstructure. Have fin stabilizers.
Combat systems: Have the Thales NCCS combat system, a version of the TAVITAC-NT weapons-control system with three Matra Défense Calisto multifunction display consoles and a Model "Y" datalink to other units of the class. The Seaspray radar/Sea Skua missile suite is a stand-alone system not integrated into the main weapons-control system. The Matra Défense Najir M42 optronic director with IR, daylight t.v., and laser rangefinder sensors controls the 40-mm AA, which has a 450-rpm firing rate. Plans to install a Sadral SAM launcher and a Salamandre jammer have been dropped, but the systems may be acquired later. A Marconi Hazeltine TPX-54(V) Mk XII IFF transponder is fitted.

♦ 1 FPB 57 class
Bldr: Lürssen, Bremen-Vegesack, Germany (In serv. 9-8-83)

P 5702 Istiqlal

Istiqlal (P 5702)—following 2005 modernization Frank Findler, 5-05

Istiqlal (P 5702)—post modernization Frank Findler, 5-05

D: 353 tons (398 fl) **S:** 36 kts **Dim:** 58.10 (54.40 wl) × 7.62 × 2.83
A: 4 MM 40 Exocet SSM; 1 76-mm 62-cal. OTO Melara DP; 1 twin 40-mm 70-cal. OTO Melara AA; 2 single 7.62-mm mg
Electronics:
Radar: 1 Decca 1226C nav.; 1 Ericsson Sea Giraffe 50HC surf./air search; 1 Saab 9LV 228 f.c.
EW: Racal RDL-2 intercept; Racal Cygnus jammer; 1 330- to 340-round Matra Défense Dagaie decoy RL
M: 4 MTU 16V538 TB92 diesels; 4 props; 14,000 bhp
Electric: 405 kw (3 × 135 kw) **Range:** 1,00/30 **Fuel:** 90 tons
Crew: 4 officers, 35 enlisted

Remarks: Two ordered in 1980 to function as leaders for the six TNC-45 class. Name means "Freedom." Sister *Sabhan* (P 5704) was captured by Iraqi forces in 8-90 and sunk by UN Coalition forces 29-1-91. Was laid up in reserve for a decade prior to being modernized and fitted with new diesels in Germany between 3-03 and 8-05. Also used for training purposes.

♦ 1 TNC-45 class
Bldr: Lürssen, Bremen-Vegesack, Germany

	L	In serv.
P 4505 Al Sanbouk (ex-*Jalboot*)	5-82	26-4-84

D: 231 tons (259 fl) **S:** 41.5 kts **Dim:** 44.90 (42.30 wl) × 7.00 × 2.40
A: 4 MM 40 Exocet SSM; 1 76-mm 62-cal. OTO Melara DP; 1 twin 40-mm 70-cal. OTO Melara AA; 2 single 7.62-mm mg
Electronics:
Radar: 1 Decca 1226 nav.; 1 Ericsson Sea Giraffe 50 surf./air search; 1 Saab 9LV 200 f.c.
EW: Racal RDL-2 intercept
M: 4 MTU 16V538 TB92 diesels; 4 props; 15,600 bhp (15,000 sust.)
Electric: 369 kw tot. (3 × 123 kw) **Range:** 500/38.5; 1,500/16
Crew: 5 officers, 27 enlisted

Al Sanbouk (P 4505) Edward B. McDonnell, 7-04

Remarks: Ordered 1980. Refitted by Lürssen in 1995–96 and again during 2005.
Combat systems: Carries 250 rounds of 76-mm and 1,800 rounds of 40-mm ammunition. Has a Matra Défense Lynx optronic gun director for the 40-mm mount, a Saab 9LV 200 control system for the 76-mm gun and missiles, and a flare rocket launcher amidships.
Losses: Five sisters were captured by invading Iraqi forces in 8-90 and subsequently sunk by UN Coalition forces (one on 18-1-91, one on 30-1-91; dates for the others uncertain): *Al Boom* (P 4501, ex-*Werjiya*), *Al Betteen* (P 4503, ex-*Mashuwah*), *Al Saadi* (P 4507, ex-*Istiqlal*), *Al Ahmadi* (P 4509), and *Al Abdali* (P 4511, ex-*Al Mubareki*).

PATROL BOATS [PB]

Note: In addition to the units listed below, about a dozen other small ex-Iraqi or former private craft have been pressed into service for patrol or utility duties.

Although 12 Manta-class patrol boats were ordered for $1.5 million during 6-98 from Simonneau S.A. Marine, Fontenay-le-Comte, France, the craft were found to be defective on delivery and have not entered service; the 12 Star Naja boats ordered earlier from the same builder were returned. The *Manta*-class hull numbers were in the IB1501 series, and the 40-kt boats were equipped with one 12.7-mm machinegun.

♦ 0 (+ 12) Mk V-C Pegasus-class Special Operations Craft [PB]
Bldr: Trinity-Halter Marine, Gulfport, Miss or Trinity-Equitable SY, New Orleans, La. (In serv. 2007– . . .)

D: 57 tons (68 fl) **S:** 50× kts (30 sust.) **Dim:** 24.99 × 5.33 × 1.32
A: 1 single 27-mm Mauser MLG 27 AA
Electronics: Radar: 1 Furuno . . . nav.
M: 2 MTU 16V396 TE94 diesels; 2 KaMeWa K50S waterjets; 4,570 bhp
Electric: 50 kw tot. (2 × 25 kw diesel sets) **Range:** 500/50; 550/35
Fuel: . . . tons (2,600 gallons) **Crew:** 5 tot. × 16 personnel

Remarks: Requested from the United States 12-05 via the Foreign Military Sales program. Slightly modified "C" variant of the U.S. Navy SEAL's *Pegasus*-class Mk V special operations craft.
Hull systems: Aluminum construction.. Each boat can launch and retrieve four inflated rubber raiding craft. The open cockpit can be covered by removable hard canopies. All seating is shock mounted. The hull is designed for minimum radar and heat signature. Hull molded depth is 2.36 m. Can tow two 9.14-m rigid inflatable raider boats at 50 kts and can operate in Sea State 3 at 35 kts. A 220 gallon/day potable water generator is fitted.
Combat systems: Kuwaiti versions are to be fitted with a single 27-mm AA gun, rather than five weapons mounting positions as in U.S. Navy variants.

SERVICE CRAFT

♦ 2 Hadiya-class logistics support lighters [YFU]
Bldr: Vosper Pty, Singapore (In serv. 1979)

Hadiya Ceriff

D: 320 tons (fl) **S:** 9 kts **Dim:** 32.3 × 7.5 × 2.5
A: None **Electronics:** Radar: 1 Decca . . . nav.
M: 2 Rolls-Royce CBM-410 diesels; 2 props; 750 bhp
Range: 1,500/8 **Crew:** 1 officer, 6 enlisted

Remarks: Captured by Iraq during 1990–91 and returned in poor condition in 1993; since then, refitted for local logistic support duties. An unusual design, with a stern vehicle ramp intended to allow them to back onto shore to load or unload cargo.

♦ 1 logistics support lighter [YFU]
Bldr: Vosper Pty, Singapore (In serv. 1975)

55 Fareed

D: 170 tons (fl) **S:** 10 kts **Dim:** 27.0 × 6.9 × 1.3
A: None **Electronics:** Radar: 1 . . . nav.
M: 2 Rolls-Royce C8M-410 diesels; 2 props; 750 bhp
Range: 1,500/9 **Crew:** 9 tot.

Remarks: Captured by Iraq and returned in poor condition in 1993. Has been rehabilitated and is used to supply offshore islands. Can carry 40 tons of vehicles or dry cargo on deck, plus liquid cargo of 24,224 liters fuel and 35,579 liters potable water. Has a bow ramp.

♦ 1 Sawahil 35–class self-propelled barracks craft [YPB]
Bldr: Inchon SB & Eng., South Korea (In serv. 1986)

S 5509 Al Dorrar (ex-*Qarq*, ex-*Sawahil 35*)

D: Approx. 1,800 tons (fl) **S:** 8 kts **Dim:** 55.0 × 20.0 × 2.0
A: 2 12.7-mm mg **Electronics:** Radar: 1 Decca . . . nav.
M: 2 diesels; 2 props; 2,400 bhp **Crew:** 40 tot.

SERVICE CRAFT *(continued)*

Al Dorrar (S 5509) Peter Voss, 11-92

Remarks: 545 dwt. The name has also been transliterated as *Qaruh.* Built for the Kuwait Shipbuilding and Repair Ministry for use as oilfield barracks. Escaped capture during the 1990–91 war and operated in support of Free Kuwaiti naval forces as a supply tender, carrying food, fuel, water, and ammunition. Refitted in 1996–97. Has a 20 × 20-m helicopter deck. Sisters *Sawahil 40* and *Sawahil 43* were lost during the war, and *Sawahil 50* served the Kuwaiti Coast Guard until recently.

COAST GUARD

Personnel: Approx. 500 uniformed personnel, plus 600 civilians

Bases: Shuwaikh and Umm al-Hainan

Note: Most of the craft built by Cougar Marine listed below were ordered in 1-91 by the then government-in-exile and were delivered after the 1991 liberation of Kuwait. All craft are painted dark gray and have a bright-red paired diagonal stripe on either beam.

PATROL CRAFT [WPC]

♦ 3 Al Shaheed FPB 100 class
Bldr: OCÉA, St. Nazaire, France

	In serv.
P 305 AL SHAHEED	7-97
P 306 BAYAN	25-5-99
P 307 DASMAN	8-6-01

Dasman (P 307) Bernard Prézelin, 8-01

D: 90 tons (115 fl) **S:** 30 kts **Dim:** 33.30 (27.6 wl) × 7.00 × 1.15
A: 3 12.7-mm mg
Electronics:
Radar: 1 Decca 20V90 nav.; 1 Decca C 252/8 nav.
E/O: 1 FLIR
M: 2 MTU 12V396 TE94 diesels; 2 waterjets; 4,400 bhp
Range: 360/25 **Crew:** 11 tot.

Remarks: P 307 ran trials in 6-01. The aluminum-construction hull has a notch amidships to permit easier rescue of persons in the water.

♦ 10 Subahi FPB 110 class
Bldr: OCÉA, St. Nazaire, France

	In serv.		In serv.
P 300 RAYYAN (ex-*Taroub,* 317)	23-8-05	P 312 NAIF	4-3-04
P 308 SUBAHI	6-8-03	P 313 DHAFIR	7-04
P 309 JABERI	12-03	P 314 MARZOUG	9-04
P 310 SAAD	2-04	P 315 MASH'HOOR	1-05
P 311 AHMEDI	13-1-04	P 316 WADDAH	3-05

D: 90 tons (115 fl) **S:** 30 kts **Dim:** 35.20 (29.85 wl) × 6.80 × 1.25
A: 3 12.7-mm mg
Electronics:
Radar: 2 Decca Bridgemaster-E nav.
E/O: 1 FLIR
M: 2 MTU 12V4000 M70 diesels; 2 waterjets; 4,600 bhp
Range: 500/20 **Crew:** 16 tot.

Rayyan (P 300)—used as Coast Guard flagship, upperworks are painted white. Bernard Prézelin, 8-05

Ahmedi (P 311) Bernard Prézelin, 2-04

Remarks: Slightly modified versions of the Al Shaheed class listed above. Ordered late in 2002, the class employs the AMARIS stabilized IR surveillance system, voyage management system, and other navigational systems. The aluminum-construction hull has a notch amidships to permit easier rescue of persons in the water. P 300 is equipped to serve as flagship for the Kuwaiti Coast Guard with upperworks painted white instead of a uniform gray.

♦ 4 ASI OPV 310 class
Bldr: Transfield ASI Pty, South Coogie, Australia (In serv. 11-92)

	In serv.		In serv.
P 301 INTTISAR	20-1-93	P 303 MAIMON	30-6-93
P 302 AMAN	20-1-93	P 304 MOBARK	30-6-93

Mobark (P 304) U.S. Navy, 9-95

D: 148 tons (165 fl) **S:** 28 kts
Dim: 32.60 (31.50 hull; 28.60 wl) × 8.20 × 1.60 (hull)
A: 1 12.7-mm mg; 2 single 7.62-mm mg
Electronics: Radar: 1 . . . nav.
M: 2 MTU 16V396 TB94 diesels; 2 props; . . . bhp—1 MTU 8V183 TE62 diesel for loiter; 1 Hamilton 422 waterjet; . . . bhp
Electric: 116 kw (2 × 50-kw Caterpillar 3304 diesels; 1 × 16 kw)
Range: 300/28; 2,500/12 **Fuel:** 27.9 tons **Endurance:** 8–10 days
Crew: 3 officers, 8 enlisted

Remarks: Ordered 7-90. Modified standard Australian foreign aid patrol boat design, with less draft and fuel and a third engine added centerline for cruising. Carry a 5-m rigid inflatable boarding boat. Builder has an option for a third pair. Sisters serve the Hong Kong Police.

PATROL BOATS [WPB]

♦ 3 Austal patrol and personnel transport boats
Bldr: Image Marine, Henderson, Australia (In serv. 2004)

T 205 KASSIR T 210 DASTOOR T 215 MAHROOS

COAST GUARD PATROL BOATS [WPB] *(continued)*

22-meter patrol boat—those in Kuwaiti service are painted gray with two red-orange stripes at the bow Image Marine, 2003

D: . . . **S:** 25 kts sust. **Dim:** 21.60 (19.60 wl) × 5.96 × 1.50 (hull)
A: Small arms **Electronics:** Radar: 1 . . . nav.
M: 2 M.A.N. D2842 LE 408 diesels; 2 props; 1,970 bhp
Electric: 80 kVA tot. (2 × 40-kVA diesel sets)
Range: 325/25 **Fuel:** 6,000 liters **Crew:** 3 tot. + 41 passengers

Remarks: Ordered 7-1-03 from Image Marine, a division of Austal Ships Pty. Operate in Arabian Sea waters in up to Force 6 winds. The passenger compartment is located directly below the pilothouse and has 41 individual seats. Painted gray with two red-orange stripes at the bow.

♦ 16 Type 46 fast patrol boats
Bldr: Victory Team shipbuilders, Dubai (In serv. 2005–6)

D: . . . **S:** 52 kts **Dim:** 14.2 × . . . × . . .
A: 2 single 12.7-mm mg **Electronics:** Radar: . . .
M: 2 Yanmar diesels; 2 props
Electric: . . .
Range: 200/50 **Fuel:** . . . **Crew:** 4 tot.

Remarks: Ordered 4-04.

♦ 4 . . . class
Bldr: FB Design, Annone Brianza, Italy (In serv. 2001)

D: 4.5 tons light **S:** 54 kts **Dim:** 13.00 × 2.70 × . . .
A: 2 single 12.7-mm mg
M: 2 Yanmar . . . diesels; 2 5-bladed Rolla surface-piercing props; 840 bhp
Range: 300/40; 480/25 **Fuel:** 260 gallons **Crew:** 4 tot.

Remarks: Deep-vee hull formed of Kevlar composite over a balsawood core. The machinegun mounts are side-by-side forward of the amidships conning position.

♦ 6 Enforcer 40 Mk 2B class
Bldr: Cougar Marine, Warsash, U.K. (In serv. 6-96 to 11-99)

Kuwaiti Coast Guard Enforcer 40 Mk 2B–class unit 465 Cougar Marine, 1996

D: 5.5 tons light **S:** 45 kts **Dim:** 12.19 × 2.74 × 0.76
A: 2 single 7.62-mm mg **Electronics:** Radar: 1 . . . nav.
M: 2 Ford Sabre 380S diesels; 2 Arneson ASD 8 outdrives with Rolla props; 760 bhp
Range: 300/35 **Fuel:** 818 liters **Crew:** 4 tot.

Remarks: Monohull form, constructed of GRP and Kevlar over a foam and plywood core. Can accommodate up to 300 kg of weapons.

♦ 23 28-foot class
Bldr: Al-Shaali Marine, Dubai (In serv. 7-92)

Remarks: GRP construction, ordered in early 1992. Powered by two Yamaha 200-bhp outboard engines. Have an APELCO navigational radar. No other details available.

♦ 10 33-foot class
Bldr: Al-Shaali Marine, Dubai (In serv. 7-92– . . .)

Remarks: GRP construction. Powered by two Yamaha 200-bhp outboard engines. Have an APELCO navigational radar. No other details available.

♦ 3 UFPB 1300 class
Bldr: Cougar Marine, Washington, U.K. (In serv. 6-91)

D: . . . tons (fl) **S:** . . . kts **Dim:** 13.0 × . . . × . . . **A:** 1 7.62-mm mg
M: 2 Ford Sabre 380C diesels; 2 Arneson surface-piercing props; 760 bhp

♦ 4 UFPB 1200 class
Bldr: Cougar Marine, Washington, U.K. (In serv. 6-91)

D: . . . tons (fl) **S:** . . . kts **Dim:** 12.0 × . . . × . . . **A:** 1 7.62-mm mg
M: 2 Ford Sabre 380C diesels; 2 Arneson surface-piercing props; 760 bhp

♦ 3 UFPB 1100 Predator-class GRP-hulled
Bldr: Cougar Marine, Washington, U.K. (In serv. 6-91)

D: . . . tons (fl) **S:** . . . kts **Dim:** 11.0 × . . . × . . . **A:** 1 7.62-mm mg
M: 2 Yamaha 200B gasoline outboards; 400 bhp

♦ 3 UFPB 1000–class GRP-hulled
Bldr: Cougar Marine, Washington, U.K. (In serv. 4-91)

D: . . . tons (fl) **S:** . . . kts **Dim:** 10.00 × . . . × . . . **A:** 1 7.62-mm mg
M: 2 Yamaha 200B gasoline outboards; 400 bhp

♦ 3 Cat 900–class catamarans
Bldr: Cougar Marine, Washington, U.K. (In serv. 5-91)

D: 2 tons (fl) **S:** 35 kts **Dim:** 9.0 × . . . × . . . **A:** 1 7.62-mm mg
M: 2 Yamaha 200B gasoline outboards; 400 bhp

SERVICE CRAFT

♦ 1 PVF 512 Sea Truck–class launch [WYFL]
Bldr: RTK Marine, Poole, U.K. (In serv. 6-94)

D: 9 tons (fl) **S:** 26 kts **Dim:** 12.7 × 3.2 × . . .
Electronics: Radar: 1 . . . nav.
M: 2 Yamaha diesels; 2 outdrive props; . . . bhp
Crew: 2 tot. + 14 passengers.

Remarks: Ordered 2-94 with an option for a second (not yet taken up). GRP construction. Can be beached to disembark passengers.

♦ 2 Al Tahaddy–class logistics support craft [WYFU]
Bldr: Singapore SB & Eng., Johore (L: 15-4-94; in serv. 7-94)

L 401 Al Tahaddy L 402 Al Soumood

Al Soumood (L 402) Maritime Photographic, 1-99

D: 215 tons (fl) **S:** 13 kts **Dim:** 43.0 × 10.0 × 1.5 **A:** . . .
Electronics: Radar: 1 Decca . . . nav.
M: 2 MTU . . . diesels; 2 props; . . . bhp

Remarks: Utility landing craft–typed craft. Capable of transporting vehicle and dry cargo up to 80 tons total. Have a bow ramp and a firefighting monitor atop the pilothouse.

♦ 1 Loadmaster Mk II logistics support landing craft [WYFU]
Bldr: Fairey Marine, Cowes (In serv. 1984–85)

L 403 Saffar

D: 175 tons light; 320 tons normal (420 fl) **S:** 10.5 kts (10.0 sust.)
Dim: 33.00 (30.00 pp) × 10.20 × 1.75
A: None **Electronics:** Radar: 1 Decca . . . nav.
M: 2 Caterpillar 3412 DITA, V-12 diesels; 2 Kort-nozzle props; 1,214 bhp (1,010 sust.)
Electric: 72 kw tot. **Range:** 1,000/10 **Fuel:** 30 tons
Crew: 1 officer, 6 enlisted

Remarks: Ordered in 1983. Captured by Iraqi forces, 8-90; recovered postwar, rehabilitated, and reactivated in 1992. Cargo includes 150 tons on deck, or 90 tons on deck and 60 tons liquid cargo. Can accommodate two 60-ton tanks. Sisters *Al Seef* (L 102) and *Al Badani* (L 104) were lost during the Iraqi war.

LAOS

Lao People's Democratic Republic

ARMY MARINE SECTION

Personnel: Approx. 600 total

PATROL BOATS [WPB]

♦ Approx. 40 river patrol craft

Remarks: Reported by press to have been a gift of the USSR in 1985. No other data available.

Note: Also possibly in service are four small landing craft. A number of locally built riverine craft are also in use.

LATVIA

Latvian Republic

LATVIAN NAVY

(*Latvijas Juras Speki*)

Personnel: Approx. 800 total (including 400 coast guard personnel)

Bases: Headquarters at Riga; bases at Liepaja, Bolderaja, and Ventspils

Organization: The fleet is divided into three coast guard divisions: the First Coast Guard Division, headquartered at Liepaja; the Second Coast Guard Division, headquartered at Bolderaja; and the Third Coast Guard Division at Ventspils. The First Division incorporates the coast guard ship division at Bolderaja and a coast defense company with rifle and communications platoons; another rifle platoon is at Ainazi. The Second Division incorporates a combat ship division at Liepaja, a coast guard ship division at Liepaja, and the coast defense battalion (with companies at Kolka, Liepaja, and Pavilosta). The newly created (1998) Third Division operates a single craft at Ventspils, along with a coast defense battalion company.

The Latvian Coast Guard is subordinated to the navy and shares personnel and base resources. Craft of the former Center for Search and Rescue Coordination were transferred to the navy in 2001, the first craft to transfer being the *Astra,* a former Finnish rescue ship purchased in 1996, on 13-3-01.

PATROL CRAFT [PC]

♦ 4 ex-Norwegian Storm class
Bldr: Bergens Mekaniske Verksted, Bergen (In serv.: P 03: 1967)

P-01 Zibens (ex-*Djerv,* P 966)
P-02 Lode (ex-*Hvass,* P 972)
P-03 Linga (ex-*Gnist,* P 979)
P-04 Bulta (ex-*Traust,* P 973)

Lode (P 02) Michael Winter, 6-05

Lode (P-02) Leo Van Ginderen, 5-05

Zibens (P-01) Martin Mokrus, 6-04

D: 105 tons (125 fl) **S:** 37 kts **Dim:** 36.53 × 6.3 × 1.8
A: P-04: 1 40-mm 60-cal. Bofors Mk 3 AA—others: 1 76.2-mm 50-cal. Bofors low-angle; 1 40-mm 70-cal. Bofors L70 AA
Electronics: Radar: P-04: Decca TM 1226 nav.—others: 1 Furuno . . . nav.
M: 2 Maybach MB 872A (MTU 16V538 TB90) diesels; 2 props; 7,200 bhp
Range: 550/36 **Crew:** 22 tot.

Remarks: P-04, launched 18-11-66, was stricken from the Norwegian Navy during 1993, rehabilitated during 1994, transferred 13-12-94 with the armament systems deleted, and recommissioned 1-2-95. An old Bofors hand-operated 40-mm AA was mounted aft during 1998. P 01, transferred in 2001, was incorrectly reported as the ex-*Josepf Schares* in previous editions. P-02 and P-03 were recommissioned 11-6-01 after transfer from Norway; their original gun armament was retained, along with a Bofors TVT300 optical director without the WM-22 gun fire-control system. All are based at Liepaja.

♦ 5 Pilica class (Project 918M)
Bldr: Stocznia Marynarki Wojennej, Gdynia (In serv. 1977–83; transferred 2006)

D: 85.62 tons std., 86.88 tons normal (93.03 normal fl; 100 max. fl)
S: 27.8 kts (25 cruise) **Dim:** 28.85 × 5.76 × 1.36 (hull)
A: 1 twin 23-mm 87-cal. ZU-23-2M Wrobel-1 AA; 2 fixed 533-mm OTAM-53 TT (2 SET-53M homing torpedoes)
Electronics:
Radar: 1 SRN-301 nav.
Sonar: MG-329M portable dipping set; SP-4301 echo sounder
M: 3 M-50F-5 diesels; 3 props; 3,600 bhp **Range:** 340/25; 1,160/11.4
Endurance: 5 days **Crew:** 3 officers, 9–11 enlisted

Remarks: Ordered on 28-12-04, transferred during 2006. Have steel hull, aluminum alloy superstructure, and GRP mast. Data listed above reflect the vessels while still in Polish service.

MINE-COUNTERMEASURES SHIPS

♦ 1 (+ 4) Alkmaar ("Tripartite")-class coastal minehunters [MHC]
Bldr: Van der Giessen de Noord, Alblasserdam (Transferred 2006–8)

	Laid down	L	In serv.
. . . (ex-*Alkmaar,* M 850)	30-1-79	18-5-82	28-5-83
. . . (ex-*Dalfzijl,* M 851)	29-5-80	29-10-82	17-8-83
. . . (ex-*Dordrecht,* M 852)	5-1-81	26-2-83	16-11-83
M 04 . . . (ex-*Harlingen,* M 854)	30-11-81	9-7-83	12-4-84
. . . (ex-*Scheveningen,* M 855)	25-5-82	8-12-83	18-7-84

D: 510 tons (540 fl) **S:** 15 kts (7 hunting)
Dim: 51.6 (47.1 pp) × 8.96 × 2.45 (2.6 max.)
A: 1 20-mm 90-cal. GIAT 20F-2 AA
Electronics:
Radar: 1 Decca TM 1229C or Consilium Selesmar NN 950 nav.
Sonar: Thales DUBM-21B
M: 1 Brons-Werkspoor A-RUB 215 × 12 diesel; 1 CP prop; 1,900 bhp—2 75-shp bow-thrusters; 2 120-shp ACEC active rudders
Electric: 970 kw tot. (3 × 270 kw, gas-turbine driven; 1 × 160-kw diesel set)
Range: 3,500/10 **Endurance:** 15 days **Crew:** 34–42 tot.

Remarks: Same basic design as the Tripartite minehunters for France and Belgium. These vessels were retired from Dutch service between 2000 and 2004 without having received the upgrades and modernizations planned for those remaining in Dutch service, though Latvia may elect to do so at a later date.
Hull systems: Hull is made of a compound of glass fiber and polyester resin. Have active tank stabilization. The 5-ton modular van abaft the superstructure can contain a decompression station, communications equipment, drone control gear, and so forth.
Combat systems: Mine-countermeasures equipment includes two PAP 104 Mk 4 remote-controlled submersibles, the EVEC 20 plot table, autopilot, Toran and Sydelis radio navaids, and the Decca HiFix Mk 6 precision navigation system. Can also tow a mechanical drag sweep and carry OD-3 mechanical sweep gear. The DUBM-21B sonar can detect mines in waters up to 80-m depth, at slant ranges up to 500 m.

♦ 1 ex-German Type 331B minehunter [MHC]

	Bldr	L	In serv.
M-03 Nemejs (ex-*Völklingen,* M 1087)	Burmester, Bremen	20-10-59	21-5-60

D: 388 tons (402 fl) **S:** 16.5 kts
Dim: 47.45 × 8.5 × 2.8 (3.68 with sonar extended)
A: 1 40-mm 70-cal. Bofors AA

MINE-COUNTERMEASURES SHIPS *(continued)*

Nemejs (M-03) Michael Nitz, 7-05

Nemejs (M-03) Michael Nitz, 7-05

Electronics:
Radar: 1 Raytheon SPS-64(V) nav.
Sonar: DSQS-11A HF minehunting
M: 2 MTU 16V538 TB90 diesels; 2 CP props; 5,000 bhp **Electric:** 220 kw tot.
Range: 1,400/16; 3,950/9 **Crew:** 5 officers, 29 enlisted + 6 divers

Remarks: Stricken from the German Navy 23-3-99, transferred 24-3-99, and formally commissioned at Riga 1-10-99 after an extensive refit in Germany.
Hull systems: Wooden construction, with nonmagnetic engines. Minehunting speed is 6 kts on two 50-kw electric motors.
Combat systems: Six divers and two French PAP-104 remote-controlled minehunting devices can be carried. Has no mechanical sweep gear. The 40-mm gun is controlled by a lead-computing optical director on the bridge.

♦ 2 ex-East German Kondor-II-class (Project 89.2) minesweepers [MSC]
Bldr: VEB Peenewerft, Wolgast

	Original in serv.	Transferred	In serv.
M-01 Viesturs (ex-*Kamenz,* 351)	24-7-71	30-8-93	4-94
M-02 Imanta (ex-*Röbel,* 324)	1-12-71	30-8-93	5-94

Viesturs (M-01) Michael Winter, 6-04

D: 414 tons (479 fl) **S:** 18 kts **Dim:** 56.52 × 7.78 × 2.46
A: 1 twin 23-mm 87-cal. Wrobel ZSU-23-2 AA; 2 single 20-mm 90-cal. Rh-202 AA
Electronics: Radar: TSR-333 nav.
M: 2 Type 40DM diesels; 2 CP Kort-nozzle props; 4,400 bhp
Electric: 625 kw tot. (5 × 125-kw diesel sets)
Range: 2,000/15 **Endurance:** 10 days **Crew:** 6 officers, 24 enlisted

Remarks: Transferred 21-7-93 and delivered 31-8-93 at Riga after removal of all armament and portable mine-countermeasures equipment. Had been out of service in reserve since 1-12-81 and 3-10-90, respectively. The similar former East German Kondor-class torpedo retriever *Libben* (V 662) was acquired in mid-1995 for cannibalization to support these two units. M-02 was initially armed with three Polish-supplied gunmounts; two have now been distributed to other units. Both received German 20-mm AA mounts during 2000. Surplus German sweep gear was acquired for both in 1996. Based at Liepaja. Expected to decommission by 2008, to be replaced by the Dutch Alkmaar class.

AUXILIARIES

♦ 1 ex-Norwegian Vidar-class fleet flagship [AGF]
Bldr: Mjellem & Karlsen, Bergen

	Laid down	L	In serv.
A 53 Virsaitis (ex-*Vale,* N 53)	1-2-76	5-8-77	10-2-78

Virsaitis (A 53) Chris Sattler, 7-05

Virsaitis (A 53) Leo Van Ginderen, 6-05

D: 1,500 tons (1,722 fl) **S:** 15 kts **Dim:** 64.80 (60.00 pp) × 12.00 × 4.00 (hull)
A: 2 single 40-mm 70-cal. Bofors AA; 320 mines
Electronics:
Radar: 2 Decca TM 1226 nav.
Sonar: Simrad SQ3D hull-mounted HF
M: 2 Wichmann 7AX diesels; 2 props; 4,200 bhp—425-shp bow-thruster
Electric: 1,000 kw tot. **Range:** . . . / . . . **Fuel:** 247 tons **Crew:** 50 tot.

Remarks: Former minelayer transferred by donation 27-1-03 for use as a fleet flagship and tender to patrol craft. Capable of serving as a minelayer (mines carried on three decks, with electric elevators to first platform deck and upper deck, and three mine-laying rails) and torpedo-recovery ship as well as a personnel and cargo transport. Has TVT300 optronic directors for the 40-mm AA. Antisubmarine armament of two triple Mk 32 ASW TT and two d.c. racks has been removed, as was the Mistral point-defense missile system.

♦ 1 Ex-Dutch Blommendal-class hydrographic survey ships [AGS]
Bldr: Boele's Scheepswerven en Machinefabriek BV, Bolnes

	Laid down	L	In serv.
A 90 Varonis (ex-*Buyskes,* 904)	31-1-72	11-7-72	9-3-73

Varonis (A 90) Jaroslaw Malinowski, 11-04

AUXILIARIES *(continued)*

D: 867 tons (1,025 fl) **S:** 14 kts **Dim:** 58.80 × 11.13 × 3.70
Electronics:
Radar: 1 Decca TM 1226 nav.; 1 Decca 1229 nav.
Sonar: Thales Bathyscan hull-mounted HF side-scanning; 2 STN Atlas Elektronik DESO-25 precision echo-sounders
M: 3 Paxman 12 RPHCZ7 diesels (742-bhp each), Smit electric drive; 1 prop; 1,100 shp
Electric: 745 kw tot. **Range:** 7,000/10 **Crew:** 6 officers, 37 enlisted

Remarks: Decommissioned from Dutch service on 11-12-03, transferred to Latvia 5-11-04, and formally recommissioned on 27-11-04. Hull and superstructure are painted white, the stacks and masts yellow.

SERVICE CRAFT

♦ **1 Soviet Nyryat-1-class diving tender [YDT]**
Bldr: . . . Russia (In serv. ca. 1960)

A-51 Lidaka (ex-*Gefests,* A 101)

Lidaka (A-51) Stefan Marx, 2002

D: 92 tons (116.1 fl) **S:** 11 kts **Dim:** 28.58 × 5.20 × 1.70
A: 1 12.7-mm mg **Electronics:** Radar: 1 SNN-7 nav.
M: 1 Type 6CSP 28/3C diesel; 1 prop; 450 bhp
Range: 1,500/10 **Crew:** 1 officer, 5 enlisted

Remarks: Ex-civilian unit of the class, based at Ventspils and taken over in 1992, not a former Russian Navy unit. Based at Liepaja.

♦ **1 ex-Polish Goliat-class (Project H300/II) small harbor tug [YTL]**
Bldr: Gdynska Stocznia Remontowa Nauta, Gdynia (In serv. 20-1-63)

A-18 Perkons (ex-H 18)

D: 112 tons (fl) **S:** 10 kts **Dim:** 21.4 × 5.8 × 2.1
M: 1 Buckau-Wolf 8NVD36 diesel; 1 prop; 300 bhp
Range: 300/9 **Crew:** 3 officers, 9 enlisted

Remarks: Donated by Poland 16-11-93. Based at Liepaja.

Note: Also taken over were two Soviet Army pontoon bridge erection boats, renumbered RK-104 and RK-105; one is in land storage and the other acts as a painting float. A former Soviet PO-2 (Project 376) utility launch named *Roze* was transferred to the navy from the Latvian Maritime Board at Ventspils for possible future activation.

Perkons (A-18) Hartmut Ehlers, 4-95

COAST GUARD
(Latvijas Kara Flotes)

Note: The coast guard is subordinate to the navy, and its personnel totals are included in the naval listing above.

PATROL CRAFT [WPC]

♦ **1 ex-Finnish Valpas class**
Bldr: Laivateollisuus Oy, Turku

	Laid down	L	In serv.
Valpas	20-5-70	22-12-70	21-7-71

Valpas—painted with green hull, red and white stripes and gray superstructure Jaroslaw Cislak, 5-03

D: 545 tons **S:** 15 kts **Dim:** 48.3 × 8.7 × 4.0
A: Provision for 1 twin 23-mm 60-cal. Sako AA
Electronics: Radar: 2 . . . nav.—Sonar: Simrad SS 105 (14 kHz)
M: 1 Werkspoor TMABS-398 diesel; 1 CP prop; 2,000 bhp **Crew:** 22 tot.

Remarks: Ice-strengthened; equipped for towing, firefighting, and salvage duties. Transferred from Finland 25-9-02.

♦ **1 Ribnadzor-4-class fisheries protection patrol boat**
Bldr: Rybinsk Sudostroitel'niy Zavod (In serv. 1979)

KA-03 Kometa (ex-103, ex-*Ribnadzor*-2)

Kometa (KA-03) Hartmut Ehlers, 9-96

COAST GUARD PATROL CRAFT [WPC] *(continued)*

D: 143 tons (173.3 fl) **S:** 15 kts **Dim:** 34.40 × 5.80 × 2.45
A: 1 12.7-mm mg **Electronics:** Radar: 1 Mius (Spin Trough) nav.
M: 1 Type 40DM-M3 diesel; 1 prop; 2,200 bhp **Range:** . . . / . . .
Crew: 4 officers, 13 enlisted

Remarks: Taken over and recommissioned for naval use 5-5-92. Based at Bolderaja. Sister *Spulga* (KA-02) went aground at Karlskrona 2-11-00 and sank while under tow on 6-11-00.

♦ 1 ex-Finnish Tiira-class training launch [YXT]
Bldr: Valmet-Laivateollisuus, Turku

	L	In serv.
. . . (ex-*Tiira*)	5-9-85	1-11-85

D: 65 tons (fl) **S:** 25+ kts **Dim:** 26.80 (24.20 pp) × 5.50 × 1.40 (1.85 props)
A: Provision for: 1 or 2 twin 23-mm 60-cal. Sako AA
Electronics:
Radar: 1 . . . nav.
Sonar: Simrad SS-242 hull-mounted
M: 2 MTU 8V396 TB82 diesels; 2 props; 2,286 bhp
Electric: 62 kVa tot. **Fuel:** 8 tons **Crew:** 2 officers, 6 enlisted

Remarks: Transferred from Finland in 2001.

PATROL BOATS [WPB]

♦ 5 ex-Swedish Coast Guard Kbv 236 class (In serv. 1970)

	Transferred	Base
KA-01 Kristaps (ex-Kbv 244)	5-2-93	Bolderaja
KA-06 Gaisma (ex-Kbv 249)	9-11-93	Bolderaja
KA-07 Ausma (ex-Kbv 260)	9-11-93	Liepaja
KA-08 Saule (ex-Kbv 256)	27-4-94	Ventspils
KA-09 Klints (ex-Kbv 250)	27-4-94	Bolderaja

Saule (KA-08) H&L Van Ginderen, 10-00

Klints (KA-09)—with larger pilothouse Hartmut Ehlers, 4-95

D: 17 tons (fl) **S:** 22 kts **Dim:** 19.2 × 4.0 × 1.3
A: Small arms **Electronics:** Radar: 1 . . . nav.
M: 2 Volvo Penta TAMD 120A diesels; 2 props; 700 bhp
Crew: 1 officer, 2 enlisted

Remarks: Sisters transferred to Estonia and Lithuania also. KA-07 has a slightly higher pilothouse, while KA-09 has a larger pilothouse with a second (Furuno) radar atop it. All carry a rigid inflatable inspection dinghy aft.

♦ 1 ex-Russian Aist-class (Project 1398) patrol launch
Bldr: Svetenskiy Zavod, Kokue (In serv. 1975–86)

KA-12 Granata

Granata (KA-12) Hartmut Ehlers, 4-95

D: 3.55 tons (5.8 fl) **S:** 20 kts **Dim:** 9.50 × 2.60 × 0.50
A: Small arms **Electronics:** Radar: none
M: 1 3D-20 diesel; 1 prop; 235 bhp **Fuel:** 0.37 tons **Crew:** . . . tot.

Remarks: Transferred in 1994. Had been used by Russian Maritime Border Guard. Refitted in Latvia prior to recommissioning circa 5-95. Based at Liepaja.

♦ 2 former Russian Navy officers launches (Project 371U)
KA-10 KA-11

KA-11—KA-10 has a smaller cockpit aft and a smaller pilothouse Hartmut Ehlers, 9-96

D: 9.41 tons (fl) **S:** 13.5 kts **Dim:** 12.61 × 3.23 × 0.6 (1.00 over prop)
A: Small arms **Electronics:** Radar: 1 Furuno . . . nav.
M: 1 Type 3D6S diesel; 1 prop; 150 bhp **Range:** 140/13.5
Crew: 1 officer, 2 enlisted

Remarks: Built during the early 1950s. Both had been used by the DOSAAF (Soviet Communist Youth League) Technical Center for Diving at Riga. KA-11 was refitted at Riga in 1995. Both are based at Bolderaja. Have steel hulls and wooden superstructure, with KA-11 having had the cover over the after cockpit and the pilothouse enlarged while in Soviet service.

♦ 1 . . . -class salvage craft
Bldr: . . . Finland (In serv: 12-3-01)

KA-14 Astra

D: 22 tons (fl) **S:** 25 kts **Dim:** 22.8 × 5.5 × 2.8
A: . . . **Electronics:** Radar: 1 Furuno . . . nav.
M: 3 Saab-Scania D91-1467 diesels; 3 props; 1,850 bhp **Range:** 525/25
Crew: 1 officer, 3 enlisted

Remarks: No other data available.

LEBANON

Republic of Lebanon

Personnel: Approx. 1,100 total

Bases: Beirut and Jounieh

PATROL BOATS [PB]

♦ 7 Tracker Mk II class
Bldr: Fairey Allday Marine, Hamble, U.K.

	In serv.
301 Trablous (ex-*Attacker,* P 281)	11-3-83
302 Jounieh (ex-*Fencer,* P 283)	21-3-83
303 Batroun (ex-*Safeguard*)	1978
304 Jebail (ex-*Chaser,* P 282)	11-3-83
306 Saïda (ex-*Striker,* P 285)	7-83
307 Sarafand (ex-*Swift*)	1978
309 Arz (ex-*Hunter,* P 284)	21-3-83

PATROL BOATS [PB] *(continued)*

Trablous (301) French Navy, 5-96

D: 34.54 tons (fl) **S:** 21 kts **Dim:** 20.0 (19.25 wl) × 5.18 × 1.50
A: 3 single 12.7-mm mg **Electronics:** Radar: 1 Decca 1216 nav.
M: 2 G.M. 12V71 TI diesels; 2 props; 1,300 bhp **Electric:** 30 kw tot.
Range: 650/20 **Crew:** 11 tot.

Remarks: The five former Royal Navy units were purchased in 7-92, having been paid off in 1991–92. GRP hull construction. *Batroun* and *Sarafand* were purchased in 3-94 after retirement from the British Customs Service; they have Decca 2690 radars and have been fitted with twin 23-mm AA mounts on the bow.

♦ **27 ex-U.S. Bridge Erection Boats** (14 in reserve)
Bldr: Fairey Marintechnik, Cowes, U.K. (In serv. 1980s)

D: 6 tons (fl) **S:** 22 kts **Dim:** 8.2 × 2.5 × 0.6
A: 2 single 7.62-mm mg **M:** 2 Ford Sabre 212 diesels; 2 waterjets; 424 bhp
Range: 154/22 **Crew:** 3 tot.

Remarks: Transferred 1-94, but 14 remain in land storage. Originally intended for freshwater service on European rivers in support of pontoon bridge erection units, but used by Lebanon for inshore patrol duties. Aluminum construction. No radar.

AMPHIBIOUS WARFARE CRAFT

♦ **2 French EDIC-III-class utility landing craft [LCU]**
Bldr: SFCN, Villeneuve-la-Garenne

21 Sour (In serv. 1-85) 22 Damour (L: 11-12-84)

Damour (22) French Navy, 5-96

D: 375 tons (712 fl) **S:** 10 kts **Dim:** 59.00 (57.00 pp) × 11.90 × 1.67 (1.10 light)
A: 2 single 20-mm 70-cal. Oerlikon Mk 10 AA; 1 81-mm mortar
Electronics: Radar: 1 Decca 1226 nav.
M: 2 SACM MGO 175-V12-A diesels; 2 props; 1,040 bhp
Range: 1,800/10 **Fuel:** 35 tons **Crew:** 18 tot. + 33 troops

Remarks: Ordered 30-7-83 as aid from the French government. *Sour* replaced an earlier EDIC (L 9096) of the same name that had been loaned 7-11-83. Can carry 11 trucks or 5 armored personnel carriers.

Note: Also in use is the yacht *Imanuella* (501), a captured drug runner; no details available. The customs service operates two Tracker Mk II patrol boats, the *Erez-II* and the *Lebanon-II,* with the same characteristics data as those for the naval units.

LIBYA

Socialist People's Libyan Arab Jamahiriya

Personnel: Approx. 8,000 total, including the Coast Guard

Bases: Ships based at Al Khums, Ras Hilal, and Tobruq; naval air base at Al Girdabiyah; naval infantry at Sidi Bilal

Naval Aviation: About five AS.316B Alouette-III and seven Super Frelon helicopters.

Coastal Defense: Some truck-mounted batteries with twin launchers for Russian P-20 Termit (SS-C-3) antiship missiles may still be operable. There is also an extensive force of beach patrol troops under naval control.

Note: The recent easing of economic sanctions on Libya has had a marked impact on their naval forces as numerous warships, long considered nonoperational, are returned to service.

SUBMARINES [SS]

Note: Although the hulks of Soviet-supplied Foxtrot-class (Project 641) diesel submarines *Al Ahad* (313), *Al Mitraqah* (314), *Al Khyber* (315), and *Al Hunayn* (316) remain more or less afloat at Tobruq, none has operated even on the surface since 1995, and the last known submergence by a Libyan submarine took place 19 or more years ago. Sister *Al Badr* (311) sank alongside in harbor in 1993 and has not been repaired, while *Al Fateh* (312) was sent to the Baltic in 1987 for an overhaul and was later scrapped in Russia. Montenegrin technicians were said to be traveling to Libya to attempt repair and activation of one or more submarines as of late 7-99, but such vital components as batteries are very difficult to obtain, and the boats are almost certainly beyond repair.

FRIGATES [FF]

♦ **2 Soviet Modified Koni class (Project 1159TR)**
Bldr: Krasniy Metallist Zavod, Zelnodol'sk, Russia

	Laid down	L	In serv.
212 Al Hani	10-1-85	27-4-85	28-6-86
213 Al Ghardabia	18-4-85	27-4-86	24-10-87

Al Ghardabia (213) Leo Van Ginderen, 5-05

Al Ghardabia (213) Anthony Vella, 5-05

D: 1,440 tons light; 1,596 tons normal (1,676 fl)
S: 27 kts (29.67 on trials; 22 on diesels)
Dim: 96.51 × 12.55 × 4.12 (mean hull; 5.72 over sonar)
A: 4 P-20/21 Termit (SS-N-2C Styx) SSM; 1 2-rail Osa-M (SA-N-4) SAM syst. (20 9M-33 Gecko missiles); 2 twin 76.2-mm 59-cal. AK-726 DP; 2 twin 30-mm 65-cal. AK-230 AA; 1 12-round RBU-6000 ASW RL (60 RGB-60 rockets); 4 fixed 400-mm ASW TT
Electronics:
Radar: 1 Don-2 nav.; 1 MR-302 (Strut Curve) surf./air search; 1 Koral-E (Plank Shave) surface target detection/desig.; 1 MPZ-301 (Pop Group) SAM f.c.; 1 MR-105 Turel' (Hawk Screech) 76.2-mm gun f.c.; 1 MR-104 Rys' (Drum Tilt) 30-mm gun f.c.
Sonar: MG-322T hull-mounted MF; HF f.c.
EW: 2 Bizan'-series (Watch Dog) intercept; 1 Cross Loop-A MFD/F; 2 16-round PK-16 decoy RL
M: CODAG: 1 M-813 gas turbine (18,000 shp), 2 Type 68B diesels (9,000 bhp each); 3 props; 36,000 hp
Range: 4,546/14.98 **Crew:** 96 tot.

Remarks: Were the 11th and 12th units built of this export class. These were the only version of the Koni (NATO "Koni-III") to be built with antiship missiles and ASW torpedoes, at the expense of one ASW rocket launcher. After several years of inactivity 213 was recently reactivated and visited Malta during 5-05.
Hull systems: The deckhouse amidships is continuous in order to accommodate additional air-conditioning equipment. The centerline propeller is of fixed pitch, while the outboard propellers are controllable pitch.
Combat systems: The Koral-E radar acts as surface search and acquisition for the Termit missiles and can also function in the passive intercept mode. The MPZ-301 track-while-scan radar controls the Osa-M SAMs; the MR-105 Turel' (with two pedestal-type optical target designators) handles the 76.2-mm guns; and the MR-104 Rys' radar director (again with two visual backup directors) serves the 30-mm guns.

FRIGATES [FF] *(continued)*

Note: The Vosper Mk 7 frigate *Dat Assawari* (211), removed from a Genoese shipyard while partially finished with an overhaul, was returned to Tripoli in 1992 and is a nonoperational training hulk along with the Vosper Mk 1B corvette *Tobruk* (411).

GUIDED-MISSILE PATROL COMBATANTS [PGG]

♦ 2 Nanuchka-II class (Project 1234E)

Bldr: Sudostroitel'noye Obyedineniye "Almaz," Petrovskiy SY, St. Petersburg, Russia

	Laid down	L	In serv.
416 Tariq-ibn Ziyad (ex-*Ain Mara;* ex-MPK-9)	21-4-79	10-1-81	27-5-81
418 Ain Zaara (ex-MPK-25)	27-5-81	21-7-82	19-1-83

Tariq-ibn Ziyad (416) H&L Van Ginderen, 7-91

D: 560 tons (660 fl) **S:** 30 kts **Dim:** 59.3 × 12.6 × 2.4 (3.1 max.)
A: 6 P-20/21 Termit (SS-N-2C Styx) SSM; 1 2-rail Osa-M (SA-N-4) SAM syst. (20 9M-33 Gecko missiles); 1 twin 57-mm 70-cal. AK-727 DP
Electronics:
Radar: 1 Don-2 nav.; 1 Rangout (Square Tie) surf. missile target detection/desig.; 1 MPZ-301 (Pop Group) SAM f.c.; 1 MR-103 Bars (Muff Cob) radar-E/O gun f.c.
EW: 1 Bell Tap intercept; 2 16-round PK-16 decoy RL
M: 3 M-521 diesels; 3 props; 25,996 bhp
Range: 900/30; 2,500/12 (on 1 engine) **Endurance:** 10 days
Crew: 7 officers, 42 enlisted

Remarks: Sister *Ain Zaquit* (419) was sunk 24-3-86 by U.S. aircraft. 416, damaged the next day by U.S. aircraft, was sent to the Baltic for an extensive repair/overhaul in 1990, returning to Libya in 2-91. *Ain al Gazala* (417) was cannibalized during the 1990s to keep the other two marginally operable.
Hull systems: Considered to be poor sea boats by some customers, with unreliable propulsion plants (M-521 is a tropicalized version of the M-507, which is a paired M-504 42-cylinder radial diesel sharing a common gearbox).
Combat systems: The MR-103 radar director for the 57-mm gunmount has a t.v. adjunct. The Rangout radar's antenna is mounted within the radome named Band Stand by NATO and can also function in a passive mode as a target radiation intercept system.

GUIDED-MISSILE PATROL CRAFT [PTG]

♦ 8 Combattante-II class

Bldr: CMN, Cherbourg, France

	Laid down	L	In serv.
518 Sharara (ex-*Beir Grassa*)	13-3-78	28-6-79	9-2-82
522 Shehab (ex-*Beir Gzir*)	10-6-78	22-1-80	3-4-82
524 Wahg (ex-*Beir Gtifa*)	30-1-79	20-5-80	29-5-82
525 Shouaiai (ex-*Beir Algandula*)	12-2-79	14-1-81	5-9-82
532 Shoula (ex-*Beir Alkitan*)	17-12-79	22-4-81	29-10-82
534 Shafak (ex-*Beir Alkirim*)	11-3-80	23-6-81	17-12-82
538 Rad (ex-*Beir Alkur*)	20-10-80	30-11-81	10-5-83
542 Laheeb (ex-*Beir Alkuesat*)	20-1-81	9-1-82	29-7-83

Shafak (534)—visiting Malta Anthony Vella, 6-01

D: 258 tons (311 fl) **S:** 39 kts **Dim:** 49.00 (46.20 pp) × 7.10 × 2.00
A: 4 Otomat Mk 1 SSM; 1 76-mm 62-cal. OTO Melara Compact DP; 1 twin 40-mm 70-cal. Breda-Bofors AA
Electronics: Radar: 1 Decca 1226 nav.; 1 Thales Triton surf./air search; 1 Thales Castor IIB gun f.c.
M: 4 MTU MD 20V538 TB 91 diesels; 4 props; 18,000 bhp
Range: 1,600/15 **Crew:** 8 officers, 19 enlisted

Laheeb (542) Anthony Vella, 6-01

Remarks: Delivery was embargoed from 27-2-81 to 12-81 by the French government. Had been laid up for many years for lack of spares, but 522, 534, and 542 visited Malta in fall 2001, indicating that the relaxation on embargoes against Libya has resulted in the reactivation of at least three. *Rad* (538), previously thought to have retired, was sighted in service during 5-05.
Disposals: *Waheed* (526) was sunk by U.S. forces on 24-3-86. *Bark* (536, ex-*Beir Alkardmen*) is reportedly beyond repair, although she may still be afloat and used as cannibalization spares source.
Combat systems: The gun fire–control system is the Thales Vega II. The Otomat missiles for these ships have long ago passed their shelf lives, but the missile launch canisters remain aboard; the missiles may no longer be usable.

♦ 5 Soviet Osa-II class (Project 205EM)

513 Al Zuara 523 Al Fikah 531 Al Bitar
515 Al Ruha 525 Al Sakab

Al Zuara (513)—in dry dock at Malta H&L Van Ginderen, 1986

D: 184 tons (226 normal fl, 245 overload) **S:** 40 kts (35 sust.)
Dim: 38.6 (37.5 wl) × 7.6 (6.3 wl) × 2.0 (hull; 3.1 props)
A: 4 P-15M/20/21 Termit (SS-N-2B/C Styx) SSM; 2 twin 30-mm 65-cal. AK-230 AA

GUIDED-MISSILE PATROL CRAFT [PTG] *(continued)*

Electronics: Radar: 1 Rangout (Square Tie) surf. search/target detection;
1 MR-104 Rys' (Drum Tilt) gun f.c.
M: 3 M-504 or M-504B diesels; 3 props; 15,000 bhp **Electric:** 400 kw tot.
Range: 500/34; 750/25 **Endurance:** 5 days **Crew:** 4 officers, 24 enlisted

Remarks: Probably built at Rybinsk. One delivered in 1976, four in 1977, one in 1978, three in 1979, and three in 1980. Reportedly, the original order was reduced from 24 to 12. Names and numbers above represent the latest available listing; numbers are changed from time to time. The survivors rarely put to sea. During 1993, they were repainted with blue hulls and white superstructures.
Disposals: By 1998, *Al Katum* (511), *Al Baida* (517), *Al Nabha* (519), *Al Safra* (521), *Al Mosha* (527), *Al Mathur* (529), and *Al Sadad* (533) had been relegated to cannibalization spares.
Combat systems: The Rangout radar can probably also be operated in the passive mode to detect target radiations. Can carry 2,000 rounds of 30-mm ammunition. The reliability of any remaining P-15M missiles is suspect.

Note: Of the upwards of 125 radio-controlled, GRP-hulled suicide boats of Libyan, Swedish, and Cypriot construction acquired during the early 1980s for coast defense service, most are probably no longer operable. No details are available except that speeds of 30 kts were attainable and that the Cyprus-built craft were 7.92 m long and those built in Sweden were 9.45 m o.a.

MINE WARFARE SHIPS

♦ 5 Soviet Natya-class (Project 266ME) fleet minesweepers [MSF]
Bldr: Sudostroitel'noye Obyedineniye "Almaz" (Sredniy Neva), Kolpino

111 Al I'sar (ex-*Ras el Gelais*)
113 Al Tayyar (ex-*Ras Hadad*)
117 Ras al Falluga
119 Ras al Oula
123 Ras Massad

Libyan Navy Natya—painted with blue hull and white superstructure 1993

D: 750 tons std., 804 tons normal (873 max.) **S:** 17.6 kts (16 sust.)
Dim: 61.00 (57.6 wl) × 10.20 × 2.98 (hull)
A: 2 twin 30-mm 65-cal. AK-230 AA; 2 twin 25-mm 80-cal. 2M-3 AA—123 only: 2 4-round SA-N-8 SAM syst. (18 Igla-1 missiles)—all: 2 5-round RBU-1200 ASW RL (60 RGB-12 rockets); 2 mine rails (8 UDME mines)
Electronics:
Radar: 1 Don-2 nav.; 1 MR-104 Rys' (Drum Tilt) f.c.
Sonar: MG-89 HF hull-mounted
M: 2 M-503B-3E diesels; 2 shrouded CP props; 5,000 bhp (4,500 sust.)
Electric: 600 kw tot. (3 × 200-kw DGR-200/1500 diesel sets)
Range: 1,800/16; 3,000/12; 5,200/10 **Fuel:** 87 tons **Endurance:** 10–15 days
Crew: 8 officers, 59 enlisted

Remarks: Survivors of 12, the first pair delivered 3-81, the second pair in 2-83, the fifth unit 3-9-83, the sixth during 2-84, the seventh 20-1-85, and the last five in 10-86. Names on the first two were changed after delivery but not, apparently, the remainder. Are used primarily for coastal patrolling and rarely, if ever, exercise their mine-warfare capabilities. Were repainted with blue hulls and white superstructures around 1993. 123 conducted a cadet training cruise during 1997.
Hull systems: Like the units built for India, they lack the ramp at the stern found on Soviet units. Stem is cut back sharply below the waterline. Have a low-magnetic-signature, aluminum-steel alloy hull and a DGR-450/1500P diesel-driven degaussing system. The engines are a derated version of the same high-speed, multirow diesels that power the Osa-class guided-missile patrol boats. Have enhanced air-conditioning capacity over their Russian Navy sisters and also have about 100 kw more generator capacity. Carry 45 tons of water but do not have distilling equipment. Navigational equipment includes a GKU-2 gyrocompass, NELMZB echo sounder, Rumb MFD/F, Pirs-1M receiver for Decca radio navaid, and AP-4 automatic position plot. Khmel-1 infrared position-keeping and signaling equipment is carried.
Combat systems: The RBU-1200 ASW rocket launchers are also used for detonating mines. Sweep gear includes GKT-2 mechanical, AT-2 acoustic, and TEM-3 magnetic arrays. The sonar incorporates a downward-looking, high-frequency, bottomed-mine detection component with a range of 350–400 m. Some 2,149 rounds are carried for each 30-mm gunmount.
Disposals: *Ras al Hamman* (115), *Ras al Dawar* (121), and *Ras al Hani* (125) had been hulked by 1998 as cannibalization spares sources and are not likely to operate again.

AMPHIBIOUS WARFARE SHIPS

Disposal note: Of the Polnocny-C-class (Project 773KL) medium landing craft delivered 1977–79, *Ibn al Qyis* (113) was lost in 9-78 through fire while at sea, and *Ibn al Hadrani* (112), *Ibn el Omayar* (116), and *Ibn el Farat* (118) had ceased to be functional by 1999, although perhaps one could be reactivated; they remain afloat.

♦ 2 Ibn Ouf-class tank landing ship [LST] Bldr: C.N.I.M., La Seyne

	Laid down	L	In serv.
132 Ibn Ouf	1-4-76	22-10-76	11-3-77
134 Ibn Harissa	18-4-77	18-10-77	10-3-78

Ibn Harissa (134) Anthony Vella, 5-05

Ibn Harissa (134) Frank Behling, 5-05

D: 2,800 tons (fl) **S:** 15 kts **Dim:** 100 × 15.65 × 2.6
A: 6 40-mm 70-cal. OTO Melara AA—1 81-mm mortar
Electronics: Radar: 1 Decca 12216 nav.
M: 2 SEMT-Pielstick 16 PA4 V185 diesels; 2 CP props; 5,340 bhp
Range: 4000/14 **Crew:** 35 crew + 240 troops

Remarks: Though long thought retired from the Libyan Navy, 134 resurfaced in the Mediterranean in early 2003 and visited Malta during 5-05. *Ibn Ouf* (132) appears to have also returned to service by 2005. Cargo: 570 tons, including up to 11 tanks. Helicopter platform aft. Operational utility of the vessel is unknown. Painted light blue-green with a black waterline.

♦ 4 Turkish Ç 107-class utility landing craft [LCU]
Bldrs: Taskizak SY, Istanbul, and Gölçük Naval SY

130 Ibn al Idrissi (ex-Ç 130)
131 Ibn Marwhan (ex-Ç 131)
132 Ras el Hillel (ex-Ç 132)
133 El Kobayat (ex-Ç 133)

D: 280 tons (600 fl) **S:** 10 kts (8.5 loaded) **Dim:** 56.56 × 11.58 × 1.25
A: 2 single 20-mm 70-cal. Oerlikon AA
Electronics: Radar: 1 . . . nav.
M: 3 G.M. Detroit Diesel 6-71TI diesels; 3 props; 900 bhp
Range: 600/10; 1,100/8 **Crew:** 15 tot.

Remarks: Former Turkish Navy units transferred 7-12-79. As many as 50 were to be acquired, with two Turkish yards each building 25, but it now appears that only the initial increment was ever received. Design follows that of the World War II–era British LCT(4) class. Cargo: up to 350 tons (five heavy tanks, up to 100 troops). Cargo deck: 28.5 × 7.9 m. One of the above may have been discarded, and the others seldom operate.

AUXILIARIES

Disposal note: Small combatant support ship *Zeltin* (711) had been retired from service as of 2005.

Note: The three following ships are registered as merchant vessels and operate for the Libyan government–controlled General National Maritime Transportation Co., homeported at Tripoli; all three, however, have performed both overt and covert military missions and can thus be said to be military vessels in fact if not in name.

♦ 1 vehicle transport [AK]
Bldr: Naikai SB & Eng., Setoda, Japan (In serv. 1973)

Garyounis (ex-*Mashu*)

D: Approx. 15,000 tons (fl) **S:** 20.5 kts **Dim:** 166.53 (155.00 pp) × 24.36 × 6.47
Electronics: Radar: . . .
M: 2 Nippon Kokan-Pielstick 16 PC2 5V400 diesels; 2 props; 20,800 bhp—bow-thruster
Electric: 1,860 kw (3 × 620 kw) **Range:** . . . / . . . **Crew:** . . .

Remarks: 6,561 grt/2,593 dwt. Former Ro/Ro passenger ferry with accommodations for up to 679 passengers. Employed as a naval cadet training ship during 1989. The stern ramp can be used for minelaying.

AUXILIARIES *(continued)*

♦ 1 Ro/Ro vehicle carrier [AK]
Bldr: Nystads Varv A/B, Nystad, Finland (In serv. 1-75)

GHAT

D: Approx. 6,200 tons (fl) **S:** 18 kts **Dim:** 118.60 (106.79 pp) × 16.13 × 5.57
M: 2 Wärtsilä-Pielstick 8 PC2 2L400 diesels; 2 CP props; 8,000 bhp—bow-thruster
Electric: 1,560 kw tot. (3 × 520-kw diesel sets)
Range: . . . / . . . **Fuel:** 461 tons heavy oil/75 tons diesel **Crew:** . . .

Remarks: 2,412 grt/3,266 dwt. Stern door only. Has been used to transport military cargoes and to lay mines. Can carry several hundred mines on temporary rails in the vehicle deck or several hundred troops. Has side vehicle doors and can carry up to 300 automobiles.

♦ 1 Ro/Ro vehicle carrier [AK]
Bldr: C.N. Luigi Orlando, Livorno, Italy (In serv. 1971)

EL TEMSAH (ex-*Espresso Veneto*)

D: Approx. 5,600 tons (fl) **S:** 19 kts
Dim: 105.36 (96.55 pp) × 19.51 (17.51 wl) × 5.11
M: 2 Fiat B300.16V diesels; 2 CP props; 8,000 bhp
Electric: 520 kw tot. (4 × 130-kw diesel sets)
Range: . . . / . . . **Fuel:** 199 tons **Crew:** . . .

Remarks: 4,567 grt/2,926 dwt. Acquired in 1972; in addition to commercial ventures, has been used to transport military cargoes and to lay mines. Was burned out in a 1986 accident but has been restored to active service. Has a 20-m-long stern vehicle ramp, which is also useful for laying mines, and there are a total of 720 m of vehicle parking lanes and two side-loading vehicle doors.

♦ 1 Yugoslav Spasilac-class training ship [AXT]
Bldr: Tito SY, Belgrade (In serv. 1982)

722 AL MUNJED (ex-Yugoslav *Zlatica*)

D: 1,590 tons (fl) **S:** 13.4 kts **Dim:** 55.50 × 12.00 × 3.84 (4.34 max.)
A: 4 twin 14.5-mm 93-cal. mg **Electronics:** Radar: 1 . . . nav.
M: 2 diesels; 2 Kort-nozzle props; 4,340 bhp **Electric:** 540 kVA
Range: 4,000/13.4 **Crew:** 53 tot. (72 accomm.)

Remarks: Acquired in 1982. Resembles an oilfield supply vessel, with low freeboard aft. Sister *Aka* was in the Iraqi Navy, and another is in reserve in Croatia. Was used as submarine support ship when the Foxtrots were operational, then was laid up until used in 1998 for a cadet training cruise; has not been reported at sea since then, however.
Hull systems: Equipped for underwater cutting and welding, towing, salvage lifting, firefighting, and other salvage tasks. Can carry up to 250 tons of deck cargo, transferring 490 tons of cargo fuel, 48 tons of cargo water, and 5 tons of lube oil. Can support divers to 300 m with a three-section decompression chamber. Also has the capability to support a small rescue submersible. Has a bow-thruster and can lay a four-point moor.

SERVICE CRAFT

♦ 1 Soviet Yelva-class (Project 535M) diving tender [YDT]
Bldr: Gorokhovtse Zavod (In serv. 19-12-77)

AL MANOUD (ex-VM 917)

D: 279 tons (300 fl) **S:** 12.4 kts **Dim:** 40.90 (37.00 pp) × 8.00 × 2.02
Electronics: Radar: 1 Mius (Spin Trough) nav.—Sonar: MGA-1 HF
M: 2 Type 3D12A diesels; 2 props; 600 bhp **Electric:** 200 kw tot.
Range: 1,870/12 **Endurance:** 10 days **Crew:** 24 tot.

Remarks: Can support seven hard-hat divers working at 60 m and has a submersible decompression chamber supported by a 2.5-ton derrick. Relegated to harbor service by the mid-1990s.

♦ 1 small floating dry dock [YFDL]
Bldr: Blohm + Voss, Hamburg (In serv. 1984)

Lift capacity: 3,200 tons **Dim:** 105.20 × 26.00 × 6.40

Remarks: Ordered 20-2-84, laid down 17-4-84.

♦ 1 Soviet Poluchat-I-class torpedo retriever [YPT]

723

D: 84.7 tons (92.8 fl) **S:** 21.6 kts **Dim:** 29.60 × 5.98 × 1.56 (hull)
A: 1 twin 14.5-mm 93-cal. 2M-7 AA
Electronics: Radar: 1 Mius (Spin Trough) nav.
M: 2 M-50F-4 diesels; 2 props; 2,400 bhp **Electric:** 14 kw tot.
Range: 250/21.6; 550/14; 900/10 **Crew:** 3 officers, 12 enlisted

Remarks: Delivered 20-5-85. Has a stern ramp for torpedo recovery. May no longer be operational.

♦ 4 Ras el Helal–class large harbor tugs [YTB]
Bldr: Mondego, Foz, Portugal

	In serv.		In serv.
A 31 RAS EL HELAL	22-10-77	A 33 AL SHWEIREF	17-2-78
A 32 AL KERIAT	17-2-78	A 34 AL TABKAH	29-7-78

D: 200 grt **S:** 14 kts **Dim:** 34.8 × 9.0 × 4.0 (molded depth)
M: 2 diesels; 2 props; 2,300 bhp

♦ 3 harbor tugs [YTM]
Bldr: Jonker & Stans SY, the Netherlands (In serv. 1980)

A 33 A 34 A 35

D: 150 grt **S:** . . . **Dim:** 26.60 × 7.90 × 2.48
M: 2 diesels; 2 Voith-Schneider vertical cycloidal props; . . . bhp

Remarks: Two 17.00 × 6.25 × 2.75-m harbor tugs were delivered at the same time as A 33–A 34. All the tugs listed serve naval and commercial vessels at Libyan ports.

Note: The Libyan customs service operates up to four Swedish-built Boghammar patrol launches of 5.5 tons displacement and may still have six Yugoslav PB 90–class 90-ton patrol boats in service.

LITHUANIA

Lithuanian Republic

LITHUANIAN REPUBLIC NAVAL FLOTILLA

(Lietuvos Respublikas Karines Juru Pajegos)

Personnel: 710 total including 300 conscripts

Base: Klaipeda, with Coastal Radar Service stations at Klaipeda, Nida, and Palanga

CORVETTES [FFL]

♦ 2 Grisha-III class (Project 1124M) Bldr: Zelenodol'sk Zavod

	In serv.
F 11 ZEMAITIS (ex-MPK-108, *Komsomolets Latviy*)	1-10-81
F 12 AUKŠTAITIS (ex-MPK-44)	15-8-80

Zemaitis (F 11) Frank Findler, 6-05

Zemaitis (F 11) Leo Van Ginderen, 6-05

D: 860 tons light, 954 tons normal (990 fl)
S: 32 kts (21 on gas turbine alone, 16 on diesels)
Dim: 71.20 (66.90 wl) × 10.15 (9.50 wl) × 3.40 (hull)
A: 1 twin-rail Osa-2M (SA-N-4) SAM syst. (20 9M-33 Gecko missiles); 1 twin 57-mm AK-725 DP; 1 30-mm 54-cal. AK-630M gatling AA; 2 12-tubed RBU-6000 ASW RL (96 RGB-60 rockets)
Electronics:
Radar: 1 Terma Scanter Mil 009 nav.; 1 Decca RM 1290 nav.; 1MR-302 (Strut Curve) air/surf. search; 1 MPZ-310 (Pop Group) SAM f.c.; 1 MR-123 Vympel (Bass Tilt) gun f.c.
Sonar: MGK-335MC Pirhana (Bull Nose) hull-mounted MF, Argun' (Elk Tail) MF through-hull dipping
EW: Vympel-R2 intercept, with 2 Bizan'-4 (Watch Dog) (2–18 GHz)
M: CODAG: 1 M-88 gas turbine (18,000 shp), 2 Type M507A diesels (10,000 bhp each); 3 props; 38,000 hp—2 maneuvering propellers
Electric: 1,000 kw (1 × 500-kw, 1 × 300-kw, 1 × 200-kw diesel sets)
Range: 950/27; 2,750/14; 4,000/10 **Fuel:** 130 tons + 13 tons overload
Endurance: 9 days **Crew:** 5 officers, 43 enlisted (accomm. for 83)

Remarks: Transferred and commissioned 6-11-92. Are planned to remain in service to 2007–10.
Combat systems: The torpedo tubes were removed from F 12 in 1995 and F 11 in 1996 as Lithuanian waters are too shallow for successful use of torpedoes (of which none had been furnished by the Russians, anyway). Reported to carry 1,000 rounds of 57-mm and 2,000 rounds of 30-mm gun ammunition. Depth charge racks have been removed, and there are no mines available for the deck rails. A Danish radar replaced the original Don-2 navigational/surface-search set in 1998.

PATROL CRAFT [PC]

♦ 3 ex-Norwegian Storm class
Bldr: Bergens Mekaniske Verksted, Bergen (In serv. 1966–67)

	L
P 31 DZŪKAS (ex-*Kjekk,* P 965)	27-9-65
P 32 SELIS (ex-*Skudd,* P 967)	25-3-66
P 33 SKALVIS (ex-*Steil,* P 969)	20-9-66

PATROL CRAFT [PC] *(continued)*

Skalvis (P 33)—alongside sisters, note the new 76.2-mm gun forward
Hartmut Ehlers, 6-03

D: 105 tons (125 fl) **S:** 37 kts **Dim:** 36.53 × 6.30 × 1.55
A: 1 76.2-mm 50-cal. Bofors low-angle; 1 40-mm 70-cal. Bofors L70 AA
Electronics: Radar: P 31: 1 Decca TM 1226 nav.—others: 1 Furuno . . . nav.
M: 2 Maybach MB 872A (MTU 16V538 TB90) diesels; 2 props; 7,200 bhp
Range: 550/36 **Crew:** 3 officers, 15 enlisted

Remarks: P 31 was transferred 10-00 as a spare parts source, refitted, and placed in service 8-01. P 32 and P 33 were transferred and recommissioned 21-6-01; their original WM-22 radar gun f.c.s. was deleted prior to transfer.

PATROL BOATS [PB]

♦ 1 former Russian Navy officers launch (Project 371U)

VYTIS-01

D: 9.41 tons (fl) **S:** 13.5 kts **Dim:** 12.61 × 3.23 × 0.6 (1.00 over prop)
A: Small arms **Electronics:** Radar: 1 Furuno. . . nav.
M: 1 Type 3D6S diesel; 1 prop; 150 bhp **Range:** 140/13.5
Crew: 1 officer, 2 enlisted

Remarks: Same type of launch once carried aboard Soviet *Sverdlov*-class cruisers and also used as personnel launches at naval bases. Two sisters are in Latvian service.

MINE-COUNTERMEASURES SHIPS

♦ 2 ex-German Type 331B minehunters [MHC]

Bldr: Burmester, Bremen

	L	In serv.
M 51 KURŠIS (ex-*Marburg,* M 1080)	4-8-58	11-6-59
M 52 SŪDUVIS (ex-*Koblenz,* M 1071)	6-5-57	8-7-58

Kuršis (M 51) Leo Van Ginderen, 6-05

Sūduvis (M 52) Michael Nitz, 7-05

D: 388 tons (402 fl) **S:** 16.5 kts
Dim: 47.45 × 8.5 × 2.8 (3.68 with sonar extended)
A: 1 40-mm 70-cal. Bofors AA
Electronics:
Radar: 1 Raytheon SPS-64(V) nav.
Sonar: EFS DSQS-11A HF minehunting
M: 2 MTU 16V538 TB90 diesels; 2 CP props; 5,000 bhp **Electric:** 220 kw tot.
Range: 1,400/16; 3,950/9 **Crew:** 5 officers, 29 enlisted + 6 divers

Remarks: M 52 was decommissioned from the German Navy 22-6-99, donated and transferred in 9-99, and commissioned on 4-12-99. M 51, decommissioned from German service 25-5-00, was donated during 11-00 and recommissioned in 4-01 after a refit at Krögerwerft, Rendsburg.
Hull systems: Wooden construction, with nonmagnetic engines. Minehunting speed is 6 kts on two 50-kw electric motors.
Combat systems: Have no mechanical sweep gear. Six divers and two French PAP-104 remote-controlled minehunting devices are carried. The 40-mm gun is controlled by a lead-computing optical director on the bridge.

AUXILIARIES

♦ 1 ex-Soviet Valerian Uryvayev–class training ship [AXT]

Bldr: Khabarovsk Shipyard (In serv. 1977)

A 41 VĖTRA (ex-*Rudolf Samoylovich*)

Vėtra (A 41) Marian Wright, 6-04

D: 1,050 tons (fl) **S:** 11.75 kts **Dim:** 55.66 × 9.53 × 4.16
A: 2 single 12.7-mm mg; 2 single 45-mm KM-21 saluting cannon
Electronics: Radar: 1 Decca RM 1290 nav.
M: 1 Deutz–Karl Liebnecht 6NVD48A-2U diesel; 1 CP prop; 875 bhp
Electric: 450 kw tot. **Range:** 10,000/11 **Endurance:** 40 days
Crew: 8 officers, 26 enlisted

Remarks: 694 grt/350 dwt. Transferred to Lithuanian control in 11-91 from the former Soviet Hydrometeorological Service, which had operated her from St. Petersburg. Belongs to the Ministry of the Environment but is leased by the Lithuanian Navy; initially used as a fisheries protection and inspection vessel, she is now employed as fleet training ship and also for coastal survey work. Has an ice-strengthened hull, a bow-thruster, and two 1.5-ton derricks serving a small hold aft. Sister *Vėjas* (ex-Soviet *Lev Titov*) is operated by the Ministry of the Environment.

SERVICE CRAFT

♦ 1 coastal survey craft [YGS]

H 21 HK 21 (ex-*Vilnele*)

HK 21—at pier side Hartmut Ehlers, 6-03

D: 88 tons (fl) **S:** 12 kts **Dim:** 23.1 × 5.8 × 1.8
A: 1 12.7-mm mg **Electronics:** Radar: 1 . . . nav.
M: 2 diesels; 2 props; 600 bhp **Crew:** 1 officer, 6 enlisted

Remarks: A former pilot boat acquired in 1992. Served until 1994 as tender to the *Vėtra* and later as a patrol launch. Now used mostly as an inshore survey craft. The pennant number was changed in 2001.

♦ 1 ex-Swedish Navy small harbor tug [YTL]

Bldr: . . . (In serv. 1975)

H 22 (ex-*Atlas,* A 330)

D: 35 tons (fl) **S:** 9 kts **Dim:** . . . × . . . × . . .
M: 1 . . . diesel; 210 bhp

Remarks: Donated by Sweden in 2000; had been laid up at Karlskrona since 1995.

SERVICE CRAFT *(continued)*

H 22—small harbor tug Hartmut Ehlers, 6-03

STATE BORDER POLICE
(Pasienio Policija)

Note: Established in 1996 to serve as a form of coast guard.

Personnel: Approx. 80 total

SURFACE-EFFECT PATROL BOATS [WPBA]

♦ **1 Type 2000TDX Mk 2**
Bldr: Griffon Hovercraft, Southampton, U.K. (In serv. 2000)

CHRISTINA

D: 5 tons (fl) **S:** 40 kts **Dim:** 12.6 × 6.1 × . . .
Electronics: Radar: 1 Furuno 100C nav.
M: 1 Deutz BF8L diesel; 1 CP shrouded prop; 355 bhp **Crew:** 3 tot.

Remarks: Ordered in 1999 for inshore and shallow-water patrol duties.

PATROL BOATS [WPB]

♦ **1 ex-Finnish Tiira class**
Bldr: Valmet-Laivateollisuus, Turku

	Laid down	L	In serv.
102 KIHU	7-4-86	7-86	17-12-86

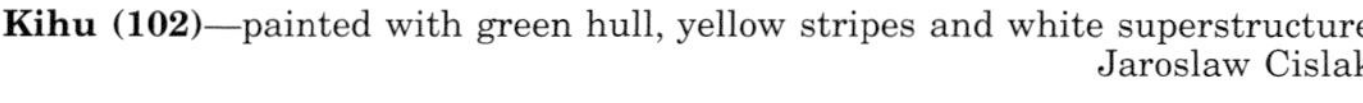

Kihu (102)—painted with green hull, yellow stripes and white superstructure
Jaroslaw Cislak, 5-03

D: 65 tons (fl) **S:** 25+ kts **Dim:** 26.80 (24.20 pp) × 5.50 × 1.40 (1.85 props)
A: None **Electronics:** Radar: 1 . . . nav.
M: 2 MTU 8V396 TB82 diesels; 2 props; 2,286 bhp **Electric:** 62 kVa tot.
Fuel: 8 tons **Crew:** 2 officers, 4 enlisted

Remarks: Donated late in 1997 from the Finnish Frontier Guard. Aluminum construction, with hard-chine hullform. Sonar was removed prior to transfer.

Disposal note: The nine ex-Polish Border Guard Project S-3 (Szkwal) patrol launches donated on 5-8-96 were never put into service and were discarded in 2000.

♦ **1 ex-Swedish Kbv 041–class former oil-spill cleanup boat**
Bldr: Karlstad Varv, Karlstad (In serv. 1972)

042 MADELEINE (ex-Kbv 041)

Madeleine (042) Hartmut Ehlers, 6-03

D: 70 tons (fl) **S:** 11 kts **Dim:** 18.4 × 5.4 × 1.3
M: 2 diesels; 2 props; 450 bhp **Crew:** 8 tot.

Remarks: Transferred in 4-95 for use in patrolling Coronian Lagoon, near Klaipeda. Was originally to have gone to the navy as P 41. Carries a rigid inflatable inspection boat.

♦ **1 ex-Swedish Kbv 101 class** Bldr: Karlskronavarvet (In serv. 1969)

101 LILIAN (ex-Kbv 101)

Lilian (101) Hartmut Ehlers, 6-03

D: 50 tons (fl) **S:** 22 kts **Dim:** 24.90 × 5.00 × 1.10
Electronics: Radar: 1 . . . nav.
M: 2 MTU 8V331 TC82 diesels; 2 props; 1,866 bhp **Electric:** 60 kVA tot.
Range: 1,000/15 **Fuel:** 11 tons **Crew:** 7 tot.

Remarks: Donated by the Swedish Coast Guard in 6-96. Has a small, high-frequency, hull-mounted sonar.

Disposal note: Former Russian Navy officers launch *Vytis-02* is no longer in service as of 9-03.

♦ **1 ex-Danish Home Guard patrol boat** Bldr: Gillelje (In serv. 1941)

S 07 LOKYS (ex-*Apollo,* MHV 56)

Lokys (S 07) Hartmut Ehlers, 6-03

D: 30 tons (35 fl) **S:** 10 kts (9 sust.) **Dim:** 18.4 (17.0 pp) × 6.0 × 2.2
A: 2 single 7.62-mm mg **Electronics:** Radar: 1 Decca RM 1290S nav.
M: 1 Alpha diesel; 1 prop; 165 bhp **Crew:** 7 tot.

Remarks: Donated 7-97. Wooden-hulled former fishing boat.

Note: The Lithuanian Fisheries Inspection Service operates the former Swedish Coast Guard Kbv 236–class patrol boat *Victoria* (245, ex-Kbv 245), transferred 16-2-93.

MADAGASCAR

Democratic Republic of Madagascar

MALAGASY AERONAVAL FORCE

Personnel: 500 total including approx. 100 Marines. The former navy and air force were united in 1991 as the Malagasy Aeronaval Force.

Bases: Principal base at Diego-Suarez, with minor facilities at Fort Dauphin, Majunga, Manakara, Nossi-Be, Tamatave, and Tulear

AMPHIBIOUS WARFARE CRAFT

♦ 1 French EDIC-class utility landing craft [LCU]
Bldr: C.N. Franco-Belges (In serv. 1964)

AINA VAO VAO (ex-EDIC L 9082)

D: 250 tons (670 fl) **S:** 8 kts **Dim:** 59.00 × 11.95 × 1.30 (1.62 max.)
A: 1 12.7-mm mg **Electronics:** Radar: 1 Decca 1226 nav.
M: 2 MGO diesels; 2 props; 1,000 bhp **Range:** 1,800/8 **Crew:** 17 tot.

Remarks: Transferred 27-9-85, having been laid up at Tahiti since being stricken from the French Navy in 1981. Can carry 11 trucks. Given a minor refit by French Navy personnel during 3-96.

AUXILIARIES

♦ 1 Chamois-class local support tender [AG]
Bldr: Ch. de la Perriere, Lorient

	L	In serv.
MATSILO (ex-*Chamois,* A 767)	30-4-76	24-9-76

Matsilo CF Stephen A. Frebourg, 10-97

D: 305 tons light (500 fl) **S:** 14.5 kts **Dim:** 41.60 (36.96 pp) × 7.5 × 3.18
A: 2 single 12.7-mm mg **Electronics:** Radar: 1 Decca 1226 nav.
M: 2 SACM-Wärtsilä UD30 V16M3 diesels; 2 CP Kort-nozzle props; 2,800 bhp
Range: 7,200/12 **Fuel:** 92 m^3 **Crew:** 2 officers, 8 petty officers, 10 ratings

Remarks: Stricken from the French Navy 1-9-95 and transferred to Madagascar 5-96 as a general-purpose cargo transport, patrol, and training ship. Has a 5.6-ton crane and a 50-ton stern gallows crane. Can carry 100 tons dry cargo on deck, or 125 tons of fuel and 40 tons of water, or 65 tons of fuel and 125 tons of water. Has two rudders and an 80-hp bow-thruster. The stern winch has a 28-ton bollard pull. Can also be used as transport for 28 passengers.

SERVICE CRAFT

♦ 1 coastal tug [YTB]
Bldr: SECREN, Antsiranana (In serv. 1982)

TROZONA

D: 400 tons (fl) **S:** 11.5 kts **Dim:** 30.0 (27.0 pp) × 8.0 × 4.5
A: 1 12.7-mm mg **Electronics:** Radar: 1 Decca 110 nav.
M: 1 SACM-Wärtsilä UD30 V16 ASHR diesel; 1 prop; 1,000 bhp
Electric: 120 kw tot. **Range:** 5,000/9.5
Crew: 3 officers, 9 petty officers, 14 ratings

Remarks: Acquired in 1995, refitted, and commissioned 10-97. Employed on patrol duties. Bollard pull: 17.5 tons. A firefighting monitor is mounted atop the pilothouse.

Trozona CF Stephen A. Frebourg, 10-97

♦ 3 ex-French Aigrette-class small harbor tugs [YTL]

ENGOULVENT (ex-Y 723) TOURTERELLE (ex-Y 643)
MARTIN-PECHEUR (ex-Y 675)

Martin-Pecheur (left) and Engoulvent CF Stephen A. Frebourg, 10-97

D: 56 tons (fl) **S:** 9 kts **Dim:** 18.4 × 5.7 × 2.5
M: 1 Poyaud diesel; 1 prop; 250 bhp **Range:** 1,700/9 **Crew:** 5 tot.

Remarks: *Tourterelle,* donated in 1995, had been out of service since 1980. The other two were donated in 1996. Bollard pull: 10 tons. Sister *Bouleau* had been stricken by 1997. Have no armament and no radars.

♦ 7 ex-U.S. Coast Guard 44-foot rescue launches [YH]

D: 14.9 tons light (17.7 fl) **S:** 13 kts **Dim:** 13.44 × 3.87 × 1.19
Electronics: Radar: 1 . . . nav.
M: 2 G.M. Detroit diesel 6V53 diesels; 2 props; 372 bhp
Range: 200/11 **Fuel:** 1.2 tons **Crew:** 3–4

Remarks: Transferred 2003. "Unsinkable" design can carry up to 21 rescued personnel. No names or numbers have yet been announced.

MALAWI

Republic of Malawi

MALAWI POLICE

Personnel: Approx. 220 total

Base: Monkey Bay, Lake Malawi; a small facility is available on Lake Nyasa

PATROL BOATS [WPB]

Note: *Antares*-class patrol boat *Kasungu* (P 703, ex-*Chikala*), which has been out of service since 1993, is still afloat at Monkey Bay and may eventually be repaired.

PATROL BOATS [WPB] *(continued)*

♦ **1 Namicurra-class launch**
Bldr: Tornado Products, South Africa (In serv. 1980–81)

P 704 KANING'A (ex-Y 1520)

Kaning'a (P 704) Malawi Police, 1997

D: 4 tons light (5.2 fl) **S:** 30 kts **Dim:** 9.5 × 2.5 × 0.8
A: 1 12.7-mm mg; 1 twin 7.62-mm mg; small arms
Electronics: Radar: 1 . . . nav.
M: 2 BMW inboard-outboard gasoline engines; 2 props; 380 bhp **Crew:** 4 tot.

Remarks: Donated to Malawi 29-10-88 by South Africa. Radar-equipped, GRP-hulled, catamaran harbor craft, which can be land-transported by trailer. When fitted, the 7.62-mm twin mount is positioned aft in the cockpit, while the 12.7-mm mg is located at the aft edge of the pilothouse; normally only the 12.7-mm mg is carried, in the aft position. Refitted in 1997.

SERVICE CRAFT

♦ **1 Type . . . LCM**
Bldr: Rotork Marine, U.K. (In serv. . . .)

P 702 CHIKOKO I

D: 9 tons (fl) **S:** 24 kts **Dim:** 12.7 × 3.2 × 0.5 **A:** 3 single 7.62-mm mg
Electronics: Radar: 1 . . . nav.
M: 2 Volvo . . . diesels; 2 props; 260 bhp
Range: 3,000/15 **Crew:** 8 tot.

Remarks: No additional data available.

♦ **12 Buccaneer Legend RIB personnel launches [WYFL]**
Bldr: Buccaneer Inflatables, Glenvista, South Africa (In serv. 1993)

D: 1.2 tons light (3.5 tons fl) **S:** 37 kts **Dim:** 8.00 × 2.60 × . . .
A: 1 12.7-mm mg **M:** 1 Cummins . . . diesel; 1 prop; 320 bhp
Crew: 4 + 18 troops

Remarks: Ordered late 1992. Have semi-rigid aluminum lower hull with flexible upper collar.

MALAYSIA

ROYAL MALAYSIAN NAVY
(Tentera Laut Diraja)

Personnel: 15,000 total plus about 1,000 reserves. Included in this total are 160 naval aviation personnel and an unknown number of special forces naval commandos.

Bases: KD *Malaya,* at Perak on Telok Muroh, is headquarters and base for Lumut Headquarters, Region 1. The headquarters and base for Region 2 is at Tanjung Lembung, Labuan, and establishment of a new Region 3 continues, with headquarters at Langkawi. A fourth region is to be established at Sarawak later. Small facilities are located at Kuantan on the east coast of the Malay Peninsula, KD *Sri Sandakan* on the Sulu Sea coast of Borneo, Sungei Antu in Sarawak on Borneo, and Layang-Layang in the Spratly Islands (with smaller detachments on Ubi and Mantanani Islands). A new submarine and patrol boat base is being built at Teluk Sepanggar, near Kota Kina-bulu in Sabah, to replace the Labuan Island facility. An air station is to be built at Sitiawan, Perak. The principal naval dockyard at Lumut was sold to Penang Shipbuilding Corp. on 8-12-95. Work on an underground submarine base was begun at Kampung Sepanggar, Sabah, during 12-02 with construction expected to be completed during 2007. The naval air base, KD *Rajawali,* is to be moved to a new facility at Sungai Wangi, Sitiawan.

Naval Aviation: Six AS.355 Fennec helicopters based at Lumut had been delivered by 2004; they employ a Thales-EADS Ocean Master radar, Honeywell–Rolls Royce LHTEC CTS800-4N turboshaft engines and are armed with torpedoes and Sea Skua ASMs and are used for ASW as well as missile targeting, training, vertical replenishment, cargo transport, SAR, and medical evacuation. Six AgustaWestland Super Lynx Series 300 helicopters were ordered 7-9-99 with all delivered by 10-03. On 11-10-01, Matra-BAe Systems Sea Skua missiles were ordered for use with the Super Lynx 300 helicopters.

Malaysian Navy Super Lynx 300 Hartmut Ehlers, 9-03

The Royal Malaysian Air Force operates four Beech Super King Air B200T coastal maritime surveillance aircraft. For maritime strike duties, 18 Hawk 200 single-seat and 10 two-seat Hawk 100 light fighters are equipped with Sea Eagle missiles. Eight AGM-84C Harpoon–equipped F/A-18D fighter-bombers are also capable of maritime strike; some 25 missiles are available.

Note: Warship names are prefixed by KD (*Kapal DiRaja,* or King's Ship).

ATTACK SUBMARINES [SS]

Note: Although the Netherlands Rotterdamse Droogdok Maatschappij (RDM) transported its two former Netherlands Navy *Zwaardvis*-class submarines to Lumut on 20-10-00 (arriving 14-12-00) with the intent of having them overhauled at Lumut as training submarines for the Malaysian Navy, no contract has yet been signed.

♦ **0 (+ 2) Scorpène class**

	Bldr	Laid down	L	In serv.
S . . .	DCN, Cherbourg	2005	2007	2008
S . . .	Navantia (formerly Izar), Cartagena	. . .	. . .	7-09

Cutaway model of the Scorpène-class submarine Hans Karr, 5-05

D: 1,586 tons surf./1,745 tons sub. **S:** 12 kts surf./20× kts sub.
Dim: 66.40 × 6.20 × 5.8 (surf.)
A: 6 bow 533-mm TT (18 WASS Black Shark wire-guided torpedoes and Aérospatiale SM 39 Exocet antiship missiles)
Electronics:
Radar: 1 . . . nav./surf. search
Sonar: Thales . . . suite, with passive flank and towed arrays
EW: . . . intercept
M: Diesel electric: 4 MTU . . . diesels (840 bhp each), Jeumont axial-flux permanent magnet electric motor; 1 prop; 3,800 shp
Range: 6,500/8 (surf.); 550/4 (sub.) **Endurance:** 50 days
Crew: 6 officers, 26 enlisted

Remarks: Two were ordered on 5-6-02 for $1.1 billion, along with the free transfer of the retired French Navy *Agosta*-class *Ouessant.* Original plans called for the class to be delivered in 2007, but the program was delayed during 2005. Both will be based at a new facility in Teluk Sepanggar, near Kota Kina-bulu in Sabah.
Hull systems: Employ HLES 80 steel in the pressure hull, permitting diving depths in excess of 320 m. No air-independent propulsion system was ordered. A 360-cell battery is employed. All machinery is "rafted" for sound isolation. Only nine personnel will be on watch under normal conditions.
Combat systems: The UDS International SUBTICS (Submarine Tactical Information and Command System) weapons-control system would be similar to the French Navy's SET (*Système d'Exploitation Tactique*) and would have six two-screen display consoles. The sonar suite would include a cylindrical bow transducer array, an active array, a passive ranging array, acoustic intercept system, and passive flank arrays. Black Shark torpedoes were ordered for the class late in 2002.

♦ **1 Agosta class**
Bldr: DCN, Cherbourg

	Laid down	L	In serv.
. . . (ex-*Ouessant,* S 623)	1974	23-10-76	27-7-78

Agosta-class submarine ex-*Ouessant*—The submarine will remain in French waters until 2009 while Malaysian sailors receive onboard training for duty in their new Scorpène-class submarines. Bernard Prézelin, 9-05

ATTACK SUBMARINES [SS] *(continued)*

D: 1,250 tons std; 1,510 tons surf./1,760 tons sub.
S: 12.5 kts surf./20.5 kts sub. (5 min), 17.5 kts sub. (1 hr)
Dim: 67.57 × 6.80 × 5.40
A: 4 bow 550-mm TT (20 torpedoes and/or SM 39 Exocet antiship missiles)
Electronics:
Radar: 1 Thales DRUA 33C nav./search
Sonar: Thales DUUA 2D active (8 kHz); Thales DSUV 22C multifunction passive; Thales DUUX 21 intercept; Thales DSUV 62A towed linear passive array
EW: Thales ARUR 12 and ARUD (Thales DR-4000U and DR-2000U) intercept
M: 2 SEMT-Pielstick 16 PA4 V185 VG diesel generator sets (850 kw each); 1 3,500-kw electric propulsion motor (2,200 kw sust.); 1 prop; 4,600 shp—23-shp creep electric creep motor
Range: 8,500/9 snorkel; 178/3.5, 280/3 sub. on creep motor; 17.5/17.5 sub.; 7,900/12 surf.
Fuel: 185 tons **Endurance:** 45 days
Crew: 7 officers, 24 petty officers, 23 other enlisted

Remarks: Ordered from France on 5-6-02; after refit, will operate in French waters training Malaysian crews for four years and then transit to Malaysia in 2009. All data above pertain to the submarine in French Navy service. Had been retired from the French Navy on 1-7-01.
Hull systems: Max. operating depth: 320 m. Mixed-transit range with 21% indiscretion rate is said to be 10,000 n.m. at 7 kts. Is air-conditioned.
Combat systems: Has the DLA D3 weapons-control system. The torpedo tubes accept torpedoes of either 550-mm or 533-mm diameter. The submarine is equipped to carry mines.

FRIGATES [FF]

♦ 2 Yarrow Frigate 2000 class
Bldr: GEC-Yarrow SB, Scotstoun, Glasgow, Scotland

	Laid down	L	In serv.
29 Jebat	11-94	27-5-95	18-11-99
30 Lekiu	3-94	3-12-94	7-10-99

Jebat (29) Hartmut Ehlers, 9-03

Lekiu (30) Hartmut Ehlers, 9-03

Lekiu (30)—note the helicopter hangar and the very low freeboard at the stern
Brian Morrison/H&L Van Ginderen, 11-99

D: 1,845 tons (2,270 fl) **S:** 28.5 kts (27 sust.)
Dim: 105.50 (97.50 pp) × 12.75 × 3.80 (hull)
A: 8 MM 40 Exocet Block 2 SSM; 1 16-cell Sea Wolf SAM vertical-launch group; 1 57-mm 70-cal. Bofors SAK 57 Mk 2 DP; 2 single 30-mm MSI DS30B REMSIG AA; 2 triple 324-mm WASS B-515/3 ASW TT (Sting Ray torpedoes); 1 AS.355MN Fennec helicopter
Electronics:
Radar: 1 Decca . . . nav.; 1 Ericsson Sea Giraffe 150HC surf./air search; 1 Thales DA-08 air search; 2 GEC-Marconi Type 1802 SW f.c.
Sonar: Thales Spherion hull-mounted MF
EW: Marconi Mentor-2(V)1 intercept; Thorn-EMI Scimitar jammer; 2 12-round Wallop SuperBarricade decoy RL; Graseby Sea Siren torpedo decoy syst.
E/O: 1 Rademac System 2400 optronic f.c. and surveillance; 1 GEC-Marconi Type V3901 IR surveillance
M: 4 MTU 20V1163 TB 93 diesels; 2 CP props; 40,000 hp (33,300 sust.)
Range: 5,000/14 (diesel) **Crew:** 19 officers, 127 enlisted

Remarks: Ordered 31-3-92; first steel cut for first unit 3-93. Were originally to have been commissioned 2-96 and 5-96, respectively, but experienced significant weapons-control system integration problems. Both are named for warriors of the Melaka Empire; 29, although newer, has the lower number as she is intended to be the senior ship.
Hull systems: Special attention was paid to shaping the hull and superstructure to reduce radar signature, but there are no special radar-absorption coatings.
Combat systems: Have the GEC-Marconi Nautis-F weapons-control system and EADS HF/VHF/UHF integrated communications suite. The Thales ITL 70 launch-control system is fitted for the Exocet missiles. The Rademac System 2400 electro-optical director is mounted atop the pilothouse as backup control for the 57-mm gun, which also has a local control system. Have Thales Link Y Mk 2 combat datalink capabilities. The 30-mm guns are in remotely operated mountings using inputs from the main gun fire-control system and the Rademac electro-optical director. The AMS Nautis 2 communications suite is fitted.

Note: Two units of an "improved Lekiu" class were reportedly ordered in late 2006. No additional information is yet available.

♦ 2 Kasturi class (Type FS-1500)
Bldr: Howaldtswerke, Kiel

	Laid down	L	In serv.
25 Kasturi	31-1-83	14-5-83	15-8-84
26 Lekir	31-1-83	14-5-83	15-8-84

D: 1,690 tons (1,900 fl) **S:** 28 kts **Dim:** 97.30 (91.80 pp) × 11.30 × 3.50 (hull)
A: 4 MM 38 Exocet SSM; 1 100-mm 55-cal. Creusot-Loire Compact DP; 1 57-mm 70-cal. Bofors SAK 57 Mk 1 DP; 2 twin 30-mm 75-cal. Emerlec AA; 1 2-round 375-mm Bofors ASW RL; 1 AS.355MN Fennec helicopter

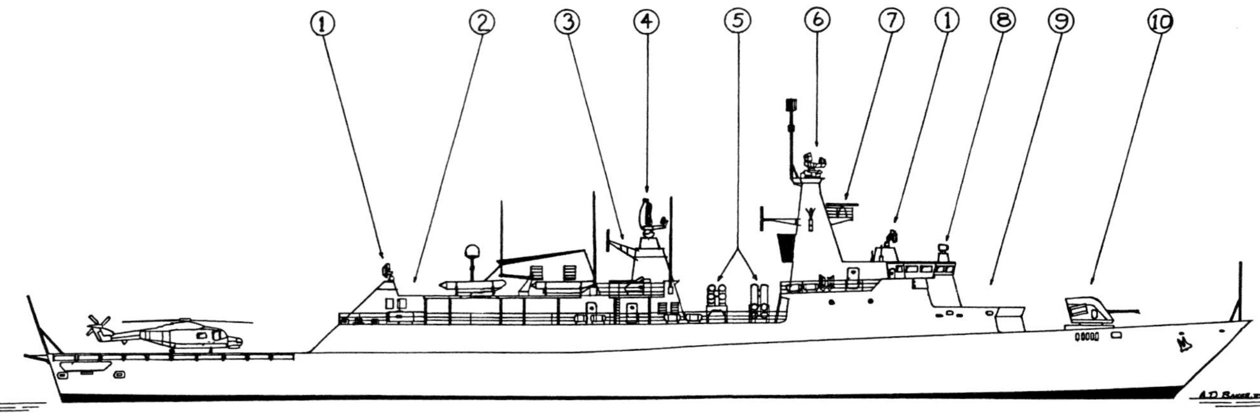

Lekiu (30) 1. Type 1802 SW radar f.c. directors 2. Triple 324-mm ASW TT 3. 30-mm AA 4. DA-08 air-search radar 5. MM 40 Exocet SSM canister launchers 6. Sea Giraffe 150HC surface/air-search radar 7. Navigational radar 8. System 2400 optronic f.c. director 9. Sea Wolf SAM vertical-launch group 10. 57-mm 70-cal. Bofors DP gun
Drawing by A. D. Baker III

FRIGATES [FF] *(continued)*

Kasturi (25) Hartmut Ehlers, 9-03

Lekir (26) Ralph Edwards, 10-01

Kasturi (25) Mitsuhiro Kadota, 9-02

Electronics:
Radar: 1 Decca TM 1226C nav.; 1 Thales DA-08 air search; 1 Thales WM-22 f.c.
Sonar: STN Atlas Elektronik DSQS-21 hull-mounted MF
EW: Racal Rapids intercept; Racal Scimitar jammer; EADS Telegon-8 HFD/F; 2 330- to 340-round Matra Défense Dagaie decoy RL
E/O: 2 Thales LIOD optronic gun directors
M: 4 MTU 20V1163 TB92 diesels; 2 CP props; 21,460 bhp
Electric: 1,392 kVA tot. **Range:** 3,600/18; 7,000/14 **Fuel:** 200 tons
Crew: 13 officers, 111 enlisted

Remarks: Ordered 10-6-81 and arrived in Malaysia 23-11-84. Are rated by Malaysia as corvettes. Four similar, but slightly smaller and differently equipped, near-sisters were built for Colombia. 25 is being used in trials of "smart ship" concepts to increase automation and reduce crew requirements.

Hull systems: Can make 23 kts on two diesels. There is no hangar, although provision was made to install a telescoping one. Have proven poor sea boats in anything above a State 2 sea due to the low bow freeboard, and maintenance access is poor.

Combat systems: Have the Thales SEWACO MA combat data system and are equipped for Link 5 and Thales Link Y Mk 1 datalink. The SEWACO system was updated during 1999 and later refits. There are flare rocket launchers on the sides of the 57-mm mount. The 100-mm guns were upgraded to Mk 2 configuration, with improved reliability, during 1994. In the EW suite, RAPIDS = Radar Passive Identification System, and SCIMITAR = System for Countering Interdiction Missiles and Target Acquisition Radars. The MM 38 Exocet missiles will shortly be time-expired.

Modernization: Both are planned to be updated with improved antiair and ASW capabilities to serve past 2010, funds permitting. A CIWS system and a medium-range SAM system would be added, and the ASW rocket launcher would be replaced with ASW torpedo tubes, while the EW system, internal communications system, and datalinks would be replaced; the 100-mm and 30-mm guns may be replaced as well.

Disposal note: *Yarrow*-class frigate *Rahmat* (24, ex-*Hang Jebat*) was decommissioned and turned into a museum ship during 2004.

PATROL SHIPS [PS]

♦ 2 (+ 4 + 21) MEKO 100 RMN class

Bldr: 171–172: Blohm + Voss, Hamburg; 173–174: NDSB Lumut, Perak; 175–176: PSC–Naval Dockyard Sdn Bhd

	Laid down	L	In serv.
171 Kadah	13-11-01	21-3-03	2-06
172 Pahang	21-12-01	2-10-03	2006
173 Perak	2-1-03	. . .	. . .
174 Terengganu	8-04	. . .	. . .
175 Kelantan	7-05	. . .	. . .
176 Selangor	7-06	. . .	2012

Kadah (171)—following launch Michael Nitz, 3-03

Pahang (172)—preparing for transport to Malaysia Michael Nitz, 10-03

Kadah (171) Michael Nitz, 3-03

D: 1,650 tons (fl) **S:** 22+ kts
Dim: 91.10 (82.80 wl) × 12.85 (11.80 waterline) × 3.40 (mean hull)
A: 1 76-mm 62-cal. OTO Melara Rapid DP; 1 30-mm 80-cal. OTO Melara–Mauser AA; 2 single 12.7-mm mg; 1 . . . ASW helicopter (see Remarks)
Electronics:
Radar: 1 STN Atlas . . . nav.; 1 EADS TRS-3D 3-D/16ES surf./air search
Sonar: ELAC WDS 3060 obstacle-avoidance
EW: Thales . . . intercept/jamming syst.; ALEX decoy syst. (2 . . . -round RL)
E/O: TMEO electro-optical gun f.c. director
M: 2 Caterpillar 3616 diesels; 2 CP props; 16,000 bhp (14,600 sust.)
Electric: 1,600 kw tot. (4 × 400 kw; Caterpillar 3412A diesels driving)
Range: 6,050/12 **Endurance:** 21 days **Crew:** 78 tot. (accomm. for 93)

PATROL SHIPS [PS] *(continued)*

Remarks: Originally referred to as the New-Generation Patrol Vessel (NGPV) for use in offshore patrol, antipollution, oil-spill cleanup, and search-and-rescue duties; an ASW role was added late in 2002. On 13-10-97, a consortium of Blohm + Voss Industrie GmbH, Howaldtswerke Deutsche Werft AG (HDW), Thyssen Rheinstahl Technik GmbH, and Ferrostaal AG was selected, but the letter of intent to order was not signed until 27-2-99 for an initial six units with an option for 21 more; the construction contract was not signed until 11-00. The total program cost is to be $1.42 billion. First steel was cut 7-6-01 at Blohm + Voss. In mid-2003 Blohm + Voss provided fully outfitted, prefabricated sections for the first two ships to be fully assembled in Malaysia, with the next four to be built primarily by PSC-NDSB with German technical assistance; prime contractorship will devolve on PSC-NDSB for any units past the first six. During 9-05 the Malaysian government assumed control of PSC-NDSB shipyard following numerous delays and difficulties. The full 27-unit program is expected to take place over 15 years. 171 arrived in Malaysia during 12-03. Both 171 and 172 failed their initial 2005 acceptance trials and required additional funding to complete, due largely to command-and-control suite difficulties. As of early 2006 construction on 173 and 174 was reportedly 45% complete, while 175 and 176 were less than 10% complete.
Hull systems: Either diesel can drive either propeller, or both. Fin stabilizers are fitted. The hull and superstructure have been shaped to reduce radar signature. A hangar and flight deck large enough to accommodate a Sikorsky S-70 (SH-60)–series helicopter are fitted, as is a landing and deck-traversing system.
Combat systems: STN Atlas Elektronik is providing technical assistance with combat systems integration; the combat data system is to be the Oerlikon-Contraves COSYS 110 M1, and a standard MICE/DAIL databus interface is to be employed. Are to have a Thales-AMS Link Y Mk 2 datalink system. The EW suite will be of Argo-Systems, Elettronica, GEC-Marconi (Type UAG), or Litton-Racal (Sceptre X) manufacture. Rhode & Schwarz will provide communications systems. Although an official Malay Navy announcement on 1-3-01 stated that ASW torpedo tubes would be fitted, it does not appear that they will be aboard initially, and no ASW sonar equipment is planned. Provision has been made for later installation of two MM 40 Exocet antiship missiles, and a 21-round Mk 49 launcher for the U.S. RIM-116 RAM SAM system may later be installed forward of the bridge.

They were originally to have carried a Super Lynx 300 or AS.355MN Fennec utility helicopter, but their mission was changed to include ASW late in 2002, and helicopters under consideration included the Super Lynx 3000, Kaman SH-2G Super SeaSprite, EADS-Eurocopter Panther, and Sikorsky S-70B.

♦ 2 Musytari class

	Bldr	L	In serv.
160 Musytari	Korea SB & Eng., Pusan, South Korea	19-7-84	19-12-85
161 Marikh	Malaysian SY & Eng., Pasir Gudang	21-1-85	8-12-87

Marikh (161) Hartmut Ehlers, 10-03

Musytari (160) Hartmut Ehlers, 10-03

D: 1,000 tons (1,300 fl) **S:** 22 kts **Dim:** 75.00 × 10.80 × 3.70
A: 1 100-mm 55-cal. Creusot-Loire Compact Mk 2 DP; 1 twin 30-mm 75-cal. Emerlec AA
Electronics:
Radar: 1 Decca TM 1226 nav.; 1 Thales DA-05 air search; 1 CelsiusTech 9GA 600 f.c.
EW: Racal Cutlass intercept; DaimlerChrysler Telegon-4 HFD/F
M: 2 SEMT-Pielstick diesels; 2 props; 12,720 bhp
Range: 6,000/20 **Crew:** 10 officers, 66 enlisted

Remarks: Ordered 6-83. A planned third unit was canceled. Intended to patrol the 200-n.m. economic zone. Names mean "Jupiter" and "Mars."
Combat systems: The CelsiusTech 9LV 230 radar/electro-optical combat system for the 100-mm gun has both a target detection and designation radar atop the foremast and a radar/electro-optical director atop the pilothouse to control the 100-mm gun. Have a large helicopter deck aft but no hangar. The 100-mm guns were upgraded to Mk 2 configuration, with improved reliability, during 1994.

GUIDED-MISSILE PATROL COMBATANTS [PGG]

♦ 4 ex-Iraqi Wadi M'ragh class
Bldr: Fincantieri, Muggiano, Italy

	Laid down	L	In serv.
134 Laksamana Hang Nadim (ex-*Kalid ibn al Walid,* F 216)	3-6-82	5-7-83	28-7-97
135 Laksamana Tun Abdul Gamil (ex-*Saad ibn abi Wakkad,* F 218)	17-8-82	30-12-83	28-7-97
136 Laksamana Muhammad Amin (ex-*Abdullah ibn abi Serh,* F 214)	22-3-82	5-7-83	7-99
137 Laksamana Tun Pusman (ex-*Salah Aldin Ayoobi,* F 220)	17-9-82	30-3-84	7-99

Laksamana Tun Pusman (137) Hartmut Ehlers, 10-03

Laksamana Tun Pusman (137) Ralph Edwards, 10-01

Laksamana Hang Nadim (134) Brian Morrison, 11-99

D: 630 tons (705 fl) **S:** 37.5 kts **Dim:** 62.30 (57.80 pp) × 9.30 × 2.80 (hull)
A: 6 Otomat Mk 2 Block IV SSM; 1 4-round Albatros SAM syst. (12 tot. Aspide missiles); 1 76-mm 62-cal. OTO Melara SuperRapid DP; 1 twin 40-mm 70-cal. OTO Melara Dardo AA; 2 triple 324-mm ILAS-3 ASW TT
Electronics:
Radar: 1 Kelvin-Hughes 1007 nav.; 1 AMS RAN-12L/X surf./air search; 1 AMS Orion RTN-10X f.c.
Sonar: STN Atlas Elektronik ASO 84-41 hull-mounted (11–13 kHz)
EW: Elettronica INS-3B intercept; 1 20-round OTO Melara SCLAR decoy RL
M: 4 MTU 20V956 TB92 diesels; 4 props; 24,400 bhp (20,400 sust.)
Electric: 650 kw tot. (3 × 200-kw, 1 × 50-kw diesel sets)
Range: 1,200/31; 4,000/18 **Fuel:** 126 tons **Endurance:** 5 days **Crew:** 51 tot.

Remarks: Ordered for Iraq during 2-81, along with two helicopter-equipped half-sisters; completed in 1987 and laid up after trials. 134 and 135 were purchased by Malaysia 27-10-95 and refitted at La Spezia beginning in 1-96. The other two were purchased 20-2-97 and handed over 31-7-99 after overhauls. 136 had been used as a demonstrator for the sale of the class by Fincantieri and was actually complete as of 1987, while 137 had never been entirely completed before work had been suspended. The first firing of an Otomat Mk 2 missile by one of this class took place 8-6-00. These four vessels constitute the 24th Corvette Squadron.

GUIDED-MISSILE PATROL COMBATANTS [PGG] *(continued)*

Combat systems: Under a 4-02 $15-million contract with AMS (BAE Systems and Finmeccanica, Italy), the IPN-10 combat data systems in 134 and 135 were to be upgraded to IPN-S (IPN-20) configuration, with two CO 3 optronic backup directors and two radar directors; funding shortfalls left the original IPN-10 system in 136 and 137. The reload Aspide missiles can only be placed in the quadruple launcher by a manually operated shipboard crane. During the reactivation refit, the 76-mm gun was upgraded, access to the 40-mm mount was improved, Link Y replaced the original combat datalink, UHF ship-to-ship communications and Inmarsat UHF SATCOM gear were added, and a GPS receiver was added. They normally operate with only two Otomat missiles aboard.

GUIDED-MISSILE PATROL BOATS [PTG]

♦ 4 Spica-M class
Bldr: Karlskrona Varvet, Karlskrona, Sweden

	Laid down	L	In serv.
3511 Handalan	24-5-77	11-11-78	26-10-79
3512 Perkasa	27-6-77	11-11-78	26-10-79
3513 Pendikar	15-7-77	11-11-78	26-10-79
3514 Gempita	21-10-77	11-11-78	26-10-79

Pendikar (3513) Ralph Edwards, 10-01

Gempita (3514) Hartmut Ehlers, 9-03

D: 240 tons (268 fl) **S:** 37.5 kts (34.5 sust.)
Dim: 43.62 (41.00 pp) × 7.00 × 2.40 (aft)
A: 4 MM 38 Exocet SSM; 1 57-mm 70-cal. Bofors SAK 57 Mk 1 DP; 1 40-mm 70-cal. Bofors AA
Electronics:
Radar: 1 Decca 1226 nav.; 1 CelsiusTech 9LV 200 Mk 2 syst. (9LV 212 tracker, 9GR 600 search radar)
EW: Decca RDL or Cutlass intercept; MEL SUSIE-1 analyzer
M: 3 MTU 16V538 TB91 diesels; 3 props; 10,800 bhp **Electric:** 400 kVA tot.
Range: 1,850/14 **Fuel:** 80 tons **Crew:** 6 officers, 34 enlisted

Remarks: Ordered 13-8-76, arriving together in Malaysia 26-10-79. 3511 is the squadron flagship. Have 103-mm rocket flare launchers on the 57-mm mount and 57-mm RL on the 40-mm mount. The tracking radar at the masthead has a stabilized antenna. The Simrad SU scanning sonar has been removed. The MM 38 Exocet missiles will shortly be time-expired.

♦ 4 French Combattante II 4AL class
Bldr: CMN, Cherbourg

	L	In serv.		L	In serv.
3501 Perdana	31-5-72	21-12-72	3503 Ganas	26-10-72	28-2-73
3502 Serang	22-12-71	31-2-73	3504 Ganyang	16-3-72	20-3-73

D: 234 tons (265 fl) **S:** 36.5 kts **Dim:** 47.00 × 7.10 × 2.50 (fl)
A: 2 MM 38 Exocet SSM; 1 57-mm 70-cal. Bofors SAK 57 Mk 1 DP; 1 40-mm 70-cal. Bofors AA
Electronics:
Radar: 1 Decca 626 nav.; 1 Thales Triton THD1040 surf./air search; 1 Thales Pollux f.c.
EW: Thales DR-2000 intercept
M: 4 MTU MB 870 diesels; 4 props; 14,000 bhp
Range: 800/25; 1,800/15 **Fuel:** 39 tons **Crew:** 4 officers, 26 enlisted

Remarks: All left France for Malaysia 2-5-73. Have steel hulls and aluminum-alloy superstructure. Six 103-mm rocket flare launchers on the 57-mm mount, four 57-mm RL on the 40-mm mount. Have the Thales Vega gun fire-control system. There are long-term plans to upgrade their missile systems, but the craft are nearing the end of their useful lives (and the MM 38 missiles are likely time-expired).

Ganas (3503) Hartmut Ehlers, 10-03

Ganyang (3504) Chris Sattler/H&L Van Ginderen, 1-00

PATROL CRAFT [PC]

♦ 6 Jerong class
Bldr: Hong Leong–Lürssen, Butterworth

	L	In serv.		L	In serv.
3505 Jerong	28-7-75	23-3-76	3508 Yu	17-7-76	15-11-76
3506 Tudak	16-3-76	16-6-76	3509 Baung	5-10-76	11-7-77
3507 Paus	2-6-76	18-8-76	3510 Pari	1-77	23-3-77

Pari (3510) H&L Van Ginderen, 5-90

Tudak (3506) Mike Louagie, 5-90

D: 210 tons (255 fl) **S:** 32 kts **Dim:** 44.90 × 7.00 × 2.48 (props)
A: 1 57-mm 70-cal. Bofors SAK Mk 1 DP; 1 40-mm 70-cal. Bofors AA
Electronics: Radar: 1 Decca 1226 nav.
M: 3 MTU MB 870 diesels; 3 props; 10,800 bhp **Electric:** 384 kVA tot.
Range: 700/31.5; 2,000/15 **Crew:** 5 officers, 31 enlisted

Remarks: Lürssen FPB 45 design. Rocket flare launchers are fitted on both gunmounts. Have a Matra Défense Naja electro-optical director for the 57-mm gun. Fin stabilizers are fitted. Reassigned to Naval Region 2 in 1995 and based at Sandakan. Under a "preliminary agreement" signed during 10-01, the entire class is to be refitted and modernized by Russia's Almaz Design Bureau at St. Petersburg.

PATROL CRAFT [PC] *(continued)*

♦ 17 Vosper 103-foot class

Bldr: Vosper Ltd., Portsmouth, U.K.

	L		L
Third group:			
34 Kris	11-3-66	43 Kerambit	20-11-66
36 Sundang	22-5-66	44 Baladau	11-1-67
37 Badek	8-5-66	45 Kelewang	31-1-67
38 Renchong	22-6-66	46 Rentaka	15-3-67
39 Tombak	20-6-66	47 Sri Perlis	26-5-67
40 Lembing	22-8-66	49 Sri Johor	21-8-67
42 Panah	10-10-66		
Second group:			
3144 Sri Sabah	30-12-63	3146 Sri Negri Sembilan	17-9-64
3145 Sri Sarawak	20-1-64	3147 Sri Melaka	2-11-64

Baladau (44)—third group of Vosper 103-foot patrol craft Piet Sinke, 8-95

Sri Negri Sembilan (3146)—second group of Vosper craft Hartmut Ehlers, 9-03

D: 96 tons (109 fl) **S:** 27 kts **Dim:** 31.39 (28.95 pp) × 5.95 × 1.65
A: 2 single 40-mm 70-cal. Bofors L70 AA; 2 single 7.62-mm mg
Electronics: Radar: 1 Decca 616 nav.
M: 2 Bristol-Siddeley or Maybach MD 655/18 diesels; 2 props; 3,550 bhp
Range: 1,400/14 (3144–3147: 1,660/14) **Crew:** 3 officers, 19–20 enlisted

Remarks: Welded hulls. Vosper antiroll stabilizers. Second group was ordered in 3-63, third group in 1965. Of the original group ordered in 9-61, *Sri Kegah* (3138) and *Sri Pahang* (3141) were stricken in 1976; *Sri Perek* (3140) foundered in 1-84; and *Sri Selangor* (3139), *Sri Kelantan* (3142), and *Sri Trengganu* (3143) were stricken 1995–96, and *Sarampang* (41) was retired on 19-1-04. The survivors have all been refitted for further service but are long overdue for replacement. 3147 is detached to Sabah, and eight others are based at Sandakan. Four (40, 43, 44, 47) are assigned to training duties.

Hull numbers 36, 42 and 3145 may have been transferred to the New Maritime Enforcement Agency in late 2006.

MINE WARFARE SHIPS

♦ 4 Italian Lerici-class coastal minehunters [MHC]

Bldr: Intermarine, Sarzana

	L	In serv.		L	In serv.
11 Mahamiru	24-2-83	11-12-85	13 Ledang	14-7-83	11-12-85
12 Jerai	8-12-83	11-12-85	14 Kinabulu	19-3-83	11-12-85

D: 578 tons (610 fl) **S:** 16 kts **Dim:** 51.00 (46.50 pp) × 9.56 × 2.85
A: 1 40-mm 70-cal Bofors AA
Electronics: Radar: 1 Decca 1226 nav.—Sonar: Thales TSM 2022
M: 2 MTU 12V396 TC82 (DB512) diesels; 2 CP props; 2,630 bhp (2,394 sust.)—2 electric retractable auxiliary props; 240 shp (for 7-kt sweep speed)
Electric: 1,000 kw (4 MTU V396 TC52 gen. sets)
Range: 1,400/14; 2,000/12 **Fuel:** 46 tons **Endurance:** 14 days
Crew: 5 officers, 37 enlisted

Remarks: Ordered 2-81 and arrived in Malaysia 28-3-86. Also used for patrol duties. Are based two each at Labuan and Lumut to provide mine-countermeasures services on both coasts of the Malay Peninsula. Plans to acquire four more have been canceled, but these four are planned to be updated with a more modern tactical data system.

Ledang (13) Brian Morrison, 11-99

Kinabulu (14) Chris Sattler/H&L Van Ginderen, 11-99

Hull systems: Glass-reinforced plastic construction. Have a different main engine, armament, and sonar than their Italian Navy sisters. Range at 12 kts can be extended to 4,000 n.m. by using the passive antirolling tanks to carry fuel.
Combat systems: The Thales IBIS II minehunting system and TSM 2060 autopilot are fitted. Have two PAP-104 remote-controlled minehunting devices, good in depths up to 300 m, and U.K. Oropesa Mk 4 mechanical sweep gear. A Draeger Duocom decompression chamber is fitted for embarked mine disposal divers. Decoy or illumination rocket launchers are mounted on the sides of the 40-mm AA gunmount. One French ECA Olister remotely operated mine countermeasures vehicle system was ordered for use with this class during mid-2002.

AMPHIBIOUS WARFARE SHIPS

Note: An amphibious transport ship, possibly a former U.S. Navy unit, is planned for acquisition.

♦ 1 ex-U.S. Newport-class tank landing ship [LST]

Bldr: National Steel SB, San Diego

	Laid down	L	In serv.
1505 Sri Inderapura (ex-*Spartanburg County,* LST 1192)	7-2-70	11-11-70	1-9-71

Sri Inderapura (1505) H&L Van Ginderen, 5-95

D: 4,975 tons light (8,576 fl) **S:** 22 kts (20 sust.)
Dim: 159.2 (171.3 over horns) × 21.18 × 5.3 (aft; 1.80 fwd)
A: 1 20-mm Mk 15 Phalanx gatling CIWS; 4 single 12.7-mm mg
Electronics:
Radar: 1 Raytheon SPS-64(V)9 nav.; 1 Raytheon SPS-10F surf. search
EW: No intercept; Mk 36 RBOC decoy syst. (2 6-round Mk 137 RL)

AMPHIBIOUS WARFARE SHIPS *(continued)*

M: 6 Alco 16-251 diesels; 2 CP props; 16,500 bhp
Range: 14,250/14 **Fuel:** 1,750 tons
Crew: 13 officers, 174 enlisted + troops: 20 officers, 294 enlisted (+ 72 emergency accomm.)

Remarks: Decommissioned 16-12-94 from the USN and purchased for $18.7 million, transferring the same date and commissioning in the Malaysian Navy 31-1-95. Given a major refit at Johor Baharu before entering service in 1998. The 1998 USN offer to sell sister *Barbour County* (LST 1195) was not accepted. *Sri Inderapura* was badly damaged by an engine-room fire on 16-12-02, with extensive repairs required. There has been talk of removing her from service altogether and purchasing a new unit from the United States, though this seems unlikely and repairs appear to be moving forward.
Hull systems: Can transport 2,000 tons of cargo, or 500 tons for beaching, on 1,765 m^2 of deck space. A side-thruster propeller forward helps when marrying to a causeway. There is a 34-m-long, 75-ton-capacity mobile aluminum ramp forward, which is linked to the tank deck by a second from the upper deck. Aft is a 242-m^2 helicopter platform and a stern door for loading and unloading vehicles. The tank deck, which has a 75-ton-capacity turntable at both ends, can carry 29 M 48 tanks or 41 2.5-ton trucks, while the upper deck can accept 29 2.5-ton trucks. Carries three LCVPs and one LCP in Welin davits. Has two 10-ton cranes. Carries 141,600 gallons of vehicle fuel.
Combat systems: The Mk 63 radar gunfire-control systems were removed 1977–78, and the two twin 76.2-mm guns were removed prior to transfer.

Note: The two multipurpose ships of the *Sri Indera Sakti* class can also be used for amphibious warfare purposes.

♦ 2 Sri Gaya–class Fast Troop Vessels (FTV) [LCP]
Bldr: PSC–Naval Dockyard, Lumut

331 Sri Gaya (In serv. 5-01) 332 Sri Tiga (In serv. 2001)

Sri Tiga (332) Ralph Edwards, 10-01

D: 116.5 tons (fl) **S:** 25 kts (loaded) **Dim:** 37.50 (30.30 wl) × 7.00 × 2.50
A: 2 single 7.62-mm mg **Electronics:** Radar: 1 . . . nav.
M: 4 M.A.N. D2842 LE408 diesels; 4 Hamilton Type 521 waterjets; 3,940 bhp tot.
Electric: 160 kw tot. (2 × 80 kw, Cummins diesels driving)
Range: . . . / . . . **Crew:** 8 total + 200 passengers

Remarks: Fully air-conditioned craft of aluminum construction, with the design based on that of the Australian WaveMaster commercial fast ferry. Can carry 4 tons of cargo (some of it refrigerated) in addition to the passengers.

♦ 1 rigid inflatable personnel special forces craft [LCP]
Bldr: Mara Shipyard & Engineering, Terengganu (In serv. 1999)

D: 3.7 tons (fl) **S:** 48 kts (37 cruising) **Dim:** 7.62 (5.80 wl) × 2.72 × 0.60
A: 1 7.62-mm mg; small arms
Electronics: Radar: 1 Furuno FR-1721 Mk II nav.
M: 2 Yamaha gasoline outboards; 400 bhp
Range: 150/37 **Fuel:** 600 liters **Crew:** 3 tot. + 12 troops

Remarks: Composite hull structure. Painted black to reduce visibility. Troops are carried in six rows of two seats abaft the cockpit, while the gunner is seated forward. Additional units may be ordered.

♦ 16 Swedish CB 90H personnel landing craft [LCP]
Bldr: Dockstavarvet, Sweden (In serv. 1998–99; 2000–2002)

11–15, 21–24, 32–34, 41–44

CB 90H landing craft Brian Morrison, 12-99

D: 14.5 tons light (19 fl) **S:** 40+ kts (35 loaded)
Dim: 14.90 (13.00 wl) × 3.80 × 0.84 **A:** 1 12.7-mm mg; 2 mine rails
Electronics: Radar: 1 Decca BridgeMaster RD 360 nav.
M: 2 Saab Scania 8V DSI-14 diesels; 2 KaMeWa FF 410 waterjets; 1,256 bhp
Range: 260/20 **Fuel:** 2.5 tons **Crew:** 4 tot. + 20 troops

Remarks: The plan to procure 100 or more of the larger Enforcer CB 90NEX–class patrol boats designed by Storebro and to have been built by Perusahaan Sadur Timah in Malaysia for the navy and national maritime police has not gone forward on schedule due to the financial situation, but by 11-99, five were in service with the navy as special forces insertion craft. Eleven more had been built by 2002. They are used primarily as patrol and logistic support craft operating from Borneo.
Hull systems: Can maintain 20 kts in 1.5-m seas, and the hull can withstand at least 25 groundings without significant damage. In lieu of troops, can carry up to 2.8 tons of cargo. The 12.7-mm mg will employ a U.S.-made stabilized mounting ordered in 2002.

AUXILIARIES

♦ 2 multipurpose support ships [AG]

	Bldr	Laid down	L	In serv.
1503 Sri Indera Sakti	Bremer-Vulcan, Bremen, Germany	15-2-80	1-7-80	24-10-80
1504 Mahawangsa	Hanjin Industrial SB, Masan, South Korea	. . .	. . .	16-5-83

Sri Indera Sakti (1503) Ralph Edwards, 10-02

Mahawangsa (1504)—note the higher helicopter platform Maritime Photographic, 4-97

D: 2,000 tons light (4,300 fl) **S:** 16.8 kts **Dim:** 100.00 (91.20 pp) × 15.00 × 4.75
A: 1 57-mm 70-cal. Bofors SAK-57 Mk 1 DP
Electronics: Radar: 1 Decca TM 1226 nav., 1 . . . surf. search
M: 2 Deutz-KHD SBV 6M540 diesels; 2 CP props; 5,986 bhp—bow-thruster
Electric: 1,200 kw tot. **Range:** 14,000/15 **Fuel:** 1,350 tons (max.)
Endurance: 60 days **Crew:** 14 officers, 122 enlisted + 75 passengers

Remarks: 1,800 dwt. 1503 ordered 10-79, 1504 in 2-81. Intended to perform a variety of tasks, including providing support (including up to 1,300 tons of fuel and 200 tons of water) to deployed small combatants or mine-countermeasures ships; acting as flagships; performing as vehicle and troop transports in amphibious operations; and acting as cadet training ships.
Hull systems: 1504 is 103.00 m o.a., draws 5.00 m, displaces 5,000 tons (fl), and can reach 15.5 kts; she is configured to carry 410 tons of ammunition. The ship lacks a funnel, thus effectively doubling the area of the helicopter deck, which is also positioned higher than on 1503. Both have 1,000 m^3 of cargo space for spare parts, and 10 standard 20-ft cargo containers can be carried on deck amidships. They can carry 17 tanks, while 1504 can also stow 11 3-ton trucks on deck beneath the helicopter platform. Vehicle holds aft are reached by ramps on either side of the stern. They can carry 600 troops on the 680-m^2 vehicle deck. Extensive repair facilities and divers' support equipment are provided. Provisions spaces total 300 m^3, including 100 m^3 of refrigerated stores. A 16-ton crane is installed amidships.
Combat systems: The stern-mounted second 57-mm gun was removed from 1504 by 4-97, and neither carries the two 20-mm AA originally fitted. Have a Matra Défense Naja optical gun director. Chaff and illumination rocket launchers are mounted on the sides of the gunmount. Can embark a Malaysian Army Sikorsky S-61 helicopter. Have been fitted with an S-band surface-search radar and a commercial SATCOM system.

Disposal note: U.S. LST 542–class support ship and former landing ship *Sri Banggi* (1501; ex-*Henry County,* LST 824) was stricken during 2000; sister *Rajah Jarom* (1502; ex-*Sedgewick County,* LST 1123) was stricken 9-9-99.

AUXILIARIES *(continued)*

♦ 1 hydrographic survey ship [AGS]
Bldr: Hong Leong–Lürssen, Butterworth (In serv. 12-10-98)

153 Perantau

Perantau (153)—white hull, buff stack and mast, pennant number not worn Hartmut Ehlers, 9-03

D: 1,996 tons (fl) **S:** 16.3 kts **Dim:** 67.80 (62.40 pp) × 13.28 × 4.00
A: None
Electronics:
Radar: 1 STN Atlas nav.
Sonar: STN Atlas Elektronik Fansweep and Hydrosweep multibeam mapping
M: 2 Deutz SBV8 M628 diesels; 2 Berg CP props; 4,760 bhp—1 Schottel 3-ton-thrust bow-thruster
Electric: 1,950 kw (3 × 600-kw MWM V8616 diesel-driven sets, 1 × 150 kw)
Range: 6,000/10 **Crew:** 17 officers, 77 enlisted

Remarks: 506 dwt. Ordered in fall 1996 for delivery 8-97—a very tight schedule that was not met. The ship is capable of producing high-precision underwater topography charts. Design by Krögerwerft, Germany. A near-sister was completed in 1997 for the German Hydrographic Institute.
Hull systems: STN Atlas Elektronik provided the NACOS 55 integrated navigation system, Hydrosweep MD-2 multibeam sonar, and Hydromap hydrographic evaluation system. Other survey equipment includes differential GPS, medium-range and short-range radio position-fixing systems, combined side-scan sonar and bottom-profiling system, deep-sea echo sounders, acoustic doppler current profilers, gravity corer and bottom sampling equipment, recording current meters, tide gauges, and an underwater camera. Has two 8-ton cranes aft. Carries two survey launches (with Fansweep 20 portable survey sounders), two general-purpose launches, and two rigid inflatables.

♦ 1 oceanographic research and hydrographic survey ship [AGS]
Bldr: Hong Leong–Lürssen, Butterworth (In serv. 12-1-78)

152 Mutiara

Mutiara (152)—does not wear her pennant number Hartmut Ehlers, 10-03

D: 1,905 tons (fl) **S:** 16 kts **Dim:** 70.0 (64.0 pp) × 13.0 × 4.0
A: 2 twin 20-mm 70-cal. Oerlikon Mk 24 AA
Electronics: Radar: 1 Decca 1226 nav.; 1 Decca 1229 nav.
M: 1 Deutz SBA-12M-528 diesel; 1 CP prop; 2,000 bhp
Range: 4,500/16 **Crew:** 14 officers, 141 enlisted

Remarks: Ordered in 1975. Carries six small survey launches and has a small helicopter platform aft. White hull, buff stack.

♦ 1 British-built training ship [AXT]
Bldr: Yarrow Shipbuilders, Scotstoun, Glasgow

	Laid down	L	In serv.
76 Hang Tuah (ex-*Mermaid*)	1965	29-12-66	16-5-73

D: 2,300 tons (2,520 fl) **S:** 22 kts **Dim:** 103.40 × 12.20 × 4.80
A: 1 57-mm 70-cal. Bofors SAK 57 Mk 1 DP; 2 single 40-mm 70-cal. Bofors L70 AA; 1 3-round Limbo Mk 10 ASW mortar (51 projectiles)
Electronics:
Radar: 1 Decca 1226 nav.; 1 Plessey AWS-1 air search
Sonar: Graseby Type 174 hull-mounted (14–22 kHz) search; Graseby Type 170 hull-mounted attack (15 kHz)
EW: None
M: 2 Stork-Wärtsilä 12SW28 diesels; 2 CP props; 9,928 bhp
Electric: . . . kw tot. (3 × . . . kw, Wärtsilä 12V UD 25 diesels driving)
Range: 4,800/15 **Fuel:** 230 tons **Crew:** 210 tot.

Hang Tuah (76) Brian Morrison, 11-99

Remarks: Former frigate, used as fleet training ship after a 1991–92 refit. Ordered for Ghana in 1964 as a frigate-cum-yacht. Because of a change in government in Ghana, the ship was not delivered and at the end of 1971 she was purchased by the British government. Was sold to Malaysia in 5-77 and delivered 8-77 after a refit. Extensively upgraded, rearmed, and re-engined during a 1995 to 2-97 refit at Malaysian SB & Eng., Johor Baharu.
Hull systems: Has a helicopter pad but no hangar. Fin stabilizers are fitted. Originally had the same machinery (eight Admiralty Standard Range-I diesels, totaling 14,400 bhp) and has the same below-waterline hullform as the British *Leopard-* and *Salisbury*-class frigates; was given three new diesel generators during the 1995 to 2-97 refit.
Combat systems: The twin 102-mm 45-cal. Vickers Mk 19 gunmount was removed from the forecastle during the 1995–97 refit and replaced with the after 57-mm mounting from *Mahawangsa* (1504). The original 40-mm 60-cal. Mk 6 AA mounts were replaced with Bofors L70 weapons. All three gunmounts have fixed rocket flare launchers on their sides, and the 57-mm mount is controlled by a Matra Défense Naja optical director. The Limbo ASW mortar has a range of 400–914 m and fires a pattern of three 177-kg time-fuzed projectiles. The sonar suite may have been updated, although one source states that the Limbo mortar is no longer operational.

SERVICE CRAFT

Disposal note: Diving tender [YDT] *Duyong* (1109) was retired during 2000.

♦ 1 fast personnel ferry [YFL]
Bldr: . . . (In serv. 2001)

332 Tiga

Remarks: High-speed, waterjet-propelled personnel ferry, probably adapted from a commercial design. No data available.

♦ 5 miscellaneous launches [YFL]

Kempong Mangkasa Patak Sellar Tepuruk

Remarks: No data available.

♦ 2 Lang Tiram–class large harbor tugs [YTB]
Bldr: Penang SY, Pulau Jerejah (In serv. 1981–82)

Lang Tiram Lang Siput

D: . . . **S:** 12.5 kts **Dim:** 29.0 × 7.0 × 2.0
M: 2 Ruston-Paxman diesels; 2 props; 1,800 bhp

Remarks: Sisters *Lang Hindek* and *Lang Kangok* were transferred to Malaysian Marine Department in 1992.

♦ 3 Tunda Satu 1–class large harbor tugs [YTB]
Bldr: Ironwood SY, Malaysia (In serv. 1978–79)

A 1 Tunda Satu 1 A 2 Tunda Satu 2 A 3 Tunda Satu 3

Tunda Satu 1 (A 1) H&L Van Ginderen, 5-90

D: 150 tons **S:** . . . **Dim:** 26.0 × . . . × . . .
M: 1 Cummins diesel; 1 prop: . . . bhp

♦ 8 miscellaneous tugs [YTB/YTM/YTL]

A 4 Penyu (ex-*Salvigilant*)
A 5 Kupang
A 6 Sotong (ex-*Asiatic Charm*)
A 7 Ketam
A 8 Kepah (ex-*Arctic Supplier*)
A 9 Siput
A 10 Teritup
A 11 Belankas

SERVICE CRAFT *(continued)*

Penyu (A 4) Hartmut Ehlers, 10-03

Remarks: A 4 is a 398-grt salvage tug, built in 1976 and purchased in 1980. A 6 is a 233-grt tug, built in 1976 and purchased in 1980. A 7 is a salvage and firefighting tug. A 8 is a 432-grt tug, built in 1974 and purchased in 1980.

♦ **1 sail-training brigantine [YTS]**
Bldr: Brooke Marine, Lowestoft, U.K.

	Laid down	L	In serv.
A 13 Tunas Samadura	1-12-88	4-8-89	16-10-89

Tunas Samadura (A 13)—white-painted and without pennant number
Hartmut Ehlers, 9-03

D: 239 tons (fl) **S:** 10 kts power/14 kts sail **Dim:** 44.00 (35 pp) × 7.8 × 4.0
M: 2 Perkins diesels; 2 props; . . . bhp **Crew:** 6 officers, 21 enlisted + 24 trainees

Remarks: Operated by the navy, but trains all Malaysian sea services. Foremast is 30 m high, mainmast 32.6 m. Steel construction hull.

MALAYSIAN ARMY

LANDING CRAFT [LCP]

♦ **165 Damen 540 class**
Bldrs: 65 by Damen, Gorinchem, Netherlands; 100 by Limbougan Timor, Kuala Trengganu (In serv. 1986–87)

D: . . . **S:** 25–30 kts **Dim:** 5.4 × 1.83 × . . .
M: 1 40-bhp outboard **Crew:** 2 crew, 10 troops

Remarks: Ordered 10-85. Transferred from the navy in 1993. About 250–300 other small river-crossing assault boats are available.

MALAYSIAN MARITIME ENFORCEMENT AGENCY

Note: In March 2005 the Malaysian Maritime Enforcement Agency (MMEA) was formed, combining units from the Fisheries Department, Royal Customs and Excise Department, and Sabah police. The MMEA took over law enforcement, search-and-rescue, pollution-control, counter-drug and antipiracy operations inside Malaysia's economic exclusion zone. The new force will eventually operate a minimum of six helicopters, a number of fixed wing aircraft, and as many as 80 patrol craft of varying size, including those listed below.

PATROL CRAFT [WPC]

♦ **6 Brooke Marine 29-meter design**
Bldr: Penang SY, Pulau Jerejah (In serv. 1982–83)

PX 28 Sangitan, PX 29 Sabahan, PX 30 Sri Dungun, PX 31 Sri Tioman, PX 32 Sri Tumpar, PX 33 Segama

Sri Tioman (PX 31) NAVPIC Holland, 9-94

D: 114 tons **S:** 36 kts **Dim:** 29.0 (26.5 pp) × 6.0 × 1.7
A: 1 20-mm 70-cal. Oerlikon AA; 2 single 7.62-mm mg
Electronics: Radar: 1 . . . nav.
M: 2 Paxman Valenta 16 RP 200M diesels; 2 props; 8,000 bhp
Range: 1,200/24 **Crew:** 4 officers, 14 constables

Remarks: Ordered in 1980. Design evolved from that of the PX 26 class. Carry 2,000 rounds of 20-mm ammunition.

♦ **14 PZ class**
Bldr: Hong Leong–Lürssen, Butterworth (In serv. 1981–83)

PZ 1 Lang Hitan, PZ 2 Lang Malam, PZ 3 Lang Leban, PZ 4 Lang Kuik, PZ 5 Balong, PZ 6 Berlian, PZ 7 Kurita, PZ 8 Serangan Batu, PZ 9 Harinan Bintang, PZ 11 Harinan Belang, PZ 12 Harimau Akar, PZ 13 Parangan, PZ 14 Marsusi, PZ 15 Alu Alu

Lang Hitan (PZ 1) Hartmut Ehlers, 9-03

D: 188 tons (205 fl) **S:** 34 kts **Dim:** 38.50 (36.00 wl) × 7.00 × 2.20
A: 1 40-mm 70-cal. Bofors AA; 1 20-mm 70-cal. AA; 2 single 7.62-mm mg
Electronics: Radar: 1 Kelvin-Hughes 14/9 nav.
M: 2 MTU 20V538 TB92 diesels; 2 props; 9,000 bhp **Electric:** 130 kVA tot.
Range: 550/31.5; 1,100/16 **Crew:** 4 officers, 34 constables

Remarks: Lürssen FPB 38 design. Ordered in 1979; first delivered 8-81. Sister *Harimau Kumbang* (PZ 10) has been stricken. Have two rocket flare launchers. Carry 1,000 rounds of 40-mm and 2,000 rounds of 20-mm ammunition. A near-sister was delivered to Bangladesh in 1999.

PATROL BOATS [WPB]

♦ **10 Penyengat-class fast patrol boats**
Bldr: MSET, Pulau, Mambing (In serv. 2001–2)

Camar Sepuluh, PSC 6, PSC 7, PSC 16, PSC 17, PSC 29, and 4 others

Remarks: No additional data available.

♦ **2 Camar . . . class**
Bldr: . . ., Malaysia (In serv. 1997)

PA 20 Camar 6, PA 30 Camar 8

D: 44 tons **S:** 35 kts **Dim:** 21.0 × . . . × . . .
M: 2 MWM TBD 616 V16 diesels (3,000 bhp each)

Remarks: No additional data available.

PATROL BOATS [WPB] *(continued)*

♦ **4 Swedish IC 16 class**
Bldr: DNSS, Sarawak (In serv. 2003–4)

D: 13 tons (20 fl) **S:** 50 kts **Dim:** 15.9 (13.0 wl) × 3.80 × 1
Electronics: 1 Furuno . . . nav.
M: 2 M.A.N. D2842 LE 410 diesels; 2 KaMeWa waterjets; 2,200 bhp
Range: 240/30 **Crew:** 6 tot.

Remarks: Based on the Swedish SRC 90E class. Served with Customs Service prior to formation of the MMEA.

♦ **1 9.65-meter class**
Bldr: DMS, Johor Baharu (In serv. 1990s)

D: . . . tons (fl) **S:** 61 kts **Dim:** 9.65 × . . . × . . .
A: 2 single 7.62-mm mg **M:** 3 MerCruiser outboards; 3 props; 415 bhp
Crew: . . .

♦ **1 prototype Swiss-built**
Bldr: Friedrich Fassmer Werft, Berne/Motzen (In serv. 12-96)

PX . . .

D: 44 tons (fl) **S:** 35 kts **Dim:** 21.0 × . . . × . . .
A: small arms **Electronics:** Radar: 1 . . . nav.
M: 2 MWM TBD616V16 diesels; 2 props; 3,000 bhp
Range: . . . / . . . **Crew:** . . . tot.

Remarks: Aluminum alloy construction.

♦ **23 Simonneau SM 465 class**
Bldr: Hong Leong–Lürssen, Butterworth (In serv. 1992–93)

PC 6 through PC 28

Simonneau SM 465–class PC 6 Maritime Photographic, 4-97

D: 18 tons (at half load) **S:** 40+ kts **Dim:** 14.00 × 4.00 × 0.75
A: 2 single 12.7-mm mg **Electronics:** Radar: 1 Furuno . . . nav.
M: 2 MTU 12V183 TE92 diesels; 2 props; 2,000 bhp
Fuel: 2,000 liters **Crew:** 6 tot.

Remarks: Aluminum construction. Have one diesel generator and are air-conditioned. Carry an outboard-powered inspection craft.

♦ **12 7.5-meter class**
Bldr: Destination Marine, Johor Baharu (In serv. 1990–91)

D: . . . tons (fl) **S:** 45 kts **Dim:** 7.5 × 2.5 × 1.0
A: 2 single 7.62-mm mg **M:** 2 gasoline outboards; 550 bhp **Crew:** . . .

Remarks: Ordered 6-89 for antipiracy duties. Six were intended for service at Sabah.

♦ **3 PX 25 class**
Bldr: Hong Leong–Lürssen, Butterworth (In serv. 1973–74)

PX 25 Sri Gaya PX 26 Sri Kudat PX 27 Sri Tawau

D: 92.5 tons **S:** 25 kts **Dim:** 28.0 × 5.4 × 1.6
A: 1 20-mm 70-cal. Oerlikon Mk 10 AA; 2 single 7.62-mm mg
Electronics: Radar: 1 Furuno . . . nav.
M: 2 MTU MB820Db diesels; 2 props; 2,460 bhp
Range: 1,050/15 **Crew:** 2 officers, 17 constables

Remarks: An improved version of the PX 21 class, with increased range.

♦ **4 PX 21 class**
Bldr: Vosper Pty, Singapore (In serv. 1973–74)

PX 21 Kuala Trengganu PX 23 Sri Menanti
PX 22 Johore Bahru PX 24 Kuching

D: 92 tons (fl) **S:** 25 kts **Dim:** 27.3 × 5.8 × 1.5
A: 2 single 20-mm 70-cal. Oerlikon Mk 10 AA; 2 single 7.62-mm mg
Electronics: Radar: 1 Furuno . . . nav.
M: 2 MTU MB820Db diesels; 2 props; 2,460 bhp
Range: 750/15 **Crew:** 2 officers, 17 constables

♦ **2 PX 1 class**
Bldr: Vosper Pty, Singapore (In serv. 1963–69)

PX 19 Alor Star PX 20 Kota Bahru

D: 85 tons (fl) **S:** 25 kts **Dim:** 26.29 × 5.70 × 1.45
A: 1 20-mm 90-cal. Oerlikon GAM-B01 AA; 2 single 7.62-mm mg
Electronics: Radar: 1 Furuno . . . nav.

Kota Bahru (PX 20) NAVPIC Holland, 8-96

M: 2 MTU MB820Db diesels; 2 props; 2,460 bhp
Range: 550/20; 700/15 **Crew:** 2 officers, 13 constables

Remarks: Sisters *Mahkota* (PX 1), *Temenggong* (PX 2), *Hulubalang* (PX 3), *Maharajesetia* (PX 4), *Bentara* (PX 7), *Periwa* (PX 8), *Pekan* (PX 13), and *Kelang* (PX 14) were stricken during 1992–93, sisters PX 5 through PX 18 had been retired by 2005.

SERVICE CRAFT

♦ **2 miscellaneous personnel ferries [WYFB]**
Bldr: Brooke Dockyard, Sarawak (In serv. 1985)

PT 1 Penjaga PT 2 Margherita

Remarks: Are about 30 m long and appear to be intended primarily for riverine service. PT 2 is the more modern and may be somewhat smaller than PT 1. Also in service are smaller transports PLC 1–PLC 4, completed in 1980 by Pasir Gudang, and large personnel launches PA 39 and PA 53.

MALDIVE ISLANDS

Republic of Maldives

COAST GUARD

Personnel: Approx. 400 total, including shore-based constabulary

Base: Male

Note: The digits in the pennant numbers all add up to 7.

PATROL CRAFT [WPC]

♦ **1 ex-Indian Modified SDB Mk 3 class**
Bldr: Garden Reach SB & Eng., Calcutta

	L	In serv.
Hurawee (ex-*Tillanchang,* T 62)	10-11-99	4-01

D: 260 tons (fl) **S:** 35 kts **Dim:** 46.0 × . . . × . . .
A: 2 single 30-mm Medak AA
Electronics: Radar: 1 Bharat 1245 nav.
M: 3 MTU 16V 396 TB94 diesels; 2 props; 10,500 bhp
Range: 1,500/ . . . **Crew:** 35 tot.

Remarks: Transferred from India on 16-4-06. Intended for coastal patrol, smuggling interdiction, fisheries protection, and policing duties.

PATROL BOATS [WPB]

♦ **2 Israeli Shaldag class**
Bldr: Colombo Dockyard, Colombo, Sri Lanka

700 Iskandhar (In serv. 1999) Ghazee (In serv. 2002)

D: 40 tons (56 fl) **S:** 46 kts **Dim:** 24.37 (20.07 pp) × 6.00 × 1.15 (1.26 max.)
A: 2 single 12.7-mm mg
Electronics: Radar: 1 Koden Mk 2 nav.
M: 2 Paxman . . . diesels; 2 waterjets; 4,250 bhp
Electric: 50 kw tot. (2 × 25-kw, 440-V a.c. diesel sets)
Range: 850/16 **Endurance:** 2–3 days **Crew:** 18 tot.

Remarks: First unit was ordered in 1997. Has a deep-vee, aluminum-construction hull and five watertight compartments. Air-conditioned.

PATROL BOATS [WPB] *(continued)*

♦ **1 21-meter Tracker class**
Bldr: Fairey Marine, Cowes, U.K. (In serv. 4-87)

106 Nirolhu

Nirolhu (106) H&L Van Ginderen, 4-94

D: 35 tons (38 fl) **S:** 25 kts **Dim:** 21.00 × 5.18 × 1.45
A: 1 12.7-mm M2 mg; 1 7.62-mm FN mg
Electronics: Radar: 1 Koden Mk 2 nav.
M: 2 G.M. 12V71 TI diesels; 2 props; 1,300 bhp
Range: 450/20 **Endurance:** 7 days **Crew:** 10 tot.
Remarks: Ordered 6-85. Used for fisheries protection. GRP construction.

♦ **3 ex-U.K. Tracker II class**
Bldr: Fairey Marine, Hamble (In serv. 1978–79)

133 Kaani 142 Kuredhi 151 Midhili

Kaani (133)—with Dagger-class launch *Funa* (124) and Tracker-class *Nirolhu* (106) in the background Laurent Morlion, via Paolo Marsan, 2000

D: 31 tons (34.5 fl) **S:** 21 kts **Dim:** 20.00 (19.30 pp) × 5.18 × 1.45
A: 1 12.7-mm M2 mg; 1 7.62-mm FN mg
Electronics: Radar: 1 Koden Mk 2 nav.
M: 2 G.M. 12V71 TI diesels; 2 props; 1,300 bhp **Electric:** 30 kw tot.
Range: 650/20 **Endurance:** 7 days **Crew:** 10 tot.

Remarks: Transferred by the U.K. in 7-89; left for the Indian Ocean via heavy-lift ship. Formerly operated by H.M. Customs and Excise as *Active, Challenge,* and *Champion,* but correlation to the new names is not available. GRP hull construction. The radar has been removed from 142.

♦ **1 17-meter class**
Bldr: Cheverton, Cowes, U.K. (In serv. 1984)

115 Burevi (ex-7)

D: 22 tons (24 fl) **S:** 23.6 kts **Dim:** 17.00 × 4.50 × 1.20
A: 1 12.7-mm M2 mg; 1 7.62-mm FN mg
Electronics: Radar: 1 Koden Mk 2 nav.
M: 2 G.M. 8V71 TI diesels; 2 props; 850 bhp
Range: 790/18; 1,000/12 **Crew:** 9 tot.

Remarks: Originally completed in 1980 for Kiribati, but not delivered. Purchased in 1984 for the Maldives. GRP hull and aluminum superstructure.

♦ **1 Dagger class**
Bldr: Fairey Marine, Cowes, U.K. (In serv. 1982)

124 Funa

D: 20 tons (fl) **S:** 35 kts **Dim:** 11.2 × 3.4 × 1.2
A: 1 7.62-mm mg **Electronics:** Radar: 1 Furuno . . . nav.
M: 2 Ford Sabre diesels; 2 props; 660 bhp **Crew:** 6 tot

Remarks: GRP construction.

SERVICE CRAFT

♦ **1 . . . -class utility landing craft [WLCM]**
Bldr: Colombo Dockyard, Sri Lanka (In serv. 2000)

Remarks: 33 tons displacement, no additional information in available. A second unit is planned.

Note: A number of other small boats are also in service including the Coast Guard fire and rescue craft *"E-9"* and several RHIBs.

MALI

Republic of Mali

Personnel: About 50 total

Bases: Bamako, Mopti, Segou and Timbuktu

PATROL BOATS [PB]

♦ **2 small river patrol craft**
Bldr: . . . , France (In serv. 7-99)

Remarks: For service on the Niger river.

♦ **2 Yugoslav-built, for the Niger River**

Remarks: Transferred in 1974 via Libya. Current operating condition is unknown.

MALTA

Republic of Malta

MARITIME SQUADRON

Personnel: Approx. 200 total

Organization: The Maritime Squadron is a part of the 2nd Regiment of the Armed Forces of Malta, which also includes the Air Flight and the Air Defense Battery.

Base: Valletta

Aviation: The Aviation Flight, 2nd Regiment, Armed Forces of Malta operates two Pilatus-Britten-Norman BN-2B-26 twin-engine light maritime patrol aircraft, five ex-RAF Bulldog T.1 light observation aircraft, two Nardi-Hughes NH-500M, two Agusta-Bell AB-47G-2, and five Aérospatiale AS.316B/D Alouette-III helicopters.

PATROL CRAFT [PC]

♦ **1 Modified Italian Ubaldo Diciotti class**
Bldr: Fincantieri, Muggiano

	L	In serv.
P 61	24-6-05	4-11-05

P 61 Leo Van Ginderen, 10-05

D: 390 tons light (450 fl) **S:** 23 kts **Dim:** 53.4 × 8.10 × . . .
A: 1 25-mm OTO Melara KBA AA
Electronics: Radar: 2 ... nav.
M: 2 Isotta-Fraschini V1716 T2MSD diesels; 2 props; 6,225 bhp
Range: 2,100/16 **Crew:** 4 officers, 21 enlisted

Remarks: Ordered 11-3-04. Fitted with a stern ramp that can handle a Zodiac type, RHIB. Capable of refueling a small helicopter.

PATROL CRAFT [PC] *(continued)*

♦ 3 ex-German Kondor-I class
Bldr: VEB Peenewerft, Wolgast

	Laid down	L	In serv.
P 29 (ex-*Boltenhagen,* BG 31, ex-GS 09)	8-10-69	22-5-70	19-9-70
P 30 (ex-*Ueckermünde,* GS 01, ex-G 411)	20-8-68	27-2-69	27-6-69
P 31 (ex-*Pasewalk,* GS 05, ex-G 423)	12-12-68	18-6-69	18-10-69

P 29 Leo Van Ginderen, 2005

P 30 Ralph Edwards, 2-04

D: 339 tons (361 fl) **S:** 20 kts **Dim:** 51.98 × 7.12 × 2.30
A: 1 quadruple 14.5-mm 93-cal. mg
Electronics: Radar: 1 Furuno FR 80310 nav.; 1 Decca 1229 nav.
M: 2 Kolomna Type 40DM diesels; 2 CP props; 4,408 bhp (4,000 sust.)
Range: 1,800/15 **Crew:** 20 tot.

Remarks: After the unification of Germany, had been incorporated in the German Maritime Border Guard (*Bundesgrenzschutz-See*) but were not used operationally. P 30 and P 31 transferred to Malta in 7-92. P 29 was transferred 24-7-97; the reported name *La Vallette* is in error. The 23-mm gunmount has an on-mount lead-computing sight and replaced two single 12.7-mm mg in 1999.

PATROL BOATS [PB]

♦ 2 U.S. Coast Guard Marine Protector class
Bldr: Bollinger Shipyards, Lockport, La. (In serv. P 51: 25-10-02; P 52: 7-7-04)

P 51 (ex-WPB 87351) P 52

P 51 Leo Van Ginderen, 2005

D: 91.1 tons (fl) **S:** 27 kts **Dim:** 26.52 (24.87 pp) × 5.94 × 1.75
A: 2 single 12.7-mm M2 mg **Electronics:** Radar: 1 Hughes Aircraft SPS-73 nav.

P 52 Leo Van Ginderen, 10-05

M: 2 MTU 8V396 TE94 diesels; 2 props; 2,950 bhp (2,680 sust.)
Electric: 120 kw tot. (2 × 60-kw Stamford sets, M.A.N. D 0824 diesel-driven)
Range: 882/10 **Fuel:** 2,800 gal. **Endurance:** 10 days (5 days' provisions)
Crew: 10 tot. (accomm. for 11 tot.)

Remarks: P 51 was ordered 30-7-01 for $5.5 million using a U.S. fund grant for delivery 15-11-02, but the craft was delivered 25-10-02. P 52 was built during 2003 and delivered in 2004. Over 50 serve in the U.S. Coast Guard.
Hull systems: Hullform is based on Netherlands builder Damen's STANPAT 2600 design, which has been employed on a number of Hong Kong police patrol boats built since 1980. Steel-hull construction with Russian-made extruded aluminum panel superstructure. Use a stern ramp to launch and recover a 4.6-m aluminum-construction rigid inflatable inspection/rescue boat in seas up to 2.5 m high; the Ambar AM 550-CPB inspection launch is powered by a 100-bhp Yanmar diesel driving a North American Marine Jet waterjet for 30-kt top speeds. Has an integrated pilothouse with radar, echo sounder, GPS receiver, and other sensors linked to a central Sperry Electronic Chart Display and Information System. Tankage for 1,500 liters of potable water, with 750 liters/day distillation capacity. Is able to operate safely in water as shallow as 2 m, can maneuver at 4 kts, and is considered safe to operate in seas up to 9 m high. Crew have two-person staterooms.

♦ 2 ex-German Bremse (GB 23) class
Bldr: VEB Yachtswerf, Berlin (In serv. 1971–72)

P 32 (ex-GS 20, ex-G 733) P 33 (ex-GS 22, ex-G 722)

P 33 Ralph Edwards, 2-04

D: 25 tons light (48 fl) **S:** 17 kts **Dim:** 22.59 (20.97 wl) × 4.70 × 1.60
A: 1 12.7-mm mg **Electronics:** Radar: 1 Furuno FR 80310 nav.
M: 1 Motorenwerke Rosslau Type 6VD 18/15 AL 1 diesel; 1 prop; 510 bhp
Range: 300/12 **Fuel:** 485 liters **Crew:** 6 tot.

Remarks: Former East German Border Guard patrol craft acquired from the German Sea Border Guard (*Bundesgrenzschutz-See*) in 7-92. Are to receive new engines in the near future.

♦ 2 ex-U.S. Swift Mk II class
Bldr: Sewart Seacraft, Berwick, La. (In serv. 1968)

P 23 (ex-U.S. 50NS6823) P 24 (ex-U.S. 50NS6824)

P 24 A. A. de Kruijf, 9-05

PATROL BOATS [PB] *(continued)*

D: 22.5 tons (fl) **S:** 25 kts **Dim:** 15.6 × 4.12 × 1.5
A: 1 12.7-mm mg **Electronics:** Radar: 1 Furuno FR 80310 nav.
M: 2 G.M. Detroit Diesel 12V71T diesels; 2 props; 960 bhp **Electric:** 6 kw tot.
Range: 400/22 **Endurance:** 24–36 hr **Crew:** 6 tot.

Remarks: Donated in 1-71. The twin 12.7-mm mg mount atop the pilothouse is no longer carried, the combination mortar/12.7-mm mount aft has been reduced to a single 12.7-mm mount, the radar has been replaced, and an Adcock-type VHFD/F antenna has been added.

Disposal note: U.S.-donated launch P 26 was sold in 2000 for use as a fishing boat.

SERVICE CRAFT

♦ **1 ex-U.S. Navy LCVP Mk 7 utility launch [WYFL]**
Bldr: Gulfstream Corp. (In serv. 1965)

L 1 (ex-36VP6564)

L 1 Ralph Edwards, 2-04

D: 13.5 tons (fl) **S:** 9 kts **Dim:** 10.90 × 3.21 × 1.04 (aft)
M: 1 G.M. Gray Marine 64HN9 diesel; 1 prop; 225 bhp
Range: 110/9 **Crew:** 4 tot.

Remarks: Donated by the U.S. Navy in 1-87. GRP construction. Can carry 36 personnel or 3.5 tons of cargo in the 5.24 × 2.29-m cargo well, which has a bow ramp. Used for local transportation at Valletta. Was in poor condition by 1-99 but has since been refurbished and returned to service.

Note: The Maltese Protezzjoni Civili, based at Valletta, operates sister 12.5-ton, 33-kt self-righting search-and-rescue lifeboats *Melita I* and *Melita II* and small outboard-powered runabouts RDT I and RDT II. Also based at Valletta are government-operated pollution cleanup craft *Pupilla, Ambjent,* and *Monka* and the service craft *Miggi.*

Search-and-rescue craft Melita II A. A. de Kruijf, 9-05

MARSHALL ISLANDS

Republic of the Marshall Islands

GOVERNMENT OF THE MARSHALL ISLANDS MARITIME AUTHORITY

Personnel: 60 total

Base: Majuro

Note: Ship names are preceded by RMIS (Republic of the Marshall Islands Ship)

PATROL BOATS [WPB]

♦ **1 ASI 315 design**
Bldr: Transfield ASI Pty, South Coogie, Western Australia (In serv. 29-6-91)

03 Lomor (ex-*Ionmeto 3*)

Lomor (03) W. D. Souter, 12-92

D: 165 tons (fl) **S:** 21 kts **Dim:** 31.50 (28.60 wl) × 8.10 × 2.12
A: 3 single 12.7-mm mg **Electronics:** Radar: 1 Furuno 1011 nav.
M: 2 Caterpillar 3516 diesels; 2 props; 2,820 bhp **Electric:** 116 kw tot.
Range: 2,500/12 **Fuel:** 27.9 tons **Endurance:** 10 days
Crew: 3 officers, 14 enlisted

Remarks: "Pacific Patrol Boat" design winner for the Australian foreign aid program. Ordered in 1989. Sisters are in service with Papua New Guinea, Vanuatu, Fiji, Western Samoa, and the Solomon Islands. Guns not normally mounted. Is to be refitted in Australia during 2008 to extend service to 2021.

Note: Former U.S. Navy landing craft–type ferries YFU 76 and YFU 77 were acquired 1-12-87 from the U.S. Department of the Interior (which received them from the USN on 1-12-84) for use by a Marshall Islands government civil agency for interisland public transportation. Also in use by the civil agency are former LCU 1552 and LCM(8)-class LCMs 6057 and 15967. The U.S. Coast Guard donated White (133-ft.)-class navaids tender *White Lupine* (WLM 546) to the private Marshall Islands Diabetics Reversal Program in 1998–99. The U.S. Army maintains Halter Marine Interceptor 41–class patrol craft HSPC 1 and HSPC 2 in the Marshall Islands to patrol its facilities there.

MAURITANIA

Islamic Republic of Mauritania

NAVY

Personnel: Approx. 620 total (including approx. 200 marines)

Bases: Headquarters and dockyard at Port Friendship, Nouakchott, with minor facilities at Port Etienne, Nouadhibou, and several coastal radar stations

Maritime Aviation: Two Piper Cheyenne II twin-turboprop aircraft were delivered in 1981 for coastal surveillance duties. Capable of 7-hour, 1,525-n.m. patrols, they have a belly-mounted Bendix RDR 1400 radar.

PATROL CRAFT [PC]

♦ **1 Chinese . . . class**
Bldr: . . . (In serv. 20-4-02)

P 601 Liman el Hadrami

D: 430 tons (fl) **S:** 20 kts **Dim:** 60.20 × 8.20 × . . .
A: 2 twin 37-mm AA; 2 twin 24.5-mm 93-cal. mg
M: 3 MTU 12V4000 M90 diesels; 3 props; . . . bhp

Remarks: Donated by China. Standard customs patrol boat design.

♦ **1 French PATRA class**
Bldr: C.N. Auroux, Arcachon

	Laid down	L	In serv.
P-411 Ennasr (ex-*Dix Juillet;* ex-*Rapière,* P 674)	15-2-81	3-6-81	1-11-81

D: 115 tons (148 fl) **S:** 26.3 kts **Dim:** 40.70 (35.40 wl) × 5.90 × 1.55
A: 1 40-mm 60-cal. Bofors AA; 1 20-mm 70-cal. Oerlikon Mk 10 AA; 2 single 12.7-mm mg
Electronics: Radar: 1 Decca 1226 nav.
M: 2 Wärtsilä UD 33V12 diesels; 2 CP props; 5,000 bhp (4,340 sust.)
Electric: 120 kw tot. **Range:** 750/20; 1,500/15; 1,750/10
Crew: 2 officers, 18 enlisted (accomm. for 27 tot.)

PATROL CRAFT [PC] *(continued)*

Ennasr (P-411) Y. Keraütret, 3-98

Remarks: Built on speculation, acquired by French Navy 1-11-81, and then sold to Mauritania, commissioning 14-5-82. Renamed in 1988. Overhauled and re-engined in 1993–94. Name was reported as El Nasr in previous editions.

PATROL BOATS [PB]

♦ **4 Indian Mandovi class**
Bldr: Garden Reach DY, Calcutta (In serv. 1990)

D: 15 tons (fl) **S:** 24 kts **Dim:** 15.0 × 3.6 × 0.8
A: 1 7.62-mm mg **Electronics:** Radar: 1 Furuno FR 8030 nav.
M: 2 MWM TD-232 VI 2 diesels; 2 Hamilton waterjets; 750 bhp
Range: 240/12 **Crew:** 8 tot.

Remarks: Same basic design was also built for Mauritius by the designer, Mandovi Marine.

MINISTRY OF FISHERIES

(Délégation à la Surveillance des Pêches et au Contrôle en Mer)

Note: The ships are painted gray and carry the words "Surveillance Maritime" in large black letters on either side amidships.

FISHERIES PATROL SHIP [WPS]

♦ **1 Arguin class**
Bldr: Fassmer Werft, Berne/Motzen, Germany (In serv. 17-7-00)

ARGUIN

Arguin Fassmer, 7-00

D: Approx. 1,000 tons (fl) **S:** 16 kts (13.6 on one engine)
Dim: 54.50 (48.00 pp) × 10.60 × 4.90 (max.)
M: 2 MaK 6M20 diesels; 1 Lips CP prop; 2,736 bhp—200-shp Schottel bow-thruster
Electric: 522 kw tot. (3 × 174 kw, Caterpillar 3306 DI diesels driving)
Range: 15,000/ . . . **Endurance:** 22 days
Crew: 13 tot. (accomm. for 32)

Remarks: Ordered 10-98; hull subcontracted to Yantar Verf, Kaliningrad, Russia. Has a 9.8 × 3.4-m, 25-kt Fassmer Type MP990 "daughter boat" inspection launch on a centerline ramp at the stern; the craft is propelled by two 230-bhp diesels driving waterjets. Based at Nouadhibou. Special sand filters are fitted to protect the machinery. Is equipped for fire fighting with a 200-m^3/min firepump.

Disposal note: Fisheries patrol vessel *N'Madi* (ex-*Criscella,* ex-*Jura*) was sold commercial during 2001.

♦ **1 ex-Spanish former submarine rescue ship**
Bldr: Izar, La Carraca, Cádiz

	Laid down	L	In serv.
B-551 VOUM-LEGLEITA (ex-*Poseidón*, A 12; ex-AS 01; ex-BS 1; ex-RA 6)	28-11-61	21-3-62	8-8-64

D: 951 tons (1,107 fl) **S:** 15 kts **Dim:** 55.90 (49.80 pp) × 10.00 × 4.80
A: 2 single 20-mm 70-cal. Oerlikon Mk 10 AA
Electronics: Radar: 2 Decca TM 626 nav.
M: 2 Izar-Sulzer 6MG42 diesels; 1 CP prop; 3,200 bhp tot.
Range: 4,640/14 **Fuel:** 190 m^3
Crew: 6 officers, 54 enlisted (in Spanish service)

Remarks: Former submarine rescue ship, salvage ship, and diving tender, retired from the Spanish Navy in 1997. Transferred 1-00 after a refit for use as an offshore patrol vessel and fisheries patrol ship. Is equipped for fighting fires aboard other ships and has an ocean towing capability and salvage pumps.

FISHERIES PATROL CRAFT [WPC]

♦ **1 French modified Espadon 50 class**
Bldr: Leroux & Lotz, Lorient (In serv. 3-94)

541 ABU BEKR BEN AMER

Abu Bekr ben Amer (541) Bernard Prézelin, 3-01

D: 290 tons (360 fl) **S:** 22 kts **Dim:** 54.00 (48.50 pp) × 9.80 × 2.30 (2.75 props)
A: 2 single 12.7-mm mg **Electronics:** Radar: 1 Decca 2690 ARPA nav.
M: 2 SACM-RVR UD 33V 12M6 diesels; 2 CP props; 5,700 bhp—2 90-kw electric auxiliary propulsion motors; 250 shp (7.5 kts)
Electric: 370 kw tot. (2 × 150-kw, 1 × 70-kw diesel-driven sets)
Range: 1,400/23; 4,500/12; 14,000/7.5 (electric power)
Fuel: 55 tons **Endurance:** 21 days
Crew: 4 officers, 9 petty officers, 6 ratings (39 tot. accomm.)

Remarks: Ordered 8-92. Known colloquially as the "*Abba.*" Commercial design, employing a deep-vee hullform capable of operating at speed in a State 4 sea. Originally ordered for the French Navy, but construction was delayed by the closing of the original contract yard and the transfer of part of the contract to CMN, which also acquired the design rights. Refitted in 2001 at DCN, Lorient.
Hull systems: Has a stern embarkation ramp for an EDL 700 7-m rigid inflatable, waterjet-propelled inspection boat capable of 30 kts. Can also carry up to 22 passengers. A 400-m^3/hr firefighting monitor is installed, and there are two 7-m^3-capacity spill recovery holding tanks.

Note: The Customs Service also operates the 20.5-ton, 14-m Amgram 14–class patrol boat *Dah Ould Bah,* delivered in 3-96 and the 18.3-m RPB 18-class patrol boat *Yaboub Ould Rajel*, delivered in 2000.

MAURITIUS

NATIONAL COAST GUARD ORGANIZATION

Personnel: Approx. 500 total.

Base: Port Louis, plus 21 small coastal surveillance detachments.

Maritime Aviation: One Hindustan Aeronautic–built Dornier Do-228 with MEL surveillance radar and one Pilatus-Britten-Norman Defender are in use for coastal surveillance. Two Aérospatiale AS.316B Alouette-III helicopters are in service along with three Chetak light helicopters provided by India.

Dornier DO 228 Arjun Sarup, 10-04

Note: All patrol craft and boats have the words "Coast Guard" painted in large white letters on their sides. Pennant numbers are no longer worn. India is providing assistance with the establishment of a coastal radar surveillance system.

PATROL SHIP [WPS]

♦ 1 Vigilant class
Bldr: ASMAR, Talcahuano, Chile

	Laid down	L	In serv.
21 VIGILANT	7-94	6-12-95	10-5-96

Vigilant Arjun Sarup, 8-02

D: 1,350 tons (1,650 fl) **S:** 18 kts
Dim: 75.00 (70.50 wl; 67.50 pp) × 14.00 × 3.90
A: 1 twin 40-mm 60-cal. Mk 5 Bofors AA; 2 single 12.7-mm M2 mg; 1 AS.350B Écureuil helicopter
Electronics: Radar: 2 Kelvin-Hughes . . . nav.
M: 4 Caterpillar 3516 diesels; 2 CP props; 11,780 bhp—670-shp azimuthal bow-thruster
Electric: 1,625 kw tot. (3 × 500 kw, Caterpillar 3412 diesels driving; 1 × 125 kw, Caterpillar 3306 diesel driving; all 380 V, 50 Hz)
Range: 8,000/19 **Endurance:** 30 days
Crew: 8 officers, 45 enlisted + 2 aircrew + 20 passengers or 100 survivors

Remarks: Ordered in spring 1994 for $14.6 million, with an option for a second and plans for a possible additional two; constructed in cooperation with Western Canada Marine Group. Designed by Polar Associates, Canada. Intended for fisheries and economic exclusion zone patrol, search-and-rescue duties, pollution control, and emergency towing. A half-sister was built in Ireland for the Irish Navy in 1998–99. Refitted at Mumbai Naval Dockyard, India, from 12-99 to 11-4-00 to correct propeller shaft problems and other engineering deficiencies; shaft seals were again repaired at Mumbai from 3-01 to 9-01.
Hull systems: Has a deep-vee hullform with twin rudders and a signature-reduction superstructure shape to reduce radar signature when ship is coming toward the radar. There are a hangar and flight deck for one small helicopter, although the hangar is said to be cramped. Two fire monitors are fitted atop the hangar, with a single 600-m^3/hr firepump. Has a Flume-type stabilization system and a four-berth sick bay. Was originally intended to achieve 22 kts but can reach only 18.
Combat systems: The 40-mm gunmount was donated by India and is locally controlled.

PATROL CRAFT [WPC]

♦ 1 ex-Indian SDB Mk 3 class
Bldr: Garden Reach Dockyard, Calcutta (In serv. 1984)

GUARDIAN (ex-*Ajay,* T . . .)

Guardian Arjun Sarup, 4-05

D: 167 tons (210 fl) **S:** 30 kts (28 sust.) **Dim:** 37.80 (32.20 pp) × 7.50 × 1.85
A: 2 single 40-mm 60-cal. Bofors Mk 3 AA
Electronics: Radar: 1 Bharat 1245 nav.
M: 2 MTU 16V 538 TB92 diesels; 2 props; 6,820 bhp **Crew:** 32 tot.

Remarks: Donated in 1993 by India. May also have a centerline cruise diesel engine, as on earlier Indian Navy craft of this general type. Refitted in 2001.

PATROL BOATS [WPB]

♦ 8 Type . . . heavy duty boat RIB patrol launches
Bldr: Kay Marine, Malaysia (In serv. 2002)

05 through 12

D: 5 tons **S:** 45 kts **Dim:** 8.85 × 3.2 × 0.5
M: 2 Suzuki gasoline outboard motors; 450 hp tot.
Crew: 2

♦ 5 Type . . . heavy duty boat RIB patrol launches
Bldr: M/S Praga Marine, India (In serv. 2000)

HDB 01 through HDB 05

HDB 03—painted bright orange Arjun Sarup, 6-05

D: 5 tons (fl) **S:** 45 kts **Dim:** 8.90 × 3.50 × 0.45
M: 2 Johnson gasoline outboards; 400 bhp
Range: 300/35 **Crew:** 4 tot. + 4 passengers

Remarks: Are used for search-and-rescue and patrol/interception duties. Painted bright orange. An option exists for the purchase of six more.

♦ 1 leased Indian P-2000 class
Bldr: Anderson Marine Pty, Kadras/Goa SY (In serv. 16-10-97)

OBSERVER (ex-C 139)

Observer Arjun Sarup, 8-05

D: 49 tons (fl) **S:** 40 kts **Dim:** 20.80 (18.00 pp) × 5.80 × 1.00
A: 1 7.62-mm mg **Electronics:** Radar: 1 Furuno . . . I-band nav.
M: 2 Deutz-MWM TBD 234 V12 diesels outboard (823 bhp each), 1 Deutz-MWM TBD 234 V8 550-bhp loiter diesel centerline; 3 Hamilton 402-series waterjets; 2,200 bhp
Range: 600/15 **Crew:** 4 officers, 6 enlisted

Remarks: Leased and recommissioned in 4-01 as an "Interceptor Boat." One of 10 ordered in 9-90 for the Indian Coast Guard. Built in cooperation with Seaking Industries, with design services from Amgram, Ltd., Sussex, U.K. GRP hulls laid up by Anderson Marine employ molds originally built by Watercraft, Shoreham, U.K., for the Royal Navy *Archer* class.

♦ 2 Soviet Zhuk class (Project 1400M) (In serv. 3-12-89)

RESCUER RETRIEVER

D: 35.9 tons (39.7 fl) **S:** 30 kts
Dim: 23.80 (21.70 wl) × 5.00 (3.80 wl) × 1.00 (hull)
A: 2 twin 12.7-mm 79-cal. Utës-M mg
Electronics: Radar: 1 Furuno . . . nav.
M: 2 M-401B diesels; 2 props; 2,200 bhp
Electric: 48 kw total (2 × 21-kw, 1 × 6-kw diesel sets)
Range: 500/13.5 **Endurance:** 5 days **Crew:** 3 officers, 10 enlisted

Remarks: Were a gift of the Soviet Union originally offered in the early 1980s. Only one engine was operable on the *Rescuer* as of 4-01, and both are to be docked and overhauled.

PATROL BOATS [WPB] *(continued)*

Retriever—note two twin 12.7-mm machine guns fitted fore and aft
Arjun Sarup, 7-03

♦ **5 Mandovi class**
Bldr: Garden Reach SY, Calcutta (In serv. 1989–90)

BARRACUDA CASTOR MARLIN POLARIS SIRIUS

D: 15 tons (fl) **S:** 24 kts **Dim:** 15.0 × 3.6 × 0.8
A: 1 7.62-mm mg **Electronics:** Radar: 1 Furuno FR 8030 nav.
M: 2 Deutz-MWM TD-232 V-12 diesels; 2 Hamilton waterjets; 750 bhp
Range: 240/12 **Crew:** 8 tot.

Remarks: Nine were ordered 24-7-87; two were delivered during 1-89, the rest 19-1-90. Designed by Mandovi Marine Private, Ltd. Resemble oilfield crewboats and have "Coast Guard" painted on sides. By late 1998 only five remained in inventory, and of those, two were inactive for lack of spares.

SERVICE CRAFT

♦ **4 Ramped Logistic Support Boat class**
Bldr: Vosper Thornycroft–Halmatic, Portsmouth, U.K. (In serv. 2002–3)

13 14 15 16

Logistic Support Boat 16—painted orange with white pilothouse
Arjun Sarup, 8-03

D: 3.45 tons (empty) **S:** 35+ kts **Dim:** 8.7 × 3.2 × 1.0
M: 2 gasoline outboard motors; 400 hp tot.

Remarks: Ordered 16-8-02 for police duty. Have a bow ramp and can beach carrying craft up to Land Rover size; maximum payload is 1800 kg. Have GRP construction and planing catamaran hulls, with a vehicle cargo well and enclosed pilothouse aft. A high degree of reserve buoyancy enables the craft to remain afloat when fully swamped.

Note: Also in service are an unknown patrol boat displaying the number 01, two Rover 663 FPC RIB launches donated by Australia, and 30 other outboard-powered, Avon, Halmatic, and Zodiac RIBs for search-and-rescue duties.

MEXICO

United Mexican States

MARINA NACIONAL

Personnel: 37,000 total, including 8,700 marines

Bases/Organization: The Mexican Navy is divided between the Gulf of Mexico and Pacific Commands, with headquarters at Veracruz and Acapulco, respectively. Within the two commands are three naval regions, each further divided into zones and sectors.

The Gulf Command consists of the North Naval Region at Veracruz, with Naval Zone I at Ciudad Madero (sectors at Matamoros and La Pesca) and Naval Zone III at Veracruz (sectors at Tuxpan and Coatzacoalos); the Eastern Naval Region at Frontera, with Naval Zone V at Frontera and Naval Zone VII at Lerma (sectors at Champotón and Ciudad del Carmen); and the Caribbean Naval Region at Chetumal, with Naval Zone IX at Yucalpetén (sector at Progreso) and Naval Zone XI at Chetumal (sectors at Isla Mujeres and Cozumel).

The Pacific Command includes the Northwest Naval Region at Mazatlán, with Naval Zone II at Ensenada, Naval Zone IV at La Paz (with sectors at Puerto Cortés and Santa Rosalia), Naval Zone VI at Guaymas (sector at Puerto Peñasco), and Naval Zone VIII at Mazatlán (sector at Topolobampo); the Western Naval Region at Lázaro Cárdenas, with Naval Zone X at San Blas, Naval Zone XII at Puerto Vallarta, Naval Zone XIV at Manzanillo (sector at Isla Socorro), and Naval Zone XVI at Lázaro Cárdenas; and the Southwestern Naval Region at Acapulco, with Naval Zone XVIII at Acapulco (sector at Ixtapa-Zihuatanejo), Naval Zone XX at Salina Cruz (sector at Puerto Angel), and Naval Zone XXII at Puerto Madero. Naval air bases are located at Mexico City, Campeche, Las Bajadas, Tulúm, Chetumal, Puerto Cortés, Isla Mujeres, La Paz, Salina Cruz, and Tapachula. The three separately administered naval bases are at Tuxpan (Veracruz), Ensenada (Baja California), and Lázaro Cárdenas (Michoacán).

Marines: Headquarters for the marines is at Mexico City. Reorganized again in 1998, the marine corps now has three infantry brigades, each with three battalions: the 1st Brigade, headquartered at Veracruz; the 2nd, headquartered at Acapulco; and the 4th, headquartered at Manzanillo. In addition, there are nine infantry battalions assigned one-each at Mexico City (the Guardias Presidenciales 24th Battalion), Ensenada, La Paz, Guaymas, Lerna, Mazatlán, Yucalpetén, Chetumal, and Lázaro Cárdenas. There is also the 1st Parachute Naval Fusilier Brigade at Mexico City and a Coastal Defense Group headquartered at Veracruz with its 1st Artillery Battalion at Frontera and 2nd Artillery Battalion at Puerto Madero.

Naval Aviation: The Mexican Navy operates three E-2C Hawkeye radar surveillance aircraft (transferred and refurbished by Israel; delivered in 2004 and equipped with APS-125 radar), eight CASA 212-200 coastal surveillance aircraft (one equipped as a VIP transport), one de Havilland DHC-5D Buffalo, one Fokker F-27, 2 Antonov An-32, and 43 light fixed-wing aircraft, including one Learjet 24D, 12 Beech B-55, one Cessna 402, one Beech King Air 90, four Rockwell Turbo-Commander 1000, one Piper Aztec, one Grumman HU-16 Albatross amphibian, one Cessna 337G, one Beech D590, one Cessna 206A, one Cessna 441, 13 Maule MX-7-180, three Beech T-34 Mentor, and two Mexican-designed Tonatiuh II. A Bombardier DHC-8 Q200 turboprop transport (with option for a second) was ordered 9-00 and is based at Mexico City. Helicopters include 10 MD 90 Explorers, three MD 90 Combat Explorers, 12 Mil Mi-8/17, four Mil Mi-2 Hoplite, four Eurocopter AS.355 Fennec, 11 MBB BO-105CB, four McDonnell-Douglas MD 500E and one MD 500, three Hughes 269A, two Aérospatiale Alouette-III, one Robinson R44 Clipper, and two Bell UH-1H, plus 10 Aérospatiale AS.315 Lama helicopters for search-and-rescue duties and two float-equipped Robinson R22 Mariner and one RotorWay International Exec 162F trainers. Two AS.565MB Panther helicopters were ordered during 10-03 and delivered during 6-05. The Mexican variant of the aircraft are fitted with two Turbomeca Arriel 2C turbine engines.

An additional 12 Mi-8 and/or Mi-17 helicopters are to be procured from Russia, and 10 more MD 90 Explorers may be purchased. All Explorers are to be armed with 70-mm rocket pods and 12.7-mm gatling machineguns.

Mexican Navy E-2C Hawkeye Mexican Navy via Brooks Rowlett, 2004

Mexican Navy AN-32 Mexican Navy, 2002

MARINA NACIONAL *(continued)*

Mexican Navy Mi-8 U.S. Navy, 9-05

Naval aviation is organized into six operational squadrons, a search-and-rescue squadron, and three training squadrons. Air bases are located at Mexico City, Las Bajadas, Tulúm, Campeche, Chetumal, Puerto Cortés, Isla Mujeres, La Paz, Salina Cruz, and Tapachula, with detachments of two Mil Mi-2 Hoplite SAR helicopters each at Acapulco and Veracruz. Aircraft are organized as follows:

1st Grupo Aeronaval at Veracruz:
- 1 EAEPM (*Escuadrón Aeronaval Embarcado de Patrulla Aeronaval*): BO-105CB and AS.355 Fennec helicopters
- 3 EA (*Escuadrón Aeronaval*): King Air 90, CASA 212, and PA-23 Aztec light transports
- 1 EATL (*Escuadrón de Apoyo Táctico y Logistico*): Mi-8MTV-1 helicopters
- EBS (*Escuadrón de Búsqueda y Salvamento*): BO-105CB SAR helicopters

2nd Grupo Aeronaval at Chetumal:
- 1 EA: CASA 212, PA-23 Aztec, Maule M-6, Aero Commander 680T, Tonatiuh II
- 3 EATL: Mi-8MTV-1 helicopters
- 4 EBR (*Escuadrón de Búsqueda y Rescate*): UH-1H, MD 500 helicopters

Independent detachments:

- 2 EA, Mexico City: Learjet 24D VIP transports, CASA 212-200, King Air 90, DHC-5D, and Turbo-Commander 1000 light transports
- 2 EATL, Teacapan: Mi-8MTV-1 helicopters
- 4 EA, La Paz: Cessna 182, Cessna 206, Cessna 210, Cessna 337G, B-55 Baron, CASA 212, and Twin Bonanza light transports; BO-105CB, AS.319B Alouette-III helicopters; 1 HU-16 Albatross amphibian
- 5 EA, Campeche: CASA 212, Cessna 402B, Cessna 404 light transports
- 6 EA, Tapachula: B-55 Baron light transports

Escuela de Aviación Naval, Veracruz:
- *Escuadrón Primario:* Maule MX-7-180
- *Escuadrón Basico:* F33A/C Bonanza fixed-wing, MD 500E and UH-12E helicopters
- *Escuadrón Avanzado:* B-55 Baron

Coastal Defense: The Mexican Navy and Marine Corps are responsible for coast defense. U.S.-supplied 20-mm Mk 68 AA guns are mounted on Gama Goat vehicles and surplus 40-mm Bofors AA on M35 trucks to provide coastal region defenses. To defend naval bases, the marines have eight OTO Melara M56 howitzers and FIROS 6 rocket launchers mounted on trucks.

Note: Pennant numbers, and many names, were changed during 2001. Officially, all ship names should be preceded by Armade República Mexicana (ARM). Unofficially, ships are known by their last names if the full names contain multiple words.

The two *Gearing*-class and one *Fletcher*-class destroyers have been retyped as patrol ships for this edition, due to their greatly reduced speeds and the loss of their ASW capabilities.

FRIGATES [FF]

♦ 4 ex-U.S. Knox class

Bldrs: F-211: Lockheed SB, Seattle; F-213: Avondale SY, Westwego, La.; others: Todd SB, Seattle

	Laid down	L	In serv.
F-211 Ignacio Allende (ex-E-50; ex-*Stein,* FF 1065)	1-6-70	19-12-70	8-1-72
F-212 Mariano Abasolo (ex-E-51; ex-*Marvin Shields,* FF 1066)	12-4-68	23-10-69	10-4-71
F-213 Guadalupe Victoria (ex-E-52; ex-*Pharris,* FF 1094)	11-2-72	16-12-72	26-1-74
F-214 Amiral Francisco Javier Mina (ex-*Whipple,* FF 1062)	24-4-67	12-4-68	22-8-70

D: 3,130 tons light (4,260 fl) **S:** 27+ kts
Dim: 134.00 (126.49 wl) × 14.33 × 4.77 (7.83 over sonar)
A: 1 127-mm 54-cal. Mk 42 DP; 2 paired, fixed 324-mm Mk 32 Mod. 9 ASW TT; 1 . . . helicopter
Electronics:
Radar: 1 Raytheon SPS-64(V)9 nav.; 1 Raytheon SPS-10 surf. search; 1 Lockheed SPS-40B air search; 1 Western Electric SPG-53F gun f.c.
Sonar: EDO-G.E. SQS-26CX bow-mounted LF
TACAN: SRN-15A
EW: Raytheon SLQ-32(V)2 intercept; Mk 36 SRBOC decoy syst. (2 6-round Mk 137 RL); T Mk 6 Fanfare towed acoustic torpedo decoy

Ignacio Allende (F-211) Mexican Navy, 2004

Mariano Abasolo (F-212) Christopher P. Cavas, 3-02

M: 1 set Westinghouse geared steam turbines; 1 prop; 35,000 shp
Boilers: 2 Combustion Engineering VsM, M-Type (F-211, F-214: Babcock & Wilcox D-Type); 84 kg/cm², 510° C
Electric: 3,000 kw tot. (3 × 750-kw turbogenerators, 1 × 750-kw diesel set)
Range: 4,300/20 **Fuel:** 750 tons max. **Crew:** 20 officers, 268 enlisted

Remarks: In late 1996 the U.S. Congress approved the transfer by sale of the first two during U.S. FY 97; they had been in reserve since 19-3-92 and 2-7-92, respectively. The two were formally transferred for $7 million each on 29-1-98 and underwent reactivation refits in Mexico. Mexico declined the offer of sister *Roark* (FF 1053), for spares, late in 1998; instead, the *Pharris,* in reserve since 15-4-92, was purchased on 2-2-00 and towed to Manzanillo, arriving 8-3-00 for reactivation in Mexico. The *Whipple,* placed in reserve on 14-2-92 by the U.S. Navy, was offered to Mexico in 1999 and arrived under tow at Manzanillo on 3-5-02 to begin reactivation. With their relatively light effective armament, the ships are essentially gunboats. Redesignated *Fragatas* in 2001.

FRIGATES [FF] *(continued)*

Hull systems: Bow bulwarks and a spray strake have been added forward to reduce deck wetness, a problem in this class; the addition added 9.1 tons and extended the overall length from the original 133.59 m. Antirolling fin stabilizers are fitted. The Prairie/Masker bubbler system is fitted to hulls and propellers to reduce radiated noise.
Combat systems: Carry a Mk 68 gunfire-control system with SPG-53F radar. SLQ-32(V)1—later upgraded to (V)2—replaced WLR-1C as the EW suite. The Mk 15 Phalanx CIWS was not transferred with the ships. Instead, on F-211 only, a Mk 128 octuple launcher for the no-longer-operational U.S. Mk 25 Basic Point Defense System Sea Sparrow SAM was installed on the fantail in its place, and the equally obsolete radar director was reinstalled atop the hangar; the system is not operational, and no missiles were transferred. Although the Mk 112 octuple missile launcher for the ASROC ASW missile system was retained, no missiles were acquired for it. The ASW torpedo tubes are fixed in the forward end of the hangar superstructure, aimed outboard at an angle of 45°. Have the Mk 114 ASW fire-control system. Only F-213 had SPS-67 in place of SPS-10 radar, and it was replaced by an SPS-10 set prior to transfer. F-213 has the Mk 68 Mod. 13 gun f.c.s.; the others have Mk 68 Mod. 11.

♦ 2 ex-U.S. Bronstein class
Bldr: Avondale SY, New Orleans

	Laid down	L	In serv.
F-201 Nicolás Bravo (ex-E-40; ex-*McCloy,* FF 1038)	15-9-61	9-6-62	21-10-63
F-202 Hermenegildo Galeana (ex-E-42; ex-*Bronstein,* FF 1037)	16-5-61	31-5-62	16-6-63

Nicolás Bravo (F-201) Mexican Navy, 2002

D: 2,360 tons (2,650 fl) **S:** 24 kts **Dim:** 113.23 (106.68 wl) × 12.34 × 7.00
A: 1 twin 76.2-mm 50-cal. Mk 33 DP; 2 triple 324-mm Mk 32 ASW TT; 1 M-60 Explorer helicopter
Electronics:
Radar: 1 . . . nav; 1 . . . surf. search; 1 Raytheon SPS-10F surf. search; 1 Lockheed SPS-40D air search; 1 Mk 35 f.c.
Sonar: SQS-26AXR bow-mounted LF
EW: removed
M: 1 set de Laval geared steam turbines; 1 prop; 20,000 shp
Boilers: 2 Foster-Wheeler; 42.2 kg/cm^2, 440° C
Range: 3,900/15 **Fuel:** 480 tons **Crew:** 17 officers, 190 enlisted

Remarks: First offered to Mexico in 1991; transferred 16-11-93 primarily for training duties. Had been decommissioned from the USN on 13-12-90 and 14-12-90, respectively. Redesignated *Fragatas* in 2001. Based at Manzanillo.
Hull systems: The portside Welin davit and boat have been removed.
Combat systems: The 76.2-mm gunmount is controlled by a Mk 56 gun fire-control system. The helicopter facility on both is hampered by the lack of a full-sized hangar. Have a Mk 114 Mod. 7 ASW weapons-control system, but the ASW features have not been activated, as the SQS-26CX sonar was an early, developmental model of the system and is no longer supportable; the Mk 112 ASROC ASW missile launchers remain aboard, however, and there are probably no torpedoes available for the two triple mountings. WLR-1 and WLR-3 intercept equipment, the Mk 34 RBOC decoy rocket system, and the T Mk 6 Fanfare homing torpedo decoy system have been removed. Two modern navigation and search radars have been added to supplement the U.S. system aboard at transfer. The Bofors 57-mm 70-cal. Mk 3 DP gunmount added aft during the late 1990s had been removed by mid-2002.

PATROL SHIPS [PS]

Note: The four U.S. *Abnaki*-class oceangoing tugs [ATA] are also used for ocean patrol work; see data under Auxiliaries.

♦ 4 Oaxaca class
Bldrs: P-162, P-164: Tampico Naval SY, Tamanlipas; P-161, 163: Salina Cruz Naval SY, Salina Cruz

	Laid down	L	In serv.
P-161 Oaxaca	17-12-01	11-4-03	2004
P 162 Baja California	13-12-01	21-5-03	2004
P-163 . . .	11-4-03	2004	2005
P-164 . . .	21-5-03	2004	2005

Baja California (P-162) Mexican Navy, 2004

D: 1,680 fl) **S:** 20 kts **Dim:** 86.0 × 10.5 × 3.57
A: 1 76-mm 62-cal. OTO Melara DP; 1 25-mm OTO Melara AA; 1 helicopter
Electronics: Radar: 2 Terma Scanter 2001 nav./surf. search
M: 2 Caterpillar 3916 V16 diesels; 2 props
Crew: 77 total

Remarks: Enlarged version of the *Durango*-class patrol ships, T-type *Durango*. Have a hangar and flight deck for one helicopter. The class also carries a small 11-m fast launch.

♦ 4 Durango class
Bldrs: P-151, P-153: Tampico Naval SY No. 1, Tamanlipas; P-152, P-154: Salina Cruz Naval SY No. 8, Salina Cruz

	Laid down	L	In serv.
P-151 Durango (ex-*Miguel Lerdo de Tejada*)	3-99	2000	11-9-00
P-152 Sonora (ex-*Melchor Ocampo*)	3-99	2000	4-9-00
P-153 Guanajuato	2000	2001	13-12-01
P-154 Veracruz	2000	2001	17-12-01

Sonora (P-152) Mexican Navy, 2004

D: 1,135 tons (1,340 fl) **S:** 18 kts **Dim:** 74.4 × 10.5 × 2.90 (3.5 over props)
A: 1 57-mm 70-cal. Bofors Mk 3 DP; 1 MD 90 helicopter
Electronics:
Radar: 1 . . . nav. (X-band); 1 . . . surf./air search (S-band)
E/O: 1 Saab Dynamics EOS-450 optronic f.c. for 57-mm gun
M: 2 Caterpillar 3616 V16 diesels; 2 props; 12,394 bhp
Range: 3,830/18 **Fuel:** 227.4 tons **Endurance:** 20 days
Crew: 11 officers, 65 enlisted + 16 passengers

PATROL SHIPS [PS] *(continued)*

Remarks: An improved version of the *Sierra* class, but with a gunmount aft instead of a helicopter facility. Four Bofors 57-mm Mk 3 DP gunmounts were ordered for units of the class early in 2000; the ships are being fitted with Saab Dynamics EOS-450 E/O directors.

♦ 4 Sierra (Holzinger 2000) class

Bldrs: P-141, P-143: Tampico Naval SY No. 1, Tamanlipas; P-142, P-144: Salina Cruz Naval SY No. 8, Salina Cruz

	Laid down	L	In serv.
P-141 Justo Sierra Méndez (ex-C-2001)	19-1-98	1-6-98	1-6-99
P-142 Benito Juárez (ex-C-2002, ex-*Rosas Coria*)	19-1-98	23-7-98	1-6-99
P-143 Guillermo Prieto	1-6-98	16-4-99	18-9-99
P-144 Matias Romero	23-7-98	16-4-99	17-9-99

Matias Romero (P-144) Mexican Navy, 2004

Justo Sierra Méndez (P-141) Mexican Navy, 2004

D: 1,135 tons (1,340 fl) **S:** 18 kts **Dim:** 74.4 × 10.5 × 2.90 (3.5 over props)
A: 1 57-mm 70-cal. Bofors Mk 3 DP; 1 MD-902 Explorer helicopter
Electronics:
Radar: 1 . . . nav. (X-band); 1 . . . surf./air search (S-band)
E/O: 1 Saab Dynamics EOS-450 optronic f.c. for 57-mm gun
M: 2 Caterpillar 3616 V16 diesels; 2 props; 12,394 bhp
Range: 3,830/18 **Fuel:** 227.4 tons **Endurance:** 20 days
Crew: 11 officers, 65 enlisted + 16 passengers

Remarks: Ordered in spring 1997. Planned class total was 16 but has been reduced to eight, with the second group of four now considered to be a separate class.
Hull systems: Essentially a repeat of the *Águila* class but with a flush-decked hull of slightly greater beam and greater freeboard and a superstructure with a shape intended to reduce radar signature. The boats are carried in pockets on either beam, and fin stabilizers are fitted. A Boston Whaler Piranha-class chase boat can be carried at the stern. Have the Vosper VT300 fin stabilization system. The first unit at completion was some 165 tons heavier than designed.
Combat systems: The first two were initially equipped with twin Bofors 40-mm Mk 1 Mod. 2 guns and Elsag electro-optical directors.

♦ 4 Águila class

Bldrs: P-131, P-133: Tampico Naval SY No. 1; P-132, P-134: Salina Cruz Naval SY No. 20

	Laid down	L	In serv.
P-131 Sebastián José Holzinger (ex-C-01, ex-*Capitán de Navio Sebastián José Holzinger*, ex-*Uxmal*)	1-6-86	1-6-88	23-11-91
P-132 Blas Godinez (ex-C-02, ex-*Capitán de Navio Blas Godinez Brito*, ex-*Mitla*)	7-86	1-6-88	21-4-92
P-133 José María de la Vega Gonzalez (ex-C-03, ex-*Brigadier José María de la Vega Gonzalez*, ex-*Peten*)	. . .	22-3-92	6-3-94
P-134 Gral. Felipe Berriozabal (ex-C-04, ex-*Anahuac*)	. . .	21-4-91	5-5-93

José María de la Vega Gonzalez (P-133) Mexican Navy, 2002

Blas Godinez (P-132) Mexican Navy, 2002

D: 1,022 tons (1,290 fl) **S:** 22 kts **Dim:** 74.4 (70.0 pp) × 10.35 × 3.4 (max.)
A: 1 twin 40-mm 60-cal. Mk 1 Mod. 2 Bofors AA; 1 BO-105CB helicopter
Electronics: Radar: 2 Raytheon SPS-64(V)6A nav.
M: 2 MTU 20V956 TB92 diesels; 2 props; 13,320 bhp (10,140 sust.)
Range: 3,830/18 **Fuel:** 227.4 tons **Endurance:** 20 days
Crew: 11 officers, 64 enlisted + 16 passengers

Remarks: A smaller variant of the Spanish-built *Halcón* design, with higher speed. Plans announced 23-6-83 called for construction of nine units at four naval shipyards, but the total was reduced to four in 10-84.
Hull systems: Have a smaller helicopter deck than the *Halcón* class, less topweight, and two engine rooms (vice one). Displacement grew by 115 tons during construction. P-133 and P-134 have fin stablization systems.
Combat systems: Were to have had an AMS NA-18 optronic fire-control system and Bofors 57-mm 70-cal. DP gun, but weight considerations forced installation of an older, locally controlled weapon and the 57-mm guns have since been mounted on destroyers.

♦ 6 Halcón class

Bldr: Navantia, (formerly Izar, formerly E.N. Bazán), San Fernando, Cadiz, Spain

	Laid down	L	In serv.
P-121 Virgilio Uribe (ex-C-11, ex-*Cadete Virgilio Uribe Robles*)	1-7-81	13-12-81	10-9-82
P-122 José Azueta (ex-C-12, ex-*Teniente José Azueta Abad*)	7-9-81	29-1-82	15-10-82
P-123 Pedro Sainz de Barbranda (ex-C-13, ex-*Capitán de Fragata Pedro Sainz de Barbranda Borreyo*)	22-10-81	26-2-82	3-83
P-124 Carlos Castilio Bretón (ex-C-14, ex-*Comodoro Carlos Castilio Bretón Barrero*)	11-11-81	26-2-82	9-6-82
P-125 Othón P. Blanco (ex-C-15, ex-*Vice Almirante Othón P. Blanco Nuñez de Caceres*)	18-12-81	26-3-82	24-2-83
P-126 Angel Ortiz Monasterio (ex-C-16, ex-*Contralmirante Angel Ortiz Monasterio*)	30-12-81	23-4-82	24-3-83

José Azueta (P-122)—with MD 90 helicopter on deck Mexican Navy, 2002

D: 845 tons (988 fl) **S:** 21 kts **Dim:** 67.00 (63.00 pp) × 10.50 × 3.50 (max.)
A: 1 40-mm 70-cal. Bofors AA; 1 BO-105CB liaison helicopter
Electronics:
Radar: 1 Decca AC 1226 nav.
TACAN: SRN-15
E/O: 1 Matra Défense Naja optronic gun f.c.
M: 2 MTU 20V956 TB91 diesels; 2 props; 13,320 bhp **Electric:** 710 kw
Range: 5,000/18 **Crew:** 10 officers, 42 enlisted

PATROL SHIPS [PS] *(continued)*

Angel Ortiz Monasterio (P-126)—with BO 105 helicopter on deck
Mexican Navy, 2002

Remarks: Ordered in late 1980 for use in patrolling the 200-n.m. economic zone. Generally identical to ships built for Argentina, but with more-powerful engines and a longer helicopter deck. Names were revised in 1993. Commissioning of P-124 was delayed by an accident; originally completed 4-11-82. Pennant numbers were changed from GH-01 through GH-06 in 1992 and from the C (*Corbeta*) series in 2001.

♦ 1 ex-U.S. Gearing FRAM I class

Bldr: Bethlehem Steel, Staten Island, N.Y.

	Laid down	L	In serv.
D-102 Netzahualcóyotl (ex-E-11; ex-E-04; ex-*Steinaker,* DD 863)	1-9-44	13-2-45	26-5-45

Netzahualcóyotl (D-102) Mexican Navy, 2002

D: 2,448 tons light (3,690 fl) **S:** Approx. 15 kts
Dim: 119.03 × 12.52 × 4.60 (6.55 sonar)
A: 2 twin 127-mm 38-cal. Mk 38 DP
Electronics:
Radar: 1 Kelvin-Hughes 17/9 nav.; 1 Raytheon SPS-10 surf. search; 1 Westinghouse SPS-37 air search; 1 Western Electric Mk 25 f.c.
EW: WLR-1 intercept
M: 2 sets G.E. geared steam turbines; 2 props; 60,000 shp
Boilers: 4 Babcock & Wilcox; 43.3 kg/cm^2, 454° C **Electric:** 1,200 kw tot.
Range: 1,500/31; 5,800/12 **Fuel:** 650 tons **Crew:** approx. 275 tot.

Remarks: Transferred to Mexico 24-2-82 by sale, as intended replacement for a *Fletcher*-class destroyer. Renumbered during 1993. After FRAM conversion, could make 30 kts, but has lost a great deal of speed in recent years, probably due to boiler problems. Name and pennant number were again changed in 2001. D = *Destructore.*
Combat systems: Has the Mk 37 gun fire-control system with one radar director to control the 127-mm guns. A modern Bofors 57-mm gun was added forward of the bridge during the early 1990s but had been removed by 8-02, and the Mk 112 ASROC ASW missile launcher and two triple Mk 32 ASW torpedo tube sets had been removed by 9-94. The helicopter facility is no longer used. While the SQS-23 sonar set may still be aboard, it is no longer functional.
Disposals: Sister *Quetzalcóatl* (D-101; ex-*Ilhuaicamina,* E-10; ex-*Quetzalcóatl,* E-03; ex-*Vogelgesang,* DD 862) had been discarded and hulked at Manzanillo as of 8-02 for spares.

Disposal note: U.S. *Fletcher*-class patrol ship (ex-destroyer) *Cuitlahuac* (E-01; ex-*John Rodgers,* DD 574) was stricken 16-7-01. U.S. *Charles Lawrence*–class patrol ship *Coahila* (E-21; ex-*Vincente Guerrero;* ex-*Coahila,* B-07; ex-*Barber,* APD 57, ex-DE 161) was also stricken 16-7-01, along with U.S. *Crosley*-class patrol ships *Usumacinta* (E-20; ex-*Miguel Hidalgo;* ex-*Usumacinta,* B-06; ex-*Don O. Woods,* APD 118, ex-DE 721) and *Chihuahua* (E-22; ex-*José María Morelos y Pavon;* ex-*Chihuahua,* B-08; ex-*Rednour,* APD 102, ex-DE 529).

♦ 11 ex-U.S. Auk-class former fleet minesweepers

Bldrs:; A: Savannah Machine & Foundry Co., Savannah, Ga.; B: General Engineering and Drydock Co., Alameda, Calif.; C: Gulf Shipbuilding; D: J. H. Mathis, Camden, N.J.; E: Winslow Marine Railway and Shipbuilding, Seattle, Wash.

	Bldr	L
P-102 Juan de la Barrera (ex-C-71; ex-*Guillermo Prieto;* ex-*Symbol,* MSF 123)[1]	A	2-7-42
P-103 Maríano Escobedo (ex-C-72; ex-*Champion,* MSF 314)[2]	B	12-12-42
P-104 Manuel Doblado (ex-C-73; ex-*Defense,* MSF 317)[2]	B	18-2-43
P-106 Santos Degollado (ex-C-75; ex-*Gladiator,* MSF 319)[2]	B	7-5-43
P-108 Juan N. Alvarez (ex-C-77; ex-*Ardent,* MSF 340)[2]	B	22-6-43
P-109 Manuel Gutiérrez Zamora (ex-C-78; ex-*Melchior Ocampo,* G-10; ex-*Roselle,* MSF 379)[3]	C	29-8-45
P-110 Valentín Gómez Farias (ex-C-79, ex-*Starling,* MSF 64)[4]	B	15-2-42
P-112 Francisco Zarco (ex-C-81; ex-*Threat,* MSF 124)[1]	A	15-8-42
P-113 Ignacio L. Vallarta (ex-C-82; ex-*Velocity,* MSF 128)[1]	C	19-4-42
P-114 Jésus Gonzalez Ortega (ex-C-83; ex-*Chief,* MSF 315)[2]	B	5-1-43
P-117 Mariano Matamoros (ex-C-86; ex-*Hermenegildo Galeana;* ex-*Sage,* MSF 111)[5]	E	21-11-42

Santos Degollado (P-106) Mexican Navy, 2004

Jésus Gonzalez Ortega (P-114) Mexican Navy. 2004

D: 890 tons (1,250 fl) **S:** 17 kts **Dim:** 67.4 (65.5 wl) × 9.8 × 3.28
A: 1 76.2-mm 50-cal. U.S. Mk 22 DP; 2 twin 40-mm 60-cal. Mk 1 Mod. 2 Bofors AA—some also: 2 single 20-mm 70-cal. Oerlikon Mk 10 AA
Electronics: Radar: 1 Kelvin-Hughes 14/9 nav.
M: 2 diesels, electric drive (see remarks); 2 props; 2,976, 3,118, or 3,532 bhp
Electric: 300–360 kw tot. **Range:** 4,300/10 **Fuel:** 216 tons
Crew: 9 officers, 96 enlisted

Remarks: All transferred in 1973. All ASW and all minesweeping gear except the winch has been removed. Sister *Ponciano Arriaga* (G-04; ex-*Competent,* MSF 316) was stricken in 1988. One other unit, *Mariano Matamoros* (ex-*Herald,* MSF 101), was converted for use as a surveying ship and has since been stricken. Some have a small deckhouse between the stacks; some have no main deck bulwarks. New radars have been added. Names and hull numbers were revised in 1993; they had been numbered G-01 through G-19. P-103, P-104, and P-110 have been modernized with a helicopter platform aft; these units now also carry a 9-ton, 12.2-m patrol craft capable of 26 kts, carrying a crew of five, and armed with two single 12.7-mm mg and a U.S. Mk 19 40-mm grenade launcher.
Propulsion systems: The superscript numbers after the ships' names refer to five different diesels used in the propulsion plants: 1 = G.M. 12-278; 2 = Baldwin VO-8; 3 = G.M. 12-278A; 4 = Alco 539; 5 = Busch-Sulzer 539. Diesels 1 and 3 produce 3,532 bhp, 4 and 5 produce 3,118 bhp total, and 2 produces 2,976 bhp. The modernized units have been re-engined.
Combat systems: All fire-control director systems have been removed.
Disposal note: Sisters *Leandro Valle* (P 101, ex-C-70; ex-Pioneer, MSF 105), *Sebastian Lerdo de Tejada* (P 105, ex-C-74, ex-*Devastator,* MSF 318), *Ignacio de La Llave* (P-107, ex-C-76; ex-*Spear,* MSF 322), *Ignacio Manuel Altamirano* (P-111, ex-C-80; ex-*Sway,* MSF 120), *Felipe Xicotencatl* (115, ex-C-84; ex-*Melchior Ocampo,* ex-*Gutierrez Zamora;* ex-*Scoter,* MSF 381), and *Juan de Aldama* (P-116, ex-C-85; ex-*Pilot,* MSF 104) had been retired from service by 2004.

Of the units of the U.S. Admirable class, *General Miguel Negrete* (C-50; ex-DM 01; ex-*Jubilant,* MSF 255), *General Felipe Xicoténcatl* (C-53; ex-DM 06; ex-*Scuffle,* MSF 298), *Cadete Augustin Melgar* (C-54; ex-DM 11; ex-*Device,* MSF 220), *Teniente Juan de la Barrera* (C-55; ex-DM 12; ex-*Ransom,* MSF 283), *Cadete Juan Escutia* (C-56; ex-DM 13; ex-*Knave,* MSF 256), and *Cadete Francisco Marquez* (C-59; ex-DM 17; ex-*Diploma,* MSF 221) were stricken during 2000. *General Juan N. Mendez* (C-51; ex-DM 03; ex-*Execute,* MSF 232), *General Manuel E. Rincon* (C-52; ex-DM 04; ex-*Specter,* MSF 306), *Cadete Fernando Montes de Oca* (C-57; DM 14; ex-*Rebel,* MSF 284), and *General Ignacio Zaragoza* (C-60; ex-DM 18; ex-*Invade,* MSF 254) were stricken 16-7-01, as was training ship–designated *Cadete Vicente Suarez* (A-06; ex- C-61; ex-DM 19; ex-*Intrigue,* MSF 253). *Guanajuato*-class gunboat *Guanajuato* (C-07) was also stricken 16-7-01; sisters *Potosi* and *Queretaro* had been scrapped during the mid-1970s.

♦ 1 ex-U.S. Edsall-class training patrol ship [PST]

Bldr: Brown SB, Houston, Texas

	Laid down	L	In serv.
D-111 Comodoro Manuel Azueta Perillos (ex-E-30; ex-*Manuel Azueta,* A-06, ex-*Hurst,* DE 250)	27-1-43	14-4-43	30-8-43

PATROL SHIPS [PS] *(continued)*

Comodoro Manuel Azueta Perillos (D-111) Mexican Navy, 2002

D: 1,200 tons (1,590 fl) **S:** 18 kts **Dim:** 93.26 × 11.15 × 3.73
A: 3 single 76.2-mm 50-cal. U.S. Mk 26 DP; 2 twin 40-mm 60-cal. Bofors Mk 1 Mod. 2 AA; 4 single 40-mm 60-cal. Bofors Mk 3 AA; 2 single 20-mm 70-cal. Oerlikon Mk 10 AA; 2 single 37-mm saluting cannon
Electronics: Radar: 1 Kelvin-Hughes 14/9 nav.; 1 Kelvin-Hughes 17/9 nav.
M: 4 Fairbanks-Morse 38D8⅛-10 diesels; 2 props; 6,000 bhp **Electric:** 680 kw tot.
Range: 13,000/12 **Fuel:** 258 tons **Crew:** 15 officers, 201 enlisted

Remarks: Transferred 1-10-73. Former destroyer escort, used as training ship for the Gulf Fleet. Pennant number was changed in 2001. D = *Destructore.*
Combat systems: In 1994 three Mk 26 single-fire 76.2-mm guns were removed and replaced with a 76-mm 62-cal. OTO Melara Compact, controlled by an electro-optical director; a quadruple 40-mm AA mount replaced the superfiring 76.2-mm DP forward. The original armament layout, however, was restored by 1998. The Mk 52 radar director for the 76.2-mm guns, three Mk 51 Mod. 2 directors for the 40-mm AA, and all antisubmarine equipment have been removed, leaving all weapons locally controlled.

PATROL CRAFT [PC]

♦ 1 (+ 1) Centenary class
Bldr: Varadero Nacional No. 6, Guaymas, Sonora

	Laid down	L	In serv.
P-241 Demócrata (ex-C-101)	1997	16-10-97	9-7-98
P-242 Tempico	2002	. . .	2007

Demócrata (P-241) Mexican Navy, 2004

D: 400 tons (450 fl) **S:** 30 kts **Dim:** 52.50 × 9.00 × 2.60
A: 1 twin 40-mm 60-cal. Bofors Mk 1 Mod. 2 AA
Electronics: Radar: 3 . . . nav./surf. search
M: 2 MTU 20V956 TB92 diesels; 2 props; 12,238 bhp (11,700 sust.)
Range: . . . / . . . **Crew:** 13 officers, 23 enlisted

Remarks: Intended to be a series production class to replace the *Auk* and *Admirable* class, but only two have been ordered thus far. Carries a Boston Whaler *Piranha*-class armed inspection launch and two rescue RIBs. Pennant number was changed in 2001.

♦ 2 Ex-Israeli Aliyah (Sa'ar 4.5) class
Bldr: Israel SY, Haifa

	L	In serv.
301 Huracan (ex-*Aliyah*)	10-7-80	8-80
302 Tormenta (ex-*Geoula*)	10-80	31-12-80

D: 500 tons (fl) **S:** 31 kts (29 sust.) **Dim:** 61.70 (58.21 wl) × 7.62 (7.09 wl) × 2.78
A: Fitted to carry 4 RGM-84C Harpoon SSM; 4 Gabriel-II SSM; 1 20-mm Mk 15 Phalanx CIWS; 2 single 20-mm 70-cal. Oerlikon AA; 4 single 12.7-mm mg; 1 light helicopter

Huracan (301) (Sa'ar 4.5)-class patrol craft—with Dolphin helicopter, shown while still in Israeli service Israeli Navy, 1989

Electronics:
Radar: 1 Thales TH-D 1040 Neptune surf./air search; 1 Alenia Orion RTN-10X f.c.
EW: Elisra NS 9003/5 intercept/jammer system; NATACS comms intercept; Elisra NS 9010 D/F; 1 45-tube trainable decoy RL; 4 24-tube chaff RL; 4 single smoke RL
M: 4 MTU 16V956 TB91 diesels; 4 props; 14,000 bhp
Range: 1,500/30; 4,000/17 **Fuel:** 116 tons **Crew:** 53 tot.
Remarks: Transferred from the Israeli Navy during 8-04 without Harpoon missiles. The helicopter was intended to provide an over-the-horizon targeting capability to utilize fully the range capabilities of the Harpoon missiles, which, in Israeli service, were mounted athwartships in the gap between the fixed hangar and the bridge superstructure. The Gabriel missile launch containers were mounted forward between the CIWS and the bridge superstructure. U.S. Mk 15 CIWS replaced original 40-mm mount forward. Current combat configuration in the Mexican Navy is unknown.

♦ 20 Azteca class
Bldrs: A: Ailsa SB Co., Troon; B: Scott & Sons, Bowling; C: J. Lamont; D: Veracruz NSY; E: Salina Cruz NSY

	Bldr	In serv.
P-202 Matias de Cordova (ex-*Guayacura,* P-02; ex-*Matias de Cordova*)	B	22-10-74
P-206 Ignacio López Rayón (ex-*Tarahumara,* P-06; ex-*Ignacio López Rayón*)	A	19-12-74
P-207 Manuel Crescencio Rejón (ex-*Tepehuan,* P-07; ex-*Manuel Crescencio Rejón*)	A	4-7-75
P-208 Antonio de la Fuente (ex-*Mexica,* P-08; ex-*Antonio de la Fuente*)	A	4-7-75
P-209 León Guzmán (ex-*Zapoteca,* P-09; ex-*León Guzman*)	B	7-4-75
P-210 Ignacio Ramírez (ex-*Huasteca,* P-10; ex-*Ignacio Ramírez*)	A	17-7-75
P-211 Ignacio Mariscal (ex-*Mazahua,* P-11; ex-*Ignacio Mariscal*)	A	23-9-75
P-212 Heriberto Jara Corona (ex-*Huichol,* P-12; ex-*Heriberto Jara Corona*)	A	7-11-75
P-214 Felix Romero (ex-*Yaqui,* P-14; ex-*Felix Romero*)	B	23-6-75
P-215 Fernando Lizardi (ex-*Tlapaneco,* P-15; ex-*Fernando Lizardi*)	A	24-12-75
P-216 Francisco J. Múgica (ex-*Tarasco,* P-16; ex-*Francisco J. Mújica*)	A	21-11-75
P-218 José María del Castillo Velasco (ex-*Otomi,* P-18; ex-*José María del Castillo Velasco*)	C	14-1-75
P-220 José Natividad Macias (ex-*Pimas,* P-20; ex-*José Natividad Macias*)	C	2-9-76
P-223 Tamaulipas (ex-*Mazateco,* P-23; ex-*Tamaulipas*)	D	18-5-77
P-224 Yucatán (ex-*Tolteca,* P-24; ex-*Yucatán*)	D	3-7-77
P-225 Tabasco (ex-*Maya,* P-25; ex-*Tabasco*)	E	1-1-79
P-226 Veracruz (ex-*Cochimie,* P-26; ex-*Veracruz*)	E	1-1-79
P-228 Puebla (ex-*Totonaca,* P-28; ex-*Puebla*)	E	1-6-82
P-230 Leona Vicario (ex-*Olmeca,* P-30; ex-*Leona Vicario*)	D	1-5-77
P-231 Josepha Ortiz de Dominguez (ex-*Tlahica,* P-31; ex-*Josepha Ortiz de Dominguez*)	E	1-6-77

Matias de Cordova (P-202) Mexican Navy, 2004

D: 115 tons (165 fl) **S:** 23 kts **Dim:** 36.50 (30.94 pp) × 8.6 × 2.0
A: 1 40-mm 60-cal. Bofors Mk 3 AA *or* 1 7.62-mm mg
Electronics: Radar: 1 . . . nav.
M: 2 Ruston–Paxman-Ventura 12-cyl. diesels; 7,200 bhp **Electric:** 80 kw
Range: 2,500/12 **Crew:** 2 officers, 22 enlisted

Remarks: The original order for 21 was placed 27-3-73 with Associated British Machine Tool Makers, Ltd., which subcontracted the actual construction in the U.K. and later assisted with the construction of another 10 in Mexico. The 21 built in the U.K. were rehabilitated in Mexico with British assistance for 10 more years' service, beginning in 1987. Very lightly constructed. All were renamed for Mexican tribal groups during 1993, but the original names were restored and pennant numbers changed during 2001.

PATROL CRAFT [PC] *(continued)*

Combat systems: The original armament, where fitted, consisted of one 40-mm 60-cal. AA and one 20-mm 70-cal. AA; most now have only the single light machinegun.
Disposals: *Esteban Baca Calderón* (P-221; ex-*Chichimeca,* P-21; ex-*Esteban Baca Calderón*) was stricken during 2001. *Andres Quintana Roo* (P-201), *Manuel Damos Arizpe* (P-203), *Jose Maria Izazago* (P-204), *Juan Bautista Morales* (P-205), *Jose Maria Mata* (P-213), *Pastor Rouaix Jose Maria* (P-217), *Luis Manuel Rojas* (P-219), *Ignacio Zaragoza* (P-222), *Campeche* (P-227), and *Margarita Maza de Juarez* (P-229) had all been decomissioned by 2005.

♦ 3 ex-U.S. Coast Guard Cape class
Bldr: Coast Guard Yard, Curtis Bay, Md.

	In serv.	Recommissioned
P-271 Corrientes (ex-*Cabo Corrientes,* P-42; ex-Jalisco; ex-*Cape Carter,* WPB 95309)	7-12-53	1-4-90
P-272 Corzo (ex-*Cabo Corzo,* P-43; ex-*Nayarit;* ex-*Vanguard;* ex-*Cape Hedge,* WPB 95311)	21-12-53	21-4-90
P-273 Catoche (ex-*Cabo Catoche,* P-44; ex-*Cape Hattaras,* WPB 95305)	28-7-53	18-3-91

Corrientes (P-271) Mexican Navy, 2002

D: 87 tons (106 fl) **S:** 20 kts **Dim:** 28.96 × 6.10 × 1.55
A: 1 20-mm 70-cal. Oerlikon Mk 10 AA; 2 single 12.7-mm mg
Electronics: Radar: 1 Raytheon SPS-64(V)1 nav.
M: 2 G.M. 16V 149TI diesels; 2 props; 2,470 bhp **Electric:** 60 kw
Range: 550/20; 1,900/11.5 **Endurance:** 5 days **Crew:** 1 officer, 14 enlisted

Remarks: Re-engined during the 1980s. P-272 had been transferred to the U.S. Navy as a pilot boat after being stricken from the U.S. Coast Guard 7-1-87 and was transferred to Mexico in 1-90. P-271 was stricken 19-1-90 from the U.S. Coast Guard and transferred 2-90. P-273 was transferred after striking from the U.S. Coast Guard in 1991. "*Cabo*" was dropped from the names during 2001, when the pennant numbers were again changed. P = *Patrulla.*

♦ 8 Acuario class
Bldr: Astrimar, Coatzacualcos (In serv. 2004)

1301 Acuario	1302 Aguila	1303 Aries
1304 Auriga	1305 Cancer	1306 Capricorno
1307 Centauro	1308 Gemini	

D: 19 tons (fl) **S:** 47 kts **Dim:** 15.9 × 3.8 × 0.8
A: 1 12.7-mm mg **Electronics:** 1 Decca BridgeMaster E nav.
M: 2 Caterpillar 3406 E diesels; 2 props; 2 KaMeWa waterjets 1,582 bhp

Remarks: Modified versions of the Stridsbåt 90H class.

♦ 44 Stridsbåt 90H class
Bldrs: PL-1101 through PL-1140: Dockstavarvet, Docksta, and Gotlands Varvet (In serv. 2-00 to 12-01); PL-1141 through PL-1144: Astrimar, Coatzacualcos (In serv. 2004)

PI-1101 Polaris	PI-1116 Acrux	PI-1131 Hamal
PI-1102 Sirius	PI-1117 Spica	PI-1132 Suhail
PI-1103 Capella	PI-1118 Hadar	PI-1133 Debhe
PI-1104 Canopus	PI-1119 Shaula	PI-1134 Denebola
PI-1105 Vega	PI-1120 Mirfak	PI-1135 Alkaid
PI-1106 Achernar	PI-1121 Ankaa	PI-1136 Alphecca
PI-1107 Rigel	PI-1122 Bellatrix	PI-1137 Eltanin
PI-1108 Arcturus	PI-1123 Elnath	PI-1138 Cochab
PI-1109 Alpheratz	PI-1124 Alnilán	PI-1139 Enif
PI-1110 Procyón	PI-1125 Peacock	PI-1140 Schedar
PI-1111 Avior	PI-1126 Betelgeuse	PI-1141 Markab
PI-1112 Deneb	PI-1127 Adhara	PI-1142 Megrez
PI-1113 Formalhaut	PI-1128 Alioth	PI-1143 Mizar
PI-1114 Póllux	PI-1129 Rasalhague	PI-1144 Phekda
PI-1115 Régulus	PI-1130 Nunki	

Achernar (PI-1106) and Suhail (PI-1132) Martin Mokrus, 4-02

Alpheratz (1109)—close-up view Sygrid Gilliot via Paolo Marsan, 2-03

D: 13.2 tons light (18.7 fl) **S:** 45 kts **Dim:** 15.90 (13.00 wl) × 3.80 × 0.80
A: 1 12.7-mm mg
Electronics: Radar: 1 Decca Bridgemaster-E nav.
M: 2 Caterpillar 3406E diesels; 2 KaMeWa waterjets; 1,582 bhp
Electric: 8 kw tot. (1 × 8-kw Onan set)
Range: 160/40; 240/20 **Fuel:** 1.5 tons **Crew:** 4 tot. + 21 troops

Remarks: First four were built by the Gotlands Varvet division of Djupviks, which was to build another 12; the others were built by Dockstavarvet. Twelve were ordered 15-4-99, eight on 29-7-99, and 20 on 1-2-00. Intended to combat smugglers. PI = *Patrulla Interceptora.* Pennant numbers were changed from I-101 through I-140 during 2001, when they were named. The newest four were constructed in Mexico.
Hull systems: Aluminum construction. Have a 14-m^3 troop compartment (with disembarkation ramp over the bow). Have a Simrad compass, log, and echo sounder. A Transas Navi Sailor electronic chart system is fitted.

♦ 40 or more 35-foot Interceptor class
Bldr: . . ., Mexico (In serv. 1998– . . .)

C-101-01 series

D: . . . tons **S:** 50 kts **Dim:** 10.67 × . . . × . . .
A: 2 single 7.62-mm mg
M: 2 MTU . . . diesels; 2 HamiltonJet HJ 321 waterjets; . . . bhp

Remarks: Locally designed and built. Intended to intercept narcotics in inshore waters. Their subordination is not certain; they may belong to the army or the coast guard, but are said to be operated by "troops." Forty are based in the Baja California Peninsula and Gulf of California and the rest in the Yucatán Peninsula area. Operate under control of mobile four-wheel vehicles on land. Date above refers to ceremonial inauguration of the program; many of the boats had actually become operational sometime earlier. No further information available. No radar is fitted. The guns are mounted in cockpits recessed into the bow and atop the pilothouse, facing aft.

Note: An antidrug force of "144" craft was inaugurated 8-5-99; the craft may include the class above, plus the Piranha class below and an unknown number of Sea Force 730 rigid inflatable boats acquired in 1995–96. Also in use are an unknown number of 8.8-m Mako Marine (Miami, Fla.)–built patrol launches with two 200-bhp Mercury gasoline outboard engines.

♦ 4 XFPB class
Bldr: Trinity-Equitable, New Orleans (In serv. 1993–94)

	Laid down	L	In serv.
P-1201 Isla Coronado (ex-P-51)	1-93	6-93	9-93
P-1202 Isla Lobos (ex-P-52)	3-93	9-93	11-93
P-1203 Isla Guadalupe (ex-P-53)	8-93	12-93	1-94
P-1204 Isla Cozumel (ex-P-54)	8-93	3-94	3-94

Isla Coronado (P-1201) Mexican Navy, 2002

D: 52 tons (fl) **S:** 50 kts (40 sust.) **Dim:** 25.00 × 5.48 × 1.33
A: 1 12.7-mm M2HB mg; 2 single 7.62-mm M60 mg
M: 3 G.M. Detroit Diesel 16V92TA diesels; 3 Arneson outdrives with Rolla surface-piercing props; 4,350 bhp
Electric: 50 kw tot. (2 × 25-kw diesel sets)
Range: 500/35; 1,200/30 **Fuel:** 8,667 liters **Crew:** 1 officer, 8 enlisted

PATROL CRAFT [PC] *(continued)*

Remarks: First three ordered in 11-92, fourth in 5-93. Similar to six sisters built for Sri Lanka. Specifically intended for antidrug interception. All are based in the Caribbean at Isla Mujeres. Pennant numbers were changed during 2001. P = *Patrulla.*
Hull systems: Kevlar-reinforced GRP hull can be operated in up to Sea State 3. Have a 220-gallon/day potable water generator.
Combat systems: P-1204 was tested with a twin launcher for Aérospatiale MM 15 missiles at the time of completion, but the weapon was not procured. Were planned to be rearmed with one 40-mm 60-cal. Bofors Mk 3 and one 20-mm 70-cal. U.S. Mk 68 AA gun, but the change has yet to be made.

♦ 36 U.S. Piranha-class riverine patrol launches
Bldr: Boston Whaler, Edgewater, Fla. (In serv. 1990– . . .)

G-01 through G-36

Mexican Navy Piranha-class patrol launch Julio Montez, 9-02

D: 1.6 tons **S:** 37 kts **Dim:** 6.40 × 2.30 × 0.30
A: 1 7.62-mm mg; 1 40-mm Mk 19 grenade launcher
Electronics: Radar: 1 Raytheon . . . nav.
M: 2 Johnson gasoline outboards; 280 bhp
Range: 144/28 **Crew:** 2 tot. + 4 passengers

Remarks: Original plans called for procuring a total of 50. GRP construction. Outfitted at the Acapulco Naval Shipyard and intended to be carried aboard Halcón-, Águila-, and *Auk*-class patrol ships, as well as serving as local patrol craft in various ports. Are equipped with GPS receivers.

♦ 13 Olmeca class
Bldr: Acapulco NSY (In serv. 1979–84)

P-301 Arrecife Alacran (ex-P-90; ex-AM 11; ex-F-21)
P-302 Arrecife Sisal (ex-P-91; ex-AM 12; ex-F-22)
P-303 Arrecife Tanuijo (ex-P-92; ex-AM 13; ex-F-23)
P-304 Arrecife Cabezo (ex-P-93; ex-AM 14; ex-F-24)
P-305 Arrecife Santiaguillo (ex-PC-94; ex-AM 15; ex-F-25)
P-306 Arrecife Palancar (ex-PC-95; ex-AM 16; ex-F-26)
P-307 Arrecife la Galleguilla (ex-PC-96; ex-AM 17; ex-F-27)
P-308 Arrecife la Blanquilla (ex-PC-97; ex-AM 18; ex-F-28)
P-309 Arrecife Anegada de Adentro (ex-PC-98; ex-AM 19; ex-F-29)
P-310 Arrecife Rizo (ex-PC-99; ex-AM 20; ex-F-30)
P-311 Arrecife Pajaros (ex-P-100; ex-AM 21; ex-F-31)
P-312 Arrecife de Enmedio (ex-P-101; ex-AM 22; ex-F-32)
P-313 Arrecife de Hornos (ex-P-102; ex-AM 23; ex-F-33)

D: 18 tons (fl) **S:** 20 or 25 kts **Dim:** 16.7 × 4.4 × 2.4
A: 1 12.7-mm mg **Electronics:** Radar: 1 Raytheon 1900 nav.
M: First six: 2 Cummins UT-series diesels; 800 bhp—others: 2 G.M. Detroit Diesel 8V92 TI diesels; 2 props; 1,140 bhp
Range: 460/15 **Crew:** 2 officers, 13 enlisted

Remarks: One vessel (name unknown) sank off the Yucatán in 9-03. GRP construction. Last unit of the initial six with Cummins diesels was delivered 22-2-83. Five additional, with G.M. diesels, were ordered 23-6-83 and delivered by end-1984. Have a firefighting water monitor forward. All were renumbered and renamed for Mexican reefs during 1993. Pennant numbers were again changed during 2001.

♦ 2 ex-U.S. Coast Guard Point class
Bldr: Coast Guard Yard, Curtis Bay, Md.

	In serv.
PC-281 Punta Morro (ex-PC-60; ex-*Point Verde,* WPB 82311)	15-3-61
PC-282 Punta Mastún (ex-PC-61; ex-*Point Herron,* WPB 82318)	14-6-61

D: 64 tons (67 fl) **S:** 23.7 kts **Dim:** 25.30 × 5.23 × 1.95
A: 2 single 12.7-mm mg **Electronics:** Radar: 1 SPS-64(V)1 nav.
M: 2 Cummins VT-12-M diesels; 2 props; 1,600 bhp
Range: 490/23.7; 1,500/8 **Fuel:** 5.7 tons **Crew:** 1 officer, 7 enlisted

Remarks: Donated by the U.S. government for antidrug patrol duties, PC-281 on 19-7-91 and P-282 on 26-7-91. The engines are controlled from the bridge. Are equipped for towing. Were renumbered from P-45 and P-46, respectively, during 1993. Pennant numbers were again changed during 2001. PC = *Patrulla Costera.*

♦ 3 Polimar class
Bldr: Ast. de Tampico (PC-292: Iscacas SY, Guerrero)

	In serv.
PC-291 Laguna de Tamiahua (ex-P-70, ex-*Poluno,* ex-*Polimar-I*)	1-10-62
PC-292 Laguna de Lagartos (ex-P-71, ex-*Poldos,* ex-*Polimar-II*)	1968
PC-293 Laguna de Cuyutlan (ex-P-73, ex-*Polcinco,* ex-*Polimar-IV*)	28-7-53

D: 57 tons (fl) **S:** 16 kts **Dim:** 20.5 × 4.5 × 1.3
A: 1 twin 12.7-mm mg **M:** 2 diesels; 2 props; 456 bhp

Remarks: All were given new names and hull numbers during 1993; they had been F-01 through F-05. Pennant numbers were again changed during 2001. Have small navigational radars. PC = *Patrulla Costera.* Sisters *Laguna de Kana* (P-72, ex-*Poltres,* ex-*Polimar-III*) and *Villalpando* (ex-*Laguna de Mandinga,* P-74; ex-*Aspirante José V. Rincon*) were stricken 16-7-01.

♦ 2 Lago class
Bldr: Ast. de Tampico and Veracruz NSY (L: 1959–61)

PC-321 Lago de Pátzcuaro (ex-P-80, ex-AM 04)
PC-322 Lago de Chapala (ex-P-81, ex-AM 05)

Lago de Chapala (PC-322) Mexican Navy, 2002

D: 37 tons (fl) **S:** 6 kts **Dim:** 17.7 × 5.0 × . . .
A: Small arms **Electronics:** Radar: 1 . . . nav.
M: 1 diesel; 1 prop; 320 bhp **Crew:** 5 tot.

Remarks: Riverine patrol craft with low freeboard and bulwarks surrounding hull. Sisters AM 01–AM 03 and AM 09 had been stricken by 1986, AM 10 in 1988. The survivors were renumbered in 1993. Pennant numbers were again changed during 2001. PC = *Patrulla Costera.* Sisters *Lago de Texcoco* (P-82, ex-AM 06) and *Lago de Janitzio* (P-83, ex-AM 07) were stricken 16-7-01. *Lago de Cuitzeo* (P-323) was retired by 2004.

♦ 2 ex-U.S. 64-foot Distribution Box (L-Type) Boat class

PC-294 Laguna de Alvarado (ex-P-75, ex-*Polsiete,* ex- . . .)
PC-295 Laguna de Catemaco (ex-P-76, ex-*Polocho,* ex- . . .)

D: 72.3 tons (fl) **S:** 9.5 kts **Dim:** 19.58 × 5.72 × 1.83
A: 2 single 12.7-mm mg **Electronics:** Radar: 1 . . . nav.
M: 1 G.M. Detroit Diesel 64HN11 diesel; 1 prop; 165 bhp **Range:** 110/9.5

Remarks: Acquired 1-1-89 and 15-12-90, with one having been used by the U.S. Marines as a recreational craft under the name *Retreat Hell.* Were built to set and recover mine distribution boxes for controlled minefields but are now used as general-purpose tenders and patrol boats. Had 2.5-ton crane forward, now replaced by a machinegun. Built during the early 1950s. Pennant numbers were changed during 2001. PC = *Patrulla Costera.*

Note: The Mexican Navy also employs a number of locally built, shallow-draft launches driven by air-screw propellers as "chase boats" to pursue smugglers in shallow, vegetation-choked coastal waters and rivers; they normally have a crew of two.

AUXILIARIES

♦ 1 oceanographic research ship [AGOR]
Bldr: Ochida Zosen, Ise, Japan (In serv. 1978)

BI-02 Onjuku (ex-H-04)

D: 494 tons (fl) **S:** 10.5 kts **Dim:** 36.91 (33.15 pp) × 8.01 × 3.55
Electronics: Radar: 1 Furuno . . . nav.

AUXILIARIES *(continued)*

Onjuku (BI-02)—with old pennant number H&L Van Ginderen, 4-99

M: 1 Yanmar 6UA-UT diesel; 1 CP prop; 700 bhp **Electric:** 240 kw tot.
Range: 5,645/10.5 **Crew:** 4 officers, 16 enlisted

Remarks: 282 grt/263 dwt. Former stern-haul trawler, acquired in 1987. Equipped with a Furuno fish-finding sonar. Intended primarily for fisheries research; retains fishing gear. Based at Ciudad del Carmen. Pennant number was changed in 2001. BI = *Buque de Investigación.*

♦ 1 oceanographic research ship [AGOR]
Bldr: J. G. Hitzler Schiffswerft und Maschinenfabrik, Lauenburg, Germany (In serv. 1970)

BI-01 Alejandro de Humboldt (ex-H-03)

D: 585 tons (700 fl) **S:** 12.5 kts **Dim:** 42.27 (34.55 pp) × 9.61 × 3.25
M: 1 M.A.N. 8-cyl. diesel; 1 CP prop; 1,150 bhp **Electric:** 251 kw tot.
Crew: 4 officers, 16 enlisted

Remarks: 459 grt. Former German stern-haul trawler, acquired in 1982 and commissioned 22-6-87 for hydrographical and acoustic properties research. Homeported at Mazatlán. Pennant number was changed during 2001. BI = *Buque de Investigación.*

♦ 1 ex-U.S. oceanographic research ship [AGOR]
Bldr: Halter Marine, New Orleans (In serv. 1966)

BI-06 Río Ondo (ex-H-08; ex-*Deer Island,* YAG 62)

Río Ondo (BI-06)—with old pennant number H&L Van Ginderen, 4-99

D: Approx. 400 tons (fl) **S:** 10.5 kts **Dim:** 36.58 × 8.53 × 2.13
Electronics: Radar: 2 . . . nav. **M:** 2 diesels; 2 props; . . . bhp
Range: 6,200/10.5 **Crew:** 20 tot.

Remarks: 172 grt/117 nrt. Purchased 2-8-96, having been stricken in 1995 from the U.S. Navy, which used her in support of sound-quieting trials. Former tug/supply vessel acquired by the USN 15-3-83. Pennant number was changed during 2001. BI = *Buque de Investigación.*

♦ 1 ex-U.S. Robert D. Conrad–class oceanographic research ship [AGOR]
Bldr: Christy Corp., Sturgeon Bay, Wis.

	L	In serv.
BI-03 Altair (ex-H-05; ex-*James M. Gillis,* AGOR 4)	19-5-62	5-11-62

D: 1,200 tons (1,380 fl) **S:** 13.5 kts **Dim:** 63.7 (58.30 pp) × 11.37 × 4.66
Electronics: Radar: 1 Raytheon TM 1600/6X; 1 TM 1660/123
M: 2 Caterpillar D-378 diesels, electric drive; 1 prop; 2,000 bhp—bow-thruster
Electric: 850 kw tot. **Range:** 10,000/12 **Fuel:** 211 tons
Crew: 12 officers, 14 enlisted + 18 scientists

Remarks: 965 grt/355 dwt. Returned to the U.S. Navy by the University of Miami in 1980 and laid up until leased to Mexico on 15-6-83; Mexico bore the expense of subsequent reactivation. The large stack contains a 620-shp gas-turbine generator to drive the main shaft at speeds up to 6.5 kts for experiments requiring "quiet" sea conditions. Also has a retractable electric bow-thruster/propulsor, which can drive the ship to 4.5 kts. Refitted and recommissioned on 27-11-84. Pennant number was changed during 2001. BI = *Buque de Investigación.*

Altair (BI-03) Rahn, 8-02

♦ 1 ex-U.S. YW 83–class oceanographic research ship [AGOR]
Bldr: Zenith Dredge Co., Duluth, Minn.

	Laid down	L	In serv.
BI-05 Río Suchiate (ex-H-07; ex-A-27; ex-*Monob One,* YAG 61; ex-IX 309; ex-YW 87)	1-12-42	3-4-43	11-11-43

Río Suchiate (BI-05) Mexican Navy, 2002

D: 1,142 tons (fl) **S:** 11 kts **Dim:** 58.5 × 10.1 × 7.1
Electronics: Radar: 1 . . . nav.
M: 1 Caterpillar D 398 diesel; 1 Harbormaster swiveling prop; 580 bhp
Range: 2,500/9 **Crew:** 27 tot.

Remarks: Purchased 2-8-96. Former U.S. Navy water lighter, modified in 1959 to support the ballistic-missile submarine silencing program. In USN service, had four laboratories totaling 279 m^2. Stern was extended to support the new propulsion plant. Had been stricken from U.S. service 4-4-95. Pennant number was changed in 2001. BI = *Buque de Investigación.*

♦ 1 ex-U.S. Kellar-class hydrographic survey ship [AGS]
Bldr: DeFoe SB, Bay City, Mich.

	Laid down	L	In serv.
BI-04 Antares (ex-H-06; ex-*Samuel P. Lee;* ex-*S. P. Lee,* T-AG 192, ex-T-AGS 31)	27-6-66	19-10-67	2-12-68

Antares (BI-04)—as *S. P. Lee* (T-AGS 31) U.S. Navy, 10-68

D: 1,297 tons (fl) **S:** 13.5 kts **Dim:** 63.50 (58.00 pp) × 11.90 × 4.32
M: 2 Caterpillar D-378 diesels, electric drive; 1 prop; 2,000 shp
Fuel: 211 tons **Crew:** 12 officers, 22 enlisted

AUXILIARIES *(continued)*

Remarks: Until retirement and transfer to Mexico on 7-12-92, had been on loan to the Pacific Branch, U.S. Geological Survey, since 27-2-74; prior to that, she performed survey work and acoustic research for the U.S. Navy. The Mexican Navy has added a large charting laboratory built from beam to beam at the aft end of the forecastle deck. Pennant number was changed in 2001. BI = *Buque de Investigación.*

♦ 1 cargo ship [AK]
Bldr: Solversborgs Varv A/B, Solversborg, Sweden (In serv. 1962)

ATR-03 TARASCO (ex-*Río Lerma,* A-22; ex-*Tarasco,* A-25; ex-*Sea Point;* ex-*Tricon;* ex-*Marika;* ex-*Arneb*)

D: 1,970 tons (approx. 3,200 fl) **S:** 14.5 kts **Dim:** 86.01 × 12.60 × 4.69
M: 1 Klöckner-Humboldt-Deutz diesel; 1 prop; 2,100 bhp
Range: . . . / . . . **Crew:** . . .

Remarks: 2,969 grt/2,500 dwt. Former commercial dry cargo vessel, acquired in 1990 and commissioned 1-3-90 without significant modification. A three-hold dry cargo ship with two electric cranes and superstructure aft. Cargo capacity: 780 tons. Renamed and renumbered during 1993 and again in 2001, when retyped ATR (*Auxiliar Transporte*).

♦ 1 cargo ship [AK]
Bldr: . . . (In serv. 1962)

ATR-01 MAYA (ex-*Río Nautla,* A-20; ex-*Maya,* A-23)

D: 924 tons (fl) **S:** 12 kts **Dim:** 48.8 × 11.8 × 4.9
M: 1 M.A.N. diesel; 1 prop; . . . bhp **Crew:** 8 officers, 7 enlisted

Remarks: Former lighthouse supply vessel, taken over in 1988 and commissioned 1-6-88. Renamed and renumbered during 1993 and again in 2001, when retyped ATR (*Auxiliar Transporte*).

Disposal note: Transport tanker [AOT] *Portrero del Llano* (A-42, ex-*Avaro Obregon*) was stricken 16-7-01.

♦ 2 Huasteco-class transports [AP]
Bldr: Ast. de la Secretaud de Marina, Guaymas

	In serv.
AMP-01 HUASTECO (ex-*Río Usumacinta,* A-10; ex-*Huasteco,* A-21)	21-5-86
AMP-02 ZAPOTECO (ex-*Río Coatzacoalcos,* A-11; ex-*Zapoteco,* A-22)	1-6-86

Huasteco (AMP-01) Alexandre Sheldon-Duplaix, 8-02

D: 1,854 tons (2,650 fl) **S:** 17 kts **Dim:** 72.3 (69.2 pp) × 12.8 × 5.5
A: 1 40-mm 60-cal. Mk 3 Bofors AA **Electronics:** Radar: 2 . . . nav.
M: 1 G.M. Electromotive Division EMD-series diesel; 1 prop; 3,600 bhp
Range: 5,500/14 **Crew:** 57 ship's company + up to 300 troops

Remarks: Ordered in 1984 as troop transports, vehicle carriers, and transports for construction materials, food, and hospital equipment and to act as floating infirmaries and civil disaster relief ships. Helicopter platform can accept a BO-105CB and has been enlarged on the AMP-01. Renamed and renumbered during 1993 and again in 2001, when retyped AMP (*Auxiliar Multipropósito*).

♦ 2 ex-U.S. Newport-class transports [AP]
Bldr: Philadelphia Naval Shipyard, Philadelphia

	Laid down	L	In serv.
A-411 PAPALOAPAN (ex-*Sonora,* A-04; ex-*Newport,* LST 1179)	1-11-66	3-2-68	7-6-69
A-412 USUMACINTA (ex-*Frederick,* LST 1184)	13-4-68	8-3-69	11-4-70

D: 4,975 tons light (8,576 fl) **S:** 23 kts (20 sust.)
Dim: 159.2 (171.3 over horns) × 21.18 × 5.3 (aft; 1.80 fwd)
A: 4 single 12.7-mm mg
Electronics: Radar: 1 Raytheon SPS-64(V)9 nav.; 1 Raytheon SPS-10F surf. search
M: 6 G.M. Electromotive Div. 16-645-E5 diesels; 2 CP props;16,500 bhp—bow-thruster
Electric: 2,250 kw tot. (3 × 750 kw, Alco 251-E diesels driving; 450 V, 60 Hz a.c.)
Range: 14,250/14 **Fuel:** 1,750 tons
Crew: 15 officers, 247 enlisted + troops: 20 officers, 294 enlisted + 72 emergency accomm.

Remarks: A-411 was sold to Mexico 18-1-01 and transferred 23-5-01. A-412 was decommissioned 5-10-02 and sold to Mexico 9-12-02. Name and pennant number of A-411 were changed after delivery. A-411 was decommissioned 30-9-92 from the U.S. Navy. Primarily intended as transports. A = *Anfibia.*
Hull systems: Can transport 2,000 tons of cargo (500 tons for beaching) on 1,765 m² of deck space. There is a 34-m-long, 75-ton-capacity mobile aluminum ramp forward, which is linked to the tank deck by a second from the upper deck. Aft is a 242-m² helicopter platform and a stern door for loading and unloading vehicles. The tank deck, which has a 75-ton-capacity turntable at both ends, can carry 23 armored personnel carriers or 29 light tanks or 41 2.5-ton trucks, while the upper deck can accept 29 2.5-ton trucks. Can carry three LCVPs and one LCP in Welin davits. Are fitted with two 10-ton cranes. Can carry 141,600 gallons of vehicle fuel.

Papaloapan (A-411) U.S. Navy, 9-05

Combat systems: The Mk 63 radar gunfire-control systems were removed 1977–78 and the two twin 76.2-mm DP gunmounts during the early 1990s. No Phalanx CIWS mount was transferred with either ship.

Disposal note: Small transport [AP] *Río Tehuantepec* (A-24; ex-*Zacatecas,* B-02) was stricken 16-7-02.

♦ 1 ex-U.S. Fabius-class transport [AP]
Bldr: American Bridge Co., Ambridge, Pa.

	Laid down	L	In serv.
A-403 VICENTE GUERRERO (ex-*Río Grijalva,* A-03; ex-*General Vicente Guerrero,* A-05; ex-*Megara,* ARVA 6; ex-LST 1095)	22-1-45	25-3-45	27-6-45

Vicente Guerrero (A-403)—with old pennant number H&L Van Ginderen, 7-84

D: 4,100 tons (fl) **S:** 11.6 kts **Dim:** 100.0 (96.3 wl) × 15.24 × 3.4
A: 2 quadruple 40-mm 60-cal. Mk 2 Bofors AA
Electronics: Radar: 1 . . . nav.
M: 2 G.M. 12-567A diesels; 2 props; 1,700 bhp **Electric:** 520 kw
Range: 10,000/10 **Fuel:** 474 tons **Crew:** 28 officers, 85 enlisted

Remarks: Transferred 1-10-73. Originally one of two U.S. Navy tank landing ships converted while under construction to act as airframe repair ships. Has one 10-ton boom and two Mk 51 Mod. 2 gun f.c.s. for the 40-mm AA. Normally carries two U.S. LCVP personnel landing craft. Renamed and renumbered during 1993 and again in 2001. A = *Anfibia.* Used primarily as a transport.

Disposal note: Both remaining ex-US LST 542–class transports, *Río Panuco* (A-401) and *Río Papaloapan* (A-402), have been removed from service as of 2003.

♦ 6 miscellaneous seagoing tugs [ATA]
Bldr: . . .

ARE-05 IZTACCÍHUATL (ex-R-60)
ARE-06 POPOCATÉPETL (ex-R-61)
ARE-07 CITLALTÉPETL (ex-R-62)
ARE-08 XINANTÉCATL (ex-R-63)
ARE-09 MATLALCUEYE (ex-R-64)
ARE-10 TLÁLOC (ex-R-65)

Popocatépetl (ARE-06) Mexican Navy, 2004

AUXILIARIES *(continued)*

Xinantécatl (ARE-08)—painted blue with gold stripes and stack
Mexican Navy, 2004

Remarks: No data available. Some are painted blue with gold stacks and two stripes. ARE = *Auxiliar Remolcador.*

♦ 4 ex-U.S. Abnaki-class fleet tugs [ATA]

Bldr: Charleston SB & DD, Charleston, S.C. (ARE-01: United Engineering, Alameda, Calif.)

	Laid down	L	In serv.
ARE-01 Otomi (ex-*Kukulkan,* R-52, ex-A-52; ex-*Otomi,* A-17; ex-*Molala,* ATF 106)	26-7-42	23-12-42	29-9-43
ARE-02 Yaqui (ex-*Ehactl,* R-53, ex-A-53; ex-*Yaqui,* A-18; ex-*Abnaki,* ATF 96)	28-11-42	22-4-43	15-11-43
ARE-03 Seri (ex-*Tonatiuh,* R-54, ex-A-54; ex-*Seri,* A-19; ex-*Cocopa,* ATF 101)	23-5-43	5-10-43	25-3-44
ARE-04 Cora (ex-*Chac,* R-55, ex-A-55; ex-*Cora,* A-20; ex-*Hitchiti,* ATF 103)	24-8-43	29-1-44	27-5-44

Yaqui (ARE-02)
Mexican Navy, 2004

D: 1,325 tons (1,675 fl) **S:** 10 kts **Dim:** 62.48 × 11.73 × 4.67
A: 1 76.2-mm 50-cal. Mk 22 DP; 2 single 20-mm 70-cal. Oerlikon Mk 10 AA
Electronics: Radar: 1 Canadian Marconi LN-66 nav.
M: 4 Caterpillar D-399 diesels, electric drive; 1 prop; 3,000 shp
Electric: 400 kw **Range:** 7,000/15; 15,000/8 **Fuel:** 304 tons
Crew: 75 tot.

Remarks: ARE-01 was purchased 1-8-78, the others on 30-9-78. Were unarmed on delivery. Used on patrol duties and as rescue tugs. Radar may have been replaced. Renamed and renumbered during 1993; reverted to the original names in 2001. ARE = *Auxiliar Remolcador.* Were re-engined in the 1970s while in U.S. service; originally had Busch-Sulzer BS-539 diesels.

Disposal note: U.S. 143-ft. ATA-class fleet tugs *Quetzalcoatl* (A-50; ex-*Mayo,* A-12; ex-R-2; ex- . . .) and *Huitilopochtli* (A-51; ex-*Mixteco,* A-13; ex-R-3; ex- . . .) were stricken 16-7-01.

♦ 1 sail-training ship [AXT]

Bldr: Ast. y Talleres Celaya, Bilbao, Spain

	Laid down	L	In serv.
BE-01 Cuauhtémoc (ex-A-07)	27-4-81	1-82	11-12-82

D: 1,200 tons (1,800 fl) **S:** 15 kts **Dim:** 90.0 (67.0 pp) × 10.6 × 4.2
M: 1 G.M. Detroit Diesel 12V149 diesel; 1 prop; 750 bhp—2,368 m^2 max. sail area
Crew: 20 officers, 165 enlisted + 90 cadets

Cuauhtémoc (BE-01)
Jaroslaw Cislak, 7-03

Remarks: Ordered in 1980. Three-masted bark. Equipped with commercial SATCOM gear. BE = *Buque Escuela.*

♦ 1 ex-U.S. Admirable-class training ship [AXT]

Bldr: Willamette Iron & Steel, Ore.

	Laid down	L	In serv.
BE-02 Aldebaran (ex-*General Pedro María Anaya,* A-08; ex-H-02; ex-*Oceanográfico;* ex-DM 20; ex-*Harlequin,* MSF 365)	3-8-43	3-6-44	28-9-45

Aldebaran (BE-02)—with old pennant number
H&L Van Ginderen, 4-99

D: 615 tons (910 fl) **S:** 15 kts **Dim:** 56.24 (54.86 wl) × 10.06 × 2.80
A: 1 76.2-mm 50-cal. U.S. Mk 22 DP; 2 single 40-mm 60-cal. Bofors Mk 3 AA; 4 single 20-mm 70-cal. Oerlikon Mk 10 AA
Electronics: Radar: 1 Kelvin-Hughes 14/9 nav.; 1 . . . nav.
M: 2 Cooper-Bessemer GSB-8 diesels; 2 props; 1,710 bhp
Electric: 280 kw tot. **Range:** 4,300/10 **Fuel:** 138 tons
Crew: 12 officers, 50 enlisted

Remarks: Former fleet minesweeper, converted 1976–78 for use as an oceanographic research ship, with armament deleted, oceanographic winches and davits installed, and space at the aft end of the forecastle employed for portable research containers. Named during 1993. Reclassified as a training ship during the late 1990s and rearmed.

Note: Also in use as a training ship is the *Moctezuma II* (BE-03, ex-A-09); no data available.

Disposal note: Training ship [AXT] *Durango* (B-01) was stricken 16-7-01.

SERVICE CRAFT

♦ 1 ex-U.S. pile driver [YAG] (Leased 8-68)

. . . (ex-YPD 43)

♦ 7 ex-U.S. floating cranes [YD]

. . . (ex-YD 156)	. . . (ex-YD 179)	. . . (ex-YD 183)	. . . (ex-YD 203)
. . . (ex-YD 157)	. . . (ex-YD 180)	. . . (ex-YD 194)	

Remarks: Transferred 1964–71; purchased 7-78 (except ex-YD 179 and ex-YD 194).

♦ 2 ex-U.S. ARD 12–class floating dry docks [YFDL]
Bldr: Pacific Bridge, Alameda, Calif.

	In serv.
ADI-03 (ex-AR-15, ex-ARD 15)	1-44
ADI-04 (ex-AR-16; ex-*San Onofre,* ARD 30)	1945

Lift capacity: 3,500 tons **Dim:** 149.87 × 24.69 × 1.73 (light)

Remarks: ADI-03 was transferred in 4-71 on loan and purchased in 1981. ADI-04 was offered for sale to Mexico in 1999 and purchased 20-3-01. Were renumbered in the ADI (*Auxiliar Dique Flotante*) series in 2001.

♦ 2 ex-U.S. ARD 2–class floating dry docks [YFDL]
Bldr: Pacific Bridge, Alameda, Calif.

	In serv.
ADI-01 (ex-DF 01, ex-ARD 2)	4-42
ADI-02 (ex-DF 02, ex-ARD 11)	10-43

Lift capacity: 3,500 tons **Dim:** 148.0 × 21.64 × 1.6 (light)

Remarks: Transferred 8-63 and 6-74. Were renumbered in the ADI (*Auxiliar Dique Flotante*) series in 2001.

Disposal note: Ex-U.S. small auxiliary floating dry dock ex-AFDL 28 appears to have been retired from service as of 2001 and she no longer appears on the official fleet list.

♦ 1 general-purpose tender [YFU]
Bldr: Ast. Angulo Ciudad del Carmen (In serv. 27-2-85)

ATR-02 Progreso (ex-*Río Tonala,* A-21; ex-*Progreso,* A-24)

D: 152 grt **S:** 10 kts **Dim:** 22.4 × 6.5 × 1.5
A: 1 20-mm 70-cal. Oerlikon AA **M:** 1 diesel; 1 prop; . . . bhp

Remarks: Acquired in 1988 and recommissioned 27-3-89. Can carry 57 tons of package cargo and a small number of passengers. Has a fishing boat hull. Renamed and renumbered in 1993 and again in 2001, when retyped ATR (*Auxiliar Transporte*).

♦ 6 Laguna-series miscellaneous dredges [YM]

ADR-12 Laguna Farrallón (ex-D-26)
ADR-13 Laguna de Chairel (ex-D-27)
ADR-14 Laguna de San Andrés (ex-D-28)
ADR-15 Laguna de San Ignacio (ex-D-29)
ADR-16 Laguna de Términos (ex-D-30)
ADR-17 Laguna de Teculapa (ex-D-31)

Remarks: Acquired in 1994 from a Spanish builder. Consist of several different types. Typical of the group is ADR-14 which measures 32.1 m o.a., displaces 151.6 tons, and has a crew of 30. The Mexican Navy is responsible for dredging and aids-to-navigation maintenance. Received new pennant numbers in the ADR (*Auxiliar Draga*) series in 2001. Are painted blue with gold diagonal stripes.

♦ 11 Bahía-series miscellaneous dredges [YM]

ADR-01 Bahía de Banderas (ex-D-01; ex-*Chiapas,* A-30)
ADR-02 Bahía Magdalena (ex-D-02; ex-*Cristobol Colón,* A-32)
ADR-03 Bahía Kino (ex-D-03, ex- . . .)
ADR-04 Bahía Yavaros (ex-D-04; ex- . . .)
ADR-05 Bahía Chamela (ex-D-05, ex- . . .)
ADR-06 Bahía Tepoca (ex-D-06)
ADR-07 Bahía Todos Santos (ex-D-07; ex-*Mazatlán,* A-31)
ADR-08 Bahía Asunción (ex-D-22; ex-*Isla del Carmen,* A-33)
ADR-09 Bahía Almejas (ex-D-23, ex-*Isla Azteca,* A-34)
ADR-10 Bahía de Chacagua (ex-D-24)
ADR-11 Bahía de Coyuca (ex-D-25)

Bahía Chamela (ADR-05)—painted blue with gold diagonal stripes
Mexican Navy, 2002

Remarks: Acquired in 1985, with five renamed in 1993. Consist of several different types, ranging in dimensions from the smallest (ADR-11), with 45.8 m o.a. and 326.4 tons displacement, to the largest (ADR-03), with 113.5 m o.a. and 12,540 tons displacement. Painted blue with gold diagonal stripes.

♦ 2 ex-U.S. 174-foot-class fuel lighters [YO]
Bldrs: ATQ-01: J. H. Mathis, Camden, N.J.; ATQ-02: George Lawley, Neponset, Mass.

	L	In serv.
ATQ-01 Aguascalientes (ex-*Las Chopas,* A-45; ex-*Aguascalientes,* A-03; ex-YOG 6)	3-4-43	15-11-43
ATQ-02 Tlaxcala (ex-*Amatlan,* A-46; ex-*Tlaxcala,* A-04; ex-YO 107)	3-11-43	27-11-43

D: 440 tons (1,480 fl) **S:** 8 kts **Dim:** 53.0 × 9.75 × 2.5
A: 1 20-mm 70-cal. Oerlikon Mk 10 AA
M: 1 Fairbanks-Morse 38D8⅛ diesel; 1 prop; 500 bhp
Crew: 5 officers, 21 enlisted

Remarks: Purchased in 8-64 and commissioned in 11-64. Cargo capacity: 980 tons (6,570 bbl). Both were renamed and renumbered during 1993 and again in 2001. ATQ = *Auxiliar Tanque.*

♦ 2 yard tugs [YTL]

Patron Pragmar

Remarks: Bought in 1973. No data available.

♦ 10 shallow-draft push-tugs [YTL]

Remarks: No data available. Entered service in 1994 for use in swampy and shallow water service.

COAST GUARD

Note: The Mexican Coast Guard is essentially a customs service. Ten U.S. Mako 295–class patrol launches built by Mako Marine International, Miami, are in service, with the first four having been shipped 28-11-95 and the remainder 15-12-95; they are powered by Mercury gasoline outboard engines.

ARMY

♦ 144 25 Sport–class special forces craft
Bldr: Pro-Line Boats, Crystal River, Fla. (In serv. 2001)

D: 1.63 kg hull only (approx. 2.2 tons fl) **S:** 40+ kts **Dim:** 7.75 × 2.59 × 0.36
A: Small arms **Electronics:** Radar: . . .
M: 2 Mercury gasoline outboard motors; 400 bhp
Range: . . . / . . . **Fuel:** 545 liters **Crew:** 4 tot.

Remarks: GRP-construction open sport fishing boats, known as the "240 Sport" model when ordered late in 2000. Assigned to the 36th Grupo Anfibios de Fuerzas Especiales. Sixty operate from San Felipe and the others from Tampico, all painted olive green. Have 7.66 m^2 of cockpit area. Were delivered along with 144 Dodge Ram pickup trucks and boat tow-trailers.

Note: Also in service are 108 rigid inflatable launches with outboard motors of between 40 and 105 bhp.

MICRONESIA

Federated States of Micronesia

DIVISION OF SURVEILLANCE ATTORNEY GENERAL'S OFFICE

Personnel: Approx. 120 total
Bases: Principal facility at Kolonia, with outposts at Kosral, Moen, and Takatik

Note: Micronesia, which became independent on 10-5-89, consists of the Caroline Islands archipelago islands of Kosrae, Pohnpei, Truk, and Yap. The United States retains the responsibility to provide defense against external threat. Ship names are preceded by FSS (Federated States Ship).

PATROL CRAFT [WPC]

♦ 3 ASI-315 Pacific Forum class
Bldr: Transfield ASI Pty, Ltd., South Coogie, Western Australia

	Laid down	L	In serv.
FSM 01 Palakir	19-6-89	. . .	28-4-90
FSM 02 Micronesia	22-1-89	. . .	3-1-90
FSM 05 Independence	. . .	. . .	22-5-97

D: 165 tons (fl) **S:** 21 kts **Dim:** 31.50 (28.60 wl) × 8.10 × 2.12 (1.80 hull)
A: 2 single 12.7-mm mg **Electronics:** Radar: 1 Furuno 1011 nav.
M: 2 Caterpillar 3516 diesels; 2 props; 2,820 bhp (2,400 sust.)
Electric: 116 kw (2 × 50 kw, Caterpillar 3304 diesel sets; 1 × 16 kw)
Range: 2,500/12 **Fuel:** 27.9 tons **Endurance:** 8–10 days
Crew: 3 officers, 14 enlisted

Remarks: First two arrived at Port Kolonia on 7-6-90 and 25-1-91, respectively. The third was ordered in 1996. Standard Australian foreign aid patrol boat design. All three have undergone minor refits, but are due to be modernized between 2007 and 2012 to extend service life through 2020.
Hull systems: Carry a 5-m rigid inflatable boarding boat. Have an extensive navigational suite, including Furuno FSN-70 NAVSAT receiver, Furuno 525 HFD/F, Furuno 120 MF–HFD/F, FE-881 echo sounder, Furuno 500 autopilot, DS-70 doppler log, and a Weatherfax receiver. Differ from earlier units of the class in having a spray strake forward on the hull sides.

PATROL CRAFT [WPC] *(continued)*

Palakir (FSM 01) RAN, 5-90

♦ **2 ex-U.S. Coast Guard Cape class**
Bldr: Coast Guard Yard, Curtis Bay, Md.

	In serv.
FSM 03 Paluwlap (ex-*Cape Cross*, WPB 95321)	20-8-58
FSM 04 Constitution (ex-*Cape Corwin*, WPB 95326)	14-11-58

Constitution (FSM 04)—stack painted blue, with four white stars *Ships of the World,* 2-98

D: 87 tons (106 fl) **S:** 20 kts **Dim:** 28.96 × 6.10 × 1.55
A: Provision for 2 single 12.7-mm M2 mg
Electronics: Radar: 1 Raytheon SPS-64(V)9 nav.
M: 2 G.M. 16V 149TI diesels; 2 props; 2,470 bhp **Electric:** 60 kw tot.
Range: 550/20; 1,900/11.5 **Endurance:** 5 days **Crew:** 1 officer, 14 enlisted

Remarks: Transferred by the U.S. government 30-3-90 as Grant-Aid. Planned transfer of a third unit, the ex-*Cape George* (WPB 95306) was canceled, and the craft went to Palau as FSM 05. Both were re-engined and otherwise modernized, completing 16-4-82 and 15-10-82, respectively; the original four Cummins VT-12-M-700 diesels produced 18 kts from 2,324 bhp. Can make 24 kts, but are restricted due to likelihood of hull damage at speeds over 20 kts. The craft normally do not carry armament.

MONTSERRAT

Crown Colony of Montserrat

MONTSERRAT POLICE FORCE

Base: Plymouth

PATROL BOATS [WPB]

♦ **1 M 160 class**
Bldr: Halmatic, Havant, U.K. (In serv. 16-1-90)

Shamrock

Shamrock—with Montserrat's Pacific 22–class RIB at left P. H. Nargeolet, 1998

D: 17.3 tons (light) **S:** 27 kts **Dim:** 15.40 (12.20 pp) × 3.86 × 1.15
A: 1 7.62-mm mg **Electronics:** Radar: 1 Decca 370 BT nav.
M: 2 G.M. Detroit Diesel 6V92 TA diesels: 2 props; 1,100 bhp (770 sust.)
Range: 300/20; 500/17 **Fuel:** 2,700 gallons **Crew:** 6 tot.

Remarks: GRP construction, provided by the U.K. as a replacement for patrol craft *Emerald Star,* lost by grounding 6-1-87. Has semi-rigid inflatable rescue dinghy at stern. Sister to Anguilla's *Dolphin,* British Virgin Islands' *St. Ursula,* and the Turks and Caicos' *Sea Quest.*

SERVICE CRAFT

♦ **1 Pacific 22–class rigid inflatable launch [YFL]**
Bldr: Osborne, U.K (In serv. 2-96)

D: 1.75 tons light **S:** 30 kts **Dim:** 6.8 × . . . × . . .
M: 2 gasoline outboard motors; 120 bhp
Range: 85/26 **Crew:** 2 tot. + up to 12 personnel

MOROCCO

Kingdom of Morocco

MARINE ROYALE MAROCAINE

Personnel: Approx. 7,800 total, including 1,500 marines

Bases: Principal base at Casablanca, with facilities at Agadir, Al Hoceima, Dakhla, Kenitra, Safa, and Tangier

Maritime Aviation: Two AS.565MA Panther helicopters are assigned to naval liaison duties. The Ministry of Fisheries and Merchant Marine operates 11 Pilatus-Britten-Norman BN2T Defender light maritime patrol aircraft for economic exclusion zone patrol.

FRIGATES [FF]

♦ **1 Spanish Descubierta class**
Bldr: Izar (formerly E.N. Bazán), El Ferrol

	Laid down	L	In serv.
501 Lieutenant Colonel Errhamani	20-3-79	26-2-82	28-3-83

Lieutenant Colonel Errhamani (501) Guy Schaeffer via Paolo Marsan, 6-05

Lieutenant Colonel Errhamani (501)—note Albatros SAM system and two 40mm mounts Bernard Prézelin, 7-05

D: 1,270 tons (1,479 fl) **S:** 26 kts **Dim:** 88.88 (85.8 pp) × 10.4 × 3.25 (3.7 fl)
A: 1 8-round Albatros SAM syst. (24 Aspide missiles); 1 76-mm 62-cal. OTO Melara Compact DP; 2 single 40-mm 70-cal. Bofors L70 AA; 1 2-round 375-mm Bofors SR 375 ASW RL (24 Erika rockets); 2 triple 324-mm U.S. Mk 32 Mod. 5 ASW TT (Mk 46 Mod. 2 torpedoes)
Electronics:
Radar: 1 . . . nav.; 1 Thales ZW-06 surf. search; 1 Thales WM-25 Mod. 41 f.c.
Sonar: Raytheon DE 1160B hull-mounted MF
EW: Elettronica ELT 715 intercept/jammer; 2 330- to 340-round Matra Défense Dagaie decoy RL
M: 4 Izar-MTU 16MA956 TB91 diesels; 2 CP props; 18,000 bhp
Electric: 1,810 kw tot. **Range:** 4,000/18 (one engine) **Fuel:** 150 tons
Crew: 10 officers, 110 enlisted

FRIGATES [FF] *(continued)*

Remarks: Ordered 14-6-77. Refitted fall 1995 in Spain, when a towing winch was added at the stern. Has fin stabilizers.
Combat systems: Has the Thales Nederland SEWACO-MR combat data system, but the combat information center is now equipped primarily as VIP quarters. Provision was made to carry four MM 38 Exocet missiles, but they were never installed. The 40-mm guns have been enclosed with Mauser mountings of the type employed on German Type 148 missile boats and are controlled by a single optical director; a second optical director serves as backup for the WM-25 system. Can carry 600 rounds of 76-mm ammunition. The DA-05 surface/air-search radar was removed during 1997 but restored in 1999, and a small navigational radar is now carried on a pole mast atop the pilothouse. A commercial SATCOM terminal is fitted.

PATROL SHIPS [PS]

♦ 2 Floréal class

Bldr: Chantiers de l'Atlantique, St. Nazaire, France

	Laid down	L	Del.
611 Mohammed V	10-00	9-3-01	12-3-02
612 Hassan II	2001	7-12-01	22-5-03

Mohammed V (611) Derek Fox, 6-05

Hassan II (612) Bernard Prézelin, 1-04

Mohammed V (611) Leo Van Ginderen, 6-05

D: 2,600 tons (2,950 fl) **S:** 20 kts **Dim:** 93.50 (85.20 pp) × 14.00 × 4.40
A: 2 MM 38 Exocet SSM; 1 76-mm 62-cal. OTO Melara Compact DP; single 20-mm 90-cal. GIAT F2 AA; 1 AS.565MA Panther helicopter
Electronics:
Radar: 1 Decca BridgeMaster-E ARPA nav.; 1 Thales DRBV-21A surf./air search; Thales WM-25 track-while-scan f.c.
E/O: Matra Najir 2000 gun director
M: 4 SEMT-Pielstick 6 PA6 L280 BTC diesels; 2 CP props; 9,600 bhp—250-kw bowthruster
Electric: 1,770 kw (3 × 590-kw sets, 3 Baudouin 12 P15 2SR diesels driving)
Range: 10,000/15 **Fuel:** 390 tons **Endurance:** 50 days
Crew: 11 officers, 109 enlisted

Remarks: Ordered 26-10-98. Intended primarily for economic exclusion zone patrol, fisheries protection, and maritime policing duties. Were originally to have been delivered in 10-00 and 6-01. Six sisters serve in the French Navy.
Hull systems: Constructed to Veritas commercial standards. Has an emphasis on seaworthiness, with helicopter operations possible up to Sea State 5. Equipped with fin stabilizers. Have accommodations for 123 personnel total. The 23 × 14-m flight deck can accommodate a 9-ton helicopter and has a Samahé landing and deck transit system; there is also a hangar.
Combat systems: There is no combat data system. One of the two Decca radars is mounted aft for helicopter control. The Exocet missiles, 76-mm gun, and WM-25 radar were recycled from units of the *Lazaga* class and were installed at Casablanca.

PATROL COMBATANTS [PG]

♦ 5 OPV 64 class

Bldr: Lorient Naval Industries, Lanester, France

	L	In serv.
318 Raïs Bargach	9-10-95	14-12-95
319 Raïs Britel	19-3-96	14-5-96
320 Raïs Charkaoui	26-9-96	15-12-96
321 Raïs Maaninou	7-3-97	21-5-97
322 Raïs al Mounastiri	15-10-97	17-12-97

Raïs Charkaoui (320) Ralph Edwards, 5-04

Raïs Maaninou (321) Bernard Prézelin, 9-05

D: 580 tons (650 fl) **S:** 25 kts (22 sust.)
Dim: 64.00 (59.00 pp) × 11.42 × 3.00 (over props)
A: 2 single 20-mm 90-cal. AA; 2 single 12.7-mm mg
Electronics: Radar: 1 Decca 2090-series BridgeMaster I-band nav.; 1 Decca 2090-series BridgeMaster-E ARPA nav.
M: 2 Wärtsilä-Nohab 16V25 diesels (900 rpm); 2 KaMeWa CP props; 10,000 bhp—2 160-shp Leroy-Somer electric auxiliary drives (8 kts max.)
Electric: 480 kw tot. (2 × 200 kw, Wärtsilä UD19 L6 diesels driving; 1 × 80 kw, Wärtsilä UD16 L6 diesel driving)
Range: 4,000/12 **Endurance:** 10 days
Crew: 6 officers, 10 petty officers, 30 nonrated (accomm. for 54 tot.)

Remarks: First two ordered from Leroux & Lotz (now LNI/Lorient Naval Industries) in late 1993 for delivery by end-1994, but the program was delayed. The other three were ordered in 10-94. Intended for fisheries patrol duties. Are somewhat less capable than the version originally offered.
Hull systems: Hullform features a double chine forward. There are eight watertight compartments. Flume-type passive stabilization tanks are fitted fore and aft. Have a helicopter platform on the stern and a stern recovery/deployment ramp for an internally stowed rigid inflatable inspection craft. Has electric drive to both propellers for low-speed operations (6–8 kts). Equipped with a 400-m^3/hr firefighting water monitor driven by a 200-kw diesel engine. For pollution control, have two 5-m^3 dispersant tanks and two 8-m-long dispersant booms. Navigation equipment includes a GPS receiver and autopilot.
Combat systems: One 40-mm gun was to have been added in Morocco from existing stocks but has not yet been installed.

♦ 4 Osprey 55 class

Bldr: Danyard A/S, Frederikshavn, Denmark

	L	In serv.		L	In serv.
308 El Lahiq	7-87	11-87	316 El Hamiss	4-90	8-90
309 El Tawfiq	10-87	2-88	317 El Karib	7-90	12-90

D: 420 tons (500 fl) **S:** 19 kts (18 sust.)
Dim: 54.75 (51.83 pp) × 10.50 (9.15 wl) × 2.75

PATROL COMBATANTS [PG] *(continued)*

El Hamiss (316) Bernard Prézelin, 5-02

A: 1 40-mm 70-cal. Bofors AA; 2 single 20-mm 90-cal. AA
Electronics: Radar: 2 Decca . . . nav.
M: 2 M.A.N.–Burmeister & Wain Alpha 12V.23/30 DVO diesels; 2 CP props; 4,960 bhp
Electric: 268 kw/316 kVA tot. (2 MWM TD232-V8 diesels driving)
Range: 4,500/16 **Fuel:** 95 tons **Crew:** 15 tot. + 16 passengers

Remarks: First two ordered early in 1986 for fisheries protection and search-and-rescue duties; second pair ordered 30-1-89. A third pair was reportedly ordered in 6-90, but the contract was not consummated. Similar ships operate in Greek, Myanmar, Namibian, and Senegalese service. Armament was not mounted at time of delivery. 317 carries the Danyard Oil Containment System with Desmi skimmer capable of accumulating 40–70 m^3/hr of oil containment. All have a stern ramp and door for launching a 6.5-m rigid inflatable rescue/inspection craft. 308 is equipped with U.S.-made mapping sonars and navigational equipment and has conducted hydrographic surveys between Jorf las Par and Casablanca and between Rabat and Tangier. All can carry 27 tons of fresh water.

PATROL CRAFT [PC]

♦ 6 Vigilance class
Bldr: Izar (formerly E.N. Bazán), Cadiz

	L	In serv.
310 Lieutenant de Vaisseau Rabhi	23-9-87	16-9-88
311 Errachiq	23-9-87	16-12-88
312 El Akid	29-3-88	4-4-89
313 El Maher	29-3-88	20-6-89
314 El Majid	21-10-88	26-9-89
315 El Bachir	21-10-88	19-12-89

El Akid (312)—shown undergoing modernization in Lorient
Bernard Prézelin 2-05

D: 307 tons (425 fl) **S:** 22 kts **Dim:** 58.1 (54.4 pp) × 7.60 × 2.70
A: 1 40-mm 70-cal. Bofors AA; 2 single 20-mm 90-cal. Oerlikon AA
Electronics: Radar: 2 Decca . . . nav.
M: 2 MTU 16V956 TB82 diesels; 2 props; 7,600 bhp (sust.)
Range: 3,800/12 **Endurance:** 10 days
Crew: 4 officers, 32 enlisted + 15 passengers

Remarks: Three ordered 2-10-85, with an option for three more taken up shortly thereafter. "Series P200/D" design, a reduced-power version of the *Lazaga* design for 200-n.m. economic zone patrol. Have a Matra Défense Naja optronic director for the 40-mm gun. 312 underwent modernization in France during 2005.

♦ 4 Spanish Lazaga class
Bldr: Izar (formerly E.N. Bazán), Cadiz

	In serv.
304 Commandant el Khattabi	3-6-81
305 Commandant Boutouba	11-12-81
306 Commandant el Harti	25-2-82
307 Commandant Azouggarh	2-8-82

Commandant Azouggarh (307) Martin Mokrus, 12-03

D: 303 tons (420 fl) **S:** 29.6 kts **Dim:** 57.40 (54.4 pp) × 7.60 × 2.70
A: 1 76-mm 62-cal. OTO Melara DP; 1 40-mm 70-cal. Bofors–OTO Melara AA; 2 single 20-mm 90-cal. Oerlikon GAM-B01 AA
Electronics: Radar: 1 Decca . . . nav.; 1 Thales ZW-06 surf. search; 1 Thales WM-25 track-while-scan f.c.
M: 2 Izar-MTU MA16V956 TB91 diesels; 2 props; 7,780 bhp
Electric: 405 kVA **Range:** 700/27; 3,000/15 **Crew:** 41 tot.

Remarks: Ordered 14-6-77; first unit launched 21-7-80. Have added fuel capacity over the former Spanish Navy version. Although thought to have been stricken during 2001, 304 and 305 were sighted in service during 12-03.
Combat systems: Were originally equipped to carry four MM 38 Exocet antiship missiles but normally carried only two; since the mid-1990s, they have carried none at all, and the operational missiles have been rehabilitated and transferred to the new *Floréal*-class patrol ships, which also received the 76-mm guns from the first two units of this class. Can carry 300 rounds of 76-mm, 1,472 rounds of 40-mm, and 3,000 rounds of 20-mm ammunition. Have a Matra Défense Naja optical director aft for the 40-mm gun. The 40-mm mounting has been enclosed and a small navigational radar has been added.

♦ 2 French Type PR 72
Bldr: SFCN, Villeneuve-la-Garenne

	L	In serv.
302 Okba	10-10-75	16-12-76
303 Triki	2-2-76	12-7-77

Okba (302) Bernard Prézelin, 1-05

D: 370 tons (440 fl) **S:** 28 kts (at 413 tons) **Dim:** 57.0 (54.0 pp) × 7.6 × 2.5
A: 1 76-mm 62-cal. OTO Melara Compact DP; 1 40-mm 70-cal. Bofors AA; 2 single 12.7-mm mg
Electronics:
Radar: 1 Decca 1226 nav.; 1 . . . nav.
E/O: 2 Matra Défense Panda optronic f.c. directors
M: 4 SACM AGO 195V16 SZSHR diesels; 2 props; 11,040 bhp
Electric: 360 kw tot. **Range:** 2,500/16 **Crew:** 5 officers, 48 enlisted

Remarks: Ordered in 6-73. A second navigational radar has been added.

♦ 1 ex-Spanish Barceló class
Bldrs: Izar, La Carraca, Cádiz

	L	In serv.
. . . (ex-*Javier Quiroga*, P 13)	16-12-75	1-4-77

D: 110 tons (134 fl) **S:** 36.5 kts **Dim:** 36.2 (43.2 pp) × 5.8 × 1.75 (2.15 props)
A: 1 40-mm 70-cal. Bofors AA; 1 20-mm 70-cal. Oerlikon Mk 10 AA; 2 single 12.7-mm mg
Electronics: Radar: 1 Raytheon 1620/6 nav.
M: 2 Bazán-MTU 16V538 TB90 diesels; 2 props; 7,320 bhp (6,120 sust.)
Electric: 220 kVA tot. **Range:** 600/33.5; 1,200/16 **Fuel:** 18 tons
Crew: 3 officers, 16 enlisted

Remarks: Transferred from Spain 28-4-05.

PATROL BOATS [PB]

♦ 6 French Type P 32
Bldr: CMN, Cherbourg

	L	In serv.		L	In serv.
203 El Wacil	12-6-75	9-10-75	206 El Khafir	21-1-76	16-4-76
204 El Jail	10-10-75	3-12-75	207 El Haris	31-3-76	30-6-76
205 El Mikdam	1-12-75	30-1-76	208 Essahir	2-6-76	16-7-76

El Haris (207) Carlo Martinelli, 9-96

D: 89.5 tons (fl) **S:** 29 kts **Dim:** 32.20 (30.00 pp) × 5.35 × 1.85
A: 2 single 20-mm 70-cal. Oerlikon Mk 10 AA
Electronics: Radar: 1 Decca . . . nav.
M: 2 SACM-Wärtsilä UD30 V16 diesels; 2 props; 2,700 hp
Range: 1,200/12 **Crew:** 12 tot.

Remarks: Ordered 2-74. Have a GRP-sheathed, laminated wood-construction hull. The customs service operates sisters *Erraid* (209), *Erracel* (210), *El Kaced* (211), and *Essaid* (212), all ordered during 6-85.

PATROL BOATS [PB] *(continued)*

♦ **2 French RPB class**
Bldr: CNB-Bénéteau, L'Herbaudière, Noirmoutier (In serv. 2006)

. . .   . . .

D: 40 tons (fl) **S:** 28 kts **Dim:** 20.00 (17.25 pp) × 5.39 × 1.45
A: 2 single 7.62-mm mg **Electronics:** Radar: 1 Furuno . . . nav.
M: 2 M.A.N. 2842 LE 413 diesels; 2 props; 2,000 bhp
Range: 500/15 **Crew:** 8 tot.

Remarks: Same design as the French *Elorne*-class patrol boats ordered in 2005.

AMPHIBIOUS WARFARE SHIPS AND CRAFT

♦ **1 ex-U.S. Newport-class tank landing ship [LST]**
Bldr: National Steel Shipbuilding, San Diego

	Laid down	L	In serv.
407 Sidi Mohammed ben Abdallah (ex-*Bristol County,* LST 1198)	13-2-71	4-12-71	5-8-72

Sidi Mohammed ben Abdallah (407) French Navy, 10-98

D: 4,975 tons light (8,576 fl) **S:** 22 kts (20 sust.)
Dim: 159.2 (171.3 over horns) × 21.18 × 5.3 (aft; 1.80 fwd)
A: 1 20-mm Mk 15 Phalanx gatling CIWS; 4 single 12.7-mm mg
Electronics: Radar: 1 Decca . . . nav.; 1 Raytheon SPS-64(V)9 nav.; 1 Raytheon SPS-10F surf. search
M: 6 Alco 16-251 diesels; 2 CP props; 16,500 bhp—bow-thruster
Range: 14,250/14 **Fuel:** 1,750 tons
Crew: 13 officers, 174 enlisted + troops: 20 officers, 294 enlisted (+ 72 emergency accomm.)

Remarks: After decommissioning 15-7-94 from the U.S. Navy, was transferred 16-8-94 as a gift under the Grant-Aid program. Based at Casablanca. Refitted during fall 1995 in Spain.
Hull systems: Can transport 2,000 tons of cargo (500 tons max. for beaching) on 1,765 m^2 of deck space. A side-thruster propeller forward helps when marrying to a causeway. There is a 34-m-long, 75-ton-capacity mobile aluminum ramp forward, which is linked to the tank deck by a second from the upper deck. Aft is a 242-m^2 helicopter platform and a stern door for loading and unloading vehicles. The tank deck, which has a 75-ton-capacity turntable at both ends, can carry 229 M 48 tanks or 41 2.5-ton trucks, while the upper deck can accept 29 2.5-ton trucks. Normally carries three LCVPs and one LCP in Welin davits. Has two 10-ton cranes. Can carry 141,600 gallons of vehicle fuel.

♦ **3 French Champlain-class medium landing ships [LSM]**
Bldr: Dubigeon, Normandy

	In serv.
402 Daoud ben Aicha	28-5-77
403 Ahmed es Sakali	9-77
404 Abou Abdallah el Ayachi	12-78

Abou Abdallah el Ayachi (404) Martin Mokrus, 12-03

D: 750 tons (1,305 fl) **S:** 16 kts **Dim:** 80.0 (68.0 pp) × 13.0 × 2.4 (mean)
A: 2 single 40-mm 70-cal. Bofors AA; 2 single 12.7-mm mg; 2 single 81-mm mortars
Electronics: Radar: 1 Decca 1226 nav.; 1 . . . nav.
M: 2 SACM V-12 diesels; 2 CP props; 3,600 bhp
Range: 4,500/13 **Crew:** 30 officers, 54 enlisted

Remarks: First two ordered 12-3-75, third on 19-8-75. 402 refitted in France during 1995. Can carry 133 troops and about 12 vehicles; has a 330-ton beaching capacity. Can also carry 208 tons of potable water in ballast tanks. Have a helicopter platform aft.

♦ **1 French EDIC-class utility landing craft [LCU]**
Bldr: C.N. Franco-Belges (In serv. 1965)

401 Lieutenant Malghagh

D: 292 tons (642 fl) **S:** 8 kts **Dim:** 59.0 × 11.95 × 1.3 (1.62 fl)
A: 2 single 20-mm 70-cal. Oerlikon AA; 1 120-mm mortar

Lieutenant Malghagh (401)—with old pennant number 1977

Electronics: Radar: 1 Decca 1226 nav.
M: 2 MGO diesels; 2 props; 1,000 bhp **Range:** 1,800/8 **Crew:** 16 tot.

Remarks: Ordered in 1963. Can carry 11 trucks in the open vehicle well; has a bow ramp.

♦ **1 ex-French LCM(8)-class landing craft [LCM]**
Bldr: CMN, Cherbourg

. . . (ex-CTM 5)

D: 56 tons light (150 fl) **S:** 9.5 kts **Dim:** 23.80 × 6.35 × 1.25
A: 2 single 12.7-mm mg **Electronics:** Radar: 1 . . . nav.
M: 2 Poyaud 520 V8 diesels; 2 props; 480 bhp **Range:** 380/8
Fuel: 3.4 tons **Endurance:** 48 hr (at half power) **Crew:** 6 tot.

Remarks: Transferred 8-00. Cargo capacity: 90 tons.

AUXILIARIES

♦ **1 Robert D. Conrad–class oceanographic research ship [AGOR]**
Bldr: Northwest Marine, Portland, Ore.

	L	In serv.
702 Abou el Barakat al Barbari (ex-*Bartlett,* T-AGOR 13)	24-3-66	15-4-69

Abou el Barakat al Barbari (702) H&L Van Ginderen, 11-99

D: 1,088 tons light (1,643 fl) **S:** 13.5 kts
Dim: 63.7 (59.7 pp) × 11.4 × 4.9 (6.3 max. over sonar domes)
Electronics: Radar: 1 Raytheon 1650/SX nav.; 1 Raytheon 1660/12S nav.
M: 2 Cummins diesels, electric drive; 1 prop; 1,000 shp—1 350-shp JT700 Omnithruster (4.5 kts)
Electric: 850 kw tot. **Range:** 9,000/12; 8,500/9.5
Fuel: 211 tons **Endurance:** 45 days
Crew: 9 officers, 17 enlisted + 15 scientists/technicians

Remarks: Transferred 26-7-93. Renamed for a famous 12th-century Arab navigator. Formerly operated by MAR, Inc., Rockville, Md., under contract to the U.S. Military Sealift Command. The large stack contains a 620-hp gas-turbine generator set used to drive the main shaft at speeds up to 6.5 kts for experiments requiring "quiet" conditions. Sisters and near-sisters serve in Chile, Portugal, New Zealand, Tunisia, Brazil, and Mexico.

♦ **1 vehicle cargo ship [AK]**
Bldr: LNI (Lorient Naval Industries), Lanester, France (In serv. 1-8-97)

408 Ad Dakhla

Ad Dakhla (408) Bernard Prézelin, 7-97

AUXILIARIES *(continued)*

D: 1,105 tons light (2,160 fl) **S:** 12.5 kts (12 sust.)
Dim: 69.00 (64.00 wl) × 11.50 × 4.20 **A:** 2 12.7-mm mg
Electronics: Radar: 1 Decca BridgeMaster C181/6 nav.; 1 Decca BridgeMaster C324/8 nav.
M: 1 Wärtsilä Nohab 8V25 diesel; 1 CP prop; 2,693 bhp
Electric: 600 kVA tot. (2 × 300-kVA Leroy alternators, Wärtsilä-Scania UD19 L06 S4D diesels driving)
Range: 4,300/12 **Fuel:** 165 tons **Crew:** 24 tot. (accomm. for 46)

Remarks: 1,500 dwt. Ordered in 1995 to replace older support ships. The stern was built at the former Leroux & Lotz yard at St. Malo and the bow at Lanester; launched 6-97 at St. Malo, the ship was fitted out at Lorient.
Hull systems: Cargo: 800 tons max., including cargo fuel in the lower tanks. Has two folding hatch covers to permit carrying containerized cargo and can also load vehicles. Has one 17-ton electrohydraulic crane, mounted to starboard between the two cargo hatches. The hold has a continuous deck just above the waterline that is served by a 3.5-m-wide by 2.5-m-high vehicle door to starboard; vehicles can also be carried in the two lower holds. Carries 50 tons of fresh water (75 in emergencies).

♦ 1 former Danish cargo ship [AK]
Bldr: Fredrikshavn Værft & Tjrdok, Frederikshavn

405 El Aigh (ex-*Merc Caribe*) (In serv. 1972)

D: Approx. 2,000 tons (fl) **S:** 12 kts **Dim:** 76.61 × 12.30 × 3.47
A: 2 single 20-mm 70-cal. Oerlikon AA
Electronics: Radar: 2 . . . nav.
M: Burmeister & Wain Alpha, 10-cyl. diesel; 1 prop; 1,250 bhp
Range: . . . **Crew:** . . .

Remarks: 499 grt/326 nrt/1,327 dwt. Has an ice-strengthened hull with pronounced bulbous bow, two holds, and four 5-ton cranes. Acquired in 1981 to provide logistic support for operations along Saharan coast. Originally built for Per R. Henriksen P/R, Copenhagen. Bought in 1981 by the Moroccan Ministry of Travel and Commerce, then transferred to the navy. Sister *El Dakhla* (406; ex-*Anglian Merchant;* ex-*Merc Nordia*) was stricken during 1996.

SERVICE CRAFT

♦ 1 diving tender [YDT]

803 . . . (ex-14)

Remarks: Former small stern-haul fishing trawler, used for diver support and stores transport duties; no data available.

♦ 1 floating dry dock [YFDL] (Acquired from France in 1990)

Lift capacity: 4,500 tons **Dim:** 126.00 × 28.75 × . . .

♦ 1 royal yacht [YFL]
Bldr: C.N. Pise, Italy (In serv. 1981)

Oued Eddahab (ex-*Akhir*)

♦ 1 Spanish Y 171–class medium harbor tug [YTM]
Bldr: Izar (In serv. 12-93)

D: 10.5 tons **S:** 9 kts **Dim:** 9.5 × 3.1 × 0.9
M: 2 diesels; 2 waterjets; 400 bhp **Range:** 440/9

♦ 2 miscellaneous sail training craft [YTS]

Al Massira Boujdour

CUSTOMS SERVICE

Note: The Moroccan Customs Service cooperates with the navy in performing coastal patrol duties.

PATROL BOATS [WPB]

♦ 4 French Type P 32
Bldr: CMN, Cherbourg

	Laid down	L	In serv.
209 Erraid	4-86	26-12-87	18-3-88
210 Erracel	30-6-86	21-1-88	15-4-88
211 El Kaced	1-12-86	10-3-88	16-6-88
212 Essaid	. . .	19-5-88	4-7-88

Essaid (212) Carlo Martinelli, 9-96

D: 24 tons light (88.7 fl) **S:** 29 kts
Dim: 32.00 (30.09 pp) × 5.35 (4.92 wl) × 1.42 (hull)
A: 1 20-mm 90-cal. Oerlikon GAM-B01 AA
Electronics: Radar: 1 . . . nav.
M: 2 SACM-Wärtsilä UD30 V16 M7 diesels; 2 props; 2,540 bhp
Range: 1,200/12 **Crew:** 12 tot.

Remarks: Ordered 6-85. Wooden construction. Six near-sisters serve in the navy. One 20-mm AA has been removed, and the forward mount has been replaced by a newer weapon.

♦ 18 Arcor 46 class
Bldr: Arcor, C.N. d Aquitane, La Teste, France (In serv. 1987–88)

D 01 through D 18

Arcor 46–class D 08 Carlo Martinelli, 9-96

D: 12.3 tons (15.1 fl) **S:** 33 kts **Dim:** 14.50 × 4.00 × 1.20
A: 1 12.7-mm mg **Electronics:** Radar: 1 Furuno 701 nav.
M: 2 Poyaud-Wärtsilä UD18 V8 diesels; 2 props; 1,120 bhp
Range: 300/20 **Crew:** 6 tot.

Remarks: Ordered 6-85. Glass-reinforced plastic construction.

SERVICE CRAFT

♦ 2 Al Amane search-and-rescue craft [WYFL]
Bldr: Armon, . . . Spain (In serv. 3-03)

2344 Al Amane 2345 Al Baamrane

D: 68 tons (fl) **S:** 34 kts **Dim:** 15.75 × 4.48 × 1.05
M: 2 Volvo Penta D 12 diesels; 2 waterjets; 1,300 bhp **Crew:** 4 tot.

♦ 2 Al Whada search-and-rescue craft [WYFL]
Bldr: Auxnaval, . . . Spain (In serv. 2004)

1264 Al Whada 1265 Sebou

D: 70 tons (fl) **S:** 20 kts **Dim:** 20.7 × 5.8 × 1.8
M: 2 M.A.N. D2842 diesels; 2 props; 2,000 bhp **Crew:** 4 tot.

♦ 3 Assa-class search-and-rescue craft [WYFL]
Bldr: Schweers, Bardenfleth (In serv. 1991)

Assa Haouz Tariq

D: 40 tons (fl) **S:** 20 kts **Dim:** 19.4 × 4.8 × 1.3
M: 2 . . . diesels; 2 props; 1,400 bhp **Crew:** 6 tot.

♦ 5 Arcor 17 launches [WYFL]
Bldr: Arcor, C.N. d Aquitaine, La Teste, France (In serv. 1989–90)

D: . . . **S:** 50 kts **Dim:** 5.5 × 2.2 × 0.8
A: 1 7.62-mm mg **M:** . . .

Note: The gendarmerie also operates the search-and-rescue craft *Dghira*, *Loukouss*, *Rif*, *Souss*, *Al Dida*, 15 Arcor 55–class patrol boats delivered in 1992–95 and *Al Fida*, a 17-m craft delivered in 8-02.

MOZAMBIQUE

People's Republic of Mozambique

MARINHA MOÇAMBIQUE

Personnel: Approx. 200 total

Bases: Headquarters at Maputo, with minor facilities at Beira, Nacala, and Pemba and at Metangula on Lake Malawi

♦ 2 ex-South African Namicurra class
Bldr: Tornado Products, South Africa (In serv. 1980–81)

. . . (ex-Y 1507) . . . (ex-Y 1530)

D: 4 tons light (5.2 fl) **S:** 30 kts **Dim:** 9.5 × 2.7 × 0.8
A: 1 12.7-mm mg; 1 twin 7.62-mm mg;
Electronics: Radar: 1 Furuno . . . nav.
M: 2 Yamaha inboard-outboard gasoline engines; 2 props; 380 bhp
Range: 180/20 **Crew:** 4 tot.

Remarks: Glass-reinforced, plastic-hulled, catamaran-hulled harbor craft that can be land-transported on trailers. Both were transferred from South Africa on 14-9-04 with the electronics and propulsion systems donated by France. When fitted, the 7.62-mm twin mount is positioned aft in the cockpit, while the 12.7-mm mg is located at the aft edge of the pilothouse

Note: In 12-95 Portugal donated the new 11.2-m fisheries patrol and research launch *Alcantara Santos* for use by a government agency other than the navy; the craft has a beam of 3.69 m and a draft of 0.7 m and is powered by two Volvo Penta 63P diesels of 375 bhp each for speeds of up to 33 kts.

MYANMAR

Socialist Republic of the Union of Myanmar (formerly Burma)

TAMDAW LAY

Personnel: Approx. 13,000 total, including 800 naval infantry. There is also a reserve force with about 2,000 personnel available.

Bases: Headquarters at Yangon (formerly Rangoon), with facilities at Bassein, Hanggyi Island, Kyaukphu Island, Zadetkale (St. Luke's) Island, Mergui, Moulmein, Seikyi, and Sinmalaik. A Chinese-made maritime surveillance radar set was installed at Zadetkale Island during 2001.

Note: Many of the various radar systems listed on the ships and craft described below are probably no longer operational.

PATROL SHIPS [PS]

♦ **3 . . . -class 77-meter patrol ships**
Bldr: . . . China and Sinmalaik, Yangon

	In serv.
771 . . .	2001
. . .	2002
. . .	2003

D: 1,200 tons **S:** . . . kts **Dim:** 77.0 × . . . × . . .
A: 1 76-mm 62-cal. OTO Melara Compact DP; 2 single 40-mm . . . AA
Electronics: Radar: 1 . . . nav.

Remarks: May be fitted to carry antiship missiles. Hull is constructed in China with final assembly taking place in Myanmar.

Disposal note: The Ex-U.S. *Admirable*-class patrol ship *Yan Gyi Aung* (ex-*Creddock*, MSF 356) and ex-U.S. PCER 848–class patrol ship *Yan Taing Aung* (41; ex-*Farmington*, PCER 894) have both been retired by 2005. The former British River-class frigate *Mayu* (ex-*Fal*), acquired in 1947 and retired in 1979, is maintained on land as a museum and training facility at the Yangon Naval Base.

PATROL COMBATANTS [PG]

♦ **1 Danish Osprey class**
Bldr: Danyard AS, Frederikshavn (In serv. 5-80)

55 In Daw

In Ya (57)—since stricken NAVPIC Holland, 3-94

D: 385 tons (505 fl) **S:** 20 kts **Dim:** 49.95 (45.80 pp) × 10.5 (8.8 wl) × 2.75
A: 1 40-mm 60-cal. Bofors AA; 2 single 20-mm 70-cal. Oerlikon AA
Electronics: Radar: 1 . . . nav.
M: 2 Burmeister & Wain Alpha 16V23L-VO diesels; 2 CP props; 4,640 bhp
Electric: 359 kVA tot. **Range:** 4,500/16 **Crew:** 5 officers, 15 enlisted

Remarks: Operated by the navy for the People's Pearl and Fisheries Ministry on fisheries protection and economic exclusion zone patrol. Sister to the Namibian *Tobias Hainyeko*. Was armed in Myanmar. The helicopter flight deck aft is now cluttered with equipment and apparently not used. A rescue launch is recessed into the inclined ramp at stern.
Disposals: Sister *In Ma* (56) sank in 1987 and was not raised, and *In Ya* (57) remains in unmaintained reserve at Yangon, in poor condition.

GUIDED-MISSILE PATROL CRAFT [PTG]

♦ **6 Chinese Houxin (Type 343M or 037-II)**
Bldr: Qiuxin SY, Shanghai (In serv. 1996– . . .)

471 Maga	473 Duwa	475 . . .
472 Saittra	474 Zeyda	476 . . .

D: 430 tons (478 fl) **S:** 32 kts **Dim:** 62.00 × 7.20 × 2.24 (mean hull)
A: 4 C-801 SSM; 2 twin 37-mm 63-cal. Type 76A AA; 2 twin 14.5-mm 93-cal. Type 61 AA
Electronics: Radar: 1 Type 756 nav./surf. search; 1 Type 352C (Square Tie) missile targeting; 1 Type 341 (Rice Lamp) gun f.c.
M: 4 diesels; 4 props; 13,200 bhp **Range:** 750/18; 2,000/14 **Crew:** . . . tot.

Remarks: Two delivered early in 1996, two in 11-96, and two in 4-97. Are named for stars. The unsophisticated design is based on the obsolescent Haizhu-class subchaser/patrol boat. 475 was reportedly damaged in a collision during builder's trials in 8-96. Were not delivered with missiles aboard, and no missiles may have been provided.

Myanmar Houxin-class missile craft 475 or 476—during delivery voyage; note that the antiship missile racks at the stern do not have canister launchers fitted
92 Wing Det. A, RAAF, 4-97

Duwa (473)—moored with Hainan-class *Yan Aye Aung* (449) and *Yan Zwe Aung* (450)
NAVPIC Holland, 10-98

PATROL CRAFT [PC]

♦ **5 45-meter gunboats**
Bldr: Naval Dockyard, Yangon (In serv. 1996–2000)

551 through 555

D: 213 tons (fl) **S:** 30 kts **Dim:** 45.0 × 7.0 × 2.5
A: 2 single 40-mm 70-cal. Bofors AA; 3 triple
M: 2 MTU . . . diesels; 2 props; . . . bhp
Range: . . . / . . . **Crew:** 7 officers, 27 enlisted

Remarks: Construction reportedly begun in 1991. Steel-hulled craft.

♦ **10 Chinese Hainan class (Project 037)** (In serv. 1964–87)

441 Yan Sit Aung	446 Yan Min Aung
442 Yan Myat Aung	447 Yan Paing Aung
443 Yan Nyein Aung	448 Yan Win Aung
444 Yan Khwinn Aung	449 Yan Aye Aung
445 Yan Ye Aung	450 Yan Zwe Aung

Yan Nyein Aung (443)—moored with a sister and repair tender *Yan Long Aung* (200) NAVPIC Holland, 8-98

Yan Khwinn Aung (444) NAVPIC Holland, 3-94

PATROL CRAFT [PC] *(continued)*

D: 375 tons (392 fl) **S:** 30.5 kts **Dim:** 58.77 × 7.20 × 2.20 (hull)
A: 2 twin 57-mm 70-cal. DP; 2 twin 25-mm 80-cal. 2M-3M AA; 4 5-round RBU-1200 ASW RL; 2 BMB-2 d.c. mortars; 2 d.c. racks
Electronics:
Radar: 1 Type 756 nav.; 1 Pot Head surf. search
Sonar: Tamir-11 hull-mounted HF
M: 4 Type 12VEZ3025/Z diesels; 4 props; 8,800 bhp
Range: 2,000/14 **Crew:** 70 tot.

Remarks: Six delivered in 1-91 were refurbished PLAN units rather than new construction, and they were in poor material condition. Four additional, equally decrepit units were transferred in 3-94. All systems are obsolescent.

♦ 5 PGM 412 class
Bldr: Naval Dockyard, Yangon (In serv. 1983–88)

412 413 414 415 416

D: 128 tons (fl) **S:** 16 kts **Dim:** 33.5 × 6.7 × 2.0
A: 2 single 40-mm 60-cal. Bofors Mk 3 AA; 2 single 12.7-mm mg
M: 2 Deutz SBA 16MB216 LLKR diesels; 2 props; 2,720 bhp
Range: 1,400/14 **Crew:** 17 tot.

Remarks: Design was heavily influenced by the U.S.-built PGM 43 class, but they have a hull knuckle at the bow. Two additional units, completed 27-6-93 by the Myanmar Shipyard and named *Thihayarsar I* and *Thihayarsar II,* were assigned to the customs service.

♦ 2 U.S. 105-foot Commercial Cruiser aluminum patrol craft
Bldr: Swiftships, Morgan City, La.

422 (In serv. 31-3-79) 423 (In serv. 28-9-79)

D: 103 tons (111 fl) **S:** 24 kts **Dim:** 31.5 × 7.2 × 2.1
A: 2 single 40-mm 60-cal Mk 3 Bofors AA; 2 single 20-mm 70-cal. Oerlikon Mk 10 AA; 2 single 12.7-mm mg
Electronics: Radar: 1 . . . nav.
M: 2 MTU 12V331 TC81 diesels; 2 props; 1,920 bhp
Range: 1,200/18 **Fuel:** 21.6 tons **Crew:** 25 tot.

Remarks: Reportedly acquired via Vosper Pty, Singapore. Aluminum construction. Had a Raytheon 1500 Pathfinder navigational radar at delivery in 1980. Sister 421 was lost at sea in the early 1990s.

♦ 6 U.S. PGM 43 class
Bldr: Marinette Marine, Marinette, Wis. (405, 406: Peterson Bldrs, Sturgeon Bay, Wis.)

	In serv.		In serv.
401 (ex-PGM 43)	8-59	404 (ex-PGM 46)	9-59
402 (ex-PGM 44)	8-59	405 (ex-PGM 51)	6-61
403 (ex-PGM 45)	9-59	406 (ex-PGM 52)	6-61

U.S.-built PGM 43–class unit in Myanmar service NAVPIC Holland, 10-98

D: 100 tons (141 fl) **S:** 17 kts **Dim:** 30.81 × 6.45 × 2.30
A: 1 40-mm 60-cal. Mk 3 Bofors AA; 2 twin 20-mm 70-cal. Mk 24 Oerlikon AA; 2 single 12.7-mm M2 mg
Electronics: Radar: 1 EDO 320 (405, 406: Raytheon 1500 Pathfinder) nav.
M: 8 G.M. 6-71 diesels; 2 props; 2,040 bhp
Range: 1,000/16 **Fuel:** 16 tons **Crew:** 17 tot.

♦ 2 improved Y 301–class riverine patrol craft
Bldr: Similak, Burma (In serv. 1967)

Y 311 Y 312

D: 250 tons (fl) **S:** 14 kts (12 sust.) **Dim:** 37.0 × 7.3 × 1.1
A: 2 single 40-mm 60-cal. Bofors Mk 3 AA; 2 single 20-mm 70-cal. Oerlikon Mk 10 AA
M: 2 MTU–Mercedes-Benz diesels; 2 props; 1,000 bhp **Crew:** 37 tot.

Remarks: Differ in appearance from the Y 301 class in not having a funnel and in carrying both 40-mm AA on the main deck. All gunmounts have bulletproof shields.

♦ 10 Y 301–class riverine patrol craft
Bldr: Uljanik SY, Pula, Yugoslavia (In serv. 1957–60)

Y 301 through Y 310

D: 120 tons (150 fl) **S:** 13 kts **Dim:** 32.0 × 7.25 × 0.9
A: 2 single 40-mm 60-cal. Bofors Mk 3 AA
M: 2 Mercedes-Benz diesels; 2 props; 1,100 bhp **Crew:** 29 tot.

Remarks: At least one (Y 304) has a Vickers 2-pdr. (40-mm 45-cal.) AA on the forecastle vice one 40-mm Bofors. Do not have a radar.

Y 301 class

PATROL BOATS [PB]

♦ 6 Carpentaria-class fisheries patrol boats
Bldr: De Havilland Marine, Homebush Bay, Sydney, Australia (1979–80)

112 113 114 115 116 117

Carpentaria-class patrol boat in Myanmar service H&L Van Ginderen, 1980

D: 27 tons (fl) **S:** 27 kts **Dim:** 16.0 × 5.0 × 1.2
A: 1 20-mm 70-cal. Oerlikon Mk 10 AA or 12.7-mm mg
Electronics: Radar: 1 Decca 110 nav.
M: 2 G.M. 12V71 TI diesels; 2 props; 1,120 bhp **Range:** 700/22 **Crew:** 10 tot.

Remarks: Operated by the navy for the People's Pearl and Fisheries Ministry. Ordered 12-78. Sisters are in Indonesian and Solomon Islands forces. Aluminum construction.

♦ 4 18.3-meter-class riverine patrol boats
Bldr: Naval Dockyard, Yangon (In serv. 11-4-90)

Remarks: No data available, except that they are armed with three single 12.7-mm machineguns and displace 37 tons.

♦ 3 Yugoslav PB-90-class riverine patrol boats
Bldr: Brodotehnika, Belgrade (In serv. 1990)

424 425 426

D: 80 tons (90 fl) **S:** 32 kts (26 sust.) **Dim:** 27.35 × 6.55 × 1.15 (2.20 props)
A: 2 quadruple 20-mm 90-cal. M-75 AA
Electronics: Radar: 1 Decca 1226 nav.
M: 3 diesels; 3 props; 4,350 bhp
Range: 400/25 **Endurance:** 5 days **Crew:** 17 tot.

Remarks: Have four illumination/chaff RL on the foredeck.

♦ 9 30-ton-class riverine patrol boats
Bldr: Naval Dockyard, Yangon, Myanmar (In serv. 1980s)

11 12 13 14 15 16 17 18 19

D: 30 tons (37 fl) **S:** 10 kts **Dim:** 15.2 × 4.3 × 1.1
A: 1 20-mm 70-cal. Oerlikon Mk 10 AA
M: 2 Thornycroft RZ 6 diesels; 2 props; 250 bhp
Range: 400/8 **Crew:** 8 + 30–40 troops

Remarks: Low-freeboard-aft, high-forecastle craft capable of carrying a squad of troops.

♦ 6 U.S. PBR Mk II–class GRP-hulled patrol boats
Bldr: Uniflite, Bellingham, Wash. (In serv. 1978)

211 212 213 214 215 216

D: 8.9 tons (fl) **S:** 24 kts **Dim:** 9.73 × 3.53 × 0.81
A: 1 twin and 1 single 12.7-mm mg; 1 60-mm mortar
Electronics: Radar: 1 Raytheon 1900 nav.
M: 2 G.M. GV53N diesels; 2 waterjets; 430 bhp
Range: 150/23 **Crew:** 4–5 tot.

♦ 8 miscellaneous fisheries protection boats

511 520 521 522 523 901 905 906

Remarks: Typical Burmese fishing boats. 901 is of about 200 tons displacement, while the others are of about 50–80 tons. Each carries at least one machinegun.

PATROL BOATS [PB] *(continued)*

Naval modified fishing boat patrol boat 511 NAVPIC Holland, 9-98

AMPHIBIOUS WARFARE CRAFT

♦ 4 Aiyar Maung–class utility landing craft [LCU]

Bldr: Yokohama Yacht, Japan (L: 3-69)

604 AIYAR MAI 606 AIYAR MIN THA MEE
605 AIYAR MAUNG 607 AIYAR MIN THAR

Aiyar Maung (605) Yokohama Yacht, 1959

D: 250 tons (fl) **S:** 10 kts **Dim:** 38.25 × 9.14 × 1.4
M: 2 Kubota diesels; 2 props; 560 bhp **Cargo:** 100 tons **Crew:** 10 tot.

♦ 2 Sinde-class utility landing craft [LCU]

Bldr: Yokohama Yacht, Japan (In serv. 1978)

601 SINDE 602 HTONBO

Sinde (601) Yokohama Yacht, 1968

D: 220 tons (fl) **S:** 10 kts **Dim:** 29.50 × 6.72 × 1.4
M: 2 Kubota diesels; 2 props; 300 bhp **Cargo:** 50 tons, 30 passengers

♦ 1 U.S. LCU 1610–class utility landing craft [LCU]

Bldr: Southern SB (In serv. 10-67)

603 AIYAR LULIN (ex-U.S. LCU 1626)

D: 190 tons (342 fl) **S:** 11 kts **Dim:** 41.0 × 9.0 × 2.0
A: 2 single 20-mm 70-cal. Oerlikon Mk 10 AA
M: 4 G.M. Detroit Diesel 12007T diesels; 2 props; 1,000 bhp
Range: . . . / . . . **Fuel:** 10 tons **Crew:** 14 tot.

Remarks: Used as a transport. Transferred on completion; one of only two ships built to this design. Cargo capacity: 170 tons. Has bow and stern ramps.

♦ 10 ex-U.S. LCM(6) Mk 2–class landing craft [LCM]

701 through 710

D: 24 tons (64 fl) **S:** 10.2 kts (light) **Dim:** 17.07 × 4.37 × 1.22 (fwd.; 1.52 aft)
M: 2 G.M. Gray Marine 64HN9 diesels; 2 props; 330 bhp
Range: 140/10 (loaded) **Crew:** 4–5 tot.

LCM(6) landing craft in Myanmar Navy service NAVPIC Holland, 8-98

Remarks: Origins unknown. Can carry 34 tons of cargo or 80 fully equipped troops for short distances in the 11.43 × 3.35-m cargo well, which has a total area of 38.37 m^2 of usable space. Not discarded in 1996 as reported earlier.

♦ 8 riverine troop ferries [LCP]

Bldr: . . ., Yangon (In serv. 1960s)

SABAN SEINMA SETYAHAT SHWETHIDA
SAGU SETHAYA SHWEPAZUN SINMIN

D: 99 tons (fl) **S:** 12 kts **Dim:** 28.8 × 6.7 × 1.4 **A:** see remarks
M: 1 Crossley ERL-6 diesel; 1 prop; 160 bhp **Crew:** 23–32 + . . . troops

Remarks: *Seinma, Shwethida,* and *Sinmin* carry one 20-mm Oerlikon AA; *Sagu* is equipped with three single 20-mm AA and differs from the others in lacking a full permanent awning above the upper deck. Typical riverine passenger vessels, with low freeboard and open superstructure (with many sections protected by light plating).

AUXILIARIES

♦ 1 coastal hydrographic survey ship [AGS]

Bldr: Miho Zosen, Shimizu, Japan (In serv. 20-6-69)

802 . . . (ex-*Changi*)

D: Approx. 900 tons (fl) **S:** 13 kts **Dim:** 47.0 × 8.7 × 3.6
A: 2 single 20-mm 70-cal. Oerlikon Mk 10 AA
M: 1 Niigata diesel; 1 prop; . . . bhp **Crew:** 35 tot.

Remarks: 387 grt/118 dwt. Former Singapore-registry stern-haul fisheries research trawler, arrested 8-4-74 and commissioned for service as a survey vessel.

♦ 1 hydrographic survey ship [AGS]

Bldr: Tito SY, Belgrade, Yugoslavia (In serv. 1965)

801 THU TAY THI

Thu Tay Thi (801)

D: 1,100 tons (1,271 fl) **S:** 15 kts **Dim:** 62.21 (56.80 pp) × 11.00 × 3.60
A: 2 single 40-mm 60-cal. Bofors Mk 3 AA; 2 single 20-mm 70-cal. Oerlikon Mk 10 AA
M: 2 MB820Db diesels; 2 props; 1,710 bhp **Crew:** 7 officers, 92 enlisted

Remarks: Carries two inshore survey craft. Armament had been added by 6-93, with one mount in the center of what had been intended as a helicopter platform.

♦ 1 coastal cargo ship [AK]

Bldr: A/S Nordsøværftet, Ringkobing, Norway (In serv. 1975)

. . . PYI DAW AYE

Pyi Daw Aye (. . .) NAVPIC Holland, 8-98

D: Approx. 850 tons (fl) **S:** 11 kts **Dim:** 49.71 (44.46 pp) × 8.34 × 3.46
M: 1 . . . diesel; 1 prop; 600 bhp **Crew:** 12 tot.

Remarks: 300 grt/699 dwt. Has two cargo holds and two light cargo derricks. Remains in commission in very poor condition.

AUXILIARIES *(continued)*

♦ **1 coastal tanker [AOT]**
Bldr: Shimoda Dockyard, Shimoda, Japan (In serv. 1974)

609 . . . (ex-*Seria Maru*)

Myanmar Navy tanker 609 NAVPIC Holland, 10-98

D: Approx. 2,600 tons (fl) **S:** 10 kts **Dim:** 68.66 × 11.00 × 5.00
M: 1 Daihatsu diesel; 1 prop; 1,300 bhp
Range: . . . / . . . **Crew:** . . . tot.

Remarks: 972 grt/2,034 dwt. Former Japanese coastal fuels tanker, acquired around 1986.

♦ **1 coastal tanker [AOT]**
Bldr: Watanabe Zosen K.K., Hakata, Japan (In serv. 1969)

608 . . . (ex-*Inter Bunker,* ex-*Shamrock Ace,* ex-*Bunker SPC VI,* ex-*Naniwa Maru No. 33*)

Myanmar Navy tanker 608 NAVPIC Holland, 10-98

D: Approx. 2,800 tons (fl) **S:** 11.5 kts **Dim:** 70.69 (65.00 pp) × 11.00 × 4.93
M: 2 Daihatsu 8-cyl. diesels; 1 prop; 1,860 bhp
Electric: 128 kw tot (2 × 64-kw diesel sets)
Range: 5,400/11.5 **Fuel:** 98.5 tons **Crew:** 15 tot.

Remarks: 992 grt/2,209 dwt. Honduran-registry commercial vessel owned by Thai company Suphachal Chareonsri, arrested 10-91 and taken over for Myanmar Navy service. No underway replenishment capability. Has cargo expansion trunk over cargo tank area.

SERVICE CRAFT

♦ **1 presidential yacht [YAG]**
Bldr: . . . (In serv. 1980s)

Ya Dana Bon

Remarks: Three-decked, white-painted riverine transport for use on the Irrawaddy River. Operated by the navy. Reported to carry two single 7.62-mm mg.

♦ **1 diving and repair tender [YDT]**
Bldr: . . ., Japan (In serv. 1967)

200 Yan Long Aung

Yan Long Aung (200)—alongside a Hainan-class patrol craft NAVPIC Holland, 10-98

D: 536 tons (fl) **S:** 12 kts **Dim:** 54.6 × 9.1 × 2.4
A: 1 40-mm 60-cal. Mk 3 Bofors AA; 2 single 12.7-mm mg
M: 2 . . . diesels; 2 props; . . . bhp **Crew:** 88 tot.

Remarks: Formerly a torpedo retriever and torpedo boat tender. Carries a landing craft–type workboat on the starboard quarter.

♦ **25 30- to 40-ton river launches [YFL]**
Bldr: Yugoslavia (In serv. 1965)

Naval personnel launch 053 NAVPIC Holland, 10-98

Remarks: No data available. There are likely also numerous locally built launches and service craft for which no information is available.

♦ **1 riverine hydrographic survey boat [YGS]**
Bldr: Netherlands (In serv. 1957)

807 Yay Bo

D: 108 tons (fl) **S:** 10 kts **Dim:** 30.0 × 6.8 × 1.5
A: 1 12.7-mm mg **M:** 2 . . . diesels; 2 props; . . . bhp
Crew: 2 officers, 32 enlisted

NAMIBIA

FISHERIES PROTECTION SERVICE

Personnel: Approx. 200 total

Bases: Walvis Bay and Lüderitz

Maritime Aviation: Five ex-U.S. Air Force Cessna O-2A observation aircraft, transferred 26-6-94, operate from Eros Airport, Windhoek, as maritime surveillance and antipoaching patrol assets.

Note: All ships and craft carry "Fisheries Patrol" on the sides of their superstructures.

PATROL SHIPS [PS]

♦ **1 Imperial Marinheiro class**
Bldr: L. Smit, Kinderdijk, Netherlands

	L	In serv.
C 11 Lt Gen Jeromboam Dimo Hamaambo (ex-*Purus*)	6-11-54	4-55

Lt Gen Jeromboam Dimo Hamaambo (C 11) Piet Sinke, 10-05

D: 911 tons (960 fl) **S:** 15 kts **Dim:** 55.72 × 9.55 × 3.6
A: 1 . . .-mm AA; see remarks **Electronics:** Radar: 1 Decca . . . nav.
M: 2 Sulzer diesels; 2 props; 2,160 bhp
Range: . . . / . . . **Fuel:** 135 tons **Crew:** 5 officers, 65 enlisted

Remarks: Transferred from Brazil in 2004. Oceangoing tug design with 15-ton bollard pull towing capacity. While in Brazilian service, the vessel was fitted with one 76.2-mm 50-cal. U.S. Mk 26 DP and 4 single 20-mm 70-cal. Oerlikon Mk 10 AA. Current armament fit is still unknown.

PATROL CRAFT [PC]

♦ **1 Graúna class** Bldr: INACE, Fortaleza, Ceará (In serv. 2006)

Brendan Simbwaye

Graúna-class patrol craft—artist's rendering Brazilian Navy, 2003

D: 213 tons light, 242 tons normal (263 fl) **S:** 24.3 kts (22 sust.; 26.5 on trials)
Dim: 46.50 (42.50 pp) × 7.50 × 2.30
A: 1 40-mm 70-cal. Bofors 40L/70350 AA and 2 single 20-mm 90-cal. Oerlikon
Electronics: Radar: 1 Decca 1290A nav. (I-band)
M: 2 MTU 16V396 TB94 diesels; 2 props; 6,688 bhp (5,560 sust.)
Electric: 300 kw tot. (2 × 100-kw diesel sets, 1 × 100-kw shaft generator)
Range: 2,200/12 **Fuel:** 23.25 tons **Endurance:** 18 days
Crew: 4 officers, 25 enlisted

Remarks: Ordered in 2003, the vessel was newly constructed, rather than transferred from Brazil. Used for fisheries patrol duty.

PATROL COMBATANTS [PG]

♦ **2 Nathaniel Maxuilili–class fisheries protection ships**

	Bldr.	In serv.
Nathaniel Maxuilili	Moen Slip A/S, Kolvereid, Norway	14-5-02
Anna Kakurukaze Mungunda	Freire, Vigo, Spain	10-2-04

Anna Kakurukaze Mungunda Piet Sinke, 10-05

Anna Kakurukaze Mungunda Piet Sinke, 10-05

D: 1,500 tons **S:** 17 kts **Dim:** 57.6 × 12.5 × 4.2
A: 1 12.7-mm mg **Electronics:** Radar: 2 . . . nav./surf. search
M: 2 . . . diesels; . . . props; 2,040 bhp

Remarks: First unit ordered 9-99. Financed by the Norwegian development aid agency NORAD. Has a helicopter deck aft and carries two RIB inspection craft. *Anna Kakurukaze Mungunda* is 59-m long.

♦ **1 Danish Osprey-class fisheries protection ship**
Bldr: Danyard A/S, Frederikshavn (In serv. 1979)

Tobias Hainyeko (ex-*Havørnen*)

Tobias Hainyeko Piet Sinke, 10-05

D: 320 tons (506 fl) **S:** 18 kts **Dim:** 49.98 (45.80 pp) × 10.50 × 2.75
A: 1 12.7-mm mg
Electronics: Radar: 1 Furuno FRM 64 nav.; 1 Furuno FR 1525 ARPA surf. search
M: 2 Burmeister & Wain Alpha 16V23L-VO diesels; 2 CP props; 4,640 bhp
Range: 4,500/16 **Crew:** 15 tot. (accomm. for 35)

Remarks: Donated by the Danish government and transferred in fall 1993. Had been operated since completion by the Danish Ministry of Fisheries. Has a stern hangar and ramp for a 6.5-m rubber inspection dinghy. Built to mercantile specifications. Has a helicopter deck, but the original hangar has been blanked off. Five Danish naval officers formed part of the complement through 1998. Was unarmed in Danish service.

PATROL CRAFT [PC]

♦ **1 fisheries patrol craft/yacht**
Bldr: Burmester Yacht und Bootswerft, Bremen, Germany (In serv. 5-75)

P 01 Oryx (ex-*S To S*)

Oryx (P 01) Piet Sinke, 10-05

D: 406 tons (fl) **S:** 14 kts **Dim:** 45.67 (40.95 pp) × 9.12 × 2.94
A: 1 12.7-mm mg
Electronics: Radar: 1 Furuno FR 1525 ARPA nav.; 1 Furuno FR 805D nav.
M: 2 Deutz RSBA16M528 diesels; 1 CP prop; 2,000 bhp—bow-thruster
Electric: 184 kw tot. (2 × 92-kw diesel sets)
Range: 4,100/11 **Crew:** 6 officers, 14 enlisted

Remarks: 454 grt. Transferred at independence from the South African government 12-02 and is based at Walvis Bay and used for fisheries patrol. Formerly the yacht of the managing director of Fiat, Italy. Bow built by Abeking & Rasmussen, Lemwerder. Machinery is aft.

PATROL BOATS [PB]

♦ **4 Tracker-20-class patrol craft**
Bldr: Estaleiro do Sul, Porto Alegre, Brazil (In serv. 2005–6)

D: 39 tons (45 fl) **S:** 25 kts **Dim:** 20.90 (19.3 pp) × 5.18 × 1.55
A: 2 single 12.7-mm M2 mg **Electronics:** Radar: 1 Decca RM 1070A nav.
M: 2 MTU 8V396 TB83 diesels; 2 props; 2,000 bhp
Electric: 40 kw (2 × 20 kw) **Range:** 450/15
Fuel: 4.66 tons **Endurance:** 5 days **Crew:** 2 officers, 6 enlisted

Remarks: Ordered in 2003, these vessels were newly constructed units, rather than transfers from Brazil.

♦ **2 ex-South African Namicurra class**
Bldr: Tornado Products, South Africa (In serv. 1980–81)

Y 01 (ex-Y 1501) Y 10 (ex-Y 1530)

PATROL BOATS [PB] *(continued)*

Y 10 Piet Sinke, 10-05

D: 4 tons light (5.2 fl) **S:** 30 kts **Dim:** 9.5 × 2.7 × 0.8
A: 1 12.7-mm mg; 1 twin 7.62-mm mg;
Electronics: . . .
M: 2 Yamaha inboard-outboard gasoline engines; 2 props; 380 bhp
Range: 180/20 **Crew:** 4 tot.

Remarks: Glass-reinforced, plastic-hulled, catamaran-hulled harbor craft that can be land-transported on trailers. Both were transferred from South Africa on 29-10-02. When fitted, the 7.62-mm twin mount is positioned aft in the cockpit, while the 12.7-mm mg is located at the aft edge of the pilothouse

AUXILIARIES

♦ 1 fisheries research ship [WAGOR]
Bldr: Barens SB, Durban, South Africa (In serv. 10-68)

BENGUELA

D: Approx. 850 tons (fl) **S:** 12 kts **Dim:** 44.20 (37.50 pp) × 9.48 × 3.67
M: 2 Burmeister & Wain Alpha 406-26VO diesels; 1 CP prop; 1,200 bhp—2 bow-thrusters
Electric: 500 kw tot. (2 × 250-kw diesel sets)
Range: . . . / . . . **Fuel:** 122 tons **Crew:** . . . tot.

Remarks: 486 grt/142 dwt. Transferred by the government of South Africa at independence and is based at Walvis Bay and used for fisheries patrol. Stern-haul trawler design.

Note: Other small government fisheries research craft, for which no data are available, include the *Kuiseb, Nautilus II,* and *Welwitschia.*

SERVICE CRAFT

♦ 2 Buccaneer Legend rigid inflatable launches [WYFL]
Bldr: Buccaneer Inflatables, Glenvista, South Africa (In serv. 1993)

D: 1.2 tons light (3.5 tons fl) **S:** 37 kts **Dim:** 8.00 × 2.60 × . . .
A: 1 12.7-mm mg **M:** 1 Cummins . . . diesel; 1 prop; 320 bhp

Remarks: Ordered in late 1992 for rescue and patrol duties. Have a semi-rigid aluminum lower hull with flexible upper collar.

NATO
North Atlantic Treaty Organization

Note: The vessels described below are the only vessels "owned" jointly by the NATO nations. There are, however, two standing NATO Response Force Maritime Groups (SNMG) each of six to ten frigates and destroyers, which can be augmented in time of war by warships from the major signatory nations, and two standing NATO Response Force Mine Countermeasures Groups (SNMC-MG) which generally contain seven mine-countermeasures vessels plus a single command ship.

AUXILIARIES

♦ 1 Alliance-class research ship [WAGE]

	Bldr	L	In serv.
A 1956 ALLIANCE	Fincantieri, Muggiano	9-7-86	6-5-88

D: 2,466 tons (3,180 fl) **S:** 17 kts (16.3 sust.)
Dim: 93.00 (82.00 pp) × 15.20 × 5.10
Electronics:
Radar: 2 Qubit–Kelvin-Hughes Nucleus 6000 nav. (X- and S-band)
Sonar: STN Atlas Elektronik Hydrosweep mapping (50 kHz)
M: 2 GMT B.230.12M diesels, AEG CC 3127 generators, electric drive: 2 AEG 1,470-kw motors; 2 props; 4,000 shp—side-thrusters fore and aft
Electric: 1,850 kw tot. (including 1 1,605-kw Kongsberg gas-turbine set)
Range: 8,000/12 **Crew:** 10 officers, 17 unlicensed + 23 scientists

Remarks: 3,200 grt/533 dwt. Based at Naples and operated for the NATO ASW Research Center, La Spezia, by U.K. Denholm SERCO Ship Management, with German Naval Auxiliary Service officers and multinational nonrated personnel. Flies the German flag. Sister *Ta Kuan* was delivered to Taiwan in 1995, and a near-sister, configured as an intelligence collector, is in service with the Italian Navy.

Alliance (A 1956)—white painted, with buff-colored stacks and foremast; does not wear pennant number Martin Mokrus, 2-04

Hull systems: Has 6,100 m^2 of total working deck space and 400 m^2 of lab space. Has a towing winch, with 20-ton bollard pull, and 6,000 m of 50-mm cable. Also has a 1,000-kg oceanographic crane with telescopic arm. Special attention is paid to quieting. Has Flume-type passive tank stabilization. Pennant number (not borne) is from a block assigned to the German Navy. During 1991, began trials with a 64-hydrophone vertical-array towed passive sonar system. An STN Atlas Elektronik Hydrosweep MD multibeam echo sounder was ordered for the ship during 3-93; it covers a swath 2 km wide in waters up to 1 km deep. Other modernizations effected were substitution of Qubit–Kelvin-Hughes radars and installation of a Magnavox precision navigation system, Qubit–Kelvin-Hughes TRAC integrated navigation and information management systems, two GPS receivers, two LORAN-C receivers, and a Decca radio-navigation chain receiver. The modernization was completed during 4-95. Trials were conducted during 1995 with a 4-tonne, dual-frequency (200 Hz, 4 kHz) towed vertically directive source developed by the U.S. Office of Naval Research and Naval Undersea Warfare Center.

The Ultra Electronics Deployable Undersea Sensing System (DUSS) began trials in the ship during mid-2002. The system employs an active transmitter combined with a number of receive buoys linked by the SATCOM array and wideband terrestrial communications.

SERVICE CRAFT

♦ 1 oceanographic tender [YAGE]
Bldr: McTay Marine, Liverpool, U.K. (In serv. 6-9-02)

LEONARDO

Leonardo Luciano Grazioli, 9-04

D: 393 tons (fl) **S:** 11.5 kts sust. **Dim:** 28.60 × 9.00 × 2.50
Electronics: Radar: 1 Sperry X-band E 250 nav.; 1 Sperry S-band E 250 nav.
M: 2 Cummins . . . diesels, electric drive; 2 Schottel azimuthal props; . . . shp—azimuthal bow-thruster
Range: 1,500/11 **Crew:** 5 + a scientific party of up to 7

Remarks: Ordered 19-12-00. The hull was built in Poland by Remontowa Ship Repair, Gdansk, for fitting out in the U.K. An A-frame gallows crane has been installed at the stern. This craft replaces the *Manning* (ex-U.S. Army T-514), which was retired early in 2002. Used for studies of the effect of the sea floor on acoustic energy, propagation studies, and demonstration projects. Is actually owned by the Italian Ministry of Defense. Navigation equipment includes a Sperry SR180 Mk 1 gyrocompass, Navipol fluxgate compass, Navitwin III universal data repeater, and Kongsberg Simrad navigation system.

SERVICE CRAFT *(continued)*

Note: The NATO Submarine Rescue System (NSRS), expected in service by early 2007 is being built by Rolls-Royce and is financed primarily by the United Kingdom, France, and Norway. Expected to displace 2.4 tons and measure 2.8-m long, the NSRS, will be based at Faslane, Scotland, and replace the British LR5 now operational with the British Royal Navy.

NETHERLANDS

Kingdom of the Netherlands

NAVY

Personnel: 8,080 total including 950 naval aviation personnel, plus 3,100 marines and 5,000+ reservists

Bases: Headquarters at The Hague, with the main naval base at Den Helder and helicopter facilities at de Kooij Naval Air Station, near Den Helder. Minor facilities are also located at Curaçao in the Caribbean. Bases at Valkenberg and Vlissingen were closed during 2005. The Belgian naval staff was formally integrated with that of the Netherlands at Den Helder on 28-3-95.

Naval Aviation: Due to budget cuts, the last remaining P-3C Orion maritime patrol aircraft were retired in 2005 (eight were sold to Germany and five to Portugal). 20 Westland SH-14D Lynx helicopters are in service and are eventually to be replaced by 22 NH-90 helicopters, between 2007 and 2012. Seven Netherlands Army 300 Squadron Cougar helicopters have been adapted for use from the *Rotterdam* (L 800).

SH-14D Lynx Frank Findler, 7-05

Royal Netherlands Marines: Bases at Rotterdam, Doorn, and Texel (where landing craft are maintained) and training facilities at Amsterdam. Detachment at Aruba. Organized into four combat battalions, one combat support battalion (with two motorized companies, one landing craft company, and a special boat section), and one logistic support battalion.

WEAPONS AND SYSTEMS

A. MISSILES

♦ Surface-to-air missiles

U.S. SM-2 MR Block IIIA on the *De Zeven Provinciën*–class frigates. U.S. RIM-7M Sea Sparrow on the *Karel Doorman*–class frigates. RIM-7P Evolved Sea Sparrow in the *De Zeven Provinciën*–class frigates. Data for all can be found in the U.S.A. section.

♦ Surface-to-surface missiles

U.S. RGM-84 Harpoon on the *De Zeven Provinciën* and *Karel Doorman* classes. Sub-Harpoon was not acquired for the submarines. In 11-05, 30 Tomahawk Block IV land-attack cruise missiles were ordered from the United States. The missiles will begin arming the first two *De Zeven Provinciën*–class frigates (*De Zeven Provinciën* and *Tromp*) in 2008.

B. GUNS

127-mm 54-cal. OTO Melara DP: On the *De Zeven Provinciën*–class guided-missile frigates. These are refurbished mountings previously used aboard the Canadian Tribal class. See the Italy section for data.

76-mm OTO Melara Compact: On the *Karel Doorman*–class frigates. Upgraded to fire at 100 rds/min. See the Italy section for further data.

30-mm SGE-30 Goalkeeper: Uses the U.S. General Electric GAU-8A 30-mm gatling gun and EX-30 mounting, co-mounted with a Thales Nederland (formerly Hollandse Signaal-Apparaaten/H.S.A.) track-while-scan radar fire-control system. The latter uses independent I-band search/acquisition and I/K-band tracking radars. The seven-barreled gatling gun has a 4,200-rd/min maximum rate of fire; 1,190 rounds are carried on-mount. Muzzle velocity is 1,021 m/sec. Total weight, with ammunition, is 6,372 kg.

20-mm 90-cal. Oerlikon AA: In modern GIAT 20F-2 mountings on mine-countermeasures vessels (to be replaced by two single 12.7-mm Browning M2 mg during 2004); old Oerlikon 70-cal. weapons in U.S.-style Mk 10 pintle mountings on frigates, minesweepers, and auxiliaries.

C. ANTISUBMARINE WEAPONS

U.S. Mk 46 Mod. 5 torpedoes on ships and aircraft, and U.S. NT-37C/D/E (reworked Mk 37) and Mk 48 Mod. 4 torpedoes on submarines.

D. RADARS

All designed and manufactured by Thales Nederland (formerly the Hollandse Signaal-Apparaaten [H.S.A.] division of Thomson-CSF). Thales Nederland and the multinational EADS established ET Marinesysteme GmbH on 19-4-01 to maintain existing H.S.A. combat systems on German and Dutch naval units, develop the combat system for the German Type 130 corvette program, continue development of the APAR radar, and cooperate on development of a joint Maritime Tactical Ballistic Missile Defence system.

Name	*Type*	*Band*
ZW-07	Submarine nav./surf. search	I
LW-08	Long-range air search	D
DA-08	Medium-range air search	E/F
MW-08*	Air search, multitrack	G
SEAPAR**	ESSM Sea Sparrow f.c.	X (I/J-band)
Scout	Low-interceptable nav./search	X; 1 mw to 1 w output
SMART*	3-D air search	L (F)
STING	Lightweight automatic f.c.	I/K dual-freq.
STIR***	Missile and gunfire control	I/K (X + Ka)
Surf	Low-interceptable air/surf. search	4-watt max. output; 30-km range
LIROD-8	Radar, optronic weapon control	K

***SMART-L (Signaal Multibeam Acquisition Radar for Targeting, L-band):** Delivery of 20 successor SMART-L sets began in the late 1990s. Range against an air target is 400 km, and up to 1,000 targets can be tracked. MW-08 is essentially a G-band variant and can detect and track up to 20 air and 10 surface contacts simultaneously.

****SEAPAR (Self-defense ESSM Active Phased-Array Radar):** Being developed by a Raytheon/Thales Nederland consortium for the NATO Sea Sparrow Project Office as a fire-control radar to take advantage of the longer-range ESSM version of the Sea Sparrow missile. It will employ technology developed for Raytheon's SPY-3 and the Thales Nederland APAR radar.

*****STIR (Separate Tracking and Illumination Radar):** Has 1.8- or 2.9-m-dia. parabolic dish antennas and a co-mounted t.v. camera.

APAR (Active Phased Array Radar): Under development in cooperation with Canada and Germany for use on future frigates. As APAR STIR, it would employ four fixed faces and act as part of the weapons-control system.

Seven Thales Squire battlefield surveillance radar sets were ordered for the Royal Netherlands Marines late in 2000.

E. ELECTRO-OPTICAL DEVICES

IRSCAN: Omnidirectional passive surveillance system by Thales Nederland. Rotates at 78 rpm and has a range of 15 km against aircraft and 12 km against missiles. Total system weighs only 560 kg.

Mirador: Developed by Thales Nederland for use in detecting, tracking, and identifying targets in poor visibility. Can perform three-dimensional target acquisition and tracking using two daylight t.v. cameras, a thermal imager, a laser rangefinder, and a low-light t.v. camera, all on a common mounting.

F. SONARS

DSQS-24C: STN Atlas Elektronik hull mounted sonar carried in *De Zeven Provinciën* class
ALF: Active Low Frequency towed sonar being developed for the *De Zeven Provinciën* class
DUBM-21: Thales HF minehunting array
DUUX-5: Thales Fenelon passive-ranging
Octopus: Active/passive submarine array on the *Walrus* class, derived from the Thales TSM-2272 Eledone
PHS-32, MF: Export sonar, hull-mounted or VDS (9.3, 10.5, or 11.7 kHz)
PHS-36, MF: License-built Canadian SQS-509 on the *Karel Doorman*–class frigates (5.5, 6.5, 7.5 kHz)
Type 2026: British passive linear towed hydrophone array for submarines

G. ELECTRONIC WARFARE

In use are the British Scimitar J-band deception and jamming system, Rapids I 18-GHz passive intercept array, and Ramses I/J-band passive and deceptive repeater equipment. Boeing Argo Systems APECS-2/AR-700 intercept equipment is installed on *Karel Doorman*–class frigates.

ATTACK SUBMARINES [SS]

♦ 4 Walrus class

Bldr: Rotterdamse Droogdok Maatschappij, Rotterdam

	Laid down	L	Trials	In serv.
S 802 Walrus	11-10-79	28-10-85	12-9-90	25-3-92
S 803 Zeeleeuw	24-9-81	20-6-87	28-10-88	25-4-90
S 808 Dolfijn	12-6-86	25-4-90	10-9-91	29-1-93
S 810 Bruinvis	14-4-88	25-4-92	5-3-93	5-7-94

ATTACK SUBMARINES [SS] *(continued)*

Bruinvis (S 810) Frank Findler, 1-05

Dolfijn (S 808) Leo Van Ginderen, 6-05

Walrus (S 802) Derek Fox, 4-04

D: 1,900 tons light, 2,465 tons surf./2,800 tons sub.
S: 13 kts surf./21 kts sub. **Dim:** 67.73 × 8.40 × 7.00
A: 4 bow 533-mm TT (20 Mk 48 Mod. 4 and NT-37D torpedoes or 40 mines)
Electronics:
Radar: 1 ZW-07 (Decca Type 1001) nav./surf. search
Sonar: Thales Octopus (TSM 2272 Eledone) active/passive; GEC Avionics Type 2026 linear clip-on passive array; Thales DUUX-5 Fenelon passive-ranging
EW: Boeing ArgoSystems AR 700 intercept
M: 3 SEMT-Pielstick 12 PA4V 200VG (S 808, S 810: Brons-Werkspoor 0-RUB 215X121) diesels (2,300 bhp each), 3 Holec Type 304 980-kw alternators, 1 Holec motor; 1 7-bladed prop; 3,950 shp surf./5,430 shp sub.
Range: 10,000/9 (snorkel) **Fuel:** 310 tons **Endurance:** 60 days
Crew: 7 officers, 45 enlisted

Remarks: First two were ordered 19-6-78 and 17-12-79, respectively. Second pair was authorized 5-1-84, with S 808 ordered 16-10-84 and S 810 on 16-8-85. Construction of the first pair was delayed by the need to lengthen the hull after the keels had been laid in order to accommodate larger diesel generator sets. S 802 was severely damaged by fire 14-8-86, returned to land 2-5-87 for repairs, and relaunched 13-9-89. Plans to construct two more units were canceled in 7-88. Active units operate at sea about 120 days per year. Hairline cracks in the inboard section of diesel-exhaust piping caused a halt to submerged operations during 10-00; S 808 returned to full service on 25-11-00, S 810 in 12-00, and S 802 in mid-2001, while S 803 completed a refit in 2-01. Are planned to receive midlife modernizations, possibly with a section added to contain an air-independent auxiliary propulsion plant, starting in 2009. S 810 was damaged in a collision with a surface ship on 25-10-01, S 808 suffered rudder damage 14-6-03 while operating submerged southwest of England.
Hull systems: Propulsion plant is on resilient mountings to reduce noise emissions. Each Holec ac/dc generator has built-in rectifiers and produces 980 kw. There are three 140-cell batteries. Diving depth: 300 m; periscope depth: 18 m. Has X-configuration stern control surfaces and sail-mounted bow planes. Hull construction is of MAREL steel, with single-hull midbody and double-hull ends; reserve buoyancy is 12%. S 803 was equipped with an enlarged snorkel exhaust defuser at the aft end of the sail during a 1996 yard period; the others now have it as well.
Combat systems: First two have the SEWACO VIII combat data system with seven-console GIPSY (*Geïntegreerd In Formatie en Presentatie Systeem*) data display system; the second pair have the SEWACO VII data system with SMR-MV data processor. All are equipped with the Sperry Mk 29 Mod. 2A inertial navigation system and receivers for GPS and have NATO Link 11 datalink capabilities, using a 450-m floating wire antenna. Torpedo tubes are of the U.S. Mk 67 "water-slug" type, capable of launching at any operational depth. They are fitted to launch UGM-84-series Sub-Harpoon antiship missiles, but none have been procured. The Eledone sonar suite includes a medium-range active sonar, flank passive arrays, and a sonar intercept array. Have Kollmorgen Model 76 search and attack periscopes, with integral ranging radar and intercept antennas.

GUIDED-MISSILE FRIGATES [FFG]

♦ 4 De Zeven Provinciën class
Bldr: Schelde Shipbuilding, Vlissingen

	Laid down	L	In serv.
F 802 De Zeven Provinciën	1-9-98	8-4-00	26-4-02
F 803 Tromp	3-9-99	7-4-01	14-3-03
F 804 De Ruyter	1-9-00	13-4-02	22-4-04
F 805 Evertsen	6-9-01	19-4-03	10-6-05

De Zeven Provinciën (F 802) Leo Van Ginderen, 4-05

Evertsen (F 805) Frank Findler, 4-05

De Zeven Provinciën (F 802) Leo Van Ginderen, 4-05

D: 4,400 tons (6,200 fl) **S:** 30 kts (19 on diesels)
Dim: 144.24 (130.20 pp) × 18.82 (17.15 wl) × 5.18 (mean hull)
A: 8 RGM-84F Harpoon Block ID SSM; 40-cell Mk 41 VLS (32 Standard SM-2 Block IIIA and 32 RIM-162 Evolved Sea Sparrow SAM); 1 127-mm 54-cal. OTO Melara DP; 2 30-mm Goalkeeper CIWS; 2 single 12.7-mm Browning M2 mg; 4 fixed, paired 324-mm Mk 32 Mod. 9 ASW TT (Mk 46 Mod. 5 torpedoes); 1 SH-14D Lynx helicopter; F 802 and F 803 only: Tomahawk Block IV from 2008
Electronics:
Radar: 1 Thales Scout nav/surf. search; 1 Thales APAR 3-D phased-array target desig. and tracking; 1 Thales SMART-L early warning
Sonar: STN Atlas Elektronik DSQS-24C hull-mounted LF; provision for active towed linear array
TACAN: Thales Vesta

GUIDED-MISSILE FRIGATES [FFG] *(continued)*

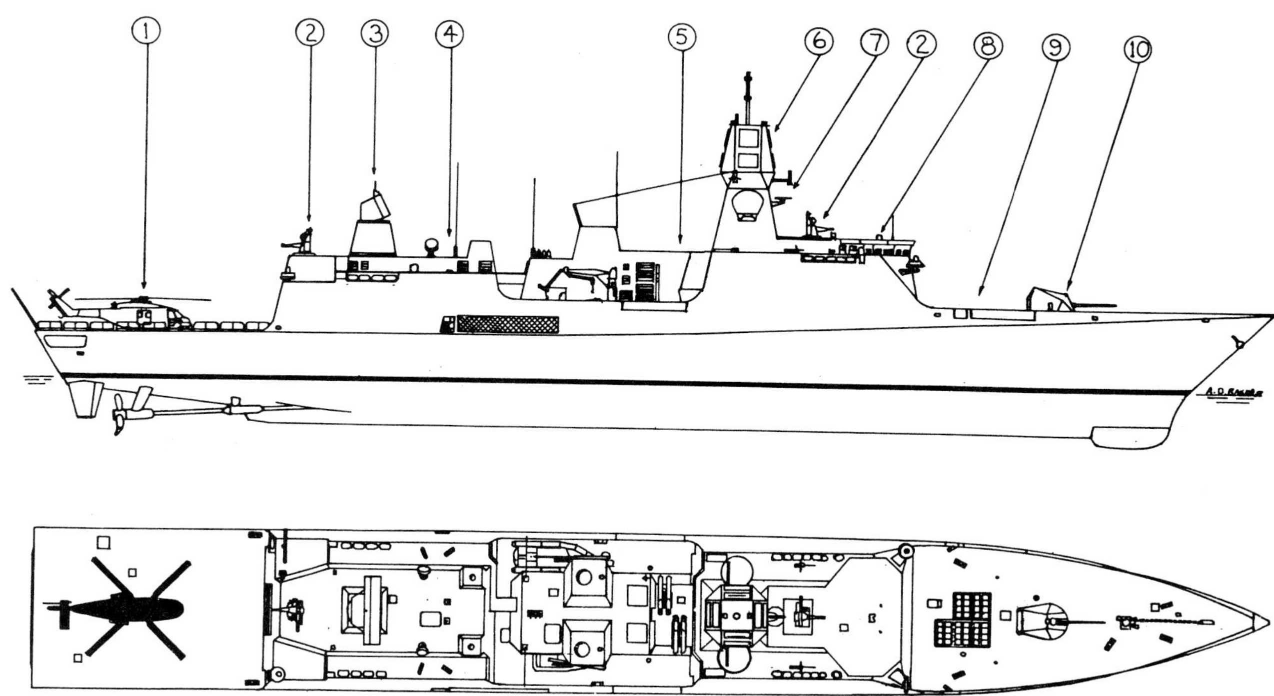

De Zeven Provinciën (F 802) 1. NH-90 helicopter 2. 30-mm Goalkeeper CIWS 3. SMART-L early-warning radar 4. Paired ASW torpedo tubes (on main deck, within the small opening in the hull side) 5. Harpoon SSM, in quadruple sets, behind radar reflection reduction paneling (see plan view) 6. APAR 3-D phased-array target-designation and tracking radar 7. Scout navigational radar 8. SIRIUS infrared surveillance and tracking sensor 9. Mk 41 VLS (40 cells) 10. 127-mm 54-cal. OTOBreda DP gun

Drawing by A. D. Baker III

EW: Racal Spectre (U.K. UAT) intercept (0.5–18 GHz)/jamming (7.5–18 GHz); Mk 36 SRBOC decoy syst. (4 6-round Raytheon Mk 137 RL); 4 twin Nulka offboard jammer RL; SLQ-25A Nixie towed acoustic torpedo decoy
E/O: Thales Mirador-FD surveillance, tracking, and gun f.c.; Thales SIRIUS surveillance

M: CODOG: 2 Rolls-Royce SM-1C Spey gas turbines (26,140 shp each), 2 Stork-Wärtsilä 16V6ST diesels (5,630 bhp each); 2 CP props

Electric: 6,600 kw tot. (4 × 1,650-kw sets, 4 GEC-Alstom Paxman 12VP185 diesels driving)

Range: 5,000/18 **Endurance:** 21 days

Crew: F 802, 803: 32 officers, 47 petty officers, 123 ratings (232 accomm.)—F 804, 805: 182 tot.

Remarks: Were to have been a cooperative venture with Germany and Spain under an agreement signed 27-1-94, but the German ship design differs and Spain later withdrew. First two are designated LCF (*Luchtverdedigings en Commando Fregat*, or Air-Defense and Command Frigate) and were ordered 3-6-95; they were to cost $829 million for both. Authorization for a second pair was granted by the parliament 24-10-96, and they were ordered 2-5-97 for $375 million each. The total four-ship procurement to cost an estimated $1.61 billion.

Hull systems: Employ twin rudders with rudder roll stabilization. Ship's boats are rigid inflatables stowed behind bulwarks. Reduced radar and infrared signature measures have been extensively employed. Electrical power is 220- and 115-V, 60-Hz a.c., and 24- and 28-V, 400-Hz a.c. Have six "autonomous internal zones" divided by PriMa flexible, watertight, blast- and fragmentation-resistant bulkheads.

Combat systems: The combat system is the Thales SEWACO IX, with Link 11 and 16 datalink capability; 36 Protec-II reconfigurable display and operations consoles per ship are installed. The SMART-L radar will be able to maintain up to 1,000 tracks, while APAR can maintain 200 tracks and provide guidance illumination for more than 30 (the combat system allows for 16 air targets to be attacked at once, along with two surface and two subsurface contacts). The orientation of the four phased-array faces of the APAR radar was changed late in 1997 to fore and aft, port and starboard, rather than at 45° off the centerline as originally intended.

Each Mk 41 VLS cell can hold one Standard or four Sea Sparrow missiles. Beginning in 2008, the first two units will be fitted to carry Tomahawk Block IV land attack cruise missiles. The forward Goalkeeper CIWS may be replaced later by a U.S. RAM point-defense missile system with RIM-116 missiles.

The hull-mounted sonar was ordered 5-98, with the towed array decision to be made in 1999 between the STN Atlas Elektronik ATASS, Honeywell Low Frequency Active Towed Array, and Thales Combined Active-Passive Towed Array systems after competitive trials.

The first two were originally to have had twin 120-mm gunmounts recycled from the *Tromp* class (and before that aboard the destroyer *Gelderland*). The OTO Melara mounts for the first two ships were ordered 12-12-96 (with an option for two more) in order to take advantage of planned developments in U.S. 127-mm extended range guidance munitions (ERGM); all four are refurbished ex-Canadian mountings from the *Tribal* class. The helicopters carry ASW and antiship weapons, and the magazines will stow up to 24 ASW torpedoes and 12 antiship missiles; the DCN Samahé helicopter landing system will be installed on the 27-m-long flight deck. Terma, Denmark, is installing the SRBOC system, which will incorporate an on-mount round identification system. The Mirador E/O sensor is also referred to as the TEOOS (Trainable Electro-Optical Observation System), and the sensor mount has two daylight t.v. cameras, an Albatross thermal-imaging camera, and a low-light t.v. camera. Two 20-mm cannons were originally fitted were been replaced by two single 12.7-mm Browning M2 mg during 2004.

The Rhode & Schwarz integrated communications suite will include UHF/SHF SATCOM, an integrated message-handling and control system (IMUS), and cryptographic equipment. Navigational equipment will include two NAVSAT terminals, two inertial navigational systems (MINS), and a weather satellite receiver.

Disposal note: *Jacob Van Heemskerck*–class frigates *Jacob Van Heemskerck* (F 812) and *Witte de With* (F 813) were decommissioned during 2004 and transferred to Chile.

FRIGATES [FF]

Note: A new class of four patrol frigates is in the early stages of development in the Netherlands. Intended as replacement for the *Karel Doorman* class, the 90-m warships would displace 2,800-tons, be fitted with a hanger for storage of a single NH-90 helicopter and carry a crew of only 50 plus up to 40 troops or marines.

♦ 3 Karel Doorman class

Bldr: Schelde Shipbuilding, Vlissingen

	Laid down	L	In serv.
F 827 Karel Doorman	26-2-85	20-4-88	31-5-91
F 828 Van Speijk	1-10-91	26-3-94	7-9-95
F 834 Van Galen	7-6-90	21-11-92	1-12-94

Willem van der Zaan (F 829)—since decommissioned Frank Findler, 9-05

D: 2,800 tons light (3,320 fl) **S:** 29 kts (21 on diesels)

Dim: 122.25 (114.40 pp) × 14.37 (13.10 wl) × 4.30 (6.05 sonar)

A: 4 RGM-84A/C Harpoon SSM; 16-cell Mk 48 Mod. 1 VLS (16 RIM-7M NATO Sea Sparrow SAM); 1 76-mm 62-cal. OTO Melara DP; 1 30-mm Goalkeeper gatling CIWS; 2 single 12.7-mm Browning M2 mg; 4 fixed, paired 324-mm Mk 32 Mod. 9 ASW TT (Mk 46 Mod. 5 torpedoes); 1 SH-14D Lynx ASW helicopter

FRIGATES [FF] *(continued)*

Karel Doorman (F 827)—note the protective covering carried over the vertical-launch SAM system on the port side of the helicopter hangar
Anthony Vella, 10-04

Karel Doorman (F 827) Rob Cabo, 1-05

Electronics:
Radar: 1 Decca 1690/9 nav.; 1 Thales Scout nav./surf. search; 1 Thales SMART-S 3-D air search; 1 Thales LW-08 early warning; 2 Thales STIR-18 missile f.c.; 1 Thales Goalkeeper f.c. array
Sonar: PHS-36 (SQS-509) hull-mounted MF—last four also: provision for Thales Anaconda (DSBV-61A) towed array
EW: ArgoSystems APECS-II intercept and AR-740 jammer; Mk 36 SRBOC decoy syst. (2 6-round Raytheon Mk 137 RL); SLQ-25 Nixie towed acoustic torpedo decoy syst.
M: CODOG: 2 Stork-Wärtsilä 12 SWD 280 V-12 cruise diesels (4,225 bhp each), 2 Rolls-Royce Spey RM-1A or C gas turbines; 2 CP props; 48,252 (F 827: 37,530) shp max.
Electric: 2,720 kw (4 × 650-kw diesel sets, Stork-Wärtsilä DRo 218K diesels driving; 1 × 120-kw diesel set)
Range: 5,000+/18 **Endurance:** 30 days
Crew: 16 officers, 138 enlisted (163 max. accomm.)

Remarks: Originally known as the "M" class. First four were ordered 29-2-84, three years earlier than planned, to help the shipbuilding industry, and a second group of four was ordered 10-4-86. Accommodations for female crew members are incorporated, plus bunks for 30 marines. Two of the remaining four units are to be decomissioned in the near future.
Hull systems: Have a computer-controlled rudder roll-stabilization system instead of fins. Carry three RIBs. Have the Spey RM-1C gas turbines operating at 24,126 shp each.
Combat systems: Have the Thales DAISY VII/SEWACO VII(B) data system with full Link 10, 11, and 16 capability. The 76-mm gun fires at up to 100 rds/min. Some, and possibly all, were updated with radar reflection-reducing panels outboard of the vertical missile launchers, Thales Scout low-probability-of-intercept surface-search radars (with the Decca navigational radar relocated atop the pilothouse), and Inmarsat commercial SATCOM. The long-range LR-IRSCAN infrared surveillance and tracking system is to be installed on all. The 20-mm cannon were replaced by two single 12.7-mm Browning M2 mg during 2004.
Disposals: *Tjerk Hiddes* (F 830) and *Abraham Van der Hulst* (F 832) were decommissioned during 2004 and transferred to Chile. *Willem van der Zaan* (F 829) decommissioned on 25-8-06, and *Karel Doorman* (F 827) is expected to decommission by 2007. Both are to be transferred to Belgium by 2008. *Van Amstel* (F 831) and *Van Nes* (F 833) decommissioned during 2006-7. *Bloys Van Treslong* (F 824), the last remaining *Kortenaer*-class frigate in Dutch service, was decommissioned on 17-12-03 for transfer to Greece.

Note: Four corvette-sized patrol ships were reportedly ordered from Royal Schelde on 19-5-06 with delivery expected during 2-10-2011. Additional data is not yet available.

MINE WARFARE SHIPS

♦ 9 Alkmaar ("Tripartite")-class coastal minehunters [MHC]
Bldr: Van der Giessen de Noord, Alblasserdam

	Ordered	Laid down	L	In serv.
M 853 Haarlem	23-1-79	16-6-81	9-7-83	12-1-84
M 856 Maassluis	16-12-81	7-11-82	5-5-84	12-12-84
M 857 Makkum	16-12-81	28-2-83	27-9-84	13-5-85
M 858 Middelburg	21-7-82	11-7-83	18-2-85	10-12-86
M 859 Hellevoetsluis (ex-*Scheveningen*)	21-7-82	12-12-83	18-7-85	20-2-87
M 860 Schiedam	5-12-83	6-5-84	26-4-86	9-7-86
M 861 Urk	5-12-83	30-9-84	4-10-86	10-12-86
M 862 Zierikzee (ex-*Veere*)	3-7-84	25-2-85	4-10-86	7-5-87
M 864 Willemstad	3-7-84	3-10-86	27-1-89	20-9-89

Urk (M 861) Leo Van Ginderen, 6-05

Makkum (M 857) Frank Findler, 7-05

Urk (M 861) Bernard Prézelin, 7-05

D: 510 tons (540 fl) **S:** 15 kts (7 hunting)
Dim: 51.6 (47.1 pp) × 8.96 × 2.45 (2.6 max.)
A: 1 20-mm 90-cal. GIAT 20F-2 AA
Electronics:
Radar: 1 Decca TM 1229C or Consilium Selesmar NN 950 nav.
Sonar: Thales DUBM-21B
M: 1 Brons-Werkspoor A-RUB 215 × 12 diesel; 1 CP prop; 1,900 bhp—2 75-shp bow-thrusters; 2 120-shp ACEC active rudders
Electric: 970 kw tot. (3 × 270 kw, gas-turbine driven; 1 × 160-kw diesel set)
Range: 3,500/10 **Endurance:** 15 days **Crew:** 34–42 tot.

Remarks: Same basic design as the Tripartite minehunters for France and Belgium. The original *Willemstad* (M 864) was sold to Indonesia while under construction in 1985 and replaced with a later unit.
Hull systems: Hull is made of a compound of glass fiber and polyester resin. Have active tank stabilization. The 5-ton modular van abaft the superstructure can contain a decompression station, communications equipment, drone control gear, and other equipment.
Combat systems: Mine-countermeasures equipment includes two PAP 104 Mk 4 remote-controlled submersibles, the EVEC 20 plot table, autopilot, Toran and Sydelis radio navaids, and the Decca HiFix Mk 6 precision navigation system. Can also tow a mechanical drag sweep and carry OD-3 mechanical sweep gear. The DUBM-21B sonar can detect mines in waters up to 80-m depth, at slant ranges up to 500 m. Are being fitted with new Consilium Selesmar NN 950 navigational radars, commencing in 1999.

MINE WARFARE SHIPS *(continued)*

Modernization: The surviving units are being modernized to serve until 2020 with upgrades performed at Den Helder between 2004 and 2009. Known as the PAM (Project Adaptations Mine Warfare) program, improvements include new sonars and command and control systems supplied by STN Atlas Elektronik under a 10-12-01 contract; six Belgian units of the class will also be upgraded under the same contract. Both a hull-mounted VDS sonar and the STN Atlas Seafox self-propelled minehunting ROV are included as part of the refit. Five Bofors Double Eagle Mk II mine-disposal ROVs have been ordered for the ships. Also to be carried will be a "One-Shot Mine Disposal System," using disposable wire-guided, self-powered submersibles. A minesweeping capability will be added, but a plan to procure up to a dozen 270-ton, 40-m mine countermeasures drones to be operated by the Tripartite ships has been reduced to nine, with the first to be ordered during 2007 and deliveries to come 2010–15.
Disposals: Of the first three completed, *Alkmaar* (M 850) was retired 12-5-01, *Delfzijl* (M 851) on 19-6-01, and *Dordrecht* (M 852) on 5-7-01; *Scheveningen* (M 855; ex-*Hellevoetsluis*) was retired on 4-12-02 and *Harlingen* (M 854) in 2004. The five were sold to Latvia in 2005. *Vlaardingen* (M 863) was damaged beyond repair in a collision on 29-4-02.

AMPHIBIOUS WARFARE SHIPS AND CRAFT

♦ 1 Johan de Witt–class amphibious transport ship [LPD]
Bldr: Schelde Shipbuilding, Vlissingen

	Laid down	L	In serv.
L 801 Johan de Witt	18-6-03	13-5-06	3-07

Johan de Witt (L 801) A.A. de Kruijf, 9-06

Johan de Witt (L 801) A.A. de Kruijf, 9-06

D: 16,000 tons (fl) **S:** 19 kts **Dim:** 176.35 × 29.2 × 5.90
A: 2 single 30-mm Goalkeeper CIWS; 4 single 12.7-mm Browning M2 mg; up to 6 Netherlands Army Cougar helicopters
Electronics:
Radar: 2 Thales Pilot nav.; 1 Thales DA-08 surf./air search; 2 Thales Goalkeeper f.c.
TACAN: Thales Vesta transponder
EW: . . . intercept; Mk 36 SRBOC decoy syst. (4 6-round Raytheon Mk 137 RL); SLQ-25A Nixie acoustic torpedo decoy syst.
E/O: Thales IRSCAN surveillance and tracking
M: 4 Stork Werkspoor 12SW28 diesel generator sets (3,650 kw each), 2 Holec electric motors; 2 fixed-pitch podded props; 16,628 shp—2 600-shp electric motors for slow-speed operations—248-shp bow-thruster
Electric: . . .
Range: 10,000/12 **Crew:** 146 tot. + up to 400 staff or approx. 550 troops

Remarks: What had been intended as a repeat *Rotterdam* (L 800) transformed into a larger vessel intended to transport logistic and combat support elements of a Royal Netherlands Marine battalion, whereas the earlier *Rotterdam* can carry the combat units when both ships are available. Originally known as the ATS-2-class, the vessel has facilities for 400 flag and force command personnel and can also be used for humanitarian operations, disaster relief, and emergency evacuations. Ordered 3-5-02, with sea trials taking place in 2006. The hull was constructed at Damen Shipyard Galatz, Romania.
Hull systems: The design is an enlarged version of the *Rotterdam* able to dock British LCU Mk 10 landing craft and operate four British Army EH.101 heavy-lift or six NH-90 medium helicopters. The docking well is 1 m broader but considerably shorter than the one in *Rotterdam*, while the superstructure is enlarged to accommodate the command facilities; two LCU-1-class landing craft can be stowed in davits and two in the docking well. A large medical complex, including an operating theater, is fitted.
Combat systems: Has a Thales SEWACO combat system, similar to that on the *Rotterdam*. The ship has both Link 11 and Link 16 combat datalink capabilities, with provision to replace Link 11 with Link 22 when it is available.

♦ 1 Rotterdam-class amphibious transport ship [LPD]
Bldr: Schelde Shipbuilding, Vlissingen (hull by B.V. De Merwede, Hardinxveld-Giessendam)

	Laid down	L	In serv.
L 800 Rotterdam	23-2-96	22-2-97	18-4-98

Rotterdam (L 800) Derek Fox, 7-05

Rotterdam (L 800) Bernard Prézelin, 9-04

Rotterdam (L 800) Leo van Ginderen, 6-04

D: 10,800 tons (12,750 fl) **S:** 19 kts
Dim: 166.20 (142.4 wl; 139.55 pp) × 25.0 (23.26 wl) × 5.23 (5.90 max.)
A: 2 single 30-mm Goalkeeper CIWS; 4 single 12.7-mm Browning M2 mg; up to 6 Netherlands Army Cougar helicopters
Electronics:
Radar: 2 Thales Pilot nav.; 1 Thales DA-08 surf./air search; 2 Thales Goalkeeper f.c.
TACAN: Thales Vesta transponder
EW: . . . intercept; Mk 36 SRBOC decoy syst. (4 6-round Raytheon Mk 137 RL); SLQ-25A Nixie acoustic torpedo decoy syst.
E/O: Thales IRSCAN surveillance and tracking
M: 4 Stork Werkspoor 12SW28 diesel generator sets (3,650 kw each), 2 Holec electric motors; 2 fixed-pitch props; 16,628 shp—2 600-shp electric motors for slow-speed operations—1 248-shp bow-thruster
Electric: 3,650 kw from main generators; 1,000-kw diesel-driven harbor set (see Remarks)
Range: 6,000/12
Fuel: 830 tons + 200 tons aviation and vehicle fuel + 50 tons for landing craft
Endurance: 30 days (with embarked troops)
Crew: 13 officers, 23 chief petty officers, 77 other enlisted + marines: 41 officers, 156 senior petty officers, 414 other enlisted (+ 150 additional for 24 hours)

Remarks: The final design, prepared by Schelde and Spain's Izar (formerly E.N. Bazán), was approved late in 5-93, with two sisters also built in Spain. Ordered 25-4-94. Up to 20% of the crew can be female.
Hull systems: Built to merchant marine standards but has degaussing coils and a gas-tight citadel. Ballast tanks (to flood down the docking well) accommodate 4,000

AMPHIBIOUS WARFARE SHIPS AND CRAFT *(continued)*

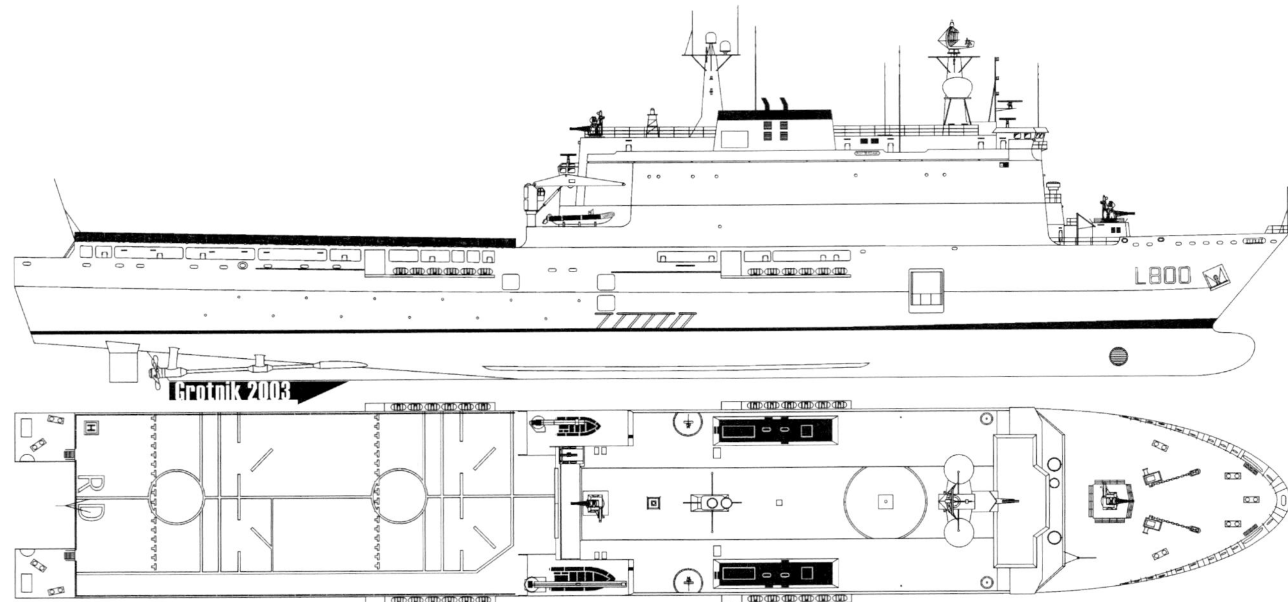

Rotterdam (L 800) Drawing by Tomasz Grotnik, 2003

tons of seawater. Carries 300 tons of potable water. Is able to operate in Sea State 6. The main diesel generator system provides both propulsion and ship's service power. Hospital facilities include two operating rooms, 100 beds, and 10 intensive-care berths.

Combat systems: Has the Thales SEWACO combat data system, with Link 11 combat datalink capability. Has a dual helicopter hangar totaling 510 m^2 and two landing spots on the 60 × 25-m helicopter deck. There is 903 m^2 of internal vehicle parking space and the 885-m^2 docking well can also be used for additional vehicles; further vehicles can be carried on the 1,340-m^2 helicopter deck. Has 627 m^3 of general stores capacity (136 m^3 refrigerated), 630 m^3 of marine equipment capacity, and 320 m^3 of ammunition storage. One 25-ton and one 2.5-ton capacity cranes are fitted. Is able to carry up to 30 Leopard-2 battle tanks or 160 armored personnel carriers. Two Leopard tanks have been altered to function as Beach Armored Recovery Vehicles for use with the ship, which also can carry two portable road-layers. Vehicles can be moved from below decks to the helicopter deck by a 25-ton-capacity elevator. The docking well can accommodate six LCVP Mk 3 or four Dutch LCU-1 or four British LCU Mk 9 or four U.S. LCM(8) landing craft. There are three side doors per side, with the forward door usable for vehicle loading and debarking. To support ASW helicopters, the magazine accommodates 30 Mk 46 torpedoes and 300 sonobuoys.

Embarked troop Stinger shoulder-launched SAMs contribute to ship defenses. Has SHF military SATCOM capability and Inmarsat commercial SATCOM facilities and over 40 radio transceivers and receivers. NATO Link 11 and Link 14 datalinks are fitted. The DA-08 radar uses the antenna from a DA-05 set and was recycled from one of the *Jacob Van Heemskerck*–class frigates. During 2003 the four 20-mm Mk 10 cannon were replaced by four 12.7-mm machineguns.

♦ 5 LCU-1-class utility landing craft [LCU]
Bldr: Visser, Den Helder

	Laid down	L	In serv.
L 9525	28-4-97	9-8-97	7-4-98
L 9526	28-9-98	25-6-99	31-7-99
L 9527	28-9-98	30-8-99	24-9-99
L 9528	. . .	22-10-99	17-12-99
L 9529	. . .	12-11-99	20-12-99

L 9526—lengthened unit A. A. de Kruijf, 7-05

D: 200 tons (fl) **S:** . . . kts **Dim:** 27.30 (23.80 wl) × 6.84 × 1.55
A: 2 single 12.7-mm mg **Electronics:** Radar: 1 Furuno . . . nav.
M: 2 Caterpillar 3412C D1-T diesels driving Stamford 543.F1 generators (565 kVA each), 2 Alconza D.400.M6 electric motors (400 kw each); 2 Schottel SJP.82.T vertical-cycloidal props; 1,400 shp
Electric: 70 kw tot. (1 × 70 kw, Perkins T4.236 diesel driving)
Range: 400/8 **Endurance:** 14 days **Crew:** 5 tot. + 130 troops

Remarks: Four were ordered 18-4-97 for use with *Rotterdam* (L 800), with an option for the fifth later taken up. Originally were to have had hulls built in Romania, but the hulls were instead built at Roermond and fitted out at Den Helder. Visser is a subsidiary of the Damen group. Assigned directly to the Royal Netherlands Marine Corps. Painted green, they are based at Texel.

L 9529 Michael Nitz, 3-05

Hull systems: Unusually deep 4.4-m molded depth to hull, which has vehicle ramps fore and aft. Able to carry 130 troops or three 4-ton trucks or two 10-ton trucks or four BV 206 tracked personnel carriers or 6–8 jeeps or two Warrior armored fighting vehicles; can also carry one beach armored recovery vehicle (BARV). Ballast tanks aft are used to alter the hull trim for beaching. The propellers are mounted fore and aft. Electric power is taken from one of the main generators, and there is also a Perkins diesel-powered emergency set. The articulating radar mast is raised or lowered pneumatically. L 9526 and later have improved machinery arrangements. L 9526 was lengthened by 8.5 meters during 2004 and is now 35.3-m long with a reduced draft. She is officially known as an "LCU Mk.2" craft

♦ 6 LCA Mk 3 landing craft [LCVP]
Bldr: Van der Giessen de Noord, Alblasserdam

	In serv.		In serv.
L 9536	16-10-90	L 9539	10-4-92
L 9537	12-12-92	L 9540	13-3-92
L 9538	26-11-91	L 9541	19-10-92

L 9539 Camil Busquets i Vilanova, 2005

AMPHIBIOUS WARFARE SHIPS AND CRAFT *(continued)*

L 9538 Michael Nitz, 3-05

D: 23 tons (28.5 fl) **S:** 18 kts (light; 13 loaded) **Dim:** 16.90 × 4.77 × 1.10
A: 2 single 7.62-mm FN FAL mg **Electronics:** Radar: 1 Furuno . . . nav.
M: 2 DAF-Turbo DKS-1160M diesels; 2 Schottel swiveling props; 520 bhp
Range: 220/13 **Crew:** 3 tot. + 34 troops

Remarks: Ordered 10-12-88. L 9536 laid down 10-8-89, L 9540 on 16-5-91, and L 9541 on 4-9-91. GRP construction. Can carry 7 tons of cargo or two Land Rover light trucks or a BV 202E Snowcat tracked vehicle. The cargo deck is covered with GRP segments that slide aft for stowage.

♦ 6 LCA Mk 2 landing craft [LCVP]
Bldr: Naval Shipyard, Den Helder

	In serv.		In serv.
L 9530	10-10-84	L 9533	13-12-85
L 9531	20-12-84	L 9534	13-12-85
L 9532	4-7-85	L 9535	5-1-86

L 9534 Rob Cabo, 7-05

D: 8.5 tons (13.6 fl) **S:** 11 kts **Dim:** 16.0 × 4.4 × 1.3
A: 1 7.62-mm FN FAL mg **Electronics:** Radar: 1 Furuno . . . nav.
M: 1 DAF-Turbo diesel; 1 Schottel swiveling prop; 260 bhp
Range: 220/11 **Crew:** 3 tot. + 25 troops

Remarks: GRP construction. Were originally to have been a dozen. Can carry a Land Rover truck or a BV 202E Snowcat tracked snow vehicle in place of the 25 troops. The machinegun is mounted to port of the ramp at the bow. L 9533 has been disarmed and equipped as a fireboat at Den Helder; she is painted red.

♦ 23 U.S. Whaler assault craft [LCP]
Bldr: Boston Whaler, Edgewater, Fla. (In serv. 10-3-92)

WM9-9201 through WM9-9223

Netherlands Marines Boston Whaler assault launch H&L Van Ginderen, 7-97

D: 2 tons (fl) **S:** 30 kts **Dim:** 6.50 × 2.35 × . . .
A: . . . **M:** 2 gasoline outboards; 140 bhp
Range: 100/30 **Crew:** 8 marines

Remarks: WM = Watertransport Motor. Purchased in 1992. Foam-core GRP construction. Also accepted for service on the same date were three 13-ft. Boston Whalers (WM9-9224 through WM9-9226) for use by the Dutch Marines in the West Indies.

♦ 29 RIB assault launches [LCP]
Bldr: Mulder & Rijke, IJmuiden (In serv. 2-89 through 1-2-96)

WM8-8801, WM8-8803, WM8-8804, WM8-8902 through WM8-8909, WM8-9001 through WM8-9009, WM8-9101, WM8-9102, WM8-9201, WM8-9202, WM8-9501 through WM8-9505

Rigid inflatable assault launches WM8-9007 and 9005 Paolo Marsan, 7-04

D: 1.62 tons **S:** 26 kts **Dim:** 7.00 × 2.60 × 0.80
M: 1 Volvo Penta TAMD 32A diesel outboard; 110 bhp

Remarks: WM = Watertransport Motor. For transport aboard frigates, etc., and used by Dutch Marines. WM8-8700 was transferred to Pakistan in 7-94, and WM8-8802 and WM8-8901 were transferred to Greece in 1995.

Note: The Royal Netherlands Marines also employ a number of smaller Zodiac RIBs capable of carrying four armed commandos in addition to the coxswain. One-man assault paddle-kayaks are also available.

Royal Netherlands Marines in a Zodiac assault RIB Rob Cabo, 7-03

AUXILIARIES

♦ 1 support ship for the Netherlands Antilles [AG]
Bldr: Damen, Gorinchem

	Laid down	L	In serv.
A 804 PELIKAAN	25-8-05	7-2-06	6-06

Pelikaan (A 804) A.A. de Kruijf, 6-06

AUXILIARIES *(continued)*

D: 1,400 tons **S:** 14.5 kts **Dim:** 65.4 × 13.25 × 3.0
A: 2 single 12.7-mm mg
Electronics: Radar: 1 . . . nav.
M: 2 Caterpillar . . . diesels; 2 fixed-pitch props; 4,000 bhp
Crew: 14 tot. + 57 troops

Remarks: Ordered 10-1-05 as replacement for the previous *Pelikaan* (A 801). Designed for use as a general-purpose tender/supply ship in the Netherlands Antilles and for transporting marines, as required. Has a large electrohydraulic crane forward that can handle small assault boats stowed on deck.

Disposal note: The previous Netherlands Antilles support ship, also named *Pelikaan* (A 801, ex-*Kilindoni*), was decomissioned in 2006.

♦ 1 torpedo-trials ship [AGE]
Bldr: Schelde Shipbuilding, Vlissingen

	Laid down	L	In serv.
A 900 MERCUUR	6-11-85	25-10-86	21-8-87

Mercuur (A 900) Leo van Ginderen, 6-05

D: 1,200 tons (1,500 fl) **S:** 14 kts **Dim:** 64.85 × 12.00 × 4.30
A: 2 fixed, underwater 533-mm TT; mines
Electronics:
Radar: 1 Decca TM 1229 nav.
Sonar: SQR-01 bow-mounted active and passive
M: 2 Brons-M.A.N. 61-20/27 diesel generator sets (650 kw each), electric drive; 2 props; 1,100 shp—bow-thruster
Crew: 6 officers, 30 enlisted + 3 trials personnel

Remarks: Ordered 13-6-84. An ASW escort version of the design was unsuccessfully offered commercially. Has a helicopter vertical-replenishment deck above the torpedo workshop. The sonar array is in a large bow-mounted dome that protrudes well below the keel; the two underwater torpedo tube muzzles exit near the bow. Two 20-mm Oerlikon Mk 10 AA originally fitted have been removed, as has been the triple 324-mm ASW torpedo tube mounting.

♦ 2 Snellius-class hydrographic survey ships [AGS]
Bldr: Damen–Royal Schelde, Vlissingen (hulls by Damen SY Galati, Romania)

	Laid down	L	Commissioned
A 802 SNELLIUS	6-01	13-9-03	18-12-03
A 803 LUYMES	6-02	17-1-04	3-6-04

D: 1,875 tons (fl) **S:** 13 kts **Dim:** 81.42 × 13.1 × 4.0
Electronics: 1 . . . nav.; Furuno . . . sonar
M: 3 Caterpillar 3412 diesels, electric drive; 1 prop; 1,565 shp—bow-thruster
Crew: 12 tot. + 6 hydrographers (42 accomm.)

Remarks: Replaced *Tydeman* (A 906) and *Buyskes* (A 904). Each has three crews to permit near-continuous operations. Are used in home waters and in the Netherlands Antilles and also perform surveillance and coast guard duties. Have a helicopter landing deck but no hangar.

Snellius (A 802) Frank Findler, 6-04

Disposal note: *Blommendal*-class hydrographic survey ship *Buyskes* (A 904) was decommissioned 18-12-03 and transferred to Latvia. *Tydeman*-class hydrographic survey ship *Tydeman* (A 906) was retired on 3-6-04.

Note: Damen Polycat harbor launch Y 8200 is used for inshore survey work.

Luymes (A 803) A. A. de Kruijf, 7-05

♦ 1 (+ 1) Patiño-class underway replenishment ships [AOR]
Bldr: Schelde Shipbuilding, Vlissingen (hull by B.V. De Merwede, Hardinxveld-Giessendam)

	Laid down	L	In serv.
A 836 AMSTERDAM	25-5-92	11-9-93	2-9-95

Amsterdam (A 836) Rob Cabo, 7-05

D: 17,040 tons (fl) **S:** 21 kts (20 sust.)
Dim: 165.84 (156.00 wl) × 23.70 (22.00 wl) × 8.00
A: 1 30-mm Goalkeeper CIWS; 2 single 12.7-mm Browning M2 mg; 2–3 helicopters (see Remarks)
Electronics:
Radar: 2 Kelvin-Hughes . . . F-band nav.; 1 Kelvin-Hughes Type 1007 nav.
TACAN: Thales Vesta beacon
EW: Ferranti AWARE-4 radar warning; Mk 36 SRBOC decoy syst. (4 6-round Raytheon Mk 137 RL); SLQ-25 Nixie towed acoustic torpedo decoy syst.
E/O: Thales IRSCAN surveillance syst.
M: 2 Izar–Burmeister & Wain V16V-40/45 diesels; 1 5-bladed, 5.7-m-dia. CP prop; 26,240 shp
Electric: 4,000 kw tot. (4 × 1,000-kw Izar–Burmeister & Wain sets)
Range: 13,440/20 **Endurance:** 30 days
Crew: 23 officers, 137 enlisted + 70 spare berths

Remarks: A 836 was ordered during 10-91 to replace *Poolster;* the order for a planned second ship has been delayed several times. Joint design between Netherlands' Nevesbu and Spain's E.N. Bazán (now Izar) design bureaus. Twenty percent of the crew can be women. Commenced sea trials 3-4-95 and was accepted for service 10-7-95. The 20-mm cannon were replaced by two single 12.7-mm Browning M2 mg during 2004. A second unit of the class, built to an improved design, was ordered on 16-5-06 and is expected in service around 2010.
Hull systems: Has four 2-ton-capacity dual-purpose and two 250-kg solid-stores alongside replenishment stations on each side and a VERTREP position forward/ Cargo deadweight: 10,300 tons, including 6,700 tons fuel, 1,660 tons aviation fuel, 178.8 tons fresh water, 180.9 tons ammunition, 18.6 tons sonobuoys, 83.3 tons provisions, and 9 tons spare parts. Fuel transfer rate is 1,000 m^3 per hour to port and 600 m^3 per hour to starboard, and 200 m^3 per hour for aviation fuel on either beam; there is provision for fueling astern at 450 m^3/hr. There are repair shops to assist other vessels. Crew figure above includes an aviation complement of 24. Is able to carry three Lynx or two Merlin/Sea King–size helicopters. Has a gas-tight citadel. Capable of operating in up to Sea State 6. Equipped for NATO Link 11.

♦ 1 improved Poolster-class underway replenishment ship [AOR]
Bldr: Verolme, Alblasserdam

	Laid down	L	In serv.
A 832 ZUIDERKRUIS	16-7-73	15-10-74	27-6-75

AUXILIARIES *(continued)*

Zuiderkruis (A 832) Bernard Prézelin, 9-04

Zuiderkruis (A 832) Rob Cabo, 5-05

D: 17,357 tons **S:** 21 kts **Dim:** 169.59 (157.00 pp) × 20.3 × 8.4 (max.)
A: 1 30-mm Goalkeeper gatling CIWS; 2 single 12.7-mm Browning M2 mg; up to 3 SH-14D Lynx helicopters
Electronics:
Radar: 2 Decca TM 1226C nav.; 1 Thales Scout nav./surf. search; 1 Decca 2459 surf. search
EW: Ferranti AWARE-4 radar warning; Mk 36 SRBOC decoy syst. (4 6-round Raytheon Mk 137 decoy RL)
E/O: Thales IRSCAN surveillance and tracking
M: 2 Werkspoor TM 410 16-cyl. diesels; 1 prop; 21,000 bhp
Electric: 3,000 kw tot. **Crew:** 17 officers, 249 enlisted

Remarks: Expected to retire by 2015.
Hull systems: Cargo capacity: 9,000 tons fuel, 400 tons JP-5 aviation fuel, 200 tons fresh water, spare parts, ammunition. Can carry ASW torpedoes and other stores to support ASW helicopters. Has two fueling stations per side, amidships, and one sliding-stay, constant-tension, solid transfer station each side, forward.

SERVICE CRAFT

♦ 1 trials barge [YAGEN]

Y 8100 (In serv. 14-7-95)

Trials barge Y 8100 H&L Van Ginderen, 7-97

Remarks: Ordered 31-8-94. Non-self-propelled. No data available.

♦ 1 floating boathouse barge [YAGN]

Y 8066 (In serv. 1994)

♦ 1 work platform barge [YC]

Bldr: Rijkswerf, Den Helder (In serv. 11-8-95)

Y 8119 Neelte Jans

Neelte Jans (Y 8119) Paolo Marsan, 7-04

Remarks: Ordered 31-8-94 and laid down 2-1-95. Non-self-propelled.

♦ 3 work platform barges [YC]

Bldr: . . . (In serv. 1995)

Y 8116 Y 8117 Y 8118

Remarks: Ordered 11-94. Non-self-propelled.

♦ 13 miscellaneous deck-cargo barges [YC] (In serv. 1900–1992)

Y 8322, Y 8331, Y 8332, Y 8334, Y 8337–Y 8341, Y 8343–Y 8345, Y 8377

Deck-cargo barge Y 8343 A. A. de Kruijf, 7-05

Remarks: Y 8377 is ex-Army RV 141, transferred in 10-89 for use by marines in ship-to-shore transits. Y 8345 is used as a dirty water–receiving craft.

♦ 26 miscellaneous mooring pontoons [YC]

	In serv.		In serv.
Y 8578	20-10-87	Y 8600–8603	3-2-81 to 1984
Y 8595	1956	Y 8604–8610	1983–85
Y 8597	. . .	Y 8611–8613	23-6-86
Y 8598	1971	Y 8614–8617	Acquired 25-9-86
Y 8599	1977	Y 8712–8714	1940

Remarks: Y 8597, Y 8598, Y 8599, and Y 8600 through Y 8603 are used with submarines. Y 8711 was stricken 4-12-96. Y 8713 carries extra accommodations huts and is moored with accommodations barge *Thetis* (A 887).

♦ 1 towed-array cable pontoon [YC]

Y 8577 (In serv. 18-12-92)

Towed-array cable pontoon Y 8577 A. A. de Kruijf, 7-05

Remarks: Employed to replace towed linear hydrophone sonar arrays in frigates.

SERVICE CRAFT *(continued)*

♦ 1 miscellaneous barge [YC]

Y 8715 (In serv. 1983)

♦ 1 floating crane [YD]

Y 8514 (In serv. 1974)

♦ 4 Cerberus-class diving tenders [YDT]

Bldr: Scheepswerf Visser, Den Helder

	Laid down	L	In serv.
A 851 Cerberus	15-4-91	18-12-91	28-2-92
A 852 Argus	16-9-91	14-3-92	2-6-92
A 853 Nautilus	16-3-92	10-6-92	18-9-92
A 854 Hydra	11-6-92	11-9-92	20-11-92

Nautilus (A 853) A. A. de Kruijf, 7-05

Hydra (A 854)—as lengthened H&L Van Ginderen, 7-99

D: 200 tons (233 fl) **S:** 10.25 kts
Dim: 27.30 (26.00 pp) × 8.76 (8.50 wl) × 1.50 (see Remarks)
Electronics: Radar: 1 Decca . . . nav.
M: 2 Volvo Penta TAMD-122A diesels; 2 props; 760 bhp
Electric: 144 kVA tot. (2 × 72 kVA, DAF DH-825 MGK diesels driving)
Range: 750/10 **Crew:** 2 officers, 6 unlicensed + 6 divers

Remarks: First three ordered 29-11-90, the fourth later. Have an electrohydraulic crane with 8-m max. reach and 2-ton max. capacity aft to tend divers and a rigid inflatable boat. Can support two hard-hat divers simultaneously at 50 m. Crews are civilian. Between 2-8-97 and 12-3-98, A 854 was lengthened by 10.5 m under a 26-5-97 contract by Visser SY, Den Helder, to provide increased accommodations; she was relaunched 5-3-98 and recommissioned 13-3-98 and now displaces about 310 tons (fl).

♦ 6 miscellaneous diving pontoons [YDTN]

	In serv.		In serv.
Y 8579	30-5-86	Y 8582	28-5-86
Y 8580	18-12-85	Y 8583	. . .
Y 8581	2-4-86	Y 8590	1952

Diving Pontoon Y 8581 Paolo Marsan, 7-04

Remarks: Y 8584, 8588, and 8592 were transferred to the Sea Scouts in 1993. Y 8586 was stricken 22-2-95, and Y 8585 and 8589 had been discarded by 1999.

♦ 6 Polycat-class harbor launches [YFL]

Bldr: Mulder & Rijke, IJmuiden

	In serv.		In serv.
Y 8200	15-11-89	Y 8203	16-3-90
Y 8201	8-12-89	WM1-9001 Jonge Prins 3	27-4-90
Y 8203	16-2-90	WM1-9002	8-12-90

Polycat launch Y 8200 A. A. de Kruijf, 7-05

D: 4.75 tons (fl) **S:** 14.5 kts **Dim:** 9.50 × 3.70 × 1.45
Electronics: Radar: 1 Furuno . . . nav.
M: 1 Volvo Penta TAMD 41 diesel; 1 waterjet; 170 bhp **Crew:** 4–6 tot.

Remarks: First four ordered 12-1-89; fifth and sixth later. Damen Polycat glass-reinforced plastic hulls. Y 8200 is used for inshore survey work.

♦ 1 public relations launch [YFL]

Bldr: Akerboom, Leiden (In serv. 1972)

Y 8005 Nieuwediep (ex-*Spido 11*)

Nieuwediep (Y 8005) Rob Cabo, 7-05

D: Approx. 50 tons (fl) **S:** . . . kts **Dim:** 17.75 × 3.75 × 1.45
Electronics: Radar: 1 Furuno . . . nav.
M: 2 Volvo Penta diesels; 2 props; 300 bhp **Crew:** 4 tot. + 50 passengers

Remarks: Acquired 10-2-92 and stationed at Den Helder to provide transportation for public visitors.

♦ 4 WM7-class personnel launches [YFL]

Bldr: Victoria

	In serv.		In serv.
WM7-9301 Plancius	1993	WM7-9303 Douwes	1993
WM7-9302 Waghenaer	1993	WM7-9501 Fortuin II	1995

D: 3.0 tons **S:** . . . kts **Dim:** 8.55 × 2.72 × 1.60
M: 1 . . . diesel; 1 prop; . . . bhp

Remarks: WM = Watertransport Motor. Polyester construction.

♦ 10 WM4-class personnel launches [YFL]

Bldr: Rijkswerf Den Helder

	In serv.
WM4-9801 (ex- . . .)	. . .
WM4-9802 (ex-WM4-7001)	1970
WM4-9901 (ex-WM4-7501)	1975
and seven others	

D: first four: 6.26 tons—others: 5.98 tons **S:** . . . kts **Dim:** 11.18 × 3.27 × 1.84
M: 1 . . . diesel; 1 prop; . . . bhp

Remarks: WM = Watertransport Motor. Polyester plastic hulls. One is carried aboard the replenishment oiler *Zuiderkruis* (A 832); the others are assigned to shore stations. All received a CUP (Capability Update Program) refit to keep them in service through 2010, with new numbers being assigned as they are completed (e.g., WM4-9802). WM4-9901 completed the CUP update 28-5-99 and was renumbered at that time.

SERVICE CRAFT *(continued)*

WM4-series launch WM4-9801 Rob Cabo, 3-05

♦ 18 miscellaneous personnel launches [YFL]

13 WM2-7303 class:
WM2-7402 through WM2-7404, WM2-7501, WM2-7502, WM2-7603, WM2-7605 through WM2-7608, WM2-7610, WM2-7901, WM2-7903
5 miscellaneous:
WM1-8405, WM1-9001 Jonge Prinz, WM3-8001 Tjarda, WR1-8802, WR1-8804

WM2-7303-class launch WM2-7606 Rob Cabo, 7-98

Remarks: WM = Watertransport Motor. No data available. Completed in the years signified by the first two digits of the second set of numbers.

♦ 4 survey launches [YGS]

WM2-7601 WM2-7602 WM2-8901 WM2-8902

Remarks: Last two are 9.5 × 3.8 m, with 1 Volvo Penta diesel (170 bhp for 15 kts).

♦ 5 fast self-propelled target craft [YGT]

Bldr: . . . (In serv. Y 8704: 5-86; Y 8699: 1994; Y 8695: 1995)

Y 8695 Y 8696 Y 8698 Y 8699 Y 8704

Remarks: Sister Y 8697 transferred to Pakistan in 7-94.

♦ 2 target barges [YGTN]

Y 8700 Y 8705

♦ 1 fuel lighter [YO]

Bldr: Scheepswerf DeHoop B.V., Schiedam

	Laid down	L	In serv.
Y 8760 Patria	10-7-97	10-11-97	9-4-98

Patria (Y 8760) Rob Cabo, 7-05

D: 680 tons (fl) **S:** 8 kts **Dim:** 44.25 (42.00 pp) × 6.50 × 2.80
Electronics: Radar: 1 . . . nav.
M: 1 Volvo Penta TAMD 122A diesel; 1 prop; 375 bhp—1 147-shp azimuthal bow-thruster
Electric: 41 kw tot. (1 diesel set) **Crew:** 2 tot.

Remarks: Ordered 26-6-97 for service at Den Helder. The hull was assembled by Made Shipyard in two sections that were towed to de Hoop's facility on 10-10-97 and 30-10-97. Received an extensive refit in 2004, at which time she was painted dark blue and given a redesigned bridge layout. Other improvements included an improved loading/off-loading system and bow thruster.
Hull systems: Carries 250 m^3 of fuel in four tanks and 175 m^3 of potable water; three 10-m^3 tanks can carry oil sludge or spoil-water from submarines. Pumping rate is 150 m^3/hr, with the same diesel engine that powers the bow-thruster also being employed to drive the pump. Hull molded depth is 2.0 m.

♦ 1 non-self-propelled accommodations barge [YPBN]

Bldr: Koninklijke Maatschappij de Schelde, Vlissingen (In serv. 27-6-85)

A 887 Thetis

Thetis (A 887)—with barge alongside Rob Cabo, 7-05

D: 1,000 tons (fl) **Dim:** 68.47 (62.85 pp) × 12.82 × 1.60

Remarks: Launched 1-83. Three floating fenders, delivered in 1986. Stationed at Den Helder.

♦ 1 ex-German Type 430 torpedo recovery craft [YPT]

Bldr: Burmester, Bremen

	Laid down	L	In serv.
Y . . . (ex-TF 1; Y 851, ex-W 70)	4-1-65	13-10-65	24-3-66

D: 56 tons (63.5 fl) **S:** 17 kts **Dim:** 25.22 (23.50 pp) × 5.40 (5.00 wl) × 1.60
Electric: 36 kw tot. (2 × 18-kw diesel sets)
M: 1 MWM 12-cyl. diesel; 1 prop; 1,000 bhp **Crew:** 6 tot.

Remarks: Stricken from the German Navy 24-5-95 and sold to the Netherlands in 1998. Wooden construction. Has a stern ramp for torpedo recovery.

♦ 2 sludge barges [YRG]

Bldr: Scheepswerf DeHoop B.V., Lobith (Both in serv. 3-9-86)

Y 8351 Y 8352

Sludge barge Y 8352—in light condition H&L Van Ginderen, 7-99

D: Approx. 460 tons (fl) **Dim:** 25.25 × 6.24 × 3.30

Remarks: Ordered 14-2-86 and laid down 4-4-86.

♦ 5 Linge-class coastal tugs [YTB]

Bldr: Delta SY, Sliedrecht (hulls for A 874, A 875 by Scheepswerf Bijlsma B.V., Wartena; hull for A 878 by Made Scheepswerf, Made)

	Laid down	L	In serv.
A 874 Linge	12-6-86	15-11-86	20-2-87
A 875 Regge	23-6-86	10-1-87	6-5-87
A 876 Hunze	17-12-86	9-6-87	20-10-87
A 877 Rotte	17-12-86	23-6-87	20-10-87
A 878 Gouwe	13-5-96	25-11-96	21-2-97

D: Approx. 500 tons (fl) **S:** 12.5 kts **Dim:** 27.45 (26.30 pp) × 8.30 × 3.80
Electronics: Radar: 1 Decca TM 1229 nav.
M: 2 Stork-Werkspoor Type DRO 218 K (A 878: Caterpillar . . .) diesels; 2 Kort-nozzle props; 1,632 bhp
Electric: 192 kw **Fuel:** 55 tons **Crew:** 7 tot.

Remarks: First two ordered 16-4-86. All based at Den Helder. A 878, ordered 9-5-96, replaced *Westgat* (A 872); she was originally launched 12-9-96 and then returned to the building slip for further work.

SERVICE CRAFT *(continued)*

Hunze (A 876) A. A. de Kruijf, 7-05

♦ 2 Breezand-class harbor tugs [YTM]
Bldr: Deltawerf, Sliedrecht

	In serv.
Y 8018 Breezand	12-89
Y 8019 Balgzand	12-1-90

Breezand (Y 8018) Rob Cabo, 7-04

D: Approx. 90 tons (fl) **S:** 10 kts **Dim:** 16.52 × 5.32 × 1.80
Electronics: Radar: 1 . . . nav.
M: 2 Volvo Penta TAMD-122A diesels; 2 props; 760 bhp

Remarks: Ordered 5-12-88. Y 8018 was launched 22-11-89, Y 8019 on 27-12-89.

♦ 5 DT-2750-class steel tug/workboats [YTL]
Bldr: Deltawerf, Sliedrecht

	In serv.		In serv.
Y 8055 Schelde	18-2-87	Y 8058 Zuidwal	5-12-86
Y 8056 Wierbalg	18-2-87	Y 8059 Westwal	29-12-86
Y 8057 Malzwin	24-12-86		

Westwal (Y 8059) Rob Cabo, 11-03

D: Approx. 35 tons (fl) **S:** . . . **Dim:** 10.80 × 3.76 × 1.60
M: 1 DAF diesel; 1 prop; 115 bhp

Remarks: Y 8058 is based at Vlissingen, the others at Den Helder.

♦ 1 LCA Mk 2 fireboat [YTR]
Bldr: Naval Shipyard, Den Helder (In serv. 13-12-85)

L 9533

Fireboat L 9533—painted red Rob Cabo, 7-05

D: 8.5 tons (13.6 fl) **S:** 11 kts **Dim:** 16.0 × 4.4 × 1.3
Electronics: Radar: 1 Furuno . . . nav.
M: 1 DAF-Turbo diesel; 1 Schottel swiveling prop; 260 bhp
Range: 220/11 **Crew:** 3 tot.

Remarks: Replaced the older L 9515 as fireboat at Den Helder in 2000; painted red. Glass-reinforced plastic construction.

♦ 1 sail-training ketch [YTS]
Bldr: Haarlemse Scheepsbouw Mij., Haarlem

	L	In serv.
Y 8050 Urania (ex-*Tromp*)	1929	23-4-38

Urania (Y 8050) Leo van Ginderen, 6-05

D: 76.4 tons (fl) **S:** 5 kts (10 under sail) **Dim:** 23.94 × 5.29 × 3.15
M: 1 Kromhout diesel; 1 prop; 65 bhp—625 m^2 sail area **Crew:** 17 tot.

Note: There are also 24 small sport and training oar-and-sail boats with hull numbers in the WR1 series under naval control.

♦ 1 seamanship training craft [YXT]
Bldr: Vervako SY, Heusden

	Laid down	L	In serv.
A 902 Van Kinsbergen	5-11-98	23-4-99	2-11-99

D: . . . tons **S:** . . . kts **Dim:** 41.51 (35.87 pp) × 9.20 × 3.30
Electronics: Radar: . . .
M: 2 . . . diesels; 2 props; . . . bhp—bow-thruster

Remarks: Ordered 15-6-98 as a replacement for *Zeefakkel* (A 903). Fitted out by Damen at Gorinchem after launching.

Disposal note: Seamanship training craft *Zeefakkel* (A 903) was retired during 2000.

SERVICE CRAFT *(continued)*

Van Kinsbergen (A 902)—painted white with yellow mast and stack
Leo Van Ginderen, 4-05

ROYAL NETHERLANDS ARMY

AMPHIBIOUS WARFARE CRAFT

♦ 1 RV 40–class tank landing craft [WLCU]
Bldr: Grave B.V. (In serv. 22-11-79)

RV 40

D: 815 tons **S:** 9.4 kts **Dim:** 45.8 × 9.5 × 2.20
M: 2 Mercedes-Benz OM404 diesels; 2 props; 654 bhp **Crew:** 4 tot.

♦ 58 Type ASA-540 aluminum river assault boats [WLCP]
Bldr: Damen, Gorinchem (In serv. 1980s)

D: 1.8 tons (fl) **S:** 25–30 kts **Dim:** 5.40 × 1.83 × 0.10
M: 1 25- to 40-bhp diesel outboard **Crew:** 4–8 tot.

♦ 49 or more Type 700 Bridge Support Boats [WLCP]
Bldr: Damen, Gorinchem

D: 6 tons (fl) **S:** 8.6 kts **Dim:** 7.00 × 2.90 × 0.75
M: 1 Deutz BF 8L 513 diesel; 2 props; 250 bhp

Remarks: Steel construction, intended for transport by DAF YGZ 2300 trucks and used in assembling and positioning pontoon bridges. Have 2.6-ton bollard pull. Props are full-swiveling and ducted.

SERVICE CRAFT

♦ 1 diving tender [WYDT]
Bldr: Werf Vervaco, Heusden (In serv. 3-11-89)

RV 50

Army diving tender RV 50 IJ Plokker, 10-04

D: Approx. 400 tons (fl) **S:** 9 kts **Dim:** 37.00 × 9.00 × 1.50
Electronics: Radar: 1 AP Mk 4 nav.
M: 2 . . . . . . diesels; 2 props; 476 bhp **Crew:** 21 tot.

Remarks: Launched 8-9-89. Has a “moonpool” aft beneath the gantry for a 50-m-depth-capable diving bell. Equipped with a decompression chamber.

COAST GUARD

The Netherlands Coast Guard, established 26-2-87, is actually a cooperative of several departments each performing a traditional coast guard mission such as search and rescue, maritime traffic research, seaway marking, maritime traffic control, customs control, environmental control, fisheries inspection, navigation control, and border patrol at sea. The Royal Military Police is classified under the coast guard.

The coast guard has no vessels of its own but employs ships, boats, and craft supplied by other services. Vessels available for use include some 60 rescue craft from the Royal Netherlands Lifeboat Service, as well as five river and harbor police patrol craft, several multipurpose patrol vessels from the Department of Public Works, and other air and maritime assets. Units in coast guard use continue to carry their original markings while adding diagonal red, white, and blue stripes, the Netherlands Coast Guard shield, and the word “Kustwacht” on their hull sides. The Coast Guard Operations Center was collocated with the combined Belgian-Netherlands Maritime Headquarters at Den Helder in 1997, with a staff of 30. The Netherlands Antilles Coast Guard is described separately.

NETHERLANDS ANTILLES AND ARUBA

COAST GUARD

Personnel: Approx. 160 total

Organization: Formally established 1-1-98. Headquartered at the Royal Netherlands Perera Naval Base at Curaçao, the Netherlands Antilles and Aruba (NAA) Coast Guard is intended primarily to combat the drug trade in the Caribbean. Smaller facilities are maintained at Aruba and St. Maarten. The Royal Netherlands Navy supplies 23 of the personnel total. The coast guard is subordinate to the Royal Netherlands Navy, reporting to the senior commander in the area. The Netherlands Antilles and Aruba remain colonial possessions of the Netherlands, with Aruba enjoying increasing autonomy.

Maritime Aviation: Heliholland, at Curaçao, provides one Eurocopter AS.355 and one Schweizer helicopter for SAR duties as requested; they are normally engaged in training Royal Netherlands Navy helicopter pilots.

Note: Craft are painted gray, with a broad yellow hull diagonal stripe followed by narrow blue, white, and red diagonals on the hull sides. In 1999, the crest of the Netherlands Antilles was added on the yellow diagonal.

PATROL CRAFT [WPC]

♦ 3 Patrol 4100 class
Bldr: Damen Shipyards, Gorinchem, the Netherlands

	Laid down	L	In serv.
P 810 Jaguar	18-8-97	31-3-98	2-11-98
P 811 Panter	20-9-97	19-5-98	18-1-99
P 812 Poema	5-1-98	7-1-99	14-3-99

Poema (P 812) A. A. de Kruijf, 5-03

Jaguar (P 810)—with fire monitor spraying A. A. de Kruijf, 5-03

D: 170 tons light (204.7 fl) **S:** 26 kts (27.8 on trials; 24 sust.)
Dim: 42.80 (40.00 wl; 39.00 pp) × 6.71 (5.99 wl) × 2.52 (props)
A: 1 12.7-mm mg
Electronics:
Radar: 1 Kelvin-Hughes Type 1007 nav.; 1 Thales Scout nav./surf. search
EW: VHF–UHFD/F
M: 2 Caterpillar 3516 DI-TA diesels; 2 Lips CP props; 5,600 bhp—bow-thruster
Electric: 262 kVA tot. (2 × 131 kVA, 2 Caterpillar 3304B DI-T diesels driving)
Range: 600/23; 2,000/12 **Fuel:** 27.15 m^3 **Endurance:** 7 days
Crew: 3 officers, 8 enlisted + 6 constable officer passengers

Remarks: Ordered 1-5-97 for $23 million. P 810 ran trials on 14/15-10-98 and was handed over about five months behind schedule; she left for the Caribbean during 1-99. P 810 suffered a serious fire on 23-5-99 and was repaired by the builder. Are stationed at Curaçao, Aruba, and St. Maarten, respectively.

PATROL CRAFT [WPC] *(continued)*

Hull systems: Are able to operate in State 4–5 seas. Carry a video camera, audio recording equipment, chemical and gas sensors, and firefighting equipment (including a firefighting monitor on the forecastle and a 2.68-m^3 foam tank). Thermal-imaging and image-intensification sensors, a secure communications suite, and a gas-tight citadel are fitted. The six-man inspection RIB is carried on an inclined ramp at the stern and can achieve 45 kts on its inboard diesel/waterjet propulsion plant; also carried is a 3.8-m dory with a 25-bhp outboard.

Combat systems: Have a variant of the Thales SEWACO combat data system to coordinate the various sensor data.

PATROL BOATS [WPB]

♦ **4 PB 1 class**
Bldr: Schottel, Warmond (In serv. 1970s)

PB 1 PB 2 PB 3 PB 4

PB 2—with original number Hartmut Ehlers, 11-90

D: 50 tons (fl) **S:** 18 kts **Dim:** 17.48 × 4.77 × 1.6
A: 1 12.7-mm mg **Electronics:** Radar: 1 Decca . . . nav.
M: 2 MTU 12V183 TC91 diesels; 2 props; 1,190 bhp **Crew:** 6 tot.

Remarks: Former police craft previously assigned to the Curaçao area. Were originally numbered P 1 through P 4.

♦ **6 Ribsea 700DOB-class rigid inflatable launches**
Bldr: Mulder & Rijke, IJmuiden (In serv. 13-9-97)

D: 3.1 tons (fl) **S:** 50 kts (40 sust.) **Dim:** 7.20 × 2.60 × 0.42
A: Small arms **M:** 2 Mercury gasoline outboards; 400 bhp
Range: 180/ . . . **Crew:** 2 tot. + 4 passengers

Remarks: Were acquired with one trailer each and a total of three towing vehicles. Are used for inshore patrol duties. Stationed at Aruba and St. Maarten.

NEW ZEALAND

Dominion of New Zealand

Personnel: 1,980 total plus 370 reservists

Bases: Ships are based at HMNZS *Philomel,* Devonport Naval Base, Auckland; since 20-11-00, HMNZS *Philomel* has also incorporated the naval college.

Naval Aviation: Five SH-2G(NZ) Super SeaSprite helicopters are flown by RNZN crews but maintained by six-man RNZAF detachments. The first two SH-2G(NZ) helicopters arrived at Auckland on 6-6-01. The SH-2G(NZ) is optimized for surface-surveillance and surface-attack duties and carries AGM-65D(NZ) Maverick antiship missiles or two Mk 46 torpedoes or two Mk 11 depth charges; they are also equipped with a single 7.62-mm MAG58 machinegun.

RNZN SH-2G(NZ) Super SeaSprite—with an AGM-65D(NZ) Maverick missile Kaman, 2001

Six Lockheed P-3K Orion maritime patrol aircraft belong to No. 5 Sqn., RNZAF. During 10-04 a $352-million (NZ dollar) program was announced to upgrade the P-3 fleet. Improvements include new communications equipment, imaging radar, video and infrared sensors and mission managements systems. Modernization work began in late 2005 with delivery of the final aircraft scheduled for 2010. In 2003 P-3Ks were fitted with the BattleMap tactical display system, which includes the Link-11 communications medium. Two leased Beech King Air B200 light transports are used for training and transport.

Weapons and Sensors: Obsolescent U.S. Mk 44 antisubmarine torpedoes were replaced by Alliant Techsystems Mk 46 Mod. 5 torpedoes, and current Mk 46 Mod. 2 torpedoes are being upgraded to Mod. 5. New ASW torpedoes are to be purchased, with the Eurotorp MU-90, Raytheon Mk 54, and Bofors Weapons System 90 under consideration.

FRIGATES [FF]

♦ **2 ANZAC frigate (MEKO 200ANZ) class**
Bldr: Transfield Shipbuilding, Williamstown, and Newcastle, N.S.W., Australia

	Laid down	L	In serv.
F 77 Te Kaha	19-9-94	22-7-95	22-7-97
F 111 Te Mana	18-5-96	10-5-97	10-12-99

Te Mana (F 111) Chris Sattler, 3-05

Te Kaha (F 77)—with SeaSprite helicopter on the flight deck Chris Sattler, 1-05

Te Mana (F 111) Chris Sattler, 3-05

D: 3,200 tons (3,500 fl) **S:** 28 kts (20 on diesel)
Dim: 117.50 (109.50 pp) × 14.80 (13.80 wl) × 5.99 (4.12 hull)
A: 1 Mk 41 Mod. 5 8-celled VLS module (8 RIM-7P Sea Sparrow missiles); 1 127-mm 54-cal. Northern Ordnance Mk 45 Mod. 2 DP; 1 20-mm Mk 15 Phalanx Block I CIWS; 6 single 12.7-mm mg; 1 SH-2G Super SeaSprite helicopter
Electronics:
Radar: 1 STN Atlas Elektronik 9600-M ARPA nav.; 1 Ericsson Sea Giraffe 150HC target desig.; 1 Raytheon SPS-49(V)8 early warning; 1 CelsiusTech 9LV 200 Sea Viking f.c.
Sonar: Thomson-Marconi Spherion-B hull-mounted (7 kHz)
EW: Racal-Thorn Sceptre XL intercept; EADS Telegon-10/Maigret HFD/F; Mk 36 Mod. 1 SRBOC decoy syst. (4 6-tubed Mk 137 RL); SLQ-25 Nixie towed acoustic torpedo decoy syst.
M: CODOG: 2 MTU 12V1163 TB83 diesels (4,420 bhp each), 1 G.E. LM-2500-30 gas turbine (30,152 shp); 2 CP props
Electric: 2,480 kw (4 × 620-kw MTU 8V396 TE54 diesels driving Siemens generator sets; 400 V, 60 Hz)
Range: 900/27 (gas turbine); 6,000/18, 10,000/13 (1 diesel) **Fuel:** 423 tons
Crew: 22 officers, 118 enlisted

Remarks: Contract was awarded 14-8-89 for eight sisters for the Royal Australian Navy, with options for two or four more for New Zealand, which decided in 9-89 initially to order only two, at a cost of about $420 million (U.S.) each. The New Zealand government decided in 11-97 not to order two additional units. *Te Kaha* means "The Strength" and *Te Mana* "The Power" in Maori.

Hull systems: Were originally to have had two G.E. LM-2500 gas turbines and a maximum speed of 31.75 kts; the starboard turbine was eliminated to save money. Either diesel can drive either or both shafts. Fin stabilizers are fitted. Endurance is

FRIGATES [FF] *(continued)*

considerably greater than in other countries' units of this class, due to the enhanced fuel supply. Carry 29 m^3 of dry provisions, 26 m^3 of refrigerated provisions, and 54 tons of fresh water. Infrared-absorbent exterior paint is employed.
Combat systems: Have the CelsiusTech 9LV 453 Mk 3 combat data/fire-control system, with only one Ceros 200 director (although space for a second is present); the director has television and infrared tracking, as well as a J-band radar and a laser rangefinder. There are seven dual-screen Type IIA combat system displays, and the 9LV 453 system employs no fewer than 55 Motorola 6820 and 68040 processors using Ada software. Also carried is an N-FOCSS command decision support system. The ships have NATO Link 11 data-sharing. The G-band Sea Giraffe radar employs a CelsiusTech 9GA XYZ antenna. The SPS-49(V)8 radar's antenna mounts the antenna for the Cossor IFF interrogator. The Spherion-B sonar has "triple-rotation direct transmission" to increase the radiated sound level by 6 dB and incorporates a torpedo warning feature. The Dowty FMS 15 towed linear hydrophone sonar system may be added later. ASW torpedo tubes will probably be added in the future, and the ships will probably be fitted to carry several 12.7-mm machineguns. Have Raytheon Mk 73 control system for the SAM installation. There is space for a second vertical-launch Sea Sparrow module. The U.S. Mk 15 CIWS from *Wellington* (F 69) was fitted to F 77 early in 1999. Evolved Sea Sparrow missiles are planned to eventually replace the present RIM-7P missiles, potentially quadrupling the missile load. Employ a harpoon-type helicopter haul-down system but do not have a deck-traversing system. Are equipped with Plessey GPS satellite receivers and have two Sperry Mk 49 inertial navigational systems. The 127-mm gun on F 111 has a radar-cross-section-reduction gunhouse, the first of its type on a Mk 45 gunmount in any navy. Two Ferranti FMS 15/2 towed passive sonar arrays and U.S. Whittaker Corp. DLS (Data Link Set), originally ordered for the *Leanders* below, may later be installed in these ships, but plans also call for the addition of an active low-frequency towed array. Also planned for both are an E/O surveillance system and a UHF SATCOM terminal. Consideration is being given to acquiring U.S. RGM-84 Harpoon or Kongsberg Penguin missiles for the ships to give them an antiship capability.

Disposal note: The broad-beam *Leander*-class frigate *Canterbury* (F 421) was decomissioned on 31 March 2005 after 34 years of service and scuttled in 2006 to form an artificial reef.

PATROL SHIPS [PS]

♦ 0 (+ 2) offshore patrol vessels
Bldr: Tenix Defence Systems, Williamstown, Australia

	Laid down	L	In serv.
. . . Otago	2005	11-06	4-07
. . . Wellington	2005	2007	10-07

Offshore Patrol Vessel—computer rendering Tenix, 2004

D: 1,600 tons **S:** 22 kts **Dim:** 85 × 14 × 3.6
A: 1 DS-25 25-mm DP; 2 single 12.7-mm mg
Electronics: . . .
M: 2 M.A.N. 12 RK280 diesels; 2 props
Range: 6,000/15 **Crew:** 35 total (+ 34 additional passengers)

Remarks: Part of the RNZN, "Project Protector," effort. Contract was awarded to Tenix, Australia, on 30-7-04. Based on the Irish *Roísín*-class patrol ships, each vessel is intended to conduct maritime surveillance and EEZ patrol duties on average 210 days per year, usually in conjunction with maritime aviation assets. Will be fitted with one hangar and helicopter for flight operations and carry two rigid inflatable boats at the stern. The command and control suite will include a combined air/surface-search radar. The ships are to be capable of operations in Sea State 6. The 25-mm gun system employs the Alliant Tech Systems M242 Bushmaster cannon.

♦ 1 (+ 3) inshore patrol vessels
Bldr: Tenix Defence Systems, Wihangarei

	Laid down	L	Delivered
. . . Rotoiti	3-3-06	2006	1-07
. . . Hawea	2006	2006	5-07
. . . Pukaki	2006	2006	9-07
. . . Taupo	2006	2007	12-07

D: 340 tons **S:** 25 kts **Dim:** 55 × 9 × 2.9
A: 2 single 12.7-mm mg
Electronics: . . .
M: 2 M.A.N. 12 VP 185 diesels; 2 props
Range: 3,000/15 **Crew:** 20 total (+ 16 additional passengers)

Inshore Patrol Vessel—computer rendering Tenix, 2004

Remarks: Part of the RNZN, "Project Protector," effort. Contract was awarded to Tenix, Australia, on 30-7-04. Based on the Philippine Coast Guard *San Juan*–class search-and-rescue craft. Will conduct maritime surveillance and patrol in support of civil agencies, including law enforcement support, out to 24nm from shore with each craft sailing on average 237 days a year. The ships are capable of patrolling in Sea State 5 and surviving in Sea State 8. Can carry two rigid inflatable boats at the stern, but no helicopter landing deck is fitted.

PATROL CRAFT [PC]

♦ 4 Moa-class naval reserve training/mine warfare craft
Bldr: Whangarei Engineering Co., Auckland

	L	In serv.		L	In serv.
P 3553 Moa	16-7-83	19-2-84	P 3555 Wakakura	29-10-84	26-3-85
P 3554 Kiwi	7-5-84	2-9-84	P 3556 Hinau	8-5-85	4-10-85

Hinau (P 3556) Ralph Edwards, 10-01

Moa (P 3553) Rob Cabo, 12-02

PATROL CRAFT [PC] *(continued)*

D: 91.5 tons light (112.2 fl) **S:** 12 kts **Dim:** 26.82 (24.38 wl) × 6.10 × 2.18
A: Provision for 1 12.7-mm Browning M2 mg
Electronics: Radar: 1 Decca 916 nav.—Sonar: Klein 595 Tracpoint side-scan
M: 2 Cummins KT-1150M diesels; 2 props; 710 bhp
Range: 1,000/11 **Fuel:** 11 tons **Crew:** 5 officers, 13 enlisted

Remarks: Ordered 11-2-82. Design derived from that of an Australian 88-ft. torpedo retriever; the training craft [YXT] *Kahu* and the now-stricken survey craft *Takapu* and *Tarapunga* were built to the same basic design. Based as follows for naval reserve training: P 3553 at HMNZS *Toroa,* Dunedin; P 3554 at HMNZS *Pegasus,* Christchurch; P 3555 at HMNZS *Olphert,* Wellington; and P 3556 at HMNZS *Ngapona,* Auckland. In 1991, they received side-scan sonars and enhanced navigation equipment to permit use as "Q-route" (cleared passage) mine survey boats and are planned to receive influence mine-countermeasures gear at a later date. On 1-1-96 were assigned to the new Maritime Mine Warfare Force. Are to be "upgraded" for further service, although there are plans to replace them with more capable craft.

AMPHIBIOUS WARFARE SHIPS

♦ 1 Canterbury-class multirole vessel
Bldr: Merwede, Rotterdam the Netherlands

	Laid down	L	In serv.
L 421 CANTERBURY	6-9-05	11-2-06	1-07

Canterbury (L 421) RNZN, 2006

D: 9,000 tons **S:** 19 kts **Dim:** 131.2 × 23.4 × 5.6
A: 1 25-mm DS-25 DP; 2 single 12.7-mm mg; provision for 1 SH-26 and 4 NH-90 helicopters
Electronics: . . .
M: 2 Wärtsilä 9V32 diesel diesels; 2 CP props; 12,240 bhp
Range: 8,000/16
Crew: 53 total +250 troops and 10 aircrew

Remarks: Compromises the sealift portion of the "Project Protector" effort. Built in the Netherlands under subcontract from Tenix, Australia. A modified version of the 12,500-grt Dutch-built commercial roll-on/roll-off ferry *Ben My Chree*, military alterations include a flight deck and helicopter hangar for two helicopters and the ability to carry two 23m LCMs, two 11m and two 7.4m RIBs for boarding duties. Capable of offloading cargo and troops directly ashore when port facilities are not available.

AUXILIARIES

♦ 1 ex-U.S. Stalwart-class hydrographic survey ship [AGS]
Bldr: Halter Marine, Moss Point, Miss.

	Laid down	L	In serv.
A 14 RESOLUTION (ex-*Tenacious,* T-AGOS 17, ex-*Intrepid*)	26-2-88	17-2-89	29-9-89

Resolution (A 14)—as modified, with tripod mainmast aft removed, new tripod mast added atop the pilothouse, and RIB launches added aft to starboard and amidships to port; the ship does not wear her pennant number RNZN, 10-00

D: 1,600 tons light (2,300 fl) **S:** 11 kts
Dim: 68.28 (62.10 wl) × 13.10 × 4.54 (6.54 over sonar)
Electronics:
Radar: 2 Raytheon . . . nav.
Sonar: STN Atlas Elektronik Hydrosweep MD-2-30 multibeam mapping (30 kHz); Swath-E multibeam echo sounder; Ferranti Marine FMS 15/2 towed passive array
M: 4 Caterpillar D398B 800-bhp diesels, G.E. electric drive; 2 4-bladed props; 2,200 shp (1,600 sust.)—550-hp bow-thruster
Electric: 1,500 kVA from main generators + 265-kw emergency set
Range: 15,000/11 **Fuel:** 904 tons **Endurance:** 98 days
Crew: 7 officers, 14 enlisted + 30 scientific party

Remarks: 1,486 grt/786 dwt. Had been in reserve since 14-2-95 at San Diego. Was purchased 10-10-96 for $22.1 million and refitted at Portland, Ore., 21-10-96 through 20-12-96; commissioned 13-2-97, departing U.S. waters 17-2-97 and arriving in Auckland 29-3-97; and reconfigured as a survey vessel between 7-97 and 9-2-98. Became fully operational as of 7-98 and was "rededicated" on 27-11-98. She is intended to be used some 300 days per year (130 days in survey work, 60 days on acoustic research, 50 days of unspecified naval tasking, and 60 days for other agencies) and is expected to serve until 2020. Previously painted white with buff stacks but repainted gray during 2003.
Hull systems: Has a flat-chine hullform without bilge keels, which are planned to be added later in New Zealand. Has passive tank roll stabilization. There are outstanding endurance and recreational facilities for the crew. Main-engine motor/generator sets also supply ship's-service power. Inshore survey craft and an enlarged charthouse have been fitted for the survey role.
Electronics systems: The UQQ-2 SURTASS (Surveillance Towed Array Sensor) has been removed, as has its associated WSC-6 satellite communications datalink system. The multibeam mapping sonar was added between 5-98 and 6-98, along with an Atlas Hydromap data system and Hydromap Caris geographic data management and processing system. The mapping sonar, with transducers mounted in a large pod below the hull, covers a swath 4,000 m wide in 1,000-m-deep water and can be employed in waters up to 5,000 m deep. A differential GPS system, the inshore survey launch *Adventure,* and additional davits and winches were also added. Late in 1998, she was fitted to tow an FMS 15 linear passive acoustic array for trials purposes. Other navigational and mission equipment includes a TSS POS/MV 320 motion sensor, Trimble 4000SE positioning equipment, Trimble Centurion nine-channel GPS, and Omni-STAR wide-area differential GPS.

♦ 1 small replenishment oiler [AOR]
Bldr: Hyundai SY, Ulsan, S. Korea

	Laid down	L	In serv.
A 11 ENDEAVOUR	10-4-87	8-87	8-4-88

Endeavour (A 11) Chris Sattler, 1-05

D: 7,300 tons (12,390 fl) **S:** 14 kts
Dim: 138.05 (128.00 pp) × 18.40 × 7.20 (4.50 light)
A: Provision for 2 single 20-mm 70-cal Oerlikon AA
Electronics: Radar: 1 Decca-Racal RM-1290A/9 nav.; 1 Decca-Racal ARPA-1690S nav.
M: 1 Hyundai–Burmeister & Wain 12V-32/36 diesel; 1 CP prop; 5,300 bhp—Lips 600-shp bow-thruster
Electric: 1,920 kw tot. (3 × 600-kw alternators; 3 Daihatsu 6DL-20 890-bhp diesels driving; 1 × 120-kw Cummins diesel-driven emergency set)
Range: 8,000/14 **Fuel:** 400 tons **Crew:** 11 officers, 39 enlisted

Remarks: 8,400 dwt/6,990 grt. Ordered 28-7-86. Launch and completion dates were delayed by shipyard labor and machinery problems; was to have been delivered 20-1-88. Left Ulsan 14-4-88 and arrived in New Zealand 25-5-88. Has operated with as few as 30 in the crew. Was given a four-month refit during 2001, during which the engine and generators were overhauled, safety measures improved, and the ship's launch relocated to the container deck.
Hull systems: Cargo: 7,500 tons fuel, 100 tons aviation fuel, and 100 tons water in five tanks. Has deck storage for four 20-ft. refrigerated cargo containers. There are single fueling stations to port and starboard, plus an over-the-stern fueling rig. Has a Magnavox 2290 NAVSAT receiver. Helicopter hangar is incorporated within the starboard side of the superstructure; the hangar may not be able to accommodate the new SH-2F/G helicopter, however.

Disposal note: Under a decision announced 8-5-01, the troop and vehicle transport *Charles Upham* (A 02, ex-*Mercandian Queen II*), which had been on charter to Spanish operator Contenemar S.A. since 25-6-98, was sold to the charterer for $8 million.

♦ 1 salvage ship [ARS]
Bldr: Alexander Cochrane SB, Selby, Yorkshire, U.K. (In serv. 5-79)

A 09 MANAWANUI (ex-*Star Perseus*)

D: 911 tons (fl) **S:** 10.7 kts **Dim:** 43.97 (38.25 pp) × 9.86 × 3.31 **A:** none
Electronics:
Radar: 2 Decca . . . nav.
Sonar: Klein 595 Tracpoint towed side-scan
M: 2 Caterpillar D379TA diesels; 2 CP props; 1,130 bhp—1 55-ton-thrust bow-thruster
Range: 5,000/10.7; 8,000/10 **Endurance:** 130 days
Crew: 2 officers, 22 enlisted

Remarks: 480 grt/396 dwt. Oilfield service and diving tender, purchased 3-88 from Star Offshore Service Marine, Ltd., and commissioned in the RNZN 5-4-88 for use as a seagoing diving tender. On 1-1-96, was assigned to the Maritime Mine Warfare Force.

AUXILIARIES *(continued)*

Manawanui (A 09) RNZN, 2000

Hull systems: Capable of four-point mooring. Can support three divers working at 76 m and has a triple-lock decompression chamber. Has an electrohydraulic 13-ton crane on the after deck and can carry 150 tons of deck cargo. A 1994 refit saw the installation of the side-scan sonar, a GPS receiver, Inmarsat satellite communications equipment, and an MCIAS data recording system. During a 1997 refit was equipped with oceanographic equipment, including a U-frame gantry, winches, and additional capstans.

SERVICE CRAFT

♦ 1 air-support training craft [YFL]

Bldr: Naval DY, HMNZS Philomel, Auckland (In serv. 4-84)

MATUA

D: 8 tons **S:** 14 kts **Dim:** 12.0 × . . . × . . .
M: 2 Perkins diesels; 2 props; . . . bhp
Range: 200/14 **Crew:** 2–4 tot.

Remarks: Plywood hull. Used for parachute recovery, helicopter winch training, diver support, patrol, and rescue duties at Naval Air Support Unit, Hobsonville. The same organization also operates two 12.2-m, 16-kt. crash boats and one 10-m, 8-kt. personnel launch.

♦ 1 catamaran inshore survey launch [YGS]

Bldr: Bladerunner Boats, Kumeu (In serv. 11-99)

ADVENTURE

Adventure—on land for maintenance Ralph Edwards, 10-01

D: 6.5 tons (fl) **S:** 25 kts **Dim:** 9.70 × . . . × . . .
Electronics: Radar: 1 . . . nav.—Sonar: 1 multibeam echo sounder
M: . . . **Crew:** 5 tot.

Remarks: All-aluminum-construction catamaran. Intended to operate with the *Resolution* (A 14), which will process the data obtained and stored by the small boat's multibeam echo sounder. Is also employed on commercial harbor survey work and is assigned to the Hydrographic Business Unit.

Disposal note: Inshore survey craft *Takapu* (A 07) and *Tarapunga* (A 08) were stricken during 9-00, with A 07 sold commercial on 25-9-00.

♦ 4 Chico-40-class sail-training sloops [YTS] (L: 21-5-90)

6911 PAEA II 6912 MAKO II 6913 MANGA II 6914 HAKU II

D: 7.3 tons (fl) **S:** 7 kts (under power) **Dim:** 12.00 (9.80 wl) × 3.90 × 2.00
M: 1 diesel; 1 prop; . . . bhp—80 m² sail area **Crew:** 10 max.

Remarks: Kept at Auckland, for seamanship proficiency training and recreation.

♦ 1 basic-training boat [YXT] Bldr: Whangarei Eng. Ltd.

	L	In serv.
A 04 KAHU (ex-*Manawanui*)	8-12-78	28-5-79

Kahu (A 04) Ralph Edwards, 10-01

D: 91.5 tons (110 fl) **S:** 12 kts **Dim:** 26.82 (24.38 wl) × 6.10 × 2.20
Electronics: Radar: 1 Decca 916 nav.
M: 2 Cummins KT 1150M diesels; 2 props; 730 bhp
Range: 1,000/12 **Crew:** 16 max.

Remarks: Built as a diving tender; renamed and reassigned as a basic navigational and maneuvering training craft at HMNZS *Taranaki* training center on acquisition of the "new" *Manawanui* (A 09) in 1988. Same basic design as the *Moa*-class patrol/training craft and the stricken survey craft *Takapu* and *Tarapunga* but has a light tripod mast and derrick aft.

Note: The New Zealand Customs Service received a Hawk IV–class patrol boat for smuggling interdiction purposes in 1999; the 14.9 × 5.0-m, 24-kt craft has twin Saab Scania 400-bhp diesel engines and an endurance of 1,000 n.m. at 15 kts.

NICARAGUA

Republic of Nicaragua

FUERZA NAVAL-EJERCITO DE NICARAGUA

Personnel: Approx. 800 total

Bases: The fleet is organized into an Atlantic Naval District, with headquarters at Bluefields, and a Pacific District, with headquarters at Puerto Corinto. Atlantic bases include Puerto Cabezas and El Bluff, and in the Pacific are Puerto Corinto and San Juan del Sur.

PATROL BOATS [PB]

♦ 3 ex-Israeli Dabur class

Bldr: Israeli Aircraft Industries, Be er Sheva (In serv. 1973–77)

GC-201 GC-203 GC-305

Dabur-class GC-201 Fuerza Naval, via Julio Montes, 1-01

D: 25 tons (35 fl) **S:** 19 kts **Dim:** 19.8 × 5.8 × 0.8
A: 2 twin 23-mm ZSU-23 AA; 2 single 14.5-mm 93-cal. AA
Electronics: Radar: 1 Decca Super 101 Mk 3 nav.
M: 2 G.M. Detroit Diesel 12V71 TI diesels; 2 props; 960 bhp
Electric: 20 kw tot. **Range:** 1,200/17 **Crew:** 2 officers, 7 enlisted

Remarks: These three former Israeli Navy units were acquired during 11-95, delivered after overhaul in 6-96, and recommissioned on 13-8-96. Two survivors of a group of four sisters delivered in 5-78, GC-231 and GC-235, were refitted in Cuba in 1995 but had been discarded by 1998. Aluminum construction. Could make 25 kts when new. Range may have been reduced to 450 n.m. at 13 kts. The twin 14.5-mm mg mount was added on the bow in 1998. All three are based at El Bluff.

PATROL BOATS [PB] *(continued)*

Disposal note: GC 301 and GC 302, the last two survivors of the 11 Soviet Zhuk-class (Project 1400) patrol boats, had been retired by 2005.

♦ **2 ex-North Korean Sin Hung class**
Bldr: . . ., North Korea (In serv. 1960s)

GC-408 GC-412

Sin Hung–class GC-410—now out of service, flanked by two sisters
Julio Montes, 2-96

D: 25 tons **S:** . . . kts **Dim:** 18.3 × 3.4 × 1.7
A: 2 twin 14.5-mm 93-cal. 2M-7 AA **Electronics:** Radar: 1 Furuno . . . nav.
M: 2 MTU . . . diesels; 2 props; . . . bhp **Crew:** 10 tot.

Remarks: Survivors of ten, of which two were delivered in 10-83, two in 1984, and six in 3-89. Former torpedo boats, delivered without the tubes. Had been discarded around 1998, but in 2000 two of the boats were reactivated, with their M-50-series high-speed diesels replaced by MTU truck diesels. Have a lightly built, stepped-hydroplane, aluminum-alloy hull.

♦ **Up to 54 Eduardoño class** Bldr: . . ., Colombia (In serv. . . .)

A camouflaged Eduardoño and its heavily armed crew of seven
Julio Montes, 9-00

D: Approx 4 tons (fl) **S:** . . . kts **Dim:** . . . × . . . × . . .
A: 1 12.7-mm mg; 2 single 7.62-mm mg
M: 2 gasoline outboard motors; 2 props; 300 bhp

Remarks: Ex-drug runners captured by the government, eight in 1998 and another 46 by the end of 2000. Do not carry pennant numbers. They are in two sizes, with one version being 10.0 m o.a. Some have been equipped with Furuno navigational radars and/or GPS terminals.

Note: Also in use are five captured Miami-built "cigarette boats" (two others are used by the Nicaraguan Police).

♦ **Up to 12 locally built GRP-hulled patrol launches**
Bldr: . . ., Nicaragua

L/E-016 and others

Locally built GRP launch L/E-016 Julio Montes, 9-00

Remarks: Prototype was completed in 1994 to begin replacement of earlier wooden-hulled craft. Use a glass-reinforced plastic hull supplied by Cuba, are powered by a single 150-bhp gasoline outboard, and are armed with one 12.7-mm mg. Have yellow, green, brown, and mauve camouflage. All have been relegated to secondary duties with the acquisition of large numbers of captured drug craft.

Disposal note: Soviet Yevgenya-class (Project 1258) inshore minesweepers BM-501 and BM-510 were no longer in service as of 2005.

SERVICE CRAFT

♦ **1 medium harbor tug [YTM]**
Bldr: . . ., U.S. (In serv. 13-8-96)

XV Aniversario

D: 110 tons (fl) **S:** 13 kts **Dim:** 22.0 × 6.1 × . . .
A: 2 single 7.62-mm mg **Electronics:** Radar: 1 Furuno . . . nav.
M: 2 G.M. Detroit Diesel 6-71-series diesels; 2 props; 600 bhp **Crew:** 8 tot.

Remarks: Is naval-operated but is also employed for commercial tug duties.

NIGERIA

Republic of Nigeria

NAVY

Personnel: Approx. 7,000 total in the navy and coast guard

Bases: The Western Naval Command has its base at NNS *Olokin,* Apapa, Lagos, with dockyard facilities at Wilmot Point, Victoria Island, near Lagos. The Eastern Naval Command base is at NNS *Anansa,* Calabar. Minor facilities exist at NNS *Okemini,* Okemini; NNS *Akaso,* Port Harcourt; and NNS *Umalokun,* Warri. Principal training facilities are located at NNS *Quorra,* Lagos. A new base is planned at Bonny to combat unrest and piracy in Bayelsa.

Naval Aviation: Two Lynx Mk 89 ASW helicopters with Gem 3, 1,128-hp turbines for use aboard *Aradu* (F 89), two armed AgustaWestland A-109 for shore-based patrol, and two BO-105 light helicopters for shore-based liaison. The air force has three Fokker F 27 Maritime patrol aircraft, delivered 1983–84 for coastal surveillance; 14 Dornier Do-128-6MPA twin-engine aircraft used for coastal patrol and smuggling interdiction; and 12 MBB BO-105C light helicopters that can be used for search-and-rescue work.

Note: The current material condition of virtually all Nigerian Navy ships and craft is poor at best, and none have fully operational combat systems. However, a major effort began during 2003 to bring an increasing number of ships back to operational status. Ship names are prefixed by NNS (Nigerian Naval Ship).

FRIGATES [FF]

♦ 1 MEKO 360 class
Bldr: Blohm + Voss, Hamburg

	Laid down	L	In serv.
F 89 Aradu (ex-*Republic*)	1-12-78	25-1-80	20-2-82

Aradu (F 89) Leo Van Ginderen, 6-05

Aradu (F 89) Chris Sattler, 7-05

D: 3,360 tons (fl) **S:** 30.5 kts (18 on diesels)
Dim: 125.90 (119.00 pp) × 15.00 (14.00 wl) × 4.32 (5.80 props)
A: 1 8-round Albatros Mk 2 Mod. 9 SAM syst. (8 Aspide missiles; probably nonoperational); 1 127-mm 54-cal. OTO Melara DP; 4 twin 40-mm 70-cal. OTO Melara Dardo AA; 2 triple 324-mm STWS-1B ASW TT (18 A-244S torpedoes); 1 d.c. rack (6 d.c.); 1 Lynx Mk 89 helicopter
Electronics:
Radar: 1 Decca 1226 nav.; 1 Plessey AWS-5D surf./air search; 1 Thales STIR-18 SAM f.c.; 1 Thales M 25 gun f.c.
Sonar: STN Atlas Elektronik EA80 hull-mounted MF
TACAN: Thales Vesta beacon
EW: Decca RDL-2 intercept; Decca RCM-2 jammer; 2 20-round OTO Melara 105-mm SCLAR trainable decoy RL
M: CODOG: 2 Rolls-Royce Olympus TM-3B gas turbines (25,440 shp each), 2 MTU 20V956 TB92 diesels (5,210 bhp each); 2 KaMeWa CP props; 50,880 bhp max.
Electric: 4,120 kVA tot. **Range:** 4,500/18; 6,500/15 **Fuel:** 440 tons
Crew: 26 officers, 169 enlisted

Remarks: Ordered 3-11-77. Renamed 1-11-80 (the name means "Thunder"). Ran aground in the Congo River during 7-87, collided with a pier in 8-87 at Lagos, and also suffered a collision at sea that same year. Refitted at Victoria Island Naval Dockyard, Lagos, from 10-90 to 2-94 but by 1995 was again inoperable and was employed primarily as a brothel. Went to sea briefly in 1995 and again in 1998, when she was stranded for two months in Liberia by engine failures. Builder reportedly assisted with repairs in 1998–99, but few, if any, of the sensors and combat systems function. Previously thought nonoperational, F 89 sailed to the United Kingdom during 2005 to take part in 200th anniversary celebrations commemorating the battle of Trafalgar.

Combat systems: Has the Thales SEWACO combat data system. Although the launch canister racks remain aboard, the eight Otomat Mk 1 antiship missiles long ago became time-expired and have not been replaced. Can carry 460 rounds of 127-mm and 10,752 rounds of 40-mm ammunition and 120 rounds for the decoy launchers.

PATROL COMBATANTS [PG]

♦ 2 Erin'mi class (Vosper Mk 9) (nonoperational)
Bldr: Vosper Thornycroft, Portsmouth, U.K.

	Laid down	L	In serv.
F 83 Erin'mi	14-10-75	20-1-77	29-1-80
F 84 Enymiri	11-2-77	9-2-78	2-5-80

Enymiri (F 84) H&L Van Ginderen, 5-82

D: 850 tons (fl) **S:** 27 kts **Dim:** 69.0 (64.0 pp) × 9.6 × 3.0 (3.6 max.)
A: 1 76-mm 62-cal. OTO Melara DP; 1 40-mm 70-cal. Bofors AA; 2 single 20-mm 70-cal. Oerlikon Mk 10 AA; 1 2-round 375-mm Bofors ASW RL

Electronics:
Radar: 1 Decca TM 1226 nav.; 1 Plessey AWS-2 air search; 1 Thales WM-24 f.c.
Sonar: Plessey PMS-26 hull-mounted MF (10 kHz)
EW: Decca Cutlass intercept; 2 Protean decoy RL
M: 4 MTU 20V956 TB92 diesels; 2 CP props; 20,512 bhp
Electric: 889 kw (3 × 260-kw MTU 6V51 sets, 1 × 109-kw emergency set)
Range: 2,200/14 **Endurance:** 10 days **Crew:** 90 tot.

Remarks: By 1989 F 83 was in marginal condition with many systems inoperative, and by 1993 she was unseaworthy; the ship was refitted in 1994–95 and participated in a 12-95 exercise at sea. By 1997 F 83 was again out of service; she was said to have been at sea once in 1998, but probably not since. F 84 had been considered beyond repair by 1996 but was seen in refit at Lagos during 2000. F 84 suffered a major engine-room explosion on 22-12-04, killing one and injuring dozens.
Hull systems: Could sustain 20 kts on two diesels. Funnel was heightened after initial trials. Have Vosper gyro-controlled fin stabilizers.
Combat systems: Can carry 750 rounds of 76-mm ammunition and 24 ASW rockets. Have two 50-mm flare rocket launchers. The Sea Cat point-defense missile system (with lightweight triple launcher and 15 total missile magazine capacity) is inoperable, and replacement missiles are unavailable; the sonar set and ASW rocket launcher system are also likely to be beyond repair.

PATROL CRAFT [PC]

♦ 3 Combattante IIIB class (1 nonoperational)
Bldr: CMN, Cherbourg, France

	Laid down	L	In serv.
P 181 Siri	15-5-79	3-6-80	19-2-81
P 182 *Ayam*	7-9-79	10-11-80	11-6-81
P 183 Ekun	14-11-79	11-2-81	18-9-81

Ekun (P 183) French Navy, 5-97

D: 376 tons light (430 fl) **S:** 37 kts
Dim: 56.0 (53.0 pp) × 8.16 (7.61 wl) × 2.15 (hull)
A: 1 76-mm 62-cal. OTO Melara DP; 1 twin 40-mm 70-cal. OTO Melara–Bofors AA; 2 twin 30-mm 75-cal. Emerlec EX-30 AA
Electronics:
Radar: 1 Decca 1226 nav.; 1 Thales Triton surf./air search; 1 Thales Castor-II f.c.
EW: Decca RDL intercept
M: 4 MTU 16V956 TB92 diesels; 4 props; 20,840 bhp (17,320 sust.)
Range: 2,000/15 **Crew:** 42 tot.

Remarks: Three were ordered 11-77. Remained at Cherbourg until 9-5-82 because of a payment dispute. Official commissioning date was 6-2-82 for all. Refitted 1986–88 by builder, but the ships remained in France through 9-92 because of nonpayment for the work. *Siri* (P 181) was inoperable and used for cannibalization from 1995 to 2003 but was again active by 2005.
Combat systems: Have the Thales Vega gun and missile f.c.s., with two Matra Défense Panda gun directors also fitted. The U.S.-made 30-mm guns have a range of 6 km and fire at 1,200 rds/min per mount. Although they are capable of carrying four MM 38 Exocet missiles, all of Nigeria's Exocets have exceeded their shelf lives and are unusable.

♦ 3 FPB 57 class (nonoperational)
Bldr: Friedrich Lürssen Werft, Bremen-Vegesack, Germany

	Laid down	L	In serv.
P 178 Ekpe	17-2-79	17-12-79	8-80
P 179 Damisa	17-2-79	27-3-80	4-81
P 180 Agu	17-2-79	7-11-80	4-81

Damisa (P 179)—outboard *Agu* (P 180) Gilbert Gyssels, 6-81

D: 373 tons light (436 fl) **S:** 35 kts **Dim:** 58.1 (54.4 wl) × 7.62 × 2.83 (props)
A: 1 76-mm 62-cal. OTO Melara DP; 1 twin 40-mm 70-cal. OTO Melara–Bofors AA; 2 twin 30-mm 75-cal. Emerlec EX-30 AA
Electronics:
Radar: 1 Decca TM 1226C nav.; 1 Thales WM-28 track-while-scan f.c.
EW: Decca RDL intercept
M: 4 MTU 16V956 TB92 diesels; 4 props; 20,840 bhp (17,320 sust.)
Electric: 405 kVA tot. **Range:** 1,600/32; 3,000/16 **Crew:** 40 tot.

PATROL CRAFT [PC] *(continued)*

Remarks: Of the three German-built FPB 57–class guided-missile patrol craft, P 180 was cannibalized in the early 1990s to provide spares for the other two. P 178 and 179 were refitted at Lagos in 1995 but by 1997 had again become inoperable. P 178 made a deployment to Sierra Leone in 1997 but broke down en route. During 9-01, the builder received a contract to overhaul all three in Germany. The time-expired Otomat Mk 2 antiship missiles have been removed.

PATROL BOATS [PB]

♦ 15 Defender-class (25-foot) response boats
Bldr: Safe Boats, Port Orchard, Wash. (In serv. 2004–5)

P 313–P 327

D: . . . tons **S:** 40+ kts **Dim:** 7.62 × 2.59 × 1.0
A: 1 7.62-mm mg; **Electronics:** 1 Raytheon Raymarine . . . nav.
M: 2 Honda BF225 4-stroke gasoline outboards; 450 bhp **Range:** 175/35
Fuel: 125 gals. Crew: 3 total

Remarks: Ordered 12-04. Can operate efficiently in shallow 60-cm water, 30mph winds and 6-foot seas. Hundreds of this class are operated by the U.S. Coast Guard.

MINE-COUNTERMEASURES SHIPS

♦ 2 Italian Lerici-class minehunters [MHC]
Bldr: Intermarine, Sarzana

	Laid down	L	Del.	In serv.
M 371 Ohue	23-7-84	22-11-85	28-5-87	4-88
M 372 Maraba	11-3-85	6-6-86	25-2-88	4-88

Maraba (M 372) Carlo Martinelli, 6-87

D: 470 tons (550 fl) **S:** 15.5 kts **Dim:** 51.00 (46.50 pp) × 9.56 × 2.80
A: 1 twin 30-mm 75-cal. Emerlec EX-30 AA; 2 single 20-mm 90-cal. Oerlikon GAM-B01 AA
Electronics:
Radar: 1 Decca 1226 nav.
Sonar: Thales TSM 2022 variable-depth HF
M: 2 MTU 12V396 TC83 diesels; 2 Turbomeccanica PG2000 waterjets; 2,840 bhp
Electric: 600 kw (2 × 300 kw, MTU 6V396 TC diesels driving)
Range: 2,500/12 **Endurance:** 14 days **Crew:** 5 officers, 45 enlisted

Remarks: First ship was ordered 9-4-83, the second in 5-84; an option for two more was not taken up. Difficulties in obtaining an export license delayed delivery. Both were out of service by 1996 but began refits at Lagos during 1999 and are probably back in service.
Hull systems: GRP construction throughout. For free running, the swiveling waterjets are locked centerline, and twin rudders are used for steering; when minehunting, the waterjets are swiveled for steering. Range at 12 kts can be extended to 4,000 n.m. by using the passive roll stabilization tanks as fuel tanks.
Combat systems: Can support 6–7 mine-disposal divers. Carry two Gaymarine Pluto remote-controlled minehunting submersibles, Oropesa Mk 4 mechanical sweep gear, and the Thales IBIS-V minehunting control system. Have Galeazzi two-man decompression chambers for mine-disposal divers.

AMPHIBIOUS WARFARE SHIPS

♦ 2 German Type-502 medium landing ships [LSM] (1 inoperable)
Bldr: Howaldtswerke, Hamburg

	Laid down	L	In serv.
L 1312 Ambe	3-3-78	7-7-78	11-5-79
L 1313 *Ofiom*	15-9-78	7-12-78	7-79

Ambe (L 1312) French Navy, 5-97

D: 1,190 tons light; 1,470 tons normal (1,750 fl) **S:** 17 kts
Dim: 86.9 (74.5 pp) × 14.0 × 2.30
A: 1 40-mm 70-cal. OTO Melara AA; 2 single 20-mm 90-cal. Oerlikon GAM-B01 AA
Electronics: Radar: 1 Decca 1226 nav.
M: 2 MTU 16V956 TB92 diesels; 4 props; 7,000 bhp
Electric: 900 kw tot. **Range:** 5,000/12
Crew: 6 officers, 53 enlisted + 540 troops (1,000 for short distances)

Remarks: The design was originally prepared for the German Navy, which did not order any. L 1313 went aground in 1992 and was not immediately repaired; a 1999 contract to repair and reactivate the ship was canceled in 4-01 when only 50% complete, due to major cost overruns. L 1312 remains marginally operational but can no longer be beached.
Hull systems: Cargo: 400 tons of vehicles plus troops (typically five 40-ton tanks or seven 18-ton tanks plus four 45-ton trucks). Have an articulated bow ramp (now welded shut) and a short stern ramp for loading from a pier. Each engine drives two props.

AUXILIARIES

Note: Nigeria reportedly purchased the 90-m *Tydeman*-class hydrographic survey ship *Tydeman* (A 906) from the Netherlands during 2004. However, payment for the vessel was never received so the decommissioned craft remains pierside at the naval base in Den Helder, Netherlands.

♦ 1 U.K. Bulldog-class survey ship [AGS]
Bldr: Brooke Marine Ltd., Lowestoft, U.K.

	Laid down	L	In serv.
A 498 Lana	5-4-74	4-3-76	15-7-76

D: 800 tons (1,100 fl) **S:** 16 kts **Dim:** 60.95 (57.80 pp) × 11.43 × 3.70
A: 2 single 20-mm 70-cal. Oerlikon Mk 7 AA
Electronics: Radar: 1 Decca 1226 nav.
M: 4 Lister-Blackstone ERS-8-M turbocharged diesels; 2 KaMeWa CP props; 2,640 bhp
Electric: 720 kw tot. (4 × 180 kw, Lister Blackstone ERS4M diesels driving)
Range: 4,500/12 **Fuel:** 139 tons **Endurance:** 90 days
Crew: 5 officers, 34 enlisted

Remarks: Although reported out of service and irreparable by the late 1990s, the ship was reported to be in "reasonable condition" as of 2001 and had probably been overhauled at Lagos. Has a passive-tank stabilization system and can carry one 8.7-m survey launch.

♦ 4 ex-U.S. Coast Guard Balsam-class patrol ships/buoy tenders [AGL]
Bldr: Marine Iron SB Co. (A 503: Duluth Iron Works)

	Laid down	L	In serv.
A 501 Kyanwa (ex-*Sedge,* WLB 402)	6-10-43	27-11-43	5-7-44
A 502 Ologbo (ex-*Cowslip,* WLB 277)	16-9-41	11-4-42	17-10-42
A 503 Nwambe (ex-*Firebush,* WLB 393)	12-11-43	3-2-44	20-7-44
A 504 Obula (ex-*Sassafras,* WLB 401)	16-8-43	5-10-43	23-5-44

Nwambe (A 503) George R. Schneider, 7-03

Kyanwa (A 501) George R. Schneider, 2-03

AUXILIARIES *(continued)*

D: 697 tons light (1,038 fl) **S:** 12–14 kts **Dim:** 54.9 (51.8 pp) × 11.3 × 4.0
A: Small arms
Electronics: Radar: 1 Hughes-Furuno SPS-73 nav.
M: 2 G.M. EMD 645 diesels, electric drive; 1 prop; 1,070 shp
Electric: 400 kw tot. **Range:** 5,500/12 **Crew:** 42 tot.

Remarks: A 501 was decommissioned from the U.S. Coast Guard 15-11-02 and was transferred 21-12-02; A 502 was decommissioned 11-12-02 and transferred 26-1-03; A 503 was decommissioned and transferred 30-6-03; A 504 was decommissioned 31-10-03 and transferred to Nigeria during 2004. All three are intended for general logistic support duties. Very robustly constructed vessels that still have a number of years' service remaining despite their advanced age. Received major service-life extension program overhauls between 1983 and 1991. Are used for maritime law enforcement, training, and search-and-rescue in Nigerian service. Were transferred free of charge by the United States with grants of $750K per ship to outfit them and train their crews in the U.S. Were transferred unarmed, although the Nigerians will probably arm them.

SERVICE CRAFT

♦ **2 Commander Apayi Joe–class large harbor tugs [YTB]**
Bldr: Scheepswerf de Wiel BV, Asperen, the Netherlands

A 499 Commander Apayi Joe (In serv. 9-83)
A 500 Commander Rudolf (In serv. . . .)

Commander Rudolf (A 500) H&L Van Ginderen, 7-84

D: 310 tons (fl) **S:** 11 kts **Dim:** 23.17 × 7.19 × 2.91
M: 2 M.A.N. diesels; 2 props; 1,510 bhp

Remarks: 130 grt. *Commander Rudolf* was completed but not paid for and was retained by the builder for commercial use; by 1995, however, the craft had been delivered. Their operational status remains unknown, but at least one is probably capable of getting to sea.

♦ **1 water lighter [YW]**

Water Barge One

Remarks: Self-propelled. Current status unknown.

Disposal note: Training craft *Ruwan Yaro* (A 497; ex-*Ogina Bereton*) was sunk by scuttling on 1-12-01.

Note: There were also 44 service launches built by Fairey Marine, Hamble, U.K.: 2 of 10 m, 22 of 7 m, 15 of 6.7 m, and 5 of 5.5 m. Four Cheverton 8.2-m launches are also in use. Eight Flight Refueling Sea Flash 8.5-m, radio-controlled target boats were delivered in 1987. Two 11.75-m torpedo retrievers were delivered by Crestitalia, Ameglia, Italy, in 1986. Damen SY, Gorinchem, the Netherlands, delivered two 27-m fuel lighters and two small PushyCat 46 tugs early in 1986 for naval use. The operational status of all of these craft is unknown.

NIGERIAN COAST GUARD

Note: The coast guard is under the operational control of the navy, and naval personnel man its craft. One source reports that none of the craft listed below remain operational.

PATROL BOATS [WPB]

♦ **6 Type SM-500**
Bldr: Simonneau, Fontenay-le-Comte, France (In serv. 1986–87)

P 233 P 234 P 235 P 236 P 237 P 238

D: 22 tons (25 fl) **S:** 33 kts **Dim:** 15.80 (14.05 wl) × 4.60 × 0.90 (1.80 props)
A: 2 single 7.62-mm mg **Electronics:** Radar: 1 Decca 976 nav.
M: 2 MTU 6V396 TC82DE diesels; 2 props; 2,400 bhp
Range: 375/25 **Fuel:** 2,500 liters **Crew:** 6 tot.

Remarks: Aluminum construction. The first delivered in 5-86, the second in 6-86.

P 234 Simmoneau, 1986

♦ **6 Stan Pat 1500 patrol craft**
Bldr: Damen, Gorinchem, the Netherlands

P 227 through P 229 (In serv. 4-86) P 230 through P 232 (In serv. 6-86)

P 230 Damen, 7-86

D: 16 tons (fl) **S:** 32 kts **Dim:** 15.11 (13.57 wl) × 4.45 × 1.40 (0.75 mean hull)
A: 1 7.62-mm mg **Electronics:** Radar: 1 Decca . . . nav.
M: 2 MTU 6V331 TC82 diesels; 2 props; 2,250 bhp **Fuel:** 2 m^3 **Crew:** 6 tot.

Remarks: Several may be nonoperational.

Note: The civilian marine police organization, with approximately 1,600 personnel, is headquartered at Lagos and operates a number of launches on the Niger River and Lake Chad. Ten 7.62-m, 35-kt, aluminum-hulled launches (PAD.42 through PAD.51) were delivered for police use by Abels Boatyard, Bristol, U.K., on 19-10-99; the boats are powered by two 80-bhp Yamaha gasoline outboards. The customs service also has several small launches.

NORWAY

Kingdom of Norway

NORSKE MARINE

Personnel: Approx. 4,500 tot. plus about 270 in the Coast Guard and 160 in Coast Artillery units. The Naval Home Guard has a mobilization strength of about 4,900 officers and personnel with access to some 235 boats.

Bases: Headquarters, Eastern District, is at *Karl Johans* Vern (base), Horten. Headquarters, Western District, is at Haakonsvern, Bergen. Other district bases are located at Ramsund, Harstad, and at Olavsvern, Tromsø. Submarine repair and maintenance are carried out at Laksevag.

Organization: Command of naval forces and coastal artillery forts is divided between Commander, Naval Forces South Norway (with naval district commands Østlandet, Sørlandet, Rogaland, Vestlandet, and Trøndelag), and Commander, Naval Forces North Norway (with naval district commands Halogaland and Tromsø). Naval forces are subordinate to Commanders, Allied Forces South Norway and North Norway, who are in turn subordinate to the Chief of Defense Norway.

NORSKE MARINE *(continued)*

Under the new defense reductions begun in 2002, Olavsvern, Hysnes, Ulsnes, Marvika, and Karljohansvern Naval Bases will be closed; the Officer Candidate School will be established at Horten and existing naval and coast artillery officer candidate schools closed; the Clearance Diver Command is being established at Haakonsvern; and the number of enlisted personnel to be trained at the KNM *Harald Hårfagre* Naval Training Center has been reduced. Also, three Coastal Artillery–controlled minefields, three land-based torpedo batteries, and all nine coastal artillery forts are to be mothballed, while the Coast Artillery's separate training fort and training units will be disestablished. A new Coastal Ranger Command is being established at Trondenes to train and support the new Coastal Ranger squads.

Maritime Aviation: The Royal Norwegian Navy itself operates no aircraft. Six WG-13 Lynx helicopters are used by the coast guard. The Royal Norwegian Air Force can use its F-16 fighters in a maritime strike role, using Penguin Mk 3 missiles. For maritime surveillance duties, four P-3C Update III Orions are operated by Royal Norwegian Air Force 333 Sqn.; the aircraft began an Update Improvement Program in 1-98, receiving APS-137(V)5 inverse synthetic aperture radars, OASIS-III (Over-the-Horizon Airborne Sensor Information System) and SATCOM gear, upgrades to the AAR-36 infrared detection system, ARN-151 GPS, AAR-47 missile-warning gear, and the ALE-47 decoy system. In addition, the air force operates eight Mk 43, one Mk 43A, and two Mk 43B Westland Sea King and 20 Bell UH-1D helicopters in search-and-rescue duties. Earlier Sea King variants are being updated to Mk 43B configuration with roof-mounted Bendix RSR 1500 radar, nose-mounted Bendix RDR 1300 radar, and FLIR 2000. On 13-9-01, 14 NH-90 helicopters were ordered for shipboard service, with six to be configured for ASW and the others for search-and-rescue duties; the contract also contained an option for a further 10 SAR versions; deliveries began in 2006 and will continue through 2009.

The maritime squadrons of the Royal Norwegian Air Force are:

Aircraft	*Squadron*	*Bases*
Sea King	330 Sqn.	Banak, Bodø, Ørland, Sola
Orion	333 Sqn.	Andøya
Lynx	337 Sqn.	Bardufoss
UH-1D	719 Sqn.	Bodø
UH-1D	720 Sqn.	Rygge

Coast Artillery: Norway's coastline near important ports and harbors is heavily fortified. Existing facilities employ 75-mm 60-cal. Bofors guns acquired during the 1960s, shore-mounted torpedo tubes, Penguin antiship missiles, and Swedish RBS-70 surface-to-air missiles. The Bofors 120-mm automatic ERSTA coast defense gun was ordered in 1981 and first firings took place at Trondheim in 1991; the weapon has a 27-km range and fires 24.5- or 24.6-kg shells at 25 rds/min. Bofors Weapon Systems has supplied 400 RBS-17 Hellfire coast defense missiles and 60 launchers to equip 12 mobile missile batteries under a 1-96 contract; the missiles replace old German fixed 105-mm coast defense guns. Shore-mounted artillery was to be discarded between 2002 and 2005, but the parliament (*Storting*) required on 3-7-01 that nine coastal forts be retained in "mothballed" condition; nonetheless, three controlled minefields, three shore-based torpedo batteries, and all nine coastal artillery forts are to be mothballed.

Note: Names to naval ships are prefixed by KNM (*Kgl. Norske Marine*), while those of coast guard vessels are prefixed by K/V (*Kystvakt*). Kvaerner Mandal shipyard was sold to Umø A/S early in 2000.

WEAPONS AND SYSTEMS

The name of the principal Norwegian armaments and military electronics manufacturer was restored to Kongsberg A/S in mid-1995; from 1987, the company was known as Norsk Fortvartechnologi A/S (NFT).

The Norwegian Navy uses mostly British, American, and Swedish weapons and systems, but it has built two systems of its own, the Terne automatic ASW rocket system and the Penguin surface-to-surface missile, which are described below. The French Mistral point-defense SAM was selected for fleet-wide use in 1-93. Six launchers and 200 RIM-116 RAM point-defense missiles were requested from the United States in 1996 for use on the five new frigates.

Submarines are equipped with Swedish Tp 617 (45 kts, 20,000-m range) or American NT-37C (20,000-m range) and Mk 37 Mod. 2 wire-guided torpedoes. On 16-12-91, 146 German DM-2A3 wire-guided torpedoes were ordered for the *Ula*-class submarines. Some 190 British Stingray ASW torpedoes were delivered 1990–92 for use on P-3C Orion aircraft. Norway has also developed its own radar and electro-optical gun and missile fire-control systems. Sonars are manufactured by Kongsberg Simrad Mesotech, which has exported a number of small, high-frequency sets for naval use.

Terne-3 Mk 10 (ASW): Mfr: Kongsberg Defence & Aerospace A/S (KDA). Developed by Kongsberg, the sextuple launcher mount weighs a little less than 3 tons and ripple-launches its rockets at 45° to 75° elevation, the latter for minimum range. Reloads automatically in 40 seconds. The rocket is 1.97 m in length, 0.2 m in diameter, and 120 kg in weight (warhead: 48 kg), and has a combination timed and proximity fuze. Employed on the *Oslo* class. Received "Mk 10" upgrade 1991–93. Maximum range: 900 m.

NSM (Nytt Sjomalsmissil): Mfr: Kongsberg Defence & Aerospace A/S (KDA). A new-generation, subsonic, turbojet-powered, GPS and infrared-homing replacement for the Penguin series; in development. The decision was made in 1995 not to go ahead with a coast-defense, land-launched version. A contract was let 24-12-96 for the research and development program; Kongsberg was working in cooperation with Aérospatiale under a 1-9-97 agreement but teamed with Germany's DaimlerChrysler Aerospace (now EADS) and TDW in 5-00 for the development of the missile. The launch canister is 4.0 m long and 81 × 80 cm in cross section. The missile airframe incorporates signature-reduction measures. First launch was on 24-10-00 with deliveries beginning in 2005–6. The missile is intended to equip *Skjold-* and *Fridtjof Nansen*–class warships.

Length: 3.95 m (with booster) **Wingspan:** 1.4 m (0.7 folded)
Weight: 412 kg (with 65-kg booster) **Warhead:** 120 kg
Propulsion: Microturbo TRI-40 turbofan **Speed:** high subsonic
Max. range: 200+ km **Guidance:** imaging infrared and GPS

Penguin Mk 1: Mfr: Kongsberg Defence & Aerospace A/S (KDA). The missile is protected by a fiberglass container that also serves as a launcher. No longer in production, and most, if not all, have been removed from the ships and craft that carried them.

Length: 2.95 m **Diameter:** 0.28 m **Wingspan:** 1.42 m
Weight: 330 kg **Speed:** Mach 0.7
Max. range: 20,000 m **Guidance:** Infrared homing

Penguin Mk 2: Mfr: Kongsberg Defence & Aerospace A/S (KDA). An Mk 2 Mod. 7 helicopter-launched version was developed for the U.S. Navy.

Length: 3.00 m **Diameter:** 0.28 m **Wingspan:** 1.42 m
Weight: 340 kg **Warhead:** 120-kg Bullpup Mk 19 (50-kg explosive)
Speed: Mach 0.8
Max. range: 26,000 m **Guidance:** infrared homing

Penguin Mk 3 (air-launched): Mfr: Kongsberg Defence & Aerospace A/S (KDA). Penguin Mk 3 can be launched at altitudes of 150 to 30,000 ft.

Length: 3.20 m **Diameter:** 0.28 m **Wingspan:** 1.00 m
Weight: 360 kg (400 with launcher)
Warhead: 120 kg (50-kg explosive) **Speed:** Mach 0.8
Max. range: 40,000+ m **Guidance:** infrared homing

Mines: Existing Mk 2 and Mk 51 controlled mines have been modernized with new fuzing and a command-and-control system linked to shore-based surveillance radars under Project Ida. The Project 6033 New Independent Mine was approved 7-92 and may result in a deepwater rising mine; BAE Systems in the U.K., Bofors Underwater Systems, and Kongsberg are competing to design the system, in conjunction with other partners. Initial production model deliveries would come after 2004.

Mine countermeasures: Kongsberg Simrad Mesotech, Norway, has developed the SM 2000, a 200-kHz, multibeam, obstacle-avoidance sonar that can also be employed in a mine-countermeasures role. Its range is 400 m, and the system can be used at speeds up to 4 kts. Six sets for shipboard use are believed to have been delivered by 2000. Kongsberg manufactures the Minesniper (ex-Hugin-I) remotely operated mine detection and disposal vehicle; weighing about 30 kg and being about 2 m long, it has been ordered by the Spanish Navy. On 11-2-03, Kongsberg received a development prototype for the Hugin 1000, which will have an endurance of 20 hours and be able to operate to 600-m depths; the craft's sensor package will enable it to be used for seabed route surveys and mine detection and classification.

ATTACK SUBMARINES [SS]

Note: Norway withdrew from the now-defunct Viking submarine project during 7-02 and may not order new submarines until the mid-2020s.

♦ 6 Ula class (Project 6071/German Type 210)
Bldr: Thyssen Nordseewerke, Emden

	Laid down	L	In serv.
S 300 Ula	29-1-87	28-7-88	27-4-89
S 301 Utsira	15-6-90	21-11-91	30-4-92
S 302 Utstein	6-12-89	25-4-91	14-11-91
S 303 Utvaer	8-12-88	19-4-90	8-11-90
S 304 Uthaug	15-6-89	18-10-90	7-5-91
S 305 Uredd	23-6-88	22-9-89	3-5-90

Ula (S 300) Derek Fox, 8-04

Utsira (S 301) Eivind Rodlie, 6-02

Utstein (S 302)—during NATO exercise "Odin-One" U.S. Navy, 8-03

D: 940 tons std.; 1,040 tons surf./1,150 tons sub.
S: 11 kts surf./23 kts sub. **Dim:** 59.00 × 5.40 × 4.60
A: 8 bow 533-mm TT (14 DM-2A3 Seehake wire-guided torpedoes)

ATTACK SUBMARINES [SS] *(continued)*

Electronics:
Radar: 1 Kelvin-Hughes Type 1007 nav./surf. search
Sonar: STN Atlas Elektronik DBQS-21F (CSU-83) suite; Thales passive conformal arrays
EW: Racal Sealion intercept
M: 2 MTU 16V652 MB diesels (1,260 bhp each), 2 × 870-kw, 3-phase NEBB generator sets, 1 Siemens electric motor; 1 prop; 6,000 shp
Range: 5,000/8 snorkel **Fuel:** 100 tons **Endurance:** 40 days
Crew: 3 officers, 15–17 enlisted

Remarks: Six were ordered 30-9-82; an option to order two more was later dropped. Reportedly, the ships were plagued with noisy machinery and weapons system control problems and were initially the source of considerable dissatisfaction. S 300 was to commission 4-90 after one year of trials, which began 27-4-89; she was placed in reserve 15-11-91 to 1994, pending delivery of torpedoes. S 304 collided with an uncharted rock while submerged 2-12-94, and grounded later the same day while returning to port. Only four are active at any given time, with the others decommissioned for overhaul.
Hull systems: Normal operating depth: 250 m. Have Anker batteries. All but S 300 have pressure hulls built by Kværner Brug, Oslo. Have X-form stern control surfaces.
Combat systems: The Kongsberg MSI-90U torpedo f.c.s. are being updated under a 5-95 contract, with completions between 1998 and 2005. Fitted with the Carl Zeiss SERO 40 periscope suite, with SERO 14 optronic search periscope and SERO 15 attack periscope with laser rangefinder; also have a GPS terminal. Use Riva Calzoni Trident non-pressure-hull-penetrating radio masts. A LOFAR (LOw-Frequency Active Ranging) sonar system is to be added.

Disposal note: Modernized Type 207 submarines *Skolpen* (S 306), *Stord* (S 308), *Svenner* (S 309), and *Kunna* (S 319) were withdrawn from service at the end of 2001 and were transferred to Poland between mid-2002 and 2004.

FRIGATES [FF]

♦ 2 (+ 3) Fridtjof Nansen class (Project 6088)
Bldr: Navantia (formerly Izar), El Ferrol

	Laid down	L	In serv.
F 310 Fridtjof Nansen	9-4-03	3-6-04	5-4-06
F 311 Roald Amundsen	3-6-04	25-5-05	9-06
F 312 Otto Sverdrup	28-5-05	28-4-06	9-07
F 313 Helge Ingstad	28-4-06	2007	2008
F 314 Thor Heyerdahl	2007	2008	2009

D: 4,681 tons (5,130 fl) **S:** 27 kts (18 cruise on diesels)
Dim: 132.00 (120.39 wl) × 16.80 (15.90 wl) × 4.90 (mean hull)
A: 8 NSM SSM; 8-cell Mk 41VLS (32 RIM-7P ESSM Sea Sparrow missiles); 1 76-mm 62-cal. OTO Melara SuperRapid DP; 4 single 12.7-mm mg; 4 fixed, paired 324-mm ASW TT (Stingray torpedoes); 1 or 2 d.c. racks; 1 NH-90 helicopter
Electronics:
Radar: 3 Decca BridgeMaster . . . ARPA nav. (2 X-band, 1 S-band); 1 Lockheed Martin SPY-1F 3-D tracking, target-desig., and weapons control; 2 Raytheon SPG-62 target illuminators
Sonar: Thales TSM 2633 (MRS 2000) Spherion hull-mounted MF; Thales CAPTAS Mk 2(V)1 active/passive towed linear array.
EW: Condor CS-3701 active/passive suite; 2 12-round Terma DL-12T decoy RL; Loki torpedo decoy syst.; EADS COLDS laser countermeasure
E/O: Sagem VIGY 20 IR and optical surveillance and tracking syst.

Fridtjof Nansen (F 310) Wikimedia.org, 2006

M: CODAG: 2 Izar Bravo 12-cyl. diesels (6,000 bhp each), 1 G.E. LM-2500 gas turbine (28,832 shp); 2 CP props; 40,832 hp max.—1 1,340-shp retractable bow-thruster
Electric: 3,600 kw tot. (4 × 900-kw alternators, MTU 12V 396 diesels driving)
Range: 4,500/16 **Crew:** 120 tot. (accomm. for 146)

Remarks: Spain's Empresa Nacional Bazán, later Izar and now Navantia, teamed with Lockheed Martin Government Systems, won the design competition in 5-99, with the selection of the Bazán offer of its F 310 design confirmed 29-2-00. Permission to go ahead with the program was given by the parliament 31-5-00, and the construction contract was signed 23-6-00. The program is expected to cost over $2 billion (U.S.) and is the single largest Norwegian defense project ever undertaken. Some of the armament and sensor systems may have been transferred from the *Oslo* class. Though the 4th and 5th units were to have originally been completed in Norway, plans were altered during 2004 and all units are being constructed in Spain. While having sophisticated sensor and combat data systems, the ships are not heavily armed.
Hull systems: Steel hull and superstructure. Manufactured from 24 modules. Hulls have 13 watertight compartments. Able to operate with no personnel in the engine rooms, with the plant operated from the bridge or main engineering control room. There are two 690-V main and two 450-V ship's service electric switchboards, with two 690/450-V, 2,000-kVA transformers. Signature-reduction measures include topside shaping, acoustically hooded machinery and equipment, an IR suppression system, a wet-down spray system, degaussing, propeller shaft grounding, and a flexible drive train. Extensive medical facilities are carried. There are four damage-control stations and a complete NBC warfare defense system. The vessels are able to remain mobile with two compartments flooded. The originally planned electric drive system was eliminated to save costs, and the electrical generation plant is considerably less powerful than the 8,200-kw total originally envisaged.
Combat systems: Lockheed Martin is responsible for combat systems integration in conjunction with Kongsberg; the Aegis combat system, SPY-1F, is a scaled version of the SPY-1D radar found on *Arleigh Burke*–class DDGs. The combat system has Kongsberg SC 3100 and SC 3200 operator consoles instead of the UYQ-70 terminals used by the U.S. Navy. Equipped to operate with Link 11, with provisions for Link 16 and Link 22 when available. The Kongsberg-Thales MSI-2005F ASW weapons-control

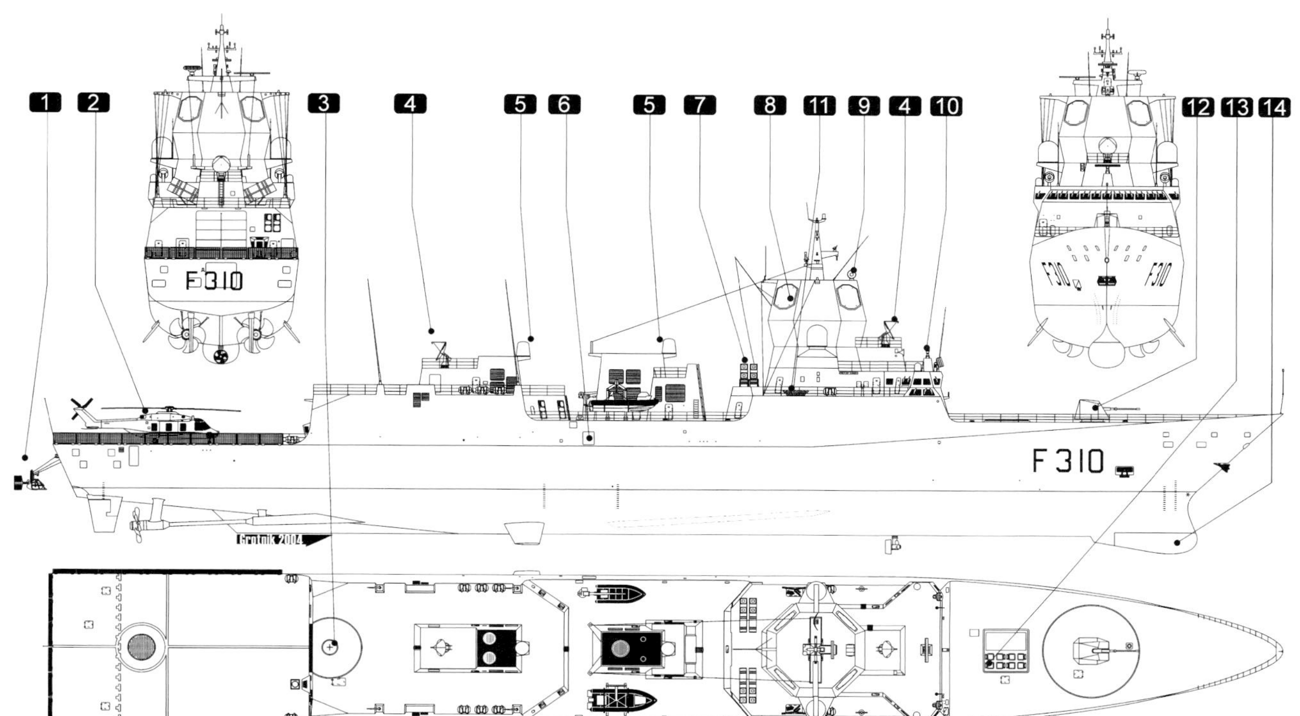

Fridtjof Nansen (F 310) 1. CAPTAS Mk II V1 towed array 2. NH-90 ASW helicopter 3. Provision for CIWS AA gun 4. SPG-62 target illuminator 5. CS-3701 EW antennas 6. 324 mm ASW torpedo tubes 7. NSM antiship missiles 8. SPY-1F Aegis antenna arrays 9. VIGY 20 electro-optical fc. system 10. Bridge Master nav. radar 11. Terma DL-12T decoy launcher 12. 76-mm 62-cal. OTO Melara DP 13. Mk 41 vertical-launch system 14. TSM 2633 Spherion sonar Drawing by Tomasz Grotnik, 2004

FRIGATES [FF] *(continued)*

system will be integrated into the main system. The COLDS (Common Opto-electronic Laser Detection System) detects missile laser seekers and directs a laser beam of equivalent pulse repetition frequency against a safe spot on the ocean to spoof the missile. Space and weight are reserved for a second eight-cell Mk 41 VLS, but there are no immediate plans to incorporate the Standard SM-2 missile. As delivered there are two positions for close-in AA defense weapons to be added later. All units of the class are fitted to carry the Loki offboard torpedo defense system launched from a 130-mm rocket launcher. NH-90-series helicopters are expected to be procured for the ships, and accommodations are provided for a 10-strong aviation personnel group. A proposal was made during 2002 to install a 127-mm gun instead of the 76-mm weapon and to add a second Mk 41 VLS.

♦ 2 Oslo class

Bldr: Marinens Hovedverft (Naval Dockyard), Horten

	Laid down	L	In serv.	Mod. completed
F 302 Trondheim	1963	4-9-64	2-6-66	30-11-87
F 304 Narvik	1964	8-1-65	30-11-66	21-10-88

Trondheim (F 302) Bernard Prézelin, 2-05

Trondheim (F 302) Bernard Prézelin, 2-05

Trondheim (F 302) Rob Cabo, 4-05

D: 1,670 tons (1,970 fl) **S:** 25 kts
Dim: 96.62 (93.87 pp) × 11.17 × 4.52 (5.62 over prop)
A: 1 8-round Mk 29 SAM launcher (24 RIM-7M Sea Sparrow missiles); 1 twin 76.2-mm 50-cal. U.S. Mk. 33 DP; 1 40-mm 70-cal. Bofors AA; 1 6-round Terne-3 Mk 10 ASW RL; 2 triple 324-mm Mk 32 Mod. 5 ASW TT (6 Stingray torpedoes); 1 d.c. rack (6 d.c.)
Electronics:
Radar: 1 Decca . . . nav.; 1 Decca TM 1226 nav./surf. search; 1 Siemens-Plessey AWS-9(2D) air search; 1 CelsiusTech 9LV 200 Mk 2 gun f.c.; 1 Raytheon Mk 95 SAM f.c.
Sonar: Thales TSM 2633 (Spherion Mk 1) hull-mounted and VDS (7 kHz); Kongsberg Terne-3 hull-mounted HF attack
EW: ArgoSystems APECS intercept; Nera SR-1A intercept; 2 . . . decoy RL
M: 1 set Laval-Ljungstrom PN 20 geared steam turbines; 1 prop; 20,000 shp
Boilers: 2 Babcock & Wilcox; 42.18 kg/cm^2, 454° C **Electric:** 1,100 kw tot.
Range: 4,500/15 **Crew:** 11 officers, 19 senior petty officers, 90 other enlisted

Remarks: Half of the construction cost was financed by the United States. Rebuilt during the late 1970s with the Penguin antiship missile, NATO Sea Sparrow point-defense SAM, and ASW torpedo tubes. All were modernized again between 1987 and 1988.
Hull systems: Design is based on the U.S. *Dealey* class, but with higher freeboard forward and many European subsystems. Due to excessive weights aft and resultant hull cracking, the stern of F 304 was strengthened during an overhaul completed late in 1994, adding some 200 tons to the displacement; the alteration was made to the other one and restrictions on their open-ocean operations were lifted. They are equipped with UFAS Sjøbjørn-25-class aluminum-hulled, rigid inflatable personnel launches powered by a 350-bhp Yanmar 6LY-UTE diesel driving a Hamilton 273 waterjet for speeds up to 33 kts.
Combat systems: By the end of 1998, all had received Siemens-Plessey AWS-9 (2-D) air-search radars in place of the previous Siemens MPDR-45 sets; also installed was the Siemens-Plessey ODIN command and fire-control system as a subsystem to the existing NFT MSI-3100 combat control system. Have NATO Link 11 and Link 14 datalink capability. Two 20-mm 90-cal. Rheinmetall AA have been removed from the after superstructure, and Penguin antiship missiles are no longer carried. Use the Raytheon Mk 91 Mod. 0 control system for the NATO Sea Sparrow SAM system, with a twin-antenna Mk 95 radar director (mounted on a pylon atop the missile-reload magazine). Mounted just forward of the Mk 29 missile launcher is a TVT-300 lead-computing optronic director for the 40-mm AA gun.
Disposals: Sister *Oslo* (F 300) ran aground 24-1-94 and sank the next day after having been pulled off the shore. *Stavanger* (F 303) was placed in reserve in 4-99 and was sunk as a target on 14-6-02, and *Bergen* (F 301) was decommissioned during 8-05. The remaining two are due to be replaced by the *Fridtjof Nansen* class by 2008.

AIR-CUSHION GUIDED-MISSILE PATROL BOATS [PTGA]

♦ 1 (+ 5) Skjold class (Project 6081)

Bldrs: P 960: Kværner Mandal A/S, Mandal; others: Umoe Mandal A/S, Mandal

	Laid down	L	In serv.
P 960 Skjold	8-97	22-9-98	17-4-99
P 961 Storm	2006	2007	2-08
P 962 Skudd	2006	2007	7-08
P 963 Steil	2006	2007	11-08
P 964 Glimt	2007	2008	3-09
P 965 Gnist	2007	2008	7-09

Skjold (P 960)—painted in a splinter camouflage scheme U.S. Navy, 11-01

Skjold (P 960)—during trials with OTOMelara 76-mm gun aboard KNM Tordenskjold, 9-99

D: 260 tons (fl) **S:** 55 kts (57.1 on trials)
Dim: 46.79 (41.50 pp) × 13.50 × 2.25 (0.83 on cushion)
A: Provision for 8 NSM SSM; 1 76-mm 62-cal. OTO Melara SuperRapid DP; 1 2-round Simbad point-defense SAM launcher (Mistral missiles)
Electronics:
Radar: 1 Ericsson Sea Giraffe surf./air search; 1 CelsiusTech CEROS 200 f.c. (P 960 only: 2 Decca 1229 nav., no search or f.c. radars)
EW: . . . intercept (P 960: none)
E/O: SAGEM VIGY 20 optronic f.c.
M: CODOG: 2 Rolls-Royce–Allison 571-KF9 gas turbines (8,160 shp each), 2 MTU 6R183 TE92 auxiliary diesels (500 bhp each); 2 KaMeWa 80S2 waterjets; 16,320 shp—2 MTU 12V183 TE92 diesels (985 bhp each) driving lift fans
Electric: 456 kw tot (2 MTU 6R183 TE52 diesels driving)
Range: . . . / . . . **Endurance:** 14 days **Crew:** 4 officers, 11 enlisted

Remarks: *Skjold* means "Shield." Originally to have been a class of 24 to replace the *Storm* and *Snögg* classes. Kværner Mandal received the $30-million prototype contract on 30-8-96, and five to seven production versions were to have been ordered in 1999 after 15 months of trials (with the prototype later to refit to production standard); the final unit would have been delivered in 2004. The start for the production version was delayed to 2006 in 1-97 but restored to 2000 in mid-1998 to preserve industrial capabilities; then the order for six was eliminated from the 1999 budget. The navy then

AIR-CUSHION GUIDED-MISSILE PATROL BOATS [PTGA] *(continued)*

announced a desire to order the seven additional units in 2003, but the program was recommended for cancellation by the chief of defense in 6-00 and the prototype was to have been stricken during 2002; instead, however, the U.S. Navy leased the craft and the services of a Norwegian crew from 6-9-01 to 5-9-02, and during that time, the Norwegian Parliament convinced the government to fund construction of five more. P 960 averaged 49 kts while under way during her transatlantic voyage in 9-01.
Hull systems: Foam-core GRP-construction, rigid-sidewall surface effect ship, with infrared and radio energy shielding molded into the structure to reduce signature. Has an automatic ride control system. Production versions may have a different propulsion system with Rolls-Royce–Allison 571-KF11 gas turbines of up to 16,400 kw total output to sustain 55 kts. The prototype was to be able to sustain 44 kts in a State 3 sea. Can operate in waters as shallow as 1 m.
Combat systems: The SENIT 2000 combat system, ordered 26-6-97, is to be made by a consortium of Kongsberg and Simrad with DCN, France, and will be a variant of DCN's SENIT 8 system; there are six display consoles. The principal radar is to be a two-dimensional system vice the originally planned 3-D radar. The communications system includes HF through UHF radios, cryptographic systems, and Link 11. The missile launchers are to be recessed into the stern area, and decoy rocket launchers are to be recessed into the bow area. Aboard in 9-99 was an experimental, reduced radar reflectivity OTO Melara 76-mm mount; the mount was returned to OTO Melara early in 10-99. During her U.S. Navy charter in 2001–2, P 960 was completely unarmed; she carried two Decca 1226 navigational radars and no EW equipment, while the combat center was largely empty of equipment.

GUIDED-MISSILE PATROL CRAFT [PTG]

♦ 14 Hauk class
Bldr: Bergens Mekaniske Verksteder (last four: Westamarin A/S, Alta)

	In serv.		In serv.
P 986 HAUK	17-8-78	P 993 LOM	15-1-80
P 987 ØRN	19-1-79	P 994 STEGG	18-3-80
P 988 TERNE	13-3-79	P 995 FALK	30-4-80
P 989 TJELD	25-5-79	P 996 RAVN	20-5-80
P 990 SKARV	17-7-79	P 997 GRIBB	10-7-80
P 991 TEIST	11-9-79	P 998 GEIR	16-9-80
P 992 JO	1-11-79	P 999 ERLE	10-12-80

Hauk (P 986)—note penguin missile canisters — Frank Behling, 2003

Jo (P 992) — Frank Findler, 4-03

D: 130 tons (155 fl) **S:** 35 kts **Dim:** 36.53 × 6.3 × 1.65
A: Provision for 4 Penguin Mk 2 SSM—fitted with 1 40-mm 70-cal. Bofors AA; 1 2-round Simbad point-defense SAM launcher (Mistral missiles); 2 fixed 533-mm TT (2 Bofors Tp 61 wire-guided torpedoes)
Electronics:
Radar: 1 Decca TM 1226 nav., 1 . . . surf. search
Sonar: Simrad SQ3D/SF hull-mounted HF
EW: Racal Matilda radar intercept
E/O: MSI-80S director
M: 2 MTU 16V538 TB92 diesels; 2 props; 7,340 bhp
Range: 440/34 **Crew:** 6 officers, 18 enlisted

Remarks: A modernization program at Umoe-Mandal Shipyard is all but completed, with P 991, P 992, and P 994 accepted on 9-11-01 and the others apparently completed by the end of 2003. Crews include nine conscripts; some women also serve aboard. P 992 ran hard aground at 25 kts early in 2-02 but was not badly damaged and returned to service within a month.
Hull systems: P 989 has been fitted with a wave-piercing bow to provide a 0.5-kt speed increase and improved propulsion efficiency.
Combat systems: Have the Kongsberg MSI-80S fire-control system, which uses two Decca radars plus a Phillips TVT-300 electro-optical tracker and an Ericsson laser rangefinder. Have two 50-mm flare RL. During 1992–94 refits, received one Simbad twin-launcher for Mistral surface-to-air missiles in place of the 20-mm AA gun. The torpedoes have a 25-km range. Penguin missiles are not normally carried.
Modernization: The modernization program includes substituting the SENIT 2000 combat system chosen for the *Skjold* class, replacing the MSI-80S optronic director with a SAGEM VIGY 20, upgrading the 40-mm gun with an autoloader system, replacing the radar and EW system, installing new decoy rocket launchers, and adding a new communications suite with a NATO Link 11 capability.

PATROL BOATS [PB]

♦ 6 Harek class (Type 1300 Mk 2)
Bldr: . . . , Ålesund (In serv. 2003–4)

SHV 101 HAREK	SHV 104 KVITSØY
SHV 102 . . .	SHV 105 . . .
SHV 103 . . .	SHV 106 . . .

Kvitsøy (SHV-104) — *Okrety Wojenn* via Jaroslaw Malinowski, 2004

D: 10 tons **S:** 40 kts **Dim:** 13.30 × 3.65 × 0.75)
A: 2 single 12.7-mm M2 mg
Electronics: Radar: 1 . . . nav.
M: 2 Volvo-Penta TAMD 74EDC diesels; 2 waterjets; 900 bhp **Crew:** 2

Remarks: Ordered 2003 for antiterrorism operations. Assigned to the Naval Home Guard. Patrol boats numbered SHV-101 through SHV-103 are built to a slightly modified design.

♦ 7 Gyda class (Type 1290)
Bldr: . . . , Ålesund (In serv. 2003–4)

L 4540	L 4543	L 4545
L 4541	L 4544	L 4546
L 4542		

D: 7 tons **S:** 42 kts **Dim:** 12.9 × 3.5 × 0.75)
A: 2 single 12.7-mm M2 mg
Electronics: Radar: 1 . . . nav.
M: 2 Volvo TAMD 74 C diesels; 2 waterjets; 900 bhp **Crew:** 2

Remarks: Ordered 2003 for anti-terrorism operations. Assigned to the Naval Home Guard.

MINE WARFARE SHIPS

♦ 1 Vidar-class minelayer [MM]
Bldr: Mjellem & Karlsen, Bergen

	Laid down	L	In serv.
N 52 VIDAR	1-3-76	18-3-77	21-10-77

D: 1,500 tons (1,722 fl) **S:** 15 kts **Dim:** 64.80 (60.00 pp) × 12.00 × 4.00 (hull)
A: 2 single 40-mm 70-cal. Bofors AA; 1 2-round Simbad point-defense SAM launcher (Mistral missiles); 320 mines
Electronics:
Radar: 2 Decca TM 1226 nav.
Sonar: Simrad SQ3D hull-mounted HF
M: 2 Wichmann 7AX diesels; 2 props; 4,200 bhp—425-shp bow-thruster
Electric: 1,000 kw tot. **Range:** . . . / . . . **Fuel:** 247 tons **Crew:** 50 tot.

Remarks: Ordered 11-6-75. Was modified 5-98 with additional command-and-control facilities as flagship of NATO's ComStanNavForLant. Is to operate until 2008.
Combat systems: Capable of serving as a minelayer (mines carried on three decks, with electric elevators to first platform deck and upper deck, and three mine-laying rails), torpedo-recovery ship, personnel and cargo transport, fisheries-protection ship, and ASW escort. Has TVT-300 optronic directors for the 40-mm AA. Antisubmarine armament of two triple Mk 32 ASW TT and two d.c. racks has been removed.
Disposals: Sister *Vale* (N 53) was retired and donated to Latvia 27-1-03.

MINE WARFARE SHIPS *(continued)*

Vidar (N 52) Michael Nitz, 12-04

Vidar (N 52) Frank Findler, 6-04

♦ 1 controlled minefield tender [MM]

Bldr: Voldnes Skipsverft A/S, Fosnavåg (In serv. 1981)

N 50 TYR (ex-*Standby Master*)

Tyr (N 50) Eivind Rodlie, 4-98

D: 495 tons (650 fl) **S:** 13 kts **Dim:** 42.25 (36.02 pp) × 10.10 × 4.20
A: . . . mines
Electronics: Radar: 1 Furuno FR711 nav., 1 Furuno 1011 nav.
M: 2 Deutz SBA12M816 diesels; 1 CP prop; 1,370 bhp—1 650-shp azimuth thruster forward, 1 250-shp thruster aft
Electric: 684 kw tot. (2 × 320-kw shaft generators, 1 × 44-kw diesel set)
Range: . . . / . . . **Fuel:** . . . tons **Crew:** 7 officers, 15 enlisted

Remarks: 497 grt. Former oilfield standby safety and pollution-control ship, acquired 12-93 from K/S Strand Sea Service A/S, Ålesund, for conversion from 1994 to 1-95 by Mjellum & Karlsen, Bergen, as a replacement for the controlled minefield tender *Borgen* (N 51). Received a new crane, additional superstructure to accommodate mines being transported or repaired, a remotely operated submersible (ROV) and its control system, a new bow-thruster, and a workboat. Commissioned 7-3-95. The parliament specifically required active retention of this ship on 3-7-01.

Note: The Norwegian Navy also intends to employ civilian passenger/vehicle ferries as minelayers in wartime. As an example, the 1,435-grt/841-dwt ferry *Stavanger,* delivered 31-3-90 by Myklebust Mekaniske Verksted, is intended for wartime use in such a role.

♦ 8 Oksøy/Alta-class minehunter/minesweepers [MHC/MSC]

Bldr: Kværner Mandal A/S, Mandal

	In serv.		In serv.
4 Minehunters [MHC]:			
M 340 OKSØY	15-8-94	M 342 MÅLØY	24-3-95
M 341 KARMØY	9-1-95	M 343 HINNØY	8-9-95
4 Minesweepers [MSC]:			
M 350 ALTA	12-1-96	M 352 RAUMA	2-12-96
M 351 OTRA	8-11-96	M 353 GLOMMA	1-7-97

Otra (M 351)—minesweeper variant Leo van Ginderen, 5-06

Hinnøy (M 343)—minehunter variant Frank Findler, 6-04

Alta (M 350)—minesweeper variant Guy Schaeffer via Paolo Marsan, 6-04

D: 275 tons light, 343 tons std. (375 fl) **S:** 30 kts (20.5 cruising)
Dim: 55.20 (52.00 pp) × 13.55 (13.30 wl) × 2.15 (0.87 on cushion)
A: 12-round Simbad SAM syst. (Mistral missiles); 2 single 20-mm 90-cal. Rheinmetall AA; 2 single 12.7-mm M2 mg
Electronics:
Radar: 2 Decca RN 88 nav. with DB-2000 ARPA displays
Sonar: minesweepers: Simrad SA-950 hull-mounted mine-avoidance (95 kHz)—minehunters: Thales TSM-2023N variable-depth HF
M: 2 MTU 12V396 TE94 propulsion diesels (2,040 bhp each), 2 MTU 8V396 TE54 diesels for lift fans (940 bhp each); 2 Kværner Eureka waterjets; 4,160 bhp—jet-vane bow-thruster
Electric: 500 kw tot. (2 MTU 12V183 TE51 diesels driving)
Range: 1,500/20 **Fuel:** 73,000 liters
Crew: Minehunters: 12 officers, 26 enlisted; minesweepers: 10 officers, 22 enlisted

Remarks: Approved 3-8-87 by the Ministry of Defense and ordered 9-11-89. M 340 was laid down 1-12-90, launched 8-3-93, and declared fully operational in 5-95. Entire program is said to have cost $437.5 million, including a $156.3-million overrun. One of the minesweepers is to be reconfigured as a mine-clearance, diver-support ship. M 340 suffered moderate damage during 2-05 when she ran aground.

MINE WARFARE SHIPS *(continued)*

Hull systems: Rigid-sidewall air-cushion vehicle design. The cushion area is 48.50 × 10.00 × 2.35 (high) m. Have hydraulic drive for low-speed operations. Design limits rolling to 2°–3° in Sea State 3. All machinery is installed on the main deck, which reduces the magnetic and acoustic signatures. Have Cirrus automated air-cushion ride control and Simrad Albatross dynamic positioning system. One-ton-thrust air jets near the bow provide precise maneuvering capability. The lift fan capacity is inadequate, limiting their endurance. There is a two-man divers' decompression chamber. The standard of accommodations is very high.
Combat systems: The minehunters carry two Gayrobot Pluto Plus 41 submersibles and are equipped with the Thales/ASM/Simrad MICOS minehunting system. On both versions, the sonar transducers are mounted on pivoting arms mounted between the hulls. All have Seatex GPS receivers. The minesweepers are able to tow the AGATE (Air-Gun And Transduce Equipment) high-speed acoustic array with air-gun and transducer noisemakers; the system entered service in mid-2002. The minesweepers also have Elma magnetic sweep gear and Oropesa size 4 wire sweep arrays but do not carry mine disposal divers. M 341 conducted successful trials of the Kongsberg-Simrad Hugin-I autonomous underwater vehicle in a minehunting configuration during 12-01; Hugin has been renamed Minesniper and has been ordered by Spain. M 341 conducted trials with an upgraded version, Hugin 1000, during 2004–5.
Disposals: *Orkla* (M 353) suffered a catastrophic fire and subsequently sank at sea 19-11-02.

AMPHIBIOUS WARFARE CRAFT

♦ 20 CB-90N-class landing craft [LCP]
Bldrs: Dockstavarvet, Sweden; Mjellem & Karlsen, Norway; and Westamarin, Norway (In serv. 7-96 to 1998)

L 4510 TRONDERNES (ex-KA 1)
L 4511 HYSNES (ex-KA 2)
L 4512 HELLEN (ex-KA 3)
L 4513 TORÅS (ex-KA 4)
L 4514 MØVIK (ex-KA 5)
L 4520 SKROLSVIK (ex-KA 11)
L 4521 KRÅKENES (ex-KA 12)
L 4522 STANGNES (ex-KA 13)
L 4523 KJØKØY (ex-KA 14)
L 4524 MØRVIKA (ex-KA 15)
L 4525 KOPÅS (ex-KA 16)
L 4526 TANGEN (ex-KA 17)
L 4527 ODDANE (ex-KA 18)
L 4528 MALMØYA (ex-KA 19)
L 4529 BRETTINGEN (ex-KA 21)
L 4530 LØKHAUG (ex-KA 22)
L 4531 SØRVIKNES (ex-KA 23)
L 4532 OSTERNES (ex-KA 31)
L 4533 FJELL (ex-KA 32)
L 4534 LERØY (ex-KA 33)

Lerøy (L 4534)—with old pennant number Eivind Rodlie, 6-01

D: 14.5 tons light (19 fl) **S:** 40+ kts (35 loaded)
Dim: 14.90 (13.00 wl) × 3.80 × 0.84
A: 2 twin and 1 single 12.7-mm mg; provision for RBS-17 Hellfire SSM, 1 81-mm mortar, 4 mines, or 6 d.c.
Electronics: Radar: 1 Decca BridgeMaster RD 360 nav.
M: 2 Saab Scania 8V DSI-14 diesels; 2 KaMeWa FF 450C or FF 410 waterjets; 1,104 or 1,256 bhp (see Remarks)
Electric: 5 kw tot. (1 × 5-kw diesel set; 230/400 V a.c.)
Range: 260/20 **Fuel:** 2.5 tons **Crew:** 4 tot. + 20 troops

Remarks: Same basic design is used as Sweden's Stridsbåt-90H (Combat Boat 90H) class. Organized into four-boat battery groups, each with three launcher boats (each with four missiles and one launcher) and one command boat. The class were renumbered during 2005.

First four were ordered in 11-95 and delivered between 7-96 and 10-96 by the Swedish design yard for trials; three more were delivered in 1997, 13 during 1998, and two more early in 1999. An option for 14 more has not been exercised. Intended as transports for Coastal Artillery mobile RBS-17 Hellfire coast-defense missile batteries.
Hull systems: Can maintain 20 kts in 1.5-m seas, and the hull can withstand at least 25 groundings without significant damage. In lieu of troops, can carry up to 2.8 tons of cargo. Fuel capacity has been increased over the Swedish version. KA 5 and later have uprated engines (1,256 bhp tot.) and employ KaMeWa FF 410 waterjets. Navigation equipment includes two GPS receivers, Seapath 200/M and Sealog 100/M computer navaids, a Simrad EQ30 log, and an echo sounder. There are two radar displays. The troop compartment is higher than in the Swedish Artillery Service units to permit standing.

Disposal notes: Sisters *Bjørgvin* (KA 30), *Nodaros* (KA 20), and *Trondarnes* (KA 10) were no longer in service as of 2003. The three remaining *Reinøysund*-class utility landing craft, *Sørøysund* (L 4503), *Maursund* (L 4504), and *Tjeldsund* (L 4506), had been retired from service by 2005.

Note: Norwegian special forces employ several high-speed, waterjet-driven RIB assault landing craft equipped with a small Raytheon radar but not armed; no other data available. The Norwegian Army has six M.A.N. GHH MLC 60 bridging ferries of 26-m span, propelled by Schottel pumpjets; the craft are named *Håling-I* through *Håling-VI*.

AUXILIARIES

Note: The 14,989-grt auto/passenger ferry *Peter Wessel* was acquired by the government in 9-85 for conversion to a casualty evacuation ship with a medical staff of 450 and facilities for 800 seriously wounded and 1,200 lightly wounded troops; she is not under naval control and normally operates in commercial service.

♦ 1 general-purpose operational support ship [AG]
Bldr: Ulstein Hatlo A/S, Ulsteinvik (In serv. 1981)

A 535 VALKYRIEN (ex-*Far Senior*, ex-*Stad Senior*)

Valkyrien (A 535) Marian Wright, 12-04

Valkyrien (A 535)—with containerized cargo on the working deck Dieter Wolf, 5-00

D: Approx. 3,000 tons (fl) **S:** 16 kts **Dim:** 68.03 (59.02 pp) × 14.71 × 4.77
A: None **Electronics:** Radar: 2 Furuno . . . nav.
M: 4 Bergens Normo KVMB-12 diesels, electric drive; 2 CP props; 11,600 shp (10,560 sust.)—2 800-shp bow-thrusters—1 800-shp stern-thruster
Electric: 3,000 kw (2 × 1,256-kw shaft generators, 2 × 244-kw diesel sets)
Range: 10,000/10 **Fuel:** 1,000 tons **Crew:** 13 tot. (23 accomm.)

Remarks: 491 grt/1,112 dwt. Former anchor-handling tug/supply vessel, purchased 12-93 from Sverre Farstad & Co., A/S, Ålesund. Converted during 1994 to 1-95 to perform such varied duties as torpedo recovery, ocean towing, target towing, transportation of troops and cargo to naval exercises, training for civilian crews of merchant vessels likely to be taken up from trade in an emergency, target service, search and rescue, support to small combatants, and pollution control; in wartime will also be able to act as a minelayer. Has an ice-strengthened hull and extensive navigational aids. Is equipped with oil-recovery gear and pollution-control equipment and can carry up to 700 tons of cargo on the open after deck. Bollard pull: 128 tons.

Note: A new repair tender for the *Fridtjof Nansen*–class frigates has been proposed; the ship would enter service after 2008.

♦ 1 royal yacht [AG]
Bldr: Camper & Nicholsons, Gosport, U.K. (L: 17-2-37)

A 533 NORGE (ex-*Philante*)

D: 1,786 tons (fl) **S:** 17 kts **Dim:** 76.27 × 8.53 × 4.65
Electronics: Radar: 2 Decca . . . nav.
M: 2 Bergen KRMB-8 diesels; 2 props; 4,850 bhp **Electric:** 300 kw tot.
Range: 9,900/17 **Fuel:** 175 tons **Crew:** 18 officers, 32 enlisted

Remarks: Built as a yacht for aviation pioneer T. O. M. Sopwith, then used by the British Royal Navy as an ASW escort 1940–43, later as a training ship; purchased by Norway in 1948. Can carry 50-passenger royal party. Suffered a severe fire 8-3-85 but was repaired by summer 1986.

AUXILIARIES *(continued)*

Norge (A 533)—white hull, yellow funnel, pennant number not worn
Ralph Edwards, 10-05

♦ 1 intelligence collection ship [AGI]
Bldr: Tangen Verft A/S (In serv. 11-93)

MARJATA

Marjata R.Nor.N., 1995

D: 5,300 tons (7,560 fl) **S:** 15 kts **Dim:** 81.50 (72.00 pp) × 39.90 × 6.00
Electronics: Radar: 2 . . . nav.—EW: various intercept arrays
M: 2 MTU 16V396 TE diesels, 2 Siemens generators, electric drive; 2 Schottel SRP 3030 azimuth props aft; 8,160 shp—1 bow Schottel azimuthal prop (2,720 shp)
Electric: 7,200 kw tot. (2 × 3,600-kw Dresser Rand gas turbine sets)
Crew: 14 crew + 31 technicians

Remarks: Owned by the Ministry of Defense vice the navy proper. Built under subcontract from Langsten Slip og Båtbyggeri A/S. Aerial A/S, Horten, Ramform M7 design. Replaced a smaller vessel of the same name completed in 1976. Will have three large radomes covering collection antennas and a sonar installation at the stern. Has an unusual wedge-shaped hullform to provide stability in the rough seas in which she will operate. Has a large helicopter deck aft. Originally painted with gray hull, white superstructure, and yellow masts, but now painted all white. The civilian geophysical research ship *Ramform Challenger* is a sister that differs in having a raised helicopter deck aft and a much smaller antenna array.

♦ 1 logistics support ship [AGP]
Bldr: Horten Verft, Horten

	Laid down	L	In serv.
A 530 HORTEN	28-1-77	12-8-77	9-6-78

Horten (A 530) Eivind Rodlie, 6-02

D: 2,500 tons (fl) **S:** 16.5 kts **Dim:** 87.0 (82.0 pp) × 13.7 × . . .
A: 2 single 40-mm 70-cal. Bofors AA; mines
Electronics: Radar: 3 Decca . . . nav.
M: 2 Wichmann 7AX diesels; 2 props; 4,200 bhp **Crew:** 86 tot.

Remarks: Used to support submarines and small combatants. Can accommodate up to 45 additional personnel and has messing facilities for 190 additional. Has a helicopter deck and bow-thruster. Expected to retire in the near future.

SERVICE CRAFT

Note: Until 1-98, smaller service craft were identified by a pennant number system employing three letters to identify their naval district subordination, plus a one- or two-digit number. They are now identified by function: HD for diving tenders, HM for multirole tenders, HP for personnel launches, HR for rescue craft, HS for tugs, and HT for torpedo retrievers.

♦ 1 relic/training tender [YAG]
Bldr: Fisher Boat Works, Detroit, Mich.

	Laid down	L	In serv.
HP 15 HITRA (ex-U.S. SC 718)	22-9-42	31-3-43	25-5-43

Hitra (HP 15) Eivind Rodlie, 9-05

D: 95 tons light (148 fl) **S:** 15 kts
Dim: 33.80 (32.77 wl) × 5.18 × 1.98
A: 1 40-mm Mk 3 AA; 2 single 20-mm Oerlikon Mk 10 AA
Electronics: Radar: 1 . . . nav.
M: 2 MTU 8V183 TE72 diesels; 2 props; 1,100 bhp
Fuel: 16 tons **Crew:** . . .

Remarks: Survivor of the ships and craft that served Free Norwegian naval forces during World War II. Reacquired 8-5-87 for restoration to operational service as a cadet training craft and museum ship; the original engines were located and reinstalled. Operational during the summer months. Wooden construction. Does not carry a pennant number. In original World War II configuration, she had a third 20-mm gun aft and was also fitted with two Mk 20 Mousetrap ASW RL, two Mk 6 d.c. mortars, and two d.c. racks. The original G.M. diesels have been replaced by newer MTU diesels.

Disposal note: *Reinøysund*-class diving tenders *Reinøysund* (L 4502) and *Rotsund* (L 4505) had been retired from service by 2005.

♦ 1 small miscellaneous diving tenders [YDT]

HD 2 VIKEN (In serv. 1984)

Remarks: Can also carry four tons of general cargo or up to 40 passengers. Sister *Rya* (HD 1) had been retired from service by 2005.

♦ 3 Torpen-series stores tenders [YF]

	Bldr	In serv.
HM 1 ROTVAER (ex-NSD 35)	Båtservice Verft, Mandal	3-78
HM 2 KRØTTØY (ex-HSD 15)	Voldnes Skipsverft, Fosnavåg	6-78
HM 3 TORPEN (ex-VSD 4)	Båtservice Verft, Mandal	15-12-77

Torpen (HM 3) Eivind Rodlie, 9-02

D: Typical: 215 tons (300 fl) **S:** 11 kts **Dim:** 29.0 × 6.4 × 2.57
A: 1 12.7-mm mg **Electronics:** Radar: 1 Decca 1226 nav.
M: 1 MWM TBD 601-6K diesel; 1 CP prop; 530 bhp
Range: 1,200/11 **Fuel:** 11 tons **Crew:** 6 enlisted + 100 passengers

SERVICE CRAFT *(continued)*

Remarks: Basically similar craft, tailored to a variety of duties, including logistics support, ammunition transport, personnel transport (31 to 75, depending on configuration), and divers' support. Cargo capacity: 80 to 100 tons. Sisters *Wisting* (ØSD 2) and *Viken* (VSD 5) had been stricken by 1-98, and by 1-02, *Tautra* (HM 5, ex-TSD 5) and *Ramnes* (HM 6, ex-ROS 23) were no longer in service. Sister *Arnøy* (HP 9) is rated as a personnel ferry.

♦ **1 logistics support tender [YF]** (In serv. 1969)

HM 7 KJEØY

D: 190 tons **S:** 10.7 kts **Dim:** 20.90 × . . . × . . . **M:** 1 diesel; . . . bhp

Remarks: Generally similar to the craft of the *Torpen* series. Can carry 80 tons of cargo and 30 passengers.

♦ **1 Hysnes-class personnel launch [YFL]**
Bldr: . . . (In serv. 1985)

SHV 109 FOSNA (ex-*Hysnes*, HP 3; ex-*Øysprint*)

Fosna (SHV 109) Eivind Rodlie, 8-03

D: Approx. 38 tons (fl) **S:** 32 kts (26 cruise) **Dim:** 15.54 × 4.88 × 1.10
Electronics: Radar: 2 Decca . . . nav.
M: 2 Saab Scania DSI 14 diesels; 2 props; 1,250 bhp
Crew: 2 tot. + 30 passengers

Remarks: Acquired by late 1999, renamed in 2003. GRP construction. Had been re-engined in 1991.

♦ **1 HP 20–class harbor personnel launch [YFL]**

HP 20 ELLIDA

Remarks: A request for contract tenders for one harbor personnel transport capable of breaking light ice was issued in 3-98; HP 20 was in service by 7-99. Has a small bow ramp for mating to a pier, and there is a small crane forward of the passenger cabin, which can accommodate 24 persons seated. Can achieve 24 kts. No other data available.

♦ **1 Welding-class personnel launch [YFL]**
Bldr: Fjellstrand, Omastrand (In serv. 1-11-74)

HP 8 WELDING (ex-ØSD 1)

D: 27.5 tons **S:** 17 kts **Dim:** 16.3 × 5.3 × 1.2
A: 1 12.7-mm mg **Electronics:** Radar: 1 Decca . . . nav.
M: 2 G.M. Detroit Diesel 6V-71 diesels; 2 props; 800 bhp
Crew: 4 tot. + 14 passengers

Remarks: Sister *Brimse* (RSD 23, ex-TSD 1) was stricken during 1998.

♦ **8 miscellaneous personnel launches [YFL]**

	In serv.	Kts	Passengers
HP 1 MÅGØY (ex-HSD 10)	1989	20	12
HP 2 FJØLØY	1993	16	26
HP 4 ODIN (ex-TSD 3, ex-ØSD 6)	1989	17	9
HP 5 RAMNES	1994	12	35 (+ 120 tons cargo)
HP 6 WISTING (ex-*Oscarsborg*, ØSD 11)	1968	9	75
HP 7 NORDEP I (ex-ØSD 15)	1987	12.5	60 (+ 6 tons cargo)
HP 9 ARNØY (ex-ØSD 5)	1978	13.5	50
HP 14 MARSTEINEN (ex-VSD 6)	1994	12	7

Remarks: HP 9 is a sister to the *Torpen*-series YFs. No data are available for the others, except that HP 6 displaces 23 tons. *Folden* (HP 10, ex-ØSD 10) and *Gleodden* (HP 13, ex-SSD 3) were no longer in service as of 1-01.

Ramnes (HP 5) Eivind Rodlie, 7-04

♦ **4 miscellaneous rescue launches [YFL]**

HR 1 MARINEJ 1 HR 2 MARINEJ 2 HR 3 HR 4

Remarks: No data available. Are probably RIBs assigned to shore stations.

♦ **1 torpedo retriever and oil-spill cleanup ship [YPT]**
Bldr: Fjellstrand, Hardinger (In serv. 10-78)

HT 1 VERNØY (ex-VSD 1)

D: 150 grt **S:** 12 kts **Dim:** 31.30 × 6.67 × 2.00
M: 2 MWM diesels; 2 Schottel azimuthal props; . . . bhp **Crew:** 5 tot.

Remarks: Is also equipped for fire fighting. Has an articulating electrohydraulic crane aft to handle torpedoes.

♦ **1 small torpedo retriever [YPT]**
Bldr: P. Høivolds, Kristiansand (In serv. 7-78)

HT 3 KARLSØY (ex-TRSD 4)

Karlsøy (HT 3) Eivind Rodlie, 9-02

Remarks: Can also be employed to transport 87 tons of general cargo and 31 passengers. Capable of 11.5 kts.

♦ **2 large harbor tugs [YTB]** Bldr: Vaagland Båtbyggeri

H 54 SLEIPNER (ex-*Boa Sleipner*) H 55 MJØLNER (ex-*Boa Mjølner*)

D: . . . **S:** 12.5 kts **Dim:** 24.0 × 9.0 × 3.5
M: 2 Caterpillar . . . diesels; 2 props; 3,000 bhp

Remarks: Purchased 20-12-02 and based at Haakonvaerft.

♦ **1 large harbor tug [YTB]**
Bldr: Haugesund Slip, Haugesund (In serv. 1979)

HS 1 KVARVEN (ex-VSD 2, ex-*Oscar Tybring*)

Kvarven (HS 1)—with old pennant number Lt. Arild Engelsen, R.Nor.N., 3-88

SERVICE CRAFT *(continued)*

D: Approx. 170 tons (fl) **S:** 11 kts **Dim:** 22.50 × 6.30 × . . .
M: 1 G.M. Detroit Diesel 16V-149 diesel; 1 prop; 1,175 bhp (900 sust.)

Remarks: 97 grt. Acquired in 1988. Built originally as a rescue ship. Can carry 12 passengers.

♦ 2 miscellaneous medium harbor tugs (YTM)

HS 2 Bogøy (ex-VSD 10) HS 3

Remarks: HS 2 is capable of 10.5 kts and can carry four tons of general cargo; completed in 1993. HS 3, built in 1967, can achieve 9 kts. No other data available.

♦ 2 navigational training craft [YXT]

Bldr: Fjellstrand, Omastrand (In serv. 1-78)

P 358 Hessa (ex-*Hitra,* ex-*Marsteinen,* VSD 2)
P 359 Vigra (ex-*Kvarven,* VSD 6)

Hessa (P 358) Eivind Rodlie, 8-99

D: 40 tons (fl) **S:** 22 kts **Dim:** 23.20 × 5.00 × 1.10
A: 1 12.7-mm mg **Electronics:** Radar: 1 Decca . . . nav.
M: 2 G.M. 12V71 diesels; 2 props; 1,800 bhp **Crew:** 5 crew + 13 cadets

Remarks: Aluminum construction. For use at the naval academy. Renamed and renumbered in 1981. P 358 was again renamed in 5-87 to free the name for the relic/training tender *Hitra* (HP 15). The gun is not usually mounted.

COAST GUARD

(Kystvakt)

The Norwegian Coast Guard was established in 4-77 to perform fisheries-protection duties, patrol the waters in the vicinity of offshore oil rigs, and maintain surveillance over the 200-n.m. economic zone. The civilian-manned, semiautonomous Fishing Equipment Patrol (*Bruksvakt*) operates smaller units to inspect fishing gear. The Inner Coastal Surveillance System (SIKO) was established 1-1-97.

Bases and Organization: Coast Guard Squadron North is based at Sortland, and Coast Guard Squadron South at Håkonsvern, near Bergen.

Coast Guard Aviation: The Royal Norwegian Air Force operates six WG-13 Lynx Mk 86 helicopters and two Lockheed P-3N Orion maritime patrol aircraft in support of the coast guard. Several additional helicopters are sought.

Note: Ships of the coast guard proper have W-series pennants, while the Inner Coastal Surveillance System units have pennants in the KV series In some instances, a dash connects the "W" and the number in the pennants. All ships and craft carry the word *Kystvakt* (Coast Guard) on their sides. The old 40-mm 60-cal. Mk 3 Bofors AA guns are being replaced by 40-mm 70-cal. Bofors L70 mounts removed from stricken Norwegian Navy units.

PATROL SHIPS [WPS]

♦ 5 leased Type ST 610

Bldr: Gryfia, Szczecin, Poland (In serv. 2006–7)

D: 3,130 tons (fl) **S:** 19 kts **Dim:** 83.0 × 15.50 × 6.0
A: 1 57-mm 70-cal. Bofors DP
Electronics: Radar: . . .
M: 2 Bergen B 32/40 L diesels; 2 CP azimuthal props; 10,800 shp
Range: 10,000/13 **Crew:** 26 tot. (+ 9 others)

Remarks: Ordered under a 15-year lease agreement from a Fosnavåg-based firm. First unit delivered 2-06 with the fifth unit expected by 12-07. Are capable of operating 330 days a year. Carry 2 RIB launches.

♦ 1 Type UT 512

Bldr: Aker Tulcea, Romania

	L	In serv.
W 318 Herstad	2004	1-05

D: 3,130 tons (fl) **S:** 18 kts **Dim:** 83.0 × 15.50 × 6.0
A: 1 57-mm 70-cal. Bofors DP
Electronics: Radar: . . .
M: 2 Bergen B 32/40 L diesels; 2 CP azimuthal props; 10,800 shp
Range: 10,000/13 **Crew:** 26 tot. (+ 9 others)

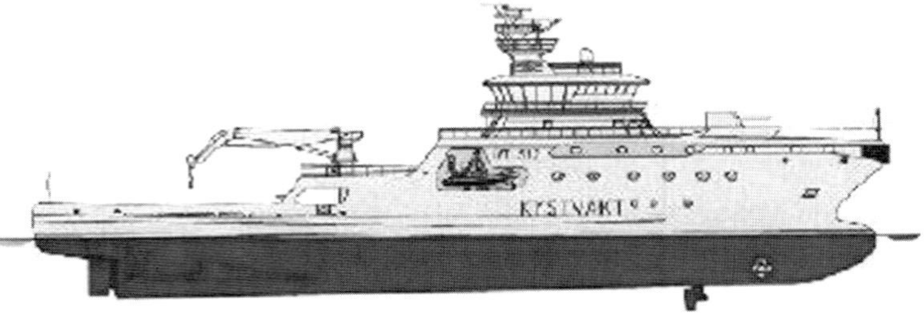

UT 512 Design Rolls Royce, 2003

Remarks: Ordered 11-03. Owned by Remon shipping, this is the first armed Kystvakt vessel built on a "built and charter" basis. Designed by Rolls-Royce Marine for firefighting, environmental, law enforcement, push and pull tug, and rescue/lifesaving operations and is also compatible with NATO submarine rescue operations.

♦ 1 Svalbard class

Bldr: Tangen Verft, Krager, division of Langsten Slip & Båtbyggeri A/S, Tomrefjord

	L	In serv.
W 303 Svalbard	2-01	3-02

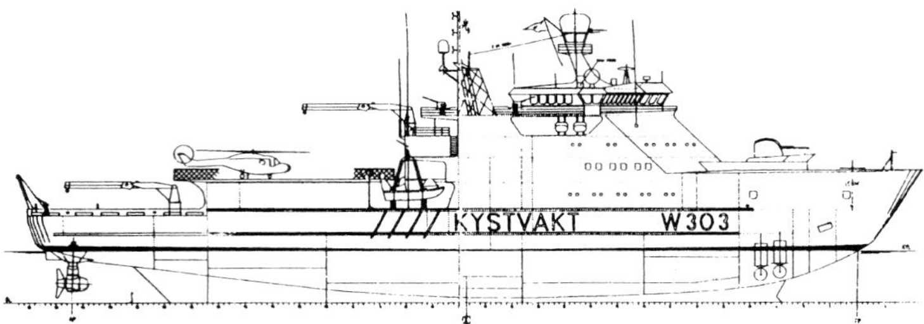

Svalbard (W 303) R.Nor.N., 1996

D: 6,100 tons (fl) **S:** 18 kts (17 sust.) **Dim:** 103.70 × 19.10 × 6.50
A: 1 57-mm 70-cal. Bofors DP; 1 2-round Simbad SAM syst. (Mistral missiles)
Electronics: Radar: 1 . . . surface search; 1 . . . nav.
M: 4 diesels, electric drive; 2 CP azimuthal props; 10,700 shp—2 bow tunnel-thrusters
Range: 10,000/13 **Crew:** 56 tot.

Remarks: Ordered 7-1-00. Intended for northern service, with an icebreaker hull capable of breaking 1-m ice. Has a helicopter deck and hangar and passive tank stabilization. Will be operated with two crews to ensure maximum sea time. Will employ an EDO combat system like that being backfitted to the *Norkapp* class.

♦ 3 Norkapp (Type 320) class

	Bldr	L	In serv.
W 320 Norkapp	Bergens Mek. Verksted, Bergen	2-4-80	25-4-81
W 321 Senja	Horten Verft, Horten	16-3-80	8-3-81
W 322 Andennes	Haugesund Verksted, Haugesund	21-3-81	30-1-82

Senja (W 321) Werner Globke, 6-05

Andennes (W 322) Eivind Rodlie, 10-99

COAST GUARD PATROL SHIPS [WPS] *(continued)*

D: 2,201 tons light (3,276 fl) **S:** 23 kts **Dim:** 105.00 (97.50 pp) × 13.85 × 4.55
A: 1 57-mm 70-cal. Bofors DP; 1 2-round Simbad SAM syst. (Mistral missiles); 3 single 20-mm 90-cal. Rheinmetall AA; 1 d.c. rack (6 d.c.); 1 WG-13 Lynx helicopter—provision for 2 triple 324-mm Mk 32 Mod. 5 ASW TT
Electronics:
Radar: 2 Decca TM 1226 nav.; 1 Decca RM 914 nav.; 1 Plessey AWS-4 air search; 1 CelsiusTech 9LV 218 f.c.
Sonar: Simrad SS105 hull-mounted MF (14 kHz)
EW: . . . intercept; 2 . . . decoy RL
EO: Thorn-EMI SM 8312 infrared surveillance syst.
M: 4 Wichmann 9-AXAG diesels; 2 CP props; 14,400 bhp
Electric: 1,600 kw tot. **Range:** 7,500/15 **Fuel:** 350 tons
Crew: 42 ship's company + 6 helicopter crew (109 tot. accomm.)

Remarks: Program was delayed by design changes and lack of funding; four additional units were canceled. W 321 was used in trials of a two-crew operational concept in 1994–95.
Hull systems: Carry three 300-m^3/hr water cannon for fire fighting and have meteorological reporting gear. Have fin stabilizers. Carry one UFAS Sjøbjørn 25–class, aluminum-hulled, rigid inflatable personnel launch powered by a 350-bhp Yanmar 6LY-UTE diesel driving a Hamilton 273 waterjet for speeds up to 33 kts. Also have one Yanmar Searaider (85 bhp outboard) rigid inflatable inspection boat.
Combat systems: In time of conflict, six Penguin Mk 2 antiship missiles can be added. The Kongsberg MSI-80S NAVKIS data system with MFC 2000S display consoles is fitted. The weapons-control system was updated in 1996–97 by adding the Thorn-EMI Marine Electro-Optical Surveillance System (MEOSS). The Simbad point-defense SAM launch position is mounted on a raised pedestal in place of the starboard aft 20-mm mounting atop the hangar.
Modernization: EDO is supplying a new command-and-control system for the class under a 7-98 contract; included are a DRS Technologies SPS-67(V)3 surface-search radar, IFF system, integrated E/O f.c. and surveillance sensor, hull-mounted sonar, and integrated bridge control and display suite. The combat data system will employ four to six multifunction display consoles. Installations began during 2001. Will likely remain in service until 2020.

♦ 1 Tromsø-class leased fisheries patrol vessel
Bldr: Naval Shipyard Gdynia, Gdynia, Poland (In serv. 4-96)

W 313 Tromsø

Tromsø (W 313) Eivind Rodlie, 10-99

D: 2,100 tons (fl) **S:** 17 kts **Dim:** 70.0 (51.40 pp) × 12.40 × 5.50
A: 1 40-mm 70-cal. Bofors L70 AA **Electronics:** Radar: 2 . . . nav.
M: 1 . . . diesel; 1 CP prop; 3,600 bhp—690-shp azimuthal bow-thruster—400-shp stern side-thruster
Electric: 2,100 kw tot. (1 × 1,000-kw shaft generator, 2 × 500-kw diesel sets, 1 × 100-kw emergency diesel set)
Range: . . . / . . . **Fuel:** 400 m^3
Crew: 5 officers, 10 enlisted, 5 civilians (26 tot. accomm.)

Remarks: Ordered 11-95 and operated under 10-year charter (with option to purchase after five years) from Tromsø Dampskibsselskab, using owner's crews in part. Has two crews. Intended to operate around northern Norway; has an ice-strengthened hull and helicopter deck. An 800-m^3-total oil recovery/seawater ballast tankage system is included, and the ship is equipped for fire fighting. Carries 150 m^3 of fresh water. Equipped with a rigid inflatable boarding boat and an inspection launch and has a 3.5-ton-capacity (at 12-m radius) electrohydraulic crane aft. Has an environmental cover for the 40-mm gun.

♦ 1 Ålesund-class leased fisheries patrol vessel
Bldr: Myklebust Mek. Verksted, Gurskebotn (In serv. 4-96)

W 312 Ålesund

D: 1,470 tons (fl) **S:** 18 kts **Dim:** 63.20 (57.00 pp) × 11.50 × 4.67
A: 1 40-mm 70-cal. Bofors L70 AA
Electronics: Radar: 1 . . . nav.; 1 . . . nav.
M: 1 Wichmann 8V28B diesel; 1 Wichmann PR 82/4I CP prop; 3,600 bhp—bow- and stern-thrusters
Electric: . . . kw tot. (1,440-kw main shaft generator, 2 × . . . -kw emergency sets)
Range: 20,600/13 **Endurance:** 200 days
Crew: 5 officers, 15 enlisted, 3 civilians (32 tot. accomm.)

Remarks: Ordered 11-95 and operated under 10-year charter (with option to purchase after five years) from Remøy Shipping. Construction contracted to Myklebust Mek

Ålesund (W 312) Elvind Rodlie, 3-04

Verksted, which subcontracted the forward portion of the hull to Voldnes Skipsverft and the stern to Ulstein Vannylven. Has a stern-haul trawler hullform with bulbous forefoot. Uses two alternating crews. Helicopter facilities are fitted. Two semi-rigid inflatable inspection boats are carried, with the Springer 25 to port capable of 36 kts and a 120-n.m. range on its Hamilton waterjet propulsion system; both are handled by an electrohydraulic crane. Has a 37-ton-bollard-pull hydraulic towing winch. There is an 800-ton-capacity spilled oil recovery tank. The crew are berthed in 12 single and 10 two-person cabins.

Note: The 63-meter, 1,141-ton leased patrol vessel *Eigun* (W 310) is also in service.

Disposal note: Leased fisheriers patrol vessel *Nysleppen* (W 318) and leased hydrographic research vessel *Lance* (W 311) were retired from service by 2005.

♦ 1 stern-haul purse seiner
Bldr: Brødrene Lothes, Haugesund (In serv. 7-78)

W 317 Lafjord

Lafjord (W 317) Frank Findler, 8-04

D: Approx. 1,800 tons (fl) **S:** 14.5 kts **Dim:** 55.40 (48.11 pp) × 9.86 × 6.18
A: 1 40-mm 60-cal. Mk 3 Bofors AA **Electronics:** Radar: . . .
M: 1 Wichmann 7AXA diesel; 1 prop; 2,100 bhp
Electric: 419 kw tot. (2 × 160-kw, 1 × 99-kw diesel sets)
Range: 7,700/14.5 **Fuel:** 189.5 tons heavy oil, 36 tons diesel **Crew:** . . . tot.

Remarks: 814 grt/1,000 dwt. Chartered in 1980 from K/S Lafjord & Co., Bergen. Has side-thrusters fore and aft and an ice-strengthened hull.

♦ 1 stern-haul purse seiner
Bldr: Cochrane & Sons Ltd., Selby

W 316 Malene Østervold

Malene Østervold (W 316) Eivind Rodlie, 9-05

D: Approx. 1,680 tons (fl) **S:** 16 kts **Dim:** 69.2 × 11.6 × 7.0
A: 1 40-mm 60-cal. Mk 3 Bofors AA **Electronics:** Radar: 1 . . . nav.
M: 1 . . . diesel; 1 prop; 2,650 bhp
Electric: 540 kw tot.

Remarks: Charted in 2002. Built in 1965.

♦ 1 leased stern-haul purse seiner
Bldr: Smedvik Mek. Verksted A/S, Tjørvåg (In serv. 4-78)

W 315 Nordsjøbas

COAST GUARD PATROL SHIPS [WPS] *(continued)*

D: Approx. 1,780 tons (fl) **S:** 13.5 kts **Dim:** 52.05 (44.73 pp) × 10.01 × 6.37
A: 1 40-mm 60-cal. Mk 3 Bofors AA **Electronics:** Radar: . . .
M: 1 MaK 6M453AK diesel; 1 CP prop; 2,400 bhp
Electric: 920 kw tot. (1 × 752-kw, 1 × 168-kw diesel sets)
Range: 8,300/13.5 **Fuel:** 180 tons **Crew:** . . . tot.

Remarks: 814 grt/1,087 dwt. Chartered in 1980 from Nordsjøbas A/S, Ålesund. Has side-thrusters fore and aft.

Disposal note: Leased purse seiner *Stålbas* (W 314) had been retired by 2004 and former naval fisheries protection ship *Nornen* (W 300) was retired during 2000.

AUXILIARIES

♦ **1 H. U. Sverdrup II–class ocean surveillance ship [WAGI]**
Bldr: Kaldnes Industrier A/S, Tønsberg (completed by Sigbj. Iversen A/S Flekkefjord, 6-90)

H. U. Sverdrup II

H. U. Sverdrup II H&L Van Ginderen, 9-90

D: 1,387 grt **S:** . . . kts **Dim:** 55.00 × 13.00 × 5.38
M: 1 Bergen 8-cyl. diesel; 1 prop; 2,000 bhp

Remarks: Operated for the Forsvarets Forskingsinstitut (Military Research Institute) by the coast guard. White hull, red pilothouse and masts, red-blue-red diagonal hull stripe. Equipped with Marisat satellite communications equipment, stern-haul trawl equipment, and a large oceanographic crane aft. Russian official sources have referred to this ship (probably erroneously) as an intelligence collector.

INNER COASTAL SURVEILLANCE SYSTEM

An organization formed on 1-1-97 to provide closer-in patrol of Norwegian offshore interests. Its unarmed ships and craft carry the word *Kystvakt* on their sides, and the organization is subordinate to the main coast guard.

	In serv.	Tonnage
KV 1 Titran	1992	184 grt
KV 3 Sture Gøran	1969	193 grt
KV 5 Agder	1974	140 grt
KV 6 Garsøy	1988	195 grt
KV 7 Åhav	1987	50 grt

Titran (KV 1) Eivind Rodlie, 8-04

Remarks: KV 6 can make 20 kts on two 1,142-bhp Deutz-MWM TBD 04 V8 diesels and is 34.00 (o.a.) × 6.00 × 1.80 m (KV 1 is similar); the ship has one X-band and one S-band navigational radar. KV 7 can reach 25 kts on two 1,100-bhp G.M. diesels and is 27.00 (o.a.) × 5.80 × 1.50 m.

FISHING EQUIPMENT PATROL

(*Bruksvakt*)

Also subordinated to the coast guard is the unarmed Fishing Equipment Patrol, which operates eight chartered former fishing craft and oilfield support craft, all repainted a uniform naval gray:

	In serv.	Tonnage
KV 21 Polarvakt	1965	290 grt
KV 22 Barentshav	1957	318 grt
KV 23 Norvakt	1959	197 grt
KV 24 Lofothav	1954	271 grt
KV 25 Sjøveien	1966	339 grt
KV 27 Sjøfareren	1966	180 grt
KV 28 Nysleppen	1967	343 grt
KV 29 Peter Jarl (ex-*Havkyst,* KV 26)	1965	320 grt

Peter Jarl (KV 29) Eivind Rodlie, 9-02

Sjøfareren (KV 27) A. A. de Kruijf, 4-00

Remarks: KV 27 can make 12 kts on her one G.M. 16V149 TI, 1,200-bhp diesel and is 28.36 × 7.71 × 3.70 m. *Havkyst,* reported in the last edition to have left the service, was sighted with a new name and number in 9-02; KV 29, a former stern trawler, is 38.1 × 8.01 × 4.87 m and has one 900-bhp Wichmann diesel and an ice-strengthened hull.

MINISTRY OF THE ENVIRONMENT

(*Kystverket*)

The Ministry of the Environment has a fleet of seven ships and craft operated by its own personnel: *Sjøtroll* (80 tons, in serv. 1976), *Johan Hjort* (2,000 tons, in serv. 12-90), the tug/supply vessel *Geofjord* (1,615 grt, ex-*Aldona,* acquired 11-91 as an oil-spill recovery ship), and the pollution-control tenders *Oljevern 01* through *Oljevern 04* (completed in 1978, 200 tons, with crews of two officers and six unlicensed personnel each).

OMAN

Sultanate of Oman

ROYAL NAVY OF OMAN

Personnel: 4,200 total

Bases: Headquarters at Muaskar al Murtafa'a. The principal base is at Qa'Adat Said bin Sultan Albahria Base, Wudam, with lesser facilities at Minah Rasyut and Jazorat Ghanam, Musandam.

Maritime Aviation: Two Royal Omani Air Force Dornier Do-228-100 light maritime surveillance aircraft are used for coastal patrol. Air force Super Puma and Sea King helicopters can land aboard platforms on several of the larger ships. Sixteen AgustaWestland Super Lynx 300 helicopters were ordered during 1-02, with two intended for shipboard use; deliveries started in 2004.

Note: Ship and craft names are prefixed RNOV (Royal Navy of Oman Vessel).

CORVETTES [FFL]

Note: Three 2,500-ton corvettes of a new class are to be built by Vosper Thornycroft, Portsmouth, UK. Dubbed "mini-frigates" by Oman, the final contract is expected in 2007 with deliveries to begin by 2010.

♦ 2 Vigilance class (Project Muheet)
Bldr: Vosper Thornycroft, Woolston, Southampton, U.K.

	Laid down	L	In serv. (accepted)
Q 31 Qahir al Amwaj	17-5-93	21-9-94	3-9-96
Q 32 Al Mua'zzar	4-4-94	26-9-95	26-11-96

Al Mua'zzar (Q 32) Leo van Ginderen, 6-05

Al Mua'zzar (Q 32) Leo van Ginderen, 6-05

Al Mua'zzar (Q 32) Chris Sattler, 6-05

D: 1,185 tons (1,450 fl) **S:** 31 kts **Dim:** 83.70 (78.50 pp) × 11.50 × 3.50 (hull)
A: 8 MM 40 Exocet Block II SSM; 1 8-round Crotale NG SAM syst. (16 Crotale VT-1 missiles); 1 76-mm 62-cal. OTO Melara SuperRapid DP; 2 single 20-mm 90-cal. Oerlikon GAM-B01 AA; 2 single 7.62-mm mg
Electronics:
Radar: 1 Kelvin-Hughes Type 1007 nav.; 1 Thales MW-08 3-D surf./air search; 1 Thales Castor-IIJ MRR (TRS-5204) f.c.; 1 Thales Sting f.c.
Sonar: see Remarks
EW: Thales DR-3000S1 Compact intercept (1–18 GHz); Furuno FD527 comms D/F; 2 12-round Wallop SuperBarricade decoy RL
E/O: Thales IRSCAN surveillance/tracking
M: 4 Crossley–SEMT-Pielstick 16 PA6 V280 STC diesels; 2 KaMeWa CP props; 32,000 bhp (28,160 sust.)
Electric: 1,270 kw tot. (3 × 400-kw MTU RV183 TF51 diesel-powered sets; 1 × 70-kw MTU 6V 183 AA51 diesel emergency set)
Range: 5,500/12 **Fuel:** 156 tons **Crew:** 14 officers, 62 enlisted (accomm.)

Remarks: Ordered 5-4-92. Names mean "Conqueror of the Waves" and "The Supported," respectively. Q 31 departed for Oman 18-6-96 and Q 32 on 20-3-97. Are being operated with crews totaling around 60 each.
Hull systems: Have fin stabilizers. The aluminum alloy superstructure is shaped to reduce radar signature and has been coated with radar-absorbent materials. Stack has an infrared-suppressant system. Have a helicopter deck, but no hangar. Carry 19 tons of fresh water.
Combat systems: Have the Thales SEWACO-FD combat system (based on the TACTICOS C2 system). The Thales SINCOS communications suite is fitted. The Sting radar-E/O gun director incorporates radar, laser rangefinder, and low-light-level t.v. sensors. Planned installation of a towed active linear sonar array and two sets of ASW torpedo tubes did not take place, and the ships have no ASW capability.

PATROL SHIPS [PS]

♦ 1 Al Mabrukah class
Bldr: Brooke Marine, Lowestoft, U.K.

	L	In serv.
Q 30 Al Mabrukah (ex-A 1, ex-*Al Said*)	7-4-70	1971

Al Mabrukah (Q 30) Omani Navy, 1996

D: 785 tons (930 fl) **S:** 17 kts **Dim:** 61.47 (55.63 pp) × 10.70 × 3.05
A: 1 40-mm 70-cal. Bofors AA; 2 single 20-mm 90-cal. RO-Oerlikon GAM-B01 AA
Electronics:
Radar: 1 Decca TM 1226 nav.; 1 Decca . . . nav.
EW: Racal Cutlass radar intercept; 2 9-round Wallop Barricade decoy RL
M: 2 Paxman Ventura 12YJCM diesels; 2 props; 2,580 bhp
Electric: 500 kw tot. (2 × 250-kw diesel sets)
Crew: 11 officers, 23 enlisted + 37 passengers/trainees

Remarks: 990 grt/290 dwt. Renamed and converted from royal yacht to fleet training ship at builders, 1-83 to 4-84; received new accommodations arrangements, communications suite, and armament and the helicopter deck was enlarged. Had increasingly been used on patrol duties and was formally redesignated a "corvette" in 1997.

GUIDED-MISSILE PATROL CRAFT [PTG]

Note: All patrol craft were given pennant numbers starting with Z around 2002–3.

♦ 4 Province class
Bldr: Vosper Thornycroft, Portchester, U.K.

	Laid down	L	In serv.
Z 10 Dhofar (ex-B 10)	30-9-80	14-10-81	7-8-82
Z 11 Al Sharquiyah (ex-B 11)	10-81	2-12-82	5-12-83
Z 12 Al Bat'nah (ex-B 12)	9-12-81	11-82	18-1-84
Z 14 Mussandam (ex-B 14)	8-10-87	19-3-88	31-3-89

Al Bat'nah (Z 12) French Navy, 1995

Mussandam (Z 14) French Navy, 4-93

D: 311 tons light (394 fl) **S:** 40 kts **Dim:** 56.70 (52.00 pp) × 8.20 × 2.40 (hull)
A: 6 or 8 MM 40 Exocet SSM; 1 76-mm 62-cal. OTO Melara Compact DP; 1 twin 40-mm 70-cal. OTO Melara AA; 2 single 12.7-mm mg
Electronics:
Radar: Z 11: 1 Decca 1226 nav.; 1 Plessey AWS-4 air search—others: 1 Decca TM 1226 nav.; 1 Plessey AWS-6 air search; 1 CelsiusTech 9LV 300 f.c.s.
EW: Racal 242 suite (Cutlass intercept, Scorpion jammer, Sadie processor); 2 9-round Wallop Barricade decoy RL
M: 4 Paxman Valenta 18RP200 diesels; 4 props; 17,900 bhp (15,000 sust.)—2 80-hp electric outdrives
Electric: 420 kw tot. **Range:** 2,000/15 **Fuel:** 45.5 tons
Crew: 5 officers, 40 enlisted + 14 trainees

Remarks: Z 10 was ordered in 1980, Z 11 and Z 12 in 1-81, and Z 14 on 3-1-86. Z 10 sailed for Oman 21-10-82. Similar ships are operated by Egypt and Kenya.
Combat systems: Z 10 has the Sperry Sea Archer Mk 2 gun fire-control system, with two optical trackers. The other three can carry eight MM 40 Exocets in two sets of four but usually carry only six; they also have the CelsiusTech 9LV 300 f.c.s. with I-band search radar and J-band radar/electro-optical fire-control director forward and a separate t.v./IR director aft for the 40-mm AA. The Exocet launchers have now been "boxed-in" with metal heat shielding.

PATROL CRAFT [PC]

♦ 3 Vigilante 400 class (Project Mawj)
Bldr: CMN, Cherbourg

	Laid down	L	In serv.
Z 1 Al Bushra (ex-B 1)	16-2-94	14-3-95	15-6-95
Z 2 Al Mansoor (ex-B 2)	12-4-94	3-5-94	10-8-95
Z 3 Al Najah (ex-B 3)	27-6-94	5-3-96	5-96

Al Najah (Z 3) Ralph Edwards, 2-01

Al Najah (Z 3) Brian Morrison, 2-01

D: 373 tons (477 fl) **S:** 24 kts (22 sust.)
Dim: 54.50 (50.00) × 8.00 (7.70 wl) × 2.54
A: 1 76-mm 62-cal. OTO Melara Compact DP; 2 single 20-mm 90-cal. RO-Oerlikon GAM-B01 AA; 2 single 12.7-mm M2 mg
Electronics:
Radar: 1 Kelvin-Hughes Type 1007 ARPA nav.
E/O: CelsiusTech 9LV 207 optronic director
M: 2 MTU 16V538 TB93 diesels; 2 CP props; 8,400 bhp
Electric: 360 kw tot. (3 × 120 kw) **Range:** 2,400/15 **Fuel:** 73 tons
Endurance: 15 days **Crew:** 3 officers, 21 enlisted + 20 passengers

Remarks: Ordered 1-9-93; another five to be equipped with ASW weapons and sensors were proposed but not ordered. Names repeat those of the stricken 37.5-m-class patrol boats. Fitting out was completed at the Royal Dockyard, Muscat. First two arrived in Oman 28-9-95, the third on 29-6-96. Have two 35-m^3 cargo holds.
Combat systems: The 76-mm guns were to have been taken from the gunboats of the Brooke Marine 37.5-m class, but new mounts were instead provided to replace the French 40-mm mountings installed at launch. Provision was made for later installation of up to eight MM 15 short-range antiship missiles, four fixed 324-mm ASW torpedo tubes, and the Thales ATAS towed active sonar array, but the plan to give them an ASW capability has been canceled. Also omitted was the planned Thales DR-3000S1 Compact intercept system and two 9-round Wallop Barricade decoy rocket launchers.

PATROL BOATS [PB]

♦ 4 Al Seeb class
Bldr: Vosper Pty, Singapore (In serv. 15-3-81)

Z 20 Al Seeb (ex-B 20)
Z 21 Al Shinas (ex-B 21)
Z 22 Al Sadah (ex-B 22)
Z 23 Al Khasab (ex-B 23)

Al Seeb (Z 20) Omani Navy, 1996

D: 60.7 tons (75 fl) **S:** 26 kts **Dim:** 25.00 (23.00 pp) × 5.80 × 1.50
A: 1 20-mm 90-cal. Oerlikon GAM-B01 AA; 2 single 7.62-mm mg
Electronics: Radar: 1 Decca 1226 nav.
M: 2 MTU 12V331 TC92 diesels, plus 1 Cummins N855M cruise diesel (197 bhp); 3 props; 3,072 bhp
Range: 750/14; 2,300/8 **Crew:** 13 tot.

Remarks: Ordered 24-4-81. Craft had been completed in 1980 on speculation by builder. Glass-reinforced plastic hulls. Have five spare berths. Maximum speed on cruise diesel is 8 kts. Renumbered during 2002 or 2003.

AMPHIBIOUS WARFARE SHIPS AND CRAFT

Note: The large troop and vehicle transport *Fulk al Salamah* is subordinated to the Royal Yacht Squadron (q.v.). Amphibious warfare ships L 2 through L 10 were renumbered A 2 through A 10 around 2002–3.

♦ 1 Nasr al Bahr–class landing ship [LST]
Bldr: Brooke Marine, Lowestoft, U.K.

	L	In serv.
A 2 Nasr al Bahr (ex-L 2)	16-5-84	13-2-85

Nasr al Bahr (A 2) French Navy, 3-95

D: 2,500 tons (fl) **S:** 15.5 kts **Dim:** 93.00 (80.00 pp) × 15.50 × 2.3 (mean)
A: 2 twin 40-mm 70-cal. OTO Melara Dardo AA; 2 single 20-mm 90-cal. Oerlikon GAM-B01 AA
Electronics:
Radar: 1 Decca 1226 nav.; 1 Decca 1290 nav.
EW: . . . intercept; 2 18-round Wallop Super Barricade decoy RL
M: 2 Paxman Valenta 18RP200CM diesels; 2 CP props; 7,800 bhp
Range: 4,000/13 **Endurance:** 28 days (10 with troops)
Crew: 13 officers, 16 chief petty officers, 52 other enlisted + 240 troops: 13 officers, 16 noncommissioned officers, 211 other enlisted

Remarks: Ordered 18-3-82. Two sisters were built for Algeria. Name means "Sea Lion."
Hull systems: Vehicle deck is 75 × 7.4 m, with a 30 × 7-m cargo hatch; bow ramp is 18 m long by 4.5 m wide and stern ramp is 5 by 4 m. Intended to land 450 tons of cargo or seven main battle tanks on a gradient of up to 1:40. Two Sea Truck LCVPs carried. Has a helicopter deck for one Sea King/Commando or Super Puma helicopter. A traveling 16-ton crane spans the cargo deck forward. Max. cargo: 650 tons. A new, taller funnel was fitted during a 1997 refit.
Combat systems: Has the CelsiusTech 9LV 200 weapons-control system with one Matra Défense Lynx electro-optical gun director. Carries 2,000 rounds of 40-mm and 2,450 rounds of 20-mm ammunition and 244 chaff rounds.

Disposal note: Logistic support landing ship *Al Munassir* (L 1), placed in reserve during the mid-1990s, was stricken by 2005.

♦ 1 Mahmal-class utility landing craft [LCU]
Bldr: Abu Dhabi SB

	L	In serv.
Al Munassir	17-5-06	12-06

Al Munassir Abu Dhabi Ship Building, 5-06

D: 800 (fl) **S:** 10 kts **Dim:** 64.0 × . . . × . . .
M: 2 Caterpillar . . . diesels

Remarks: New 64-meter landing craft built to Omani design specifications and ordered on 2-28-05. Can carry 50 troops or 46 tons of cargo.

♦ 3 Saba al Bahr–class utility landing craft [LCU]
Bldr: Vosper Pty, Singapore

	Laid down	L	In serv.
A 8 Saba al Bahr (ex-L 8)	. . .	30-6-81	17-9-81
A 9 Al Doghas (ex-L 9)	9-7-82	12-11-82	10-1-83
A 10 Al Temsah (ex-L 10)	8-9-82	15-12-82	12-2-83

D: 230 tons (fl) **S:** 8 kts **Dim:** 33.0 (27.84 pp) × 8.18 × 1.51
A: None **Electronics:** Radar: 1 Furuno 701 nav.
M: 2 Caterpillar 3408TA diesels; 2 props; 762 bhp
Electric: 180 kw tot. **Range:** 1,800/8 **Crew:** 11 tot.

AMPHIBIOUS WARFARE SHIPS AND CRAFT *(continued)*

Al Temsah (A 10) Omani Navy, 1996

Remarks: A 8: 170 grt/100 dwt; A 9, 10: 191 grt/155 dwt. A 8 was ordered 24-4-81, A 9 and A 10 in 7-82. Cargo: 100 tons of vehicles or stores, or 45 tons of deck cargo plus 50 tons of fresh water (and 35 tons of water ballast). L 8 is 30.00 m o.a./24.85 pp. Pennant numbers were changed briefly from C-series to L-series in 2000 before changing to the "A" letter prefix.

♦ 1 landing craft [LCM]
Bldr: Lewis Offshore, Stornaway, Scotland (In serv. 1979)

A 7 Al Neemran (ex-L 7)

Al Neemran (A 7) Omani Navy, 1994

D: Approx. 140 tons (fl) **S:** 8 kts (7 loaded) **Dim:** 25.5 × 7.4 × 1.8
A: None **Electronics:** Radar: 1 Furuno . . . nav.
M: 2 . . . diesels; 2 props; 300 bhp **Crew:** 6 tot.

Remarks: 85 dwt. Cargo: approx. 75 tons. Pennant changed briefly from C 7 to L 7 in 2000 before changing to the current "A" letter prefix.

AUXILIARIES

♦ 1 dry cargo ship [AK]
Bldr: Scheepswerf G. Bijlsma & Zn. B.V., Wartena, the Netherlands

	L	In serv.
T 1 Al Sultana (ex-A 2, ex-T 2)	18-5-75	4-6-75

Al Sultana (T 1) Guy Schaeffer via Paolo Marsan, 4-02

D: Approx. 1,700 tons (fl) **S:** 11.25 kts **Dim:** 65.69 (59.90 pp) × 10.83 × 4.13
A: None **Electronics:** Radar: 1 Decca TM 1226 nav.
M: 1 Mirrlees-Blackstone ESL8 Mk. 2 diesel; 1,120 bhp
Electric: 192 kw tot. (2 × 76-kw, 1 × 40-kw diesel sets)
Fuel: 82.5 tons **Crew:** 20 tot.

Remarks: 909 grt/1,495 dwt. Traveling 1-ton crane straddles the 33.6 × 7.7-m hatch to one continuous 40.4-m-long hold. Was replaced in the training role by *Al Mabrukah* (Q 30). Refitted 1992; given new pennant number in 1997 and again around 2002.

SERVICE CRAFT

♦ 1 Sea Truck–type divers' support launch [YDT]
Bldr: Rotork, U.K. (In serv. 1991)

R 1

D: 13 tons (fl) **S:** 20 kts **Dim:** 18.0 × 3.8 × 1.1
A: 2 single 7.62-mm mg **Electronics:** Radar: none
M: 2 Volvo Penta AQD70D diesels; 2 props; 430 bhp **Crew:** 4 tot.

Remarks: Supports combat swimmers rather than hard-hat divers. Sister *Zahra 27* serves the Royal Oman Police.

♦ 11 miscellaneous workboats [YFL]
Bldr: Cheverton, Cowes, U.K. (In serv. 4-75)

W 4 W 5 W 7 through W 11 WF 41 through WF 44

D: 3.5 tons **S:** 25 kts **Dim:** 8.28 × 2.7 × 0.8 **M:** 2 diesels

Remarks: WF 41 through WF 44 are 12.0 m o.a. and displace about 5.5 tons (fl).

♦ 1 inshore survey craft [YGS] Bldr: Watercraft, U.K. (In serv. 4-81)

M 1 Al Rahmanniya (ex-H 1)

D: 23.6 tons (fl) **S:** 13.5 kts **Dim:** 15.5 (14.0 pp) × 4.0 × 12.5
Electronics: Radar: 1 Decca 101 nav.
M: 2 Volvo TMD 120A diesels; 2 props; 520 bhp **Electric:** 25 kVA
Range: 500/12 **Crew:** 10 tot.

Al Rahmanniya (M 1) Omani Navy, 1996

Remarks: Glass-reinforced plastic construction. Raytheon DE 719B and Kelvin-Hughes MS 48 echo sounders, a Decca DMU transponder and Sea Fix receiver, and a Hewlett-Packard 9815A data-storage computer are fitted. Renumbered during 2002 or 2003.

Note: Two small U.S. Navy survey launches from the survey ship *Harkness* (T-AGS 32) were left in Oman during 11-92 but do not seem to have been put into service.

♦ 1 or more Sea Flash radio-controlled target boats [YGT]
Bldr: Flight Refuelling, U.K. (In serv. 1987)

♦ 2 PushyCat 1500–class small tugs [YTL]
Bldr: Scheepswerf Damen B.V., Gorinchem, the Netherlands (In serv. 1990)

T 2 T 3

PushyCat tug T 3 Hartmut Ehlers, 10-92

Remarks: Dimensions: 15.0 × 4.75 × 1.90. Sister T 1 was lost overboard on delivery voyage and was replaced by T 3.

♦ 1 sail-training craft [YTS]
Bldr: Hard & MacKenzie, Buckie, Scotland (In serv. 1971)

S 1 Shabab Oman (ex-*Captain Scott*)

D: 386 tons (fl) **S:** 10 kts (on diesels) **Dim:** 43.90 × 8.59 × 4.65
M: 2 Gardner 8-cyl. diesels; 2 props; 460 bhp
Crew: 5 officers, 15 enlisted + 3 officer/instructors, 24 trainees

Remarks: 264 grt. Three-masted, wooden-hulled barkentine, purchased in 1977 in the U.K. for training Omani youth in seamanship; commissioned in 1979. Operated by the navy for the Ministry of Youth Affairs. Name means "Youth of Oman."

Disposal note: Brooke Marine 37.5-m patrol craft *Al Wafi* (B 4) and *Al Fulk* (B 5) were placed in reserve in 1995 with the intent of reactivating the pair eventually for use as training craft; the plan did not come to fruition, and the craft are now probably beyond reclamation. Their sisters *Al Mujahid* (B 6) and *Al Jabhar* (B 7) were stricken during 1994.

SERVICE CRAFT *(continued)*

Shabab Oman (S 1) Michael Nitz, 8-05

ROYAL YACHT SQUADRON

Note: An entirely separate organization from the navy, the Royal Yacht Squadron, with around 150 personnel, bases its ships at Mina al Qaboos. In addition to the two large, modern units below, the squadron also operates the elegant wooden-hulled, three-masted, lateen-rigged sailing dhow *Zinat al Bihar.*

♦ 1 royal yacht [WAG] Bldr: C.N. Picchiotti, Viareggio, Italy (In serv. 7-82)

AL SAID

Al Said Peter Voss, 9-94

D: 3,250 tons (fl) **S:** 18 kts **Dim:** 103.82 (85.91 pp) × 16.24 × 4.72
Electronics: 1 Decca TM 1226C nav; 1 Decca ACS 1230C nav.
M: 2 GMT A420.6L diesels; 2 CP props; 8,400 hp—bow-thruster
Electric: 2,142 kw tot. (3 × 714-kw diesel sets) **Crew:** 16 officers, 140 enlisted

Remarks: 4,442 grt/1,320 dwt. Replaced former *Al Said* (now training ship *Al Mabrukah* [Q 30]). Has a helicopter pad aft, VHF SATCOM, and fin stabilizers. Carries one Rotork LCVP and three Puma-C-class personnel launches.

♦ 1 troop and vehicle transport [WAP]
Bldr: Bremer-Vulkan, Bremen-Vegesack, Germany

	Laid down	L	In serv.
FULK AL SALAMAH (ex-*Ghubat al Salamah*, ex-*Tulip*)	17-1-86	29-8-86	3-4-87

Fulk al Salamah French Navy, 7-96

D: Approx. 10,000 tons (fl) **S:** 19.5 kts **Dim:** 136.33 (125.02 pp) × 21.04 × 5.30
A: None **Electronics:** Radar: 2 Decca . . . nav.
M: 4 G.M.T. A420.6 diesels; 2 CP props; 16,800 bhp
Electric: 3,780 kw tot. (3 × 1,260-kw diesel sets)
Range: . . . **Crew:** . . .

Remarks: 10,864-grt/5,186-nrt combination attack transport/logistic support vessel. Has VHF SATCOM equipment, a hangar and flight deck for two AS.332C Super Puma transport helicopters, two Sea Truck landing craft in davits below the helicopter deck, a large cargo hold forward with a 22.4 × 7.0-m hatch, accommodations for at least 240 troops, and a large vehicle loading door to starboard (plus four personnel/stores doors through the hull sides). *Tulip* was the cover name assigned while the ship was building. Was attached to UNESCO during 1991 as an "investigation ship."

ROYAL OMAN POLICE

Personnel: About 400 total

Bases: Principal base at Mina al Qaboos, with craft also stationed at Sidab

Aviation: Two EADS CN-235 maritime patrol and transport aircraft; two Pilatus-Britten-Norman BN-2T Maritime Defender transport and search-and-rescue aircraft; two Agusta-Bell AB-205 and three AB-214 utility helicopters.

PATROL BOATS [WPB]

Note: Patrol boats Haras I through X and Zahra 14, 15, 17, 18, and 21 received new hull pennant numbers during 2002–3.

♦ 0 (+ 3) 27-meter . . . class
Bldr: U.S. Marine, New Orleans, La. (In serv. 2007)

Remarks: Ordered 6-05 for delivery during 2007. 27-meter GRP hull, 50 knots top speed. Lengthened and modified version of the XFPB-class patrol boats in service with Mexico. Up to ten additional units may be purchased.

♦ 2 Type D 59116, GRP-hulled
Bldr: Yokohama Yacht, Japan (In serv. 1988)

DHEEB AL BAHAR II DHEEB AL BAHAR III

Dheeb al Bahar III Hartmut Ehlers, 6-03

D: 65 tons (fl) **S:** 36 kts **Dim:** 23.00 × 5.20 × 1.20
A: 1 12.7-mm mg
Electronics: Radar: 1 Furuno FR-711-2 nav.; 1 Furuno 2400 nav.
M: 2 MTU 12V396 TB93 diesels; 2 props; 3,260 bhp
Range: 420/30 **Crew:** 11 tot.

♦ 1 P 2000 class Bldr: Watercraft Ltd., Shoreham, U.K. (In serv. 12-84)

DHEEB AL BAHAR I

Dheeb al Bahar I Hartmut Ehlers, 6-03

D: 80 tons (fl) **S:** 38 kts **Dim:** 20.80 (18.00 pp) × 5.80 × 1.50
A: 1 20-mm 90-cal. Oerlikon GAM-B01 AA; 2 single 7.62-mm mg
Electronics: Radar: 1 Furuno FR-701 nav.
M: 2 MTU 12V396 TB93 diesels; 2 props; 3,920 bhp (3,260 sust.)
Range: 423/35; 660/22 **Crew:** 8 tot.

Remarks: GRP construction with aluminum superstructure. Equipped with a navigational satellite receiver and an MFD/F loop.

♦ 1 Type PT 1903 Mk III patrol craft
Bldr: Le Comte, Vianen, the Netherlands (In serv. 8-81)

H 8 HARAS VIII

D: 30 tons (33 fl) **S:** 30 kts **Dim:** 19.27 × 4.95 × 1.25
A: 2 single 12.7-mm mg **Electronics:** Radar: 1 Decca 1226C nav.
M: 2 MTU 8V331 TC92 diesels; 2 props; 1,770 bhp
Range: 1,650/17; 2,300/12 **Crew:** 10 tot.

♦ 3 CG 29 class Bldr: Karlskrona Varvet, Karlskrona, Sweden

H 7 HARAS VII (In serv. 6-81) H 10 HARAS X (In serv. 14-4-82)
H 9 HARAS IX (In serv. 1982)

ROYAL OMAN POLICE PATROL BOATS [WPB] *(continued)*

Haras X (H 10) Omani Navy, 1998

D: 84 tons (fl) **S:** 25 kts **Dim:** 28.9 × 5.4 × 1.3
A: 2 single 20-mm 90-cal. Oerlikon GAM-B01 AA
Electronics: Radar: 1 Decca 1226C nav.
M: 2 MTU 8V331 IC82 diesels; 2 props; 1,866 bhp
Range: 600/15 **Crew:** 13 tot.

Remarks: GRP construction. Enlarged version of a design built for Liberia. *Haras IX* has also been reported to have MTU 12V396 diesels.

♦ 1 CG 27–class GRP-hulled Bldr: Karlskrona, Sweden (In serv. 1980)

H 6 Haras VI

D: 53 tons (fl) **S:** 27 kts **Dim:** 24.0 × 5.5 × 1.0
A: 1 20-mm 90-cal. Oerlikon GAM-B01 AA
Electronics: Radar: 1 Decca 1226C nav.
M: 2 MTU 12V331 diesels; 2 props; 2,800 bhp **Crew:** 11 tot.

♦ 5 Haras I–class GRP-hulled Bldr: Vosper Pty., Singapore

H 1 Haras I, H 2 Haras II, H 3 Haras III, and H 4 Haras IV
(In serv. 22-12-75)
H 5 Haras V (In serv. 11-78)

Haras II (H 2) Hartmut Ehlers, 10-92

D: 45 tons (50 fl) **S:** 24.5 kts **Dim:** 22.9 × 6.0 × 1.5
A: 1 20-mm 90-cal. Oerlikon GAM-B01 AA
Electronics: Radar: 1 Decca 101 nav.
M: 2 Caterpillar D348 diesels; 2 props; 1,450 bhp
Range: 600/20; 1,000/11 **Crew:** 11 tot.

♦ 2 Zahra 18 class Bldr: Emsworth SY, U.K. (In serv. 1987)

Z 18 Zahra 18 Z 21 Zahra 21

Zahra 18 (Z 18) Hartmut Ehlers, 10-92

D: 18 tons (21 fl) **S:** 22 kts **Dim:** 16.0 × 4.2 × 1.2
A: 1 or 2 single 7.62-mm mg **Electronics:** Radar: 1 Decca 101 nav.
M: 2 Cummins VTA-903M diesels; 2 props; 643 bhp
Range: 700/20; 510/22 **Crew:** 6 tot.

Remarks: GRP hulls molded by Watercraft, Shoreham, and completed by Emsworth.

♦ 3 Zahra 14 class
Bldr: Watercraft, Shoreham (In serv. 1981)

Z 14 Zahra 14 Z 15 Zahra 15 Z 17 Zahra 17

Zahra 17 (Z 17)—alongside *Zahra 14* Hartmut Ehlers, 6-03

D: 17.25 tons (fl) **S:** 22 kts **Dim:** 13.9 (12.6 wl) × 4.3 × 1.1
A: 1 or 2 single 7.62-mm mg **Electronics:** Radar: 1 Decca 101 nav.
M: 2 Cummins VTA-903M diesels; 2 props; 643 bhp
Range: 700/20; 510/22 **Crew:** 6 tot.

Remarks: The GRP hulls were molded to a standard Keith Nelson pilot/patrol boat design. *Zahra 17* has a higher pilothouse than the others.

♦ 20 Cougar Enforcer 33 Ultra Fast Boats
Bldr: Vosper Thornycroft Halmatic, Portsmouth, U.K. (In serv. 2003)

D: 5.4 tons **S:** 45+ kts **Dim:** 10.88 (8.5 wl) × 2.84 × 0.75
A: Small arms **Electronics:** . . .
M: 2 Yanmar 6 cyl. marine diesels; 2 Hamilton waterjets
Range: 120/45+ **Crew:** . . .

Remarks: Perform coastal patrol duties. All delivered during 2003. VT Halmatic provides operational and maintenance training in the U.K., with follow-on training in Oman.

♦ 14 Rodman 58 patrol craft
Bldr: Rodman Polyship S.A., Vigo, Spain (In serv. 2003–4)

D: 19 tons **S:** 34 kts **Dim:** 18.0 × 4.9 × 1.2
A: Small arms **Electronics:** . . .
M: 2 . . . diesels; 2 . . . waterjets
Range: 345/17 **Crew**: 5 total

Remarks: Ordered 11-1-02; total program cost was $15.1 million.

SERVICE CRAFT

♦ 1 Zahra 16–series diving tender [WYDT]
Bldr: Rotork, U.K. (In serv. 1981)

Z 27 Zahra 27

Zahra 27 (Z 27) Hartmut Ehlers, 6-03

D: 11 tons (23 fl) **S:** 20 kts **Dim:** 18.0 × 3.0 × 0.5
A: 2 single 7.62-mm mg
M: 2 Volvo Penta AQD 70/750 diesel outdrives; 430 bhp **Crew:** 4 tot.

Remarks: Received a new hull pennant number during 2002–3. Sisters *Zahra 16, Zahra 20,* and *Zahra 22* have been retired. Sister R 1 serves the navy.

Note: A new *Zahra 16* was photographed in service during 2003; no additional information is available.

PAKISTAN

Islamic Republic of Pakistan

NAVY

Personnel: About 24,000 total, including 1,400 marines and 2,000 assigned to the Maritime Security Agency. The navy also operates all customs service patrol boats.

Bases: Major base and repair facilities at Karachi and Ormara; minor facilities at Gwadar and Port Qasim

Naval Aviation: The Naval Air Arm consists of 10 P-3C Orion (8 were acquired in 2006–7), three Atlantic Mk 1, and one Fokker F-27-400M maritime patrol aircraft; three Westland Lynx HAS.3 and seven AS.316 Alouette-III shipboard helicopters; five Westland Sea King Mk 45 and Sea King Mk 45C land-based helicopters armed with AM-39 Exocet antiship missiles; four Fokker F-27-200 and two HAMC Y-12-II transports; and two Cessna liaison aircraft. The P-3 Orions are armed with A 244 torpedoes and Harpoon antiship missiles.

Pakistani Navy P-3C Orion Lockheed Martin, 1993

Pakistani Navy Atlantic Mk 1 U.S. Navy, 5-95

All naval aircraft are based at PNS *Mehran* and are assigned to the following squadrons: Sea Kings to 111 Sqn., Lynxes to 222 Sqn., Alouettes to 333 Sqn., Orions to 28 Sqn., and Atlantics to 29 Sqn.

Thales Ocean Master radars have been installed in the Atlantic Mk 1s; one Fokker F-27-200 has also been equipped with Ocean Master, plus DR-3000A intercept equipment. All five Sea King helicopters have been fitted with GEC-Marconi AQS-928G acoustic processors and Type 2069 dipping sonars. Three ex-French Navy Atlantic Mk 1 reconnaissance aircraft donated during 1996 have been used for cannibalization spares. Twelve air force Mirage-V fighters are equipped to launch AM 39 Exocets for maritime strike missions.

Weapons and Sensors: Italian WASS heavyweight torpedoes are on order to replace older French torpedoes. 60 Harpoon Block II antiship missiles (40 air launched and 20 ship-launched) were requested from the United States in 2005.

Note: Ship names are preceded by PNS (Pakistani Naval Ship).

ATTACK SUBMARINES [SS]

♦ 2 (+ 1) French Agosta-90B class
Bldr: DCN, Cherbourg (S 139: Karachi NSY)

	Laid down	L	In serv.
S 137 KHALID	15-7-95	18-12-98	21-12-99
S 138 SAAD	6-98	24-8-02	12-12-03
S 139 HAMZA	3-1-97	10-8-06	2008

Khalid (S 137) Pakistani Navy, 2000

Khalid (S 137) DCN, 1999

D: 1,250 tons std.; 1,570 tons surf./1,760 tons sub. **S:** 12.5 kts surf./20 kts sub.
Dim: 67.57 (S 139: 77.57) × 6.80 × 5.40
A: 4 bow 550-mm TT (16 F 17P Mod. 2 torpedoes and/or SM 39 Exocet SSM)
Electronics:
Radar: 1 Kelvin-Hughes Type 1007 nav./surf. search
Sonar: Thales: TSM 2233 Advanced Eledone; DUUX-5 (TSM 2055) passive ranging; TSM 2933 towed linear passive array
EW: Thales DR-3000U intercept
M: 2 SEMT-Pielstick A16 PA4 185 diesels (850 kw each), Jeumont-Schneider electric motor; 1 prop; 3,000 shp—1 23-hp cruise motor—S 139 only: MESMA air-independent auxiliary power system (200 kw)
Range: 7,900/10 snorkel; 178/3.5 sub. **Fuel:** 200 tons
Endurance: 68 days **Crew:** 7 officers, 29 enlisted

Remarks: Ordered 21-9-94. The first unit was built entirely in France. The three prefabricated sections for S 138 were fabricated in France between 9-95 and 5-98 and were shipped to Karachi 29-4-98 for outfitting and assembly. The third is being constructed and fitted out at Karachi (where the program was officially inaugurated 3-1-97 by the Pakistani president), with about 20% of the components and material coming from France, where hull section fabrication had begun on 13-2-99. The program is to cost $950 million total, plus another $100 million for the SM39 Exocet missiles. Pakistan has offered to provide S 139 to Malaysia, with a replacement to be built for the Pakistani Navy. S 137 was delivered in France 13-9-99, arrived at Karachi 16-12-99, and is assigned to Submarine Squadron 5. Completion of S 138 was delayed from 12-02 by the local security situation and the withdrawal of many French technicians during 5-02.

Hull systems: Agosta-90B is an updated version of the original *Agosta* with smaller crew, greater automation, an inertial navigation system, an integrated weapon system with optronic periscope, and the French MESMA (*Module d'Énergie Sous-Marine Autonome*) air-independent propulsion system (which is to be installed in the third unit in an 8-m extra section to the pressure hull and backfitted to the other two later). MESMA burns diesel oil and oxygen in a high-pressure combustion heat-generating loop, transferring the heat to a secondary Rankine-cycle heat transference loop. The complete MESMA system weighs some 30 tons but produces only 200 kw of electricity; enough fuel for 18 days of operations is carried. The hull sections to accommodate the MESMA system were fabricated in France, with the first completed 6-00.

The pressure hulls are built of HLES 80 (*Haute Limite Elastique Soudable*), a U.S. HY 100–equivalent steel. The batteries are supplied by CEAC. Operating functions will be controlled by a SAGEM SS Mk 1 control system. The integrated navigational suite includes Minicin Mod. 3 inertial navigation, radio navigation receivers, CGM 5 gyro, and LH 92 automatic log. Safare Crouzet provided a self-noise monitoring system. Normal maximum operating depth: 320 m.

Combat systems: The sonar arrays are an integral function of the UDS International SUBTICS (Submarine Tactical Information and Command System) weapons-control system, which is similar to the French Navy's SET (*Système d'Exploitation Tactique*) and has six two-screen display consoles. SOPELEM search and attack periscopes are fitted, as is an "electromagnetic detection system." S 137 launched an SM 39 Exocet missile on 10-3-01 while submerged.

♦ 2 French Agosta class
Bldr: Dubigeon, Nantes

	Laid down	L	In serv.
S 135 HASHMAT (ex-*Astrant*)	15-9-76	14-12-77	17-2-79
S 136 HURMAT (ex-*Adventurous*)	18-9-77	1-12-78	18-2-80

Hurmat (S 136) 92 Wing Det. A, RAAF, 1998

ATTACK SUBMARINES [SS] *(continued)*

D: 1,230 tons std.; 1,480 tons surf. (max.)/1,725 tons sub.
S: 12.5 kts surf./20.5 kts sub. **Dim:** 67.90 × 6.80 × 5.40
A: 4 bow 550-mm TT (20 F 17P torpedoes and UGM-84A Harpoon SSM)
Electronics:
Radar: 1 Thales DRUA-33 nav./surf. search
Sonar: Thales DUUA-2A/B active/passive search/attack (8 kHz); Thales DSUV-2H passive; Thales DUUX-2A passive-ranging
EW: ARUR intercept; ARUD intercept
M: 2 SEMT-Pielstick A16 PA4 185 diesels, electric drive; 1 prop; 4,600 shp—1 23-hp cruise motor
Range: 7,900/10 snorkel; 178/3.5 sub. **Fuel:** 200 tons
Crew: 7 officers, 47 enlisted

Remarks: Originally ordered for South Africa, but the sale was canceled in 1977 due to the arms embargo and completion slowed. Sold to Pakistan in 11-78. Diving depth: 300 m. Battery capacity is twice that of the previous *Daphné* class. Were fitted to launch U.S. Sub-Harpoon antiship missiles in 1984–85, but the missiles are now past their shelf lives. Are assigned to Submarine Squadron 5.

Disposal note: *Daphné*-class submarines *Hangor* (S 131), *Shushuk* (S 132), *Mangro* (S 133), and *Ghazi* (S 134) were decomissioned on 2-1-06.

MIDGET SUBMARINES [SSM]

♦ 3 MG-110-class midget submarines
Bldr: Pakistan NDY, Karachi (In serv. 1988–92)

Pakistani Navy MG-110 midget submarine French Navy, 1994

D: 110 tons surf./130 tons sub. **S:** 9 kts surf./7 kts sub.
Dim: 27.8 × 2.02 × 5.60 (high)
A: 2 533-mm SUT wire-guided torpedoes or 8 Mk 414 300-kg mines in drop gear
M: 1 diesel generator set, 1 electric motor; 1 3-bladed prop; . . . shp
Range: 1,600/7 surf.; 8.5/6, 60/4.5 sub. **Endurance:** 20 days
Crew: 6 crew + 8 combat swimmers

Remarks: Assembled with components supplied by COS.M.O.S., Livorno, Italy. A lengthened version of the same builder's S.X. 756 class. Began delivery in 1988 to replace the earlier S.X. 404–class midget subs, which have all been retired; a third MG-110 was lost in 1995, and further construction was abandoned. Diving depth: 150 m max. Have a Pilkington CK 39 periscope. A number of COS.M.O.S. CF2 FX60, two-man swimmer delivery vehicles ("chariots") from the same builder are also in service, and two can be carried in lieu of torpedoes or mines on each MG-110.

FRIGATES [FF]

♦ 0 (+ 4) Modified Jiangwei-II class (F 22P)

	Bldr.	Laid down	L	In serv.
. . .	Houdong, SY Shanghai	2006	2007	2008
. . .	Houdong, SY Shanghai	. . .	. . .	. . .
. . .	Karachi SY & Eng. Wks., Karachi	. . .	. . .	. . .
. . .	Karachi SY & Eng. Wks., Karachi	. . .	. . .	2013

D: 150 tons (185 fl) **S:** 23 kts **Dim:** 114.5 (108.0 wl) × 12.4 (12.2 wl) × 3.6 (hull)
A: 8 C-802 YJ-2 (CSS-N-8 Saccade) SSM; 1 8-round HQ-7 SAM system (16 missiles); 1 twin 100-mm 55-cal. ENG-2 DP; 4 30-mm AA; 1 helicopter
Electronics:
Radar: 1 Type 517H-1 (Knife Rest) long range 2-D air search; 1 Type . . . nav.; 2 . . . missile fc; 1 Type . . . gun f.c.
Sonar: . . .
M: . . .
Range: . . . / . . . **Crew:** . . .

Remarks: Plans to purchase up to four Chinese-built frigates of the Jiangwei-II class were made public in 3-95. An agreement to build four frigates was signed with China 12-4-00, but funding for the project (which cost about $600 million) was not available until the order was finalized on 4-4-05. Current plans call for the first two to be built in China and the rest at the Naval Dockyard, Karachi. The design is known as the F-22P class in Pakistan. Pakistan may install western electronics, communications, and weapon systems rather than the Chinese equipment listed above.

♦ 6 ex-U.K. Amazon class (Type 21)
Bldr: Yarrow (Shipbuilders) Ltd., Scotstoun, Glasgow, Scotland (D 182, 185: Vosper Thornycroft, Woolston)

	Laid down	L	In serv.
D 181 TARIQ (ex-*Ambuscade*, F 172)	1-9-71	18-1-73	5-9-75
D 182 BABUR (ex-*Amazon*, F 169)	6-11-69	26-4-71	11-5-74
D 183 KHYBER (ex-*Arrow*, F 173)	28-9-72	5-2-74	29-7-76
D 184 BADR (ex-*Alacrity*, F 174)	5-3-73	18-9-74	2-7-77
D 185 TIPPU SULTAN (ex-*Active*, F 171)	23-7-71	23-11-72	17-6-77
D 186 SHAHJAHAN (ex-*Avenger*, F 185)	30-10-74	20-11-75	19-7-78

D: 3,210 tons (3,710 fl) **S:** 30 kts
Dim: 117.04 (109.70 pp) × 12.7 × 4.8 (6.4 over sonar)

Tippu Sultan (D 185) Leo van Ginderen, 6-05

Tippu Sultan (D 185) Frank Findler, 6-05

Babur (D 182) U.S. Navy, 11-04

Shahjahan (D 186) U.S. Navy, 6-05

A: D 181, 183, 185: 1 6-round LY-60N SAM syst.; 1 114-mm 55-cal. Vickers Mk 8 DP; 1 20-mm Mk 15 Phalanx gatling CIWS (D 185 only: 2 single 20-mm 85-cal. Oerlikon AA but no Phalanx)—D 183 only: 2 fixed 400-mm ASW TT (Bofors Tp 43X2 torpedoes)—D 182, 184, 186: 4 RGM-84 Harpoon SSM; 1 114-mm 55-cal. Vickers Mk 8 DP; 1 20-mm Mk 15 Phalanx gatling CIWS—D 184, 186 only: 2 triple 324-mm STWS.1 ASW TT (U.S. Mk 46 torpedoes)—D 182 only: 2 fixed 400-mm ASW TT (Bofors Tp 43X2 torpedoes)—all: 1 Lynx helicopter
Electronics:
Radar: 1 Kelvin-Hughes Type 1006 nav.; 1 Marconi Type 992R (D 181, 183, 185: Thales DA-08) surf./air search—D 182, 184, 186 only: 1 AESN RTN-10X Orion gun f.c.; General Dynamics Mk 90 Phalanx f.c.—D 181, 183, 185 only: 1 LL-1 f.c. (with laser and IR sensors)
Sonar: Graseby Type 184P hull-mounted search; Kelvin-Hughes Type 162M bottomed-target classification (50 kHz); Type 185 underwater telephone
EW: Thales DR-3000S1X intercept; FH-12 HFD/F; 2 8-round Corvus decoy RL—D 183, 185 also: 4 4-round decoy RL—all: Type 182 towed acoustic torpedo decoy
E/O: 1 Matra Défense Najir Mk 2 optronic f.c.

FRIGATES [FF] *(continued)*

M: COGOG: 2 Olympus TM-3B gas turbines (25,000 shp each), 2 Tyne RM-1A gas turbines (4,250 shp each); 2 CP props; 50,000 shp max.
Electric: 3,000 kw tot. (4 × 750-kw diesel sets; 450 V, 3-phase, 60-Hz a.c.)
Range: 1,200/30; 4,500/17 **Endurance:** 60 days **Crew:** 13 officers, 164 enlisted

Remarks: D 181 transferred 28-7-93 and formally commissioned 20-11-93 at Karachi. D 182 retired from the Royal Navy 30-9-93 and transferred same date, commissioning 18-1-94. D 183 and D 184 were transferred 1-3-94, D 185 on 29-7-94, and D 186 on 23-9-94. Designed jointly by Vosper Thornycroft and Yarrow under a 27-2-68 contract. All are assigned to Destroyer Squadron 25.
Hull systems: The ships have been criticized for fragility and vulnerability and for being overloaded and top-heavy; permanent ballast had to be added, and in RN service none could carry the full originally intended weapon and sensor suite. The hulls were strengthened during the early 1980s, due to cracking during the Falklands War; doubler plates were added amidships and other work added some 350 tons to displacement and cost at least 2 kts in maximum speed. New equipment added in Pakistan has not helped their stability. Remote control of the engine room is accomplished from the bridge. Have retractable fin stabilizers.
Combat systems: As transferred, had the CAAIS DBA-2 combat data system and a Ferranti WSA.4 digital fire-control system employing two Selenia RTN-10X radar directors (U.K. Type 912) for the 114-mm gun and the since-removed Sea Cat SAM system; the after radar director has been removed in all, and the forward one has been replaced by a Chinese LL-1 set in D 181, 183, and 185. The CAAIS DBA-2 combat data system is a separate entity whose data are automatically transmitted to the WSA.4.

CelsiusTech of Sweden received a contract on 16-9-94 to reequip four of the ships (probably D 181–183 and 185) with the 9LV Mk 3 combat system, but the work does not appear to have been done; the same four ships were to receive tubes for Bofors Tp 43X2 ASW torpedoes, but only D 183 is *confirmed* to have received the tubes, mounted one on either side of the hangar at the forecastle deck level and aimed aft. Two Thales/BAE Systems ATAS (Active Towed Acoustic System) sets were ordered in 11-93 for these ships, but, again, the equipment has not been installed.

Four Thales DR-3000S EW systems were ordered to replace the original UAA-1 intercept arrays. The Thales LW-08 radar was selected to replace the Type 992R air-search radar in 9-94, but only the three ships with the Chinese SAM system have it; in those ships, the Chinese LL-1 radar director controls both the gun and the missiles. All six ships were to receive the Matra Défense Najir Mk 2 electro-optical backup 114-mm gun director. Chinese-made twin 25-mm AA were mounted just abaft the bridge on D 182, 184, and 186, but they were later removed, as have been the two single 20-mm Oerlikon Mk 4 mountings from all. D 185 (and possibly others) has an additional navigational radar set. All six have been modified to accept a 20-mm Phalanx gatling CIWS atop the helicopter hangar; the mounts are moved from ship to ship, as there are not enough for all of them. Likely upgrades include Phalanx block 1B CIWS and Harpoon Block II antiship missiles.

♦ 1 ex-U.K. Broad-Beam Leander class

Bldr: Yarrow, Scotstoun, Glasgow, Scotland

	Laid down	L	In serv.
F 263 Shamsher (ex-*Diomede,* F 16)	30-1-68	15-4-69	2-4-71

Shamsher (F 263) Rahn, 12-01

D: 2,660 tons (3,120 fl) **S:** 27 kts
Dim: 113.38 (109.73 pp) × 13.12 × 4.50 (5.49 props)
A: 1 twin 114-mm 45-cal. Vickers Mk 6 DP; 3 twin 25-mm 80-cal. Type 61M AA; 1 3-round Limbo Mk 10 ASW mortar; 1 AS.319B Alouette-III helicopter
Electronics:
Radar: 1 . . . nav.; 1 Kelvin-Hughes Type 1006 nav.; 1 Plessey Type 994 surf./air search; 1 Marconi Type 965 early warning; 1 Plessey Type 903 gun f.c.
Sonar: Graseby Type 184P hull-mounted MF search; Graseby Type 170B hull-mounted HF attack; Kelvin-Hughes Type 162M bottomed-target classification
EW: UA-8/9 intercept; Type 668 jammers; FH-12 HFD/F; 2 8-round Corvus decoy RL; Type 182 towed acoustic torpedo decoy
M: 2 sets White–English Electric geared steam turbines; 2 5-bladed props; 30,000 shp
Boilers: 2 Babcock & Wilcox 3-drum; 38.7 kg/cm^2, 450° C
Electric: 2,500 kw tot. **Range:** 4,500/12 **Fuel:** 500 tons
Crew: 15 officers, 220 enlisted

Remarks: F 263 was decommissioned 7-7-88 and sold to Pakistan 15-7-88. Although among the newest Royal Navy *Leanders,* it had not been modernized. Is assigned to Destroyer Squadron 18 and used primarily for training.
Disposals: Sister *Zulfiqua* (F 262) was decommissioned during 2002 and is used for cannibalization spares for F 263.
Combat systems: The Sea Cat point-defense SAM system and the associated Type 904 radar director were no longer aboard as of 1994. The 20-mm gunmounts have been removed, and twin Chinese 25-mm gunmounts have been substituted for them just abaft the pilothouse and on the former Type 904 radar director platform atop the helicopter hangar. A second navigational radar antenna has been stepped on a pole mast atop the pilothouse, to port.

GUIDED-MISSILE PATROL CRAFT [PTG]

♦ 0 (+ 2) Improved Turkish MRTP33-class (KAAN 33)

Bldr: Yonca Technical Investment Co., Tuzla, Turkey (In serv. 2008)

D: . . . **S:** 60 kts (gas turbines); 28 kts (diesels) **Dim:** 33.0 × . . . × . . .
A: . . . SSM; 1 single 30-mm . . . AA; 2 single 12.7-mm mg
M: CODOG: 1 Honeywell TF-50 gas-turbine, 2 MTU . . . diesels; 2 MJP waterjets
Range: 970/15; 850/36 **Crew:** 20 total

Remarks: Ordered 8-06, expected in service by 2008.

♦ 5 Jalalat class

Bldrs: P 1029, P 1030: Karachi NDY; others: Karachi SY & Eng. Wks.

	L	In serv.
P 1029 Jalalat (ex-P 1022)	17-11-96	15-8-97
P 1030 Shujaat	6-3-99	30-9-99
P 1031 Haibat	2004	9-04
P 1032 Jurat	9-9-04	2005
P 1033 Quwwat	13-9-04	9-05

Jalalat (P 1029) Pakistani Navy, 2000

D: 150 tons (185 fl) **S:** 23 kts **Dim:** 39.0 × 6.7 × 1.8
A: 4 C-801 (CSS-N-4 Sardine) SSM; 1 twin 37-mm 63-cal. Type 76A AA
Electronics:
Radar: 1 Type 756 nav.; 1 Type SR-47A/R missile target detection and tracking; 1 Type 47G gun f.c.
EW: . . . radar threat warning, 4 4-round decoy RL
M: 2 MTU . . . diesels; 2 props; 5,984 bhp
Range: 2,000/17 **Crew:** 3 officers, 28 enlisted

Remarks: Design is based on that of the patrol craft *Larkana* (q.v.), but with Chinese-supplied armament and sensors. The second and any later units were to carry C-802 missiles and will have intercept and jamming equipment. P 1030 was laid down during 6-98. Are assigned to Patrol Squadron 10.

Disposal note: Ex-Chinese Huangfeng class (Chinese Project 21) guided-missile patrol craft *Deshat* (P 1026), *Himmat* (P 1027), and *Quwwat* (P 1028) were no longer in service as of 2005. Sister *Azmat* (P 1025) was stricken during 1998.

PATROL CRAFT [PC]

♦ 1 Larkana class Bldr: Karachi NDY (L: 6-6-94)

P 157 Larkana

Larkana (P 157) French Navy, 9-97

D: 150 tons (180 fl) **S:** 24 kts **Dim:** 39.0 × 6.7 × 1.7
A: 1 twin 37-mm 63-cal. Type 74 AA; 2 twin 25-mm 80-cal. Type 61M AA; 2 Mk 64 d.c. racks
Electronics: Radar: 1 Type 756 nav.
M: 2 MTU . . . diesels; 2 props; 5,984 bhp
Range: 2,000/17 **Crew:** 3 officers, 22 enlisted

Remarks: First combatant built in Pakistan; keel laid 1991. Three more were built as *Jalalat*-class guided-missile patrol craft. Hull lines enlarged from those of the *Rajshahi* (P 140).

PATROL CRAFT [PC] *(continued)*

♦ **1 32-meter class** Bldr: Brooke Marine, Lowestoft, U.K. (In serv. 1965)

P 140 Rajshahi

D: 115 tons (143 fl) **S:** 24 kts **Dim:** 32.62 (30.48 pp) × 6.10 × 1.55
A: 2 single 40-mm 60-cal. Bofors Mk 9 AA; 2 single 14.5-mm 93-cal. AA
Electronics: Radar: 1 . . . nav.
M: 2 MTU 12V538 diesels; 2 props; 3,400 bhp **Crew:** 19 tot.

Remarks: Last survivor of a class of four. A sister operates in the Bangladeshi Navy.

PATROL BOATS [PB]

♦ **2 MRTP 15 class (Interceptor)**
Bldr: Yonca Technical Investment Co., Tuzla, Turkey (In serv. 2004)

P 01 P 02

P 01 Yonca/Onuk via Mritunjoy Mazumdar, 6-04

D: 19 tons (fl) **S:** 54 kts **Dim:** 15.40 × 4.04 × 0.92 **A:** 2 single 12.7-mm mg
Electronics: Radar: 1 Raytheon . . . nav.
M: 2 MTU 12V183 TE93 diesels; 2 props; 2,300 bhp
Range: 300/40 **Crew:** 2 tot.

Remarks: More than a dozen are in service with the Turkish Coast Guard. First unit delivered 8-04, next eight weeks later. Assigned to the Navy's Special Services Group unit.

♦ **4 . . . -class assault boats**
Bldr: Karachi NDY (In serv. 2004–5)

Remarks: Based on a Thai design. First unit delivered 12-04. No additional data available.

AIR-CUSHION PATROL CRAFT [PBA]

♦ **2 (+ 2) 2000-TDX(M)–class assault hovercraft**
Bldr: Karachi NDY (In serv. 2004–)

D: 7 tons (fl) **S:** 40 kts **Dim:** 11.7 × 4.6 × 0.50
M: 1 Deutz FB 8 L-513 diesel; 1 props; 320 bhp

Remarks: First unit entered service during 12-04. GRP construction hull. Designed by Griffon Hovercraft, Ltd., Salisbury Green, U.K.

MINE WARFARE SHIPS

♦ **3 Tripartite-class minehunters [MHC]**
Bldr: DCN Lorient (M 163: fitted out by Karachi NDY)

	Laid down	L	In serv.
M 163 Muhafiz (ex-M 654, ex-*Moshad*)	7-4-94	8-7-95	15-5-96
M 164 Mujahid (ex-*Mahmoud*)	8-4-94	28-1-97	9-7-98
M 166 Munsif (ex-*Sagittaire,* M 650)	13-11-85	9-11-88	27-7-89

Muhafiz (M 163)—with *Khyber* (D 183) in the background Rahn, 3-02

D: 535 tons (605 fl) **S:** 15 kts (on main engine; 7 while hunting)
Dim: 51.6 (47.1 pp) × 8.96 × 2.49 (hull; 3.50 max.)
A: 1 20-mm 90-cal. GIAT 20F2 AA; 2 single 12.7-mm mg

Electronics:
Radar: 1 Kelvin-Hughes Type 1007 (M 166: Decca 1229) nav.
Sonar: Thales DUBM-21D (M 166: DUBM-21B)
M: 1 Brons-Werkspoor A RUB 215V12 diesel; 1 CP prop; 1,900 bhp—2 ACEC electric maneuvering props (120 shp each)—bow-thruster
Electric: 750 kw tot. **Range:** 3,000/12
Crew: 5 officers, 23 petty officers, 21 ratings

Remarks: Ordered 17-1-92; an option for three additional was not taken up. The first ship was transferred from the French Navy in 9-92 and left for Pakistan 27-11-92, the second was built at Lorient and arrived in Pakistan 18-9-96, and the hull for the third was shipped to Karachi 19-4-95 for fitting out with French assistance. Are assigned to Minesweeper Squadron 21.
Hull systems: Built of glass-reinforced polyester plastic. Have a six-man portable decompression chamber module at the aft end of the forecastle deck.
Combat systems: Have one mechanical drag sweep, and may also have the AP-4 acoustic sweep. Have an EVEC 20 automatic plotting table, Decca HiFix and Sydelis radio precision navigation equipment, and two PAP-104 remote-controlled minehunting submersibles. M 163 and M 164 have the digital DUBM-21D sonar, with hybrid circuitry, Mustang computer, higher-definition displays, built-in test equipment, and integration into the tactical system; they also have the Thales TSM 2061 Mk II tactical data system and the Finnish Elesco Family of Integrated Minesweeping Systems (FIMS) sweep array with MRK-960 three-electrode magnetic sweep and MKR-400 pipe-type noncontrollable noisemaker.

AUXILIARIES

♦ **1 oceanographic research ship [AGOR]**

	Bldr	Laid down	L	In serv.
Behr Paima	Ishikawajima Harima, Tokyo	16-2-82	. . .	17-12-82

D: Approx. 1,400 tons (fl) **S:** 13.75 kts **Dim:** 61.02 (55.00 pp) × 11.82 × 3.71
M: 2 Daihatsu 6DSM-22 diesels; 2 CP props; 2,000 bhp—bow-thruster
Electric: 960 kw tot. (3 × 320-kw, 410-V, 50-Hz a.c. diesel sets)
Range: 5,400/12 **Crew:** 16 officers, 68 enlisted

Remarks: 1,183 grt./400 dwt. Ordered 15-4-81. Operated by the navy for the Ministry of Communications, Ports, and Shipping. Carries two hydrographic survey launches. White painted.

♦ **1 Chinese Fuqing-class replenishment oiler [AOR]**

	Bldr	L	In serv.
A 47 Nasr	Dalian SY	. . .	31-7-87

Nasr (A 47)—with Phalanx CIWS visible abaft the stack and a Sea King helicopter on the flight deck Hartmut Ehlers, 9-03

D: 14,600 tons (21,740 fl) **S:** 18.6 kts **Dim:** 160.82 (157.00 pp) × 21.80 × 9.40
A: 2 twin 37-mm 63-cal. Type 74 AA; 1 20-mm Mk 15 Phalanx CIWS gatling AA; 2 single 14.5-mm 93-cal. AA
Electronics: Radar: 2 Decca 1226 nav.; 1 General Dynamics Mk 90 Phalanx f.c.
M: 1 Dalian-Sulzer 8 RLB 66 diesel; 1 prop; 17,400 bhp (15,000 sust.)
Electric: 2,480 kw tot. **Range:** 18,000/14.6 **Crew:** 26 officers, 120 enlisted

Remarks: Has equipment similar to U.S. Navy transfer systems: two liquid replenishment stations per side, with constant-tension solid transfer stations each side just forward of the stack. Helicopter deck can accommodate a Sea King or Alouette-III, but there is no hangar. Four electric cranes and two derricks for cargo handling. Can carry 11,000 tons of fuel oil, 1,000 tons of diesel fuel, 200 tons of feedwater, 200 tons of potable water, and 50 tons of lube oil. A U.S. Phalanx antimissile gun system was added abaft the funnel in 1995; the mount was probably removed from the discarded County-class destroyer *Babur.* A 47 was rammed by the commercial tanker *Sun Marsat* at Karachi on 21-10-98, with minor damage.

♦ **1 ex-Dutch Poolster-class replenishment oiler [AOR]**
Bldr: Rotterdamse Droogdok Maatschappij, Rotterdam

	Laid down	L	In serv.
A 20 Moawin (ex-*Poolster,* A 835)	18-9-62	16-10-63	10-9-64

Moawin (A 20) Edward McDonnell, 5-05

D: 16,836 tons (fl) **S:** 21 kts **Dim:** 168.41 (157.00 pp) × 20.33 × 8.24
A: 2 single 20-mm 70-cal. Oerlikon Mk 10 AA; 1 d.c. rack (8 d.c.)

AUXILIARIES *(continued)*

Moawin (A 20) Michael Winter, 6-05

Electronics:
Radar: 1 Decca TM 1229 nav.; 1 Decca 2459 surf. search
Sonar: 1 CWE-610 hull-mounted MF (probably nonoperational)
EW: SLQ-32(V)1 intercept; Mk 36 SRBOC decoy syst. (4 6-round Raytheon Mk 137 RL)
M: 2 sets geared steam turbines; 1 prop; 22,500 shp **Boilers:** 2
Electric: 2,100 kw **Crew:** 17 officers, 183 enlisted

Remarks: Purchased 22-6-94, transferred 27-7-94, and departed Dutch waters 3-8-94. Officially recommissioned on 15-9-94. Is also a combat supply ship capable of participating effectively in antisubmarine warfare. For short distances, she can carry 300 troops.
Hull systems: Cargo capacity: 10,300 tons, including 8,000 tons of fuel. Has a hangar for three small helicopters or one Sea King helicopter.
Combat systems: U.S. EW equipment has been substituted in Pakistan for the Netherlands Navy Ferranti AWARE-4 array.

SERVICE CRAFT

♦ 1 degaussing tender [YDG]
Bldr: Karachi SY & Eng. Wks. (In serv. 1979)

D: 260 tons (fl) **S:** 10 kts **Dim:** 35.22 (34.0 wl) × 7.00 × 2.4
M: 1 diesel; 1 prop; 375 bhp **Crew:** 5 tot.

Remarks: Built with French technical assistance and very similar in design to French Navy's Y 732. Wooden hull.

♦ 1 floating dry dock [YFDL]
Bldr: Karachi SY & Eng. Wks. (In serv. 1995)

Lift capacity: 4,000 tons **Dim:** 166.0 × 28.0 × . . .

Remarks: Four-section dock, with last module launched 31-12-94.

♦ 1 floating dry dock [YFDL]
Bldr: Karachi SY & Eng. Wks. (In serv. 1981)

Lift capacity: 2,000 tons

♦ 1 U.S. ARD 2–class floating dry dock [YFDL]
Bldr: Pacific Bridge, Alameda, Calif. (In serv. 4-43)

Peshawar (ex-ARD 6)

Lift capacity: 3,500 tons **Dim:** 148.03 × 21.64 × 1.6 (light)

Remarks: Transferred 6-61. May have been replaced by the new 4,000-ton dock.

♦ 1 1,200-ton-capacity floating dry dock [YFDL] (In serv. 1974)

FC II

♦ 2 logistics craft [YFL]
Bldr: Le Comte, Vianen, the Netherlands (In serv. 18-2-82)

D: 13 tons (fl) **S:** 21 kts **Dim:** 18.1 × 3.8 × 0.9
M: 2 Volvo Penta AQAD 40 diesels; 2 outdrives; 520 bhp

Remarks: GRP-hulled landing craft. Names and numbers not known.

♦ 2 logistics craft [YFL]
Bldr: Le Comte, Vianen, the Netherlands (In serv. 18-2-82)

D: 13 tons (fl) **S:** 21 kts **Dim:** 18.1 × 3.8 × 0.9
M: 2 Volvo Penta AQAD 40 diesels; 2 outdrives; 520 bhp

Remarks: GRP-hulled landing craft. Names and numbers not known.

♦ 2 Gwadar-class liquid cargo lighters [YO/YW]
Bldr: Karachi SY & Eng. Wks.

A 49 Gwadar (In serv. 1984) A 21 Kalmat (In serv. 29-8-92)

D: Approx. 1,400 tons (fl) **S:** 10 kts **Dim:** 62.84 (57.92 pp) × 11.31 × 3.03
A: 2 single 14.5-mm 93-cal. mg **Electronics:** Radar: 2 Decca . . . nav.
M: 1 Sulzer diesel; 1 prop; 550 bhp **Crew:** 25 tot.

Remarks: A 49 (831 grt) is configured to carry fuel, while A 21 (885 grt) is a water tanker. Both carry about 350 m^3 of liquid cargo and also have an electrohydraulic crane to permit carrying dry cargo on deck. A 21 was laid down 23-2-90 and launched 11-6-91. A 21 has a simplified superstructure with freestanding stack, while A 49's stack fairs into the pilothouse structure.

Gwadar (A 49)—note Maritime Security Agency ship *Nazim* (D 156) and patrol craft *Barkat* (P 1060) and *Vehdat* (P 1063) in background Pakistani Navy, 2000

♦ 1 Attock-class liquid cargo lighter [YO]
Bldr: . . ., Trieste, Italy (In serv. 1957)

A 40 Attock (ex-U.S. YO 249)

D: 600 tons light (1,225 fl) **S:** 8 kts **Dim:** 54.0 × 9.8 × 4.6
M: 2 GMT diesels; 2 props; 800 bhp **Crew:** 18 tot.

Remarks: Built with U.S. Mutual Defense Assistance Program funds. Cargo: 6,500 bbl (about 550 tons). Two single 20-mm AA guns and the navigational radar have been removed. Sister *Zum Zum* (A 44), configured as a water tanker, was stricken during 1996.

♦ 1 ex-U.K. O-class accommodations barge hulk [YPBN]
Bldr: John Brown & Co., Clydebank

	Laid down	L	In serv.
A 260 (ex-*Tippu Sultan*, ex-*Onslow*, ex-*Pakenham*)	1-7-40	31-3-41	8-10-41

D: Approx. 2,000 tons (fl) **Dim:** 105.16 (103.18 pp) × 10.67 × . . .

Remarks: Transferred to Pakistan 30-9-49 as a destroyer and later converted to a Type 16 antisubmarine frigate with U.S. funds. Had two sets Parson geared turbines (40,000 shp) and two Admiralty 3-drum boilers, the latter probably still in use to provide hotel services. Used since deactivation in 1980 as a berthing hulk, small combatant support ship, and supply barge at Gwadar.

♦ 2 Rustom-class harbor tugs [YTB]
Bldr: Karachi SY & Eng. Wks., Karachi (In serv. 2001)

Rustom Joshila

D: . . . tons **S:** . . . **Dim:** 25.0 × 8.5 × 3.4
M: 2 12-cyl. Caterpillar . . . diesels; 2 props; . . . bhp

Remarks: 239 grt.

♦ 2 Bholu-class harbor tugs [YTB]
Bldr: Damen, Hardinxveld, the Netherlands (In serv. 4-91)

A 44 Bholu A 45 Gama

D: 265 tons (fl) **S:** 12 kts **Dim:** 26.00 (24.36 pp) × 6.81 × 2.15
Electronics: Radar: 1 . . . nav.
M: 2 Cummins KTA-38M diesels; 2 props; 1,900 bhp
Fuel: 36 tons **Crew:** 6 tot.

Remarks: Replaced two former U.S. small harbor tugs with the same names. Equipped for fire fighting.

♦ 2 large harbor tugs [YTB]
Bldr: Karachi SY & Eng. Wks.

Delair (In serv. ca. 2000) Janbaz (In serv. 1990)

D: 282 grt **S:** . . . kts **Dim:** 35.01 (32.62 pp) × 9.30 × 3.90
M: 2 Niigata diesels; 2 props; . . . bhp

Remarks: *Janbaz* has also been reported to be a fuel lighter, and the two may be of differing designs.

♦ 1 small pusher tug [YTL]
Bldr: Karachi SY & Eng. Wks. (In serv. 11-1-83)

Goga

Remarks: No data available. Also in service is the small tug *Jhara*.

Note: Two locally built multipurpose 38-m, 250-ton auxiliary craft entered service during 2003–4. No additional data are available.

MARITIME SECURITY AGENCY

Note: The Maritime Security Agency (MSA) was established 1-1-87 to patrol the maritime exclusion zone. Its personnel were transferred from the navy, to which it is subordinated. The MSA's ships and boats are painted white, with red and blue diagonal stripes and "MSA" on the side. Most craft operate from Karachi.

Personnel: About 2,000 total (all seconded from the navy)

Aviation: Two Pilatus-Britten-Norman BN-2T Maritime Defender light maritime reconnaissance aircraft assigned to 93 Sqn. at PNS *Mehran* are dedicated to fisheries patrol and search-and-rescue work; the second was delivered in mid-1994.

MARITIME SECURITY AGENCY *(continued)*

Maritime Security Agency BN-2T Maritime Defender U.S. Navy, 1-96

DESTROYERS [WDD]

♦ **1 ex-U.S. Gearing FRAM I class**
Bldr: Todd Pacific SY, Seattle

	Laid down	L	In serv.
D 156 Nazim (ex-*Tughril,* D 167; ex-*Henderson,* DD 785)	27-10-44	28-5-45	4-8-45

Nazim (D 156)—with patrol craft *Rafaqat* (P 68) alongside Rahn, 12-01

D: 2,425 tons (3,460 fl) **S:** 30 kts **Dim:** 119.00 × 12.45 × 5.80 (max.)
A: 1 twin 127-mm 38-cal. Mk 38 DP; 4 quadruple 14.5-mm 93-cal. ZPU-4 AA
Electronics:
Radar: 1 Decca 1226 nav.; 1 Raytheon SPS-10B surf. search; 1 Lockheed SPS-40 air search; 1 Western Electric Mk 25 gun f.c.
EW: ArgoSystems APECS-II suite with AR 700 intercept
M: 2 sets G.E. geared steam turbines; 2 props; 60,000 shp
Boilers: 4 Babcock & Wilcox; 43.3 kg/cm^2, 454° C **Electric:** 1,300 kw tot.
Range: 2,400/25; 4,800/15 **Fuel:** 600 tons **Crew:** 27 officers, 247 enlisted

Remarks: Transferred from the Pakistani Navy in 1998 to replace the identically named and numbered unit resubordinated in 1993 (ex-*Tuppu Sultan,* D 168; ex-*Damato,* DD 871). Serves as flagship of the Maritime Security Agency and seldom, if ever, moves under her own power. The quadruple machinegun mounts are not always installed. The helicopter facility aft remains usable. The Harpoon missiles, Phalanx CIWS, and torpedo tubes were removed, and the sonar is probably nonoperational. The after twin 127-mm gunmount has been removed.

PATROL CRAFT [WPC]

♦ **4 Barkat class**
Bldr: Huangpu SY, China

	In serv.		In serv.
P 1060 Barkat	1-90	P 1062 Nusrat	8-90
P 1061 Rehmat	1-90	P 1063 Vehdat	8-90

D: 390 tons (435 fl) **S:** 27 kts **Dim:** 58.77 × 7.20 × 2.40 (mean hull)
A: 1 twin 37-mm 63-cal. Type 74 AA; 2 twin 14.5-mm 93-cal. AA
Electronics: Radar: 2 Fujitsu OPS-9 or Anritsu ARC-32A nav.
M: 4 MTU 16V396 TB93 diesels; 4 props; 8,720 bhp
Range: 1,500/12 **Crew:** 5 officers, 45 enlisted

Remarks: First two were delivered 29-12-89 for commissioning in Pakistan. Are built on Hainan-class naval patrol boat hulls. Sisters operate in Chinese police and customs forces.

♦ **2 Chinese Shanghai-II class**

P 66 Sabqat P 68 Rafaqat

D: 122.5 tons normal (134.8 fl) **S:** 28.5 kts **Dim:** 38.78 × 5.41 × 1.55 (hull)
A: 2 twin 37-mm 63-cal. Type 74 AA; 2 twin 25-mm 80-cal. Type 61M AA
Electronics: Radar: 1 Anritsu ARC-32A nav.
M: 2 Type L12-V180 (M-50F-4) diesels (1,200 bhp each), 2 L12-180Z (12D6) diesels (910 bhp each); 4 props; 4,220 bhp
Electric: 39 kw tot. **Range:** 750/16.5 **Endurance:** 7 days **Crew:** 36 tot.

Sabqat (P 66) French Navy, 1995

Remarks: Transferred from China in 1972 or 1973. P 66 and P 68 were commissioned in the Maritime Security Agency during 4-92. Have been renovated and given new electronics. Sisters *Pishin* (P 65) and *Bahawalpur* (P 69) had been retired by 2005. *Quetta* (P 141), *Bannu* (P 154), *Kalat* (P 156), and *Sahival* (P 160), officially in reserve since 1982, were renovated and transferred to the MSA on 1-1-87 but stricken in 1990.

COAST GUARD

Note: The coast guard, organized in 1985, is manned by Pakistani Army personnel and subordinated to the Ministry of the Interior. All of the craft listed below have GRP hulls.

PATROL BOATS [WPB]

♦ **1 Swallow class**
Bldr: Swallowcraft/Kangnam SB, Pusan, South Korea (In serv. 3-86)

Saif

D: 32 tons (fl) **S:** 25 kts **Dim:** 20.0 × 4.7 × 1.3
A: 2 single 12.7-mm mg
M: 2 G.M. Detroit Diesel 12V71 TI diesels; 2 props; 1,060 bhp
Range: 500/20 **Crew:** 8 tot.

♦ **4 Italian MV 55 class**
Bldr: Crestitalia, Ameglia (In serv. 1987)

P 551 Sadd P 552 Shabaz P 553 Waqir P 554 Burq

D: 22.8 tons (fl) **S:** 35 kts **Dim:** 16.50 × 5.20 × 0.88
A: 1 20-mm AA **Electronics:** Radar: 1 . . . nav.
M: 2 MTU diesels; 2 props; 2,200 bhp **Range:** 425/25 **Crew:** 5 tot.

CUSTOMS SERVICE

Note: Pakistani Customs Service craft are naval-manned and would come under naval control in wartime. The service operates 18 MV 55–class patrol boats, P 551 through P 568, which are identical to the Maritime Security Agency units of that class, except that they have a single 14.5-mm machinegun and are powered by two 800-bhp diesels for 30-kt maximum speed.

PALAU

Republic of Palau

BUREAU OF PUBLIC SAFETY
DIVISION OF LAW ENFORCEMENT

Note: The Republic of Palau in the western Caroline Islands consists of 343 islands and became fully independent on 1-10-94. Craft are identified by a broad blue and narrow yellow diagonal hull stripe abreast the pilothouse. Craft names are preceded by PSS (Palau State Ship).

PATROL CRAFT [WPC]

♦ **1 Australian ASI 315 class**
Bldr: Transfield ASI Pty, Ltd., South Coogie, W.A. (In serv. 25-7-96)

001 President H. I. Remeliik

D: 148 tons (165 fl) **S:** 21 kts **Dim:** 31.50 (28.60 wl) × 8.10 × 2.12 (1.80 hull)
A: 2 single 7.62-mm mg **Electronics:** Radar: 1 Furuno 1011 nav.
M: 2 Caterpillar 3516 diesels; 2 props; 2,820 bhp (2,400 sust.)
Electric: 116 kw (2 × 50-kw Caterpillar 3304 diesel sets; 1 × 16 kw)
Range: 2,500/12 **Fuel:** 27.9 tons **Endurance:** 8–10 days
Crew: 3 officers, 12 enlisted + 7 Marine Patrol Police constables

Remarks: Standard Australian foreign aid patrol boat design. Named for Haruo I. Remeliik, Palau's first president. Ran trials in 5-96. Underwent a refit during 2003. A major refit is planned for 2011 in Australia.
Hull systems: Carries a 5-m rigid inflatable boarding boat. Has an extensive navigational suite, including Furuno FSN-70 NAVSAT receiver, Furuno 525 HFD/F, Furuno 120 MH-HFD/F, FE-881 echo sounder, Furuno 500 autopilot, DS-70 doppler log, and Weatherfax receiver. Differs from earlier units of the class in having a spray strake forward on the hull sides.

PATROL CRAFT [WPC] *(continued)*

President H. I. Remeliik (001) ABPH Darren Yates, RAN, 5-96

PANAMA

Republic of Panama

NATIONAL MARITIME SERVICE

Personnel: Approx. 400 total

Base: Flamenco Island, Colón. There are repair facilities at Coco Solo and a small facility at Quebrada de Piedra. A repair and training facility is located at Remo Largo, Cativa, Colón and another facility at Balboa.

Maritime aviation: The air force operates a number of aircraft with a secondary maritime patrol role, including two DHC Twin Otter, three CASA C-212, one Pilatus-Britten-Norman BN-2T Islander, two Cessna U-17, and one Cessna 172. Air force helicopters include eight Bell UH-1B, nine UH-1H, and four UH-1N. Larger fixed-wing transports include one L-188 Electra, four C-47s, one Shorts Skyvan, and one Falcon 20 for VIP transport. Aircraft are based at Quebrada de Piedra, and a small airport facility at Kuna Yala.

PATROL SHIPS [PS]

♦ **1 ex-U.S. Coast Guard Balsam class**
Bldr: Marine Iron SB Co.

	Laid down	L	In serv.
401 Independencia (ex-*Sweetgum*, WLB 309)	21-2-43	15-4-43	20-11-43

D: 697 tons light (1,038 fl) **S:** 12.8–13 kts
Dim: 54.9 (51.8 pp) × 11.3 × 4.0 **A:** 2 single 12.7-mm M2 mg
Electronics: Radar: 1 Hughes-Furuno SPS-73 nav.
M: 2 diesels, electric drive; 1 prop; 1,200 shp
Electric: 400 kw tot. **Range:** 4,600/12 **Crew:** 6 officers, 47 enlisted

Remarks: Decommissioned 15-2-02 and transferred the same day for use as an offshore patrol ship. Very robustly constructed vessel that still has a number of years' service remaining despite her advanced age; unlike most of the class, however, the ship has never been extensively updated. Has a 20-ton derrick and a large cargo hold originally intended to accommodate navigational aids buoys.

PATROL CRAFT [WPC]

♦ **2 U.K. Vosper 103-foot class**
Bldr: Vosper Thornycroft, Portsmouth (In serv. 3-71)

P-301 Panquiaco (ex-GC 10) P-302 Ligia Elena (ex-GC 11)

D: 96 tons (123 fl) **S:** 18 kts **Dim:** 31.25 × 6.02 × 1.98
A: 2 single 7.62-mm mg **Electronics:** Radar: 1 Raytheon 2600 nav.
M: 2 G.M. Detroit Diesel 16V71 TI diesels; 2 props; 2,500 bhp
Electric: 80 kVA tot. **Range:** 1,400/14 **Crew:** 3 officers, 14 enlisted

Remarks: Launched 22-7-70 and 25-8-70, respectively. P-302 was sunk by U.S. forces during the 12-89 invasion and P-301 had been discarded by late 1991, but both began extensive overhauls in Panama in 9-92 (including re-engining) and have been returned to service. Have Vosper fin stabilizers, steel hulls, and aluminum alloy superstructures. Both are assigned to the Pacific coast.

Ligia Elena (P-302) H&L Van Ginderen, 4-97

♦ **1 former oceanographic research support craft**
Bldr: Equitable Equipment Co., New Orleans (In serv. 1965)

P-303 Naos (ex-*Erline,* 105UB821; ex-M/V *Orrin*)

Naos (P-303) Panamanian Navy, 12-98

D: 96 tons (120 fl) **S:** 10 kts **Dim:** 32.00 × 6.31 × 1.80
A: 2 single 7.62-mm mg **Electronics:** Radar: 1 Raytheon 920 nav.
M: 2 Caterpillar . . . diesels; 2 props; approx. 1,000 bhp
Range: 550/8 **Crew:** 2 officers, 9 enlisted

Remarks: Former offshore crew boat, acquired in 1967 and operated by the U.S. Naval Underwater Systems Center at Tudor Hill, Bermuda, until transferred to Panama in 7-92. Commissioned in 12-92 after an overhaul and employed in local patrol duties, based on the Pacific coast. Re-engined in 1997.

♦ **1 former drug runner**
Bldr: . . . (In serv. . . .)

P-305 Escudo de Verguas (ex-*Aun Sin Nombre,* ex-*Kathyuska Kelly*)

Escudo de Verguas (P-305) Panamanian Navy, 11-98

D: 158 tons (fl) **S:** 10 kts **Dim:** 27.6 × 7.3 × 1.9
A: 1 12.7-mm mg **Electronics:** Radar: 1 Raytheon . . . nav.
M: 2 G.M. Detroit Diesel 12V71 TI diesels; 1,020 bhp (840 sust.)
Crew: 2 officers, 8 enlisted

Remarks: Confiscated in 1996. Operates in the Caribbean. Resembles a fishing boat.

♦ **1 ex-U.S. mine route survey craft** (In serv. . . .)

A-402 Flamenco (ex-P-304, 103WB 831, ex-*Scherazade,* CT-3; ex-*Scherazade*)

Flamenco (P-304)—as *Scherazade* (CT-3) H&L Van Ginderen, 8-88

PATROL CRAFT [WPC] *(continued)*

D: 220 tons (fl) **S:** 9 kts **Dim:** 30.8 × 7.6 × 2.1
A: 2 single 7.62-mm mg **Electronics:** Radar: 1 Furuno 1411 nav.
M: 2 Caterpillar diesels; 2 props; . . . bhp **Crew:** 2 officers, 9 enlisted

Remarks: Transferred 22-7-92. Wooden-hulled former shrimp boat, later used for U.S. Naval Reserve COOP (Craft Of Opportunity Program) mine-route survey work and then as a workboat. Had been acquired for USN service 28-6-85.

PATROL BOATS [WPB]

♦ 3 ex-U.S. Sea Spectre PB Mk IV class
Bldr: Atlantic Marine, Ft. George Island, Fla.

	Laid down	L	In serv.
P-841 Chiriqui (ex-68PB841)	24-12-84	23-9-85	2-1-86
P-842 Veraguas (ex-68PB842)	25-3-85	11-11-85	2-1-86
P-843 Bocas Del Toro (ex-68PB843)	17-6-85	31-12-85	15-2-86

D: 42.25 tons (46 fl) **S:** 20 kts **Dim:** 120.85 × 5.50 × 1.07 (hull; 1.80 props)
A: 2 single 7.62-mm mg **Electronics:** Radar: 1 Furuno 1411 nav.
M: 3 G.M. 12V71 TI diesels; 3 props; 1,950 bhp **Endurance:** 3 days
Range: 450/26; 2,000/. . . **Crew:** 1 officer, 6 enlisted

Remarks: Transferred without armament as grant-aid in 3-98. Aluminum construction. Were able to reach 30 kts when new. Had intricate camouflage paint schemes as of late 1998.

♦ 1 U.S. Swiftships 65-foot class
Bldr: Swiftships, Morgan City, La. (In serv. 7-82)

P-201 General Esteban Huertas (ex-*Comandante Torrijos,* GC 16)

General Esteban Huertas (P-201)—with old pennant number U.S. Navy, 1983

D: 31.1 tons (35 fl) **S:** 23 kts (13 sust.) **Dim:** 19.81 (17.90 wl) × 5.64 × 1.83
A: 2 single 7.62-mm mg **Electronics:** Radar: 1 Raytheon . . . nav.
M: 2 G.M. Detroit Diesel 12V71 TI N75 diesels; 2 props; 1,020 bhp
Electric: 20 kw tot. **Range:** 500/8 **Fuel:** 6 tons **Crew:** 2 officers, 8 enlisted

Remarks: Badly damaged in the 12-89 invasion, but has been restored to service. Sister *Presidente Porras* (P-202) was sunk. Aluminum construction. Operates in the Caribbean.

♦ 1 former oilfield crew boat
Bldr: . . .

P-203 Cacique Nome (ex-*Negrita*)

Cacique Nome (P-203)—on land for overhaul Panamanian Navy, 12-98

D: 68 tons (fl) **S:** 13 kts **Dim:** 24.4 × 4.6 × 1.8
A: 2 single 7.62-mm mg **Electronics:** Radar: 1 Raytheon 1900 nav.
M: 2 G.M. Detroit Diesel 12V 71-series diesels; 2 props; 1,680 bhp
Range: 250/10 **Crew:** 2 officers, 6 enlisted

Remarks: Typical oilfield crew boat of U.S. construction. Refitted at Coco Solo and commissioned 5-5-93. Operates on the Pacific coast.

♦ 5 U.S. Coast Guard 82-foot Point class
Bldr: J. Martinac SB, Tacoma, Wash. (P-206, P-207: U.S. Coast Guard Yard, Curtis Bay, Md.)

	In serv.
P-204 3 de Noviembre (ex-*Point Barrow,* WPB 82348)	4-10-66
P-206 28 de Noviembre (ex-*Point Huron,* WPB 82357)	17-2-67
P-207 10 de Noviembre (ex-*Point Francis,* WPB 82356)	3-2-67
P-208 4 de Noviembre (ex-*Point Winslow,* WPB 82360)	3-3-67
P-209 5 de Noviembre (ex-*Point Hannon,* WPB 82355)	23-1-67

D: 64 tons (69 fl) **S:** 23.7 kts **Dim:** 25.30 × 5.23 × 1.95
A: 2 single 12.7-mm mg
Electronics: Radar: 1 Raytheon SPS-64(V)1 (P-208, P-209: Hughes-Furuno SPS-73(V)) nav.
M: P-204: 2 Cummins VT-12-M diesels; 2 props; 1,600 bhp—others: 2 Caterpillar 3412 diesels; 2 props; 1,480 bhp
Range: 490/23; 1,500/8 **Fuel:** 5.7 tons **Crew:** 1 officer, 9 enlisted

Remarks: P-204 was transferred 7-6-91, P-206 and P-207 on 22-4-99, P-208 on 20-9-00, and P-209 on 11-1-01. Well equipped with navigational and salvage equipment; can tow small craft.

♦ 1 ex-U.S. MSB 29–class former minesweeping boat
Bldr: John Trumpy, Annapolis, Md. (In serv. 1954)

P-205 Punta Mala (ex-MSB 29)

D: 80 tons (fl) **S:** 12 kts **Dim:** 25.0 × 5.8 × 1.7
A: 2 single 7.62-mm mg **Electronics:** Radar: 1 Raytheon 1900 nav.
M: 2 Packard 2D850 diesels; 2 props; 600 bhp
Range: 1,500/10 **Crew:** 2 officers, 9 enlisted

Remarks: Transferred to Panama 3-3-93 for use as a patrol craft. Wooden construction. Was the only unit of its class. Operates on the Pacific coast.

♦ 2 ex-U.S. LCPL Mk 11 class

P-101 Panama P-102 Calamar (ex-PC-3602)

D: 9.75 tons light (13 fl) **S:** 19 kts (15 sust.) **Dim:** 10.98 (9.26 pp) × 3.97 × 1.13
A: 1 7.62-mm mg **Electronics:** Radar: none
M: 1 G.M. 8V71 TI diesel; 350–425 bhp
Range: 160/12 **Fuel:** 630 liters **Crew:** 5 tot.

Remarks: Former U.S. Navy personnel landing craft. P-101 was acquired in 2-98 and P-102 in 12-92. GRP construction. Can also carry up to 2 tons of cargo or 15 passengers. Sisters *Barracuda* (PC-3601) and *Centollo* (PC-3603) were stricken in 1997.

♦ 6 19-foot Guardian-class patrol launches
Bldr: Boston Whaler, Edgewater, Fla. (In serv. 11-95 through 12-98)

BPC-1801 through BPC-1806

D: 0.79 tons light (1.59 fl) **S:** 35 kts **Dim:** 5.64 × 2.18 × 0.25
A: 1 7.62-mm mg **M:** 2 Johnson gasoline outboard motors; 150 bhp
Fuel: 239 liters **Crew:** 4 tot.

Remarks: GRP foam-core construction. No radar fitted.

♦ 5 22-foot Pirana-class patrol launches
Bldr: Boston Whaler, Edgewater, Fla. (In serv. 6-91 through 10-92)

BPC-2201 through BPC-2205

D: 1.5 tons (2 fl) **S:** 35 kts **Dim:** 6.81 × 2.26 × 0.60
A: 1 7.62-mm mg **M:** 2 Johnson gasoline outboard motors; 360 bhp
Range: 167/40 **Crew:** 4 tot.

Remarks: GRP foam-core construction. No radar fitted.

♦ 10 BPC-3201-class patrol launches
Bldr: . . . (In serv. 6-95 to 10-98)

BPC-3201 through BPC-3210

D: 7 tons (fl) **S:** 35 kts **Dim:** 10.2 × 2.3 × 0.6
A: 1 7.62-mm mg **Electronics:** Radar: none
M: 2 Yamaha gasoline outboards; 400 bhp **Crew:** 4 tot.

Remarks: Skiff-hulled craft of GRP construction. All serve in the Caribbean.

Note: Also used for patrol are the open launches BPC-2902 and BPC-2903, 9-m craft that operate in the Pacific and were acquired during the mid-1990s.

SERVICE CRAFT

Note: A single Sonic Jet Performance, Inc., PRJ-1200 patrol/rescue launch, with a top speed of 45+ kts and dimensions of 3.65 × 2.4 × 0.36 m, was delivered to an unnamed Panamanian agency during 2-03.

♦ 1 ex-U.S. MSB 5–class logistics support craft [WYF]

L-16 Nombre de Dios (ex-MSB 28)

D: 30 tons light (44 fl) **S:** 12 kts **Dim:** 17.45 × 4.83 × 1.2
A: 1 7.62-mm mg **Electronics:** Radar: 1 Raytheon . . . nav.
M: 2 G.M. Detroit Diesel 6-71 diesels; 2 props; 600 bhp
Crew: 1 officer, 5 enlisted

Remarks: Survivors of a class of 47 minesweeping boats built between 1952 and 1956. Have wooden hulls and nonmagnetic machinery. Transferred to Panama 3-3-93 and used in logistic support duties on the Pacific coast. Armament, all sweep gear, and radar were removed. Sister *Santa Clara* (L-15, ex-MSB 25) was stricken during 1996. Sister *Bastimentos* (L-17) was retired in 2003.

♦ 1 logistic support craft [WYF]

L-11 Trinidad (ex-*Endeavour*)

SERVICE CRAFT *(continued)*

D: 120 tons (fl) **S:** 12 kts **Dim:** 22.9 × 4.3 × 2.1
Electronics: Radar: 1 Furuno . . . nav.
M: 1 Caterpillar . . . diesel; 1 prop; 365 bhp **Crew:** 1 officer, 6 enlisted

Remarks: Acquired in 9-91 and entered service in 5-92.

♦ 5 miscellaneous support launches [WYFL]

BA-051 Bucaro (ex-*Orient Express*)
BA-054 Orca
BA-055 Dorado I
BA-056 Dorado II
BA-057 Anguilla

Remarks: BA-051, employed for training, is a former drug-running, 19-m sailing sloop captured in 1996. BA-054, acquired in 1997, is used for rescue duties on the Pacific coast. BA-055 and BA-056, acquired in 2-98, are 40-kt, outboard-powered open launches used for logistics support. BA-057 is another former drug runner, put in service in 11-98, and is capable of 50 kts.

Note: The Panamanian Customs Service received 16-m, Dutch-built (Delta, Sliedrecht) launches *Hornerito* and *Surubi* in 9-95; no other data available.

PAPUA NEW GUINEA

DEFENCE FORCE MARITIME ELEMENT

Personnel: Approx. 400 total

Bases: Headquarters at Port Moresby. One patrol boat each is deployed to Buka and Alotau. There is also a facility at Lombrun on Manus Island.

Maritime Aviation: The Papua New Guinea Defence Force operates six Nomad N.22B light transports, one Beech Super King Air 200, and one Gulfstream-II transport for coastal patrol and logistics duties.

Note: Ship names are preceded by HMPNGS (Her Majesty's Papua New Guinea Ship).

PATROL CRAFT [PC]

♦ 4 ASI 315 class

Bldr: Transfield ASI Pty, Ltd., South Coogie, Western Australia

	Laid down	L	In serv.
P 01 Tarangau	. . .	1987	16-5-87
P 02 Dreger	12-1-87	7-9-87	29-10-87
P 03 Seeadler	21-3-88	21-9-88	28-10-88
P 04 Basilisk	19-10-88	7-5-89	1-7-89

Basilisk (P 04) LSPH W. McBride, RAN, 7-89

D: 165 tons (fl) **S:** 21 kts (20 sust.)
Dim: 31.50 (28.60 wl) × 8.10 × 2.12 (1.80 hull)
A: 1 20-mm 90-cal. Oerlikon GAM-B01 AA; 2 single 12.7-mm M2 mg
Electronics: Radar: 1 Furuno. . . nav.
M: 2 Caterpillar 3516TA diesels; 2 props; 2,820 bhp (2,400 sust.)
Electric: 116 kw (2 × 50-kw Caterpillar 3304 diesels; 1 × 16 kw)
Range: 2,500/12 **Fuel:** 27.9 tons **Endurance:** 8–10 days
Crew: 3 officers, 14 enlisted

Remarks: First two ordered 19-3-85, the other pair 3-10-85. Australian foreign aid program Pacific Patrol Boat, with sisters in a number of Southwest Pacific–area island nation forces. Carry a 5-m aluminum boarding boat. Have an extensive navigational suite, including Furuno FSN-70 NAVSAT receiver, Furuno 525 HFD/F, Furuno 120 MF–HFD/F, FE-881 echo sounder, and DS-70 doppler log. The original Furuno radar was replaced in all during 1997 refits in Australia; the navigational systems were also updated.

AMPHIBIOUS WARFARE SHIPS

♦ 2 ex-Australian Balikpapan-class utility landing craft [LCU]

Bldr: Walkers Ltd., Maryborough

31 Salamaua (In serv. 19-10-73) 32 Buna (In serv. 7-12-73)

Salamaua (31) Gilbert Gyssels, 1980

D: 316 tons (503 fl) **S:** 8 kts **Dim:** 44.5 × 10.1 × 1.9
A: 2 single 12.7-mm M2 mg **Electronics:** Radar: 1 Decca RM 916 nav.
M: 3 G.M. Detroit Diesel 12V71 diesels; 3 props; 675 bhp
Range: 1,300–2,280/10 (depending on load) **Crew:** 2 officers, 11 enlisted

Remarks: Entered service in 1972 and transferred in 1975. Cargo: 140–180 tons. Refitted 1985–86.

SERVICE CRAFT

♦ 1 ex-Australian small harbor tug [YTL]

Bldr: Perrin Eng., Brisbane (In serv. 1972)

HTS 503

D: 47.5 tons **S:** 9 kts **Dim:** 15.4 × 4.6 × 1.1
M: 2 G.M. Detroit Diesel 3-71 diesels; 2 props; 340 bhp
Range: 710/9 **Crew:** 3 tot.

Remarks: Transferred in 1974. Retains Royal Australian Navy pennant number.

PARAGUAY

Republic of Paraguay

ARMADA NACIONAL DE PARAGUAY

Personnel: 3,600 total, including 100 naval aviation, 900 marines, and the coast guard (*Prefectura General Naval*).

Bases: On the Río Paraguay: Base Naval de Bahía Negra (BNBN); on the Río Parana: Base Naval Ciudad del Este (BNCE), Base Naval de Encarnación (BNE), Base Naval de Salto del Guairá (BNSG), and Base Naval de Ita-Piru (BNIP). Repairs and maintenance are performed at the Arsenal de Marina, Puerto Sajonia, near Asunción.

Organization: The principal commands include the Cuartel General, Comando de la Flota, Comando de la Infantería de Marina, Comando de la Aviación Naval, Comando de Apoyo de Combate, Comando de Institutos Navales de Ensenanza, Prefectura General Naval, Dirección de Apoyo de Servicio, and Dirección del Material.

Naval Aviation: Fixed-wing assets include two Cessna 310 and one Cessna 150M light utility aircraft. Helicopters include two Helibras AS.350B Esquilo (referred to locally as HB-350, or UH-50). Fixed-wing aircraft are based at Asunción International Airport and helicopters at Puerto Sajonia, near Asunción.

Paraguayan Navy AS.350B Esquilo helicopter Hartmut Ehlers, 5-00

PATROL COMBATANTS [PG]

♦ 1 Brazilian Roraima class
Bldr: Ars. de Marinha do Rio de Janeiro

	Laid down	L	In serv.
P 05 ITAIPÚ	3-3-83	16-3-84	2-4-85

Itaipú (P 05)—alongside *Nanawa* (P 02) Hartmut Ehlers, 4-03

D: 220 tons light (384 fl) **S:** 14.5 kts **Dim:** 46.3 (45.0 pp) × 8.45 × 1.42 (max.)
A: 1 40-mm 60-cal. Bofors Mk 3 AA; 2 single 12.7-mm M2 mg; 2 81-mm mortar/12.7-mm mg combination mounts
Electronics: Radar: 1 . . . nav.
M: 2 M.A.N. V6V 16/18 TL diesels; 2 props; 1,824 bhp (1,732 sust.)
Range: 4,500/11 **Endurance:** 30 days
Crew: 9 officers, 31 enlisted + 30 marines

Remarks: Order was announced 11-4-83. Has small helicopter deck and can accommodate one of the AS.350 helicopters. Carries medical personnel for civic action duties.

♦ 2 ex-Argentinian Bouchard class
Bldr: Rio Santiago NY, Argentina

	L	In serv.
P 02 NANAWA (ex-*Bouchard*)	20-3-36	16-5-37
P 04 TENIENTE FARINA (ex-*Py*)	31-3-38	1-7-38

Nanawa (P 02) Hartmut Ehlers, 5-00

D: 450 tons (650 fl) **S:** 16 kts **Dim:** 59.5 × 7.3 × 2.6
A: 2 twin 40-mm 60-cal. Bofors AA; 2 single 12.7-mm mg
Electronics: Radar: 1 . . . nav.
M: 2 M.A.N. diesels; 2 props; 2,000 bhp **Range:** 3,000/12 **Crew:** 70 tot.

Remarks: Former ocean minesweepers. P 02 was donated in 1-64 and P 04 was purchased 6-3-68. Sister *Capitán Meza* (P 03, ex-M 2, ex-*Seaver*) is now employed as an immobile barracks hulk.

♦ 1 Paraguay class
Bldr: Cantieri Odero, Genoa, Italy (In serv. 5-31)

C 1 PARAGUAY (ex-*Comodoro Meyo*)

D: 636 tons light; 745 normal (856 fl) **S:** 17.5 kts **Dim:** 70.15 × 10.70 × 1.65
A: C 1: 2 twin 120-mm 50-cal. Ansaldo Model 1926 low-angle; 3 single 76-mm 40-cal. Odero-Terni Model 1917 AA; 2 single 40-mm 39-cal. Odero-Terni Model 1928 2-pdr. AA; fittings for 2 single 20-mm Oerlikon AA
Electronics: Radar: 1 . . . nav.
M: 2 sets Parsons geared steam turbines; 2 props; 3,800 shp **Boilers:** 2
Range: 1,700/16 **Fuel:** 170 tons **Crew:** 86 tot.

Remarks: Configuration has changed very little from when first delivered nearly 70 years ago. Have light armor: 12.7-mm to sides and 7.6-mm to decks. The boilers have become unreliable, and the propulsion plant may eventually be replaced with diesel engines.

Paraguay (C 1)—alongside *Teniente Farina* (P 04) Hartmut Ehlers, 4-03

Combat systems: The 120-mm mounts were developed for use on late-1920s Italian destroyer classes. An optical rangefinder serves each of the two 120-mm gunmounts. The 76-mm guns are not U.S. mounts as previously listed but are instead high-angle mounts of Italian origin. The 40-mm AA on C 1 are the last of their type on an active warship in any navy.
Disposals: *Humita* (C 2, ex-*Capitán Cabral*) was retired during 2001 and relegated to floating museum status.

♦ 1 former tug
Bldr: Werf Conrad, Haarlem, the Netherlands (In serv. 1908)

P 01 CAPITÁN CABRAL (ex-*Triunfo*, ex-*Adolfo Riquelme*)

Capitán Cabral (P 01) Hartmut Ehlers, 4-03

D: 180 tons (206 fl) **S:** 8 kts **Dim:** 34.50 (30.00 pp) × 7.10 × 1.71
A: 1 40-mm 60-cal. Mk 3 Bofors AA; 2 single 20-mm 70-cal. Oerlikon AA; 2 single 12.7-mm M2 mg
Electronics: Radar: 1 . . . nav.
M: 1 Caterpillar 3408 diesel; 1 prop; 336 bhp **Crew:** 25 tot.

Remarks: Steel or iron hull (not wood as previously reported). Originally reciprocating steam-powered, she was re-engined and rearmed in the late 1980s. Operates from Puerto Sajonia, Asunción.

PATROL BOATS [PB]

Note: Two Rodman 101–class and five Rodman 55–class patrol launches ordered from Spain 19-9-95 were never delivered due to payment problems; the craft were eventually sold to Surinam by the builder.

♦ 2 Yhaguy class
Bldr: . . ., Taiwan (In serv. 23-6-99)

P 08 YHAGUY P 09 TEBICUARY

Tebicuary (P 09) Hartmut Ehlers, 4-03

PATROL BOATS [PB] *(continued)*

D: 20 tons (fl) **S:** 40 kts **Dim:** 16.5 × . . . × . . .
A: 2 single 12.7-mm mg **Electronics:** Radar: 1 . . . nav.
M: 2 gasoline inboard engines; 800 bhp **Crew:** 12 tot.

Remarks: Donated by Taiwan. GRP construction. Two sisters delivered to Gambia in 1999.

♦ **5 P 07 class**
Bldr: Arsenal de Marina, Asunción

	L
LP 07 (ex-P 07)	3-89
LP 08 (ex-P 08)	2-90
LP 09 (ex-P 09)	2-90
LP 10 (ex-P 10)	10-91
LP 11 (ex-P 11)	10-91

LP 10 Hartmut Ehlers, 4-03

D: 18 tons (fl) **S:** 12 kts **Dim:** 14.70 × 3.06 × 0.85
A: 2 single 12.7-mm mg **Electronics:** Radar: none
M: 2 G.M. 6-71 diesels; 2 props; 340 bhp **Range:** 240/12 **Crew:** 4 tot.

Remarks: Originally to have consisted of 13 units, but construction was stopped in 1991 with only five vessels. Steel construction units, designed by the Paraguayan Navy and built at its own facilities to save funds. Replaced six small patrol craft delivered by the U.S. in 1967–71. Operated by the Prefectura General Naval.

♦ **2 ex-Taiwanese Tzu Chiang class**
Bldr: China Shipbuilding Corp., Kaohsiung (In serv. 31-12-77)

P 06 Capitán Ortiz (ex-FABG 3) P 07 Teniente Robles (ex-FABG 4)

Capitán Ortiz (P 06)—alongside sister Hartmut Ehlers, 4-03

D: 47 tons (fl) **S:** 38 kts **Dim:** 22.86 × 5.49 × 0.94 (1.82 props)
A: 1 20-mm 70-cal. Oerlikon AA; 1 12.7-mm mg
Electronics: Radar: 1 Decca 926 nav.
M: 3 MTU 12V331 TC81 diesels; 3 props; 4,020 bhp
Electric: 30 kw tot. (1 × 30-kw Ford diesel set)
Range: 700/32; 1,200/17 **Crew:** 12 tot.

Remarks: Former prototype guided-missile patrol boats, with a design based on the Israeli *Dvora* class but with slightly different hullform, three engines, and a tall pylon mast. Were decommissioned in 1994, disarmed, and donated to Paraguay in 11-94. Aluminum construction.

♦ **5 LP 101 class**
Bldr: Sewart Seacraft, Berwick, La. (In serv. 1967–71)

LP 101 LP 102 LP 103 LP 104 LP 106

D: 15 tons (fl) **S:** 20 kts **Dim:** 13.1 × 3.9 × 0.9
A: 2 single 12.7-mm mg **Electronics:** Radar: none
M: 2 G.M. Detroit Diesel 6-71 diesels; 2 props; 500 bhp **Crew:** 7 tot.

Remarks: Survivors of six delivered 1967–71. All five are operated by the Prefectura General Naval. Aluminum construction.

LP 104 Hartmut Ehlers, 4-03

AMPHIBIOUS WARFARE CRAFT

♦ **3 U.S. LCVP Mk 7 class [LCVP]**

	Builder	L
EDVP 01	Arsenal de Marina, Asunción	9-93
EDVP 02	Arsenal de Marina, Asunción	9-93
EDVP 03	. . . , Ladario, Brazil	1981

EDVP 03 Hartmut Ehlers, 4-03

D: 9 tons (13 fl) **S:** 8 kts **Dim:** 10.90 × 3.21 × 1.04 (aft)
M: 1 Saab Scania D11 diesel; 157 bhp

Remarks: All three have steel hulls. Can carry 36 troops or 3.5 tons of cargo. Cargo deck is 5.24 × 2.29 m, with a 2.00-m-wide access through the bow ramp.

AUXILIARIES

Disposal note: Ex-U.S. LSM 1–class headquarters ship *Boqueron* (BC 1, ex-*Teniente Pratt Gil,* ex-*Corrientes,* ex-LSM 86) had been removed from service by 12-97 but remains afloat as a hulk.

♦ **1 cargo ship [AK]**
Bldr: Ast. de Tomás Ruiz de Velasco, Bilbao, Spain (In serv. 2-68)

Guarani

Guarani Hartmut Ehlers, 4-03

D: Approx. 1,700 tons (fl) **S:** 12.2 kts **Dim:** 73.61 (65.61 pp) × 11.13 × 3.67
Electronics: Radar: 1 . . . nav.
M: 1 MWM diesel; 1 prop; 1,300 bhp
Electric: 162 kw tot. (3 × 54-kw diesel sets) **Crew:** 21 tot.

Remarks: 714 grt/1,047 dwt. Transferred from the Flota Mercante de Estado and now operated as a commercial cargo carrier between Asunción, Buenos Aires, and Montevideo with a naval crew. The ship has been stripped of much equipment but is still officially in service.
Hull systems: Cargo: approx. 900 tons. Has two holds totaling 2,455 m^3 grain/ 2,212 m^3 bale capacity. There are two hatches (11 × 5.4 m and 19.6 × 5.4 m), four 5-ton derricks, and two 3-ton derricks.

SERVICE CRAFT

♦ 1 river transport [YF]
Bldr: Arsenal de Marina, Asunción (In serv. 1964)

T 1 Teniente Herreros (ex-*Presidente Stroessner*)

D: 420 tons (fl) **S:** 10 kts **Dim:** 37.8 × 9.0 × 2.2
M: 2 MWM diesels; 2 props; 330 bhp

Remarks: 150 grt. Cargo: 120 tons. Has a single 1-ton electrohydraulic crane amidships and superstructure near the stern. There are also several very small stores carriers in service.

Disposal note: U.S. LCU 501–class ferry BT 1 was no longer in service as of 2004.

♦ 1 ex-U.S. floating dry dock [YFDL]
Bldr: Doullut & Ewin, Mobile, Ala. (In serv. 6-44)

DF 1 (ex-AFDL 26)

DF 1 Hartmut Ehlers, 4-03

Lift capacity: 1,000 tons **Dim:** 60.96 × 19.5 × 1.04 (light)

Remarks: Transferred in 3-65.

♦ 1 presidential yacht [YFL]
Bldr: Arsenal de Marina, Asunción (In serv. 5-02)

3 de Febrero (ex-*26 de Febrero*)

3 de Febrero Hartmut Ehlers, 4-03

D: 98.5 tons **S:** 11.3 kts (cruising speed) **Dim:** 28.1 × 6.0 × 1.6
M: 2 Rolls-Royce diesels, each 258 hp; 2 shafts
Range: 1349/11 **Crew:** 6 + 8 guests

Remarks: Low-freeboard, white-painted craft operated by the navy.

♦ 1 utility launch [YFL]

L 01 Teniente Cabrera

Remarks: Marine Infantry tender. No additional data available.

♦ 1 Columbian Nodriza-class riverine support lighter [YFU]
Bldr: Cartagena Naval SY (In serv. . . . 2002)

D: 260 tons **S:** 9 kts **Dim:** 38.4 × 9.5 × 2.8
A: 8 single 12.7-mm mg **Electronics:** Radar: 1 . . . nav.
M: 2 diesels; 2 props; 880 bhp **Crew:** 18 + 82 troops

Remarks: Has 80-mm armor to the hull sides below the waterline. Medical facilities are fitted. The "2.8-m" figure in the dimensions may refer to molded depth rather than draft. A helicopter deck is fitted.

♦ 1 survey launch [YGS]

LH 1 Suboficial Rogelio Lesme

D: 16 tons **S:** 13 kts **Dim:** 14.5 × 3.1 × 0.8
M: 1 Mercedes-Benz diesel **Crew:** 5

Remarks: Built in 1958. Uses the same hull as the LP 07–class patrol boats.

Note: The non-self-propelled dredger *Teniente Oscar Carreras Saguier* (D-2), built in Argentina during 1958, was transferred to Paraguay in 1969. She displaces 140 tons, measures 20.5 × 7.0 × 1.2, and remains under navy control. The non-self-propelled floating crane *Grua Flotante* (G-1) was built in the Netherlands in 1907; she displaces 85 tons and measures 22.0 × 7.7 × 0.9. In addition, two non-self-propelled transport barges, *Ybycu'i* (CH-1) and *Paraguaari* (CH-8), remain in service.

Suboficial Rogelio Lesme (LH 1) Hartmut Ehlers, 5-00

♦ 1 ex-U.S. YTL 422–class tug
Bldr: Gunderson Bros. Eng. Corp., Portland, Ore.

	Laid down	L	In serv.
R 4 Triunfo (ex-YTL 567)	5-3-45	17-8-45	30-10-45

Triunfo (R 4) Hartmut Ehlers, 4-03

D: 85 tons (fl) **S:** 9 kts **Dim:** 20.17 × 5.18 × 1.50
M: 1 Scania DSI 14 M03 diesel; 1 prop; 357 bhp **Crew:** 5 tot.

Remarks: Transferred 4-74. Had been reported stricken but was noted in service during 2000. May have been re-engined and modified as per the *Angostura* (R 5).

♦ 1 ex-U.S. YTL 131–class tug [YTL]
Bldr: Robert Jacob, Inc., Staten Island, N.Y.

	Laid down	L	In serv.
R 5 Angostura (ex-YTL 211)	26-12-41	20-6-42	21-8-42

Angostura (R 5)—at right, with two R 2–class tugs; note the extended funnel and new pilothouse atop the old on the *Angostura* Hartmut Ehlers, 12-97

D: 82 tons **S:** 9 kts **Dim:** 20.2 (19.5 wl) × 5.5 × 2.4
M: 1 Scania DSI 14 M03 diesel; 1 prop; 357 bhp **Crew:** 5 tot.

Remarks: Transferred by lease in 3-65. Has been re-engined in Paraguay, and a pilothouse has been added above the original pilothouse.

♦ 1 R 2–class small tugs [YTL]

R 7 Esperanza

Remarks: Locally built, 20-ton craft.

Note: Pushboat *Arsenal 2* (A 2, ex-*4 de Mayo*) and the ex-R 9 (current name unknown) are also in service, and the Prefectura General Naval also operates the outboard motor–propelled PGN 214.

PERU

Republic of Peru

MARINA DE GUERRA DEL PERÚ

Personnel: 25,000 total (including 1,000 coast guard and 400 naval aviation personnel and 4,000 marines)

Bases: Callao (with dockyard), San Lorenzo (submarines), Chimbote, Paita, and San Juan, with river bases at Iquitos and on the Río Madre de Dios and the Lake Titicaca base at Puno. Minor bases are located at El Salto, Bayovar, Pimental, Pacasmayo, Salaverry, Mollendo, Matarani, Ilo, Inambari, Pucallpa, and El Estrecho. The naval academy is located at La Punta, Callao.

Organization: Organized into two commands: Pacific Naval Force, headquartered at Callao, and Amazon River Force, headquartered at Iquitos. The Pacific Naval Force is subdivided into five naval forces: Surface, Submarine, Naval Aviation, Infantry, and Special Operations. Planning for a reorganization began during 2001. Operations are geographically divided into five naval zones: I Zone at Piura, II Zone at Callao, III Zone at Arequipa, IV Zone at Pucallpa, and V Zone at Iquitos.

Naval Aviation: Fixed-wing, land-based aircraft include five Beech Super King Air 200T maritime patrol aircraft; one Fokker F-27-200, one Fokker F-27-500, one Fokker F-27-600, and two Antonov An-32B transports; three Beech T-34C trainers; and one Cessna 206 light liaison aircraft. Helicopters include three AM 39 Exocet SSM–equipped ASH-3D Sea King, five Agusta-Bell AB-212AS, four Bell 206B JetRanger, one Bell 205A, and three Mil Mi-8T Hip.

Peruvian Fokker F-27-200 Peruvian Navy, 2000

Peruvian ASH-3D Sea King—aboard frigate *Mariategui* (FM 54) Peruvian Navy, 4-01

Peruvian Agusta-Bell AB-212 U.S. Navy, 7-05

Peruvian Bell 206B JetRanger Peruvian Navy, 2001

Peruvian Mil Mi-8T Hip Peruvian Navy, 2001

Marines: The 5,000-strong naval infantry force is headquartered at Ancón and is divided into the *Guarnición de Marina* 1st Battalion and *Guardia Chalaca* 2nd Battalion at Ancón; *Punta Malpelo* 3rd Battalion at Tumbes; and *Ucayali* 4th Battalion at Pucallpa. The force is equipped with armored cars and with light amphibious vehicles.

Weapons systems: The navy's Centro de Fabricación de Armas (CEFAR) division of the SIMA shipyard group has designed and deployed the MGP-86 (*Marina de Guerra del Perú*) quadruple SAM launcher, which employs manned, open launchers similar to those developed for the Russian Navy to launch 9M-39 Igla (NATO SA-16 Gimlet) heat-seeking SAMs purchased from Nicaragua in 1994. The same launcher is also being deployed in land-based batteries.

Note: Ship names are preceded by BAP (*Buque Armada Peruana,* or Peruvian Naval Ship).

ATTACK SUBMARINES [SS]

♦ 6 German Type 209/1200
Bldr: Howaldtswerke, Kiel

	L	In serv.
SS 31 Angamos (ex-*Casma*)	31-8-79	19-12-80
SS 32 Antofagasta	19-12-79	14-3-80
SS 33 Pisagua (ex-*Blume*)	19-5-81	8-4-82
SS 34 Chipana (ex-*Pisagua*)	7-8-81	12-7-83
SS 35 Islay	11-10-73	23-1-75
SS 36 Arica	5-4-74	4-4-75

Angamos (SS 31) Vladimir Lemonos, 2-03

Antofagasta (S 32) Vladimir Lemonos, 2-03

ATTACK SUBMARINES [SS] *(continued)*

Chipana (SS 34)—taking part in exercise "Silent Force" U.S. Navy, 6-03

D: 1,000 tons surf. std.; 1,180 tons fl/1,285 tons sub.
S: 11 kts surf./12 kts snorkel/21 kts sub. (for 5 min) **Dim:** 55.90 × 6.30 × 5.50
A: 8 bow 533-mm TT (14 tot. German SST-4 Mod. 0 wire-guided torpedoes)
Electronics:
Radar: 1 Thales Calypso nav./surf. search
Sonar: SS 31, 32: STN Atlas Elektronik CSU 3-Z active; PRS 3-4 passive—SS 33–36: STN Atlas Elektronik CSU-83 active/passive suite—all: Thales DUUX-2C intercept
EW: . . . intercept
M: 4 MTU Type 12V493 AZ80 GA31L diesels, each linked to a 450-kw Siemens alternator, 1 Siemens electric motor; 1 prop; 4,600 shp
Range: 11,300/4 surf.; 28/20, 460/4 sub. **Fuel:** 63 tons
Endurance: 40 days **Crew:** 5 officers, 30 (SS 35, 36: 26) enlisted

Remarks: SS 31 and SS 32 were ordered 12-8-76, two others in 3-77. Delivery of SS 33 was delayed by a collision 2-4-82. SS 32 completed an overhaul at SIMA, Callao, in 10-96. SS 31 was renamed on 19-8-98.
Hull systems: SS 33 and later are 56.1 m o.a., 1,185 tons surf./1,290 tons sub. Diving depth: 250 m. The battery has four groups of 120 cells, weighs 257 tons, and produces 11,500 amp-hr.
Combat systems: All now have the Sepa Mk 3 torpedo fire-control system.

CRUISERS [CL]

♦ 1 ex-Dutch De Ruyter–class light cruiser
Bldr: Wilton-Fijenoord, Schiedam

	Laid down	L	In serv.
CLM 81 Almirante Grau (ex-*De Ruyter*, ex-*De Zeven Provinciën*)	5-9-39	24-12-44	18-11-53

Almirante Grau (CLM 81) Vladimir Lemonos, 4-03

Almirante Grau (CLM 81) Vladimir Lemonos, 4-03

D: 9,681 tons (12,165 fl) **S:** 32 kts **Dim:** 187.32 (182.4 pp) × 17.25 × 6.72
A: 8 Otomat Mk 2 SSM; 4 twin 152-mm 53-cal. Bofors DP; 2 twin 40-mm 70-cal. OTO Melara AA; 4 single 40-mm 70-cal. Bofors AA
Electronics:
Radar: 1 Decca 1226 nav.; 1 Thales DA-08 surf. search; 1 Plessey AWS-1 air search; 1 Thales WM-25 track-while-scan gun/missile f.c.; 1 Thales STIR-24 SAM illuminator; 2 Thales LIROD-8 gun f.c.
EW: Thales Rapids intercept; CME Scimitar deceptive jammer; 1 Matra Défense Sagaie decoy RL; 2 Matra Défense Dagaie decoy RL
M: 2 sets Parsons geared steam turbines; 2 props; 85,000 shp
Boilers: 4 Yarrow-Werkspoor, three-drum **Electric:** 4,000 kw tot.
Range: 2,100/32; 6,900/12 **Crew:** 49 officers, 904 enlisted

Remarks: Purchased 7-3-73, recommissioned 23-5-73. Completion of refitting at Amsterdamse Droogdok Maatschappij planned for 26-3-85 to 1987 was delayed. Left the Netherlands 22-1-88 and was officially recommissioned 7-89 in Peru, but without many of the weapons and systems planned for her modernization. The modernization was eventually completed in 1994 at SIMA, Callao. Currently active as flagship of the Fuerza de Superficie. Is the world's last operational gun cruiser. Expected to retire by 2008.
Hull systems: Armor consists of a 76- to 102-mm belt and 20 to 25 mm on two decks; the 152-mm gunhouses are lightly armored.
Combat systems: During modernization, was fitted with the Thales SEWACO-PE combat system. Four twin 57-mm Bofors DP were removed prior to departure for Europe, and eight single 40-mm AA were also removed; the 57-mm guns remain, but in 1994 eight single 40-mm weapons and eight Otomat cruise missile containers were installed. The four forward 40-mm single mounts were replaced in 1995 by the two twin OTO Melara Dardo mountings removed from the *Daring*-class destroyer *Palacios*. Was to have received two octuple Albatros SAM launchers for Aspide SAMs during the refit in the Netherlands, but although the foundations were added, the launchers were not, and the after position now accommodates a radome housing an SHF SATCOM antenna. Can carry 3,250 rounds of 152-mm and 16,000 rounds of 40-mm ammunition. The original CWE-10N sonar was removed during modernization. The antenna for a Panamax SATCOM system is mounted in a larger radome on the after superstructure. The Thales LW-08 early warning radar was replaced by a Plessey AWS-1 air search radar during 2004.

Disposal note: Ex-British *Daring*-class destroyer *Ferré* (DM 74) was retired during 2006.

FRIGATES [FF]

♦ 8 Italian Lupo class
Bldrs: FM 51, 52, 56–58: Fincantieri, Riva Trigoso; FM 53, 54: SIMA, Callao; FM 55: CNR, Muggiano

	Laid down	L	In serv.
FM 51 Carvajal	8-10-74	17-11-76	5-2-79
FM 52 Villavisencio	6-10-76	7-2-78	25-6-79
FM 53 Montero	16-6-76	8-10-82	29-7-84
FM 54 Mariategui	13-8-76	8-10-84	28-12-87
FM 55 Aguirre (ex-F 567 *Orsa*)	1-8-77	1-3-79	1-3-80
FM 56 Palacios (ex-F 564 *Lupo*)	8-10-74	29-7-76	20-9-77
FM 57 Bolognesi (ex-F 566 *Perseo*)	28-2-77	8-7-78	1-3-80
FM 58 Quiñones (ex-F 565 *Sagittario*)	4-2-76	22-6-77	18-11-78

Carvajal (FM 51)—with AB-212AS helicopter on the lengthened flight deck aft U.S. Navy, 7-05

Mariategui (FM 54) U.S. Navy, 8-04

D: 2,208 tons (2,500 fl) **S:** 32 kts **Dim:** 108.4 (106.0 pp) × 11.28 × 3.66
A: 8 Otomat Mk 2 SSM; 1 127-mm 54-cal. OTO Melara DP; 1 8-round Albatros SAM syst. (8 Aspide missiles); provision for 2 4-round MGP-86 SAM syst. (9M-39 Igla missiles); 2 twin 40-mm 70-cal. OTO Melara Dardo AA; 2 triple 324-mm Mk 32 ASW TT (WASS A-244 torpedoes); 1 AB-212 (FM 51, 54: ASH-3D Sea King with AM 39 Exocet missiles) ASW helicopter
Electronics:
Radar: 1 S.M.A. 3RM20 nav.; 1 AMS RAN-11LX surface search; 1 AMS RAN-10S air search (Thales LW-08 in 51); 1 AMS RTN-10X f.c.; 2 AMS RTN-20X f.c.; 1 AMS RTN-30X f.c.
Sonar: EDO 610E hull-mounted (6, 7, 8 kHz)
EW: Elettronica Lambda intercept; 2 20-round 105-mm OTO Melara SCLAR decoy RL
M: CODOG: 2 Fiat-G.E. LM-2500 gas turbines (25,000 shp each), 2 GMT A230-20M diesels (3,900 bhp each); 2 CP props
Electric: 3,120 kw tot.
Range: 900/35 (on gas turbines); 3,450/20.5 (on diesels)
Crew: 20 officers, 165 enlisted

FRIGATES [FF] *(continued)*

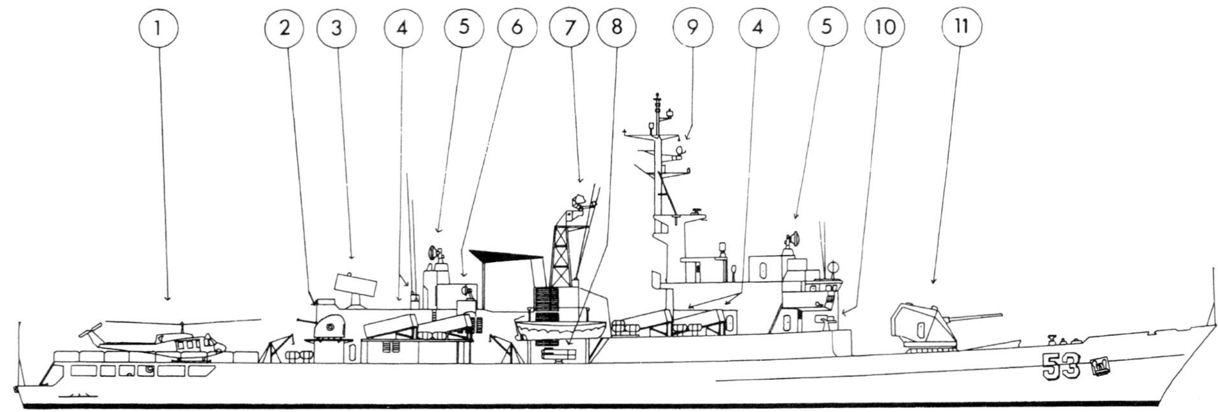

Montero (FM 53) 1. AB-212AS helicopter on original-length helicopter platform 2. Twin 40-mm OTO Melara Dardo AA 3. 8-round Albatros system SAM launcher 4. Otomat Mk 2 antiship missile launch canisters 5. RTN-10X gun (forward) and RTN-30X SAM f.c. radars 6. RTN-20X radar gun f.c. directors port and starboard for 40-mm AA 7. RAN-10S air-search radar 8. Triple ASW torpedo tubes 9. RAN-11LX surface-search radar 10. 20-round SCLAR decoy rocket launcher 11. 127-mm 54-cal. OTO Melara DP gun

Drawing by Robert Dumas, from *Flottes de Combat*

Carvajal (FM 51) Vladimir Lemonos, 5-03

Remarks: 51–54 differ from the others in having a fixed (vice telescoping) hangar and a step down to the hull at the stern; the Dardo 40-mm mounts are one deck higher, and the SAM fire-control system also differs. 55 and 56 were transferred from Italy without missiles during 5-05. 57 and 58, originally to have been renamed *Ferré* and *Almirante Grau,* were transferred and commissioned into Peruvian service at La Spezia, Italy, on 23-1-06 and renamed *Bolognesi* and *Quiñones*.

Combat systems: Selenia IPN-10 data system is fitted. There are no reloads for the Albatros SAM system. The helicopter provides over-the-horizon targeting and mid-course guidance for the Otomat missiles. In 1989, were fitted with equipment to permit refueling hovering Sea King helicopters. One unit was used in trials during 1996 with a single MGP-86 manned SAM launcher for Russian 9M-39 Igla (NATO SA-16 Gimlet) missiles, and the others have since been backfitted to accept the launchers, two of which are installed during periods of crisis. FM 51 and 54 were modified at SIMA, Callao, in 1997–98 with helicopter decks extended right to the stern to accommodate a Sea King helicopter; the hangars remained unaltered, however. The AMS RAN-10S air search radar was replaced by the Thales LW-08 radar aboard *Carvajal* during 2004.

GUIDED-MISSILE PATROL COMBATANTS [PGG]

♦ 6 French PR-72-560 class

Bldr: SFCN, Villeneuve-la-Garenne (hulls of CM 21, 23, 25 by Arsenal de Lorient)

	L	In serv.
CM 21 Velarde	16-9-78	25-7-80
CM 22 Santillana	11-9-79	25-7-80
CM 23 De los Heros	20-5-79	17-11-80
CM 24 Herrera	16-2-79	26-2-81
CM 25 Larrea	20-5-79	16-6-81
CM 26 Sanchez Carrion	28-6-79	14-9-81

D: 470 tons light; 560 tons normal (610 fl) **S:** 37 (CM 21–23: 34) kts
Dim: 64.0 (59.0 pp) × 8.35 × 2.60 (max.)
A: 4 MM 38 Exocet SSM; 1 76-mm 62-cal. OTO Melara Compact DP; 1 twin 40-mm 70-cal. OTO Melara–Bofors AA; 1 4-round MGP-86 SAM launcher (9M-39 Igla/ SA-16 Gimlet missiles); 2 single 7.62-mm mg
Electronics:
Radar: 1 Decca TM 1226 nav.; 1 Thales THD 1040 Triton air/surf. search; 1 Thales Castor-II f.c.
EW: Thales DR-2000 intercept
M: CM 21–23: 4 MTU 12V595-series diesels; 4 props; 17,424 bhp—CM 24–26: 4 SACM AGO 240 V-16 M7 diesels; 4 props; 22,000 bhp
Electric: 560 kw tot. **Range:** 1,200/30; 2,500/16 **Crew:** 36 tot. (accomm. for 46)

Remarks: Originally numbered P 101–P 106. Were refitted, re-engined, and given new engine controls and monitoring systems (resulting in 45% better fuel economy) between 1999 and 2002.

Herrera (CM 24) U.S. Navy, 8-06

Sanchez Carrion (CM 26) Peruvian Navy, 6-01

Hull systems: A helicopter VERTREP (VERTical REPlenishment) station is painted on the fantail, to starboard.

Combat systems: Have the Thales Vega weapons-control system, with a Matra Défense Panda backup optical gun director. During modernization refits, are being fitted to accept the portable, Peruvian-developed MGP-86 point-defense SAM launcher, which uses 9M-39 Igla missiles purchased secondhand from Nicaragua in 1994.

PATROL CRAFT [PC]

♦ 2 Marañon-class river gunboats

Bldr: John I. Thornycroft, Woolston, U.K.

	Laid down	L	In serv.
CF 13 Ucayali (ex-CF 401)	4-50	7-3-51	3-10-51
CF 14 Marañon (ex-CF 402)	4-50	23-4-51	3-10-51

D: 350 tons (365 fl) **S:** 12 kts **Dim:** 47.22 × 9.75 × 1.22
A: 1 76.2-mm 50-cal. U.S. Mk 26 DP; 2 single 40-mm 60-cal. Bofors Mk 3 AA; 2 single 20-mm 70-cal. Oerlikon Mk 10 AA
Electronics: Radar: 1 . . . nav.
M: 2 British Polar M441 diesels; 2 props; 800 bhp
Range: 5,000/10 **Crew:** 4 officers, 36 enlisted

PATROL CRAFT [PC] *(continued)*

Marañon (CF 14) Peruvian Navy, 1999

Remarks: Based at Iquitos for service on the upper Amazon. Steel hulled with aluminum-alloy superstructures. The after 76.2-mm mount was replaced by a second 40-mm mounting, and the twin 20-mm mounts have been replaced by singles.

♦ 2 Amazonas-class river gunboats

Bldr: Electric Boat Co., Groton, Conn. (In serv. 1934)

CF 11 Amazonas (ex-CF 403) CF 12 Loreto (ex-CF 404)

Amazonas (CF 11) Peruvian Navy, 1999

D: 250 tons **S:** 15 kts **Dim:** 46.7 × 6.7 × 1.2
A: 1 76.2-mm 50-cal. U.S. Mk 26 DP; 3 single 40-mm 60-cal. Mk 3 Bofors AA; 2 single 20-mm 70-cal. Oerlikon AA
M: 2 diesels; 2 props; 750 bhp **Range:** 4,000/10 **Crew:** 5 officers, 30 enlisted

Remarks: Based at Iquitos on the upper Amazon. The 40-mm AA mounts have shields, and a third 40-mm mount has replaced the after 76.2-mm weapon. Do not have radars.

Note: The old river gunboat *America* (15), nonoperational since 1981, is retained as a museum at Iquitos. The former U.S. *Cannon*-class frigate *Castilla* (ex-*Bangust,* DE 739) is hulked at Iquitos on the upper Amazon as headquarters and training ship for the Amazon Flotilla.

AMPHIBIOUS WARFARE SHIPS

♦ 4 ex-U.S. Terrebonne Parish–class tank landing ships [LST]

Bldr: Ingalls SB, Pascagoula, Miss. (DT 144: Bath Iron Works, Bath, Maine)

	L	In serv.
DT 141 Paita (ex-*Walworth County,* LST 1164)	18-5-53	26-10-53
DT 142 Pisco (ex-*Waldo County,* LST 1163)	17-3-53	17-9-53
DT 143 Callao (ex-*Washoe County,* LST 1165)	14-7-53	30-11-53
DT 144 Eten (ex-*Traverse County,* LST 1160)	3-10-53	19-12-53

D: 2,590 tons (6,225 fl) **S:** 13 kts
Dim: 117.35 × 16.76 × 3.70 (mean; 5.18 max. aft)
A: 5 40-mm 60-cal. Bofors AA (2 twin U.K. Mk 5 or U.S. Mk 1 Mod. 2; 1 U.S. Mk 3)
Electronics: Radar: 1 . . . nav.
M: 4 G.M. 16-278A diesels; 2 CP props; 6,000 hp **Electric:** 600 kw tot.
Range: 6,000/9 **Fuel:** 1,060 tons **Crew:** 116 tot.

Paita (DT 141) Vladimir Lemonos, 5-03

Callao (DT 143) Werner Globke, 11-04

Remarks: Originally leased from the U.S. for five years on 7-8-84. Reactivated from Maritime Administration reserve by Todd SY, San Francisco, Calif., and delivered mid-10-84; all were officially recommissioned 4-3-85. DT 142, formerly used for cannibalization spares, has been restored to full service.
Hull systems: Have a bow ramp and accommodations for 395 troops. Cargo: approx. 2,200 tons, carried in the tank deck and on the upper deck, forward (with a ramp to the lower deck).
Combat systems: Having been in Military Sealift Command service from 1972 until deactivated, they were unarmed at time of transfer. All received 40-mm AA after arrival in Peru. DT 142 has twin U.S. Mk 1 Mod. 2 40-mm mountings forward vice the twin, shielded Mk 5 mounts on others of the class.

AUXILIARIES

♦ 1 oceanographic research ship [AGOR]

Bldr: SIMA, Callao

	Laid down	L	In serv.
Humboldt	3-1-77	13-10-78	1980

Humboldt—red hull and masts, cream-colored superstructure Peruvian Navy, 2001

D: 1,200 tons (1,980 fl) **S:** 14 kts **Dim:** 76.21 (66.02 pp) × 12.68 × 4.40
A: None **Electronics:** Radar: 2 . . . nav.
M: 2 Burmeister & Wain Alpha 10V23L-VO diesels; 2 CP props; 3,000 bhp
Crew: 53 tot.

Remarks: 1,731 grt/600 dwt. Modified stern-haul factory trawler design, well equipped for oceanographic and fisheries research.

♦ 1 ex-Netherlands Dokkum-class survey ship [AGS]

Bldr: Gusto/F.A. Smulders, Schiedam

	Laid down	L	In serv.
AH 171 Carrasco (ex-*Abcoude,* M 810; ex-MSC 176)	10-11-53	2-9-55	18-5-56

D: 373 tons (453 fl) **S:** 15 kts **Dim:** 46.62 × 8.75 × 2.28
A: 2 single 20-mm 70-cal. Mk 10 Oerlikon AA
Electronics: Radar: 1 Decca TM 1229C nav.
M: 2 Fijenoord-M.A.N. V 64 diesels; 2 props; 2,500 bhp
Range: 2,500/10 **Crew:** 27–36 tot.

Remarks: Former minesweeper, decommissioned from the Netherlands Navy 5-11-93, stricken 16-7-94, and purchased 12-7-94. Typed as a *Buque Hidrográfico* and employed both in hydrographic survey and training duties. Wooden construction. Funded by the United States, hence the MSC-series hull number assigned during building. Reports that sisters *Drachten* and *Naaldwijk* were purchased in 1996 were in error.

AUXILIARIES *(continued)*

Carrasco (AH 171) Vladimir Lemonos, 2-03

♦ **1 Ilo-class cargo ship [AK]**
Bldr: SIMA, Callao (In serv. 15-12-71)

ATC 131 Mollendo (ex-*Ilo*)

Mollendo (ATC 131) U.S. Navy, 1-06

Mollendo (ATC 131) Vladimir Lemonos, 4-03

D: 18,400 tons (fl) **S:** 15.6 kts **Dim:** 153.88 (144.56 pp) × 20.48 × 9.39
M: 1 Burmeister & Wain 6K47EF diesel; 1 prop; 11,600 bhp
Electric: 1,140 kw (3 × 380-kw diesel sets) **Crew:** 60 tot.

Remarks: 8,621 grt/13,450 dwt. Typed as a *Buque Transporte de Carga,* ATC 131 (renamed 10-3-00) is used primarily to carry commercial cargo by the Oficina Naviera Comercial. The engine room flooded 1-91 while carrying 11,000 tons of sugar, and she has had numerous engineering problems since. Sister *Rimac* is in commercial service for the state shipping company. Began operating as a training ship during 2005, carrying 300 cadets, officers, and crew.
Hull systems: Has five holds with a total 19,563 m^3 grain and 18,082 m^3 bale capacity. Has five hatches (of 7.0, 12.8, 12.8, 18.2, and 10.4 × 6.5 m, respectively), one 3-ton crane, and two 50-ton, six 10-ton, and six 5-ton derricks.

♦ **1 ex-U.S. Sealift-class oiler [AO]**
Bldr: Bath Iron Works, Bath, Maine

	L	In serv.
ATP 153 Lobitos (ex-*Santa Chiara;* ex-*Sealift Caribbean,* T-AOT 174)	8-6-74	6-11-74

Lobitos (ATP 153) Maritime Photographic, 6-01

D: 33,000 tons (fl) **S:** 16 kts **Dim:** 178.92 (170.80 pp) × 25.61 × 10.50
Electronics: Radar: 1 Raytheon TM 1650/6X nav.; 1 Raytheon TM 1645 nav.
M: 2 Colt-Pielstick 14 PC2 V400, 14-cyl., 520-rpm diesels; 1 CP prop; 14,000 bhp—bow-thruster
Electric: 2,000 kw tot.
Range: 12,000/16 **Fuel:** 3,440 tons **Crew:** . . . tot.

Remarks: 17,157 grt/27,217 dwt. Purchased from commercial operator Santa Sopia S.A., Panama, in 2-98; had been stricken from U.S. Military Sealift Command service on completion of a 20-year charter in 10-95, during which time the ship had been operated in freighting service by commercial contract crews. Is typed as a *Buque Transporte de Petroleo.* Was provided with an underway refueling capability in a refit completed in 11-98 and is also operated in revenue commercial service. Cargo: 225,154 barrels liquid. In U.S. MSC service, was operated with a crew of nine officers and 17 unlicensed personnel.

♦ **1 Talara-class transport oiler [AOT]**
Bldr: SIMA, Callao

	Laid down	L	In serv.
ATP 152 Talara	1975	9-7-76	23-1-78

Talara (ATP 152) Peruvian Navy, 2000

D: 30,000 tons (fl) **S:** 16.25 kts **Dim:** 171.18 (161.55 pp) × 25.38 × 9.53
M: 1 Burmeister & Wain 6K 47EF diesel; 1 prop; 11,600 bhp
Electric: 1,890 kw tot. **Crew:** . . . tot.

Remarks: 16,633 grt/25,648 dwt. Cargo: 35,642 m^3. Typed as a *Buque Transporte de Petroleo.* Sister *Trompeteros* is operated by Petroperu, the state fuel monopoly, which transferred this ship to the navy's Oficina Naviera Comercial upon completion.

♦ **1 ex-U.S. Sotoyomo-class ocean tug [ATA]**
Bldr: Levingston SB Co., Orange, Texas

	Laid down	L	In serv.
AMB 160 Unanue (ex-*Wateree,* ATA 174)	5-1-43	18-11-43	20-7-44

Unanue (AMB 160) Peruvian Navy, 1999

D: 835 tons (fl) **S:** 13 kts **Dim:** 43.59 (40.70 pp) × 10.31 × 3.96
A: None **Electronics:** Radar: 2 . . . nav.
M: 2 G.M. Electromotive Div. 12-278A diesels, electric drive; 1 prop; 1,500 shp
Electric: 120 kw tot. **Range:** 8,000/8 **Fuel:** 158 tons **Crew:** 45 tot.

Remarks: Purchased from the U.S. in 11-61 and employed on salvage and search-and-rescue duties. Typed *Buque Madrina de Buzos.*

AUXILIARIES *(continued)*

♦ 1 ex-U.S. Cherokee-class ocean tug [ATA]
Bldr: Cramp SB, Philadelphia

	Laid down	L	In serv.
ARA 123 Guardian Rios (ex-*Pinto,* ATF 90)	10-8-42	5-1-43	1-4-43

Guardian Rios (ARA 123) Vladimir Lemonos, 3-03

D: 1,235 tons (1,675 fl) **S:** 16.5 kts **Dim:** 62.48 (59.44 pp) × 11.73 × 4.67
A: 4 single 20-mm 70-cal. Oerlikon AA **Electronics:** Radar: 2 . . . nav.
M: 4 G.M. 12-278 diesels, electric drive; 1 prop; 3,000 shp
Electric: 260 kw tot. **Range:** 6,500/16; 13,000/10 **Crew:** 99 tot.

Remarks: Loaned in 12-60 and purchased outright 17-5-74. Used for salvage and rescue duties.

SERVICE CRAFT

♦ 1 riverine supply craft [YF]

Remarks: One 35-m, self-propelled supply lighter is employed on the upper Amazon. The craft displaces about 230 tons (fl) and can carry about 50 troops in addition to around 80 tons of supplies.

♦ 1 floating dry dock [YFDM]
Bldr: SIMA, Callao (In serv. 2-91)

ADF 104

Lift capacity: 4,500 tons **Dim:** 115.8 × 30.1 × 12.5 (max., flooded)

Remarks: Launched 12-12-90. Designed by Senermar, Spain. Intended for use at Callao. Internal dimensions: 99.8 × 23.8 m. Is also used for commercial repair work.

♦ 1 ex-U.S. ARD 2–class floating dry dock [YFDM]
Bldr: Pacific Bridge Co., Alameda, Calif. (In serv. 8-43)

ADF 107 (ex-WY 20, ex-ARD 8)

Lift capacity: 3,500 tons **Dim:** 148.03 × 21.64 × 1.60 (light)

Remarks: Transferred in 2-61 and purchased outright in 1981. Is also used for commercial repair work.

♦ 1 small floating dry dock [YFDL]
Bldr: John I. Thornycroft, Southampton (In serv. 1951)

ADF 108

Small floating dry dock ADF 108—with patrol craft *Marañon* (CF 14) aboard Peruvian Navy, 2001

Lift capacity: 600 tons **Dim:** 59.13 × 18.7 × . . .

Remarks: Serves the Amazon Flotilla at Iquitos, assigned to SINAI (*Servicio Industrial de la Marina-Iquitos*).

♦ 1 ex-U.S. AFDL 7–class floating dry dock [YFDL]
Bldr: Foundation Co., Kearny, N.J. (In serv. 10-44)

ADF 106 (ex-WY 19, ex-AFDL 33)

Lift capacity: 1,900 tons **Dim:** 87.78 × 19.51 × 0.99 (light)

Remarks: Transferred in 7-59.

♦ 2 Dutch Van Straelen–class inshore survey craft [YGS]
Bldr: De Vries–Leutsch, Amsterdam

	Laid down	L	In serv.
AH 175 Carrillo (ex-*Icaro,* ex-*Van Hamel,* M 871)	27-4-59	28-5-60	14-10-60
AH 176 Melo (ex-*Van der Wel,* M 878)	30-5-60	3-5-61	6-10-61

Carrillo (AH 175) Vladimir Lemonos, 2-03

D: 151 tons (171 fl) **S:** 13 kts **Dim:** 33.08 (30.30 wl) × 6.88 × 1.80
A: 1 20-mm 70-cal. Oerlikon Mk 10 AA
Electronics: Radar: 1 Decca TM 1226 nav.
M: 2 G.M. Detroit Diesel 16V92N diesels; 2 props; 1,400 bhp
Crew: 2 officers, 15 enlisted

Remarks: Former inshore minesweepers, purchased 23-2-85 for conversion in Peru to inshore survey duties. Received the Interplot 200 survey system and new engines. Wooden construction. Bridge on AH 175 has been modified and enlarged.

♦ 1 coastal survey craft [YGS]
Bldr: SIMA, Chimbote (In serv. 1982)

EH 174 Macha

D: 49 tons (53 fl) **S:** 13 kts **Dim:** 19.8 × 5.2 × 0.9
M: 2 Caterpillar 3406-TA diesels; 2 props; 534 bhp
Range: 533/10.5 **Crew:** 2 officers, 4 enlisted

Remarks: Has side-looking sonar for bottom mapping to 1,200-m depths. EH = *Embarcación Hidrográfica.*

♦ 1 river survey craft [YGS]
Bldr: MacLaren, Niteroi, Brazil (In serv. 1981)

AH 172 Stiglich

Stiglich (AH 172) Peruvian Navy, 1991

D: 230 tons (250 fl) **S:** 9 kts **Dim:** 31.40 × 8.00 × 1.54
Electronics: Radar: 1 . . . nav.
M: 2 Caterpillar 3304 diesels; 2 props; 250 bhp
Range: 8,000/9 **Crew:** 2 officers, 20 enlisted

Remarks: Operates on the Amazon from Iquitos. White-painted. Classed as a *Buque Hidrográfico.*

♦ 1 river survey craft [YGS]
Bldr: SIMA, Iquitos (In serv. 1981)

AEH 173

SERVICE CRAFT *(continued)*

D: 12 tons (fl) **S:** 7 kts **Dim:** 10.0 × 3.7 × 1.4
M: 2 Volvo Penta AQD-series diesels; 2 props; . . . bhp

Remarks: GRP construction. Operates on the Amazon from Iquitos. White-painted. Classed as a *Buque Hidrográfico.*

Note: Also reported in use for riverine survey duties is the 5-ton, 40-kt launch AH 177.

♦ **1 hospital craft for Amazon service [YH]**
Bldr: SIMA, Iquitos (In serv. 13-5-76)

ABH 302 MORONA

Morona (ABH 302) Peruvian Navy, 1999

D: 150 tons (fl) **S:** 12 kts **Dim:** 30.0 × 6.0 × 0.6
M: Diesels; . . . bhp **Range:** 5,864/6.4 **Crew:** . . . tot.

Remarks: Based at Iquitos on the upper Amazon River. Refitted mid-1990s with enlarged superstructure. There are also several smaller hospital launches on the Amazon.

♦ **1 hospital craft for Lake Titicaca service [YH]**
Bldr: Cammell-Laird, Birkenhead, U.K. (In serv. 1879)

ABH 306 PUNO (ex-*Yapura*)

Puno (ABH 306) Peruvian Navy, 2000

D: 500 grt **S:** . . . kts **Dim:** 38.10 × 6.10 × 3.96
Electronics: Radar: 1 Raytheon 1500B Pathfinder nav.
M: 1 Paxman-Ricardo V-12 gasoline engine; 1 prop; 410 bhp

Remarks: Reacquired by the navy 17-3-76 and converted to a hospital ship. Sister *Chuquito* (ARB 19, ex-*Yavari*) was stricken in 1990 after 119 years' service and is now used as a museum ship.

♦ **1 coastal light fuels tanker [YO]**
Bldr: Gerhard Voldnes A/S Skps, Fosnavåg, Norway (In serv. 1965)

ACP 157 SUPE (ex-*Taxiarchis,* ex-*Cryla,* ex-*Gevotank*)

D: 1,400 tons (fl) **S:** 10 kts (9 loaded) **Dim:** 66.81 (63.68 pp) × 9.53 × 3.95
A: None **Electronics:** Radar: 2 . . . nav.
M: 1 MaK 6-cyl. diesel; 1 CP prop; 1,100 bhp
Electric: 128 kw tot. (2 × 56-kw, 1 × 16-kw emergency diesel sets; 220 V a.c.)
Range: . . . / . . . **Fuel:** 38 tons **Crew:** 17 tot.

Supe (ACP 157) Maritime Photographic, 6-01

Remarks: 497 grt/1,138 dwt. Former commercial vegetable oil tanker, acquired 29-8-95 and intended for revenue-producing service, delivering parcel cargoes to coastal ports and fueling fishing fleets at sea. Has an ice-strengthened hull. Cargo: 1,200 tons (1,437 m^3) liquid in eight tanks. Typed as a *Buque Transporte de Petroleo.*

♦ **2 ex-U.S. 174-foot-class yard oilers [YO]**
Bldrs: ACP 118: Jeffersonville Boat & Mach., Ind.; ACP 119: RTC Shipbuilding, Camden, N.J.

	Laid down	L	In serv.
ACP 118 NOGUERA (ex-YO 221)	15-1-45	22-5-45	31-8-45
ACP 119 GAUDEN (ex-YO 171)	18-3-44	20-7-44	15-11-44

Noguera (ACP 118) Peruvian Navy, 1999

D: 440 tons light (1,390 fl) **S:** 10 kts (9 loaded) **Dim:** 53.04 × 9.75 × 3.96
A: None **Electronics:** Radar: 1 Raytheon . . . nav.
M: 2 G.M. diesels; 2 props; 540 bhp **Electric:** 80 kw tot.
Range: 2,000/8 **Crew:** 20 tot.

Remarks: ACP 118 transferred in 2-75; ACP 119 was purchased 26-1-81. Cargo: approximately 900 tons (6,570 barrels). Typed as *Buques Cisterna de Petroleo.* Have black hulls and dark gray superstructures.

♦ **4 Río Comaina–class Amazon River fuel lighters [YO]**
Bldr: SIMA, Iquitos (In serv. 1975–76)

ABP 336 RÍO COMAINA
ABP 337 RÍO HUAZAGA
ABP 338 RÍO CHINGANAZA
ABP 339 RÍO CENEPA

D: Approx. 165 tons (fl) **S:** 7.5 kts **Dim:** 30.0 × 6.0 × 1.0
M: 2 Caterpillar D 3304 diesels; 2 props; 250 bhp

Remarks: Typed as *Cisternas de Petroleo,* as are the five Peruvian YONs.

♦ **2 ABP 342–class Amazon River fuel barges [YON]**
Bldr: SIMA, Iquitos (In serv. 1974)

ABP 342 ABP 343

D: Approx. 210 tons (fl) **Dim:** 60.3 × 12.1 × 0.3

♦ **1 ABP 344–class Amazon River fuel barge [YON]**
Bldr: Conrad Industries, Morgan City, La. (In serv. . . .)

ABP 344

D: Approx. 150 tons (fl) **Dim:** 42.6 × 12.1 × 0.3

♦ **1 ABP 345–class Amazon River fuel barge [YON]**
Bldr: SIMA, Iquitos (In serv. 1974)

ABP 345

D: Approx. 270 tons (fl) **Dim:** 48.7 × 12.0 × 0.3

♦ **1 ABP 346–class Amazon River fuel barge [YON]**
Bldr: Conrad Industries, Morgan City, La. (In serv. . . .)

ABP 346

D: Approx. 320 tons (fl) **Dim:** 45.7 × 12.1 × 0.6

♦ **1 floating forward riverine base [YPL]**
Bldr: SIMA, Iquitos (In serv. 7-98)

ABF 401 (ex-B6-01)

Remarks: Dimensions are 45.7 × . . . × 10. Designed by the U.S. Army Corps of Engineers to provide a floating accommodations, command, and logistics support base for Peruvian National Police, Navy, and Coast Guard personnel on the 10,000-km Peruvian Amazon basin network. Capable of supporting eight 25-ft patrol craft with food, water, fuel, maintenance, and lodging for two months. Resembles a two-deck houseboat.

SERVICE CRAFT *(continued)*

Forward riverine base ABF 401 Peruvian Navy, 7-98

♦ 1 torpedo retriever [YPT]
Bldr: Friedrich Lürssen Werft, Vegesack, Germany (In serv. 18-7-81)

ART 322 San Lorenzo

San Lorenzo (ART 322) Vladimir Lemonos, 3-03

D: 51.5 tons (65.5 fl) **S:** 19 kts **Dim:** 25.35 (23.47 pp) × 5.62 × 1.68
M: 2 MTU 8V396 TC82 diesels; 2 props; 1,590 bhp
Range: 500/15 **Fuel:** 14 tons **Crew:** 9 tot.

Remarks: Can stow four long or eight short torpedoes on the ramp aft. Typed as a *Lancha de Rescate de Torpedos.*

♦ 1 ex-U.S. YR 24–class floating workshop [YR]
Bldr: DeKom SB, Brooklyn, N.Y.

	Laid down	L	In serv.
ART 105 (ex-YR 59)	3-11-43	22-4-44	24-8-44

D: 520 tons (770 fl) **Dim:** 45.72 × 10.36 × 1.8
Electric: 220 kw tot. **Fuel:** 75 tons **Crew:** 47 tot.

Remarks: Transferred 8-8-61. Typed as a *Taller Flotante de Reparaciones.*

♦ 1 large harbor tug [YTB]
Bldr: . . ., U.S. (In serv. 1984)

ARB 126 Dueñas

D: 869 tons (fl) **S:** 11 kts **Dim:** 40.99 × 11.58 × . . .
M: 2 Fairbanks 38D8⅛ × 10 diesels; . . . props; 3,400 bhp

Remarks: Acquired in 1984 from Belco Petroleum Co. and put into service 6-5-85. Typed as a *Remolcador de Bahía*. Based at Callao.

♦ 2 Selendon-class harbor tugs [YTM]
Bldr: Ruhrorter, Duisburg, Germany (In serv. 1967)

ARB 128 Olaya ARB 129 Selendon

Selendon (ARB 129) Peruvian Navy, 1999

D: 80 grt **S:** 10 kts **Dim:** 18.7 × 6.2 × 2.3
M: 1 diesel; 1 prop; 600 bhp **Range:** 1,500/12; 2,000/8

♦ 2 Mejia-class small harbor tugs [YTL]
Bldr: Fabrimet, Callao (In serv. 1974)

ARB 120 Mejia ARB 121 Huerta

Mejia (ARB 120) Peruvian Navy, 1999

D: 19.9 tons (fl) **S:** 10 kts **Dim:** . . . × . . . × . . .
M: 1 G.M. Detroit Diesel 6H-12-V71 diesel; 1 prop; 340 bhp
Range: 850/8; 1,000/6 **Crew:** . . . tot.

Remarks: Typed as *Remolcadores de Bahía.* Are also equipped to transport personnel locally. Based at Callao.

♦ 1 Tapuima-class riverine push-tug [YTL]
Bldr: Gonzales SY, Houston, Texas (In serv. 1973)

AER 180 Tapuima

D: Approx. 60 tons (fl) **S:** . . . kts **Dim:** 13.1 × 5.5 × 1.2
M: 2 G.M. Detroit Diesel 8V71 diesels; 2 props; 600 bhp

Remarks: Serves on the upper Amazon. Acquired in 1982.

♦ 2 Gaudin-class riverine push-tugs [YTL]
Bldr: SIMA, Iquitos

	In serv.
AER 186 Gaudin	1975
AER 187 Zambrano	1977

D: Approx. 45 tons (fl) **S:** 5 kts **Dim:** 16.2 × 6.5 × 1.2
M: 2 Caterpillar D334 6-cyl. diesels; 2 props; 450 bhp

Remarks: Serve on the upper Amazon. Less than 50 tons displacement.

♦ 1 sail training craft [YTS]
Bldr: Hattaras Yachts, High Point, N.C.

ALY 311 Neptuno

D: 26 tons **S:** 19 kts **Dim:** 16.1 × 4.7 × 3.4
M: 2 G.M. Detroit Diesel 6V71 TI diesels; . . . bhp

Remarks: Although typed as an *Embarcación de Instrucción,* is used more as a yacht. No information available on rig or sail area.

♦ 1 sail training craft [YTS]
Bldr: James O. Rasborough, Halifax, Canada (In serv. 1974)

ALY 313 Marte

Marte (ALY 313) Peruvian Navy, 2000

D: 55 tons **S:** 8 kts **Dim:** 20.30 × 5.18 × 1.95
Electronics: Radar: 1 Furuno . . . nav.
M: 2 Perkins 130C 6-cyl. diesels; 2 props; 260 bhp
Endurance: 7 days **Crew:** 2 officers, 3 enlisted, 21 cadets

Remarks: Used for cadet instruction at the naval academy.

SERVICE CRAFT *(continued)*

♦ 1 ex-U.S. 174-foot water tanker [YW] Bldr: Leatham D. Smith, Wis.

	Laid down	L	In serv.
ACA 111 CALOYERAS (ex-YW 128)	9-4-45	22-5-45	28-7-45

Caloyeras (ACA 111) Vladimir Lemonos, 4-03

D: 440 tons (1,390 fl) **S:** 7 kts **Dim:** 53.04 × 9.75 × 4.0
M: 1 G.M. diesel; 1 prop; 640 bhp **Fuel:** 25 tons **Crew:** 23 tot.

Remarks: Purchased 26-1-81. Cargo: 930 tons. Sister *Mantilla* (ACA 110, ex-YW 122) was stricken in 1997. Resembles the 174-ft.-class yard oilers *Noguera* (ACP 118) and *Gauden* (ACP 119).

♦ 1 water barge [YWN] Bldr: SIMA, Iquitos (In serv. 1972)

ABA 332

Remarks: 330 tons (fl). Serves at the Base Naval del Callao. Typed as a *Barcaza Cisterna de Agua.*

COAST GUARD
(*Guardacosta*)

Note: The Peruvian Coast Guard was established in 1975 and is intended to patrol to the extent of the 200-n.m. economic zone. Pennant numbers are prefaced by letter designations indicating subordination to the Coastal Patrol (PC), Lake Patrol (PL), Port Patrol (PP), or River Patrol (PF). Larger craft carry a red-white-red diagonal striping on the hull side.

Maritime Aviation: One de Havilland Twin Otter DHC-6-100 floatplane transport (transferred from the navy)

Peruvian Coast Guard DHC-6-100 Twin Otter floatplane Peruvian Navy, 2001

PATROL CRAFT [WPC]

♦ 5 Río Cañete class Bldr: SIMA, Chimbote

	In serv.		In serv.
PC 243 RÍO NEPEÑA	1-12-81	PC 246 RÍO HUARMEY	8-10-82
PC 244 RÍO TAMBO	10-3-82	PC 247 RÍO ZAÑA	12-2-85
PC 245 RÍO OCOÑA	14-7-82		

Río Zaña (PC 247) Vladimir Lemonos, 10-03

D: 296 tons (fl) **S:** 22 kts (17 sust.) **Dim:** 50.98 (49.10 pp) × 7.40 × 1.70
A: 1 20-mm 70-cal. Oerlikon Mk 10 AA; 2 single 12.7-mm mg
Electronics: Radar: 1 JRC 5256 nav.—EW: . . . intercept
M: 4 Izar-MTU V8V 16/18 TLS diesels; 2 props; 5,640 bhp
Electric: 170 kw tot. **Range:** 3,000/17 **Endurance:** 20 days
Crew: 4 officers, 26 enlisted

Remarks: Have steel hulls and aluminum superstructure. The 40-mm gun formerly mounted aft has been removed. PC 245 completed a one-year overhaul at SIMA in 1996, in which a distilling plant was installed, as was a VHF/UHF SATCOM transceiver; the others followed in 1996–98. Class prototype *Río Cañete* (PC 248) was stricken in 1990.

♦ 1 U.S. PGM 71 class
Bldr: SIMA, Callao (In serv. 5-9-71)

PC 223 RÍO CHIRA (ex-PGM 11)

Río Chira (PC 223) Peruvian Navy, 1999

D: 130 tons (145 fl) **S:** 17 kts **Dim:** 30.80 (30.20 wl) × 6.40 × 1.85 (2.31 props)
A: Removed **Electronics:** Radar: 1 JRC 5256 nav.
M: 8 G.M. Detroit Diesel 6-71 diesels; 2 props; 2,200 hp
Electric: 120 kw tot. **Range:** 1,500/10 **Crew:** 4 officers, 18 enlisted

Remarks: Transferred from the navy in 1975. Built with U.S. aid and equipment but did not receive a U.S. hull number. U.S.-built sister *Río Sama* (PC 222, ex-U.S. PGM 78) has been stricken. The armament of one 40-mm 60-cal. Bofors Mk. 3, three single 20-mm Oerlikon, and two 12.7-mm machineguns has been removed.

PATROL BOATS [WPB]

♦ 12 Modified 40-foot Dauntless class
Bldr: SIMA, Callao (In serv. 2003–4)

PP 222 ZORRITOS	PP 226 . . .	PP 230 . . .
PP 223 . . .	PP 227 . . .	PP 231 . . .
PP 224 PUNTA ARENAS	PP 228 . . .	PP 293 JULI
PP 225 SANTA ROSA	PP 229 . . .	PP 294 MOHO

PP 230 Werner Globke, 11-04

D: . . . tons **S:** 25 kts **Dim:** 12 × 3 × . . . **A:** . . .
Electronics: Radar: 1 . . . nav.
M: 2 Caterpillar 275 diesels; 2 props; 550 bhp

Remarks: Modified *Dauntless*-class built indigenously. *Zorritos* entered service 23-9-03.

♦ 6 U.S. 40-foot Dauntless class
Bldr: SeaArk, Monticello, Ark. (In serv. 6-00 through 11-00)

PP 216 CHICAMA	PP 218 HORRILLOS	PP 220 CAMANÁ
PP 217 HUANCHACO	PP 219 CHANCAY	PP 221 CHALA

D: 12.25 tons (fl) **S:** 28 kts
Dim: 12.19 (11.13 wl) × 4.27 × 1.32 (max.; 0.69 hull)
A: 2 single 12.7-mm mg; 2 single 7.62-mm mg
Electronics: Radar: 1 Furuno 821 nav.
M: 2 Caterpillar 3208TA diesels; 2 props; 870 bhp (720 sust.)
Electric: 10 kw tot. (1 × 10-kw generator; 220 V, 60 Hz a.c.)
Range: 200/30; 400/22 **Fuel:** 500 gallons **Crew:** 5 tot.

Remarks: Ordered 2-00 via the U.S. DoD. Have aluminum-construction hull and superstructure, with bunks for four. Are fitted with Magellan 315 GPS and Motorola Astro Spectra VHF radio.

COAST GUARD PATROL BOATS [WPB] *(continued)*

Huanchaco (PP 217) Vladimir Lemonos, 4-03

♦ 2 Cougar 42–class port patrol launches
Bldr: Cougar Marine, Miami, Fla. (In serv. 1992–93)

PP 210 Río Supe PP 211 Río Vitor

Río Supe (PP 210) Peruvian Navy, 1999

D: 2.5 tons (fl) **S:** 40 kts **Dim:** 12.80 × 3.60 × 1.80
A: Small arms **Electronics:** Radar 1 . . . nav.
M: 2 Volvo Penta TAMD 62A outdrive diesels; 2 props; 500 bhp
Range: 240/ . . . **Crew:** 6 tot.

Remarks: Typed as *Patrulleras Interceptoras.* Resemble U.S. "cigarette boat" racing launches. GRP construction.

♦ 3 Cougar 25–class port patrol launches
Bldr: Cougar Marine, Miami, Fla. (In serv. 1992–93)

PP 212 Mancora PP 213 Huara PP 214 Quilca

Mancora (PP 212)—aboard *Callao* (DT 143) Vladimir Lemonos, 11-03

D: 1.5 tons (fl) **S:** 35 kts **Dim:** 6.80 × 2.20 × 0.40
A: Small arms **Electronics:** Radar: 1 . . . nav.
M: 1 Volvo Penta AD 41B outdrive diesel; 1 prop; 200 bhp
Range: 207/ . . . **Crew:** 3 tot.

Remarks: GRP construction. Typed as *Patrulleras de Puerto.*

♦ 1 Pucusana-class port patrol launch
Bldr: Construcciones Nauticas, Callao (In serv. . . .)

PP 215 Pucusana

D: 3.5 tons (fl) **S:** 30 kts **Dim:** 9.10 × 3.30 × 1.10
A: Small arms **Electronics:** Radar: . . .
M: 1 Volvo Penta KAD 42PA outdrive diesel; 1 prop; 230 bhp
Range: 500/ . . . **Crew:** 6 tot.

♦ 8 Cougar 22–class harbor patrol launches
Bldr: Cougar Marine, Miami, Fla. (In serv. 1992–93)

DCB 350 La Cruz DCB 353 Samanco DCB 356 Ancón
DCB 351 Cabo Blanco DCB 354 Besique DCB 357 Paracas
DCB 352 Colan DCB 355 Salinas

D: 1.5 tons (fl) **S:** 30 kts **Dim:** 6.60 × 2.20 × 0.90
A: Small arms **Electronics:** Radar: . . .
M: 1 Evinrude gasoline outboard; 200 bhp
Range: 120/ . . . **Crew:** 4 tot.

Remarks: GRP construction. Typed as *Embarcaciones de Control de Bahía.*

♦ 3 La Punta–class (Anchova design) port patrol
Bldr: MacLaren Estaleiros e Serviços Marítimos, Niteroi, Brazil (In serv. 1981–82)

PP 232 Río Santa PP 235 Río Viru PP 236 Río Lurin

Río Lurin (PP 236) Peruvian Navy, 2001

D: 43 tons (fl) **S:** 25 kts **Dim:** 18.6 × 5.35 × 1.6
A: 1 12.7-mm mg **Electronics:** Radar: 1 Raytheon . . . nav.
M: 2 G.M. Detroit Diesel 12V-71 T1 diesels; 2 props; 1,800 bhp
Range: 700/15 **Crew:** 7 tot.

Disposal note: The patrol launch *Río Surco* (PP 237) and three sisters had been withdrawn from service by 2004.

♦ 4 Río Santiago–class riverine patrol boats
Bldr: SIMA, Iquitos (In serv. . . .)

PF 260 Río Huallaga PF 262 Río Putumayo
PF 261 Río Santiago PF 263 Río Nanay

D: 4.2 tons (fl) **S:** 25 kts **Dim:** 10.00 × 2.55 × 1.55
A: 2 single 12.7-mm mg
M: 1 Volvo Penta KAD 42B outdrive diesel; 230 bhp
Range: 470/ . . . **Crew:** 4 tot.

Remarks: Aluminum construction. PF 263 has an Evinrude engine of 150 bhp and is consequently slower. Typed as *Patrulleras Fluviales.*

♦ 4 Río Napo–class riverine patrol boats
Bldr: SIMA, Iquitos (In serv. . . .)

PF 264 Río Napo PF 266 Río Matador
PF 265 Río Yavari PF 267 Río Pachitea

D: 1.8 tons (fl) **S:** 35 kts **Dim:** 6.75 × 2.28 × 0.60 **A:** Small arms
M: 2 Evinrude SE-150 WTPLY outboards; 300 bhp
Range: 200/ . . . **Crew:** 5 tot.

Remarks: Aluminum construction. Typed as *Patrulleras Fluviales.*

♦ 4 Río Itaya–class riverine patrol boats
Bldr: SIMA, Iquitos (In serv. . . .)

PF 270 Río Itaya PF 272 Río Zapote
PF 271 Río Patayacu PF 273 Río Chambira

D: 0.8 tons (fl) **S:** 20 kts **Dim:** 5.80 × 2.10 × 1.00
A: Small arms **M:** 1 Evinrude SE-150 WTPLY outboard; 150 bhp
Range: 140/ . . . **Crew:** 4 tot.

Remarks: Aluminum construction. PF 271 has two engines for 300 bhp total. Typed as *Patrulleras Fluviales.*

♦ 1 Río Tambopata–class riverine patrol boat
Bldr: SIMA, Iquitos (In serv. . . .)

PF 274 Río Tambopata

D: 1.5 tons (fl) **S:** 40 kts **Dim:** 8.30 × 2.20 × 0.90
A: Small arms **M:** 1 Evinrude SE-200 WTPLG outboard; 200 bhp
Range: 360/ . . . **Crew:** 5 tot.

COAST GUARD PATROL BOATS [WPB] *(continued)*

Remarks: Aluminum construction. Typed as *Patrulleras Fluviales.* Operates on the Río Madre de Dios.

♦ 3 P 33 class
Bldr: American Shipbuilding & Designs, Miami, Fla.

	In serv.
PL 290 Río Ramis (ex-P-33)	15-9-82
PL 291 Río Ilave	20-11-82
PL 292 Río Azangaro	4-2-83

Río Ramis (PL 290)—with previous pennant number American Shipbuilding, 1982

D: 4.8 tons (fl) **S:** 27 kts **Dim:** 10.06 (9.19 pp) × 3.35 × 0.76
A: 1 or 2 single 12.7-mm mg
Electronics: Radar: 1 Raytheon 2800 nav.
M: 2 Perkins ST-6-354-4M diesels; 2 props; 480 bhp
Range: 450/27 **Crew:** 4 tot.

Remarks: GRP construction with Kevlar armor. Employed on Lake Titicaca.

♦ 1 Río Zarumilla class
Bldr: Korody Marine, Viareggio, Italy (In serv. 5-9-60)

PC 242 Río Piura

D: 37 tons (fl) **S:** 18 kts **Dim:** 20.00 × 5.20 × 1.10
A: 1 20-mm 70-cal. Oerlikon Mk 10 AA; 1 12.7-mm mg
Electronics: Radar: 1 Raytheon 1900 Pathfinder nav.
M: 2 G.M. Detroit Diesel 8V71 diesels; 2 props; 1,200 bhp
Range: 1,000/14 **Crew:** 1 officer, 7 enlisted

Remarks: Sister *Río Zarumilla* (PC 240) was stricken in 1990 and *Río Tumbes* (PC 241) in 1994. The forward 40-mm gunmount was replaced by the 20-mm AA in 1992, and the after mounting has been replaced by the 12.7-mm mg.

SERVICE CRAFT

♦ 1 Largato-class ferry boat [WYFB]

MD 147 Lagarto

D: 30 tons (fl) **S:** . . . kts **Dim:** 16.0 × 9.0 × 1.2
M: 2 Harbormaster azimuthal drive diesels; 150 bhp

Remarks: Transferred from the *Ministerio de Transportes y Comunicaciones* during 3-79. Used as a ferry at Puerto Maldonado on the Río Madre de Dios.

PHILIPPINES

REPUBLIC OF THE PHILIPPINES

NAVY

Personnel: Approx. 24,000 total, including 7,600 marines. About 15,000 serve in the naval reserve force.

Organization and Bases: Headquarters at Manila. Principal base and repair facilities at Cavite on Manila Bay. In 1995, the navy was reorganized into a naval base at Cavite, plus four naval force bases: Naval Force North, headquartered at Cagayan; Naval Force West, at Palawan; Naval Force South, at Tawi-Tawi; and Naval Force Central, at Mactan. The Naval Station San Miguel, Zambales, is used for training. Naval Reservation Ternate is used for marine corps headquarters and training. Smaller outposts are located at Bonifacio, Cebu, Davao, Legaspi, Poro, and Zamboanga.

Naval Aviation: Four Philippine-assembled Pilatus-Britten-Norman BN-2 Defender light maritime patrol aircraft, two Cessna 117s and four MBB BO-105 helicopters. The air force has two Fokker F-27 Maritime patrol aircraft. Two of four refurbished former RAF C-130K Hercules transports ordered in 3-01 from Lockheed Martin for the Philippine Air Force are equipped with portable "interim long-range patrol" modules for coastal patrol and SAR missions.

Marine Corps: The force of three brigades and 10 battalions was reduced to two brigades and six battalions in 1995. Headquarters is at Ternate on Manila Bay, with major forces deployed to Mindanao and Palawan Islands. The marine corps operates U.S.-supplied LVTP-7 armored amphibious personnel carriers.

Note: Ship names are preceded by BRP (*Barko ng Republika ng Pilipinas,* or Ship of the Republic of the Philippines). In 3-03, the head of the Philippine House of Representatives, Defense Committee, revealed that only 56% of the fleet was operational.

PATROL SHIPS [PS]

♦ 1 ex-U.S. Cannon class
Bldr: Federal SB & DD Co., Newark, N.J.

	Laid down	L	In serv.
PF 11 Rajah Humabon (ex-*Hatsuhi;* ex-*Atherton,* DE 169)	14-1-43	27-5-43	29-8-43

Rajah Humabon (PF 11) John Mortimer, 5-98

D: 1,240 tons (1,620 fl) **S:** 20 kts **Dim:** 93.27 (91.44 wl) × 11.15 × 3.56 (hull)
A: 3 single 76.2-mm 50-cal. Mk 26 DP; 3 twin 40-mm 60-cal. Mk 1 Mod. 2 AA; 6 single 20-mm 70-cal Oerlikon Mk 10 AA; 4 single 12.7-mm mg
Electronics: Radar: 1 Raytheon SPS-64(V)11 nav.; 1 . . . nav.; 1 . . . nav.
M: 4 G.M. Electromotive Div. 16-278A diesels, electric drive; 2 props; 6,000 shp
Electric: 680 kw tot. **Range:** 11,600/11 **Fuel:** 260 tons **Crew:** 165 tot.

Remarks: Stricken in 1993 but restored to service at Cavite Dockyard in 1995, recommissioning during 1-96. Had been transferred to Japan from the USN on 14-6-55 and stricken 6-75, reverting to U.S. ownership. Sold to the Philippines 23-12-78, she remained laid up in Japan until towed to South Korea for overhaul in 1979. Sister *Datu Kalantiaw* (PS 76; ex-*Booth,* DE 170) was lost in a typhoon 21-9-81, and *Datu Sikatuna* (ex-*Amick,* DE 168) was stricken and discarded in 1989.
Combat systems: The entire ASW suite, with EDO SQS-17B hull-mounted sonar, a Mk 10 Hedgehog spiggot mortar, six Mk 6 depth charge mortars, and one Mk 9 depth charge rack, was removed prior to 1995. The obsolete 76.2-mm gun control systems have all been removed, and all guns are locally controlled using ringsights. As of 1998 it was planned to add antiship missiles to this aged unit, but none has been purchased to date.

♦ 2 ex-U.S. Auk-class former minesweepers
Bldrs: PS 70: Associated SB, Seattle, Wash.; PS 74: Savannah Machinery & Foundry, Savannah, Ga.

	Laid down	L	In serv.
PS 70 Quezon (ex-*Vigilance,* MSF 324)	28-11-42	5-4-43	28-2-44
PS 74 Rizal (ex-PS 69; ex-*Murrelet,* MSF 372)	24-8-44	29-12-44	21-8-45

Quezon (PS 70) John Mortimer, 5-98

D: 890 tons (1,250 fl) **S:** 18 kts **Dim:** 67.39 (65.53 wl) × 9.80 × 3.28
A: 2 single 76.2-mm 50-cal. Mk 26 DP; 2 twin 40-mm 60-cal. Mk 1 Mod. 2 AA; 2 single 20-mm 70-cal. Oerlikon Mk 4 AA; 4 single 12.7-mm mg
Electronics: Radar: 1 Raytheon SPS-64(V)11 nav.; 1 . . . nav.; 1 . . . nav.
M: 4 G.M. Electromotive Div. 12-278 diesels, electric drive; 2 props; 3,532 shp
Electric: 360 kw tot. **Range:** 4,300/10 **Fuel:** 216 tons **Crew:** 100 tot.

Remarks: PS 74 was transferred 18-6-65 and PS 70 on 19-8-67. Had been stricken at the end of 1994, but both were refitted at Cavite Dockyard during 1995. PS 74 completed restoration in 1-96 and was renumbered prior to recommissioning; PS 70 completed a rehabilitation overhaul in 4-96. They differ visually in that PS 70 has bulwarks to the hull sides amidships, while PS 74 does not. PS 74 sank a Chinese fishing boat in a collision on 23-5-99 off Scarborough Bank.

PATROL SHIPS [PS] *(continued)*

Rizal (PS 74) NAVPIC Holland, 11-00

Combat systems: All ASW equipment has been removed, though it is planned to add antiship missiles to these ships. The machineguns are mounted on the fantail and bridge wings; the remaining 20-mm mounts are before the pilothouse. There is no weapons-control system, and all guns are ringsight aimed.

♦ 6 ex-U.S. PCE 827 and PCER 848 classes

Bldrs: PS 19, 23: Pullman Standard Car Co., Chicago; PS 28: Albina Eng. & Machine Wks., Portland, Ore.; others: Willamette Iron & Steel Corp., Portland, Ore.

	Laid down	L	In serv.
PS 19 Miguel Malvar (ex-*Ngoc Hoi;* ex-*Brattleboro,* EPCER 852)	28-10-43	1-3-44	26-5-44
PS 22 Sultan Kudarat (ex-*Dong Da II;* ex-*Crestview,* PCE 895)	2-12-42	18-5-43	30-10-44
PS 23 Datu Marikudo (ex-*Van Kiep II;* ex-*Amherst,* PCER 853)	16-11-43	18-3-44	16-6-44
PS 28 Cebu (ex-PCE 881)	11-8-43	10-11-43	31-7-44
PS 31 Pangasinan (ex-PCE 891)	28-10-42	24-4-43	15-6-44
PS 32 Iloilo (ex-PCE 897)	16-12-42	3-8-43	6-1-45

Miguel Malvar (PS 19) NAVPIC Holland, 11-97

D: 903 tons (fl) **S:** 15 kts **Dim:** 56.24 (54.86 wl) × 10.08 × 2.87
A: 1 76.2-mm 50-cal. Mk 26 DP—PS 19 only: 2 twin 40-mm 60-cal. Mk 1 Mod. 2 AA—others: 3 single 40-mm 60-cal. Bofors Mk 3 AA; 4 single 20-mm 70-cal. U.S. Mk 68 AA; 4 single 12.7-mm mg
Electronics: Radar: 1 SPS-64(V)11 nav.; 1 SPS-64(V) . . . nav.
M: PS 22, 23, 32: 2 G.M. 12-278A diesels; 2 props; 2,000 bhp—PS 19, 28, 31: 2 G.M. 12-567A diesels; 2 props; 1,800 bhp
Electric: 240–280 kw tot. **Range:** 9,000/10 **Fuel:** 125 tons
Crew: 7 officers, 70 enlisted

Remarks: PS 28 through PS 32 were transferred in 7-48; one of these, *Leyte* (PS 30, ex-PCE 885), was lost by grounding in 1979. PS 19, 22, and 23 were transferred to South Vietnam 11-7-66, 29-11-61, and 6-70, respectively, and escaped Vietnam in 5-75; PS 19 and 22 were sold to the Philippines in 11-75, PS 23 on 5-4-76. PS 19 and PS 23 were built with longer forecastles as rescue ships. Sister *Negros Occidental* (PS 29, ex-U.S. PCE 884) was discarded during 1995 but remains afloat.
Combat systems: PS 19, 22, 31, and 32 completed two-year rehabilitations 1990–92 with revised armament and new radars and communications gear; PS 23 and PS 28 were refitted to the same standard in 1992–93. There is no weapons-control system; all guns are ringsight aimed.

♦ 1 ex-U.S. Admirable-class former minesweeper

Bldr: Winslow Marine Railway, Seattle

	Laid down	L	In serv.
PS 20 Magat Salamat (ex-*Chi Lang;* ex-*Gayety,* MSF 239)	14-11-43	19-3-44	23-9-45

Magat Salamat (PS 20) Philippine Navy, 1997

D: 650 tons light (905 fl) **S:** 14 kts **Dim:** 56.24 (54.86 wl) × 10.06 × 2.87
A: 1 76.2-mm 50-cal. Mk 26 DP; 2 single 40-mm 60-cal. Mk 3 AA; 4 single 20-mm 70-cal. Mk 68 AA; 4 single 12.7-mm mg
Electronics: Radar: 1 SPS-64(V)11 nav.
M: 2 . . . diesels; 2 props; 1,710 bhp **Electric:** 280 kw tot.
Range: 9,000/10 **Fuel:** 140 tons **Crew:** 7 officers, 70 enlisted

Remarks: Rehabilitated at Cavite Dockyard beginning late in 1995. Had been transferred to Vietnam in the mid-1960s, escaping to the Philippines in 4-75, and was formally acquired 11-75. The original Cooper-Bessemer GSD-8 diesels have probably been replaced.
Combat systems: There is no weapons-control system; all guns are ringsight aimed. The 76.2-mm gunmount has been provided with a shield.

PATROL COMBATANTS [PG]

♦ 3 ex-U.K. Peacock class

Bldr: Hall Russell, Aberdeen, Scotland

	Laid down	L	In serv.
PS 35 Emilio Jacinto (ex-*Peacock,* P 239)	29-1-82	1-12-82	12-10-83
PS 36 Apolinario Mabini (ex-*Plover,* P 240)	13-5-82	12-4-83	20-7-84
PS 37 Artemio Ricarte (ex-*Starling,* P 241)	9-9-82	7-9-83	10-8-84

Emilio Jacinto (PS 35) Navpic-Holland, 1-02

Apolinario Mabini (PS 36) Stefan Karpinski, 6-02

PATROL COMBATANTS [PG] *(continued)*

Apolinario Mabini (PS 36) Stefan Karpinski, 6-02

D: 664 tons (712 fl) **S:** 28 kts+ (25 sust.) **Dim:** 62.60 (60.00 pp) × 10.00 × 2.72
A: 1 76-mm 62-cal. OTO Melara Compact DP; 1 25-mm Bushmaster AA; 4 single 7.62-mm mg
Electronics:
Radar: 1 Kelvin-Hughes Type 1006 nav.
E/O: 1 Radamec 1500 tracking and surveillance
M: 2 APE-Crossley SEMT-Pielstick 18 PA6 V280 diesels; 2 3-bladed props; 14,188 bhp—1 Schottel S103 LSVEST drop-down, shrouded loiter prop; 181 shp
Electric: 755 kw tot. **Range:** 2,500/17 **Fuel:** 44 tons
Crew: 6 officers, 25 enlisted (44 tot. accomm.)

Remarks: Purchased 4-97 for about $20 million total, with turnover on 1-8-97 and recommissioning 4-8-97. Had been built for service at Hong Kong and became surplus when the colony was handed back to China on 30-6-97. Sisters *Swallow* (P 242) and *Swift* (P 243) returned to the U.K. 3-9-88 and were paid off and sold to Ireland 8-10-88.

During a two-year modernization program for the class begun during 2005 and completed by 12-06, all received a 25-mm 75-cal. Bushmaster gun aft, along with new electric and navigation systems, including a Rademac 1500 optronic fire-control system in place of the older Sea Archer fire-control radar. Later planned updates include new engines and new safety and training equipment.
Hull systems: Carry two Avon Searaider 5.4-m, 30-kt, 10-man semi-rigid rubber inspection dinghies and a small "fast patrol craft." Have two rudders. Reported to be bad rollers, requiring deeper bilge keels to be fitted.
Combat systems: Some 450 rounds of 76-mm ammunition can be carried, with the gun controlled by a GSA7 Sea Archer Mk 1 electro-optical director, to which a G.E.C. V3800 thermal imager was added in 1987. Have 2 50-mm rocket flare projectors. The Philippine Navy plans to add some sort of antiship missile to the ships, but due to top-weight problems, it would have to be a lightweight system such as Sea Skua; no missiles have been ordered to date.

PATROL CRAFT [PC]

♦ 1 ex-U.S. Cyclone class
Bldr: Bollinger Machine Shop & SY, Lockport, La.

	Laid down	L	In serv.
PS 38 General Mariano Alverez (ex-*Cyclone,* PC 1)	22-6-91	1-2-92	7-8-93

General Mariano Alverez (PS 38)—ex-*Cyclone,* shown while still in U.S. Service U.S. Navy

D: 352 tons light (387 fl) **S:** 35 kts (25 cruise) **Dim:** 54.36 (50.74 wl) × 7.62 × 2.44
A: 1 25-mm Mk 88 Bushmaster in in Mk 38 low-angle mount forward; 1 25-mm Bushmaster gun in Mk 96 stabilized mount aft
Electronics:
Radar: 1 Sperry Rascar 3400C X-band nav./surf. search; 1 Sperry Rascar 3400C S-band nav./surf. search
Sonar: Wesmar side-scanning hull-mounted HF
EW: APR-39(V)1 Privateer radar warning; Mk 52 Mod. 0 decoy syst. (2 6-round Mk 137 RL)
E/O: Marconi Vistar FLIR
M: 4 Paxman Valenta 16V RP-200 CM diesels; 4 5-bladed props; 13,400 bhp
Electric: 310 kw tot. (2 × 155-kw Caterpillar 3306 DIT Series C diesel sets)
Range: 595/35; 3,000+/12 **Fuel:** 40 tons
Endurance: 10 days **Crew:** 4 officers, 24 enlisted

Remarks: Decommissioned from the USN on 29-2-00 and transferred to the U.S. Coast Guard 1-3-00 but immediately laid up due to lack of operating funds. Transferred to the Philippines on 6-3-03.
Hull systems: Has Vosper fin stabilization system and a stern wedge to improve trim at high speeds. Kevlar armor is fitted to the command space. Minimum speed is 3 kts. Prior to final delivery, the vessel received a "stern ramp" modification upgrade known as the Combat Craft Retrieval System (CCRS) and previously applied to four of the USN's *Cyclone*-class fleet in order to accommodate an RIB on the ramp.
Combat systems: The Sperry Vision 2100M combat system employs the navigational radars and the Sperry Voyage Management System integrated navigation and control system as a combat data suite. Has a Sperry Marine automated Integrated Bridge System (IBS). Navigation systems include GPS and Loran receivers. Radio gear includes LST-5C SATCOM/line-of-sight UHF transceiver, A5 Spectra VHF radio, ICM120 Marine Band radio, and RF 5000 HF, VRC-92A VHF, and VRC-83(V)2 VHF/UHF transceivers. SAT-2A infrared signaling systems are fitted, and the Marconi Vistar stabilized FLIR sensor with integral low-light-level television camera is mounted on the mast. The sonar transducer is retracted within the hull at speeds above 14 kts.

♦ 2 (+ 1 + 3) Gen. Emilio Aguinaldo class
Bldr: Cavite NSY

	Laid down	L	In serv.
PG 140 Gen. Emilio Aguinaldo	. . .	23-6-84	21-11-90
PG 141 Gen. Antonio Luna	2-12-90	23-6-92	1999
PG 142 . . .	14-2-94	4-00	. . .

Gen. Antonio Luna (PG 141)—being moved by two Philippine Navy tugs while still not quite complete Leo Dirkx, 5-99

D: 215 tons (279 fl) **S:** 18 kts **Dim:** 44.0 × 6.2 × 1.6
A: 2 single 40-mm 60-cal. Bofors Mk 3 AA; 2 single 20-mm 70-cal. Oerlikon AA; 4 single 12.7-mm mg
Electronics: Radar: 1 . . . nav.
M: 4 G.M. Detroit Diesel 12V92 TA diesels; 4 props; 2,040 bhp
Range: 1,100/18 **Crew:** 6 officers, 52 enlisted

Remarks: PG 140 was originally to have carried antiship missiles; press reports indicate she was not finally commissioned until 6-92, and no missiles have been carried since. PG 141 was launched as indicated but did not begin fitting out until 1994 budget funding was provided; she has yet to be formally commissioned. PG 142 was officially begun 23-6-92, but little work has been accomplished. Three more are planned, and if funds are available, their armament would be changed to one 76-mm OTO Melara Compact DP and an OTO Melara twin 25-mm AA; due to the extensive superstructure and its attendant topweight, however, the installation of additional armament does not seem practicable. The design is overloaded and underpowered; the basic hull design was evolved from that of the *Katapangan* class.

♦ 3 Katapangan class

	Bldr	In serv.
P 101 Kagitingan	W. Müller, Hameln, Germany	9-2-79
P 102 Bagong Lakas	W. Müller, Hameln, Germany	9-2-79
P 103 Katapangan	Cavite NSY	1982

D: 132 tons (150 fl) **S:** 16 kts **Dim:** 37.0 × 6.2 × 1.7
A: 1 twin 30-mm 75-cal. Emerlec EX-31 AA; 4 single 12.7-mm mg; 2 single 7.62-mm mg
Electronics: Radar: 1 . . . nav.
M: 2 MTU MB 12V493 TZ60 diesels; 2 props; 2,050 bhp
Crew: 4 officers, 26 enlisted

Remarks: Unsuccessful design that could not approach designed speed of 28 kts. Had been discarded by 1992, but were rehabilitated under the 1994 budget. A fourth unit, *Bagong Silang,* was never completed at Cavite.

♦ 5 ex-South Korean Sea Dolphin class (PKM 200 series)
Bldrs: Korea-Tacoma SY, Chinhae, and Korea SB & Eng., Masan (In serv. 1970s–80s)

PG 110 Tomas Batillo
PG 111 Boni Serrano
PG 112 Bienvenido Salting
PG 114 Salvador Abcede
PG 115 Ramon Aguirre

D: 113 tons (143 fl) **S:** 38 kts **Dim:** 33.10 (31.25 wl) × 6.92 × 1.75 (2.45 props)
A: 1 40-mm 60-cal. Bofors Mk 3 AA; 1 twin 30-mm 90-cal. Emerlec AA; 2 single 20-mm 70-cal. Oerlikon Mk 10 AA; 2 single 7.62-mm M2 mg
Electronics: Radar: 1 Raytheon 1645 nav./surf. search
M: 2 MTU 16V538 TB90 diesels; 2 props; 10,800 bhp (9,000 sust.)
Electric: 100 kw tot. (2 × 50-kw diesel sets)
Range: 500/32; 1,000/20 **Fuel:** 15 tons **Crew:** 5 officers, 26 enlisted

PATROL CRAFT [PC] *(continued)*

Sea Dolphin–class unit in South Korean service—Philippine Navy version has an open 40-mm mount on fantail, a twin 30-mm mount forward (as here), and single 20-mm mounts on bridge wings; the masts have also been changed to four-legged lattice structures H&L Van Ginderen, 5-97

Remarks: Five units from the PKM 200 series—the former PKM 225, 226, 229, 231, and 235—were transferred to the Philippines 15-6-95 and arrived 8-95. After refurbishment PG 110–112 and PG 114 were recommissioned 22-5-96. Two more were apparently employed as cannibalization spares. Designed for 38 kts; can now make only 32 kts continuous.

PATROL BOATS [PB]

♦ 22 U.S. 78-foot class

Bldrs: PG 370–381 and five others: Trinity-Equitable SY, New Orleans; others: Marine Division, Atlantic, Gulf & Pacific Co. (AG&P SY), Manila

	In serv.
PG 370 Jose Andrada	8-90
PG 371 Enrique Jurado	24-6-91
PG 372 Alfredo Peckson	24-6-91
PG 374 Simeon Castro	24-6-91
PG 375 Carlos Albert	1-92
PG 376 Heracleo Alano	1-92
PG 377 Liberato Picar	1-92
PG 378 Hilario Ruiz	1-6-95
PG 379 Rafael Pargas	1-6-95
PG 380 Nestor Reinoso	1-6-95
PG 381 Dioscoro Papa	1-6-95
PG 383 Ismael Lomibao	1995
PG 384 Leovigildo Antioque	22-5-96
PG 385 Federico Martir	22-5-96
PG 386 Filipino Flojo	22-5-96
PG 387 Anastacio Cacayorin	1996
PG 388 Manuel Gomez	1996
PG 389 Teotimo Figuracion	1996
PG 390 José Loor Sr.	1997
PG 392 Juan Magluyan	3-98
PG 393 Florenca Nuño	5-98
PG 395 Felix Apolinario	1999

Florenca Nuño (PG 393)—with 25-mm gun forward H&L Van Ginderen/C. Delgoffe, 5-00

Hilario Ruiz (PG 378) H&L Van Ginderen/Brian Morrison, 5-98

D: 56.4 tons (fl) **S:** 28 kts **Dim:** 23.66 × 6.06 × 1.01 (hull; 1.76 props)
A: Five or more: 1 25-mm 75-cal. Mk 38 Mod. 0 Bushmaster low-angle—all: 2 or 4 single 12.7-mm M3 mg; 2 single 7.62-mm mg
Electronics: Radar: 1 Raytheon SPS-64(V)11
M: 2 G.M. 16V92 TAB diesels; 2 props; 2,800 bhp
Electric: 70 kw (2 × 35-kw diesel sets) **Range:** 600/24, 1,200/12
Fuel: 18,950 liters **Endurance:** 5 days **Crew:** 2 officers, 8 enlisted

Remarks: First four were ordered in 9-89 for $9.4 million; the fifth was ordered in 4-90 and three more in 8-90. In 3-93 Halter received a $36.2 million (U.S.) contract to build four more in the U.S., provide four kits to a yard in the Philippines, and assist in the construction of three more in a Philippine yard; in 6-94 another 12 were ordered for $27.5 million, with seven to be built by AG&P Shipyard in the Philippines. DF 379 and 380 were launched 29-4-95 by AG&P. The original goal was 35 total, but that was curtailed for lack of funds. Were originally intended to operate in flotillas of seven, each attached to a larger patrol boat acting as leader.
Hull systems: Aluminum construction. A 4-m rigid inflatable boat powered by a 40-bhp outboard motor is stowed amidships.
Combat systems: The design made provision to install a 40-mm Mk. 3 gun on the foredeck and an 80-mm mortar aft, but current plans call for eventual installation of a 25-mm mount forward on all. Carry 4,000 rounds of 12.7-mm and 2,000 rounds of 7.62-mm ammunition. Usually carry two "big eyes" binoculars on tripod mounts, one on the forecastle and one just abaft the mast. Some have a second navigational radar. PG 383 and PG 392 were photographed during 12-03 with what appeared to be a bulletproof covering over the pilothouse windows.

♦ 4 U.S. Swift Mk III class

Bldr: Peterson Bldrs, Sturgeon Bay, Wis. (In serv. 1975–76)

PCF 351 PCF 352 PCF 353 PCF 354

PCF 351—with guns temporarily dismounted H&L Van Ginderen/Brian Morrison, 5-98

D: 28 tons (36.7 fl) **S:** 30 kts **Dim:** 19.78 × 5.5 × 1.8
A: 1 twin and 2 single 12.7-mm mg **Electronics:** Radar: 1 Koden . . . nav.
M: 3 G.M. 8V71 TI diesels; 3 props; 1,950 bhp **Range:** 500/30 **Crew:** 8 tot.

Remarks: Aluminum construction. Pilothouse offset to starboard. Ten sisters serve in the Philippine Coast Guard.

♦ 10 South Korean Schoolboy/Sea Hawk class

Bldrs: Korea SB & Eng., Masan, and Korea-Tacoma SY, Chinhae (In serv. 1974–79)

PG 841 Conrado Yap
PG 842 Tedorico Dominado Jr.
PG 843 Cosme Acosta
PG 844 José Artiaga Jr.
PG 846 Nicanor Jimenez
PG 847 Léopoldo Regis
PG 848 Léon Tadina
PG 849 Loreto Danipog
PG 851 Apollo Tiano
PG 853 Sulpicio Fernandez

D: 72 tons (80 fl) **S:** 40 kts **Dim:** 25.37 × 5.40 × 1.20
A: 1 40-mm/60-cal. Bofors Mk 3 AA; 2 single 20-mm 70-cal. Oerlikon Mk 10 AA; 2 single 12.7-mm mg; 2 single 7.62-mm mg
Electronics: Radar: 1 Raytheon 1645 nav.
M: 2 MTU 16V538 TD90 diesels; 2 props; 5,200 bhp
Range: 500/20; 600/17 **Crew:** 6 officers, 19 enlisted

Remarks: Transferred to the Philippines as the result of an agreement reached in late 5-93 for a token $100 (U.S.) each. Eight were commissioned in the Philippines 23-6-93, the others on 23-6-94. Have been rearmed with spare weapons from Philippine Navy inventory. Two sisters, to have been numbered PG 845 and PG 852, have not yet been reactivated and were probably employed as cannibalization spares.

♦ 2 ex-U.S. Coast Guard 82-foot Point class

Bldr: PG 394: J. Martinac SB, Tacoma, Wash. (PG 396: U.S. Coast Guard Yard, Curtis Bay, Md.)

	In serv.
PG 394 Alberto Navaret (ex-*Point Evans,* WPB 82354)	10-1-67
PG 396 Abraham Campo (ex-*Point Doran,* WPB 82375)	1-6-70

D: 64 tons (66 fl) **S:** 23.7 kts **Dim:** 25.3 × 5.23 × 1.95
A: 2 single 12.7-mm M2 mg
Electronics: Radar: 1 Hughes-Furuno SPS-73 nav.
M: 2 Cummins VT-12-M diesels; 2 props; 1,600 bhp—*or* 2 Caterpillar 3412 diesels; 2 props; 1,480 bhp
Range: 490/23.7; 1,500/8 **Fuel:** 5.7 tons **Crew:** 1 officer, 7 enlisted

Remarks: PG 394 was transferred by donation 1-12-99 and PG 396 on 6-3-01 (and recommissioned 5-12-01 in the Philippines). Mild steel hull. High-speed diesels are controlled from the bridge. PG 396 displaces 69 tons (fl), can achieve 22.6 knots, and has a range of 320 n.m. at 22.6 kts or 1,200 n.m. at 8 kts. The armament listed is that aboard in USCG service; it may be augmented with additional 12.7-mm and/or 7.62-mm mg in Philippine service.

AMPHIBIOUS WARFARE SHIPS

♦ 2 U.S. Army Gen. Frank S. Besson–class vehicle landing ships [LST]
Bldr: Halter Marine–Moss Point Marine, Escatawpa, Miss.

	In serv.
LC 550 Bacolod City	3-12-93
LC 551 Dagupan City (ex-*Cagayan de Oro*)	23-6-94

Dagupan City (LC 551) Takatoshi Okano, 10-98

D: 1,678 tons light (4,265 fl) **S:** 12 kts (11.6 sust.)
Dim: 83.14 (78.03 pp) × 18.28 (18.16 wl) × 3.66 (max.)
A: 2 single 20-mm 70-cal. Oerlikon Mk 10 AA; 2 single 12.7-mm M2 mg
Electronics: Radar: 1 Raytheon SPS-64(V)2 nav.; 1 Raytheon SPS-64(V)2 nav.
M: 2 G.M. EMD 16-645-E2 diesels; 2 props; 3,900 bhp—bow-thruster (250 shp)
Electric: 500 kw (2 × 250-kw diesel sets) **Range:** 8,358/11
Fuel: 524 tons **Endurance:** 38 days **Crew:** 6 officers, 24 enlisted

Remarks: Ordered 3-4-92 under the U.S. Aid Program, with the contract administered by the U.S. Army. Design is based on the Australian roll-on/roll-off beachable cargo ship *Frances Bay.* Built to commercial specifications.
Hull systems: Can transport up to 1,815 metric tons of vehicles or cargo containers on the 975-m^2 cargo deck; beaching load is 900 tons on a 1:30 gradient. Can also carry up to 122 tons of potable water. Have a bow ramp of 8.23-m width, but no stern ramp as on U.S. Army examples; instead, the pair have a helicopter deck and accommodations for 150 troops aft. Carry two LCVP landing craft in davits amidships.

♦ 5 ex-U.S. LST 1– and LST 542–class landing ships [LST]
Bldrs: LT 86, 87: Bethlehem Steel, Hingham, Mass.; LT 501: American Bridge, Ambridge, Pa.; LT 504: Missouri Valley Bridge & Iron Co., Evansville, Ind.; LT 516: Dravo Corp., Pittsburgh, Pa.

	In serv.
LT 86 Zamboanga del Sur (ex-*Marion County,* T 975)	3-2-45
LT 87 Cotabato del Sur (ex-*Thi Nai;* ex-*Cayuga County,* LST 529)	28-2-44
LT 501 Laguna (ex-T-LST 230)	3-11-43
LT 504 Lanao del Norte (ex-T-LST 566)	29-5-44
LT 516 Kalinga Apayo (ex-AE 516; ex-*Can Tho;* ex-*Garrett County,* AGP 786, ex-LST 786)	28-8-44

Lanao del Norte (LT 504) C. Schaefer, 3-97

D: 1,620 tons (4,080 fl) **S:** 11 kts **Dim:** 99.98 (96.32 wl) × 15.24 × 4.29
A: LT 86, 87, 516 only: 2 twin 40-mm 60-cal. Mk 1 Mod. 2 Bofors AA; 2 single 40-mm 60-cal. Bofors Mk 3 AA—all: 4 single 20-mm 70-cal. Oerlikon AA
Electronics: Radar: 1 Raytheon SPS-64(V)11 nav.
M: 2 G.M. 12-567A diesels; 2 props; 1,700 bhp **Electric:** 300 kw tot.
Range: 15,000/9 **Fuel:** 570 tons **Crew:** 60–100 tot.

Remarks: LT 86 was transferred 15-10-76; later deactivated, she was recommissioned 21-11-90. LT 87 escaped from South Vietnam (to which she had been transferred in 12-63) in 4-75 and was officially transferred to the Philippines 17-11-75; stricken in 1993, she was restored to service in 1995 and is now configured as a command center for disaster relief operations. LT 501 and LT 504 were purchased in 1976, having previously been stricken by the USN and laid up in Japan. LT 516 was transferred to South Vietnam in 4-71, escaped in 4-75, and was purchased by the Philippines 13-9-77. LT 501 and LT 504 were rehabilitated during 1992–93; none of the other survivors are in good condition.
Hull systems: LT 516 was converted during the mid-1960s to serve as a smallcraft tender; she retains operational bow doors, but much of the cargo deck is filled with repair shops and bins for spare parts. The ship has a helicopter deck amidships and a 10-ton derrick tending an enlarged hatch.
Disposals: Stricken have been *Agusan del Sur* (LT 54; ex-*Nha Trang;* ex-*Jerome County,* LST 848), *Mindoro Occidental* (LT 93, ex-T-LST 222), *Suragao del Norte* (LT 94, ex-T-LST 488), *Suragao del Sur* (LT 95, ex-T-LST 546), *Maquindanao* (LT 96; ex-*Caddo Parish,* LST 515), *Cagayan* (LT 97; ex-*Hickman County,* LST 825), *Ilocos Norte* (LT 98; ex-*Madeira County,* LST 905), *Tarlac* (LT 500, ex-T-LST-47), *Samar Oriental* (LT 502, ex-T-LST 287), *Lanao del Sur* (LT 503, ex-T-LST 491), *Leyte del Sur* (LT 505, ex-T-LST 607), *Davao Oriental* (LT 506; ex-*Oosumi;* ex-*Daggett County,* LST 689), *Aurora* (LT 508; ex-*Harris County,* T-LST 822), *Samar del Norte* (LT 510; ex-*Shiretoko;* ex-*Nansemond County,* LST 1064), *Cotabato del Norte* (LT 511; ex-*Orleans Parrish,* T-LST 1069, ex-MCS 6, ex-LST 1069), and *Tawi-Tawi* (LT 512, ex-T-LST 1072). The *Sierra Madre* (LT 57; ex-AL 57; ex-*Dumaguet;* ex-South Vietnamese *My Tho;* ex-U.S. *Harnett County,* AGP 821; ex-LST 821) ran aground in 1999 on the Spratley Islands, where the hulk is now employed as a observation station. *Benguet* (LT 507; ex-*Davies County,* T-LST 692) grounded on Scarborough Shoal in the South China Sea 3-11-99; she was pulled off on 30-11-99 but found not worth repairing and stricken during 2000.

♦ 7 U.S. LCM(8)-class landing craft [LCM]

LCM 260 through LCM 266

D: 118 tons (fl) **S:** 9 kts **Dim:** 22.43 × 6.42 × 1.4 (aft)
M: 4 G.M. 6-71 diesels; 2 props; 600 bhp **Range:** 140/9 **Crew:** 3 tot.

Remarks: Transferred 19-3-75. Cargo capacity: 54 tons or 120 troops. LCM 260 sank during a typhoon 13-11-90 but was restored to service.

♦ 11 ex-U.S. LCM(6)-class landing craft [LCM]

D: 24 tons (56 fl) **S:** 10 kts **Dim:** 17.07 × 4.37 × 1.17 (aft)
M: 2 G.M. Gray Marine 64HN9 diesels; 2 props; 330 bhp
Range: 130/9 **Crew:** 3 tot.

Remarks: Transferred 1955–75. Cargo capacity: 30 tons or 80 troops. Sixty-nine others have been discarded or converted to service craft.

♦ 7 U.S. Mini-ATC class [LCP]
Bldr: Tacoma BY, Tacoma, Wash. (In serv. 1978)

D: 9.3 tons light (13 fl) **S:** 28.5 kts **Dim:** 10.97 × 3.89 × 0.30
A: Up to 4 single 12.7-mm mg; 1 40-mm Mk 19 grenade launcher; 1 60-mm M 60 mortar
M: 2 G.M. 8V53N diesels; 2 Jacuzzi 14Y waterjets; 566 bhp
Range: 37/28 **Crew:** 2 tot. + 15 troops

Remarks: Aluminum construction; rectangular planform. Can carry small radar. Very quiet in operation. Three others have been discarded.

♦ 2 Aquatrack amphibious vehicles [LCP]
Bldr: GKN Defence, Telford, U.K. (In serv. 1995)

D: 13.5 tons (fl) **S:** 6 kts in water/40 kph on land
Dim: 9.21 × 3.20 × 3.15 (high)
M: 1 Deutz BF8L513 diesel; 2 CP props; 315 bhp
Range: 500 km/40 kph (on land) **Crew:** 2 tot. + 2 passengers

Remarks: Operated by the Philippine Marines for the Mount Pinatubo Rescue Team. Running gear duplicates that of an M 113 armored personnel carrier, and the tracks contribute to afloat propulsion. Able to beach through 3-m seas. Can operate in Sea State 5. Has a 4.3 × 2.6-m open cargo deck and stern ramp aft, capable of carrying 5 tons of cargo or a light truck.

AUXILIARIES

♦ 1 ex-U.S. Alamosa-class cargo ship [AK]
Bldr: Froemming Bros., Milwaukee, Wis. (In serv. 22-9-45)

AC 90 Mactan (ex-TK 90; ex-*Kukui,* WAK 186; ex-*Colquitt,* AK 174)

Mactan (AC 90) Douglas A. Cromby, 9-92

D: 4,900 tons (7,450 fl) **S:** 12 kts **Dim:** 103.18 (97.54 pp) × 15.24 × 6.43
A: 2 single 20-mm 70-cal. Oerlikon Mk 10 AA; 2 single 12.7-mm mg
Electronics: Radar: 1 Raytheon SPS-64(V)11 nav.; 1 . . . nav.
M: 1 Nordberg TSM6 diesel; 1 prop; 1,750 bhp **Electric:** 500 kw tot.
Fuel: 350 tons **Crew:** 85 tot.

Remarks: 6,071 dwt. Built for the U.S. Maritime Commission, taken over by the USN on completion, then transferred to the U.S. Coast Guard 24-9-45. Transferred to the Philippines on 29-2-72. Was to have been stricken during 1994 but remains in commission. The first platform deck in the cargo hold was converted to passenger accommodations while the ship was in USCG service. Is employed as a military transport, supply ship, and lighthouse tender and normally stows one LCM(6) or LCVP landing craft amidships for use as a supply tender.

♦ 1 troop transport [AP]
Bldr: Ishikawajima-Harima, Tokyo (In serv. 1959)

AT 25 Ang Pangulo (ex-TP 777, ex-*The President,* ex-*Roxas,* ex-*Lapu-Lapu*)

AUXILIARIES *(continued)*

Ang Pangulo (AT 25) Leo Dirkx, 5-99

D: 2,239 tons (2,727 fl) **S:** 18 kts **Dim:** 83.84 (78.50 pp) × 13.01 × 6.4
A: 2 single 20-mm 70-cal. Oerlikon Mk 10 AA—2 single 12.7-mm mg
Electronics: Radar: 2 . . . nav.
M: 2 Mitsui–Burmeister & Wain DE 642 VBF 75 diesels; 2 props; 5,000 bhp
Electric: 820 kw tot. **Range:** 6,900/15
Crew: 8 officers, 73 enlisted + 48 passengers

Remarks: Built as part of Japan's war reparations. Initially employed as a presidential yacht and command ship. Was in Hong Kong for sale in 1986 and remained away from the Philippines during the initial period of former President Marcos's exile. On return to Philippine waters was redesignated a troop transport, a role for which she is not particularly well equipped. By 5-96 she was again being referred to as the presidential yacht.

♦ 1 ex-U.S. Achelous-class repair ship [AR]
Bldr: Chicago Bridge & Iron Co., Seneca, Ill.

	L	In serv.
AD 617 Yakal (ex-AR 517; ex-*Satyr,* ARL 23; ex-LST 852)	13-11-44	24-11-44

D: 3,960 tons (fl) **S:** 11.6 kts **Dim:** 99.98 (96.32 wl) × 15.24 × 3.71
A: 1 quadruple 40-mm 60-cal. Bofors Mk 2 AA; 5 twin 20-mm 70-cal. Oerlikon Mk 24 AA
Electronics: Radar: 1 Raytheon SPS-64(V)11 nav.
M: 2 G.M. 12-567A diesels; 2 props; 1,800 bhp **Electric:** 420 kw tot.
Fuel: 620 tons **Crew:** 250 tot.

Remarks: Transferred 24-1-77. Was converted during construction to serve as a repair ship, with shops installed in the former tank deck and wing compartments.
Hull systems: Has a 60-ton capacity A-frame lift boom to port, one 10-ton derrick, and one 20-ton derrick. The bow doors have been welded shut.
Disposals: *Kamagong* (AR 67; ex-*Aklan;* ex-*Romulus,* ARL 22; ex-LST 926) was discarded during 1989 and *Narra* (AR 88; ex-*Krishna,* ARL 38; ex-LST 1149) during 1992.

Note: Two small vessels described as "research ships" were acquired in 1993: *Fort San Antonio* (AM 700) and *Fort Abad* (AM 701); no data available.

SERVICE CRAFT

♦ 1 ex-U.S. YCV 3–class former aircraft transport barge [YC]
Bldr: Pearl Harbor NSY (In serv. 25-11-43)

YB 206 (ex-YCV 7)

Dim: 33.53 × 9.14 × . . . **Cargo capacity:** 250 tons

Remarks: Transferred 5-63. Used as a general-purpose barge.

♦ 2 ex-U.S. Navy barges [YC]

	Transferred
YC 227 (ex-YC 1402)	8-59
YC 301 (ex-YC 1403)	8-71

Dim: 24.38 × 8.73 × 1.22

♦ 1 ex-U.S. 30-ton-capacity floating crane [YD]

	In serv.	Transferred
YU 206 (ex-YD 163)	12-5-46	1-71

D: 650 tons (fl) **Dim:** 36.58 × 13.72 × 2.13

♦ 1 ex-U.S. 60-ton-capacity floating crane [YD]

	In serv.	Transferred
YU 207 (ex-YD 191)	3-52	8-71

D: 920 tons (fl) **Dim:** 36.58 × 18.24 × 2.13

♦ 1 ex-U.S. Army 230-class 100-ton-capacity floating crane [YD]

	L	Transferred
YD 202 (ex-BCL 1791)	1943	7-49

D: 2,100 tons (fl) **Dim:** 64.0 × 12.5 × 3.4

♦ 2 ex-U.S. AFDL floating dry docks [YFDL]
Bldr: V.P. Loftis, Wilmington, N.C. (In serv. 1944–45)

YD 205 (ex-AFDL 44) YD . . . (ex-AFDL 40)

Lift capacity: 2,800 tons **Dim:** 118.6 × 25.6 × 3.1 (light)

Remarks: YD 205 was transferred during 9-69 and purchased outright on 1-8-80. Ex-AFDL 40 was purchased on 30-6-90.

♦ 2 ex-U.S. AFDL 1–class floating dry docks [YFDL]

	Bldr	In serv.
YD 200 (ex-AFDL 24)	Doullet & Ewin, Mobile, Ala.	1-44
YD 204 (ex-AFDL 20)	G. D. Auchter, Jacksonville, Fla.	6-44

Lift capacity: 1,000 tons **Dim:** 60.96 × 19.51 × 1.04 (light)

Remarks: YD 200 was transferred during 7-48. YD 204 was loaned during 10-61 and purchased 1-8-80.

♦ 1 Ang Pinuno–class presidential yacht [YFL]
Bldr: Vosper Pty., Singapore (In serv. 12-77)

TP 77 Ang Pinuno

D: 150 tons **S:** 28.5 kts **Dim:** 37.9 × 7.2 × . . .
M: 3 MTU 12538 TB91 diesels; 3 props; 7,500 bhp

Remarks: Stricken in 1995 but restored to service in 1998–99 at Cavite. Painted white.

♦ 1 or more converted LCM(6) personnel launches [YFL]

286 and others

D: 24 tons (56 fl) **S:** 10 kts **Dim:** 17.07 × 4.37 × 1.17 (aft)
M: 2 G.M. Gray Marine 64HN9 diesels; 2 props; 330 bhp
Range: 130/9 **Crew:** 3 tot.

Remarks: Former U.S.-built landing craft, with the tank deck enclosed to accommodate seated passengers and the bow ramp plated up.

♦ 1 dredge [YMN]

SDP-1

Naval dredge SDP-1 Leo Dirkx, 5-99

Remarks: No data available.

♦ 2 ex-U.S. 174-foot YOG-class small tankers [YO]
Bldr: Puget Sound NSY, Bremerton, Wash.

	Laid down	L	In serv.
AF 72 Lake Taal (ex-YO 72, ex-YOG . . .)	. . .	. . .	14-4-45
AF 78 Lake Buhi (ex-YO 78, ex-YOG 73)	15-12-43	23-2-44	28-11-44

D: 445 tons light (1,420 fl) **S:** 8 kts **Dim:** 53.04 × 10.01 × 4.27
A: 1 20-mm 70-cal. Mk 10 Oerlikon AA **Electronics:** Radar: 1 . . . nav.
M: 2 G.M. 8-278A diesels; 2 props; 640 bhp **Fuel:** 25 tons
Crew: 5 officers, 25 enlisted

Remarks: Transferred 7-67; had been used as gasoline tanker by the USN. Ex-U.S. YOG 33 and YOG 80, which escaped from Vietnam, were used for cannibalization spares. Cargo capacity: 985 tons. Sister *Lake Mainit* (YO 35) was stricken during 1979 and *Lake Naujan* (YO 43, ex-YO 173) in 1989.

♦ 1 or more medium harbor tugs [YTM]

YQ . . . Lilimbon

Lilimbon—tug assigned to the Philippine Navy Seabees Leo Dirkx, 5-99

Remarks: No characteristics data available. Is attached to the Philippine Navy Construction Corps.

♦ 2 ex-U.S. YTL 442–class small harbor tugs [YTL]
Bldr: Everett-Pacific Co., Everett, Wash.

YQ 223 Tagbanua (ex-YTL 429) YQ 225 Ilongot (ex-YTL 427)

SERVICE CRAFT *(continued)*

YTL 442–class tug—renumbered 2000 and equipped for firefighting
H&L Van Ginderen/Brian Morrison, 5-98

D: 70 tons (80 fl) **S:** 9 kts **Dim:** 20.17 × 5.18 × 1.5
M: 1 Hamilton 685A diesel; 300 bhp

Remarks: Built 1944–45; transferred 5-63 and 8-71. At least one is now equipped as a fireboat; renumbered 2000 in 1998, the craft has two firefighting monitors.

♦ 1 ex-U.S. YTM 764–class fireboat [YTR] (In serv. 1945)

YQ . . . Fire Tug (ex-*Hiamonee,* YTM 776)

Fire tug—the former U.S. *Hiamonee* (YTM 776), still without a Philippine Navy pennant number H&L Van Ginderen/Brian Morrison, 5-98

D: 260 tons (350 fl) **S:** 11 kts **Dim:** 30.8 × 8.5 × 3.7
M: 2 Enterprise diesels; 1 prop; 1,270 bhp **Crew:** 8 tot.

Remarks: Purchased 30-6-90; had been stricken from the USN 30-11-86. Is employed as a fireboat and general-purpose tug, although only one firefighting monitor is fitted, atop the pilothouse.

♦ 2 ex-U.S. 174-foot YW-class water tankers [YW]

Bldrs: AW 33: Marine Iron & SB Co., Duluth, Minn.; AW 34: Leatham D. Smith SB, Sturgeon Bay, Wis.

	Laid down	L	In serv.
AW 33 Lake Buluan (ex-YW 111)	30-9-44	16-12-44	1-8-45
AW 34 Lake Paoay (ex-YW 130)	14-5-45	24-6-45	28-8-45

Lake Paoay (AW 34)—with patrol boat *Teotimo Figuracion* (PG 389) alongside
NAVPIC Holland, 12-97

D: 440 tons light (1,390 fl) **S:** 8 kts **Dim:** 53.04 × 10.01 × 4.0
A: 1 40-mm 60-cal. Bofors Mk 3 AA; 1 20-mm 70-cal Oerlikon AA
Electronics: Radar: 1 . . . nav.
M: 2 G.M. 8-278A diesels; 2 props; 640 bhp **Electric:** 80 kw
Fuel: 25 tons **Crew:** 5 officers, 25 enlisted

Remarks: Transferred 16-7-75. Cargo capacity: 930 tons. Sister *Lake Lanao* (YW 42, ex-U.S. YW 125) was stricken during 1989.

COAST GUARD

Note: Given autonomous status from the Philippine Navy and transferred from the Department of National Defense to the Department of Transportation and Communication on 23-11-96, the size of the Philippine Coast Guard has fluctuated widely since its establishment in the early 1970s. At one time, it had responsibility for maintaining navigational aids and included many of the tenders now returned to the navy. Up to 60 new patrol craft are desired, but funds are lacking. The coast guard has eight districts comprising a total of 60 stations. In addition to the units listed, many adapted wooden-hulled native smallcraft are employed for local logistic and patrol service; no characteristics are available for these. There are also a number of powered fishing craft and coastal commercial craft enrolled in the Philippine Coast Guard Auxiliary.

Personnel: Approx. 3,000 active, plus 4,000 ready reserve

PATROL CRAFT [WPC]

♦ 4 35-meter class

Bldr: Tenix Defense Systems, South Coogie, Australia

	In serv.
3501 Ilocos Norte	9-5-03
3502 Nueva Vizcaya	8-8-03
3503 Romblon	20-10-03
3504 Davio Del Norte	16-1-04

Romblon (3503)—at launching Tenix, 10-03

D: 115 **S:** 25 kts (on water jets) **Dim:** 35 × 7.3 × 2.3
A: 2 12.7-mm mg **Electronics:** Radar: 1 . . . nav.
M: 2 . . . diesel main engines and 1 water jet for loiter capability; 2 fixed pitch props

Remarks: Construction of four, with an option for ten more, was authorized 10-12-01. The design is an updated version of the ADI 315 design built for southeast Asian island countries and for Kuwait. All are aluminum construction designed for search-and-rescue missions.

♦ 4 San Juan–class search-and-rescue craft

Bldr: Tenix Defense Systems, South Coogie, Australia

	In serv.
AU 001 San Juan	21-7-00
AU 002 Edsa II (ex-*Don Emilio*)	12-00
AU 003 Pampanga	30-1-03
AU 004 Batangas	8-8-03

San Juan (AU 001)—with UH-1 helicopter on deck Tenix, 2001

COAST GUARD PATROL CRAFT [WPC] *(continued)*

San Juan (AU 001)—alongside *Edsa II* (AU 002) Stefan Karpinski, 2002

D: 540 tons (fl) **S:** 24.5 kts **Dim:** 56.00 (51.00 wl) × 10.55 × 2.50 (max.)
A: Small arms **Electronics:** Radar: 2 Furuno . . . nav.
M: 2 Caterpillar 3612 diesels; 2 CP props; 10,890 bhp
Electric: 690 kw tot. (2 × 260 kw, Caterpillar 3406 diesels driving; 1 × 170 kw; Caterpillar 3306T diesel driving; 60 Hz a.c.)
Range: 1,000/24; 2,000/15 **Fuel:** 88 tons + 3 tons helicopter fuel
Crew: 8 officers, 30 enlisted + 300 survivors

Remarks: Built with Australian government financial assistance. The second pair was ordered on 10-12-01. AU 002 was launched 4-10-00. AU 001 is based at Manila and AU 002 at Cebu City. Have medical facilities and carry a medical officer. Helicopter deck can accept a Sikorsky S-76 or Bell UH-1H, but there is no hangar. Navaids include Furuno FS-1800 GPS set and Furuno Felcom-81A Inmarsat commercial SATCOM. Employ a single-chine planing hull. Carry a 6.5-m rescue RIB on the stern launch/recovery ramp and four 4.5-m RIBs handled by two cranes. A divers' recompression chamber is fitted, and the ships are equipped with pollution-control gear. Delivered unarmed, but may be fitted with 12.7-mm mg. Are painted white.

♦ 2 Bessang Pass–class search-and-rescue craft (1 *nonoperational*)
Bldr: Sumidagawa, Tokyo (In serv. 1976–77)

AU 75 Bessang Pass (ex-SAR 99) AU 100 Tirad Pass (ex-SAR 100)

Bessang Pass (AU 75) (ex-SAR 99, ex-. . . 77) H&L Van Ginderen, 1986

D: 275 tons (fl) **S:** 30 kts (27.5 sust.) **Dim:** 44.0 × 7.4 × 1.5
A: 2 twin 12.7-mm mg **Electronics:** Radar: 1 . . . nav.
M: 2 MTU 12V538 TB82 diesels; 2 props; 4,030 bhp
Range: 2,300/14 **Crew:** 32 tot.

Remarks: Although AU 75 was reported to have run aground and been lost in 9-83, she was to have been refitted and returned to service as of 8-98. Since 2001, at which time she was still nonoperational, no additional information has become available. AU 100 has also been refitted for antipiracy patrol duties. Similar craft were constructed for the Indian Coast Guard. Are painted white.

♦ 4 ex-U.S. PGM 39 class
Bldr: Tacoma Boat, Tacoma, Wash.

	In serv.
PG 61 Agusan (ex-PGM 39)	3-60
PG 62 Catanduanes (ex-PGM 40)	3-60
PG 63 Romblon (ex-PGM 41)	3-60
PG 64 Palawan (ex-PGM 42)	6-60

D: 122 tons **S:** 17 kts **Dim:** 30.6 × 6.4 × 2.1 (props)
A: 2 single 20-mm 70-cal. Oerlikon Mk 10 AA
Electronics: Radar: 1 Raytheon 1500 nav.
M: 2 MTU 12V493 TY57 (MB 820) diesels; 2 props; 1,900 bhp
Range: 1,400/11 **Crew:** 15 tot.

Remarks: Transferred from Philippine Navy service by 1992.

PATROL BOATS [WPB]

♦ 11 CGC 103–class patrol launches
Bldr: Cavite NY (In serv. 1984– . . .)

CGC 103 CGC 115 CGC 129 CGC 132 CGC 134 CGC 136
CGC 110 CGC 128 CGC 130 CGC 133 CGC 135

D: 13 tons (fl) **S:** 28 kts **Dim:** 12.2 × 4.1 × 0.9
A: 1 12.7-mm mg; 1 7.62-mm mg **Electronics:** Radar: none
M: 2 G.M. Detroit Diesel 6-71 diesels; 2 props; 560 bhp
Range: . . . / . . . **Crew:** 5 tot.

Remarks: Used for harbor police work. GRP construction. One was stricken in 1994.

♦ 3 Mk II design
Bldr: Cavite NY (In serv. 7-85 to 1986)

DF 314 DF 315 DF 316

D: 24.6 tons (fl) **S:** 36 kts **Dim:** 16.7 × 5.0 × 1.3
A: . . . **Electronics:** Radar: 1 . . . nav.
M: 2 MTU 8V396 TB93 diesels; 2 props; 2,400 bhp

Remarks: Improved version of the DB 411 class. GRP hull. There were to have been 55 built under an 18-6-82 order, but by 1986 only four hulls were ready and no more were built.

♦ 10 DB 411 class
Bldr: Marcelo Fiberglass Corp., Manila (In serv. 1975–76)

DB 411 DB 417 DB 422 DB 429 DB 432
DB 413 DB 419 DB 426 DB 431 DB 433

DB 431 RAN, 6-82

D: 15 tons (21.75 fl) **S:** 20 kts **Dim:** 14.07 × 4.32 × 1.04 (1.48 props)
A: 1 twin and 1 single 12.7-mm mg
Electronics: Radar: 1 Canadian Marconi LN-66 nav.
M: 2 MTU 8V-331 TC80 diesels; 2 props; 1,800 bhp **Electric:** 7.5 kVA tot.
Range: 200/36 **Crew:** 6 tot.

Remarks: Eighty were ordered in 8-75, but of 25 hulls completed during 1975, 12 were destroyed by fire and the program was terminated. Since then, at least two others have been discarded. The twin machinegun mount is recessed into the forecastle. Later examples employ Cummins diesels. Were originally intended to achieve 46 kts. Formerly numbered in the PC series.

♦ 6 Australian fiberglass-hulled
Bldr: De Havilland Marine, Sydney (In serv. 20-11-74 to 8-2-75)

DF 318 DF 321 DF 326 DF 328 DF 330 DF 331

DF 318 Leo Dirkx, 5-99

D: 16.5 tons (fl) **S:** 25 kts **Dim:** 14.0 × 4.6 × 1.0
A: 2 single 12.7-mm mg **M:** 2 Caterpillar D348 diesels; 2 props; 740 bhp
Range: 500/12 **Crew:** 8 tot.

Remarks: Design very similar to the U.S. Patrol Boat Mk 1 class.

♦ 14 U.S. Swift Mk III class
Bldr: Peterson Bldrs, Sturgeon Bay, Wis. (In serv. 1975–76)

DF 325 through DF 332 DF 347 DF 352 DF 354
DF 334 DF 351 DF 353

D: 28 tons (36.7 fl) **S:** 30 kts **Dim:** 19.78 × 5.5 × 1.8
A: 1 twin and 2 single 12.7-mm mg
Electronics: Radar: 1 Canadian Marconi LN-66 nav.
M: 3 G.M. 8V71 TI diesels; 3 props; 1,950 bhp
Range: 500/30 **Crew:** 8 tot.

Remarks: Aluminum construction. Pilothouse offset to starboard. Sisters PCF 351 though PCF 354 serve in the Philippine Navy, and three others have been discarded. DF 347, and possibly others, has had the twin 12.7-mm mg position atop the pilothouse removed.

COAST GUARD PATROL BOATS [WPB] *(continued)*

DF 334—painted white H&L Van Ginderen/Brian Morrison, 5-98

♦ 12 ex-U.S. Swift Mk I and Mk II classes
Bldr: Sewart Seacraft, Berwick, La. (In serv. 1966–70)

Mk I: DF 300, DF 301, DF 302, DF 303
Mk II: DF 305, DF 307 through DF 313

DF 313—black hull, red-superstructure Stefan Karpinski, 2002

D: 22.5 tons (fl) **S:** 25 kts **Dim:** 15.6 × 4.12 × 1.5
A: 1 twin 12.7-mm mg; 1 combination 81-mm mortar/12.7-mm mg
Electronics: Radar: 1 Canadian Marconi LN-66 nav.
M: 2 G.M. 12V71T diesels; 2 props; 960 bhp **Electric:** 6 kw tot.
Range: 400/22 **Endurance:** 24–36 hr **Crew:** 6–8 tot.

Remarks: Aluminum construction. Data apply to Mk II version; Mk I is 15.2 m o.a. and has a flush-decked hull, while the Mk II has a low forecastle to improve seaworthiness. Formerly numbered in the PCF series. Six others, including the Philippine-built, ferroconcrete-hulled PCF 317, have been discarded.

AUXILIARIES

♦ 1 Corregidor-class navigational aids tender [WAGL]
Bldr: Niigata Eng., Niigata, Japan

	Laid down	L	In serv.
AG 891 Corregidor	8-7-97	5-11-97	2-3-98

Corregidor (AG 891) Stefan Karpinski, 2002

D: Approx. 1,130 tons (fl) **S:** 13.4 kts **Dim:** 56.92 (50.00 pp) × 11.00 × 3.75
A: None **Electronics:** Radar: 1 . . . nav.
M: 2 Niigata . . . diesels; 2 props; . . . bhp **Range:** 4,000/11.7
Fuel: 87.1 m^3 **Endurance:** 15 days **Crew:** 37 tot. (+ 8 spare)

Remarks: 835 grt/731 dwt. Lighthouse and buoy tender. Has a 418.8-m^3 buoy hold and 87.6-m^3 cargo hold. Carries 106 m^3 of fresh water and up to 383 m^3 of ballast water. Crew includes a maintenance team from the Department of Transportation and Communications. Is painted white.

♦ 1 ex-U.S. Coast Guard Balsam-class navigational aids tender [WAGL] Bldr: Marine Iron & SB Corp., Duluth, Minn. (In serv. 2-5-44)

AG 89 Kalinga (ex-TK 89; ex-*Redbud,* WAGL 398; ex-T-AKL 398; ex-AG 398)

D: 935 tons (1,020 fl) **S:** 13 kts **Dim:** 54.86 × 11.28 × 3.96
A: 1 12.7-mm mg **Electronics:** Radar: 1 . . . nav.
M: 2 . . . diesels, electric drive; 1 prop; 1,200 shp
Range: 3,500/7.5 **Crew:** 53 tot.

Remarks: Built for the U.S. Coast Guard, then transferred to the USN on 25-3-49 as AG 398 and to the Military Sealift Command on 10-49 as T-AKL 398, and returned to the U.S. Coast Guard 20-11-70. Transferred to the Philippines 1-3-72. Has a 20-ton buoy derrick. Refitted at Cavite Dockyard in 1995, recommissioning in 11-95; the original Cooper-Bessemer GSD-8 diesels were replaced. Has a helicopter platform and an ice-breaking bow.

♦ 2 ex-U.S. Army FS 381–class navigational aids tenders [WAGL]
Bldr: Ingalls, Pascagoula, Miss. (In serv. 1943–44)

AE 71 Mangyan (ex-AS 71, ex-*Miho,* ex-FS 524)
AE 79 Limasawa (ex-TK 79; ex-*Nettle,* WAK 169; ex-FS 396)

D: 473 tons light (950 fl) **S:** 12 kts **Dim:** 53.8 (50.27 pp) × 9.75 × 3.05
A: 2 single 12.7-mm mg **Electronics:** Radar: 1 . . . nav.
M: 2 G.M. 6-278A diesels; 2 props; 1,000 bhp **Electric:** 225 kw tot.
Range: 3,700/11; 4,150/10 **Fuel:** 67 tons **Crew:** 50 tot.

Remarks: AE 79 was loaned in 1-68 and purchased outright 31-8-78. AE 71 was purchased 24-9-76 after having served in the Japanese Navy as a mine countermeasures support ship; she was refitted and recommissioned during 1979. Both serve as buoy tenders and lighthouse supply ships, with AE 71 having had a deckhouse built over the after half of the cargo area. Cargo capacity: 345 tons. Speed reduced to 8 kts in AE 71; AE 79 has been overhauled and the engines renewed. Sister *Badjao* (AE 59, ex-AS 59, ex-Japanese *Nasami,* ex-U.S. Army FS 408) was stricken during 1996.

♦ 1 ex-U.S. Army FS 330–class navigational aids tender [WAGL]
Bldr: Higgins, Inc., New Orleans (In serv. 1944)

AE 46 Cape Bojeador (ex-TK 46, ex-FS 203)

D: 420 tons (742 fl) **S:** 10 kts **Dim:** 51.77 (48.77 pp) × 9.75 × 2.43
A: 2 single 12.7-mm mg **Electronics:** Radar: 1 . . . nav.
M: 4 Buda-Lanova 6 DHMR-1879 diesels; 2 props; 680 bhp
Electric: 225 kw tot. **Range:** 3,830/10 **Fuel:** 50 tons **Crew:** 50 tot.

Remarks: Decommissioned in 1988 but refitted for further service and recommissioned 21-11-90; may have been re-engined as well, as obtaining parts for the engines listed above would be extremely difficult. Had been transferred from the U.S.A. in 2-50. Cargo capacity: 150 tons. Sister *Lauis Ledge* (TK 45, ex-FS 185) was stricken in 1988.

SERVICE CRAFT

♦ 2 ex-U.S. YTL 442–class small harbor tugs [WYTL]
Bldrs: YQ 222: Winslow Marine Railway & SB, Winslow,Wash.;
YQ 226: Everett-Pacific Co., Everett, Wash.

YQ 222 Igorot (ex-YTL 572) YQ 226 Tasaday (ex-YTL 425)

D: 70 tons (80 fl) **S:** 9 kts **Dim:** 20.17 × 5.18 × 1.5
M: 1 Hamilton 685A diesel; 300 bhp

Remarks: Built 1944–45. YQ 222 was transferred during 7-48 by grant. YQ 226 was transferred on loan in 12-69 and purchased outright 1-8-80. Two sisters serve in the Philippine Navy proper.

Note: Also in use for logistic services are two large landing craft (B 124, B 244), LCM(6)-class landing craft BM 270, LCVP BV 182, and around 80 "Banca"-type native launches with outboard propulsion.
The Ministry of Defense operates the ships and craft of the Coast and Geodetic Survey, including *Hydrographer Ventura* (1,169 grt; completed in 1999 in Spain); *Atyimba* (686 tons fl; completed in 1969); and 245-ton sisters *Arinya* (completed in 1962) and *Alunya* (completed in 1964). An environmental patrol and fisheries protection patrol boat, *Bantay Kalikasan,* commissioned 2-2-95, may also be operated by this agency, as may the sister "research ships" *Fort San Antonio* (AM 700) and *Fort Abad* (AM 701), which were acquired in 1993.

POLAND

Republic of Poland

POLSKA MARYNARKA WOJENNA

Personnel: 12,300 total, plus 12,000 reservists

Organization and Bases: The major commands are the two coastal defense flotillas, one warship flotilla, and the naval air brigade. The 3rd Warship Flotilla is located at Gdynia-Oksywie naval base, the 8th Coast Defense Flotilla at Świnoujście and Kołobrzeg naval bases, and the 9th Coast Defense Flotilla at Hel Peninsula. Ships of the Hydrographic Protection Squadron are based at Gdynia-Oksywie while the Naval Aviation Brigade is based at Gdynia–Babie Doly air station. The naval academy and the warrant officers school are at Gdynia, while the career noncommissioned officers school is at Ustka. The 1st Naval Regiment of Riflemen (*Morski Pulk Strzelcow*) is based at Gdynia-Witomin and the 11th Naval Communications Regiment (*11 Pulk Lacznosci MW*) at Wejherowo. The 7th Naval Hospital is at Gdańsk-Oliwa and the 115th Military Hospital on the Hel Peninsula.
Plans call for the establishment of a marine battalion around 2008.

POLSKA MARYNARKA WOJENNA *(continued)*

Naval Aviation: The Naval Aviation Brigade (*Brygada Lotnictwa Marynarki Wojennej*) operates six TS-11Rbis DF Iskra reconnaissance jets, 12 TS-11bis D/DF Iskra jet trainers, five An-2 Colt light transports, one An-28 transport, six An-28B-1R Bryza maritime surveillance aircraft, four SH-2G SeaSprite shipboard ASW helicopters, two Mi-2 helicopters, 10 Mi-14PL land-based ASW helicopters (all of which have been updated to carry new ASW equipment and A-244S Mod. 3 ASW torpedoes), three Mi-14PS SAR helicopters, two W-3 Sokol transport helicopters, seven W-3RM Anakonda SAR helicopters, and two Mi-17 transport helicopters.

The first two SH-2G SeaSprite helicopters were delivered on 27-9-02 and the second pair during 6-03; they are equipped to launch A-244S and MU-90 Impact torpedoes and are assigned to the 1st Naval Aviation Division.

TS-11Rbis Iskra reconnaissance aircraft Jaroslaw Cislak, 6-02

An-28B-1R Bryza maritime surveillance aircraft Jaroslaw Cislak, 7-05

Mi-14PL ASW helicopter Jaroslaw Cislak, 7-05

Mi-17 helicopter—painted gray Jaroslaw Cislak, 7-05

Aviation elements are the 7th Special Air Force Regiment at Siemirowice, 34th Fighter Regiment at Gdynia–Babie Doly, and 40th Helicopter Squadron for Combating Submarines and Rescue at Darlowo.

Some 27 Iryada combat training aircraft, completed in 1996 but stored, may be acquired and completed to the Oryada Orkan M-93 configuration as replacements for the 21 MiG-21bis and five MiG-21UM fighters transferred to the Polish Air Force during 2001.

W-3RM Anakonda SAR helicopter Jaroslaw Cislak, 7-05

SH-2G SeaSprite Jaroslaw Cislak, 7-05

Coastal Defense: In use to defend major ports and naval facilities are long-range artillery and SS-C-3 Styx truck-mounted antiship missiles. The 1st Naval Regiment of Riflemen (*Morski Pulk Strzelcow,* or Marine Rifle Regiment) is based at Gdynia-Witomin, while the 8th Coastal Defense Flotilla is protected by the 8th Antiaircraft Artillery Battalion at Miedzyzdroje and the 9th Coastal Defense Flotilla is protected by the 7th Antiaircraft Artillery Battalion and the 55th ABC Defense Company at Ustka. The 8th Kolobrzkeski Sappers Battalion and 4th Mine-laying Battalion at Dziwnow carry out engineering tasks in support of the 8th Flotilla. CRM-100 naval covert coastal surveillance radars built by Przemyslowy Instytut Telekomuniacji (PIT), Warsaw, began delivery late in 1999; they have a range of about 24 n.m. and are linked to the Leba automated command and control system (the radar may later be adapted for surface ships and for use on offshore platforms).

WEAPONS AND SENSORS

While most weapon and sensor systems are of Soviet origin, Poland manufactures some under license and has introduced its own navigational radars as a result of its extensive merchant ship and fishing boat construction industry. A naval gunmount manufactured by the Cenzin Foreign Trade Enterprise is the twin 23-mm Wrobel-2MR, a water-cooled variant of the Soviet ZU-23-2 mount that can also be equipped to carry two 9K-32M Strela heat-seeking missiles:

Length: 2,608 m **Bore:** 23 mm
Mount weight: 2,500 kg **Muzzle velocity:** 970 m/sec
Rate of fire: 1,600–2,000 rds/mount/min (800 practical)
Effective range: 2,000 m **Effective altitude:** 1,500 m

On-mount ammunition supply is 200 rounds per barrel. The 9K-32M missiles have a length of 1,440 mm and a diameter of 72 mm and have a cruise velocity of 500 m/sec; the infrared seeker has a 40° field of view. Also available from the same manufacturer are the 12.7-mm Drop and Ohar naval heavy machinegun mountings.

Soviet-era torpedoes still available are the Type 53-56, Type 53-65K oxygen-powered, SET-53 and SET-53M electric ASW homing; and TEST-71 wire-guided electric ASW—all of 533-mm diameter. During 2000, 10 A-244S ASW torpedoes were acquired from Italy for use with Mi-14 PL helicopters. Some 30 Eurotorp MU-90 Impact ASW torpedoes were ordered on 18-2-02.

The Polish T.MMD-2 mine weighs 640 kg (warhead: 240 kg) and is some 1,815 m long and 572 mm in diameter. As of 2-01, 252 operational and 15 exercise versions had been ordered for the Polish Navy (with an option for 248 more), and the U.S. Navy had ordered 100.

Note: All ship names are prefixed by ORP (*Okret Rzeczpospolitej Polskiej,* or Ship of the Republic of Poland).

ATTACK SUBMARINES [SS]

♦ 1 Soviet Kilo class (Project 877E)

Bldr: United Admiralty SY, St. Petersburg (In serv. 29-4-86)

291 ORZEL (ex-B-800)

ATTACK SUBMARINES [SS] *(continued)*

Orzel (291) Jaroslaw Cislak, 6-04

D: 2,325 tons surf. (2,460 with emergency fuel)/3,180 tons sub.
S: 10 kts surf./9 kts snorkel/17 kts sub.
Dim: 72.60 (70.0 wl) × 9.90 (12.80 over stern planes) × 6.60 (fwd.; 6.20 mean)
A: 6 bow 533-mm TT (18 Type 53-65K and TEST-71ME torpedoes, or up to 24 Type MDT mines); 1 Fasta-M shoulder-launched SAM position (8 9K-32M Strela-2M missiles)
Electronics:
Radar: 1 MRK-50 Tobol (Snoop Tray-2) nav./search
Sonar: MGK-400 Rubikon (Shark Gill) LF active/passive suite; MG-53 passive hull array; MG-519 Arfa (Mouse Roar) HF active classification/mine avoidance; MG-553 sound-velocity measuring; MG-512 own-ship's cavitation detection
EW: MRP-25 Ankier intercept; Type 6701E Iva (Quad Loop) HFD/F
M: 2 Type 4-2DL42M diesels driving 30DG generator sets (1,825 bhp/1,500 kw at 700 rpm), electric drive: 1 PG-141 motor; 1 6-bladed prop; 5,900 shp—1 130-shp PG-142 electric low-speed motor on main shaft—2 PG-140 low-speed maneuvering motors; 2 ducted props; 204 shp (3 kts)
Range: 6,000/7 snorkel; 400/3 sub. **Fuel:** 172 tons
Endurance: 45 days **Crew:** 16 officers, 44 enlisted

Remarks: *Orzel* was the first Kilo to be exported from the then-USSR. Additional units were planned to complete replacement of the quartet of Whiskey-class submarines then in service, but lack of funds forced the leasing of two, now retired, Foxtrots instead. Based at Gdynia-Oksywie. Communications and data-sharing systems were updated in 1999–2000 to allow the ship to operate with NATO forces, and the submarine was thoroughly overhauled for continued service.
Hull systems: Propulsion plant is on isolation mounts for silencing. Hull has 32% reserve buoyancy at surfaced displacement. At rest on the surface, the submarine trims down 0.4 m by the bow. Maximum diving depth is 300 m, normal maximum operating depth 240 m, and periscope depth 17.5 m. Has an anechoic hull coating. Two Type 446 batteries, each with 120 cells, provide 9,700 kwh and weigh 446 tons total. Hull has six watertight compartments.
Combat systems: Combat system, designated Murena or MVU-110EM, has two operator consoles and can conduct two simultaneous attacks while tracking three other targets manually. The SAM launch position is located in the after portion of the sail. Only two of the torpedo tubes can accept wire-guided torpedoes.

♦ 4 ex-Norwegian modernized German Type 207
Bldr: Rheinstahl-Nordseewerke, Emden

	Laid down	L	In serv.	Mod. completed
294 SOKOL (ex-*Stord,* S 308)	1-4-66	2-9-66	9-2-67	26-10-90
295 SEP (ex-*Skolpen,* S 306)	1-11-65	24-3-66	17-8-66	10-89
296 BIELEK (ex-*Svenner,* S 309)	8-9-66	27-1-67	1-7-67	10-93
297 KONDOR (ex-*Kunna,* S 319)	3-3-64	16-7-64	1-10-64	12-91

Bielek (296) Michael Nitz, 2-05

D: 469 tons surf./524 tons sub. **S:** 12 kts surf./17 kts sub.
Dim: 47.41 (296: 48.41) × 4.60 × 3.80
A: 8 bow 533-mm TT (8 Bofors Tp 61 or DM-2A3 Seehake wire-guided torpedoes)
Electronics:
Radar: 1 Kelvin-Hughes Type 1007 nav.
Sonar: STN Atlas Elektronik DBQS-21F (CSU-83) suite (active and passive)
EW: ArgoSystems AR 700 intercept
M: 2 MTU 12V493 AZ 80 GA31L diesels (600 bhp each), 2 405-kw generators, 1 1,100-kw motor; 1 2.3-m-dia. prop; 1,700 shp
Range: 5,000/8 snorkel; 14/17, 141/6 sub. **Crew:** 5 officers, 13 enlisted

Remarks: Originally a class of fifteen, financed by the U.S. Modernized by Mjellum and Karlsen, Urivale, Bergen. 296 is configured for training duties. Were to be retired from Norwegian service over the 2002–5 period. Instead, they were decommissioned at the end of 2001 and Poland agreed to acquire them on 15-2-02. The transfer contract was signed on 13-5-02 at a cost of only $17.4 million, which included training, spares, and some 30 Tp 613 and NT37C wire-guided torpedoes. 294 arrived at Oksywie on 29-5-02 and was recommissioned on 4-6-02; 295 was transferred during 7-02 and commissioned 16-8-02; 296 was recommissioned on 8-10-03 and 297 in the spring of 2004 after refits in Norway. Sister *Kobben* was transferred during 7-02 as a stationary training platform under the name *Jastrzab.*

Sokol (294) Jaroslaw Cislak, 6-03

Hull systems: Design is based on the German Type 205, but these are deeper diving. Were lengthened 2 m and re-engined during modernization. Operating depth: 190 m. 296 was built 1 m longer than her sisters and is equipped with a second Pilkington CK 30 periscope for training; she displaces about 14 additional tons.
Combat systems: During modernization, received MSI-90U combat data systems in place of MSI-70U, new sonar and communications suites, Thorn-EMI D-3 data-distribution systems, new radar, and new EW gear. The MSI-90U systems have been modified to permit the submarines to launch the DM-2A3 torpedo, which has not been transferred to Poland.

Disposal note: Foxtrot-class (Project 641K) submarines *Wilk* (292, ex-B-38) and *Dzik* (293, ex-B-40) were placed up for sale for $15 million each at the end of 2001; they were stricken during the fourth quarter of 2003.

GUIDED-MISSILE FRIGATES [FFG]

♦ 2 ex-U.S. Oliver Hazard Perry class

	Bldr:	Laid down	L	In serv.
272 GEN. K. PULASKI (ex-*Clark,* FFG 11)	Bath Iron Works, Bath, Maine	17-7-78	24-3-79	9-5-80
273 GEN. T. KOSCIUSZKO (ex-*Wadsworth,* FFG 9)	Todd Shipyards, San Pedro, Calif.	13-7-77	29-7-78	28-2-80

Gen. K. Pulaski (272) Ralph Edwards, 5-04

Gen T. Kosciuszko (273) Michael Winter, 6-05

D: 2,769 tons light (3,658 fl) **S:** 29 kts (30.6 on trials)
Dim: 135.64 (125.9 wl) × 13.72 × 5.8 (6.7 max.)
A: 1 Mk 13 Mod. 4 launcher (4 Harpoon and 36 Standard SM-1 MR Block VIB missiles); 1 76-mm 62-cal. Mk 75 DP; 1 20-mm Mk 15 Phalanx gatling CIWS; 2 triple 324-mm Mk 32 Mod. 5 (273: Mod 17) ASW TT (6 A-244 Mod. 3 torpedoes); 1 or 2 SH-2G Super SeaSprite ASW helicopters (A-244Z and/or MU-90 Impact torpedoes)
Electronics:
Radar: 1 Cardion SPS-55 surf. search; 1 Raytheon SPS-49(V)4 air search; 1 Lockheed-Martin Mk 92 Mod. 2 missile/gun f.c.; 1 Lockheed-Martin STIR missile/gun f.c.
Sonar: SQQ-89(V)2 (273: SQQ-89(V)9) suite: Raytheon SQS-56 hull-mounted LF
TACAN: URN-25
EW: Raytheon SLQ-32(V)2 intercept; Mk 36 SRBOC decoy syst. (2 6-round Raytheon Mk 137 launchers); SLQ-25 Nixie towed acoustic torpedo decoy

GUIDED-MISSILE FRIGATES [FFG] *(continued)*

Gen T. Kosciuszko (273) Frank Findler, 6-05

M: 2 G.E. LM-2500 gas turbines; 1 5.5-m-dia. CP, 5-bladed prop; 41,000 shp (40,000 sust.)—2 drop-down electric propulsors; 720 shp
Electric: 3,000 kw tot. (3 × 1,000 kw, diesels driving)
Range: 4,200/20; 5,000/18 **Fuel:** 587 tons + 64 tons helicopter fuel
Crew: 16 officers, 198 enlisted

Remarks: 272 was transferred 15-3-00 as a gift and was recommissioned in Poland on 25-6-00, the 80th anniversary of the establishment of the Polish Navy; the full names (not borne on the nameplates) are *General Kazimierz Pulaski* and *General Thadeuz Kosciuszko.* 273 was transferred on 28-6-02 and recommissioned on 25-10-02. Both ships are named for Polish officers who assisted in the U.S. Revolution.
Hull systems: Has 19-mm aluminum-alloy armor over the magazine spaces, 16-mm steel over the main engine-control room, and 19-mm Kevlar plastic armor over vital electronics and command spaces. Because of a hull twisting problem, doubler plates have been added over the hull sides amidships just below the main deck. Speed on one turbine alone is 25 knots. The auxiliary power system uses two retractable pods located well forward and can drive the ships at up to 6 knots. Have fin stabilizers. No helicopter haul-down and deck traversal system is fitted.
Combat systems: The ships have the Mk 13 weapons-direction system. The Mk 92 Mod. 4 fire-control system controls missile and 76-mm gun fire; it uses a STIR (modified SPG-60) antenna amidships and a U.S.-built version of the WM-28 radar forward and can track four separate targets, while there are two missile illumination channels.
Delivered with 272 were 18 Standard SM-1 MR Block VI missiles (one a dummy training round), two RGM-84 Harpoon Block IG antiship missiles, and six ASW torpedoes. The Mk 75 gun is a license-built version of the OTO Melara Compact. Two Mk 24 optical missile and gun target designators are mounted in tubs atop the pilothouse. A total of 24 ASW torpedoes can be carried for helicopters and the shipboard tubes. The SQQ-89(V) sonar suite incorporates a UYQ-25A sonobuoy processor; the towed linear passive hydrophone arrays were not transferred with the ships.

FRIGATES [FF]

♦ 0 (+ 4 + 2) MEKO A-100 class (Project 621)
Bldr: Stocznia Marynarki Wojennej, Gdynia

	Laid down	L	In serv.
241 Islazak	28-10-01	2005	2007
242 Kujawiak	2003	2006	. . .
243 Krakowiak	. . .	. . .	. . .
244 Mazur	. . .		. . .

Project 621 (MEKO A-100)—builders model Hans Karr, 2004

Project 621 (MEKO A-100)—builders model Hans Karr, 2004

D: 1,690 tons (2,090 fl) **S:** 30+ kts
Dim: 95.20 (86.40 pp) × 13.30 (12.50 wl) × 3.35 (mean hull; 4.55 over sonar)
A: 8 Saab Bofors RBS-15 Mk 3 SSM; 1 8-cell Mk 41 VLS (32 RIM-162 Evolved Sea Sparrow or 8 RIM-7M Sea Sparrow missiles); 1 21-round RAM Mk 31 SAM syst. (RIM-116A Block 0 missiles); 1 76-mm 62-cal. OTO Melara SuperRapid DP; 2 6-round Bofors ASW-610 ASW mortars; 2 triple 324-mm ASW TT; 4 mine rails; 1 10-ton helicopter
Electronics:
Radar: 1 . . . nav.; 1 EADS MRS-3D 3-D search; 2 . . . f.c.
Sonar: . . .
EW: . . . intercept; 2 . . . decoy RL
M: CODAG: 1 LM 2500 gas turbine (18,800 shp), 2 . . . diesels (4,346 bhp each); 2 CP props
Electric: 2,200 kw tot. (2 × 550 kw, diesel-powered sets)
Range: 4,000/15 **Crew:** 74–90 tot.

Remarks: Offered as a cooperative program replacing the original Polish Navy concept of building up to seven modified versions of the *Kaszub* class (Project 620 II). The navy hopes to build six units. Also known as the Gawron class. 241 was ordered during 2001 at a cost of about $150 million.
Hull systems: Will have fin stabilizers. Two RIBs will be carried in recessed, screened pockets, one per side.
Combat systems: CTM, Gdynia, and PIT, Warsaw, will perform combat system integration for the class. The ships are to have a Thales TACTICOS combat system compatible with NATO weapon and sensor systems. MOC Mk 3 combat system operator consoles will be fitted. Will have SCOT 3 VHF SATCOM. The armament suite listed above is the preferred one, but funding constraints may result in the fitting of a single SAM system, possibly the French Mica VLS, with 16 missiles.

CORVETTES [FFL]

♦ 1 Kaszub class (Project 620)
Bldr: Stocznia Pótnocna, Gdańsk

	Laid down	L	In serv.
240 Kaszub	11-5-85	4-10-86	15-3-87

Kaszub (240) Michael Winter, 6-05

D: 1,051 tons (1,183 fl) **S:** 26.2 kts
Dim: 82.34 (77.83 pp) × 10.00 × 2.93 (hull; 4.9 over sonar)
A: 1 76.2-mm 59-cal. AK-176 DP; 2 4-round Fasta-4M SAM syst. (16 9K-32M Strela-2M missiles); 3 twin 23-mm 87-cal. ZU-23-2M Wrobel-I AA; 2 12-round RBU-6000 Smerch ASW RL (98 RGB-60 rockets); 2 twin 533-mm DTA 53-620 TT (SET-53M torpedoes); 2 d.c. racks (6 B-1 or B-2 d.c. each); 2 mine rails (4–20 tot. Type 08/39, AGSB, or JaM mines)
Electronics:
Radar: 1 SRN-741XT nav.; 1 SRN-7453 Nogat surf. search; 1 MR-302 Rubka (Strut Curve) surf./air search
Sonar: MG-322T Argun hull-mounted MF; MG-329M Shelon HF dipping (at stern); MG-16 underwater telephone
EW: No intercept; 1 122-mm Jastrzab-2 decoy RL; 2 9-round 81-mm Derkacz-2 decoy RL
M: 4 Cegielski-Sulzer 16ASV25/30 diesels; 2 CP, 250-rpm props; 16,890 bhp
Electric: 800 kw tot. (4 × 200-kw diesel sets)
Range: 840/26; 2,000/18; 3,480/14 **Crew:** 9 officers, 71 enlisted

Remarks: First seagoing combatant designed and built in Poland since prior to World War II. Work began 9-6-84. Was found to have a warped hull and shafts after launch and had to be repaired at the Gdynia naval yard. Was loaned to the border guard from the fall of 1990 for use as a flagship; returned to naval service 1-91. Communications and data-sharing systems were updated in 1999–2000 to allow the ship to operate with NATO forces. Is attached to the 11th Patrol Boat Squadron.
Combat systems: The helicopter-type dipping sonar is located in the cabinet at the extreme stern; the ship must be dead in the water to use it. Main gun forward was not mounted until 9-91 and still lacks a fire-control director; it is locally controlled. During foreign port visits, has carried two 45-mm saluting cannon on the forecastle. Carries three smoke floats each side at the stern. Has the Drakon torpedo fire-control system for the two torpedo tube sets, which train out several degrees to fire.

GUIDED-MISSILE PATROL CRAFT [PTG]

♦ 3 Orkan (ex-East German Sassnitz) class (Project 660)
Bldr: VEB Peenewerft, Wolgast/Stocznia Pótnocna, Gdańsk

	Laid down	L	In serv.
421 Orkan	13-9-89	29-9-90	18-9-92
422 Piorun	10-7-89	7-7-90	11-3-94
423 Grom (ex-*Huragan*)	18-9-89	11-12-90	28-3-95

D: 331 tons (369 fl) **S:** 38.5 kts **Dim:** 48.90 (45.00 pp) × 8.65 × 2.20
A: 8 RBS-15 Mk 3 SSM; 1 76.2-mm 59-cal. AK-176 DP; 1 30-mm 54-cal. AK-630M gatling AA; 1 4-round FAM-14 SAM syst. (8 9K-32M Strela-2M missiles)

GUIDED-MISSILE PATROL CRAFT [PTG] *(continued)*

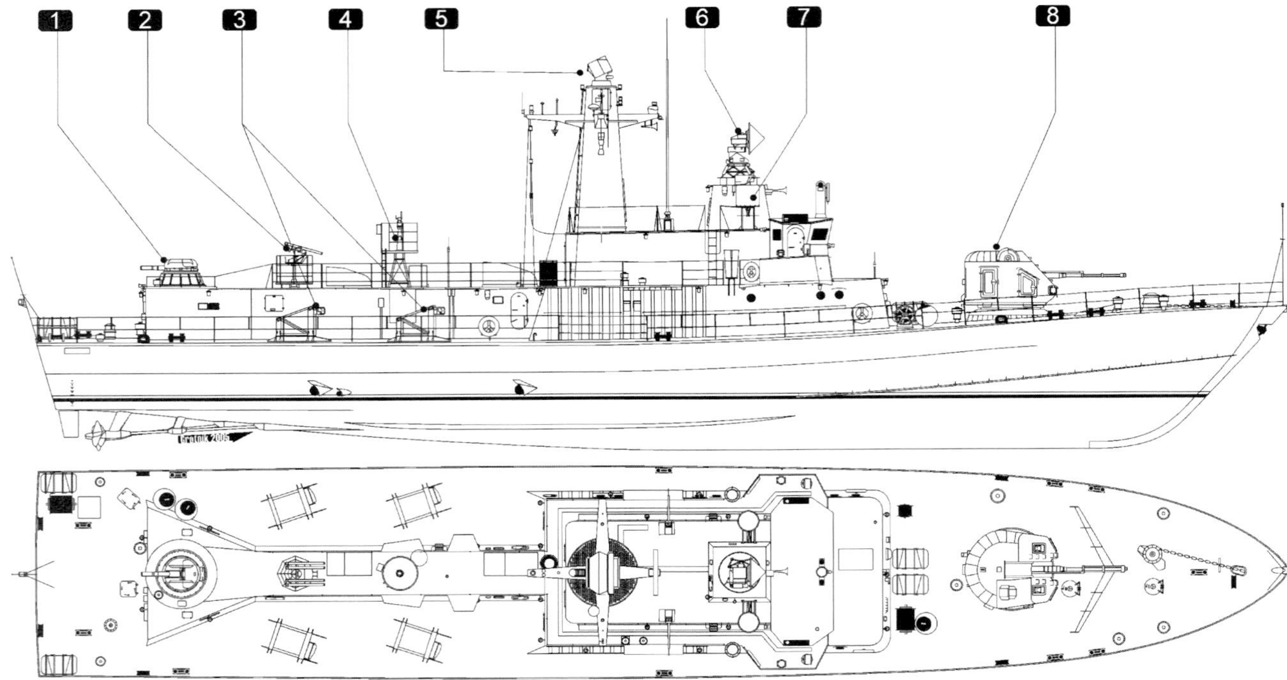

Orkan class—post-modernization 1. 30 mm AK-630M AA gun 2. FAM-14 SAM system for Strela-2M missiles 3. Provision for RBS-15 SSM 4. Kolonka-2 target designator 5. Sea Giraffe AMB 3-D radar 6. Sting EO fc. system 7. EW antenna suite 8. 76.2 mm AK-176 DP gun. Drawing by Tomasz Grotnik, 2005

Piorun (422)—undergoing modernization Jaroslaw Cislak, 6-05

Electronics: Radar: 1 Ericsson Sea Giraffe AMB 3-D system; 1 CRM-200 nav.; 1 MR-123 Vympel-AME (Bass Tilt) gun f.c.; 1 Thales Sting-EO f.c.
M: 3 M-520T diesels; 3 props; 16,183 bhp (14,685 sust.)
Electric: 439 kw (1 × 183-kw, 2 × 128-kw diesel sets)
Range: 1,619/38; 1,600/18; 2,400/13 **Endurance:** 5 days
Crew: 4 officers, 32 enlisted

Remarks: East German project number was 151A. Were purchased incomplete without engines or armament just prior to the unification of Germany; transferred 3-10-90. Name for 423 was changed in 1994. 421 had her communications and datalink systems updated during 1999–2000 to allow her to operate with NATO forces. All three received significant modernizations between 2001 and late 2006. Are attached to the 3rd Flotilla Patrol Boat Squadron, based at Gdynia-Oksywie.
Hull systems: Each "star radial" M-520 diesel has eight rows of seven cylinders. Have steel hulls and aluminum superstructures. The bare hulls were constructed in Germany; the rest of the construction took place in Poland.
Combat systems: Under a $15.5-million contract signed 29-6-01, the three were modernized by Thales Nederland and Stocznia Marynarki Wojennej, Gdynia, with the Thales TACTICOS combat data system, Sting radar/electro-optical gun fire-control system, Focon digital fiber-optic data network, and NATO Link 11 capability added. The class retain their German Rhode & Schwarz radio communications gear. The search radar has been replaced by the Ericsson Sea Giraffe AMB 3-D system, and the Przemyslowy Instytut Telekomuniacji (PIT) ESM system and PIT's CRM-200 navigational radar replaced older equipment. The three also have provision to launch eight Saab RBS-15 Mk 3 antiship missiles. Modernization work began during 7-01 and was completed by late 2006. Have Kolonka-2 manned ringsight directors for the AK-630 AA mounts.

◆ 2 Soviet Tarantul-I (Russian Molnaya-1) class (Project 1241RE)
Bldr: Volodarskiy SY 341, Rybinsk

	In serv.
436 Metalowiec	13-2-88
437 Rolnik	4-2-89

D: 385 tons light, 420 tons normal (455 fl) **S:** 43 kts
Dim: 56.90 (49.50 pp) × 10.20 (9.40 wl) × 2.14 (hull; 3.59 props)
A: 4 P-20/21 Termit (SS-N-2C Styx) SSM (KT-138E launchers); 1 76.2-mm 59-cal. AK-176 DP; 1 4-rail MTU-40S (SA-N-8) SAM syst. (12 9K-32M Strela-2 missiles); 2 single 30-mm 54-cal. AK-630 gatling AA

Rolnik (437) Jaroslaw Cislak, 5-05

Electronics:
Radar: 1 Kivach-2 (436, 437: Pechora) nav.; 1 Garpun-E (Plank Shave) targeting; 1 MR-123 Vympel-A (Bass Tilt) f.c.
EW: 2 PK-16 decoy syst. (2 16-round KL-101 RL)
M: M-15E COGAG plant: 2 DMR-76 cruise gas turbines (4,000 shp each), 2 PR-77 boost gas turbines (12,000 shp each); 2 props; 32,000 shp
Electric: 500 kw tot. (2 × 200-kw, 1 × 100-kw diesel sets)
Range: 400/43; 2,200/14 **Fuel:** 50 tons (122,634 liters)
Endurance: 10 days **Crew:** 6 officers, 40 enlisted

Remarks: Names mean "Metalworker" and "Farmer," respectively. Both are based at Gdynia-Oksywie.
Hull systems: Stainless-steel-alloy, seven-watertight-compartments hull with aluminum alloy superstructure, decks, and internal bulkheads. Very strongly constructed. Have difficulty maneuvering below 10 kts. Range has also been stated to be 2,350 n.m. at 12–13 kts (at 34° C) with a maximum speed of 43 kts at 15° C (35 kts at 34° C).
Combat systems: Carry 252 ready-service rounds and another 150 in reserve for the 76.2-mm gun. The Zvezdochka-1241RE weapons system employs digital computers and has many backup features. The target-designation radar can be used in the passive mode to provide target bearings and threat warning. A PMK-453 lead-computing backup optical director can control the 30-mm guns, and the 76.2-mm mount can be locally controlled.
Disposals: Sisters *Górnik* (434) and *Hutnik* (435) were retired during 2005 and will likely be sold abroad. 436 and 437 are expected to retired by 2008.

◆ 2 Soviet Osa-I (Russian Moskit) class (Project 205)
Bldr: . . ., Russia

	In serv.
431 Świnoujście	13-1-73
433 Wladyslawowo	13-11-75

GUIDED-MISSILE PATROL CRAFT [PTG] *(continued)*

Wladyslawowo (433) Jaroslaw Cislak, 5-05

Wladyslawowo (433)—note Styx missile launchers, aft 30-mm gun and radars Jaroslaw Cislak, 6-04

D: 165 tons light, 209.5 normal (220 fl)
S: 38.5 kts (36 sust.) **Dim:** 38.6 × 7.6 × 1.73
A: 4 P-15U Termit (SS-N-2A Styx) SSM; 1 4-round Fasta-4M SAM syst. (8 Strela-2M missiles); 2 twin 30-mm 65-cal. AK-230 AA
Electronics: Radar: 1 SRN-207M nav.; 1 Rangout (Square Tie) surf. search/target desig.; 1 MR-104 Rys' (Drum Tilt) gun f.c.
M: 3 M-503A2 diesels; 3 props; 12,000 bhp
Range: 400/34; 750/25 **Crew:** 4 officers, 18 enlisted

Remarks: Built in the USSR during the early 1960s and transferred on the dates listed above. All are named for coastal cities and are based at Gdynia-Oksywie. Were refitted for further service during the early 2000s and are currently employed primarily in training roles.
Disposals: *Hel* (421), *Gdańsk* (422), and *Kołobrzeg* (. . .) have been discarded, the latter on 18-9-92. *Ustka* (428) and *Oksywie* (429) were stricken 2-10-00. Sisters *Gdynia* (423), *Szczecin* (425), and *Elblag* (426) were converted as patrol boats for the border guard beginning in 1989 and have since been stricken. *Puck* (427) and *Darlowo* (430) were stricken 31-1-03 and *Dziwnów* (432) was retired in 2004.

PATROL CRAFT [PC]

♦ 4 KP-166 (Pilica) class (Project 918M)
Bldr: Stocznia Marynarki Wojennej, Gdynia

	In serv.		In serv.
KP-167	28-1-78	KP-171	8-1-82
KP-168	28-1-78	KP-174	22-9-82

KP-171 Jaroslaw Cislak, 2000

D: 85.62 tons std., 86.88 tons normal (93.03 normal fl; 100 max. fl)
S: 27.8 kts (25 cruise) **Dim:** 28.85 × 5.76 × 1.36 (hull)
A: 1 twin 23-mm 87-cal. ZU-23-2M Wrobel-1 AA; 2 fixed 533-mm OTAM-53 TT (2 SET-53M homing torpedoes)
Electronics:
Radar: 1 SRN-301 nav.
Sonar: MG-329M portable dipping set; SP-4301 echo sounder
M: 3 M-50F-5 diesels; 3 props; 3,600 bhp **Range:** 340/25; 1,160/11.4
Endurance: 5 days **Crew:** 3 officers, 9–11 enlisted

Remarks: Transferred to the navy in 1991 from the Ministry of the Interior's border guard. Now considered to be ASW patrol boats. All are based at Kołobrzeg in the 16th ASW Division, 8th Coastal Defense Flotilla.
Hull systems: Have steel hull, aluminum alloy superstructure, and GRP mast.
Combat systems: Carry 2–4 Type MDS smoke floats at the stern. Two different torpedo tube mounts, removed from discarded P-6-class torpedo boats, were installed; they are angled 7° outboard. The original Soviet twin 25-mm 2M-3M gunmounts were replaced 1986–90.
Disposals: K-166, -169, -170, -172, -173, -175, and -176 were decomissioned during 2004–5. KP-161 through KP-165 were returned to the coast guard in 1992 as SG-161 through SG-165. All six remaining *Groźny* (Modified Obluze)-class (Project 912M) patrol craft had been stricken by 2006.

MINE WARFARE SHIPS

♦ 0 (+ 5) Kormoran-class (Project 257) coastal minehunters [MHC]
Bldr: Stocznia Marynarki Wojennej, Gdynia

D: . . . tons **S:** . . . kts **Dim:** . . . × . . . × . . .
A: 1 twin 23-mm 87-cal. ZU-23-2MR Wrobel-2MR AA; 1 4-round Fasta-4M SAM syst. (8–12 tot. 9M-32M Strela-2M missiles)
Electronics:
Radar: 1 Decca Bridgemaster-E ARPA nav.
Sonar: AkMor SHL-100AM hull-mounted HF; AkMor SHL-200M-1 towed side-scan VHF
M: . . . diesels; 1 prop—active rudder stern-thruster—bow-thruster
Range: . . . / . . . **Crew:** . . .

Remarks: Detail design work on a new, enlarged variant of the Notec-class minehunters began sometime after 2001. The hull-mounted sonar dome is to be retractable. The first of the class was planned to be laid down in 2003, but the design remains on the drawing board. Thales Underwater Systems received an order during 3-02 for one TSM 2022 Mk III acoustic array for use with the "SHL-101T" sonar suite on this class. The first unit is unlikely to enter service before 2009.

♦ 3 Krogulec-class (Project 206FM) minehunters [MHC]
Bldr: Stocznia imeni Komuny Pariskej, Gdynia

	Laid down	L	In serv.
621 Flaming	. . .	5-5-65	11-11-66
623 Mewa	18-7-66	22-12-66	9-5-67
624 Czajka	12-9-66	17-12-66	17-6-67

Czajka (624) Martin Mokrus, 8-04

D: 426 tons light; 472.1 tons normal (507 fl) **S:** 18 kts
Dim: 60.00 (58.20 pp) × 7.97 (7.70 wl) × 2.14 (hull)
A: 1 twin 23-mm 87-cal. ZU-23-2MR Wrobel-2MR AA (4 9M-32M Strela-2M SAM on mount); 2 Fasta-4M SAM launchers (16 tot. 9M-32M Strela-2M missiles); 2 d.c. racks (12 B-1 or B-2 d.c. tot.); 2 mine rails (8 AMD-1000 or 16 08/39 mines)
Electronics:
Radar: 1 Decca Bridgemaster-E ARPA nav.
Sonar: AkMor SHL-100AM hull-mounted HF; AkMor SHL-200M-1 towed side-scan VHF
EW: PIT Bren intercept; 6 9-round, Derkach 81-mm decoy RL

MINE WARFARE SHIPS *(continued)*

Mewa (623) Leo van Ginderen, 10-05

M: 2 Sulzer-Cegielski ATL25/30 diesels; 2 Lips-Schelde CP props; 3,740 bhp
Electric: 160 kw tot. (4 × 40-kw [55 kw max.] Leyland–Huta Stalowa Wola SW 400 diesel generator sets)
Range: 2,000/12 **Fuel:** 45 tons **Endurance:** 12 days
Crew: 5 officers, 48 enlisted (incl. 5 mine-disposal divers)

Remarks: Named for birds. Have been extensively overhauled and modernized by Stocznia Marynarki Wojennej, Gdynia, with communications and datalink systems updated to allow them to operate with NATO forces; work on 623 was completed 16-5-99, and the ship was recommissioned during 12-99. 624 completed modification 26-5-99, 621 in 2001. The trio are planned to operate through 2010. 623 joined the NATO Mine Countermeasures Force North on 12-10-02, the first Polish Navy warship assigned to NATO.
Combat systems: Are now equipped with the Pstrokosz integrated mine-countermeasures command, control, and communications system and carry Polish-designed Ukwial remotely operated sonar- and t.v.-equipped submersibles and new sonars to enable them to act as minehunters. They are also fitted with the MT-2 mechanical sweep with Bofors explosive cutters and have had the TEM-PE-2M magnetic sweep gear updated so that it can operate concurrently with a new BGAT acoustic sweep gear set, with both handled by a new, smaller sweep winch. A two-compartment decompression chamber and semi-rigid inflatable launch were added for the mine-disposal divers, and 10 ZNH-230 sonobuoys are also carried. They can detect moored mines at a range of 1,600 m and bottom mines at 600 m. ATO-compatible Suprasl IFF systems and the Pstroksz precision navigation system are fitted. During modernization, they also received a new degaussing system, overhauled engines, a new NBC warfare protection system, and NATO-compatible fueling connections. The Polish Navy hopes to acquire Russian Igla SAMs to replace the Strela-2Ms.
Disposals: *Orlik* (613), *Krogulec* (614), *Jastrzab* (615), and *Kormoran* (616) were stricken during 6-93; *Czapla* (617) and *Pelikan* (619) during 12-93; *Albatros* (618) during 1995; and *Tukan* (620) on 2-10-00. *Rybitwa* (622) was employed as an accommodations hulk until stricken 5-2-02.

♦ 17 Notec-class (Project 207D, 207P, and 207M) coastal minehunter/minesweepers [MHC]

Bldr: Stocznia Marynarki Wojennej, Gdynia

	L	In serv.		L	In serv.
630 Goplo	16-4-81	13-3-82	639 Necko	21-11-88	9-5-89
631 Gardnó	23-6-83	31-3-84	640 Naklo	29-5-89	2-3-90
632 Bukowo	28-7-84	23-6-85	641 Drużno	29-11-89	21-9-90
633 Dąbie	24-5-85	11-5-86	642 Hańcza	9-7-90	1-3-91
634 Jamno	11-2-86	11-10-86	643 Mamry	20-9-91	25-9-92
635 Mielno	27-6-86	9-5-87	644 Wigry	28-11-92	14-5-93
636 Wicko	20-3-87	12-10-87	645 Śniardwy	20-6-93	28-1-94
637 Resko	1-10-87	26-3-88	646 Wdzydze	24-6-94	2-12-94
638 Sarbsko	10-5-88	12-10-88			

Sarbsko (638) Jaroslaw Cislak, 6-04

D: 208 tons light; 213 tons normal (225 fl) **S:** 14.5 kts
Dim: 38.46 (36.50 pp) × 7.35 (7.15 molded breadth) × 1.78 (hull)
A: 1 twin 23-mm 87-cal. ZU-23-2MR Wrobel-2MR AA; 2 d.c. racks (12 d.c. tot.); 2 mine rails (6–24 mines, depending on type)
Electronics:
Radar: 1 SRN-302 nav.
Sonar: AkMor SHL-100 Flaming-A; AkMor SHL-200 hull-mounted HF mine-location
M: 2 Type M-401A diesels; 2 Kort-nozzle 5-bladed, CP, 241-rpm props; 2,000 bhp (1,600 sust.)—1 150-kw, 514-rpm tunnel-thruster fwd
Electric: 60 kw tot. (2 × 30-kw Wola 71H6 diesel-driven sets)
Range: 950/14; 1,100/9 **Endurance:** 5 days
Crew: 4 officers, 6 warrant officers, 20 enlisted

Remarks: Named for lakes. 630 (Project 207D) is used as a trials ship for sweep gear and sonars and is based at Gdynia-Oksywie. Project 207P units 631–642 are assigned to the 12th Division, 8th Coastal Defense Flotilla, Świnoujście. Project 207M units 643–646 are assigned to the 13th Minesweeping Division, 9th Coastal Defense Flotilla, Hel. Plans for a fifth Project 207M unit were canceled in 1993. 643 had communications and datalink systems updated during 1999–2000 to allow her to operate with NATO forces.
Hull systems: Have 20-mm-thick GRP hull-construction. All are capable of hunting for or sweeping mines in waters 5–20 m deep in conditions up to Sea State 3 and winds at 4–5 Beaufort. The Project 207M quintet have a longer pilothouse. The final four have 230 kVA total alternator capacity from two Wola 71H6 diesel-driven, 400-V, 50-Hz alternator sets; also fitted are two 30-kw d.c. sweep current generators. Normally carry crews of only 24 total.
Combat systems: SHL-100 Flaming-A is a forward-looking mine-avoidance sonar, while SHL-200 is a side- and aft-looking mine-location set operating at 100 kHz. The ships are equipped with mechanical, acoustic, and magnetic sweep gear. The first two were initially fitted with the Type 23-2PM gunmount until the Wrobel-2MR mount was available; the SAM-launching feature of the gunmounts is not used in these ships. Are eventually to be equipped with more modern sweep gear. The depth charge racks are bolted to the mine rails when installed.
Disposal note: Leniwka-class (Project B-410S-IVS) minesweeping boats TR-25 (625) and TR-26 (626) were retired during 2005.

AMPHIBIOUS WARFARE SHIPS

♦ 5 Lublin-class (Project 767) minelayer/landing ships [LSM]

Bldr: Stocznia Pótnocna, Gdańsk

	L	In serv.		L	In serv.
821 Lublin	12-7-88	12-10-89	824 Poznań	5-1-90	8-3-91
822 Gniezno	7-12-88	23-2-90	825 Torań	8-6-90	24-5-91
823 Kraków	7-3-89	27-6-90			

Poznań (824) Michael Nitz, 8-05

Lublin (821) Frank Findler, 10-05

D: 1,210 tons std.; 1,350 tons normal (1,675 fl) **S:** 16.5 kts
Dim: 95.80 (91.20 hull; 81.00 pp) × 10.80 × 2.40
A: 4 twin 23-mm 87-cal. ZU-23-2MR Wrobel-2MR combination AA/SAM syst. (24 Strela-2M missiles); 9 elongated explosive charges for beach clearing; up to 134 mines on tank deck
Electronics:
Radar: 1 SRN-7453 nav.; 1 SRN-443XTA surf. search.
EW: No intercept; 12 9-round, 81-mm Derkach-2 decoy RL
M: 3 Sulzer-Cegielski 6ATL25D diesels; 3 Kort-nozzle props; 5,400 bhp
Electric: 750 kVA tot. (3 × 250-kVA, ZMiN-Wola, 400-V, 50-Hz diesel sets)
Range: 850–1,400/16.25 (depending on load) **Endurance:** 5 days
Crew: 5 officers, 2 warrant officers, 8 petty officers, 22 other enlisted + 135 troops

Remarks: 465 dwt. Officially retyped as minelayers in mid-1992, but remain configured primarily for an amphibious role. A planned sixth unit was canceled. 821 has been employed as a combat diver support ship since at least 1998. Two were refitted in 1998.
Hull systems: The 600-m^2 open cargo deck can accommodate nine 45-ton tanks in one row or two rows of 2.5-m-wide vehicles for a maximum vehicle load of 465 tons; maximum cargo load is 536 tons. Have hydraulic-snub cargo tie-down system. Vehicle deck has 4.2-m clearance at the ends, and the two-part folding bow ramp is 20 m long when extended. Equipped with an automated ballast system for use when discharging or loading cargo off a beach. Have Decca AD-2 and BRAS radio navaid receivers.

Combat systems: In the minelaying role, a mezzanine deck can be added in the vehicle cargo space to increase stowage. 824 was initially equipped with ZU-23-2 Wrobel-1 gunmounts vice the combination gun/missile mounting. Each 23-mm mount has 200 ready-service rounds.

♦ 3 Deba-class (Project 716) utility landing craft [LCU]

Bldr: Stocznia Marynarki Wojennej, Gdynia

	In serv.
851 KD-11	7-8-88
852 KD-12	2-1-91
853 KD-13	3-5-91

KD-11 (851) Jaroslaw Cislak, 9-03

D: 164 tons normal (176 fl) **S:** 20 kts
Dim: 37.23 (33.60 wl) × 7.27 (6.27 wl) × 1.67
A: 1 twin 23-mm 87-cal. ZU-23-2 Wrobel-1 AA; 2 PW-LWO line-charge RL; mines
Electronics: Radar: 1 SRN-207A nav.
M: 3 M-401A diesels; 3 props; 3,150 bhp
Electric: 104 kVA tot. (2 × 52-kVA diesel alternator sets; 400 V, 50 Hz)
Range: 500/16 **Fuel:** 9.4 tons **Crew:** 12 tot. + 50 troops

Remarks: Built as landing craft but redesignated as patrol boats during 1992, although they remain configured for amphibious warfare. Original plans to build 12 were reduced to five and finally to three. Are based at Świnoujście.
Hull systems: Can carry a 20-ton payload, including one armored personnel carrier and 50 troops (in a special compartment).

AUXILIARIES

♦ 2 Mrówka-class (Project 208) degaussing/deperming tenders [ADG]

Bldr: Stocznia Marynarki Wojennej, Gdynia

	In serv.
SD-11	10-10-71
SD-13	16-12-72

SD-13 IJ. Plokker, 2004

D: 550 tons (600 fl) **S:** 9.5 kts **Dim:** 44.23 × 8.12 × 2.54
A: 1 twin 25-mm 80-cal. 2M-3 AA
Electronics: Radar: 1 RN-231 nav.
M: 1 Wola 6ND36 diesel; 1 prop; 335 bhp
Range: 1,000/9.5 **Endurance:** 14 days **Crew:** 25 tot.

Remarks: SD = *Stacja Demagnetyzacyjna* (degaussing station). Name "*Wrona,*" associated with SD-11, is unofficial. Can deperm ships of up to 6,000 tons.

Disposal note: Sister SD-12 was retired during 2005. The Polnocny-B (Project 771A) former medium landing ship *Cedynia* (810), used in recent years as a munitions and cargo transport [AE], was stricken 7-4-01 for scrapping.

♦ 1 Bereza (SR-28)-class (Project 130Z Malz) fleet support ship [AG]

Bldr: Stocznia Pótnocna, Gdańsk

	L	In serv.
511 Kontradmiral Xawery Czernicki (ex-SR-253)	16-11-00	1-9-01

D: 2,049 tons (2,390 fl) **S:** 13.8 kts (12 sust.) **Dim:** 72.90 × 13.80 × 4.50
A: 1 twin 23-mm 87-cal. ZU-23-2MR Wrobel-2MR AA; 2 4-round WM-4 launchers for Strela-2M point-defense SAMs

Kontradmiral Xawery Czernicki (511) Jaroslaw Cislak, 6-05

Electronics:
Radar: 1 Decca BridgeMaster C341 ARPA nav., 1 Radwar . . . surf. search
EW: Jastrzab intercept; ORLO laser detector; 6 9-round, WNP 81/9, 81-mm Jastrzab decoy RL
M: 2 Zgoda-Sulzer 8AL25D, 750-rpm diesels; 2 CP Kort-nozzle props; 2,896 bhp—bow-thruster
Electric: 1,185 kVA + 1,550 kw tot. (2 × 480 kVA, 1 × 225 kVA; 2 × 645 kw, 1 × 260 kw)
Range: 7,000/12 **Endurance:** 30 days (14 with troops aboard)
Crew: 7 officers, 3 warrant officers, 7 senior petty officers, 21 ratings + 140 troops

Remarks: Originally ordered as the 19th Project 130 deperming tender [ADG] for the Soviet Navy and left incomplete when the Russians were unable to continue payments; significantly reconfigured and completed as a troop or military cargo ship, underway support ship, and intelligence collection vessel (using special containerized equipment in the latter role). Project name means "Mollusk." Work began 16-8-00. Based at Świnoujście and assigned to the 2nd Transport-Mineship Squadron, 8th Coast Defense Flotilla, Świnoujście.
Hull systems: Has been reconfigured to carry 140 troops with full equipment, 10 20-ft. cargo containers (150 tons max. total), or four 20-ft. containers and six Star 266 trucks. A 16-ton hydraulic crane is fitted, and there is a ramp at the stern for vehicles. A 20 × 12-m helicopter deck for one Anakonda-size helicopter is fitted above the fantail, and helicopter fueling facilities are provided. Has NBC warfare protection equipment and a GPS navigational aid. Achieved 14.1 kts on trials in light condition. A bow bulb was added to the hull during modifications for her new role. Two rudders are fitted.
Combat systems: The LN-10 Leba command and communication system is fitted, as are a SATCOM terminal and a RADWAR Suprasl IFF interrogator. For intelligence collection missions, the ship can carry a PIT Srokosz modular communications and signals intercept system mounted in a 20-ft. container positioned on the helicopter deck.

♦ 1 Polnocny-C-class (Project 776) command ship [AGF]

	Bldr.	L	In serv.
811 Grunwald	Stocznia Pótnocna, Gdańsk	16-9-72	21-4-73

Grunwald (811) Jaroslaw Cislak, 9-03

D: 1,060 tons light; 1,233 tons normal (1,314 fl) **S:** 16.3 kts
Dim: 81.30 (76.00 pp) × 9.30 × 1.20 (fwd./2.60 aft)
A: 2 twin 30-mm 65-cal. AK-230 AA; 2 4-round Fasta-4M SAM syst. (Strela-2M missiles); 2 18-round 140-mm MW-18M RL
Electronics: Radar: 1 SRN-207 nav.; 1 SRN-433XTA nav.; 1 SRN-7453 Nogat surf. search; 1 MR-104 Rys' (Drum Tilt) f.c.
M: 2 Type 40DM diesels; 2 props; 4,400 bhp
Range: 1,200/16; 2,600/12 **Endurance:** 30 days
Crew: 45 tot. + 54 command staff and vehicle crew

Remarks: The only unit of her type built as a command ship. Currently is in the 8th Flotilla but is used primarily for hydrographic survey work. Ships of this general design serve in the Russian Navy in landing-ship configuration (Project 773), and modified versions with a helicopter deck ("Polnocny-D" Projects 773K, 773KL, 773M, and 773IM) were built for export to Iraq, Libya, and India. Based at Świnoujście.
Hull systems: The normal belowdecks vehicle deck was configured with permanent command and accommodations facilities, with space left at the forward end only to transport one 15-ton armored personnel carrier or two light trucks or jeeps. Hull has a sharp, reinforced "beak" at the bow to facilitate beaching. The upper deck cannot be used to carry cargo.

AUXILIARIES *(continued)*

♦ 2 modified Moma-class (Project 863) intelligence collectors [AGI]
Bldr: Stocznia Pótnocna, Gdańsk (In serv. 1975–76)

262 Nawigator (In serv. 17-2-75) 263 Hydrograf (In serv. 8-5-75)

Nawigator (262) Jaroslaw Cislak, 2-05

D: 1,467 tons std. (1,675 fl) **S:** 17 kts
Dim: 73.30 × 12.00 (11.20 wl) × 3.82 (4.20 max.)
A: Provision for 4 twin 25-mm 80-cal. 2M-3 AA
Electronics:
Radar: 1 SRN-623 nav.; 1 SRN-7453 Nogat surf. search
EW: . . . intercept; . . . jammer
M: 2 Zgoda-Sulzer 6TD48 diesels; 2 CP props; 3,600 bhp
Range: 8,700/11 **Endurance:** 30 days **Crew:** 87 tot.

Remarks: At one time, were euphemistically described as "navigational training ships," but are now openly listed as radioelectronic collection ships (*okret dozoru radioelektronicznego*). Both based at Gdynia-Oksywie. Crane is omitted, superstructure is lengthened, and lattice mainmast is as on the *Piast* class. In 262, the forecastle is the original length, and the radome is cylindrical; in 263, the forecastle has been extended aft to the bridge face and the radome atop the pilothouse has a rounded top.

♦ 2 Heweliusz-class (Project 874) hydrographic survey ships [AGS]
Bldr: Stocznia Pótnocna, Gdańsk

	Laid down	L	In serv.
265 Heweliusz	5-6-81	20-11-81	27-11-82
266 Arctowski	5-6-81	20-11-81	27-11-82

Heweliusz (265) Jaroslaw Cislak, 5-05

D: 1,145 tons std. (1,218 fl) **S:** 13.7 kts (12 sust.)
Dim: 61.60 × 11.20 (10.80 wl) × 3.50
Electronics: Radar: 1 SRN-743X nav., 1 SRN-7453 Nogat surf. search
M: 2 Cegielski-Sulzer 6AL25/30 diesels; 2 1.9-m-dia., 320-rpm CP props; 1,920 bhp—2 140-kw electric auxiliary drive motors—bow-thruster
Electric: 675 kVA tot. **Range:** 5,900/11 **Crew:** 10 officers, 39 enlisted

Remarks: 751 grt, 250 dwt. Modified version of the Finik class built for the Soviet Navy. Named for an astronomer and an explorer. Civilian sisters *Planeta* (launched 21-5-82) and *Zodiak* (launched 28-8-82) are subordinated to the Maritime Agency at Szczecin. The two naval units are based at Gdynia-Oksywie.
Hull systems: Are able to link via chain drag for clearance surveys. Have four precision echo sounders. Unlike their Russian Navy sisters, have forecastle extended nearly to stern (providing additional accommodations spaces) and no buoy-handling capability. Carry two small survey launches aft. STN Atlas Elektronik DESO 20 precision echo sounder, RALOG 20 radio navigation receiver, and DOLOG 12D doppler log are fitted.
Disposal note: Soviet Moma-class (Project 861K) hydrographic survey ship *Kopernik* (261) was retired during 5-05.

♦ 1 ZP-1200-class small replenishment oiler [AO]
Bldr: Stocznia Marynarki Wojennej, Gdynia (In serv. 11-3-91)

Z-1 Baltyk

D: 1,984 tons (2,984 fl) **S:** 15.7 kts
Dim: 84.70 (79.00 pp) × 13.10 (12.80 wl) × 4.80
A: 2 twin 23-mm 87-cal. ZU-23-2 Wrobel-1 AA
Electronics: Radar: 1 SRN-443XTA nav.; 1 SRN-7453 Nogat surf. search
M: 2 Sulzer-Cegielski 8ASL25D diesels; 2 props; 4,025 bhp
Range: 4,250/12 **Endurance:** 20 days **Crew:** 4 officers, 28 enlisted

Remarks: Based at Gdynia-Oksywie. Was originally to have been the first of a class of four. Communications and datalink systems were updated during 1999–2000 to allow her to operate with NATO forces.
Hull systems: Has replenishment stations port and starboard and is also able to conduct astern refueling. Z = *Zbiornikowiec* (tanker). Cargo capacity: 1,184 tons fuel in seven tanks, 97.5 tons lube oil in four tanks, 26 tons residual oil, and 28 tons used oil.

Baltyk (Z-1) Jaroslaw Cislak, 2-05

♦ 3 Moskit-class (Project B-199 and ZW-2) coastal oilers [AO]

	Bldr.	Laid down	L	In serv.
Z-3	Stocznia Rzeczna, Wroctaw	12-67	22-7-69	23-9-70
Z-8	Stocznia Rzeczna, Wroctaw	. . .	14-9-69	23-7-70
Z-9	Stocznia Wista, Gdańsk	. . .	1-8-70	15-5-71

D: 700 tons light (1,225 fl, except Z-9: 1,180 tons fl) **S:** 10 kts
Dim: 57.7 (55.87 wl) × 9.50 (9.30 wl) × 3.32 (Z-9: 3.60)
A: 2 twin 23-mm 87-cal. ZU-23-2 (Z-9: 25-mm 80-cal. 2M-3M) AA; provision for 2 4-round Fasta-4M SAM syst. (Strela-2M missiles)
Electronics: Radar: 1 SRN-206 nav.
M: 1 Magdeburg (Z-9: Model 6NVD 48A-ZU) diesel; 1 CP prop; 845 (Z-9: 1,054) bhp
Range: 1,200/12 **Endurance:** 10 days **Crew:** 2 officers, 21 enlisted

Remarks: Z = *Zbiornikowiec* (tanker). The names associated with these ships, "*Krab,*" "*Meduza,*" and "*Slimak,*" are unofficial. Z-9 is considered to be of the separate ZW-2 class. Based at S´winoujs´cie, Hel, and Gdynia-Oksywie, respectively. Wrobel-1 mounts have replaced the twin 25-mm 2M-3 mounts previously installed, except in Z-9, which retains the 25-mm mounts. The gunmounts are not always fitted, and the missile systems do not seem to have been mounted. Cargo: Z-3, Z-8: 656.5 tons; Z-9: 598.6 tons.

Z-8 Jaroslaw Cislak, 7-04

♦ 2 Piast-class (Project 570) salvage ships [ARS]
Bldr: Stocznia Pótnocna, Gdańsk

281 Piast (In serv. 26-1-74) 282 Lech (In serv. 30-11-74)

Lech (282) Jaroslaw Cislak, 5-04

D: 1,697 tons std. (1,887 fl) **S:** 15.5 kts
Dim: 72.64 (67.20 pp) × 12.00 (11.60 wl) × 4.60
A: 2 4-round Fasta-4M SAM launchers (8 Strela-2M missiles)—provision for 2 twin 25-mm 80-cal. 2M-3 AA; 2 twin 23-mm 87-cal. ZU-23-2 Wrobel-1 AA
Electronics: Radar: 2 SRN-7453 Nogat nav./surf. search
M: 2 Sulzer-Zgoda 6TD48, 225-rpm diesels; 2 CP, 225-rpm props; 3,600 bhp
Electric: 900 kVA tot. (3 × 300-kVA diesel sets)
Range: 3,000/12 **Endurance:** 25 days **Crew:** 8 officers, 49 enlisted + 12 divers

Remarks: A variation of the Moma design for salvage and rescue duties. Based at Gdynia-Oksywie. 282 had her communications systems updated during 1999–2000 to allow her to operate with NATO forces. Sister *Vanguardia* (ex-East German *Otto von Guericke*) is in service with the Uruguayan Navy.
Hull systems: Have extensive firefighting facilities: three foam/water monitors, two firepumps, and two portable firefighting pumps; total pump capacity is 1,960 m^3/hour. Capable of ocean-towing. Have a 60-m-capable, three-person diving bell and a six-place decompression chamber. 281 deployed with UN Coalition forces to the Mideast 12-90 to

AUXILIARIES *(continued)*

20-5-91, armed with four twin 25-mm AA and equipped with a Navstar 2000 GPS receiver, Navtex facsimile receiver, and Kelvin-Hughes collision avoidance system. Both have been refitted with a dynamic positioning system with heavier anchors forward and two anchors mounted aft in order to provide a four-point mooring capability. 281 has a light helicopter platform mounted atop the salvage equipment aft.

♦ 1 Wodnik-class (Project 888) training ships [ATS]
Bldr: Stocznia Pótnocna, Gdańsk

	L	In serv.
251 Wodnik	29-11-75	28-5-76

Wodnik (251) Leo van Ginderen, 2-06

D: 1,489 tons (1,745 fl) **S:** 15.5 kts **Dim:** 72.24 × 12.00 (11.60 wl) × 4.13
A: 2 twin 30-mm 65-cal. AK-230 AA; 2 twin 23-mm 87-cal. ZU-23-2MR Wrobel-2MR combination AA/SAM syst. (Strela-2M missiles)
Electronics: Radar: 1 SRN-7453 Nogat nav./surf. search
M: 2 Sulzer-Cegielski 6TD48 diesels; 2 CP props; 3,600 bhp **Range:** 7,800/15
Endurance: 30 days **Crew:** 24 officers, 32 enlisted + 13 instructors, 87 cadets

Remarks: Nearly identical to the former East German *Wilhelm Pieck* and similar to the *Luga* and *Oka* in the Soviet Navy. Based at Gdynia-Oksywie. Name means "Water Elf." From 12-90 to 5-91, 251 operated as an unarmed hospital ship in support of UN Coalition forces in the Mideast, reconverting to training ship on return. 251 had communications and other systems updated during 1999–2000 to allow her to operate with NATO units.

Wodnik (251) Leo van Ginderen, 2-06

Hull systems: Developed from the Moma navigational aids tender design. As a hospital ship, *Wodnik* had berths for 84 patients (plus facilities for 30–50 ambulatory patients) and carried 10 medical personnel in addition to an operating crew of 63; to assist her deployment, she received new radios, a Navstar 2000 GPS receiver, a Navtex facsimile receiver, and Kelvin-Hughes collision avoidance equipment.
Combat systems: The MR-104 Rys' (Drum Tilt) gun fire-control radar formerly carried at the top of the lattice mast has been removed from both, and individual ringsight directors now control the 30-mm guns. A helicopter deck was added aft on 251 in 1991 and has been retained in place of the 30-mm mount originally fitted there.
Disposals: Sister *Gryf* (252) was decomissioned during 2005.

Note: The merchant marine sail training ship *Dar Mlodziezy* occasionally carries naval cadets among her trainees.

SERVICE CRAFT

♦ 1 pollution control lighter [YAG]
Bldr: Stocznia Pótnocna, Gdańsk (In serv. 14-7-61)

B-7 (ex-Z-7)

B-7 Jaroslaw Cislak, 9-05

D: 615 tons (fl) **S:** 8 kts **Dim:** 44.2 × 7.6 × 3.1 (max.)
M: 1 Wola diesel; 1 prop; 300 bhp **Crew:** 7 tot.

Remarks: Former Project 500 fuel lighter, converted as an oil-spill collection craft by Nauta Repair Yard, Gdynia. The single Wola diesel has reportedly been removed.

♦ 1 B-600-class cargo lighter [YF]

B-9 (In serv. 9-10-70)

B-9 Dieter Wolf, 9-03

Remarks: B = *Barka* (dumb barge or self-propelled lighter for dry or liquid cargo). Is self-propelled and has a small navigational radar. Originally constructed as a river barge in 1954.

♦ 1 miscellaneous barge [YC]

B-6 (In serv. 1-11-54)

Remarks: Barge B-5 was reportedly removed from service in 1998.

B-6 Jaroslaw Cislak, 5-02

♦ 2 Project KH-K-class communications launches [YFL]
Bldr: Wroclawska Stocznia Rzeczna, Wroctaw

K-20 (In serv. 15-5-89) K-21 (In serv. 19-2-90)

K-21—communications launch Jaroslaw Cislak, 9-03

D: 12.25 tons (fl) **S:** 8.4 kts **Dim:** 9.00 × 3.00 × 0.83 **Crew:** 3

Remarks: Also capable of light towing. K = *Kuter* (general-purpose craft).

♦ 3 Project 4142-class passenger launches [YFL]
Bldr: Tczewska Stocznia Rzeczna, Tczewie

K-5 (In serv. 15-2-88) K-7 (In serv. 15-12-88) K-9 (In serv. 25-9-89)

K-5 Jaroslaw Cislak, 7-05

SERVICE CRAFT *(continued)*

D: 45 tons (50 fl) **S:** 9.1 kts **Dim:** 18.88 × 4.42 × 1.60
M: 1 Wola diesel; 1 prop; 100 bhp **Range:** 85/8 **Crew:** 4 tot.

Remarks: Similar to survey launches K-4 and K-10. K = *Kuter* (general-purpose craft).

♦ 1 Project B-574 passenger launches [YFL]
Bldr: Wroclawska Stocznia Rzeczna, Wroctaw

K-13 (In serv. 26-7-78)

K-13 Jaroslaw Cislak, 5-05

D: 45 tons (50 fl) **S:** 9.1 kts **Dim:** 18.88 × 4.42 × 1.60
M: 1 Wola diesel; 1 prop; 100 bhp **Range:** 85/8 **Crew:** 4 tot.

Remarks: Similar to Project 4142, but with wooden hull. Can also be used as tugs. K = *Kuter* (general-purpose craft).

Disposal note: Sisters K-12 and K-14 were retired during 2005.

♦ 1 Project B-447 passenger launches [YFL]
Bldr: Wroclawska Stocznia Rzeczna, Wroctaw (In serv. 11-7-76)

K-2

K-2 Jaroslaw Cislak, 5-05

D: 45 tons (50 fl) **S:** 9.1 kts **Dim:** 18.88 × 4.42 × 1.60
M: 1 Wola diesel; 1 prop; 100 bhp **Range:** 85/8 **Crew:** 4 tot.

Remarks: Similar to Project B-574. Also usable as inshore survey craft. K = *Kuter* (general-purpose craft). Sister K-1 was stricken from service 31-3-03.

♦ 1 SMK-75-class multipurpose launch [YFL]
Bldr: Stocznia Marynarki Wojennej, Gdnyia (In serv. 15-2-86)

M-41

D: 1.5 tons (fl) **S:** . . . kts **Dim:** 6.35 × 1.95 × 0.68

Remarks: M = *Motorwka* (general-purpose harbor-service motorboat).

♦ 3 M-35/MW-class multipurpose launches [YFL]
Bldr: Tczewska Stocznia Rzeczna, Tczewie

	In serv.		In serv.
M-12	12-10-83	M-22	10-11-84
M-21	29-12-83		

D: 28.66 tons (fl) **S:** 8.3 kts **Dim:** 10.75 × 4.0 × 1.5
M: 3 diesels; 3 props; 450 bhp **Crew:** 3 tot.

Remarks: One sister was delivered to the coast guard in 1991 as SG-036. M = *Motorwka* (general-purpose harbor-service motorboat).

Disposals: Sisters M-5, M-29, and M-30 were decommissioned during 2005.

M-22 Jaroslaw Cislak, 3-02

♦ 1 MG-600/MW-class multipurpose launch [YFL]
Bldr: Stocznia Wista, Gdańsk (In serv. 20-4-77)

M-32

M-32 Jaroslaw Cislak, 9-03

D: 40 tons (fl) **S:** 14.7 kts **Dim:** 20.61 × 4.59 × 1.15
Crew: 5 + up to 8 passengers

Remarks: M = *Motorwka* (general-purpose harbor-service motorboat).

Disposal note: Both remaining Project B-306 multipurpose launches (M-2 and M-28) were stricken from service 31-03-03.

♦ 2 Project Delfin motor launches [YFL]
Bldr: Stocznia Ustka, Ustka (In serv. 8-3-71)

M-25 M-26

D: . . . tons **S:** . . . kts **Dim:** 8.52 × 3.2 × 0.60

Remarks: M = *Motorwka* (general-purpose harbor-service motorboat). Can carry up to 32 passengers.

♦ 1 Project MS-3600 commander-in-chief's yacht [YFL]
Bldr: Stocznia Marynarki Wojennej, Gdynia

	Laid down	L	In serv.
M-1	10-9-69	25-2-70	26-6-70

M-1—blue hull, white superstructure as commander-in-chief's yacht
Jaroslaw Cislak, 11-04

D: 74.4 tons (fl) **S:** 27.6 kts **Dim:** 28.70 × 5.80 × 1.20
M: 3 Soviet M-50-FS diesels; 3 props; 3,600 bhp **Crew:** 8 tot.+ 30 passengers

Remarks: Has a steel hull and aluminum superstructure. M = *Motorwka* (general-purpose harbor-service motorboat).

Disposal note: Project M-600/II staff motorboat *M-3* was decomissioned during 2005.

♦ 1 M-150-class motor launch [YFL]
Bldr: Stocznia Marynarki Wojennej, Gdynia (In serv. 29-1-66)

M-6

D: 10 tons (fl) **S:** 12.3 kts **Dim:** 13.95 × 3.75 × 0.80
Crew: 5 + up to 10 passengers

SERVICE CRAFT *(continued)*

Remarks: M = *Motorwka* (general-purpose harbor-service motorboat).

Disposal note: Russian Kometa-M-class (Project 342 MT) passenger hydrofoils *Pogwizd, Zodiak,* and *Zefir* had all been decomissioned by 2006.

♦ 2 Project 4234 inshore survey craft [YGS]
Bldr: Stocznia Wista, Gdańsk

K-4 (In serv. 25-9-89) K-10 (In serv. 6-2-89)

K-4 Jaroslaw Cislak, 6-04

D: 45 tons (50 fl) **S:** 9.1 kts **Dim:** 18.88 × 4.42 × 1.60
Electronics: Radar: 1 SRN-207A nav.
M: 1 Wola DM 150 diesel; 1 prop; 165 bhp
Range: 85/8 **Crew:** 10 tot. + 4 passengers

Remarks: Similar to passenger launches K-5, K-7, and K-9. GRP construction. K = *Kuter* (general-purpose craft).

♦ 5 MH-111-class hydrographic launches [YGS]
Bldr: Stocznia Marynarki Wojennej, Gdynia

	In serv.		In serv.
M-35	12-7-84	M-39	18-1-84
M-37	18-1-84	M-40	24-10-84
M-38	18-1-84		

M-39—on land storage Jaroslaw Cislak, 6-04

D: 9.1 tons (10 fl) **S:** 8.6 kts **Dim:** 10.72 × 4.06 × 0.60
Electronics: Radar: 1 SRN-207A nav.
M: 1 Puck-Rekin SW 400/MZ diesel; 95 bhp
Range: 184/8.4 **Crew:** 4 + 8 survey party

Remarks: Resemble cabin cruisers. M = *Motorwka* (general-purpose harbor-service motorboat).

♦ 3 45-meter fuel barges [YON]
Bldr: . . .

B-11 (In serv. 31-12-79) B-12 (In serv. 1-8-80) B-13 (In serv. 20-6-81)

Dim: 65.0 × 9.26 × 3.0 **Crew:** 6 tot.

Remarks: B = *Barka* (dumb-barge or self-propelled lighter for dry or liquid cargo). Is not fitted with a propulsion system.

Disposal note: Project PR-5–class fuel barge B-2 was removed from service 31-1-03.

B-12 Jaroslaw Cislak, 7-04

♦ 1 Project BPZ-500A/MW fuel barge [YON]
Bldr: Tczewska Stocznia Rzeczna, Tczewie (In serv. 25-7-88)

B-3

Remarks: Dimensions are 35.0 × 8.9 × 2.5. B = *Barka* (dumb-barge or self-propelled lighter for dry or liquid cargo). Based at Kołobrzeg. Can carry 600 tons of cargo.

♦ 1 Pajak-class (Project Kormoran) torpedo retrievers [YPT]
Bldr: Stocznia Marynarki Wojennej, Gdynia

	L	In serv.
K-8	26-8-70	3-7-71

D: 110 tons light; 133 tons std. (149 fl) **S:** 21 kts (19.3 sust.)
Dim: 34.92 (33.70 wl) × 6.60 (6.02 wl) × 1.72
A: 1 twin 23-mm 87-cal. ZU-23-2 Wrobel-1 AA
Electronics: Radar: 1 SRN-206 nav.
M: 2 M-50F-5 diesels; 2 props; 2,370 bhp
Range: 256/17.5; 660/9.5 **Endurance:** 5 days **Crew:** 18 tot.

Remarks: The name associated with this ship, *"Kormoran-I,"* is unofficial. K = *Kuter* (general-purpose craft). Is based at Gdynia-Oksywie. Has a 3-ton-capacity crane with 8-m radius and a stern recovery ramp. Can stow eight 533-mm torpedoes on deck.

Disposal: Sister K-11 was decomissioned in 2005.

♦ 2 Zbyszko-class (Project B-823) salvage tenders [YRS]
Bldr: Stocznia Ustka, Ustka

	Laid down	L	In serv.
R-14 Zbyszko	5-90	12-90	8-11-91
R-15 Maćko	10-90	2-91	20-3-92

Maćko (R-15)—alongside sister *Zbyszko* (R-14) Jaroslaw Cislak, 5-04

D: 380 tons (fl) **S:** 11 kts **Dim:** 35.00 (30.00 pp) × 8.00 × 3.00
Electronics: Radar: 1 SRN-402X nav.
M: 1 Sulzer-Ceglielski 6AL20/24D diesel; 1 Kort-nozzle, CP, 458-rpm, 1.58-m-dia. prop; 750 bhp (530 sust.)
Electric: 144 kw tot. (3 × 48-kw Wola SW400 diesel sets)
Range: 3,000/10 **Crew:** 15 tot.

Remarks: Operated by the Naval Rescue and Salvage Service. R = *Okret Ratownicz* (salvage tug, salvage craft, or diving tender). Are able to support two divers to a depth of 45 m simultaneously and have 100-m-depth decompression chambers. Equipped with two DWP-16 firefighting water cannon. Based at Kołobrzeg.

♦ 2 Pluskwa-class (Project R-30) salvage tugs [YRS]
Bldr: Stocznia Marynarki Wojennej, Gdynia

R-11 Gniewko (In serv. 29-9-81) R-13 Semko (In serv. 9-5-87)

D: 321 tons (369 fl) **S:** 12 kts **Dim:** 32.38 (28.50 pp) × 9.00 (8.20 wl) × 3.06
Electronics: Radar: 1 SRN-823 nav.
M: 1 Sulzer-Cegielski 6AL25/30 diesel; 1 Kort-nozzle prop; 1,470 bhp
Electric: 363 kw tot. (3 × 121 kw; 3 Wola H-6 165-bhp diesels driving)
Range: 4,600/7 **Fuel:** 43 tons **Endurance:** 6 days
Crew: 18 tot. (incl. 5 divers)

Remarks: R-11 was launched 26-10-80 and commenced sea trials 7-7-81. R = *Okret Ratownicz* (salvage tug, salvage craft, or diving tender). Are attached to the 41st Salvage and Rescue Division, R-11 based at Hel and the other at Świnoujście. Can recover objects from depths up to 60 m and are equipped to support salvage divers and conduct fire fighting.

Disposals: Sister *Bolko* (R-12) was retired during 5-05.

SERVICE CRAFT *(continued)*

Gniewko (R-11) Jaroslaw Cislak, 6-04

♦ 2 Project H-960-class large harbor tugs [YTB]
Bldr: Gdynska Stocznia Remontowa Nauta, Gdynia

H-6 (In serv. 25-9-92) H-8 (In serv. 19-3-93)

H-8 Jaroslaw Cislak, 9-05

D: 310 tons (332 fl) **S:** 12 kts **Dim:** 27.80 × 8.40 (8.00 wl) × 3.00
Electronics: Radar: 1 SRN-401XA nav.
M: 1 Sulzer-Cegielski 6ATL25D diesel; 1 Kort-nozzle, CP, 247-rpm prop; 1,280 bhp
Range: 1,150/12 **Crew:** 1 officer, 16 enlisted

Remarks: Ordered in 1988. H-6 was launched 11-5-91, H-8 on 15-11-92. H = *Holownik* (tug). H-6 is based at Hel, H-8 at Gdynia-Oksywie.

Disposal note: Motyl-class (Project 1500) large harbor tugs H-12 and H-20 were stricken 31-3-03.

♦ 2 Project B-820 medium harbor tugs [YTM]
Bldr: Stocznia Ustka, Ustka

H-9 (In serv. 27-6-93) H-10 (In serv. 24-6-93)

H-9 Jaroslaw Cislak, 5-04

D: 149.3 tons (fl) **S:** 10.8 kts **Dim:** 22.01 (18.50 pp) × 6.40 × 2.30
M: 1 Cegielski-Sulzer 6AL20/24 diesel; 1 CP prop; 570 bhp
Endurance: 4 days **Crew:** 4–6 tot.

Remarks: 75 kilonewton bollard pull. H = *Holownik* (tug).

♦ 4 Bucha-class (Project H-900/II) medium harbor tugs [YTM]
Bldr: Stocznia Remontowa Nauta, Gdynia

	In serv.		In serv.
H-3	3-12-79	H-5	15-6-81
H-4	10-2-80	H-7	19-7-81

D: 220 tons (310 fl) **S:** 12 kts **Dim:** 26.30 (25.40 pp) × 7.10 × 2.80
Electronics: Radar: 1 SRN-206 nav.
M: 1 Cegielski-Sulzer 6AL20/24H diesel; 1 CP prop; 760 bhp
Electric: 76 kw tot. **Fuel:** 20 tons **Crew:** 15 tot.

Remarks: Class was also built for civil use. H = *Holownik* (tug). Bollard pull: 10 tons. H-3 is based at Hel, H-4 at Świnoujście, and H-5 and H-7 at Gdynia-Oksywie.

H-7 Jaroslaw Cislak, 9-05

♦ 2 Project H-800/IV medium harbor tugs [YTM]
Bldr: Stocznia Remontowa Nauta, Gdynia

H-1 (In serv. 30-12-70) H-2 (In serv. 28-2-79)

H-2 Jaroslaw Cislak, 9-03

D: 218 tons (fl) **S:** 11 kts **Dim:** 25.6 × 6.8 × 2.8
Electronics: Radar: 1 SRN-206 nav.
M: 1 Magdeburg 6NVD48 diesel; 1 Kort-nozzle prop; 800 bhp
Range: 1,500/9 **Crew:** 17 tot.

Remarks: Bollard pull: 12 tons. H = *Holownik* (tug).

♦ 1 Project B-79/II sail-training craft [YTS]

	Bldr.	Laid down	L	In serv.
Iskra	Stocznia Gdańsk	11-11-81	6-3-82	11-8-82

D: 381 tons (498 fl) **S:** 10.2 (under power)
Dim: 49.00 (42.70 hull; 36.00 pp) × 8.00 × 3.70
Electronics: Radar: 1 SRN-206 nav.
M: 1 Wola 68H12 diesel; 1 CP, 356-rpm, 1.5-m-dia. prop; 310 bhp—sail area: 1,038 m^2 max.; 960 m^2 normal
Crew: 5 officers, 8 petty officers, 50 cadets

Remarks: The three-masted barkentine's name means "Spark." Has 63 total berths. Can also be used for oceanographic research. Is operated by the Polish Naval Academy (*Akedemia Marynarki Wojennej*). Circumnavigated the globe in 1995–96. Sister *Pogoria* is civilian subordinated, as is the much larger sail-training ship *Dar Mlodziezy,* also completed in 1982. Sister *Kaliakra* is operated by Bulgaria.

Disposal note: *Bryza*-class (Project OS-1) navigational training craft *Bryza* (K-18), *Podchorąży* (711), *Kadet* (712), and *Elew* (713) were retired by 2005.

SERVICE CRAFT *(continued)*

Iskra Leo van Ginderen, 7-05

POLISH BORDER GUARD
(*Straz Graniczna Rzeczpospolitej Polskiej*)
MINISTRY OF THE INTERIOR

Established 19-5-91 under the Ministry of the Interior from the assets of the former Sea Border Brigade, which had earlier been known as the Border Guard (*Wojska Ochrony Pogranicza*), and several other maritime agencies. Ships and craft are marked *"Straz Graniczna RP,"* and their dark blue hulls carry a red diagonal stripe with a yellow edge. Pennant numbers begin with SG (*Strazy Granicnej*). Most ships are based at Gdańsk. The fleet is organized into two squadrons, the Kaszubski Dywizjon Strazy Granicznej (Kashubian Squadron of the Border Guard) and the Pomorski Dywizjon Strazy Granicznej (Pomeranian Squadron). The Baltycki Dywizjon Strazy Granicznej (Baltic Squadron) was disestablished on 1-1-00.

Maritime Aviation: Four PZL-104M Wilga 2000 light observation aircraft and one PZL M20 Mewa (license-built Piper PA 34 Seneca-II) light patrol aircraft

Construction Program: Plans call for the construction of two 400- to 500-ton, 50- to 60-m-long, 25-kt patrol craft armed with a 25-mm gun and equipped with a helicopter platform. Also planned are two more SAR 1500 rescue launches, two air-cushion craft, and five smaller support launches.

PATROL CRAFT [WPC]

♦ 2 SKS-40-class fisheries patrol boats Bldr: Stocznia Wista, Gdańsk

	In serv.
SG-311 Kaper-1	21-1-91
SG-312 Kaper-2	1-10-94

Kaper-1 (SG-311) Jaroslaw Cislak, 5-04

D: 470 tons (fl) **S:** 17.6 kts
Dim: 42.60 (38.76 pp) × 8.38 (7.70 wl) × 2.80 (3.00 max.)
A: 2 single 7.62-mm mg
Electronics: Radar: 1 Decca . . . nav.; 1 SRN-231 nav.
M: 2 Sulzer-HCP 8ATL25D diesels; 2 CP, 1.65-m-dia., 493-rpm props; 4,790 bhp
Electric: 290 kw tot. (2 × 145 kw, Wola 72H6 diesels driving)
Range: 2,800/14 **Endurance:** 8 days **Crew:** 11 crew + 2 inspectors

Remarks: 376 grt. Begun for the Maritime Office of Inspections (*Urzed Morski*) but incorporated instead into the new border patrol agency. *Kaper* means "Privateer." SG-312 was launched 3-4-92. As of 4-02, SG-311 was attached to the Kashubian Squadron and based at Gdańsk, while SG-312 was attached to the Pomeranian Squadron and based at Kołobrzeg. SG-311 carries Project M-4500 RIB SG-027 on deck aft.

♦ 2 Obluze class (Project 912)
Bldr: Stocznia Marynarki Wojennej, Gdynia

	In serv.
SG-323 Zefir	10-6-67
SG-325 Tęcza	31-1-68

Zefir (SG-323) Jaroslaw Cislak, 5-04

D: 212 tons (237 fl) **S:** 24 kts **Dim:** 41.40 (39.50 pp) × 5.80 × 1.90 (hull)
A: 2 twin 30-mm 65-cal. AK-230 AA; 4 d.c. racks (2 internal, 2 on deck aft; 24 tot. d.c.); 4 AMD-1000 mines in lieu of topside d.c. racks
Electronics:
Radar: 1 SRN-207 nav.
Sonar: Tamir-11 hull-mounted HF searchlight
M: 2 Type 40DM diesels; 2 props; 4,000 bhp **Electric:** 150 kw
Range: 1,220/12 **Fuel:** 25 tons **Crew:** 20 tot.

Remarks: Names mean "Zephyr" and "Rainbow," respectively. Five additional units with more-powerful engines and fire-control radars for the 30-mm AA serve in the Polish Navy. Both are attached to the Pomeranian Squadron and are based at Kołobrzeg.

Disposals: *Fala* (SG-321) and *Szkwal* (SG-322) were stricken 16-2-96, with *Fala* destined to become a museum ship in Kołobrzeg. *Zorza* (SG-324) was stricken 22-10-98.

PATROL BOATS [WPB]

♦ 2 SAR-1500SG patrol launches
Bldrs: Alu International, Gdańsk (hulls), and Damen Shipyard Polska, Gdynia (fitting out)

	In serv.
SG-211 Strażnik-1	29-4-00
SG-212 Strażnik-2	9-7-00

Strażnik (SG-211) Jaroslaw Cislak, 2-05

D: . . . tons **S:** 35 kts **Dim:** 15.20 (14.6 hull; 11.80 wl) × 5.39 (4.20 hull) × 0.90
A: 1 7.62-mm PKMS mg **Electronics:** Radar: 1 Decca BridgeMaster-E ARPA nav.
M: 2 M.A.N. 2848LE 401 diesels; 2 waterjets; 1,340 bhp
Range: 170/20 **Fuel:** 1.56 m^3 **Crew:** 1 officer, 3 enlisted + 8 passengers

Remarks: Two ordered 5-10-99, with the pair laid down 7-10-99 and 5-11-99, respectively. Two more may be procured. SG-211 is attached to the Kashubian Squadron and based at Gdańsk; SG-212 is attached to the Pomeranian Squadron. Have aluminum hulls with an inflated collar surrounding the hull. Design is based on the Dutch SAR 1500 lifeboat *Graf Van Bylandt.* Can carry up to 75 people in an emergency.

♦ 2 Pilica class (Project 918M)
Bldr: Stocznia Marynarki Wojennej, Gdynia

	In serv.
SG-161	6-6-73
SG-164	3-10-74

D: 79.7 tons (86.9 fl) **S:** 28 kts **Dim:** 28.59 × 5.76 × 1.30
A: 1 twin 23-mm 87-cal. Wrobel-2M AA
Electronics: Radar: 1 RN-231 nav.
M: 3 M-50F-4 diesels; 3 props; 3,600 bhp **Crew:** 13 tot.

Remarks: Differ from the eight naval-subordinated units in lacking torpedo tubes and in having an A-frame gantry crane aft to assist in towing and rescue work. SG-161 is attached to the Kashubian Squadron and based at Gdańsk. Sisters SG-162 and SG-163 were stricken 19-2-99.

POLISH BORDER GUARD PATROL BOATS [WPB] *(continued)*

SG-164 Jaroslaw Cislak, 9-03

◆ **6 Wisloka class (Project 90)** Bldr: Stocznia Wista, Gdańsk

	In serv.		In serv.
SG-142	20-1-74	SG-146	24-10-75
SG-144	1-2-75	SG-150	23-4-77
SG-145	27-7-75	SG-152	5-8-77

SG-145 Jaroslaw Cislak, 5-04

D: 42 tons (50 fl) **S:** 12 kts **Dim:** 22.8 × 5.0 × 1.2
A: 1 twin 12.7-mm M1 mg **Electronics:** Radar: 1 SRN-207 nav.
M: 2 Wola 31 ANM28 H12A diesels; 2 props; 1,006 bhp
Range: 500/18 **Crew:** 9 tot.

Remarks: SG-142 and SG-150 are attached to the Kashubian Squadron and based at Gdańsk, the others to the Pomeranian Squadron, based at Świnoujście. Sister SG-141 was stricken 19-2-99, while SG-147, SG-148, SG-149, and SG-151 had already been stricken by that date. SG-150 carries Project MR-4800 RIB SG-025 on deck aft.

SERVICE CRAFT

◆ **1 (+ 1) Griffon 2000 TD Mk III–class air cushion vehicles**
Bldr: Griffon Hovercraft, Salisbury Green, Southampton, U.K. (In serv. 2006–)

SG 411 SG 412

SG-411 *Okrety Wojenne* via Jaroslaw Malinowski, 2006

D: 7.5 tons (fl) **S:** 30 kts **Dim:** 12.7 × 6.1 × 3.9
A: Provision for 1 7.62-mm mg **Electronics:** Radar: 1 . . . nav.
M: 1 Deutz BF8L513 diesel; 1 shrouded CP airscrew; 320 bhp
Range: 300/25 loaded **Crew:** 2 tot. + 12 troops

Remarks: Ordered 7-05. Can carry 2,200-kg cargo in lieu of troops. GRP construction hull.

◆ **1 MI-6-class launches [WYFL]**
Bldr: Stocznia Wista, Gdańsk (In serv. 1988–90)

SG-008

D: 13.8 tons (17.9 fl) **S:** 11 kts **Dim:** 14.05 (13.00 pp) × 3.52 × 1.20

Remarks: Attached to the Kashubian Squadron, based at Gdańsk. Sister SG 006 was stricken in 2005, SG-015 on 19-2-99, and SG-016 and SG-017 on 25-6-99.

SG-008 Jaroslaw Cislak, 5-03

◆ **1 M-35/MW-class launch [WYFL]**
Bldr: Tzcewska Stocznia Rzeczna, Tzcewcie (In serv. 25-12-85)

SG-036

SG-036 Jaroslaw Cislak, 5-03

D: 28.66 tons (41 fl) **S:** 8.3 kts **Dim:** 10.75 × 4.4 × 1.6
M: 1 Wola DM 150 diesel; 1 prop; 150 bhp **Crew:** 4 tot.

Remarks: Attached to the Kashubian Squadron and based at Gdańsk.

Note: Also in service are the following RIBs: four Project S-7500 and S-7500/K: SG-002, SG-003, SG-004, and SG-005; seven Project MR-4800 and MR-4800/B: SG-020 through SG-026; three Project M-4500: SG-027, SG-029, and SG-030; and six Project S-6100: SG-061 through SG-066. Sail-training craft *Galeon* (in serv. 29-7-86) and *Karawela II* (in serv. 15-7-81) of, respectively, Conrad 46 and Conrad 45 type are also in service.

Project S-6100 launch SG-066 Jaroslaw Cislak, 11-04

PORTUGAL

Portuguese Republic

MARINHA PORTUGUESA

Personnel: 10,950, including 1,980 marines. 930 personnel are in the naval reserve force.

Bases: Principal base at Alfeite, which also has a well-equipped dockyard; smaller facilities at Ponta Delgada, Portimão, Porto, and Funchal (Madeira)

Naval Aviation: Five Lynx Mk 95 ordered 10-90 were delivered during 1993 to form a naval aviation organization (three are new construction, and the other two are rebuilt, ex-RN HAS.3s); the helicopters carry Bendix 1500 radars and AQS-18 dipping sonars. Naval aircraft are based at Montijo, near Lisbon.

MARINHA PORTUGUESA *(continued)*

Portuguese Navy Lynx Mk 95—aboard *Alvares Cabral* (F 331)
Ben Sullivan, 11-03

Seven Air Force CASA 212-200 Aviocar light transports (four with photo equipment) are equipped for maritime reconnaissance and fisheries protection duties. Six ex-Australian P-3B-II Orions are operated by Esquadra de Reconhecimento Maritimo 601 from Montijo. An additional five P-3C Orions were purchased from the Netherlands during 2005. Five C-130H Hercules transports and 10 AS.330C Puma helicopters are used for search and rescue. The Pumas are to be replaced by 12 AgustaWestland EH.101 helicopters ordered 3-12-01; deliveries of the first EH.101s began in 2005. Two CASA 212-300s were ordered in early 1993 for fisheries patrol duties to begin replacement of the CASA 212-200s.

Note: Ship names are preceded by NRP (*Navio Republicano Portugues*).

ATTACK SUBMARINES [SS]

♦ 0 (+ 2) German Type 209 PN class

	Bldr	Laid down	L	In serv.
S . . .	Howaldtswerke, Kiel	. . .	. . .	2009
S . . .	Nordseewerke, Emden	. . .	. . .	2010

D: 1,740 tons surf./2,011 tons sub.
S: 12 kts surf./22 kts sub. (max.) **Dim:** 65 × 6.30 × 5.50
A: 8 bow 533-mm TT (16 Black Shark wire-guided torpedoes and UGM-84 Harpoon missiles)
Electronics:
Radar: 1 . . . nav.
Sonar: . . .
EW: . . .
M: Diesel-electric, with Siemens Polymer Electrolytic Membrane fuel cells for air-independent cruising, 2 MTU 16V396 diesels (2,000 kw), 1 7-bladed prop
Range: 13,000/4; 7,900/8 **Crew:** 27 total

Remarks: Replacements for the *Daphné*-class submarines; were ordered 4-04. To be fitted with Air Independent Propulsion. Operating depth will be 350 m. The class represents a compromise between the older Type 209 and more modern Type 212/214-class submarines. Will carry the STN Atlas Elektronik ISUS 90 combat data system. Option for a third unit may be exercised at a later date.

♦ 2 French Daphné class
Bldr: Dubigeon-Normandy, Nantes

	Laid down	L	In serv.
S 164 Barracuda	19-10-65	24-4-67	4-5-68
S 166 Delfim	14-5-67	23-9-68	1-10-69

Barracuda (S 164) Bernard Prézelin, 9-05

Barracuda (S 164) Bernard Prézelin, 9-05

D: 746 tons std.; 868 tons surf./1,038 tons sub.
S: 13.5 kts surf./15 kts sub. **Dim:** 57.78 × 6.75 × 4.62
A: 12 550-mm TT (8 fwd, 4 aft; 12 ECAN E 14 or E 15 torpedoes—no reloads)
Electronics:
Radar: 1 Kelvin-Hughes Type 1007 nav./search
Sonar: Thales DUUA-2 active (8.4 kHz); Thales DSUV-2 passive
EW: ARUR and ARUD intercept
M: Diesel-electric propulsion: 2 SEMT-Pielstick 12PA1 diesels, 2 × 450-kw generator sets, 2 Jeumont-Schneider 800-shp (1,300 shp for short periods) motors; 2 props
Range: 2,710/12.5 surf.; 9,430/ . . . surf.; 2,130/10, 4,300/7.5 snorkel
Crew: 5 officers, 45 enlisted

Disposals: *Cachalote* (S 165) was purchased by the Pakistani Navy in 1975. *Albacora* (S 163) was stricken 14-7-00. S 166 is expected to decomission during 2006–7 and S 164 will follow in 2009.
Hull systems: Operating depth was originally 300 m, but they probably do not attempt that depth anymore.
Combat systems: The sonar suite has been updated, but not to the extent performed on sisters in other navies. The after torpedo tubes are external to the pressure hull. Were to be modernized under the 1992–95 budgetary period, probably with French sonars, but funds were not available; they did receive new radars in 1994.

GUIDED-MISSILE FRIGATES [FFG]

♦ 0 (+ 2) ex-U.S. Oliver Hazard Perry class
Builder: Todd, San Pedro, Calif.

	Laid down	L	In serv.
. . . (ex-*George Philip,* FFG 12)	14-12-77	16-12-78	15-11-80
. . . (ex-*Sides,* FFG 14)	7-8-78	19-5-79	30-5-81

D: 2,769 tons light (3,658 fl) **S:** 29 kts (30.6 on trials)
Dim: 135.64 (125.9 wl) × 13.72 × 5.8 (6.7 max.)
A: 1 Mk 13 Mod. 4 launcher (4 Harpoon and 36 Standard SM-1 MR missiles); 1 76-mm 62-cal. Mk 75 DP; 1 20-mm Mk 15 Phalanx gatling CIWS; 2 triple 324-mm Mk 32 Mod. 5 ASW TT (6 A244 Mod. 3 torpedoes); 1 or 2 helicopters
Electronics:
Radar: 1 Cardion SPS-55 surf. search.; 1 Raytheon SPS-49(V)4 air search; 1 Lockheed-Martin Mk 92 Mod. 2 missile/gun f.c.; 1 Lockheed-Martin STIR missile/gun f.c.
Sonar: SQQ-89(V)2 suite: Raytheon SQS-56 hull-mounted LF
TACAN: URN-25
EW: Raytheon SLQ-32(V)2 intercept; Mk 36 SRBOC decoy syst. (2 6-round Raytheon Mk 137 RL); SLQ-25 Nixie towed acoustic torpedo decoy syst.
M: 2 G.E. LM-2500 gas turbines; 1 5.5-m-dia., CP, 5-bladed prop; 41,000 shp (40,000 sust.)—2 drop-down electric propulsors; 720 shp
Electric: 3,000 kw tot. (3 × 1,000 kw, diesels driving)
Range: 4,200/20; 5,000/18 **Fuel:** 587 tons + 64 tons helicopter fuel
Crew: 16 officers, 198 enlisted

Remarks: Expected to transfer during 2007.
Hull systems: Have 19-mm aluminum-alloy armor over magazine spaces, 16-mm steel over the main engine-control room, and 19-mm Kevlar plastic armor over vital electronics and command spaces. Speed on one turbine alone is 25 kts. The auxiliary power system uses two retractable pods located well forward and can drive the ships at up to 6 kts. Have fin stabilizers. Do not have a helicopter haul-down and deck traversal system.
Combat systems: Have the Mk 13 weapons-direction system. The Mk 92 Mod. 4 fire-control system controls missile and 76-mm gunfire; uses a STIR (modified SPG-60) antenna amidships and a U.S.-built version of the Hollandse Signaal Apparaaten (H.S.A., now Thales) WM-28 radar forward and can track four separate targets; there are two missile illumination channels per ship.
The Mk 75 gun is a license-built version of the OTO Melara Compact. Two Mk 24 optical missile and gun target designators are mounted in tubs atop the pilothouse. A total of 24 ASW torpedoes can be carried for helicopters and the shipboard tubes. The SQQ-89(V) sonar suite incorporates a UYQ-25A sonobuoy processor; the towed linear passive hydrophone arrays were not transferred.

FRIGATES [FF]

♦ 3 MEKO 200 class

	Bldr	Laid down	L	In serv.
F 330 Vasco da Gama	Blohm + Voss, Hamburg	2-2-89	26-6-89	20-11-90
F 331 Alvares Cabral	Howaldtswerke, Kiel	2-6-89	2-5-90	18-1-91
F 332 Corte Real	Howaldtswerke, Kiel	20-10-89	2-5-90	22-11-91

Alvares Cabral (F 331) Leo van Ginderen, 6-05

Corte Real (F 332) Leo van Ginderen, 9-05

D: 2,920 tons (3,200 fl) **S:** 31.75 kts (18 on diesel)
Dim: 115.90 (109.00 pp) × 14.80 (13.80 wl) × 5.97 (4.10 hull)

FRIGATES [FF] *(continued)*

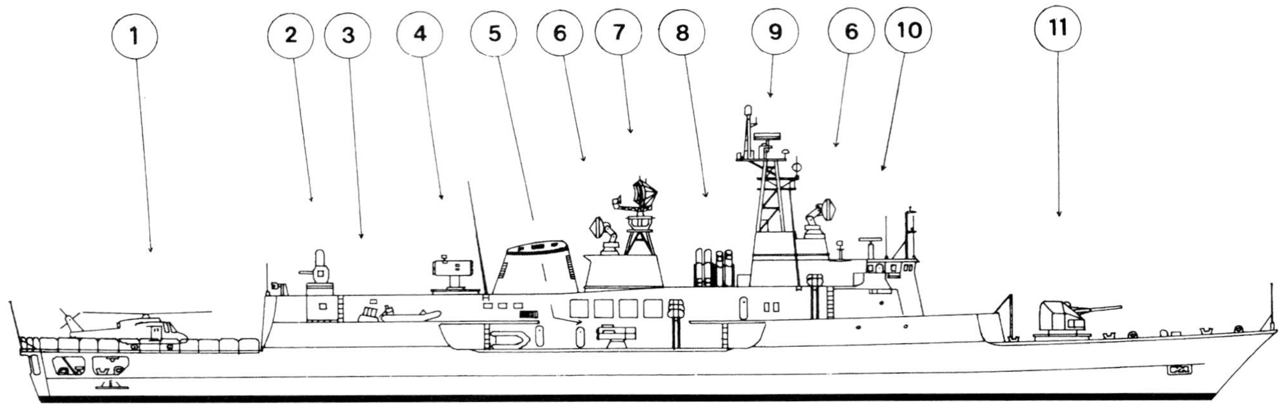

Vasco da Gama (F 330) 1. Lynx Mk 95 helicopter 2. Mk 15 Phalanx CIWS 3. Mk 137 launchers for the Mk 36 SRBOC decoy system 4. 8-round Mk 29 launcher for Sea Sparrow missiles 5. Triple Mk 32 Mod. 5 ASW TT. 6. STIR-18 fire-control/illumination radars 7. DA-08 early-warning radar 8. RGM-84 Harpoon SSM 9. MW-08 surface/air-search radar 10. Type 1007 navigational radar 11. 100-mm 55-cal. Model 1968 CADAM DP gun Drawing by Robert Dumas, from *Flottes de Combat*

Corte Real (F 332) Leo van Ginderen, 9-05

A: 8 RGM-84C Harpoon SSM; 1 8-round Mk 29 SAM launcher (8 RIM-7M Sea Sparrow missiles); 1 100-mm 55-cal. Model 1968 CADAM DP; 1 20-mm Mk 15 Phalanx gatling CIWS; 2 single 20-mm 70-cal. Oerlikon Mk 4 AA; 2 triple 324-mm Mk 32 Mod 5 ASW TT (U.S. Mk 46 Mod. 5 torpedoes); 1 Lynx Mk 95 ASW helicopter

Electronics:

Radar: 1 Kelvin-Hughes Type 1007 nav.; 1 Thales MW-08 Mod. 3 3-D surf./air search; 1 Thales DA-08 early warning; 2 Thales STIR-18 f.c.; 1 General Dynamics Mk 90 Phalanx f.c.

Sonar: Computing Devices Canada SQS-510(V) hull-mounted (6.4–8.0 kHz)

EW: ArgoSystems APECS-II/AR-700 intercept/jammer suite; Mk 36 Mod 1 SRBOC decoy syst. (2 6-round Raytheon Mk 137 RL); SLQ-25 Nixie towed acoustic torpedo decoy syst.

M: CODOG: 2 MTU 12V1163 TB83 diesels (4,420 bhp each), 2 G.E. LM-2500-30 gas turbines (30,000 shp each); 2 Escher-Weiss CP props

Electric: 2,480 kw (4 × 620-kw diesel sets)

Range: 900/31.75; 4,100/18 (2 diesels) **Fuel:** 300 tons

Crew: 23 officers, 44 petty officers, 115 ratings (incl. 4 officers, 5 petty officers, and 9 ratings in helicopter detachment) + 16 flag staff

Remarks: Ordered 25-7-86. Financed 60% by the U.S., Canada, West Germany, Norway, and the Netherlands and 40% by Portugal. Equipped to accommodate a flag officer staff. F 330 completed a 6-month overhaul at the Arsenal do Alfeite on 19-4-01, with all electronics systems overhauls under a contract with Thales Nederland; the other two ships are to follow.

Hull systems: Have fin stabilizers and the NAUTOS propulsion control system. Are to receive an infrared signature reduction system for the funnels.

Combat systems: Have Thales SEWACO (Sensor Weapon, Control and Command System), STACOS tactical command system, and Vespa datalink transponder. NATO Link 11 and Link 14 datalinks, the Sicom 200 integrated communications suite, and an MNS 2000 navigation suite are fitted. Are fitted for later installation of a towed linear hydrophone array (TASS). One set of UHF SATCOM equipment, using the British SCOT system, is rotated among the three, and all have been equipped with Inmarsat-B commercial UHF SATCOM, electronic chart displays, and a laser gyro inertial guidance system since completion.

During modernizations planned for the 2009–14 timeframe, vertically launched Evolved Sea Sparrow missiles may be substituted for the Mk 29 launcher; the Phalanx may be upgraded to Block IB; and Harpoon Block II missiles, Thales/Raytheon SEAPAR multifunction radar, and RAM or SEARAM point-defense SAM systems may be added.

♦ 3 French Commandant Riviere class

Bldr: A.C. de Bretagne, Nantes

	Laid down	L	In serv.
F 480 Comandante João Belo	6-9-65	22-3-66	1-7-67
F 481 Comandante Hermengildo Capelo	13-5-66	29-11-66	26-4-68
F 483 Comandante Sacadura Cabral	18-8-67	15-3-68	25-11-69

Comandante João Belo (F 480) Frank Findler, 7-05

Comandante Sacadura Cabral (F 483) Leo van Ginderen, 6-05

D: 1,760 tons (2,250 fl) **S:** 25 kts (26.6 on trials)

Dim: 102.70 (98.00 pp) × 11.80 × 3.80 (hull; 4.35 max.)

A: 2 single 100-mm 55-cal. Model 1953 DP; 2 single 40-mm 60-cal. Bofors AA; 2 triple 324-mm Mk 32 Mod. 5 ASW TT (Mk 46 Mod. 5 torpedoes)

Electronics:

Radar: 1 Kelvin-Hughes Type 1007 nav.; 1 Thales DRBV-22A air search; 1 Thales DRBV-50 surf./air search; 1 Thales DRBC-31D f.c.

Sonar: Computing Devices Canada SQS-510(V) hull-mounted

EW: ArgoSystems APECS-II/700 intercept/jamming suite; Mk 36 SRBOC decoy syst. (2 6-round Raytheon Mk 137 RL); SLQ-25(V) Nixie acoustic torpedo decoy syst.

M: 4 SEMT-Pielstick 12 PC2.2 V400 diesels; 2 props; 16,000 bhp

Electric: 1,280 kw tot. (4 × 320-kw diesel sets)

Range: 2,300/25; 7,500/15 **Fuel:** 210 tons **Crew:** 14 officers, 183 enlisted

Remarks: As completed, were generally similar to sisters built for the French Navy. They were modernized under the 1992–95 budget and will likely remain in service through 2010. F 481 completed the first modernization refit in 10-95 with accommodations for 15 female personnel added. Sister *Comandante Roberto Ivens* (F 482) was to have been adapted for cadet training duties but was instead stricken during 1997.

Combat systems: Modernization included installing the Thales SEWACO-FD- derived combat data system, adding a NATO Link 11 datalink capability, and substituting the SQS-510(V) sonar for the original SQS-17A and DUBA-3 suite, U.S. Mk 32 Mod. 5 tubes and Mk 46 Mod 5 torpedoes for the French 550-mm tubes, and the ArgoSystems APECS-II/700 EW suite for ARBR-10. The U.S. SLQ-25 Nixie towed torpedo decoy system was added, while the 305-mm mortar and after, superfiring, 100-mm gunmount were removed. A planned helicopter platform addition was omitted.

PATROL SHIPS [PS]

♦ 2 (+ 2) Baptiste de Andrade class

Bldr: Estaeiros Navais, Viana do Castelo

	L	In serv.
. . . Viana do Castelo	. . .	2006
. . . Ponta Delgada	. . .	2006
. . .	. . .	2007
. . .	. . .	2008

PATROL SHIPS [PS] *(continued)*

D: 1,300 tons (1,540 fl) **S:** 20 kts **Dim:** 83.1 (79.8 pp) × 12.95 × 3.7
A: 1 40-mm . . . AA
Electronics: Radar: 2 . . . nav.
M: 2 . . . diesels; 2 props; 10,560 bhp
Range: 5,000/15 **Endurance:** 30 days **Crew:** 5 officers, 30 enlisted

Remarks: First two units were ordered 10-02 and the second two followed in 5-04. Up to six additional units are sought to replace the *Baptiste de Andrade–* and *João Coutinho–*class patrol ships and the *Cacine*-class patrol craft. The class has a helicopter landing platform (but no hangar) and can carry up to 32 additional personnel in addition to the regular crew. Two ships of the class will likely operate as navigational aids tenders and a third unit is to be configured as a pollution-control ship with a crane fitted aft.

♦ 3 Baptiste de Andrade class
Bldr: Izar (formerly E.N. Bazán), Cartagena, Spain

	Laid down	L	In serv.
F 486 Baptiste de Andrade	1-9-72	13-3-73	19-11-74
F 487 João Roby	1-12-72	3-6-73	18-3-75
F 488 Afonso Cerquiera	10-3-73	6-10-73	26-6-75

Baptiste de Andrade (F 486) Winter & Findler, 8-98

D: 1,252 tons (1,348 fl) **S:** 21 kts **Dim:** 84.59 (81.0 pp) × 10.3 × 3.3
A: 1 100-mm 55-cal. Model 1968 DP; 2 single 40-mm 60-cal. Bofors AA
Electronics:
Radar: 1 Decca TM626 nav.; 1 Plessey AWS-2 air search; 1 Thales Pollux f.c.
Sonar: Removed—EW: None
M: 2 OEW-Pielstick 12PC2 V400 diesels; 2 props; 10,560 bhp
Electric: 1,100 kVA **Range:** 5,900/18 **Crew:** 11 officers, 111 enlisted

Remarks: Developed version of the *João Coutinho* class with more modern weapons and electronics. F 488 began stripping mid-12-93 for striking 3-1-94 but was given a refit in 1997 and returned to service. Since 1999, the class has been employed for "public interest tasks" (i.e., fisheries patrol), and the ASW capability has been deleted, as in the *João Coutinho* class.
Combat systems: Have a Thales Vega gun-control system with Pollux radar and a backup C.S. Défense Panda optical director for the 100-mm gun and two lead-computing directors for the 40-mm AA. Have a helicopter deck fitted atop the after deckhouse, but no landing aids or hangar. The Thales Diodon hull-mounted sonar and two triple Mk 32 ASW torpedo tube sets were removed during 1999–2000; the air-search radar may also have been deleted. Data about fisheries activities are exchanged via a satellite communications system to a shore database.
Disposals: Sister *Oliveira E. Carmo* (F 489) had been stricken by 2004.

♦ 4 João Coutinho class
Bldrs: F 475–477: Blohm + Voss, Hamburg; others: Izar (formerly E.N. Bazán), Cartagena, Spain

	Laid down	L	In serv.
F 471 Antonio Enes	10-4-68	16-8-69	18-6-71
F 475 João Coutinho	24-12-68	2-5-69	7-3-70
F 476 Jacinto Candido	10-2-68	16-6-69	10-6-70
F 477 General Pereira d'Eca	21-4-69	26-7-69	10-10-70

Augusto de Castilho (F 484)—since retired ABBw/FAFIO, 5-00

D: 1,252 tons (1,401 fl) **S:** 24.4 kts **Dim:** 84.59 (81.0 pp) × 10.30 × 3.30
A: 1 twin 76.2-mm 50-cal. U.S. Mk 33 DP; 1 twin 40-mm 60-cal. Bofors AA
Electronics:
Radar: 1 Decca RM 1226C nav.; 1 Kelvin-Hughes . . . surf. search
Sonar: Removed—EW: None
M: 2 OEW-Pielstick 12PC2 V280 diesels; 2 props; 10,560 bhp
Electric: 900 kw tot. **Range:** 5,900/8 **Crew:** 9 officers, 68 enlisted

Remarks: Former corvettes. Primarily used for fisheries patrol duties, with ASW capabilities deleted, resulting in a saving of 23 enlisted personnel billets. Can also carry 34 marines.
Hull systems: F 475 made 25 kts on original trials. The helicopter deck has a removable hatch.
Combat systems: ASW armament of one Mk 10 Hedgehog mortar, two Mk 6 d.c. mortars, and two d.c. racks had been deleted by 1987. During the early 1990s, the obsolete MLA-1B air-search radar was replaced by a Kelvin-Hughes surface-search set. The SPG-34 gunfire-control radar and Mk 63 Mod. 21 gun f.c.s. had been removed by 1994, leaving the 76.2-mm mount dependent on local control. The 40-mm mount has an associated Mk 51 Mod. 2 lead-computing director just abaft the stack. Can carry 1,200 rounds of 76.2-mm ammunition. Data about fisheries activities are exchanged via satellite communications system to a shore database.
Disposals: *Honorio Barreto* (F 485) was decomissioned in 2003 and *Augusto de Castilho* (F 484) retired during 2004.

PATROL CRAFT [PC]

♦ 4 Cacine class
Bldrs: P 1140, 1144, 1146: Arsenal do Alfeite; P 1161: Est. Nav. do Mondego

	In serv.		In serv.
P 1140 Cacine	5-69	P 1146 Zaire	11-70
P 1144 Cuanza	30-5-69	P 1161 Save	5-73

Cacine (P 1140) Martin Mokrus, 12-03

Cacine (P 1140) Martin Mokrus, 12-03

D: 292.5 tons (310 fl) **S:** 20 kts **Dim:** 44.00 × 7.67 × 2.20
A: 1 40-mm 60-cal. Bofors AA; 1 20-mm 70-cal. Oerlikon AA
Electronics: Radar: 1 Kelvin-Hughes Type 1007 nav.
M: 2 MTU 12V538 TB80 diesels; 2 props; 4,400 bhp (3,750 sust.)
Range: 4,400/12 **Crew:** 3 officers, 30 enlisted

Remarks: P 1161, built by Estalieros Navais do Mondego, has low bulwarks at the bow; the others do not. All carry radio signal direction-finding equipment. Rigid inflatable inspection dinghies, tended by a small electrohydraulic crane, have replaced the after 40-mm gun and two d.c. racks. The original Maybach 12V528 diesels have been replaced.

Disposals: *Mandovi* (P 1142) was retired in 1997, *Rovuma* (P 1143) in 2000, *Geba* (P 1145) in 2003, and *Zambeze* (P 1147) and *Limpopo* (P 1160) were stricken in 2004.

PATROL BOATS [PB]

♦ 4 Centaro class
Bldrs: P 1157, 1158: CONAFIL, Vila Real de Santo Antonio; others: Arsenal do Alfeite

	In serv.		In serv.
P 1155 Centaro	1-2-00	P 1157 Pegaso	27-3-01
P 1156 Orion	3-4-00	P 1158 Sagitario	27-3-01

D: 82 tons (94 fl) **S:** 26 kts (28 on trials) **Dim:** 28.40 × 5.95 × 1.45
A: 1 20-mm 70-cal. Oerlikon Mk 4 AA **Electronics:** Radar: 1 . . . nav.
M: 2 Cummins KTA50-M2 diesels; 2 props; 3,600 bhp
Electric: 150 kw tot. (2 × 75 kw, Cummins 6BT5.9D(M) diesels driving)
Range: 640/20 **Crew:** 2 officers, 8 enlisted

Remarks: Ordered in 1998 as an improved version of the *Argos* class for use in fisheries protection, search and rescue, and general inshore patrol work. Aluminum construction. A 4-m inspection and rescue launch is carried on a launch and recovery ramp at the stern.

PATROL BOATS [PB] *(continued)*

♦ **1 river patrol boat** Bldr: Arsenal do Alfeite (In serv. 1-8-91)

P 370 Rio Minho

Rio Minho (P 370) H&L Van Ginderen, 8-94

D: 57 tons (72 fl) **S:** 10 kts **Dim:** 22.4 (20.0 pp) × 5.5 × 0.8
A: 1 7.62-mm mg **Electronics:** Radar: 1 Furuno FR-1505 DA nav.
M: 2 Deutz diesels; 2 Schottel waterjets; 664 bhp
Range: 420/7 **Crew:** 1 officer, 7 enlisted

Remarks: Replaced the craft *Atria* (P 360) as Rio Minho patrol vessel.

♦ **5 Argos class**
Bldrs: CONAFIL, Vila Real de Santo Antonio, and Arsenal do Alfeite

	In serv.		In serv.
P 1150 Argos	2-7-91	P 1153 Cassiopeia	11-11-91
P 1151 Dragão	18-10-91	P 1154 Hidra	18-12-91
P 1152 Escorpião	26-11-91		

Hidra (P 1154) Leo Van Ginderen, 1-01

D: 84 tons (94 fl) **S:** 28 kts **Dim:** 27.20 (25.20 pp) × 5.90 × 1.40
A: 2 single 12.7-mm mg **Electronics:** Radar: 1 Furuno FR-1505 DA nav.
M: 2 MTU 12V396 TE84 diesels; 2 props; 3,700 bhp
Range: 1,350/15; 200/28 **Crew:** 1 officer, 8 enlisted

Remarks: Hulls for first two were delivered to Arsenal do Alfeite early in 1991 for fitting out; the other three were built entirely at Alfeite. P 1150 was struck by a Cacine-class patrol craft on 7-7-95 and suffered severe damage.
Hull systems: GRP construction with seven watertight compartments. Have a ramp at the stern for a 4.0-m rigid inflatable inspection boat. Have Tayo VHF-Plus radio D/F.

♦ **3 Albatroz class** Bldr: Arsenal do Alfeite

	In serv.
P 1165 Aguia	28-2-75
P 1167 Cisne	31-3-76
UAM 630 Condor (ex-P 1166)	23-4-75

D: 45 tons (fl) **S:** 20 kts **Dim:** 23.6 (21.88 pp) × 5.25 × 1.6
A: 1 20-mm 70-cal. Oerlikon AA; 2 single 12.7-mm mg
Electronics: Radar: 1 Decca 316P nav.
M: 2 Cummins diesels; 2 props; 1,100 bhp
Range: 450/18; 2,500/12 **Crew:** 1 officer, 7 enlisted

Remarks: *Condor* was relegated to harbor duties in 1992 and no longer carries fixed armament; she is operated by the naval police.

Note: Units with UAM-series pennants are all assigned to harbor patrol duties and are assigned to the naval police. UAM = *Unitad Auxiliaria da Marinha* (Naval Auxiliary Unit).
Disposals: Sister *Andorhina* (P 1164) was decommissioned during 2003. *Albatroz* (P 1162) and *Acor* (P 1163) were transferred to East Timor on 12-1-02.

Albatroz (P 1162)—since decommissioned and transferred abroad
Leo Van Ginderen, 1-01

♦ **8 Spanish Bazán 39–class harbor patrol boats**
Bldr: Rodman-Polyships, Vigo

	In serv.		In serv.
UAM 642 Calmaria	30-11-93	UAM 646 Suão	9-94
UAM 643 Cirro	30-11-93	UAM 647 Macareo	9-94
UAM 644 Vendeval	18-1-94	UAM 648 Preia-Mar	10-94
UAM 645 Moncão	8-94	UAM 649 Baixa-Mar	11-94

Calmaria (UAM 642) Antonio Scrimali via L. Grazioli, 2-02

D: 12 tons (15.7 fl) **S:** 32 kts **Dim:** 11.9 × 3.8 × 0.7
A: 1 7.62-mm mg **Electronics:** Radar: 1 Furuno 1830 nav.
M: 2 Izar-M.A.N. D2866 LXE diesels; 2 waterjets; 881 bhp
Range: 275/20 **Crew:** 3 tot.

Remarks: Ordered 8-1-93 to the same design as the Spanish Guardia Civil del Mar boats for use by the Brigada Fiscal (Customs Brigade) for drug control work. GRP construction. Design is also known as the Saeta 12 10T.

♦ **4 Surriada-class harbor patrol boats**
Bldr: Cheverton, Cowes, U.K. (In serv. 1982)

UAM 602 Surriada	UAM 612 Bonança
UAM 605 Mareta	UAM 613 Mar Chão

Mareta (UAM 605) Leo Van Ginderen, 1-01

D: 9 tons (fl) **S:** 20 kts **Dim:** 12.0 × 3.6 × 1.0
A: small arms **Electronics:** Radar: 1 Decca 110 nav.
M: 2 Volvo Penta TAMD 66B outdrive diesels; 2 props; 426 bhp **Crew:** 4 tot.

Remarks: First pair delivered in 5-82, the others in 7-82. Intended to patrol on the Tagus in the Lisbon area. GRP hulls. Have service craft pennant numbers.

PATROL BOATS [PB] *(continued)*

♦ 30 miscellaneous harbor patrol boats

UAM 608 MARESIA

D: . . . **S:** . . . **Dim:** 12.0 × 2.7 × 1.8
M: 2 Rolls-Royce Sabre 212 diesels; 2 props; 424 bhp

UAM 611 BOLINA

D: 15 tons (fl) **S:** 14 kts **Dim:** 12.57 × 3.64 × 1.10
M: 2 Rolls-Royce Sabre 212 diesels; 2 props; 424 bhp

UAM 631 LEVANTE

D: . . . **S:** . . . **Dim:** 12.0 × 3.8 × . . .
M: 2 Volvo Penta diesels; 2 props; 520 bhp

UAM 636 VENTANTE

Ventante (UAM 636) Guy Schaeffer, via Paolo Marsan, 9-98

D: 7.8 tons (fl) **S:** 32 kts **Dim:** 12.0 × 3.8 × 0.5
Electronics: Radar: 1 Decca . . . nav.
M: 2 AIFO 8361/SR diesels; 2 Castoldi 06 waterjets; 580 bhp
Range: 224/28 **Fuel:** 0.6 tons **Crew:** 5 tot.

UAM 601 BALUARTE
UAM 603 MELIDES
UAM 604 MAR DE SESIBRA
UAM 607 ROAZ
UAM 610 COLFINHO
UAM 614 BALANÇO
UAM 616 SATITANTE
UAM 617 TENEBROSA
UAM 618 TERESA PAULA
UAM 619 PERRARIA
UAM 620 CAPITANIA
UAM 621 SAN LOURENÇO
UAM 622 SALGA
UAM 623 SERRETA
UAM 624 DIOGO DE TEIVE
UAM 625 COMANDANTE NEWTON
UAM 626 ESPALAMACA
UAM 627 CARÇA
UAM 628 MARVÃO
UAM 629 MAR DA BARCA
UAM 632 ARRÁBIDA
UAM 633 SANTA CATARINA
UAM 634 SIROCCO
UAM 635 BRISA
UAM 639 TUFÃO
UAM 640 CICLONE

Satitante (UAM 616) Leo Van Ginderen, 1-01

Remarks: UAM 636 is a sister to the Italian Customs Service's V.5500 class, built by Crestitalia, Ameglia, around 1980 and is of GRP construction. UAM 611 is a typical U.K. Keith Nelson GRP-hulled pilot launch. No data available for the other units. All are attached to various port and harbor facilities.

AMPHIBIOUS WARFARE SHIPS

♦ 1 Modified Dutch Rotterdam Class [LPD]

Bldr: Estaeiros Navais, Viana do Castelo

	Laid down	L	In serv.
. . .	2007	2009	2011

D: 10,500 tons (12,750 fl) **S:** 19 kts
Dim: 163.0 × 25.0 × 5.23
A: 1 30-mm Goalkeeper CIWS and/or 1 21-round Mk 49 RAM point-defense SAM launcher (RIM-116A missiles)
Electronics:
Radar: . . .
E/O: Thales IRSCAN surveillance and tracking
M: . . . diesel generator sets, . . . electric motors; 2 props
Range: 6,000/15
Fuel: . . .
Crew: 150 total (+ 654 troops)

Remarks: Based on the Dutch *Rotterdam*-class LPD design. Ordered during 2-05, the ship is known as the NAVPOL (Navio Polivalente Logistico = Versatile Logistics Ship) in Portugal. Has a helicopter hangar capable of carrying six helicopters with two landing spots on deck. Over 100 vehicles can be carried on deck along with 20+ vehicles carried internally. The 880 m^2 docking well can accommodate four U.S. LCM landing craft. Hospital facilities include 35 beds. Four additional LCMs will likely be ordered for use aboard ship.

♦ 1 Bombarda-class utility landing craft [LCU]

Bldr: Arsenal do Alfeite (In serv. 1985)

LDG 203 BACAMARTE

Bacamarte (LDG 203) H&L Van Ginderen/F. Heine, 1-00

D: 285 tons (652 fl) **S:** 11 kts (9.5 loaded) **Dim:** 59.0 (52.88 pp) × 11.91 × 1.6
A: 2 single 20-mm 70-cal. Oerlikon AA
Electronics: Radar: 1 Decca RM 316P nav.
M: 2 MTU MD 225 diesels; 2 props; 910 bhp
Range: 1,800/8 **Crew:** 3 officers, 18 enlisted

Remarks: Design based on the French EDIC series. Cargo: 350 tons. Sisters *Bombarda* (LDG 201) and *Alabarda* (LDG 202) were retired during 1997.

AUXILIARIES

Note: All survey ships and craft are subordinated to the Hydrographic Institute (*Instituto Hidrográfico*).

♦ 2 ex-U.S. Stalwart-class survey ships [AGS]

Bldr: Tacoma Boat, Tacoma, Wash.

	Laid down	L	In serv.
A 522 DOM CARLOS I (ex-*Audacious*, T-AGOS 11; ex-*Dauntless*)	29-2-88	28-1-89	12-6-89
A 523 ALMIRANTE GAGO COUTINHO (ex-*Assurance*, T-AGOS 5)	31-5-84	12-1-85	1-5-85

Almirante Gago Coutinho (A 523) George R. Schneider, 1-00

D: 1,600 tons light (2,285 fl) **S:** 11 kts **Dim:** 68.28 (62.10 wl) × 13.10 × 4.57
Electronics: Radar: 2 . . . nav.
M: 4 Caterpillar-Kato D-398B 800-bhp diesels, G.E. electric drive; 2 4-bladed props; 2,200 shp (1,600 sust.)—550-hp bow-thruster
Electric: 1,500 kVA from main generators + 265-kw emergency set
Range: 3,000/11 + 6,480/3 **Fuel:** 834 tons **Endurance:** 98 days
Crew: 6 officers, 6 petty officers, 19 junior enlisted + 15 technicians

Remarks: 1,472 grt/786 dwt. Built as an ocean surveillance ship to tow a long linear passive hydrophone array and placed in reserve by the U.S. Navy on 30-11-95, A 522 was transferred 9-12-96 as Grant-Aid for use as a hydrographic survey ship to replace *Almeida Carvalho;* she was recommissioned 28-2-97 and was in refit and conversion through mid-1998 in Portugal. A 523 was transferred 28-10-99 and recommissioned 26-1-00; the ship is employed primarily for oceanographic research. A 522 carries the survey craft *Mergulitão*.

AUXILIARIES *(continued)*

Hull systems: Have a flat-chine hullform without bilge keels. Have passive tank roll stabilization. Originally intended to conduct 60- to 90-day patrols and to be at sea 292 days per year, they have outstanding endurance and recreational facilities for crews but are considered to be rough-riding vessels during the winter months in higher latitudes. Main-engine motor/generator sets also supply ship's service power.
Mission systems: The UQQ-2 SURTASS (Surveillance Towed Array Sensor) was removed prior to transfer, as was the WSC-6 satellite communications system. Are now equipped with survey and oceanographic sensors, wet and dry laboratories, a chartroom, a survey launch, new cranes, and space to accept a portable container.

♦ 2 Andromeda-class hydrographic survey ships [AGS]
Bldr: Arsenal do Alfeite

	Laid down	L	In serv.
A 5203 Andromeda	1984	12-12-85	1-2-87
A 5205 Auriga	6-84	1986	1-7-87

Andromeda (A 5203) H&L Van Ginderen, 8-97

D: 230 tons (270 fl) **S:** 12 kts **Dim:** 31.50 (28.00 pp) × 7.74 × 2.50
Electronics: Radar: 1 Racal-Decca RM 914C nav.
M: 1 MTU 12V396 TC 82 diesel; 1 prop; 1,200 bhp (1,030 sust.)
Electric: 160 kw (1 × 100-kw diesel set, 1 × 60-kw shaft generator)
Range: 1,100/12; 1,980/10 **Fuel:** 35.5 tons **Crew:** 3 officers, 14 enlisted

Remarks: Intended to replace the U.K. *Bay*-class survey ship *Alfonso de Albuquerque* (A 526), stricken in 1983. Also used for oceanographic research. A 5205 carries a Phantom S2 remotely piloted submersible and a Klein towed side-scan sonar.

♦ 1 U.K. Rover-class oiler [AO]
Bldr: Swan Hunter, Hebburn-on-Tyne

	Laid down	L	In serv.
A 5210 Bérrio (ex-*Blue Rover,* A 270)	18-1-69	11-11-69	15-7-70

Bérrio (A 5210) Ben Sullivan, 7-04

D: 4,763 tons light (11,585 fl) **S:** 19.25 kts (17 sust.)
Dim: 140.62 (131.07 pp) × 19.26 × 7.14
A: 2 single 20-mm 70-cal. Oerlikon Mk 7A AA
Electronics: Radar: 1 Kelvin-Hughes Type 1006 nav.; 1 Decca TM 1226 nav.; 1 Decca 1229 nav.
M: 2 Crossley-Pielstick 16 PA4 diesels; 1 CP prop; 15,360 bhp—bow-thruster
Electric: 2,720 kw tot. (8 × 340-kw diesel sets)
Range: 14,000/15 **Fuel:** 965 tons heavy oil + 123 tons diesel
Crew: 7 officers, 11 petty officers, 36 ratings

Remarks: 7,513 grt/7,042 dwt. Purchased and transferred 31-3-93. Sisters operate in Indonesian and British service.
Hull systems: Has 13 cargo tanks totaling 8,155 m^3 and one 387-m^3 dry cargo hold. Cargo capacity includes 4,500 tons of fuel, 460 tons of aviation fuel, 325 tons of water, 10 tons of lube oil, 120 tons of stores, and 25 tons of munitions. Has a helicopter deck but no hangar. Re-engined in 1973–74. Has two stern anchors.

♦ 1 lighthouse tender and seagoing tug [ATA]
Bldr: Arsenal do Alfeite

	Laid down	L	In serv.
A 521 Schultz Xavier	2-70	1972	14-7-72

Schultz Xavier (A 521) Stefan Karpinski, 2003

D: 900 tons (fl) **S:** 14 kts **Dim:** 56.1 × 10.0 × 3.8
M: 2 diesels; 1 prop; 2,400 bhp **Range:** 3,000/12.5
Crew: 4 officers, 50 enlisted

♦ 1 ex-German Horst Wessel–class sail-training ship [AXT]
Bldr: Blohm + Voss, Hamburg

	L	In serv.
A 520 Sagres (ex-*Guanabara,* ex-*Albert Leo Schlageter*)	30-10-37	1-2-38

Sagres (A 520) Michael Nitz, 8-05

D: 1,725 tons (1,940 fl) **S:** 10.5 kts (18 under sail)
Dim: 90.00 (75.90 hull; 70.40 pp) × 11.90 × 5.30
A: 2 single 47-mm saluting guns **Electronics:** Radar: 2 Decca . . . nav.
M: 2 MTU 12V183 TE92 diesels; 1 prop; 750 bhp—sail area: 2,355 m^2 max.
Range: 5,450/7.5 (under power) **Crew:** 12 officers, 150 enlisted + . . . cadets

Remarks: Acquired by the U.S. Navy as war reparations in 1945; was sold to Brazil in 1948 and then to Portugal in 1962, commissioning 2-2-62. Height of mainmast: 43.3 m. Sisters are U.S. Coast Guard's *Eagle,* Romania's *Mircea,* Germany's *Gorch Fock,* and Russian merchant training vessel *Tovarisch.* Was refitted and the hull renewed at Arsenal do Alfeite 2-87 to 1988 and again refitted in 1991–92, when she was also re-engined.

♦ 1 sail-training schooner [AXT]
Bldr: . . ., Lisbon (In serv. 1937)

UAM 201 Creoula

D: 818 tons (1,055 fl) **S:** . . . kts **Dim:** 67.4 × 9.9 × 4.2
M: 1 MTU 8V183 TE92 diesel; 1 prop; 480 bhp **Crew:** . . .

Remarks: Former four-masted Grand Banks fishing schooner, acquired in 1976 as a museum by the Portuguese Department of Fisheries; turned over to the navy and commissioned for active seagoing training in 1987. Refitted and re-engined in 1992, when accommodations were also improved.

AUXILIARIES *(continued)*

Creoula (UAM 201) Paolo Marsan, 8-04

SERVICE CRAFT

Note: UAM stands for *Unitad Auxiliaria da Marinha* (Naval Auxiliary Unit). Harbor patrol boats with UAM-series pennant numbers are listed above under patrol boats.

♦ 2 environmental protection launches [YAG]
Bldr: Aqua-Guard, Vancouver, Canada (In serv. 1994)

UAM 688 Enchente UAM 886 Vazante

D: 14 tons (fl) **S:** 10 kts **Dim:** 8.84 × 3.00 × 0.96
M: . . . diesels; . . . props; . . . bhp **Range:** 60/5 **Crew:** 2 tot.

Remarks: Bought through the European Community ENVIREG (Environmental Regulation) program and used in the Lisbon area. Transport floating pollution barriers and can extract debris from the water.

Note: The small dredger UAM 687 is also in service.

♦ 2 miscellaneous ammunition lighters [YE]
UAM 304 Marateca UAM 305 Mouro

Mouro (UAM 305) H&L Van Ginderen, 3-91

♦ 1 yacht/tender [YFL]
Bldr: Halmatic, U.K. (In serv. 10-84)

UAM 901 Alva

D: 6.5 tons (fl) **S:** 20 kts **Dim:** 10.62 (9.37 wl) × 3.50 × 0.84
M: 2 Volvo TAMD 60C diesels; 2 props; 420 bhp

Remarks: GRP construction. Based at Lisbon and used as commander-in-chief's yacht. Carries 12 passengers.

Alva (UAM 901) H&L Van Ginderen, 3-91

♦ 9 miscellaneous harbor personnel transports [YFL]

UAM 907 Coura UAM 910 Tamega UAM 913 Zezere
UAM 908 Paiva UAM 911 Tua UAM 915 Nabão
UAM 909 Sorraia UAM 912 Vascão UAM 916 Muge

Coura (UAM 907)—*Paiva* (UAM 908) is identical Bernard Prézelin, 3-98

Remarks: Attached to the Lisbon Naval Base. The Portuguese Air Force also operates at least one personnel ferry, F-A 1, in the Lisbon area.

♦ 3 miscellaneous personnel launches [YFL]

UAM 831 Tainha UAM 905 Caia UAM 906 Corgo

Remarks: Employed as flag officers' barges at Lisbon. UAM 831 was completed 6-12-93.

♦ 1 aquarium service craft [YFL]

UAM 852 Albacora II

Albacora II (UAM 852) Stefan Karpinski, 2003

Remarks: Attached to the Vasco da Gama Aquarium (*Aquário Vasco da Gama*). No data available.

♦ 1 catamaran river navigational aids tender [YGL]
Bldr: San Jacinto, Aveiro (In serv. 30-1-85)

UAM 676 Guia

D: 70 tons **S:** 8.5 kts **Dim:** 22.0 × 7.9 × 2.2
M: 1 Deutz SBA 6M 816U diesel; 1 Schottel prop; 350 bhp—1 Harbor Master 50 F76 maneuvering unit (3.5 kts)

Remarks: Subordinated to the Lighthouse Service (*Direcção de Faróis).*

SERVICE CRAFT *(continued)*

Guia (UAM 676) Mike Louagie, 3-91

♦ **6 miscellaneous navigational aids tenders [YGL]**

UAM 675 Berlenga
UAM 677 Esteiro
UAM 678 Bugio
UAM 679 Giralta
UAM 681 São Vicente
UAM 780 Santa Maria II

Navigational aids tender Esteiro (UAM 677) Leo Van Ginderen, 1-01

Remarks: No other data available.

♦ **3 Coral-class inshore survey/lighthouse tenders [YGS]**

UAM 801 Coral UAM 802 Atlanta (ex-*Hidra*) UAM 805 Fisália

Remarks: GRP construction. Are 36 tons (fl). Launched in 1980. UAM 805 has a larger, glassed-in cabin forward of the pilothouse. No other data available.

Disposal note: Inshore lighthouse tender/survey craft *Savel* (UAM 630), *Actinia* (UAM 803), and *Sicandra* (UAM 804) were stricken during 2000.

♦ **28 miscellaneous port lifeboats [YH]**

UAM 650 Aguda
UAM 651 Almirante Jaime Afreixo
UAM 652 Almirante Ferreira do Amaral
UAM 655 Commandante Couceiro
UAM 656 Patrão Ezequiel Seabra
UAM 657 Gomes de Amorim
UAM 658 Nossa Senhora de Conceição
UAM 659 Patrão António Faustino
UAM 660 Patrão Quirino Lopes
UAM 661 Patrão Rabumba
UAM 662 Patrão Chalandra
UAM 663 Rainha Don Amélia
UAM 664 Rei Don Carlos I
UAM 665 Santa Maria
UAM 667 Patrão António Simóes
UAM 668 Patrão João Rangel
UAM 669 Vila Chã
UAM 670 Patrão Henrique Faleiro
UAM 671 Patrão Cesar Martins
UAM 672 Patrão João da Silva
UAM 673 Patrão Joaquim Casaca
UAM 674 Patrão Joaquim Lopes
UAM 682 Patrão Arnaldo dos Santos
UAM 685 Patrão José André dos Santos
UAM 689 Rainha D. Amelia
UAM 690 Patrão Moisés Macatrão
UAM 691 Nossa Senhora da Boa Viagem
UAM 692 Duque da Ribeira

Remarks: All subordinated to the Naval Rescue Service (*Instituto de Socorros a Náufragos*). Painted white and orange and have "*Salva-Vidas*" (Life-Saving) on the side. UAM 690 was completed 18-4-97: built of GRP, she displaces 11.12 tons, can achieve 21 kts (18 sust.), is 13.5 (11.8 pp) × 3.8 × 0.62, and is based at Ribeira da Foz. UAM 689, UAM 690, UAM 691 (in serv. 1997), and UAM 692 (in serv. 17-5-98) are 17 m long and have a 350-bhp diesel engine. No further data available.
Disposals: *Sota Patrão Anónio Crista* (UAM 666) had been discarded by 1-01.

Patrão Cesar Martins (UAM 671) Guy Schaeffer, via Paolo Marsan, 9-98

Patrão Moisés Macatrão (UAM 690)—UAM 691 and UAM 692 are sisters
Guy Schaeffer, via Paolo Marsan, 9-98

♦ **1 accommodations barge [YPB]**

UAM 854 Barrocas

Remarks: Attached to the Arsenal do Alfeite. No data available.

♦ **1 ex-U.S. Army Design 3004 medium harbor tug [YTM]**
Bldr: . . . (In serv. 1954)

UAM 914 Nisa (ex-RB 2, ex-ST 1996)

D: 100 tons light (122 fl) **S:** 12 kts **Dim:** 21.31 × 5.94 × 2.50
M: 1 diesel; 1 prop; 600 bhp
Range: 3,500/12 **Fuel:** 15 tons **Crew:** 6 tot.

Remarks: Transferred 2-3-62. Sister RB 1 was stricken in 1984.

♦ **1 sail-training sloop [YTS]**

A 5201 Vega (ex-*Arreda*)

D: 60 tons **S:** . . . **Dim:** 19.8 × 4.3 × 2.5

♦ **1 sail-training yacht [YTS]**

A 5204 Polar (ex-*Anne Linde*)

Polar (A 5204) Carlo Martinelli, 7-96

SERVICE CRAFT *(continued)*

D: 70 tons **S:** . . . **Dim:** 22.9 × 4.9 × 2.5

Remarks: Acquired in trade for the large sail-training ship *Sagres I,* now a museum ship at Hamburg. Both A 5204 and *Vega* (A 5201) have Raytheon commercial navigational radar sets.

♦ 3 Rodman 700–class seamanship training craft [YXT]
Bldr: Rodman Polyships, Vigo, Spain (In serv. 1996)

UAM . . . Mindelo UAM . . . Cacheu UAM . . . Niassa

D: 2 tons **S:** 22 kts **Dim:** 6.98 × 2.80 × 0.70
M: 1 Volvo Penta AQAD 40 diesel; 1 prop; 130 bhp
Range: . . . / . . . **Fuel:** 200 liters **Crew:** . . . tot.

Remarks: Acquired for the naval school to teach trainees from Portuguese-speaking African nations. GRP construction.

Disposal note: Chinese-style motor lorcha *Macau* (UAM 202) had been sold for commercial use by 2005.

Note: The Portuguese Customs Brigade (*Brigada Fiscal*) operates a considerable number of small harbor launches without fixed armament. To replace older units, a dozen 45-kt, 16.36-m, GRP-construction launches were ordered from CONAFIL, Vila Real de Santo Antonio, early in 2000, with deliveries commencing in 9-00.

QATAR

State of Qatar

Personnel: Approx. 1,800 total, including the marine police

Bases: Principal base at Doha, with a small facility at Halul Island

Maritime Aviation: Five Agusta-built SH-3D Sea King helicopters of the Air Force's No. 8 Squadron are in service for search-and-rescue duties; of these, two are equipped to launch AM 39 Exocet missiles.

Coast Defense: There are three truck-mounted batteries of MM 40 Exocet antiship missiles, with four missiles per truck.

Note: Ship names are prefixed by QENS (Qatari Emiri Navy Ship).

CORVETTES [FFL]

GUIDED-MISSILE PATROL CRAFT [PTG]

♦ 4 Vita class
Bldr: Vosper Thornycroft, Portchester, U.K.

	L	In serv.
Q 04 Barzan	1-4-95	9-5-96
Q 05 Huwar	15-7-95	6-6-96
Q 06 Al Udeid	21-3-96	16-12-96
Q 07 Al Debeel	31-8-96	3-7-97

Huwar (Q 05) French Navy, 1998

Al Debeel (Q 07)—with *Al Udeid* (Q 06) in background Vosper Thornycroft, 1997

D: 376 tons light (480 fl) **S:** 38 kts (35 sust.)
Dim: 56.50 (52.00 wl) × 9.00 (8.2 wl) × 2.25 (hull; 2.50 max.)
A: 4 MM 40 Exocet SSM; 1 76-mm 62-cal. OTO Melara SuperRapid DP; 1 6-round Sadral point-defense SAM syst. (Mistral missiles); 1 30-mm Goalkeeper SGE-30 CIWS; 2 single 12.7-mm mg
Electronics:
Radar: 1 Kelvin-Hughes Type 1007 nav.; 1 Thales MRR 3-D surf./air search; 1 Thales Sting gun f.c.; 1 Thales Goalkeeper f.c.
EW: Thales DR-3000S1 Compact intercept (1–18 GHz); Dassault Salamandre jammer; 1 330- to 340-round Matra Défense Dagaie decoy RL
E/O: Thales IRSCAN surveillance and tracking
M: 4 MTU 20V538 TB93 diesels; 4 props; 18,800 bhp (15,020 sust.)
Electric: 780 kw tot. (3 × 260-kw Stansfield alternators, 3 MWM TB234V-8 diesels driving—412 bhp each)—135-kw emergency set
Range: 1,800/12 **Fuel:** 44 tons **Crew:** 7 officers, 24 enlisted, 4 trainees

Remarks: Design derived from Vosper Thornycroft's "Vita" concept. Ordered 4-6-92. First two departed for Qatar 18-7-97, the second pair 30-4-98.
Hull systems: Have accommodations for a total of 47 personnel. Equipped with fin stabilizers.
Combat systems: Have the Thales SEWACO-FD combat data system. The Sting radar gun director has radar and television sensors. Employ the C.S. Défense Sidewinder EW suite control system, and use the Thorn-EMI shipboard data distribution system. The MRR radar operates in G band and is used for close- and medium-range target detection and designation.

♦ 3 French Combattante III class
Bldr: CMN, Cherbourg

	Laid down	L	In serv.
Q 01 Damsah	6-5-81	17-6-82	10-11-82
Q 02 Al Ghariyah	26-8-81	23-9-82	10-2-83
Q 03 Rbigah	27-10-81	22-12-82	11-5-83

Damsah (Q 01) CMN, 1982

D: 395 tons (430 fl) **S:** 38.5 kts
Dim: 56.00 (53.00 pp) × 8.16 × 2.15 (hull; 2.50 max.)
A: 8 MM 40 Exocet SSM; 1 76-mm 62-cal. OTO Melara Compact DP; 1 twin 40-mm 70-cal. OTO Melara AA; 2 twin 30-mm 75-cal. Emerlec EX-30 AA
Electronics:
Radar: 1 Decca 1226 nav.; 1 Thales Pollux search; 1 Thales Castor-II gun f.c.
EW: Racal Cutlass intercept; 1 330- to 340-round Matra Défense Dagaie decoy RL
M: 4 MTU 20V538 TB93 diesels; 4 props; 19,300 bhp (15,020 sust.)
Range: 2,000/15 **Crew:** 6 officers, 41 enlisted

Remarks: Ordered 10-80. Very similar in appearance and equipment to the three Nigerian units of the class. Arrived at Doha in 7-83. Refitted 1996–98.
Combat systems: Have the Thales Vega weapons-control system, with two Matra Défense Panda optical backup gun directors. During planned refits, the 30-mm AA are to be replaced by two Simbad twin launchers for Mistral infrared-homing SAMs and the intercept array is to be replaced by the Thales DR-3000 system.

PATROL CRAFT [PC]

♦ 4 Vosper 103-foot class
Bldr: Vosper Thornycroft, Portchester, U.K.

	In serv.
Q 13 That Assuari	3-10-75
Q 14 Al Wussail	28-10-75
Q 15 Fateh al Khatab	22-1-76
Q 16 Tariq	1-3-76

That Assuari (Q 13)—with a sister in the background L. V. Bonneau, 2001

PATROL CRAFT [PC] *(continued)*

D: 120 tons (fl) **S:** 27 kts **Dim:** 32.40 (31.10 pp) × 6.30 × 1.60 (hull)
A: 1 twin 30-mm 75-cal. Oerlikon GCM-A03-2 AA; 1 single 20-mm 70-cal. Oerlikon AA
Electronics: Radar: 1 Decca 1226 nav.
M: 2 Paxman Ventura 16RP200 diesels; 2 props; 6,250 bhp **Crew:** 25 tot.

Remarks: Were to have been retired upon arrival of the new Vita-class missile craft but remain active. Sisters *Barzan* (Q 11) and *Huwar* (Q 12) were stricken in 1996. The original twin 30-mm gunmounts were replaced by single 20-mm mounts during early 1990s refits, but had been restored by 2001. Probably can no longer make the indicated maximum speed.

PATROL BOATS [PB]

♦ **6 CMN 15-60 class**
Bldr: CMN, Cherbourg, France (In serv. 2006)

D: 12 tons (fl) **S:** 60 kts (55 sust.) **Dim:** 15.50 (12.00 pp) × 3.00 × 0.80
A: 1 12.7-mm mg **Electronics:** Radar: 1 Furuno . . . nav.
M: 2 . . . diesels; 2 props; 1,680 bhp
Range: 500/35 **Crew:** 6 tot.

Remarks: Four were ordered on 4-2-03, with an option for two more. Referred to by the builder as an "ultra-fast interceptor" for police, antismuggling, surveillance, special forces, strike, and liaison duties. GRP hull and superstructure. Equipped with GPS receiver, computer-aided navigation system, and HF/VHF/UHF transceivers. Six sisters serve in Yemen.

♦ **Up to 3 Polycat 1450 class**
Bldr: Damen, Gorinchem, the Netherlands (In serv. 1980)

Q 31 series

D: 18 tons (fl) **S:** 26 kts **Dim:** 14.5 × 4.7 × 1.5
A: 1 12.7-mm mg **Electronics:** Radar: 1 Decca . . . nav.
M: 2 G.M. Detroit Diesel 12V71 TI diesels; 2 props; 1,300 bhp
Range: 650/20 **Crew:** 11 tot.

Remarks: Ordered 2-83. GRP construction. Of the original six, one was out of service in 1997 and two more by 1999.

SERVICE CRAFT

♦ **1 logistics landing craft [YFU]**
Bldr: . . ., Singapore (In serv. 1987)

Rabha

D: . . . **S:** 9–10 kts **Dim:** 48.8 × . . . × . . .
M: 2 diesels; 2 props; . . . bhp

Remarks: Reportedly capable of transporting three tanks and 110 troops.

♦ **1 inshore survey craft**
Bldr: . . . . . . (In serv. 2000)

Mukhtabar Albihar

Note: The marine police, with a total of about 800 personnel, operate nine patrol boats:

- **3 M 160 class** (In serv. 12-96): 19 tons (fl), 24 kts, 1 12.7-mm mg
- **4 MV 45 class** (In serv. 1989): 17 tons (fl), 32 kts, 2 single 7.62-mm mg
- **2 P 1200 class** (In serv. 1980): 12.7 tons (fl), 29 kts, 2 single 7.62-mm mg

Qatari Marine Police M 160–class patrol boat Halmatic, 12-96

There is also a customs service patrol launch force.

ROMANIA

Republic of Romania

NAVY

Personnel: 7,200 total plus about 600 marines.

Organization: Reorganized into one naval operational command and one riverine flotilla.

Bases: Headquarters, principal base, and training facilities at Mangalia, with other facilities at Constanta, Tulcea, and Braila.

Naval Aviation: Five Soviet Mi-14PL Haze-A land-based ASW helicopters and six Romanian-built IAR-316 Alouette-III shipboard helicopters are in service, operated by the air force. Seventeen IAR-330L Puma helicopters are assigned to the search-and-rescue role and carry the legend "Coast Guard" on their sides.

Naval Infantry: Reduced to one battalion of roughly 600 marines. Equipment includes 13 TAB-71 and TABC-79 armored personnel carriers.

ATTACK SUBMARINES [SS]

♦ **1 Soviet Kilo class (Project 877E)** (Nonoperational)
Bldr: United Admiralty SY, St. Petersburg (In serv. 12-86)

521 Delfinul

Delfinul (521) *Ships of the World,* 1998

D: 2,325 tons surf.; 2,450 tons with emergency fuel/3,076 tons sub.
S: 10 kts surf./17 kts sub.
Dim: 72.60 (70.0 wl) × 9.90 (12.80 over stern planes) × 6.60 (fwd.; 6.20 mean)
A: 6 bow 533-mm TT (18 torpedoes or 24 mines); 1 Fasta-4 SAM shoulder-launched SAM syst. (8 9K-32M Strela missiles)
Electronics:
Radar: 1 MRK-50 Tobol (Snoop Tray-2) nav./search
Sonar: MGK-400 Rubikon (Shark Gill) LF active/passive suite; passive hull array; MG-519 Arfa (Mouse Roar) HF active classification/mine avoidance; MG-553 sound-velocity measuring; MG-512 cavitation detection
EW: Brick Pulp or Squid Head intercept; 6701E (Quad Loop) D/F
M: 2 Type 4-2DL42M diesel generator sets (1,825 bhp/1,500 kw at 700 rpm), electric drive: 1 motor; 1 6-bladed prop; 5,900 shp—1 130-shp low-speed motor—2 low-speed maneuvering motors; 2 ducted props; 204 shp (3 kts)
Range: 6,000/7 snorkel; 400/3 sub. **Fuel:** 172 tons **Endurance:** 45 days
Crew: 12 officers, 41 enlisted

Remarks: Named for Romania's first submarine, which was commissioned in 1936. Is said to be in need of a major overhaul and has not been operational since at least mid-1996.
Hull systems: Propulsion plant is suspended for silencing. Hull has 32% reserve buoyancy at 2,350 m^3 surfaced displacement. At rest on the surface, the submarine trims down 0.4 m by the bow. Maximum diving depth is 300 m, normal depth 240 m, and periscope depth 17.5 m. Has an anechoic hull coating. Two batteries, each with 120 cells, provide 9,700 kwh. Hull has six watertight compartments.
Combat systems: The combat system, designated Murena or MVU-110EM, can conduct two simultaneous attacks while tracking three other targets manually. The SAM launch position is located in after portion of the sail. Weapons carried can include Type E-53 wire-guided, E-53-60 and E-53-85 wake-homing, and E-53-67 acoustic homing torpedoes and KMD-500, KMD-1000, KMD-II-500, KMD-II-1000, and UMD mines.

DESTROYER [DD]

♦ **1 Muntenia class**
Bldr: Santierul Naval 2 Mai, Mangalia

	Laid down	L	In serv.
111 Marasesti (ex-*Muntenia*)	1979	4-81	5-8-85

Marasesti (111) Cem D. Yaylali, 6-04

D: 5,400 tons (5,790 fl) **S:** 27 kts **Dim:** 144.60 (139.00 pp) × 14.80 × 4.90 (hull)
A: 4 twin P-20/21 Termit (SS-N-2C Styx) SSM launchers; 2 twin 76.2-mm 59-cal. AK-726 DP; 4 single 30-mm 54-cal. AK-630 gatling AA; 2 quadruple SA-N-5 Grail SAM launchers (9K-32M Strela short-range missiles); 2 triple 533-mm TT (Russian 53-65 wake-homing torpedoes); 2 12-tubed RBU-6000 ASW RL; 2 IAR-316 Alouette-III helicopters; 1 IAR-330 Puma helicopter

DESTROYER [DD] *(continued)*

Electronics:
Radar: 1 Nayada nav.; 1 MR-302 Rubka (Strut Curve) air/surf. search; 1 Garpun (Plank Shave) missile target desig.; 1 Fut-B (Hawk Screech) 76.2-mm gun f.c.; 2 MR-104 Rys' (Drum Tilt) 30-mm gun f.c.
Sonar: . . . MF hull-mounted search; . . . HF f.c.
EW: . . . intercept; 2 16-tubed PK-16 decoy RL
M: 4 6-cyl. diesels; 4 3-bladed props; 32,000 bhp
Range: . . . / . . . **Crew:** 25 officers, 245 enlisted

Remarks: Reportedly was laid down in 1981 and launched by 1983. Laid up in 6-88, shortly after completion, she may never have operated in her original configuration; major modifications were completed 15-8-92, after which she made several Mediterranean cruises. A planned second unit does not seem to have been laid down. The ship was offered for sale in 2-93 but remains in commission. Has elaborate flag/head-of-state accommodations. The original Romanian type designation, *Destrugator* (Destroyer), was changed to *Fregate* (Frigate) in 3-01. Based at Mangalia. Underwent modernizations during 2006.
Hull systems: When advertised for sale, was said to be all-diesel, but one source indicates that she has two Russian boost gas turbines, and another says that there are four propeller shafts. Although much topweight was removed during postcompletion modifications, she retains excess topweight.
Combat systems: During the reconstruction, the four twin antiship missile launchers were repositioned one deck lower and the original tower masts were replaced by lighter and lower lattice masts in order to improve stability; in addition, the two quintuple-tubed RBU-1200 ASW rocket launchers were replaced by RBU-6000 launchers mounted forward of the bridge. Combat systems are mostly autonomous, without a central combat control center. Four radomes of differing sizes for probable EW intercept antennas are mounted on the foremast; these replaced the original Bizan'-series (Watch Dog) arrays. The manned SAM launchers flank the base of the foremast. The Garpun (Plank Shave) antiship missile target designation radar has its antenna mounted on the foremast; the device can also be employed as a passive receiver for target emissions.
During the 2000–2020 program, is being given GPS navigation gear, an underway replenishment capability, and new communications equipment (including Inmarsat SATCOM); the radar and sonar systems are to be integrated with a combat data system, using a locally developed system employing commercial computers running Microsoft Windows programming.

FRIGATES [FF]

♦ 2 ex-UK Boxer-class (Type 22 Batch 2) ASW
Bldr: F 221: Swan Hunter (Shipbuilders) Ltd., Wallsend-on-Tyne; F 222: Yarrow, Scotstoun, Glasgow

	Laid down	L	In serv.
F 221 Regele Ferdinand (ex-*Coventry*, F 98)	29-3-84	8-4-86	24-10-88
F 222 Regina Maria (ex-*London*, F 95)	23-2-82	27-10-84	5-6-87

Regele Ferdinand (F 221) Ben Sullivan, 10-04

Regina Marina (F 222) Frank Findler, 6-05

D: 4,250 tons (4,850 fl) **S:** 30 kts (18 on cruise engines)
Dim: 148.10 (140.00 pp) × 14.75 × 4.30 (hull; 6.00 max.)
A: 1 76-mm 62-cal. OTO Melara Compact DP; 2 single 20-mm 90-cal. Oerlikon GAM-B01 AA; 2 triple 324-mm STWS.2 ASW TT; 2 . . . helicopters

Regina Marina (F 222) A. A. de Kruijf, 7-05

Electronics:
Radar: 1 Kelvin-Hughes Type 1007 nav.; 1 Marconi Type 967M-968 surf./air search
Sonar: Plessey Type 2016 hull-mounted (4.5–7.5 kHz)
EW: Racal UAA(2) intercept; Terma DLT-12 decoy RL syst.; Type 2070 towed torpedo decoy
E/O: BAE Systems 2500 surveillance, tracking, and f.c.
M: COGAG: 2 Rolls-Royce Spey SM-1A gas turbines (18,770 shp each), 2 Rolls-Royce Tyne RM-1C gas turbines (5,340 shp each); 2 CP props; 48,220 shp max.
Electric: 4,000 kw (4 × 1,000-kw Paxman Valenta 12PA 200CZ diesel-driven sets)
Range: 7,000/18; 12,000/14 (one shaft) **Fuel:** 700 tons + 80 tons aviation fuel
Crew: 203 total

Remarks: The sale, reportedly costing $186.5 million, was agreed to on 1-3-02 and finalized on 14-1-03. Following modernization in the U.K., F 221 was transferred during 9-04 and F 222 in 4-05. *London* was decommissioned from the Royal Navy on 11-6-99, and *Coventry* was retired on 28-2-02. Between 2008 and 2009, a further refit in Romania is to begin, with enhanced command and control systems to be added to permit them to be used as flagships, along with new EW equipment and possibly a SAM and antiship missile system.
Hull systems: Two auxiliary boilers and two 50-ton/day flash evaporators are installed. Water-displacement fuel tanks are used.
Combat systems: In U.K. service, had the CACS-1 data system, with 26 operators and 16 displays. Are NATO Link 11 and Link 14 compatible. During refits in the U.K., the CACS-1 system is being updated and the NAUTIS 3 fire-control computer system added. The two Sea Wolf GWS.25 Mod. 3 SAM systems and their Type 911 radar illuminator/trackers have been removed. The 76-mm gun will initially be controlled by the E/O director only.

♦ 2 Tetal-II class (Project 1048M)
Bldr: Santierul Naval 2 Mai, Mangalia

	L	In serv.
264 Contre-Amiral Eustatiu Sebastian	1988	30-12-89
265 Contre-Amiral Horia Macellariu	1991	29-9-96

Contre-Amiral Horia Macellariu (265) Cem D. Yaylali, 9-02

Contre-Amiral Horia Macellariu (265) Cem D. Yaylali, 4-05

D: 1,540 tons (1,660 fl) **S:** 24 kts **Dim:** 92.42 (89.40 pp) × 11.40 × 3.75
A: 1 twin 76.2-mm 59-cal. AK-176 DP; 2 single 30-mm 59-cal. AK-630 gatling AA; 2 twin, trainable 533-mm ASW TT; 2 12-tubed RBU-6000 ASW RL; 2 d.c. racks; 1 IAR-316B Alouette-III helicopter
Electronics:
Radar: 1 Nayada nav.; 1 MR-302 Rubka (Strut Curve) surf./air search; 1 MR-123 Vympel (Bass Tilt) f.c.
Sonar: Hull-mounted MF search and HF f.c.; HF dipping sonar at stern
EW: 2 Bizan'-4 (Watch Dog) intercept (2–18 GHz); 2 16-tubed PK-16 decoy RL
M: 4 . . . diesels; 4 props; 17,612 bhp (13,140 sust.)
Electric: 700 kw tot. (4 × 175-kw diesel sets)
Range: 1,500/ . . . **Endurance:** 10 days **Crew:** 7 officers, 70 enlisted

FRIGATES [FF] *(continued)*

Remarks: Employ same hull and propulsion as the original Tetal-I variant but substitute a helicopter deck (with no hangar or haul-down system) for the after 76.2-mm gunmount and have improved weapons. The "M" in the project number stands for *Modernizata*. A planned third unit was reportedly laid down, but work seems to have been canceled. Both are based at Constanta.
Combat systems: Although listed as being of the AK-630 model, the 30-mm gatling guns, which are mounted abreast the stack, may be of the lighter-weight AK-306 model. There are Kolonka-2 manned ringsight directors for the AK-230 AA mounts, and the 76.2-mm mount can be controlled locally. The MR-123 director can control the 76.2-mm and AK-630/306 gunmounts.

♦ 2 Tetal-I class (Project 1048)
Bldr: Santierul Naval 2 Mai, Mangalia

	L	In serv.
260 Amiral Petre Barbuneanu	1981	4-2-83
263 Vice-Amiral Eugeniu Rosca	1985	23-4-87

Amiral Petre Barbuneanu (260) Cem D. Yaylali, 9-98

D: 1,480 tons (1,600 fl) **S:** 24 kts **Dim:** 92.42 (89.40 pp) × 11.40 × 3.60
A: 2 twin 76.2-mm 59-cal. AK-726 DP; 2 twin 30-mm 65-cal. AK-230 AA; 4 twin 14.5-mm 93-cal. AA; 2 16-tubed RBU-2500 ASW RL; 2 twin, trainable 533-mm TT; 2 mine rails
Electronics:
Radar: 1 Nayada nav.; 1 MR-302 Rubka (Strut Curve) surf./air search; 1 Fut-B (Hawk Screech) f.c.; 1/MR-104 Rys' (Drum Tilt) f.c.
Sonar: . . . hull-mounted MF
EW: 2 Bizan'-4 (Watch Dog) intercept (2–18 GHz); 2 16-tubed PK-16 decoy RL
M: 4 . . . diesels; 4 props; 17,612 bhp
Electric: 700 kw tot. (4 × 175-kw diesel sets)
Range: 1,500/ . . . **Endurance:** 10 days **Crew:** 7 officers, 70 enlisted

Remarks: "Tetal" is the NATO code name for this class, which is entirely of Romanian design. First unit was laid down in 1980; program was slowed by economic problems. Romanian ship-type designation: *Fregate* (Frigate). Both are based at Constanta.
Hull systems: Have also been reported as having four 3,250-bhp diesels.
Combat systems: The Fut-B (Hawk Screech) radar director for the 76.2-mm gunmounts has two associated manned target designators on the bridge wings. The MR 104 Rys' (Drum Tilt) radar director controls both 30-mm mounts, and Kolonka-1 ringsight backup directors are carried on platforms flanking the mast. The torpedo tubes can probably accommodate both antiship and antisubmarine torpedoes. Are planned to be updated with NATO-compatible communications and IFF systems, an E/O adjunct to the weapons-control system, and, possibly, improved weapons and other sensors.
Disposals: Sisters *Vice-Amiral Vasile Scodrea* (261) and *Vice-Amiral Vasile Urseanu* (262) were decomissioned during 2004.

GUIDED-MISSILE PATROL BOATS [PTG]

♦ 3 Soviet Tarantul I class (Project 1241E)
Bldr: Volodarskiy Zavod, Rybinsk

	In serv.
188 Zborul	12-90
189 Pescarusul	12-91
190 Lastunul	12-91

D: 385 tons light (455 fl) **S:** 43 kts
Dim: 56.10 (49.50 pp) × 10.20 (9.40 wl) × 2.14 (hull; 3.59 props)
A: 4 P-20/21 Termit (SS-N-2C Styx) SSM; 1 76.2-mm 59-cal. AK-176 DP; 1 4-round MTU-40S (SA-N-8) SAM syst. (12 9K-32M Strela missiles); 2 single 30-mm 54-cal. AK-630 gatling AA
Electronics:
Radar: 1 Kivach-2 nav.; 1 Garpun (Plank Shave) targeting; 1 MR-123 Vympel (Bass Tilt) f.c.
EW: 2 16-round PK-16 decoy RL
M: M-15E COGAG plant: 2 DMR-76 cruise gas turbines (4,000 shp each), 2 PR-77 boost gas turbines (12,000 shp each); 2 props; 32,000 shp
Electric: 500 kw tot. (2 × 200-kw, 1 × 100-kw diesel sets)
Range: 760/43; 1,400/13 **Fuel:** 50 tons (122,634 liters)
Endurance: 10 days **Crew:** 7 officers, 32 enlisted

Remarks: Romanian ship-type designation: *Nave Purtatoare de Racchete* (Missile-carrying Ship). Based at Mangalia.
Hull systems: Stainless-steel-alloy, seven-watertight-compartment hull with aluminum alloy superstructure, decks, and internal bulkheads. Very strongly constructed and rugged. Have difficulty maneuvering below 10 kts, due to small size of the rudders.
Combat systems: Do not have a combat system per se; each weapons system is independently controlled by analog computers, although there are backup control systems for each. Carry 152 ready-service rounds and can carry another 150 in reserve for the 76.2-mm gun, which can be operated in local mode as well as under director control. Normally carry two infrared-homing and two radar-homing antiship missiles. The Plank Shave radar can be used in the passive mode to determine target bearing. There is otherwise no intercept system other than a small MFD/F.

Lastunul (190) Romanian Navy, 1995

Disposal note: The remaining three ex-Soviet Osa-I class (Project 205) guided-missile patrol boats, *Vulturul* (195), *Eretele* (198), and *Albatrosul* (199), were retired from service by 2005.

TORPEDO BOATS [PT]

♦ 4 Naluca class
Bldr: Santierul Naval 2 Mai, Mangalia

	In serv.		In serv.
202 Smeul	25-10-79	209 Vulcanul	26-10-81
204 Vijelia	7-2-80	212 Tornada	5-10-82

D: 215 tons (fl) **S:** 38 kts **Dim:** 38.60 × 7.60 × 1.85 (hull)
A: 2 twin 30-mm 65-cal. AK-230 AA; 4 fixed 533-mm TT
Electronics: Radar: 1 Baklan (Pot Drum) nav./surf. search; 1 MR-104 Rys' (Drum Tilt) f.c.
M: 3 M-503A2 diesels; 3 props; 12,000 bhp (8,025 sust.) **Electric:** 200 kw tot.
Range: 500/34; 750/25 **Endurance:** 5 days **Crew:** 4 officers, 18 enlisted

Remarks: Design is based on Osa class, essentially an Osa-I with torpedo tubes substituted for the missile launchers. NATO nickname for the class was "Epitrop." Romanian ship-type designation: *Vedete Torpiloare Mari* (Large Torpedo Boat). All are based at Mangalia.
Disposals: Sisters *Naluca* (201), *Viforul* (203), *Viscolul* (205), *Virtejul* (206), *Fulgerul* (207), *Vintul* (208), *Furtuna* (210), and *Trasnetul* (211) were retired from service by 2005.

♦ 6 Chinese Huchuan-class (Project 834) semi-hydrofoils
Bldrs: Dobreta SY, Turnu, and Santierul Naval 2 Mai, Mangalia
(In serv. 1973–83, 1988–90)

From among 51 through 74, 320 through 325

Huchuan-class 320—outboard three sisters Arsenalul Armatei, 1999

D: 37 tons (43 fl) **S:** 52 kts **Dim:** 22.50 × 6.26 (3.80 deck) × 1.15 (1.11 foiling)
A: 2 twin 14.5-mm 93-cal. Type 81 AA; 2 fixed 533-mm TT; 4 d.c. in tilt racks
Electronics: 1 Type 756 nav.
M: 3 Type L-12V-180 diesels; 3 props; 3,600 bhp **Electric:** 5.6 kw tot.
Range: 500/30 **Endurance:** 2 days **Crew:** 11 tot.

Remarks: Romanian ship-type designation: *Vedete Torpiloare Mici* (Small Torpedo Boat). Three others, built in China, were later deleted, as have been nine Romanian-built craft. 320–325 were completed 1988–90 by Santierul Naval 2 Mai, Mangalia. Sisters *Jupiter* and *Marte* had the torpedo tubes and hydrofoils removed and were assigned for use as search-and-rescue craft [YH]. All use Chinese-made, side-by-side, powered gunmounts. The diesel engines are a Chinese version of the Russian M-50F-4. All are based at Mangalia.

MINE WARFARE SHIPS

♦ 1 Cosar-class minelayers [MM]
Bldr: Santierul Naval 2 Mai, Mangalia

274 VICE-AMIRAL CONSTANTIN BALESCU (In serv. 16-11-81)

D: 1,450 tons (fl) **S:** 19 kts **Dim:** 79.0 × 10.6 × 3.6
A: 1 57-mm 70-cal. DP; 2 twin 30-mm 65-cal. AK-230 AA; 2 twin 14.5-mm 93-cal. Type 81 AA; 2 5-round RBU-1200 ASW RL; 2 mine rails (200 mines)
Electronics:
Radar: 1 Nayada nav.; 1 MR-302 Rubka (Strut Curve) surf./air search; 1 MR-103 Bars (Muff Cob) f.c.; 1 MR-104 Rys' (Drum Tilt) f.c.
Sonar: Probable Tamir-11 (MG-11)-derivative hull-mounted searchlight (25–30 kHz)
EW: 2 Bizan'-4 (Watch Dog) intercept (2–18 GHz)
M: 2 . . . diesels; 2 props; 6,400 bhp **Crew:** 75 tot.

Remarks: "Cosar" is the NATO nickname. Romanian ship-type designation: *Puitoare de Mine* (Minelayer). Also useful as ASW escorts. Share the same hull as the oceanographic research ship *Grigore Antipa* and intelligence collection ship *Emil Racovita.*
Combat systems: The MR-105 radar/electro-optical director controls the semiautomatic 57-mm gun; the MR-104 radar f.c.s. controls the 30-mm AA, for which there are also Kolonka-1 backup ringsight directors on platforms on the lattice mast.
Disposals: Sister ship *Vice-Amiral Ioan Murgescu* (271) was retired during 2004.

♦ 4 Musca-class oceangoing minesweepers [MSF]
Bldr: Cala de Adocare, Mangalia

	Laid down	L	In serv.
24 LOCOTENANT REMUS LEPRI	1984	. . .	23-4-87
25 LOCOTENANT LUPU DINESCU	. . .	8-86	6-1-89
29 LOCOTENANT DIMITRIE NICOLESCUE	1985	. . .	7-12-89
30 SUBLOCOTENANT ALEXANDRU AXENTE	. . .	. . .	7-12-89

Locotenant Dimitrie Nicolescue (29) Cem D. Yaylali, 4-05

D: 710 tons (790 fl) **S:** 17 kts **Dim:** 60.80 (59.20 wl) × 9.50 × 2.70
A: 2 twin 30-mm 65-cal. AK-230 AA; 4 quadruple 14.5-mm 93-cal. AA; 2 4-round SA-N-5 SAM syst. (. . . 9K-32M Strela missiles); 2 5-round RBU-1200 ASW RL; 2 mine rails (50 mines)
Electronics:
Radar: 1 Nayada nav.; 1 Kivach nav.; 1 MR-104 Rys' (Drum Tilt) f.c.
Sonar: Tamir-11 (MG-11)-derivative hull-mounted HF searchlight
M: 2 . . . diesels; 2 props; 4,800 bhp **Range:** . . . **Crew:** 60 tot.

Remarks: Romanian ship-type designation: *Dragoare Maritime* (Seagoing Minesweeper). Steel-hulled. Carry an unusually large number of danbuoy swept channel markers and may have magnetic and acoustic sweep gear in addition to mechanical sweeping equipment. The point-defense SAM launchers are mounted abaft the forward 30-mm mount on the forecastle and just abaft the stack.

Disposal note: Four remaining German M-40-class minesweepers, in service since the 1950s, were retired by 2005.

AUXILIARIES

♦ 1 intelligence collection ship [AGI]
Bldr: Drobeta Severin SY (In serv. 30-10-77)

EMIL RACOVITA

D: 1,900 tons (fl) **S:** 11 kts **Dim:** 70.1 × 10.0 × 3.0
M: 1 diesel; 1 prop; 3,285 bhp **Crew:** 80 tot.

Remarks: Although designed as an oceanographic research ship, is used primarily as an intelligence collector. Based at Constanta. Other sources list this unit as a near-sister to the salvage and oceanographic research ship *Grigore Antipa.*

♦ 2 Croitor-class small-combatant tenders [AGP]
Bldr: Santierul Naval Braila, Braila

	In serv.
281 CONSTANTA	15-9-80
283 MIDIA	26-2-82

D: 2,850 tons (fl) **S:** 16 kts **Dim:** 108.0 × 13.5 × 3.8
A: 1 twin 57-mm 70-cal. DP; 2 4-round SA-N-5 SAM syst. (16 9K-32M Strela missiles); 2 twin 30-mm 65-cal. AK-230 AA; 2 twin 14.5-mm 93-cal. AA; 2 5-round RBU-1200 ASW RL; 1 IAR-316 Alouette-III helicopter
Electronics:
Radar: 1 Kivach nav.; 1 MR-302 Rubka (Strut Curve) surf./air search; 1 MR-103 Bars (Muff Cob) f.c.; 1 MR-104 Rys' (Drum Tilt) f.c.
Sonar: Tamir-11 (MG-11) derivative hull-mounted HF searchlight
EW: 2 Bizan'-series (Watch Dog) intercept (2–18 GHz)
M: 2 diesels; 2 props; 6,500 bhp **Crew:** 150 tot.

Remarks: "Croitor" is the NATO nickname. Have a helicopter hangar and flight deck aft. Crane forward of bridge tends the magazine for torpedoes and Termit-series anti-ship missiles. The SA-N-5 rack launchers are mounted atop the helicopter hangar.

Midia (283) H&L Van Ginderen, 8-99

Constanta (281) Guy Schaeffer, via Paolo Marsan, 6-01

♦ 1 Dolj-class general cargo ship [AK]
Bldr: Santierul Naval Braila, Braila (L: 1977)

ALBATROS (ex-*Dej*)

D: 8,750 tons (fl) **S:** 16 kts (15.5 sust.)
Dim: 130.8 (121.21 pp) × 17.71 × 8.10 (max.; 6.60 normal)
Electronics: . . .
M: 1 Cegielski-Sulzer 5RD68 diesel; 1 prop; 6,100 bhp
Electric: 600 kw tot. (3 × 200-kw diesel sets)
Range: . . . / . . . **Fuel:** 1,148 tons heavy oil **Crew:** . . . tot.

Remarks: 4,399 grt/6,253 dwt. Acquired 6-95 from Intreprinderea de Exploratore a Floti Maritime NAVROM, Constanta. Has been largely inactive. Has an ice-strengthened hull, four holds, and five 3-ton cranes. Grain capacity is 11,980 m^3; bale capacity 11,067 m^3.

♦ 1 small seagoing tanker [AO] Bldr: Tulcea SY (In serv. 24-12-92)

TM 532 TULCEA

Tulcea (TM 532)—note bulbous bow form French Navy, 8-96

D: 2,170 tons (fl) **S:** 16 kts **Dim:** 76.3 × 12.5 × 5.0
A: 1 twin 30-mm 65-cal. AK-230 AA; 2 twin 14.5-mm 93-cal. AA
Electronics: Radar: 1 . . . nav.
M: 2 diesels; 2 props; 4,800 bhp **Crew:** . . . tot.

Remarks: Has one replenishment station per side. Cargo: 1,200 tons. Work on a proposed second unit has ceased.

♦ 2 coastal tankers [AO]
Bldr: Santierul Naval Braila, Braila (In serv. 15-6-71)

TM 530 TM 531

D: 1,042 tons (fl) **S:** 12.5 kts **Dim:** 55.2 × 9.4 × 4.1
A: 1 37-mm 63-cal. AA; 2 single 12.7-mm mg
M: 2 diesels; 2 props; 1,800 bhp **Cargo:** 500 tons

♦ 1 submersible tender/salvage ship [ARS]
Bldr: Cala de Adocare, Mangalia (In serv. 25-5-80)

GRIGORE ANTIPA

AUXILIARIES *(continued)*

Grigore Antipa—white-painted and with no pennant number
Romanian Navy, 1995

D: 1,450 tons (fl) **S:** 19 kts **Dim:** 79.0 × 10.6 × 3.6
A: None **Electronics:** Radar: 1 Nayada nav.
M: 2 diesels; 2 props; 6,400 bhp **Crew:** 75 tot.

Remarks: Employs same hull and propulsion plant as the Cosar-class minelayers. Carries the SM358 manned salvage submersible at the stern and a submersible decompression chamber beneath a gantry to starboard, aft. Equipped to lay a four-point mooring. Based at Constanta and may also be employed in intelligence collection. Painted white, with deck equipment in red. Has a commercial SATCOM terminal.

♦ 2 Grozavu-class ocean tugs [ATA]
Bldr: Olteniza SY

RM 500 Grozavu (In serv. 29-6-93) RM 501 Hercules (In serv. 29-9-96)

Grozavu (RM 500) *Ships of the World,* 1998

D: 3,600 tons (fl) **S:** 12 kts **Dim:** 64.8 × 14.6 × 5.5
A: 1 twin 30-mm 65-cal. AK-230 AA; 4 twin 14.5-mm 93-cal. AA
M: 2 diesels; 2 props; 5,000 bhp **Crew:** . . .

Remarks: RM = *Remorcher de Mare* (seagoing tug). Also capable of salvage duties.

♦ 1 German Horst Wessel–class sail-training ship [AXT]
Bldr: Blohm + Voss, Hamburg

	Laid down	L	In serv.
A 288 Mircea	15-4-38	22-9-38	29-3-39

Mircea (A 288) Leo van Ginderen, 7-05

D: 1,604 tons (fl) **S:** 12 kts (13 under sail)
Dim: 81.28 (67.84 o.a. hull; 62.80 wl) × 12.50 × 5.02
Electronics: Radar: 1 Decca 202 nav.; 1 Nayada nav.
M: 1 MaK 6M 451 AK diesel; 1 prop; 1,100 bhp—max. sail area: 5,739 m^2
Range: 5,000/13 (on sail and engine); 3,000/12 (engine alone)
Crew: 5 officers, 17 warrant officers, 38 enlisted + 120–140 cadets

Remarks: Three-masted bark. Fore- and mainmast are 44 m above the waterline, the mizzenmast 39 m. Can carry a total of 23 sails (4 jibs, 6 staysails, 10 square sails, and 3 gaff sails). Sister to U.S. Coast Guard *Eagle,* Russian merchant training vessel *Tovarisch,* German *Gorch Fock,* and Portuguese *Sagres.* Navigation equipment includes a Rumb-16 D/F loop, MEL-25 log, and DT-700 echo sounder. Refitted by builder, 1966–67. Based at Constanta.

SERVICE CRAFT

♦ 2 degaussing tenders [YDG]

	Bldr	In serv.
Energerica	Santierul Naval Braila, Braila	20-10-73
Magnetica	Santierul Naval 2 Mai, Mangalia	18-12-89

D: 160 tons (fl) **S:** 12.5 kts **Dim:** 38.0 × 5.5 × 1.4
A: 1 twin 14.5-mm 93-cal. AA; 2 single 12.7-mm 79-cal. mg
M: 1 diesel (800-bhp) generator set, electric motor; 1 prop; 600 shp

Remarks: *Magnetica* is larger: 299 tons (fl); 40.8 × 6.6 × 3.2 (molded depth). All are capable of providing deperming services to ships of up to 3,000 tons displacement.
Disposals: Sisters *Automatice* and *Electronica* appear to have retired from service by 2005.

♦ 1 commander-in-chief's yacht [YFL]
Rindunica

Rindunica U.S. Navy, 1992

D: 40 tons (fl) **S:** 28 kts **Dim:** 24.0 × 5.0 × 1.1
Electronics: Radar: 1 . . . nav.
M: 2 M-50F-series diesels; 2 props; 2,200 bhp **Crew:** 6 tot.

♦ 4 small fuel lighters [YO]
Bldr: Braila SY (In serv. 1986–87)

MM 132 MM 133 MM 136 MM 137

D: 190 tons (fl) **S:** 10 kts **Dim:** 29.6 × 6.9 × 2.5
M: 2 Type 3D6 diesels; 2 props; 300 bhp **Cargo:** 80 tons

Remarks: Sister MM 131 was retired during 2001.

♦ 5 small harbor tugs [YTL]

SRS 570 SRS 571 SRS 572 SRS 577 SRS 675

Tug SRS 570 French Navy, 9-94

Remarks: Carry one twin and one single 14.5-mm mg. Some may have been retired. No further data available.

DANUBE FLOTILLA

RIVER MONITORS [PM]

♦ 3 Mihail Kogalniceanu class (Project 1310)
Bldr: Santierul Naval Turnu Severin, Mangalia (In serv. 1993–98)

	In serv.
45 Mihail Kogalniceanu	19-12-93
46 I. C. Bratianu	28-12-94
47 Lascar Catargiu	1998

D: 474 tons (550 fl) **S:** 18 kts **Dim:** 62.00 × 7.60 × 1.60
A: 2 single 105-mm tank guns; 1 quadruple and 2 twin 14.5-mm 93-cal. AA; 2 4-round SA-N-5 SAM syst. (16 9K-32M Strela missiles); 2 40-round 122-mm BM-21 artillery RL (. . . reloads)
Electronics: Radar: 1 Mius (Spin Trough) nav.
M: 2 . . . diesels; 2 props; 3,800 bhp **Crew:** 52 tot.

DANUBE FLOTILLA RIVER MONITORS [PM] *(continued)*

Mihail Kogalniceanu (45) Romanian Navy, 1991

Remarks: Romanian ship-type designation: *Minitoare* (Monitor). Carry inspection dinghies on stern. The BM-21 rocket launchers retract within the superstructure for reloading. There are no mine rails. All are based at Braila. A fourth unit is said to be under construction, though an estimated completion date is unknown.

♦ **5 Brutar-II class**
Bldr: Santierul 2 Mai, Mangalia

	In serv.		In serv.
176 Rahova	14-4-88	179 Posada	14-5-92
177 Opanez	24-7-90	180 Rovine	30-7-93
178 Smardan	24-7-90		

Rahova (176) Siegfried Breyer Collection

D: 370 tons (fl) **S:** 16 kts **Dim:** 50.7 × 8.0 × 1.5
A: 1 105-mm tank gun; 1 twin 23-mm AA; 2 quadruple and 2 twin 14.5-mm AA; 1 4-round SA-N-5 SAM syst. (. . . 9K-32M Strela missiles); 2 40-round 122-mm BM-21 artillery RL (. . . reloads); 2 mine rails (. . . mines)
Electronics: Radar: 1 . . . nav.
M: 2 diesels; 2 props; 2,700 bhp

Remarks: "Brutar" is the NATO nickname. Romanian ship-type designation: *Vedete Blindante Mari* (Large Armored Boat). Very low-lying craft, with armored tank turret and machinegun turrets. They are about 5 m longer than the *Grivita* (94) and also feature sloped armor on the sides in the region of the artillery rocket launchers, increasing their maximum beam by about 1 m. The BM-21 rocket launchers are retracted into the hull for reloading. Four of the 14.5-mm mg mounts are mounted in twin armored turrets abreast the tank turret; the others are in standard Romanian open quadruple mountings. The mine rails are considerably longer than in the *Grivita.*

♦ **1 Brutar-I class**
Bldr: Santierul 2 Mai, Mangalia (In serv. 21-11-86)

94 Grivita

D: 320 tons (fl) **S:** 18 kts **Dim:** 45.7 × 8.00 × 1.5
A: 1 105-mm tank gun; 1 twin 14.5-mm 93-cal. AA; 2 4-round SA-N-5 SAM syst. (. . . 9K-32M Strela missiles); 2 40-round 122-mm BM-21 artillery RL; 2 mine rails (. . . mines)
Electronics: Radar: 1 . . . nav.
M: 2 M-50-series diesels; 2 props; 2,400 bhp

Remarks: Has virtually no superstructure but is equipped with two periscopes and a conning station forward of and below the armored turret. The BM-21 rocket launchers are retracted into the hull for reloading.

Disposal note: All eighteen VB 76–class river monitors have been retired from service.

PATROL CRAFT [WPC]

♦ **4 ex-German Neustadt class**
Bldr: Lürssen, Vegesack

	Laid down	L	In serv.
10 General Paraschiv Vasilescu (ex-*Bayreuth,* BG 17)	15-9-69	9-1-70	1970
. . . (ex-*Alsfeld,* BG 16)	31-5-69	11-11-69	1970
. . . (ex-*Bad Bramstedt,* BG 12)	10-1-69	2-4-69	1969
. . . (ex-*Eschwege,* BG 15)	27-3-69	16-9-69	19-3-70

D: 191 tons (218 fl) **S:** 30 kts **Dim:** 38.50 (36.00 pp) × 7.00 × 2.15
A: 2 7.62-mm mg—provision for 1 40-mm 70-cal. Bofors AA
Electronics: Radar: 1 Selenia ARP 1645 nav., 1 . . . nav.
M: 2 Maybach 16-cyl. diesels; 2 props; 7,200 bhp—cruise engine: 1 MWM cruise diesel; 1 prop; 685 bhp
Electric: 156 kw tot. **Range:** 450/27 **Fuel:** 15 tons **Crew:** 24 tot.

General Paraschiv Vasilescu (10)—painted blue with white superstructure
Frank Behling, 12-03

Remarks: Ex-*Bayreuth* transferred 1-04, remaining three were transferred during 2005–6. Operated by the Romanian Border Guard; homeport is in Constanta.

PATROL BOATS [PB]

♦ **3 U.S. 27-foot Vigilant class**
Bldr: Boston Whaler, Edgewater, Fla. (In serv. 4-93)

D: 2.27 tons light (4.0 fl) **S:** 36 kts **Dim:** 8.10 × 3.05 × 0.48
A: 1 7.62-mm mg **Electronics:** Radar: 1 Furuno . . . nav.
M: 2 Evinrude gasoline outboards; 450 bhp **Fuel:** 545 liters **Crew:** 3 tot.

Remarks: Transferred for use in enforcing the UN embargo against Serbia on the Danube. Foam-core GRP "unsinkable" hulls.

Note: A small, locally designed air-cushion vehicle [PBA] was completed for the Danube River Flotilla in 1998 by the shipyard at Mangalia; no data available.

MINE WARFARE CRAFT

♦ **6 river minesweepers [MSI]**
Bldr: Turnu-Severin SY (In serv. 1975–84)

VD 147 through VD 151 and VD 157

River minesweeper VD 148—alongside a sister Romanian Navy, 1991

D: 97 tons (fl) **S:** 13 kts **Dim:** 33.3 × 4.0 × 0.89
A: 2 twin 14.5-mm 93-cal. Type 81 AA; 2 mine rails (6 mines)
Electronics: Radar: 1 Nayada nav. **M:** 2 diesels; 2 props; 870 bhp

Remarks: Resemble the VB 76–class monitors. Seven based at Galati, four at Giurgiu, three at Sulina, four at Tulcea, and seven at Turnu-Severin. Ninteen of the class had been retired by 2005.

Note: Also in service at the Danube River facilities and at the naval base at Constanta are several barges, ferries, launches, and a number of tugs. Vessel numbers include 591, 596, 341, 342, and others.

RUSSIA

Russian Federation

ROSIYSKIY VOENNOMORSKIY FLOT

Personnel: About 142,000 total including 35,000 naval aviation personnel and 9,500 naval infantry

Organization and Bases: Naval headquarters is in Moscow. The headquarters for the Northern Fleet is at Severomorsk in the Kola Inlet. Major ship bases in the Northern Fleet area are located at Gadzhgiyevo, Gremikha, Litsa Zaliv, Motovskij Zaliv, Nerpichija Guba (submarine facility), Olenija Guba (submarine facility), Andreeva Bay (spent nuclear fuel storage facility), Ara Guba (submarine storage facility),

ROSIYSKIY VOENNOMORSKIY FLOT *(continued)*

Yagelnaja, Polyarnyy, Murmansk (Rosta shipyard), and Arkhangel'sk (Naval Infantry). Late in 2000, mention began to be made of a separate "Kola Fleet" assigned to the protection of the Barents Sea and charged with protecting ships and submarines deploying beyond local waters, with its units based at Severomorsk and Polyarnyy, though as of 2006 this has yet to be established. Pacific Fleet headquarters is at Vladivostok (which also has the major repair yards for the area), with major facilities at Petropavlovsk-na-Kamchatskiy and Sovetskaya Gavan, and minor facilities at Komsomol'sk for the Amur River Flotilla; there are numerous detachments elsewhere in the area. The Baltic Fleet headquarters is at Kaliningrad, with the principal bases at Bal'tiysk in the Kaliningrad oblast and at Kronshtadt Island, west of St. Petersburg; minor facilities are located at Lomonosov, Primorsk, and Vyborg. The former Leningrad Naval Base command was incorporated into the Baltic Fleet command structure during 1993. The Black Sea Fleet headquarters remains at Sevastopol', which is leased from the Ukraine until 2017. Ukraine has stated that it will not renew the lease so the Headquarters and Base facilities will have to be established at another location on or about that time. Smaller facilities remain at Novorossiysk (which is to be expanded) and at Temryuk. The Caspian Flotilla headquarters was removed to Astrakhan during 1992, but most ships are based at Makhachkala.

Russia continues to keep a ship on station in Syria, although its navy now only rarely appears in the Mediterranean. The formerly significant (but recently all-but-abandoned) Russian naval base at Cam Ranh Bay, Vietnam, was closed 1-7-02 due to Russian inability to pay the rent.

As the result of an inspection made during 1-02, all remaining active Pacific Fleet submarine resources are being consolidated at Sovetskaya Gavan, near Vladivostok.

Note: Russian shipyards Baltiisky Zavod and Severnaya Verf reached a five-year deal in 2005 indicating that Baltiisky Zavod will build only civilian ships while rival Severnaya Verf will work exclusively on military projects through 2010. By the end of 2006 the major St. Petersburg naval shipbuilding yards, Admiralty, Baltic, and Northern were combined into a single new shipbuilding facility on the site of the former Northern Shipyard. Ship repair facilities at St. Petersburg's Kronshtadtskiy Morskoy Zavod are to be reorganized into separate naval and commercial ship repair facilities.

Coastal Defense: During 2001 the remaining coastal missile defense forces were placed in cadre status, with only 50 troops manning the missile regiments in each of the major fleets. The P-20/21 Rubezh-A (SSC-3) and P-35 Redut (SSC-1B) missiles and their transporters were placed in a state of preservation, although there are plans to conduct one test firing per fleet per year for each system type.

Note on ship names and types: Prior to 1991, the pennant numbers on the sides of Russian combatants were temporary tactical numbers denoting administrative subordination and were changed wholesale from time to time for security reasons. Since that time, however, the numbers have been relatively stable, and for that reason they are now included here, prefixing warship names and/or the alphanumeric names applied to small combatants, mine warfare units, and amphibious warfare units. Submarines normally do not wear pennant numbers.

The class names used herein are for the most part those used by NATO, with Russian class nicknames following in parentheses and the official permanent project number assigned to the design following the class name. The Russian Navy has a number of unique ship-type classifications; these are translated, where applicable, in the individual class entries.

WEAPONS AND SYSTEMS

Note: Nuclear warheads were widely deployed in the past on Soviet Navy missiles and other ordnance, especially submarine-deployed weapons. In 1991 in response to an initiative by U.S. President George H. W. Bush, it was announced that tactical nuclear weapons would be removed from Soviet warships, with the intent that only strategic ballistic submarines would have nuclear warheads in the future.

The navy announced in 1-01 that two of seven "missile systems," four of seven air-defense missile systems, and three of seven shipboard artillery systems in use would be retired by the end of the year.

Dates in parentheses following system names below are for acceptance into service.

A. MISSILES

♦ Submarine-launched ballistic missiles

Note: CEP = Circular Error Probable (i.e., half of all missiles launched will fall within this radius). The RSM-series designations for ballistic missile systems are apparently used only in diplomatic negotiations.

SS-N-18 Stingray (Russian RSM-50/R-29DU Volna) (8-77)

Two-stage missile employed on the Delta-III class. CEP is estimated at 1,100 m (Mod. 1). Mods. 2 and 3 are no longer in service. Production designation was 4K-75DU. Overall missile system designation is D-9DU. Designed by the Makeyev Bureau. The proposed commercial space-booster variant has the program name Volna. Capable of depressed-trajectory firing, which reduces detectability. The missiles employ an astral-radio correction flight trajectory, employing data from navigational satellites to correct the inertially set path while in flight.

Length: 14.10 m **Diameter:** 1.80 m **Weight:** 35,300 kg
Range: 3,510 n.m. (3 × 550-kg MIRV warheads)

SS-N-20 Sturgeon (Russian R-39) (. . .)

Cover designation RSM-52 was used for diplomatic purposes; production designation for the missile was 3M-20. Now carried only by one active Project 941 (Typhoon)-class submarine. Solid-fueled missile using liquid-fueled thrusters to alter flight trajectory, based on inputs to the inertial guidance system from navigational satellites. Each missile carries 10 warheads.

Length: 16.0 m **Diameter:** 2.40 m
Weight: 90,000 kg (incl. 6,000-kg launch-assist device and 2,500-kg reentry vehicle)
Range: 4,480 n.m. (10 × 255-kg MIRV warheads)

SS-N-23 Skiff (Russian RSM-54/R-29RM) (2-86)

Three-stage weapon, originally with a payload of up to 10 (Mod. 1) or four (Mod. 2) MIRV warheads, carried by the six Delta-IV class SSBNs. Designed by the Makeyev Bureau. CEP is estimated at 500 m. The first stage weighs 22,300 kg at launch. Overall missile system designator: D-9RM. The commercial space-booster variant has the program name Shtil. Production was restarted under a 1999 order. A new version with 10 independently targeted warheads, called Sineva, is under development by the Makeyev Bureau, with missile production to span 2002–7. During Russian wargame tests in 2-04, a Sineva missile veered off course and was forced to self-destruct.

Length: 14.8 m **Diameter:** 1.90 m **Weight:** 40,300 kg
Range: 4,860 nm (4 × 700-kg MIRV warheads)

SS-NX-30 (Russian Bulava) (2007)

Replacement for the solid-fueled Makeyev Bureau SS-NX-28 (Russian R-39UTTKh Grom or 3M-91 Izdelie) missile that was formally canceled early in 1998 after three unsuccessful flights. The SS-NX-30 (X because it is still experimental and not yet operational) was designed by another agency for use with the incomplete SSBN *Yuriy Dolgorukiy* and the modernized Project 941–class TK-208. It will be a navalized version—known as Bulava (Mace)—having 70 percent commonality with the Topol-M, which entered service late in 1998 with land-based rocket forces. A successful unpowered test launch from the Typhoon-class SSBN *Dmitriy Donskoy* was completed on 23-9-04. The first successful full flight test flight was conducted on 27-9-05. Flight tests continued into 2006 and current plans call for initial deployments to begin during 2008. The missile is claimed to be capable of defeating any U.S. ballistic-missile defense system, probably indicating that it will employ decoys. Data for the land-based version of the three-stage, solid-fueled Topol-M include:

Length: 22.7 m **Diameter:** 1.86 m **Weight:** 47,200 kg **Range:** 11,000 km

♦ Surface-to-surface cruise missiles

SS-N-2A/SS-N-2B Styx (Russian P-15/P-15U Termit) (1960/1965)

P-15, the original fixed-wing missile, is dubbed SS-N-2A by NATO and uses the hooded 4S-30 launcher; P-15U Termit-U, with folding wings, is called SS-N-2B and uses the cylindrical KT-67B or KT-67ER launcher. Production designation for the P-15 was 4K-40 or 4K-40T, while for P-15U it was 4K-40U. Liquid-propulsion rocket with solid booster. I-band active radar guidance in targeting, with infrared *or* radar homing. Altitude can be preset at 100, 150, 200, 250, or 300 m. Installed in Osa-I and Osa-II guided-missile boats. No longer used by the Russian Navy, but still in foreign service. Designed by MKB Raduga.

Length: 6.665 m **Diameter:** 0.8 m **Wingspan:** 2.5 m
Weight: 2,523 kg **Warhead:** 480 kg **Speed:** Mach 1.3 (320 m/sec)
Range: 80 km max. (50–60 effective)/8 km min.

SS-N-2C Styx (Russian P-15M Termit-M; export: P-20/21/22 Rubezh) (1972)

The basic weapon, the P-15M, has folding wings and an improved radar seeker. The P-20 Rubezh series export versions included the basic radar-homing P-20; the P-20K, with an improved radar altimeter to permit lower cruise flight; and the P-20M, with range extended to 45 n.m. The P-21 is an infrared-homing version of the P-20, and the P-22 is an infrared-homing version of the extended-range P-20M. In order to employ fully the over-the-horizon maximum range of the SS-N-2C, it is necessary to have a forward observer. The SS-N-2C is carried by Tarantul-I and -II guided-missile patrol craft, using KT-138 launchers. Missile production designation is 4K-40M. Widely exported. A land-based version, the SSC-3, is carried in pairs on special truck launchers.

Length: 6.5 m **Diameter:** 0.8 m **Wingspan:** 2.5 m
Weight: 2,500 kg **Warhead:** 500 kg armor-piercing **Speed:** Mach 1.3

SS-N-2D Styx (Russian P-27 Termit-R) (1980s?)

The latest variant of the Styx family, equipped with a new L-band seeker and, like the P-20M, capable of 45-n.m. flights. Missile production designation is 3M-51; the overall system is the 4K-51. Made by the Progress airframe plant, Khabarovsk, but no longer in production. It is uncertain whether it was ever used by the Russian Navy, which has almost no craft left that could launch it.

Note: With the retirement of the last warship equipped to launch it, the SS-N-3B Shaddock (Russian P-6 Progress) has effectively been retired.

SS-N-9 Siren (Russian P-120 Malakhit) (1972)

Features inertial guidance, with active radar or infrared homing to the target. Has a 500-kg conventional or nuclear warhead. Developed by the Chelomey Bureau (now NPO Mashinostroeniya) and installed in Nanuchka-I- and -III-class guided-missile patrol combatants. A submerged-launch version (P-120L) was carried by Charlie-II submarines. Missile production designation is 4K-85, and the launcher is designated KT-84.

Length: 8.84 m **Diameter:** 0.80 m **Wingspan:** 1.6 m
Weight: 5,400 kg **Speed:** Mach 0.9
Range: 30 n.m. (64.8 n.m. with a forward observer or video datalink)

SS-N-12 Sandbox (Russian P-500 Bazal't) (1975)

Has a 1,000-kg conventional or nuclear warhead. Developed by the Chelomey Bureau. Now carried only by *Slava*-class cruisers. Missile production designation: 4K-80.

Length: 12.4 m **Diameter:** 0.88 m **Wingspan:** 1.8 m
Weight: 4,800 kg **Speed:** Mach 2.5 **Range:** 300 n.m.

Note: The SS-N-14 Silex, a dual-purpose antisubmarine and antiship missile, is described in the antisubmarine weapon section.

SS-N-19 Shipwreck (Russian P-700 Granit) (1981)

Designed by the Chelomey (OKB-52, now Mashinostroeniya) design bureau and carried by the *Kirov*-class cruisers and Oscar-class nuclear-powered submarines (from which it is submerged launched). The missile's manufacturing designation is 3M-45, and it is also referred to as the P-50 missile. Originally intended to be launched

WEAPONS AND SYSTEMS *(continued)*

by salvo against aircraft carriers detected and tracked via the datalinked, nuclear-powered Legenda radar surveillance satellite system, which is no longer in use, nor is the missile version with the original 500-kiloton nuclear warhead. A rear-mounted solid-fuel booster is employed for the submerged launch, with a KR-93 turbojet engine providing sustained flight (ramjet propulsion has also been reported, and the external configuration would support either method). Has double-folding wings and folding tail surfaces.

Length: 10.5 m **Diameter:** 0.88 m **Wingspan:** 2.6 m
Weight: 7,000 kg **Warhead:** 750 kg
Speed: Mach 2.5 max. **Range:** 550 km

SS-N-21 Sampson (RPK-55 Granat) (1988)

A torpedo-tube-launched strategic land target weapon similar in concept to the U.S. Tomahawk. It was withdrawn from service in 1991, but numerous examples remain in land storage. Developed by the Novator Bureau. Submerged launched from submarines. Employ a terrain-following, low-altitude (190–200 m) flight pattern. Production designation was 3M-10. Has a nuclear warhead. A "stealth"-type nosecone fairing is fitted. The turbojet sustainer engine is extended from the lower, aft end of the missile after launch. The projected land-launch variant was designated SSC-4 Slingshot by NATO, although it does not seem to have entered production.

Length: 8.09 m (8.39 with canister) **Diameter:** 0.51 m (0.65 with canister)
Wingspan: 0.30 m **Weight:** 1,700 kg (2,440 with canister)
Speed: Mach 0.7 **Range:** 1,620 n.m.

SS-N-22 Sunburn (Russian P-270 Moskit/P-100 Moskit-M) (1984)

Missile production designation: 3M-80; export version: 3M-80E. Designed by Raduga OKB, with production integration by Altair State Research and Development Corp. and production by the Progress airframe plant, Khabarovsk. A successor to the SS-N-9, but not used by submarines. At launch, climbs to 32–70 m altitude. Descends to 10–15 m (20 m for export versions) at 17 km after launch. At 7.5 km from the predesignated target, climbs to 20 m to activate its radar seeker. At 1 km from the target, pops up to 24 m in active mode or descends to 3 m in passive mode. Can be programmed to pull 15-g., 200-m-radius evasive turns until 7 km from the target. Capable of being launched up to 60° off target azimuth and at 5-second intervals. Minimum range is 7 km.

Carried by *Sovremennyy*-class destroyers and by Tarantul-III- and Dergach-class guided-missile patrol combatants. The design has been sold to Boeing for target drone use by the U.S. Navy. Some 841 were said to be in Russian and Ukrainian hands as of 6-94, by which time production had probably ceased. In 7-98, 48 new Moskit-M surface-launched missiles were ordered for China (the only export customer to date). Additional orders may follow.

Propulsion is rocket-ramjet, with an internal rocket booster that is ejected through the exhaust as the ramjet sustainer ignites. The P-100 Moskit-M version (of which only a few were made for Russian Navy use) has a 129-km range. An air-launched version, the Kh-41, was first launched during 1998 but has yet to enter service.

Length: 9.385 m **Diameter:** 0.52 m (1.3 over folded fins)
Wingspan: 2.10 m (1.30 folded)
Weight: 3,950 kg **Warhead:** 300 kg (150 kg of explosive)
Speed: Mach 2.5 **Range:** 100 km

SS-N-25 Switchblade (Russian Kh-35 Uran) (1997)

A Harpoon- or Exocet-size antiship weapon intended to be booster-launched from canisters mounted in quadruple nests; the design was originally intended for air launch. Design bureau: Zvezda OKB. Only one Russian Navy combatant, Matka-class trials craft R-44, has launched the weapon. The missile has been purchased by India, where it entered service in 1998. Cruise altitude is 5–10 m, descending to 3–5 m during final approach. Production designation: 3M-24 (3M-24E for export). The 3Ts-25E target-seeker radar can be used in active and passive modes and can detect and home on a 10,000-m^2 target at a range of 40–45 km in normal conditions. Under ideal conditions, ranges increase to 85–90 km.

Length: 3.75 m (4.7 with booster) **Diameter:** 470 mm
Wingspan: 930 mm
Weight: 603 kg (incl. 120-kg booster) **Warhead:** 145 kg
Speed: Mach 0.9 (280–300 m/sec) **Range:** 5–130 km

An improved version, the 3M-24M1, with a GPS receiver and a range of 250 km is planned, and another variant with an infrared seeker may be developed.

SS-N-26 Yakhont/Sapless (Russian P-800 Oniks/3M-55) (1999)

Offered by NPO Mashinostroeniya (successor to the Chelomey Bureau) is the ramjet-powered P-800 Oniks, which makes its Mach-2.5 terminal attack at 5- to 15-m sea-skimming height. Production designation: 3M-55. Can be vertically launched from a submerged submarine, launched horizontally from 650-mm-diameter torpedo tubes, or launched by aircraft (two per MiG-29, three per Su-27, and eight per Tu-142) or land batteries. It employs an integral solid-rocket booster. A longer-range version with solid-fuel propulsion, Yashma, was offered for export development in 6-95, but apparently has fostered no interest. Yakhont is evidently the export name, with Oniks the name of the domestic version. The radar seeker has a range of 75 km and is said to be able to distinguish targets by position and radar cross section or to home on electromagnetic radiation. A proposed coast-defense version has been designated SSC-5 by NATO. Data for the submarine- and ship-launched versions are:

Length: 8.90 m **Diameter:** 650 mm (container)
Weight: 3,900 kg (2,550 air-launched) **Warhead:** 200 kg
Speed: Mach 2.0–2.5 **Range:** 120 km low/300 km high
Cruise altitude: 5–14,000 m

A longer-range (300-kw) variant of the Yakhont is in development as the Brahmos. Capable of vertical launch from surface ships and submarines or of being launched by aircraft, the Brahmos is to have a warhead weight of up to 300 kg, a maximum altitude of 15,000 m, and a length of 9.0 m.

SS-N-27 Novator Al'fa (Russian P-10 Biryuza/3M-54) (. . .)

Novator Design Bureau offers the Biryuza antiship missile for air launch, for submarine launch (via capsule), in a shipboard-launch version, or in a six-tube mobile land launcher (as the Al'fa system) At the onset of terminal run-in, beginning about 60 km from the target, the missile ejects a terminal-homing, Mach-2.5, rocket-powered payload vehicle that travels at about 10 m altitude. The weapon is still in competition with the P-800 Oniks for possible Russian Navy service but is being sold in quantity to the Indian Navy as the 3M-54E Club for surface-ship (3M-54E) and submarine (3M-54TE) use. Data for the original version include:

Length: 8.22 m **Diameter:** 533 mm
Weight: 1,900 kg (2,500 with solid booster) **Warhead:** 200 kg
Speed: Mach 0.6–0.8 (3.0 attack) **Range:** 220 km

The subsonic 3M-54E1 variant of the system employs an airframe derived from that of the RPK-55 Granat (NATO SS-N-21) and resembles the U.S. Tomahawk. Both 3M-54E and 3M-54E1 employ the same 400- to 500-kg-thrust Baranov TRDD-50 turbojet cruise engine. The 3M-54E1 is intended to fit in a standard 533-mm torpedo tube. Cruise altitude is 10–15 m, and during terminal phase, it flies at 5 m altitude; there is no detaching terminal-phase vehicle. India purchased 30 of the missiles during 2000 for $2.5 million each and China is said to have ordered the weapon for submarine use; trials in India during 5-02 showed the weapon to have deficient range performance.

Length: 6.20 m **Diameter:** 533 mm
Weight: 1,780 kg (at launch) **Warhead:** 450 kg
Speed: Mach 0.6–0.8 (180–240 m/sec) **Range:** Approx. 300 km

An ASW version designated 91RE1 is in development for launch from 533-mm submarine torpedo tubes at depths to 150 m and with the submarine traveling at speeds up to 15 kts; it would weigh 2,050 kg (including a homing torpedo payload) and have a range of 35 km. The 91RE2 ASW version would be fired from surface ships and would have a weight of 1,200 kg and a range of 40 km; it could be launched from vertical tubes or inclined canister launchers.

Note: Further development of the NPO Mashinostroeniya Al'fa missile has apparently been terminated.

Vikhr' (. . .)

Vikhr' is an adaptation of a helicopter-borne antitank missile system. Offered for export, a full system would consist of four missile canisters co-mounted on a standard AK-306 or AK-630 gatling gun mount and controlled by an electro-optical director. Range is about 8–10 km.

♦ Coast-defense missiles

Note: The Coastal Missile and Artillery regiments were stood down during 2001, and all remaining launchers and missiles assigned to Russian coastal missile regiments were placed in preservation.

♦ Surface-to-air missiles

SA-N-1 Goa (Russian M-1Volna system) (1962)

A naval version of the land-based SA-3. Now fitted on one Kashin-class destroyer and one Kynda-class cruiser in the Russian Navy and on five Kashin-class destroyers in the Indian Navy. Also has a surface-to-surface capability. Uses Yatagan (Peel Group) radar directors and the ZIF-101 or ZIF-102 cross-level stabilized twin-launcher. All versions have 16 missiles per magazine. Can handle aerial targets at speeds of 100–600 m/sec. System reaction time is 16–18 seconds. Designed by the Fakel Engineering Design Bureau with system integration by the Altair Bureau. Is obsolescent and reportedly was never considered satisfactory in service; may have been removed from Russian service by 2000.

Length: 5.948 m overall (1st stage: 1.871 m; 2d stage: 4.131 m)
Diameter: 1st stage: 552 mm; 2d stage: 390 mm
Weight: 960 kg (1st stage: 532 kg; 2d stage: 428 kg) **Warhead:** 72 kg
Speed: 730 m/sec
Range: 24 km slant range (3.5 min.); 17 km surface-to-surface
Altitude: 0.1–14 km

SA-N-3 Goblet (Russian M-11 Shtorm system) (1967)

Twin Type B-187 or Type B-192A launcher with V-611 (4K-60 and 4K-65) missiles. Guidance is via radar/command by Head Lights–series (Grom) radar director. Now fitted only on one Kara-class destroyer. Has an anti–surface target capability. Designed by Fakel Engineering Design Bureau, with Altair Bureau providing system integration. Mimimum range is 7 km. System reaction time is 25 seconds, and the missile can be used against targets traveling up to 700 m/sec.

Weight: 550 kg **Warhead:** Approx. 60 kg
Speed: Mach 2.5 **Range:** 30 km **Altitude:** 300–80,000 ft.

SA-N-4 Gecko (Russian Osa-M, Osa-2M, and Osa-MA systems) (1968)

The twin ZIF-122 (also known as the 4S-33) launcher elevates from a cylindrical magazine holding 20 9M-33M missiles on four rings of five. The missile was designed by Fakel Engineering Design Bureau, with Altair State Research and Development Corp. providing system integration. All versions of the system are designated RZ-13 by the navy, but production numbers assigned were 4K-33 for the original Osa-M system, 4K-33M for the Osa-2M (which can also use 9M-33M3 or 9M-33M5 missiles), and the Koni-class export frigates (with 9M-33M missiles). Guidance is radar/command via Pop Group (MPZ-301) radar director. Has a conventional warhead. Fitted in *Kirov*-class cruisers, Kara-class destroyers, Krivak-series frigates, Grisha-series corvettes, Nanuchka-series guided-missile patrol combatants, and *Ivan Rogov*–class landing ships. The system reaction time is 20 seconds, and only one target can be engaged at a time by each director. Can be used against surface targets.

Length: 3.16 m **Diameter:** 0.21 m **Weight:** 126 kg
Warhead: 14.2 kg **Range:** 1.2–10 km **Altitude:** 80–16,400 ft.

WEAPONS AND SYSTEMS *(continued)*

SA-N-5 Grail (Russian Strela-2 and Strela-2M systems) (1969)

A naval version of the SA-7 Grail (Russian 4K-32 or 4K-32M Strela) missile. Formerly carried on Pauk- and Tarantul-class small combatants, landing ships, some minesweepers, and many auxiliaries. Either employs a four-missile launch rack with operator or is shoulder-launched singly from a 9P-53 or 9P-58 launch/storage tube. East German–built quadruple launchers were designated the Fasta-4M system, with the launcher apparently designated the MTU-4US. The visually aimed, IR-homing Strela-2M entered service in 1974. Both variants have been almost entirely superseded in naval service by the Strela-3 series (SA-N-8), but some may remain in foreign navies.

Length: 1.44 m **Weight:** 15 kg (with launch tube)
Speed: 500 m/sec **Range:** 4.4 km **Altitude:** up to 7,800 ft.

SA-N-6 Grumble (Russian S-300F Fort and S-300FM Fort-M) (1983)

A navalized version of the land-based SA-10. The export naval version is known as Rif; an updated version of the system, the Rif-M, was announced 9-4-01. Designer: Fakel Engineering Design Bureau, with system integration by the Altair State Research and Development Corp. Range is up to 100 km, depending on the type of missile launched; altitude is up to 90,000 ft. Range against incoming missiles at 25-m altitude is 25 km; targets at 2,000 m and higher can be engaged to 90 km. Can handle targets moving at up to 2,268 kts (4,200 km/hr). The initial version on cruisers *Azov* and *Admiral Ushakov* used hot launch, but all current missiles employ vertical cold-launch from eight-missile 3S-41 rotating magazines (with the missiles in individual containers) and use track-via-missile guidance via the Top Dome (3P-41 Volna) radar system; each Top Dome can reportedly track six targets simultaneously, directing two missiles per target, provided they are within the same 60° arc. Launch interval is 3 seconds. Carried by *Kirov*- and *Slava*-class cruisers. Also has an antiship capability. Land-based S-300 version has been exported. Three different missiles are used: 5V-55K with a range of 45 km; 5V-55RM with a 75-km range; and the new 5V-55U missile (equivalent to the land-based S-300PMU) with 100-km range (the missile has also been referred to as the 48N6E2 and in the Fort-M version on *Petr Velikiy* is said to have a range of 150 km).

Data for the 5V-55RM missile include:

Length: 7.25 m **Diameter:** 508 mm **Wingspan:** 1.124 m
Weight: 1,664 kg **Warhead:** 133 kg
Speed: 2,000 m/sec **Range:** 5–75 km **Altitude:** 25–25,000 m

SA-N-7 Gadfly (Russian M-22 or ZR-90 Uragan system) (1981)

A navalized version of the land-based Buk-1M (SA-11), employing MS-196 single-armed launchers. Designer: Novator Bureau, with system integration by Altair State Research and Development Corp. Used on *Sovremennyy*-class and Indian Navy Project 15 destroyers and Indian Project 11356 frigates. The export version is referred to as the Shtil (Stiletto) system. Has 24 single-stage Type 9M-38M1 or 9M-38M13 single-stage missiles per magazine, 12 each on two side-by-side rings (only the prototype ZS-90 launchers had a ring of eight missiles surrounded by a ring of 12). Each launcher group requires a crew of 19 and weighs 49 tons. The launcher elevates to 70° maximum. The missiles can maneuver at up to 20 g. and employ semiactive homing guidance via Front Dome (OP-3) radar illuminators. The missiles can handle aircraft targets traveling 420–830 m/sec and missiles moving 330–830 m/sec, and the system probably has a secondary antiship capability. System reaction time is 16–19 seconds, and advertised kill percentage is 81–96% for a two-missile salvo. The similar but improved and longer-range 9M-38E1 Yozh missile for the land-based Buk-2M/Ural (SA-X-17 Grizzly) is believed to be used on the 16th-built and later units of the *Sovremennyy* class; it was to replace the 9M-30-series missiles on earlier ships of the class, but funding was not available.

Length: 5.55 m **Diameter:** 400 mm **Wingspan:** 860 mm
Weight: 690 kg **Warhead:** 70 kg **Speed:** Mach 3.0 (830 m/sec)
Range: 25 km max./3 km min. against aircraft; 3.5–12 km against missiles
Altitude: 15–15,000 m against aircraft; 10–10,000 m against missiles

SA-N-8 Gremlin (Russian Strela-3) (1986?)

A navalized version of the SA-14 (Russian 9M-36 Strela-3), the cooled-seeker successor to the SA-7 Grail. Developed by KBM, Kolomna. Uses either the same Fasta-4M system with MTU-4US, four-round manned launcher as the Strela-2/2M (SA-N-5) or a shoulder-launcher. A twin, manned lightweight launcher nicknamed the Dzhigit is on offer for export but has not been seen on Russian warships. Has slightly greater range than the SA-N-5, from which it is virtually indistinguishable while in the launch tube, which has a slightly larger control section than that of the SA-N-5 launch tube. Weight: 9.9 kg; length: 1.3 m. The launchers are also able to employ the SA-16 Igla-I (9M-313) missile, an improved version of the SA-14 that entered service around 1985, and can also accept the SA-18 Grouse (9M-39 Igla).

SA-N-9 Gauntlet (Russian Kinzhal) (1984)

A vertically launched, short-range system intended as a successor to SA-N-4; naval variant of the SA-15 Tor. Export name is Klinok. Designer: Fakel Engineering Design Bureau, with system integration by Altair State Research and Development Corp. The 9M-330 (naval production designation: 3M-95) missiles are carried in groups of eight in 2-m-diameter 3S-95 launch cylinders aboard *Udaloy*-class destroyers, carriers *Admiral Gorshkov* and *Admiral Flota Sovetskogo Soyuza Kuznetsov,* and other new-construction ships. Maximum flight time is 20 seconds, with a 10-second max. motor burn. Can be used against targets traveling at up to 700 m/sec. Response time is 8–24 seconds, and one missile can be launched every 3 seconds. Uses a gas-ejection launch system, with the missile engines igniting when the missiles are about 20 m above the launcher. Each system can track and attack four targets within a 60°-wide by 60°-high field. Command guided by Cross Sword radar directors, which have a co-mounted target detection and designation radar, an illumination radar, and an electro-optical backup feature and can control two missiles simultaneously. The control system may be designated ZR-90. Appears to have had developmental problems, as the first ships to carry it were completed as much as eight years before it was available for installation. Each Kinzhal installation weighs 41 tons and requires a crew of 13.

Weight: 165 kg **Warhead:** 15 kg
Speed: 850 m/sec **Range:** 1.5–15 km **Altitude:** 32–19,700 ft.

SA-N-11 Grison close-in weapons system (Russian Kortik) (1988)

A naval version of the land-based Tunguska (2S-6) system. *Kortik* means "dagger." The export version is known as Kashtan ("Chestnut Tree"). Referred to by NATO as the CADS-1 (Close Air Defense System-1). Designer: KB Priborstroyeniye, Tula, with shipboard system integration by Altair State Research and Development Corp. Carried on the carrier *Admiral Flota Sovetskogo Soyuza Kuznetsov,* cruisers *Admiral Nakhimov* and *Petr Velikiy,* frigate *Neustrashimyy,* and one Tarantul-II-class guided-missile craft (for trials). Uses the radar-guided 9M-311 Vikhr'-K missile (a navalized SA-19), launched from a disposable tube. Mount carries up to eight missiles, two 30-mm Type GSH-6-30L gatling AA guns (each with 500 rounds in a linkless feed system), and an on-mount Hot Flash (3P-87) search-and-track radar system with electro-optical backup; a separate Pozitiv-M-series target detection and tracking radar is normally associated with the system. Missiles can be auto-reloaded from a below-decks magazine that holds 48 missiles per mount. The 30-mm gatling guns are essentially the same as those used in the AK-630 mount, except for provision of a water cooling jacket and flash shield. They can be used against targets at up to 3,000 m altitude and ranges from 500 to 1,500 m (4,000 m max. range); rate of fire is 2,500 rds/min/barrel, and muzzle velocity is 960 m/sec (1,100 m/sec for armor-piercing rounds). The entire Kortik/Kashtan mount weighs 13,500 kg, is 2.25 m high, and sweeps a 2.76-m radius. Production ceased in 1993. The Kashtan-M, with 100–200% improved system reliability and reduced reaction time, was offered for export in 2000. Characteristics for the 9M-311 Vikhr'-K missile include:

Length: 2.562 m **Diameter:** 170 mm **Wingspan:** 225 mm
Weight: 43.6 kg **Warhead:** 9 kg
Speed: 900 m/sec initial; 600 m/sec in sustained flight after 800 m
Range: 1.5–10 km **Altitude:** 15–6,000 m

Note: The Arena anti–cruise missile defense system for warships was said to be in development as of 2-01. Based on a reactive armor concept developed for armored vehicles, Arena would be a kind of reactive skin to vital sections of a ship that would detonate or slow armor-piercing missile warheads. It would probably be too heavy and too expensive to cover more than a small percentage of the surface of a warship.

♦ Air-to-surface missiles

AS-4 Kitchen (Russian Kh-22) (1967)

Developed by the Raduga MKB. The Kh-22M missile uses a 1,000-kg conventional warhead; the Kh-22N had a nuclear warhead. The Kh-22MP variant was an antiradar weapon. Uses inertial guidance with radar-terminal homing. Was in service on Backfire-B aircraft. Has reportedly been put back into production, possibly in expectation of sales to India.

Length: 11.1 m **Diameter:** 0.87 m **Wingspan:** 4.8 m
Weight: 6,400 kg **Speed:** Mach 2.5–3.5
Range: 240 n.m. high-launch/146 n.m. low-launch

AS-7 Kerry (Russian Kh-23M Grom) (late 1970s)

A tactical weapon, designed by Zvezda OKB. Uses solid-fuel propulsion and has command guidance and a 110-kg conventional warhead. Can be carried by the land-based Su-25 Frogfoot; was formerly used on carrier-based Yak-38 Forger aircraft. The updated Grom-M version is designated Kh-66; an antiradar version was designated Kh-24. Now used primarily for training.

Length: 3.5 m **Diameter:** 305 mm **Wingspan:** 0.95 m
Weight: 287 kg **Speed:** 1,895 kts **Range:** 1–6 n.m.

Note: The AS-9 Kyle (Russian Kh-28 and Kh-28E) missile system is believed to have been retired from service by 2001.

AS-11 Kilter (Russian Kh-58 series) (1985)

Variants include Kh-58A, -58E, and -58U. Designed by Raduga MKB. Has passive home-on-electromagnetic-emissions (ARM) guidance with a shutdown memory feature but is not tunable in flight. Flies a modified ballistic flight path. Roughly comparable to the U.S. AGM-88 HARM.

Weight: 780 kg **Warhead:** 170 kg
Speed: 2,008 kts **Range:** 70–180 km

AS-13 Kingbolt (Russian Kh-59 Ovod) (. . .)

Similar to the U.S. Maverick in concept; uses electro-optical control with lock-on-after-launch capability. Designed by Zvezda OKB. Used with the APK-9 datalink pod for maximum range. Usable only in clear-air, daylight conditions.

Weight: 875 kg **Warhead:** 250 kg
Speed: . . . kts **Range:** 32 n.m.

AS-14 Kedge (Russian Kh-29 series) (. . .)

Made in three versions: the television-guided Kh-29T, laser-guided Kh-29ML, and home-on-electromagnetic-radiation (ARM) Kh-29P. Designed by Molniya OKB. Flies a modified ballistic flight path. Kh-29T is usable in daylight only. The Kh-29MP probably uses the same seeker as the AS-12 Kegler and requires the use of a belly-mounted guidance pod.

Weight: 680 kg **Warhead:** 320 kg
Speed: 660 kts **Range:** 4.3–5.4 n.m. (Kh-29MP: 18.9 n.m.)

AS-16 Kickback (Russian Kh-15P/S) (1992)

Short-range, inertially guided, rocket-powered missile with an active millimeter-wave terminal seeker. Designed by Raduga OKB. Equivalent to the U.S. Air Force SRAM, which it somewhat resembles. Carried by Tu-22M3 Backfire-C bombers. The terminal-homing antiship version is the Kh-15S; the Kh-15P has a passive antiradar seeker. Is capable of a Mach 5 terminal dive.

Length: 4.78 m **Diameter:** 455 mm **Wingspan:** 0.92 m
Weight: Approx. 1,200 kg **Warhead:** 150 kg

WEAPONS AND SYSTEMS *(continued)*

AS-17 Krypton (Russian Kh-31A/P) (1993?)

Ramjet-powered with alternate antiship or anti–land target seekers. Designed by Zvezda OKB. Also used by Russian Air Force in a radiation-seeking variant. Data for Kh-31P:

Length: 5.20 m **Diameter:** 0.36 m **Wingspan:** 779 mm
Weight: 600 kg **Warhead:** 90 kg
Speed: Mach 2.9 **Range:** 70 n.m.

AS-X-18 Kazoo (Russian Kh-59M Ovod-M) (. . .)

Turbojet-powered, t.v.-command-guided antiship weapon with 7–1,000 m preset cruise altitude. Another design by the Zvezda OKB. Derived from the Kh-59 (AS-13). Has not yet entered active service.

Length: 5.1–5.3 m **Weight:** 850 kg (air-launched)/1,000 kg (ship-launched)
Warhead: 315-kg armor-piercing or 280-kg canister
Speed: Mach 0.9 **Range:** 150 km max.

AS-20 Kayak (Russian Kh-35 Uran) (1998–99?)

Air-launched version of the Kh-35 Uran (SS-N-25 Switchblade). Designed by Zvezda OKB. Has been offered for export for several years but does not seem to have entered service yet in Russia.

Note: Laser-guided and conventional free-fall bombs in 500-, 750-, and 1,000-kg sizes are also available.

♦ Air-to-air missiles

AA-10 Alamo (Russian R-27) (. . .)

Carried by Su-27K/Su-33 Flanker-D shipboard fighters. Available in active, semi-active, and passive-homing versions. Developer: Vympel Bureau, in cooperation with Artem, Ukraine. The R-27P1 passive-homing variant has a maximum range of 80 km and the 347-kg passive-homing R-27EP1 has a range of 110 km; both home on radiations from the target aircraft.

AA-11 Archer (Russian R-73, R-73M) (. . .)

Carried by Su-27K/Su-33 Flanker-D shipboard fighters. Developer: Vympel Bureau.

AA-12 Adder (Russian R-77) (1993)

A medium-range weapon that is also being developed in vertical-launched land and shipboard versions. Can be used by naval Su-27K/Su-33 Flanker-D carrier aircraft. Roughly equivalent to the U.S. AMRAAM. All versions use the Belotsevkovskiy folding control surfaces. A longer-range rocket-ramjet-powered version is in development. Developer: Vympel Bureau.

Weight: 175 kg **Warhead:** 18 kg
Speed: 1,721 kts **Range:** 43.2 n.m.

Note: Novator Design Bureau offers the 400-km-range KS-172 Al'fa AAM with active radar homing and midcourse correction capability for antimissile and anti-AWACS use. The two-stage missile is 7.4 m long, including the 1.4-m booster; seven can be carried by an Su-33 Flanker-D, but the system has not yet been procured for the Russian Navy. Development status is uncertain.

B. ARTILLERY ROCKET SYSTEMS

140-mm Ogon

Made by Start Zavod, Yekaterinburg, and used only on the Zubr (NATO Pomornik) surface-effect landing craft class (Project 12322). Employs 22-tube, autoloading, retractable launchers that, when closed, have a cover that fits flush with the upper deck of the launch craft. A truck-mounted coast-defense version of the system is offered for export as the Daraba.

140-mm UMS-73 Grad-M

Employed only on a few Ropucha- and Alligator-class tank landing ships and the *Ivan Rogov*–class dock landing ships. A twin-armed launcher hoists two 20-round magazine clips from below decks for salvo launching.

122-mm WM-18

A manually loaded system employed on Polnocny-series landing ships. Each launcher holds 18 rockets.

C. GUNS

130-mm/54-caliber twin, dual-purpose (Russian AK-130)

A fully automatic gun for surface, shore-bombardment, and aerial targets. Fitted on *Sovremennyy-* and *Admiral Chabanenko*–class destroyers, *Slava*-class cruisers, and later *Kirov*-class cruisers. Made by Yurga Engineering Plant, Yurga. Water cooled. Uses a modified Kite Screech (MR-184) dual-band radar director with electro-optical (t.v. and laser rangefinder) backup or local control by on-mount operator. The export version has a reduced firing rate of 35–60 rounds per mount per minute. Can train and elevate at 25°/sec. Uses AR-32 influence and DVM-60M time-fuzed AA ammunition as well as high-explosive surface-target projectiles. There are 180 ready-service rounds per mount. The fire-control system is designated T-91. A single-barreled, mobile coast-defense system, Bereg, using the same gun, is offered for export.

Mount weight: 98 metric tons without ammunition
Projectile weight: 32 kg (+ 21-kg cartridge)
Muzzle velocity: 950 m/sec **Rate of fire:** 60+ rds/min/barrel max.
Arc of elevation: –15° to +85° **Max. range for surface fire:** 28,000 m

100-mm/55-caliber single-purpose (Russian U-5 TS)

An armored T-55 tank turret-mounted gun carried on Yaz-class and Vosh-class river monitors.

Muzzle velocity: 780 m/sec **Rate of fire:** 4 rds/min max.
Arc of elevation: –4° to +17° **Max. range:** 4,800 m

100-mm/59-caliber automatic dual-purpose (Russian AK-100)

A single-barreled, water-cooled gun in an enclosed, manned mounting found on *Udaloy*-class destroyers, and *Neustrashimyy-,* Krivak-II-, and Krivak-III-class frigates. Designed by Ametist Central Design Bureau and made by Topaz. Uses a Kite Screech (MR-145 Lev) radar director (75-km range) with electro-optical backup or local control by on-mount operator. Fires high-explosive shells with impact, proximity, or time fuzing. The ZIF-91 mount carries 175 ready-service rounds and can traverse through ±200°. System weight is 8 metric tons, and the gunhouse is armored. The gun mounting is designated the A-190.

Mount weight: 49 tons empty **Projectile weight:** 15.6 kg
Muzzle velocity: 880 m/sec **Rate of fire:** 60 rds/min
Arc of elevation: –10° to +85° **Training speed:** 30°/sec
Elevation speed: 20°/sec **Max. theoretical range:** 21,500 m

76.2-mm/59-caliber single automatic dual-purpose (Russian AK-176)

A fully automatic gun with on-mount crew, designed as the A-221 by Burevestnik Central Scientific Research Institute and since manufactured by Topaz. Entered service on 22-6-79. The AK-176M version has an armored gunhouse; used on larger ships, it is outwardly identical to the AK-176. Carried by Grisha-V- and Parchim-II-class corvettes; Nanuchka-III-, Pauk-, and Tarantul-class guided-missile patrol combatants; Matka-class guided-missile hydrofoils; and others. Requires a crew of six, with two on mount. Employs Bass Tilt (MR-123 or MR-123-02 Vympel/Koral) radar/electro-optical director or Rakurs electro-optical director or local, on-mount control. The automatic magazine below the gun rotates with the mount and holds 152 rounds. Fires high-explosive shells with impact or proximity fuzing.

Weight: 11.2 tons empty, 13.1 tons with ready-service ammunition
Projectile weight: 5.9 kg **Muzzle velocity:** 850 m/sec
Rate of fire: 120 rds/min **Arc of elevation:** –15° to +85°
Training speed: 35°/sec **Elevation speed:** 30°/sec
Theoretical max. range for surface fire: 15,500 m
Practical range for antiaircraft fire: 6,000–7,000 m

76.2-mm/59-caliber twin dual-purpose (Russian AK-726)

Installed on Kara- and Kashin-class destroyers, Krivak-I-class frigates, *Smol'nyy*-class training ships, and *Ivan Susanin*–class patrol icebreakers. Employs an Owl Screech (MR-105 Turel'), Hawk Screech (Fut-B), or Kite Screech-A (MR-114 Yakhont) radar director, with Fut-B used in conjunction with a separate ringsight target designator. The twin gunmount is designated ZIF-67 and has 5-mm bulletproof plating. In larger ships, the normal ammunition allowance is 300 rounds per barrel. The normal gun crew is nine per mount.

Mount weight: 26,000 kg **Projectile weight:** 12.8 kg
Muzzle velocity: 980 m/sec **Rate of fire:** 90–107 rds/min/barrel
Arc of elevation: –10° to +85°
Max. range for surface fire: 15.7 km (13.2 effective)
Max. range for antiaircraft fire: 11,000 m (6,000–7,000 effective)

76.2-mm/48-caliber single-purpose (Russian D-56 TM)

Tank turret–mounted weapon used on Shmel'-class river gunboats (same mount and turret as used by PT-76 amphibious tank).

Muzzle velocity: 680 m/sec **Rate of fire:** 15 rds/min max.
Arc of elevation: –4° to +30° **Max. effective range:** 8,000 m

57-mm/70-caliber twin automatic dual-purpose (Russian AK-725)

Automatic weapon with no on-mount crew, installed on Grisha-II- and -III-class corvettes, Nanuchka-I guided-missile patrol combatants, and Ropucha-series LSTs. Has water-cooled barrels. The mount is designated ZIF-72. Employs a Muff Cob (MR-103 Bars) radar/electro-optical or Bass Tilt (MR-123 Vympel/Koral) radar director. Barrels have a life of 1,500 rounds. Maximum range is 12.7 km, but the shells self-destruct at 6.7 km.

Mount weight: 14,500 kg **Rate of fire:** 200 rds/min/barrel max.
Max. effective range: 6,700 m

Note: The twin, manned 57-mm/70-cal. open ZIF-31B mounting is still found on Alligator-class landing ships and one Don-class submarine tender. It can be locally controlled. Maximum effective range: 8,400 m.

37-mm/63-caliber twin AA (Russian V-11M)

No longer in Russian service but is still found on foreign ships, particularly Chinese-built version, Type 74. Uses either hand-cranked cross-leveling or power cross-leveling. Control by on-mount lead-computing sight.

Muzzle velocity: 880 m/sec **Rate of fire:** 160 rds/min/barrel max.
Arc of elevation: 0° to +85° **Max. range:** 9,500 m (2,500 effective)

30-mm/54-caliber single gatling AA (Russian AK-630 and AK-630M)

Designed to fire a great number of rounds at an extremely high rate in order to intercept a cruise missile at a relatively short distance. Manufactured by Mashzavod imeni Ryabakov, Tula. In service on numerous classes, installed in mounts similar to those of the 30-mm AK-230 double-barreled automatic guns. The GSh-6-30K gatling gun has six 30-mm barrels; 2,000 rounds are carried on-mount, with another 1,000 per mount normally maintained in reserve. Nicknamed the "Metallorezka." The system cannot engage targets flying below 10 m in altitude. The often-used incorrect designation "ADMG-630" is an early NATO nickname.

The AK-630M is an updated variant with an improved magazine feed. A version known as AK-213M with a different magazine shape apparently never entered production. An over-and-under, twin gatling mount was offered in 1993 as the AK-630M1-2

WEAPONS AND SYSTEMS *(continued)*

Roy, but only one was built and it was installed only in one Matka-class trials ship; its data are similar to the AK-630 and AK-630M, except for higher weight (2.5 tons empty, 6.5 loaded) and greater rate of fire (4,000 rds/min). Maximum burst duration for AK-630 and AK-630M1-2 mounts is 400 rounds.

In 1997 a new twin variant was offered as the Palma, using two AO-18KD guns mounted on either side of a central pedestal that also carries an E/O tracker. The guns would have an 1,100-m/sec muzzle velocity, and a full 10,000 rounds of ammunition per mount (6.9 tons) would be carried. Palma would have a 3- to 5-second response time and would employ an MR-700-series Fregat target-designation radar and MR-123 Vympel fire-control radar.

AK-630-series mounts are normally controlled by a Bass Tilt (MR-123-02 Vympel) radar director, with an SP-521 Rakurs (NATO Kolonka-2) remote manned backup director (on the carrier *Admiral Flota Sovetskogo Soyuza Kuznetsov,* the gun is controlled by the Hot Flash radar system on nearby Kortik gun/missile close-in-defense systems). Data for the basic AK-630 are:

Mount weight: 3,814 kg complete **Projectile weight:** 0.834 kg
Muzzle velocity: 880–900 m/sec **Rate of fire:** 4,000–5,000 rds/min max.
Arc of elevation: –12° to +88°
Traverse rate: 70°/sec **Elevation rate:** 50°/sec
Max. range for antiaircraft fire: 4,000–5,000 m

30-mm/54-caliber single lightweight gatling AA (Russian AK-306)

Lightweight version of the AK-630 series, using the electrically driven AO-18L gun with a rate of fire of 600–1,000 rds/min. Has 500 rounds on mount. Elevates to 85°. Used on late-construction Natya (Project 266ME)-, all Sonya-, and all Lida-class minesweepers and some riverine combatants. Mount weighs 1,000 kg empty, vice the 1,850 kg of the heavyweight version, and has no cooling system.

30-mm/65-caliber twin automatic AA (Russian AK-230)

Manufactured by Mashzavod imeni Ryabakov, Tula. Installed on many classes of ships—cruisers, destroyers, guided-missile boats, supply ships, and so on. Widely exported. Employs Drum Tilt (MR-104 Rys') radar director or Kolonka-1 remote ringsight director. Replaced in production by the AK-630/306 gatling gun system.

Mount weight: 1,905 kg **Muzzle velocity:** 1,050 m/sec
Rate of fire: 1,000 rds/min/barrel max.
Max. range for antiaircraft fire: 4,000 m

25-mm/80-caliber twin AA (Russian 2M-3M)

Still found on exported ships and a few Russian Navy units, the manned mount employs two superimposed guns, with an on-mount ringsight for control. Widely employed on Chinese and other former Soviet-client naval ships. The twin 2M-8 version of this mount was used on submarines in the 1950s, and the 2M-3 was an early, unpowered mounting.

Muzzle velocity: 900 m/sec **Rate of fire:** 150–200 rds/min/gun max.
Arc of elevation: –10° to +83° **Max. range:** 3,000 m

14.5-mm/93-caliber twin machine gun (Russian 2M-7)

Found in over-and-under twin open mountings.

Muzzle velocity: 1,000 m/sec **Rate of fire:** 150 rds/min/gun
Arc of elevation: –5° to +90° **Max. range:** 7,000 m

Note: Also still in use are 1930s-design, twin, over-and-under 12.7-mm 79-cal. 2M-1 machinegun mounts and the Utës-M twin 12.7-mm 60-cal. manned side-by-side mounting on Zhuk-class patrol boats, river monitors, and surface-effect amphibious craft; Utës-M has a combined 1,200 rds/min rate of fire. The original Utës version has a single 12.7-mm mg.

For saluting purposes, old Type 21KM 45-mm guns have been adapted and are installed semipermanently in larger combatants.

D. ANTISUBMARINE WEAPONS

♦ Missiles

SS-N-14 Silex (Russian URPK-3/4 Metel'/URK-5 Rastrub) (1973/1984)

Two versions of this missile entered service, both given the same basic designation by NATO. The original URPK-3 system employed the Type 83R Metel' ("Snowstorm") missile with a 450-mm AT-1 (NATO E45-70A) homing torpedo payload carried below the fuselage. The AT-1 was replaced by the 533-mm AT-2UM (NATO 53-72) torpedo in 1973 and the missile was redesignated the Type 84R Metel'-M; the new torpedo had a range of 8 km with a 23-kt search speed and 40-kt attack speed and was effective to 400-m depths. The URPK-3 employed fixed quadruple KT-100M launchers and the Grom-M (NATO Head Lights-B) control radar for guidance. The URPK-4 version for the Krivak-series (Project 1135) frigates employed a quadruple trainable KTM-100-1135 launcher and was controlled by the MR-212 Drakon (NATO Eye Bowl) radar.

The original URPK-3 and URPK-4 were superseded in 1984 by the URK-5 Rastrub ("Bell") system, which used a "universal missile," the Type 83R, against either submarines or surface targets; for the latter mission, the missile body itself was fitted with a warhead. The homing torpedo payload is the UMGT-1 (NATO E45-75A), with an operating depth to 500 m, a maximum speed of 41 kts, and a range of 8 km. In the ASW mode, the missile cruises at 400-m altitude at Mach 0.95; in the antiship mode, the missile descends to 15 m in the terminal phase to deliver a 185-kg shaped hollow-charge warhead (in addition to the 60-kg warhead within the torpedo). The missile uses two solid drop-off boosters and a solid rocket sustainer and has folding wings and fins. The Type 85RUS variant is also equipped with an infrared terminal seeker. Also offered for export was a *shore*-launched version. The data below refer to the URK-5 system/Type 85R missile version:

Length: 7.205 m **Diameter:** 0.574 m (upper body) **Height:** 1.35 m
Weight: 3,930 kg **Speed:** 290 m/sec **Range:** 5–50 km

SS-N-15a/b Starfish (Russian RPK-6 Vodopad/Vodoley) (1981)

Antisubmarine missile very similar in concept and design to the former U.S. Navy UUM-44 SUBROC. Designed by Novator Bureau, Sverdlovsk. Submerged-launched from 533-mm submarine torpedo tubes on the Victor-, Akula-, and Sierra-series submarines and from torpedo tubes on later *Kirov*-class cruisers and on the frigate *Neustrashimyy.* Also usable against surface targets. The RPK-6 Vodopad ("Waterfall") uses Type 83R and 83RN (SS-N-15a) missiles, while the surface-launch version, referred to as Vodoley, uses Type 84R and nuclear-warhead 84RN (SS-N-15b) missiles. Launch depth is 50–150 m for the Vodopad, and launch preparations for both versions take only 10 seconds.

Length: 8.166 m **Diameter:** 533 mm **Weight:** 2,445 kg
Payload: 742-kg UMGT-1 homing torpedo with 100-kg warhead
Range: 10–35 km

Note: The weapon originally assigned the SS-N-15 Starfish designation by NATO was the now-retired RPK-2 V'yuga, which used the Type 81R missile and carried a 200-kT nuclear depth charge to a range of 10–35 km; V'yuga entered service in 1969.

SS-N-16a/b Stallion (Russian/RPK-7 Veter/Vodopad-MK) (1984)

Derived from the SS-N-15 system but uses 650-mm tubes and has roughly twice the range. Employs the Type 86R (B-255) missile to transport a 742-kg UMGT-1 acoustic homing torpedo, which has a range of 8 km, a maximum speed of 41 kts, a 100-kg warhead, and a sensor range of up to 1,500 m. Has a range of around 100 km, and the course reportedly can be command-changed in flight. Can be launched between 50 and 350 m depth. RPK-7 Veter is 11 m long. The Type 88R version (SS-N-16b) carries a nuclear depth bomb.

SS-NX-29 Medvedka (Russian Medvedka)

A small-ship antisubmarine missile system developed by Moscow Thermal Engineering Institute and under trial in the now-retired prototype Babochka-class hydrofoil *Aleksandr Kunakhovich* beginning in 1994; as of 10-00, funds were said to be unavailable to complete state trials for the missile, which has not yet entered production. Would be manufactured by Votinsky Zavod. Launches a rocket with a 2.8-m-long, 320-mm-diameter parachute-retarded homing Gidropribor Central Research Institute UTST-95 Kolibri thermal-propulsion torpedo payload. The rocket has a variable-thrust solid-fuel motor to variable ranges. Prototypes are four-tube, elevatable mountings, but the system is also offered in twin-tube and four-tube fixed launchers and rotatable two- or four-tube installations for larger ships. The fire-control system, developed by Granit Research and Production Association, electronically compensates for ship stabilization errors. A Mach 2 antiship variant is offered for development that would employ a two-stage solid rocket with active or passive terminal seeker and a range of 50 km. The launcher, with four missiles, weighs 9,500 kg.

Length: 5.35 m **Diameter:** 400 mm **Weight:** 750 kg
Range: 8–23 km **Depth of target:** 15–500 m

SS-NX- . . . (Russian Type 91RE2)

Offered for export by the Novator Experimental Machine-Design Bureau in 5-99. Designed for vertical or inclined launch. Has a solid-fueled APR-3ME torpedo payload. Would employ booster for launch and use a parachute to lower the torpedo after separation. The torpedo is 3.2 m long by 350 mm in diameter and weighs 450 kg, with a 76-kg warhead; it has a target-detection range of 2,000 m and a maximum attack depth of 800 m. Up to four missiles could be directed at one target. Missile data include:

Length: 6.20 m **Diameter:** 51.4 cm **Weight:** 1,200 kg **Range:** 40 km

♦ Rockets

Note: RBU = *Raketnaya Bombometnaya Ustanovka* (Rocket Depth-charge Launcher)

RPK-5 Liven' (1982)

A 10-tube weapon system similar in configuration to the RBU-6000 but launching a considerably larger Type 89R rocket with a range of up to 3,000 m (100 m minimum range) against submarines at down to 600-m depths. Manufacturer: Splav Research Enterprise, Tula. The export system is referred to as the UDAV-1 and the system has been referred to by NATO—inaccurately—as the RBU-12000. Primarily an antitorpedo system, with secondary ASW and antiswimmer functions. Launcher designation is KT-153. Found to date on the carriers *Admiral Gorshkov* and *Admiral Flota Sovetskogo Soyuza Kuznetsov* and the *Kirov*-class cruisers *Admiral Nakhimov* and *Petr Velikiy.* Original trials were in a six-tube variant on Grisha-class corvette MRK-5. Primarily intended as a torpedo countermeasure launcher, with UDAV-1M-system projectiles in Type 111SZ simple explosive (232.5 kg each), 111SG acoustic-fuzed, or 111SO decoy rockets (201 kg each); the decoy rockets are fired in pairs, followed by the floating barrage rocket and simple barrage rockets. The system is said to have a reaction time of 15 seconds. The rockets are 300 mm in diameter, and the launcher weighs 6,600 kg.

RBU-6000 Smerch-2/RPK-8 Zapad

The 3,100-kg mount has 12 barrels, 2.00 m in length and 212 mm in diameter, arranged in a horseshoe and normally fired in paired sequence. Has a vertical automatic loading system, loading barrel by barrel. Can be trained and elevated. Maximum range: 6,000 m. Normal allowance is 192 rockets for each pair of two. Installed in *Slava* and *Kirov* cruisers; *Udaloy-,* Kara-, and Kashin-class guided-missile destroyers; Krivak- and *Neustrashimyy*-class frigates; and Grisha-class corvettes. Uses the PUS-B Burya fire-control system and requires three personnel: one operator and two to load hoists in the magazine. The standard RGB-60 round is 1,830 mm long and weighs 110 kg; the warhead weighs 25 kg and has impact and time/impact fuzes. Can also be employed as a torpedo countermeasure, using RPK-8 rounds.

The RPK-8 Zapad antisubmarine rocket system uses the same launcher as the RBU-6000 system, but with the 90R missile, a 112.5-kg, 212-mm-diameter acoustic-homing round made by Splav State Research and Production Association that can detect targets up to 130 m away and can deflect from its ballistic descent after striking the water; the 90R has a 19-kg warhead and is said to be able to attack submarines at 1,000-m depths or defeat torpedoes at depths of up to 10 m. The 90R rocket, said to be 80% effective and eight times more effective than the RGB-60, has been bought by India and Algeria and is said to be in production for the Russian Navy.

WEAPONS AND SYSTEMS *(continued)*

RBU-2500

Made up of two horizontal rows of eight barrels each, approximately 1.6 m in length, which can be trained and elevated. Manual reloading. Range: 2,500 m. Has a 21-kg warhead. Now carried only by two *Smol'nyy*-class training ships and a handful of ships in foreign navies. Probably also usable as a torpedo countermeasure launcher.

RBU-1200 Uragan

Made up of two horizontal rows of short, superimposed barrels, three atop two. Tube diameter: 253.5 mm; length: 1.380 m. The 71.5-kg (34-kg warhead) rocket is 1.228 m long and 252 mm in diameter. Range: 1,200 m. Early installations were fixed in train and their tubes had to be manually loaded at 40° elevation, but systems in Natya and Pauk classes can be trained for firing and must be trained 90° outboard for loading from deckhouse magazines.

RBU-1000 Smerch-3

Primarily a torpedo countermeasure launcher, but can be used against submarines operating at up to 500-m depth, submarine countermeasures, and even frogmen. The stabilized 1,800-kg launcher is made up of six barrels arranged in two vertical rows of three and fired in order at 1-second intervals, with vertical automatic loading. Installed in Kara-, *Sovremennyy*-, and Kashin-class destroyers. Uses the PUS-B Burya fire-control system. Trainable. Tube diameter: 300 mm. Length: 2.165 m. Range: 1,000 m. Rocket weighs 195 kg (100-kg warhead). Normal allowance is 24 rounds per launcher.

DP-64

Handheld rocket-grenade launcher. A twin-barreled weapon launching 0.65-kg FG-45 high-explosive or SG-45 marker grenades to a range of 400 m. Said to have a 14-m destructive radius with the 0.18-kg explosive in the FG-45. Intended for use on classes of ships and submarines and also by shore personnel against combat swimmers.

DP-65

Lightweight rocket-grenade launcher. A 10-barreled launcher for 55-mm-diameter RG-55 rocket grenades, with a range of 5–500 m. Can be remotely aimed and elevated and uses acoustic target cueing to detect combat swimmers.

MRG-1

Seven-barreled, pedestal-mounted portable rocket grenade launcher intended for use by surface ships and harbor defenses against combat swimmers. Has a range of 50–500 m and employs 55-mm-diameter RG-55 grenades. Firing is cued by acoustic sensors.

♦ Depth charges

The successor to the long-standard PLAB depth bomb is the S3V (or KAB-250PL), which weighs 94 kg (with 50 kg of explosive) and has a length of 1.30 m and a diameter of 211 mm. The weapon has an active sonar fuzing system and can change its underwater trajectory by up to 60° off the initial path, sinking to a depth of 600 m in 16.2 seconds, at which point it can be up to 520 m offset from the original drop point. The S3V sinks at the rate of 16.2 m/sec. The PLAB-10K (RBK-11) is a cluster depth bomb with six small depth charges.

Note: Many of the weapons described in the Mines section are intended for use against submarines as well as surface ships.

E. TORPEDOES

Note: Although a great many different torpedoes have been produced over the past 40 years for submarine, surface-ship, and aircraft use, the number actually in widespread service is not as great, and many of those offered for export since 1990 exist only as paper designs or in prototype status. The listing below contains both service and export models but may not be exhaustive.

DST-90: Long-range, wake-homing torpedoes for submarine use. Maximum firing depth is 100 m, and the torpedo runs at a depth of 20 m. The gas-turbine propulsion system is fueled by a mix of kerosene and high-test hydrogen peroxide. May be related to SET-92K and APSET-92 torpedoes. Probably only a prototype system.

Diameter: 650 mm **Length:** 11.000 m **Weight:** 4,750 kg
Warhead weight: 557 kg **Speed/range:** 35 kts/50 km

DT: Long-range, submarine-launched export torpedo with active acoustic homing, although the illustration in a brochure showed it being used in what appeared to be a wake-homing mode (as well as in a preprogrammed mode against a harbor). Gas turbine; wakeless propulsion. Offered for export in 1993, although Russia does not export submarines with 650-mm torpedo tubes! May be only a paper project.

Diameter: 650 mm **Length:** 11.000 m **Weight:** 4,500 kg
Warhead weight: 445 kg **Speed/range:** 50 kts/50 km; 30 kts/100 km

65-76: Wake-homing weapon made by Dvigatel Zavod, St. Petersburg, and launched from Victor-III and all later submarines with 650-mm tubes. Probably available originally in both conventional and nuclear-warhead versions. The standard 650-mm long-range, wake-homing torpedo aboard Russian Navy nuclear-powered attack submarines. Entered service in 1957. The latest version, with hydrogen peroxide fuel, was removed from service in 2-02 as a result of the *Kursk* disaster. The torpedo is known as the "Kit" (Kite).

Diameter: 650 mm **Length:** 9.140 m
Warhead weight: 900 kg **Speed/range:** 50 kts/50 km; 30 kts/100 km

UMGT-1: Antisubmarine torpedo made by Dvigatel Zavod, St. Petersburg, and used as payload for RPK-6 Vodopad and RPK-7 Veter submarine missiles. An acoustic-homing weapon with a range of 8 km at 41 kts, a sensor range of 1,500 m, and a 100-kg warhead. Can be launched at depths up to 150 m.

UGST: Antisurface torpedo with pumpjet propulsor and unitary-fueled reciprocating engine. In development by Region and Mortep since the 1980s and offered for export; may not have entered production for Russian Navy use. Can attack submarines at depths to 500 m. Has magnetic and acoustic fuzes. Also offered with a television, wire-guided homing system for use against surface ships.

Diameter: 534.4 mm **Length:** 7.200 m **Weight:** 2,200 kg
Warhead weight: 200 kg **Speed/range:** 35–50 kts/20–35 km

TEST-71M: Wire-guided antisubmarine and antisurface torpedo from Dvigatel Zavod, St. Petersburg. Electrical propulsion. Has both acoustic proximity and contact fuzes. The silver-zinc battery has a 1-year shelf-life aboard submarines. Available for export in a 7.935-m-long version as TEST-71ME and TEST-71MVE, the latter for antisubmarine use. A practice variant weighing 1,480 kg or 1,445 kg is also available. Can be used against submarines operating down to 400 m in depth. Related to the SET-65E. The latest variant, TEST-71MK, remains in service and incorporates a wire-guidance feature.

Diameter: 534.4 mm **Length:** 8.260 m
Weight: 1,840 kg **Warhead weight:** 205 kg
Speed/range: 40 kts/20 km max. (cruise speed: 24 kts)

TEST-96: Multipurpose ship- and submarine-launched wire-guided export torpedo with active/passive homing, impact and proximity fuzes, and electric propulsion.

Diameter: 533 mm **Length:** 8.000 m **Weight:** 1,800 kg
Warhead weight: 250 kg **Speed/range:** . . . / . . .

ET-80A: Wire-guided, improved version of the SET-65 with 400-m depth capability. Electric propulsion. For use by submarines and surface ships.

Diameter: 533 mm **Length:** 7.800 m
Warhead weight: 272 kg **Speed/range:** 35 kts/15 km; . . . /12 km

53-68: Modernized, nuclear-warhead version of the 53-65 with 100-m launch depth and 300-m maximum operating depth. Straight runner with wakeless HTP fuel propulsion. No longer deployed, but may be retained in storage at land depots.

Diameter: 533 mm **Length:** 7.200 m
Warhead: 20 kT nuclear **Speed/range:** 45 kts/14 km

53-65K: Wake-homing anti–surface ship weapon with a closed-cycle turbine engine. Runs at 4- to 14-m depths and can successfully attack ships moving at up to 35 kts. Operational in 1968. Export version is 53-65KE. The practice version has a range of 12 km.

Diameter: 533.4 mm **Length:** 7.945 m **Weight:** 2,100 kg
Warhead weight: 300 kg **Range:** 55 kts/19 km; 40 kts/24 km

SET-65: Submarine torpedo with passive acoustic homing and electric propulsion and 400-m operating capability, operational in 1967. The practice version weighs 1,362 kg. A 2001 Russian brochure gives the SET-65E export version's speed as 40 kts and its maximum range as 16 km.

Diameter: 533.4 mm **Length:** 7.800 m **Weight:** 1,738 kg
Warhead weight: 205 kg **Speed/range:** 35 kts/10 km; 24 kts/15 km

53-83: Thermal engine–propelled, surface- and submarine-launched wake-homing weapon. Other than its diameter (533 mm), no data are available.

ET-80(66): Nuclear-warhead submarine torpedo with silver-zinc battery electric propulsion and a 300-m operating depth. Straight runner. No longer deployed, but may be retained in storage at land depots.

Diameter: 533 mm **Length:** 7.700 m
Warhead: 20 kT nuclear **Speed/range:** 35 kts/10 km; 20 kts/40 km

SAET-50/SAET-60M/USET-80: Referred to by NATO as the ET-80A. Entered service in 1961 as the first Soviet passive acoustic homing torpedo, intended for use by submarines against surface targets; runs at 5- to 14-m depths. The initial Soviet designation was probably SAET-50, while SAET-60 is a higher-performance version that appeared around 1966 and has a range of 15 km at 35 kts; both weapons use a 46-cell battery. The current version, known as the USET-80, is said to be only 10% reliable, although it is the most widely deployed torpedo on Russian submarines; it may have been the cause of the demise of the submarine *Kursk*.

Diameter: 534.4 mm **Length:** 7.800 m **Weight:** 1,855 kg
Warhead weight: 205 kg **Speed/range:** SAET-50: 23.3 kts/7.3 km

E53-75, E53-79: Electric torpedoes for air and missile delivery. May no longer be in use.

53-66: Electric-propelled straight and pattern-running torpedo for surface ship and submarine use. May no longer be in use.

53-57: Antiship torpedo for surface ships, introduced in 1957. May no longer be in use.

Diameter: 533 mm **Length:** . . .
Warhead weight: 300 kg **Speed/range:** 45 kts/18 km

53-56V, VA: Standard export torpedo boat weapon, either straight or pattern running with reciprocating air/steam propulsion. Entered service during the 1950s. A nuclear-warhead version with a 15-kT warhead was developed for Soviet submarine use but is no longer deployed.

Diameter: 533 mm **Length:** 7.000 m
Warhead weight: 400 kg **Speed/range:** 51 kts/4 km; 41 kts/8 km

SET-53M: Active acoustic antisubmarine torpedo, introduced in 1953 for use in surface ships. Probably long out of service in Russia but still may appear in foreign fleets.

Diameter: 533 mm **Length:** . . .
Warhead weight: 100 kg **Speed/range:** 29 kts/14 km

E45-75A: An improved E45-70 with a 300-m operating depth and electric propulsion, for delivery by SS-N-14 or aircraft. A modified, 4.6-m-long version is also in use which presumably has a longer range. E45-75A replaced the slower E45-70A.

Diameter: 450 mm **Length:** 3.900 m
Warhead weight: 90 kg **Range:** 38 kts/8 km

WEAPONS AND SYSTEMS *(continued)*

APSET-95: Russian Navy designation: UMGT-1 (NATO E40-79). Air-dropped ASW torpedo usable against 2- to 400-m-deep submarine targets. Parachute retarded. Uses active/passive homing and electric propulsion. An improved version, APSET-96, has also been offered for export.

Diameter: 400 mm **Length:** 3.845 m **Weight:** 650–720 kg
Warhead weight: 60 kg **Speed/range:** 24 or 40 kts/up to 20 km

USET-95 (Mod. 3): Multipurpose ship-, aircraft-, and submarine-launched export torpedo with active/passive acoustic homing for use against submarine and surface targets. Electric propulsion. Can be launched from 534.4-mm tubes using liners.

Diameter: 400 mm **Length:** 4.700 m **Weight:** 650–720 kg
Warhead weight: 60 kg **Speed/range:** 50 kts/ . . .

SET-40: Active/passive-acoustic-homing, surface-launched antisubmarine torpedo with battery power. Seeker range is 585 m. Entered service around 1960 and has largely been succeeded by the SET-65. Also serves as the payload of the PMT-1 moored antisubmarine mine.

Diameter: 400 mm **Length:** 4.500 m **Weight:** 530 kg
Warhead weight: 80 kg **Speed/range:** 28 kts/8 km
Depth of target: Up to 200 m

APR-2: Intended for dropping by helicopters and aircraft against submarines at depths of up to 600 m and moving at up to 43 kts. Has a solid-rocket propulsion system that continues to function underwater, and employs active acoustic homing with a range of 1,500 m. In effect, it is a cross between a homing torpedo and a self-propelled depth charge.

Diameter: 350 mm **Length:** 3.7 m **Weight:** 575 kg
Warhead: 100 kg Trotyl equivalent
Speed: 62 kts **Endurance:** 1–2 min

APR-3: A developmental, updated version of the APR-2 under development that will use pumpjet propulsion vice the APR-2's rocket; it will be effective to 800-m depths. The APR-3E is offered for export. For both, the seeker sensor is a multichannel active sonar with 1.5–2.0° bearing accuracy, and the guidance system employs two-plane adaptive lead-angle computation. The APR-3 searches in an 1,800- to 2,000-m-diameter circle and has a 2,000-m detection range. It is offered as the payload for the Type 91RE2 antisubmarine missile system (see description under antisubmarine missiles).

Diameter: 350 mm **Length:** 3.20 m **Weight:** 450 kg
Warhead: 76 kg TNT equivalent
Speed: 65 kts search, 100 kts attack **Endurance:** . . .

GPD-3: Decoy device designed to be carried two per torpedo tube. Russian designation: MG-74. Nickname: "Impostor." Each 3.9-m-long, 533-mm-diameter, 797-kg device can be instructed to perform noise jamming, selective jamming of active sonars, or echo simulation and can be used at up to 250-m depths. Developed by Gidropribor Central Research Institute. A 400-mm-diameter, 4.5-m-long decoy device with a weight of 497 kg is also still in use.

VA-111 Shkval: A 533-mm-diameter, 195-kt, rocket-propelled weapon that travels in a supercavitating vacuum bubble. Made by Region. Its maximum range is only 7–10 km. Probably intended as a countermeasure against torpedo attack, using a nuclear warhead to destroy not only the enemy torpedoes but also the launch platform. Entered service in 1977 but was removed from service in 1991 and stored for possible future use. A version with a speed of 300 kts is in development, with initial sea trials conducted in spring 1998; a Shkval-E variant with a 210-kg-TNT warhead is offered for export, and the new version is equipped with a target sensor of unspecified variety. The weapon's diameter would preclude its being launched from a conventional 533-mm torpedo tube, thus limiting its use to the Russian Navy. Shkval-E uses both a contact and a probable laser fuze. The Kazakhstani factory in 1999 sold China a number of Shkvals but not the fire-control system, rendering them useless. The earlier RAT-52 air-dropped rocket torpedo has been retired. Data for the export Shkval-E include:

Diameter: 534.4 mm **Length:** 8.2 m
Weight: 2,700 kg **Warhead:** 210 kg TNT equivalent
Speed: 90–100 m/sec **Max. effective range:** 10 km

Note: For launching 400-mm-diameter torpedoes from surface ships, single 402-mm OTA-40 fixed tubes are employed; the tubes are 4.90 m long and weigh 475 kg empty. They employ gunpowder ejection. For surface ships with 533-mm weapons, the 536-mm-diameter, 8.525-m-long PTA-series trainable or fixed tubes are used; they also employ gunpowder ejection and are electrically trained.

F. MINES

Russia has a vast inventory of air-, surface-, and submarine-launched mines, using mechanical (contact), acoustic, magnetic, and possibly pressure fuzing. Older mines still available include the M12, M16, M26, M31, KB1, MAG, AMAG1, PLT-G, PL-150, KRAB, MIRAB, MKB-3, MAG, and MYaM. Specific details are unavailable for the modern systems, such as the KMD and AMD, which have 300-kg explosive charges, and the rocket-propelled rising mines known by NATO as "Cluster Bay" and the deep-water "Cluster Gulf," which have 230 kg of explosives. The RMZ and YaRM mines are small antimine countermeasures and anti-invasion weapons. There may also be stocks of nuclear-armed mines.

Mines offered for export include:

KPM: Surface ship–launched moored anti-invasion beach defense mine designed to be laid by small craft moving at up to 6 kts. Weighs 745 kg, has a 480-kg TNT-equivalent warhead, and can be moored in waters 5–20 m deep. Length: 1.40 m; width: 0.7 m; height: 0.745 m.

MDM-1: Electromagnetic and acoustic influence bottom mine launched by submarines traveling at up to 8 kts or surface ships moving at up to 15 kts. Weighs 960 kg and has an explosive charge equivalent to 1,120 kg of TNT. Measures 2.860 m long by 533 mm in diameter. Can be emplaced in waters 12–120 m deep.

MDM-2: Surface-launched bottom mine with three-channel acoustic exploder, detonation delay setting, ship counter, and self-destruction feature. Weight: 1,413 kg with 950-kg TNT-equivalent warhead. Measures 2.30 m long by 790 mm in diameter (atop cart). Can be laid in waters 12–35 m deep (125 m for use as an antisubmarine mine).

MDM-3: Aircraft- or surface-launched three-channel fuzed (acoustic/electromagnetic/pressure) bottom mine. In the surface-launched version, the device weighs 635 kg with cart and is 1.525 m long; air launched (at up to 540 kts), it weighs 525 kg and is 1.58 m long. Both variants carry 300-kg-TNT-equivalent warheads. Can be emplaced in waters up to 35 m deep.

MDM-4: Aircraft- or surface-launched three-channel fuzed (acoustic/electromagnetic/pressure) bottom mine. In the surface-launched version, the device weighs 1,420 kg with cart and is 2.30 m long; air launched (at up to 540 kts), it weighs 1,370 kg and is 2.785 m long. Both variants carry 950-kg-TNT-equivalent warheads. Can be emplaced in waters up to 50 m deep (125 m surface-launched or 250 m air-dropped as an antisubmarine mine).

MDM-5: Aircraft- or surface-launched three-channel fuzed (acoustic/electromagnetic/pressure) bottom mine. In the surface-launched version, the device weighs 1,470 kg with cart and is 2.40 m long; air launched (at up to 540 kts), it weighs 1,500 kg and is 3.055 m long. Both variants carry 1,350-kg-TNT-equivalent warheads. Can be emplaced in waters up to 60 m deep (300 m for use as an antisubmarine mine).

MDM-6: Offered in 3-94, it can be launched by surface ships traveling 4–15 kts or submarines traveling 4–8 kts, can be laid in waters as shallow as 12 m or as deep as 120 m, and has a 1-year in-water life. Seeker is similar to that of the larger MDM-5. Weighs 960 kg and is 2.860 m long by 533 mm in diameter.

MDS: Mobile bottom mine laid by submarines. Resembles a torpedo and has contra-rotating propellers. Employs an influence sensor and can be laid in waters more than 8 m deep. Weight: 1,380 kg; length: 7.9 m; diameter: 534 mm.

MShM: A 4.00-m-long export rising mine, said also to be torpedo tube–launched and to be intended for emplacement in waters 60–300 m deep. The payload is rocket driven, with the rocket ejected from the cylindrical, 533-mm-diameter capsule. The entire weapon weighs 820 kg, and the rocket has a 250-kg warhead. The rocket uses an acoustic target sensor, and one is capable of covering an area of 882,000 m^2.

RMK-1: A 1,850-kg, 7.83-m-long by 533-mm-diameter, tethered antisubmarine mine moored in depths from 200 to 400 m. Releases a rocket-powered homing device with a 350-kg warhead. Offered for export as the RMR-2. Entered service in 1983 as a replacement for the RMT-1. It can be emplaced from air, surface, or submarine platforms.

RMT-1: Moored antisubmarine mine that releases a SET-40 homing torpedo, equivalent to the U.S. Navy's CAPTOR system and said to be superior in performance. Entered service in 1972. The torpedo, at the top of the array, is launched horizontally.

RM-2: Rocket-assisted submarine- or ship-laid moored mine with influence sensors; the activated mine launches the stabilized, solid-fuel rocket, which has both impact and influence fuzing. Can be laid in depths up to 450 m. Weight: 870 kg; length: 3.850 m; diameter: 534 mm.

SMDM: Submarine torpedo tube–launched mine. Version 1 is 533 mm in diameter, weighs 7,900 kg, has a 480-kg warhead, and can be emplaced in waters 4–100 m deep. Version 2 is 650 mm in diameter, weighs 5,500 kg, has an 800-kg warhead, and can be emplaced in waters 8–150 m deep. Propelled by a torpedo afterbody to a predetermined location. An "SMDM-4," offered in 3-94, can be emplaced in waters as shallow as 4 m or as deep as 150 m and has an explosive weight equivalent to 480 kg of TNT and a working life of 1 year.

UDM/UDM-2/UDM-500: Antisurface and antisubmarine magnetic influence mines intended for air drop or surface launch. Usable in waters more than 8 m deep. UDM and UDM-2 have fin stabilizers, while UDM-500 has a braking parachute. UDM weighs (surface launch/aircraft launch) 1,420/1,320 kg and is 2.100/2.785 m long by 790/630 mm in diameter. UDM-2 weighs 1,470/1,500 kg and is 2.400/3.055 m long by 630 mm in diameter. UDM-500 weighs 635/575 kg and is 1.525/1.500 m long by 600/450 mm in diameter.

G. RADARS

Note: Radars are listed by their NATO names, although because those names were based on appearance rather than performance characteristics, there is not always a direct correlation to the actual Russian designation and name, which, where known, are given. In the ship listings, the Russian designations and names are given first, with the NATO names in parentheses. For some radars, there appears to be more than one nickname; while this may be a case of there being both domestic and export system names, it may also indicate that there are capability and/or configurational differences as well.

♦ Navigational

The most widely used are the X-band Don-2, Mius (Spin Trough), Volga (Don-Kay), and MR-212/201 Vaygach and Vaygach-U (Palm Frond). Kivach-3 and MR-312 Nayada are Russian designators (also used by NATO) for small sets used on recent small combatants and auxiliaries. Many ships carry two or three navigational sets (port-and-starboard antennas normally operate together with a single display).

♦ Surface search

Submarines carry the MRK-50 Albatros/Tobol series (Snoop Tray, Snoop Slab, Snoop Plate, or Snoop Pair), all operating in the X band. Submarines also carry ranging radars mounted on their attack periscopes.

♦ Long-range air search

Big Net: Russian designation: MR-500 Kliver ("Jib"). A large L-band (850-MHz) radar fitted on the two surviving Kashin destroyers. Its detection range on an aircraft is probably more than 100 miles.

Flat Screen: Russian MR-700 Podberezovik. Made by Salyut, Moscow, and offered for export as the Podberezovik-ET1 and -ET2. C-band, planar array, rotating 3-D long-range air-search radar found only aboard the Kara-class destroyer *Kerch'*. Has 300-km range against a 7-m^2 target at 1,500-m altitude, with a 5-km minimum range. Can track a 500-m^2 surface target at 30 km. Rotates at 12 rpm. System weighs 13 tons with a 3-ton antenna and requires 110 kw.

WEAPONS AND SYSTEMS *(continued)*

Half Plate: Russian MR-755 Fregat-MA. Made by Salyut Moscow Production Association. Single-antenna, phased array set on two modernized Krivak-I frigates and some Grisha-V corvettes. Said to have a range of 150 km against air targets within a 55° vertical swath. Rotates at 15 rpm and has a system weight of 6,500 kg.

Head Net-C: Russian MR-310U Angara-M. S-band radar with an antenna consisting of two Head Net-A antennas mounted back to back, one in a horizontal plane, the other tilted about 30°. Once widely used on cruisers and destroyers. The Head Net–series radars use a band that gives a 60- to 70-mile detection range on an attack bomber flying at high altitude.

Peel Cone: Russian Reyd. Small air/surface-search combined radar used on Maritime Border Guard Muravey-, Stenka-, and Pauk-class patrol craft and on naval Pauks and Mukha-class hydrofoils.

Plate Steer: Russian M-700-series Fregat-M. S band. Top Steer and Strut Curve antennas combined in a back-to-back array on two early *Sovremennyy*-class destroyers and the carrier *Admiral Flota Sovetskogo Soyuza Kuznetsov.*

Sky Watch: Russian Mars-Passat. The Russian Navy's first fixed, planar-array, early-warning radar, employing four arrays. Apparently unsuccessful and probably not operational (provision was made for it on the carrier *Kuznetsov,* but it does not seem to have been installed).

Slim Net: Russian Fut-N. An early-model S-band radar fitted on Petya-class corvettes and no longer in Russian Navy service.

Strut Curve: Russian MR-302 Rubka. S-band set on early Grisha-series corvettes. Widely exported.

Strut Pair: Russian MR-320M Topaz/Topaz-M/V. S band. Mounted on the carrier *Kuznetsov,* early *Udaloy*-class destroyers, and early Grisha-V corvettes. Employs pulse compression. The antenna is essentially two Strut Curve reflectors back to back. Manufactured by Typhoon Instrument Building Plant, Kaluga.

Top Pair: Russian MR-800 Flag or Voskhod. C/F-band, 3-D radar using a Top Sail and a Big Net antenna mounted back to back. Used on the *Kirov* and *Slava* classes, always accompanied by a Top Steer backup radar. Said to have a range of 500 km against aerial targets. Antenna rotates at 3–12 rpm, and system weight is 43,500 kg.

Top Plate: Russian MR-750 Fregat-MA; the version on the frigate *Neustrashimyy* is designated MR-760 and Top Plate-B (Russian MR-710 Fregat-MA) is on the *Slava*-class cruisers *Varyag* and *Admiral Flota Lobov.* MR-750 is an E-band radar with identical back-to-back, phased-array, 3-D radar antennas on *Udaloy*-class destroyers *Marshal Vasilevskiy, Admiral Zakharov,* and later. Can detect a 7-m^2 target at a range of 130 km at 5,000 m altitude or a 300-m^2 ship at 30 km. Rotates at 15 rpm. Requires 30 kw of 380-V, 50-Hz current. System weighs 7.5 tons with a 2.2-ton antenna. Associated with the Poima-E data processor, which can track 20 targets simultaneously. Export version is Fregat-MAE. Related to the single-antenna MR-755 Fregat-MA (Half Plate).

Top Sail: Russian MR-600 Voskhod ("Dawn"). S-band, 3-D radar now installed only on two Kara-class destroyers. Uses a very large, heavy, stabilized antenna.

Top Steer: Russian MR-700 Fregat. S-band, back-to-back, 3-D radar antenna using one Top Steer and one Top Plate antenna, on later *Sovremennyy*-class destroyers.

♦ Missile tracking and control

Band Stand: Russian Monolit (although the nickname "Mineral" appears to be applied when the dome is associated with the SS-N-22 missile system and "Titanit" when it is associated with SS-N-9). On *Sovremennyy* destroyers and Tarantul-II and Nanuchka guided-missile combatants, the radome covers an L-band, tropospheric-scatter radar for antiship missile target acquisition, tracking, and control. Housed in a large radome. In export ships (and possibly some Russian installations), "Band Stand" covers a Square Tie missile target acquisition radar, associated with the SS-N-2 Styx family; later classes may have Band Stand radomes over Plank Shave antiship missile target-designation radars.

Cross Dome: Russian MR-352 Pozitiv series. Manufactured by Typhoon Instrument Building Plant, Kaluga. Separate target detection and tracking radar for the Kortik/Kashtan gun-and-missile CIWS, with antennas mounted in a hemispherical radome. Export versions are Pozitiv-E, Pozitiv-E1.1, etc. Three-dimensional system with a range from 15 to 110 km and capable of tracking 30 targets simultaneously.

The Pozitiv-ME1.2 version does not employ a radome and is a true 3-D radar. Employing a mechanically stabilized, rotating, single-pane phased-array antenna with IFF interrogation antenna on the lower edge, the radar is tailored to act as the target detection and designation set for the Kashtan CIWS. The first customer was Algeria.

Cross Sword: Russian MR-350 or MR-360 Podkat. Manufactured by Typhoon Instrument Building Plant, Kaluga. Ku- and X-band, multiarray missile guidance director for the SA-N-9 SAM system. Incorporates both detection/tracker radar and illuminator/tracker antennas. Probably has an electro-optical backup. Can track and attack four targets simultaneously within a 60°-wide by 60°-high field.

Eye Bowl: Russian MR-212 Drakon or Musson. F band. A smaller version of the command antenna component of Head Lights, installed in *Udaloy*-class destroyers and Krivak-series frigates (which do not have Head Lights). Command radar for the SS-N-14 antisubmarine/antiship missile system.

Front Dome: Russian OP-3. X-band target illuminator for the SA-N-7 SAM system in the *Sovremennyy*-class destroyers (which have six) and on Indian Navy Project 15 destroyers and Project 1135 frigates. Resembles the gun fire-control radar Bass Tilt and is very compact. Each director can track two targets simultaneously if the targets are reasonably close together.

Head Lights-C: Russian Grom. F-, G-, H-, and D-band antenna now mounted only on two Kara-class guided-missile destroyers. Similar to Peel Group, with an assembly of tracking radar for the target and guidance radar for the missile. Used for guidance for the Goblet missile of the SA-N-3 system and for the surface-to-underwater missiles of the SS-N-14 system. Formerly found in several versions, designated Head Lights-A, -B, and -C, the last being equipped to provide tracking and control of SS-N-14 missiles.

Hot Flash: Russian 3P-87. Multiantenna radar weapons-control system found on the Kortik combined SA-N-11 SAM/twin 30-mm gatling AA close-in defense system mounting. Controls the guns and provides target designation to the missiles.

Peel Group: Russian Yatagan. Now found only on the two surviving Kashin-series destroyers. The antenna assembly is made up of two groups of large and small reflectors, in both horizontal and vertical orientation, with parabolic design (S-band tracker; X-band tracker). Maximum range is approximately 30–40 miles. Used for guidance of the Goa missile in the SA-N-1 system.

Plank Shave: Russian 3Ts-25 Garpun ("Harpoon"), designed by the Granit Central Research Institute and manufactured by Typhoon Instrument Building Plant, Kaluga. Employed as an active and passive target detection and designation system for shorter-range antiship missile systems of the Termit (SS-N-2) and Kh-35 Uran (SS-N-25) series; it is also capable of being employed as a surface- and air-search radar. A successor to Square Tie, acting as air/surface search and missile target acquisition and tracking radar. The latest export variant is known as Garpun-Bal E1 (3Ts-25E1) and is said to have a range of 45 km in active mode and 70–500 km in passive intercept mode; the system has a 0.2–1.5° bearing accuracy in passive mode and 1° bearing accuracy when active and can track six targets simultaneously.

Pop Group: Russian MPZ-301 Baza (export name: Korund). F-, H-, and I-band missile guidance set for the SA-N-4 system. Upper component rotates independently and serves as a target acquisition radar; lower portion is used for missile control and can handle two missiles at once. Latest version appears to have an electro-optical backup.

Square Tie: Russian Rangout. Employed for SS-N-2-series missile target detection and designation. Also acts as a surface-search radar and probably can be used as a passive radar intercept receiver. Found on exported Osa-series small missile combatants and also used by the Chinese Navy.

Top Dome: Russian Volna. X-band director associated with the SA-N-6 vertically launched SAM system in the *Kirov*- and *Slava*-class cruisers. Employs a 4-m-diameter hemispheric radome, fixed in elevation but mechanically steerable in azimuth. Three smaller dielectric radomes are mounted on the face of its mounting pedestal, and there is also a smaller hemispheric radome below it. Can reportedly track six targets at once, although probably only if all are within about a 60° cone.

Trap Door-C: Russian Argon. Used for tracking the SS-N-12 missiles on the *Slava*-class cruisers (with the Argon-1164 antenna mount fixed on the mast).

♦ Gunfire control

Bass Tilt: Russian MR-123 Vympel; export name: Koral-E. X(I)-band radar director used with paired AK-630 gatling guns fitted in *Kiev* carriers and Kara cruisers, as well as in Grisha-III corvettes, where it also controls the twin 57-mm, and in Nanuchka-III corvettes and Matka guided-missile patrol craft, where it also controls the 76.2-mm gun. Tracking ranges are up to 45 km (30 km with MTI). Peak power output: 250 kw with 1.8° beamwidth. Normally rotates at 15 rpm until going into target tracking mode. System weight: 5.2 tons. The latest version, MR-123-02, incorporates a television camera and laser rangefinder.

Drum Tilt: Russian MR-104 Rys'. C- and X-band radar director installed on ships and craft fitted with 30-mm AK-230 twin-barrel AA.

Hawk Screech: Russian Fut-B. X-band director for 76.2-mm DP guns; always found in conjunction with optical director/target designators. Obsolescent.

Kite Screech-A, -B, -C: Russian MR-114, MR-145, and MR-184 Lev. X- and Ka-band director to control 100-mm AK-100 and 130-mm AK-130 twin DP. There is a television backup and laser rangefinder adjunct in Kite Screech-B. Can track targets to 75 km and tracks its own shells for correction, employing a digital computer. Elevates to 75°. System weight: 8.0 tons. Has MTI and ECCM features. Beamwidth: 1° in X band and 0.25° in Ka band. Peak output power: 300 kw in X band, 25 kw in Ka band. MR-184 Kite Screech-C is used with 130-mm guns, while MR-145 Kite Screech-B is used with 100-mm mounts in recent classes and MR-114 Kite Screech-A was found only in the Krivak-II-class frigates.

Muff Cob: Russian MR-103 Bars. C-band director for 57-mm AA twin automatic guns. Has a television camera attachment.

Owl Screech: Russian MR-105 Turel'. X-band director for 76.2-mm DP guns. An improved version of Hawk Screech, without the associated manned target designators.

Note: A new radar gunfire-control system nicknamed Laska was offered for export in 4-97 by the Topaz Moscow State Industrial Complex.

♦ Datalink antennas

Light Bulb: Russian Pricep. Spherical radomes found only on SS-N-22 Sunburn anti-ship missile–equipped *Sovremennyy*-class destroyers (two antennas) and Tarantul-III missile boats (one antenna). Apparently performs a datalink function with the missiles.

Note: The Russian Navy also employs numerous other datalink systems, for which details are unavailable. Such datalinks include systems permitting aircraft to provide targeting data to surface ships and submarines for over-the-horizon launching of antiship missiles. Some of the Bell-series radomes usually associated with EW functions may actually house directional datalink antennas tailored to specific weapons systems or functions such as ASW.

H. SONARS

Until the late 1950s, the Soviet Navy showed little interest in antisubmarine warfare or, of course, submarine detection. Most of its ships were equipped with HF sonars (Tamir-11 or -11M, Pegas, Herkules) of World War II–era concept. New or modernized ships have much-improved sensors. Where known, actual Russian nomenclature is employed in the ship data sections; most sonars have alphanumeric designators beginning with "MG-."

♦ For surface ships

MG-7: Used on Yevgenya (Project 1258) inshore minesweepers and as a static swimmer and chariot detection set, lowered on a cable while at moorings. HF (above 100 kHz).

WEAPONS AND SYSTEMS *(continued)*

MG-11 Tamir-11 (NATO Stag Ear): HF (24.5–30 kHz) searchlight set, no longer used by the Russian Navy but still found in smaller export craft in Third World fleets
MG-26 Khrom, Khrom-K, or Khrom-2M: standard underwater telephone set
MG-35 Shtil: MF underwater communications set used in the Kara and Krivak-III classes and on most submarine classes. MG-35E is an export version offered by the Akhtuba Instrumentation Plant; it has 6-kw transmission power.
MG-69 and -69M: Made by Priboy. Mine-countermeasures sonars, with the MG-69M (offered for export in 2000) having a bottom-mine detection capability and incorporating digital technology and a new signal processor.
MG-79 Mizen: A further improvement on the MG-16 Lany (NATO Stag Ear), used in Natya-class minesweepers. Range against bottom mines in up to 100 m of water is said to be as much as 400 m, with 1.5° bearing accuracy.
MG-89 and -89M Serna: Made by Priboy. Combined MF/HF set used in late and export Natyas for minehunting and mine avoidance. Range: 1,500 m against moored mines or 500 m against bottom mines, with 1.5° bearing accuracy. MG-89M, offered for export in 2000, employs digital technology and a new signal processor.
MG-311 Vychegda (NATO Wolf Paw): Used in the Kashin, Koni, and Petya classes for ASW search
MG-312 Titan (NATO Bull Nose): MF ASW set in the Kashin and Koni classes
MG-322: Possible designation for the search component of the set in the one Bulgarian Koni. MG-322T is used in the Parchim-class units now in Indonesian service.
MG-325 Vega (NATO Mare Tail): VDS on older major combatants
MG-332 Titan-2 (NATO Bull Nose): Hull or bow mounted; the main search set in the Kara class
MG-335 Platina (NATO Bull Horn): In the *Kuznetsov, Slava,* and *Sovremennyy* classes
MG-335M Argun': Hull-mounted LF set used in Grisha-series corvettes and the nuclear-powered intelligence collector *Ural*
MG-509 Radian (NATO Mouse Roar): Mine-avoidance sonar fitted on submarines with the Kerch and Rubin sonar suites
MG-519 Arfa: Mine-avoidance sonar fitted to submarines with the Rubikon or Skat-series sonar suites
MG-747 Amulet: HF dipping sonar on the nuclear-powered intelligence collector *Ural* and possibly other units
MGK-345 Bronza: Said to have a range of 4.6 km hull-mounted, 5.5 km as a towed VDS, and 7 km in the dipping version. Operates at center frequencies of 6.5, 7.0, and 7.5 kHz, with 1% range accuracy and 0.7° bearing accuracy. Has range scales up to 32 km. A component of the Zvezda M-1 sonar suite (NATO Rat Tail).
MGK-335MS Pirhana: May be the designation for the VDS version of Platina used on Krivak-I and -II. The VDS version can be towed at up to 150-m depths.
MGK-355 Polinom (NATO Horse Jaw/Horse Tail): Active bow-mounted and VDS suite on the *Kirov*-class cruisers and *Udaloy*-class destroyers
MGK-365 Zvezda M-1 (NATO Ox Yoke/Ox Tail): LF active/passive bow array on the carrier *Kuznetsov,* frigate *Neustrashimyy,* and two Krivak frigates. The destroyer *Admiral Chabanenko* has the Zvezda M-2 variant.

♦ For submarines

Systems currently employed include:

MGK-400 Rubikon: Sonar suite on Tango- and Kilo-class diesel submarines and Delta-III SSBNs
MGK-503 Skat-KS (NATO Shark Gill): Sonar suite on Victor-III and Sierra-I SSNs. SKAT-BDRM is on the Delta-IV-class SSBNs. An upgraded version of the basic MGK-500 Skat. The system includes passive detection arrays, sound intercept warning system, communications system, MG-512 self-noise measurement set, MG-518 upward-beam echo sounder for ice navigation, MG-519 mine-detection/avoidance active set, MR-553 sound-velocity measurement device, NOR-1 ice-free lane detection set, and NOK-1 safe-surfacing set to detect overhead obstacles.
MGK-540 Skat-3 (NATO Shark Gill): Sonar suite on Akula-I, Akula-II, and Sierra-II SSNs and Oscar-II SSGNs; the first Russian all-digital sonar system
MGK- . . . Lira: New sonar suite for the Lada-class SS
MGK- . . . Irtysh Amfora: Sonar suite for the *Severodvinsk*-class SSN; uses a spherical bow array
MGS-30: Emergency pinger for sunken submarines, effective to 6,000 m and with a range of 10 km; can be interrogated up to nine months after sinking

♦ For aircraft

Ka-27PL Helix ASW helicopters carry dipping sonars, which are also used aboard smaller ASW patrol craft such as the Turya and Stenka classes. Land-based maritime patrol/ASW aircraft (Bear-F, May) carry an extensive family of sonobuoys.

♦ Fixed sea-based

Numerous fixed hydrophone arrays are installed to protect Soviet naval bases and harbors. The Cluster Lance planar arrays are used in the Pacific area.

I. ELECTRONIC WARFARE

The large number of radomes of every description that can be seen on Soviet ships, especially on the newest and most important types (helicopter and guided-missile cruisers, for example) is an indication of the attention the Russian Navy gives to electronic warfare. NATO code names for the antenna arrays for intercept or jamming radars include the Side Globe intercept/jamming; Top Hat-A intercept; Top Hat-B jamming; Bell Thump/Bell Bash intercept/jamming; Bell Shroud/Bell Squat intercept; Rum Tub intercept; Bell Clout intercept; Cage Pot intercept; Sprat Star VHF intercept; Grid Crane VHF–UHF intercept; Site Crane VHF intercept; and Watch Dog intercept. Literally hundreds of antennas have received NATO nicknames, and it is not possible to list them all here; the individual antennas are listed by name and correlated to Russian system names (where known) on the ship data pages.

Submarine EW systems employ the following NATO-designated antenna arrays:

Bald Head: Russian Bukhta system. Large radome combined with Snoop Head radar array on Oscar-II-class SSGNs.
Brick Pulp: Russian MRP-10 Zaliv-P or Buleva system. Plain radome on Delta-III and Delta-IV SSBNs and Victor-III SSNs.
Rim Hat: Truncated conical radome combined with Snoop Pair radar on Akula- and Sierra-class SSNs
Squid Head: Russian MRM-25EM system. Thimble radome atop ring of small disc antennas on the Kilo and Tango classes.
Stop Light-A: Russian Nakat. Older system (1–18 GHz) on export Kilo-class SSs.

Russian designations for EW systems offered for export (but not correlated to NATO-designated system nicknames) include:

MR-401S/MP-401MS: Integrated intercept and jamming system for surface ships, with a 7–30° bearing accuracy, five operating personnel, and a system weight of 6,100 kg
MR-405: Integrated intercept/jamming system that also cues launch of decoys from the PK-16 weapons system. The active component offers repeater, masking, spot, and barrage jamming and provides 360° coverage. The system weighs 2,000 kg and requires two operators.
MR-407: Integrated intercept/jamming system that also cues decoy launch from PK-2 and PK-16 launchers. The system weighs 6,500 kg and has three operators. May equate to NATO Foot Ball radome array on *Sovremennyy*-class destroyers.

Three types of decoy rocket launchers are employed:

PK-2: Twin-tube, autoloading 140-mm ZIF-121 launcher, mechanically elevated and trained, with AZ-TSP-47 (36.1-kg chaff), AZ-TST-47 (37.5-kg infrared), and AZ-TSO-47 (38.5-kg combined chaff/IR) rounds; all varieties are 1.105 m long. Entering service is the AZ-TSTV-47 round, which floats and dispenses a 6,000-m-long aerosol cloud to defeat laser rangefinders. Each system weighs 15,000 kg, and 100 rounds per launcher are carried. Can fire at 15 rds/min. Requires a crew of five to seven personnel. Used on Maritime Border Guard Amur River Flotilla Yaz-class monitors as an artillery device, firing antipersonnel grenades.
PK-10: Ten-tube, 120-mm, fixed elevation and train, with SR-50 (25.5-kg chaff), SOM-50 (25-kg infrared- and laser-fuzed decoy), and SK-50 (25-kg chaff/IR/laser combined) rounds; all rounds are 1.226 m long. The system first appeared on a *Udaloy* in 1989 and is now widely deployed. The launcher itself, which weighs 205 kg, is designated KT-216; as many as 16 can be controlled from one console on a large ship.
PK-16: East German–designed, 16-round, 82-mm bore, fixed-train, mechanically elevated, with TSP-60U (8.3-kg chaff) and TSP-60U (8.5-kg infrared) rounds; both varieties are 653 mm long. The launcher designation is KT-101. A 32-round version, PK-32, was installed on East German–built *Sassnitz*-class patrol boats.

TACAN systems include the large cylindrical Cake Stand array on aircraft carriers, and the various forms of the paired cylindrical Privod (NATO Round House) array on the *Kirov, Udaloy,* and other classes. A variety of microwave automatic aircraft landing system arrays are used on modern carriers, cruisers, destroyers, and *Neustrashimyy*-class frigates.

J. COMMUNICATIONS

All Russian Navy warships are equipped to transmit and receive MF through VHF communications, while submarines have a VLF capability (using towed buoy antennas) and UHF equipment is coming into wider use in surface ships. VHF antennas in use include Cage Bare, Cage Cone, Cage Stalk, and the older Straight Key. Major warships usually have a Pop Art VHF antenna. Submarines rely on VLF, using towed wire and/or towed buoy antennas, and a land-based ELF submarine communications alerting station entered service in the early 1990s. Tu-142 Bear-J aircraft were equipped with a trailing wire antenna strategic submarine communications system analogous to the U.S. TACAMO system.

K. SATELLITES

The Russians had hoped to maintain an ocean surveillance ELINT satellite system whose data were to be transmitted either to ground stations or directly to ships equipped with the SS-N-12 and SS-N-19 cruise-missile systems, but recent economic problems have made it difficult to sustain the necessary satellite constellation; the system is thus only intermittently operational at best. The receiving antenna is mounted in a large cylindrical radome termed Punch Bowl. Many other ships can apparently also employ Russian and Western commercial communications and navigational satellites.

L. INFRARED AND ELECTRO-OPTICAL SYSTEMS

Cod Eye: Radiometric sextant used on ballistic-missile submarines for precision navigation
Half Cup: Russian Spektr-F. A laser detection system seen increasingly on combatants and intelligence collection ships. The fixed devices are normally installed in pairs and have a 20- to 25-km range against the infrared emissions from an incoming missile. Made by the Industrial Amalgam Zagorskiy Optika-Mekhanichevkyy Zauro.
Squeeze Box: Installed on *Sovremennyy*-class destroyers and on *Ivan Rogov*–and Alligator-class landing ships with 140-mm artillery rocket launchers. A lightweight version is used on Pomornik-class surface-effect landing craft. Believed to incorporate television, laser rangefinder, and infrared sensors and used in artillery rocket fire control.
Tee Plinth: Russian MT-45. Heavyweight television sensor installed in large ships in the 1960s and 1970s.

Note: Also in use are smaller, fixed television surveillance devices such as Tilt Pot and periscopes mounted atop pilothouses to permit operations in biological or chemical warfare conditions and poor weather. The "Tall View" periscope in the *Sovremennyy* class probably provides the commanding officer with his own view when he is in the command center during combat operations; there are similar "CIC periscopes" in other large combatants. All combatant submarines carry both a wide-field-of-view search periscope and a higher-magnification, narrow-view attack periscope, the latter probably fitted with a laser and/or radar rangefinder.

GUIDED-MISSILE AIRCRAFT CARRIERS [CVG]

♦ 1 Kuznetsov (Orel) class (Project 11435)

Bldr: Chernomorskiy (Nosenko) SY 444, Nikolayev, Ukraine

	Laid down	L	In serv.
063 ADMIRAL FLOTA SOVETSKOGO SOYUZA KUZNETSOV (ex-*Tbilisi*, ex-*Leonid Brezhnev*, ex-*Riga*)	1-9-82	4-12-85	29-1-91

Admiral Flota Sovetskogo Soyuza Kuznetsov (063)—with Flanker, Helix and Frogfoot aircraft on deck Boris Lemachko

Admiral Flota Sovetskogo Soyuza Kuznetsov (063) Boris Lemachko

D: 43,000 tons light; 55,000 tons std. (59,100 fl; 65,000 max.) **S:** 29 kts
Dim: 306.45 (270.00 wl) × 72.30 (68.5 flight deck; 35.41 wl) × 9.14 (10.00 max.)
Air group: 18 Su-33 Flanker-D interceptors; 4 SU-25UTG Frogfoot; 15 Ka-27PL Helix-A ASW helicopters; 2 Ka-29RLD AEW helicopters; 2 Ka-27PS Helix-C SAR helicopters
A: 12 P-700 Granit (SS-N-19 Shipwreck) SSM; 24 Kinzhal (SA-N-9) VLS SAM syst. (192 9M-330 Gauntlet missiles); 8 Kortik CIWS (256 tot. 9M-311/SA-N-11 Grison missiles, plus 2 single 30-mm gatling AA per mount); 6 single 30-mm 54-cal. AK-630 gatling AA; 2 10-round RPK-5 Liven' (UDAV-1) ASW/antitorpedo RL (60 tot. rockets)
Electronics:
Radar: 3 MR-212/201 Vaygach-U (Palm Frond) nav.; 2 MR-320M Topaz-M (Strut Pair) air search; 1 Mars-Passat (Sky Watch) 3-D early warning (nonoperational); 1 MR-710 Fregat-MA (Top Plate-B) 3-D air search; 4 MR-360 Podkat (Cross Sword) f.c.; 8 3P-87 (Hot Flash) f.c. (on Kortik mounts); 2 Fly Trap CAC
Sonar: MGK-365 Zvezda M-1 hull-mounted LF; MG-35 underwater telephone
TACAN: Cake Stand

Admiral Flota Sovetskogo Soyuza Kuznetsov (063)—at sea, with four Su-33 fighters and one Ka-27 helicopter on deck TASS, 2000

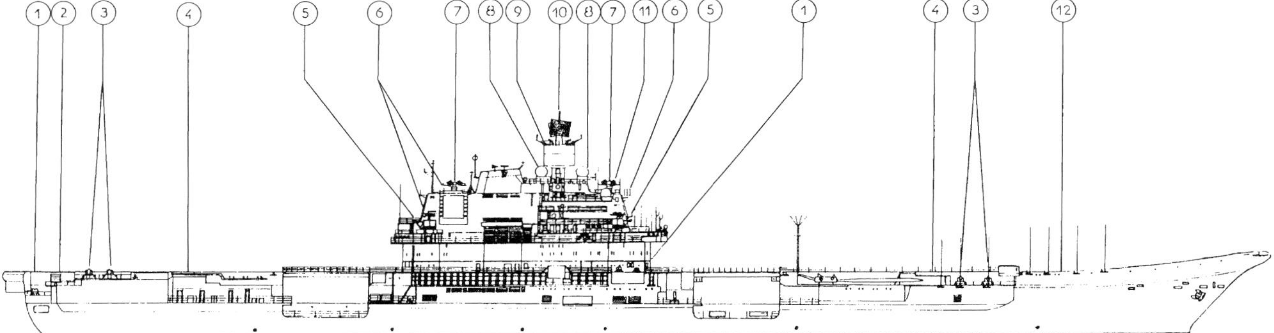

Admiral Flota Sovetskogo Soyuza Kuznetsov (063) 1. 30-mm AK-630M gatling AA 2. RPK-5 Liven' ASW RL 3. Kortik CIWS (with twin 30-mm gatling AA and 8 SAM rails per mount) 4. Kinzhal SAM system silos 5. MR-360 Podkat radar directors for the Kinzhal system 6. Mars-Passat early-warning radar arrays (nonoperational) 7. MR-320M Topaz-M surf./air-search radars 8. Low Ball SATCOM antenna radomes 9. Cake Stand TACAN antenna array 10. MR-710 Fregat-MA 3-D air-search radar 11. Punch Bowl radar surveillance datalink antenna radomes (nonoperational) 12. P-700 Granat antiship missile launchers (recessed into the flight deck)
Drawing by Lucien Gassier, from *Flottes de Combat*

GUIDED-MISSILE AIRCRAFT CARRIERS [CVG] *(continued)*

EW: Sozbezie-BR suite: 8 Wine Glass; 4 Flat Track, 8 Bell Push, and 4 Bell Nip intercept/jamming; 3 Cross Loop D/F; 2 twin PK-2 decoy RL; 10 fixed 10-round PK-10 decoy RL
E/O: 1 Bob Tail telescoping; 3 Tin Man t.v./IR/laser; 5 fixed t.v.; 4 optical periscopes; 4 or more Spektr-F (Half Cup) laser warning
M: 4 sets TV12-4 geared steam turbines; 4 props; 200,000 shp
Boilers: 8 KVG-4 turbopressurized, 64 kg/cm^2
Electric: 22,500 kw tot. (9 × 1,500-kw turboalternators, 6 × 1,500-kw diesel sets)
Range: 3,850/29; 8,500/18; 12,000/10 **Fuel:** 3,100 tons
Endurance: 45 days (provisions limited)
Crew: 518 officers, 1,442 enlisted ship's company + 626 air group + 40 flag staff

Remarks: Design began in 1974, with the ship intended primarily to carry interceptor fixed-wing aircraft with no ground or ship attack role. The original name was changed to *Leonid Brezhnev* 26-11-82, to *Tbilisi* 11-8-87, and for the third time 4-10-90. Deployed without an air group from the Black Sea bound for the Northern Fleet to serve as flagship 2-12-91. Deployed to the Mediterranean 12-95 to 3-96 with about 14 fixed-wing pilots. Refitted again at Rosta 7-96 to 1-7-98 and officially rejoined the Northern Fleet 3-11-98. Was briefly at sea during 6-99 to conduct carrier compatibility tests with the Sukhoi Su-27KUB two-seat trainer and again in 9-00. Entered overhaul in 2000 which was completed in late 2003. During post-overhaul sea trials in 10-03, she was damaged by a fire. Took part in Northern Fleet exercises in 8-05. During 9-05 conducted carrier qualification trials for her air wing in the North Atlantic losing one Su-33 plane in the process.

The second ship of the class (Project 1143.6), *Varyag,* also initially named *Riga,* was laid down 6-12-85 and launched 6-12-88. Fitting out had ceased by 11-92, and the ship was stricken 30-7-93. The largely stripped hulk was sold by Ukraine and left Mikolayiv 14-6-00 for China for scrapping; not until 4-11-01, however, was the tow permitted to pass through the Bosporus. The ship currently lies at Dalian Shipyard in China; her future is uncertain.

Hull systems: The propulsion plant is essentially a duplicate of that used in the *Kiev* class, with standard vertical turbopressurized boilers upgraded to produce up to 115 tons/hr of steam. There are 3,857 compartments within the hull and island. Has 27 decks from keel up. Trims down by the stern by about 2 m. Has the Kaskad automatic degaussing system.

Aviation systems: Is rated to carry a maximum of 52 aircraft (36 Su-33 fighters, 16 Ka-27 ASW helicopters, and 5 other helicopters), but the nominal actual combat air group is not large.

Flight deck area totals 14,700 m^2. The aircraft landing system employs four cross-deck wires spaced at 14-m intervals near the after end of the 220-m, 5.5°-angled deck, and aircraft are guided to the deck by an automatic radar-controlled landing system employing two Fly Trap-B microwave automatic landing control devices; there is also a Luna-3 mirror landing system. Aircraft take off up the 15° ramp from any of three detent positions (two with a 105-m run and one to port with a 195-m run), where they are held firmly in check until full engine afterburner thrust is developed. A great many objects protrude above the flight deck, including decoy rocket launchers, a fixed navigational light mast to starboard, and a number of firefighting foam cannon. There are but two aircraft elevators, 20 m long by 15 m wide and capable of lifting about 40 tons each. Belowdecks aircraft accommodations are limited by the 153-m-long by 26.0-m-wide by 7.2-m-high hangar and by the installation of 12 inclined launch tubes for antiship missiles that take up space that could have been employed for additional aircraft stowage; there are very few flight deck aircraft tiedown positions, and all aircraft are intended to be hangared. The hangar is equipped with four fore-and-aft tracks for maneuvering and securing aircraft. Carries 2,500 tons aviation fuel.

Combat systems: The heavy shipboard armament suite, aside from the dozen antiship missiles, is strictly for short-range self-defense. The six individual AK-630 gatling guns are controlled by the Kortik CIWS fire-control systems or by remote backup optical directors. In all, 24,000 rounds of 30-mm ammunition are carried for the AK-630 mounts and 48,000 rounds for the Kortik mountings. The SA-N-9 rotating silo launchers are arranged in groups of six, and the Kortik CIWS systems are paired to cover the four "corners" of the ship. The RPK-5 Liven ASW rocket launchers are installed aft, primarily as torpedo-countermeasures launchers.

The Mars-Passat (Sky Watch) four-panel fixed planar array three-dimensional air-search radar in *Kuznetsov* was not a success and is not operational. The communications suite is called Buran-2. Satellite communications antenna systems include two Low Ball communications arrays and two Punch Bowl over-the-horizon targeting data reception antennas, although the associated radar satellites are no longer operating. Navigation equipment includes Kurs-10A-1 and 10A-2 gyrocompasses; an ILE-1 electrodynamic log; a Beysur navigation system; an RYu-02 radionavigation aid; GEL-3, NEL-M1, and NEL-M2 echo sounders; and an AP-5 automatic plot.

Disposal note: The Modified *Kiev*-class (Project 11434) VTOL aircraft carrier, *Admiral Gorshkov* (ex-*Baku*), inoperable since 1991, was transferred to India 20-1-04 following more than a decade of negotiations. Delivery of the vessel to India is not expected until around 2008. Of the three aviation cruisers [CVHG] of the *Kiev* class, *Kiev* was stricken 31-8-94 and began a tow to China for scrapping 21-5-00. *Minsk* and *Novorossiysk* were stricken 30-7-93. *Novorossiysk* eventually was sold to an Indian breaker, while the stripped hulk of the *Minsk* was sold to a Chinese firm in 9-98 for use as a floating exhibition and theme park near Hong Kong.

MARITIME AVIATION (*Morskaya Aviatsiya*)

Naval aviation is an integral part of the Russian Navy. Organization and ranks are the same as those of the Russian Air Force. Current first-line active aircraft totals are estimated as follows: *fixed-wing:* about 50 Backfire bombers, including five for reconnaissance duties (not all are flyable), 29 Su-33 Flanker-D shipboard interceptors, 30 Su-24 Fencer-C and -D land-based strike fighters, 10 SU-25 Frogfoot ground attack, three Il-20 Coot-A and -B and seven An-12 Cub electronic surveillance, 28 Tu-142 Bear-F maritime reconnaissance and ASW, and 35 Il-18 May medium-range maritime reconnaissance and ASW; *helicopters:* 80 Ka-27PL Helix-A ASW (includes an unknown number of Ka-27PS Helix-D SAR/utility and Ka-27RTs targeting variant), two Ka-27RLD Helix aerial surveillance, 30 Ka-29TB Helix-B assault. There are also an unknown number of training and transport aircraft.

COMBAT AIRCRAFT

Note: In the following entries, the "operational radius" is roughly 60% of the maximum radius given by half of the range. The aircraft are arranged alphanumerically by design bureau designation.

Fixed-wing aircraft:

♦ Il-38 May antisubmarine patrol aircraft
Design Bureau: Ilyushin

Il-38 May maritime patrol aircraft 1994

IOC: 1969 **Wingspan:** 37.40 m **Length:** 39.60 m **Height:** 10.2 m
Weight: 33.70 tons empty (66.00 max.) **Wing area:** 140 m^2
Speed: 372 kts max. (354 cruise, 162–216 during patrol)
Engines: 4 Ivechenko AI-20M turboprops (4,250 shp each)
Ceiling: 26,000–33,000 ft. **Range:** 7,100 km ferry; 6,500 km normal patrol
Operational radius: 1,700 km (11 hr) **Fuel:** 35,153 liters (all internal)
Armament: 8,000 kg weapons, flares, and sonobuoys (2 AT-1 or AT-2 torpedoes and 10 PLAB-250-120 d.c. or 8 AMD-2-500 mines)
Avionics: TSV-264 (Wet Eye) surveillance radar, MAD boom, sonobuoy processor, etc.

Remarks: Development began in 1960, using the airframe from the Il-18D transport with the wings moved 3 m forward on the fuselage to offset the weight of the radar, additional fuel tanks, and the Berkut-38 combat system. Conducted first flight 27-9-61; entered service 17-1-69. Crew of seven. Znamya Truda (now MiG-MAPO) built 57 total, of which five were later sold to India.

Are equipped with the Put-4B-2K navigational aid system, AP-6E autopilot, and ARK-B radio compass. Sonobuoys carried normally include 144 RGB-1 passive nondirectional, 10 RGB-2 passive directional, and 3 RSB-3 active/passive. Takeoff distance is 1,200 m, landing distance 850 m.

The prototype Il-38N conversion update first flew early in 2001 and was to be equipped with a chin-mounted FLIR and a new EW intercept array mounted in a large pod on stilts atop the forward fuselage. The modernized aircraft carries the Novella combat data system in place of the original Berkut. Production modification Il-38N update aircraft would be flown until 2010–12.

♦ Su-24 Fencer maritime fighter-bomber
Design Bureau: Sukhoi-Beriev

IOC: 1985 **Wingspan:** 17.63 m (10.36 m fully swept) **Length:** 22.67 m
Height: 5.92 m **Weight:** 39,700 kg max. (35,910 normal)
Speed: 1,320 kts at sea level; 1,550 kts at 36,000 ft. (Mach 1.35)
Engines: 2 Lyulka AL-21F-3 turbojets (11,200 kg thrust each)
Ceiling: 36,000 ft. **Range:** 2,750 km ferry
Operational radius: 3,390 km low-low-low; 1,300 km high-low-high
Fuel: 9,850 kg internal; 14,900 kg with three external tanks **Crew:** 2
Armament: 4 Kh-25L, 3 Kh-29L/T, 2 Kh-31P, or 2 Kh-59 missiles or up to 8 tons KAB-500KR or KAB-1500L guided bombs; 1 23-mm cannon (500 rds)

Russian Navy Su-24 Fencer strike fighter—taking part in exercise BALTOPS 2003 U.S. Navy, 6-03

Remarks: Fencer-A, -B, and -D strike fighters were transferred from the Soviet Air Force in 1989–90 to avoid CFE limitations. Variable-geometry, swing-wing design (with four positions: 16°, 35°, 45°, and 69°). Takeoff run: up to 1,400 m from a concrete runway; landing run: 950 m.

♦ Su-25UTG Frogfoot shipboard trainer
Design Bureau: Sukhoi-Beriev

IOC: 1978 **Wingspan:** 14.36 m **Length:** 15.55 m
Weight: 12.7 tons max. **Speed:** Mach 0.8 (520 kts)
Engines: 2 Tumanskiy R-195 turbojets (4,500 kg thrust each)
Ceiling: 7,000 m **Operational radius:** 280 km (900 with four external tanks)

Remarks: A navalized carrier familiarization variant of the two-seat Su-28 Frogfoot trainer, the Su-25UTG, was tested aboard the carrier *Admiral Flota Sovetskogo Soyuza Kuznetsov* in 11-89. The 10 delivered in 1989–90 are now mostly nonoperational.

COMBAT AIRCRAFT *(continued)*

Su-25UTG Frogfoot shipboard trainer 1990

♦ Su-33 Flanker-D shipboard interceptors
Design Bureau: Sukhoi-Beriev

Su-33 Flanker-D shipboard fighter [no credit or date]

Wingspan: 14.70 m (10.00 folded) **Length:** 21.93 m **Height:** 5.90 m
Wing area: 62 m^2 **Speed:** Mach 2.35 (1,550 kts) max.; 702 kts at sea level
Engines: 2 Lyulka AL-31F turbofans (7,598 kg thrust each; 12,500 kg with afterburning)
Altitude: 56,000 ft. **Operational radius:** 1,500 km (4,000 max.)
Armament: 10 AA-10 Alamo and/or AA-11 Archer AAM (6,500 kg max.); 1 30-mm GSh-301 gatling gun (150 rds)
Avionics: Track-while-scan, look-down/shoot-down radar with 130-km range

Remarks: Design bureau designation is Su-27K. In addition to 20 production aircraft delivered 1993–95 (out of 24 originally ordered), five prototypes had been produced by end-1991, including a single side-by-side, Su-27IB two-seat trainer version. Shipboard acceptance trials for the production aircraft were conducted in 7-94.

The navalized Flanker has folding wings and an upward-folding radome for carrier stowage, canard winglets, a shorter "stinger" radome protruding from the aft end, a tailhook (which eliminates one stores position), upgraded engines, 10 tons of internal fuel capacity for 4,000-km ferry range, and aerial refueling capability. The Su-33 weighs 2,500 kg more than the land-based version of the aircraft in light condition. Landing speed is 240 kph. The folding portion of the wing was intended to have six stores positions. The Su-33 has been seen carrying the "ASM-MSS" air-to-ground missile, an apparent air-launched version of the SS-N-22.

♦ Tu-22M3 Backfire-C medium-range bomber
Design Bureau: Tupolev

Tu-22M3 Backfire-C bomber

IOC: 1984 **Wingspan:** 34.28 m (23.30 fully swept)
Length: 42.60 m **Height:** 11.60 m **Weight:** 124.0 tons max.
Speed: Mach 2.0 (2,000 kph) at 50,000 ft. max.; Mach 1.3 at 3,000 ft.
Engines: 2 Samara NK-25 turbojets (30,000-kg/245-kN thrust each)
Ceiling: 46,000 ft. service
Operational radius: (with/without refueling) 3,485/2,250 km supersonic, 6,300/5,320 km subsonic (6,000-kg load)
Fuel: 53.0 tons max. **Crew:** 4
Armament: 24,000-kg bombs; or 3 AS-4, 6 AS-6, or 6 AS-9 missiles; or mines; 2 23-mm cannon (twin)
Avionics: Down Beat navigation and bombing radar; optical bombsight; Fan Tail tailgun radar; ECM/ECCM suite

Remarks: Have variable-geometry swept wings, which sweep to three positions only: 20°, 30°, and 65°. The Backfire-C has raked engine air inlets and more powerful engines than the preceding Backfire-B, all of which are believed to have been retired from naval service. Naval aviation units carry no refueling probes, and very little flight time has been accomplished in recent years. Takeoff speed is 200 kts with a 2,000–2,100 m run; landing speed is 154 kts with a 1,200–1,300 m run at 88 tons landing weight. Cruising speed is said to be 486 kts. External weapons loads can consist of 2 FAB-3000, 8 FAB-1500, 42 FAB-500, or 69 FAB-250 or FAB-100 bombs or 8 1,500 kg or 18 500-kg mines.

♦ Tu-142M3 Bear-F maritime reconnaissance and ASW aircraft
Design Bureau: Tupolev

Tu-142 Bear-F ASW aircraft Werner Globke, 6-03

IOC: 1975 **Wingspan:** 51.10 m **Length:** 49.50 m **Height:** 12.12 m
Weight: 185 tons max. (91.8 empty) **Speed:** 462 kts (397 cruise)
Engines: 4 Kuznetsov NK-12MV turboprops (15,000 shp each); 4 8-bladed AV-60K counterrotating props
Ceiling: 36,000 ft. **Operational radius:** 4,000 km
Endurance: 16.75 hrs unrefueled **Fuel:** 86 tons
Armament: 2 23-mm cannon (twin); 9,000-kg (max.) torpedoes, air-dropped stores
Avionics: Wet Eye (Berkut or Korshun-K) surveillance radars; ECM/ECCM suite

Remarks: The Bear-F (Tu-142M) ASW patrol aircraft has also been exported to India. Length over the refueling probe is 53.088 m. The wings are swept at 33° 33′ and have an area of 289.9 m^2. Takeoff run at maximum load is 2,530 m. The current version of the Bear-F said to be able to find and track submarines operating 800 m below the surface; a crew of 10 can be carried. The surviving Tu-142M3 aircraft are planned to be retained until at least 2016. All Bear-J communications relay aircraft are believed to have been retired.

Helicopters:

♦ Ka-27PL Helix-A antisubmarine helicopter
Design Bureau: Kamov

Ka-27PL Helix shipboard ASW helicopter Leo van Ginderen, 6-05

IOC: 1982 **Rotor diameter:** 15.90 m **Length:** 11.30 m (12.23 rotors deployed)
Weight: 11,500 (Ka-32T: 12,600) kg max.
Speed: 143 kts (124 with 5,000-kg payload)

COMBAT AIRCRAFT *(continued)*

Engines: 2 Isotov TV3-117VK turboshafts (2,200 shp each) (Ka-28PL:TVZ-117MA, 2,350 shp each; Ka-29TB: TV3-117VK, 2,400 shp each; Ka-32: 2,225 shp each)
Ceiling: 2,950 m hovering; 6,000 m max. **Range:** 540 n.m. max.
Operational radius: 375 km (2.0–2.5 hr) (Ka-32: 800 km/4.5 hr)
Fuel: 3,270 liters (internal)
Armament: 800 kg max.: 2 ASW torpedoes or PLAB-250-120 d.c. or OMAB bombs; 2 UV-26 countermeasures dispensers (32 decoys each)—Ka-29TB: 1 7.62-mm gatling gun; 8 AT-6 Spiral antitank missiles; 2 80-mm rocket pods (20 each) or 57-mm rocket pods (32 each); 8–10 troops
Avionics: Osminog radar; VGS-3 Ros-V dipping sonar; NKV-252 navigation system; PKV-252 flight control system

Remarks: Prototype first flew in 12-74. Various versions, by maker's designation, have included the Ka-27L transport, Ka-27PL ASW (Helix-A), Ka-27PS utility (Helix-C), Ka-27PSD search and rescue (Helix-D), Ka-28 export version of Ka-27PL, Ka-29TB naval infantry transport (Helix-B), Ka-31 export aerial surveillance, Ka-32T civil transport/naval utility, and Ka-32S civilian search and rescue. The Ka-27PL can cover 1,200 km^2 of ocean during an operational sortie. Maximum payload is 800 kg and maximum endurance is 5.2 hours. Several Ka-27 airframes were equipped to provide targeting services for antiship missile–launching cruisers and destroyers and are designated Ka-27RTs. The Ka-27PS utility variant can carry 5,000 kg of cargo internally, while the Ka-27PSD SAR variant has a 300-kg electric hoist and carries 4,830 kg of internal fuel.

Ka-29TB Helix-B shipboard assault helicopter Rozvoorouzhenie, 1995

Ka-29RLD AEW helicopter prototype—with radar antenna deployed 1995

The Ka-29TB armed combat transport variant can carry 16 fully equipped troops or 10 stretchers. It is equipped with FLIR and low-light television sensors. The Ka-29TB has a maximum takeoff weight of 11,500 kg and a combat payload of 1,800 kg. Its ferry range is 740 km (with two 500-liter fuel tanks in the weapons bay in lieu of torpedoes) and maximum speed is 151 kts (130 cruise). Some 59 were built, but only about 16 remain in service.

SUBMARINES

NUCLEAR-POWERED BALLISTIC-MISSILE SUBMARINES [SSBN]

(RPKSN + Raketnyy Podvodnyy Kreyser Strategicheskogo Naznacheniya, or Strategic Missile Submarine Cruiser; formerly PLARB + Podvodnaya Lodka Atomnaya Raketnaya Ballisticheskaya, or Nuclear-Powered Ballistic-Missile Submarine)

♦ 0 (+ 3 + ?) Borey class (Project 955)

Bldr: Sevmashpredpriyatiye, Severodvinsk (Severodvinsk SY 402)

	Laid down	L	In serv.
K- . . . YURIY DOLGORUKIY (ex-*Sankt Petersburg*)	2-11-96	12-06	2007
K- . . . ALEKSANDER NEVSKY	19-3-04	2007	2008
K- . . . VLADIMIR MONOMACH	1-06	. . .	. . .

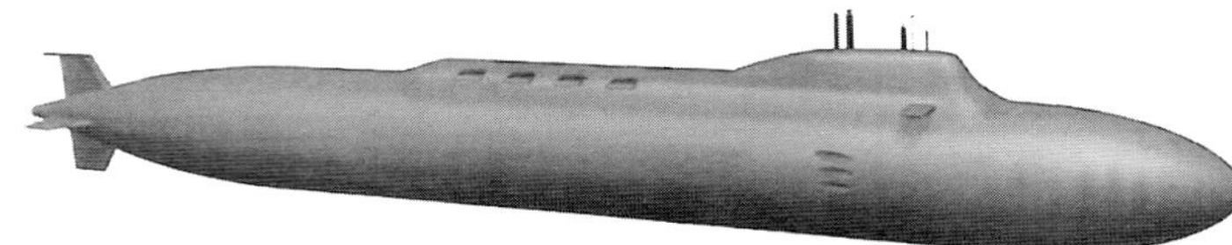

Borey class (Project 955), original configuration—artist's conjecture U.S. Navy, 1996

D: 14,720 tons surf./19,400 tons sub. **S:** 15 kts surf./29 kts sub.
Dim: 170.00 × 13.50 × 9.00
A: 12 SS-N-30 (Bulava) ballistic missiles; 4 533-mm TT (12 tot. UGST and SAET-60M torpedoes, Type 86R/SS-N-16 Stallion ASW missiles); 1 shoulder-launched SAM system (8 Igla-M missiles)
Electronics:
Radar: . . .
Sonar: MGK-540 Skat-3M suite with towed array
M: 2 OK-650B pressurized-water nuclear reactors (190 Mw each), 2 Type OK-9 steam turbines; 2 7-bladed props; 98,000 shp—2 500-shp d.c. electric emergency props
Electric: 7,400 kw tot. (2 × 3,200-kw turboalternators, 2 × 500-kw diesel sets)
Endurance: 100 days **Crew:** 55 officers, 52 enlisted

Remarks: Program commenced in 1982 under chief designer Vladimir N. Zdornov of the Rubin Central Naval Technology Design Bureau (TsKB-18). The original reported project nickname, Grom ("Thunder"), was applied to the missile system. The overall project name is Borey ("Cold Northern Wind"). The first unit is named for the founder of Moscow, "George Long-Arm." Was to have been the 1,001st submarine built in Russia since the Soviet Revolution of 1917. However, was only 2–3% complete as of mid-1998, by which time construction had halted. The associated SS-N-28 Grom missile program was canceled early in 1998, and the design of the submarine had to be recast to accommodate the new, smaller Bulava missile. Russian plans call for up to 12 of the class to enter service by 2021.
Hull systems: Diving depth: 380 m normal, 450 m maximum operational. A detachable crew rescue chamber is built into the central portion of the sail. The hullform incorporates a Double Hogner stern, as in the Delta-IV SSBNs and the retired Papa-class SSGN. The overall design was very conservative and appears to have evolved from that of Project 667BDRM (the Delta-IV class).
Combat systems: Was to have had the Omnibus combat direction system, the Molnaya-M communications suite, and the Medveditsa-M navigation systems suite. The planned SS-N-28 Grom ballistic missile, an improved version of the SS-N-20, is to be replaced by the smaller Bulava, a submerged launch–capable variant of the SS-25 Topol-M (NATO SS-25 Sickle).

♦ 6 Delta-IV (Del'fin) class (Project 667BDRM)

(1 *out of service/in refit*)
Bldr: Sevmashpredpriyatiye, Severodvinsk (Severodvinsk SY 402)

	Laid down	L	Del.	In serv.	Fleet
827 K-51 VERKHOTUR'E (ex-*Imeni XXVI Sezda KPSS*)	23-2-81	2-84	28-12-84	29-12-85	Northern
807 K-84 YEKATERINBURG	17-2-82	1-85	30-12-85	7-87	Northern
805 K-114 TULA	3-84	3-12-86	14-11-87	22-4-88	Northern
820 *K-117 BRYANSK*	3-85	12-87	17-10-88	3-90	Northern
839 K-18 KARELIYA	7-2-86	3-2-89	17-6-89	11-10-89	Northern
849 K-407 NOVOMOSKOVSK	3-87	14-2-90	30-12-90	20-2-92	Northern

Kareliya (K-18) Boris Lemachko, 7-99

Kareliya (K-18) at left, Verkhotur'e (K-51) at right Boris Lemachko, 8-00

NUCLEAR-POWERED BALLISTIC-MISSILE SUBMARINES [SSBN] *(continued)*

Delta-IV-class (Project 667BDRM) SSBN Boris Lemachko, 7-00

D: 11,740 tons surf./15,500 tons sub. **S:** 14 kts surf./24 kts sub.
Dim: 167.00 (158.0 wl) × 12.20 × 8.80
A: 16 R-29RM (SS-N-23 Skiff) ballistic missiles; 4 bow 533-mm TT (12 torpedoes and/or Type 83RN and 84RN/SS-N-15 Starfish missiles)
Electronics:
Radar: 1 Albatros'-series (Snoop Tray) nav./surface search
Sonar: MGK-500-series Skat-BDRM (Shark Gill) LF active/passive suite; MGK-519 active mine-avoidance; Pelamida towed passive array; MG-512 cavitation monitor; MG-518 upward-looking echo sounder; MG-519 mine detection; MG-533 sound-velocity measurement; NOR-1 active ice-lane detector; NOK-1 active surface warning
EW: MRP-10 Zaliv-P (Brick Pulp) intercept; Park Lamp D/F
E/O: Cod Eye radiometric sextant; 2 periscopes
M: 2 VM-4SG pressurized-water nuclear reactors (90 Mw each), 2 sets Type OK-700A geared steam turbines; 2 5-bladed props; 60,000 shp—2 306-shp electric low-speed motors
Electric: 6,920 kw tot. (2 × 3,000-kw turbogenerators; 2 × 460-kw diesel sets)
Endurance: 80 days **Crew:** 41 officers, 94 enlisted

Remarks: The ultimate expansion of the original Yankee (Project 667A) design. All are in the Northern Fleet, based at Gadshievo, on the Olen'ya Guba. At least two additional units were being built when production was halted by order of former President Yeltsin. Designed at TsKB Rubin under S. N. Kovalev. On 7-12-89, K-84 attempted to launch 16 missiles in succession while in the White Sea; the third launch failed and 13 of the crew were injured, apparently by the falling missile. One unit was damaged 20-3-93 in a collision with the U.S. submarine *Grayling.* K-407 was employed to launch a commercial-configured RSM-54 missile with a German Tubsat-M telecommunications satellite on 8-7-98. The service life of this class is approx. at 20–30 years. All are assigned to the 13th Division in the Northern Fleet.

A number of the class are undergoing refits and modernizations, though these may not include refueling for budgetary reasons. K-51 was refitted from 1993 to 12-99 at Zvezdochka Verf, Severodvinsk, and is expected to operate through 2007. K-84, out of service since 1996, completed a refueling refit at Zvezdochka on 16-4-02, with the submarine entering service in 2003 following a 5-02 relaunch. K-114 and K-117 started refit at Severodvinsk in 12-04 followed by K-18 in 2005, with refit of K-114 completed by 10-05. K-117 and K-18 are expected back in service by 2007. K-407 had completed refit at Zvezdochka with another scheduled to follow in 2008.

K-18 was named in 8-96, K-114 was named on 12-10-97, K-407 was renamed on 17-9-97, and K-51 and K-84 were renamed during 4-99.

K-18 successfully launched two missiles 12-9-00, although no new/rotation missiles may have been loaded on any Russian SSBN since 2-99, when all shoreside missile-handling cranes were declared unsafe.

Hull systems: The design was initially distinguishable from the Delta-III class by markedly fewer limber holes at the base of the missile tube "hump," the presence of a towed passive hydrophone array dispenser tube atop rudder, and, on K-51 only, a pyramidal housing at the aft end of the missile turtledeck; many of the surviving Delta-IIIs, however, have now been backfitted with towed array fittings, and some had the limber hole openings covered in the missile bay area. Capable of operating under the Arctic ice pack and breaking through to launch weapons. Normal operating depth: 380 m; maximum: 450 m. Have bow and stern side-thrusters. May have a detachable crew escape chamber abaft the missile tubes. Hull beam also reported as 12.2 m, surfaced displacement as 9,210 tons, and submerged displacement as 11,740 tons. Although the class is usually said to have seven-bladed propellers, *Yekaterinburg* had two very conventional five-bladed screws when photographed at Severodvinsk as of 5-02.

Combat systems: The ballistic-missile launch complex is known as D-9RM. Have a Pert Spring antenna for the Tsunami SATCOM system, a Tobol-M navigational system, and the Molnaya-M communications suite. The missiles are launched while the submarine is at 55-m depth, traveling at up to 6 kts. All missiles now employ four warheads. Were to have been adapted to launch the since-canceled SS-N-28 Grom ballistic missile.

Disposals: The unnamed K-64, the third Delta-IV completed, was declared for scrap during 2-01.

♦ 3 Typhoon (Akula) class (Projects 941 and 941U*)
(1 *nonoperational*)
Bldr: Sevmashpredpriyatiye, Severodvinsk (Severodvinsk SY 402)

	Laid down	L	In serv.	Fleet
834 TK-208 DMITRIY DONSKOY*	30-6-76	27-9-80	27-12-81	Northern
818 *TK-17 ARCHANGEL'SK*	24-2-85	12-12-86	15-12-87	Northern
806 TK-20 SEVERSTAL'	6-1-86	7-88	4-9-89	Northern

Two Project 941 Typhoon-class SSBNs at their Northern Fleet base Boris Lemachko

Typhoon-class SSBN *Ships of the World*

D: 23,200 tons surf./33,800 tons sub. (see Remarks)
S: 12 kts surf./25 kts sub. **Dim:** 172.8 (165.0 wl) × 23.2 × 11.5

NUCLEAR-POWERED BALLISTIC-MISSILE SUBMARINES [SSBN] *(continued)*

A: TK-20: 20 R-39 (SS-N-20 Sturgeon) ballistic missiles—TK-208: provision for 20 Bulava-30 ballistic missiles—all: 6 bow 533-mm TT (22 Type 53-65K, SET-65, and SAET-60M torpedoes and Type 83RN and 84RN/SS-N-15 Starfish missiles); 1 shoulder-launched SAM syst. (8 Igla-M missiles)
Electronics:
Radar: 1 Albatros'-series (Snoop Pair) nav./search
Sonar: Skat-series (Shark Gill) LF active/passive suite; MG-519 Alfa active mine avoidance; MG-518 Sever echo sounder
EW: Nakat-M (Rim Hat) intercept (on Tobol mast); Park Lamp D/F
E/O: Cod Eye radiometric sextant; 2 periscopes
M: 2 OK-650 pressurized-water nuclear reactors (190 Mw each), 2 sets steam turbines; 2 shrouded 7-bladed props; 100,000 shp—2 516-shp low-speed electric motors on main shafts; 2 1,020-shp drop-down emergency propulsors (bow and stern)
Electric: 14,300 kw tot. (4 × 3,200-kw turbogenerators, 2 × 750-kw diesel sets)
Endurance: 120 days **Crew:** 52 officers, 85 warrant officers, 42 enlisted

Remarks: Submarine class code name is Akula ("Shark") in Russia; Tayfun is the overall project code name for the submarine *and* its missiles. Designed at TsKB Rubin, St. Petersburg, under Sergei N. Kovalev. These are the world's largest submarines by a considerable margin, intended to operate beneath the Arctic ice pack, breaking through to launch missiles.

The first built, TK-208 (named during 10-00), commenced modernization and refueling at Severodvinsk in 10-90 to carry the since-canceled SS-N-28 Grom missile; she has instead been fitted to carry the smaller Bulava-30 missile. She was "relaunched" on 26-6-02 and began Bulava missile testing on 30-6-02. She will be unavailable for operational deployment until 2006–7, at which time Bulava testing will have been completed. As of 2006, TK-20 was undergoing overhaul with TK-17 (currently in reserve) to follow upon completion. Plans call for both to be fitted with the Bulava SLBM system.

Hull systems: Maximum safe diving depth is 400 m. The volume within the outer hull and appendages is 49,800 m^3. Surfaced displacement has also been reported as being 28,500 tons. Design incorporates two parallel 8.5-m-diameter (6.0 forward) pressure hulls within the outer hull, with the massive sail being an additional pressure vessel; another pressure vessel centerline forward accommodates the torpedo tubes, while a fifth, small one is located centerline at the stern for the rudder and stern-plane machinery. There are 19 watertight compartments. Flanking the sail are two cylindrical crew escape modules. Hull has massive bilge keels to reduce rolling, an unusual feature in a modern submarine. On TK-208 only, abaft the communications buoy hatches were pyramidal protrusions that probably served as flow trim devices; these may now have been removed. Telescoping masts from fore to aft include two periscopes, radio sextant, radar, radio, and D/F. Officers live in two- and four-man cabins, and crew amenities include a gymnasium, solarium, swimming pool, sauna, and pet facilities.

TK-208 was fitted with what appeared to be Kort-nozzle-mounted harbor maneuvering propellers mounted at the ends of the stern planes when rolled out in 6-02; the top of the lower rudder, both ends of each of the moving portions of the stern planes, and the fixed ends of the stern planes had been fitted with flow plates, and six-bladed, highly-skewed propellers had been fitted.

Combat systems: The forward location of the missile tubes between two parallel pressure hulls is unique. All have two large hatches abaft the sail for deploying towed communications buoys. The Rim Hat EW intercept array surrounds the base of the back-to-back radar antenna, which also has a directional EW mode. Have the Tobol-941 navigation system. The ballistic-missile launch complex in TK-20, in which the missiles are suspended from rings around their upper ends, is known as D-19; all missiles now carry 10 warheads. The solid-fueled R-39 missiles employ liquid-fuel thrusters for in-flight course correction. The torpedo tubes are arranged two abreast and three high, above the bow active/passive sonar array; they are stated to be able to launch mines, and one official source indicates that at least two are of 650-mm diameter. Have the Molnaya-L1 communications suite (with Tsunami SATCOM) and Symfoniya navigational suite. The MTK-100 underwater television system is fitted. Were all to have been adapted to launch the now-canceled SS-N-28 Grom ballistic missile. In 5-04 it was reported that the TK-20 carried a rationed 10 rather than the full load of 20 SLBMs.

Disposals: The incomplete TK-210 was broken up on the ways in 1990. TK-202 and TK-12 (the second and third built) were discarded 31-7-96 for lack of funds to refit them; with U.S. financial and technical assistance, TK-202 began scrapping in 1999. TK-13, inactive since 1998 (and previously reported as TK-17), began scrapping late in 8-01. TK-12 was stricken in 1998 and had been scrapped at Zvezdochka by 2004.

♦ 7 Delta-III (Kal'mar) class (Project 667BDR)

Bldr: Sevmashpredpriyatiye, Severodvinsk (Severodvinsk SY 402)

	Laid down	L	In serv.	Fleet
915 K-487 Podol'sk	4-75	4-77	25-12-77	Northern
864 K-496 Borisoglebsk	7-75	8-77	28-10-78	Pacific
912 K-506 Zelenograd	11-75	12-77	8-12-78	Pacific
. . . K-223 Kizlovodsk	2-77	4-79	3-12-79	Pacific
938 K-180 Petropavlovsk-Kamshatskiy	8-77	1-80	2-12-80	Northern
993 K-433 Svyotoy Giorgiy Pobedonosets	8-78	6-80	19-12-80	Pacific
862 K-44 Ryazan	6-79	1-82	14-12-82	Northern

Delta-III class (Project 667BDR) JMSDF via *Ships of the World,* 2005

Delta-III class (Project 667BDR) JMSDF via *Ships of the World,* 2005

Delta-III class (Project 667BDR) Boris Lemachko, 2-01

D: 10,600 tons surf./13,050 tons sub. **S:** 14 kts surf./24 kts sub.
Dim: 155.00 × 11.70 × 8.70
A: 16 R-29DU (SS-N-18 Stingray) SLBM; 4 533-mm bow TT (12 torpedoes and/or Type 83RN and 84RN/SS-N-15 Starfish missiles); 2 402-mm OTA-40 bow TT (4 MG-14 or MG-44 active decoys)
Electronics:
Radar: 1 MRK-50-series (Snoop Tray) nav./search
Sonar: MGK-400 Rubikon LF active/passive suite; MGK-519 active mine avoidance; Pelamida towed passive array in some; MG-512 cavitation monitor; MG-518 upward-looking echo sounder; MG-533 sound-velocity measurement; NOR-1 active ice-lane detector; NOK-1 active surface warning
EW: MRP-10 Zaliv-P (Brick Pulp) intercept; Park Lamp D/F
E/O: Cod Eye radiometric sextant; 2 periscopes
M: 2 VM-4S pressurized-water nuclear reactors (89.2 Mw each), 2 Type OK-700A steam turbines; 2 5-bladed props; 52,000 shp—2 306-shp electric low-speed motors on main shafts
Electric: 6,920 kw tot. (2 × 3,000-kw a.c. alternators, 2 × 460-kw diesel sets)
Endurance: 80 days **Crew:** 40 officers, 90 enlisted

Remarks: Survivors of 18 completed. All Pacific Fleet ballistic-missile submarines were named on 1-7-98, but the following names have not yet been correlated to the K-series hull numbers: *Dmitrov, Krasnogorsk, Noginsk, Serpukhov,* and *Voskresensk.* K-44 was named on 19-3-98 and K-496 on 11-1-99. K-496 was the submarine from which a failed launch attempt to place a solar monitoring satellite in orbit occurred during 7-01. A press report on 19-7-99 stated that only one or two of the Pacific Fleet units, all of which are based at Petropavlovsk-na-Kamchatskiy, could go to sea. K-487 launched an exercise missile on 18-9-01. According to a 23-4-99 statement by Russian Navy C-in-C Fleet Admiral Kuroyedov, all Pacific Fleet units were to be retired by 2005, but during 7-99, he said that all surviving units of the class were to be extended in service indefinitely. On 12-7-02, K-44 launched a Volna booster missile with a "Demonstrator-2" inflatable space station payload recovery system. K-433 underwent refit from 2-93 to 8-03 at Zvezda. K-44 and K-180 are based at Saida Guba in the Northern Fleet; the remaining five at Tarya Bay in the Pacific. K-44 began a refit at Zvezdochka shipyard in Severodvinsk during late 2005.

Hull systems: Has a higher turtledeck than the Delta-II to accommodate longer ballistic-missile tubes. The pressure hull is 9.8 m in diameter, has 211 external frames, and has 11 watertight compartments; the missile compartment is 45 m long. Height from keel to top of sail is 17.65 m. Primary ship's service electric power is delivered at 380 V/50 Hz. Test diving depth is 580 m, normal operating depth 320 m. The bow-planes rotate to vertical in order to facilitate breaking through ice; the submarines normally break through up to 0.9 m of ice but can surface through 1.8 m ice in an emergency. Have bow and stern side-thrusters. Crew amenities include a gymnasium and solarium.

Combat systems: The Molnaya-M communications suite incorporates towed VLF communications buoys and a Pert Spring antenna for the Tsunami SATCOM system, and there is a towed communications buoy stowed beneath a hatch just abaft the missile tubes. The navigational suite is known as Tobol-M. Were being backfitted with towed passive linear sonar arrays, as on the Delta-IV class, from which they were becoming difficult to distinguish, but the updating program has probably ended. Some are fitted with the MGK-400 Rubikon active sonar. The ballistic-missile launch complex is known as D-9R. The surviving units were to have been adapted to launch the now-canceled SS-N-28 Grom ballistic missile. All remaining R-29DU missiles employ three warheads.

Disposals: K-424, the class prototype, was stricken in 1996, along with the second unit, K-441 (named *Imeni XXVI Sezda K.P.S.S.* until 8-92). Three more Pacific Fleet units had been stricken by 1998. Northern Fleet unit K-129, the 13th unit of the class, which had suffered bow damage in a collision in 1993 and was reported to have been stricken 1-9-95, was instead converted to a submersible tender, relaunched 29-12-00 and returned to service in 2003 and is due to replace the Yankee Stretch–class mothership submarine for the Paltus submersible. Pacific Fleet units K-211 and K-498 have been laid up in reserve since 2001 and are unlikely to see further service.

Disposal note: The four Delta-II (Murena-M)-class (Project 667BD) ballistic-missile submarines (K-182, K-92, K-193, and K-421) were discarded from the Northern Fleet 31-7-96. K-421 began scrappng at Zvezdochka Verf, Severodvinsk, during 2-00.

Of the 18 units of the Delta-I (Murena) class (Project 667B), class prototype K-279 was stricken 24-1-91; Pacific Fleet unit K-477 on 5-7-94; Northern Fleet units K-450, K-385, K-453, K-460, K-472, and K-475 and Pacific Fleet units K-171, K-417, K-497, K-512, and K-523 on 31-3-95; and Northern Fleet units K-447 and K-457 in 1998. Pacific Fleet K-500 (ex-*60 Letiye Velikogo Oktyabrya*) and K-530 were reportedly still in commission as of 8-00, but all Delta-I SSBNs were to have been retired by the end of 2001.

NUCLEAR-POWERED CRUISE-MISSILE ATTACK SUBMARINES [SSGN]

(PLARK + Podvodnaya Lodka Atomnaya Raketnaya Krylataya, or Nuclear-Powered Cruise-Missile Submarine)

♦ 9 (+ 1) Oscar-II (Antey-II) class (Project 949A) (1 in *reserve*)

Bldr: Sevmashpredpriyatiye, Severodvinsk (Severodvinsk SY 402)

	Laid down	L	In serv.	Fleet
929 K-132 Irkutsk	1983	1986	1-87	Pacific
812 K-119 Voronezh	25-2-86	1987	29-12-89	Northern
919 *K-173 Krasnoyarsk*	4-8-83	1987	30-12-88	Pacific
816 K-410 Smolensk	9-12-86	1988	28-12-90	Northern
904 K-442 Chelyabinsk	21-5-87	1989	28-12-90	Pacific
920 K-456 Vilyuchinsk (ex-*Kasatka*)	9-2-88	1990	18-8-92	Pacific
847 K-266 Orël (ex-*Severodvinsk*)	19-1-89	22-5-92	30-12-92	Northern
947 K-186 Omsk	13-7-89	8-5-93	10-12-93	Pacific
902 K-150 Tomsk	21-8-91	18-7-96	30-12-96	Pacific
. . . K-135 Volgograd	2-9-93	. . .	. . .	. . .

Irkutsk (K-132) JMSDF, 11-01

D: 14,700 tons surf./19,400 tons sub. **S:** 15 kts surf./31 kts sub.
Dim: 154.0 × 18.2 (20.1 over stern planes) × 9.2
A: 24 P-700 Granit (SS-N-19) SSM; 4 bow 533-mm and 4 bow 650-mm TT (24 Type 86R and/or 88R/SS-N-16 Stallion and Type 83RN and 84RN/SS-N-15 Starfish missiles and/or 65-76, USET-80, and Shkval torpedoes, and 4 MG-14 or MG-44 programmable torpedo decoys)
Electronics:
Radar: 1 Albatros'-series (Snoop Pair) nav./search
Sonar: MGK-540 Skat-3 (Shark Gill) LF active/passive suite; Pelamida towed passive array; MG-512 cavitation monitor; MG-518 upward-looking echo sounder; MG-519 active mine detection; MG-533 sound-velocity measurement; NOR-1 ice-lane detector; NOK-1 surface warning
EW: Bald Head intercept; . . . D/F
M: 2 OK-650B pressurized-water reactors (190 Mw each), 2 sets Type OK-9 steam turbines; 2 7-bladed props; 98,000 shp—2 electric low-speed motors for speeds up to 5 kts
Electric: 6,780 kw tot. (2 × 3,200-kw turboalternators, 2 × 190-kw diesel sets)
Endurance: 120 days **Crew:** 52 officers, 55 enlisted

Remarks: Type designation: *Atomnie Podvodnie Kreysery 1 Ranga* (Nuclear-Powered Submarine Cruiser, 1st Class). Lengthened version of the Oscar-I, on which design development began in 1967 at the Rubin Design Bureau under P. O. Pustyntsev (later I. L. Baranov). There were originally to have been 20 units. Work on *Belgorod* ceased around 1994 but resumed during 9-00 as a replacement for the lost *Kursk*. A 13th unit, to have been named *Pskov,* was canceled in 1996, although the ship was "dedicated" in 5-96 and was probably partially assembled.

K-456 was renamed on 4-5-97. K-150 transited under the polar icecap to the Pacific Fleet, arriving at Petropavlovsk-na-Kamchatskiy 24-9-98. K-132 and K-173, the latter out of service since 1995, were laid up with skeleton crews awaiting funding for recoring and refit; K-132 began a minor refit near Vladivostok during 12-01.

Hull systems: The enveloped volume submerged displacement is 23,860 tons. The missile tubes provide a 3.5-m standoff between the outer hull and pressure hull. Maximum operational diving depth is 500 m. There are 10 watertight compartments within the pressure hull. All machinery employs two-stage sound isolation mountings. Crew amenities include a gymnasium, solarium, swimming pool, sauna, and pet facilities. The additional length over that of the two stricken Project 949 Oscar-I-class units is employed for combat data systems and improved degaussing systems.

Combat systems: The missile tubes are arranged in two rows of 12 flanking the pressure hull and fixed at an elevation of about 40°; six doors cover each row of 12. To achieve their maximum combat usefulness, the submarines were intended to employ their Punch Bowl antennas to receive radar satellite targeting data from a system that never went into service, but they can employ ELINT-derived target data from satellites of the Legend system, whose final satellite was launched 21-12-01. They also have a Pert Spring antenna for the Molnaya-M SATCOM system. The 650-mm torpedo tubes may be used to launch the RPK-7 Veter (or Vodopad-MK) system's Type 88R antisubmarine missiles. All have a towed linear passive hydrophone array, with the cable deploying from the top of the vertical stabilizer at the stern. A towed VLF communications buoy is housed in the hump abaft the sail; it is deployed via a double-doored 7.5 × 2.5-m hatch. The integrated navigational system is termed Symfoniya-U, and the communications suite designation is Tsunami. The "Rim Hat" EW intercept array surrounds the base of the search radar radome.

Losses and disposals: The newest Northern Fleet unit, *Kursk* (K-141), sank on 12-8-00 in the Barents Sea after a Type 65-76A exercise torpedo exploded, with the loss of 118 crew. The submarine had made a cruise to the Mediterranean in the fall of 1999. In the fall of 2001, the Dutch Mammoet-Smit consortium raised all but the bow of the submarine. The following summer the Russian Navy raised the remaining bow portion of the submarine, which was scrapped following an inspection. *Krasnodor* (K-148) was decommissioned during 2002. Though 80% complete, *Belgorod* (K-139) was canceled during 7-06. Funding will instead be used to overhaul several surface warships.

Yankee-Notch-class (Project 667AT) strategic cruise missile submarine K-395 was stricken during 2004. Modified Charlie-II (Skat-M/Project 0674040) cruise-missile trials submarine *Novogord Velikiy* (B-452; ex-*Berkut,* K-452), retained in commission in reserve for more than five years, was to have been retired "by 2002"; the submarine had been reconfigured to launch the Oniks (Yakhont) supersonic antiship cruise missile, but it is unclear whether any at-sea launches were ever carried out. The other five units of the Charlie-III class were discarded 1992–95: B-458 (in serv. 29-12-75), B-479 (in serv. 29-9-77), B-503 (in serv. 31-12-78), B-508 (in serv. 15-3-80), and B-209 (in serv. 31-12-80 and stricken 1-9-95).

Oscar-I (Antey)-class (Project 949) units *Arkhangel'sk* (K-525) and *Murmansk* (K-206, ex-*Minskiy Komsomolets*) were stricken 7-11-99 and 7-1-98, respectively. Although the pair's impending scrapping was announced in 11-98, work did not begin on defueling the *Murmansk* until 20-7-01.

The inactive, experimental Yankee Sidecar–class (Project 667) cruise-missile submarine KS-420 was decommissioned during 2002.

The single Papa-class (Project 661) nuclear-powered cruise-missile submarine, K-162, was decommissioned during 1991 and is stored at Severodvinsk, officially in reserve. The world's fastest submarine, K-162 achieved a sustained speed of 44.9 kts during trials on the power from two 88.7-Mw reactors.

Of the 11 Charlie-I (Skat)-class (Project 670) cruise-missile submarines, K-429 sank 1-6-83 in the Pacific and was subsequently raised, but sank again 13-8-85 and was not returned to service; another, leased to India 5-1-88 for three years under the name *Chakra,* was returned to the Soviet Pacific Fleet in 1-91 and was discarded; Pacific Fleet units B-201 and B-320 were stricken 5-7-94; and the last to be retired, B-212, was stricken from the Pacific Fleet 1-9-95.

Echo-II-class cruise-missile submarine *Krasnogardets* (B-222) was refitted during 2002 for use as a museum exhibit; the reactor is still aboard.

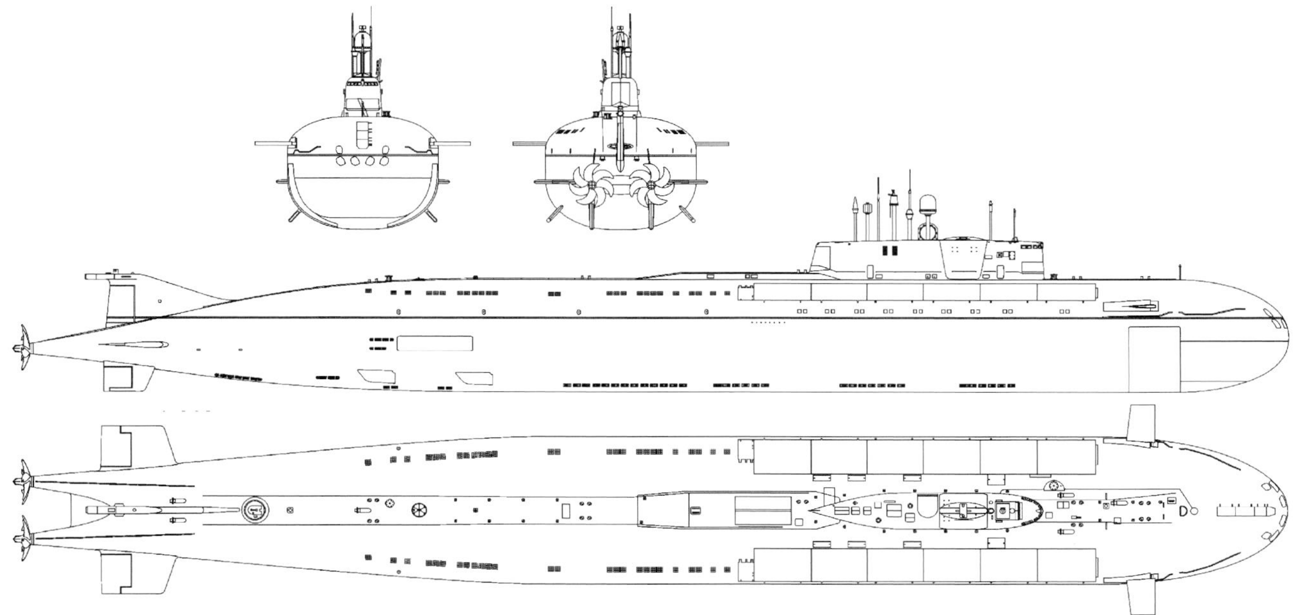

Oscar-II Class Drawing by T. Grotnik, 2001

NUCLEAR-POWERED ATTACK SUBMARINES [SSN]

(PLA + Podvodnaya Lodka Atomnaya, or Nuclear-Powered Submarine)

♦ 0 (+ 1 + 2) Severodvinsk (Yasen') class (Project 885)

Bldr: Sevmashpredpriyatiye, Severodvinsk (Severodvinsk SY 199)

	Laid down	L	In serv.
K-329 Severodvinsk	21-12-93	2006	2007

Severodvinsk (Project 885)—artist's conjecture, showing a bow-mounted Irtysh-Amfora sonar array, amidships torpedo tubes, and standard propeller at the stern
U.S. Navy, 1996

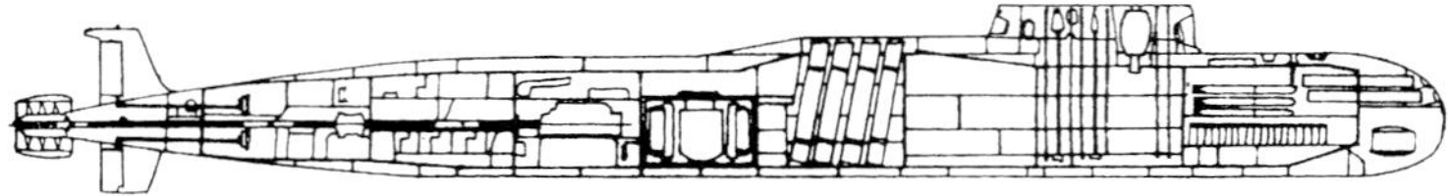

Severodvinsk (Project 885)—internal arrangement drawing, showing older-type cylindrical sonar array beneath bow-mounted torpedo tubes and a pump-jet propulsor aft; note also the slightly angled missile tubes abaft the sail
A.S. Pavlov, *Voennie Korabli Rossie,* 1997–98

D: 9,500 tons surf./11,800 tons sub. **S:** 16 kts surf./31 kts sub.
Dim: 120.00 × 15.0 × 10.0
A: 6 multipurpose inclined launch tubes (up to 24 Oniks antiship missiles); 10 533-mm TT (32 tot. Type 83RN and 84RN/SS-N-15 Starfish missiles, USET-80 and UGST torpedoes, MDM-6 and MShM mines, etc.)
Electronics:
Radar: 1 MRK-50 Albatros'-series (Snoop Pair) nav./search
Sonar: Irtysh-Amfora system, with bow-mounted spherical active/passive array or Skat-3 syst. with cylindrical bow array; active arrays; flank array; towed linear passive array
EW: . . . intercept syst.; 6 533-mm external bow tubes for 12 MG-104 and/or MG-114 programmable torpedo decoys (2 per tube)
M: 1 OK-650KPM pressurized-water nuclear reactor (200 Mw), 2 sets steam turbines; 1 pump-jet prop; 50,000 shp
Electric: . . . tot. (2 × . . . turboalternators, 1 × 700-kw diesel set, 1 × 300-kw diesel set)
Endurance: 100 days **Crew:** 32 officers, 53 enlisted

Remarks: A total of seven was reportedly planned. Work on the first, which was ordered 22-1-93, had halted as of 2-11-96; at that time, only fabrication of the sternmost third of the hull had been accomplished. The Russian Navy C-in-C, however, claimed during 2001 that work was still under way on the *Severodvinsk.* Designed by Malakhit Central Design Bureau 16 (TsKB-16) under V. N. Pyalov. Crew was originally to have been 22 officers and 28 enlisted, indicating that some planned degree of automation was later sacrificed.
Hull systems: Propulsion plant is said to be substantially the same as in the Project 971 (Akula SSN) submarines but was probably to have had enhanced noise-reduction features. One published Russian report stated in 4-96 that the submarine would have a maximum speed between 35 and 40 kts and a maximum quiet-operating speed of 20 kts (implying that the quiet-operating speed of the previous Akula series is less than that). The normal maximum operating depth was to be 520 m, with a maximum of 600 m.
Combat systems: Speculation as to what might be carried in the vertical launch tubes includes possible stowage of the Novator Al'fa (SS-N-27) antiship cruise missile, although it can also be accommodated by normal 533-mm torpedo tubes, or the supersonic, ramjet-propelled Yakhont export antiship missile system (domestic nickname: Oniks), a competitor to the Al'fa.
The expected Irtysh-Amfora bow sonar array was thought to resemble the array of the U.S. BQQ-2, in which a spherical active/passive array is flanked by passive receiving hydrophone arrays, but a drawing of the ship published in 1996 showed a standard Russian-style cylindrical bow array (the system dubbed Skat-3) with the torpedo tubes above it. Resource constraints may have forced Russia to abandon the more complex spherical array, which is installed in Yankee Big-Nose trials submarine *Kazan* (KS-403). Locating a spherical sonar array at the bow requires the torpedo tubes to be relocated farther aft, angled outboard, as in U.S. submarine designs since the late 1950s; if the design has been altered to employ a cylindrical array, however, then the tubes will likely have been relocated at the bow. Was to have been fitted with the Medveditsa-M navigation suite and the Paravan towed communications buoy.

♦ 2 (+ 2) Akula-II class (Project 0971A)

Bldr: Sevmashpredpriyatiye, Severodvinsk (Shipyard 402)

	Laid down	L	In serv.	Fleet
890 K-157 Vepr'	13-7-90	10-12-94	25-11-95	Northern
835 K-335 Gepard	23-9-91	18-9-99	4-12-01	Northern
. . . K-337 Kuguar	1992	22-1-98	. . .	Northern
. . . K-333 Rys'	1994	6-10-98	. . .	. . .

Vepr' (K-157) Bernard Prézelin, 9-04

D: 9,830 tons surf./ . . . tons sub. **S:** 10 kts surf./33–35 kts sub.
Dim: 114.30 × 13.60 (15.40 over stern planes) × 9.68
A: 4 bow 650-mm TT (Type 86R and 88R/SS-N-16 Stallion missiles and/or Type 65-76 or UGST torpedoes); 4 bow 533-mm TT (Type 83RN and 84RN/SS-N-15 Starfish and RPK-55 Granat/SS-N-21 Sampson missiles; USET-80 torpedoes; mines); 1 shoulder-launched SAM syst. (18 Strela-2M or Igla-M missiles)

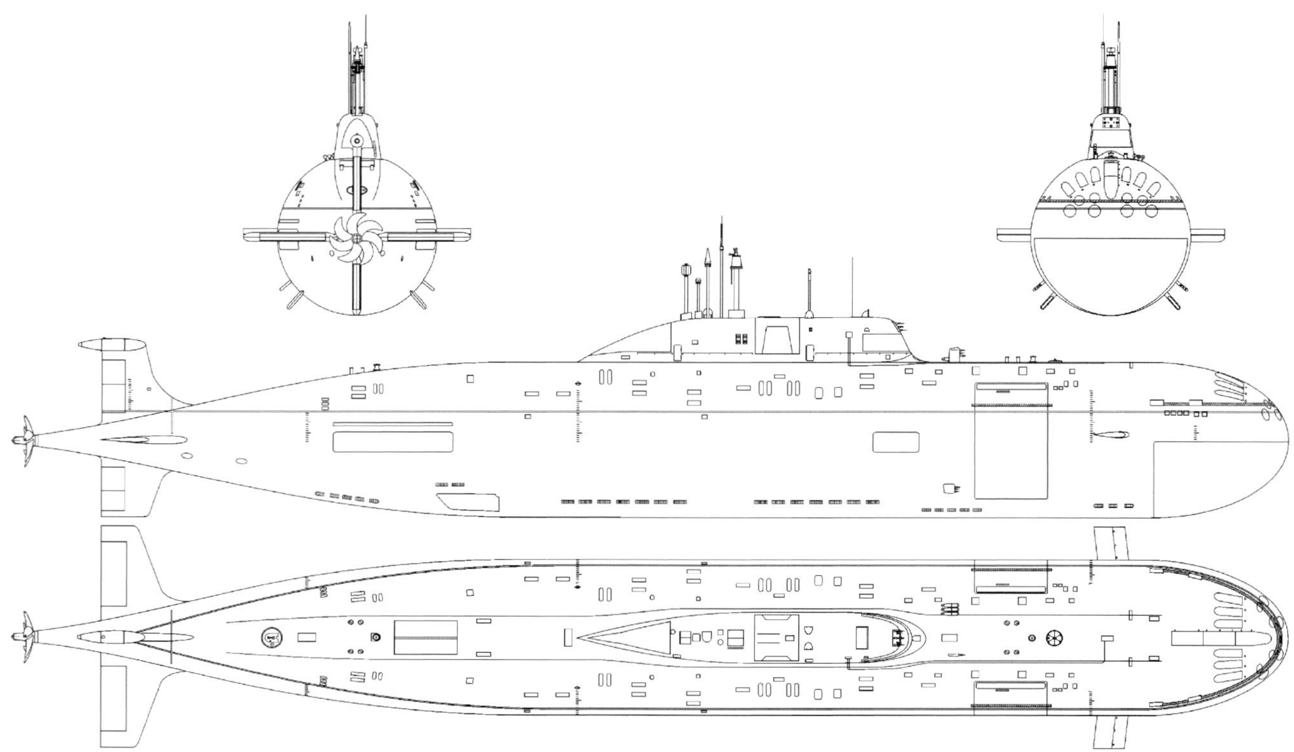

Akula-II class Gepard (K-335)—This unit is not fitted with a towed array pod atop the vertical stabilizer. Instead the sail is elongated to accommodate a towed array winch
Drawing by T. Grotnik, 2002

NUCLEAR-POWERED ATTACK SUBMARINES [SSN] *(continued)*

Vepr' (K-157) Bernard Prézelin, 9-04

Electronics:
Radar: 1 MRK-50 Albatros'-series (Snoop Pair) nav./search
Sonar: MGK-540 Skat-3 (Shark Gill) suite: MGK-503 LF active/passive; large-aperture passive flank array; MG-519 HF mine-avoidance; large-aperture towed passive LF linear hydrophone array
EW: Amber Light intercept; Rim Hat intercept; Park Lamp D/F; 6 533-mm external bow tubes for 12 MG-104 and/or MG-114 programmable torpedo decoys (2 per tube)
M: 1 OK-9BM pressurized-water nuclear reactor (190 Mw), steam turbines; 1 7-bladed prop; 47,600 shp—2 410-shp dc electric low-speed motors (3–4 kts)
Electric: 1,500 kw (2 × 750-kw diesel emergency sets)
Endurance: 100 days **Crew:** 31 officers, 22 enlisted

Remarks: Designed by Firma Malakhit, St. Petersburg, under G. N. Chernishov. The lengthened Akula-II class incorporates further quieting measures and a greater degree of automation over the Improved Akula-I (Project 971U). Work on K-335 (with reactor installed and fueled and a crew assigned since 1998), K-337, and K-333 at Severodvinsk had ceased by early 1997, but construction on the then-80%-complete K-335 was restarted in 9-97, builder's trials began 15-9-00, and acceptance trials started 7-12-00. K-333 and K-337 were offered to India in 2004 on a five-year lease, though transfer of the boats has not yet occurred and Akula-I may be transferred instead. A fifth unit of the class was canceled. K-337 and K-333 are expected to complete once funding becomes available. *Vepr'* translates as "wild boar," *Gepard* as "cheetah," and *Kuguar* as "cougar."
Hull systems: Enveloped volume submerged displacement for the Akula-II version is 12,770 tons. K-157 appears to be about 4 m longer than the Akula-I series between the after edge of the sail and the towed communications buoy hatch; with the additional length being in the engineering area abaft the probable reactor spaces, it is most likely associated with further quieting measures in the main engine suspension system. See also the hull systems remarks under the Akula-I class.
Combat systems: Have nonacoustic submarine detection system arrays mounted on the forward edge of the sail and on the casing forward of the sail. K-335 lacks the towed array pod atop the vertical stabilizer at the stern (the towed array is streamed from a small tube at the top of the vertical stabilizer, with the winch and drum relocated within the lengthened sail). A total of 40 torpedo tube–launched weapons can be carried. See also the combat systems remarks under the Akula-I class.

♦ 11 (+ 2) Akula-I (Shchuka-B) class (Projects 971 and 971U*) (2 *nonoperational*)

Bldrs: A: Zavod imeni Leninskiy Komsomol (Shipyard 199), Komsomol'skna-Amur; B: Sevmashpredpriyatiye, Severodvinsk (Shipyard 402)

	Bldr	Laid down	L	In serv.	Fleet
974 K-263 Barnaul Del'fin	A	1981	15-7-84	12-85	Pacific
985 *K-322 Kashalot*	A	1982	1985	1986	Pacific
990 K-391 Bratsk (ex-*Kit*)	A	1982	1985	1987	Pacific
997 K-331 Magdan (ex-*Navral*, ex-*Rys*')*	A	1983	1986	1989	Pacific
860 K-480 Ak-Bars (ex-*Kazan*, ex-*Bars*)	B	22-2-85	16-4-88	29-12-88	Northern
878 K-317 Pantera	B	6-11-86	11-3-90	27-12-90	Northern
867 K-461 Volk*	B	14-11-87	11-6-91	29-12-91	Northern
951 K-419 Kuzbass (ex-*Morzh*)*	A	1984	11-6-91	1992	Pacific
872 K-328 Leopard*	B	26-10-88	28-6-92	30-12-92	Northern
853 K-154 Tigr ("Tiger")*	B	10-9-89	26-6-93	5-1-94	Northern
970 *K-267 Samara* (ex-*Drakon*)*	A	1985	15-7-94	28-7-95	Pacific
. . . K-152 Nerpa*	A	1986	. . .	2007	Pacific
. . . K- . . . Kaban *	A	1992	. . .	. . .	Pacific

Akula-I-class (Project 971)—note the nonacoustic ASW sensors on the casing forward of the sail U.S. Navy, 1994

Improved Akula-I class (Project 971U)—note the covers over the decoy launching tubes, three on either side of the torpedo-loading hatch fairing at the bow M.O.D. U.K., via Norman Polmar, 1994

D: 8,140 tons surf./ . . . tons sub. **S:** 10 kts surf./33–35 kts sub.
Dim: 110.30 × 13.60 (15.40 over stern planes) × 9.68
A: 4 bow 650-mm TT (Type 86R and 88R/SS-N-16 Stallion missiles and/or Type 65-76 torpedoes); 4 bow 533-mm TT (Type 83RN and 84RN/SS-N-15 Starfish and RKP-55 Granat/SS-N-21 Sampson missiles; USET-80 torpedoes; mines); 1 shoulder-launched SAM syst. (18 Strela-2M or Igla-M missiles)
Electronics:
Radar: 1 MRK-50 Albatros'-series (Snoop Pair) nav./search
Sonar: MGK-540 Skat-3 (Shark Gill) suite: MGK-503 LF active/passive; . . . passive flank array; MG-519 HF active mine avoidance; . . . large-aperture towed passive LF linear hydrophone array
EW: Amber Light intercept; Rim Hat intercept; Park Lamp D/F—K-317 and later: 6 533-mm external tubes for MG-104 and MG-114 programmable torpedo decoys (2 per tube)
M: 1 OK-9BM pressurized-water nuclear reactor (190 Mw), steam turbines; 1 7-bladed prop; 47,600 shp—2 410-shp dc electric low-speed motors (3–4 kts)
Electric: 1,500 kw (2 × 750-kw diesel emergency sets)
Endurance: 100 days **Crew:** 33 officers, 40 enlisted

Remarks: Designed by Firma Malakhit, St. Petersburg, under G. N. Chernishov. In 8-98, the local government of Samara pledged funds for the completion of K-267, which although delivered in late 1995 had not yet been fully paid for; in return for a 2-year sponsorship, the boat was renamed *Samara.* K-154 was in refit at Sevmashpredpriyatiye from 1997 to 2003. K-322 had been laid up by the end of 1998 for lack of funds to recore her. The crew of K-331 has requested yet another renaming, to *Magadan.* K-317 began a refit at Sevmashpredpriyatiye late in 2001 for completion in 2006, allowing the submarine to operate for an additional 5–8 years. K-263 and K-331 were renamed during 2004–5. K-480 has been in reserve since 1998 while K-322 and K-263 have been non-operational since 2002, all are three are awaiting overhaul.

Komsomol'sk-built units are all to the original design. K-331 and later Severodvinsk-built units have significant sound quieting improvements over the earlier boats and are referred to by NATO as the Improved Akula-I class and in Russia as Project 971U. Two Improved Akula-I units laid down in 1986 and 1987 remain incomplete within the building hall at Komsomol'sk, with K-152 82% finished and having already had the reactor installed and fueled and *Kaban* about 25% complete; work had ceased around 9-95 on both due to lack of payments. During 1-00, however, the government provided funds for further work on K-152.

Though initially rejected by India, negotiations on the lease of two submarines were soon renewed between the two nations due to slippages in development and construction of the Indian ATV program. Reports during early 2006 indicate that Russia has agreed to lease India the two incomplete Improved Akula-I Class SSN's

NUCLEAR-POWERED ATTACK SUBMARINES [SSN] *(continued)*

(or Akula-IIs according to some reports) for 10 years at a cost of US$25 million a year per ship with a later option to purchase the boats outright. Initial outlays required by the Indian Navy may be as high as US$1.0 billion for the completion of construction and training of crews for two SSNs.

Hull systems: Akulas differ in appearance from the Sierras in having a longer, much more streamlined sail. They also have a steel pressure hull vice titanium on the Sierra. A detachable crew-escape compartment is located within the sail. Maximum operating depth is 520 m, with normal operating depth of 400–450 m and crush depth reported as 900 m. Sound-quieting measures on all include double isolation of mechanical noise sources; all machinery is mounted on isolated foundations which are in turn mounted on rafts isolated from the inner hull structure by rubber pneumatic blocks. There are six main watertight compartments and four internal decks in the ship control space area (Compartment II) and auxiliary machinery spaces (Compartment III). The propulsion plant includes four steam generators, with two circulating pumps for the first and fourth loops and three pumps for the third; the steam turbine plant includes two a.c. turboalternators, each with two feed and two condensor pumps. Sufficient diesel fuel is available to operate the two diesel generator sets for 10 days. There are two electric battery groups. Class prototype K-284 had a 190-Mw OK-650M.01 reactor.

Combat systems: The combat system is named Omnibus and the navigation suite Medveditsa-971. The Snoop Pair radar and Rim Hat intercept array are on the same telescoping mast, with the Rim Hat array surrounding the base of the radar antenna. All have a pod-mounted towed linear hydrophone array dispenser atop the vertical stabilizer. A total of 40 torpedo tube–launched weapons can be carried. K-419 and later units have six external horizontal tubes flanking the loading hatch atop the pressure hull at the bow; each tube holds two programmable torpedo decoys. The earlier units probably carry up to four decoys internally in lieu of weapons. All are said to be able to accommodate 28 RPK-55 Granat strategic cruise missiles, a subsonic weapon with a 200-kT nuclear warhead that was supposed to have been placed in land storage after an agreement with the U.S.A. in 1991.

All but K-284 have nonacoustic submarine detection system arrays mounted on the forward edge of the sail and on the casing forward of the sail. The sonar hydrophone array includes a massive active/passive cylindrical bow array beneath the torpedo tubes, large rectangular conformal arrays on either side of the hull forward of the sail, a smaller linear flank array on either beam between the sail and the stern, passive arrays on the forward and after edges of the sail, an active array in the sail, and a towed passive linear array housed in the pod atop the vertical fin at the stern. The Molnaya-M communications suite includes a towed antenna buoy. Have a Pert Spring SATCOM antenna. K-284 and K-322 lack hydroacoustic countermeasures systems.

Disposals: The unnamed class prototype K-284, commissioned in the Pacific Fleet only on 31-12-88 after a protracted series of trials, was reportedly stricken in 12-95; the hulk remains afloat, and plans to repair, refuel, and reactivate the submarine were announced during 2002, though funding shortages may make this goal impossible.

♦ 2 Sierra-II (Kondor) class (Project 945A)

Bldr: Krasnoye Sormovo Zavod 112, Nizhniy Novgorod

	Laid down	L	In serv.	Fleet
602 K-534 Nizhniy Novgorod (ex-*Zubatka*)	6-86	6-88	28-12-90	Northern
663 K-336 Pskov (ex-*Okun'*)	5-90	6-92	12-8-93	Northern

Pskov (K-336) TASS, 2000

Nizhniy Novgorod (K-534)—note the large, broad-topped sail with sensor masts offset to starboard and nonacoustic ASW sensors on projection to starboard at the fore end of the sail M.O.D. U.K., 1992

D: 6,470 tons surf. /8,500 tons sub. **S:** 12 kts surf. /33.6 kts sub.
Dim: 110.50 × 12.22 (16.50 over horizontal stabilizers) × 9.40
A: 6 533-mm bow TT (40 Type 83RN and 84RN/SS-N-15 Starfish ASW missiles; VA-111 Shkval rocket torpedoes; USET-80 torpedoes; or up to 42 mines in lieu of other weapons); 1 shoulder-launched SAM syst. (8 Strela-2M or Igla-M missiles)
Electronics:
Radar: 1 MRK-50 Albatros'-series (Snoop Pair) nav./search
Sonar: MGK-540 Skat-3 (Shark Gill) LF suite; passive flank arrays; MG-519 active HF mine avoidance; large-aperture towed passive hydrophone array
EW: Rim Hat intercept; Park Lamp D/F
M: 1 pressurized-water OK-650B nuclear reactor (190 Mw), 1 steam turbine; 1 7-bladed prop; 48,000 shp—2 496-shp auxiliary propulsion motors—2 185-shp retractable electric maneuvering propulsors
Electric: 4,700 kw tot. (2 × 1,600-kw turboalternators, 2 × 750-kw diesel generator sets)
Endurance: 100 days **Crew:** 32 officers, 29 enlisted

Remarks: Designed by Lazurit Central Design Bureau 112. Both are in the Northern Fleet, with K-336 based at Ara Guba and K-534 at Litsa Guba. Nonoperational since 6-97, K-534 began overhaul and recoring during 2003. The incomplete hull of K-536, a modified Project 945B (Project Mars) variant, was canceled during 7-92 and scrapped in 1993.

Hull systems: Have seven watertight compartments in the pressure hull, vice six in the earlier Sierra-I (Project 945), to incorporate improved sound quieting and crew amenities. The Sierra-II is 5 m longer than the Sierra-I and has a 6-m-longer sail that is also broader, with a conspicuously blunt forward edge; the Sierra-II sail has the telescoping masts mounted on the starboard side, while the port side appears to incorporate two detachable crew buoyant rescue chambers. Like Sierra-I, Sierra-IIs have titanium pressure hulls. Maximum depth: 600 m; normal operating depth: 520 m. The propulsion plant includes four steam generators, with two circulating pumps for the first and fourth loops and three pumps for the third; the steam turbine plant includes two a.c. turboalternators, each with two feed and two condensor pumps. Sufficient diesel fuel is available to operate the two diesel generator sets for 10 days. There are two electric battery groups. Two retractable underhull maneuvering propulsors are fitted.

Combat systems: Two additional 533-mm torpedo tubes were added to the original design, in part to be able to launch the Granat (SS-N-21) strategic cruise missile but also because the larger bow cylindrical sonar array precluded installation of 650-mm tubes. The sonar suite includes the passive cylindrical bow array, three active planar arrays (two flank, one in the sail), and large vertical Shark Rib flank arrays. In addition to the hydroacoustic arrays, also carry a nonacoustic antisubmarine sensor system incorporating some 12 probes, nine on the forward edge of the sail and three on a protrusion to starboard from the forward end of the sail. The combat system is called Omnibus, the communications suite Molnaya-MTs, and the navgation suite Symfoniya.

♦ 2 Sierra-I (Barrakuda) class (Project 945) (1 in *reserve*)

Bldr: Krasnoye Sormovo Zavod 112, Nizhniy Novgorod

	Laid down	L	In serv.	Fleet
648 *K-239 Kostroma* (ex-*Karp*)	8-5-82	29-7-83	21-9-84	Northern
622 K-276 Krab	8-83	4-84	9-87	Northern

Sierra-I class (Project 945) Norwegian Air Force

D: 6,300 tons surf./8,300 tons sub. **S:** 12 kts surf./33.6 kts sub.
Dim: 107.00 × 12.22 (16.50 over stern stabilizers) × 8.80
A: 2 bow 650-mm and 4 bow 533-mm TT (40 Type 83RN and 84RN/SS-N-15 Starfish and Type 86R and 88R/SS-N-16 Stallion ASW missiles; VA-111 Shkval rocket torpedoes; and/or USET-80 and 65-76 torpedoes; or up to 42 mines in lieu of other weapons)
Electronics:
Radar: 1 MRK-50 Albatros'-series (Snoop Pair) nav./search
Sonar: MGK-503 Skat-KS (Shark Gill) suite; Paravan towed passive hydrophone array
EW: Rim Hat intercept, Park Lamp D/F
M: 1 OK-650A pressurized-water nuclear reactor (180 Mw), 1 steam turbine; 1 7-bladed prop; 43,000 shp—2 496-shp auxiliary propulsion motors
Electric: 3,800 kw tot. (2 × 1,600-kw turboalternators; 2 × 300-kw diesel generator sets, 750-bhp diesels driving)
Endurance: 90 days **Crew:** 31 officers, 28 warrant officers

Remarks: Design initiated 3-72 at TsKB-122 Lazarit Design Bureau under N. I. Kvash. The submarines were transferred via river/canal system to Severodvinsk for final fitting out. K-239, renamed during 1996, was in a collision with the U.S. submarine *Baton Rouge* 11-2-92 and has been laid up at Ara Guba since 1998 awaiting funding for a recoring overhaul.

Hull systems: Sierras differ from Akulas in having a significantly blunter sail shape, although the Sierra-I has a smaller and more streamlined sail than does the later Sierra-II. K-239 has a low extension to the after end of the sail not found on the K-276. Normal operating depth is 480 m, maximum 550 m. The propulsion plant includes four steam generators, each with two circulating pumps for the first and fourth loops and three pumps for the third; the steam turbine plant includes two a.c. turboalternators, each with two feed and two condensor pumps. Sufficient diesel fuel is available to operate the two diesel generator sets for 10 days. There are two electric battery groups. Maximum speed is also reported to be 35.5 kts. They probably do not have the crew escape pod system incorporated in the later Sierra-II pair.

NUCLEAR-POWERED ATTACK SUBMARINES [SSN] *(continued)*

The titanium pressure hull has a yield strength of 70–72 kg/mm^2, a hemispheric end cap, and six watertight compartments. The use of titanium for the pressure hull was intended to reduce the magnetic signature and to permit a lighter, river-transportable submarine. A solid-fuel pyrotechnic gas generator system can be used to blow the two main ballast tanks in an emergency.
Combat systems: Carry environmental sensors on the sail for nonacoustic submarine detection and are equipped with a mast-mounted Pert Spring communications satellite antenna. The combat system is called Omnibus, the communications suite Molnaya-MTs, and the navigation suite Symfoniya. Are not equipped with a portable SAM system like the later Sierra-II.

♦ 5 Victor-III class (Project 671RTMK/671.7) (1 in *refit*)
Bldr: Admiralteiskiye Verfi 194, St. Petersburg

	Laid down	L	In serv.
667 *K-292 Perm*	15-4-86	29-4-87	27-11-87
654 K-388 Petrozavodsk	8-5-87	3-6-88	30-11-88
618 K-138 Obninsk	7-12-88	5-8-89	10-5-90
671 K-414 Daniil Moskovskiy	1-12-88	31-8-90	30-12-90
661 K-448 Tambov'	31-1-91	17-10-91	24-9-92

Victor-III class (Project 671RTMK)—at Severodvinsk Boris Lemachko, 8-99

Victor-III class—note the slab-sided outer hull casing amidships and the several missing anechoic tiles Boris Lemachko, 2-01

D: 4,950 tons light surf.; 6,990 tons normal surf./ 7,250 tons sub.
S: 11.6 kts surf./31 kts sub.
Dim: 107.20 × 10.78 (16.48 over stern planes) × 7.90 (fwd; 7.80 aft)
A: 2 bow 650-mm TT (8 Type 88R/SS-N-16 Stallion missiles and/or Type 65-76 torpedoes); 4 bow 533-mm TT (16 Type 82RN and 84RN/SS-N-15 Starfish and Type 53-65K and USET-80 torpedoes, VA-111 Shkval rocket torpedoes, MG-74 Korund and Siren decoys, or up to 36 mines)
Electronics:
Radar: 1 MRK-50 Albatros'-series (Snoop Tray-2) nav./search
Sonar: MGK-503 Skat-KS (Shark Gill) suite: LF active/passive; passive flank array; Barrakuda towed passive linear array; MT-70 active ice avoidance (see remarks)
EW: MRP-10 Zaliv-P/Buleva (Brick Pulp) intercept; Park Lamp D/F
M: 2 VM-4P pressurized-water nuclear reactors (75 Mw each), 2 sets OK-300 steam turbines; 1 7-bladed prop; 31,000 shp at 290 shaft rpm—2 low-speed electric cruise motors; 2 small props on stern planes; 1,020 shp at 500 rpm
Electric: 4,460 kw tot. (2 × 2,000-kw, 380-V, 50-Hz a.c. OK-2 turbogenerators, 1 × 460-kw diesel emergency set)
Endurance: 80 days **Crew:** 27 officers, 34 warrant officers, 35 enlisted

Remarks: Survivors of 26 Project 671–series units; as of 7-00, four were active in the Northern Fleet and none in the Pacific, where the one remaining unit, K-292, was laid up at Strelok. Project 671RTM was approved in 6-75. Launchings resumed at St. Petersburg in 7-85 with the 22nd Project 671 unit, modified as Project 671RTMK (or 671.7) to enable launching Granat strategic cruise missiles. Hull number prefixes were originally "B," but were changed to "K" on 29-8-91 when the class was redesignated Large Nuclear-Powered Submarines, First Rank. A Northern Fleet unit of this class suffered a gas leak accident in 1-98, killing the commanding officer and injuring four enlisted personnel. K-448 was named on 10-4-95. Northern Fleet unit K-388 conducted trials in carrying commercial cargo in the Arctic region in 1995. K-292 began an overhaul in 2004.

Hull systems: Pressure hull is fabricated from AK-29 steel. Initially employed an unusual eight-bladed propeller, consisting of two tandem four-bladed props oriented 22.5° apart and co-rotating; all survivors have a standard seven-bladed prop. Diving depth is 400 m normal/600 m maximum operational. Are more highly automated than earlier versions of the Victor series, permitting smaller crews, although complements have grown as new systems have been added. There are two 112-cell battery groups with 8,000 Amp-hr capacity. Reserve buoyancy is 28%.
Combat systems: The late-construction Project 671RTMK Victor-IIIs employed the Varyag command system, which has four computers, four command consoles, three combat data consoles, three sonar operator consoles, and three weapons/countermeasures consoles; they were the only units equipped to launch the RPK-55 Granat (SS-N-21 Sampson) strategic cruise missile, now no longer in service. One periscope is Type PZKG-10. The ASW missile system is known as the RPK-6 Vodopad or RPK-7 Veter, depending on whether 533-mm-diameter Type 86R or 650-mm Type 88R missiles are carried (presumably, both can be). VA-111 Shkval rocket-powered torpedoes, with nuclear warheads, were meant as "revenge" weapons against submarines that had fired on Soviet boats and are probably no longer carried, since tactical nuclear weapons were removed from Russian warships in 1991. Torpedoes can be launched at depths up to 250 m.

The standard communications suite is the Molnaya-L, with Kiparis, Anis, and Sintez antennas and the Paravan towed VLF wire antenna, which is deployed from the casing abaft the sail. The Tsunami-B SATCOM system (with Pert Spring antenna) is fitted to all. The navigation suite is designated Medveditsa-671RTM.

The Project 671RTMK units have Skat-series sonar suites with the Barrakuda LF active/passive bow array (with a nominal range of 230 km), Akula flank arrays, Chanel passive sonar intercept, a passive ranging array, the Pithon towed array (with towing winch and cable reel housed in the 7.8-m-long by 2.2-m-diameter fairing atop the vertical stabilizer aft), an active HF fire-control set, a mine-avoidance active set, and an underwater telephone. Also carried on a few is a nonacoustic wake-sensing system with sensors mounted on the starboard side of the sail.
Disposals: Among the 21 Project 671RTM units deactivated and/or stricken due to the lack of overhaul and recoring funds were K-182 (stricken 31-7-96); K-218, *50 Let Komsomol'skiy na Amur* (K-242) (stricken 30-5-98); K-251 (stricken 30-5-98); K-254, K-298, K-305 (stricken 30-5-98); K-324, K-355 (stricken 30-5-98); K-358 (ex-*Murmanskiy Komsomolets*), K-360 (stricken 30-5-98); K-412, K-492 (stricken 31-7-96); K-507 (stricken 30-5-98); K 524 (ex-*60 Let Sheftstva V.L.K.S.M.*); and K-527. *Volgograd* (K-502) has been retired by 2006.

ATTACK SUBMARINES [SS]
(PL = Podvodnaya Lodka, or Submarine)

♦ 1 (+ 2 + ?) Lada class (Projects 677 and 677E*)
Bldr: Admiralteiskiye Verfi 194, St. Petersburg

	Laid down	L	In serv.
B-100 Sankt Peterburg	26-12-97	26-10-04	2006
B- . . . Kronshtadt	27-7-05	. . .	. . .
B . . . Petrozavodsk	2006	. . .	. . .

Sankt Peterburg (B-100) *Ships of the World,* 2005

Lada class (Project 677) Firma Rubin

D: 1,765 tons surf. normal/2,700 tons sub. **S:** 11 kts surf./22 kts sub.
Dim: 67.00 × 7.20 × 4.40
A: 6 bow 533-mm TT (18 tot. P-10 Biyuza antiship missiles, Type 91RE1 Klub ASW missiles, SET-80 torpedoes, VA-111 Shkval rocket torpedoes, or up to 22 DM-1 and/or RM-2G mines)

Electronics:
Radar: 1 . . . nav./search
Sonar: Lira suite: bow active; bow and flank passive; towed linear passive array; active bow mine-avoidance set; passive rangefinding array; self-noise measurement
EW: . . . intercept

ATTACK SUBMARINES [SS] *(continued)*

Sankt Peterburg (B-100) *Ships of the World,* 2005

M: 2 Type 2D-42-series diesel generator sets, 1 2,000-kw electric motor generator; 1 7-bladed prop; 2,700 shp—possible Kristal-27E fuel-cell auxiliary propulsion syst.; 400 shp
Range: 6,000/. . . snorkel; 650/3 sub. **Endurance:** 50 days
Crew: 41 tot.

Remarks: B-100 was ordered in 8-97 for the Russian Navy, while a similar Project 677E (Amur 1650) unit was financed as an export demonstrator by the Korskaya Tekhika financial consortium (Rubin Design Bureau, Admiralty Shipyard, National Reserve Bank, Amur Shipyard, Zvezdochka State Engineering Co., the Ministry of Defense First Central Research Institute, and Rosvoorouszhenie, the state military export firm). Both units are versions of the Rubin Central Design Bureau's Amur 1650, on which design work began in 1989. Project Amur is available in versions from 550 to 2,000 tons surfaced displacement (see table below). A second unit was laid down during 12-97, but will reportedly be sold to a foreign customer.
Hull systems: Modern Russia's first single-hulled submarine, the Lada is a conservative design, with sail-mounted bow planes and cruciform stern control surfaces. Intended to operate 10 years between overhauls. Two battery groups. Said to be "8–10 times" quieter than the Project 877 Kilo and will have an anechoic hull coating. To use brushless generators to reduce noise. Will have an inertial navigational system. Crew figure given is with three-section watch; with a two-section watch, the crew can be reduced to 34. Accommodations are in separate cabins. All waste products will be retained aboard until return to port. Normal operating depth limit is 200 m, with 250-m maximum. The proposed air-independent propulsion system would use two vertical cryogenic pressure containers, one for hydrogen and one for oxygen; it is uncertain whether it will be aboard B-100.
Combat systems: The attack periscope is to have night-vision features and a laser rangefinder. The search periscope will be non-hull-penetrating. Will have a trailing-wire communications antenna. The radar and intercept antennas will be on the same mast, and the radar will have a low-power mode for concealed operations.
Variants offered: Amur 1450, the export variant about which most information has been published (as it would be expected to offer the greatest chance for foreign purchase interest), would have one 2,000-kw electric motor developing 2,700 shp, a range of 4,000 n.m. on snorkel and 300 n.m. at 3 kts submerged, and an endurance of 30 days and carry a crew of 34–41. The Amur 1850 variant would have more battery capacity than the Amur 1450 and a more powerful electric motor; its endurance would also be extended. The Amur 1650 variant announced in 1997 appears to have been tailored to Indian requirements. Basic data for the variants offered to date include:

Amur variant	*550*	*750*	*950*	*1450*	*1650*	*1850*
Displacement (m^3)						
Normal surfaced	550	750	950	1,450	1,765	1,850
Full, submerged	700	900	1,300	2,100	2,300	2,600
Length (m)	46	48	56	58	67	68
Beam (m)	4.4	5.0	5.6	7.2	7.1	7.2
Normal depth (m)	200	200	250	250	250	250
Armament						
Tubes/dia. (mm)	4/400	4/400	4/533	6/533	6/533	6/533
Total weapons	8	16	12	16	18	16
Speed, sub. (kts)	18	17	19	17	21	22
Range (n.m.)						
Submerged (at 3 kts)	250	250	350	300	650	500
Snorkeling	1,500	3,000	4,000	4,000	6,000	6,000
Endurance (days)	20	20	30	30	40	50
Crew (tot.)	18	21	21	34	. . .	37

Note: In 1998, the Rubin Design Bureau announced the development of the Project 636M design, said to be the third generation of the basic Kilo concept. Project 636M would feature a "missile complex," an inertial navigational system, a night-vision periscope with television and laser rangefinder, a towed VLF and ELF communications antenna, a "more powerful" sonar suite, and a battery with 2.5 times the service life of current Russian submarine batteries (which are short-lived in comparision with foreign submarine batteries). Project 636M is intended to be competitive in the export market through 2010 and will be able to accept further new systems as they are developed. No customers have materialized to date, although it may be this version that was unsuccessfully offered to South Korea in 1999.

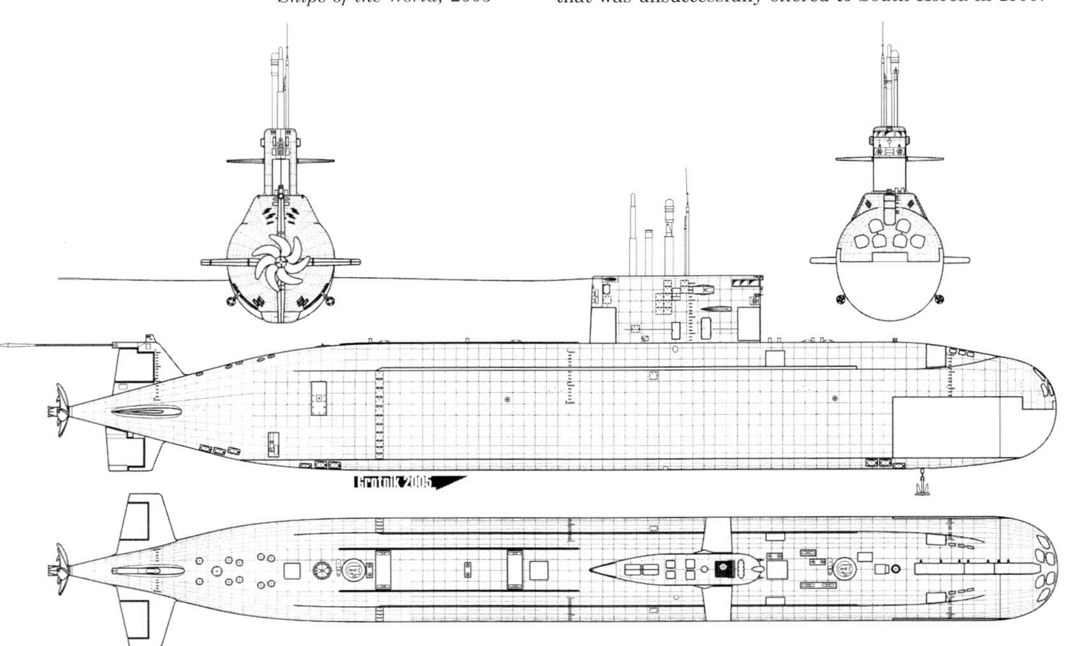

Sankt Peterburg (B-100) Drawing by Tomasz Grotnik, 2005

ATTACK SUBMARINES [SS] *(continued)*

♦ **5 Improved Kilo class (Project 636)** (1 in *reserve*)
Bldrs: A: Krasnoye Sormovo Zavod 199, Nizhniy Novgorod; B: Zavodni Leninskiy Komsomol 112, Komsomol'sk-na-Amur

	Bldr	Laid down	L	In serv.	Fleet
429 B-177 Lipetsk	A	11-84	1-9-85	29-9-00	Northern
431 *B-459 Vladikavkaz*	A	3-90	15-7-91	2-92	Northern
529 B-187 . . .	B	3-10-90	10-91	1-93	Pacific
521 B-190 . . .	B	10-91	8-5-92	12-94	Pacific
507 B-345 . . .	A	22-4-93	1993	22-1-94	Pacific

B-345 (507) Mitsuhiro Kadota, 9-02

B-187 (529) Boris Lemachko via Werner Globke, 5-03

D: 2,350 tons surf./3,126 tons sub. **S:** 11 kts surf./19.8 kts sub.
Dim: 73.80 × 9.90 × 6.60 (max. surf.)
A: 6 bow 533-mm TT (18 Type 86R/SS-N-16 Stallion missiles, torpedoes, and/or up to 24 mines); 1 shoulder-launched SAM syst. (6 Igla-M missiles)
Electronics:
Radar: MRK-50 Albatros' (Snoop Tray-2) nav./search
Sonar: MGK-400 Rubikon (Shark Gill) LF active/passive suite: passive hull array; MG-519 active object avoidance; MG-553 sound-velocity measurement; MG-512 self-cavitation measurement
EW: MRM-25EM (Squid Head) intercept
M: 2 Type 4-2AA-42M turbocharged diesel generator sets (1,500 kw each at 700 rpm), 2 PG-141M electric motors; 1 7-bladed prop; 5,500 shp—1 MT-140 electric low-speed motor (183 shp)—2 MT-168 internal electric creep/maneuvering motors; 2 ducted props; 204 shp (for 3 kts)
Range: 7,500/7 snorkel; 400/3 sub. **Endurance:** 45 days
Crew: 13 officers, 12 warrant officers, 12 petty officers, 15 nonrated

Remarks: An across-the-board improvement over the standard Project 877–series Kilo that has been offered for foreign sale as the Project 636 since 1993 but is also in service with the Russian Navy. Two export Type 636 Kilos were built for China at Admiralty Shipyard, St. Petersburg.
Hull systems: Have improved sound quieting over the earlier Project 877 series and a greater degree of automation. The electric propulsion motor is mounted on a flexible raft, and the maximum shaft rpm has been halved to 250 rpm. Maximum snorkeling speed is 8–10 kts. The bow has been reshaped to improve flow and some auxiliary machinery has been moved aft from the bow compartment to reduce noise interference with the passive bow sonar array. A more efficient model of the diesel generator set has been employed. The 7.2-m-diameter pressure hull has been lengthened to 53.0 m to accommodate the rafted main engines and also allowing tankage for additional diesel fuel. Pressure-hull thickness is 24–27 mm, except in some reinforced areas, where it is 30–35 mm thick. There are three 614-mm-diameter access hatches. The outer hull is coated with 0.8-m-square rubber anechoic tiles, attached with glue over special studs. The stern planes, rudder, and bow planes mounted just forward of the sail are controlled by a Pirit-23 hydraulic system. The two maneuvering propellers are mounted in internal ducts just forward of the stern planes, with the shafts to the motors protruding directly aft through the after pressure bulkhead. The export version of Project 636 has been offered with an air-independent propulsion system in a lengthened hull.

There are two attack periscopes with 1.5× and 6× magnification. Have two 120-cell Type 446 lead-acid batteries. Height from keel to the top of the 5-m-high sail is 14.7 m. Diving depth is 240 m normal/300 m maximum, and periscope depth is 17.5 m. Require 120 seconds to submerge. The hull has 30% reserve buoyancy in surfaced condition.
Combat systems: Only the two outer torpedo tubes in the lower row can accommodate TEST-71ME wire-guided torpedoes, while all tubes can launch 53-65KE, 53-56B, 53BA, and SET-53ME torpedoes; an automatic reload system permits reloading within 3 minutes. Torpedoes can be launched down to 240-m depth. With 12 in the torpedo tubes and 12 in the racks, 24 Type AM-1 mines can be carried in lieu of some torpedoes; mines can be laid only with the submarine at a depth of not more than 50 m.

The combat system is the digital MVU-110EM, which has three computer/processors; five targets can be tracked simultaneously (two automatically). The MGK-400 sonar suite is said to be able to detect submarines at a range of 16–20 km and surface ships at 60–80 km. Radio communication gear fitted includes two P-654-MP transmitters, three P-680-1 HF/VHF receivers, one P-683-1 LF receiver, one P-625 UHF transceiver, and one P-608H portable set. The MPM-25EM intercept array incorporates the transponder for the Khrom-K IFF system.

♦ **12 Kilo (Paltus) class (Projects 877 and 877KM)**†
Bldrs: A: Zavod imeni Leninskiy Komsomol 112, Komsomol'sk-na-Amur; B: Krasnoye Sormovo Zavod 199, Nizhniy Novgorod

	Bldr	Laid down	L	In serv.	Fleet
504 B-260 Razboynik	A	9-80	19-8-81	10-81	Pacific
469 B-227 . . .	A	9-81	1-9-82	11-82	Baltic
554 B-871 Alrosa*	B	1-83	1-3-84	6-84	Black Sea
545 B-439† . . .	A	1985	1986	1986	. . .
487 B-806 Tur	B	9-85	7-86	8-87	Baltic
425 B-808 Jaroslav	B	. . .	. . .	1988	. . .
403 B-401 Novorossiysk	B	6-88	8-89	4-1-90	Northern
405 B-402 Vologda	B	11-88	9-89	1990	Northern
547 B-464† Ust-Kamsatsk	A	11-88	9-89	6-91	Pacific
409 B-471 Magnitogorsk (ex-B-489, ex-448)	B	10-89	10-90	1991	Pacific
549 B-494 Ust-Bolsheretsk	A	1989	1990	1990	. . .
440 B-800 Kaluga	B	1989	1990	1990	. . .

* Converted to Project 877VD with pumpjet

B-402 Vologda (405) Jürg Kürsener, 5-03

B-439 (545) Boris Lemachko via Werner Globke, 5-03

D: 2,325 tons surf. (2,450 with emergency fuel)/3,076 tons sub.
S: 10 kts surf. /17 kts sub.
Dim: 72.60 (70.0 wl) × 9.90 (12.80 over stern planes) × 6.60 (fwd; 6.20 mean)

ATTACK SUBMARINES [SS] *(continued)*

B-439 (545) Boris Lemachko via Werner Globke, 5-03

A: 6 bow 533-mm TT (18 Type 86R/SS-N-16 Stallion missiles, torpedoes, and/or up to 24 mines); 1 shoulder-launched SAM syst. (6 Igla-M missiles)
Electronics:
Radar: 1 MRK-50 Albatros' (Snoop Tray-2)nav./search
Sonar: MGK-400 Rubikon (Shark Gill) LF active/passive suite; passive hull array; MG-519 Arfa (Mouse Roar) HF active target classification/mine avoidance; MG-553 sound-velocity measuring; MG-512 cavitation detection—some also: MG-53 sonar intercept
EW: MRM-25EM (Squid Head) intercept; 6701E (Quad Loop) D/F
M: 2 Type 4-2DL42M diesel generator sets (1,825 bhp/1,500 kw at 700 rpm), electric drive: 1 motor; 1 6-bladed prop (B-871: pumpjet); 5,900 shp—1 130-shp low-speed motor; 2 low-speed maneuvering motors; 2 ducted props; 204 shp (3 kts)
Range: 6,000/7 snorkel; 400/3 sub. **Fuel:** 172 tons
Endurance: 45 days **Crew:** 12 officers, 41–45 enlisted

Remarks: Informally known as the Warshavyanka class, as they were originally intended to be built in numbers for the Warsaw pact navies; Paltus is the official project code name. Begun in 1974 at Firma Rubin, the design effort was headed by Yu. N. Kormilitsyn. Black Sea Fleet unit B-871 began an overhaul and conversion at Sevastopol' on 9-9-90 and has been fitted with a pumpjet propulsor; the submarine remained nonoperational until 7-99 for lack of batteries but returned to sea during 2000. Baltic Fleet unit B-227 was given new batteries late in 2000; the boat is used primarily to train foreign crews. B-806 was refitted at St. Petersburg from 10-01 to 5-02 and is used to train foreign crews. During 2004 B-871 was named *Alrosa* in honor of the private corporation that serves as her sponsor.
Exports: More than a half-dozen foreign customers (Projects 877E and 877EKM) including India, Algeria, Poland, Romania, Iran, and China. Export models on offer have included Projects 877M with six 533-mm internal tubes; 877EM, 73.2 m long with two tubes capable of firing wire-guided torpedoes; 877MK, with an improved combat data system; and 877EKM, with all tubes capable of launching wire-guided torpedoes. Export-configured units have had a longer walking deck abaft the sail than the Russian Navy version.
Hull systems: Propulsion plant is suspended for silencing. Hull has 32% reserve buoyancy at 2,350 m^3 surfaced displacement and 26% at 2,450 m^3. Surfaced draft at 2,450 tons with emergency fuel and antisonar coating installed is 6.60 m forward, 6.70 m aft. Enveloped volume submerged is 4,200 m^3. Maximum diving depth is 300 m, normal depth 240 m, and periscope depth 17.5 m; can submerge in 120 seconds. Can sustain 8 kts on surface in the heaviest sea conditions and can achieve 400 n.m. submerged at 3 kts if the air-conditioning system is off. Have an anechoic hull coating like larger nuclear submarines. Two battery groups, each with 120 cells, provide 9,700 kw-hr at 100 Amp. The 51.8-m-long pressure hull has six watertight compartments. The air regeneration system provides enough breathable atmosphere for 260 hours of operations with a full crew. Carry 10 tons of lube oil, 8.5 tons of provisions, 19.3 tons of fresh water, and 4 tons of distilled water. Have the Pirit-2E automated maneuvering system.
Combat systems: The combat system, designated MVU-110EM, can conduct two simultaneous attacks while tracking three other targets manually. The sonar suite is supplemented by MG-519 active mine-avoidance set, MG-553 sound velocity meter, and MG-512 own-ship cavitation detector. The shoulder-fired SAM launch position is located in the after portion of the sail. Torpedo tube–launched weapons carried can include TEST-71M wire-guided, E53-65K and SET-53M wake-homing, and E53-56B acoustic homing torpedoes; KMD-500, KMD-1000, KMD-II-500, KMD-II-1000, and UMD mines; and Type 83R and 84R (SS-N-15 Starfish) antisubmarine missiles. Full mine load is carried two in each tube plus 12 in the torpedo reload compartment. Can launch torpedoes via compressed air in waters up to 240 m deep. On the six Project 877KM units, the lower, outboard tubes are equipped to launch wire-guided torpedoes, of which up to six may be carried. Torpedoes are launchable by the Murena-M torpedo launch system within two minutes of alert; reload of all six tubes takes only five minutes. There are two PZKG periscopes. Communications equipment includes Type IVA-MV for shortwave and Type ANIS-M-B for VHF and UHF.
Hull systems: Hull is sheathed in an anechoic sonar-absorbent rubber compound. Have significantly greater battery capacity than the Foxtrot class and their greater internal volume provides more space for weapons reloads. Diving depth: 300 m maximum, 240 m normal operating. Total volume enveloped by outer hull, the sail, and all appendages is 4,600 m^3.
Combat systems: Have the Most-641B navigation/data system and the Uzel combat data system with Vol'fram torpedo f.c. computer and Pirit autopilot. EW arrays vary; some had the later Squid Head array. B-437 was fitted with a towed linear passive sonar array at Kronshtadt during the mid-1990s, with the cable reel in a drum forward of the sail and the array exiting a tube above the stern; a second unit was supposed to have received it, but the work was not completed.
Disposals: Northern Fleet units B-290, B-303, and B-519, at Kronshtadt for overhauls, were stricken 1-9-95. B-319 and B-386 were stricken from the Northern Fleet 31-7-96 (with B-386 becoming a museum exhibit at Severodvinsk on 12-1-01). Baltic Fleet unit B-312 was deactivated 1-5-98 and stricken during 1999; Baltic Fleet unit B-307 had been stricken earlier. Baltic Fleet unit B-303 was towed away for scrap 1-7-99 and B-519 and B-290 two days later. Black Sea Fleet unit B-380 (ex-*Gor'hovskiy Komsomolets*) was inactivated 10-1-96 and was turned down by Ukraine for transfer; the submarine remains afloat at Sevastopol', however, but is unlikely to be refitted and reactivated. B-30, B-97, B-215, B-504, and B-546 remain afloat at various Northern Fleet bases but are are out of commission and unlikely to return to service. Former Northern Fleet unit B-434 was refitted at Severodvinsk during 2002 for use as a museum exhibit at Hamburg, Germany. Northern Fleet units B-307 and B-515 were being scrapped at Belokamenka as of 7-02. All Russian Project 877 units, other than those listed above, have been withdrawn from service.

Disposal note: The last Tango (Som) class (Project 641B) *B-380*, ex-*Magnetogorskiy Komsomolets*, was retired during 2005.

NUCLEAR-POWERED AUXILIARY SUBMARINES [SSAN]

♦ 2 Uniform (Kashalot) class (Project 1910) (1 *nonoperational*)
Bldr: Admiralteiskiye Verfi 196 (Sudomekh Division), St. Petersburg

	Laid down	L	In serv.
AS-13	20-10-77	25-11-82	31-12-86
AS-15	23-2-83	29-4-88	30-12-91

Uniform class (Project 1910) M.O.D. U.K., 1992

D: 1,390 tons surf./1,580 tons sub. **S:** 10 kts surf./30 kts sub.
Dim: 69.0 × 7.0 × 5.2 **A:** None
Electronics: Radar: Snoop Slab search—Sonar: HF active arrays
M: 1 1.5-Mw pressurized-water nuclear reactor; 1 prop; 10,000 shp
Crew: 36 tot.

Remarks: Apparently intended for research or special operations on the ocean floor. The first Soviet single-hulled nuclear-powered submarines. Fitting-out work on a third unit of the class, numbered AS-12, had ceased by 10-98.
Hull systems: Titanium-construction, single-hulled design with an operating diving depth of up to 700 m. Have fairings on the hull side abreast the sail house maneuvering thrusters.

♦ 2 Paltus (Nelhma) class (Project 1851)
Bldr: Admiralteiskiye Verfi 196 (Sudomekh Division), St. Petersburg

	Laid down	L	In serv.
AS-21	26-12-84	29-4-91	28-12-91
AS-35	20-12-89	29-9-94	12-10-95

D: 730 tons sub. **S:** 6 kts sub. **Dim:** 53.0 × 3.8 × 5.3
M: 1 10-Mw pressurized-water reactor, 1 diesel generator set; 1 prop; 300 shp
Crew: 14 tot. (all officers)

Remarks: Other sources give the Paltus class as Project 1083.1. Reportedly yet another small submarine intended for special operations on the sea floor. Equipped with two manipulators forward and maneuvering thrusters abreast the sail. Operating depth said to be 1,000 m. Work on a reported third unit had ceased by 10-98 (and probably well before that).

♦ 1 Delta Stretch class (Project . . .)
Bldr: Sevmashpredpriyatiye, Severodvinsk (Severodvinsk SY 402)

	Laid down	L	In serv.
BS-136 (ex-BS-129; ex-K-129)	2-79	3-81	19-11-81

D: 10,600 tons surf./13,050 tons sub. **S:** 14 kts surf./24 kts sub.
Dim: . . . × 11.70 × 8.70 **A:** probably none

NUCLEAR-POWERED AUXILIARY SUBMARINES [SSAN]
(continued)

Electronics:
Radar: 1 MRK-50-series Albatros' (Snoop Tray) nav./search
Sonar: MGK-500-series Skat-2 (Shark Gill) LF active/passive suite: MGK-519 (Mouse Roar) active mine avoidance; MG-512 cavitation monitor; MG-518 active upward-looking echo sounder; MG-519 mine detection; MG-533 sound-velocity measurement; NOR-1 ice-lane detector; NOK-1 surface warning
EW: MRP-10 Zaliv-P (Brick Pulp) intercept; Park Lamp D/F

M: 2 VM-4S pressurized-water nuclear reactors (89.2 Mw each), 2 Type OK-700A steam turbines; 2 5-bladed props; 52,000 shp—2 306-shp electric low-speed motors on main shafts
Electric: 6,920 kw tot. (2 × 3,000-kw a.c. alternators, 2 × 460-kw diesel sets)
Endurance: 80 days **Crew:** . . . tot.

Remarks: Relaunched 29-12-00 after undergoing conversion since 1995 at Severodvinsk as a *Sverkhmalaya Podvodnavy Lodka* ("Super-Small Submarine") tender for the Paltus class (Project 1851). Had been in a collision with a U.S. submarine during 1993 and was then considered for conversion as a civilian oceanographic research submarine.
Hull systems: The 32.5-m mid-body, originally intended for a second Yankee Stretch conversion, replaced the original 45-m-long ballistic-missile section, but the new overall dimension is not known and could be as long as the 162.5 m of the Yankee Stretch. The pressure hull is 9.8 m in diameter. Primary ship's service electric power is delivered at 380 V/50 Hz. Test diving depth is 580 m, normal operating depth 320 m. Has bow and stern side-thrusters. Is probably able to accommodate a Paltus SSAN within the new mid-body.
Combat systems: The Molnaya-M communications suite incorporates towed VLF communications buoys and a Pert Spring antenna for the Tsunami SATCOM system.

Disposal note: Yankee Stretch conversion (Project 09774) *Orënburg* (BS-411) and Yankee Big Note (Akson-2) conversion (Project 09790) *Kazan* (KS-403) were decommissioned during 2005.

AUXILIARY SUBMARINES [SSA]

Disposal note: The sole Beluga (Russian Makrel')-class (Project 1710) trials submarine, SS-533, inactive at Sevastopol' since 1997, was stricken during late 2001.

Of the four Bravo (Kefal')-class (Project 690) target submarines, Northern Fleet unit BS-368 was stricken 3-7-92; Black Sea Fleet unit SS-256, stricken 10-1-96 and offered to Ukraine (which did not accept her), was towed to Kerch' for scrapping 29-10-99; and Black Sea Fleet unit SS-226 was flooded out and foundered 17-1-99 but was later refloated, leaving only SS-310, used as a stationary training device at Sevastopol', remaining on the fleet list but unlikely to be returned to service.

Of the two India (Lenok)-class (Project 940) salvage submarines, Pacific Fleet unit BS-486 (ex-*Komsomolets Uzbekhistana*) was stricken 17-11-94 and was towed away for scrap 20-9-00. The Northern Fleet's India, BS-257, has been immobilized since 1990 in need of a major overhaul but is still considered a unit of the fleet, although unlikely ever to operate again.

MIDGET SUBMARINES [SSM]

Disposal note: Losos (Pirhana)-class (Project 865) combatant midget submarines MS-520 and MS-521, in reserve since 7-92, were stricken during 1997, but one may have been retrieved during 1999–2000 and upgraded to serve as a technology and sales demonstrator by the St. Petersburg Maritime Machine-Building Bureau, which is offering variants of the design for export with submerged displacements of 130, 170, 220, 400, 550, and 750 tons; gas turbine–powered generators are offered, and a crew of nine plus six combat swimmers could be carried.

Swimmer-delivery vehicles are discussed in the amphibious warfare section under [LSDV]. Salvage and research submarines [YSS] are listed with service craft.

NUCLEAR-POWERED GUIDED-MISSILE CRUISERS [CGN]

♦ 2 Kirov (Orlan) class (Project 1144.2) (1 *nonoperational/refit*)
Bldr: Ob'yedineniye Baltiyskiye Verf (Baltic Yard), St. Petersburg, Russia

	Laid down	L	In serv.	Fleet
080 ADMIRAL NAKHIMOV (ex-*Kalinin*)	17-5-83	25-4-86	30-12-88	Northern
099 PETR VELIKIY (ex-*Yuri Andropov*)	25-8-86	24-4-89	18-4-98	Northern

Petr Velikiy (099)—launching 9M330 Gopher SAM Boris Lemachko, 8-00

Admiral Nakhimov (080) Boris Lemachko, 2-00

D: 24,300 tons std., 24,500 normal (26,396 fl)
S: 32 kts (17 on conventional steam power)
Dim: 251.20 (228.00 wl) × 28.50 (24.00 wl) × 9.10 (mean hull; 10.33 max.)
A: *Nakhimov:* 20 P-700 Granit (SS-N-19 Shipwreck) SSM (20 inclined SM-233 launch tubes); 12 6-round Fort (SA-N-6) SAM syst. (96 5V-55U/Grumble missiles; 12 B-203A vertical launchers); 2 twin-rail Osa-M (SA-N-4) SAM syst. (4K-33/Gecko missiles); 1 twin 130-mm 70-cal. AK-130 DP (840 rounds); 6 Kortik CIWS (each with 8 missile rails and 2 30-mm gatling AA (192 9M-311/SA-N-11 Grison missiles; 24,000 30-mm rounds); 2 quintuple 533-mm TT (20 torpedoes and/or Type 86R Vodopad-MK/SS-N-16 Stallion missiles); 1 10-round RPK-5 Liven' ASW RL (40 rockets); 2 6-round RBU-1000 ASW RL (102 rockets); 2 Ka-27PL Helix-A ASW helicopters; 1 Ka-27RTs Helix-A targeting helicopter
Petr Velikiy: 20 P-700 Granit (SS-N-19 Shipwreck) SSM (20 inclined SM-233 launch tubes); 12 6-round S-300F/FM Fort/Fort-M (SA-N-6) SAM syst. (48 48N6E and 48N6E2/Grumble missiles; 12 B-203A vertical launchers); 16 8-round Kinzhal (SA-N-9) SAM syst. (128 9M-330/Gopher missiles); 6 Kortik CIWS, each with 8 missile rails and 2 30-mm gatling AA (192 9M-311/SA-N-11 Grison missiles; 24,000 30-mm rounds); 1 twin 130-mm 70-cal. AK-130 DP (840 rounds); 2 quintuple 533-mm TT (20 torpedoes and/or Type 86R Vodopad-MK/SS-N-16 Stallion missiles); 1 10-round RPK-5 Liven' ASW RL (40 rockets); 2 6-round RBU-1000 ASW RL (102 rockets); 2 Ka-27PL Helix-A ASW helicopters; 1 Ka-27RTs Helix-A targeting helicopter

Electronics:
Nakhimov:
Radar: 3 MR-212/201 Vaygach-U (Palm Frond) nav.; 1 MR-800 Voskhod (Top Pair) 3-D early warning; 1 MR-710 Fregat-MA (Top Plate-B) 3-D air search; 2 Volna (Top Dome) SA-N-6 f.c.; 2 MPZ-301 Baza (Pop Group) SA-N-4 f.c.; 1 MR-184 Lev (Kite Screech-C) gun f.c.; 6 3P-87 (Hot Flash) Kortik CIWS f.c.; 1 Fly Screen landing aid
Sonar: MGK-355 Polinom suite: MGK-335 Platina (Horse Jaw) bow-mounted LF; Orion (Horse Tail) LF VDS; MG-35 underwater telephone; MGK-355TA torpedo detection
TACAN: 2 Privod-B (Round House)
EW: Kantata-M suite: 8 Foot Ball intercept; 4 Bell Bash jammers; 4 Bell Nip; 4 Bell Push; 4 Bell Thumb; 2 PK-2 decoy syst. (2 twin ZIF-121RL; 400 rockets)
E/O: 4 Tin Man stabilized multisensor surveillance
Petr Velikiy:
Radar: 3 MR-212/201 Vaygach-U (Palm Frond) nav.; 2 MR-320M Topaz-M (Strut Pair) surf./air search; 1 MR-800 Voskhod (Top Pair) 3-D early warning; 1 MR-710 Fregat-MA (Top Plate-B) 3-D air search; 1 Volna (Top Dome) SA-N-6 f.c.; 1 F1M (Tomb Stone) SA-N-6 f.c.; 2 Podkat (Cross Sword) SA-N-9 f.c.; 1 MR-184 (Kite Screech-C) 130-mm gun f.c.; 6 3P-87 (Hot Flash) Kortik CIWS f.c.; 1 Fly Screen landing aid
Sonar: MGK-355 Polinom suite: MGK-335 Platina (Horse Jaw) bow-mounted LF; Orion (Horse Tail) LF VDS; MG-35 underwater telephone; MGK-355TA torpedo detection
TACAN: 2 Privod (Round House)
EW: Kantata-M suite: 8 Foot Ball intercept; 4 Bell Bash jammers; 4 Bell Nip; 4 Bell Push; 4 Bell Thumb; 2 PK-2 decoy syst. (2 twin ZIF-121 RL; 400 rockets); 12 10-round PK-10 fixed decoy RL
E/O: 4 Tin Man stabilized multisensor surveillance; . . . Spektr-F (Half Cup) laser warning

M: CONAS (Combined Nuclear and Steam): 2 KN-3 nuclear reactors (300 Mw each) + 2 oil-fired boilers, steam turbines; 2 4-bladed props; 140,000 shp
Electric: 18,000 kw tot. (4 × 3,000-kw turboalternators, 4 × 1,500-kw diesel sets)
Range: 14,000/30 (on nuclear plant); 1,300/17 (on steam plant)
Fuel: 1,120 tons + 58 tons aviation fuel **Endurance:** 60 days
Crew: 105 officers, 550 enlisted (accomm. for 120 officers, 640 enlisted)

Remarks: The type-designation applied has been RKR (*Raketnyy Kreyser,* Missile Cruiser) or, on occasion, *Atomnaya Raketnyy Kreyser.* Designed under Gennadiy Starshinov. A 6-96 Russian technical paper stated that these ships have only one-twentieth the combat potential of a single U.S. nuclear-powered aircraft carrier, though it is probably even less. The names were changed under a 27-5-92 decree by President Yeltsin.
Status: *Admiral Ushakov,* the former *Kirov,* is no longer in service and has been deleted from the Russian Navy list. Sovremennyy class destroyer *Besstrashnyy* (434) has been named *Admiral Ushakov.*

Admiral Lazarev, which arrived in the Pacific Fleet 9-10-85, was reported in the Russian press to be for sale for scrap in 7-94, and a formal decision to decommission the ship for disposal was reportedly made 10-12-94; in 2-95, however, the Russian Navy vigorously denied that the ship was for sale, although admitting that she had not gone to sea in five years. Late in 1997, it was announced that the *Lazarev* would be decommissioned shortly, which finally happened 18-6-99. Though some work on an overhaul began in 2000 funding has since dried up and the warship is to be stricken.

Admiral Nakhimov underwent a short refit during mid-1996 at Rosta but was said to be unable to go to sea as of 6-98; a further refit was to start at Severodvinsk in 12-98, using components scavenged from the ex-*Kirov,* but the ship did not arrive at Severodvinsk to begin the work until 21-8-99 and remained there into 2003 when steps were taken to begin reactor reactivation. Additional work on the warship is to take place during 2006–7, at which time a new computerized management system and Onyx missiles may be fitted.

NUCLEAR-POWERED GUIDED-MISSILE CRUISERS [CGN] *(continued)*

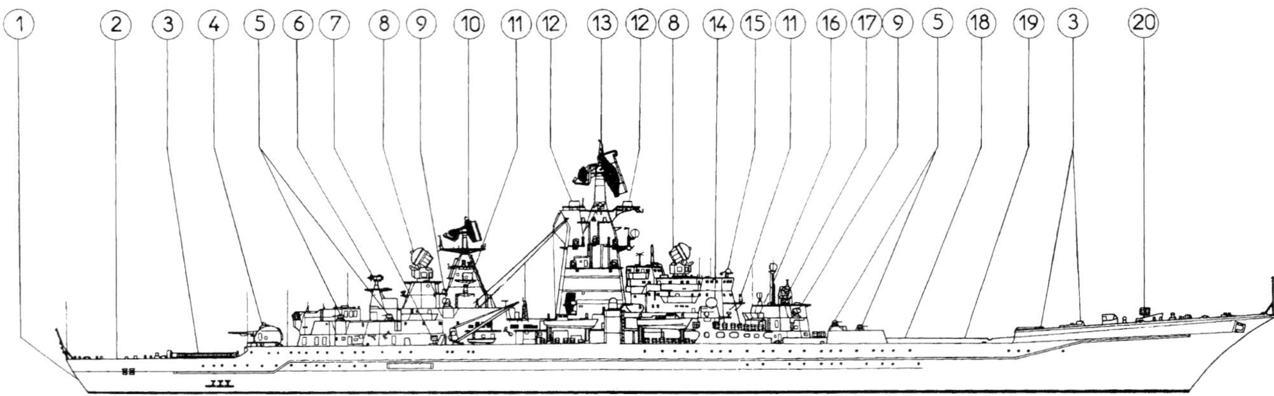

Admiral Lazarev (015) Since retired. 1. VDS housing 2. helicopter pad 3. planned location for Kinzhal SAM system (never installed) 4. twin 130-mm AK-130 DP gunmount 5. 30-mm AK-630M gatling AA 6. MR-184 Lev radar director for 130-mm gunmount 7. RBU-1000 ASW/torpedo countermeasures RL 8. Volna radar director for Fort SAM system 9. MR-123 Vympel radar director for 30-mm gatling AA 10. MR-700M Fregat 3-D air-search radar 11. Tin Man optronic sensor 12. Privod TACAN 13. MR-800 Voskhod 3-D early-warning radar 14. Big Ball SATCOM antenna radome 15. MR-212/201 Vaygach-U nav./surf.-search radars 16. Osa-M SAM system launchers 17. MPZ-301 Baza radar directors for the Osa-M SAM system. 18. P-700 Granit antiship missile launchers (recessed into deck) 19. Fort SAM VLS 20. RBU-6000 ASW RL
Drawing by Louis Gassier, from *Flottes de Combat*

Petr Velikiy began sea trials 8-6-96. During subsequent sea trials in the Baltic on 27-10-96, a steam pipe ruptured, killing four personnel. The ship departed the Baltic late in 11-96 for further trials in the Barents Sea but was laid up on arrival 24-11-96 and remained inactive until late 1997. When finally commissioned, she was placed in the Northern Fleet rather than the Pacific, as originally intended. The ship was dry docked for minor overhaul as of 8-01 but appears to be active.

Construction of a fifth unit, to have been named *Admiral Flota Sovetskogo Soyuza Kuznetsov* (following initial plans to name her *Dzerzhinskiy* and then *Oktyabrskaya Revolutsiya*), was authorized 31-12-88, but the ship was officially canceled 4-10-90 shortly after the keel had been laid.

Hull systems: A long, raised strake down either side of the hull on both acts as an external hull stiffener, as on some smaller Russian warship classes. The helicopter hangar is beneath the forward portion of the fantail, with an elevator delivering the aircraft to the flight deck. The steeply raked stern has a 9-m-wide centerline recess for the VDS installation. Two solid-stores replenishment stations are fitted: one amidships to port and one folding station forward to port, abreast the SA-N-6 system; both employ the sliding-stay, constant-tension concept. Oil and water replenishments are handled at stations on either beam abreast the Kite Screech gun f.c. radar. The forward reload missile transfer equipment is considerably more compact on later units than it was on ex-*Kirov*. Have 100-mm armor on the reactor compartment's sides and 35-mm on its ends, 70-mm on the sides and 50-mm on the upper deck of the steering machinery compartment, and 80-mm on the conning position. Amenities include a sauna with 6-m pool, a saloon and billiard room for the officers, and a 200-seat enlisted "club" that converts to a gymnasium. The ships have their own television studio and printing plant and are equipped with a two-deck clinic. Firefighting capabilities are said to be deficient.

Propulsion systems: The two circular reactor access hatches can be seen amidships, just abaft the enormous twin exhaust uptakes for the unusual CONAS (Combined Nuclear and Steam) propulsion system. The oil-fired boilers provide steam to completely separate turbines, which are geared to the same drive shafts as the nuclear-supplied turbines. The starboard stack uptake serves the oil-fired boilers, while the port uptake serves to ventilate the reactor spaces.

Combat systems: The combat direction system is called Lesorub 44. The launch tubes for the 20 P-700 antiship missiles are buried within the hull at a fixed elevation angle of 40–45°, in four rows of five, forward of the superstructure. Before these are the 12 vertical launchers for the long-range SAM system; each has a door, beneath which is a rotating magazine containing eight missiles. Targeting data for the P-700 missile, with its 300-n.m. maximum range, was to come either from land-based aircraft, a helicopter embarked on the ship, or radar satellites via the Punch Bowl satellite communications antennas on either side of the ship (but the satellite system never became operational). The gatling gun mounts on the first two are paired and located so as to cover all four quadrants; each pair is served by a Bass Tilt radar director and a manned, SP-521 Rakurs (Kolonka-2) ringsight backup director.

On *Nakhimov*, eight SA-N-9 launchers were intended to be fitted within the forecastle, while eight more were to be located flanking the helicopter elevator, four per side (the gatling guns are mounted on the after superstructure); they have never been installed. The intended two Cross Sword directors for SA-N-9 were never mounted; they were to have been positioned abaft the Kite Screech aft and between the two Pop Group directors forward. The two MR-320M Topaz-M (Strut Pair) radars in *Petr Velikiy* provide target designation services to the two Cross Sword radar tracker/directors for the SA-N-9 SAM system. *Nakhimov* and *Petr Velikiy* have the new RPK-5 Liven' ASW/countertorpedo rocket launcher vice the RBU-6000 and mount the new Kortik combined twin long-barrel 30-mm gatling gun and octuple, reloadable SA-N-11 missile system vice the 30-mm AK-630 mounts.

Petr Velikiy initially had two Top Dome radar directors for the Fort (SA-N-6) surface-to-air missile system, but by 7-96, the forward one had been replaced by a modified Tomb Stone director adapted from a mobile land-based system; one Russian publication stated that a different missile variant is used with each director.

As might be expected, the communications antenna array is extensive and diverse and includes satellite communications equipment and long-range HF gear. The first two were given the Tsunami-BM SATCOM system and the later pair the Kristall-BK system. *Petr Velikiy* has two large, thimble-shaped radomes for the Legenda SATCOM system on pylons forward of the boat davits amidships and two smaller Punch Bowl spherical radomes just below the Korall-BN (Low Ball) SATCOM radomes. The four stabilized Tin Man electro-optical sensors cover all four quadrants, and there are also several smaller remote t.v. cameras. Two Bob Tail radiometric sextant antennas are housed in spherical enclosures. The Fly Screen microwave landing-approach radar is mounted on a starboard platform on the after tower mast. The VDS employs a lens-shaped "fish" about 4 m in diameter to house the transducer and has a twin boom-mounted empennage with horizontal and vertical control surfaces. In addition to a low-frequency bow-mounted sonar, there is probably an MF set for fire-control purposes (including depth determination) for the ASW rocket launchers (which also have a torpedo-countermeasures function). The EW devices listed here as Wine Flask have also been referred to as Modified Foot Ball; they appear to be combined receiver/jammers.

GUIDED-MISSILE CRUISERS [CG]

♦ 3 Slava (Atlant) class (Project 1164)

Bldr: 61 Kommunara SY 445, Nikolayev, Ukraine

	Laid down	L	In serv.	Fleet
121 Moskva (ex-*Slava*)	5-11-76	27-7-79	7-2-83	Black Sea
055 Marshal Ustinov (ex-*Admiral Flota Lobov*)	5-10-78	25-2-82	21-9-86	Northern
011 Varyag ("Viking," ex-*Chervona Ukraina*)	27-7-79	28-8-83	25-12-89	Pacific

Moskva (121) Luciano Grazioli, 2-06

Varyag (011) Brian Morrison, 10-02

D: 9,380 tons std. (11,280 normal fl; 11,490 max. fl) **S:** 32.5 kts (30 sust.)
Dim: 186.40 (170.00 wl) × 20.80 (19.20 wl) × 6.23 (mean hull; 8.40 over sonar dome)

GUIDED-MISSILE CRUISERS [CG] *(continued)*

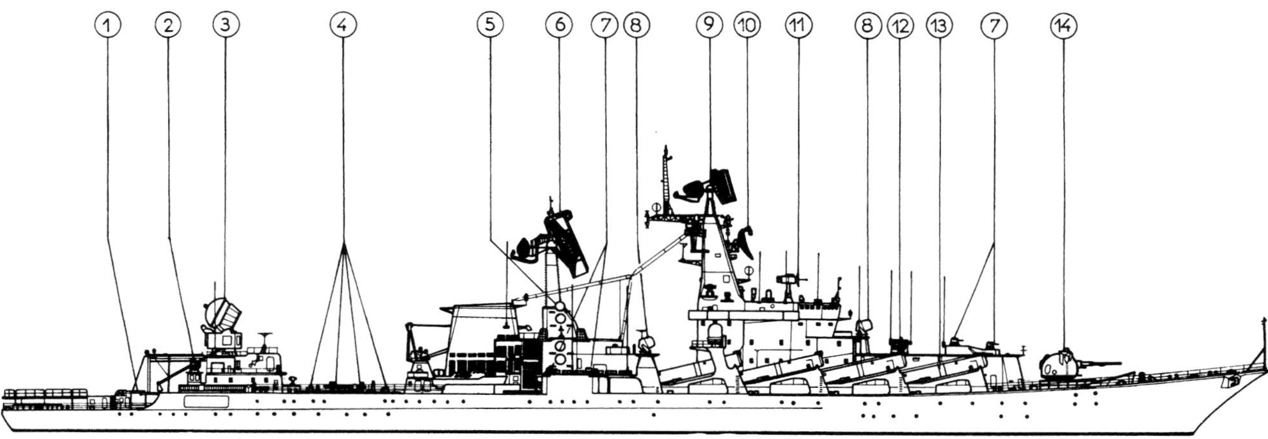

Moskva (121) 1. Osa-MA SAM launchers (port and starboard, flanking helicopter hangar) 2. MPZ-301 Baza director for Osa-M system 3. Volna radar director for Fort SAM system 4. Fort SAM VLS (recessed into deck) 5. Gurzhor-A and -B EW antennas 6. MR-600 Voskhod 3-D 3-D early-warning radar 7. 30-mm AK-630M gatling AA 8. MR-123 Vympel radar directors for 30-mm gatling AA 9. MR-700 Fregat 3-D air-search/target-designation radar 10. Argon-1164 tracking and telemetry array for P-500 Bazal't missiles 11. MR-184 Lev radar director for 130-mm gunmount 12. RBU-6000 ASW RL 13. Four twin launchers per side for P-500 Bazal't antiship missile system 14. Twin 130-mm AK-130 DP gunmount
Drawing by Louis Gassier, from *Flottes de Combat*

Varyag (011) Brian Morrison, 10-02

Marshal Ustinov (055) Boris Lemachko, 2002

A: 16 P-500 Bazal't (SS-N-12 Sandbox) SSM (4K-80 missiles); 8 8-round Fort (SA-N-6) vertical-launch SAM groups (64 S-300MPU/3R-41 or 5V-55/Grumble missiles; 8 B-203A rotating vertical launchers); 2 twin-rail Osa-MA SAM syst. (40 9M-33M5/Gecko missiles); 1 twin 130-mm 70-cal. AK-130 DP (600 rounds); 6 single 30-mm 54-cal. AK-630M gatling AA (48,000 rounds); 2 quintuple 533-mm TT; 2 12-round RBU-6000 ASW RL (144 rockets); 1 Ka-27PL ASW or Ka-2RTs Helix targeting helicopter

Electronics:

Radar: 3 MR-212/201 Vaygach-U (Palm Frond) nav.; 1 MR-600 Voskhod (Top Pair) 3-D early warning; 1 MR-700 Fregat (Top Steer) (*Varyag:* MR-710 Fregat-MA (Top Plate-B) 3-D air search); 1 Volna (Top Dome) SA-N-6 f.c.; 2 MPZ-301 Baza (Pop Group) SA-N-4 f.c.; 1 MR-184 Lev (Kite Screech-C) 130-mm gun f.c.; 3 MR-123 Vympel (Bass Tilt) 30-mm f.c.; 1 Argon-1164 (Front Door-C) SS-N-12 tracking and telemetry

Sonar: Bull Nose hull-mounted LF, Platina (Horse Tail) MF VDS

EW: *Moskva, Ustinov,* and *Varyag:* Kol'cho suite: 8 MR-401 Gurzhor-A and -B (Side Globe) intercept; 4 MR-404 Ograda (Rum Tub) jammers; 2 Bell Crown; 2 Bell Push; . . . Bell-series; 2 PK-2 decoy syst. (2 twin ZIF-121 trainable RL; 400 rockets)—*Varyag* also: 12 10-round PK-10 fixed decoy RL—*Ustinov:* 2 MP-405M Start-2 syst.: MRP-11M/12M (Bell Shroud) intercept; 2 Bell Squat; 4 Foot Ball-B; 2 PK-2 trainable decoy syst. (2 twin ZIF-121 trainable launchers; 400 rockets); 12 10-round PK-10 fixed decoy RL

E/O: *Moskva* only: 2 Tee Plinth stabilized t.v. surveillance

M: COGOG M-21 plant: 4 M8KF boost gas turbines (22,500 shp each); 2 M-70 cruise gas turbines (10,000 shp each); 2 exhaust-gas cruise turbines (1,500 shp each); 2 props; 113,000 shp
Electric: 8,250 kw tot. (3 × 1,500-kw, 3 × 1,250-kw gas turbine sets)
Range: 2,200/32; 8,070/18 **Fuel:** . . . tons + 17.5 tons aviation fuel
Endurance: 30 days **Crew:** 62 (*Moskva:* 66) officers, 64 *michmen,* 355 enlisted

Remarks: Initially referred to by the NATO code name "BLK-COM-1" and later, briefly, as the "Krasina" class. Typed *Raketnyy Kreyser* (Missile Cruiser) by the Russian Navy. Chief designer was V. Mutikhin. Fitted as flagships, in which role they carry up to 27 additional officers and 24 additional enlisted. Are unusual in having considerable equipment that was not the latest of its type in Soviet service even when the class was introduced.

Status: *Moskva* (named *Slava* until 14-7-95) began an overhaul in 12-90 at 61 Kommunara Zavod, Nikolayev; the work was 70% complete as of 7-98 but was not completed due to nonpayment of debts by Russia. The ship was returned to Russian Navy control 16-7-99 for further work at Sevastopol' before recommissioning during 4-00; she became flagship of the Black Sea Fleet 26-10-00. A missile from the *Moskva* hit a Ukrainian passenger ship during 4-00.

Marshal Ustinov entered the Baltic for an overhaul in 1994 and reentered service 13-1-98, returning to the Northern Fleet. *Varyag* (name changed 9-2-96) remains in commission with a reduced crew; she visited Japan during 2002.

The fourth ship of the class, the *Ukrayina,* was the last combatant warship to be built by 61 Kommunara Shipyard and was delayed in completion by the economic turmoil in Russia and Ukraine. As of 1-4-93, when the ship was taken over by Ukraine, it was reported that she would be completed for the Ukrainian Navy, but an agreement was reached during 8-95 (at which time she was said to be 94.2% complete) for the ship to be completed for the Russian Navy as the *Admiral Flota Lobov.* Lack of funds, however, again precluded any work being done, and the ship remained Ukrainian property. Ukrainian President Kuchma then decreed on 17-2-99 that she would be completed for the Ukraine Navy, and the Ukrainian flag was raised aboard her 17-6-99. By 8-00, however, work on completing the ship had again halted for lack of funds, and on 28-9-01, Kuchma offered to sell her to Russia, which rejected the offer during 1-02.

A fifth, revised Project 11641 unit, to have been named *Rossiya* (later changed to *Oktyabrskaya Revolutsiya*), and a sixth, to have been named *Admiral Flota Sovetskogo Soyuza Gorshkov,* were canceled 4-10-90. The pair would have displaced an additional 200 tons, would have been 6 m longer than the earlier group, and would have had the Platina sonar system (without towed array) and the canceled R-1000 Vulcan missile system.

Hull systems: Have retractable fin stabilizers. Each of the paired stack uptakes on the first three incorporates one cruise-turbine exhaust, two boost-turbine exhausts, and two gas-turbine generator exhausts. Gas turbine exhaust waste-heat boilers provide steam to two auxiliary turbines to improve crusing range by about 12%. Unlike the first three ships of the class, the *Marshal Ustinov* has a single large stack uptake, with a smaller crane offset to starboard. Officer accommodations are opulent by Western standards, even to the extent of installing a waterfall-equipped belowdecks swimming pool and sauna, but enlisted quarters are spartan; in general, the ships contain a great deal of flammable material and appear to lack adequate damage-control features. A one-man elevator is installed to take the commanding officer from the central command post to the bridge. Have operated with as few as 38 officers.

Combat systems: Only one director is provided for the Fort SAM system, limiting its flexibility and restricting target tracking to six aircraft at a time, all within a 60° bearing. The torpedo tubes are mounted behind shutters in the ship's sides, near the stern. The hangar floor is one half-deck below the flight deck, which is reached via an inclined ramp, the helicopter being maneuvered by a chain-haul system. In *Varyag,* the Top Steer paired radar was replaced by Top Plate, and 10 PK-10 fixed decoy rocket launchers were added. Two Punch Bowl antennas for the Korvet-5 satellite targeting datalink system are fitted. *Ustinov* has the radomes for two Korvet-5 SATCOM system antennas, but may not have the actual system; the ship's EW suite is simplified from that of the three earlier ships.

Disposal note: The last Kynda-class (Project 58) guided-missile cruiser, the *Admiral Golovko* (ex-*Doblestnyy*), was retired during fall 2002. Baltic Fleet sister *Groznyy* was stricken 24-6-91; the Pacific Fleet's *Varyag* (ex-*Soobrazitel'niy*) was laid up 29-4-90 and stricken 21-5-91; and Pacific Fleet unit *Admiral Fokin* (ex-*Vladivostok,* ex-*Steregushchiy*) was stricken 30-7-93 and scrapped in India in 1995.

GUIDED-MISSILE DESTROYERS [DDG]

♦ **10 Sovremennyy (Sarych) class (Projects 956 and 956A)**
(5 in overhaul*, 1 *nonoperational*)
Bldr: Severnaya Verf 190, St. Petersburg

	Laid down	L	In serv.	Fleet
Project 956:				
720 Boyevoy	26-3-82	4-8-84	28-9-86	Pacific
778 Burnyy	4-11-83	30-12-86	30-9-88	Pacific
429 Gremyashchiy* (ex-*Vedushchiy*)	23-11-84	30-5-87	14-1-89	Northern
715 Bystryy*	29-10-85	28-11-87	30-9-89	Pacific
420 *Rastoropnyy**	15-8-86	4-6-88	30-12-89	Northern
754 Bezboyaznennyy*	8-1-87	18-2-89	23-12-90	Pacific
406 Bezuderzhanyy	24-2-87	30-9-89	25-6-91	Northern
Project 956A:				
620 Bespokoynyy*	18-4-87	22-2-92	29-12-93	Baltic
610 Nastoychivyy (ex-*Moskovskiy Komsomolets*)	7-4-88	15-2-92	27-3-93	Baltic
434 Admiral Ushakov (ex-*Beestrashnyy*)	16-4-88	31-12-92	17-4-94	Northern

Nastoychivyy (610)—Project 956A — Frank Findler, 6-05

Nastoychivyy (610) — Leo van Ginderen, 6-05

Bespokoynyy (620)—Project 956A — Jürg Kürsener, 5-03

D: 6,500 tons light, 7,940 tons normal (8,480 fl) **S:** 33.4 kts (32.7 sust.)
Dim: 156.37 (145.00 wl) × 17.19 (16.30 wl) × 5.99 (mean hull; 7.85 max.)
A: 8 P-270 Moskit or P-100 Moskit-M (SS-N-22 Sunburn) SSM (3M-80 or 3M-82 missiles); 2 ZR-90 Uragan (SA-N-7) SAM syst. (2 single-rail MS-196 launchers; 48 9M-38 Buk-M1 or 9M-38M1 Smerch/Gadfly missiles); 2 twin 130-mm 54-cal. AK-130 DP (2,000 rounds); 4 single 30-mm 54-cal. AK-630M gatling AA (16,000 rounds); 2 twin 533-mm DTA-53 TT; 2 6-round RBU-1000 ASW RL (48 RGB-10 rockets); 2 mine rails (up to 40 tot. mines); 1 Ka-27PL Helix-A ASW or Ka-27RTs targeting helicopter
Electronics:
Radar: 3 MR-212/201 Vaygach-U (Palm Frond) nav.; 1 MR-760MA Fregat-MA (Top Plate-B) 3-D air search; 6 OP-3 (Front Dome) SA-N-7 f.c.; 1 MR-184M Lev (Kite Screech-C) 130-mm f.c.; 2 MR-123 Vympel (Bass Tilt) 30-mm f.c.; 1 Mineral surf. target tracking and desig.
Sonar: MG-335MS Platina-S (Bull Horn) MF bow-mounted; MG-7 (Whale Tongue) HF f.c.
EW: MP-405M Start-2 or MR-401 intercept syst.: 2 MRP-11M/12M (Bell Shroud); 2 Bell Squat; 4 Foot Ball-B; MR-407 jamming syst; 2 PK-2M trainable decoy syst. (2 twin-tube ZIF-121 launchers; 200 rockets)—all except *Boyevoy:* 8 10-round PK-10 fixed decoy RL
E/O: 2, 4, or 8 Spektr-F (Half Cup) laser warning; 1 Squeeze Box multisensor; 1 Tall View periscope; 2 Watch Box bridge periscopes
M: 2 sets TV-12 geared steam turbines; 2 4-bladed props; 110,000 shp (99,500 sust.)
Boilers: 4 turbopressurized Type KVN-98/64, 640 kg/cm^2, 500° C
Electric: 4,900 kw tot. (2 × 1,250-kw turboalternators, 4 × 600-kw diesel sets)
Range: 1,345/32.7; 3,920/18 (5,340/18.4 with overload fuel)
Fuel: 1,740 tons + 5 tons aviation fuel **Endurance:** 30 days
Crew: 25 officers, 271 enlisted (accomm. for 38 officers, 330 enlisted)

Remarks: Type designation: EM (*Eskhadrennyy Minonosets,* Destroyer). Project name, Sarych, means "Buzzard." Chief designer was I. Rubis. Design derived from the Kresta-I and -II series built at the same shipyard; uses a similar hullform and the same propulsion plant. Formerly called the "BAL-COM-2" class by NATO. Primarily intended for surface warfare tasks, including antiship, shore bombardment, and antiair defense; the minimal ASW capability is primarily for self-defense. Two units were ordered from 61 Kommunara Zavod, Nikolayev: *Vnushitel'nyy* ("Imposing") was laid down in 1982 and launched 17-10-87 but never completed (the hulk has been used as a floating storage barge), and the second unit was not begun. *Bespokoynyy,* the first of the Project 956A variant (see below), suffered a serious fire at Baltiysk 13-8-92, delaying her departure for the Pacific; she was instead assigned to the Baltic Fleet at Baltiysk with *Nastoychivyy. Rastoropnyy* entered the Baltic at the end of 11-00 and proceeded to Svernyy Werf, St. Petersburg, reportedly to undergo a major overhaul and modernization. The modernization was canceled soon thereafter, however, and the warship now lies derelict at the yard. Pacific Fleet unit *Bystryy,* placed in reserve early in 1999 with three of her boilers unserviceable, entered Dalzavod Shipyard during 5-02 for a refit which continued into 2006. Northern Fleet unit *Gremyashchiy* was also in overhaul as of 2005–6. *Bezboyaznennyy* began an overhaul in 2002 and remained at the yard through 2006 while sister *Bespokoynyy* began overhaul at Yantar in 2004.

The first planned Project 956U unit, to have carried the Kortik point-defense system, was the scrapped 20th hull and was to have been named *Vechniy.* A total of 28 of all versions of the basic design was to have been completed. Instead, it was announced in 8-95 that only 19 would be completed, with components assembled for later units, including the 20th, *Buynyy,* to be discarded. In 1-96, however, with no funds available for further work on the class, it was announced that two units of the class, the 18th, *Yekaterinburg* (ex-*Vazhniy*), and 19th, *Aleksandr Nevskiy* (ex-*Vdumchivyy*), would be sold to China. *Besstrashnyy* was renamed *Admiral Ushakov* during 2004, taking the name of the now-retired ex-*Kirov*.

Hull systems: The propulsion plant is essentially the same as that of the preceding Kresta-I and -II classes and employs turbopressurized boilers. Retractable fin stabilizers are fitted. Export versions are offered with a propulsion plant said to produce 73,500 kw (98,578 shp).

Combat systems: The combat system is named Sapfir-U. Early units, now stricken, had a variety of radar installations, but the survivors are more standardized.

The helicopter hangar is partially telescoping, extending aft from the stack structure, and the helicopter facilities are less elaborate than in other contemporary Russian classes, with no support or weapons stowage for an ASW helicopter provided.

The Ka-25RTs Hormone-B helicopter (which was seldom carried) could provide targeting data for the Moskit (SS-N-22) missiles, and the ships also have the large Monolit (Band Stand) radome associated with missile targeting. In recent years, when a helicopter has been aboard, it has been either a Ka-27PL ASW or a utility version of the Helix. There are also two small spherical Pricep (Light Bulb) datalink radomes on

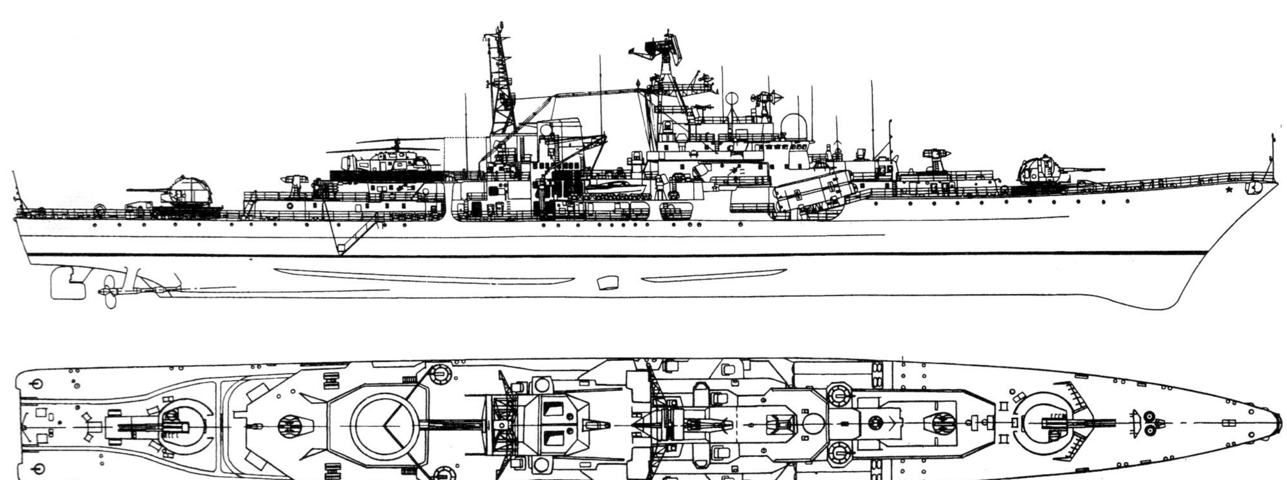
Sovremennyy class (Project 956) — Rosvoorouzhenie, 2000

GUIDED-MISSILE DESTROYERS [DDG] *(continued)*

the sides of the stack that are associated with the Moskit missile system, which uses quadruple KT-190 fixed launchers. The twin-tube, trainable launchers for the PK-2 decoy systems are at the extreme stern, and all except *Boyevoy* have eight additional 10-round PK-10 fixed launchers (six on the bridge level, two aft).

The MS-196 SAM launchers are apparently limited to launch arcs within 30° of the centerline. Maximum launch rate is five rounds per minute per launcher. The 130-mm guns, in ZIF-94 mountings, are of a fully automatic, water-cooled model, capable of AA or surface fire; they are restricted to firing arcs of 40° each side of the centerline. The AK-630 guns are restricted to firing arcs of –5° (off the centerline) through 160° for the forward mounts and 15° off centerline forward through 170° for the after mounts. The Lev-series radar gun directors in the final three units have laser rangefinder attachments.

Squeeze Box is an optronic gun fire-control director combining a laser rangefinder, low-light-level television, and infrared devices. *Nastoychivyy* appears to substitute two Soup Cup EW antennas for two Foot Ball-B and also has a Trawl Net intercept antenna and a Long Head IFF transponder. *Bezboyaznennyy* and *Nastoychivyy* have two Chop Dish small SATCOM antennas.

Bespokoynyy and later are designated Project 956A and have longer cruise-missile tubes to accept the extended-range P-100 Moskit-M system's 3M-82 missile; Project 956A ships are also said to carry a naval version of the 9M-38E1 Yozh (NATO SA-17 Grizzly) land-based SAM vice the Uragan system's original 9K-37 Smerch missiles.

Offered for export construction is an 8,700-ton variant with 16 Kh-35 Uran (SS-N-25 Switchblade) antiship missiles in place of the eight SS-N-22 missiles, two Kortik CIWS flanking the aft end of the helicopter deck, and omission of the AK-630 gatling guns. A 9,000-ton variant has also been offered with 24 unidentified vertically launched antiship missiles replacing the aft 130-mm gunmount and four Kortik mounts (the forward pair would replace the tube-launched cruise missile launcher installations abreast the bridge). Export versions are also offered with the SSN-137 towed sonar array.

Disposals: *Sovremennyy,* which began a never-completed overhaul at Rosta in 1988, was allocated for cannibalization in 8-98 and stricken during 11-98; she remains afloat at Rosta as a spares source. The disarmed and partially stripped *Otlichnyy* was placed in technical reserve at Severomorsk in 11-94 under constant pumping to control flooding; she was stricken in 1998 and later scrapped. Pacific Fleet unit *Otchayannyy* and Northern Fleet units *Otlichniy* and *Okrylennyy* were stricken 16-8-97, with the latter being scrapped beginning 10-00 at Murmansk. Northern Fleet unit *Bezuprechniy* began a yard period at Rosta in 1992 but was laid up 1-11-93; in 8-94 the ship was sent to Severnaya Werf, St. Petersburg, for conversion to Project 956A configuration, but the work never commenced and she is now essentially derelict, having been stripped of useful parts to assist in outfitting the two sold to China. Pacific Fleet unit *Stoikiy* flooded and capsized during spring 1999 while in reserve; a sailor had stolen the flooding valve castings. Pacific Fleet unit *Osmotritel'nyy,* in reserve for some years, is under consideration for scrapping.

♦ 2 Kara (Berkut-B) class (Project 1134B) (1 in *reserve/overhaul*)

Bldr: 61 Kommunara SY 445, Nikolayev, Ukraine

	Laid down	L	In serv.	Fleet
707 Ochakov	19-12-69	30-4-71	4-11-73	Black Sea
713 *Kerch'*	30-4-71	21-7-72	25-12-74	Black Sea

Kerch' (713) Boris Lemachko, 9-02

D: 6,590 tons light (8,470 normal fl, 8,825 max. fl)
S: 32.7 kts (30 sust., 18 on cruise turbines)
Dim: 173.40 (162.00 wl) × 18.50 (16.80 wl) × 6.35 (max.; 5.74 max. hull)
A: 8 URK-5 Rastrub (SS-N-14 Silex) ASW/antiship SSM (2 4-round KT-100 launchers, 8 Type 83R and 83RUS missiles); 2 twin-rail M-11 Shtorm (SA-N-3) SAM syst. (80 V-611/Goblet missiles); 2 twin-rail Osa-M (SA-N-4) SAM syst. (40 9M-33/Gecko missiles); 2 twin 76.2-mm 59-cal. AK-726 DP (2,400 rounds); 4 single 30-mm 54-cal. AK-630M gatling AA (8,000 rounds); 2 quintuple 533-mm TT; 2 12-round RBU-6000 ASW RL (144 RGB-60 rockets); 2 6-round RBU-1000 ASW RL (60 RGB-10 rockets); 1 Ka-27PL Helix-A helicopter
Electronics:
Radar: 1 Don-2 or MR-212/201 Vaygach-U (Palm Frond) nav.; 2 Volga (Don-Kay) nav.; 1 MR-700 Podberezovik (Flat Screen) 3-D early warning; 1 MR-310U Angara-M (Head Net-C) air search; 2 Grom (Head Lights-C) cruise missile f.c.; 2 MPZ-301 Baza (Pop Group) SA-N-4 f.c.; 2 MR-105 Turel' (Owl Screech) 76.2-mm f.c.; 2 MR-123 Vympel (Bass Tilt) 30-mm f.c.
Sonar: MG-332 Titan-2T (Bull Nose) hull-mounted MF; MG-325 Vega (Mare Tail) MF VDS
EW: Kol'cho-series suite: 8 MR-401 Gurzhor-A/B (Side Globe) intercept; 4 MR-404 (Rum Tub) jammers; 2 PK-2 trainable decoy syst. (2 twin ZIF-121 RL)
E/O: 2 Tee Plinth t.v. surveillance
M: COGOG M-5 plant: 4 M-8E (GTU-12A) boost gas turbines, 20,000 shp each; 2 M-62 cruise gas turbines, 6,000 shp each; 2 props; 92,000 shp max.
Electric: 5,600 kw tot. (4 × 1,250-kw, 1 × 600-kw gas turbine sets)
Range: 2,270/32.7; 7,100/18; 9,000/14
Fuel: 1,830 tons + 16.8 tons aviation fuel **Endurance:** 30 days
Crew: 47 officers, 47 warrant officers, 286 enlisted

Remarks: Type designation: BPK (*Bol'shoy Protivolodochnyy Korabl',* Large Antisubmarine Ship), a type considered by the Russian Navy to be more in the destroyer than cruiser category; the commanding officers have normally been commander-equivalents. *Kerch'* had completed a minor refit at Sevastapol' by 2004 at which time she received the gas turbine engines from the Ukrainian frigate *Sevastopol'*; she was decommissioned during 1-05 and is currently awaiting overhaul at Novorossisk. Sister *Ochakov* underwent overhaul between 2000 and 2005 at Sevastapol'.
Hull systems: Have retractable active fin stabilization systems.
Combat systems: The missile systems all can also be used against surface targets, and the RBU weapons have a countertorpedo capability. The helicopter hangar is at main-deck level, the helicopter being raised to the flight deck by means of an inclined elevator. Six ASW torpedoes are carried for the helicopter. Received the new MR-700 Podberezovik (Flat Screen) rotating, phased planar array, 3-D air-search radar in place of MR-600 Voskhod (Top Sail) during a late-1980s overhaul; the radar has not been fitted to any other class.
Disposals: Pacific Ocean Fleet units *Nikolayev* and *Tashkent* returned to the Black Sea for overhauls in the late 1980s; both were stricken 3-7-92 and sold for scrap during 1994, with the *Nikolayev* having sunk in the Red Sea while under tow to India and the *Tashkent* having been scrapped at Alang, India, in 12-94. *Vladivostok* (ex-*Tallin*), in reserve at Sevastopol' since the early 1990s, was stricken on 5-7-94 and scrapped 12-94 at Alang. Pacific Fleet unit *Petropavlovsk* was stricken on 17-11-94. The Modified Kara–class Black Sea Fleet destroyer *Azov* (Project 1134.7BF) was stricken 10-12-98, having already been stripped of useful equipment.

♦ 1 Kashin class (Project 61)

Bldr: 61 Kommunara Zavod 445, Nikolayev, Ukraine

	Laid down	L	In serv.	Fleet
810 Smetlivyy	26-8-67	15-6-68	21-10-69	Black Sea

Smetlivyy (810) Anthony Vella, 9-04

D: 3,550 tons std.; 4,030 tons normal (4,510 fl) **S:** 34 kts (35.5 on trials)
Dim: 144.00 (132.20 wl) × 15.80 (14.00 wl) × 4.45 (hull; 6.0 max.)
A: 2 twin-rail SA-N-1 Volna SAM syst. (2 ZIF-101 launchers; 32 V-601/Goa missiles); 1 twin 76.2-mm 59-cal. AK-726 DP; 1 quintuple 533-mm PTA-53-61 TT; 2 12-round RBU-6000 ASW RL (192 RGB-60 rockets); 2 mine rails (. . . mines)
Electronics:
Radar: 2 Volga (Don-Kay) or Vaygach-U (Palm Frond) nav.; 1 MR-310U Angara-M (Head Net-C) air search; 1 MR-500 Kliver (Big Net) early warning; 1 Yatagan (Peel Group) SA-N-1 f.c.; 1 MR-105 Turel' (Owl Screech) gun f.c.
Sonar: MIK-300 suite: MG-332 Titan-2 bow sonar and MG-325 Vega VDS (see remarks)
EW: 2 Start-1 (Bell Shroud) intercept; 2 . . . (Bell Squat) jammers; 4 16-round PK-16 fixed decoy RL; 2 10-round PK-10 fixed decoy RL
E/O: 2 trainable Tee Plinth t.v.; 4 Tilt Pot fixed t.v.; 2 Watch Box bridge periscopes
M: COGAG M-3 plant: 4 Type M-8E gas turbines, 2 3-bladed props (300 rpm max.); 96,000 shp (72,000 sust.)
Electric: 2,800 kw tot. (4 × 600-kw gas turbine sets, 2 × 200-kw diesel sets)
Range: 1,000/35; 2,000/30; 3,500/18 **Fuel:** 940 tons + 6 tons aviation fuel
Crew: 22 officers, 266 enlisted

Remarks: Program initiated 8-56; design completed 11-59. Was in overhaul and modification 1987–96; after departing the yard, was briefly laid up for lack of funds to complete the final 5% of the overhaul, which included a new sonar suite, the addition of antiship missiles, and improved EW equipment. Is assigned to the Black Sea Fleet. Was demoted from *Bol'shoy Protivolodochnyy Korabl'* (Large Antisubmarine Ship) to *Storozhevoy Korabl'* (Patrol Ship) in 1992.
Hull systems: Original displacement was 3,400 tons standard, 4,390 full load. There are 14 main watertight compartments, including five main engineering compartments: forward and after paired main engine compartments (each with one main engine, two gas turbine generators, and a diesel generator) and an auxiliary compartment. The service life of the main engines is nominally 3,000 hours. Were among the world's first ships to pay attention to sound and heat radiation reduction, and the superstructure and stacks were shaped to reduce radar return; stack effluent temperature is 180° C at full power. Superstructure and masts were built of AMG-5V light alloy. Hull has a double bottom over 80% of length. Manned spaces are pressurized against NBC warfare attack; the washdown system supplies 700 tons/hr of salt water. Has retractable fin stabilizers. Original provisions endurance was only 10 days; 70 tons of fresh water are carried.
Combat systems: Can carry 2,400 rounds of 76.2-mm ammunition; the twin 76.2-mm guns are in a ZIF-67 mounting. The Volna SAM system, which uses ZIF-101 triaxially stabilized twin-armed launchers, has never been considered satisfactory and may no longer be operational. During 1990s refit, the RBU-1000 ASW rocket launchers were replaced by racks port and starboard for quadruple Kh-35 Uran (SS-N-25) missile launchers (not actually installed until 2000 and then removed again after a port visit to Turkey), a variable-depth sonar was added at the stern, and the after 76.2-mm gunmount and its associated f.c. radar were deleted. Other changes included the installation of a modern EW suite and increased officer accommodations within the forward superstructure block, but planned replacement of the 533-mm torpedo tube mount by a seven-tube 402-mm OTA-40 mounting was not carried out.
Disposals: Class prototype *Komsomolets Ukrainyy* was laid down 15-9-59, launched 31-12-60, and commissioned 31-12-62. Of 20 originally completed during 1962–73, six were converted or completed to the "Modified Kashin" design (Projects 61M and

GUIDED-MISSILE DESTROYERS [DDG] *(continued)*

61MP). *Otvazhnyy* (ex-*Orel*) sank 20-8-74 after a SAM magazine explosion and fire. *Provornyy* was converted during the 1970s as trials ship for the SA-N-7 SAM system and was stricken in 10-90. *Komsomolets Ukrainyy* was stricken 24-1-91, *Soobrazitel'ny* on 3-7-92, and *Odarennyy, Steregushchiy,* and *Strogiy* on 30-7-93. *Sposobnyy* returned to the Black Sea 30-7-87 for a refit and conversion as Project 01091 sonar trials ship at Sevmorzavod, Sevastopol', but was officially stricken 6-1-93 and towed away for scrap 2-4-95 (in 4-93, Ukraine had made a claim to the ship but was rebuffed by Russia). *Obratsovyy* was stricken 30-7-93 and *Krasnyy Krym* on 24-6-91. *Reshitel'niy,* long out of service, was not stricken until 16-8-97 and was scrapped in Turkey in 1999. *Krasny Kavkaz* was stricken 26-5-98 and *Skoryy* by mid-1999.

Disposal note: The remaining Modified Kashin (Project 61M), the Black Sea Fleet's *Sderzhannyy,* began stripping of armament and antennas for later disposal on 29-5-01 and was scrapped at Mikolayiv, Ukraine, during 2002. *Smel'yy* was transferred to Poland during 12-87; *Ognevoy* was scrapped in Turkey in 10-90; *Slavnyy* was stricken 24-6-91; *Stroynyy* was scrapped in Turkey in 1-91; and *Smyshlennyy* was stricken 22-2-93.

DESTROYERS [DD]

♦ 1 Admiral Chabanenko ("Udaloy-II") class (Project 11551)

Bldr: Yantar Zavod 820, Kaliningrad

	Laid down	L	In serv.	Fleet
650 Admiral Chabanenko (ex-*Admiral Basistiy*)	28-2-89	14-12-92	28-1-99	Northern

Admiral Chabanenko (650) Bernard Prézelin, 9-04

Admiral Chabanenko (650) Bernard Prézelin, 9-04

D: 7,750 tons (8,950 fl) **S:** 29.5 kts
Dim: 163.0 (150.0 wl) × 19.3 (17.8 wl) × 6.2 (8.0 max.)
A: 8 P-100 Moskit-M (SS-N-22 Sunburn) SSM (2 quadruple KT-190M launchers); Kinzhal (SA-N-9) SAM syst. (8 8-round PU 4S-95 VLS; 64 9M-330 Tor-M1/ Gauntlet missiles); 1 twin 130-mm 70-cal. AK-130 DP; 2 Kortik CIWS (each with 8 missile tubes and 2 30-mm GSH-6-30L gatling AA; 64 tot. 9M-311 Vikhr'-K/ SA-N-11 Grison missiles); 2 10-round RPK-5 Liven' ASW RL; 2 quadruple 533-mm TT (Type 86R Vodopad-NK [SS-N-16] ASW missiles and torpedoes); 2 mine rails (. . . mines); 1 Ka-27PL Helix-A ASW helicopter; 1 Ka-27RTs Helix targeting helicopter
Electronics:
Radar: 3 MR-212/201 Vaygach-U (Palm Frond) nav.; 1 MR-760 Fregat-MA (Top Plate) 3-D air search; 1 MR-320M Topaz-V (Strut Pair) surf./air search; 1 MR-184 Lev (Kite Screech-C) 130-mm f.c.; 1 Garpun-BAL (in Monolit/ Band Stand radome) antiship missile targeting; 2 MR-360 Podkat (Cross Sword) SA-N-9 f.c.; 2 3P-87 (Hot Flash) Kortik CIWS f.c.; 1 Fly Screen-B helicopter landing aid
Sonar: Zvezda-M2 suite: . . . (Ox Yoke) bow-mounted LF; MGK-345 Bronza (Rat Tail) LF VDS
TACAN: 2 Privod-B (Round House)
EW: Start-series suite: 2 Wine Glass intercept; 2 MP-401 (Bell Shroud) intercept; 2 Bell Squat; 2 PK-2 decoy syst. (2 twin, trainable ZIF-121 RL); 10 10-round PK-10 fixed decoy RL
E/O: 4 Spektr-F (Half Cup) laser detection
M: COGAG M-9 plant: 2 M8KF boost gas turbines (22,500 shp each), 2 M-62 cruise gas turbines (7,500 shp each); 2 props; 60,000 shp max.
Electric: 6,000 kw tot. (4 × 1,500-kw gas turbine sets)
Range: 5,700/18 **Fuel:** 2,000 tons **Endurance:** 30 days
Crew: 32 officers, 264 warrant officers and enlisted

Remarks: Two ships of this design were originally intended for the KGB Maritime Border Guard but after the 1991 revolution were bequeathed to the navy. Completion of the first was delayed by the economic and social turmoil within Russia, and the second, *Admiral Kucharov* (later named *Admiral Basistiy*), was scrapped in 3-94, prior to launch. *Admiral Chabanenko* was handed over to the Russian Navy in 10-96 but was not commissioned for two additional years; she departed Baltiysk 24-2-99 and arrived at Severomorsk 10-3-99 for duty with the Northern Fleet. As of 12-00, the ship was assigned to the "Kola Fleet" and based at Severomorsk.
Hull systems: Hull and propulsion plant essentially dupicate those of the *Udaloy* class, although the forecastle deck has been extended further aft. One source indicates that the gas turbine engines are uprated over those in the *Udaloys,* producing a total output of 65,000 shp and an unlikely maximum speed of 32 kts. Maximum propeller rpm is 327.
Combat systems: Electronics equipment not listed above includes two Chop Dish SATCOM antennas mounted abreast the hangar and two Pricep (Light Bulb) datalink antennas, associated with the Moskit missile system. The sonar suite probably duplicates that of the frigate *Neustrashimyy;* the bow-mounted sonar dome is unusually long, extending aft to beneath the 130-mm mount and containing a second, possibly flank, transducer array, but one source indicates that a planned, even larger array was not installed. The torpedo tubes are mounted behind shutters in the hull sides, and there may be a complete set of reloads. Carries 350 rounds of 130-mm and 12,000 rounds of 30-mm gun ammunition. The RBU-6000 rocket launchers are described as being intended primarily as antitorpedo countermeasures in this ship. The 130-mm gun fire-control radar is a dual-frequency set with laser rangefinder and television adjuncts. The Type 2S95 vertical SAM launchers provide up to a 24 launch/min rate of fire.

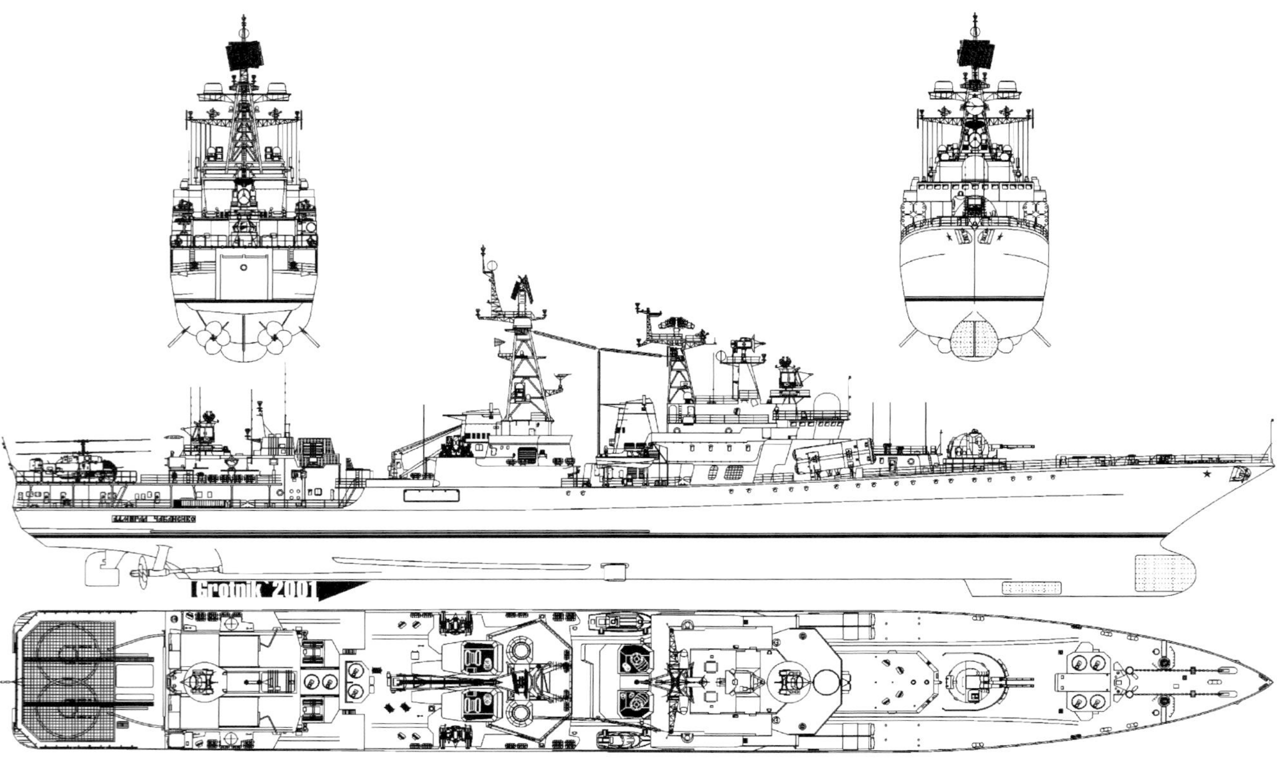

Udaloy-II class—project 11551 Drawing by T. Grotnik, 2001

DESTROYERS [DD] *(continued)*

♦ **8 Udaloy (Fregat) class (Project 1155R)** (3 in *reserve*)
Bldrs: A: SevernayaVerf 190, St. Petersburg; B: Yantar Zavod 820, Kaliningrad

	Bldr	Laid down	L	In serv.	Fleet
400 *Vitse-Admiral Kulakov*	A	4-11-77	16-5-80	10-1-82	Northern
564 Admiral Tributs	A	19-4-80	26-3-83	30-12-85	Pacific
543 Marshal Shaposhnikov	B	8-5-83	30-12-84	30-12-85	Pacific
619 Severomorsk (ex-*Simferopol'*, ex-*Marshal Zhukov*, ex-*Marshal Budenniy*)	B	12-6-84	24-12-85	30-12-87	Northern
605 Admiral Levchenko (ex-*Khabarovsk*)	A	27-1-82	21-2-85	30-9-88	Northern
572 *Admiral Vinogradov*	B	5-2-86	4-6-87	30-12-88	Pacific
678 Admiral Kharlamov	B	7-8-86	29-6-88	30-12-89	Northern
548 *Admiral Panteleyev*	B	28-4-88	7-2-90	19-12-91	Pacific

Admiral Levchenko (605) Michael Winter, 6-05

Admiral Levchenko (605) Bernard Prézelin, 6-05

D: 6,930–6,945 tons std.; 7,570–7,585 tons normal (8,404 max. fl)
S: 29.5 kts (29 sust.)
Dim: 163.50 (145.00 wl) × 19.00 (17.20 wl) × 5.19 (hull; 7.80 max.)
A: 8 URK-5 Rastrub (SS-N-14 Silex) ASW and antiship SSM (2 quadruple KT-100 launchers; 8 Type 83R and 83RUS missiles); 8 Kinzhal (SA-N-9) SAM syst. (8 8-round PU 4S-95 VLS; 64 9M-330 Tor M1/Gauntlet missiles); 2 single 100-mm 70-cal. AK-100 DP (1,200 tot. rounds); 4 single 30-mm 54-cal. AK-630M gatling AA (12,000 rounds); 2 12-round RBU-6000 ASW RL (96 RGB-12 rockets); 2 quadruple 533-mm CLTA-53-1155 TT; 2 mine rails (. . . mines); 2 Ka-27PL Helix-A ASW helicopters

Admiral Levchenko (605) Leo van Ginderen, 6-05

Marshal Shaposhnikov (543) U.S. Navy, 3-06

Electronics:
Radar: 3 MR-212/201 Vaygach-U (Palm Frond) nav.—all but *Shaposhnikov:* 1 MR-320M Topaz-V (Strut Pair) surf./air search; 1 MR-760MA Fregat-MA (Top Plate) 3-D air search; 2 Drakon (Eye Bowl) f.c. for ASW/antiship missiles; 1 MR-145 Lev (Kite Screech-B) 100-mm f.c.; 2 MR-360 Podkat (Cross Sword) SAM f.c.; 2 MR-123 Vympel (Bass Tilt) 30-mm f.c.; 1 . . . (Fly Screen-B) microwave helicopter landing aid
Sonar: MGK-355 Polinom suite: MGK-335 Platina (Horse Jaw) bow-mounted LF; Orion (Horse Tail) LF VDS; MG-35 underwater telephone; MGK-355TA torpedo detection
TACAN: 2 Privod (Round House)
EW: 2 Start-2 (Bell Shroud); 2 Bell Squat; 4 Bell Crown; 2 twin PK-2 decoy RL (ZIF-121 launchers; 400 rockets)—later ships also: 10 10-round PK-10 fixed decoy RL
E/O: 6 Spektr-F (Half Cup) laser warning
M: COGAG M-9 plant : 2 M-8KF boost gas turbines (22,500 shp each), 2 M-62 cruise gas turbines (7,500 shp each); 2 5-bladed props; 60,000 shp max.
Electric: 5,000 kw tot. (4 × 1,250-kw gas turbine sets)
Range: 2,550/29; 7,700/18; 6,882/14 **Fuel:** 1,500 tons + 40 tons aviation fuel
Endurance: 30 days **Crew:** 29 officers, 191 enlisted

Remarks: Class initally had the NATO nickname "BAL-COM-3." Type designation is BPK (*Bol'shoy Protivolodochnyy Korabl'*, Large Antisubmarine Ship). Project name Fregat means "Frigate bird." This class saw relatively little operational use during the 1990s because of the difficulty in obtaining spare gas turbines, which have had to be imported from Ukraine; the Rybinsk Motors factory began repairing the existing engines in 1999 and is developing the capability to manufacture replacements. Increased funding has permitted an increasing number of refits and ships of the class are now much more extensively employed in operations.
Status: *Admiral Tributs* had a serious shipyard fire at Vladivostok 18-7-91 and was placed in reserve in 1995; she had another fire in 9-95 and began repairs during 1-98 at Dalzavod Shipyard, Vladivostok, where repairs were completed in 2001. *Simferopol'* was renamed *Severomorsk* on 21-1-96, she began a major refit at Severnaya Verf, St. Petersburg, arriving in 7-98 but with work not commencing until fall 1999 and completing 30-8-00; her departure for the Northern Fleet was delayed by a fire at St. Petersburg in 9-00, and the ship left Bal'tysk 5-11-00. *Admiral Levchenko* arrived in 2-00 at the same yard for refit and replacement of engines and returned to the Northern Fleet at the end of 9-01, and *Admiral Kharlamov* was refitted at Northern Fleet area facilities during 1999–2001. The refit of *Vitse-Admiral Kulakov,* at Kron-

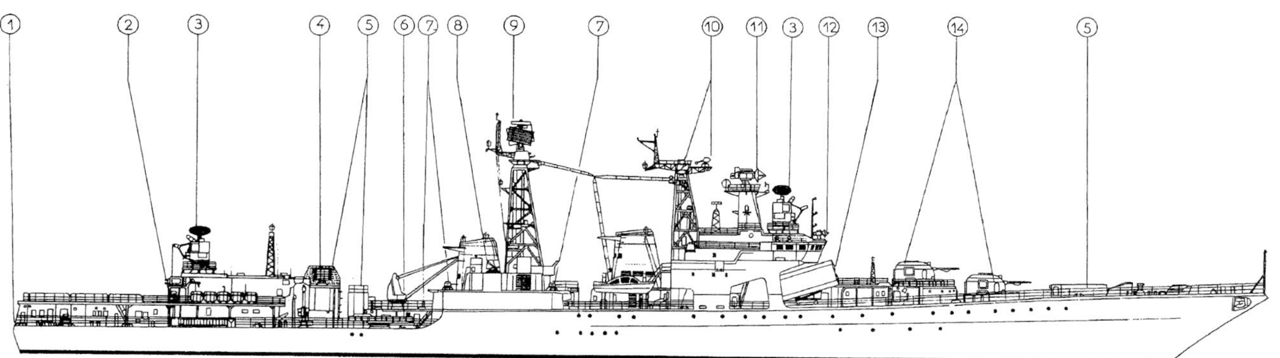

Udaloy class 1. VDS housing beneath helicopter flight deck 2. Dual helicopter hangars 3. MR-360 Podkat radar director for Kinzhal SAM system 4. RBU-6000 ASW RL 5. Rotating vertical launch cells for Kinzhal SAM system 6. Quadruple 533-mm TT (port and starboard) 7. 30-mm AK-630 gatling AA 8. MR-123 Vympel radar director for 30-mm AA 9. MR-760MA Fregat-MA 3-D air-search radar 10. MR-212/201 Vaygach-U nav./surf.-search radars (the platform above these is now occupied by the antenna for the MR-320M Topaz-V surf./air-search radar) 11. MR-145 Lev radar director for the 100-mm guns 12. Drakon radar director/trackers for URK-5 Rastrub ASW/antiship missiles 13. Quadruple launch containers for URK-5 ASW/antiship missiles 14. 100-mm AK-100 DP guns
Drawing by Lucien Gassier, from *Flottes de Combat*

DESTROYERS [DD] *(continued)*

shtadt since 1992, was moved in 6-00 to Severnaya Verf, St. Petersburg, where work resumed in 2002 and completed in 2005. *Vitse-Admiral Kulakov, Admiral Vinogradov,* and *Admiral Panteleyev* were placed in reserve status during 2005.
Hull systems: Were originally to have had a more-powerful propulsion plant totaling 72,000 shp, but the intended boost turbine component was not developed. Either cruise turbine can drive either or both shafts via a common gearbox. Maximum propeller rpm is 327. Have automated controls for the propulsion and auxiliary plants. Fitted with retractable fin stabilizers. The sonar dome is 30 m long and 5.1 m wide and imposes a considerable performance penalty. In overload condition, up to 1,700 tons of fuel can be carried.
Combat systems: The combat system is named Lesorub-5. Four vertical launchers for the Kinzhal SAM system have a combined rate of fire of up to 24 per minute and are located on the raised portion of the forecastle, two more are disposed athwartships in the small deckhouse between the torpedo tubes, and two are arranged fore and aft in the deckhouse between the RBU-6000 ASW RL mounts; each rotating cylinder holds eight missiles. All normally carry four antiship and four antisubmarine torpedoes in the 533-mm tubes; there are no reloads.

The two hangars are side by side and use inclined elevator ramps to raise the aircraft to the flight deck; the hangar roofs slide forward in two segmented sections to clear the rotors. From the third unit on, the helicopter deck was wider, extending to the sides of the ship. Two Privod (Round House) TACAN radomes are mounted on yards on the after mast, while the Fly Screen microwave landing-control radar is beside the starboard hangar. Four ASW torpedoes, 72 air-dropped rocket-propelled depth charges, and 20 standard depth charges can be carried for the helicopters.

The EW suite is incomplete, with several empty platforms on the after mast, except for *Severomorsk,* which has four Foot Ball (Start-series) radomes on the after mast. *Vitse-Admiral Kulakov* was to have had the radar suite updated to later class standard during her current, protracted overhaul. *Marshal Shaposhnikov* still lacks the antenna for the MR-320M Topaz-V air-search radar atop the foremast.
Disposals: Class prototype *Udaloy* was stricken from the Northern Fleet 31-8-98. *Admiral Zakharov,* completed in 1983, suffered an engine room explosion and fire 17-2-92, was stricken 29-9-94, and was later scrapped in South Korea. *Admiral Spiridonov,* placed in 2nd Class Reserve at Vladivostok 31-8-98 after several years of inactivity, was being used as a spare parts source until she was scrapped during 2005. The overhaul of *Marshal Vasil'yevskiy* ceased during 2002 and the vessel was reportedly decommissioned during 2006.

GUIDED MISSILE FRIGATES [FFG]

♦ 0 (+ 1 + 1 + ?) Serguei Gorshkov class (Project 22350)
Bldr: Severnaya Verf, St. Petersburg

	Laid down	L	In serv.
. . . Serguei Gorshkov	2-2-06	. . .	2009

D: 4,500 tons **S:** 30 kts **Dim:** 132. × . . . × . . .
A: 8 Onyx (3M55) SSM missiles; 1 ZR-90 Uragan (SA-N-7) SAM syst. (1 single-rail MS-196 launcher; 1 130-mm DP; SS-NX-29 ASW missiles; 1 helicopter

Remarks: Data listed above is speculative. Though large enough to be considered destroyers, the vessels have reportedly been classified as frigates for political reasons. Each unit will cost US$300-$400 million to build. A maximum of 20 units of this class are projected.

FRIGATES [FF]

♦ 0 (+ 3 + 1) Steregushchiy class (Project 20380)
Bldr: Severnaya Verf, St. Petersburg

	Laid down	L	In serv.
. . . Steregushchiy	21-12-01	16-5-06	2007
. . . Soobraziltel'nyy	20-05-03	2007	2008
. . . Boikiy	26-7-05	. . .	. . .

Model of the Russian Project 20380 frigate Alexandre Sheldon-Duplaix, 6-03

D: 1,850 tons (2,100 fl) **S:** 26 kts **Dim:** 111.6 × 14.0 × 3.7 (mean hull)
A: 8 Kh-35 Uran SSM; 1 3R87ME Kortik-M CIWS syst. (64 9M-311 missiles; 2 30-mm gatling AA); 1 100-mm 59-cal. A-190 DP; 2 single 30-mm 54-cal. AK-630M AA; 2 pair 533-mm TR-203 TT (Type 83RN and 84R Vodopad-NK ASW missiles or Type 53-65N and SET-65 torpedoes); 1 Kamov Ka-27PL Helix-A ASW helicopter
Electronics:
Radar: 2 MR-231 nav./surf. search; 1 Pozitiv-M1 3-D air search; 1 Garpun SSM target desig.
Sonar: Zarya hull-mounted LF; Minotaur towed VDS
EW: TK-25 intercept/active suite; 4 10-round PK-10 fixed decoy RL
M: 4 Kolomenskiy 16D49 diesels; 2 CP props; 33,188 bhp—drop-down electric azimuthal bow-thruster
Electric: 2,000 kw tot. (4 × 500-kw Kolomenskiy 22-26DG diesel sets)
Range: 3,600/15 **Fuel:** . . . tons + 20 tons aviation fuel
Endurance: 15 days **Crew:** 14 officers, 86 enlisted (with air crew)

Remarks: Are initially to be used in the Caspian Flotilla, according to statements by the commander-in-chief of the Russian Navy, Adm. Kuroyedov, and the chief of the Main Navy Staff, Adm. Kravchenko. The design was approved by the Russian Navy during 2-01, at which time a unit cost of $50 million was expected. The construction contract was given to Severnaya Verf on 25-5-01. Although the goal is 20 ships in the class and the Russian Navy C-in-C announced that 10 were in the original order, the number was reduced to four as of 15-6-01, and the price had risen to about $120 million each. During 10-01 an export version, Project 20282, was offered to Iran for $150 million.
Hull systems: Will have fin stabilizers and bow bulwarks. No hangar is to be fitted, but there will be a helicopter weapons reload and fueling capability. The hull and superstructure do not appear to have had much radar signature reduction effort. The boat to starboard and RIB to port are carried behind low bulwarks.
Combat systems: The 30-mm gatling guns appear to have only lead-computing ringsight directors. The Kortik SAM launcher sets are recessed into the deck just forward of the helicopter platform, while the SSM missiles are vertically launched from cells just abaft the 100-mm gun. It is possible that the weapons fit has not yet been finalized.

Note: Cancellation of the frigate *Novik* (Project 12441) at Yantar Zavod, Kaliningrad, was announced 30-10-01. The ship had been laid down 26-7-97 but was canceled on 22-1-98. Some $3.16 million was provided in the FY 01 defense budget to restart construction, however, and the ship was about 10% completed, but the age of the design and the projected expense involved in building only one ship to the now-aging design evidently proved too much. Despite the cancellation, however, the yard was reportedly continuing work into 2002, though the funding was intermittent at best throughout 2006–7.

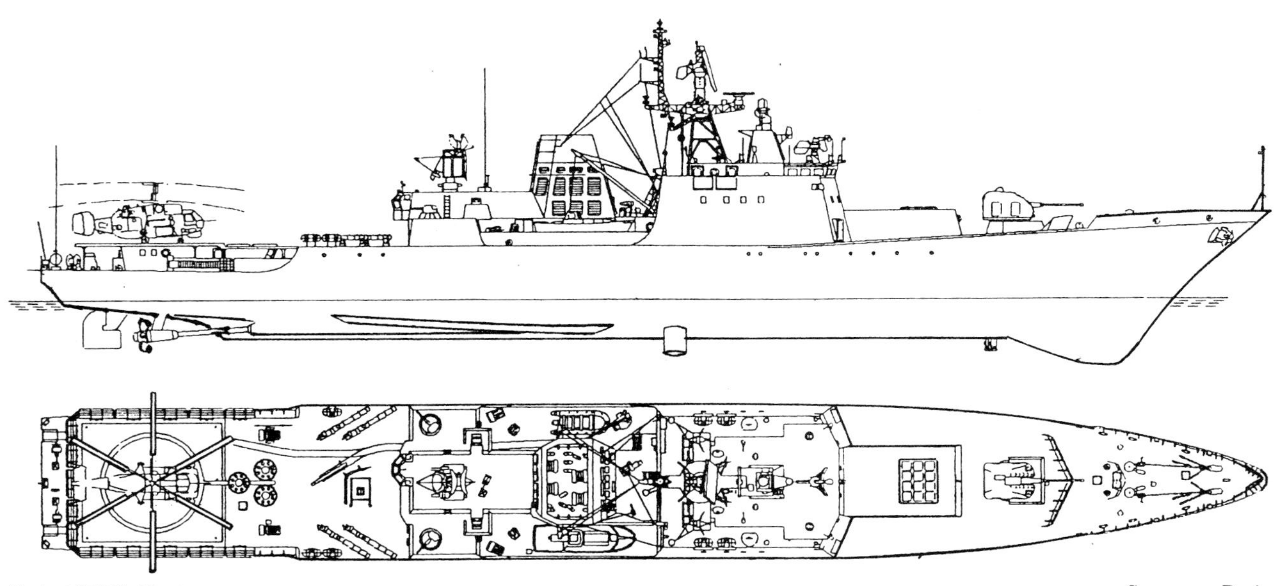

Drawing of the Project 20380 frigate Severnoye Design Bureau, 2001

FRIGATES [FF] *(continued)*

♦ 1 (+ 1) Gepard (Yastreb) class (Project 11661)
Bldr: Zelenodol'sk Zavod, Kazan, Tatarstan

	Laid down	L	In serv.	Fleet
691 TATARSTAN (ex-*Yastreb*, ex-SKR-200)	15-9-92	7-93	12-7-02	Caspian
. . . DAGESTAN (ex-*Burevestnik*, ex-*Gepard*, ex-*Albatros*, ex-SKR-201)	1994	15-8-05	2007	. . .

Tatarstan (691) Zelenodol'sk Zavod via Werner Globke, 6-03

D: 1,600 tons (2,090 fl) **S:** 27 kts (20 on diesel)
Dim: 102.14 (93.50 wl) × 13.09 × 3.60 (5.30 over sonar dome)
A: 8 Kh-35 Uran (SS-N-25 Switchblade) SSM; 1 twin-rail Osa-M (SA-N-4) SAM syst. (20 9M-33/Gecko missiles); 1 76.2-mm 59-cal. AK-176 DP; 2 single 30-mm 54-cal. AK-630 gatling AA; 2 twin 533-mm TT; 1 12-round RBU-6000 ASW RL; 2 mine rails (12–20 mines)
Electronics:
Radar: 1 . . . nav.; 1 MR-352 Pozitiv (Cross Dome) surf./air search; 1 MPZ-301 Baza (Pop Group) SA-N-4 missile f.c.; 1 Monolit (Band Stand) cruise missile target desig.; 1 MR-123 Vympel (Bass Tilt) 30-mm f.c.
Sonar: Zarnitsa suite: . . . MF hull mounted; . . . MF VDS
EW: 2 Bell Shroud intercept; 2 Bell Squat jammers; 4 16-round PK-16 fixed decoy RL
M: CODOG: 2 gas turbines (29,300 shp each), 1 Type 61D diesel (8,000 bhp); 2 props
Electric: 1,800 kw tot. (3 × 600-kw, 380-V, 50-Hz a.c. diesel alternator sets)
Range: 950/27; 3,500/14; 4,000/10 (5,000/10 at overload displacement)
Endurance: 15 days **Crew:** 15 officers, 94 enlisted (accomm. for 131 tot.)

Remarks: Has also been listed as Project 11660. Characteristics above are for the basic version, of which the first, *Tatarstan,* was essentially complete by late 1995. *Burevestnik* was to be of a modified design, optimized for patrol duties, and was to have a helicopter hangar if completed. Funds had reportedly been found during 12-99 to complete three ships, which were said at that time to be 93%, 67%, and 40% complete. Funding for completion of the first unit was requested from Tatarstan, for which the ship was formally named on 17-4-02, and she was delivered to the Caspian Flotilla during 7-02. The third unit may have been scrapped, although a 5-02 press report indicated that it was still at the yard. No additional information has since been made available.

The design is offered for export in the following variations: Gepard 1, with a helicopter platform (but no hangar) atop a deckhouse at the stern replacing the VDS housing; Gepard 2, with a helicopter hangar in place of the SA-N-4 SAM system and VDS deleted; Gepard 3, with greater beam (13.8 m) and displacement (2,100 tons fl), a Kortik CIWS in place of the forward 30-mm gatling gun, the other gatling guns eliminated, the missile tubes raised one deck, the torpedo tubes moved near the stern, and a helicopter deck and hangar above a VDS housing; Gepard 4, configured as a rescue ship with no armament (although mounting positions as in the basic design would be fitted forward) and with a hangar and flight deck as in the Gepard 2; and Gepard 5, with helicopter deck, no hangar, and reduced gun armament (one 76.2-mm and two 30-mm gatling) as a patrol ship, with extended range (6,000 n.m. at 10 kts) but reduced speed of 23 kts from two 8,000-bhp diesels and no gas turbine.

Hull systems: Molded depth amidships: 7.25 m; height above waterline: 25.00 m. Capable of employing weapons in up to Sea State 5. Steel hull and superstructure, with some use of aluminum-magnesium alloy in the upper superstructure. To carry 13 10-man life rafts. Hull is equipped with fin stabilizers and has twin rudders. Either the gas turbines or the diesel is used for propulsion, but not all together; in an emergency, the diesel can drive one shaft and one gas turbine the other.

Combat systems: To carry a sonobuoy receiver/processor for working with ASW aircraft. A tactical data system is planned. The hull-mounted sonar dome is located below and just forward of the bridge. The large Monolit (Band Stand) radome atop the pilothouse probably contains a target detection and designation radar for the Kh-35 Uran antiship missiles. The sonar dome is mounted below and just forward of the bridge. To carry 500 rounds of 76-mm and 4,000 rounds of 30-mm ammunition.

♦ 2 (+ 1) Neustrashimyy class (Project 11540)
Bldr: Yantar Zavod 820, Kaliningrad

	Laid down	L	In serv.	Fleet
712 NEUSTRASHIMYY ("Fearless")	25-3-87	25-5-88	24-1-93	Baltic
. . . YAROSLAV MUDRYY (ex-*Nepristupnyy*)	27-5-88	5-91	2006	. . .
. . . TUMAN (ex-300 *Let Rossiyskomy Flot*)	9-90	6-11-98	. . .	. . .

Neustrashimyy (712) Michael Nitz, 9-05

Neustrashimyy (712) Frank Findler, 6-05

D: 3,210 tons light; 3,590 tons std. (4,350 fl) **S:** 29 kts (31+ on trials)
Dim: 129.63 (123.00 wl) × 15.60 (14.30 wl) × 4.26 (mean hull; 8.35 over sonar dome)
A: 4 Kinzhal (SA-N-9) SAM syst. (4 8-round PU 4S-95 VLS; 32 9M-330 Tor-M1/Gauntlet missiles); 1 100-mm 59-cal. AK-100 DP (350 rounds); 2 Kortik CIWS (each with 8 missile tubes and 2 30-mm GSH-6-30L gatling AA; 64 tot. 9M-311 Kormuk/SA-N-11 Grison missiles); 6 fixed 533-mm fixed TT (12 RPK-6 Vodopad/SS-N-16 missiles and/or SET-65 and 53-65K torpedoes); 2 12-round RBU-6000 ASW RL (96 RGB-60 rockets); 1 Ka-27PL Helix-A helicopter; 2 mine rails (. . . mines)
Electronics:
Radar: 1 MR-312 Nayada nav.; 1 MR-212/201 Vaygach-U (Palm Frond) nav.; 1 MR-760MA Fregat-MA (Top Plate) 3-D air search; 1 MR-352 Pozitiv (Cross Dome) target desig.; 1 MR-360 Podkat (Cross Sword) SAM f.c.; 1 MR-145 Lev (Kite Screech-B) 100-mm f.c.; 2 3P-87 (Hot Flash) Kortik f.c.
Sonar: MGK-365 Zvezda M-1 suite: . . . (Ox Yoke) bow-mounted LF; MGK-345 Bronza (Rat Tail) LF VDS; MG-35 Shtil underwater telephone
EW: MR-407 Vympel-R2 suite: 2 . . . (Foot Ball-A) intercept; 2 . . . (Half Hat-B) intercept; 2 . . . (Cage Flask) intercept; 2 . . . (Bell Squat) jammer; 2 16-round PK-16 fixed decoy RL (400 rockets); 8 10-round PK-10 fixed decoy RL

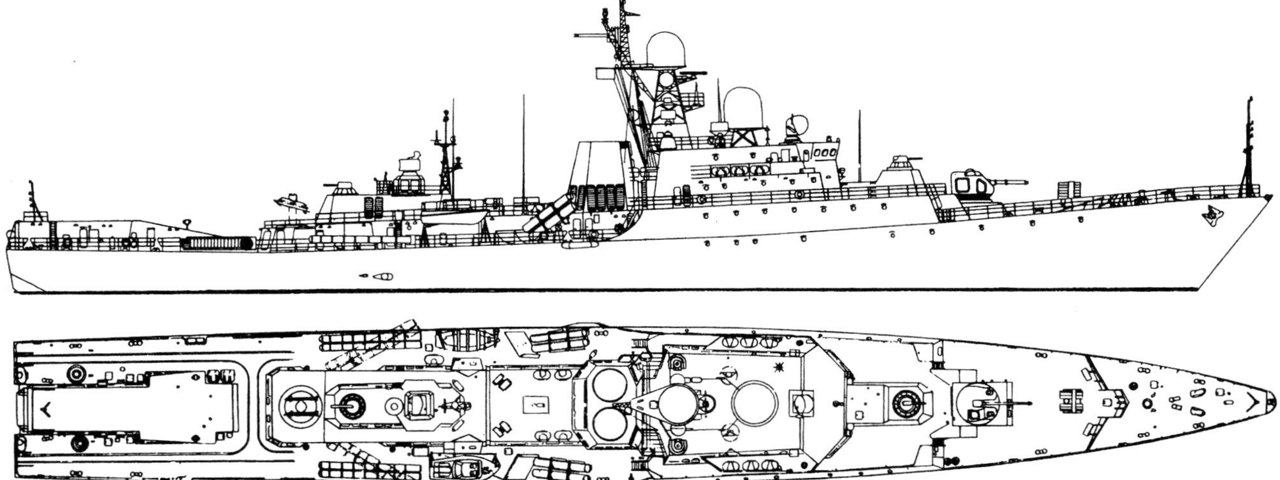

Tatarstan (Project 11661) Rozvoorouzhenie, 1993

FRIGATES [FF] *(continued)*

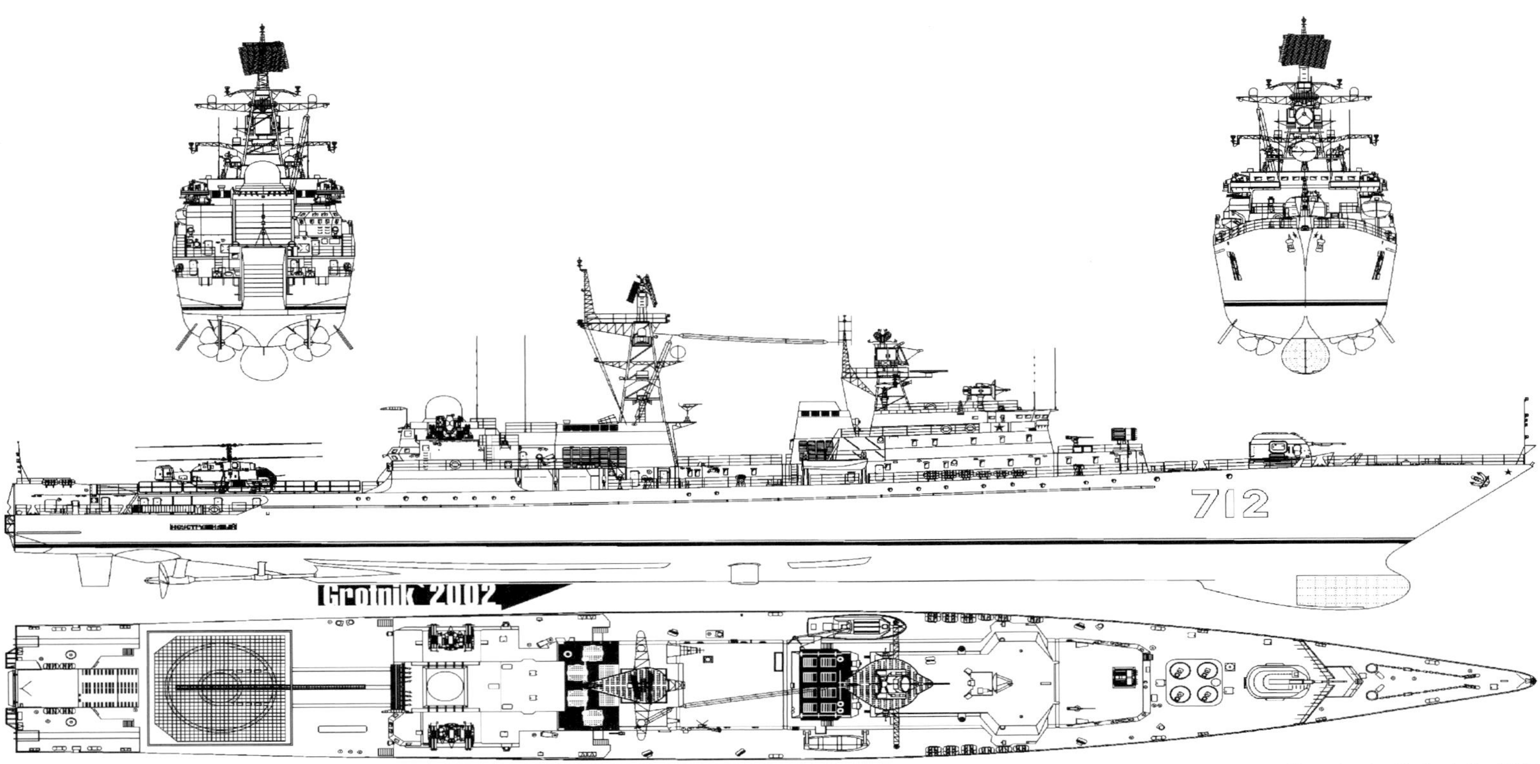

Neustrashimyy (712) Drawing by T. Grotnik, 2002

M: COGAG: 2 M-70 cruise gas turbines (9,000 shp each), 2 M-90 boost gas turbines (19,500 shp each); 2 props; 57,000 shp max.
Electric: 3,050 kw tot. (1 × 1,250-kw and 1 × 600-kw gas turbine sets, 2 × 600-kw diesel sets; 380 V a.c.)
Range: 700/30; 2,900/18 **Fuel:** 580 tons **Endurance:** 30 days
Crew: 35 officers, 34 warrant officers, 141 enlisted

Remarks: Ordered 3-2-97. *Neustrashimyy* began sea trials during 12-89 but was not commissioned until more than three years later, after a number of alterations had been performed. She has been largely inactive since 1995 but completed a three-month refit at Yantar Zavod, Kaliningrad, during 7-00. The design is optimized for ASW and was originally intended to be a successor to the much smaller Grisha series. At least four were planned, with the fourth, *Nepokornyy* ("Unruly"), to have been of a modified design (Project 1154.1). *Yaroslav Mudryy* and unlaunched sister ex-*Tuman* were stricken 22-10-98; the *Mudryy*'s incomplete hull remained at the shipyard, which hopes to complete her either for export or for the Russian Navy, while the ex-*Tuman* was launched 6-11-98 only to clear the ways for merchant ship repair work and began scrapping on 29-3-99. Funding for work on the *Mudryy* was provided in the 2002 Russian defense budget, and the still-afloat hulk of the ex-*Tuman* was moved to a fitting-out pier during 7-02. It remains unclear if or when the third unit will enter Russian naval service.

An export version, dubbed the Korsar class (Project 11541), would have a Sigma-E combat data system and would be armed with Kh-35 Uran or with Yakhont antiship missiles but would otherwise be equipped like the *Neustrashimyy.*

Hull systems: Is of steel construction, with very little use of light alloys in the superstructure. Special care has been taken in the design to reduce radar and infrared emissions. The above water hullform has a flat flare over its entire length, while the low superstructure has each level broken by flat convex planes to disperse radar returns. The stacks feature complex eductors and are shaped to reduce radar returns; the after stack (just abaft the mainmast) was originally so low as to be barely higher than the hangar. Between initial trials and 10-91, baffle plates were added abreast the stack exhausts, the eight exhausts in the forward stack were raised slightly and angled aftward, and the formerly flat door covering the variable-depth sonar housing was given a sawtooth angular surface—all to reduce infrared signature further. Most of the superstructure is sheathed in radar-absorbent material; the effectiveness of the signature-reduction effort is spoiled somewhat, however, by the design of the lattice mast and a plethora of bulky antennas. Has fin stabilizers, and flow fins have been added to the hull bottom just outboard the propellers. The generator plant has also been described as consisting of five diesel sets with a total output of 3,500 kw.

Combat systems: The combat system is designated Tron and was reportedly the first fully integrated Russian Navy computerized system. The six torpedo tubes flanking the hangar are fixed at about a 15° outboard angle and can launch the Type 86R antisubmarine missiles of the RPK-6 Vodopad system as well as wire-guided torpedoes. The designation Zvezda M-1 applies to the entire hull-mounted and variable depth sonar suite; there is no provision for a towed linear passive hydrophone array. The sonar dome projects well ahead of the keel and extends aft nearly as far as the RBU-6000 ASW rocket launcher, indicating the likely presence of passive flank arrays. The RBU-6000 ASW rocket launcher can function as a torpedo countermeasure system. The ASW weapons-control system name is Purga. There are none of the bridge periscopes found in other modern Russian designs. Amidships there are provisions for later installation of four quadruple launchers for the Kh-35 Uran (NATO SS-N-25 Switchblade) antiship missile system. The communications suite is referred to as Buran-6.

Yaroslav Mudryy and *Tuman* will reportedly be equipped with 3M-54E or 3M-54E1 Klub-S antiship missiles with vertical launch systems. Unconfirmed reports indicate that *Mudryy* may have been renamed *Nadezhda.*

Note: The Krivak-III-class frigates are described in the Federal Border Guard section.

♦ 3 Krivak-II (Burevestnik-M) class (Project 1135M) *(1 nonoperational)*
Bldr: Yantar Zavod 820, Kaliningrad

	Laid down	L	In serv.	Fleet
731 NEUKROTIMYY (ex-*Komsomolets Litviy*, ex-*Neukrotimyy*)	22-1-76	27-6-77	30-12-77	Baltic
662 *REVNOSTNYY*	27-6-79	23-4-80	27-12-80	Pacific
808 PYTLIVYY	27-6-79	16-4-81	30-11-81	Black Sea

Pytlivyy (808) Cem D. Yaylali, 5-05

Pytlivyy (808) Cem D. Yaylali, 5-05

D: 2,945–3,075 tons light; 3,305 tons normal (3,505 max. fl) **S:** 30.6 kts
Dim: 123.10 (113.00 wl) × 14.20 (13.20 wl) × 4.57 (mean hull; 7.3 over sonar dome)
A: 4 URK-5 Rastrub (SS-N-14 Silex) SSM (1 quadruple KT-106 launcher; 4 Type 83R and 83RUS missiles); 2 twin-rail Osa-M (SA-N-4) SAM syst. (40 9M-33/Gecko missiles); 2 single 100-mm 59-cal. AK-100 DP (1,200 rounds); 2 12-round RBU-6000 ASW RL (144 RGB-60 rockets); 2 quadruple 533-mm UTA-53-1135 TT (4 SET-65 and 4 53-65K torpedoes); 2 mine rails (12–20 mines)

FRIGATES [FF] *(continued)*

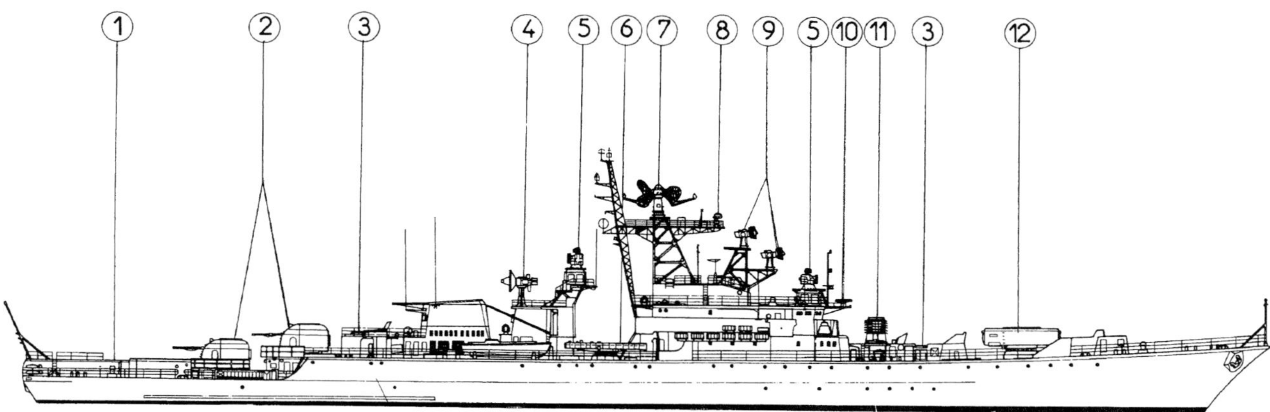

Krivak-II class 1. VDS housing 2. 100-mm AK-100 DP guns 3. launchers for Osa-M SAM system (shown retracted) 4. MR-114 Lev radar director for 100-mm guns 5. MPZ-301 Baza radar director for Osa-M SAM system 6. Quadruple 533-mm TT 7. MR-310U Angara-M surface/air-search radar 8. Voga or Vaygach-U nav./surface-search radar 9. Drakon radar directors for URK-5 Rastrub ASW/antiship missile system 10. Mius navigational radar 11. RBU-6000 ASW RL 12. Quadruple KT-106 launcher for URK-5 Rastrub missiles
Drawing by Lucien Gassier, from *Flottes de Combat*

Electronics:
Radar: 1 MR-212/201 Vaygach-U (Palm Frond) or Volga (Don-Kay) nav.; 1 Mius (Spin Trough) or Don-2 nav.; 1 MR-310U Angara-M (Head Net-C) air search; 2 . . . Drakon (Eye Bowl) SS-N-14 f.c.; 2 MPZ-301 Baza (Pop Group) SA-N-4 f.c.; 1 MR-114 Lev (Kite Screech-A) 100-mm gun f.c.
Sonar: MGK-332MC Titan-2 (Bull Nose) hull-mounted MF; MG-325 Vega (Mare Tail) MF VDS; MG-26 underwater telephone
EW: Smerch suite: 2 Bell Shroud intercept; 2 Bell Squat jammers; 4 16-round PK-16 fixed decoy RL (128 rockets); 2 towed torpedo decoys—*Revnostnyy* and possibly others also: 4 10-round PK-10 fixed decoy RL
E/O: some: 2 Spektr-F (Half Cup) laser warning
M: COGAG M-7 plant: 2 M-62 cruise gas turbines (7,475 shp each), 2 M-8K boost gas turbines (20,000 shp each); 2 props; 54,950 shp tot.
Electric: 3,000 kw (5 × 600-kw diesel sets)
Range: 640/30; 4,000/14 **Endurance:** 30 days
Crew: 23 officers, 28 warrant officers, 130 enlisted (accomm. for 194 tot.)

Remarks: Type designation: SKR (*Storozhevoy Korabl',* Patrol Ship), formerly BPK (*Bol'shoy Protovolodochnyy Korabl',* Large Antisubmarine Ship). The VDS housing at the stern is somewhat larger than on the Krivak-I, but the principal difference between the two classes is the substitution of two single 100-mm for the two twin 76.2-mm guns. *Neukrotimyy* was renamed in 1988 for the Communist Youth League of Lithuania but renamed again in 1990 when that country demanded independence. Repairs on *Neukrotimyy* were suspended in mid-1995 when 90% complete and were not completed until 2000. On 30-7-05 she was damaged by the accidental explosion of a practice mine that flooded her engineering spaces. Raised, she was towed to Sevemaya Verf Shipyard for repairs. A refit of the *Revnostnyy* was at a standstill at Dalzavod repair yard in 5-00, with 80% of the work complete; the ship appears to be in very poor condition but remains in commission.
Hull systems: Were designed to be 2,870 tons standard, 3,430 tons full load, but one source indicates that displacements have grown to 3,170 tons standard and 3,670 tons full load. There are 14 watertight compartments. The superstructure is built of aluminum-magnesium alloy, welded to the hull with bimetallic inserts. Type UKA-135 fin stabilizers are fitted. The propulsion plant originally delivered 45,570 shp normal/51,200 shp max. total (with the cruise turbines operating at 6,000 shp each and the boost turbines at 18,000 each), but the output was later increased. Hull block coefficient is 0.46, very fine for this type of vessel. For slow speeds, any one of the engines can drive both propellers.
Combat systems: The combat system is known as Planshet-35 and the ASW weapons-control system as Purga. Carry 1,200 rounds of 100-mm ammunition. The chaff/decoy rocket launchers were moved from the stern to the 01 level, abreast the aft SA-N-4 launcher. *Revnostnyy* has four four-tube decoy RL mounted between the torpedo tubes, in addition to her normal chaff RL system. Can carry 12 KSM, 14 KRAB, or 16 IGDM-500 mines. The bow sonar initially installed was designated MG-332T. The hoist gear for the VDS is designated POUKB-1.
Disposals: *Gordelivyy* was reported in mid-1992 to have begun an overhaul that could not be completed for lack of funds; the ship was instead placed in reserve and stricken 5-7-94. Pacific Fleet unit *Grozyashchiy* was stricken 17-11-94 and *Rezkiy* on 1-9-95. Black Sea Fleet unit *Razitel'nyy* was stricken from the Black Sea Fleet 10-1-96 and was to have been transferred to Ukraine 1-4-96, but was not transferred until 6-97. Pacific Fleet unit *R'yannyy* and Northern Fleet units *Gromkiy* and *Bessmennyy* were stricken 16-8-98. *Rezvyy,* decommissioned during the 1990s, sank at her berthing pier while laid up awaiting overhaul. She was later raised but deemed unworthy of repair and stricken during 2005.

♦ 2 Modified Krivak-I class (Project 11352) (1 in *reserve*)

Bldr: Severnaya Verf 190 (ex-Zhdanov Zavod 190), St. Petersburg

	Laid down	L	In serv.	Converted	Fleet
930 *Legkiy* (ex-*Leningradskiy Komsomolets*)	22-4-76	1-4-77	29-9-77	12-87 to 3-90	Northern
702 *Pylkiy*	6-5-77	20-8-78	28-12-78	1990 to 17-3-94	Baltic

D: 3,175 tons (3,675 fl) **S:** 30.6 kts
Dim: 126.0 (116.9 wl) × 14.2 (13.2 wl) × 4.7 (mean hull; 8.0 over sonar)

Pylkiy (702) French Navy, 3-96

Legkiy (930)—showing how the enlarged VDS housing severely restricts arcs of fire for the after twin 76.2-mm gunmount *Ships of the World,* 1997

A: 4 URK-5 Rastrub-B (SS-N-14 Silex) SSM (1 quadruple KT-106 launcher; Type 83R and 83RUS missiles); 2 twin-rail Osa-M (SA-N-4) SAM syst. (40 9M-33/Gecko missiles); 2 twin 76.2-mm 59-cal. AK-726 DP; 2 quadruple 533-mm UTA-53-1135 TT (4 SET-65 and 4 53-65 torpedoes); 2 mine rails (12–16 mines)
Electronics:
Radar: 2 MR-212/201 Vaygach-U (Palm Frond) nav.; 1 MR-755 Fregat-M2 (Half Plate) surf./air search; 2 . . . Drakon (Eye Bowl) SS-N-14 f.c.; 2 MPZ-301 Baza (Pop Group) SA-N-4 f.c.; 1 MR-105 Turel' (Owl Screech) gun f.c.
Sonar: MGK-365 Svezda M-1 suite: MG-335S Platina-C hull-mounted LF; MGK-345 Bronza LF VDS; MG-35 Shtil underwater telephone
EW: 2 Start-2 (Bell Shroud) intercept; 2 MP-401 Start (Bell Squat-A/B) jammers; 4 16-round PK-16 fixed decoy RL (128 rockets); 2 towed torpedo decoys; 3 sets corner-reflector decoys
E/O: 6 Spektr-F (Half Cup) laser warning
M: COGAG M-7 plant: 2 M-62 cruise gas turbines (7,475 shp each), 2 M-8K boost gas turbines (20,000 shp each); 2 props; 54,950 shp tot.
Electric: 3,000 kw (5 × 600-kw diesel sets)
Range: 640/30; 4,000/14 **Endurance:** 30 days
Crew: 22 officers, 198 warrant officers and enlisted

Remarks: This modernization program was initiated in 1985–86 for the original version of the Krivak class, but lack of funds halted the program with only two units fully

FRIGATES [FF] *(continued)*

converted. It had originally been intended to construct new Project 1135 units to the modified design. *Legkiy* was modernized to Project 11352 configuration at Severnaya Verf, St. Petersburg, followed by *Pylkiy* at Yantar Zavod 820, Kaliningrad, completed during 1994. Krivak-I-class *Letuchiy* was to have begun a similar modernization in 3-87 for completion 4-90 at the Far East Shipbuilding Plant 202, Vladivostok, but the work was not performed. *Pylkiy* began a refit at Yantar Zavod, Kaliningrad, fall 2000, and was in dry dock at Baltiysk during 6-01. *Legkiy* was decommissioned during 12-03, most likely to enter reserve status.

Hull systems: One semiofficial source gives the revised displacement as 3,000 tons standard and 3,350 tons full load. The bow appears to have been lengthened by about 3 m to accommodate the new bow-mounted sonar. See the remarks under the Krivak-I class for additional information.

Combat systems: The full conversion performed provided an improved sonar suite (with enlarged VDS housing), while the RBU-6000 ASW rocket launchers replaced by as-yet-vacant racks for two quadruple Kh-35 Uran (SS-N-25) antiship cruise-missile launchers, the Angara-M (Head Net-C) air-search radar was replaced by Fregat-M2 (Half Plate) atop a new lattice foremast with an additional deckhouse level at its base, and eight 10-tube fixed decoy rocket launchers were added to the four 16-tube launchers already mounted; also added were the six Spektr-F laser detectors. The communications suite was updated to Buran-6 standard. The ASW weapons-control system name is Purga.

♦ 3 Krivak-I (Burevestnik) class (Project 1135 and 11353*)

(2 in *reserve*)

Bldrs: A: Yantar Zavod 820, Kaliningrad; B: Severnaya Verf 190 (ex-Zhdanov Zavod 190), St. Petersburg; C: Zaliv Zavod 532, Kerch', Ukraine

	Bldr	Laid down	L	In serv.	Fleet
937 *Zharkiy**	A	16-4-74	3-11-75	29-6-76	Northern
955 Zadornyy	B	10-11-77	25-3-79	31-8-79	Baltic
801 *Ladnyy*	C	25-5-79	7-5-80	29-12-80	Black Sea

Ladnyy (801) Hartmut Ehlers, 7-00

D: 2,810 tons std.; 3,200 tons normal (3,420 fl) **S:** 30.6 kts (32.5 on trials)
Dim: 123.00 (113.00 wl) × 14.20 (13.20 wl) × 4.48 (hull; 7.30 max.)
A: 4 URK-5 Rastrub (SS-N-14 Silex) SSM (1 quadruple KT-106 launcher; 4 Type 83R and 83RUS missiles); 2 twin-rail SA-N-4 Osa-M SAM syst. (ZIF-122 launchers; 40 9M-33/Gecko missiles); 2 twin 76.2-mm 59-cal. AK-726 DP (2,000 rounds); 2 12-round RBU-6000 ASW RL (144 RGB-60 rockets); 2 quadruple 533-mm UTA-53-1135 TT (4 SET-65 and 4 53-65 torpedoes); 2 mine rails (12–16 mines)
Electronics:
Radar: 1 Don-2 or Mius (Spin Trough) nav.; 1 Volga (Don-Kay) or MR-212/201 Vaygach-U (Palm Frond) nav.; 1 MR-310U Angara-M (Head Net-C) air search; 2 . . . Drakon (Eye Bowl) SS-N-14 f.c.; 2 MPZ-301 Baza (Pop Group) SA-N-4 f.c.; 1 MR-105 Turel' (Owl Screech) gun f.c.
Sonar: MG-332 Titan-2 (Bull Nose) hull-mounted MF; MG-325 Vega (Mare Tail) MF VDS; MG-26 underwater telephone; NEL-5 echo sounder
EW: 2 Start-2 (Bell Shroud) intercept; 2 MP-401 Start (Bell Squat-A/B) jammers; 4 16-round PK-16 fixed decoy RL (128 rockets); 2 towed torpedo decoys; 3 sets corner-reflector decoys
E/O: some: Spektr-F (Half Cup) laser warning
M: COGAG M-7 plant: 2 M-62 cruise gas turbines (7,475 shp each), 2 M-8K boost gas turbines (20,000 shp each); 2 props; 54,950 shp tot.
Electric: 3,000 kw tot. (5 × 600-kw diesel sets)
Range: 1,290/30; 4,995/14 **Fuel:** 348 tons normal (515 max.)
Endurance: 30 days **Crew:** 22 officers, 23 warrant officers, 145 enlisted

Remarks: Designed at Northern Planning and Design Office (TsKB-53) by a team headed by Prof. V. Yukhnin, with Nikolay Pavlovich Sobelev as chief designer. Keel for class prototype *Bditel'nyy* was laid 21-7-68. In 1978, the Krivak-I and Krivak-II classes were rerated from second-class BPK (*Bol'shoy Protivolodochnyy Korabl',* Large Antisubmarine Ship) to SKR (*Storozhevoy Korabl',* Patrol Ship), a demotion prompted perhaps by their limited endurance at high speeds, speed, and size.

Status: *Zharkiy* has not operated since the early 1990s and at one point was offered for scrap, but seems still to be at least nominally in service. *Ladnyy* was under overhaul at Sevastopol' during 2001.

Hull systems: Were designed to be 2,735 tons standard, 3,100 tons full load, but one source reports that displacements have grown to 3,075 tons standard and 3,575 tons full load. There are 14 watertight compartments. The superstructure is built of aluminum-magnesium alloy, welded to the hull with bimetallic inserts. Type UKA-135 fin stabilizers are fitted. The propulsion plant originally delivered 45,570 shp normal/51,200 shp max. total (with the cruise turbines operating at 6,000 shp each and the boost turbines at 18,000 each), but the total output was later increased. Hull block coefficient is 0.46, very fine for this type of vessel. For slow speeds, any one of the engines can drive both propellers. All have UKA-135 retractable fin stabilizers and a single rudder.

Combat systems: The combat system is designated Planshet-35. The bow sonar operates at 4.5, 5.0, or 5.5 kHz, with a 380-Hz bandwidth; pulse repetition rates are 30, 60, or 120 msec, and the set employs rotating directional transmission (RDT), with either CW or FM transmission. The VDS is apparently an independent system, and its towed "fish" is said to suffer from directional instability. There is a separate high-frequency tilting-stave sonar linked to the Purga fire-control system to provide targeting for the RBU-6000 ASW rocket launchers. *Zharkiy* was modified during the mid-1980s with a new VDS housing and possible new bow sonar, an installation that probably duplicates that in the two Modified Krivak-I-class frigates. All can carry 2,000 rounds of 76.2-mm ammunition, and the two mine rails can accommodate 12 KSM, 14 KRAB, or 16 IGDM-500 mines.

Disposals: Pacific Fleet sister *Razyashchiy* and Northern Fleet unit *Doblestnyy* were stricken 3-7-92, with the former towed away for scrap 8-93 and the latter in 12-96. Northern Fleet unit *Dostoynyy* was stricken 22-2-93, Baltic Fleet units *Sil'nyy* and *Svirepyy* on 30-7-93, and *Bditel'nyy* and *Bodryy* on 31-7-96 (scrapped at Kiel, Germany, beginning on 14-10-97, and at Yantar Zavod, Kaliningrad, in 1998, respectively). Pacific Fleet unit *Poryvistyy* was relegated to service as a museum ship during 1995 and sister *Retivyy* was stricken 1-9-95. Black Sea Fleet sister *Deyatel'nyy* was stricken 5-7-94 and was towed through the Bosporus bound for scrapping during 5-97. Black Sea Fleet units *Bezzavetnyy* and *Bezukoriznennyy* (both stricken 10-1-96) were to have been transferred to Ukraine 1-4-96, but the transfer was not carried out until 6-97; they have since been stricken. Pacific Fleet unit *Razumnyy* had been stricken by 1998. Baltic Fleet unit *Druzhnyy* was retired 3-10-02 to become a museum exhibit at St. Petersburg. *Storozhevoy* (663) has been scrapped as of 2003 and is being broken up at a Kamchatka Peninsula base. *Letuchiy* (661) was retired by 2006.

CORVETTES [FFL]

Note: Most of the Russian "corvette" classes are under the normal 1,000-ton full-load displacement figure differentiating patrol combatants [PG] from corvettes [FFL]. They are nonetheless retained here in the corvette category by convention, as their displacements had originally been considerably overestimated by NATO intelligence agencies.

♦ 11 Parchim-II class (East German Project 133.1M)

Bldr: VEB Peenewerft, Wolgast, Germany

	Laid down	L	In serv.
304 MPK-192	26-2-85	29-8-85	11-4-86
311 MPK-205 Kazanets	4-1-85	28-12-85	11-4-86
301 MPK-67	28-3-85	19-4-86	30-6-87
308 MPK-99 Zelenodolsk	25-6-85	12-8-86	28-12-87
245 MPK-105	30-12-85	20-11-86	16-3-88
222 MPK-213	8-4-86	28-2-87	29-7-88
258 MPK-216	22-6-86	25-6-87	30-9-88
243 MPK-227	2-9-87	16-8-88	20-2-89
244 MPK-228 Bashkortostan	20-11-87	31-10-88	20-2-89
232 MPK-229 Kalmykiya	23-2-88	30-1-89	20-2-89
218 MPK-224 Aleksin	28-2-87	30-3-88	31-3-89

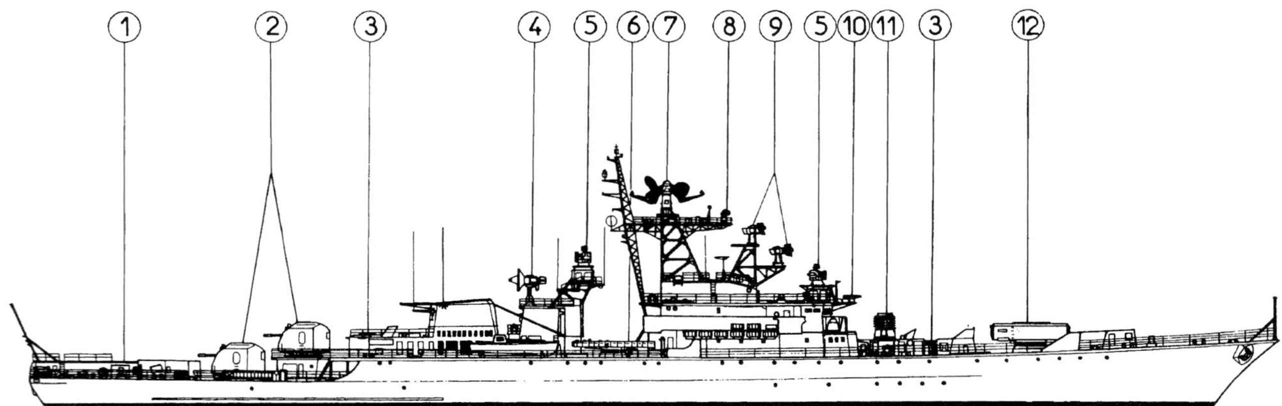

Krivak-I class 1. VDS housing 2. Twin 76.2-mm DP gunmounts 3. Launchers for Osa-M SAM system (shown retracted) 4. MR-105 Turel' radar director for 76.2-mm guns 5. MPZ-301 Baza radar directors for Osa-M SAM system 6. Quadruple 533-mm TT 7. MR-310U Angara-M surface/air-search radar 8. Volga or Vaygach-U navigational/surface-search radar 9. Drakon radar directors for URK-5 Rastrub ASW/antiship missile system 10. Mius navigational radar 11. RBU-6000 ASW RL 12. Quadruple KT-106 launcher for the URK-5 Rastrub missile system Drawing by Lucien Gassier, from Flottes de Combat

CORVETTES [FFL] *(continued)*

MPK-67 (301) Boris Lemachko, 6-00

MPK-229 Kalmykiya (232) Jaroslaw Cislak, 6-04

D: 790 tons light; 865 tons normal (935 fl) **S:** 24.5 kts
Dim: 75.20 (69.00 pp) × 9.78 (8.50 wl) × 2.80 (hull; 4.55 max.)
A: 1 76.2-mm 59-cal. AK-176 DP; 1 30-mm AK-630 gatling AA; 2 4-round Strela-3 (SA-N-8) SAM syst. (24 Gremlin missiles); 2 twin 533-mm TT; 2 12-round RBU-6000 ASW RL (96 RGB-60 rockets); 2 d.c. racks (12 d.c. tot.); 2 mine rails
Electronics:
Radar: 1 Mius (Spin Trough) nav.; 1 MR-352 Pozitiv (Cross Dome) air search; 1 MR-123 Vympel (Bass Tilt) gun f.c.
Sonar: MGK-335MC (Bull Horn) hull-mounted (3 kHz); Ros'-K HF dipping
EW: Vympel-R2 suite: 2 Bizan'-4 (Watch Dog) intercept (2–18 GHz); 2 16-round PK-16 fixed decoy RL
M: 3 Type M-504A-3 diesels; 3 props (centerline only: CP); 14,250 bhp
Electric: 900 kw tot. (1 × 500-kw, 2 × 200-kw diesel sets)
Range: 1,200/20; 2,200/12 **Endurance:** 10 days **Crew:** 9 officers, 71 enlisted

Remarks: Type designation: MPK (*Malyy Protivolodochnyy Korabl',* Small Antisubmarine Ship). An improved version of the former East German Navy's *Parchim* class (all of whose members are now in the Indonesian Navy), with later armament, a more powerful sonar, and a new 75-n.m.-range MR-352 Pozitiv radar. As this design was inferior in most respects to the contemporary Grisha-V, its acquisition may have been a form of aid to the East German shipbuilding industry. Commenced refitting in order of construction during 9-94 at the building yard in Germany, with all completed by 10-95. All are in the Baltic Fleet. MPK-229 was named during 12-96 under an agreement whereby the Kalmyk Republic would provide financial assistance and draftees to the Baltic Fleet. MPK-205 was named on 10-2-98. MPK-228 was damaged by fire during 1999 but has been repaired. The three ships with 300-series pennant numbers are based at Kronshtadt, while the others are based at Baltiysk.
Hull systems: Due to engine cooling problems, these ships can only operate for 30 minutes at speeds between 8 and 12 kts.
Combat systems: The dipping sonar deploys through the forewardmost of the two doors on the starboard side of the main deck superstructure. The d.c. racks exit through ports in the stern. The ASW weapons-control system name is Drakon. The first 10 did not initially carry the antenna for the MR-352 radar within the large masthead radome, due to developmental problems; the antenna was later backfitted.

♦ 25 Grisha-V class (Projects 1124MEh, 1124MU, and 1124.4)

Bldrs: A: Leninskaya Kuznitsa SY No. 302, Kiev; B: Zelenodol'sk Zavod No. 340, Kazan; C: Khabarovsk SY No. 368, Khabarovsk

	Bldr.	Laid down	L	In serv.	Fleet
064 MPK-134 Muromets (ex-*Kievskiy Komsomolets,* ex-MPK-64)	A	5-80	5-82	10-12-82	Black Sea
071 MPK-118 Suzdalets (ex-*Komsomolets Moldaviy*)	A	1-8-81	27-3-83	30-10-83	Black Sea
129 MPK-139	A	8-4-82	18-2-84	2-8-84	Northern
055 MPK-199 Kasimov (ex-*Komsomolets Armenii*)	A	20-2-84	7-12-85	7-10-86	Black Sea
354 MPK-221 Stelyak	. . .	. . .	. . .	29-12-87	. . .
171 MPK-113	A	2-11-85	31-7-87	5-8-88	Northern
199 MPK-194 Brest (ex-*Brestkiy Komsomolets*)	B	11-5-87	30-7-88	27-9-88	Northern
133 MPK-196	B	11-5-87	30-7-88	30-12-88	Northern
053 MPK-207 Povorino	A	12-6-86	6-5-88	3-4-89	Black Sea
106 MPK-197	B	27-10-87	8-4-89	25-10-89	Northern
390 MPK-222 Koreyets	C	7-1-87	27-4-89	20-12-89	Pacific
054 MPK-217 Eysk	A	16-3-87	12-4-89	26-12-89	Black Sea
396 MPK-28	C	2-9-87	9-9-89	27-12-89	Pacific
113 MPK-203 Yunga	B	26-3-88	19-7-89	28-12-89	Northern
138 MPK-130 Naryan-Mar (ex-*Arkhangelskiy Komsomolets*)	B	17-8-88	9-3-90	28-9-90	Northern
332 MPK-107 (ex-*Irkutskiy Komsomolets*)	C	22-2-88	5-6-90	14-12-90	Pacific
155 MPK-56	B	12-4-89	30-6-90	29-12-90	Northern
323 MPK-64 Metel	C	4-1-88	2-10-90	31-12-90	Pacific
375 MPK-82	A	20-4-89	20-4-91	26-9-91	Pacific
362 MPK-17	C	22-1-90	28-8-91	30-12-91	Pacific
190 MPK-14 Monchegorsk	B	27-3-91	6-6-92	31-5-93	Northern
196 MPK-59 Snezhnogorsk	B	20-11-90	22-5-93	12-8-94	Northern
137 MPK-69 . . .	. . .	. . .	. . .	. . .	. . .
164 MPK-7 Onega	. . .	. . .	. . .	. . .	. . .
350 MPK-214 Leninskay Kuznitsa	. . .	. . .	. . .	. . .	. . .

MPK-214 Leninskay Kuznitsa (350) JMSDF via *Ships of the World,* 2005

MPK-222 Koreyets (390)—firing her RBU-6000 rocket launcher *Ships of the World, 2005*

MPK-118 Suzdalets (071) Boris Lemachko, 3-06

D: 876–930 tons std. (1,030–1,070 fl)
S: 32 kts (21 on gas turbine; 16 on diesels)
Dim: 71.20 (66.90 wl) × 10.15 (9.50 wl) × 3.54–3.72 (hull)
A: 1 twin-rail Osa-M (SA-N-4) SAM syst. (20 9M-33/Gecko missiles); 1 76.2-mm 59-cal. AK-176 DP (304 rounds); 1 30-mm 54-cal. AK-630M gatling AA (3,000 rounds); 2 shoulder-launched Strela-3 (SA-N-8) SAM positions (20–24 Gremlin shoulder-launched missiles); 2 twin 533-mm TT; 1 12-round RBU-6000 ASW RL (48 RGB-60 rockets; see remarks); 2 d.c. racks (6 d.c. each) or up to 18 mines
Electronics:
Radar: 1 MR-312 Nayada nav.; 1 MR-320 Topaz-M (Strut Pair) (late units: MR-755 Fregat-M2 Half Plate-B) surf./air search; 1 MPZ-301 Baza (Pop Group) SA-N-4 f.c.; 1 MR-123 Vympel (Bass Tilt) gun f.c.
Sonar: MGK-335MC Platina (Bull Horn) hull-mounted (3 kHz); Shelon' (Elk Tail) dipping (7.5 kHz)
EW: 2 Bizan'-4B (Watch Dog) intercept (2–18 GHz); 2 16-round PK-16 fixed decoy RL—some also: 4 10-round PK-10 fixed decoy RL
E/O: some: 4 Spektr-F (Half Cup) infrared detectors

CORVETTES [FFL] *(continued)*

M: CODAG: 1 M-8M gas turbine (18,000 shp), 2 Type M-507A diesels (10,000 bhp each); 3 props; 38,000 hp—2 maneuvering propellers
Electric: 1,000 kw tot. (1 × 500-kw, 1 × 300-kw, 1 × 200-kw diesel sets)
Range: 950/27; on diesels alone: 2,500/14; 4,000/10 **Fuel:** 143 tons
Endurance: 9 days **Crew:** 9 officers, 77 enlisted

Remarks: Type designation: MPK (*Malyy Protivolodochnyy Korabl',* Small Antisubmarine Ship). Sister *Stelyak* was built for the Federal Border Guard. MPK-194 was named *Brest* during 7-00 and is reportedly numbered 199, not 250 as was reported in previous editions. MPK-217 was named on 9-9-99, MPK-203 on 2-2-90, and MPK-14 on 17-8-99. One as-yet-unidentified Northern Fleet unit was named *Yekatarinskiy Gavan* during 7-00; MPK-59 was named 2-6-01.
Hull systems: There are two drop-down harbor maneuvering propulsors at the extreme stern, as in the now-stricken Petya class (Project 159 series). Carry 10.5 tons of lube oil and 27.2 tons of fresh water. Maximum propeller rpm is 585 on the diesels.
Combat systems: This final production variant of the basic Grisha design substituted the MR-320M Topaz-M (Strut Pair) radar for MR-302 Rubka (Strut Curve) and a 76.2-mm gun for the twin 57-mm mount, with one RBU-6000 ASW RL removed as weight compensation (the surviving mount is carried in the port position). Beginning in the late 1980s, the MR-755 Fregat-M2 (Half Plate-B) radar (whose antenna consists of one half of the back-to-back Top Plate 3-D radar) was substituted for MR-320M on new-construction units.

Two launch positions for shoulder-fired point-defense SAMs have been added at the break of the 01 level superstructure, just forward of the stack. Just abaft the mast is a manned SP-521 Rakurs (Kolonka-2) backup ringsight director for the 30-mm gun. The ships can carry 550 rounds of 76-mm and 2,000 rounds of 30-mm ammunition. The torpedo tubes have been modified to launch wire-guided torpedoes. The dipping sonar is housed in the after superstructure, lowering through the hull between the starboard and centerline propeller shafts. The d.c. racks are mounted atop the mine rails and must be removed to carry mines (which is rarely—if ever—done).
Disposals: Northern Fleet units MPK-142, MPK-190, MPK-198, and MPK-202 were stricken 16-3-98, Pacific Fleet unit MPK-89 on 17-7-97, and MPK-20 on 20-8-92 while building at Khabarovsk. *Lutsk* was transferred to Ukraine 12-2-94 while building at Kiev. A Northern Fleet unit with pennant number 178 was scrapped during 2002. Pacific Fleet unit MPK-125 and Northern Fleet unit MPK-10 were stricken by 2005.

♦ 2 Grisha-III class (Project 1124MP)
Bldr: A: Khbarovsk SY No. 368, Khabarovsk; B: Leninskaya Kuznitsa SY No. 302, Kiev

	Bldr	Laid down	L	In serv.	Fleet
059 MPK-49	C	23-3-80	14-2-82	31-8-82	Black Sea
369 MPK-191	A	30-11-82	7-5-85	21-12-85	Pacific

MPK-191 (369)—Grisha-III class JMSDF via *Ships of the World,* 2005

D: 860 tons light; 954 tons normal (990 fl)
S: 34 kts (21 on gas turbine alone; 16 on diesels)
Dim: 71.20 (66.90 wl) × 10.15 (9.50 wl) × 3.40 (hull)
A: 1 twin-rail Osa-M (SA-N-4) SAM syst. (20 9M-33/Gecko missiles); 1 twin 57-mm AK-725 DP (1,100 rounds); 1 30-mm 54-cal. AK-630M gatling AA (2,000 rounds); 2 12-round RBU-6000 ASW RL (96 RGB-60 rockets); 2 twin 533-mm TT; 2 d.c. racks (12 d.c.) or up to 18 mines
Electronics:
Radar: 1 Don-2 nav.; 1 MR-302 Rubka (Strut Curve) surf./air search; 1 MPZ-301 Baza (Pop Group) SA-N-4 f.c.; 1 MR-123 Vympel (Bass Tilt) gun f.c.
Sonar: MGK-335M Argun' (Bull Nose) hull-mounted MF; Shelon' (Elk Tail) MF through-hull dipping
EW: 2 Bizan'-4B (Watch Dog) intercept (2–18 GHz)
M: CODAG: 1 M-8M gas turbine (18,000 shp), 2 Type M-507A diesels (10,000 bhp each); 3 props; 38,000 hp—2 maneuvering propellers
Electric: 1,000 kw (1 × 500-kw, 1 × 300-kw, 1 × 200-kw diesel sets)
Range: 950/27; on diesels alone: 2,750/14; 4,000/10
Fuel: 130 tons + 13 tons overload **Endurance:** 9 days
Crew: 9 officers, 74 enlisted

Remarks: Russian type: MPK (*Malyy Protivolodochnyy Korabl',* Small Antisubmarine Ship). Survivors of 22 built for the Soviet Navy. Although considered to be in commission. Sisters *Bezuprechniy, Zorkiy,* and *Smelyy* are in service with the Federal Border Guard in the Pacific area.
Hull systems: Have retractable fin stabilizers. Said to consume 450 kg of fuel per hour at 14 kts on diesel propulsion. Maximum propeller rpm is 585 on the diesels.
Combat systems: The MR-123 Vympel (Bass Tilt) fire-control radar, which is atop a small deckhouse to port on the aft superstructure, has been substituted for the MR-103 Bars (Muff Cob) fire-control radar fitted in earlier variants of the Grisha series, while a gatling gun has been mounted in the space occupied by MR-103 in the Grisha-I and -II. Some may have two Strela-3 (SA-N-8) SAM launch positions, as on the Grisha-V. Can carry 1,000 rounds of 57-mm and 2,000 rounds of 30-mm gun ammunition. The d.c. racks are mounted atop the mine rails and must be removed to carry mines (which is rarely—if ever—done).

Disposals: Pacific Fleet units: MPK-81 was stricken 11-2-94, MPK-122 and MPK-155 on 5-7-94, MPK-143 and MPK-4 on 17-7-97, MPK-37 and MPK-145 on 4-8-95, MPK-170 on 31-7-96, and MPK-101 (ex-*Zaporozhkiy Komsomolets*) on 16-3-98. Northern Fleet: MPK-138 was stricken 3-7-92, MPK-40 on 25-1-94, and MPK-141 and MPK-152 on 5-7-94. Baltic Fleet: MPK-44 (ex-*Komsomolets Latvii*) and MPK-108 were stricken 28-4-93 and transferred to Lithuania. Black Sea Fleet: MPK-6 was stricken 16-3-98 and scrapped at Inkerman beginning 9-12-98. MPK-178 and MPK-127 (ex-*Komsomolets Gruziy*) had both been stricken by 2005.

Disposal note: The last two of 15 Grisha-I (Albatros)-class units, MPK-33 and MPK-31, were stricken 7-2-95. The sole Grisha-IV-class (Project 1124K) unit, MPK-104, was stricken from the Black Sea Fleet 16-3-98.

GUIDED-MISSILE PATROL COMBATANTS (AIR-CUSHION) [PGGA]

♦ 2 Dergach (Sivuch)-class (Project 1239) surface-effect ships
Bldr: Zelenodol'sk Zavod, Kazan

	In serv.	Fleet
615 MRK-27 Bora	12-5-97	Black Sea
616 MRK-17 Samum (ex-575)	26-2-00	Black Sea

MRK-17 Samum (616)—in gray paint, with previous pennant number. Stern area is painted black to cover exhaust staining

MRK-27 Bora (615)—in black and gray-toned camouflage Boris Lemachko, 5-03

D: 850 tons light; 910 tons std. (1,050 fl) **S:** 53 kts (45 sust.; 20 hullborne)
Dim: 65.60 (63.90 hull) × 17.20 × 3.05 (1.70 on cushion)
A: 8 P-270 Moskit (SS-N-22 Sunburn) SSM (2 quadruple KT-190 launchers); 1 twin-rail Osa-MA 1 (SA-N-4) SAM syst. (20 9M-33M/Gecko missiles); 1 76.2-mm 59-cal. AK-176M DP (345 rounds); 2 single 30-mm 54-cal. AK-630 gatling AA (6,000 rounds)
Electronics:
Radar: 1 SRN-207 Ekran (Curl Stone-B) nav.; 1 MR-352 Pozitiv (Cross Dome) surf./air search; 1 Monolit-M (Band Stand) active/passive surf. target detection, tracking, and targeting; 1 MPZ-301 Baza (Pop Group) SA-N-4 f.c.; 1 MR-123-1 Vympel-AM (Bass Tilt) gun f.c.
EW: Vympel-R2 suite: 2 MRP-11/12M intercept; 2 MP-405 intercept; 1 Rumb MFD/F; 2 10-round PK-10 fixed decoy RL; 2 16-round PK-16 decoy RL
M: CODOG M-10 plant: 2 M-10-1 gas turbines for propulsion (20,000 shp each); 2 Zvezda M-511A diesels (10,000 bhp each) for hullborne operations; 2 Zvezda M-504 diesels (rated at 3,300 bhp each) for lift fans; 2 4-bladed tandem props (on Z-drive pylons) for on-cushion propulsion; 2 4-bladed props for hullborne propulsion
Electric: 800 kw tot. (4 × 200-kw diesel sets)
Range: 800/45 on cushion; 2,500/12 hullborne
Endurance: 10 days **Crew:** 9 officers, 59 enlisted

GUIDED-MISSILE PATROL COMBATANTS (AIR-CUSHION) [PGGA] *(continued)*

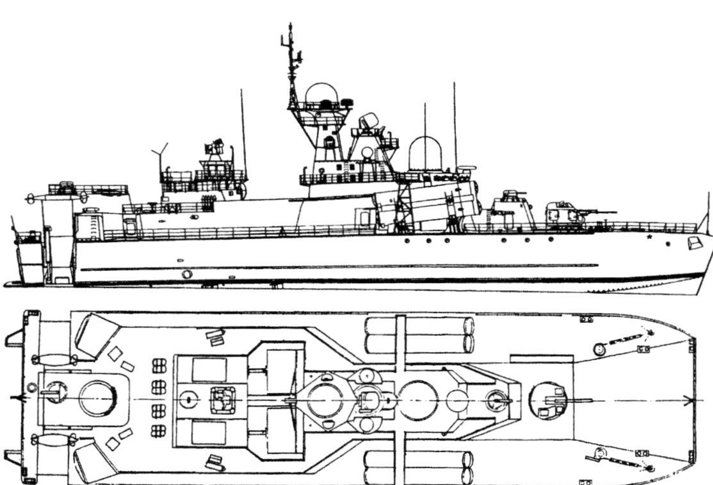

Dergach class (Project 1239) Rozvoorouzhenie, 1995

Remarks: Project nickname is Sivuch ("Beaver"). Chief designer was L.V. El'skiy of the Almaz Design Bureau, succeeded by Valery I. Korolkov. A programmed third unit was canceled. Intended for 15-year service lives, the ships are said to be expensive to operate, mechanically unreliable, and plagued by vibration at high speeds. Both were named on 18-3-92. Program authorized 24-12-80. MRK-27 was delivered 30-12-89 but not accepted for operational service until 1997; the ship is homeported at Sevastopol'. MRK-17, launched 12-10-92, was delivered to the Baltic Fleet 31-12-95 but remained uncommissioned for more than four years; the ship was transferred to the Black Sea Fleet during 6-02 and given a new pennant number. Additional ships of the class may be built.

Hull systems: Rigid sidewall–type surface-effect ships, the largest ever built, with semirigid bow and stern seals that did not need replacement during the mere 1,250 hours the *Bora* operated 1989–2000. Have an aluminum-magnesium alloy hull. The propellers are mounted in tandem at the end of struts that can be swung completely out of the water; there are diesel-powered hull-mounted propellers for harbor maneuvering. One set of propulsion engines must be stopped before the other can be engaged. The M-511A is a twin variant of the M-504 radial diesel. Using the cushion pressurization engines alone, the air exhausting from the stern can produce speeds of 3 kts for local maneuvering. The commanding officer has a BCh-5 automated shipboard equipment monitoring display console.

Combat systems: The ships have a Monolit-M (Band Stand) radome and two Pricep (Light Bulb) datalink radomes, equipment associated with the Moskit supersonic, sea-skimming missile system; Monolit can operate in either active or passive intercept mode. All eight antiship missiles can be salvoed within 35 seconds. The control system for the Osa-M SAM system has also been referred to as the 4R-33A. The Vympel radar director can control the 76-mm and/or 30-mm guns simultaneously against a single target; there are two manned SP-521 Rakurs (Kolonka-2) ringsight backup directors for the gatling guns. The communications suite is named Buran-7.

Disposal note: Of the two Utka (Lun')-class (Project 903) wing-in-ground-effect craft, the missile-armed unit, MD-160, was no longer in service as of 1999, while the search-and-rescue-configured *Spasatel'* had not been completed and has probably been abandoned.

GUIDED-MISSILE PATROL COMBATANTS [PGG]

Note: Tarantul-class variants are listed under Guided-Missile Patrol Craft [PTG], as all but one variant built to date displace less than 500 tons full load.

♦ 16 Nanuchka-III and -IV* class (Project 1234.1 and 1234.7*)
(2 in *reserve*)

Bldrs: Sudostroitel'noye Obyedineniye "Almaz," Petrovskiy SY, St. Petersburg; Vladivostokskiy Sudostroitel'nyy Zavod (Ulis),Vladivostok

	Laid down	L	In serv.	Fleet
566 Burun	1975	1977	17-2-78	Baltic
555 Geyzer	21-12-87	28-8-89	28-2-90	Baltic
551 Liven'	28-9-88	8-5-91	11-2-92	Baltic
590 Meteor	13-11-84	16-9-87	19-2-88	Baltic
617 Mirazh	30-8-83	19-8-86	24-2-87	Black
409 Moroz	17-2-85	23-9-89	28-2-90	Pacific
526 Nakat*	4-11-82	16-4-87	30-12-87	Northern
570 Passat	27-5-88	13-6-90	14-3-91	Baltic
562 Priliv	29-4-82	26-4-85	7-1-86	Baltic
520 Rassvet	29-9-86	22-8-88	1-3-89	Northern
450 *Razliv*	1-11-86	24-8-91	11-2-92	Pacific
620 Shtil' (ex-*Komsomolets Mordovii*, ex-*Zyb'*)	28-6-76	23-10-78	16-2-79	Black
423 *Smerch*	16-11-81	16-11-84	4-3-85	Pacific
533 Tucha	4-5-77	29-4-80	24-10-80	Northern
505 Urugan	1-8-80	27-5-83	15-12-83	Northern
560 Zyb'	26-8-86	28-2-89	31-10-89	Baltic

D: 610 tons light; 639 tons std. (730 fl; 790 max.) **S:** 34 kts
Dim: 59.30 (54.85 wl) × 11.80 (8.86 wl) × 3.08 (normal)
A: 6 P-120 Malakhit (SS-N-9 Siren) SSM (2 triple KT-84 launchers); 1 twin-rail Osa-M (SA-N-4B) SAM syst. (20 9M-33M5/G`ecko missiles); 1 76.2-mm 59-cal. AK-176 DP (304 rounds); 1 30-mm 65-cal. AK-630 gatling AA (3,000 rounds)

Passat (570) Ralph Edwards, 6-03

Geyzer (555) Michael Winter, 7-06

Electronics:
Radar: 1 or 2 MR-312 Nayada nav. (not in all); 1 Dubrava (Peel Pair) nav./surf. search (not in all); 1 Titanit (Band Stand) target desig.; 1 MPZ-301 Baza (Pop Group) SAM f.c.; 1 MR-123 Vympel (Bass Tilt) gun f.c.
EW: Vympel-R2 suite: 2 Half Hat-B intercept; 2 Foot Ball-A intercept; 2 16-round PK-16 decoy RL; 4 10-round PK-10 decoy RL
M: 3 M-521 diesels; 3 props; 30,000 shp
Electric: 700 kw tot. (2 × 300-kw, 1 × 100-kw diesel sets)
Range: 415/34; 2,100/18; 3,500/12 (1 engine)
Fuel: 132 tons **Endurance:** 10 days
Crew: 7 officers, 42 enlisted (accomm. for 10 officers, 55 enlisted)

Remarks: Type designation: MRK (*Malyy Raketnyy Korabl',* Small Missile Ship). *Burun,* the first built, was commissioned 17-2-78. One Northern Fleet unit, *Nakat,* sometimes referred to as the Nanuchka-IV (Project 1234.7), was modified while under construction with two sextuple racks for P-800 Oniks (SS-N-26 Sapless/Yakhont) antiship missiles in place of the SS-N-9 SSM. The *Moroz* acted as host to Japanese ships visiting Petropavlovsk-na-Kamchatka during 9-00, and the 450 and 423 are laid up there.

Combat systems: The single 76.2-mm DP was substituted for the Nanuchka-II's twin 57-mm AA aft, the gatling gun is in the position occupied by Muff Cob in the Nanuchka-I, and Bass Tilt is situated atop a new deckhouse abaft the mast. The 30-mm gatling gun is off centerline to starboard. Two Fish Bowl or Pricep (Light Bulb) radomes on the mast are believed to house SS-N-9 missile datalink antennas. Intercept arrays vary considerably: early units had a Peel Pair target-designation and tracking radar atop the mast, while later units lack the Peel Pair, add two Light Bulb missile datalink antenna radomes on the sides of the mast, and have one or two MR-312 Nayada navigational radars. Late units also had four 10-round PK-10 fixed decoy rocket launchers in addition to the two 16-round launchers.

Disposals: Black Sea Fleet unit *Mirazh* was not transferred to Ukraine in 1997 as reported in the last edition. Pacific Fleet unit *Purga,* Northern Fleet unit *Priboi,* and Black Sea Fleet unit *Iney* (ex-*XX Syezd V.L.K.S.M.*) had been stricken by late 1998. A unit named *Perekat,* laid down in 1988, was broken up in 1992. Northern Fleet unit *Veter* was stricken 4-8-95. The hull of another (to have been named *Koreyets*) was broken up before completion on the ways at the Petrovskiy facility in 1991. Northern Fleet unit *Aysberg* was stricken by 2005.

♦ 1 Nanuchka-I (Ovod) class (Project 1234)

Bldr: Sudostroitel'noye Obyedineniye "Almaz," Petrovskiy SY, St. Petersburg

	Laid down	L	In serv.	Fleet
621 Zarnitsa	27-7-70	28-4-73	26-10-73	Black Sea

D: 610 tons light; 639 tons std. (700 fl; 760 max.) **S:** 35 kts
Dim: 59.30 (54.00 wl) × 11.80 (8.86 wl) × 3.02 (normal)
A: 6 P-120 Malakhit (SS-N-9 Siren) SSM (2 triple KT-84 launchers); 1 twin-rail Osa-M (SA-N-4) SAM syst. (20 4K-33/Gecko missiles); 1 twin 57-mm 70-cal. AK-725 DP (1,100 rounds)
Electronics:
Radar: 1 Dubrava (Peel Pair) nav./surf. search; 1 Titanit (Band Stand) missile target desig.; 1 MPZ-301 Baza (Pop Group) SA-N-4 f.c.; 1 MR-103 Bars (Muff Cob) gun f.c.
EW: Zaliv suite: 4 . . . intercept; 2 16-round PK-16 decoy syst. RL
M: 3 M-507A diesels; 3 props; 30,000 bhp
Electric: 750 kw tot. (2 × 300-kw, 2 × 75-kw diesel sets)
Range: 900/30; 2,500/12 (1 engine) **Fuel:** 132 tons **Endurance:** 10 days
Crew: 7–10 officers, 42–50 enlisted

GUIDED-MISSILE PATROL COMBATANTS [PGG] *(continued)*

Zarnitsa (621)—the surviving Black Sea Fleet Nanuchka-I; note the 57-mm gunmount aft and the large radome for the Titanit targeting sensor mounted abaft the pilothouse Hartmut Ehlers, 7-00

Remarks: Survivors of a class of 17. Design approved 17-8-65. Type designation: MRK (*Malyy Raketnyy Korabl',* Small Missile Ship). *Zarnitsa* is assigned to the 166th Novorossiysk Red Banner Small Rocket Ship Division of the 41st Fast Rocket Craft Brigade.
Hull systems: Are reported to be very bad seaboats, with pronounced heaving motion, but are nonetheless claimed to be operable in seas up to State 5 (State 4 for weapons operations). Engines are reported to be unreliable.
Combat systems: Overhauled during 2004–5. May have been equipped to carry the Yakhont/Sapless (SS-N-26) missile system. In this class, the Band Stand radome contains the antenna for the Titanit SSM target-designation system. The communications system can maintain seven circuits simultaneously.
Disposals: Pacific Fleet unit *Musson* sank 16-4-87 after being hit by a target drone; 39 were killed. Black Sea Fleet unit (and class prototype) *Burya* was stricken 24-6-91. Also stricken have been Pacific Fleet unit *Briz* and Black Sea Fleet unit *Groza* on 3-7-92; *Bora* and *Grom* on 5-7-94; *Volna* and *Zarya* on 31-7-96; Baltic Fleet sisters *Grad, Raduga, Shkval,* and *Shtorm* on 5-7-94, 10-12-95, 1-9-95, and 16-3-98, respectively; Pacific Fleet units *Vikhr* on 5-7-94, *Tsiklon* on 17-11-94, and *Tayfun* on 1-9-95; and Northern Fleet unit *Metel'* on 16-3-98. Baltic Fleet unit *Molniya* was scrapped at Yantar Shipyard, Kaliningrad, during 2002.

GUIDED-MISSILE PATROL CRAFT [PTG]

Note: The Katran-class program (Project 20970) has been abandoned in favor of more modern designs.

♦ 0 (+ 1 + . . .) Skorpion class (Project 12300)
Bldr: Vympel Zavod, Rybinsk

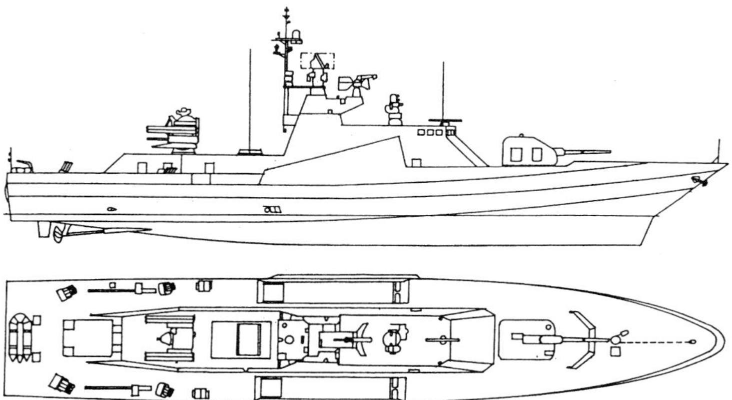

Skorpion (Project 12300) design concept *Voenniy Parad,* 1-00

D: 456 tons (470 fl) **S:** 38 kts **Dim:** 56.8 × 10.8 × 2.7
A: 4 P-800 Oniks (SS-N-26 Sapless) SSM; 1 100-mm A-190 DP; 2 Kashtan-1 CIWS (2 30-mm GSH-6-30L gatling AA and 32 9M-311 Vikhr'-K/SA-N-11 Grison missiles each; 6,000 total rounds 30-mm)
Electronics:
Radar: 1 Pozitiv-ME1.1 search radar; 1 Monument-E1 surface target-tracking and datalink; 1 Puma-E gun f.c.
Sonar: Anapa hull-mounted
EW: . . . intercept, 4 10-round PK-10 decoy RL
M: CODAG: 1 M-70FR gas turbine (16,000 shp), 2 MTU 16V4000 M-90 diesels; 3 props; 20,900 hp max.
Range: 2,200/12 **Endurance:** 10 days
Crew: 37 tot.

Remarks: A "stealth" design by the Central Maritime Design Office. A privately funded prototype was laid down 5-6-01. Though expected to have been ready for trials during 2005, there are no indications they have yet taken place. Also offered is the Project 12301 variant with Kh-35 Uran antiship missiles, and Project 12301P for potential Russian Federal Border Guard purchase. The price is said to be about $35 million per boat, and the builder hopes to sell 10 to the Russian Navy, 10 to the Federal Border Guard, and 28 abroad.

Combat systems: Will have vertical launchers for the SSMs. The Sigma combat system, Gorizont-25 integrated navigational system, and Buran-6E automatic communications suite will be fitted.

♦ 1 (+ . . .) Tarantul-IV class (Project 12421)
Bldr: Vympel Zavod, Rybinsk (In serv. 26-2-00)

. . . R-5

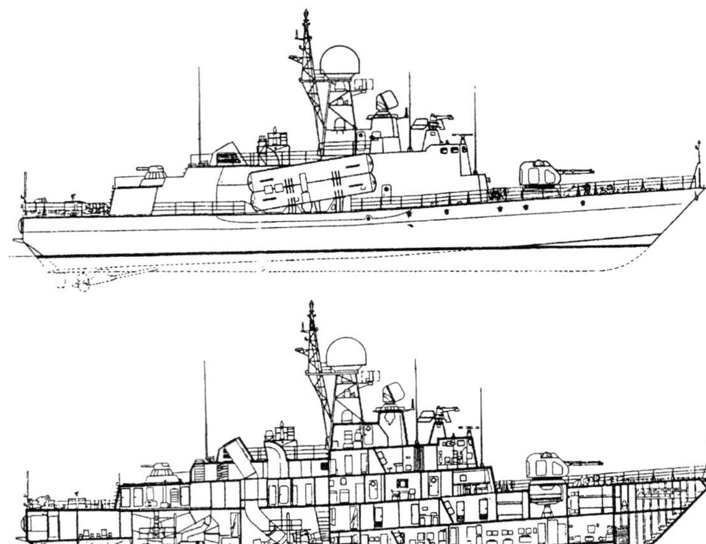

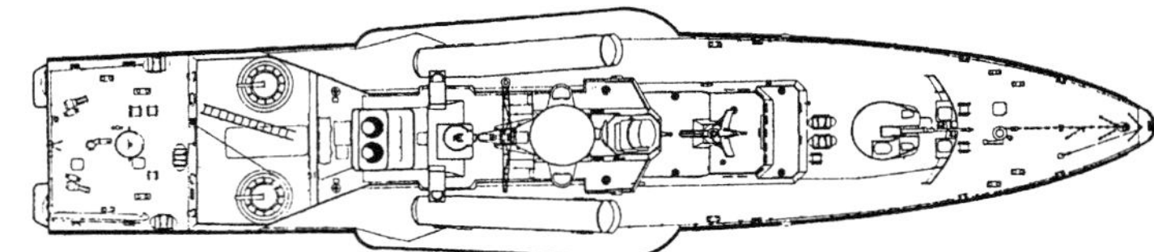

R-5—the Tarantul-IV (Project 12421) Rozvoorouzhenie, 1995

D: 450 tons (550 fl) **S:** 38 kts (35 sust.)
Dim: 56.9 × 13.00 (max.; 8.75 wl) × 2.65 (hull; 4.51 props)
A: 4 P-270 Moskit (SS-N-22 Sunburn) SSM; 1 76.2-mm 59-cal. AK-176 DP; 1 4-round Fasta-4M (SA-N-8) SAM syst. (12 Igla-M/Gremlin missiles); 2 single 30-mm 54-cal. AK-630M gatling AA
Electronics:
Radar: 1 Kivach-3 nav.; 1 MR-352 Pozitiv surf./air search; 1 Garpun-Bal target detection/desig.; 1 MR-123-02 Vympel (Bass Tilt) gun f.c.
EW: 2 Half Hat-B intercept; 2 Foot Ball-A intercept, 2 10-round PK-10 decoy RL
M: 2 gas turbines (16,000 shp each); 2 props; 32,000 shp
Electric: 455 kw tot. (2 × 180-kw, 1 × 95-kw, 380-V, 50-Hz diesel sets)
Range: 2,400/12 **Crew:** 44 tot.

Remarks: Prototype of the latest export offering in the basic Tarantul series, with addition of MR-352 Pozitiv surface- and air-search radar set and the elimination of the cruise diesels. Launched in 9-97. May be owned by the Almaz design bureau as an export demonstrator rather than the Russian Navy itself, although it was said to have been assigned to the Baltic Fleet as of 5-00. No further units have been ordered. Missile-firing trials were to begin during 10-99. Although *Molnaya* ("Lightning") has been given as the actual name for the craft, it may be a reference to the overall project name, which is also Molnaya. The same basic design is offered with 16 Kh-35 Uran (SS-N-25) antiship missiles as Project 12418. Sredniy Neva Shipyard was expecting an order for a ship of this class as of 1-02.
Hull systems: Maximum speed listed is achievable in 15° C air temperature.
Combat systems: The Garpun-Bal radar system can track 15 targets simultaneously and can also be used in passive mode to track and target emitting platforms.

♦ 20 Tarantul-III (Molnaya-M) class (Project 1241.1RZ)
Bldrs: Sudostroitel'noye Obyedineniye "Almaz," Petrovskiy SY, St. Petersburg, and Sredniy Neva SY, Kolpino; Vladivostokskiy Sudostroitel'nyy Zavod (Ulis), Vladivostok

	In serv.		In. serv.
819 R-42 (ex-*Tamborvskiy Komsomolets*)	1987	971 R-298	1990
955 Burya R-60	1987	825 R-291 Dmitrovgrad	1991
991 R-261	1988	940 R-11	9-91
953 R-239 Groza	1989	924 R-14	12-91
909 R-271	1989	874 R-293 Morashansk	1992
855 R-187	1989	937 R-18	9-92
954 R-334 Ivanovets	12-89	978 R-19	12-92
999 R-442	12-89	921 R-20	12-93
952 R-109	1990	946 R-24	1994
951 R-297	1990	916 R-29	. . .

D: 436 tons light (493 fl) **S:** 38 kts (41 light)
Dim: 56.10 (49.50 pp) × 10.20 (8.74 wl) × 2.47 (hull; 4.33 props)

GUIDED-MISSILE PATROL CRAFT [PTG] *(continued)*

R-29 (916) Takatoshi Okano, 9-04

R-60 Burya (955) Boris Lemachko, 2006

A: 4 P-270 Moskit (SS-N-22 Sunburn) SSM (3M-80 missiles); 1 76-mm 59-cal. AK-176 DP (152 rounds); 1 4-round Fasta-4M (SA-N-8) SAM syst. (16 9M-36 Strela-3M/Gremlin missiles); 2 single 30-mm 54-cal. AK-630M gatling AA (4,000 rounds)

Electronics:

Radar: 1 Kivach-3 nav.; 1 Mineral (Band Stand) missile target detection/desig.; 1 MR-123-02 Vympel (Bass Tilt) gun f.c.

EW: MP 405-1 Vympel-R2 suite: 2 Half Hat-B intercept; 2 Foot Ball-A intercept; 2 16-round PK-16 decoy RL; 2 or 4 10-round PK-10 decoy RL

M: CODAG: 2 M-70 (PR-76) gas turbines (12,000 shp each), 2 Type M-510 diesels (5,000 bhp each; 4,000 sust.); 2 props; 34,000 hp max.

Electric: 500 kw tot. (2 × 200-kw, 1 × 100-kw diesel sets)

Range: 400/36; 1,600/20; 2,400/12 **Fuel:** 50 tons **Endurance:** 10 days

Crew: 8 officers, 33 enlisted

Remarks: Although a prototype Tarantul configured with four SS-N-22 supersonic sea-skimming missiles appeared in the early 1980s, not until 1987 was what appears to be a production version sighted. The original program goal was 44 units. Four are in the Baltic Fleet based at Baltiysk, three are assigned to the Caspian Flotilla, and there are also units in the Pacific (including R-297 and R-298) and Black Sea Fleets (including R-60, R-239, and R-334).

Hull systems: The propulsion system differs from that of earlier Tarantuls in that diesels were substituted for the cruise turbines to improve cruising range.

Combat systems: A single Pricep (Light Bulb) missile datalink antenna radome is located atop a vertical lattice mast. The antenna within the Band Stand radome provides active and passive targeting for the antiship missiles; the EW suite is integrated with the active radars and can track 15 targets simultaneously to 120 km actively and 500 km passively. There is a backup lead-computing optical director for the six-barrel, 30-mm gatling guns. Carry a total of 152 rounds of 76.2-mm and 4,000 rounds of 30-mm ammunition (including 2,000 rounds of 30-mm ready-service on-mount). The communications suite permits maintaining seven circuits simultaneously.

Disposals: R-63 (ex-*Kuybyshevskiy Komsomolets*) had been transferred to Ukraine by 8-97 and has since been scrapped. Five others, mostly from the Black Sea Fleet, have been retired for lack of overhaul funds. R-240 of this class was stricken by 2005.

♦ 5 Tarantul-II (Molnaya) class (Project 1241.1/2 or 12411M)

Bldrs: Sudostroitel'noye Obyedineniye "Almaz," Petrovskiy SY, St. Petersburg, and Sredniy Neva SY, Kolpino; Vladivostokskiy Sudostroitel'nyy Zavod (Ulis), Vladivostok

	In serv.		In. serv.
709 R-101	1985	820 R-255 (ex-*Kronshtadtskiy Komsomolets*)	1981
852 R-129	1985		
962 R-71	1985	705 R-49 Stupinets	. . .

D: 329 tons light; 436 tons std. (469 fl) **S:** 42 kts

Dim: 56.10 (49.50 pp) × 10.20 (8.74 wl) × 2.38 (hull; 4.15 props)

A: 4 P-15M Termit (SS-N-2C Styx) SSM; 1 76.2-mm 59-cal. AK-176 DP; 1 Fasta-4M (SA-N-8) SAM syst. (16 9M-36 Strela-3M/Gremlin missiles)—all except R-71: 2 single 30-mm 54-cal. AK-630M gatling AA—R-71 only: 1 Kortik CIWS (with 8 missile tubes and 2 30-mm GSH-6-30L gatling AA; 8 tot. 9M-311 Vikhr'-K/ SA-N-11 Grison missiles—see remarks)

Electronics:

Radar: 1 Kivach-3 nav., 1 Monolit (Band Stand) missile target detection and tracking; 1 MR-123 Vympel (Bass Tilt) gun f.c.—R-71 also: MR-352 Pozitiv (Cross Dome) surf./air search; 1 3P-87 (Hot Flash) Kortik f.c.

EW: No intercept; 2 16-round PK-16 decoy RL

R-71 (962) Boris Lemachko, 3-06

R-71 (962) Boris Lemachko, 2005

M: COGAG M-15 plant: 2 M-75 (DMR-76) cruise gas turbines (5,000 shp each), 2 M-70 (PR-77) boost gas turbines (12,000 shp each); 2 props; 32,000 shp (23,700 shp at 34° C air and 30° C water temperature)

Electric: 700 kw tot. (2 × 200-kw, 1 × 300-kw diesel sets)

Range: 760/43; 1,400/13 **Fuel:** 50 tons **Endurance:** 10 days

Crew: 5 officers, 36 enlisted

Remarks: The initial large-scale production variant of the Tarantul design for the Soviet Navy. The considerably modified R-71 is a trials ship (Project 1241.7) in the Black Sea Fleet, the unit with pennant number 705 is assigned to the Caspian Flotilla, and R-255 and possibly two others are assigned to the Baltic Fleet and based at Baltiysk.

Hull systems: The cruise gas turbines exhaust through a stack, while the high-speed turbines exhaust through the transom stern, adding their residual thrust to the propulsive power; all four engines are employed simultaneously for maximum power. One unit of the class is said to have had the same CODAG propulsion plant as the Tarantul-III variant.

Combat systems: A Pricep (Light Bulb) cruise missile datalink antenna has been added at the masthead, while the Band Stand radome conceals a missile target acquisition and tracking radar that can also be employed in passive mode. There are four unoccupied positions for EW antennas. Some 152 rounds of 76.2-mm and 4,000 rounds of 30-mm ammunition are normally carried, although there is emergency stowage for an additional 162 rounds of 76-mm ammunition. R-71 has been equipped with a Kortik twin 30-mm cannon/9M-311 missile launcher (with missile racks but without missile reload facilities) and an MR-352 Pozitiv surface/air-search target detection, designation, and tracking radar set.

Disposals: Caspian Flotilla sister *Poltavskiy Komsomolets* and one Black Sea Fleet unit were transferred to Bulgaria in 1992. One Baltic Fleet unit had been stricken by 7-96 at Kronshtadt, and three others are believed to have been retired as well. Pacific Fleet unit R-46 was stricken 5-7-94. Black Sea Fleet unit R-54 (ex-*Krasnodarskiy Komsomolets*) was transferred to Ukraine in 6-97. Pacific Fleet units R-45, R-66, and R-69 were stricken 1-9-95, R-76 and R-158 on 31-7-96, and R-113 and R-230 during 1997. Another five had been retired by 1999, mostly from the Black Sea Fleet. R-42 was stricken by 2005.

Disposal note: Tarantul-I-class (Project 1241.1) guided-missile craft R-26 (860) appears to have been retired in 2000; others were built for export to Poland (4), East Germany (5), India (5; plus others built indigenously), and Vietnam (2).

♦ 2 Matka (Vikhr')-class (Project 206MR) semi-hydrofoil

Bldr: Sudostroitel'noye Obyedineniye "Almaz" (Sredniy Neva), Kolpino

702 R-27 Borovsk (In serv. 1977) 966 R-44 Kosar (In serv. 1978)

D: 230 tons (257 fl; 268 max.) **S:** 42 kts

Dim: 38.60 (37.50 wl) × 12.5 (7.6 hull; 5.9 wl) × 2.10 (hull; 3.26 over foils)

A: R-27: 2 P-15 Termit (SS-N-2C Styx) antiship missiles; 1 76.2-mm 59-cal. AK-176 DP; 1 30-mm 54-cal. AK-630M gatling AA—R-44: 8 Kh-35 Uran (SS-N-25 Switchblade) SSM; 1 76.2-mm 59-cal. AK-176 DP; 1 twin 30-mm 54-cal. AK-630M1-2 Roy gatling AA

Electronics: Radar: 1 Cheese Cake nav.; 1 Garpun (Plank Shave) target detection/tracking; 1 MR-123 Vympel-AM (Bass Tilt) gun f.c.

GUIDED-MISSILE PATROL CRAFT [PTG] *(continued)*

R-44 Kosar (966)—note the quadruple launchers for Kh-35 Uran missiles to stern Boris Lemachko, 2002

M: 3 M-520TM5 diesels; 3 props; 16,200 bhp (14,400 sust.)
Electric: 300 kw tot. (1 × 100-kw DGF-2A-100/1500 and 1 × 200-kw DRGA-2A-200/1500 diesel sets; 380 V, 50 Hz a.c.)
Range: 600/35; 1,200/22–24; 1,800/10–12 **Fuel:** 38 tons max., overload
Endurance: 8 days **Crew:** 25–28 tot.

Remarks: Essentially a missile-armed version of the Turya-class hydrofoil torpedo boat, with larger superstructure, a 76.2-mm gun forward, and missiles and gatling gun aft. Designed by the Almaz Bureau. Black Sea Fleet unit R-44 is equipped for trials and sales demonstration work with Kh-35 Uran antiship missiles and is based at Karanhinnaya Bay, Sevastopol'. R-27 retains the original armament and is based in the Caspian Sea at Astrakhan.
Hull systems: Steel hull with aluminum/magnesium-alloy superstructure. Appear to be overloaded, and construction ceased in favor of the Tarantul series. As with Turya class, the stern planes on the surface while the bow is supported by the hydrofoils at high speeds. Both the foils and the transom stern flap are remotely controlled via a Baza 02065 gyro system to improve the ride. In colder waters (below 25° C), the craft could make 43–45 kts on foil.
Combat systems: In 1987–88, R-44 had her P-15M Termit (SS-N-2B Styx) missile launchers replaced with two quadruple tubes for Kh-35 Uran (SS-N-25 Switchblade) antiship missiles; the ship also carries the prototype AK-630M1-2 twin 30-mm gatling gun mounting in place of the original AK-630M and has small portable deckhouses just forward of the Kh-35 installation. R-44's missile tubes were temporarily removed during 2000 and put aboard the destroyer *Smel'yy* but were reinstalled at Feodosiya in spring 2001. Positions for EW intercept antennas remain empty. Carries 152 rounds of 76.2-mm and 2,000 rounds of 30-mm ammunition. SPO-3 radiation-warning equipment and the R-784 automated radio system are fitted.
Disposals: At least five Baltic Fleet units had been discarded by 1995 (including R-254 on 5-7-94), and R-25, R-30, R-50, and R-221, which had been in storage at Kronshtadt since the mid-1990s. Four Black Sea Fleet units (R-251, R-260, R-262, and R-265) were transferred to Ukraine 10-1-96 and another, R-15, on a later date.

TORPEDO BOATS [PT]

Disposal note: The sole Bogomol-class (Project 02065; Project Vikhr'-3) training torpedo boat, Pacific Fleet unit T-229, was offered for sale in 7-99 and is no longer in service. Turya-class (Project 206M) torpedo boats T-75 and T-118 had been retired from the Caspian Flotilla by 2001.

PATROL CRAFT, HYDROFOIL [PCH]

♦ 1 Mukha (Sokol) class (Project 11451)
Bldr: More Zavod, Feodosiya, Ukraine

	Laid down	L	In serv.
060 MPK-220 Vladimirets	12-5-84	20-8-90	14-3-91

MPK-220 Vladimirets (060) Hartmut Ehlers, 3-02

D: 320 tons light; 362 tons std.; 415.1 tons normal (468.1 fl)
S: 50 kts (12.2 on cruise diesels)
Dim: 49.97 (46.3 wl) × 9.9 (hull; 21.2 over foils; 9.20 wl) × 4.5 (mean hull; 7.26 over foils)
A: 1 76.2-mm 59-cal. AK-176 DP; 2 single 30-mm 54-cal. AK-630M gatling AA; 2 quadruple 224-mm TR-224 ASW TT
Electronics:
Radar: 1 Don-2 nav.; 1 Reyd (Peel Cone) nav./surf. search; 1 MR-123 Vympel (Bass Tilt) f.c.
Sonar: Zvezda-M1 through-hull variable-depth dipping sonar amidships
EW: No intercept equipment; 2 16-round PK-16 decoy RL
M: CODAG: 2 NK-12M boost gas turbines (18,000 shp each); 2 M-401 diesels (1,200 bhp each); 3 tandem 4-bladed propellers; 38,400 shp max.—2 Kort-nozzle low-speed thrusters
Electric: 400 kw tot. (2 × 200-kw diesel sets)
Range: 750/50; on one diesel: 1,200/12; 2,000/8 **Endurance:** 7 days
Crew: 5 officers, 34 enlisted

Remarks: A production version of the 1978-vintage Babochka prototype (Project 1141.1), with heavier armament and a less powerful propulsion plant. Assigned to the Black Sea Fleet. Named during 7-98. Was under refit at Sevastopol' during 2001. Sister MPK-215 (wearing pennant 056) was scrapped at Sevastopol' late during 2001. A third unit, MPK-231, was not completed and was stricken 28-7-94. Three further units were being built for the Ukraine Navy, but construction was abandoned.
Hull systems: A true hydrofoil, with fixed foils fore and aft. One semiofficial source gives the displacement as 364 tons light and 475 tons full load. An export version has been offered by Ukraine with one Ukraine Central Machinery gas turbine on the centerline (4,000 shp) and two PR-77 boost gas turbines (12,100 shp each), at a cost of $25 million per ship.
Combat systems: The combat system is designated Gangut-1141 and the communications suite Buran-7. The small-diameter torpedo tubes must be trained outboard about 40° to launch; what torpedo is carried is not known.

Disposal note: Prototype hydrofoil antisubmarine warfare craft *Aleksandr Kunakhovich* (NATO Babochka class, Project 1141.1) had been stricken by 2001.

Note: All Muravey (Antarets)-class (Project 133) patrol hydrofoils are subordinated to the Federal Border Guard and are discussed in that section.

PATROL CRAFT [PC]

Note: See also under the Federal Border Guard for additional patrol craft and patrol boat designs.

♦ 3 Svetlyak class (Project 1041.0)
Bldrs: Vladivostokskiy Sudostroitel'nyy Zavod (Vostochnaya Verf), Ulis, Vladivostok; Sudostroitel'noye Obyedineniye "Almaz," Petrovskiy SY, St. Petersburg

	In serv.
301 AKA-235	1991
361 AKA-275	1992
. . . AKA-300 Let Rossiyskomu Flotu	1997

D: 328 tons (365 normal fl; 382 max.) **S:** 32 kts (31 sust.)
Dim: 49.50 (45.00 wl) × 9.20 × 2.14 (hull; 2.50 props)
A: 1 76.2-mm 59-cal. AK-176M DP; 1 30-mm 54-cal. AK-630M gatling AA; 16 Igla-series (SA-14/16) shoulder-launched SAM; 1 or 2 AGS-17 grenade launchers; 1 DP-64 antiswimmer grenade launcher; 2 fixed 402-mm OTA-40 ASW TT; 2 d.c. racks (6 d.c. each)
Electronics:
Radar: 1 Reyd (Peel Cone) nav./surf. search; 1 MR-123 Vympel-AM (Bass Tilt) f.c.
Sonar: Uzh HF helicopter dipping sonar at stern
EW: Slyabing intercept; MFD/F loop; 2 16-round PK-16 decoy RL
M: 3 M-520B diesels; 3 props; 15,000 bhp
Electric: 400 kw tot. (1 × 200-kw, 2 × 100-kw diesel sets; 380 V, 50 Hz a.c.)
Range: 1,500/31–32; 2,200/12–13 **Endurance:** 10 days
Crew: 4 officers, 4 warrant officers, 20 enlisted (41 tot. accomm.)

Remarks: Type designation: AKA (*Artilleriyskiy Kater,* Gunboat). Design, by Almaz Central Marine Design Bureau, was tailored to extended patrolling for Federal Border Guard use, but three have been assigned to the navy: AKA-235 in the Baltic, AKA-275 in the Black Sea, and *300 Let Rossiyskomu Flotu* ("300 Years of the Russian Navy") to the Northern Fleet. The Federal Border Guard operates others. Five had been ordered for the navy from the Almaz yard, but the navy could not pay and the units were exported.
Hull systems: Semi-planing, round-bilge hull with low spray chine forward. Propellers do not project below the keel. Have a steel hull with magnesium/aluminum-alloy superstructure. Can survive with two compartments flooded. Have NBC warfare protection. The engine room is coated with vibration-damping material. The pilothouse is equipped with a centerline periscope.
Combat systems: There is an SP-521 Rakurs (Kolonka-2) ringsight backup director for the 30-mm gun, and the 76.2-mm mount can be operated in local control and has an integral electro-optical sighting system. Carry 152 rounds of 76-mm ammunition (all on-mount) and up to 3,000 rounds of 30-mm. Navigational equipment includes a NAVSAT receiver, radio navaid receiver, automatic plot, and echo sounder. There is no hull-mounted sonar; the dipping sonar is extended from a compartment to port of the centerline at the stern.

Disposal note: Tyulen'-class patrol tug (Project 2035) *PRDK-179* and Pauk-I (Molnaya-2) class (Project 1231.2) boat *MPK-144* had been stricken by 2005.

♦ 1 Stenka (Tarantul) class (Project 205M)
Bldr: Sudostroitel'noye Obyedineniye "Almaz," Petrovskiy SY, St. Petersburg

375 AKA-232 (In serv. . . .)

D: 170 tons light; 211 tons std. (245 fl) **S:** 35 kts
Dim: 39.80 (37.50 wl) × 7.60 (5.90 wl) × 1.96
A: 2 twin 30-mm 65-cal. AK-230 AA; 4 fixed 402-mm OTA-40 TT (4 SET-40 ASW torpedoes); 2 d.c. racks (6 BB-1 d.c. each)
Electronics:
Radar: 1 Reyd (Peel Cone) nav./surf. search; 1 MR-104 Rys' (Drum Tilt) gun f.c.
Sonar: Bronza hull-mounted HF; HF helicopter dipping-type
EW: SPO-3 intercept
M: 3 M-504B or M-520 diesels; 3 props; 15,000 bhp
Range: 500/35; 800/20; 1,500/11.5 **Endurance:** 10 days
Crew: 4–5 officers, 26–27 enlisted

PATROL CRAFT [PC] *(continued)*

Remarks: The majority of the 117 built for Russia served as Project 205P in the Federal Border Guard, which still has 23 in service (which see for appearance). AKA-232 operates in the Caspian Flotilla.

PATROL BOATS [PB]

Note: Most surviving craft in this category appear to be assigned either to the Federal Border Guard or to the customs service.

♦ 5 Zhuk (Gryf) class (Project 1400 or 1400M)

Bldr: More Zavod, Feodosiya, Ukraine (In serv. 1971–86)

AKA-11 AKA-38 AKA-49 AKA-326 AKA-388

Russian Navy Zhuk Pennant 050—assigned to the Caspian Flotilla
Boris Lemachko, 2000

D: 35.9 tons (39.7 fl) **S:** 30 kts
Dim: 23.80 (21.70 wl) × 5.00 (3.80 wl) × 1.00 (hull; 1.90 max.)
A: 1 twin 14.5-mm 93-cal. 2M-7 AA *or* 1 twin 12.7-mm 60-cal. Utës-Ma mg
Electronics: Radar: 1 Lotsiya nav.
M: Project 1400M: 2 M-401 diesels; 2 props; 2,200 bhp—Project 1400: 2 M-50F4 diesels; 2 props; 2,400 bhp
Electric: 48 kw tot. (2 × 21-kw, 1 × 6-kw diesel sets)
Range: 700/28; 1,100/15 **Endurance:** 5 days **Crew:** 1 officer, 6 enlisted

Remarks: More than 110 others of this class were exported, 26 remain in Federal Border Guard service, and at least 10 were built as naval officers' yachts [YFL] (q.v.). Have an aluminum alloy hull. Capable of operating in up to Sea State 4 or 5. These units may have been retired as their status remains unknown.

Disposal note: The surviving Poluchat-I (TL-1) Class unit AKA-527 was stricken by 2005.

RIVER MONITORS [WPM]

Note: The Yaz (Project 1208)-, Pivyaka (Project 1212)-, and Vosh (Project 1248)-class river monitors are subordinated to the Federal Border Guard (q.v.).

♦ 15 Shmel'-class (Project 1204)

Bldrs: Kamysh Burun Zavod, Kerch', and 61 Kommunara Zavod, Nikolayev, Ukraine (In serv. 1967–74)

AK-201	AK-247	AK-489	and three others
AK-202	AK-249	AK-507	
AK-208	AK-407	AK-508	
AK-245	AK-409	AK-509	

Shmel' class pennant 141 Boris Lemachko, 2001

D: 77.4 tons (fl) **S:** 24 kts **Dim:** 27.70 × 4.32 × 0.90 (2.00 molded depth)
A: 1 76.2-mm, 48-cal. D-56TM low-angle (in a PT-76 tank turret); 1 twin 25-mm 80-cal. 2M-3M AA; 1 7.62-mm mg (in tank turret); 1 17-round 140-mm BM-14-17 artillery RL (36 rockets); 2 mine rails (up to 8 mines)
Electronics: Radar: 1 Donets-2 nav.
M: 2 M-50F-4 diesels; 2 props; 2,400 bhp
Electric: 50 kw tot. (2 × 25-kw DG-25 diesel sets)
Range: 240/20; 600/10 **Fuel:** 4.75 tons **Endurance:** 7 days
Crew: 1 officer, 2 warrant officers, 11 enlisted

Remarks: Survivors of 65 built for the Soviet Navy; 53 others were for the Maritime (now Federal) Border Guard. Units built at Nikolayev were prefabricated and later assembled at Khabarovsk for Border Guard use on the Amur-Ussuri River system, where 16 remain in service. Naval type designation: AK (*Artilleriyskiy Kater,* Artillery Cutter). Designed by TsKB-5 (the current Firma Almaz) design bureau under L. V. Ozimov. AK-208, -245, -247, -407, -409, -489, -507, -508, and -509 are in the Baltic Fleet (most stored ashore in reserve); the others are in the Caspian Flotilla. Two units are maintained on Lake Pripus on the Estonian border. Only two pennant numbers are available: AK-509 is 112 and AK-407 is 148.
Hull systems: The screws are mounted in tunnels to reduce draft. Armor includes 10-mm over the pilothouse and gun barbettes, 8-mm over the hull and internal bulkheads, and 5-mm over the deck and pilothouse. Have a Gradus-2 gyrocompass and NEL-7 echo sounder.
Combat systems: Early units had a twin 14.5-mm machinegun mount aft that resembled a tank turret, and some have also carried up to four 30-mm BL-30 Plamya grenade launchers and four pintle-mounted 7.62-mm machineguns. The 7.62-mm machinegun is mounted coaxially with the 76-mm gun (for which 40 rounds are carried on-mount); up to four others fire through slits in the sides of the open-topped redoubt forward of the artillery RL. Mine loads vary from four UDM-500 or two UDM-1000 to six KPM or eight YaM mines.
Disposals: Four were transferred to Kampuchea 1984–85. Former Danube River Flotilla units AKA-211, -246, and -563 were transferred to Ukraine 1-5-95; other units of the Danube Flotilla, including AK-209, -223, -224, -225,-248, -397, -506, -527, -564, -582, -583, -598, -599, and -602, were also transferred to Ukraine in 1995, along with other assets of the former Russian Danube Flotilla. Pacific Fleet Amur River Flotilla units AK-354 and -587 were stricken 3-7-92 and 9-10-92, respectively, followed by sisters AKA-203, -242, -314, -316, -317, -318, -384, -387, -581, and -584 on 30-7-93 and AKA-197, -198, -205, -385, -398, -399, -408, -585, -588, and -589 on 5-7-94.

MINE WARFARE SHIPS

♦ 2 Gorya-class (Project 1266.0) minehunting ships [MHS]

Bldr: Sudostroitel'noye Obyedineniye "Almaz" (Sredniy Neva), Kolpino

	Laid down	L	In serv.
812 Vladimir Gumanenko	15-9-85	4-3-91	9-1-94
901 Zheleznyakov	28-2-85	17-7-86	30-12-88

Zheleznyakov (901) Boris Lemachko, 5-03

D: 780 tons light; 1,070 tons std. (1,228 fl) **S:** 15.7 kts
Dim: 67.80 × 10.95 × 3.65 (4.35 over sonar)
A: 1 76.2-mm 59-cal. AK-176 DP; 1 30-mm 54-cal. AK-630M gatling AA; 2 4-round Fasta-4M (SA-N-8) SAM syst. (16 9M-39 Igla/Gremlin missiles); 8 fixed 402-mm Ketmen' special TT
Electronics:
Radar: 1 MR-312 Nayada nav.; 1 MR-212/201 Vaygach-U (Palm Frond) nav.; 1 MR-123 Vympel (Bass Tilt) f.c.
Sonar: Kabarga-A3 HF minehunting
EW: No intercept arrays; 2 16-round PK-16 decoy RL
M: 2 M-503B-37 diesels; 2 CP props; 5,100 bhp—bow- and stern-thrusters
Range: 1,500/12 **Endurance:** 15 days **Crew:** 7 officers, 63 enlisted

Remarks: Metal-hulled combined minehunter/minesweeper design possibly originally intended for locating and neutralizing U.S. Captor deep-laid torpedo-launching mines. Twenty were to have been built. *Zheleznyakov* was transferred to the Black Sea Fleet during 8-89 and is based at Novorossiysk. *Vladimir Gumanenko* was initially attached to the Baltic Fleet but was transferred to the Northern Fleet in 1996 or 1997, although not arriving from the Baltic until 11-00; she is assigned to the "Kola Fleet" and based at Severomorsk. Construction of a third was canceled.
Combat systems: The very cramped mine-countermeasures working area accommodates several standard acoustic mine-countermeasures devices, including KTK-1, TEM-3M, AT-3, and SHZ-3. The 76.2-mm gun is limited to less than 180° in horizontal train. The ship tows a remote-controlled Paltus minehunting submersible with 3,100 m of control cable. For mine disposal, two 100-kg depth bombs and 20 smaller charges are carried. The sliding doors at the 02 level on the hull sides aft cover the quadruple launch tubes for the special minehunting torpedoes, which are fired in pairs linked by a cable to engage mine anchor cables. Employ the Buran-6 communications suite.

♦ 1 Natya-II (Akvamarin-2)-class (Project 266.6) minehunting ship [MHS] (in *reserve*)

Bldr: Sudostroitel'noye Obyedineniye "Almaz" (Sredniy Neva), Kolpino

960 *Strelok* (In serv. 1982)

D: 750 tons std., 804 tons normal (873 fl) **S:** 17.6 kts (16 sust.)
Dim: 61.00 (57.60 wl; 56.00 pp) × 10.20 (9.80 wl) × 2.98 (hull; 3.45 max.)

MINE WARFARE SHIPS *(continued)*

Strelok (960)—with original pennant number U.S. Navy, 2-86

A: 2 twin 30-mm 65-cal. AK-230M AA; 2 Fasta-4M (SA-N-8) SAM syst. (16 Strela-3 or Igla-M/Gremlin missiles)
Electronics: Radar: 1 Don-2 nav.—Sonar: MG-89 Serna HF hull-mounted
M: 2 M-503B-3E diesels; 2 CP props; 5,000 bhp
Electric: 600 kw tot. (3 × 200-kw DGR-200/1500 diesel sets)
Range: 1,800/16; 3,000/12; 5,200/10 **Fuel:** 87 tons **Endurance:** 10–15 days
Crew: 8 officers, 59 enlisted

Remarks: Single-unit prototype believed intended for trials with a minehunting system deployed from a deckhouse on the fantail; the equipment replaced the standard Natya mine-countermeasures winch. Retains articulated sweep gear davits at the stern, but no countermeasures gear is visible on deck. Omitted were the normal ASW RL and two twin 25-mm AA. Transferred to the Black Sea Fleet in 7-85, she is based at Novorossiysk and has been in reserve for over a decade.

♦ 14 Natya-I (Akvamarin)-class (Project 266M and 266ME*) fleet minesweepers [MSF] (4 or more *nonoperational*)
Bldr: Sudostroitel'noye Obyedineniye "Almaz" (Sredniy Neva), Kolpino

	In serv.	Fleet
718 MT-265*	12-89	Pacific
738 MT-264*	9-89	Pacific
770 Valentin Pikul'*	20-1-02	Black Sea
806 Motorisk	1976	. . .
834 Pulemetchik	1975	. . .
855 Mashinist	1975	Northen
854 Marsoviy	1986	Northern
855 Kontradmiral Vlasov	1972	Northern
909 Vitse-Admiral Zhukov (ex-*Ehlektrik*)	1977	Black Sea
911 *Radist* (ex-*Kharkovskiy Komsomolets*)	1973	Black Sea
912 *Turbinist*	1975	Black Sea
913 *Kovorovyets* (ex-*Kurskiy Komsomolets*, ex-*Navodchik*)	30-12-74	Black Sea
919 *Snayper*	1976	Black Sea
. . . Vitse-Admiral Zakhar'in*	2005	. . .

Radist (911) Boris Lemachko, 3-06

Valentin Pikul (770) Cem D. Yaylali, 5-06

D: Project 266M: 715 tons light, 735–750 tons std., 804–812 tons normal—Project 266ME: 745 tons (804 fl; 873 max.)
S: 17.6 kts (16 sust.)
Dim: 61.00 (57.60 wl; 56.00 pp) × 10.20 (9.80 wl) × 2.98 (hull; 3.60 max.)
A: Project 266M: 2 twin 30-mm 65-cal. AK-230M AA; 2 twin 25-mm 80-cal. 2M-3M AA; 2 4-round Fasta-4M (SA-N-8) SAM syst. (16 Strela or 20 Igla-M/Gremlin missiles); 2 5-round RBU-1200M ASW RL (30 RGB-12 projectiles); 1 mine rail (7 KMD-100 mines or 32 BB-1 d.c.)—Project 266ME: 2 single 30-mm 54-cal. AK-306 gatling AA; 2 4-round Fasta-4M (SA-N-8) SAM syst. (20 Strela-3 or Igla-M/Gremlin missiles); 2 5-round RBU-1200M ASW RL (30 RGB-12 projectiles); 1 mine rail (7 KMD-100 mines or 32 BB-1 d.c.)
Electronics:
Radar: 1 or 2 Don-MN (Don-2) nav.—Project 266M only: 1 MR-104 Rys' (Drum Tilt) f.c.
Sonar: Project 266M: MG-69 Lan' or MG-79 Mizen' search; MG-26 underwater telephone—Project 266ME: MG-89 minehunting; MG-35 underwater telephone; NEL-MZB echo sounder
M: 2 M-503B-3E diesels; 2 shrouded CP props; 5,000 bhp
Electric: 600 kw tot. (3 × 200-kw DGR-200/1500 diesel sets; 380 V, 50 Hz a.c.)
Range: 1,800/16; 2,700/12; 5,200/10 **Fuel:** 48 tons normal, 87 tons max.
Endurance: Project 266M: 10 days—Project 266ME: 15 days
Crew: 6 officers, 8 warrant officers, 54 enlisted

Remarks: Type designation: MT (*Morskoy Tral'shchik,* Seagoing Minesweeper). Equipped also to serve as ASW escorts, with the RBU-1200 rocket launchers also used for detonating mines. Designed under T. D. Pokhodun. Khabarovsk SY completed only five in 1972–76, of which none remain in service. The first unit, *Semen Roshal',* was completed for the Baltic Fleet in fall 1970. Post-1980 Project 266ME production was both for domestic use and for export, with one unit delivered to Syria with no ASW ordnance or minesweeping gear in 1985 as a training ship, 12 for India, eight for Libya, one for Ethiopia, and one for Yemen (the latter two to a modified design; see below). Of the active survivors, at least four are in the Northern Fleet, four or more in the Pacific Fleet, one in the Baltic Fleet, and five in the Black Sea Fleet. The *Kovorovyets,* along with *Radist, Snayper,* and *Turbinist,* had been reduced to cadre crew status by the summer of 2001, with only 10 crew aboard each.

Beginning in 1989, four units of a new variant with single 30-mm AK-306 gatling guns substituted for the twin 30-mm AK-230 mounts, but without 25-mm guns, Rys' (Drum Tilt) fire-control radar, or net trawl facilities, were completed; MT-264 and MT-265 were transferred from the Baltic to the Pacific Fleet, and one each was sold to Ethiopia and Yemen. Two more in the same configuration were reported under construction for export as of 1-94, and of those, *Valentin Pikul'* (launched 31-5-00 at Sredniy Neva Zavod) was to be assigned to the Northern Fleet after trials but was instead sent to the Black Sea Fleet during 7-02; the *Vitse-Admiral Zakhar'in* was launched during spring 2002.

Hull systems: The stem is cut back sharply below the waterline, as in the earlier T-43 and Yurka classes. Have low magnetic signature, with an aluminum/steel-alloy hull and the DGR-450/1500P diesel-driven degaussing system. Endurance at 12 kts with normal 48-ton fuel load is 1,500 n.m.; with 80-ton overload fuel load, 2,700 n.m. All living spaces are air-conditioned.

Combat systems: Two quadruple point-defense SAM launchers have been added to a number of units of the class (but not all), just abaft the lattice mast. Some also have an extra navigational radar atop the pilothouse, usually a Mius (Spin Trough). Sweep gear includes SEMP-3 magnetic and MPT-3 mechanical arrays and a net trawl deployed over the stern ramp. The sonar incorporates a downward-looking, high-frequency, bottomed-mine detection component. Can deploy television minehunting equipment. Have NEL-5 echo sounders. Ships completed through 1980 had rigid 2.5-ton-capacity davits aft; later units had articulated KBG-5-TMI jib cranes in the same position. *Valentin Pikul'* is said to be equipped with an MKT-210 towed television minehunting system, BKT or AT-3, AT-5, TEM-4, PMR-2, and PMT sweep arrays, and the Mikron sweep-operating system.

Disposals: Black Sea Fleet units *Ivan Maslov* and *Schitchik* and Baltic Fleet unit MT-159 have been stricken (dates unknown). Pacific Fleet units *Kontradmiral Pershin, Paravan,* and *Tral* were stricken 30-7-93; Black Sea Fleet units *Dizelist* and *Signal'shchik* and Pacific Fleet unit *Kontradmiral Khoroshkhin* on 5-7-94; Black Sea unit *Rulevoy* by 1995; Baltic Fleet unit *Semen Roshal'* on 1-9-95; and Pacific Fleet unit *Yakor'* on 1-9-95 (sunk as a missile target 25-4-96). Pacific Fleet Project 265ME unit *Zaryad* was stricken 31-7-96 after only five years' service. Sister *Torpedist* was redesignated experimental ship OS-99 in 1990 and stricken in 1995. *Zapad, Raketchik,* and Pacific Fleet unit *Zapal* were stricken during 1997. Black Sea Fleet units *Razvedchik* and *Zenitchik* were transferred to Ukraine in 1997. Baltic Fleet unit *Dmitry Lysov* was placed in reserve in 1998 and is unlikely to return to service. *Artillerist* and *Desantnik* were no longer in service as of 2001. *Svyazist* (610) was reported to have been scrapped by 2003.

♦ 25 Sonya (Yakhont)-class (Project 1265 and 1265.5*) coastal minesweepers [MSC]
Bldrs: Avangard Zavod, Petrozavodsk; Vladivostokskiy Sudostroitel'niy Zavod (Ulis),Vladivostok

	In serv.	Fleet
402 BT-97 Polyarnyy	1984	. . .
411 BT-111 Kolomna	1986	Northern
418 BT-22 . . .	1981	Northern
425 BT-31	1981	Northern
426 BT-241 Mineral'nie Vodi	1985	Black Sea
438 BT-40 Lt. Iun	1982	Black Sea
443 BT-152	. . .	. . .
454 BT- . . . Yelnya	. . .	. . .
501 BT-244	1987	Caspian
505 BT-. . . Aleksey Lebedev*	1989	Baltic
510 BT-230	1987	Baltic
513 BT-48	1987	Baltic
522 BT-157 Sergei Kolbas'ev	1989	Baltic
525 BT-232	1989	Pacific
532 BT-88 Jusup Akajev	1988	Caspian
533 BT-245	1989	Pacific
554 BT-96	12-83	Pacific
561 BT-115	1993	Baltic
565 BT-100	2-85	Pacific
568 BT-94	1983	Baltic
580 BT-132	1-81	Pacific
563 BT-44	1985	. . .
592 BT-114	11-87	Pacific
593 BT-215	1991	Pacific
598 BT-51	12-86	Pacific

MINE WARFARE SHIPS *(continued)*

BT-230 (510) Boris Lemachko, 4-06

BT-241 Mineral'nie Vodi (426) Boris Lemachko, 5-03

D: 401–427 tons (430–460 fl) **S:** 14 kts
Dim: 48.80 (46.00 wl) × 10.20 (9.20 wl) × 2.40–2.50 (mean hull; 2.75–2.85 max.)
A: Project 1265: 1 twin 30-mm 65-cal. AK-230M AA; 1 twin 25-mm 80-cal. 2M-3M AA—some also: 1 or 2 4-round Fasta-4M (SA-N-8) SAM syst. (up to 15 Strela-3 or Igla-M missiles); up to 5 mines—Project 1265.5: 2 single 30-mm 54-cal. AK-306 gatling AA: 1 or 2 4-round Fasta-4M (SA-N-8) SAM syst. (up to 15 Strela-3 or Igla-M missiles); up to 5 mines
Electronics:
Radar: 1 Mius (Spin Trough) nav.
Sonar: MG-69, -79, or -89 Serna HF hull-mounted; MG-26 or -35 underwater telephone; NEL-MZB echo sounder (see remarks)
M: 2 DRA-210-A or -B diesels; 2 3-bladed CP props; 2,200 or 2,000 bhp—2 low-speed thrusters
Electric: 350 kw tot. (3 × 100-kw, 1 × 50-kw diesel sets; 380 V, 50 Hz a.c.)
Range: 1,700/10 **Fuel:** 27.1 tons **Endurance:** 15 days
Crew: 5–6 officers, 26–40 enlisted (45 tot. accomm.)

Remarks: Type designation: BT (*Basovyy Tral'shchik,* Base Minesweeper), 3rd Rank. *Yakhont,* the program name, refers to a kind of sapphire. Designed in 1968 under D. I. Rudakov and, later, Valeriy Ivanovich Nemudrov at the Western Design Bureau, St. Petersburg. Construction ceased at Vladivostok in 1991 after 22 had been built. BT-115 was the last completed at Petrozavodsk, with work on BT-116 suspended until restarted for completion in 1998. Two incompete Petrozavodsk units were sold to the Mediterranean Tourism Investment Corp., a French firm, and were to be completed starting in 6-01 as tour boats for service on the Côte d'Azur. Two new Project 1265E export units were transferred to Cuba in 1980 and two more in 1985; other new units have gone to Bulgaria (4), Syria (1), and Vietnam (2). One Northern Fleet unit has been renamed the *Yadrin.* Caspian Sea Flotilla unit BT-88 is used as a patrol craft, the reason for her combatant-series pennant number. A replacement design was planned to enter service in 1996 but has been indefinitely postponed due to financial problems. BT-88 and BT-244 may be subordinated to the Federal Border Guard.
Hull systems: Wooden construction with glass-reinforced plastic hull sheathing. Bollard pull: 10 tons at 9 kts. Endurance is five days longer than with Project 1265E export variant, and range is 200 n.m. greater at 10 kts. Later series-construction units have the 1,000-bhp DRA-210A main propulsion diesels, which have the alternative designation 12ChPN 18/20. Early units were fitted with the older Type 9D diesel, and some have two 100-kw and one 200-kw diesel generator sets.
Combat systems: Carry AT-5 acoustic, PEMT-4 magnetic loop, and BKT-2 mechanical sweep equipment. Can tow CT-2 solenoidal magnetic minesweeping buoys and also net-sweep arrays and can lay linear mine disposal charges. Are also able to employ KIU-1 or KIU-2-2m underwater television mine location and destruction equipment. Export variants carry the GKT-2 contact sweep; ST-2, AT-2, and PEMT-2 influence sweeps; and an IT-3 mine detector/expoder. Are equipped with an underwater telephone. The 25-mm mount is aimed by the operator, while the 30-mm mount is controlled by a Kolonka-1 ringsight director; 1,000 rounds of 30-mm and 2,000 rounds of 25-mm ammunition are normally carried. The Project 1265.5 units were built with two 30-mm AK-630M gatling AA in place of the original armament; they also have MG-69 or MG-79 Mizen sonars in place of MG-89 Serna and employ two SP-521 Rakurs (Kolonka-2) 19-1 simple remote directors to control the gunmounts. The sonar dome pivots at the after end to retract within the hull in all variants. Manned launchers for point-defense missiles began to be added to these ships in the early 1980s, initially just one to port or starboard of the after gunmount, but later two, flanking the gunmount.
Disposals: Caspian Flotilla units BT-16 (ex-*Astrakhanskiy Komsomolets*), -103, and -155 were transferred to Azerbaijan 3-7-92. One Northern Fleet unit was declared for scrap in 1991, and Baltic Fleet units BT-123 and -342 were offered for scrap in 1992. Baltic Fleet units BT-77, -258, -260, -291, -320, and -324 were stricken 30-7-93. Pacific Fleet units stricken: BT-266 and -327 on 30-7-93 (BT-327 relegated to service as a berthing barge); BT-734 on 5-7-94; BT-347 and -438 on 1-9-95; BT-267 on 31-7-96; and BT-38, -56, -78, -121, and -470 on 16-8-97. Black Sea Fleet unit BT-79 (ex-*Khersonskiy Komsomolets*) was transferred to Ukraine 30-12-95, followed in mid-1997 by BT-126 (ex-*Orensburgskiy Komsomolets*), which had been stricken 10-1-96. Northern Fleet units BT-206, -261, -263, -270, -294, -296, -298, -302, and -325; Baltic Fleet units BT-252, -315, -317, -328, -329, -330, and -350; and BT-343 (fleet unknown) have either been discarded or placed in unmaintained reserve since 1998. Thirteen additional units had been stricken by 2005.

♦ 8 (+ 1) Lida (Sapfir)-class (Project 10750) inshore minesweepers [MSI]

Bldr: Sudostroitel'noye Obyedineniye "Almaz" (Sredniy Neva), Kolpino

	Laid down	L	In serv.
206 RT-249	9-4-87	27-7-90	29-12-90
210 RT-273	29-3-88	11-12-91	30-9-92
219 RT-231	28-7-88	19-8-92	25-8-93
239 RT-252	12-10-87	27-9-91	30-12-91
300 RT-233	20-10-88	8-7-93	9-9-94
316 RT-57	20-10-86	29-7-87	12-12-89
348 RT-248	16-3-87	6-2-90	29-9-90
372 RT-234	27-4-89	31-3-94	28-8-96

RT-231 (219)—at Astrakhan Boris Lemachko, 7-00

RT-57 (316)—at St. Petersburg Rozvoorouzhenie, 7-96

D: 85 tons light; 131 tons normal (135 fl; 137 max.) **S:** 12.5 kts
Dim: 31.45 × 6.50 × 1.58
A: 1 30-mm 54-cal. AK-306 gatling AA; 5 Igla-M (SA-14/16) shoulder-launched SAMs; 2 mine rails (. . . mines)
Electronics:
Radar: 1 Liman nav.
Sonar: Kabarga-A1 HF hull-mounted minehunting
M: 3 Type 3D-12MM diesels; 3 props; 900 bhp
Electric: 150 kw tot. (3 × 50-kw diesel sets)
Range: 210/12.5; 400/10 (650/10 with overload fuel) **Endurance:** 5 days
Crew: 1 officer, 13 enlisted

Remarks: Intended as the successor to the Yevgenya class. Offered for export as Project 10750E or for coproduction. Designed by V. I. Nemudrov and A. A. Forst of the Western Design Bureau, St. Petersburg (now the Zapadnoye PKB). Intended to counter mines in waters up to 80 m deep. RT-233 has been transferred to the Caspian Flotilla. Three units of the class begun at Petrozavodsk Zavod prior to 1991 remained suspended at the yard as of 5-01, and one other was said to be nearing completion at Sredniy Neva, Kolpino, during early 2002.

MINE WARFARE SHIPS *(continued)*

Hull systems: Glass-reinforced plastic construction with frames at 400-mm spacing (300 mm aft). Main and auxiliary machinery is sound mounted, and special attention has been paid to reducing acoustic and magnetic signatures. A degaussing system is fitted. Berthing spaces are air-conditioned. Navigation equipment includes NEL-M3B echo sounder, LGT-1 pressure log, and GKU-2 gyrocompass. An infrared signaling system is fitted.
Combat systems: Mine-countermeasures equipment includes a towed television hunting system (as on the Yevgenya class), an AT-6 acoustic sweep, one or two magnetic sweeps (one an SEMT-1 coil array), and one GKT-3MO deep contact wire sweep. Have an LES-67 minesweeping winch with three drums and a bollard pull of 5.3 tons at 9 kts. Have an SP-521 Rakurs (Kolonka-2) pedestal director for the gunmount, for which 500 rounds are normally carried (1,000 in emergency).
Disposals: RT-341 (331) was reportedly no longer operational and was being cannabalized for spares as of mid-2003.

Disposal note: Remaining Yevgenya (Korund)-class (Project 1258) inshore minesweepers, Olya (Malakhit)-class (Project 1259) minesweepers and Tanya (Chelnok)-class (Project 1300.0) drones had been retired from service by 2005.

♦ 1 Barentsevo More–class (Project 1332) auxiliary minesweeper [MSA] (In *reserve*)

Bldr: Baltiya Zavod, Klaypeda, Estonia (In serv. 12-73)

844 *MT-434*

MT-434 (844)—while active Boris Lemachko, 7-93

D: 1,290 tons (1,889 fl) **S:** 13.3 kts **Dim:** 58.82 × 12.99 × 5.10
A: 2 twin 25-mm 80-cal. 2M-3M AA; 2 7-round MRG-7 grenade launchers
Electronics: Radar: 1 Don-2 nav.—Sonar: . . .
M: 1 Zgoda-Sulzer Type 6L-525 diesel; 1 CP prop; 2,200 bhp
Electric: 300 kw tot. (2 × 150-kw diesel sets)
Range: 10,000/13 **Fuel:** 231 tons **Endurance:** 36 days **Crew:** 39 tot.

Remarks: Converted in 1984 from one of 65 units of the *Barentsevo More* class as a prototype for adapting Russia's numerous fish factory trawler fleet for mine-countermeasures duties in wartime. Is assigned to the Northern Fleet and was formerly operated in the White Sea in support of nuclear submarine trials. Considered to be a Seagoing Base Minesweeper. Was in reserve as of 12-98.

AMPHIBIOUS WARFARE SHIPS

♦ 1 Ivan Rogov (Yedinorog)–class (Project 1174) dock landing ship [LSD]

Bldr: Yantar Pribaltiyskiy Zavod 820, Kaliningrad

	L	In serv.	Fleet
020 Mitrofan Moskalenko	1988	12-89	Northern

Mitrofan Moskalenko (020)—on delivery to the Northern Fleet M.O.D. Bonn, 3-92

D: 8,260 tons light (11,580 without combat load; 14,060 fl) **S:** 21 kts (19 sust.)
Dim: 157.50 (149.90 wl) × 23.80 (22.00 wl) × 4.20 (6.70 flooded down)
A: 1 twin-rail Osa-M (SA-N-4) SAM syst. (20 4K-33/Gecko missiles); 1 twin 76.2-mm 59-cal. AK-726 DP; 2 4-round Fasta-4M (SA-N-8) SAM syst. (16–20 Igla-M/Gremlin missiles); 4 single 30-mm 54-cal. AK-630 gatling AA; 1 40-round 122-mm UMS-73 Grad-M artillery RL (1,320 BM-21 rockets); 4 Ka-29TB Helix-B helicopters
Electronics:
Radar: 2 MR-212/201 Vaygach-U (Palm Frond) nav.; 1 MR-710 Fregat-MA (Top Plate-A) air search; 1 MR-10 Turel' (Owl Screech) 76.2-mm gun f.c.; 1 MPZ-301 Baza (Pop Group) SAM f.c.; 2 MR-123 Vympel (Bass Tilt) 30-mm gun f.c.; 1 Fly Screen microwave helicopter landing aid

Mitrofan Moskalenko (020) Boris Lemachko Collection, 2002

TACAN: Privod (Round House)
EW: No intercept or jammers; 4 16-round PK-16 decoy RL; 10 10-round PK-10 decoy RL
E/O: 1 Squeeze Box multisensor artillery rocket f.c. and surveillance
M: COGAG M-12 plant: 2 M-8K gas turbines; 2 props (260 rpm max.); 36,000 shp
Electric: 3,000 kw tot. (6 × 500-kw diesel sets)
Range: 4,000/18 (7,200/18 with emergency fuel); 7,500/14.5 (6,000/14 loaded)
Endurance: 30 days (15 with 500 landing force aboard)
Crew: 37 officers, 202 enlisted + troops: 46 officers, 519 enlisted

Remarks: Type designation: BDK (*Bol'shoy Desantnyy Korabl',* Large Landing Ship). Designed under N.V. Maksimov. A planned fourth unit was canceled. The ability to use helicopters, to beach, and to deploy air-cushion vehicles gave a versatility unmatched by any other Russian amphibious-warfare ship; those capabilities were combined with an organic shore fire-bombardment capability and very extensive command, control, and surveillance facilities. *Mitrofan Moskalenko,* while in commission, seldom operates.
Hull systems: The hull has a pronounced bulb projecting forward below the waterline. Is equipped with bow doors and a 32-m-long articulating ramp leading to a 54-m-long by 12.3-m-wide by 3-m-high vehicle cargo deck (660 m^2 total parking area) in the forward part of the hull, while a stern door provides access to a 75-m-long by 12.8-m-wide by 8.2-m-high floodable docking well intended to accommodate up to three Lebed-class (Project 1206) air-cushion landing craft (q.v.) or six Ondatra-class (Project 1176) or T-4 (Project 1785) landing craft. The massive superstructure incorporates a helicopter hangar with a steep ramp leading downward to a helicopter pad on the foredeck and doors aft that lead to a second helicopter platform over the stern. There are also hydraulically raised ramps leading from the upper deck forward of the superstructure to both the bow doors and the docking well. Cargo capacity: 2,500 tons maximum; capable of transporting an entire naval infantry battalion and its vehicles, including 53 tanks or 80 armored personnel carriers, and trucks (load reduced to 25 tanks if landing craft are carried). The normal load is 440 troops and 79 vehicles, or a tank unit with 46 main battle tanks.
Combat systems: The Grad-M rocket launcher has a range of 20 km; each rocket produces 356 shrapnel fragments. The rockets are carried in a drum magazine and automatically loaded in two packets of 20 each. A total of 1,200 rounds are carried for the twin 76.2-mm, ZIF-67 gunmount and 16,000 rounds for the 30-mm guns. The Osa-M SAM system uses the standard ZIF-122 launcher. Each Ka-29 helicopter can transport 16 fully equipped troops and provide its own fire support, with rockets, missiles, and guns.
Disposals: *Ivan Rogov* was laid up by 1994, stricken 1-9-95, and being scrapped at Vladivostok as of 5-99. *Aleksandr Nikolayev* was under refit at Vladivostok for possible sale to Indonesia in mid-1999, but the offer was not accepted and work has since halted. She remains in reserve at Vladivostok.

♦ 0 (+ 1 + 5) Ivan Gren-class (Project 1171.1) tank landing ships [LST]

Bldr: Yantar Zavod, Kaliningrad

	Laid down	In serv.
(. . .) BDK- . . . Ivan Gren	23-12-04	2008
(. . .) BDK- . . .	. . .	. . .
(. . .) BDK- . . .	. . .	. . .
(. . .) BDK- . . .	. . .	. . .
(. . .) BDK- . . .	. . .	. . .
(. . .) BDK- . . .	. . .	2012

AMPHIBIOUS WARFARE SHIPS *(continued)*

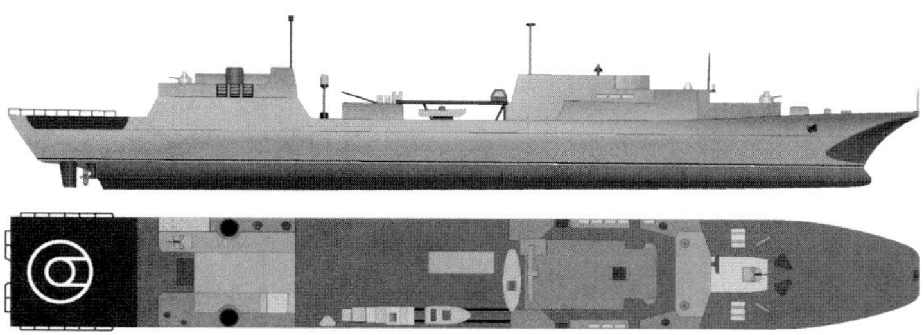

Project 1171.1E tank landing ship Computer rendering by J.M. Caiella, 2006

D: Approx. 5,000 tons **S:** . . . kts **Dim:** 120.0 × 16.5 × 3.6 **S:** 18 kts
A: 2 18-round 140-mm WM-18 barrage RL; 1 76.2-mm 59-cal. AK-176M DP; . . . 30-mm 54-cal. AK-630M gatling AA; 1 KA-29 helicopter
Electronics: . . .
M: 2 . . . diesels
Electric: . . .
Range: 3,500/16 **Endurance:** 30 days **Crew:** . . .

Remarks: New construction LST intended to replace the Alligator class. Five units are planned with a total estimated program cost of about US $1.8 billion. Will have a cargo capacity of 13 60-ton tanks or 36 armored personnel carriers and up to 300 troops. To be fitted with a helicopter landing deck.

♦ 3 Ropucha-II-class (Project 775.2) tank landing ships [LST]

Bldr: Stocznia Polnocna, Gdansk, Poland

	In serv.	Fleet
077 BDK-11	2-91	Pacific
130 BDK-61 Korolev	4-91	Baltic
151 BDK-54 Azov	20-4-90	Black Sea

BDK-11 (077) U.S. Navy, 3-06

BDK-54 Azov (151) Luciano Grazioli, 2-06

D: 2,768 tons light; 3.450 tons std. (4,080 fl) **S:** 17.8 kts
Dim: 112.50 (105.00 wl) × 15.00 × 3.70 (aft)
A: 1 76.2-mm 59-cal. AK-176M DP; 2 single 30-mm 54-cal. AK-630M gatling AA; 2 40-round 122-mm UMS-73 Grad-M artillery RL (320 BM-21 rockets); 2 mine rails (up to 90 1-ton mines)
Electronics:
Radar: 2 Don-2 nav.; 1 MR-352 Pozitiv (Cross Dome) surf./air search; 1 MR-123 Vympel (Bass Tilt) gun f.c.
E/O: 1 Squeeze Box surveillance/rocket f.c.; 2 bridge periscopes
M: 2 Type 16 VB40/48 16-cyl., 500-rpm diesels; 2 props; 19,200 bhp
Electric: 1,920 kw tot. (3 × 640 kw; Cegielski-Sulzer 6A25 diesels driving)
Range: 3,500/16; 6,000/12 **Endurance:** 30 days (with landing force)
Crew: 8 officers, 79 enlisted (accomm. for 17 officers, 81 enlisted) + 225 troops

Remarks: Variant of the basic Ropucha design, substituting later defensive armament and sensors. Only three were built. Hull system data for Ropucha-I class (q.v.) apply. BDK-54 (laid down 22-11-98 and launched 19-5-89) was named on 10-12-98; the ship had visited Greece during 10-98. BDK-54 was named and renumbered from BDK-122 during 2000.

♦ 13 Ropucha-I-class (Project 775) tank landing ships [LST]

(1 in *reserve*)
Bldr: Stocznia Polnocna, Gdansk, Poland

	In serv.	Fleet
012 BDK-91 Olenogorskiy Gornyak	1976	Northern
016 BDK-45 Georgy Pobedonsets	5-3-85	. . .
027 BDK-182 Kondopoga	1976	Northern
031 BDK-55 Aleksandr Otrakovskiy	1978	Northern
055 BDK-98 . . .	. . .	Pacific
066 BDK-101 Mokhar Avezov	19-12-81	Pacific
050 *BDK-14 . . .*	31-8-81	Pacific
102 BDK-58 Kaliningrad	9-12-84	Baltic
110 BDK-100 Aleksandr Shabalin	1985	Baltic
127 BDK-43 Minsk	1983	Baltic
142 BDK-46 Novocherkassk	11-87	Black Sea
156 BDK-67 Yamal	1988	Black Sea
158 BDK-64 Tsezar' Kunikov	1986	Black Sea

BDK-64 Tsezar' Kunikov (158) Cem D. Yaylali, 4-05

BDK-43 Minsk (127) M. Wright, 2004

BDK-58 Kaliningrad (102) Jaroslaw Cislak, 6-05

D: 2,768 tons light (4,080 fl) **S:** 17.5 kts
Dim: 112.50 (105.00 wl) × 15.00 × 3.70 (aft, loaded)
A: 2 twin 57-mm 70-cal. AK-725 DP—some: 4 4-round Fasta-4M SAM syst. (32 Strela-3 or Igla-M/Gremlin missiles)—some also: 2 40-round 122-mm UMS-73 Grad-M artillery RL (360 BM-21 rockets)—all: 2 mine rails (up to 92 1-ton mines)
Electronics: Radar: 2 Don-2 or MR-212/201 Vaygach-U (Palm Frond) nav.; 1 MR-302 Rubka (Strut Curve) surf./air search; 1 MR-103 Bars (Muff Cob) gun f.c.
M: 2 Type 16ZVB 40/48 16-cyl., 500-rpm diesels; 2 props; 19,200 bhp
Electric: 1,920 kw tot. (3 × 640 kw; Cegielski-Sulzer 6A25 diesels driving)
Range: 3,500/16; 6,000/12 **Endurance:** 30 days (with landing force)
Crew: 8 officers, 79 enlisted (accomm. for 17 officers, 81 enlisted) + 150 troops

Remarks: Russian type designation: BDK (*Bol'shoy Desantnyy Korabl',* Large Landing Ship). Builder's Project B-23. BDK-64 was refitted at Varna, Bulgaria, from 1996 to 12-98; a Baltic Fleet unit of the class was refitted at Rostock, Germany, beginning in 3-98; and BDK-182 began a refit at St. Petersburg during 7-98. BDK-58, refitted at Rostock in 1999, was named on 2-7-99. Some 40 enlisted personnel on BDK-101 mutinied on 18-7-00 against beatings and other cruel treatment; the offending officers and sailors were arrested. Black Sea Fleet unit BDK-46, thought to have been stricken by 1999, was undergoing reactivation overhaul at Sevastopol' during 2001. BDK-67 was named *Yamal* during 1-02.
Hull systems: The six units in the group built 1980–85 had angled hances to the corners of the main-deck superstructure, a stern ramp with no external web reinforcing, and reinforcing gussets around the forward 57-mm gun platform. The hull has

AMPHIBIOUS WARFARE SHIPS *(continued)*

a molded depth of 8.65 m amidships and is equipped with a "beak" bow projection to aid in beaching. Fully degaussed. Have a forced ventilation system with NBC warfare filters. No vehicle cargo is carried on the upper deck; the hatch serves for loading vehicles by crane and for ventilation when vehicle motors are running. Bow and stern doors permit roll-on/roll-off loading. Cargo capacity: 482 tons; usable deck space: 540 m^2 on a full-length vehicle deck that is 95 m long and 4.5 m high, with a width of 6.5 m for the forward 55 m, narrowing to 4.5 m beneath the superstructure to the stern. Alternate cargo loads are 10 41-ton tanks with 40 vehicle crew and 150 troops; 12 amphibious tanks with 36 vehicle crew; or a mix of three 41-ton tanks, three 120-mm mine throwers, three armored cars, four trucks, five light vehicles, and 123 troops. One Pacific Fleet unit had a crane on the foredeck.
Combat systems: Several received four quadruple point-defense SAM launchers, although these may later have been removed. The entire class was intended to receive two UMS-73 barrage rocket launchers on the forecastle, but only the six most recently completed actually carried the weapons, and several of these ships have been discarded; the rockets are carried in a drum magazine, are loaded in two packets of 20 each, have a range of up to 20 km, and are fired at 0.5-second intervals. Although equipped to receive the accompanying Squeeze Box electro-optical rangefinder/director, none of the ships yet has it. Some 20 smoke floats can be carried aft. Mines can only be carried when there is no amphibious cargo. The communications suite can accommodate 15 simultaneous channels.
Disposals: Pacific Fleet unit BDK-48 was stricken during 1994, followed by Pacific Fleet units BDK-63, -90, -181, and -197 on 5-7-94. Baltic Fleet unit BDK-47 was stricken 1-9-95, and Northern Fleet unit BDK-200 was stricken 30-7-98. BDK-119 was transferred to then–Southern Yemen in 1979 (and stricken there by 1999), and *Konstantin Ol'shanskiy* (BDK-56) was transferred to Ukraine 12-3-96. BDK 105 was scrapped in 2002. BDK-32 was retired during 2003 and BDK-183 began decommissioning during 12-05.

♦ 5 Alligator (Tapir)-class (Project 1171) tank landing ships [LST]

Bldr: Yantar Zavod, Kaliningrad

	Laid down	L	In serv.	Fleet
081 BDK-104 NIKOLAY VILKOV	3-9-71	30-11-73	30-7-74	Pacific
119 BDK-. . . DONETSKIY SHAKHTER	5-9-68	10-3-69	31-12-69	Baltic
148 BDK-69 ORSK	30-8-67	29-2-68	31-12-68	Black Sea
150 BDK-65 SARATOV (ex-*Voronezhskiy Komsomolets,* ex-BDK-10)	5-2-64	1-7-64	18-8-66	Black Sea
152 BDK-. . . NIKOLAY FIL'CHENKOV	30-1-74	29-3-75	30-12-75	Black Sea

BDK-69 Orsk (148) Harmut Ehlers, 3-02

BDK-104 Nikolay Vilkov (081)—the Pacific Fleet's only Alligator JMSDF, 3-94

D: 2,760 tons light; 2,905 tons std. (4,360 fl) **S:** 16.5 kts (16 sust.)
Dim: 113.1 (105.0 pp) × 15.6 × 4.10 (mean hull; 6.15 aft, loaded)
A: 1 twin 57-mm 70-cal. ZIF-31B DP—BDK-104 and *Fil'chenkov* only: 2 twin 25-mm 2M-3M AA; 3 4-round Fasta-4M SAM syst. (24 Strela-3 or Igla-M missiles)—BDK-104 and *Fil'chenkov* only: 1 40-round 122-mm UMS-73 Grad-M artillery RL (160 rockets)
Electronics:
Radar: 2 Don-2 and/or Mius (Spin Trough) nav.
E/O: BDK-104 and *Fil'chenkov* only: 1 Squeeze Box multisensor surveillance/rocket f.c.
M: 2 Type 58A diesels; 2 props; 9,000 bhp
Electric: Early units: 740 kw tot. (2 × 270-kw, 2 × 100-kw diesel sets)—BDK-104 and *Fil'chenkov:* 900 kw tot. (3 × 300-kw DRG300/500-1 diesel sets)
Range: 3,500/16.5; 8,000/15
Endurance: 15 days (20 for BDK-104 and *Fil'chenkov;* 10 with landing force)
Crew: 5 officers, 50 enlisted + 440 troops (313 in BDK-65)

Remarks: Soviet type designation: BDK (*Bol'shoy Desantnyy Korabl',* Large Landing Ship). The design, by TsKB-50, was initially approved on 14-2-62 but evolved continually during the time these ships were built. Also known as the Nosorog class in Russia. Survivors of 14 completed; a 15th unit, to have been named *Nikolay Golubkov,* was canceled in 1975 while under construction. Although the former *Donetskiy Shakhter* had been reported stricken on 1-9-95, the ship remained in service and underwent a refit at Baltiysk during 2000–2001; she is used primarily to ferry vehicles and equipment between Kaliningrad and St. Petersburg/Kronshtadt; a report that she was to be stricken during 2002 appears to have been in error. BDK-69 began an overhaul during 4-01. The class will eventually be replaced by the new *Ivan Gren* class (Project 1171.1) on a one-to-one basis.
Hull systems: Have ramps fore and aft. Their cargo hoisting equipment varies (one or two 5-ton KE26TD cranes, one 7.5-ton KE29 crane): Type I unit BDK-65 has two cranes forward; later ships had one less crane. Cargo capacity is about 600 tons for beaching and 1,750 tons in freighting service; can carry 20 tanks, plus lighter vehicles on upper decks. The tank deck is 90 m long and totals 850 m^2 in area. Nominal vehicle capacity is 20 MAZ-543 or 52 ZIL-131, or 85 GAZ-66 trucks. Troops are accommodated below the tank deck under cramped conditions in the lower, No. 3 hold. The engines are Model 58A-4 in BDK-104.
Combat systems: In Type IV pair (BDK-104 and *Fil'chenkov*), a 40-tube, 140-mm UMS-73 rocket launcher forward for shore bombardment was added; they also have two twin 25-mm AA mounts aft in addition to the other armament. The open 57-mm gun mounting is locally controlled; 1,200 rounds of ammunition are normally carried. The communications suite can handle six channels simultaneously.
Disposals: Black Sea unit *Krymskiy Komsomolets* (BDK-6) was stricken in 1992, Baltic Fleet unit *Krasnaya Presnaya* on 17-11-94, and Pacific Fleet units BDK-25 (ex-*Tomskiy Komsomolets,* ex-BDK-13), BDK-80 (ex-*Petr Il'ichev*), *Sergei Lazo,* and *Aleksandr Tortsev* on 17-11-94. BDK-25 was sold for scrap in 4-95. Baltic Fleet unit BDK-62 (ex-*Komsomolets Kareliy*) was stricken during 1998 and BDK-77 (ex-*50 Let Shefstva V.L.M.S.M.*) prior to 2001. The last remaining Polnovny-C-class (project 773) medium landing ship, SDK-154, was retired during 2005.

Note: The two remaining Polnocny-B-class (Project 771) medium landing craft have been redesignated as cargo transports and can be found under [AK].

♦ 3 Pomornik (Zubr)-class (Project 1232.2) air-cushion vehicle landing craft [LCUA]

Bldr: Sudostroitel'noye Obyedineniye "Almaz," Dekabristov SY, St. Petersburg

	In serv.
770 MDK-118 EVGENY KOCHESHKOV	1991
782 MDK-94 MORDOVIA	15-10-91
795 MDK-108	10-8-94

MDK-118 Evgeny Kocheshkov (770) Ralph Edwards, 6-03

MDK-118 Evgeny Kocheshkov (770) Alexandre Sheldon-Duplaix, 6-03

D: 340 tons light; 415 tons normal (550 fl) **S:** 63 kts (55 sust.)
Dim: 57.3 (56.2 hull) × 25.6 (22.0 hull) × 21.9 (high)
A: 2 4-round Fasta-4M (SA-N-8) SAM syst. (32 Igla-M/Gremlin missiles); 2 single 30-mm 54-cal. AK-630M gatling AA; 2 22-round 140-mm MS-227 Ogon' retractable artillery RL (132 rockets); up to 80 mines in lieu of vehicle cargo, using portable rails
Electronics:
Radar: 1 SRN-207 Ekran (Curl Stone-B) nav.; 1 MR-123-2 Vympel (Bass Tilt) gun f.c.
E/O: 1 DVU-3 (Quad Look) multisensor surveillance and rocket f.c.
M: 5 NK-12MV (M-70) gas turbines (12,100 shp each/10,000 shp sust.; 2 to power lift fans); 3 ducted 5.5-m-dia. CP airscrew propellers, 4 NO-10 2.5-m-dia. lift fans; 36,300 shp for propulsion

AMPHIBIOUS WARFARE SHIPS *(continued)*

Electric: 300 or 400 kw tot. (4 × 75- or 100-kw GTG-110 gas turbine sets)
Range: 300/55 with 130-ton payload; 1,000/55 light **Fuel:** 56 tons (180 m^3)
Endurance: 5 days (1 with full troop complement)
Crew: 4 officers, 7 warrant officers, 20 enlisted + 140–360 troops

Remarks: Project name is *Zubr* ("Bison"). Are too large for shipboard transportation and are intended for short-range independent assault operations. Hull numbers are in the MDK (*Mal'yy Desantnyy Korabl',* Small Landing Ship) category. There are apparently significant reliability problems with the design; they were originally intended to have a 16-year service life. The only remaining units serve in the Baltic Fleet, where one has been in reserve and the other operates only twice per year; they are to be refitted using the profits from the sale of two to Greece, which has purchased one new unit (begun as MDK-107 for the Russian Navy) and the refurbished Baltic Fleet unit MDK-50 from Russia and two refurbished units from Ukraine. MDK-118 was renamed the *Evgeny Kocheshkov* early in 2002, and MDK-94 was named *Mordovia* during 6-02. MDK-118 began a refit at St. Petersburg late in 2002.
Hull systems: The complex hull structure employs light alloys, some of which are flammable. The vehicle deck can hold up to 10 BTR-70 armored amphibious personnel transport vehicles or three T-80B main battle tanks plus a detachment of infantry—or up to 140 troops and 130 tons of combat cargo. Have small bow and stern ramps. Navigational equipment includes a gyrocompass, Decca radio navigation system receiver, drift indicator, and NAVSAT receiver.
Propulsion systems: Three of the gas-turbine engines are mounted on pylons and drive airscrew propellers; they are equipped with exhaust thrust diverters to enhance mobility. The two lift-fan gas turbines drive four blowers to maintain skirt pressure and are mounted near the stern in the wing compartments; they exhaust through the stern.
Combat systems: The Quad Look electro-optical device is a modified Squeeze Box that has no weather cover; there is also a television camera mounted just below the pilothouse. The navigational radar is mounted within a lozenge-shaped radome. The retractable MS-227 artillery rocket launchers are located near the bow in the hull wing-walls and are reloaded below decks. The rockets have a range of 4.5–10 km, depending on type, and are ripple fired at 0.2-second intervals; they are launched via the DVU-3 control system.
Disposals: Work on two others at St. Petersburg had been halted for about two years as of 7-95, and attempts were being made to sell them for commercial purposes; approval to scrap them was given early in 7-97, and one was sold to Greece during 6-99 and delivered during 9-01. The class prototype, assigned to the Baltic Fleet, had been scrapped by mid-1998, and two others followed by 1999. Black Sea Fleet units MDK-57, -93, and -123 were transferred to Ukraine 1-3-96.

♦ 6 Aist (Dzheryan)-class (Project 1232.1) air-cushion vehicle amphibious landing craft [LCUA]

Bldr: Sudostroitel'noye Obyedineniye "Almaz," Dekabristov SY, St. Petersburg (In serv. 1970–85)

608 MDK . . .	610 MDK . . .	722 MDK-113
609 MDK . . .	700 MDK . . .	730 MDK-89

MDK-113 (722)—on beaching pad at Baltiysk Hartmut Ehlers, 9-95

D: 231 tons light; 298 tons std. (355 fl) **S:** 70 kts light (50 sust., loaded)
Dim: 47.80 (45.50 hull) × 17.50 × 0.3 (1.3 at rest)
A: 2 4-round Fasta-4M (SA-N-8) SAM syst. (32 9M-36 Strela-3 or Igla-M/Gremlin missiles); 2 twin 30-mm 65-cal. AK-230 AA
Electronics:
Radar: 1 Mius (Spin Trough) nav.; 1 MR-104 Rys' (Drum Tilt) f.c.
EW: No intercept; 2 16-round PK-16 decoy RL
M: 2 DT-4 gas turbines; 4 AV-70 airscrew props, 2 lift fans; 31,558 shp
Electric: 60 kw (2 × 30-kw diesel sets)
Range: 100/45; 208/40 **Fuel:** 47 tons **Endurance:** 5 days
Crew: 3 officers, 18 enlisted + up to 220 troops

Remarks: Eighteen were built. Typed MDK (*Mal'yy Desantnyy Korabl',* Small Landing Ship). The designed service life was not more than 16 years. Three Black Sea Fleet units were transferred to the Federal Border Guard around 1996 and are now employed as patrol craft in the Caspian Sea. MDK-113 was active as of 7-00, based at Baltiysk.
Hull systems: Have bow and stern ramps. Cargo capacity: 74 tons (2 T-62 or T-64 tanks, or 4 PT-76 tanks, or 5 BTR-60 armored personnel carriers), plus 220 troops; normal load, however, is around 50 tons. The DT-4 gas turbines are marinized versions of the NK-12 aircraft engine. Early units had riveted aluminum hulls, later ones welded; the hull structure experienced considerable corrosion in service.
Combat systems: Carry 2,000 rounds of 30-mm ammunition. Early units did not have the point-defense SAM launchers.

Disposal note: Baltic Fleet units VP-103 and VP-117 were for sale for scrap in 1992, and two more Baltic units were discarded during 1993. All fourteen remaining units of the Vydr-class (Project 106K) utility landing craft—MDK-23, MDK-175, MDK-200, MDK-155, MDK-181, MDK-176, MDK-193, MDK-159, MDK-190, MDK-192, MDK-173, MDK-170, MDK-191 and MDK-168—had been retired

♦ 3 Lebed (Kal'mar)-class (Project 1206) air-cushion landing craft [LCMA]

Bldr: Sudostoitel'noye Obyedineniye "Almaz," Dekabristov SY, St. Petersburg, or Yuzhnaya Tochka Zavod, Feodosiya, Ukraine

	In serv.		In serv.
557 D-146	1983	602 D-141	1982
600 D-457	1985		

Lebed class—typical unit, since retired from the Northern Fleet 7-94

D: 70 tons (87 fl) **S:** 70 kts max. **Dim:** 24.8 × 10.8 × 1.3 (at rest)
A: 1 twin 12.7-mm Ütes-M mg **Electronics:** Radar: 1 . . . nav.
M: 2 AL-20K gas turbines; 2 shrouded airscrew props; 20,000 shp (16,000 sust.)
Range: 100/60 **Fuel:** 12.7 tons **Crew:** 2 officers, 4 enlisted + 120 troops

Remarks: Entire class of 20 had been believed to have been retired by end-1997, but it was reported in 2000 that four remained in the Northern Fleet, of which D-454 (pennant 543) was photographed on 21-7-00 loading for transit via the canal and river system from the Northern Fleet for operations with the Federal Border Guard in the Caspian. Of the remainder, one was transferred to Vietnam and the others had been retired by the late 1990s. Can carry one or two armored personnel carriers or 120 troops or about 35 tons of cargo. Have a bow ramp only.

Note: Ten Tsaplya-class (Project 1206.1) air-cushion landing craft are operated by the Federal Border Guard.

♦ 1 Serna-class (Project 1177.0) fast landing craft [LCM]

Bldr: Volga Zavod, Nizhniy Novgorod

747 DKA-67 (In serv. 4-5-95)

DKA-67 (747)—with a Ropucha-class LST in the background Hartmut Ehlers, 7-96

D: 53 tons light (105 fl) **S:** 30 kts **Dim:** 25.65 × 5.85 × 1.52 (1.30 at speed)
A: Shoulder-launched Strela-3 (SA-16) SAMs; 3 single 7.62-mm PKMB mg
Electronics: Radar: 1 Liman nav.
M: 2 Zvezda M-503A-3 diesels; 2 shrouded props; 3,300 bhp
Electric: 32 kw tot. (2 × 16-kw DGR-16/1,500 diesel sets)
Range: 100/30 loaded; 600/30 half-load **Crew:** 4 tot.

Remarks: Private venture design by the R. Alekseyev Central Hydrofoil Design Bureau. Five were built, two of which were sold to a commercial operator in the United Arab Emirates in 1994, one was sold to Estonia in 1994, DKA-67 was delivered to the Baltic Fleet, and a second naval unit was intended for use by the Caspian Flotilla. "Serna" is the builder's project name and is also used as the NATO nickname.
Hull systems: Have a useful load of 45–50 tons on the 13 × 4 × 2.5-m cargo deck that extends about 2 m beneath the pilothouse. A portable canopy and seats for 100 personnel can be installed on the vehicle deck. The semi-planing hull incorporates an air cavity to provide underhull lubrication. Aluminum/magnesium-alloy construction. Have an articulating bow ramp. Range with half load of 600 n.m. can be achieved by using reserve void tanks to carry fuel.

AMPHIBIOUS WARFARE SHIPS *(continued)*

♦ 4 Ondatra (Akula)-class (Project 1176) landing craft [LCM]
(In serv. 1979–91)

640 DKA-704 672 DKA-295
713 DKA-286 795 DKA-325

D: 90 tons normal (107.3 fl) **S:** 11.5 kts **Dim:** 24.50 × 6.00 × 1.55
A: None **Electronics:** Radar: 1 Mius (Spin Trough) nav. (portable)
M: 2 Type 3D12 diesels; 2 props; 600 bhp **Range:** 330/10; 500/5
Endurance: 2 days **Crew:** 5 tot. (enlisted)

Remarks: Typed DKA (*Desantnyy Kater,* Landing Craft). In all, 29 were built for use aboard the *Ivan Rogov*–class landing ships. Two were transferred to Yemen in 1983, one is in Georgian service, and DKA-305 and DKA-455 were transferred to Ukraine in 1997. The cargo well is 13.7 × 3.9 m and can accommodate one 40-ton tank or up to 50 tons of general cargo; some 20 troops/vehicle crew can be carried.

DKA-286 (713)—at St. Petersburg Hartmut Ehlers, 7-96

Disposals: DKA-182, DKA-148, DKA-464, DKA-337, DKA-52, DKA-423, DKA-277, DKA-424, DKA-426, DKA-347, DKA-143, DKA-702, DKA-295, DKA-348, DKA-70, DKA-343, DKA-536, DKA-142, DKA-512 and DKA-288 were all retired by 2005.

♦ Up to 73 T-4-class (Project 1785) landing craft [LCM]
Bldr: . . . (In serv. 1968–74)

T-4 class—standard-configuration, hull number 22 Boris Lemachko, 7-01

D: 35 tons light (93 fl) **S:** 10 kts (light) **Dim:** 20.4 × 5.4 × 1.2 (max. aft)
M: 2 Type 3D6 diesels; 2 props; 300 bhp
Range: 300/8 **Endurance:** 2 days **Crew:** 2 tot.

Remarks: Can accommodate up to 50 tons of cargo on the 9.5 × 3.9-m vehicle deck. D-305 and D-455 of the Black Sea Fleet were transferred to Ukraine in 1996–97.

Note: Two other LCM designs, the Project 1733 Vostok class and Project 20150 Slavyanka class, now seem to be used only for service craft functions and are listed below under [YFU].

♦ 4 Gus (Skat)-class (Project 1205) air-cushion personnel landing craft [LCPA]
Bldr: Sudostroitel'noye Obyedineniye "Almaz," Dekabristov Zavod, St. Petersburg (In serv. 1969–76)

631 D-357 634 D-732 650 D- . . . 698 D-448

D: 17 tons light (27.2 fl) **S:** 49 kts (loaded) **Dim:** 21.3 × 8.4 × 0.2 (at rest)
M: 2 TVD-10 turboprop engines; 2,340 shp—1 TVD-10 gas turbine lift-fan engine; 780 shp
Range: 185/50 light; 230/43 loaded **Crew:** 7 tot. + 24 troops

Remarks: Survivors of 32 built. A small number had a second control cab above and behind the normal one, for training purposes. Troops debark via two ladders on either side forward.

Gus class—in camouflage paint scheme H&L Van Ginderen, 1992

SWIMMER DELIVERY VEHICLES [LSDV]

♦ Up to 24 Triton-II (Project 908) special forces submersibles
B-520 through B-543 series

D: 5.7 tons sub. **S:** 6 kts sub.
Dim: 9.50 × 1.90 × 1.60 **M:** 1 electric motor; 1 prop; . . . shp
Range: 60/6 **Endurance:** 12 hours **Crew:** 6 tot. combat swimmers

Remarks: Triton-II was offered for export in 1994 and is also in use by Russian special forces (Spetsnaz), who employ several different types of swimmer delivery vehicles. Designed by Firma Malakhit, St. Petersburg, under Yu. K. Mineyev. Diving depth: 40 m.

Note: LSDV designs offered for foreign sale include the Project 907 Triton, a 1.6-ton, 5.0-m-long device with a speed of 6 kts for 6 hours and capable of carrying two combat swimmers. A total of eight Triton vehicles are said to have been constructed, B-483 through B-490. The Sirena-UME combat diver chariot can be launched from a 533-mm torpedo tube and is 11.3 m long; displacing 1.6 tons submerged, it has a range of 8 n.m. at 4 kts and can dive to 40 m.

AUXILIARIES

Note: The numbers of ships remaining within the various auxiliary and service craft classes are more difficult to determine because they tend not to be sold abroad for scrapping to the same extent as are combatants (which have the more valuable metals in greater proportion). Further, many such units are kept in commission for accommodations use but no longer perform their primary functions.

♦ 14 Bereza (SR-28)-class (Polish Project 130) deperming ships [ADG] (1 or more in *reserve*)
Bldr: Stocznia Polnocna, Gdansk, Poland (In serv. 1984–91)

SR-28	SR-216	SR-569	SR-938
SR-74	SR-245	SR-570	SR-939
SR-120	SR-479	SR-933	
SR-137	SR-541	SR-936	

Caspian Flotilla Bereza SR-933 Boris Lemachko, 7-95

D: 1,850 tons (2,051 fl) **S:** 13.8 kts **Dim:** 69.50 × 13.80 × 3.99
Electronics: Radar: 1 Mius-M (Kivach) nav.
M: 2 Zgoda-Sulzer 8AL25/30, 750-rpm diesels; 2 CP Kort-nozzle props; 2,940 bhp—bow-thruster
Electric: 1,185 kVA + 1,550 kw tot. (2 × 480 kVA, 1 × 225 kVA, 2 × 645 kw, 1 × 260 kw)
Range: 1,000/13.8 **Endurance:** 30 days **Crew:** 50 tot. (civilian)

Remarks: SR = *Sudno Razmagnichivanya* (Deperming Vessel); intended for "degaussing surface ships and submarines, conducting magnetic field measurements of ships and vessels, [and] regulating ground fault neutralizers." SR-28, -120, -245, -479, -570, and -936 are assigned to the Baltic Fleet; SR-137, -541, and -939 to the Black Sea Fleet; and all others to the Northern Fleet. Polish sources indicate that only 17 were built for Russia, and it is possible that some of the SR-series numbers noted above may have been changes rather than additional ships.
Hull systems: Data listed above are from a Polish source; Russian Navy data indicate a displacement of 2,090 tons full load. Can service two ships simultaneously. Have three laboratories, a machine shop, and a cable hold. A large crane is fitted aft to handle deperming cables.

AUXILIARIES *(continued)*

Disposals: One sister was delivered to Bulgaria in mid-1989. Of two more that were building at the time of the collapse of the Soviet Union, one remained nearly complete at the builder's yard as of 7-98 and has been altered for Polish Navy service. Sister SR-568 was stricken from the Black Sea Fleet on 10-1-96 and was in Ukraine service as of 8-97. SR-548 was no longer in service as of 2001. SR-23, SR-59, SR-253, and SR-278 were stricken in 2005.

♦ 21 Pelym (SR-218)-class (Project 1799 and 1799A) deperming ships [ADG] (5 or more in *reserve*)

Bldr: Khabarovsk (14 units) and Gorokhovtse Shipyards (In serv. 1971–87)

SR-26 SR-180 SR-218 SR-276 SR-344 SR-455
SR-77 SR-188 SR-220 SR-280 SR-370
SR-111 SR-203 SR-221 SR-281 SR-373
SR-179 SR-215 SR-233 SR-334 SR-409

Pacific Fleet Pelym-class SR-111—a late-construction unit with the forecastle deck extended to the stern Boris Lemachko, 2002

D: 1,050 tons (1,200 fl) **S:** 13.5 kts **Dim:** 64.06 × 11.71 × 3.51
Electronics: Radar: 1 Donets-2 nav.
M: 1 1,200-kw diesel generating set, 2 300-kw diesel generating sets, electric drive; 1 prop; 1,740 shp (1,536 sust.)
Range: 1,000/13.5; 2,500/12 **Endurance:** 15 days **Crew:** 43 tot. (civilian)

Remarks: SR = *Sudno Razmagnichivanya* (Deperming Vessel). Late units have a tripod mast aft to support radio antenna wires; early ships had an aerial spreader on the stack. The final variant (Project 1799A) had the forecastle deck extended right aft to the stern to provide stowage for a rectangular raft of unknown function. As of 2000, SR-215, -218, -220, -276, -280, -334, -409, and -455 were in the Northern Fleet; SR-203 in the Baltic Fleet; SR-26 and -344 in the Black Sea Fleet; and SR-77, -111, -180, -188, -221, -233, -281, -370, and -373 in the Pacific.
Disposals: One was transferred to Cuba in 2-82. Pacific Fleet unit SR-191 was stricken 5-7-94, and Baltic Fleet unit SR-70 on 1-9-95. Baltic Fleet unit SR-241 sank at Kronshtadt during the winter of 1998–99, and SR-407 was stripped and readied for scrapping by 8-00; others also may have been discarded or be in reserve. SR-222 has been stripped of her deperming equipment but may be used as a barracks hulk.

Note: The surviving Sekstan-class (Project 220) deperming tenders are listed under [YDG] in the Service Craft section.

♦ 1 Finik-class (Project 872) munitions transport [AE]

Bldr: Stocznia Polnocna, Gdansk, Poland (In serv. 1979–81)

VTR-75 (ex-OS-265, ex-GS-265)

Finik-class VTR-75—with T-43GKS-class signature-monitoring ship SFP-17 alongside Hartmut Ehlers, 7-00

D: 950 tons (1,186 fl) **S:** 13.8 kts **Dim:** 61.30 × 11.80 (10.80 wl) × 3.28
Electronics: Radar: 2 Don-2 nav.
M: 2 Cegielski-Sulzer diesels; 2 CP props; 1,920 bhp—2 75-kw electric motors for quiet, 6-kt operations—130-kw bow-thruster
Electric: 675 kVA tot. **Range:** 3,000/13; 4,800/11 **Endurance:** 15 days
Crew: 5 officers, 23 unlicensed (civilian)

Remarks: Polish B-91 design. Black Sea Fleet unit built as a hydrographic survey ship and navigational aids tender, later employed as a trials ship (OS-265), and by 7-00 redesignated as a munitions carrier. Based at Sevatstopol'.
Hull systems: Intended for navigational buoy-tending and hydrographic survey duties, for which four echo sounders are fitted. Up to three fiberglass 3-dwt utility landing craft can be stowed on the buoy working deck beneath the 7-ton crane.

♦ 3 Amga-class (Project 1791) ballistic-missile transports [AEM] (2 in *reserve*)

Bldr: Krasnoye Sormovo SY, Nizhniy Novgorod

Amga (In serv. 12-72) Daugava (In serv. 30-12-80) *Vetluga* (In serv. 1976)

Daugava—with new missile-handling crane Boris Lemachko, 2000

D: *Amga:* 3,300 tons light (4,480 fl) **S:** 15.5 (*Amga:* 14.5) kts
Dim: *Amga:* 102.00 × 17.80 × 4.50 (see Remarks)
A: 2 twin 25-mm 80-cal. 2M-3M AA **Electronics:** Radar: 1 Don-2 nav.
M: 2 Type 67B (12DRPN 23/2 × 30) (*Amga:* Type 37D) diesels; 2 props; 7,500 (*Amga:* 4,000) bhp
Range: 4,500/12 (*Amga:* 4,000/12) **Endurance:** 20 days **Crew:** 56 tot.

Remarks: Have ice-reinforced hulls and one 55-ton crane with a reach of 34 m. Intended to transport ballistic missiles for strategic submarines. *Vetluga* (Project 1791M) is 109.8 m o.a. *Daugava* (Project 1791P) is 113.2 m long and displaces 6,200 tons (fl); since delivery in 1976, she has been equipped with a new, more robust missile-handling crane boom. *Vetluga* and *Daugava* are in the Pacific Fleet; *Amga,* which has a lower-powered propulsion plant, is in the Northern Fleet, in reserve. An RSN-50 ballistic missile was dropped alongside the *Vetluga* at Konyushkov Bay, 60 km east of Vladivostok, on 16-6-00, causing a fire and smoke that severely injured a dozen or more personnel.

♦ 2 Lama-class (Project 323B) cruise missile transports [AEM]

Bldr: Chernomorets Zavod, Nikolayev, Ukraine

	In serv.
General Ryabakov (ex-PRTB-13, ex-PM-873, ex-PM-877)	1979
VTR-33 (ex-PRTB-33, ex-*Voronezh*, ex-PM-874, ex-PM-873)	1972

VTR-33 Boris Lemachko, 5-03

D: 4,045 tons (5,000 fl) **S:** 13 kts **Dim:** 112.80 × 15.50 × 4.40
A: *Ryabakov* only: 1 twin 57-mm 70-cal. AK-725 DP
Electronics: Radar: *Ryabakov:* 2 Don-2 nav.; 1 MR-302 Rubka (Strut Curve) air search; 1 MR-103 Bars (Muff Cob) f.c.—VTR-33: 2 Don-2 nav.; 1 Fut-N (Slim Net) surf./air search
M: 2 Type 1D-46 (6DN 39/45) diesels; 2 props; 2,600 bhp
Range: 2,000/10 **Endurance:** 15 days **Crew:** up to 154 civilians

Remarks: Designation as PRTB (*Plavuchaya Raketno-Tekhnicheskaya Basa,* Floating Missile Technical Base) indicates that the ships are capable of servicing nuclear warheads. Are survivors of seven Project 323-series units built. Both are stationed in the Black Sea Fleet at Sevastopol' and are operated by civilian crews. VTR-33 was most recently renamed during 8-99.
Hull systems: VTR-33 was designed to serve small missile craft and could carry 12 Styx-series reload missiles; the ship has two 10-ton precision cranes. *General Ryabakov* has larger cranes and was originally intended to transport SS-N-3-series missiles.

AUXILIARIES *(continued)*

Combat systems: The former armament of one twin 57-mm 70-cal. ZIF-31B DP and two twin 25-mm 2M-3M AA has been removed from VTR-33, and the armament on *Ryabakov* is probably nonoperational.
Disposals: Northern Fleet unit PRTB-15 (ex-PM-44, ex-PM-93) was offered for scrap during 1992. Pacific Fleet unit PRTB-20 (ex- . . .) was stricken 30-7-93 and PRTB-24 (ex-PM-150) and PRTB-43 (ex-PM-150) on 5-7-94; PRTB-8 (ex- . . .) was also stricken in 1994. *Kolomiya* (U 533, ex-PRTB-13) was transferred to Ukraine in 1996 but was later scrapped at Inkerman, beginning late in 1999.

♦ 4 Mayak-class (Project 502R) provisions transports [AFT]
Bldrs: Dnepr SY, Kiev; Volgograd; Khabarovsk; and Yaroslavl (In serv. 1965–70)

LAMA MIUS UL'MA VYTEGRA

Mius Hartmut Ehlers, 3-02

D: 770 tons (950 fl) **S:** 12.1 kts (11 sust.) **Dim:** 54.3 × 9.3 × 3.6
Electronics: Radar: 1 Mius (Spin Trough) nav.
M: 1 8NVD 48AU diesel; 800 bhp **Electric:** 300 kw tot. (3 × 100-kw diesel sets)
Range: 6,000/11; 8,300/9 **Fuel:** 127 tons **Endurance:** 30 days
Crew: 29 tot. (civilian)

Remarks: 690 grt. Former trawlers. Refrigerated fish holds were converted to carry provisions for deployed forces. *Vytegra* is assigned to the Northern Fleet, *Ul'ma* to the Pacific Fleet, and *Lama* and *Mius* to the Black Sea Fleet. Some, including both Black Sea Fleet units, may be inactive.
Disposals: Sisters *Rioni* and *Neman* were stricken during 2005.

♦ 2 Tomba-class (Project 802) generator ships [AG]
(1 *nonoperational*)
Bldr: A. Warski SY, Szczecin, Poland (In serv. 1978)

ENS-244 ENS-348

Tomba-class ENS-244—under tow, with an Okhtenskiy-class tug alongside aft
Boris Lemachko, 2000

D: 4,101 tons (5,411 fl) **S:** 12.5 kts **Dim:** 108.60 × 16.50 × 4.50
Electronics: Radar: 1 Don-2 nav.; 1 Mius (Spin Trough) nav.
M: 1 Zgoda-Sulzer 6TAD-48 diesel; 1 prop; 3,000 bhp
Electric: 6,400 kw tot. (8 × 800-kw diesel sets)
Range: 23,800/12 **Fuel:** 405 tons **Endurance:** 30 days
Crew: 3 officers, 46 enlisted

Remarks: ENS = *Elektrostantsiye Nativatel'noye Sudno* (Electric Power Station and Steam-Source Ship). Have two stacks and a "mack" on the forecastle, all containing diesel-engine exhausts, while the stack amidships also has the uptake from a large auxiliary boiler. Have two 1.5-ton cranes. ENS-348 is in the Pacific Fleet and may be being used to provide power to facilities ashore; ENS-244 is based at Severomorsk and appears to be nonoperational.

♦ 2 Vytegrales-class (Project 1998) search-and-rescue ships [AG]
Bldr: Zhdanov Zavod, St. Petersburg (In serv. 1964–66)

506 DAURIYA (ex-*Vyborglets*) 508 APSHERON (ex-*Vagalets*)

D: 4,760 tons (7,230 fl) **S:** 15 kts **Dim:** 126.00 (114.00 pp) × 16.70 × 5.60
Electronics:
Radar: 2 MR-212/201 Vaygach-U (Palm Frond) nav./surf. search (*Dauriya:* 2 Don-2 nav.)—*Apsheron* only: 1 Fly Screen landing aid
TACAN: *Apsheron* and *Sevan* only: 2 Privod (Round House)

Dauriya (506)—hull is painted black, superstructure white, and masts gold
Boris Lemachko, 2002

Dauriya (506)—at Sevastopol' Boris Lemachko, 2002

M: 1 Bryansk–Burmeister & Wain 950 VTBF 110 diesel; 1 prop; 5,200 bhp
Range: 7,380/14.5 **Fuel:** 462 tons **Endurance:** 60 days **Crew:** 90 tot. (naval)

Remarks: Originally built as Project 596P merchant timber carriers, then converted as space-event support ships by the addition of more communications facilities and a helicopter platform over the stern—consequently losing access to the after hold. Although they have been used as fleet supply ships and flagships, they are still considered to be search-and-rescue vessels. *Apsheron* (painted white) and *Dauriya* (with black hull and white superstructure) are assigned to the Black Sea Fleet. *Sevan* (painted white) was resubordinated to the Baltic Fleet Search and Rescue Brigade in 7-97.
Hull systems: In 1991, *Apsheron* completed an extensive refit and alteration at Sevastopol' and was equipped with a 13 × 11.5 × 6-m hangar for two helicopters and new electronics including two Vaygach-U (Palm Frond) radars in place of Don-2, Round House helicopter-control TACAN, and Fly Screen helicopter landing aid radar antennas. *Dauriya* has been given two large parabolic reflector antennas abreast the signal mast but otherwise is little altered since the original conversion.
Disposals: Black Sea Fleet sister *Dikson* (ex-*Vostok-3*) was further converted to a weapons trials ship (Project 59610); she was stricken 30-7-93 and scrapped in 1995. *Donbass* (ex-*Vostok-4*) was stricken 30-7-93 and towed to Turkey for scrapping in 2-95. Sister *Yamal* was reconverted to a standard commercial cargo ship during 1995 at Kaliningrad and was no longer naval by 1-02. *Baskunchak* (ex-*Kirishi*) and *Taman'* (ex-*Suzdal'*) were stricken 10-1-96 and transferred to Ukraine on 12-3-96. Seven sisters, all now stricken, were converted to serve the Academy of Sciences as satellite-tracking ships.

♦ 15 Onega-class (Project 1806 and 1806.1) environmental-monitoring ships [AG] (9 *nonoperational*)
Bldr: Zelenodol'sk Zavod (In serv. 9-73 to 1996)

AKADEMIK ISANIN (ex-GKS-83)
AKADEMIK SEMENIKHIN
SFP-224 (ex-GKS-224)
SFP-240 (ex-GKS-240)
SFP-286 (ex-GKS-286)
INZHENER AKULOV
SFP-95 (ex-GKS-95)
SFP-173
SFP-177
SFP-183
SFP-283 (ex-GKS-283)
SFP-295
SFP-511
SFP-542
VLADIMIR PEREGUDOV (ex-SFP-562)

Baltic Fleet Onega-class SFP-283—an early-construction unit with pylon masts and a stand-alone after deckhouse Boris Lemachko, 2000

AUXILIARIES *(continued)*

Black Sea Fleet Onega-class SFP-183—a late-construction unit with lattice masts, the stack set much farther aft, and an air-sampling station emplaced abaft the stack Hartmut Ehlers, 7-00

D: 1,300–1,350 tons (1,410–1,460 fl) **S:** 14 kts
Dim: 80.00 × 11.60 × 3.17–3.27
Electronics:
Radar: 1 Don-2 nav.—some also: 1 . . . nav.
Sonar: Arktika-M passive array; active dipping set
M: 2 diesels; 2 props; 2,800 bhp **Electric:** 800 kw tot. (4 × 200-kw diesel sets)
Range: 1,000/10 **Endurance:** 15 days **Crew:** 45 tot.

Remarks: GKS = *Gidroakusticheskoye Kontrol'noye Sudno* (Hydroacoustic Monitoring Ship); SFP (*Sudna Fizicheskiy Postroeniy,* Physical Fields Measuring Post) on later and redesignated units indicates a somewhat different mission and sensors. Officially said to be intended to "measure acoustic, magnetic, low-frequency, electromagnetic, electric, and heat fields set up by surface ships and submarines for compliance with existing standards and specifications." SFP-173 and SFP-177 were delivered in 1991. *Akademik Semenikhin,* which is in the GKS configuration, was commissioned 15-10-92, and the similar *Akademik Isanin* and *Inzhener Akulov* in 1994 and 1996, respectively; SFP-95, GKS-240, SFP-283, and *Isanin* are assigned to the Northern Fleet; SFP-173, SFP-224, SFP-295, and SFP-542 to the Pacific Fleet; SFP-177 and SFP-183 to the Black Sea Fleet; and *Akulov* and *Semenikhin* to the Baltic Fleet. Northern Fleet unit SFP-562 was renamed the *Vladimir Peregudov* in 1998.
Hull systems: Later ships (Project 1806.1) have the after deckhouse farther forward, abutting the stack, and have lattice vice pylon masts. SFP-designated units are usually seen with two side-by-side modular structures topped with two rectangular air vents mounted at the forward end of the after deckhouse platform (which was originally intended to be a helicopter platform); the devices may be employed in air sampling.
Disposals: Pacific Fleet unit SFP-340 was stricken in 1990 after a fire, and Pacific Fleet sister SFP-343 was stricken in 9-95. Black Sea Fleet unit SFP-322 was stricken 10-1-96 and transferred to Ukraine in 1997. Baltic Fleet unit SFP-511 was derelict at Kronshtadt as of 1998. SFP-52 (ex-GKS-52) had been stricken by 2001. The last surviving T-43GKS-class (Project 513M) environment-monitoring ship, SFP-17 (ex-GKS-17) had been retired by 2005.

♦ 5 Dobrynya Nikitich–class (Project 97 and 97AP/2*) port icebreakers [AGB]
Bldr: Admiralty SY, St. Petersburg (In serv. 1960–74)

	Laid down	L	In serv.	Fleet
Dobrynya Nikitich	20-12-59	10-5-60	31-12-60	Black Sea
Purga*	31-5-60	10-12-60	23-10-61	Baltic
Buran	21-1-66	16-5-66	24-10-66	Baltic
Sadko*	22-6-67	28-6-68	6-11-68	Pacific
Peresvet*	10-7-68	29-1-69	28-7-70	Northern

Sadko U.S. Navy, 9-91

D: 2,300–2,520 tons (2,700–2,940 fl) **S:** 14.5 kts **Dim:** 67.70 × 18.30 × 5.50
Electronics: Radar: 1 or 2 Don-2 nav.
M: 3 13D100 diesels, electric drive; 3 props (1 fwd); 5,400 shp
Electric: 700 or 1,200 kw tot. **Range:** 5,500/12; 13,000/9.4
Fuel: 580 tons **Endurance:** 30 days **Crew:** 39–48 tot.

Remarks: Twenty of this class were built for the Soviet Navy and civilian service. *Peresvet, Purga,* and *Sadko* were built to Project 97AP/2 patrol and hydrographic survey configuration and were armed with one twin 57-mm ZIF-31B AA and one twin 25-mm 2M-3M AA, since removed; they displace 3,600 tons (fl) and have a range of 6,800 n.m. at 12 kts. All can carry 170 tons of fresh water and 27 tons of lubricants.
Disposals: Pacific Fleet sisters *Vyuga* and *Il'ya Muromets* were stricken in 1991 and on 30-7-93, respectively.

Disposal note: *Kamchatka*-class (Project 10221) sonar trials ship *Kamchatka* (SSV-679, ex-SSV-391), placed in reserve since around 1993, appears to again be in good condition and may have reentered service.

♦ 1 Potok (Smen')-class (Project 1236) torpedo trials ship [AGE]
Bldr: Zelenodol'sk SY (In serv. 1971–74)

OS-114

Potok-class OS-225—since stricken [no date or credit]

D: 750 tons (860 fl) **S:** 17 kts **Dim:** 72.1 × 9.4 × 2.5
A: 1 533-mm TT; 1 406-mm TT
Electronics: Radar: 1 Don-2 nav.
M: 2 Type 40-D diesels; 2 props; 4,000 bhp
Range: 2,500/12 **Endurance:** 5 days **Crew:** 30 tot.

Remarks: OS = *Opitnoye Sudno* (Experimental Vessel). The design closely resembles that of a T-58-class minesweeper, but the forecastle extends farther aft, nearly to the stern. The trainable torpedo tubes are on the bow. A large crane aft is used for retrieval of expended weapons. Operated on Lake Ladoga, east of St. Petersburg.
Disposals: Black Sea Fleet sisters OS-149 and OS-225 were stricken 1-9-95; OS-100 was transferred to Ukraine 1-8-97 but was scrapped at Feodosiya during 2002.

♦ 1 Volgograd-class (Project 593) trials tender [AGE]
Bldr: . . . Zavod, Volgograd (In serv. 10-64)

OS-248 Volgograd

D: 1,200 tons (fl) **S:** 16 kts **Dim:** 82.40 × 13.90 × 3.55
M: 4 Type 5D-50 diesel generator sets, 2 electric motors; 2 props; 2,800 shp
Electric: 740 kw tot. (4 × 160-kw, 1 × 100-kw diesel sets)
Range: . . . / . . . **Fuel:** 68 tons **Crew:** . . . tot.

Remarks: Former passenger vessel, taken over for Caspian Sea service in 1992. Function uncertain. Has folding masts for riverine navigation.

♦ 7 Vishnaya (Meridian)-class (Project 864) intelligence collectors [AGI]
Bldr: Stocznia Polnocna, Gdansk

	In serv.
407 SSV-169 Tavriya	1986
425 SSV-175 Odograf	1988
437 SSV-201 Priazov'ye	14-6-87
756 SSV-208 Kuril'y	16-10-86
402 SSV-231 Vasiliy Tatishchev (ex-*Pelengator*)	21-8-88
411 SSV-520 Meridian	1985
761 SSV-535 Kareliya	5-6-86

Baltic Fleet Vishnaya-class SSV-520 Meridian (411)—with a single radome Boris Lemachko, 7-00

Pacific Fleet Vishnaya-class SSV-208 Kuril'y (756)—with two spherical radomes on the mounting platforms atop the bridge JMSDF, 10-01

AUXILIARIES *(continued)*

D: 2,690 tons light; 3,100 tons std. (3,470 fl)—see Remarks **S:** 16 kts
Dim: 94.40 (88.00 wl) × 14.60 × 4.50
A: 2 single 30-mm 54-cal. AK-630 gatling AA; 2 4-round Fasta-4M (SA-N-8) SAM (16 Igla-1M missiles)
Electronics:
Radar: 2 Volga (Don-Kay) nav.
Sonar: Pamyat hull-mounted array; HF dipping sonar
EW: Various intercept arrays
M: 2 Cegielski-Sulzer 12AV 25/30, 750-rpm diesels; 2 CP props; 4,400 bhp—2 140-shp electric auxiliary low-speed drives
Electric: 2,000 kw tot. (4 × 500 kw) **Range:** 7,900/12.5
Endurance: 45 days **Crew:** 30 officers, 121 enlisted

Remarks: SSV-208 and -535 are in the Pacific Fleet, SSV-201 is in the Black Sea Fleet, SSV-169 and -175 are in the Northern Fleet, and SSV-231 and -520 are in the Baltic Fleet. SSV-231 was renamed early in 2000. SSV-520 was sequestered at Nauta Ship Repair Yard in Poland during 1992 for nonpayment of repair fees; the ship completed a refit at Rostock NIR-Reparaturwerft, Germany, in 4-99. The ships are now only rarely deployed, and then only in local waters; as yet, they have not been photographed wearing the pennant numbers listed above. SSV-231 completed her 13th deployment, a reconnaissance voyage to the Atlantic, on 6-11-01.
Hull systems: Displacements are reported to have risen to 2,980 tons light/3,996 full load in service.
Combat systems: There are two Rakurs-series lead-computing directors for the 30-mm guns mounted forward. The point-defense SAM launchers are aft. The dipping sonar installation is mounted within the stern, deploying the transducer through a door in the transom. Two large circular radome foundations atop the forward superstructure support a variety of antenas; SSV-201 and -231 have two large radomes, and SSV-175 and -520 have one, while SSV-169 has exposed parabolic-mesh antennas on the after of the two platforms and no antennas on the forward one. Neither Pacific Fleet unit has large radomes.

♦ 3 Al'pinist-class (Project 503M) intelligence collectors [AGI]
Bldr: Leninskaya Kuznetsa Zavod, Kiev, Ukraine

	In serv.
739 GS-7	1979
314 GS-19 Zigulrovsk	1980
317 GS-39 Syzran	1981

Al'pinist-class GS-39 (317) Frank Findler, 6-02

D: 810 tons light (1,140 fl) **S:** 12.6 kts **Dim:** 53.70 (46.20 pp) × 10.50 × 4.10
A: GS-19 and GS-39 only: 2 Fasta-4M (SA-N-8) SAM syst. (16 Strela-2M or Igla-1M missiles)
Electronics: Radar: 1 Don-2 nav.—Sonar: Paltus-MP
M: 1 Type 8NVD48-2U diesel; 1 CP prop; 1,320 bhp
Electric: 450 kw tot. (1 × 300-kw, 1 × 150-kw diesel sets)
Range: 7,600/12.5 **Fuel:** 162 tons **Endurance:** 25 days **Crew:** 24 tot.

Remarks: Selected from a class of several hundred 322-dwt Project 503 stern-haul trawlers and modified as intelligence collectors. The Russian Navy also used an *Al'pinist* in an experimental role (OS-104, now stricken), and several have been used in civilian oceanographic research. GS-19 and GS-39 are in the Baltic Fleet, GS-7 in the Pacific Fleet, from which sister GS-8 was stricken 5-7-94. GS-7 operated in the South China Sea during summer 1998.
Hull systems: The 218-m^3 former fish hold may provide electronics and/or additional accommodations spaces. Have a bow-thruster.
Mission systems: During 1988 GS-19 and GS-39 had their forecastle decks extended to the stern, point-defense launchers added fore and aft, and their collection antenna suites greatly enhanced: a series of planar antennas surround the ships at upper deck level, and an elaborate VHFD/F array surmounts the after goalpost mast. GS-7 has had the forecastle extended, but not all the way to the stern. GS-19 is equipped with a Stop Light submarine-type intercept array, GS-39 carries two Bizan'-4-series (Watch Dog) intercept arrays, and GS-7 has a Squid Head submarine-type antenna array.

♦ 2 Bal'zam (Aziya)-class (Project 1826) intelligence collectors [AGI]
Bldr: Yantar Zavod 820, Kaliningrad

	In serv.
696 SSV-80 Pribaltika	28-7-84
463 SSV-571 Belomor'ye	1986

D: 3,100 tons (4,900 fl) **S:** 22 kts (20 sust.) **Dim:** 105.0 × 15.5 × 5.6
A: 1 30-mm 54-cal. AK-630 gatling AA; 2 4-round Fasta-4M SAM syst. (16 Strela-series or Igla-1M missiles)

SSV-571 Belomor'ye (463) French Navy, 5-96

Electronics:
Radar: 2 Volga (Don-Kay) nav.
Sonar: Hull-mounted MF; possible passive hull arrays; Uzh HF dipping
EW: 2 Cage Pot; 1 Twin Wheel D/F; 1 Log Maze D/F; 1 Fir Tree; 1 Wing Fold; 1 Trawl Net; 2 Sprat Star; 1 Cross Loop-A MFD/F; 1 High Ring-C HFD/F; 1 Park Plinth VHFD/F
M: 2 Type 58D (16DRPN 23/2 × 30) diesels; 2 props; 9,000 bhp
Range: 7,000/16, 10,000/14 **Endurance:** 60 days
Crew: 189 tot. (accomm. for 220)

Remarks: SSV = *Sudno Svyazyy* (Communications Vessel). These were the first built-for-the-purpose intelligence-collection and -processing ships, wholly military in concept. SSV-571 is active in the Northern Fleet; SSV-80, in the Pacific Fleet, has been laid up since the 1990s. Reports concerning her 2002 reactivation appear to have been incorrect.
Hull systems: Equipped to refuel under way and to transfer solid cargo and personnel via constant-tension rigs on either side of the after mast.
Combat systems: There is only a remote SP-521 Rakurs (Kolonka-2) pedestal director for the gatling gun. The two spherical radomes probably house satellite transmitting and receiving antennas. Have Prim Wheel and Soup Cup satellite antennas. Russian designations for the special antennas (uncorrelated) are Prokhlada, Buksir-N, Rotor-H, Oktava, and Pamyat.
Disposals: Northern Fleet sister (and class prototype) *Lira* (SSV-516) had become derelict by the end of 1996 and was stricken during 1998. Pacific Fleet unit *Aziya* (SSV-493), laid up at Vladivostok since the mid-1990s, had been stricken by 2001.

♦ 2 converted Yug-class (Project 0862.1 and 0862.2) intelligence collectors [AGI]
Bldr: Stocznia Polnocna, Gdansk

	In serv.
SSV-703 Temryuk (ex-SSV-328, ex-*Yug*)	5-78
SSV-704 (ex-*Mangyshlak*)	4-11-83

Yug-class SSV-704 J. G. Stemmelin, 5-97

D: 1,960 tons (2,490 fl) **S:** 15.6 kts **Dim:** 82.50 (75.80 pp) × 13.50 × 3.97
A: 2 twin 12.7-mm 59-cal. Utës-M mg
Electronics:
Radar: 2 Don-2 nav.
Sonar: Uzh HF dipping
EW: 2 Bizan'-4 (Watch Dog) intercept; 1 HFD/F loop
M: 2 Zgoda-Sulzer 12AB 25/30 diesels; 2 CP props; 4,400 bhp (3,600 sust.)—2 125-shp electric low-speed motors—300-shp bow-thruster
Electric: 3,600 kw tot. (4 × 500-kw, 4 × 400-kw diesel sets)
Range: 4,430/17; 10,850/13 **Fuel:** 343 tons (406 max.) **Endurance:** 45 days
Crew: 4 officers, 54 enlisted

Remarks: Conversion of SSV-703 from an existing Black Sea Fleet oceanographic research ship was completed in summer 1989 and that of SSV-704 by 1990. The forecastle deck was extended to the stern, and the sides plated in; the 01- and 02-level superstructures were also extended aft, presumably to allow for an increase in accommodations and for electronics spaces. Both are in the Northern Fleet. SSV-703 wore tactical pennant 700 when entering the Baltic in 10-00.
Combat systems: The machinegun mounts are mounted abaft the boats. The large radome on the cylindrical stalk between the stack and the foremast was also found on the giant *Ural* (SSV-33). There is, however, a paucity of other electromagnetic signal collection antennas, and the ships may have a more specialized intelligence collection role, perhaps in acoustics.

Disposal note: Of the six *Primor'ye*-class (Project 394B) intelligence collection ships, *Zabaykal'ye* (SSV-464), stricken 30-7-93, was scrapped in India early in 1995; *Primor'ye* (SSV-465) was stricken 5-7-94 from the Pacific Fleet; Northern Fleet unit *Zakarpat'ye* (SSV-502) was stricken 31-12-93 and scrapped during 1995; Northern Fleet unit *Zaporozh'ye* (SSV-501) was stricken 31-7-96; Black Sea Fleet unit *Krym* (SSV-590) was towed from Sevastopol' for scrapping on 26-1-00; and *Kavkaz* (SSV-591) was reassigned as a floating barracks and staff headquarters hulk during 2001.

♦ 4 Moma-class (Project 861M) intelligence collectors [AGI]
Bldr: Stocznia Polnocna, Gdansk, Poland (In serv. 1968–74)

SSV-418 Ekvator	SSV-512 Kil'din
SSV-506 Nakhodka	SSV-824 Liman

D: 1,080 tons light; 1,260 tons std. (1,560 fl) **S:** 16 kts
Dim: 73.30 (64.20 pp) × 11.20 (10.80 wl) × 3.90

AUXILIARIES *(continued)*

SSV-418 Ekvator—note large HFD/F loop aft, two mFD/F loops on the mast, and the removal of the buoy crane forward Boris Lemachko, 1998

A: 2 4-round Fasta-4M (SA-N-8) SAM syst. (16 Strela and/or Igla-series missiles)
Electronics: Radar: 2 Don-2 nav.—Sonar: Bronza array
M: 2 Zgoda-Sulzer 6TD48 diesels; 2 CP props; 3,600 bhp
Range: 9,700/11 **Endurance:** 35 days
Crew: *Liman* and *Kil'din:* 15 officers, 12 warrant officers, 43 enlisted

Remarks: Former survey ship/navigational buoy tenders. Black Sea Fleet navigational aids tender variant *Liman* was redesignated an intelligence collector in 1999 and deployed as such to the Adriatic in 4-99; she was relieved by Black Sea Fleet sister *Kil'din* 19-5-99 and returned to Sevastopol' 16-7-99. Another, the *Okean,* is reported to serve as SSV-518 in the Black Sea Fleet, but other sources state that she was transferred to civilian control in 1992. *Ekvator* is assigned to the Pacific Fleet. Reports that *Nakhodka* had been stricken by 2001 proved incorrect.
Disposals: Northern Fleet unit *Archipelag* (SSV-512) was stricken 5-7-94. Black Sea Fleet unit *Yupiter* was stricken 10-1-96 and transferred to Ukraine 12-3-96. Pacific Fleet units *Il'men'* (SSV-472), *Pelorus* (SSV-509), and *Seliger* were stricken 30-7-93, and *Vega* (SSV-474) was stricken 1-9-95.

♦ 7 Kashtan-class (Project 141) mooring-buoy tenders [AGL]
Bldr: VEB Neptunwerft, Rostock, East Germany

	In serv.
Alexandr Pushkin (ex-KIL-926)	1988
KIL-143	1989
KIL-158	. . .
KIL-164	1989
KIL-168	5-10-90
KIL-498	1990
KIL-927	1988

KIL-158 Boris Lemachko, 7-03

D: 4,200 tons (5,250 fl) **S:** 13.75 kts **Dim:** 113.00 (97.82 pp) × 18.22 × 3.71
Electronics: Radar: 1 Mius (Spin Trough) nav.; 1 Don-2 nav.
M: 2 Karl Liebnecht–M.A.N. 8VDS 26/20AL-1 diesels (2,991 bhp each), 2 generator sets, electric drive; 2 props; 4,200 shp (3,000 sust.)—bow-thruster
Range: 4,000/11 **Endurance:** 45 days
Crew: 44 tot. (accomm. for 18 officers, 36 unlicensed civilians)

Remarks: 4,400 grt/1,000 dwt. *Aleksandr Pushkin* is based in the Baltic; KIL-168, KIL-498, and KIL-927 are homeported at Vladivostok; and KIL-143 and KIL-164 are homeported at Murmansk. KIL-158, reportedly transferred to Ukraine in 1993 and used in commercial service, appeared to be back in Russian Navy service as of 2000 and relieved Amur-class repair ship PM-56 as station ship at Tartus, Syria, during 9-00. The Pacific Fleet units have been employed in carrying commercial vehicle, timber, and finished lumber cargoes since 1992. KIL-926 was refitted at Rostock, Germany, during 1999; she was renamed *Aleksandr Pushkin* on completion of the overhaul on 5-6-99.
Hull systems: Have 100-ton German Stülcken heavy-lift gantry at the stern for lifting mooring buoys and for salvage assignments, a 12-ton electrohydraulic crane to starboard, and a 60-ton derrick amidships. Like the preceding Sura class (of which this design is an obvious development), these also have a 300-ton liquid-cargo capacity.
Disposals: Baltic Fleet unit KIL-140 was renamed SS-750 during 1995 and is equipped to serve as a salvage and rescue submersible tender (see under [ARS]).

♦ 4 Sura-class (Project 145) mooring-buoy tenders [AGL]
Bldr: VEB Neptunwerft, Rostock, East Germany (In serv. 1965–72, 1976–78)

KIL-22 KIL-25 KIL-27 KIL-31

KIL-31 M.O.D. U.K., 5-90

D: 2,260 tons (3,150 fl) **S:** 13.2 kts
Dim: 87.30 (80.20 hull; 68.00 pp) × 14.80 × 5.10
Electronics: Radar: 2 Don-2 nav.
M: 4 diesels, electric drive; 2 props; 2,240 shp (1,780 sust.)
Range: 4,000/10 **Endurance:** 20 days **Crew:** 45 tot. (civilian)

Remarks: 2,366 grt. KIL = *Kilektor* (Mooring Tender). KIL-22 and -31 are assigned to the Northern Fleet; KIL-27 to the Pacific and KIL-25 to the Black Sea. KIL-25 was refitted in Bulgaria in 1996.
Hull systems: Can carry 460 tons of cargo in the hold amidships and 300 tons of cargo fuel. The stern rig, which can lift 65 tons, is used for buoy-handling and salvage. Mooring buoys are stowed amidships and moved aft for handling by the stern gallows rig via a chain-haul system. There are also a 5-ton electric crane to port and a 65-ton heavy-lift boom amidships, the latter tending the buoy stowage holds. The diesel propulsion generator plant is forward.
Disposals: Pacific Fleet unit KIL-32 was stricken in 3-95 and sold to China, probably for scrapping. Black Sea Fleet unit KIL-33 was stricken 10-1-96 and transferred to Ukraine during summer 1997. KIL-2, KIL-23, and KIL-29, long in reserve, were stricken by 2005.

♦ 1 Marshal Nedelin–class (Project 1914.1) missile range instrumentation ship [AGM]
Bldr: United Admiralty SY, St. Petersburg

	Laid down	L	Del.	In serv.
Marshal Krylov	24-7-82	24-7-87	31-12-89	23-2-90

Marshal Krylov JMSDF, 7-90

D: 18,360 tons light; 23,800 tons normal (23,780 fl)
S: 22.7 kts **Dim:** 211.20 × 27.70 × 8.30
A: Provision for 3 single 30-mm 54-cal. AK-630 gatling AA
Electronics:
Radar: 3 MR-212/201 Vaygach-U (Palm Frond) nav.; 1 MR-750 Fregat (Top Plate) surf./air search; 1 Fly Screen helicopter control; 1 End Tray balloon tracking; 1 Ship Globe missile tracking
Sonar: MGK-335-series Platina-S LF hull-mounted; Uzh dipping sonar
TACAN: 2 Privod-B (Round House)
M: 2 Type 68E (DGZA-6U or 18DRN 23/2 × 30) diesels; 2 props; 16,000 shp
Range: 20,000/15.5 **Endurance:** 120 days
Crew: 81 officers, 82 warrant officers, 240 enlisted (accomm. for 106 officers, 311 enlisted)

Remarks: Was intended to begin replacement of the since-stricken *Desna-* and *Sibir'*-class range-tracking ships, but was equipped also to serve in a space-tracking and communications role. Named for a pioneer leader of the Soviet ballistic-missile program. Pacific Fleet unit *Marshal Nedelin* was reported stricken in 1997 and was towed away to India for scrapping 4-4-00. A planned third ship, *Marshal Biryuzov,* was canceled. An incomplete, greatly modified, civilian-subordinated version of the class, *Akademik Nikolay Pilyugin,* was sold incomplete and converted to a cruise liner. *Marshal Krylov* was assigned to the Pacific Fleet 23-2-90.

AUXILIARIES *(continued)*

Hull systems: Twin hangars can accommodate 2 Ka-32 Helix utility helicopters. Hull has a bulbous bow form. Has a swimming pool just abaft the stack.
Sensor systems: Has one Quad Leaf, three Quad Wedge, four Quad Rods, and six telemetry reception arrays. Is equipped with the Tayfun-2 SATCOM and Shtorm communications suite.

♦ 2 Sibiryakov-class (Project 873) oceanographic research ships [AGOR] Bldr: Stocznia Polnocna, Gdansk, Poland

	Laid down	L	In serv.
ROMUALD MUKHLEVICH	1988	1990	12-91
SIBIRYAKOV	8-88	5-89	7-90

Sibiryakov H&L Van Ginderen, 3-95

Romuald Mukhlevich NAVPIC Holland, 10-01

D: 2,280 tons light (3,450 fl) **S:** 16 kts (14 sust.)
Dim: 85.65 (75.60 pp) × 15.00 × 4.80
Electronics: Radar: 2 MR-312 Nayada nav.—Sonar: . . .
M: 2 Cegielski-Sulzer Type 12 ASV25D 1,000-rpm diesels, electric drive: 2 2,400-kw motors; 2 CP props; 6,480 shp—2 Type 6AL20D 750-rpm auxiliary diesels, 2 420-kw motors for low-speed propulsion—bow and stern tunnel-thrusters
Electric: 2,780 kVA tot. (3 Sulzer 6AL25D diesel-driven sets)
Range: 11,520/12 **Endurance:** 40 days
Crew: 58 tot. + 12 scientists/technicians

Remarks: 1,950 dwt. Ordered 1-89 to explore for mineral resources at depths up to 6,000 m. *Sibiryakov* is assigned to the Baltic Fleet and *Romuald Mukhlevich* to the Northern Fleet. Each ship carries two submersibles.
Hull systems: Can carry two 18-ton submersibles and have 14 laboratories, including hydrographic, meteorological, magnetometeric, geologic, gravimetric, and photographic facilities. Model photos indicate presence of a broad-swath echo-sounder mapping system, with conformal transducer windows forward, amidships, and aft. Designed full load displacement was 3,422 tons.
Combat systems: Provision was made at the bow for a twin 30-mm AK-230 AA gunmount with optical director, and the ships have an NBC defense filter system and internal degaussing.

♦ 11 Yug-class (Project 862) oceanographic research ships [AGOR] (4 in *reserve*)
Bldr: Stocznia Polnocna, Gdansk, Poland (In serv. 5-78 to 6-9-83)

DONUZLAV	*PERSEY*
GIDROLOG	*SENEZH*
GORIZONT	STVOR
MARSHAL GELOVANI	VITSE-ADMIRAL VORONTSOV (ex-*Briz*)
NIKOLAY MATUSEVICH	*VIZIR*
PEGAS	

D: 1,960 tons (2,490 fl) **S:** 15.6 kts **Dim:** 82.50 (75.80 pp) × 13.50 × 3.97
Electronics: Radar: 2 Don-2 nav.
M: 2 Zgoda-Sulzer 12AB 25/30 diesels; 2 CP props; 4,400 bhp (3,600 sust.)—2 125-shp electric low-speed motors—300-shp bow-thruster
Electric: 3,600 kw tot. (4 × 500-kw, 4 × 400-kw diesel sets)

Donuzlav—at Sevastopol' Hartmut Ehlers, 7-00

Stvor Boris Lemachko, 2002

Range: 4,430/17; 10,850/13 **Fuel:** 343 tons (406 max.) **Endurance:** 45 days
Crew: 4 officers., 54 enlisted (accomm. 8 officers, 38 unlicensed civilians, 20 scientists + 4 spare)

Remarks: Stated to be intended for "complex oceanographic research; exploration of the sea bed and sampling of soils; gravimetric studies; hydrographic and geophysical research, including the removal and implanting of oceanographic buoys; collection of navigational and hydrographic data; and inshore hydrographic surveys by [use of the] embarked two Project 727 glass-reinforced plastic-hulled cutters." *Briz* was renamed *Vitse-Admiral Vorontsov* in 1985. *Stvor* and *Donuzlav* are assigned to the Black Sea Fleet and *Gorizont* and *Vizir* to the Northern Fleet, with the latter inactive. *Nikolay Matusevich* and *Persey* are laid up at Kronshtadt; and *Pegas* is active in the Pacific Fleet. *Marshal Gelovani* began a 45-day environmental survey of the Sea of Okhotsk in 10-00 under the joint Russian-German Kuriles and Sea of Okhotsk Experiment program; as of 4-00, she was the only active Pacific Fleet oceanographic research ship. Even those still nominally in commission seldom operate.
Hull systems: As completed were 1,842 tons light, 2,435 fl. Have a quadrantial davit over the stern ramp with 4-ton lift, two 5-ton booms, several oceanographic davits, three echo sounders, and six laboratories. Have deck reinforcements for three twin 25-mm 80-cal. 2M-3M AA. *Zodiak* was fitted about 1985 with a large gantry at the stern to handle a towed object and had the main deck superstructure extended aft.
Disposals: Class name–ship *Yug* was converted to an intelligence collector by 1989, followed by *Mangyshlak* by 1990 (see under [AGI]). *Pluton* and *Strelets* of this class, previously assigned to the Baltic Fleet, were transferred to the Federal Border Guard in 8-97 and are now based at Murmansk, from where they are used to conduct economic exclusion zone (EEZ) patrols; see under [WPS]. *Gals* appears to have been discarded by 2001. *Tayga* and the decommissioned *Zodiak* had been stricken by 2005.

♦ 2 Akademik Krylov–class (Project 852 and 856) oceanographic research ships [AGOR] (In *reserve*)
Bldr: A. Warski SY, Szczecin, Poland

	In serv.
ADMIRAL VLADIMIRSKIY	1974
LEONID DEMIN	1979

Leonid Demin—in Baltic while escorting Kilo-class submarine *Yunes* to Iran M.O.D. Bonn, 12-96

D: 6,580 tons (9,120 fl) **S:** 20.4 kts (19 sust.) **Dim:** 147.80 × 18.60 × 6.26–6.40
Electronics: Radar: 3 Don-2 nav.
M: 4 diesels; 2 props; 16,000 bhp
Range: 18,000/15 **Endurance:** 45 days
Crew: 90 tot. (civilian) + 80 scientists (accomm. for 250 tot.)

Remarks: Among the largest ships of their type in any navy. *Leonid Demin* escorted the third Iranian Kilo-class submarine from the Baltic to Iran between 11-96 and 1-97 but has not operated since returning to Kronshtadt. *Admiral Vladimirskiy* has not operated since at least the mid-1990s.
Hull systems: Equipped with a helicopter hangar and flight deck, two Project 726 survey launches, and 26 laboratories totaling 900 m^2. Have two cargo holds and a 7-ton cargo crane forward. *Demin,* delivered in 1978, has a pointed stern, adding about 2 m to the overall length listed above.
Disposals: Black Sea Fleet unit *Akademik Krylov* was sold to a Greek commercial operator in 1993, Baltic Fleet unit *Mikhail Krupskiy* was stricken 1-9-95, and Pacific Fleet unit *Leonid Sobelyev* was stricken 31-7-96 (and sold to India for scrap in 8-97). *Ivan Kruzhenstern* was placed in unmaintained reserve at Kronshtadt during 10-98 and has apparently since been stricken.

AUXILIARIES *(continued)*

♦ 3 Nikolay Zubov–class (Project 850M) oceanographic research ships [AGOR] (1 in *reserve*)
Bldr: A. Warski SY, Szczecin, Poland

	In serv.
ANDREY VIL'KITSKIY	1966
BORIS DAVYDOV	1967
SEMEN DEZHNEV	1968

Andrey Vil'kitskiy—visiting St. Petersburg H&L Van Ginderen, 1995

D: 2,674 tons (3,021–3,123 fl) **S:** 16.5 kts **Dim:** 89.70 × 13.00 × 4.80
Electronics:
Radar: *Vil'kitskiy:* 2 Don-2 nav.—*Dezhnev:* 2 MR-212/201 Vaygach-U (Palm Frond) nav.
Sonar: MG-329 hull-mounted HF; NEL-5 and NEL-6 echo sounders
M: 2 Zgoda-Sulzer 8TD-48 diesels; 2 props; 4,800 bhp
Electric: 960 kw tot. (3 × 320-kw diesel sets)
Range: 9,000/15.3; 10,000/13 **Endurance:** 40 days
Crew: 68 tot. (civilian) + up to 26 scientific party (146 tot. accomm.)

Remarks: Assigned to the Northern Fleet.
Hull systems: Could originally carry four Project 727U or 338M survey launches, but now have only two. Have nine laboratories, totaling 120 m^2, along with two 7-ton and two 5-ton booms, nine 0.5- to 1.2-ton oceanographic-equipment davits, and 600 m^3 capacity total in two holds. The after platform, *not* for helicopters, was larger in the later ships.
Disposals: Sister *Vasiliy Golovnin* was stricken from the Black Sea Fleet in 1991 and later taken over by Ukraine under the name *Sviatov Nikolay;* by 8-94, the ship was in derelict condition at Sevastopol'. Northern Fleet unit *Aleksey Chirikov* was stricken 30-7-93, and Pacific Fleet unit *Fedor Litke* on 31-7-96. *Faddey Bellingsgauzen* and *Nikolay Zubov* have also been retired. Three others, now stricken, served as intelligence collectors.

♦ 1 Modified Sorum–class (Project 1454) hydrographic survey ship [AGS]
Bldr: Yaroslavl Zavod (In serv. 30-10-87)

GS-31 (ex-OS-572)

GS-31—as OS-572 M.O.D. U.K., 6-88

D: 1,250 tons (1,696 fl) **S:** 14 kts **Dim:** 59.10 (55.50 pp) × 12.60 × 4.60
Electronics: Radar: 2 Don-2 nav.
M: 2 Type 25-DB 2 (6ChN 30/38) diesels, electric drive; 1 prop; 2,500 shp (1,850 sust.)
Range: 6,700/13 **Fuel:** 322 tons **Crew:** 60 tot. (accomm.)

Remarks: Built as a trials platform for towed passive linear hydrophone (towed array) research and development. Variant of a standard ocean tug design, but with the forecastle deck extended to the stern, where a raised poop housed the array and towing winch. After several years of inactivity, was redesignated a hydrographic survey vessel in 1997 and now presumably operates in that role. Assigned to the Northern Fleet.

♦ 20 Finik-class (Project 872) hydrographic survey ships [AGS] (7 in *reserve*)
Bldr: Stocznia Polnocna, Gdansk, Poland (In serv. 1979–81)

GS-44	GS-87	GS-294	*GS-392*	*GS-402*
GS-47	*GS-270*	GS-297	GS-397	*GS-403*
GS-84	GS-272	*GS-301*	*GS-399*	GS-404
GS-86	GS-278	GS-388	*GS-400*	GS-405

Finik-class GS-86—at Sevastopol', with black hull and white superstructure Hartmut Ehlers, 8-00

Finik-class GS-294—note the beachable workboat stowed athwartships abaft the buoy hatch JMSDF, 10-94

D: 950 tons (1,186 fl) **S:** 13.8 kts **Dim:** 61.30 × 11.80 (10.80 wl) × 3.28
Electronics: Radar: 2 Don-2 nav.
M: 2 Cegielski-Sulzer diesels; 2 CP props; 1,920 bhp—2 75-kw electric motors for quiet, 6-kt operations—130-kw bow-thruster
Electric: 675 kVA tot. **Range:** 3,000/13; 4,800/11 **Endurance:** 15 days
Crew: 5 officers, 23 unlicensed (civilian)

Remarks: Polish B-91 design. GS = *Gidrograficheskoye Sudno* (Hydrographic Survey Ship). Fleet assignments include GS-44, -47, -84, -270, -272, -397, and -404 in the Pacific Fleet; GS-301 in the Caspian Flotilla; and GS-87, -278, -297, -388, -392, -399, -400, -403, and -405 in the Northern Fleet. One was built for East Germany and four for Poland (two civilian). Black Sea Fleet unit GS-265 was redesignated OS-265 as a trials ship for service as ammunition transport VTR-75. Several Pacific Fleet units, including GS-47 and GS-84, have been employed carrying commercial cargoes.
Hull systems: Intended for navigational buoy-tending and hydrographic survey duties, for which four echo sounders are fitted. Up to three fiberglass 3-dwt utility landing craft can be stowed on the buoy working deck beneath the 7-ton crane. Have hydrological, hydrographic, and cartographic facilities.

Note: The Russian Navy Hydrographic Service ships of the Finik, Moma, Biya, Kamenka, Samara, and other classes are used as hydrographic survey ships and navigation tenders, handling buoys, marking channels, and so forth. They set and retrieve some 2,000 buoys and 4,000 spar buoys that are taken up for the winter months and, prior to 1992, supported and maintained 600 lighthouses, 150 noise beacons, and 8,000 navigation buoys. Most can carry from two to six navigation buoys. In addition, they are equipped to take basic oceanographic and meteorological samplings.
The two Ayristo (NATO Vinograd)-class inshore survey ships can now be found under [YGS] in the Service Craft section.
Disposals: GS-401 is now in commercial service in the Ukraine. GS-260, -280 and -398 had been stricken by 2005.

♦ 6 Biya-class (Project 871) hydrographic survey ships [AGS] (1 in *reserve*)
Bldr: Stocznia Polnocna, Gdansk, Poland (In serv. 1972–76)

GS-200	*GS-206*	GS-214
GS-202	GS-210	GS-273

Biya-class GS-214—note that the buoy crane is mounted at the forecastle break in this class M.O.D. Bonn, 7-91

D: 600 tons (723 fl) **S:** 13 kts **Dim:** 54.30 × 9.56 × 2.65
Electronics: Radar: 1 Don-2 nav.
M: 2 diesels; 2 CP props; 1,100 bhp **Range:** 2,000/11
Fuel: 90 tons **Endurance:** 15 days **Crew:** 25 tot. (civilian)

AUXILIARIES *(continued)*

Biya-class GS-273—at Sevastopol', with a Flamingo-class launch alongside
Boris Lemachko, 5-00

Remarks: GS = *Gidrograficheskoye Sudno* (Hydrographic Survey Ship). Eighteen were originally built for Soviet Navy use. GS-202 is assigned to the Caspian Flotilla, GS-273 to the Black Sea Fleet, GS-200 and -210 to the Pacific Fleet, and the others to the Northern Fleet.
Hull systems: Similar to the Kamenka class, but with a longer superstructure and less buoy-handling space. Carry one survey launch and have one 5-ton crane. Laboratory space: 15 m^2.
Disposals: One unit was transferred to Guinea-Bissau, one (GC-186) to Cuba in 1980, and one to Cape Verde in 1980. GS-275 was stricken from the Baltic Fleet 3-7-92 and GS-198 from the Pacific Fleet 5-7-94. GS-82 was stricken 10-1-96 and transferred to Ukraine in 1997. GS-204 and -208 were stricken during 1994 and GS-212 in 1996. GS-193 and -194 had been stricken by 2005.

♦ 7 Kamenka-class (Project 870) hydrographic survey ships [AGS] (6 in *reserve*)
Bldr: Stocznia Polnocna, Gdansk, Poland (In serv. 1968–72)

GS-66	*MGS-113* (ex-*Bel'bek*)	*GS-211*
GS-78	*GS-118*	
GS-107	*GS-199*	

Kamenka-class GS-118—laid up at Kronshtadt Boris Lemachko, 2000

D: 590 tons (703 fl) **S:** 13.7 kts **Dim:** 53.50 × 9.40 × 2.62
Electronics: Radar: 1 Don-2 nav.
M: 2 Cegielski-Sulzer 6 NVD-48 diesels; 2 CP props; 1,765 bhp
Range: 1,720/13 **Endurance:** 15 days **Crew:** 24 tot. (civilian)

Remarks: GS = *Gidrograficheskoye Sudno* (Hydrographic Survey Ship). Similar to the Biya class (Project 871), but with more facilities for stowing and handling buoys. Have no survey launch. One 5-ton crane is fitted. GS-103 is in the Black Sea Fleet; GS-66 and GS-107 in the Baltic Fleet; GS-78 and -118 in the Northern Fleet; and MGS-113 and GS-199 and -211 in the Pacific Fleet. All except GS-78 remain in reserve status.
Disposals: One sister, *Buk,* formerly served in the East German Navy and now is employed by the German Water Navigation Board Maritime Police (*Schiffahrtspolizei*). Northern Fleet unit GS-74 was stricken 5-7-94. The naval-manned Pacific Fleet unit *Astronom* was stricken 30-7-93 and sold commercial. Baltic Fleet unit GS-207 was stricken 1-9-95. Sister *Vern'er* (GS-108) was transferred to Estonia as EVA-108, and Black Sea Fleet unit GS-273 was stricken 10-1-96 and had been transferred to Ukraine by summer 1997. GS-103, GS-194, GS-198 and GS-269 were stricken during 2004–5.

♦ 6 Moma-class (Project 861) hydrographic survey ships [AGS] (1 in *reserve*)
Bldr: Stocznia Polnocna, Gdansk, Poland (In serv. 1967–74)

Andromeda	*Askol'd*
Antares	Kril'on
Antarktida	Mars

Moma-class Mars—off Murmansk NAVPIC-Holland, 10-01

D: 1,140 tons (1,502 fl) **S:** 15 kts
Dim: 73.30 (64.20 pp) × 11.20 (10.80 wl) × 3.80
Electronics: Radar: 2 Don-2 nav.
M: 2 Zgoda-Sulzer 6TD48 diesels; 2 CP props; 3,600 bhp
Range: 8,000/11 **Endurance:** 25 days **Crew:** 41 tot. (civilian)

Remarks: Carry one survey launch and a 7-ton crane, and have four laboratories, totaling 35 m^2.
Disposals: *Okean* (ex-SSV-518) and *Berezan'* were transferred prior to 1992 to the custody of cities in the Ukraine for use as navigational aids tenders, with the former scrapped during 7-01 and the latter transferred to the Ukrainian Navy. Sister *Sever* was stricken from the Pacific Fleet in 1988, and *Anadyr'* was stricken in 1984 after going aground. Pacific Fleet unit *Zapol'yare* was stricken 5-7-94, Northern Fleet unit *El'ton* on 1-9-95, and Pacific Fleet unit *Al'tayr* on 31-7-96. The Pacific Fleet's *Rybachiy* (ex-*Odograf*), modified with oceanographic research equipment and naval manned, was stricken 16-8-97. Sister *Liman* was redesignated as an intelligence collector in 1999. Black Sea unit *Arktika* capsized and sank in port at Novorossiysk on 10-12-02 due to high winds and ice accretion; there were no personnel losses. *Cheleken, Kolguyev, Morzhovets,* and *Taymyr* were stricken by 2005.

♦ 3 Ob'-class (Project B-320/B-320 II) hospital ships [AH]
Bldr: A. Warski SY, Szczecin, Poland

	In serv.
Irtysh	10-8-90
Svir'	7-89
Yenisey	1-81

Yenisey—at Sevastopol' Hartmut Ehlers, 3-02

Svir'—at Severomorsk Boris Lemachko, 2000

D: 9,430 tons (11,623–11,977 fl) **S:** 20 kts (19.8 sust.)
Dim: 152.60 (142.00 pp) × 19.40 × 6.39
Electronics: Radar: 3 Don-2 (*Irtysh:* MR-312 Nayada) nav.
M: 2 Type 12 ZV 40/48, 12-cyl., 750-rpm diesels; 2 CP props; 15,600 bhp
Electric: 5,000 kVA tot. (4 × 1,250-kVA diesel sets)
Range: 8,000/19; 10,000/14 **Fuel:** 2,125 tons **Endurance:** 40 days
Crew: 124 ship's crew + 83 medical personnel, up to 300 patients, or up to 650 passengers

Remarks: Intended to "provide medical and recreational facilities." Have also been employed as personnel transports. Have civilian crews but carry uniformed naval medical personnel. Later two are Project B-320 II, implying a modification to the basic design; external differences are minor. *Irtysh* is in the Pacific Fleet, *Svir'* in the Northern Fleet, and *Yenisey* in the Black Sea Fleet. The ships are on offer for charter for humanitarian purposes. *Svir'* had a serious fire 10-3-99, with three deaths. Were being maintained with crews of 75 in 1998.

AUXILIARIES *(continued)*

Hull systems: Normally have 100 sick beds, plus 200 berths for recuperating personnel that can be converted to sickbeds; in an emergency, another 150 can be added. There are seven operating rooms and five laboratories. The ships have a decompression chamber and a sauna, as well as a collapsable swimming pool that is deployed over the side. Degaussing gear and NBC warfare filters are fitted. The hangar aft can accommodate a Hormone-C or Helix-D utility helicopter. Bow-thrusters fitted, as are fin stabilizers. There are a physical therapy facility, two gymnasiums, two pools, a library, and a 100-seat auditorium. Are equipped with Rumb radio direction-finder, M3-B echo sounder, KEL-1 automatic log, and Kurs-10A-1 gyrocompass. One source gives the radar designations as MR-212, MR-216, and MR-250.
Disposals: Class name-ship *Ob'* (commissioned 28-3-80) was stricken 16-8-97.

♦ 2 Neon Antonov–class (Project 1595) cargo ships [AK]
Bldr: Nikolayevsk-na-Amur Zavod

	In serv.
DVINA	. . .
IRBIT	1975

Dvina—at Severomorsk Boris Lemachko, 5-00

D: 2,420 tons light (4,040 fl) **S:** 18 kts **Dim:** 96.30 (87.20 pp) × 14.50 × 5.10
Electronics: Radar: 1 Volga (Don Kay) nav.; 1 Mius (Spin Trough) nav.
M: 2 Type 67B (12DRPN 23/2 × 30) diesels; 1 prop; 7,500 bhp
Range: 5,000/18; 8,750/14 **Endurance:** 25 days
Crew: 45 tot. + 18 passengers

Remarks: Specialized supply ships for remote garrisons in the Pacific region. Both were chartered commercial in 1992, but *Dvina* now serves the Northern Fleet and *Irbit* has apparently been returned from the charterer. Eight sisters operate with the Federal Border Guard in the Pacific area.
Hull systems: Carry one Project 1785 logistics landing craft (36 tons light, 78.2 tons fl; 21.90 × 5.81 × 1.00 m; one 470-bhp diesel for 9.8 kts) starboard aft and a workboat port aft, with a 50-ton boat derrick to handle them. The hull has a bulbous forefoot and two cargo holds forward, tended by only two 5-ton derricks. The pilothouse is equipped with MPK-455M navigational periscopes port and starboard. Cargo capacity: 804 tons.
Combat systems: The armament of one twin 30-mm 65-cal. AK-230 AA gunmount and two twin 12.7-mm Ütes-M machinegun mounts was removed by 1992.

♦ 3 Yuniy Partizan–class (Project 740/2B) cargo ships [AK] (1 in *reserve*)
Bldr: Turnu-Severin SY and Oltenitza SY, Romania (In serv. 1975–78)

	In serv.
PECHORA	1976
TURGAY	1975
UFA	30-6-77

Turgay—laid up at Sevastopol' Hartmut Ehlers, 7-00

D: 2,800 tons std. (3,947 fl) **S:** 12.8 kts **Dim:** 88.75 (80.25 pp) × 12.80 × 4.60
Electronics: Radar: 1 Don-2 nav.
M: 1 Zgoda-Sulzer 8 TAD 36 diesel; 1 prop; 2,080 bhp **Electric:** 306 kw tot.
Range: 4,800/10 **Fuel:** 125 tons **Endurance:** 20 days **Crew:** 35 tot. (civilian)

Remarks: 2,079 grt/2,150 dwt. Sister *Pinega,* converted to a missile transport (Project 10680) and renamed *Vitse-Admiral Fomin,* was scrapped in 1995. Pacific Fleet unit *Ufa,* still naval owned, has been employed in commercial cargo-carrying since 1992. *Turgay* is laid up at Sevastopol', and *Pechora* is assigned to the Northern Fleet. Twenty sisters were constructed for civilian service.
Hull systems: Have three 10-ton cranes, one of which can be rigged to lift 28 tons. Cargo volume: 3,200 m^3. Originally intended to be able to carry 58 standard cargo containers.

Note: Cargo ships and larger dry cargo-carrying service craft are usually referred to as VTR (*Voyenyy Transport,* Military Transport).

♦ 1 Amguema-class (Project 550) icebreaking cargo ship [AK]
Bldr: Kherson SY (In serv. 9-74)

YAUZA

Yauza 1976

D: 5,118 tons light (14,470 fl) **S:** 15 kts
Dim: 133.10 (123.00 pp) × 18.80 (18.50 wl) × 7.60 (max.)
Electronics: Radar: 2 Don-2 nav.
M: 4 Type 3D-100 diesels, electric drive; 1 prop; 7,200 shp
Electric: 880 kw tot. (4 × 220-kw diesel sets) **Range:** 7,000/15
Fuel: 1,000 tons **Endurance:** 90 days **Crew:** 58 tot. (civilian)

Remarks: 6,280-dwt passenger/cargo ship, assigned to the Northern Fleet. Not sighted in many years but reportedly still in use. Can break 0.6-m ice. Two 60-ton, two 10-ton, and six 5-ton cranes. Navigational equipment includes an SRP-5 HFD/F, NEL-5 echo sounder, and Kurs-3 gyrocompass.

♦ 2 Polnocny-B-class (Project 771A) vehicle cargo ships [AK]
Bldr: Stocznia Polnocna, Gdansk, Poland (In serv. 15-6-67 to 30-11-70)

VTR-140 (ex-MDK- . . .) VTR-141 (ex-MDK- . . .)

D: 558 tons light; 640 tons std. (884 fl) **S:** 18 kts
Dim: 75.00 (70.00 wl) × 9.00 (8.60 wl) × 1.20 (fwd; 2.40 aft; 2.07 mean)
A: 1 twin 30-mm 65-cal. AK-230 AA
Electronics: Radar: 1 Mius (Spin Trough) nav.; 1 MR-104 Rys' (Drum Tilt) gun f.c.
M: 2 Type 40DM diesels; 2 props; 4,400 bhp **Range:** 700/18; 2,000/16
Crew: 5 officers, 32 enlisted + 60–180 troops

Remarks: Former medium landing ships redesignated as cargo ships. VTR = *Voyenyy Transport* (Military Transport). Survivors of 13 Project 771 and 12 Project 771A units delivered to the Soviet Union 1967–70. Assigned to the Black Sea Fleet. A third unit may be in service, assigned to the Northern Fleet
Hull systems: Differed from the Polnocny-A (Project 770D and 770MA) in having concave bow-flare. Has a door only in the bow, and the hull has a "beak" projecting forward below the waterline at the bow to aid in beaching. Hatches to the upper deck are for loading and ventilation only. Cargo: 237 tons max., including six tanks or 180 troops and their equipment; 30 vehicle crew are carried with the tank loadout. The vehicle deck is 44.3 m long, 5.3 m wide, and 3.6 m high.

Disposal notes: *Vytegrales*-class cargo ship *Yamal* (ex-*Tosnolets*), reconverted from a "rescue ship" in 1995, had ceased to be under naval ownership by 1-02. The last MP-6-class (Project 572) cargo ship, *Khoper*, was stricken by 2005. Pacific Fleet sister *Bureya* (ex-VTR-296) was sold in Japan in 1993, while Baltic Fleet *Bira* (ex-OS-10) was stricken in 1996, and *Vologda* was stricken 1-9-95 and sold for commercial service. Keyla-class (Project 1849) cargo ship *Tvertsa* was stricken from the Pacific Fleet 24-6-91, *Ussuri* was reportedly sold commercial during 1992, and *Mezen'* was stricken from Black Sea Fleet 10-1-96 and transferred to Ukraine. *Ritsa* was converted as a training ship for intelligence collection personnel and was derelict at Sevastopol' by mid-1997. *Ponoy, Severka, Unzha,* and *Yeruslan* had all been stricken by 2004.

♦ 1 Kaliningradneft'-class oiler [AO]
Bldr: Rauma-Repola, Rauma, Finland (In serv. 5-83)

VYAZ'MA (ex-*Katun*)

D: 3,150 tons light; 4,820 tons std. (8,913 fl) **S:** 14.4 kts
Dim: 115.50 (112.00 pp) × 17.00 × 7.00
Electronics: Radar: 1 Okean-A nav.; 1 Okean-B nav.
M: 1 Russkiy–Burmeister & Wain 5 DKRP 50/110-2 diesel; 1 prop; 3,850 bhp
Electric: 805 kw tot. **Range:** 5,000/14 **Fuel:** 452 tons **Endurance:** 50 days
Crew: 12 officers, 28 unlicensed (all civilians)

Remarks: 4,821 grt/5,873 dwt. One of the last two built of a class that had more than two dozen units delivered to the USSR Ministry of Fisheries 1979–82. Assigned to the Northern Fleet.

AUXILIARIES *(continued)*

Vyaz'ma—at Severomorsk Boris Lemachko, 2000

Hull systems: Is not capable of alongside refueling but does have two over-the-stern liquid replenishment rigs, although she can refuel ships moored alongside, dead in the water. There is no provision for underway solid stores replenishment. Carries 5,750 m^3 (5,263 tons) of liquid cargo in 10 tanks and 80 m^3 of dry cargo in one hold within the forecastle. Two cargo pumps have combined 400-m^3/hr capacity. Has a 1,600-ton water ballast capacity.
Disposals: *Argun'* (ex-*Kallevere*), which formerly operated with the Pacific Fleet, was chartered to the Far East Shipping Line during 1991 and was sold to a commercial operator in 1996; the ship was arrested at Cape Town in 1999 and auctioned to pay debts on 23-5-00.

♦ 2 Dubna-class oilers [AO]

Bldr: Rauma-Repola, Rauma, Finland

	In serv.
DUBNA	1974
PECHENGA	1978

Pechenga JMSDF, via *Ships of the World,* 2005

D: 4,300 tons light (11,140 fl) **S:** 15.5 kts
Dim: 130.10 (126.30 pp) × 20.00 × 7.20
Electronics: Radar: 2 Don-2 nav.
M: 1 Russkiy Dizel 8DRPH 23/230, 8-cyl. diesel; 1 prop; 6,000 bhp
Electric: 1,485 kVA tot. **Range:** 7,000/16; 8,200/12
Fuel: 1,056 m^3 **Endurance:** 60 days **Crew:** 62 tot. (civilian)

Remarks: 6,022 grt/6,500 dwt. Soviet type designation: VTR (*Voyenyy Tanker,* Military Tanker). Both are assigned to the Pacific Fleet. *Pechenga* had the solid stores transfer system removed during 1993–94 and is employed primarily in carrying commercial liquid cargoes.
Hull systems: Cargo capacity is 5,300 tons total: 2,100 tons fuel oil, 2,080 tons diesel, 120 tons lube oil (in four grades), 900 tons fresh water, 50 tons provisions, and 50 tons spares. Have 27 cargo tanks. There are four 250-ton/hr, two 100-ton/hr, and two 20-ton/hr cargo pumps. *Dubna* (but not *Pechenga*) can transfer 1-ton loads from constant-tension stations forward. Supply liquid replenishment from one station on port and starboard, amidships, and over the stern. Additional berths are provided for "turnover crews." The original commercial Okean-series radars were replaced.
Disposals: Black Sea Fleet unit *Sventa* had become the Ukrainian *Kerch'* (U 758) by 8-97. Pacific Fleet unit *Irkut* was stricken 31-7-96 and sold for commercial service.

♦ 5 Boris Chilikin–class (Project 1559V and 1593*) replenishment oilers [AO] (1 in *reserve*)

Bldr: Baltic Zavod, St. Petersburg

	In serv.		In serv.
BORIS BUTOMA*	1978	SERGEY OSIPOV (ex-*Dnestr*)	1977
GENRIKH GASANOV	1975	VLADIMIR KOLYACHITSKIY	1972
IVAN BUBNOV	1974		

Vladimir Kolyachitskiy JMSDF, via *Ships of the World,* 1-01

D: 6,950 tons light (22,460 fl) **S:** 16.7 kts (16 sust.)
Dim: 162.36 (150.02 pp) × 21.41 × 9.04
Electronics: Radar: 2 Volga (Don-Kay) nav.
M: 1 Cegielski-Sulzer 6 DKRN-74/160, 6-cyl. diesel; 1 prop; 9,600 bhp
Electric: 1,200 kw tot. (1 × 500-kw gas turbine set; 2 × 300-kw, 1 × 100-kw diesel sets)
Range: 10,000/16 **Endurance:** 90 days **Crew:** 75 tot. (civilian)

Remarks: 16,300 dwt. Soviet type designation: VTR (*Voyenyy Tanker,* Military Tanker). Naval version of the merchant *Velikiy Oktyabr* class. *Dnestr* was renamed on 5-4-97 in honor of the former civilian captain of the *Genrikh Gasanov,* who died aboard his ship in 11-96 after more than 20 years aboard her. *Boris Butoma,* completed 30-10-78, differs from the others in minor detail. She and *Vladimir Kolyachitskiy* are assigned to the Pacific Fleet, *Ivan Bubnov* to the Black Sea Fleet, and the other two to the Northern Fleet.
Hull systems: Equipment varies: early units had solid-stores, constant-tension rigs on both sides forward; later units had the rig only to starboard, with a liquid transfer station to port. All have port and starboard liquid-replenishment stations amidships and can replenish liquids over the stern. Cargo: 8,250 tons fuel oil, 2,050 tons diesel fuel, 1,000 tons jet fuel (kerosene), 450 tons fresh water, 450 tons boiler feedwater, 250 tons lube oil, and 220 tons dry cargo (primarily provisions). There are two 3-ton electric cranes forward.
Combat systems: *Bubnov* and *Gasanov* were the last completed and appeared in merchant colors, without two twin 57-mm automatic gunmounts, MR-302 Rubka (Strut Curve) air/surface-search radar, or MR-103 Bars (Muff Cob) fire-control radars; that equipment was removed from the other ships by the end of the 1970s, although several retained their gunhouses for a short period.
Disposals: Black Sea Fleet unit *Boris Chilikin* had become the Ukrainian U 757 by 8-97.

♦ 4 Altay-class (Project 160) oilers [AO]

Bldr: Rauma-Repola, Rauma, Finland

	In serv.	Fleet		In serv.	Fleet
ILIM	1971	Pacific	PRUT	1972	Northern
KOLA	1967	Northern	YEL'NYA	1971	Baltic

Kola H&L Van Ginderen, 1-97

D: 2,828 tons light (7,225 fl) **S:** 14.2 kts
Dim: 106.07 (97.00 pp) × 15.40 × 6.75
Electronics:
Radar: 2 Don-2 nav.
Sonar: MGL-25 underwater telephone; NEL-5 echo sounder
M: 1 Valmet–Burmeister & Wain BM-550 VTBN-110 diesel; 1 prop; 3,250 bhp (2,900 sust.)
Electric: 638 kw tot. (2 × 260-kw, 1 × 22-kw diesel sets; 1 × 96-kw turbogenerator
Range: 6,000/12 **Fuel:** 264 tons **Endurance:** 20 days **Crew:** 52 tot. (civilians)

Remarks: 3,670 grt/5,045 dwt. More than two dozen sisters served in the Soviet merchant marine. *Yel'nya* was stricken in 1992 and the hulk was briefly seized by Ukrainian dissidents at Sevastopol' during 4-93; she was subsequently refitted for further service and in 7-96 transited to the Baltic Fleet and is now based at Baltiysk, from which she is primarily employed in fueling the Russian fishing fleet, although she was reported in 11-01 to be badly in need of a refit.
Hull systems: An A-frame kingpost forward was added to *Izhora, Ilim,* and *Prut* during the late 1970s, permitting them to refuel one ship at a time on either beam; the others could only fuel alongside while dead in the water. Transfer gear, however, has been removed from *Ilim* and probably the others as well. All are also able to replenish over the stern. Have 10 cargo tanks and were originally equipped to transport 1,300 tons of heavy oil, 2,700 tons of distilled fuel, 200 tons of water, and 100 tons of lube oil. Differ in details, heights of masts, etc. The main propulsion engine bears the Russian designation 5DKRN-50/100. They carry 95 tons potable water for own use.
Disposals: Pacific Fleet unit *Yegorlik* was sold commercial in 1996. Black Sea Fleet unit *Izhora* was chartered commercial 17-7-91 but may remain naval property.

♦ 2 Olekma-class oilers [AO]

Bldr: Rauma-Repola, Rauma, Finland (In serv. 1964)

IMAN OLEKMA

Iman Hartmut Ehlers, 3-02

D: 2,300 tons light (6,440 fl) **S:** 14 kts **Dim:** 105.40 × 14.80 × 6.20
Electronics: Radar: 1 Don-2 nav.; 1 . . . nav.
M: 1 Burmeister & Wain 550 VTBF-110 diesel; 1 prop; 2,900 bhp
Electric: 295 kw tot. (2 × 120-kw diesel sets, 1 × 55-kw emergency diesel set)

AUXILIARIES *(continued)*

Range: 4,000/14; 6,000/10 **Fuel:** 257 tons **Endurance:** 20 days
Crew: 40 tot. (accomm. for 52)

Remarks: 3,360 grt/4,400 dwt. Assigned to the Black Sea Fleet. Near-sister *Pevek*-class *Zolotoi Rog* was stricken in 1994 and sold for scrap in Turkey.
Hull systems: *Olekma* was modernized in 1978 with an A-frame abaft the bridge to permit underway fueling of one ship at a time on either beam; can also refuel over the stern. Cargo capacity is 4,482 tons total: 1,500 tons fuel oil, 1,500 tons diesel, 150 tons lube oil, 500 tons fresh water, 50 tons dry stores. There are two 250 ton/hr cargo pumps and one 3-ton and three 1-ton cargo derricks.

♦ 5 Uda-class (Project 577) oilers [AO]
Bldr: Karamaki Zavod, Vyborg SY (In serv. 1962–67)

	In serv.	Fleet		In serv.	Fleet
DUNAY	12-65	Pacific	TEREK	7-62	Northern
KOIDA	7-66	Black Sea	VISHERA	6-67	Pacific
LENA	12-66	Baltic			

Lena—with extra A-frame kingpost amidships to support refueling hoses
South African Navy, 4-97

D: 2,910 tons light (7,160 fl) **S:** 17 kts **Dim:** 121.2 × 15.8 × 6.3
Electronics: Radar: 2 Don-2 nav.—*Lena* also: 1 MR-212/201 Vaygach-U (Palm Frond) nav.
M: 2 Type 58D (16DPN 23/2 × 30) diesels; 2 props; 9,000 bhp
Range: 4,000/14 **Endurance:** 30 days **Crew:** 74 tot. (civilians)

Remarks: Type designation: VTR (*Voyenyy Tanker,* Military Tanker). Three others were transferred to Indonesia during the early 1960s and later scrapped. *Lena* cruised to Cape Town and back during 1997. *Koida* was stricken 30-7-93 but was refitted late in the 1990s and is based at Sevastopol'.
Hull systems: *Dunay, Vishera,* and *Lena* have been equipped with a second A-frame kingpost amidships for underway liquid replenishment. Cargo capacity includes 2,000 tons of fuel oil, 800 tons of distillate fuel, 100 tons of lube oil, 300 tons of feedwater, 200 tons of potable water, and 100 tons of stores.
Combat systems: Equipped to carry eight 57-mm AA, but none has been mounted since the early 1960s.

Disposal note: Sister *Sheksna* was retired by 2005. The *Berezina* class (Project 1833) replenishment oiler *Berezina* (154) was scrapped in Turkey during 2003.

♦ 2 Belyanka-class (Project 1151.0) nuclear waste–disposal ships [AOS]
Bldr: Karamaki Zavod, Vyborg

	In serv.
AMUR	29-11-87
PINEGA	17-7-87

Amur Boris Lemachko, 1991

D: 6,680 tons std. (8,250 fl) **S:** 15.3 kts **Dim:** 130.3 (123.10 pp) × 17.34 × 6.95
Electronics: Radar: 2 Kivach nav.
M: 2 Type 58E (16DPN 23/2 × 30) diesels; 1 prop; 9,000 bhp
Range: 4,000/14 **Endurance:** 25 days **Crew:** 86 tot. (civilian)

Remarks: Intended as waste nuclear-reactor plant coolant-water collection and spent fuel rod transport ships. *Amur,* based at Severodvinsk, has been employed to dump radioactive waste liquids into the Kara Sea east of Novaya Zemlya. *Pinega,* based in the Pacific Fleet area, has been converted with Japanese assistance for use in the at-sea disposal of low-level radioactive waste. A third unit was begun at Severodvinsk but was not completed.
Hull systems: Have a large electrohydraulic crane to handle containers with spent reactor rods. Cargo capacity: 1,070 tons. The 10.5 × 14.5 × 6.0-m cargo hold is tended by one KE39, 16-ton, 20-m-reach electrohydraulic crane.

♦ 4 Luza-class (Project 1541) missile fuel transports [AOS]
Bldr: Karamaki Zavod,Vyborg (In serv. 1960–62)

ALAMBAY BARGUZIN DON SELENGA

Alambay Boris Lemachko, 2002

Alambay JMSDF, 10-94

D: 926 tons light, 1,140 tons normal (1,540 fl) **S:** 12.2 kts
Dim: 62.20 × 10.00 × 3.63 **Electronics:** Radar: 1 Don-2 nav.
M: 2 diesels; 2 props; 1,600 bhp **Range:** 2,000/11 **Endurance:** 10 days
Crew: 4 officers, 36 unlicensed (civilian)

Remarks: Survivors of nine built. Originally designed to carry volatile liquids, including 357 tons of oxidizer and 152 tons of missile fuel, in 10 vertical cylindrical isolation tanks. *Alambay* and *Barguzin* (refitted in 1995) are in the Pacific Fleet, *Don* in the Black Sea Fleet, and *Selenga* in the Baltic. Some of these may be inactive or stricken.
Disposals: Northern Fleet units *Aragvi* and *Kama* were stricken 1-9-95, and three others had been retired by the early 1990s (*Oka, Sasima,* and *Yenisey,* the latter in 1978 after an accident).

♦ 4 Vala-class (Project 1783A) nuclear waste transports [AOS]
Bldr: Karamaki Zavod,Vyborg, and . . . Zavod, Vladivostok (In service: 1961–71)

TNT-11 TNT-19 TNT-23 TNT-29

Northern Fleet Vala-class unit—with pennant 12 NAVPIC-Holland, 10-01

AUXILIARIES *(continued)*

D: 1,080 tons light (2,310 fl) **S:** 11 kts **Dim:** 74.40 × 11.50 × 3.95
A: Provision for 2 twin 12.7-mm Utës-M mg
Electronics: Radar: 1 Don-2 nav.
M: 2 Type 1D46 (6DN 39/45) diesels; 2 props; 2,600 bhp
Range: 1,000/9 **Endurance:** 20 days **Crew:** 4 officers, 29 enlisted

Remarks: Carry up to 906 tons of waste liquids from nuclear propulsion plants and have been used for open-ocean dumping of low-level radioactive materials. All active units are assigned to the Northern Fleet. Several of these are inactive, and all are in need of replacement (and are reported to be significantly radioactive).
Disposals: Pacific Fleet unit TNT-27, which dumped radioactive materials in the Sea of Japan in 10-93, is no longer operational. TNT-25 has been derelict at Zvezdochka repair yard, Yagriy Island, Severodvinsk, since 1994, still with 450 tons of radioactive waste aboard. TNT-5, -8, -17, -22, and -42 have been stricken.

Note: Also used for nuclear waste transport and disposal are as many as two units (TNT-12 and -42) of the Zeya class (Project 1783), essentially a non-self-propelled version of the Vala class, and the smaller PEK-50-class barges, which hold only 50 tons of radioactive liquid each. Most of the survivors are in poor condition, and many are radioactively contaminated.

♦ 13 Amur-class (Project 304 and 304M*) repair ships [AR]
Bldr: A. Warski SY, Szczecin, Poland (In serv. 1968–78, 1981–88)

PM-30	PM-69*	PM-138
PM-34	PM-82	PM-140
PM-40	PM-86*	PM-156
PM-59*	PM-97*	
PM-64	PM-129	

Amur-class PM-138 Boris Lemachko Collection, 2001

Amur-class PM-86—a Baltic Fleet Project 304M Jaroslaw Cislak, 2000

D: 4,000 tons (5,490 fl) **S:** 14 kts **Dim:** 121.70 × 17.00 × 4.63
Electronics: Radar: 1 Don-2 nav.
M: 2 diesels; 1 prop; 2,990 bhp
Range: 7,800/10; 13,200/8 **Endurance:** 40 days
Crew: 208 tot. + up to 300 passengers

Remarks: PM = *Plavuchaya Masterskaya* (Floating Workshop). Early units did not have the passenger facilities. Serve surface ships and submarines with basic repair facilities and 280 tons of spare parts. Have two 3-ton cranes and, usually, one 1.5-ton crane. The fourth series (Project 304M or NATO Amur-II), consisting of PM-59, -69, -86, and -97, had an extra deckhouse atop the superstructure forward of the stack, squared-off stacks, a slightly flattened face to the forward side of the bridge superstructure, and only two new-style cranes. There are a great many more minor variations within the class. In addition to the units listed above, a PM-30 has been photographed in the Baltic, possibly a renumbering. PM-82 and PM-86 remain in use in the Baltic Fleet area, primarily as housing for officers and their families. Several of the above listed craft may no longer be operational.
Disposals: PM-94 and -164 had been stricken by 1996. Northern Fleet units PM-163 and -161 were stricken on 22-2-93 and 1-9-95, respectively, and PM-49 was derelict at Pavlowskaya Bukhta as of 10-96. Black Sea Fleet unit PM-9 was transferred to Ukraine 1-8-97. PM-5, -37, -81, and -92 (all but the latter having been nonoperational for several years) had been stricken by 2001. PM-56 and PM-75 had been scrapped by 2004.

♦ 6 Oskol class (Projects 300 and 303) [AR] (4 *nonoperational*)
Bldr: A. Warski SY, Szczecin, Poland (In serv. 1963–67)

PM-20	*PM-51*	*PM-63*
PM-26	*PM-62*	PM-146

Oskol-class PM-146—a flush-decked Project 303 unit French Navy, 1991

D: 2,034–2,100 tons (2,521–2,800 fl) **S:** 14 kts
Dim: 88.6 × 13.60 (12.00 wl) × 3.80–3.90
Electronics: Radar: 2 Don-2 nav.
M: 1 Zgoda-Sulzer 6TAD-48 diesel; 1 prop; 2,250 bhp
Range: 3,000/10 **Crew:** 60 tot. (137 accomm.)

Remarks: PM = *Plavuchaya Masterskaya* (Floating Workshop).Thirteen were built: six Project 300 (2,078 tons std./2,690 tons fl); two armed Project 301T (2,100 tons std./2,700 tons fl); and five flush-decked Project 303 (2,034 tons std./2,521 tons fl), of which PM-146 is one. All have one or two 3-ton cranes. PM-26 is assigned to the Black Sea Fleet and is berthed in the Sovetskaya Bukhta, Sevastopol'.
Disposals: Project 303/2 sister PM-147 was stricken from the Pacific Fleet 3-7-92. Black Sea Fleet unit PM-2 was transferred to the Ministry of Shipbuilding (and offered to Ukraine in 1997 but not accepted). PM-28 had been discarded by 1996. Pacific Fleet unit PM-148 was stricken 31-7-96. The remaining armed unit, Black Sea Fleet unit PM-24, was scrapped in Turkey beginning 15-10-97. PM-21 was deployed to Yemen at Aden during the late 1980s but returned to the Black Sea in 1991 and has since been stricken. The only Baltic Fleet unit (PM-68) was being scrapped as of 5-02.

♦ 2 Biriusa-class (Project 1175) cable layers [ARC] (1 *nonoperational*)
Bldr: Wärtsilä SY, Turku, Finland

	L	In serv.
Biriusa	29-11-85	20-6-86
Kem'	23-11-85	24-11-86

Kem'—at Vladivostok Boris Lemachko, 2000

D: 2,370 tons (fl) **S:** 11.8 kts **Dim:** 86.10 (78.70 pp) × 12.6 × 3.10
Electronics: Radar: 2 Mius (Spin Trough) nav.
M: Diesel-electric: 2 Wärtsilä Vasa 8R22 diesels; 2 Schottel azimuthal props; 1,700 shp—bow tunnel thruster
Crew: 48 tot. (civilian)

Remarks: 2,650 grt. Ordered 1-85. Both are in the Pacific Fleet. *Kem'* was overhauled in South Korea in 1994, but *Biriusa* was laid up by 1997 awaiting funding for a badly needed overhaul.
Hull systems: A lengthened version of the *Emba* class, with more-powerful engines, carrying twice as much cable (600 tons: 518 m^3 coiled, in two cable tanks), and equipped with a gantry over the bow cable. Have three 2-m-diameter bow cable sheaves and two 2-m-diameter cable drums. Propellers swivel through 360°.

♦ 2 Emba-class (Project 1172) cable layers [ARC] (1 *nonoperational*)
Bldr: Wärtsilä SY, Turku, Finland

	L
Nepryadva	24-4-81
Setun'	29-4-81

Setun'—at Sevastopol' Hartmut Ehlers, 7-00

AUXILIARIES *(continued)*

D: 1,443 tons (2,145 fl) **S:** 11.8 kts **Dim:** 75.90 (68.50 pp) × 12.60 × 3.10
Electronics: Radar: 2 Mius (Spin Trough) nav.
M: Diesel-electric: 2 Wärtsilä Vasa 6R22 diesels; 2 shrouded Schottel props; 1,360 shp—bow tunnel thruster
Range: 7,000/7 **Endurance:** 25 days **Crew:** 38 tot. (civilian)

Remarks: 1,910 grt. Cargo: 300 tons cable. Intended for use in shallow coastal areas, rivers, and harbors. Have one 5-ton crane. *Setun'* is in the Black Sea Fleet. Baltic Fleet unit *Nepryadva* was reported sold to Estonia in 1997 but is still laid up at Lomonosov. Caspian Flotilla unit *Emba* was transferred to Azerbaijan after 1992.

♦ 4 Klaz'ma-class (Projects 1112 and 1274*) cable layers [ARC]
Bldr: Wärtsilä SY, Turku, Finland

	Laid down	L	In serv.
Donets	17-12-67	1968	1968
Inguri	21-10-76	7-10-77	1978
Yana*	4-5-61	1-11-62	9-7-63
Zeya	1968	1969	1970

Donets Jaroslaw Cislak, 7-01

D: 3,800–3,910 tons (6,810–6,920 fl) **S:** 14 kts
Dim: 130.4 (120.0 pp) × 16.0 × 5.75 **Electronics:** Radar: 2 Don-2 nav.
M: 5 Wärtsilä 624TS diesels (1,000 bhp each), electric drive; 2 props; 2,150 shp—475-shp active rudder, 640-shp bow-thruster
Range: 12,000/14 **Fuel:** 250 tons **Endurance:** 30 days
Crew: 85–118 tot. (civilian)

Remarks: Type designation: KS (*Kabel'noye Sudno,* Cable Ship). *Yana* has an all-naval crew and reportedly can be employed as a minelayer. Plans to replace these worn-out ships with eight larger, 4,000-dwt cable layers to be built in Finland foundered with the collapse of the USSR, and their present operational condition is unknown. *Donets* is assigned to the Baltic Fleet, and the others to the Northern Fleet.
Hull systems: *Yana* (Project 1274) has four 2,436-bhp diesel generator sets and a longer forecastle, and is 5,645 grt/3,400 dwt (6,810 tons fl). All have ice-strengthened hulls. In the 5,760-grt/3,750-dwt later units (Project 1112), the diesel engines drive five 680-kw generators, which provide power for propulsion and for all auxiliary functions. All cable machinery was built by Submarine Cables, Ltd., Great Britain. *Inguri, Tavda,* and *Zeya* carry 1,850 m^3 of cable and displace 7,885 tons (fl), drawing 5.76 m. The other two have three cable tanks totaling 1,600 m^3.
Disposals: Black Sea Fleet sister *Tsna* was stricken 10-1-96 and transferred to Ukraine between 6-97 and 8-97; she has since been stricken. Pacific Fleet units *Katun'* and *Ingul* (Project 1274) were stricken in 1995 and on 31-7-96, respectively. *Tavda* was transferred to the Ukraine in 1997 and has been up for sale since 2000.

♦ 3 Malina-class (Project 2020) nuclear-powered-submarine propulsion plant tenders [ARR] *(nonoperational)*
Bldr: Chernomorskiy Zavod, Nikolayev, Ukraine

	In serv.
PT'-5 *PM-63*	6-84
PT'-6 PM-74	14-9-85
PT'-7 PM-12	9-90

Malina-class PM-74 (PT'-6) JMSDF, 8-95

D: 10,435 tons (12,983 fl) **S:** 11.5 kts **Dim:** 138.4 (123.0 wl) × 21.0 × 6.86
Electronics: Radar: 2 MR 212/201 Vaygach (Palm Frond) nav. (PM-12: 2/MR-312 Nayada nav.)
M: 4 diesels, 4 PG-112-1 generator sets, electric drive; 1 prop; 2,700 shp
Range: 13,000/10 **Endurance:** 45 days **Crew:** 33 officers, 191 enlisted

Remarks: PM = *Plavuchaya Masterskaya* (Floating Workshop). Second unit began trials in spring 1985, the third in 11-90. A fourth, PM-16, was launched in 1-92 to clear the ways; after massive modifications, she was completed in 5-96 as the Swan Hellenic cruise liner *Minerva.* Northern Fleet units PM-12 and PM-63 are assigned to the civilian nuclear-powered icebreaker fleet at Murmansk and to Sevmash at Severodvinsk, respectively. PM-74 was delivered to the Pacific Fleet late in 1985 and is used to transport nuclear fuel in Shkotovo. PM-63 completed an overhaul at Severodvinsk 17-12-94, but it was reported in 1998 that her propulsion system was inoperable. PM-12 was refitted from 8-98 to 6-10-00, using U.S. funds to improve the security of nuclear materials; the ship is based at Nerpa Zavod, near Murmansk.
Hull systems: The unusual hullform, with no curved surfaces, indicates that the ships were not intended to move very often. They were designed to serve nuclear-powered submarines, as evidenced by the mooring pockets along the hull sides and the two 16-ton-capacity, specialized reactor recoring cranes. Have 450 m^3 of radioactive liquid storage tankage and are capable of accommodating 1,400 fuel rods—the equivalent of six reactor recorings.

♦ 1 Khoper-class (Project 16570) salvage tug [ARS]
Bldr: Svirsk Zavod, Nikol'sk (In serv. 7-96)

SB-931

D: 1,960 tons light (2,883 fl) **S:** 12+ kts
Dim: 63.75 (57.57 pp) × 14.26 × 5.61 (max.)
A: 1 twin 25-mm 80-cal. Type 2M-3M AA
Electronics: Radar: . . .
M: 2 Type 6R32 diesels; 2 CP props; 5,900 bhp
Range: 12,000/12 **Crew:** 25 tot. (accomm. for 37)

Remarks: Prototype was laid down in 1995 as a general salvage and rescue tug design capable of supporting divers to 45-m depths and equipped for a wide variety of salvage and underwater work duties. To date, no further units have been announced. Carries a rescue lifeboat, a divers' workboat, and diver recovery and decompression systems. Also equipped for firefighting and water-blast cleaning. Hull has seven watertight compartments and an icebreaking bow. Was initially assigned to the Northern Fleet but may now be in the Baltic.

♦ 1 Kashtan-class rescue submersible tender [ARS]
Bldr: VEB Neptunwerft, Rostock, East Germany (In serv. 1990)

SS-750 (ex-KIL-140)

Kashtan-class SS-750 2000

D: 4,200 tons (5,250 fl) **S:** 13.75 kts **Dim:** 113.00 (97.82 pp) × 18.22 × 3.71
Electronics: Radar: 1 Mius (Spin Trough) nav., 1 Don-2 nav.
M: 2 Karl Liebnecht–M.A.N. 8VDS 26/20AL-1 diesels (2,991 bhp each), 2 generator sets, electric drive; 2 props; 4,200 shp (3,000 sust.)—bow-thruster
Range: 4,000/11 **Endurance:** 45 days
Crew: 44 tot. (accomm. for 18 officers, 36 unlicensed civilians)

Remarks: 4,400 grt/1,000 dwt. Renamed during 1995. Is used to transport and support two salvage submersibles, AS-22 and AS-26 (see under [YSS]). Is based in the Baltic and acted as trials tender to the deep salvage submersible *Rus'* during 6-00. Seven sisters remain in service as mooring buoy tenders.
Hull systems: Has a 100-ton German Stülcken heavy-lift gantry at the stern for lifting mooring buoys and for salvage assignments, a 12-ton electrohydraulic crane to starboard, and a 60-ton derrick amidships. The external appearance was not extensively altered from the standard appearance for the class.

Disposal note: Of the two *Nikolay Chiker*–class (Project 5757) salvage tugs, *Fotiy Krylov* (SB-135) was stricken 3-7-92. She was sold to Alexander G. Tsavliris & Sons, Piraeus, Greece, early in 1993 as *Tsavliris Giant;* the Russian government subsequently declared the sale to have been invalid, recovered ownership of the vessel, and then leased her to Tsavliris Salvage Group, which operates her from Singapore on charter. Sister *Nikolay Chiker* (SB-131) was long-term chartered to the same company (now trading as Tsavliris Russ) during 7-00; remaining under the Russian flag, she was refitted late in 2000 and is now stationed in the Far East.

♦ 3 Sliva-class (Project 712) salvage tugs [ARS]
Bldr: Rauma-Repola Oy, Uusikaupunki/Nystad, Finland

	Laid down	L	In serv.	Fleet
SB-406	. . .	6-7-83	20-2-84	Northern
SB-921	17-8-84	28-12-84	5-7-85	Baltic
Shakhter (ex-SB-922)	31-8-84	3-5-85	20-12-85	Black Sea

D: 2,170 tons (2,980 fl) **S:** 16.1 kts **Dim:** 68.81 (60.13 pp) × 15.40 × 5.40
Electronics: Radar: 2 MR-312 Nayada-5 nav.

AUXILIARIES *(continued)*

Sliva-class SB-921 H&L Van Ginderen, 3-90

M: 2 SEMT-Pielstick/Russkiy Dizel 6 PC2.5 L400 (TS HN40/46) diesels; 2 CP props; 7,800 bhp—bow-thruster
Range: 6,120/15 **Endurance:** 30 days
Crew: 43 crew + 10 salvage party (all civilian)

Remarks: 2,050 grt/810 dwt. The similar icebreaking rescue ships of the *Stroptivyy* class are civilian subordinated. SB-922 was renamed *Shakhter* ("Miner") in 1987.
Disposals: Sister SB-408 was sold to Alexander G. Tsavliris & Sons, Piraeus, Greece, and renamed *Tsavliris Challenger* early in 1993 for use as a station salvage ship based in Sri Lanka; the Russian government subsequently declared the sale to have been invalid and recovered ownership, after which she was chartered to Tsavliris, for whom she still operates.
Hull systems: Bollard pull: 90 tons. Ice-reinforced hull. Able to support divers to 60 m. Have four water monitors, one 60- and one 30-ton winch, a unique 350-m floating power cable to support vessels in distress, a 5-ton electrohydraulic crane, and two cargo holds (100 m^3 and 50 m^3).

♦ 3 Goryn'-class (Project 563S) rescue tugs [ARS]
Bldr: Rauma-Repola, Rauma, Finland (In serv. 1982–83)

SB-521 (ex-MB-61) SB-522 (ex-MB-62) SB-523 (ex-MB-64)

Goryn'-class SB-522 JMSDF, via *Ships of the World,* 2005

D: 1,650 tons light; 2,240 tons normal (2,600 fl) **S:** 13.5 kts
Dim: 63.50 × 14.30 (13.80 wl) × 5.20
Electronics: Radar: 2 Don-2 nav.
M: 1 Russkiy Dizel Type 67N diesel; 3,500 bhp
Range: 8,000/12 **Endurance:** 40 days **Crew:** 43 tot. (civilian)

Remarks: SB = *Spastel'niy Buksir* (Rescue Tug). Former fleet tugs, redesignated as salvage tugs; have also been referred to as Project 714. SB-365, -522, and -523 can be distinguished from the standard tug version by the electrohydraulic crane and small tripod mast abaft the stack, and they have probably been fitted with MG-26 underwater telephones. SB-523 is in the Northern Fleet, SB-522 in the Pacific Fleet, and SB-36 (redesignated from MB-36 prior to 7-00) in the Black Sea Fleet.
Disposals: Sister SB-524 (ex-MB-108) of the Black Sea Fleet was stricken during 1996 and transferred to Ukraine in 1997. SB-365 (ex-MB-29) was out of service by 2001.

♦ 4 Pionier Moskvyy–class (Project 05360 and 05361*) salvage submersible tenders [ARS] (1 in *reserve*)
Bldr: Karamaki Zavod, Vyborg

	In serv.
Mikhail Rudnitskiy	1979
Giorgiy Koz'min	1980
Giorgiy Titov	1983
*Sayany**	1984

D: 6,100 tons (7,960 fl) **S:** 15.75 kts **Dim:** 130.30 (119.00 pp) × 17.30 × 5.90
Electronics:
Radar: 2 Okean-M nav.
Sonar: MGA-21 (*Sayany:* MG-89 Mezen') MF/HF active; MGV-5N underwater communications
M: 1 5DKRN 62/140-3 diesel; 1 prop; 6,100 bhp
Electric: 1,500 kw tot. **Range:** 12,000/15.5 **Endurance:** 45 days
Crew: 10 officers, 12 warrant officers, 40 enlisted + 40 naval salvage/submersible operations party

Mikhail Rudnitskiy NAVPIC-Holland, 10-01

Remarks: Type designation: *Sudno-baza Podvodnikh Issledovaniy* (Underwater Research Support Ship). First three carry the ensign of the Naval Salvage and Rescue Service and are named for important developers of research/salvage submersibles; *Sayany* was configured for scientific research submersible support and was laid up, although in commission. *Mikhail Rudnitskiy* and *Giorgiy Titov* serve in the Northern Fleet and the other two in the Pacific Fleet. *Giorgiy Titov* serves as tender for the rescue submersible AS-28.
Hull systems: Modification of a standard merchant timber-carrier/container-ship design, retaining two holds. The former after hold area has two superstructure levels built over it, and the former small hold forward has been plated over. Retain two 50-ton and two 20-ton derricks and have had heavy-cable fairleads cut in the bulwarks fore and aft and a number of boat booms added to starboard; the heavy-lift system is stabilized. *Titov* has a larger superstructure built over the no. 3 hold than do the first two and carries two Pisces submersibles with 2,000-m depth capability. *Rudnitskiy* carries the Poisk-2-class (Project 1839) three-man salvage submersible [YSS] *Bester* (AS-34), plus underwater search and exploration equipment; during 8-00, she also operated the Project 1855 rescue submersible *Priz* (AS-32). *Sayany,* painted in white and gray, has had the forecastle and poop decks extended, the deckhouse amidships raised one deck higher, and a two-level deckhouse built over the forward hold area; she appears intended for a research role and is equipped with a high-frequency sonar of the type used on Russian Navy minesweepers. All are equipped with bow- and stern-thrusters and can be attached to a four-point salvage moor.

♦ 4 Ingul (Pamir)-class (Project 1452) salvage tugs [ARS]
Bldr: United Admiralty SY, St. Petersburg

	Laid down	L	In serv.	Fleet
Alatau	23-3-82	21-4-83	29-12-83	Pacific
Altay (ex-*Karabakh*)	14-2-85	18-4-87	21-10-87	Northern
Mashuk	7-6-74	27-6-75	25-12-75	Pacific
Pamir	2-4-73	28-5-74	26-12-74	Northern

Altay NAVPIC-Holland, 10-01

Altay NAVPIC-Holland, 10-01

AUXILIARIES *(continued)*

D: 3,320 tons (4,040 fl) **S:** 20 kts (18.75 cruise)
Dim: 92.79 (80.40 pp) × 15.63 × 5.85
Electronics: Radar: 2 Don-2 or Okean nav.
M: 2 Type 58D-4R, 16-cyl. diesels; 2 CP props; 9,000 bhp
Electric: 1,300 kw (4 × 300-kw, 1 × 100-kw diesel sets)
Range: 9,000/18.7; 15,000/12 **Fuel:** 675 tons heavy oil, 155 tons diesel
Endurance: 60 days **Crew:** 70 tot. (civilian) + 18 salvage party

Remarks: Two sisters, *Yaguar* and *Bars* (2,781 grt/1,140 dwt), were built for the merchant marine and had 35-man crews, plus bunks for 50 rescued personnel; *Bars* was sold to China in 1997. *Altay* was renamed in 1994.
Hull systems: Very powerful tugs with a constant-tension highline personnel rescue system, salvage pumps, firefighting equipment, and complete diving gear, capable of supporting divers to 60-m depths from two stations. Have 94-ton bollard pull and are equipped with one 60-ton and one 30-ton towing winch. An NK-300 submersible television camera system is installed. Have four 500-m^3/hr firefighting pumps. Carry one-each Project 1393A, 1394A, and 338PKV motorboats. Have three cargo holds (400 m^3 aft, 300 m^3 forward, and 120 m^3 rescue equipment stowage). The hull has a large bulbous bow. *Altay* has Intelsat SATCOM equipment and may have more elaborate salvage capabilities. All can carry 182 tons of potable water.
Combat systems: Provision was made to install a twin 57-mm AA mount and two twin 25-mm AA mounts, but none has ever carried armament.

♦ 4 Okhtenskiy (Goliat)-class (Project 733S) rescue tugs [ARS]
Bldr: Petrozavod SY, St. Petersburg (In serv. 1958–early 1960s)

SB-4 Kodor SB-5 SB-9 SB-171 Loksa

Okhtenskiy-class rescue tug SB-9 Boris Lemachko, 2002

D: 759 tons (934 fl) **S:** 13.2 kts **Dim:** 47.30 (43.00 pp) × 10.30 × 4.20
Electronics:
Radar: 1–2 Don-2 or Mius (Spin Trough) nav.
Sonar: Kama hull-mounted underwater telephone
M: Diesel-electric: 2 Type D5D50 (6ChN 30/38) diesels, 2 generator sets (950 kw each); 1 prop; 1,500 shp
Electric: 340 kw tot. **Range:** 8,000/11 **Fuel:** 197 tons
Endurance: 25 days **Crew:** 51 tot. (civilian + naval diving party)

Remarks: SB = *Spastel'niy Buksir* (Rescue Tug), hence the "S" suffix to the project number. Principal characteristics are essentially identical to the general fleet-tug version, except that they are equipped to support divers and have an underwater telephone. Bollard pull is 20 tons. There is a 5-ton derrick. SB-5 deployed to the Mediterranean during 6-98 to tow home Amur-class repair ship PM-56 from Syria. SB-9 is in the Northern Fleet based at Arkhangel'sk, SB-4 and -5 are in the Black Sea Fleet, and SB-171 is in the Baltic Fleet.
Disposals: Northern Fleet sister SB-3 was for sale for scrap in 1992, Pacific Fleet SB-28 was stricken 3-7-92, and SB-163 (ex-MB-163) had been retired by 2001. Black Sea Fleet unit *Moshniy* (SB-6) was stricken 5-7-94. Black Sea Fleet unit SB-15 was stricken 10-1-96 and transferred to Ukraine 1-8-97. Northern Fleet unit SB-11 had reverted to fleet tug status as MB-11 by 2001. The last two Roslavl-class (Project AT-202) salvage ships, SB-41 and SB-46, were stricken by 2005.

♦ 4 Iva-class (Polish Project B-99) firefighting tugs [ARS]
Bldr: Stocznia Polnocna, Gdansk, Poland

	L	In serv.		L	In serv.
Vikhr-5	11-5-84	30-11-84	Vikhr-8	22-12-84	31-5-85
Vikhr-6	4-9-84	28-2-85	Vikhr-9	18-6-85	29-3-86

D: 2,299 tons (fl) **S:** 16 kts **Dim:** 72.30 (63.00 pp) × 14.30 × 4.56
M: 2 Cegielski-Sulzer 16 AV 25/30 diesels; 2 CP props; 5,880 bhp—2 500-shp side-thrusters
Electric: 740 kw (2 × 370-kw diesel sets) **Range:** 2,500/12 **Fuel:** 186 tons
Crew: 26 ship's company, 18 rescue team + 50 evacuees

Remarks: 2008 grt/317 dwt. Eight others (all with "*Vikhr*"-series names) are civilian units serving offshore oilfields. Have water, foam, and chemical firefighting systems with a total pumping capacity of 4,000 m^3/hr.
Disposals: *Vikhr-2* was transferred to Vietnam in 5-92. *Vikhr-4* was sold to the Norwegian firm Echo Shipping in 2000 as the *Echo Fighter* and placed on long-term charter to Greenpeace as the *Esperanza* as of 1-01.

Vikhr-5 H&L Van Ginderen, 1998

♦ 4 Katun'-II (Ikar)-class (Project 1993) seagoing fireboats [ARS]
Bldr: Srednyy Neva Zavod, Kolpino, St. Petersburg (In serv. 1978–80)

PZhS-64 PZhS-92 PZhS-95 PZhS-219

D: 1,065 tons (1,255 fl) **S:** 17 kts **Dim:** 65.40 × 10.20 × 3.19
Electronics:
Radar: 1 Mius (Spin Trough) nav.
Sonar: MGA-21 HF hull-mounted object avoidance
M: 2 Type 6DR-42 diesels; 2 props; 5,000 bhp
Electric: 500 kw tot. (2 × 200-kw, 1 × 100-kw diesel sets)
Range: 2,000/17 **Endurance:** 20 days **Crew:** 38 tot.

Remarks: Enlarged version of the Katun'-I design (Project 1893). One source says only two were built. Have two 1,000-m^3/hr and four 500-m^3/hr fire and salvage pumps. PZhS-64 and -92 operate in the Northern Fleet, PZhS-95 and -219 in the Pacific.

♦ 9 Katun'-I-class (Project 1893) seagoing fireboats [ARS]
Bldr: Srednyy Neva Zavod, Kolpino, St. Petersburg (In serv. 1970–78)

PZhS-96 PZhS-123 PZhS-209 PZhS-279 PZhS-551
PZhS-98 PZhS-124 PZhS-273 PZhS-282

Katun'-I-class PZhS-98—at Murmansk NAVPIC-Holland, 10-01

D: 883 tons (930 fl) **S:** 18 kts **Dim:** 62.60 × 10.20 × 3.19
Electronics:
Radar: 1 Mius (Spin Trough) or Don-2 nav.
Sonar: MGA-21 HF hull-mounted object avoidance
M: 2 Type 40DM (12DRN 23/30) diesels; 2 props; 4,400 bhp
Range: 1,800/12 **Endurance:** 20 days **Crew:** 32 tot. (civilian; accomm. for 45)

Remarks: Originally designated PDS (*Pozharno-Degazatsionnoye Sudno,* Firefighting and Decontamination Ship) and later revised to PZhS (*Pozharnoye Sudno,* Firefighting Ship). There are several civilian sisters, including the *General Gamidov.* Fleet assignments include PZhS-96, -124, -282, and -551 in the Baltic; PZhS-98 in the Northern; PZhS-123 in the Black Sea; PZhS-209 in the Pacific; and PZhS-273 and -279 in the Caspian Flotilla. PZhS-123 carries the local unofficial name *Dunay.*
Hull systems: Have extensive firefighting gear, including an extendable boom-mounted monitor, and can fight fires on land up to 200 m from the water. Also intended for use in decontaminating surface ships and submarines. Have an 8-ton bollard-pull towing hook. Are equipped with four 1,000 m^3/hr firefighting and salvage pumps, one 1,000-m^3/hr and seven 500-m^3/hr firefighting monitors, high-pressure air and portable electric power supplies, a tank to hold 15 tons of foam agent, and a Project 1395 motorboat equipped with a towing hook.

Note: See also harbor fireboat entries under [YTR].

Disposal note: Ugra-class (Project 1886.1) submarine tender *Vladimir Yegorov* (ex-PB-82) was scrapped in 1993; Black Sea Fleet unit *Volga,* used in recent years as a stationary staff headquarters and accommodations hulk at Sevastopol', had been discarded by mid-2001 and began scrapping at Mikolayiv, Ukraine, during 7-02. Pacific Fleet Don-class (Project 310) submarine tender PB-9 (ex-*Kamchatskiy Komsomolets,* ex-PKZ-124, ex-*Batur*) may still be performing a similar role as a hulk.

AUXILIARIES *(continued)*

Modified Dnepr–class (Project 725A) submarine tenders PM-130 and PM-135 are apparently no longer in service. Standard Dnepr (Project 725) unit PM-17 was scrapped at Byelokamenka during mid-2002.

♦ 0 (+ 1 + 1) Igor Belousov–class (Project 23100) submarine rescue ship [ASR]
Bldr: Admiralty SY, St. Petersburg

	Laid down	L	In serv.
Igor Belousov	2004	12-05	2009

D: Approx. 5,300 tons (fl) **S:** 16 kts **Dim:** 107.0 × . . . × . . .
Electronics: Radar: 2 . . . nav.
M: . . . **Electric:** . . .
Range: 3,000/16 **Crew:** . . .

Remarks: Intended primarily for deepwater salvage and submarine rescue. Will be equipped with a DSRV-type submersible capable of operating to depths of at least 700 m. The ships will also be equipped with remotely operated vehicles, special-purpose deep diving equipment and a helicopter deck. Initial plans call for two ships to be built, one each for the Northern and Pacific Fleets.

♦ 1 El'brus (Osminog)-class (Project 537) submarine rescue ship [ASR]
Bldr: Zavod imeni 61 Kommunara, Nikolayev, Ukraine

	L	In serv.
Alagez	1984	28-1-89

Alagez—with a Krivak-I-class frigate alongside Boris Lemachko, 7-98

Alagez H&L Van Ginderen, 2-92

D: 12,430 tons (14,300 fl) **S:** 20 kts (17 sust.)
Dim: 175.00 (156.00 wl) × 25.10 (24.80 wl) × 7.50
A: Provision for 4 single 30-mm 54-cal. AK-630 or AK-306 gatling AA
Electronics:
Radar: 1 Don-2 nav.; 2 MR-212/201 Vaygach-U (Palm Frond) nav.
Sonar: MGA-6 Gamma hull-mounted HF search suite
M: 4 Type 68G (18DN 23/2 × 30) diesels (7,250 bhp each), electric drive; 2 props; 24,900 shp
Electric: 3,200 kw tot. (4 × 800-kw diesel sets)
Range: 5,000/20; 15,000/10 **Endurance:** 60 days
Crew: 312 tot. + 106 passengers

Remarks: Far and away the world's largest and most elaborate submarine salvage-and-rescue ship. Deployed to the Pacific Fleet on completion. Reactivated during 2000–2001 as a result of the loss of the cruise-missile submarine *Kursk.* Based at Vladivostok. Suffered a fire while undergoing refit during 2004, though the extent of damage remains unknown. Photos viewed during 6-04 fail to indicate external damage.
Hull systems: Has an icebreaking hull. The large hangar aft of the stack was intended to hold one Poisk-2-class (Project 1839) and two Priz-class (Project 1855) salvage-and-rescue submersibles, which are moved forward on rails for launching by an extendable overhead 100-ton gantry crane that can be deployed on either side in sea states up to 5. Has a hangar for one Helix helicopter, with the hangar door pivoting downward to form a ramp leading to the helicopter flight deck. Can lay and retrieve a four-point moor. The 3-ton crane on the port quarter has a very long folding arm. Has submersible decompression and observation chambers, firefighting equipment, and five 500-m^3/hr salvage pumps.

Disposal notes: Older sister *El'brus*—which made one brief deployment from 12-81 to 1-82 and then returned to the Black Sea, emerged again briefly in 5-84, and has not been deployed since—was stricken between 8-97 and 5-98 and was towed to India for scrapping in 2-00.The incomplete hull of a third unit, *Ayudag,* was launched 1-95 to clear the ways and was approved for scrapping in 8-95. Following the *Kursk* disaster, Nepa-class (Project 530) submarine rescue ship *Karpaty* began a reactivation overhaul. Insufficient funds caused cancellation of the project and *Karpaty* was stricken during 2002.

♦ 2 Prut-class (Project 05275* and 527M) submarine rescue ships [ASR]
Bldr: Zavod imeni 61 Kommunara, Nikolayev, Ukraine

	In serv.	Fleet
EPRON (ex-SS-26, ex-MB-26)*	29-10-59	Black Sea
SS-83 (ex-SS-24)	1961	Pacific

EPRON—at Sevastopol' Hartmut Ehlers, 7-00

D: 2,120 tons light; 2,770 tons std. (3,330–3,380 fl) **S:** 18.8 (SS-83: 17.8) kts
Dim: 89.70 (85.00 wl) × 14.30 (14.00 wl) × 5.20–5.40 (6.57 max.)
Electronics:
Radar: 2 Don-2 nav.
Sonar: MGA-6 suite (probable HF search); MG-26 underwater telephone
M: 4 3D-100M diesels (1,800 bhp each), 4 PGK-215/55 generator sets (1,250 kw each), electric drive; 2 props; 7,000 shp
Electric: 1,740 kw tot. (7 × 220-kw diesel sets)
Range: 2,500/16.5; 10,500/11.3 **Fuel:** 260.2 tons **Endurance:** 35 days
Crew: 129–135 tot.

Remarks: SS = *Spasitel'noye Sudno* (Rescue Ship). SS-83 was modernized during 1969–74 to Project 527M status. *EPRON* is an acronym for *Ekspeditskaya Podvodnik Rabot Ososbogo Nazhnacheniya,* the Russian Navy's submarine rescue service, and was assigned in 1969; the ship underwent a refit at Sevastopol' during 1999.
Hull systems: Have one 12-ton derrick, two or three special carriers for rescue chambers, a submersible decompression chamber for divers, and salvage observation bells. Four anchor buoys are stowed on inclined racks on the after deck. Earlier units had tripod foremasts; these survivors have quadripod foremasts and smaller mooring buoys. Can tow ships of more than 15,000 tons displacement.
Disposals: Northern Fleet sister *Altay* (SS-22) burned out in 1969 and was scrapped; SS-44 was lost in 1973 in a grounding; SS-23 was scrapped around 1987; Black Sea Fleet unit SS-21 was stricken 7-1-92 and became the commercial *Podvodnik Marinesko;* Pacific Fleet unit *Zhiguli* (ex-SS-25) was stricken 30-7-93 and sold to China, probably for scrapping; Northern Fleet unit *Beshtau* (ex-SS-44, ex-MB-11; not the same unit as the SS-44 lost in 1973) was stricken 22-2-93; and Northern Fleet unit *Vladimir Trefol'ev* (ex-SS-87, ex-SS-28) was stricken 1-9-95.

♦ 2 Neftegaz-class (Polish Project B-92) oilfield tug/supply vessels [ATA]
Bldr: A. Warski SY, Szczecin, Poland (In serv. 1983–90)

	In serv.
Ilga	3-11-83
Kalar	5-02-90

Kalar—gray hull, white superstructure, black funnels, red mast
JMSDF, via *Ships of the World,* 2005

D: 3,080 tons (4,013 fl) **S:** 15 kts **Dim:** 80.70 (71.50 pp) × 16.30 (15.0 wl) × 5.00
Electronics: Radar: 2 MR-312 Nayada nav.
M: 2 Zgoda-Sulzer diesels; 2 CP props; 7,200 bhp
Electric: 1,200 kw tot. (3 × 400-kw diesel sets)
Range: 5,000/12 **Fuel:** 533 tons **Endurance:** 30 days
Crew: 23 tot. (civilian) + 12 passengers

Remarks: 2,372 grt/1,396 dwt. Survivors of a class of 43 oilfield supply tugs ordered in 1982. Cargo: up to 600 tons of dry cargo on deck, plus 1,000 m^3 of liquid cargo. Can act as tugs and have four firefighting water monitors. Have a bow-thruster. *Ilga*

AUXILIARIES *(continued)*

has carried a large missile-range telemetry tracking antenna aft and operates in the Northern Fleet, primarily in cargo service; *Kalar* is in the Pacific Fleet and is used as a rescue tug. Black Sea Fleet sister *Aleksandr Kortunov* had been discarded or sold commercial by 2001.

Disposal note: MB-331-class oceangoing tug MB-331 had either been stricken or transferred to commercial service by 2001; sister MB-330, in poor condition, was operating on charter to the Far Eastern Shipping Co. (FESCO) by 1996.

♦ 7 Goryn'-class (Project 563) seagoing tugs [ATA]

Bldr: Rauma-Repola, Finland (In serv. 1982–83)

MB-15	MB-32	MB-119 (ex-*Bilbino*)	Yevgeniy Khorov (ex-MB-35)
MB-18	MB-38	SB-36 (ex-MB-36)	

SB-36 Cem D. Yaylali, 2-06

D: 1,650 tons light, 2,240 tons normal (2,600 fl) **S:** 13.5 kts
Dim: 63.50 × 14.30 (13.80 wl) × 5.20
Electronics: Radar: 2 Don-2 nav.
M: 1 Russkiy Dizel Type 67N diesel; 3,500 bhp
Range: 8,000/12 **Endurance:** 40 days
Crew: 43 tot. (civilians) + 18 passengers

Remarks: 1,600 grt. Russian type designation: MB (*Morskoy Buksir,* Seagoing Tug). Intended for ocean towing, salvage, and fire fighting. Four others were converted as rescue tugs (SB—*Spastel'noye Buksir*). MB-38 is in the Northern Fleet, and *Yevgeniy Khorov* (delivered 15-9-82 and renamed late in 2001) and MB-119 (delivered 20-3-78) are in the Baltic Fleet, with MB-15, MB-18, and MB-32 in the Pacific Fleet. Black Sea Fleet unit MB-36 was redesignated SB-36 prior to 7-00.
Hull systems: Early units had 35-ton bollard pull. The later units have a Type 671 diesel and produce 43 tons bollard pull. The two series can be distinguished visually by the overlapping rubbing strakes at the forecastle break in the early units and the sloping connecting strake in late units.
Disposals: MB-105 (ex-*Baykalsh*) was sold to Vietnam for commercial use in 8-95.

♦ 12 Sorum-class (Project 745) seagoing tugs [ATA]

Bldr: Yaroslavl Zavod (In serv. 1973–92)

MB-4	MB-56	MB-76	MB-110
MB-28	MB-58	MB-99	MB-148
MB-37	MB-61	MB-100	MB-304

Sorum-class MB-99 JMSDF, via *Ships of the World,* 2005

D: 1,140–1,210 tons (1,512–1,656 fl) **S:** 13.8 kts
Dim: 58.30 (55.50 pp) × 12.60 × 4.60
Electronics: Radar: 2 Don-2 nav.
M: 2 Type 25-DB 2 (6ChN 30/38) diesels, electric drive; 1 prop; 2,500 shp (1,850 sust.)
Range: 6,200/11 **Fuel:** 297 tons **Endurance:** 40 days
Crew: 35 tot. (civilian + 40 passengers/rescuees)

Remarks: MB = *Morskoy Buksir* (Seagoing Tug). MB-110, the final unit, was completed 31-8-91. Armed versions of the design serve the Federal Border Guard as patrol ships [WPS], and another, OS-572, was a trials ship [AGE] and now operates as survey vessel GS-31. Reported fleet assignments: MB-28, -56, -58, -110 and -100 in the Northern Fleet; -37, -61, -76, and -148 in the Pacific Fleet; and MB-4 in the Baltic Fleet.

Sorum-class MB-37 Boris Lemachko, 1998

A modified version with larger superstructure and an A-frame kingpost aft is used by the Ministry of Fisheries as a rescue tug, prominently displaying *Spastel'* ("Rescue") on the black hull sides; known as the *Almaz* class, it includes *Almaz, Ametist, Kapitan Beklemishev,* and *Neustrashimyy,* with sister *Purga* having been sold to the Turkish Navy in 1999. One unit of the class, possibly a civilian *Almaz,* has been transferred to Vietnam. Soviet Naval Auxiliary Service units are unarmed but do have blanking plates for two twin 30-mm AA mount positions forward. Most units recently sighted have a radome for a commercial SATCOM system antenna atop the after mast.
Disposals: Black Sea Fleet sister MB-30 was stricken 10-1-96, and MB-30 was transferred to Ukraine on 1-8-97; the remaining Black Sea Fleet unit, MB-31, was sunk as a missile target during 2001. By 2001, Northern Fleet units MB-6, -13, -19, and -307 had been stricken, while sisters MB-70 and -175 had earlier been discarded or sold commercial.

♦ 19 Okhtenskiy (Goliat)-class seagoing tugs (Project 733) [ATA]

Bldr: Petrozavod SY, St. Petersburg (In serv. 1958–66)

	Fleet		Fleet
MB-5	Northern	MB-164	Northern
MB-8	Northern	MB-165 Serdity	Baltic
MB-11	Pacific	MB-166	Pacific
MB-12	Pacific	MB-169 Pochaetnyi	. . .
MB-16	Pacific	MB-173 50 Let Oktyabrskiy	Black Sea
MB-21	Northern	MB-175	Pacific
MB-23	Black Sea	MB-176	Pacific
MB-52	Northern	MB-178 Saturn	Baltic
MB-160	Black Sea	RB-187	Pacific
MB-162	Baltic		

Okhtenskiy-class MB-21—a Northern Fleet unit NAVPIC-Holland, 10-01

D: 717 tons (890 fl) **S:** 13.3 kts **Dim:** 47.30 (43.0 pp) × 10.30 × 4.14
Electronics: Radar: 1–2 Don-2 or Mius (Spin Trough) nav.
M: Diesel-electric: 2 Type D5D50 (6ChN 30/38) diesels, 2 generator sets (950 kw each); 1 prop;1,500 shp
Electric: 340 kw tot. **Range:** 6,000/13; 7,800/7 **Fuel:** 197 tons
Endurance: 30 days **Crew:** 31 tot. (civilian) + 40 passengers/rescuees

Remarks: MB = *Morskoy Buksir* (Seagoing Tug); sisters designated SB (*Spastel'noye Buksir,* Rescue Tug) are listed under [ARS]. Two have been demoted to *Rednyy Buksir* (Roadstead Tug) status, but their former MB-numbers are not known. Most units with names vice MB-series names were civilian, but the names listed above are applied to naval units.
Hull systems: Bollard pull: 27 tons initial/17 tons sustained. Have a 5-ton derrick.
Disposals: A number of the 40 naval (including eight Project 733S rescue tugs [ARS]) and 23 civilian units completed have been stricken. Pacific Fleet sister *Alatyr',* laid up in 1990, was stricken 5-9-94. Black Sea Fleet units *Tyulen* (MB-171) and *Volkhov* were stricken 5-7-94 and 31-7-96, respectively. Pacific Fleet units MB-24 and -170 were stricken 31-7-96 for commercial employment. Others known to have been retired by 2005 are *Stoikiy, Strogiy,* MB-2, MB-24, MB-64, MB-86, MB-95, MB-151, MB-152, MB-172, MB-196, and *Sil'niy* (MB-152). One Pacific Fleet unit was transferred to Vietnam in 5-92, and MB-51 was transferred to Ukraine on 1-8-97.

AUXILIARIES *(continued)*

♦ 7 Roslavl-class (Project 730) seagoing tugs [ATA]
Bldr: Dalyan' Zavod, Riga (In serv. 1953–60)

MB-45	MB-102	MB-145	MB-951
MB-69	MB-134	MB-147	

Roslavl-class MB-145—at Makhachkala on the Caspian Sea
Boris Lemachko, 1997

D: 470 tons (625 fl) **S:** 12 kts **Dim:** 44.5 × 9.5 × 3.5
Electronics: Radar: 1 Don-2 nav.
M: 2 Type 6DR-30/50 diesels; 2 props; 1,200 bhp
Electric: 125 kw tot. (1 × 100-kw, 1 × 25-kw diesel sets) **Range:** 6,000/11
Fuel: 86.8 tons **Endurance:** 10 days **Crew:** 30 tot. (civilian)

Remarks: Predecessor to the Okhtenskiy class; project number has also been said to be A-202. Two others, SB-41 and SB-46, remain in service as rescue tugs, and two, named *Bodriy* and *Nevel'skoy,* are assigned to another government agency. Two others were built in Romania. MB-102 is assigned to the Northern Fleet and MB-145 to the Caspian Flotilla; fleet assignments for the others are not available.
Disposals: Black Sea Fleet unit *Dzhambul* and MB-158 were stricken 3-7-92. Baltic Fleet units MB-91 and MB-94 were stricken 22-2-93 and 1-9-95, respectively. Northern Fleet unit MB-116 was stricken 22-2-93, and MB-125 has either been discarded or never existed.

♦ 1 Manych-class (Project 1549) water tanker [AW]
Bldr: Karamaki Zavod, Vyborg (In serv. 1972)

Manych

Manych—with munitions carrier *General Ryabakov* in background
Hartmut Ehlers, 7-00

D: 3,065 tons light (5,800 fl) **S:** 17 kts **Dim:** 114.5 × 15.9 × 5.8 (max.)
A: Provision for 2 twin 57-mm 70-cal AK-725 DP
Electronics:
Radar: 2 Volga (Don-Kay) nav.; 1 MR-302 Rubka (Strut Curve) surf./air search; 2 MR-103 Bars (Muff Cob) gun f.c. (nonfunctional)
M: 2 Type 58D diesels; 2 props; 9,000 bhp
Range: 6,000/14 **Endurance:** 30 days **Crew:** 79 tot.

Remarks: Was refitted in Bulgaria in the mid-1990s. Is in service, based at Sevastopol', although the ship has not been known to get under way for some time. Retains fire-control radars, but the two twin 57-mm DP gunmounts were removed in 1981. Sister *Tagil* was discarded from the Pacific Fleet in 1996.
Hull systems: Cargo capacity: 1,800 tons potable or boiler water, 20 tons distilled water, and 180 tons provisions.

♦ 4 Voda (MVT-6)-class (Project 561) water tankers [AWT]
Bldr: Yantar Zavod, Kaliningrad (In serv. 1953–60)

MVT-16 MVT-20 MVT-136 (ex-*Vodoley-21*) MVT-148

D: 982 tons light (2,255 fl) **S:** 12 kts **Dim:** 81.30 × 11.40 × 3.44 (1.65 light)
Electronics: Radar: 1 Don-2 or Mius (Spin Trough) nav.
M: 2 Russkiy Dizel 8DR30/50 diesels; 2 props; 1,600 bhp
Electric: 150 kw tot. (1 × 100-kw, 1 × 50-kw diesel sets; 380 V, 50 Hz)
Range: 2,900/10; 3,500/7 **Endurance:** 15 days **Crew:** 38 tot.

Remarks: 1,000 grt. Seventeen were completed, of which several were equipped with working decks to permit their use as underway water replenishment ships for deployed steam-powered warships. The five above were still in limited use in the late 1990s.
Hull systems: Cargo: 700 tons feedwater, 300 tons potable water. Have one 3-ton derrick for hose handling.

Voda-class MVT-136—a Pacific Fleet unit Boris Lemachko, 5-96

Disposals: Baltic Fleet unit MVT-138 was stricken 3-7-92. Black Sea Fleet unit *Abakan* (ex-MVT-9) was stricken 30-7-93 (but remains hulked at Sevastopol'); sister *Sura* (ex-MVT-19) was stricken 10-1-96 and transferred to Ukraine in 1997. Pacific Fleet unit MVT-135 (ex-*Vodoley-12*) was stricken 31-7-96 for scrapping but may be the unit now in Vietnamese Navy service. Also reported discarded between 1989 and 1997 were MVT-6, -10, -17, -18, -134, and -428.

♦ 2 Smol'nyy class (Project 887) [AXT]
Bldr: A. Warski SY, Szczecin, Poland (In serv. 1976–78)

200 Perekop (In serv. 1-1-78) 210 Smol'nyy (In serv. 1976)

Smol'nyy (210) Dieter Wolf, 6-03

Smol'nyy (210) Dieter Wolf, 6-03

D: 5,659 tons light; 6,120 tons std. (7,270 fl) **S:** 20 kts
Dim: 138.00 × 17.20 × 5.53
A: 2 twin 76.2-mm 59-cal. AK-726 DP; 2 twin 30-mm 65-cal. AK-230 AA; 2 12-round RBU-2500 ASW RL (128 RGB-25 rockets); 2 45-mm Type 21-KM saluting cannon
Electronics:
Radar: 1 Volga (Don-Kay) nav.; 2 Don-2 nav.; 1 Mius (Spin Trough) nav.; 1 MR-310 Angara-M (Head Net-C) surf./air search; 1 MR-105 Turel' (Owl Screech) f.c.; 1 MR-104 Rys' (Drum Tilt) AA f.c.
Sonar: Shelon hull-mounted MF search; searchlight HF attack
EW: 2 Bizan'-4 (Watch Dog) intercept (2–18 GHz)
M: 2 16-cyl. diesels; 2 props; 16,000 bhp
Electric: 2,560 kw tot. (4 × 640-kw diesel sets; 400 V, 50 Hz)
Range: 10,870/14 **Fuel:** 1,050 tons **Endurance:** 40 days
Crew: 12 officers, 121 enlisted + 30 instructors and 300 cadets

Remarks: Built to relieve the *Sverdlov*-class cruisers that were formerly used for cadet training. Both are based at Kronshtadt. *Smol'nyy* was refitted at Rostock, Germany, from 4-98 through 2000. Most weapon and sensor equipment is obsolescent.

AUXILIARIES *(continued)*

Hull systems: Carry six rowboats aft for exercising the cadets. Have numerous duplicate navigational training facilities for training purposes. Carry 396 tons of potable water, 35 tons of lubricating oil, and 61.2 tons of provisions. Also said to carry 14 instructors and 330 cadets.
Combat systems: Carry 700 rounds of 76.2-mm and 4,000 rounds of 30-mm ammunition.
Disposals: *Khasan* was decommissioned 1-10-95, stricken 31-10-98, and scrapped at Yantar Shipyard, Kaliningrad, beginning in 11-99.

Disposal note: *Luga*-class cadet-training ship *Luga,* laid up at Kronshtadt since the mid-1990s, had reached derelict condition by 2000 and is unlikely to see further service. Sister *Oka* was based at the now-Azerbaijani port of Baku in the Caspian to support the Kirov Naval Academy and was transferred to Azerbaijan in 1992 or 1993.

SERVICE CRAFT

Note: Classes listed below are those for which data have been published. There are additionally large numbers of yardcraft in such categories as floating cranes [YD], floating dry docks [YFDB, YFDL, YFDM], covered and open barges [YC, YFN], and fuel barges [YON] and innumerable small launches [YFL]; illustrations for examples of some of these are provided, where available.

♦ **10 Razvedchik-class (Project 1388M) environmental monitoring craft [YAG]** Bldr: Sosnovka Zavod (In serv. 1983–87)

KRKh-321	KRKh-559	KRKh-1374	KRKh-1884
KRKh-528	KRKh-579	KRKh-1668	
KRKh-536	KRKh-959	KRKh-1821	

Razvedchik-class KRKh-1821 Ralph Edwards, 6-03

D: 220 tons (270 fl) **S:** 31 kts **Dim:** 46.0 × 6.0 × 2.1
Electronics: Radar: 1 Mius (Spin Trough) nav.
M: 2 M-504-series diesels; 2 props; 9,000 bhp
Range: 1,500/10 **Endurance:** 10 days **Crew:** 14 tot.

Remarks: Intended for radiological and environmental pollutant monitoring. A variant of the NATO-designated Shelon'-class (Project 1388) torpedo retriever, with a full-height after deckhouse containing laboratory spaces and no torpedo retrieval ramp. KRKh-536, -559, and -959 are in the Northern Fleet; KRKh-321 is in the Black Sea Fleet; KRKh-1821 is in the Baltic Fleet; and KRKh-528 and -579 are in the Pacific Fleet. KRKh-213 has been reconfigured as officer's yacht KSV-213. Sister KRKh-1208 was derelict at Kronshtadt by 1999.

♦ **1 Rossiya-class (Project 785) fleet staff support craft [YAG]**
Bldr: . . ., Czech Republic (In serv. 1952)

AZERBAYZHAN

Azerbayzhan H&L Van Ginderen, 5-95

D: 1003 tons (fl) **S:** 11 kts **Dim:** 78.00 × 12.20 × 1.90
M: 2 diesels; 2 props; 800 bhp

Remarks: One of a class of 36 large river passenger craft. Acquired from the Kama Shipping Co. and adapted to serve as the headquarters ship for the Caspian Flotilla. Has berthing for 233 passengers and can carry 25 tons cargo.

♦ **2 Muna-class trials craft [YAGE]**
Bldr: . . . SY, Nikolayev, Ukraine (In serv. 1966–85)

OS-114 (ex-MBSS- . . .) OS-220 (ex-MBSS- . . .)

D: 457 tons (688 fl) **S:** 11 kts **Dim:** 51.50 × 8.40 × 2.70
A: OS-220 only: 2 bow . . .-mm TT (underwater)
Electronics: Radar: 1 Mius (Spin Trough) nav.

Muna-class trials craft OS-220 Hartmut Ehlers, 9-98

M: 1 Type 6DR 30/50 diesel; 1 prop; 600 bhp
Range: 1,700/10 **Endurance:** 15 days **Crew:** 15 tot. (+ 7 passengers)

Remarks: Former munitions carriers reconfigured for trials service. OS-220, based at Balaklava in the Black Sea Fleet, is equipped to launch and recover torpedoes.
Hull systems: Have a single 3.2-ton-capacity electric crane.

♦ **1 missile trials barge [YAGE]**

BGP-60

Submersible missile-trials platform BGP-60 Hartmut Ehlers, 9-98

Remarks: No data available. Was in storage at Balaklava as of 9-98. Appears to be a roughly square barge complete with a vertical launch tube for ballistic missiles, covered by a partial section of submarine outer hull structure. A tower structure on one corner provides an observation post. The craft is submersible. Moored with the craft was another test barge, possibly configured for launching cruise missiles.

♦ **. . . miscellaneous floating cranes [YD]**

Floating crane PK-21500—with Flamingo-class workboat RK-290 alongside
Hartmut Ehlers, 9-95

SERVICE CRAFT *(continued)*

Remarks: The Russian Navy and the Ministry of Shipbuilding have a large number of floating cranes, most equipped with auxiliary propulsion systems to permit local movement at bases and in harbors.

♦ 4 Sekstan-class (Project 220) deperming tenders [YDG]

Bldr: Laivateolissus SY, Turku, Finland (In serv. 1953–57)

SR-127 SR-144 SR-151 SR-154

Sekstan-class SR-154—alongside Bereza-class deperming tender SR-137 at Sevastopol' Werner Globke, 8-97

D: 280 tons (400 fl) **S:** 9 kts **Dim:** 40.6 × 9.3 × 4.3
Electronics: Radar: 1 Don-2 or Mius (Spin Trough) nav.
M: 1 diesel; 1 prop; 400 bhp
Range: 8,000/9 **Endurance:** 37 days **Crew:** 24 tot.

Remarks: Survivors of 72 built as war reparations. Several were transferred abroad and others were converted as cargo lighters. Wooden construction. Among recent disposals, Baltic Fleet unit SR-176 was stricken 22-2-93 and SR-160 and SR-171 were abandoned in Latvia in 2-94. SR-144 is in the Northern Fleet, SR-154 in the Black Sea Fleet, and the other two in the Pacific Fleet.

♦ 1 (+ 2) new-construction diving tenders (Project 11980) [YDT]

Bldr: Sudostroitel'nyy Zavod "Slip," Rybinsk (In serv. 2004– . . .)

VM-596 (In serv.: 28-11-04)

D: Approx. 300 tons (fl) **S:** 11 kts **Dim:** 38.00 × 7.70 × 1.90
Electronics: Radar: 1 . . . nav.
M: 2 diesels; 2 props; 600 bhp **Electric:** 150 kw tot. (3 × 50-kw diesel sets)
Range: 500/11 **Endurance:** 5 days **Crew:** 16 tot. (incl. 6 divers)

Remarks: The first unit was to have been completed in 1996, if funds for construction had been made available, but not until late 2002 was there a report of any actual construction progress, when it was said that the first ship would be delivered during 2003. Intended to begin replacement of the remaining Project 376 and 1415 diving tenders. Will be able to support divers to depths of 60 m and can use remote controlled salvage gear down to 300.0 meters.

♦ 28 Flamingo (Tanya)-class (Project 1415.1 and 1415.2) diving tenders [YDT]

Bldr: Sosnovka Zavod, Rybinsk; Yaroslavl Zavod; and others (In serv. 1976–90s)

RVK-114	RVK-557	RVK-1209	RVK-1390	RVK-1893	RVK-2058
RVK-125	RVK-576	RVK-1250	RVK-1405	RVK-1943	RVK-2059
RVK-187	RVK-615	RVK-1251	RVK-1480	RVK-1944	RVK-2072
RVK-344	RVK-717	RVK-1254	RVK-1886	RVK-2029	
RVK-511	RVK-1080	RVK-1376	RVK-1887	RVK-2048	

Flamingo-class diving tender RVK-344—with bulwarks at bow and stern; some diving-tender units have continuous bulwarks running from bow to stern Stefan Marx, 2001

D: 42 tons (54 fl) **S:** 11 kts **Dim:** 21.20 × 3.93 × 1.40
Electronics: Radar: 1 Lotsiya nav. (not always fitted)
M: 1 Type 3D-12A or 3D-12L diesel; 1 prop; 300 bhp
Electric: 12 kw tot. (DGR 1A-16/1500 generator)
Range: 200/11 **Endurance:** 5 days **Crew:** 3 tot. + 5 divers

Flamingo-class diving tender RVK-2059 Stefan Marx, 2001

Remarks: Designed by Redan Central Design Bureau. RVK probably stands for *Rednyy Vodolanyy Kater* (Roadstead Diving Cutter). Can support divers to 45 m. Up to 50 sisters are assigned to the Federal Border Guard as patrol boats and are known in Russia as the Kulik class (q.v.). Others are equipped as workboats [YFL] or inshore survey craft [YGS]. The bulwarks around the hull vary in extent, with some having full bulwarks, others various cut-outs, and others bulwarks only at the bow and stern.

♦ 28 Yelva (Krab)-class (Project 535M) diving tenders [YDT]

Bldr: Gorokhovtse Zavod (In serv. 1971–83)

VM-20	VM-250	VM-409	VM-420	VM-809	VM-915
VM-72	VM-263	VM-413	VM-425	VM-907	VM-916
VM-146	VM-268	VM-414	VM-429	VM-908	VM-919
VM-153	VM-270	VM-415	VM-725	VM-909	
VM-154	VM-277	VM-416	VM-807	VM-910	

Yelva-class diving tender VM-416—off Sevastopol'; note gantry for submersible diver's decompression chamber to port at the aft end of the superstructure Boris Lemachko, 2000

VM-413 Boris Lemachko, 2-06

D: 279 tons (300 fl) **S:** 12.4 kts **Dim:** 40.90 (37.00 pp) × 8.00 × 2.02
Electronics: Radar: 1 Don-2 or Mius (Spin Trough) nav.—Sonar: MGA-1 HF
M: 2 Type 3D-12A diesels; 2 props; 600 bhp **Electric:** 200 kw tot.
Range: 1,870/12 **Endurance:** 10 days **Crew:** 24 tot. + 4 divers

Remarks: Can support two divers at once to 60 m. Have a built-in decompression chamber; some (but not all) also have a submersible decompression chamber. Have one 2.5-ton-capacity derrick. Endurance has also been reported as 1,500 n.m. at 10 kts. Additional units are in civilian service. Known fleet assignments: VM-153, -277, -414, -425, -429, -725, -809, -908, -915, and -916 in the Northern Fleet; VM-146, -263, -270, -409, -415, -420, -807, and -910 in the Pacific; VM-250, -268, and -909 in the Baltic; and VM-154, -413, and -416 in the Black Sea.
Disposals: Baltic Fleet units VM-143 and -266 were stricken 22-2-93 and Pacific Fleet unit VM-251 on 5-7-94. VM-152 was stricken from the Black Sea Fleet 10-1-96 and transferred to Ukraine. Several were exported, including VM-917 to Libya in 1973 and two to Cuba (in 1973 and 1978; one later lost).

SERVICE CRAFT *(continued)*

♦ up to 54 Nyryat'-1-class (Project 522) diving tenders [YDT]
(In serv. 1955–mid-1960s)

From among:

VM-1	VM-72	VM-88	VM-122	VM-153	VM-203
VM-7	VM-73	VM-89	VM-125	VM-155	VM-260
VM-9	VM-74	VM-91	VM-126	VM-159	VM-261
VM-10	VM-75	VM-93	VM-129	VM-189	VM-277
VM-33	VM-76	VM-99	VM-142	VM-191	
VM-34	VM-77	VM-103	VM-147	VM-192	
VM-48	VM-79	VM-107	VM-148	VM-193	
VM-65	VM-80	VM-113	VM-149	VM-194	
VM-70	VM-82	VM-115	VM-150	VM-195	
VM-71	VM-87	VM-116	VM-151	VM-201	

Nyryat'-1-class diving tender VM-9—with enclosed pilothouse added atop the original position Boris Lemachko, 2000

D: 105.4 tons (115 fl) **S:** 10 kts **Dim:** 28.50 × 5.50 × 1.70
Electronics: Radar: 1 Mius (Spin Trough) nav. or none
M: 1 Type 6CSP 28/3C diesel; 1 prop; 450 bhp
Range: 900/9 **Endurance:** 10 days **Crew:** 15–22 tot.

Remarks: VM = *Vodolaznyy Morskoy* (Seagoing Diving Tender). Survivors of about 60 built for Soviet Navy. Same hull was used for the GPB-480-class inshore survey craft. Others were built for export. The commanding officer is usually an experienced *michman* (warrant officer). Can support hard-hat divers to 20-m depths. As built, could be equipped with one 12.7-mm mg. Black Sea Fleet unit VM-122 bears the name *Udomlya.*
Disposals: Northern Fleet units VM-105 and -121 were offered for scrap in 1992. VM-84, -106, and -127 were stricken from the Baltic Fleet 22-2-93. VM-5, -14, -114, and -230 were stricken from the Black Sea Fleet 10-1-96 and transferred to Ukraine. VM-125 was mistakenly accidentally attacked and sunk by Syrian aircraft during 1989, but the craft was evidently salvaged, as she was listed as active as of 2000.

♦ . . . Nyryat'-2 (Yaroslavets)-class (Project 376) diving tenders [YDT]
Bldr: Yaroslavl Zavod (In serv. 1950s–90) and Sosnnovskiy Sudostroitel'nyy Zavod (1995– . . .)

From among:

RVK-220 through RVK-257	RVK-1159
RVK-259 through RVK-500	RVK-1349
RVK-617	RVK-1446
RVK-667	RVK-1893
RVK-780 through RVK-790	RVK-1947
RVK-850 through RVK-900	RVK-2081
RVK-920	

Black Sea Fleet Nyryat'-2-class diving tender RVK-617—with the characteristic bulwarks from bow to stern that distinguish this variant of the ubiquitous Project 376 launch Hartmut Ehlers, 7-00

D: 32.2 tons (38.2 fl) **S:** 9–10 kts **Dim:** 21.00 × 3.90 × 1.40 (max.; 1.26 mean)
Electronics: Radar: 1 Spin Trough nav. or none
M: 1 Type 3D-6S1 diesel; 1 prop; 150 bhp
Electric: 10 kw tot. (1 × 10 kw, DGPN-8/1500 diesel driving)
Range: 1,600/8 **Fuel:** 1.5 tons **Endurance:** 5 days
Crew: 10 tot. as diving tender

Remarks: Over 600 Project 376 launches have been built to the same general design for military and civilian use, of which 400 were said still to be in military service as of 1998. Nyryat'-2 was a NATO nickname applied to PO-2-class workboats configured as diving tenders with bow or full-length bulwarks (see under [YFL]), but some diving tenders do not have any bulwarks at all. Can support hard-hat divers to 20-m depths. All-steel construction. Can be operated safely in Force 8 winds and 2-m seas and can break light ice.

♦ 11 Muna-class (Project 1823, 1823B, 1824B, and 1824T) ammmunition lighters [YE]
Bldr: . . . SY, Nikolayev, Ukraine, and Nakhodka SY (In serv. 1966–85)

VTR-6	VTR-85	VTR-91
VTR-28	VTR-87	VTR-94
VTR-76	VTR-89	VTR-148
VTR-83	VTR-90	

Muna-class munitions lighter VTR-83 Boris Lemachko, 2002

D: 457 tons (688 fl) **S:** 11 kts **Dim:** 51.50 × 8.40 × 2.70
Electronics: Radar: 1 Mius (Spin Trough) nav.
M: 1 Type 6DR 30/50 diesel; 1 prop; 600 bhp
Range: 1,700/10 **Endurance:** 15 days **Crew:** 15 tot. + 7 passengers

Remarks: Built in several different configurations: some as torpedo transports, others to carry surface-to-air missiles. The newest, VTR-76, was completed 17-12-85. Originally carried MBSS (*Morskaya Barzha Samokhodnaya Sukhogruznaya,* Seagoing Self-Propelled Dry Cargo Lighter)-series pennants but now have VTR (*Voyennyy Transport,* Military Transport)-series pennants. Two others were converted into coastal survey ships (since stricken) and another two into trials craft [YAGE] OS-114 and OS-220 (q.v.). VTR-76, -85, -87, -89, -90, and -91 are assigned to the Pacific; VTR-94 remains in Black Sea Fleet service, and subordination of the others listed is not available. The Federal Border Guard operates several others.
Hull systems: Usually have a single 3.2-ton-capacity electric crane positioned between two or four small holds. Deadweight cargo capacity is 175 tons.
Disposals: VTR-93 was stricken 10-1-96 and was in Ukraine Navy service as of 8-97. VTR-32, -39, -48, -77, -81, -86, -92 and -97 were stricken by 2005.

♦ 1 Vydra-class (Project 106K) cargo lighter [YF]
Bldr: . . . (In serv. 1967–69)

BSS-705200 (ex-MDK- . . .)

D: 308 tons light (550 fl) **S:** 10.5 kts
Dim: 54.50 (50.00 pp) × 7.70 (7.50 wl) × 2.25 (mean hull)
Electronics: Radar: 1 Don-2 nav.
M: 2 Type 3D-12 diesels; 2 Kort-nozzle props; 600 bhp
Range: 1,400/10 (loaded) **Endurance:** 8 days **Crew:** 12 tot.

Remarks: The only current unit to have been redesignated as a service craft out of 15 survivors of the 46 built for Russian use as utility landing craft. Assigned to the Black Sea Fleet. The cargo deck is 30.0 × 4.5 m and can accommodate up to 176 tons of vehicles or cargo (6 ZIL-131 or 10 GAZ-66 trucks).

♦ 1 or more SMB-1-class (Project 106) cargo lighters [YF]
Bldr: . . . (In serv. 1958–65)

MBSS-233200

D: 180 tons light; 280 tons std. (356 fl) **S:** 10.5 kts
Dim: 48.20 (44.40 pp) × 6.70 (5.50 wl) × 1.90 (mean hull)
M: 2 Type 3D-12 diesels; 2 props; 600 bhp
Range: 1,200/10 (loaded) **Endurance:** 5 days **Crew:** 12 tot.

Remarks: Former utility landing craft employed as local-service supply craft, the survivors of 20 built. Assigned to the Caspian or the Black Sea. The cargo deck is 25.0 × 4.0 m and can accommodate up to 176 tons of vehicles or cargo (6 ZIL-131 or 10 GAZ-66 trucks).

SERVICE CRAFT *(continued)*

SMB-1-class cargo lighter MBSS-233200 Boris Lemachko, 1999

♦ 12 Project 411B dry cargo lighters [YF]
Bldr: Vyborg Zavod (In serv. 1958–61)

MBSN-405250	MBSN-449250	MBSN-465250	MBSN-804250
MBSN-430250	MBSN-452250	MBSN-466250	MBSN-815250
MBSN-437250	MBSN-454250	MBSN-802250	MBSN-818250

D: 320 tons (fl) **S:** 9 kts **Dim:** 35.0 × . . . × . . .
M: 1 Type 3D-12 diesel; 1 prop; 300 bhp **Range:** 1,150/9 **Crew:** 8 tot.

Project 411B dry cargo lighters MBSN-454250 and MBSN-4532250—modified to drip four drum-shaped buoys to establish a 4-point moor, probably in support of salvage work Boris Lemachko, 1999

Remarks: Either the above list is incomplete or some of these craft have had their pennant numbers changed over the years (as evidenced by the photo of an MBSN-4532250).

♦ 2 Lentra (Logger)-class cargo lighters [YF]
Bldr: Leningradskaya Kuznitsa Zavod, Kiev, Ukraine (In serv. 10-55)

Alma Pakhra

Lentra-class cargo lighter Alma Hartmut Ehlers, 7-00

D: 250 tons (479 fl) **S:** 10 kts **Dim:** 39.20 × 7.30 × 2.80
Electronics: Radar: 1 Mius (Spin Trough) nav.
M: 1 Type 8 NVD-36 diesel; 1 prop; 300 bhp
Range: 6,900/9 **Fuel:** 41.7 tons **Crew:** 21 tot.

Remarks: Modified fishing craft employed as local cargo transports, *Pakhra* in the Caspian Flotilla and *Alma* in the Black Sea Fleet. Can carry up to 55 tons of liquid cargo in addition to solid stores stowed in two holds.

♦ 1 or more Shalanda (BSS-53150)-class (Project 431) cargo lighters [YF]
Bldr: . . . (In serv. 1951 to late 1950s)

MNS-30150

D: 158 tons light (326 fl) **S:** 8.2 kts **Dim:** 36.00 × 6.90 × 2.00
M: 1 Type 3D-12 diesel; 1 prop; 300 bhp
Range: 500/8 **Endurance:** 10 days **Crew:** 8 tot.

Shalanda-class lighter MNS-30150—at Sevastopol' Boris Lemachko, 7-00

Remarks: Although many have been discarded, a few of the 60 built may still be in service. The standard version could carry 150 tons of dry cargo and was normally equipped with one 3-ton electric crane. Some were configured as slaked lime transports in support of the now-discarded Quebec-class (Project A615), Kreislauf-cycle submarines.

Note: Some 150 floating dry docks served the Soviet Navy at the end of the 1980s (of which all but about 30 were the property of the Ministry of Shipbuilding), but only five of them had capacities of 25,000 tons or more; many of the older ones have since been abandoned, but newer units are listed below. Most Russian floating dry docks were built in Yugoslavia. PD = *Plavuchiya Dok* (Floating Dry Dock). See also [YRD] for specialized transport docks. An unfinished 13,500-ton-capacity floating dock was purchased from the Kherson Shipyard during 7-97 for use in scrapping discarded nuclear-powered submarines in the Northern Fleet area; the craft has steel sidewalls and a reinforced concrete pontoon hull.

A new floating dry dock for use in scrapping retired Pacific Fleet nuclear-powered submarines was delivered by Pallada Shipyard, Ukraine, on 25-4-02; it had been begun in 1993.

♦ 1 PD-50-class large floating dry dock [YFDB]
Bldr: Götaverken, Arendal, Sweden (In serv. 1980)

PD-50

Capacity: 80,000 tons **Dim:** 330.00 × 67.00 × 6.10

Remarks: Assigned to the Northern Fleet. Has been employed for docking aircraft carriers and was used for docking the salvaged hulk of the submarine *Kursk*. Has one 50-ton and one 30-ton traveling crane. Flooded draft over blocks is 15 m. Has a crew of about 175 tot.

♦ 1 PD-41-class large floating dry dock [YFDB]
Bldr: Ishikawajima-Harima Heavy Industries, Tokyo (In serv. 10-78)

PD-41

Capacity: 80,000 tons **Dim:** 305.00 × 67.00 × 6.00

Remarks: Assigned to the Pacific Fleet and has been employed for docking aircraft carriers. Has two 30-ton traveling cranes. Flooded draft over blocks is 15 m. Has a crew of about 175 tot.

♦ 2 PD-81-class large floating dry docks [YFDB]
Bldr: . . . (In serv. 1979–80)

PD-81 PD- . . .

Capacity: 29,300 tons **Dim:** 250.00 × 38.30 × 5.20

Remarks: One is assigned to the Pacific Fleet at Vladivostok. Have one 20-ton and one 15-ton traveling cranes. Flooded draft over blocks is 11.4 m.

♦ 1 Project 2121-class large floating dry dock [YFDB]
Bldr: . . . (In serv. 1980)

Sukhona

Capacity: 25,000 tons **Dim:** 199.0 × 42.0 × 7.0

Remarks: Assigned to the Northern Fleet and has been employed for docking *Kiev*-class aircraft carriers. Has two 25-ton traveling cranes. Flooded draft over blocks is 13 m and distance between wing walls is 27 m.

♦ 1 Shilka-class (Project 1780) medium floating dry dock [YFDM]
Bldr: Amur Shipyard (In serv. . . .)

Shilka

Capacity: 12,000 tons
Dim: 180.00 × 35.00 (24.00 dock floor width) × 16.80 (max.)

Remarks: Covered, climate-controlled dock built for Russian Navy Pacific Fleet submarine use on the Kamchatka Peninsula. Has 10-m maximum water depth above keel blocks when flooded. There are two 10-ton, two 8-ton (2.3-ton at maximum reach), and three 0.5-ton cranes. Diesel generators are fitted. The design is also offered for export.

SERVICE CRAFT *(continued)*

♦ . . . Project 1760 medium floating dry docks [YFDM]
Bldr: . . . (In serv. . . .)

Capacity: 8,500 tons **Dim:** 155.0 × 32.4 × 4.5

Remarks: Concrete construction. Have two 5-ton traveling cranes. Flooded draft over blocks is 7.0 m and width between wing walls is 23.4 m.

♦ 3 Project 823 medium floating dry docks [YFDM]
Bldr: . . . (In serv. 1965– . . .)

PD-3 . . . . . .

Capacity: 6,500 tons **Dim:** 155.0 × 31.0 × 5.0

Remarks: Concrete construction. Have two 5-ton traveling cranes. Flooded draft over blocks is 8.5 m and width between wing walls is 22.5 m.

Project 823 medium floating dry dock PD-3—under tow in the Sea of Japan; note the extensive superstructure atop one side of the dockwall and the traveling crane on the other; stowed horizontally atop the long superstructure is a tall, slender vent stack, an indication that the dock is intended to service nuclear-powered submarines
JMSDF

♦ 2 Project 122A medium floating dry docks [YFDM]
Bldr: . . .

PD-27 (In serv. 1954) . . . (In serv. 1960)

Capacity: 6,000 tons **Dim:** 140.0 × 32.0 × 4.4

Remarks: Have two 5-ton traveling cranes. Flooded draft over blocks is 7.0 m and width between wing walls is 21.3 m.

♦ 1 Project 782 medium floating dry dock [YFDM]
Bldr: . . . (In serv. 1954)

PD-45

Capacity: 8,000 tons **Dim:** 120.0 × 37.4 × 4.3

Remarks: Steel construction. Has two 3-ton traveling cranes. Flooded draft over blocks is 8.0 m and width between wing walls is 24.4 m.

Note: The following three dock classes were typed PDE and were better equipped to perform more complex repairs.

♦ 1 Project 13560 medium repair floating dry dock [YFDM]
Bldr: . . . (In serv. 1985)

PD- . . .

Capacity: 8,500 tons **Dim:** 148.7 × 35.0 × 5.2

Remarks: Concrete construction. Has two 12-ton and two 10-ton traveling cranes. Flooded draft over blocks is 10.0 m and width between wing walls is 20.0 m.

♦ 1 Project 1780 medium repair floating dry dock [YFDM]
Bldr: . . . (In serv. 1977)

PD-71

Capacity: 13,400 tons **Dim:** 180.0 × 35.0 × 6.2

Remarks: Steel construction. Has two 10-ton and four 8-ton traveling cranes. Flooded draft over blocks is 10.0 m and width between wing walls is 20.6 m.

♦ 3 Project 1777 medium repair floating dry docks [YFDM]
Bldr: . . . (In serv. 1973–78)

PD-73 . . . . . .

Capacity: 9,100 tons **Dim:** 160.0 × 32.4 × 7.3

Remarks: Concrete construction. Have two 10-ton and two 8-ton traveling cranes. Flooded draft over blocks is 9.1 m and width between wing walls is 21.4 m.

♦ . . . Project 1758 small floating dry docks [YFDL]
Bldr . . . (In serv. 1970s)

Capacity: 4,500 tons **Dim:** 118.0 × 29.6 × 3.3

Remarks: Concrete construction. Have two 5-ton traveling cranes. Flooded draft over blocks is 6.3 m and width between wing walls is 20.0 m.

♦ 1 Project 765 small floating dry dock [YFDL]
Bldr: . . . (In serv. 1967)

PD-6

Capacity: 2,000 tons **Dim:** 91.0 × 15.0 × 6.0

Remarks: Steel construction. Has two 5-ton traveling cranes. Flooded draft over blocks is 6.5 m.

♦ 45 Flamingo (Tanya)-class (Project 1415.1) workboats [YFL]
Bldr: Sosnovka Zavod, Rybinsk; Yaroslavl Zavod; and others (In serv. 1976–90s)

6 BSK-series:

BSK-2	BSK-12	BSK-15
BSK-3	BSK-14	BSK-16

17 RK (Rednyy Kater, *Roadstead Cutter*)-series:

RK-78	RK-676	RK-963	RK-1206	RK-1394	RK-1886
RK-340	RK-931	RK-994	RK-1214	RK-1403	RK-1978
RK-413	RK-962	RK-995	RK-1243	RK-1664	

18 PRDKA (Protivodiversionniye Kater, *Counterswimmer Cutter*)-series:

PRDKA-316	PRDKA-391	PRDKA-407	PRDKA-1356
PRDKA-331	PRDKA-400	PRDKA-409	PRDKA-1376
PRDKA-333	PRDKA-402	PRDKA-419	PRDKA-1978
PRDKA-372	PRDKA-404	PRDKA-838	
PRDKA-376	PRDKA-405	PRDKA-885	

4 named units:

H. Bezhlivtsev	M. Naumov
I. Paskirev	N. Rudenko

Flamingo-class workboat RK-1243 Boris Lemachko, 2003

D: 42 tons (54 fl) **S:** 11 kts **Dim:** 21.20 × 3.93 × 1.40
Electronics: Radar: 1 Lotsiya nav. (not always fitted)
M: 1 Type 3D-12A or 3D-12L diesel; 1 prop; 300 bhp
Electric: 12 kw tot. (DGR 1A-16/1500 generator)
Range: 200/11 **Endurance:** 5 days **Crew:** 4 tot. + 27 passengers

Remarks: Designed by Redan Central Design Bureau. RK (*Reydnyy Kater*) workboat version has a capacity for 27 passengers or 17 tons of cargo. Others are equipped as diving tenders [YDT] and inshore survey craft [YGS] (q.v.), while additional units are assigned to the border guard as patrol boats, and one, TS-581, is used by the customs service. The numbers painted on the craft may change with varying assignments or changes of basing, as few photos show craft with any of the numbers listed above.

♦ 1 (+ 4) Project 21270 flag officers' yachts [YFL]
Bldr: Severnaya Verf, St. Petersburg (In serv. 25-6-03-. . .)

Burevstnik

D: 85 tons (fl) **S:** 25+ kts **Dim:** 32.0 (27.4 pp) × 6.5 (6.2 wl)
Electronics: Radar: 1 . . . nav.
M: 2 Zvezda . . . diesels; 1 prop; . . . bhp
Crew: 6 tot. + 20 passengers

Remarks: A contract for two was announced in 9-00, later increased to five. Will replace aging craft now in use as flag officer barges and are known as "parade motorboats." The first two will be assigned to the Kronshtadt Naval Base, which placed the initial building order. The first unit was laid down 28-4-01 and launched during 4-03.

♦ 1 Razvedchik-class (Project 1388M) flag officers' yacht [YFL]
Bldr: Sosnovka Zavod (In serv. 1983–87)

KSV-213

Officers' yacht KSV-213 NAVPIC Holland, 10-01

SERVICE CRAFT *(continued)*

D: 220 tons (270 fl) **S:** 31 kts **Dim:** 46.0 × 6.0 × 2.1
Electronics: Radar: 1 Mius (Spin Trough) nav.
M: 2 M-504-series diesels; 2 props; 9,000 bhp
Range: 1,500/10 **Endurance:** 10 days **Crew:** 14 tot.

Remarks: KSV = *Katera Svyazi* (Communications Cutter). Adapted from the version of Project 1388 configured as a radiological monitoring craft [YAG]. Has a a full-height after deckhouse and no torpedo retrieval ramp.

♦ **14 Project 14670 officers' yachts [YFL]**
Bldr: Yuzhnaya Tochka Zavod, Feodosiya, Ukraine (In serv. 1985–88)

KSV-9 Sokol	KSV-1499	Chaika
KSV-316 Gurzuf	KSV-1537	Kronshtadt
KSV-1135 Berkut	KSV-1594	Lastochka
KSV-1380	KSV-1754	Lebed'
KSV-1460	Burun	

Burun—Project 14670 officers' yacht Boris Lemachko, 2001

D: 38 tons (49 fl) **S:** 31 kts **Dim:** 24.0 × 5.2 × 1.9
A: None **Electronics:** Radar: 1 . . . nav.
M: 2 M-50F-series diesels; 2 props; 2,400 bhp
Range: 700/29; 1,100/15 **Endurance:** 5 days **Crew:** 12 tot.

Remarks: KSV = *Katera Svyazi* (Communications Cutter); used for local control and liaison activities. One source says only eight were built, so the named units may duplicate known KSV numbers. Design is based on the Zhuk-class (Project 1400) patrol boat hull. *Lebed'* and *Kronshtadt* are in the Baltic Fleet; KSV-1594 is in the Caspian Flotilla; and the other three fleets are said to have one or two each. Sister *Pogranichnik* ("Border Guardsman") is assigned to the Federal Border Guard

♦ **4 Project 360 flag officers' yachts [YFL]**
Bldr: Sudostroitel'noye Obyedineniye "Almaz," Petrovskiy SY, St. Petersburg (In serv. 1961–64)

KSV-11 KSV-12 KSV-21 Shtorm

Shtorm—Project 360 flag officers' yacht Boris Lemachko Collection, 2003

D: 136.7 tons (149.6 fl) **S:** 35.6 kts **Dim:** 37.15 × 7.50 × 2.41
Electronics: Radar: 1 . . . nav.
M: 2 M-503-series radial diesels; 2 props; 6,600 bhp
Range: 460/26 **Endurance:** 5 days **Crew:** 13 tot.

Remarks: KSV = *Katera Svyazi* (Communications Cutter). Yacht version of the Project 205–series (NATO Osa-class) missile boat design. KSV-11 is in the Baltic Fleet and *Shtorm* in the Pacific Fleet; the subordination of the others is not available. Black Sea Fleet sister *Merkuriy* was transferred to Georgia during 1998 and is now used as a patrol boat.

♦ **4 Al'batros-class (Project 183Sh) flag officers' yachts [YFL]**
Bldr: Sudostroitel'noye Obyedineniye "Almaz," Petrovskiy SY, St. Petersburg (In serv. ca. 1964–75)

Shkval Tayfun Tsiklon Uragan

Project 183Sh officers' yacht Shkval NAVPIC-Holland, 10-01

D: 56.6 tons (68 fl) **S:** 39 kts **Dim:** 23.7 × 6.1 × 1.3
Electronics: Radar: 1 . . . nav.
M: 4 M-50F-1 diesels; 4 props; 4,800 bhp
Range: 320/32 **Fuel:** 7.2 tons **Endurance:** 5 days **Crew:** 11 tot.

Remarks: Able to accommodate about 40 personnel for short trips. The hullform is derived from that of the wooden-hulled P-6 torpedo boat. *Shkval* is in the Northern Fleet, the others in the Pacific Fleet.
Disposals: Baltic Sea Fleet unit *Al'batros,* Black Sea Fleet unit *Burevestnik,* and Northern Fleet unit *Chayka* have been stricken since 1999. Black Sea Fleet unit *Sokol* (KSV-9) was transferred to Ukraine. *Berkut* (ex-KSV-1135) was stricken in 1994 and is now in private hands at Balaklava.

♦ **12 Polish Bryza-class (Project 772) personnel ferries [YFL]**
Bldr: Stocznia Wisla, Gdansk, Poland, and Neftegaz Zavod (In serv. 1967–79)

MK-55	MK-326	PSK-49	PSK-228
MK199	PSK-43	PSK-55	PSK-236
MK-321	PSK-44	PSK-58	PSK-537

Bryza-class PSK-537—at Sevastopol' Boris Lemachko, 7-99

D: 134 tons (144.5 fl) **S:** 10.5 kts **Dim:** 28.82 × 6.30 × 2.00
Electronics: Radar: 2 . . . nav.
M: 2 Type 3-D6 or Wola DM-150 diesels; 2 props; 300 bhp
Electric: 84 kw tot. **Range:** 1,100/10 **Crew:** 11 tot. + . . . passengers

Remarks: Six others of the slightly different Project 772U are employed as training craft [YXT]. Dozens of this class have been retired.

♦ **37 Nazhimovets-class (Project 286) personnel ferries [YFL]**
Bldr: . . . (In serv. 1954–64)

MK-31	PSK-1993 (ex-PK-1)
MK-38	PSK-2005 (ex-MK-22)
MK-45 through MK-60	PSK-2006
PK-6 through PK-19	PSK-2007
PSK-1991 (ex-MK-4)	

Nazhimovets-class personnel ferry 1679—at Murmansk NAVPIC-Holland, 10-01

SERVICE CRAFT *(continued)*

D: 87 tons (105 fl) **S:** 11.2 kts **Dim:** 26.90 × 5.30 × 1.85
M: 1 Type 3D-12 diesel; 1 prop; 300 bhp
Endurance: 5 days **Crew:** 5 tot. + 123 passengers

Remarks: Several have local names. Most seem to have been assigned to the Pacific Fleet, from which PSK-12 was stricken in 1995.

♦ . . . PO-2 (Yaroslavets)-class (Project 376) workboats [YFL]
Bldr: Yaroslavl Zavod (In serv. 1950s–90) and Sosnovskiy Sudostroitel'nyy Zavod (1995 . . .)

P-376	RK-45	RK-518	RK-1116	RK-636
RK-25	RK-162	RK-778	RK-1818	and others

RK-636 Boris Lemachko, 7-06

D: 32.2 tons (38.2 fl) **S:** 9–10 kts **Dim:** 21.00 × 3.90 × 1.40 (max.; 1.26 mean)
Electronics: Radar: 1 Mius (Spin Trough) nav. or none
M: 1 Type 3D-6S1 diesel; 1 prop; 150 bhp
Electric: 10 kw tot. (1 × 10 kw, DGPN-8/1500 diesel driving)
Range: 1,600/8 **Fuel:** 1.5 tons **Endurance:** 5 days
Crew: 4–6 tot. as utility craft

Remarks: RK = *Reydniy Kater* (Roadstead Cutter). More than 600 have been built to the same general design for military and civilian use, of which 390 were said still to be in military service as of 2001; some were configured as Nyryat'-2-class diving tenders [YDT] and others as survey craft [YGS] and training craft [YXT] (q.v.). All-steel construction. Can be operated safely in Force 8 winds and 2-m seas and can break light ice. Are rail transportable. The craft remain under construction at Sosnovka for military and civil use. P-376 is used as a patrol boat in the Pacific Fleet and may mount a 12.7-mm 2M-1 or 14.5-mm 2M-7 twin machinegun.

♦ Up to 65 Admiralets-class (Project 371bis and 371U) workboats [YFL]
Bldr: . . . (In serv. 1956– . . .)

P-721 through P-730	RK-1101	RK-1351	RK-1781
RK-1009	RK-1107	RK-1513	RK-1821
RK-1048	RK-1119	RK-1585	RK-2084
RK-1049	RK-1159	RK-1645	RK-210
RK-1050	RK-1189	RK-1709	RK-2113
RK-1056	RK-1194	RK-1728	RK-2271
RK-1070	RK-1238	RK-1733	RK-2323
RK-1088	RK-1341	RK-1757	

D: 9.41 tons (fl) **S:** 13.5 kts **Dim:** 12.61 × 3.23 × 1.10
M: 1 3D-6 diesel; 1 prop; 150 bhp **Range:** 140/13 **Crew:** 2 tot.

Remarks: Units with P-series pennants are probably used for harbor patrol duties; the others are *Reydniy Katera* (Roadstead Cutters) used as general-utility launches.

Note: Also in service in 2001 were up to 82 harbor utility craft of Projects T-63, -73, -351, and -433; all had Type 3D-6 diesel engines of 150 bhp, but no further information is available.

♦ Up to 32 Slavyanka-class (Project 20150) harbor utility craft [YFU]
Bldr: . . ., Slavyanka (In serv. 1979–98)

Slavyanka-class harbor utility craft BSS-050 Hartmut Ehlers, 7-96

D: 36 tons light (78.2 fl) **S:** 9.8 kts **Dim:** 21.90 × 5.81 × 1.00
M: 1 diesel; 1 prop; 470 bhp **Crew:** 2 tot.

Remarks: Resemble vehicle landing craft and have a bow ramp. Used for local stores transport. Some have BSS-series pennants (including BSS-74050) and others have pennants in the RBK series (including RBK-2019).

♦ Up to 35 Vostok-class (Project 1733) harbor utility craft [YFU]
Bldr: . . . (In serv. 1969–80)

D: 18.56 tons light (38.9 fl) **S:** 8.2 kts **Dim:** 16.50 (pp) × 4.78 × 1.00
M: 1 diesel; 1 prop; 235 bhp **Crew:** 2 tot.

Remarks: Resemble vehicle landing craft and have a bow ramp. The open vehicle/cargo compartment forward is 9.5 m long by 3.9 m wide.

♦ 2 BGK-1701-class (Project 16611) inshore-survey craft [YGS]
Bldr: Vympel Zavod, Rybinsk (In serv. 1996)

GS-438 (In serv. 1996) GS-439 (In serv. 1997)

BGK-1701-class survey craft GS-439 —at Kronshtadt; note the extendible side-looking bottom-mapping sonar support boom in stowed position, folded aft along the side of the craft, which has a black hull and white superstructure
Boris Lemachko, 1998

D: 310 tons light (384.7 fl) **S:** 11.5 kts
Dim: 39.80 (37.76 wl) × 7.80 (9.80 over survey sonar supports) × 2.20
Electronics: Radar: 1 . . . nav.
M: 2 DRA-525 diesels; 2 Kort-nozzle props; 400 bhp—bow-thruster
Range: . . . / . . . **Endurance:** 10 days **Crew:** 22 tot.

Remarks: Intended for sea bottom surveys in coastal regions and probably to have been a replacement for the GPB-480 design. Are equipped with booms on either beam to support towed mapping sonar arrays; when extended, the array is 42.6 m wide and permits surveying at 6 kts. No further construction has been reported.

♦ 2 Vinograd (Ayristo)-class coastal survey ships [YGS]
Bldr: Rauma-Repola SY, Savonlinna, Finland

GS-525 (In serv. 12-11-85) GS-526 (In serv. 17-12-85)

Vinograd-class survey craft GS-525—in refit at Rostock, Germany
Hartmut Ehlers, 6-98

D: 372 tons light (499 fl) **S:** 10 kts (8.5 sust.)
Dim: 32.30 (28.60 pp) × 9.60 × 2.60
Electronics: Radar: 1 Mius (Spin Trough) nav.
M: 2 Baykal 300 diesels; 2 CP props; 598 bhp
Range: 1,000/6 **Endurance:** 10 days **Crew:** 19 tot. (civilian)

Remarks: Have small side-scan sonars that lower from recesses on the hull sides amidships. Data are processed and recorded by electronic computer, the first such system on a Russian survey ship class. GS-525 is in the Baltic Fleet, GS-526 in the Northern Fleet. GS-525 was refitted at Neptunwerft, Rostock, during 1998.

♦ 26 Flamingo (Tanya)-class (Project 1415.2) inshore survey craft [YGS]
Bldr: Sosnovka Zavod, Rybinsk; Yaroslavl Zavod; and others (In serv. 1976–90s)

BGK-193	BGK-817	BGK-1512	BGK-1627	BGK-1938
BGK-326	BGK-1373	BGK-1515	BGK-1631	BGK-1939
BGK-498	BGK-1416	BGK-1554	BGK-1641	
BGK-585	BGK-1417	BGK-1557	BGK-1642	
BGK-717	BGK-1506	BGK-1567	BGK-1919	
BGK-799	BGK-1507	BGK-1596	BGK-1937	

SERVICE CRAFT *(continued)*

Flamingo-class survey craft BGK-1631—at St. Petersburg, with a surveyors' reference pole lashed to the mast — Boris Lemachko, 2000

D: 42 tons (54 fl) **S:** 11 kts **Dim:** 21.20 × 3.93 × 1.40
Electronics: Radar: 1 Lotsiya nav. (not always fitted)
M: 1 Type 3D-12A or 3D-12L diesel; 1 prop; 300 bhp
Electric: 12 kw tot. (DGR 1A-16/1500 generator)
Range: 200/11 **Endurance:** 5 days **Crew:** 4 tot.

Remarks: BGK = *Bol'shoye Gidrograficheskoye Kater* (Large Hydrographic Cutter). Designed by Redan Central Design Bureau. Have hull bulwarks cut down amidships. Others of this class are configured as diving tenders [YDT] and workboats [YFL] and as patrol boats for the Federal Border Guard.

♦ Up to 69 GPB-480-class (Project 1896 and 1896U) inshore survey craft [YGS]

Bldr: Vympel Zavod, Rybinsk (In serv. 1955–60s)

From among:

BGK-53	BGK-171	BGK-310	BGK-597	BGK-697	BGK-796
BGK-54	BGK-172	BGK-312	BGK-613	BGK-705	BGK-835
BGK-73	BGK-185	BGK-327	BGK-625	BGK-752	BGK-885
BGK-74	BGK-188	BGK-333	BGK-626	BGK-754	BGK-886
BGK-77	BGK-191	BGK-359	BGK-627	BGK-755	BGK-1505
BGK-102	BGK-192	BGK-462	BGK-628	BGK-767	BGK-1511
BGK-137	BGK-193	BGK-478	BGK-629	BGK-768	BGK-1529
BGK-140	BGK-197	BGK-480	BGK-632	BGK-785	BGK-1550
BGK-161	BGK-209	BGK-487	BGK-635	BGK-786	BGK-1554
BGK-162	BGK-210	BGK-498	BGK-652	BGK-789	UK-231
BGK-163	BGK-212	BGK-551	BGK-663	BGK-792	
BGK-167	BKG-214	BGK-574	BGK-682	BGK-793	
BGK-168	BGK-218	BGK-586	BGK-683	BGK-794	
BGK-169	BGK-244	BGK-596	BGK-685	BGK-795	

GPB-480-class BGK-785 — Boris Lemachko, 7-01

D: 92 tons (116.1 fl) **S:** 12.5 kts (11.8 sust.) **Dim:** 28.58 × 5.20 × 1.70
Electronics: 1 SNN-7 nav.
M: 1 Type 6CSP 28/3C diesel; 1 prop; 450 bhp (300 sust.)
Range: 1,500/10 **Endurance:** 10 days **Crew:** 14–15 tot.

Remarks: BGK = *Bol'shoye Gidrograficheskoye Kater* (Large Hydrographic Cutter). Also referred to as the GS-204 class. Were earlier numbered in the GPB (*Gidrograficheskoye Pribezhnyy Bot,* Coastal Hydrographic Survey Boat) series. BGK-218, -632, -685, and -886 are in the Caspian Flotilla; BGK-171, -214, -312, -613, -767, -1511, and -1529 are in the Baltic Fleet; BGK-77, -244, -333, -635, -697, and -775 in the Black Sea Fleet; BGK-73, -137, -172, -191, -192, -193, -197, -212, -310, -327, -462, -478, -487, -551, -574, -596, -597, -625, -626, -663, -754, -755, -768, -835, -885, -1505, -1550, and -1554 in the Northern Fleet; and BGK-53, -54, -74, -102, -140, -161, -162, -163, -167, -168, -169, -185, -188, -209, -210, -359, -480, -586, -627, -628, -629, -652, -682, -683, -705, -752, -785, -786, -789, -792, -795, and -796 and training unit UK-231 in the Pacific Fleet.
Disposals: Several others have been stricken, including Pacific Fleet units BGK-362, -481, -508, and -788 (the last on 5-7-94) and Black Sea Fleet units BGK-247, -716, -186, -631, -930, and -1629 (the last four on 30-7-93). BGK-37, -246, -248, -334, -650, -714, and -1589 were stricken 10-1-96 and later transferred to Ukraine. Black Sea unit BGK-775 capsized and sank in port at Novorossiysk 10-12-02 due to high winds and ice accumulation.
Hull systems: There are a 6-m^2 charthouse/laboratory and two 1.5-ton derricks. Most employ a dual side-looking mapping sonar system using transducers mounted on swinging-arm davits amidships. Displacements have grown with age, and some are as much as 98 tons light, 126 full load.

♦ 2 Gornostai-class (Project . . .) inshore survey craft [YGS]

BGK-22 BGK-28

Gornostai-class survey craft BGK-22—at Sevastopol' — Hartmut Ehlers, 8-00

Remarks: No data available. Modified fishing boats, resembling smaller versions of the GPB-480 class. BGK-22 is in the Black Sea Fleet, BGK-28 in the Baltic Fleet.

♦ 20 GPB-710 (Kayra)-class (Project 1403A) survey launches [YGS]

Bldr: . . . (In serv. 1969– . . .)

MGK-252	MGK-710	MGK-760	MGK-954	MGK-1273
MGK-352	MGK-749	MGK-771	MGK-1001	MGK-1659
MGK-657	MGK-751	MGK-840	MGK-1002	MGK-1804
MGK-678	MGK-753	MGK-879	MGK-1099	MGK-1805

D: 7 tons (fl) **S:** 10 kts **Dim:** 11.0 × 3.0 × 0.7
M: 1 diesel; 1 prop; 90 bhp **Range:** 150/10 **Endurance:** 2 days **Crew:** 6 tot.

Remarks: MGK = *Mal'yy Geografischeskoye Kater* (Small Hydrographic Cutter). GRP construction. For use either independently or transported aboard larger hydrographic survey ships.
Disposals: MGK-150, -175, -258, -912, -913, and -1098 were transferred to Ukraine 10-1-98.

♦ 16 MGK-1019 (Drofa)-class (Project 16830) survey launches [YGS]

Bldr: . . . (In serv. . . .)

MGK-1019	MGK-1782	MGK-2106
MGK-1236	MGK-2075	and others

D: 5.5 tons (fl) **S:** 7.5 kts **Dim:** 9.1 × 2.90 × 0.70
M: 1 Type 6CHSP-9.5/11 diesel; 1 prop; 65 bhp
Range: 150/7.5 **Endurance:** 1 day **Crew:** 2 tot.

Remarks: MGK = *Mal'yy Geografischeskoye Kater* (Small Hydrographic Cutter). All serve in the Caspian Flotilla. Two others, MGK-112 and MGK-1889, were transferred to Ukraine 10-1-98.

♦ . . . PO-2 (Yaroslavets)-class (Project G-376) survey launches [YGS]

Bldr: Yaroslavl Zavod (In serv. 1958–90)

BGK-11 BGK-466 BGK-747 and others

PO-2-class survey craft BGK-11 — H&L Van Ginderen, 7-00

SERVICE CRAFT *(continued)*

D: 32.2 tons (38.2 fl) **S:** 9–10 kts **Dim:** 21.00 × 3.90 × 1.40 (max.; 1.26 mean)
Electronics: Radar: 1 Mius (Spin Trough) nav. or none
M: 1 Type 3D-6S1 diesel; 1 prop; 150 bhp
Electric: 10 kw tot. (1 × 10 kw, DGPN-8/1500 diesel driving)
Range: 1,100/8 **Fuel:** 1 ton **Endurance:** 3 days **Crew:** 4–6 tot.

Remarks: More than 600 have been built to the same general design for military and civilian use. Are rail transportable. All-steel construction. Have reduced range compared with other PO-2 variants (see under [YFL] and [YXT] and under the Nyryat'-2 class [YDT]). Were originally numbered in the MGK-511 through MGK-726 series. Baltic Fleet units BGK-466 and BGK-747 have bulwarks extending from the bow to just forward of the pilothouse.

♦ 6 Burunduk-class (Project 1392V) target-control boats [YGT]
Bldr: Zelenodol'sk Zavod (In serv. 1966–70)

KVM-119 KVM-332 KVM-543 KVM-684 KVM-702 KVM-732

Burunduk-class target-control craft KVM-702 H&L Van Ginderen, 10-91

D: 160 tons (200 fl) **S:** 17 kts **Dim:** 38.60 (37.50 wl) × 7.80 (6.30 wl) × 1.44 (hull)
Electronics: Radar: 1 Rangout (Square Tie) surf. search/target detection
M: 3 M-50F-series diesels; 3 props; 3,600 bhp
Range: 300/17 **Endurance:** 5 days **Crew:** 12 tot.

Remarks: Are from among the 49 Osa (Project 205) hulls adapted for target service use. In this configuration, they are employed to operate unmanned Project 1392 target craft via the Fialka radio control system. Black Sea Fleet KVM-702 was reportedly stricken on 30-7-93 but was reported to be operational in the Black Sea Fleet again as of 1-99.
Disposals: Baltic Fleet unit KVM-659 was stricken 1-9-95.

♦ 12 Lotsman-class (Project 1392B) missile targets [YGT]
Bldr: Zelenodol'sk Zavod (In serv. 1966–70)

KM-76 KM-159 KM-447 KM-593 KM-654 KM-731
KM-102 KM-330 KM-541 KM-594 KM-730 KM-897

Lotsman-class target craft KTs-593 H&L Van Ginderen, 1995

D: 160 tons (200 fl) **S:** 17 kts **Dim:** 38.6 (37.5 wl) × 7.8 (6.3 wl) × 1.44 (hull)
M: 3 M-50F-series diesels; 3 props; 3,600 bhp
Range: 300/17 **Endurance:** 5 days **Crew:** 12 tot. (see remarks)

Remarks: Formerly designated KTs (*Kontrol'naya Tsel',* Controlled Target); designation was changed to KM (expansion not available) by 1-99. Survivors of 20 built. Employ the Osa (Project 205) missile boat hull but have a much less powerful propulsion plant. Crew disembarks when the craft is in operation. Can be equipped with radar corner reflectors to strengthen target and two heat-generator chimneys to attract infrared homing missiles. KM-593 and KM-731 are in the Black Sea Fleet.
Disposals: Black Sea Fleet units KTs-895 and -1207 were stricken 3-7-92 and KTs-332 on 30-7-93. KTs-543 and -896 had been discarded or sunk by 2001. Some or all of the above may by now have been stricken as well.

Note: The Russian Navy also employs large numbers of non-self-propelled target barges, all specially constructed for the role. Two variants predominate: the 107-m missile-target design with a tapered, ship-like hull, and the 64-m catamaran-hulled gunnery-target barge.

♦ 12 SK-620 (Drakon)-class (Project 620) ambulance craft [YH]
Bldr: Stocznia Wisla, Gdansk, Poland (In serv. 1978–84)

MK-391 MK-1408 PSK-1411 SN-401
MK-1303 MK-1409 SN-126 SN-1320
MK-1407 PSK-382 SN-128 SN-1520

SK-620-class PSK-405—since retired Frank Findler, 6-02

D: 306.6 tons light (341 fl) **S:** 11.2 kts **Dim:** 39.41 (36.00 pp) × 8.40 × 2.15
Electronics: Radar: 1 or 2 Mius (Spin Trough) nav.
M: 2 Wola 56ANM30-H12, 1,600-rpm diesels; 2 props; 620 bhp
Electric: 156 kVA tot. (3 × 52 kVA, Wola SW400/E53 diesel-driven)
Range: 1,000/10 **Endurance:** 6 days (with 32 persons aboard)
Crew: 14 tot. + 3 medical personnel and 15 patients (25 in emergency)

Remarks: A total of 35 were built. Pennant numbers were initially in the SK-600 series (SK = *Sanitarnyy Kater,* Clinical Cutter); the 12 later units were designated MK (*Mestaya Kater,* . . . Cutter). Those with PSK-series pennants have been used as personnel ferries. Ambulance craft are white painted and have NBC warfare defensive measures, a sick bay with 12 berths, an isolation space with two berths, an operating room, a disinfection chamber, a first-aid station, and medical equipment storerooms. Very similar to the slightly smaller Petrushka-class training craft by the same builder.
Disposals: PSK-405 and PSK-673 were no longer in service as of 2003.

♦ 30 Toplivo-2 (Kair)-class (Project 1844 and 1844D*) liquid cargo lighters [YO]
Bldrs: Kherson SY; Khabarov SY; and Alexandria SY, Egypt (In serv. 1958–84)

MNS-35500 VTN-34 VTN-46 VTN-66 VTN-82*
PUS-1 VTN-35 VTN-48 VTN-68 VTN-95
VTN-24 VTN-36 VTN-53 VTN-71 VTN-96
VTN-26 VTN-37 VTN-58 VTN-72 VTN-98
VTN-28 VTN-39 VTN-60* VTN-75 VTN-99
VTN-30 VTN-45 VTN-64 VTN-78 VUS-22

Toplivo-2-class fuel lighter VTN-28 Boris Lemachko, 9-01

D: 466–547 tons (1,140–1,180 fl) **S:** 10 kts
Dim: 54.26 (49.40 pp) × 7.40 × 3.10–3.44
Electronics: Radar: 1 Mius (Spin Trough) or Don-2 nav.
M: 1 Russkiy Dizel 6 DR30/50-5-2 diesel; 1 prop; 600 bhp **Electric:** 250 kw tot.
Range: 1,500/10 **Fuel:** 19 tons **Endurance:** 20 days **Crew:** 20–24 tot.

Remarks: 308 grt/508 dwt. The series built in Egypt was terminated by Soviet expulsion. VTN-64, -66, and -96 are assigned to the Black Sea Fleet; VTN-28, -37, -60, and -82 to the Pacific Fleet; VTN-24 and -30 to the Baltic Fleet; VTN-45 and -95 to the Caspian Flotilla; and the others to the Northern Fleet. VTN-60 and -82 (completed 16-7-84) are of Project 1844D, differences unknown. PUS-1 and VUS-22 serve as special liquid cargo lighters. MNS-35500 has for some reason been relegated to harbor service.
Disposals: Black Sea Fleet sisters VTN-38 and -81 were stricken 10-1-96 and transferred, probably in 6-97, to Ukraine. Pacific Fleet unit VTN-43 was stricken 31-7-96 and sold for commercial use. Baltic Fleet unit VZS-431 was stricken by 1994 and is used as a fuel barge at Admiralty Shipyard, Sudomekh division.
Hull systems: Have four cargo tanks, totaling 606 m^2. As fuel lighters, can carry up to 495 tons fuel oil. Fully seagoing, if required. Have one 0.5-ton hose-handling crane.

SERVICE CRAFT *(continued)*

♦ up to 12 Khobi-class (Project 437M) base tankers [YO]
Bldr: . . . SY, St. Petersburg (In serv. 1957–59)

From among:

	Fleet		Fleet
CHEREMSHA	Northern	SHACHA	Northern
INDIGA	Black	SHELON'	Pacific
KHOBI	Caspian	SISOLA	Northern
METAN	Northern	SOS'VA	Baltic
ORSHA	Baltic	TARTU	Northern
SEYMA	Black	TUNGUSKA	Pacific

Seyma Boris Lemachko, 6-06

D: 690 tons light; 768 tons std. (1,520 fl) **S:** 13 kts
Dim: 67.40 (63.20 pp) × 10.10 × 3.63
Electronics: Radar: 1 Don-2 nav.
M: 2 Type 8DR 30/50 diesels; 2 props; 1,600 bhp
Range: 2,000/10 **Endurance:** 10 days **Crew:** 33 tot.

Remarks: Although antiquated, a number of this class reportedly remain in local service. Baltic Fleet sister *Lovat'* was stricken 1-9-95; the *Moksha* was no longer in service as of 2003. Three others were built for Indonesia and two for Albania. Cargo is either 700 tons fuel oil or 550 tons diesel fuel, although in recent years at least one has been used as a sludge lighter: the *Cheremsha* was used to steal 1,197.5 tons of fuel from Northern Fleet ships during 1996–97 while supposedly pursuing her normal activity of collecting waste water.

Disposal note: *Irtysh*-class base tanker *Narva; Konda*-class base tankers *Konda, Sayaniy,* and *Yakhroma;* and *Nercha*-class (Project 931) base tankers *Klyaz'ma* and *Nercha* are no longer in service.

♦ 1 ex-German Dora-class base tanker [YO]
Bldr: D. W. Kramer Sons, Elmshorn, Germany (In serv. 1941)

ISTRA (ex-German *Elsa*)

Istra—at Sevastopol' Boris Lemachko, 7-00

D: 973 tons (1,200 fl) **S:** 12 kts **Dim:** 61.00 (56.65 pp) × 9.00 × 2.75
A: None **Electronics:** Radar: 1 . . . nav.
M: 2 M.A.N. 6-cyl. diesels; 2 3-bladed props; 900 bhp
Range: 1,200/12 **Crew:** 20 tot.

Remarks: Former German *Luftwaffe* aviation fuel lighter, captured by Great Britain in 5-45 and assigned to Russia as war reparations in 1946. Cargo: 331 tons liquid, 17.5 tons dry stores. Baltic Fleet sister *Izhma* (ex-*Empire Togonto,* ex-*Dora*) had been stricken by 2001, and two others were stricken several decades ago.

♦ Up to 30 Toplivo-3-class harbor fuel lighters [YO]
Bldr: . . . (In serv. 1950s)

VTN-3 VTN-24 and others

Toplivo-3-class fuel lighter VTN-3—alongside icebreaker *Purga* at Lomonosov Boris Lemachko, 1999

D: 1,200 tons (fl) **S:** 9 kts **Dim:** 52.7 × 10.0 × 3.0
M: 1 3D-12 diesel; 1 prop; 300 bhp

Remarks: Low-freeboard, low-superstructure harbor craft. A number of the 47 built have been discarded, including Northern Fleet units VTN-1, -7, -22, and -35 on 1-9-95.

♦ 2 Bolva-series (Project 5-Ya) accommodations barges [YPB]
Bldr: Valmet Oy, Helsinki, Finland (In serv. 1983)

IPKZ-100 IMATRA MIASS

Imatra (IPKZ-100)—moored at Sevastopol' Hartmut Ehlers, 3-02

D: 2,500 tons (3,573 fl) **Dim:** 113.50 (110.90 pp) × 13.80 × 2.80
Endurance: 30 days **Crew:** 40 tot. + 394 passengers

Remarks: 4,448 grt/1,000 dwt. Of the total of 48 built, only two late units went to naval service. The first series of eight Bolva-I units were built 1960–63; the second series of 30 Bolva-IIs, built 1963–72, had a hangar-like auditorium built atop the superstructure aft; and the Bolva-IIIs were built 1971– . . . , with 10 completed. The last three civil units were ordered in 1983. IPKZ-100 is stationed at Sevastopol', *Miass* at Kaliningrad.

♦ 2 Volna-class accommodations barges [YPB]

S-920 VOLNA

Volna Ralph Edwards, 6-03

Remarks: Have been used to accommodate crews of submarines fitting out at Admiralty Shipyard, St. Petersburg, since the 1960s. They have at least four diesel generator sets but do not appear to have been fitted with propulsion systems.

Disposal note: Accommodations hulk *PKZ-14* (ex-yacht *Angara,* ex-*Nadir,* ex-German *Hela*) was placed up for sale at the end of 2002.

Note: Retired combatant ships employed as floating barracks are common in the Russian Navy. All bear hull numbers in the PKZ (*Plavuchiya Kazerna,* Floating Barracks) series. Many of the larger oceanographic research ships have been employed as floating quarters for officers and their families.

SERVICE CRAFT *(continued)*

♦ 23 Shelon' (TL-1127)-class (Project 1388) torpedo retrievers [YPT]
Bldr: Sosnovka Zavod (In serv. 1978–84)

TL-270	TL-1003	TL-1271	TL-1551	TL-1717
TL-287	TL-1126	TL-1302	TL-1596	TL-2021
TL-288	TL-1127	TL-1474	TL-1597	TL-2023
TL-289	TL-1128	TL-1478	TL-1603	
TL-704	TL-1134	TL-1536	TL-1666	

Shelon'-class torpedo retriever TL-1478 Boris Lemachko, 4-02

D: 270 tons (fl) **S:** 30 kts **Dim:** 46.0 × 6.0 × 2.0
Electronics: Radar: 1 Kuban nav.—Sonar: Oka-1 HF dipping
M: 2 M-504 diesels; 2 props; 10,000 bhp
Range: 1,500/10 **Endurance:** 10 days **Crew:** 20 tot.

Remarks: Have a high-speed hull with a covered torpedo-recovery ramp aft. Eight others were completed 1983–87 as Razvedchik-class (Project 1388M) environmental monitoring ships [YAG] (q.v.). TL-1128 is equipped with a twin 25-mm 80-cal. 2M-3M gunmount on the forecastle, and the others have a pedestal on which to place the gunmount. Fleet assignments include: TL-287 in the Black Sea Fleet; TL-270, -1003, -1126, -1128, -1474, -1478, -1536, -1596, and -1666 in the Northern Fleet; TL-1127, -1603, and -1717 in the Baltic Fleet; and TL-1134, -1302, -1551, -2021, and -2023 in the Pacific Fleet.
Disposals: Black Sea Fleet units TL-1374, -1476, and -1602 were stricken 3-7-92, and sisters TL-1005 and -1616 were stricken 10-1-96 and transferred to Ukraine in 1997; Black Sea Fleet unit TL-1626 was stricken for disposal 31-7-96. Pacific Fleet unit TL-827 was stricken 8-2-98. One unit was reportedly transferred to Azerbaijan during 1992. TL 1590 was no longer in service as of 2003.

♦ 13 Poluchat-I (TL-1)-class (Project 368T) torpedo retrievers [YPT]
Bldrs: Sosnovka Zavod and Nikolayevsk-na-Amure Zavod (In serv. 1960–77)

TL-119	TL-720	TL-843	TL-980	TL-998
TL-184	TL-826	TL-854	TL-994	
TL-373	TL-842	TL-923	TL-997	

Poluchat-I-class torpedo retriever TL-843 Boris Lemachko, 7-02

D: 84.7 tons (92.8 fl) **S:** 21.6 kts
Dim: 29.60 × 6.10 (5.80 wl) × 1.56 (1.90 props)
Electronics: Radar: 1 Don-2 or Mius (Spin Trough) nav.
M: 2 M-50F-4 diesels; 2 props; 2,400 bhp **Range:** 250/21.6; 550/14
Crew: 1 officer, 2 warrant officers, 12 enlisted

Remarks: TL = *Torpedolov* (Torpedo Retriever). Have a recovery ramp aft. Export units had lower-powered M-50-series diesels and could achieve only 18 kts. One other is configured as patrol boat AKA-527 in the Caspian Flotilla, and at least one other has been converted as an officers' yacht. Large numbers have been retired in recent years. Have a Gira-KM gyrocompass and NEL-3 echo sounder. The hull has seven watertight bulkheads.

Note: The classes that follow under the [YRD] designation were all intended to transport new warships (primarily submarines) from inland yards through the extensive Soviet river and canal network to coastal facilities with sufficient water depth to permit them to be floated for final fitting out. All of them were of steel construction, and all were characterized by having the forward end enclosed, as in the World War II–era U.S. ARD classes. They are not equipped with cranes, and they are proportionately much narrower than normal floating dry docks. Often a small superstructure to house the tow crew is fitted at the forward, enclosed end. The Russian designation is TPD, wherein the "T" stands for "Transport" and the "PD" for *Plavuchiya Dock* (Floating Dock).

♦ 1 Project 20230 transport dock [YRD]
Bldr: . . . (In serv. 1983)

OKA-2

Capacity: 5,200 tons **Dim:** 135.4 × 14.0 × 3.6

Remarks: Flooded draft over blocks is 9.0 m and width between wing walls is 11.2 m.

♦ 1 Project 1767 transport dock [YRD]
Bldr: . . . (In serv. 1972)

TPD-70

Capacity: 4,700 tons **Dim:** 134.6 × 14.0 × 3.6

Remarks: Flooded draft over blocks is 8.8 m and width between wing walls is 12.0 m.

♦ 3 Project 1757 transport docks [YRD]
Bldr: . . . (In serv. 1969–75)

TPD-59 2 others

Capacity: 8,500 tons **Dim:** 165.0 × 23.5 × 3.9

Remarks: Flooded draft over blocks is 10.6 m and width between wing walls is 14.5 m.

♦ 7 Project 1753 transport docks [YRD]
Bldr: . . . (In serv. 1963–67)

TPD-9 6 others

Capacity: 3,600 tons **Dim:** 135.0 × 14.0 × 3.2

Remarks: Flooded draft over blocks is 7.6 m and width between wing walls is 1.4 m.

♦ 2 Project 769A transport docks [YRD]
Bldr: . . . (In serv. 1964)

TPD-14 1 other

Capacity: 4,500 tons **Dim:** 144.0 × 18.4 × 3.8

Remarks: Flooded draft over blocks is 8.9 m and width between wing walls is 13.2 m.

Note: Examples of some of the older transport docks that may still be available include Project 769 (three built; characteristics as for Project 769A except only 131 m long and 3,700 tons capacity); Project 768 (1,300 tons capacity, 77.2 m long); Project 764 (three built 1956–59, 1,700 tons capacity, 110.0 m long).

♦ 1 Landysh-class nuclear waste–processing barge [YRRN]
Bldr: . . ., Japan (In serv. 16-8-00)

LANDYSH

Remarks: Rectangular barge, with a processing plant capable of handling 7,000 m^3 of nuclear waste per year. Built for the Pacific Fleet with Japanese financial and technical assistance. Placed in operation at Zvezda Zavod, Bol'shoy Kamen, near Vladivostok, on 22-11-01, the facility also includes several buildings and can treat up to 7,000 m^3 of nuclear waste water annually.

♦ 1 nuclear support barge [YRRN]
Bldr: Rauma-Repola, Savonlinna, Finland (In serv. 9-86)

ROSTA-1

D: 1,700 tons (fl) **Dim:** 63.00 × 12.00 × 2.30

Remarks: Launched 21-3-86. Intended to provide radiation-hazard disposal, decontamination, laboratory services, and refit assistance to nuclear-powered ships at Murmansk.

♦ 2 PM-124-class (Project 326 and 326M) nuclear support barges [YRRN]
Bldr: . . . (In serv. 1960– . . .)

PM-78 PM-125

D: 3,300 tons (4,000 fl) **Dim:** 92.00 × 13.40 (12.00 wl) × 4.50
Endurance: 15 days **Crew:** 59 tot.

Remarks: Originally constructed as non-self-propelled freight barges for war reparations in the early 1950s; adapted from 1960 on to support nuclear submarine construction and repair. Employ the same hull as the Vyn-class accommodations barges. Two were Project 326 and six were Project 326M. Have two 12-ton recoring cranes and storage space for 560 used nuclear fuel rods. Northern Fleet unit PM-124 has been discarded. Pacific Fleet units PM-48, -80, and -133 were contaminated with nuclear radiation and have been discarded, and Northern Fleet unit PM-78 was said to be contaminated as of 9-00 but was still being used for used nuclear fuel rod storage. Pacific Fleet unit PTB-24 was stricken 5-7-94.

♦ 1 salvage lifting ship [YSD]
Bldr: De Schelde, Vlissingen, the Netherlands

	Laid down	L	In serv.
KOMMUNA (ex-*Volkhov*)	1912	30-11-13	27-7-15

SERVICE CRAFT *(continued)*

Kommuna—at Sevastopol' Hartmut Ehlers, 8-00

D: 2,450 tons (fl) **S:** 10.2 kts **Dim:** 96.0 × 20.4 × 4.7
A: None **Electronics:** 1 . . . nav.
M: 2 diesels; 2 props; 1,200 bhp **Range:** 1,700/6 **Fuel:** 82 tons
Crew: 250 tot. (when manned)

Remarks: Although "retired" during 1978, was refitted 1980–84 and remains in service at Sevastopol' to support submersibles. Catamaran hulled. Intended to raise sunken submarines by means of four 250-ton-capacity lifting rigs above and between the hulls.

♦ 0 (+ 1) submarine scrapping support barge [YSDN]
Bldr: Palada Zavod, Kherson, Ukraine (In serv. . . .)

Remarks: A large barge was ordered in 1996, intended to provide support during the scrapping of nuclear-powered submarines. As of 30-8-00, it was 98.5% complete, but the Russian government had not found a satisfactory way to pay for it and was trying to obtain delivery by promising to pay for half the work; no reports of a delivery have been received.

♦ 0 (+ 1) submarine rescue submersible [YSS]
Bldr: Rybinskiy Zavod, Rybinsk (In serv. 2002)

Remarks: Laid down in 1993. The work pace increased in response to the loss of the submarine *Kursk,* but funding shortages halted work during 2-01. No data are available, but she is said to be able to work in depths to 100 m and to be used for repairs on external, underwater features of surface ships and submarines as well as to rescue submariners. Has a crew of 16, plus six divers in repair mode.

♦ 2 Rus'-class (Project 1681) salvage submersibles [YSS]
Bldr: Admiralty Shipyard, St. Petersburg

	Laid down	L	In serv.
Rus'	1-6-92	20-5-00	2000
Konsul	1997	. . .	12-00

D: 24 tons (surf.) **S:** 3 kts **Dim:** 8.0 × 2.1 × 3.7 (high)
M: 6 electric maneuvering motors
Endurance: 80 hrs **Crew:** 2–3 tot.

Remarks: Designed by the Malakhit Design Bureau. Capable of diving to 6,000 m. Crew is carried in a 2.1-m-diameter titanium alloy sphere. The sonar system can detect objects to 750-m ranges, and the manipulator can lift objects weighing up to 400 kg. Sea trials for the *Rus'* began from Baltiysk during 10-99. *Rus'* was to be used to dive on the Yankee-class (Project 667AU) SSBN K-219, which sank 6-10-86 east of Bermuda. *Konsul* was to have been completed by 12-00, but no reports to that effect have been received and the craft may still be undelivered.

♦ 5 Priz-class (Project 1855) salvage submersibles [YSS]
Bldr: Krasnoye Sormovo Zavod 112, Nizhniy Novgorod (In serv. 1986– . . .)

AS-26 AS-28 AS-30 AS-32 Priz and one other

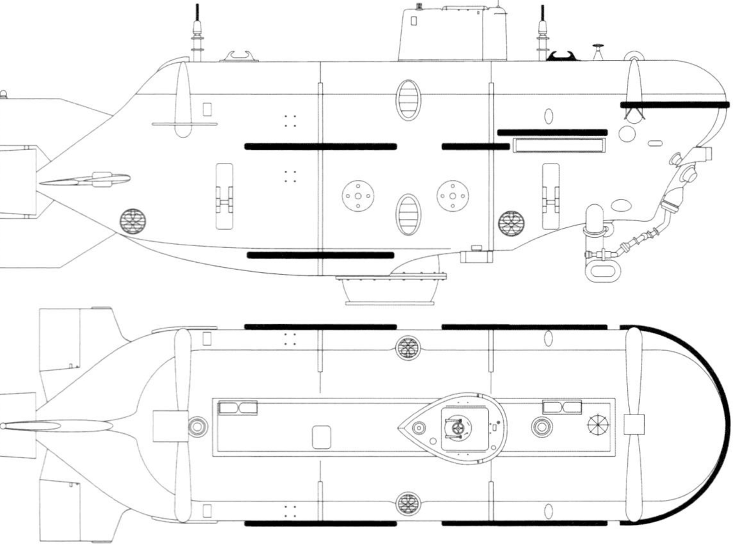

Submersible AS-28 Drawing by T. Grotnik, 2005

D: 50 tons sub. **S:** 3.3 kts **Dim:** 13.5 × 3.8 × 4.6 **Crew:** 4 + 20 passengers

Remarks: Intended for salvage and bottom work. Diving depth: 1,000 m. Have a titanium pressure hull and two manipulators (each can lift 55 kg). *Priz* took part in the unsuccessful rescue attempts for the submarine *Kursk* during 8-00. The craft are painted with red and white vertical stripes. During 8-05 AS-28 was rescued by the British submersible *Scorpio 45* after becoming entangled in a hydrophone array 190 meters underwater off the Russian coast. All are to undergo a 14-month modernization by Nizhniy Novgorod SY at which time they are to receive state-of-the-art electronics and improvements. Reportedly only the outside hulls will remain the same. No dates have yet been reported for the modernizations to complete.

♦ 4 Sever-class (Project 1832) research submersibles [YSS]
Bldr: Admiralteiskiye Verfi 196 (Sudomekh Division), St. Petersburg

LS-8 LS-17 LS-28 LS-34

D: 28 tons surf./40 tons sub. **S:** 4 kts sub. **Dim:** 12.5 × 2.7 × 3.8 (high)
Crew: 5 tot.

Remarks: Capable of diving to 2,000 m. Some may have been discarded.

♦ 18 Poisk-2 (Project 1839 and 1839.2) rescue and salvage submersibles [YSS]
Bldr: Admiralteiskiye Verfi 196 (Sudomekh Division), St. Petersburg

ARS-1	ARS-7	ARS-13	ARS-29	ARS-35
ARS-2	ARS-9	ARS-14	ARS-30	ARS-36
ARS-3	ARS-10	ARS-15	ARS-31	
ARS-4	ARS-12	ARS-16	ARS-34 Bester	

D: 46 tons sub. **S:** 3.9 kts sub. **Dim:** 13.60 × 3.49 × 4.87 (high)
Electronics: Sonar: MGA-8 search; MGS-29 noisemaking beacon; MGA-2 underwater telephone (8.2 kHz); MGV-55 underwater telephone (34.5–39.9 kHz)
M: electric motors; 1 prop—2 vertical thrusters—2 horizontal thrusters
Range: 16/2 **Endurance:** 48 hours **Crew:** 3 tot.

Remarks: Can be carried by the rescue ship *Alagez* and several other salvage and rescue ships. Diving depth: 500 m. ARS = *Avtonomiy Rabochniy Snaryad* (Autonomous Utility Craft). Have an SP-200M battery complex with three groups of 116 cells at 220 V and four groups of 14 cells at 27 V. Have two periscopes and four viewing ports and are equipped with an MGP-30/600 underwater manipulation system. There are also three anchors. ARS-34, which took part in the unsuccessful rescue attempts on the submarine *Kursk* during 8-00, is named *Bester;* the craft operated from the salvage ship *Mikhail Rudnitskiy.*

♦ Up to 9 Project 1837 and 1837K rescue and salvage submersibles [YSS]
Bldr: Admiralteiskiye Verfi 196 (Sudomekh Division), St. Petersburg

AS-5 AS-11 AS-18 AS-20 through AS-27 series

D: 45 tons sub. **S:** 3.6 kts sub. **Dim:** 12.7 × 3.9 × 5.4 (high)
Electronics: Sonar: MGA-5 search; MGS-29 noisemaking beacon; MGA-2 underwater telephone (8.2 KHz); MGV-55 underwater telephone (34.5–39.9 kHz)
M: 6 electric motors; 2 propulsion props—2 vertical thrusters—2 horizontal thrusters
Range: 16.5/2 **Endurance:** 48 hours (10 with rescued personnel aboard)
Crew: 3 tot.

Remarks: Can (or could) carry up to 11 personnel and were used for rescue duties. Normal operating depth: 500 m. Pressue hull is constructed of AK-29 steel. SP-200M lead-acid battery complex has three groups of 16 cells at 220 V and four groups with 27 V output. Have three periscopes and an RSU-1D radio set. Equipped with a bow manipulator and two sets of lifting pistons. In the Black Sea Fleet, were based with old rescue ship *Kommuna,* the rescue ship *El'brus,* and the trials craft OS-3; were also carried by India (Project 940) salvage submarines. Several of the total of 12 built have been discarded: Pacific Fleet sister A-3 was stricken 30-7-93 and AS-14 and AS-19 on 31-7-96.

Note: Also in service are (or were) four Poisk-class (Project 1806) rescue and salvage submersibles (AGS-6, -17, -37, and -38) with a diving depth of 4,000 m.

♦ 3 OT-2400-class (Project N-3291) large riverine push-tugs [YTB]
Bldr: Obuda SY, Budapest, Hungary (In serv. 1988)

RB-346 RB-347 RB-348

D: 725 tons (923 fl) **S:** 13 kts **Dim:** 51.5 × 12.0 × 2.3
Electronics: Radar: 1 . . . nav.
M: 2 Type G-70 diesels; 2 props; 2,400 bhp **Range:** . . . / . . .
Fuel: 200 tons **Endurance:** 15 days **Crew:** 16 tot. (civilian)

OT-2400-class river tug RB-346 Boris Lemachko, 1999

SERVICE CRAFT *(continued)*

Remarks: Employed as push-tugs for submarine transportation docks and barges on the canal system linking the St. Petersburg area with the Northern Fleet. Assigned to the Baltic Fleet. Have rectangular barge-like hulls with twin barge push-pylons at the bow.

♦ 9 Stividor (MB-70)-class (Project 192 and 192A*) large harbor tugs [YTB]

Bldr: . . ., Yugoslavia (In serv. 1970–89)

RB-22* RB-108 RB-136 RB-280* RB-326
RB-40* RB-109 RB-167 RB-325

Northern Fleet Stividor-class tug RB-108 NAVPIC-Holland, 10-01

D: 451 tons (575 fl) **S:** 13 kts **Dim:** 35.7 × 9.5 × 4.6
M: 2 ASL-25D diesels; 2 Kort-nozzle props; 2,520 bhp—bow-thruster
Electric: 340 kw tot. (2 × 125-kw, 2 × 45-kw diesel sets)
Range: . . . / . . . **Fuel:** 76 tons **Endurance:** 10 days **Crew:** . . . tot.

Remarks: Bollard pull: 35 tons. Carry 14 tons of potable water, 3.6 tons of lubricants. Have three firefighting water monitors. Late-construction units RB-22 (In serv. 1989) and RB-280 are Project 192A, differences unknown (there are no external differences). The engines were built in the former East Germany. RB-40, -108, and -109 are in the Northern Fleet; RB-22, -280, -325, and -326 in the Pacific; and RB-136 in the Black Sea.

♦ 19 Prometey (Anton Mazin)-class (Project 498, 04983, and 04985) large harbor tugs [YTB]

Bldrs: Petrozavod SY, St. Petersburg; Gorokhovets SY (In serv. 1973–83)

RB-1 RB-98 RB-201 RB-262 RB-327
RB-7 RB-158 RB-202 RB-265 RB-360
RB-57 RB-173 RB-217 RB-296 RB-362
RB-68 RB-179 RB-239 RB-314

Prometey-class large harbor tug RB-239—with much rust on hull
Boris Lemachko, 4-01

D: 257 tons light; 305 tons normal (364 fl) **S:** 11 kts
Dim: 29.30 (28.2 pp) × 8.30 × 3.20
Electronics: Radar: 1 Mius (Spin Trough) nav.
M: 2 6DR 30/50 diesels; 2 Kort-nozzle props; 1,200 bhp (see Remarks)
Electric: 50 kw tot. **Range:** 1,800/12 **Fuel:** 30 tons **Crew:** 3–5 tot.

Remarks: More than 100 were built since 1971, most of which went into civilian service. Some have been exported. Known fleet subordinations: RB-7, -173, -179, -217, and -239 are in the Pacific Fleet; RB-68 and -158 in the Northern Fleet; RB-314 and -327 in the Baltic Fleet; and RB-98 and -201 in the Black Sea Fleet.
Disposals: RB-69, -295, and -308 of this class were stricken from the Black Sea Fleet 10-1-96 and later transferred to Ukraine.
Hull systems: Have a 14-ton bollard pull and an ice-strengthened hull. The more powerful Project 498T (or 04983) series (of which RB-239 is one) have two 800-bhp Type 8ChNP-25/30 diesels and displace 319 tons full load; they are 29.80 m long and draw 3.40 m. RB-217 is of the later Project 04985, differences unknown.

♦ 34 Sidehole-I and -II (Peredovik)-class (Project 737K and 737M) medium harbor tugs [YTM]

Bldr: Petrozavod SY, St. Petersburg (In serv. 1973–83)

From among . . .

BUK-600 RB-25 RB-49 RB-194 RB-233 RB-248
RB-2 RB-26 RB-51 RB-197 RB-237 BR-250
RB-5 RB-29 RB-52 RB-198 RB-240 RB-256
RB-17 RB-43 RB-168 RB-199 RB-244 RB-310
RB-20 RB-44 RB-192 RB-212 RB-246 RB-311
RB-23 RB-46 RB-193 RB-232 RB-247

Sidehole-II-class tug RB-250 Ralph Edwards, 6-03

Northern Fleet Sidehole-class tug RB-51 NAVPIC-Holland, 10-01

D: 183 tons (206 fl) **S:** 10 kts **Dim:** 24.2 × 7.0 × 3.4
Electronics: Radar: 1 Mius (Spin Trough) nav.
M: 2 Type 6 CHN25/34 diesels; 2 vertical cycloidal props; 900 bhp
Electric: 37 kw tot. (1 × 37-kw diesel set)
Range: 130/9.5 **Fuel:** 17.4 tons **Endurance:** 6 days **Crew:** 4 tot.

Remarks: Others are employed in civil use. Bollard pull: 10.5 tons. Naval units have RB (*Rednyy Buksir,* Roadstead Tug) pennants, except BUK-600, whose designation indicates "Tug-Cutter." The NATO nickname "Sidehole" derived from the distinctive cutout in the sides of the first level of the superstructure abreast the side-by-side stacks in the initial production variant. Known fleet assignments include: RB-232, -233, -240, -310, and -311 and BUK-600 in the Pacific Fleet; RB-248 and -256 in the Caspian Flotilla; RB-44, -193, -199, -237, -244, and -247 in the Black Sea Fleet; and RB-2, -29, -43, -49, -50, -168, -246, and at least one other in the Northern Fleet.
Hull systems: Twenty-six early Project 737 units displaced 150 tons light (178 fl) and were powered by 300-bhp 6 CH-25/34 diesels; some of the units listed above are probably of that variant. Can carry 3.6 tons potable water and 0.5 tons lube oil.
Disposals: Northern Fleet unit RB-290 was stricken 3-7-92. Black Sea Fleet units RB-245 and -255 were stricken 5-7-94, and the same fleet's RB-27 was stricken 10-1-96 and later transferred to Ukraine. All remaining units of the Tugur-class (Project 730) medium harbor tugs had been stricken by 2001, as had been the former German tug RB-65, a unit of what NATO called the Scholle class but which was actually one of six World War II *Geier*-class tugs taken over by Russia in 1946.

SERVICE CRAFT *(continued)*

♦ 30 Project 1496 small harbor tugs [YTL]
Bldr: Sovetskaya Govan' Zavod, Azove (In serv. 1966–80)

BUK-1393	RB-10	RB-158	RB-222	RB-288	RB-303
MB-301	RB-14	RB-179	RB-243	RB-290	RB-312
MB-315	RB-51	RB-185	RB-254	RB-293	RB-313
MB-317	RB-63	RB-195	RB-259	RB-297	RB-399
MB-322	RB-66	RB-215	RB-263	RB-298	RB-410

Project 1496 tug-cutter designated BUK-1240 Boris Lemachko, 1995

D: 91.3 tons (108.5 fl) **S:** 10.5 kts **Dim:** 23.40 × 5.87 × 1.87
Electronics: Radar: 1 Lotsiya nav.
M: 1 Type 8 ChSN 18/22-1 diesel; 1 shrouded prop; 315 bhp
Electric: 18 kw tot. **Range:** 1,450/10.5 **Fuel:** 8.3 tons
Endurance: 6 days **Crew:** 8 tot.

Remarks: Eleven others serve the Federal Border Guard in the Pacific region. Most are designated RB (*Rednyy Buksir,* Roadstead Tug); four are designated MB (*Morskoy Buksir,* Seagoing Tug) and one BUK, which stands for "Tug-Cutter." All are in the Northern Fleet, except RB-259 in the Caspian Flotilla and MB-301, RB-14, and RB-399 in the Pacific Fleet.
Disposals: RB-83, -139, -161, -197, and -270 have been stricken since 1999.

♦ . . . Vyun-class (Project 1664.0) firefighting launches [YTR]
Bldr: . . . Russia (In serv. 1995– . . .)

D: 67.4 tons (fl) **S:** 19.4 kts **Dim:** 30.80 × 5.00 × 0.81 (fwd; 0.75 aft)
Electronics: Radar: 1 . . . nav.
M: 2 Type M-419A diesels; 2 waterjets; 2,170 bhp
Fuel: 3 tons **Crew:** 2 tot. + 6 firemen

Remarks: Firefighting launch, designed by Vympel Joint Stock Co., with at least one prototype (*Vyun-I*) completed by 1997. Has four PN-60B main firepumps of 60-liter/sec capacity each and three 216-m^3/hr-capacity fire monitors, plus two portable firepumps, a water curtain system, and foam blanket–generating equipment. Intended for harbor, lake, and riverine service. It is not known if any are in naval service, but the design could serve as a replacement for earlier such craft.

♦ 15 Morkov-class (Project 14611) fireboats [YTR]
Bldr: Vympel Zavod, Rybinsk (In serv. 1984–92)

PZhK-415	PZhK-1378	PZhK-1545	PZhK-1680
PZhK-417	PZhK-1514	PZhK-1546	PZhK-1859
PZhK-900	PZhK-1515	PZhK-1547	PZhK-2055
PZhK-1296	PZhK-1544	PZhK-1560	

Morkov-class fireboat PZhK-900—with all monitors spraying Stefan Marx, 2001

D: 280 tons (320 fl) **S:** 12.5 kts **Dim:** 41.00 (36.53 pp) × 7.80 × 2.14
Electronics: Radar: 1 Mius (Spin Trough) nav.
M: 2 Barnaul' 3KD 12N-520 diesels; 2 CP props; 1,040 bhp—bow-thruster
Electric: 400 kw tot. **Range:** 250/12.5 **Endurance:** 5 days **Crew:** 15 tot.

Remarks: PZhK-900 is based at St. Petersburg, and PZhK-415 and -1680 are also in the Baltic Fleet. Other fleet assignments include PZhK-1296, -1378, -1545, -1546, and -2055 in the Northern; PZhK-417, -1515, -1544, -1547, -1560, and -1859 in the Pacific. Four similar Mars-class (Project 14613) craft had been completed by 1996, and five more have been built for Turkey, but none seem to have entered Russian Navy service to date. Sister PZhK-1819 was stricken from the Black Sea Fleet 10-1-96 and later transferred to Ukraine.
Hull systems: Have four firefighting water monitors, two with 220-m^2/hr capacity and two of 500 m^3/hr, driven by two 750-m^3/hr diesel-powered pumps; in some, there are four 720-m^3/hr fire monitors. Have both foam and Freon extinguishing systems, with 20 tons of foaming agent carried. Can spray a water curtain to protect themselves. Can also be used for towing.
Disposals: PZhK-638 had been stricken by 2005.

♦ 20 Pozharnyy-I (PZhK-1)-class (Project 364) fireboats [YTR]
Bldrs: Volodarskogo Zavod, Rybinsk; Kirova Zavod, Khabarovsk; and Nikolayevskna-Amure (In serv. 1954–67)

From among:

PZhK-3	PZhK-36	PZhK-46	PZhK-59	PZhK-84
PZhK-5	PZhK-37	PZhK-47	PZhK-64	PZhK-86
PZhK-17	PZhK-41	PZhK-49	PZhK-66	
PZhK-30	PZhK-42	PZhK-53	PZhK-68	
PZhK-31	PZhK-43	PZhK-54	PZhK-79	
PZhK-32	PZhK-44	PZhK-55	PZhK-82	

Pozharnyy-I-class fireboat PZhK-5 H&L Van Ginderen, 7-00

D: 145.9 tons (179–181 fl) **S:** 15.7 kts
Dim: 34.90 (31.90 wl) × 6.50 (6.20 wl) × 1.84
Electronics: Radar: 1 Mius (Spin Trough) or Don-2 nav. or none
M: 2 Type M-50F-1 diesels (900 bhp each), 1 Type . . . diesel (450 bhp); 3 props; 2,250 bhp
Range: 284/15.7; 1,050/10 **Fuel:** 12 tons **Endurance:** 5 days **Crew:** 26 tot.

Remarks: As many as 84 were built, some for civilian organizations.
Disposals: Black Sea Fleet unit PZhK-50 sank during a storm while in port in 1992. Known strikes include PZhK-45 in 1991. PZhK-4, PDK-15, PDK-71, PZhK-429, and PZhK-432 were transferred to other agencies. PZhK-12 and -170 were stricken from the Baltic Fleet 3-7-92. PZhK-20 and -38 were stricken 10-1-96 and later transferred to Ukraine. One other was built for export to Iraq.

♦ 1 Modified Toplivo-2-class (Project 1844.4) water lighter [YW]
Bldr: Khabarovsk SY (In serv. 1993)

MVT-17

MVT-17 Boris Lemachko, 2003

D: 625 tons (1,204 fl) **S:** 10 kts **Dim:** 54.54 × 9.70 × 3.51
A: None **Electronics:** Radar: 1 . . . nav.
M: 1 6-DR-series diesel; 1 prop; 600 bhp
Range: 1,000/10 **Endurance:** 15 days **Crew:** 21 tot.

Remarks: Final variant of the numerous Toplivo-2 series. Assigned to the Pacific Fleet and given a seagoing water tanker pennant, probably indicating use in transporting potable water to offshore facilities. Differs in external appearance from earlier units primarily in having an enlarged superstructure aft. No further sisters have been built.

♦ 8 Project 1580 harbor water lighters [YW]
Bldr: . . . SY, Yugoslavia (In serv. 1988–91)

PPSK-10	PPSK-16	PPSK-20	PPSK-27
PPSK-15	PPSK-18	PPSK-25	PPSK-28

D: 447 tons (553 fl) **S:** 11 kts **Dim:** 45.0 × 8.0 × 2.1
M: 1 . . . diesel; 1 prop; 600 bhp **Endurance:** 5 days **Crew:** 21 tot.

Remarks: Sister PPSK-17 has been stricken from the Baltic Fleet.

SERVICE CRAFT *(continued)*

♦ Up to 30 Toplivo-1-class (Project 5) water lighters [YW]
Bldr: Lenin Shipyard, Gdansk, Poland (In serv. 1959–62)

MNS-8240 MNS-8250 MNS-25250 and others

MNS-25250 Boris Lemachko, 5-06

D: 420 tons (600 fl) **S:** 10 kts **Dim:** 34.40 (33.00 pp) × 7.00 × 3.10
M: 1 Type 3D-12 diesel; 1 prop; 300 bhp **Fuel:** 6 tons **Crew:** . . . tot.

Remarks: Harbor water lighters. Hull numbers in the MNS series. A number have been discarded, and some may have been converted to transport fuel. MNS-8250 is based at Kronshtadt and MNS-25250 at Sevastopol'.

♦ 12 Petrushka-class (Project TS-39 or UK-3) training cutters [YXT]
Bldr: Stocznia Wisla, Gdansk (In serv. 1978–84)

MK-157	MK-207	MK-1277	PSK-1519	PSK-1562	UK-216
MK-194	MK-288	PSK-1304	PSK-1556	PSK-2017	UK-240

Petrushka-class training cutter MK-207 Boris Lemachko, 2002

D: 338.2 tons normal (345.4 fl) **S:** 12 kts **Dim:** 39.27 (36.00 pp) × 8.60 × 2.55
Electronics: Radar: 2 Mius (Spin Trough) nav.
M: 2 Wola H12, 1,000-rpm diesels; 2 props; 610 bhp
Electric: 180 kw tot. (2 × 90 kw, Wola H6 diesels driving)
Range: 1,000/10 **Crew:** 13 tot. + 30 instructors and students

Remarks: Hull numbers were all originally in the UK (*Uchebniy Kater,* Training Cutter) series. The first delivery of a second series, ordered during 4-91, was halted by the collapse of the Soviet Union. Have two classrooms and a navigational training facility on the bridge, and an MFD/F loop on a short mast aft. Are equipped with NBC warfare defense measures. Very similar to the SK-620-class ambulance craft from the same builder. Have an echo sounder, gyrocompass, MFD/F, and electromagnetic log. Two 23-person-capacity workboats are carried. UK-230 of this class was transferred to the Brigantina youth training organization during 1999. PSK-designated units are used as personnel ferries; the function of the MK-designated units is not available.

♦ 6 Polish Bryza-class (Project 772U) training cutters [YXT]
Bldrs: Stocznia Wisla, Gdansk, Poland; Neftegaz Zavod (In serv. 1967–79)

UK-214 UK-222 UK-230 UK-232 UK-236 UK-687

D: 135 tons (142 fl) **S:** 10.5 kts **Dim:** 28.82 × 6.60 × 1.86
Electronics: Radar: 2 . . . nav.
M: 2 Type 3-D6 or Wola DM-150 diesels; 2 props; 300 bhp
Electric: 84 kw tot. **Range:** 1,100/10 **Crew:** 11 tot. + 28 students

Bryza-class training cutter UK-537—since stricken Boris Lemachko, 1998

Remarks: Used at naval training centers for basic navigation and maneuvering training. Some 25 others remain in service as personnel ferries [YFL] with numbers in the MK and PSK series (q.v.). All are in the Baltic Fleet except UK-687, which is in the Caspian Flotilla.
Disposals: Black Sea Fleet unit UK-190 was stricken 5-7-94 and transferred to Ukraine.

♦ Up to 20 PO-2 (Yaroslavets)-class (Project 376U) training launches [YXT]
Bldr: Yaroslavl Zavod (In serv. 1950s–90)

UK-190 through UK-193 UK-195 through UK-210

D: 32.2 tons (38.2 fl) **S:** 9–10 kts **Dim:** 21.00 × 3.90 × 1.40 (max.; 1.26 mean)
Electronics: Radar: 1 Mius (Spin Trough) nav. or none
M: 1 Type 3D-6S1 diesel; 1 prop; 150 bhp
Electric: 10 kw tot. (1 × 10 kw, DGPN-8/1500 diesel driving)
Range: 1,600/8 **Fuel:** 1.5 tons **Endurance:** 5 days
Crew: 4–6 tot. + . . . trainees

Remarks: More than 600 have been built to the same general design for military and civilian use (see under [YFL] and [YGS] and under the Nyryat'-2 class [YDT]). Can be operated safely in Force 8 winds and 2-m seas and can break light ice. The Project 376U variant is employed for navigational and maneuvering training duties.

Note: In use as immobile training hulks are a number of former combatants. They can be distinguished by the use of UTS (*Uchebnoye/Trenoye Sudno*)-series hull numbers. Former T-43-class minesweeper UTS-306 was refitted at Kaliningrad in 1995, early-model sister UTS-415 was still in use at Sevastopol' as of 2000, and long-hull T-43 training barge UTS-433 was moored at Donuzlav in 2000.

FEDERAL BORDER GUARD

(Naval Forces of the Federal Border Guard Service)

The former KGB Maritime Border Service fleet was reorganized in 1994 as the Naval Forces of the Federal Border Guard Service with the assigned duties of defending Russia's borders, defending the Russian Economic Exclusion Zone (EEZ), providing fisheries protection services (in conjunction with the Ministry of Fisheries), and providing protection to the resources of the Far North and continental shelves of Russian territory (in conjunction with the Ministry of Ecology and Natural Resources). The Federal Border Guard is attempting to evolve into more of a coast guard–like organization, although it continues to have the mission of protecting the security of Russia's maritime borders. Its officers are trained at the regular naval academies, and its enlisted personnel are almost all conscripts. In wartime, the organization's ships and craft would come under the control of the navy, which in peacetime has been accused of not providing the necessary support to maintain their combat systems. The fisheries patrol ships and craft of the Ministry of Fisheries were taken over by the Federal Border Guard in 8-98. The service has been subordinated to the Russian Federal Security Service since 11-3-03.

Personnel: About 8,600 total. Ships and craft are operating with 50% crew complements.

Organization: There are two Maritime Regional Directorates, Arctic and Pacific, to which are subordinated 10 Coastal Border Guard Regions, as follows: the 1st, Murmansk; 2nd, Arkhangelsk; 3rd, St. Petersburg; 4th, Kaliningrad; 5th, Novorossiysk; 6th, Caspian Sea; 7th, Nakhodka; 8th, Sakhalin Island; 9th, Kuril Islands; and 10th, Kamchatka. Each region is divided into sectors dependent on the numbers and types of ships and craft assigned. Ships and craft are categorized by descending size and capability as 1st class, EEZ patrol ships; 2nd class, coastal border guard ships; 3rd class, ships and boats for port and roadstead patrol; 4th class, ships and boats for river and lake patrol; and 5th class, support craft. By 2010, the Federal Border Guard hopes to have 300 patrol ships, 650 smaller boats of all types, and 50 support ships and craft—a seemingly unattainable goal.

Maritime Aviation: The Federal Border Guard operates over 200 aircraft including Mi-8, Mi-24, and Ka-27 helicopters, An-24 and Tu-134 transports, Be-12PSS Mail SAR amphibians, and An-26 and An-72P Coaler maritime surveillance aircraft. Only 48% of the border guard aircraft inventory was reported as flyable. Reports that all border guard Mi-8 and Mi-24 helicopters and Tu-134 and An-24 transports had been retired by 1998 are incorrect. The approximately 25 border guard Be-12PSS (Poiskovo Spasatelnyi) Mail amphibians have had their weapons systems and submarine detection gear removed. Plans call for adding helicopter decks to the larger ("1st through 3rd Rate") ships to accommodate rescue helicopters.

Coastal Defense: Troop detachments are stationed at various island and mainland coastal locations considered vulnerable to assault. Coastal surveillance radar systems cover most areas, with the Gorizont Nayada-5 radar in the process of being replaced by the Nayada-5PV.

Note: While "naval" ship and craft types carry pennant numbers, those ships and craft transferred from the Ministry of Fisheries do not. Most units now carry diagonal stripes of red, blue, and white on the hull sides, but on some the red stripes lead, while on other units the blue stripes lead.

FRIGATES [WFF]

Note: Future plans call for the acquisition of an unspecified number of the ocean patrol version of the naval Gepard-class (Project 1166.0) small frigate (see under Russian Navy section).

♦ 7 Krivak-III (Nerey) class (Project 11351BPB)

(1 or more *nonoperational*) Bldr: Zaliv Zavod 532, Kerch', Ukraine

	Laid down	L	In serv.
113 *Menzhinskiy*	14-8-81	31-12-82	29-12-83
158 Dzerzhinskiy	11-1-84	2-3-84	29-12-84
156 Orël (ex-*Yuriy Andropov*, ex-*Imeni XXVII S'yezda K.P.S.S.*)	26-9-83	2-11-85	30-9-86
104 Pskov (ex-*Imeni 70 Letiya VchK-KGB*)	. . .	1987	30-12-87
060 Anadyr (ex-*Imeni 70 Letiya Pogranvoysk*)	22-10-87	28-3-88	16-8-89
103 Kedrov	5-11-88	30-4-89	20-11-90
052 Vorovskiy	20-2-90	28-7-90	29-12-90

Orël (156) Boris Lemachko, 1999

Kedrov (103) French Navy, 10-90

D: 3,274 tons std.; 3,458 tons normal (3,642 fl; 3,774 max.) **S:** 31 kts (30 sust.)
Dim: 122.98 (113.00 pp) × 14.20 (13.2 wl) × 4.72 (hull; 6.20 over sonar dome)
A: 1 twin-rail Osa-MA (SA-N-4) SAM syst. (20 9M-33/Gecko missiles); 1 100-mm 59-cal. AK-100 DP (2,000 rounds); 2 single 30-mm 54-cal. AK-630M gatling AA (12,000 rounds); 1 . . . grenade launcher; 2 12-round RBU-6000 ASW RL (96 RGB-60 rockets); 2 quadruple 533-mm UTA-53-1135 TT (4 SET-65 and 4 53-65K torpedoes); 1 Ka-27PS Helix-A helicopter
Electronics:
Radar: 1 Vaygach-U (Palm Frond) nav.; 1 Volga (Don-Kay) or Nayada-1 nav.; 1 Nayada-2 helicopter control; 1 MR-760 Fregat-MA (Top Plate) 3-D (*Menzhinskiy:* MR-310U Angara-M/Head Net-C) air search; 1 MPZ-301 Baza (Pop Group) missile f.c.; 1 MR-114 Bars (Kite Screech-A) 100-mm f.c.; 1 MR-123 Vympel (Bass Tilt) 30-mm f.c.
Sonar: MGK-335S Platina-C hull-mounted LF; MG-345 Bronza LF VDS; MG-26 underwater telephone
EW: 2 Start-2 (Bell Shroud) intercept; 2 MP-401 Start (Bell Squat A/B) jammer; 4 16-round PK-16 fixed decoy RL (128 rockets); 2 towed torpedo decoys; 3 sets floating corner-reflector decoys
E/O: . . . Spektr-F (Half Cup) laser warning
M: COGAG M-7 plant: 2 M-62 cruise gas turbines (7,475 shp each), 2 M-8K boost gas turbines (20,000 shp each); 2 props; 54,900 shp max.
Electric: 2,500 kw tot. (5 × 500-kw diesel sets)
Range: 1,146/30; 3,636/14 **Fuel:** . . . tons + 22 tons aviation fuel
Endurance: 30 days
Crew: 26 officers, 29 warrant officers, 143 enlisted (incl. 12 in aviation group)

Remarks: Revised version of basic Krivak design for Federal Border Guard service in the Far East. Design approved 6-80. Typed PSKR (*Pogranichnyy Storozhevoy Korabl',* Border Patrol Ship). First two are named for prominent KGB "heroes." The original name for the *Orël* ("Eagle") meant "In Honor of the 27th Congress of the Communist Party of the Soviet Union," and that of the *Pskov* "In Honor of the 70th Anniversary of the KGB." The sixth is named for Mikhail Sergeyevich Kedrov (1878–1941), a pioneer member of the NKVD and later a member of the Soviet supreme court; and the seventh is named for a World War II–era KGB leader. The eighth unit, to have been named *Kirov* and then (after the 1991 revolution) *Latsis,* was taken over in 3-93 by Ukraine and completed as *Hetman Sagaidachnyy.* A ninth, begun as the *Krasniy Vympel* ("Red Banner") was to be completed for Ukrainian service as *Hetman Vyshnevetsky,* but work ceased. *Dzerzhinskiy* completed a modernization overhaul at Vladivostok in 1999. The ships are seldom operated, due to the expense, and not all of their combat systems are operational; full crews are not carried.
Hull systems: There are 14 watertight compartments. The superstructure is built of aluminum-magnesium alloy, welded to the hull with bimetallic inserts. Type UKA-135 fin stabilizers are fitted. The propulsion plant originally delivered 45,570 shp normal/51,200 shp max. total (with the cruise turbines operating at 6,000 shp each and the boost turbines at 18,000 shp each), but the output was later increased. Hull block coefficient is 0.46, very fine for this type of vessel. For slow speeds, any one of the engines can drive both propellers.
Combat systems: The combat system is designated Sapfir-U7; the ASW weapons control system name is Purga, the antisubmarine missile control system is called Musson, and the communications suite is the Tayfun-3. The addition of a helicopter facility (with simple deck-transit system) and helicopter weapons reload magazines cost two gunmounts and one SA-N-4 position aft, while the Krivak-I/II SS-N-14 dual- purpose missile system was replaced by a 100-mm gun, more useful for the patrol mission of these ships. Two six-barrel gatling guns were added to improve close-in defense. The Nayada-2 radar mounted atop the helicopter hangar serves in flight control.

CORVETTES [WFFL]

♦ 1 Grisha-V class (Project 1124MU)

Bldr: Shipyard No. 368, Khabarovsk

	Laid down	L	In serv.
354 Stelyak (ex-MPK-221)	8-2-85	29-4-87	29-12-87

D: 930 tons std. (1,070 fl) **S:** 32 kts (21 on gas turbine; 16 on diesels)
Dim: 71.20 (66.90 wl) × 10.15 (9.50 wl) × 3.72 (hull)
A: 1 twin-rail Osa-M (SA-N-4) SAM syst. (20 9M-33/Gecko missiles); 1 76.2-mm 59-cal. AK-176 DP (304 rounds); 1 30-mm 54-cal. AK-630M gatling AA (3,000 rounds); 2 point-defense shoulder-launched SAM positions (20–24 Igla-M missiles); 2 twin 533-mm TT; 1 12-round RBU-6000 ASW RL (48 RGB-60 rockets); 2 d.c. racks (6 d.c. each) or up to 18 mines
Electronics:
Radar: 1 MR-312 Nayada nav.; 1 MR-755 Topaz-2B (Half Plate-B) surf./air search; 1 MPZ-301 Baza (Pop Group) SAM f.c.; 1 MR-123 Vympel (Bass Tilt) gun f.c.
Sonar: MGK-335MC Platina (Bull Nose) hull-mounted (3 kHz); Shelon' (Elk Tail) dipping (7.5 kHz)
EW: 2 Bizan'-4B (Watch Dog) intercept (2–18 GHz); 2 16-round PK-16 fixed decoy RL
M: CODAG: 1 M-8M gas turbine (18,000 shp), 2 M-507A diesels (10,000 bhp each); 3 props; 38,000 hp
Electric: 1,000 kw tot. (1 × 500-kw, 1 × 300-kw, 1 × 200-kw diesel sets)
Range: 950/27; on diesels alone: 2,500/14; 4,000/10 **Fuel:** 143 tons
Endurance: 9 days **Crew:** 9 officers, 77 enlisted

Remarks: Assigned to the Federal Border Guard on completion. Operates in the Pacific region. A reported second unit of this design named *Poryvistry* apparently never existed.
Hull systems: There are two drop-down harbor maneuvering propulsors at the extreme stern, as in the now-stricken Petya (Project 159–series) class. Carries 10.5 tons of lube oil and 27.2 tons of fresh water.

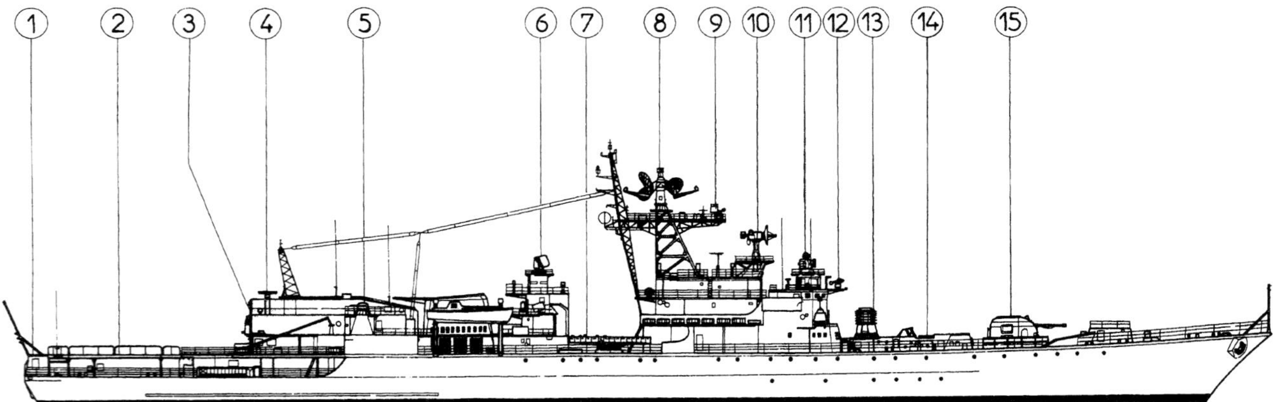

Krivak-III Menzhinskiy (113) 1. VDS sonar housing 2. Helicopter platform 3. Helicopter hangar 4. Nayada-2 radar for helicopter landing and take-off control 5. 30-mm AK-630 gatling AA 6. MR-123 Vympel radar director for 30-mm guns 7. Quadruple 533-mm TT 8. MR-310U Angara-M (MR-750MA Fregat-MA on others of the class) air-search radar 9. Volga navigational and surface-search radar 10. MR-114 Bars radar director for 100-mm gun 11. MPZ-301 radar director for Osa-M SAM system 12. Nayada-1 nav. radar 13. RBU-6000 ASW RL 14. Osa-M SAM launcher (shown retracted) 15. 100-mm AK-100 DP gun Drawing by Lucien Gassier, from *Flottes de Combat*

BORDER GUARD CORVETTES [WFFL] *(continued)*

Combat systems: Two launch positions for shoulder-fired point-defense SAMs have been added at the break of the 01 level superstructure, just forward of the stack. Just abaft the mast is an SP-521 Rakurs (Kolonka-2) backup ringsight director for the 30-mm gun. The torpedo tubes have been modified to launch wire-guided torpedoes. The dipping sonar is housed in the after superstructure, lowering through the hull between the starboard and centerline propeller shafts.

♦ 3 Grisha-III class (Projects 1124M and 1124MP)
Bldr: Vladivostokskogo SSZ, Novolitovsk

	Laid down	L	In serv.
. . . Bezuprechniy	7-79	5-81	19-12-81
058 Zorkiy	15-2-80	2-11-81	29-10-82
153 Smel'yy	18-3-81	7-5-83	15-12-83

Smel'yy (153)—a second boat has been added to port of the stack on this unit U.S. Navy, 1985

D: 860 tons light; 954 tons normal (990 fl)
S: 32 kts (21 on gas turbine; 16 on diesels)
Dim: 71.20 (66.90 wl) × 10.15 (9.50 wl) × 3.40 (hull)
A: 1 twin-rail Osa-M (SA-N-4) SAM syst. (20 9M-33/Gecko missiles); 1 twin 57-mm AK-725 DP (1,100 rounds); 1 30-mm 54-cal. AK-630M gatling AA (2,000 rounds); 2 12-round RBU-6000 ASW RL (96 RGB-60 rockets); 2 twin 533-mm TT; 2 d.c. racks (6 d.c. each)
Electronics:
Radar: 1 Don-2 nav.; 1 MR-302 Rubka (Strut Curve) surf./air search; 1 MPZ-301 Baza (Pop Group) SAM f.c.; 1 MR-123 Vympel (Bass Tilt) gun f.c.
Sonar: MGK- . . . Argun' (Bull Nose) hull-mounted MF; Shelon' (Elk Tail) MF through-hull dipping
EW: 2 Bizan'-4B (Watch Dog) intercept (2–18 GHz)
M: CODAG: 1 M-8M gas turbine (18,000 shp), 2 M-507A diesels (10,000 bhp each); 3 props; 38,000 hp—2 maneuvering propellers
Electric: 1,000 kw (1 × 500-kw, 1 × 300-kw, 1 × 200-kw diesel sets)
Range: 950/27; 2,750/14; 4,000/10 **Fuel:** 130 tons + 13 tons overload
Endurance: 9 days **Crew:** 9 officers, 74 enlisted

Remarks: Survivors of five built for the KGB Border Guard. All serve in the Pacific region.
Hull systems: Have retractable fin stabilizers. Said to consume 450 kg of fuel per hour at 14 kts. *Smel'yy* has had an extra boat added to port of the stack, stowed on an 01-level platform.
Combat systems: The d.c. racks are mounted on the aft end of the mine rails. Some may have two SAM launch positions, as on the Grisha-V.
Disposals: *Bditel'nyy* and *Reshitel'nyy* were stricken 13-6-98; three others, *Bravyy, Vernyy,* and *Strogiy,* were stricken 10-2-92 and broken up while under construction. *Bezuprechniy* may also no longer be in service.

♦ 4 Grisha-II class (Project 1124P) Bldrs: Zelenodolsk Zavod 340, Kazan

	Laid down	L	In serv.
. . . Izumrud	8-2-73	3-2-74	28-12-74
. . . Predaniy	18-3-82	16-4-83	30-9-83
. . . Nadezhnyy	19-9-82	25-2-84	20-9-84
. . . Dozorniy	28-6-83	1985	26-12-85

Northern Fleet area Grisha-II class M.O.D. U.K., 9-87

D: 890 tons (1,010 fl) **S:** 32 kts
Dim: 71.10 (66.90 wl) × 10.15 (9.50 wl) × 3.60 (hull)
A: 2 twin 57-mm AK-257 DP (2,200 rounds); 2 12-round RBU-6000 ASW RL (96 RGB-60 rockets); 2 twin 533-mm DTA-53-1124 TT; 2 d.c. racks (20 tot. d.c.) or mines
Electronics:
Radar: 1 Don-2 nav.; 1 MR-302 Rubka (Strut Curve) surf./air search; 1 MR-103 Bars (Muff Cob) f.c.
Sonar: MGK-355M Argun' (Bull Nose) hull-mounted (3 kHz); Shelon' (Elk Tail) through-hull dipping (7.5 kHz)
EW: 2 Bizan'-4B (Watch Dog) intercept (2–18 GHz)

Northern Fleet area Grisha-II class M.O.D. U.K., 5-90

M: CODAG: 1 M-8M (M-813) gas turbine (18,000 shp), 2 M-507A diesels (10,000 bhp each); 3 props; 38,000 hp—2 maneuvering propellers
Electric: 1,000 kw (1 × 500-kw, 1 × 300-kw, 1 × 200-kw diesel sets)
Range: 950/27; 2,750/14; 4,000/10
Fuel: 130 tons + 13 tons overload (see remarks) **Endurance:** 9 days
Crew: 9 officers, 70 enlisted

Remarks: Survivors of 12 built for the KGB Maritime Border Guard. All are active in the Northern Fleet, although probably not for much longer. The names *Korund, Malachit,* and *Primernyy* associated with this class were apparently in error.
Hull systems: Can achieve 7 kts on one diesel, 16 kts on both diesels, and 22 kts on gas turbine alone. Fin stabilizers are fitted. There is tankage for 22.2 tons of fresh water and 10.5 tons of lube oil.
Combat systems: A second twin 57-mm gun (with 500 rounds per mount) was substituted for the Osa-M SAM system forward, and the missile-control radar was not installed.
Disposals: *Brilliant* was stricken 13-3-95, *Zhemchug* on 4-10-95, *Rubin* on 15-6-92, *Ametist* on 23-5-97, *Sapfir* on 13-6-98, and *Provorniy* on 4-8-98. Black Sea Fleet units *Dnepr* and *Izmail* were transferred to Ukraine 26-11-92.

PATROL SHIPS [WPS]

Note: In order to carry out its new fisheries patrol duties, the Federal Border Guard has taken over an unknown number of patrol ships from the Ministry of Fisheries; most would fit in the Patrol Ship [WPS] category. In addition to the classes described below, a Northern Fleet–area unit named *Syktyvkar* was taken over in 8-98 from the Ministry of Fisheries; no data available. A fisheries protection ship named *Berkut* was added to the Baltic-area fleet 1-7-98; again, no data available. A Pacific-area fisheries patrol craft named *A. Pyn'ko* has been named in the press.

♦ 1 (+ 2 + 7) Sprut class (Project 6457S)
Bldr: Yantar Verf, Kaliningrad

	Laid down	L	In serv.
. . . Sprut	28-5-02	. . .	2005

Sprut Class—builder's model Alexandre Sheldon-Duplaix, 6-03

D: 800 tons (fl) **S:** 21.5 kts **Dim:** 65.90 × 10.60 × 3.20
A: 2 single 7.62-mm mg **Electronics:** Radar: 2 . . . nav.
M: 1 MTU 16V1163 TB37L diesel, electric drive; 1 prop; 6,974 bhp—1 1,073-shp electric motor for cruising
Range: 6,500/12 **Endurance:** 30 days **Crew:** 14 tot.

Remarks: Described as an "environmental patrol ship." Fitted with a helicopter deck. Aluminum-alloy superstructure with a steel hull. Used for EEZ and pollution-control and maritime safety and security duties. They carry a 30-kt RIB. The hulls and superstructures for three sisters for the German Federal Border Guard were built by Yantar Verf for Abeking and Rasmussen as the *Bad Bramstedt* class; data above reflect the German version.

♦ 8 Al'pinist class (Project 503POS)
Bldr: Volgograd Zavod (*Argal, Bars:* Khabarovsk; two new units: Yaroslavl Zavod)

	In serv.		In serv.		In serv.
Antias	1997	Paliya	1998	Grinda	9-01
Argal	1998	Parella	1999	Kurs	12-01
Bars	1989	Diana	2000		

D: 810 tons light (1,140 fl) **S:** 12.6 kts **Dim:** 53.70 (46.20 pp) × 10.50 × 4.10
Electronics: Radar: 2 Don-2 nav.
M: 1 Type 8NVD48-2U diesel; 1 CP prop; 1,320 bhp—bow-thruster
Electric: 450 kw tot. (1 × 300-kw, 1 × 150-kw diesel sets)
Range: 7,000/12.5 **Fuel:** 162 tons **Endurance:** 25 days **Crew:** 44 tot.

Remarks: A standard 704-grt/308-dwt long-lines fishing trawler design, acquired and adapted for use as fisheries patrol ships. The Russian Navy uses three sisters as intelligence collectors. *Antias* had a confrontation with a U.S. Coast Guard cutter in Bering Sea waters during 1999. *Bars* was transferred to Federal Border Guard control in 1998 and operates in the Pacific, as will the two new units ordered from Yaroslavl Zavod during 10-00.

BORDER GUARD PATROL SHIPS [WPS] *(continued)*

♦ 4 Komandor-class fisheries protection ships
Bldr: Danyard, Frederikshavn, Denmark

	L	In serv.
Komandor	12-88	8-89
Shkiper Gek	4-89	20-12-89
Kherluf Bidstrup	8-89	2-90
Manchzur	4-5-90	6-7-90

Kherluf Bidstrup Boris Lemachko, 3-01

Manchzur—with a commercial vehicle cargo; note that the engine exhaust stack is near the stern in this class, abaft the helicopter deck JMSDF, 4-94

D: 2,425 tons (fl) **S:** 20 kts (19.2 cruising)
Dim: 88.90 (82.20 wl) × 13.60 × 4.70 (mean)
A: None; 1 Ka-32S Helix-D SAR helicopter
Electronics: Radar: 3 . . . nav. (1 Furuno)
M: 2 Russkiy Dizel–Pielstick 6 PC2.5 L400 diesels; 1 4-bladed CP prop; 7,786 bhp—1 500-shp bow-thruster
Electric: 1,840 kw (1 × 600-kw shaft generator, 2 × 620-kw diesel sets)
Range: 7,000/19.2 **Crew:** 42 tot.

Remarks: 2,800 grt/534 dwt. Ordered 11-11-87. Operated for and by the Ministry of Fisheries in the Northern Pacific area until 8-98 when transferred to the Federal Border Guard. The helicopter is stored in a two-deck-high hangar beneath the flight deck, which is 14 m long and has folding sides to increase its width. Have Blohm + Voss folding fin stabilizers. Carry two unsinkable GRP lifeboats and two rigid inflatables—one of which is for inspection duties. All are based in the Pacific.

♦ 1 Akademik Fersman class (Project B-93)
Bldr: A. Warski SY, Szczecin, Poland

	L	In serv.
Spastel' Proconchik (ex-*Akademik Fersman*)	24-1-85	10-5-86

D: 3,250 tons (fl) **S:** 14.5 kts **Dim:** 81.87 (73.51 pp) × 14.83 × 5.00
Electronics: Radar: 2 . . . nav.
M: 1 Zgoda-Sulzer 6 ZL 40/48 diesel; 1 Kort-nozzle CP prop; 4,200 bhp—bow-thruster
Electric: 2,208 kw tot. (1 × 1,200-kw shaft alternator, 2 × 504-kw diesel sets)
Range: 12,000/14.5 **Fuel:** 700 m^3 heavy oil, 170 m^3 diesel
Crew: 31 tot. + 29 passengers (as research ship)

Remarks: 2,833 grt/1,283 dwt. Sold to Russian government early in 1997 by the Yuzhmorneftegeofizika trust, which had used her as a seismic research ship. The new name indicates employment in search-and-rescue service, for which her long range is well suited.

♦ 2 Yug class (Project 862)
Bldr: Stocznia Polnocna, Gdansk, Poland (In serv. 1978–83)

025 Pluton 028 Strelets

D: 1,960 tons (2,490 fl) **S:** 15.6 kts **Dim:** 82.50 (75.80 pp) × 13.50 × 3.97
A: Probably none
Electronics: Radar: 2 Don-2 nav.
M: 2 Zgoda-Sulzer 8TD48.2 diesels; 2 CP props; 4,400 bhp (3,600 sust.)—2 100-kw low-speed electric motors—300-shp bow-thruster
Electric: 1,920 kVA tot.
Range: 9,000/13 **Fuel:** 343 tons **Endurance:** 40 days
Crew: 8 officers, 38 unlicensed (civilian), 20 scientists + 4 spare

Remarks: Built as oceanographic research and hydrographic survey vessels. Transferred to the Federal Border Guard in 1997, arriving at Murmansk, where they are now based, in 8-97. Are used to conduct EEZ patrols. Thirteen sisters remain in the Russian Navy configured as oceanographic research ships, and two others were converted as intelligence collection ships.

Strelets (028)—while still in naval service Hartmut Ehlers, 7-93

Hull systems: Have a quadrantial davit over stern ramp with 4-ton lift, two 5-ton booms, several oceanographic davits, three echo sounders, and six laboratories. Have deck reinforcements for three twin 25-mm AA. Carry two Project 727 GRP-hulled inshore survey launches.

♦ 6 Ivan Susanin–class (Project 97P/8) patrol icebreakers
Bldr: Admiralty SY, St. Petersburg (In serv. 1975–81)

	Laid down	L	In serv.	Fleet area
093 Ivan Susanin	31-7-72	38-2-73	12-73	. . .
161 Aysburg	17-10-73	27-4-74	26-12-74	Pacific
173 Anadyr' (ex-*Imeni XXV S'yezda K.P.S.S.*, ex-*Dnepr*)	16-7-75	14-2-76	30-9-76	. . .
018 Murmansk (ex-*Dunay*)	24-12-76	5-8-77	30-12-77	Pacific
170 Neva	23-11-77	28-7-78	29-12-78	Pacific
183 Volga	27-2-79	19-4-80	26-12-80	Pacific

Murmansk (018) Boris Lemachko, 7-02

D: 2,785 tons (3,710 fl) **S:** 14 kts **Dim:** 70.0 (62.0 pp) × 18.1 (17.5 wl) × 6.60
A: 1 twin 76.2-mm 59-cal. AK-276 DP; 2 single 30-mm 54-cal. AK-630 gatling AA
Electronics:
Radar: 2 Volga (Don-Kay) nav.; 1 MR-302 Rubka (Strut Curve) surf./air search; 1 MR-105 Turel' (Owl Screech) 76.2-mm gun f.c.
M: 3 Type 13D-100 diesels, electric drive; 2 props; 4,800 shp
Electric: 1,200 kw tot. **Range:** 5,500/14.5; 13,000/9.4 **Fuel:** 580 tons
Endurance: 50 days **Crew:** 9 officers, 33 enlisted (accomm. for 123 tot.)

Remarks: Built for KGB Maritime Border Service use and designated PSKR (*Pogranichnyy Storozhevoy Korabl'*, Border Patrol Ship). Sister *Ruslan* has been stricken. *Ivan Susanin*, thought to have been retired, is apparently still in service. *Anadyr'* was given its current name in 11-4-92 and *Murmansk* in 5-96; the latter was refitted from 7-97 to 1-00.
Hull systems: Can carry 170 tons of fresh water and 27 tons of lubricants. The hull is divided into eight watertight compartments. The bow propeller was omitted in this variant and the motor compartment used to accommodate two diesel generator sets.
Combat systems: The 30-mm gatling AA guns are controlled only by two SP-521 Rakurs (Kolonka-2) ringsight directors. Have a helicopter deck aft but no hangar. *Murmansk* and *Neva* also have two positions for shoulder-launched surface-to-air missiles.

♦ 17 Sorum-class (Project 745P) armed tugs
Bldr: Yaroslavl Zavod (In serv. 1974–1997)

	In serv.	Fleet
073 Zabaykal'ye	1979	Pacific
067 Chukotka	1981	Pacific
022 Zapolyare	29-9-82	Northern
110 Kareliya	30-9-83	Northern
142 Aldan (ex-*Bug*)	25-11-85	Pacific

BORDER GUARD PATROL SHIPS [WPS] *(continued)*

	In serv.	Fleet
016 Ural	30-9-86	Northern
030 Yenisey	5-11-87	Northern
. . . Vyatka (ex-*Viktor Kingisepp*)	30-9-88	Baltic
101 General Armii Matrosov (ex-*Taymir*)	1992	Caspian
103 Don	24-10-97	Baltic
043 Amur	. . .	Pacific
105 Baykal(ex-*Yan Bergin*)	. . .	Baltic
135 Brest	. . .	Pacific
172 Primor'ye (ex-159)	. . .	Pacific
124 Sakhalin	. . .	Pacific
198 Kamchatka	. . .	Pacific
058 Ladoga	. . .	Northern

Primor'ye (172) *Ships of the World,* 2005

Primor'ye (172) Mitsuhiro Kadota, 2002

D: 1,210 tons (1,656 fl) **S:** 14 kts **Dim:** 58.3 (55.5 pp) × 12.6 × 4.6
A: *Don, Sakhalin,* and *Vyatka:* 2 single 20-mm 54-cal. AK-306 gatling AA—others: 2 twin 30-mm 65-cal. AK-230 AA
Electronics: Radar: 2 Don-2 nav.
M: 2 Type 5-2D42 (6ChN 30/38) diesels, 2 generators (950 kw each), electric drive; 1 prop; 2,500 shp (1,850 sust.)
Range: 6,750/13 **Fuel:** 297 tons **Endurance:** 40 days
Crew: 3 officers, 37 enlisted

Remarks: Typed PSKR (*Pogranichnyy Storozhevoy Korabl',* Border Patrol Ship). Armed units of a standard naval/commercial Project 745 seagoing tug, used by the Federal Border Guard for patrol duties. Because these ships are inexpensive to operate and can accommodate deck cargo, they are widely used by the Border Guard, especially in the Pacific region. Retain all towing, firefighting, and salvage facilities. A new series of five was ordered during 5-94. Two more were ordered fall 1998. *Don* was laid down 18-12-91 but not launched until 8-96; the keel for another was laid down in 5-97.
Hull systems: The output of the propulsion plant is listed as less than that of the Project 745 ocean tug version, which is credited with 3,000 shp. Carry 89 tons of potable water.
Combat systems: On all, the guns are controlled by a single SP-521 Rakurs (Kolonka-2) manned director.
Disposals: Sisters *Vitim, Stavropol,* and *Nevel'sk* had been stricken by 2005. Pacific area unit *Neman* was stricken 16-7-96.

PATROL CRAFT, HYDROFOIL [WPCH]

♦ 5 Muravey (Antarets) class (Project 133)
Bldr: Yuzhnaya Tochka Zavod, Feodosiya, Ukraine (In serv. 1983–92)

P101 . . . . . . Del'fin
P104 . . . . . . Riba
. . . Tuapse

Black Sea Muravey-class pennant 136 French Navy, 1997

Black Sea Muravey-class pennant 025 [no credit or date]

D: 180 tons light; 195 tons std. (220 fl) **S:** 65 kts (60 sust.)
Dim: 40.30 (39.60 hull; 34.40 wl) × 8.00 (12.0 over foils; 7.30 wl) × 1.90 (hull; 4.55 over foils)
A: 1 76.2-mm 59-cal. AK-176 DP; 1 30-mm 54-cal. AK-630 gatling AA; 2 fixed 402-mm OTA-40 ASW TT; 1 d.c. rack (6 d.c.); 1 55-mm grenade launcher (70 projectiles)
Electronics:
Radar: 1 Reyd (Peel Cone) nav./surf. search; 1 MR-123 Vympel (Bass Tilt) gun f.c.
Sonar: Ros'-K HF dipping at stern
M: COGAG M-20 plant: 2 M-70 gas turbines; 2 props; 22,600 shp (20,000 sust.)
Range: 410/45–50 **Endurance:** 5 days **Crew:** 5 officers, 20 enlisted

Remarks: Thirteen were built for the KGB Maritime Border Service. Designed under B. F. Orlov at Alekseyev Central Hydrofoil Design Bureau. One of the units listed above may have been renamed *Riba.* The survivors serve in the Baltic and Black Sea. Commercial versions equipped to carry 150 passengers and six automobiles or 300 passengers are offered for export.
Hull systems: Foil system uses fixed, fully submerged bow and stern sets, with an automatically adjusted amidships surface-piercing set beneath the bridge to control the ride. There is a single step to the hull aft. Both propeller shafts are sharply angled downward and are supported by the stern foil struts assembly. Can maintain 50 kts in Sea State 4 and operate hullborne in up to Sea State 7. Hull is hard-chine in form and made of aluminum-magnesium alloy.
Combat systems: The dipping sonar deploys through a hatch in the transom stern. There is an SP-521 Rakurs (Kolonka-2) ringsight backup director for the 30-mm gatling gun aft. The d.c. rack is on the starboard quarter. The grenade launcher is intended to combat underwater swimmers.
Disposals: Black Sea sisters P-103, -105, and -108 were stricken 5-7-94 after having been transferred to Ukraine in 4-94; P-115 was in Ukraine service by 1997. Black Sea unit P-102 was stricken for disposal on 23-9-94. P-106, -107, P-109 through P-111, -117 and -118 have been stricken

PATROL CRAFT [WPC]

♦ 1 (+ 4 + 3) Buyan class (Project 21630)
Bldr: Sudostroitel'noye Obyedineniye "Almaz," Petrovskiy SY, St. Petersburg

	Laid down	L	In serv.
. . . Astrakhan	30-1-04	7-10-05	12-05
. . . Kaspiysk	25-2-05	2006	2007
. . . Moskovityanin	. . .	. . .	. . .
. . .	. . .	. . .	. . .
. . .	. . .	. . .	. . .

D: 500 tons **S:** 20 kts
Dim: 51.2 × . . . × . . .
A: 1 100-mm 59-cal. A-190 DP; 2 single 30-mm 54-cal. AK-630M gatling AA; 1 twin 12.7-mm mg; 3 single 7.62-mm mg; 1 . . . -round 122-mm UMS-73 Grad-M artillery RL (. . . rockets)
Electronics: Radar: 1 . . . nav.; 1 MR-123 Vympel (Bass Tilt) f.c.
M: 2 . . . diesels; 2 waterjets
Range: . . . / . . .

Remarks: Ordered during 2004. All are to be assigned to the Caspian Sea. Fitted with a stern ramp.

BORDER GUARD PATROL CRAFT [WPC] *(continued)*

Buyan-class patrol craft Astrakhan—at launching *Ships of the World,* 2005

Astrakhan—stern view *Ships of the World,* 2005

♦ 3 Merkuriya class (Project 14232)

Bldr: Yaroslavskiy SB, Yaroslavl (In serv. 2000–2003)

PETR MATVEEV PAVEL VERESHCHAGIN VITALIY KIRSANOV

D: 90 tons (99 fl) **S:** 50 kts **Dim:** 35.40 × 8.30 × 2.00 (props)
A: 1 30-mm 54-cal. AK-306 gatling AA; 1 14.5-mm AA; 1 Kornet or Metis-M SAM syst. (4 missiles; see remarks)
Electronics:
Radar: 1 . . . nav.
EW: . . . intercept; 1 10-round PK-10 decoy RL

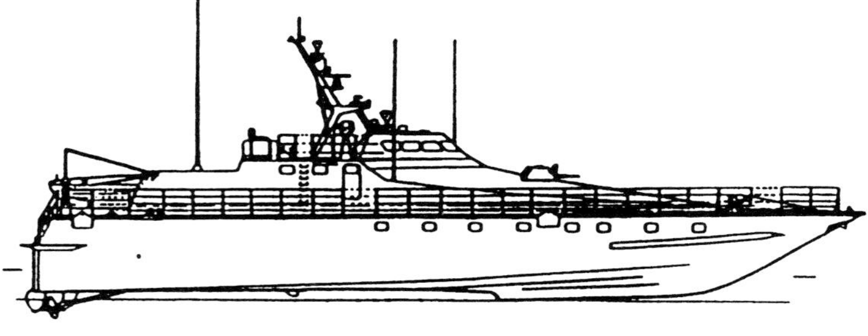

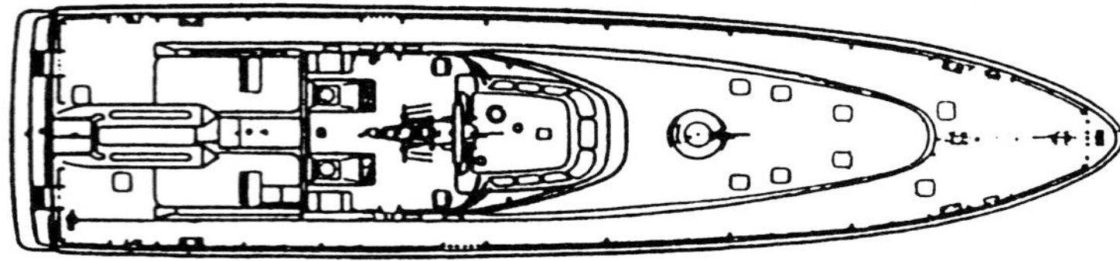

Merkuriya-class—armed Border Guard variant (Project 14232) Aleksey Bureau

M: 2 Zvezda M-504B-4 diesels; 2 props; 9,980 bhp
Range: 500/30 **Endurance:** 5 days **Crew:** 16 tot.

Remarks: Typed as a "4th Rank Border Guard Ship" and referred to as the *Sokzhoi* class in recent literature. Designed by Alekseyev Central Hydrofoil Design Bureau, Nizhniy Novgorod, for the customs service, for which the prototype *Petr Matveev* (TS-100) and *Pavel Vereshchagin* (TS-101; in serv. 5-11-00) operate; they were built by Yaroslavskiy Shipbuilding. The design is also offered for export as a high-speed yacht with MTU 16V396 TV94 diesels as an alternative propulsion plant.
Hull systems: Originally reported to displace 102 tons full load. Range is also given as 800 n.m. Uses an air cavity beneath the aluminum-magnesium alloy hull to enhance planing lift. Can operate in State 6 seas and at 30 kts in 1.5-m waves.
Combat systems: The 30-mm gun is controlled by a Kolonka-219 lead-computing ringsight director. The design is also offered for export with a 7.62-mm mg added to the 30-mm mount, firing coaxially, plus two to four antiship missiles of unspecified type, while six Igla shoulder-launched SAMs can supplement or replace the Kornet or Metis-M system (for which no data are available; they may have been programs that have not reached production stage).

♦ 3 (+ . . .) Mirazh class (Project 14310)

Bldr: Vympel Zavod, Rybinsk

	In serv.
PK-500	12-9-01
PK-501	2002
117 PK- . . .	2003

Mirazh-class patrol craft pennant 117 Boris Lemachko, 6-05

D: 109 tons light; 120 tons normal (121.1 fl) **S:** 50 kts
Dim: 34.95 × 6.79 (6.60 wl) × 2.10 (hull; 2.70 props)
A: 1 30-mm 54-cal. AK-306 gatling AA; 1 twin 14.5-mm mg; 2 triple 9M-114 Shturm SSM launchers (6 9M-120 Ataka or 9M-121 Vikhr' short-range missiles); 1 twin point-defense SAM launcher position (8 Igla-M missiles); 1 DP-64 handheld grenade launcher
Electronics: Radar: 1 Decca BridgeMaster C181/4 AT nav.
M: 2 Zvezda M-520B diesels; 2 props; 10,800 bhp
Electric: 125 kw tot. (2 × 50-kw, 1 × 25-kw, 380-V, 50-Hz diesel sets)
Range: 1,500/8 **Fuel:** 16.2 tons **Endurance:** 5 days
Crew: 2 officers, 3 warrant officers, 7 enlisted

Remarks: Offered for export in 2-93; construction of three was authorized in 1993, but only one was launched, in 1988. After lack of success in selling the craft, the yard presented it to the Federal Border Guard on 18-7-01 for service in the Caspian Sea, where it was commissioned into the Astrakhan Brigade. Another boat was laid down on 8-1-01. Designed by Firma Almaz, St. Petersburg. Funds permitting, the border guard would like to acquire 20 additional units.
Hull systems: Have an aluminum-magnesium alloy hull, with a stepped design and the hull bottom equipped with "interceptors" to minimize roll and improve the hull planing effect. Underhull air lubrication reduces the lift-to-drag ratio by between 5% and 30%. Can operate in Sea State 5. Fully armed, the craft would displace 126 tons full load. Equipped with the tropicalized M-520 TM5 engine, the craft would have a maximum speed of 48 kts.
Combat systems: Said to be able to carry 500 rounds of 30-mm ammunition and 2,000 rounds of machinegun ammunition. The export version was offered with six 9M-120 Ataka (NATO AT-6 Spiral) missiles; these were originally designed for antitank use and have a range of 6 km. The 30-mm gunmount has 500 rounds on-mount.

♦ 20 Svetlyak class (Projects 1041.0)

Bldrs: Vladivostokskiy Sudostroitel'nyy Zavod (Vostochnaya Verf), Ulis, Vladivostok (In serv. 1988– . . .); Sudostroitel'noye Obyedineniye "Almaz," Petrovskiy SY, St. Petersburg (In serv. 1991– . . .); Yaroslavskiy SB, Yaroslavl (6 units, in serv. 1990–95)

	In serv.		In serv.
017 PSKR-920 PODOL'SK	1994	099 . . . PITERSKIY ALMAZ	. . .
023 PSKR-915 NEVEL'SK	1993	100 PSKR-902 STAVROPOL'	1989
026 PSKR-918 YUZHNO-SAKHALINSK	1994	102 PSKR-931 KIZLYAR	23-12-97
	8-2-92	106 PSKR-912 DERBENT	1994
028 PSKR-906 SOCHI	1991	119 PSKR-914 KORSAKOV	1992
042 PSKR-911 SIKTIVKAR	1994	126 PSKR-923	1996
044 PSKR-917 YAMALETS	1990	141 PSKR-909 VYBORG	1992
065 PSKR-908 BRIZ	12-6-00	143 PSKR-913 ALMAZ	15-10-93
076 PSKR-919 STOROSHEVIK	1989	. . . RASUL GAMZATOV	. . .
077 NEPTUN	. . .	. . . KANIN	. . .
088 PSKR-903 KHOLMSK			

D: 328 tons light (365–375 normal fl, 382–390 max.) **S:** 32 kts (31 sust.)
Dim: 49.50 (45.00 wl) × 9.20 × 2.14 (hull; 2.50 props)
A: 1 76.2-mm 59-cal. AK-176M DP (not in PSKR-931 and unnamed unit); 1 (PSKR-913 and unnamed unit: 2) single 30-mm 54-cal. AK-630M gatling AA; 1 or 2 AGS-17 grenade launchers; 1 DP-64 antiswimmer grenade launcher; 2 fixed 402-mm OTA-40 ASW TT (4 SET-40 torpedoes); 2 d.c. racks (6 BB-1 d.c. each)

BORDER GUARD PATROL CRAFT [WPC] *(continued)*

PSKR-909 Vyborg (141) Ralph Edwards, 6-03

PSKR-923 (126) *Ships of the World,* 2004

Electronics:
Radar: 1 Reyd (Peel Cone) and/or Mius (Spin Trough) nav./surf. search; 1 MR-123 Vympel-AM (Bass Tilt) f.c.
Sonar: Uzh HF helicopter dipping sonar at stern (not in PSKR-931 and one other)
EW: Slyabing intercept; . . . MFD/F loop; 2 16-round PK-16 fixed decoy RL
M: 3 Zvezda M-520B diesels; 3 props; 15,000 bhp
Electric: 400 kw tot. (1 × 200-kw, 2 × 100-kw diesel sets; 380 V, 50 Hz a.c.)
Range: 1,500/31–32; 2,200/12–13 **Endurance:** 10 days
Crew: 4 officers, 4 warrant officers, 20 enlisted (41 tot. accomm.)

Remarks: Design, by Almaz Central Marine Design Bureau, is tailored to extended patrolling. Three sisters serve in the Russian Navy. The NATO nickname means "Firefly." The initial Project 1041.0–series units were built for service in the Far East. The first Petrovskiy-built unit (probably PSKR-913) was launched 28-7-92 and delivered 25-2-93; the same yard launched its seventh unit 10-12-96, the only naval surface combatant launched in Russia that year. PSKR-906 was delivered by Almaz 27-5-99 and is assigned to the Black Sea. Two sisters may have been ordered by Vietnam.

Project 1041.2 is offered as an export version without ASW equipment. The design is also offered as Project 1041.1 at 390 tons full load, with a 30-kt maximum speed and eight SS-N-25 missiles. The patrol version has been offered to Sri Lanka and to Equatorial Guinea at $25 million per unit.
Hull systems: Semi-planing, round-bilge hull with low spray chine forward. Propellers do not project below the keel. Have a steel hull with aluminum-magnesium alloy superstructure. Can survive with two compartments flooded. Have NBC warfare protection. The engine room is coated with vibration-damping material. The pilothouse is equipped with a centerline periscope.
Combat systems: There is an SP-521 Rakurs (Kolonka-2) ringsight backup director for the 30-mm gun; the 76.2-mm mount can be operated in local control and has an integral electro-optical sighting system. Carries 152 rounds of 76-mm (all on-mount) and up to 3,000 rounds of 30-mm ammunition. Navigational equipment includes a NAVSAT receiver, radio navaid receiver, automatic plot, and echo sounder. The design is also offered with a quadruple SAM launcher (and 16 Igla-series heat-seeking missiles) atop an enlarged dipping sonar housing at the stern, but none has yet been seen with the feature installed; the dipping sonar is extended from a compartment to port of the centerline at the stern, and there is no hull-mounted set. Some also have an additional Vaygach or MR-312 Nayada navigational radar. PSKR-931, *Pikul',* and a unit fitting out at Vladivostok during 2000 received a 30-mm AK-630M gatling gun forward instead of the standard 76-mm mount.

♦ 2 Modified Pauk II class (Project 1241PE)
Bldr: Yaroslavskiy SB, Yaroslavl

	Laid down	L	Del.	In serv.
093 Novorossiysk (ex-MPK-291)	11-4-90	23-4-91	30-3-97	12-5-97
149 Kuban' (ex-MPK-292)	20-7-90	. . .	31-12-97	9-4-98

D: 425 tons (495 fl) **S:** 32 kts (28 sust.)
Dim: 58.5 (49.5 pp) × 10.2 (9.4 wl) × 2.16 (hull; 3.61 props)
A: 1 76.2-mm 59-cal. AK-176 DP; 1 4-round Fasta-4M SAM syst. (16 Igla-M/Gremlin missiles); 1 30-mm 54-cal. AK-630 gatling AA; 2 5-round RBU-1200 ASW RL (30 RGB-12 rockets); 4 fixed 533-mm TT (2 SET-65E ASW and 2 Type 53-65KE antiship torpedoes); 2 d.c. racks (6 BB-1 d.c. each)

Modified Pauk-II Novorossiysk (093)—prior to delivery 1991

Novorossiysk (093) and Kuban'—at their builder's, prior to delivery Yaroslavskiy Zavod, 10-96

Electronics:
Radar: 1 Pechora nav.; 1 MR-352 Pozitiv (Cross Dome) air/surf. search; 1 MR-123 Vympel-AM (Bass Tilt) gun f.c.
Sonar: MGK-345 MF hull-mounted and MF dipping system
EW: 2 16-round PK-16 fixed decoy RL
M: 2 M-521-TM5 diesels; 3 props; 17,330 bhp
Range: 2,000/20; 3,000/12 **Fuel:** 50 tons **Endurance:** 10 days
Crew: 7 officers, 32 enlisted

Remarks: Are of the export Pauk-II variant of the type delivered to India (4) and Cuba (1); they were originally intended for delivery to Iraq, along with MPK-293, which was not completed. They differ from the standard Russian Navy version in having a larger pilothouse, incorporating Cross Dome radar, and using 533-mm torpedo tubes (which are able to carry antiship as well as ASW torpedoes) vice 402-mm ASW TT. MPK-291 was named on 24-8-96 and MPK-292 on 10-9-97 when they were transferred to the border guard; they operate in the Black Sea.
Hull systems: The large housing for a dipping sonar system projects 1.5 m out from the stern. The large hull-mounted sonar dome is located approximately beneath the gun fire-control radar. The hull is constructed of mild steel, while the middle part of the deck plating, some internal bulkheads, and much of the superstructure are made of aluminum-magnesium alloy. Range with normal fuel allowance is only 1,600 n.m. at 12 kts.
Combat systems: The combat data system is designated SU-580E. There is an SP-521 Rakurs (Kolonka-2) backup ringsight director for the single gatling AA gun; Bass Tilt can control both the 76.2-mm and 30-mm guns. The normal ammunition load is 152 rounds of 76-mm (all ready-service, on-mount) and 2,000 rounds of 30-mm. The torpedo tubes must be trained out to launch. The sonar suite is nicknamed Bronza; MGK-345 applies to both the hull-mounted and dipping sonars, and the dipping sonar transducer can be lowered to 200 m.

♦ 2 Bogomol (Vikhr'-III) class (Project 2061)
Bldr: Vladivostokskiy Sudostroitel'nyy Zavod, Ulis, Vladivostok

070 PSKR-900 (In serv. 1988) 075 PSKR-902 (In serv. 1989)

D: 215 tons (251 fl) **S:** 36 kts **Dim:** 40.15 × 7.60 × 2.80
A: 1 76.2-mm 59-cal. AK-176M DP; 1 30-mm 54-cal. AK-306M AA
Electronics:
Radar: 1 MR-102 (Pot Drum) surf. search; 1 MR-123 Vympel (Bass Tilt) f.c.
EW: Nakat intercept; SPO-3 jammer
M: 3 M-520TM-5 diesels; 3 props; 14,400 bhp
Electric: 300 kw tot. (1 × 200-kw; 1 × 100-kw diesel sets)
Range: 400/36; 1,700/12 (2,500/12 with emergency fuel stowage)
Endurance: 9 days **Crew:** 5 officers, 32 enlisted

Remarks: Originally ordered for Iraq, but retained for use in the Pacific area, initially to train foreign crews, and then transferred to the Federal Border Guard in 1997. One was numbered T-229 in Russian Navy service.

♦ 18 Pauk-I (Molnaya-2) class (Project 1241.2P)
Bldr: Yaroslavl Zavod; Vladivostokskiy Sudostroitel'nyy Zavod, Ulis, Vladivostok

	In serv.		In serv.
021 PSKR-804 Tol'yatti	1984	065 PSKR-806 Minsk (ex-*Yaguar*)	1984
023 PSKR-818 Nakhodka	1986	077 PSKR-815 Nikolay Kaplunov (ex-*Sobol'*)	1985
024 PSKR-802 Kaliningrad (ex-*Kunitsa*)	1982	078 PSKR-807 Kobchik	1985
031 PSKR-810 Yaroslavl	1986	099 PSKR-809 Krechet	1987
037 PSKR-816 Yastreb	1992	130 PSKR-803 Kondor	1983
040 PSKR-811 Sarych	. . .	152 PSKR-800 Berkut	1981
041 PSKR-808 Grif	1986	161 PSKR-805 Korshun	1984
042 PSKR-814 Orlan	1989	163 PSKR-801 Voron	1982
052 PSKR-817 Cheboksary	1992		
063 PSKR-812 Sokol	1989		

BORDER GUARD PATROL CRAFT [WPC] *(continued)*

PSKR-806 Minsk (065) Jaroslaw Cislak, 5-03

PSKR-809 Krechet (099)—temporarily displaying the hull number 134 Boris Lemachko, 1998

D: 415 tons (475 fl) **S:** 32 kts (28 sust.)
Dim: 57.60 (49.50 pp) × 10.40 (8.74 wl) × 2.14 (hull; 3.59 props)
A: 1 76.2-mm AK-176 DP; 1 4-round Fasta-4M (SA-N-8) SAM syst. (16 9M-313 Igla/Gremlin missiles); 1 30-mm 54-cal. AK-630 gatling AA; 2 5-round RBU-1200 ASW RL (30 RGB-12 projectiles); 4 fixed 402-mm OTA-40 ASW TT (4 SET-40 torpedoes); 2 d.c. racks (6 BB-1 d.c. each)
Electronics:
Radar: 1 Mius (Spin Trough) nav.; 1 Reyd (Peel Cone) nav./surf. search; 1 MR-123 Vympel-AM (Bass Tilt) f.c.
Sonar: MGK-345 Bronza MF hull-mounted and MF dipping (6.5/7.0/7.5 kHz)
EW: Vympel-R2 suite: 2 Half Hat-B intercept (not in all); 2 16-round PK-16 fixed decoy RL—some also: 2 10-round PK-10 fixed decoy RL
M: 2 Zvezda M-517 or M-507A twin diesels; 2 props; 20,800 bhp (16,180 sust.)
Electric: 500 kw tot. (2 × 200-kw, 1 × 100-kw diesel sets)
Range: 2,000/20; 2,600/14; 1,600/12 (normal fuel; 3,000/12 with max. fuel)
Fuel: 50 tons normal **Endurance:** 10 days **Crew:** 5–7 officers, 31–32 enlisted

Remarks: Use the same hull as the Tarantul-class missile corvette but have ASW armament vice antiship missiles and an all-diesel propulsion plant vice the Tarantul's COGAG/CODOG system. Another two are operated by the Russian Navy. PSKR-802, -804, -810, -815, and -817 serve in the Baltic area; PSKR-808 and -814 in the Black Sea; and the others in the Pacific.
Hull systems: A large housing for a dipping sonar system projects about 1.5 m out from the stern. The large hull-mounted sonar dome is located approximately beneath the gun fire-control radar. The hull is constructed of mild steel, while the middle part of the deck plating, some internal bulkheads, and much of the superstructure are made of aluminum-magnesium alloy.
Combat systems: The combat data system is designated SU-580. There is an SP-521 Rakurs (Kolonka-2) backup ringsight director for the single gatling AA gun. The Bass Tilt radar director can control both the 76.2-mm and 30-mm guns. The normal ammunition load is 152 rounds of 76-mm (all ready-service, on-mount) and 2,000 rounds of 30-mm. The sonar suite has a range of about 7 km for the dipping component; MGK-345 applies to both the hull-mounted and dipping sonars, and the dipping sonar transducer can be lowered to 200 m.
Disposals: Federal Border Guard sisters *Gregoriy Gnatenko, Grigoriy Kuropyatnikov,* and PSKR-813 were transferred, probably on loan, to the Ukraine Maritime Border Service in 2-92; they were permanently transferred during 4-94 but not officially stricken until 5-7-94.

♦ 1 Project 1330 fisheries protection craft
Bldr: Vympel Joint Stock Co., Rybinsk (In serv. 1983)

ZOGOTITSA

D: 124.7 tons (183.1 fl) **S:** 9.5 kts **Dim:** 26.40 × 6.50 × 2.70
M: 1 diesel; 1 prop; 225 bhp **Range:** 1,800/9.5 **Crew:** 11 tot.

Remarks: Standard small fishing boat design adapted by the Ministry of Fisheries as a fisheries inspection craft.

♦ 19 Stenka (Tarantul) class (Project 205P)
Bldrs: Sudostroitel'noye Obyedineniye "Almaz," Petrovskiy SY, St. Petersburg; Yaroslavl Zavod; and . . ., Vladivostok (In serv. 1977–90)

014 PSKR-714	129 PSKR-690
035 PSKR-724	139 PSKR-659
044 PSKR-660	. . . PSKR-667
047 PSKR-700	. . . PSKR-695
048 PSKR-715	. . . PSKR-708
078 PSKR-717	and seven others
097 PSKR-712	

D: 170 tons light; 211 tons std. (245 fl) **S:** 35 kts
Dim: 39.80 (37.50 wl) × 7.60 (5.90 wl) × 1.96
A: 2 twin 30-mm 65-cal. AK-230 AA; 4 fixed 402-mm OTA-40 TT (4 SET-40 ASW torpedoes); 2 d.c. racks (6 BB-1 d.c. each)

Stenka-class PSKR-659 (139) JMSDF, 1994

Electronics:
Radar: 1 Baklan (Pot Drum) or Peel Cone nav./surf. search; 1 MR-104 Rys' (Drum Tilt) gun f.c.
Sonar: Bronza hull-mounted HF; HF helicopter dipping-type
EW: SPO-3 intercept
M: 3 M-504B or M-520 diesels; 3 props; 15,000 bhp
Range: 500/35; 800/20; 1,500/11.5 **Endurance:** 10 days
Crew: 4–5 officers, 26–27 enlisted

Remarks: Survivors of some 117 built for the KGB Maritime Border Service 1967–90. Construction continued for more than 20 years, although at a low rate in later years, and new units continued to enter service to replace early craft being discarded until the early 1990s. Late-construction units had Peel Cone navigational radar vice Pot Drum. Only a small number were exported: four to Cuba, four to Cambodia, two to Azerbaijan in 7-92 (ex-Russian AK-234 and AK-374), and several to Vietnam. Units are assigned to the Pacific, Baltic, Black, and Caspian Sea fleets.
Disposals: From the Pacific Fleet, PSKR-680 and -691 were stricken 31-1-91; PSKR-681 through -684 on 10-9-92; P-685, -686, -687, -699, and -698 on 30-7-93; and P-693 on 5-7-94 for disposal. In 2-92, 13 Black Sea area units (PSKR-635, -636, -637, -639, -642, -650, -702, -705, -709, -720, -722, and one other) were transferred on loan to Ukrainian control; three more (probably PSKR-629, -630, and -643) were offered but not accepted and were stricken on 5-7-94 along with several others. Black Sea unit PSKR-651 was stricken in 1998 at Novorossiysk. Baltic-region units PSKR-667 and -699 were awaiting scrapping as of late 1998. PSKR-638 and -692 were transferred to Georgia late in 1999. Stricken since 1999 have been PSKR-694, -704, and -725.

AIR-CUSHION PATROL BOATS [WPBA]

♦ 4 Chilim class (Project 20910)
Bldr: Yaroslavskiy Sudostroitelniy Zavod (In serv. 2000–2001)

. . . PSKR-500 CHILIM (In serv. 20-9-00)	. . . PSKR-502
. . . PSKR-501	. . . PSKR-504

Chilim-class patrol hovercraft FPS RF, via M. Schiele, 2001

D: 8.6 tons (9.4 fl) **S:** 37.8–43.2 kts (light)
Dim: 12.0 × 5.6 (5.9 over skirts) × . . .
A: 1 7.62-mm PKMB mg (600 rounds); 1 RPG-7 grenade launcher; 1 . . . -mm OKM mg; 7 AK-47 rifles; . . . /Igla-M shoulder-launched SAMs
Electronics: Radar: 1 . . . nav.
M: 2 Deutz BF8M513 diesels; 2 lift fans and 2 airscrew propellers; 506 bhp (430 sust.)
Electric: 9 kw tot. (2 × 3-kw shaft generators, 1 × 3-kw diesel set)
Range: 162/38 (calm water; 350/38 with ferry fuel load)
Fuel: 425 kg normal **Crew:** 2 tot. + 6 troops

Remarks: Ordered in fall 1997 for delivery by mid-1998 but delayed by funding problems; first unit was laid down 24-2-98 and ran trials on the Volga 25-1-00. Designed by Almaz Central Marine Construction Bureau under W. A. Abramovskiy. Have GPS receivers, a radar, an MK-69-M2 magnetic compass, two IFF transponders, and an infrared detector. Can maintain 27–32 kts in a State 3 sea. Originally were to have been engined with Deutz BF6M1013 engines of 215 bhp each. Payload is 800 kg maximum.

PATROL BOATS [WPB]

♦ 1 (+ 8) Mangust class (Project 12150)
Bldr: Vympel Joint Stock Co., Rybinsk (In serv. 20-8-01 to . . .)

601 . . .

Mangust-class patrol boat 601 Boris Lemachko, 6-05

D: 27.2 tons (fl) **S:** 53 kts **Dim:** 19.45 × 4.40 × 1.20 (max.; 1.13 hull)
A: 2 single 14.5-mm mg; 1 Igla-M shoulder-launched SAM launch position; 2 single AGS-17 grenade launchers; 1 DP-64 antiswimmer grenade launcher
Electronics: Radar: 1 . . . nav.
M: 2 Zvezda M-470K diesels; 2 props; 3,000 bhp
Range: 230/35–40 **Endurance:** 48 hours **Crew:** 6 tot.

Remarks: Design was first announced in the early 1990s; the prototype, TS-300, was completed in 1998 for the customs service. The first unit completed for the Federal Border Guard was assigned to the Caspian Sea region. A second unit was launched during 8-01, and the builder has the capacity to build five per year. Design name *Mangust* means "Mongoose." GRP construction. Has a SATCOM terminal. Nine units are planned.

Note: Also in service are two 19-m, 30-ton Garpun-class (A-77) patrol boats built by Vyborg SY during 2003–4 and a 17-m, 26-ton Type A-125 patrol boat named *Valentin Chuikin*, delivered during 2004 by Almaz.

♦ 3 (+ . . .) Teryer class (Project 14170)
Bldr: Zelenodol'sk Zavod

TERYER-1 (In serv. 16-9-00) TERYER-2 TERYER-3

D: 8.3 tons **S:** 32 kts **Dim:** 11.52 × 3.14 × 0.56
A: Small arms **Electronics:** Radar: 1 . . . nav.
M: 2 . . . diesels; 2 waterjets; 464 bhp
Range: 120/30 **Crew:** 6 tot.

Remarks: *Teryer* means "Terrier." Prototype ran trials in 1998 but was not accepted by the border guard until 9-00. Zelenodol'sk Marine Design Bureau is developing a more powerful version with two 300-bhp diesels and a range of 480 n.m.

♦ 11 Sobol' class (Project 12200)
Bldr: first 6: Sosnovka Zavod, Rybinsk (In serv. 1999–2001); others: Sudostroitel'noye Obyedineniye "Almaz," Dekabristov SY, St. Petersburg (In serv. 2003–4)

BSK-1 through BSK-11

D: 57 tons (fl) **S:** 47 kts **Dim:** 27.96 × 4.40 × 1.34 amidships
A: 1 30-mm 54-cal. AK-306 gatling AA; 4 Igla-M SAMs; 1 14.5-mm 93-cal. mg; 1 30-mm AGS-17 Plamya grenade launcher
Electronics: Radar: 1 . . . nav.
M: 2 Deutz TBD616 V16 diesels; 2 Arneson ASD 14 outdrive props; 3,650 bhp (3,350 bhp sust.)
Electric: 60 kw tot. (2 × 30-kw Deutz sets)
Range: 500/40 **Fuel:** 6.8 tons **Crew:** 6 tot.

Remarks: A seventh unit was ordered from Almaz and laid down 24-1-03. Aluminum alloy construction with single-step hull bottom. Have an ST60 integrated navigational system and VNTsU-UV3450 E/O surveillance and targeting sensor. The AK-306 mounting has four launch tubes for Igla-M IR-homing SAMs mounted on its sides; 500 rounds of 30-mm ammunition are carried.

♦ 3 Mustang-2 class (Project 18623)
Bldr: Yaroslavskiy SB, Yaroslavl (In serv. 2000)

817 BSK-19 . . . . . .

Mustang-2 class patrol boat BSK-19 Ralph Edwards, 6-03

D: 35.5 tons (fl) **S:** 40 kts **Dim:** 20.0 × 4.5 × 1.1
A:1 14.5-mm 93-cal. AA; 1 30-mm AGS-17 Plamya grenade launcher
Electronics: Radar: 1 . . . nav.
M: 2 Zvezda M-470 diesels; 2 KaMeWa FF-550 waterjets; 2,950 bhp
Range: 250/30 **Crew:** 6 tot.

Remarks: Originally intended for police duties and ordered by the Ministry of Fisheries, whose fisheries patrol duties were absorbed by the Federal Border Guard in 8-98. Aluminum alloy hull. Made 48 kts on trials. Can operate in State 5 sea. Designed by Redan Bureau, St. Petersburg.

♦ 2 Mustang class (Project 18627)
Bldr: Yaroslavskiy SB, Yaroslavl

PMK-1 (In serv. 1999) PMK-2 (In serv. 2000)

D: 18 tons (21.2 fl) **S:** 40 kts **Dim:** 15.80 × 3.80 × 0.70
A: 1 14.5-mm 93-cal. AA; 2 shoulder-launched Igla-M SAMs; 1 30-mm AGS-17 Plamya grenade launcher
Electronics: Radar: 1 . . . nav.
M: 1 Zvezda M-470 diesel; 1 KaMeWa FF-550 waterjet; 1,500 bhp
Range: 500/37 **Crew:** 1–2 tot.

Remarks: Originally intended for police duties and ordered by the Ministry of Fisheries, whose fisheries patrol duties were absorbed by the Federal Border Guard in 8-98. First unit launched 7-7-97. Aluminum alloy hull. Made 48 kts on trials. Can operate in State 5 seas. Designed by Redan Bureau, St. Petersburg.

♦ 1 Mustang-99 class (Project 18629)
Bldr: Yaroslavskiy SB, Yaroslavl (In serv. 12-99)

PMK-3

D: 30.8 tons (fl) **S:** 50 kts **Dim:** 19.60 × 3.90 × 0.90
A: 1 14.5-mm 93-cal. AA **Electronics:** Radar: 1 . . . nav.
M: 2 . . . diesels; 2 KaMeWa waterjets; 3,200 bhp
Range: 350/45 **Crew:** 4 tot.

♦ 3 (+ 9) Ogonek-class (Project 12130)
Bldr: Khabarovskiy Sudostroytel'niy Zavod, Khabarovsk (In serv. 4-12-98 to . . .)

. . . STRELETS . . . . . .

D: 91 tons (98 fl) **S:** 25.2 kts **Dim:** 33.40 × 4.20 × 0.81
A: 1 30-mm 65-cal. AK-306 gatling AA; 1 4-round Fasta-4M (SA-N-8) SAM syst. (. . . Igla-M missiles); 1 14.5-mm AA
Electronics: Radar: . . .
M: 2 . . . diesels; 2 props; 2,200 bhp
Range: 270/20 **Crew:** 2 officers, 1 warrant officer, 14 enlisted

Remarks: Intended to patrol the Amur and Ussuri River borders with China. Two or three more of the class were to be built after 2000, and up to 12 may ultimately be constructed. The enclosed 14.5-mm mg mount is mounted aft and the 30-mm gatling gun forward. The third unit was delivered during 2004.

♦ 5 (+ . . .) Yastreb class (Project 1226.0)
Bldr: Yaroslavskiy Shipbuilding Plant OJSC, Yaroslavl

	Laid down	L	In serv.
RUS'	3-1-97	22-5-97	19-9-97
. . .	3-97	. . .	4-98
. . .	3-7-97	. . .	10-98
. . .	29-10-97	. . .	11-98
. . .	. . .	. . .	1998

Yastreb-class Rus' Yaroslavskiy SB, 9-97

D: 9.75 tons (fl) **S:** 40 kts
Dim: 13.50 (12.97 pp) × 3.42 (3.20 wl) × 0.85 (0.66 hull)
A: 1 7.62-mm mg **Electronics:** Radar: 1 . . . nav.
M: 2 diesels; 2 KaMeWa waterjets; 880 bhp
Range: 200/35 **Endurance:** 1 day **Crew:** 2 tot. + 6 troops

Remarks: GRP construction. First craft may have been built on speculation. The design, by Almaz Central Design Bureau, is also offered for export.

♦ 3 (+ . . .) Boyets class (Project 13987)
Bldr: Redan Joint Stock Co., St. Petersburg (In serv. 7-96 to . . .)

S-1 S-2 S-3

D: 5.9 tons (6.6 fl) **S:** 40 kts **Dim:** 10.20 × 3.10 × 0.51
A: Small arms **Electronics:** Radar: 1 . . . nav.
M: 2 Volvo Penta TAMD 63L diesels; 2 KaMeWa waterjets; 630 bhp
Range: 250/40 **Crew:** 2 tot. + 8 passengers

Remarks: S-1 is used as part of the security service for the Russian president. The craft are intended for riverine, lake, and coastal service. Can mount a 12.7-mm mg. GRP construction.

♦ 17 Kulik class (Project 1415PV)
Bldr: Sosnovka Zavod, Rybinsk; Yaroslavl Zavod; and others (In serv. 1976–90s)

PSKA-200 through PSKA-250 series

BORDER GUARD PATROL BOATS [WPB] *(continued)*

Kulik-class BGK-1631—at Kronshtadt Boris Lemachko, 7-00

D: 42 tons (54 fl) **S:** 10.8 kts **Dim:** 21.20 × 3.93 × 1.40
A: Small arms **Electronics:** Radar: 1 Lotsiya nav. (not always fitted)
M: 1 Type 3D-12A or 3D-12L diesel; 1 prop; 300 bhp
Electric: 12 kw tot. (DGR 1A-16/1500 generator)
Range: 200/11 **Endurance:** 5 days **Crew:** 4 tot.

Remarks: Assigned as harbor patrol and utility craft for the Federal Border Guard; some 95 others serve as naval service craft, where they are known as the Tanya (NATO Flamingo) class. Designed by the Redan Central Design Bureau. Are rail transportable. The craft do not wear their PSKA numbers; some have pennant numbers in the BGK series, while others wear only a number, without the BGK prefix.

♦ 23 Zhuk (Gryf) class (Project 1400 or 1400M)
Bldr: More Zavod, Feodosiya, Ukraine (In serv. 1971–86)

637 PSKA-545	648 PSKA-51	661 PSKA-576	671 PSKA-530
639 PSKA-513	652 PSKA-500	662 PSKA-577	679 PSKA-532
640 PSKA-516	657 PSKA-510	663 PSKA-128	. . . PSKA-52
641 PSKA-553	658 PSKA-520	664 PSKA-139	. . . PSKA-548
642 PSKA-554	659 PSKA-525	665 PSKA-109	. . . PSKA-560
643 PSKA-563	660 PSKA-559	666 PSKA-111	

D: 35.9 tons (39.7 fl) **S:** 30 kts
Dim: 23.80 (21.70 wl) × 5.00 (3.80 wl) × 1.00 (hull; 1.90 max.)
A: 1 twin 14.5-mm 93-cal. 2M-7 AA *or* 1 twin 12.7-mm 60-cal. Utës-Ma mg
Electronics: Radar: 1 Lotsiya nav.
M: Project 1400: 2 M-50F-4 diesels; 2 props; 2,400 bhp—Project 1400M: 2 M-401 diesels; 2 props; 2,200 bhp
Electric: 48 kw total (2 × 21-kw, 1 × 6-kw diesel sets)
Range: 700/28; 1,100/15 **Endurance:** 5 days **Crew:** 1 officer, 6 enlisted

Zhuk-class PSKA-545 (637) —with Russian Navy Moma-class survey ships in the background French Navy, 1997

Remarks: Ten operated by the Soviet GRU military intelligence service had hull numbers and, in several cases, names, including *Sokol* (KSV-9), KSB-12, *Chayka* (KSV-485), *Berkut* (KSV-1135), *Gurzuf* (KSV-1499), and KSV-1754. Twenty-three Black Sea–area Federal Border Guard units (PKSA-53, -54, -125, -141, -501 through -509, -511, -512, -517, -519, -523, -524, -526, and -534) were stricken 5-7-94 and transferred to the Ukraine Border Guard, and PSKA-527 was transferred to the Ukraine Navy. One Caspian area unit was to have transferred to Kazakhstan in 1996. One semiofficial source states that only 30 were built for the Federal Border Guard. More than 110 others have been exported. At least ten others were built as naval (vice border guard) officers' yachts.
Hull systems: Aluminum alloy hull. Capable of operating in up to Sea State 4 or 5. Range also reported as 700 n.m. at 28 kts and 1,100 n.m. at 15 kts.
Combat systems: Most export units were armed with two 12.7-mm 60-cal. Utës-M, side-by-side turreted gunmounts; earlier nonexport units have one (or occasionally two) over-and-under 14.5-mm 93-cal. 2M-7 gunmounts, while many retained for border guard service now have the twin 12.7-mm Utës-M machinegun mounting forward and a searchlight aft.

♦ 30 Saygak-class (Project 14081 and 14081M)
Bldr: Kama Zavod, Perm; . . ., Moscow (In serv. 1986–99)

PSKA-400 through PSKA-429

Saygak-class PSKA-419 (652)—in camouflage paint scheme Boris Lemachko, 5-98

D: 11.5 tons (13 fl) **S:** 38 kts (35 sust.) **Dim:** 14.05 × 3.50 × 0.65
A: Small arms **Electronics:** Radar: 1 . . . nav.
M: 1 Zvezda M-401B (12CHSN18/20) diesel; 1 waterjet; 1,000 bhp
Electric: 8 kw (1 Type DGK8/1500 diesel driving; 27 V)
Range: 135/35 **Fuel:** 1.15 tons **Crew:** 2 tot. + 4–8 police personnel

Remarks: Offered for foreign sale in 1993 and typical of current Russian small personnel launch design. Rail transportable, the craft are intended for riverine and lake use and in coastal waters in seas up to Sea State 3. Aluminum alloy construction. Sisters TS-501 through TS-505 are used by the customs service. One additional unit was built as a prototype radio-controlled target (Project 14082), and two have been built in Kazakhstan. As many as fifteen may be in reserve.

♦ 30 Aist-class (Project 1398) launches
Bldr: Svetenskiy Zavod, Kokue (In serv. 1975–86)

PMK-18 PMK-21 PMK-50 PMK-51 and others

D: 3.55 tons (5.8 fl) **S:** 20 kts **Dim:** 9.50 × 2.60 × 0.50
A: Small arms **Electronics:** Radar: none
M: 1 3D-20 diesel; 1 waterjet; 235 bhp **Fuel:** 0.37 tons **Crew:** . . . tot.

Remarks: Employed on the Amur-Ussuri River network in the Russian Far East. Rail transportable. One former Maritime Border Service unit was transferred to Latvia in 1995, four are operated by the Georgian Navy, and others are used by the customs service. Designed by Redan Central Design Bureau, St. Petersburg, in 1968.

♦ 15 PO-2 (Yaroslavets) class (Project P-376)
Bldrs: Yaroslavl Zavod (In serv. 1958–90); Sosnovskiy Sudostroitel'nyy Zavod (In serv. 1995– . . .)

PSKA-580	PSKA-586	PSKA-591	PSKA-594	PSKA-597
PSKA-581	PSKA-587	PSKA-592	PSKA-595	PSKA-598
PSKA-582	PSKA-590	PSKA-593	PSKA-596	PSKA-599

D: 32.2 tons (38.2 fl) **S:** 9–10 kts **Dim:** 21.00 × 3.90 × 1.40 (max.; 1.26 mean)
A: 1 twin 12.7-mm 79-cal. mg
Electronics: Radar: 1 Mius (Spin Trough) nav. or none
M: 1 Type 3D-6S1 diesel; 1 prop; 150 bhp
Electric: 10 kw tot. (1 × 10 kw, DGPN-8/1500 diesel driving)
Range: 1,600/8 **Fuel:** 1.5 tons **Endurance:** 5 days
Crew: 2 warrant officers (*michman*), 6 enlisted

Remarks: More than 600 have been built to the same general design for military and civilian use. Are rail transportable and all-steel construction. Can be operated safely in Force 8 winds and 2-m seas and can break light ice. The majority of the Federal Border Guard units are in the Pacific region, most on the Amur-Ussuri River network.

RIVER MONITORS [WPM]

♦ 2 Yaz' (Slepen') class (Project 1208)
Bldr: Khabarovsk Zavod

	Laid down	L	In serv.
066 Blagoveshchensk (ex-*60 Let VChK*)	14-10-76	15-10-77	28-6-79
106 Shkval (ex-MAK-11)	27-2-79	28-10-80	30-5-81

Yaz'-class Blagoveshchensk (066) H&L Van Ginderen, 5-95

D: 390 tons light; 423 tons std. (447 fl) **S:** 24.3 kts (23 sust.)
Dim: 55.20 (53.30 wl) × 9.14 (8.48 wl) × 1.44
A: 2 single 100-mm D-10T2S low-angle (in T-55 tank turrets); 2 single 30-mm 54-cal. AK-630M gatling AA; 2 twin 12.7-mm 60-cal. Utës-M mg; 2 single 7.62-mm mg (in 100-mm turrets); 1 twin 140-mm ZIF-121M Sneg artillery RL; 2 30-mm BP-30 Plamya grenade launchers; shoulder-launched point-defense SAMs

BORDER GUARD RIVER MONITORS [WPM] *(continued)*

Electronics: Radar: 1 Mius (Spin Trough) or Kivach nav.; 1 MR-123 Vympel (Bass Tilt) f.c.
M: 3 M-512B diesels; 3 props; 11,400 bhp
Range: 550/20; 1,000/10 **Endurance:** 10 days **Crew:** 4 officers, 28 enlisted

Remarks: Survivors of 11 built. Low-freeboard monitors, designed at TsKB-5 under M. V. Koshkin. Some were reportedly assembled at Vladivostok. Both are assigned to the Amur-Ussuri River network.
Hull systems: Have cutaway bows to improve navigation in light ice. The three propellers and three rudders are mounted in a "tunnel" to reduce the draft. Are extensively armored, with 35-mm armor on the superstructure, pilothouse, and weapons-control stations; 8- to 20-mm side plating; 100- to 200-mm on the citadel; and 35-mm decks.
Combat systems: The ZIF-121M rocket launcher amidships is essentially the same autoloading device employed on major seagoing combatants as a decoy rocket launcher; in these ships, it reportedly launches artillery rockets, although it may also be used for illumination rockets. The 7.62-mm machineguns are coaxially mounted with the 100-mm cannon. Do not have mine rails.
Disposals: Since the mid-1990s, *Groza* (ex-MAK-4), *Smerch* (ex-MAK-6), *Tayfun* (ex-MAK-7), *Shtorm* (ex-MAK-7), *Vikhr'* (ex-*Khabarovsk*, ex-MAK-2), *V'yuga* (ex-MAK-3), and *Uragan* (ex-MAK-8) have been placed in disposal reserve. MAK-1 was discarded in 1992.

♦ 4 Vosh (Moskit) class (Project 1248.1)
Bldr: Svetenskiy Zavod, Kokue (In serv. 1988–91)

056 Storm | 057 Groza | 137 Khabarovsk | 138 Vasiliy Poyarkov

Vosh-class unit—possibly named *Vasiliy Poyarkov* Boris Lemachko, 6-01

D: 150 tons light; 213 tons std. (223–230 fl) **S:** 17.5 kts
Dim: 38.90 (37.50 wl) × 6.1 × 1.27
A: 1 100-mm D-10T2S low-angle (in a T-55 tank turret); 1 30-mm 54-cal. AK-630M gatling AA; 1 twin 12.7-mm 60-cal. Utës-M mg; 1 twin 140-mm ZIF-21M Sneg artillery RL; 1 30-mm BP-30 Plamya grenade launcher
Electronics: Radar: 1 Mius (Spin Trough) nav.
M: 3 M-401B diesels; 3 props; 3,300 bhp
Range: 500/10 **Endurance:** 7 days **Crew:** 3 officers, 31 enlisted

Remarks: Employed on the Amur and Ussuri River borders with China. Also known as the PSKR-300 class. The 100-mm gun is mounted coaxially with the 7.62-mm machinegun in an armored turret salvaged from a T-55 tank. Do not have mine rails. Have 100- to 200-mm armor over vital areas.

♦ 8 Piyavka class (Project 1249)
Bldr: Khabarovsk Zavod (In serv. 1979–84)

013 PSKR-55	093 Kazak Ussuriyskiy	123 PSKR-58
058 PSKR-57 (ex-PSKR-56)	146 PSKR-54	189 PSKR-59
065 PSKR-53	117 PSKR-52	

Piyavka-class PSKR-58 (123) Boris Lemachko, 2002

D: 150 tons light; 216 tons std. (229 fl) **S:** 17.5 kts
Dim: 41.90 (40.00 wl) × 6.1 × 1.23
A: 1 30-mm 54-cal. AK-630M gatling AA; 1 twin 12.7-mm 60-cal. Utës-M mg; 1 30-mm BP-30 Plamya grenade launcher
Electronics: Radar: 1 Mius (Spin Trough) nav.
M: 3 M-401B diesels; 3 props; 3,300 bhp **Range:** 500/10 **Endurance:** 7 days
Crew: 2 officers, 26 enlisted + 12 troops

Remarks: Like the Vosh class, are intended for duty on the Amur-Ussuri River system to police the border with China, but are configured to carry a dozen constabulary personnel in addition to the crew and can also carry up to 12 tons of supplies. Are not armored. 093 was named *Kazak Ussuriyskiy* in 1996.

♦ 16 Shmel'-class (Project 1204)
Bldr: Kamysh Burun Zavod, Kerch' (98 units), and 61 Kommunara Zavod, Nikolayev, Ukraine (In serv. 1967–74)

019 PSKR-341	080 PSKR-347	094 PSKR-365	149 PSKR-374
033 PSKR-358	085 PSKR-355	107 PSKR-375	179 PSKR-366
034 PSKR-359	089 PSKR-357	113 PSKR-346	181 PSKR-342
049 PSKR-377	091 PSKR-350	147 PSKR-376	187 PSKR-367

Shmel'-class PSKR-374 (145)—at Blagoveshensk, with Border Guard PO-2 patrol launch in the background Boris Lemachko, 1998

D: 77.4 tons (fl) **S:** 24 kts **Dim:** 27.70 × 4.32 × 0.90 (2.00 molded depth)
A: 1 76.2-mm, 48-cal. D-56TM (in a PT-76 tank turret); 1 twin 25-mm 80-cal. 2M-3M AA *or* 1 twin 14.5-mm 93-cal. 2M-7 AA; 1 7.62-mm mg (in tank turret); 2 mine rails (up to 4 mines each)
Electronics: Radar: 1 Donets-2 nav.—Sonar: NEL-7 echo sounder
M: 2 M-50F-4 diesels; 2 props; 2,400 bhp
Electric: 50 kw tot. (2 × 25-kw diesel sets)
Range: 240/20; 600/10 **Fuel:** 4.75 tons **Endurance:** 7 days
Crew: 1 officer, 2 warrant officers, 11 enlisted

Remarks: Survivors of 53 built for the KGB Border Guard; 16 of the 65 built for the Soviet Navy are also still in service. Designed by TsKB-5 (the current Firma Almaz) design bureau under L. V. Ozimov. Units built at Nikolayev were prefabricated and later assembled at Khabarovsk. Three former Federal Border Guard units based on Lake Peipus in western Russia (including PSKR-389) are now in Belorussian hands, while four others may be in Ukraine service. Danube Flotilla units AKA-506, -564, -583, and -602 were stricken 31-7-96 and scrapped. All remaining Federal Border Guard units operate on the Amur-Ussuri River border between China and Russia.
Hull systems: The screws are mounted in tunnels to reduce draft. Armor includes 10-mm over the pilothouse and gun barbettes, 8-mm over the hull and internal bulkheads, and 5-mm over the deck and pilothouse. Have a Gradus-2 gyrocompass and NEL-7 echo sounder.
Combat systems: Some have also carried up to four 30-mm Plamya grenade launchers and four pintle-mounted 7.62-mm machineguns. One 7.62-mm machinegun is mounted coaxially with the 76-mm gun (for which 40 rounds are carried on-mount). Mine loads vary from four UDM-500 or 2 UDM-1000 to six KPM or eight YaM mines.

AMPHIBIOUS WARFARE CRAFT

Disposal note: The three Aist (Dzheryan)-class air-cushion landing craft (Project 1232.1), transferred to the Border Guard from the Black Sea Fleet in 1995–96, have been stricken due to age and maintenance problems.

♦ 1 Vydra class (Project 106KM) utility landing craft [WLCU]
Bldr: . . . (In serv. 1967–69)

610 MDK-174

D: 308 tons light (550 fl) **S:** 10.5 kts
Dim: 54.50 (50.00 pp) × 7.70 (7.50 wl) × 2.25 (mean hull)
Electronics: Radar: 1 Don-2 nav.
M: 2 Type 3D-12 diesels; 2 Kort-nozzle props; 600 bhp
Range: 1,400/10 (loaded) **Endurance:** 8 days **Crew:** 1 officer, 11 enlisted

Remarks: Assigned to the Amur-Ussuri River network as supply craft. The cargo deck measures 30.0 × 4.5 m and can accommodate up to 176 tons of vehicles or cargo (6 ZIL-131 or 10 GAZ-66 trucks). Bulgaria received 21 sisters and Egypt 10.

♦ 7 Tsaplya (Murena)-class (Project 1206.1) air-cushion vehicle landing craft [WLCMA]
Bldr: Yuzhnaya Tochka SY, Feodosiya; Ussuri SY, Khabarovsk

	In serv.		In serv.
659 DK-143	1992	680 DK-285	1988
665 DK-259	9-10-87	688 DK-458	2-4-87
668 DK-453	1985	699 DK-447	1989
670 DK-323	1990		

D: 80 tons light; 104 tons std. (135 normal; 149 fl)
S: 55 kts (empty; 50 with 24-ton load)
Dim: 31.60 (over skirt) × 12.90 (14.80 over skirt) × 1.6 (at rest)
A: 2 single 30-mm 54-cal. AK-306 gatling AA; 1 shoulder-launched SAM position (. . . Igla-M missiles); 1 twin 12.7-mm Utës-M mg; 2 40-mm BP-30 Plamya grenade launchers (1,800 grenades); 10–24 mines in lieu of vehicles

BORDER GUARD AMPHIBIOUS WARFARE CRAFT *(continued)*

Tsaplya-class DK-323 (670) H&L Van Ginderen, 5-95

Electronics: Radar: 1 SRN-207 Ekran (Curl Stone-B) nav.
M: 2 PR-77 gas turbines; 2 3.5-m-dia. airscrew props; 8,000 shp—2 2.2-m-dia. axial lift fans (powered by main engines)
Range: 500/50; with 24-ton payload: 200/55 **Endurance:** 1–3 days
Crew: 3 officers, 8 enlisted + 80–130 troops

Remarks: Rated as DKA (*Desantny Kater,* Landing Craft), 3rd class. Design is essentially that of the Lebed (Project 1206), but lengthened; intended for riverine service. Are operated on the Amur-Ussuri River system in the Far East. The design has been offered for foreign sale without artillery rockets as Project 1206.1E. A mine warfare variant, Pelikan (Project 1206T), was also built, but both units have been discarded. Although one source reported that 10 were built, the total may only have been the seven still in service. Sister DK-142 was transferred to South Korea during late 2002 in part payment for Russian loan debts.
Hull systems: Cargo: 24 tons of cargo under normal conditions, but up to 40–42 tons with a 10-kt speed reduction: one amphibious tank plus 80 troops, or 25 tons of stores and 160 soldiers, or 225 soldiers. Other cargo: 1 T-72M or T-80 tank or two PT-76 amphibious tanks or three BTR-70 armored personnel carriers. The bow ramp is 5.5 m long by 5.0 m wide. The cargo deck has about 130 m^2 of useful space. Light alloy hull with detachable, rubberized, flexible cloth skirts that are cylindrical in section. Can maintain 50 kts in Sea State 2 or 30 kts in Sea State 3. The gas turbine plant is also reported as two MT-70R installations; the engines drive an integrated lift/propulsion plant with one axial lift fan and one airscrew propeller on either side. Can cross 1-m obstacles and ditches up to 4–5 m wide.
Combat systems: The gatling guns are controlled by SP-521 Rakurs (Kolonka-2) ringsight directors on platforms abaft the pilothouse. The grenade launchers flank the bow ramp. May also carry "AGS-17" rockets. Carry 1,000 rounds of 30-mm and 1,000 rounds of 12.7-mm ammunition.

♦ 1 Lebed (Kal'mar)-class (Project 1206) air-cushion landing craft [WLCMA]
Bldr: Sudostoitel'noye Obyedineniye "Almaz," Dekabristov SY, St. Petersburg, or Yuzhnaya Tochka Zavod, Feodosiya, Ukraine (In serv. 1984)

543 D-454

D: 70 tons (87 fl) **S:** 70 kts max. **Dim:** 24.8 × 10.8 × 1.3 (at rest)
A: 1 12.7-mm Ütes-M mg **Electronics:** Radar: 1 . . . nav.
M: 2 AL-20K gas turbines; 2 shrouded airscrew props; 20,000 shp (16,000 sust.)
Range: 100/60 **Fuel:** 12.7 tons **Crew:** 2 officers, 4 enlisted + 120 troops

Remarks: The entire class had been reported retired by the end of 1997, but it was reported in 2000 that four remained in the Northern Fleet, of which D-454 was photographed on 21-7-00 loading for transit via the canal and river system from the Northern Fleet for operations with the Federal Border Guard in the Caspian. Used for patrolling oilfields and shallow waters. Can carry one or two armored personnel carriers or 120 troops or about 35 tons of cargo. Has a bow ramp only.

AUXILIARIES

♦ 8 Neon Antonov–class (Project 1595) cargo ships [WAK]
Bldr: Nikolayevsk-na-Amur Zavod (In serv. 1978–87)

090 Nikolay Sipyagin
105 Ivan Yevteyev
115 Ivan Lednev
119 Nikolay Starshinov
143 Sergey Sudyeskiy
154 Vasiliy Sutsov
176 Vyacheslav Denisov
184 Mikhail Konovalov

Vyacheslav Denisov (176)—at Vladivostok Boris Lemachko, 2000

D: 2,420 tons light (4,040 fl) **S:** 18 kts **Dim:** 96.30 (87.20 pp) × 14.50 × 5.10
A: 1 twin 30-mm 65-cal. AK-230 AA; 2 twin 12.7-mm 60-cal. Utës-M mg
Electronics: Radar: 2 Vaygach-U (Palm Frond) or 1 Volga (Don-Kay) and 1 Mius (Spin Trough) or Don-2 nav.
M: 2 Type 67B (12DRPN 23/2 × 30) diesels; 1 prop; 7,500 bhp
Range: 5,000/18; 8,750/14
Endurance: 25 days **Crew:** 45 tot. + 18 passengers

Mikhail Konovalov (184) Boris Lemachko, 2002

Remarks: Specialized supply ships for remote garrisons of the Federal Border Guard in the Pacific area. Built in the Far East. Some may be nonoperational. Sisters *Dvina* and *Irbit* are assigned to the Russian Navy Pacific Fleet. The initial ship of the class was named *Neon Antonov;* either the ship has been stricken or one of the units listed above is that ship renamed.
Hull systems: Carry one Project 1785 logistics landing craft aft to starboard (36 tons light/78.2 tons fl; 21.90 × 5.81 × 1.00 m; one 470-bhp diesel for 9.8 kts) and a workboat to port, aft, with a 50-ton boat derrick to handle them. The hull has a bulbous forefoot. There are two cargo holds forward, tended by only two 5-ton derricks. The pilothouse is equipped with MPK-455M navigational periscopes port and starboard. Cargo capacity: 804 tons.
Combat systems: The 30-mm gunmount is controlled by a Rakurs-series (Kolonka-1) remote ringsight director mounted in an enclosed shelter, which must limit its effectiveness. The machineguns are in enclosed mounts like those mounted on Zhuk-class patrol craft.

♦ 1 Baskunchak-class (Project 1545) oiler [WAO]
Bldr: Zaliv Zavod, Kerch' (In serv. 1966–68)

102 Sovetskiy Pogranichnik

Sovetskiy Pogranichnik (102)—at Vladivostok Boris Lemachko, 4-01

D: 1,260 tons light (2,940 fl) **S:** 13.2 kts **Dim:** 83.60 (74.00 pp) × 12.00 × 3.80
Electronics: Radar: 1 Don-2 nav.
M: 1 Type 8DR 43/61W diesel; 1 prop; 2,220 bhp (2,000 sust.)
Electric: 325 kw tot. **Range:** 5,000/12 **Fuel:** 124 tons **Crew:** 30 tot.

Remarks: 1,768 grt/1,660 dwt. The name means "Soviet Border Guardsman" and has not yet been changed. Operates in the Pacific, primarily employed in transporting fuels to outlying Federal Border Guard outposts. Sister *Ivan Golubets* had been discarded by 2001 and replaced with the new, smaller *Ishim* (see under [WYO]). One sister, *Usedom,* was formerly in the East German Navy; 16 others served in the Soviet merchant marine. Has an ice-reinforced hull. Cargo: 1,490 tons (9,993 bbl.) of up to four different types.

♦ 2 Okhtenskiy (Goliat)-class (Project 733) patrol tugs [WATA]
Bldr: Petrozavod SY, St. Petersburg (In serv. 1958–66)

PB-187 PB-196

Border Guard Okhtenskiy-class seagoing tug pennant 033—with a cargo of automobiles and vans on deck aft JMSDF, 12-95

BORDER GUARD AUXILIARIES *(continued)*

D: 717 tons (890 fl) **S:** 13.3 kts **Dim:** 47.30 (43.0 pp) × 10.30 × 4.14
A: Small arms
Electronics: Radar: 1 or 2 Don-2 or Mius (Spin Trough) nav.
M: Diesel-electric: 2 Type D5D50 diesels; 1 prop; 1,500 shp **Electric:** 340 kw
Range: 6,000/13; 7,800/7 **Fuel:** 197 tons **Endurance:** 30 days
Crew: 31 tot. (civilian) + 40 passengers/rescuees

Remarks: Standard seagoing tug design, of which five were assigned to the KGB Maritime Border Guard in the Far East (including ex-MB-36 and ex-MB-163) and were at one time armed with a twin 57-mm ZIF-31B gunmount forward. Sister PSKR-3 (ex-MB- . . .) was stricken 5-7-94. Bollard pull: 27 tons initial/17 sustained. Have a 5-ton derrick. A number of naval sisters remain in service as tugs and as rescue tugs.

SERVICE CRAFT

♦ Up to 4 Muna-class (Project 1823) ammmunition lighters [WYE]
Bldr: Nakhodka SY (In serv. 1966–85)

036 PSKR-451 . . . PSKR-452 . . . PSKR-454 . . . PSKR-460

Muna-class PSKR-451 (036) Boris Lemachko, 5-98

D: 457 tons (688 fl) **S:** 11 kts **Dim:** 51.50 × 8.40 × 2.70
Electronics: Radar: 1 Mius (Spin Trough) nav.
M: 1 Type 6DR 30/50 diesel; 1 prop; 600 bhp
Range: 1,700/10 **Endurance:** 15 days **Crew:** 15 tot. + 7 passengers

Remarks: Munitions lighters, adapted as local cargo transports. PSKR-451 is based at Vladivostok, and the others, if still in service, probably also operate in the Far East region.
Hull systems: Have a single 3.2-ton-capacity electric crane positioned between two small holds. Cargo capacity: 175 tons.

♦ 0 (+ 2) . . . -class (Project . . .) cargo lighters [WYF]
Bldr: Sudoverf, Rybinsk (In serv. . . .)

D: 114 tons (fl) **S:** 9 kts **Dim:** 24.00 × 5.20 × 1.52
Electronics: . . .
M: 2 . . . diesels; 2 azimuthal, Kort-nozzle props; 296 bhp

Remarks: Ordered 7-00 for local river ferry and coastal service. Have a 12.5 × 3.6-m cargo deck suitable for carrying two 25-ton trucks and have a bow ramp. Can be used to tow barges. The yard was previously known as Rybinsk Shipyard.

♦ 6 Kanin-class (Project 16900A) cargo lighters [WYF]
Bldr: Zvezdochka State-Run Machine Building Enterprise, Severodvinsk

	In serv.		In serv.
PSKR-490 Kanin	1994	PSKR-. . . Yurga	12-97
PSKR-491 Urengoy	1995	PSKR-. . . Ogra	1998
PSKR-. . . Khanty-Mansiysk	28-3-97	PSKR-. . . Arkhangel'sk	1999

Kanin (PSKR-490)—at Gelendzhik Boris Lemachko, 7-00

D: 748 tons (920 fl) **S:** 9.5 kts **Dim:** 45.45 × 8.80 × 2.50
Electronics: Radar: 1 . . . nav.
M: 2 . . . diesels; 1 prop; 800 bhp
Range: 2,200/8 **Endurance:** 10 days **Crew:** 22 tot.

Remarks: 396 dwt. Originally completed for commercial service but acquired for the Federal Border Guard after completion. *Khanty-Mansiysk* is assigned to the Black Sea, PSKR-490 and one other to the Barents Sea area. Bows are reinforced for Arctic navigation. Have two holds and a single electrohydraulic crane. Three sisters were under construction for merchant service in 1998. The shipyard is also known as the Zvezdochka Scientific Industrial Association. A seventh unit may have entered service in 2002.

♦ 1 Chaika-class (Project 1360) presidential yacht [WYFL]
Bldr: Sudostroitel'noye Obyedineniye "Almaz," Petrovskiy SY, St. Petersburg (In serv. 1980)

Kavkaz

D: 158 tons (220 fl) **S:** 32 kts **Dim:** 45.50 × 8.0 × 2.50 (mean hull)
M: 2 M-503A radial diesels: 2 props; 8,000 bhp
Range: 500/35 **Fuel:** 40 tons **Crew:** 32 tot.

Remarks: Built on the Osa (Project 205) missile-boat hull but with a two-level, streamlined superstructure. Operated in the Black Sea by the Federal Border Guard. White painted. A refit by the builder was completed 24-5-02. To be replaced in 2007. Sister *Krym* was transferred to Ukraine 1-5-95.

♦ 1 Project 14670 officers' yacht [WYFL]
Bldr: . . . (In serv. 1985–88)

Pogranichnik

Pogranichnik—at Kronshtadt, with memorial submarine D-2 in background Boris Lemachko, 2000

D: 38 tons (49 fl) **S:** 31 kts **Dim:** 24.0 × 5.2 × 1.9
A: none **Electronics:** Radar: 1 . . . nav.
M: 2 M-50F-series diesels; 2 props; 2,400 bhp
Range: 700/29; 1,100/15 **Endurance:** 5 days **Crew:** 12 tot.

Remarks: Some 13 sisters serve naval officers. The design is a variant of the Zhuk-class patrol boat.

♦ 1 Project 12210 fuel lighter [WYO]
Bldr: Zvenigov Zavod, . . . (In serv. 2001)

D: 2,350 tons (fl) **S:** 10 kts **Dim:** 72.30 × 12.00 × 4.30
M: 2 diesels; 2 props; 2,800 bhp **Range:** 1,500/10 **Crew:** 7 tot.

Remarks: Probably intended for riverine service in the Far East.

♦ 1 Project 15010 fuel lighter/supply ship [WYO]
Bldr: Nikolayevske-na-Amur Zavod (In serv. 2001)

Ishim

D: 960 tons light (2,450 fl) **S:** 14 kts **Dim:** 80.00 × 12.00 × 3.70
M: 1 diesels; 1 prop; 2,800 bhp **Crew:** 35 tot.

Remarks: Intended to support offshore and coastal bases. Cargo: 1,115 tons distillate fuel, 600 tons kerosene, 430 tons gasoline, 80 tons lube oil, 75 tons potable water, and 50 tons of provisions.

♦ 5 Bis-class (Project 1481) riverine fuel lighters [WYO]
Bldr: Sventenskiy Zavod, Kokue (In serv. 1974–76)

VNS-180150 VNS-182150 VNS- . . .
VNS-181150 VNS-183150

Three Bis-class fuel lighters—note the extremely shallow draft Boris Lemachko, 10-00

D: 600 tons (fl) **S:** 10 kts **Dim:** 57.8 × 9.5 × 1.2
M: 2 Type 3D-12 diesels; 2 props; 600 bhp
Endurance: 6 days **Crew:** 7 tot.

Remarks: Operate on the Amur and Ussuri Rivers. Have sufficient communications facilities to be used as command ships.

BORDER GUARD SERVICE CRAFT *(continued)*

♦ **Up to 27 Project 1496 small harbor tugs [WYTL]**
Bldr: Sovetskaya Govan' Zavod, Azove (In serv. 1966–80)

600 PSKA-272	620 PSKA-582	648 PSKA-585	663 PSKA-589
603 PSKA-584	621 PSKA-594	651 PSKA-588	664 PSKA-597
604 PSKA-583	624 PSKA-274	654 PSKA-278	671 PSKA-590
608 PSKA-599	626 PSKA-277	655 PSKA-275	673 PSKA-282
614 PSKA-595	633 PSKA-586	656 PSKA-279	681 PSKA-273
615 PSKA-581	636 PSKA-592	657 PSKA-276	697 PSKA-587
617 PSKA-580	642 PSKA-591	659 PSKA-281	

Project 1496 tug PSKA-588 (651) Boris Lemachko, 2002

D: 91.3 tons (108.5 fl) **S:** 10.5 kts **Dim:** 23.40 × 5.87 × 1.87
Electronics: Radar: 1 or 2 Lotsiya and/or Mius (Spin Trough) nav.
M: 1 Type 8 ChSN 18/22-1 diesel; 1 shrouded prop; 315 bhp
Electric: 18 kw tot.
Range: 1,450/10.5 **Fuel:** 8.3 tons **Endurance:** 6 days **Crew:** 8 tot.

Remarks: All serve in the Pacific region as tugs and local stores and personnel transports. Another 35 are in naval service (q.v.). Have a NEL-10 echo sounder. Carry 4.4 tons potable water.

CUSTOMS SERVICE

Note: Little information is available about the structure or composition of the Russian Federation Customs Service, but it has become apparent that it operates patrol craft independent of the Russian Navy and the Federal Border Guard. Known classes are listed below.

PATROL CRAFT [WPC]

♦ **2 (+ . . .) Merkuriya-class (Project 14232)**
Bldr: Yaroslavskiy SB, Yaroslavl

TS-100 Petr Matveyev (L: 10-96)
TS-101 Pavel Vereshchagin (In serv. 5-11-00)

Pavel Vereshchagin (TS-101) Ralph Edwards, 6-03

D: 90 tons (99.3 fl) **S:** 50 kts **Dim:** 35.40 × 8.30 × 2.00 (props)
A: 1 14.5-mm AA; 2 single 7.62-mm mg
Electronics: Radar: 1 . . . nav.
M: 2 M-504B-4 diesels; 2 props; 9,980 bhp (8,000 sust.)
Range: 600/30 **Endurance:** 5 days **Crew:** 16 tot.

Remarks: Designed by Alekseyev Central Hydrofoil Design Bureau, Nizhniy Novgorod, for the customs service, replacing the initial Ikar project. The design is also offered for export as a high-speed yacht, with MTU 16V396 TV94 diesels as an alternative propulsion plant. Uses an air cavity beneath the aluminum-magnesium alloy hull to enhance planing lift. Can operate in State 6 seas and at 30 kts in 1.5-m waves. Armament can also be a coaxial dual 14.5-mm and 7.62-mm machinegun mount, as in the prototype, or a 30-mm AK-306 lightweight gatling gunmount. The prototype was to be delivered to Vladivostok in 12-96 for use as a customs service patrol craft from Novorossiysk. A modified and more heavily armed sister named *Al'batros* (ex-*Sokzhoi*) was completed for the Federal Border Guard.

PATROL BOATS [WPB]

♦ **1 (+ . . .) Mangust class (Project 1215.0)**
Bldr: Yaroslavskiy SB, Yaroslavl (In serv. 1998– . . .)

TS-300

D: 26.1 (27.2 fl) **S:** 53 kts **Dim:** 19.50 (17.10 wl) × 4.60 (4.40 wl) × 1.15
A: 2 Igla shoulder-launched SAMs; 1 14.5-mm mg; 1 7.62-mm mg; 1 30-mm AGS-17 Plamya grenade launcher
Electronics: Radar: 1 . . . nav.
M: 2 M-470K diesels; 2 Arneson outdrive props; 1,500 bhp
Electric: 16 kw tot. (1 × 16-kw diesel set)
Range: 350/40; 430/37 **Fuel:** 3.5 tons **Endurance:** 2 days **Crew:** 6 tot.

Remarks: GRP construction. First craft may have been built on speculation, but has been assigned to the customs service. The design, by Almaz Central Design Bureau, is also offered for export. Constructed of aluminum-magnesium alloy. The propulsion drive system is made in the U.S.A. See entry for this class in the Federal Border Guard section for appearance.

♦ **5 Saygak class (Projects 1408.1 and 1408M)**
Bldr: Kama Shipyard, Perm (Permskiy Sudostroitel'nyy Zavod) (In serv. 1986– . . .)

TS-501 TS-502 TS-503 TS-504 TS-505

D: 13 tons (fl) **S:** 38 kts (35 sust.) **Dim:** 14.05 × 3.50 × 0.65
A: Small arms **Electronics:** Radar: 1 . . . nav.
M: 1 M-401B (12CHSN18/20) diesel; 1 waterjet; 1,000 bhp
Electric: 8 kw (1 Type DGK8/1500 diesel driving; 27 V)
Range: 135/35 **Fuel:** 1.15 tons **Crew:** 2 tot. + 4–8 police personnel

Remarks: Offered for foreign sale in 1993 and typical of current Russian small personnel launch design. Rail transportable, the craft are intended for riverine and lake use and in coastal waters in seas up to Sea State 3. Aluminum alloy construction. TS-505 is assigned to Kaliningrad. The Moscow Shipyard (Moskovskiy Sudostroitel'nyy Zavod) is also to build the design, if demand warrants, and two are being built in Kazakhstan.

ST. KITTS AND NEVIS

Federation of Saint Kitts and Nevis

ST. CHRISTOPHER–NEVIS COAST GUARD

Personnel: 45 total

Base: Basseterre

PATROL CRAFT [WPC]

♦ **1 U.S. 110-ft. Commercial Cruiser design**
Bldr: Swiftships, Inc., Morgan City, La. (In serv. 7-85)

C 253 Stalwart

Stalwart (C 253) Mike Louagie, 1995

D: 99.8 tons (fl) **S:** 24 kts (21 cruise) **Dim:** 33.53 × 7.62 × 2.13
A: 2 single 12.7-mm M2 mg; 2 single 7.62-mm mg
Electronics: Radar: 1 Raytheon . . . nav.
M: 4 G.M. Detroit Diesel 12V71 TI diesels; 4 props; 2,400 bhp (1,680 sust.)
Range: 1,800/15 **Fuel:** 31,608 liters **Crew:** 11 tot.

Remarks: Aluminum construction. Acquired with U.S. financial assistance. The weapons are normally not mounted.

PATROL BOATS [WPB]

♦ **1 U.S. Dauntless 40-ft. class**
Bldr: SeaArk, Monticello, Ark. (In serv. 8-8-95)

C 421 Ardent

D: 15 tons (fl) **S:** 28 kts **Dim:** 12.19 (11.13 wl) × 3.86 × 0.69 (hull)
A: 1 7.62-mm mg **Electronics:** Radar: 1 Raytheon R40X nav.
M: 2 Caterpillar 3208TA diesels; 2 props; 850 bhp (720 sust.)
Range: 200/30; 400/22 **Fuel:** 250 gallons **Crew:** 4 tot.

Remarks: Ordered 4-94. Aluminum construction. C. Raymond Hunt, "Deep-Vee" hull design.

PATROL BOATS [WPB] *(continued)*

Ardent (C 421) SeaArk, 8-95

♦ **1 Spear-class** Bldr: Fairey Marine, U.K. (In serv. 10-9-74)

RANGER I

D: 4.3 tons (fl) **S:** 20 kts **Dim:** 9.1 × 2.8 × 0.8
A: 2 single 7.62-mm mg
M: 2 Ford Mermaid diesels; 2 props; 360 bhp **Crew:** 2 tot.

Remarks: GRP construction. Does not have a radar.

SERVICE CRAFT

♦ **2 Whaler utility launches [WYFL]**
Bldr: Boston Whaler, Rockland, Mass. (In serv. 5-88)

C 078 ROVER II C 087 ROVER I

D: 1.5 tons light (2 fl) **S:** 35 kts **Dim:** 6.81 × 2.26 × 0.60
M: 1 Johnson V6-2500CC gasoline outboard, 223 bhp **Range:** 70/35
Crew: 2 tot.

Remarks: U.S. government funded. Foam-core GRP construction.

ST. LUCIA

State of Saint Lucia

COAST GUARD

Personnel: 49 total

Base: Castries

Note: The Coast Guard is subordinated to the Comptroller of Customs and Excise.

PATROL BOATS [WPB]

♦ **1 U.S. Dauntless 40-ft. class**
Bldr: SeaArk Marine, Monticello, Ark. (In serv. 9-10-95)

P-04 PROTECTOR

Protector (P-04) SeaArk, 10-95

D: 15 tons (fl) **S:** 28 kts **Dim:** 12.19 (11.13 wl) × 3.86 × 0.69 (hull)
A: 1 7.62-mm mg **Electronics:** Radar: 1 Raytheon R40X nav.
M: 2 Caterpillar 3208TA diesels; 2 props; 850 bhp (720 sust.)
Range: 200/30; 400/22 **Fuel:** 250 gallons **Crew:** 5 tot.

Remarks: Ordered 4-94 under U.S. Foreign Military Sales aid program. Aluminum construction. C. Raymond Hunt, "Deep-Vee" hull design.

♦ **1 U.S. 65-ft. Commercial Cruiser design**
Bldr: Swiftships, Inc., Morgan City, La. (In serv. 3-5-84)

P-02 DEFENDER

Defender (P-02) Maritime Photographic, 11-93

D: 35 tons (fl) **S:** 23 kts **Dim:** 19.96 × 5.59 × 1.52 **A:** Small arms
Electronics: Radar: 1 Raytheon 1210 nav.
M: 2 G.M. Detroit Diesel 12V71 TI diesels; 2 props; 1,350 bhp
Electric: 20 kw **Range:** 500/18 **Crew:** 5 tot.

Remarks: Aluminum construction. Ordered 9-11-83 with U.S. financial aid. Blue hull, white superstructure.

♦ **1 ex-U.S. Coast Guard 82-ft Point class**
Bldr: J. Martinac SB, Tacoma, Wash. (In serv. 14-4-67)

P-01 ALPHONSE REYNOLDS (ex-*Point Turner,* WPB 82365)

D: 64 tons (69 fl) **S:** 23 kts **Dim:** 25.3 × 5.23 × 1.95
A: 2 single 12.7-mm M2 mg
Electronics: Radar: 1 Raytheon SPS-64(V)1 nav.
M: 2 Caterpillar 3412 diesels; 2 props; 1,480 bhp
Range: 490/23.7; 1,500/8 **Fuel:** 5.7 tons **Crew:** 1 officer, 7 enlisted

Remarks: Decommissioned from U.S. Coast Guard service on 3-4-98 and donated to St. Lucia on 15-4-98. Is in excellent condition and was re-engined early in the 1990s.
Hull systems: Hull in mild steel. High-speed diesels controlled from the bridge. Well equipped for salvage and towing.

Note: Also in service are Mako Marine–built, GRP-hulled launches P-06 and P-07 and the 35-kt, rigid-inflatable Hurricane search-and-rescue launch P-05.

ST. VINCENT

State of Saint Vincent and the Grenadines

COAST GUARD

Personnel: 60 total

Base: Calliaqua

Note: Formerly named the Marine Wing of the State of Saint Vincent and the Grenadines Police Force. The prefix "SVG" in pennant numbers stands for "Saint Vincent Government."

PATROL CRAFT [WPC]

♦ **1 120-ft. Commercial Cruiser class**
Bldr: Swiftships, Inc., Morgan City, La.

	L	In serv.
SVG-01 CAPTAIN MULZAC	6-6-86	13-6-87

Captain Mulzac (SVG-01) Alexandre Sheldon-Duplaix, 1-92

PATROL CRAFT [WPC] *(continued)*

D: 101 tons light (. . . fl) **S:** 21 kts **Dim:** 35.56 × 7.62 × 2.10
A: 2 single 12.7-mm M2 mg; 2 single 7.62-mm mg
Electronics: Radar: 1 Furuno 1411 Mk II nav.
M: 4 G.M. Detroit Diesel 12V71 TI diesels; 4 props; 2,700 bhp
Range: 1,800/15 **Crew:** 4 officers, 10 enlisted

Remarks: Ordered 8-86 with U.S. financial aid. Aluminum construction. Former oil-field pipe carrier, converted for patrol duties.

PATROL BOATS [WPB]

♦ **1 U.S. Dauntless 40-ft. class**
Bldr: SeaArk Marine, Monticello, Ark. (In serv. 8-6-95)

SVG-04 Hairoun

D: 15 tons (fl) **S:** 28 kts **Dim:** 12.19 (11.13 wl) × 3.86 × 0.69 (hull)
A: 1 7.62-mm mg
Electronics: Radar: 1 Raytheon R40X nav.
M: 2 Caterpillar 3208TA diesels; 2 props; 850 bhp (720 sust.)
Range: 200/30; 400/22 **Fuel:** 250 gallons **Crew:** 4 tot.

Remarks: Ordered 4-94. Aluminum construction. C. Raymond Hunt, "Deep-Vee" hull design.

♦ **1 U.K.-built patrol boat**
Bldr: Vosper Thornycroft, Portchester (In serv. 23-3-81)

SVG-05 George McIntosh

George McIntosh (SVG-05) H&L Van Ginderen, 3-81

D: 70 tons (fl) **S:** 24.5 kts **Dim:** 22.86 × 7.43 × 1.64
A: 1 20-mm 90-cal. Oerlikon AA
Electronics: Radar: 1 Furuno 1411 Mk II nav.
M: 2 Caterpillar 12V D348 TA diesels; 2 props; 1,840 bhp (1,450 sust.)
Electric: 24 kw tot. **Range:** 600/21; 1,000/11 **Crew:** 3 officers, 8 enlisted

Remarks: Glass-reinforced plastic, Keith Nelson–designed hull.

Note: Also used for local service are the U.S.–supplied Zodiac rigid inflatable launch SVG-03 and the 1994-vintage Boston Whaler–built launch *Chatham Bay* (SVG-08).

SAMOA

Independent State of Samoa

Base: Apia Harbor

Note: The name of the country was changed from Western Samoa during 8-97.

PATROL CRAFT [PC]

♦ **1 Australian ASI 315 class**
Bldr: Transfield-ASI, South Coogie, Western Australia

	Laid down	L	In serv.
Nafanua	20-5-87	18-2-88	19-3-88

D: 165 tons (fl) **S:** 20 kts **Dim:** 31.5 (28.6 wl) × 8.1 × 2.12
A: Small arms **Electronics:** Radar: 1 Furuno 1011 nav.
M: 2 Caterpillar 3516 diesels; 2 props; 2,820 bhp **Electric:** 116 kw tot.
Range: 2,500/12 **Fuel:** 29 tons **Crew:** 3 officers, 14 enlisted

Remarks: Provided under the Australian Defense Cooperation Program. Ordered 3-10-85. Sisters built for other Southwest Pacific nations. Underwent a major life-extension refit in 2006 to extend service through 2018. Extensive navigational suite, including Furuno FSN-70 NAVSAT receiver, 525 HF/DF, 120 MF/HFD/F, FE-881 echo sounder, and DS-70 doppler log.

Nafanua H&L Van Ginderen, 1-96

SÃO TOME AND PRINCIPE

Republic of São Tome and Principe

Personnel: 50–75 total

PATROL BOATS [PB]

♦ **1 U.S. 2810-V Protector Class**
Bldr: SeaArk Marine, Monticello, Ark. (In serv. 11-1-92)

Falcão

D: . . . tons (fl) **S:** 38 kts **Dim:** 8.69 × 3.56 × 0.56 **A:** Small arms
Electronics: Radar: 1 Furuno . . . nav.
M: 2 Volvo AQAD 41/290 outdrive diesels; 2 props; 400 bhp **Crew:** 4 tot.

Remarks: U.S. donation. Aluminum construction. Formally dedicated 20-1-92.

SAUDI ARABIA

Kingdom of Saudi Arabia

NAVY

Personnel: Approx. 15,500 total, including 3,000 Marines

Bases: Headquarters at Riyadh. Principal bases at Jiddah (Red Sea) and Al Jubail (Persian Gulf). Other facilities exist at Dammam.

Naval Aviation: 15 AS.365 F/AS Dauphin-2 for ship- and shore-based ASW and ship attack, and 4 SA-365N Dauphin-2 configured for search-and-rescue duties, with Omera DRB 32 search radar. The Frontier Force, Border Guard, and Police Division of the Ministry of the Interior share six AS.332F1 Super Puma helicopters equipped with AM 39 Exocet antiship missiles or a 20-mm cannon. NH-90 helicopters will likely be ordered in the near future.

♦ **AS.365 Dauphin-2 helicopter:**

Rotor diameter: 13.29 m **Fuselage length:** 11.41 m **Height:** 4 m
Weight: light: 1,850 kg; max.: 3,900 kg **Speed:** 130 kts max.
Propulsion: 2 Turbomeca Arriel 1C turbines, 710 bhp each
Radius of action: 100 nautical miles with 4/AS-15; 140 nautical miles with 2/AS-15
Endurance: 2 hours with 4/AS-15; 3 hours with 2/AS-15
Armament: 2 or 4 Aerospatiale AS-15 antiship missiles or 2 Mk 36 ASW torpedoes.

Remarks: The AS-15 missile has a range of 15 km, weighs 96 kg, and is 2.16 m long. The helicopter carries an Agrion-15 frequency-agile, pulse-doppler radar to provide missile targeting and to permit the helicopter to provide mid-course guidance update information to the ship-launched Otomat Mk 2 (Erato) missiles, which have a range of 90 nautical miles, weigh 780 kg, and carry a 210-kg warhead.
Coast defense: Several batteries of truck-mounted Otomat Mk 2 (Erato) antiship missiles are reportedly available.

NAVY *(continued)*

Saudi Navy AS.365 Dauphin-2 French Navy, 1996

GUIDED MISSILE FRIGATES [FFG]

♦ 3 Al Riyadh (F-3000S) class   Bldr: DCN, Lorient

	Laid down	L	In serv.
812 Al Riyadh	29-9-99	1-8-00	26-7-03
814 Makkah	25-8-00	20-7-01	3-4-04
816 Al Dammam	26-8-01	7-9-02	23-10-04

D: 3,800 tons normal (4,650 fl) **S:** 25 kts
Dim: 133.00 (128.00 pp) × 17.00 (13.80 wl) × 4.40 (hull)
A: 8 MM-40 Exocet Block 2 SSM; 2 8-cell Sylver A43 vertical launch SAM group (16 Aster 15 missiles); 1 76-mm 62-cal. OTO Melara SuperCompact DP; 2 single 20-mm 90-cal. GIAT F-2 AA; 2 single 12.7-mm mg; 4 fixed 533-mm ASW TT (F 17P wire-guided heavyweight ASW torpedoes); 2 AS.365F/AS Dauphin-2 helicopters (with AS.15 antiship missiles)
Electronics:
Radar: 2 Decca 20V90 nav.; 1 Thales DRBV-26D Jupiter early warning; 1 Thales Arabel missile f.c.; 1 Thales Castor-IIJ/C gun f.c.
Sonar: Thales Spherion bow-mounted and CAPTAS 20 towed array
EW: Thales DR 3000S2 intercept (1-18 gHz); Dassault Salamandre B2 jammer; Altesse communications intercept and D/F; TRC 281 comms jammer; 2 330-340-round Matra Défense Dagaie Mk 2 decoy RL
E/O: 2 Matra Défense Najir target designation and f.c.
M: 4 SEMT-Pielstick 16 PA 6 BTC diesels; 2 CP props; 31,800 bhp—drop-down, azimuthal bow-thruster
Electric: 3,000 kw (3 × 1,000 kw diesel sets) **Range:** 7,000/15; 8,000/12
Fuel: . . . tons **Endurance:** 50 days
Crew: 25 officers, 155 enlisted (accomm. for 190 tot.)

Al Dammam (816) Bernard Prézelin, 8-04

Makkah (814) Bernard Prézelin, 3-04

Al Riyadh (812) Bernard Prézelin, 4-04

Remarks: A project definition contract was granted to France on 11-6-89, but a letter of agreement was not signed until 22-11-94 and then for only two ships under the "Sawari-2" program, which also called for the construction of a fully equipped naval training center and major technical support services in addition to the two frigates. The third unit was ordered on 21-5-97. During 9-01, 812 began sea trials and was delivered on 27-7-02; the ship spent two years based at Toulon for crew training, prior to sailing for home waters. On 3-12-04, *Makkah* suffered major damage after

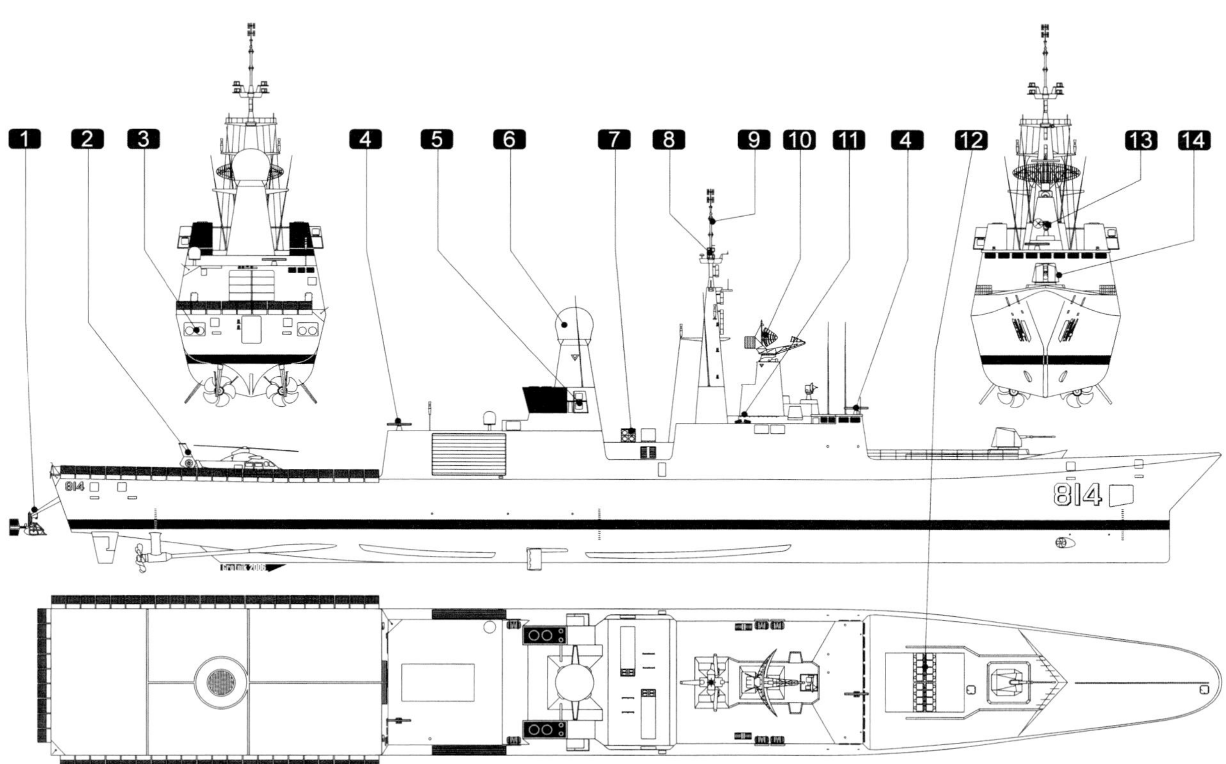

Makkah (814) 1. CAPTAS 20 variable-depth sonar 2. Dauphin 2 ASW helicopter 3. Stern 533-mm torpedo tubes 4. Racal Decca 20V90 navigation radar. 5. Salamandre B2 EW jammer array 6. Arabel target detection and tracking 7. MM 40 Exocet antiship missiles 8. Thales DR 3000S2 intercept array 9. Atlesse communications intercept 10. DRBV-26D early warning radar 11. Dagaie Mk 2 decoy launcher 12. Sylver vertical launch system for Aster-15 missiles 13. Castor-II J/C fire control 14. 76 mm OTO Melara DP Gun
Drawing by T. Grotnik, 2006

GUIDED MISSILE FRIGATES [FFG] *(continued)*

Makkah (814) Bernard Prézelin, 3-04

grounding on a coral reef while traveling near top speed. Damage from the accident resulted in complete flooding of the engine room and numerous injuries to the crew. Extensive repairs are expected.

Hull systems: A particular effort has been made to reduce the ships' signatures; the diesel propulsion engines are mounted in pairs on isolation platforms, and the superstructure, masts, and forecastle are covered with radar-absorbant GRP-resin compound. The superstructure is built primarily of steel. Vertical hull and superstructure surfaces are slanted at plus or minus 10 degrees to reduce radar reflectivity. They are also fitted with degaussing equipment and extensive NBC warfare protection.

Special steel armor is provided for the magazines. Hull plating is 10-mm steel. All chocks, bollards, and boat recesses are covered to reduce radar reflectivity. Modified deep-vee hull form, fin stabilizers, and rudder-controlled roll reduction are employed to improve seaworthiness. There are two rudders, and the hull form incorporates twin skegs aft. Hull has 11 watertight compartments. The helicopter can be launched and recovered in up to Sea State 6, and the SAMAHE deck traversing and landing system is fitted. Boats are stowed in superstructure recesses that are covered with sliding doors to reduce radar reflection.

Combat systems: The Thales SENIT 7 (TAVITAC 2000) combat control system with nine VISTA display consoles and two tactical plotting tables is installed. The ships have Link 11 connectivity with Saudi AWACS aircraft. The first two were originally to have had Crotale-NG SAM systems as an interim measure until the Aster 15 system was available, but delays in the start of the program have permitted all three to be built with the same equipment. Provision has been made for doubling the number of Sylver vertical missile launch cells, and the ships may eventually carry the longer-ranged Aster 30 missile as well as the Aster 15. 812 was completed with a GIAT 100-mm Compact gunmount, but it was replaced during a summer 2004 refit at Lorient; the other two will have the low-reflectivity 76-mm mount installed prior to delivery; the associated Castor-IIJ/C radar director also has IR and low light-level television sensors. The planned two Sadral point-defense SAM systems have been dropped from all three.

Hofouf (704)—with Dauphin-2 helicopter on deck. Hartmut Ehlers, 9-03

Hofouf (704)—note stern torpedo tubes and variable depth sonar Hartmut Ehlers, 9-03

Taif (708) Rob Cabo, 1-00

FRIGATES [FF]

♦ 4 Al Madinah class

	Bldr	Laid down	L	In serv.
702 Al Madinah	Arsenal de Lorient	15-10-81	23-4-83	4-1-85
704 Hofouf	CNIM, La Seyne	14-6-82	24-6-83	31-10-85
706 Abha	CNIM, La Seyne	7-12-82	23-12-83	4-4-86
708 Taif	CNIM, La Seyne	1-3-83	25-5-84	29-8-86

D: 2,000 tons (2,250 normal, 2,610 fl) **S:** 30 kts
Dim: 115.00 (106.50 pp) × 12.50 wl × 3.40 (4.65 over sonar)
A: 8 Otomat Mk 2 Erato SSM; 1 8-round Crotale EDIR SAM syst. (26 missiles); 1 100-mm 55-cal. Compact DP; 2 twin 40-mm 70-cal. OTO Melara Dardo AA; 4 fixed 533-mm ASW TT (F17P wire-guided torpedoes); 1 SA 365F Dauphin-2 helicopter

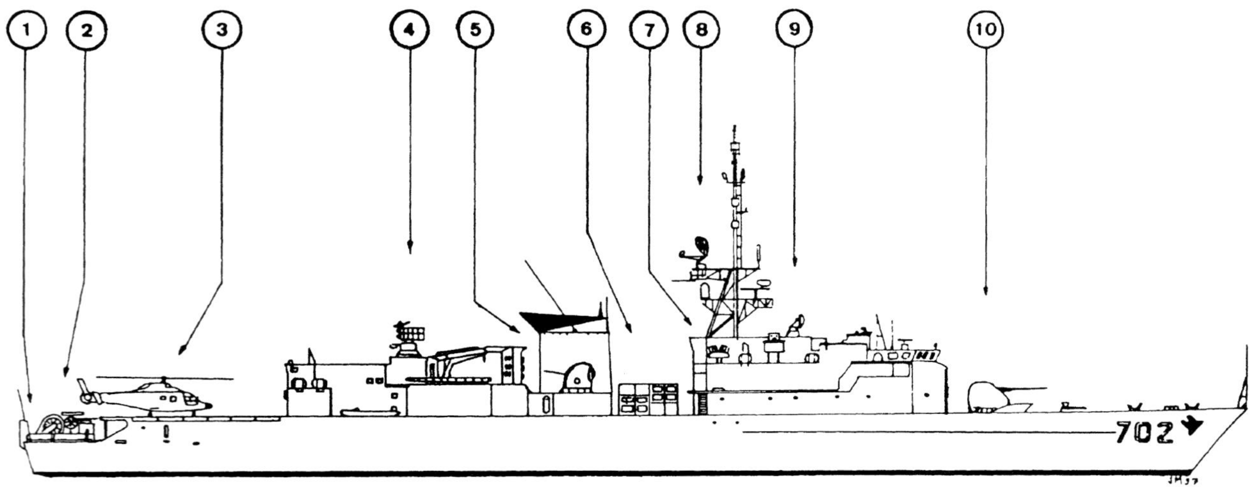

Al Madinah (702) 1. Stern 533-mm torpedo tubes 2. Sorel variable-depth sonar 3. Dauphin-2 helicopter 4. Crotale EDIR SAM launcher 5. Twin 40-mm OTOBreda AA 6. Otomat antiship missiles 7. Dagaie Mk 2 decoy RL 8. Sea Tiger (DRBV-15) air-search radar 9. Castor-IIC gun f.c. radar 10. 100-mm Compact DP gun
Drawing by Jean Moulin, from *Flottes de Combat*

FRIGATES [FF] *(continued)*

Electronics:
Radar: 2 Decca TM 1226 nav.; 1 Thales Sea Tiger (DRBV-15) air-search; 1 Thales Castor IIC gun f.c.; 1 Thales DRBC-32E missile f.c.
Sonar: Thales TSM 2630 (Diodon) hull-mounted; Thales TSM 2630 (Sorel) VDS
EW: Thales DR 4000S intercept syst.; Thales Janet jammer; EADS Telegon VI D/F; 2 330-340-round Matra Défense Dagaie Mk 2 decoy RL
E/O: 1 Contraves LSEOS Mk II gun f.c.; 2 Matra Défense Naja gun optronic f.c.
M: 4 SEMT-Pielstick 16 PA 6 BTC diesels/2 props; 32,500 bhp
Electric: 2,560 kw (4 × 480-kw diesel sets; 2 × 320-kw diesel sets)
Range: 6,500/18; 8,000/15 **Fuel:** 370 tons **Endurance:** 30 days
Crew: 15 officers, 50 petty officers, 114 enlisted

Remarks: Ordered 10-80 as part of the Sawari program. Under a 2-94 agreement, were given extensive overhauls in France under the Mouette program. Work began in France 12-95 with 702, which departed for Saudi Arabia on 8-4-97; 704 arrived in Toulon on 1-10-96; 706 completed summer 1999; and 708 finished on 21-3-00. All are based at Jiddah.
Hull systems: Have an NBC warfare defense citadel. There are 13 main watertight bulkheads to the hull, which is equipped with retractable fin stabilizers. During refits, the NBC defense system was improved, as were self-maintenance capabilities.
Combat systems: Have Thales TAVITAC computer data system, with two Type 15M 125F computers, nine BarcoView Texen Vista display consoles (one on the bridge), and two E7000 tactical tables; the combat datalink operates with NATO Link 11 and Royal Saudi Air Force aircraft. The Otomat missiles have the Erato (Extended Range Automated Targeting) feature, using the combat data system and helicopter-derived target data. Have the Alcatel Type DLA torpedo f.c.s. Sorel is a VDS version of the Diodon sonar; both operate at 11, 12, or 13 kHz. Carry 500 rds 100-mm ammunition, 6,300 rds 40-mm. During the modernization refits, the fire-control radars were updated, and the original helicopter deck-handling system was replaced by the DCN SAMAHE system; the Otomat Mk 2 Erato missiles were also overhauled. Are equipped with Matra Défense Sylosat NAVSAT receivers.

CORVETTES [FFL]

♦ 4 U.S. PCG class
Bldr: Tacoma Boatbuilding, Tacoma, Wash.

	Laid down	L	In serv.
612 Badr (ex-PCG 1)	30-5-79	26-1-80	28-9-81
614 AL Yarmook (ex-PCG 2)	13-12-79	13-5-80	10-5-82
616 Hitteen (ex-PCG 3)	19-5-80	5-9-80	12-10-82
618 Tabuk (ex-PCG 4)	22-9-80	18-6-81	10-1-83

Al Yarmook (614) —with frigate *Taif* (708) in background
A. A. Alleyne, U.S. Navy, 1998

D: 903 tons (1,038 fl) **S:** 30 kts on gas turbine, 21 kts on diesels
Dim: 74.68 × 9.60 × 2.59 (hull)
A: 8 RGM-84C Harpoon SSM; 1 76-mm 62-cal. U.S. Mk 75 DP; 1 20-mm Mk 15 Block 0 Phalanx CIWS; 2 single 20-mm 70-cal. Oerlikon AA; 1 81-mm mortar; 2 single 40-mm Mk 19 grenade launchers; 2 triple 324-mm Mk 32 Mod. 5 ASW TT (Mk 46 Mod. 2 torpedoes)
Electronics:
Radar: 1 Cardion SPS-55 nav./surf. search; 1 Lockheed Martin SPS-40B air-search; 1 Sperry Mk 92 Mod. 5 f.c.; 1 General Dynamics Mk 90 Phalanx f.c.
Sonar: SQS-56 (Raytheon DE-1160B) hull-mounted (5.6, 7.5, 8.4 kHz)
EW: SLQ-32 (V)1 intercept; Mk 36 SRBOC decoy syst. (2 6-round Mk 137 RL)
E/O: Safire infrared surveillance and tracking
M: CODOG: 1 G.E. LM-2500 gas turbine (23,000 shp); 2 MTU 12V652 TB91 diesels (3,058 bhp tot.); 2 CP props
Electric: 1,200 kw tot. **Range:** 4,000/20 **Crew:** 7 officers, 51 enlisted

Remarks: Ordered 30-8-77. Program completed well behind schedule, with the ships considerably overweight. Have fin stabilizers. Have one Mk 24 optical target designation transmitter. The Mk 309 ASW f.c.s. is fitted. Given a commercial combat information datalink system (Link W) during the late 1990s. All based at Al Jubail on the Persian Gulf and are supported by U.S. contractors.

GUIDED-MISSILE PATROL COMBATANTS [PTG]

♦ 9 U.S. PGG class
Bldr: Peterson Builders, Sturgeon Bay, Wisc.

	Laid down	L	In serv.
511 As Siddiq (ex-PGG 1)	30-9-78	22-9-79	15-12-80
513 Al Farouq (ex-PGG 2)	12-3-79	17-5-80	22-6-81
515 Abdul Aziz (ex-PGG 3)	19-10-79	23-8-80	3-9-81
517 Faisal (ex-PGG 4)	4-3-80	15-11-80	23-11-81
519 Khalid (ex-PGG 5)	27-6-80	28-3-81	11-1-82
521 Amr (ex-PGG 6)	21-10-80	13-6-81	21-6-82
523 Tariq (ex-PGG 7)	10-2-81	23-9-81	16-8-82
525 Oqbah (ex-PGG 8)	8-5-81	12-12-81	18-10-82
527 Abu Obaidah (ex-PGG 9)	4-9-81	3-4-82	6-12-82

Khalid (519) Leo Dirkx, 11-98

Oqbah (525) H&L Van Ginderen, 1-00

D: 425 tons (495 fl) **S:** 34 kts on gas turbine, 16 kts on diesels
Dim: 58.02 × 8.08 × 1.95 (hull)
A: 4 RGM-84C Harpoon SSM; 1 76-mm 62-cal. U.S. Mk 75 DP;1 20-mm Mk 15 Block 0 Phalanx CIWS; 2 single 20-mm 70-cal. Oerlikon AA; 1 81-mm mortar; 2 single 40-mm Mk 19 grenade launchers
Electronics:
Radar: 1 Cardion SPS-55 nav./surf. search; 1 Sperry Mk 92 Mod. 5 f.c.; 1 General Dynamics Mk 90 Phalanx f.c.
EW: SLQ-32 (V)1 intercept; Mk 36 SRBOC decoy syst. (2 6-round Mk 137 RL)
E/O: Safire infrared surveillance and tracking
M: CODOG: 1 G.E. gas turbine (23,000 shp); 2 MTU 12V652 TB91 diesels (3,058 bhp tot.); 2 CP props
Electric: 800 kw **Range:** 600/30; 2,900/14 **Crew:** 5 officers, 33 enlisted

Remarks: Ordered 16-2-77. Fin stabilizers fitted. Delivered behind schedule and considerably over designed displacement. Have one Mk 24 optical target designation transmitter. Given a commercial combat information datalink system (Link W) during the late 1990s. 521 and 523 are based at Jiddah on the Red Sea, the others in the Persian Gulf at Al Jubail.

PATROL BOATS [PB]

♦ 17 U.S. 78-ft. PCF class
Bldr: Trinity-Equitable SY, New Orleans, La. (In serv. 1-93)

52 through 68

D: 56.4 tons (fl) **S:** 28 kts **Dim:** 23.66 × 6.06 × 1.01 hull (1.76 props)
A: 2 single 25-mm 87-cal. U.S. Mk. 38 low-angle chain guns; 2 single 7.62-mm mg
Electronics: Radar: 1 Raytheon SPS-64(V)1 nav.
M: 2 G.M. Detroit Diesel 16V92 TAB diesels; 2 props; 2,800 bhp
Electric: 70 kw (2 × 35 kw) **Range:** 600/24, 1,200/12 **Fuel:** 18,950 liters
Endurance: 5 days **Crew:** 2 officers, 6 enlisted

Remarks: Ordered 12-90. Referred to locally as PCF—Fast Patrol Craft. Aluminum construction. A 4-m rigid inflatable boat powered by a 40 bhp outboard motor is stowed amidships. Even-numbered boats serve on the Red Sea coast, with six at Jiddah and three at Jizen; the other eight are based at Al Jubail on the Persian Gulf coast. Sisters serve in the Philippine Navy.

♦ 40 Naja ASD 12 class
Bldr: Simonneau S.A. Marine, Fontenay-le-Comte, France (In serv. 1988–89, 1991)

D: 7.5 tons (fl) **S:** 50 kts **Dim:** 12.80 (10.20 pp) × 4.00 × 0.50
A: 1 20-mm 90-cal. GIAT F-2 AA; 2 single 7.62 GIAT mg
Electronics: Radar: 1 Furuno . . . nav.
M: 4 OMC gasoline outboard motors; 1,200 shp
Range: 350/35 **Fuel:** 1,700 liters **Crew:** 4 tot.

Remarks: First group of 20 ordered 6-6-88, second in 10-90. Of the first group, one was lost during shipment but was replaced by the builder. Aluminum construction. Employed by naval special forces personnel.

PATROL BOATS [PB] *(continued)*

Naja ASD 12 class—on trials Simonneau, 1988

MINE WARFARE SHIPS

♦ 3 U.K. Sandown-class minehunters [MHC]

Bldr: Vosper Thornycroft, Woolston

	Laid down	L	In serv.
420 Al Jawf (ex-*Inverness*)	. . .	2-8-89	21-12-91
422 Shaqra	14-5-90	15-5-91	8-2-93
424 Al Kharj	4-90	9-2-93	9-94

Shaqra (422) Maritime Photographic, 5-96

Al Kharj (424) Maritime Photographic, 3-96

D: 378 tons light (465 fl) **S:** 15 kts (13 sust.)/6.5 hunting
Dim: 52.50 (50.00 pp) × 10.50 (9.00 wl) × 2.30
A: 1 twin 30-mm 75-cal. Emerlec EX-74
Electronics:
Radar: 1 Kelvin-Hughes Type 1007 nav.
Sonar: 1 Plessey-MUSL 2093 variable-depth minehunting
EW: Thales Shiploc intercept; Mk 36 RBOC decoy syst. (2 6-round Mk 137 RL)
E/O: Oerlikon-Contraves Sea Hawk Mk 2 TMEO optronic surveillance/f.c.
M: 2 Paxman Valenta 6 RPA 200-E diesels; 2 Voith-Schneider 16 G.S. 5-bladedvertical cycloidal props; 1,500 bhp (1,360 sust.)—2/200-shp electric motors (7 kt max)—2 Schottel electric bow-thrusters
Electric: 750 kw (3 × 250 kw Mawdsley generators; 3 Perkins V8-250G diesels driving [335 bhp each])
Range: 3,000/12 **Crew:** 7 officers, 40 enlisted

Remarks: Ordered 3-12-88. A planned second batch of three was canceled. 420 did not depart for Saudi Arabia until 3-11-95, four years after completion; 422 departed 1-12-96 and 424 on 7-8-97 after completion of vibration trials.
Hull systems: Constructed of GRP and are cramped internally.
Combat systems: The Plessey NAUTIS-M navigation/minehunting data system is fitted. The sonar uses a variable-depth vertical lozenge-shaped towed body lowered beneath the hull; it has search, depth-finder, classification, and route survey modes. All have the RN Remote-Controlled Mine Disposal System Mk 2, using two French PAP-104 Mk 5 submersibles and carry mine disposal divers. Also have Racal Hyperfix, QM 14, and Navigator Mk 21 radio navaids. Are capable of dealing with mines to 200 m depths.

♦ 4 U.S. MSC 322–class minesweepers [MSC]

Bldr: Peterson Builders, Sturgeon Bay, Wisc.

	Laid down	L	In serv.
412 Addiriyah (ex-MSC 322)	12-5-76	20-12-76	6-7-78
414 Al Quysumah (ex-MSC 323)	24-8-76	26-5-77	15-8-78
416 Al Wadeeah (ex-MSC 324)	28-12-76	6-9-77	7-9-78
418 Safwa (ex-MSC 325)	5-3-77	7-12-77	20-10-78

Al Quysumah (414) H&L Van Ginderen, 1996

D: 320 tons (407 fl) **S:** 14 kts **Dim:** 46.63 × 8.29 × 4.06 max.
A: 1 20-mm 70-cal. Mk 67 AA
Electronics:
Radar: 1 Cardion SPS-55 nav./surf. search
Sonar: G.E. SQQ-14 VDS minehunting HF
M: 2 Waukesha L1616 diesels; 2 props; 1,200 bhp
Electric: 2,150 kw tot. (1 × 1,750 kw a.c. sweep generator, 2 × 200 kw, all diesel)
Crew: 4 officers, 35 enlisted

Remarks: Ordered 30-9-75. Longer than other standard U.S. export coastal minesweepers of the period. Wooden construction. Used primarily as patrol boats and played very little part in clearing Iraqi-laid mines during and after the 1991 Gulf War. 412 is based at Jiddah, the others at Al Jubail.

AMPHIBIOUS WARFARE CRAFT

♦ 4 U.S. LCU 1646 class utility landing craft [LCU]

Bldr: Newport SY, Newport, R.I. (In serv. 1976)

212 Al Qiaq (ex-SA 310) 216 Al Ulu (ex-SA 312)
214 As Sulayel (ex-SA 311) 218 Afif (ex-SA 313)

D: 173 tons light (375 fl) **S:** 11 kts **Dim:** 41.07 × 9.07 × 2.00
A: 2 single 20-mm 70-cal. U.S. Mk 67 AA
Electronics: Radar: 1 Canadian Marconi LN-66 nav.
M: 4 G.M. Detroit Diesel 6-71 diesels; 2 Kort-nozzle props; 900 bhp
Electric: 80 kw tot. **Range:** 1,200/10
Crew: 2 officers, 12 enlisted + 20 passengers

Remarks: Standard units of the class, with a cargo capacity rated at 168 tons on the open 30.5 × 5.5-m cargo deck; have ramps fore and aft. Used as logistics transports. Based at Al Jubail.

♦ 4 U.S. LCM(6)-class landing craft [LCM]

Bldr: Marinette Marine, Marinette, Wisc. (In serv. 7-80)

220 Dhuba 222 Umlus 224 Al Leeth 226 Al Quonfetha

D: 24 tons (57.5 fl) **S:** 13 kts **Dim:** 17.07 × 4.37 × 1.14
A: 2 single 40-mm Mk 19 grenade launchers
M: 2 G.M. Detroit Diesel 6V71 diesels; 2 props; 450 bhp
Range: 130/9 (loaded) **Crew:** 5 tot.

Remarks: Four others received in 7-77 have been cannibalized. Cargo: 30 tons or 80 troops. Cargo well: 11.9 × 3.7.

AUXILIARIES

♦ 2 underway replenishment oilers [AOR]

Bldr: CN la Ciotat, Marseilles

	Laid down	L	In serv.
902 Boraida	13-4-82	22-1-83	29-2-84
904 Yunbou	9-10-83	20-10-84	29-8-85

Boraida (902) Hartmut Ehlers, 9-03

D: 10,500 tons (trials) **S:** 20.5 kts **Dim:** 135.0 × 18.7 × 7.0
A: 2 twin 40-mm 70-cal. OTO Melara Dardo AA
Electronics:
Radar: 2 Decca TM 1226 nav.
E/O: 2 Matra Défense Naja optical f.c.s.

AUXILIARIES *(continued)*

Boraida (902) Carlo Martinelli, 3-97

M: 2 SEMT-Pielstick 14 PC 2.5V400 diesels; 2 CP props; 13,200 bhp
Electric: 3,400 kw tot. **Range:** 7,000/17 **Endurance:** 30 days
Crew: 140 tot. + 55 cadets

Remarks: Ordered 10-80 as part of the Sawari program. 902 left France 3-8-84 for Saudi Arabia. Design is a reduced version of the French *Durance* class. Act as training ships as well as replenishment vessels. 902 began refit at Toulon during 3-96, completing in 5-97; 904 was refitted from 5-97 to 3-99. Both based at Jiddah.
Hull systems: Cargo includes 4,350 tons of diesel fuel; 350 tons of aviation fuel; 140 tons potable water; 100 tons provisions; 100 tons munitions; and 70 tons spares. One replenishment station per side, plus over-the-stern refueling. Can transfer 1.7-ton solid loads. Have electrical, mechanical, and metal workshops.
Combat systems: The two AS.365N Dauphin-2 helicopters can also carry ASW and antiship weapons.

SERVICE CRAFT

♦ **2 U.S. YTB 760–class tugs [YTB]** (In serv. 15-10-75)

EN 111 Tuwaig (ex-YTB 837) EN 112 Dareen (ex-YTB 838)

D: 291 tons (356 fl) **S:** 12 kts **Dim:** 33.22 × 9.30 × 4.14
A: 2 single 20-mm 70-cal. Mk 67 AA
Electronics: Radar: 1 Canadian Marconi LN-66 nav.
M: 1 Fairbanks-Morse 38D8Q diesel; 1 prop; 2,000 bhp
Electric: 120 kw tot. **Range:** 2,000/10 **Crew:** 4 officers, 8 enlisted

Remarks: 25-ton bollard pull. Intended for target towing, firefighting, torpedo recovery, and local patrol duties. EN 111 is based at Al Jubail, EN 112 at Jiddah (to assist the yacht squadron).

ROYAL YACHT SQUADRON

Note: Considered a separate command, but personnel are drawn from the Saudi Navy. The yachts are based at Jiddah.

AUXILIARIES

♦ **1 ex-Iraqi presidential yacht [AG]**
Bldr: Elsinore SB & Eng., Denmark (L: 10-80; In serv. 1981)

Al Yamana (ex-*Qadissayat Saddam*)

Al Yamana Elsinore SB, 1980

D: 1,660 tons (fl) **S:** 19.3 kts **Dim:** 82.00 × 13.00 × 3.30
M: 2 MTU 12V1163 TB82 diesels; 2 CP props; 6,000 bhp **Electric:** 1,095 kVA

Remarks: 2,282 grt. Because of the Iran-Iraq War, was never delivered to Saddam Hussein, who gave it as a present to King Fahd in 1987. Can carry 56 passengers (74 additional on short cruises). Has Sperry retractable fin stabilizers. 300-hp bowthruster. Helicopter deck aft above swimming pool.

♦ **1 royal yacht [AG]**
Bldr: Helsingor Vaerft, Denmark (In serv. 12-83)

Abdul Aziz

Abdul Aziz Leo van Ginderen, 7-06

D: approx. 5,200 tons (fl) **S:** 22 kts **Dim:** 147.00 (126.00 pp) × 18.00 × 4.90
M: 2 Lindholmen-Pielstick 12 PC 2-5V400 diesels; 2 props; 15,600 bhp
Fuel: 640 tons **Crew:** 65 crew, plus 4 royalty, plus 60 passengers

Remarks: Delivered by builders 4-83 to Vosper Shiprepairers, Southampton, for final fitting out and ran post-outfitting trials 15-5-84. Has a stern ramp leading to vehicle garage, a swimming pool, and a helicopter hangar forward, beneath the forecastle.

♦ **1 Jetfoil-type hydrofoil royal yacht tender [AG]**
Bldr: Boeing, Seattle, Wash. (In serv. 8-85)

Al Aziziah

D: 115 tons (fl) **S:** 46 kts
Dim: 27.4 (foils down) × 9.1 × 1.9 hull (5.2 foils down at rest/2.0 foiling)
A: 2 single 20-mm G.E. Sea Vulcan gatling AA (I × 2), with 2 Stinger missiles co-mounted
Electronics: Radar: 1 . . . nav.
M: 2 Allison 501-KF20A gas turbines; 2 Rocketdyne R-20 waterjet pumps; 9,000 shp (7,560 sust.)—2 G.M. 8V92 TI diesels; 2 props; 900 bhp for hullborne cruise
Range: 890/40; 1,500/15 (hullborne) **Fuel:** 33 tons **Crew:** . . .

Remarks: Aluminum construction. Subcontracted to Boeing by Lockheed. Has a Kollmorgen HSV-20NCS electro-optical GFCS with Mk 35 Mod. L3 electro-optical sight for the gun mounts. Acts as tender and escort craft for the larger yachts.

BORDER GUARD
MINISTRY OF THE INTERIOR

Personnel: Approx. 4,500 tot.

Base: Headquarters at Azizah, with minor facilities at Al Dammam, Al Qatif, Al Sharmah, Al Wajh, Haqi, Ras al-Mishab, Ras Tanura, Qizan, and Yanbu' al-Bahr.

PATROL CRAFT [WPC]

♦ **4 Al Jouf class** Bldr: Blohm + Voss, Hamburg

	In serv.		In serv.
351 Al Jouf	15-6-89	353 Hail	20-8-89
352 Turaif	15-6-89	354 Najran	20-8-89

Turaif (352) Gilbert Gyssels, 6-89

D: 210 tons (fl) **S:** 38 kts **Dim:** 38.80 (36.20 pp) × 7.90 × 1.90
A: 2 single 20-mm 90-cal. Oerlikon GAM B-01 AA; 2 single 12.7-mm mg
Electronics: Radar: 1 Decca RM 1290A nav.; 1 Decca ARPA S-1690 surf. search
M: 3 MTU 16V538 diesels; 3 props; 11,260 bhp **Electric:** 321 kVa tot.
Range: 1,900/15 **Crew:** 4 officers, 16 enlisted

Remarks: Ordered 9-86. Steel hulls, aluminum superstructures. Have a 300-liter/min. firefighting monitor and carry a radio direction-finder. Two based at Jiddah on the Red Sea and two at Al Dammam on the Persian Gulf.

PATROL BOATS [WPB]

♦ **6 Stan Patrol 2606 class**
Bldr: Damen Shipyards, Gorinchem, the Netherlands (In serv. 2002–3)

317 Assir	319 Al Kharj	321 . . .
318 Al Dhahran	320 Arar	322 . . .

Al Dhahran (318)—with *Assir* (317) in background IJ Plokker, 8-02

D: 55 tons **S:** 30 kts **Dim:** 26.0 × 6.0 × 1.80
M: 2 MTU 12V396 TE94 diesels; 2 props; 4,430bhp
Electronics: Radar: 1 . . . nav.

Remarks: The first two ran trials during 1-02. Aluminum construction.

BORDER GUARD PATROL BOATS [WPB] *(continued)*

♦ 2 Sea Guard SM742 class

Bldr: Simonneau S.A. Marine, Fontenay-le-Comte, France (In serv. 4-92)

304 AL RIYADH   305 ZULURAB

Zulurab (305)—in missile trials configuration   Simonneau, 1992

D: 52.5 tons (fl) **S:** 35+ kts **Dim:** 22.50 × 5.60 × 1.70
A: 1 20-mm 90-cal. GIAT F-2 AA; 2 single 7.62 GIAT mg
Electronics: Radar: 1 Furuno . . . nav.
M: 2 MTU 12V396 TB92 diesels; 2 props; 2,920 bhp
Range: . . . / . . . **Fuel:** 6,500 liters **Crew:** 10 tot.

Remarks: Ordered 1992. Aluminum construction. Used for wire-guided missile trials in France before delivery, but Saudi Arabia did not buy the missile system. Based at Jiddah.

♦ 30 SM 331 Tom Cat–class patrol launches

Bldr: Simonneau S.A. Marine, Fontenay-le-Comte, France (In serv. 1992)

SM 331 Tom Cat class   Simonneau

D: 4.65 tons (fl) **S:** 40 kts **Dim:** 9.30 × 3.04 × 0.45 **A:** 1 7.62-mm mg
Electronics: Radar: 1 Furuno . . . nav.
M: 2 Johnson 6-cyl, gasoline outboards; 500 bhp
Fuel: 500 liters **Crew:** 4 tot.

Remarks: Aluminum construction.

♦ 2 CGV-26 Explorer class

Bldr: Abeking & Rasmussen, Lemwerder, Germany

	Laid down	L	In serv.
AL JUBATEL	1-3-86	3-87	4-87
SALWA	1-3-86	3-87	4-87

D: 80 tons (95 fl) **S:** 34 kts **Dim:** 26.60 (23.00 pp) × 6.50 × 1.80 (props)
A: 2 single 20-mm 90-cal. Oerlikon GAM-B01 AA; 2 single 12.7-mm mg
Electronics: Radar: 1 Decca AC 1290 nav.
M: 2 MTU 16V396 TB94 diesels; 2 props; 6,340 bhp
Range: 1,100/25 **Crew:** 4 officers, 8 enlisted

Remarks: Ordered 11-8-85. Steel construction. Based at Qizan and Al Wajh, respectively.

Disposal note: All remaining units of the *Scorpion*-class patrol boats had been retired by 2006.

Al Jubatel   Abeking & Rasmussen, 1987

♦ 12 Rapier class

Bldr: Halter Marine, New Orleans, La. (In serv. 1976–77)

127–138

D: 26 tons (fl) **S:** 28 kts **Dim:** 15.24 × 4.57 × 1.35 **A:** 2 single 7.62-mm mg
Electronics: Radar: 1 . . . nav. **M:** 1 G.M. 12V71 TI diesels; 2 props; 1,300 bhp
Electric: 20 kw tot. **Crew:** 1 officer, 8 enlisted

♦ 60 Whaler patrol launches

Bldr: Boston Whaler, Rockland, Mass. (In serv. 1980s)

D: 1.5 tons light (2 fl) **S:** 30 kts **Dim:** 8.30 × 2.00 × 0.60
M: 2 Johnson V6, 2.5-liter gasoline outboards; 310 bhp **Range:** 70/35
Crew: 2 tot.

AUXILIARIES

♦ 1 training ship [WAXT]

Bldr: Bayerische Schiffsbau, Erlenbach, Germany (In serv. 12-77)

TEBUK

D: 600 tons (750 fl) **S:** 20 kts **Dim:** 60.0 (55.5 pp) × 10.0 × 2.50
A: 1 20-mm Oerlikon GAM-B01 AA **Electronics:** Radar: 1 Decca TM 1226 nav.
M: 2 MTU 16V538 TB81 diesels; 2 props; 5,260 bhp (4,800 sust.)
Electric: 1,040 kVA tot. **Range:** 2,400/18; 3,900/12
Crew: 24 crew + 36 trainees

SERVICE CRAFT

♦ 5 Type 8000TD(M) hovercraft launches [WYFLA]

Bldr: Griffon Hovercraft, Ltd., Woolston, U.K. (In serv. 2001–2)

D: 27 tons (fl) **S:** 42 kts **Dim:** 21.15 (19.85 hull) × 11.30 (8.70 hull) × 0.30
A: 1 12.7-mm mg **Electronics:** Radar: 1 Raytheon R-80 nav.
M: 2 MTU 12V183 TB32 diesels; 2 ducted CP airscrew props; 1,600 bhp
Range: 365/42; 500/ . . . **Fuel:** 2,000 liters **Crew:** 4 tot + 16 passengers

Remarks: Ordered 10-00. Maximum hover height: 1.25 m. Can make 50 kts in light condition, can carry an 8-ton payload, will have a single firefighting monitor, and can be operated on one engine. A 1-ton crane is fitted, and the vehicle well forward can accommodate a jeep or Land Rover. Three are based on the Red Sea coast and two on the Persian Gulf coast.

♦ 3 Type SAH-2000 hovercraft launches [WYFLA]

Bldr: Slingsby, U.K. (In serv. 1991–92)

D: 6 tons **S:** 40 kts **Dim:** 10.6 × 4.2 × 0.50 **A:** 1 7.62-mm mg
M: 1 Deutz BF6L913C diesel for lift and propulsion; 1 ducted airscrew; 190 bhp
Range: 500/40 **Crew:** 2 + 16 passengers

Remarks: Have Kevlar armor.

♦ 3 ramped personel launches [WYFL]

Bldr: Rotork, U.K. (In serv. 1991)

AL FAISAL   AL HAMZA   AL HASSHIM

D: 9 tons (fl) **S:** 28 kts **Dim:** 12.7 × 3.2 × 0.9 **M:** 2 diesels; 2 props; 240 bhp
Crew: 3 + 28 troops

♦ 1 yacht [WYFL]

AL TAIF

D: 75 tons (fl) **S:** 15 kts **Dim:** 21.4 × 5.8 × 1.7
Electronics: Radar: 1 Decca 101 nav.
M: 2 Deutz SBF 12M716 diesels; 2 props; . . . bhp

Remarks: Used primarily for training and based at Jiddah.

♦ 3 fuel lighters [WYO]

AL FORAT   AL NIL   DAJLAH

D: 233 tons (fl) **S:** 12 kts **Dim:** 28.70 (27.00 pp) × 6.50 × 2.10
Electronics: Radar: 1 Decca 110 nav.
M: 2 Caterpillar D343 diesels; 2 props; . . . bhp
Range: 500/12 **Crew:** . . . tot.

Remarks: Based at Jiddah (*Al Nil* at Azizah).

BORDER GUARD SERVICE CRAFT *(continued)*

♦ **3 harbor tugs [WYTM]**

D: 210 tons (fl) **S:** 13 kts **Dim:** 25.7 × 7.2 × 2.9
M: 1 Deutz SBA 16M816 diesel; 1 prop; . . . bhp **Range:** 1,200/12

♦ **1 fireboat [WYTR]**
Bldr: Vosper Pty, Singapore (In serv. 1982)

JUBAIL 2

Jubail 2 H&L Van Ginderen, 1-97

D: Approx. 210 tons (fl) **S:** 18 kts (17 sust.) **Dim:** 32.4 × 7.2 × 2.0
Electronics: Radar: 1 Decca 090 nav.
M: 2 MWM TBD 603 V16 diesels; 2 props; . . . bhp
Range: 950/16 **Fuel:** 25 tons **Crew:** 10 tot. (accommodations for 13)

Remarks: 183 grt. Has six firefighting monitors. The largest, atop the pilothouse, has a volume of 16,000 liters/min, while three atop the mast each can pump 5,000 liters/min and two aft can each pump 8,000 liters/min. The craft is protected by spray screens and carry foam and Halon spray facilities. It can also support divers and have portable salvage pumps. An extensive navigation equipment suite is provided.

SENEGAL

Republic of Senegal

Personnel: About 950 total

Bases: Headquarters, principal base, and dockyard at Dakar, with facilities also on the Casamance River.

Maritime Aviation: The Air Force operates one Canadian de Havilland DHC-6-300M Twin Otter for maritime patrol.

Note: Due to maintenance problems, only a fraction of vessels remain operational.

PATROL COMBATANTS [PG]

♦ **1 Osprey 55 design**
Bldr: Danyard A/S, Frederikshavn, Denmark

	Laid down	L	In serv.
FOUTA	11-86	3-87	1-6-87

Fouta Bernard Prézelin, 2-01

D: 500 tons (fl) **S:** 20.2 kts; 19 sust.
Dim: 54.75 (50.83 pp) × 10.50 (9.15 wl) × 2.55 hull
A: 1 40-mm 70-cal. Bofors AA; 1 20-mm 90-cal. GIAT F2 AA
Electronics: Radar: 1 Furuno FR-1411 nav.; 1 Furuno FR-1221 nav.
M: 2 M.A.N.-Burmeister & Wain Alpha 12V.23/30-DVO diesels; 2 CP props; 4,960 bhp
Electric: 359 kw tot. **Range:** 4,500/16 **Fuel:** 95 tons
Crew: 4 officers, 34 enlisted + 8 trainees

Remarks: Ordered early 1986; financed by the Ministry of Equipment. Thornycroft-Giles "short, fat ship" hull. Near-sisters in Mauritanean, Moroccan, Greek, and Myanmar service. Used for 200-n.m. economic zone and fisheries patrol. Armed after delivery. No helicopter facility. Berths for 20 rescued personnel. A stern docking well holds a 6.5-m Watercraft RI-22 inspection/rescue boat. Carries 27 tons fresh water.

PATROL CRAFT [PC]

♦ **1 French PR 72 MS class** Bldr: SFCN, Villeneuve-la-Garenne

	Laid down	L	In serv.
NJAMBUUR	5-80	23-12-80	2-83

Njambuur Bernard Prézelin, 2-03

Njambuur Paolo Marsan Collection, 1-05

D: 381 tons light (451 fl) **S:** 24 kts **Dim:** 58.70 (54.0 pp) × 8.22 × 2.18
A: 2 single 76-mm 62-cal. OTO Melara Compact; 2 single 12.7-mm mg
Electronics:
Radar: 2 Furuno 1421 nav.
E/O: 2 Matra Défense Naja optical gun f.c.
M: 2 SACM-Wärtsilä UD30V16 diesels; 2 props; 5,900 bhp
Range: 2,500/16 **Crew:** 39 tot. + 7 passengers

Remarks: Ordered 1979. No longer carries pennant P 773. Was towed to Raidco Marine, Lorient, France, late in 2001 for a major overhaul and modernization that was completed during 1-03; diesel engines were replaced, an engine exhaust stack was fitted, and the 20-mm guns were replaced by 12.7-mm mountings.

♦ **2 PR-48 class** Bldr: SFCN, Villeneuve-la-Garenne

	Laid down	L	In serv.
POPENGUINE	12-73	22-3-74	10-8-74
PODOR	12-75	20-7-76	13-7-77

Popenguine—with two sisters and the *Njambuur* in the background
Bernard Prézelin, 2-01

PATROL CRAFT [PC] *(continued)*

D: 250 tons (fl) **S:** 23 kts **Dim:** 47.5 (45.5 pp) × 7.1 × 2.5
A: 1 single 40-mm 70-cal. Bofors AA; *Podor* only: 1 single 20-mm 90-cal. GIAT F2 AA; 2 single 12.7-mm mg
Electronics: Radar: 1 Furuno 1421 nav.
M: 2 SACM-Wärtsilä UD30V12 diesels; 2 props; 4,350 bhp
Range: 2,000/16 **Crew:** 3 officers, 22 enlisted

Remarks: Steel construction. Both were re-engined and had received a stack by 2004. *Podor's* aft 40-mm Bofors gun aft was replaced by a single 20-mm AA. Sister *Saint Louis* had been retired from service by 2004 and is now used for spare parts.

PATROL BOATS [PB]

♦ 2 French Elorn (RPB 20) class
Bldr: CNB-Bénéteau, L'Herbaudière, Noirmoutier

	L	In serv.
Enseigne de Vaisseau Alphonse Faye	5-7-04	2004
Baye Sogui	2005	5-05

D: 40 tons (fl) **S:** 25 kts **Dim:** 20.00 (17.25 pp) × 5.39 × 1.45
A: 1 7.62-mm mg **Electronics:** Radar: 1 Furuno . . . nav.
M: 2 MAN V12 diesels; 2 props; 2,000 bhp
Range: 500/15 **Crew:** 8 tot.

Remarks: Same design as the French *Elorne*-class patrol boats. One firefighting monitor is fitted, and a 4.7-m rigid-inflatable rescue boat is stowed on a launch-and-recover ramp at the stern. The option for a third unit of the class may be exercised in the future. Expected to remain in service through at least 2025.

♦ 2 U.S. 51-ft. class
Bldr: Peterson Bldrs., Sturgeon Bay, Wis.

	In serv.
Matelot Alioure Samb	28-10-93
Matelot Oumar Ndoye	4-11-93

Matelot Alioure Samb French Navy, 6-97

D: 22 tons (24 fl) **S:** 24 kts **Dim:** 15.54 × 4.47 × 1.30
A: 1 twin 12.7-mm M2 mg; 2 single 7.62-mm mg
Electronics: Radar: 1 Furuno . . . nav.
M: 2 G.M. Detroit Diesel 6V-92TA diesels; 2 props; 900 bhp **Electric:** 15 kw tot.
Range: 500/20 kts **Fuel:** 800 U.S. gallons **Crew:** 6 tot.

Remarks: Are from among a group of five ordered 25-9-92 by the U.S. Navy for transfer to African countries. Cost $925,000 each. Aluminum construction. Carry a 4.27-m rigid inflatable inspection craft (with 50 bhp outboard motor) on the stern.

♦ 1 Interceptor class
Bldr: Turbec Ltd., St. Catharines, Canada

Sénégal 2

Sénégal 2 Bernard Prézelin, 2-01

D: 52 tons (61.7 fl) **S:** 32 kts **Dim:** 26.5 × 5.81 × 1.60
A: 1 20-mm 90-cal. GIAT F-2 AA **Electronics:** Radar: 1/JRC 3610 nav.
M: 2 diesels; 2 props; 2,700 bhp **Crew:** . . .

Remarks: In service 2-79. Used for fisheries protection patrol. Sisters *Siné Saloum* and *Casamance 2* were retired during 2003.

♦ 4 Tender One–class rigid inflatable boats
Bldr: Raidco Marine, Lorient (In serv. 2005)

P 16 Ibra Faye	P 18 El Hadji Mbor Diagne
P 17 Ousmane Diop Coumba Pathe	P 19 Alieu Condou N'doye

D: 8 tons (9.5 fl) **S:** 29 kts (27 without waterjets) **Dim:** 11.6 × 3.7 × 0.75
A: . . . **Electronics:** Radar: 1 Furuno nav.
M: 2 Cummins diesels; 2 waterjets (2 props in P 18 & P 19); 630 bhp
Range: 250/27 **Crew:** 4

Remarks: GRP Shell construction. P 16 and P 17 are slightly faster and have waterjets while P 18 and 19 are fitted with props.

AMPHIBIOUS WARFARE CRAFT

♦ 1 French EDIC 700-class tank landing craft [LCU]
Bldr: SFCN, Villeneuve-la-Garenne

	Laid down	L	In serv.
Karabene	23-4-85	6-3-86	23-6-86

Karabene Paolo Marsan Collection, 1-05

D: 410 tons light (730 fl) **S:** 12 kts **Dim:** 59.00 (52.90 pp) × 11.90 × 1.69 (max.)
A: 2 single 20-mm 90-cal. GIAT F-2 AA; 1 81-mm mortar
Electronics: Radar: 1 Furuno RDP 118 nav.
M: 2 UNI UD30.V12 (SACM-MGO 175 V12 ASH) diesels; 2 props; 1,400 bhp (1,040 sust.)
Range: 1,800/8 **Crew:** 18 tot.

Remarks: Ordered 3-6-85 and arrived during 8-86. Cargo: 340 tons, carried in 28.50 × 8.0-m vehicle well: eleven trucks or five light tanks.

♦ 1 French EDIC-class tank landing craft [LCU]
Bldr: SFCN, Villeneuve-la-Garenne (L: 30-3-67)

Faleme-II (ex-*Javeline,* L 9070)

Faleme-II Bernard Prézelin, 2-01

D: 280 tons light (670 fl) **S:** 8 kts loaded
Dim: 59.00 × 11.95 × 1.30 (1.62 max. fl)
A: 2 single 20-mm 70-cal. Oerlikon AA **Electronics:** Radar: 1 Decca 1229 nav.
M: 2 SACM-MGO 175 V12 ASH diesels; 2 props; 1,040 bhp
Range: 1,800/8 **Crew:** 5 petty officers, 12 ratings (in French service)

Remarks: Stricken from French Navy in 1998 and transferred to Senegal on 12-1-00. EDIC = *Engins de Débarquement pour Infantrie et Chars.* Can carry 11 trucks or 5 armored personnel carriers.

♦ 1 ex-French LCM (8)–class landing craft [LCM]
Bldr: CMN, Cherbourg, France

. . . (ex-CTM 5)

Ex-CTM 5 Bernard Prézelin, 2-01

AMPHIBIOUS WARFARE CRAFT *(continued)*

D: 56 tons light (150 fl) **S:** 9.5 kts **Dim:** 23.80 × 6.35 × 1.25
A: 2 single 12.7-mm mg
Electronics: Radar: 1 . . . nav. **M:** 2 Poyaud 520 V8 diesels; 2 props; 480 bhp
Range: 380/8 **Fuel:** 3.4 tons **Endurance:** 48 hours at half power
Crew: 6 tot.

Remarks: Transferred 5-99 from the French Navy. Cargo capacity: 90 tons. The machineguns are usually not mounted.

SERVICE CRAFT

♦ 1 small oceanographic research ship [YAG]
Bldr: . . ., Japan (In serv. 2001)

ITAF DEME

Itaf Deme Bernard Prézelin, 2-01

D: 318 tons (fl) **S:** 12 kts **Dim:** 38 × 8.03 × 3.4
Electronics: 2 . . . Furuno nav.
M: 1 Yanmar diesel; 1 CP prop; 1,100 bhp **Crew:** 18 tot.

Remarks: Ordered during 2000 as a replacement for oceanographic research ship *Louis Sauger*. A modified purse-seiner used mainly for fisheries research. Naval-crewed.

♦ 1 French Oiseau-class small harbor tug [YTL]

CHEIK OUMAR FALL (ex-*Olivier,* Y 719)

Cheik Oumar Fall Bernard Prézelin, 2-01

D: 56 tons **S:** 9 kts **Dim:** 18.4 × 5.7 × 2.5
M: 1 Poyaud diesel; 1 prop; 250 shp
Range: 1,700/9 **Crew:** 4 tot.

Remarks: On loan from the French Navy; arrived 1990. Bollard pull: 3.5 tons. Given new name in 2000. Sister *Ibis* has been discarded, and *Aigrette,* on loan since 1990, was stricken in 1998.

SERBIA & MONTENEGRO

The State of Serbia & Montenegro

Note: On 21-5-06, Montenegro voted to secede from Serbia and form a separate nation now known as the Republic of Montenegro. How this will impact the disposition of naval forces remains to be seen. Data listed here represents those assets in service immediately prior to the June 2006 dissolution of the united State of Serbia and Montenegro.

Personnel: Approx. 2,900 total, plus 900 marines

Bases: Tivat is the only actual naval base remaining, though some vessels remain stationed at Bar. Plans to construct a new base at Valdamos have been canceled. All aircraft are based at Podgorica, Montenegro. Repair facilities are inadequate.

Organization: The Fleet was reorganized 1-01 into the Rocket Ships Flotilla (frigates and missile craft), Coastal Flotilla, and Submarine Flotilla.

Naval Aviation: Helicopters: One squadron of 2 Ka-27PL Helix-A ASW and up to 20 Mi-8 Hip utility. Fixed wing: two DHC-2 Beaver utility, four CL-215 firefighting/SAR. The remaining Ka-25 Hormone helicopters were reported discarded as of 5-00, and the remaining Mi-14PL Haze ASW helicopters were destroyed by NATO bombing at Podgorica in 1999.

Coast Defense: Several mobile SSC-3 batteries are believed still to be operational. Also employed for coast defense are mobile 88-mm and fixed 130-mm artillery.

Armament Systems: Ships and craft are primarily equipped with imported weapon and sensor systems, but the M-71 single and M-75 quadruple 20-mm AA mountings were license-produced in the former Yugoslavia as copies of Hispano-Suiza weapons. The former Yugoslavia also has made some of its own mines.

ATTACK SUBMARINES [SS]

♦ 1 Sava class
Bldr: Brodosplit, Split, Croatia

	Laid down	L	In serv.
P 831 SAVA	1977	1982	1982

Sava (P 831) *Ships of the World,* 1988

D: 770 tons surf./964 tons sub. **S:** 10 kts surf./16 kts sub. **Dim:** 55.8 × 7.2 × 5.5
A: 6 bow 533-mm TT (10 total Soviet Type 53 or Swedish TP-61 wire-guided torpedoes or 20 mines)
Electronics:
Radar: 1 Flag (Snoop Plate) search—EW: Stop Light intercept (2-18 gHz)
Sonar: STN-Atlas Elektronik PRS-3 active/passive suite (see Remarks)
M: 2 Sulzer diesels (1,600 bhp each), 2 generators (1,000 kw each), 1 electric motor; 1 5-bladed prop; 1,560 shp
Endurance: 28 days **Crew:** 35 tot.

Remarks: P = *Podmornica* (submarine). Carries a mixture of Soviet and Western European equipment. Attached to the 88th Brigade. Had been laid up for lack of batteries and spare parts around 1993 but was reportedly again operational by 3-04. Plans to refit the submarine have been canceled due to lack of funds. Sister *Drava* (832) was retired during 2003.
Hull systems: Pressure hull steel is of 56 kg/cm^2 strength. Maximum diving depth: 300 meters. Outer hull is said to have been fabricated of glass-reinforced plastic.
Combat systems: Sonar suite also reported to be Soviet-supplied MG-15 Herkules active and MG-10 Feniks-M passive array.

MIDGET SUBMARINES [SSM]

♦ 3 Una (M-100D) class (all nonoperational)
Bldr: Brodosplit, Split, Croatia

	In serv.
913 ZETA	1985
915 KUPA	1988
916 VRBAS (ex-*Vardar*)	1989

Una (M-100D)-class midget submarine—laid up, in land storage
E. Sieche via Werner Globka, 5-04

MIDGET SUBMARINES [SSM] *(continued)*

D: 76 tons surf./88 tons sub. **S:** 8.0 kts surf./11.0 kts sub.
Dim: 18.8 (16.5 wl) × 3.0 × 2.5
A: 6 mines or 4 R1 swimmer-delivery vehicles, externally carried
M: Electric only: two 18-kw motors; 1 5-bladed prop
Electronics:
Radar: None
Sonar: STN-Atlas Elektronik PP-10 active, PSU 1-2 passive
Range: 250/3 (sub.) **Crew:** 4 crew + 6 swimmers

Remarks: Typed *Diverzantska Podmornica.* Sister *Soca* (914) was captured by Croatia in 1991 and put into service in 9-93; she was later lengthened and relaunched in 1996. *Tisa* (911) and *Una* (912) have been discarded. 913, 915, and 916 were nonoperational as of 2004, though one or more may have been reactivated.
Hull systems: Have no on-board generators; power is supplied by two shore-charged 128-cell, 1,450 amp./hr (5-hour rate) batteries. Working depth is 105 m, with test depth at 120 m and estimated collapse depth of 182 m. Theoretically capable of remaining submerged for 96 hours. The R1 swimmer-delivery vehicles each weigh 145 kg, are 3.7 m long by 0.52 m diameter, and have a range of 12 n.m. at 3 kts.

FRIGATES [FF]

♦ 2 Kotor class
Bldr: Tito SY, Kraljevica, Croatia

	L	In serv.
VPB 33 Kotor	21-5-85	1-87
VPB 34 Novi Sad (ex-*Pula*)	18-12-86	11-88

Novi Sad (VPB 34) ANBw/FAFIO, 3-99

Novi Sad (VPB 34) Frane Moric, via Dr. Zvonimir Freivogel, 5-92

D: 1,492 tons (1,850 fl) **S:** 27 kts
Dim: 96.70 (91.80 wl) × 11.70 × 3.55 (5.80 over sonar)
A: 4 P-20/21 Rubezh (SS-N-2C Styx) SSM; 1 2-round Osa-M (SA-N-4) SAM syst. (20 Gecko missiles); 1 twin 76.2-mm 59-cal. AK-726 DP; 2 4-round Fasta-4M SAM syst. (Grail missiles); twin 30-mm 65-cal. AK-230 AA; 2 single 20-mm 90-cal. M 71 AA; 2 12-round RBU-6000 SW RL
Electronics:
Radar: 1 Vaygach (Palm Frond) nav.; 1 MR-302 Rubka (Strut Curve) surf./air-search; 1 PZ-301 (Pop Group) SAM f.c.; 1 CelsiusTech 9LV200 Mk 1 76.2-mm gun f.c.; 1 MR-104 Rys' Drum Tilt) 30-mm gun f.c.
Sonar: MG-322T hull-mounted MF search, HF attack
EW: 2 intercept arrays, VHFD/F, 2 18-round Wallop Barricade decoy RL
M: CODAG: 2 SEMT-Pielstick 12 PA6V280 diesels (4,800 bhp each), 1 Soviet gas turbine 19,000 shp); 3 props (CP outboard); 28,600 shp
Electric: 1,350 kw tot. **Crew:** Approx. 90 tot.

Remarks: VPB—*Veliki Patrolni Brod* (Large Patrol Ship). VPB 33 was damaged by Croatian shore batteries fall 1991 but appeared to be intact and in service as of 5-99. Design is Yugoslavian and is not a modification of the somewhat similar Koni class, which has an entirely different hull form and layout. The name *Novi Sad* has also been attributed to a Yugoslav minesweeper.
Hull systems: The main-propulsion diesels were ordered in 6-80 (two to be built under license), and the first was delivered 31-3-81; the propulsion concept (but not layout) duplicates the arrangement in the Koni class. Two sets of Italian-made ILAS-3 ASW torpedo tubes, to have been mounted on the fantail, were not installed.

Disposal note: Koni-class frigate *Beograd* (VPB 31, ex-*Split,* ex-Soviet *Sokol*) was stricken during 2002 along with sister *Podgorica* (VPB 32, ex-*Koper,* ex-Soviet SKR-481), which had been out of service since 1997.

GUIDED-MISSILE PATROL CRAFT [PTG]

♦ 4 Rade Končar (Type 240) class (1 in *reserve*)
Bldr: Tito SY, Kraljevica, Croatia

	L	In serv.
RT 401	15-10-76	4-77
RT 404	9-11-78	11-79
RT 405	26-4-79	8-79
RT 406	23-11-79	11-80

RT 404 E. Sieche via Werner Globka, 5-04

D: 242 tons (fl) **S:** 39 kts (37 sust.) **Dim:** 45.00 × 8.00 × 1.80 (2.50 props)
A: 2 P-20/21 Rubezh (SS-N-2B Styx) SSM; 2 single (RT 401:1) 57-mm 70-cal. Bofors SAK 57 Mk 1 DP; RT 401 only: 1 30-mm AK-630 gatling AA
Electronics:
Radar: 1 Decca 1226 nav.; 1 CelsiusTech 9LV200 Mk II target detection/f.c.
EW: 2 18-round Wallop Barricade decoy RL
M: CODAG: 2 Rolls-Royce Proteus gas turbines (4,500 shp each); 2 MTU 20V538 TB92 diesels (3,600 bhp each); 4 CP props; 16,200 hp max.
Electric: 300 kVA tot. **Range:** 880/23; 1,650/15 **Endurance:** 7 days
Crew: 5 officers, 10 petty officers, 15 enlisted

Remarks: RT = *Raketna Topovnjaca.* Of Yugoslav design, using Swedish fire control and guns and Soviet missiles. The names may have been changed, as they commemorate naval figures of Croatian, Bosnian, and Albanian ethnic origin. Names had been deleted by 3-04.
Hull systems: Steel hull, aluminum superstructure. Have NBC warfare protection.
Combat systems: In RT 401 and RT 402 (ex-*Vlado Četkovič,* now *Šibenik* under Croation control), the after 57-mm mount was removed and replaced with a Soviet-supplied 30-mm gatling gun to improve antimissile defenses; the gatling gun, however, is controlled only by a Kolonka-II ringsight director mounted in a cupola just abaft the mast.
Disposals: *Ramiz Sadiku* (RT 403) was stricken during 2002.

Disposal notes: Osa-I (Project 205) guided missile patrol boats *Steven Filipovič-Seljo* (RČ 304), *Zikica Jovanovic Spanac* (RČ 305, ex-*Velimir Skorpik*), *Nikola Martinovič* (RČ 306), and *Josip Mazar Sosa* (RČ 307) were stricken in 2002 and offered for sale; sisters *Mitar Acev* (RČ 301) and *Zihaca Jovanovic-Spanac* (RČ 310) came under Croatian control. *Karlo Rojc* (RČ 308) was heavily damaged and has not been repaired.

PATROL CRAFT [PC]

♦ 4 Mirna (Type 140) class
Bldr: Tito SY, Kraljevica, Croatia (In serv. 1981–82)

	L		L
PČ 174 (ex-*Učka*)	5-3-82	PČ 178 Kosmaju	9-9-83
PČ 175 Grmec	23-7-82	PČ 179 Zelengora	15-12-83

Kosmaju (PČ 178)—with quadruple 20-mm AA mount aft
Feda Klaric, via Dr. Zvonimir Freivogel, 10-91

D: 125.3 tons (142.3 fl) **S:** 30 kts
Dim: 32.00 (29.25 pp × 6.68 × 1.76 (2.41 max.)
A: 1 40-mm 70-cal. Bofors L70 AA; 1 4-round Fasta-4M (SA-N-5) SAM syst. (12 missiles); 1 20-mm 90-cal. M-71 AA; 8 Type MDB-MT3 d.c.

PATROL CRAFT [PC] *(continued)*

Electronics:
Radar: 1 Decca 1216C nav.
Sonar: Simrad 5Q3D/SF hull-mounted HF
M: 2 SEMT-Pielstick 12 PA4 200GDS diesels; 2 props; 6,000 bhp electric motors for low speeds (6 kts)
Range: 400/20 **Fuel:** 16.2 tons **Crew:** 3 officers, 4 petty officers, 12 enlisted

Remarks: PČ = *Patrolni Čamac.* Sisters *Koprivnik,* (PČ 171), *Mukos* (PČ 176), *Cer* (PČ 180), and *Kozolo* (or *Durmitor,* PČ 181) are in Croatian hands, while PČ 173 (name uncertain) has been cannibalized and discarded; ex-*Pohorje* (PČ 172) and *Fruska-Gora* (PČ 177) were reported inoperable and have probably been discarded.
Hull systems: The first ten propulsion diesels were ordered in 1979, for license production in Yugoslavia. Endurance at 20 kts can be increased to 530 n.m. in emergencies using void tankage. Peacetime endurance is four days; wartime is eight days.
Combat systems: Have two 4-rail, S-2M, 128-mm M66 illumination rocket launchers amidships. There are also four chaff or illumination rocket rails on the sides of the 40-mm AA. The aftermost gunmount in some was originally a quadruple 20-mm M-75 mounting, and some may still have it vice the single mount listed.

PATROL BOATS [PB]

♦ 6 Type 20 riverine
Bldr: . . ., Beograd (In serv. 1980–84)

PČ 211 through PČ 216

PČ 216 *Front*, via Dr. Zvonimir Freivogel

D: 52 tons (56 fl) **S:** 16 kts **Dim:** 21.27 (20.06 wl) × 7.50 × 1.20
A: 2 single 20-mm 90-cal. M-71 AA; mines **Electronics:** Radar: 1 Decca 110 nav.
M: 2 diesels; 2 props; 1,156 bhp **Range:** 200/15 **Crew:** 11 tot.

Remarks: Steel hull, glass-reinforced plastic superstructure. All employed by the River Flotilla on the Danube and tributaries. Can carry four R-1 or six KMD-2-500 mines.

♦ 1 Botica-class (Type 16) riverine
Bldr: . . ., Tivat (In serv. 1970)

PČ 302

PČ 302 E. Sieche via Werner Globka, 5-04

D: 22.96 tons (24.07 fl) **S:** 15.1 kts
Dim: 17.04 × 3.60 × 0.85 mean hull (1.60 max.)
A: 1 20-mm 90-cal. M-71 AA; 7 single 7.62-mm mg
Electronics: Radar: 1 Decca 101 nav.
M: 2 diesels; 2 props; 464 bhp **Range:** 1,460/11.6
Crew: 7 crew + 30 troops or combat swimmers

Remarks: *Botica* is the NATO class nickname. Intended for patrol, troop transport, and logistic support duties, with up to 3 tons of cargo. All had been employed on lakes and rivers in Macedonia. PČ 302 was sighted under way during 2004.

Disposal note: Sister PČ 305 was transferred to Tanzania, and PČ 301 was stricken 1992–93; PČ 303 and PČ 304 were stricken during 1995. All Type 15 riverine and lake patrol craft had been retired by 2005.

♦ 1 ex-U.S. Rhine River patrol boat
Bldr: Theodor Hitzler Werft, Regensburg, Germany (In serv. 1956)

RPČ 111

D: 27.5 tons (29 fl) **S:** 17.8 kts **Dim:** 26.00 (24.10 pp) × 4.13 (3.90 wl) × 0.93
A: 2 single 20-mm 90-cal. M-71 AA **M:** 2 MWM diesels; 2 props; 440 bhp
Range: 870/14.6 **Crew:** 6 tot.

Remarks: Built for U.S. Navy's Rhine River Patrol and transferred to Yugoslavia during late 1950s. One sister remains in service in the Belgian Navy. Probably does not have radar.

MINE WARFARE SHIPS

♦ 2 French Sirius-class coastal minesweepers/minehunters [MHC] (1 *nonoperational*)
Bldrs: A. Normand, Le Havre, France

	In serv.
M 152 Podgora (ex-*Smeli*, ex-MSC 230)	9-57
M 153 Blitvenica (ex-*Slobodni*, ex-MSC 231)	9-57

Blitvenica (M 153) H&L Van Ginderen, 10-99

D: 400 tons (440 fl) **S:** 15 kts (sweeping: 11.5) **Dim:** 46.4 (42.7 pp) × 8.55 × 2.5
A: 1 twin 20-mm 70-cal. Oerlikon Mk 24 AA
Electronics:
Radar: 1 DRBN-30 nav.
Sonar: Thales TSM 2022 minehunting
M: 2 SEMT-Pielstick 16 PA1-175 diesels; 2 props; 2,000 bhp **Electric:** 375 kw tot.
Range: 3,000/10 **Fuel:** 48 tons **Crew:** 40 tot.

Remarks: M = *Minolovac.* Built with U.S. Offshore Procurement funds. Sister *Vukov Klanac* (M 151, ex-*Hrabri,* ex-U.S. MSC 229) was extensively damaged 9-91, captured by Croatia, and later stricken. *Gradac* (M 161, ex-*Snazhi*) was stricken and scrapped during 1993, and M 153 may be in reserve or stricken. Have wooden-planked hulls with metal framing.
Combat systems: Have French PAP-104 remote-controlled minehunting/disposal submersibles, and Decca Hifix precision navigation systems. New minehunting sonars replaced Plessey Type 193M on both after 1988.

♦ 7 Nestin-class (Type 50) river minesweepers [MSB]
Bldr: Brodotehnika, Belgrade

	L		L
RML 331 Nestin	20-12-75	335 Vucedol	1979
RML 332 Motajica	18-12-76	336 Djerdap	1980
RML 333 Belegis	1-77	341 Novi Sad	8-6-96
RML 334 Bosut	1978		

D: 57.31 tons light, 68 tons std. (79.6 fl) **S:** 14 kts (11.9 sust.)
Dim: 27.00 × 6.50 × 1.08 (1.18 max.)
A: 1 quadruple 20-mm 90-cal. M-75 AA; 2 single 20-mm 90-cal. M-71 AA; 1 4-round MTU-4 SAM syst. (Strela-2M missiles); 24 R-1 moored or 18 AIM-M-82 acoustic bottom mines or 30 mine-destruction charges
Electronics:
Radar: 1 Decca RM 1216R nav. (RML 341: RR 205 DMT nav.)
Sonar: PP-10M high-frequency hull-mounted
M: 2 Torpedo B.539RM/22 diesels; 2 props; 512 bhp **Range:** 1,720/11.9
Fuel: 10.7 tons **Endurance:** 15 days **Crew:** 17 tot.

Remarks: RML = *Recni Minolovac.* Used on the Danube. RML 341 (Project S-25N) is the first warship built for the Federal Yugoslav Navy. The name *Novi Sad* duplicates that of one of the Kotor-class frigates. Three sisters were built for Iraq and six for Hungary. Sister *Panonsko More* (RML 337) was stricken in 1997.
Hull systems: Aluminum alloy construction. Navigation equipment includes Anschutz-12 gyrocompass and STN-Atlas 240 (RML 341: Ultrasound D-15) echo sounder. Can make 9.7 kts against the average Danube current or 14 kts downstream. Turning radius is 60 meters. RML 341 has reduced magnetic signature, increased hull strength, improved accommodations, air-conditioning, and the addition of a smoke-screen generator. Can carry 100 troops for short distances.
Combat systems: Sweep gear includes type PEAM-1A towed magnetic solenoid and acoustic sweep pontoon, Type AEL-1 explosive sweep (using 15-charge line charges), and Types MDL-1 or MDL-2R mechanical sweeps. Two illumination chaff rocket launchers are fitted. Armament listed is that mounted on RML 341, but the others probably have been brought up to the same standard. Alternate mine loads include 24 P-1 contact or 18 AIM-M.82 acoustic, or 24 Rokan GM-100 magnetic, or 36-48 PLRM-1A free-floating contact/timed. The PEAM-1A towed mine-countermeasures pontoon is 18.1 meters long by 1.22 m beam and displaces 16.47 metric tons; it incorporates an acoustic generator in the bow and magnetic coils amidships, the latter energized by a 16 kw diesel generator, and the device is towed some 220 meters abaft the minecraft.

AMPHIBIOUS WARFARE SHIPS

♦ 1 Silba-class tank landing craft/minelayer [LSM] (In reserve)
Bldr: Brodosplit, Split, Croatia (In serv. 1990)

DBM 241 Silba

D: 700 tons (880 fl) **S:** 12 kts **Dim:** 49.70 (43.90 pp) × 10.20 × 2.60 max.
A: 2 twin 30-mm 65-cal. AK-230 AA; 1 quadruple 20-mm 90-cal. M-75 AA; up to 94 Type SAG-1 mines
Electronics: Radar: 1 Decca 1290A nav.
M: 2 Burmeister & Wain Alpha 10V23L-VO diesels; 2 CP props; 3,100 bhp
Range: 1,200/12 **Crew:** 3 officers, 30 enlisted + up to 300 troops

AMPHIBIOUS WARFARE SHIPS *(continued)*

Silba (DBM 241)—when active ANBw/FAFIO, via Siegfried Breyer, 1998

Remarks: DBM 241 was laid up at Tivat as of 10-98. Two sisters serve in the Croatian Navy.
Hull systems: Has bow and stern ramps, with continuous covered vehicle deck also used for portable minerails. Cargo capacity: 460 tons or four medium tanks or up to seven armored personnel carriers.
Combat systems: Has two 128-mm rocket flare launchers. The 30-mm gunmounts are mounted port and starboard, just abaft the bridge, while the 20-mm mount is located near the stern.

♦ 6 DJČ 621–class (Type 22) landing craft [LCM]
Bldr: Gleben SY, Vela Luka, Korčula (In serv. 1983–85)

DJČ 621 DJČ 625 DJČ 628 DJČ 630 DJČ 631 DJČ 632

DJČ 621–class DJČ 627—since lost Yugoslav Navy, 1989

D: 48 tons (fl) **S:** 30 kts **Dim:** 22.30 × 4.84 × 1.07 (1.58 props)
A: 2 single 20-mm 90-cal. M-71 AA; 1 30-mm PB-30 grenade launcher
Electronics: Radar: 1 Decca 101 nav. **M:** 2 MTU diesels; 2 waterjets; 1,740 bhp
Range: 320/22 **Crew:** 8 tot. + 40 troops

Remarks: DJČ = *Desantni Jurisni Čamac.* All are assigned to the riverine flotilla. One sister is in Croatian Navy, one in Croatian police service, and three others are used by Croatia as civilian fireboats. Additional power permits the hull to plane, greatly increasing speed over the Type 21 design. Are of glass-reinforced-plastic construction with a bow ramp. Can carry vehicles totaling 15 tons in 32-m^2 cargo area. The waterjet propulsion system is said to be less than successful, and it is likely that some or all of these craft have been laid up or discarded.

♦ 3 DJČ 613–class (Type 21) vehicle/personnel landing craft [LCM]
Bldr: Gleben SY, Vela Luka, Korčula (In serv. 1978)

DJČ 614 DJČ 616 DJČ 618

D: 32 tons (38 fl) **S:** 25 kts **Dim:** 21.30 × 4.84 × 1.07 (1.58 props)
A: 1 20-mm 90-cal. M-71 AA; 1 30-mm PB-30 grenade launcher
Electronics: Radar: 1 Decca 101 nav.
M: 2 MTU 12V331 TC81 diesels; 2 props; 2,500 bhp
Range: 320/22 **Crew:** 7 tot. + 40 troops

Remarks: DJČ = *Desantni Jurisni Čamac.* Seven others damaged or sunk during combat in 1991–92. Glass-reinforced-plastic construction. Design is very similar to the earlier Type 11, but the propulsion plant is more powerful. Bow ramp. Can carry vehicles totaling 6 tons in 32-m^2 cargo area. Sister DJČ 617 was retired in 2004.

♦ 3 DJČ 601–class (Type 11) landing craft [LCM]
Bldr: Gleben SY, Vela Luka, Korčula (In serv. 1976–77)

DJČ 604 DJČ 605 DJČ 608

D: 32 tons (38 fl) **S:** 23.5 kts (21 sust.) **Dim:** 21.30 × 4.84 × 1.07 (1.58 props)
A: 1 20-mm 90-cal. M-71 AA; 1 30-mm PB-30 grenade launcher
Electronics: Radar: 1 Decca 101 nav.
M: 1 MTU 12V331 TC81 diesel; 1 prop; 1,450 bhp
Range: 320/22 **Crew:** 7 tot. + 40 troops

Remarks: DJČ = *Desantni Jurisni Čamac.* Glass-reinforced-plastic construction. Sister DJČ 603 and two others were captured by Croatia and a number of others were sunk.

♦ 2 DČ 101–class personnel landing craft [LCP]
Bldr: Vela Luca, Korčula (In serv. 1982)

DČ 101 DČ 102

D: 5.5 tons light (11 fl) **S:** 25 kts (20 sust.)
Dim: 11.30 × 3.10 × 0.32 **A:** 1 7.62-mm mg
Electronics: Radar: 1 Decca 101 nav.
M: 2 diesels; 2 waterjets *or* 2 outdrives; 260 bhp
Range: 100/15 **Crew:** 2 tot.

Remarks: DČ = *Desantni Čamac.* For riverine use. Can carry up to 30 troops.

♦ 2 BDČ 91–class personnel landing craft [LCP]
Bldr: . . ., U.K. (In serv. 1976)

BDČ 91 BDČ 92

D: 2.5 tons (2.8 fl) **S:** 37.8 kts **Dim:** 7.37 × 3.00 × 0.75
M: 3 Mercedes Benz gasoline engines; 3 props; 221 bhp
Range: 108/27 kts **Crew:** 3 tot.

Remarks: For transporting special forces personnel on the river system. GRP construction.

AUXILIARIES

Disposal note: City-class command ship and smallcraft tender *Vis* (PB 25) was stricken around 2001 and sold to a private buyer. Riverine command ship *Kozara* (RPB 30, ex-PB 30; ex-U.S. *Oregon;* ex-German *Kriemhild*) was reportedly stricken during 2000.

♦ 1 Lubin-class multipurpose cargo transport [AK]
Bldr: Brodosplit, Split, Croatia (In serv. mid-1980s)

PO 91 Lubin

Lubin (PO 91)—recently reactivated E. Sieche via Werner Globka, 5-04

D: 600 tons (882 fl, 1,000 max.) **S:** 16.2 kts (14.3 sust.)
Dim: 58.20 × 11.00 × 2.75 (mean)
A: 1 40-mm 60-cal. Bofors Mk 3 AA; 1 quadruple 20-mm 90-cal. M-75 AA; 2 shoulder-fired Strela-2M SAM launch positions
Electronics: Radar: 1 . . . nav. **M:** 2 diesels; 2 CP props; 3,480 bhp
Range: 1,500/14.3 **Endurance:** 10 days
Crew: 34 crew + 150 fully equipped troops, 6 vehicle drivers

Remarks: PO = *Pomocni Oruzar* (Ammunition Auxiliary). Reactivated in 2004 after more than a decade out of service. Intended to supply combatants with missiles, torpedoes, mines, and other ordnance, using two slewing cranes on upper deck. Sister *Ugor* (PO 92), laid up since 1991, was transferred to the Montenegrin government for commercial use or scrapping. *Kit* (PO 93) was retired in 2000.
Hull systems: Continuous cargo deck can accommodate up to six tanks; have a visor-type bow and extendable bow ramp, two electrohydraulic cranes. As ammunition transports, can carry up to 20 torpedoes or 40 sea mines. Have two S-2M, 128-mm M66 illumination rocket launchers.

SERVICE CRAFT

♦ 1 riverine degaussing craft [YDG]
Bldr: Brodotehnika, Belgrade (In serv. 1984)

RSRB 36 Sabac

D: 107.2 tons (115.8 fl) **S:** 11.9 kts **Dim:** 32.20 × 7.05 × 1.27
A: 2 single 20-mm M-71 AA; 1 4-round MTU-4 SAM syst. (Strela-2M missiles)
Electronics: Radar: 1 Decca 1216A nav. **M:** 2 diesels; 2 props; 790 bhp
Range: 716/10.8 **Crew:** 16 tot.

Remarks: Patrol boat–type hull, with superstructure set well aft. Acts as deperming tender for Danube River Flotilla craft.

♦ Up to 5 BRM 81–class diving tenders [YDT]
Bldr: Punat SY, Punat (In serv. 1978–84)

BRM 81 BRM 85 BRM 86 BRM 87 BRM 88

BRM 81 class Punat SY, via Dr. Zvonimir Freivogel, ca. 1978

D: 46 tons light (65 fl) **S:** 10.5 kts **Dim:** 22.10 (20.50 pp) × 5.66 × 1.90
A: 2 single 20-mm 90-cal. M-71 AA **Electronics:** Radar: 1 Decca 101 nav.
M: 2 diesels; 2 props; 320 bhp **Range:** 400/12 **Crew:** 8 tot.

SERVICE CRAFT *(continued)*

Remarks: Resemble the survey craft BH 11 and BH 12 and training craft BS 21 and BS 22, except that there is a low deckhouse forward of the pilothouse. Sister BRM 84 was lost to a mine on 25-9-91. The armament may have been reduced or removed.

♦ **2 inshore survey craft [YGS]**
Bldr: . . . SY, Yugoslavia (In serv. mid-1980s)

BH 11 (ex-BH 1) BH 12 (ex-BH 2)

D: 46 tons light (65 fl) **S:** 10.5 kts **Dim:** 22.10 (20.50 pp) × 5.66 × 1.90
Electronics: Radar: 1 Decca 101 nav. **M:** 2 diesels; 2 props; 320 bhp
Range: 400/12 **Crew:** 4 tot.

Remarks: Same basic design as PT 82–series transports. Carry six survey personnel in addition to listed crews.

Note: Also reported in use is the 4.5-ton survey launch CH 1.

♦ **1 Drina-class fuel lighters [YO]** (in reserve)
Bldr: Tito SY, Kraljevica (In serv. 1989)

PN 27 Sipa (L: 16-9-88)

Sipa (PN 27) ANBw/FAFIO, via Siegfried Breyer, 1998

D: Approx. 600 tons (fl) **S:** . . . kts **Dim:** . . . × . . . × . . .
A: 1 quadruple 20-mm M-75 AA; 2 single 20-mm M-71 AA
Electronics: Radar: 1 . . . nav.
M: 1 . . . diesel; 1 prop; . . . bhp

Remarks: PN = *Pomocni Nafta* (Oil Fuel Auxiliary). Drina is the NATO nickname. Names mean “Cuttlefish.” Based at Tivat. *Lignja* (PN 26) was retired during 2004.

♦ **2 PR 37–class coastal tugs [YTM]**
Bldr: Split SY, Croatia (In serv. 1950s)

PR 37 Zubatac PR 38 . . .

D: 550 tons (fl) **S:** 11 kts **Dim:** 32.0 × 8.0 × 5.0 **M:** 2 diesels; 2 props; . . . bhp
Crew: 18 tot.

Remarks: PR = *Pomorski Remorker* (Auxiliary Tug). Originally reciprocating steam-propelled; re-engined with diesels. Sister *Dupin* (PR 36) was captured by Croatia but was not placed in service.

♦ **2 LR 67–class harbor tugs [YTM]**
Bldr: Split SY, Croatia (In serv. 1960s)

LR 72 LR 77

D: 130 tons (fl) **S:** 13 kts **Dim:** 21.4 × 4.9 ×2.1
A: 1 single 20-mm 90-cal. M 71 AA **M:** 1 diesels; 1 prop; . . . bhp **Range:** 1,400/7

Remarks: LR = *Lucki Remorker* (Harbor Tug).

♦ **2 training craft [YXT]** (In serv. mid-1980s)

BS 21 BS 22

D: 46 tons light (65 fl) **S:** 10.5 kts **Dim:** 22.10 (20.50 pp) × 5.66 × 1.90
Electronics: Radar: 1 Decca 101 nav. **M:** 2 diesels; 2 props; 320 bhp
Range: 400/12 **Crew:** 2 officers, 18 cadets

Remarks: Same basic design as BRM 81–series diving tenders and the survey craft BH 11 and BH 12.

♦ **1 sail-training ship [YTS]**
Bldr: Blohm Voss, Hamburg

	L	In serv.
Jadran (ex-*Marco Polo*)	25-6-31	1932

Sail training craft Jadran Michael Winter, 6-05

D: 720 tons (800 fl) **S:** 8 kts **Dim:** 60.00 (50 pp) × 8.80 × 4.20
A: 2 single 47-mm saluting guns **Electronics:** Radar: 2 Decca . . . nav.
M: 2 . . . diesels; 1 prop; 750 bhp—sail area: 933 m2
Range: 5,450/7.5 (under power) **Crew:** 12 officers, 150 enlisted . . . cadets

Remarks: Was again operational by 2002, following several years out of service.

SEYCHELLES

Republic of Seychelles

SEYCHELLES COAST GUARD

Personnel: Approximately 220 tot., including 20 in Air Wing and 80 marines

Base: Port Victoria, Mahé.

Maritime Aviation: 1 Britten-Norman BN-42 B/T Maritime Defender.

Note: The Seychelles People’s Navy and People’s Air Force were combined into a single Coast Guard service during 12-92.

PATROL CRAFT [WPC]

♦ **1 Modified SDB Mk 3 class**
Bldr: Garden Reach SB & Eng., Calcutta

	L	In serv.
. . . Topaz (ex-*Tarmugli*, T 64)	6-99	28-9-00

D: 260 tons (fl) **S:** 35 kts **Dim:** 46.0 × 7.5 × 3.9
A: 1 single 30-mm Medak AA
Electronics: Radar: 1 Bharat 1245 nav.
M: 3 MTU 16V 396 TB94 diesels; 2 props; 10,500 bhp
Range: 2,000/12 **Crew:** 35 tot.

Remarks: Transferred from India 16-2-05. An enlarged version of the four built in the 1980s. Intended for coastal patrol, smuggling interdiction, fisheries protection, and policing duties.

♦ **1 FPB 42 class**
Bldr: C.N. Picchiotti, Viareggio, Italy (In serv. 10-1-83)

605 Andromache

Andromache (605) Stefan Karpinski, 2003

D: 240 tons (268 fl) **S:** 28 kts **Dim:** 41.80 × 8.00 × 2.50 (props; 1.70 hull)
A: 2 single 7.62-mm mg **Electronics:** Radar: 2 Furuno . . . nav.
M: 2 Paxman Valenta 16 RP200 CM diesels; 2 props; 6,800 bhp (5,700 sust.)
Range: 3,000/16 **Crew:** 3 officers, 19 enlisted

Remarks: Ordered 8-10-81. Also used as a personnel transport. Refitted 1985–86 in Italy. Planned second unit not ordered. The 20-mm Oerlikon AA mounting formerly on the bow has been removed.
Disposals: Russian-built Turya-class (Project 206ME) hydrofoil torpedoboat *Zoroaster* (606), in reserve since 1992, has been deleted here due to the unlikelihood of spares being obtainable to repair her; she remains afloat as a training hulk, with the 57-mm gunmount, fire-control radar, and torpedo tubes removed. The remaining Russian-donated Zhuk-class (Project 1400M) patrol boat, *Fortune* (604), had been retired by mid-2000.

PATROL BOAT [WPB]

♦ **1 Junion class**
Bldr:. . . (In serv. 2003)

602 Junion

PATROL BOAT [WPB] *(continued)*

D: 40 tons fl **S:** 20 kts **Dim:** 18.3 × 5.1 × 1.8
A: . . . **Electronics:** Radar: 1 Furuno . . . nav.
M: 2 . . . diesels; 2 props;
Range: . . . / . . . **Crew:** 5 tot.

Remarks: Delivered in 2003. No additional data available.

SERVICE CRAFT

♦ **5 ex-U.S. Coast Guard 44-ft Motor Life Boat–class lifeboats [WYH]** Bldr: U.S.C.G. Yard, Curtis Bay, Md. (In serv. 31-3-61 to 8-5-73)

Aries (ex-44 . . .) Libra (ex-44 . . .) Pisces (ex-44 . . .)
Taurus (ex-44 . . .) Virgo (ex-44 . . .)

Former U.S. Coast Guard lifeboat 44311—aboard USS *Anchorage* (LSD 36) for shipment to the Seychelles George R. Schneider, 7-00

D: 14.9 tons light (17.7 fl) **S:** 13 kts (11.8 sust.) **Dim:** 13.44 × 3.87 × 1.19
Electronics: Radar: 1 JRC . . . nav.
M: 2 G.M. Detroit Diesel 6V53 diesels; 2 props; 372 bhp
Range: 185/11.8; 200/11 **Fuel:** 1.2 tons **Crew:** 4 tot.

Remarks: Transferred 7-00. "Unsinkable" design. Can carry up to 21 rescued personnel. Are the former U.S. Coast Guard vessels 44305, 44311, 44336, 44347, and 44393.

Note: Also operated by the Coast Guard are the small presidential yacht *Gemini* and a sailing schooner with auxiliary propulsion, *Arc en Ciel,* which is used as a local logistics support craft. The 855-ton (full load) logistics landing craft *Cinq Juin* is operated by the Ministère de la Cooperation in commercial service but is available for government cargoes.

SIERRA LEONE

Republic of Sierra Leone

Personnel: Approx. 200 total

Base: Freetown

PATROL CRAFT [PC]

♦ **1 Chinese Haizhui class**
Bldr: Guijian SY (In serv. 1-1-97)

PB 103 Alimany Rassin

D: 150 tons (170 fl) **S:** 29 kts **Dim:** 41.0 × 5.41 × 1.80
A: 1 twin 37-mm 63-cal. Type 76 AA; 1 twin 25-mm 80-cal. Type 81 AA; 2 twin 14.5-mm 93-cal. AA
Electronics: Radar: 1 Anritsu 726 UA nav./surf-search
M: 4 Type L12-180Z diesels; 4 props; 4,800 bhp (4,400 bhp sust.)
Range: 750/16 **Crew:** 4 officers, 24 enlisted

Remarks: A new-construction unit transferred 11-96 to replace the inoperable Shanghai-II-class patrol boats *Moa* and *Naimbana,* which in turn had been transferred in 3-87 as replacements for a trio of Shanghai-IIs delivered in 1976. By 1998 was inoperable but photos taken during 2002 show her in good condition. Has gyro-controlled fin stabilizers. Sisters operate in the Sri Lankan Navy.

Disposal note: The U.S. 110-ft. Commercial Cruiser–class patrol craft *Farandugu* had been hulked by 2000 and is probably beyond repair. Two Cougar Cat 900S patrol launches acquired in 1998 quickly became inoperable and will probably not be returned to service. Chinese Yuhai-class utility landing craft *Tiwai Island* (104) was no longer considered operational by 2001.

SINGAPORE

Republic of Singapore

NAVY

Personnel: Approximately 2,200 total (including 1,800 conscripts); 9,000 active reservists are also available in emergency.

Bases: Primary bases are located at Changi (RSS Panglima), near the eastern end of the Johore Strait and Tuas, on the Johore Strait.

Organization: Operational missile combatants and the latest patrol craft are assigned to the 1st Flotilla, while antisubmarine patrol craft and the tank landing ships are assigned to the 3rd Flotilla. The Naval Logistics Command (NALCOM) is responsible for repairs, maintenance, and supply. Base defense is handled by Base Defence Squadrons, medical care by Medical Centers, and material and personnel transportation by the Naval Material and Transport Base. There is also a Coastal Command (COSCOM); six inshore patrol craft and the mine-countermeasures units are assigned to it. The Training Command (TRACOM) is responsible for all training and is responsible for the Institute of Naval Technology and Operations, Institute of Maritime Systems, Tactical Training Centers at Brani and Tuas, and the Institute of Maritime Warfare at Tuas.

Maritime Aviation: There is no naval-subordinated aviation arm. The Singapore Air Force 125 Squadron maintains helicopters available for maritime support missions including: 18 AS-332M Super Puma helicopters equipped for ASW and troop carrying, 19 Bell UH-1H helicopters, six AS-350B Écureuil light helicopters, and 20 AS-550 Fennec attack helicopters (10 with Helitow antitank/ship missiles and 20-mm rocket pods, 10 in utility configuration). Six Sikorsky S-70B helicopters were ordered during 1-05 for delivery between 2008 and 2010; they operate from the new frigates. Five Fokker 50 Maritime Enforcer maritime patrol aircraft are assigned to 121 Squadron; they have APS-134 surveillance radars and Honeywell P-650 weather radar, AQR-185(V) sonobuoy receivers, GEC V00-1069 infrared sensors, ASQ-504(V) magnetic anomaly detectors, an extensive EW suite, and Litton LTN 92 inertial navigation systems. Weapons can include two fuselage-mounted Harpoon antiship missiles and four wing-mounted ASW torpedoes. Four other Fokker 50 aircraft serve in logistic support roles.

The Singapore Air Force also operates 4 E-2C Hawkeye radar surveillance aircraft and some 50 A-4 Skyhawk fighter-bombers capable of maritime strike. Eight F-16A/B fighters were delivered in 1988. In addition to tracking aerial contacts, the Hawkeyes are capable of providing over-the-horizon targeting data for Harpoon missiles aboard naval units.

Note: The name for the principal local warship builder, Singapore SB & Eng., has been changed to Singapore Technologies Marine. Ship names are prefixed by RSS—Republic of Singapore Ship. Pennant numbers no longer are preceded by a type-letter when painted on the ships, but the prefixes remain in effect for administrative purposes.

ATTACK SUBMARINES [SS]

♦ **0 (+ 2) ex-Swedish Västergötland class (Type A-17)**
Bldrs: Kockums, Malmö, and Karlskronavarvet, Karlskrona

	Laid down	L	In serv.
. . . (ex-*Västergötland*)	10-1-83	17-9-86	27-11-87
. . . (ex-*Hälsingland*)	1-1-84	31-8-87	20-10-88

D: 990 tons light, 1,070 tons surf./1,143 tons sub. **S:** 11 kts (surf.)/20 kts (sub.)
Dim: 48.50 × 6.06 × 5.60 (surf.)
A: 6 bow 533-mm TT (12 Tp 613 torpedoes); 3 bow 400-mm TT (6 Tp 422 or Ty 45 torpedoes); 22 mines in external portable containers
Electronics:
Radar: 1 Terma . . . nav./surf. search
Sonar: Atlas CSU-83 suite (DBQS-21active/passive, FAS 3-1 flank arrays, towed array)
EW: ArgoSystems AR-700-S5 intercept
M: 2 Hedemora V12A/15-Ub (VA 185) diesels (1,080 bhp each); 2 Jeumont-Schneider 760-kw generators; 1 ASEA electric motor; 1/5-bladed prop; 1,800 shp
Endurance: 45 days **Crew:** 5 officers, 15 enlisted (25 accomm.)

Remarks: Purchase from Sweden announced 4-11-05. Expected to enter service in 2010. Following modifications to operate in tropical waters they may also be fitted with air independent propulsion systems. Intended to replace some of the older Sjöormen-class submarines now in service. Design by Kockums. Ships ordered for Sweden 8-12-81, with Kockums building the mid-bodies and Karlskronavarvet building the bows and sterns. Two younger sisters will remain in Swedish service to receive AIP upgrades with 100-kw Stirling Mk 3 air-independent auxiliary engines.
Hull systems: Can operate at 300 meters. Have only 7% reserve bouyancy. Employ sail-mounted forward control planes and cruciform stern control surfaces. Have six berthing compartments, with five spare berths for trainees. Two Tudor 84-cell lead-acid battery sets are fitted. Sperry Mk 29 gyrocompass. Two main watertight compartments. Have an anechoic hull coating. Have a single crew escape chamber, fitted with a mating coaming for rescue submersibles or diving bells.
Combat systems: The torpedo tubes are arranged with the row of six 533-mm tubes above the three short 400-mm tubes. Use Ericsson IPS-17 combat data/fire-control system (Swedish Navy designation SESUB 900A). Two Barr & Stroud CK038 periscopes are fitted; in the pair being modernized, these are being equipped with a thermal imager and an enhanced image intensifier by Thales Optronics, Glasgow.

♦ **4 ex-Swedish Sjöormen (Type A-11B) class**
Bldrs: Kockums AB, Malmo (ex-Sjöhästen: Karlskronavarvet)

	Laid down	L	In serv.
S . . . Centurion (ex-*Sjöormen*)	1965	25-1-67	31-7-67
S . . . Chieftain (ex-*Sjöhunden*)	1966	21-3-68	25-6-69
S . . . Challenger (ex-*Sjöhästen*)	1966	9-1-68	15-9-69
S . . . Conqueror (ex-*Sjölejonet*)	1966	29-6-67	16-12-68

ATTACK SUBMARINES [SS] *(continued)*

Chieftain NAVPIC-Holland, 5-02

Conqueror Brian Morrison, 8-00

Ex-Swedish Sjöormen class Singapore Navy

D: 1,130 tons surf./1,400 tons sub. **S:** 10 kts surf./20 kts sub.
Dim: 50.5 × 6.1 × 5.1
A: 4 bow 533-mm TT (8 Tp 613 torpedoes or mines); 2 bow 400-mm TT (4 Tp 431 ASW torpedoes)
Electronics: Radar: 1 Terma . . . search
Sonar: STN Atlas CSU-83 suit
EW: . . .
M: Diesel-electric: 4 Hedemora-Pielstick PV/12PA2, 525-bhp diesel generator groups (600 kw each), 1 ASEA electric motor; 1 5-bladed prop; 1,500 shp
Endurance: 21 days **Crew:** 7 officers, 21 enlisted

Remarks: The contract to acquire the *Sjöhunden* was announced 23-9-95 for transfer 4-96 for use in training submariners in Swedish waters; the submarine was refitted at Karlskrona from 2-96 to 26-9-97 and originally was to have left for Singapore late in 2-98 but was retained in Sweden for training (along with *Challenger*) until 2003. On 31-7-97, three more former Swedish Navy units were ordered under "Project Riken," all to be refurbished at Kockums AB, Malmo, for delivery in 1999 to 2001. *Conqueror* and *Centurion* were officially transferred on 28-5-99 to begin their refit and tropicalization modifications. The remaining unit of the class, *Sjöbjornen,* was also purchased for cannibalization. The active four are not expected to be fully combat-ready until 2004, at which point they will be nearly 35 years old. Two of the class are expected to decommission upon arrival of the newer ex-Swedish Västergöth and class bonds. *Conqueror* was commissioned in Singapore on 2-7-00 as the first unit of 171 Squadron, and *Chieftain* was relaunched on 23-5-01, arrived in Singapore on 3-5-02, and was recommissioned on 25-8-02. The other two arrived from Sweden during 1-04.
Hull systems: Maximum diving depth 300 meters; 150-m normal. In Swedish service, the pressure hulls were not stressed by deep diving, leaving them in excellent condition at retirement. Have four battery compartments and the stern planes are in X-configuration with bow planes on the sail. During modifications for Singapore service, piping and valves were replaced for operations in higher-salinity waters, and the air conditioning system was enhanced.
Combat systems: *Challenger* was modernized 1984–85 with Ericsson IBS-A17 combat data/fire-control system with a Cesnor 932 computer and two operator consoles, but a French UDS International SUBTICS (Submarine Tactical Integrated Combat System) has apparently replaced the original IBS-A12 system on the others and probably on *Challenger* as well.

FRIGATES [FF]

◆ **3 (+ 3) Trident class**
Bldr: First unit: DCN, Lorient; others: Singapore Technologies Marine, Jurong

	Laid down	L	In serv.
68 FORMIDABLE	14-11-02	7-01-04	5-05 (del.)
69 INTREPID	08-3-03	7-04	2005
70 STEADFAST	2003	28-1-05	2006
71 TENACIOUS	2004	15-7-05	2007
72 STALWART	2005	2006	2008
73 SUPREME	2006	9-5-06	2009

Formidable (68) Bernard Prézelin, 5-05

Formidable (68) Bernard Prézelin, 6-04

Formidable (68) Bernard Prézelin, 5-05

FRIGATES [FF] *(continued)*

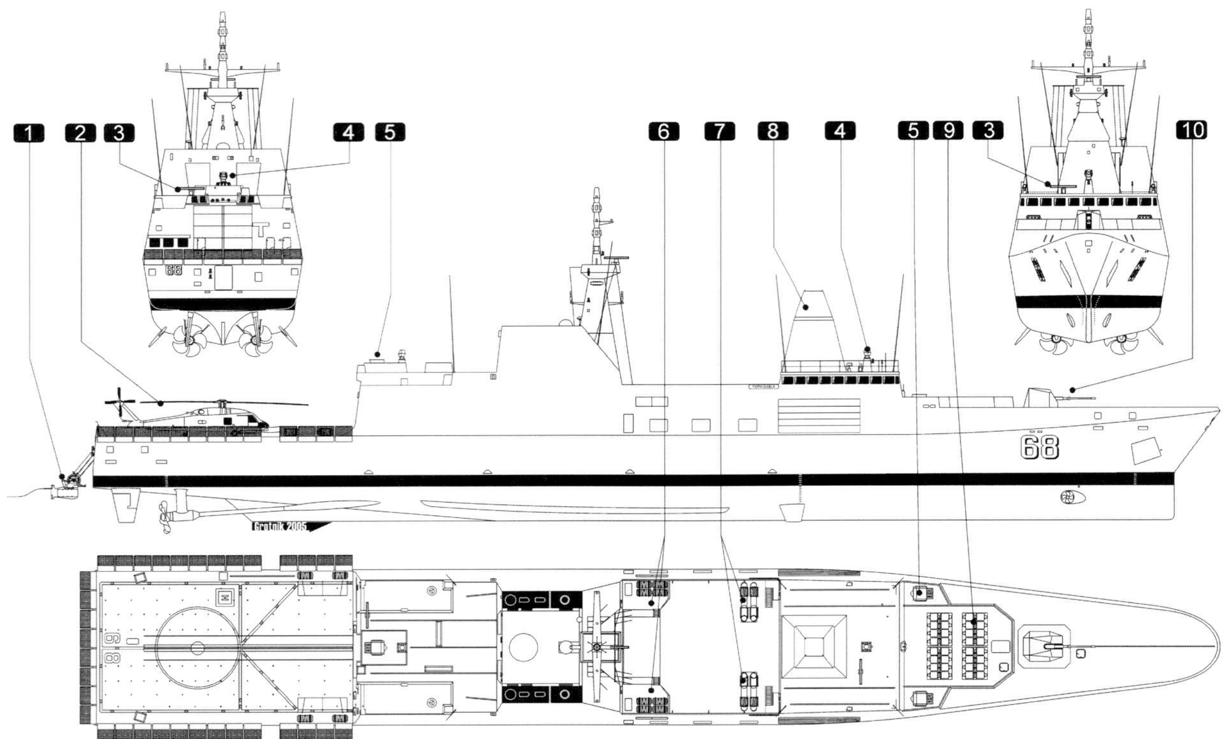

Formidable (68) 1. EDO 980 LF VDS 2. SH-70 Seahawk helicopter 3. Terma Scanter 2001 nav./surf. search 4. Najir optronic f.c. radar 5. EADS NGDS decoy launcher (8 barreled) 6. 2 triple 324 mm ASW torpedo tubes 7. RGM 84C Harpoon SSM (two quadruple sets) 8. Thales Herakles 3-D multi function radar 9. Sylver vertical launch system for Aster-15 missiles 10. 76-mm OTO Melara SuperRapid DP gun Drawing by T. Grotnik, 2005

D: 3,800 tons (fl) **S:** 31 kts **Dim:** 114.8 × 16.3 × 6.0
A: 8 RGM-84C Harpoon SSM; 4 8-cell Sylver A43 vertical launch SAM group (32 Aster 15 missiles); 1 OTO Melara 76-mm 62-cal. Super Rapid DP; 2 single 20-mm . . . AA; 2 single 12.7-mm mg; two triple fixed 324-mm Type B515 TT (Eurotorp A-244 wire-guided torpedoes); 1 S-70 Seahawk helicopter
Electronics:
Radar: 2 Terma Scanter 2001 nav./surf. search; 1 Thales Herakles 3-D surf./air search and f.c.
Sonar: Bow-mounted LF, EDO 980 LF VDS, towed passive array
EW: . . . intercept; . . . 8-round EADS NGDS decoy syst.
E/O: 1 EADS Najir 2000 optronic director and surveillance
M: CODAD: 4 MTU 20V8000 M90 diesels, electric drive; 2 props; 44,600 shp
Range: 5,000/15 **Crew:** 86 tot.

Remarks: Initially known as the New Generation Patrol Vessel (NGVP). Originally planned to be ordered late 1997/early 1998 as a class of eight 1,000-ton missile corvettes, the program was delayed to incorporate new technologies from abroad, and the ship size has grown from 75–90 m overall to as large as 110 m overall, placing it in the frigate category. A contract to design the class and build the first unit was given to DCN, France, on 3-3-00. First steel was cut for the second and third ships on 2-10-02.
Hull systems: Was originally to have employed a trimaran hull constructed of GRP, with Kevlar armor, but as size has nearly tripled, will be a monohull built of conventional materials, with considerable effort made at signature reduction. Fin stabilizers and twin rudders are fitted.
Combat systems: The combat system is to be provided by Singapore Technologies Electronics and will incorporate an integrated ship command and operation system, fiber-optic data transfer, multifunction operating consoles, an integrated communications suite, and automation of functions so as to reduce personnel requirements. Reloads are planned for the fixed torpedo tubes. The Matra Aster 15 SAM system, using Sylver VLS, was selected instead of the Barak SAM system. The two Terma navigation and search radars will be integrated through a Thales Bridgemaster integrated ship control system

GUIDED-MISSILE PATROL COMBATANTS [PGG]

♦ 6 Victory (MGB 62) class

Bldr: P 88: Lürssen, Vegesack, Germany; others: Singapore Technologies Marine, Jurong

	L	In serv.		L	In serv.
P 88 Victory	8-6-88	18-8-90	P 91 Valiant	22-7-89	25-5-91
P 89 Valour	10-12-88	18-8-90	P 92 Vigour	1-2-89	25-5-91
P 90 Vigilance	27-4-89	18-8-90	P 93 Vengeance	23-2-90	25-5-91

D: 550 tons normal (600 fl) **S:** 35 kts **Dim:** 62.95 (59.90 pp) × 9.30 × 2.60
A: 8 RGM-84C Harpoon SSM; 2 Barak VLS SAM groups (16 missiles); 1 76-mm 62-cal. OTO Melara Super Rapid DP; 4 single 12.7-mm mg; 2 triple 324-mm ILAS-3 ASW TT (WASS A-244S torpedoes)
Electronics:
Radar: 1 Kelvin-Hughes Type 1007 nav.; 1 Ericsson Sea Giraffe 150HC surf./air search; 2 Elta EL/M-2221 GM STGR f.c.
Sonar: Thales Salmon VDS
EW: Rafael SEWS 1101 intercept; MBAT/RAN-1010 jammer; Alenia-Marconi Shield III decoy syst. (2 6-round RL); Mk 36 RBOC decoy syst. (2 6-round Mk 137 RL)

Vengeance (P 93) John Mortimer, 8-01

Vigour (P 92) John Mortimer, 8-01

M: 4 MTU 20V538 TB93 diesels; 4 props; 18,740 bhp (15,020 sust.)
Electric: 408 kw tot. **Range:** 700/34; 4,000/16 **Crew:** 8 officers, 41 enlisted

Remarks: First unit ordered 6-86. Transferred to the new Coastal Command 10-91 for antipiracy, fisheries protection, and search-and-rescue duties. They constitute 188 Squadron, 1st Flotilla.
Hull systems: Same hull as a pair built for Bahrain, but without helicopter facilities. Received Van Rieetschoten & Houwens ARSA (Adaptive Rudder-roll Stabilizing Autopilot) rudder roll-stabilization system during 1992. Have experienced stability problems due to the weight of the large tower mast structure.

GUIDED-MISSILE PATROL COMBATANTS [PGG] *(continued)*

Combat systems: Have CelsiusTech 9LV 200 combat system and Israeli NATACS command system. The navigation radar incorporates a combat data plotting system. EW suite intercept band covers 1–18 GHz, and jammer covers 7.5–18 GHz, using two stabilized antennas. There is also a communications D/F capability. Barak point-defense missile systems were ordered for all in 4-96 after successful trials in P 89; the two eight-cell launch groups are recessed into the main deck on either side near the stern, and a second weapons control radar has been added abaft the tower mast. Normally, only two Harpoon missiles are aboard.

PATROL COMBATANTS [PG]

♦ 11 Fearless class

Bldr: Singapore Technologies Marine, Jurong

	L	In serv.		L	In serv.
P 82 Resilience	23-11-96	7-2-98	P 94 Fearless	18-2-95	5-10-96
P 83 Unity	19-7-97	7-2-98	P 95 Brave	9-9-95	5-10-96
P 84 Sovereignty	19-7-97	7-2-98	P 97 Gallant	27-4-96	3-5-97
P 85 Justice	18-10-97	7-2-98	P 98 Daring	27-4-96	3-5-97
P 86 Freedom	18-10-97	22-8-98	P 99 Dauntless	23-11-96	3-5-97
P 87 Independence	4-98	22-8-98			

Fearless (P 94)—ASW variant, with VIGY-10 optronic surveillance sensor on mast platform Brian Morrison, 8-00

Brave (P 95)—ASW variant, now with triple torpedo tube mounts port and starboard; note the pipe guards over the waterjet exhausts at the stern Brian Morrison, 8-00

Resilence (P 82)—gunboat variant Hans Karr, 5-05

D: 500 tons (fl) **S:** 36 kts **Dim:** 55.0 × 8.60 × 2.20 hull
A: 1 2-round Sadral point-defense SAM syst. (. . . Mistral missiles); 1 76-mm 62-cal. OTO Melara Super Rapid DP; 4 single 7.62-mm mg; P 94–99 only: 2 triple 324-mm ILAS-3 ASW TT (WAAS A-244S torpedoes)
Electronics:
Radar: 1 Kelvin-Hughes Type 1007 nav.; 1 Elta EL/M-2228X surveillance/f.c.
Sonar: P 94–99 only: Thales TSM-2362 Gudgeon MF hull-mounted
EW: Elisra NS-9010C intercept; Alenia-Marconi Shield III decoy syst. (2 6-round RL)
E/O: Elbit MSIS optronic gun f.c.
M: 2 MTU 12V595 TE90 diesels; 2 KaMeWa waterjets; 8,430 bhp
Range: . . . / . . . **Crew:** 5 officers, 22 enlisted

Remarks: Contract for first six assigned to Singapore Shipbuilding and Engineering in mid-1994. An order for the second six was announced 18-2-94. P 94–99 constitute the 189 Squadron, while P 82–87 are the 82 Squadron. Roughly half are termed APV (Antisubmarine Patrol Vessels), while the others are OPV (Offshore Patrol Vessels). P 83 is used to test new equipment as the "naval technology evaluation ship."
Combat systems: Have the Elbit ST 3100 WCS combat data system. Second group of six were to carry four to six Gabriel-II antiship missiles in lieu of antisubmarine torpedo tubes, but they were completed without the missiles, which are no longer planned to be added. The sonar is derived from Thales' Spherion series; it has a retractable transducer. All 12 carry a rigid-inflatable inspection launch aft; in P 82–87, it is handled by a large electrohydraulic crane. P 94 had been fitted with a Sagem VIGY-10 electro-optical surveillance system by mid-2000, with the sensor mounted on a new platform on the mast.
Disposals: Sister *Courageous* (P 96) was severely damaged in a collision with a 52,000-ton merchant ship on 3-1-03; four crewmembers were killed and the stern half of the ship was utterly destroyed, she was subsequently stricken.

GUIDED MISSILE PATROL CRAFT [PTG]

♦ 6 Sea Wolf (FPB 45) class

Bldrs: P 76, P 77: Lürssen, Vegesack, Germany; others: Singapore Technologies Marine, Jurong

	In serv.		In serv.
P 76 Sea Wolf	1972	P 79 Sea Tiger	1974
P 77 Sea Lion	1972	P 80 Sea Hawk	1975
P 78 Sea Dragon	1974	P 81 Sea Scorpion	29-2-76

Sea Tiger (P 79)—with two Harpoon and two Gabriel-I missile canisters aboard Stefan Karpinski, 2002

Sea Scorpion (P 81) Stefan Karpinski, 2002

D: 226 tons (254 fl) **S:** 35 kts **Dim:** 44.90 (42.30 wl) × 7.00 × 2.48
A: 2 or 4 RGM-84C Harpoon SSM; 2 Gabriel I SSM; 1 57-mm 70-cal. Bofors SAK-57 Mk 1 DP; 1 2-round Simbad point-defense SAM syst. (. . . Mistral missiles); 2 single 12.7-mm mg
Electronics:
Radar: 1 Decca TM 626 nav.; 1 Thales WM-28 f.c.
EW: Rafael SEWS 1101 intercept/jammer suite, Mk 36 RBOC decoy syst. (4 6-round Mk 137 RL)
M: 4 MTU 16V538 TB92 diesels; 4 props; 14,400 bhp (13,640 sust.)
Range: 950/30; 2,000/15 **Crew:** 7 officers, 33 enlisted

Remarks: Ordered in 1970. Class constitutes 185 Squadron, 1st Flotilla. Are to be maintained active until at least 2004. Are somewhat overloaded.

GUIDED MISSILE PATROL CRAFT [PTG] *(continued)*

Combat systems: Four Harpoon SSM replaced the former Gabriel triple, trainable SSM mount aft, but normally only two are carried; in 1988, P 80 was the first to complete modernization; P 76, the last, completed updating early in 1991. The remaining two fixed Gabriel launchers will be removed when the missiles have reached the end of their shelf lives. Two multiple 57-mm flare launchers are carried on the 57-mm mount. Carry 504 rounds 57-mm. The Simbad manned launcher for Mistral missiles has replaced the 40-mm mount formerly on the fantail; the decoy rocket launchers flank the Simbad launcher. Intercept equipment on tripod topmast added 1980–81.

PATROL BOATS [PB]

♦ 12 FB-series inshore patrol craft (In reserve)
Bldr: Singapore Technologies Marine, Jurong (In serv. 1990–91)

FB 31 through FB 42

FB 35 Ralph Edwards, 10-01

D: 20 tons (fl) **S:** 30 kts **Dim:** 14.5 × 4.1 × 1.1 **A:** 1 7.62-mm mg
Electronics: Radar: 1 Decca . . . nav.
M: 2 MTU 12V183 TC 91 diesels; 2 Hamilton waterjets; 1,200 bhp **Crew:** 4 tot.

Remarks: Similar to the Police Coast Guard PT 12 class, they were formerly based at Brani as part of 186 Coastal Patrol Squadron but have been retained in land storage at Tuas for several years.

MINE WARFARE SHIPS

♦ 4 Swedish Landsort-class minehunters [MHC]
Bldr: Karlskronavarvet, Karlskrona, Sweden (see Remarks)

	Laid down	L	In serv.
M 105 Bedok	17-10-91	24-6-93	7-10-95
M 106 Kallang	. . .	29-1-94	7-10-95
M 107 Katong	. . .	8-4-94	7-10-95
M 108 Punggol	. . .	16-7-94	7-10-95

Bedok (M 105) Martijn Westers via A.A. de Kruijf, 8-06

D: 310 tons (360 fl) **S:** 15 kts **Dim:** 47.50 (45.00 pp) × 9.60 × 2.30
A: 1 40-mm 70-cal. Bofors L70 AA; 4 single 7.62-mm mg; portable minerails
Electronics:
Radar: 1 Norcontrol DB 2000 nav.; 1 Thales WM-20 gun f.c.
Sonar: Thales TSM 2022 variable-depth HF minehunting
E/O: CelsiusTech 9LV100 optronic gun f.c.
M: 4 Saab-Scania DSI-14 diesels; 2 Voith-Schneider vertical cycloidal props; 1,440 bhp
Electric: 585 kVA tot. **Range:** 2,500/12 **Crew:** 7 officers, 32 enlisted

Punggol (M 108)—note mine-clearance swimmer access platform recessed into the port side of the transom stern Martijn Westers via A.A. de Kruijf, 8-06

Remarks: First two ordered 4-91, with option for two more. M 105 was built entirely in Sweden; hulls for the others were built in Sweden for outfitting in Singapore by Singapore Technologies Marine, Jurong, with M 108 leaving Sweden on 17-8-93 as deck cargo. M 106 began sea trials 11-94. All were commissioned together as 194 Mine Countermeasures Squadron, based at Tuas under the Coastal Command.
Hull systems: Glass-reinforced-plastic construction. Have 2 × 225 kVA and 1 × 135 kVA diesel generator sets, all mounted on the upper deck to reduce noise signature.
Combat systems: Have the Thales TSM 2061 mine countermeasures information system with IBIS plot. Carry two PAP 105 Mk 5 remote-controlled mine-disposal vehicles. The Y-shaped portable mine-rail arrangement provides a single laying point. Are equipped with a Racal precision navigation system and a Magnavox GPS system.

AMPHIBIOUS WARFARE SHIPS AND CRAFT

♦ 4 Endurance-class tank landing ships [LST]
Bldr: Singapore Technologies Marine, Jurong

	L	In serv.
L 207 Endurance	14-3-98	18-3-00
L 208 Resolution	1-8-98	18-3-00
L 209 Persistence	13-3-99	7-4-01
L 210 Endeavour	13-2-00	7-4-01

Persistence (L 209) RAN, 10-04

Endeavour (L 210) Hartmut Ehlers, 9-03

D: 6,000 tons (8,500 fl) **S:** 15+ kts **Dim:** 141.0 × 21.0 × 5.0 mean
A: 2 2-rail Simbad point-defense SAM syst. (. . . Mistral missiles); 1 76-mm 62-cal. OTO Melara SuperRapid DP; 2 single 12.7-mm mg
Electronics:
Radar: 1 Kelvin Hughes Type 1007 ARPA nav.; 1 Elta STAR surf./air-search
EW: Rafael RAN 1101 intercept; . . . jammer; Alenia-Marconi Shield III decoy syst. (2 6-round RL)
E/O: 1 EADS Najir 2000 optronic director and surveillance
M: 2 Ruston 16RK270 diesels, electric drive; 2 KaMeWa CP props; 13,400 shp—bow-thruster
Electric: 2,800 kw tot (4 × 700 kw/875 kVA diesel sets)
Range: 5,000+/15; 10,400/12
Crew: 65 tot. (accomm. for 100) + 350 troops

Remarks: Ordered 8-96 as replacements for the U.S.-built LSTs for use in logistics support duties. L 207 was laid down on 26-3-97. Builder's class name is "STEM 1400 LST." Designed in cooperation with Ingalls Shipbuilding, Pascagoula, Mississippi. They form the 3rd Flotilla's 191 Squadron and operate from Tuas Naval Base.

AMPHIBIOUS WARFARE SHIPS AND CRAFT *(continued)*

Resolution (L 208) Ralph Edwards, 10-02

Hull systems: Have 60-ton capacity, 4.05-m-wide, 16.8-m-long bow ramp; a stern docking capacity for up to four landing craft on the main vehicle deck; and two 22-ton capacity, 18-m-long by 6-m-wide internal elevators between the vehicle deck and the upper deck. The stern door is 15.6 m wide by 8 m high and swings down to form a 7-m, 66-ton capacity vehicle ramp. Two 25-ton cranes are fitted. Cargo capacity includes up to 18 tanks, 20 other vehicles, and 350 troops, for a total of more than 1,080 tons. Four EP-02-class landing craft (LCVP) and two RIBs are carried in quadrantial davits. Have an integrated bridge system to enable one operator to control ship speed and direction. There is a prominent bow bulb, which may interfere with beaching. The engine rooms are designed for full-time unmanned operation. Twin rudders are fitted.
Combat systems: Were originally to have had two eight-cell vertical launchers for Barak SAMs, and a planned twin 40-mm OTO Melara Compact and 30-mm Goalkeeper SGE-30 CIWS were also omitted from the armament suite. A twin helicopter landing and deck traversing system is installed on the flight deck, and two AS.332M Super Puma helicopters can be carried. An integrated communications system with fiber-optic local area network is fitted, and there is an integrated combat information center. The previously listed Ericsson Sea Giraffe radar was never installed; the Elta STAR was substituted during the construction phase.

Disposal note: LST 542–class vehicle landing ships *Excellence* (L 202; ex-T-LST 629) and *Intrepid* (L 203; ex-T-LST 579) were decommissioned and stricken on 23-11-00. They, along with sisters *Endurance* (L 201, ex-*Holmes County,* LST 836) and *Persistence* (L 205, ex-T-LST 613), which were stricken during 1998, remain afloat. U.K. *Sir Lancelot*–class vehicle cargo ship *Perseverance* (L 206) was decommissioned during 10-01 and sold for use as a civilian-manned antipirate maritime surveillance asset.

♦ 4 RPL 60–class utility landing craft [LCU]

	Bldr.	Laid down	L	In serv.
RPL 60	North SY, Singapore	. . .	11-85	1986
RPL 61	North SY, Singapore	. . .	11-85	1986
RPL 62	Singapore Technologies Marine	5-85	10-85	2-11-85
RPL 63	Singapore Technologies Marine	5-85	10-85	2-11-85

RPL 60 John Mortimer, 8-01

D: 151 tons (approx. 330 fl) **S:** 10 kts **Dim:** 36.0 (33.0 pp) × 8.5 × 1.8
A: None **Electronics:** Radar: 1 . . .
M: 2 Deutz-M.A.N. D2540MLE diesels; 2 Schottel vertical cycloidal props; 860 bhp
Crew: 6 tot.

Remarks: Ordered 28-2-85. Differ in detail, by builder. Cargo capacity: 110 tons max. Can carry 450 standing troops or two AMX13 tanks. Cargo deck: 26.5 × 6.6 m. Painted green; assigned to Naval Logistics Command. Construction of two additional units was canceled.

♦ 30 EP 02–class vehicle and personnel landing craft [LCVP]
Bldr: Singapore Technologies Marine, Jurong (In serv. 1993– . . .)

D: 38 tons (fl) **S:** 20 kts **Dim:** 21.0 × 5.6 × 0.7 **A:** 2 single 12.7-mm mg
M: 2 M.A.N. D2866 LE diesels; 2 KaMeWa waterjets; 880 bhp
Range: 100/20 **Crew:** 4 + 30 troops

Remarks: Enlarged version of EP 01 class with greater freeboard and an 18-ton cargo capacity. Numbered in 300 series.

EP 02–class landing craft 377 Hartmut Ehlers, 10-03

♦ 10 U.S. 22-ft. Whaler class [LCP]
Bldr: Boston Whaler, Rockland, Mass. (In serv. 1989)

D: 1.5 tons light (2.25 fl) **S:** 40 kts **Dim:** 6.81 × 2.26 × 0.36
A: 1 12.7-mm mg; 1 40-mm Mk 19 grenade launcher
M: 2 Johnson OMC gasoline outboard engines; 360 bhp
Range: 167/40; 750/ . . . **Fuel:** 243 liters **Crew:** 3 tot.

Remarks: GRP-hulled open launches. Used by Naval Diving Unit combat swimmer group.

♦ 100 EP 01–class personnel landing craft [LCP]
Bldr: Singapore Technologies Marine, Jurong (In serv. 1980s–1990s)

EP 01–class landing craft L 210-1—assigned to the landing ship *Endeavour* (L 210) Brian Morrison, 10-01

D: 4 tons (fl) **S:** 20 kts **Dim:** 13.6 × 3.7 × 0.6
M: 2 M.A.N. D2866 LE diesels; 2 Hamilton 362 waterjets; 816 bhp
Range: 100/20 **Crew:** 2 tot. + 30 troops

Remarks: Typed "Fast Craft, Equipment and Personnel." Aluminum construction craft with cargo well and bow ramp. Can carry one platoon of troops or a light vehicle. Are assigned to 195 Squadron. Now numbered in the 500 and 800 series, except for those carried aboard the larger tank landing ships, which wear the same pennant number as their hosts.

SERVICE CRAFT

♦ 2 floating dry docks [YFDL]
Bldr: Singapore Technologies Marine, Jurong (In serv. 1994)

FD 1 FD 2

FD 1 Stefan Karpinski, 2002

Remarks: 600-ton capacity. FD 1 at Tuas, FD 2 at Brani.

♦ 2 ALC-1800-class personnel launches [YFL]
Bldr: Le Comte, Vianen, the Netherlands (L: 16-10-85; In serv. 1-11-85)

FL 1 FL 2

Remarks: No data available. Ordered 10-4-85 and laid down 12-6-85 and 4-7-85, respectively.

Disposal note: Route survey craft and diving tender *Jupiter* (A 102) was decommissioned during 9-01 and transferred to Indonesia on 21-3-02.

♦ 1 fuel lighter [YO]
Bldr: Siong Huat SY, Singapore (In serv. 1-9-87)

JOLLY RODGER II

D: 800 dwt **S:** . . . **Dim:** . . . × . . . × . . .

M: 2 MWM TPK-6K diesels; 2 props; 2,060 bhp

Remarks: Laid down 8-6-87, launched 11-8-87.

SERVICE CRAFT *(continued)*

◆ **1 training craft** Bldr: . . . (In serv. . . .)

A . . . Avatar (ex- . . .)

Remarks: Purchased and commissioned on 30-1-02 as training craft for 192 and 193 Squadrons. No data available other than that she is diesel-powered. Some reports indicate that the craft may be a chartered merchant ship.

POLICE COAST GUARD

PATROL BOATS [WPB]

Note: Under the 1999 contract for the Southerly 18-m-class small patrol boats, two 20-meter, 30-knot command boats are also to be constructed; no data yet available. Also to be acquired are six rigid inflatable patrol launches.

◆ **32 (+ 8) Southerly 10.5-m-class small patrol RIBs**
Bldr: Chuan Hup Holdings Asia-Pacific Geraldton Pte. Shipyards, Singapore (In serv. 2002–4)

PC 201 through PC 232

D: . . . tons **S:** 52 kts **Dim:** 10.80 × 3.3 × 0.5
M: 3 Marcury gasoline outboards; 3 props; 750 bhp
Range: . . . / . . . **Fuel:** 880 liters **Crew:** 3

Remarks: First 20 ordered fall 2000, others in 1-02. Produced in cooperation with Australian Motor Yachts, Coomera. Have an aluminum alloy core structure.

◆ **30 Southerly 18-m-class small patrol boats**
Bldr: Asia-Pacific Shipyards, Singapore (In serv. 1998–2000)

PT 20 Manta Ray
PT 21 . . . Ray
PT 22 . . . Ray
PT 23 Bull Ray
PT 24 Butterfly Ray
PT 25 Cownose Ray
PT 26 . . . Ray
PT 27 Electric Ray
PT 28 . . . Ray
PT 29 . . . Ray
PT 30 Eagle Ray
PT 31 Giant Reef Ray
PT 32 River Ray
PT 33 . . . Ray
PT 34 . . . Ray
PT 35 . . . Ray
PT 36 . . . Ray
PT 37 . . . Ray
PT 38 . . . Ray
PT 39 . . . Ray
PT 40 . . . Ray
PT 41 . . . Ray
PT 42 . . . Ray
PT 43 . . . Ray
PT 44 . . . Ray
PT 61 . . . Ray
PT 62 . . . Ray
PT 63 . . . Ray
PT 64 . . . Ray
PT 65 . . . Ray

PT 26—armed with single 7.62-mm mg Stefan Karpinski, 2002

PT 64 Stefan Karpinski, 2002

D: . . . tons **S:** 40+ kts **Dim:** 18.0 × 5.4 × 0.9
A: 1 7.62-mm mg **Electronics:** Radar: 1 . . . nav.
M: 2 . . . diesels; 2 waterjets 400 bhp **Crew:** 5 tot.

Remarks: Contract for 18 units was awarded during 9-97 to Geraldton Boat Builders, Geraldton, Western Australia, which built the boats at Asia-Pacific's Singapore yard; a contract for the 19th through 25th units was issued during 1-00 with additional units following. Aluminum construction. Can reach 40 kts on 80% power. Two of the total, PT 20 and PT 30, were configured as command and control boats.

Manta Ray (PT 20)—command craft, with larger pilothouse Brian Morrison, 8-00

◆ **11 Fish-class fast interceptors**
Bldr: Greenbay Marine, Green Bay, Wisc. (In serv. 5-95–96)

PK 10 Sailfish
PK 20 Spearfish
PK 21 White Marlin
PK 22 Silver Marlin
PK 23 Striped Marlin
PK 24 Black Marlin
PK 25 Blue Marlin
PK 26 Jumping Marlin
PK 30 Billfish
PK 40 Swordfish
PK 50 Spikefish

Sailfish (PK 10) Brian Morrison, 8-00

White Marlin (PK 21) Brian Morrison, 8-00

D: . . . tons **S:** 50 kts **Dim:** 12.8 × 3.2 × 0.5 **A:** 1 7.62-mm mg
Electronics: Radar: 1 Furuno . . . nav.
M: 3 MerCruiser 502 Magnum diesel outdrive engines; . . . bhp

Remarks: Designed by Philip Curran. No longer carry the standard white-red-white diagonal hull striping of the Singapore Police Coast Guard, in order to reduce their visibility. PK 21 through PK 24 were built in Singapore to a slightly different design.

◆ **8 PT 12 class**
Bldr: Singapore Technologies Marine, Jurong

	In serv.		In serv.
PT 12 . . .	2-87	PT 16 . . .	21-1-89
PT 13 . . .	2-87	PT 17 Striped Marlin	3-89
PT 14 . . .	21-1-89	PT 18 . . .	3-89
PT 15 Todak	21-1-89	PT 19 Dorado	3-89

D: 21 tons (fl) **S:** 30 + kts **Dim:** 14.80 × 4.23 × 1.20
A: 2 single 7.62-mm mg **Electronics:** Radar: 1 Decca . . . nav.
M: PT 12–15: 2 M.A.N. D2840 LE diesels; 2 props; 1,252 bhp; PT 16–19: 2 MTU 12V183 TC 91 diesels; 2 props; 1,182 bhp
Range: 310/22 **Fuel:** 2,000 liters **Crew:** 4 tot.

Remarks: Updated version of PT 1 class. The final two are configured as "command boats" and have air-conditioned seating for 10 passengers. All have names.

COAST GUARD PATROL BOATS [WPB] *(continued)*

Striped Marlin (PT 17) Douglas A. Cromby, 6-00

♦ 11 PT 1 class
Bldr: Singapore SB & Eng., Jurong

	Laid down	L	In serv.
PT 1 Amberjack	21-7-83	19-12-83	14-1-84
PT 2 . . .	25-7-83	6-1-84	17-2-84
PT 3 . . .	28-7-83	16-1-84	13-3-84
PT 4 . . .	1-8-83	23-3-84	6-4-84
PT 5 Cosby	15-9-83	23-4-84	15-5-84
PT 6 Dolphin	30-9-83	14-5-84	1-6-84
PT 7 Leatherjacket	11-10-83	30-5-84	19-6-84
PT 8 . . .	14-10-83	16-6-84	5-7-84
PT 9 . . .	21-12-83	4-7-84	1-8-84
PT 10 Pari Burong	6-1-84	23-7-84	24-8-84
PT 11 Piranha	19-1-84	10-8-84	5-9-84

Leatherjacket (PT 7) Brian Morrison, 8-00

D: 20 tons **S:** 30 kts **Dim:** 14.54 × 4.23 × 1.20 (props) **A:** 1 7.62-mm mg
Electronics: Radar: 1 Decca . . . nav.
M: 2 M.A.N. D2542 MLE diesels; 2 props; 1,076 bhp
Range: 310/22 **Fuel:** 2,600 liters **Crew:** 7 tot.

Remarks: Aluminum construction. Four near-sisters built for Singapore Customs (CE 5–CE 8, delivered 6-2-87), and seven were built for Brunei.

♦ 12 Swift class
Bldr: Singapore Technologies Marine, Jurong (In serv. 20-10-81)

PH 50 Hammerhead Shark (ex-*Swift Lancer,* P 12)
PH 51 Mako Shark (ex-*Swift Swordsman,* P 14)
PH 52 White Shark (ex-*Swift Archer,* P 16)
PH 53 Blue Shark (ex-*Swift Combatant,* P 18)
PH 54 Tiger Shark (ex-*Swift Knight,* P 11)
PH 55 Basking Shark (ex-*Swift Warrior,* P 15)
PH 56 Sandbar Shark (ex-*Swift Conqueror,* P 21)
PH 57 Thresher Shark (ex-*Swift Chieftain,* P 23)
PH 58 Whitetip Shark (ex-*Swift Warlord,* P 17)
PH 59 Blacktip Shark (ex-*Swift Challenger,* P 19)
PH 60 Goblin Shark (ex-*Swift Cavalier,* P 20)
PH 61 School Shark (ex-*Swift Centurion,* P 22)

D: 45.7 tons (fl) **S:** 33 kts (31 sust.) **Dim:** 22.7 (20.0 pp) × 6.2 × 1.6 (3.0 props)
A: 1 20-mm 90-cal. Oerlikon GAM B-01 AA; 2 single 7.62-mm mg
Electronics: Radar: 1 Decca 1226 ARPA nav.
M: 2 Deutz SBA-16M816 diesels; 2 props; 2,660 bhp
Range: 550/20; 900/10 **Fuel:** 8.6 tons **Crew:** 3 officers, 9 enlisted

Remarks: The first unit was launched on 8-6-80. On 15-2-93, the first four were transferred to the Police Coast Guard; four more followed in 1994; and the final four were transferred and recommissioned on 22-1-97.
Hull systems: Design based on Australian de Havilland Capricornica design. Aluminum construction. Carry two tons fresh water and have two generator sets.

Mako Shark (PH 51) Brian Morrison, 8-00

Disposal note: The 24 patrol launches of the PX 1 class were retired by 2002 and the 37 PC 32–class patrol launches were decommissioned during 2004.

Note: There are additional Police Coast Guard launches in service, including at least four in the PL series. Also in operation are number of service craft, including the push-tug *Pilot Whale.*

SINGAPORE ARMY

♦ Up to 450 assault-personnel landing craft [LCP]
Bldr: Singapore Technologies Marine, Jurong (In serv. 1980s)

D: . . . **S:** 12 kts **Dim:** 5.3 × 1.8 × 0.7 (molded depth)
M: 1 outboard motor; 50 shp **Crew:** 12 troops

Remarks: Man-portable craft.

CUSTOMS AND EXCISE SERVICE

Note: The Singapore Customs and Excise Service operates at least 28 patrol launches, including the large CE 8, 20-ton sisters CE 5 through CE 7, four CE 1–class launches (CE 1 through CE 4), and 20 or more C 70–class launches. Customs and Excise craft are painted gray; the five large units can mount a single 7.62-mm mg. A new class of 12-m, 50-kt fast patrol RIB launches powered by four Yamaha 250-bhp gasoline outboards began delivery during 2001 from Lita Ocean, Singapore, employing prefabricated kits supplied by Marine Kits Australia.

Customs and Excise patrol boat CE 7 NAVPIC-Holland, 9-98

Customs and Excise patrol boat CE 3 Chris Sattler, 8-00

Customs and Excise patrol launch C 78 NAVPIC-Holland, 9-98

SINGAPORE PORTS AUTHORITY

Note: The Singapore Ports Authority operates 18 GP-50-class pilot launches, the hydrographic survey craft *Mata Ikan* (103 tons, built 1967), and survey launches *Discovery* and *Investigator* (31 tons, built 1980).

SLOVENIA

Republic of Slovenia

SLOVENE NATIONAL POLICE
(*Nasi Mornarji*)

Personnel: 47 tot.

Base: Isola, near Koper

Note: Officially formed 30-1-93 at the time of the launch of the first ship built for it, the training vessel *Sinji Galeb,* Slovenia's maritime force was officially referred to as the 430th Coastal Defense Unit of the Slovene Army, but in mid-1996, the entire organization was transferred to the Slovene National Police.

PATROL BOATS [WPB]

♦ **1 Israeli Super Dvora Mk II class**
Bldr: RAMTA-Israeli Aircraft Industries, Be'er Sheva (In serv. 1-8-96)

HPL 21 Ankaran (ex-P 112)

Ankaran (HPL 21)—Super Dvora Mk II class
Slovenska Vojska, via Dr. Zvonimir Freivogel

D: 48 tons (54 fl) **S:** 42 kts **Dim:** 22.40 × 5.49 × 1.00
A: 2 single 20-mm 70-cal. Oerlikon Mk 10 AA; 2 single 12.7-mm mg
Electronics:
Radar: 1 Koden MD 3220 nav.
E/O: 1 Elop MSIS surveillance
M: 2 MTU 8V396 TE94 diesels; 2 props; 3,000 bhp
Electric: 30 kw **Range:** 700/14 **Crew:** 3 officers, 9 enlisted

Remarks: Ordered 9-95. Aluminum construction. Negotiations to purchase a second were under way as of 11-97, but no order followed.

♦ **1 GC 20 class** Bldr: Aviotechnica, Viareggio, Italy (In serv. 21-6-95)

P 111 Ladse

Ladse (P 111) H&L Van Ginderen, 1998

D: 44 tons (fl) **S:** 40 kts **Dim:** 19.86 × 5.00 × 0.90 (hull) **A:** 1 7.62-mm mg
Electronics: Radar: 2 Furuno . . . nav.
M: 2 MTU 8V396 TE 84 diesels; 2 props; 2,400 bhp
Electric: 32 kw tot. (2 × 16 kw sets) **Range:** 270/35 **Crew:** 9 tot.

Remarks: Aluminum-magnesium alloy hull and superstructure. Not considered to be suitable for open-sea work.

SERVICE CRAFT

♦ **1 training launch [WYXT]**
Bldr: . . . (In serv. 30-1-93)

P 101 Sinji Galeb

Sinji Galeb (P 101) H&L Van Ginderen, 1998

Remarks: A 12-m, GRP-construction cabin cruiser; no other data available.

Note: Several small patrol boats and rigid inflatable patrol launches are in service. There is also a Slovene Customs Service, which also operates several small patrol boats.

SOLOMON ISLANDS

Republic of the Solomon Islands

ROYAL SOLOMON ISLANDS POLICE SERVICE

Personnel: 14 officers, 60 constables

Note: Vessel names are prefaced by "RSIPV" (Royal Solomon Islands Police Vessel).

PATROL CRAFT [WPC]

♦ **2 ASI 315 design**
Bldr: Transfield ASI Pty. Ltd., South Coogee, Western Australia

	Laid down	L	In serv.
03 Lata	12-9-87	19-5-88	3-9-88
04 Auki	23-1-91	1991	2-11-91

Lata (03) Chris Sattler, 4-06

Auki (03) Chris Sattler, 6-06

PATROL CRAFT [WPC] *(continued)*

D: 165 tons (fl) **S:** 21 kts **Dim:** 31.50 (28.60 wl) × 8.10 × 2.12
A: 3 single 12.7-mm mg
Electronics: Radar: 1 Furuno 1011 nav.
M: 2 Caterpillar 3516 diesels; 2 props; 2,820 bhp
Electric: 116 kw tot. **Range:** 2,500/12 **Fuel:** 27.9 tons **Endurance:** 10 days
Crew: 1 officer, 4 noncommissioned, 9 constables

Remarks: "Pacific Patrol Boat" design for Australian foreign aid program. First unit ordered 3-10-85. Both were modernized between 2004–7 for service through 2018. Carry a 5-m aluminum boarding boat. Extensive navigational suite, including Furuno FSN-70 NAVSAT receiver, 525 HF/DF, 120 MF/HF/DF, FE-881 echo-sounder and DS-70 doppler log. Sisters in service in Papua New Guinea, Vanuatu, Fiji, and Samoa.

Note: Also in service are several RIBS and the police patrol craft *Jackpot*.

Police patrol craft Jackpot Chris Sattler, 4-06

DEPARTMENT OF FISHERIES

PATROL BOATS [WPB]

♦ **1 Carpentaria class**
Bldr: De Havilland Marine, Homebush Bay, Australia (In serv. 30-3-79)

01 Tulagi

Tulagi (01) H&L Van Ginderen, 1989

D: 27 tons (fl) **S:** 27 kts **Dim:** 16.0 × 5.0 × 1.2
A: 2 single 7.62-mm mg
Electronics: Radar: 1 Decca 110 nav.
M: 2 G.M. Detroit Diesel 12V71 TI diesels; 2 props; 1,120 bhp
Range: 700/22 **Crew:** 10 tot.

Remarks: Operated by the Department of Fisheries for fisheries patrol.

Note: Oceanographic research craft *Solomon Atu* and *Solomon Kariqua* are operated by other Solomon Islands government agencies, as are utility landing craft *Ligumo III* and *Ulushaghe*.

SOUTH AFRICA

Republic of South Africa

NAVY

Personnel: Approx. 4,500 total plus about 2,000 civilians. There are also about 1,300 naval reserves.

Bases: Headquarters at Pretoria. Other principal facilities are located at Simon's Town and Salisbury Island, Durban.

Oryx helicopter—aboard SAS *Drakensberg* (A 301) Leo van Ginderen, 6-05

Naval Aviation: A South African Air Force detachment is available to assist the navy and can provide 12 AS.316 Alouette-III and 9 Oryx (Cougar Mk 1) helicopters for shipboard operations. Five C-47TP transports are used for maritime surveillance. Four GKN Westland Super Lynx 300 helicopters, for service on the new frigates, were ordered in August 2003 with delivery in 2007.

Weapons and sensors: Most equipment is of European and Israeli origin. Stocks of U.S.-supplied Mk 44 ASW torpedoes are being upgraded as the A44 and fitted with a 61-kg Sochem directed-energy warhead and a new homing head; a running time of 6 minutes at 32 kts is claimed.

The twin 35-mm 35DP6 gunmount is under development as an antiaircraft weapon; mounting two Vektor GA 35 guns with 1,175-m/sec muzzle velocity and a firing rate of 550 rounds per gun per minute, the mount will also have a t.v./infrared sight, and the guns may be adapted to fire the Oerlikon-Contraves AHEAD (Advanced Hit Efficiency And Destruction) round. The weapons are planned to be mounted on the new frigates.

The Skorpioen antiship missile is a license-built version of the Israeli Gabriel-II. A new warhead for backfitting to existing missiles has been developed by Somchem; it consists of a steel casing containing 35 self-forging fragment explosive charges, with the voids filled with PBX explosive. The warhead weighs 150 kg, of which 99 kg is explosive.

The SAMCON 600 naval mine is offered for export and may be purchased for domestic use; it can be launched by aircraft, submarines, and surface ships.

Denel announced late in 1998 development of the Umkhonto-IR vertically launched shipboard SAM for service entry circa 2004. Intended for use on new South African Navy frigates, the missile employs command to line-of-sight guidance, using a shipboard tracking radar and command guidance to bring it in range of its integral heat-seeking sensor. Missiles are to be carried in groups of four launchers. Flight trials during 5-02 and through 2006 proved successful; the missile was also ordered for the Finnish Navy on 18-10-02. Data for the Umkhonto-IR, the design of which is based on the Crotale NG, include:

Length: 3,300 mm **Diameter:** 180 mm **Wingspan:** 400 mm
Weight: 125 kg **Warhead:** 23 kg blast/fragmentation **Speed:** Mach 2.4
Range: 800-m min./12,000-m max. **Max. altitude:** 10,000 m

Note: Ship names are prefaced by SAS—South African Ship.

ATTACK SUBMARINES [SS]

♦ **2 (+ 1) German Type 209/1400 MOD class**
Bldr: German Submarine Consortium (First two units: HDW, Kiel; third unit: Blohm + Voss, Hamburg)

	Laid down	L	In serv.
S 101 Manthtisi	2004	15-6-04	3-11-05
S 102	. . .	4-5-05	9-06
S 103	. . .	2006	9-07

Manthtisi (S 101) South African Navy via David Shirlaw, 10-05

D: 1,472 tons surf./1,594 tons sub. **S:** 11.0 kts surf./21.5 kts sub.
Dim: 62.00 × 6.20 (7.60 over stern planes) × 5.50
A: 8 bow 533-mm TT (14 torpedoes and/or mines)
Electronics:
Radar: 1 Thales . . . nav.
Sonar: STN Atlas Elektronik CSU-90 suite; HDW-WASS C303/S Circe torpedo decoy system
EW: Grintek . . . intercept
M: 4 MTU 12V396 SE84 AG diesels (800 bhp each), 4 405-kw generator sets, 1 Siemens electric motor; 1 prop; 5,000 shp
Range: 10,000/8 snorkel; 230/8, 390/4, 25/21.5 sub. **Endurance:** 45 days
Crew: 30 tot. (+ 5 trainees)

ATTACK SUBMARINES [SS] *(continued)*

S 102—during sea trials Michael Nitz, 3-06

S 102—during sea trials Michael Nitz, 3-06

Remarks: Design selected 12-11-98 to replace the *Daphné* class; an agreement to purchase the submarines from the German Submarine Consortium (Howaldtswerke Deutsche Werft AG, Thyssen Nordseewerke GmbH, and Ferrostaal AG) for 4.5 billion rand (about $750 million) was concluded on 16-6-99, with final contract signed on 7-7-00. Construction on the first unit was begun by HDW on 22-5-01, and fabrication of the first stern section was begun by Kockums during 4-01.
Hull systems: Normal operating depth 200 m max.
Combat systems: Will have STN Atlas ISUS-90-45 combat system, non-hull-penetrating Zeiss OMS 100 optronic sensor mast, Zeiss SERO 400 electro-optic periscope system, and Grintek Communications comms equipment.

Disposal note: All three remaining *Daphné*-class submarines, *Spear* (S 97), *Umkhonto* (S 98), and *Assegaai* (S 99) were retired from South African service by 12-03.

FRIGATES [FF]

♦ 4 (+ 1) MEKO A-200SAN (Valour-class) frigates

Bldrs: A: Blohm + Voss AG, Hamburg; B: HDW, Kiel

	Bldr	Laid down	L	In serv.
F 145 Amatola	A	2-8-01	7-6-02	25-9-05
F 146 Isandlwana	B	26-10-01	22-11-02	12-05
F 147 Spioenkop	A	28-2-02	2-8-03	7-06
F 148 Mendi	B	28-6-02	24-11-03	12-06

Mendi (F 148) Martin Mokrus, 8-04

Spioenkop (F 147) Martin Mokrus, 5-04

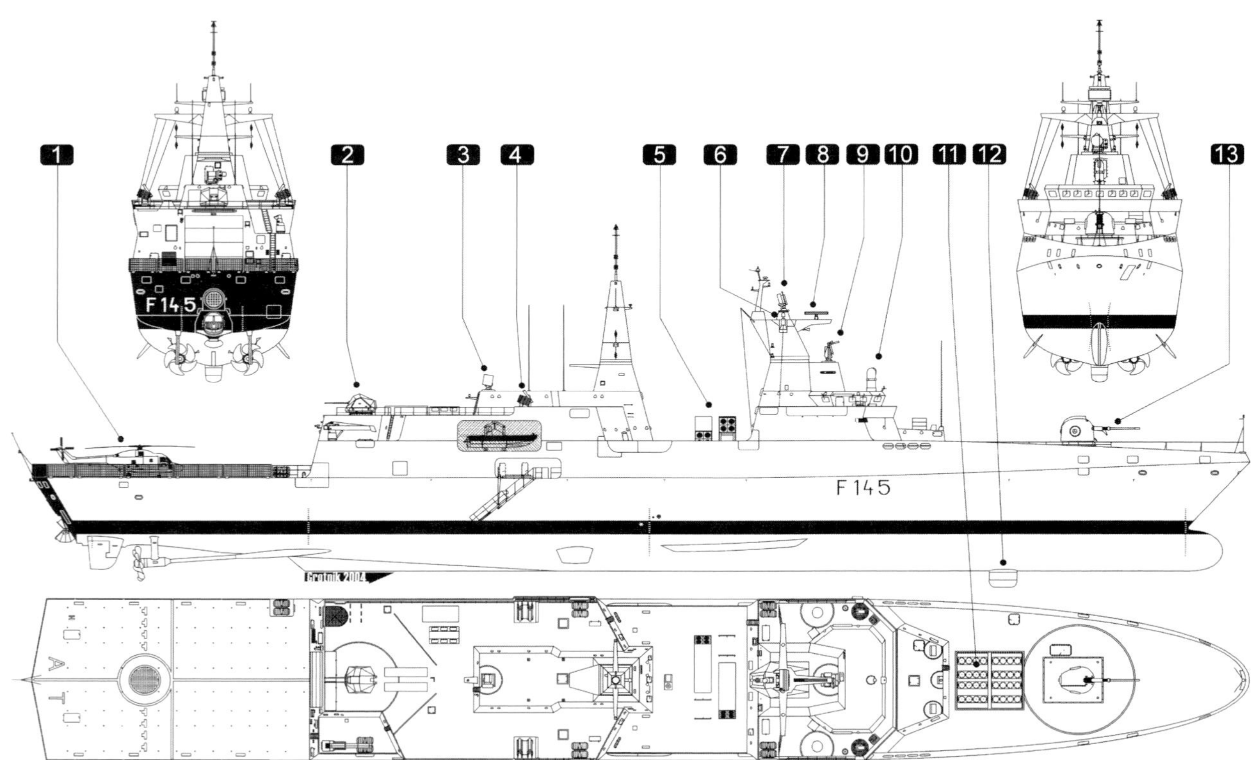

Amatola (F 145) 1. Super Lynx or SeaSprite helicopter 2. 35-mm Denel AA 3. Reutech Electro Optical Tracker 4. Wallop Grintec Ultra Barricade decoy launcher 5. MM 40 Exocet antiship missiles 6. Avitronics Shrike EW 7. Thales MRR 3-D radar 8. Navigation radar 9. Reutech RTS-6400 fc. radar 10. Provision for ECM system (not fitted) 11. Denel Umkhonto-IR VLS SAM system (16 cells) 12. Thales Kingklip LF hull mounted sonar 13. 76-mm OTO Melara DP gun Drawing by T. Grotnik, 2005

FRIGATES [FF] *(continued)*

Isandlwana (F 146) Bernard Prézelin, 9-04

D: 3,590 tons (fl) **S:** 28 kts **Dim:** 121.00 (105.20 wl) × 16.34 × 4.40 hull mean
A: 8 MM 40 Exocet Block 2 SSM; 16 Denel Umkhonto-IR VLS SAM—1 76-mm 62-cal. OTO Melara DP; 1 twin 35-mm Denel AA; 2 single 20-mm 90-cal. Rheinmetall AA; 2 twin 324-mm TT; 1 or 2 Super Lynx 300 or SH-2G Super SeaSprite helicopter (with Mokapa antiship missiles)
Electronics:
Radar: 1 Thales Scout nav.; 1 Thales MRR 3-D search; 2 Reutech ORT RTS-6400 f.c.
Sonar: Thales Kingklip hull-mounted LF
TACAN: Thales Vesta beacon
EW: Avitronics Shrike electronic and laser signal warning; 2 Wallop-Grintek UltraBarricade decoy syst. (2 24-round trainable RL)
E/O: 1 Reutech . . . tracking; 2 M-Tek target-designation sights
M: CODAG: 1 G.E. LM-2500 gas turbine (26,824 shp), 2 MTU 16V1163 TB93 diesels (7,940 bhp each); 1 KaMeWa waterjet centerline, 2 Lips CP props outboard
Electric: 2,200 kw tot. (4 × 550 kw, MTU . . . diesels driving)
Range: 7,000/15 **Endurance:** 28 days
Crew: 115 total (124 tot. accomm.)

Remarks: The Blohm + Voss design was selected on 12-11-98 and ordered on 3-12-99. Work on the first began on 28-2-01 and on the third on 28-8-01. F 147 began sea trials 4-5-04. A fifth unit was ordered on 12-9-06.
Hull systems: Hull shaped to reduce radar signature. Fin stabilizers. The propulsion system is described as being of CODAG-WARP (Combined Diesel and Gas turbine—Waterjet and Refined Propellers), with the cross-connected diesels driving the two CP props and the gas turbine the waterjet. One diesel can drive both propeller shafts for economic cruising up to 20 kts. The gas turbine and diesels exhaust out the stern of the ship, providing some residual thrust and signature reduction benefits. Twin rudders are fitted. The helicopter hangar accommodates one Oryx or two smaller helicopters. F 145 had to have its communications cabling replaced, delaying delivery. Well suited for rough seas in the South Atlantic.
Combat systems: Have a Thales Tavitac combat data system. The 76-mm guns are recycled from older SAN ships. The Umkhonto missiles are carried in four quadruple vertical launch modules. The decoy launchers carry 24 102-mm Wallop SuperPallisade and SuperStockade decoy rockets plus two tubes for larger decoys. No EW jamming system is carried. Two indigenously made 25-mm LIW GA35 guns are to replace the 20-mm mounts later. Have the locally developed Grinaker Seacon-1 external and Thales FOKON internal communications suites. The Kentron Mokapa antiship missile for the helicopters has a range of 12 n.m.

GUIDED-MISSILE PATROL CRAFT [PTG]

♦ 2 Israeli Reshev ("Warrior") class
Bldrs: Sandock Austral SY, Durban

	L	In serv.
P 1567 Galeshewe (ex-*Hendrik Mentz*)	26-3-82	11-2-83
P 1569 Makhanda (ex-*Magnus Malan*)	27-3-86	4-7-86

Adam Kok (P 1563), since stricken, and Makhanda (P 1569) Edward McDonnell, 2003

D: 415 tons (450 fl) **S:** 34.5 kts (32 sust.)
Dim: 58.10 (54.10 pp) × 7.62 × 2.35 (fwd.)/2.69 (aft)
A: 6 Skorpioen SSM; 2 single 76-mm 62-cal. OTO Melara Compact DP; 2 single 20-mm 90-cal Oerlikon GAM-B01 AA; 4 single 12.7-mm mg
Electronics:
Radar: 1 Thales THD-1040 Neptune surf./air search; 1 Alenia RTN-10X Orion f.c.
EW: P 1563: Grintek MN-21 intercept; Systel Kondor comms intercept; ADS signal warning and analysis processor; ADS decoy control system; others: Elta MN-53 intercept; Elta EA-2118 comms intercept; Elta Rattler jammer; all: 4 ACDS decoy RL
M: 4 MTU 16V538 TB91 diesels; 4 props; 12,000 bhp
Electric: 352 kw tot. (4 × 88 kw) **Range:** 1,500/30; 3,000/20; 5,000/15
Endurance: 10 days **Crew:** 8 officers, 44 enlisted

Remarks: Two surviving units of the class were ordered 15-11-77. Originally referred to as the "Minister" class and named for former ministers of defense, the ships were renamed on 1-4-97 after South African military heroes, and the official class name was also altered. P 1567 was refitted from 1997 to 3-98, but without the electronics upgrade. The last of the class is to be stricken in 2008.
Hull systems: Have a water washdown system to permit operating in NBC warfare conditions. Engines exhaust either above or below waterline, the latter employed to reduce infrared signature. Have six spare berths for trainees. Have strengthened hulls and some changes in the electronics suite, but they have been severely stressed by the heavy seas off South Africa's coast.
Combat systems: The Skorpioen antiship missile is a license-built version of the Israeli Gabriel II; range is 20 n.m. at Mach 0.7. Carry 500 rds 76-mm ammunition.
Disposals: *Jan Smuts* (P 1561) decommissioned to reserve on 20-3-98 but has been stripped of useful equipment and will not likely be returned to service. *René Sethren* (P 1566, ex-*Oswald Pirow*) was stricken on 12-10-01. *Shaka* (P 1562), *Adam Kok* (P 1563), *Sekhukhuni* (P 1564), *Isaac Dyobh* (P 1565), and *Job Masego* (P 1568) were retired by 2006.

PATROL BOATS [PB]

♦ 24 Namicurra class
Bldr: Tornado Products, South Africa (In serv. 1980–81)

Y 1502 through Y 1505
Y 1508 through Y 1509
Y 1511 through Y 1519
Y 1521 through Y 1529

Namicurra-class patrol boat Edward McDonnell, 2003

D: 4 tons light (5.2 fl) **S:** 30 kts **Dim:** 9.5 × 2.7 × 0.8
A: 1 12.7-mm mg; 1 twin 7.62-mm mg; 1 shotgun
Electronics: Radar: 1 Furuno . . . nav.
M: 2 BMW or Yamaha inboard-outboard gasoline engines; 2 props; 380 bhp
Range: 180/20 **Crew:** 4 tot.

Remarks: Radar-equipped, glass-reinforced, plastic-hulled, catamaran-hulled harbor craft that can be land-transported on trailers. When fitted, the 7.62-mm twin mount is positioned aft in the cockpit, while the 12.7-mm mg is located at the aft edge of the pilothouse; normally only the 12.7-mm mg is carried, in the aft position. Now carry only the letter "Y" and the last two digits of the pennant number on each side of the pilothouse.
Disposals: Sister Y 1520 was transferred to Malawi on 29-10-88, and Y 1506 was lost off Port Elizabeth (date not available). Y 1501 and Y 1510 were transferred to Namibia in 2003. Y 1507 and Y 1530 were transferred to Mozambique during 2004.

MINE WARFARE SHIPS

♦ 4 River-class coastal minehunters [MHC]
Bldrs: First two: Abeking & Rasmussen, Lemwerder, Germany; others: Sandock Austral SY, Durban

	In serv.
M 1142 Umzimkulu (ex-*Navors III*)	30-10-81
M 1212 Umhloti (ex-*Navors IV*)	26-11-81
M 1213 Umgeni (ex-*Navors II*)	23-3-81
M 1499 Umkomaas (ex-*Navors I*)	13-2-81

Umhloti (M 1212) H&L Van Ginderen, 4-00

D: 380 tons (fl) **S:** 16.5 kts
Dim: 48.10 (44.50 pp) × 8.45 × 2.10 (fwd.)/2.50 (aft)
A: 1 20-mm 90-cal. Oerlikon GAM-B01AA; 2 single 12.7-mm mg

MINE WARFARE SHIPS *(continued)*

Electronics:
Radar: 1 Decca . . . nav.
Sonar: 1 Simrad . . . hull-mounted HF, 1 Klein towed side-looking HF
M: 2 MTU 12V652 TB81 diesels; 2 Voith-Schneider vertical cycloidal props; 3,156 bhp—2 85-kw electric motor/shaft generators for minehunting operations (7 kts max.)
Electric: 618 kw tot. (2 × 165 kw 12-cyl., diesel sets, 1 × 118 kw diesel set, 2 × 85 kw shaft generators
Range: 2,000+/13 **Fuel:** 55 tons **Crew:** 7 officers, 33 enlisted

Remarks: Ordered 1978. The first two hulls were built in West Germany ostensibly as "hydrological and geophysical research ships" and delivered to Sandock Austral Shipyard, Durban, in 1980 for outfitting. Last unit was launched 31-7-81. All were originally painted with blue hulls and white superstructures; they were repainted gray during 1-82, but were not officially acknowledged as naval vessels until 28-1-88. Form the Mine Countermeasures Squadron, at Simon's Town. They are to serve through 2010.
Hull systems: Wooden construction, with GRP hull sheathing below waterline. Have four rudders.
Combat systems: Have Minehunting System Mk 2, including two French PAP-104 remote-controlled submersibles per ship. Were designed to carry Thales DUBM-21 minehunting sonar, but a Simrad retractable 2-frequency set was fitted instead. Navigational equipment includes MRD1 precision radio-navigation set, gyrocompass, doppler log, and echo sounder. Have a mine disposal divers' rigid inflatable boat aft and a decompression chamber for the six-man mine disposal diver team. Thales-African Defence Systems data plotting and recording systems are being installed under a 5-99 contract.

♦ 4 ex-German Type 351 minesweepers [MSC] (2 in *reserve*)
Bldr: Burmester, Bremen

	L	In serv.
M 1222 Tshwane (ex-Schleswig, M 1073)	2-10-57	30-10-58
M 1223 Kapa (ex-*Düren*, M 1079)	12-6-58	22-4-59
M 1224 Mangaung (ex-Konstanz, M 1081)	30-9-58	23-7-59
M 1225 Thekwini (ex-*Wolfsburg*, M 1082)	10-12-58	8-10-59

D: 488 tons (fl) **S:** 16.5 kts **Dim:** 47.50 × 8.50 × 2.75
A: 1 40-mm 70-cal. Bofors AA
Electronics:
Radar: 1 STN Atlas Elektronik TRS-N nav.
Sonar: DSQS-11A
M: 2 MTU MD 871 UM/1D diesels; 2 CP props; 3,300 bhp **Range:** 2,200/16
Electric: 195 kw tot. **Crew:** 4 officers, 40 enlisted

Remarks: Transferred 15-1-01 and departed 19-1-01 for Simonstown on a pontoon barge under tow with sisters *Paderborn* (M 1076, stricken 24-11-99) and *Ulm* (M 1083, stricken 21-9-99), which were transferred for cannibalization. First two were recommissioned on 5-9-01, and the second pair were recommissioned in 2002. Locally referred to as the "City class," they carry the tribal names for Durban, Kapstadt, Johannesburg, and Pretoria. They are former Type 320 minesweepers, each converted to control three F-1 Troika drone magnetic/acoustic minesweepers, completing on 19-3-81, 7-11-83, 24-5-82, and 4-3-82, respectively. South Africa also requested two *Seehund* drones, but Germany was not able to oblige; the ships are thus initially of little use except as patrol craft, but additional mine-countermeasures equipment may be installed in South Africa.
Hull systems: Wooden construction, with original nonmagnetic engines.
Combat systems: As transferred, could carry and tow an Oropesa sweep rig and stow numerous channel-marking (dan) buoys. Were each intended to be able to control three German *Seehund*-class minesweeping drones. The 40-mm gun is controlled by a remote lead-computing optical director.

Disposal note: All remaining units of the former UK Ton-class minesweeper/minehunters operated by South Africa have been discarded as of 2002.

AMPHIBIOUS WARFARE CRAFT

♦ 6 Lima-class personnel landing craft [LCP]
Bldr: . . . (In serv. 2003)

L 29 through L 34

D: 4.2 tons **S:** 38 kts **Dim:** 9.1 × . . . × . . . **A:** Small arms
M: 2 gasoline outboard motors **Range:** 65/26
Crew: . . . (can carry up to 24 troops)

Remarks: GRP construction. Two are carried aboard *Drakensberg* (A 301).

Disposal note: The eight Delta 80–class personnel landing craft have reportedly been removed from service and replaced by the Lima class.

AUXILIARY SHIPS

♦ 1 U.K. Hecla-class hydrographic survey ship [AGS]
Bldr: Yarrow, Scotstoun

	Laid down	L	In serv.
A 324 Protea	20-7-70	14-7-71	23-5-72

D: 1,930 tons (2,750 fl) **S:** 14 kts **Dim:** 79.25 (71.63 pp) × 14.94 × 4.57
A: 2 single 20-mm 70-cal. Oerlikon AA; 2 single 12.7-mm mg
Electronics:
Radar: 1 Kelvin-Hughes Type 1006 nav.
Sonar: STN Atlas Elektronik Hydrosweep MD multi-beam mapping; STN Atlas Elektronik Deso 25 survey echo sounder; EG&G sidescan mapping
M: 3 MTU . . . diesels (1,280 bhp each), 3 generator sets; 1 motor; 1 CP prop; 2,000 shp—bow-thruster
Range: 12,000/11 **Fuel:** 560 tons **Crew:** 18 officers, 114 enlisted + 4 aircrew

Protea (A 324)—white hull, buff funnel and mast, pennant number not displayed
Ralph Edwards, 4-00

Remarks: Ordered 7-11-69. Equipped during 1983 refit for electronic surveillance duties and carries an extensive communications suite. Re-engined during refit 1995–96 and now expected to operate until at least 2009. White-painted, with "buff" stack and mast.
Hull systems: Hull reinforced for navigating in ice. Bow-thruster and antiroll tanks fitted. During 1996 refit, the air-conditioning and refrigeration plants were upgraded, and a new steam boiler and evaporators were fitted.
Mission systems: Has Polaris survey system, with automated data storage, both for the ship and for the two survey launches. Navigational equipment includes an STN Atlas Elektronik Dolog 22 doppler log, a ship-motion sensor, a bathymetric probe, and automated tide gauge, Racal Hyderlink long-range radio position fixing, Del Norte transponder short-range radio position fixing, and differential GPS. Both survey launches have GPS and Deso 25 echo sounders; each can tow the sidescan mapping sonar. Also carried is a suite of land survey equipment. Can carry an Alouette III helicopter for aerial survey work and buoy and transponder placement. Communications intercept equipment was removed during the 1996 refit.

Disposal note: Ex-Ukrainian Ivan Papanin–class fleet supply ship *Outeniqua* (A 302) was retired during 7-04 and sold for commercial use.

♦ 1 fleet replenishment ship [AOR] Bldr: Dorbyl Marine, Durban

	Laid down	L	In serv.
A 301 Drakensberg	3-8-84	24-4-86	11-11-87

Drakensberg (A 301) Michael Winter, 6-05

Drakensberg (A 301) Michael Nitz, 2-06

D: 6,000 tons light (12,500 fl) **S:** 20+ kts **Dim:** 146.30 × 19.50 × 7.90
A: 4 single 20-mm 90-cal. Oerlikon GAM-B01 AA; 6 single 12.7-mm M2 mg; 2 AS.330H/J Puma helicopters
Electronics: Radar: 2 . . . nav.
M: 2 12-cyl. SEMT-Pielstick diesels; 1 CP prop; 16,320 bhp—bow-thruster
Range: 8,000/15 **Endurance:** 90 days
Crew: 10 officers, 86 enlisted + 10 SAAF aviation complement, 22 trainees

Remarks: Ordered 22-9-84. Largest ship ever built in South Africa; builder formerly known as Sandock Austral. Is used for patrol and SAR duties and is considered by some to be South Africa's most capable naval ship.
Hull systems: Can carry 5,500 tons cargo fuel, 208 tons potable water, 100 tons dry provisions, 33 tons frozen foods, 230 tons of containerized cargo, and 1,000 tons of palletized and general cargo and munitions. Helicopter decks fore and aft, hangar aft only; when Puma helicopters are embarked, 10 SAAF personnel are aboard. One dual refueling/solid transfer station is located on each beam, and the ship is also capable of over-the-stern refueling. Equipped with tunnel-thruster in the pronounced bulbous bow. Has five generator sets. Four desalinization plants can produce 70,000 liters potable water per day. Has davits port and starboard to handle Delta 80, 37-knot assault boats. Has additional navigational training equipment, an extensive infirmary, and can accommodate more than 200 additional personnel, if required. Two rigid inflatable boats, two landing craft, and two diving service boats are carried. The helicopter deck traversing system has been removed.

SERVICE CRAFT

♦ 3 Coastguard T 2212–class hydrofoil rescue craft [YHH]
Bldr: T-Craft International, Capetown

P 1552 Tobie (In serv. 6-92)
P 1553 Tern (In serv. 6-96)
P 1554 Tekane (In serv. 12-96)

Tekane (P 1554) SAN, 4-97

D: 23 tons (45 fl) **S:** 41 kts **Dim:** 22.00 × 7.00 × 0.90 **A:** 1 12.7-mm mg
Electronics: Radar: 1 . . . nav.
M: 2 MTU 12V183 TE92 diesels; 2 Castoldi waterjets; 2,000 bhp
Range: 525/30 **Crew:** 4 tot. + 12 passengers

Remarks: Trials with a prototype were undertaken during summer 1991 under temporary pennant number T 2201. Three production versions were ordered 10-91, but one was initially rejected. Were intended to serve as air-sea rescue craft in support of the South African Air Force, based at Saldanha Bay. The South African Police Coast Guard also uses units of this design, and three were sold to Israel in 11-97.
Hull systems: Unusual catamaran hull form with hydrofoils between the hulls. GRP construction. Have accommodations for 16 but can be operated with as few as four personnel. Were intended to be able to maintain 37 kts in Sea State 5. Carry a 3.4-m rigid inflatable rescue boat aft in a recess between the hulls.

Disposal note: Air-sea rescue craft P 1551 (ex-R 31), in reserve since 1997, went aground while under tow on 23-5-02 and was lost.

Disposal note: Diving tender and torpedo-recovery craft *Fleur* (P 3148) was no longer in service as of 2006.

♦ 1 large harbor tug [YTB] Bldr: . . ., Singapore (L: 1995)

K 230 Umalusi (ex-*Golden Energy*)

D: 490 tons (fl) **S:** 13 kts **Dim:** 30.00 (28.84 wl) × 10.00 × 4.90 max.
Electronics: Radar: 1 Furuno 1941 nav.
M: 2 Caterpillar 3516TA diesels; 2 Aquamaster Model 1401 Kort-nozzle 4-bladed azimuth props; 3,620 bhp
Electric: 212 kVA tot. (2 × 106 kVA, Caterpillar 3304T diesel sets driving)
Range: . . . / . . . **Fuel:** 60 m^3 **Crew:** 12 tot.

Remarks: One large firefighting harbor tug was purchased from Tai Kong Trading Co., Singapore, in 3-97, for $4.48 million to replace the *De Noord.* The new name, the subject of a public contest, means "Shepherd" in Bantu.
Hull systems: Has a 42-ton bollard pull capacity and is equipped with an 80-ton double-drum towing winch, two 13,000 liter/min. fire monitors, a 50 m^3/hr oil dispersant system with 7.6 m^3 capacity.

♦ 1 large harbor tug [YTB] Bldr: Dorman Long, Durban

	L	In serv.
De Mist	21-12-78	23-12-78

De Mist—black hull, buff superstructure Peter Froud, 4-97

D: 275 tons (fl) **S:** 12.5 kts **Dim:** 34.3 (32.3 pp) × 7.8 × 3.4
M: 2 Mirrlees-Blackstone ESL-8-MGR diesels; 2 Voith-Schneider vertical cycloidal props; 2,440 bhp
Crew: 5 officers, 6 unlicensed (civilian)

Remarks: Bollard pull: 25 tons. Has two firefighting monitors and carries 20,000 liters lightwater foam. Based at Simon's Town Dockyard. Is fully seagoing, if required.

♦ 1 large harbor tug [YTB]
Bldr: Globe Eng. Wks., Capetown

	Laid down	L	In serv.
De Neys	7-67	7-69	23-7-69

De Neys French Navy, 4-97

D: 282 tons (fl) **S:** 11.5 kts **Dim:** 28.65 (27.0 wl) × 8.23 × 4.72
M: 2 Lister-Blackstone ERS-8-M diesels; 2 Voith-Schneider vertical cycloidal props; 1,268 bhp
Crew: 10 tot. (civilian)

Remarks: 180 grt. 14-ton max. bollard pull. Steel construction, with wooden decks. Based at Simon's Town Dockyard. Has a single firefighting monitor.

♦ 3 miscellaneous dockyard tugs [YTM]

DL 2 DL 4 E.L.S. Sylvester DL 5

DL 2 Peter Froud, 4-97

E.L.S. Sylvester (DL 4) Peter Froud, 4-97

Remarks: All three are used at Simon's Town Dockyard. DL 2 was built around 1940 in Scotland, DL 4 was launched 5-2-73 at Simon's Town, and DL 5 was built during the 1960s in South Africa at Globe Engineering Works. No data available.

POLICE COAST GUARD

(*Kuswag*)

The South African Police Water Wing was renamed the Police Coast Guard in 1995 and is equipped with a number of miscellaneous small craft and launches and at least one T-Craft catamaran hydrofoil launch of the type used by the navy. Hulls are painted red, superstructures white, and either diagonal hull stripes or stack stripes of blue-yellow-blue are carried.

♦ 1 OPV Fisheries and Environmental Protection Ship [WPS]
Bldr: Schelde, Shipbuilding, Vlissingen

	Laid down	L	In serv.
Sarah Baartman	10-03	9-04	10-1-05

POLICE COAST GUARD *(continued)*

Sarah Baartman Damen, 2004

D: . . . **S:** 22 kts (20 sust.) **Dim:** 82.90 × 13.00 × 6.80 **A:** . . .
Electronics: Radar: X- and S-band nav. **M:** 2 Wärtsilä 12V26A; 2 CP props; 11,100 shp
Range: 12,000/15 **Fuel:** . . .
Endurance: 45 days **Crew:** 29 tot.

Remarks: The main task of the Offshore Patrol Vessel is fishery and environmental protection, assistance in operations, oil-spill cleanup, search and rescue, and limited towing and fire fighting. Humanitarian assistance can be provided where required. Has a landing pad and can accommodate one helicopter. Fitted with SATCOM and an echo sounder.

♦ 3 (+ 1) 45-meter coastal patrol boats [WPB]
Bldr: Far Ocean Marine, Durban

	In serv.
LILLIAN NGOYI	2005
RUTH FIRST	2005
VICTORIA MXENGE	2005
. . .	2007

D: . . . **S:** 25 kts **Dim:** 45.0 x . . . x . . . **A:** . . .
Electronics: . . . **M:** . . .
Range: 3,500/15 **Endurance:** 14 days **Crew:** 13 tot. (+ 2 fisheries inspectors)

Remarks: Built under the same 2002 contract as Fisheries and Environmental Protection Ship *Sarah Baartman*. Designed to operate up to 200 n.m. offshore but operate mostly within 50–80 miles off the coast with general patrol and environmental protection duties.

Note: The 5,353 grt/3,035 dwt Department of Transport–operated Antarctic survey and supply ship *S.A. Agulhas* has not been operated by the Navy since 1989. Other government-owned vessels include fisheries research ships *Africana, Algoa,* and *Sardinops* and fisheries protection ships *Jasus, Patella,* and *Pelagus.*

SPAIN

Spanish State

ARMADA ESPAÑOLA

Personnel: 19,455 total including 5,300 marines and 814 naval aviation personnel; plus 9,000 naval reservists.

Bases: Primary facilities are located at El Ferrol, Rota, Cartagena, Las Palmas in the Canary Islands and Mahón on Minorca and Porto Pi on Majorca

Naval Aviation: Four EAV-8B Harrier V/STOL fighter-bombers and 12 EAV-8B+ Harrier are operated by the Ninth Aircraft Squadron in service for use on the carrier *Príncipe de Asturias*. The EAV-8Bs are being re-equipped as EAV-8B+ with the APG-65 radar. Spanish Harriers carry AIM-120 AMRAAM and AIM-9L Sidewinder air-to-air missiles and AGM-65F Maverick air-to-ground missiles.

The *Arma Aerea de la Armada* also operates 12 SH-60B Seahawk, nine Augusta-Bell AB-212 (three are equipped with Elettronica "Gufo" 2000 EW intercept gear and 11 have a datalink), eight Sikorsky SH-3D Sea King, three SH-3D AEW conversions, and 10 Hughes 369-HM(500M) Cayuse helicopters, plus three Cessna 550 Citation-II, liaison aircraft. All AB-212 and SH-3 helicopters are expected to be replaced by 32 NH-90 helicopters (20 transport, 6 AEW, and 6 ASW) between 2015–2020. The SH-60Bs have been equipped to launch Kongsberg Penguin Mk 2 Mod. 7 antiship missiles, 20 of which were ordered in 6-00. The final six SH-60Bs were delivered 2002–3 and are equipped to fire the Hellfire missile.

The Spanish Air Force performs the maritime surveillance mission, using two P-3A and five P-3B Orions. Between 2002 and 2006, the Orions were updated with five multifunction data display stations each and new weapons and ASW sensor management systems. Additional P-3CB improvements include a new radar, ESM, IFF interrogator, Link 11 capability, inertial navigation and GPS receiver, new communications suite, and ground support center.

Spanish Navy EAV-8B+ Harrier Neill Rush, 10-05

Spanish Navy AB-212 Martin Mokrus, 4-05

Air Force CASA C-212 Aviocar with APS-128 radar, Fokker F-27-200MPA fixed-wing aircraft, and AS.332B Super Puma helicopters are used for search-and-rescue work. Air Force F/A-18 Hornet fighter-bombers are equipped for maritime strike with AGM-84 Harpoon missiles. The search-and-rescue service (*Servicio de Busqueda y Salvamento*) has 9 AS.332F Super Puma helicopters for rescue duties and two configured as VIP transports.

The CASA CN-235M is Spain's current-production maritime surveillance aircraft and has been widely exported. The following is a description of the version delivered to the Irish Air Corps in 11-94:

Wingspan: 25.8 m **Length:** 21.3 m **Weight:** 13,600 kg max
Wing area: 60 m^2 **Speed:** 282 kts (cruise)
Engines: 2 G.E. CT7-9C turboprop; 3,500 shp tot. **Range:** 1,038 n.m.
Crew: 6 tot. **Avionics:** Litton APS-504(V)5 INS, FLIR, radar

Marine Corps: The *Tercia de Armada* (TEAR), was re-formed in 1968 from the *Grupo Especial de Infanteria de Marina,* which had been established in 1957. Artillery support consists of one battery of six U.S. M109, self-propelled 155-mm guns and six M-56 105-mm towed howitzers. Also available are 16 M-60A3 medium tanks and 18 Piranha armored personnel carriers. For amphibious assault, there are 19 AAVP-7A1 tracked armored personnel vehicles, all updated from LVTP-7-series configuration from 11-97 to mid-2000. Antitank equipment consists of 24 TOW-2 missile launchers, while 12 Mistral lightweight SAM systems (50 missiles total) provide air defense.

WEAPONS AND SYSTEMS

Except for naval guns, which are domestically manufactured, most of the weapon systems in use are of American or French manufacture. In use are U.S. RGM-84A and RGM-84C Harpoon antiship missiles and Mk 46 Mod. 5 antisubmarine torpedoes. Spanish Air Force F/A-18 Hornets can carry AGM-84C Harpoon missiles for maritime strikes. AGM-65F Maverick missiles were ordered for use with AV-8B+ Harrier aircraft. The Spanish Navy continues to express interest in the Tomahawk land attack missile for possible use in S 80 submarines and F 100 frigates.

The Meroka antiaircraft/antimissile point-defense system consists of two rows of six 20-mm Oerlikon guns:

Length: 120 calibers **Round weight:** 320 gr. all-up
Projectile weight: 102 gr. **Muzzle velocity:** 1,200m/sec.
Maximum rate of fire: 9,000 rd/min **Maximum effective range:** 2,000 m

Meroka employs a Lockheed Martin VPS-2 Sharpshooter I-band monopulse radar on the mount, with target designation by the ship's AESN RAN-12L/X dual-frequency search radar and an AESN PDS-10 TDS console. The 20 Mod. 2A mounts procured carry 720 rounds each and have a thermal imager; the later Mod. 2B version has 2,160 rounds. In 1993, three Mod. 2B mounts with digital data processors, automatic target acquisition, improved performance against sea-skimming targets, a more powerful, PRF-agile AESN RTN-30X radar using Moving-Target Indication (MTI), and built-in test equipment were procured; all Mod. 2A mounts are being upgraded to the same standard.

Under development for use on the F-100 and succeeding F-110-class frigates is the Bazán-FABA DORNA (*Dirección de tiro Optrónica y Radárica Naval*) gun fire-control system with co-mounted K-band radar and laser rangefinder; it can be used independently of the main weapons control system to control 40-, 76-, and 127-mm guns.

Mines made by SAES, Madrid, include:

- MILA-6B: Limpet mine with time fuze; also usable as demolition charge.
- MIM-90: Cylindrical submarine-laid mine with same detection systems as the MO-90.

WEAPONS AND SYSTEMS *(continued)*

- MO-90: 1,000 kg (with 300 kg HBX-3 charge) moored mine capable of being laid in depths from 15 to 350 m at speeds of up to 30 kts by surface craft. Height: 1.90 m, width: 1.10 m. Lethal to 40-m range. Has minesweeping countermeasures features and can be programmed to sterilize in 0 to 720 days. First deliveries began in 12-92.

There are two fixed ground stations for the SECOMSAT (*Sistema Español de Comunicaciones Militares por Satélite*) military SATCOM system, which employs the commercial Hispisat communications satellite constellation. Shipboard terminals had been installed by early 1997 in the carrier *Príncipe de Asturias,* the frigate *Navarra,* and the transport *Aragón,* and the Marines have a mobile terminal; the other *Perry*-class frigates are also to receive the system. Twenty Leica GPS MX 412B 12-channel differential GPS sets were delivered early in 1998 for shipboard use.

Note: Pennant numbers on all seagoing ships have been toned down to a dark gray. The major state-owned shipyards, Astilleros Españoles SA (AESA) and E.N. Bazán, were combined in 7-00, with the new firm known as Izar Construcciones Navales, S.A. (Izar, for short). Late in 2004 the company was restructured and is now called Navantia.

V/STOL AIRCRAFT CARRIER [CVV]

♦ 1 Modified U.S. Sea Control Ship design

Bldr: Izar, Ferrol

	Laid down	L	In serv.
R 11 Príncipe de Asturias (ex-*Canarias,* ex-*Almirante Carrero*)	8-10-79	22-5-82	30-5-88

Príncipe de Asturias (R 11) U.S. Navy, 7-04

Príncipe de Asturias (R 11) Michael Nitz, 7-05

Príncipe de Asturias (R 11) Leo van Ginderen, 6-05

D: 15,912 tons (17,188 fl) **S:** 26 kts
Dim: 195.1 (187.5 pp) × 24.4 (30.0 flight deck) × 6.7 (9.4 over prop)
Air Group: 6–8 EAV-8B Harrier V/STOL fighters; 2 SH-60B, 6-10 SH-3D/G, and 2-4 AB-212 helicopters
A: 4 12-barrel 20-mm Meroka Mod. 2A CIWS
Electronics:
Radar: 1 Cardion SPS-55 surf. search; 1 Hughes SPS-52C 3-D air search; 1 ITT SPN-35A air control; 1 Selenia RAN-11 L/X target designation; 4 Lockheed VPS-2 f.c. (on Meroka mounts)
TACAN: URN-25
EW: Elettronica Nettunel intercept; Mk 36 Mod. 2 SRBOC decoy syst. (6 6-round Mk 137 RL); SLQ-25 Nixie towed torpedo decoy syst.
M: 2 G.E. LM-2500 gas turbines; 1 CP prop; 46,400 shp—2/800-shp retractable Pleuger electric auxiliary props (4.5 kts)
Electric: 7,500 kw (3 Allison 501-K17 gas turbine-driven 2,500-kw sets)
Range: 6,500/20
Crew: 90 officers, 465 enlisted + 201 air group and flag staff of 7

Remarks: Ordered 29-6-77. Design is essentially that of the final version of the U.S. Navy's canceled Sea Control Ship concept, with a 12-degree ski-jump bow added. Serves as flagship of *Grupo Aeronaval* Alfa and is based at Rota. Mid-life modernization, begun during 2006, is expected to complete by 2008.
Hull systems: Has two pair Denny-Brown fin stabilizers. U.S. Prairie/Masker hull and propeller air bubble system installed to reduce radiated noise. Boats include two LCVP-type landing craft. Has been modified to accommodate female crewmembers.
Aviation systems: The flight deck is 175.3 × 29 m and is served by two elevators, one at the extreme aft end and the other to starboard of the flight path, forward of the island. Takeoff pattern from the 12-degree ski-jump is angled to starboard. The hangar provides a total of 2,300 m^2 parking space. In a 1990 refit, a parallel fuel distribution system with 37,000-m^3 tank capacity was installed to permit carrying a

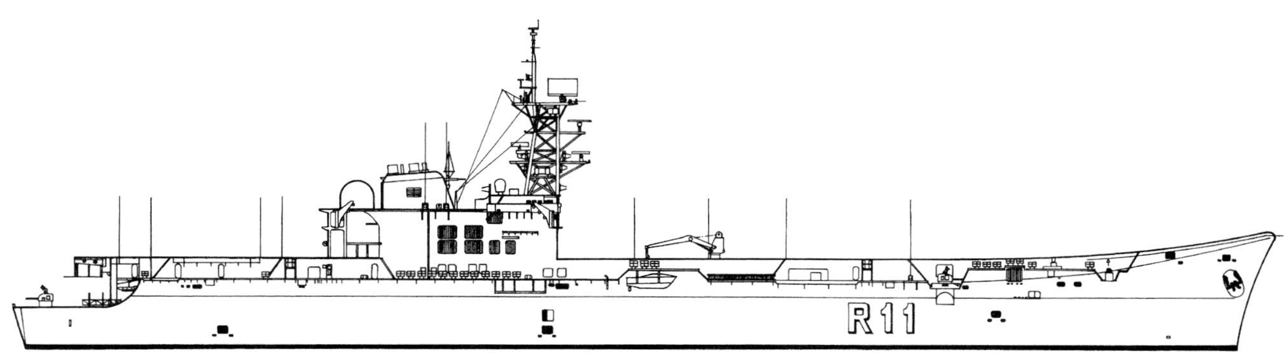

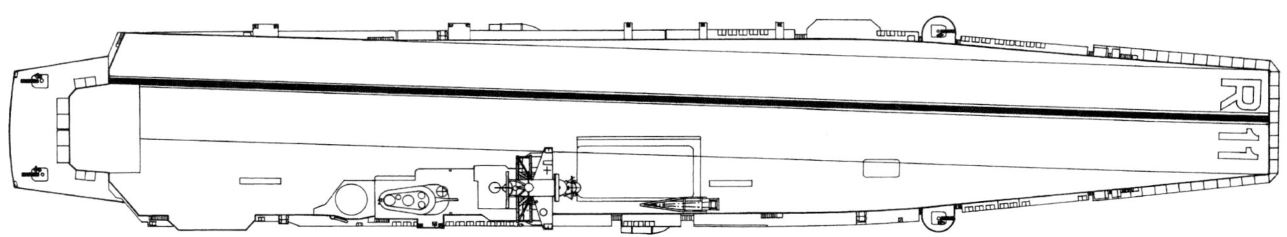

Príncipe de Asturias (R 11) *Ships of the World,* 2002

V/STOL AIRCRAFT CARRIER [CVV] *(continued)*

fuel load of 40% aviation fuel/60% DFM propulsion fuel; at the same time, the island superstructure was enlarged to port at its aft end to incorporate a briefing room, the flying control central was enlarged, and accommodations for six additional officers and 30 additional enlisted were added. A Marconi Deck Approach Projector Sight (DAPS) has been added to facilitate Harrier landings.
Combat systems: The Tritan combat data system employs two Unisys UYK-43 and two UYK-20 computers; Link 11 and Link 14 data link and U.S. FLEETSATCOM are installed, as are the Saturn 3S and SECOMSAT (*Sistema Español de Comunicaciones Militares por Satélite*) SATCOM system, both of which share two SCOT radome-covered dish antennas. Has U.S. UPX-25 and UPX-28 IFF equipment, Raylass navigation system with Magnavox MX1105 NAVSAT/Omega receiver, and two Sperry HK inertial navigation systems (SINS). The SPS-52C radar was updated to SPS-52D in 1990. Two Rheinmetall 37-mm saluting cannon are mounted on the fantail.

ATTACK SUBMARINES [SS]

♦ 0 (+ 4) (S-80) Program   Bldr: Navantia, Cartagena

	Laid down	L	In serv.
S 81 . . .	2007	2010	2011
S 82 . . .	2008	2011	2012
S 83 . . .	2009	2012	2013
S 84 . . .	2010	2013	2014

D: 2,120 tons surf. fl/2,425 tons sub. **S:** 12 kts surf./20 kts sub.
Dim: 71.1 × 8.4 × 7.3
A: 6 533-mm bow TT (18 DM-2A4 wire-guided torpedoes and UGM-84 Harpoon missiles)
Electronics:
Radar: . . .
Sonar: . . .
M: 2 × 1,100 kw diesel generator sets, 1 electric motor; 1 prop; 3,800 shp
Range: 6,500/8 (snorkel); 750/4 (sub.) **Endurance:** 50 days **Crew:** 32-35 tot.

Remarks: Intended to replace *Daphné* class. Cooperative design effort between Izar and DCN, France. In 9-03, the Spanish government formally authorized the construction of the first four submarines. Will be fitted with Air Independent Propulsion (AIP) systems.
Hull systems: These are the first Spanish boats to be fitted with air-independent propulsion (AIP). Range on the Rankine-cycle AIP system (probably Bertin's MESMA system) would be 750/4. Diving depth: 300–350 m.
Combat systems: Are planned to employ the Kongsberg Defence and Aerospace MSI-90U combat data system, using multiple-function, flat-screen displays. Will carry a modernized version of the French DSUV-22 sonar.

♦ 4 French Agosta (S-70) class   Bldr: Izar, Cartagena

	Laid down	L	In serv.
S 71 Galerna	5-9-77	5-12-81	22-1-83
S 72 Siroco	27-11-78	13-11-82	5-12-83
S 73 Mistral	30-5-80	14-11-83	5-6-85
S 74 Tramontana	18-12-81	30-11-84	27-1-86

Galerna (S 71) Bernard Prézelin, 6-05

Galerna (S 71) Bernard Prézelin, 6-05

D: 1,230 tons std.; 1,490 tons surf./1,750 tons sub. **S:** 12 kts surf./20.5 kts sub.
Dim: 67.90 × 6.80 × 5.40
A: 4 550-mm bow TT (20 ECAN F 17 Mod. 2, E 18, and L 5 Mod. 3 and 4 torpedoes or up to 19 mines with 9 torpedoes)

Galerna (S 71) Bernard Prézelin, 6-05

Electronics:
Radar: 1 DRUA-33C search/nav.—EW: Thorn-EMI Manta-E intercept
Sonar: S 71, 72, 74: Thales DUUX-2A passive ranging; DUUX-5 passive ranging; S 73: Thales DUUA-2A/2B active, Thales DSUV-22 passive search and attack; SOLARSUB towed passive linear array
M: 2 SEMT-Pielstick 16 PA4 185 diesel generator sets (850 kw each); 1 prop; 4,600 shp main engine—1 32-shp cruising engine
Range: 8,500/9 (snorkel); 17.5/17.5 (sub.); 350/3.5 (sub.) **Fuel:** 185 tons
Endurance: 45 days **Crew:** 6 officers, 48 enlisted

Remarks: Built with technical assistance from DCN, France. First two were ordered 9-5-75, the second pair on 29-6-77. S 73 may not receive new equipment added to the others. All are based with *Flotilla de Submarinos* at Cartagena.
Hull systems: Can dive to 300 m. During recent modernizations to all but S 73, the periscopes were modified for night vision, new tubular-plate batteries were substituted, new diesel engine exhaust valves were fitted, and noise-reduction measures were undertaken.
Combat systems: All but S 73 have received mid-life "ACRUX" refits beginning 3-93 with S 71; in addition, the DLA-2A (CIMSA 15/Mitra-125) torpedo fire-control system was modified to launch the F-17 Mod. 2 torpedo, and the sonar suites were upgraded. S 73 ran trials during spring 1991 with the Thales clip-on DSUV-62 towed passive linear hydrophone array, but it was not purchased; instead, the SOLARSUB (*Sonar de Largo Alcance Remolcado Submarino,* or Long-Range Towed Sonar, Submarine) was developed and installed on the class during 2004–5.

Disposal note: *Daphné* (S-60)-class submarine *Tonina* (S 62) was retired on 30-9-05 and sister *Marsopa* (S 63) was stricken during 4-06. *Narval* (S 64) decommissioned on 23-1-03; *Delfín* (561) was decommissioned in 2003.

GUIDED-MISSILE FRIGATES [FFG]

Note: Preliminary design work is also ongoing on a follow-on F-110 guided-missile ship design that would have many features and systems similar to those of the F-100 but would have additional gun firepower.
The private Advanced Frigate Consortium (Izar, with Lockheed Martin Naval Electronics and Surveillance Systems, and General Dynamics Bath Ironworks) is designing for potential export (and possible Spanish Navy) purchase a 130-m overall, 4,600-ton frigate to be equipped with the reduced-size and weight SPY-1K Aegis radar system and the COMBATSS (Component-Based Total Ship System) combat data suite; also to be carried would be Mk 41 VLS, a 76-mm DP gun with backup E/O director, ASW torpedo tubes, a helicopter with hangar, and a hull-mounted sonar; a variety of propulsion options are to be offered.

♦ 4 (+ 1 + 1) Álvaro de Bazán–class (Project F-100)
Bldr: Navantia (ex-Izar), Ferrol

	Laid down	L	In serv.
F 101 Álvaro de Bazán	14-6-99	27-10-00	19-9-02
F 102 Almirante Juan de Borbón (ex-*Roger de Lauria*)	27-10-00	28-2-02	3-12-03
F 103 Blas de Lezo	28-2-02	16-5-03	16-12-04
F 104 Méndez Nuñez	16-5-03	12-11-04	28-2-06
F 105 Roger de Lauria	2008	2009	2011

Almirante Juan de Borbón (F 102) Leo van Ginderen, 3-06

Blas de Lezo (F 103) Michael Winter, 6-05

GUIDED-MISSILE FRIGATES [FFG] *(continued)*

Álvaro de Bazán (F 101) U.S. Navy, 7-05

Blas de Lezo (F 103) Leo van Ginderen, 6-05

D: 4,555 tons (5,802 fl) **S:** 28.5 kts (27 kts sustained)
Dim: 146.72 (133.20 pp) × 18.60 (17.50 wl) × 4.75 (4.84 at full load)
A: 8 RGM-84F Harpoon Block 1D SSM; 48-cell Mk 41 VLS syst. (32 Standard SM-2 Block IIIA and 64 RIM-162 Evolved Sea Sparrow SAM); 1 127-mm 54-cal. Mk 45 Mod. 2 DP; 1 12-barreled 20-mm Meroka-2B CIWS; 2 single 20-mm 90-cal. AA; 2 pair fixed 324-mm Mk 32 Mod. 9 ASW TT; 1 SH-60B Seahawk LAMPS III Block II ASW helicopter
Electronics:
Radar: 1 Thales Scout nav./surf. search; 1 Raytheon SPS-67(V)4 surf. search; 1 Lockheed Martin SPY-1D 3-D tracking, target-designation, and weapons control; 2 Raytheon SPG-62 target illuminators; 1 AESN RAN-30L/X Meroka f.c, 1/FABA Dorna gun f.c.
Sonar: ENOSA-Raytheon DE 1160LF (I) hull-mounted; EDO UQN-4 deep-water echo sounder; EDO Model 5400 underwater telephone; provision for active/passive towed linear hydrophone array
EW: Indra SLQ-380 Aldebarán intercept/jammer suite; CESELSA Elnath Mk 9500 comms intercept; . . . laser detection and countermeasure syst.; Mk 36 Mod. 2 SRBOC decoy RL syst. (4 6-round Mk 137 RL); SLQ-25A Enhanced Nixie acoustic torpedo decoy syst.
E/O: Thales SIRIUS optronic surveillance; FABA Dorna radar/optronic weapons f.c.s.
M: CODOG: 2 G.E. LM 2500 gas turbines (23,324 shp each), 2 Bazán-Caterpillar 3600-series low-r.p.m. diesels (6,000 shp each); 2 LIPS 4.65-m dia., 5-bladed CP props; 46,648 shp max.
Electric: 4,400 kw tot. (4 × 1,100 kw Bazán-MTU 12C396 diesel sets)
Range: 5,000/18 **Endurance:** 21 days
Crew: 35 officers, 215 enlisted (including 11 air unit; accomm. for 250, including 16 flag group)

Remarks: Were to have been constructed under a 27-1-94 cooperative venture with Germany and the Netherlands. Spain, however, withdrew from the radar and weapons control portions of the agreement on 6-6-95. Authority to construct four was granted by the Council of Ministers on 24-1-97, the contract was placed on 31-1-97, and fabrication of modules began during 11-97. Cost about $540 million each. Intended to serve for 30 years. The Standard SAM system provides AAW coverage out to 150 km. All are based at Rota. A fifth unit of the class was ordered during 6-05. A sixth unit is planned.
Hull systems: Have fin stabilizers. The ships are to be able to operate in 100-kt winds. A design growth margin of 450 tons was provided, and maximum permissible displacement will be 6,250 tons. The hull has four internal decks and is built of AH-36 high-tensile steel. The hangar can accommodate two SH-60-sized helicopters, but only one will be assigned to each ship; the flight deck will be 26.4 m long. Fireproof internal paneling is employed, and special efforts have been made to reduce radar, acoustic, and heat signatures. Are to have Sperry MarineWQN-2 doppler speed and motion logs.
Combat systems: The SPY-1D Aegis radar system has the Lockheed Martin Distributed Advanced Naval Combat System with much the same Aegis Baseline 5 Phase III system used on current-construction U.S. *Arleigh Burke*–class destroyers, but the Spanish version will have a federated data-distribution architecture, giving it some features of the later Aegis Baseline 6 Phase I on the first two ships and Baseline 7 Phase 1 on the latter two. F 105 is expected to have more advanced antiballistic missile capabilities than the earlier units. Hardware and software requirements are being defined by Fábrica de Artillería de Bazán (FABA) so as to integrate Spanish- and U.S.-origin equipment via a redundant local-area net. Hewlett-Packard 743 VME processors are being used. There are 14 SAINSEL CONAM2000 color command consoles and two integrated command display consoles. The ships have NATO Link 11 and Link 16 datalink. WSC-3 UHF SATCOM and a Spanish SHF SATCOM will be fitted.
Also incorporated in the combat system is FABA's DORNA optronic and radar naval fire-control system. The torpedo fire-control system will be the SAINSEL DLT 309. SAINSEL, CESELSA, and ENOSA are all part of the Indra Electronics Group. The U.S. UPX-29 fixed-array IFF interrogation system with Sanders OE-120/UPX electronically-steered interrogation antenna is installed, as is the Lucent UYS-2A(V) DEM E electronic and acoustic intercept signal processing system. Space is provided for later installation of a towed linear sonar array.
The point-defense RIM-7PTC Evolved Sea Sparrow Missiles will be carried in "quad-packs," four per Mk 41 launch cell, and Standard SM-2 Block IIIA missiles will be used for area air-defense. May later be equipped to carry U.S. BGM-109C Tomahawk land-attack missiles. The 127-mm guns are surplus U.S. Navy mountings from *Tarawa*-class LHAs upgraded to Mod. 2 by Izar's FABA armament division. Plans to install ABCAS ASW mortars have been canceled. The Aegis system will provide target cueing for the CIWS. The ships will have a full LAMPS-III ASW helicopter capability, with the SQQ-28 LAMPS-III electronics package and SRQ-4 datalink.

♦ 6 U.S. Oliver Hazard Perry class Bldr: Izar, Ferrol

	Laid down	L	In serv.
F 81 Santa María	22-5-82	24-11-84	12-10-86
F 82 Victoria	16-8-83	23-7-86	11-11-87
F 83 Numancia	8-1-86	29-1-87	17-11-89
F 84 Reina Sofia (ex-*América*)	12-10-87	19-7-89	30-10-90
F 85 Navarra	15-4-91	23-10-92	30-5-94
F 86 Canarias	15-4-92	21-6-93	14-12-94

Canarias (F 86) Bernard Prézelin, 2-05

Navarra (F 85) U.S. Navy, 9-04

Reina Sofia (F 84) Cem D. Yaylali, 5-05

D: F 81–84: 2,851 tons light, 3,610 standard (4,017 fl); F 85, 86: 4,107 tons (fl)
S: 29 kts max. **Dim:** 138.80 (125.90 wl) × 14.30 × 4.52 (6.60 sonar dome)
A: 1 Mk 13 Mod. 4 missile launcher (8 RGM-84C Harpoon SSM and 32 Standard SM-1 MR Block V SAM); 1 76-mm 62-cal. U.S. Mk 75 DP; 1 20-mm Meroka Mod. 2A or B CIWS; 2 triple 324-mm Mk 32 Mod. 5 ASW TT (Mk 46 Mod. 5 torpedoes); 1 SH-60B Seahawk LAMPS-III ASW helicopter
Electronics:
Radar: 1 Raytheon 1650/9xR nav.; 1 Cardion SPS-55 nav./surf.-search; 1 Raytheon SPS-49(V)4 or 5 air-search; 1 Lockheed-Martin Mk 92 Mod. 2 or 6 CAS track-while-scan gun/missile f.c.; 1 Lockheed STIR Mk 54 Mod. 0 or Mod 1 missile/gun f.c.; 1 AESN RAN-12 L/X Meroka CIWS target designation; 1 Lockheed Martin VPS-2 CIWS f.c. (being replaced by AESN RTN-30X)
Sonar: Raytheon DE 1160 hull-mounted MF; Gould SQR-19(V)2 TASS

GUIDED-MISSILE FRIGATES [FFG] *(continued)*

Canarias (F 86) Bernard Prézelin, 9-05

TACAN: URN-25
EW: Elettronica Nettunel MK-3000 active/passive suite; Mk 36 Super RBOC decoy syst. (2 6-round Mk 137 RL); SLQ-25 Nixie torpedo decoy syst.
M: 2 Fiat-G.E. LM-2500 gas turbines; 1 CP prop; 41,000 shp—2/350-shp retractable, rotatable electric auxiliary propulsion motors
Electric: 4,000 kw (4 × 1,000-kw Kato-Allison 114-DOOL diesel sets)
Range: 5,000/18 **Fuel:** 587 tons **Crew:** 13 officers, 210 enlisted

Remarks: First three were ordered on 29-6-77, the fourth on 19-6-86, and the fifth and sixth on 26-10-89. F 85 began sea trials 10-93. They form the 41st Escort Squadron and are assigned to Aviation Group Alfa, based at Rota.
Hull systems: All have the longer hull used in U.S. FFG 36–61. Last two were built with accommodations for female crewmembers, and the others were similarly modified. The U.S. Prairie/Masker bubble noise reduction system is fitted, as are fin stabilizers. F 85 and F 86 have hydrodynamic flow fins added at the waterline aft to improve fuel economy by about 6%.
Combat systems: Have NATO Link-11 datalink equipment and Saturn 3S SATCOM gear. The hull-mounted sonar is essentially the same as the U.S. Navy's SQS-56. Have RAST helicopter deck-handling system to handle SH-60B LAMPS-III helicopters. F 83 and later were completed with the SSQ-28 LAMPS-III datalink, backfitted to the others. Although twin hangars can accommodate two SH-60B, only one per ship is carried. F 81 through F 84 have Mk 92 Mod. 2 f.c.s. and SPS-49(V)4 radars; the other two, with the CORT update, have Mk 92 Mod. 6 f.c.s. and SPS-49(V)6 radars. F 85 and F 86 also have the improved Mod. 2B Meroka CIWS, Sainsel-Ceselsa-Inisel 3-operator CONAM combat data display systems, and an integrated GPS/inertial navigation system. F 81–84 have SPS-49(V)4 search radars and Mk 92 Mod. 2 fire control systems, while the other two have SPS-49(V)5 and Mk 92 Mod. 6. F 83 and F 86 had terminals for the Hispisat SATCOM system installed by 1997, and the others are to be similarly backfitted. F 85 received Matra-Marconi SCOT antennas for the Hispisat SHF SATCOM system in 1998.
Modernization: All may receive the INISEL/FABA DORNA (*Direccion de tiro Optrónica y Radárica Naval*) weapons direction system, with Thales Nederland Sting radar tracker, infrared camera, laser rangefinder, and high-definition t.v. in place of the original U.S. Mk 92 systems; trials commenced with a containerized system on the helicopter deck of F 83 in 4-96. All are also to receive the Ensa Elnath communications intercept system. The original VPS-2 radars for the Meroka system are to be replaced by an AESN RTN-30X radar.

Disposal note: All remaining *Baleares*-class frigates, *Extremadura* (F 75), *Catalina* (F 73), *Andalucía* (F 72), and *Asturias* (F 74), had been decommissioned by 2006.

PATROL SHIPS [PS]

♦ 0 (+ 4 + 6) BPC-47(BAM) class
Bldr: Navantia, Puerto Real (In serv. 2008)

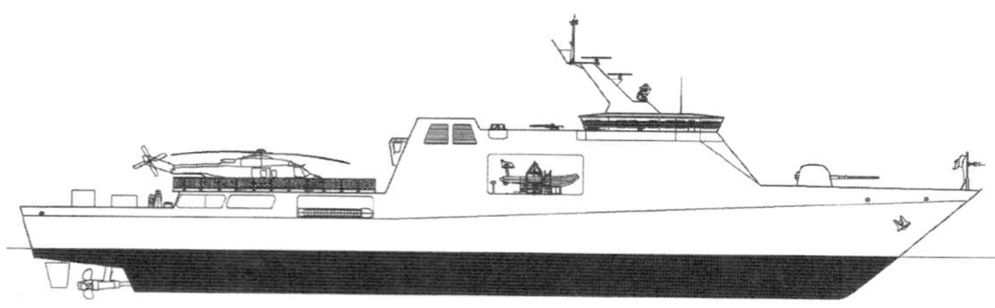

BPC-47(BAM)-class patrol ship—official drawing
Navantia via Antoni Casinos, 2004

D: 2,900 tons (fl) **S:** 20 kts **Dim:** 93.5 × 14.2 × 4.2
A: 1 76-mm 62-cal. OTO Melara SuperRapid DP; 1 helicopter
Electronics: Radar: 2 . . . nav.
M: 2 . . . diesels; 2 props
Range: 8,000/. . . **Crew:** 40 tot. (+ 20 passengers)

Remarks: BAM = Buque de Acción Marítima (Maritime Action Ship). New class of 2,900-ton patrol ships are as large as frigates, though less heavily armed and built to a modular design. Will be fitted with helictoper landing platform and hangar. Up to 16 may be built. Intended to replace the Barcelo and Anaga classes.

♦ 2 Arnomendi-class fisheries patrol ship
Bldr: Construcciones Navales P. Freire, S.A., Vigo

	In serv.
P 63 Arnomendi	20-1-01
P 64 Tarifa	5-7-04

Arnomendi (P 63) Ralph Edwards, 8-01

D: 1,500 tons (fl) **S:** 16.02 kts (trials)
Dim: 66.50 × 10.50 × 4.35 **A:** 1 12.7-mm mg
Electronics: Radar: 1 . . . nav.
M: 1 MaK 8M-25 diesel; 1 CP prop; 3,265 bhp—bow-thruster
Range: 22,000/16 **Crew:** 44 tot. (naval and civilian)

Remarks: P 63 was built for the Secretaría General de Pesca Marítima but transferred to the Navy on 17-1-01 by the Ministerio de Agricultura, Pesca, y Alimentación. Carry Ministry of Agriculture, Fisheries, and Food civilian personnel for inspection duties. Based at Las Palmas, Canary Islands.
Hull systems: Has helicopter platform but no hangar. Is equipped with a hook for towing and carries two 6.2-m RIBs, each with two waterjet engines. Two fire monitors are located atop the foremast, and the ship is equipped to support divers. There are two electric generators.

♦ 1 Alborán-class fisheries patrol ship
Bldr: C.N. P. Freire, Vigo (In serv. 8-1-97)

P 62 Alborán

Alborán (P 62) Dieter Wolf, 2-99

D: 1,356 tons (1,848 fl) **S:** 15 kts (13 sust.) **Dim:** 65.92 (57.00 pp) × 10.50 × 4.35
A: 1 12.7-mm mg
Electronics: Radar: 1 Furuno FAR.2825 nav.; 1 Furuno FR-2130S nav.
M: 1 MaK 6M 453C diesel; 1 CP prop; 3,000 bhp (2,447 bhp sust.)—electric emergency propulsion system; 350 shp (5 kts)—bow-thruster
Electric: 1,040 kw tot (1 × 400 kw diesel set, 2 × 320 kw diesel sets)
Range: 20,000/11 **Fuel:** 575 tons + 15 tons JP-5 aviation
Crew: 7 officers, 30 enlisted + 14 passengers (see Remarks)

Remarks: New construction 1,123 grt/900 dwt stern-haul trawler hull taken over for use as an oceangoing fisheries protection ship. Funded by the *Subsecretaria de la Marine Mercante* for the Ministry of Agriculture, Fisheries, and Food (MAPA). Is based at Cartagena and operates primarily in the Mediterranean. Normal passenger complement includes two physicians and four fisheries inspectors.
Mission systems: Is equipped with Inmarsat SATCOM terminal. The helicopter deck large enough to accommodate an AB-212 is built over the stern and is 10.53 m above the normal waterline. A recreational gymnasium is fitted. Navigation equipment includes a TD-L 1620 MFD/F and FD-160 VHFD/F, Furuno FE-881 Mk II echo sounder, Furuno FCV-780 underwater television, Robertson RGC-11 gyrocompass, DS-70 doppler log, AP-9 Mk II-GA automatic pilot, FAX-208 meteorological fax, and two Furuno GPS receivers. Has 670 m^3 stores capacity, including 20 m^3 refrigerated storage.

♦ 4 Serviola class (Type B-215)
Bldr: Izar, Ferrol

	Laid down	L	In serv.	Based
P 71 Serviola	7-10-89	10-5-90	22-3-91	Ferrol
P 72 Centinela	19-1-90	30-10-90	24-9-91	Las Palmas
P 73 Vigía	6-6-90	12-4-91	24-3-92	Cádiz
P 74 Atalaya	30-10-90	22-11-91	29-6-92	Ferrol

D: 826 tons light (1,270 fl) **S:** 20 kts **Dim:** 68.65 (63.00 wl) × 10.40 × 3.40
A: 1 76.2-mm 50-cal U.S. Mk 26 DP; 2 single 12.7-mm mg

PATROL SHIPS [PS] *(continued)*

Vigía (P 73) Camil Busquets i Vilanova, 1-99

Electronics: Radar: 1 Decca 2690BT ARPA nav.; 1 Decca 2459F/I nav.
M: 2 Bazán-MTU 16V956 TB91 diesels; 2 CP props; 7,500 bhp
Electric: 468 kW tot. (3 Bazán-MAN R6V 16/18 diesel sets)
Range: 8,000/12 **Fuel:** 247 tons **Endurance:** 30 days
Crew: 8 officers, 34 enlisted + 6 spare berths

Remarks: Ordered 2-89 for use as offshore patrol vessels. A planned fifth unit was not ordered. Design based on the *Águila* class for the Mexican Navy. Originally referred to as the Milano class while under construction.
Hull systems: Platform for an AB-212-sized helicopter, but no hangar. Have nonretractable fin stabilizers. Carry two rigid inflatable inspection boats and have three 80-m^3/hr firefighting pumps. Are being modified to accommodate female crewmembers.
Combat systems: The 76.2-mm gun, from surplus stocks, is controlled by an Alcor-C optronic director or locally. P 73 has been equipped with an MSP-4000 optronic surveillance device for trials. Can carry 200 rounds 76.2-mm and 7,000 rounds 12.7-mm ammunition. Are equipped with Saturn 3S SATCOM transceivers.

♦ 1 Chilreu-class fisheries patrol ship
Bldr: Naval Gijon S.A., Gijón (L: 2-5-88)

P 61 Chilreu (ex-*Pescalonso 2*)

Chilreu (P 61) Camil Busquets i Vilanova, 5-01

D: 1,157 tons (2,101 fl) **S:** 15 kts (12.5 sust.)
Dim: 67.78 (57.82 pp) × 11.02 × 4.66
A: 1 12.7-mm mg **Electronics:** Radar: 2 Decca . . . nav.
M: 1 MaK 6M 453AK diesel; 1 CP prop; 2,460 bhp
Electric: 1,040 kw tot (1 × 400 kw diesel set, 2 × 320 kw diesel sets)
Range: 15,000/12 **Endurance:** 90 days **Crew:** 6 officers, 26 enlisted

Remarks: 1,316 grt/1,080 dwt former commercial stern-haul trawler transferred from the Ministry of Agriculture, Fisheries, and Food and commissioned into the Spanish Navy on 30-3-92. Retains refrigerated cargo hold and is equipped with INMARSAT terminal. Based at Ferrol.

Disposal note: All five remaining *Descubierta*-class patrol ships, *Descubierta* (P 75), *Infanta Elena* (P 76), *Infanta Cristina* (P 77), *Cazadora* (P 78), and *Vencedora* (P 79) had been decommissioned by 2006. Uruguay has expressed interest in purchasing ships of the class.

PATROL CRAFT [PC]

♦ 9 Anaga class
Bldr: Izar, San Fernando, Cádiz

	L	In serv.
P 21 Anaga	14-2-80	14-10-80
P 22 Tagomago	14-2-80	30-1-81
P 23 Marola	. . .	4-6-81
P 24 Mouro	. . .	14-7-81
P 25 Grosa	15-12-80	15-9-81
P 26 Medas	15-12-80	16-10-81
P 27 Ízaro	15-12-80	9-12-81
P 28 Tabarca	15-12-80	30-12-81
P 30 Bergantín	24-11-81	30-7-82

Ízaro (P 27) Stefan Karpinski, 2002

Deva (P 29)—since retired Camil Busquets i Vilanova, 6-00

D: 296.5 tons (350 fl) **S:** 20 kts **Dim:** 44.4 (40.0 pp) × 6.6 × 2.6
A: 1 76.2-mm 50-cal. U.S. Mk 22 DP; 1 20-mm 70-cal. Oerlikon Mk 10 AA
Electronics: Radar: 2 Decca 1226 nav.
M: 1 Bazán-MTU 16V956 SB90 diesel; 1 CP prop; 4,800 bhp (4,000 sust.)
Range: 4,000/13 **Crew:** 3 officers, 22 enlisted

Remarks: Ordered 22-7-78. P 21 laid down 4-79. P 30 originally numbered PVZ 210 and the others PVZ 21–29. Named for small islands. Carry rescue and firefighting equipment. Intended primarily as fisheries protection patrol craft. Two 7.62-mm mg can also be mounted. To be replaced by the BPC 47 (BAM) Program.
Disposals: Sister *Deva* (P 29) was retired on 23-7-04.

♦ 5 Barceló class
Bldrs: P 11: Lürssen, Vegesack, Germany; others; Izar, La Carraca, Cádiz

	L	In serv.
P 11 Barceló	6-10-75	26-3-76
P 12 Laya	16-12-75	23-12-76
P 14 Ordóñez	10-9-76	7-6-77
P 15 Acevedo	10-9-76	14-7-77
P 16 Candido Perez	3-3-77	25-11-77

Barceló (P 11) Leo Dirkx, 4-01

D: 110 tons (134 fl) **S:** 36.5 kts **Dim:** 36.2 (43.2 pp) × 5.8 × 1.75 (2.15 props)
A: 1 40-mm 70-cal. Bofors AA; 1 20-mm 70-cal. Oerlikon Mk 10 AA; 2 single 12.7-mm mg
Electronics: Radar: 1 Raytheon 1620/6 nav.
M: 2 Bazán-MTU 16V538 TB90 diesels; 2 props; 7,320 bhp (6,120 sust.)
Electric: 220 kVA tot. **Range:** 600/33.5; 1,200/16 **Fuel:** 18 tons
Crew: 3 officers, 16 enlisted

Remarks: Lürssen FPB 36 design. Carry 750 rounds 40-mm, 2,500 rounds 20-mm ammunition. A Matra Défense optical director is fitted for the 40-mm gun. To be replaced by the BPC 47 (BAM) Program.
Disposals: Sister *Javier Quiroga* (P 13) was decommissioned 28-4-05 and transferred abroad.

PATROL BOATS [PB]

♦ 4 Conejera class

Bldr: Izar, San Fernando, Cádiz

	L	In serv.
P 31 CONEJERA (ex-LVE 1)	9-81	31-12-81
P 32 DRAGONERA (ex-LVE 2)	9-81	31-12-81
P 33 ESPALMADOR (ex-LVE 3)	11-1-82	10-5-82
P 34 ALCANADA (ex-LVE 4)	10-2-82	10-5-82

Espalmador (P 33) Frank Behling, 9-02

Alcanada (P 34) Camil Busquets i Vilanova, 5-01

D: 85 tons (fl) **S:** 25 kts **Dim:** 32.15 (30.0 pp) × 5.30 × 1.42
A: 1 20-mm 70-cal. Oerlikon Mk 10 AA; 1 12.7-mm mg
Electronics: Radar: 1 Furuno . . . nav.
M: 2 Bazán-M.A.N. V8V16/18 TLS diesels; 2 props; 2,800 bhp (2,450 sust.)
Range: 1,200/15 **Crew:** 12 tot.

Remarks: Ordered 1978; first two laid down 20-12-79. Jointly funded by the Navy and the Ministry of Commerce for fisheries patrol duties. Aluminum construction. A planned further six were not built.

♦ 2 small fisheries patrol boats

Bldr: Ast. Viudes, Barcelona

	In serv.
P 81 TORALLA	29-4-87
P 82 FORMENTOR	23-6-89

Toralla (P 81) Dieter Wolf, 1-01

D: 56 tons (78 fl) **S:** 19.75 kts **Dim:** 28.50 (25.00 wl) × 6.50 × 1.45
A: 1 12.7-mm mg
Electronics: Radar: 1 Decca RM 1070 nav.; 1 Decca RM 270 nav.
M: 2 Bazán-MTU 8V396 TB93 diesels; 2 props; 2,200 bhp
Range: 1,000/12 **Crew:** 13 tot.

Remarks: GRP-sheathed wooden hulls. A planned third was not ordered.

♦ 1 P 101 class

Bldr: Aresa, Arenys del Mar, Barcelona (In serv. 1981–88)

P 114 (ex-Y 528, ex-P 111, ex-LVC 11)

D: 16.9 tons (21.7 fl) **S:** 27 kts **Dim:** 15.90 (13.7 pp) × 4.36 × 1.33
A: 1 12.7-mm mg **Electronics:** Radar: 1 Decca 110 nav.
M: 2 Baudouin-Interdiesel DNP-8 MIR diesels; 2 props; 1,024 bhp
Electric: 12 kVA tot. **Range:** 430/18
Fuel: 2.2 tons **Crew:** 2 officers, 4–5 enlisted

Remarks: Ordered 13-5-77. Jointly funded by the Navy and the Ministry of Commerce. Glass-reinforced-plastic construction. Seven other P 101–class units, reclassified as personnel launches, are also in service.
Disposal: Sister P 103 stricken 1990; P 115 damaged by fire late 1991 but not stricken until 1-5-93. Eighteen others stricken 1993. Y 528 was again redesignated P 114 on 15-2-96 to replace P 104, stricken that date.

♦ 1 Cabo Fradera–class river patrol boat

Bldr: Izar, La Carraca, Cádiz (In serv. 11-1-63)

P 201 CABO FRADERA (ex-PVI 01, ex-V 22)

D: 21 tons (28 fl) **S:** 10 kts **Dim:** 17.80 × 4.20 × 0.82 **A:** 1 7.62-mm mg
Electronics: Radar: 1 Furuno . . . nav.
M: 2 diesels; 2 props; 280 bhp **Crew:** 9 tot.

Remarks: Based at Tuy on the Río Miño border with Portugal.

Disposal notes: The last P 202–class patrol launch, P 221, was stricken 24-5-00.

MINE WARFARE SHIPS

♦ 1 Descubierta-class mine-countermeasures support ship [MCS]

Bldr: Izar, Cartagena

	Laid down	L	In serv.
M 11 DIANA (ex-F 32)	18-7-75	26-1-76	30-6-79

Diana (M 11) Luciano Grazioli, 2-03

D: 1,408 tons (1,620 fl) **S:** 26 kts **Dim:** 88.88 (85.80 pp) × 10.40 × 3.90
A: 1 76-mm 62-cal. OTO Melara Compact DP
Electronics:
Radar: 1 . . . nav. (X-band); 1 . . . nav. (S-band)
Sonar: Removed
EW: Removed
M: 4 MTU-Bazán 16MA956 TB91 diesels; 2 CP props; 18,000 bhp
Electric: 1,810 kw tot. **Range:** 6,100/18; 7,500/12
Fuel: 250 tons **Crew:** 10 officers, 108 enlisted

Remarks: Ordered on 7-12-73 as a small frigate; converted in 2000 at Cartagena to serve as a mine-countermeasures support ship and renumbered M 11 on 15-6-00.
Hull systems: Has fin stabilization, plus U.S. Prairie/Masker bubble system to reduce radiated noise below the waterline.
Combat systems: During conversion, the Albatros SAM system, two 40-mm AA, all ASW and ESM equipment, Harpoon missiles, and some radars were removed. Additional navigational radars were added, along with a divers' decompression chamber and foundations for four portable mine-countermeasures repair shop modules. Is equipped with a Saturn 3S SATCOM transceiver.

♦ 6 Segura-class minehunters (M-3 program) [MHC]

Bldr: Izar, Cartagena

	Laid down	L	In serv.
M 31 SEGURA	30-5-95	25-7-97	27-4-99
M 32 SELLA	12-96	6-7-98	28-5-99
M 33 TAMBRE	12-97	5-3-99	18-2-00
M 34 TURIA	11-98	22-11-99	6-12-01
M 35 DUERO	2002	28-4-03	5-7-04
M 36 TAJO	2003	10-6-04	10-1-05

D: 520 tons (550 fl) **S:** 14.5 kts **Dim:** 54.00 (51.00 pp) × 10.70 × 2.15
A: 1 20-mm 85-cal. Oerlikon GAM B01 AA
Electronics:
Radar: 1 Kelvin-Hughes 1007 nav.
Sonar: Indra-Raytheon-Thomson-Marconi SQQ-32(SP) variable-depth minehunting (HF)
E/O: Alcor-C optronic gun director

MINE WARFARE SHIPS *(continued)*

Duero (M 35) Leo van Ginderen, 4-05

Sella (M 32) Ralph Edwards, 2-04

M: 2 MTU 12V396 TB84 diesels; 2 Voith-Schneider vertical cycloidal props; 1,120 bhp—2 168-shp electric motors for 7-kt hunting speeds—2 74-shp bow-thrusters
Electric: 810 kw tot. (3 × 270 kw diesel sets) **Range:** 2,000/12
Crew: 7 officers, 26 enlisted (40 tot. accommodations)

Remarks: Construction of first four enlarged versions of the British *Sandown*-class minehunter design at Izar, Cartagena, was initially authorized 26-10-92 and confirmed by the Spanish cabinet on 7-5-93. Two more minehunters were ordered on 29-12-00. Construction technology assistance was provided by France's DCN under a 12-93 contract.
Combat systems: The SMYC CM (*Sistema de Mando Y Control para Cazaminas*) minehunting data and command system is based on the GEC-Marconi NAUTIS-M; it has three CM-1 operator consoles and is integrated with the FABA PN/UDDB navigation system. The first four carry two Gayrobot Pluto Plus mine detection and disposal vehicles, while later units will carry Kongsberg Minesniper mine-disposal ROVs (which will be backfitted in the earlier ships); an order for four additional ship-sets was placed on 8-1-03. A FABA ICCS 4 integrated communications system is fitted.

Disposal notes: Of the four ex-U.S. Navy *Aggressive*-class minesweepers transferred to Spain in 1971, *Guadalete* (M 41, ex-PVZ 41, ex-M 41, ex-*Dynamic,* MSO 432) was retired on 15-7-98; *Guadiana* (M 44, ex-*Vigor,* MSO 473) in 1999; *Guadalquivir* (M 43, ex-*Persistent,* MSO 491) on 13-10-00; and *Guadalmedina* (M 42, ex-*Pivot,* MSO 463) on 2-4-00. Two ex-U.S. MSC 268 and *Redwing*-class coastal minesweepers *Ebro* (M 22, ex-M 26, ex-MSC 269) and *Odiel* (M 26, ex-M 32, ex-MSC 288) were decommissioned on 25-2-05. Sister *Sil* (M 27) was decommissioned on 14-3-03. Ex-U.S. *Adjutant*-class units *Duero* (M 23, ex-M 28, ex-*Spoonbill,* MSC 202) and *Miño* (M 28, ex-PVZ 53, ex-M 25, ex-MSC 266) were retired during 1999. *Adjutant*-class *Júcar* (M 21, ex-M 23, ex-MSC 220) and MSC 268–class *Tajo* (M 24, ex-M 30, ex-MSC 287) were retired during 12-01. *Genil* (M 25) was retired 16-1-04.

AMPHIBIOUS WARFARE SHIPS

♦ 0 (+ 1) amphibious assault ship [LHD]
Bldr: Navantia, Ferrol

	Laid down	L	In serv.
L 53 Juan Carlos I	20-5-05	11-07	2009

D: 27,082 tons (fl) **S:** 21.5 kts **Dim:** 230.8 × 32 × 7.7
Air group: Up to 12 helicopters or 8 Harrier attack fighters
A: . . . point defense SAM; system; 4 20-mm 90-cal. Oerlikon GAM-B01 AA; 2 single 12.7-mm mg
Electronics: . . .
M: CODLAG (COmbined Diesel-eLectric and Gas turbine): 2 G.E. LM 2500 gas turbines; 2 M.A.N. . . . diesels; 2 electric azimuthal thrusters; . . . shp—bow-thruster
Electric: Main engines plus 1 × 650 kw emergency diesel-driven set
Range: 9,000/15 **Crew:** 243 tot. + 1,200 troops and 199 naval and amphibious staff

Remarks: Known as the Strategic Projection ship. The Spanish government formally authorized construction during 9-03. Izar received the design contract on 5-2-03. Will be the largest warship ever built for Spain. To replace two *Newport*-class LSTs.

Rendering of Juan Carlos I (L 53) Navantia (formerly Izar), 2002

Hull systems: Will have an island superstructure offset to starboard on the full-length helicopter deck. To have a surface-piercing bow bulb. The floodable stern well will accommodate four LCM(8)-sized landing craft or one LCAC. Cargo capacity: 6,000 tons. There will be two 3,000-m^2 parking decks for helicopters, vehicles, and containerized cargo. Will have extensive medical facilities.
Aviation features: Will have 202-m long flight deck with landing spots for either four CH-47, six NH-90, or eight AB-212 helicopters. The hangar will accommodate 12 helicopters or eight Harrier V/STOL attack aircraft. There will be two 25-ton capacity aircraft elevators.

♦ 2 Rotterdam-class dock landing ships [LPD]
Bldr: Izar, Ferrol

	Laid down	L	In serv.
L 51 Galicia	31-5-96	21-7-97	30-4-98
L 52 Castilla	11-12-97	14-6-99	26-6-00

Galicia (L 51) Anthony Vella, 4-05

Castilla (L 52) Martin Mokrus, 4-05

Castilla (L 52) Martin Mokrus, 4-05

D: 9,500 tons std.; 11,200 tons normal (13,815 fl) **S:** 20 kts
Dim: 163.12 (145.00 wl; 142.2 pp) × 25.00 (23.26 wl) × 5.23 (5.90 props)
Air group: 6 helicopters
A: 2 twin 20-mm 70-cal. Oerlikon Mk 24 AA; provision for: 2 20-mm Meroka Mod. 2B CIWS

AMPHIBIOUS WARFARE SHIPS *(continued)*

Electronics:
Radar: 3 Kelvin-Hughes . . . ARPA nav.; 2 Lockheed VPS-2 Meroka f.c.; L 52 also: DaimlerChrysler TRS-3D/16-ES 3-D air/surf.-search and target designation
EW: Indra SLQ-380 Aldebaran intercept; Mk 36 SRBOC decoy syst. (4 6-round Mk 137 RL)
M: 4 Bazán-MAN-Burmeister & Wain 40/54Adiesels; 2 props; 19,000 shp—2/680 shp side-thrusters
Electric: 6,800 kw tot. (4 × 1,500 kw diesel sets; 2 × 400 kw emergency diesel sets)
Range: 6,000/12
Fuel: 800 tons + 200 tons aviation and vehicle fuel + 50 tons for landing craft
Crew: L 51: 13 officers, 100 enlisted + troops: 41 officers, 570 enlisted; L 52: 179 crew + 65 Marine Corps staff + 404 troops

Remarks: L 51 ordered 8-94 for $169 million. Approval to construct L 52 was granted by Council of Ministers on 9-5-97. The design was prepared by Royal Schelde and Spain's Izar. Sister *Rotterdam* was built for Netherlands Navy service, and similar ships are on order for the UK, with others possibly to be ordered by Belgium and Germany. L 52 has enhanced command and control capabilities for service as an amphibious force flagship; this is to result in fewer troops but a larger staff being accommodated. L 51 and L 52 are based at Rota.
Hull systems: Built to merchant marine standards but have degaussing coils and a gas-tight citadel. The Spanish Navy version has straight diesel propulsion, whereas the Dutch version has a diesel-electric propulsion plant and different weapon and sensor systems. L 51 has accommodations for up to 127 ship's company. Have dual helicopter hangar (510 m^2 tot.) and two landing spots on 60 × 25 m (1,340 m^2) helicopter deck; can carry up to six helicopters in the hangars. Have 1,010 m^2 internal vehicle parking space and can use 885 m^2 docking well (55 × 16 m) for additional vehicles; further vehicles can be carried on the helicopter deck and in the helicopter hangar. Normal vehicle load expected to be five M60A3 tanks, three LVTP-7 amphibious armored personnel carriers, 10 trucks with trailers, 31 light vehicles with trailers, two ambulances, one crane, one push-truck, and one forklift; 33 M60 tanks alone could be carried. Maximum cargo is 2,488 tons. Docking well to accommodate four LCM (8) landing craft (up to 347 tons) or up to 818 tons of vehicles. Carry 300 tons potable water. Ballast tanks (to flood down docking well) accommodate 4,000 tons seawater. Troop cargo includes 400 m^3 total equipment stowage plus 30 m^3 (about 112 tons) ammunition storage. Hospital facilities in L 51 include two operating rooms, 100 beds, and 10 intensive-care berths.
Combat systems: Have an infrared surveillance system and some form of combat data system. Are NATO Link 11–compatible. To permit use as secondary ASW platforms, are equipped with a sonobuoy and weapons storage compartment capable of accommodating 25 tons of stores. L 52 has the SICOA (*Sistema de mando y Control para Operaciones Anfibias*) command and control system and enhanced communications and support facilities for a 65-person Marine Corps staff (at the expense of some troop berthing) and an enhanced radar suite.

♦ 1 ex-U.S. Newport-class tank landing ships [LST]
Bldr: National Steel SB, San Diego, Calif.

	Laid down	L	In serv.
L 42 Pizarro (ex-*Harlan County,* LST 1196)	7-11-70	24-7-71	8-4-72

Pizarro (L 42) Bernard Prézelin, 6-02

Hernán Cortés (L 41)—since stricken Bernard Prézelin, 6-02

D: 4,975 tons light, 6,800 std. (8,550 fl) **S:** 22 kts (20 sust.)
Dim: 159.2 (171.3 over horns) × 21.18 × 5.3 (aft) × 1.80 (fwd)
A: 1 20-mm Mk 15 Phalanx gatling CIWS; 2 single 20-mm 85-cal. Oerlikon GAM B01 AA; 4 single 12.7-mm mg
Electronics: Radar: 1 Canadian Marconi LN-66 nav.; 1 Raytheon SPS-10 surf. search
M: 6 Alco 16-251 diesels; 2 CP props; 16,500 bhp—bow-thruster
Range: 14,250/14 **Fuel:** 1,750 tons
Crew: 15 officers, 25 petty officers, 215 nonrated + 374–431 troops

Remarks: Transferred on 14-4-95, with 50-month lease, with option to purchase. Attached to the *Grupo Anfibio* Delta and based at Rota. Expected to serve until 2010.
Hull systems: Can transport 2,000 tons cargo, or, for beaching, 500 tons of cargo, on 1,765 m^2 of deck space. There is a 34-m long, 75-ton capacity mobile aluminum ramp forward, which is linked to the tank deck by a second from the upper deck. Aft is a 242 m^2 helicopter platform and a stern door for loading and unloading vehicles. Four pontoon causeway sections can be carried on the hull sides. The tank deck, which has a 75-ton-capacity turntable at both ends, can carry 23 AAV-7A1 armored personnel carriers or 29 M 48 tanks or 41 2.5-ton trucks, while the upper deck can accept 29 2.5-ton trucks. Now carry two LCVP and two LCP in Welin davits. Has two 10-ton cranes. Carry 141,600 gallons vehicle fuel. Transferred with six pontoon sections, two of them powered. In emergency situation, can transport up to 1,610 troops for a brief time, in lieu of vehicles.
Combat systems: Is now equipped with Saturn 3S SATCOM system. The Phalanx CIWS is said to be nonoperational. Is operated with three AB-212 helicopters each, although there is no hangar.

Disposal notes: Sister *Hernán Cortés* (L 41) was stricken in 2006. Ex-U.S. Navy *Paul Revere*–class amphibious transport *Aragón* (L 22, ex-*Francis Marion,* LPA 249, ex-*Prairie Mariner*) was stricken on 17-11-00; sister *Castilla* (ex-*Paul Revere,* LPA 248, ex-*Diamond Mariner*) was stricken on 16-6-98. Ex-U.S. LCU 1466–class utility landing craft L 71 and L 72 were retired during 2004.

♦ 2 (+ 10) LCM-1E-class landing craft
Bldr: Izar, La Carraca, San Fernando (In serv. 2001–. . .)

L 601 through L 612

D: 52 tons light (108 fl) **S:** 20 kts **Dim:** 23.30 × 6.40 × 2.8 (loaded)
M: 2 Bazán-MTU . . . diesels; 2 waterjets; 2,200 bhp
Range: 190/ . . . **Crew:** 3 tot.

Remarks: Carried by the new *Rotterdam*-class dock landing ships. Steel construction. Have 56-ton capacity (100 tons in overload condition) on a 100 m^2 vehicle deck. Bow and stern ramps are fitted.

♦ 1 amphibious warping tugs [LCM]
Bldr: . . . (In serv. 19-10-95)

L 92

Remarks: U.S.-type tug pontoons, powered by modular diesel outdrives. Assigned with six ex-U.S. pontoon sections to the Grupo Naval de Playa at Puntales Naval Base, Cádiz, for use aboard the two *Newport*-class LSTs. No data available. Sister L 91 was retired in 2005.

♦ 8 U.S. LCM(8)-class landing craft [LCM]
Bldr: L 81–86: Oxnard Boat, Calif. (In serv. 1975); others: Izar, La Carraca, San Fernando (In serv. 1988)

L 81 through L 86 (ex-LCM 81–86) L 87 L 88

D: 58.8 tons (116 fl) **S:** 10 kts **Dim:** 22.40 × 6.42 × 1.83 (aft)
M: 2 G.M. Detroit Diesel 6-71 diesels; 2 props; 600 bhp
Range: 150/9.2 (loaded) **Fuel:** 2.4 tons **Crew:** 5 tot.

Remarks: First six transferred 7-75 to 9-75. Two others built in Spain. Carry up to 53.5-tons cargo. Assigned to the Grupo Naval de Playa at Puntales Naval Base, Cádiz. To be replaced by the LCM-1E class by 2010.

♦ 14 LCM(6)E-class landing craft [LCM]
Bldr: Izar, San Fernando (In serv. 1985–89)

L 161 to L 167 L 261 to L 267

D: 24 tons (56 fl) **S:** 10.2 kts **Dim:** 17.07 × 4.37 × 1.52 (props)
M: 2 Gray Marine 64HN9 or G.M. 6V71 diesels; 2 props; 330 bhp
Range: 130/10 **Crew:** 3 tot. + 80 troops

Remarks: Cargo: 34 tons.

♦ 4 LCVP Mk 7E landing craft [LCVP]
Bldr: Ast. y Talleres Ferrolanos S.A. (In serv. 1987)

D: 11.77 tons (fl) **S:** . . . **Dim:** . . . × . . . × . . . **M:** . . .

Remarks: Attached to the carrier *Príncipe de Asturias.*

♦ Up to 14 ex-U.S. LCVP [LCVP]

D: 13 tons (fl) **S:** 9 kts **Dim:** 10.90 × 3.21 × 1.04 (aft)
M: 1 Gray Marine 64HN9 diesel; 225 bhp **Range:** 110/9

Remarks: Survivors of 20 transferred with larger ships. Glass-reinforced-plastic hulls. Can carry 36 troops or 3.5 tons cargo. Cargo deck is 5.24 × 2.29 m, with 2.00-m-wide access through the bow ramp.

AUXILIARY SHIPS

♦ 1 stores transport [AFT]
Bldr: Eriksbergs M/V AB, Göteborg, Sweden (In serv. 5-53)

A 01 Contramaestre Casado (ex-*Thanasis K.,* ex-*Fortuna Reefer,* ex-*Bonzo,* ex-*Bajamar,* ex-*Leeward Islands*)

D: Approx. 5,300 tons (fl) **S:** 16 kts **Dim:** 104.20 (96.12 pp) × 14.36 × 6.11
A: 2 single 20-mm 70-cal. Oerlikon Mk 10 AA
Electronics: Radar: 1 Decca 626 nav.; 1 Decca TM 1226 nav.
M: 1 Eriksberg 7-cyl. heavy-oil diesel; 1 prop; 3,600 bhp **Electric:** 660 kw tot.
Range: 18,600/16 **Fuel:** 727 tons **Crew:** 72 tot.

AUXILIARY SHIPS *(continued)*

Contramaestre Casado (A 01)—with portable tracking array on the helicopter platform aft Bernard Prézelin, 5-00

Remarks: 2,272 grt/2,743 dwt former commercial refrigerated cargo ship impounded for smuggling and turned over to the Spanish Navy to supply the Canary Islands; commissioned 15-12-82. Four cargo holds. Two 5-ton derricks. Helicopter platform at stern. The guns are mounted on the main deck, abreast the forward cargo crane.

♦ 1 ex-German Darss-class intelligence collector [AGI]

Bldr: VEB Schiffswerft Neptun, Rostock (In serv. 6-85)

A 111 Alerta (ex-*Jasmund,* D 41)

Alerta (A 111) Dieter Wolf, 1-01

D: 2,292 tons (fl) **S:** 12 kts **Dim:** 76.52 × 12.37 × 4.15
A: 2 single 12.7-mm mg **Electronics:** Radar: 1 Decca . . . nav.
M: 1 12-cyl. Kolomna Type 40 DM diesel; 1 CP Kort-nozzle prop; 2,200 bhp
Electric: 520 kw (4 × 130 kw) **Range:** 1,000/12
Endurance: 14 days **Crew:** 60 tot.

Remarks: Purchased late 1992 and commissioned 6-12-92 prior to sailing to Spain for refit. Begun as a cargo vessel, but converted for use as an intelligence collector by the former East German *Volksmarine.* Five sisters, all now stricken, served as cargo vessels in the *Volksmarine* and *Bundesmarine.* Transferred without intelligence equipment, which was developed by Spain; also used for trials with new radar and EW equipment. Has Saturn 3S SATCOM terminal.

♦ 1 Antarctic oceanographic research ship [AGOR]

Bldr: Izar, San Fernando

	Laid down	L	In serv.
A 33 Hespérides (ex-*Mar Antártico*)	1989	12-3-90	1991

Hespérides (A 33)—red hull, foremast and stacks, white superstructure Leo van Ginderen, 9-02

D: 1,983 tons (2,750 fl) **S:** 15 kts **Dim:** 82.48 (77.74 pp) × 14.33 × 4.48 **A:** None
Electronics:
Radar: 1 Decca 2690 ARPA nav.; 1 Decca 2690 ACS nav.
Sonar: All Simrad: EM-12 deep-sea multibeam echo sounder (13 kHz/11,000-m depth); EM-1000 multibeam echo sounder (95 kHz/5,800-m depth); EK-500 fisheries research echo sounder (38, 120, and 200 kHz); EA-500 hydrographic echo sounder (12 and 200 kHz); SL-490 obstacle-avoidance sonar (49 kHz); and VD-280 towed transducer platform
M: 2 Bazán-M.A.N. Burmeister & Wain 14V 20/27 diesels (1,904 bhp each) and 2 Bazán-M.A.N. Burmeister & Wain 7L 20/27 diesels (884 bhp each) in two generator set pairs; 2 A.E.G. 1,400 kw electric motors; 1 prop; 3,800 shp—350 shp bow- and stern-thrusters
Range: 12,000/13 **Endurance:** 120 days
Crew: 9 officers, 30 enlisted + 30 scientists

Remarks: Ordered 7-88. Paid for by Ministry of Foreign Affairs; operated by Navy and subordinated to the Straits Zone. Intended for geophysical, magnetic, and biological research. Painted with red hull and white superstructure. Underwent modernization during 2004. Suffered minor damage during a 4-05 collision.
Hull systems: Has icebreaker bow for duties in support of Spain's Livingston Island, Antarctica, station. Helicopter deck and telescopic hangar for one Augusta-Bell 212. Diver-support to 200 m. Twelve laboratories total 330 m^2. In addition to the main generator complexes, also has a 120-kw emergency diesel generator set. All of the sonar equipment, except the towed transducer, has transducers mounted in a 12 × 3 m keel dome. There is a complete automated data reduction and storage system.

♦ 2 Malaspina-class hydrographic survey ships [AGS]

Bldr: Izar, La Carraca, Cádiz

	L	In serv.
A 31 Malaspina	14-8-73	21-2-75
A 32 Tofiño	22-12-73	23-4-75

Tofiño (A 32)—white-painted Dieter Wolf, 1-01

Tofiño (A 32) Camil Busquets i Vilanova, 5-00

D: 820 tons (1,090 fl) **S:** 15 kts **Dim:** 57.7 (51.4 pp) × 11.7 × 3.64
A: 2 single 20-mm 70-cal. Oerlikon Mk 10 AA
Electronics:
Radar: 1 Raytheon 1620/6XB nav.
Sonar: STN Atlas Elektronik DESO-10 AN 1021 echo sounders, Burnett 538-2 deep-sounding echo sounder, Egg Mk 8 side-scanning mapping sonar
M: 2 San Carlos-MWM TbRHS-345-6I diesels; 2 CP Props; 2,700 bhp—active rudder with electric motor for slow-speed operations
Electric: 780 kVA tot. **Range:** 3,140/14.5; 4,000/12
Crew: 9 officers, 54 enlisted

Remarks: Formerly AH 31 and AH 32, redesignated 1986. Have Magnavox Transit satellite navigation system, Omega, Raydist, and a Hewlett-Packard 2100AC computer.

♦ 2 Castor-class survey ships [AGS]

Bldr: Izar, La Carraca, Cádiz

	L	In serv.
A 23 Antares	5-3-73	21-11-74
A 24 Rigel	5-3-73	21-11-74

D: 354.5 tons (383.4 fl) **S:** 11.5 kts
Dim: 38.36 (33.84 pp) × 7.60 × 3.10 max. **A:** None
Electronics: Radar: 1 Raytheon 1620 nav.
M: 1 Echevarria-Burmeister & Wain Alpha 408-26VO diesel; 1 prop; 800 bhp (A 21 and 22: 720 bhp)
Range: 3,000/11.5 **Fuel:** 52.9 tons **Crew:** 4 officers, 34 enlisted

AUXILIARY SHIPS *(continued)*

Cástor (A 21)—since retired Martin Mokrus, 9-02

Remarks: Redesignated A 23–24 from AH 23–24 in 1986. Produced in pairs, the later units having full main-deck bulwarks and the earlier pair cleared fantail to allow use of Oropesa floats to support towed side-looking mapping sonar arrays. Have Raydist navigation system, Omega receivers, three echo sounders, and a Hewlett-Packard 2100A computer. Subordinated to the Straits Zone. Sisters *Cástor* (A 21) and *Póllux* (A 22) were retired on 17-10-04 and 22-1-03 respectively.

♦ 1 roll-on/roll-off vehicle and container carrier [AK]
Bldr: Cia. Comercio e Navegação Maua, Niteroi, Brazil (In serv. 10-84)

A 05 El Camino Español (ex-*Cindya,* ex-*Mercantil Mage,* ex-*Araguary*)

El Camino Español (A 05) Dieter Wolf, 1-01

D: 4,560 tons (fl) **S:** 15 kts (12.4 kts sust.) **Dim:** 93.53 (80.02 pp) × 18.24 × 4.61
A: None **Electronics:** Radar: 2 . . . nav.
M: 2 M.A.N.-Sulzer 6L25/30 diesels; 2 props; 6,482 bhp—bow-thruster
Electric: 600 kw tot. (3 × 200 kw, 220/440-v, 50 Hz sets) **Range:** . . . / . . .
Fuel: 382.5 tons heavy oil, 106.5 tons diesel **Crew:** . . . tot.

Remarks: 1,329 grt/3,502 dwt. Acquired 5-3-98 from Scheepvaartmij Unidor N.V., Willemstad, Netherlands Antilles, to carry military vehicles and cargo for the Spanish Army. Commissioned on 27-9-99. The officers are naval personnel and the enlisted are army personnel.
Hull systems: Combination vehicle, heavy lift, and container carrier, with cargo deck and single 8.0-m long by 11.5-m wide, combination stern door/vehicle ramp aft. Has two internal vehicle cargo decks (40.2 m and 39.0 m long, both 12.5-m wide by 6.1-m high, with a total lane-length of 344 m. Can also be used to carry up to 260 standard 20-ft. cargo containers and has two 25-ton capacity cranes mounted on the port side.

♦ 1 vehicle carrier [AK]
Bldr: Soc. Met. Duro Felguera, Gijon, Spain (In serv. 1973)

A 04 Martín Posadillo (ex-ET 02, ex-*Cala Portals,* ex-*Rivanervión*)

Martín Posadillo (A 04) Dieter Wolf, 1-01

D: 1,920 tons (fl) **S:** 14 kts **Dim:** 75.01 (68.03 pp) × 13.01 × 4.27 **A:** None
Electronics: Radar: . . . nav. **M:** 1 MWM RHS345AU diesel; 1 prop; 2,400 bhp
Electric: 264 kw tot. (2 × 132 kw diesel-driven sets; 380 V 50Hz. a.c.)
Range: . . . / . . . **Crew:** 18 tot.

Remarks: 684 grt/1,283 dwt. Former commercial vehicle ferry. Acquired by the Spanish Army (*Ejército Español,* hence the former Army pennant number ET 02) to support troops at Ceuta and Melilla in North Africa. Commissioned 15-2-00. Although she remains an Army-owned ship, the vessel is naval crewed and operated.
Hull systems: Cargo: up to 42 trucks and 25 jeeps. Has a single, nonslewing centerline vehicle ramp at the stern and two cargo decks.

Note: Another Spanish Army vehicle transport, the *Santa Teresa de Avila* (ET 01) may now operate in Spanish Navy service or may have been sold; the craft was much smaller than the previous pair, being only 17.6 m overall, by 6.3 m beam and 2.3 m molded depth.

♦ 1 replenishment oiler [AO]
Bldr: Izar, Ferrol

	Laid down	L	In serv.
A 11 Marqués de la Ensenada (ex-*Mar del Norte*)	16-11-89	3-10-90	3-6-91

Marqués de la Ensenada (A 11) Guy Schaeffer via Paolo Marsan, 12-04

D: 13,592 tons (fl) **S:** 16 kts **Dim:** 123.21 (115.00 pp) × 19.50 × 7.98
A: 2 single 7.62-mm mg
Electronics: Radar: 1 Decca 2690/9 ARPA nav.; 1 Decca 2459 surf. search
M: 1 Bazán-M.A.N. 18V40/54A diesel; 1 prop; 11,250 bhp
Electric: 2,520 kw tot. (4 × 630 kw Bazán-MTU V8V 16/18 TL diesels driving)
Range: 10,000/15 **Crew:** 11 officers, 69 enlisted

Remarks: Commercial-design tanker ordered 12-88, initially as an interim replacement for the retired *Teide* until the *Patiño* (A 14) was available. Based at Las Palmas.
Hull systems: Helicopter platform aft and VERTREP positions fore and aft. Cargo: 7,498 tons distillate fuel, 1,746 tons JP-5, 2,878 tons water, 10 tons spares, plus six 20-foot refrigerated containers. Can accept 1,000 tons additional cargo fuel in an emergency. Liquid supply stations port and starboard can transfer 680 m^3 per hour, while solid transfer stations port and starboard can handle 250 kg loads. Has three 120-m^3/hr cargo pumps and an 18 ton/day distiller. Medical facilities are provided.
Combat systems: Provision was made for later installation of a Meroka CIWS aft and four Mk 137 decoy RL.

♦ 1 (+ 1) Patiño-class/modified Patiño-class* replenishment oiler [AOR]
Bldr: A 14: Izar, Ferrol; A 15: Navantia, Puerto Real

	Laid down	L	In serv.
A 14 Patiño (ex-*Mar del Sur*)	1-7-93	22-6-94	16-6-95
A 15 Cantabria*	2006	7-06	12-08

Patiño (A 14) Bernard Prézelin, 4-05

D: 17,045 tons (fl) **S:** 21 kts (20 sust.)
Dim: 165.84 (156.00 wl) × 23.70 (22.00 wl) × 8.00
A: 2 single 20-mm 85-cal. Oerlikon GAM-B01 AA; 2 single 12.7-mm mg; up to 3 SH-3D Sea King helicopters
Electronics:
Radar: 1 . . . nav.; 2 Decca 2690 nav. and helicopter control
TACAN: URN-25A
EW: Indra SLQ-380 Aldebarán intercept; Mk 36 SRBOC decoy syst. (6 6-round Mk 137 RL); SLQ-25A Nixie towed torpedo decoy syst.

AUXILIARY SHIPS *(continued)*

Patiño (A 14) Bernard Prézelin, 4-05

M: Diesel-electric: 4 Bazán-M.A.N. V16V-40/45 diesels, 2 motors; 2 props; 26,240 shp
Range: 13,500/20 **Endurance:** 30 days
Crew: 143 tot. + 19 air complement + 20 spare berths

Remarks: A 14 ordered 26-12-91. Officially rated as a *Buque de Aprovisionamiento de Combate* (Combat Supply Vessel) and also known as the AOR 90 class. *Cantabria* (A 15) will be similar in capability to the *Patiño* (A 14) but will also be able to carry and land assault troops. A 14 was initially a joint design between Netherlands' Nevesbu and Spain's Bazán design bureaus under agreement signed 11-88. Sister *Amsterdam* (A 836) was built in the Netherlands and operates in the Netherlands Navy. Based at Rota. A 14 is expected to undergo an extensive modernization beginning in 2009.
Hull systems: Have four 2-ton capacity dual-purpose and two 250-kg solid stores alongside replenishment stations, a VERTREP position forward, and can refuel over the stern at 450 m^3/hr. Cargo deadweight: 10,300 tons, including 6,700 tons ship fuel, 1,660 tons JP-5, 180 tons water, 20 tons ammunition, 100 tons dry stores, 25 tons of sonobuoys, and 9 tons spare parts. Have repair and medical facilities. Can accommodate up to 50 female crewmembers. *Cantabria* (A 15) is fitted with a double hull.
Combat systems: As of 2006, the planned Meroka Mod. 2B CIWS had not been installed. Four decoy launchers are mounted abreast the stack on the after superstructure and two more atop the pilothouse.

♦ 1 salvage and rescue tug [ARS]
Bldr: Duro Felguera, Gijón (In serv. 24-3-75)

A 101 Mar Caribe (ex-*Amatista*)

Mar Caribe (A 101) Camil Busquets i Vilanova, 5-00

D: 1,860 tons (fl) **S:** 13.5 kts **Dim:** 58.48 (52.61 pp) × 11.86 × 4.21 **A:** None
Electronics: Radar: 2 . . . nav.
M: 2 Echevarría-Burmeister & Wain Alpha 18V 23/30 diesels; 2 props; 4,860 bhp—bow-thruster
Electric: 660 kw (3 × 220 kw diesel sets) **Range:** 6,000/10
Fuel: 361 tons **Crew:** 44 tot.

Remarks: Former oilfield supply tugs purchased and commissioned 14-12-88. Assigned to the amphibious forces. In 1997, sister *Mar Rojo* (A 102, ex-*Amapola*) was redesignated a submarine rescue ship, and the ship was renamed *Neptuno* (A 20) in 1999; see under [ASR].
Hull systems: Has 80-ton bollard pull.

♦ 1 submarine rescue ship [ASR]
Bldr: Duro Felguera, Gijón (In serv. 24-3-75)

A 20 Neptuno (ex-*Mar Rojo,* A 102; ex-*Amapola*)

Neptuno (A 20) Leo van Ginderen, 4-05

D: 1,860 tons (fl) **S:** 13.5 kts **Dim:** 58.48 (52.61 pp) × 11.86 × 4.21 **A:** None
Electronics: Radar: 2 . . . nav.
M: 2 Echevarría-Burmeister & Wain Alpha 18V 23/30 diesels; 2 props; 4,860 bhp—bow-thruster
Electric: 660 kw (3 × 220 kw diesel sets) **Range:** 6,000/10
Fuel: 361 tons **Crew:** 44 tot.

Remarks: Former oilfield supply tug purchased and commissioned 14-12-88. Replaced the *Poseidón* (A 12) as submarine rescue ship in 1997 and was renamed and renumbered during 1999.
Hull systems: Has 80-ton bollard pull. Completed conversion at Cartagena Navy Yard as a diving tender and diving training ship in 1-91; has been equipped to support divers to 200 m and carries a 600-m-capable Vosma submersible that will later be replaced by a deep submergence submarine rescue vehicle. Also equipped with a dynamic positioning system and a high-frequency object avoidance sonar.

♦ 1 ex-commercial seagoing tug [ATA]
Bldr: Astilleros Luzuriaga S.A., Pasajes, San Sebastián (In serv. 1982)

A 53 La Graña (ex-Y 119, ex-*Punta Amer*)

La Graña (A 53) Bernard Prézelin, 4-05

D: 480 tons (fl) **S:** 14 kts **Dim:** 31.24 (29.00 pp) × 8.40 × 3.16
M: . . . diesels; 2 Voith-Schneider vertical cycloidal props; 3,240 bhp
Range: 1,750/12 **Crew:** 28 tot.

Remarks: 292 grt/205 dwt. Redesignated as a seagoing tug during 1994. Sister Y 120 was stricken during 1993.

♦ 2 Mahón-class seagoing tugs [ATA]
Bldr: Astilleros Atlantico, Santander (In serv. 1978)

A 51 Mahón (ex-*Circos*) A 52 Las Palmas (ex-*Somiedo*)

Mahón (A 51) French Navy, 9-97

AUXILIARY SHIPS *(continued)*

D: 1,437 (A 52: 1,450) tons (fl) **S:** 14 kts **Dim:** 41.0 × 11.6 × 5.5
A: 2 single 12.7-mm mg **Electronics:** Radar: 2 Decca . . . nav.
M: 2 AESA-Sulzer 16 ASV 25/30 diesels; 2 props; 7,744 bhp
Range: 27,000/12 (A 52) **Crew:** 8 officers, 25 enlisted

Remarks: 700 dwt. Former oilfield support tugs purchased from Compañía Hispano Americana de Offshore SA and commissioned 30-7-81. Redesignated from AR 51 and 52 in 1986. A 52 was modified in 1988 to serve as Antarctic exploration ship with bow strengthened, space for two scientific vans on fantail, additional fuel tankage, and accommodations for 22 scientists; was relieved during 1992 in that role by the new *Hespérides* and is now based at Las Palmas as a general-purpose ocean tug, although she is still painted in high-visibility colors.

Disposal note: *Cádiz*-class ocean tug *Ferrol* (A 43, ex-AR 43, ex-AR 45, ex-RA 5) was decommissioned during 2-04.

♦ 1 sail-training ship [AXT]
Bldr: Ast. Echevarrieta, Cádiz

	Laid down	L	In serv.
A 71 Juan Sebastián de Elcano	24-11-25	5-3-27	17-8-28

Juan Sebastián de Elcano (A 71) Bernard Prézelin, 6-02

D: 3,420 tons (3,754 fl) **S:** 10 kts **Dim:** 94.11 (82.00 pp) × 13.6 × 6.95
A: 2 single 37-mm saluting cannon **Electronics:** Radar: 2 Decca TM 626 nav.
M: 1 Deutz-MWM RBV 6M diesel; 1 prop; 1,500 bhp—2,467 m^2 max. sail area
Range: 10,000/9.5; 13,000/8 **Fuel:** 230 tons **Crew:** 224 tot. + 80 cadets

Remarks: Four-masted topsail schooner. Renumbered from A 01 in 1986, but the pennant number is not worn. Re-engined 1992. Based at Cádiz.

SERVICE CRAFT

♦ 13 miscellaneous barges [YC]

Y 308, Y 309, Y 314, Y 316, Y 318, Y 319, Y 323, Y 331, Y 341, Y 343, Y 351, Y 354, Y 365

♦ 2 YGR 23–class floating cranes [YD] (In serv. 1954)

Y 384 (ex-YGR 23) Y 383 (ex-YGR 22)

D: 470–490 tons (fl) **Dim:** 22.5 × 14.0 × 3.0 **Capacity:** 30 tons

♦ 1 miscellaneous floating crane [YD] (In serv. 1953)

Y 385 (ex-YGR 31)

D: 272 tons **Dim:** 19.0 × 11.7 × 2.4 **Capacity:** 15 tons

♦ 2 small diving tenders [YDT]
Bldr: Ast. y Talleres Ferrolanos, La Graña (In serv. 6-86)

Y 583 (ex-YBZ 83) Y 584 (ex-YBZ 84)

Remarks: No data available.

♦ 1 small diving tender [YDT]
Bldr: . . . (In serv. 9-9-82)

Y 579 (ex-YBZ 61)

D: 8 tons **S:** 12 kts **Dim:** 11.0 × 4.0 × 0.8 **M:** diesels; waterjets

♦ 1 small diving tender [YDT] (In serv. 15-6-83)

Y 580 (ex-YBZ 71)

D: 13.7 tons **S:** 7 kts **Dim:** 10.9 × 3.8 × 0.8 **M:** 1 diesel; 70 bhp

♦ 5 ammunition lighters [YE]
Bldr: Cartagena Naval Dockyard (In serv.: Y 365: 1986; others: 1991)

Y 365 Y 421 Y 422 Y 423 Y 424

Ammunition lighter Y 365 Camil Busquets i Vilanova, 5-01

D: 53 tons light (140 fl) **S:** . . . kts **Dim:** 22.3 × 8.7 × 0.8
M: 2 Harbormaster diesel azimuthal outdrive engines; 600 bhp

Remarks: The data do not apply to the slightly smaller Y 365, which was ordered 30-12-85 and launched 25-9-86. All have rectangular barge-like hulls, a single hold, and an articulating electrohydraulic crane.

♦ 7 P 101–class harbor patrol launches [YFL]
Bldr: ARESA, Arenys del Mar, Barcelona (In serv. 1978–82)

Y 521 (ex-P 102), Y 522 (ex-P 107), Y 523 (ex-P 121), Y 524 (ex-P 122), Y 525 (ex-P 101), Y 526 (ex-P 118), Y 527 (ex-P 119)

P 101–class patrol launch Y 525—white-painted Guy Schaeffer, 9-98

D: 16.9 tons (21.7 fl) **S:** 26 kts **Dim:** 15.90 (13.70 pp) × 4.36 × 1.33
A: 1 12.7-mm mg **Electronics:** Radar: 1 Decca 110 nav.
M: 2 Baudouin-Interdiesel DNP-8 MIR diesels; 2 props; 768 bhp
Electric: 12 kVA tot. **Range:** 430/18
Fuel: 2.2 tons **Crew:** 2 officers, 4–5 enlisted

Remarks: Ordered 13-5-77; funded jointly by navy and Ministry of Commerce. Redesignated late in 1993 from patrol craft to "Small Transport Craft" but retain a port patrol function, and sister Y 528 was redesignated P 114 again on 15-2-96. Three operate on the Río Miño. Originally numbered in LVC-series.
Hull systems: Y 523 and Y 524 have supercharged engines producing 1,024 bhp total and a maximum speed of 27 kts. Glass-reinforced plastic hull construction.

♦ 4 P 202–class harbor patrol craft [YFL]
Bldr: Rodman-Polyships, Vigo (In serv. 1978–80)

Y 545 (ex-P 202) Y 546 (ex-P 204) Y 547 (ex-P 211) Y 548 (ex-P 220)

D: 3 tons (4.2 fl) **S:** 18 kts **Dim:** 9.0 × 3.1 × 0.8 **A:** 1 7.62-mm mg
Electronics: Radar: see Remarks
M: 2 Ebro MH-58 inboard/outboard diesels; 2 props; 240 bhp
Range: 120/18 **Crew:** 6 tot.

Remarks: Retyped "Small Transport Craft" late in 1993 from patrol craft, but are still used in harbor patrol work. Glass-reinforced plastic construction. Originally numbered in the PVI-series. May have Decca 060 navigational radars. Sister P 221 was stricken 24-5-00.

♦ 5 Y 531–class personnel launches [YFL]
Bldr: Rodman, Vigo (In serv. 1980–81)

Y 531–535 (ex-QF 01–05)

SERVICE CRAFT *(continued)*

Y 531–class personnel launch Y 533—outboard LCP(L) Mk 11E launch Y 505
H&L Van Ginderen, 5-94

D: 3 tons (4.2 fl) **S:** 17 kts **Dim:** 9.0 × 3.1 × 0.8
M: 2 Volvo-Penta inboard/outboard diesels; 2 props; 240 bhp **Range:** 120/18

Remarks: GRP construction. Similar to the P 202 class. Miscellaneous personnel launch Y 515 is also in service. EDIC-class logistics support craft A 07 (ex-LCT 7) was stricken during 1998; sisters A 06 (ex-LCT 6) and A 08 (ex-LCT 8) were retired during 2004.

♦ **1 suction dredge [YM]**
Bldr: IHC, the Netherlands (In serv. 2-12-81)

Y 441 (ex-YDR 11)

Suction dredge Y 441 Camil Busquets i Vilanova, 1-99

D: 150 tons (fl) **S:** . . . **Dim:** 25.2 × 5.8 × 1.0 **M:** 1 diesel; 530 bhp

♦ **1 fuel lighter [YO]**
Bldr: Izar, San Fernando (In serv. 1980)

Y 231 (ex-YPF 21, ex-PP 6)

Fuel lighter Y 231 Camil Busquets i Vilanova, 1-99

D: 523 tons (fl) **S:** 10.8 kts **Dim:** 24.0 × 7.0 × 3.0
M: 2 Harbormaster diesel azimuthal outdrive units; 600 bhp

Remarks: Cargo: 300 tons.

♦ **1 fuel lighter [YO]**
Bldr: Izar, San Fernando (In serv. 1980)

Y 232 (ex-YPF 31, ex-PP 23)

D: 830 tons (fl) **S:** 10.7 kts **Dim:** 42.8 × 8.4 × 3.1
M: 1 diesel; 1 prop; 600 bhp **Cargo:** . . . tons

Note: Also in service is fuel lighter Y 221, a rectangular barge hull with two Harbormaster diesel outdrives; no other data available.

Fuel lighter Y 221 Camil Busquets i Vilanova, 1-99

♦ **1 diesel-fuel lighter [YO]**
Bldr: Izar, Cartagena (In serv. 1981)

Y 254 (ex-YPG 41)

D: 214 grt **S:** 10.7 kts **Dim:** 24.0 × 5.5 × 2.2
M: 1 M.A.N. diesel; 1 prop; 400 bhp **Cargo:** 100 tons

♦ **1 diesel-fuel lighter [YO]**
Bldr: Izar, Cádiz (In serv. 1980)

Y 255 (ex-YPG 51)

D: 520 grt **S:** . . . **Dim:** 34.0 × 7.0 × 2.9
M: 1 diesel; 1 prop; . . . bhp **Cargo:** . . .

♦ **3 YPG 21–class diesel-fuel lighters [YO]**
Bldr: Izar, Cádiz (In serv. 1963–65)

Y 237 (ex-YPG 22) Y 252 (ex-YPG 21) Y 253 (ex-YPG 23)

D: 337 grt **S:** 10.7 kts **Dim:** 34.3 × 6.2 × 2.3
M: 1 diesel; 1 prop; 220 bhp **Cargo:** 100 tons

♦ **1 YPG 01–class diesel-fuel lighters [YO]**
Bldr: Izar, Ferrol (In serv. 1956, 1959)

Y 251 (ex-YPG 11, ex-YPG 01)

D: 200 grt **S:** 10 kts **Dim:** 34.0 × 6.0 × 2.7 **M:** 1 diesel; 1 prop; . . . bhp
Cargo: 193 tons

Remarks: Formerly numbered in the PB series. Sister YPG 02 stricken 1982 and Y 236 had been retired by 2006.

♦ **2 non-self-propelled fuel oil barges [YON]** (In serv. . . .)

Y 202 (ex-YPFN 31) Y 211 (ex-YPGN 01)

♦ **1 oil-spill recovery storage barge [YOSN]**

Y 411

Remarks: No data available. Sister Y 412 stricken 1994.

♦ **1 barracks barge [YPB]**
Bldr: Pullman Std. Car Co., Chicago, Ill. (In serv. 1944)

Y 601 (ex-YFCN 01, ex-LSM 329 or 331)

D: 1,095 tons (fl) **Dim:** 62.03 (59.89 wl) × 10.52 × 2.54

Remarks: Former medium landing ship, transferred 5-60. Hulked and employed as an accommodations ship at Ferrol.

♦ **2 Y 122–class coastal tractor tugs [YTB]**
Bldr: Izar, Ferrol (In serv. 1991)

Y 122 Y 123

Tug Y 123 Camil Busquets i Vilanova, 5-00

SERVICE CRAFT *(continued)*

D: 423 tons (fl) **S:** 12 kts **Dim:** 29.50 (28.00 pp) × 11.00 × 4.00
Electronics: 1 Decca RM 770 nav.
M: 2 Caterpillar diesels; 2 Voith-Schneider Type 26 II/165 vertical cycloidal props; 3,000 bhp
Range: 1,000/12 **Fuel:** 58.3 tons **Crew:** 8 tot.

Remarks: Bollard pull of 35 tons. Have two 1,200-m^3/hr firefighting monitors and a 1-ton crane.

♦ **2 Y 118–class large harbor tugs [YTB]**
Bldr: Izar, . . . (In serv. 1988–91)

Y 118 Y 121

Tug Y 121 Camil Busquets i Vilanova, 1-99

D: 220 tons (236 fl) **S:** 14 kts **Dim:** 22.5 × 7.5 × . . .
M: 2 MTU diesels; 2 Voith-Schneider 21 Gil/135 vertical cycloidal props; 1,768 bhp (1,560 sust.)
Range: 1,560/14

Remarks: Are equipped with two firefighting water monitors and have an electro-hydraulic crane on the fantail for torpedo recovery.

♦ **2 coastal tugs [YTB]**
Bldr: Izar, Ferrol

	In serv.
Y 116 (ex-YRR 21, ex-YRR 71)	10-4-81
Y 117 (ex-YRR 22, ex-YRR 72)	1-6-81

D: 422 tons (fl) **S:** 12.4 kts **Dim:** 28.0 × 8.0 × 3.8
M: 2 diesels; 2 Voith-Schneider vertical cycloidal props; 1,500 bhp
Range: 3,000/10

Disposal notes: YRR 53–class coastal tug Y 115 (ex-YRR 16, ex-YRR 55, ex-RR 55) was stricken during 1998 and sister Y 114 (ex-YRR 15, ex-YRR 54, ex-RR 54) during 2001.

♦ **2 large harbor tugs [YTB]**
Bldr: Izar, Ferrol (In serv. 1983)

Y 144 (ex-*Bellatrix*) Y 145 (ex-*Procyon*)

Tug Y 145 Camil Busquets i Vilanova, 1-99

D: 195 tons **S:** 13 kts **Dim:** 26.8 × 7.9 × 3.2 **M:** 2 diesels; 2 props; 2,030 bhp

Remarks: Former merchant tugs. Have been equipped with roller fenders on the superstructure to permit coming alongside the carrier *Príncipe de Asturias.*

♦ **2 Y 141–class large harbor tugs [YTB]**
Bldr: Izar, Cartagena (In serv. 1981)

Y 141 Y 142

D: 195 tons (229 fl) **S:** 12 kts **Dim:** 28.0 × 7.5 × 3.4
M: 2 diesels; 1 prop; 950 bhp
Range: 2,030/11

♦ **1 submarine-support push-tug [YTM]**
Bldr: Izar, La Carraca (In serv. 1-99)

Y 174

Submarine-support push-tug Y 174—just prior to launch
Camil Busquets i Vilanova, 1-99

D: 17 tons (fl) **S:** 9 kts **Dim:** 8.40 × 3.80 × 0.70
M: 2 Guascor H74TA diesels; 2 Hamilton waterjets; 536 bhp
Range: 75/8 **Crew:** 2 tot.

Remarks: First of new series intended to replace earlier, less-powerful push-tugs listed under YTL.

♦ **1 medium harbor tug [YTM]**
Bldr: Izar, San Fernando (In serv. 14-4-87)

Y 147

Medium harbor tug Y 147 Ralph Edwards, 8-01

D: . . . tons **S:** 10 kts **Dim:** 16.5 × . . . × . . . **M:** 1 diesel; 1 prop; 400 bhp
Range: 400/10

Remarks: 87 grt. Ordered 18-12-85; launched 25-2-87. Has one water monitor for fire fighting. Based at Las Palmas, Canary Islands.

♦ **1 medium harbor tug [YTM]**
Bldr: S. España d. C.N. Cádiz (In serv. 1965)

Y 146 (ex-YRP 61)

D: 173 tons (fl) **S:** 10 kts **Dim:** 23.3 × 6.0 × 2.9 **M:** 1 diesel; 1 prop; 825 bhp
Range: 830/10

Remarks: Entered naval service 27-10-83.

Disposal notes: YRR 50–class coastal tug Y 111 (ex-YRR 11; ex-YRR 31; ex-RR 50) was retired during 2001.

SERVICE CRAFT *(continued)*

♦ **1 U.S. Army Design 3004 medium harbor tug [YTM]**
(In serv. 27-12-61)

Y 143 (ex-YRP 41, ex-RP 40, ex- . . .)

D: 111 tons light (133 fl) **S:** 12 kts **Dim:** 21.31 × 5.94 × 2.50
M: 1 diesel; 1 prop; 600 bhp **Range:** 600/10 **Fuel:** 15 tons **Crew:** 6 tot.

♦ **2 YRP 01–class small harbor tugs [YTL]**
Bldr: Izar, La Carraca (In serv. 1965–67)

Y 131 (ex-YRP . . .) Y 140 (ex-YRP . . .)

D: 65 tons (fl) **S:** 9 kts **Dim:** 18.45 (16.75 pp) × 4.72 × 1.57 max.
M: 1 diesel; 1 Kort-nozzle prop; 200 bhp **Range:** 200/8 **Crew:** 6 tot.

Remarks: Sister YRP 10 stricken 11-6-84, YRP 11 on 6-7-82, and Y 136 in 1992. Seven other had been retired by 2006.

♦ **3 submarine-support push-tugs [YTL]**

	In serv.
Y 171 (ex-YRS 01)	3-11-82
Y 172 (ex-YRS 02)	5-85
Y 173 (ex-YRS 03)	6-85

Submarine-support push-tug Y 171—on land for maintenance
Camil Busquets i Vilanova, 5-01

D: 9.8 tons (fl) (Y 171: 10.5 tons) **S:** 11 kts **Dim:** 9.5 (Y 171: 8.3) × . . . × . . .
M: 2 diesels; 2 waterjets; 400 bhp **Range:** 440/11

♦ **4 miscellaneous sail training craft [YTS]**

	In serv.	D (tons fl)	Rig
A 72 Arosa	1-4-81	52	Ketch
A 74 La Graciosa (ex-*Dejá Vu*)	1931	. . .	Schooner
A 75 Sisargas	19-9-95	90	Ketch
A 76 Giralda	10-9-93	25	Ketch

Remarks: All are attached to the Naval Academy (*Escuela Naval Militar*). A 72, 22.84 m o.a., was built in Portsmouth, U.K., by Inglaterra. A 75 is on loan from a private individual. A 76 was donated by King Juan Carlos I on 23-8-93; built in the U.K. by Morris & Mortimer, Argull, she is 25.0 × 6.0 m, has two 114-bhp Gardner diesels, and can achieve 14 kts. Sloop *Hispania* (A 73) was stricken on 5-7-01.

Disposal note: Large water lighter *Condestable Zaragoza* (A 66) was retired in late 2004.

♦ **1 large water lighter [YW]**
Bldr: Izar, San Fernando

	L	In serv.
A 65 Marinero Jarano (ex-AA 31, ex-A 31)	1-7-81	16-3-81

Marinero Jarano (A 65) Ralph Edwards, 8-01

D: 535 tons (fl) **S:** 10.8 kts **Dim:** 34.0 × 7.0 × 3.03
M: 1 diesel; 1 prop; 600 bhp **Cargo:** 300 tons

♦ **4 Guardiamarina Barrutia–class navigational training tenders [YXT]** Bldr: Izar, Cartagena

	L	In serv.
A 82 Guardiamarina Salas	26-1-83	10-5-83
A 83 Guardiamarina Godínez	9-5-83	4-7-83
A 84 Guardiamarina Rull	19-1-84	11-6-84
A 85 Guardiamarina Chereguini	29-3-84	11-6-84

Guardiamarina Barrutia (A 81)—since retired Spanish Navy, 1992

D: 90 tons (fl) **S:** 12.5 kts **Dim:** 21.89 × 5.10 × 1.52 **A:** None
Electronics: Radar: 1 Halcon 948 nav. **M:** 2 MTU diesels; 2 props; 800 bhp
Range: 1,000/ . . . **Crew:** . . . tot. + 1 instructor and 12–21 cadets

Remarks: Tenders to the Escuela Naval Militar. Have Magnavox NAVSAT receiver, Decca 21 Navigator. Formerly numbered YE 02–05 and AI 02–05. Sister *Guardiamarine Barrutia* (A 81) was retired in 2004.

AIR FORCE

The Spanish Air Force operates three 11-meter Rodman 38–class GRP air/sea rescue boats built by Polyships at Vigo in 1991. Launch EA-01 is assigned to the Puerto Pollenca airbase.

Note: All Spanish Army logistics support craft have either been transferred to the Navy or disposed of.

GUARDIA CIVIL SERVICIO MARÍTIMO

Originally subordinated to the Spanish Army, the *Guardia Civil* has been given port security and antiterrorist responsibilities and plans to expand its afloat forces to a total of 12 30-meter, 36 18-meter, and 39 12-meter patrol boats, supported by some 2,000 personnel. In wartime, the organization would come under the Ministry of Defense. Facilities are located at Corunna, Santander, Murcia, Barcelona, Algeciras, Almeira, Malaga, and Pontevedra. Craft are painted green and white, with a red- yellow-red diagonal abaft the green-painted bows. The Guardia Civil also operates a number of MBB BO-105 light SAR helicopters.

Personnel: Approx 1,000 tot.

PATROL BOATS [WPB]

♦ **11 Rodman 101 class**
Bldr: Rodman-Polyships, Vigo (In serv. 2001–5)

A 05 Rio Palma	A 09 Rio Nervion	A 13 Rio Ara
A 06 Rio Andarax	A 10 Rio Guardalaviar	A 14 Rio Adaja
A 07 Rio Guadalupe	A 11 Rio Cabriel	A 15 Rio Duero
A 08 Rio Almanzora	A 12 Rio Cervantes	

Rio Guadalupe (A 07) A. A. de Kruif, 9-04

D: 110 tons (fl) **S:** 30 kts **Dim:** 30 × 5.8 × 1.8
M: 2 G.M. Detroit Diesel 16V92 A; 2 props; 2,900 bhp
Range: 800/12 **Crew:** 12 tot.

Remarks: GRP construction. Fitted with stern ramp for the launch and recovery of a small RIB inspection and rescue launch.

GUARDIA CIVIL PATROL BOATS [WPB] *(continued)*

♦ 3 Rodman 82 class
Bldr: Rodman-Polyships, Vigo (In serv. 2001–2)

A 02 Rio Guadario (ex-*Seriola*)   A 03 Rio Puiserga   A 04 Rio Nalon

Rio Guadario (A 02)—with old name   Camil Busquets i Vilanova, 5-01

D: 61 tons (fl)   **S:** 26.5 kts   **Dim:** 26 × 6 × 1.5   **Electronics:** Radar: 1 . . . nav.
M: 2 diesels; 2 waterjets; 1,400 bhp   **Range:** 720/17   **Crew:** 9 tot.

Remarks: Has a stern ramp for the launch and recovery of a small RIB inspection and rescue launch.

♦ 11 Bazán 39 class
Bldr: Izar, Cartagena (In serv. 1993–94)

L 01, L 02, L 04 through L 12

Bazán 39–class L 09   Daniel Ferro, 1-06

D: 14 tons (fl)   **S:** 38 kts   **Dim:** 11.9 × 3.8 × 0.7   **A:** 1 7.62-mm mg
Electronics: Radar: 1 Ericsson . . . nav.
M: 2 M.A.N. D2848 LXE diesels; 2 Hamilton waterjets; 1,360 bhp   **Range:** 300/25
Crew: 4 tot.

Remarks: GRP hulls. The design is based on that of the civil Saetta-II yacht; 24 more were planned. L 03 is no longer in service.

♦ 12 Rodman 55 HJ class
Bldr: Rodman-Polyships, Vigo (In serv. 1999–2005)

M 17 through M 28

D: 18.5 tons (fl)   **S:** 50 kts   **Dim:** 17.5 × 3.8 × 0.7   **A:** 1 7.62-mm mg
Electronics: Radar: 1 Ericsson . . . nav.
M: 2 Bazán-M.A.N. D2842 LXE diesels; 2 Hamilton waterjets; 2,480 bhp
Crew: 5 tot.

Remarks: Larger, faster and more powerful than the Rodman 55 class listed below. Have names beginning with "Rio."

♦ 16 Rodman 55 class
Bldr: Rodman-Polyships, Vigo (In serv. 1992–96)

M 01 through M 16

D: 15.7 tons (fl)   **S:** 40 kts   **Dim:** 16.5 × 3.8 × 0.7   **A:** 1 12.7-mm mg
Electronics: Radar: 1 Ericsson . . . nav.
M: 2 Bazán-M.A.N. D2848 LXE diesels; 2 Hamilton waterjets; 1,360 bhp
Range: 500/25   **Crew:** 7 tot.

Rodman 55–class M 04   A. A. de Kruijf, 9-04

Remarks: Completed five in 1992, three in 1993, and the rest in 1995–96. GRP construction. Have a VHFD/F array. M 01 was lengthened by 2.5 meters in 2003. M 15 is named *Tineycheide* and M 16 *Almirante Diaz Pimienta*. Both may be of a slightly larger variant

Note: The Guardia Civil also employs an unreported number of RIB patrol and inspection launches.

CUSTOMS SERVICE
(*Servicio de Vigilancia Aduanera*)

Aviation: Three MBB BO-105CB helicopters, one BK-117, and one Dauphin helicopter.

Note: Ships and craft have very dark blue hulls and narrow-broad-narrow diagonal white hull stripes with the Customs Service shield superimposed. Smaller units carry "*Aduanas*" (Customs) on hull sides.

Ships and craft in service include:

	In serv.	Displ.	Kts	bhp	Dim.
Águila	1974	80	29	2,750	32.00 × 5.75 × 1.60
Albatross III	1-7-70	84.7	29	2,700	32.25 × 5.86 × 1.85
Alca I and III	1989	24	35	2,000	16.98 × 4.70 × 0.79
Alcaraván I–V	1984–87	71.5	28	3,920	28.50 × 6.50 × 1.80
Alcaudon II	1999	22	50	2268	17.26 × 4.96 × . . .
Alcotan II	1997	22	55	3057	17.26 × 4.96
Arao	2003	87	35	5,520	31.36 × 6.00 × 1.10
Colimbo II and IV, HJ-1	1999–2003	22	50	2268	17 × 4 × . . .
Cormorán	20-2-90	22	65	2,970	17.00 × 4.00 × 1.00
Fenix	1998	22	55	2268	17.26 × 4.96 × . . .
Gavilán II–IV	1977–87	65	22.5–31	2,750	28.00 × 5.15 × 1.30
Gerifalte I	8-01	87	35	5,520	31.36 × 6.00 × 1.10
Halcón II and III	1980, 83	73	28	3,200	24.50 × 6.08 × . . .
HJ A	1994	20	50	1980	14.1 × 3.95 × . . .
HJ I, III–X	1986–90	20	45–50	2,970	14.00 × 3.80 × 0.70
IMP I and III	1989–90	5	65–70	400	9.60 × 2.85 × . . .
IPP I and III	1989	2	65–70	400	6.35 × 2.40 × . . .
Nebli	1993	51	50	3,480	22.55 × 6.47 × 1.65
Milano II	. . .	. . .	. . .	. . .	. . .
Petrel I	1994	1,600	12	1,200	72.5 × 12.0 × . . .
Petrel II	2004	1,150	. . .	6,866	61 × 10 ×
VA II–V	1984–85	23.7	28	1,400	15.7 × 4.1 × 1.2
X Aniversario	8-01	87	35	5,520	31.36 × 6.00 × 1.10

VA II–series customs launch VA-III   Leo van Ginderen, 5-05

Note: There are also a large number of RIBs in service including the large *Bill* (1997, 3t, 600 hp, 10 m × 2.5 m) and *Oceanic* (1995, 12t, 1040 hp, 11.68 m × 3.4 m).

CUSTOMS SERVICE *(continued)*

Milano II Neill Rush, 10-05

SOCIETY FOR MARITIME RESCUE AND SAFETY
(Sociedad de Salvamento y Seguridad Marítima: SeaSeMar)

Established in 1995 by the Spanish Government to coordinate the existing rescue system. Employs chartered salvage and rescue units, and the fleet changes composition frequently. Ships and craft are painted a brilliant red-orange and have one broad and one diagonal hull stripe. In 2006 the force included emergency towing vessels, chartered rescue tugs, high-speed rapid-intervention craft, and pollution-control vessels in service. Ten depots have been established on the coast to store oil-recovery gear, and 12 ports have been equipped with oil-skimming craft. Also in use are SH-3 Sea King helicopters. In 2000, the three-digit pennant numbers formerly applied to salvage tugs had been replaced by two-digit numbers prefixed by "BS-," while smaller rescue craft bore "ES-"-series numbers.

GALICIAN STATE FISHERIES PROTECTION SERVICE
(Servicio de Inspección e Vigilancia Pesqueira)

Note: Operated by the Xunta de Galacia, with bases at Vigo, Portonovo, Vilaxoán, Riveira, Portosín, Sada, and Celeiro; additional bases are to be built on the Costa da Morte. Similar organizations operate craft in Andalucía, Catalunya, Asturias, and in the Basque area; no data available. Craft are painted with aquamarine-blue bow, dark-blue stern, and aquamarine-and-white superstructures. The Galician State Fisheries Protection Service operated roughly two dozen small launches, most of which displace fewer than 10 tons full load.

SRI LANKA

Republic of Sri Lanka

NAVY

Personnel: About 15,000 total, including 2,400 Sri Lanka Naval Reserve personnel

Bases: The fleet is divided into four Area Commands: North, East, South, and West. Principal naval base is located at Trincomalee with other facilities at Kankesanthurai, Galle, Medawachiya, and Colombo.

Maritime Aviation: One Beech Super King Air was acquired in 1986 by the Air Force for maritime surveillance, which also operates six Bell 214 helicopters for land-based maritime patrol and attack duties.

Note: Ship names are prefaced by SLNS (Sri Lanka Naval Ship). During 2005–6 the Sri Lankan Navy expressed interest in purchasing a number of foreign vessels including two retired Koni-class frigates from Serbia Montenegro, a *Sir Galahad*–class tank landing ship, and a *Castle*-class offshore patrol vessel from the United Kingdom along with a number of smaller patrol boats from other nations. It remains to be seen whether financial or other realities will scuttle these efforts.

Tamil rebel forces operate a large number of very small, outboard-powered craft for raiding purposes; no details are available.

PATROL SHIPS [PS]

♦ 1 ex-Indian Sukanya class
Bldr: Hindustan SY, Vishakhapatnam

	Laid down	L	In serv.
P 620 SARAYU (ex-*Sharada*, P 55)	9-88	22-8-90	27-10-91

Sarayu (P 620) Brian Morrison, 8-01

Sarayu (P 620)—displaying old pennant number (P 55), and carrying an Indian Chetak helicopter on deck Werner Globke collection, 7-02

D: 1,650 tons (1,890 fl) **S:** 21.7 kts **Dim:** 101.95 (96.00 pp) × 11.50 × 3.40
A: 1 40-mm Bofors 60-cal. Mk 3 AA; 2 twin 25-mm 80-cal. Type 61 AA; 4 single 12.7-mm mg
Electronics:
Radar: 1 Bharat 1245 nav.; 1 . . . nav.; 1 Decca 2459 surf. search
EW: . . . intercept
M: 2 Kirloskar-SEMT-Pielstick 16PA 6V280 diesels; 2 props; 12,800 bhp
Range: 7,000/15 **Fuel:** 300 tons + 40 tons aviation fuel **Endurance:** 60 days
Crew: 10 officers, 60 enlisted (accomm. for 16 officers, 141 enlisted)

Remarks: Purchased for $20 million and transferred 9-12-00. Plans for a second, new-construction unit of the class were canceled during 7-01. The pennant number is not carried.
Hull systems: Has fin stabilizers and a towing capability. Carries 60 tons fresh water and 9 tons lube oil. Some helicopter-related equipment was removed prior to transfer.
Combat systems: The 40-mm guns are simple Mk 3 powered mountings with local control only; two additional mounts were added abreast the hangar after delivery. Also added have been a third navigational radar and a radar intercept array. Has a helicopter hangar and flight deck.

GUIDED MISSILE PATROL CRAFT [PTG]

♦ 2 Reshev (Sa'ar IV) class
Bldr: Israel SY, Haifa

	L	In serv.
P 701 NANDIMITHRA (ex-*Moledet*)	22-3-79	5-79
P 702 SURANIMILA (ex-*Komemiyut*)	19-7-79	8-80

Nandimithra (P 701) Hartmut Ehlers, 10-03

D: 415 tons (450 fl) **S:** 32 kts **Dim:** 58.10 × 7.62 × 2.40
A: 4 Gabriel II SSM; 2 single 76-mm 62-cal. OTO Melara Compact DP; 2 single 20-mm Rafael Typhoon gatling AA
Electronics:
Radar: 1 Thales Neptune TH-D 1040 surf./air search; 1 Alenia Orion RTN-10X gun f.c.
EW: Elisra NS 9003/5 intercept/jammer suite
E/O: Elop MSIS IR/t.v. surveillance and tracking
M: 4 MTU 16V956 TB91 diesels; 4 props; 14,000 bhp (10,680 sust.)
Range: 1,650/30; 4,000/17.5 **Crew:** 45 tot.

GUIDED MISSILE PATROL CRAFT [PTG] *(continued)*

Remarks: Purchased during 2000 and recommissioned in Sri Lanka on 9-12-00.
Hull systems: Quarters are air-conditioned.
Combat systems: Original missile armament was seven fixed Gabriel launchers. The 76-mm guns have been especially adapted for shore bombardment. The armament was revised prior to delivery.

PATROL CRAFT [PC]

Note: In 7-99 it was reported that negotiations were under way with Russia for the purchase of a Svetlyak-class patrol craft, a Bogomol-class torpedo boat, and a Pauk-I-class antisubmarine patrol craft; the discussions, however, came to nothing.

♦ 1 ex-U.S. Coast Guard Reliance (210-ft) class
Bldr: U.S. Coast Guard Yard, Curtis Bay, Md.

	Laid down	L	In serv.
P 621 SAMUDURA (ex-*Courageous,* WMEC 622)	1-7-66	29-4-67	8-12-68

D: 879 tons (1,050 fl) **S:** 18 kts **Dim:** 64.16 (60.96 pp) × 10.36 × 3.25
A: 2 single 12.7-mm M2 mg; 1 helicopter
Electronics: Radar: 2 Hughes-Furuno SPS-73 nav.
M: 2 Alco 16V-251B diesels; 2 CP props; 5,000 bhp **Electric:** 500 kw tot.
Range: 2,700/18; 6,100/14 **Endurance:** 30 days
Crew: . . . tot. (accomm. for 12 officers, 72 enlisted)

Remarks: Transferred on 24-6-04, decommissioned from U.S. Coast Guard Service 9-01.

♦ 1 . . . -class requisitioned patrol boat
Bldr: Stocznia imeni Komuny Pariskej, Gdynia (In serv. 1972)

. . . (ex-*Simon Keghian,* ex-*Thierry Pascal*)

D: . . . tons **S:** 14 kts. **Dim:** 54.3 × 11.0 × 5.2
A: None
M: 1 . . . diesel, 2,000 bhp

Remarks: Donated by a French humanitarian association to a local group of Sri Lankan fisherman in 2-05 after the 12-04 Tsunami. Requisitioned by the Sri Lankan government in 3-05 for use as a patrol and training vessel.

♦ 2 Chinese Lushun class (Project 062-1-G)
Bldr: Lushun Dockyard, China (In serv. 2-3-98)

P 340 PRATHPA P 341 UDARA

D: 212 tons (fl) **S:** 28 kts **Dim:** 45.50 × 6.40 × 1.70
A: 2 twin 37-mm 63-cal. Type 76 AA; 2 twin 14.5-mm 79-cal. Type 81 AA
Electronics: Radar: 1 Decca RM 1070A nav.
M: 4 Type Z12V 190 BCJ diesels; 4 props; 4,800 bhp **Range:** 750/16
Crew: 3 officers, 27 enlisted

♦ 1 Chinese Haiqing class (Project 037-I)
Bldr: Qingdao SY (In serv. 22-5-96)

P 351 PARAKRAMABAHU

Parakramabahu (P 351) Sri Lankan Navy, 5-96

D: 440 tons (478 fl) **S:** 28 kts **Dim:** 62.0 × 7.20 × 2.24 (hull)
A: 2 twin 57-mm Type 66 AA; 2 twin 14.5-mm 79-cal. Type 81 AA; 4 5-round Type 87 ASW RL; 2 BMB-2 d.c. mortars; 2 d.c. racks; 2 minerails
Electronics:
Radar: 1 Anritsu RA 273 nav./surf. search
Sonar: HF hull-mounted
M: 4 PR 230ZC diesels; 4 props; 13,200 bhp
Range: 750/18; 1,300/15 **Crew:** 70 tot.

Remarks: First unit delivered new 13-12-95 but not commissioned until later. Acquisition of two more was canceled. Has an optical f.c. director. Range can be extended to 1,800 n.m. by using void tankage. Suffered significant damage during the 12-04 Tsunami.

♦ 1 Jayesagara class
Bldr: Colombo Dockyard

	Laid down	L	In serv.
P 601 JAYESAGARA	5-82	26-5-83	9-12-83

Jayesagara (P 601) Mike Louagie, 5-90

D: 315 tons (330 fl) **S:** 15 kts **Dim:** 39.80 × 7.00 × 2.20
A: 1 twin 25-mm 80-cal. Type 61 AA; 1 twin 14.5-mm 79-cal. Type 81 AA
Electronics: Radar: 1 Anritsu RA 273 nav./surf-search
M: 2 M.A.N. 8L 20/27 diesels; 2 props; 2,040 bhp
Electric: 220 kw tot. **Range:** 3,000/11
Endurance: 30 days **Crew:** 4 officers, 48 enlisted

Remarks: Two were ordered 31-12-81; three more authorized 8-84 but not built. Sister *Sagarawardene* (P 602) was sunk by two Tamil Tiger insurgent explosive suicide boats on 19-9-94. The 25-mm gunmount is to be replaced by a more modern weapon. P 601 was undergoing an overhaul during 8-03, which was likely completed in 2004–5.

♦ 7 (+ . . .) Chinese Haizhui class
Bldr: Guijian SY (P 317–319: Qinxin SY)

	In serv.		In serv.
P 317 EDITHARD II	8-98	P 330 RANAJAYA	9-9-96
P 318 WICKRAMA II	8-98	P 331 RANADEERA	9-9-96
P 319 . . .	8-98	P 332 RANAWICKREMA	9-9-96
P 322 RANARISI	14-7-92		

Ranajaya (P 330)—as deck cargo on heavy-lift ship *Gajah Borneo*
92 Wing Det. A, RAAF, 8-95

D: 150 tons (170 fl) **S:** 29 kts **Dim:** 41.0 × 5.41 × 1.80
A: P 317–319: 2 twin 20-mm 75-cal. Oerlikon/Royal Ordnance GCM-A03-2 AA; 2 twin 14.5-mm 93-cal. AA; P 322–332: 1 twin 37-mm 63-cal. Type 76 AA; 1 twin 25-mm 80-cal. Type 81 AA; 2 twin 14.5-mm 93-cal. AA
Electronics:
Radar: P 322–332: 1 Anritsu 726 UA nav./surf-search; P 317–319: 1 Koden MD 3220 Mk 2 nav.; 1 Furuno 825 nav.
M: 4 Type L12-180Z diesels; 4 props; 4,800 bhp (4,400 bhp sust.) **Range:** 750/16
Crew: 4 officers, 24 enlisted

Remarks: P 322, delivered 11-91, is of a slightly different design, closer to the original Shanghai-II in appearance. Her sister *Ranasura* (P 320) was lost on 13-4-95, and *Rana Viru* (P 321) was sunk by Tamil forces on 19-7-96. P 330–332 were delivered by Chinese heavy lift ships from 9-95 through 22-5-96 and have a flush-faced leading edge to the superstructure, which in both variants includes an enclosed pilothouse. Two more were ordered during 12-00, though they have not yet been constructed. P 330–332 have fin stabilizers. The third group, P 317–319 (and presumably the pair ordered in 12-00), have twin British-made AA mountings fore and aft and twin Chinese semi-enclosed 14.5-mm mg. mountings amidships. At least three were damaged during the 12-04 tsunami.

♦ 2 Chinese Shanghai-II class

P 311 WEERAYA (ex-P 3141)
P 315 JAGATHA (ex-P 3145)

D: 122.5 tons (135 fl) **S:** 28.5 kts **Dim:** 38.78 × 5.41 × 1.55
A: 2 twin 20-mm 90-cal. Royal Ordnance GCM-AO3 AA; 2 twin 14.5-mm 93-cal. Type 81 mg
Electronics: 1 Furuno FR 8250 nav.
M: 2 Type L12-180 diesels (1,200 bhp each), 2 Type L12-180Z diesels (910 bhp each); 4 props; 4,220 bhp
Electric: 39 kw **Range:** 750/16.5 **Endurance:** 7 days **Crew:** 34 tot.

PATROL CRAFT [PC] *(continued)*

Weeraya (P 311)—with twin 25-mm AA mount forward, twin 37-mm mount aft, and two twin 14.5-mm mounts amidships Sri Lankan Navy, 1990

Remarks: 311 was transferred in February 1972; *Jagatha* was transferred 1980, commissioning 30-11-80.
Hull systems: The L12-180 diesel is a copy of the Russian M50-F4 engine, and the L12-180Z is a copy of the 12D6 engine.
Combat systems: Original group were delivered armed with 2 twin 37-mm AA and 2 twin 25-mm AA and equipped with Pot Head radars.
Disposals: Of original group, *Daksaya* was stricken during 1983, *Balawitha* (P 3144) was stricken during 1991, *Suraya* (P 310) was lost 13-4-95, and *Rakshaka* (P 316), damaged the same date, was stricken during 1996. *Ranakami* (P 312) was sunk by Tamil forces in 2000.

PATROL BOATS [PB]

♦ 5 Mk V-A Pegasus class

Bldr: Halter Marine Equitable SY, New Orleans, La. (In serv. 1997)

P 480 P 481 P 483 P 484 P 485

Mk V-A Pegasus class Sri Lankan Navy, 11-96

D: 57 tons (68 fl) **S:** 47 kts (40 sust.) **Dim:** 24.99 × 5.33 × 1.32
A: 2 single 20-mm 90-cal Oerlikon AA; 2 single 12.7-mm M2 mg; 2 single 7.62-mm M-60 mg; 1 40-mm Mk 19 grenade launcher
Electronics: Radar: 1 Raytheon R 1210 nav.
M: 2 MTU 16V396 TE94 diesels; 2 Arneson outdrives with Rolla surface-piercing props; 4,570 bhp
Electric: 50 kw tot. (2 × 25 kw diesel sets) **Range:** 500/35; 1,200/30
Fuel: 8,667 liters **Crew:** 12 tot.

Remarks: Three ordered 3-96, with option for three more, taken up 12-96. First two delivered 8-11-96, third during 12-96, and the other three in 9-97. Five more were to be ordered early in 2001, at $3.8 million each, but the order was not placed. P 482 was lost to Tamil sabotage on 7-4-00 and another may have been damaged. Similar craft operate in the U.S. Navy. Have Kevlar-reinforced GRP hull. Have a 220-gallon/day potable water generator. Heavier armament is to be added later, probably to include U.S. 25-mm Bushmaster guns in place of one or both 20-mm mounts.

♦ 11 Israeli Shaldag class

Bldr: P 470–472 and 1 other: Israel Shipyards, Haifa; others: Colombo Dockyard

	In serv.		In serv.		In serv.
P . . .	5-1-02	P 454	1997	P 472	16-2-00
P 451 (ex-P 494)	1997	P 455	1997	P 495	1998
P 452 (ex-P 495)	1997	P 470 (ex-P 491)	5-90	P 497	1999
P 453	1998	P 471 (ex-P 492)	20-7-96		

Shaldag-class P 470—Israeli-built version Sri Lankan Navy, 1996

D: 40 tons (56 fl) **S:** 46 kts **Dim:** 24.37 (20.07 pp) × 6.00 × 1.15 (1.26 max.)
A: 1 20-mm Rafael Typhoon gatling AA; 1 20-mm 90-cal. Oerlikon; 4 single 7.62-mm mg; 4 40-mm Mk 19 grenade launchers
Electronics: Radar: 1 Furuno FR 8250 or Koden Mk 2 nav.
M: P 470–472: 2 Deutz-MWM TBD 604 B V16 diesels; 2 waterjets; 5,000 bhp; others: 2 MTU 12V396 TE 94 diesels; 2 waterjets; 4,570 (3,260 sust.) bhp
Electric: 50 kw tot. (2 × 25 kw, 440 V AC diesel sets) **Range:** 850/16
Endurance: 2–3 days **Crew:** 15 tot.

Shaldag class—Sri Lankan–built, "Colombo-class" version Sri Lankan Navy, 1996

Remarks: First unit was a builder-funded prototype that was not accepted by the Israeli Navy; trials by the U.S. Navy, mandated by the U.S. Congress, found the craft unacceptable as well. Sri Lanka bought the prototype on 24-1-96 along with P 471; a third Israeli-built unit, P 472, was acquired in 2000. The Sri Lankan–built units, known locally as the "Colombo class," are a modified version with improved hull strength, smaller superstructure, different engines, and built with Israeli technical assistance at Colombo Dockyard; two were also built at Colombo for the Maldive Islands.
Hull systems: Deep-vee, aluminum-construction hull. Five watertight compartments. Air-conditioned. Range for P 470 and P 471 also reported as 640 n.m. at 45 kts.
Combat systems: The armament described previously was seen on several units of the class as of 2000; some may retain the original 20-mm Oerlikon gun on the bow.
Disposals: P 494 and P 496 were lost to Tamil rebel forces during 2000, and several others have been damaged, some severely.

♦ 4 Sea Sentinel 508 class

Bldrs: Simonneau Marine, Fontenay-le-Comte, France (In serv. 1993–95)

P 410 (ex-P 483) P 411 (ex-P 484) P 412 (ex-P 485) P 413 (ex-P 486)

Sea Sentinel 508–class P 410—with original pennant number French Navy, 1993

D: 28 tons (fl) **S:** 45 kts (42 sust.) **Dim:** 17.3 × 4.9 × . . .
A: 1 20-mm 90-cal. GIAT F-2 AA; 1 12.7-mm mg; 2 single 7.62-mm mg
Electronics: Radar: 1 . . . nav.
M: 2 MTU 12V183 TE93 diesels; 2 Hamilton waterjets; 2,300 bhp **Range:** 500/35
Crew: 8 tot.

Remarks: Ordered 3-93, with the second pair of hulls fitted out at Colombo; first two completed 11-93 and 12-93. Nine more were ordered 1996 from Colombo Dockyard and referred to as the UFAC (Ultra-Fast Attack Craft) class, but they were later canceled, as was a plan to build up to an additional 96. Aluminum construction.

♦ 3 Killer class

Bldr: Korea SB & Eng., Pusan (In serv. 2-88)

P 430 (ex-P 473) P 431 (ex-P 474) P 432 (ex-P 475)

Killer-class P 430—with original pennant number Sri Lankan Navy, 1996

D: 56 tons (fl) **S:** 40 kts **Dim:** 23.0 × 5.4 × 1.8
A: 2 single 20-mm 90-cal. Oerlikon AA; 2 single 12.7-mm mg
Electronics: Radar: 1 Decca 926 nav.
M: 2 MTU 8V396 TB93 diesels; 2 props; 3,260 bhp **Crew:** 12 tot.

Remarks: Ordered 10-86. A planned additional three were not ordered.

PATROL BOATS [PB] *(continued)*

♦ 7 Israeli Super Dvora class
Bldr: RAMTA-Israeli Aircraft Industries, Be'er Sheva (In serv. 1987–97)

	In serv.		In serv.
P 440 (ex-P 465)	1987	P 460 (ex-P 441)	5-11-95
P 441 (ex-P 466)	1987	P 461 (ex-P 496)	30-4-96
P 442 (ex-P 467)	1987	P 462 (ex-P 497)	22-6-96
P 443 (ex-P 468)	1987		

Super Dvora–class P 441 Sri Lankan Navy, 1996

D: 48 tons (54 fl) **S:** 36 (P 460-462: 46) kts **Dim:** 22.40 × 5.49 × 1.00
A: 2 single 20-mm 70-cal. Oerlikon AA; 2 single 12.7-mm mg
Electronics: Radar: 1/Decca 926 (P 460–462: Koden MD 3220) nav.
M: 2 MTU 12V396 TB93 or TB94 diesels; 2 props; 3,260 bhp (see Remarks)
Electric: 30 kw tot. **Range:** 700/14 **Crew:** 1 officer, 9–11 enlisted

Remarks: Improved version of basic Dvora design. First four are from a group ordered 10-86. Second group (P 460–462) are Mk II version with slightly more powerful engines and an improved fire-control and surveillance system.
Hull systems: Engines in P 460–462 are rated at 2,285 bhp each, producing a top speed of around 46 kts, while the engines in the first four produce speeds of about 36 kts.
Combat systems: P 460–462 have an Elop MSIS optronic director.
Disposals: P 463 and one other were lost in action on 5-6-00. On 20-3-01 one was sunk by Sri Lankan Air Force fire and another to Tamil Rebel action.

♦ 3 Israeli Dvora class
Bldr: Israeli Aircraft Ind., Be'er Sheva (In serv. 1984–86)

P 420 (ex-P 453) P 421 (ex-P 454) P 422 (ex-P 455)

Dvora-class P 457—lost on 25-10-96 Sri Lankan Navy, 8-91

D: 47 tons (fl) **S:** 36 kts **Dim:** 21.62 × 5.49 × 0.94 (1.82 props)
A: 2 single 20-mm 70-cal. Oerlikon AA; 2 single 12.7-mm mg
Electronics: Radar: 1 Decca 926 nav.
M: 2 MTU 12V331 TC81 diesels; 2 props; 2,720 bhp
Electric: 30 kw **Range:** 700/32; 1,200/17 **Crew:** 12 tot.

Remarks: First six ordered late 1984. Aluminum construction.
Disposals: P 456 lost 29-8-95, P 457 on 25-10-96, and P 458 on 30-3-96. Two others had been lost earlier. One Dvora or Super Dvora was sunk on 18-10-97.

♦ 4 P 445 class
Bldr: Colombo Dockyard

	L	In serv.		L	In serv.
P 241	. . .	20-9-82	P 244	27-8-82	1982
P 242	. . .	17-9-82	P 245	20-9-82	1982

P 445–class P 241 Sri Lankan Navy, 1993

D: 40 tons (44 fl) **S:** 22 kts **Dim:** 20.0 (18.3 pp) × 5.1 × 1.3
A: 1 20-mm 70-cal. Oerlikon AA; 2 single 12.7-mm mg
Electronics: Radar: 1 Furuno FR 2010 nav.
M: 2 G.M. Detroit Diesel 12V71 TI diesels; 2 props; 1,300 bhp (840 sust,)
Range: 1,200/14 Fuel: 10 tons **Endurance:** 14 days **Crew:** 1 officer, 9 enlisted

Remarks: Steel construction. Sister P 243 was lost to a limpet mine on 11-6-96.

♦ 4 P 201 class
Bldr: Colombo Dockyard (P 201 in serv. 1981; P 211 in 6-86; others: . . .)

P 201 P 211 P 214 P 215

D: 15 tons (22 fl) **S:** 20 kts **Dim:** 13.73 × 3.63 × 0.90 **A:** 1 12.7-mm mg
Electronics: Radar: 1 Furuno FR 2010 nav.
M: 2 G.M. Detroit Diesel 8V71 TI diesels; 2 props; 800 bhp (460 sust.)
Electric: 1 kw **Range:** 450/14
Fuel: 2.5 tons **Crew:** 1 officer, 5 enlisted

Remarks: Also employed for customs inspection. Sister P 203 sank during 1989.

♦ 4 Belikawa class
Bldr: Cheverton, Cowes, U.K. (In serv. 4-77 to 10-77)

P 221 P 222 P 223 P 224

D: 22 tons (fl) **S:** 23.6 kts **Dim:** 17.0 × 4.5 × 1.2 **A:** 1 12.7-mm mg
Electronics: Radar: 1 Decca 110 nav.
M: 2 G.M. Detroit Diesel 8V71 TI diesels; 2 props; 800 bhp
Range: 790/18, 1,000/12.2 **Crew:** 7 tot.

Remarks: GRP construction. Originally intended for customs duties but used as patrol craft. Originally named *Belikawa, Diyakawa, Korawakka,* and *Seruwa,* respectively, with hull numbers P 421–424. Sister *Tarawa* (P 225, ex-P 425) has been discarded.

♦ 25 P 151 class
Bldr: P 151, 152: TAOS Yacht, Colombo (In serv. 1991); others; Blue Star Marine, Colombo (In serv. 1994–95, 1997–98)

P 151 P 161 through P 173 P 189 through P 194
P 152 P 180 P 196 through P 198

P 151–class P 161 Sri Lankan Navy, 1996

D: 7 tons (9 fl) **S:** 33 kts **Dim:** 9.8 × 2.1 × 0.5 **A:** 1 12.7-mm mg
Electronics: Radar: 1 Furuno 1941 nav.
M: 2 Cummins 6BTA5.9-M2 diesels; 2 waterjets; 584 bhp
Range: 330/25 **Crew:** 5 tot.

Remarks: GRP construction. Sister P 174 lost early in 1999. P 183 was lost during 2000. More were to be built, but the program seems to have ceased by the end of 1998.

♦ 5 P 140 class
Bldr: Blue Star Marine, Colombo (In serv. 1988)

P 145 through P 149

P 140–class P 149 Sri Lankan Navy, 1990

D: 3.5 tons (5 fl) **S:** 30 kts **Dim:** 12.8 × 2.4 × 0.5 **A:** 1 12.7-mm mg
Electronics: Radar: None **M:** 2 gasoline outboard motors; 280 bhp **Crew:** 4 tot.

Remarks: Designed to operate from the "deckship" command vessels. Sister P 150 was lost 8-91 to a mine, P 143 was lost in 1996, and three others have been lost or discarded. Seven others may also have been stricken.

♦ 3 P 111 class
Bldr: Consolidated Marine Eng., Sri Lanka (In serv. 1988–94)

P 111 P 112 P 113

PATROL BOATS [PB] *(continued)*

P 111–class P 112 Sri Lankan Navy, 1996

D: 3.5 tons (5 fl) **S:** 26 kts **Dim:** 13.4 × 3.0 × 0.5 **A:** 1 12.7-mm mg
Electronics: Radar: None
M: 2 Yamaha D343 K diesels; 2 props; 324 bhp **Crew:** 4–5 tot.

Remarks: Nine delivered 1988, four in 1992, and two in 1994. Designed to operate from the "deckship" command vessels. Wooden construction. A dozen have been lost in action or discarded, and the three listed previously may no longer be in service.

♦ 3 Cougar Cat 900 patrol craft
Bldr: Cougar Marine, Netley, U.K. (In serv. 1984–85)

P 102 P 107 P 109

Cougar Cat 900–class P 106—since stricken Sri Lankan Navy, 1990

D: 4.5 tons (7.4 fl) **S:** 30 kts **Dim:** 10.40 × 2.89 × 0.78 (0.48 at speed)
A: 1 12.7-mm mg **Electronics:** Radar: None
M: 2 Ford Sabre diesels; 2 Type 290P outdrives; 500 bhp
Range: 150/32 **Crew:** 3–8 tot.

Remarks: First unit, purchased 1984 for evaluation in operations from mother ships, was 9.20 m o.a. Glass-reinforced-plastic construction. Eight more ordered 1-85 and delivered by 10-85. Five or more have been lost or discarded. P 101 had been lost to Tamil action by 2004.

AMPHIBIOUS WARFARE CRAFT

♦ 1 Chinese Yuhai-class utility landing craft [LCU]
Bldr: Wuhu SY (In serv. 22-5-96)

L 841 Shakhti

Shakhti (L 841) Sri Lankan Navy, 5-96

D: 799 tons (fl) **S:** 14 kts **Dim:** 58.4 × 10.4 × 2.7
A: 5 twin 14.5-mm 93-cal. Model 81 AA; 6 single 12.7-mm mg
Electronics: Radar: 1 Type 756 nav.
M: 2 M.A.N. 8L 20/27 diesels; 2 props; 4,900 bhp
Range: 1,000/12 **Crew:** 56 tot.

Remarks: Delivered 13-12-95. A reported second unit was for a different country. Essentially an enlarged LCU and appears to have been designed for commercial rather than military service. Bow ramp only. Cargo capacity is two tanks and 250 troops or up to 150 tons of miscellaneous cargo. The 12.7-mm mg were added in Sri Lanka.

♦ 2 Kandula-class utility landing craft [LCU]
Bldr: Colombo Dockyard

	In serv.
L 836 Ranavijaya	21-7-94
L 839 Ranagaja (ex-*Gajasingha*)	15-11-91

D: 200 tons (268 fl) **S:** 8 kts **Dim:** 33.00 (30.00 pp) × 8.00 × 1.50
A: 4 14.5-mm 93-cal. AA—2 12.7-mm mg
Electronics: 1 Furuno FCR 1421 nav.
M: 2 Caterpillar 3408 TA diesels; 2 props; 1,524 bhp
Range: 1,800/8 **Crew:** 2 officers, 10 enlisted + 54 troops

Remarks: Vosper Singapore–built sisters *Kandula* (A 537) and *Pabbatha* (L 838, ex-A 538) were lost 1992 and 24-2-98, respectively; a second landing craft (class unspecified) was also lost on the latter date. L 839 was begun for a civilian customer and taken over for the navy; the craft was badly damaged by gunfire during 10-95, with 54 personnel casualties.

♦ 1 M-10-class air-cushion landing craft [LCMA]
Bldr: Vosper Thornycroft, Portchester, U.K. (In serv. 6-98)

A 530

M-10-class hovercraft A 530 ABS Hovercraft, 6-98

D: 28 tons (fl) **S:** 35 kts loaded **Dim:** 18.84 × 8.80 × 0.35 at rest
A: 1 12.7-mm mg **Electronics:** Radar: 1 . . . nav.
M: 2 Deutz BF12L513C diesels; 2 lift fans, 2 air-screw props; 1,050 bhp
Range: 600/30 **Fuel:** 4,600 liters **Crew:** 1 officer, 2 enlisted + 56 troops

Remarks: Designed by ABS Hovercraft, U.K. Arrived in Sri Lanka during 12-98. Is capable of carrying one tracked vehicle, or 56 seated troops, or one 20-ft. cargo container, or 20 stretcher cases. The hull is constructed of GRP, with a GRP/foam sandwich deck and Kevlar-reinforced superstructure. Can clear 1-m obstacles and can operate in 2.5-m seas.

♦ 2 Chinese Yuqin-class landing craft [LCM]

L 820 (In serv. 6-91) L 821 (In serv. 5-95)

Yuqin-class landing craft L 820 Sri Lankan Navy, 1992

D: 60 tons light (110 fl) **S:** 11.5 (9.5 loaded) kts **Dim:** 24.1 × 5.2 × 1.1
A: 2 twin 14.5-mm 93-cal. AA **Electronics:** Radar: 1 Fuji . . . nav.
M: 2 Type 12V50 diesels; 2 props; 600 bhp **Range:** 500/10
Crew: 2 officers, 10 enlisted

Remarks: Cargo: 46 tons.

♦ 1 catamaran personnel transport [LCP]
Bldr: International Catamarans, Hobart, Tasmania (In serv. 20-12-87)

A 540 Hansaya (ex-*Offshore Pioneer*)

Lihinaya (A 541)—lost in 2000 Sri Lankan Navy, 1990

AMPHIBIOUS WARFARE CRAFT *(continued)*

D: 153.2 tons (fl) **S:** 32 kts **Dim:** 30.00 × 11.20 × 2.34
A: 1 20-mm 70-cal. Oerlikon AA; 2 single 12.7-mm mg
Electronics: Radar: 1 Furuno 1012 nav. **M:** 2 MTU diesels; 2 props; 3,560 bhp
Crew: 2 officers, 10 enlisted

Remarks: 169 grt. Cargo: 60 tons stores or 120 troops. Acquired 1-86 and converted by Sing Koon Seng SY, Singapore, when they were lengthened 5 m and had additional superstructure added. Originally built as oilfield supply boats. *Lihinaya* (A 541, ex-*Offshore Pride*) was sunk by Tamil forces on 23-10-00.

SERVICE CRAFT

♦ 2 personnel launches [YFL]

A 542 A 543

Remarks: No data available.

SUDAN

Republic of the Sudan

Personnel: Approx. 1,800 total

Bases: Kosti, Flamingo Bay, for Red Sea units; Khartoum for River Nile units.

Aviation: Two CASA Aviocar C-212-200.

Note: Due to operating conditions and the withdrawal of traditional sources of aid, the material condition of the units of the Sudanese fleet is seriously deficient. A number of patrol craft are no longer operable, and all auxiliaries have been discarded. Iran has supplied several small patrol craft and some technical aid.

PATROL BOATS [PB]

♦ 8 Iranian Ashoora-I-class patrol launches
Bldr; IRI Marine Industries, Iran (In serv. 1992)

D: 3 tons (fl) **S:** 42 kts **Dim:** 8.1 × 2.4 × 0.5 **A:** 1 14.5-mm 93-cal. Mg
M: 2 Yamaha gasoline outboards; 400 bhp **Crew:** 3 tot.

Remarks: GRP construction. Based on the Red Sea coast at Kosti.

Disposal notes: The two remaining ex-Iranian 70-ton patrol boats, *Kader* (129, ex-*Shahpar*) and *Karari* (130, ex-*Shakram*), have been inoperable at Flamingo Bay since 1995 and are unlikely to see further service.

♦ 4 Yugoslav Type 15 riverine patrol launches
Bldr: . . . (In serv. 18-5-89)

502 Kurmuk 503 Qaysan 504 Rumbek 505 Mayom

D: 19.5 tons (fl) **S:** 16 kts **Dim:** 16.87 × 3.90 × 0.65 (0.70 props)
A: 1 20-mm 90-cal. Hispano-Suiza M-71 AA; 2 single 7.62-mm mg
Electronics: Radar: None **M:** 2 diesels; 2 props; 330 bhp
Range: 160/12 **Crew:** 6 tot.

Remarks: Design originally intended for riverine and lake use by Yugoslavia. Were a gift; intended for use on the White Nile and are based at Khartoum.

♦ 4 ex-Iranian U.S. 40-ft. Commercial Cruiser class
Bldr: Sewart Seacraft, Berwick, La. (In serv. 1963)

1161 Maroub 1162 Fijab 1163 Salak 1164 Halote

D: 10 tons **S:** 30 kts **Dim:** 12.2 × 3.4 × 1.1 **A:** 1 12.7-mm mg
Electronics: Radar: None **M:** 2 G.M. Detroit Diesel 6-71 diesels; 2 props; 348 bhp

Remarks: Donated by Iran in 1978 and thought to have been stricken circa 1990, but at least three said to be in service on the Red Sea as late as 1992, and all four were operable as of 1998.

AMPHIBIOUS WARFARE CRAFT

♦ 4 Yugoslav DC 101–class personnel landing craft [LCVP]
Bldr: Vela Luca, Korcula Island, Yugoslavia

D: 5.5 tons light (11 fl) **S:** 25 kts (20 sust.)
Dim: 11.30 × 3.10 × 0.32 **A:** 1 7.62-mm mg
Electronics: Radar: 1 Decca 101 nav.
M: 2 diesels; 2 waterjets *or* 2 outdrives; 260 bhp
Range: 100/15 **Crew:** 2 tot.

Remarks: Delivered by air in 1991 and assembled in Sudan. Based at Kosti on Flamingo Bay. Glass-reinforced-plastic construction. Misidentified as Type 11 landing craft in earlier editions. Can carry two jeeps or 30 troops, for a total of 4.8 tons.

SURINAME

Republic of Suriname

Personnel: 240 tot.

Base: Kruktu Tere, Paramaribo

Naval Aviation: The Air Force uses two CASA C-212-400 transports for coastal patrol.

PATROL BOATS [PB]

♦ 3 Rodman 101 class
Bldr: Rodman-Polyships, Vigo, Spain (In serv. 2-99 to 4-99)

P 01 Jarrabakka P 02 Spari P 03 Gramorgu

D: 46 tons (fl) **S:** 33 kts **Dim:** 30.00 (24.96 pp) × 6.51 (6.00 wl) × 1.50
A: 1 12.7-mm mg
Electronics: Radar: 1 Furuno . . . nav.
M: 2 MTU 12V2000 diesels; 2 Hamilton HM-571 waterjets; 2,900 bhp (2,760 bhp sust.)
Electric: 42 kw (2 × 21 kw diesel sets) **Range:** 800/25 **Crew:** 9 tot.

Remarks: Ordered 12-97. GRP construction.

♦ 5 Rodman 55 class
Bldr: Rodman-Polyships, Vigo, Spain (In serv. 10-98 to 4-99)

P 04 through P 08

D: 15.7 tons (fl) **S:** 25 kts **Dim:** 16.50 × 3.80 × 0.7 **A:** 1 7.62-mm mg
Electronics: Radar: 1 Decca. . . nav.
M: 2 Bazán-M.A.N. D2848 LXE diesels; 2 Hamilton waterjets; 1,360 bhp (1,216 sust.)
Range: 500/25 **Crew:** 7 tot.

Remarks: Ordered 12-97; had originally been ordered for Paraguay. GRP construction.

SWEDEN

Kingdom of Sweden

SVENSKA MARINEN

Personnel: 4,280 total, including 2,000 draftees and 320 naval aviation personnel. There are also about 1,300 personnel in the Naval Brigade (ex-Coastal Artillery Service) About 27,000 reservists are available for the navy and Naval Brigade (about 3,000 total for the latter).

Bases: Principal base at Muskö, with other facilities at Karlskrona and Göteborg.

Naval Aviation: 320 personnel and the following helicopters: five Agusta Bell 206-A JetRanger (HKP-6) and 14 Vertol 107-II-4 (3 HKP-4B for minesweeping and 11 HKP-4C for rescue and ASW, with six depth charges or up to four Tp 422 torpedoes, AS-380 dipping sonar). Of three CASA C-212-200 Aviocar light transports in service, two are used by the Coast Guard and one by the Navy. Eleven AS.332M1 Super Puma (HKP-10) are used by the Swedish Air Force for search-and-rescue duties. The 14 HKP-4 helicopters, refitted and given new doppler navigation systems by late 2001, are due to be replaced between 2006 and 2011 by eight NH-90 (HKP-14) helicopters, five of which will be fitted with the Thales FLASH dipping sonar, APS-143B(v)3 radar and provisions for launching air-to-surface missiles. Three of the NH-90s will be equipped for SAR duties. Nine Augusta A-109 (HKP-15) helicopters were ordered in 2001 and began replacing the HKP-4 helicopters in 2005.

WEAPONS AND SYSTEMS

A. MISSILES

RBS-12, the infrared-homing Norwegian Kongsberg Penguin Mk 2 missile, is in use on board the *Kaparen*-class guided-missile patrol boats. It has a 120-kg warhead.

Length: 3.0 m **Diameter:** 280 mm **Wingspan:** 1.4 m
Weight: 340 kg **Warhead weight:** 120 kg
Speed: Mach 0.7 **Max. range:** 30 km at an altitude of 60–100 m

RBS-15, made by Saab Dynamics, became operational in 1985. The missile has a solid rocket booster and a turbojet sustainer. A sea-skimmer, it has a terminal-homing guidance system. The RBS-15F is launched from Air Force Viggen jet fighters. Under a 1994 contract, all missiles were upgraded to Mk 2 status by the end of 1997. A submarine-launched version is being studied. The Mk 3 version has a range of 200 km, programmable flight waypoints, reduced radar cross-section, a re-attack capability, a 200-kg warhead, greater maneuverability, and greater resistance to countermeasures; it can be used for land attack. Data for the Mk 2 version:

Length: 4.350 m **Diameter:** 0.500 m
Wingspan: 0.85 m (folded); 1.4 (extended)
Weight: 598 kg (770 kg with booster) **Speed:** Mach 0.8
Range: 80–100 km at an altitude of 10–20 m **Altitude:** 10–20 m

RBS-17, a version of the U.S. Laser-Hellfire, procured for use by the Naval Brigade.

Length: 1.625 m **Weight:** 48 kg (71 with launcher) **Range:** 5+ km

WEAPONS AND SYSTEMS *(continued)*

RBS-70, a shoulder-launched SAM made by Bofors, entered development in 1983 as a weapon for surface combatants in a version known as the RBS-70 SLM. Replaced Army and Coast Artillery 40-mm AA during 1990–92.

Length: 1.735 m **Diameter:** 152 mm **Weight:** 25 kg
Launcher weight: 150 kg (loaded)
Range: 5–6 km **Altitude:** 3 km

RBS-90 is basically a longer-ranged RBS-70 Mk 2 with a night sight; it is offered with a remote-controlled octuple launcher. Range is 8 km and altitude 5 km.

B. GUNS

Note: All guns, except the Patria Hägglands 120-mm mortar, are manufactured by Saab AB under its Bofors trademark.

120-mm SSG 120 twin, automatic mortar: Contracts let 19-6-02 for installation on a new Dockstavarvet-built Stridsbåt 90H assault boat under the AMOS (Advanced Mortar System) program. The autoloading mortars are installed in a single turret and are to have a range of 10 km (5.4 n.m.) and an associated fire-control system capable of direct and indirect fire.

57-mm single-barrel automatic SAK 57 Mk 3: Employs shaped GRP gunhouse lengthened to conceal gun barrel at low depression to reduce radar signature and incorporates fold-out decoy rocket launchers. The mount has 120 rounds on board, with 40 ready to fire and uses cassettes to reduce reload time to 8 seconds. As with the other 57-mm mounts, it has a backup local control capability. The 57-mm 3P (Prefragmented, Programmable, Proximity-fused) round weighs 2.4 kg, with 2,400 tungsten pellets and .46 kg Octol explosive as payload. The HCER-BB (High Capacity Extended Range—Base-Bleed) round, with a range of 21 km and muzzle velocity of 950 m/sec, is also available.

57-mm single-barrel automatic SAK 57 Mk 2: Entered service in 1985. Carries 120 rounds ready service within the low, streamlined gunhouse, automatically loading clips of 20 rounds each. Can be upgraded to Mk 3 version (see previous entry).

Mount weight: 6 tons
Shell weight: AA: 5.8 kg (projectile: 2.4 kg); Surface fire: 6.8 kg
Muzzle velocity: 1,020 m/sec **Max. rate of fire:** 220 rounds/min
Train speed: 55 deg./sec **Elevation:** –10 deg./+85 deg.
Range: 14,000 m max. horizontal

57-mm single-barrel automatic SAK 57 Mk 1: Installed on the *Kaparen*-class missile boats and Spica-II torpedo boats.

Mount weight (without ammunition): 6 tons
Max. rate of fire: 200 rounds/min **Train speed:** 55 deg./sec
Elevation: –10 deg./+75 deg. **Elevation speed:** 20 deg./sec

40-mm single-barrel semi-automatic L70: 40-mm, 70-cal., 3.7-ton Trinity mounting has a 1,025-m/sec muzzle velocity, a 4-km range, and a 330-rpm firing rate from a 100-round magazine; fitted with an integral radar, the Trinity fires a .975-kg 3-P (Prefragmented, Preprogrammable, Proximity-fused) round with 1,000 tungsten pellets. Basic Trinity version, E1, has on-mount radar and laser rangefinder; E1 Optronic version lacks the radar; the S1 variant uses a remote-control director and has no on-mount operator. A Mk 3 version, using the Trinity mount but without the fire-control system, is being developed. Characteristics for the standard Bofors L70 gunmount include:

Barrel length: 70 caliber **Mount weight:** 2.8 to 3.3 tons without ammunition
Muzzle velocity: 1,005–1,025 m/sec **Elevation:** –10 deg/+90 deg
Training rate: 85 deg./sec **Effective range:** 4 km

C. TORPEDOES

All produced by Saab Bofors Underwater Systems AB, Motala (formerly Bofors Sutec; formerly Underwater Division, Swedish Ordnance; and formerly FFV Ordnance).

Tp 62 (Torpedo 2000): New-generation heavyweight torpedo to follow the Tp 61 series. First order placed 17-12-97 and first example delivered 12-6-01. The weapon is wire-guided, with active, passive, and combined active/passive homing modes. It has eight interchangeable modules, is powered by a hydrogen peroxide–fueled engine, and has contact and influence fuses. Maximum operating depth is 500 m. The weapon has also been ordered by Brazil. An Autonomous Underwater Vehicle (AUV 62) surveillance version is under study.

Diameter: 533.4 mm **Length:** 5,990 mm **Weight:** 1,450 kg
Warhead: . . . **Speed:** 60 kts max. **Range:** 45 km max.

Tp 61 series: The wire-guided Tp 61 is used for antisurface duties from surface ships and submarines. The weapon entered service in 1977 and is now employed in the Tp 613 version, with a wakeless hydrogen peroxide engine. The Tp 617 is a 6.98-m-long export version weighing 1,850 kg and having a 20,000-m range. Characteristics for the Tp 613 include:

Diameter: 533.4 mm **Length:** 7,025 mm **Weight:** 1,765 kg
Warhead: 240 kg **Range:** 30,000 m

Note: Development of the Tp 46 Grampus lightweight torpedo was canceled during 2002.

Tp 45: Evolved from the Tp 431 program and formerly known as Tp 43X2, the Tp 45 was to enter service in the mid-1990s.

Diameter: 400 mm **Length:** 2,800 mm **Weight:** 310 kg **Range:** 20,000 m

Note: Due to the delay in the availability of the Type 45, 50 Whitehead A-244 lightweight torpedoes were ordered from Italy in 1990.

Tp 42/43 series: The lightweight Tp 42 torpedo is wire-guided and has acoustic homing, for use by submarines, surface ships, and aircraft against submarines. It was developed from the similar Tp 41. The Tp 422 entered Swedish service in 1983; a reduced-charge warhead is available for peacetime use against intruders. Data for the Tp 422 include:

Diameter: 400 mm
Length: 2,600 mm (2,440 mm without wire-guidance attachment)
Weight: 298 kg **Warhead:** 50 kg **Range:** 20,000 m (10,000 at high speed)

D. ASW WEAPONS

ALECTO: Under development by Saab Bofors Dynamics for use on the *Visby* class. Has a six-barreled, trainable 127-mm launcher capable of firing ASW, passive torpedo-defense, and offboard air-defense decoy rounds. Range originally was to be 150–1,200 meters, but as of 2000, the planned range was to be up to 6,000 m, and torpedo countermeasure, ECM, and sonobouy payloads are foreseen.

ASW 600: A Saab Bofors Dynamics–made rocket launcher firing 100-mm-dia. M83 charges to ranges of 350–400 m in patterns of 9, 18, 27, or 36 grenades when installed in the normal four-unit suite. Formerly named Elma LLS-920. Each grenade weighs 4.2 kg and has a shaped-charge warhead. A shallow-water (10-m minimum) version entered service in 1986, followed by chaff and IR decoy rounds. A 600-meter-ranged hard-kill version of the ASW 600 round, the M90, with a larger rocket engine, is now available, as is a decoy round called EWS-900E. The current missile system is officially known as RBS-12. The ASW-601 system, which used a trainable launcher, was not put into production.

Bofors 375-mm ASW rocket launcher: No longer in Swedish Navy service, was once widely used in foreign navies in two-, four-, or six-tubed versions. Two types of rockets were furnished: the Erika, with ranges from 600–1,600 m, and the Nelli, with ranges from 1,600–3,600 m. The SR-375 twin-tubed launcher has a 24-round auto-loading magazine.

Note: During 1992, Saab Missiles announced a depth charge with a Dowty active acoustic sensor (100–200 kHz) and control fins; charges missing a target by more than 5 m would sink without detonating. Helicopters can employ the Malin ASW depth charge.

E. MINES

Submarines employ the Saab Bofors Underwater Systems Mine 42, a 533-mm dia., converted Tp 27 straight-running heavyweight torpedo equipped with influence fuzing; these are launched from 533-mm torpedo tubes. Also used by submarines are portable mine-belt mine containers, two per submarine, each holding 22 influence mines.

F. SENSORS

The Ericsson Sea Giraffe 150-series C-band radars are offered for export in various models and provide for air and surface search via two separate channels. The digital, pulse-compression radar is offered at 15- to 60-kw power with differing antenna gains. A new variant with agile, multibeam transmission was offered in 1997; it can track 100 targets at up to 70 degrees elevation and has new ECCM features. Five Sea Giraffe AMB sets were ordered in 1-98 for the *Visby* class; the radar is based on the variant used with the land-based RBS-23 Bamse air-defense missile system.

Seven sets of U.S. Klein sidescan high-frequency sonars were purchased in 1984 to assist in locating intruding submarines.

Saab Bofors Dynamics AB offers a mobile underwater acoustic, magnetic, pressure, and electric field-data acquisition system; data are sent to a portable land evaluation station via fiberoptic cable, and there is also a television camera to permit monitoring the area above the array.

Note: In the ship name and hull number lists that follow, also given is a three-letter condensed form of the ship's name used when pennant numbers have been painted out.

ATTACK SUBMARINES [SS]

Note: Swedish submarine builder Kockums was taken over by Howaldtswerke Deutsche Werft (HDW), Kiel, on 21-9-99, but the trademark is maintained. The joint Swedish-Norwegian-Danish *Viking* submarine project is no longer a viable option. Denmark and Norway have both withdrawn from the project and Sweden is unlikely to continue unilateral design and development of the class and may instead opt for a modified German Type 214 submarine.

♦ 3 Gotland class (Type A-19)

Bldr: Kockums, Mälmo

	Symbol	Laid down	L	Trials	In serv.
Gotland	Gld	27-11-92	2-2-95	1-7-95	9-99 (del. 2-9-96)
Halland	Hnd	7-94	27-9-96	15-3-97	9-99 (del. 1-10-97)
Uppland	Upd	14-1-94	9-2-96	1-8-96	9-99 (del. 1-5-97)

Gotland (Gld) Ralph Edwards, 10-05

D: 1,384 tons surf./1,494 tons sub. **S:** 10 kts surf./10 kts snorkel/20 kts sub.
Dim: 60.60 × 6.06 × 5.60 (surf.)
A: 4 bow 533-mm TT (12 Tp 613 or 62 torpedoes); 2 bow 400-mm TT (4 Tp 422 or Tp 45 ASW torpedoes); 48 Bunny or Tp 42 mines in external belt
Electronics:
Radar: 1 Terma . . . nav./surf. search—EW: Thorn-EMI Manta intercept
Sonar: STN Atlas Elektronik CSU-90-2 suite (PRS 3-15 panoramic passive ranging, FAS 3-1 LF flank arrays)

ATTACK SUBMARINES [SS] *(continued)*

Gotland (Gld)—arriving in San Diego aboard a heavy lift ship for operations with the U.S. Navy U.S. Navy, 6-05

M: 2 Hedemora V12A/15-Ub (VA 185) diesels (1,300 bhp each); 2 Jeumont-Schneider 760 kw generators; 1 ASEA electric motor; 1 7-bladed prop; 1,800 shp—2 Stirling V4-275R Mk II 75 kw air-independent generator sets
Range: . . . / . . . **Crew:** 23 tot.

Remarks: Ordered 28-3-90, although not funded until the 1992 budget. Order change placed 5-9-91 to incorporate Stirling-cycle external-combustion engines, resulting in 200-ton increase in displacement and 7.5-m increase in length; original displacement was to have been 1,240 tons surfaced, 1,350 tons submerged. Plans to construct two more were abandoned. Can reportedly stay submerged for three weeks using AIP systems. *Halland* was equipped during 2001 with improved air conditioning and enhanced communications systems to permit her operating with foreign navies in "warmer" waters; the submarine had made a very successful cruise to the Mediterranean during 2000, the first-ever visit there by a Swedish submarine. Under a 31-3-05 bilateral 4-year lease agreement between Sweden and the United States, *Gotland* and her crew are being homeported in the United States at San Diego through 2009. While there, the submarine and Swedish crew serve as the opposing force-OPFOR-during at-sea antisubmarine warfare exercises for U.S. aircraft carrier and expeditionary strike groups and also assist with various antisubmarine training opportunities. The lease has proven very successful and will likely be extended.

Hull systems: Design is essentially an updated Tp A-17 with Stirling-cycle air independent auxiliary low-speed propulsion and improved electronics. The Stirling engines, which can operate the submarines at up to 6 kts, are extremely quiet running, radiating less noise than a household appliance; about 24 tons of liquid oxygen are carried for the engines, which also burn standard diesel fuel. Employ Varta batteries. The hull has a rubberized anechoic coating. Normal diving depth 200 m. Employ a SAGEM gyrocompass, Differential GPS receiver, and inertial navigation system and have a Polyamp-FMV magnetic sensor to permit automatic control adjustment of the degaussing system to deal with local magnetic-field variations.
Combat systems: Have Saab 9SCS Mk 3 (Swedish Navy designation SESUB 940A) submarine command, control, communications, and weapons control system with three Terma Tp IID multifunction operator consoles; the system is a variant of the 9LV Mk 3 and can display 272 and track 95 targets simultaneously. The data system was updated starting in 1998 to permit employment of the new Tp 62 torpedo, whose onboard sonar can relay target data to the submarine's fire-control system. The Tp 45 lightweight torpedo is to replace the Tp 431 initially carried. Have one Kollmorgen Model 76 and one CK083 periscope, with the latter being upgraded by Thales Optronics, Glasgow, with a thermal imager and enhanced image intensifier. Torpedo tubes are of the swim-out configuration, and two torpedoes per tube are carried in the 400-mm tubes. A VLF communications set is fitted. There are no plans to fit a towed array sonar, but an active mine-avoidance set is to be added. U.S. Signal Processing Systems acoustic intercept arrays and signal analysis systems have been added. The external mine belt, which can be dropped after emptying, can be reloaded with 48 mines in only two hours.

♦ 2 Västergötland class (Type A-17)

Bldrs: Kockums, Malmö, and Karlskronavarvet, Karlskrona

	Symbol	Laid down	L	In serv.
SÖDERMANLAND	SÖD	1985	12-4-88	21-4-89
ÖSTERGÖTLAND	ÖGD	1986	9-12-88	10-1-90

Södermanland (Söd)—post–AIP modernization Michael Nitz, 5-06

D: 1,250 tons surf./1,500 tons sub. **S:** 11 kts (surf.)/20 kts (sub.)
Dim: 60.50 × 6.06 × 5.60 (surf.)
A: 6 bow 533-mm TT (12 Tp 613 torpedoes); 3 bow 400-mm TT (6 Tp 422 or Ty 45 torpedoes); 22 mines in external portable containers
Electronics:
Radar: 1 Terma . . . nav./surf. search
Sonar: Atlas CSU-83 suite (DBQS-21active/passive, FAS 3-1 flank arrays, towed array)
EW: ArgoSystems AR-700-S5 intercept

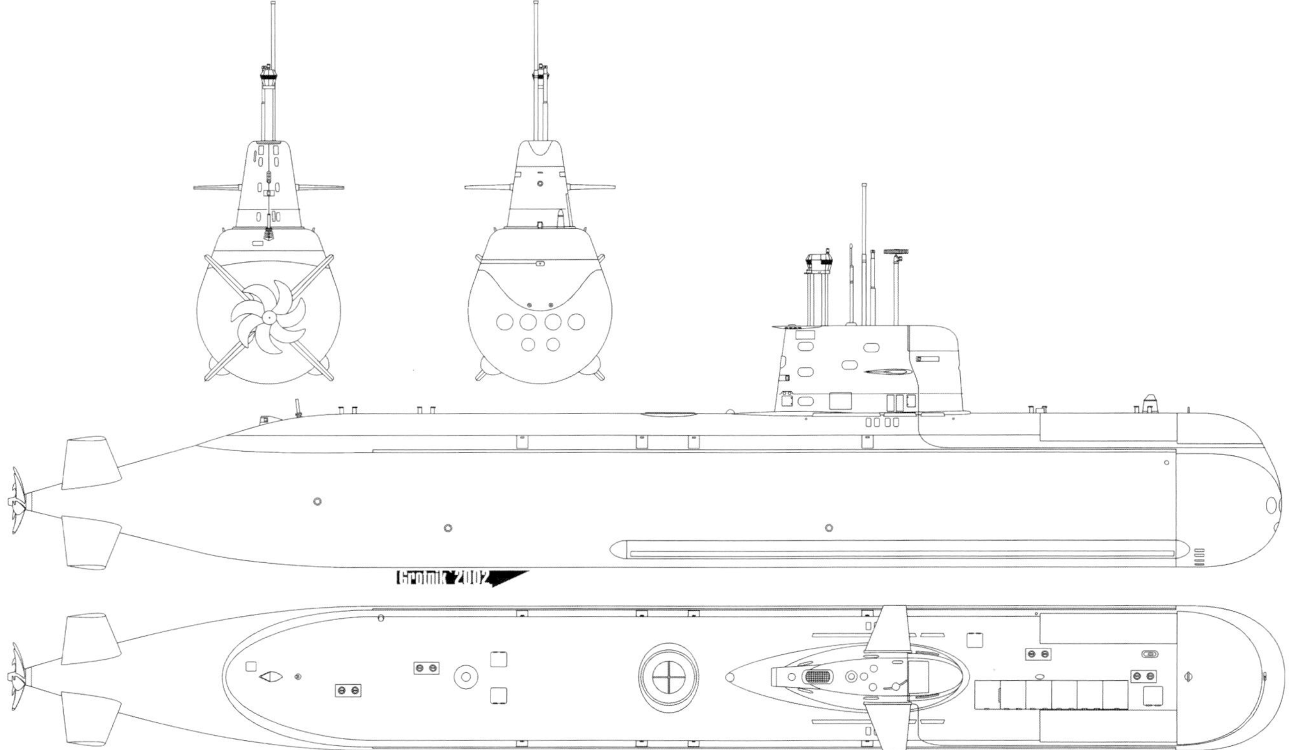

Gotland-class submarine Drawing by T. Grotnik, 2002

ATTACK SUBMARINES [SS] *(continued)*

Södermanland (Söd)—note that the hull has been lengthened by 10 meters to allow for the insertion of a Stirling air-independent propulsion system Michael Nitz, 5-06

M: 2 Hedemora V12A/15-Ub (VA 185) diesels (1,080 bhp each); 2 Jeumont-Schneider 760-kw generators; 1 ASEA electric motor; 1/5-bladed prop; 1,800 shp—2 Stirling V4-275R Mk II 75 kw air-independent generator sets
Endurance: 45 days **Crew:** 5 officers, 15 enlisted (25 accomm.)

Remarks: Design by Kockums under 17-4-78 contract. Ships ordered 8-12-81, with Kockums building the mid-bodies and Karlskronavarvet building the bows and sterns. *Södermanland* and *Östergötland* were given 100-kw Stirling Mk 3 air-independent auxiliary engines and lengthened by 10-m under an 11-99 contract with Kockums. They returned to service during 7-04 and 7-05 respectively.
Hull systems: Can operate at 300 meters. Have only 7% reserve bouyancy. Employ sail-mounted forward control planes and cruciform stern control surfaces. Have six berthing compartments, with five spare berths for trainees. Two Tudor 84-cell lead-acid battery sets are fitted. Sperry Mk 29 gyrocompass. Two main watertight compartments. Have an anechoic hull coating. Have a single crew escape chamber, fitted with a mating coaming for rescue submersibles or diving bells.
Combat systems: The torpedo tubes are arranged with the row of six 533-mm tubes above the three short 400-mm tubes. Use Ericsson IPS-17 combat data/fire-control system (Swedish Navy designation SESUB 900A), which will eventually be replaced by the SESUB 960. Two Barr & Stroud CK038 periscopes are fitted; these are being equipped with a thermal imager and an enhanced image intensifier by Thales Optronics, Glasgow. U.S. Signal Processing Systems acoustic intercept arrays and signal analysis systems are being added to *Östergötland* and *Södermanland,* which will also receive active mine-avoidance sonars. Plans to add a land-attack missile-launching capability appear to have been dropped.

Disposal notes: Sisters *Västergötland* and *Hälsingland* were not modified with AIP systems and were decommissioned on 31-12-05 and sold to Singapore. Following modifications for tropical water operations, they will be transfered during 2010. Of the five units of the *Sjöormen* class, *Sjöhunden* was sold to Singapore 23-9-95 for training purposes; and *Sjöormen, Sjölejonet,* and *Sjöhästen* were sold to Singapore on 31-7-97 for refurbishment and delivery, along with the *Sjöbjornen,* which was cannibalized in Sweden for spares.

MIDGET SUBMARINES [SSM]

♦ **1 intruder simulator** Builder: K.A. Johanssons AB (L: 19-6-90)

SPIGGEN

Spiggen Curt Borgenstam Jr., 8-97

D: 12 tons surf./14 tons sub. **S:** 6 kts surf./3-5 kts sub.
Dim: 11.00 × 1.70 × 2.70 (high) **A:** None
M: 1 Volvo Penta diesel, electric drive; 1 prop; . . . shp
Range: 27/5 (sub.) **Endurance:** 2 days **Crew:** 2 tot.

Remarks: Intended to simulate foreign submarines long believed to have been operating in Swedish waters. Named for a British X-craft midget submarine acquired by the Swedish Navy after World War II. Began trials 1-91. Refitted by Kockums during 1995. Diving depth: 100 m.

GUIDED-MISSILE PATROL COMBATANTS [PGG]

♦ **4 (+ 1) Visby (YS 2000)-class multipurpose**
Bldr: Karlskronavarvet, Karlskrona

	L	In serv.
K 31 VISBY	8-6-00	2-05
K 32 HELSINGBORG	27-6-03	7-05
K 33 HÄRNÖSAND	16-12-04	1-06
K 34 NYKÖPING	18-8-05	7-06
K 35 KARLSTAD	24-8-06	1-07

Helsingborg (K 32) Kockums via David Shirlaw, 2006

Visby (K 31) Dieter Wolf, 6-02

Visby (K 31) Frank Behling, 6-02

D: 650 tons (fl) **S:** 40 kts (34 kts sust.; 15 kts on diesels)
Dim: 72.80 (63.00 wl, 61.50 pp) × 10.40 × 2.40
A: Fitted with: 1 57-mm 70-cal. Bofors Sak 57 Mk 3 DP—provision for: 8 RBS-15 Mk 3 SSM; 4 fixed 400-mm ASW TT (4 Tp 45 torpedoes); 2 6-round 127-mm ALECTO ASW RL; 1 Hkp-15 helicopter
Electronics:
Radar: 1 . . . X-band nav.; 1 . . . S-band surf. search; 1 Ericsson Sea Giraffe AMB 3-D C-band surveillance; 1 Saab CEROS 200 radar/E/O f.c.
Sonar: CDC Hydra suite: . . . hull-mounted; . . . 2-frequency variable-depth; . . . towed linear passive array
EW: Condor Systems CS-3701 intercept (2-18 gHz); . . . comms intercept; 127-mm passive torpedo and antimissile decoys launched by the ALECTO launchers
E/O: . . . IRST
M: CODOG: 4 Honeywell-Vericor TF50A gas turbines (5,365 shp each); 2 MTU 16V 2000 N90 diesels (1,740 bhp each); 2 KaMeWa 125 SII waterjets; 21,460 shp max.—bow-thruster
Electric: 810 kw tot. (3 × 270 kw Isotta Fraschini V1308 T2ME-1550 diesel alternator sets)
Range: . . . / . . . **Crew:** 21 officers, 20 enlisted + small flag staff

GUIDED-MISSILE PATROL COMBATANTS [PGG] *(continued)*

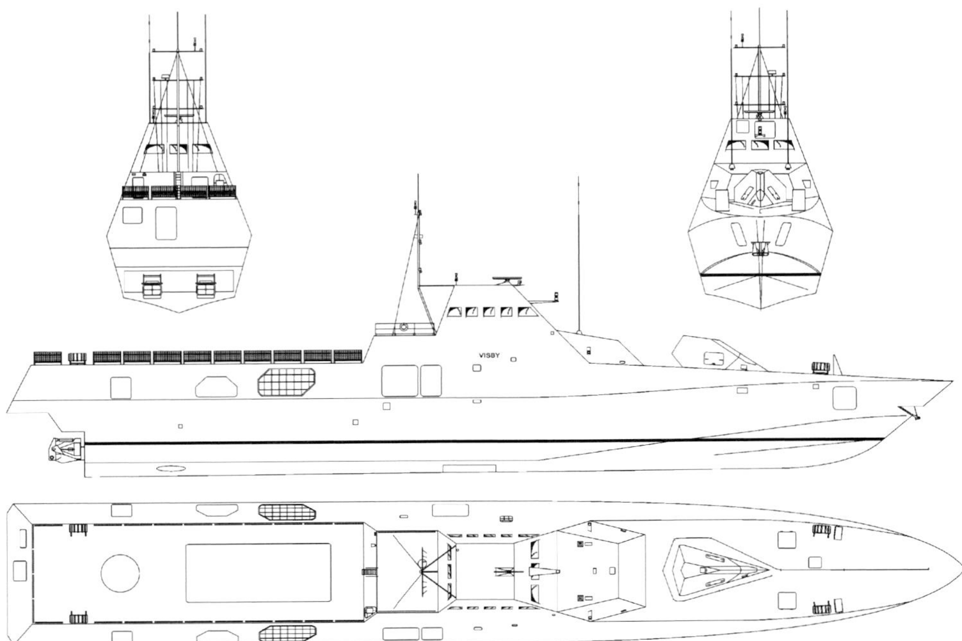

Visby (K 31) Drawing by T. Grotnik, 2003

Remarks: YS stands for *Ytsridsfartyg;* they are also known as the YSM class. Funding requested 8-93 for the first four; program delayed two years in 10-93, but reinstated in 9-6-94. Contract reduced to two with option for two more when let on 12-10-95; the second pair was ordered 17-12-96 and a third pair early in 9-99. The first four were delivered in mine-countermeasures configuration. The third pair is to be equipped with eight antiship missiles. The original class total was to have been 20, reduced to 14 in 1996, and then six. In 9-01, the sixth unit, *Uddevalla* (K 36), was canceled due to significant program cost overruns, although an option to build the ship later remains. The design grew by several hundred tons in the final, contract version, and the launch date for the *Visby* had slipped a year from the originally announced 4-6-99; builder's sea trials began on 7-12-01.

Hull systems: Measures taken during design and construction to reduce radar cross-section; infrared, magnetic, hydroacoustic, visual, airborne acoustic, laser cross-section, and electrical signatures; hydroacoustic target strength; wake; and directionally-emitted signals. Although initially planned to be rigid-sidewall air-cushion vehicles, these ships are instead conventional monohulls. The multi-axial carbon-reinforced glass- and carbon-fiber sandwich plastic construction will provide low radar and magnetic signature and will be composed of patent MAX-CF HS carbon/glass hybrid reinforcement with vinylester-polyester matrix and ductile PVC foam. The helicopter hangar is below the flight deck, but K 33 will be the first to be capable of operating helicopters. Fin stabilizers are fitted. Will have carbon-fiber power shafts.

Combat systems: Employ the Saab 9LV CETRIS combat system, which is based on the 9LV Mk 3E; there are 16 multipurpose display/action terminals. The Danish INFOCOM ICS2000 integrated communications system is employed. Weight and space is reserved for a point-defense SAM system. Have GPS navigation capability, and use external target location sensor information datalinked to the ships. The 57-mm gun employs Bofors 3P (Prefragmented, Programmable, Proximity-fused) ammunition.

The first four carry a minehunting sonar and two Bofors Double Eagle mine-location ROVs and two STN Elektronik Seafox remotely operated vehicles for mine disposal; the ROVs are deployed through doors in the side of the hull amidships, and a third, Swedish-developed ROV-S reconnaissance submersible will also eventually be carried. In the K 35, the mine-countermeasures submersible installation will be replaced by four below-decks launchers for antiship missiles per side; the Bamsea navalized version of the low-signature RBS-23 Bamse missile or the Raytheon ESSM are under consideration and may be backfitted into the original four at a later date. Have an infrared scanner and two weapons control directors. The Hydra sonar suite is supported by a Computing Services Canada NECTA (Naval Environmental Command Tactical Aid) underwater environment modeling system with 3-D color displays. The Computer Devices Canada integrated hull-mounted and towed array sonar suite, ordered 29-9-97, is used for both ASW and mine countermeasures. An active radar jammer may be fitted later. Are fitted with Knudsen, Canada, 320B echo-sounders.

GUIDED-MISSILE PATROL CRAFT [PTG]

♦ 4 Göteborg class (KKV-90 design)

Bldr: Karlskronavarvet, Karlskrona

	Symbol	Laid down	L	In serv.
K 21 GÖTEBORG	GBG	10-2-86	12-4-89	15-2-90
K 22 GÄVLE	GLE	10-9-88	12-8-89	1-2-91
K 23 KALMAR	KMR	10-9-88	1-11-90	1-9-91
K 24 SUNDSVALL	SVL	10-3-89	29-11-91	7-7-93

D: 380 tons (425 fl) **S:** 32 kts **Dim:** 57.0 (50.0 wl) × 8.0 (7.3 wl) × 1.93

A: 8 RBS-15 SSM; 1 57-mm Bofors 70-cal. SAK-57 Mk 2 DP; 1 40-mm 70-cal. Bofors L70 AA; 4 fixed 400-mm ASW TT (Type 45 torpedoes); 4 9-round Saab ASW 600 ASW RL; 2 mine rails (40 or more mines)

Sundsvall (K 24) Bernard Prézelin, 8-04

Gävle (K 22) Ralph Edwards, 5-04

Electronics:

Radar: 1 Terma PN-612 nav.; 1 Saab Pilot surf. search; 1 Ericsson Sea Giraffe 150 HC surf./air-search; 2 Saab 9GR-400 f.c.

Sonar: Simrad SS 304 Spira hull-mounted (34 kHz); Thales TSM 2643 Salmon dismountable VDS (MF)

EW: ArgoSystems AR-700 intercept/deception syst.; IR detector; Saab 9CM-300 decoy syst. (2 36-round RL)

M: 3 MTU 16V396 TB94 diesels; 3 KaMeWa 80-S62/6 waterjets; 8,640 bhp (6,390 sust.)—K 22 only: bow thruster

Range: . . . / . . . **Electric:** 855 kVA tot. (3 × 285 kVA diesel alternator sets)

Crew: 7 officers, 36 enlisted (46 tot. accomm.)

Remarks: Ordered 1-12-85; two others, to have been named *Helsingborg* and *Härnösand,* were not ordered. Considered to be "corvettes." Modernization refits began in late 1998 with K 22. Under a 28-6-01 contract, the class are to have their communications suites, combat data systems, and after fire-control directors upgraded. Expected to remain in service through at least 2015.

Hull systems: Steel hull, aluminum superstructures. Have fin stabilizers. Infrared, radar, and noise signature suppression measures are incorporated. K 22 during modernization had radar signature-suppression measures added, including reconfiguring the deckhouse, replacing the lifelines with nonreflective ones, and extension of the bridge wings; the others are to be similarly updated.

Combat systems: Have Saab 9LV Mk 3 weapons control system, with six multifunction operator consoles. The Saab 9LV 450 gunfire-control system uses the ARTE-726E

GUIDED-MISSILE PATROL CRAFT [PTG] *(continued)*

Gävle (K 22) Martin Mokrus, 5-04

gun-control system, RCI-400 missile fire-control, TORPE torpedo-control, 9AU-300 ASW fire-control, and 9CM-300 EW-control systems. The EW suite includes an ArgoSystems CAROL intercept receiver and deception transmitter, with Thorn-EMI Sceptre XL analyzer. The two optronic weapons directors have co-mounted t.v., IR, laser, and 9GR-400 radars. The four fixed ASW TT are mounted two firing aft, two forward, on the starboard side mine rails for wire-guided Tp 45 ASW torpedoes. GEC-Marconi AQS-928G/SM acoustic processors are fitted and can monitor up to eight LOFAR passive omnidirectional and four DIFAR or VLAD passive directional, two DICASS (active directional), and one bathythermal buoys simultaneously. The PN-612 navigational radar is the same equipment as the Scanter Mil 009 radar used by the Danish Navy. Beginning in 1995 K 22 was used in trials with an STN Atlas Elektronik passive towed linear sonar array, with the winch and drum mounted to starboard of the VDS installation; after the 1998–2001 refit K 22 has a new gunhouse for the 40-mm mount, shortened mine rails, and a new ESM suite. One ship of this class tested the Thales IRSCAN infrared search-and-track system during 1999–2000.

♦ 2 Stockholm class (Spica III/YA-81 design)

Bldr: Karlskronavarvet, Karlskrona

	Symbol	Laid down	L	In serv.
K 11 STOCKHOLM	STO	1-8-82	24-8-84	1-3-85
K 12 MALMÖ	MMÖ	14-3-83	21-3-85	10-5-85

Malmö (K 12) Bernard Prézelin, 8-04

D: 310 tons (335 fl) **S:** 30 kts (20 kts on diesels)
Dim: 50.5 (46.6 wl) × 7.5 (6.8 wl) × 2.0 (hull)

Stockholm (K 11) Leo van Ginderen, 6-05

A: 8 RBS-15 SSM; 1 57-mm Bofors 70-cal. SAK-57 Mk 2 DP; 4 fixed 400-mm ASW TT (Type 45 torpedoes); 2 6-round 127-mm ALECTO ASW RL; 2 mine rails (40 or more mines)
Electronics:
Radar: 1 Terma PN-612 nav.; 1 Ericsson Sea Giraffe 50HC surf./air search; 1 Saab 9LV 200 Mk 2 f.c.
Sonar: Simrad SS 304 Spira hull-mounted (34 kHz); Thomson-CSF TSM 2642 Salmon dismountable MF VDS
EW: Saab-Scania EWS-905 intercept; 2 36-round Saab Philax decoy RL
M: CODAG: 1 Vericor TF50 gas turbine (5,364 shp); 2 MTU 16V396 TB94 diesels (2,095 bhp each); 3 CP props
Electric: 648 kw tot. **Range:** . . . **Crew:** 7 officers, 23 enlisted

Remarks: Ordered 9-81. Both underwent midlife modernizations under an 11-99 contract with Kockums. Work on K 12 was completed during 10-02, and K 11 was redelivered on 31-1-03. Both vessels operate as part of the Third Surface Combat Flotilla in Karlskrona.
Hull systems: During modernization, the original Allison 570KF gas turbine (7,170 shp max./6,000 shp sust.) was replaced by a TF50 engine in K 12 in 9-01 and K 11 a month later; the gearbox was also changed, and newer versions of the diesel engines were substituted. The superstructure configuration has been significantly altered to reduce radar and infrared signatures, and a pylon mast is replacing the original lattice structure.
Combat systems: As completed, had the Ericsson MARIL 880 weapons-control system, with an SRA Censor 932E computer, but a new system based on the Saab AB 9LV Mk 3 was installed during modernization. The 9LV300 gunfire-control system incorporates a 9LV200 radar director forward and a 9LV100 optronic director on the aft face of the main mast. During modernization, the 40-mm 70-cal. Bofors AA mount aft was removed, as was the provision to launch wire-guided Tp 61 antiship torpedoes; four 400-mm fixed ASW torpedo tubes may be incorporated in the modified design.

Disposal notes: The *Kaparen*-class patrol craft have all been retired. This includes *Vale* (P 155), *Mjölner* (P 157), and *Mysing* (P 158), stricken in 1995, and *Hugin* (P 151), *Munin* (P 152), *Mode* (P 154), and *Vidar* (P 156) on 1-7-01. The remaining units, *Jägaren* (V 150), *Magne* (P 153), *Kaparen* (P 159), *Väktaren* (P 160), *Snapphanen* (P 161), *Spajaren* (P 162), *Styrbjöbrn* (P 163), *Starkodder* (P 164), *Tordön* (P 165), and *Tirfing* (P 166), were retired by the end of 2006. All units of the Spika-II class have also been retired. *Norrtälje* (R 133), *Varberg* (R 134), *Västerås* (R 135), *Västervik* (R 136), *Umeå* (R 137), and *Strömstad* (R 141) were retired in 1998. *Luleå* (R 139) and *Halmstad* (R 140) were retired in 2002, *Nynäshamn* (R 132) and *Pteå* (R 138) in 2005, while *Norrköping* (R 131) and *Ystad* (R 142) were stricken in 2006. *Dalarö*-class patrol boats *Dalarö* (V 09), *Sandhamn* (V 10), and *Östhammar* (V 11) were retired by 2003.

MINE WARFARE SHIPS

♦ 1 fleet minelaying/training ship

Bldr: Karlskronavarvet, Karlskrona

	Symbol	Laid down	L	In serv.
M 04 CARLSKRONA (ex-*Karlskrona*)	CKR	1980	28-5-80	19-3-82

Carlskrona (M 04) Arjun Sarup, 4-01

D: 3,300 tons (3,550 fl) **S:** 20 kts **Dim:** 105.70 (97.50 pp) × 15.2 × 4.00
A: 2 single 57-mm 70-cal. Bofors SAK 57 Mk 1 DP; 2 single 40-mm 70-cal. Bofors L 70 AA; 105 large mines
Electronics:
Radar: 1 Terma Scanter 009 nav.; 1 Raytheon . . . nav.; 1 Ericsson Sea Giraffe 50HC surf./air search; 2 Saab 9LV200 Mk 2 f.c. (9LV400 system)
EW: ArgoSystems AR-700 intercept; 2 36-round Saab Philax decoy RL

MINE WARFARE SHIPS *(continued)*

Carlskrona (M 04) Camil Busquets i Vilanova, 5-00

M: 4 Nohab-Polar F212-D825, 12-cyl. diesels; 2 CP props; 10,560 bhp—bow-thruster
Electric: 2,570 kVA tot.
Crew: As training ship: 43 officers, 40 cadets, 92 enlisted + accomm. for 136 cadets, 46 instructors

Remarks: Ordered 25-11-77 as *Karlskrona.* Name spelling changed to honor the current Swedish king. Intended to act as a mine-countermeasures ship support tender and submarine torpedo hard target in peacetime, when not conducting the annual cadet training cruise. If used as a minelayer, the ship would carry 118 personnel total. Completed a 12-month refit by Kockums on 20-12-02 and is expected to remain in service until 2022.
Hull systems: Reinforced below waterline to permit exercise torpedo hits; there are 14 watertight compartments. Has Roll-Nix rudder roll-control, providing a 40% reduction in roll. An improved helicopter pad was added during the 2001 refit, and measures were taken to improve the ship's stability.
Combat systems: Extensive navigational systems. Raised helicopter deck above fantail. There are two lead-computing optical directors to control the 40-mm AA and two radar/optronic 9LV200 Mk 2 directors for the 57-mm guns. The Simrad SQ3-D/SF hull-mounted sonar has been removed. A large radome was added abaft the after gun director for the ship's 2000 cruise; it contains the antenna for a SATCOM system.

♦ 1 Älvsborg-class minelayer
Bldr: Karlskronavarvet, Karlskrona

	Symbol	Laid down	L	In serv.
A 265 VISBORG (ex-M 3)	VBG	16-10-73	22-1-75	6-2-76

Visborg (A 265) Michael Nitz, 4-06

D: 2,450 tons (fl) **S:** 16 kts **Dim:** 92.4 (83.3 pp) × 14.7 × 4.0
A: 3 single 40-mm 70-cal. Bofors SAK 40/48 AA; up to 300 mines
Electronics:
Radar: 1 Terma Scanter 009 nav.; 1 Raytheon . . . nav.; 1 Ericsson Sea Giraffe 50HC surf./air search; 1 Saab 9LV 200 f.c.
EW: ArgoSystems AR-700 intercept; 2 36-round Saab Philax decoy RL
M: 2 Nohab-Polar 112VS, 12-cyl. diesels; 1 CP prop; 4,200 bhp—350 shp bow-thruster
Electric: 1,200 kw tot.
Crew: 20 officers, 70 enlisted + 158 flag staff accomm.

Remarks: Is equipped as Flagship, Coastal Fleet. Has a helicopter deck; two triple 103-mm flare rocket launchers. Sister *Älvsborg,* laid up at the end of 1993, was sold to Chile in 10-96.

♦ 1 Kbv 171–class mine-countermeasures support ship [MCS]
Bldr: Karlskronavarvet, Karlskrona

	L	In serv.
A 262 SKREDSVIK (ex-M 70, ex-Kbv 172)	13-9-80	10-81

D: 335 tons (375 fl) **S:** 20 kts **Dim:** 49.90 (46.00 pp) × 8.52 × 2.40 **A:** None
Electronics:
Radar: 1 Decca . . . nav.
Sonar: Simrad Subsea hull-mounted HF searchlight-type

Skredsvik (A 262) H&L Van Ginderen, 12-94

M: 2 Hedemora V16A/15 diesels; 2 KaMeWa CP props; 4,480 bhp—bow-thruster
Electric: 340 kVA **Range:** 500/20; 3,000/12 **Crew:** 14 tot.

Remarks: Former Swedish Coast Guard class "A" cutter laid up in 1990 and leased to the navy in 1991. Refitted 12-92 to 2-93 to act as mine clearance divers' support ship and command vessel for mine-countermeasures operations. Sister Kbv 171 was sold to Belgium in 1998.
Hull systems: Glass-reinforced-plastic sandwich hull construction originally developed for the not-built M 70–class naval minesweeper. Former helicopter platform now used to stow rigid-inflatable divers' workboats. Has Roll-Nix rudder roll-control system. A firefighting water monitor is located on the 01 level, forward of bridge.

Disposal note: Mine-countermeasures support ship *Utö* (A 261) was sold for commercial use in 2004.

♦ 7 Landsort (M80)-class coastal minesweeper/hunters [MHC]
Bldr: Karlskronavarvet, Karlskrona

	Symbol	Laid down	L	In serv.
M 71 LANDSORT	LDO	5-10-81	22-11-82	19-3-84
M 72 ARHOLMA	ARH	13-2-82	10-10-84	23-11-84
M 73 KOSTER	KSR	1-9-84	16-1-86	30-5-86
M 74 KULLEN	KLN	1-1-85	15-8-86	3-7-87
M 75 VINGA	VIN	27-4-86	14-8-87	22-11-87
M 76 VEN	VEN	15-5-87	18-8-88	12-12-88
M 77 ULVÖN	ULN	2-1-88	10-89	9-10-92

Ven (M 76) Michael Winter, 5-04

Ven (M 76) Curt Borgenstam Jr., 5-97

D: 310 tons (360 fl) **S:** 15 kts **Dim:** 47.50 (45.00 pp) × 9.60 × 2.30
A: 1 40-mm 70-cal. Bofors SAK 40/48 AA; . . . RBS-70 shoulder-launched SAM; 2 single 7.62-mm mg; 4 9-round Saab ASW 600 ASW RL; . . . mines (portable rails)
Electronics:
Radar: 1 Terma Scanter 009 nav.
Sonar: Thales TSM 2022 variable-depth minehunting (250–525 kHz)
EW: . . . Matilde intercept; 2 36-round Saab Philax decoy RL
M: 4 Saab-Scania DSI-14 diesels; 2 Voith-Schneider vertical cycloidal props; 1,456 bhp

MINE WARFARE SHIPS *(continued)*

Electric: 468 kw tot. (2 × 180 kw alternators, 1 × 108 kw alternator)
Range: 2,000/12 **Crew:** 12 officers, 14 enlisted

Remarks: First pair ordered 25-2-81. Next four ordered 31-1-84 and one more in 10-88. Plans to order an eighth canceled. Four sisters were built for Singapore. During 2003 *Kullen* (M 74) and *Ven* (M 76) underwent a modernization refit at Karlskrona for participation in international peacekeeping missions. M 73 and M 77 are undergoing modernization between 2005 and 2009 and M 75 will follow soon thereafter.
Hull systems: Glass-reinforced-plastic construction, using same mold as Swedish Coast Guard's patrol cutter Kbv 171. The diesel generator sets are all mounted on the upper deck to reduce the noise signature.
Combat systems: Have 9MJ-400 computerized integrated navigational/mine system and a Saab 9LV-100 gun-control system with TVT-100 optronic director for the 40-mm gun. Carry two Sutec Sea Owl or Double Eagle Mark-III remote-controlled mine-disposal vehicles, as well as controlling up to three SAM, glass-reinforced-plastic, self-propelled magnetic/acoustic catamaran minesweeping devices. The EW intercept gear is a Swedish-built variant of the Thorn-EMI Matilda. Have Y-shaped portable mine rail arrangement with single laying-point.

Ulvön was used in 9-95 to demonstrate the Bofors-Sutec Ibis VII Propelled Variable-Depth Sonar system, which uses a Sutec Double Eagle remotely operated vehicle and a Thales TSM 2022 Mk3 sonar. One unit has been equipped for trials with the Finnish Elesco Family of Integrated Minesweeping Systems (FIMS) sweep array with MRK-960 3-electrode magnetic sweep and MKR-400 pipe-type noncontrollable noisemaker; the data processing system is Elesco's SSCP, with differential GPS. Are being fitted with new integrated mine-countermeasures system and sonar during post 2006 modernizations.

♦ 4 Styrsö-class inshore minesweeper/minehunters [MHI]
Bldr: Karlskronavarvet, Karlskrona

	L	In serv.		L	In serv.
M 11 Styrsö	8-3-96	20-9-96	M 13 Skaftö	20-1-97	13-6-97
M 12 Spårö	30-8-96	21-2-97	M 14 Sturkö	27-6-97	19-12-97

Sturkö (M 14) Curt Borgenstam Jr., 5-01

Skaftö (M 13) Curt Borgenstam Jr., 8-97

D: 175 tons (200 fl) **S:** 13 kts
Dim: 36.00 (33.00 wl; 32.00 pp) × 7.90 × 2.20 (2.00 hull)
A: 2 12.7-mm mg—mines
Electronics:
Radar: Decca Bridgemaster ARPA nav./surf.-search
Sonar: Terma RESON hull-mounted mine-avoidance, EG&G DF1000 towed side-looking, Tritech SE 500 (in ROV)
M: 2 Saab Scania DSI-14 diesels; 2 fixed-pitch props; 728 bhp—bow-thruster
Electric: 828 kw tot. (2 × 414 kw diesel sets) **Range:** 1,500/12 **Fuel:** 20 m^3
Endurance: 7 days **Crew:** 7 officers, 8 enlisted + 2 spare berths

Remarks: YSB = *Ytsridfartyg Bevakning* (Surface Combat Vessel). Also able to be employed as coastal patrol craft. First four ordered 11-2-94, with work on first actually having begun during 7-93. Are capable of minesweeping as well as minehunting. The first of two planned additional batches of four was to be equipped for minehunting and would have carried mine-disposal divers; a third batch of four was planned to replace the existing mine-disposal diver support ships. No further contracts have been placed, however.
Hull systems: Employ GRP construction and "stealth" signature-reductions features tested in the trials ship *Smyge,* but have conventional monohulls. Have full NBC protection system, including sprinkler systems and a filtered citadel.
Combat systems: The Erisoft ERIMIS (Erisoft Maritime Information System) mine countermeasure command system employs six multi-function command modules, with inputs from the sonar suite, the radar, a GPS receiver, laser rangefinder, the gyro, and the log. Mine-countermeasures suite includes two Bofors Sea Eagle remotely operated submersibles equipped with a t.v. camera and the Tritech SE 500 high-definition sonar. Much of the sweep gear comes from discarded units of the *Arkö* class; included are Tp AK-90 acoustic sweep and EL-90 magnetic sweep gear. A 40-mm gun can be retrofitted, and RBS-70 SAMs may later be carried. The ships are able to control SAM-series mine-countermeasures drones.

♦ 1 Viksten-class inshore minesweeper [MSI]

	Symbol	Bldr	L	In serv.
M 33 Viksten	Vsn	Karlskronavarvet	18-4-74	1-7-74

Viksten (M 33) H&L Van Ginderen, 8-93

D: 115 tons (130 fl) **S:** 11 kts **Dim:** 25.3 × 6.6 × 2.5
A: 1 20-mm 70-cal. Oerlikon AA
Electronics: Radar: 1 Terma Scanter 009 nav.
M: 1 diesel; 1 prop; 460 bhp **Crew:** 9 tot.

Remarks: The hull is made of glass-reinforced plastic; she was intended to serve as the prototype for a new class of 300-ton, 43-meter coastal minesweepers that were not built.

Disposal note: *Gillöga*-class inshore minesweepers *Gillöga* (M 47) and *Svartlöga* (M 49) were stricken during 1997 and sister *Rödlöga* (M 48) during 1998; *Gåssten*-class inshore minesweeper *Gåssten* (M 31) was stricken during 2000, and sister *Norsten* (M 32) was sold in 1998–99 for use as a fishing boat.

♦ 1 Danish SF 100–class drone minesweeper [MSD]
Bldr: Danyard, Aalborg (In serv. 12-01)

Sökaren

D: 102 tons (125 fl) **S:** 12 kts (11 sust.)
Dim: 26.50 (24.15 wl; 23.90 pp) × 7.00 × 2.20
Electronics:
Radar: 1 . . . nav.
Sonar: Thales STS 2054 towed sidescan HF
M: 2 Saab Scania DSI 14.74.M diesels; 2 Schottel SPJ.82T azimuthal waterjets; 960 bhp—bow-thruster
Range: 420/10 **Crew:** 3–4 tot. (for transits; accomm. for 11 tot.)

Remarks: Ordered 2-01 for comparative trials with the Swedish SAM-II class. GRP construction. Can be operated by crews as inshore minehunter/minesweepers or by remote control. The Danish Navy operates four configured as minehunting drones and plans to acquire more equipped as patrol craft.
Combat systems: Employs the IN-SNEC sonar and television datalink and INFOCOM low-rate craft command datalink. Uses containerized mine-countermeasures equipment. Can be used to deploy Bofors Double Eagle mine location and disposal ROVs or to stream sweep gear. Has a 7-kN bollard pull at 8.5 kts.

♦ 5 SAM-01–class radio-controlled mine countermeasures craft [MSD]
Bldr: Karlskronavarvet, Karlskrona

	In serv.		In serv.
SAM 01	29-3-83	SAM 04 Paddington	26-5-83
SAM 02	29-3-83	SAM 05 Samanta	1992
SAM 03 Sammy	1992		

Paddington (SAM 04) Curt Borgenstam Jr., 8-93

MINE WARFARE SHIPS *(continued)*

D: 15 tons (20 fl) **S:** 8 kts **Dim:** 18.0 × 6.10 × 0.70 (1.60 prop)
M: 1 Volvo-Penta TAMD 70D diesel; 1 Schottel shrouded prop; 210 bhp
Range: 330/7

Remarks: The catamarans also automatically lay eight swept-channel danbuoy markers. An eventual total of 20 SAMs was planned at one time. Two sisters—the original SAM 03 and SAM 05—were sold to the U.S. Navy for use in the Persian Gulf in 3-91; replacements named *Sammy* and *Samanta* were completed in 1992. Six others were delivered to Japan during 1998–99.

♦ 1 mine warfare diver support tender [MSS]
Bldr: Båtservice A/S, Mandal, Norway (in serv. 1984)

A 212 Ägir (ex-*Bloom Surveyor*)

Ägir (A 212) Curt Borgenstam Jr., 8-94

D: 240 tons (fl) **S:** 11 kts **Dim:** 24.35 (21.50 pp) × 7.60 × 1.28 **A:** None
Electronics: Radar: 1 Terma Scanter 009 nav.; 1 . . . nav.
M: 2 G.M. Detroit Diesel diesels; 2 props; 1,540 bhp

Remarks: 117 grt. Acquired 1989 from a Norwegian oilfield company. Has portable decompression chamber, stern diver support gallows crane, extensive communications gear, and bow-thruster. Reclassified from diving tender to mine warfare tender at the end of 1996.

Disposal notes: *Hisingen*-class mine-countermeasures diver support craft [MSS] *Hisingen* (M 43), *Blackan* (M 44), *Dämmen* (M 45), and *Galten* (M 46) were stricken during 2000.

♦ 0 (+ 5) . . .-class mine-countermeasures training craft [MSSS]
Bldr: Swedeship Marine AB, Djupviks Varv (In serv. 2008–. . .)

D: 80 tons **S:** 24 kts **Dim:** 28.9 × 6.0 × . . .
A: . . . **M:** 2 . . . diesels; 2 props **Crew:** 4 total + 6 cadets

Remarks: Ordered 12-5-06. Intended to replace the M 15 class mine-countermeasures support craft.

♦ 5 M 15–class mine-countermeasures diver support craft [MSS]
Bldr: . . . (All L: 1941)

M 20 (ex-*Skuld,* A 242) M 21 M 22 M24 M25

D: 70 tons (93 fl) **S:** 12–13 kts **Dim:** 27.7 × 5.05 × 1.4 (2.0 props)
A: Fitted for: 1 20-mm 70-cal. Oerlikon AA **M:** 2 diesels; 2 props; 320–430 hp
Crew: 10 tot.

Remarks: Wooden hulls. M 21, M 22, and M 25 are used as tenders for mine-clearance divers. All were to be replaced by the *Styrsö* class, but they remain in service. The gun is not normally mounted. No radar. M 20 was returned to the mine-countermeasures category in 1993 after having served as a trials tender; the craft retains an additional deckhouse abaft the pilothouse.

M 22 H&L Van Ginderen, 10-96

AUXILIARIES

♦ 1 intelligence collection ship [AGI]
Bldr: Karlskronavarvet, Karlskrona

	Symbol	Laid down	L	In serv.
A 201 Orion	Ori	23-4-82	30-11-83	7-6-84

Orion (A 201) Curt Borgenstam Jr., 7-01

D: 1,400 tons (fl) **S:** 15 kts **Dim:** 61.3 × 11.0 × 4.2 **A:** none
Electronics:
Radar: 1 Terma Scanter 009 nav.; 1 Raytheon . . . nav.
Sonar: SEA Sonar 088
EW: . . .
M: 2 Hedemora V8A/135 diesels; 1 CP prop; 1,840 bhp **Crew:** 35 tot.

Remarks: Ordered 25-6-81. Expected to last 30 years. Signal collection antennas beneath a large glass-reinforced plastic radome atop full length of the superstructure. Has a commercial SATCOM antenna atop after lattice mast and a helicopter platform at the stern.

In 2002, received a SEA Sonar 088 sonar system recycled from a submarine; the equipment was fitted with a sonobuoy processing capability.

♦ 1 ex-Russian Modified Akademik Shuleykin–class patrol boat tender [AGP]
Bldr: Laivateollisuus, Turku, Finland

	L
A 264 Trossö (ex-*Livonia,* ex-*Ar'nold Veymer*)	14-2-88

Trossö (A 264) Jaroslaw Cislak, 6-03

Trossö (A 264) Jaroslaw Cislak, 6-02

AUXILIARIES *(continued)*

D: 2,554 tons (fl) **S:** 14 kts **Dim:** 74.50 (64.3 pp) × 14.70 × 4.50
Electronics: Radar: 1 Okean-M4 nav.; 1 Okean-B nav.
M: 2 S.E.M.T.-Pielstick 6PC2.5 L400 diesels; 2 CP props; 3,500 bhp—200-shp bow-thruster
Electric: 600 kVA tot. **Range:** 14,000/12 **Endurance:** 50 days **Crew:** 64 tot.

Remarks: 1,650 grt/600 dwt. A 264 was purchased around 9-96 from the Estonian Marine Institute. Originally configured for general oceanography, the ship was subordinated to the Estonian S.S.R. Academy of Sciences. The ship was transferred to Estonia in 1991 under the name *Livonia* and was adapted as a pollution patrol and cleanup vessel and for use in fisheries protection duties before being assigned to the Estonian Marine Institute. Converted in Sweden during 1997 to serve as a depot and headquarters ship for the surface attack flotilla based at Karlskrona. A second ship was to be acquired during 2000 as tender to the surface attack flotilla at Berga Naval Base, but no announcement has yet been made.
Hull systems: Has Decca Arkas autopilot, Rumb MFD/F loop, NEL-M2B echo sounder, ELAC ENIF deep echo sounder, ELAC bottom profiler, Furuno doppler log, 1 EL-2 electromagnetic log, and Furuno FSN-200 NAVSAT receiver; can be fitted with INTELSAT SATCOM. The radars may have been replaced during the 1997 refit.

♦ 1 patrol craft tender [AGP]
Bldr: Sterkoder M/V A/S, Kristiansund, Norway

A 263 GÅLÖ (ex-*Herjolfur*)

Gålö (A 263) Curt Borgenstam Jr., 5-01

D: Approx. 1,600 tons (fl) **S:** 14 kts **Dim:** 60.36 (53.01 pp) × 12.01 × 4.55
A: None **Electronics:** Radar: 1 . . . nav.
M: 1 Wichmann 9AXA diesel; 1 CP prop: 2,400 bhp—bow and stern thrusters
Range: . . . / . . . **Crew:** 24 tot.

Remarks: 1,037 grt/200 dwt. Former Ro-Ro vehicle cargo and passenger ferry purchased in 1993 from Herjolfur H/f, Vestmannaeyjar, Iceland, for conversion as a patrol boat tender. Has one 5-ton crane. As a ferry, had 17 cabins with 34 total berths.

♦ 1 general-purpose cargo transport [AK]
Bldr: Mjellem & Karlsen A/S, Bergen (In serv. 1980)

A 343 SLEIPNER (ex-*Ardal*)

D: 1,049 tons (fl) **S:** 12 kts **Dim:** 49.66 (45.12 pp) × 11.03 × 3.55
A: Provision for: 2 single 20-mm 70-cal. Oerlikon AA
Electronics: Radar: 2 . . . nav.
M: 1 Bergens Normo LDM-8 diesel; 1 prop; 1,300 bhp—bow-thruster
Electric: 236 kw tot. (2 × 118 kw diesel sets) **Range:** . . . / . . . **Crew:** 12 tot.

Remarks: 448 grt/825 dwt. Former Ro-Ro vehicle cargo and container carrier purchased 1992 from Fylkesbåtane i Sogn og Fjordane, Florø, Norway, for use as a general-purpose supply ship. Has ice-strengthened hull, 45 meters of vehicle cargo lane (8.0 m wide and 2.3 m high), 1 cargo hold (with 6.4 × 2.9 m hatch), one 10-ton electrohydraulic crane, and one 20-ton derrick. There is a stern ramp for vehicle loading, plus one side door. Cargo capacity: 1,130-m^3 bale.

Sleipner (A 343) Curt Borgenstam, Jr., 8-00

♦ 1 submarine rescue and salvage ship [ASR]
Bldr: Scheepswerf de Hoop, Lobith, the Netherlands (In serv. 1985)

A 214 BELOS (BEL) (ex-*Energy Supporter*)

Belos (A 214)—with rescue submersible URF on deck. Note also helicopter platform at the bow Jaroslaw Cislak, 5-04

D: Approx. 5,600 tons (fl) **S:** 13.26 kt **Dim:** 104.91 (85.91 pp) × 18.45 × 5.10
A: Fitted for: 2 single 20-mm 70-cal. Oerlikon AA
Electronics:
Radar: . . . nav.
Sonar: . . . hull-mounted HF; . . . towed sidescan
M: Electric drive: 5 Brons-M.A.N. 9LV 25.30 diesels (2,250 bhp each), 5 generators, 2 motors; 2 Azimuth props; 5,110 shp—3/ CP bow-thrusters
Electric: Main generators + 1 × 304 kw emergency diesel set **Range:** . . . / . . .
Fuel: . . . tons **Crew:** 25 ship's company + up to 40 salvage party, including divers

Remarks: 5,069 grt. Former oilfield supply, firefighting, and diver maintenance support vessel purchased 2-4-92 from Italian company S.A.N.A. and refitted at Rio de Janeiro before proceeding to Sweden and commissioning 15-10-92. Has medical and berthing facilities for 35 rescued submariners.
Hull systems: A dynamic positioning system is fitted. Has 22-m helicopter deck raised above forecastle. Hull has two moonpool calm-water diving accesses through the hull bottom. A Mantis one-man tethered submersible, handled by an A-frame crane to starboard, is used to reconnoiter bottomed submarines and has a 760-m max. depth; the Mantis can also be used as a remotely operated vehicle. The ship also carries a three-man diving bell capable of operating in depths up to 1,500 m and a divers' "wet bell" usable to 60-m depths and Sea Owl remotely operated submersibles. There are one six-man and one eight-man decompression chambers for divers and a 35-man hyperbaric chamber for rescued submariners.

SERVICE CRAFT

♦ 4 Ejdern-class sonobuoy monitoring boats [YAG]
Bldr: Djupviks Varv, Tjörn

	In serv.		In serv.
B 01 EJDERN	23-4-91	B 03 SVÄRTAN	1991
B 02 KRICKAN	1991	B 04 VIGGEN	1992

Ejdern (B 01) Curt Borgenstam Jr., 5-97

D: 34 tons (36 fl) **S:** 15 kts **Dim:** 19.00 (17.40 pp) × 4.98 × 1.00
A: Provision for: 1 20-mm 70-cal. Oerlikon AA **Electronics:** Radar: 1 . . . nav.
M: 2 Volvo Penta TAMD-122A diesels; 2 props; 800 bhp
Crew: 3 officers, 7 enlisted

Remarks: Aluminum construction. Equipped to deploy six recoverable hydrophones for use in detecting intruders in Swedish waters. Have G.E.C. AQS-928 sonobuoy acoustic data processors. Gun not normally mounted.

Disposal note: *Hanö*-class service craft *Tjurkö* (V 53) and *Sturkö* (V 54) were no longer in service by 2002. Trials craft *Urd* (A 241) was retired in 2004.

♦ 1 diving tender [YDT]
Bldr: . . ., Sweden (L: 1983)

A 213 NORDANÖ (ex-*Sjöjungfrun*)

D: Approx. 240 tons (fl) **S:** 10 kts **Dim:** 24.4 × 7.6 × 2.7 **A:** None
Electronics: Radar: none **M:** 2 Volvo Penta TAMD diesels; 2 props; 767 bhp
Crew: 15 tot.

Remarks: 148 grt. Acquired 1992.

SERVICE CRAFT *(continued)*

♦ 3 diving tenders [YDT]
Bldr: Storebro Bruks AB (In serv. 1980)

D: 7 tons (fl) **S:** 24 kts **Dim:** 10.35 × 3.30 × 1.0
Electronics: Radar: 1 Decca 091 nav.
M: 2 Volvo Penta TAMD 60C diesels; 2 props; 370 bhp

Remarks: Fold-down door at stern. 1.7-ton useful load.

♦ 1 Loke-class ferry [YFB]
Bldr: Oskarshamms (In serv. 1994)

A 344 Loke

Loke (A 344) H&L Van Ginderen, 10-96

D: 455 tons (fl) **S:** 12.5 kts **Dim:** 35.90 × 9.00 × 2.68 **A:** None
Electronics: Radar: 1 Terma Scanter 009 nav.
M: 2 Saab Scania . . . diesels; 2 props; . . . bhp
Crew: 8 tot.

Remarks: Was to have been the first of a new class of coastal transports for the Coastal Artillery Service, but no additional units were ordered. Is equipped with a bow ramp for vehicle cargo and an electrohydraulic crane amidships for cargo pallets. Can carry 50 personnel for short voyages or 200 persons in local, harbor service. Cargo capacity is 50 tons on deck. Not equipped for minelaying.

♦ 1 Stridsbåt-90H-class senior officer's launch [YFL]
Bldrs: Dockstavarvet, Docksta (In serv. 1999)

Blåtunga

Blåtunga Curt Borgenstam Jr., 6-00

D: 18 tons light (fl) **S:** 40 kts **Dim:** 15.90 (13.00 wl) × 3.80 × 0.80
Electronics: Radar: 1 Decca RD 360 nav.
M: 2 Saab Scania 8V DSI-14 diesels; 2 FF Jet FF 450 waterjets; 1,256 bhp
Range: 160/40; 240/20 **Fuel:** 1.5 tons **Crew:** 4 tot. + 21 troops

Remarks: Has flag officer and staff accommodations in the space occupied by the troop compartment in the boats of this class built for the Coastal Artillery Force. Aluminum construction.

♦ 1 personnel ferry [YFL]
Bldr: . . ., Gryt (In serv. 1984)

Rödnäbba (ex-*Långvik*)

Remarks: Acquired in 1990 for use in local transportation of naval personnel. Former coastal passenger vessel.

♦ 2 range safety boats [YFL]
Bldr: Storebro Bruks AB (In serv. 1980)

D: 5.5 tons (7 fl) **S:** 24 kts **Dim:** 10.35 × 3.30 × 1.0
Electronics: Radar: 1 Decca 091 nav.
M: 2 Volvo Penta TAMD 60C diesels; 2 props; 370 bhp

Remarks: Fold-down door at stern. 1.7-ton useful load.

♦ 3 personnel launches [YFL]
Bldr: Storebro Bruks AB (In serv. 1980)

1298 1300 1310

Personnel launch 1298 Gilbert Gyssels, 8-90

D: 5.5 tons (7 fl) **S:** 24 kts **Dim:** 9.30 × 3.30 × 1.0
Electronics: Radar: 1 Decca 091 nav.
M: 2 Volvo Penta TAMD 60C diesels; 2 props; 370 bhp

Remarks: Builder's Tp 31 design; glass-reinforced-plastic construction. Can carry 25 personnel or six stretchers. Can reach 27 kts in light condition.

♦ 7 603-class utility craft [YFU]
Bldrs: Djupviks, Tjörn; Oskarhamms; Marinvarvet, Fårösund (In serv. 1986–87)

652 Almö	654 . . .	656 . . .	658 . . .
653 Donsö	655 . . .	657 Bollö	

Bollö (657) Frank Findler, 7-02

D: 20 tons (53 fl) **S:** 8–10 kts **Dim:** 21.0 (20.0 pp) × 7.2 × 0.7 **A:** None
Electronics: Radar: 1 Decca RM 914C nav.
M: 2 Saab-Scania DSI-11/40-M20 diesels; 2 Schottel props; 340 bhp
Cargo: 25 tons deck cargo or 30 tons liquid **Crew:** . . .

Remarks: Classified as "support boats" (*Trossbåt*). The prototype (since discarded) was delivered in 1978. The Naval Brigade operates sisters as landing craft. Have a stores-handling crane and bow ramp and can be beached.

Disposal note: Harbor fuel lighter *Eldaren* (A 229; ex-*Brotank*) was stricken during 2000.

♦ 1 torpedo- and missile-recovery craft [YPT]
Bldr: Lunde Varv & Verkstads AB, Kramfors

	Symbol	L	In serv.
A 248 Pingvinen	Pin	26-9-73	3-75

D: 191 tons (fl) **S:** 13 kts **Dim:** 33.0 × 6.1 × 1.8
Electronics: Radar: 1 Terma Scanter 009 nav.
M: 2 MTU 12V493 diesels; 2 props; 1,040 bhp
Crew: 14 tot.

Pingvinen (A 248) Werner Schiefer, 10-96

♦ 1 torpedo- and missile-recovery craft [YPT]
Bldr: Djupviksvarvet, Rönnäng (L: 9-63)

A 247 Pelikanen (Pel)

SERVICE CRAFT *(continued)*

Pelikanen (A 247) Jaroslaw Cislak, 9-98

D: 130 tons **S:** 15 kts **Dim:** 33.0 × 5.8 × 1.8
Electronics: Radar: 1 Terma Scanter 009 nav.
M: 2 MTU 12V493 diesels; 2 props; 1,040 bhp
Crew: 14 tot.

◆ 1 salvage and rescue submersible [YSS]
Bldr: Kockums, Malmö (L: 17-4-78)

URF

URF—suspended from the dynamic-positioning stern crane of the *Belos* (A 214) Jaroslaw Cislak, 9-98

D: 52 tons (surfaced) **S:** 3 kts **Dim:** 13.9 × 43.2 × 2.9 **Crew:** 3 tot.

Remarks: *URF* is an acronym for *Ubåts Räddnings Farkost* (Submarine Rescue Craft). Two projected sisters were not built. Sweden and Norway signed agreement in early 1995 for the *URF* to provide rescue services for Norwegian submarines. Based at the Naval Diving Center, Berga. The submarine rescue ship *Belos* (A 214) acts as tender and transport. *URF* can mate while submerged with the British submarine rescue craft LR5.
Hull systems: Can be towed at up to 10 kts to the scene of an accident. Has a depth capability of 460 meters and can accommodate up to 25 persons rescued from a bottomed submarine. Lockout capability to support two divers to 300 meters. Pressure hull of HY 130 steel; normal maximum depth 460 meters and collapse depth of 900 meters.

Note: Kockums in 5-01 announced development of a second-generation *URF* capable of rescuing up to 35 persons from a submarine sunk to a depth of 700 meters and listing at up to 45 degrees. There is no immediate customer for the craft.

◆ 1 Achilles-class icebreaking tug [YTB]
Bldr: Åsiverken, Åmål (L: 1962)

A 251 Achilles

D: 450 tons **S:** 12 kts **Dim:** 35.5 (33.15 pp) × 9.5 × 3.9
Electronics: Radar: 1 or 2 Decca 1226C nav.
M: 1 diesel; 1 prop; 1,650 bhp **Crew:** 12 tot.

Remarks: Sister *Ajax* (A 252) stricken 1994. Capable of light icebreaking.

◆ 1 Herkules-class icebreaking tug [YTM]
Bldr: Åsiverken, Åmål

A 324 Hera (L: 1971)

Hera (A 324) Gilbert Gyssels, 8-90

D: 127 tons **S:** 11.5 kts **Dim:** 21.4 × 6.9 × 3.7 **M:** Diesels; 615 bhp
Disposals: Sister *Herkules* (A 323) was no longer in service as of 2004.

◆ 2 Hermes-class icebreaking tugs [YTM] (L: 1953–57)

A 253 Hermes (Hem) A 322 Heros (Her)

Hermes (A 253) Curt Borgenstam Jr., 6-94

D: 185 tons **S:** 11 kts **Dim:** 24.5 (23.0 pp) × 6.8 × 3.6 **M:** Diesel; 600 bhp
Remarks: Sister *Hector* (A 321) was stricken during 1991.

◆ 6 small harbor tugs/tenders [YTL]
Bldr: Lundevarv (In serv. 1978–79)

A 751 . . . A 754 Björkö
A 752 Willy A 755 . . .
A 753 Ran A 756 . . .

D: 42 tons (fl) **S:** 9.5 kts **Dim:** 15.5 × 5.0 × 2.7 **M:** 1 diesel

Remarks: Can break thin ice. Carry 40 passengers. Sisters are used by the Naval Brigade.

Willy (A 752) Curt Borgenstam Jr., 8-97

SERVICE CRAFT *(continued)*

♦ **2 sail-training schooners [YTS]**
Bldr: Naval Dockyard, Stockholm (L 1947, 1948)

S 01 GLADAN (GAD)   S 02 FALKEN (FAK)

Gladan (S 01) Ralph Edwards, 6-03

D: 220 tons **S:** 6 kts **Dim:** 42.5 (34.4 hull; 28.3 pp) × 7.27 × 4.2
M: 1 diesel auxiliary; 1 prop; 220 bhp; sail area: 711 m^2
Crew: 8 officers, 8 enlisted + 28 cadets

♦ **1 Arkö-class training craft [YXT]**
Bldr: Karlskronavarvet, Karlskrona (In serv. 1964)

M 67 NÄMNDÖ

D: 285 tons (300 fl) **S:** 14.5 kts **Dim:** 44.4 × 7.5 × 2.5 (3.0 props) **A:** None
Electronics: Radar: 1 . . . nav. **M:** 2 MTU 12V 493 diesels; 2 props; 1,000 bhp
Crew: . . . tot.

Remarks: Former minesweeper converted during the early 1990s for use as a navigational training tender. Stack raised to keep exhaust from the open bridge area. Wooden construction.

NAVAL BRIGADE

The Coastal Artillery Service was renamed the Naval Brigade in 2001–2. Consisting of some 1,300 active personnel plus reservists, the force is equipped with 24 Bofors 120-mm 55-cal. KARIN/CD-80 mobile guns, six missile trucks (each with four RBS-15 Mk 2 launchers), three+ Mowag wheeled armored vehicles, in addition to a number of self-propelled Bofors TriKA 40-mm AA batteries and associated Ericsson ARTE 740 (Giraffe CD) radars. Also in service are laser-guided RBS-17 (modified Hellfire) launchers and missiles, RBS-70 SAM systems and 81-mm and 120-mm mortars. Some fixed 75- and 120-mm gun batteries remain in service though all 152-mm gun batteries have been retired.

PATROL BOATS [PB]

♦ **12 Tapper class (Bevakningsbåt 2000 or Type 80)**
Bldr: Djupviks Varv, Tjörn

	In serv.		In serv.		In serv.
81 TAPPER	4-2-93	85 TRYGG	1995	89 STOLT	6-97
82 DJÄRV	1993	86 MODIG	1995	90 ÄRLIG	12-97
83 DRISTIG	1994	87 HURTIG	12-95	91 MUNTER	1998
84 HÄNDIG	1994	88 RAPP	12-96	92 ORÄDD	5-99

D: 54 tons (60 fl) **S:** 28 kts (25 sust.) **Dim:** 21.85 (19.73 pp) × 5.40 × 1.05
A: 2 single 12.7-mm mg; 4 9-round Saab ASW 600) ASW RL; 8 d.c. in individual racks; 1 mine rail
Electronics:
Radar: 2 Decca. . . nav.
Sonar: Simrad . . . HF hull-mounted searchlight
M: 2 MWM TBD 234 V16 diesels; 2 waterjets; 2,440 bhp (2,090 sust.)—bow-thruster
Electric: 40 kVA tot. **Crew:** 8 tot

Remarks: First seven ordered 1991 to begin replacement of the Type 72 class; five more ordered 1994. Design based on same builder's Kbv 290 for the Swedish Coast Guard. Aluminum alloy construction. Have GPS navigational system. Normally carry a Phantom HD-2 remotely operated submersible equipped with a Tritech ST 525 HF imaging sonar for sea-bottom surveillance.

Disposal note: All remaining Type 72–class patrol boats (numbers 61 through 77) had been retired by 2006.

Modig (86) Photo via Brooks Rowlett, 5-03

MINE WARFARE SHIPS

♦ **1 MUL 20–class minelayer [MM]** Bldr: Åsiverken, Åmål

	Symbol	L	In serv.
MUL 20 FURUSUND	FUR	16-12-82	10-10-83

Furusund (MUL 20) Royal Swedish Navy, 1984

D: 225 tons (245 fl) **S:** 11 kts **Dim:** 32.4 (30.0 pp) × 8.4 × 1.8
A: 1 20-mm 70-cal. Oerlikon AA; 2 7.62-mm mg; . . . mines
Electronics: Radar: 1 Decca RM 1226C nav.
M: 2 Saab-Scania GASI-14 diesels (335 bhp each), ASEA 300 kVA electric drive; 2 props; 420 shp + 1 125-hp maneuvering prop
Electric: 73 kw tot. **Crew:** 24 tot. (10 peacetime)

Remarks: Ordered 23-6-81. Nine more were planned, but the builder went bankrupt after only the one was completed and no more were ordered. Can carry up to 24 tons of mines on two deck rails.

♦ **3 MUL 12–class mine planters [MM]** (In serv. 1952–56)

MUL 12 ARKÖSUND (ARK)   MUL 18 FÅRÖSUND (ex-*Öresund*)
MUL 15 GRUNDSUND (GRU)

Kalmarsund (MUL 13)—since retired Curt Borgenstam Jr., 8-94

NAVAL BRIGADE MINE WARFARE SHIPS *(continued)*

D: 200 tons (245 fl) **S:** 10.5 kts **Dim:** 31.18 (29.0 pp) × 7.62 × 3.1
A: 2 single 12.7-mm mg; . . . mines **Electronics:** Radar: 1 Decca RM 1226C nav.
M: 2 Nohab or Saab-Scania diesels; 2 props; 460 bhp **Crew:** 24 tot.

Remarks: These craft are used for placing and maintaining controlled mine fields. Given names 1985–86. Can carry up to 26 tons of mines on two deck rails.

Disposal note: Sisters *Fårösund* (MUL 16) and *Alnösund* (MUL 14) were stricken during 1995–96. *Karlmarsund* (MUL 13), *Skramsösund* (MUL 17), and *Barösund* (MUL 19) were retired between 2002 and 2004. Coastal mine planter *Kalvsund* (MUL 11) was retired in 2002.

♦ 6 small minelaying launches [MM]
Bldr: Marinvarvet, Fårösund

1879–1881 (In serv. 4-7-83) 1882–1884 (In serv. 23-1-84)

Remarks: Displacement 2.5 tons; waterjet-powered: 20 kts. Ordered 27-11-82.

AMPHIBIOUS WARFARE CRAFT

♦ 1 M-10X-class air-cushion landing craft [LCMA]
Bldr: Karlskronavarvet and ABS Hovercraft, UK (In serv. 26-6-98)

M-10X prototype Curt Borgenstam Jr., 6-98

D: 26 tons (fl) **S:** 50 kts light/35 kts loaded **Dim:** 20.6 × 8.80 × 0.35 at rest
A: 1 12.7-mm mg **Electronics:** Radar: 1 . . . nav.
M: 2 Deutz BF12L513C diesels; 2 lift fans, 2 airscrew props; 1,050 bhp
Range: 600/30 **Fuel:** 4,600 liters **Crew:** 1 officer, 2 enlisted

Remarks: Designed by ABS Hovercraft, which also provided the machinery and skirts. Ordered 1997 with an option for six more, but when the government attempted to order three more in 11-01, Kockums, the corporate successor, refused the business.
Hull systems: Capable of carrying one tracked vehicle, 50 seated troops, one 20-ft. cargo container, or 20 stretcher cases. The hull is constructed of GRP carbon fiber and vinyl laminate, with a GRP/foam sandwich deck and Kevlar-reinforced superstructure. Can clear 1-m obstacles and can operate in 2.5-m seas.

Disposal note: *Grim*-class utility landing craft *Bore*, *Grim,* and *Heimdal* had been retired by 2006.

♦ 16 Trossbåt-class vehicle/personnel landing craft [LCM]
Bldr: First two: Homsvarvet (1st in serv. 1-91, 2nd late 1993); others: Djupviks, Tjörn (In serv. 1996–98)

662 through 677

D: 30 tons (45 fl) **S:** 30 kts (23 loaded) **Dim:** 24.00 × 5.40 × 1.20
A: 1 12.7-mm mg; mines (on portable rails)
Electronics: Radar: 1/Terma Scanter 009 nav.
M: 3 Saab Scania 8V DSI-14 diesels; 3 Alumina FF450 waterjets; 1,380 bhp
Range: 150/15 (loaded) **Fuel:** 15,000 liters **Crew:** 4 tot. + 17 troops

Remarks: *Trossbåt* means "Support Boat." Aluminum construction. Cargo: 15 tons on 14.0 × 4.5–m deck area, or 2 m^3 water and 9 tons cargo, 8 m^3 diesel fuel, or 7 m^3 of water and no deck cargo. Have folding bow ramp and a small crane. Considered to be capable of operating in light ice. A dozen sisters were ordered on 22-1-02 from Abu Dhabi Ship Building for use by the United Arab Emirates Navy. Ten had been retired by 2006.

Trossbåt 662—the bow swings upward to permit the vehicle ramp to be extended
Curt Borgenstam Jr., 9-00

Trossbåt 673 Stefan Karpinski, 7-05

♦ 10 603-class vehicle landing craft [LCM]
Bldrs: Djupviks, Tjörn; Oskarhamms; Marinvarvet, Fårösund (In serv. 1984–87)

603 through 612

603-class landing craft 610 Curt Borgenstam Jr., 7-94

D: 20 tons (53 fl) **S:** 8–10 kts **Dim:** 21.0 (20.0 pp) × 7.2 × 0.7 **A:** None
Electronics: Radar: 1 Decca RM 914C nav.
M: 2 Saab-Scania DSI-11/40-M20 diesels; 2 Schottel props; 340 bhp
Cargo: 25 tons deck cargo or 30 tons liquid **Crew:** . . .

Remarks: The prototype (since discarded) was delivered in 1978; classified as "support boats" (*Trossbåt*). 603 was delivered 2-4-84 by Marinvarvet; 604 and 605 delivered 1-10-84 by Djupviks. 607 in service 1-9-86; 608 on 22-9-86; 609 on 12-3-87; 610 on 27-4-86; and 612 delivered 1987. The navy proper operates sisters as service craft.

♦ 3 (+ . . .) Transportbåt 2000–class personnel landing craft [LCP]
Bldr: Djupviks Varv, Tjörn (In serv. 11-98 to 1-99)

451 452 453

Transportbåt 2000–class 452 Eivind Rodlie, 2001

D: 43 tons (fl) **S:** 25 kts (loaded) **Dim:** 23.5 × 5.1 × 1.0
A: 2 single 12.7-mm mg; 2 mine rails **Electronics:** Radar: 1 Terma . . . nav.
M: 451: 3 Saab Scania DSI 14 diesels; 3 FF Jet 450 waterjets; 1,194 bhp;
452: 2 Volvo Penta 163 diesels; 3 KaMeWa K40 waterjets; . . . bhp
Range: . . . / . . . **Crew:** 3 tot.

Remarks: Aluminum-hulled prototypes ordered 9-97 to evaluate proposed program for about 12 additional craft to deliver from 2003 to 2010, but no further orders have been announced. One is configured to carry 45 fully equipped troops or 10 tons of stores and the other as a mobile brigade headquarters. Production version may be built of GRP and may have a different propulsion system. The machineguns are carried on training rings above the bridge and on the stern.

NAVAL BRIGADE AMPHIBIOUS WARFARE CRAFT *(continued)*

◆ **27 CB 90-class fast personnel landing craft [LCP]**
Bldrs: Dockstavarvet, Docksta and Gotlands Varvet (In serv. 2002–3)

948 through 974

D: 17.6 tons light (22.6 fl) **S:** 41 kts **Dim:** 16.10 × 3.24 × 0.90
A: 2 fixed and 1 flexible 12.7-mm mg
Electronics: Radar: 1 Decca 189 nav.
M: 2 Saab Scania DSI-14/52 M 23 diesels; 2 Kamewa waterjets; 1,256 bhp
Range: . . . / . . . **Fuel:** . . . tons **Crew:** 4 tot. + 18 troops

Remarks: Modified versions of the Stridsbåt-90H-class fast personnel landing craft with improved armor and NBC protection equipment, similar to those delivered in the newer 90H units.

◆ **145 Stridsbåt 90H–class fast personnel landing craft [LCP]**
Bldrs: Dockstavarvet, Docksta, and Gotlands Varvet (In serv. 10-12-92 to 1-03)

803 through 947

Stridsbåt 90H–class 903 Stefan Karpinski, 7-05

Stridsbåt 90H–class 884 Michael Winter, 5-04

D: 13.2 tons light (18 fl) **S:** 40 kts **Dim:** 15.90 (13.00 wl) × 3.80 × 0.80
A: 2 fixed and 1 flexible 12.7-mm mg—provision for: RBS-17 Hellfire SSM, 1 81-mm mortar, 4 mines (2.8 tons), or 6 d.c.
Electronics: Radar: 1 Decca RD 360 (final 27: Decca BridgeMaster E ARPA) nav.
M: 2 Saab Scania 8V DSI-14 diesels; 2 FF Jet FF 450 waterjets; 1,256 bhp
Range: 160/40; 240/20 **Fuel:** 1.5 tons **Crew:** 4 tot. + 21 troops

Remarks: The first batch of 12 was begun during 9-90 by Dockstavarvet; the Batch II order, placed 23-1-92, was shared by the two yards cited previously (Gotlands Varvet is a subsidiary of Djupviks), with the final 29 delivered by 2003 to a modified design intended for peacekeeping operations; these craft have enhanced personnel protection, biological and chemical warfare protection, and air conditioning to permit them to operate in a Mediterranean climate. Aluminum construction. The basic design has also been an export success, with units sold to Norway, Malaysia, and Mexico. A near-sister operates as the VIP launch *Blåtunga* for the Swedish Navy. Sisters 801 and 802 were retired during 2004.
Combat systems: The single 12.7-mm mg (which can be replaced by a 40-mm grenade launcher) is mounted on a ring atop the troop compartment. Two units completed in 1993 and four more of the batch converted in 1995–96 are designated CB-90L and are configured as Battalion Command Centers; they have two 7.5-kVA generator sets and 220/380 V, 48-Hz electrical installations to support nine workstations and a unit commander in the reconfigured troop compartment; 10 additional radio antennas are fitted. 801 (since retired) was fitted with a Patria Vammas-Hägglunds AMOS (Advanced Mortar Sytem) twin 120-mm mortar in an armored turret mounted abaft the pilothouse late in 1999 for trials; a similar mounting was placed aboard an operational unit under a 6-02 contract, and additional boats may be similarly converted. The final 27 have Transas Scandinavia AB Navsystem 3000 automated navigations systems and Decca BridgeMaster-E radars.

◆ **52 SRC 90E–class ambulance craft [LCP]**
Bldr: Storebro Bruks AB, Storebro (In serv. 15-8-95 to end-1998)

103 through 154

SRC 90E–class 103 Storebro, 1995

D: 6.5 tons light (9.5 fl) **S:** 40 kts (37 loaded)
Dim: 11.88 (10.88 hull) × 2.90 × 0.70
M: 2 Saab Scania DSI-1 V-8 diesel; 1 KaMeWa FF-410 waterjet; 560 bhp (at 3,800 r.p.m.; 340 bhp sustained)
Range: 215/40 **Fuel:** 650 liters **Crew:** 2 tot.

Remarks: Ambulance craft capable of carrying one ton of cargo in addition to 10 troops or seated casualties or four to five stretcher cases. Prototypes, 101 and 102, delivered 1994. First series order for 39 came in 11-94; 13 more were ordered early in 1997. At least one (Kbv 414) was also procured for the Coast Guard. A further prototype for an improved version capable of 50 kts was launched on 28-10-98.
Hull systems: Hulls constructed of carbon-fiber reinforced vinyl ester sandwich with a foam core. Cabin and piloting station are vibration-isolated from the rest of the hull. Bow folds down to become a step.

◆ **21 200-class large personnel landing craft [LCP]**
Bldrs: Lundevarv Verkstads and Marinteknik, Öregrund (In serv. 1957–77)

208	234–237	258
215	241	261
223	247–248	263–264
230–232	252	267–269

200-class 258 H&L Van Ginderen, 1-98

D: 31 tons (fl) **S:** 17 kts **Dim:** 21.4 × 4.2 × 1.3
A: 2 or 3/6.5-mm mg—mines
Electronics: Radar: 1/Decca RM 914C nav.
M: 3 Saab-Scania 6 DS-11 diesels; 3 props; 705 bhp **Crew:** 5 crew, 40 troops

Remarks: 267 through 269 have Volvo Penta diesels. Patrol-boat-like bow opens to permit extension of ramp from troop compartment below decks. Twin machinegun to port, plus single mount aft in some. Mine rails can be laid from the pilothouse over the stern. All were refitted during the 1990s. Numbers missing in sequence have been stricken.

◆ **120 G-båt raiding launches [LCP]**
Bldr: Marine Alutech Oy, Teijo, Finland (In serv. 1993–99)

G-båt raiding launch Stefan Marx, 1998

D: 1.75 tons (3 fl) **S:** 30 kts **Dim:** 8.10 (6.50 pp) s 2.10 × 0.50
M: 1 Volvo TAMD 42WJ diesel; 1 FF-Jet waterjet; 230 bhp (at 3,800 r.p.m. 170 bhp sustained)
Fuel: 250 liters **Crew:** 1 + 8 troops

NAVAL BRIGADE AMPHIBIOUS WARFARE CRAFT *(continued)*

Remarks: Designed by FMV. Aluminum construction. Typed *"Gruppbåt."* The 53rd was completed 6-94 and the 100th during 1999. Cargo capacity is 1 ton.

Note: A number of very small vessels, including more than 50 outboard-powered canoes/kayaks are also in service with amphibious units for special operations use.

SERVICE CRAFT

♦ **5 support tugs [YTL]** Bldr: Djupviks, Tjörn (In serv. 1982–85)

701 through 705

Support tug 702 Curt Borgenstam Jr., 6-94

D: 42 tons **S:** 9.5 kts **Dim:** 15.5 × 5.0 × 2.7 **M:** 1 diesel; 1 prop; . . . bhp

Remarks: Can be used to transport cargo and personnel, to plant mines, or as tugs. Bulwarks at bow open to permit debarking personnel over a beach. Several sisters serve the Swedish Navy proper.

SWEDISH MARITIME ADMINISTRATION

(Sjöfartsverket)

AUXILIARIES

Note: The Swedish Maritime Administration operates all icebreakers and hydrographic research vessels. Ships and craft have black hulls and buff-colored superstructures; the stacks are white and bear the organization's seal.

♦ **1 Oden-class icebreaker [WAGB]** Bldr: Götaverken, Arendal

	Laid down	L	In serv.
Oden	19-10-87	5-8-88	29-1-89

Oden Stefan Karpinski, 7-05

D: 10,300 tons (12,900 fl) **S:** 17 kts free (3 kt through 1.8-m ice)
Dim: 107.80 (93.20 pp) × 31.00 max (29.40 over "reamers"; 25.00 wl) × 7.00 (8.50 max.)
A: Provision for: 4 single 40-mm 70-cal. Bofors L70 AA; . . . mines
Electronics: Radar: 2 . . . nav.
M: 4 Cegielski-Sulzer 8ZAL-40S diesels, geared drive; 2 shrouded CP props; 24,480 bhp—bow and stern thrusters
Electric: 4,800 kw (4 NEBB 1,200 kw alternators, Sulzer AT-25H diesels, 1,750 bhp each, driving)
Range: 30,000/13 **Fuel:** 2,917 tons heavy oil, 854 tons diesel
Crew: 32 tot. + 17 spare berths

Remarks: 9,436 grt/4,906 dwt. Ordered 1-87. Is available for Arctic-service commercial charter in summer and was commercially crewed for a North Polar expedition in 1996. A second unit, to be named *Thule,* is planned but has not yet been funded.
Hull systems: Unique hull form, designed by Canadian Marine Drilling Co., is nearly rectangular in plan form and has a barge-like bow, with beam-wise extensions. Has 150-ton towing winch, 10-ton crane, and 390-m^2 helicopter deck aft. Carries up to 3,650-m^3 ballast water and has a heeling pump system, hull wash, and jet-mister to assist in ice conditions.
Combat systems: The 40-mm guns can be mounted at the corners of the superstructure. Can be equipped as a minelayer.

♦ **3 Finnish Urho-class icebreakers [WAGB]**
Bldr: Wärtsilä, Helsinki, Finland

	Laid down	L	In serv.
Atle	10-5-73	27-11-73	21-10-74
Frej	. . .	3-6-74	30-9-75
Ymer	12-2-76	3-9-76	26-10-77

Atle H&L Van Ginderen, 5-95

D: 7,900 tons (9,500 fl) **S:** 18.5 kts
Dim: 104.70 (96.02 pp) × 23.86 (22.5 wl) × 8.40
A: 4 single 40-mm 70-cal. Bofors L70 AA; 3 mine rails
M: 5 Wärtsilä-Pielstick 12PC2.5 V400 diesels (4,650-bhp each), 5 generators, 4 Strömberg electric motors; 2 fixed-pitch props fwd, 2 CP props aft; 22,000 shp
Crew: 16 officers, 38 enlisted

Remarks: 6,844 grt. Helicopter platform. All personnel live and normally work above the main deck. *Frej* was given permanent gun armament, mine rails, and fuel facilities for two helicopters in 10-83 and the others in 1984. The guns are mounted atop the hangar and forward of the pilothouse.

♦ **1 Ale-class lake icebreaker [WAGB]**
Bldr: Wärtsilä, Helsinki, Finland

	L	In serv.
Ale	1-6-73	12-12-73

Ale H&L Van Ginderen, 9-98

D: 1,550 tons (fl) **S:** 14 kts **Dim:** 46.0 × 13.0 × 5.0
A: Provision for: 1 40-mm 70-cal. Bofors L 70 AA (not normally aboard)
M: 2 diesels, electric drive; 2 props; 4,750 shp **Crew:** 8 officers, 24 enlisted

Remarks: Built for service on Lake Vänern in central Sweden, also used for hydrographic survey in summer.

Note: In addition to the *Ale,* three 3,000-dwt commercial combination icebreaker/oilfield anchor-handling tugs ordered 7-98 for delivery in 2000–2001 will be employed from January to March for 15 years by the Board of Navigation as icebreakers in Swedish waters. Ordered by Bylock & Nordsjofrakt, Sweden, and Viking Supply Ships, Norway, under the consortium name B&N Viking Icebreaking & Offshore AS, the ships are being built by Kvaerner Kleven Leirvik, Norway. The ships will have a bollard pull of 200 tons on 18,500 bhp and will be able to break 1-m ice at 3 knots continuous.

♦ **2 Baltica-class harbor icebreaker/navigational tenders [WAGL]**
Bldr: Åsiverken AB, Åmål

Baltica (In serv. 26-2-82) Scandica (In serv. 27-1-83)

D: 1,238 tons (fl) **S:** 15 kts **Dim:** 54.92 (50.12 pp) × 12.04 × 2.70
Electronics: Radar: 1 Decca ARPA; 1 Decca Clearscan nav.
M: 2 Hedemora V16A/10 diesels; 1 CP prop; 3,520 bhp—300 shp bow and stern tunnel-thrusters
Electric: 1,100 kw tot. (5 × 220 kw diesel sets) **Fuel:** 140 tons **Crew:** 12 tot.

Remarks: 856 grt/350 dwt. Twelve-ton electrohydraulic crane serving combination buoy hold/workshop. Can tow at 50-ton bollard pull. Capable of operating in light ice conditions. Civilian-manned.

SWEDISH MARITIME ADMINISTRATION AUXILIARIES *(continued)*

Scandica—black hull, cream upperworks Curt Borgenstam Jr., 6-00

♦ **1 lighthouse supply ship [WAGL]**
Bldr: AB Åsiverken, Åmål (In serv. 22-1-81)

FYRBJÖRN

D: . . . tons **S:** 12.5 kts **Dim:** 40.05 (39.50 pp) × 10.50 × 3.30
M: 1 Hedemora V12A/13.5 diesel; 1 prop; 1,360 bhp

Remarks: 430 grt. Molded depth of hull: 4.9 meters.

♦ **1 lighthouse supply ship [WAGL]**
Bldr: Sigbjörn Iversens Mek. Verkstad, Flekkefjord, Norway (In serv. 14-12-76)

FYRBYGGAREN

Fyrbyggaren Curt Borgenstam Jr., 5-99

D: . . . tons **S:** . . . kts **Dim:** 41.8 × 10.0 × . . .
M: 1 Wichmann 5AX diesel; 1 prop; 1,500 bhp **Crew:** 8 tot.

Remarks: 499 grt. Molded depth of hull: 4.9 meters.

SERVICE CRAFT

♦ **1 catamaran-hulled hydrographic survey craft [WYGS]**
Bldr: Oskarshamms Varv (In serv. 28-6-85)

NILS STRÖMKRONA (NSA)

D: 175 tons **S:** 12 kts **Dim:** 30.00 (27.61 pp) × 10.0 × 1.60
M: 4 Saab Scania 8-cyl. diesels; 2 CP props; 1,729 bhp—bow and stern thrusters
Range: . . . / . . . **Fuel:** 17 tons **Crew:** 5 officers, 9 enlisted

Remarks: 311 grt. Built to replace 1894-vintage unit with the same name. Each aluminum-construction hull has 3.9-m beam. Based at Norrköping.

Nils Strömkrona Curt Borgenstam Jr., 8-93

♦ **1 coastal survey boat [WYGS]**
Bldr: Djupviks, Rönnäng (In serv. 10-82)

JACOB HÄGG (JHÄ)

Jacob Hägg Jaroslaw Cislak, 5-98

D: 130 tons (fl) **S:** 16.5 kts **Dim:** 36.50 × 7.50 × 1.65
M: 4 Saab-Scania DSI-14 diesels; 2 props; 1,684 bhp (1,300 sust.)

Remarks: Aluminum construction. The same builder also delivered a 42-ton, 400-hp hydrographic survey launch in 1983.

COAST GUARD

Personnel: Approx. 600 total.

The Swedish Coast Guard became independent from the Swedish Customs Service on 1-7-88. It now is responsible for fisheries regulation, customs patrol, pollution and dumping monitoring and cleanup and other environmental considerations, and merchant traffic regulation. All units now have dark blue–painted hulls with a yellow diagonal stripe and white superstructures. None are armed. All boat pennants were changed 7-88 from "Tv"—*Tullverket* (Central Customs Office) prefix—in 1988 to "Kbv"—*Kustbevakning* (Coast Guard).

Organization: The Coast Guard fleet is organized into four regions, with a total of 15 districts; each district has two to four stations, with craft based at 30 locations.

Maritime Aviation: Two CASA C-212-200 Aviocar patrol aircraft with side-looking radar (SLAR) and four BO-105 helicopters are in service. Bombardier Dash 8 transport and patrol aircraft will begin replacing the two Casa C-212s beginning in 2007–8.

PATROL SHIPS [WPS]

♦ **1 modified Finnish Tursas class**
Bldr: Rauma Oy, Uusikaupunki, Finland

Kbv 181 GOTLAND (In serv. 30-11-90)

Gotland (Kbv 181) Hartmut Ehlers, 6-96

D: 800 tons (fl) **S:** 16 kts **Dim:** 56.00 (49.80 pp) × 10.20 × 4.00
Electronics:
Radar: 2 Decca . . . nav.
Sonar: Simrad Subsea hull-mounted HF searchlight-type

COAST GUARD PATROL SHIPS [WPS] *(continued)*

M: 2 Wärtsilä Vasa 8R22 diesels; 2 props; 3,800 bhp—bow-thruster
Electric: 700 kW tot. **Range:** 2,800/15; 6,100/8 **Fuel:** 82 m^2 **Crew:** 11 tot.

Remarks: Ordered 10-89 as flagship and command vessel for search-and-rescue and oil-spill cleanup operations. Lengthened over the Finnish prototype to accommodate a second hold to stow oil-spill cleanup gear. Can be armed with one 20-mm 70-cal. Oerlikon AA. Can make 12 kts through 0.2-m ice. Equipped 1994 with Russian GLONASS navigational satellite receiver.

PATROL CRAFT [WPC]

♦ **2 Kbv 201 class**
Bldr: Kockums, Karlskrona

Kbv 201 (In serv. 10-01) Kbv 202 (In serv. 25-1-02)

Kbv 201—at builder's Curt Borgenstam Jr., 9-01

D: 468 tons (fl) **S:** 22 kts (20 sust.) **Dim:** 52.0 (50.0 pp) × 8.6 × 2.3
Electronics: Radar: 1 . . . nav; 1 . . . nav.
M: 2 MWM 620-series 16-cyl diesels; 2 props; 2 CP props: 7,500 bhp— 2/bow-thrusters
Range: 2,000/16 **Endurance:** 5 days **Crew:** 8 tot.

Remarks: Ordered 9-98 with option for two more possible in the future. Design prepared by Marintek, Norway. Have spilled-oil recovery system with two storage tanks. A ramp is incorporated in the stern for a high-speed RIB. A towing winch is installed aft, and there is a firefighting monitor on the forecastle. There are two flapped rudders, and fin stabilizers are fitted. Cabins for each crewmember. Oil recovery system with two tanks totaling 100-tons capacity. Integrated bridge controls for maneuvering, navigation, and communications. Are capable of breaking 0.3 m of ice.

PATROL BOATS [WPB]

♦ **16 Kbv 301 class**
Bldr: Kbv 301: Djupviks, Tjörn/Rönnäng; others: Karlskronavarvet, Karlskrona (In serv. 1993–98)

Kbv 301 through Kbv 316

Kbv 301 H&L Van Ginderen, 2-95

D: 34 tons light (47 fl) **S:** 38 kts (34 sust.) **Dim:** 19.95 × 4.65 × 1.02
Electronics: Radar: 1 Furuno FR 7010 nav.; 1 Furuno 2011 surf. search
M: 2 MTU 12V183 TE92 diesels; 2 KaMeWa waterjets; 2,000 bhp
Range: 250/34; 500/ 25 **Crew:** 3–4 tot.

Remarks: Design evolved from Kbv 290. Aluminum alloy construction. Prototype Kbv 301 was completed in 1993; Kbv 302 was completed on 17-2-95 and Kbv 306 on 22-8-96, with later units completed during 1997–98. Navigational equipment includes Furuno FCV 561 echo sounder, Robertson RGC50 gyro, GPS receiver, Decca Navigator radio navaid receiver, autopilot, and a data-recording computer. An image-intensifier surveillance device is fitted.

♦ **1 Kbv 290 class**
Bldr: Djupviks, Tjörn/Rönnäng (In serv. 6-12-90)

Kbv 290

Kbv 290 H&L Van Ginderen, 12-97

D: 45 tons (51fl) **S:** 28 kts **Dim:** 21.85 (19.73 pp) × 5.40 × 1.05
Electronics: Radar: 1 . . . nav.
M: 2 MWM TBD 234 V16 diesels; 2 props; 2,120 bhp
Range: 400/ . . . **Fuel:** 5,000 liters **Crew:** 4 tot.

Remarks: Aluminum construction. Intended as prototype for new class to replace older patrol craft; production version became the Kbv 301 class.

♦ **2 Kbv 288 class** Bldr: Djupviks, Tjörn/Rönnäng (In serv. ca. 1990)

Kbv 288 Kbv 289

Kbv 288 H&L Van Ginderen, 1-95

D: 53 tons (fl) **S:** 24 kts **Dim:** 21.85 × 5.40 × 1.80
Electronics: Radar: 1 Furuno FR2011 nav.; 1 Furuno FR7040R nav.
M: 2 Cummins KTA 38M diesels; 2 props; 2,080 bhp **Electric:** 60 kVA tot.
Range: 300/ . . . **Crew:** 5 tot.

Remarks: Improved version of Kbv 281 class with lower superstructure. Have Plath gyrocompass and autopilot, Furuno FCV 665 and FUS 200 echo-sounders, Decca Mk 53 radio navaid receiver, Furuno GP500 GPS receiver, Wesmar S5400 imaging sonar, fax and t.v. receivers, in a navigation suite typical of those fitted to modern Swedish Coast Guard patrol boats.

♦ **7 Kbv 281 class** Bldr: Djupviks, Tjörn/Rönnäng

	In serv.		In serv.		In serv.
Kbv 281	1979	Kbv 284	30-1-84	Kbv 287	2-2-87
Kbv 282	. . .	Kbv 285	2-5-84		
Kbv 283	1980	Kbv 286	21-8-86		

Kbv 287 Paolo Marsan, 5-04

D: 37 tons (42 fl) **S:** 30+ kts **Dim:** 21.85 × 5.00 × 1.70
Electronics: Radar: 1 Furuno FR2011 nav.; 1 Furuno FR7040R nav.
M: 2 Cummins KTA 38M diesels; 2 props; 2,100 bhp **Crew:** 5 tot.

Remarks: Class "B" cutters. Aluminum construction. Kbv 286 and 287 ordered 1-9-85. Kbv 286 launched 14-6-86, Kbv 287 on 25-1-87; they lack the flying bridge atop the pilothouse of the other five.

COAST GUARD PATROL BOATS [WPB] *(continued)*

♦ **2 Kbv 102 class** Bldr: Djupviks, Tjörn (In serv. 1972–73)

Kbv 104 Kbv 105

D: 53 tons (fl) **S:** 22 kts **Dim:** 26.72 × 5.23 × 1.13
M: Kbv 104: 2 MTU 8V331 TC82 diesels; 2 props; 1,866 bhp **Electric:** 60 kVA
Range: 1,000/15 **Fuel:** 11 tons **Crew:** 6 tot.

Remarks: Class "A" cutters. Aluminum construction. Three sisters were built for the Liberian Coast Guard. Kbv 105 was re-engined in 1987 with two Cummins KTA 38M diesels. Sister Kbv 102 was retired in 10-01 and Kbv 103 during 1-02.

SERVICE CRAFT

♦ **1 Class A pollution-control depot ship [WYAG]**
Bldr: Lunde Varv & Verkstads, Ramvik (L: 24-3-85)

Kbv 006

D: 450 tons (fl) **S:** 15 kts **Dim:** 37.35 (33.70 pp) × 8.80 × . . .
M: 2 Cummins KTA-2300M diesels; 2 rudder props; 2,100 bhp **Fuel:** 30.5 tons
Crew: 6 tot.

Remarks: Similar to Kbv 004 design; ordered 12-84.

Note: Also in service is the 650-ton pollution-control depot ship Kbv 005, built in Sweden in 1980 and purchased in 1993, for which no additional data are available.

♦ **1 Class A pollution-control depot ship [WYAG]**
Bldr: Lunde Varv & Verkstads, Ramvik (In serv. 1980)

Kbv 004

D: 450 tons (fl) **S:** 12 kts **Dim:** 35.5 × 8.0 × 3.0
M: 2 diesels; 2 props; 1,200 bhp **Electric:** 224 kVA **Crew:** 10 tot.

Remarks: Helipad on fantail, 200-hp bow-thruster, 30-kt workboat, 80-m^3 oil-containment tanks, 500-m^3 containment boom stowage, oil-spill skimming equipment, firefighting gear. Has salvage diver support capabilities.

Disposal note: Class A pollution-control depot ship *Rivöfjord* (Kbv 003) was transferred to Estonia during 2002.

♦ **2 Kbv 050–class Class B Sea Truck pollution-control craft [WYAG]** Bldr: Lunde Varv & Verkstads, Ramvik (In serv. 20-9-83 and 6-83)

Kbv 050 Kbv 051

Kbv 051 Leo van Ginderen, 9-05

D: 340 tons (fl) **S:** 9.5 kts **Dim:** 39.15 × 8.50 × 2.40 **M:** Diesels
Range: 2,000/9 **Crew:** . . .

Remarks: Enlarged version of Kbv 045 class. Have bow ramps and can beach.

♦ **5 Kbv 045–class Class B Sea Truck pollution-control craft [WYAG]** Bldr: Lunde Varv & Verkstads, Ramvik (In serv. 1980–83)

Kbv 045 Kbv 046 Kbv 047 Kbv 048 Kbv 049

Kbv 048 Martin Mokrus, 6-03

D: 133 tons (230 fl) **S:** 11 kts **Dim:** 28.9 (24.80 pp) × 6.5 × 1.9
M: 2 Saab-Scania DST-11 diesels; 2 props; 540 bhp
Electric: 300 kw **Fuel:** 18 tons **Crew:** 4 tot.

Remarks: Resemble landing craft, with bow ramp. 110-m^3 total tankage for recovered oil. Hydraulic thrusters fore and aft. Stowage for 800-m oil-spill containment booms. Endless belt-type oil-recovery device. Kbv 045 lengthened to 36.4 m overall by Öregrund Marinteknik Verkstad during 1993 to increase recovered waste capacity to 150 m^3; she now displaces 340 tons full load.

♦ **1 Class B Sea Truck–type oil-spill cleanup boat [WYAG]**
Bldr: Djupviks, Rönnäng (In serv. 1976)

Kbv 044

Kbv 044 H&L Van Ginderen, 5-96

D: 76 tons (100 fl) **S:** 12 kts **Dim:** 25.0 × 6.0 × 1.5
M: 2 Volvo Penta diesels; 2 props; 580 bhp

Disposal note: Oil-spill cleanup craft Kbv 059 and Kbv 041–class cleanup craft Kbv 041 and Kbv 043 were out of service by 1999.

♦ **1 Kbv 010–class Class C oil-spill cleanup base craft [WYAG]**
Bldr: Lunde Varv & Verkstads AB, Ramvik (In serv. 1985)

Kbv 010

Kbv 010 Curt Borgenstam Jr., 6-00

D: 400 tons (fl) **S:** 12 kts **Dim:** 46.10 × 8.60 × 3.50
M: 2 . . . diesels; 2 props; . . . bhp

♦ **1 Class D1 catamaran oil-spill cleanup craft [WYAG]**
Bldr: Djupvik, Tjörn (In serv. 8-6-82)

Kbv 02011

D: 60 tons (fl) **S:** 27 kts **Dim:** 27.6 × 9.2 × 1.5
M: 2 MTU 12V396 TB82 diesels; 2 props; 2,600 bhp

Remarks: Drum-type skimmer mounted forward between the hulls can recover up to 40 tons/hr., or a belt-type cleaner can recover 10–20 tons/hr. Design is Westermoen of Norway's Type 88.

♦ **1 Kbv 015–class Class C oil-spill cleanup base craft [WYAG]**
(In serv. 1971)

Kbv 015

D: 140 tons (fl) **S:** . . . **Dim:** 23.0 × 5.5 × . . .

♦ **3 miscellaneous Class D2 catamaran oil-spill cleanup craft [WYAG]**

	In serv.	D:	Dim:
Kbv 021	1973	30 tons (fl)	14.0 × 7.0
Kbv 022	1973	30 tons (fl)	14.0 × 7.0
Kbv 023	1975	30 tons (fl)	16.5 × 7.5

♦ **6 Class E Skerry-boat shore-cleaning boats [WYAG]**
(In serv. 1979–82)

From among Kbv 701–712 series

D: 9 tons **S:** . . . **Dim:** 9.0 × 3.1 × . . .

♦ **1 or more SRC 90E–class personnel launches [WYFL]**
Bldr: Storebro Bruks AB, Storebro (In serv. . . .)

Kbv 414

COAST GUARD SERVICE CRAFT *(continued)*

Kbv 414 Storebro

D: 6.5 tons light (9.5 fl) **S:** 40 kts (37 loaded)
Dim: 11.88 (10.88 hull) × 2.90 × 0.70
M: 2 Saab Scania DSI-14 V-8 diesel; 1 KaMeWa FF-410 waterjet; 560 bhp (at 3,800 r.p.m.; 340 bhp sustained)
Range: 215/40 **Fuel:** 650 liters **Crew:** 2 tot. + 10 passengers

Remarks: Sister to a large group being procured for the Naval Brigade, but is used by the Coast Guard for personnel transportation and SAR duties.
Hull systems: Hulls constructed of carbon-fiber reinforced vinyl ester sandwich with a foam core. Cabin and piloting station are vibration-isolated from the rest of the hull. Capable of carrying 4 stretchers and/or 10 seated casualties.

♦ 1 Kbv 416–class launch [WYFL]
Bldr: Aluminumbåtar, Gryt (In serv. 1981)

Kbv 416

D: 6.8 tons (fl) **S:** 33 kts **Dim:** 10.20 × 3.15 × . . .
Electronics: Radar: 1/Anritsu . . . nav.
M: 2 Volvo Penta AQAD 41 diesel outdrives; 2 props; . . . bhp

Remarks: Is equipped with a Shipmate RS 5700 GPS receiver.

♦ 8 Kbv 401–class launches [WYFL] (In serv. 1994–95)

Kbv 401 through 408

♦ 3 8100 TD–class air-cushion vehicles [WYFLA]
Bldr: Griffon Hovercraft, Salisbury Green, Southampton, U.K. (In serv. 2006–7)

. . . .

D: . . . **S:** 42 kts **Dim:** 22.50 × 11.0 × . . .
Electronics: Radar: 1 . . . nav.
M: 2 Iveco diesels; 2 CP airscrews; 2,000 bhp
Crew: . . . tot.

Remarks: Ordered as part of the Swedish Navy's "Hovercraft 2000" program. First unit entered service during 10-06 and third during 3-07.

♦ 3 2000 TDX–class air-cushion vehicles [WYFLA]
Bldr: Griffon Hovercraft, Salisbury Green, Southampton, U.K.

	In serv.
Kbv 591	1992
Kbv 592	1992
Kbv 593	10-9-93

D: 6.75 tons (fl) **S:** 35 kts **Dim:** 11.04 × 4.60 × 0.52
Electronics: Radar: 1 Furuno . . . nav.
M: 1 Deutz BF8L-513 diesel driving lift fan and 1 CP airscrew; 320 bhp
Fuel: 284 liters **Crew:** 3 tot.

Note: Also in service are about one dozen miscellaneous speedboats.

SWITZERLAND
Swiss Confederation

SWISS ARMY

PATROL BOATS [WPB]

♦ 11 Patrouillenboat 80 class
Bldr: Müller AG, Spiez (In serv. 1978–84)

A 462001 Antares	A 462005 Orion	A 462009 Sirius
A 462002 Aquarius	A 462006 Perseus	A 462010 Uranus
A 462003 Castor	A 462007 Pollux	A 462011 Venus
A 462004 Mars	A 462008 Saturn	

D: 5.2 tons (5.9 fl) **S:** 30 kts **Dim:** 10.7 × 3.3 × 0.9 (0.6 hull)
A: 2 single 12.7-mm mg
Electronics: Radar: 1 JFS Electronic 364 nav.
M: 2 Volvo Penta KAD 42 diesels; 2 props; 460 shp **Crew:** 8 tot.

Perseus (A 462006) H&L Van Ginderen, 3-98

Remarks: Glass-reinforced-plastic construction, wooden superstructure. Replaced a group of wooden-hulled craft built in 1942. Employed on Lakes Constance, Geneva, and Maggiore. *Aquarius* completed in 1978, *Pollux* in 1984, the rest in 1981. Modernized starting in 1998, receiving diesels in place of the original gasoline engines at the cost of about 5 kts maximum speed.

Notes: Swiss police agencies operate six 10-m and one 12-m patrol launches.

SYRIA
Syrian Arab Republic

Personnel: Approx. 7,600 total, plus 4,000 reserves

Bases: Principal base at Tartus, with other facilities at Al Mina al Bayda, Baniyas, and Latakia.

Naval Aviation: Helicopters: 5 Kamov Ka-28PL Helix-A ASW and 12 Mi-14PL Haze-A ASW.

Coastal Defense: Twelve batteries of SSC-1B Shaddock (possibly no longer operational) and SSC-3 Styx missiles have been transferred from the former USSR; they are located in mobile batteries at Tartous, Baniyas, and Latakia. Coast defense artillery includes 130-mm and 100-mm guns, served by a network of radar surveillance and radar fire-control equipment.

CORVETTES [FFL]

♦ 2 ex-Soviet Petya-I class (Project 159E)
Bldr: Khabarovsk Zavod

	Laid down	L	In serv.
1/508 . . . (ex-12, ex-SKR . . .)	. . .	. . .	. . .
2/508 Al Hirasa (ex-14, ex-SKR-95)	10-3-67	15-5-68	13-3-69

Al Hirasa (2/508) H&L Van Ginderen, 9-81

D: 938 tons (1,077 fl) **S:** 29 kts
Dim: 81.80 (78.00 pp) × 9.20 (8.90 wl) × 2.85 (hull)
A: 2 twin 76.2-mm 59-cal. AK-276 DP; 4 12-round RBU-2500 ASW RL; 1 triple 533-mm TT; 2 d.c. racks (6 d.c. each); 2 mine rails
Electronics:
Radar: 1 Don-2 nav.; 1 Fut-N (Slim Net) air/surf. search; 1 Fut-B (Hawk Screech) gun f.c.
Sonar: Titan hull-mounted MF; Vychegda HF searchlight attack
M: CODOG: 1 Type 61-D3 diesel (6,000 bhp), 2 M-2 gas turbines (15,000 shp each); 3 props (centerline CP)—2/75 kw auxiliary electric motors: 3 kts
Range: 450/29; 4,800/10 **Crew:** 8 officers, 84 enlisted

Remarks: Transferred 7-75 and 3-75, respectively. Based at Tartous. Both were operational in 2001, although how much longer that can be maintained is questionable.

GUIDED-MISSILE PATROL CRAFT [PTG]

♦ 8 ex-Soviet Osa-II class (Project 205ME)

33 34 35 36 37 38 39 40

D: 184 tons (226 fl; 245 overload) **S:** 40 (35 sust.) kts
Dim: 38.6 (37.5 wl) × 7.6 (5.9 wl) × 2.01 hull
A: 4 P-15M Termit (SS-N-2C Styx) SSM; 2 twin 30-mm 65-cal. AK-230 AA; 1 4-round Fasta-M point-defense SAM syst.

GUIDED-MISSILE PATROL CRAFT [PTG] *(continued)*

Syrian Osa-II French Navy, 1983

Electronics:
Radar: 1 Rangout (Square Tie) surf. search/target-detection; 1 MR-104 Rys' (Drum Tilt) gun f.c.
EW: 2 16-round PK-16 decoy RL
M: 3 M504B diesels; 3 props; 15,000 bhp **Electric:** 400 kw tot.
Range: 500/34; 750/25 **Endurance:** 5 days **Crew:** 4 officers, 24 enlisted

Remarks: Two transferred 1978, four in 1979, two in 1982, two in 5-84, two in 1985; four had been deleted by 1987. The pair delivered in 1984 were each equipped with two 16-tubed PK-16 decoy rocket launchers and a Grail point-defense SAM launcher; the others have presumably been backfitted. All are based at Latakia. As few as two may be operational.

PATROL BOATS [PB]

♦ 1 35-meter class Bldr: OCÉA, St. Nazaire, France

	In serv.
. . . PALMYRA	2005

D: 90 tons (115 fl) **S:** 30 kts **Dim:** 35.20 (29.85 wl) × 6.80 × 1.25
A: . . .
Electronics: . . .
Radar: 1 Decca 20V90 nav.; 1 Decca C 252/8 nav.
M: 2 MTU 12V396 TE94 diesels; 2 waterjets; 4,400 bhp

Remarks: Based on the *Al Shaheed* class in Kuwait coast guard service. The aluminum-construction hull has a notch amidships to permit easier rescue of persons in the water. May also operate as a navigational aids tender.

♦ 8 Soviet Zhuk (Gryf) class (Project 1400M)

1/8 2/8 3/8 4/8 5/8 6/8 7/8 8/8

D: 35.9 tons (39.7 fl) **S:** 30 kts
Dim: 23.80 (21.70 wl) × 5.00 (3.80 wl) × 1.00 (hull; 1.90 max.)
A: 2 twin 12.7-mm 60-cal. Utës-M mg **Electronics:** Radar: 1 Lotsiya nav.
M: 2 M-401 diesels; 2 props; 2,200 bhp
Electric: 48 kw total (2 × 21 kw, 1 × 6 kw diesel sets
Range: 500/13.5 **Endurance:** 5 days **Crew:** 1 officer, 9 enlisted

Remarks: Three delivered new 12-83, three in 12-84, three in 1-85; one has been stricken. Based at Tartous.
Hull systems: Aluminum alloy hull. Capable of operating in up to Sea State 4 or 5. Range also reported as 700 n. m. at 28 kts, 1,100 n.m. at 15 kts.

MINE WARFARE SHIPS AND CRAFT

♦ 1 Soviet Sonya-class (Project 1265E) coastal minesweeper [MSC] Bldr: Avangard Zavod, Petrozavodsk

532

D: 401 tons (430 fl) **S:** 14 kts
Dim: 48.80 (46.00 wl) × 10.20 (9.20 wl) × 2.40-2.50 mean hull (2.75-2.85 max.)
A: 1 twin 30-mm 65-cal. AK-230 AA; 1 twin 25-mm 80-cal. 2M-3M AA; 1 4-round Fasta-M point-defense SAM syst.; up to 5 mines
Electronics:
Radar: 1 Mius (Spin Trough) nav.
Sonar: MG-89 Serna HF hull-mounted; MG-35 underwater telephone; NEL-MZB echo sounder (see Remarks)
M: 2 DRA-210-A or DRA-210-B diesels; 2 3-bladed CP props; 2,200 or 2,000 bhp—2 low-speed thrusters
Electric: 350 kw tot. (3 × 100 kw, 1 × 50 kw diesel sets; 380 V 50 Hz a.c.)
Range: 1,700/10 **Fuel:** 27.1 tons **Endurance:** 15 days
Crew: 5–6 officers, 26–40 enlisted (45 tot. accomm.)

Remarks: Arrived in Syria 1-86. Based at Tartous.
Hull systems: Wooden construction with glass-reinforced plastic hull sheathing. Bollard pull: 10 tons at 9 kts.
Combat systems: Carries acoustic, loop and towed solenoidal magnetic, and net-sweep and mechanical sweep equipment and can lay linear mine-disposal charges. Carries GKT-2 contact sweep; ST-2, AT-2, PEMT-2 influence sweeps, and an IT-3 mine detector/exploder. The 25-mm mount is aimed by the operator, while the 30-mm mount is controlled by a Kolonka-1 ringsight director. The point-defense SAM launcher is mounted to port of the 25-mm mount. 1,000 rounds 30-mm and 2,000 rounds 25-mm are normally carried. The sonar dome pivots at the after end to retract within the hull.

♦ 3 Soviet Yevgenya-class (Project 1258) inshore minesweepers [MSI]
Bldr: Sudostroitel'noye Obyedineniye "Almaz" (Sredniy Neva), Kolpino

6/507 7/507 8/507

D: 88.5 tons light, 94.5 normal (97.9 fl) **S:** 11 kts
Dim: 26.13 (24.20 wl) × 5.90 (5.10 wl) × 1.38
A: 1 twin 25-mm 80-cal. 2M-3M AA; 4 d.c. (+ 8 emergency stowage)
Electronics:
Radar: 1 Mius (Spin Trough) nav.
Sonar: MG-7 HF dipping
M: 2 Type 3D12 diesels; 2 props; 600 bhp—hydraulic slow-speed drive
Electric: 100 kw tot. (2 × 50 kw diesel sets) **Range:** 400/10 **Fuel:** 2.7 tons
Endurance: 3 days **Crew:** 1 officer, 9 enlisted (+ 2–3 clearance divers)

Remarks: First unit transferred 1978, second in 1981, the third and fourth arrived on 15-2-85, and the fifth on 19-1-86. Sisters 4/507 and 5/507 had been stricken by the end of 1997. Based at Tartous.
Hull systems: Glass-reinforced plastic hull. Navigational equipment includes Girya-MA gyrocompass and NEL-7 echo sounder. The last two delivered had tripod masts.
Combat systems: Can employ a Neva-1 television minehunting system useful to 30 m depths that dispenses marker buoys to permit later disposal of mines by divers or explosive charges. The sonar is lowered via one of the stern davits. Carry VKT-1 mechanical, AT-2 acoustic, and SEMT-1 solenoid coil sweep gear.

AMPHIBIOUS WARFARE SHIPS AND CRAFT

♦ 3 Soviet Polnocny-B-class (Project 771) medium landing ships [LSM] Bldr: Stocznia Polnocna, Gdansk

1/114 2/114 3/114

D: 558 tons light, 640 tons std. (884 fl) **S:** 18 kts
Dim: 75.00 (70.00 wl) × 9.00 (8.60 wl) × 1.20 fwd/2.40 aft (2.07 mean)
A: 1 or 2 twin 30-mm 65-cal. AK-230 AA; 2 18-round 140-mm WM-18 barrage RL (180 rockets); 2 or 4 4-round Fasta-M point-defense SAM syst.
Electronics: Radar: 1 Mius (Spin Trough) nav.; 1 MR-104 Rys' (Drum Tilt) f.c.
M: 2 Type 40DM diesels; 2 props; 4,400 bhp **Range:** 700/18; 2,000/16
Crew: 5 officers, 32 enlisted + 60–180 troops

Remarks: One transferred from USSR 15-1-84, two in 2-85. Based at Tartous and used primarily as coastal logistics support transports.
Hull systems: Have a bow-door only, and the hull has a "beak" projecting forward below the waterline at the bow to aid in beaching. Hatches to upper deck are for loading and ventilation only. Cargo: 237 tons max., including six tanks or 180 troops and their equipment; 30 vehicle crew are carried with tank loadout. Vehicle deck is 44.3 m long by 5.3 m wide and 3.6 m high.

AUXILIARIES

♦ 1 modified Soviet Natya-class (Project 266E) oceanographic research ship [AGOR]
Bldr: Sudostroitel'noye Obyedineniye "Almaz" (Sredniy Neva), Kolpino (In serv. 1985)

642

Syrian Natya 642—prior to conversion from training ship to oceanographic research vessel French Navy, 1985

D: 750 tons std., 804 tons normal **S:** 17.6 kts (16 sust.)
Dim: 61.00 (57.6 wl) × 10.20 × 2.98 hull **A:** Removed
Electronics: Radar: 1 Don-2 nav.; 1 MR-104 Rys' (Drum Tilt) f.c.
M: 2 M-503B-3E diesels: 2 shrouded CP props; 5,000 bhp
Electric: 600 kw tot. (3 × 200 kw DGR-200/1500 diesel sets)
Range: 1,800/16; 3,000/12; 5,200/10 **Endurance:** 10–15 days
Crew: 8 officers, 59 enlisted

COAST GUARD PATROL BOATS [WPB] *(continued)*

Remarks: Built specifically as a training ship, with no ASW ordnance or mine-countermeasures systems, arriving from the USSR in 1-85. Converted to serve as an oceanographic research ship during early 1990s and now painted white.
Hull systems: Low magnetic signature, aluminum-steel alloy hull.
Combat systems: Delivered armed with two twin 30-mm AK-230 and two twin 25-mm 2M-3M AA mounts, now removed, but retains the MR-104 Rys' radar associated with the 30-mm mounts.

♦ **1 training ship/transport [AXT]**
Bldr: Stocznia Pólnocna SY, Gdansk (In serv. 1989)

AL ASSAD

Al Assad Bernard Prézelin, 7-03

D: Approx. 7,500 tons (fl) **S:** 16 kts **Dim:** 115.90 (106.93 pp) × 18.02 × 6.01
A: None **Electronics:** Radar: 2 . . . nav.
M: 2 Zgoda-Sulzer 6ZL 40/48 diesels; 2 props; 8,700 bhp—bow-thruster
Electric: 1,512 kw tot. (3 × 504 kw diesel sets; 400 V, 50 Hz a.c.)
Range: 12,500/15 **Crew:** 56 tot. + 140 trainees

Remarks: 7,191 grt/3,459 dwt. Ordered at the beginning of 1984 and launched 8-2-87. Combination naval and merchant marine training ship and vehicle and personnel transport. Can carry 60 standard 20-ft. cargo containers and has 3,606-m^3 bale cargo capacity. Has stern ramp for vehicle cargo. Based at Latakia.

SERVICE CRAFT

♦ **3 survey launches [YGS]**
Bldr: ARCOR, La Teste, France (In serv. 1985)

D: 9 tons (fl) **S:** 25 kts **Dim:** 9.80 (8.50 pp) × 3.40 × 0.90
M: 2 Volvo Penta AQAD-40 diesels; 2 props; 310 bhp **Range:** 300/ . . .
Crew: 4 tot.

Remarks: Ordered in 12-84. GRP construction.

TAIWAN

Republic of China

Personnel: 45,000 total navy including 15,000 Marines; plus approximately 67,000 naval reservists and Marine reservists.

Bases: Organized into three Naval Districts: First Naval District, with headquarters at Tsoying and naval shipyard at Kaohsiung; Second Naval District, with headquarters and naval shipyard at Makung in the Pescadores Islands; and Third Naval District, with headquarters and naval shipyard at Keelung. Other naval facilities at Anping, Hualien, Kuhai, Suao, and Wuchi.

Naval Aviation: The Naval Aviation Command's equipment includes eight McDonnell Douglas MD-500/ASW and 19 Sikorsky S-70C(M)-1 Thunderhawk helicopters for land-based use (the MD-500s occasionally are deployed aboard destroyers and frigates). The S-70C(M)-1 helicopter is an export-version of the U.S. Navy SH-60B Seahawk and is equipped with APS-128PC radar, ASN-150 tactical navigation system, ALR-606 ESM gear, one or two ARR-84 99-channel sonobuoy receivers, and MAD gear. Two Thunderhawks have been reconfigured as SIGINT collectors. The MD-500s have ASQ-81(V)2 MAD gear and can lift one torpedo. Eleven S-70C(M)2 helicopters configured for shipboard service were ordered on 26-6-97 for use in the new *La Fayette*–class frigates. Negotiations to acquire a dozen ex-USN SH-2F SeaSprite shipboard helicopters for service aboard the *Knox*-class have been under way for at least five years, without result. A dozen ex-USN MH-53E mine-countermeasures helicopters have also been ordered and delivery will likely occur around 2010.

S-2T Tracker *DTM,* 1-01

S-70C(M)-1 Thunderhawk *DTM,* 7-00

MD-500/ASW—with torpedo and MAD gear aboard *DTM,* 1-01

The Grumman S-2E Trackers of the ROCAF's 439th Composite Wing were transferred to the ROCN on 1-7-98. Two Trackers were modernized in 1991 by Grumman to S-2T standard with Garrett TPE-331-15AW turboprops (1,640 shp each), AQS-902F digital sonobuoy processor, ARR-84 99-channel sonobuoy receiver, DIFAR and CODAR capability, Litton APS-504 radar, ASQ-504 MAD, and AAS-40 FLIR (in place of the former searchlight); 18 other aircraft were modernized by Chung-Shan Institute of Science and Technology at Taichung. Two S-2Es are fitted for EW vice ASW duties. The surviving S-2 airframes are to be replaced by 12 P-3C Orions delivered between 2009 and 2011.

The Republic of China Air Force (ROCAF) operates six Grumman E-2T Hawkeye APS-145 radar-equipped airborne early warning and air control aircraft. A number of ROCAF are equipped for a maritime strike role with Hsiung Feng II air-to-surface missiles. In 9-98, the U.S. sold Taiwan 58 air-launched AGM-84 Harpoon antiship missiles for launch from ROCAF F-16 fighters.

Marine Corps: The Marine Corps has some 150 U.S.-built LVT-5 tracked amphibious vehicles (in troop-carrying, command, and beach salvage variants), plus 155-mm and 105-mm artillery. 60 AAV7A1 amphibious tracked personnel carriers were purchased during 2003 with delivery commencing in 2005. Shore-based antiship missile systems, transferred to the Marine Corps in 2003, include land-based mobile batteries with Hsiung Feng II antiship missiles.

WEAPONS AND SYSTEMS

A. MISSILES

♦ **Surface-to-surface missile systems:**

Gabriel Mk II: An unknown number of Israeli-provided Gabriel Mk II antiship missiles remain in inventory; they can be launched by the same launchers used for the Hsiung Feng I system.

Harpoon (RGM-84A): Imported U.S. weapon, launched from U.S.-supplied *Knox*-class frigates; 41 were purchased in 1993, 58 AGM-84A air-launched variants were ordered in 1998 for the Air Force, and 71 RGM-84L Block 2 variants of the missile were requested during 9-00, plus six training missiles and ten launch command sets, for use on the PFG-2 class. In 6-03 it was announced that 32 RGM-84L Block II Harpoon missiles would be delivered in stages for use by the ex-*Kidd*-class DDGs. In 2005 Taiwan announced that the missile would also begin arming the Hai Lung–class submarines. See data in U.S. section.

Hsiung Feng I: Indigenously developed and based on the Gabriel Mk II, with numerous improvements. *Hsiung Feng* means "Mighty Wind."

Length: 3.43 m **Diameter:** 0.34 m **Wingspan:** 1.366 m **Weight:** 537.5 kg
Warhead: 180 kg **Speed:** Mach 0.7 **Range:** 36–40 km **Altitude:** 1–3 m

Hsiung Feng II: Developed by the Chung-Shan Institute of Science and Technology. Powered by a turbojet, it has a mid-course guidance provision and an active X-band radar seeker *plus* IR seekers. The weapon is capable of air, surface, and land launch and may be adapted for submarine launch. First air launches were made in 1993, using an AT-3 jet trainer to carry the missile and an F-104 fighter to provide targeting. Shipboard launched from quadruple box launchers oriented athwartships. Mobile land

WEAPONS AND SYSTEMS *(continued)*

launchers for the missile were to enter service during 6-02, but the first land-launch did not take place until 16-5-02. Powered by a Microturbo 078 turbojet. Missiles being produced as of 2001 have a range of 170 km, an improved imaging infrared seeker, and a self-forging fragmentation warhead.

Length: 4.845 m **Diameter:** 0.4 m **Wingspan:** 1.15 m **Weight:** 695 kg
Warhead: 190 kg **Speed:** Mach 0.85 **Range:** 150–170 km **Altitude:** 5–7 m

Note: A 300-km-ranged, supersonic, land-attack Hsiung-III missile is under development.

♦ Surface-to-air missile systems:

Sea Chaparral: Manned, quadruple launcher for the MIM-72F adaptation of the heat-seeking AIM-9D Sidewinder AAM. Originally developed during Vietnam War for the U.S. Navy. Used on Taiwanese Navy frigates, amphibious ships, and auxiliaries; the normal outfit is 16 missiles per launcher. Missile data:

Length: 2.908 m **Diameter:** 0.127 m **Wingspan:** 0.701 m
Weight: 85.7 kg **Warhead:** 11.34 kg **Speed:** Mach 1.7–2.5
Range: 1.2–9.4 km **Altitude:** 4,755 m max.

RAM: In 2-93 it was announced that the U.S. was planning to sell the RIM-116A RAM point-defense SAM system to Taiwan, possibly for use aboard the planned new class of medium-sized patrol ships; no mounts have been ordered to date, however.

Standard SM-1MR: U.S.-made; used aboard *Knox*-class FFGs and PFG-2 FFGs. In 1992 204 SM-1 Block VI missiles were ordered for use aboard the new frigates.

Standard SM-2MR: U.S.-made; to be carried in the ex-*Kidd*-class DDGs. In 6-03 an order was concluded for purchase of 148 SM-2 Block IIIA missiles.

B. SHIPBOARD GUNS:

U.S-made guns in use include 127-mm Mk 42 Mod. 9 single DP; 76.2-mm Mk 33 twin DP; 76-mm Mk 75 DP (or the original Italian-made OTO Melara version); 40-mm 60-cal. Bofors AA in single Mk 3, twin Mk 1 Mod. 2, and quadruple Mk 2 mountings; 20-mm Mk 11 Mod. 0 Phalanx close-in weapons systems (CIWS); and a few 20-mm 70-cal Oerlikon AA in U.S. Mk 10 single or Mk 24 twin mountings. The indigenously developed 580-kg T75 AA mounting employs 20-mm 68-cal. M39A2 or M39A3 aircraft cannon, which have a 2,000-m practical range when used on ships.

The Taiwanese Mk 62 gun fire-control system uses existing U.S. Mk 51 Mod. 2 and Mk 52 fire-control system with stabilization added to enable them to be employed against surface targets; a total of 38 systems were manufactured in the 1960s, and these have been recycled to newer ships. Other weapons control systems are of U.S. and French origin.

C. TORPEDOES:

In use are U.S.-made Mk 44 and Mk 46 antisubmarine torpedoes. In 9-98, 131 Alliant Mk 46 Mod. 5A(S) ASW torpedoes were ordered from the United States, primarily for use with helicopters; another 41 were ordered during 3-99. Taiwan's Wang Siang Guan underwater ordnance laboratory is working on the Kang Lung (Proud Dragon) heavyweight, 533-mm wire-guided torpedo project. A 7-02 press report revealed that U.S. Mk 48 Mod. 3 wire-guided torpedoes had been in service since the early 1990s and that existing stocks were to be augmented by the Mod. 4 version.

D. ASW ORDNANCE:

The U.S. Mk 16 Mod. 8 ASROC system, with eight-celled Mk 112 launchers, is installed on *Knox*-class frigates, and missiles with Mk 46 Mod. 5 torpedo payloads have been acquired. Many ships are equipped with U.S. Mk 9–design racks for Mk 9 quick-sinking depth charges (154.2 kg weight, with 88.45 kg explosive payload). The cylindrical Mk 6 depth charge is also still in use: 190.5 kg with 136.1 kg explosive payload.

E. MINES:

Mk 6 Mod. 14: Bottom-moored spherical mechanical contact mine of U.S. design. Diameter 105.41 cm, weighing 635 kg with Mk 6 Mod. 5 or Mod. 16 anchor and with 136 kg of explosives. Some are equipped with a contact buoy tethered to the top of the mine casing.

WSM 110: Air-dropped or surface-launched cylindrical bottom influence mine. 1690 mm long by 485 mm diameter; weighs 635 kg with 295-kg explosive payload.

WSM 111: A moored, rocket-assisted rising mine for antisubmarine use. In development 2001 by Chungshan Institute of Science and Technology.

WSM 210: Spindle-shaped bottom influence mine with 295-kg explosive payload. Intended for launch from surface ships and can be laid in waters from 30 to 120 m deep. WS-II-series mines made after 1990 have a microprocessor, use multi-influence sensors, and can be laid in shallower water.

F. SENSORS AND COUNTERMEASURES:

To date, most shipboard equipment has been of U.S. and French design and manufacture. Locally developed have been the Tacheng combat data link system (also known as "Link-T"), which is hosted on an off-the-shelf Acer personal computer system, and the CR-201 King Feng 127-mm countermeasures rocket launcher, which uses a 16-tubed trainable launcher. Litton WD-2A radar-warning equipment (equivalent to ALR-66 aircraft gear) is being employed on smaller combatants and auxiliaries, and the U.S. Mk 36 Mod. 1 and 2 SRBOC (Super Rapid Blooming Offboard Countermeasures) launch system is used on newer ships. The French Matra Défense Dagaie Mk II decoy launcher is aboard the *La Fayette*–class frigates, along with French/ European sensors.

Note: China Shipbuilding Corporation, with yards at Kaohsiung and Keelung, was for sale as of 6-00 but continues to operate.

ATTACK SUBMARINES [SS]

Note: U.S. President George W. Bush announced on 24-4-01 that the U.S. would provide eight conventionally powered diesel-electric submarines for Taiwan, but almost immediately the governments of the Netherlands, Australia, and Germany, in order to appease China, declared that their submarine builders could not participate. As of late 2006, the deal remained on hold due to a number of political and international issues.

♦ 2 Hai Lung class

Bldr: Wilton Fijenoord, Schiedam, the Netherlands

	Laid down	L	Delivered	In serv.
793 Hai Lung	12-82	4-10-86	9-10-87	9-10-87
794 Hai Hu	12-82	20-12-86	9-4-88	4-7-88

Hai Lung (793)—in dry dock *Ships of the World,* 2005

Hai Lung (793) *Ships of the World*

D: 2,370 tons max. surf./2,657 tons sub. **S:** 11 kts (surf.)/20 kts (sub.)
Dim: 66.92 × 8.40 × 6.70
A: 6 bow 533-mm TT fwd (28 German SUT and/or U.S. Mk 48 Mod. 3 wire-guided torpedoes or Harpoon SSM)
Electronics:
Radar: 1 Thales ZW-06 nav./surface search
Sonar: Thales SIASS-Z integrated passive/active suite
EW: Elbit TIMNEX 4 CH(V)2 intercept (2–18 gHz)

ATTACK SUBMARINES [SS] *(continued)*

M: 3 Brons/Stork-Werkspoor 12 ORUB 215 diesels (1,350 bhp each); 2 922-kw Holec DG.110/47/90 alternator groups, 1 Holec 3,800-kw motor; 1 5-bladed prop; 5,100 shp sub./1,400 shp surf.
Range: 10,000/9 (surf.) **Fuel:** 310 tons **Crew:** 8 officers, 59 enlisted

Remarks: Ordered late 1980, over mainland China's protests. The design, which is based closely on that of the Dutch *Zwaardvis* class, is also referred to as the "Sea Dragon" class, as the names mean "Sea Dragon" and "Sea Tiger," respectively. Request for two more (and option for fifth and sixth) turned down by Dutch government in 1984, due to Chinese pressure. Highly automated design. 794 ran aground while submerged early in 10-01 but was not seriously damaged. Will likely be fitted with an air-independent-propulsion system in the future.
Hull systems: Two 196-cell batteries. Normal operational diving depth: 240 m.
Combat systems: SINBADS-M, eight-target track data system, Sperry Mk 29 Mod. 2A inertial navigation system. A submerged-launch variant of the Hsiung Feng II antiship missile is in development for use by these and any later submarines. Have the Carl Zeiss SERO 40 periscope suite, with AS 40 attack and BS 40 attack periscopes. In 2005 Taiwan announced the capability to launch the Harpoon SSM from the class.

AUXILIARY SUBMARINES [SSA]

♦ 2 ex-U.S. GUPPY II class

	Bldr	Laid down	L	In serv.
791 HAI SHIH (ex-*Cutlass,* SS 478)	Portsmouth, NSY, Portsmouth, N.H.	22-7-44	5-11-44	17-3-45
792 HAI PAO (ex-*Tusk,* SS 426)	Cramp SB Philadelphia, Pa.	23-8-43	8-7-45	11-4-46

Hai Pao (792) *Taiwan Defense Review,* 8-98

D: 1,517 tons (std.); 1,870 tons (surf.)/2,440 tons (sub.)
S: 18 kts (surf.)/16 kts (sub.) **Dim:** 93.57 × 8.33 × 5.18
A: 10 533-mm TT (6 fwd, 4 aft; 22 torpedoes—but may have none)
Electronics:
Radar: 1 SS-2 search—EW: WLR-1G, WLR-3 intercept
Sonar: BQR-2B passive, BQS-4C active (7 kHz), DUUG-1B sonar intercept
M: Diesel-electric propulsion: 4 Fairbanks-Morse 38D8Q diesels; 2 electric motors; 2 props; 4,610 bhp (surf.)/5,200 shp (sub.)
Range: 10,000/10 (surf.); 95/5 (sub.) **Fuel:** 330 tons
Crew: 11 officers, 70 enlisted

Remarks: Transferred 12-4-73 and 18-10-73, for ASW training. Four 126-cell batteries. Source of torpedoes, if any, uncertain: may use old Japanese or U.S. Mk 14 World War II–era straight-runners, Indonesian-supplied German SUT, or U.K. Mk 24 Tigerfish; the tubes were welded shut at time of delivery but may have been made operational again. Diving depth originally limited to 122 m but is probably much less now. New propeller shafts were ordered from the U.S. for both in 1999, indicating an intention to keep them in service.

GUIDED-MISSILE DESTROYERS [DDG]

♦ 4 ex-U.S. Kidd class
Bldr: Northrop Grumman Ingalls SB, Pascagoula, Miss.

	Laid down	L	In serv.
1801 KEELUNG (ex-Chiteh, ex-*Scott*, DDG 995)	12-2-79	1-3-80	24-10-81
1802 SUAO (ex-Mingteh, ex-*Callaghan*, DDG 994)	23-10-78	1-12-79	29-8-81
1803 TSOYING (ex-Tongteh, ex-*Kidd*, DDG 993)	26-6-78	11-8-79	27-6-81
1805 MAKUNG (ex-Wuteh, ex-*Chandler*, DDG 996)	7-5-79	24-5-80	13-3-82

D: 7,326 tons light (9, 950 fl) **S:** 30+ kts
Dim: 171.70 (161.23 fl) × 16.76 × 7.01 (10.06 over sonar)

Makung (1805)—while still in U.S. Navy service H&L Van Ginderen, 3-98

Suao (1802)—while still in U.S. Navy service 93 Wing Det. A, RAAF, 3-94

A: 2 2-rail Mk 26 missile launchers (68 Standard SM-2MR Block IIIA missiles); 8 RGM-84L Block II Harpoon SSM; 2 single 127-mm 54-cal. Mk 45 Mod. 1 DP; 2 20-mm Mk 15 Phalanx gatling CIWS; 2 triple Mk 32 Mod. 5 ASW TT (24 Mk 46 Mod. 5 torpedoes); 1 . . . helicopter
Electronics:
Radar: 1 Raytheon SPS-64(V)9 nav.; 1 Cardion SPS-55 surf. search; 1 Raytheon SPS-49(V)5 air search; 1 ITT SPS-48E 3-D early warning; 2 Raytheon SPG-51D missile illumination; 1 Lockheed Martin SPG-60 illumination/gun f.c.; 1 Lockheed Martin SPQ-9A surf. gun f.c.; 2 General Dynamics Mk 90 Phalanx f.c.
Sonar: EDO-G.E. SQS-53A bow-mounted LF
EW: Raytheon SLQ-32(V)5 passive, with Sidekick jammer; Mk 36 SRBOC decoy syst. (4 6-round Mk 137 RL); SLQ-25 Nixie towed torpedo decoy TACAN: URN-25
M: 4 G.E. LM-2500 gas turbines; 2 5-bladed props; 86,000 shp (80,000 shp sust.)
Electric: 6,000 kw tot. (3 × 2,000 kw Allision 501K gas turbine-driven alternators; 360–400 Hz)
Range: 3,300/30; 6,000/20 **Fuel:** 1,534 tons + 72 tons aviation fuel
Crew: 28 officers, 320 enlisted

Remarks: Named after Taiwanese port cities and numbered in accordance with their order of reactivation. Offered by the U.S. on 1-1-01. Reactivation and refit (performed at Detyens Shipyard in South Carolina) cost approximately $800 million. The first to be reactivated, *Keelung* and *Suao*, sailed for Taiwan in November 2005. The remaining two units, *Tsoying* and *Makung*, entered Taiwanese service in 2006. Characteristics and equipment listed previously describe the ships in U.S. Navy service; they may have been considerably altered during reactivation. Permission to buy the ships was obtained from the legislature during 11-02. Transferred with the ships were 248 Standard SM-2 Block IIIA and 32 RGM-84L Block II Harpoon missiles.
Hull systems: Extensive use of Kevlar and aluminum armor raised their displacements by around 1,000 tons.
Combat systems: All four received the New Threat Upgrade improvements between 1988 and 1990 and are equipped with the Mk 14 weapons direction system. They also have the Naval Tactical Data System (NTDS), with Links 4A, 11, and 14. Two Mk 74 missile fire-control systems employ the two SPG-51D missile illuminators and the SPG-60 gun fire-control radar to enable attacking three aerial targets simultaneously; there are four SYR-1 missile telemetry receivers. The Mk 86 Mod. 5 gun fire-control system uses the SPQ-9A radar for surface fire and the SPG-60 radar for AA fire. The Mk 116 underwater fire-control system handles ship-launched ASW torpedo launching (and formerly ASROC ASW missile launching). Mk 41 vertical launch systems may be selected to replace the Mk 26 launchers at a later date.

Disposal note: The seven remaining ex-U.S. *Gearing* FRAM-I–class Wu Chin III conversion destroyers, *Chien Yang* (912), *Liao Yang* (921), *Shen Yang* (923), *Te Yang* (925), *Yun Yang* (927), *Chen Yang* (928), and *Shao Yang* (929), were retired by 2005.

GUIDED-MISSILE FRIGATES [FFG]

♦ 8 PFG-2 class (Kuang Hua I program)

Bldr: China SB Corp., Kaohsiung

	Laid down	L	In serv.
1101 Cheung Kung	2-12-90	27-10-91	7-5-93
1103 Cheng Ho	21-12-91	15-10-92	28-3-94
1105 Chi Kuang	4-10-92	27-9-93	4-3-95
1106 Yueh Fei	5-9-93	26-8-94	7-2-96
1107 Tzu I	7-8-94	13-7-95	9-1-97
1108 Pan Chao	7-95	3-7-96	16-12-97
1109 Chang Chien	6-96	14-5-97	1-12-98
1110 Tian Dan	4-01	17-10-02	3-04

Pan Chao (1108) Chris Sattler, 4-02

Pan Chao (1108)—note the Hsiung Feng II ASM box launchers abaft the bridge Chris Sattler, 4-02

D: 3,207 tons light (4,104 fl) **S:** 27.5 kts
Dim: 138.07 (125.90 wl) × 14.31 (13.72 wl) × 5.70 (8.60 max.)
A: 8 Hsiung Feng II SSM; 1 Mk 13 Mod. 4 guided-missile launch syst. (40 Standard SM-1 MR SAM and RGM-84L Harpoon SSM); 1 76-mm 62-cal. OTO Melara DP; 2 single 40-mm 70-cal. Bofors AA; 1 20-mm Mk 15 Phalanx gatling CIWS; 3 single 20-mm 68-cal. Type 75 AA; 2 triple Mk 32 Mod. 5 ASW TT (Mk 46 Mod. 5 torpedoes); 1 S-70C(M)-2 Thunderhawk ASW helicopter
Electronics:
Radar: 1 Cardion SPS-55 surf. search; 1 Raytheon SPS-49(V)5 air-search; 1 Raytheon Mk 92 Mod. 6 f.c.; 1 Thales STIR-24 missile f.c.; 1 General Dynamics Mk 90 Phalanx f.c.
Sonar: Raytheon DE-1160B hull-mounted MF; provision for: EDO SQR-18A(V)2 towed passive linear hydrophone array or Thales ATAS/Lamproie towed passive/active linear hydrophone array
EW: Chang Feng IV suite (SLQ-32(V)5 intercept, Sidekick jammer); Mk 36 SRBOC decoy syst. (2 6-round Mk 137 RL); SLQ-25A Nixie towed acoustic torpedo decoy

Cheung Kung (1101) H&L Van Ginderen, 1-99

M: 2 G.M. LM-2500 gas turbines; 1 CP prop; 40,420 shp—2 drop-down electric propulsors; 720 shp
Electric: 4,000 kw tot. (4 × 1,000-kw diesel alternator sets)
Range: 4,200/20; 5,000/18 **Fuel:** 587 tons + 64 tons helicopter fuel
Crew: 13 officers, 193 enlisted + 19 air group

Remarks: Ordered 8-5-89. Design is a slightly modified version of the "long-hulled" U.S. Navy *Oliver Hazard Perry* class. Named for Chinese maritime heroes. Construction of the first two aided by "kits" supplied by Bath Iron Works, which also provided technical assistance in constructing the others. Detail design by Gibbs & Cox. Originally only four were to have been built to the basic design, but development of the phased-array radar and vertically launched SAM for the Batch II, updated variant lagged, and the Batch II program was canceled altogether in 10-94. Are all assigned to the 124th Frigate Squadron. Funds to construct the eighth unit were provided in the 1999 budget; the ship had earlier been canceled in 10-94 and was to be reordered during 1-99, but the actual contract was delayed to 12-00.
Hull systems: Have fin stabilizers, rudder roll-control, and the Prairie/Masker acoustic sound signature reduction air-bubble generation system.
Combat systems: The U.S. Norden Systems SYS-2(V)2 sensor data fusion system is installed, as is the Vitro Cando off-the-shelf computerized data system, which assists the Mk 92 weapons control system. A RAST helicopter hold-down and transfer system is fitted. *Chi Kuang* (1105) was the first of the class to have a data link, backfitted into the earlier pair. The Hsiung Feng II missiles are carried in box launchers atop the superstructure, abaft the bridge; they are launched by a U.S. Hughes-supplied missile-control system that can also control the 40-mm guns. The 40-mm mounts cannot be manned when the 76-mm gun is firing, due to blast effects. The 20-mm guns are modified M-39 aircraft cannon and are mounted atop the hangar (flanking the Phalanx) and forward of the Mk 92 fire-control system radome. The towed sonar array will not be installed until later; the EDO system offered would incorporate an AMSP2 processor, while the Thales system would have both active and passive capabilities. To be used by the Mk 13 launcher, 71 RGM-84L Harpoon Block II missiles were requested from the U.S. for this class in 9-00; they will replace the Hsiung Feng II launchers, which will be mounted ashore for coastal defense and aboard *Jing Jiang*–class patrol combatants. The class may be fitted with a Mk 49 RAM SAM launcher and RIM-116 missiles at a later date.

FRIGATES [FF]

♦ 6 La Fayette class (Project Kuang Hua II)

Bldr: DCN, Lorient

	Laid down	L	In serv.
1202 Kang Ting	1-9-93	12-3-94	24-5-96
1203 Hsi Ning	28-3-94	5-11-94	12-10-96
1205 Kun Ming	7-11-94	13-5-95	26-2-97
1206 Ti Hua	1-7-95	25-11-95	14-8-97
1207 Wu Chang	1-7-95	25-11-95	16-12-97
1208 Cheng De	27-12-95	26-7-96	9-3-98

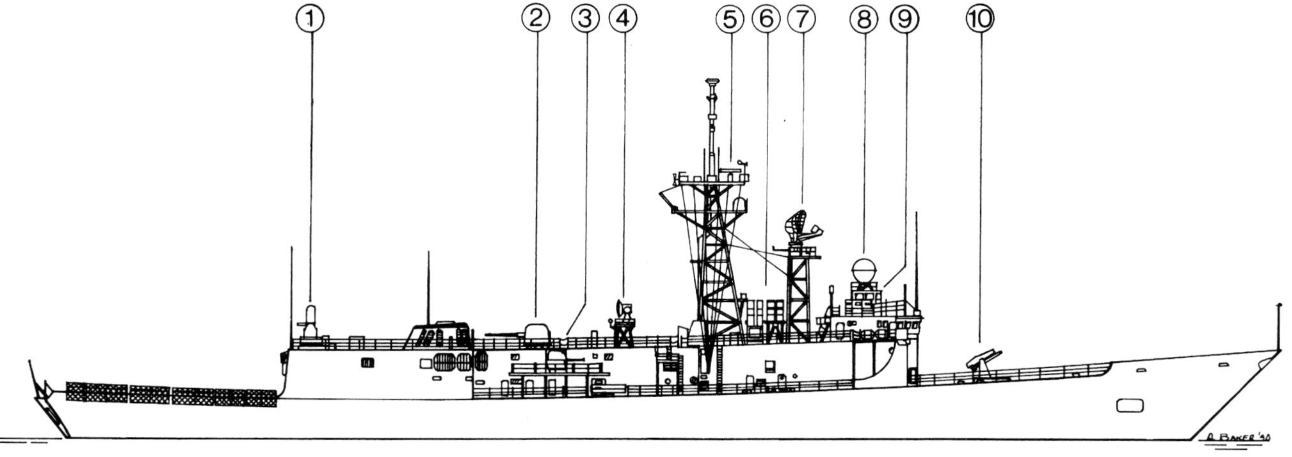

Cheung Kung (1101) 1. 20-mm Mk 15 Phalanx CIWS 2. 76-mm 62-cal. OTO Melara DP 3. 40-mm 70-cal. Bofors AA 4. STIR-24 weapons-control radar 5. SPS-55 surface-search radar 6. Hsiung Feng II antiship missile launch canisters (to be removed) 7. SPS-49(V)5 air-search radar 8. Mk 92 Mod. 6 weapons-control radar 9. Chang Feng IV/SLQ-32(V)5 EW system antenna group 10. Mk 13 Mod. 4 missile launcher
Drawing by A. D. Baker III

FRIGATES [FF] *(continued)*

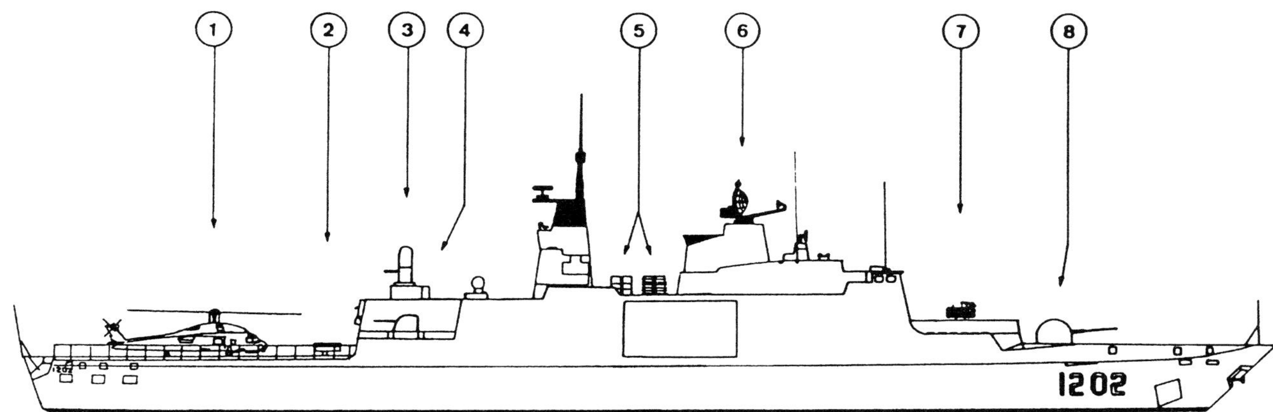

Kang Ting (1202) 1. S-70C(M)-1 Thunderhawk helicopter 2. Triple Mk 32 ASW TT 3. 20-mm Mk 15 Phalanx CIWS 4. 40-mm 70-cal. Bofors AA 5. Hsiung Feng II antiship missiles 6. Jupiter air-search radar 7. Launcher for Sea Chaparral SAM system 8. 76-mm 62-cal. OTO Melara DP Drawing by Jean Moulin, from *Flottes de Combat*

Ti Hua (1206) Chris Sattler, 4-06

Ti Hua (1206) Chris Sattler, 4-06

Ti Hua (1206) Chris Sattler, 4-06

D: 3,680 tons (fl) **S:** 28 kts **Dim:** 125.00 × 15.40 (13.80 wl) × 4.00 hull
A: 8 Hsiung Feng II SSM; 1 4-round Sea Chaparral SAM syst. (16 MIM-72F missiles); 1 76-mm 62-cal. U.S. Mk 75 DP; 2 single 40-mm 70-cal. Bofors AA; 1 20-mm Mk 15 Mod. 11 Block 1A Phalanx CIWS; 2 triple 324-mm Mk 32 Mod. 5 ASW TT (Mk 46 Mod. 5 torpedoes); 1 S-70C(M)-1 Thunderhawk ASW helicopter
Electronics:
Radar: 2 Decca 20V90 nav.; 1 Thales Triton-G surf. search; 1 Thales Jupiter air-search; 2 Thales Castor-IIC f.c.; 1 General Dynamics Mk 90 Phalanx f.c.
Sonar: Thales TSM 2633 Spherion-B hull-mounted (MF); provision for: Thales ATAS (V)3 ALOSE/Lamproie active towed linear array (3 kHz)
EW: . . . intercept/jamming; 2 33-340-round Matra Défense Dagaie Mk. 2 decoy RL
E/O: 2 Matra Défense Najir target designation and gun f.c.

M: 4 SEMT-Pielstick 16 PA 6 BTC diesels; 2 CP props; 31,800 bhp
Electric: 2,250 kw tot. (3 × 750 kw diesel alternator sets)
Range: 7,000/15; 9,000/12 **Fuel:** . . .
Endurance: 50 days **Crew:** 20 officers, 156 enlisted

Remarks: Also referred to by Taiwan as the PF class and by the builders as the FL-3000 class or MOP-1 class. Project definition contract granted to France 11-6-89; construction contract signed 27-9-91. Originally, France was to deliver the first six hulls without weapons or sensors to Taiwan for fitting out (earlier it had been proposed to deliver the hulls in prefabricated sections). In mid-1993, however, it was decided to build the six ships under contract entirely in France, saving about $120 million. In 1-94 France and the People's Republic of China announced that no more orders would be accepted, but that was later clarified to mean that no more beyond the total of 14 on option, but no more have been ordered. The ships are named for the capital cities of mainland Chinese provinces. 1202 arrived 18-5-96 and required only a week to outfit with armament prior to commissioning. They constitute Frigate Squadron 124 and are based at Tsoying.
Hull systems: A particular effort has been made to reduce the ships' signatures; the diesel propulsion engines are mounted in pairs on isolation platforms, and the superstructure, masts, and forecastle are covered with radar-absorbent GRP-resin compound. Much of the superstructure is built of GRP. Vertical hull and superstructure surfaces are slanted at plus or minus 10 degrees to reduce radar reflectivity. The ships are also fitted with degaussing equipment and extensive NBC warfare protection. Special armor is provided for the magazines. All chocks, bollards, and boat recesses are covered to reduce radar reflectivity. Employ a modified deep-vee hull form, fin stabilizers, and rudder-controlled roll reduction to improve seaworthiness. There are two rudders, and the hull form incorporates twin skegs aft. Hull has 11 watertight compartments. The French SAMAHE helicopter deck downhaul and deck transiting system turned out to be incompatible with the S-70C(M)1 helicopter and has been modified; the helicopter can be launched and recovered in up to Sea State 6. Boats are stowed in superstructure recesses that are covered to reduce radar reflection. One Taiwanese source states that SEMT-Pielstick 12PA 6V 280STC diesels are installed, for a total of 21,000 bhp and a maximum speed of only 25 kts.
Combat systems: The ships have the Thomson-CSF TAVITAC 2000 fully distributed combat data system with five Vista display consoles and a Precilec DHS plotting table. The Sea Chaparral system will likely be replaced by a more modern SAM system in the near future. The 76-mm guns were made by OTO Melara, but to the U.S. Mk 75 pattern. The Jupiter radar employs the antenna from the Thales LW-08 radar. 1207 has a Taiwanese-developed EW system for trials. At least one unit had what appeared to be the French ARBB 33 Salamandre active jamming system in 1999, but none has yet been fitted with the planned SLQ-32(V)5 suite, a torpedo decoy system, or the planned ATAS (Active Towed-Array Sonar) active/passive linear hydrophone array with Mustang acoustic processor.

♦ 8 ex-U.S. Knox class

Bldr: Avondale SY (now Northrop Grumman SB), Westwego, La. (932: Lockheed SB, Seattle, Wash.)

	Laid down	L	In serv.
932 Chi Yang (ex-*Robert E. Peary*, FF 1073; ex-*Conolly,* FF 1073)	20-12-70	23-6-71	23-9-72
933 Feng Yang (ex-*Brewton*, FF 1086)	2-10-70	24-7-71	8-7-72
934 Fen Yang (ex-*Kirk*, FF 1087)	4-12-70	25-9-71	9-9-72
935 Lan Yang (ex-*Joseph Hewes*, FFT 1078)	15-5-69	7-3-70	24-4-71
936 Hae Yang (ex-*Cook*, FF 1083)	20-3-70	23-1-71	18-12-71
937 Hwai Yang (ex-*Barbey*, FF 1088)	5-2-71	4-12-71	11-11-72
938 Ning Yang (ex-*Aylwin*, FF 1081)	13-11-69	29-8-70	18-9-71
939 Yi Yang (ex-*Valdez*, FF 1096)	30-6-72	24-3-73	27-7-74

D: 3,075 tons light, 3,877 tons std. (4,260 fl) **S:** 27.5 kts
Dim: 134.0 (126.5 wl) × 14.33 × 4.60 (7.55 over sonar) (see Remarks)
A: 4 RGM-84A Harpoon SSM (from ASROC launcher); 2 triple and two paired, fixed SAM launchers (10 Standard SM-1 MR SAM/SSM); 1 127-mm 54-cal. Mk 42 Mod. 9 DP; 1 20-mm Mk 15 Phalanx CIWS; 4 single 20-mm 68-cal. T75AA; 2 single 12.7-mm M2 mg; 1 8-round Mk 16 ASROC ASW syst. (Mk 112 launcher; 12 reloads); 4 paired, fixed 324-mm Mk 32 Mod. 9 fixed TT (Alliant Mk 46 Mod. 5 torpedoes); 1 MD-500 helicopter
Electronics:
Radar: 1 Raytheon SPS-64(V)9 nav.; 1 Raytheon SPS-10F (937, 939: Norden SPS-67(V)1) surf. search; 1 Thales DA-08/2 air search; 1 Thales STIR-18 missile f.c.; 1 General Dynamics Mk 90 Phalanx f.c.

FRIGATES [FF] *(continued)*

Yi Yang (939) William H. Clarke, 7-99

Hwai Yang (937) *DTM,* 1998

Sonar: SQS-26CX hull-mounted (3.5 kHz); SQS-35 VDS (see Remarks); EDO SQR-18A(V)1 towed linear passive hydrophone array
TACAN: SRN-15
EW: SLQ-32(V)1 or 32(V)2 intercept; Mk 36 SRBOC decoy syst. (2 6-round, Mk 137 RL), T-Mk 6 Fanfare towed acoustic torpedo decoy

M: 1 set Westinghouse geared steam turbines; 1 prop; 35,000 shp
Boilers: 2 Combustion Eng (932: Babcock & Wilcox) D-Type; 84 kg/cm^2, 510° C
Electric: 3,000 kw tot. (3 × 750 kw turboalternators, 1 × 750 kw diesel set)
Range: 2,750/27.5; 4,300/20 **Fuel:** 750 tons
Crew: 17–20 officers, 255–265 enlisted

Remarks: The first three were transferred on lease on decommissioning from the U.S. Navy on 7-8-92, 23-7-92, and 6-8-93, respectively. The lease cost only $14.5 million, but the complete training, overhaul, modification, and technical support package came to $236.19 million. They arrived at Tsoying on 27-9-93 and were commissioned 6-10-93. 935 transferred on decommissioning from the U.S. Navy on 30-6-94, while 936 and 937 were transferred 31-5-94 and 21-6-94, respectively; all three left U.S. waters on 2-7-95 and were formally recommissioned on 4-8-95. Permanent transfer by sale for the first six was approved under the U.S. Defense Authorization Act for FY 99.

A third group of three was planned for acquisition by sale during 1996; all had been in reserve for several years and needed reactivation refits prior to delivery, and the final arrangement, made in 1998, resulted in the purchase of 938 and 939 on 28-4-98. After activation refits at Detyens SY, Charleston, S.C., they arrived in Taiwan on 4-10-99 and were commissioned on 18-10-99.

Hull systems: Nonretractable antirolling fin stabilizers are fitted in all. Prairie/Masker bubbler system fitted to hulls and propellers to reduce radiated noise.

Combat systems: All units of the class are undergoing a major equipment modernization between 2005 and 2007 using electronics and weapons from the decommissioned ex-U.S. *Gearing*-class destroyers. Modifications include replacement of the SPS-40 with a DA-08 radar, replacement of the SPG-53 with the STIR 1.8 fire control, and the addition of 10 SM-1MR missile launch canisters—two double canisters atop the helicopter hangar and two triple canisters between the hangar and stack. The current 127-mm guns may also be replaced by 76-mm OTO Melara guns from the decommissioned *Gearing* class. 933 was the first to complete modernization in 2005. All have the C-STEM tactical data plotting system. The ASROC system has an automatic reloading magazine beneath the bridge; the two starboard cells and the two corresponding reload magazine positions are employed for Harpoon missiles. The ships have the SWG-1A Harpoon firing system. The ASW torpedo tubes are fixed, in the forward end of the hangar superstructure, aimed outboard at an angle of 45 degrees. The SQS-35 towed VDS was restored to service prior to transfer from the U.S., but it is apparently now used only to stream the SQR-18A(V)1 towed array. 937 tested the CS/MPQ-78 fire-control system in 1999 as possible replacement for the Mk 68 system; the device is based on the Contraves Skyguard system. Have Mk 114 ASW fire-control system. All received the ASWTDS (ASW Tactical Data System) during the 1980s. 935–937 were equipped with latest model Mk 15 Mod. 11 Block 1A Phalanx CIWS, with 4,500 r.p.m. firing rate and additional on-mount ammunition; they also carry a Tai Yang Technologies commercial SATCOM system. 938 and 939 were fitted with McDonnell Douglas Astronautics Mast-Mounted Sight (a modified helicopter electro-optical device) during their reactivations in the U.S.; the spherical antennas are mounted on the forward face of the pilothouse.

GUIDED-MISSILE PATROL COMBATANTS [PGG]

♦ 12 Jing Chiang class (Project Kuang Hua III)

Bldr: 603: United (Lien-Ho) SB, Kaohsiung; others: China SB Corp., Kaohsiung

	Laid down	L	In serv.
603 Jing Chiang	18-8-93	27-6-94	1-12-94
605 Dang Chiang	1-9-97	18-6-98	7-9-99
606 Sing Chiang	1-9-97	14-8-98	7-9-99
607 Feng Chiang	1-98	22-10-98	29-10-99
608 Tzeng Chiang	1-98	12-98	29-10-99
609 Kao Chiang	6-98	3-99	11-99
610 Jin Chiang	6-98	13-5-99	15-2-00
611 Hsiang Chiang	10-98	7-99	5-00
612 Tze Chiang	10-98	9-99	21-7-00
613 Po Chiang	3-99	11-99	21-7-00
615 Chang Chiang	3-99	3-00	21-7-00
617 Chu Chiang	3-99	5-00	21-7-00

Jing Chiang (603)—with Hsiung Feng I missiles *DTM*

Hsiang Chiang (611)—outboard a sister *DTM,* 7-00

D: 500 tons light (680 fl) **S:** 25.1 kts **Dim:** 61.41 × 9.50 × 2.5
A: 1 40-mm 70-cal. Bofors AA; 1 20-mm 68-cal. T 75 AA; 2 single 12.7-mm mg; 2 d.c. racks (4 Mk 6 d.c. each); 2 mine rails (8 tot. mines)—603 only: 4 Hsiung Feng-I SSM (see Remarks)
Electronics:
Radar: 1 Decca Bridgemaster 250 (603: CS/UPS-60X) nav.; 605 and later: Terma Scanter Mil 009 surf. search; 603 only: 1 CS/SPG-21A missile f.c.
Sonar: Simrad SS-247 hull-mounted HF (24 kHz active/passive)
EW: Litton WD-2A intercept; DLT-6 130-mm decoy syst. (2 6-round RL)
E/O: all but 603: Contraves Brashear LSEOS Mk IIA f.c.; 603 only: El-Op Sea Eye FLIR

GUIDED-MISSILE PATROL COMBATANTS [PGG] *(continued)*

M: 2 MTU 16V1163 TB93 diesels; 2 props; 15,020 bhp (12,800 bhp sust.)
Range: 3,600/15 **Crew:** 7 officers, 25 enlisted (accommodations for 50 tot.)

Remarks: Prototype 603 was ordered on 25-6-93, with work commenced 18-8-93 as part of the naval Kuang Hua III (Second Generation Combatant III) program. To have been a class of 12 naval patrol boats for the planned Coastal Patrol Administration, which was never organized. In mid-1995 it was announced that the remaining 11 would be built after all. The contract was tendered 19-6-96 and then canceled over alleged financial irregularities; it was reinstated on 26-6-97. Cost for first unit was $19 million, and the remaining 11 were to cost about $15 million each. All are named for Taiwanese rivers. The failure of the U.S.-made gun fire-control system to pass trials delayed the commissioning of the first five units into 9-99. A sister is operated by the Coast Guard as the *Taipei* (116).
Hull systems: Fin stabilizers are fitted. 605 and later have Sperry Mk 39 ring-laser gyros and SRD-331M doppler speed logs.
Combat systems: Most armament and other combat systems on 603 were recycled from a retired destroyer. 603 carries two inspection boats and is equipped with two firefighting water cannon. The surface search radar on 603 is a license-built version of the Canadian Marconi LN-66. While 603 is normally equipped with four missiles, the others had only weight and space provision; as of 2001, it was planned to mount Hsiung Feng II antiship missiles removed from PFG-2-class frigates. The E/O fire-control system in 605 and later controls the 40-mm AA gun and has a low-light t.v. and infrared sensors and a laser rangefinder on the stabilized director. 603 has a Kollmorgen Mk 985 periscopic backup gun director, but the gun is primarily locally controlled. German Buck Mk 245 Giant IR and Mk 214 Sea Gnat radar decoy rockets are used with Danish-made decoy system.

GUIDED-MISSILE PATROL CRAFT [PTG]

♦ 1 (+ 29) Kuang Hua VI project

Bldr: 1st unit: Tsoying Logistics Command, Kaohsiung (In serv. 10-03); others: China SB, Kaohsiung, with Jong Shyn SB Co. Ltd. and Ching Fu SB Co. Ltd.

FACG 60

Kuang Hua VI project—official model of the original, smaller concept *DTM,* 1996

D: 150 tons (180 fl) **S:** 33 kts **Dim:** 34.2 × 7.0 × . . .
A: 4 Hsiung Feng II antiship missiles; 2 single 20-mm 68-cal. T 75 AA
Electronics: Radar: . . . **M:** 3 diesels; 3 outdrive CP props; . . . bhp
Range: 800/30 **Crew:** . . . tot.

Remarks: Program approved 7-96, and design is in development as a one-for-one replacement for the Hai Ou class, but with only 30 to be built; as of late 1998, plans called for building and testing a prototype before committing to series production, and during 4-99 it was announced that only the prototype would be ordered initially.

Design, developed by the ROCN's Ship Development Center, employs stealth techniques to reduce radar and infrared signatures and was enlarged in 1997 from the original 34.5-m, 150-ton concept. The prototype was launched on 2-10-02 and was seen active during 9-03 exercises.
Combat systems: Employs the Taiwanese-developed Ta-Cheng tactical data system and a ship-to-shore datalink. A new stand-alone fire-control system for the missiles, with a single display and command console, is to be employed. The antiship missiles are to be mounted in pairs, athwartships behind sloped bulwarks to reduce radar signature. The 40-mm mount is to be placed forward but may be replaced by another weapon; at the stern, either a 20-mm T75S AA gun or a point-defense SAM system may be installed.

♦ 46 Hai Ou class

Bldr: China SB, Kaohsiung (In serv. 1980–84)

FABG 9 through 12
FABG 14 through 21
FABG 23 through 30
FABG 32 through 39
FABG 41 through 58

D: 47 tons (56 fl) **S:** 40 kts **Dim:** 22.87 × 5.50 × 1.00 (2.02 props)
A: 2 Hsiung Feng I SSM; 1 20-mm 68-cal. T 75 AA; 2 single 12.7-mm mg
Electronics:
Radar: 1 CS/UPS-60X nav.; 1 Lockheed Martin HR-76C5 (CS/SPG-21A) missile target-designation
EW: Litton WD-2A intercept; 2 paired AV-2 decoy RL
M: 2 MTU 12V331 TC92 diesels; 2 props; 2,605 bhp
Electric: 30 kw tot. **Range:** 700/32
Crew: 2 officers, 8 enlisted

Remarks: Design based closely on an original pair of imported Israeli Dvora class; class name means "Seagull." All are attached to the Hai Chiao (Sea Dragon) division, homeported at Makung, Tsoying, Anping, Wuchi, Keelung, and Suao. Two similar, earlier craft of Taiwanese design and construction were disarmed and transferred to Paraguay in 11-94.

Hai Ou–class FABG 52 *Ships of the World,* 1-98

Hai Ou–class FABG 10 *DTM,* 10-98

Hull systems: Aluminum construction. Made 45 kts light on trials but are now capable of only 25–30 kt maximum speeds. Hull form differs from that of the Dvora class and provides greater speed on less horsepower.
Combat systems: The fire-control radar is a variant of the HR-76 C2 used on destroyers and it is accompanied by a Kollmorgen Mk 35 optical sight projecting through the pilothouse roof. Early units had a pylon mast and the missile launchers situated near the stern; late units (the majority) have a lattice mast and the missile launchers located closer to amidships. Shoulder-launched Stinger point-defense SAMs may also be carried. FABG 11 has Israeli-made missile-control equipment and an Israeli fire-control radar.

♦ 2 Lung Chiang class

	Bldr	In serv.
601 Lung Chiang	Tacoma Boatbldg, Tacoma, Wash.	15-5-78
602 Sui Chiang	China SB Corp., Kaohsiung	6-83

Sui Chiang (602) *Ships of the World,* 1996

D: 218 tons (240 fl) **S:** 36.2 kts
Dim: 50.14 (46.94 pp) × 7.26 × 1.65 (hull; 3.05 max.)
A: 4 Hsiung Feng I SSM; 1 76-mm 62-cal. OTO Melara DP; 1 40-mm 70-cal. Bofors L 70 AA; 2 single 12.7-mm mg
Electronics:
Radar: 1 Goldstar . . . nav.; 1 Raytheon SPS-58C surf./air-search; Lockheed Martin HR-76 f.c.
EW: WD-2A intercept, 2 paired AV-2 (602: SMOC-4) decoy RL
M: CODOG: 3 G.M. 12V149 TI diesels (1,800 bhp each), 3 AVCO-Lycoming TF-40A gas turbines (5,000 shp each); 3 CP props; 15,000 shp max.
Range: 700/36 (gas turbines), 1,900/30 (3 diesels); 2,700/12 (1 diesel)
Fuel: 14,869 gallons **Crew:** 6 officers, 32 enlisted

Remarks: Design is a variation of Tacoma Boatbuilding (U.S.) PSMM Mk-5 design. Second unit is of revised design, with fin stabilizers; a planned six additional were canceled. Both had been brought up to the same standard of equipment by 1990. 601 is to be decommissioned soon and may be transferred abroad.
Combat systems: The HR-76 radar for the H-930 Mod. 2 weapons-control system is mounted in a radome atop the mainmast, and the antenna for the SPS-58A radar is on a stub mast forward of the exhaust stack. The original twin Emerlec 30-mm AA mount has been replaced by a 40-mm mount.

PATROL CRAFT [PC]

♦ 8 32-meter class
Bldr: China SB, Kaohsiung (In serv. 1987–90)

PCL-1 Ning Hai	PCL-5 . . . Hai	PCL-8 . . . Hai
PCL-2 Ann Hai	PCL-6 . . . Hai	PCL-9 . . . Hai
PCL-3 . . . Hai	PCL-7 . . . Hai	

PCL-8 *DTM,* 8-99

D: 100 tons (143 fl) **S:** 40 kts **Dim:** 32.10 × 8.99 × 1.80
A: 1 40-mm 60-cal. Bofors AA; 1 20-mm 68-cal. T75 AA; 2 d.c. racks (4 d.c. each)
Electronics:
Radar: 1 Decca . . . nav.
Sonar: . . . hull-mounted HF
M: 3 MTU 12V396 TB93 diesels; 3 props; 5,880 bhp **Range:** . . . **Fuel:** 36 tons
Crew: 3 officers, 13 enlisted

Remarks: Designed by Vosper-QAF, Singapore. Intended for harbor and coastal patrol service. Assigned to the Coastal Patrol Command under the tactical control of various naval bases and have a Gemini dinghy on davits aft. *Hai* means "sea." The 40-mm gun is on a locally made power-driven mounting. A 20-mm mount was added on the fantail around 1994 in place of the original two single 12.7-mm mg.

Note: At least six small, GRP-hulled armed launches were in use for escort duties in the Matsu Island region as of 4-01; armed with either a 40-mm Mk 19 grenade launcher or a 12.7-mm mg and crewed by two or three, the white-painted craft are powered by two gasoline outboard engines and have a JRC navigational radar.

MINE WARFARE SHIPS

♦ 4 MWW 50–class coastal minehunters [MHC]
Bldr: Abeking & Rasmussen, Lemwerder, Germany

	Laid down	L	In serv.
1301 Yung Feng (ex-*Explorer-I*)	26-4-90	29-10-90	12-7-91
1302 Yung Chia (ex-*Explorer-II*)	26-4-90	29-10-90	12-7-91
1303 Yung Nien (ex-*Explorer-III*)	22-10-90	2-5-91	12-7-91
1305 Yung Shun (ex-*Explorer-IV*)	22-10-90	2-5-91	12-7-91

Yung Feng (1301) *DTM,* 1998

D: 464.5 tons (558.3 fl) **S:** 15 kts **Dim:** 49.90 × 10.80 (9.80 wl) × 2.80
A: 1 20-mm 68-cal. T75 AA; 2 single 12.7-mm mg
Electronics:
Radar: 1 Decca . . . nav.
Sonar: Thales TSM 2022 through-hull VDS
M: 2 MTU 8V396 TB 93 diesels; 2 props; 2,180 bhp **Range:** 2,500/12
Crew: 5 officers, 40 enlisted

Remarks: Two ordered 14-9-88 and two on 23-3-89. Were delivered without armament or mine-countermeasures equipment in blue hull/white superstructure paint scheme and lettered "CPC Offshore" on sides for the China Petroleum Corporation, which had ostensibly ordered them as "multipurpose offshore vessels" intended to "support oilrigs, oceanographic research, firefighting, pollution control, and search-and-rescue."

Yung Shun (1305) *DTM,* 1998

Not formally commissioned until 3-95. Planned order for up to eight more canceled due to a procurement scandal over spare parts for the first four, which have proven difficult to maintain.
Hull systems: Wooden hull construction. At least one has suffered from mechanical problems.
Combat systems: Have Thales IBIS-V mine-countermeasures data system. Each can carry one Pinguin A1 search/classification and one Pinguin B3 mine localization and disposal ROV. In 6-97, a 20-mm AA replaced the firefighting monitor formerly mounted on the foredeck.

♦ 4 ex-U.S. Aggressive-class minehunter/minesweepers [MHS]
Bldrs: 1306: Wilmington Boat Works, Wilmington, Calif.; others: J.M. Martinac, Tacoma, Wash.

	Laid down	L	In serv.
1306 Yung Yang (ex-*Implicit*, MSO 455)	29-10-51	1-8-53	10-3-54
1307 Yung Tzu (ex-*Conquest*, MSO 488)	26-3-53	20-5-54	20-7-55
1308 Yung Ku (ex-*Gallant*, MSO 489)	21-5-53	4-6-54	14-9-55
1309 Yung Teh (ex-*Pledge*, MSO 492)	24-6-54	20-7-55	20-4-56

Yung Ku (1308) *DTM,* 1998

Yung Tzu (1307) C. Chung, 7-96

D: 716 tons light; 857 tons std. (920 fl) **S:** 14 kts **Dim:** 52.42 × 10.97 × 4.2
A: 2 single 12.7-mm M2 mg
Electronics:
Radar: 1 Raytheon SPS-64(V)9 nav.
Sonar: SQQ-14 variable-depth minehunting (350 kHz)
M: 4 Waukesha L-1616 diesels; 2 CP props; 2,400 bhp **Range:** 3,300/10
Fuel: 48 tons **Crew:** 10 officers, 68 enlisted

Remarks: 1307–1309 transferred 3-8-94, 1306 on 30-9-94. All had outer hull planking replaced prior to delivery in Taiwan; they were formally commissioned at Kaohsiung on 1-3-95.

MINE WARFARE SHIPS *(continued)*

Hull systems: Wooden construction; nonmagnetic, stainless-steel machinery. All were given very thorough rehabilitations during the early to mid-1970s, receiving semi-enclosed bridges, enlarged superstructures abaft the bridge, SQQ-14 minehunting sonars, new communications gear, and upgraded accommodations.
Combat systems: Have the SLQ-37(V) magnetic sweep system, incorporating A Mk 4(V) and A Mk 6(B) acoustic arrays and the SLQ-38 wire sweep. Hoist machinery for the SQQ-14 minehunting sonar occupies the position of the former 40-mm AA gun. Plans to update their mine countermeasures systems have not reached fruition.

♦ 4 ex-Belgian Adjutant and U.S. MSC 268*–class coastal minesweepers [MSC]

	Bldr	In serv.
158 Yung Chuan (ex-MSC 278)*	Tacoma Boat, Wash.	10-6-59
162 Yung Fu (ex-*Diest,* ex-MSC 77)	Adams Yacht, Quincy, Mass.	5-53
167 Yung Ching (ex-*Eekloo,* ex-MSC 101)	Hodgdon Bros., Maine	5-53
168 Yung Chen (ex-*Maaseick,* ex-MSC 78)	Adams Yacht, Quincy, Mass.	7-53

Yung Chuan (158) *DTM,* 4-98

D: 167, 168: 337 tons (385 fl); 158: 335 tons (378 fl) **S:** 13.6 kts
Dim: 167, 168: 43.92 (41.50 wl) × 8.26 × 2.17 (2.62 max.); 158: 44.45 × 8.50 × 2.59 max.
A: 1 twin 20-mm 70-cal. Oerlikon Mk 24 AA
Electronics:
Radar: 1 Decca 707 nav.
Sonar: Simrad SA950 hull-mounted (95 kHz)
M: 2 G.M. 8-268A diesels; 2 props; 1,200 bhp (158: 4 G.M. Detroit Diesel 6-71 diesels; 2 props; 890 bhp)
Range: 2,500/12; 3,500/7 **Fuel:** 40 tons **Crew:** 6 officers, 35 enlisted

Remarks: Wooden hulls. 158 transferred on completion; the ex-Belgian ships were transferred in 7-69 to 11-69. The survivors have been modernized and rehabilitated under the Fu Yung program: 158 in 1983–84 and the others by 1987. MSC 158 has a lower bridge structure than the others. Carry A Mk4(V) acoustic mine countermeasure.
Disposals: Sister *Yung Ping* (156, ex-MSC 140) stricken 1982; *Yung Chi* (166, ex-*Charleroi,* ex-MSC 152), and *Yung Nien* (479, ex-MSC 277) by 1991; *Yung Ju* (159, ex-MSC 300) ran aground off west coast of Taiwan and was stricken in 1992; *Yung Sui* (164, ex-*Diksmuide;* ex-MSC 65) had been stricken by 1994; *Yung Shan* (165, ex-MSC 63), and *Yung Jen* (163, ex-MSC 64) were stricken during 5-95.

AMPHIBIOUS WARFARE SHIPS

♦ 1 command ship/tank landing ship [LCC]
Bldr: Dravo Corp., Neville Island, Pittsburgh, Pa.

	L	In serv.
LCC-1 Kaohsiung (ex-219, ex-*Chung Hai,* LST 229; ex-*Dukes County,* LST 735)	11-3-44	26-4-44

Kaohsiung (LCC-1) *DTM,* 1998

D: 1,653 tons (3,675 fl) **S:** 11 kts **Dim:** 99.98 × 15.24 × 4.27
A: 2 twin 40-mm 60-cal. Bofors Mk 1 Mod. 2 AA; 2 single 40-mm 60-cl. Bofors Mk 3 AA: 2 single 20-mm 68-cal. T75 AA; 4 single 12.7-mm mg
Electronics:
Radar: 1 CS/UPS-60 nav.; 1 Raytheon SPS-10 surf.-search; 1 Lockheed Martin (R.C.A.) SPS-6C air-search
M: 2 G.M. 12-567A diesels; 2 props; 1,700 bhp **Electric:** 300 kw tot.
Range: 15,000/9 **Crew:** 11 officers, 100 enlisted

Remarks: Transferred 21-5-57 and converted to a command ship in 1964, with additional communications gear and radars. Is assigned to the 205th Squadron. Retains bow doors. An SPS-6C radar antenna has replaced the original SPS-12; the actual set installed may be a variant of the SPS-58. Has one Taiwanese Mk 62 and two U.S. Mk 51 optical gun f.c. directors.

♦ 1 ex-U.S. Anchorage-class dock landing ship [LSD]
Bldr: General Dynamics, Quincy, Mass.

	Laid down	L	In serv.
193 Shui Hai (ex-*Tan Hai,* ex-*Pensacola,* LSD 38)	12-3-69	11-7-70	27-3-71

Shui Hai (193) William H. Clarke, 4-00

D: 8,200 tons light (13,680 fl) **S:** 22 kts
Dim: 168.66 (162.80 wl) × 25.90 × 5.60 (6.10 max.)
A: 2 20-mm Mk 15 Phalanx gatling CIWS; 6 single 12.7-mm M2 mg
Electronics:
Radar: 1 Raytheon SPS-64(V)9 nav.; 1 Raytheon SPS-10F surf.-search; 1 Lockheed Martin SPS-40D air-search
EW: Raytheon SLQ-32(V)1 intercept; Mk 36 SRBOC decoy syst. (4 6-round Mk 137 RL); SLQ-25 Nixie towed torpedo decoy system
M: 2 sets de Laval geared steam turbines; 2 props; 24,000 shp
Boilers: 2 Foster-Wheeler; 42.3 kg/cm^2, 467° C
Range: 14,800/12 **Fuel:** 2,750 tons
Crew: 18 officers, 303–304 enlisted + troops: 25 officers, 311 enlisted

Remarks: Transferred on 22-9-99. Was assigned to the new Fast-Response Amphibious Group on 1-5-00, prior to arrival on 2-6-00.
Hull systems: Can accommodate (with/without portable mezzanine deck installed) 1–3 LCU, 6–9 LCM(8), 12–18 LCM(6), or 50 LVT in the 131.06 × 15.24 m well deck. One LCM(6), one LCP, and two LCPL can be stowed on deck, handled by the two 50-ton cranes. Have 1,115 m^2 of vehicle parking space forward of the docking well. The helicopter deck is removable and has one landing spot. Carries 90 tons of JP-5 fuel for helicopters.
Combat systems: Mk 56 and Mk 63 gun directors were removed in 1977, two twin 76.2-mm gunmounts by 1990, and the remaining 76.2-mm mounts in 1993–94.

♦ 1 ex-U.S. Cabildo-class dock landing ship [LSD]
Bldr: Newport News SB & DD, Newport News, Va.

	Laid down	L	In serv.
191 Chung Cheng (ex-*Comstock,* LSD 19)	3-1-45	28-4-45	2-7-45

Chung Cheng (191) H&L Van Ginderen, 1-97

D: 4,790 tons (9,375 fl) **S:** 15.6 kts **Dim:** 139.52 (138.38 wl) × 22.0 × 5.49
A: 1 4-round Sea Chaparral point-defense SAM syst. (16 MIM-72F missiles); 4 quadruple 40-mm 60-cal. Bofors Mk 2 AA
Electronics: Radar: 1 Canadian Marconi LN-66 nav.; 1 Raytheon SPS-5 surf.-search
M: 2 sets geared steam turbines; 2 props; 9,000 shp
Boilers: 2 single-drum; 17.5 kg/cm^2
Range: 8,000/15; 16,675/9.5 **Fuel:** 1,758 tons
Crew: 17 officers, 230 enlisted + up to 1,200 troops

AMPHIBIOUS WARFARE SHIPS *(continued)*

Remarks: Acquired in 1985 from a scrap dealer for cannibalization but found to be in good condition and was recommissioned during 9-2-86, followed by a refit that ended in 1-87; took the name and number of the former *Ashland*-class LSD *White Marsh* (LSD 8), which had been transferred on loan 17-11-60 and purchased outright during 5-76. Sister *Chen Hai* (LSD 192, ex-*Fort Marion,* LSD 22), transferred by sale on 15-4-77, was stricken on 1-6-99. 191 is employed in resupply service to Pratas Reef Islands in South China Sea.
Hull systems: Helicopter platform over 119.5 × 13.4-meter docking well, which can accommodate three LCUs, 18 LCMs, or 32 amphibious armored troop carriers. The boilers do not have superheat.
Combat systems: Has four U.S. Mk 51 and one Taiwanese Mk 62 lead-computing gun f.c.s, with the latter employing stabilization and range information from the surface-search radar for use against surface and shore targets.

◆ 2 ex-U.S. Newport-class tank landing ships [LST]
Bldr: Philadelphia Naval Shipyard

	Laid down	L	In serv.
232 Chung Ho (ex-*Manitowoc*, LST 1180)	1-2-67	4-6-69	24-1-70
233 Chung Ping (ex-*Sumter*, LST 1181)	14-11-67	13-12-69	20-6-70

Chung Ho (232) Chris Sattler, 6-00

Chung Ho (232) Chris Sattler, 6-00

D: 4,975 tons light (8,576 fl) **S:** 22 kts (20 sust.)
Dim: 159.2 (171.3 over horns) × 21.18 × 5.3 (aft)/1.80 (fwd)
A: 2 twin 40-mm 60-cal. Bofors Mk 1 Mod. 2 AA; 1 20-mm Mk 15 Phalanx CIWS; 2 single 12.7-mm mg
Electronics:
Radar: 1 Raytheon SPS-64(V)9 nav.; 1 Raytheon SPS-10F surf. search
TACAN: SRN-15A
M: 6 G.M. Electromotive Div. 16-645-E5 diesels; 2 CP props; 16,500 bhp—bow-thruster
Electric: 2,250 kw tot. (3 × 750 kw, Alco 251-E diesels driving; 450 V 60 Hz a.c.)
Range: 14,250/14 **Fuel:** 1,750 tons
Crew: 13 officers, 174 enlisted + troops: 20 officers, 294 enlisted + 72 emergency accomm.

Remarks: Were to transfer on lease 7-1-95 but reactivation for transfer was not begun until mid-1996 at Newport News Shipbuilding & Dry Dock, Virginia; they had been decommissioned 30-6-93 and placed in reserve on 30-9-93. The official transfer took place on 18-4-97 at Guam, and the ships were formally commissioned on 8-5-98 at their base at Tsoying. Both were purchased outright on 29-9-00.
Hull systems: Can transport 2,000 tons of cargo, or, for beaching, 500 tons of cargo on 1,765 m^2 of deck space. A side-thruster propeller forward helps when marrying to a causeway. There is a 34-m long, 75-ton capacity mobile aluminum ramp forward, which is linked to the tank deck by a second from the upper deck. Aft is a 242-m^2 helicopter platform and a stern door for loading and unloading vehicles. Four pontoon causeway sections can be carried on the hull sides. The tank deck, which has a 75-ton-capacity turntable at both ends, can carry 23 AAV-7A1 armored personnel carriers, 29 M 48 tanks, or 41 2.5-ton trucks, while the upper deck can accept 29 2.5-ton trucks. Normally carry three LCVP and one LCP in Welin davits. Have two 10-ton cranes. Carry 141,600 gallons vehicle fuel.
Combat systems: Mk 63 radar gunfire-control systems removed 1977–78, but unlike other units of their class retained the two twin 76.2-mm gunmounts on delivery; by 10-98 233 had the 76.2-mm mounts replaced by two twin 40-mm 60-cal. AA mounts. A TACAN antenna has been added atop the mainmast.

◆ 11 ex-U.S. LST 1- and LST 542–class tank landing ships [LST]

	Bldr	In serv.
201 Chung Hai (ex-LST 755)	American Br., Ambridge, Pa.	29-7-44
205 Chung Chien (ex-LST 716)	Jeffersonville B & M, Ind.	18-8-44
208 Chung Shun (ex-LST 732)	Dravo, Pittsburgh, Pa.	10-4-44
216 Chung Kuang (ex-LST 503)	Jeffersonville B & M, Ind.	14-12-43
217 Chung Suo (ex-*Bradley County,* LST 400)	Newport News SB & DD, Va.	7-1-43
218 Chung Chi (ex-LST 279)	American Br., Ambridge, Pa.	25-10-43
221 Chung Chuan (ex-*Wan Tu,* ex-LST 640)	Chicago Bridge & Iron, Seneca, Il.	18-9-44
226 Chung Chih (ex-*Sagadohoc County,* LST 1091)	American Br., Ambridge, Pa.	6-4-45
227 Chung Ming (ex-*Sweetwater County,* LST 1152)	Dravo, Pittsburgh, Pa.	13-4-45
230 Chung Pang (ex-LST 578)	Missouri Valley Bridge & Iron, Evansville, Ind.	15-7-44
231 Chung Yeh (ex-*Sublette County,* LST 1144)	Chicago Bridge & Iron, Seneca, Ill.	28-5-45

Chung Pang (230)—with two pair of Welin davits per side, aft *DTM,* 1-98

Chung Suo (217)—with unique lattice mast aft *DTM,* 1996

D: 1,653 tons (4,080 fl) **S:** 11.6 kts **Dim:** 99.98 × 15.24 × 3.40
A: 2 twin 40-mm 60-cal. Bofors Mk 1 Mod. 2 AA; 2 single 40-mm 60-cal. Bofors Mk 3 AA; 2 or 4 single 20-mm 68-cal. T 75 AA; 2 or 4 12.7-mm mg
Electronics: 1 CS/UPS-60X nav. **M:** 2 G.M. 12-567A diesels; 2 props; 1,700 bhp
Electric: 300 kw tot. **Range:** 15,000/9 **Fuel:** 569 tons **Crew:** 100–125 tot.

Remarks: Three of the class are reportedly in reserve status. 201 transferred 29-5-46, 205 on 12-6-46, 208 on 29-5-46, 216 on 4-4-55, 217 and 218 on 30-6-55, 221 on 29-5-46, 226 on 21-10-58, 227 on 24-10-58, 230 on 21-9-58, and 231 on 21-9-61. All were re-engined and extensively rebuilt during the late 1960s, in many cases becoming almost new ships. A further modernization from 1992 on under the Chung Hsing program provided new engines, generators, and air-conditioning systems, plus rebuilt bridge superstructures. 226 was to have been converted as a command ship (LCC 2) and did receive the same large lattice mast as LCC 1 (see entry above).
Combat systems: Have two U.S. Mk 51 and one Taiwanese Mk 62 g.f.c.s, with the latter employing stabilization and range information from the surface-search radar for use against surface and shore targets. Most have four sets of Welin davits, although 226 has six and 205 has two; each set handles one LCVP landing craft. All carry Tai Yang Co. commercial SATCOM telephone equipment.
Disposals: *Chung Cheng* (224, ex-*Lafayette County,* LST 859) was stricken during 1989. Between 1984 and 1991, six others had also been laid up at Kaohsiung: *Chung Ting* (203, ex-LST 537), *Chung Chi* (206, ex-LST 1017), *Chung Lien* (209, ex-LST 1050), *Chung Chiang* (225, ex-*San Bernardino County,* LST 1110), *Chung Shu* (228, ex-LST 520), and *Chung Wan* (229, ex-LST 535); all were discarded during 1993. *Chung Sheng* (222, ex-LST(H) 1033) ran aground near Keelung on 5-10-95 and was stricken and scrapped on-site. Stricken for scrap on 8-11-97 were *Chung Hsing* (204, ex-LST 557), *Ching Yung* (210, ex-574), and *Chung Fu* (223, ex-*Iron County,* LST 840).

◆ 4 ex-U.S. LSM 1–class medium landing ships [LSM]

	Bldr	L	In serv.
341 Mei Chin (ex-LSM 155)	Charleston NY, S.C.	19-6-44	26-7-44
347 Mei Sung (ex-LSM 457)	Western Pipe & Steel, San Pedro, Calif.	28-1-45	28-3-45
353 Mei Ping (ex-LSM 471)	Brown SB, Houston, Tex.	17-2-45	23-2-45
356 Mei Lo (ex-LSM 362)	Brown SB, Houston, Tex.	9-12-44	11-1-45

Mei Ping (353) *DTM,* 10-98

D: 513 tons light, 743 std. (1,095 fl) **S:** 12.5 kts
Dim: 62.03 (59.89 wl) × 10.52 × 2.20 (2.54 max.)
A: 2 twin 40-mm 60-cal. Bofors Mk 1 Mod. 2 AA; 4 single 20-mm 68-cal. T 75 AA; 4 single 12.7-mm mg

AMPHIBIOUS WARFARE SHIPS *(continued)*

Electronics: Radar: 1 CS/UPS-60X nav.
M: 2 G.M. Electromotive Div. 16-278A (353, 356: 2 Fairbanks-Morse 38D8 1/8 × 10) diesels; 2 props; 2,800 bhp
Electric: 240 kw tot. **Range:** 5,000/7 **Fuel:** 165 tons
Crew: 8–13 officers, 35–56 enlisted

Remarks: 341 and 347 transferred in 1946, 353 in 11-56, and 356 in 5-62. Have been extensively modernized; the original cylindrical pilothouse and bridge replaced with larger, rectangular structure, and a twin 40-mm AA mount was added aft. Have one U.S. Mk 51 and one Taiwanese Mk 62 g.f.c.s, with the latter employing stabilization and range information from the surface-search radar for use against surface and shore targets. Pennant numbers were changed from the 600-series during modernizations.

♦ 2 U.S. LCU 1610–class utility landing craft [LCU]
Bldr: China SB Corp., Kaohsiung (In serv. 1979)

LCU-497 Ho Fong LCU-498 Ho Hu

Ho Fong (LCU-497) *DTM,* 1998

D: 190 tons std. (390 normal, 437 fl) **S:** 11 kts **Dim:** 41.07 × 9.07 × 2.08
A: 2 single 20-mm 68-cal. T 75 AA; 2 single 12.7-mm mg
Electronics: Radar: 1 CS/UPS-60X nav.
M: 4 G.M. Detroit Diesel 6-71 diesels; 2 Kort-nozzle props; 1,200 bhp
Electric: 40 kw tot. **Range:** 1,200/8
Fuel: 13 tons **Crew:** 4 officers, 15 enlisted

Remarks: Built under license from the United States. Cargo capacity is 180 tons; cargo space, 36.9 × 7.62 m max. (4.5-m-wide bow ramp). Up to 400 troops can be accommodated for short periods on deck. Drive-through feature permits marrying bow and stern to other landing craft or causeways. Have kedging anchor starboard side aft to assist in extraction from beaches.

♦ 6 ex-U.S. LCU 1466–class utility landing craft [LCU]
Bldr: Ishikawajima, Harima, Japan (In serv. 3-55)

LCU-488 Ho Shan (ex-LCU 1596) LCU-491 Ho Meng (ex-LCU 1599)
LCU-489 Ho Chuan (ex-LCU 1597) LCU-492 Ho Mou (ex-LCU 1600)
LCU-490 Ho Seng (ex-LCU 1598) LCU-493 Ho Shou (ex-LCU 1601)

Ho Chuan (LCU-489) *DTM,* 1998

D: 180 tons light (347 fl) **S:** 8 kts **Dim:** 35.08 × 10.36 × 1.60 (aft)
A: 2 single 20-mm 68-cal. T 75 AA; 2 single 12.7-mm mg
Electronics: Radar: 1 CS/UPS-60X nav.
M: 3 G.M. Gray Marine 64 YTL diesels; 3 props; 675 bhp **Electric:** 40 kw tot.
Range: 1,200/6 (700/7 loaded) **Fuel:** 11 tons **Crew:** 4 officers, 15 enlisted

Remarks: Built under U.S. Offshore Procurement Program. Cargo: 150 tons or 300 troops on 15.8 × 9.0 m deck, with 4.3-m-wide bow ramp.

♦ 11 ex-U.S. LCU 501 (LCT(6))–class utility landing craft [LCU]

	In serv.
LCU-401 Ho Chi (ex-LCU 1212)	16-8-44
LCU-402 Ho Huei (ex-LCU 1218)	25-8-44
LCU-403 Ho Yao (ex-LCU 1244)	22-9-44
LCU-406 Ho Chao (ex-LCU 1429)	8-12-44
LCU-481 Ho Shun (ex-LCU 1225)	4-9-44
LCU-484 Ho Chung (ex-LCU 849)	7-8-44
LCU-494 Ho Chun (ex-LCU 892)	27-7-44
LCU-495 Ho Yung (ex-LCU 1271)	19-8-44
LCU-496 Ho Chien (ex-LCU 1278)	22-7-44
SB 1 Ho Chie (ex-LCU 700)	18-4-44
SB 2 To Ten (ex-1367)	1944

D: 158 tons (286 fl) **S:** 10 kts **Dim:** 36.3 (32.0 wl) × 9.96 × 1.27 (max. aft)
A: 2 single 20-mm 68-cal. T 75 AA; 2 single 12.7-mm mg
Electronics: Radar: 1 CS/UPS-60X nav.

Ho Chun (LCU-494) *Ships of the World,* 2001

M: 3 G.M. 6-71 diesels; 3 props; 675 bhp **Electric:** 20 kw tot.
Fuel: 10.5 tons **Crew:** 4 officers, 15 enlisted

Remarks: Six transferred between 1946 and 1948, the others between 1958 and 1959. SB 1 has served in an auxiliary role since delivery, and one of the other units has been redesignated SB 2.

Disposals: Sister *Ho Deng* (LCU-404, ex-LCU 1367) sank after collision in Makung Harbor during a typhoon on 22-8-86. *Ho Geng* (LCU-405, ex-LCU 1397), *Ho Teng* (LCU-407, ex-LCU 1452), *Ho Tsung* (LCU 482, ex-LCU 1213), and *Ho Chang* (LCU-485, ex-LCU 512) had all been decommissioned by 2005.

♦ 170 LCM(6)-class landing craft [LCM] Bldrs: U.S. and Taiwan

LCM(6) 2228—with transport Yuen Feng (AP 524) in background *DTM,* 5-00

D: 26.7 tons light (62.35 fl) **S:** 9 kts **Dim:** 17.07 × 4.37 × 1.52 (max. aft)
A: 1-2 single 12.7-mm mg in some
M: 2 G.M. Gray Marine 64HN9 diesels; 2 props; 450 bhp
Range: 130/9 **Crew:** 5–9 tot.

Remarks: can carry 34 tons of cargo. About 80 have been retired.

♦ About 100 U.S. LCVP class [LCVP]

LCVP—from the since-stricken landing ship *Chung Fu* (223) C. Chung

D: 13 tons (fl) **S:** 9 kts **Dim:** 10.9 × 3.21 × 1.04
A: 2 single 7.62-mm mg M: 1 G.M. Gray Marine 64HN9 diesel; 225 bhp
Range: 110/9 **Crew:** 3 tot.

Remarks: Many of the total are assigned to the LSTs. Wooden construction. Cargo: 36 troops or 4 tons. Some 25–30, known as Type 272, were built in Taiwan in the 1970s. Some are equipped with radar and two 7.62-mm mg for use as beach reconnaissance craft.

AUXILIARIES

♦ 1 Alliance-class oceanographic and hydrographic research ship [AGOR] Bldr: Fincantieri, Muggiano, La Spezia, Italy

	Laid down	L	In serv.
AGS 1601 Ta Kuan	8-4-94	17-12-94	26-9-95

D: 2,466 tons (3,180 fl) **S:** 17 kts (16.3 sust.)
Dim: 93.00 (82.00 pp) × 15.20 × 5.10 **A:** None
Electronics:
Radar: 1 Sperry Marine . . . nav.; 1 . . . nav.
Sonar: Simrad EM 1200

AUXILIARIES *(continued)*

Ta Kuan (AGS 1601) ROCN, via *DTM,* 8-97

M: 2 GMT B.230.12M diesels, AEG CC 3127 generators, electric drive: 2 AEG 1,470-kw motors; 2 props; 4,000 shp—side-thrusters fore and aft
Electric: 1,850 kw tot. (including 1/1,605-kw gas-turbine set) **Range:** 12,000/15.5
Crew: 82 tot., including 20 scientists

Remarks: Ordered 10-6-93 for use by the Ministry of Transport and Communications. Design based closely on that of the NATO research ship *Alliance* but is capable of arctic operations. Is employed primarily in oceanographic research in support of antisubmarine warfare at the underwater sound range off Suao, eastern Taiwan.
Hull systems: Has about 6,100 m^2 total working deck space, 400 m^2 lab space. Towing winch, 20-ton bollard pull, with 6,000 m of 50-mm cable. Also has 1,000-kg oceanographic crane with telescopic arm. Special attention paid to quieting. Has Flume-type passive tank stabilization.

♦ 1 underway-replenishment ship [AOR]
Bldr: China SB Corp., Keelung

	Laid down	L	In serv.
AOE 530 Wu Yi	25-6-88	4-3-89	23-6-90

Wu Yi (AOE 530) Chris Sattler, 4-06

Wu Yi (AOE 530) Chris Sattler, 4-06

D: 7,700 tons light (17,000 fl) **S:** 20.8 kts **Dim:** 162.12 × 22.00 × 8.60
A: 1 4-round Sea Chaparral SAM syst. (16 MIM-72F missiles); 2 single 40-mm 60-cal. Bofors Mk 3 AA; 2 single 20-mm 68-cal. T 75 AA; 4 single 12.7-mm mg
Electronics:
Radar: 1 GoldStar . . . nav.; 1 CS/UPS-60X nav.; 1 . . . nav.
TACAN: SRN-15
M: 2 Mitsubishi-M.A.N. 14-cyl. diesels; 2 props; 25,000 bhp **Range:** 8,000/17.5
Crew: 18 officers, 146 enlisted

Remarks: Designed in U.S. by Rosenblatt & Son. Helicopter deck at stern is capable of handling two CH-47- or S-70C-sized helicopters. Capable of underway replenishment on both sides; has four fueling and two solids transfer stations. Carries 9,300 tons of fuel and water, 600 tons munitions and provisions. Largest naval unit yet built in Taiwan. Reportedly, the hull was found to be warped after launch and has a permanent list, the ship is underpowered, and there are gearbox and steering equipment problems.
Combat systems: The original Bofors L70 AA mounts (which were locally controlled) were replaced by elderly, hand-operated 40-mm 60-cal. mountings in 1999.

♦ 2 ex-U.S. Patapsco-class transport tankers [AOT]
Bldr: Cargill Inc., Savage, Minn.

	Laid down	L	In serv.
AOG 507 Chang Bai (ex-*Elkhorn*, AOG 7)	7-9-42	15-5-43	12-2-44
AOG 517 Hsing Lung (ex-*Pecatonia*, AOG 57)	6-12-44	17-3-45	28-11-45

Chang Bai (AOG 507) *Ships of the World,* 1996

D: 1,850 tons light (4,335 fl) **S:** 14 kts **Dim:** 94.72 (89.0 wl) × 14.78 × 4.78
A: 2 twin 40-mm 60-cal. Bofors Mk 1 Mod 2 AA; 2 single 20-mm 68-cal. T 75 AA; 4 single 12.7-mm mg
Electronics: Radar: 1 CS/UPS-60X nav.
M: 2 G.M. 16-278A diesels; 2 props; 3,300 bhp
Electric: 460 kw tot. **Range:** 4,880/14; 6,940/10
Fuel: 314 tons **Crew:** 76 tot.

Remarks: Former gasoline tankers now used for supplying offshore islands. Cargo: 2,040 tons. 507 transferred on 1-7-72. Both purchased outright 19-5-76. Sister *Lung Chuan* (515, ex-New Zealand *Endeavour,* ex-*Namakagon,* AOG 53) has been stricken.
Combat systems: Have one U.S. Mk 51 and one Taiwanese-developed Type 62 g.f.c.s. for the 40-mm guns.

♦ 3 Yuen Feng–class transports [AP]
Bldr: Tsoying Naval SY

	Laid down	L	In serv.
AP 524 Yuen Feng	16-12-81	6-4-82	10-9-82
AP 525 Wu Gang	26-10-83	26-4-84	9-10-84
AP 526 Hsin Kang	. . .	1988	11-88

Hsin Kang (AP 526) *DTM*

Yuen Feng (AP 524) *Ships of the World,* 2000

D: 524: 2,070 tons light, 3,040 tons std. (4,600 fl); others: 2,804 tons (4,845 fl)
S: 524: 20.4 kts; others: 20 kts **Dim:** 101.78 × 524: 18.0 (others: 16.46) × 4.57
A: 1 4-round Sea Chaparral point-defense SAM syst. (16 MIM-72F missiles); 2 single 40-mm 60-cal. Bofors Mk 3 AA; 4 single 12.7-mm mg
Electronics:
Radar: 1 Goldstar . . . nav.
EW: Litton WD-2A intercept; Mk 36 SRBOC decoy syst. (2 6-round Mk 137 RL)
M: 2 diesels; 2 props; . . . bhp—bow-thruster
Range: 524: 5,600/18; others: 5,600/16
Crew: 524: 11 officers, 84 enlisted; others: 11 officers, 50 enlisted

Remarks: Transports to serve Quemoy and Matsu garrisons, replacing stricken LSTs. Stern truncated to fit small berthing area; do *not* have stern vehicle ramp. Can carry more than 600 passengers, except AP 524: 500. AP 525 and AP 526 have smaller cargo cranes. AP 526 was hit aft by a South Korean merchant ship at Kaohsiung on 21-3-97; the severe damage was repaired by 13-5-97. Although they had been ordered, AP 527 through AP 529 may have been canceled in 1998 when the government directed the ROCN to use commercial vessels to transport troops and supplies whenever possible; there is no evidence of their completion.

Disposal note: Ex-U.S. *Bolster*-class salvage ship *Ta De* (ARS 550) was retired by 2003. *Tai Wu*–class transport *Tai Wu* (AP 518) was decommissioned during 2004. *Wan An*–class transport *Wan An* (AP 523) was no longer in service by 2005.

♦ 1 ex-U.S. Diver-class salvage ship [ARS]
Bldr: Basalt Rock Co., Napa, Calif.

	Laid down	L	In serv.
ARS 552 Tai Hu (ex-*Grapple*, ARS 7)	8-9-42	31-12-42	16-12-43

AUXILIARIES *(continued)*

Tai Hu (ARS 552) H&L Van Ginderen, 1-99

D: 1,478 tons (1,745 fl) **S:** 14.8 kts
Dim: 65.08 (63.09 wl) × 12.40 (11.89 wl) × 4.11
A: 2 single 20-mm 68-cal. T 75 AA **Electronics:** Radar: 1 CS/UPS-60X nav.
M: 4 Caterpillar D-399 diesels, electric drive; 2 props; 3,000 shp
Electric: 460 kw tot.
Range: 9,000/13; 14,700/7 **Fuel:** 283 tons **Crew:** 85 tot.

Remarks: Transferred on 1-12-77. May be retired during 2004–5 as a cost-saving measure.

♦ **5 ex-U.S. Cherokee-, Abnaki-* and Achomawi**-class fleet tugs [ATA]** Bldrs: 548, 551: United Eng., Alameda, Calif.; 555: Cramp SB &DD Co., Philadelphia, Pa.; others: Charleston SB & DD, Charleston, S.C.

	Laid down	L	In serv.
ATF 551 Ta Wan (ex-*Apache*, ATF 67)	8-11-44	8-5-45	12-12-45
ATF 553 Ta Mo (ex-*Tawakoni*, ATF 114)*	19-5-43	28-10-43	15-9-44
ATF 554 Ta Tu (ex-*Achomawi*, ATF 148)**	15-1-44	10-9-44	11-11-44
ATF 555 Ta Feng (ex-*Narragansett*, ATF 88)	31-2-42	8-8-42	15-1-43
ATF 563 Ta Tai (ex-*Shakori*, ATF 162)**	9-5-45	9-8-45	20-12-45

Ta Feng (ATF 555)—*Cherokee* class *DTM,* 1998

Ta Tu (ATF 554)—*Achomawi* class *DTM,* 1998

D: 1,235 tons (1,731 fl); 554, 563: 1,640 tons (2,130 fl) **S:** 15 kts
Dim: 62.48 (59.44 wl) × 11.73 × 4.93 max. (554, 563: 5.18 max.)
A: 1 40-mm 60-cal. Bofors Mk 3 AA; 1 twin 20-mm 70-cal. AA; 2 single 12.7-mm mg
Electronics: Radar: 1 CS/UPS-60X nav.
M: 4 G.M. 12-278 (ATF 554: 12-278A; ATF 553: Caterpillar D399) diesels, electric drive; 1 prop; 3,000 shp
Electric: 260 or 400 kw tot. **Fuel:** 295 tons **Range:** 6,500/16; 15,000/8
Crew: 11 officers, 76–78 enlisted

Remarks: ATF 551 was transferred on 30-6-74 and ATF 553 on 1-9-78. The others were purchased 20-6-91 unarmed from the U.S. Maritime Administration along with ex-*Wenatchee* (ATF 118), which was to be used for cannibalization spares. ATF 551 went aground 15-3-87 but was salvaged for further service. Sister *Ta Tung* (ATF 548, ex-*Chickasaw,* ATF 83) was stricken on 16-7-99.

SERVICE CRAFT

♦ **1 ex-U.S. medium auxiliary floating dry dock [YFDM]**
Bldr: Everett Pacific, Calif. (In serv. 6-44)

Fo Wu 7 (ex-*Competent,* AFDM 6, ex-YFD 62)

Dim: 189.6 × 37.8 (28.3 clear width) × 1.9 (16.1 max flooded)
Capacity: 18,000 tons

Remarks: Transferred by sale during 1999. Had been retired from USN during 7-97 at Pearl Harbor.

♦ **1 ex-U.S. ARD 12–class floating dry dock [YFDL]**
Bldr: Pacific Bridge, Alameda, Calif.

Fo Wu 6 (ex-*Windsor,* ARD 22)

Dim: 149.86 × 24.69 × 1.73 (light) **Capacity:** 3,500 tons

Remarks: In service 4-44, transferred on lease 19-5-76; purchased outright in 1996.

♦ **1 ex-U.S. ARD 2–class floating dry dock [YFDL]**
Bldr: Pacific Bridge, Alameda, Calif.

Fo Wu 5 (ex-ARD 9)

Dim: 148.03 × 21.64 × 1.75 (light) **Capacity:** 3,500 tons

Remarks: In service 9-43, transferred on 12-1-77; purchased outright 1981.

♦ **2 ex-U.S. floating dry docks [YFDL]**
Bldr: V. P. Loftis, Wilmington, N.C.

Han Jih (ex-AFDL 34) Hay Tan (ex-AFDL 36)

Dim: 73.15 × 19.69 × 1.3 (light) **Capacity:** 1,000 tons

Remarks: In service 6-44 and 5-44, transferred in 7-59 and 3-47, respectively.

♦ **1 ex-U.S. floating dry dock [YFDL]**

Kim Men (ex-AFDL 5)

Dim: 60.96 × 19.5 × 1.04 **Capacity:** 1,000 tons

Remarks: Built in 1944, transferred in 8-58.

♦ **1 personnel ferry [YFL]** Bldr: . . .

	Laid down	L	In serv.
. . .	16-10-96	27-3-97	15-5-97

D: 339 tons (fl) **S:** 12 kts **Dim:** 41.15 × . . . × . . .
Electronics: Radar: 1 Goldstar . . . nav.
M: . . . diesels; . . . props; . . . bhp **Range:** 1,200/12
Crew: 10 tot. + 350 passengers

♦ **1 German Seahorse-class research submersible [YSS]**
Bldr: . . ., Germany (In serv. 1984)

D: 52 tons (sub.) **S:** 5 kts (sub.) **Dim:** 14.5 × 2.3 × . . .
M: Battery-powered electric motor; 1 prop; 107 shp **Range:** 400/5 (sub.)
Crew: 4 + 2 divers

Remarks: Delivery of a second canceled by German government. Ostensibly intended for underwater research, but probably employed in clandestine operations.

♦ **4 YTB 50–class large harbor tugs [YTB]**
Bldr: Chung Fu SB CO., Kaohsiung

	In serv.		In serv.
YTB 50	15-7-99	YTB . . .	13-9-99
YTB . . .	15-8-99	YTB . . .	15-10-99

YTB 50 *DTM,* 6-00

SERVICE CRAFT *(continued)*

D: Approx. 360 tons (fl) **S:** 10.5 kts **Dim:** 28.0 × 8.0 × 3.8
M: 2 Cummins V12 KTA38M2 diesels; Ulstein azimuthal props; 2,400 bhp
Crew: 10–12 tot.

Remarks: First four ordered 7-98 to begin replacement of the remaining U.S.-built harbor tugs; four or five more planned under Kuang Hua V Program, with another ten possibly to be built later. Are equipped for firefighting (with a telescoping mast to support a firefighting monitor) and oil-spill recovery. Have a 23-ton bollard pull capability.

♦ **1 or more YTB-48-class large harbor tugs [YTB]**
Bldr: . . . (In serv. . . .)

YTB 48

YTB 48 *DTM,* 1998

D: 286 tons (356 fl) **S:** 12.5 kts **Dim:** 33.05 × 9.30 × 4.14
M: 1 Fairbanks-Morse 38D8 1/8 × 12 diesel; 1 prop; 2,000 bhp
Electric: 120 kw tot. **Range:** 2,000/12 **Crew:** 12 tot.

♦ **3 YTL 41–class medium harbor tugs [YTM]**
Bldr: . . ., Taiwan (In serv. 1990–91)

YTL 41 YTL 43 YTL 45

YTL 43 C. Chung, 2-93

Remarks: No data available. Replaced the former U.S. Navy small harbor tugs with the same numbers that had been transferred in 1963–64. Are equipped for firefighting, with monitors atop mast, two atop pilothouse, and one on after superstructure.

♦ **3 ex-U.S. Army Design 3004 medium harbor tugs [YTM]**

YTL 34 (ex-ST-2002) YTL 36 (ex-ST-2004) YTL 38 (ex-ST-2008)

D: 100 tons light (122 fl) **S:** 12 kts **Dim:** 21.31 × 5.94 × 2.50
M: 1 diesel; 1 prop; 600 bhp **Range:** 3,500/12 **Fuel:** 15 tons **Crew:** 6 tot.

Remarks: Transferred 3-62; were built around 1954.

COAST GUARD

Personnel: Approximately 26,500 personnel total, including 22,000 assigned to the Coast Guard, 650 in customs enforcement, and 1,000 maritime police personnel

Note: Established 28-1-00, when the eight largest ships of the Customs Service were transferred to the new agency. During 2001 the Coast Guard was effectively combined with the National Police Administration, the National Fire Administration, and the Fisheries Administration. The craft and personnel of the former Maritime Security Police Coastal Patrol Command were integrated into the Coast Guard during 2002. Subordinated to the Navy in time of war.

PATROL SHIPS [WPS]

♦ **2 Ho Hsing class**
Bldr: China Shipbuilding, Keelung

	In serv.
101 Ho Hsing	1992
102 Wei Hsing	1992

Wei Hsing *Ships of the World,* 2000

D: 1,795 tons (fl) **S:** 22 kts **Dim:** 82.29 × 11.59 × 4.14
A: 2 single 12.7-mm mg
Electronics: Radar: 2 Decca . . . nav.
M: 2 MTU 16V1163 TB93 diesels; 2 CP props; 13,122 bhp—bow-thruster
Electric: 1,050 kw tot. (3 × 350 kw diesel alternator sets)
Range: 7,000/16 **Fuel:** 290 tons
Crew: 18 officers, 62 enlisted

Remarks: Ordered 11-1-90. Planned to deliver both on 1-7-91 but were delayed by German embargo on the engines. Nearly complete, *Ho Hsing* capsized 18-8-91 in a typhoon and was salvaged. Have accommodations for two senior personnel in addition to listed crew. Taken over from Customs Service during 1-00. Very similar to U.S. Coast Guard *Bear*-class, 270-ft cutters, but carry no heavy armament and substitute four high-speed interceptor craft in individual davits (two per side) for a helicopter facility. The eight interceptor craft were delivered 7-91 from Hood Military Vessels of the U.S.: 12.19 m overall, six crew, two 300-bhp Cummins diesels driving Arneson outdrives for 35 kts, range: 382 nautical miles at 35 kts, 466 nautical miles at 30 kts.

FISHERIES PATROL SHIPS [WPS]

Note: The ships and craft in this category were taken over from the Maritime Security Police and prior to that, from the Ministry of Agriculture. Currently in use are: *Shun Hu No. 1* (785 tons; 58.8 m overall; 16 kts), *Shun Hu No. 2* and *Shun Hu No. 3* (496 tons; 45.2 m overall; 16 kts), *Shun Hu No. 5* (131 tons; 31.5 m overall; 20 kts), and *Shun Hu No. 6* (200 tons); no other data are available for these units.

Shun Hu No. 3 *Ships of the World,* 2001

Shun Hu No. 1 Mitsuhiro Kadota, 9-01

COAST GUARD FISHERIES PATROL SHIPS [WPS] *(continued)*

Shun Hu No. 5 *Ships of the World,* 2001

PATROL COMBATANTS [WPG]

♦ 4 Tai Chung class

Bldr: Ching-Fu Shipbuilding Corp., Kaohsiung

	In serv.		In serv.
117 TAI CHUNG	20-1-01	119 HUALIEN	5-01
118 KEELUNG	3-01	120 PENGHU	30-6-01

Tai Chung (117) *Ships of the World,* 2001

D: 500 tons (630 fl) **S:** 30 kts **Dim:** 63.50 × 9.28 × 2.70
A: 1 20-mm 68-cal. T 75 AA
Electronics: Radar: 1 JRC . . . X-band nav., 1 JRC . . . S-band surf. search
M: 2 MTU 16V1163 TB93 diesels; 2 props; 15,608 bhp **Range:** 2,400/18
Crew: 9 officers, 37 enlisted

Remarks: Referred to as the *Hsiung Hsing* class in previous editions.

♦ 1 Jing Chiang class

Bldr: China SB Corp., Kaohsiung (In serv. 20-3-00)

116 TAIPEI

Taipei (116) *Ships of the World,* 2001

D: 500 tons light (680 fl) **S:** 30.9 kts **Dim:** 61.41 × 9.50 × 2.5
A: 2 single 12.7-mm mg
Electronics: Radar: 1 Decca Bridgemaster 250 nav.; 1 Terma Scanter Mil 009 surf. search
M: 2 MTU 16V1163 TB93 diesels; 2 props; 15,020 bhp (12,800 bhp sust.)
Range: 3,600/15 **Crew:** 7 officers, 25 enlisted

Remarks: Differs from naval sisters in having only light mg armament and in carrying two RIB inspection/rescue aft in davits.

♦ 2 Mou Hsing class

Bldr: Wilton-Fijenoord, Schiedam, the Netherlands

	L	In serv.
MOU HSING	13-2-88	14-6-88
FU HSING	13-2-88	14-6-88

Mou Hsing Fu S. Mei, 1-93

D: 700 tons light (917 fl) **S:** 28 kts (25 sust.) **Dim:** 66.10 × 9.60 × 3.22
A: 2 single 12.7-mm mg **Electronics:** Radar: 2/ . . . nav.
M: 3 MTU 16V538 TB93 diesels; 3 props; 13,200 bhp (11,040 sust.)
Range: 4,500/12 **Crew:** 54 tot.

Remarks: Ordered 4-86. Taken over from Customs Service during 1-00.

♦ 1 Yun Hsing class

Bldr: China SB, Keelung (In serv. 28-12-87)

YUN HSING

Yun Hsing H&L Van Ginderen, 5-97

D: 900 tons (964 fl) **S:** 24 kts **Dim:** 65.0 × 10.0 × 2.9
A: 2 single 12.7-mm mg Electronics: Radar: 2 JRC . . . nav.
M: 2 M.A.N.-Sulzer 12 VSA 25/30 diesels; 2 props; 7,200 bhp **Crew:** 67 tot.

Remarks: Taken over from Customs Service during 1-00. Carries two U.S. 26-ft motor whaleboats as inspection boats.

♦ 3 Chin Hsing class

Bldr: China SB, Keelung

	In serv.
107 PAO HSING	11-86
108 CHIN HSING	23-5-85
109 TEH HSING	11-86

D: 550 tons (fl) **S:** 24 kts **Dim:** 57.8 × 7.8 × 2.1 **A:** 2 single 12.7-mm mg
Electronics: Radar: 2 JRC . . . nav.
M: 2 M.A.N. 12V 25/30 diesels; 2 props; 7,200 bhp **Crew:** 40 tot.

Remarks: A flush-decked design resembling South Korean Coast Guard "Sea Whale" design, but somewhat smaller. *Chin Hsing* launched 26-12-84. Former armament of one 40-mm and two single 20-mm AA removed.

PATROL CRAFT [WPC]

♦ 13 PP-901 class

Bldr: Lung Teh Shipbuilding, Kaohsiung (In serv. 9-96 to 1-97)

PP-6001	PP-6006	PP-6011	PP-6016
PP-6002	PP-6007	PP-6012	
PP-6003	PP-6009	PP-6014	
PP-6005	PP-6010	PP-6015	

D: 91 tons (102 fl) **S:** 42 kts **Dim:** 30.50 (28.00 pp) × 6.20 × 1.30 (2.40 over props)
A: 2 single 12.7-mm mg **Electronics:** Radar: 2 . . . nav.

COAST GUARD PATROL CRAFT [WPC] *(continued)*

PP-6002—note rigid inflatable fender around hull *Ships of the World,* 2001

M: 2 Paxman 12VP185 diesels; 2 4-bladed props; 6,552 bhp
Electric: 96 kw tot. (2 × 48 kw Alsthom sets, diesel driven) **Range:** 600/25
Fuel: 17 m^3 **Crew:** 12 tot.

Remarks: Ordered 10-95. Kevlar structure, with deep-vee hull form. Have X-band navigational radar, video plot, Global Positioning System receiver, D/F, and echo sounder. Carry a 6.5-m RIB inspection craft. Propulsion plant also reported to be two MTU diesels of 3,070 bhp each for a maximum of 30 kts (28 sust.) and to have been constructed of steel, with aluminum superstructures by TMMC Shipyard, Kaohsiung.

♦ 15 PP-1001 class
Bldr: China SB Corp., Kaohsiung (In serv. 8-12-92 to 11-98)

PP-1001–PP-1003, PP-1005–PP-10013, PP-10017–PP-10019

PP-10011 *Ships of the World,* 2001

D: 140 tons (fl) **S:** 30 kts **Dim:** 27.40 × 8.70 × 1.60 **A:** 2 single 12.7-mm mg
Electronics: Radar: 1 Decca . . . nav.
M: 2 MTU diesels; 2 props; 6,000 bhp **Crew:** 12 tot.

Remarks: First two were built for the ROCN and transferred to the new Maritime Security Police on completion.

♦ 1 Hsun Hsing class
Bldr: China SB, Kaohsiung (In serv. 15-12-86)

Hsun Hsing

D: 239 tons (264 fl) **S:** 28 kts **Dim:** 44.5 × 7.5 × 1.7 **A:** 3 12.7-mm mg
Electronics: Radar: 2 . . . nav.
M: 3 MTU 16V396 TB93 diesels; 3 props; 8,160 bhp **Crew:** 41 tot.

Note: Also in service are two or more 25-m patrol craft in the PP-5000 pennant number series; capable of 32 kts, they appear to be of recent construction.

PATROL BOATS [WPB]

♦ 1 (+ 16) PP-2001 class
Bldr: Lung-The Shipbldg., Dong-Shan (In serv. 2002)

PP 2003

D: 21 tons (fl) **S:** 39 kts **Dim:** 15.00 (13.80 wl) × 4.60 × 0.80 **A:** . . .
Electronics: Radar: . . .
M: 1 M.A.N. 2840-LE401 diesel; 1 Hamilton HM.461 waterjet; 820 bhp
Range: 350/25 **Fuel:** 3,000 liters **Crew:** 6 tot.

Remarks: Prototype delivered and sixteen more ordered early in 2002. GRP construction.

♦ 5 or more PP-3538 class
Bldr: Lung-The Shipbldg., Dong-Shan (In serv. . . .)

PP-3538 PP-3539 PP-3551 PP-3552 PP-3553

D: 55.7 tons (fl) **S:** 28 kts **Dim:** 20.0 × . . . × . . . **A:** 2 single 12.7-mm mg
M: 2 . . . diesels; 2 props; . . . bhp

♦ 7 PP-701 class
Bldr: Lung Teh Shipbuilding (In serv. 1994–95)

PP-701 through PP-703 PP-705 through PP-708

D: 29 tons (fl) **S:** 45 kts **Dim:** 20.00 × 4.80 × 0.72 **A:** . . . small arms
Electronics: Radar: 1 . . . nav.
M: 3 M.A.N. . . . diesels; 3 Servogear 4-bladed props; 3,320 bhp
Range: 400/30 **Crew:** 8 tot.

Remarks: Single-skin GRP deep-vee hull using PVC core with Kevlar and E-glass reinforcement; a semi-rigid inflatable fender surrounds the hull. Capable of maintaining 30 kts in 2-meter waves and Force 8 wind. Intended for antismuggling patrol off the northeast coast of Taiwan.

♦ 23 PP-501 class
Bldr: prototype: Vosper Pty, Singapore; others: China SB, Kaohsiung (In serv. 1989– . . .)

PP-501	PP-603	PP-607	PP-611	PP-615	PP-619	PP-623	PP-628
PP-502	PP-605	PP-609	PP-612	PP-616	PP-620	PP-625	PP-630
PP-602	PP-606	PP-610	PP-613	PP-618	PP-621	PP-627	

PP-501 *Ships of the World*

D: 28 tons (fl) **S:** 40+ kts **Dim:** 21.00 (16.60 wl) × 4.80 × 1.00
A: 2 single 12.7-mm mg **Electronics:** Radar: 1/Decca 170 nav.
M: 2 G.M.-Stewart & Stevenson 16V92 TMAB diesels; 2 Arneson ASD 14 surface-piercing outdrives; 2,700 bhp
Electric: 18 kw tot. **Range:** 400/ . . . **Crew:** 8 tot.

Remarks: Aluminum construction. Previously referred to as the "PBC 3501" class.

♦ 10 PP-820 class
Bldr: China Shipbuilding Corp., Kaohsiung (In serv. 1989–91)

PP-820–PP-823, PP-825–PP-830

D: 100 tons (fl) **S:** 30 kts **Dim:** 27.4 (26.2 wl) × 8.7 × 1.8
A: 2 single 12.7-mm mg **Electronics:** Radar: 1 . . . nav.
M: 3 Isotta Fraschini diesels; 3 Castoldi waterjets; 3,000 bhp

Remarks: Used mainly for fisheries patrol and counterinsurgency missions; have a large searchlight atop the pilothouse.

♦ 12 PP 801 class
Bldr: China Shipbuilding Corp., Kaohsiung

PP-801	PP-803	PP-808	PP-810	PP-812	PP-815
PP-802	PP-807	PP-809	PP-811	PP-813	PP-816

D: 55 tons (fl) **S:** 25 kts **Dim:** 18.3 × . . . × . . . **A:** 2 single 12.7-mm mg
M: 2 diesels; waterjet drive

Remarks: Were built around 1971. Aluminum construction. Sister PP-805 was lost during 11-97.

♦ 22 Type 42 class
Bldr: . . ., Taiwan (In serv. 1970s)

D: 10.5 tons (fl) **S:** 32 kts **Dim:** 12.8 × . . . × . . . **A:** 1 12.7-mm mg
Electronics: Radar: 1 . . . nav.
M: 2 G.M. diesels; 2 Arneson surface-piercing outdrives; 1,300 bhp
Range: 400/ . . .

Remarks: GRP construction, C. Raymond Hunt design.

♦ 20 M-4 Jet-Boat riverine patrol craft

PP-301 through PP-320

Remarks: Employed for harbor and river-mouth antismuggling patrol. Gasoline outboard-propelled.

CUSTOMS SERVICE

Subordinate to the Ministry of Finance in peacetime and to the navy in time of war. Ships and craft are painted white, and seagoing units bear the legend "Customs Preventive Ship" on their sides in English. All ships and craft of more than 100 tons full-load displacement were transferred to the new Coast Guard on 28-1-00.

TANZANIA

United Republic of Tanzania

NAVY

Personnel: About 1,000 total

Bases: Headquarters, principal base at Dar Es Salaam, other facilities are located at Zanzibar and at Mwanza on Lake Victoria.

Coastal Defense: There is a battery of mobile 85-mm artillery.

PATROL CRAFT [PC]

♦ 2 Chinese Shanghai-II class

P 67 Mzizi (ex-JW 9867) P 68 Mzia (ex-JW 9868)

Tanzanian Shanghai-II—one of the now-stricken group delivered 1970–71 H&L Van Ginderen, 1984

D: 122.5 tons (134.8 fl) **S:** 28.5 kts
Dim: 38.78 × 5.41 × 1.49 (hull; 1.554 full load)
A: 2 twin 37-mm 63-cal. Type 74 AA; 2 twin 25-mm 80-cal. Type 61M AA
Electronics: Radar: 1 Type 756 nav.
M: 2 Type L12-180 (M50F-4) diesels (1,200 bhp each), and 2 Type 12D6 diesels (910 bhp each); 4 props; 4,200 bhp
Electric: 39 kw tot. **Range:** 750/16.5 **Endurance:** 7 days **Crew:** 36 tot.

Remarks: Delivered 6-92 and were probably refurbished ex–Chinese Navy units rather than new construction. Of seven other new units delivered 1970–71, the last was out of service by early 1992. The 910-bhp diesels are used for cruising. P 68 was in good condition as of spring 2002.

TORPEDO BOATS [PT]

♦ 2 Chinese Huchuan class (Project 026)
Bldr: Hudung SY, Shanghai

P 43 (ex-JW 9843) P 44 (ex-JW 9844)

Huchuan-class JW 9842—since stricken 1976

D: 39 tons (45.8 fl) **S:** 50 kts **Dim:** 22.50 × 3.80 × 1.146
A: 2 fixed 533-mm TT; 2 twin 14.5-mm 93-cal. Type 81 mg
Electronics: Radar: 1 Skin Head nav. **M:** 3 M50F-4 diesels; 3 props; 3,600 bhp
Electric: 5.6 kw **Range:** 500/30 **Crew:** 11 tot.

Remarks: Survivors of four delivered new in 1975. Unlike most Chinese Navy Huchuans, these craft had no hydrofoils. Are late-model Project 026 units with one gunmount forward and one aft. All four were operational in 1993, having undergone an overhaul at Dar Es Salaam in 1991–92, but by 1998 JW 9841 and JW 9842 had been stricken to provide a source of spares for the other two; the operational units are based on Lake Tanganyika at Kigoma, where there are few, if any, targets for their torpedoes (assuming any are still operable) and the radars are probably no longer functioning.

PATROL BOATS [PB]

♦ 2 (+ 2) ex-British Protector class
Bldr: PB 19: Babcock Marine, Cowes, U.K.; PB 20: Fairey Marine, Cowes, U.K.

PB 19 Ngunguri (ex-*Vincent*) PB 20 Mamba (ex-*Vigilant*)
. . . (ex-*Valiant*) . . . (ex-*Venturous*)

D: 100 tons (fl) **S:** 25 kts **Dim:** 25.70 × 6.20 × 1.7
A: . . .
Electronics: Radar: 2 Decca nav.
M: 2 Paxman 12 . . . diesels; 2 props; 2,880 bhp—1 Perkins 6/3544 auxiliary propulsion diesel; 1 waterjet
Range: 500/30 **Crew:** 11 tot.

Mamba (PB 20)—while still in British service Derek Fox, 9-02

Remarks: Purchased 9-05 from the British Customs and Marine Excise Branch; ex-*Valiant* and ex-*Venturous* will follow by 2007.

♦ 2 70-ton class
Bldr: Vosper Thornycroft, Portchester, U.K.

D: 70 tons **S:** 24.5 kts **Dim:** 22.9 × 6.0 × 1.5
A: 2 single 20-mm 90-cal. Oerlikon GAM-B01 AA
Electronics: Radar: 1 Furuno . . . nav.
M: 2 diesels; 2 props; 1,840 bhp **Range:** 800/20 **Crew:** 11 tot.

Remarks: The first two of four units were delivered 6-7-73, the others during 1974, but one had been retired around 1997 and one was inoperable as of 1999. Glass-reinforced-plastic construction. Keith Nelson hull design. Are both assigned to Zanzibar.

AMPHIBIOUS WARFARE CRAFT

♦ 2 Chinese Yuchin (Type 069)-class landing craft [LCM]
Bldr: Kailing SY, Zhoushen (L: 8-4-95)

L 08 Pono L 09 Kibua

Kibua (L 09) M.O.D. Bonn, 4-97

D: 85 tons (fl) **S:** 11.5 kts **Dim:** 24.1 × 5.2 × 1.2
M: 2 M.A.N. . . . diesels; 2 props; 600 bhp **Range:** 700/11.5 (light) **Crew:** 8 tot.

Remarks: New export version of design with greater molded depth to improve cargo capacity, air-conditioning, and improved steering system. Intended primarily for logistics support. Based at Dar-es-Salaam.

THAILAND

Kingdom of Thailand

NAVY

Personnel: 70,600 total (including 1,941 in Naval Air Arm, 23,000 Marines and the Coast Defense Command)

NAVY *(continued)*

Bases: Fleet headquarters, dockyard, and principal base at Bangkok, with other bases at Phang-Nga, Sattahip, and Songkhla at Thap Lamu

Naval Aviation: Naval aviation forces include: seven AV-8S Matador V/STOL fighters and two TAV-8A Harrier V/STOL trainers, being replaced by Sea Harrier FA.2 fighters in 2006–7; 14 A-7E and four TA-7C Corsair-II land-based attack aircraft (in 2003 it was announced that only four Corsairs will remain in service through 2008 with the remaining aircraft to be used for spares); three P-3B Orion, two Fokker F-27-400M and three Fokker F-27-200 Marine, six Dornier Do-228-212, nine GAF N-24L Searchmasters for maritime surveillance; two CL-215-III firefighting amphibians; 11 Summit Sentry O2-377 Sentry light attack aircraft; one UP-3A Orion, two Fokker F27-400M; 10 Cessna O-1G Bird Dog observation aircraft; nine U-17B Skywagon utility aircraft; two Super Lynx 300, six Sikorsky S-70B-7 Seahawk, five Sikorsky S-76B, and five Bell 212 and five Bell 214 helicopters. The U.S. Navy has offered 10 SH-2F SeaSprite SH02F helicopters and eight of these will likely be delivered as improved SH-2G variants during 2007–8. The F-27-200 patrol aircraft are equipped to launch AGM-84C Harpoon missiles and Stingray ASW torpedoes.

Thai Navy AV-8S Matador Royal Thai Navy, 1996

Coast Defense Command: The Royal Thai Marines are stationed in the eastern coastal area of the country for coastal defense duties. Emplaced artillery includes 155-mm and 105-mm guns and numerous smaller caliber AA guns available for air defense.

Note: Ship names are preceded by HTMS (His Thai Majesty's Ship).

AIRCRAFT CARRIER, V/STOL [CVV]

♦ 1 Chakri Naruebet class

Bldr: Izar (formerly E.N. Bazán), Ferrol, Spain

	Laid down	L	In serv.
911 Chakri Naruebet	12-7-94	20-1-96	10-8-97

Chakri Naruebet (911)—with container ship visible over the bow in the background Royal Thai Navy, 8-97

Chakri Naruebet (911) Royal Thai Navy, 8-97

Chakri Naruebet (911) Izar, 1997

D: 11,486 tons (fl) **S:** 27.5 kts (26.2 kts sust.; 17.2 kts on diesels)
Dim: 182.65 (174.10 flight deck; 164.10 pp) × 30.50 (22.50 wl) × 6.12
Air Group: 6 AV-8S Matador V/STOL fighters; 4 S-70B-7 Seahawk helicopters (up to 18 total helicopters max.)
A: 3 6-round Sadral point-defense SAM syst. (Mistral missiles); 2 single 20-mm AA; 2 single 12.7-mm mg; see Remarks
Electronics:
Radar: 2 Kelvin-Hughes 1007 nav.; 1 Hughes SPS-52C 3-D air search; 1 Kelvin-Hughes . . . air-control;
TACAN: SRN-15A
EW: See Remarks
M: CODOG: 2 Bazán-MTU 16V1163 TB83 diesels (5,600 bhp each), 2 G.E. LM2500 gas turbines (22,125 shp each); 2 5-bladed CP props; 44,250 shp max.
Electric: 4,800 kw tot. (4 × 1,200 kw MAN diesel alternator sets)
Range: 7,150/16.5; 10,000/12
Crew: 62 officers, 393 enlisted + up to 146 aircrew + up to 675 troops

Remarks: Ordered 28-3-92. Delivered 27-3-97. Builder's BSAC 160 design. Name means "In Honor of the Chakri Dynasty." Intended for disaster relief duties in peacetime and was originally to have had a civilian crew. The ship arrived in Thailand 10-8-97. Due to funding shortages, the ship operates infrequently, reportedly only one day per month, within the confines of the naval base harbor at Sattahip, to exercise the air group.

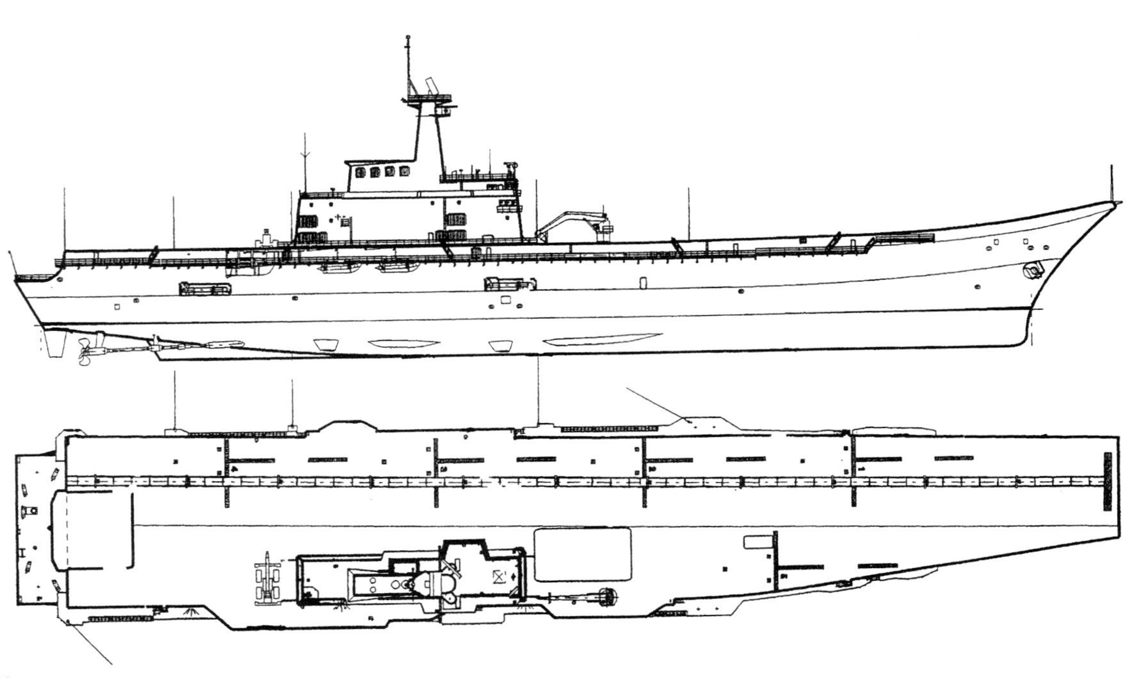

Chakri Naruebet (911) Izar, 1995

AIRCRAFT CARRIER, V/STOL [CVV] *(continued)*

Combat systems: Three sextuple Sadral launchers for Mistral heat-seeking SAMs were added in 2001. Reports indicate that one Mk 48 Sea Sparrow VLS SAM launch group with eight RIM-7M missiles, four Phalanx CIWS AA guns; one or two STIR 1.8 fire-control radar and a SLQ-32(V)3 and Indra SLQ-380 Aldebarán intercept/jammer suite may have been added by 2006–7, though this remains unconfirmed. Combat data and control system based on Spanish Tritan, with UYK-3 and UYK-20 computers.
Hull systems: The hull has 14 watertight compartments, and the ship is built to Lloyd's RS commercial standards. Has two pair of fin stabilizers. The hullform includes a wedge at the stern to improve speed and economy. Normal troop accommodation total is 455. Has accommodations for the Thai royal family. There is stowage for 99 m^3 of refrigerated and 300 m^3 dry stores, 60 tons aviation fuel, and 100 tons aviation ordnance. Evaporators producing 90 tons of water per day are fitted. There are two rudders.
Aviation systems: Up to five CH-47 Chinook-sized helicopters can be accommodated on the after portion of the flight deck. The 100 × 20.5–m hangar below is able to hold 10 Sea Harrier V/STOL fighters or 15 Sea King–sized helicopters or 30 or more personnel carriers. The 165 × 30.5–m flight deck is served by two 13.5 × 13.5–m, 20-ton elevators (one centerline at the stern) and a 16-ton crane. There are two weapons elevators.

FRIGATES [FF]

♦ 2 Chinese Type 25T
Bldr: Zhonghua SY, Shanghai

	Laid down	L	In serv.
421 Naresuan	11-91	7-93	15-12-94
422 Taksin	1991	23-7-94	28-9-95

Taksin (422) Chris Sattler, 8-05

Taksin (422) Chris Sattler, 9-05

Taksin (422) Chris Sattler, 8-05

D: 2,590 tons (2,980 fl) **S:** 32 kts **Dim:** 120.50 × 13.40 × 3.85 (hull)
A: 8 RGM-84A Harpoon SSM; 1 Mk 48 Sea Sparrow VLS SAM launch group with 8 RIM-7M missiles; 1 127-mm 54-cal. U.S. Mk 45 Mod. 2 DP; 2 twin 37-mm 76-cal. Type 76A AA; 2 triple 324-mm Mk 32 Mod. 5 ASW TT (Mk 46 Mod. 5 torpedoes); 1 Super Lynx helicopter
Electronics:
Radar: 1 Raytheon SPS-64(V)15 nav.; 1 Raytheon SPS-64(V)5 helo control; 1 Chinese Type 360 surf./air-search; 1 Thales LW-08 air-search; 1 Thales STIR-1.8 gun and SAM f.c.; 1 Chinese Type 347G gun f.c. (for 37-mm AA)
Sonar: Chinese SJD-7 bow-mounted (MF)
EW: Chinese Mirage NRJ-5 intercept and Model 945 GPJ passive jammer; . . . active jammer; 4 26-round Type 945 decoy RL
E/O: JM-83H optronic gun f.c.

M: CODOG: 2 G.E. LM-2500 gas turbines (27,500 shp each), 2 MTU 20V1163 TB 83 diesels (8,000 bhp each/7,385 bhp sust.); 2 CP props; 55,000 shp max.
Electric: 1,760 kw tot. (4 × 440 kw, MTU 12V396 TM 53 diesels driving)
Range: 4,000/18 **Endurance:** 15 days **Crew:** 24 officers, 144 enlisted

Remarks: Ordered 21-9-89. First unit handed over 15-12-94 for final fitting out with Western-supplied electronics and weapons in Thailand, completing 10-95; only the Chinese-made armament and electronic equipment listed previously was aboard at time of delivery. Very lightly built, with the firing of the 127-mm gun causing structural damage forward.
Hull systems: Have fin stabilizers. Damage control is considerably improved over earlier Chinese designs.
Combat systems: There is a helicopter hangar, and each can carry a Super Lynx 300 helicopter. One source indicates that "Mirage" EW system is a copy of the Elettronica Newton-Beta system. There is one Chinese JM-83H optical backup director for the 37-mm guns, mounted atop the after edge of the helicopter hangar; the Type 347G radar director is said to be a license-built version of the Selenia RTN-20S. The Raytheon DE-1160C hull-mounted LF (5.6/7.5/8.4 kHz) sonar may be substituted later for the Chinese set installed at delivery. Were recently fitted with the Mk 48 VLS SAM system and Sea Sparrow missiles.

♦ 4 Chinese Jianghu III Class (Project 053HT and 053HTH*)
Bldr: Zhonghua SY, Shanghai

	Laid down	L	In serv.
455 Chao Phraya	4-89	24-6-90	5-4-91
456 Bangpakong	1989	24-7-90	20-7-91
457 Kraburi*	1990	28-12-90	16-1-92
458 Saiburi*	1990	29-6-91	4-8-92

Bangpakong (456) Brian Morrison, 10-02

Chao Phraya (455)—with two 100-mm gunmounts Ralph Edwards, 10-01

Bangpakong (456) Brian Morrison, 10-02

D: 1,676 tons (1,924 fl) **S:** 31 kts (30 sust.) **Dim:** 103.20 × 10.83 × 3.10 (hull)
A: 4 C-801 SSM; 1 (455, 456: 2) twin 100-mm 56-cal. DP; 4 twin 37-mm 63-cal. Type 74 AA; 2 5-round Type 86 ASW RL
Electronics:
Radar: 1 Decca RM 1290A/D ARPA nav.; 1 Type 354 (MX-902/Eye Shield) air search; 1 Type 352C (Square Tie) missile target acquisition and tracking; 1 Type 343 (Sun Visor) gun f.c.; 1 Type 341 (Rice Lamp) gun f.c.
Sonar: Type SJD-5A bow-mounted searchlight (HF)
EW: Elettronica Newton-Beta suite (Type 211 intercept, Type 318 noise jammer, Type 521 deception jammer); 2 26-round Type 945 decoy RL

FRIGATES [FF] *(continued)*

Saiburi (458)—with helicopter deck aft Takatoshi Okano, 6-00

M: 4 MTU 20V1163 TB83 diesels; 2 CP props; 26,750 bhp sust.
Electric: 1,600 kw (4 × 400 kw, MTU 8V396-series diesel-driven sets)
Range: 3,500/18 **Endurance:** 15 days
Crew: 22 officers, 146 enlisted (accomm. for 24 officers, 182 enlisted)

Remarks: First two ordered 18-7-88, second pair 8-89. Are employed primarily for antipiracy and marine police functions. Plans to modernize the ships with Western weapons and sensors have been dropped. 457 suffered serious damage during the 12-04 tsunami and may be disposed of rather than repaired.
Hull systems: Said to be flimsily constructed and to have very poor damage-control features. Have fin stabilization system. May be able to reach only 28 kts.
Combat systems: The EW suite employs Type 923 omnidirectional antennas for the Type 521 deception jammer, and Type 981 omnidirectional and Type 929 directional antennas, all mounted on the mast and superstructure sides; the equipment is of Italian design, license-built in China. The 100-mm guns are controlled by the Wok Won director atop the pilothouse (with integral Type 343 Sun Visor radar), while the Type 341 radar aft provides range inputs to the 37-mm guns, which are aimed via ringsights and are arranged to cover one quadrant for each mount. The 100-mm guns have a rate of fire of 25 rounds per minute and a range of 16 km and employ a French-designed autoloader. 457 and 458 have a helicopter platform raised above the fantail at forecastle level and omit the after twin 100-mm gunmount, but there is no hangar; Bell UH-1 helicopters can be accommodated.

♦ 1 Yarrow Frigate class
Bldr: Yarrow, Scotstoun, Glasgow, Scotland

	Laid down	L	In serv.
433 Makut Rajakumarn	11-1-70	18-11-71	7-5-73

Makut Rajakumarn (433) Takatoshi Okano, 7-98

Makut Rajakumarn (433) *Ships of the World,* 7-98

D: 1,650 tons (1,900 fl) **S:** 26 kts (gas turbines)/18 kts (diesel)
Dim: 97.56 (92.99 pp) × 10.97 × 5.5 (over sonar)
A: 2 single 114-mm 55-cal. Vickers Mk 8 DP; 1 twin 40-mm 70-cal. OTO Melara Compact AA; 1 twin 20-mm AA; 2 single 12.7-mm mg; 2 triple 324-mm PMW 49A ASW TT (6 Stingray torpedoes); 1 d.c. rack (6 d.c.)
Electronics:
Radar: 1 Decca . . . nav.; 1 Thales ZW-06 surf. search; 1 Thales DA-05 surf./air-search; 1 Thales WM-22 Mod. 61 f.c.
Sonar: STN-Atlas Elektronik DSQS-21C hull-mounted MF
EW: Elettronica Newton intercept; FH-4 HFD/F
M: CODOG: 1 Rolls-Royce Olympus TBM 3B gas turbine (23,125 shp), 1 Crossley-Pielstick 12 PC2V diesel (6,000 bhp); 2 CP props
Electric: 2,200 kw tot. **Range:** 1,000/25; 4,000/18
Crew: 16 officers, 124 enlisted

Remarks: Ordered 21-8-69. Similar to the Malaysian *Rahmat* but longer and more heavily armed. Used primarily as a training ship. Modernized 1985–88 after a serious fire in 2-84: a new sonar and air-search radar were fitted, and the engineering plant was renewed.
Combat systems: During a 1993 refit, the Sea Cat missile launcher and director were deleted and replaced with two single 40-mm AA. In 1997 two sets of ASW TT (with U.K. Stingray torpedoes) replaced the single 40-mm mounts, a new EW suite was fitted, and a twin 40-mm AA mount with an optical director was situated aft. A twin 20-mm AA gun had been fitted by 2005. The original Limbo triple ASW mortar remains aboard but is nonoperational. Has a Thales SEWACO TH combat data system. The WM-22 track-while-scan radar controls the 114-mm guns, and there are two optical backup directors.

♦ 2 ex-U.S. Knox class
Bldr: Avondale Marine, Westwego, La.

	Laid down	L	In serv.
461 Phuttha Yotfa Chulalok (ex-*Truett,* FFT 1095)	27-4-72	3-2-73	1-6-74
462 Phuttha Loetla Naphalai (ex-*Ouellet,* FF 1077)	15-1-69	17-1-70	12-12-70

Phuttha Loetla Naphalai (462) H&L Van Ginderen, 8-98

Phuttha Yotfa Chulalok (461) *Ships of the World,* 1998

D: 3,130 tons light (4,260 fl) **S:** 29 kts
Dim: 134.00 (126.49 wl) × 14.33 × 4.77 (7.83 over sonar)
A: 4 RGM-84C Harpoon SSM (using Mk 112 ASROC launcher system); 1 127-mm 54-cal. Mk 42 Mod. 10 DP; 1 20-mm Mk 15 Phalanx CIWS; 4 single 12.7-mm M2 mg; 1 8-round Mk 16 Mod. 8 ASROC ASW syst. (Mk 112 launcher); 4 fixed 324-mm Mk 32 Mod. 9 ASW TT (Mk 46 Mod. 5) torpedoes; 1 . . . helicopter
Electronics:
Radar: 1 Raytheon SPS-64(V)9 nav.; 1 Raytheon SPS-10F surf. search; 1 Lockheed Martin SPS-40D air search; 1 Western Electric SPG-53F gun f.c.; 1 General Dynamics Mk 90 Phalanx f.c.
Sonar: G.E. SQS-26CX bow-mounted LF; EDO SQR-18(V)1 (462: SQR-18A(V)2) towed linear passive array
TACAN: SRN-15A
EW: SLQ-32(V)2 intercept; Mk 36 SRBOC decoy syst. (4 6-round Mk 137 RL); T-Mk 6 Fanfare towed acoustic torpedo decoy
M: 1 set Westinghouse geared steam turbines; 1 prop; 35,000 shp
Boilers: 2 Combustion Engineering V2M M-Type (462: Babcock & Wilcox D-Type); 84 kg/cm^2, 510-deg. C
Electric: 3,000 kw tot. (3 × 750 kw turbogenerators, 1 × 750 kw diesel set)
Range: 4,300/20 **Fuel:** 750 tons max. **Crew:** 17 officers, 271 enlisted

Remarks: 461 transferred on decommissioning from U.S.N. on 31-7-94; 462, in reserve since 6-8-93, was leased 27-11-96 and transferred 5-98 after reactivation and refit by Cascade General at Portland, Oregon, arriving in Thailand during 11-98. Both were on five-year lease, but 461 was donated outright during U.S. Fiscal Year 2000.

FRIGATES [FF] *(continued)*

Hull systems: Bow bulwarks and a spray strake were added forward to reduce deck wetness, a problem in this class; the addition added 9.1 tons and extended the overall length from the original 133.59 m. 461 has a TEAM (SM-5) computer system for the continual monitoring of the ship's electronic equipment. Anti-rolling fin stabilizers are fitted to both. The Prairie/Masker bubbler system is fitted to the hull and propellers to reduce radiated noise.
Combat systems: The ASROC system has an 18-weapon automatic reloading magazine beneath the bridge; it is also used to stow the Harpoon missiles, which are launched from the starboard pair of eight launcher cells. The ASW torpedo tubes are fixed, in the forward end of the hangar superstructure, aimed outboard at an angle of 45-degrees; a total of 24 Mk 46–series torpedoes can be carried, including those intended to be carried by the helicopter. Both have Mk 114 Mod. 6 ASW fire-control systems and a Mk 68 Mod. 3 gunfire-control system with SPG-53F radar. During reactivation overhaul, 462 was equipped with SQR-18(V)2 Towed Array Sonar System (TASS), while 461 retains the SQR-18(V) system, which uses the winch and deactivated VDS "fish" from the inactivated SQS-35 VDS system to tow the linear array. A Marisat SATCOM system has replaced the WSC-3 UHF SATCOM system in both.

CORVETTES [FFL]

♦ 2 U.S. PFMM Mk 16 class
Bldr: Tacoma Boatbldg., Tacoma, Wash.

	Laid down	L	In serv.
441 Ratanakosin	6-2-84	11-3-86	26-9-86
442 Sukhothai	26-3-84	20-7-86	19-2-87

Ratanakosin (441)—note single 76-mm and twin 40-mm guns Hans Karr, 11-03

D: 840 tons normal (960 fl) **S:** 26 kts **Dim:** 76.82 × 9.55 × 2.44 (hull)
A: 8 RGM-84A Harpoon SSM; 1 8-round Albatros SAM system (24 Aspide missiles); 1 76-mm 62-cal. OTO Melara Compact DP; 1 twin 40-mm 70-cal. OTO Melara Compact AA; 2 single 20-mm 90-cal. Oerlikon GAM-B01 AA; 2 triple 324-mm Mk 32 Mod. 5 ASW TT (6 Stingray torpedoes)
Electronics:
Radar: 1 Decca 1226 nav.; 1 Thales ZW-06 surf. search; 1 Thales DA-05 surf./ air-search; 1 Thales WM-25 Mod. 41 f.c.
Sonar: STN-Atlas Elektronik DSQS-21C hull-mounted MF
EW: Elettronica Newton intercept; 1 330-340-round Matra Défense Dagaie Mk 2 decoy RL
E/O: Thales LIROD-8 f.c.

Sukhothai (442) Stefan Karpinski, 5-02

M: 2 MTU 20V1163 TB83 diesels; 2 props; 16,000 bhp (14,730 sust.)
Range: 3,000/16 **Crew:** 15 officers, 72 enlisted

Remarks: Ordered 9-5-83. Plans to build a third ship in Thailand were canceled. Enlarged version of U.S.-built Saudi Arabian PCG class. Have the Thales Mini-SADOC weapons control system. The LIROD-8 optronic backup director for the 76-mm gun has radar, infrared, and low-light-level t.v. sensors. 442 performed the first Thai Navy launch of a Harpoon missile on 23-5-02.

♦ 2 ex-U.S. PF 103 class

	Bldr	Laid down	L	In serv.
431 Tapi (ex-PF 107)	American SB, Toledo, Ohio	1-4-70	17-10-70	1-11-71
432 Khirirat (ex-PF 108)	Norfolk SB & DD, Va.	18-2-72	2-6-73	10-8-74

Tapi (431) J & P Van Raemdonck, 3-04

Khirirat (432) Arjun Sarup, 4-01

CORVETTES [FFL] *(continued)*

D: 893 tons light (1,172 fl) **S:** 20 kts **Dim:** 84.04 × 10.06 × 3.05 (4.27 sonar)
A: 1 76-mm 62-cal. OTO Melara Compact DP; 1 40-mm 70-cal. Bofors L70 AA; 2 single 20-mm 90-cal. Oerlikon GAM B01 AA; 2 single 12.7-mm mg; 2 triple 324-mm Mk 32 Mod. 5 ASW TT (6 Mk 46 mod. 2 torpedoes); 1 Mk 9 d.c. rack (7 Mk 9 d.c.)
Electronics:
Radar: 1 Raytheon . . . nav.; 1 Westinghouse SPS-6C air-search; 1 Thales WM-22 Mod. 61 f.c.
Sonar: Krupp-Atlas DSQS-21C hull-mounted MF
M: 2 Fairbanks-Morse 38TD8⅛ × 10 diesels; 2 props; 5,300 bhp
Electric: 750 kw tot. **Range:** 2,400/18 **Fuel:** 110 tons
Crew: 15 officers, 120 enlisted

Remarks: Ordered 27-6-69 and 26-6-71, respectively. Four sisters were also built for the Iranian Navy. *Tapi* completed modernization in 1983 with the OTO Melara gun replacing the forward U.S. 76.2-mm mount, a Bofors 40-mm on a raised bandstand replacing the aft 76.2-mm mount, two single 20-mm AA replacing the original twin 40-mm mount, an H.S.A. WM-22 track-while-scan radar director being mounted above the bridge, and a new sonar in place of the original U.S. SQS-17A; the Hedgehog ASW spiggot mortar was removed. *Khirirat* received similar modernization in 1985–87, and both received further updates to the communications suites in 1988–89. The main engines are turbopressurized.

PATROL SHIPS [PS]

♦ 2 (+ . . .) Chinese . . . class
Bldr: Qiuxin SY, Shanghai

	Laid down	L	In serv.
511	2003	19-9-04	11-05
512	2004	2005	2006

D: 1,500 tons (fl) **S:** 25 kts **Dim:** 95.5 × 11.6 × 3.1
A: . . . SSM; 1 76-mm 62-cal. OTO Melara Compact DP; 1 twin 23-mm AA; 1 helicopter
Electronics: Radar: Alenia Marconi RAN 30 surf./air search
M: 2 Ruston . . . diesels; 2 CP props; 15,660 bhp
Range: 3,500/15 **Crew:** 18 officers, 60 enlisted

Remarks: The construction contract was awarded on 21-12-02, with both units built in China. Intended to replace retired offshore patrol vessels and supplement existing patrol assets, with an eventual possible 12-unit construction program.
Combat systems: The ships have the STN-Atlas COSYS combat control system, Oerlikon Contraves gun f.c.s, Rohde & Schwarz integrated communications system, and Raytheon integrated navigation system.

GUIDED-MISSILE PATROL BOATS [PTG]

♦ 3 Ratcharit class
Bldr: C.N. Breda, Venice, Italy

	L	In serv.
321 Ratcharit	30-7-78	10-8-79
322 Witthayakom	2-9-78	12-11-79
323 Udomet	28-9-78	21-2-80

Udomet (323) Stefan Karpinski, 5-02

Udomet (323) Stefan Karpinski, 5-02

D: 235 tons light (270 fl) **S:** 36 kts **Dim:** 49.80 (47.25 pp) × 7.50 × 1.68 (hull)
A: 4 MM 38 Exocet SSM; 1 76-mm 62-cal. OTO Melara Compact DP; 1 40-mm 70-cal. OTO Melara AA
Electronics:
Radar: 1 Decca 1226 nav.; 1 Thales WM-25 track-while-scan f.c.
EW: Decca RDL-2 intercept
M: 3 MTU MD20 V538 TB91 diesels; 3 CP props; 13,500 bhp
Electric: 440 kw tot. **Range:** 650/36; 2,000/15 **Crew:** 7 officers, 38 enlisted

Remarks: Formerly numbered 4, 5, and 6. Ordered 23-7-76. Builder's BMB 230 design. Can make 30 kts on two engines.

♦ 3 Prabrarapak class
Bldr: Singapore Technologies Marine, Jurong, Singapore

	L	In serv.
311 Prabrarapak	29-7-75	28-7-76
312 Hanhak Sattru	28-10-75	6-11-76
313 Suphairin	20-2-76	1-2-77

D: 224 tons (260 fl) **S:** 41 kts **Dim:** 44.9 × 7.0 × 2.1 (2.46 props)
A: 5 Gabriel-I SSM (2 fixed, 1 triple trainable launchers); 1 57-mm 70-cal. Bofors Mk 1 DP; 1 40-mm 70-cal. Bofors L70 AA; 2 single 12.7-mm mg
Electronics:
Radar: 1 Decca TM 626 nav.; 1 Thales WM-28 Mod. 5 track-while-scan f.c.
EW: Decca RDL-2 intercept
M: 4 MTU 16V538 TB92 diesels; 4 props; 14,000 bhp **Electric:** 405 kVA tot.
Range: 500/38.5; 1,500/16 **Crew:** 5 officers, 36 enlisted

Remarks: Built under license from Friedrich Lürssen Werft, Germany, and are similar to the Singapore Navy's FPB-45-design boats. The missiles are no longer mounted and may have become time-expired; a replacement system is being sought. Six 103-mm rocket flare launch rails are mounted on the sides of the 57-mm mount.

PATROL COMBATANTS [PG]

♦ 3 Hua Hin class
Bldr: Asia Marine, Samut Prakau (543: Bangkok Naval Dockyard)

	Laid down	L	In serv.
541 Hua Hin	3-97	3-3-99	25-3-00
542 Klaeng	5-97	19-4-99	17-1-01
543 Si Racha	12-97	6-9-99	17-1-01

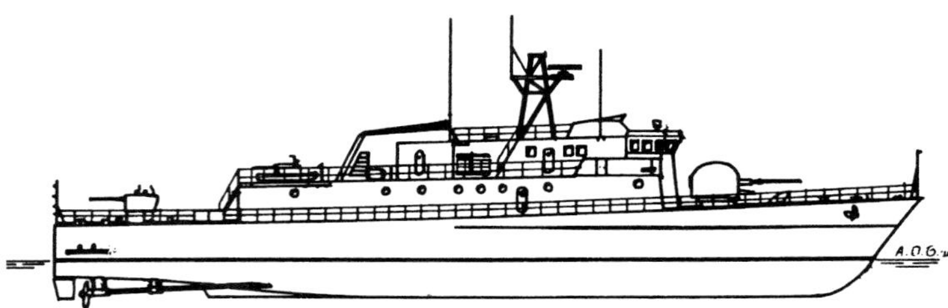
Hua Hin (541) A. D. Baker III, 1997

D: 645 tons (fl) **S:** 25 kts **Dim:** 62.0 (56.7 pp) × 8.9 × 2.7 (hull)
A: 1 76-mm 62-cal. OTO Melara Compact DP; 1 40-mm 70-cal. Bofors L70 AA; 2 single 20-mm 90-cal. Oerlion GAM-B01 AA; 2 single 12.7-mm mg
Electronics: Radar: 1 Sperry SM5000 APAR nav. 1 Sperry RASCAR nav.
M: 3 Paxman 12VP 185 diesels; 3 props (CP on centerline); 10,372 bhp sust.
Range: 2,500/15 **Crew:** 11 officers, 34 enlisted

Remarks: Ordered 9-96 from Silkline, but the contract was canceled for lack of performance and reissued as cited. Very similar to the *Khamronsin* design following, but lack ASW equipment. A single optical director is fitted for the 76-mm gun; the 40-mm mount is locally controlled.

♦ 3 Khamronsin class

	Bldr	Laid down	L	In serv.
531 Khamronsin	Italthai, Bangkok	15-3-88	15-8-89	29-7-92
532 Thayanchon	Italthai, Bangkok	20-4-88	7-12-89	5-9-92
533 Longlom	Royal Thai Naval Dockyard, Bangkok	15-3-88	8-8-89	2-10-92

Longlom (533) Hartmut Ehlers, 9-03

D: 362 light (475 half load; approx. 630 fl) **S:** 25 kts
Dim: 62.0 (56.7 pp) × 8.26 × 2.50 (hull)
A: 1 76-mm 62-cal. OTO Melara Compact DP; 1 twin 30-mm 70-cal. OTO Melara AA; 4 single 12.7-mm mg; 2 triple 324-mm BAE Systems PMW-49A ASW TT (Stingray torpedoes); 2 d.c. mortars; 1 d.c. rack; . . . mines
Electronics:
Radar: 1 Decca 1226 nav.; 1 BAE Systems AWS-4 surf./air-search
Sonar: Krupp-Atlas DSQS-21C hull-mounted MF
M: 2 MTU 12V1163 TB93 diesels; 2 CP props; 7,340 bhp **Range:** 2,500/15
Fuel: . . . **Crew:** 6 officers, 51 enlisted

PATROL COMBATANTS [PG] *(continued)*

Longlom (533) Ralph Edwards, 10-01

Remarks: First three ordered 29-9-87; a fourth in a simplified version was ordered in 9-89 for the Marine Police.
Combat systems: Have BAE Systems Sea Archer 1A Mod. 2 optronic (t.v./IR/laser) gun f.c.s. and the BAE Systems (ex-Plessey) NAUTIS-P combat data system. Are unusual among modern warships in having depth charge mortars installed (on the fantail, forward of the single centerline depth charge rack, which is flanked by short mine rails).

♦ 3 MV 400 design
Bldr: C.N. Breda, Porto Marghera, Venice, Italy

	Laid down	L	In serv.
331 Chonburi	15-8-81	7-6-82	22-2-83
332 Songkhla	15-9-81	6-9-82	16-7-83
333 Phuket	15-12-81	3-2-83	13-1-84

Chonburi (331) Hartmut Ehlers, 9-03

Phuket (333) Ralph Edwards, 10-01

D: 400 tons (450 fl) **S:** 30 kts **Dim:** 60.40 (57.50 pp) × 8.80 × 1.95 (hull)
A: 2 single 76-mm 62-cal. OTO Melara Compact DP; 1 twin 40-mm 70-cal. OTO Melara-Bofors AA; 2 single 12.7-mm mg
Electronics:
Radar: 1 Thales ZW-06 surf. search; 1 Thales WM-22 mod. 61 track-while-scan f.c.
EW: Elettronica Newton intercept; Mk 36 SRBOC decoy syst. (4 6-round Mk 137 RL)
M: 2 MTU 20V538 TB92 diesels; 3 CP props; 15,000 bhp (12,600 sust.)
Electric: 800 kw tot. **Range:** 900/29; 2,500/18 **Crew:** 7 officers, 35 enlisted

Remarks: Ordered 11-79. Steel hull and aluminum-alloy superstructure. Able to accommodate antiship missiles, but none have been installed. Have a Thales LIROD-8 optronic backup director for the 76.2-mm guns.

PATROL CRAFT [PC]

♦ 3 PC 30 class
Bldr: Silkline International, Pranburi

	Laid down	L	In serv.
T 81	3-97	. . .	7-99
T 82	. . .	1999	9-12-99
T 83	. . .	1999	29-8-00

T 81—on trials Silkline, 3-99

D: 105 tons (120 fl) **S:** 27 kts (25 sust.) **Dim:** 31.00 (28.00 pp) × 6.50 × 1.80
A: 1 40-mm 60-cal. Bofors Mk 3 AA; 1 20-mm 90-cal. Oerlikon GAM-B01 AA; 2 single 12.7-mm mg
Electronics: Radar: 1 Sperry SM5000 nav.
M: 2 MTU 16V2000 N90 SR diesels; 2 props; 3,600 bhp
Electric: 160 kw (2 × 80 kw diesel sets) **Range:** 1,300/15 **Fuel:** 26,000 liters
Endurance: 7 days **Crew:** 3 officers, 26 enlisted

Remarks: First three ordered 9-96, with 15 more planned, but the builder went bankrupt and no more have been ordered. Designed and constructed in partnership with Australian Submarine Corporation. Are used for Economic Exclusion Zone patrol. The "T" in the pennant number is rendered in Sanskrit. Aluminum construction.

♦ 6 Sattahip class
Bldr: Italthai SY, Samutprakarn, Bangkok

	L	In serv.		L	In serv.
521 Sattahip	27-7-83	16-9-83	524 Kantang	26-10-84	14-10-85
522 Klongyai	9-3-84	7-5-84	525 Thepa	1985	17-4-86
523 Takbai	25-5-84	18-7-84	526 Thai Muang	12-85	17-4-86

Thepa (525)—with old 76.2-mm Mk 22 gun forward NAVPIC-Holland, 2-97

Sattahip (521)—with 76-mm OTO Melara gun forward NAVPIC-Holland, 8-96

D: 270 tons (300 fl) **S:** 22 kts **Dim:** 50.14 (47.22 wl) × 7.30 × 1.58 (1.80 props)
A: 521–523: 1 76-mm 62-cal. OTO Melara Compact DP; 1 40-mm 70-cal. Bofors L70 AA; 2 single 20-mm 90-cal. Oerlikon GAM-B01 AA; 2 single 12.7-mm mg—524–526: 1 76.2-mm 50-cal. U.S. Mk 22 DP; 1 40-mm 60-cal. Bofors Mk 3 AA; 2 single 20-mm 90-cal. Oerlikon GAM-B01 AA; 2 single 12.7-mm mg
Electronics: Radar: 1 Decca 1226 nav.
M: 2 MTU 16V538 TB91 diesels; 2 props; 6,840 bhp
Electric: 420 kw tot. **Range:** 2,500/15 **Fuel:** 80 tons **Crew:** 56 tot.

Remarks: First four ordered 9-9-81, others on 27-12-83 and 31-8-84 to a Lürssen design. First three have Italian NA 18 optronic director for the 76-mm gun. The 76.2-mm guns in the final three came from discarded U.S.-built ships.

♦ 7 T 93 class
Bldr: Royal Thai Naval Dockyard, Bangkok

	In serv.		In serv.
T 93	1973	T 97	16-9-83
T 94	16-9-81	T 98	1984
T 95	1981	T 99	5-87
T 96	1982		

D: 117 tons (125 fl) **S:** 25 kts **Dim:** 34.00 (32.00 wl) × 5.70 × 1.40 (1.65 props)
A: 2 single 40-mm 60-cal. Bofors Mk 3 AA; 2 single 12.7-mm mg
Electronics: Radar: 1 Decca . . . nav.
M: 2 MTU 12V538 TB81 diesels; 2 props; 3,300 bhp **Crew:** 23–25 tot.

PATROL CRAFT [PC] *(continued)*

T 93–class T 96 Ralph Edwards, 10-01

T 93–class T 98 Hartmut Ehlers, 9-03

Remarks: Revised version of T 91 design. T 99 has 20-mm gun aft and has a BAe Systems Sea Archer Mk 1A optronic director for the 40-mm gun, which is a Bofors 70-cal. power-operated weapon. The "T" in the pennant number is rendered in Sanskrit.

♦ 2 T 91 class
Bldr: Royal Thai Naval Dockyard, Bangkok

T 91 (L: 1965) T 92 (L: 1973)

T 91 NAVPIC-Holland, 9-96

T 92 NAVPIC-Holland, 12-96

D: 87.5 tons (100 fl) **S:** 25 kts **Dim:** 31.8 × 5.36 × 1.5
A: T 91: 1 40-mm 60-cal. Bofors Mk 3 AA; 1 20-mm 90-cal. Oerlikon GAM-B01 AA—T-92: 2 single 40-mm 60-cal. Mk 3 AA
Electronics: Radar: 1 Decca . . . nav. **M:** 2 MTU diesels; 2 props; 3,300 bhp
Range: 700/21 **Crew:** 21 tot.

Remarks: T 91 has a longer superstructure and lower spray strakes on the hull sides forward. Both were refitted 1984–85. The "T" in the pennant number is rendered in Sanskrit.

♦ 10 ex-U.S. PGM 71 class
Bldr: Peterson Builders, Sturgeon Bay, Wisc.

	L	In serv.
T 11 (ex-PGM 71)	22-5-65	1-2-66
T 12 (ex-PGM 79)	18-12-65	1967
T 13 (ex-PGM 107)	13-4-67	28-8-67
T 14 (ex-PGM 113)	3-6-69	18-8-69
T 15 (ex-PGM 114)	24-6-69	18-8-69
T 16 (ex-PGM 115)	24-4-69	12-2-70
T 17 (ex-PGM 116)	3-6-69	12-2-70
T 18 (ex-PGM 117)	24-6-69	12-2-70
T 19 (ex-PGM 123)	4-5-70	25-12-70
T 110 (ex-PGM 124)	22-6-70	10-70

PGM 71–class T 17 NAVPIC-Holland, 2-97

D: 130 tons (144 fl) **S:** 17 kts **Dim:** 30.81 × 6.45 × 2.30
A: 1 40-mm 60-cal. Mk 3 Bofors AA; 1 twin 20-mm 70-cal. Oerlikon Mk 24 AA; 2 single 12.7-mm M2 mg; 1 81-mm mortar
Electronics: Radar: 1 Decca 202 (T 11, 12: Decca 303) nav.
M: 8 G.M. Detroit Diesel 6-71 diesels; 2 props; 2,040 bhp **Range:** 1,000/12
Crew: 23–25 tot.

Remarks: The twin 20-mm mount on the fantail has been replaced by an 81-mm mortar. The "T" in the pennant number is rendered in Sanskrit.

HYDROFOIL PATROL BOATS [PBH]

♦ 1 Hysucat 18 catamaran hydrofoil
Bldr: Tecnautic, Prapradaeng, Bangkok (L: 21-9-86)

T 231

T 231—with original armament Tecnautic, 1986

D: 41 tons (fl) **S:** 31 kts **Dim:** 18.25 × 6.57 × 1.61 (props)
A: 1 20-mm 90-cal. Oerlikon GAM-B01 AA **Electronics:** Radar: 1 . . . nav.
M: 2 MWM TBD 234 V-12 diesels; 2 props; 1,640 bhp **Range:** 500/36
Crew: 2 officers, 8 enlisted

Remarks: Ordered 23-9-85 after trials with a 6.5-m, 85-hp prototype. Design assisted by Friedrich Lürssen Werft, Bremen-Vegesack. Exceeded designed displacement by 5.5 tons due to water seepage between Kevlar outer sheathing and the foam-core inner hull wall and failed to make 36-kt contract speed; plans to acquire 12 more were canceled. The design employs catamaran hulls with fixed foils mounted between them. Original U.S. G.E. Vulcan 20, 20-mm gatling gun and Kollmorgen-G.E. SV-20NCS g.f.c.s. and Mk 35 Mod. L3 periscopic sight removed 1988 and replaced with 20-mm Oerlikon. May have been retired from service. Two near-sisters were completed in 3-95 for the Marine Police.

PATROL BOATS [PB]

♦ 13 T 213 class
Bldr: Italthai Development Co., Bangkok

	In serv.		In serv.		In serv.
T 213	29-8-80	T 219	16-9-81	T 223	16-9-81
T 214	29-8-80	T 220	16-9-81	T 224	19-11-81
T 216	26-3-81	T 221	16-9-81	T 225	28-3-84
T 217	26-3-81	T 222	16-9-81	T 226	28-3-84
T 218	26-3-81				

PATROL BOATS [PB] *(continued)*

T 223 Jasper van Raemdonck, 3-04

T 223 Jasper van Raemdonck, 3-04

D: 34 tons (approx. 50 fl) **S:** 22 kts (18 sust.) **Dim:** 19.8 × 5.3 × 1.5
A: 1 20-mm 90-cal. Oerlikon GAM-B01 AA; 1 12.7-mm mg/81-mm mortar combination
Electronics: Radar: 1 Decca 110 nav.
M: 2 MTU 8V396-series diesels; 2 props; 1,300 bhp
Crew: 1 officer, 7 enlisted

Remarks: Aluminum construction. Intended for fisheries protection duties. The U.S.-made combined mortar/machinegun mount is on the fantail. The "T" in the pennant number is rendered in Sanskrit or omitted. T 215 sank during the 12-04 tsunami.

♦ 3 ex-U.S. Sea Spectre PB Mk III class
Bldr: Peterson Builders, Sturgeon Bay, Wisc. (In serv. 1975)

T 210 T 211 T 212

D: 28 tons (36.7 fl) **S:** 30 kts (22 sust.) **Dim:** 19.78 × 5.50 × 1.80 (props)
A: 2 20-mm 70-cal. Mk 67 Oerlikon AA; 2 single 12.7-mm mg; 2 single 7.62-mm mg; 1 81-mm mortar
Electronics: Radar: 1 Raytheon 1500B Pathfinder nav.
M: 3 G.M. Detroit Diesel 8V71 TI diesels; 3 props; 1,800 bhp **Range:** 450/20
Endurance: 3 days **Crew:** 1 officer, 8 enlisted

Remarks: Transferred 1975. Aluminum construction. The "T" in the pennant number is rendered in Sanskrit or not displayed.

♦ 9 ex-U.S. Swift Mk II class
Bldr: Swiftships Inc., Morgan City, La.

T 21 through T 29

D: 22.5 tons (fl) **S:** 25 kts (20 sust.) **Dim:** 15.64 × 4.14 × 1.06
A: 1 twin 12.7-mm mg; 1 12.7-mm mg/81-mm mortar combined mount
Electronics: Radar: 1 Raytheon 1500B Pathfinder nav.
M: 2 G.M. Detroit Diesel 6V53 N diesels; 2 props; 860 bhp **Range:** 400/24
Crew: 1 officer, 7 enlisted

Remarks: Transferred 1968–70. Aluminum construction. Two are assigned to the Riverine Squadron and operate on the upper Mekong River. The "T" in the pennant number is rendered in Sanskrit.

Swift Mk II–class T 26—outboard T 27 Jasper van Raemdonck, 3-04

♦ 90+ assault boats
Bldr: . . ., Thailand (In serv. late 1980s)

D: 0.4 tons (fl) **S:** 24 kts **Dim:** 5.0 × 1.9 × 0.4 **A:** 1/7.62-mm mg
M: 1 gasoline outboard; . . . bhp **Crew:** 2 tot. + 4 troops

Remarks: Locally built GRP foam-core hull craft employed by the Riverine Squadron on the upper Mekong River.

♦ 13 U.S. PBR Mk II class
Bldr: Uniflite, Bellingham, Wash.

T 240 series

PBR Mk II class Royal Thai Navy, 1996

D: 8.9 tons (fl) **S:** 14 kts **Dim:** 9.73 × 3.53 × 0.81
A: 1 twin and 1 single 12.7-mm mg; 1 60-mm mortar
Electronics: Radar: 1 Raytheon 1900 (SPS-66) nav.
M: 2 G.M. 6V53N diesels; 2 Jacuzzi water jets; 420 bhp
Range: 150/23 **Crew:** 4 tot.

Remarks: Survivors of 37 transferred: 20 in 1966–67, 10 in 1972, and 7 in 1973. GRP-construction hulls with some Kevlar armor. Employed by Riverine Squadron on upper Mekong River. Are all over-age, worn out, and in need of replacement; could originally make 24 kts. The "T" in the pennant number is rendered in Sanskrit.

MINE WARFARE SHIPS

♦ 1 mine countermeasures support ship [MCS]

	Bldr	L	In serv.
621 THALANG	Royal Thai NDY, Bangkok	. . .	4-8-80

Thalang (621) NAVPIC-Holland, 9-96

D: 1,000 tons (fl) **S:** 12 kts **Dim:** 55.7 × 10.0 × 3.1
A: 1 40-mm 60-cal. Mk 3 Bofors AA; 2 single 20-mm 70-cal. Oerlikon Mk 10 AA; 2 single 12.7-mm M2 mg; . . . mines
Electronics: Radar: 1 Decca TM 1226 nav.
M: 2 MTU diesels; 2 props; 1,310 bhp **Crew:** 77 tot.

Remarks: Designed by Ferostaal, Essen, Germany. Has two 3-ton cranes on the stern and carries four sets of spare mine-countermeasures equipment for transfer to minesweepers. Also capable of use as a minelayer and can stream a mechanical minesweeping array.

MINE WARFARE SHIPS *(continued)*

◆ 2 Gaeta-class minehunter/minesweepers [MHC]
Bldr: Intermarine SpA, Sarzana, Italy

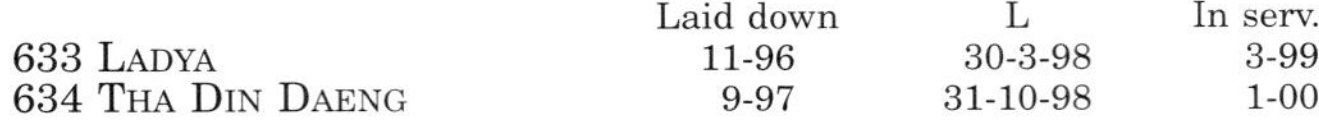

	Laid down	L	In serv.
633 Ladya	11-96	30-3-98	3-99
634 Tha Din Daeng	9-97	31-10-98	1-00

Ladya (633) John Mortimer, 5-99

D: 665 tons (697 fl) **S:** 14.3 kts **Dim:** 52.45 (46.50 pp) × 9.87 × 2.95
A: 1 30-mm Royal Ordnance DS-30B AA
Electronics:
Radar: 1 STN Atlas Elektronik 9600M ARPA nav.
Sonar: STN Atlas Elektronik DSQS-11H
M: 2 MTU 396 TE74K diesels; 2 Voith-Schneider Type 18 GH/135 vertical cycloidal props; 1,610 bhp—2 180-shp hydraulic motors for quiet running to 6 kts—180-shp bow-thruster
Electric: 900 kw tot. **Range:** 1,500/14; 2,500/12 **Fuel:** 49 tons
Crew: 8 officers, 42 enlisted

Remarks: Ordered 19-9-96. A planned third was not ordered. Sisters operate in the Italian and Australian navies.
Hull systems: GRP foam-core hull construction. Carry a two-man decompression chamber and are fitted with passive tank stabilization (using tanks for fuel, range can be extended by 1,500 n.m. at 12 kts). Crew listing includes seven mine-disposal divers.
Combat systems: Use the STN-Atlas MWS-80 mine-countermeasures operations control system. Carry two Gayrobot Pluto Plus remotely operated vehicles. Are able to stream Oropesa Mk 4 mechanical sweep gear and have the Australian Defence Industries Mini Dyad and Bofors MS 106 influence sweep systems. The sonar is planned to be upgraded to the more effective DSQS-11M version.

◆ 2 M 48–class minehunter/sweepers [MHC]
Bldr: Friedrich Lürssen Werft, Vegesack, Germany

631 Bangrachan (In serv. 29-4-87) 632 Nhongsarhai (In serv. 17-11-87)

Nhongsarhai (632) John Mortimer, 6-01

D: 414 tons light (444.3 fl) **S:** 18 kts **Dim:** 48.00 (45.70 pp) × 9.30 × 2.75
A: 3 single 20-mm 90-cal. Oerlikon GAM-B01 AA; mine rails
Electronics:
Radar: 1 Decca 1229 nav.
Sonar: Krupp-Atlas DSQS-11H hull-mounted
M: 2 MTU 16V396 TB83-DB51L diesels; 2 CP props; 3,223 bhp—auxiliary diesel low-speed (7-kt) propulsion
Electric: 620 kw tot. **Range:** 3,100/12 **Crew:** 7 officers, 33 enlisted

Remarks: First ordered 31-8-84, second 5-8-85 with option for two more not exercised. Used primarily as patrol boats. Have had problems with stability, and the ineffective sonar system may be replaced with Atlas DSQS-11M.
Hull systems: Composite hull construction: nonmagnetic metal framing with wooden skin. Have Becker flap rudders, Motorola MiniRanger navigational positioning system, and a Draeger portable decompression chamber for mine-disposal divers.
Combat systems: Krupp-Atlas MWS-80R mine-countermeasures system. Carry two Gaymarine Pluto remote-controlled minehunting/disposal submersibles, plus mechanical, magnetic, and acoustic sweep gear. Use a removable generator module when sweeping and carry SDG 31 mechanical sweep gear. Carry 7,600 rounds 20-mm ammunition and 30 mine-disposal charges.

◆ 2 ex-U.S. MSC 289–class minesweepers [MSC]

	Bldr	In serv.
612 Bangkeo (ex-MSC 303)	Dorchester SB, Camden, N.J.	9-7-65
613 Don Chedi (ex-MSC 313)	Peterson, Sturgeon Bay, Wisc.	17-9-65

Don Chedi (613)—outboard *Bangkeo* (612) Maritime Photographic, 11-01

D: 330 tons (384 fl) **S:** 13 kts **Dim:** 44.32 × 8.29 × 2.70
A: 1 20-mm 70-cal. Oerlikon Mk 10 AA
Electronics:
Radar: 1 Decca 1226 nav.
Sonar: UQS-1D hull-mounted (100 kHz)
M: 4 G.M. Detroit Diesel 6-71 diesels; 2 props; 1,000 bhp (880 sust.)
Range: 2,500/10 **Crew:** 7 officers, 36 enlisted

Remarks: Transferred on completion. Wooden construction. Re-engined and reactivated from reserve, 1987–88, but now need replacement. Sister *Tadindeng* (7, ex-U.S. MSC 301) was stricken 1992 and *Ladya* (635, ex-MSC 297) in 1995. Carry U.S. Mk 4(V), Mk 6, and Type Q2 mine-countermeasures equipment. The original twin 20-mm AA mount replaced by a single mount.

◆ 7 MSB 11–class minesweeping launches [MSB]
Bldr: . . ., Thailand (In serv. 1994 to 1998)

MSB 11 through MSB 17

D: 25 tons (fl) **S:** 8 kts **Dim:** 15.29 × 4.01 × 1.35 **A:** 2 single 7.62-mm mg
M: 1 G.M. Gray Marine 64 HN9 diesel; 1 prop; 165 bhp
Range: . . . / . . . **Crew:** 10 tot.

Remarks: Wooden construction design patterned on the U.S.-built 50-ft. class but with hull decked over forward and a pilothouse added. Equipped with generator for magnetic sweep array and able to sweep moored mechanical mines. No radar fitted, but have a large corner reflector on the mast to permit tracking by land-based radars.

◆ 5 ex-U.S. 50-foot motor-launch minesweepers [MSB]

MLM 6 through MLM 10 (ex-MSB 1 through MSB 5)

D: 21 tons (fl) **S:** 8 kts **Dim:** 15.29 × 4.01 × 1.31
A: 2 single 7.62-mm mg (I × 2) **M:** 1 Navy DB diesel; 1 prop; 85 bhp
Range: 150/8 **Crew:** 6 tot.

Remarks: Transferred 1963–64. Formerly numbered MLMS 6–10. Wooden-hulled former personnel launches, converted before transfer. Employed on the Chao Phraya River.

AMPHIBIOUS WARFARE SHIPS

◆ 2 PS 700–class tank-landing ships [LST]

	Bldr.	L	In serv.
721 Sichang	Italthai SY, Bangkok	14-4-87	9-10-87
722 Surin	Bangkok Dock Co.	12-4-88	16-12-88

Sichang (721) U.S. Navy, 5-06

D: 721: 3,540 tons (4,235 fl); 722: 4,520 tons (fl) **S:** 16 kts
Dim: 721: 103.00 (91.65 pp) × 15.65 × 3.52 (722: 109.00 overall)
A: 1 (722: 2) single 40-mm 70-cal. Bofors L70 AA; 2 single 20-mm 90-cal. Oerlikon GAM-B01 AA; 2 single 12.7-mm mg
Electronics: Radar: 1 Decca 1226 nav.
M: 2 MTU 20V1163 TB62 diesels; 2 CP props; 9,600 bhp
Range: 4,000/14; 7,000/12 **Crew:** 52 crew + 339 troops (722: 354 troops)

Remarks: 2,045 dwt. License-built French Normed design, built with technical assistance from Korea Tacoma SY. A third was ordered during 1987 but later canceled; six total were originally planned. 722 was not fully operational until 1992.
Hull systems: *Surin* was delayed after launch to include a 6-m hull "plug" to provide sufficient space for the ship to accommodate a 354-man Thai troop battalion. Cargo: 850 tons (up to thirteen 50-ton tanks, six 2-ton trucks). Have 17-m bow ramp. Beaching draft 2.88 m at 1,162 dwt. Helicopter deck aft in 722 is one deck higher, and the ship is flush-decked, whereas 721 has a forecastle.
Combat systems: Have BAE Systems Sea Archer Mk 1A Mod. 2 optronic (low-light t.v., laser, IR) f.c.s. for 40-mm guns; the additional 40-mm mount in 722 is mounted aft atop a helicopter flight deck control station.

AMPHIBIOUS WARFARE SHIPS *(continued)*

♦ 4 ex-U.S. LST 542–class tank-landing ships [LST]

	Bldr	L	In serv.
712 Chang (ex-*Lincoln Cty.*, LST 898)	Dravo, Pittsburgh	25-11-44	29-12-44
713 Pangan (ex-*Stark Cty.*, LST 1134)	Chicago Br. & Iron, Ind.	16-3-45	7-4-45
714 Lanta (ex-*Stone Cty.*, LST 1141)	Chicago Br. & Iron, Ind.	18-4-45	9-5-45
715 Prathong (ex-*Dodge Cty.*, LST 722)	Jeffersonville Br. & Mach. Co., Ind.	21-8-44	13-9-44

Chang (712) IJ Plokker, 2-02

D: 1,625 tons (4,080 fl) **S:** 11 kts **Dim:** 99.98 × 15.24 × 4.36
A: 712–713: 2 twin 40-mm 60-cal. Bofors Mk 1 Mod. 2 AA; 4 single 40-mm 60-cal. Bofors Mk 3 AA; 4 single 12.7-mm mg; 712 also: 2 single 20-mm 70-cal. Oerlikon Mk 10 AA; 714: 6 single 40-mm 60-cal. Bofors Mk 3 AA; 715: 2 single 40-mm 60-cal. Bofors Mk 3 AA
Electronics: Radar: 1 Decca 1229 nav.; 1 Decca 1226 nav.
M: 2 G.M. 12-567A diesels; 2 props; 1.700 bhp **Electric:** 300 kw tot.
Range: 15,000/9 **Fuel:** 569 tons **Crew:** 80 tot. + 348 troops

Remarks: 711 was purchased in 10-47, and 712 was transferred in 8-62, 713 in 5-66, 714 on 12-3-70 (purchased 1-3-79), and 715 on 17-12-75. 711, discarded by 1978, was restored to service in 1994–95 prior to decomissioning in 2000.
Hull systems: Cargo: 1,230 tons maximum/815 tons beaching. All but 713 carry a tracked 10-ton mobile crane on the upper deck. 712 has a reinforced bow and waterline, originally intended for arctic navigation.
Combat systems: Two Mk 51 Mod. 2 lead-computing directors for twin 40-mm AA have been removed.

♦ 1 ex-U.S. LSM 1–class medium landing ship [LSM]
Bldr: Pullman Standard Car Mfg. Co., Chicago, Ill.

	Laid down	L	In serv.
731 Kut (ex-LSM 338)	17-8-44	5-12-44	10-1-45

Kut (731) NAVPIC-Holland, 9-96

D: 743 tons (1,095 fl) **S:** 12.5 kts **Dim:** 62.03 × 10.52 × 2.54
A: 1 twin 40-mm 60-cal. Bofors Mk 1 Mod. 2 Bofors AA; 4 single 20-mm 70-cal. Oerlikon Mk 10 AA
Electronics: Radar: 1 Decca 1226 nav.
M: 2 Fairbanks-Morse 38D8⅛ × 10 diesels; 2 props; 2,800 bhp
Range: 2,500/12 **Crew:** 6 officers, 85 enlisted + 50 troops

Remarks: Formerly numbered 1 and 3. 731 transferred in 10-46, 732 on 25-5-62. Have a Mk 51 Mod. 2 optical lead-computing director for the 40-mm mount. Cargo: 452 tons. Sister *Phai* (2, ex-LSM 333) was stricken during 1990; *Kram* (732, ex-LSM 469) was scuttled as an artificial reef on 1-3-03.

♦ 1 ex-U.S. LSSL 1–class support landing craft [LCFS]
Bldr: Commercial Iron Works, Portland, Ore.

	Laid down	L	In serv.
751 Nakha (ex-*Himiwari*, ex-LSSL 102)	13-1-45	3-2-45	17-2-45

D: 233 tons (387 fl) **S:** 14 kts **Dim:** 48.16 × 10.52 × 2.54
A: 1 76.2-mm 50-cal. Mk 22 DP; 2 twin 40-mm 60-cal. Bofors Mk 1 Mod. 2 AA; 3 single 20-mm 70-cal. Oerlikon Mk 10 AA; 2 single 12.7-mm M2 mg
Electronics: Radar: 1 Decca . . . nav.
M: 8 G.M. Detroit Diesel 6051-71 diesels; 2 CP props; 1,320 bhp
Electric: 120 kw **Range:** 3,500/12.5 **Fuel:** 84 tons **Crew:** 60 tot.

Remarks: Transferred to Japan in 7-59 and to Thailand in 10-66 on return to U.S. control from Japan. Used mainly as a tender and headquarters ship for small patrol craft. The armament has been slightly reduced, and the gunmounts have locally fabricated shielding. The last of a once-numerous class.

Nakha (751) NAVPIC-Holland, 1-97

♦ 2 ex-U.S. LCI(L) 351–class infantry landing craft [LCP]
Bldrs: 741: George Lawley & Sons, Neponset, Mass.; 742: Commercial Iron Works, Portland, Ore.

	Laid down	L	In serv.
741 Prab (ex-LCI(M) 670)	21-3-44	28-3-44	1-4-44
742 Satakut (ex-LCI(M) 739)	30-1-44	27-2-44	6-3-44

Prab (741)—with old pennant number Ross Gillett, 8-89

D: 231 tons light (387 fl) **S:** 14.4 kts **Dim:** 48.46 (46.63 wl) × 7.21 × 1.73
A: 741: 1 76.2-mm 50-cal. Mk 22 DP; 742: 1 40-mm 60-cal. Bofors Mk 3 AA; both: 2 single 20-mm 70-cal. Oerlikon Mk 10 AA
Electronics: Radar: 1 Raytheon 1500B Pathfinder (SPS-53) nav.
M: 8 G.M. 6051-71 diesels; 2 CP props; 1,320 bhp **Electric:** 40 kw tot
Range: 5,600/12.5 **Fuel:** 113 tons **Crew:** 7 officers, 42 enlisted + 76 troops

Remarks: 741 was built in only 11 days. Transferred to Thailand in 10-46. Completed with four 4.2-in (107-mm) chemical mortars and with normal raised forecastle deleted, but were reconfigured to carry troops by Thailand. 741 had been out of service for several years before refit circa 1991–92; her forecastle has been removed, and the 76.2-mm gun is located on the foredeck. 742 was refitted for further service during the mid-1990s and carries the 40-mm gun atop the original forecastle. Can carry 101 tons cargo.

♦ 3 Man Nok–class utility landing craft [LCU]
Bldr: Silkline-ASC (Australian Submarine Corp) Joint Venture Co., Prandari (In serv. 2002)

	L
781 Man Nok	12-01
782 Man Klang	11-01
783 Man Nai	12-01

Man Klang (782) NAVPIC-Holland, 2002

D: 550 tons (fl) **S:** 12 kts **Dim:** 52.40 (48.00 pp) × 11.20 × 1.20
A: 2 single 20-mm 70-cal. Oerlikon Mk 10 AA
Electronics: Radar: 1 Raytheon Pathfinder nav.
M: 2 Caterpillar 3412DITA diesels; 2 Kort-nozzle props; 1,440 bhp
Electric: . . . kw (1 Caterpillar 3306DT diesel driving) **Range:** 1,500/10
Crew: 3 officers, 30 enlisted

Remarks: Ordered 10-97 for delivery within 36 months, but program was well behind schedule when the original builder defaulted. Have bow and stern vehicle ramps, and the bridge is offset to starboard. Resemble a modernized version of the *Thong Kaeo* class and were designed by Sea Transport Solutions.

AMPHIBIOUS WARFARE SHIPS *(continued)*

Man Nai (783)—taking part in exercises U.S. Marine Corps, 5-03

♦ 4 Thong Kaeo–class utility landing craft [LCU]
Bldr: Royal Thai Naval Dockyard, Bangkok

	In serv.		In serv.
771 Thong Kaeo	23-12-82	773 Wang Nok	16-9-83
772 Thonglang	19-4-83	774 Wang Nai	11-11-83

Wang Nai (774)—alongside *Surin* (722) Maritime Photographic, 5-97

D: 193 tons (396 fl) **S:** 10 kts **Dim:** 41.0 × 9.0 × 2.1
A: 2 single 20-mm 90-cal. Oerlikon GAM-B01 AA; 2 single 7.62-mm mg
Electronics: Radar: 1 Decca . . . nav.
M: 2 G.M. Detroit Diesel 16V71N diesels; 2 props; 1,400 bhp
Electric: 60 kw tot. (2 × 30 kw diesel sets)
Range: 1,200/10 **Crew:** 3 officers, 29 enlisted

Remarks: Formerly numbered 7-10. Based on U.S. LCU 1626–class design. First four ordered 1980, fifth ordered 1984 but never completed. Cargo: 143 tons, with 30.5 × 5.5–m vehicle deck.

♦ 6 ex-U.S. LCU 501–class utility landing craft [LCU]

	Bldr	L	In serv.
761 Mataphon (ex-LCU 1260)	Quincy Barge, Ill.	29-7-44	8-9-44
762 Rawi (ex-LCU 800)	Mt. Vernon Br. Co., Ohio	14-6-44	16-6-44
763 Adang (ex-LCU 861)	Darby, Kansas City, Kan.	15-2-44	22-2-44
764 Phe Tra (ex-LCU 1089)	Quincy Barge, Ill.	10-5-44	10-6-44
765 Kolum (ex-LCU 904)	Missouri Valley Bridge & Iron	13-5-44	11-3-44
766 Talibong (ex-LCU 753)	Quincy Barge, Ill.	30-3-44	10-5-44

Mataphon (761) IJ Plokker, 2-02

D: 134 tons (309 fl) **S:** 10 kts **Dim:** 36.3 × 9.96 × 1.14
A: 2 twin 20-mm 70-cal. Oerlikon Mk 24 AA
Electronics: Radar: 1 Raytheon 1500B (SPS-53) Pathfinder nav.
M: 3 G.M. 6051-71 diesels; 3 props; 675 bhp **Range:** 1,200/7
Fuel: 10.5 tons **Crew:** 13 tot.

Remarks: Transferred 10-46 to 11-47. Used as logistics transports on the Chao Phraya River. Cargo: 150 tons. 765, stricken 1984, had been rehabilitated for further service by 1993.

♦ 24 ex-U.S. LCM(6)-class landing craft [LCM]

L 14 through L 16 L 81 through L 82
L 61 through L 68 L 85 through L 87
L 71 through L 78

D: 24 tons (56 fl) **S:** 9 kts **Dim:** 17.11 × 4.27 × 1.17
M: 2 G.M. Gray Marine 64HN9 diesels; 2 props; 330 bhp
Range: 130/9 **Crew:** 5 tot.

Remarks: Transferred 2-65 to 4-69. Cargo capacity: 34 tons.

♦ 12 ex-U.S. LCVP-class landing craft [LCVP]

L 51 through L 59 L 510 through L 512

D: 12 tons (fl) **S:** 9 kts **Dim:** 10.9 × 3.21 × 1.04
M: 1 G.M. Gray Marine 64HN9 diesel; 1 prop; 225 bhp
Range: 110/9 **Crew:** 3 + 39 troops

Remarks: Transferred 3-63. The LCVPs are carried aboard the Thai LSTs.

♦ 4 armored riverine personnel transports [LCP]
Bldr: Bangkok Dock Co., Ltd. (In serv. 1984)

L 40 L 41 L 42 L 43

D: 10 tons (fl) **S:** 25 kts **Dim:** 12.0 × 3.0 × 1.0
M: 2 Ford Sabre diesels; 2 Castoldi Mod. 06 waterjets; . . . bhp
Crew: . . . tot. + 35 troops

Remarks: Based on a GRP-hulled prototype constructed in 1968.

♦ 3 Type 1000 TD hovercraft personnel transports [LCPA]
Bldr: Griffon Hovercraft, Salisbury Green, U.K. (In serv. 1990)

401 402 403

D: 4.9 tons (fl) **S:** 33 kts (27 kts loaded) **Dim:** 8.80 × 3.93 × 2.50 (high)
M: 1 Deutz BF 6L913C diesel; 1 shrouded airscrew/1 lift-fan; 192 bhp
Range: 200/27 **Crew:** 2 + 10 troops or 1,000 kg cargo

Remarks: Used primarily for search-and-rescue duties.

AUXILIARIES

♦ 1 navigational buoy tender [AGL]
Bldr: Royal Thai Naval Dockyard, Bangkok (In serv. 18-1-79)

821 Suriya

Suriya (821) NAVPIC-Holland, 8-96

D: 690 tons light (960 fl) **S:** 12 kts **Dim:** 54.2 (47.3 pp) × 10.0 × 3.0
A: 2 single 20-mm 70-cal. Oerlikon Mk 10 AA
Electronics: Radar: 1 Decca . . . nav.
M: 2 MTU diesels; 1 prop; 1,310 bhp **Electric:** 300 kw tot. **Range:** 3,000/12
Crew: 12 officers, 48 enlisted

Remarks: One 10-ton derrick serves short, very low-freeboard working deck forward. Cargo capacity: 270 tons.

♦ 1 oceanographic research ship [AGOR]
Bldr: C. Melchers, Bremen, Germany

	Laid down	L	In serv.
811 Chandhara	27-9-60	17-12-60	1961

Chandhara (811) NAVPIC-Holland, 7-01

D: 870 tons (997 fl) **S:** 13 kts **Dim:** 70.0 (61.0 pp) × 10.5 × 3.0
A: 2 single 40-mm 60-cal. Bofors Mk 3 AA **Electronics:** Radar: 1 Decca . . . nav.
M: 2 Klöckner-Humboldt-Deutz diesels; 2 props; 1,090 bhp **Range:** 10,000/10
Crew: 8 officers, 60 enlisted

Remarks: Built as a training ship and has also served as a royal yacht.

AUXILIARIES *(continued)*

♦ 1 oceanographic research and survey ship [AGS]

Bldr: Royal Thai Naval Dockyard, Bangkok

	Laid down	L	In serv.
812 SUK	27-8-79	16-9-81	3-9-82

Suk (812) H&L Van Ginderen, 5-99

D: 1,400 tons (1,526 fl) **S:** 15 kts **Dim:** 62.9 × 11.0 × 4.1
A: 2 single 20-mm 70-cal. Oerlikon Mk 10 AA; 2 single 7.62-mm mg
Electronics: Radar: 1 Decca TM 1226 nav. **M:** 2 MTU diesels; 2 props; 2,400 bhp
Crew: 20 officers, 66 enlisted

Remarks: Used primarily in oceanographic research, for which a stern gallows crane and five oceanographic cranes are fitted.

♦ 1 small oiler [AO]

	Bldr	L	In serv.
831 CHULA	Singapore Slipway & Eng.	24-9-80	1981

Chula (831)—with former pennant number Royal Thai Navy, 1996

D: 2,000 tons (fl) **S:** 14 kts **Dim:** 67.00 × 9.50 × 4.35
A: 2 single 20-mm 90-cal. Oerlikon GAM-B01 AA
Electronics: Radar: 1 Decca 1226 nav.
M: 2 MTU 12V396 TC62 diesels; 2 props; 2,400 bhp **Crew:** 7 officers, 32 enlisted

Remarks: 960 dwt. Cargo: 800 tons, transferred by means of an electrohydraulic boom supporting the hose. Formerly numbered 2.

♦ 1 Chinese-built replenishment oiler (Project R22T) [AOR]

Bldr: . . . SY, Dalien

	Laid down	L	In serv.
871 SIMILAN	12-94	9-11-95	12-8-96

Similan (871) Royal Thai Navy, 1997

D: 22,000 tons (fl) **S:** 20 kts (19 sust.) **Dim:** 171.40 × 24.16 × 9.00
A: 4 single 20-mm 90-cal. Oerlikon GAM-B01 AA
Electronics: Radar: 1 Decca 1290 ARPA nav.
M: 2 SEMT-Pielstick 16PC2 6V400 diesels; 2 KaMeWa CP props; 24,000 bhp
Range: 10,000/15 **Crew:** 19 officers, 138 enlisted + 26 passengers

Remarks: Ordered 29-9-93. Much-modified, flush-decked version of the Fuqing class built for Chinese Navy and merchant marine and for the Pakistani Navy; layout resembles a French *Durance*-class ship.
Hull systems: Has hangar for one Sikorsky S-70 helicopter to provide vertical replenishment of solid stores, two refueling stations on either beam. Carries 11,400 tons cargo, including 7,900 tons diesel fuel, 2,500 tons aviation fuel, 250 tons fresh water, 70 tons lube oil, and 680 tons dry cargo, ammunition, and stores.
Combat systems: The planned Chinese-made armament of four twin 37-mm Model 76A AA and their associated Type 341 Rice Lamp radar f.c. director were not mounted, nor was the Type 354 (Eye Shield) search and target designation radar.

Disposal note: British *Algerine*-class training ship *Phosamton* (415, ex-*Minstrel*) was decommissioned during 2005.

♦ 1 ex-U.S. Cannon-class training ship [AXT]

Bldr: Western Pipe & Steel, Los Angeles, Calif.

	Laid down	L	In serv.
413 PIN KLAO (ex-*Hemminger,* DE 746)	8-5-43	27-12-43	30-5-44

Pin Klao (413)—with old pennant number *Ships of the World,* 4-92

D: 1,240 tons (1,620 fl) **S:** 20 kts **Dim:** 93.27 (91.44 wl) × 11.15 × 3.56 (hull)
A: 3 single 76.2-mm 50-cal. Mk 22 DP; 3 twin 40-mm 60-cal. Mk 2 Mod. 5 AA; 2 triple 324-mm Mk 32 Mod. 5 ASW TT (6 Mk 46 Mod. 2 torpedoes); 1 24-round Mk 10 Hedgehog fixed ASW spiggot mortar; 8 Mk 6 d.c. mortars (3 Mk 9 d.c. each); 2 Mk 9 d.c. racks (7 Mk 9 d.c. each)
Electronics:
Radar: 2 . . . nav.; 1 Westinghouse SPS-6C air-search
Sonar: SQS-11 hull-mounted MF
M: 4 G.M. 16-278A diesels, electric drive; 2 props; 6,000 shp
Electric: 680 kw tot. **Range:** 11,600/11
Fuel: 260 tons **Crew:** 14 officers, 178 enlisted

Remarks: Transferred 7-59 and purchased 6-6-75, after which the ship underwent an extensive overhaul at Guam. Relegated to cadet training service in 1991 and has made several Asian training cruises since. Mk 52 AA radar gun director for 76.2-mm guns has been removed, as have one Mk 63 radar director and two Mk 51 Mod. 2 lead-computing directors for the 40-mm guns, but the optical rangefinder for the 76.2-mm guns has been retained. During 6-02, was said to be nearing retirement.

SERVICE CRAFT

♦ 3 Samed-class harbor oilers [YO]

Bldr: Royal Thai Naval Dockyard, Bangkok

	In serv.
834 PROET	16-1-70
835 SAMED	15-12-70
842 CHIK	1970

Samed (835) NAVPIC-Holland, 7-96

D: 360 tons (485 fl) **S:** 9 kts **Dim:** 39.0 (36.6 pp) × 6.1 × 2.8 **A:** None
Electronics: Radar: 1 . . . nav. **M:** 1 G.M. 8-268A diesel; 500 bhp **Crew:** 20 tot.

Remarks: Formerly numbered 9–11. All designed to mount 2/20-mm AA but do not carry them. Cargo: 210 tons.

♦ 1 ex-U.S. YO 57–class fuel lighter [YO]

Bldr: Albina Engineering and Mechanical Works, Portland, Ore. (In serv. 1944)

832 SAMUI (ex-YOG 60)

D: 445 tons light (1,420 fl) **S:** 8 kts **Dim:** 53.03 × 9.75 × 4.27
A: 2 single 20-mm 70-cal. Oerlikon Mk 10 AA
Electronics: Radar: 1 Raytheon 1500B Pathfinder (SPS-53) nav.
M: 1 Union diesel; 1 prop; 560 bhp **Fuel:** 25 tons **Crew:** 29 tot.

SERVICE CRAFT *(continued)*

Samui (832) NAVPIC-Holland, 3-95

Remarks: Transferred post–World War II. 832 had been hulked during 1980s but was restored to service circa 1991 after a refit; a flying bridge has been added above the original pilothouse. Cargo: 985 tons.

♦ **1 Prong-class fuel lighter [YO]** Bldr: . . . (In serv. 1938)

833 Prong

D: 150 tons (fl) **S:** 10 kts **Dim:** 29.0 × 5.5 × 2.3
M: 1 diesel; 1 prop; 150 bhp **Crew:** 14 tot.

Remarks: Had been hulked many years ago but was reported restored to service by 1995.

♦ **2 Samaesan-class firefighting large harbor tugs [YTB]**
Bldr: Oakwell Engineering, Bangkok (In serv. 28-2-95)

855 Samaesan 856 Raet

Raet (856) Royal Thai Navy, 1994

D: 300 tons (fl) **S:** 10 kts **Dim:** 25.00 × 8.50 × 2.40 **A:** none
Electronics: Radar: 1 . . . nav.
M: 2 Caterpillar 3512TA diesels; 2 Aquamaster US 901 azimuthal props; 2,350 bhp
Range: . . . / . . . **Crew:** 6 tot.

Remarks: Formerly numbered 7 and 8. Ordered 23-9-92 and launched 12-93. Twin stacks, all-round view pilothouse. Have two water monitors atop the pilothouse and a third atop the tall mast. Serve at the Sattahip Naval Base.

♦ **2 Rin-class coastal tugs [YTB]**
Bldr: Singapore SB & Eng. (In serv. 9-80)

	L
853 Rin	14-6-80
854 Rang	12-6-80

Rang (854) NAVPIC-Holland, 9-96

D: 250 tons (300 fl) **S:** 12 kts **Dim:** 32.3 × 9.0 × . . .
M: 1 MWM TBD 441V/12K diesel; 1 prop; 2,100 bhp **Electric:** 233 kw
Range: 1,000/10 **Crew:** 16 tot.

Remarks: Formerly numbered 5 and 6. Bollard pull: 22 tons. Have four firefighting monitors, including one atop the unusually tall mast.

♦ **2 ex-Canadian small harbor tugs [YTL]**
Bldr: Central Bridge Co., Trenton, Ontario (In serv. 1943–44)

851 Klueng Baden 852 Marin Vichai

Klueng Baden (851)—alongside oiler *Proet* (834) and fuel lighter *Prong* (833) Maritime Photographic, 5-97

D: 63 grt **S:** 8 kts **Dim:** 19.8 × 5.0 × 1.8 **M:** 1 diesel; 240 bhp

Remarks: Formerly numbered 2 and 3. Acquired in 1953.

♦ **1 Charn-class water lighter [YW]**
Bldr: Royal Thai Naval Dockyard, Bangkok (L: 14-1-65)

841 Chuang

Chuang (841) J & P van Raemdonck, 3-04

D: 355 tons (485 fl) **S:** 11 kts **Dim:** 42.0 × 7.5 × 3.1
M: 1 G.M. diesel; 500 bhp **Crew:** 29 tot.

Remarks: Formerly numbered 5. Can carry one 20-mm AA. No radar fitted.

♦ **1 . . . -class transportation lighter [YC]**
Bldr: . . . (In serv. 1948)

861 Kled Keo (ex-7, ex-*Norfrost*)

D: 450 tons (fl) **S:** 12 kts **Dim:** 46.0 × 7.6 × 4.3
M: 1 diesel; 1 prop; 900 bhp **Crew:** 7 officers + 47 enlisted

Remarks: Retired from Norwegian service and transferred in 1966. Retired in 1990 but put back in service during 1996.

♦ **1 Daxin-class naval cadet training ship [AXT]**

	Bldr	L	In serv.
937 . . .	Qiuxin SY, Shanghai	2005	2006

D: 4,500 tons (5,448 fl) **S:** 15 kts **Dim:** 119 × 15.80 × 5.30
A: 4 twin 37-mm Type 76A AA
Electronics:
Radar: 1 Type 363 early warning; 1 Type 354 Eye Shield air/surface-search radar
M: 2 . . . diesels; 2 props
Range: 5,000/15 **Crew:** . . .

Remarks: A sister serves with the Chinese fleet.

Note: The personnel transport numbered 131 has also been reported in service, no additional information is available. In addition to the larger service craft listed and described previously, the Royal Thai Navy operates numerous small personnel launches, stores transports, and fuel and water lighters in local, base-support service.

ROYAL THAI MARINE POLICE

Performing duties analogous to those of a coast guard, the Royal Thai Marine Police has absorbed the former Customs Service fleet. The organization operates a number of aircraft and helicopters. In addition to the vessels listed below, the Thai Marine Police also use numerous outboard-powered launches.

PATROL CRAFT [WPC]

♦ 1 modified Khamronsin class
Bldr: Italthai Marine, Bangkok (In serv. 4-92)

1804 Srinakarin

Srinakarin (1804)—with patrol boat *Sriyanont* (901) alongside IJ Plokker, 2-02

D: 362 light (475 fl) **S:** 25 kts **Dim:** 62.0 (56.7 pp) × 8.26 × 2.50 (hull)
A: 1 30-mm 82-cal. OTO Melara AA; 2 single 20-mm 90-cal. Oerlikon GAM-B01 AA
Electronics: Radar: 1 Decca 1226 nav.
M: 2 Deutz-M.W.M. BV 16M 628 diesels; 2 CP props; 9,980 bhp **Range:** 2,500/15
Fuel: . . . **Crew:** 6 officers, 51 enlisted

Remarks: Simplified version of Thai Navy *Khamronsin*-class patrol craft design. First unit ordered in 9-89 and a second in 1991, but the latter was canceled.

♦ 2 Damrong Rachanuphat class
Bldr: Schiffwerft Hameln, Germany

	In serv.
1802 Damrong Rachanuphat	3-1-69
1803 Lopburi Ramas	10-12-72

Lopburi Ramas (1803) H&L Van Ginderen, 2-88

D: 430 tons (fl) **S:** 23 kts **Dim:** 56.7 × 8.1 × 2.4
A: 1 twin 30-mm 75-cal. Oerlikon GCM-A03 AA; 2 single 20-mm 90-cal. Oerlkon GAM-B01 AA
Electronics: Radar: 1 Decca 1226 nav.; 1 Decca . . . nav.
M: 4 MTU diesels; 2 props; 4,400 bhp **Crew:** 45 tot.

Remarks: The original armament has been recently updated.

♦ 2 Chasanyabadee class
Bldr: Sumidagawa, Tokyo, Japan

1101 Chasanyabadee (In serv. 8-72) 1103 Phromyothee (In serv. 5-73)

Phromyothee (1103) J & P van Raemdonck, 3-04

D: 130 tons (fl) **S:** 32 kts **Dim:** 34.0 × 5.8 × 2.8
A: 2 single 20-mm 70-cal. Oerlikon Mk 10 AA
Electronics: Radar: 1 Decca . . . nav.
M: 3 Ikegai diesels; 3 props; 4,050 bhp

♦ 1 Chawengsak Songkram class
Bldr: Yokohama Yacht, Japan (In serv. 13-4-73)

1102 Chawengsak Songkram

D: 190 tons (fl) **S:** 32 kts **Dim:** 37.0 (35.5 pp) × 6.80 × 1.50
A: 2 single 20-mm 70-cal Oerlikon Mk 10 AA **Electronics:** Radar: 1 . . . nav.
M: 4 Ikegai diesels; 2 props; 5,400 bhp **Crew:** 4 officers, 12 enlisted

Remarks: Unnamed sister 1201 is assigned to customs duties.

PATROL BOATS [WPB]

♦ 1 Sriyanont class
Bldr: Italthai Marine, Bangkok (In serv. 12-6-86)

901 Sriyanont

D: 52 tons light (approx. 90 fl) **S:** 23 kts **Dim:** 27.4 × 4.9 × 2.0
A: 1 20-mm 90-cal. Oerlikon GAM-B01 AA; 2 single 7.62-mm mg
Electronics: Radar: 1 Decca . . . nav.
M: 2 Deutz SBA 16M 816CH diesels; 2 props; 2,680 bhp **Crew:** 14 tot.

♦ 3 U.S. Cutlass class
Bldr: Halter Marine, New Orleans, La. (In serv. 9-3-69)

807 Phra Ong Chao Khamrop 808 Picharn Pholakit 809 Ram Inthra

Picharn Pholakit (808)—outboard *Phra Ong Chao Khamrop* (807) NAVPIC-Holland, 8-96

D: 34 tons (fl) **S:** 25 kts **Dim:** 19.66 × 5.18 × 1.12
A: 1 20-mm 70-cal. Oerlikon Mk 10 AA; 2 single 7.62-mm mg
M: 3 G.M. Detroit Diesel 12V71 TI diesels; 2 props; 1,530 bhp **Fuel:** 2.7 tons
Crew: 15 tot.

♦ 3 27-meter class
Bldr: Tecnautic, Bangkok (In serv. 1984)

810 811 812

810 and 812—with 18-meter-class 619 alongside Maritime Photographic, 5-97

D: 50 tons (fl) **S:** 27 kts **Dim:** 27.00 × 5.85 × 1.90
A: 1 20-mm 90-cal. Oerlikon GAM-B01 AA; 2 single 7.62-mm mg
M: 3 Isotta-Fraschini diesels; 3 Castoldi 07 waterjets; 2,500 bhp

♦ 6 24.6-meter class
Bldr: Marsun, Bangkok (In serv. 27-3-1991–1996)

630 631 632 633 634 635

D: 60 tons (fl) **S:** 38 kts **Dim:** 24.60 × 6.00 × 1.10 **A:** 1 12.7-mm mg
Electronics: Radar: 1 . . . nav.
M: 2 G.M. Detroit Diesel 16V149 TI diesels; 2 props; 4,000 bhp **Crew:** 12 tot.

Remarks: Kevlar/GRP sandwich hull. Launched 11-2-91.

MARINE POLICE PATROL BOATS [WPB] *(continued)*

635—outboard *Damrong Rachanuphat* (1802) Maritime Photographic, 11-01

♦ 5 19.5-meter class
Bldr: Italthai Marine, Bangkok (In serv. 1987–90)

625 626 627 628 629

629 John Bouvia, 1990

D: 42 tons (fl) **S:** 27 kts **Dim:** 19.5 × 5.3 × 1.5 **A:** 1 12.7-mm mg
Electronics: Radar: 1 . . . nav. **M:** 2 M.A.N. D2842LE diesels; 2 props; 1,520 bhp

Remarks: Sisters are also operated by the Fisheries Patrol service.

♦ 17 18-meter class
Bldr: Tecnautic, Bangkok (In serv. 1983–19-2-86)

608 through 624

619—outboard two 27-meter-class patrol boats IJ Plokker, 2-02

D: 30 tons (fl) **S:** 27 kts **Dim:** 18.30 × 4.45 × 0.90 **A:** 1 12.7-mm mg
Electronics: Radar: 1 . . . nav.
M: 2 Isotta-Fraschini ID 368V diesels; 2 Castoldi 07 waterjets; 1,930 bhp

♦ 2 17.4-meter class
Bldr: Marsun, Bangkok (In serv. 26-3-86)

539 540

D: 30 tons (fl) **S:** 25 kts **Dim:** 17.4 × 4.9 × 0.9 **A:** 1 12.7-mm mg
Electronics: Radar: 1 . . . nav.
M: 2 G.M. Detroit Diesel 12V71 TI diesels; 2 props; 1,500 bhp **Crew:** 8 tot.

539—outboard a 16.6-meter patrol boat Maritime Photographic, 5-97

♦ 26 16.6-meter class
Bldrs: 513–533: Sumidigawa, Tokyo, Japan; others: Captain Co., Bangkok,Thailand (In serv. 1978–79)

513 through 538

526 Maritime Photographic, 11-01

D: 18 tons (fl) **S:** 23 kts **Dim:** 16.5 × 3.8 × 0.70 **A:** 1 12.7-mm mg
M: 2 Cummins diesels; 800 bhp

♦ 26 12.2-meter class
Bldr: Camcraft, Crown Point, La.

415 through 440

435 NAVPIC-Holland, 8-96

D: 13 tons (fl) **S:** 25 kts **Dim:** 12.2 × 3.7 × 1.0 **A:** Small arms
M: 2 G.M. Detroit Diesel 6-71 diesels; 2 props; 540 bhp

♦ 1 11.5-meter GRP-hulled prototype
Bldr: SEAT Co., Bangkok (In serv. 1990)

339

339 Maritime Photographic, 5-97

MARINE POLICE PATROL BOATS [WPB] *(continued)*

D: Approx. 5 tons (fl) **S:** 60 kts (57 sust.) **Dim:** 11.58 × 2.73 × . . .
M: 5 gasoline outboards motors; 1,000 bhp

♦ **38 11.3-meter river patrol boats**
Bldr: . . .

301 through 338

324 Jasper van Raemdonck, 3-04

D: 5 tons (fl) **S:** 25 kts **Dim:** 11.3 × 3.4 × . . . **A:** Small arms
M: 2 . . . diesels; 2 props; . . . bhp

♦ **22 Typhoon-class rigid inflatable boats**
Bldr: Task Force Boats, U.K. (In serv. 1990–91)

Remarks: Two 225 bhp Johnson gasoline outboards: 50 kts (40 kts with 12 police aboard).

Note: Also in service are patrol craft numbered 111, 212, 214, 220, and 222. The vessels are painted white and bear a broad diagonal red strip (with Marine Department insignia badge) followed by a narrow white and narrow blue strip.

Patrol craft 111 Jasper van Raemdonck, 3-04

TOGO

Republic of Togo

Personnel: 200 total (including marine infantry)

Base: Lomée

PATROL BOATS [PB]

♦ **2 wooden hulled**
Bldr: C. N. de l'Estérel, Cannes, France

P 761 Kara (L: 18-5-76) P 762 Mono (L: 1976)

D: 80 tons (fl) **S:** 30 kts **Dim:** 32.00 × 5.80 × 1.50
A: 1 40-mm 60-cal. Mk 3 Bofors AA; 1 20-mm 70-cal. Oerlikon Mk 10 AA
Electronics: Radar: 1 Furuno . . . nav.
M: 2 MTU 12V493 TY60 diesels; 2,700 bhp
Range: 1,500/15 **Crew:** 1 officer, 17 enlisted

Mono (P 762) French Navy, 12-96

Remarks: Wooden construction. The 20-mm gun is on the forecastle; the 40-mm gun aft.

Notes: There are also two smaller patrol launches in service; no data available.

TONGA

Kingdom of Tonga

TONGAN DEFENCE SERVICE
MARITIME DEFENCE DIVISION

Personnel: 118 total (19 officers), plus Royal Tongan Marines: 4 officers, 46 enlisted

Base: HMNB *Masefield,* Touliki Base, on Nuku'alofa

Note: Ship names are preceded by VOEA—*Vaka Oe Ene Afio.*

PATROL CRAFT [PC]

♦ **3 ASI 315 design**
Bldr: Transfield-ASI, Ltd., South Coogie, Australia

	Laid down	L	In serv.
P 201 Neiafu	30-1-89	21-9-89	30-10-89
P 202 Pangai	2-10-89	1990	30-6-90
P 203 Savea	2-90	1991	23-3-91

Savea (P 203) H&L Van Ginderen, 9-99

D: 165 tons (fl) **S:** 21 kts **Dim:** 31.50 (28.60 wl) × 8.10 × 2.12
A: 2 single 12.7-mm mg **Electronics:** Radar: 1 Furuno 1101 nav.
M: 2 Caterpillar 3516 diesels; 2 props; 2,820 bhp
Electric: 116 kw tot. **Range:** 2,500/12 **Fuel:** 27.9 tons
Endurance: 10 days **Crew:** 4 officers, 9 enlisted

Remarks: Australian government "Pacific Patrol Boat" grant-aid design, donated to a number of Southwest Pacific island states. P 203 was refitted 5-99 to 8-99 by Port Macquerie Sliways, Australia. P 201 and P 202 are to be modernized between 2007 and 2008 and all three are expected to remain in service through 2019.
Hull systems: Aluminum construction. Carry a 5-m aluminum boarding boat. Extensive navigational suite, including Furuno FSN-70 NAVSAT receiver, 525 HF/DF, 120 MF/HFD/F, FE-881 echo sounder, and DS-70 doppler log. P 203 is additionally equipped to perform hydrographic survey work.

SERVICE CRAFT

♦ **1 royal yacht [YFL]**
Titilupe

SERVICE CRAFT *(continued)*

Titilupe H&L Van Ginderen, 8-99

D: 10 tons (fl) **S:** 8 kts **Dim:** 10.4 × 3.0 × 1.0
M: 1 Ford Sabre diesel; 1 prop; . . . bhp

Remarks: 10.4-m glass-reinforced plastic craft capable of 8 kts; also used in patrol work.

♦ 6 4.90-meter aluminum utility launches [YFL]

Remarks: Powered by 30 bhp outboard motors.

♦ 1 Australian-built U.S. LCM(8)-class landing craft [YFU]

Bldr: North Queensland Eng., Cairns

C 315 Late (ex-Australian Army 1057)

Late (C 315) H&L Van Ginderen, 1-94

D: 34 tons light (116 fl) **S:** 12 kts **Dim:** 22.70 × 6.41 × 1.37 **A:** 1 7.62-mm mg
Electronics: Radar: 1 Koden MD 305 nav.
M: 2 G.M. Detroit Diesel 12V71 diesels; 2 props; 600 bhp
Range: 480/10 **Crew:** 5 tot.

Remarks: Transferred to Tonga 1-9-82. Cargo: 55 tons. Has been fitted with a pilothouse and navigational radar and is used for interisland logistic support.

Note: The Tonga Marine and Wharf Department operates the 1,119 grt/2,889 dwt tanker *Lomipeau* (A 301; ex-French Navy *Punaruu,* A 632; ex-Norwegian merchant chemical tanker *Bow Cecil*), transferred from the French Navy on 28-9-95. The 5.4-ton Sea Truck logistic landing craft *Fangailifuka* and *Alo-i-Talau* are operated by the governors of Ha'apaik and Vavau Islands, respectively, but can be recalled for Tonga Navy service if necessary.

TRINIDAD AND TOBAGO

Republic of Trinidad and Tobago

COAST GUARD

Personnel: Approx. 700 total (including 50 in the Coast Guard air wing)

Bases: Headquarters at Staubles Bay, Chauguaramas. Stations at Hart's Cut, Port Fortin, Tobago, Point Galeota (Mayaro), and Piarco International Airport (Trinidad).

Aviation: The Coast Guard operates one Cessna 402B light transport for maritime surveillance and has two Piper Navajo, two C-26, and one Cessna 310-II aircraft for liaison and training. The private National Helicopter Services Ltd, which supports search-and-rescue service, provides one B0-105 helicopter in support of the Trinidad and Tobago Police Service and the armed forces and also has available two S-76, one S-76A+, and three other Bo-105 helicopters.

Note: Ship names are preceded by TTS (Trinidad and Tobago Ship).

PATROL SHIPS [PS]

Note: Three 80-meter patrol ships with a helicopter landing deck and capable of carrying a small RIB are planned for service entry during 2007–8. Current bidders for the project include Blohm + Voss (Meko 100 design), Fincantieri (Siro-class), and Vosper-Thornycroft (with a variant of the River-class patrol craft).

♦ 1 ex-U.K. Island-class offshore patrol vessel

Bldr: Hall Russell, Aberdeen

	L	In serv.
CG 20 Nelson (ex-*Orkney*, P 299)	29-6-76	25-2-77

Nelson (CG 20) Ben Sullivan, 1-01

D: 998 tons (1,280 fl) **S:** 16.5 kts **Dim:** 61.10 (51.97 pp) × 11.00 × 4.27
A: 1 20-mm 90-cal. Oerlikon GAM-B01 AA; 2 single 7.62-mm mg
Electronics:
Radar: 1 Kelvin-Hughes Type 1006 nav.
Sonar: Simrad SU "Sidescan"
M: 2 Ruston 12RK3CM diesels (750 rpm); 1/CP prop; 5,640 bhp (4,380 sust.)
Electric: 536 kw tot. (3 × 162 kw, 1 × 50 kw diesel sets; 440 V a.c.)
Range: 11,000/12 **Fuel:** 310 tons
Crew: 4 officers, 29 enlisted (accomm. for 57 tot.)

Remarks: Retired from the Royal Navy on 27-5-99 and transferred to Trinidad and Tobago on 18-12-00, recommissioning on 22-2-01.
Hull systems: Has fin stabilizers and can maintain 12–15 kts in a Force 8 gale. Two Avon Searaider semi-rigid dinghies are carried for inspection purposes. Can carry 28.6 tons detergent (a 6-hr supply) for oil-spill cleanup.
Combat systems: The Racal CANE DEA-1 combat data system is fitted. The 30-mm gun was removed prior to transfer, but a 20-mm gun may have been substituted.

PATROL CRAFT [WPC]

♦ 2 CG 40 class (nonoperational)

Bldr: Karlskronavarvet, Karlskrona, Sweden (Both in serv. 15-6-80)

CG 5 Barracuda CG 6 Cascadura

Cascadura (CG 6) Maritime Photographic, 1-94

D: 210 tons (fl) **S:** 32 kts (27 sust.) **Dim:** 40.60 × 6.70 × 1.70
A: 1 40-mm 70-cal Bofors L70 AA; 1 20-mm 90-cal. Oerlikon GAM-B01 AA
Electronics: Radar: 1 Decca TM 1226 nav.
M: 2 Paxman Valenta 16RP200 CM diesels; 2 props; 8,000 bhp (6,700 sust.)
Range: 2,200/15 **Crew:** 22 tot. (+ 9 spare berths)

Remarks: Ordered 8-78. Have an optronic f.c.s. for the 40-mm AA. A rescue dinghy is carried on the stern. Have HF and VHF D/F gear, pollution-spill control equipment. Refitted 1988–89. Both were placed ashore for refits during 1999, but only CG 6 appears near completion.

PATROL BOATS [WPB]

♦ 3 U.S. Dauntless class
Bldr: SeaArk, Monticello, Ark. (In serv. 14-6-95)

CG 38 Soldado CG Roxborough 39 CG 40 Mayaro

Soldado (CG 38) SeaArk, 5-95

D: 11 tons (15 fl) **S:** 28 kts **Dim:** 12.19 (11.13 wl) × 3.86 × 0.69 (hull)
A: 1 7.62-mm mg **Electronics:** Radar: 1 Raytheon R40X nav.
M: 2 Caterpillar 3208TA diesels; 2 props; 850 bhp (720 sust.)
Range: 200/30; 400/22 **Fuel:** 250 gallons **Crew:** 5 tot.

Remarks: Ordered 4-94. Last unit completed 4-95, and all were delivered together as part of a U.S. aid package. Based at Cedros, Tobago, and Galeota, respectively. Aluminum construction. C. Raymond Hunt, deep-vee hull design.

♦ 2 31-ft. Interceptor class
Bldr: Bowen Boats, Port-of-Spain (In serv. 5-91)

CG 001 CG 002

D: . . . tons **S:** 46 kts **Dim:** 9.45 × . . . × . . . **A:** Small arms
Electronics: Radar: 1 Raytheon . . . nav.
M: 2 gasoline outboards; . . . bhp **Crew:** 2–3 tot.

Remarks: Aluminum construction. Attached to Special Squadron for antidrug work.

♦ 2 Wasp 20-m class
Bldr: W. A. Souter & Sons, Cowes, U.K. (In serv. 12-82)

CG 31 Kairi (ex-*Sea Bird*) CG 32 Moriah (ex-*Sea Dog*)

Moriah (CG 32) Trinidad & Tobago C.G., 1989

D: 32 tons (fl) **S:** 36 kts (30 sust.) **Dim:** 20.0 × 5.0 × 1.5
A: 2 single 7.62-mm mg
Electronics: Radar: 1 Decca 150 nav.
M: 2 G.M. 16V92 TI diesels; 2 props; 2,400 bhp
Range: 450/30 **Crew:** 2 officers, 4 enlisted

Remarks: Ordered 30-9-81. Transferred from Police in 6-89. Aluminum hulls. Both had fallen into disrepair by the mid-1990s but were refurbished and restored to service during 1999.

♦ 4 Wasp 17-m-class patrol craft
Bldr: W. A. Souter & Sons, Cowes, U.K. (In serv. 27-8-82)

CG 27 Plymouth CG 28 Caroni CG 29 Galeota CG 30 Moruga

D: 19.25 tons (fl) **S:** 28 kts (25 sust.) **Dim:** 16.76 (13.90 wl) × 4.20 × 1.40
A: 2 single 7.62-mm mg **Electronics:** Radar: 1 Decca 150 nav.
M: 2 G.M.-Stewart and Stevenson 8V92 MTAB diesels; 2 props; 1,470 bhp
Range: 500/18 **Crew:** 2 officers, 4–6 enlisted

Remarks: Glass-reinforced-plastic construction. Ordered 8-81. Sister *Cedros* (CG 35, ex-Marine Police *Sea Erne*) was stricken in 1997. CG 28, CG 29, and CG 30, after lying ashore in neglect during the mid-1990s, were refurbished and returned to service during 1999.

Disposal notes: Patrol launch *Carenage* (CG 37, ex-*Sea Dragon*) was stricken during 1999.

Plymouth (CG 27) H&L Van Ginderen, 2-94

♦ 1 aluminum-hulled
Bldr: SeaArk Marine, Monticello, Ark. (In serv. 5-79)

CG 33 Matelot (ex-*Sea Scorpion*)

Matelot (CG 33) Maritime Photographic, 1-94

D: 15.5 tons (fl) **S:** 28 kts **Dim:** 13.7 × 4.1 × 1.3 **A:** 1 7.62-mm mg
Electronics: Radar: 1 . . . nav.
M: 2 G.M. Detroit Diesel 8V92 diesels; 2 props; 850 bhp
Range: 500/20 **Crew:** 6 tot.

Remarks: Transferred from police 30-6-89. Sister *Mathura* (CG 34, ex-*Sea Spray*) stricken 1990. CG 33 was refitted during 1998.

♦ 4 ex-U.S. Coast Guard 82-ft Point class
Bldr: CG 7 and CG 9: J. Martinac SB, Tacoma, Wash.; CG 8 and CG 10: Coast Guard Yard, Curtis Bay, Md.

	In serv.
CG 7 Corozal Point (ex-*Point Bennett*, WPB 82351)	19-12-66
CG 8 Crown Point (ex-*Point Heyer*, WPB 82369)	3-8-67
CG 9 Galera Point (ex-*Point Bonita*, WPB 82347)	12-9-66
CG 10 Bacolet Point (ex-*Point Highland*, WPB 82333)	27-6-62

Crown Point (CG 8) Leo Dirkx, 9-00

D: 64 tons (69 fl) **S:** 23.7 kts **Dim:** 25.3 × 5.23 × 1.95
A: Provision for: 2 single 7.62-mm M2 mg
Electronics: Radar: 1 Hughes-Furuno SPS-73 nav.

PATROL BOATS [WPB] *(continued)*

M: 2 Caterpillar 3412 diesels; 2 props; 1,480 bhp
Range: 490/23.7; 1,500/8 **Fuel:** 5.7 tons
Crew: 1 officer, 7 enlisted

Remarks: CG 7 and CG 8 were transferred by donation on 12-2-99, having been stricken from U.S. Coast Guard service during 1998; CG 9 was donated on 14-11-00 and CG 10 on 24-7-01.
Hull systems: Hull built of mild steel. High-speed diesels controlled from the bridge. Well equipped for salvage and towing. Although elderly, are in excellent condition but are considered to be heavy rollers.

SERVICE CRAFT

♦ 3 Hurricane 733–class rigid-inflatable launches [WYFL]

CG 003 CG 004 CG 005

Remarks: Delivered in 1993 as U.S. aid. Are 25-ft., GRP-hulled craft with inflatable rubber collars powered by two Johnson V6 gasoline outboards. Equipped with Raytheon navigational radar. One other has been stricken.

♦ 1 service launch [WYFL]
Bldr: Tugs & Lighters, Ltd., Port-of-Spain (In serv. 15-8-76)

A 01 Naparima (ex-CG 26)

D: 21.4 tons **S:** 10 kts **Dim:** 15.2 × 4.9 × 2.4
M: 2 G.M. Detroit Diesel 6V71 diesels; 2 props; 460 bhp
Range: 400/10 **Crew:** 6 tot.

♦ 1 small launch [WYFL]

A 04 Reform

Remarks: Transferred from Prison Authority in 1989.

TUNISIA

Republic of Tunisia

NAVY

Personnel: Approx. 4,800 total

Bases: Principal base and headquarters at Bizerte, with additional facilities at Kilibia, La Galité, and Sfax.

Maritime Aviation: The Air Force acquired 10 surplus ex-U.S. Navy SH-3H and HH-3E Sea King helicopters in 1995 for search-and-rescue duties.

GUIDED-MISSILE PATROL CRAFT [PTG]

♦ 3 Combattante-III class
Bldr: CMN, Cherbourg, France

	Laid down	L	In serv.
P 501 La Galité	26-5-82	16-6-83	27-2-85
P 502 Tunis	28-9-82	27-10-83	28-3-85
P 503 Carthage	6-1-83	24-1-84	29-4-85

Carthage (P 503) Bernard Prézelin, 4-05

Carthage (P 503) Guy Schaeffer via Paolo Marsan, 8-04

D: 395 tons (425 fl) **S:** 38.5 kts
Dim: 56.80 (53.00 pp) × 8.16 × 2.15 (2.50 props)
A: 8 MM 40 Exocet SSM; 1 76-mm 62-cal. OTO Melara Compact DP; 1 twin 40-mm 70-cal. Melara AA; 2 twin 30-mm 75-cal. Oerlikon AA
Electronics:
Radar: 1 Decca . . . nav.; 1 Thales Triton-S surf./air-search;1 Thales Castor-IIB gun f.c.
EW: Thales DR2000 intercept, 1 330-340-round Matra Défense Dagaie decoy RL
M: 4 MTU 20V538 TB93 diesels; 4 props; 19,300 bhp **Electric:** 405 kVA tot.
Range: 700/33; 2,800/10 **Crew:** 35 tot.

Remarks: Ordered 27-6-81. Are said to be in need of refits, but all are operating.
Combat systems: Have Thomson-CSF TAVITAC combat direction system with Vega-II control system for missiles, 76-mm and 40-mm guns; two Matra Défense Naja optronic gun directors atop pilothouse control the 30-mm mounts and/or the 40-mm mount. The Matra Défense Sylosat satellite navigational system is fitted.

♦ 6 Type 143
Bldrs: A: Lürssen, Vegesack; B: Krögerwerft, Rendsburg

	Bldr	Laid down	L	In serv.
P 505 Hamilcar (ex-*Sperber,* P 6115)	B	18-1-73	15-1-74	27-9-76
P 506 Hannon (ex-*Greif,* P 6116)	A	12-12-73	4-9-75	25-11-76
P 507 Hamilcon (ex *Geier,* P 6113)	A	14-2-73	18-9-74	2-6-76
P 508 Hannibal (ex-*Seeadler,* P 6118)	A	12-6-74	17-11-75	28-3-77
P 509 Hasdrubal (ex-*Habicht,* P 6119)	B	25-1-74	5-6-75	23-12-77
P 510 Giscon (ex-*Kormoran,* P 6120)	A	26-11-74	14-4-76	29-7-77

Hannibal (P 508) Frank Findler, 10-05

Hannon (P 506) A.A. de Kruijf, 7-05

D: 300 tons (393 fl) **S:** 36 kts (32 fl) **Dim:** 57.6 (54.4 pp) × 7.76 × 2.82 (2.56 hull)
A: Provision for 4 MM 38 Exocet SSM; 2 single 76-mm 62-cal. OTO Melara DP; 2 Stinger point-defense SAM launch positions; 2 single 12.7-mm mg; 2 fixed, aft-launching 533-mm TT (Seeal wire-guided torpedoes; no reloads)
Electronics:
Radar: 1 SMA 3RM 20 nav.; 1 Thales WM-27 track-while-scan f.c.
EW: Racal Octopus suite: Cutlass intercept and Scorpion jammer; 2 6-round Buck-Wegmann Hot Dog/Silver Dog decoy RL; Wolke chaff dispenser
M: 4 MTU 16V956 TB91 diesels; 4 props; 16,000 bhp (at 1,515 rpm)
Electric: 540 kw **Range:** 600/30; 2,600/16 **Fuel:** 116 tons
Crew: 4 officers, 19 petty officers., 17 ratings

Remarks: Transferred from Germany in three batches. 505 and 506 were transferred on 4-5-05, 507 and 508 on 30-5-05, and 509 and 510 were turned over on 13-12-05. Exocet missiles were carried while in German service but no missiles were included in the 2005 transfers. Originally ordered for Germany in 1972.
Hull systems: Wood-planked, round-bilge hull with steel frames.
Combat systems: During 1988–92, the WM-27 radar fire-control systems were updated and various ECCM measures were added. There is a secondary OGR-7/3 optical f.c.s. for the aft 76-mm gun.

PATROL CRAFT [PC]

♦ 3 Chinese Type 62-1–class patrol boats
Bldr: . . . (In serv. 3-94)

P 207 Utique P 208 Jerba P 209 Kuriat

D: 120 tons (fl) **S:** 32 kts (28 sust.) **Dim:** 35.0 × 5.4 × 1.8
A: 2 twin 25-mm 80-cal. Type 81 AA **Electronics:** Radar: 1 Type 756 nav.

PATROL CRAFT [PC] *(continued)*

Jerba (P 208) Leo van Ginderen, 3-02

M: 4 MWM TBD604 BV12 diesels; 4 props; 4,400 bhp
Range: 750/17 **Crew:** 39 tot.

Remarks: Delivered via heavy lift ship 1-94. Shortened version of Shanghai-II design, with larger superstructure, lighter armament, and German-made diesels.

♦ 3 French P 48 class
Bldr: SFCN, Villeneuve-la-Garenne

	L	In serv.
P 301 Bizerte	20-11-69	10-7-70
P 302 Horria (ex-*Liberté*)	19-2-70	10-70
P 304 Monastir	25-6-74	25-3-75

Bizerte (P 301) H&L van Ginderen/Camil Busquets i Vilanova, 7-98

D: 250 tons (fl) **S:** 22 kts **Dim:** 48.0 (45.5 pp) × 7.1 × 2.25
A: 2 twin 37-mm 63-cal. Model 74 AA; 2 4-round SS-12 wire-guided missile launchers
Electronics: Radar: 1/Decca TM 1226 nav.
M: 2 MTU 16V652 TB81 diesels; 2 props; 4,600 bhp **Range:** 2,000/16
Crew: 4 officers, 30 enlisted

Remarks: Rearmed with guns from discarded Shanghai-II-class patrol craft in 1994. The missile system (command-guided from a station on the bridge) may no longer be functional and is considered unreliable except against large, nearby targets.

PATROL BOATS [PB]

♦ 4 French 32-meter class
Bldr: C.N. de l'Estérel, Cannes

	In serv.		In serv.
P 201 Istiklal (ex-French VC 11)	1957	P 203 Al Jala	11-63
P 202 Joumhouria	1-61	P 204 Remada	7-67

Joumhouria (P 202) B. Laffont, 5-99

D: 60 tons (82 fl) **S:** 28 kts **Dim:** 31.45 × 5.75 × 1.7
A: 2 single 20-mm 70-cal. Oerlikon AA **Electronics:** Radar: 1 Decca 1226 nav.
M: 2 MTU 12V493 TY70 diesels; 2 props; 2,700 bhp (2,200 sust.)
Range: 1,400/15 **Crew:** 3 officers, 14 enlisted

Remarks: Wooden construction. P 201 was launched on 25-5-57 and transferred in 3-59.

♦ 6 French 25-meter class
Bldr: C.N. de l'Estérel, Cannes (In serv. 1961–63)

V 101 through V 106

V 105 Bernard Prézelin, 4-05

D: 38–39 tons **S:** 23 kts **Dim:** 25.0 × 4.75 × 1.25
A: 1 20-mm 70-cal. Oerlikon AA
Electronics: Radar: 1 Decca 1226 nav.
M: 2 G.M. 12V71 TI diesels; 2 props; 940 bhp
Range: 900/16 **Crew:** 11 tot.

♦ 9 44-foot ex-U.S. Coast Guard motor life boats [YH]
Bldr: USCG Yard, Curtis Bay, Md.

132-24 and eight others

132-24 Bernard Prézelin, 4-05

D: 14.9 tons light (17.7 fl) **S:** 13 kts (11.8 sust.)
Dim: 13.44 × 3.87 × 1.19 **Electronics:** Radar: 1/SPS-57 nav.
M: 2 G.M. Detroit Diesel 6V53 diesels; 2 props; 372 bhp
Range: 185/11.8; 200/11 **Fuel:** 1.2 tons **Crew:** 4 tot.

Remarks: Built during the 1960s and 1970s. Transferred from the U.S. Coast Guard during 2003–4. "Unsinkable" design. Can carry up to 21 rescued personnel.

AUXILIARIES

♦ 1 buoy tender and pollution-control ship [AGL]
Bldr: Damen SY, Gorinchem, the Netherlands (In serv. 3-98)

A 802 Sidi bou Said

Sidi bou Said (A 802) *Marines*/J. Carney, 1998

D: Approx. 640 tons (fl) **S:** 10.4 kts **Dim:** 38.80 × 10.25 × 2.80 **A:** None
Electronics: Radar: . . . **M:** 2 Caterpillar 3406C TA/B diesels; 2 props; 800 bhp
Electric: . . . kw tot. (2 × . . ., Caterpillar 3304 B/T-SR4 diesels driving)
Range: . . . / . . . **Crew:** 18 tot.

Remarks: Ordered 12-96 as a "buoy-laying, towing, and pollution control vessel" to Damen's Stan Carrier 3910 design. Can carry a 50-ton deck cargo and up to 200 m^3 of fuel oil and water. Bollard pull is 8 tons. Has a 20-ton deck crane and an A-frame gantry with 50-ton capacity.

AUXILIARIES *(continued)*

♦ 1 ex-U.S. Robert D. Conrad–class oceanographic research ship [AGOR]
Bldr: Northwest Marine, Portland, Ore.

	L	In serv.
A 701 N.H.O. SALAMMBO (ex-*De Steiguer*, T-AGOR 12)	3-6-66	28-2-69

N.H.O. Salammbo (A 701) Luciano Grazioli, 2-01

D: 1,088 tons light (1, 643 fl) **S:** 13.5 kts
Dim: 63.51 (58.32 pp) × 11.89 × 4.97 (6.3 m max. over sonar domes)
Electronics: Radar: 1 Raytheon 1650/SX nav.; 1 Raytheon 1660/12S nav.
M: 2 Cummins diesels, electric drive; 1 prop; 1,000 shp—JT700 Omnithruster; 350 shp
Electric: 850 kw **Range:** 9,000/12 **Fuel:** 211 tons **Endurance:** 45 days
Crew: As U.S. ship: 9 officers, 17 unlicensed, 15 scientists/technicians

Remarks: 1,143 grt./355 dwt. Transferred 2-11-92. New name commemorates a major oceanographic research center in Tunisia. Left for Tunisia 9-11-92. To be used for foreign cruising as well as for oceanographic research in Tunisian waters. Large stack contains 620-hp gas-turbine generator set used to drive main shaft at speeds up to 6.5 kts for experiments requiring "quiet" conditions. Also has retractable electric bow-thruster/propulsor, which provides up to 4.5 kts.

♦ 1 ex-Italian Simeto-class water transport tanker [AWT]
Bldr: CINET, Molfetta

	Laid down	L	In serv.
AIN ZAGHOUAN (ex-*Simeto*, A 5375)	14-3-86	4-2-88	9-7-88

D: 1,914 tons (fl) **S:** 13 kts **Dim:** 68.35 (63.60 pp) × 10.06 × 3.90
A: 2 single 7.62-mm mg **Electronics:** Radar: 1 SMA SPN-748 nav.
M: 2 Wärtsilä NSD B 230.6 diesels; 1 prop; 2,400 bhp—125-shp bow-thruster
Electric: 420 kw (3 × 140 kw Isotta-Fraschini ID30SS6L diesel sets)
Range: 1,650/12 **Crew:** 2 officers, 24 enlisted

Remarks: Retired from the Italian Navy during 2002 and transferred 30-6-03. Cargo: 1,200 tons.

♦ 1 ex-U.S. Silas Bent–class training ship [AXT]
Bldr: Defoe SB, Bay City, Mich.

	L	In serv.
A 700 KHEIREDDINE (ex-*Wilkes*, T-AGS 33)	31-7-69	28-6-71

Kheireddine (A 700) Anthony Vella, 8-03

D: 1,915 tons (2,565 fl) **S:** 15 kts **Dim:** 86.9 (80.8 pp) × 14.6 × 4.6
Electronics: Radar: 1 Raytheon RM 1650/9X nav.; 1 Raytheon TM 1660/12S nav.
M: 2 Alco diesels, electric drive: Westinghouse or G.E. motor; 1 CP Prop; 3,600 shp (plus 350-hp bow-thruster)
Electric: 960 kw tot. **Range:** 5,800–6,300/14.5; 8,000/13 **Fuel:** 461 tons
Crew: 35 crew + 26–30 scientists

Remarks: Deactivated 8-9-95 from U.S. Navy and transferred 29-9-95 as Grant Aid to Tunisia. Used primarily as training ship for the Tunisian Naval Academy but also performs oceanographic research work in the Mediterranean. Retains bathymetric and acoustic doppler current profiling equipment.

SERVICE CRAFT

♦ 2 Diving Tenders [YDT]

A 707 DEGGA A 708 EL JEM

El Jem (A 708)—diving tender Guy Schaeffer via Paolo Paolo Marsan, 7-02

Remarks: No data available.

♦ 1 ex-Italian MEN 215–class personnel launch [YFL]
Bldr: Intermarine-Crestitalia, Ameglia, La Spezia (In serv. 1986)

. . . (ex-MEN 215)

D: 82 tons (fl) **S:** 28 kts (23 sust.) **Dim:** 27.28 × 6.98 × 1.10
Electronics: Radar: 1 SMA SPN-732 nav.
M: 2 Isotta Fraschini ID 36 SS 12V diesels; 2 props; 3,200 bhp
Electric: 50 kVA (2 × 25 kVA gen.) **Range:** 250/14
Crew: 4 tot., + 250 passengers

Remarks: Stricken from Italian Navy 17-12-02 and transferred during 2003. Originally built to be carried by the carrier *Giuseppe Garibaldi* as commando transports for search-and-rescue, disaster relief, and other transport duties. GRP construction. Since completion, however, had been used as a personnel ferry.

♦ 2 ex-U.S. Army LCM(8) Mod. 1–class utility craft [YFU]
(In serv. 1954)

. . . (ex-LCM 8265, ex-C200779) . . . (ex-LCM 8268, ex-C200782)

D: 58.8 tons light (116 fl) **S:** 9.2 kts (loaded) **Dim:** 22.40 × 6.42 × 1.40 (mean)
M: 2 G.M. Detroit Diesel 6-71 diesels; 2 props; 600 bhp **Range:** 150/9.2 (loaded)
Fuel: 2.4 tons **Crew:** 2–4 tot.

Remarks: Donated to Tunisia on 17-11-00. Former U.S. Army landing craft originally built for the U.S. Navy. Cargo: 60 tons or 150 personnel for short distances in 12.8 × 4.3 m open well with 54.6-m^2 space with bow ramp.

♦ 2 ex-U.S. Coast Guard White-class coastal buoy tenders [YGL]
Bldr: Erie Concrete & Steel Supply Co., Erie, Pa.

	Laid down	L	In serv.
A 804 TABARKA (ex-*White Heath*, WLM 545)	4-6-43	21-7-43	9-8-44
A 805 TURGUENESS (ex-*White Lupine*, WLM 546)	28-4-43	28-7-43	31-5-44

D: 435 tons (600 fl) **S:** 9.8 kts **Dim:** 40.49 × 9.14 × 2.67
M: 2 diesels; 2 props; 600 bhp **Electric:** 90 kw tot.
Range: 2,100/9.8; 4,500/5.1 **Fuel:** 40 tons **Crew:** 1 officer, 23 enlisted

Remarks: Former U.S. Navy self-propelled covered lighters YF 446 and YF 445, transferred to the U.S. Coast Guard on 3-9-47 and 9-8-47 respectively; stricken from U.S. Coast Guard on 27-2-98 and 31-3-98 and donated to Tunisia 10-6-98 for service as navigational buoy tenders. Have one 10-ton buoy-handling derrick.

♦ 1 navigational aids tender [YGL]
Bldr: . . ., the Netherlands (In serv. 1961)

BOUGHRARA (ex-*IJsselmeer*)

Boughrara B. Laffont, 5-99

D: . . . tons **S:** . . . kts **Dim:** 26.60 × 5.60 × 1.50 **M:** 1 diesel; 1 prop; . . . bhp

Remarks: Acquired 1996 from the Netherlands.

♦ 2 inshore survey launches [YGS]

GUESETTE (In serv. 1992) ALYSSA (In serv. 25-3-96)

SERVICE CRAFT *(continued)*

D: 8.5 tons (fl) **S:** 10 kts **Dim:** 11.0 × 3.8 × 1.1
M: 1 Perkins diesel; 1 prop; 200 bhp **Crew:** 6 tot.

Remarks: *Alyssa* is additionally configured for oceanographic research.

♦ 1 small harbor tug [YTL]
Sidi Mansour

Small harbor tug Sidi Mansour B. Laffont, 5-99

D: 226 tons (290 fl) **S:** 11 kts **Dim:** 28.0 (25.0 pp) × 8.0 × 4.5
M: 1 . . . diesel; 1 prop; 1,000 bhp
Range: 4,100/11 **Crew:** 12 tot.

♦ 1 ex-Italian RP 125–class small harbor tug [YTL]
Bldr: C.N. Ferrari, La Spezia (In serv. 29-3-84)

. . . (ex-RP 127, Y 480)

D: 78 tons (120 fl) **S:** 9.5 kts **Dim:** 19.85 (17.00 pp) × 5.20 × 2.10
M: 1 Fiat AIFO 828-SM diesel; 1 prop; 368 bhp **Electric:** 28 kw
Range: 400/9.5 **Crew:** 3 tot.

Remarks: 76 grt. Has one 120-m^3/hr water cannon. Transferred to Tunisia in 2003.

♦ 1 ex-Italian Porto d'Ischia–class medium harbor tugs [YTM]
Bldr: CNR, Riva Trigoso (In serv. 1969–70)

Sidi Daoud (ex-*Porto d'Ischia,* Y 436)

D: 250 tons (297 fl) **S:** 12 kts **Dim:** 25.5 × 7.1 × 3.3
M: 1 diesel; 1 CP prop; 850 bhp **Range:** 2,600/12

Remarks: Retired from Italian Navy during 2002 and transferred 2003 to Tunisia. The planned transfer of sister ex-*Riva Trigoso* (Y 443) did not come to fruition.

♦ 2 ex-Italian Aragosta-class training craft [YXT]

	Bldr	L	In serv.
A . . . (ex-*Aragosta,* A 5378, ex-M 5450)	CRDA, Monfalcone	8-56	19-7-57
A . . . (ex-*Polipo,* A 5381, ex-M 5463)	Costaguta, Voltri	15-6-57	10-7-57

D: 120 tons (178 fl) **S:** 13.5 kts **Dim:** 32.35 × 6.47 × 2.14 **A:** None
Electronics: Radar: 1 BX-732 nav.
M: 2 Fiat/MTU MB 820D diesels; 2 props; 1,000 bhp
Electric: 340 kw **Range:** 2,000/9 **Fuel:** 15 tons **Crew:** 2 officers, 13 enlisted

Remarks: Transferred by donation during 2003. Former inshore minesweepers of a design based on British "Ham"-class design. Built with U.S. Military Assistance Program funds. Wooden construction. Single 20-mm AA fwd removed. Reclassified 1984–85 for use as administrative tenders and navigational training craft at the Italian Naval Academy.

NATIONAL GUARD
(Gendarmarie Nationale—Direction Maritime)

PATROL CRAFT [WPC]

♦ 6 ex-German Kondor-I-class patrol boats
Bldr: VEB Peenewerft, Wolgast

	In serv.
601 Ras el Blad (ex-*Demmin*, GS 02, ex-G 422)	16-8-69
602 Ras Ajdir (ex-*Malchin,* GS 03, ex-G 441, ex-*Klütz*, G 13)	18-10-69
603 Ras Eddrek (ex-*Altentreptow*, GS 04, ex-G 414)	5-9-69
604 Ras Mamoura (ex-*Templin*, BG 31, ex-GS 06, ex-G 442)	20-12-69
605 Ras Enghela (ex-*Ahrenskoop*, BG 33, ex-GS 08, ex-G 421)	8-8-70
606 Ras Ifrikia (ex-*Warnemünde,* ex-*Bergen* . . .)	25-9-69

D: 225 tons light (339 fl) **S:** 20 kts **Dim:** 52.00 × 7.12 × 2.40
A: 1 twin 25-mm 80-cal. Type 61 AA (see Remarks)
Electronics: Radar: 1 (606: 2) . . . nav.
M: 2 Type 40DM diesels; 2 CP props; 4,000 bhp (sust.)
Range: 1,900/15 **Crew:** 20 tot.

Ras Enghela (605)—standard configuration H&L Van Ginderen, 3-98

Ras Ifrikia (606)—with enlarged and lengthened superstructure Bernard Prézelin, 6-00

Remarks: 601 through 604 were transferred from the German Border Guard to Tunisia in 7-92 without armament, but at least 601 had received a 25-mm mount removed from discarded Shanghai-II-class patrol boat by 1995. 605 was transferred on 5-8-97 and was not immediately armed. 606, transferred on 16-5-00, had been reconfigured as a fisheries protection and research vessel during East German service and was later employed in that capacity by the German Ministry of Food and Agriculture; her superstructure had been extended nearly to the stern and the bridge moved forward.

PATROL BOATS [WPB]

♦ 4 Gabes class
Bldr: SBCN, Loctudy, France (In serv. 1988–89)

Gabes Jerba Kelibia Tabark

D: 12 tons (fl) **S:** 35 kts **Dim:** 12.9 × 3.8 × 0.9 **A:** 2 single 12.7-mm mg
Electronics: Radar: 1 Decca . . . nav. **M:** 2 . . . diesels; 2 props; 800 bhp
Range: 250/15 **Crew:** 6 tot.

Remarks: One of the class carries the hull number GN 1202.

♦ 5 ex-East German Bremse class
Bldr: VEB Yachtswerf, Berlin (In serv. 1971–72)

Bullarijia (ex-G 36)
Sbeitla (ex-G 32)
Seleuta (ex-G 39)
Uerkouane (ex-G 38)
Utique (ex-G 37)

Utique Bernard Prézelin, 4-05

D: 25 tons light (48 fl) **S:** 17 kts **Dim:** 22.59 (20.97 wl) × 4.70 × 1.60
A: 2 single 7.62-mm mg **Electronics:** Radar: 1 Furuno FR 80310 nav.
M: 1 Motorenwerke Rosslau Type 6VD 18/15 AL 1 diesel; 1 prop; 510 bhp
Range: 300/12 **Fuel:** 485 liters **Crew:** 4 tot.

Remarks: Transferred as a gift of the German government during 5-92. Wooden hulls.

♦ 11 Assad ibn Fourrat class
Bldr: . . ., Bizert (In serv. 1986–89)

Assad ibn Fourrat GN 2004
Mohommed Brahim Rejeb GN 2005
and 7 others

D: 32 tons (fl) **S:** 28 kts **Dim:** 20.5 × 4.70 × 1.30
A: 1 single 12.7-mm mg and two single 7.62-mm mg
Electronics: Radar: 1 . . . decca nav.
M: 2 . . . diesels; 2 prop; 1,000 bhp
Range: 500/20 **Crew:** 8 tot.

Remarks: Built with South Korean assistance.

NATIONAL GUARD PATROL BOATS [WPB] *(continued)*

Assad ibn Fourrat–class patrol boat B. Laffont, 5-99

Notes: The Coast Guard also operates one locally built *Assad ibn Fourrat*–class patrol boat and the boats GN 1602, GN 1401–1403, GN 1704–1705, GN 907, and GN 1105, for which no additional data are available. The craft are painted white or gray and carry a broad red/narrow white/narrow red diagonal stripe on each side. Between 2000 and 2002, the Customs Service took delivery of four 11.6-meter, 11-ton, Rodman 38–class boats.

Rodman 38–class customs boat Leo van Ginderen, 3-02

Turkish Navy S-70B Seahawk Cem D. Yaylali, 10-03

AB-212 Cem D. Yaylali, 10-03

ATR-72—official model; deliveries are planned to begin in 2010 Cem D. Yaylali, 9-05

TURKEY

Republic of Turkey

TURKISH REPUBLIC NAVY

(Türkiye Cumhuriyeti Bahriyesi)

Personnel: 48,600 tot. (including 3,100 Marines); 55,000 are in service with the naval reserve.

Bases: Fleet Headquarters is located at the capital, Ankara. Other primary facilities are located at Gölçük, Izmir, Antalya, Aksaz, Foça, Iskenderun, Samsun, and Mersin.

Naval Aviation: The Turkish Naval Aviation Force (*Türk Donama Havaciligi*) has one operational squadron, 351, with eight S-70B Seahawk (12 more were ordered in 2005), three AB 204AS, nine AB 212ASW, and three AB-212EW helicopters. Fixed-wing pilot proficiency is maintained on six SOCATA TB-20 trainers delivered in 1995. Naval air facilities are maintained at Trabzon, Sinop, Istanbul, Çanakkale, Izmir, Antalya, Iskenderun, and Cengiz Topel Naval Air Station, Kocaeli.

The Sikorsky S-70B Seahawk ASW helicopters are equipped with AGM-114M Hellfire-II antiship missiles, HELRAS active dipping sonar, and APS-143(V) radar. Turkish Navy plans call for an eventual total of 32.

Nine (three for the Coast Guard) CASA CN-235 maritime patrol aircraft were locally assembled by Tusas Aerospace Industries, near Ankara between 2001 and 2002. Five SAR-configured Agusta-Bell 412 helicopters are also in service with the Coast Guard. Ten Alenia ATR-72 maritime patrol aircraft were ordered in 2005, with deliveries to begin in 2010.

Marines: The Turkish Marine Corps has three combat infantry battalions, one artillery battalion, a headquarters company, and various support units.

Note: Turkish Navy ship names are preceded by TCG (*Türkiye Cumhuriyeti Genisi*) (Turkish Republic Ship).

WEAPONS AND SYSTEMS

Most weapons and systems are of U.S. origin, some from Germany and France. British Sea Skua antiship missiles have been purchased for use by AB-212 helicopters. In 1991 a license was obtained from Marconi Underwater Systems to build 40 Mk 24 Mod. 2 Tigerfish wire-guided submarine torpedoes to begin replacement of German SUT and SST-4 and U.S. Mk 37 torpedoes; 20 Tigerfish were delivered by GEC-Marconi in 1998. Ten U.S. Mk 48 submarine torpedoes were ordered in 1990, and the Turkish Navy also has a considerable number of AGM-84A and AGM-84C Harpoon surface-launched antiship missiles and received UGM-84C Sub-Harpoon missiles during the mid-1990s. A July 1999 order for 16 Penguin Mk 2 Mod. 7 antiship missiles was canceled in 10-99, but in 7-00 Norway agreed to sell Turkey Penguin Mk III missiles. The corvettes purchased from France were delivered with MM 38 Exocet antiship missiles.

Some 208 pedestal-mounted Stinger point-defense SAM launch systems from ASELSAN, Turkey, were to be delivered by the end of 2000 for use on naval ships and at shore stations. Starting in 2-01, 84 AGM-114K Hellfire-II antiship missiles with blast-fragmentation warheads for antiship use began delivery for launch from SH-60B Seahawk helicopters.

All Turkish Navy major surface combatants are equipped to employ Link 11 datalink. Links 16 and 22 and the U.S. Cooperative Engagement Capability (CEC) may be incorporated in the future.

Sea Guard Close-In Weapons System—Contraves/Oerlikon

Employed only by the Turkish Navy, each Sea Guard installation has three Sea Zenith quadruple 25-mm AA with a combined rate of fire of 3,200 rounds per minute per mount. With a practical range of about 2,000 m, the mountings can depress to –15 deg. and elevate to +127 deg., with extremely rapid elevation and traversing. In the MEKO-200 class, the three mounts are controlled by two Siemens Albis radar-electro-optical directors. Sufficient ready-service ammunition is carried on-mount for 18 engagements.

Bora—ASELSAN Microwave and Systems Technologies Division

A close-defense SAM system using components from the armored vehicle Pedestal-Mounted Air Defense System (PMADS) and the smaller Zipkin system. The prototype Bora, completed in 1999, carries four Stinger heat-seeking SAMs and a 12.7-mm mg plus t.v. and infrared optical sensors and a pulse-laser rangefinder, all on a stabilized mounting. No immediate plans for shipboard installations have been announced.

WEAPONS AND SYSTEMS *(continued)*

Note: Since 1997, submarine pennant numbers are no longer displayed, and surface ship pennants have had the white component replaced with gray to reduce the contrast and thereby assist somewhat in defeating infrared-homing missiles.

ATTACK SUBMARINES [SS]

♦ 7 (+ 1) German Type 209/1400 class

Bldr: S 353–358: Gölçük Naval Shipyard, Kocaeli, Izmir; S 359 and later: Pendik Naval Shipyard, Istanbul

	Laid down	L	In serv.
S 353 Preveze	12-9-89	27-11-93	28-7-94
S 354 Sakarya	1-2-90	28-7-94	4-96
S 355 18 Mart	28-7-94	25-8-97	24-7-98
S 356 Anafartalar	1-8-95	2-9-98	22-7-99
S 357 Gür	24-7-98	25-7-01	19-2-04
S 358 Çanakkale	22-7-99	7-02	2005
S 359 Burakreis	25-7-01	2004	2006
S 360 Ikikci Inönü	25-2-02	2005	2007

Preveze (S 353) Cem D. Yaylali, 10-03

Sakarya (S 354) Boris Lemachko Collection, 6-03

D: 1,464 tons surf./1,586 tons sub. **S:** 11.0 surf./21.5 kts sub.
Dim: 62.00 × 6.20 (7.60 over stern planes) × 5.50
A: 8 533-mm bow TT (14 Mk 24 Mod. 2 Tigerfish torpedoes and UGM-84C Sub-Harpoon SSM, and/or mines (see Remarks)
Electronics:
Radar: 1 . . . nav./surf. search
Sonar: STN Atlas Elektronik CSU-83/1 suite (with flank and TAS-3 towed passive arrays)
EW: Racal Porpoise intercept suite (S 357 and later: Racal Sealion)
M: 4 MTU 12V493 A280 AG diesels (800 bhp each), 4 405-kw generator sets, 1 Siemens electric motor; 1 prop; 5,000 shp
Range: 15,000/4 surf.; 10,000/8 snorkel; 230/8, 390/4, 25/21.5 sub.
Endurance: 50 days **Crew:** 8 officers, 27 enlisted (accommodations)

Remarks: Lengthened version of the standard IKL 1400 design. First two of planned six ordered 12-11-87; second pair, ordered in 1993, was built with Howaldtswerke technical assistance. Named for battles. S 359 is to cost $556 million.
Hull systems: Diving depth: 320 m. Reserve buoyancy: 10%. Four 120-cell batteries. Have Kollmorgen Model 76-374 search and attack periscopes, with integral ranging radar and intercept antennas.
Combat systems: All have the Atlas Electronik ISUS-83-2 command and control system with four display consoles; it links radar, periscope t.v., ESM, Link 11, and sonar suite data. Four of the torpedo tubes can be used to launch missiles and four to lay mines. The Porpoise EW suite is an export version of the British Navy's UAC system. S 357 and later are to carry STN Atlas Elektronik DM2A4 wire-guided torpedoes.

♦ 6 German Type 209/1200

Bldrs: S 347, S 348, S 349; Howaldtswerke, Kiel; S 350 and later: Gölçük Naval Shipyard, Kocaeli, Izmir

	Laid down	L	In serv.
S 347 Atilay	1-12-72	23-10-74	12-3-76
S 348 Saldiray	2-1-73	14-2-75	15-1-77
S 349 Batiray	11-6-75	24-10-77	7-11-78
S 350 Yildiray	1-5-76	20-7-77	20-7-81
S 351 Doganay	21-3-80	16-11-83	16-11-85
S 352 Dolunay	16-11-83	21-7-88	29-6-90

D: 1,000 tons std./1,180 tons surf./1,285 sub. **S:** 11.5 kts surf./22 kts sub.
Dim: 55.90 × 6.30 × 5.50
A: 8 533-mm bow TT (14 SUT, SST-4 Mod. 0, and Mk 37 Mod. 2 wire-guided torpedoes, and/or mines)

Yildiray (S 350) Hartmut Ehlers, 3-96

Dolunay (S 352) Hartmut Ehlers, 10-95

Electronics:
Radar: 1 Thales Calypso-II nav/surf.-search
Sonar: STN Atlas Elektronik CSU-3 suite: AN526 passive/AN407AS active, DUUX-2 underwater telephone
EW: S 347, 348: Racal Sealion intercept; others: Racal Porpoise suite
M: 4 MTU 12V493 TY60 diesels (600 bhp each); 4 405-kw generator sets; 1 Siemens electric motor, 5,000 shp
Range: 7,800/8 surf.; 11,300/4 (surf.); 28/20 (sub.); 460/4 (sub.) **Fuel:** 185 tons
Endurance: 50 days **Crew:** 6 officers, 27 enlisted

Remarks: Are all to be modernized so as to permit retirement of the remaining ex-U.S. Navy submarines. In 2000 two submarines of this class were offered for lease to Malaysia, probably S 347 and S 348, with the pair to be replaced later by two new-construction Type 209/1400 for Malaysia.
Hull systems: Have four Hagen 120-cell lead-acid batteries, delivering 11,500 Am/hr and weighing 257 tons. Normal operating depth: 250 m.
Combat systems: First two have Thales M8 torpedo fire control; the others have the Thales SINBADS combat system. Have Kollmorgen Model 76-374 search and attack periscopes, with integral ranging radar and intercept antennas. The original Thales DR-2000 EW suite in the first two was replaced in 1999–2000.

Disposal notes: Ex-U.S. *Tang*-class *Hizir Reis* (S 342) was withdrawn from service during 2-04 and sister *Piri Reis* (S 343) was decommissioned on 9-8-04.

DESTROYERS [DD]

Note: During 2005–6 Turkey began negotiating with the U.S. Navy to purchase the retired *Spruance*-class destroyers *Cushing* (DD 985) and *O'Bannon* (DD 987). As of mid-2006, the deal appears to have been called off.

GUIDED-MISSILE FRIGATES [FFG]

♦ 8 ex-U.S. Oliver Hazard Perry class

	Bldr	Laid down	L	In serv.
F 490 Gaziantep (ex-*Clifton Sprague,* FFG 16)	Bath Iron Works	30-7-79	16-2-80	21-3-81
F 491 Giresun (ex-*Antrim,* FFG 20)	Todd, Seattle	21-6-78	27-3-79	26-9-81
F 492 Gemlik (ex-*Flatley,* FFG 21)	Bath Iron Works	13-11-79	15-5-80	20-6-81
F 493 Gelibolu (ex-*Reid,* FFG 30)	Todd, San Pedro	8-10-80	27-6-81	19-2-83
F 494 Gökçeada (ex-*Mahlon S. Tisdale,* FFG 27)	Todd, San Pedro	19-3-80	7-2-81	13-11-82
F 495 Gediz (ex-*John A. Moore,* FFG 19)	Todd, San Pedro	19-12-78	20-10-79	14-11-81
F 496 Gökova (ex-*Samuel Eliot Morison,* FFG 13)	Bath Iron Works	4-12-78	14-7-79	10-10-80
F 497 Gosku (ex-*Estocin,* FFG 15)	Bath Iron Works	2-4-79	3-11-79	10-1-81

Gelibolu (F 493) Leo van Ginderen, 3-06

GUIDED-MISSILE FRIGATES [FFG] *(continued)*

Gediz (F 495) Ralph Edwards, 5-04

Gemlịk (F 492) Bernard Prézelin, 2-05

D: 3,106 tons light (3,989 fl) **S:** 29 kts (30.6 trials)
Dim: 138.8 × 13.72 × 5.8 (6.7 max.)
A: 1 Mk 13 Mod. 4 missile launcher (4 RGM-84C Harpoon and 36 Standard SM-1 MR missiles); 1 76-mm 62-cal. Mk 75 DP; 1 20-mm Mk 15 Phalanx gatling CIWS; 2 single 12.7-mm mg; 2 triple 324-mm Mk 32 Mod. 7 ASW TT (Mk 46 Mod. 5 torpedoes); 2 S-70B Seahawk helicopter
Electronics:
Radar: 1 . . . nav., 1 Cardion SPS-55 surf. search.; 1 Raytheon SPS-49(V)4 air-search; 1 Raytheon Mk 92 Mod. 2 missile illumination/gun f.c.; 1 Lockheed Martin STIR (SPG-60 Mod.) missile illumination/gun f.c.; 1 General Dynamics Mk 90 Phalanx f.c.
Sonar: SQQ-89(V)2 suite: Raytheon SQS-56 hull-mounted LF (see Remarks)
TACAN: URN-25
EW: Raytheon SLQ-32(V)2 passive; Mk 36 SRBOC decoy syst. (2 6-round Mk 137 RL); SLQ-25 Nixie towed acoustic torpedo decoy
M: 2 G.E. LM-2500 gas turbines; 1 5.5-m diameter, 5-bladed CP prop; 41,000 shp (40,000 sust.)—2 350-shp drop-down electric propulsors
Electric: 4,000 kw tot. (4 × 1,000 kw diesel-driven alternator sets)
Range: 4,200/20; 5,000/18 **Fuel:** 587 tons + 64 tons helicopter fuel
Crew: 19 officers, 121 petty officers, 79 enlisted

Remarks: F 490 and F 491 were transferred under Grant Aid program during U.S. Fiscal Year 1996, and F 492 was transferred on lease (but was offered for outright sale for $28 million during U.S. Fiscal Year 2001). F 490 had been decommissioned from the U.S. Navy on 2-6-95, while F 491 was decommissioned on 8-5-96 and F 492 on 11-5-96. F 490 arrived in Turkey on 16-3-98, the other two on 13-4-98, and they were formally recommissioned on 24-7-98. F 493, decommissioned 25-9-98 from the USN, was transferred by sale on 5-1-99. F 494, in reserve since 27-9-96, and the ex-*Duncan* (FFG 10), purchased as a spare parts source, departed Pearl Harbor under tow on 29-1-99 for Detyens SY, Charleston, South Carolina, with F 494 arriving at Gölçük on 27-9-99. F 495 was transferred by sale on 1-9-00 and formally recommissioned in Turkey on 25-7-01. The planned sale of the *Estocin* (FFG 15) in the fall of 2001 was delayed until 3-4-03, but the FFG 13 was transferred as planned on 10-4-02. They are locally referred to as the "G class" and are named for Turkish towns.
Hull systems: Displacement figures cited apply specifically to F 496. These ships are particularly well protected against splinter and fragmentation damage, with 19-mm aluminum-alloy armor over magazine spaces, 16-mm steel over the main engine-control room, and 19-mm Kevlar plastic armor over vital electronics and command spaces. Speed on one gas turbine is 25 knots. The auxiliary power system uses two retractable pods located well forward and can drive the ships at up to 6 knots. The two fin stabilizers extend 2.36 m and are located 57.9 m abaft the bow perpendicular; F 490 and F 493 were the only units of the class never fitted with the stabilizers while in U.S. Navy service, and they still have not been added. All are equipped with the Prairie/Masker air bubbler system to reduce radiated machinery noise below the waterline.

The helicopter flight decks have been extended three meters by Pendik Naval Shipyard, Istanbul (as in later examples of the U.S. Navy's units of the class) to handle S-70 helicopters, with all of the ships modified by 2006.
Combat systems: The Mk 92 Mod. 2 fire-control system controls missile and 76-mm gunfire; it uses a STIR (modified SPG-60) antenna amidships and a U.S.-built version of the WM-28 radar forward and can track four separate targets. The Mk 75 gun is a license-built version of the OTO Melara Compact. A Mk 13 weapons-direction system is fitted. There are two Mk 24 optical missile and gun target designators mounted in tubs atop the pilothouse. The only ship-launched ASW weapons are the Mk 46 Mod. 5 torpedoes in the two triple torpedo tubes; a total of 24 torpedoes can be carried for the tubes and the helicopter. Harpoon antiship missiles are launched via the SWG-1 launch control system. F 490–495 were delivered without helicopters, SQQ-28 helicopter datalink, and towed passive sonar arrays, but a navigational radar was added. Upgrades to the combat control system are planned under the Genesis program, with contractor bids due 20-10-00; existing stand-alone displays will be replaced by multifunctional operator consoles and the combat system integrated. FFG 13 and FFG 15 were said to have been transferred with their SQR-19(V)2 towed passive sonar arrays aboard.

♦ 0 (+ 8–12) TF-2000 project
Bldr: 4 by Pendik Naval Shipyard, Istanbul (In serv. 2012– . . .)

D: Ca. 1,800 tons (fl) **S:** 28+ kts (26 sust.; 18 on diesels) **Dim:** . . . × . . . × . . .
A: . . . / . . . SSM; STANDARD SM-2 vertical-launch area air-defense missile system; Sea Sparrow ESSM SAM vertical-launch short-range air-defense missile system; RAM (RIM-116 missiles) point-defense SAM system; 1 or 2 . . .-mm DP guns; 2 single 25 to 40-mm AA; 2 triple 324-mm Mk 32 ASW TT (Mk 46 Mod. 5 torpedoes); 1 10-ton-class helicopter
Electronics:
Radar: 1 . . . nav.; 1. . . surface-search; 1 . . . 3-D air search
Sonar: . . . bow-mounted LF
EW: . . .
E/O: . . . missile-detection system, . . . t.v./LLTV/IR/laser director
M: CODOG: 2 gas turbines, 1 or 2 diesels; 2 CP props; . . . hp **Range:** 5,000/18
Endurance: 30 days **Crew:** 41 officers, 201 enlisted

Remarks: Turkey hopes to order as many as twelve replacement frigates during the near future in a program to cover a 15-year period and to cost in excess of $3 billion. The program has been ongoing since the mid-1990s, though no contract has yet been announced. The first unit could enter in service around 2012.

FRIGATES [FF]

♦ 4 MEKO 200TN Track II-A and -B* class

	Bldr.	Laid down	L	In serv.
F 244 Barbaros	Blohm + Voss, Hamburg	4-92	26-10-93	25-3-95
F 245 Oruçreis	Gölçük Naval Shipyard	23-7-92	28-7-94	10-5-96
F 246 Salihreis*	Blohm + Voss, Hamburg	16-3-95	26-9-97	17-12-98
F 247 Kemalreis*	Gölçük Naval Shipyard	3-12-96	24-7-98	8-6-00

Oruçreis (F 245)—MEKO 200TN Track II-A variant Leo van Ginderen, 6-05

Oruçreis (F 245) Leo van Ginderen, 6-05

Salihreis (F 246)—MEKO 200TN Track II-B variant with Mk 48 vertical SAM launch system abaft the twin stacks Cem D. Yaylali, 7-05

D: F 244, 245: 3,100 tons (3,350 fl); F 246, 247: 3,150 tons (3,400 fl)
S: 31.75 kts (22 max. on diesel)
Dim: F 244, 245: 116.72 (107.20 pp) × 14.80 (13.80 wl) × 6.12 max. (4.25 hull); F 246, 247: 117.72 (108.20 pp) × 14.80 (13.80 wl) × 6.12 max. (4.25 hull)
A: 8 RGM-84C Harpoon SSM; F 244, 245 only: 1 8-round Mk 29 SAM launcher (24 RIM-7M Sea Sparrow SAM); F 246, 247 only: 1 Mk 41 Mod. 8 vertical launch group (16 RIM-7P Sea Sparrow SAM); all: 1 127-mm 54-cal. Mk 45 Mod. 2A DP; 3 4-barrel 25-mm Oerlikon GM 25-52 Sea Zenith CIWS; 2 single 12.7-mm mg; 2 triple 324-mm Mk 32 Mod. 5 ASW TT; 1 AB-212 ASW helicopter

FRIGATES [FF] *(continued)*

Barbaros (F 244)—note Mk 29 Sea Sparrow missile launcher carried aft atop the helicopter hangar on MEKO 200TN Track II-A variants Rob Cabo, 8-05

Electronics:
Radar: 1 Decca 2690 BT ARPA nav.; 1 BAE Systems AWS-9 (TN) 996 air search; 1 Thales STIR-24 SAM f.c.; 1 Thales STIR-18 missile/gun f.c.; 1 Contraves TMX Dolphin CIWS target designation; 2 Contraves TMKu CIWS f.c.
Sonar: Raytheon SQS-56 (DE 1160) hull-mounted MF
TACAN: URN-25
EW: Racal Cutlass B1 intercept; Racal Scorpion B jammer; Mk 36 SRBOC decoy syst. (2 6-round Mk 137 RL); SLQ-25 Nixie towed torpedo decoy
E/O: GEC-Marconi FLIR; Ferranti laser rangefinder

M: CODOG: 2 MTU 16V1163 TB83 diesels (6,530 bhp each), 2 G.E. LM-2500-30 gas turbines (31,766 shp each); 2 KaMeWa CP props; 63,532 shp max.
Electric: 2,480 kw tot. (4 × 620-kw MTU 8V396-series diesel alternator sets)
Range: 900/31.75; 4,100/18 (2 diesels)
Fuel: 300 tons **Crew:** 24 officers, 156 enlisted

Remarks: First two of planned four ordered 19-1-90 (but contract did not go into effect until 13-3-91); letter of intent for second pair signed 14-12-92 and final contract signed with Blohm + Voss/Thyssen Rheinstahl Technik GmbH consortium on 25-11-94. First steel cut for F 244 on 5-11-91. The German subsidy for the construction of the second pair was suspended from 3-95 to 9-95 because of Turkey's intervention against Kurdish elements in northern Iraq. F 244 arrived at Gölçük on 27-6-95. Two more were on option, to be built one each in Turkey and Germany, but they were canceled in 10-99.

Hull systems: In addition to having a different propulsion system than the initial Turkish MEKO quartet, they also substitute later electronics, improved air conditioning, and better NBC warfare protection (with a complete citadel). F 246 and F 247 are 1 m longer to accommodate SH60 helicopters more easily; they also have bulwarks fitted to the bow. All four have fin stabilizers.

Combat systems: Have the Thale STACOS Mod. III FD combat data system with two Oerlikon-Contraves Ku-band radar trackers for Sea Sparrow and the Sea Guard CIWS. First two are fitted for later substitution of the Mk 41 vertical launch group for 16 Sea Sparrow missiles in place of the octuple Mk 29 launcher; later pair had Mk 41 vertical launch group aft as built and have two STIR-24 tracker/illuminators; they also have command staff facilities. When available, the folding-fin Evolved Sea Sparrow SAM will be procured, allowing 24 to be carried in the eight Mk 41 Mod. 8 VLS cells. S-70B helicopters equipped to launch AGM-114M Hellfire-II antiship missiles are to replace the older AB-212 helicopters, which are equipped to launch Sea Skua missiles. F 244 and F 245 are equipped with two antennas for the Scot 1C SHF SATCOM system and a commercial SATCOM terminal, while the other two have two commercial SATCOM antennas.

♦ 4 MEKO 200TN Track I class

	Bldr:	Laid down	L	In serv.
F 240 Yavuz	Blohm + Voss, Hamburg	31-5-85	7-11-85	17-7-87
F 241 Turgut Reis (ex-*Turgut*)	Howaldtswerke, Kiel	20-9-85	30-5-86	4-2-88
F 242 Fatih	Gölçük Naval Shipyard	1-1-86	24-4-87	22-7-88
F 243 Yildirim	Gölçük Naval Shipyard	24-4-87	22-7-88	21-7-89

Yavuz (F 240) Cem D. Yaylali, 4-05

Yildirim (F 243) Cem D. Yaylali, 8-05

Fatih (F 242) Cem D. Yaylali, 7-05

D: 2,414 tons (2,994 fl) **S:** 27 kts (20 cruise)
Dim: 110.50 (102.20 pp) × 14.20 (13.25 wl) × 4.10 (mean hull)
A: 8 Harpoon SSM; 1 8-round Mk 29 SAM launcher (16 RIM-7M Sea Sparrow missiles); 1 127-mm 54-cal. Mk 45 Mod. 1 DP; 3 4-barrel 25-mm Oerlikon-Contraves Sea Zenith GM 25 CIWS; 2 single 12.7-mm mg; 2 triple 324-mm Mk 32 Mod. 5 ASW TT (Mk 46 Mod. 5 torpedoes); 1 Agusta-Bell AB-212 helicopter with Sea Skua SSM

Electronics:
Radar: 1 Decca TM 1226 nav.; 1 BAE Systems AWS-6 (Dolphin) surf.-air search; 1 Thales DA-08 air-search; 1 Thales WM-25 track-while-scan missile/gun f.c.; 1 STIR-24 SAM illumination; 2 Siemens Albis TMKu radar/optronic f.c. (for Sea Zenith CIWS)
Sonar: Raytheon SQS-56 (DE 1160) hull-mounted MF
TACAN: Thales Vesta
EW: Thales Rapids/Ramses suite; Mk 36 SRBOC decoy syst. (2 6-round Mk 137 RL); SLQ-25 Nixie towed torpedo decoy syst.

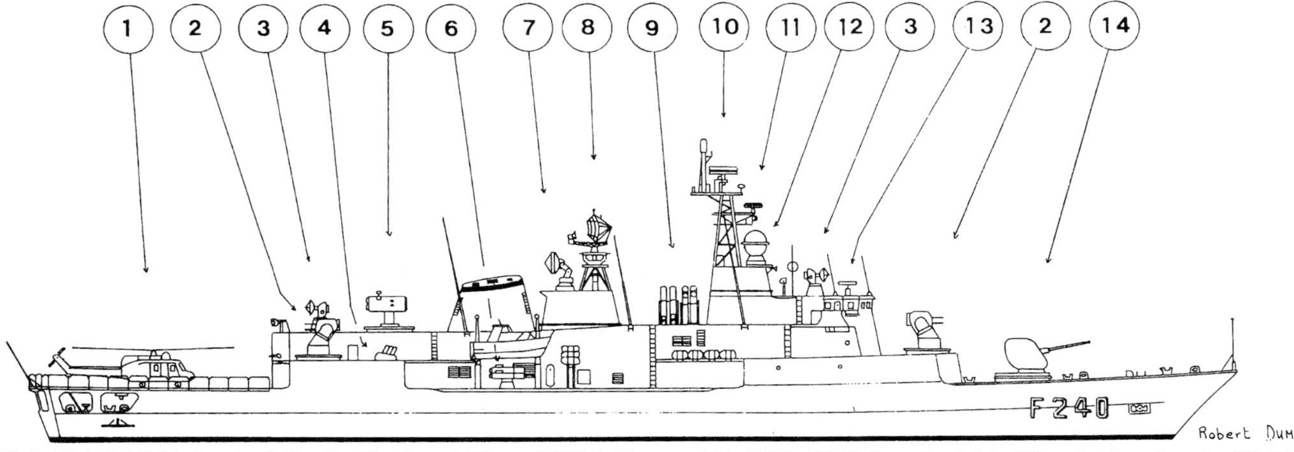

Yavuz (F 240) 1. AB-212 ASW helicopter 2. Sea Zenith 4-barrel 25-mm CIWS 3. Siemens Albis TMKu CIWS f.c. radar 4. Mk 137 rocket launchers for Mk 36 SRBOC decoy system 5. 8-round Mk 29 SAM launcher 6. Mk 32 ASW TT 7. STIR-24 tracker/illuminator radar 8. DA-08 air-search radar 9. Harpoon antiship missiles 10. WM-25 track-while-scan radar director 11. 127-mm 54-cal. DP gun Drawing by Robert Dumas, from *Flottes de Combat*

FRIGATES [FF] *(continued)*

M: 4 MTU 20V1163 TB93 diesels; 2 CP props; 35,940 bhp (29,940 sust.)
Electric: 1,440 kw tot. (3 × 480 kw MTU diesel-driven sets) **Range:** 4,000/20
Fuel: 380 tons **Crew:** 26 officers, 154 enlisted

Remarks: Ordered 4-83, with Blohm + Voss supplying technical assistance in constructing two in Turkey. Name of F 241 changed 14-2-88.
Hull systems: MEKO modular concept permits rapid changeout and installation of combat systems. Have fin stabilizers.
Combat systems: Have the Thales STACOS-TU data system. Albis, by Siemens, is a laser-radar-optronic f.c. director for the Sea Zenith guns. S-70B Seahawk helicopters equipped to launch AGM-114M Hellfire-II antiship missiles are to replace the older AB-212 helicopters.

♦ 3 ex-U.S. Knox class
Bldr: Avondale SY (now Northrop Grumman SB), Westwego, La.

	Laid down	L	In serv.
F 250 Muavenet (ex-*Capodanno,* FF 1093)	12-10-71	21-10-72	17-11-73
F 253 Zafer (ex-*Thomas C. Hart,* FF 1092)	8-10-71	12-8-72	28-7-73
F 255 Karadeniz (ex-*Donald B. Beary,* FFT 1085)	24-7-70	22-5-71	22-7-72

Mauvenet (F 250) Cem D. Yaylali, 5-05

D: 3,130 tons light (4,260 fl) **S:** 29 kts
Dim: 134.00 (126.49 wl) × 14.33 × 4.77 (7.83 over sonar)
A: 4 RGM-84C Harpoon SSM (using Mk 112 ASROC launcher); 1 127-mm 54-cal. Mk 42 Mod. 10 DP; 1 20-mm Mk 15 CIWS; Mk 16 Mod. 8 ASROC ASW RL syst. (1 8-round Mk 112 launcher); 4 single 12.7-mm mg; 2 twin, fixed 324-mm Mk 32 Mod. 9 fixed ASW TT (Mk 46 Mod. 5 torpedoes); 1 Mk 9 d.c. rack (6 Mk 9 d.c.); 1 AB-212 helicopter
Electronics:
Radar: 1 Decca TM 1226 nav.; Raytheon SPS-10F surf.-search; 1 Lockheed SPS-40D air search; 1 Western Electric SPG-53D/F gun f.c.; 1 General Dynamics Mk 90 Phalanx f.c.
Sonar: EDO-G.E. SQS-26CX bow-mounted LF
TACAN: SRN-15A
EW: Raytheon SLQ-32(V)2 intercept; Mk 36 SRBOC decoy syst. (2 6-round Mk 137 RL); T-Mk 6 Fanfare towed acoustic torpedo decoy
M: 1 set Westinghouse geared steam turbines; 1 prop; 35,000 shp
Boilers: 2 Combustion Engineering (F 252: Babcock & Wilcox) V2M D-Type; 84 kg/cm^2, 510° C
Electric: 3,000 kw tot. (3 × 750 kw turbogenerators, 1 × 750 kw diesel set)
Range: 4,300/20 **Fuel:** 750 tons max. **Crew:** 17–20 officers, 255–267 enlisted

Remarks: Transferred on lease after decommissioning from U.S. Navy: F 250 on 30-7-93, F 253 on 30-8-93 and F 255 on 20-5-94. The first set was officially commissioned in the Turkish Navy on 29-11-93 and the third on 29-7-94. Were purchased outright during 2001–2. Also transferred as Grant Aid on 13-12-93 was the former *Elmer Montgomery* (FF 1082) as a spare parts source; the ship was scrapped beginning 12-10-99 at Aliaga. Sisters *Paul* (FF 1080), *Miller* (FF 1091; delivered 8-99 and sunk during a torpedo exercise in 2001), and *W.S. Sims* (FF 1059) were transferred free on 31-12-98 for use as spare parts sources and were then to be scrapped in Turkey. The Turkish Navy is reportedly not enthusiastic about these ships, due to their light armament, age, and relatively poor condition.
Hull systems: Except on F 250 and F 255, bow bulwarks and a spray strake have been added forward to reduce deck wetness, a problem in this class; the addition added 9.1 tons and extended the overall length from the original 133.59 m. All carry a TEAM (SM-5) computer system for the continual monitoring of the ship's electronic equipment. Antirolling fin stabilizers are fitted in all. The Prairie/Masker bubbler system is installed to reduce radiated noise.
Combat systems: At least four of the class have been refitted with the Sigma K-5 command and control system and Link 11 capability. The ASROC system has an 18-weapon automatic reloading magazine beneath the bridge; it is also used to stow the Harpoon missiles, which are launched from the starboard pair of launcher cells. The ASW torpedo tubes are fixed in the forward end of the hangar superstructure, aimed outboard at an angle of 45 degrees; a total of 24 Mk 46-series torpedoes can be carried, including those intended to be carried by the helicopter. The ships have the Mk 114 Mod. 6 ASW fire-control system. In 7-93 the U.S. Congress authorized the sale of 32 Harpoon missiles, 40 Asroc ASW rockets, and 104 Mk 46 Mod. 5 ASW torpedoes to support the *Knox*-class frigates. The towed array sonars were not transferred to Turkey, and the VDS installations had been removed as well. All carry a Mk 68 Mod. 3 gunfire-control system with SPG-53D or F radar. WSC-3 UHF satellite-communications systems were replaced by a commercial MARISAT terminal prior to transfer. The LN-66 navigational radars installed at time of transfer have been replaced.
Disposals: Sister *Adatepe* (F 251, ex-*Fanning,* FF 1076) was stricken during 11-00 after suffering severe boiler problems. *Akdeniz* (F 257, ex-*Bowen,* FFT 1079) was stricken during 2001. *Kocatepe* (F 252 ex-*Reasoner*) was stricken in 2002, *Trakya* (F 254, ex-*McCandless*) in 2003, and *Ege* (F 256, ex-*Ainsworth,* FFT 1090) in 2005.

CORVETTES [FFL]

♦ 0 (+ up to 7) proposed Mil-Gem (Heybeliada class)
Bldr: . . . , Turkey

	L	In serv.
. . . Heybeliada	. . .	. . .

Mil-Gem (Heybeliada class) corvette—official model Cem D. Yaylali, 9-05

D: 2,000 tons (fl) **S:** 29+ kts **Dim:** 99.0 × 14.4 × 3.75
A: . . . Harpoon SSM; . . . point-defense air defense system; 1 76-mm DP; 2 12.7-mm mg; . . . 324-mm Mk 32 ASW TT; 1 10-ton-class helicopter
Electronics:
Radar: 1 . . . nav.; 1. . . surface-search; 1 . . . 3-D air search
Sonar: . . .
EW: . . .
E/O: . . . missile-detection system, . . . t.v./LLTV/IR/laser director
M: CODOG: 1 gas turbine, 2 diesels; 2 CP props; . . . hp **Range:** 3,500/15
Crew: About 80

Remarks: A program to construct seven corvettes in Turkey under the Mil-Gem or National Vessel Project may take precedence over future frigate construction due to budget curtailments. Data listed above are preliminary. Other proposed equipment includes Chaff, IR and torpedo decoy systems, military and commercial satellite communications systems, local area networks, 3-D search radar, laser warning receiver, and a sonar system. No additional details or firm project dates have yet been announced.

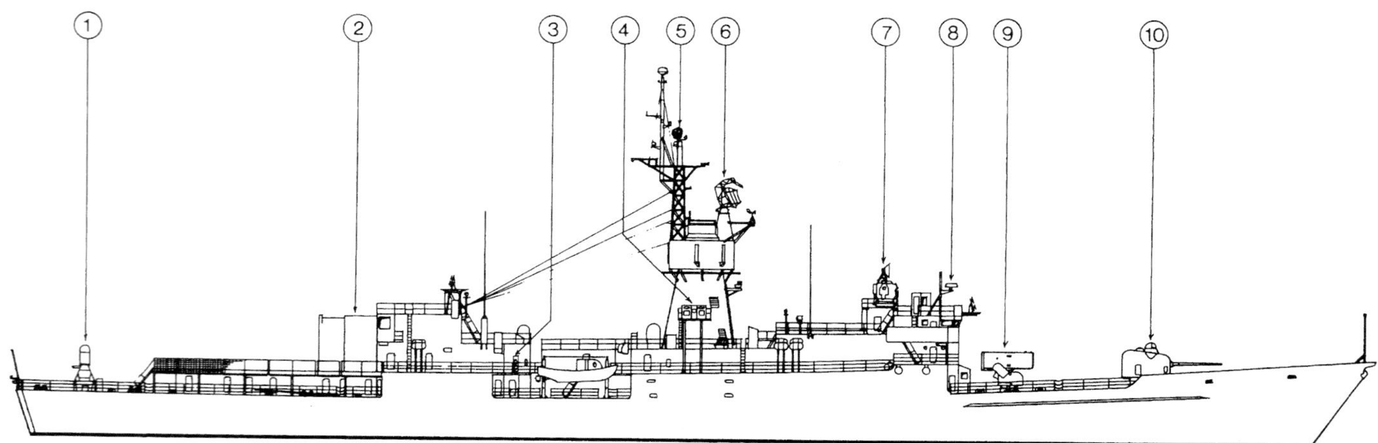

Knox class 1. 20-mm Phalanx CIWS 2. Telescoping helicopter hangar 3. Twin, fixed Mk 32 Mod. 9 ASW TT 4. SLQ-32(V)2 EW antenna group 5. SPS-10F surface-search radar 6. SPS-40D air-search radar 7. Stabilized director for Mk 68 gun fire-control system, with SPG-53F radar 8. Navigational radar 9. 8-cell Mk 112 ASROC missile launcher 10. 127-mm Mk 42 Mod. 10 DP gun
Drawing by A. D. Baker III

CORVETTES [FFL] *(continued)*

♦ 6 ex-French D'Estienne d'Orves class (Type A-69)

Bldr: DCN Lorient

	Laid down	L	In serv.
F 500 Bozcaada (ex-*Commandant de Pimodan,* F 787)	1-9-75	7-8-76	20-5-78
F 501 Bodrum (ex-*Drogou,* F 783)	15-12-74	31-1-76	30-9-76
F 502 Bandirma (ex-*Quartier Maître Anquetil,* F 786)	1-8-75	7-8-76	4-2-78
F 503 Beykoz (ex-*D'Estienne d'Orves,* F 781)	1-9-72	1-6-73	10-9-76
F 504 Bartin (ex-*Amyot d'Inville,* F 782)	11-9-73	30-11-74	13-10-76
F 505 Bafra (ex-*Second Maitre le Bihan,* F 788)	1-11-76	13-8-77	7-7-79

Bartin (F 504) Bernard Prézelin, 6-02

Bandirma (F 502) Cem D. Yaylali, 4-05

Beykoz (F 503) Bernard Prézelin, 4-02

D: 1,100 tons (1,250 fl) **S:** 23.3 kts
Dim: 80.00 (76.00 pp) × 10.30 × 3.00 (5.30 over sonar)
A: 2 MM 38 Exocet; 1 100-mm 55-cal. Model 1968 CADAM DP; 2 single 20-mm 70-cal. Oerlikon AA; 4 single 12.7-mm mg; 1 6-round 375-mm Model 1972 F1 ASW rocket launcher; 4 550-mm fixed TT for L-5 ASW torpedoes (no reloads)
Electronics:
Radar: 1 Decca 1226 nav. 1 Thales DRBV 51A surf./air search, 1 Thales DRBC 32E f.c.
Sonar: Thales DUBA 25 hull-mounted MF
EW: ARBR 16 intercept; 2 330–340-round Matra Défense AMBL 1A Dagaie decoy RL; SLQ-25 Nixie towed acoustic torpedo decoy syst.
M: 2 SEMT-Pielstick 12 PC 2 V400 diesels; 2 CP props; 12,000 bhp
Electric: 840 kw (2 × 320 kw, 1 × 200 kw diesel-driven sets) **Range:** 4,500/15
Endurance: 15–20 days **Crew:** 7 officers, 85 enlisted (in French service)

Remarks: Purchased for $60 million total (plus $150 million for overhauls), announced 11-00. Very economical and seaworthy ships designed for coastal antisubmarine warfare, but available for scouting missions, training, and showing the flag. The new names commemorate those of Turkish coastal towns. After refits at Brest, F 500 was recommissioned in the Turkish Navy on 25-7-01, F 501 on 18-10-01, and F 502 on 14-12-01. F 503 and F 504 (transferred on 6-5-02) received more extensive overhauls to engines and armament system, along with F 505, which was transferred on 26-6-02; F 501 through F 504 were officially recommissioned in Turkey on 25-7-02. Are known as the Burak class in Turkish service.
Hull systems: Do not have fin stabilizers but are nonetheless excellent seaboats.
Combat systems: The control system for the 100-mm gun consists of a DRBC 32E monopulse, X-band radar, and a semi-analog, semi-digital computer; there is also a Matra Défense Naja optical director. During refits in the late 1980s, the ships received a new 100-mm gun, U.S. SLQ-25 Nixie torpedo decoy, upgraded sonar, Dagaie launchers, L-5 ASW torpedo launching capability, and waste-processing systems. ASW rocket launchers had been removed from all but F 503 by 11-97.

GUIDED-MISSILE PATROL COMBATANTS [PGG]

♦ 6 (+ 3) Kiliç class

Bldrs: P 330, P 333: Friedrich Lürssen Werft, Bremen-Vegesack, Germany; others: Pendik Naval Shipyard, Istanbul

	Laid down	L	In serv.
P 330 Kiliç	6-96	15-7-97	24-7-98
P 331 Kalkan	5-7-96	24-9-98	22-7-99
P 332 Mizrak	1997	5-4-99	8-6-00
P 333 Tufan	25-7-01	24-2-03	11-5-05
P 334 Meltem	4-01	1-9-04	2006
P 335 Imbat	25-7-02	2005	2006
P 336 Zipkin	. . .	. . .	2007
P 337 Atka	. . .	. . .	. . .
P 338 Bora	. . .	. . .	. . .

Tufan (P 333)—note faceted gunhouse for the 76-mm gun Michael Nitz, 6-05

Kalkan (P 331)—with only two Harpoon canisters aboard Cem D. Yaylali, 7-05

Tufan (P 333) Michael Nitz, 6-05

D: 540 tons (fl) **S:** 38 kts **Dim:** 62.4 (59.0 pp) × 8.3 × 2.8
A: Up to 8 RGM-84C Harpoon SSM; 1 76-mm 62-cal. OTO Melara Compact DP; 1 twin 40-mm 70-cal. OTO Melara Compact AA; 2 single 7.62-mm mg
Electronics:
Radar: 1 Thales Scout nav/surf. search; 1 Thales MW-08 3-D air/surface search; 1 Thales STING-EO f.c.; P 333 and later: 1 Thales LIROD f.c.
EW: Racal Cutlass 1C intercept; Mk 36 SRBOC decoy syst. (2 6-round Mk 137 RL)
E/O: P 330–332: 1 Thales LIROD Mk 2 f.c.; all: 1 Thales target designation sight

GUIDED-MISSILE PATROL COMBATANTS [PGG] *(continued)*

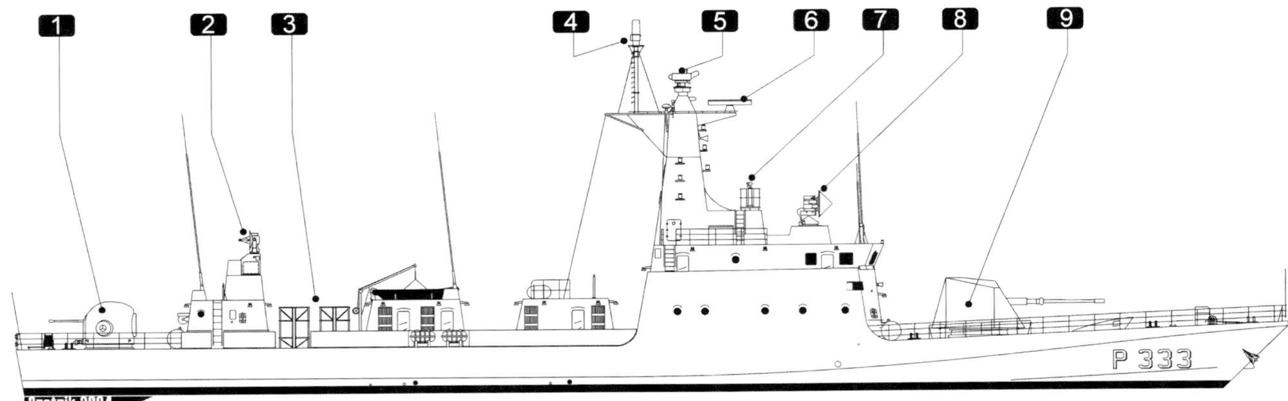

Tufan (P 333) 1. Twin OTO Melara 40-mm AA 2. Thales Lirod f.c. system 3. Harpoon antiship missile launch canisters 4. Racal Cutlass 1C EW intercept array 5. MW-08 air/surface-search radar 6. Thales Scout navigational radar 7. Thales target designation sight 8. Thales Sting EO f.c. system 9. 76-mm OTO Melara DP gun

Drawing by T. Grotnik, 2004

M: 4 MTU 16V956 TB91 diesels; 4 props; 18,000 bhp (15,120 bhp sust.)
Electric: 405 kVA tot. **Range:** 700/35; 1,600/32.5; 3,300/16
Endurance: 12 days **Crew:** 6 officers, 39 enlisted

Remarks: Enlarged version of the FPB 57 design, with an integrated weapons control system and new electronics. Three were authorized early in 1993 and were ordered 3-94. P 330 departed German waters on 28-3-98. The keel of P 335 was ceremonially laid down at Gölçük, but the ship is actually being built at Istanbul. Four more (with an option for two additional) were ordered on 19-6-00, and another order for three was placed during fall 2002, with the first to be built by Lürssen. P 333 was delivered in 2003 and underwent two years of trials and systems integration prior to 5-05 commissioning.
Hull systems: Were initially fitted with bulwarks at the bow, removed after builder's trials. One Turkish source credits them with 22,000 bhp; if so some other propulsion diesel is installed.
Combat systems: Have Thales STACOS-FD Mod. 4 combat data systems and can employ off-board targeting information via datalink. Vesta helicopter beacon is fitted. The STING-EO fire-control system for the 76-mm gun incorporates both a radar and an E/O sensor. The LIOD (LIROD, with radar, in P 333 and later) system controls the 40-mm mount. Usually carry only two or four Harpoon missiles. P 333's OTO Melara 76/62 gun is in a faceted gunhouse, reducing radar signature.

GUIDED-MISSILE PATROL CRAFT [PTG]

♦ 2 modified German FPB 57 class

Bldr: Taskizak Naval Dockyard, Istanbul

	L	In serv.
P 348 Yildiz	3-6-94	3-6-96
P 349 Karayel	20-6-95	19-9-96

Yildiz (P 348) Cem D. Yaylali, 10-03

D: 387 tons (432.4 fl) **S:** 36.5 kts **Dim:** 57.84 (54.40 pp) × 7.62 × 2.83
A: Up to 8 RGM-84C Harpoon SSM; 1 76-mm 62-cal. OTO Melara Compact DP; 1 twin 35-mm 90-cal. Oerlikon AA; 2 single 7.62-mm mg
Electronics:
Radar: 1 Kelvin-Hughes Type 1007 nav.; 1 BAE Systems AWS-6 (Dolphin) surf./air search; 1 Siemens Albis TMX-CW f.c.
EW: Racal Cutlass B1 intercept; Mk 36 SRBOC decoy syst. (2 6-round Mk 137 RL)
E/O: Thales LIOD optronic director (for 35-mm mount)
M: 4 MTU 16V956 TB91 diesels; 4 props; 18,000 bhp (15,120 sust.)
Electric: 405 kVA tot. **Range:** 700/35; 1,600/32.5; 3,300/16
Endurance: 12 days **Crew:** 6 officers, 39 enlisted

Remarks: Ordered 6-91 as an improved version of the *Dogan* series (see following entry).
Hull systems: Have steel hulls, aluminum superstructures, and NBC warfare defensive citadels.
Combat systems: Have Thales STACOS-FD Mod. 4 combat data systems and can employ offboard targeting information via datalink. A Thales Vesta helicopter beacon is fitted. Can carry 300 rounds 76-mm, 2,750 rounds 35-mm. Usually carry only two or four Harpoon missiles.

♦ 8 German FPB 57 class

Bldrs: P 340: Lürssen, Vegesack, Germany; others: Taskizak Naval Dockyard, Istanbul

	Laid down	L	In serv.
P 340 Dogan	2-6-75	16-6-76	15-6-77
P 341 Marti	1-7-75	30-6-77	28-7-78
P 342 Tayfun	1-12-75	1979	19-7-79
P 343 Volkan	. . .	1980	25-7-80
P 344 Rüzgar (ex-*Gurbet*)	30-7-81	1983	17-12-84
P 345 Poyraz	. . .	17-12-84	7-2-86
P 346 Gayret	. . .	24-7-87	22-7-88
P 347 Firtina	. . .	31-5-88	23-10-88

Dogan (P 340) Cem D. Yaylali, 7-05

Rüzgar (P 344) Hartmut Ehlers, 10-98

D: 353 tons (398 fl) **S:** 36.5 kts **Dim:** 58.1 (54.4 pp) × 7.62 × 2.83
A: Up to 8 RGM-84A Harpoon SSM; 1 76-mm 62-cal. OTO Melara Compact DP; 1 twin 35-mm 90-cal. Oerlikon AA; 2 single 7.62-mm mg
Electronics:
Radar: 1 Decca TM 1226 nav.; Thales WM-28-41 f.c.
EW: MEL SUSIE-1 intercept; 2 20-round decoy RL
E/O: P 341, 346, 347: 2 Thales LIOD-series optronic gun f.c.
M: 4 MTU 16V956 TB91 diesels; 4 props; 18,000 bhp (15,120 sust.)
Electric: 405 kVA tot. **Range:** 700/35; 1,600/32.5; 3,300/16
Endurance: 12 days **Crew:** 5 officers, 33 enlisted

Remarks: Initial series first order placed 3-8-73. Have steel hulls, aluminum superstructures.
Combat systems: The 76-mm mount had a manned local-control cupola on P 340–345, since deleted. All can carry 300 rounds 76-mm, 2,750 rounds 35-mm. Usually carry only two or four Harpoon antiship missiles aboard. P 340 through P 343 were modernized by Thales under a 9-97 contract, with the Tacticos combat data system replacing the original system and LIOD Mk 2 (LIghtweight Optronic Director) and EW intercept systems added; P 341, the first to be completed, returned to service during 12-00. P 346 and P 347 had LIOD optronic gun directors on completion. All others of the class had been similarly modified by 2004.

GUIDED-MISSILE PATROL CRAFT [PTG] *(continued)*

♦ 8 Kartal-class guided-missile and torpedo boats
Bldr: Friedrich Lürssen Werft, Vegesack, Germany (In serv. 1967–71)

	In serv.		In serv.
P 321 Denizkuşu	9-3-67	P 326 Pelikan	11-2-70
P 322 Atmaca	9-3-67	P 327 Albatros	18-3-70
P 323 Şahin	3-11-66	P 328 Şimşek	6-11-69
P 324 Kartal	3-11-66	P 329 Kasirga	25-11-67

Denizkuşu (P 321) Cem D. Yaylali, 7-00

Kartal (P 324) Cem D. Yaylali, 10-98

D: 184 tons (210 fl) **S:** 42 kts **Dim:** 42.8 × 7.14 × 2.21
A: 2 single 40-mm 70-cal. Bofors L70 AA; 4 Penguin Mk 1 SSM; 2 fixed 533-mm TT (2 wire-guided torpedoes); 4 mines (in lieu of missiles)
Electronics:
Radar: 1 Decca TM 1226 nav.
EW: . . . intercept
M: 4 MTU 16V538 diesels; 4 props; 12,000 bhp
Range: 500/39; 1,000/32 **Crew:** 39 tot.

Remarks: Have wooden planking on steel and light-metal keel and frames; the superstructure is built of aluminum alloy. Can be fitted as fast gunboats or minelayers (four mines). All now normally carry four Penguin IR-homing antiship missiles. No longer carry spare torpedoes. Sister *Meltem* (P 325) was cut in two by Soviet naval training ship *Khasan* 25-9-85 and stricken after salvage.

PATROL CRAFT [PC]

♦ 7 AB 25 class
Bldrs: AB 25–31: Haliç SY; AB 33: Camialti SY; AB 35, 36: Taşkizak Naval Shipyard, Istanbul

	In serv.		In serv.
P 127 AB 27	27-6-69	P 133 AB 33	15-5-70
P 128 AB 28	4-69	P 135 AB 35	13-4-76
P 129 AB 29	21-2-69	P 136 AB 36	13-4-76
P 131 AB 31	17-11-71		

AB 31 (P 131) Martin Mokrus, 5-05

D: 150 tons (170 fl) **S:** 22 kts **Dim:** 40.24 × 6.40 × 1.65
A: 1 40-mm 60-cal. Bofors Mk 3 AA; 1 20-mm 70-cal. Oerlikon Mk 10 AA; 2 single 12.7-mm mg; 2 4-rail Mk 20 Mousetrap ASW RL; 4 single d.c. release racks
Electronics:
Radar: 1 Decca TM 1226 nav.
Sonar: Thales PMS-26 hull-mounted HF
M: 2 SACM-AGO V16CSHR diesels; 2 props; 4,800 bhp; 2 cruise diesels; 300 bhp
Crew: 3 officers, 28 enlisted

Remarks: Fourteen others are assigned to the Coast Guard. Built with French technical assistance. AB 35 and AB 36, delivered two years later than others, have a lower hull knuckle forward and bow bulwarks. Cruise diesels are geared to the main shafts. Hull numbers revised 1-1-91; had been P 1225–1236. The forward 40-mm gun was replaced by a 20-mm mount to reduce topweight.

AB 33 (P 133) Martin Mokrus, 5-04

Disposals: AB 30 was transferred to the Georgian Navy on 5-12-98; AB 32 and AB 26 to Kazakhstan during 1999 and 2001 respectively; and AB 34 to Azerbaijan on 17-7-00. AB 25 was retired in 2003.

Disposal notes: U.S. *Asheville*-class patrol craft *Bora* (P 339, ex-*Surprise,* PG 97) and Turkish-built, German-designed PB 57–class *Girne* (P 140) were retired during 11-00. AB 25 was decommissioned during 2003.

♦ 4 ex-U.S. PGM 71 class
Bldr: Peterson Builders, Sturgeon Bay, Wisc.

	L	In serv.
P 121 AB 21 (ex-PGM 104)	4-5-67	8-67
P 122 AB 22 (ex-PGM 105)	25-5-67	9-67
P 123 AB 23 (ex-PGM 106)	7-7-67	10-67
P 124 AB 24 (ex-PGM 108)	14-9-67	5-68

AB 21 (P 121) H&L Van Ginderen, 7-95

D: 104 tons (144 fl) **S:** 17 kts **Dim:** 30.81 × 6.45 × 1.83
A: 1 40-mm 60-cal. Bofors Mk 3 AA; 2 twin 20-mm 70-cal. Oerlikon Mk 24 AA; 2 4-rail Mk 20 Mousetrap ASW RL; 2 d.c. racks (2 d.c. each)
Electronics:
Radar: 1 Raytheon 1500B nav.
Sonar: EDO SQS-17A hull-mounted MF
M: 8 G.M. Detroit Diesel 6-71 diesels; 2 props; 2,040 bhp **Electric:** 30 kw tot.
Range: 1,000/12 **Fuel:** 16 tons **Crew:** 30 tot.

Remarks: First three handed over 12-67. Hull numbers, revised 1-1-91, had been P 1221–1224. Two single 12.7-mm mg have been removed.

♦ 2 ex-U.S. PC 1638 class
Bldrs: Gunderson Bros., Portland, Ore.

	L	In serv.
P 113 Yar Hisar (ex-PC 1640)	14-5-64	9-64
P 114 Ak Hisar (ex-PC 1641)	14-5-64	3-12-64

Yar Hisar (P 113) Hartmut Ehlers, 6-98

D: 325 tons (477 fl) **S:** 19 kts **Dim:** 52.9 × 7.0 × 3.1 (hull)
A: 2 single 40-mm 60-cal. Bofors Mk 3 AA; 2 twin 20-mm 70-cal. Oerlikon Mk 24 AA
Electronics: Radar: 1/Decca TM 1226 nav.
M: 2 Alco 169 × 10 AT diesels; 2 props; 4,800 bhp
Range: 5,000/10 **Fuel:** 60 tons **Crew:** 5 officers, 60 enlisted

Remarks: Design based on the U.S. PC 461 class of World War II.
Combat systems: Until the late 1990s, were equipped with an Mk 15 trainable Hedgehog ASW spiggot mortar on the bow, four Mk 6 depth-charge mortars (with 3 rounds each), and one Mk 9 depth-charge rack (with nine d.c.). All ASW ordnance and the sonar have been removed, and a second 40-mm AA has replaced the Hedgehog forward.
Disposals: Sisters *Sultan Hisar* (P 111, ex-PC 1638), *Demir Hisar* (P 112, ex-PC 1639), and *Sivri Hisar* (P 115, ex-PC 1642) were stricken during 11-00. *Koç Hisar* (P 116) was stricken in 2002.

PATROL CRAFT [PC] *(continued)*

♦ 2 ex-German Mercure-class former coastal minesweepers
Bldr: C.N. Amiot (CMN), Cherbourg

	Laid down	L	In serv.
P 301 Kozlu (ex-M 523; ex-*Hameln,* M 1251)	20-1-58	20-8-59	15-10-59
P 302 Kuşadasi (ex-M 524; ex-*Vegesack,* M 1250)	20-12-57	21-5-59	19-9-59

D: 366 tons (383 fl) **S:** 14.5 kts **Dim:** 44.62 (42.5 pp) × 8.41 × 2.55
A: 1 twin 20-mm 70-cal. Oerlikon Mk 24 AA
Electronics:
Radar: 1 Decca 707 nav.
Sonar: Simrad . . . hull-mounted HF
M: 2 Mercedes-Benz MB-820 Db diesels; 2 KaMeWa CP props; 1,320 bhp
Electric: 776 kw tot. (2 × 320 kw, 2 × 68 kw diesel sets) **Range:** 5,000/12
Fuel: 34.9 tons **Crew:** 40 tot.

Remarks: Built for the German Navy, placed in reserve in 1963, and stricken on 31-12-73. Transferred to Turkey between 6-75 and 10-75. Converted for use as patrol craft at Taskizak in 1999. Three sisters remain as minesweepers, and one other is a salvage ship. Wooden construction.

♦ 2 ex-Canadian Bay-class former coastal minesweepers
Bldr: Davie SB, Lauzon, Quebec

	L
P 530 Trabzon (ex-M 530, ex-*Gaspé*)	20-5-53
P 531 Terme (ex-M 531, ex-*Trinity*)	31-7-53

Terme (P 531)—with former pennant number prefix Hartmut Ehlers, 10-89

D: 390 tons (412 fl) **S:** 16 kts **Dim:** 50.0 (46.05 pp) × 9.21 × 2.8
A: 1 40-mm 60-cal. Bofors AA; 2 single 12.7-mm mg
Electronics: Radar: 1 Decca TM 1226 nav.
M: 2 G.M. 12-278A diesels; 2 props; 2,400 bhp
Electric: 940-kw sweep/plus 690-kw ship's service **Range:** 4,000/10
Fuel: 52 tons **Crew:** 4 officers, 31 enlisted

Remarks: Transferred under U.S. Military Aid Program on 19-5-58. Redesignated as patrol boats in 1991 and portable sweep gear removed. Wood-planked skin on steel frame. The 40-mm gun is in a World War II–era U.K. "Boffin" mounting. Do not have a sonar.
Disposals: Sister *Tekirdag* (A 601, ex-M 533, ex-*Ungava*) was scrapped 3-02. *Tirebolu* (P 532, ex-M 532, ex-*Comox*) was stricken on 15-12-95.

Note: Mine-disposal divers' tenders of the MTB 1–class and the various antisubmarine net tenders also carry patrol-series pennant numbers.

MINE WARFARE SHIPS

Note: The *Rhein*-class training ships also have minerails, as do the *Kartal*-class guided-missile patrol boats.

♦ 1 Osman Gazi–class minelayer/landing ships [MM]
Bldr: Taskizak Naval Shipyard, Istanbul

	Laid down	L	In serv.
N^L 125 Osman Gazi	5-7-89	20-7-90	27-7-94

Osman Gazi (N^L 125) Guy Schaeffer via Paolo Marsan, 7-04

D: 3,773 tons (fl) **S:** 17 kts (15 sust.) **Dim:** 105.00 (95.50 wl) × 15.50 × 3.75
A: 2 twin 40-mm 70-cal. Bofors AA; 1 twin 35-mm 90-cal. Oerlikon AA; approx. 200 mines
Electronics: Radar: 1 Decca TM 1226 nav.
M: 4 MTU 8V396-series diesels; 2 props; 10,000 bhp
Range: 4,000/15 **Crew:** . . .

Remarks: Named for the founder of the Ottoman Empire. Construction of a second, to have been named *Orhan Gazi* (N^L 126) was canceled in 7-91. Has 50% more capacity than *Sarucabey* class, carrying 900 troops and 15 tanks. Carries four LCVP-type landing craft abreast the stack and has a helicopter platform, amphibious warfare command facilities, and full NBC warfare protection. Two ports in the stern lead to minerails on the tank deck.

♦ 2 Sarucabey-class minelayer/landing ship [MM]
Bldr: Taskizak Naval Shipyard, Istanbul

	Laid down	L	In serv.
N^L 123 Sarucabey (ex-*Karaçebey*)	25-7-80	30-7-81	26-7-84
N^L 124 Karamürselbey	26-7-83	26-7-84	27-7-85

Sarucabey (N^L 123) Cem D. Yaylali, 4-96

Karamürselbey (N^L 124)—with pilothouse one deck lower than on N^L 123 Leo Dirkx, 7-01

D: 2,600 tons (fl) **S:** 14 kts **Dim:** 92.0 × 14.0 × . . .
A: 3 single 40-mm 70-cal. Bofors L70 AA; 2 twin 20-mm 70-cal. Oerlikon Mk 24; 2 mine rails (150 mines)
Electronics: Radar: 1 Decca TM 1226 nav.
M: 3 diesels; 3 props; 4,320 bhp **Crew:** . . .

Remarks: Two LCVP stowed on deck amidships, handled by large articulated crane. Have two mine-embarkation ports on each side at tank-deck level that can also be used to disembark troops into craft alongside. Can carry 11 tanks, 12 trucks, and 600 troops. Minelaying ports in stern lead to rails on the tank deck.

Disposal note: Ex-German, ex-U.S. LST 542–class minelayer/tank landing ships *Bayraktar* (N^L 120) and *Sancaktar* (N^L 121) had both been retired by 2004.

♦ 3 (+ 3) Aydin-class coastal minehunters [MHC]
Bldr: first unit: Lürssen/Abeking & Rasmussen; others: Pendik Naval SY, Istanbul (In serv. 2005–8)

	Laid down	L	In serv.
M 265 Alanya	6-11-00	21-3-03	23-2-05
M 266 Amasra	25-7-01	10-5-04	2006
M 267 Ayvalik	25-7-02	. . .	2006
M 268 Akçakoca	27-7-02	. . .	. . .
M 269 Anamur	. . .	. . .	. . .
M 270 Akçay	. . .	. . .	2008

Alanya (M 265) Michael Nitz, 6-05

D: 500 tons (715 fl) **S:** 14 kts **Dim:** 54.46 × 9.70 (9.56 wl) × 2.50 (3.2 props)
A: 1 30-mm 80-cal. OTO Melara/Mauser AA; 2 single 12.7-mm mg; 60 mines

MINE WARFARE SHIPS *(continued)*

Alanya (M 265) Frank Findler, 5-04

Electronics:
Radar: 1 Kelvin Hughes Type 1007 nav.
Sonar: Thales Type 2093 minehunting HF VDS
EW: Thales DR 2000 intercept
M: 2 MTU 8V396 TE84K diesels; 2 Voith-Schneider vertical cycloidal props; 3,000 bhp—2 Schottel azimuthal thrusters
Electric: 690 kw tot. (3 × 230 kw; 3 MWM 6-cyl. diesels driving)
Range: . . . / . . . **Crew:** 53 tot. accommodations

Remarks: The Friedrich Lürssen Werft/Abeking & Rasmussen design, a variant of the German Navy's Type 332, was selected on 8-4-99, and the contract was signed on 30-7-99. Program to cost $625 million. The keel for M 267 was ceremonially laid at Gölçük, but the ship is actually being built at Istanbul. Three to five additional units may be ordered later. *Alanya* began sea trials 5-03.
Hull systems: Shock mountings are provided for virtually every piece of equipment and for all crew seats. Have a less-powerful propulsion plant than their German half-sisters and are beamier. A Haux portable divers' decompression chamber will be carried.
Combat systems: Will have the Alenia-Marconi Systems NAUTIS III-M command system. Are intended to carry two PAP 104 Mk 5 remote-controlled mine location/destruction submersibles and four mine-clearance divers. The Pinguin weighs 1.35 tons, is 3.5 m long, travels at up to 8 kts, and has an Atlas AIS 11 high-frequency sonar. A single Oropesa mechanical minesweeping rig will be carried.

♦ 5 ex-French Circé-class coastal minehunters [MHC]
Bldr: CMN, Cherbourg

	Laid down	L	In serv.
M 260 Edinçük (ex-*Cybèle*, M 712)	15-9-70	2-3-72	28-9-72
M 261 Edremit (ex-*Calliope*, M 713)	4-4-70	20-10-71	28-9-72
M 262 Enez (ex-*Clio*, M 714)	4-9-69	10-6-71	18-5-72
M 263 Erdek (ex-*Circé*, M 715)	30-1-69	15-12-70	18-5-72
M 264 Ermenli (ex-*Cérès*, M 716)	2-2-71	10-8-72	8-3-73

Enez (M 262) Bernard Prézelin, 2-04

D: 423 tons (508 fl) **S:** 15 kts **Dim:** 50.90 (46.50 pp) × 8.90 × 3.60 (max.)
A: 1 20-mm 90-cal. GIAT F2 AA
Electronics:
Radar: 1 DRBN 34A (Decca 1229) nav.
Sonar: Thales DUBM 21D HF VDS
M: 1 MTU diesel; 1 prop; 1,800 bhp—2 260-shp electric propulsors
Range: 3,000/12 **Crew:** 4 officers, 19 petty officers, 24 ratings

Remarks: Sold to Turkey under a 24-9-97 agreement; M 263 and M 261 were stricken from the French Navy on 13-2-97, M 262 during 3-97, M 260 on 4-7-97, and M 264 on 1-4-98. M 260 arrived in Turkey on 24-8-98, M 262 on 9-12-98; M 263 was handed over on 8-12-98 and arrived in Turkey during 1-99, and M 264 was transferred during 1-99. All were formally recommissioned on 22-7-99. Designed for the detection and destruction of mines laid as deep as 60 m.
Hull systems: Hull made of laminated wood. Design stressed low magnetic signature and silent operation. Two independent propulsion systems, one for transit and the other for minesweeping, both with remote control. Special rudders with small propellers mounted at the base of the rudder's after end and powered by a 260-hp electric motor, giving a speed of 7 knots and permitting exceptional maneuverability.
Combat systems: Prior to transfer, they were updated with the Thales MINETAC tactical data system (based on the SENIT 8.01 combat data system), PAP-Plus mine-countermeasures submersibles, and differential GPS receivers. Mines are destroyed either by divers (six in each crew) or by one of the two PAP-Plus wire-guided submersibles. The ships do not have minesweeping gear. Received updated DUBM 20A sonar with coherent processing feature during mid-1980s refits; subsequently further updated to DUBM 20B and then to DUBM 21D prior to transfer.

Ermenli (M 264) Martin Mokrus, 5-04

♦ 3 ex-German French Mercure–class coastal minesweepers [MSC]
Bldr: C.N. Amiot (CMN), Cherbourg

	Laid down	L	In serv.
M 520 Karamürsel (ex-*Wörms*, M 1253)	19-3-58	30-1-60	30-4-60
M 521 Kerempe (ex-*Detmold*, M 1252)	19-2-58	17-11-59	20-2-60
M 522 Kilimli (ex-*Siegen*, M 1254)	18-4-58	29-3-60	9-7-60

Kilimli (M 522) Hartmut Ehlers, 4-96

D: 366 tons (383 fl) **S:** 14.5 kts **Dim:** 44.62 (42.50 pp) × 8.41 × 2.55
A: 1 twin 20-mm 70-cal. Oerlikon Mk 24
Electronics:
Radar: 1 Decca 707 nav.
Sonar: Simrad . . . hull-mounted HF
M: 2 Mercedes-Benz MB-820 Db diesels; 2 KaMeWa CP props; 1,320 bhp
Electric: 776 kw tot. (2 × 320 kw sweep generators, 2 × 68 kw ship's service gen.)
Range: 5,000/12 **Fuel:** 34.9 tons **Crew:** 40 tot.

Remarks: Built for the German Navy, placed in reserve in 1963, and stricken on 31-12-73. Transferred to Turkey between 6-75 and 10-75. Sisters *Kozlu* (M 523, ex-*Hameln*) and *Kusadasi* (M 524, ex-*Vegesack*) were converted to patrol craft at Taskizak in 1999, and *Kemer* (M 525, ex-*Passau*) was stricken in 1998 but then adapted as salvage support ship A 582. Wooden construction. M 520 has been employed for minehunting trials since 1987 and is equipped with a minehunting sonar; the others had Simrad mine avoidance sonars added post-1988.

♦ 5 ex-U.S. MSC 289–class coastal minesweepers [MSC]
Bldrs: M 514, M 515; Dorchester Builders, Dorchester, N.J.; M 516 to M 518: Peterson Builders, Sturgeon Bay, Wisc.

	L	Del.	In serv.
M 514 Silifke (ex-MSC 304)	21-11-64	9-65	21-3-66
M 515 Saros (ex-MSC 305)	1-5-65	2-66	25-10-66
M 516 Sigacik (ex-MSC 311)	12-6-64	6-65	20-12-65
M 517 Sapanca (ex-MSC 312)	14-9-64	26-7-65	20-12-65
M 518 Sariyer (ex-MSC 315)	21-4-66	8-9-67	7-12-67

D: 300 tons (392 fl) **S:** 14 kts **Dim:** 44.32 × 8.29 × 2.55 (hull)
A: 1 twin 20-mm 70-cal. Oerlikon Mk 24 AA
Electronics:
Radar: 1 Decca 1226 nav.
Sonar: UQS-1D hull-mounted (100 kHz)
M: 2 Waukesha L-1616 diesels; 2 props; 1,200 bhp **Range:** 2,500/10
Fuel: 40 tons **Crew:** 4 officers, 34 enlisted

Remarks: Provided under U.S. Military Aid program. Wooden construction. Have lower pilothouse and taller stack than earlier U.S.-designed minesweepers. The sonar is primarily for detecting and avoiding moored mines and has little utility against bottom mines. Are equipped with acoustic, magnetic, and wire-sweep arrays.

MINE WARFARE SHIPS *(continued)*

Sariyer (M 518) Martin Mokrus, 5-04

Disposal note: All four remaining ex-U.S. MSC 268–class coastal minesweepers *Samsun* (M 510), *Sinop* (M 511), *Sürmene* (M 512), and *Seddulbahir* (M 513) had been retired by 2005.

♦ 4 ex-U.S. Cove-class inshore minesweepers [MSI]

Bldr: Peterson Builders, Sturgeon Bay, Wisc.

	L	In serv.
M 500 Foça (ex-MSI 15)	23-8-66	8-67
M 501 Fethiye (ex-MSI 16)	7-12-66	9-67
M 502 Fatsa (ex-MSI 17)	11-4-67	10-67
M 503 Finike (ex-MSI 18)	11-67	12-67

Fethiye (M 501) Hartmut Ehlers, 10-98

D: 203 tons (239 fl) **S:** 12.5 kts **Dim:** 34.06 × 7.14 × 2.4
A: 2 single 12.7-mm mg (I × 2)
Electronics: Radar: 1 . . . nav.
M: 4 G.M. Detroit Diesel 6-71 diesels; 2 props; 960 bhp
Electric: 120 kw tot. **Range:** 1,000/9 **Fuel:** 20 tons **Crew:** 20 tot.

Remarks: Transferred on completion. Wooden construction. Machinegun mounts are atop pilothouse and abaft stack; the actual guns are normally stowed below.

♦ 2 ex-U.S. 64-foot distribution-box minefield tenders [MSS]

Y 91 Şamandira 11 (ex-Y 1149, ex-Y 132)
Y 92 Şamandira 12 (ex-Y 1150)

D: 72 tons (fl) **S:** 9.5 kts **Dim:** 19.58 × 5.72 × 1.83
A: 1 G.M. Gray Marine 64HN9 diesel; 1 prop; 225 bhp **Crew:** 6 tot.

Remarks: Transferred in 1959. Wooden construction. Y 92 was restored to service in 1994 several years after having been discarded. Are used as controlled minefield electrical distribution box tenders. Resemble MTB 1 class below but are smaller. Sister *Şamandira 1* (Y 81) was retired in 2004.

♦ 6 MTB 1–class mine-warfare support tenders [MSS]

Bldr: . . ., U.K. (In serv. 1942)

P 313 MTB 3 P 317 MTB 7
P 314 MTB 4 P 318 MTB 8
P 316 MTB 6 P 319 MTB 9

Dalgiç 2 (P 312)—since retired Antonio Scrimali, 8-97

D: 70 tons **S:** 20 kts **Dim:** 21.8 × 4.2 × 2.6 **A:** 1 12.7-mm mg
M: 2 diesels; 2,000 bhp

Remarks: Used as general-purpose tender/supply craft at mine warfare bases. Sister MTB 10 was stricken 1987. *Dalgiç 2* (P 312) and *MTB 5* (P 315) were retired in 2004. MTB 1 was converted to diving tender *Dalgiç 1.*

♦ 2 Samandira Motoru–class small danbuoy layers [MSS]

Y 91 Şamandira Motoru 11 Y 92 Şamandira Motoru 12

Remarks: Five others of this class are laid up in land storage. No data available.

AMPHIBIOUS WARFARE SHIPS AND CRAFT

Note: The minelayer-landing ships *Osman Gazi* (N[L] 125), *Sarucabey* (N[L] 123), and *Karamürselbey* (N[L] 124) can also be employed in amphibious landings.

♦ 2 ex-U.S. Terrebonne Parish–class tank landing ships [LST]

Bldr: Christy Corp., Sturgeon Bay, Wisc.

	L	In serv.
L 401 Ertugrul (ex-*Windham County,* LST 1170)	22-5-54	15-12-54
L 402 Serdar (ex-*Westchester County,* LST 1167)	18-4-53	10-3-54

Serdar (L 402) French Navy, 1998

Ertugrul (L 401) Turkish Navy

D: 2,590 tons (5,786 fl) **S:** 15 kts **Dim:** 117.35 (112.77 pp) × 17.06 × 5.18
A: 3 twin 76.2-mm 50-cal. Mk 33 DP
Electronics: Radar: 1 Decca TM 1226 nav.; 1 SPS-10 surf. search; 2 Western Electric Mk 34 f.c.
M: 4 G.M. Electromotive Div. 16-278A diesels; 2 CP props; 6,000 bhp
Electric: 600 kw **Fuel:** 874 tons **Crew:** 116 tot. + 395 troops

Remarks: L 401 leased in 6-73 and L 402 in 8-74; both purchased 6-8-87. Cargo: 2,200 tons. Can carry four LCVPs in Welin davits. Two Mk 63 radar GFCS.

Note: The "Ç" preceding landing craft pennants stands for *Çikartma Gemisi* (landing craft).

♦ 13 Ç 139–class utility landing craft [LCU]

Bldr: Taskizak Naval Shipyard, Istanbul

	L		L		L
Ç 138	1984	Ç 143	25-7-85	Ç 147	21-7-89
Ç 139	8-84	Ç 144	25-7-85	Ç 148	21-7-90
Ç 140	8-84	Ç 145	21-7-89	Ç 149	21-7-90
Ç 141	9-84	Ç 146	21-7-89	Ç 150	7-91
Ç 142	25-7-85				

Ç 141 Hartmut Ehlers, 6-86

D: 280 tons light (600 fl) **S:** 10 kts (8.5 kts loaded)
Dim: 60.16 × 11.58 × 1.25 (aft)
A: 2 single 20-mm 70-cal. Oerlikon Mk 10 AA; 2 single 12.7-mm mg
Electronics: Radar: 1 Decca TM 1226 nav.

AMPHIBIOUS WARFARE SHIPS AND CRAFT *(continued)*

M: 2 MTU 8V396 TE-series diesels; 2 props; 1,240 bhp
Range: 600/10 (light); 1,100/8 (loaded) **Crew:** 1 officer, 16 enlisted

Remarks: Developed from the Ç 107 design, but with greater length, greater molded depth amidships, and larger superstructure. Can carry 100 troops and six M-48 tanks.

♦ 12 Ç 107–class utility landing craft [LCU]
Bldr: Gölçük Naval SY, Kocaeli (In serv. 1973–81)

Ç 120	Ç 126	Ç 129	Ç 134
Ç 123	Ç 127	Ç 132	Ç 135
Ç 125	Ç 128	Ç 133	Ç 137

Ç 120 French Navy, 1998

D: 260 tons light (580 fl) **S:** 10 kts (8.5 kts loaded)
Dim: 56.56 × 11.58 × 1.25 (aft)
A: 2 single 20-mm 70-cal. Oerlikon Mk 10 AA; 2 single 12.7-mm mg
Electronics: Radar: 1 Decca TM 1226 nav.
M: 3 G.M. Detroit Diesel 6-71 diesels; 3 props; 900 bhp (675 sust.)
Range: 600/10 (light); 1,100/8 **Crew:** 1 officer, 16 enlisted

Remarks: Design based on British LCT(4) design. Can carry 100 troops and five M-48 tanks.
Disposals: Ç 136 lost in storm 30-1-85. Ç 107 and Ç 113 were stricken in 1992, and Ç 111, 112, 115, and 116 had been deleted by 1981; Ç 110 was stricken during 1998. Ç 108, Ç 114, Ç 118, Ç 119, Ç 121, and Ç 122 were stricken early in 2000. Ç 117 and Ç 124 were retired in 2004.

♦ 17 U.S. LCM(8)-class landing craft [LCM]
Bldr: Taskizak Naval Shipyard, Istanbul (In serv. 1965–66)

Ç 303	Ç 308	Ç 313	Ç 319	Ç 329 through Ç 331
Ç 305	Ç 312	Ç 314	Ç 321 through Ç 327	

D: 34 tons light (121 fl) **S:** 12 kts **Dim:** 22.43 × 6.43 × 1.35 fwd./1.47 aft
A: 1 or 2 single 12.7-mm mg
M: 4 G.M. Detroit Diesel 6-71 diesels; 2 props; 590 bhp
Range: 190/12 (light); 140/9 (loaded) **Crew:** 5 tot. enlisted

Remarks: Cargo: 60 tons or 150 troops for short distances in 12.8 × 4.3–m open well with 54.6 m^2 space. More than a dozen sisters have been discarded, including eight in 1991, one in 1992, and Ç 316 and Ç 328 during 2000.

♦ 22 or more U.S. LCVP landing craft [LCVP]

D: 13 tons (fl) **S:** 9 kts **Dim:** 10.9 × 3.21 × 1.04 **A:** 2 single 7.62-mm mg
M: 1 G.M. Gray Marine 64HN9 diesel; 225 bhp **Range:** 110/9 **Crew:** 3 tot.

Remarks: Carried aboard the larger mine-warfare and amphibious landing ships. Wooden construction. Cargo: 36 troops or 4 tons.

Note: Also in service are a number of small RIB assault boats and at least two 15–18m GRP construction special forces landing craft.

AUXILIARIES

Disposal note: Intelligence collection ship [AGI] *Yunus* (A 590; ex-German *Alster,* A 50; ex-trawler *Mellum*) was stricken on 6-3-00 and arrived at Aliaga for scrapping on 16-11-00. Converted Canadian Bay-class intelligence collector *Tekirdag* (A 601; ex-M 533; ex-Canadian *Ungava*) was scrapped at Aliaga beginning 3-02.

♦ 1 U.S. Adjutant-class oceanographic research ship [AGOR]
Bldr: Stephen Brothers, . . . (In serv. 8-54)

Y 90 Deney (ex-*Selçuk,* M 508; ex-*Pavot;* ex-MSC 124)

D: 300 tons (392 fl) **S:** 14 kts **Dim:** 43.00 (41.50 pp) × 7.95 × 2.55 **A:** None
Electronics: Radar: 1 . . . nav.
M: 2 G.M. Detroit Diesel 8-268A diesels; 2 props; 1,200 bhp
Range: 2,500/10 **Fuel:** 40 tons **Crew:** . . . tot.

Remarks: Originally built for France but returned to U.S. control on 23-3-70 and transferred to Turkey on 4-9-70. Retired as a minesweeper in 4-98 and subsequently converted as an oceanographic research ship. Wooden construction.

♦ 1 oceanographic research and hydrographic survey ship [AGS]
Bldr: Gölçük Naval Shipyard, Kocaeli (L: 17-11-83; in serv. 7-84)

A 594 Çubuklu (ex-Y 1251)

D: 512 tons light (680 fl) **S:** 11 kts **Dim:** 40.40 (36.40 wl) × 9.60 × 3.20
A: 2 single 20-mm 70-cal. Oerlikon Mk 10 AA
Electronics: Radar: 1 Decca . . . nav.
M: 1 MWM diesel; 1 CP prop; 1,004 bhp (820 sust.)
Crew: 5 officers, 26 enlisted (39 tot. accomm.)

Çubuklu (A 594) J. G. Stemmelen, 5-97

Remarks: Carries one survey launch to port. Forecastle side plating extends to abaft boat installation on port side. Received Qubit (Australia) integrated navigation data processing system in 1990–91.

♦ 2 ex-U.S. Silas Bent–class hydrographic survey ships [AGS]
Bldr: American Shipbuilding, Lorain, Ohio

	L	In serv.
A 588 Çandarli (ex-*Kane,* T-AGS 27)	20-11-65	19-5-67
A 599 Çeşme (ex-*Silas Bent,* T-AGS 26)	16-5-64	23-7-65

Çandarli (A 588) Leo Dirkx, 7-01

D: 1,900 tons (2,743 fl) **S:** 15 kts **Dim:** 86.9 (80.8 pp) × 14.6 × 4.6 **A:** None
Electronics: Radar: 2 Raytheon . . . nav.
M: 2 Alco diesels, electric drive: Westinghouse electric motor; 1 CP prop; 3,600 shp—350 shp electric bow-thruster
Electric: 960 kw tot. **Range:** 5,800/14.5; 8,000/13 **Fuel:** 461 tons
Crew: 40 tot. + 30 scientists

Remarks: A 599 transferred to Turkey on 28-10-99 at Singapore, having been deactivated by the U.S. Military Sealift Command the same day; the ship was formally recommissioned on 8-6-00. *Çandarli* was transferred on 14-3-01 and formally recommissioned on 25-7-01.

♦ 2 Kanarya-class coastal cargo transports [AK]
Bldr: Taskizak Naval Shipyard, Istanbul (In serv. 1972–74)

A 592 Karadeniz Ereglisi (ex-Y 1157) A 593 Eceabat (ex-Y 1165)

Şarköy (A 591)—since retired, with former pennant number H&L Van Ginderen, 1991

D: 823 tons (fl) **S:** 10 kts **Dim:** 50.7 (47.4 pp) × 8.0 × . . .
A: 1 20-mm 70-cal. Oerlikon Mk 10 AA **Electronics:** Radar: 1 . . . nav.
M: 1 diesel; 1 prop; 1,440 bhp **Crew:** 3 officers, 20 enlisted

Remarks: 500 dwt. Molded depth: 3.6 m. Redesignated auxiliaries from service craft in 1991. Cargo is about 300 tons total, in two holds, tended by two 1-ton derricks. Sister *Kanarya* (ex-Y 1155) stricken 1993 and *Şarköy* (A 591, ex-Y 1156) retired in by 2006.

♦ 1 ex-U.S. AN 103–class net tender [AN]
Bldr: Krögerwerft, Rendsburg, Germany

	Laid down	L	In serv.
P 305 AG 5 (ex-AN 104)	1960	20-10-60	25-2-61

AUXILIARIES *(continued)*

D: 680 tons (975 fl) **S:** 12.8 kts **Dim:** 52.50 (48.50 hull) × 10.60 × 3.70
A: 1 40-mm 70-cal. Bofors L70 AA; 3 single 20-mm 70-cal. Oerlikon Mk 10 AA
Electronics: Radar: 1/Decca TM 1226 nav.
M: 1 M.A.N. G7V 40/60 diesel; 1 prop; 1,470 bhp
Range: 6,500/10.8 **Fuel:** 134 tons **Crew:** 5 officers, 45 enlisted

Remarks: Sister to the *Thetis* in the Greek Navy. Built with U.S. Offshore Procurement funds. Can carry 1,600 rounds 40-mm, 25,200 rounds 20-mm ammunition.

♦ 1 ex-U.S. AN 93–class net tender [AN]
Bldr: Bethlehem Steel, Staten Island, N.Y.

	L	In serv.
P 306 AG 6 (ex-*Dutch Cerberus;* ex-AN 93)	5-52	10-11-52

AG 6 (P 306) Hartmut Ehlers, 5-84

D: 780 tons (902 fl) **S:** 12.8 kts **Dim:** 50.29 (44.50 pp) × 10.20 × 3.20
A: 1 76.2-mm 50-cal. Mk 22 DP; 4 single 20-mm 70-cal. Oerlikon Mk 10 AA
Electronics: Radar: 1 Decca TM 1226 nav.
M: 2 G.M. 8-268A diesels, electric drive; 1 prop; 1,500 shp
Range: 5,200/12 **Crew:** 48 tot.

Remarks: Prototype of a class also built in France and Italy. Transferred to the Netherlands in 12-52 and returned 17-9-70; transferred to Turkey the same day.

♦ 1 Modified Akar-class replenishment oiler [AO]
Bldr: KOC-RMK Tersanesi, Tuzla, Istanbul

	Laid down	L	In serv.
A 595 Yarbay Kudret Güngör	5-11-93	10-94	24-10-95

Yarbay Kudret Güngör (A 595) ANBw/FAFIO, 10-99

Yarbay Kudret Güngör (A 595) Turkish Navy, 1995

D: Approx. 20,000 tons (fl) **S:** 15 kts **Dim:** 145.10 × 22.80 × 8.40
A: 2 twin 35-mm 90-cal. Oerlikon AA; 1 20-mm Mk 15 Phalanx CIWS
Electronics: Radar: 1 Decca TM 1226 nav.; 1 Decca . . . nav.; 1 General Dynamics Mk 90 Phalanx f.c.
M: 2 diesels; 1 prop; 6,500 bhp **Range:** 6,000/14 **Endurance:** 90 days
Crew: 14 officers, 189 enlisted

Remarks: 14,000 dwt. Ordered 5-93 as the first Turkish commercial-built ship for the Turkish Navy. Began sea trials 12-95. Is a near sister to *Akar* (A 580), as it had long been planned to build a second ship of the class, but has more modern armament and a different cargo layout. There is a civilian sister to this vessel, delivered by the builder in 1992. The builder was formerly known as SEDEF Gemi Endustrisi A.S.
Hull systems: Cargo includes 11,300 tons fuel oil, 80 tons lube oil, 2,700 tons fresh water; refrigerated cargo capacity is 250 m^3 and dry provisions capacity 250 m^3. As in *Akar,* there is one liquid fuel underway transfer station per side. An extra cargo crane has been added forward, to port. Has a helicopter deck but no hangar.
Combat systems: The 35-mm mount was recycled from a retired destroyer and may have local-only control. The Phalanx mounting is forward and has a wide arc of fire.

♦ 1 Akar-class replenishment oiler [AO]
Bldr: Gölçük Naval SY, Kocaeli

	L	In serv.
A 580 Akar	16-11-83	24-4-87

Akar (A 580) French Navy, 2-96

D: 19,350 tons (fl) **S:** 15 kts **Dim:** 145.1 × 22.8 × 8.4
A: 1 twin 76.2-mm 50-cal. Mk 33 DP; 1 twin 40-mm 70-cal. Bofors AA; 2 single 20-mm 70-cal. Oerlikon Mk 10 AA
Electronics: Radar: 1 Decca . . . nav.; 1 Decca 1226 nav.; 1 Western Electric Mk 34 f.c.
M: 1 diesel; 1 prop; 6,500 bhp **Crew:** 329 tot.

Remarks: 15,000 dwt. Construction was suspended for several years after launching.
Hull systems: Cargo: essentially the same as *Yarbay Kudret Güngör,* but less capacity for solid stores. Has one underway liquid replenishment station per side and two cranes to handle solid stores directly forward of the bridge. Has helicopter platform but no hangar.
Combat systems: Has U.S. Mk 63 gun f.c.s. for the 76.2-mm guns, with the SPG-34 radar's antenna on the gunmount.

♦ 2 Albay Hakki Burak–class transport tankers [AOT]
Bldr: KOÇ–RMK Tersanesi, Tuzla

	L	In serv.
A 571 Albay Hakki Burak	. . .	8-6-00
A 572 Yüzbazi Tolunay	21-11-99	8-6-00

Albay Hakki Burak (A 571)—in light-load condition Turkish Navy, 1999

D: 2,355 tons light (. . . fl) **S:** 15 kts **Dim:** 81.3 × . . . × . . .
A: 2 single 12.7-mm mg
Electronics: Radar: 1/ . . . nav. **M:** 2 . . . diesels; 2 props. 3,200 bhp

Remarks: 1,500 dwt. Transport tankers without underway replenishment capabilities. No other data available.

♦ 1 Taşkizak-class transport tanker [AOT]
Bldr: Taşkizak Naval Shipyard, Istanbul

	L	In serv.
A 570 Taşkizak	28-7-83	1-8-84

Taşkizak (A 570) J. G. Stemmelen, 5-97

AUXILIARIES *(continued)*

D: 1,440 tons (fl) **S:** 13 kts **Dim:** 64.6 × 9.4 × 3.5
A: 1 40-mm 60-cal. Bofors Mk 3 AA: 2 single 20-mm 70-cal. Oerlikon Mk 10 AA
Electronics: Radar: 1 Decca TM 1226 nav.
M: 1 diesel; 1 prop; 1,400 bhp **Crew:** 57 tot.

Remarks: Cargo capacity is 800 tons.

♦ 1 Binbaşi Saadettin Gürcan–class transport oiler [AOT]
Bldr: Taşkizak Naval Shipyard, Istanbul (L: 7-69)

A 573 Binbaşi Saadettin Gürcan

D: 1,505 tons (4,680 fl) **S:** 16 kts **Dim:** 89.7 × 11.8 × 5.4
A: 2 single 20-mm 70-cal. Oerlikon Mk 10 AA
Electronics: Radar: 1 Decca TM 1226 nav.
M: 4 G.M. Electromotive Div. 16-567A diesels, electric drive; 2 props; 4,400 shp
Crew: . . . tot.

Binbaşi Saadettin Gürcan (A 573)—in overhaul; the survey ship *Çubuklu* (A 594) is seen alongside H&L Van Ginderen, 7-95

Remarks: Primarily used as a transport tanker, but is capable of delivering fuel to ships alongside while dead-in-the-water. Previously carried a 40-mm 60-cal. Bofors Mk 3 AA gun.

Disposal note: Ex-German *Bodensee*-class transport oiler *Inebolu* (A 575, ex-*Bodensee,* ex-*Unkas*) was stricken during 2-04.

♦ 1 vehicle and personnel transport [AP]
Bldr: Turkiye Gemi Sanayii A.S., Camialti, Istanbul

	L	In serv.
A 1600 Iskenderun	1987	1991

D: . . . **S:** 18 kts **Dim:** 127.50 (120.00 pp) × 19.40 × 5.42 **A:** none
Electronics: Radar: . . .
M: 4 Skoda-Sulzer 6ZL 40/48 diesels; 2 props; 16,800 bhp—2 bow-thrusters
Electric: 3,192 kw tot. (3 × 1,000 kw diesel sets; 1 × 192 kw emergency diesel set)

Remarks: 10,583 grt/1,714 dwt. Purchased from T.D.I Deniz Yollari Isletmesi and recommissioned for the Turkish Navy as a vehicle and personnel carrier on 25-7-02. Polish-designed vehicle and passenger ferry. Polish-built sisters *Ankara* and *Samsun* remain in commercial service.
Hull systems: Has bow and stern vehicle cargo doors with ramps, and vehicle side doors port and starboard. There are 468 lane-meters of vehicle cargo space, sufficient for 214 automobiles; clear height in the vehicle deck is 4.2 m.

♦ 1 ex-Russian Almaz-class salvage tug [ARS]
Bldr: Okean SY, Mikolayiv, Ukraine (In serv. ca. 1974)

A 586 Akbaş (ex-*Yawa*)

Russian commercial Almaz-class salvage tug Ametist JMSDF/*Ships of the World,* 1998

D: 1,210 tons (1,656 fl) **S:** 13.25 kts sust. **Dim:** 58.55 (51.62 pp) × 12.68 × 4.67
A: . . . **Electronics:** Radar: 2 Don-2 nav.
M: Diesel-electric: 2 Type 25-DB 2 (6ChN 30/38) diesels (1,500 bhp each), 2 generators, 1 motor; 1 prop; 2,500 shp (1,850 shp sust.)
Range: 6,200/11 **Fuel:** 297 tons **Endurance:** 40 days **Crew:** approx. 35 tot.

Remarks: 1,074 grt/44 dwt. Purchased 1999 from Russia; former identity not known, but may be the former *Purga,* a former fishing fleet salvage tug. Design very similar to Russian Navy Sorum-class seagoing tug, except that the superstructure is higher and the mainmast is of A-frame configuration. Can accommodate 40 rescued personnel and is equipped for firefighting, salvage pumping, and ocean towing. Based at Aksaz.

♦ 1 ex-French Tenace-class salvage tug [ARS]
Bldr: Ch. de la Rochelle-Palice, France

	L	In serv.
A 576 Degirmendere (ex-*Centaure,* A 674)	8-1-74	15-11-74

Degirmendere (A 576) Bernard Prézelin, 4-99

D: 970 tons (1,440 fl) **S:** 13.5 kts **Dim:** 51.0 × 11.5 × 5.7 **A:** None
Electronics: 1 Decca TM 1226 nav.
M: 2 SACM AGO 240 V12 diesels; 1 Kort-nozzle CP prop; 4,600 bhp
Electric: 766 kw tot. (3 × 227, 1 × 85 kw diesel sets) **Fuel:** 500 tons
Range: 9,500/13 **Crew:** 3 officers, 34 enlisted

Remarks: Decommissioned from French Navy and sold to Turkey on 15-1-99; transferred 16-3-99 and formally recommissioned on 22-7-99. Based at Aksaz and used for salvage duties.
Hull systems: Pumps include one of 350 m^3/hr (serving two fire monitors with a range of 60 m) and one of 120 m^3/hr, plus numerous smaller salvage and firefighting pumps. Carries two semi-rigid inflatable boats. Bollard-pull: 60 tons. Living quarters air-conditioned.

♦ 1 ex-German Mercure-class salvage tender [ARS]
Bldr: C.N. Amiot (CMN), Cherbourg

	Laid down	L	In serv.
A 582 Kemer (ex-M 525; ex-*Passau,* M 1255)	19-5-58	25-6-60	15-10-60

Kemer (A 582) Cem D. Yaylali, 5-05

D: 366 tons (383 fl) **S:** 14.5 kts **Dim:** 44.62 (42.5 pp) × 8.41 × 2.55
A: 1 twin 20-mm 70-cal. Oerlikon Mk 24 AA
Electronics: Radar: 1 Decca 707 nav.
M: 2 Mercedes-Benz MB-820 Db diesels; 2 KaMeWa CP props; 1,320 bhp
Electric: 776 kw tot. (2 × 320 kw, 2 × 68 kw diesel sets)
Range: 5,000/12 **Fuel:** 34.9 tons **Crew:** 40 tot.

AUXILIARIES *(continued)*

Remarks: Built for the German Navy, placed in reserve in 1963, and stricken on 31-12-73. Transferred to Turkey between 6-75 and 10-75. Stricken 1998 but then modified as a salvage tender and recommissioned. Sisters serve as minesweepers and patrol craft. Wooden construction.

♦ 1 ex-U.S. Diver-class salvage ship [ARS]
Bldr: Basalt Rock Co., Napa, Calif.

	Laid down	L	In serv.
A 589 IŞIN (ex-*Safeguard,* ARS 25)	5-6-43	20-11-43	31-10-44

Işin (A 589) Cem D. Yaylali, 6-04

D: 1,480 tons (1,970 fl) **S:** 14.8 kts **Dim:** 65.08 (63.09 pp) × 12.5 × 4.0
A: 2 single 20-mm 70-cal. Oerlikon Mk 10 AA **Electronics:** Radar: 2 . . . nav.
M: 4 Cooper-Bessemer GSB-8 diesels, electric drive; 2 props; 3,000 shp
Electric: 460 kw tot. **Fuel:** 300 tons **Crew:** 97 tot.

Remarks: Leased 28-9-79; purchased 6-8-87. Wooden fenders add 0.6 m to beam.

Disposal notes: Submarine tender *Umurbey* (A 588; ex-German cargo ship *Dithmarschen*) was stricken 12-1-99 and arrived at Aliaga for scrapping on 18-9-99. U.S. *Bluebird*-class submarine rescue ship *Kurtaran* (A 584; ex-*Bluebird,* ASR 19; ex-*Yurok,* ATF 164) was stricken on 15-9-00 and was sunk by aircraft during an exercise in 2001.

♦ 1 ex-U.S. Chanticleer-class submarine-rescue ship [ASR]
Bldr: Moore Shipbuilding and Drydock Co., Oakland, Calif.

	Laid down	L	In serv.
A 585 AKIN (ex-*Greenlet,* ASR 10)	15-10-41	12-7-42	29-5-43

Akin (A 585) Leo Dirkx, 7-01

D: 1,770 tons (2,321 fl) **S:** 15 kts **Dim:** 76.61 (73.15 pp) × 12.8 × 4.52
A: 1 40-mm 60-cal. Bofors Mk 3 AA; 2 twin 20-mm 70-cal. Oerlikon Mk 24 AA
Electronics: Radar: 1 Decca TM 1226 nav.
M: 4 Alco 539 diesels, electric drive; 1 prop; 3,000 shp **Electric:** 460 kw tot.
Fuel: 235 tons **Crew:** 85 tot.

Remarks: Loaned on 12-6-70 and purchased outright on 15-2-73. Carries McCann rescue diving bell and four marker buoys. Can also be used for general salvage duties.

♦ 1 Darica-class seagoing tug/torpedo retriever [ATA]
Bldr: Taskizak Naval Shipyard, Istanbul

	L	In serv.
A 578 DARICA (ex-Y 1125)	27-7-87	20-7-90

D: 750 tons (fl) **S:** 14 kts **Dim:** 40.9 × 9.8 × 3.9 **A:** None
Electronics: Radar: 1 . . . nav. **M:** 2 ABC diesels; 2 props; 4,000 bhp
Range: 2,500/14

Remarks: Oilfield tug-supply type vessel, with open fantail for recovering and stowing torpedoes; is also equipped for fire fighting and salvage.

Darica (A 578) H&L Van Ginderen, 11-94

♦ 1 ex-U.S. Cherokee-class fleet tug [ATA]
Bldr: United Eng. Co., Alameda, Calif.

	Laid down	L	In serv.
A 587 GAZAL (ex-*Sioux,* ATF 75)	14-2-42	27-5-42	6-12-42

Gazal (A 587) H&L Van Ginderen, 7-95

D: 1,235 tons (1,675 fl) **S:** 16.5 kts **Dim:** 62.48 (59.44 pp) × 11.73 × 4.67
A: 1 76.2-mm 50-cal. Mk 22 DP; 2 single 20-mm 70-cal. Oerlikon Mk 10 AA
M: 4 G.M. 12-278 diesels, electric drive; 1 prop; 3,000 shp **Electric:** 260 kw tot.
Range: 6,500/16; 15,000/8 **Fuel:** 300 tons **Crew:** 85 tot.

Remarks: Transferred on 30-10-72 and purchased outright on 15-8-73. Can be used for salvage duties. Similar to submarine rescue ship *Kurtaran* (A 584).

♦ 2 Van-class water tankers [AWT]
Bldr: Gölçük Naval Shipyard, Kocaeli (In serv. 1969–70)

A 597 VAN (ex-Y 1208) A 598 ULABAT (ex-Y 1209)

Van (A 597) Martin Mokrus, 5-04

AUXILIARIES *(continued)*

D: 900 tons (1,250 fl) **S:** 10 kts **Dim:** 53.1 × 9.0 × 3.0
A: 1 20-mm 70-cal. Oerlikon Mk 10 AA **Electronics:** Radar: 1 Decca 707 nav.
M: 1 diesel; 1 prop; 650 bhp **Crew:** . . . tot.

Remarks: Cargo: 700 tons. Reclassified as auxiliaries from service craft on 1-1-91.

♦ 3 ex-German FW 1–class water tankers [AWT]

Bldrs: A 581, 598: Schichau, Bremerhaven; A 600: Jadewerft, Wilhelmshaven

	Laid down	L	In serv.
A 581 Çinar (ex-*FW 1*)	5-4-63	22-7-63	30-11-63
A 598 Söğüt (ex-Y 1217, ex-*FW 2*)	5-4-63	3-9-63	4-1-64
A 600 Kavak (ex-*FW 4*)	14-6-63	14-3-64	28-7-64

Çinar (A 581) Cem D. Yaylali, 5-05

D: 598 tons (647 fl) **S:** 9.5 kts **Dim:** 44.03 (41.4 pp) × 7.8 × 2.63
M: 1 MWM 12-cyl. diesel; 1 prop; 230 bhp **Electric:** 130 kVA tot.
Range: 2,150/9 **Fuel:** 15 tons **Crew:** 12 tot.

Remarks: A 598 transferred on 3-12-75, A 600 on 12-4-91, and A 581 early in 1996. Cargo: 343 tons of fresh water. A 598 reclassified as an auxiliary from service craft on 1-1-91.

♦ 2 ex-German Rhein-class (Type 401) training ships [AXT]

	Bldr	L	In serv.
A 577 Sokullu Mehmet Paşa (ex-*Donau,* A 69)	Schlichting, Travemünde	26-11-60	23-5-64
A 579 Cezayirli Gazi Hasan Paşa (ex-*Elbe,* A 61)	Schlieker, Hamburg	5-5-60	17-4-62

Cezayirli Gazi Hasan Paşa (A 579) Martin Mokrus, 5-05

Sokullu Mehmet Paşa (A 577) Guy Schaeffer via Paolo Marsan, 7-05

D: 2,330 tons (2,930 fl) **S:** 20 kts (22 trials)
Dim: 98.80 (92.80 pp) × 11.80 × 3.95
A: 2 single 100-mm 65-cal. Creusot-Loire Model 1953 DP; 2 twin 40-mm 70-cal. Bofors AA; 2 mine rails (70 mines max.)
Electronics:
Radar: 1 . . . nav.; 1 Thales SGR-103 surf.-search; 1 Thales SGR-105 air-search; 2 Thales M 45 f.c.
EW: . . . intercept
M: 6 MTU 16V TB81 (A 577: Maybach . . .) diesels; 2 CP props; 11,400 bhp
Electric: 2,250 kw tot. **Range:** 2,500/16 **Fuel:** 334 tons
Crew: 98 tot. (accomm. for 40 officers, 170 enlisted)

Remarks: Both were built as small combatant tenders but have been used as cadet training ships since acquired by Turkey. The current A 577 was transferred on 13-3-95 as a replacement for a near-sister ship of the same name and number (ex-*Isar,* A 54, transferred on 30-9-82). The current A 579 was decommissioned from the German Navy 17-12-92 and transferred during 1993 as a replacement for near-sister *Cezayirli Gazi Hasan Paşa* (A 579; ex-*Ruhr,* A 64). Both have two M4 radar directors for the 100-mm guns and can be employed as minelayers or escorts, if required.

SERVICE CRAFT

♦ 5 Deniz Temizleme Arac-1–class pollution-control craft [YAG]

Bldr: Y 151: . . ., Italy; others: Göçük Naval Shipyard (In serv. 1982–95)

	In serv.
Y 151 Deniz Temizleme Arac-1	1983
Y 152 Deniz Temizleme Arac-2	1992
Y 153 Deniz Temizleme Arac-3	1993
Y 154 Deniz Temizleme Arac-4	1993
Y 155 Deniz Temizleme Arac-5	1995

Pollution skimmer Deniz Temizleme Arac-5 (Y 155) Hartmut Ehlers, 10-96

D: 12.5 tons (fl) **S:** 10 kts **Dim:** 12.5 × 5.30 × . . .
M: 2 G.M. Detroit Diesel diesels; 2 props; 380 bhp

Remarks: Catamaran-hulled craft with debris and oil-spill collection sweepers between the hulls. Also have one firefighting water monitor.

♦ 1 ex-U.S. floating crane [YD]

Bldr: Odenback SB, Rochester, N.Y. (In serv. 14-8-51)

Y 60 Algarna III (ex-Y 1023, ex-YD 185)

D: 1,200 tons (fl) **Dim:** 36.6 × 13.7 × 2.7

Remarks: Transferred in 9-63. Capacity: 100 tons.

♦ 1 miscellaneous floating crane [YD]

Y 59 Levent (ex-Y 1022)

Remarks: Capacity: 600 tons.

♦ 1 Cephane-class ammunition lighter [YE]

Y 97 Cephane 2 (ex-Y 1195)

Remarks: Of about 850 tons (fl). *Cephane 1* (Y 1194) was stricken during 1987 and *Cephane 3* (Y 1197) during 1992.

♦ 4 Salopa-series stores lighters [YF]

Y 21–24 Salopa 21–24 (ex-Y 1031–1034)

Remarks: No data available; characteristics vary.

♦ 5 Layter-series stores lighters [YF]

Y 102–104, 106, 107 Layter 2–4, 6, 7 (ex-Y 1012–1014, 1016, 1017)

Remarks: No data available. Sister *Layter 1* (Y 101, ex-Y 1011) was scrapped during 2000.

♦ 16 Mavna-series miscellaneous stores launches [YF]

Y 1–4 Mavna 1–4 (ex-Y 1181–1184)
Y 7–13 Mavna 7–13 (ex-Y 1187–1193)
Y 14–18 Mavna 14–18 (ex-Y 1198–1202)

Mavna 18 (Y 18) H&L Van Ginderen, 7-95

Remarks: Small diesel-powered stores and personnel lighters; engines aft.

SERVICE CRAFT *(continued)*

♦ 12 miscellaneous floating dry docks [YFDL/YFDM]

	Capacity (tons)		Capacity (tons)
Y 121 Havuz 1 (ex-Y 1081)	16,000	Y 128 Havuz 8 (ex-Y 1088)	700
Y 122 Havuz 2 (ex-Y 1082)	12,000	Y 129 Havuz 9 (ex-Y 1089)	3,500
Y 123 Havuz 3 (ex-Y 1083)	2,500	Y 130 Havuz 10 (ex-Y 1090)	300
Y 124 Havuz 4 (ex-Y 1084)	4,500	Y 131 Havuz 11 (ex-Y . . .)	14.500
Y 125 Havuz 5 (ex-Y 1085)	400	Y 132 Havuz 12 (ex-Y . . .)	5,000
Y 126 Havuz 6 (ex-Y 1086)	3,000	Y 133 Havuz 13 (ex-Y . . .)	7,500

Remarks: Y 123 is a sectional pontoon dock built by M.A.N., Blixen, Germany, in 1958 with U.S. funds; D: 4,500 tons empty; Dim: 115.95 × 36.4 (30.50 clear width) × 9.0 max. (8.00 clear over blocks). During 7-89, Taskizak NDY delivered *Havuz 10* in 7-89, while Gölçük delivered *Havuz 9* on 21-7-89.

♦ 4 miscellaneous personnel ferry [YFL]

Y 44 . . .   Y 45 . . .   Y 46 Tersane III   Y 47 . . .

Personnel ferry Tersane III (Y 46) Cem D. Yaylali, 4-98

Remarks: Small, enclosed personnel ferry employed in the Istanbul area for local transportation.

♦ 2 miscellaneous officers' yachts [YFL]

Y 76 Gül (ex-Y 1103)   . . . Kaplan

Kaplan Cem D. Yaylali, 6-04

Gül (Y 76) H&L Van Ginderen, 7-95

Remarks: *Kaplan* is a former U.S. "63-ft. AVR" wooden-hulled air/sea rescue craft used as a flag officer barge and does not seem to have a Y-series number

♦ 7 pontoon barges [YFN]

Ponton 1–7 (ex-Y 1061–1067)

♦ 2 inshore survey craft [YGS] (In serv. 1994?)

Y 35 Mesaha 1   Y 36 Mesaha 2

Mesaha 2 (Y 36)—outboard *Mesaha 1* (Y 35) Cem D. Yaylali, 9-94

D: 38 tons (fl) **S:** 10 kts **Dim:** 15.9 × 4.5 × 1.3 **Electronics:** Radar: 1/ . . . nav.
M: 2 G.M. Detroit Diesel 6-71 diesels; 2 props; 440 bhp (348 sust.) **Range:** 600/10
Crew: 9 tot.

Note: Steel-hulled craft that replace a pair of former U.S. Navy 52-ft inshore survey boats with the same names and pennant numbers.

♦ 3 H 500–class small fuel lighters [YO]
Bldr: Taskizak Naval Shipyard, Istanbul (In serv. 1970s)

Y 140 H 500 (ex-Y 1231)
Y 141 H 501 (ex-Y 1232)
Y 142 H 503 (ex-Y 1233)

Fuel lighter H 501 (Y 141)—with former pennant number Hartmut Ehlers, 3-90

D: 300 tons **S:** 11 kts **Dim:** 33.6 × 8.5 × 1.8
M: 1 G.M. Detroit Diesel 6-71 diesel; 1 prop; 225 bhp **Cargo:** 150 tons

♦ 2 ex-U.S. APL 41–class barracks barges [YPL]
Bldr: Y 38: Puget Sound Bridge & Dredge, Seattle, Wash.; Y 39: Tampa SB, Tampa, Fla.

	L
Y 38 Yüzbaşi Nasit Öngeren (ex-Y 1204, ex-APL 47)	5-1-45
Y 39 Binbaşi Metin Sülüs (ex-Y 1205, ex-APL 53)	3-3-45

D: 2,660 tons (fl) **Dim:** 79.6 × 14.99 × 2.59 **Electric:** 300 kw **Crew:** 650 tot.

Remarks: Y 38 was leased in 10-72, Y 39 in 12-74; both purchased 6-8-87. Pennant numbers changed 1991. Nonself-propelled.

♦ 1 Turkish-built torpedo retriever [YPT]
Bldr: Gölçük Naval Shipyard, Kocaeli (In serv. 1995)

Y 44 Takip-2

Takip-2 (Y 44) Cem D. Yaylali, 9-98

Remarks: No data available. Has two cranes for retrieving weapons but no recovery ramp. Appears to be about 18 m overall and powered by two diesels.

♦ 1 ex-U.S. 72-ft.-class torpedo retriever [YPT]
Bldr: Gölçük Navy Yard (In serv. 1961)

Y 98 Takip-1 (ex-Y 1052, ex- . . .)

D: 53 tons (fl) **S:** 18 kts **Dim:** 22.17 × 5.18 × 1.68
M: 2 G.M. diesels; 2 props; 1,000 bhp **Range:** 450/18 **Crew:** 6 tot.

Remarks: Built with U.S. aid to a U.S. standard design. Wooden construction. Can carry up to 10.8 tons of weapons retrieved via stern ramp.

♦ 1 old torpedo retriever [YPT]
Bldr: Gölçük Naval Shipyard, Kocaeli (In serv. 1938)

Y 95 Torpido Tenderi 95 (ex-Y 1051)

SERVICE CRAFT *(continued)*

D: 300 tons (fl) **S:** 10 kts **Dim:** . . . × . . . × . . .
M: 1 MWM diesel; 1 prop; 1,000 bhp **Crew:** 6 tot.

Remarks: Near sister to the now-stricken munitions lighter *Bekirdere* (Y 94). Has two torpedo recovery ramps.

♦ 5 Önder-class large harbor tug [YTB]
Bldr: Alaybey SY, Izmit (In serv. Y 160: 22-7-99; others: 8-6-00)

Y 160 Önder Y 161 Öncü Y 162 Özgen Y 163 Ödev Y 164 Özgür

Özgen (Y 162) Cem D. Yaylali, 5-05

D: . . . tons **S:** 12 kts **Dim:** 28.0 (26.5 pp) × 9.0 × 4.4 (over props)
M: 2 . . . diesels; 2 Voith-Schneider Type 26 GII/165 vertical cycloidal props; 3,400 bhp
Range: 1,500/12 **Crew:** . . . tot.

Remarks: Equipped for fire fighting, with water monitors at masthead and atop the pilothouse.

♦ 1 ex-East German Project 414 large harbor tug [YTB]
Bldr: Yachtwerft/Volkswerft, Stralsund (In serv. 1989)

A 583 Aksaz (ex-*Koos,* Y 1651; ex-*Delphin,* A 08)

D: 286 tons (320 fl) **S:** 10.5 kts **Dim:** 30.87 (29.30 pp) × 8.77 × 2.50
Electronics: Radar: 1 SRN-402 nav.
M: 1 SKL 6VD26/20 AL-1 diesel; 1 Kort-nozzle prop; 1,200 bhp (720 sust.)
Electric: 150 kw tot. **Range:** 1,800/10 **Crew:** 13 tot.

Remarks: 140 grt. Acquired by Germany on unification, 10-90, as one of three completed units of a planned six-unit class. Stricken 28-9-95 and sold to Turkey on 7-10-96, departing the same date. Fitted with one water monitor for fire fighting.

♦ 1 Doganarslan-class large harbor tug [YTB]
Bldr: Taskizak Naval Shipyard, Istanbul (In serv. 25-7-85 and 1987)

Y 52 Doganarslan (ex-Y 1123)

Doganarslan (Y 52) J. G. Stemmelen, 4-97

D: 500 tons (fl) **S:** 12 kts **Dim:** . . . × . . . × . . . **M:** . . .

Remarks: No other data available.

♦ 1 Kuvvet-class larger harbor tug [YTB]
Bldr: . . . (In serv. 2-62)

Y 53 Kuvvet (ex-Y 1122)

D: 390 tons **S:** . . . kts **Dim:** 32.1 × 7.9 × 3.6 **M:** . . .

Remarks: Built in Turkey with U.S. Grant Aid funds. Pennant number changed during 1991.

♦ 1 U.S. Army–Design 3004 medium harbor tug [YTM]
Bldr: . . . (In serv. 2-62)

Y 54 Kudret (ex-Y 1229, ex-LT- . . .)

D: 100 tons light (122 tons fl) **S:** 12 kts **Dim:** 21.31 × 5.94 × 2.50
M: 1 diesel; 1 prop; 600 bhp **Range:** 3,500/12 **Fuel:** 15 tons **Crew:** 6 tot.

Remarks: Built in Turkey with U.S. Grant Aid funds. Pennant number changed 1991.

♦ 1 ex-U.S. Army 320-design small harbor tug [YTL]

Y 64 Ersen Bayrak (ex-Y 1134, ex-LT . . .)

Remarks: No data available.

♦ 1 Turkish-designed medium harbor tug [YTM]
Bldr: Gölçük Naval Shipyard (In serv. 11-5-63)

Y 55 Atil (ex-Y 1132)

D: 143.5 tons (fl) **S:** 10 kts **Dim:** 24.40 × 6.72 × 2.70
M: 1 G.M. Electromotive Div. 8-268A diesel; 1 prop; 450 bhp

♦ 47 push tugs [YTL]

Katir 1–47

Katir 38 Hartmut Ehlers, 10-89

Remarks: No data available. Are not assigned Y-series pennant numbers.

♦ 3 Russian Mars-class fireboats (Project 14613) [YTR]
Bldr: Vympel Zavod, Rybinsk

	In serv.		In serv.
A 1542 Söndüren 2	8-6-00	A 1544 Söndüren 4	8-6-00
A 1543 Söndüren 3	22-7-99		

Söndüren 2 (A 1542) Cem D. Yaylali, 5-06

D: 385 tons (fl) **S:** 11.5 kts **Dim:** 39.80 (37.76 wl, 35.20 pp) × 7.80 × 4.75 max.
Electronics: Radar: 1 Mius (Spin Trough) nav.
M: 2 Barnaul' 3KD 12N-520 diesels; 2 CP props; 1,018 bhp—bow-thruster
Electric: 400 kw tot. **Range:** 500/11.5 **Fuel:** 12.6 tons
Endurance: 5 days **Crew:** 13 tot.

Remarks: Ordered 1997. As many as five were originally planned. Have two 1,000-m^3/hr M827 diesel-driven pumps and four fire monitors (2 × 500 m^3/hr, 2 × 220 m^3/hr), plus two firehose distribution mains on the upper deck, a water curtain system, and chemical and powder fire-extinguishing systems. There are two foam generators, with articulating applicators mounted 15 m above the waterline. Can place water on fires at 200 m distance.

SERVICE CRAFT *(continued)*

♦ 1 ex-U.S. firefighting tug [YTR]

Y 51 Söndüren 1 (ex-Y 1117, ex-YTL 751)

D: 70 tons (80 fl) **S:** 8 kts **Dim:** 21.34 × 5.89 × 2.21
M: 1 diesel; 1 prop; 375 bhp **Range:** 700/8 **Crew:** 4 tot.

Remarks: Transferred in 5-54.

♦ 4 Pinar 3 class small water lighters [YW]
Bldr: Taskizak Naval Shipyard, Istanbul (In serv. ca. 1970)

Y 113 Pinar 3 Y 114 Pinar 4 Y 115 Pinar 5 Y 116 Pinar 6

Pinar 3 (Y 113) Cem D. Yaylali, 4-05

D: 300 tons **S:** 11 kts **Dim:** 33.6 × 8.5 × 1.8
M: 1 G.M. Detroit Diesel 6-71 diesel; 1 prop; 225 bhp **Cargo:** 150 tons

♦ 1 large water lighter [YW]
Bldr: Gölçük Naval Shipyard, Kocaeli (In serv. 1958)

Y 112 Pinar 2

Pinar 2 (Y 112) Paolo Marsan, 8-97

D: 1,300 tons (fl) **S:** 10 kts **Dim:** 51.0 × 8.5 × . . . **A:** None
M: 1 diesel; 1 prop; . . . bhp **Crew:** 11 tot.

♦ 1 small water lighter [YW]
Bldr: Meentzer SY, Neth. (In serv. 1938)

Y 111 Pinar 1 (ex-*Istanbul*)

D: 490 tons (fl) **S:** . . . **Dim:** . . . × . . . × . . . **M:** 1 diesel; 240 bhp

♦ 8 E-1-class cadet training craft [YXT]
Bldr: Bora Shipping Industry and Trading (Bora-Düzgit Tersanesi), Tuzla

	In serv.		In serv.
A 1531 E-1	22-7-99	A 1535 E-5	8-6-00
A 1532 E-2	22-7-99	A 1536 E-6	8-6-00
A 1533 E-3	8-6-00	A 1537 E-7	8-6-00
A 1534 E-4	8-6-00	A 1538 E-8	8-6-00

D: 93.5 tons (fl) **S:** 13 kts **Dim:** 28.80 × 6.00 × 1.20 **Electronics:** Radar: . . .
M: 2 MTU . . . diesels; 2 props; . . . bhp **Range:** 240/10 **Crew:** . . . tot.

Remarks: Ordered 12-97 for use at the Turkish Naval Academy as seamanship and navigational training boats. First unit launched 10-98, and all were to have been delivered by 8-99. The final unit was delivered in 3-00. Have aluminum hulls. Built under subcontract by Duzgit Group at Tuzla.

MINISTRY OF THE INTERIOR COAST GUARD (*Sahil Güvenlik*)

Personnel: Approx. 2,200 total (including 800 regulars and 1,400 conscripts) plus 1,050 on loan from the Navy

Aviation: Coast Guard air assets include one Maule MX-7 light fixed-wing and three CASA CN-235 maritime patrol aircraft. Three Agusta-Bell AB-206B helicopters and nine search-and-rescue configured Agusta-Bell 412 helicopters are also in service with five more ordered during 2005. The aircraft are painted white with an orange diagonal stripe.

Turkish Coast Guard AB 412 helicopter Cem D. Yaylali, 5-05

PATROL SHIPS [WPS]

♦ 0 (+ 4) new construction ocean rescue and patrol ships
Bldr: 1st unit: . . . .; others: Taskizak Naval Shipyard, Istanbul

D: 1,490 tons (fl) **S:** 22 kts (20 sust.)
Dim: 84.70 (79.80 pp) × 11.85 (10.80 wl) × 3.40 hull
A: 1 40-mm 70-cal Bofors AA; 2 single 12.7-mm mg
Electronics: Radar: 1 . . . nav.; 1 . . . surf./air search
M: 4 MTU 12V1163 TB93 diesels; 2 props; 11,534 bhp
Electric: 1300 kw tot. (2 × 600 kw, 1 × 100 kw emergency diesel sets)
Range: 3,000/15 **Fuel:** 158 tons diesel; 10 tons aviation **Endurance:** 10 days
Crew: 64 tot. (accomm. for 77 tot.)

Remarks: Two designs are under consideration, one from Italy's Fincantieri and the other from Peenewerft GmbH, Germany. Data for the German Type OPV 1400 SAR offering are given here. A helicopter deck will be fitted.

PATROL CRAFT [WPC]

♦ 12 SG 80 class
Bldr: Taskizak Naval Shipyard, Istanbul

	L	In serv.		L	In serv.
SG 80	3-6-94	6-96	SG 86	. . .	8-6-00
SG 81	3-6-94	5-7-96	SG 87	. . .	8-6-00
SG 82	20-4-95	5-97	SG 88	. . .	8-6-00
SG 83	20-4-95	5-97	SG 89	. . .	8-6-00
SG 84	5-7-96	1998	SG 90	. . .	25-7-02
SG 85	5-7-96	1998	SG 91	. . .	25-7-02

SG 90 Cem D. Yaylali, 10-03

D: 182.4 tons (195 fl) **S:** 27 kts (25 sust.) **Dim:** 40.75 (37.00 pp) × 7.05 × 2.13
A: 1 40-mm 70-cal. Bofors L70 AA; 2 single 12.7-mm mg
Electronics: Radar: 1 Decca . . . nav.
M: 2 MTU . . . diesels; 2 props; 5,700 bhp (5,040 sust.)
Range: . . . / . . . **Crew:** 24 tot.

Remarks: Designed by Taskizak Naval Dockyard with assistance from the Technical University of Istanbul. Have a more conventional hull form than the SG 71 and SAR-33 classes. A firefighting water monitor is mounted aft.

♦ 4 SG 71 class
Bldr: Taskizak Naval Shipyard, Istanbul

SG 71 (In serv.: 25-7-85) SG 73 (L: . . .)
SG 72 (L: 25-7-85) SG 74 (L: 24-7-87)

D: 210 tons (fl) **S:** 40 kts (35 sust.) **Dim:** 36.60 × 8.60 × 1.90
A: 1 40-mm 60-cal. Bofors Mk 3 AA; 2 single 7.62-mm mg
Electronics: Radar: 1 Decca TM 1226 nav.
M: 3 SACM (UNI) AGO 195 V16 CSHR diesels; 3 CP props; 12,000 bhp (7,200 sust.)
Range: 450/35; 1,000/20 **Crew:** 24 tot.

Remarks: Lengthened version of SAR-33 class, with longer superstructure. Bury bows at higher speeds and are not considered a success. The pilothouse windows slope forward on SG 71, backward on SG 74.

COAST GUARD PATROL CRAFT [WPC] *(continued)*

SG 71 Cem D. Yaylali, 8-00

♦ 10 SAR-33 class
Bldrs: SG 61: Abeking & Rasmussen, Lemwerder, Germany; others: Taskizak Naval Shipyard, Istanbul (In serv. 1978–84)

SG 61 through SG 70 (ex-J 61 through J 70)

SG 65 Cem D. Yaylali, 6-04

SG 67 Martin Mokrus, 5-04

D: 150 tons (170 fl) **S:** 40 kts **Dim:** 33.00 (29.50 wl) × 8.60 × 1.85
A: 1 40-mm 60-cal. Bofors Mk 3 AA; 2 single 76.2-mm mg
Electronics: Radar: 1 Decca TM 1226 nav.
M: 3 SACM-AGO 195 V16 CSHR diesels; 3 CP props; 12,000 bhp (7,200 sust.)
Electric: 300 kw tot. **Range:** 450/35; 1,000/20 **Fuel:** 18 tons **Crew:** 23 tot.

Remarks: SG 61 was launched on 12-12-77 and SG 62 in 7-78; SG 65 through SG 67 in service 30-7-81. Wedge-shaped hull design of remarkable seaworthiness and steadiness at high speeds in heavy weather. Turkey was also to have built 14 units of this class for Libya, but the contract was canceled circa 1986.

♦ 14 AB 25 class
Bldr: Taskizak Naval Shipyard, Istanbul (In serv. 1972–78)

SG 121 through SG 134 (ex-SG 21 through SG 34)

SG 134 Cem D. Yaylali, 6-04

D: 170 tons (fl) **S:** 22 kts **Dim:** 40.24 × 6.4 × 1.65
A: 2 single 40-mm Bofors Mk 3 AA; 1 20-mm 70-cal. Oerlikon Mk 10 AA or 2 single 12.7-mm mg
Electronics: Radar: 1 Decca TM 1226 nav.
M: 2 SACM-AGO 195 V16 CSHR diesels; 2 props; 4,800 bhp—2 cruise diesels; 300 bhp
Crew: 25 tot.

Remarks: Eleven sisters are operated by the Turkish Navy and one each by Azerbaijan, Georgia, and Kazakhstan. Built with French technical assistance. SG 30 through SG 34 are of the later variant with lower hull knuckle and low bulwarks at the bow to improve seaworthiness; they have two mg on platforms at the aft end of the superstructure, while the earlier units have a single 20-mm AA abaft the mast. 100 was added to the pennant numbers during 2002.

PATROL BOATS [WPB]

♦ 1 MRTP 33 class
Bldr: Yonca Technical Investment Co. and Onuk Vehicle Ltd., Tuzla (In serv. 7-04)

SG 301

D: 124 tons (fl) **S:** 43 kts **Dim:** 35.6 × 6.7 × 1.4 **A:** 1 20-mm AA; 1 12.7-mm mg
Electronics: Radar: 1 . . . nav.
M: 2 MTU 16V4000 M90 diesels; 2 MJP 750 waterjets; 7,300 bhp **Range:** 650/20

♦ 10 MRTP 29 class
Bldr: Yonca Technical Investment Co. and Onuk Vehicle Ltd., Tuzla (In serv. 9-98 to 8-6-00)

SG 101 through SG 110

SG 107 Martin Mokrus, 5-05

D: 90 tons (fl) **S:** 45 kts **Dim:** 29.6 × 6.3 × 1.5 **A:** 2 single 12.7-mm mg
Electronics: Radar: 1 . . . nav.
M: 2 MTU 16V4000 M90 diesels; 2 MJP 750 waterjets; 7,300 bhp **Range:** 750/30
Crew: 3 officers, 8 enlisted + 7 passengers

Remarks: Also known as the Onur class; builder's Sea Guard design. Ordered for $56 million in 5-99, with all to be delivered during 2000, but SG 103–105 were not commissioned until 25-7-02, with SG 106–110 following later. Hull built of composite materials, with replaceable armor plating, was meant also to carry a 20-mm or 30-mm gun forward, but it has not yet been mounted. Low-observable design by Kaan NZ Onuk, with noise-, electronic-, and heat-reduction measures. Also offered with an AlliedSignal TF-series gas turbine on a centerline waterjet for 55-kt maximum speeds.

♦ 7 KW 15 class
Bldr: Schweers, Bardenfleth (In serv. 1961–62)

SG 113–SG 116 and SG 118–SSG 120

SG 115 Frank Findler, 3-04

D: 70 tons (fl) **S:** 25 kts **Dim:** 28.9 × 4.7 × 1.4
A: 1 40-mm AA; 1 twin 20-mm AA
Electronics: Radar: 1 Decca nav.
M: 2 MTU 12V . . . diesels; 2 props; 2,000 bhp **Range:** 1,500/19
Crew: 15 total

COAST GUARD PATROL BOATS [WPB] *(continued)*

Remarks: Sister SG 112 was retired during 2004. Erroneously reported as having been stricken in previous editions.

♦ 4 U.S. 27-ft. Vigilant-class patrol launches
Bldr: Boston Whaler, Edgewater, Fla. (In serv. 9-99)

Remarks: Foam-core GRP hull construction; claimed to be unsinkable. Powered by twin 250-bhp Mercury gasoline outboard motors for speeds greater than 50 kts.

♦ 18 MRTP 15 class
Bldr: Yonca Technical Investment Co., Tuzla (In serv. 1998–2004)

SG 1 through SG 18

SG 11 Cem D. Yaylali, 5-05

D: 19 tons (fl) **S:** 54 kts **Dim:** 15.40 × 4.04 × 0.92 **A:** Small arms
Electronics: Radar: 1 Raytheon . . . nav.
M: 2 MTU 12V183 TE93 diesels; 2 props; 2,300 bhp
Range: 300/40 **Crew:** 2 tot.

Remarks: Have GPS receiver and an echo sounder. SG 4 made 53.7 kts on trials.

♦ 10 14.6-m class
Bldr: Gölçük Naval Shipyard, Kocaeli, and Taskizak Naval Shipyard, Istanbul

SG 50 through SG 59

SG 59 Cem D. Yaylali, 5-05

D: 25 tons (29 fl) **S:** 18 kts (15 sust.) **Dim:** 14.6 × 3.5 × 1.1 **A:** 1 12.7-mm mg
Electronics: Radar: 1 Raytheon. . . nav.
M: 2 diesels; 2 props; 700 bhp **Crew:** 7 tot.

Remarks: First three completed 20-7-90 by Taskizak, three others in 7-91. Four delivered 23-7-92 by Gölçük Naval Shipyard. SG 102 and SG 103 are no longer in service.

♦ 1 SG 42–class harbor patrol boat
Bldr: . . .

SG 42 (ex-SG 2)

D: 15 tons (fl) **S:** 18 kts **Dim:** 14.5 × 4.4 × 0.7 **A:** Small arms
Electronics: Radar: 1 . . . nav. **M:** 2 diesels; 2 props; 700 bhp **Crew:** 7 tot.

Remarks: GRP-hulled cabin cruiser, as is SG 41, in the following entry.

♦ 1 SG 41–class harbor patrol boat
Bldr: . . .

SG 41 (ex-SG 1)

D: 35 tons (fl) **S:** 20 kts **Dim:** 17.0 × 5.0 × 1.0 **A:** Small arms
Electronics: Radar: 1 . . . nav. **M:** 2 diesels; 2 props; 1,050 bhp **Crew:** 7 tot.

Note: Also in service are a number of 5.8-meter RIBs.

TURKMENISTAN

Personnel: Approx. 700 tot.

Bases: All craft are based at Türkmenbashy.

Organizations: Organized in a division of patrol "ships," one seagoing minesweeper, and two air-cushion landing craft.

PATROL BOATS [PB]

♦ 10 Kalkan-M class
Bldr: More Zavod, Feodosiya, Ukraine (In serv. 2002–3)

D: 8.6 tons (fl) **S:** 30 kts **Dim:** 11.6 × 3.3 × 0.6
A: 2 single 7.62 or 12.7-mm mg; 1 BP-30 grenade launcher
M: 1 Volvo TAMD122P diesel **Range:** 270/34

Remarks: Three were ordered early in 2002 for offshore oilfield protection duties; additional units were ordered later. Said to cost $400,000–425,000 each.

♦ 2 ex-Russian Zhuk (Gryf) class (Project 1400)
Bldr: Morye (ex-Yuzhnaya Tochka) Zavod, Feodosiya (In serv. 1970s)

. . . . . .

D: 35.9 tons (39.7 fl) **S:** 35 kts
Dim: 23.80 (21.70 wl) × 5.00 (3.80 wl) × 1.00 (hull; 1.90 max.)
A: 1 twin 14.5-mm; 1 single 12.7-mm mg **Electronics:** Radar: 1 Lotsiya nav.
M: 2 . . . diesels; 2 props; 2,200 bhp
Electric: . . . **Range:** 500/13.5
Endurance: 5 days **Crew:** 1 officer, 9 enlisted

Remarks: Transferred from the Ukraine during 6-04. Additional units may follow. Aluminum alloy hull. Capable of operating in up to Sea State 4 or 5. Range also reported as 700 n.m. at 28 knots, 1,100 n.m. at 15 kts.

♦ 1 ex-U.S. Coast Guard 82-ft Point class
Bldr: Coast Guard Yard, Curtis Bay, Md. (In serv. 3-8-70)

PB-129 Merjen (ex-*Point Jackson,* WPB 82378)

D: 64 tons (66-69 fl) **S:** 22.6 kts **Dim:** 25.3 × 5.23 × 1.95
A: 2 single 12.7-mm M2 mg
Electronics: Radar: 1 Hughes-Furuno SPS-73 nav.
M: 2 Caterpillar 3412 diesels; 2 props; 1,480 bhp
Range: 320/22.6; 1,200/8 **Fuel:** 5.7 tons **Crew:** 8–10 tot.

Remarks: Transferred after striking on 30-5-00. Hull built of mild steel. High-speed diesels controlled from the bridge. Well equipped for salvage and towing. Is equipped with 4.27 m Avon Searider rigid-inflatable boats powered by a 40 bhp outboard engine.

Notes: Several other patrol boats (some referred to as ships) are said to be in service; class and total unknown. All Skat- (NATO "Gus") class air-cushion personnel landing craft (Project 1205) have been retired from service by 2005.

TURKS AND CAICOS

British Colony

POLICE

Base: Cockburn Harbor, Grand Turk

PATROL BOATS [WPB]

♦ 1 M 160 class Bldr: Halmatic, Havant, U.K. (In serv. 9-89)

Sea Quest

Sea Quest Maritime Photographic, 1-94

PATROL BOATS [WPB] *(continued)*

D: 17.3 tons (fl) **S:** 27+ kts **Dim:** 15.40 (12.20 pp) × 3.86 × 1.15
A: 1 7.62-mm mg **Electronics:** Radar: 1 Decca 370BT nav.
M: 2 G.M. Detroit Diesel 6V92 TA diesels; 2 props; 1,100 bhp (770 sust.)
Range: 300/20; 500/17 **Fuel:** 2,700 liters **Crew:** 8 tot.

Remarks: Sister to Virgin Islands' *Ursula.* Carries rigid inflatable inspection dinghy aft.

♦ **1 Dagger class**
Bldr: Fairey Marine, Cowes, U.K. (In serv. 6-86)

SEA HAWK

Sea Hawk Maritime Photographic, 1-94

D: 8 tons light (12 fl) **S:** 24 kts **Dim:** 12.2 × 3.4 × 1.1 **A:** 1 7.62-mm mg
Electronics: Radar: 1 Decca 370BT nav.
M: 2 Perkins T6.3544M diesels; 2 props; 440 bhp (330 sust.)
Range: 540/20 **Crew:** 6 tot.

Remarks: GRP construction.

TUVALU

TUVALU POLICE FORCE MARITIME WING

Personnel: Approx. 30 total

Base: Funafuti

Note: Craft names are preceded by HMTSS—Her Majesty's Tuvalu Surveillance Ship.

PATROL CRAFT [WPC]

♦ **1 ASI 315 class**
Bldr: Transfield-ASI, South Coogie, West Australia (In serv. 8-10-94)

801 TE MATAELI

Te Mataeli (801) H&L Van Ginderen, 7-94

D: 165 tons (fl) **S:** 21 kts (20 sust.)
Dim: 31.50 (28.60 wl) × 8.10 × 2.12 (1.80 hull) **A:** Small arms
Electronics: Radar: 1 Furuno 1011 nav.
M: 2 Caterpillar 3516 diesels; 2 props; 2,820 bhp (2,400 sust.) **Range:** 2,500/12
Fuel: 27.9 tons **Endurance:** 8–10 days
Electric: 116 kw (2 × 50 kw; Caterpillar 3304 diesels; 1 × 16 kw)
Crew: 3 officers, 14 enlisted

Remarks: Australian foreign aid program "Pacific Patrol Boat," with many sisters in a number of Southwest Pacific–area island nation forces. Ordered late 1992. Name means "Knowledge-That-Brings-You-Home." Carries a 5-m aluminum boarding boat. Extensive navigational suite, including Furuno FSN-70 NAVSAT receiver, 525 HF/DF, 120 MF/HFD/F, FE-881 echo sounder, and DS-70 doppler log. Expected to undergo modernization and refit during 2011 to remain in service through 2024.

UGANDA

ARMY MARINE UNIT

Personnel: Approx. 400 total, operated largely as a paramilitary naval infantry force

Bases: Headquarters at Fort Bell, Entebbe. Minor facilities at Bukakata, Gaba, Jinja, Majinji, and Sese, all on Lake Victoria.

Notes: Operations by the Ugandan Army Marine Unit on Lake Victoria were said to be at a standstill by 9-99 due to the heavy growth of hibiscus plants in the lake. The three Yugoslav Type AL8K aluminum launches were no longer operational. Some 14 GRP-hulled craft armed with one 78.62-mm mg and powered by gasoline outboard motors may still be available, in storage; these were built by FB Marine, Italy.

UKRAINE

NAVY

Personnel: Approx. 13,500 total, including 3,000 naval infantry and up to 2,500 naval aviation personnel

Bases: Principal naval bases are located at Sevastopil (Sevastopol'), Odesa (Odessa), Donuzlav, and Kerch'. Construction and repair yards are located at Balaklava and Nikolaev.

Naval Aviation: 11 Be-12 ASW amphibians and up to 28 Ka-25 Hormone and Ka-27 Helix-series helicopters. Several An-12 Cub surveillance aircraft may also remain in service.

Note: In 1997 Ukraine and Russia signed a lease agreement that spelled out a division of the former Soviet Black Sea fleet while charging Russia an allual fee (currently approximately $98 million) for continued use of several Black Sea naval bases through 2017.

ATTACK SUBMARINES [SS]

♦ **1 Foxtrot class (Project 641K)**
Bldr: Novo Admiralteiskiye Verfi 196 (Sudomekh Division), St. Petersburg, Russia

	Laid down	L	In serv.
U 01 ZAPORIZHZHYA (ex-B-435)	24-3-70	29-5-70	6-11-70

Zaporizhzhya (U 01) Hartmut Ehlers, 8-00

D: 1,957 tons (surf.)/2,485 tons (sub.) **S:** 15.5 kts (surf.)/18 kts (sub.)
Dim: 91.30 (89.70 wl) × 7.50 × 6.06 (surf.)
A: 10 533-mm TT (6 fwd, 4 aft—14 torpedoes or 28 AMD-1000 mines)
Electronics:
Radar: 1 MRK-50 Albatros (Snoop Tray-1) nav./search
Sonar: MG-15 Herkules active; MG-100 Arktika MF active target tracking (13-16 kHz); MG-10 Feniks-M passive array
EW: 1 Stop Light intercept; Quad Loop D/F
M: 3 Type 2D-42M diesels (1,825 bhp each), 3 electric motors (1 × 2,700 shp, 2 × 1,350 shp); 3 6-bladed props; 5,400 shp (sub.)—1 100-shp low-speed electric "creep" motor on centerline shaft
Range: 4,153/16.6 (surf.); 20,000/8 (surf.); 11,500/8 (snorkel); 36/18 (sub.); 380/2 (sub.)
Fuel: 360 tons **Endurance:** 70 days **Crew:** 12 officers, 70 enlisted

ATTACK SUBMARINES [SS] *(continued)*

Remarks: U 01 was transferred and recommissioned on 1-8-97 but had not been to sea since 1995. Completed a minor refit in 8-00. Was again operational by 2003, having had outer hull plating renewed at Balaklava, hydraulics systems overhauled and a new battery set provided from Greece.
Hull systems: Four 112-cell battery groups. Can dive in as little as 45–60 seconds and has 527 tons reserve buoyancy in surfaced condition. The pressure hull has seven watertight compartments. Operating depth is 250 m; 280 m maximum. Crew size listed is maximum accommodations. One authoritative source gives the range as 30,000 n.m. at 8 kts on the surface or 17,900 n.m. at 8 kts on snorkel; this may be achievable by employing some ballast tankage for fuel stowage.
Combat systems: Uses the Leningrad mechanical analog torpedo fire-control system. Original combat load was 22 torpedoes, with eight aft; in recent years, however, the stern tubes have been loaded with countermeasures devices, and berths have replaced the reload racks in the after torpedo room. Most of the combat systems were inoperative at time of transfer.

GUIDED-MISSILE CRUISERS [CG]

Note: President Leonid Kuchma offered the incomplete *Slava* (Atlant)-class guided-missile cruiser *Ukrayina* (ex-*Admiral Flota Lobov,* ex-*Ukrayina,* ex-*Vilna Ukrayina,* ex-*Bohdan Khmenytsky,* ex-*Poltava,* ex-*Admiral Flota Lobov,* ex-*Komsomolets*) to Russia on 28-9-01, and the offer was tentatively accepted a week later only to be rejected during 1-02; work on the ship had ceased during 8-00 for lack of funds, and it was also stated that the Russians would not provide the 16 P-500 cruise missiles that were to constitute the ship's principal armament. As an alternative armament, Russia has offered to sell 3M54E Klub or Yakhont missiles for use on the ship, but it now seems likely that the *Ukrayina* will remain uncompleted. One offer to sell the ship to China during 6-02 was rejected.

FRIGATES [FF]

♦ 1 Russian Krivak-III class (Project 11351)
Bldr: Kamysh-Burun Zavod 532, Kerch'

	Laid down	L	In serv.
U 130 HETMAN SAHAYDACHNIY (ex-*Poltava,* ex-*Latsis,* ex-*Kirov*)	9-7-91	29-3-92	11-7-93

Hetman Sahaydachniy (U 130) Hartmut Ehlers, 7-00

D: 3,274 tons std., 3,458 tons normal (3,642 fl; 3,774 max.) **S:** 31 kts (30 sust.)
Dim: 122.98 (113.00 pp) × 14.20 (13.2 wl) × 4.72 hull (7.20 over sonar dome)
A: 1 twin-rail Osa-MA (SA-N-4) SAM syst. (20 9M-33/Gecko missiles); 1 100-mm 59-cal. AK-100 DP (600 rounds); 2 single 30-mm 54-cal. AK-630M gatling AA (12,000 rounds); 1 . . . grenade launcher; 2 12-round RBU-6000 ASW RL (96 RGB-60 rockets); 2 quadruple 533-mm UTA-53-1135 TT (4 SET-65 and 4 53-65K torpedoes); 1 Ka-25 Hormone or Ka-27 Helix helicopter; 2 mine rails (12–16 mines)
Electronics:
Radar: 1 MR-212/201 Vaygach-U (Palm Frond) nav.; 1 Volga (Don-Kay) nav.; 1 Nayada-2 helicopter control; 1 MR-760 Fregat-MA (Top Plate) 3-D air search; 1 MPZ-301 (Pop Group) SAM f.c.; 1 MR-114 Bars (Kite Screech-A) 100-mm f.c.; 1 MR-123 Vympel (Bass Tilt) 30-mm f.c.
Sonar: MGK-332MC Titan-2 (Bull Nose) hull-mounted MF; MG-325 Vega (Mare Tail) MF VDS; MG-26 underwater telephone
EW: Smerch suite: 2 Start-2 (Bell Shroud) intercept; 2 MP-401 Start (Bell Squat A/B) jammers; 4 16-round PK-16 fixed decoy RL (128 rockets); 2 towed torpedo decoys; 3 sets corner-reflector decoys
M: COGAG M-7 plant: 2 M62 cruise gas turbines (7,475 shp each), 2 M8K boost gas turbines (20,000 shp each); 2 props; 54,950 shp tot.
Electric: 2,500 kw tot. (5 × 500 kw diesel sets) **Range:** 1,146/30; 3,636/14
Fuel: . . . tons + 22 tons aviation fuel **Endurance:** 30 days
Crew: 18 officers, 162 warrant officers and enlisted

Remarks: Revised version of basic Krivak design for Soviet KGB Maritime Border Guard service in the Far East, where the first six now serve. U 130, the seventh unit, originally to have been named *Kirov* (and then *Latsis* after the 1991 revolution), was taken over by Ukraine and began trials, operating from Sevastopil in mid-3-93. Named for a Cossack Hetman who led incursions into Crimea and Turkey during the 18th century. The eighth, begun as the *Krasniy Vympel'* (later *Berzin,* and then *Zaliv*) was to be completed for Ukraine as the *Hetman Bayda Vyshnevetskiy* (U 131), but construction was canceled 2-96.
Combat systems: The combat system is designated Sapfir-U7; the ASW weapons control system name is Purga; and the communications suite is called Tayfun-3. The addition of a helicopter facility (with simple deck-transit system) and helicopter weapons reload magazines cost two gun mounts and one SAM position aft, while the Krivak-I/II SS-N-14 dual-purpose missile system was replaced by a 100-mm gun, more useful for the patrol mission of these ships. Two six-barreled gatling guns were added to improve close-in defense. The Nayada-2 radar mounted atop the helicopter hangar is intended to serve in landing control.

Hetman Sahaydachniy (U 130) Boris Lemachko, 2000

♦ 1 ex-Russian Krivak-II (Burevestnik-M) class (Project 1135M)
Bldr: Yantar Zavod 820, Kaliningrad, Kaliningradskiy Oblast

	Laid down	L	In serv.
U 132 SEVASTOPOL' (ex-*Razitel'nyy*)	11-2-75	1-7-76	31-12-76

Sevastopol' (U 132)—alongside Krivak-III-class frigate ***Hetman Sahaydachniy*** **(U 130)** JLC & DV via Paolo Marsan, 8-03

D: 2,945-3,075 tons; 3,305 normal (3,505 max. fl) **S:** 30.6 kts
Dim: 123.10 (113.00 wl) × 14.20 (13.2 wl) × 4.57 mean hull (7.3 over sonar dome)
A: 4 URK-5 Metel' (SS-N-14 Silex) SSM KT-106 launcher; 8 Type 83R and 83RUS Metel' missiles); 2 twin-rail Osa-M (SA-N-4) SAM systems (40 9M-33/Gecko missiles); 2 single 100-mm 59-cal. AK-100 DP (1,200 rounds); 2 12-round RBU-6000 ASW RL (144 RGB-60 rockets); 2 quadruple 533-mm UTA-53-1135 TT (4 SET-65 and 4 53-65K torpedoes); 2 mine rails (12–16 mines)
Electronics:
Radar: 1 MR-212/201 Vaygach-U (Palm Frond) nav.; 1 Don-2 nav.; 1 MR-310U Angara-M (Head Net-C) air search; 2 . . . Drakon (Eye Bowl) SSM f.c.; 2 MPZ-301 Baza (Pop Group) SA-N-4 f.c.; 1 MR-114 Lev (Kite Screech-A) 100-mm f.c.
Sonar: MGK-332MC Titan-2 (Bull Nose) hull-mounted MF; MG-325 Vega (Mare Tail) MF VDS; MG-26 underwater telephone
EW: Smerch suite: 2 Start-2 (Bell Shroud) intercept; 2 MP-401 Start (Bell Squat A/B) jammers; 4 16-round PK-16 fixed decoy RL (128 rockets); 2 towed torpedo decoys; 3 sets corner-reflector decoys

FRIGATES [FF] *(continued)*

M: COGAG M-7 plant: 2 M62 cruise gas turbines (7,475 shp each), 2 M8K boost gas turbines (20,000 shp each); 2 props; 54,950 shp tot.
Electric: 3,000 kw tot. (5 × 600 kw diesel sets) **Range:** 640/30; 4,000/14
Endurance: 30 days
Crew: 23 officers, 28 warrant officers, 130 enlisted (accomm. for 194 tot.)

Remarks: Stricken from the Black Sea Fleet on 10-1-96 and was to be transferred from the Black Sea Fleet on 1-4-96, but was withheld for a period; she was recommissioned on 24-8-97 and was in overhaul at Sevastopil during 1998–2001, with the engines removed and transferred to the Russian *Kara*-class destroyer *Kerch'*.
Hull systems: There are 14 watertight compartments. The superstructure is built of aluminum-magnesium alloy, welded to the hull via bimetallic inserts. Type UKA-135 fin stabilizers are fitted. The propulsion plant originally delivered 45,570 shp normal/51,200 shp max. total (with the cruise turbines operating at 6,000 shp each and the boost turbines at 18,000 each), but the output was later increased. Hull block coefficient is 0.46, very fine for this type of vessel. For slow speeds, any one of the engines can drive both propellers. Has UKA-135 fin stabilizers and a single rudder. Was designed to be 2,735 tons standard, 3,100 tons full load, but one source reports that displacements have grown to 3,075 tons standard and 3,575 tons full load.
Combat systems: The combat system is known as Planshet-35. The chaff/decoy rocket launchers were moved from the stern to the 01 level, abreast the aft SA-N-4 launcher. Can carry 12 KSM, 14 KRAB, or 16 IGDM-500 mines. The ASW weapons control system name is Purga. The antenna for the MR-310U air-search radar has been removed.

Disposal note: Krivak-I-class (Project 1135) frigates *Mikolayiv* (U 133, ex-*Bezukoriznennyy*) was towed from Sevastopil for scrapping during 8-01, and *Dnipropetrovsk* (U 134, ex-*Bezzavetnyy*) was stricken in 2003, though some reports indicate she may be undergoing overhaul at a Black Sea shipyard.

CORVETTES [FFL]

♦ 2 Grisha-V class (Project 1124EhM)
Bldr: Leninskaya Kuznitsa SY, Kiyiv

	L	In serv.
U 200 LUTSK	22-5-93	12-2-94
U 202 TERNOPIL	20-3-02	2004

Lutsk (U 200) Boris Lemachko Collection, 6-03

Lutsk (U 200) Cem D. Yaylali, 9-03

D: 876 tons light, 930 tons std. (1,070 fl)
S: 32 kts (21 kts on gas turbine; 16 kts on diesels)
Dim: 71.20 (66.90 wl) × 10.15 (9.50 wl) × 3.72 hull
A: 1 2-round Osa-M (SA-N-4) SAM system (20 9M-33/Gecko missiles); 1 76.2-mm 59-cal. AK-176 DP; 1 30-mm 54-cal. AK-630M gatling AA; 2 4-round Fasta-4M (SA-N-8) SAM syst. (20–24 Strela-3/Gremlin shoulder-launched missiles); 2 twin 533-mm TT; 1 12-round RBU-6000 ASW RL (48 RGB-60 rockets); 2 d.c. racks (6 d.c. each) or up to 18 mines on the two mine rails
Electronics:
Radar: 1 MR-312 Nayada nav.; 1 MR-755 Topaz-2B (Half Plate-B) surf./air search; 1 MPZ-301 Baza (Pop Group) SA-N-4 f.c.; 1 MR-123 Vympel (Bass Tilt) gun f.c.
Sonar: MGK-335MC Platina (Bull Horn) hull-mounted (3 kHz); Shelon' (Elk Tail) dipping (7.5 kHz)
EW: 2 Bizan'-4B (Watch Dog) intercept (2-18 GHz); 2 16-round PK-16 decoy RL; 4 10-round PK-10 decoy RL; 4 Spektr-F (Half Cup) infrared detectors
M: CODAG: 1 M8M (M-88) gas turbine (18,000 shp), 2 Type M-507A diesels (10,000 bhp each); 3 props; 38,000 hp—2 maneuvering propellers
Electric: 1,000 kw tot. (1 × 500 kw, 1 × 300 kw, 1 × 200 kw diesel sets)
Range: 950/27; on diesels alone: 2,500/14; 4,000/10 **Fuel:** 143 tons
Endurance: 9 days **Crew:** 9 officers, 77 enlisted

Remarks: U 200 was taken over while under construction. Announced 1993 that four more would be built, but work on *Ternopil* (U 202) was temporarily halted in 1995, while work on the other two never commenced. The *Lutsk* was overhauled at Mikolayiv from 9-00 to 5-01.
Hull systems: There are two retracting harbor-maneuvering propulsors at the extreme stern. Carries 10.5 tons of lube oil and 27.2 tons fresh water. Maximum propeller r.p.m. is 585 on the diesels.
Combat systems: Just abaft the mast is a Rakurs (Kolonka-2) backup ringsight director for the 30-mm gun. Carries 304 rounds 76-mm and 2,000 rounds 30-mm ammunition. The torpedo tubes have been modified to launch wire-guided torpedoes. The dipping sonar is housed in the after superstructure, lowering through the hull between the starboard and centerline propeller shafts. U 200 has all of the improvements fitted to late-construction examples of the class in the Russian Navy.

♦ 2 ex-Russian Grisha-II class (Project 1124A)
Bldr: Zelenodol'sk Zavod, Kazan, Russia

	Laid down	L	In serv.
U 205 CHERNIGIV (ex-*Izmail*)	12-9-78	22-6-80	28-12-80
U 206 VINNITSYA (ex-*Dnepr*)	17-6-76	12-9-76	31-12-76

Vinnitsya (U 206) Hartmut Ehlers, 8-00

Vinnitsya (U 206) Hartmut Ehlers, 8-00

D: 830 tons (990 fl) **S:** 35 kts **Dim:** 71.10 (66.90 wl) × 10.15 (9.50 wl) × 3.45 hull
A: 2 twin 57-mm AK-257 DP; 2 12-round RBU-6000 ASW RL (96 RGB-60 rockets); 2 twin 533-mm TT; 2 d.c. racks (6 d.c. each) or mines
Electronics:
Radar: 1 Don-2 nav.; 1 MR-302 Rubka (Strut Curve) surf./air search; 1 MR-103 Bars (Muff Cob) f.c.
Sonar: MGK-355M Argun' (Bull Nose) hull-mounted (3 kHz); Shelon' (Elk Tail) through-hull dipping (7.5 kHz)
EW: 2 Bizan'-4B (Watch Dog) intercept (2-18 GHz)
M: CODAG: 1 M8M (M-813) gas turbine (18,000 shp), 2 M-507A diesels (10,000 bhp each); 3 props; 38,000 hp; 2 maneuvering propellers
Electric: 1,000 kw (1 × 500 kw, 1 × 300 kw, 1 × 200 kw diesel sets)
Range: 950/27; 2,750/14; 4,000/10 **Fuel:** 130 tons + 13 tons overload
Endurance: 18 days **Crew:** 60 tot. (79 accomm.)

Remarks: Stricken from the Russian Federal Border Guard on 26-11-92 and transferred to Ukraine Maritime Border Guard on 5-7-94. Further transferred to Ukraine Navy in 1-96 and renamed. U 205 was to be stricken post-9-00 but remained in commission as of 2006.
Hull systems: An official source states that the unsupported endurance is twice that of the former naval units of the Grisha series. Fin stabilizers are fitted.
Combat systems: A second twin 57-mm was substituted for Osa-M SAM system forward; the ships can carry 2,200 rounds of 57-mm ammunition.

Disposal note: Grisha-III-class corvette *Herson* (U 210, ex-MPK 52) began scrapping at Donuslav early in 2001; the reported sister *Odessa* (U 204) evidently did not exist. Grisha-I-class (Project 1124) corvette *Sumi* (U 209, ex-MPK-43) was scrapped at Il'ychevsk beginning in 7-00. Ex-Russian Petya-III (Project 159AE) corvette U 132 was scrapped at Inkerman in 8-96. Petya-II (Project 159A) SKR-112, which defected to Ukraine at Odesa on 21-7-92 and was taken over as the first combatant ship in the new Ukrainian Navy (as U 131) was decommissioned to become a memorial at Odesa on 6-4-93.

HYDROFOIL GUIDED MISSILE PATROL CRAFT (PTGH)

♦ 2 Ex-Russian Matka (Vikhr')-class (Project 206MR) semi-hydrofoils
Bldr: Sudostroitel'noye Obyedineniye "Almaz" (Sredniy Neva), Kolpino (In serv. 1979–81)

U 153 PRYLUKY (ex-R-262)
U 154 KAKHOVKA (ex-R-265)

HYDROFOIL GUIDED MISSILE PATROL CRAFT (PTGH) *(continued)*

Kakhovka (U 154) Boris Lemachko, 1998

D: 233 tons (258 fl, 268 max.) **S:** 42 kts
Dim: 38.60 (37.50 wl) × 12.5 (7.6 hull; 5.9 wl) × 2.10 (hull; 3.26 foils)
A: 2 P-15M Termit (SS-N-2C Styx) SSM; 1 76.2-mm 59-cal. AK-176M DP; 1 30-mm 54-cal. AK-630 gatling AA; . . . SA-14/16 shoulder-launched SAMs
Electronics:
Radar: 1 . . . nav.; 1 Garpun (Plank Shave) target detection/tracking; 1 MR-123 Vympel'-AM (Bass Tilt) gun f.c.
EW: No intercept equipment; 2 16-round PK-16 decoy RL
M: 3 M-520TM5 diesels; 3 props; 14,400 bhp
Electric: 300 kw tot. (1 × 100 kw DGF2A-100/1500 and 1 × 200 kw DRGA-2A-200/1500 diesel sets; 380 V, 50-Hz a.c.)
Range: 600/35; 1,200/22–24; 1,800/11–12 **Fuel:** 38 tons max. overload
Endurance: 8 days **Crew:** 25–28 tot.

Remarks: Essentially a missile-armed version of the Turya-class hydrofoil torpedo boat, with larger superstructure, 76.2-mm gun forward, and missiles and gatling gun aft. Three were stricken from the Black Sea Fleet on 10-1-96 and transferred to Ukraine on the same date.
Hull systems: Steel hull with aluminum/magnesium alloy superstructure. The stern planes on the surface while the bow is supported by the hydrofoils at high speeds. To improve the ride, both the foils and the transom stern flap are remotely controlled via a Baza 02065 gyro system. In colder waters (below 25° C), the craft can make 43–45 kts on foil.
Combat systems: The original Cheese Cake navigational radars (so called because of their flat-topped cylindrical radomes) has been replaced by a small slotted-waveguide set. Positions for EW intercept antennas remain empty. Can employ weapons in Sea State 6. Carry 152 rds 76.2-mm and 2,000 rds 30-mm ammunition. They have SPO-3 radiation-warning equipment and the R-784 automated radio system.
Disposals: *Konotop* (U 150, ex-R-15) was transferred and recommissioned on 12-8-97 but by late 1998 was inactive at Sevastopil and was transferred to Georgia in 1998; *Tsyurupynsk* (U 151, ex-R-251) was donated to a youth training school at the end of 2001 for use as a stationary training device. *Uman'* (U 152, ex-R-260) was no longer in service as of 2002.

GUIDED-MISSILE PATROL CRAFT [PTG]

♦ 1 Tarantul-III (Molnaya) class (Project 1241.1RZ)
Bldrs: Sudostroitel'noye Obyedineniye "Almaz," Petrovskiy SY, St. Petersburg, or Sredniy Neva SY Kolpino

U 156 PRIDNIPROV'IYA (ex-*Kremenchuk,* ex-Russian R-63, ex-*Kuybyshevskiy Komsomoletsv*)

D: 436 tons light (493 fl) **S:** 38 kts (41 kts light)
Dim: 56.10 (49.50 pp) × 10.20 (8.74 wl) × 2.47 hull (4.33 props)
A: 4 P-270 Moskit (SS-N-22 Sunburn) SSM (3M80 missiles); 1 76-mm 59-cal. AK-176 DP (152 rounds); 1 4-round Fasta-4M (SA-N-8) SAM syst. (16 9M-36 Strela-3M/Gremlin missiles); 2 single 30-mm 54-cal. AK-630M gatling AA (4,000 rounds)
Electronics:
Radar: 1 Kivach-3 nav.; 1 Mineral (Band Stand) missile target detection/designation; 1 MR-123-02 Vympel (Bass Tilt) gun f.c.
EW: MP 405-1 Vympel-R2 suite: 2 Half Hat-B intercept; 2 Foot Ball-A intercept; 2 PK-16 decoy syst. (2 16-round RL); 2 or 4 PK-10 decoy syst. (2 or 4 10-round RL)
M: CODAG: 2 M70 (PR-76) gas turbines (12,000 shp each), 2 Type M-510 diesels (5,000 bhp each; 4,000 sust.); 2 props; 34,000 hp max.
Electric: 500 kw tot. (2 × 200 kw, 1 × 100 kw diesel sets)
Range: 2,400/12; 1,600/20; 400/36 **Fuel:** 50 tons **Endurance:** 10 days
Crew: 8 officers, 33 enlisted

Remarks: Transferred to Ukraine by 8-97. Was stricken around 9-00 but was refitted during 2002, renamed, and recommissioned by 9-02. Reportedly in reserve as of 2006.
Hull systems: The propulsion system differs from that of earlier Tarantuls in that diesels were substituted for the cruise turbines to improve cruising range.
Combat systems: A single Pricep (Light Bulb) missile data-link antenna radome is located atop a vertical lattice mast. The antenna within the Band Stand radome provides active and passive targeting for the antiship missiles; the EW suite is integrated with the active radars and can track 15 targets simultaneously to 120 km active and 500 km-range passive. There is a back-up lead-computing optical director for the six-barreled 30-mm gatling guns. Carry a total of 152 rounds 76.2-mm and 4,000 rounds 30-mm ammunition (including 2,000 30-mm ready-service on-mount). The communications suite permits maintaining seven circuits simultaneously.

♦ 1 Tarantul-II (Molnaya) class (Project 1241.1/2)
Bldrs: Sudostroitel'noye Obyedineniye "Almaz," Petrovskiy SY, St. Petersburg and/or Sredniy Neva SY, Kolpino (In serv. 1981–86)

	Laid down	L	In serv.
U 155 PRODNIPROV'JA (ex-*Nikopol',* ex-R-54, ex-*Krasnodarskiy Komsomolets*)	21-4-81	18-12-82	30-12-83

Prodniprov'ja (U 155) Hartmut Ehlers, 3-02

D: 329 tons light; 436 normal (469 fl) **S:** 42 kts
Dim: 56.10 (49.50 pp) × 10.20 (8.74 wl) × 2.25 hull (4.15 props)
A: 4 P-15M Termit (SS-N-2C Styx) SSM; 1 76.2-mm 59-cal. AK-176 DP; 1 4-rail Fasta-4M (SA-N-8) SAM syst. (9M-36 Strela-3M/Gremlin missiles; 2 single 30-mm 54-cal. AK-630M gatling AA
Electronics:
Radar: 1 Kivach-3 nav.; 1 Monolit (Band Stand) missile target detection and tracking; 1 MR-123 Vympel' (Bass Tilt) gun f.c.
EW: Intercept via Band Stand; 2 16-round PK-16 decoy RL
M: COGAG M-15 plant: 2 M75 (DMR-76) cruise gas turbines (5,000 shp each), 2 M70 (PR-77) boost gas turbines (12,000 shp each); 2 props; 34,000 shp
Electric: 700 kw tot. (2 × 200 kw, 1 × 300 kw diesel sets)
Range: 760/43; 1,400/13 **Fuel:** 50 tons
Endurance: 10 days **Crew:** 5 officers, 36 enlisted

Remarks: Transferred 1-8-97.
Hull systems: The cruise gas turbines exhaust through a stack, while the high-speed turbines exhaust through the transom stern, adding their residual thrust to the propulsive power; all four are employed simultaneously via planetary gearing for maximum power.
Combat systems: A Pricep (Light Bulb) cruise missile datalink antenna has been added at the masthead, while the Band Stand radome conceals a missile-target acquisition and tracking radar that can also be employed in passive intercept and tracking mode. There are four unoccupied positions for EW antennas. Some 152 rounds of 76.2-mm and 4,000 rounds of 30-mm ammunition are normally carried, and there is emergency stowage for an additional 162 rounds of 76-mm ammunition.

PATROL COMBATANTS [PG]

♦ 1 Russian Pauk-I (Molnaya-2) class (Project 1241.2)
Bldr: Yaroslavl SY, Russia

	In serv.
U 208 HMELNICHKIY (ex-*Morska Ochorona,* ex-MPK-116)	1985

Hmelnichkiy (U 208) Leo Dirkx, 7-01

D: 420 tons (475 fl, 534 max.) **S:** 32 kts (28 sust.)
Dim: 57.60 (49.50 pp) × 10.40 (8.74 wl) × 2.14 hull (3.45 max.)
A: 1 76.2-mm AK-176 DP; 1 4-round Fasta-4M (SA-N-8) SAM syst. (16 9M-313 Igla/Gremlin missiles); 1 30-mm 54-cal. AK-630 gatling AA; 2 5-round RBU-1200M ASW RL (30 RGB-12 projectiles); 4 fixed 402-mm OTA-40 ASW TT; 2 d.c. racks (12 BB-1 d.c.)

PATROL COMBATANTS [PG] *(continued)*

Electronics:
Radar: 1 Mius (Spin Trough) nav.; 1 Reyd (Peel Cone) nav./surf.-search; 1 MR-123 Vympel'-AM (Bass Tilt) f.c.
Sonar: MGK-345 Bronza MF hull-mounted and MF dipping (6.5/7.0/7.5 kHz)
EW: Vympel'-R2 suite: 2 Half Hat-B intercept; 2 16-round PK-16 decoy RL
M: 2 M-507A or M-517 twin diesels; 2 props; 20,800 bhp (16,180 bhp sust.)
Electric: 500 kw tot. (2 × 200 kw, 1 × 100 kw diesel sets)
Range: 2,000/20; 2,600/14; 1,600/12 (normal fuel; 3,000/12 with max. fuel)
Fuel: 50 tons normal **Endurance:** 10 days **Crew:** 5–7 officers, 31–32 enlisted

Remarks: Was stricken from the Black Sea Fleet on 10-1-96 and was transferred on 12-3-96 (one source indicates that U 208's strike date was 5-7-94). Three sisters are in the Border Guard (*Morska Okhorona*). U 207 appears to have been stricken by 2003.
Hull systems: The large housing for a dipping sonar system projects about 1.5 m out from the stern. The large hull-mounted sonar dome is located approximately beneath the gun fire-control radar. The hull is constructed of mild steel, although the middle part of the deck plating, some internal bulkheads, and much of the superstructure are made of aluminum-magnesium alloy.
Combat systems: The combat data system is designated SU-580. There is an SP-521 Rakurs (Kolonka-2) backup ringsight director for the single gatling AA gun; the Bass Tilt radar director can control both the 76.2-mm and 30-mm guns. Normal ammunition load is 152 rounds 76-mm (all ready-service, on-mount) and 2,000 rounds 30-mm. The sonar suite has a range of about 7 km for the dipping component; MGK-345 applies to both the hull-mounted and dipping sonars, and the dipping sonar transducer can be lowered to 200 m.

PATROL BOATS [PB]

♦ 1 ex-Russian Flamingo (Tanya) class (Project 1415)
Bldr: Sosnovka Zavod, Rybinsk, or Yaroslavl Zavod (In serv. 1980s)

U 240 Feodosiya (ex-P 99; ex-RVK-1403)

Feodosiya (U 240) Boris Lemachko, 2003

D: 42 tons (54 fl) **S:** 11 kts **Dim:** 21.20 × 3.93 × 1.40
A: Small arms; 1 AK-17 grenade launcher **Electronics:** Radar: 1 Lotsiya nav.
M: 1 Type 3D12A or 3D12L diesel; 1 prop; 300 bhp
Electric: 12 kw tot. (DGR 1A-16/1500 generator) **Range:** 200/11
Endurance: 5 days **Crew:** 3 tot. + 5 divers

Remarks: Transferred 1997. Employed as a counterswimmer harbor patrol boat (*protivodiversionniye kater*). Differs from most Project 1415 units in having continuous bulwarks surrounding the upper deck. Several others in Ukraine service are configured as diving tenders, etc.

♦ 1 ex-Russian Zhuk (Gryf) class (Project 1400M)
Bldr: Morye (ex-Yuzhnaya Tochka) Zavod, Feodosiya (In serv. 1980)

U 120 Skadovs'k (ex-PSKA-527)

Skadovs'k (U 120) Hartmut Ehlers, 7-00

D: 35.9 tons (39.7 fl) **S:** 30 kts
Dim: 23.80 (21.70 wl) × 5.00 (3.80 wl) × 1.00 (hull; 1.90 max.)
A: 1 twin 12.7-mm 60-cal. Utës-Ma mg **Electronics:** Radar: 1 Lotsiya nav.
M: 2 M-401 diesels; 2 props; 2,200 bhp
Electric: 48 kw total (2 × 21 kw, 1 × 6 kw diesel sets **Range:** 500/13.5
Endurance: 5 days **Crew:** 1 officer, 9 enlisted

Remarks: Former identification uncertain; was transferred from Russia around 1996–97. Nineteen others serve in the Border Guard (*Morska Okhorona*).
Hull systems: Aluminum alloy hull. Capable of operating in up to Sea State 4 or 5. Range also reported as 700 n.m. at 28 knots, 1,100 n.m. at 15 kts.

MINE-COUNTERMEASURES SHIPS AND CRAFT

♦ 2 ex-Russian Natya-I (Akvamarine)-class (Project 266M) fleet minesweepers [MSF]
Bldr: Sudostroitel'noye Obyedineniye "Almaz" (Sredniy Neva), Kolpino

	In serv.
U 310 Zhovti Vodi (ex-*Razvedchik*)	1977
U 311 Cherkasi (ex-*Zenitchik*)	1974

Zhovti Vodi (U 310) Cem D. Yaylali, 9-02

Cherkasi (U 311) Boris Lemachko, 2002

D: 715 tons light, 735–750 tons std., 804–812 tons normal (873 fl)
S: 17.6 kts (16 sust.)
Dim: 61.00 (57.60 wl; 56.00 pp) × 10.20 (9.80 wl) × 2.98 hull (3.60 max.)
A: 2 twin 30-mm 65-cal. AK-230M AA; 2 twin 25-mm 80-cal. 2M-3M AA; 2 5-round RBU-1200M ASW RL (30 RGB-12 rockets); 7 KMD-1000 mines or 32 mine-disposal charges
Electronics:
Radar: 1-2 Don-MN (Don-2) nav.; 1 MR-104 Rys' (Drum Tilt) f.c.
Sonar: MG-69 Lan' or MG-79 Mizen' search MG-26 underwater telephone
M: 2 M-503B-3E diesels: 2 shrouded CP props; 5,000 bhp
Electric: 600 kw tot. (3 × 200 kw DGR-200/1500 diesel sets, 380 V 50 Hz a.c.)
Range: 1,800/16; 2,700/12; 5,200/10 **Fuel:** 48 tons normal, 87 tons max.
Endurance: 10 days **Crew:** 6 officers, 8 warrant officers, 54 enlisted

Remarks: Transferred to Ukraine in 1997, with U 310 still "in reserve" in 1998 but active by 7-00. Equipped also to serve as ASW escorts, with the RBU-1200 rocket launchers also used for detonating mines. Designed under T. D. Pokhodun.

MINE-COUNTERMEASURES SHIPS AND CRAFT *(continued)*

Hull systems: Low magnetic signature, aluminum-steel alloy hull. Have DGR-450/1500P diesel-driven degaussing system. Endurance at 12 kts with normal 48-ton fuel load is 1,500 n.m.; with 80-ton overload fuel load is 2,700 n.m. All living spaces are air conditioned.
Combat systems: Sweep gear includes SEMP-3 magnetic and MPT-3 mechanical arrays and a net trawl deployed over the stern ramp. The sonar incorporates a downward-looking, high-frequency, bottomed mine detection component. Can deploy television minehunting equipment. Have NEL-5 echo sounders.

♦ 2 ex-Russian Sonya (Yakhont)-class (Project 1265) coastal minesweepers [MSC]

Bldr: Avangard Zavod, Petrozavodsk

	In serv.
U 330 MELITOPOL' (ex-BT-79, ex-*Sevastopol'skiy Komsomolets*)	1979
U 331 MARIUPOL' (ex-BT-126, ex-*Orenburgskiy Komsomolets*)	1978

Melitopol' (U 330) Boris Lemachko, 2002

Mariupol' (U 331) Boris Lemachko, 6-00

D: 401 tons (430 fl) **S:** 14 kts
Dim: 48.80 (46.00 wl) × 10.20 (9.20 wl) × 2.40 mean hull (2.75 max.)
A: 1 twin 30-mm 65-cal. AK-230M AA; 1 twin 25-mm 80-cal. 2M-3M AA; 5 mines
Electronics:
Radar: 1 Mius (Spin Trough) nav.
Sonar: MG-89 Serna HF hull-mounted; MG-35 underwater telephone; NEL-MZB echo sounder
M: 2 DRA-210-B diesels; 2 3-bladed CP props; 2,000—2 low-speed thrusters
Electric: 350 kw tot. (3 × 100 kw, 1 × 50 kw diesel sets; 380 V 50 Hz a.c.)
Range: 1,700/10 **Fuel:** 27.1 tons **Endurance:** 15 days
Crew: 5–6 officers, 26–40 enlisted (45 tot. accomm.)

Remarks: Transferred 1-10-96. Program name, *Yakhont,* is a kind of sapphire. Designed under Valeriy Ivanovich Nemudrov. U 331 was refitted during 1997–98.
Hull systems: Wooden construction with glass-reinforced plastic hull sheathing. Bollard pull: 10 tons at 9 kts.
Combat systems: Carry AT-5 acoustic, PEMT-4 magnetic loop, and BKT-2 mechanical sweep equipment. Can tow CT-2 solenoidal magnetic minesweeping buoys and also net-sweep arrays and can lay linear mine-disposal charges. Are also able to employ KIU-1 underwater t.v. mine-location equipment. Equipped with an underwater telephone. The 25-mm mount is aimed by the operator, while the 30-mm mount is controlled by an SP-521 Rekurs (Kolonka-1) ringsight director.

♦ 1 ex-Russian Yevgenya (Korund)-class (Project 1258) inshore minesweeper [MSI]

Bldr: Sudostroitel'noye Obyedineniye "Almaz" (Sredniy Neva), Kolpino (In serv. 1970–76)

U 360 GENICHESK (ex-RT-214)

D: 88.5 tons light, 94.5 normal (97.9 fl) **S:** 11 kts
Dim: 26.13 (24.20 wl) × 5.90 (5.10 wl) × 1.38
A: 1 twin 14.5-mm 93-cal. 2M-7 AA; 1 7-round MRG-1 grenade launcher; 4 depth charges (+ 8 emergency stowage)
Electronics:
Radar: 1 Mius (Spin Trough) or Kivach nav.
Sonar: MG-7 HF dipping

Genichesk (U 360) Boris Lemachko, 2003

M: 2 Type 3D12 diesels; 2 props; 600 bhp—hydraulic slow-speed drive
Electric: 100 kw tot. (2 × 50 kw diesel sets) **Range:** 400/10 **Fuel:** 2.7 tons
Endurance: 3 days **Crew:** 1 officer, 9 enlisted (+ 2–3 clearance divers)

Remarks: Transferred 12-3-96. Designed under V. I. Blinov.
Hull systems: Glass-reinforced plastic hull. Navigational equipment includes Girya-MA gyrocompass and NEL-7 echo-sounder.
Combat systems: Can employ a Neva-1 television minehunting system useful to 30 m depths that dispenses marker buoys to permit later disposal of mines by divers or explosive charges. The sonar is lowered via one of the stern davits. Carry VKT-1 mechanical, AT-2 acoustic, and SEMT-1 solenoid coil sweep gear.

AMPHIBIOUS WARFARE SHIPS AND CRAFT

♦ 1 ex-Russian Ropucha-I-class (Project 775) tank landing ship [LST]

Bldr: Stocznia Polnocna, Gdansk, Poland (In serv. 1985)

U 402 KONSTYANTYN OLSHANSKYY (ex-*Konstantin Ol'shanskiy,* BDK-56)

Konstyantyn Olshanskyy (U 402) Boris Lemachko, 2003

Konstyantyn Olshanskyy (U 402) Hartmut Ehlers, 7-00

D: 2,768 tons light; 3,450 tons normal (4,080 fl) **S:** 17.5 kts
Dim: 112.50 (105.00 wl) × 15.00 × 3.70 (aft, loaded)
A: 2 twin 57-mm 70-cal. AK-725 DP; 2 40-round 122-mm UMS-73 Grad-M artillery RL (360 BM-21 rockets); up to 92 1-ton mines
Electronics:
Radar: 2 Don-2 or Vaygach (Palm Frond) nav.; 1 MR-302 Rubka (Strut Curve) surf./air search; 1 MR-103 Bars (Muff Cob) gun f.c.
M: 2 Type 16ZVB 40/48 16-cylinder, 500 r.p.m. diesels; 2 props; 19,200 bhp
Electric: 1,920 kw tot. (3 × 640 kw; Cegielski-Sulzer 6A25 diesels driving)
Range: 3,500/16; 6,000/12 **Endurance:** 30 days (with landing force)
Crew: 8 officers, 79 enlisted (accomm. for 17 officers, 81 enlisted) + 150 troops

Remarks: Stricken from Black Sea Fleet 10-1-96 and transferred 12-3-96. Builder's Project B-23.
Hull systems: The hull has a molded depth of 8.65 m amidships and is equipped with a "beak" bow projection to aid in beaching. Fully degaussed and has forced ventilation system with NBC warfare filters. There are both bow and stern doors. No vehicle cargo is carried on the upper deck, the hatch serving for loading by crane and for ventilation when vehicle motors are running. Bow and stern doors permit roll-on/roll-off loading. Cargo capacity: 450 tons; usable deck space: 600 m^2. Alternate cargo loads are 10 41-ton tanks with 40 vehicle crew and 150 troops; 12 amphibious tanks with 36 vehicle crew; or a mix of three 41-ton tanks, three 120-mm mine throwers, three armored cars, four trucks, five light vehicles, and 123 troops.
Combat systems: Although the entire class was intended to receive two UMS-73 barrage rocket launchers on the forecastle, only the six most recently completed (among them the Ukrainian unit) actually carried the weapons. Some 20 smoke floats can be carried aft. Mines can only be carried when there is no amphibious cargo.

AMPHIBIOUS WARFARE SHIPS AND CRAFT *(continued)*

♦ 1 ex-Russian Alligator (Tapir)-class (Project 1171) tank landing ship [LST]
Bldr: Yantar Zavod, Kaliningrad, Russia

	Laid down	L	In serv.
U 762 Rivne (ex-*Il'ya Azarov,* U 401, BDK-104)	17-10-69	31-3-70	10-6-71

Rivne (U 762) Boris Lemachko, 2003

D: 2,760 tons light, 2,905 std. (4,360 fl) **S:** 16.5 kts (16 sust.)
Dim: 113.1 (105.0 pp) × 15.6 × 4.10 mean hull (6.15 loaded, aft)
A: 1 twin 57-mm 70-cal. ZIF-31B DP; 1 40-round 122-mm UMS-73 Grad-M artillery RL (160 rockets)
Electronics:
Radar: 2 Don-2 and/or Mius (Spin Trough) nav.
E/O: 1 Squeeze Box multisensor surveillance/rocket f.c.
M: 2 Type 58A diesels; 2 props; 9,000 bhp
Electric: 740 kw tot. (2 × 270 kw, 2 × 100 kw diesel sets)
Range: 3,500/16.5; 8,000/15 **Endurance:** 15 days (10 days with landing force)
Crew: 5 officers, 50 enlisted + 440 troops

Remarks: Transferred 4-96, although she had been lying unmaintained and without armament at Odesa for several years; a refit was completed during 2001, and the ship is again operational.
Hull systems: Cargo capacity is about 600 tons for beaching and 1,750 tons in freighting service; can carry 20 tanks, plus lighter vehicles on upper decks. The tank deck is 90 meters long and totals 850 m^2 in area. Has vehicle ramps fore and aft and one 7.5-ton KE29 crane. Nominal vehicle capacity is 20 MAZ-543, 52 ZIL-131, or 85 GAZ-66 trucks. Troops are accommodated below the tank deck, in considerable discomfort, in the lower No. 3 hold.
Combat systems: The open 57-mm gun mounting is locally controlled; 1,200 rounds of ammunition are normally carried. The communications suite can handle six channels simultaneously.

♦ 1 ex-Russian Polnocny-C-class (Project 774) medium landing ship [LSM]
Bldr: Stocznia Polnocna, Gdansk, Poland (In serv. 1971)

U 401 Kirovograd (ex-SDK-137)

Kirovograd (U 401)—prior to refit and activation Werner Globke, 8-97

D: 920 tons (1,192 fl) **S:** 16 kts
Dim: 81.30 (76.00 wl) × 9.30 (9.00 wl) × 1.20 fwd/2.60 aft
A: 2 twin 30-mm 65-cal. AK-230 AA; 2 18-round 140-mm WM-18 barrage RL; 4 Fasta-4M (SA-N-8) SAM syst. (32 Strela-3M/Grail missiles)
Electronics: Radar: 1 Mius (Spin Trough) nav.; 1 MR-104 Rys' (Drum Tilt) f.c.
M: 2 Type 40DM diesels; 2 props; 4,400 bhp **Range:** 900/16; 3,000/12
Endurance: 3 days **Crew:** 5 officers, 36 enlisted + 160 troops

Remarks: Transferred from Black Sea Fleet in 1994 but was not operated until a refit was completed during 2002. Lengthened and broadened version of Polnocny-B, with 53.3-m-long by 6.7-m-wide vehicle deck. Carries up to 250 tons cargo. Differs from near-sister *Grunwald* in the Polish Navy in having a full-length tank deck and no command facilities.

♦ 2 Pomornik (Zubr)-class (Project 1232.2) air-cushion vehicle landing craft [LCUA]
Bldr: Morye (ex-Yuzhnaya Tochka) Zavod, Feodosiya

	In serv.
U 420 Donets'k	26-6-93
U 424 Artemivs'k	1989

Donets'k (U 420) Boris Lemachko, 2003

D: 340 tons light, 415 normal (550 fl) **S:** 63 kts (55 sust.)
Dim: 57.3 (56.2 hull) × 25.6 (22.0 hull) × 21.9 high
A: 2 4-round Fasta-4M (SA-N-8) SAM syst. (IV × 2, 32 9M-36 Igla-1M/Gremlin missiles); 2 single 30-mm 54-cal. AK-630M gatling AA; 2 22-round 140-mm MS-227 Ogon' retractable artillery RL (132 rockets); up to 80 mines in lieu of vehicle cargo
Electronics:
Radar: 1 SRN-207 Ekran (Curl Stone-B) nav.; 1 MR-123 Vympel (Bass Tilt) gun f.c.
E/O: 1 DVU-3 (Quad Look) surveillance/f.c.
M: 5 NK-12MV (M70) gas turbines (12,100 shp each/10,000 shp sustained; 2 to power lift fans); 3 ducted CP airscrew propellers, 4 NO-10 lift fans; 36,300 shp for propulsion
Electric: 300 or 400 kw tot. (4 × 75 kw or 100 kw GTG-110 gas turbine sets)
Range: 300/55 with 130-ton payload; 1,000/55 light **Fuel:** 56 tons (180 m^3)
Endurance: 5 days (1 day with full troop complement)
Crew: 4 officers, 7 warrant officers, 20 enlisted + 140 to 360 troops

Remarks: *Donets'k* was announced to be in Ukrainian service in 1993; sister *Ivan Bohun* (U 421) was building at Morye Zavod but was left incomplete until reordered for Greece in 1999, along with *Horlivka* (U 423, ex-Russian MDK-93); the latter was scrapped late in 2002 after Greece refused delivery. Too large for shipboard transportation, they are intended for short-range independent assault operations. There are apparently significant reliability problems with the design. *Donets'k* was badly damaged 23-5-95, requiring two months of repairs; the craft has been in a shipyard since 9-00 and may be undergoing scrapping. *Artemivs'k*, mistakenly reported as having been scrapped in previous editions, remains in service
Hull systems: The dimensions given include the flexible skirt in inflated condition. Originally intended to have a 16-year service life. The vehicle deck can hold up to 10 BTR-70 armored amphibious personnel transport vehicles or three T-80B main battle tanks plus a detachment of infantry—or up to 140 troops and 130 tons of combat cargo. Have small bow and stern ramps. The vehicle cargo deck has an area of 400 m^2. Navigational equipment includes gyrocompass, Decca radio-navigation system receiver, drift indicator, and a NAVSAT receiver.
Combat systems: The Quad Look electro-optical device is a modified Squeeze Box that has no weather cover; there is also a t.v. camera mounted just below the pilothouse. The navigational radar is mounted within a lozenge-shaped radome. The retractable artillery rocket launchers are located near the bow in the hull wing-walls and are reloaded belowdecks by hand.
Propulsion systems: Three of the gas-turbine engines are mounted on pylons and drive airscrew propellers; they are equipped with exhaust thrust diverters to enhance mobility. The lift-fan gas turbines drive four blowers to maintain skirt pressure and are mounted near the stern in the wing compartments and exhaust through the stern.
Disposals: Sister *Kramators'k* (U 422, ex-MDK-57) was to be stricken post-9-00. *Ivan Bohun* (U 421) and *Horlivka* (U 423, ex-MDK-93) were refurbished in 2000–2001 for sale to Greece.

♦ 2 ex-Russian Ondatra (Akula)-class (Project 1176) landing craft [LCM]
Bldr: . . . (In serv. 1975)

U 430 Svatove U 537 Vil (ex-DK-305)

Svatove (U 430) Boris Lemachko, 3-99

D: 90 tons normal (107.3 fl) **S:** 11.5 kts **Dim:** 24.50 × 6.00 × 1.55 **A:** None
Electronics: Radar: 1 . . . nav. **M:** 2 Type 3D12 diesels; 2 props; 600 bhp
Range: 330/10; 500/5 **Endurance:** 2 days **Crew:** 6 tot. (enlisted)

Remarks: Transferred on 31-7-96. In all, 29 were built for use aboard the Russian *Ivan Rogov*–class landing ships. Cargo well is 13.7 × 3.9 m and can accommodate one 40-ton tank or up to 50 tons of general cargo; some 20 troops/vehicle crew can be carried.

AMPHIBIOUS WARFARE SHIPS AND CRAFT *(continued)*

◆ **1 T-4-class (Project 1785) landing craft [LCM]**
Bldr: . . . (In serv. 1970)

U 538 TARPAN (ex-DK-455)

Tarpan (U 538) Boris Lemachko, 2000

D: 35 tons light (93 fl) **S:** 10 kts (light) **Dim:** 20.4 × 5.4 × 1.2 max. aft
M: 2 Type 3D6 diesels; 2 props; 300 bhp **Range:** 300/8 **Endurance:** 2 days
Crew: 2–3 tot.

Remarks: Transferred to Ukraine on 31-7-96 and was under refit in 1997–98. Can accommodate up to 50 tons cargo on the 9.5 × 3.9–m vehicle deck.

AUXILIARIES

◆ **1 Bereza (SR-28)-class deperming ship (Polish Project 130) [ADG]**
Bldr: Stocznia Polnocna, Gdansk, Poland (In serv. 1987)

U 811 BALTA (ex-SR-568)

Balta (U 811) Cem D. Yaylali, 5-05

D: 1,811 tons (2,096 fl) **S:** 13.6 kts **Dim:** 69.50 × 13.80 × 3.98 **A:** None
Electronics: Radar: 1 Mius-M (Kivach) nav.
M: 2 Zgoda-Sulzer 8AL25/30, 750-r.p.m. diesels; 2 CP Kort-nozzle props; 2,940 bhp—bow-thruster
Electric: 1,185 kVA + 1,550 kw tot. (2 × 480 kVA, 1 × 225 kVA, 2 × 645 kw, 1 × 260 kw)
Range: 1,000/13.6; 1,200/10 **Fuel:** 170 tons
Endurance: 30 days **Crew:** 45 tot.

Remarks: Transferred 1-8-97. Intended for "degaussing surface ships and submarines, conducting magnetic field measurements of ships and vessels, [and] regulating ground fault neutralizers."
Hull systems: Can service two ships simultaneously. Has three laboratories, a machine shop, and a cable hold. A large crane is fitted aft to handle deperming cables.

Disposal note: Ex-Russian Lama-class missile transport [AEM] *Kolomiya* (U 533, ex-PRTB-13) was scrapped at Inkerman, beginning 1-00.

◆ **1 ex-Russian Muna-class (Project 1823) torpedo transport [AE]**
Bldr: Vympel Zavod, Nizhniy Novgorod, Russia (In serv. 1968)

U 754 DZHANKOY (ex-VTR-93, ex-VTR-69, ex-MTB-169250)

D: 441 tons light (686 fl) **S:** 11.5 kts **Dim:** 51.50 × 8.44 × 2.70 **A:** None
Electronics: Radar: 1 Mius (Spin Trough) nav.
M: 1 Type 6DR 30/50 diesel; 1 prop; 600 bhp
Range: 2,240/11.4; 4,950/9.3 **Endurance:** 15 days
Crew: 15 tot. (+ 7 passengers)

Remarks: Stricken from the Black Sea Fleet on 1-10-96 and transferred to Ukraine on 1-8-97. Has a single 3.2-ton-capacity electric crane positioned between four small holds which, on this ship, are intended to accommodate torpedoes. Cargo capacity is 175 tons.

Disposal note: Mayak-class provisions transport *Yalta* (U 755, ex-*Buzuluk*) was sold to a private firm on 8-12-00.

◆ **1 ex-Russian Onega-class (Project 1806) signature monitoring ship [AG] *(nonoperational)***
Bldr: Zelenodol'sk Zavod, Russia (In serv. 1987)

U 812 SEVERODONETS'K (ex-SFP-322)

D: 1,350 tons (1,460 fl) **S:** 14 kts **Dim:** 80.00 × 11.60 × 3.17-3.27 **A:** None
Electronics:
Radar: 1 Don-2 nav.
Sonar: Arktika-M passive array, active dipping set
M: 2 diesels; 2 props; 2,800 bhp **Range:** 1,000/10
Endurance: 15 days **Crew:** 45 tot.

Remarks: Transferred 1997. In Russian service, was officially said to be intended to "measure acoustic, magnetic, low-frequency, electromagnetic, electric, and heat fields set up by ships and submarines for compliance with existing standards and specifications." Said to be in need of a refit, and was not active as of 1998.
Hull systems: SFP-designated units were usually seen with two side-by-side modular structures topped with two rectangular air vents mounted at the fore end of the after deckhouse platform (which was originally intended to be a helicopter platform); the devices may be employed in air sampling.

Disposal note: Ex-Russian Potok (Smen')-class (Project 1236) torpedo trials ship *Artsiz* (U 863) had been retired by 2006.

◆ **1 Modified Kamchatka-class (Project 12884) fleet flagship [AGF]** Bldr: Chernomorets Zavod, Mikolayiv

	Laid down	L	In serv.
U 510 SLAVUTYCH (ex-*Pridneprovye,* SSV-189)	7-88	1-90	27-7-92

Slavutych (U 510) Cem D. Yaylali, 4-05

D: 4,460 tons (5,010 fl) **S:** 14.8 kts **Dim:** 106.02 × 16.01 × 6.00
A: 1 single 30-mm AK-306 gatling AA; 2 twin 14.5-mm 93-cal. AA; 2 4-round Fasta-4M (SA-N-8) SAM syst. (16 Strela-2M/ SA-14 Gremlin missiles); 2 single 45-mm saluting cannon
Electronics:
Radar: 2 Vaygach-U (Palm Frond) nav.
EW: . . . intercept; 2 16-round PK-16 decoy RL
M: 1 diesel; 1 prop; 5,236 bhp **Range:** 13,000/14 **Endurance:** 90 days
Crew: 19 officers, 110 enlisted

Remarks: Said to have been begun for the Soviet navy as an intelligence collector, this ship is essentially a sister to the now-stricken Russian Pacific Fleet's *Kamchatka* but lacks the tall and bulky tower mast amidships. Has been adapted to serve as the Ukrainian fleet flagship and visited New York during 2000. The lightweight gatling AA guns do not have radar directors; optical SP-521 Rekurs (Kolonka-2) lead- computing directors are mounted within nearby enclosed cupolas. Based at Sevastopil.

◆ **1 ex-Russian Amur-class (Project 304) flag and staff ship [AGF]**
Bldr: A. Warski SY, Szczecin, Poland (In serv. 1970)

U 500 DONBAS (ex-*Krasnodon*, U 803; ex-PM-9)

Donbas (U 500)—with former pennant number Hartmut Ehlers, 3-02

D: 4,000 tons (5,490 fl) **S:** 14 kts **Dim:** 121.70 × 17.00 × 4.63 **A:** None
Electronics: Radar: 1 Don-2 nav. **M:** 2 diesels; 1 prop; 3,000 bhp
Range: 7,800/10; 13,200/8 **Endurance:** 40 days **Crew:** 145 tot.

Remarks: Transferred 1-8-97. Completed overhaul and modifications during 2001 to serve as a command and staff support ship for ships based at Sevastopil. Renamed and numbered during 2003. Can serve surface ships and submarines with basic repair facilities and can carry 280 tons of spare parts. Has two 3-ton cranes and one 1.5-ton crane.

◆ **1 ex-Russian Sura-class (Project 145) mooring-buoy tender [AGL]** Bldr: VEB Neptunwerft, Rostock, East Germany (In serv. 1976)

U 852 SHOSTKA (ex-KIL-33)

D: 2,260 tons (3,150 fl) **S:** 13.2 kts
Dim: 87.30 (80.20 hull; 68.00 pp) × 14.80 × 5.10
Electronics: Radar: 2 Don-2 nav.

AUXILIARIES *(continued)*

Shostka (U 852) Boris Lemachko, 2001

M: 4 diesels, electric drive; 2 props; 2,240 shp (1,780 sust.)
Range: 4,000/10 **Endurance:** 20 days **Crew:** 40 tot.

Remarks: 2,366 grt. Stricken from the Black Sea Fleet on 10-1-96 and transferred to Ukraine 1-8-97.
Hull systems: Can carry 460 tons of cargo in hold amidships and 300 tons cargo fuel. Stern rig, which can lift 65 tons, is used for buoy-handling and salvage. Mooring buoys are stowed amidships and moved aft for handling by the stern gallows rig via a chain-haul system. There are also a 5-ton electric crane to port and a 65-ton heavy-lift boom amidships, the latter tending the buoy stowage holds. The diesel propulsion generator plant is forward.

♦ 1 Kamenka-class (Project 871) hydrographic survey ship [AGS]
Bldr: Stocznia Polnocna, Gdansk, Poland (In serv. 1979–81)

U 600 GS-82

D: 590 tons (703 fl) **S:** 13.7 kts **Dim:** 53.50 × 9.40 × 2.62
Electronics: Radar: 1 Don-2 nav.
M: 2 Cegielski-Sulzer 6 NVD-48 diesels; 2 CP props; 1,765 bhp **Range:** 2,000/11
Endurance: 15 days **Crew:** 24 tot.

Remarks: U 600 was stricken from the Black Sea Fleet on 10-1-96 and became Ukraine property in 12-3-96. Retains the original Russian alphanumeric name. Similar to the Biya-class but has more facilities for stowing and handling buoys. No survey launch is carried.

♦ 1 ex-Russian Muna-class (Project 1824B) survey ship [AGS]
Bldr: Nakhodka SY (In serv. 1970–78)

U 512 Pereyaslav (ex-*Uglomer*, GS-13)

D: 457 tons (688 fl) **S:** 11 kts **Dim:** 51.50 × 8.40 × 2.70
Electronics: Radar: 1 Mius (Spin Trough) nav.
M: 1 Type 6DR 30/50 diesel; 1 prop; 600 bhp
Range: 1,700/10 **Endurance:** 15 days **Crew:** 22 tot.

Remarks: Former ammunition lighter extensively converted at a Baltic-area shipyard to serve as a coastal survey ship and completed in 7-90; stricken 10-1-96 and later transferred to Ukraine. A small deckhouse covers the former forward ammunition hold area, while two kingposts with derricks were stepped forward of the pilothouse. The original electric crane was retained.

♦ 2 ex-Russian Biya-class (Project 870) hydrographic survey ships [AGS]
Bldr: Stocznia Polnocna, Gdansk, Poland (In serv. 1968–72)

U 601 . . . (ex-GS-212) U 603 . . . (ex-GS-273)

D: 750 tons (fl) **S:** 13 kts **Dim:** 55.0 × 9.2 × 2.6
Electronics: Radar: 1 Don-2 nav.
M: 2 diesels; 2 CP props; 1,200 bhp **Range:** 4,700/11 **Fuel:** 90 tons
Endurance: 15 days **Crew:** 25 tot.

Remarks: Stricken from the Black Sea Fleet 10-1-96. Retain their original Russian Navy alphanumeric names. Fourteen were originally built for Soviet Navy use. Have one 5-ton buoy crane. Similar to Kamenka class, but have longer superstructure and less buoy-handling space; carry one survey launch and have one 5-ton buoy crane. Laboratory space: 15 m^2.

♦ 1 ex-Russian Moma-class (Project 861) survey ship [AGS]
Bldr: Stocznia Polnocna, Gdansk, Poland (In serv. 1969)

U 602 Alchevsk (ex-*Berezan'*)

D: 1,140 tons (1,502 fl) **S:** 15 kts
Dim: 73.30 (64.20 pp) × 11.20 (10.80 wl) × 3.80
Electronics: Radar: 2 Don-2 nav.
M: 2 Zgoda-Sulzer 6TD48 diesels; 2 CP props; 3,600 bhp
Range: 8,000/11 **Endurance:** 25 days **Crew:** 41 tot. (civilian)

Remarks: *Liman, Okean,* and *Berezan'* were transferred prior to 1992 to the custody of the cities of Feodosiya, Odesa, and Kerch', respectively, for use as navigational aids tenders. *Liman* was stricken on 5-7-94 (but was active again in Russian Navy service in 4-99); *Okean* reverted to Russian control and was sold for scrap during 7-01, and *Berezan* subsequently reverted to Black Sea Fleet control and was stricken 10-1-96 and transferred to Ukraine in 1997. Sister *Simferopol'* operates as a training ship and intelligence collector (see under AXT).
Hull systems: Carries one survey launch and a 7-ton crane and has four laboratories, totaling 35 m^2.

♦ 1 ex-Russian Keyla-class (Project 740) cargo ship [AK]
Bldr: . . . SY, Budapest, Hungary (In serv. 1958–66)

U 753 Kriviy Rig (ex-*Mezen'*)

D: 854 tons light (2,178 fl) **S:** 10.7 kts **Dim:** 78.5 (71.4 pp) × 10.5 × 4.6
Electronics: Radar: 1 or 2 Don-2 or Mius (Spin Trough) nav.
M: 1 Lang 8 LD315RF diesel; 1 prop; 1,000 bhp **Electric:** 300 kw tot.
Range: 4,200/10.7 **Fuel:** 72 tons **Crew:** 26 tot.

Remarks: 1,296 grt/1,280 dwt. Stricken from Black Sea Fleet on 10-1-96 and transferred during 4-96 and recommissioned 1-8-97. Carries 1,100 tons of cargo. One 10-ton, six 2.5-ton cranes. Alternate diesel engine designation: 84RN 31.5/45.

Disposal note: Of the two Modified *Vytegrales*-class (Project 596KU) former space event support ships transferred from the Russian Black Sea Fleet during 1-96, *Chernivitsi* (U 703, ex-PSK-210, ex-*Kirishi*) and *Ivano-Frankivs'k* (U 704, ex-*Taman',* ex-*Suzdal'*) were scrapped at Aliaga, Turkey, beginning 25-9-00 and 28-10-00, respectively. *Dubna*-class oiler *Kerch'* (U 758, ex-*Sventa*), *Boris Chilikin*–class replenishment oiler *Makiievka* (U 757, ex-*Boris Chilikin*) was sold to an Italian company for commercial use during 2001 under the name *Asia,* and Klaz'ma-class cable layer *Noviy Bug* (U 851, ex-*Tsna*) was stricken by 2004.

♦ 1 ex-Russian Goryn'-class (Project 563S) rescue tug [ARS]
Bldr: Rauma-Repola, Finland (In serv. 1983)

U 705 Kremenets' (ex-SB-524, ex-MB-108)

Kremenets' (U 705) Boris Lemachko, 2003

D: 1,650 tons (2,200 fl) **S:** 13.5 kts **Dim:** 63.50 × 14.30 (13.80 wl) × 5.20
Electronics: Radar: 2 Don-2 nav. **M:** 1 Russkiy Dizel Type 67N diesel; 3,500 bhp
Range: 8,000/12 **Endurance:** 40 days **Crew:** 40 tot. (civilian)

Remarks: Former Black Sea Fleet unit stricken 10-1-96 and transferred to Ukrainian control during the summer of 1997. Former fleet tug redesignated as a salvage tug while in Russian service. Can be distinguished from standard tug version by the electrohydraulic crane and small tripod mast abaft the stack, and probably was fitted with an MG-26 underwater telephone.

♦ 1 ex-Russian Okhtenskiy (Goliat)-class (Project 733S) rescue tug [ARS]
Bldr: Petrozavod SY, St. Petersburg (In serv. 1962)

U 706 Izyaslav (ex-SB-15)

D: 759 tons (934 fl) **S:** 13.2 kts **Dim:** 47.30 (43.00 pp) × 10.30 × 4.20
Electronics: Radar: 1–2 Don-2 or Mius (Spin Trough) nav.
M: diesel-electric: 2 Type D5D50 (6ChN 30/38) diesels, 2 generator sets (950 kw each); 1 prop; 1,500 shp
Electric: 340 kw tot. **Range:** 8,000/11 **Fuel:** 197 tons **Endurance:** 25 days
Crew: 51 tot. (civilian + naval diving party)

Remarks: Stricken from Black Sea Fleet on 10-1-96 and transferred in 4-96. Former Russian designation SB—*Spastel'niy Buksir* meant Rescue Tug, hence the "S" suffix to the project number. Principal characteristics essentially identical to the general fleet-tug version, except that the rescue tugs were equipped to support divers and were able to act as submarine safety ships. Has a Kama hull-mounted underwater telephone. Bollard pull is 20 tons. There is a 5-ton derrick. Sister *Kovel'* (U 831, ex-Russian MB-51) is equipped as a standard seagoing tug.

♦ 1 ex-Russian Sorum-class (Project 745) seagoing tug [ATA]
Bldr: Yaroslavl Zavod (In serv. 1973)

U 830 Korets' (ex-MB-30)

Korets' (U 830) Hartmut Ehlers, 8-00

AUXILIARIES *(continued)*

D: 1,210 tons (1,620 fl) **S:** 13.8 kts **Dim:** 55.50 × 12.60 × 4.60
Electronics: Radar: 2 Don-2 nav.
M: 2 Type 2D42 (6ChN 30/38) diesels, electric drive; 1 prop; 2,500 shp
Range: 6,200/11 **Fuel:** 322 tons **Endurance:** 40 days
Crew: 35 tot. (civilian + 40 passengers/rescuees)

Remarks: Transferred from Black Sea Fleet 1-8-97. Russian and Ukrainian type designation MB means *Morskiye Buksir* (Seagoing Tug). Has blanking plates for two twin 30-mm AA mounts forward.

♦ **1 ex-Russian Okhtenskiy (Goliat)-class (Project 733) seagoing tug [ATA]** Bldr: Petrozavod SY, St. Petersburg (In serv. 1965)

U 831 Kovel' (ex-MB-51)

D: 759 tons (934 fl) **S:** 13.2 kts **Dim:** 47.30 (43.00 pp) × 10.30 × 4.20
Electronics: Radar: 1-2 Don-2 or Spin Trough nav.
M: Diesel-electric: 2 Type D5D50 (6ChN 30/38) diesels, 2 generator sets (950 kw each); 1 prop; 1,500 shp
Electric: 340 kw tot. **Range:** 8,000/11 **Fuel:** 197 tons
Endurance: 25 days **Crew:** 35 tot.

Remarks: Transferred 1-8-98. Sister *Izyaslav* (U 706, ex-Russian SB-15) is equipped as a submarine safety ship/rescue tug (see previous entry).

♦ **1 ex-Russian Voda-class (Project 561) water tanker [AWT]**
Bldr: Yantar Zavod 820, Kaliningrad, Russia (In serv. 1957)

U 756 Sudak (ex-*Sura,* ex-MVT-19)

Sudak (U 756) Hartmut Ehlers, 8-00

D: 982 tons light (2,255 fl) **S:** 12 kts **Dim:** 81.30 × 11.40 × 3.44 (1.65 light)
Electronics: Radar: 1 Don-2 or Mius (Spin Trough)
M: 2 Russkiy Dizel 8DR30/50 diesels; 2 props; 1,600 bhp
Electric: 150 kw tot. (1 × 100 kw, 1 × 50 kw diesel sets; 380V 50 Hz)
Range: 2,900/10; 3,500/7 **Endurance:** 15 days **Crew:** 22 tot. (40 accomm.)

Remarks: Transferred summer 1997. Russian class name: MVT-6. Cargo: 700 tons feedwater, 300 tons potable water. Has one 3-ton derrick for hose handling.

♦ **1 ex-Russian Moma-class (Project 861M) training ship [AXT]**
Bldr: Stocznia Polnocna, Gdansk, Poland (In serv. 1968–74)

U 511 Simferopol' (ex-*Yupiter*)

Simferopol' (U 511) Boris Lemachko, 12-99

D: 1,260 tons (1,600 fl) **S:** 16 kts **Dim:** 73.3 (64.2 pp) × 10.8 × 3.9
A: Removed
Electronics: Radar: 2/Don-2 nav.
M: 2 Zgoda-Sulzer 6TD48 diesels; 2 CP props; 3,600 bhp
Range: 8,000/11 **Fuel:** 220 tons **Crew:** 85 tot.

Remarks: Former intelligence collector (adapted from the standard survey/navaids tender ship design) transferred to Ukraine 1-3-96 and recommissioned same date. In Russian service, had new superstructures added in the area forward of the bridge and new masts. Ukraine Navy officially refers to the ship as a training vessel although she performed in an intelligence collection role as recently as 7-97.

SERVICE CRAFT

♦ **1 ex-Russian Vydra-class (Project 106K) trials craft [YAGE]**
Bldr: Komintern Zavod, Kherson, Ukraine (In serv. 1966)

U 862 Korosten' (ex-*Tarpan,* OS-237; ex- . . .)

Korosten' (U 862)—stern portion Werner Globke, 8-97

D: 308 tons light (442 fl) **S:** 10.5 kts
Dim: 54.50 (50.00 pp) × 7.70 (7.50 wl) × 2.25 mean hull
Electronics: Radar: 2 Don-2 nav.
M: 2 Type 3D-2 diesels; 2 Kort-nozzle props; 600 bhp **Range:** 1,400/10 (loaded)
Endurance: 8 days **Crew:** 12 tot.

Remarks: Stricken from Black Sea Fleet 10-1-96 and transferred 1997. One of 46 built for Russian use as utility landing craft, later employed in local service as a utility cargo carrier. The cargo deck is 30.0 × 4.5 m and can accommodate up to 176 tons of vehicles or cargo (6 ZIL-131 or 10 GAZ-66 trucks). Current function not known. Sister *Bilyaïvka* (U 904, ex-Russian MBSS-233200) is configured as a stores carrier [YF].

♦ **1 ex-Russian Shalanda (BSS-53150)-class (Project 431) trials craft [YAGE]** Bldr: . . . (In serv. 1958)

U 860 Kamyankha (ex-*Kasatka,* OS-94; ex-MBSS-155150)

Kamyankha (U 860) Hartmut Ehlers, 9-98

D: 158 tons light (326 fl) **S:** 8.2 kts **Dim:** 36.00 × 6.90 × 2.00
Electronics: Radar: 1 . . . nav. **M:** 1 Type 3D-12 diesel; 1 prop; 300 bhp
Range: 500/8 **Endurance:** 10 days **Crew:** 8 tot.

Remarks: Stricken from Black Sea Fleet 10-1-96. Former stores lighter (YF) altered to perform a research function; is one of a group of Shalanda-class units originally configured to transport slaked lime to support Quebec-class (Project A615) closed-cycle submarines. A deckhouse has been built forward over the original hold. The standard version could carry 150 tons of cargo and was equipped with one 3-ton electric crane.

♦ **1 ex-Russian Project D-9030 floating crane [YD]**
Bldr: . . . SY, Budapest, Hungary (In serv. 1983)

U 804 Sarni (ex-PK-112025)

Remarks: Transferred 1997. Displacement: 1,060 tons (fl). Crane can lift 25 tons. No other data available.

♦ **1 ex-Russian Yelva (Krab)-class (Project 535M) diving tender [YDT]** Bldr: Gorokhovtse Zavod (In serv. 1975)

U 700 Nikishin (ex-VM-152)

D: 295 tons (fl) **S:** 12.4 kts **Dim:** 40.90 (37.00 pp) × 8.00 × 2.07
Electronics: Radar: 1 Mius (Spin Trough) nav.
M: 2 Type 3D12A diesels; 2 props; 600 bhp
Electric: 200 kw tot. **Range:** 1,870/12
Endurance: 10 days **Crew:** 30 tot.

SERVICE CRAFT *(continued)*

Nikishin (U 700) Boris Lemachko, 1999

Remarks: Stricken from Black Sea Fleet on 10-1-96 and transferred around 4-96. Can support seven divers at once to 60 m. Has a built-in decompression chamber and probably also has a submersible decompression chamber. The name *Krab* was incorrectly ascribed to this craft in the previous edition.

♦ 5 ex-Russian Nyryat'-1-class (Project 522) diving tenders [YDT]

(In serv. 1958–60)

U 631 . . . (ex-BGK-697)
U 632 . . . (ex-BGK-334)
U 633 . . . (ex-VM-114)
U 635 Skvyra (ex-BGK-650)
U 707 Brodi (ex-VM-5)

Skvyra (U 635) Hartmut Ehlers, 7-00

D: 105.4 tons (115 fl) **S:** 10 kts **Dim:** 28.50 × 5.50 × 1.70
Electronics: Radar: 1 Mius (Spin Trough) nav.
M: 1 Type 6CSP 28/3C diesel; 1 prop; 450 bhp
Range: 900/9 **Endurance:** 10 days **Crew:** 15 tot.

Remarks: Stricken 10-1-96 from Black Sea Fleet and transferred to Ukraine; sister VM-230 was also offered but not accepted. VM—*Vodolaznyy Morskoy* (Seagoing Diving Tender). Some are used as inshore survey craft. Can support hard-hat divers to 20-meter depths. As built, could be equipped with one 12.7-mm mg.

♦ 1 ex-Russian Vydra-class (Project 106K) cargo lighter [YF]

Bldr: Komintern Zavod, Kherson, Ukraine (In serv. 1965)

U 904 Bilyaïvka (ex-MBSS-233200)

D: 301 tons light (543 fl) **S:** 10.5 kts
Dim: 54.50 (50.00 pp) × 7.70 (7.50 wl) × 2.25 mean hull
Electronics: Radar: 1 Don-2 nav.
M: 2 Type 3D12 diesels; 2 Kort-nozzle props; 600 bhp **Range:** 1,400/10 (loaded)
Endurance: 8 days **Crew:** 12 tot.

Remarks: Stricken from Black Sea Fleet 10-1-96 and transferred later. Based at Odesa. One of 46 built for Russian use as utility landing craft, employed in local service as utility cargo carries. This unit was formerly employed in trials service. The cargo deck is 30.0 × 4.5 m and can accommodate up to 176 tons of vehicles or cargo (6 ZIL-131 or 10 GAZ-66 trucks). Sister *Korosten'* (U 832; ex-Russian *Tarpan,* OS-237) is configured as a trials craft [YAGE].

♦ 1 ex-Russian Project 1526 cargo lighter [YF]

Bldr: Zavod 490, . . . (In serv. 1959)

U . . . Novgorod-Sivers'kiy (ex-MBSS-5200)

Novgorod-Sivers'kiy (U . . .)—pennant number not carried
Igor' Stelanovich, via Boris Lemachko, 8-00

Remarks: Transferred 1997. Displacement: 200 tons. Has two cargo holds and a small crane; no other data available.

♦ 1 ex-Russian Project 4116 cargo lighter [YF]

Bldr: . . . (In serv. 1952)

U . . . (ex-MBSN-405250)

Remarks: Transferred 1996–97; no data available.

♦ 1 ex-Russian Project 1141 medium floating dry dock [YFDM]

U 949 Berestechko (ex-SPD-23)

Remarks: Completed 1960. No data available. Name also reported as *Berel'nik.*

♦ 1 ex-Russian Project 1758 small floating dry dock [YFDL]

Bldr: . . . (In serv. 1970s)

U . . . (ex-PD-51)

Dim: 118.0 × 29.6 × 3.3 **Capacity:** 4,500 tons

Remarks: Concrete construction. Have two 5-ton traveling cranes. Flooded draft over blocks is 6.3 m and width between wing-walls is 20.0 m.

♦ 1 ex-Russian Project 1240 small floating dry dock [YFDL]

U 950 Khmil'nik (ex-PD-26)

Remarks: No data available.

♦ 3 ex-Russian Flamingo (Tanya)-class (Project 1415) harbor launches [YFL]

Bldr: Sosnovka Zavod, Rybinsk, or Yaroslavl Zavod (In serv. 1980s)

U 721 Volodimir-Volnidskiy (ex-RVK-1075)
U 732 . . . (ex-RVK-1403)
U 733 Tokmak (ex-RVK-1475)

Tokmak (U 733) Hartmut Ehlers, 7-00

D: 42 tons (54 fl) **S:** 11 kts **Dim:** 21.20 × 3.93 × 1.40
Electronics: Radar: 1 Lotsiya nav.
M: 1 Type 3D12A or 3D12L diesel; 1 prop; 300 bhp
Electric: 12 kw tot. (DGR 1A-16/1500 generator) **Range:** 200/11
Endurance: 5 days **Crew:** 3 tot. + 5 divers

Remarks: Transferred 1997. Employed as general-purpose launches at Kerch', Sevastopil, and Balaklava, respectively. Sister U 634 is an inshore survey craft [YGS], and *Feodosiya* (U 240, ex-P-99) is a harbor antiswimmer patrol boat.

♦ 6 ex-Russian PO-2-class (Project 376) harbor launches [YFL]

From among:

U 731 Mirgorod (ex-RVK-493)
U . . . Romni (ex-RVK-155)
U . . . (ex-RVK-5)
U . . . RK-1931
U . . . (ex-RVK-258)
U . . . (ex-RVK-761)
U . . . (ex-RVK-1473)
U 926 . . . (ex-RVK- . . .)

PO-2-class launch wearing pennant number U 172—note shield for twin 12.7-mm mg mount Boris Lemachko, 2000

SERVICE CRAFT *(continued)*

D: 32 tons (38 fl) **S:** 9–10 kts **Dim:** 21.0 × 3.90 × 1.40 max. (1.26 mean)
A: When used as patrol craft: 1 twin 12.7-mm 79-cal.mg
Electronics: Radar: 1 Mius (Spin Trough) nav. or none
M: 1 Type 3D-6S1 diesel; 1 prop; 150 bhp
Electric: 10 kw tot. (1 × 10 kw, DGPN-8/1500 diesel driving) **Range:** 1,600/8
Fuel: 1.5 tons **Endurance:** 5 days **Crew:** 4–6 tot.

Remarks: Stricken from Black Sea Fleet 10-1-96 for transfer to Ukraine. At least one of the boats listed, now numbered BG 501, serves the Border Guard. RK-1931, which retained her Russian alphanumeric name into 8-00, and U 926 operate in the Sevastopil area. A unit numbered U 172, operating at Odesa, has a twin 12.7-mm mg mount forward.

♦ **1 ex-Russian Al'batros-class (Project 183Sh) flag officers' yacht [YFL]** Bldr: Sudostroitel'noye Obyedineniye "Almaz," Petrovskiy SY, St. Petersburg (In serv. circa 1965)

U 853 . . . (ex-*Sokol,* KSV-9)

U 853—Al'batros-class flag officers' yacht Boris Lemachko

D: 56.6 tons (68 fl) **S:** 39 kts **Dim:** 23.7 × 6.1 × 1.3
Electronics: Radar: 1 . . . nav.
M: 4 M-50F-1 diesels; 4 props; 4,800 bhp **Range:** 320/32 **Fuel:** 7.2 tons
Endurance: 5 days **Crew:** 11 tot.

Remarks: Transferred 1997. Ukrainian designation: *Katera Svyazi* (Communications Cutter). Employed the wooden hull and the same propulsion plant as a P-6-class torpedo boat. Able to accommodate about 40 personnel for short trips. Four sisters remain active in the Russian Navy.

♦ **1 ex-Russian PSKL-16-class large cargo barge [YFNB]**
Bldr: . . . (In serv. 1986)

U 855 Zolotonosha (ex-PSKL-19)

Zolotonosha (U 855) Hartmut Ehlers, 3-02

D: 2,604 tons (fl?) **Dim:** . . . × . . . × . . .

Remarks: Concrete hull construction. Equipped with generators and one electrohydraulic crane. Was at one time deployed to Alexandria, Egypt, by the Soviet Navy. No other data available.

♦ **1 ex-Russian Duna-class (Project 440) floating power barge [YFP]** Bldr: . . . (In serv. 1956)

U 813 Berdichiv (ex-ENS-5)

Remarks: Nonself-propelled craft equipped with two Type 37D diesel engines (2,000 bhp each) driving generators primarily intended for charging submarine batteries.

♦ **1 ex-Russian Flamingo (Tanya)-class (Project 1415) survey craft [YGS]**
Bldr: Sosnovka Zavod, Rybinsk, or Yaroslavl Zavod (In serv. 1989)

U 634 (ex-BGK-1569)

D: 42 tons (54 fl) **S:** 11 kts **Dim:** 21.20 × 3.93 × 1.40
Electronics: Radar: 1 Lotsiya nav.
M: 1 Type 3D12A or 3D12L diesel; 1 prop; 300 bhp
Electric: 12 kw tot. (DGR 1A-16/1500 generator) **Range:** 200/11
Endurance: 5 days **Crew:** 3 tot. + 5 divers

Remarks: Transferred 1997. Based at Sevastopil.

♦ **1 ex-Russian SK-620 (Drakon)-class ambulance craft [YH]**
Bldr: Stocznia Wisla, Gdansk, Poland (In serv. 1983)

U 782 Sokal' (ex-PSK-1410)

D: 200 tons (240 fl) **S:** 10 kts **Dim:** 32.7 × 7.4 × 2.8
Electronics: Radar: 1 Mius nav.
M: 2 Wola Type 31-AMH diesels; 2 props; 620 bhp
Range: 1,000/10 **Crew:** 14 tot.

Remarks: Transferred 1997. Ukrainian designation: *Meditsinskiy Kater.* Has a hospital ward with facilities for 12 patients. In 1998, was being used as a general-purpose launch.

Sokal' (U 782) Hartmut Ehlers, 8-00

♦ **1 ex-Russian Project 1430 ambulance craft [YH]**
Bldr: . . . (In serv. 1976)

U 783 Illichivsk (ex-PSK-658)

Remarks: Transferred 1997. Displacement: 101 tons (fl); no other data available.

♦ **2 ex-Russian Toplivo-2 (Kair)-class (Project 1844) fuel lighters [YO]** Bldr: Komintern Zavod, Kherson, Ukraine (In serv. 1981, 1972)

U 760 Fastiv (ex-VTN-38) U 759 Bahmach (ex-VTN-81)

Fastiv (U 760) Boris Lemachko, 2000

D: 466 tons (1,180 tons fl) **S:** 10 kts **Dim:** 54.26 (49.40 pp) × 7.40 × 3.10-3.44
Electronics: Radar: 1 Mius (Spin Trough) or Don-2 nav.
M: 1 Russkiy Dizel 6 DR30/50-5-2 diesel; 1 prop; 600 bhp **Electric:** 250 kw tot.
Range: 1,500/10 **Fuel:** 19 tons **Endurance:** 20 days **Crew:** 24 tot.

Remarks: 308 grt/508 dwt. Transferred 1-8-97. Ukrainian type designation; *Maliye Morskiy Tanker* (Small Seagoing Tanker). Have four cargo tanks, totaling 606 m^3, and can carry up to 495 tons fuel oil. Fully seagoing if required to be. Have one 0.5-ton hose-handling crane. U 759 was badly in need of overhaul as of 2000, while U 760 was just completing an overhaul as of 8-00.

♦ **1 ex-Russian Project 14630 fuel barge [YON]**
Bldr: . . . (In serv. 1983)

U 954 (ex-MUS-482)

Remarks: Displacement: 208.8 tons.

♦ **2 ex-Russian Shelon' (TL-1127)-class (Project 1388) torpedo retrievers [YPT]** Bldr: Sosnovka Zavod, Russia (In serv. 1974, 1987)

U 890 Malin (ex-TL-1005)
U 891 Kherson (ex-*Monastirishye*, ex-TL-1616)

Kherson (U 891)—with former pennant number Boris Lemachko, 5-00

D: 270 tons (fl) **S:** 30 kts **Dim:** 46.0 × 6.0 × 2.0
Electronics:
Radar: 1 Kuban nav.
Sonar: 1 Oka-1 helicopter dipping-type
M: 2 M-504 diesels; 2 props; 10,000 bhp **Range:** 1,500/10
Endurance: 10 days **Crew:** 20 tot.

SERVICE CRAFT *(continued)*

Remarks: Stricken from the Black Sea Fleet on 10-1-96 and transferred to Ukraine summer 1997. High-speed hull with a covered torpedo-recovery ramp aft. U 891 had still not had her Russian pennant number replaced when last photographed in 5-00. May no longer be active.

♦ 1 ex-Russian Project 1784 repair barge [YR]
Bldr: . . . (In serv. 1963)

U . . . (ex-SM-15)

D: 920 tons (fl?) **Dim:** . . . × . . . × . . .

Remarks: Type designation SM (*Sudna-Misheni*) retained. Floating machine shop. No other data available; probably transferred in 1997.

♦ 1 ex-Russian Prometey-class (Project 498) large harbor tugs [YTB]
Bldr: Petrozavod SY, St. Petersburg, or Gorokhovets SY, Russia (In serv. 1971–80s)

U 947 Krasnoperekops'k (ex-RB-308)

Krasnoperekops'k (U 947) Hartmut Ehlers, 7-00

D: 262 tons (308 fl) **S:** 11 kts **Dim:** 29.30 (28.2 pp) × 8.30 × 3.30
Electronics: Radar: 1 Mius (Spin Trough) nav.
M: 2 6DR 30/50 diesels; 2 Kort-nozzle props; 1,200 bhp **Electric:** 50 kw tot.
Range: 1,800/12 **Fuel:** 30 tons **Crew:** 3–5 tot.

Remarks: Stricken from the Black Sea Fleet on 10-1-96 and transferred to Ukraine 4-96. Has 14-ton bollard pull, ice-strengthened hull.

♦ 1 ex-Russian Sidehole-II-class (Project 737K) harbor tug [YTM]
Bldr: Petrozavod SY, St. Petersburg (In serv. 1970–83)

U 953 Dubno (ex-RB-295)

Dubno (U 953) Boris Lemachko, 2003

D: 183 tons (206 fl) **S:** 10 kts **Dim:** 24.2 × 7.0 × 3.4
Electronics: Radar: 1 Mius (Spin Trough) nav.
M: 2 Type 6 CHN25/34 diesels; 2 vertical cycloidal props; 900 bhp
Range: 130/9.5 **Fuel:** 5.5 tons **Endurance:** 6 days **Crew:** 12 tot.

Remarks: Stricken from the Black Sea Fleet on 10-1-96 and later transferred to Ukraine. Russian class name: *Peredovik.* Bollard pull: 10.5 tons.

♦ 3 ex-Russian Project T63OZh small harbor tugs [YTL]
Bldr: . . . (In serv. 1954–56)

. . . (ex-BUK-239) . . . (ex-BUK-261) . . . (ex-BUK-300)

Remarks: Transferred 1997. Type designation: *Buksiriye Kater* (Tug-Cutter). Displacement: 19 tons (fl); no other data available.

♦ 1 ex-Russian Morkov-class (Project 14611) fireboat [YTR]
Bldr: . . . USSR (In serv. 1987)

U . . . (ex-PZhK-1819)

D: 280 tons (320 fl) **S:** 12.5 kts **Dim:** 41.00 (36.53 pp) × 7.80 × 2.14
Electronics: Radar: 1 Mius (Spin Trough) nav.
M: 2 Barnaul' 3KD 12N-520 diesels; 2 CP props; 1,040 bhp—bow-thruster
Electric: 400 kw tot. **Range:** 250/12.5 **Endurance:** 5 days **Crew:** 15 tot.

Remarks: Stricken from the Black Sea Fleet on 10-1-96 and later transferred to Ukraine.

Hull systems: Has four firefighting water monitors, two with 220 m^2/hr capacity and two of 500 m^3/hr, driven by two 750 m^3/hr diesel-powered pumps. Has both foam and Freon extinguishing systems, with 20 tons of foaming agent carried. Can spray a water curtain to protect herself and can also be used for towing.

♦ 2 ex-Russian Pozharnyy-I-class (Project 364) fireboats [YTR]
Bldr: . . . (In serv. 1953, 1954)

U 722 Borshchiv (ex-PZhK-20) U 728 Evpatoriya (ex-PZhK-38)

Borshchiv (U 722)—with minesweeper *Cherkasi* (U 311) and corvette *Lutsk* (U 200) in the background Leo Dirkx, 7-01

D: 145.9 tons (181 fl) **S:** 15.7 kts **Dim:** 34.9 × 6.2 × 1.8
Electronics: Radar: 1 Mius (Spin Trough)
M: 2 Type M50F-1 diesels; 2 props; 2,250 bhp (1,800 sust.)
Range: 284/15.7; 1,050/10 **Fuel:** 12 tons **Crew:** 26 tot.

Remarks: Stricken from Black Sea Fleet 10-1-96 and transferred to Ukraine in 4-96. May have had a propulsion plant consisting of two 900-bhp M50 diesels plus a centerline 450-bhp diesel. Can be armed with two twin 12.7-mm 79-cal. machinegun mounts. Both are based at Odesa.

♦ 3 Petrushka-class training cutters (Polish Project TS-39 or UK-3) [YXT]
Bldr: Stocznia Wisla, Gdansk (In serv. 1982–. . .)

U 540 Chigirin U 541 Smila U 542 Novakachovka (ex-*Darnicya*)

Chigirin (U 540) Boris Lemachko, 2000

D: 212 tons light (236 fl) **S:** 11.5 kts **Dim:** 33.00 × 7.44 × 2.44
Electronics: Radar: 2 Mius nav. (Spin Trough)
M: 2 Wola H12, 1,000 r.p.m. diesels; 2 props; 570 bhp
Electric: 250 kVA tot. (2 × 125 kVA, Wola H6 diesels driving) **Range:** 1,000/11.3
Crew: 13 tot. + 30 instructors and students

Remarks: U 541 reported transferred 1995, the others by 8-97; Two unidentified sisters may be named *Suvar* and *Akar*. Have two classrooms and a navigational training facility on the bridge. Are equipped with NBC warfare defense measures. Very similar to the slightly larger SK-620-class ambulance craft from the same builder. U 540 visited Turkey in 7-98. All three are based at Sevastopil.

♦ 3 Bryza-class training cutters (Project 772) [YXT]
Bldr: Neftegaz Zavod (In serv. 1967–79)

U 171 Gola Pristan
U 543 . . . (ex- . . .)
U 544 Voznesens'k (ex- . . .)

Voznesens'k (U 544) H&L Van Ginderen, 1998

SERVICE CRAFT *(continued)*

D: 135 tons (142 fl) **S:** 10.5 kts **Dim:** 28.82 × 6.60 × 1.86
Electronics: Radar: 2 . . . nav. **M:** 2 Type 3-D6 diesels; 2 props; 300 bhp
Electric: 84 kw tot. **Range:** 1,100/10 **Crew:** 11 tot. + 26 students

Remarks: Transferred 1994–95. One is ex-Black Sea Fleet unit UK-190, stricken on 5-7-94. Used for basic navigation and maneuvering training.

MARITIME BORDER GUARD

(*Mors'ka Okhorona*)

Note: Ships and craft were originally painted a very dark gray and had a broad yellow and narrow blue diagonal hull stripe; they are now mostly repainted with blue hull (hull areas subject to exhaust smoke staining are painted black), white superstructures, and broad yellow hull stripe. Lettered on the sides is the legend "*Mors'ka Okhorona.*" The letters BG began to precede the hull numbers early in 1999, and many of the pennant numbers initially applied began to be changed at the same time.

PATROL COMBATANTS [WPG]

♦ 3 Russian Pauk-I (Molnaya-2)-class (Project 1241.2)
Bldr: Yaroslavl SY, Russia (In serv. 1980–92)

BG 50 Grigoriy Kuropyatnikov (ex-BG 012, ex-PSKR-817)
BG 51 Poltava (ex-PSKR-813, ex-013)
BG 52 Grigoriy Gnatenko (ex-BG 014, ex-PSKR-815)

Grigoriy Gnatenko (BG 52) Boris Lemachko, 2001

Grigoriy Kuropyatnikov (BG 50) Hartmut Ehlers, 2001

D: 425 tons (495 fl, 554 max.) **S:** 32 kts (28 sust.)
Dim: 57.60 (49.50 pp) × 10.40 (8.74 wl) × 2.14 hull (4.00 props)
A: 1 76.2-mm AK-176 DP; 1 Fasta-4m (SA-N-8) SAM syst. (16 9M-313 Igla/Gremlin missiles); 1 30-mm 54-cal. AK-630 gatling AA; 2 5-round RBU-1200 ASW RL (30 RGB-12 rockets); 4 fixed 402-mm OTA-40 ASW TT; 2 d.c. racks (12 BB-1 d.c.)
Electronics:
Radar: 1 Mius (Spin Trough) nav.; 1 Reyd (Peel Cone) nav./surf.-search; 1 MR-123 Vympel'-AM (Bass Tilt) f.c.
Sonar: MGK-345 Bronza MF hull-mounted and MF dipping (6.5/7.0/7.5 kHz)
EW: Vympel'-R2 suite: 2 Half Hat-B intercept; 2 16-round PK-16 decoy RL
M: 2 M-507A or M-517 twin diesels; 2 props; 20,800 bhp (16,180 bhp sust.)
Electric: 500 kw tot. (2 × 200 kw, 1 × 100 kw diesel sets)
Range: 2,000/20; 2,600/14; 1,600/12 (normal fuel; 3,000/12 with max. fuel)
Fuel: 50 tons normal **Endurance:** 10 days **Crew:** 5–7 officers, 31–32 enlisted

Remarks: Transferred from the Russian Federal Border Guard, from which they had been stricken on 5-7-94. Both are based at Balaklava. Two sisters were transferred for service in the Navy.
Hull systems: The large housing for a dipping sonar system projects about 1.5 m out from the stern. The large hull-mounted sonar dome is located approximately beneath the gun fire-control radar. The hull is constructed of mild steel, although the middle part of the deck plating, some internal bulkheads, and much of the superstructure are made of aluminum-magnesium alloy.
Combat systems: The combat data system is designated SU-580. There is an SP-521 Rakurs (Kolonka-2) backup ringsight director for the single gatling AA gun; the Bass Tilt radar director can control both the 76.2-mm and 30-mm guns. Normal ammunition load is 152 rounds 76-mm (all ready-service, on-mount) and 2,000 rounds 30-mm. The sonar suite has a range of about 7 km for the dipping component; MGK-345 applies to both the hull mounted and dipping sonars, and the dipping sonar transducer can be lowered to 200 m.

HYDROFOIL PATROL CRAFT [WPCH]

♦ 2 ex-Russian Muravey (Antares)-class (Project 133)
Bldr: Morye (ex-Yuzhnaya Tochka) Zavod, Feodosiya, Ukraine (In serv. 1983–89)

BG 53 . . . (ex-BG 025, ex-PSKR-105)
BG 55 Galichina (ex-BG-027, ex-PSKR-115)

Galichina (BG 55) Boris Lemachko, 1999

D: 180 tons light; 195 std. (220 fl) **S:** 65 kts (60 sust.)
Dim: 40.30 (39.60 hull; 34.40 wl) × 8.00 (12.0 over foils; 7.30 wl) × 1.90 hull (4.55 over foils)
A: 1 76.2-mm 59-cal. AK-176 DP; 1 30-mm 54-cal. AK-630 gatling AA; 2 fixed 402-mm OTA-40 ASW TT; 1 d.c. rack (6 d.c.); 1 55-mm grenade launcher (70 grenades)
Electronics:
Radar: 1 Reyd (Peel Cone) nav./surf. search; 1 MR-123 Vympel (Bass Tilt) gun f.c.
Sonar: Ros'-K HF dipping at stern
M: COGAG M-20 plant: 2 M70 gas turbines; 2 props; 22,600 shp (20,000 shp sust.)
Range: 410/45–50 **Endurance:** 5 days **Crew:** 5 officers, 20 enlisted

Remarks: Thirteen Project 133 units were built for the KGB Maritime Border Guard. BG 53 was transferred to Ukraine in 4-94. BG 55 was reportedly transferred in 1996, but a reported fourth unit evidently did not transfer. Sister BG 54 (ex-BG 026, ex-PSKR-108) was reportedly stricken during 2001. A late 2001 report stated that two incomplete units of the class would eventually be finished at the Morye yard.
Hull systems: Foil system uses fixed fully submerged bow and stern sets, with an automatically adjusted amidships surface-piercing set beneath the bridge to control the ride. There is a single step to the hull aft. Both propeller shafts are sharply angled downward and are supported by the stern foil struts assembly. Can maintain 50 kts in Sea State 4 and operate hull-borne in up to Sea State 7. Hull is hard-chine in form and made of aluminum-magnesium alloy.
Combat systems: The dipping sonar deploys through a hatch in the transom stern. There is an SP-521 Rekurs (Kolonka-2) ringsight backup director for the 30-mm gatling gun aft. The depth charge rack is on the starboard quarter. The grenade launcher is intended to combat underwater swimmers.

PATROL CRAFT [WPC]

♦ 11 Stenka (Tarantul) class (Project 205P)
Bldr: Sudostroitel'noye Obyedineniye "Almaz," Petrovskiy SY, St. Petersburg (In serv. 1967–90)

BG 30 Perekop . . . (ex-21, ex-PSKR-636)
BG 31 Bukovina (ex-034, ex-PSKR-702)
BG 32 Donbas (ex-BG 035, ex-PSKR-705)
BG 57 Mikolayiv (ex-BG 033, ex-PSKR-722)
BG 61 Odesa (ex-BG 033, ex-PSKR-652)
BG 62 Podilla (ex-036, ex-PSKR-709)
BG 63 Pavel Derzhavin (ex-037, ex-PSKR-720)
BG . . . Volin (ex-20, ex-PSKR-637)
BG . . . . . . (ex-022, ex-PSKR-642)
BG . . . Zakarpattya (ex-031, ex-PSKR-648)
BG . . . Zaporiz'ka Sich (ex-032, ex-PSKR-650)

Bukovina (BG 31)—alongside sister *Pavel Derzhavin* (BG 63)
Boris Lemachko, 2006

D: 170 tons light; 211 std. (245 fl) **S:** 35 kts
Dim: 39.80 (37.50 wl) × 7.60 (5.90 wl) × 1.96
A: 2 twin 30-mm 65-cal. AK-230 AA; 4 fixed 402-mm OTA-40 ASW TT; 2 d.c. racks (12 d.c.)

BORDER GUARD PATROL CRAFT [WPC] *(continued)*

Electronics:
Radar: 1 Baklan (Pot Drum) or Reyd (Peel Cone) nav./surf. search; 1 MR-104 Rys' (Drum Tilt) gun f.c.
Sonar: Bronza hull-mounted HF; Ros'-K HF helicopter dipping-type at stern
EW: SPO-3 intercept
M: 3 M-504 or M-520 diesels; 3 props; 15,000 bhp
Range: 500/35; 800/20; 1,500/12
Endurance: 10 days **Crew:** 4–5 officers, 26–27 enlisted

Remarks: Built for the Maritime Border Guard of the KGB. Some were transferred to the Ukraine Maritime Border Guard in 2-92, possibly initially on loan. Sixteen Russian Federal Border Guard Black Sea units were stricken 5-7-94 and offered to the Ukraine Border Guard, which accepted 13, of which BG 018 (ex-PSKR-635) and BG 022 have since been stricken. The class was renumbered with two-digit numbers between 1999 and 2004. Two other names, *L'yiv* and *Kriviy Rig,* have been reported but have not yet been correlated to pennant numbers.

PATROL BOATS [WPB]

♦ 12 (+ . . .) Kalkan class (Project 50030)
Bldr: Morye Feodosiya Production Association (In serv. 1996– . . .)

BG 07 BG 304 BG 333 BG 604
BG 08 BG 310 BG 503 BG 807 Matros Mikola Mushnirov
BG 303 BG 320 BG 504 BG 808

BG 504—Kalkan-class patrol launch Boris Lemachko, 2002

D: 7 tons (fl) **S:** 30 kts **Dim:** 10.6 × 3.3 × 0.6 **A:** 1 7.62-mm mg
Electronics: Radar: None
M: 1 Type 457K diesel; 1 waterjet; 496 bhp (442 bhp sust.)
Range: 254/. . . **Crew:** 2 + 6 passengers

Remarks: Produced for harbor and riverine service, beginning in the mid-1990s. Aluminum-alloy hulls with GRP superstructures. A civilian version called the Krym-6 is also offered for service in sheltered waters. BG 303 operates from Sevastopil and BG 503 from Balaklava. BG 303 through BG 618 were not named, but later units seem to be. Sisters serve in Turkmenistan. Two were transferred to Equatorial Guinea during 2001.

♦ 17 ex-Russian Zhuk (Gryf) class (Project 1400A or 1400M)
Bldr: Morye Zavod, Feodosiya (In serv. 1971–86 and 1992–94)

From among: BG 100–107 BG 109–111
BG 115–119 and others

Zhuk-class BG 116 Boris Lemachko, 2002

D: 35.9 tons (39.7 fl) **S:** 30 kts
Dim: 23.80 (21.70 wl) × 5.00 (3.80 wl) × 1.00 (hull; 1.90 max.)
A: 1 twin 12.7-mm 60-cal. Utës-Ma mg **Electronics:** Radar: 1 Lotsiya nav.
M: Project 1400M: 2 M-401 diesels; 2 props; 2,200 bhp; Project 1400A: 2 M-50F4 diesels; 2 props; 2,400 bhp
Electric: 48 kw total (2 × 21 kw, 1 × 6 kw diesel sets)
Endurance: 5 days **Range:** 500/13.5
Crew: 1 officer, 9 enlisted

Remarks: Russian Federal Border Guard Black Sea area units P-53, -54, -125, -141, -501 through -512, -517, -519, -523 through -526, and -534 were stricken 5-7-94 and transferred to Ukraine, but most were evidently not put into service; units previously renumbered 611, 633, 634, and 635 have been stricken since transfer. An article in the Russian magazine *Tayfun* in 2-98 stated that five were completed 1992–94 at Morye Zavod, Feodosiya, where two were built for Vietnam in the mid-1990s. Two stationed at Yalta are used as escorts for the presidential yacht *Krym.* All were renumbered in the BG 100 series in 7-99, having previously been numbered in the BG 600 series. Nine are based at Odesa, five at Balaklava, and BG 118 and BG 119 at Kerch'.
Hull systems: Aluminum-alloy hull. Capable of operating in up to Sea State 4 or 5. Range also reported as 700 n.m. at 28 kts, 1,100 n.m. at 15 kts.
Combat systems: Armament seems to have been standardized at one twin 12.7-mm mount forward. Most (not BG 102) have a searchlight mounted in the after weapons mount position.

Disposal note: Two units were transferred to Equatorial Guinea between 2000 and 2003.

♦ 4 ex-Russian Shmel'-class (Project 1204M) riverine boats
Bldrs: Kamysh Burun Zavod, Kerch, and 61 Kommunara Zavod, Mikolayiv

	In serv.
BG 81 Lubni (ex-BG 171, ex-AK-211)	1972
BG 82 Kaniv (ex- BG 173, ex-AK-246)	1971
BG 83 Nizhin (ex-AK-563)	1968
BG 84 Izmayil (ex-AK-397)	1969

Kaniv (BG 82)—with former pennant number Boris Lemachko, 1999

D: 77.4 tons (fl) **S:** 24 kts **Dim:** 27.70 × 4.32 × 0.90 (2.00 molded depth)
A: 1 76.2-mm, 48 cal. D-56TM low-angle gun (in a PT-76 tank turret, with a 7.62-mm mg); 1 twin 25-mm 80-cal. 2M-3M AA; 2 mine rails (up to 8 mines)
Electronics: Radar: 1 Donets-2 nav. **M:** 2 M50F-4 diesels; 2 props; 2,400 bhp
Electric: 50 kw tot. (2 × 25 kw DG-25 diesel sets) **Range:** 240/20; 600/10
Fuel: 4.75 tons **Endurance:** 7 days
Crew: 1 officer, 2 warrant officers, 11 enlisted

Remarks: Designed in Russia by TsKB-5 (the current Almaz) design bureau under L. V. Ozimov. AKA-211, AKA-246, and AKA-563 were transferred to Ukraine in 8-95, along with other assets of the former Russian Danube Flotilla, while AKA-248, AKA-327, and AKA-397 were stricken 10-1-96 from the Black Sea Fleet and transferred later; of these, only four have been put into service. Were originally numbered in the BG 171 series by Ukraine.
Hull systems: The screws are mounted in tunnels to reduce draft. Armor includes 10-mm over the pilothouse and gun barbettes, 8-mm over the hull and internal bulkheads, and 5-mm over the deck and pilothouse.
Combat systems: One 7.62-mm machinegun is mounted coaxially with the 76-mm gun (for which 40 rounds are carried on-mount). Mine loads vary from four UDM-500 or two UDM-1000 to six KPM or eight YaM mines. Have a Gradus-2 gyrocompass, NEL-7 echo-sounder.

SERVICE CRAFT

♦ 1 ex-Russian riverine forces flagship [WYAG]
Bldr: Schiffswerf Linz AG, Germany (In serv. 1942)

BG 80 Dunay (ex-BG 500, ex-SSV-10, ex-PS-10, ex-*Prut,* ex-German *Grafenau*)

Dunay (BG 80)—with former pennant number Boris Lemachko, 1999

D: 300 tons (421 fl) **S:** 11 kts (8.5 sust.) **Dim:** 48.28 (46.60 pp) × 7.20 × 1.21
A: 3 single 14.5-mm 93-cal. mg; 2 single 45-mm saluting cannon
M: 2 Deutz RVM6M545 diesels; 2 props; 1,000 bhp (820 sust.) **Range:** 3,300/9.1
Fuel: 44 tons **Crew:** 24 tot.

Remarks: Built as one of 11 German Type N river tugs for use on the Danube. Served as flagship of the Russian Danube River Flotilla from shortly after World War II until transferred to Ukraine 1-5-95 along with other Danube Flotilla units. Retains Russian name in Ukrainian service. A sister serves as flagship of the former Yugoslav Federation forces on the Danube.

♦ 2 or more Katran-class (Project . . .) launches [WYFL]
Bldr. Morye Zavod, Feodosiya (In serv. late 1990s– . . .)

BG 316 BG 349

BORDER GUARD SERVICE CRAFT *(continued)*

Katran-class launch BG 349 Boris Lemachko, 1999

D: 13.2 tons (fl) **S:** 38 kts **Dim:** 14,30 × 3.60 × . . . **A:** Small arms
Electronics: Radar: None **M:** 1 Type 6TD diesel; 1 waterjet; 1,000 bhp
Range: 270/27 **Fuel:** 1.28 tons **Endurance:** 1 day **Crew:** 3 tot.

Remarks: Intended for harbor or lake use. Three-layer GRP construction. Can carry eight passengers or police/troops.

♦ 1 Krym-class (Project 1360) yacht [WYFL]

Bldr: Sudostroitel'noye Obyedineniye "Almaz," Petrovskiy SY, St. Petersburg (In serv. 1981)

BG 01 Krym

Krym (BG 01)—white-painted, without pennant number Boris Lemachko, 2000

D: 158 tons (220 fl) **S:** 32 kts **Dim:** 45.5 × 8.7 × 2.5 (mean hull)
M: 2 M-503A radial diesels: 2 props; 8,000 bhp **Range:** 500/35 **Fuel:** 40 tons
Endurance: 3 days **Crew:** 32 tot.

Remarks: Transferred to Ukraine on 1-5-95. Employed as the presidential yacht (*Prezidentskaya Yakhta*). Sister *Kavkaz* remains in Russian service, also on the Black Sea. White-painted; based at Yalta.

♦ 2 ex-Russian PO-2-class (Project 376) harbor launch [WYFL]

BG 501 (ex-602, ex-RVK- . . .) BG 503 (ex- . . .)

PO-2-class launch BG 501 Boris Lemachko, 1999

D: 32 tons (38 fl) **S:** 9-10 kts **Dim:** 21.0 × 3.90 × 1.40 max. (1.26 mean)
M: 1 Type 3D-6S1 diesel; 1 prop; 150 bhp
Electric: 10 kw tot. (1 × 10 kw, DGPN-8/1500 diesel driving) **Range:** 1,600/8
Fuel: 1.5 tons **Endurance:** 5 days **Crew:** 4–6 tot.

Remarks: Stricken from Black Sea Fleet 10-1-96 for transfer to Ukraine, BG 501 operates from Balaklava.

UNITED ARAB EMIRATES

NAVY

Personnel: About 2,500 tot.

Bases: Principal bases are located at Abu Dhabi, Damla, Mina Zayed, Mina Jebel, Mina Rashid, Khor Fakkan, Mina Saqr, and Mina Sultan.

Naval Aviation: Four EADS C-295 maritime patrol aircraft/ASW aircraft were delivered in 2003. Two Pilatus-Britten-Norman BN-2 Islander Maritime Defender aircraft serve for patrol duties, seven Aerospatiale AS-565SA Panther helicopters, seven Aerospatiale AS.332 Super Puma helicopters, and four Aerospatiale AS.316B Alouette-III light helicopters are also in service.

U.A.E. Navy AS.332 Super Puma U.S. Navy, 4-03

The Super Puma helicopters can launch AM 39 Exocet and the Panthers AS 15 antiship missiles. WASS A244S ASW torpedoes were selected for use with the helicopters in 1997.

Note: Incorporating the former Defense Force Sea Wing of the Abu Dhabi National Defense Force, the U.A.E. Navy was formed on 1 February 1978 as part of the federated forces of Abu Dhabi, Ajman, Dubai, Fujairah, Ras al Khaimah, Sharjah, and Umm al Qaiwan. The merchant marines of these states are also combined into a single administrative unit. Several of these nation states, including Abu Dhabi and Dubai, also operate separate Customs Services with their own patrol craft.
Coast Defense Systems: Dubai is said to have acquired 30 truck-launched Chinese HY-2 antiship missiles by 1995.

ATTACK SUBMARINES [SS]

The U.A.E. remains interested in acquiring a diesel submarine capability and most recently expressed interest in retired German Type 206A–class submarines, though no deals have yet been finalized.

FRIGATES [FF]

♦ 2 Netherlands Kortenaer class

Bldr: Royal Schelde, Vlissingen

	Laid down	L	In serv.
F 01 Abu Dhabi (ex-*Abraham Crijnssen*, F 816)	5-10-78	16-5-81	26-1-83
F 02 Al Amarat (ex-*Piet Heyn*, F 811)	28-4-77	3-6-78	14-4-81

D: 3,000 tons (3,786 fl) **S:** 30 kts (20 on 2 Tyne turbines)
Dim: 130.2 (121.8 pp) × 14.4 × 4.4 (6.0 props)
A: 8 RGM-84 Harpoon Block II SSM; 1 8-round Mk 29 missile launcher (24 RIM-7M NATO Sea Sparrow SAM); 1 76-mm 62-cal. OTO Melara DP; 1 30-mm SGE-30 Goalkeeper CIWS; 2 single 20-mm 70-cal. Oerlikon AA; 4 fixed 324-mm Mk 32 Mod. 9 ASW TT (Mk 46 Mod. 5 torpedoes); 1 . . . helicopter
Electronics:
Radar: (all Thales) 1 Scout nav.; 1 ZW-06 surf. search; 1 LW-08 early warning; WM-25 f.c.; 1 STIR-18 f.c.
Sonar: 1 Canadian Westinghouse SQS-505 hull-mounted MF
EW: Sphinx intercept; Ramses jammer; Mk 36 SRBOC decoy syst. (2 6-round Mk 137 RL); SLQ-25 Nixie towed torpedo decoy syst.

FRIGATES [FF] *(continued)*

Al Amarat (F 02) Claronav Pictures, 1-98

Abu Dhabi (F 01) *Ships of the World,* 7-01

M: COGOG: 2 Rolls-Royce Olympus TM-3B gas turbines (25,800 shp each); 2 Rolls-Royce Tyne RM-1C cruise gas turbines (4,900 shp each); 2 LIPS CP props; 51,600 shp max.
Electric: 3,000 kw tot. (4 × 750 kw, SEMT-Pielstick PA 4 diesels driving)
Range: 4,700/16 (on 1 Tyne turbine) **Crew:** 140 tot.

Remarks: Purchased 2-4-96. F 01 was transferred and recommissioned on 31-10-97 and F 02 on 29-6-98 after refits at Vlissingen that commenced summer 1996; F 02 departed for the U.A.E. on 3-7-98. F 01 had been decommissioned from the Royal Netherlands Navy in 6-96 and F 02 in 1-95. As part of the purchase agreement, training and electronics overhaul facilities were built in Abu Dhabi, and two tugs to handle the ships were bought. Are being operated with far smaller crews than when in Dutch service, where they carried 18 officers and 182 enlisted.
Hull systems: The hull is divided by fifteen watertight bulkheads. One pair of Denny-Brown, nonretracting fin stabilizers is fitted. Particular attention has been paid to habitability. Have the Sperry Mk 29 Mod. 1 inertial navigation system. The engineering plant is distributed in four compartments, forward to aft: auxiliaries; Olympus gas turbines; Tyne gas turbines plus reduction gears. There are two auxiliary boilers and two evaporators.
Combat systems: Have the Thales SEWACO-II combat data system. Normally, only one helicopter is carried, but a second can be accommodated in the hangar. The Mk 36 SRBOC chaff system replaced the original Knebworth/Corvus RL. Thales Scout low probability-of-intercept navigational radars were installed during their 1996–98 activation refits, and new Goalkeeper mountings were purchased for the ships. France's DCN and Eurosam have proposed replacing the Mk 29 box launchers with Sylver vertical launchers for Aster 15 SAMs. The Harpoon missile canisters may, in fact, be empty due to delays in acquiring the missiles from the United States.

CORVETTES [FFL]

Note: A 90-meter corvette class is planned under project LEWA-2. Requests for proposals were to be received early in 1997; no contract had been announced as of late 2003.

GUIDED-MISSILE PATROL COMBATANTS [PGG]

♦ 0 (+ 6 + 6) Baynunah (Project BR 70) class

Bldr: first unit: CMN, Cherbourg; others: Abu Dhabi SB (ADSB)

	Laid down	L	In serv.
P . . .	. . .	. . .	2008
P . . .	. . .	. . .	2008
P . . .	. . .	. . .	2009
P . . .	. . .	. . .	2009
P . . .	. . .	. . .	2010
P . . .	. . .	. . .	2010

Project Baynunah–class patrol combatant—official model Hans Karr, 2002

D: 780 tons (fl) **S:** 32 kts **Dim:** 72.0 ×11.0 × 2.8
A: 8 MM 40 Exocet SSM; 8 Mk 56 VLS cells (8 Evolved Sea Sparrow missiles); 1 76-mm 62-cal. OTO Melara Super Rapid; 2 twin 30-mm OTO-Melara AA; 1 AS.565 Panther helicopter; provision for 2 mine rails on helo deck
Electronics:
Radar: Terma Scanter 2001 nav.; EADS TRS-3D/16ES surf./air search; AMS NA-25/XM f.c.
Sonar: Provision for hull-mounted obstacle-avoidance set
EW: Eletronnica SLR-736E radar intercept; Thales Altesse communications intercept; 2 Buck MASS decoy RL
E/O: SAGEM VIGY-EOMS f.c. director; EADS COLDS laser warning
M: 4 MTU 12V595 TE90 diesels; 4 waterjets; 22,478 bhp—bow-thruster
Range: 2,400/15 **Endurance:** 14 days **Crew:** 37 tot. (plus 8 aircrew)

Remarks: Proposals requested 11-96 but the requirements were revised in 2-97 to include facilities for a helicopter and to require enhanced signature reduction measures. Initial bids were received by 2-3-97, and a winning design from CMN, Cherbourg, was selected on 23-3-01; a preliminary contract was signed during 4-02. The first four were ordered under a 1-04 contract for about $780 million. Two additional units were ordered during 7-05. First of the class is being built in France, with subsequent production taking place at Abu Dhabi Ship Building with assistance from CMN. The contract includes an option for an additional six craft.

♦ 2 German FPB 65 class

Bldr: Friedrich Lürssen Werft, Vegesack (In serv. 10-91)

PM 161 Muray Jip (ex-CM 01) PM 162 Das (ex-CM 02)

Muray Jip (PM 161)—with old pennant number French Navy, 1996

Das (PM 162)—with AS.332 Super Puma on deck French Navy, 1996

D: 590 tons (660 fl) **S:** 34 kts (32 sust.) **Dim:** 65.95 (62.90 pp) × 9.30 × 2.60
A: 8 MM 40 Exocet SSM; 1 8-round Crotale Modulaire SAM syst.; 1 76-mm 62-cal. OTO Melara Super Rapid DP; 1 30-mm Thales Goalkeeper gatling CIWS; 2 12.7-mm mg; 1 AS.316B Alouette-III helicopter
Electronics:
Radar: 1 Thales Scout nav.; 1 Ericsson Sea Giraffe 50HC surf./air-search; 1 Saab Dynamics 9LV 223 Mk. 2 f.c.; 1 Thales DRBC-51C f.c.; 1 Thales Goalkeeper f.c. array
EW: Racal Cutlass RDL-2 intercept; Racal Cygnus jammer; 2 330–340 round Matra Défense Dagaie decoy RL
M: 4 MTU 16V538 TB92 diesels; 4 props; 15,600 bhp **Electric:** 408 kw tot.
Range: 4,000/16 **Fuel:** 120 tons **Crew:** 43 tot.

Remarks: Ordered mid-1987, along with the FPB-44 class below. Design is a lengthened version of the FPB-62 class ships built for Bahrain. Launched during 1989 and completed 11-90 and 1-91, respectively; transferred after training completed. Plans to order a third were canceled.
Combat systems: In these ships, the elaborate weapons-control array includes the Saab Dynamics 9LV331 radar/optronic system for the 76-mm gun (which in this class is linked to the Sea Giraffe surveillance radar rather than the usual 9GA 209 search radar), and the self-contained track-while-scan radar array of the Goalkeeper close-in weapons system; the DRBC-51C radar provides illumination for the Crotale SAMs and is also equipped with backup optronic accessories. Goalkeeper has its own target detection/designation and tracking radars. In addition, a Matra Défense Najir optronic backup director with t.v. and infrared sensors and a laser rangefinder for the 76-mm gun is mounted on the bridge just forward of the tower mast. Have a helicopter deck with integral elevator to hangar below, as in the similar Bahraini navy units. A Thales Scout navigational radar replaced the older Decca 1226 around 2005.

GUIDED-MISSILE PATROL CRAFT [PTG]

♦ 2 German FPB-44 class

Bldr: Friedrich Lürssen Werft, Vegesack (In serv. 2-91)

P 141 Mubarraz (ex-P 41) P 142 Makasib (ex-P 42)

GUIDED-MISSILE PATROL CRAFT [PTG] *(continued)*

Makasib (P 142)—with former pennant number Steven J. Zaloga, 4-97

Makasib (P 142)—with former pennant number French Navy, 1-96

D: 210 tons (235 fl) **S:** 34 kts **Dim:** 44.0 (41.50 pp) × 7.0 × 2.2 (props)
A: 4 MM 40 Exocet; 1 6-round Sadral SAM syst. (. . . Mistral missiles); 1 76-mm 62-cal. OTO Melara Super Rapid DP; 2 single 20-mm 90-cal. Rheinmetall AA
Electronics:
Radar: 1 Thales Scout nav.; 1 Ericsson Sea Giraffe 50HC surf./air-search; 1 Saab Dynamics 9GA 331 f.c.
EW: Racal Cutlass RDL-2 intercept; Racal Cygnus jammer; 1 330–340-round Matra Défense Dagaie decoy RL
M: 2 MTU 20V538 TB92 diesels; 2 props; 10,200 bhp **Electric:** 405 kVA tot.
Range: 500/38; 1,600/16 **Crew:** 5 officers, 35 enlisted

Remarks: Order placed mid-1987. Arrived in U.A.E waters 5-91. Are an enlarged version of Lürssen's FPB-38 design rather than being further units of the TNC-45 class. Were numbered P 4401 and P 4402 until 2001.
Combat systems: The combat system is the Saab Dynamics (ex-CelsiusTech) 9LV200 Mk 2. The Sadral installation is the first export of the French system, which, in these ships, is controlled by a Matra Défense Najir optronic director abaft the mast. In order to accommodate the point-defense SAM system and the enhanced EW suite (whose spherical radome for the Cygnus jammer is mounted on the mast), a second gun position was sacrificed. A Bofors 57-mm rocket flare/chaff launcher is mounted amidships. The original Decca 1226 navigational radars were replaced with Thales low-probability-of-intercept Scout sets during 1997–98. Underwent minor modernizations in 2006.

♦ 6 German TNC-45 class
Bldr: Friedrich Lürssen Werft, Vegesack

	In serv.		In serv.
P 151 Baniyas	11-80	P 154 Shaheen	4-81
P 152 Marban	11-80	P 155 Saqar	6-81
P 153 Rodqum	4-81	P 156 Tarif	6-81

Shaheen (P 154) Steven J. Zaloga, 3-01

Marban (P 152)—with former pennant number French Navy, 1996

D: 231 tons (259 fl) **S:** 41.5 kts **Dim:** 44.90 (42.30 pp) × 7.00 × 2.46 (props)
A: 4 MM 40 Exocet; 1 76-mm 62-cal. OTO Melara Compact DP; 1 twin 40-mm 70-cal. Bofors-Breda AA; 2 single 7.62-mm mg
Electronics:
Radar: 1 Thales Scout surf. search; 1 Ericsson Sea Giraffe 50 surf./air-search; 1 Saab Dynamics 9LV 200 Mk 2 f.c. system
EW: Racal Cutlass RDL-2 intercept; 1 330–340-round Matra Défense Dagaie decoy RL
M: 4 MTU 16V538 TB92 diesels; 4 props; 15,600 bhp (13,000 sust.)
Electric: 405 kVA tot. **Range:** 500/38.5; 1,600/16 **Crew:** 5 officers, 27 enlisted

Remarks: Ordered late 1977. Refitted (without significant equipment modernization) by Abu Dhabi Ship Building, with technical assistance from Newport News Shipbuilding and Dry Dock, beginning 9-96; P 151 and P 152 were completed in 1998 and P 153 and P 154 in 10-99, and the last two were to complete in mid-2000. Previously numbered from P 4501 through P 4506, they were renumbered during 3-01.
Combat systems: The radar director is equipped with low light-level t.v. and an infrared tracker and has an associated search radar atop the mast. There is a Matra Défense Panda optical director for the 40-mm mount. Carry 350 rds 76-mm, 1,800 rds 40-mm, and 6,000 rds mg ammunition. Original navigational radar replaced by Scout during 1997–98. Received the Saab 9LV Mk 3E weapons-control system under a 2001 contract.

PATROL CRAFT [PC]

♦ 6 U.K. 110-ft. class
Bldr: Vosper Thornycroft, Portsmouth, U.K.

	L		L
P 3301 Ardhana	7-3-75	P 3304 Al Ghulian	16-9-75
P 3302 Zurara	13-6-75	P 3305 Radoom	15-12-75
P 3303 Murban	15-9-75	P 3306 Ghanadhah	1-3-76

Zurara (P 3302)—with former pennant number U.A.E. Navy, 1992

D: 110 tons (140 fl) **S:** 29 kts **Dim:** 33.5 (31.5 pp) × 6.4 × 1.7
A: 1 twin 30-mm 75-cal. BMARC/Oerlikon A32 AA; 1 20-mm 90-cal. BMARC/Oerlikon A 41A AA
Electronics: Radar: 1 Decca TM 1226 nav.
M: 2 Ruston-Paxman Valenta RP200M diesels; 2 props; 5,400 bhp
Range: 1,800/14 **Crew:** 26 tot.

Remarks: Originally operated by Abu Dhabi prior to the establishment of the U.A.E. fleet. Will likely be replaced by the new Buynunah-class corvettes. Have two U.K. 51-mm rocket flare launchers. Previously numbered 1101 through 1106, these units appear to have been renumbered during the 2000–2001 time frame.

PATROL BOATS [PB]

♦ 3 Boghammar launches
Bldr: Boghammar, Stockholm (In serv. 1986)

D: 5.5 tons (fl) **S:** 50 kts **Dim:** 13.00 × 2.66 × 0.90
M: 2 Volvo Penta TAMD-70E diesels; 2 outdrive props; 600 bhp **Range:** 500/35
Crew: 3–5 tot.

Remarks: Purchased by Abu Dhabi specifically for the defense of the Sultan's palace and are not part of the regular U.A.E. Armed Forces. Have stepped hydroplane hulls.

MINE-COUNTERMEASURES SHIPS

♦ 2 ex-Australian Bay-class catamaran minehunters
Bldr: Carrington Slipways, Tomago

	Laid down	L	In serv.
. . . (ex-*Rushcutter,* M 80)	31-5-84	8-5-86	1-11-86
. . . (ex-*Shoalwater,* M 81)	17-9-85	26-6-87	10-10-87

Ex-Shoalwater (M 81)—with former Australian pennant number
Brian Morison, 4-04

D: 100 tons (170 fl) **S:** 10 kts **Dim:** 31.00 (28.00 wl) × 9.0 × 1.90
A: 2/12.7-mm mg (I × 2)
Electronics:
Radar: 1/Kelvin-Hughes Type 1006(4) nav.
Sonar: STN Atlas Elektronik MWS-80-5 syst. (DSQS-11M sonar)
M: 2 SACM-Poyaud 520-V8-S2 325-hp diesels, hydraulic drive; 2 Schottel azimuthal props; 340 shp
Range: 1,200/10 **Crew:** 2 officers, 11 enlisted

Remarks: Decommissioned by Australia 2000–2001 and purchased by U.A.E. during 2004.
Hull systems: Glass-reinforced plastic construction; each of the two hulls is of 3.00-m beam. Main engines drive propulsion generators and ship's service generators. Reconfigured with two side-by-side exhaust funnels in 1992–93 to reduce noise. Pitch excessively in open water.
Combat systems: Sonar transducer is mounted beneath port hull. Sonar/mine-countermeasures control room in dismountable deckhouse. After trials in the early 1990s, the STN Atlas Elektronik MWS-80-5 minehunting sonar system was installed in the class. Carry two PAP-104 remote-controlled, tethered minehunting submersibles.

AMPHIBIOUS CRAFT

♦ 12 Ghannatha (Trossbåt)-class landing craft [LCVP]
Bldr: first 3: Djupviks Varv, Sweden; others: Abu Dhabi Ship Building (In serv. 2003–4)

P 201 through P 212

D: 30 tons (45 fl) **S:** 33 kts (23 loaded) **Dim:** 24.00 × 5.40 × 1.20
A: 1 12.7-mm mg **Electronics:** Radar: 1 . . . nav.
M: 2 MTU 12V 2000 diesels; 2 KaMeWa FF550 waterjets; . . . bhp
Range: 150/15 (loaded) **Fuel:** 15,000 liters **Crew:** 4 tot. + 42 troops

Remarks: Ordered 22-1-02 for $27 million under Project Ghannatha for construction under license from SwedeShip. *Trossbåt* means "Support Boat" in Swedish, and the design is used by the Swedish Coastal Artillery Service. Aluminum construction. Cargo: 15 tons on 14.0 × 4.5–m deck area or 2 m^3 water and 9 tons cargo or 8 m^3 diesel fuel or 7 m^3 of water and no deck cargo. Have folding bow ramp and a small crane. *Ghannatha* was the first to be completed at Abu Dhabi Ship Building.

AUXILIARIES

♦ 1 seagoing tug [ATA]
Bldr: Richard Dunston, Hessle, U.K. (In serv. 4-89)

A 3501 Annad

D: 795 tons (fl) **S:** 14.4 kts **Dim:** 35.00 (31.25 pp) × 9.80 × 4.15
Electronics: Radar: 1 Decca RM 2070/4 BT nav.
M: 2 Caterpillar 3606TA diesels; 2 Liaaen CP props; 4,200 bhp—Jastrum bow-thruster (3-ton thrust)
Electric: 206 kw (2 × 103 kw Siemens/Mercedes-Benz OM421 diesel sets)
Range: 2,500/14 Fuel: 143 tons **Crew:** 3 officers, 10 enlisted

Remarks: 400 grt. Fully equipped berthing/coastal tug with secondary firefighting, rescue, and salvage capabilities. Bollard pull: 55 tons. The bow-thruster is powered by a 362-bhp Caterpillar 3406TA diesel. Towing winch with 400 m of 40-mm cable, 5-ton capstan. Two 600 m^3/hr pumps for the three 200 m^3/hr and one 400 m^3/hr fire and foam monitors. Extensive navigational and communications systems. Can transport two standard containers on stern.

Annad (A 3501) R. Van Der Hoek, 1989

SERVICE CRAFT

♦ 1 diving tender [YDT]
Bldr: Crestitalia, Ameglia, La Spezia, Italy (In serv. 7-87)

D 1051 Al Gaffa

Al Gaffa (D 1051) Crestitalia, 1987

D: 100 tons (fl) **S:** 27 kts **Dim:** 31.35 × 6.90 × 1.20
Electronics: Radar: 1 . . . nav.
M: 2 MTU 12V396 TB93 diesels; 2 props; 3,950 bhp
Range: 432/18 **Crew:** 6 tot.

Remarks: Ordered 12-85. Lengthened version of the *Mario Marino* class (builder's M/V 100 design) built for the Italian Navy. GRP construction. Intended to support combat swimmers, as well as providing diving support services. Has a decompression chamber.

♦ 7 L 6401–class logistics landing craft [YFU]
Bldr: Abu Dhabi SY (In serv.: 1999; others: 2003–4)

L 64	L 66	L 68	L 70
L 65	L 67	L 69	

L 64 Steven J. Zaloga, 3-01

D: 850 tons **S:** 11 kts **Dim:** 64.0 × 12 × 2.7 **A:** 2 20-mm AA
Electronics: 1 Decca nav. **M:** 2 Caterpillar 3508 diesels; 2 props; . . .
Crew: 19 + 56 troops

Remarks: Were originally numbered L 6401 through L 6404. Two smaller 42-meter variants of this class were reportedly ordered during 2004.

SERVICE CRAFT *(continued)*

♦ **3 Al Feyi–class logistics landing craft [YFU]**
Bldrs: L 51: Siong Huat, Singapore; others: Vosper-QAF, Singapore

	L	In serv.
L 51 AL FEYI	17-4-87	4-8-87
L 52 DAYYINAH	14-10-88	12-88
L 53 JANANAH	14-10-88	12-88

D: 650 tons (fl) **S:** 11 kts **Dim:** 54.0 (50.0 pp) × 11.0 × 2.8
A: 2 single 12.7-mm mg
Electronics: Radar: 1 . . . nav. **M:** 2 MTU diesels; 2 props; 1,248 bhp
Range: 1,800/11 **Crew:** 10 tot.

Remarks: 350 dwt; can carry four medium tanks and have a large crane. Can also transport fuel and water cargo. Built at Argos Engineering Pty facilities, under lease. Were numbered L 5401 through L 5403 until 2001.

♦ **2 Pushy-Cat-class dockyard tugs [YTM]**
Bldr: Gamen, Gorinchem, the Netherlands (In serv. 1998)

2001 TEMSAH 2002 UGAAB

Temsah (2001) Maritime Photographic, 1999

D: Approx. 90 tons (fl) **S:** . . . kts **Dim:** 16.50 × 5.00 × 1.80
Electronics: Radar: 1 . . . nav.
M: 2 Volvo Penta TAMD-122A diesels; 2 props; 760 bhp **Crew:** . . . tot.

Remarks: Ordered 4-96 for service at Abu Dhabi to attend the two *Kortenaer*-class frigates. Have a firefighting monitor on a platform abaft the mast.

COAST GUARD
MINISTRY OF THE INTERIOR

Personnel: 110 officers, 1,090 enlisted

Note: Beginning in 2000, craft were being painted with a black hull (with red diagonal stripe) and white superstructure.

PATROL CRAFT [WPC]

♦ **2 Protector class**
Bldr: FBM Marine, Cowes, U.K. (In serv. fall 1999)

CG 101 (ex-P 1101) CG 102 (ex-P 1102)

D: 180 tons (fl) **S:** 35 kts **Dim:** 33.00 (29.00 pp) × 6.70 × 1.90
A: 1 20-mm 90-cal Mauser AA in Coulverine mounting; 2 single 12.7-mm mg
Electronics:
Radar: 1 . . . nav.
E/O: SAGEM optronic f.c. and surveillance
M: 2 MTU 16V396 TE94 diesels; 2 props; 5,920 bhp
Electric: 160 kw tot. (2 × 80 kw Stamford generators, MTU diesels driving)
Range: . . . / . . . **Fuel:** 15 tons **Crew:** 14 tot.

Remarks: Ordered 1-99 under Project LEWA-3. Were to be delivered fall 1999 but have probably been delayed or canceled. Aluminum construction. A Zodiac RIB with a 25 bhp Yamaha outboard motor is carried aft.

PATROL BOATS [WPB]

♦ **1 (+ up to 30) Sea Spray raiding craft [WLCP]**
Bldr: Halmatic, Southamption, U.K. (first unit); others: Abu Dhabi SY (In serv. 2000–. . .)

D: 4 tons (fl)d **S:** 38 kts **Dim:** 9.5 × 3.0 × 0.6 **A:** 1 7.62-mm mg
M: 2 . . . diesels **Crew:** 3 + 11 commandos

Remarks: Ordered for counterterrorist duties. A number of different types of RIBs are also in service.

♦ **3 18.1-meter class**
Bldr: C.N. Baglietto, Varazzo, Italy (In serv. 1993)

501 502 503

D: 22 tons (fl) **S:** 40 kts **Dim:** 18.1 × 4.3 × 0.7 **A:** 2 single 7.62-mm mg
Electronics: Radar: 1 Decca . . . nav.
M: 2 MTU 12V183 TE 92 diesels; 2 props; . . . bhp **Crew:** 6 tot.

Remarks: Ordered 1992. GRP construction.

♦ **6 GC 23 class**
Bldr: C.N. Baglietto, Varazzo, Italy (In serv. 1986–88)

758 through 763

GC 23–class 758 Maritime Photographic, 3-99

D: 40 tons light/44.50 standard (48 fl) **S:** 41.8 kts (38 sust.)
Dim: 23.00 (2.00 wl) × 5.50 × 1.17
A: 1 20-mm 90-cal. Oerlikon GAM-B01 AA; 2 single 7.62-mm mg
Electronics: Radar: 1 . . . nav.
M: 2 MTU 12V396 TB93 diesels; 2 props; 3,560 bhp (2,960 sust.)
Electric: 64 kVA **Range:** 700/20 **Fuel:** 7,500 liters
Endurance: 4 days **Crew:** 9 tot.

Remarks: Design derived from Italian Customs *Meattini* class. Aluminum-magnesium alloy hull and superstructure. First unit, paid for by Dubai, delivered 3-86. Second, paid for by Abu Dhabi, delivered 5-86. Third and fourth, paid for by Dubai, delivered 14-7-87 and 9-87. Two additional units were delivered in 1988.

♦ **12 Shark 33 class**
Bldr: Al-Shaali Marine, Dubai (In serv. 1993–94)

From among: 310 through 323

Shark 33–class 310 NAVPIC-Holland, 5-96

D: . . . tons **S:** . . . kts **Dim:** 10.06 × . . . × . . . **A:** 1 7.62-mm mg
Electronics: Radar: 1 Koden . . . nav. **M:** 2 Yamaha gasoline outboards; 500 bhp
Crew: 2–4 tot.

Remarks: Ordered 1992. GRP construction hulls. Enlarged version of the following class. Al-Shaali is the successor to Gulf Craft.

♦ **23 Shark 28 class**
Bldr: Gulf Craft, Dubai (In serv. 1992–93)

200-series

Shark 28–class 299 Maritime Photographic, 3-99

D: . . . tons **S:** . . . kts **Dim:** 8.53 × . . . × . . . **A:** 1 7.62-mm mg
Electronics: Radar: 1 Koden . . . nav. **M:** 2 Yamaha gasoline outboards; 500 bhp
Crew: 2–4 tot.

Remarks: GRP construction, ordered 1992.

♦ **16 P-63A class**
Bldr: Camcraft, New Orleans, La. (In serv. 9-78)

650 through 665

COAST GUARD PATROL BOATS [WPB] *(continued)*

P-63A-class 660 NAVPIC-Holland, 5-96

D: 50 tons (fl) **S:** 25 kts **Dim:** 19.2 × 5.5 × 1.5
A: 1 20-mm 90-cal. Oerlikon GAM-B01 AA
M: first two: 2 G.M. 12V71 TI diesels; 2 props; 1,400 bhp; others: 2 MTU 6V396 TB93 diesels; 2 props; 1,630 bhp
Crew: 8 tot.

Note: Also in use are several aluminum-hulled, outboard-powered open launches that can be transported on road trailers (200-series pennants) and several wooden-hulled dhows (100-series pennants).

SERVICE CRAFT

♦ **2 Arun-class pilot boats [WYFL]**
Bldr: Halmatic, Havant, U.K. (In serv. 1992)

NASEEM . . .

D: 37 tons (fl) **S:** 21 kts **Dim:** 18.3 × 5.34 × 1.50
M: 2 Caterpillar 3412 diesels; 2 props; 1,000 bhp
Range: 250/21 **Crew:** 5 tot.

Remarks: 34 grt. Kevlar-construction hull. Basic design, with low amidships freeboard, was intended for search-and-rescue duties but is also ideal for pilot boat use.

ARMY SPECIAL OPERATIONS COMMAND

SWIMMER DELIVERY VEHICLES [LSDV]

Note: In addition to the submersible vessels listed below, the U.A.E. has expressed interest in purchasing larger 250-ton submersibles, possibly from Fancantieri in Italy.

♦ **. . . Class 5**
Bldr: Eurotec Industries (Emirates Marine), Abu Dhabi (In serv. 1996– . . .)

D: 3.5 tons (surf. light) **S:** 7 kts sub. **Dim:** 9.1 × 1.15 × . . .
M: 1 Alstom/Parvex electric motor; 10.7 shp
Electronics: Sonar: 1 obstacle-avoidance, 1 echo sounder **Range:** 60/6
Endurance: 10 hrs **Crew:** 2

Remarks: Known as Long Range Submersible Carriers (LRSC). Have 80-mm thick hull composed of nine layers of GRP and carbon-fiber composite. Have two externally mounted nickel/cadmium batteries. Normal operating depth is 30 m; maximum diving depth is 50 m. Are equipped with GPS receiver, autopilot, and magnetic compass. The obstacle-avoidance sonar has a range of 150 m. The divers ride in cockpits; their breathing system uses either onboard or personal equipment. Payload is 450 kg. The design was ordered by two Middle East countries on 20-3-01.

♦ **. . . Class 4**
Bldr: Eurotec Industries, Abu Dhabi (In serv. 1994– . . .)

D: 1.3 tons (surf. light) **S:** 7 kts sub. **Dim:** 7.35 × 0.95 × . . .
M: 1 Alstom/Parvex electric motor; 10.7 shp
Electronics: Sonar: 1 obstacle-avoidance, 1 echo sounder **Range:** 60/6
Endurance: 10 hrs **Crew:** 2

Remarks: Known as Long-Range Submersible Carriers (LRSC). Have 80-mm thick hull composed of nine layers of GRP and carbon-fiber composite. Have two externally mounted silver-zinc batteries. Normal operating depth is 30 m; maximum diving depth is 50 m. Are equipped with GPS receiver, autopilot, and magnetic compass. The obstacle-avoidance sonar has a range of 150 m. The divers ride in cockpits; their breathing system uses either onboard or personal equipment. Payload is 200 kg.

CUSTOMS SERVICES

Several of the component states of the United Arab Emirates operate their own Customs Service patrol craft. Dubai has two U.S. Swiftships 19.8-m Commercial Cruisers. In 1992 Abu Dhabi took delivery of two 18.28-m new pilot craft with GRP hulls molded by Tyler Boats from Berthon Boat; they each have two Caterpillar 3412-DITA diesels. Sharjah received from Halter Marine, Moss Point, Mississippi, in 1987, two 70-ton, 24-kt, 23.77-m customs patrol boats of modified oilfield crewboat design.

Notes: Dubai also has a Marine Police force for harbor patrol duties. It operates at least two Magellan 36 GRP-hulled, twin Yamaha outboard-powered patrol launches (Nos. 123 and 124) and at least one smaller, aluminum-construction launch (No. 007).

UNITED KINGDOM

United Kingdom of Great Britain and Northern Ireland

ROYAL NAVY

Personnel: 40,630 total Royal Navy, including about 6,200 naval aviation personnel and 7,000 Royal Marines. Reserve forces include 26,430 naval and marine reservists. About 2,300 personnel serve in the civilian-manned Royal Fleet Auxiliary.

In July 2004, the United Kingdom announced major cuts to its armed forces. The Royal Navy was hit particularly hard with reductions of 1,500 personnel and 27 warships between 2005 and 2008. Cuts to the surface force include three Type 42–class air defense destroyers and three Type 23–class general-purpose frigates. The mine hunting force was dealt a blow by losing three *Sandown*-class and three *Hunt*-class mine-countermeasures vessels. Among submarines, three *Swiftsure*-class SSNs are expected to fall to the budget ax by 2008. It is worth noting that the Royal Navy's amphibious warfare ships escaped major cuts.

Bases: Principal naval facilities are located at Portsmouth, Devonport, Faslane, Gibraltar, Yeovilton, and the Royal Naval Air Station at Culdrose.

Naval Aviation: All Sea Harrier FA.2 V/STOL fighters were retired by 28-3-06. Twenty-four RAF GR.7 Harriers are being upgraded to GR.9 configuration for service as partial replacements for the FA.2s. Also in service are 42 Merlin HM.1 and 17 Sea King HAS.5/6 SAR helicopters, 13 Sea King ASaC 7 AEW helicopters, 42 Lynx HAS.3/HMA.8 light shipboard helicopters, and six Lynx AH.7 and nine Gazelle AH.1 assault helicopters. Land-based maritime patrol aircraft operated by the Royal Air Force include 19 Nimrod MR.2P with twelve being upgraded to MRA.4 maritime patrol aircraft. A more complete listing of aircraft, organization, and characteristics is found in the Naval Aviation section following the aircraft carrier listing.

Royal Marines: The principal operationally deployable component of the Royal Marines is 3 Commando Brigade, headquartered at Plymouth. Subordinated are 40, 42, and 45 Commando, which deploy with combat support and combat services elements seconded from the British Army: 29 Commando Regiment Royal Artillery, 59 Independent Commando Squadron Royal Engineers, and the Commando Logistic Regiment. The first Royal Marines armored vehicle, the 10.5-ton Viking armored personnel carrier, was accepted into service during 2006. The Viking carries 12 personnel, including the driver; 108 are to be built.

The Special Boat Service was differentiated from the Royal Marine Commandos in 9-02, and members of the SBS wear a special cap badge and insignia. The SBS is based at Poole, Dorsetshire.

Royal Fleet Auxiliary: Major auxiliary and supply vessels are subordinate to the Royal Fleet Auxiliary (R.F.A.), an organization manned by uniformed civil servants. The ships are built to the specifications of Lloyds of London (compartmentation, damage control, habitability) and also meet the standards of the Shipping Naval Acts of 1911 and of the Ministry of Transportation. In 1985 it was decided to reclassify all R.F.A. ships as "Government-Owned Vessels"; this was modified on 30-11-89 to place the vessels under the Director General of Supplies and Transport (Navy), Ministry of Defence (Navy). Since 1994 the head of the Royal Fleet Auxiliary has been a flag officer co-equal with other type commanders. The ships fly the blue ensign of the reserve rather than the white ensign.

Marine Services Agency: On 3-12-94 the Royal Maritime Auxiliary Service (R.M.A.S.) became the Marine Services Agency. On 28-2-96 the contract to perform most Marine Services Agency functions was let to SERCO-Denholm, effective 8-7-96, although some other specialized work is being carried out by a government-owned corporation based at Pembroke Dock, Wales. All craft operated by SERCO-Denholm were transferred to its control on 12-8-96 on bareboat charter and will continue to be U.K. government–owned, to wear former R.M.A.S. colors, and to fly the R.M.A.S. ensign. Former R.M.A.S. craft based at Gibraltar were transferred to Commander, British Forces Gibraltar and are operating with civilian crews under Marine Services Gibraltar.

Maritime Volunteer Service: At the time of its disestablishment on 1-4-94, the Royal Naval Auxiliary Service (R.N.X.S.) had 2,700 personnel at 64 ports in the United Kingdom, assigned to 12 vessels and 25 Port Headquarters. The organization was effectively reborn the same month as the nongovernment-funded Maritime Volunteer Service (M.V.S.), with around 2,000 civilian volunteers in 46 units (now 50); *Loyal Moderator* (A 220), the first of a planned 16 craft, was acquired in 3-95, and the former Thames Port Health Authority tender *Londinium I* was acquired in 9-96. Former Sea Cadet ship *Appleby* was acquired in 4-99. The craft are not considered government property. Since 7-5-98 the Royal Navy has been providing informal advisory assistance to the MVS, but not financial aid.

Shipbuilders and Major Component Mfrs.: British Aerospace (now styled BAE Systems) and GEC-Marconi Electronic Systems merged in 1999, bringing all but one major British naval shipbuilding yard under one management; BAE Systems now controls the Vickers Shipbuilding & Engineering, Ltc. (VSEL), Kvaerner Govan, and Yarrow yards and also manufactures command systems, radars, sonars, naval guns, and torpedoes; its 49.95% share in Thomson Marconi Sonar was sold to Thales in 2001. BAE Systems also owns the former Siemens Plessey and BAeSEMA concerns under its BAe Defence Systems Ltd (BAeDSL).

ROYAL NAVY *(continued)*

Vosper Thornycroft (now VT Group), Woolston, the U.K.'s only other major naval shipbuilder, purchased Halmatic on 3-11-98 and has moved Halmatic's assets to its Portchester yard. Racal Marine was purchased by Sperry Marine (a division of Litton Industries, now Northrop Grumman) in the U.S. during 1998 but is retaining its corporate identity; former owner Racal Electronics became a part of France's Thales on 11-10-00.

WEAPONS AND SYSTEMS

A. MISSILES AND BOMBS

Note: The missile design, development, and manufacturing efforts of France's Aerospatiale Matra and the U.K.'s BAE Systems (including its subsidiary Alenia Marconi Systems) were combined early in 3-01 as MBDA, which stands for Matra BAe Dynamics, Alenia Marconi Systems, and Aerospatiale Matra.

♦ Strategic Ballistic Missiles

Trident-2 D-5 Bldr: Lockheed

U.S. missile with a delivery vehicle and payload of British design and manufacture, with an independent trajectory capability (MIRV). The agreement for the acquisition of Trident was signed 14–15 July 1980. A total of 64 Trident missiles (of an originally planned 80) were acquired, and they have British-built A-90 warheads. During 7-98 submarines on patrol were limited to a maximum of about 48 warheads each. The missiles are serviced at King's Bay, Georgia, in the U.S. The RN's "fewer than 200" nuclear warheads are Britain's only nuclear weapons.

♦ Surface-to-Surface Missiles

Harpoon (RGM/UGM/AGM-84)
Bldr: Boeing

Since August 1977, 300 U.S. UGM-84 Sub-Harpoon antiship missiles have been acquired for submarine use, all of which will have been withdrawn from service by 2008. RGM-84C Harpoon Block 1C, in the GWS.60 system for surface launching, is carried aboard Type 23 "Duke"- and Type 22 *Cornwall*-class frigates and initially for the Type 45 destroyers; additional AGM-84C Harpoons have been procured for use on R.A.F. Nimrod aircraft.

All MM 38 Exocet missiles (formerly used on the Type 22–class Batch I and II frigates and on trucks based at Gibraltar for coast defense) had been retired by 1999.

Tomahawk (BGM-109 Block III/IV)
Bldr: Raytheon Systems Co. (U.S.A.)

Some 65 U.S. Tomahawk BGM-109 Block III land-attack cruise missiles were ordered 10-95 for around $280 million for use from *Swiftsure-*, *Trafalgar-*, and *Astute*-class submarines. About 70 Block III missiles were ordered since then to increase stocks and to replace those used in combat since 1999. Sixty-five Tactical Tomahawk (Block IV) missiles were ordered in 2005. See U.S. section for system details.

♦ Surface-to-Air Missiles

Note: A contract was let during 2003 for the Principal antiaircraft missile system (PAAMS) for use in the Type 45 destroyers. PAAMS is composed of the French Aster 15 and 30 missiles and the Sampson radar.

Sea Dart (GWS.30) Bldr: MBDA

A medium-range system using the Mk 30 Mod. 2 launcher on Type 42 destroyers. 1,000 had been delivered by 1985, of which 500 had been fired by late 1986. 100 more with G.Mk. 39 A1 fragmentation warheads were ordered 3-86. The Type 909 fire-control radars were updated under 5-87 contract with Marconi. It is planned to refurbish all existing airframes; an infrared fuze will be fitted, and other improvements in low-altitude capability and response time are being made. The weapons system is planned to be retired by 2015. Has a limited antiship capability, unlike its successors, Aster 15 and Aster 30. Sea Dart capability has been removed from the three *Invincible*-class carriers.

Length: 4.40 m **Diameter:** 0.42 m **Wingspan:** 0.91 m
Weight: 550 kg **Warhead:** 22.7 kg, expanding-rod
Propulsion: Solid-propellant booster, ramjet sustainer
Speed: Mach 2.5–3.0 **Range:** 35 n.m. max. **Altitude:** 100–60,000 ft.
Guidance: Semi-active homing **Fire control:** Type 909 radar

Sea Wolf (GWS.25/26) Bldr: MBDA

GWS.25 is fitted on Type 22–series frigates in a trainable launcher containing six missiles (total weight with missiles: 3,500 kg). Target designation is via the combined Type 967-968 radar. The GWS.25 Mod. 3 fire-control system employed the Marconi Type 911 (ex-805SW) search-and-track radar, with DN 181 Blindfire guidance, and upgraded features to the Type 967-968 radar.

The GWS.26 vertical-launch version is carried by the Type 23 frigates. The Block 2 variant of the missile entered service with the Royal Navy in 2005–6, with the missiles having Mk 4 SWELL (Seawolf Enhanced Low Level) dual-action fuzes, which were backfitted to existing missiles starting in 2002. Over 1000 Block 1 and 2 variants of the missile were ordered between 1995 and 2005.

Alenia Marconi Electronic Systems was selected in 9-98 (but not contracted until 12-00) to update the GWS.25 Mod. 3 and GWS.26 Mod. 1 systems; an E/O sensor is to be added to Type 911 tracking radars, while improvements to the radar trackers will increase acquisition range and improve low-altitude performance in clutter. The upgrades are being performed between 2006 and 2011. The Sea Wolf system will remain in service until at least 2025. Work on a Block 3 variant is now under way with an expected IOC around 2015. Data for the Sea Wolf GWS.25 missile include:

Length: 1.9 m **Diameter:** 0.3 m **Wingspan:** 0.56 m
Weight: 82 kg **Warhead:** 13.4 kg
Speed: Mach 2.5 **Range:** 5,000 m nominal **Guidance:** Radar

Data for the VLS Sea Wolf GWS.26 include:

Length: 3.0 m **Weight:** 140 kg **Range:** 11,000 m nominal **Guidance:** Radar
Fire control: Marconi Type 910 and 911 pulse-doppler radars, which permit control of two-missile salvos, or by electro-optical tracker

Starstreak/Seastreak (GWS . . .)
Bldr: Thales Air Defense, Belfast, Northern Ireland (formerly Short Missile Systems)

The successor to the Javelin missile, Starstreak is a Mach 0.4 missile with a range of 7 km, 1.27 m long. The first 1,000 production Starstreak missiles were ordered during 5-95 for use by the British Army and the Royal Marines.

♦ Air-to-Surface Missiles

Note: A successor to Sea Skua began initial planning in 1999 and is currently called the Future Anti-Surface Guided Weapon. The Sea Eagle antiship missile was withdrawn from service in 2000. The weapon, which has a weight of 600 kg and a range of 250 km, remains in service with India and Malaysia. In addition to the following missiles listed, RAF Nimrod aircraft can be fitted with AGM-84C Harpoon antiship missiles.

Sea Skua (CL 834) Bldr: MBDA

Developed for use by Lynx helicopters, which can carry two or four. Single-stage solid-fuel propulsion. Air-launched version has been exported to Brazil, Germany, Turkey, and South Korea. Under a 5-97 contract, existing missiles are being given life-extension overhauls. An export surface-ship version has been developed for small surface combatant use, with initial trials launches conducted late 1988 but only one sale has been made to date, to Kuwait. All are due to be retired from British service by 2012.

Length: 2.50 m **Diameter:** 0.25 m **Wingspan:** 0.72 m
Weight: 145 kg **Warhead:** 20 kg high explosive
Speed: Mach 0.8 **Range:** 15,000 m **Guidance:** Semi-active

♦ Bombs

500- and 1,000-lb conventional bombs are carried on *Invincible*-class carriers for use by Harrier fighter-bombers. Paveway precision-guided bombs are also in use and from 2006 Harriers carry Paveway IV in place of the current Paveway II.

♦ Air-to-Air Missiles

Sidewinder-1B (AIM-9L)
Bldr: Raytheon Systems Co., Tucson, Ariz.

Infrared-homing, solid-fueled, Mach 2.5 lightweight weapon employed with Harrier V/STOL aircraft.

Length: 2.90 m **Diameter:** 0.127 m **Wingspan:** 0.61 m
Weight: 84.4 kg **Speed:** Mach 2.5 **Range:** 12 nautical miles

B. GUNS

114-mm Mk 8 Bldr: Vickers

Light single-barreled gunmount with glass-reinforced plastic housing. Installed on the Type 42 destroyers and Type 23 and Type 22 Batch 3 frigates. The mounts on the Type 23 frigates are to be upgraded to Mk 8 Mod. 1 standard, with a saving of 6 tons per ship as well as reduced space requirements below decks. Several of the Type 42 destroyers (D 97, D 98) will be upgraded to Mk 8 Mod. 1 status. The weapons would lose the ready-service feed ring in favor of a hoist directly to the magazine. Development of an extended-range High Effect/Extended Range round weighing 20.6 kg, with a range of 29 km, and a muzzle velocity of 869 m/sec. was ordered from Royal Ordnance in 8-97.

Length of barrel: 55 calibers **Shell weight:** 21.0 kg
Rate of fire: 25 round/min **Arc of elevation:** –10° to +53°
Maximum effective range in surface fire: 23,000 m
Maximum effective range in antiaircraft fire: 6,000 m

30-mm twin Bldr: Oerlikon/Royal Ordnance

Twin GCM-A03-2 mounts. Eight mounts were procured during 1982 from BMARC (now Royal Ordnance) as emergency close-defense weapons for Type 42 destroyers and additional mounts were acquired later. Optical lead-computing sights. Rate of fire is 500 rds/min/barrel and effective range is 2 km.

30-mm DS-30B single Bldr: Royal Ordnance

A stabilized single mounting for the Mauser-designed 30-mm gun. Twenty-six were ordered 9-85 for the Type 23 frigates. Has 160 rounds ready service on mount. A new version, the DS-30M is under development for the Type 45 destroyers.

Projectile weight: 0.36 kg **Muzzle velocity:** 1,080 m/s
Rate of fire: 650 rds/min **Effective range:** 3 km

30-mm Goalkeeper (SGE-30) CIWS
Bldr: Thales Nederland

General Electric GAU-8A, 30-mm gatling gun in EX-30 mounting co-mounted with Thales radar detect-and-track fire-control system. Fifteen mounts have been procured. Three each have been mounted onboard HMS *Invincible* and HMS *Illustrious.* For data see Netherlands section.

20-mm Oerlikon Bldr: Royal Ordnance

Large numbers of single-barrel British-made Oerlikon GAM-B01 mountings were procured 1982–83 to augment close defense on a variety of classes. A 90-caliber weapon with 1,000-rpm firing rate and optical, lead-computing sight on mount, it has an effective range of 2 km.

20-mm Phalanx Mk 15 CIWS
Bldr: General Dynamics (U.S.)

Six U.S. Mk 15 Mod. 0 CIWS (Close-In Weapon System) mounts purchased 5-82 for use on the *Invincible*-class carriers. Additional mountings were later fitted aboard Type 42–class destroyers, amphibious warfare ship *Ocean,* the carrier *Ark Royal,* and replenishment ships *Fort Victoria* and *Fort George.* Uses six-barreled G.E. Vulcan gatling gun; see U.S. section for details.

WEAPONS AND SYSTEMS *(continued)*

7.62-mm machineguns

Standard NATO 7.62-mm light machineguns, having been found very useful in the Falklands War for disrupting low-level air attack, were added in considerable numbers to frigates and destroyers, using simple pintle mountings.

C. ANTISUBMARINE WEAPONS

Mk 10 Mortar (Limbo)

Triple-barreled mortar based on the Squid of World War II. Range: 400 to 1,000 m. Fires 177-kg time-fuzed shells, each with 94 kg of Minol explosive. Retired from Royal Navy service in 1992, but is still aboard a small number of British-built warships in the Chilean, Indian, Indonesian, Iranian, and Pakistani navies.

Mk 11 Mod. 3 depth charge

Dropped from helicopters against shallow targets. Has also been sold to Brazil, Chile, Egypt, France, India, and Pakistan.

Length: 1.4 m **Diameter:** 280 mm **Weight:** 145 kg **Warhead:** 80 kg

D. TORPEDOES

Spearfish

Bldr: BAE Systems (formerly BAe-Marconi Underwater Systems, Ltd.) (MUSL)

Heavyweight replacement for Tigerfish, began development in 1981. Has HAP (Hydrogen-Ammonium Perchlorate)-Otto fuel system and 900-shp turbine engine, with pump-jet propulsor. One hundred preproduction models, ordered in 1982, completed delivery in 1993 after protracted development and reliability problems; average cost was $14.6 million each. In 12-94 a 10-year, $950-million contract was placed for an additional 300 weapons; the first units were delivered in 9-99, the 200th was delivered during fall 2002, and the last by 2005.

Diameter: 533 mm **Length:** 8.50 m
Weight: 1,850 kg **Warhead:** 300 kg
Speed: 75 kts (55 sust.) **Range:** 40 km **Max. depth:** 900 m

Note: The last Mk 24 Tigerfish torpedoes were retired from service in 2004.

NST 75 11 Stingray

Bldr: BAE Systems (formerly BAe-Marconi Underwater Systems, Ltd.) (MUSL)

Lightweight antisubmarine torpedo replacement for Mk 44 and Mk 46 for use by surface ships and aircraft. Officially entered service in 1986, although was present during Falklands War in 1982. Electric-powered, with pump-jet propulsor. Contracts let 1996 to develop an improvement package to upgrade existing torpedoes; the upgraded Stingray Mod. 1 began entering service in 2006–7. About 3,500 Stingrays have been built for the U.K., Norway, Egypt, and Thailand.

Diameter: 325 mm **Length:** 2.60 m **Weight:** 267 kg
Warhead: 45 kg Torpex **Speed:** 45 kts max. **Range:** 8 km at 45 kts

E. MINES

Stonefish

Bldr: BAE Systems (formerly BAe-Marconi Underwater Systems, Ltd.) (MUSL)

Medium-depth modular magnetic/acoustic/pressure mine for launch by aircraft, surface ships, or submarines. Original version, described here, is being supplemented by a shorter, lighter Mk 2 version with 500-kg PBX explosive. There is also a training version. Has been bought by Australia, Finland, U.K., and two unnamed countries.

Length: 2.4 m (1.9 exercise) **Diameter:** 533 mm
Weight: 990 kg (440 kg exercise) **Warhead:** 700 kg Torpex
Life: up to 700 days in water **Shelf-life:** 20 yr.

Dragonfish

Bldr: BAE Systems (formerly BAe-Marconi Underwater Systems, Ltd.) (MUSL)

Lightweight, anti-invasion mine for use in waters to 30 m. About 85 kg in weight, it carries 80 kg of explosive and has a 200-day in-water lifetime.

Note: Also still in inventory are a number of older Mk 12, Mk 17, and Mk 28 mines (for details, see *The Naval Institute Guide to World Naval Systems* by Dr. Norman Friedman) and the Vickers Versatile Exercise Mine System, a 2.71-m × 533-mm, 560-kg device that can be laid and recovered, simulating virtually any known type of mine for training.

F. SONARS

♦ For surface ships:

Type	*Function*	*Freq. (kHz) or Band*	*Maker*
185	Underwater telephone	8–9	Graseby
193M	Minehunting	100–300	Thales
2008	Underwater telephone	HF	Admiralty
2009	Underwater telephone/IFF	HF	. . .
2015	Bathythermograph	N/A	. . .
2016	Hull, 360-deg. scan	5.5/6.5/7.5	Thales
2031(Z)	Towed passive	. . .	Thales
2034	Side-scan	110	Waverly
2048	"Speedscan," PMS 75 fwd.-looking mine avoidance	HF	Thales
2050	Hull, 360-deg. scan	4.5–7.5	Thales
2053	Side-scan mine locator	HF	. . .
2057	Towed passive 2031(Z) replacement	. . .	Thales
2059	Minehunting ROV tracker	HF	Mills Cross
2060	Bathythermograph	N/A	. . .
2065	Thinline array for 2057	. . .	. . .
2066	Torpedo expendable countermeasure system	N/A	. . .
2068	Ray path predictor (SEPADS)	. . .	. . .
2070	U.S. SLQ-25A Nixie decoy; 4 sets procured 1998	. . .	Frequency Eng. Laboratories
2080	"Talisman"—joint U.K./French design project for surface ship suite	LF	. . .
2087	Bistatic towed array	VLF	Thales
2093	Minehunting	HF	Thales
2095	Minehunting	HF	Thales
2193	Minehunting to replace 193M from 2004 on	HF	Thales

♦ For submarines:

Type	*Function*	*Freq. (kHz) or Band*	*Maker*
183	Underwater telephone	. . .	. . .
197	Echo-sounder	HF	. . .
728	Upward-looking echo sounder	HF	. . .
780	Upward-looking echo sounder	HF	. . .
2007	Passive flank array	1–3	BAC
2008	Passive flank array		
2019	PARIS Intercept	2–14	Thales
2020	Active-passive bow (sub version of 2016, uses same array as 2001; 2020EX is an upgrade)	5.5–5.7 active/ 2–16 passive	Thales
2027	Passive-ranging (uses 2001 and 2020 arrays)	. . .	. . .
2032	Bow array beam-former for 2020	VLF	. . .
2035	Sonar frequency analyzer	. . .	. . .
2039	Recording bathythermograph	N/A	. . .
2046	Processor-display/50-m towed array (27 on order)	. . .	Thales
2047	16-channel processor/freq. analyzer	. . .	. . .
2066	Bandfish torpedo-countermeasure	. . .	Dowty
2071	Noise augmentation decoy	. . .	. . .
2073	Emergency pinger	. . .	A.B. Precision
2074	Bow active/passive replacement for 2001/2020; uses 2020 array	. . .	Thales
2076	Designation for entire suite for SSNs, includes 2074, 2077, and 2081 in design	. . .	Thales
2077	Ice-navigation set for SSNs	HF	. . .
2081	Environmental sonar/nonacoustic suite	. . .	Chelsea Instr.
2082	Sonar intercept to replace 2019	. . .	Thales
2090	Integrated Bathymetric Information System	. . .	Dowty

Remarks: Type 2087 will be employed by surface ships and will incorporate an active 500-Hz LF hull sonar and a VLF passive towed-array operating down to 100 Hz and weighing around 3 tons. Current plans call for the first sonar to begin operating aboard *Westminster* (F 237) in 2008.

Two Type 2081 sensor packets are carried by SSNs; they measure water temperature, fluorescence, bioluminescence, and other ambient oceanographic phenomena.

♦ For helicopters:

Type	*Function*	*Freq. Band*	*Maker*
2069	Upgraded 195M for Sea King	HF	Thales
2095	Dipping	HF	Thales

Remarks: Type 2095 uses the FLASH (Folding Light Acoustic System for Helicopters) array in conjunction with an AQS-950 processor.

♦ Sonobuoys:

In use are the Australian SSQ-981 Barra, the U.S. SSQ-904 and SSQ-906 Jezebel, SSQ-954 and 954B Miniature DIFAR, and SSQ-963A CAMBS (Command Active Multi-Beam Sonobuoy). Some 100,000 SSQ-955 HIDAR (High Instantaneous Dynamic Range) sonobuoys were ordered from Ultra Electronics for $52 million early in 1998 for delivery from 2000 through 2003.

G. DATA SYSTEMS

ADAWS 8: On three oldest Type 42 destroyers.
ADAWS 10: Aerial and ASW defense. Fitted on the *Invincible*-class aircraft carriers; update for ADAWS 5.
ADIMP (ADAWS Improvement Program): Entered service on Type 42 destroyer *Manchester* in 1993; 14 total ordered for *Invincible* class and final eight Type 42 destroyers. Uses two F 2420 computers to sextuple processing power of earlier ADAWS 7 (itself an improved ADAWS 4). Has Raca; LFB and LFC automatic radar track recorders and LFD track combiner, as well as Ferranti LFA for the Type 996 radar interface. Supports NATO Link 10, 11, 14, and 16 datalinks.
CACS 1 (Computer-Assisted Command System): In the Type 22 Batch 3 frigates. Has two Ferranti FM 1600E computers and 12 Argus M700 miniprocessors.
CCA (Captain's Combat Aid): MUSL system for *Invincible* and Type 42 classes; being added to Type 22 frigates as well.
SAGOP (Semi-Automated Gun Course Plotting Station): Is on 18 ships equipped with 114-mm guns and was being given a naval gunfire support function as of 1998.
SSCS (Surface Ship Command System): Successor to the abortive CACS 5 for the Type 23 frigates; ordered 10-89. Has parallel processing, modular software, and Link 11 and 14 capability. Upgrades integrate the type 2087 sonar into the existing SSCS architecture.

WEAPONS AND SYSTEMS *(continued)*

Note: A number of other computerized command support and combat management systems are in development. The Pilot Flag Support System (PFSS) uses the U.S. JOTS I target position database software and acts as an intelligent datalink terminal; has been installed in Type 42 Batch C destroyers. The Fleet Ocean Surveillance Product (FOSP) provides track correlation and dynamic updating of on-board databases, in conjunction with the ship's Link 11 terminal. An Admiralty Research Establishment data fusion system has undergone trials in the Type 23 frigate *Marlborough.*

H. RADARS

♦ Navigational:

1006(1): (9,650 MHz): In submarines; navalized Kelvin-Hughes 19/9A.
1006(2, 3) (9,445 MHz): In major surface units.
1006(4) (9,425 Mhz): In mine-countermeasures ships.
1007: Kelvin-Hughes Series 1600 + Red Pac, I-band (3-cm) nav. radar with manual plot, replaces Type 1006.
1008: Racal-Decca Marine set derived from commercial BridgeMaster series (E/F-band) to supplement Type 1007 in some combatants; first orders announced 9-95. In 4-00 19 BridgeMaster E 180, X-band versions were ordered for use on support ships.

Note: Auxiliaries use a number of different commercial navigational radars, primarily the Decca 1226 and 1229 models; small craft employ Decca, Raytheon, or Furuno commercial sets.

♦ Combined air and surface search:

967/968: Paired back-to-back antennas; 967 in L-band (1,260–1,360 MHz); 968 in S-band (2,950–3,040 MHz). Employed with GWS.25 Sea Wolf system in Type 22 frigates. Type 967M has pulse-doppler to detect small targets. Rotates at 30 rpm. Incorporates Type 1010 interrogator for Mk XII IFF.
994 (S-band): BAE Systems (ex-Plessey) AWS-4 on Castle-class patrol ships and auxiliary *Argus;* uses quarter-cheese antenna from the obsolete Type 993.
996 (S-band: 2,850–3,100 Mhz): The 996/2 version is a 3-D replacement for 992Q in older ships. The 996/1 version is for Type 23–class frigates. Also used for target designation. Has stabilized antenna. BAE Systems AWS-9(3D) is the current commercial version. Being upgraded under a 5-99 contract with BAE Systems, with improved cooling systems and better target track extraction to reduce false-alarm rates. Being placed aboard most Type 23 frigates, Type 42 destroyers, *Invincible*-class carriers, and HMS *Ocean.*

♦ Air search, early warning:

965 (P-band): Long-range early warning. Still found in Indian and Chilean navies; AKE(2) antenna is a double-deck AKE(1). 965M has moving-target indicator feature.
1022 (L-band): Thales Nederland LW-08 radar with a Marconi antenna, on *Invincible* class and Type 42 destroyers. Incorporates Cossor 850 IFF interrogator. Has approximate 225 n.m. range. Rotates at 6–8 r.p.m.
ASTRAL (Air Surveillance and Targeting Radar, L-band): Uses a rotating planar array. In development as a replacement for Type 1022. To have 400 km range.
SAMPSON: Active phased-array multifunction radar developed by BAE Systems. A new semi-spherical, two-faced rotating antenna array was introduced in 1998 to reduce wind resistance and topside weight. For use in the Type 45 destroyers.
S 1850M: D-band radar for the Type 45 destroyers.

♦ Weapons control:

909: Sea Dart system (also controls the 114-mm Mk 8 gun in the Type 42 destroyers)
911: Marconi ST805 SW for Sea Wolf GWS.25 Mod. 3 system in Type 22 frigates and as 911(2) for vertical-launch Sea Wolf in the Type 23 frigates. The land-based Blindfire radar uses part of the same antenna array. To be upgraded with a new electro-optic system between 2007 and 2012.

♦ For aircraft:

Blue Kestrel: Multifunction, for Merlin helicopter.
Sea Spray: For Lynx helicopters—surface-search and target designation
Sea Searcher (I-band): For Sea King HAS.6 ASW helicopters, for use in interrogating the LAPADS sonobuoy system.
Searchwater (I-band): For surface search in Nimrod patrol aircraft and air- and surface-search in Sea King AEW.2 helicopters. Frequency-agile.
Searchwater 2000 (I-band): Racal set to be installed in updated Nimrod 2000 patrol aircraft and Sea King AEW helicopters.

I. COUNTERMEASURES

Note: The various active countermeasures systems are known as "Outfits."

♦ Surface ship and submarine systems:

Electronic Systems:

CXA(1): EADS Telegon 6 communications direction finder for submarines. Is part of the UAP(1) suite (see following). Was to have replaced all CXA(1) Telegon 6 sets by 12-96, but delays resulted in cancellation in 5-98. Now to be replaced by a new system to be built by either Raytheon E-Systems or Sanders.
Soothsayer: Lockheed Martin Systems Integration-Owego and Thales-Racal vehicle-mounted land system for Royal Marine use; formerly called EW2000, it was ordered in 2000 with service entry in 2006 and covers communications and radar frequencies in support of countermeasures.
UA-14: Racal portable radar threat warning system, for use on small craft and helicopters.
UAA(2): Covers 1–18 GHz. Used in Type 42 DDG, Type 22 FF, *Invincible*-class carriers. Made by RRDS (Racal Radar Defense Systems; now part of Thales).
UAA(3): In development to replace UAA(2).
UAD: U.S. SRD-19 direction finder portion of Outboard suite (U.S. SSQ-108 system).
UAE: ELINT array based on EM Systems S-3000 (0.5–18 GHz).
UAF(1): Thales Cutlass intercept suite for Type 23 frigates. Associated with Type 675 or commercial Cygnus jammers. Systems in *Illustrious* and early Type 23 frigates were upgraded in 1995–96.
UAG(1): Thales E-J-band (2–27 GHz) intercept on *Fort Victoria* class (Mentor 2 is the commercial name).
UAK: A component of the Outboard combat direction-finding suite. Upgraded by Sanders and Siemens-Plessey during 1996–98.
UAN(1,2): Thales Guardian shipboard version of aircraft MIR-2 Orange Crop; covers 0.6–18 GHz and is used on Castle-class patrol ships and the helicopter ship *Argus.*
UAP(1, 3): Thales suite in submarines; UAP(1) in SSNs and UAP(3) in *Vanguard*-class SSBN.
UAR(1): Thales Matilda radar warning set; covers 7.5–18 GHz and is aboard Hunt-class mine-countermeasures ships, repair ship *Diligence,* and on survey ships when used as mine-countermeasures support ships.
UAS(1): Falcon RX-740 set added to frigates and destroyers on Persian Gulf deployment; covers 1,000MHz–18 GHz.
UAT(1): Made by Thales for use on Type 23 frigates; covers 2–40 GHz, with 360° sweep from −15° to +30°; 255 track capacity, 2,000-mode threat library. Based on Sceptre XL. UAT(2) and UAT(3) are land-based prototypes and training versions.
UAT(5) and UAT(6): Thales variant in Type 22 frigates and Batch 2 and 3 Type 42 DDGs (with antenna outfit UCB[1]).
UAT(7): Replacement for UAF in early Type 23 frigates and also used on carriers and helo carrier *Ocean;* also to be in LPDs *Albion* and *Bulwark.*
UBB(1): Replacement system for Type 42 destroyers and Type 22 frigates. Will cover 0.5–18 GHz. May use existing antennas.

Jammers:

RCM-3: Gate-stealing jammer by Decca—being added to large surface combatants.

Note: The Type 670 and Type 675(2) jammers were phased out by the end of 2000 without replacement.

Decoy systems:

Bandfish: Type 2066 expendable submarine acoustic decoy.
DEC: Laser dazzling device to confuse or incapacitate aircraft pilots and IR-homing missiles.
DLB: Hunting Engineering's six-tubed, 130-mm Sea Gnat launcher, deployed in groups of four and equipped to fire Chemring Mk 214 Mod. 1 RF seduction and Royal Ordnance Mk 216 Mod. 1 RF distraction rounds and chaff mortar rounds. In some, two rear 130-mm tubes are replaced with 102-mm tubes for launching N4 broadband chaff distraction rockets. The Mk 251 Siren active decoy round completed round acceptance trials in 2002 and all RN surface combatants are being converted to employ it.
DLC: Vickers Corvus eight-tubed, 102-mm launcher, often with 50-mm flare launcher atop; fires N4 broadband chaff distraction rockets, and is mounted two per ship. No longer used by RN but is found in a few foreign fleets.
DLD: U.S. Raytheon (ex-Hycor) Mk 137, six-tubed launcher for Mk 36 SRBOC system; mounted four per ship. Fires Mk 182 chaff mortar rounds. In some auxiliaries.
DLE: Thales Shield, six-tubed 102-mm launcher, mounted four per ship and firing N5 broadband chaff rockets. Eleven systems procured.
DLF(1): Irvin Aerospace Ltd. Rubber Duck floating corner reflectors.
DLF(2): Irvin Replica floating reflector. Used by U.S. Navy as SLQ-49. Can create the illusion of a 50,000-m^2 target.
DLF(3): Replacement for DLF(2); initial order was for 16 ship sets, to include 70 buoys per ship. Can create the illusion of a 50,000-m^2 target. Uses four fixed, horizontal, tubular compressed-air launchers. Existing sets are "cross-decked" to deploying ships.
DLH: Marconi/Dassault (now Thales) SIREN offboard 7.5–17.5-gHz active parachute-retarded aerial jammer. Launched from 130-mm DLB and DLJ Sea Gnat countermeasures rocket launchers.
DLJ(1, 2): Decoy launcher outfits for large ships: DLJ(1) uses four DLB and four DLD; DLJ(2) uses eight DLB launchers and is on *Invincible, Illustrious, Fearless, Argus, Fort Victoria,* and *Fort George.*
DLK: Wallop Defence Systems Barricade 57-mm lightweight infrared and chaff decoy rocket launcher. 27 sets, each with two 18-barrel launchers, in service by 1991.

Note: Mk 8 114-mm guns can fire Chaff Charlie I- or J-band chaff rounds, and helicopters can manually drop Chaff Hotel.

Commercial equipment:

Type 242: Thales (ex-Racal) integrated intercept/jammer suite, with Cutlass, Scorpion, and Sadie processor.
Cutlass: Thales (ex-Racal) intercept 0.6–18 GHz, 5 MHz/5-deg. accuracy.
Matilda-E (Microwave Analysis Threat Indication and Launch Direction Apparatus): Lightweight, low-cost intercept system by Thales (ex-Racal). Six portable sets were on U.K. mine-countermeasures ships by 1989.
Mentor A/B/C: BAE System (ex-Marconi) intercept sets, to 40 GHz. Mentor 2002, introduced 1993, incorporated a jamming system and Shield rocket decoy launchers, and a Falcon DS-301A, 2-500 MHz communications intercept receiver is optional; the basic 2002 covered 1–18gHZ.
Sabre: Thales intercept 0.6–40 GHz, 5 MHz/2-deg. or 8° accuracy. For submarines.
Sarie: BAE Systems Selective Automatic Radar Identification Equipment; an add-on for existing EW suites.
Scorpion: Thales (ex-Racal) wide-beam jammer: can jam 5–8 targets, 50-kw output between 7.5 and 18 GHz; 1.5-sec. response time. Integrates with RN's Outfit UAF(1) console.
Shield: BAE Systems (ex-Siemens-Plessey) decoy rocket launcher. Shield I uses six-tubed launchers. Shield III, with improved central processor, comes in 12-, 18-, and 24-tube versions for different-sized ships. Launches P8 time-fuzed chaff rockets and P6 infrared decoy rockets.
Siren: BAE Systems (ex-Marconi) off-board jammer.
Sceptre: Thales (ex-CME, ex-Philips/Racal) intercept suite: Sceptre 0 for small ships, Sceptre X for corvettes, Sceptre XL for large combatants.

WEAPONS AND SYSTEMS *(continued)*

Scimitar: Thales (ex-CME, ex-Philips/Racal) deception/jammer.
UltraBarricade: Decoy launch system offered by Wallop Defence Systems and Grintek of South Africa. Has 24 chaff and dual-band IR rocket decoys on a trainable mounting that can also accommodate two tubes for larger decoys and even small surface-to-air missiles. The control system also provides optimum course-to-steer for the ship's helmsman.

Helicopter systems:

Yellow Veil: Jamming equipment on Lynx HAS.3 and Sea King HAS.6 helicopters. Derived from U.S. Whitaker ALQ-167(V). Used to protect surface ships as well as the carrying aircraft.

♦ Torpedo decoys:

SLQ-25A Nixie: U.S.-made torpedo decoy equipment. Four sets were purchased during 1997.
SSTD (Surface Ship Torpedo Defense System): Ultra Electronics was selected during 11-01 as prime contractor for the U.K. version of the SSTD which began to enter service in 2004. SSTD replaces the Type 182 decoy and uses the U.S. Frequency Engineering Laboratory SLQ-25A Nixie towed decoy, the TRAMP (Torpedo Recognition Acoustic Multi-beam Processor) sonar processor, a towed passive sonar deployed with the Nixie, and a variety of expendable countermeasures
Submarine countermeasures: 4-inch (102-mm) diameter decoy launchers are employed: Mk 6 in the *Swiftsure* class, Mk 8 in the *Trafalgar* class, and Mk 10 in the *Vanguard* class.
Type 182: An obsolete towed noisemaker, being phased out in favor of the SSTD.

J. COMMUNICATIONS

The Royal Navy employs the Skynet-5 Super-High-Frequency (SHF) satellite communications system in carriers, destroyers, and frigates, although because there are not sufficient sets, only units deploying or fully operational carry the twin SCOT (Satellite Communications Terminal) radomes, which are 1–2 m in diameter and operate in the 500-MHz band. Royal Fleet auxiliaries, hydrographic ships, and corvettes of the Castle class carry the commercial Intelsat SATCOM system. Shipboard LF/MF/HF/VHF systems are increasingly integrated and are among the best in the world; single-sideband is extensively employed. Eight frigates are equipped with the Stand-Alone Message Processing (SAMP) system. All large combatants are Link 11 equipped, and Marconi Electronic Systems (now BAE Systems) received a contract in 9-96 to provide Link 16 interoperability for the Type 42 destroyers and the *Invincible*-class carriers.

BAE Systems has developed an improved SR(S) 7392 High Frequency broadcast multichanneling capability using digital hardware and new software to permit existing equipment to increase the number of channels in operation; the system entered service in 2004. Alert Communications has supplied a Outfit SEZ HF communications set that allows up to four broadcasts to share one broadcast channel for transmission; the system has been installed in a number of ships, including submarine *Trafalgar,* mine-countermeasures ship *Brocklesby,* and RFA oiler *Gold Rover.*

AIRCRAFT CARRIERS [CVV]

♦ 0 (+ 2) Queen Elizabeth (CVF) class

Bldr: BAE Systems

	Laid down	L	In serv.
R . . . Queen Elizabeth	. . .	. . .	2014
R . . . Prince of Wales	. . .	. . .	2017

Queen Elizabeth class—computer rendering Thales, 2005

D: 65,000 tons (fl) **S:** 28 kts **Dim:** 283.0 × 79.0 (39.0 wl) × 12.0
Air Group: 40 tot., including F-35 Lightning II fixed-wing strike fighters; Merlin HM.1 helicopters; and "Maritime Airborne Surveillance and Control" (MASC) platforms
A: . . .
Electronics:
Radar: 1 Siemens-Plessey SAMPSON 3-D target-designation; 1 BAE Systems/ Thales S1850M Smartello early warning
Sonar: . . .
EW: . . . intercept; SSTD (SLQ-25A(V)) active and passive torpedo decoy system
M: 2 Rolls-Royce MT30 intercooled-recuperative gas turbines, integrated electric drive; 2 props; 100,000 shp
Electric: . . . kw tot. **Range:** 10,000/15 **Fuel:** . . . tons
Crew: 600 tot. ship's company + 1,400 command staff and air group

Queen Elizabeth class—computer rendering Thales, 2005

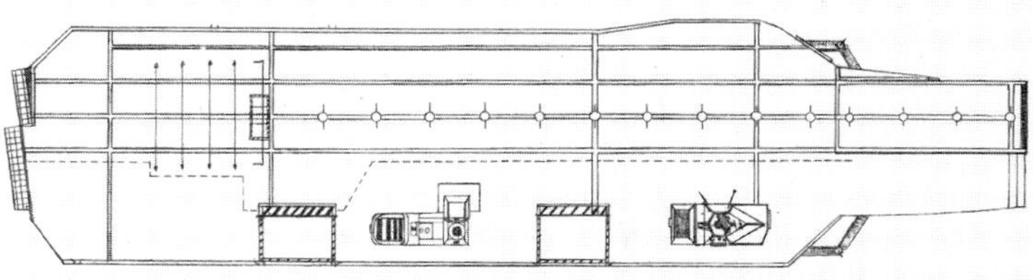

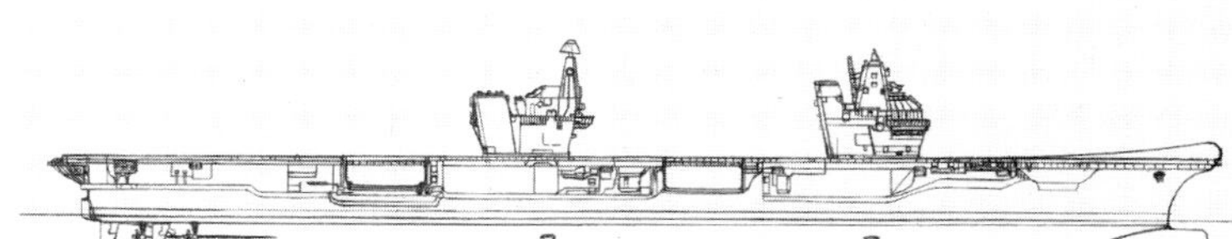

Queen Elizabeth class C.P. Vick/GlobalSecurity.org, 2006

Remarks: The 7-98 Defence White Paper confirmed that two conventional carriers would be built to replace the *Invincible* class. The U.S. F-35 Lightning II JSF (Joint Strike Fighter) will form the principal component of the air group, with the air wing likely consisting of 30–40 JSF and 4–8 helicopters. Two consortia bid on the carrier development program on 5-5-99: BAE Systems, teamed with Marconi Electronic Systems (soon thereafter owned by BAE), Rolls-Royce, and Harland & Wolff SY, against Thales UK, teamed with Lockheed Martin Naval Electronics & Surveillance Systems, Raytheon System Co., and British Marine Technology. Both consortia received preliminary design contracts on 23-11-99 and "Assessment Phase" design contracts on 21-11-01. Thales was selected on 30-1-03 to design the vessel, but with BAE Systems as prime contractor. France will also build a carrier based on the same design. The ships were originally to cost about $1.8 billion each, but the price had risen to $8.2 billion when the winning design was selected on 31-1-03. Service life is expected to be 40–50 years.

Modules for the ships will be built at three different yards (BAE Systems at Govan, Vosper Thornycroft at Portsmouth, and Babcock BES at Rosyth), with Rolls-Royce to provide the main engines and final assembly taking place at Rosyth.
Aviation systems: Although initially intended to carry the U.S. F-35 JSF STOVL strike fighter variant, which will not require catapults and arrestor gear, provision has been made in the design for later installation of non-STOVL aircraft as the F-35C CTOL variant of the JSF may later be procured. A contract to design an electromagnetic catapult for potential use in the ships let in 2001; are to be able to generate 150 combat sorties per day. As yet, there are no indications that any defensive armament system is to be installed. The hangar is to be 180 m long by 36 m broad and 7–10-m high. An additional 8–10 F-35 fighters could be added to the air group in an emergency. The ships are expected to be able to conduct campaigns of up to 150 first-day sorties or 100 sorties per day for 10 days.

♦ 3 Invincible class (1 in *reserve*)

	Bldr	Laid down	L	In serv.
R 05 Invincible	Vickers, Barrow	20-7-73	3-5-77	11-7-80
R 06 Illustrious	Swan Hunter, Wallsend	7-10-76	14-12-78	20-6-82
R 07 Ark Royal	Swan Hunter, Wallsend	14-12-78	4-6-81	1-11-85

Illustrious (R 06) Michael Winter, 6-05

V/STOL AIRCRAFT CARRIERS [CVH] *(continued)*

Illustrious (R 06) Ben Sullivan, 6-05

Invincible (R 05)—in reserve status since 2005 Derek Fox, 9-04

Ark Royal (R 07) Martin Mokrus, 3-04

Ark Royal (R 07)—after activation refit Royal Navy, 7-01

D: 16,970 tons (20,710 fl) **S:** 28 kts
Dim: 210.00 (192.87 wl) × 36.0 (27.50 wl) × 6.5 (8.8 over sonar dome)
Air Group: 16 Harrier GR.7; 4 Sea King ASaC AEW; 2 Sea King HAS.6 or Merlin HM.1
A: R 05, R 06: 3 30-mm Goalkeeper gatling CIWS; 2 single 20-mm 90-cal. Oerlikon GAM-B01 AA; R 07: 3 20-mm Mk 15 Phalanx gatling CIWS; 2 single 20-mm 90-cal. Oerlikon GAM-B01 AA
Electronics:
Radar: 2 Kelvin-Hughes Type 1007 nav.; 1 BAE Systems Type 996(1) surf./airsearch; 1 Thales Type 1022 early warning; 3 Thales Goalkeeper (R 07: General Dynamics Mk 90) f.c. suite
Sonar: BAE Systems Type 2016 hull-mounted, Type 762 echo sounder, Type 185 underwater telephone
EW: UAT(7) (R 06: UAT(8)) intercept; UAD/UAK (U.S. SSQ-108[V]2) communications intercept and D/F; 8 6-round DLJ(2) decoy RL; Type 182 towed acoustic torpedo decoy; R 05 also: UCB(1) EW Control Processor
TACAN: R 06 only: Collins AN/RN-139(V)
M: 4 Rolls-Royce Olympus TM3B gas turbines; 2 props; 112,000 shp (94,000 sust.)
Electric: 14,000 kw (8 × 1,750-kw Paxman Valenta 16-RPM 200A diesel alternator sets)
Range: 7,000/18
Crew: 60 officers, 625 enlisted (+ air group: 80 officers, 286 enlisted)

Remarks: *Invincible* was ordered on 17-4-73, *Illustrious* on 14-5-76, and *Ark Royal* in 12-78. All three are homeported at Portsmouth. Redesignated "ASW aircraft carriers" in 1980, previously having been considered a type of cruiser. The ships can embark 960 Royal Marines for short periods. During 2005 R 05 completed her final planned deployment and was placed in reserve status 3-8-05. R 06 arrived at Rosyth on 3-10-02 to begin a 23-month refit, during which new satellite and other communications equipment were fitted, the hangar deck modified and flight deck strengthened to allow for easier stowage of Harrier GR.7 and GR.9 aircraft. R 06 replaced R 05 as Royal Fleet flagship following this modernization. As of 6-06, R 07 was at Portsmouth awaiting a similar refit.
Hull systems: Modifications in 1998–99 to R 06 added about 160 tons to the displacement. All have the Prairie/Masker hull and propeller bubble system to reduce acoustic signature.
Aviation systems: *Invincible* and *Illustrious* originally had a 7° "ski jump" to assist Harrier aircraft in making rolling takeoffs at full combat load. The ramp on *Ark Royal* was inclined 12° and was 12 m longer. The ramp in R 06 is now inclined 13°, and R 07 has been altered. The 183-m-long by 13.5-m-wide flight deck was slightly angled to port to clear the now-removed Sea Dart SAM launcher. The single-level hangar has three separate bays, with the amidships bay narrower to permit passage of the gas-turbine exhaust trunks The two 9.7 by 16.7–m hydraulic, scissors-type aircraft elevators were to be replaced by Strachan & Henshaw chain-type elevators, but funds were not provided. All Sea Harrier fighters were retired in 2006 and RAF Harrier GR.7/9 strike fighters are carried in their stead. R 07 was the first RN ship to operationally deploy the new Merlin helicopter.
Combat systems: Have the ADAWS 10 combat data system, employing NATO datalinks 10, 11, and 14 (and the Link 16 JTIDS Joint Tactical Information Distribution System in R 05 and R 06). The ADIMP (ADAWS IMProvement Combat Data System) fitted in R06 and R07 was installed in R05 in 1999. The UAD/UAK communications intercept system employs the U.S. SSQ-108(V)2 Outboard COMINT intercept-D/F system, with SRD-19 direction-finder, SLR-16 intercept receiver, and OK-324/SYQ system supervisor station. Active units have two SCOT 1C antennas for the Skynet SHF SATCOM system and also have an Intelsat commercial SATCOM terminal. R 06 has a temporary TACAN capability to permit safer operation of RAF Harriers; the system was installed in 12-00 and was adapted from equipment intended for airborne use.
Modifications: The Sea Dart SAM system has been removed from all three, starting with R 06 during her 7-98 to 16-3-99 refit. R 05 was similarly altered during an 8-99 to 2-00 refit at Portsmouth but in addition had the two Type 909 missile-control radars removed and was fitted to operate Merlin helicopters. The Type 909s were originally retained on R 06 but were removed late in 2000. The vacated space has been used to enlarge the parking area of the flight deck by 8% so as better to accommodate RAF Harrier GR.7 fighter/bombers, and the Sea Dart magazine space has been converted for GR.7 weapons stowage; beneath the 23 × 18–m flight deck extension are some 22 new compartments. Additionally, R 06 received Link 16 capability, UAT(8) EW suite in place of UAF(1), and addition of the UCB(1) electronic warfare control processor and an automated command decision aid. During her reactivation overhaul at Rosyth, *Ark Royal* received the Integrated Electronic Warfare Control Processor, with UAT intercept, two Type 675 jammers (now removed), Sea Gnat, and DLH decoy equipment, as well as other modifications like those performed on *Illustrious*. The ship was also equipped to operate and maintain Merlin helicopters. The three U.S. Mk 15 Phalanx CIWS were retained but not updated.

NAVAL AVIATION

The Fleet Air Arm consists of: First-line squadrons (designation characterized by a group of three figures beginning with an 8) whose missions are attack, ASW, and helicopter assault; second-line squadrons (designation characterized by a group of three figures beginning with a 7) that are used in schools, tests, and maintenance.

Operationally assigned aircraft of the Royal Navy include:

No.	*Type*	*Function*	*Squadron*
24	RAF Harrier GR.7/GR.9	Attack /fighter	800*, 801*
42	Merlin HM.1	ASW	700, 814, 820, 824, 829
17	Sea King HAS.5/HAS.6	SAR	771
27	Sea King HC.4	Troop-carrying	845, 846, 848
13	Sea King AsaC.7	Early warning	849
42	Lynx HAS.3/HMA.8	ASW, attack, transport, training	702, 815
9	Jetstream T.2/T.3	Training/liaison	750
5	Grob Heron	Recruitment & training	727
6	Lynx AH.7	Assault	847

* 800 and 801 squadrons converted from Sea Harriers to the Harrier GR.7 in 2004 and 2006 respectively. They are now manned by 50% Royal Navy and 50% RAF personnel.

COMBAT AIRCRAFT

♦ FIXED-WING

Note: The U.S. Lockheed Martin F-35 Lightning II Joint Strike Fighter has been selected for procurement of at least four squadrons' worth of fighters. The aircraft are to be operated by the RN/RAF Joint Force 2000 from land and shipboard. The STOVL (Short Take-Off, Vertical Landing) J-35B will likely be supplemented by the conventional takeoff and landing (CTOL) U.S. Navy J-35C variant. First UK deliveries of the J-35 are expected in 2014.

♦ Harrier GR.7/GR.9

Mfr.: BAE Systems

All existing RAF Harrier GR.7 V/STOL fighter-bombers are to be upgraded to GR.9 configuration, with more powerful engines, digital weapons and navigation systems, and the ability to launch Brimstone (autonomous millimeter-wave version of the U.S. Hellfire antiarmor missile), Maverick, Paveway II (later IV), and Sidewinder AIM-9L missiles.

COMBAT AIRCRAFT *(continued)*

RAF Harrier GR.7—in Royal Navy colors Maritime Photographic, 3-98

HELICOPTERS

♦ "Maritime Airborne Surveillance and Control" (MASC) platform

Intended to replace the Sea King AEW.2A and ASaC.7 and to serve four each on the two new aircraft carriers. With the selection of the V/STOL version of the JSF fighter-bomber and the elimination of catapults for the new carriers, the MASC will now probably be a helicopter, possibly based on the Merlin, although various drone concepts are also being studied.

♦ Apache AH Mk1
Mfr.: Bell Textron

Remarks: Sixty-seven were ordered for the Army in 1995. Will achieve full operational capability by 2007 and can be carried aboard *Ocean* (L 12) and other ships assigned to amphibious warfare missions. Are essentially the same aircraft as the U.S. Army's AH-64D.

♦ Merlin HM.1
Mfr.: AgustaWestland

Rotor diameter: 18.59 m **Length:** 22.81 m (15.75 folded)
Height: 6.50 m (5.21 folded) **Weight:** 6,917 kg empty (14,600 max.)
Speed: 167 kts (150 cruise)
Propulsion: 3 Rolls-Royce/Turboméca/Piaggio RTM.322-01/8 turboshafts (2,130 shp each)
Max. ceiling: 15,000 ft
Range/endurance: 5 hr on-station (100 n.m. op. radius); 1,150 n.m. ferry range
Weapons: Four Sting Ray torpedoes or 30 troops more than 200 n.m. radius; 6,000 kg underslung to 550 n.m. range
Avionics: Marconi Electronic Systems Blue Kestrel 5000 radar, Thales Type 2095 ADS (Active Dipping Sonar) with AQS-903 acoustic processor, Racal Orange Reaper (Kestrel) ESM (0.6–18 gHz coverage)

Merlin HM.1—aboard HMS *Westminster* (F 237) Leo van Ginderen, 3-06

Remarks: On 2-9-91 44 production variants ordered from IBM-AgustaWestland consortium at a unit cost of about £97 million each, since risen to £101 million ($145 million). The last was delivered in 2002. Requires only one pilot and one systems operator in ASW role. Nine preproduction prototypes delivered 1984–90. Rather late in the game, it was discovered that the aircraft is too large to fit on the elevators of the *Invincible* class and too high to fit in Type 22 frigate hangars. In 7-98 the program was limited to 44 total airframes. An improved HM.2 variant, weighing 15,500 kg max. and with more-powerful RTM322 engines, is under consideration; to enter service around 2009, it would have an improved radar and carry the Future Air-to-Service Guided Weapon (FASGW).

♦ Lynx HAS.3, HMA.8, and AH.7
Mfr.: AgustaWestland

Rotor diameter: 12.80 m **Length:** 15.16 m **Height:** 3.60 m
Weight: 4,716 kg **Speed:** 145 kts
Propulsion: 2 Rolls-Royce Gem 4 turboshafts (1,120 shp each)
Max. ceiling: 12,000 ft
Range: 1 hr 30 min (half in transit, half hovering); 340 n.m. max.
Weapons: 2 Mk 46 or Stingray torpedoes, 2-4 Sea Skua ASM

Remarks: Data cited apply to the HAS.3 version. The HAS.3 has Sea Spray radar but no dipping sonar. Some are equipped with U.S. ALQ-167(V) Yellow Veil ECM; most have MIR.2 "Orange Crop" EW. Additional HAS.3s may be upgraded to HMA.8.

Lynx HMA.8—note the distinguishing nose sensor and EW antenna array Dave Cullen, 2-06

Lynx HAS.3 Jaroslaw Cislak, 6-02

Three Lynx began trials late 1989 as prototypes for the HMA.8 update: weight was increased to 5,125 kg, Rolls-Royce Gem 42-1 turboshafts were fitted, as were composite rotor blades, chin radome for undetermined radar, and a new tactical data system. HMA.8 Lynx also have Sea Owl infrared search and tracking equipment, CAE-made boom-mounted MAD gear, and the Sea Spray 3000 radar upgrade (which integrates the radar with the central tactical system). Lynx AH.7 helicopters serve with 847 Squadron in support of the Royal Marines; they are equipped to launch up to eight TOW antitank missiles and have a thermal-imaging sight.

♦ Sea King HC.4, HAS.5/6, and ASaC.7
Mfr.: AgustaWestland

Rotor diameter: 18.90 m **Length:** 22.15 m (17.03 fuselage; 14.40 folded)
Weight: 9,750 kg max. t.o. **Speed:** 126 kts cruise
Propulsion: 2 Rolls-Royce Gnome H.1400-1 turboshafts (1,535 shp each)
Max. ceiling: 10,000 ft. driving a 5-bladed rotor and a tail rotor
Range/Endurance: 3 hr 15 min. normal mission
Weapons: HAS.6: up to 4 Mk 46 or Stingray torpedoes or 4 Mk 11 depth charges; 1 or 2/7.62-mm mg (HC.4: 2,727 kg stores or 22 troops)

Sea King ASaC.7 Michael Winter, 6-05

Sea King HAS.6 Michael Winter, 6-05

HELICOPTERS *(continued)*

Sea King HC.4—with *Illustrious* (R 06) in background U.S. Navy, 2-02

Remarks: All HAS.2 were updated to HAS.5, and some later to HAS.6, except for 10 converted as HAS.2A (now ASaC.7) air-early-warning aircraft with Searchwater air/surface search radar (with antenna in inflating radome on pivoting arm to starboard). HAS.6 conversions and new aircraft have ASQ-504(V) MAD gear, Type 2069 dipping sonar, AQS-9026 sonobuoy processor. Most HAS.5/6 have Orange Crop EW suite. All HC.4 troop transports now come under joint operational control with British Army and RAF troop-support helicopters. All 13 AEW.2A airframes have been updated to ASaC.7 (Aerial Surveillance & Control; changed from AEW.7 during 6-02) configuration with new Searchwater 2000AEW pulse-doppler search radar; a JTIDS terminal to provide Link 16 commonality, and new IFF and communications gear. The first production conversion was delivered during 4-01.

ROYAL AIR FORCE MARITIME AIRCRAFT

The Royal Air Force (RAF) Strike Command includes the Nimrod force, search-and-rescue helicopters, and the Joint Force RN/RAF Harrier force. Maritime Patrol Aircraft include 19 (being reduced to 16) Nimrod MR.2P aircraft in Nos. 120, 201 Squadrons. Also in use are three Nimrod R.1P electronics aircraft, and two additional MR.2P are in storage. Twelve of the surviving Nimrod airframes are being rehabilitated and upgraded to Nimrod MRA.4 (formerly Nimrod 2000) configuration under a 7-96 contract, with deliveries (including three prototypes) taking place between 2006 and 2011. Twelve new construction aircraft are also being built. The program remains at least two years behind schedule. The modernized Nimrods carry new BMW-Rolls-Royce BR710 turbofans, the Racal Searchwater 2000MR surveillance radar, and a new Boeing tactical command system; the U.S. Joint Tactical Information Distribution System (JTIDS, Link 16) is also fitted.

Nimrod MR.2P Michael Winter, 6-05

Nimrod MRA.4 BAE Systems, 2005

The Raytheon/Racal Astor (Airborne Stand-Off Radar) synthetic-aperture imagery and moving-target detection radar system may be adapted for maritime.

NUCLEAR-POWERED BALLISTIC-MISSILE SUBMARINES [SSBN]

Note: Royal Navy submarines do not wear their pennant numbers. The assigned numbers are included here for reference only.

♦ 4 Vanguard class

Bldr: BAE Systems (formerly Marconi Marine-VSEL, formerly Vickers Shipbldg. & Eng., Ltd.), Barrow-in-Furness

	Ordered	Laid down	L	In serv.
S 28 Vanguard	30-4-86	3-9-86	4-3-92	14-9-93
S 29 Victorious	6-10-87	12-4-88	29-9-93	7-1-95
S 30 Vigilant	13-11-90	16-2-91	14-10-95	2-11-96
S 31 Vengeance	7-7-92	1-2-93	20-9-98	27-11-99

Vigilant (S 30) Dave Cullen, 1-06

Victorious (S 29) Bernard Prézelin, 9-00

D: 15,850 tons (submerged) **S:** 25 kts sub. **Dim:** 149.30 × 12.80 × 10.10
A: 16 Trident D5 ballistic missiles; 4 bow 533 mm TT (Spearfish torpedoes)
Electronics:
Radar: 1 Kelvin-Hughes Type 1007 nav./search
Sonar: Type 2054 suite: Type 2043 active/passive; Type 2044 towed array; Type 2045 acoustic intercept; Type 183 underwater telephone
EW: Racal UAP(3) intercept suite; 12 SSE Mk 10 countermeasures tubes (Type 2066 Bandfish and Type 2071 decoys)
M: 1 Vickers/Rolls-Royce PWR 2 pressurized-water reactor, W.H. Allen steam generators, GEC-Alstom steam turbines; 1 pump-jet; 27,500 shp—2 Paxman diesel alternator sets for emergency power: 2,700 shp
Crew: 14 officers, 121 enlisted

Remarks: Program to replace the *Resolution* class began with announcement 15-7-80 of the selection of the Trident D5 missile with eight multiple, independent re-entry vehicle (MIRV) warheads, necessitating use of U.S. *Ohio*-class midsection (although the submarines are shorter than the U.S. submarine, as eight fewer missiles are carried). Require refit and recoring only every 8–9 years. The first ship cost £1,705 million, the second £974.9 million, and the third £929 million; the fourth was expected to cost £962.6 million. S 28 was formally christened on 30-4-92, began sea trials 23-10-92, and began her first operational cruise during 12-94; S 29 followed a year later. S 31 began sea trials on 28-4-99 and entered operational service on 13-2-01. All are based at Faslane, on the River Clyde, at a facility officially opened on 14-8-93. Each of the four will undergo a three- to four-year-long overhaul period, refueling, and modernization between 2002 and 2010, during which the boats are to receive new reactors to extend the life of the class. S 28 began the overhaul at Devonport during 2-02 and was returned to service in 2005. Sisters are to follow with work completed around 2010.

Since 7-98, only one has been on patrol at a time, carrying only 48 warheads vice the 92 originally to be carried; missile launch readiness has been lowered to "days" rather than minutes of warning. In 1995 the class was given a "sub-strategic" role, with Trident D-5 missiles effectively replacing RAF-delivered WE 177 bombs, without alteration to the delivery payloads on the missiles. Have five crews among them allowing three submarines to be in commission at any one time.

Hull systems: Have anechoic hull coating. The U.S. Rockwell SINS Mk 2 inertial navigation system is installed. The two Paxman diesel alternators charge a 480-cell battery group for emergency propulsion. Bow-planes are permanently extended, an unusual and vulnerable arrangement. The hull contains some 80 km of piping and more than 500 km of cabling.

Combat systems: Have Dowty SAFS 3 fire-control system with DCC(BN) digital tactical data-handling system. Pilkington Optronics CK 51 search and CH 91 attack periscopes are fitted. A stern-arc covering sonar system is to be installed and integrated with the Type 2054 suite. The Type 2054 sonar suite had reliability problems in S 28, and the towed passive sonar array has had to be attached as a "clip-on" system in all four rather than reeled within the outer hull. An RN proposal to convert some of the ballistic missile tubes to launch Tomahawk land-attack cruise missiles was rejected during 8-02.

Note: All four decommissioned *Resolution*-class SSBNs are stored, defueled, at Rosyth, where they are planned to remain until at least 2012.

NUCLEAR-PROPELLED ATTACK SUBMARINES [SSN]

Note: The number of SSNs in service is being reduced from 12 to 8. Four of the newest *Trafalgar*-class boats are to undergo an extensive overhaul with the youngest of the class, S 93, now expected to remain in service until 2022.

♦ 0 (+ 3 + 3) Astute class

Bldr: BAE Systems Marine Barrow-in-Furness

	Laid down	L	In serv.
S 20 Astute	31-1-01	8-07	2009
S 21 Ambush	22-10-03	2008	2012
S 22 Artful	11-3-05	2008	2013
. . .			2015
. . .			. . .
. . .			. . .

Astute (S 20)—prior to launch BAE Systems, 2005

Astute (S 20)—artist's rendering BAE Systems, 2005

D: 6,690 tons surf./7,800 tons sub. **S:** 29 kts sub. **Dim:** 97.00 × 11.27 × 10.0
A: 6 bow 533-mm TT (38 total weapons: UGM-109 Tomahawk missiles, Spearfish torpedoes, mines)
Electronics:
Radar: 1 Kelvin-Hughes Type 1007 nav./search; 1 . . . bistatic radar receiver
Sonar: Type 2076 integrated suite (with Type 2074 active/passive bow array, Type 2077 HF under-ice navigational active, Type . . . towed passive array); Atlas DESO 25 echo sounder
EW: Thales UAP(4) intercept suite; DML CESM comms intercept (HF-UHF); . . . decoy launchers for SCAD 101 and SCAD 102 decoys and SCAD 200 sonar jammers
M: 1 modified Rolls-Royce PWR.2 pressurized-water reactor, 2 sets GEC-Alstom geared turbine drive; 1/pump-jet; 27,000 shp—2 Paxman auxiliary diesel alternators for emergency propulsion system, 1 retractable auxiliary electric propulsor
Crew: 12 officers, 86 enlisted (accomm. for 110 tot.)

Remarks: Originally known as the *Trafalgar* Batch-2 (B2TC) class. Requests for bids to build the class were issued to VSEL and to Marconi Electronic Systems Naval Systems on 14-7-94 for an initial three with an option for one or two more. Marconi (which formed a special subsidiary for the project and is now part of BAE Systems, as is VSEL) was the winner, and the final contract was let 17-3-97. By 2006 the program was said to cost $6.44 billion. Pressure-hull components for *Astute* began fabrication during 10-99. In 8-00, it was announced that a sixth would be sought, as a replacement for *Trafalgar* (S 107). Are to be based at Faslane. *Astute,* originally to have been delivered during 8-05, is now four years behind schedule and is not expected in service until 2009.
Hull systems: The reactor, with Type H core, is designed to operate for 25–30 years without requiring refueling. The hull form forward will resemble that of the *Vanguard* class, with nonretracting bowplanes; the stern is fuller than in previous RN submarines, in part because the pressure hull is of constant diameter throughout, and all control services are externally actuated, reducing the number of pressure hull penetrations. Will have improved accommodations over the *Trafalgar* class, although some 18 bunks will still have to be shared. Low-speed operating capabilities will also be improved, and the submarines will be capable of operating under ice and in tropical waters. Will have two 440-v a.c. Vosper Thornycroft main electrical switchboards. The originally planned submerged displacement was 6,510 tons. Normal maximum operating depth is to be 300 m. Will have Sperry Marine ring-laser gyro-based inertial navigation systems. Will have a six-man lockout chamber and can carry 12 special operations troops.
Combat systems: Will have many of the same systems as the *Trafalgar* class, although the towed array will be deployed from an onboard reel rather than clip-on, and provision for Tomahawk missiles will be built in. The BAE Systems Submarine Command System (SMCS) combat system and Thales (ex-Ferranti-Thomson) tactical weapons system data highway will be installed. Are to have Links 11 and 16 and provision for Link 22 to support surface forces. Will have provision to carry U.S.-style dry deck shelters for Special Forces equipment. Will not employ nonpenetrating optronic optical sensors, but will have two Pilkington Optronics CM010 nonhull-penetrating masts with periscope, optronics, and ESM antennas, permitting more room in the control spaces. Are to have Thales Sensors (ex-Racal) bistatic, mast-mounted radar receiver system that will allow the processing of target information from noncooperative radar sets in the vicinity of the submarine, using two Type AZE-4 antenna arrays. The first three will have the UAP(4) EW suite, with the others to get a variant of the UAT system under development. The CESM communications intercept and D/F suite is based on U.S. Argon Engineering Associates technology. The type of towed passive array has not been decided; while a "fat line" system is in development, the U.S. TB-29A "thin line" array may be selected instead.

♦ 7 Trafalgar class

Bldr: Marconi Electronic Systems Naval Systems-VSEL, Barrow-in-Furness

	Ordered	Laid down	L	In serv.
S 87 Turbulent	28-7-78	8-5-80	1-12-82	28-4-84
S 88 Tireless	5-7-79	1981	13-7-84	5-10-85
S 90 Torbay	26-6-81	12-82	8-3-85	7-2-87
S 91 Trenchant	22-3-83	28-10-85	4-11-86	14-1-89
S 92 Talent	10-9-84	1986	15-4-88	28-5-90
S 93 Triumph	3-1-86	1987	16-2-91	12-10-91
S 107 Trafalgar	7-4-77	25-4-79	1-7-81	27-5-83

Trenchant (S 91) Ben Sullivan, 4-05

Turbulent (S 87) A. A. de Kruijf, 7-05

Trenchant (S 91) Ben Sullivan, 4-05

D: 4,740 tons surf./ 5,208 tons sub. **S:** 30 kts sub.
Dim: 85.38 × 9.83 × 8.25 hull (9.50 max. surfaced)
A: 5 bow 533-mm TT (25 total weapons: UGM-109 Tomahawk land-attack missiles; UGM-84D-2 Harpoon missiles, Spearfish torpedoes, mines

NUCLEAR-PROPELLED ATTACK SUBMARINES [SSN] *(continued)*

Electronics:
Radar: 1 Kelvin-Hughes Type 1007 nav./surf. search
Sonar: Type 2020 MODEX bow MF active/passive array; Type 2072 (S 91: Type 2007) passive flank array; Type 2019 PARIS acoustic intercept array; Type 2046 (S 91: Type 2026) towed passive array; Type 2027 passive ranging; Type 2071 noise generator; Type 2077 active ice navigation; Type 2008 underwater telephone; Type 197 echo sounder; Type 728 and Type 780 upward-looking echo sounders; S 90 and S 91: Type 2076 integrated suite (with Type 2074 active/passive bow array; Type 2077 HF under-ice navigational active, Type 2081 self-noise monitoriing, Type . . . towed passive array)
EW: Thales UAP(1) intercept suite (1-18GHz); EADS CXA(1) Telegon 6 comms D/F; 4 (S 107: 10; S 93: 5) 102-mm SSE Mk 8 decoytubes (Type 2066 Bandfish and Type 2071 decoys)
M: 1 Rolls-Royce pressurized-water PWR.1 reactor; 2 W.H. Allen turbogenerator sets, GEC-Alstom geared turbine drive; 1 pump-jet; 15,000 shp—diesel-electric emergency propulsion system with 2 Paxman 400-kw diesel generator sets, 1 retractable electric propulsor
Endurance: 85 days **Crew:** 18 officers, 112 enlisted

Remarks: An improved version of the *Swiftsure* class. The active units constitute the Second Submarine Squadron, based at Devonport.

S 107 completed a 192-week refit at DML, Devonport, in 4-96; S 87 started refit in 8-93 and was recommissioned at the end of 1997. S 88 was in refit from 6-96 to 26-6-99. S 90 began a major refit in 1-98 for completion during 2-01 (delayed to 9-01 by reactor control rod failure), receiving the Type 2076 integrated sonar suite.

S 88 experienced a reactor-plant piping leak in 5-00 and did not complete repairs at Gibraltar Dockyard until 7-5-01. Others found to have the same defect were S 107, S 87, and S 90, which was already at Devonport for refit with S 91. S 90 completed modernization and refit on 23-12-02, receiving a new type 2076 sonar and weapons-control suite. S 91, 92 and 93 completed similar refit by 2006. As of 2006, plans call for S 107 to retire by 2008, S 87 in 2011, S 88 in 2013, S 90 in 2017, S 91 in 2017, and S 92 in 2019 with S 93 remaining in service until 2022.

Hull systems: Have more than 26,000 rubber anechoic coating tiles to reduce noise signature and are equipped with a degaussing system. S 107 has a standard seven-bladed propeller, while the others have pumpjet propulsors. Diving depth: 300 m. normal operating, 590 m maximum. Pressure hull built of NQ-1 (HY-80) steel. Have three internal decks and four watertight compartments. S 88 has had the sail and planes reinforced to permit under-ice operations.

Combat systems: S 91 has been backfitted with the Type DCB/DCG tactical data system; DCB employs two Ferranti F2420 computers and DCG one BAE Systems (ex-Dowty-Sema) SMCS computer. The others have the FM1600 computer, and all will standardize on the SMCS tactical data system. Under a 1997 contract, all were updated with the BAe Defence Systems Group Integrated Command Console to manage sensor employment and tactical information; the system integrates the Submarine Command System and Type 2076 sonar displays with ship-system data, periscope, and underwater t.v. camera displays. Five of the class received a new DML communications intercept system covering the HF through UHF bands, and the other two were fitted to accept the equipment. All seven are to receive the DML-Argon Engineering Associates CESM communications intercept and D/F system in place of the current CXA(1) system by 2010. Marconi Electronic Systems (now part of BAE Systems) was given a contract late in 1998 to further update the system by employing COTS (Commercial Off-The-Shelf) Sun SPARC computers with the UNIX operating system, substituting NEC 20-in., color, flat-screen displays and replacing the magnetic tape decks with digital audiotape systems, although retaining current F2420 software. Were equipped with Link 11 tactical data link by 2004 and with Link 16 satellite tactical data link (using a towed transmit/receive buoy) by 2006. Plans call for later installation of Link 22.

Mid-life refits are updating the sonar suites on the final four boats to the Thales Underwater Systems (ex-Ferranti-Thomson) Type 2076 integrated array, retaining the 2020 transducer array and including Types 2074, 2077, and 2081 sonars; although the four backfit systems were ordered 2-94, the first, on S 90, was fully operational by 2005; by end 2009, the same suite is to be have been installed on S 91, 92, and 93. S 87 conducted trials with a reelable towed array (causing the hump to her casing abaft the sail); the others employ "clip-on" arrays. The Type 2076 sonar suite has 13,000 hydrophones in its bow, flank, and towed arrays.

The centerline torpedo tube cannot launch Harpoon missiles and is angled downward by 10 degrees; the Harpoon missile is to be retired by 2008. All had been fitted to carry Tomahawk Block III and IV land attack cruise missiles by 2006. During the 2000–2002 refit of S 90, provision was made for launch and recovery of the prototype Marlin LRMS (Long Range Mine Surveillance) unmanned underwater vehicle, which uses a Spearfish torpedo body with warhead replaced by active and passive mine detection and classification sonars.

They all have Pilkington Optronics CH 34 (1 to 5X) and CK 84 (6X) periscopes, the former also carrying the AZE92 antenna for the UAB/UAP EW intercept suite and the antennas for the UHF and VHF radio receivers and NAVSAT, while the latter is equipped with t.v. and infrared intercept equipment. S 107 conducted sea trials with a prototype Pilkington Optronics CM010 nonpenetrating optronic sensor mast beginning in 3-98. S 90 and later are receiving CK 34 search and CH 84 attack periscopes and the "mini-DAMA" (Miniature Demand-Assigned Multiple Access) UHF SATCOM system (U.S. USC-42[V] set) and a DAMASCUS comms control terminal.

♦ 2 Swiftsure class

Bldr: Marconi Electronic Systems Naval Systems-VSEL, Barrow-in-Furness

	Ordered	Laid down	L	In serv.
S 104 Sceptre	1-11-71	25-10-73	20-11-76	14-2-78
S 109 Superb	20-5-70	16-3-72	30-11-74	13-11-76

D: 4,000 tons light; 4,200 tons surf./4,900 tons sub. **S:** 20 kts surf./28 kts sub.
Dim: 82.90 × 9.83 × 8.25
A: 5 bow 533-mm TT (20 Spearfish torpedoes, UGM-109 Block III Tomahawk land-attack missiles and UGM-84D-2 Sub-Harpoon missiles)

Spartan (S 105)—since retired Dave Cullen, 1-06

Superb (S 109) Ben Sullivan, 8-99

Electronics:
Radar: 1 Kelvin-Hughes 1006(1) nav./surf. search
Sonar: Type 2074 bow active/passive array; Type 2077 active classification; Type 2007 passive flank array; Type 2019 PARIS sonar intercept; Type 2046 clip-on towed passive array; Type 2035 or 2047 narrowband processor/ wideband frequency analyzer; Type 183 underwater telephone; Type 197 echo sounder
EW: Thales UAP(1) intercept; EADS CXA(1) Telegon 6 comms D/F; 2 102-mm SSE Mk 8 decoy tubes (Type 2066 Bandfish and Type 2071 decoys)
M: 1 Rolls-Royce PWR.1 pressurized-water reactor; 2 sets GEC-Alstom turbines; 1 prop or pump-jet; 15,000 shp—1 Paxman 400-kw diesel alternator set, 1 drop-down electric emergency propulsor
Crew: Accomm. for 12 officers, 85 enlisted—but up to 120 total normally aboard

Remarks: Are assigned to the 1st Submarine Squadron, Faslane. S 104 underwent a 1997–2000 major refit by Babcock Defence at Rosyth. S 109 was declared nonoperational on 7-9-00 due to concerns over the safety of the reactor system. By 1-02 problems had been repaired. S 109 is expected to remain in service until 2008, and S 104 is scheduled to decommission in 2010.

Hull systems: Have 112-cell battery. The forward diving planes are below the surfaced waterline and retract within the outer hull. Have anechoic hull and sail coatings.

Combat systems: Have DCB/DCG weapons-control system, with two Ferranti F2420 computers. Are equipped with Link 16 and are to receive Link 22 combat-information data links. Were to receive the Type 2076 integrated sonar suite and Dowty-Sema SMCS command/combat data system; Type 2074 has replaced Type 2020, Type 2082 will replace 2019, and the Type 2082 Parian ice-avoidance sonar was to be added. All carry HF, VHF, and UHF communications equipment, including U.S. WSC-3 UHF SATCOM terminals. All had the Pilkington Optronics CK 33 search periscopes updated by 1998 with GPS navigational display using antennas added to the comounted Outfit AZE(2) antenna for the UAP(1) ESM system; a CH 83 attack periscope is fitted.

Harpoon missiles are to be removed by 2008; the bow, centerline tube is angled downward and cannot be used to launch missiles.

Disposals: Sisters *Sovereign* (S 108) and *Spartan* (S 105) were retired in 2006. *Swiftsure* (S 126) was retired in 1992 and *Splendid* (S 106) in 2003.

Submarine rescue note: Submarine rescue duties are handled by the remotely operated Scorpio 45 and the manned 1978-vintage chartered rescue submersible LR5, for which a replacement is being designed in conjunction with other NATO navies. LR5 is 9.2-m long, 3.5-m high and can transport 16 survivors per trip.

GUIDED-MISSILE DESTROYERS [DDG]

♦ 0 (+ 6 + 2) Daring class (Type 45)

Bldr: BAE Systems, Govan and Vosper Thornycroft, Portsmouth

	Laid down	L	In serv.
D 32 Daring	7-03	1-2-06	5-09
D 33 Dauntless	4-10-04	2007	2010
D 34 Diamond	2005	2008	2010
D 35 Dragon	10-05	2008	2011
D 36 Defender	2006	2009	2012
D 37 Duncan	2006	2009	2013

D: 7,450 tons (fl) S: 29 kts **Dim:** 152.4 × 21.2 (18.0 wl) × 5.5
A: Provisions for 8 RGM-84C Harpoon SSM; PAAMS VLS SAM syst. (48 Sylver A50 cells; 16 Aster-30 and 32 Aster-15 missiles); 1 114-mm 55-cal.Vickers Mk 8 Mod. 1 DP; 2 single 30-mm 75-cal. DS-30M AA; 1 Lynx HMA.8 helicopter (Stingray torpedoes and Sea Skua missiles); 2 20-mm Mk 15 Mod. 1B Phalanx CIWS; 2 twin 324-mm fixed ASW TT (Stingray torpedoes); 1 Merlin or Lynx helicopter

GUIDED-MISSILE DESTROYERS [DDG] *(continued)*

Daring (D 32)—immediately following launch Dave Cullen, 2-06

Daring (D 32)—at launch Dave Cullen, 2-06

Electronics:

Radar: 2 Type 1008 nav. (E/F-band); . . . nav. (I-band); 1 Siemens-Plessey SAMPSON 3-D target-designation; 1 BAE Systems/Thales S1850M Smartello early warning

Sonar: Type 2087 suite, with Ultra-EDO MFS 7000 (EDO Model 997) hull-mounted LF; provision for low-frequency active towed linear array

E/O: Rademac 2500 surveillance and tracking

EW: UAT . . . integrated intercept and jammer suite: Minerva data processor; . . . communications intercept; 4 8-tubed DLH SIREN decoy launchers; 2 DLF(3) floating decoy launchers; SSTD (SLQ-25A(V)) or Type 2070 active and passive torpedo decoy system

M: 2 Rolls-Royce/Northrop GrummanWR-21 intercooled, recuperative gas turbines (33,530 shp each), Alstom Integrated Full-Electric Power (IFEP) drive: 2 Alstom 15-phase induction motors; 2 props; 53,648 shp—2 2,000-kw Wärtsilä 12V200 diesel-driven Hitzinger alternator sets for low-speed propulsion and/or electrical ship's service requirements

Range: 7,000+/18 **Endurance:** 45 days

Crew: 20 officers, 170 enlisted (accomm. for 235 tot., including 60 Royal Marines or commandoes)

Remarks: British participation in the 1991 Project Horizon Common New-Generation Frigate program with France and Italy was terminated on 21-4-99, but the U.K. stated a commitment to continuing the program's PAAMS (Principal Anti-Air Missile System) development effort, with the French Aster-15 and Aster-30 missile family. To meet a still-standing requirement for 8–12 new large AAW ships, a new design was prepared. Total program cost was estimated at $11.3 billion, with unit cost hoped to be around $435 million and each ship to cost about $29 million per year to operate, but by 2001, the projected unit cost had risen to more than $1 billion each. The formal order for the first six was placed on 18-2-02.

Current plans as approved by the U.K. Ministry of Defence call for the initial six destroyers to be assembled by BAE Systems, Govan. Vosper Thornycroft at Woolston will build and outfit substantial sections of the ships

Hull systems: Limiting displacement is to be 8,000 tons. Changes in the design early in 2000 brought the hull flare up to the main deck, increasing overall beam and length, while the superstructure will be more sharply sloped than had originally been planned. The design employs Lloyds commercial rather than Admiralty construction standards for warships. Range will only be about half that originally planned, and maximum speed has been reduced. The Rolls-Royce–Northrop Grumman WR-21 ICR gas turbine employs the core of the Rolls-Royce RB-211-535 aircraft engine; the plant will be fuel-efficient over a wide speed range. An integrated electric drive propulsion plant and fixed-pitch propellers will be employed, although they are designed to enable their blade pitch to be increased up to 3 degrees over the lives of the ships. Alstom Power Conversion received a contract on 31-7-00 to design and develop the electric motors for the class. Litton Marine Systems and Rockwell Automation will provide an integrated platform management system. Senior enlisted personnel will have two- and four-berth cabins and junior personnel six-berth cabins; ship's officers will have single-berth cabins and officer trainees two-berths cabins.

Combat systems: The combat system will be the BAe Defence Systems Group- Alenia Marconi Systems DNA91 (Eurocombat) and will be compatible with NATO Improved Link 11, Link 14, and Link 16; the system will incorporate mostly existing equipment. The U.S. CEC (Cooperative Engagement Capability) will not be fitted to at least the first three ships, further reducing their potential effectiveness. The ships will have a fully integrated communications system provided by Thales Communications (teamed with BAe Systems Avionics); it will include Thales SCOT 3 SHF and, possibly, EHF SATCOM systems. The Siemens-Plessey SAMPSON target tracking and illumination radar is a developed version of the Multi-function Electronically Scanned Adaptive Radar (MESAR). The radar utilizes digital adaptive beam forming, which makes it highly resistant to jamming. The S1850M Smartello long-range search radar is an improved version of the Thales SMART-L radar integrated with a new transmitter based on that of the Marconi Martello radar. Raytheon Systems will provide the navigation and integrated bridge navigational systems.

The hull-mounted sonar, a variant of the EDO Model 997 being refitted to Brazilian *Niterói*-class frigates, was selected late during 2-01.

In place of the originally selected 127-mm weapon for the *Horizon* class, the first three ships will carry Vickers 114 Mk 8 Mod. 1 mounts recycled from the Type 42 destroyers. Substitution of the new U.S. 155-mm gun had been planned for units four and later, but it may be too large and heavy. Have provisions for carrying eight Harpoon antiship missiles. Later units may be equipped with two eight-cell Mk 41 VLS so as to be able to launch Tomahawk land-attack missiles.

♦ 4 Manchester class (Type 42C)

	Bldr	Laid down	L	In serv.
D 95 MANCHESTER	Vickers (SB) Ltd. Barrow-in-Furness	19-5-79	24-11-80	16-12-82
D 96 GLOUCESTER	Vosper Thornycroft, Southampton	26-10-79	2-11-82	11-9-85
D 97 EDINBURGH	Cammell Laird, Birkenhead	8-9-80	14-4-83	18-12-85
D 98 YORK	Swan Hunter, Wallsend-on-Tyne	18-1-80	21-6-82	9-8-85

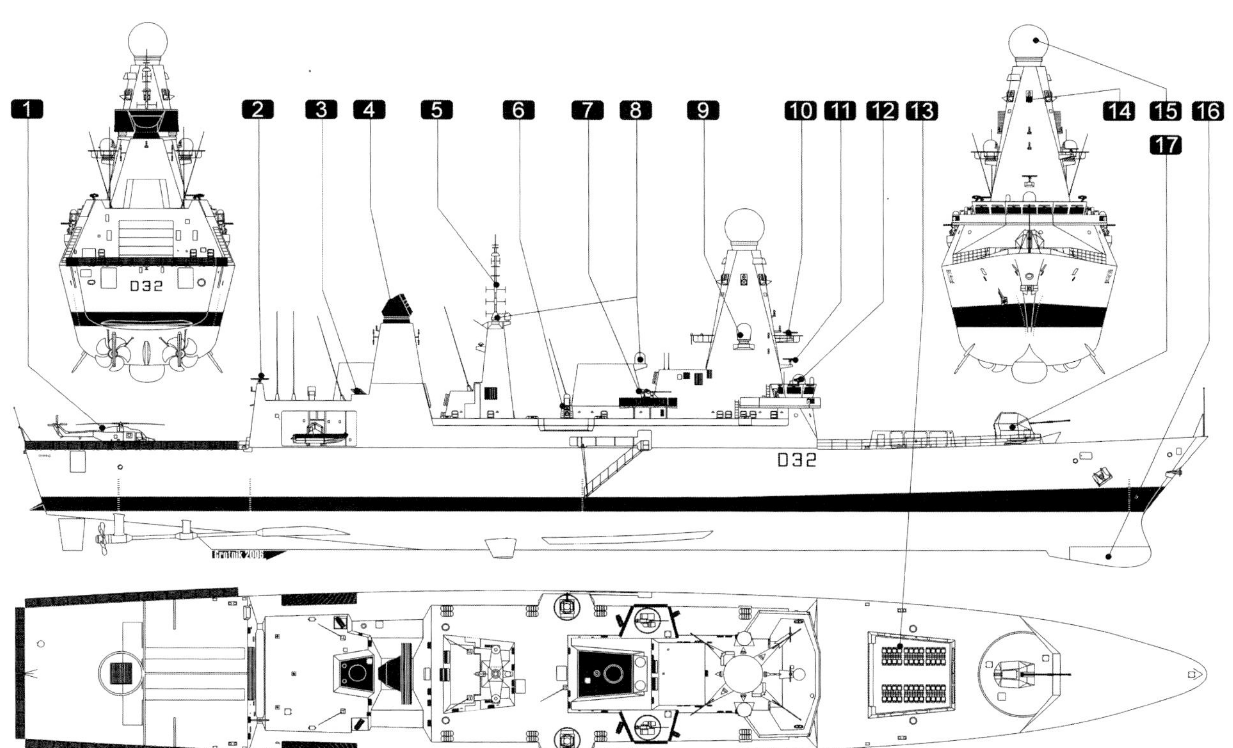

Daring (D 32) 1. Lynx (or Merlin) helicopter 2. Type 1008 navigational radar 3. DLH offboard decoy system 4. S1850M early warning radar 5. Communications antennas 6. 20-mm Phalanx CIWS 7. 30 mm DS-30M Remsig 8. EW antennas 9. Astrium SCOT 3 SATCOM antenna radomes 10. Type 1008 navigational radar 11. Unknown navigational radar 12. Radamec 2500 electro-optical surface surveillance and tracking 13. Sylver A50 VLS cells 14. EW antenna suite 15. Sampson 3-D multifunction phased array radar 16. MFS-7000 bow sonar 17. 114 mm Vickers Mk 8 Mod.1 DP gun Drawing by T. Grotnik, 2006

GUIDED-MISSILE DESTROYERS [DDG] *(continued)*

Edinburgh (D 97)—note faceted gunhouse for the Mk 8 Mod. 1 gun
Derek Fox, 10-05

York (D 98)—note heavy reinforcing strake down the sides at the main deck level
Ben Sullivan, 2-05

Edinburgh (D 97) Dave Cullen, 7-05

Manchester (D 95) Leo van Ginderen, 7-05

Gloucester (D 96) Leo van Ginderen, 7-05

D: 3,880 tons (4,775 fl) **S:** 29.5 kts (18 cruising)
Dim: 141.12 (132.3 wl) × 14.90 × 5.80 (4.20 hull)
A: 1 2-round Sea Dart GWS.30 SAM syst. (22 missiles); 1 114-mm 55-cal. Vickers Mk 8 DP (D 97 and D 98: Mk 8 Mod. 1 DP) ; 2 20-mm Mk 15 Phalanx gatling CIWS; 2 single 20-mm 90-cal. Oerlikon GAM-B01 AA; 2 triple 324-mm STWS.3 ASW TT; 1 Lynx HAS.3/HMA.8 helicopter (with Sea Skua missiles and/or Stingray ASW torpedoes)

Electronics:
Radar: 1 Kelvin-Hughes Type 1007 nav.; 1 Decca Type 1008 nav.; 1 BAE Systems Type 996(1) surf.-air search; 1 BAE Systems-Thales Type 1022 early warning; 2 BAE Systems Type 909(1) f.c.; 2 General Dynamics Mk 90 Phalanx f.c.
Sonar: BAE Systems Type 2050 hull-mounted; Kelvin-Hughes Type 162M bottomed-target classification (50 kHz); Type 185 underwater telephone
E/O: 2 Rademac 2100 optronic surveillance and target designation
EW: UAT(5) intercept; DLB decoy syst. (4 6-round Mk 137 RL); 2 DEC laser dazzler; 4 DLJ(2) floating decoy dispensers, Type 182 or Type 2070 (U.S. SLQ-25A Nixie) towed torpedo decoy syst.
M: COGOG: 2 Rolls-Royce Olympus TM3B gas turbines (27,200 shp each) for high speeds, 2 Rolls-Royce Tyne RM1C (5,340 shp each) for cruise; 2 5-bladed CP props; 54,400 shp max.
Electric: 4,000 kw (4/1,000-kw Paxman diesel sets)
Range: 4,750/18 **Fuel:** 610 tons
Crew: 27 officers, 74 senior petty officers, 184 other enlisted (D 95: 269 tot.)

Remarks: A lengthened version of the *Sheffield* class intended to provide better seaworthiness, endurance, and habitability, but having no major change in armament despite the additional 16 m in overall length. D 95 ordered 10-11-78, D 96 on 27-3-79, and D 97 and D 98 on 25-4-79. D 96 shot down an Iraqi-launched Silkworm antiship missile with a Sea Dart on 25-2-91 in the northern Persian Gulf. Based at Portsmouth. D 95 completed a 12-month refit and was reactivated on 22-7-02. D 95 and D 96 are to be retired in 2011, D 98 will follow in 2012, and D 97 in 2013.
Hull systems: Received hull strengthening strakes amidships due to weight growth and cracking. There are two pairs of fin-stabilizers. D 97 retains the bow bulwarks added when she carried a single Mk 15 Phalanx CIWS forward.
Combat systems: The ADAWS 7 combat data system initially carried has been upgraded to ADAWS 8. Missile direction system is GWS 30 Mod. 2, with GSA 1 backup system for 114-mm gun. Have NATO datalinks 10, 11, 14, and 16 JTIDS (Joint Tactical Information Distribution System). The UAT(5) EW system incorporates the UCB(1) Electronic Warfare Control Processor. The Type 675(2) active EW jammers have been deactivated or removed. All now have the CCA (Captain's Combat Aid) computerized decision-making system. D 96 and later have a larger command center. Several portable 7.62-mm machineguns are carried, including one to be fitted on each bridge wing. All carry two SCOT 1C antennas for the Skynet SATCOM system and one commercial SATCOM terminal.
In 1990 D 97 received a single 20-mm Mk 15 CIWS forward and bulwarks added at bow, though later removed; a 54-week refit 1995–96 at Rosyth brought the ship to class standard with two Phalanx mounts amidships in place of the twin 30-mm mounts. D 97 and 98 had both received the 114-mm Mk 8 Mod. 1 gunmount by 2005. The Raytheon lightweight Sea RAM point-defense missile system was installed in place of the portside Phalanx mount on D 98 from 1-2-01 to 10-01 for compatibility trials. Two single 20-mm GAM-B01 AA mounts flanking the helicopter hangar were removed from all during 2000–2001. During 2003 York became the first of many Royal Navy warships to be fitted with the SIREN off-board decoy system.

♦ 4 Sheffield class (Type 42A and 42B*)

	Bldr	Laid down	L	In serv.
D 89 Exeter	Swan Hunter, Wallsend-on-Tyne	22-7-76	25-4-78	19-9-80
D 90 Southampton	Vosper Thornycroft, Southampton	21-10-76	29-1-79	23-7-81
D 91 Nottingham	Vosper Thornycroft, Southampton	6-2-78	12-2-80	8-4-83
D 92 Liverpool*	Cammell Laird, Birkenhead	5-7-78	25-9-80	9-7-82

Nottingham (D 91) Leo van Ginderen, 6-05

Southampton (D 90) Derek Fox, 5-05

GUIDED-MISSILE DESTROYERS [DDG] *(continued)*

Nottingham (D 91) Camil Busquets i Vilanova, 2005

Liverpool (D 92) A. A. de Kruijf, 11-03

D: 3,560 tons (4,250 fl) **S:** 28 kts (18 cruising)
Dim: 125.0 (119.5 pp) × 14.34 × 5.9 (4.3 hull)
A: 1 2-round Sea Dart GWS.30 Mod. 2 SAM syst. (22 missiles); 1 114-mm 55-cal. Vickers Mk 8 DP; 2 20-mm Mk 15 Phalanx CIWS; 2 single 20-mm 90-cal. Oerlikon GAM-B01 AA; 1 Lynx HAS.3/HMA.8 helicopter (Sea Skua missiles and/or Stingray torpedoes)
Electronics:
Radar: 1 Kelvin-Hughes Type 1007 nav.; 1 Decca 1008 nav.; 1 BAE Systems Type 996(1) 3-D surf./air search; 1 BAE Systems-Thales Type 1022 early warning; 2 BAE Systems Type 909(1) f.c.; 2 General Dynamics Mk 90 Phalanx f.c.
Sonar: BAE Systems Type 2050 hull-mounted; Kelvin-Hughes Type 162M bottomed-target classification (50 kHz); Type 185 underwater telephone
EW: UAA(2) (D 89, 90: UAT[5]) intercept; DLD decoy syst. (4 6-round Mk 137 RL); 2 DEC laser-dazzlers; 4 DLF(2) or DLF(3) floating decoy launchers; Type 182 or Type 2070 towed torpedo decoy; D 89, 90 also: UCB(1) EW control syst.
M: COGOG: 2 Rolls-Royce Olympus TM3B gas turbines (27,200 shp each) for high speed; 2 Rolls-Royce Tyne RM1A (Type 42B: Tyne RM1C) cruise gas turbines (4,100 or 5,340 shp each); 2 5-bladed CP props; 54,400 shp max.
Electric: 4,000 kw (4 × 1,000-kw Paxman diesel sets) **Range:** 650/30; 4,500/18
Crew: 24 officers, 229 enlisted

Remarks: This class was found to be deficient in damage-control during the Falklands War and also to be limited in sensor capability and self-defense, although the Sea Dart system functioned effectively. D 91 completed an 18-month refit and recommissioned on 9-2-01. She subsequently went aground near Howe Island in the Tasman Sea on 7-7-02 and suffered serious flooding, she was repaired and returned to service in 2004. All of the class are based at Portsmouth.
Hull systems: Very cramped ships; can accommodate up to 312 personnel. Have Agouti bubble ejector system for propellers (which rotate inwardly) to reduce cavitation noise. Two pairs of fin stabilizers fitted. Modernizations have increased draft by .3 m and displacement by perhaps 100 tons. Have stack water spray equipment to reduce IR signature. The Type 42B have slightly less-rounded sterns.
Combat systems: Have the ADAWS 7 (D 89, 90: Mod. 1) data system with NATO Link 10, 11, 14, and 16 JTIDS (Joint Tactical Information Distribution System) datalinks and the CCA (Captain's Combat Aid) computerized decision-making system. All are equipped to carry SCOT 1C radomes for Skynet SHF satellite communications system and also carry a commercial NAVSAT terminal. The helicopter is used for surveillance and attack (Sea Skua missiles) as well as ASW. Type 965M radar was replaced by 1022 in the Type 42A ships. During refits, Type 996 radar replaced Type 992Q, except in the stricken *Birmingham.* Type 42B ships are to receive the UAT(5) EW suite, with UCB(1) Electronic Warfare Control Processor (EWCP). The Type 275 jammers were deactivated or removed by end-2000. All have two MSI-Defence Systems stabilized Director Aiming Sights. D 89–92 received Type 2050 hull-mounted sonars (4.5–7.5 kHz) during refits. Triple STWS.2 ASW torpedo tubes have been removed to save weight and to provide space for stowing rigid inflatable boats handled by the former torpedo reloading davits. The GAM-B01 mounts are on the bridge deck, abaft the pilothouse. D 89 in 1998 carried the Type 2070 torpedo decoy (U.S. SLQ-25A), but the system is cross-decked to deploying units.

Disposals and losses: Class prototype *Sheffield* (D 80) foundered 10-5-82, having been hit by an Argentine AM 39 Exocet missile on 4-5-82. *Coventry* (D 118) was lost to Argentine bombs on 25-5-82. *Birmingham* (D 86) was deactivated on 12-11-99, cannibalized for spares, and towed away for scrap on 20-10-00. *Glasgow* (D 88) was decommissioned on 22-10-04, *Newcastle* (D 87) on 5-11-04, and *Cardiff* (D 108) on 14-7-05. Current plans call for *Exeter* (D 89) to decommission in 2010, *Liverpool* (D 92) in 2009, *Southampton* (D 90) in 2011, and *Nottingham* (D 91) in 2012.

FRIGATES [FF]

♦ 13 Duke (Type 23)-class general-purpose

Bldr: Marconi Marine-Yarrow (Shipbuilders), Ltd., Scoutstoun, Glasgow (except F 237–239: Swan Hunter Shipbuilders, Ltd., Wallsend-on-Tyne)

	Laid down	L	In serv.
F 78 Kent	16-4-97	27-5-98	8-6-00
F 79 Portland	14-1-98	15-5-99	3-5-01
F 81 Sutherland	14-10-93	9-3-96	4-7-97
F 82 Somerset	12-10-92	25-6-94	20-9-96
F 83 St. Albans	5-3-99	6-5-00	6-6-02
F 229 Lancaster	18-12-87	24-5-90	1-5-92
F 231 Argyll	20-3-87	8-4-89	30-5-91
F 234 Iron Duke	12-12-88	28-3-91	20-5-93
F 235 Monmouth	1-6-89	13-11-91	24-9-93
F 236 Montrose	1-11-89	31-7-92	2-6-94
F 237 Westminster	18-1-91	4-2-92	13-5-94
F 238 Northumberland	4-4-91	4-4-92	29-11-94
F 239 Richmond	16-2-92	6-4-93	22-6-95

Sutherland (F 81) Martin Mokrus, 6-05

Westminster (F 237) Michael Winter, 6-05

Montrose (F 236) Michael Winter, 6-05

D: 3,600 tons (4,300 fl) **S:** 28 kts (F 237 on: 30 kts; all: 15 kts on electric drive)
Dim: 133.00 (123.00 pp) × 16.10 (15.00 wl) × 4.30 (5.50 max. navigational)
A: 8 RGM-84C Harpoon (GWS.60) SSM; Sea Wolf GWS.26 vertical-launch SAM syst. (32 missiles); 1 114-mm 55-cal. Vickers Mk 8 (Mk 8 Mod. 1 in F 229, F 234, F 235, F 236, F237, F 238, F 239) DP; 2 single 30-mm 75-cal. DS-30B AA; 4 fixed 324-mm Cray Marine DMTS 90 ASW TT (Stingray torpedoes); 1 Lynx HAS.3/HMA.8 helicopter (Sea Skua missiles and/or Stingray ASW torpedoes) (F 229, 234, later all: Merlin HM.1 helicopter)

FRIGATES [FF] *(continued)*

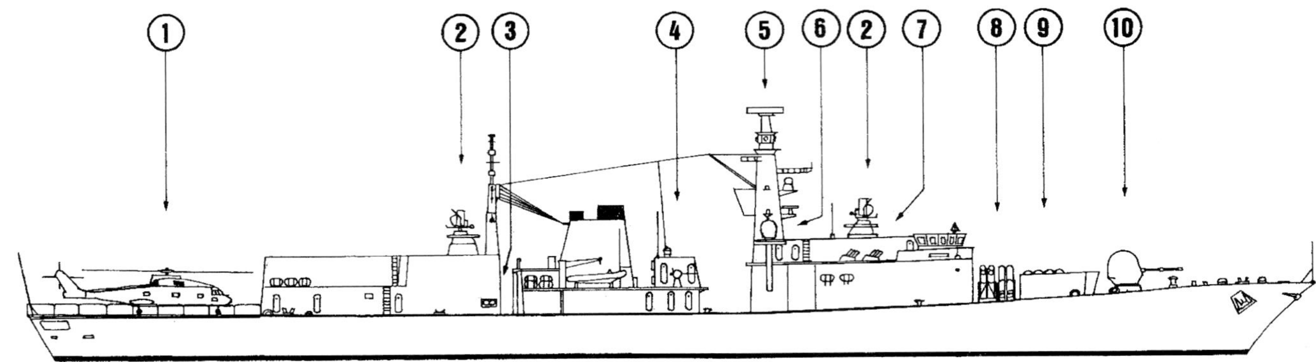

Duke (Type 23) class 1. Merlin HM.1 helicopter 2. Type 911(1) radar illuminator for Sea Wolf SAM system 3. Fixed 324-mm ASW TT (two per side) 4. 30-mm AA 5. Type 996(2) 3-D surf./air-search radar 6. SCOT-1C SHF SATCOM antenna radome (port and starboard) 7. DLB decoy launchers 8. Harpoon SSM 9. Sea Wolf GWS.26 vertical missile launch group 10. 114-mm Mk 8 DP gun
Drawing by Jean Moulin, from *Flottes de Combat*

St. Albans (F 83) Martin Mokrus, 6-05

Electronics:
Radar: 1 Kelvin-Hughes Type 1007 nav.; 1 Decca Type 1008 nav.; 1 BAE Systems Type 996(2) 3-D surf./air-search; 2 BAE Systems Type 911(1) missile/gun f.c.
Sonar: Thales Type 2050NE bow-mounted (4.5-7.5 kHz); Dowty Type 2031(Z) towed linear passive array (not in last five)
E/O: 1 GSA.8/GPEOD Sea Archer gun f.c. and surveillance
EW: Racal UAF(1) Cutlass (F 238 and later: UAT(1)) intercept; DLB decoy syst. (4 6-round RL); 2 DEC laser dazzler; 2DLF(2) floating decoy dispensers; Type 182 or Type 2070 (SLQ-25A) towed torpedo decoy syst.
M: CODLAG (COmbined Diesel-eLectric and Gas turbine): first seven: 2 Rolls-Royce SM1A Spey gas turbines (18,770 shp each, 17,000 sust.), F 237 and later: 2 Rolls-Royce SM1C Spey (26,150 shp each); all: 4 Paxman Valenta 12 RPA 200CZ diesel generator sets (5,200 kw total); 2 2,000-shp electric cruise motors; 2 props; F 229-236: 41,540 shp max./F 237-on: 52,300 shp max.
Electric: 1,890 kw tot. (see Remarks) **Range:** 7,800/17 **Fuel:** 800 tons
Crew: 17 officers, 57 senior ratings, 111 junior ratings (F 234: 150 tot.)

Remarks: Intended as lineal replacements for the *Leander*-class frigates. Originally intended to serve for only 18 years, without midlife modernization, but are now to serve longer, with upgrades begun in 2005. Each ship cost between £60 and £96 million each. Class originally was to have totaled 24. F 229 was originally given pennant F 232; changed because a "Form 232" is used to report a collision or grounding. F 229 had the hangar altered to accept the Merlin helicopter in a refit concluded in 8-99; also added were enlarged weapons sponsons amidships and improved communications systems. On 22-5-02, F 234 was rededicated after an overhaul that included substituting the Mod. 1 114-mm gun, reconfiguring the hangar to accommodate the Merlin helicopter, refurbishing the galley, installing a new interior lighting system, and overhauling the propulsion machinery; the ship can operate with a "lean-manned" crew of 150. F 235 underwent major refit and received Merlin helicopter modification in 2003; all others will eventually receive similar modifications to carry the Merlin helicopter.

F 83 was hit by the ferry *Pride of Portsmouth* on 27-10-02, causing severe damage to the frigate's bridge wing and deck fittings; repairs were completed on 12-2-03.

Hull systems: Flush-decked hull, with large helicopter hangar, helo in-haul system, and one set of fin stabilizers. The design grew considerably as a result of Falklands War "Lessons-Learned." The propulsion system permits running the shaft-concentric electric propulsion motors with the power from any combination of the four 1,300-kw ship's service generators; power from both the gas turbines and the electric motors can be obtained; ship's service power is derived from two 945-kw converter sets, and there is also a 250-kw emergency alternator powered by a Perkins CV 250GTCA diesel. Have fixed-pitch props, with astern power available only by electric drive. The more powerful engines in F 237-onward provide 1–2 knots additional speed, and F 79 made 30.8 kts during builder's trials. Superstructure external bulkheads are sloped about 7° to reduce radar signature, and radar-absorbent coatings are applied.

Combat systems: The planned Ferranti CACS 4 combat data/control system for these ships was canceled in 7-87; its replacement, the BAe Defence Systems Group (ex-Dowty-Sema-Racal) Outfit DNA(1) SSCS (Surface Ship Control System), with parallel processing, modular software, and Link 11 and 14 compatibility, was not ordered until 10-8-89. The first seagoing outfit DNA(1) was fitted in *Westminster,* and the earlier ships were severely handicapped for combat until they were backfitted. F 234 has Marconi ICS 4 integrated communications system, with U.S. URC-109 components; the others have Redifon ICS 6. All are equipped with two SCOT 1C antennas for the Skynet SATCOM system and also carry a commercial SATCOM terminal (with antenna mounted on the forward edge of the stack). There have been problems with the accuracy of the Type 996(2) radar, which also produces excess numbers of false tracks, and there have been software problems with the vertical-launch missile system. All are being equipped with the U.S. Navy's Cooperative Engagement Capability (CEC), with installation begun in 2004.

This class was equipped with the first bow-mounted sonars in the Royal Navy. The sterns have had to be strengthened to permit towing the Type 2031(Z) array; Thales Type 2087 bistatic VLF towed arrays began replacing 2031(Z) in the ships that had it around 2006 and will eventually be fitted to at least of the class; plans call for using one ship for trials with the low-frequency active towed linear array. F 234 is equipped with a prototype TRAMP (Torpedo Recognition Acoustic Multi-beam Processor) for trials in connection with the new SSTD torpedo countermeasures system.

Decca Type 1008 navigational radars have been added to all, with the antenna mounted to starboard atop the pilothouse; the antenna for the older Type 1007 radar is mounted off-center to port on the mainmast to allow an aft view for helicopter flight-control employment. F 238 and later have UAT vice UAF-1 EW equipment. The Racal 7.5–18-GHz Scorpion jammer may be added to the EW suite. UAT(7) is to replace UAF EW equipment in the first seven. The Type 275 jammers were deactivated or removed by end 2000.

On seven ships, the 114-mm guns were updated by VSEL to Mod. 1 status, saving about 6 tons in weight and considerable below-decks volume. By 2005 F 229, F 234, F 235, F 236, F237, F 238, and F 239 had received the gun modifications. The GSA.8/GPEOD Sea Archer optronic/IR director is mounted on the mast for the 114-mm gun. There is no provision for a CIWS, and until SSCS installation was completed, the ships were able to control only one Sea Wolf missile at a time.

When modernizations are complete, at least six (and possibly all 13 units) will be able to operate either the newer Merlin HM.1 helicopters or older Lynx HMA.8s. Merlin-equipped ships have the PRISM deck-handling system, a new glide-path indicator and gyro-stabilized horizon indicator, new deck lighting, modular servicing systems in the hangar, and a bridge Ship Helicopter Operating Limits Instrumentation System (SHOLIS) on the bridge.

Disposals: Sister *Norfolk* (F 230) was retired on 31-3-05, *Marlborough* (F 233) on 8-7-05, and *Grafton* (F 80) early in 2006. All three have been sold to Chile for continued service.

♦ 4 Cornwall-class (Type 22 Batch 3) general-purpose frigate

	Bldr	Laid down	L	In serv.
F 85 Cumberland	Yarrow (Shipbuilders), Scotstoun, Glasgow	12-10-84	21-6-86	10-6-89
F 86 Campbeltown	Cammell Laird, Birkenhead	4-12-85	7-10-87	27-5-89
F 87 Chatham	Swan Hunter, Wallsend-on-Tyne	12-5-86	20-1-88	4-5-90
F 99 Cornwall	Yarrow (Shipbuilders), Scotstoun, Glasgow	12-9-83	14-10-85	23-4-88

Cumberland (F 85) Michael Winter, 6-05

FRIGATES [FF] *(continued)*

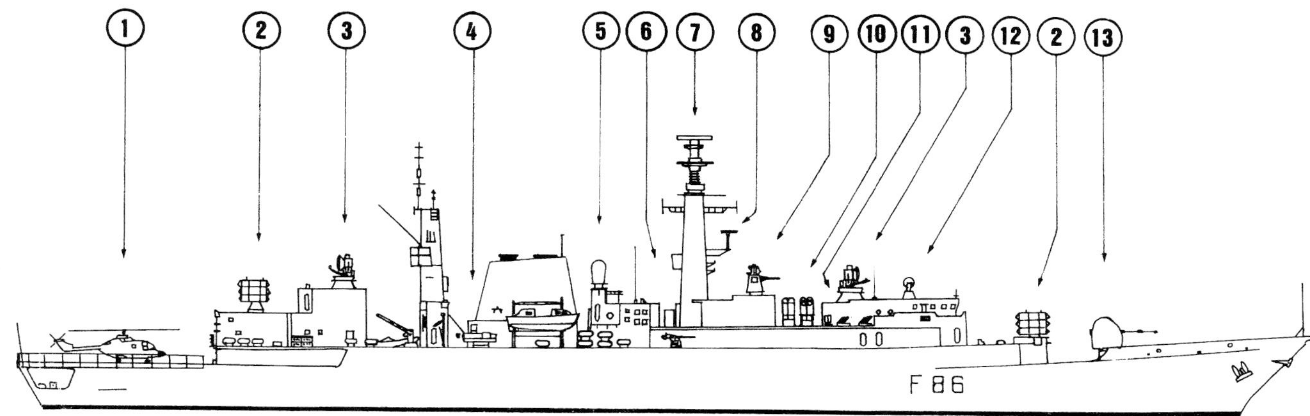

Campbeltown (F 86) 1. Lynx HAS.3 helicopter 2. Sea Wolf GWS.25 system sextuple SAM launchers 3. Type 911 radar illuminators for Sea Wolf missiles 4. triple 324-mm ASW TT 5. SCOT-1C SATCOM radomes (port and starboard) 6. 30-mm DES-30B gun 7. Type 967-968 dual surface- and air-search radars 8. Type 1006 navigational radar 9. 30-mm Goalkeeper CIWS 10. Harpoon SSM 11. DLB decoy launchers 12. Sea Archer E/O gun directors (port and starboard) 13. 114-mm Mk 8 DP gun

Drawing by Jean Moulin, from *Flottes de Combat*

Chatham (F 87) Frank Findler, 6-05

Campbeltown (F 86) Anthony Vella, 2004

D: 4,280 tons (4,850 fl) **S:** 30 kts (18 kts on Tyne gas turbines)
Dim: 148.10 (135.65 pp) × 14.75 × 5.35 hull (6.40 max.)
A: 8 RGM-84C Harpoon SSM; 2 6-round Sea Wolf GWS.25 Mod. 3 SAM systems; 1 114-mm 55-cal. Vickers Mk 8 (F 85: Mk 8 Mod. 1) DP; 1 30-mm Goalkeeper CIWS; 2 single 30-mm 75-cal. DS-30B AA; 2 triple 324-mm STWS.2 ASW TT (Stingray torpedoes); 1 or 2 Lynx HAS.3/HMA.8 helicopters (Sea Skua ASM, Stingray torpedoes) or 1 Sea King HAS.6 helicopter; F 87 also: 2 single 20-mm . . . AA
Electronics:
Radar: 1 Kelvin-Hughes Type 1006 nav.; 1 BAE Systems Type 967M-968 surf./air-search; 2 BAE Systems Type 911 f.c.; 1 Thales Goalkeeper f.c.
Sonar: Thales Type 2050 (F 99: Type 2016) hull-mounted (4.5-7.5 kHz)
EW: Racal UAT(5 or 6) intercept; UAD/UAK COBLU comms intercept; DLB decoy RL syst. (4 6-round Mk 137 RL); 2 DEC laser-dazzler; 4 DLF(2) floating decoy launchers; Type 182 towed torpedo decoy syst.
E/O: 2 GSA.8/GPEOD Sea Archer gun f.c. and surveillance
M: COGAG: 2 Rolls-Royce Spey SM.1A DR boost gas turbines (18,770 shp each) *and* 2 Rolls-Royce Tyne RM.1C gas turbines (5,340 shp each); 2 5-bladed Stone Manganese CP props; 48,220 shp max.
Electric: 4,000 kw (4 × 1,000-kw Paxman Valenta 12PA 200CZ diesel sets)
Range: 7,000/18 (on Tyne gas turbines); 12,000/14 (one shaft)
Fuel: 700 tons, plus 80 tons aviation fuel
Crew: 13 officers, 62 petty officers, 157 other enlisted (as flagships: 21 officers, 65 petty officers, 159 other enlisted)

Remarks: Third series in the Type 22/*Broadsword*-class design, with same basic hull as Batch 2/*Boxer* class, but with a 114-mm gun on the forecastle and the antiship missile launchers moved to abaft the pilothouse and oriented athwartships. The first two were ordered 14-12-82 and the third and fourth on 28-1-85. F 86 ran aground off Tromsø, Norway, on 5-9-01, damaging the starboard propeller shaft. With *Sheffield* (F 96), they form the 2nd Frigate Squadron, based at Devonport.
Hull systems: Maximum generator output is 5,200 kw for short periods. The flight deck is sized for Merlin HM.1, but the hangar reportedly is too low to accommodate the helicopter.

Combat systems: All have the DFA-7 (CACS-5) Computer-Assisted Command System, with Link 11 and 14 compatibility. The CCA (Captain's Combat Aid) computerized decision-making system has been added. They are equipped with ICS(3) communications suite and SCOT-1C SHF and Marisat SATCOM terminals. The GSA-8/GPEOD (Gun System Automation 8/General-Purpose Electro-Optical Director) t.v./IR/laser back-up directors are for the 114-mm gun. The Goalkeeper gatling AA gun mount has its own integral I-band search/tracker and I/K-band tracking radars. The Decca Type 1008 navigational radar may be added to supplement Type 1007. All four received new communications suites at Devonport Dockyard, Plymouth, during 2001. The Type 2031(Z) passive linear towed hydrophone array systems and their towing winches were removed during 1999, and the winch compartments were converted for use as gymnasiums. F 85 had the 114-mm mount replaced with a low-radar-reflective Mk 8 Mod. 1 mounting and the former towed sonar array winch room converted to a joint operations planning room during an overhaul completed 2-02. The Type 275 jammers were deactivated or removed by end-2000. The COBLU (Cooperative Outboard Logistics Update) communications intercept system is an updated version of the UAD/UAK suite aboard *Sheffield* (F 96), itself a variant of the U.S. SSQ-108(V) OUTBOARD (Organizational Unit Tactical Baseline Operational Area Radio Detection Countermeasures Exploitation System); all but F 86 had had the upgrade by end 2001.

Disposal note: The last active Type 22 Batch 2 frigate, *Sheffield* (F 96), was retired on 14-11-02 and sold to Chile. Sister *Beaver* (F 93) was decommissioned 5-2-99 and began tow to Turkey for scrapping on 21-2-01; *London* (F 95) decommissioned on 11-6-99 and *Boxer* (F 92) on 4-8-99 and was placed up for sale on 29-10-99. *Brave* (F 94) was deactivated on 1-4-99. F 92 and F 94 were sunk as targets in 2004. *Coventry* (F 98) began a five-month Caribbean deployment on 13-7-01, was paid off on 26-11-01, and decommissioned on 28-2-02; she and *London* were transferred to Romania in 2003.

PATROL SHIPS [PS]

♦ 3 (+ 1) River-class/modified river-class* patrol ships

Bldr: Vosper Thornycroft, Woolston, Southampton

	Laid down	L	In serv.
P 281 Tyne	19-9-01	29-4-02	13-1-03
P 282 Severn	2002	13-1-03	31-7-03
P 283 Mersey	2002	14-6-03	18-12-03
P 257 Clyde*	2005	6-06	2007

Tyne (P 281) Michael Winter, 6-05

D: 1,800 tons (fl) **S:** 20 kts **Dim:** 79.75 (73.60 pp) × 13.60 × 3.80
A: 1 20-mm 85-cal. Oerlikon GAM B01 AA (P 257: 1 30-mm DS-30B AA); 2 single 7.62-mm mg
Electronics: Radar: 2 Kelvin Hughes Nucleus-3 5000 ARPA nav./surf.\ search (1 X-band, 1 S-band)
M: 2 M.A.N.-Burmeister & Wain-Ruston 12RK270 diesels; 2 Lips CP props; 11,280 bhp—1 375 shp electric bow thruster

PATROL SHIPS [PS] *(continued)*

Severn (P 282) Frank Findler, 8-05

Tyne (P 281) Leo van Ginderen, 6-04

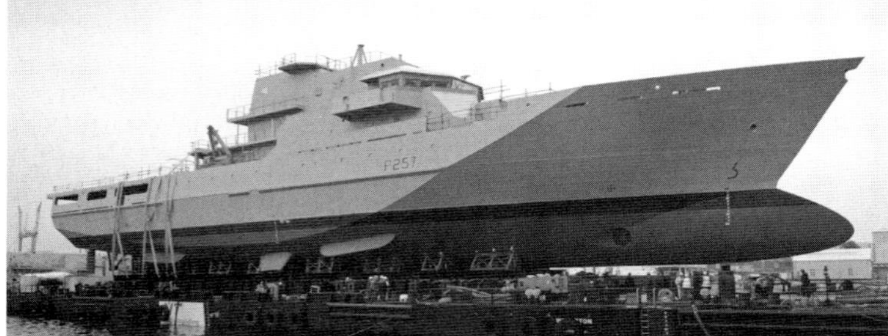

Clyde (P 257)—Falklands Islands patrol ship, preparing for launch
VT Shipbuilding via David Shirlaw, 6-06

Electric: 920 kw tot. (3 × 250-kw, 1 × 170-kw diesel alternator sets; 440 v)
Range: 5,500/15 **Fuel:** 325 tons
Endurance: 21 days **Crew:** 30 tot. + 18 Marine commandos

Remarks: First three were ordered 8-5-01 as replacements for the remaining Island-class offshore patrol ships in the fisheries protection role. The ships are RN crewed but owned by the contractor and leased to the Royal Navy for five years, with options for a 10-year renewal, purchase, or return to the builder/owner. The ships are expected to operate for 320 days per year and are based at Portsmouth. The launch of P 281 was delayed two days by industrial action and then was carried out without ceremony. P 283 is the last ship built at the UT Woolston SY. *Clyde* was ordered on 26-2-05 to replace the Castle-class patrol ships as Falklands Islands patrol vessel, she differs from previous units in having an aft helicopter deck and additional crew members.
Hull systems: Each unit will be assigned a rotating pool of 48 crew, 30 of whom will be aboard at any given time. Officers and senior enlisted will have single-berth cabins, junior ratings two-berth cabins. Two Halmatic Pacific 22 inspection RIBs will be carried, and a 25-ton capacity crane will be fitted to handle containerized disaster relief, antipollution, firefighting, rescue, and other modules. A 25-ton-capacity container crane is fitted to permit the use of special-function mission containers. The hull is designed so that a section can be inserted amidships to accommodate additional crew and equipment. The use of flat-panel hull plating results in a considerable angled knuckle abreast the pilothouse. A bow bulb is fitted. A helicopter deck capable of handling a Merlin is fitted aft on P 257 and may be added later to all units.

♦ 1 Castle-class offshore patrol vessels
Bldr: Hall Russell, Aberdeen, Scotland

	Laid down	L	In serv.
P 265 Dumbarton Castle	25-6-80	3-6-81	12-3-82

Dumbarton Castle (P 265) Marian Wright, 8-03

D: 1,350 tons (1,550 fl) **S:** 20 kts **Dim:** 81.00 (75.00 pp) × 11.50 × 3.42
A: 1 30-mm 75-cal. Oerlikon DS-30B AA; 2 single 7.62-mm mg
Electronics:
Radar: 1 Kelvin-Hughes Type 1006 nav.; 1 BAE Systems Type 994 surf./air-search
EW: RRDS UAN(1) radar warning intercept; DLE decoy RL syst. (4 6-tubed Shield RL); DLF(2) floating decoy decoy dispenser syst. (2 twin racks)
M: 2 Ruston 12 RK 320DM diesels; 2 CP props; 5,640 bhp (4,380 sust.)
Electric: 890 kw tot. (3 × 280-kw alternators, Paxman 6RPHCZ diesels, driving; 1 × 50-kw emergency set, Perkins 6.354 diesel driving; 440 v a.c.)
Range: 10,000/12 **Fuel:** 186 tons **Endurance:** 28 days
Crew: 6 officers, 39 enlisted (52 tot. accomm.)

Remarks: Ordered 8-8-80, *after* having been laid down. Based at Portsmouth. Currently serves as Falkland Islands patrol vessel. To be replaced by *Clyde* (P 257) in 2007.
Hull systems: P 265 operated at more than 2,000 tons displacement during the Falklands War. Can carry 19.5 tons helicopter fuel, 110 tons fresh water, and 30 tons of oil-spill dispersant detergent. Have Decca CANE-2 (Computer-Assisted Navigation Equipt.) NAVSAT, and Omega navigational systems. Two Avon Searaider rubber rescue/inspection dinghies are carried. Have one fire monitor and two oil-dispersing spray booms. Intended for 21-day patrols. The helicopter deck is large enough to accommodate a Sea King helicopter. Vosper Thornycroft D88 electronic machinery control systems were added during mid-1990s refits. Have additional accommodations for 25-strong Royal Marine detachment, if required.
Combat systems: Can carry acoustic and mechanical minesweeping gear as well as being able to lay mines. Carry two 50-mm rocket flare launchers. The Type 994 radar employs the antenna from the AWS-4 commercial radar. UAN(1) Orange Crop intercept equipment was developed for helicopter use and covers 0.5 to 18.0 GHz. Are equipped with a Marisat commercial SATCOM terminal. Originally had a 40-mm 60-cal. Mk 9 AA mount. On P 265, the space beneath the gunmount has been converted into a mine-countermeasures operations and planning room.

Disposal note: Sister *Leeds Castle* (P 258) was decommissioned on 12-8-05. All remaining Island-class patrol boats have been decommissioned and sold to Bangladesh and Trinidad & Tobago. *Jersey* (P 295) paid off for disposal on 16-12-93 and was sold to Bangladesh; *Orkney* (P 299) was decommissioned on 27-5-99 and sold to Trinidad & Tobago, transferring on 18-12-00. *Shetland* (P 298) was transferred to Bangladesh on 5-8-02, and the remaining units followed during 2002–3.

PATROL BOATS [PB]

♦ 2 Greyfox class
Bldr: Halmatic, Hamble (In serv. 1988)

P 284 Scimitar (ex-*Greyfox*) P 285 Sabre (ex-*Greywolf*)

Sabre (P 285) Daniel Ferro, 8-05

D: 18.5 tons **S:** 27+ kts **Dim:** 16.0 × 4.7 × 1.4 **A:** 2 7.62-mm mg
Electronics:
Radar: 1 . . . nav.
E/O: . . . FLIR
M: 2 MTU 12V193 TB92 diesels; 2 props; 2,000 bhp **Crew:** 4 tot. + 30 passengers

Remarks: Built for antiterror patrol use on Lough Neagh, Northern Island, but their existence was not disclosed until their withdrawal in 2002. Reassigned 9-02 as patrol boats at Gibraltar, where they arrived on 19-9-02 and were commissioned on 31-1-03. GRP construction with some Kevlar armor around the pilothouse. Carry two 7.62-mm pedestal-mounted machineguns aft.

PATROL BOATS [PB] *(continued)*

♦ 16 Archer (P.2000) class

Bldrs: Watercraft, Shoreham-by-Sea (last nine completed by Vosper Thornycroft); P 274 and P 275: BMT Marine Procurement Ltd.

1 patrol and search-and-rescue craft at Gibraltar:

P 293 Ranger (In serv. 3-8-88)

14 University Reserve Naval Unit training:

	In serv.	Unit Assigned
P 163 Express	26-5-88	Cardiff
P 164 Explorer	18-10-85	Northumbria
P 165 Example	16-1-86	Yorkshire
P 167 Exploit	17-8-88	Birmingham
P 264 Archer	1-3-86	Aberdeen
P 270 Biter	5-11-85	Manchester
P 272 Smiter	7-2-86	Glasgow
P 273 Pursuer	19-2-88	Sussex
P 274 Tracker	8-5-98	Portsmouth
P 279 Blazer	15-3-88	Southampton
P 280 Dasher	6-5-88	Cyprus
P 291 Puncher	13-7-88	London
P 292 Charger	8-7-88	Liverpool
P 294 Trumpeter	8-11-88	Bristol

1 Brittania Royal Naval College training tender:

P 275 Raider (In serv. 8-5-98)

Explorer (P 164) Michael Winter, 6-05

Blazer (P 279) A. A. de Kruijf, 7-05

D: 44 tons (49 fl) **S:** 22.5 kts (2 new units: 25 kts)
Dim: 20.80 (18.00 pp) × 5.80 × 1.80
A: P 293, P 294 only: 2 single 7.62-mm mg
Electronics: Radar: 1 Decca AC 1216 nav.
M: 2 Perkins CV M800T diesels; 2 props; 1,590 bhp (1,380 sust.)
Electric: 62 kVA tot. **Range:** 330/20; 550/15
Crew: 1 officer, 4 enlisted, 13 trainees

Remarks: First 14 ordered 7-84 and the other two on 2-97. Now assigned to the Inshore Training Squadron and affiliated as per the previous table. Nine were incomplete (P 273 ready for trials) when Watercraft closed. BMT (British Marine Technology) was a project management firm located at Bath that subcontracted the actual construction of P 274 and P 275, with the hulls molded by Kingfisher Boats, Falmouth, and outfitting performed by Ailsa-Troon, Scotland. P 293 has been based at Gibraltar since 1-91. P 163–165 and 167 originally bore A-series pennants as training craft for the Royal Naval Auxiliary Service; they paid off early in 1994 and recommissioned 7-94. P 275 was reassigned as navigational training tender to the Britannia Royal Naval College, Dartmouth, during 2001. P 294 replaced P 280 at Bristol, and P 280 was reassigned to the newly formed Cyprus Squadron in 2004.
Hull systems: Have GRP-construction, deep-vee, hard-chine hulls designed by Amgram, Ltd. The final pair have a modified, bulged transom stern.
Combat systems: P 293 and P 294 were re-equipped with 7.62-mm machineguns during 2002 but no longer carry a 20-mm gun forward.

Note: Patrol boats operated by the Ministry of Defence Police are listed at the end of the United Kingdom section.

MINE-COUNTERMEASURES SHIPS

Note: Under the $240-million RIMS (Replacement Influence Minesweeping System) project, the Royal Navy is exploring several unconventional concepts, including: a remote-control drone system with three 12.2-m, GRP-hulled drones controlled by a mother ship; a remotely controlled tug that would tow an influence-generating sweep; a "clip-on" sweep array; cast-concrete floating modules that could be combined to simulate specific pressure and other signatures; and helicopter-towed influence sweep arrays.

♦ 8 Sandown-class single-role minehunters (SRMH)

Bldr: Vosper Thornycroft, Woolston (Southampton) and Portsmouth

	Laid down	L	In serv.
M 104 Walney	5-90	25-11-91	20-2-93
M 106 Penzance	25-9-95	11-3-97	14-5-98
M 107 Pembroke	. . .	15-12-97	6-7-00
M 108 Grimsby	. . .	10-8-98	25-9-99
M 109 Bangor	3-98	16-4-99	26-7-00
M 110 Ramsey	. . .	25-11-99	22-6-01
M 111 Blyth	30-5-99	4-7-00	14-8-01
M 112 Shoreham	2-00	9-4-01	20-7-02

Shoreham (M 112) Frank Findler, 6-05

Walney (M 104) Leo van Ginderen, 6-05

Grimsby (M 108) Frank Findler, 6-05

D: 378 tons light, 450 tons std. (484 fl) **S:** 15 kts (6.5 max. hunting)
Dim: 52.50 (50.00 pp) × 10.50 (9.00 waterline) × 2.30
A: 1 30-mm 75-cal. DS-30B AA

MINE-COUNTERMEASURES SHIPS *(continued)*

Electronics:
Radar: 1 Kelvin-Hughes Type 1007 nav.
Sonar: Type 2093 variable-depth minehunting
EW: Fitted for: DLK decoy syst. (2 18-round Wallop Barricade 57-mm RL)
M: 2 Paxman Valenta 6RPA 200-EM 1500 diesels; 2 Voith-Schneider vertical cycloidal props; 2,024 bhp—2 200-hp electric motors (6.5 kts)—2 Schottel bow-thrusters
Electric: 750 kw tot. (3 diesel sets) **Range:** 2,600/11
Crew: 5 officers, 29 enlisted (40 accomm.)

Remarks: Pure minehunters, with no minesweeping capability. Original plan called for construction of as many as 20 for the Royal Navy. All are named for coastal resort towns. The first unit was ordered on 28-8-85 but not accepted for operational service until 12-92 because of difficulties with the sonar suite. Planned to be operational for 6,000 hours between overhauls. M 107 successfully underwent class shock trials during 5-99. M 110 cost about $46 million. Remaining units of the class have been transferred to Faslane to serve as mine-countermeasures vessels, assisting the *Vanguard*-class SSBNs. Sisters serve in Saudi Arabia and Spain.
Hull systems: Glass-reinforced-plastic construction. Use electric drive for low-speed, quiet operation. M 104 and 106 have three Mawdsley generators, each powered by a Perkins V8-250G, 335-bhp diesel. Navigational equipment includes Decca Hyperfix, QM-14, and Navigator Mk 21 radio navaids (the latter being replaced by Navigator Mk 53). M 106 and later have larger, more powerful 1.8-m-diameter cycloidal propeller sets, and their GRP superstructures were molded via the SCRIMP (Seeman Composite Resin Infusion Molding Process) method, which reduces structural weight by about 15 tons. Air conditioning was improved in M 106 onward. M 108 and later are equipped to accommodate female crewmembers.
Combat systems: Have NAUTIS-M minehunting operations system. The Type 2093 sonar uses a variable-depth vertical lozenge-shaped towed body lowered beneath the hull; it has search, depth-finder, classification, and route survey modes. The ships carry two Remote-Controlled Mine Disposal System Mk 2 (improved PAP 104 Mk 5) submersibles with up to 2,000 m of control cable and a depth capability of 300 m for mine identification and disposal. They also carry a mine-clearance diver team. M 106 and later have a new davit for the Remote-Controlled Mine Disposal System Mk 2 submersible and also carry two-man portable diver decompression chambers. Two Wallop Barricade decoy rocket launchers can be added for deployments to high-threat areas, but there is no electronic intercept equipment. M 104 received a portable decompression chamber early in 2001, doubling the depth that mine-disposal divers can work to 80 m; a second mine-countermeasures equipment crane was added aft, and the air conditioning and the ship's accommodations were improved.
Disposals: *Cromer* (M 103) was decommissioned for disposal on 26-11-01 after only nine years' service; the ship is being used as a pierside training craft at the Britannia Royal Naval College, Dartmouth, and has been named *Hindostan*. *Bridport* (M 105) was decommissioned in 2004, *Sandown* (M 101) on 19-10-04, and *Inverness* (M 102) on 15-11-04. The three were sold to Estonia in 2006.

♦ 8 Hunt-class minehunters
Bldr: Vosper Thornycroft, Woolston (except M 34: Yarrow [Shipbuilders], Scotstoun, Glasgow)

	Laid down	L	In serv.
M 30 Ledbury	5-10-77	5-12-79	11-6-81
M 31 Cattistock	20-6-79	22-1-81	16-6-82
M 33 Brocklesby	8-5-80	12-1-82	3-2-83
M 34 Middleton	1-7-80	27-4-83	15-8-84
M 37 Chiddingfold	. . .	6-10-83	26-10-84
M 38 Atherstone	9-1-84	1-3-86	30-1-87
M 39 Hurworth	1-83	25-9-84	19-7-85
M 41 Quorn	2-6-86	23-1-88	21-4-89

Cattistock (M 31) Derek Fox, 1-06

D: 625 tons (725 fl) **S:** 17 kts (15 kts sust.; 8 kts on hydraulic drive)
Dim: 60.00 (56.60 pp) × 9.85 × 2.20 hull (3.40 max.)
A: 1 30-mm 75-cal. DS-30B AA; 2 single 7.62-mm mg; provision for 2 single 20-mm 90-cal. Oerlikon GAM-B01 AA (see Remarks)
Electronics:
Radar: 1 Kelvin-Hughes Type 1006(4) or Type 1007 nav.
Sonar: Thales Type 2193 variable-depth minehunting (100-300 kHz), with Mills Cross Type 2059 submersible tracking set incorporated
EW: Provision for: MEL UAR Matilda threat warning (7.5-18 gHz); 2 2-round DLJ(2) floating radar decoy dispenser syst; DLK decoy syst. (2 18-round Wallop Barricade 57-mm RL)
M: 2 Ruston-Paxman Deltic 9-59K diesels (1,600 rpm); 2 props; 1,900 bhp (1,770 sust.); slow-speed hydraulic drive for hunting (8 kts)—bow-thruster
Electric: 1,185 kw (3 Foden FD 12 Mk 7 diesel alternators of 200 kw each for ship's service plus one 525-kw Deltic 9-55B diesel alternator for magnetic minesweeping and one 60-kw emergency set)
Range: 1,500/12 **Crew:** 5 officers, 40 enlisted

Remarks: Though capable of hunting and sweeping mines, are usually equipped solely for hunting. M 33 was laid down *prior* to ordering on 19-6-80. M 41 was ordered on 4-6-85. M 31 hit a jetty at Portsmouth on 23-11-02, putting a 60-cm hole in the hull. The remaining units of the class are to be retired between 2019 and 2023.

Ledbury (M 30) Frank Findler, 6-05

Hurworth (M 39) Leo van Ginderen, 6-05

Hull systems: Hull constructed of glass-reinforced plastic. One Deltic 9-59B diesel (645 bhp) powers the 525-kw sweep current alternator *or* four Dowty hydraulic pumps used to power the props during minehunting; the engine also provides power for the bow-thruster and the sweep winch. All are receiving the Thales VIMOS (Vibration MOnitoring System), which is expected to cut radiated noise by 3–10 dB.
Combat systems: Are equipped with CAAIS DBA-4 (64 contact-tracking) data system (upgraded to permit integration of the Navpac positioning aid) and Decca Mk 21 Hi-Fix navigation system. Most carry a Marisat SATCOM terminal. Carry six or seven divers and two French PAP 104 Mk 3 remote-controlled mine-location submersibles. Have Sperry Osborn TA 6 acoustic, M. Mk 11 magnetic loop and M. Mk 8 Orepesa wire sweeping gear as well. When deployed in high-threat areas, can be equipped with single 20-mm AA mounts on platforms abreast the stack, decoy rocket launchers, DLF-2(2) Replica floating decoys, and Matilda-E radar intercept gear. The original 40-mm 60-cal Mk 9 AA mounts have been replaced by stabilized DS-30B 30-mm AA mounts. For Northern Ireland patrol duties, M 32 and M 29 have had two Caley articulating cranes atop cylindrical bases added on the fantail to tend two Pacific and one Arctic rigid-inflatable launches, and all of their portable mine-countermeasures equipment has been removed.
Modernization: After an 18-month feasibility study, plans were dropped in 1996 for a major life-extension program to keep the ships in service for 40 years; the planned equipment changes would have been too heavy. The replacement "Hunt Minimum Update" began during 2003 and will be completed in all surviving units by 2007. Modifications include the Thales Type 2193 wideband minehunting sonar to detect bottomed mines to 80-m depths; updates to the MS 14 and MSSA Mk 1 influence sweep arrays; and substitution of a new NAUTIS III mine warfare combat data system. The program adds about 5–10 years to the ships' service lives.
Disposals: *Bicester* (M 36) was stricken on 29-6-00 and *Berkeley* (M 40) on 20-2-01; they were transferred to Greece on 31-7-00 and 28-2-01, respectively. *Brecon* (M 29), *Cottesmore* (M 32), and *Dulverton* (M 35) were retired on 28-9-05.

AMPHIBIOUS WARFARE SHIPS

Note: Landing ships and craft subordinated to the Royal Logistic Corps (formerly Royal Corps of Transport) are covered in the British Army entry at the conclusion of the United Kingdom section. *Invincible*-class aircraft carriers can also carry troops, as can the helicopter transport *Argus,* while nearly every seagoing combatant class can be adapted to carry small numbers of Royal Marines.

♦ 1 assault helicopter carrier [LPH]
Bldr: BAE Systems (formerly Kvaerner Govan, Ltd.), Govan, Scotland, and BAE Systems (formerly VSEL), Barrow-in-Furness, Scotland

	Laid down	L	In serv.
L 12 Ocean	30-3-95	11-10-95	19-3-99 (del. 30-9-98)

AMPHIBIOUS WARFARE SHIPS *(continued)*

Ocean (L 12) Leo van Ginderen, 6-05

Ocean (L 12) Camil Busquets i Vilanova, 2005

Ocean (L 12) A. A. de Kruijf, 9-03

Ocean (L 12)—with Lynx, Sea King, and Gazelle helicopters on deck
Royal Navy, 2003

D: 21,578 tons (fl) **S:** 19 kts (18 sust.)
Dim: 203.4 (193.0 pp) × 32.6 (28.5 wl; 36.1 extreme) × 6.65
Air Group: 12 Sea King HC.4 troop helicopters and 6 Lynx AH.7 or WAH-64D Apache attack helicopters
A: 5 single 20-mm GAM-B01 AA; 3 20-mm Mk 15 Phalanx gatling CIWS
Electronics:
Radar: 2 Kelvin-Hughes Type 1007 nav.; 1 BAE Systems Type 996(2) surf./air search; 3 General Dynamics Mk 90 Phalanx f.c.
EW: Racal UAT(7) intercept; DLJ(2) Sea Gnat decoy RL syst. (8 6-tubed Mk 137 launchers); 2 DLH SIREN offboard jammer launchers; provision for towed torpedo decoy
M: 2 Crossley-Pielstick 12 PC2.6 V400 diesels; 2 5-bladed props; 18,360 bhp—electric low-speed drive—Stone-Vickers bow-thruster
Electric: 8,000 kw tot. (4 × 2,000-kw Ruston 12RKC diesel sets, 1 . . .-kw Paxman Vega 12JZ emergency diesel set)
Range: 8,000/15 **Fuel:** 1,500 tons (+ 1,500 tons aviation fuel)
Crew: 311 tot. + up to 186 aircrew (461 accomm.) + 500 Royal Marine troops and 26 Royal Marine boat crew

Remarks: Originally referred to as the ASS (Aviation Support Ship) and intended to replace the vertical assault capability lost with the disposal of the carriers *Hermes* and *Bulwark*. Now referred to as an LPH. Formally ordered 1-9-93. Cost was £150.6 million. The hull was built to merchant vessel standards by Kvaerner at Govan and christened by Queen Elizabeth II on 20-2-98. During dock trials early in 4-98, the port propeller shaft and reduction gearing were damaged, delaying delivery and costing £0.5 million in repairs. Became fully operational during 3-99 after extensive trials. Does not have command and control facilities for a flag or Royal Marine brigade staff. Cannot transport heavy armored vehicles and is handicapped by low speed. Refitted 12-00 to 5-01 and given new landing craft davits, improvements to replenishment-at-sea equipment and accommodations facilities, and a new computer data network. Permanently assigned to the ship and operating the four landing craft as well as providing firefighting, security, and bridge watchstanding personnel is 9 Assault Squadron Royal Marines. Intended to operate until 2018. Based at Devonport.
Hull systems: The ship in general resembles the *Invincible* class (and has a similar underwater hullform), but with full-length flight deck without ski-jump. Four LCVP Mk 5 landing craft, each capable of carrying 35 troops and 2 tons of equipment, are carried in side embrasures. Brown Brothers folding-fin stabilizers are fitted. There is a small stern ramp for light vehicles, of which 40 half-ton trucks, 34 trailers, and six 105-mm towed guns can be carried. In an emergency, 303 additional troops can be carried, for a total of 803. There are 17 weapon and ammunition magazines, totaling 180 tons capacity. Four reverse osmosis plants can produce a total of 320 tons of potable water per day. The main engines themselves must be stopped and reversed in rotation to provide astern power.

During a refit begun fall 2002 by Fleet Support Ltd., 50-m hull blisters were added along the aft chine line on each side to improve the ship's ability to launch and recover landing craft safely; in addition, fresh water tankage was increased and a stores compartment was converted for use as a stores issuing center.
Aviation systems: The flight deck has six "spots" for Merlin-sized helicopters and can also accommodate CH-47 Chinook helicopters. The hangar can accommodate up to 12 Merlin or 12 Sea King HC.4 and six Lynx helicopters and is divided into three sections by fire curtains. Flight deck freeboard is 15.3 meters, and flight deck dimensions are 170 × 31.7 m. There are two aircraft elevators, and a vehicle ramp reaches the flight deck on the starboard side, aft. The ship was used with trials for the Apache attack helicopter during 2004 and can carry the aircraft as part of its air group.
Combat systems: The Ferranti ADAWS 2000 Mod. 1 command system is installed. Has British Aerospace DIMPS (Distributed Message Processing System), the Marconi-Matra SCOT-1D SHF SATCOM system, and a Marisat commercial SATCOM terminal. Links 11 and 14 are fitted, with provision for later installation of Link 16 (JTIDS). The three twin 30-mm 75-cal. Oerlikon GCM-B03 guns originally fitted have been replaced with 5 20-mm GAM-B01 guns.

◆ 2 Albion-class assault landing ships [LPD]
Bldr: BAE Systems (formerly Marconi Marine-VSEL), Barrow-in-Furness

	Laid down	L	In serv.
L 14 Albion	22-5-98	9-3-01	19-6-03
L 15 Bulwark	27-1-00	15-11-01	28-4-05

Bulwark (L 15) Leo van Ginderen, 7-05

Albion (L 14)—note the stern door Chris Sattler, 7-05

Albion (L 14) Michael Winter, 6-05

D: 14,600 tons (16,981 fl; 18,500 flooded) **S:** 18 kts (17.5 sust.)
Dim: 178.00 (164.7 wl; 162.0 pp) × 28.9 × 6.1
A: 2 30-mm Goalkeeper CIWS; 2 single 20-mm GAM-B01 AA; 2–3 Sea King HC.4 or Merlin HC.3 troop-carrying helicopters

AMPHIBIOUS WARFARE SHIPS *(continued)*

Electronics:
Radar: 2 Kelvin-Hughes Type 1008 nav.; 1 BAE Systems Type 996(2) surf./air search; 2 Thales Goalkeeper f.c. suite
EW: Racal UAT(7) intercept; DLJ(2) decoy syst. with DLH launch capability (8 6-round RL); towed torpedo decoy syst.
M: Diesel-electric: 2 Wärtsilä Vasa 16V32LNE diesels (8,377 bhp each) driving two 6,250-kw generators; 2 Wärtsilä Vasa 4R32LNE diesels (2,172 bhp each); driving 1,560-kw generators, 15,620 kw tot. generator output; 2 6-Mw electric motors; 2 4-m dia. props; 16,094 shp—294 shp bow-thruster
Range: 8,000/15 **Crew:** 325 tot + 305 troops (710 in emergency)

Remarks: Were originally to have been ordered in 1988 to replace *Intrepid* and *Fearless.* Design contract to Y-ARD/VSEL/Dowty-SEMA consortium 1992. The construction contract was awarded on 18-7-96 after prolonged negotiations with the only bidder. The program is now estimated to have cost about £790 million. Much of the prefabrication work for L 15 was performed at the former Kvaerner yard at Govan. The ships are based at Devonport.
Hull systems: Have two flight deck spots for Merlin-sized helicopters, four LCU Mk 10 landing craft (or two U.S. LCAC) in floodable welldeck, and four LCVP Mk 5 landing craft in davits. When fully flooded, the docking well has 3 m of water above the deck. An 11.8-m side ramp is fitted to starboard forward, and there is a small door on either beam amidships for cargo pallet loading and offloading. The 17.2-m-wide stern door articulates to form a 7.5-m-wide by 10.5-m-long vehicle ramp. Vehicle cargo capacity (twice that of *Fearless*), is six Challenger-2 main battle tanks or 16 2-ton trucks, 36 smaller vehicles, and 30 tons of stores. There are 550 linear meters of vehicle parking space, with MacGregor hoistable internal vehicle ramps from the lower vehicle deck to the upper deck aft and between the lower and mezzanine decks forward and amidships.
The hull form is adapted from that of modern commercial vehicle/passenger ferries and incorporates a bow bulb; its structure exceeds naval strength standards. A computerized ballasting system preserves trim while loading and unloading. CAE Electronics supplied an automated machinery and damage-control system.
Combat systems: Have the Marconi Electronic Systems ADAWS-2000 Mod. 1 combat data system and British Aerospace MPS2000 message-handling system. A terminal for the drone aircraft-carried Airborne Stand-Off Radar (ASTOR) is to be fitted. A Marconi-Matra SCOT-2D SHF SATCOM terminal, with two antennas, is carried. The 72-station Command Support System (CSS) is intended to support the staffs of an embarked Commander Amphibious Task Group and a Commander Land Forces.

Disposal note: *Fearless*-class amphibious assault ship *Fearless* (L 10) was decommissioned on 18-3-02, although formal retirement did not take place until 10-02. Sister *Intrepid* (L 11), in reserve at Portsmouth since late 1990, was reduced to nine-month availability reserve status on 31-8-99 and had a caretaker crew of 15; she was retired during 7-01 and is to be sold for scrap.

♦ 2 (+ 2) Largs Bay–class dock landing ships [LSD]
Bldr: First two: Swan Hunter (Tyneside), Ltd., Wallsend-on-Tyne; other two: BAE Systems, Govan, Scotland

	Laid down	L	In serv.
L 3006 Largs Bay	1-10-01	18-7-03	19-1-04
L 3007 Lyme Bay	1-10-01	2004	19-1-05
L 3008 Mounts Bay	2003	4-04	2007
L 3009 Cardigan Bay	2003	9-4-05	2007

Mounts Bay (L 3008) Dave Cullen, 10-05

D: 16,160 tons (fl) **S:** 18 kts (sust.) **Dim:** 176.6 × 26.4 × 5.8 max.
A: Provisions for 2 20-mm Mk 15 Phalanx gatling CIWS
Electronics: . . .
M: 2 Wärtsilä 12V26 and 2 Wärtsilä 8L26 diesels, 4 generator sets, electric drive; 2 ABB Azipod azimuthal props; . . . shp
Range: 8,000/15 **Crew:** 60 tot. RFA + 356 troops

Remarks: Officially styled ALSL (Alternative Landing Ship Logistic) until 7-02, when they were retyped "Landing Platform Dock (Auxiliary)." The design is based on that of Royal Schelde's *Rotterdam*-class LPD. Two new "Landing Ships Logistic" (i.e., LST) were to be procured as a result of the 1998 Defence White Paper decisions to replace *Sir Geraint* and *Sir Percivale,* but the program was expanded to four ships in 10-00, for a planned total cost of £300 million. All are operated by the Royal Fleet Auxiliary. The first two were ordered for £140 million during 12-00. The second pair were ordered for £120 million on 19-11-01, with first steel for L 3008 cut on 14-1-02. Portions of the hull structure were subcontracted to a Dutch yard.
Hull systems: Have 1,200 lane-meters of vehicle accommodation internally and on the flight deck, and are able to transport 200 tons of combat cargo such as fuel, ammunition, and stores. Two Mexiflote-powered pontoons are stowable on the hull sides. A large helicopter/vehicle/container deck is fitted, but no helicopter hangar; have one large or two small helicopter landing "spots." The ships are not capable of beaching. A stern docking well will hold one Utility Landing Craft Mk 10, though no landing craft are carried in davits. A typical vehicle load would be 36 Challenger 2 tanks or up to 150 light trucks. Employ azimuthal propellers and have no rudders. Two vehicle and cargo-handling cranes are fitted amidships.

Disposal note: *Sir Galahad*–class tank landing ship *Sir Galahad* (L 3005) was retired in 2006.

♦ 1 Sir Bedivere–class tank landing ship [LST]
Bldr: Hawthorn Leslie, Hebburn-on-Tyne

	Laid down	L	In serv.
L 3004 Sir Bedivere	10-65	20-7-66	18-5-67

Sir Bedivere (L 3004) Michael Winter, 6-05

Sir Bedivere (L 3004) Leo van Ginderen, 7-05

D: 6,700 tons (fl) **S:** 17.25 kts **Dim:** 139.02 (124.64 pp) × 17.94 (17.70 wl) × 3.90
A: Provision for 4 single 20-mm 90-cal Oerlikon GAM-B01 AA
Electronics:
Radar: 1 Kelvin-Hughes Type 1007 nav.; 1 . . . X-band nav.; 1 . . . S-band nav.
EW: . . . intercept; DLE decoy syst. (4 6-round Shield RL)
M: L 3004: 2 Stork-Wärtsilä 12SW280 diesels; 2 props; 9,840 bhp; 2 props; 9,400 bhp (8,460 sust.)—495 shp bow-thruster (L 3004: 985 shp)
Electric: 1,600 kw tot. **Range:** 8,000/15
Fuel: 811 tons
Crew: 21 officers, 44 enlisted + 402 troops

Remarks: 4473 grt/2,443 dwt. Likely to remain in service until 2011. In 1963 the Ministry of Transportation ordered the first of six specially designed LST-type ships for the British Army, chartered in peacetime to various private maritime firms. In 1970 the ships came under the control of the Royal Fleet Auxiliary Service.
Hull systems: Bow and stern ramps for vehicles, interior ramps connect the two decks. Helicopter platform and three cranes (two 8.5-ton capacity, one 20-ton). Have Marisat commercial SATCOM terminals. Can carry 2,077 tons water ballast. On L 3004 the 20-ton crane has been replaced by a 25-ton-capacity Clark Chapman crane, the amidships helicopter deck has been strengthened, and the after one lowered one deck. Most of the shade deck openings in the side were plated in and the 1-piece stern ramp replaced by an articulating two-piece ramp; the ship is able to transport 440 troops and carries four LCVP Mk 4 landing craft and one 6.5-m rigid inflatable boat. Is no longer considered suitable for beaching.
Disposals: Sisters *Sir Geraint* (L 3027), *Sir Percivale* (L 3036), and *Sir Tristram* (L 3505) were stricken by 2006. The original *Sir Galahad* (L 3005) was fatally damaged on 8-6-82 and scuttled 24-6-82.

♦ 10 LCU Mk 10 class–medium landing craft [LCM]
Bldr: BAE Systems: LCU 01, 02: Ailsa Troon Shipbuilders, Clyde; others: BAE Systems Govan, Clyde (In serv. 1999–2005)

L 1001 through L 1010

LCU Mk 10 class Frank Findler, 6-05

AMPHIBIOUS WARFARE SHIPS *(continued)*

D: 170 tons light (240 fl) **S:** 10 kts (loaded) **Dim:** 29.80 × 7.40 × 1.50
Electronics: Radar: 1 . . . nav.
M: 2 M.A.N. . . . diesels; 2 Schottel waterjets; . . . bhp—bow thruster
Electric: . . . kw tot. (2 Cummins . . . diesels driving) **Range:** 600/10
Endurance: 14 days (stores) **Crew:** 7 tot.

Remarks: For use with the new *Albion* class. Ordered 7-98 from BAE Systems for $57 million total, with construction subcontracted to Ailsa Troon. Program cost $51.2 million. First unit delivered in 1999 with subsequent units following during 2003–5; delays resulted from prototype modifications and improvements.
Hull systems: Have "drive-through" configuration, with ramps fore and aft and pilothouse to starboard, aft. Carry one heavy tank or four heavy trucks or up to 120 troops plus two snow-capable vehicles. Steel construction.

♦ 3 LCM (9) class–medium landing craft [LCM]
Bldrs L 705 and 709: Richard Dunston, Thorne; L 711: J. Bolson, Poole (In serv. 1965–66)

L 705 L 709 L 711

LCM (9)–class landing craft L 709 Ben Sullivan 6-05

D: 115 tons light (160 fl) **S:** 10 kts (9 loaded) **Dim:** 25.7 × 6.5 × 1.7
Electronics: Radar: 1 Raytheon . . . nav.
M: 2 Paxman YHXAM diesels; Kort-nozzle props; 624 bhp (474 sust.)
Range: 300/9 **Crew:** 7 tot.

Remarks: Can carry two tanks or 70 tons of cargo. Are naval manned.
Hull systems: Hull sides on all have been built up amidships, and shelter covers to the tank deck are carried. Original full-load displacement was 176 tons, but loading is now restricted. Are expected to retire in the near future.
Disposals: L 703 (F4—*Fearless* No. 4) was lost to a bomb on 8-6-82. Stricken have been class prototype L 3508 and sisters L 700, L 701, 702, 704, 706, 707, 708, 710, 713, 714, and 715.

♦ 23 LCVP Mk 5–class vehicle landing craft [LCVP]
Bldr: First 7: Vosper Thornycroft, Southampton; others: FBM Babcock Marine, Rosyth Royal Dockyard (First 7 in serv. 1-96 to 12-99; others: 2002–4)

LCVP Mk 5 class Leo van Ginderen, 6-05

D: 16 tons light (23 fl) **S:** 25 kts light; 16 kts loaded
Dim: 15.25 (14.00 pp) × 4.20 × 0.55
Electronics: Radar: 1 Raytheon . . . nav.
M: 2 Volvo Penta TAMD-72WJ diesels; 2 PP170 waterjets; 860 bhp
Range: 210/16 **Crew:** 3 tot. + 15–35 troops

Remarks: Prototype ordered 2-95. Are expected to serve for 20 years each. Can be distinguished from the LCVP Mk 4 by the six-sided pilothouse, which on the LCVP Mk 4 is rectangular.
Hull systems: Cargo capacity includes two tons of equipment in addition to 35 troops or two TUM light trucks, one 105-mm or 155-mm howitzer, or one Bv-206 Arctic tracked vehicle and trailer. Aluminum construction with planing hullform. The prototype reached 30 kts during initial trials.

♦ 19 LCVP Mk 4–class vehicle landing craft [LCVP]
Bldrs: 8301: Fairey Allday Marine, Hamble; 8401–8418: W.A. Souter, Cowes

D: 10.5 tons (16 fl) **S:** 20 kts (15 loaded) **Dim:** 13.00 (11.90 pp) × 3.20 × 0.80
A: 2 single 7.62-mm mg **Electronics:** Radar: 1 Raytheon . . . nav.
M: 2 Perkins 76-3544 diesels; 2 props; 440 bhp (8416-8418: 2 Dorman diesels; 2 CP props; . . . bhp)
Range: 150/14; 200/12 (8416–8418: 300/12) **Crew:** 3 tot. + 20–35 troops

LCVP Mk 4 class Michael Winter, 6-05

Remarks: Prototype 8301, ordered 6-2-80, is 13.50 m long by 3.50 m beam. Series units ordered 21-8-84. Have cargo well 8.80 × 2.13 m and a cargo capacity of 5.5 tons. Aluminum construction. Cargo well can be fitted with windowed, segmented cover. 8416–8418 can reach 22 kts. Four others serve the British Army's Royal Logistic Corps: LCVP 8402, 8409, 8419, and 8420. Are being replaced by the Mk 5–class landing craft. Ten have been retired by 2006.

♦ 4 Type 2000 TDX(M) assault hovercraft [LCPA]
Bldr: Griffon Hovercraft, Ltd., Salisbury Green (In serv. 1993)

C 21 C 22 C 23 C 24

Type 2000 TDX(M) assault hovercraft Michael Winter, 6-05

D: 6.75 tons (fl) **S:** 40 kts **Dim:** 11.04 × 4.60 (5.78 over skirt) × 0.52
A: 1 7.62-mm mg **Electronics:** Radar: 1 Raytheon . . . nav.
M: 1 Deutz BF8L-513 diesel driving 0.91-m diameter lift fan and 1.8-m diameter CP airscrew; 355 bhp (320 sust.)
Range: 300/40 **Fuel:** 284 liters **Crew:** 2 tot. + 16 troops

Remarks: Ordered 26-4-93. First two delivered 23-11-93. Aluminum hull structure. Payload is 16 troops or 2 tons of equipment. Maximum speed can be attained in Sea State 1, while 25 kts is maintainable in Sea State 3. The craft are able to travel over land and ice as well as water. Have GPS receivers, HF and VHF radios. Are operated by 539 Assault Squadron, Royal Marines, as part of 3 Commando Brigade. Can operate from the welldecks of utility landing craft *Fearless* (L 10). Can be accommodated in a C-130 Hercules transport. Cab top can be removed to permit carrying two 1-ton NATO standard cargo pallets.

Note: As a result of the success of the previous craft, the Royal Marines are seeking funding for several larger, "LCAC"-type air cushion landing craft capable of carrying both troops and vehicles.

Requests for bids were issued in 1-01 for a new class of "Fast Transit Craft" to replace current Royal Marine Special Boat Service craft beginning in 2007; the craft can be carried in a C-130 Hercules or beneath a CH-47 Chinook helicopter and can carry a 2.6-ton payload (10 troops and equipment) at 45 kts for 600 n.m. in a State 4 sea; the low-observable craft can also remain operable in up to State 6 seas.

Special Boat Service "Fast Transit Craft" Dave Cullen, 2006

♦ 2 FIC 145–class covert operations boats [LCP]
Bldr: Vosper Thornycroft-Halmatic, Havant (In serv. 12-94)

FIC 145-class—painted medium green Maritime Photographic, 8-01

AMPHIBIOUS WARFARE SHIPS *(continued)*

D: 9 tons light (12.5 fl) **S:** 45 kts **Dim:** 14.50 × 2.85 × 1.35 at rest
A: 2 single 12.7 or 7.62-mm mg **Electronics:** Radar: 1 Decca . . . nav.
M: 2 Seatek . . . diesels; 2 Rolla outdrive props, 1,160 bhp
Range: 225/45 **Crew:** 2 + . . . special forces

Remarks: Ordered 3-9-93. GRP and Kevlar construction, balsa-cored hulls with two hydroplane steps. Designed by Italian race boat designer Fabio Buzzi. At least two covert operations boats of an earlier design were in service by 7-93. Are operated by the Royal Marines Special Boat Service.

♦ 45 Rigid Raider assault boat Mk 3 [LCP]
Bldr: Vosper-RTK Marine, Poole, Dorset (In serv. 1996–99)

Rigid Raider assault boat Mk 3 Maritime Photographic, 8-98

D: 2.2 tons light **S:** 40 kts (36 loaded) **Dim:** 7.58 × 2.75 × . . .
M: 1 Yamaha gasoline outboard; 220 bhp **Crew:** 2 + 8 commandos

Remarks: Lengthened version of Mk 2 to improve handling. Two were donated to Georgia on 11-1-99.

Note: Procurement plans for 1999–2001 called for the acquisition of 5-m and 6.5-m Rigid Raider craft and a diesel-powered 8.5-m RIB prototype.

♦ 38 Rigid Raider assault boat Mk 2 [LCP]
Bldr: Vosper-RTK Marine, Poole, Dorset (In serv. 1993–96)

Rigid Raider assault boat Mk 2 Ben Sullivan, 6-05

D: 1.37 tons light **S:** 40 kts (30 loaded) **Dim:** 6.50 × . . . × . . .
M: 2 Suzuki gasoline outboards; 280 bhp **Crew:** 2 + 8 commandos

Remarks: Ordered late 1994. GRP hull with stainless-steel skegs and elastomer-coated foam-filled fender. Removable seats to permit transporting up to 680 kg cargo. Can reach 40 kts in light condition. Can also be operated with only one outboard motor.

♦ . . . Arctic 22 Rigid Raider inflatables [LCP] Bldr: Osborne, U.K.

Arctic 22–class Rigid Raider Leo van Ginderen, 6-05

D: 1.4 tons light **S:** 40+ kts **Dim:** 7.2 × . . . × . . .
M: 2 Mercury gasoline (or other) outboards; 280 shp **Range:** 30/40
Cargo: 15 troops or 1.12 tons stores

Remarks: Also in service are Arctic 24 and Arctic 28 RIBs.

♦ 30 or more Pacific 22 Mk II Rigid inflatables [LCP]
Bldr: Halmatic Ltd., Portchester (In serv. 2002– . . .)

Pacific 22–class Rigid Raider Daniel Ferro, 8-05

D: 1.75 tons light **S:** 32 kts **Dim:** 6.8 × . . . × . . .
M: 1 Ford Mermaid diesel; 1 waterjet; 140 bhp **Range:** 85/26
Crew: 1 + 5 passengers or 1.12 tons stores

Remarks: The prototype and four others were in service aboard landing ships as of 7-01, while two others were to be carried aboard frigates *Kent* and *Coventry* starting at the end of 6-01. Can carry 1.12 tons of stores in place of five people. Production of about 10 per year began in 2002.

Note: The Royal Navy also operates 70 Pacific 22 Mk I and Mk II RIBs as ship's boats; these have a maximum speed of 24 kts and do not have shock-resistant seating like the Royal Marine variant.

♦ 3 U.S. Mk 8 Mod. 1 swimmer delivery vehicles [LSDV]
Bldr: Maritime Special Operations Division, U.S. Naval Surface Warfare Center Coastal Systems Station, Panama City, Fla.

Remarks: Purchased 1999 to replace Mk 8 Mod. 0 craft for use by the Royal Marine Special Boat Service. Have double the range and a 50% speed increase over the Mod. 0, of which they are rebuilt examples. During reconstruction, received new motors, sonar, and navigational systems. First unit delivered 3-99 and the other two in 6-99.

♦ 35 or more Mexiflote self-propelled pontoons

Remarks: Rectangular, modular pontoon float assemblies that can be stowed vertically on the sides of landing ships. Powered by large diesel outdrives.

Mexiflote sectional pontoon—on starboard side of *Sir Tristram* (L 3505); British Army workboat *Perch* (WB 06) is visible on deck at left Douglas A. Cromby, 3-01

AUXILIARIES

The Royal Navy has expressed interest in replacing most older Royal Fleet Auxiliaries (RFA) now in service under the Military Afloat Reach and Sustainability (MARS) program. As of 2006, plans call for deliveries of five fleet tankers between 2011 and 2015, two support ships between 2017 and 2020, three joint sea-based logistics ships between 2016 and 2020, and one strike carrier support tanker in 2021. The proposed joint casuality treatment ship is not considered part of the MARS program.

Note: Ships not listed below as Royal Fleet Auxiliaries are crewed by the Royal Navy or civilian contractor personnel.

♦ 2 Fort Grange–class ammunition, food, and stores ships [AE]
Bldr: Scott-Lithgow, Greenock, Scotland

	Laid down	L	In serv.
A 385 FORT ROSALIE (ex-*Fort Grange*)	9-11-73	9-12-76	6-4-78
A 386 FORT AUSTIN	9-12-75	9-3-78	11-5-79

D: 22,749 tons (fl) **S:** 20 kts **Dim:** 183.78 (170.00 pp) × 24.06 × 9.03
A: 2 single 20-mm 90-cal Oerlikon GAM-B01 AA; 4 single 7.62-mm mg

AUXILIARIES *(continued)*

Fort Austin (A 386) Ralph Edwards, 7-03

Electronics:
Radar: 1 Type 1006 nav.; 1 Kelvin-Hughes 21/16P nav.; 1 Kelvin-Hughes 14/12 nav.
EW: DLJ(2) decoy syst. (8 6-round RL), Type 182 towed torpedo decoy
M: 1 Sulzer 8RND90 diesel; 1 prop; 23,200 bhp—2 690-shp bow-thrusters
Electric: 4,120 kw tot. (8 × 515-kw diesel sets) **Range:** 10,000/20
Crew: 31 officers, 83 unlicensed R.F.A. + 36 civilian supply staff + 45 RN flight personnel

Remarks: *Fort Rosalie:* 16,046 grt/8,300 dwt; *Fort Austin:* 16,054 grt/8,165 dwt. Ordered 11-71 and 7-72, respectively. RFA operated. The name for A 385 was changed in 6-00 at the end of a refit; the ship had been stationed at Split, Croatia, from 4-97 to 1-00, and the name change was made to avoid confusion with that of *Fort George* (A 388); the new name commemorates that of a World War II stores issue ship. Are expected to remain in service until 2013–14 respectively.
Hull systems: Four holds total 6,234 m^3 to carry guided weapons and ammunition and general stores, including 2,300 m^3 of refrigerated provisions. Have three sliding-stay, constant-tension, alongside-replenishment stations on each side. There are two 10-ton and four 5-ton electric stores cranes. Have two auxiliary boilers. In addition to the flight deck at the stern, the hangar roof can be used to operate helicopters.
Combat systems: Two additional 20-mm AA can be installed aft. Are being backfitted with Outfit DLH offboard seduction decoy launchers. One Sea King helicopter is normally carried, although up to four can be accommodated (A 386 acted as helicopter training ship while *Argus* was operating in support of UN forces in the Mideast during 1991), and they can theoretically be operated as auxiliary ASW helicopter support ships. A Marisat commercial SATCOM terminal is fitted.

Disposal note: *Throsk*-class ammunition transport *Kinterbury* (A 378) was retired during 11-04.

♦ 1 Antarctic patrol ship [AG]
Bldr: B.H. Ulstein SY, Hatlo, Norway (In serv. 1990)

A 171 Endurance (ex-A 176, ex-*Polar Circle*)

Endurance (A 171)—red hull, white superstructure, buff stack
Frank Findler, 6-05

Endurance (A 171) Derek Fox, 9-05

D: 6,500 tons (fl) **S:** 12 kts **Dim:** 91.00 (82.50 pp) × 17.90 × 6.50
A: None (see Remarks)
Electronics:
Radar: 1 Kelvin-Hughes Type 1006 nav.; 1 Furuno R 84 nav.; 1 Furuno M 34 ARG surf. search (see Remarks)
Sonar: Type 2053 echo sounder; Type 2090 echo sounder; Furuno 60-88 obstacle-avoidance
M: 2 Ulstein-Bergen BRM-8 diesels; 1 4-bladed Kort-nozzle prop; 8,152 bhp—1,000-shp bow-thruster, 775-shp stern side-thruster
Electric: 5,170 kw tot. (2 × Leroy Somer 1,980-kw shaft-generators, 2 × 605-kw Mitsubishi diesel-driven sets)
Range: 4–5,000/12 **Fuel:** 600 tons **Endurance:** 120 days
Crew: 15 officers, 97 enlisted + 14 Royal Marines

Remarks: 5,129 grt/2,200 dwt. Royal Navy–operated. Chartered 14-10-91 for one year with option to purchase from Rieber Shipping, Norway, and purchased outright on 24-1-92. The ship serves as Antarctic Territories patrol ship to guarantee the continuation of British sovereignty over the Falkland, South Georgia, and South Shetland Islands in the Antarctic Atlantic, where the ship also performs hydrographic survey duties. The original name was retained through her first deployment to south Atlantic, ending 5-92; initial pennant number changed 10-92 to commemorate her predecessor. Became subordinated to the Hydrographic Surveying Squadron summer 1995 and is expected to remain in service well into this century. Carries two shallow water survey craft (*James Caird* and *Nimrod*). Refitted by FSL, Portsmouth, from 6-99 to 10-99, with new radars and new computer. Hit uncharted rock in Antarctic waters, 21-1-03, with only minor damage.
Hull systems: Built as a combination commercial Arctic exploration and research vessel, icebreaker, and supply vessel. Able to break 3-ft. ice at 3 kts. The double-skinned hull is equipped with ice fins forward of the propeller to break up trash ice, and the rudder foundation has ice knives fitted for the same purpose. The elevator-equipped helicopter hangar is below the flight deck. During a major refit that completed 9-10-92, most of the scientific equipment (including the stern gantry) was removed and the helicopter hangar was greatly enlarged. There are a 27-ton and a 5-ton electrohydraulic cranes to handle cargo in a forward hold. Carries 78 m^3 aviation fuel and 250 m^3 potable water. Crew accommodations include a sauna, infirmary, and exercise room.
Combat systems: Has no armament and no countermeasures equipment. Navigation equipment provides fixes to 5-meter accuracy and includes two gyrocompasses, electromagnetic log, several echo sounders, Furuno object-avoidance sonar, Robertson autopilot, and a homing beacon for her Lynx HAS.3 helicopter, of which she can carry two. A commercial SATCOM terminal is fitted. The radar suite listed here is what was aboard prior to the 1999 refit.

♦ 1 special forces support ship and cable tender [AG]
Bldr: Scott-Lithgow, Greenock

	Laid down	L	In serv.
A 367 Newton	19-12-73	26-6-75	17-6-76

Newton (A 367) Bernard Prézelin, 2002

Newton (A 367)—black hull, buff superstructure Bernard Prézelin, 2002

D: 3,140 tons light (4,652 fl) **S:** 14 kts **Dim:** 98.6 (88.7 pp) × 16.15 × 5.7
Electronics:
Radar: 1 Kelvin-Hughes Type 1006 nav.
Sonar: Type 185 underwater telephone, Type 2010 and Type 2013 echo sounders
M: 3 Ruston 8RK-215 diesels (1,840 bhp each), electric drive; 1 Kort-nozzle prop; 2,680 shp—300 shp electric low-speed motor
Electric: 2,150 kw tot. **Range:** 5,000/9 **Fuel:** 244 tons
Crew: 61 total (including 12 technicians)

Remarks: Was originally intended for sonar-propagation trials and was also fitted to lay cable over the bows. She was modified to serve as a special forces support ship during a 2000–2001 refit by Cammel Laird, Birkenhead. Continues to be operated by the R.M.A.S., based at Devonport.

AUXILIARIES *(continued)*

Hull systems: Equipped with 350-hp retractable bow-thruster and passive tank stabilization system. Propulsion plant extremely quiet. Has four laboratories and seven special winches. Can carry and lay 400 tons of undersea cable and 361 tons cable repeaters. Navigation equipment includes SINS, communications and navigational satellite receivers, two optical range-finders, Decca Mk 21, and considerable other equipment. Re-engined 2000 by Ocean Fleets, Birkenhead. Has had davits added to support Special Boat Service RIB assault craft.

♦ 0 (+ 1) Joint Casualty Treatment Ship [AH]
Bldr: . . . (In serv. 2009–10)

Remarks: Was included in the 1998 Strategic Defence Review. To have been ordered in 2002 but the decision was been postponed until 2006–7 and planned delivery has been delayed to the end of the decade. The JCTS would have a 200-bed casualty facility, intensive-care units, operating theaters, a crew of about 350 (including the medical staff), and a helicopter deck with one landing and one parking spot. A side ramp will allow embarkation and debarkation of casualties while alongside a pier. Other options, including a new or converted vessel, a modular system capable of being deployed aboard a variety of commercial or naval hulls, a modified *Largs Bay*–class amphibious ship, or merely an extension of the existing standby PCRS, *Argus* (A 135), are also under consideration.

♦ 1 Aviation Training and Primary Casualty Reception Ship [AGH]
Bldr: CNR Breda, Venice, Italy

	L	In serv.
A 135 Argus (ex-*Contender Bezant*)	1981	1-6-88

Argus (A 135) Camil Busquets i Vilanova, 2005

D: 22,256 tons light (28,480 fl) **S:** 22 max. (19 sust.)
Dim: 173.01 (163.63 pp) × 30.64 × 8.20
Air Group: 6 Sea King helicopters or 12 Harrier V/STOL fighters (8 operational)
A: 2 single 20-mm 90-cal. Oerlikon GAM-B01 AA; 4 single 7.62-mm mg
Electronics:
Radar: 1 Kelvin-Hughes Type 1006 nav.; 1 Kelvin-Hughes Type 1007 nav.; 1 BAE Systems Type 994 surf./air-search
EW: UAN(1) (Racal Guardian) intercept, DLJ(2) decoy syst. (2 6-round Shield RL), Type 182 towed torpedo decoy
M: Electric drive: 2 Lindholmen-Pielstick 18PC2.5 V400 diesel generator sets, 2 Lindholmen propulsion motors; 2 props; 23,400 shp
Electric: 3,850 kw (3 × 1,200-kw diesel sets, 1 × 250-kw diesel set)
Range: 20,000/19 **Fuel:** 5,617 tons heavy oil + 3,251 tons aviation fuel
Crew: 22 officers, 58 unlicensed RFA + 3 officers, 25 enlisted RN + 42 officers, 95 enlisted RN in training detachment (up to 750 troops in emergency)

Remarks: 26,421 grt/12,221 dwt. Former roll-on/roll-off vehicle and container cargo ship purchased 2-3-84, having been on charter since 5-82, when she was used as an aircraft transport during the Falklands War. Converted at Harland and Wolff, Belfast, with vehicle cargo decks converted to a hangar and elevators added. Initially accepted 28-10-87, accepted 3-3-88, and "dedicated" 1-6-88, but continued in a trials status until completing a 17-7-89 to 3-10-89 refit. Initially intended to act as a helicopter training ship or as a transport for Harrier aircraft. Deployed twice to the Persian Gulf during the 1990–91 crisis: on 16-10-90 equipped with a 100-bed emergency hospital and carried four Sea King helicopters; and during 4-91 with 11 Sea King HC.4 and several Lynx and Gazelle helicopters. Has developed hull cracking and is generally considered not to be a successful ship. Found to be unsuitable for long-term troop deployments during operations in Adriatic in 1993. During refit from 1-01 to 5-01 at Cammell Laird, Hebburn-on-Tyne as an "Aviation Training and Primary Casualty Reception Ship," was given a permanent medical facility with beds for 90 casualties, 20 berths for intensive-care patients, and four operating theaters, all fitted into the space below the helicopter deck, which was modified to have multiple helicopter operating "spots." To be replaced by the Joint Casualty Treatment ship.
Hull systems: Passive tank stabilization added during naval conversion, watertight compartmentation improved. Can carry 5,405 tons water ballast and can also transfer fuel to ships in company. Provided with BW/CW defense system early in 2003 prior to departure for Mideast as a primary casualty treatment ship.
Aviation systems: Has space for eight Harriers and three helicopters on the hangar deck and three helicopters on deck, aft. There are two aircraft elevators. Hangar segregates into four sections. The flight deck (created by upending the former hatch covers, filling these with 1.9-m-thick concrete, and then laying over with steel for ballast and stability purposes) measures 113.52 × 28 m but is encumbered by stack and superstructure to starboard that create unpredictable airflow over the deck.
Combat systems: Racal supplied the sensors, CANE (DEB-1) data system, communications, and weapons-control package. Type 994 radar uses parabolic antenna from the AWS-4 radar. The listed gun armament is not normally carried. Two mounting positions abaft the stack for twin 30-mm 90-cal. Oerlikon AA have been empty for many years.

♦ 2 Echo-class hydrographic survey ships [AGS]
Bldr: Appledore Shipbuilders Ltd., Appledore, Devon

	Laid down	L	In serv.
H 87 Echo	10-4-01	4-3-02	3-03
H 88 Enterprise	10-4-01	24-8-02	17-10-03

Enterprise (H 88) Michael Winter, 6-05

D: 3,600 tons (fl) **S:** 15 kts **Dim:** 90.0 × 16.00 × 5.50
A: 1 20-mm Oerlikon GAM-B01 AA; 4 single 7.62-mm mg
Electronics:
Radar: 1 Decca BridgeMaster E 180 nav., 1 . . . nav.
Sonar: . . .
M: Diesel-electric drive: 2 ABB Compact Azipod electric azimuthal thrusters; 4,600 shp
Range: 9,000/12 **Crew:** 72 tot.

Remarks: Request for bids originally made 1-97 for replacements for *Roebuck, Herald, Bulldog,* and *Beagle.* The contract, for only two, was let on 21-6-00 for $197 million to Vosper Thornycroft, which also manages the operations of the ships for 25 years; the actual construction was subcontracted to Appledore. Designed by Kvaerner-Masa Marine. Will use naval crews, rotating aboard as in the *Scott* (H 131), but in three watches of 23 personnel, two being aboard and one ashore; this is intended to permit 334 days of operation per ship per year. As demonstrated during a 2003 deployment to the Persian Gulf, they can also operate as mine-countermeasures support ships, when another 35 personnel would come aboard. Both were laid down on the same day.
Hull systems: The power system can deliver anywhere from 400 kw to 3,000 kw to the propulsion plant.
Mission systems: Multibeam echo sounders and side-looking mapping sonars are fitted, and one survey launch is carried. A helicopter deck with elevator to hangar below is fitted forward of the bridge. Norway's Kongsberg Simrad supplies the integrated survey system for the two ships and their survey motor boats, including multibeam echo-sounders, processing, and data storage.

Note: Hydrographic survey ships began to be painted standard gray in 1997 in place of the traditional white with "buff" stack and masts; in 7-98 the pennant numbers were changed from "A" to "H" flag superior and are now painted on the hull sides. The Antarctic patrol ship *Endurance* (A 171) is subordinated to the Hydrographic Survey Squadron and performs surveys in the southern Atlantic region in addition to her other duties.

♦ 1 Scott-class ocean survey ship [AGS]
Bldr: Appledore Shipbuilders, Bideford

	Laid down	L	In serv.
H 131 Scott	20-1-95	13-10-96	19-9-97

Scott (H 131) Michael Winter, 6-05

D: 13,500 tons (fl) **S:** 17.6 kts (sust.) **Dim:** 131.13 × 21.50 × 8.30
Electronics:
Radar: 1 Decca 1626C ARPA nav.; 1 . . . surf. search
Sonar: SASS Mk 4 multi-beam mapping, Type 2090 echo sounder
M: 2 MaK 9M32 medium-speed diesels; 1 Lips CP prop; 10,800 bhp—1/7-ton thrust retracting azimuthal bow-thruster
Electric: 2,400 kw tot (4 × 600 kw, Cummins diesel-driven) **Range:** . . . / . . .
Endurance: 35 + days
Crew: 12 officers, 51 enlisted, including 35-person survey team (70 accomm.) (see Remarks)

Remarks: Ship ordered 20-1-95 from BAe Defence Systems Group, which subcontracted the construction to Appledore. Large size dictated by need for 8.4-m draft and flat hull bottom for mapping sonar transducer array. Intended to operate 307 days out of the year, with 42 of the total assigned crew of 63 aboard; crew members rotate aboard, 70 days on and 30 days off. Initial employment was a delineation of the boundary of the U.K.'s continental shelf. Based at Devonport. Can be equipped to support four mine-countermeasures ships with enhanced communications systems, additional stores, and an at-sea refueling system for the mine-countermeasures ships.
Hull systems: Ice-strengthened hull of 14-m molded depth, with draft maintained constant by ballasting system during survey operations. Is also equipped with oceanographic research equipment. Two large cranes aft. By 1998 the area on the upper deck forward of the boat stowage had been adapted as a helicopter pad. The Sonar Array Sounding System (SASS) Mk 4 wide-swath sonar and navigation systems are the same as those used in USN survey ships: the U.S. SQN-17 Bottom Topographic Survey System (BOTOSS) and two BQN-33 narrow-beam sonars. The keel-mounted mapping sonar covers a 5.6-km-wide, 120-deg. swath at 4,000-m depth, permitting coverage of 150 km^2 of ocean floor per hour; it has a total of 144 transmitter hydrophones on the longitudinal array and 90 on the transverse array. Gravimetric sensors with automatic data recording are also fitted. Is able to maintain 13 kts in Sea State 5. The engine room is not manned during normal operations. Personnel are accommodated in indi-

AUXILIARIES *(continued)*

vidual cabins, and a large gymnasium is fitted. Ballast tanks can hold 8,900 tons of seawater. The foredeck is strengthened to accept standard cargo containers.

♦ 1 Roebuck-class coastal survey ship [AGS]

Bldr: Brooke Marine, Lowestoft

	L	In serv.
H 130 ROEBUCK	14-11-85	30-10-86

Roebuck (H 130) Michael Winter, 6-05

Roebuck (H 130) Bernard Prézelin, 12-03

D: 1,105 tons light (1,477 fl) **S:** 15 kts **Dim:** 63.89 (57.00 pp) × 13.00 × 4.00
A: 1 20-mm Oerlikon GAM-B01 AA; 4 single 7.62-mm mg
Electronics:
Radar: 1 Decca 1626C ARPA nav.
Sonar: BAE Systems Type 2034BC Hydrosearch; Waverley Type 2033BB Side-scan
M: 4 Mirrlees ES-8 Mk 1 diesels; 2 CP props; 3,040 bhp **Range:** 4,000/10
Crew: 6 officers, 40 enlisted

Remarks: Ordered 21-5-84 as first of a planned quartet. Can theoretically be adapted to serve as a mine-countermeasures support ship but has not yet been so assigned. Underwent refit and modernization during 2004–5 and current plans call for H 130 to remain in service until 2014.
Hull systems: Three generator sets are fitted. Has Qubit SIPS (Survey Information Processing System). Other survey equipment includes Types 780AA and 778AG echo-sounders and Racal Hyperfix radio navigation aid. Hydrosearch sonar provides high-definition imaging to 600-m depths. Has A-frame at stern to tow magnetometer and the Waverley Side-scan sonar. Carries two survey launches, *Batchellor Delight* and *Jolly Prize*. Equipped with Marisat commercial SATCOM terminal.

♦ 6 Hartland Point (Ro-Ro-2700)–class vehicle cargo ships [AK]

Bldrs: First two: Harland & Wolff, Belfast, Northern Ireland; others: Flensburger Schiffsbau-Gesellschaft (FSG), Flensburg, Germany

	Laid down	L	In serv.
HARTLAND POINT	10-01	6-9-02	31-11-02
ANVIL POINT	. . .	16-1-02	1-2-03
HURST POINT	4-9-01	19-4-02	16-8-02
EDDYSTONE	. . .	16-8-02	7-11-02
LONGSTONE	. . .	8-11-02	5-2-03
BEACHY HEAD	. . .	5-2-03	1-6-03

Anvil Point—green hull, white superstructure, buff stack with green stripe Daniel Ferro, 1-06

D: 22,000 tons (fl) **S:** first three: 18 kts loaded; others: 23 kts light (21.5 kts loaded)
Dim: 193.00 (182.39 pp) × 29.99 max. (26.00 hull) × 6.60 normal (7.40 max.)
M: First three: 2 Mak-Caterpillar 7M43 heavy-oil diesels; 2 CP props; 17,500 bhp; others: 2 MaK-Caterpillar 9M43 heavy-oil diesels; 2 CP props; 21,700 bhp; all: CP bow-thruster

Hurst Point Michael Winter, 6-05

Electric: 6,850 kw tot. (2 × 1,600-kw, 2 × 1,440-kw diesel sets; 1 × 500 kVA Volvo Penta-driven emergency set)
Range: 9,200/21.5; 12,000/17.1 **Fuel:** 1,104 tons heavy oil; 113 tons diesel
Crew: 18 tot.

Remarks: 23,235 grt/13,274 dwt. Announced 7-98 that four additional roll-on/roll-off vehicle cargo ships would be acquired to support the Joint Rapid Deployment Force; the number was increased to six in 10-00, when AWSR Shipping (Andrew Weir Shipping, James Fisher, Houlder Offshore Engineering, and Bibby Line) was named as the winning bidder on the contract to operate the ships on charter for 25 years, but the 22-year, £950-million operating contract was not signed until 27-6-02. None of the three slower ships and only two of three faster ships will now be available for commercial cargoes when not carrying military cargoes and, under a 16-5-02 decision, all six will be operated at all times by British national crews. The two Harland & Wolff–built ships were ordered on 11-3-01 and the German-built quartet during 8-01. Deckhouses for all the ships were fabricated by Holm Construction, Gdansk, Poland, and delivered by barge. The design is similar to that of *Sea Centurion* (A 98), but with strengthened vehicle decks. The cost of each of the German-built ships was about $105 million. Have not been assigned pennant numbers. Commercial sisters are operated by a Turkish firm.
Hull systems: The first three have less-powerful diesel propulsion plants. Planned vehicle load is 130 armored vehicles, tracked reconnaissance vehicles, infantry fighting vehicles, armored personnel carriers, engineer vehicles, and 155-mm artillery pieces, plus 60 trucks, helicopters, and ammunition stores. The centerline stern ramp is reinforced to support heavy tanks and is 18 m long by 15 m wide; vehicles will be carried on the upper deck as well as on three cargo decks within the hull, for a total of 2,640 lane-meters capacity (189 13-m freight trailers, in commercial service). Container capacity is 656 TEU. A 40-ton crane is fitted on the starboard side. Double Flume-type passive stabilization tanks are fitted; total capacity is 792 m^3. Fuel capacity is 42 tons/day at cruise speed.

Disposal note: Vehicle cargo ship *Sea Centurion* (A 98; ex-*Stena Grecia;* ex-UND *Ausonia*) went off-charter on 28-7-03 and was returned to owner control on 25-8-03. *Celestine*-class vehicle cargo ship *Sea Crusader* (A 96) was also returned to owner control during 7-03.

♦ 2 Wave-class replenishment oilers [AO]

Bldr: A 389: BAE Systems, Barrow-in-Furness, Scotland; A 390: BAE Systems, Govan, Scotland

	Laid down	L	In serv.
A 389 WAVE KNIGHT	22-5-98	29-9-00	16-10-02
A 390 WAVE RULER	9-2-01	31-10-02	4-03

Wave Knight (A 389) Martin Mokrus, 6-04

Wave Ruler (A 390) Camil Busquets i Vilanova, 2005

AUXILIARIES *(continued)*

D: 12,500 tons light (31,500 fl) **S:** 18 kts **Dim:** 196.45 × 27.20 × 9.5
A: 2 single 30-mm 75-cal. DS-30B AA; 4 single 7.62-mm mg—provision for: 2 20-mm Mk 15 Phalanx gatling CIWS
Electronics:
Radar: 2 Kelvin Hughes 6000 ARPA nav. (E/F and I-band)
EW: . . .
M: Diesel-electric drive: 4 Wärtsilä 12V32E diesels (6,290 bhp each), 4 GECLM generator sets; 1 prop; 18,776 shp—KaMeWa bow and stern-thrusters (10-ton thrust each)
Range: 10,000/15; 8,000/18 **Crew:** 80 RFA + 22 RN aircrew

Remarks: Request for proposals issued 3-96. Both were contracted for delivery during 9-00 and 10-01, respectively. The start of A 390 was delayed, and the work was reassigned to BAE Systems' Govan facility. A 389's stern section was built by Cammell Laird, Newcastle-on-Tyne, and was attached to the ship beginning 27-1-00. Harland and Wolff, Belfast, built the cargo tankage for both ships, but A 390 was otherwise built entirely at Govan. Piping and other defects delayed sea trials for A 389 from 10-01 to 16-6-02. Sea trials for A 390 began on 17-9-02.
Hull systems: Have 16,500 m^3 total tankage for diesel (15,000 tons) and aviation fuel (3,000 m^3), lube oil, and cargo water; 500 m^3 dry cargo; and space for eight 20-ft. refrigerated provisions containers offloadable with a shipboard crane. There are three replenishment stations per side. Built to commercial standards, except for naval intact and damaged stability criteria. Double-hull construction. Have helicopter hangar and flight deck capable of handling one Merlin HM.1 helicopter. Superstructure and replenishment-rig kingposts are sloped 6° from vertical to reduce radar return. Have totally enclosed bridges with integrated controls, simplified replenishment rigs. One emergency diesel alternator set is provided.

♦ 1 Oakleaf-class replenishment oiler [AO]
Bldr: Uddevallavarvet, Uddevalla, Sweden

	L	In serv.
A 111 Oakleaf (ex-*Oktania*)	1981	14-8-86

Oakleaf (A 111) Derek Fox, 11-05

D: 49,377 tons (fl) **S:** 15.75 kts (14.5 sust.)
Dim: 173.69 (168.00 wl) × 32.26 × 11.20 max.
A: 2 single 20-mm 70-cal. Oerlikon Mk 7A AA; 2 single 7.62-mm mg
Electronics:
Radar: 2 Decca BridgeMaster Mk II ARPA (X and S-band)
EW: provision for 2 DLB decoy syst. (2 6-round Barricade RL)
M: 2 Uddevalla-Burmeister & Wain 4L80GFCA 4-cyl., 2-stroke diesels; 1 CP prop; 12,250 bhp—bow and stern tunnel-thrusters
Electric: 2,472 kw. (3 × 800-kw diesel sets, 1 × 72-kw diesel set)
Range: . . . / . . . **Crew:** 14 officers, 21 unlicensed

Remarks: 24,608 grt/34,800 dwt. Former Norwegian commercial tanker leased 7-85 to replace *Plumleaf* (A 78). Converted for naval support service by Falmouth Ship Repairers, 17-2-86 to 14-8-86. Refitted 1994–95, and charter renewed 6-97 for five years. Refitted from 4-03 to 6-03. Charter was renewed in 2002. The 20-mm AA are not always mounted. Expected to retire in 2015.
Hull systems: Cargo: 43,020 m^3 in 16 tanks; no dry cargo. Can carry up to 15,430 tons water ballast. During conversion, received two alongside fueling stations (one per side) with raised working deck, astern refueling capability, two additional generator sets, additional communications, NAVSAT equipment, and Marisat SATCOM terminal. Has three 13.7-kg/cm^2 auxiliary boilers. Retained sauna. Engineering spaces are automated and are not occupied when the ship is under way. Hull reinforced for ice navigation.

♦ 3 Leaf-class replenishment oilers [AO]
Bldr: Cammell Laird, Birkenhead

	L	In serv. (R.F.A.)
A 81 Brambleleaf (ex-*Hudson Deep*)	22-1-76	3-80
A 109 Bayleaf	27-10-81	26-3-82
A 110 Orangeleaf (ex-*Balder London*, ex-*Hudson Progress*)	. . .	2-5-84

Brambleleaf (A 81) Ben Sullivan, 4-05

D: A 109: 37,747 tons (fl); A 81, A 110: 40,870 (fl) **S:** 16.5 kts (15.5 sust.)
Dim: 170.69 (163.51 pp) × 25.94 × 11.56
A: 2 single 20-mm 90-cal. Oerlikon GAM-B01 AA; 4 single 7.62-mm mg
Electronics:
Radar: 1 Decca TM1226 nav.; 1 Decca 1229 nav.
EW: 2 DLB decoy syst. (2 6-round Barricade RL)
M: 2 Crossley-Pielstick 14PC2V-400 diesels; 1 CP prop; 14,000 bhp
Electric: 6,660 kw tot. (2 × 2,704-kw diesel sets, 2 × 626-kw diesel sets)
Range: . . . / . . . **Fuel:** 2,498 tons **Crew:** 19 officers, 37 unlicensed

Remarks: A 81: 20,440 grt/33,257 dwt; A 109: 20,086 grt/29,999 dwt; A 110: 20,284 grt/33,751 dwt. RFA-operated. A 81 acquired 1979 and refitted for naval service by Cammell Laird during 1979–80; stack raised 3.5 m, dry cargo hold added forward, replenishment-at-sea working deck added amidships, and superstructure enlarged aft. A 109, on which construction work had been suspended while still on the ways, was chartered 3-4-81 from Lombard Leasing Services and similarly altered. A 110, completed 1979 and on charter since 4-82 from Lloyds' Industrial Leasing, was re-chartered 26-3-84 and initially operated without replenishment equipment, receiving a similar conversion to that of her sisters in 1985 to 2-5-86. All are planned to be retired by 2009.
Hull systems: Liquid-cargo capacity is 32,309 m^3 (A 110: 41,881 m^3) in 24 tanks, and they normally carry 22,000 m^3 in marine-gas turbine fuel and 3,800 m^3 in aviation-gas turbine fuel; there is a small dry cargo capacity. All now have one refueling station per side, over-the-stern fueling capability, and a Marisat SATCOM terminal. Have three auxiliary boilers. A 110 received new navigational radars (probably Decca BridgeMaster Mk II ARPA, X and S-band) during a 2001 refit.
Disposals: *Appleleaf* (A 79) was leased to Australia for five years on 26-9-89 and purchased in 1994.

♦ 2 Rover-class replenishment oilers [AO]
Bldr: Swan Hunter, Hebburn-on-Tyne

	L	In serv.
A 271 Gold Rover	7-3-73	22-3-74
A 273 Black Rover	30-10-73	23-8-74

Grey Rover (A 269)—since retired M. Kadota, 2004

D: 4,700 tons light (11,522 fl) **S:** 19.25 kts (17 sust.)
Dim: 140.34 (131.07 pp) × 19.23 × 7.23
A: 2 single 20-mm 70-cal. Oerlikon Mk 7A AA; 2 single 7.62-mm mg
Electronics: Radar: 1 Kelvin-Hughes Type 1006 nav.; 1 Decca S2690 ARPA nav.; 1 Decca 1690 nav.
M: 2 SEMT-Pielstick 16PC 2 2V400 diesels; 1 CP prop; 15,360 bhp—500-shp bow-thruster
Electric: 2,720 kw tot. (8 × 340-kw diesel sets) **Range:** 14,000/15
Fuel: 965 tons heavy oil + 123 tons diesel
Crew: 18 officers, 37 unlicensed

Remarks: A 271: 7,574 grt/6,365 dwt; and A 273: 7,574 grt/6,799 dwt. R.F.A.-operated. A 271 has been used in supporting the training squadron. A 273 departed U.K. waters during 2-01 for an 11-month South Atlantic tour in support of the Falkland Islands guardship, relieving A 271. Both are scheduled to retire in 2007.
Hull systems: Cargo capacity includes 7,460 m^3 fuel, 325 m^3 water, and 70 m^3 lube oil; 600 m^3 aviation fuel or gasoline can be carried in lieu of ship fuel. Have a 25.9-m-long by 15.55-m-wide helicopter deck served by a stores elevator, but there is no hangar. Stern shapes vary, early units having had two stern anchors and later units one. A 273 has gun platforms on the forecastle.
Disposals: *Green Rover* (A 268) was placed in reserve on 30-days notice 27-5-88 and sold to Indonesia in 1-92. *Blue Rover* (A 270) was sold to Portugal and transferred 31-3-93. *Grey Rover* (A 269) was decomissioned on 28-3-06.

♦ 2 Fort Victoria–class replenishment ships [AOR]

	Bldr	Laid down	L	In serv.
A 387 Fort Victoria	Harland & Wolff, Belfast	15-9-88	12-6-90	24-6-94
A 388 Fort George	Swan Hunter, Wallsend	9-3-89	1-3-91	16-7-93

Fort George (A 388) Daniel Ferro, 1-06

AUXILIARIES *(continued)*

Fort Victoria (A 387) Bernard Prézelin, 9-05

D: 36,580 (fl) **S:** 20 kts **Dim:** 203.93 (185.00 pp) × 30.36 (28.50 wl) × 9.77
A: 2 single 30-mm 75-cal. MmSI DS-30B AA; 2 20-mm Mk 15 Phalanx gatling CIWS; 3 Sea King helicopters
Electronics:
Radar: 1 Kelvin-Hughes Type 1007 nav.; 1 Decca Type 1008 ARPA nav.; 2 General Dynamics Mk 90 Phalanx f.c.
EW: UAT intercept; DLB(1) Sea Gnat decoy syst. (4 6-round RL); Type 182 towed torpedo decoy
TACAN: Kelvin-Hughes NUCLEUS
M: 2 Crossley-Pielstick 16 PC2.6 V400 medium-speed diesels; 2 props; 25,083 bhp (23,892 sust.)
Electric: 3,900 kw tot. (6 × 650-kw Cummins KTA 386I diesel sets)
Range: . . . / . . . **Fuel:** . . . tons
Crew: 24 officers, 71 unlicensed RFA + 1 officer, 27 enlisted RN stores personnel + 28 officers, 126 enlisted RN air group

Remarks: 28,821 grt/16,967 dwt. Were to have been a class of six, to have been followed by six more of a simplified variant. A 387 was ordered 8-5-86 and A 388 on 18-12-87. Completion of A 387 was delayed by a terrorist explosion 6-9-90; the ship arrived at Cammell Laird, Birkenhead, on 7-7-92 to complete fitting out. *Fort George* underwent an eight-month refit during 2003. Expected to remain in service until 2019.
Hull systems: Can carry about 70,000 barrels (12,505 m^3) liquid cargo consisting of about 12,000 tons diesel fuel and 1,000 tons aviation fuel and 6,000 tons (6,234 m^3) of munitions, dry stores, and refrigerated cargo. They have two Clark Chapman dual-purpose liquid/solid replenishment stations per side, plus vertical replenishment and astern refueling capability; all replenishment stations are remotely controlled from a large station amidships. Have two pair of fin stabilizers. One 25-ton, two 10-ton, and two 5-ton electric cranes are fitted, with one 10-ton crane capable of supporting an additional underway-refueling rig. The large helicopter flight deck, with two landing spots, can also land Harrier attack fighters under emergency conditions. The twin hangar, which has extensive helicopter repair facilities, can accommodate up to five Sea King or Merlin helicopters, but the usual peacetime complement is three Sea Kings.
Combat systems: Planned installation of vertical launchers for 32 Sea Wolf SAMs (GWS.26 system), controlled by two Marconi Type 911 radar directors, was initially deferred and then canceled, although space and weight reservations remain available. Also omitted was the planned Type 996 air/surface-search radar. They were to have had the BAe Defence Systems Group DNA(2) Surface Ship Command System (SSCS). A 388 received two Phalanx CIWS and the UAT intercept system during a refit concluded 15-10-98; A 387 was similarly equipped during her 1-2-99 to 7-99 refit, during which the command support system was also updated. The Phalanx mounts are atop the pilothouse and atop the hangar. Can carry ASW ordnance for their helicopters. Have SCOT-1D antennas for the SHF Skynet IV SATCOM systems.

♦ 1 repair ship [AR]
Bldr: Øresundsvarvet AB, Landskrona, Sweden

	L	In serv.
A 132 Diligence (ex-*Bar Protector,* ex-*Stena Protector*)	1981	12-3-84

Diligence (A 132) Derek Fox, 6-01

D: 10,765 tons (fl) **S:** 15.5 kts **Dim:** 111.47 (101.30 pp) × 20.97 × 6.70
A: 2 single 20-mm 90-cal. Oerlikon GAM-B01 AA; 4 single 7.62-mm mg
Electronics:
Radar: 3 . . . nav.
EW: UAR(1) Matilda radar warning; DLE decoy syst. (4 6-round Shield RL)
M: 5 Nohab Polar F216V-D 16-cyl. diesels (3,600 bhp each), electric drive: 1 CP prop; 6,000 shp—2 KaMeWa 1,500-shp side-thrusters forward, 2 KaMeWa 1,500-shp rotatable thrusters aft
Electric: 4,400 kw from main engines + 2 × 208-kw emergency generators
Range: 5,000/12 **Fuel:** 837 tons
Crew: 15 officers, 26 unlicensed R.F.A.; 100 total naval repair party (total accomm.: 147 + 55 temporary)

Remarks: 6,544 grt/4,941 dwt. Built as a North Sea oilfield-support ship and chartered during the Falklands War for emergency repair work in the open sea, where she proved extremely successful as a floating maintenance depot. Purchased outright 31-10-83 from Stena (U.K.) and accepted for Royal Fleet Auxiliary service 12-3-84 after conversion to add additional repair features. Capable of being used for firefighting, towing, and salvage. Used as a submarine tender during 1997 and as a mine-countermeasures support ship in the Persian Gulf during 1998; was deployed 3-99 to the Falklands as general support ship; crew in 1999 included 38 civilians. Refitted by A&P Group, Wallsend, from 30-8-99 to 10-12-99.
Hull systems: Has an ice-strengthened hull with a centerline "moonpool" for use by divers. Flight deck atop pilothouse can accept helicopters up to Chinook-size. Has four 20- to 40-ton, one 20-ton, one 15-ton, and one 5-ton cranes. Very maneuverable and can travel 6 kts sideways. A Köngsberg Albatross dynamic positioning system and four 5-ton anchors for a four-point moor are provided. During conversion for naval use, a large hull and machinery repair workshop was added in the welldeck aft; accommodations were increased; and a saturation diving facility; armament; magazines; fuel, water, and electrical power overside transfer facilities; increased communications equipment; and additional cranes were added. Can carry 2,313-tons cargo fuel for ships moored alongside.
Combat systems: Two of the four 20-mm AA had been removed by early 2000.

♦ 2 Sal-class mooring, salvage, and net tender [ARS]
Bldr: Hall Russell, Ltd., Aberdeen, Scotland

	Laid down	L	In serv.
A 185 Salmoor	19-4-84	8-5-85	12-11-85
A 187 Salmaid	29-6-84	22-5-86	28-10-86

Salmaid (A 187) Marian Wright, 8-04

D: 1,604 tons light (2,225 fl) **S:** 15 kts **Dim:** 77.10 (65.80 pp) × 14.80 × 3.80
Electronics: Radar: 1 Decca 1226 nav.
M: 2 Ruston-Paxman 8RKCM diesels; 1 CP prop; 4,000 bhp **Range:** . . .
Crew: 4 officers, 13 unlicensed + 27 spare berths

Remarks: 1,967 grt. Ordered 29-1-84 as replacements for "Kin" class. Based on the River Clyde and operated by SERCO-Denholm. *Salmaid* (A 187) was laid up at Devonport during 2000 but was again reported to be active as of 12-02.
Hull systems: Capable of mooring, buoy tending, salvage, diving support, and fire fighting. Has a 400-ton tidal lift/200-ton deadlift capacity. Can carry 14-man salvage party.
Disposals: *Salmaster* (A 186) was placed up for sale during 2001.

SERVICE CRAFT

Note: Most service craft were operated by the Royal Maritime Auxiliary Service (RMAS) until 8-7-96, when their operation was contracted to SERCO-Denholm, which bareboat charters the craft from the government. A few units remain naval-operated or are operated for the Ministry of Defence Marine Services agency by other contractors, and several are still operated by the RMAS (primarily ships and craft engaged in hazardous activities). In most cases, craft that bore pennant numbers when in RMAS service continue to bear them. Most smaller powered craft have four-digit hull numbers, with the first two digits indicating the year of their authorization (many such craft at Portsmouth have local pennants and a few have unofficial names). Most nonself-propelled craft have numbers ending with a letter or letters in parentheses indicating their functions.

♦ 4 towed hydrophone array tenders [YAG]
Bldr: McTay Marine, Bromborough (In serv. 1986)

8611 TARV
8612 Ohm's Law
8613 Cormorant
8614 Sapper

Sapper (TRV 8614) Leo van Ginderen, 6-05

SERVICE CRAFT *(continued)*

D: . . . **S:** 12.5 kts **Dim:** 20.10 (19.88 wl) × 6.00 × . . .
Electronics: Radar: 1 Decca 150 nav.
M: 2 Perkins 6/3544 diesels; 2 Kort-nozzle props; 400 bhp **Crew:** 8 tot.

Remarks: Catamaran aluminum hulls for first three built by Hall's Aluminium Shipbuilders, Portchester. Intended to service "clip-on" linear hydrophone arrays for submarines. Towed array is stowed faked down on the deck of the craft, which can operate connected to a smaller launch (*Chaser* serves *Ohm's Law*); the submarine passes between the pair and snags the line, which is connected to the end of the array. *Ohm's Law* is at Plymouth, and *Cormorant* is at Gibraltar. *Sapper* has been reconfigured as a diving training boat.

♦ 1 trials tender [YAGE]
Bldr: Richards SB, Lowestoft

	Laid down	L	In serv.
A 368 Warden	16-8-88	29-5-89	20-11-89

Warden (A 368)—as modified — Piet Sinke, 11-00

D: 621 tons light (approx. 900 fl) **S:** 15 kts **Dim:** 48.63 (42.00 pp) × 10.50 × 3.50
Electronics:
Radar: 2 Decca RM 1250 nav.
Sonar: BAE Systems Type 2053 hull-mounted
M: 2 Ruston 8 RKCM diesels; 2 CP props; 3,800 bhp **Range:** . . .
Crew: 4 officers, 7 unlicensed

Remarks: Ordered 25-4-88. Formerly a range maintenance vessel, A 368 was converted beginning 6-10-98 as a trials vessel at A&P Appledore, Falmouth. She is operated by the RMAS at the Kyle of Lochalsh, Scotland.
Hull systems: Has two Gardner diesel alternators, two shaft-driven alternators. The large traveling quadrantial A-frame gantry on the fantail has been removed and replaced with two electrohydraulic cranes to handle RIB workboats.

♦ 1 aviation trials support ship [WAGE]
Bldr: Hall Russell, Aberdeen, Scotland (In serv. 11-66)

A 229 Colonel Templer (ex-*Criscilla*)

Colonel Templer (A 229) — Marian Wright, 9-02

D: 1,300 tons (fl) **S:** 13.6 knots **Dim:** 56.55 × 11.0 × 4.29
Electronics: Radar: 1 Decca BT 502 nav.; 1 Decca 2690 ARPA nav.
M: 2 Cummins KTA 38G4M diesels (1,260 bhp each); 2 Newage HC M734E1 generators (850 kw each); 1 Aquamaster Azimuthal thruster; 1,800 shp
Electric: 930 kw (2 × 260 kw, 2 × 180 kw, 1 × 50 kw) **Range:** 7,000/ . . .
Crew: 14 tot. + 12 scientists

Remarks: 892 grt/268 nrt. Former stern-haul trawler purchased 1980 by Royal Aerospace Establishment, Farnborough, for use in sonobuoy trials. Transferred to RMAS operational control on 1-10-88. Capsized during fire while under refit at Hull in 1-91; righted and refloated 8-2-91 and transferred to Portsmouth 30-4-91 for refit for further service; repairs completed 10-92, but not recommissioned until 10-9-93. During the repairs, the ship was altered so that it can be leased for commercial scientific work. Re-engined during 15-1-97 to 25-4-97 refit at Hull. Two moonpool openings for lowering scientific gear have been opened into the bottom. The ship is fitted with Flume passive stabilization tanks and an auxiliary propulsion system for silent running. The after deck was fitted to accept a containerized laboratory, and a 5-ton crane was installed. Has Racal MIRANS 3000 integrated navigation and bridge control system with MNS 2000 GPS receiver and VHF D/F. Carries a 9-m tender named *Quest* (Q 26). Received a pennant number after outright purchase by MoD during 9-00; is operated by the A.V. Seaworks division of Vosper Thornycroft.

Disposal note: *Triton*-class trimaran trials ship *Triton* was sold to a commercial firm during 1-05.

Note: The 8,000-ton, 108-m Ministry of Defence–owned, guided-missile trials support barge *Longbow* (ex-*Dynamic Servant*), completed 1976 and laid up at Brixham since the late 1980s, was reactivated starting in 2003 for use by a private contractor for trials with the SAM system for the new *Daring*-class (Type 45) guided-missile destroyers. She was again deactivated during 12-06.

♦ 4 200-ton stores lighters [YC]

1107(S) 1109(S) 1110(S)M 1111(S)

200-ton stores lighter 1109(S) — Mike Welsford, 7-00

Remarks: Operated by SERCO-Denholm at Devonport and Plymouth. Are 26.5 m long. Nonself-propelled. Sister 1101(S) is laid up and for sale at Portsmouth.

♦ 5 Talisman 47–class diver support craft [YDT]
Bldr: Halmatic, Northam (In serv. 1997–98)

Remarks: No data available.

♦ 2 clearance diving tenders [YDT] (1 in *reserve*)
Bldr: Halmatic, Northam

9040 Miner III (In serv. 9-93) *9041 Datchet* (In serv. 7-94)

Miner III (9040) — H&L Van Ginderen, 5-95

D: 21.5 tons (fl) **S:** 10.5 kts **Dim:** 14.20 × 4.45 × 1.60
Electronics: Radar: 1/Raytheon . . . nav.
M: 1 Ford Sabre 350C diesel; 1 prop; 350 bhp
Crew: 3 tot.

Remarks: Ordered 5-93. GRP construction. 9040 is operated by Royal Navy Southern Diving Group at Devonport, where 9041 was laid up during 1998.

♦ 4 11-meter-class diver support craft [YDT]
Bldr: Tough, Teddington (In serv.1981-82)

7646 . . . 7647 . . . 7648 Diver 8000 Reclaim

Reclaim (8000) — Ralph Edwards, 6-04

SERVICE CRAFT *(continued)*

D: 10 tons (fl) **S:** 8.5 kts **Dim:** 11.7 × 4.3 × 1.4
M: 1 Perkins 6-354.4 diesel; 1 prop; 120 bhp **Crew:** 2 crew, 12 divers

Remarks: Naval-operated: 7646 is at Portsmouth, 7647 at Pembroke Dock, 7648 at Faslane, and 8000 at Portsmouth, attached to HMS *Vernon.* GRP construction. Eight very similar craft are operated by the British Army Royal Logistic Corps.

♦ 26 200-ton ammunition lighters [YEN]

1201(A)	1209(A)	1215(A)	1225(A)	1230(A)
1202(A)	1210(A)	1216(A)	1226(A)	1232(A)
1203(A)	1211(A)	1217(A)	1227(A)	1234(A)
1205(A)	1213(A)	1223(A)	1228(A)	1235(A)
1206(A)	1214(A)	1224(A)	1229(A)	1236(A)
1207(A)				

200-ton ammunition lighter 1236(A)—being moved by a tug; note the electrohydraulic crane added to this unit A. A. de Kruijf, 9-00

Remarks: 1201(A), 1202(A), 1205(A)–1207(A), 1215(A), 1223(A), 1224(A), 1226(A), and 1236(A) are at Portsmouth; 1227(A) is at Gibraltar; and the others are at Devonport. Are 28 m long and nonself-propelled. 1236(A) has an electrohydraulic crane, but most have no cargo-handling gear of their own. Sister 1208(A) had been stricken by 8-00.

♦ 4 100-ton ammunition lighters [YEN]

329(A) 330(A) 344(A) 345(A)

Remarks: All based at Portsmouth and operated by SERCO-Denholm. Are 21.3 m long and nonself-propelled.

♦ 3 Oban-class personnel and stores lighters [YF]
Bldr: McTay Marine, Bromborough

	L	In serv.
A 283 Oban (ex-*Padstow*)	25-10-99	4-2-00
A 284 Oronsay	26-5-00	12-6-00
A 285 Omagh	14-8-00	26-9-00

Oronsay (A 284) Marian Wright, 6-05

D: approx. 320 tons (fl) **S:** 10 kts sust. **Dim:** 27.65 (25.80 pp) × 7.30 × 2.74
Electronics: Radar: 1 . . . nav.
M: 2 Cummins N14M 6-cyl. diesels; 2 Kort-nozzle props; 1,080 bhp
Electric: 218 kw tot. (2 × 109-kw diesel-driven sets) **Range:** 2,000/10
Fuel: 26 tons **Crew:** 7 + 60 passengers

Remarks: 199 grt. Ordered late 1998 to replace *Melton* (A 83), *Menai* (A 84), and *Meon* (A 87) as personnel ferries and stores carriers, based at Faslane.

Disposal note: Of the eight units of the Insect class, *Cricket* (A 229) was placed in reserve 4-2-94 and sold commercial as *Sapphire* in 6-95, along with *Gnat* (A 239), renamed *North Star; Cicala* (A 263) was sold commercial summer 1996; *Scarab* (A 272) was sold to a commercial operator on 24-9-96; *Bee* (A 216) was for sale at Portsmouth as of 8-00; *Cockchafer* (A 230) was sold to TAE Marine during 2001; and *Ladybird* (A 253) was retired in 2003.

♦ 3 Cartmel-class stores lighters [YF]
Bldrs: C. D. Holmes, Beverley

	In serv.	Based at
A 83 Melton	21-8-81	Kyle of Lochalsh
A 84 Menai	4-11-81	Devonport
A 87 Meon	9-11-82	Devonport

D: 143 tons (fl) **S:** 10.5 kts **Dims:** 24.38 (22.86 pp) × 6.40 × 1.98
Electronics: Radar: 1 Decca 360 nav.
M: 1 Lister-Blackstone ERS-4-MGR diesel; 1 prop; 330 bhp
Electric: 106 kw tot. (2 × 53-kw diesel sets)
Range: 1,000/10; 2,000/6 **Crew:** 6 tot.

Remarks: Ordered 25-2-80. Are all Government Marine Services craft operated by SERCO-Denholm, except for A 83, operated by the RMAS at Kyle of Lochalsh. All have a 2-ton stores derrick.
Disposals: Sister *Cawsand* (A 351) was placed up for sale 10-85; *Cartmel* (A 350) stricken 1989 and sold for scrap 24-6-93; *Denmead* (A 363) stricken 1991. *Criccieth* (A 391) sold 7-92; *Dunster* (A 393) and *Fotherby* (A 341) were discarded in 1993. *Froxfield* (A 354), *Clovelly* (A 389), and *Cromarty* (A 488) were sold to a French operator for commercial service during 7-94. *Glencoe* (A 392) was for sale as of late 1994. *Elsing* (A 277) was for sale at Gibraltar in mid-1995. *Dornoch* (A 490), *Felsted* (A 348), *Fintry* (A 394), *Fulbeck* (A 365), *Landovery* (A 207), and *Cricklade* (A 381) were stricken 1996 and placed up for sale for commercial use (*Fintry* was purchased in 1998 by SERCO Denholm, renamed *Eilidh-M,* and is on MOD charter at Devonport). *Elkstone* (A 353), *Epworth* (A 355), *Grasmere* (A 402), and *Holmwood* (A 1772) were laid up at Devonport as of spring 1999 and are not likely to see further service. *Harlech* (A 1768), *Hambledon* (A 1769), *Horning* (A 1773), and *Lamlash* (A 208) were deactivated and offered for sale during 2000–2001. *Lechlade* (A 211) was sold for scrap during 10-01, and *Hever* (A 1776) was laid up and for sale as of mid-2001. *Milford* (A 91) was sold fall 2001 for service on the Amazon at Iquitos, Peru, as the *Amazon Hope. Ettrick* (A 274) and *Headcorn* (A 1776) were no longer in service as of 2006.

Note: The Ministry of Defence recently acquired a large (100+) number of RIBs ranging from 5 to 9 m overall; some serve in the Royal Navy and others the Army.

♦ 4 Newhaven-class catamaran personnel ferries [YFL]
Bldr: Aluminium Shipbuilders Ltd., Fishbourne, Isle of Wight

	L	In serv.	Based at
A 280 Newhaven	10-4-00	1-8-00	Portsmouth
A 281 Nutbourne	14-8-00	10-10-00	Portsmouth
A 282 Netley	14-10-00	10-1-01	Portsmouth
A 286 Padstow	7-4-00	8-6-00	Devonport

Newhaven (A 280) Leo van Ginderen, 6-05

D: . . . tons **S:** . . . kts **Dim:** 18.0 × 7.0 × . . . **Electronics:** Radar: 1 . . . nav.
M: 2 . . . diesels; 2 props; . . . bhp **Crew:** 3 tot. + 60 passengers

Remarks: Ordered 19-2-99. All are operated by SERCO-Denholm. Have steel hulls with two-deck aluminum deckhouse.

♦ 2 Bovisand-class SWATH personnel ferries [YFL]
Bldr: FBM Babcock Marine, Cowes

A 191 Bovisand (In serv. 7-97) A 192 Cawsand (In serv. 9-97)

D: 225 tons (fl) **S:** 15.5 kts (11 sust.) **Dim:** 23.90 (21.00 wl) × 11.10 × 2.25
Electronics: Radar: 1 . . . nav.
M: 2 diesels; 2 props; 1,224 bhp **Crew:** 4 tot. + up to 75 passengers

Remarks: Ordered 5-96 for use by Flag Officer Sea Training, Devonport, to transfer crewmembers to ships undergoing training while at sea; operated by SERCO-Denholm. Are the only British units to use Small Waterplane Twin Hull (SWATH) catamaran hullform, which provides great stability in a seaway. They use a hydraulically adjusted telescopic gangways to transfer personnel in up to Sea State 3 conditions. Aluminum construction.

SERVICE CRAFT *(continued)*

Bovisand (A 191) Rob Cabo, 6-01

♦ **1 catamaran submarine support personnel ferry [YFL]**
Bldr: FBM Babcock Marine, Cowes (In serv. 18-1-93)

A 232 Adamant

Adamant (A 232) H&L Van Ginderen, 10-97

D: . . . tons **S:** 23 kts **Dim:** 30.80 (27.50 pp) × 7.80 × 1.10
Electronics: Radar: 1 Decca . . . nav.
M: 2 Cummins KTA 19MS diesels; 2 MJP J650 waterjets; 1,360 bhp
Electric: 60 kw tot. (2 × 30 kw) **Range:** 250/23; 350/ . . . **Crew:** 5 tot.

Remarks: Ordered 30-11-91 and launched 8-10-92. Marine Services craft, operated by SERCO-Denholm to serve ballistic-missile submarine crews based at Faslane, on the Firth of Clyde. Aluminum hull construction. Carries 36 personnel plus 1-ton stores. To supply submarines offshore, has an 8.1-m constant tension gangway and hydraulically operated fenders. Navigational equipment includes Shipmate GPS receiver and video position plotter, S.G. Brown 100B gyrocompass, and Furuno echo sounder.

♦ **1 catamaran harbor launch [YFL]**
Bldr: FBM Babcock Marine, Cowes (In serv. 1989)

HL 8837

D: 20.5 tons **S:** 13 kts (10 loaded) **Dim:** 15.80 (13.80 wl) × 5.50 × 1.50
Electronics: Radar: 1 Decca . . . nav.
M: Ford Mermaid Turbo-4 diesels; 2 props; 280 bhp
Range: 400/10 **Crew:** 2 crew + 30 to 60 passengers

Remarks: HL 8837 (also known as "D37") was prototype for a new series to replace the large number of outdated harbor personnel launches; no more were built. Can also carry 2 tons stores with 30 passengers. Operated by Marine Services.

Note: SERCO-Denholm also operated the 50-passenger ferry *SD 9* and the 75-passenger *SD 12* at Devonport as of 1-02. The RMAS has chartered the 32-m commercial Ro-Ro landing craft *Sara Maatje VI* from Van Stee Survey & Supply, Harlingen, the Netherlands, from 1-01 through 1-03.

HL 8837 Michael Winter, 6-05

Disposal note: *Seal*-class long-range recovery and support craft *Seal* (5000) and *Seagull* (5001) were retired during 2001.

♦ **6 Aircrew Training Vessels**
Bldr: FBM Babcock Marine*, Rosyth, Scotland, and Cebu, the Philippines (In serv. 2003)

Smit Dee*	Smit Towy	Smit Don*
Smit Spey	Smit Yare	Smit Dart*

Smit Spey Ben Sullivan, 3-05

D: . . . tons **S:** 22 kts (7 kts on cruise waterjet) **Dim:** 27.84 (24.00 wl) × 6.70 × 1.70
M: 2 Cummins KTA19M4 diesels; 2 props; 1,400 bhp—1 Cummins 6CTA 8.3M cruise diesel; 1 centerline Ultra Dynamics UJ305 cruise waterjet; 350 bhp
Range: 650/21 **Crew:** 6 tot.

Remarks: Ordered 18-1-02 by Smit International (Scotland), Ltd., Three of the craft were built in Scotland and three in the Philippines to a modified version of a 27-m patrol-boat design. There is a docking well aft for an RIB launch or for torpedo retrieval and deck space for helicopter winching training. Aluminum construction. Replace the *Spitfire* class.

Disposal note: *Spitfire*-class rescue and target-towing craft *Spitfire* (4000), *Hurricane* (4005), *Lancaster* (4006), and *Wellington* (4007) were sold in 2004. Sisters *Sunderland* (4001) and *Stirling* (4002), transferred to the navy in 8-85 as *Hart* (P 257) and *Cormorant* (P 256), were stricken during 1-91 after serving as patrol boats at Gibraltar. British Army artillery range safety craft sister *Petard* (Y 01, ex-*Alfred Herring, V.C.*) was stricken during 4-02, and her sister *Falconet* (Y 02, ex-*Michael Murphy, V.C.*) was stricken during 6-01 and sold commercially in Egypt during 10-01. *Halifax* (4003) and *Hampden* (4004) were decommissioned during 2002.

♦ **12 Talisman-49-class utility launches [YFL]**
Bldr: RSC 7713–7822: Anderson, Rigden & Perkins, Ltd; others: Halmatic Ltd., Havant

	In serv.	Based at
RSC 7713 Samuel Morley, V.C.	1980	Kyle of Lochalsh
RSC 7821 Joseph Hughes, G.C.	1981	Pembroke Dock
RSC 7822 James Dalton, V.C.	1981	Dover
RSC 8125 Sir Paul Travers	20-10-82	Pembroke Dock
RSC 8126 Sir Cecil Smith	6-7-82	Dover
RSC 8128 Sir Reginald Kerr	17-3-83	Pembroke Dock
RSC 8129 Sir Humphrey Gale	8-4-83	Portland
RSC 8487 Geoffrey Rackham, G.C.	19-12-85	Portland
RSC 8488 Walter Cleal, G.C.	1986	Dover
L.01	1-91	Portsmouth
L.02	1-91	Portsmouth
L.03	1-91	Portsmouth

D: 20.24-20.6 tons light (23.6 fl) **S:** 20-22 kts
Dim: 14.71 (13.27 wl) × 4.42 × 1.625 max.
Electronics: Radar: 1 Furuno . . . or Raytheon . . . nav.
M: 2 Fiat 828SM diesels; 2 props; 880 bhp
Range: 300/20 **Crew:** 3 tot. (civilian)

SERVICE CRAFT *(continued)*

Remarks: L.01 through L.03 were ordered during 1991 for delivery 1-91 for use as pilot boats; one of the three is named *St. Clement.* The RSCs were transferred from British Army to the RMAS on 1-10-88 and are now operated by Smit Scotland on contract. Sister *Sir William Roe* remains in Army service and others, including *Swift* and *Panther,* have been built for the Customs Service. The RSC-designated units are being retired and replaced by RIBs. RSC 7820 and RSC 8489 are no longer in naval service.
Hull systems: GRP Talisman-49 hulls. RSC 8125–8129 are 20.59 tons light displacement and are 14.90 m long by 4.66 m beam and 1.65 m max. draft. RSC 7821–7822 are 19.684 tons light displacement. The RSCs have superstructures like those of the 15-m utility launches but slightly lower; L.01–L.03 have their pilothouses near the stern.

♦ 5 15-meter utility launches [YFL]
Bldrs: Vosper Thornycroft (Halmatic), Havant (In serv. 1983–92)

8303   8304 Swift   8305 Opal   9295   9296

15-meter utility launch Swift (8304) Piet Sinke, 11-00

D: 20.6 tons (23.6 fl) **S:** 20 kts **Dim:** 14.94 (13.41 wl) × 4.65 × 1.30
Electronics: Radar: 1 Furuno . . . or Raytheon . . . nav.
M: 2 Rolls-Royce C8M410 diesels; 2 props: 820 bhp **Range:** 300/20 **Crew:** 3 tot.

Remarks: 8303, based at Portsmouth, is used on occasion as a pilot launch. 9295 and 9296, based at Faslane, are general-purpose launches. The other two are pilot boats based at Devonport. All employ the Talisman-49 GRP hull used by the 12 boats listed immediately prior. One of the class has been named *Rapid.* Sisters (8551–8556) serve the Ministry of Defence Police.

Disposal note: RAF 1300-series general-purpose launches 1374 and 1392 were for sale as of 1999.

♦ 4 14-meter target service launches [YFL]

7442   7443   8845   8846

Remarks: 7442 and 7443 are based at Rosyth; 8845 and 8846 are based on the Clyde.

♦ 5 13.90-meter harbor launches [YFL]
Bldr: R. Dunston, Hessle (In serv. 1981)

HL 8090 Cyclone   HL 8092 . . .   HL 8095 Starling
HL 8091 Sparrow   HL 8093 Metro

Starling (HL 8095) Rob Cabo, 6-01

Remarks: 8090 is based at Gibraltar; 8091 at Devonport; and 8092, 8093, and 8095 at Portsmouth. Sister 8094 was stricken by 11-93 and 8096 by 1-96. Have a small navigational radar.

♦ 8 new 11-m harbor launches [YFL]
Bldr: Holyhead Marine Services, Holyhead (In serv. 9-99 through . . . -00)

9894   9895   9896   9897   9898   . . .   .

D: . . . tons **S:** . . . **Dim:** 11.20 × . . . × 1.2
M: 1 Sabre M130C diesel; 1 prop; 130 bhp
Range: 130/8 **Fuel:** 450 liters **Crew:** . . .

Remarks: Ordered 4-99. GRP construction.

♦ Up to 7 old 11-m harbor launches [YFL] (In serv. 1979–88)

HL 7992   HL 7998   HL 8812   HL 8847 Firecrest
HL 7996   HL 8001   HL 8813

Old 11-meter harbor launch Paul C. Clift, 5-98

Remarks: HL 7998 and 8813 are based at Devonport on pollution-control duties; the others at Portsmouth for general stores and transportation duties. GRP construction.

♦ 5 10-m fast harbor launches [YFL]
Bldr: Holyhead Marine Services, Holyhead (In serv. 4-00 through . . . -00)

9893   . . .   .

D: . . . **S:** . . . **Dim:** 10.0 × . . . × . . .

Remarks: Ordered 4-99. GRP construction.

Note: Other launches in service include 10.4-m fast motor launch Mk 8 HL 7144 (based at Portsmouth); 10.4-m fast motor launches HL 6750 and HL 6754 (both based at Gibraltar); 10-m fast motor launches HL 9313–HL 9316 (two based at Portsmouth, two at Devonport); 8.53-m general service launches HL 6994, HL 8474, HL 8475, HL 8829, HL 8832, and HL 8833 (8474 and 8475 at Faslane; 6994 and 8832 at Portsmouth; 8829 and 8833 at Devonport); 7.6-m motor boats HL 7981 and HL 7989 (both at Portsmouth); 7.3-m ferry boats HL 7447 and HL 7448 (both assigned to RAF support); 6.7-m Pacific-22 rigid inflatables HL 9502 and HL 9503 (at Portsmouth); and up to 21 Searider rigid inflatables.

♦ 4 Cook-class survey boats [YGS]
Bldr: Vosper-Thornycroft (Halmatic), Northam (In serv. 1996)

3423 Nesbitt   9424 Pat Barton   9425 Cook   9426 Owen

Nesbitt (3423) Daniel Ferro, 1-06

D: 8.75 tons (11 fl) **S:** 13 kts (12 sust.) **Dim:** 8.94 (8.10 wl) × 3.60 × 0.99
M: 2 Perkins Sabre 6.3544 diesels; 2 props; 230 bhp
Electronics:
Radar: 1 . . . nav.
Sonar: STN-Atlas Elektronik Fansweep 20 mapping, Simrad EM3000 multibeam mapping
Range: 200/13; 300/8 **Crew:** 2 tot. + 10 survey party

Remarks: GRP construction. Ordered 1995 and are built on Halmatic's Nelson 35 standard GRP construction hull. Are attached to the Hydrographic School and naval-operated. Maximum survey speed is 3 kts. Have GPS receiver and are equipped with Ultra 3000 side-scan sonar and Qubit survey data recording system.

♦ 1 inshore survey craft [YGS]
Bldr: Emsworth SY, Emsworth

	L	In serv.
H 86 Gleaner	18-10-83	5-12-84

SERVICE CRAFT *(continued)*

Gleaner (H 86) Marian Wright, 6-05

D: 20 tons (22 fl) **S:** 14 kts **Dim:** 14.81 × 4.55 × 1.30
Electronics:
Radar: 1 Decca 360 nav.
Sonar: STN-Atlas Elektronik Fansweep 20 mapping; Simrad EM3000 multibeam mapping
M: 2 Rolls-Royce CG M-310 diesels; 2 props; 524 bhp; 1 Perkins 4.236 M cruise diesel on centerline; 1 prop; 72 bhp
Range: 450/10 **Crew:** 1 officer, 4 enlisted + 1 spare berth

Remarks: Referred to as HMSML (Her Majesty's Survey Motor Launch) *Gleaner* and is the smallest commissioned "ship" in the RN; intended for survey work in the Solent, Portsmouth, and Channel Islands areas. Glass-reinforced-plastic hull molded by Halmatic. Speed on cruise engine: 3–7 kts. The pennant number flag superior was changed from "A" to "H" in 7-98.

♦ 1 Oil-class fuel lighter [YO]
Bldr: Appledore SB, Appledore (L: 18-2-69)

Y 21 Oilpress

D: 208 tons light; 250 tons std. (543.2 fl) **S:** 10 kts
Dim: 42.65 (39.62 pp) × 7.87 (7.47 wl) × 2.68 max.
Electronics: Radar: 1 . . . nav.
M: 1 Lister-Blackstone ES-6-MGR diesel; 1 prop; 405 bhp
Electric: 225 kw (3 × 75 kw, 220 v d.c.; Foden FD.6 Mk VI diesels driving)
Range: 1,500/10 **Fuel:** 12 tons **Crew:** 4 officers, 7 unlicensed

Remarks: 362 grt. Cargo capacity: 250 tons. Marine Services craft operated at Devonport by SERCO-Denholm. Has two 100 ton/hr. capacity cargo pumps, and the six cargo tanks are heated.
Disposals: *Oilfield* (Y 24), in reserve since 9-5-87, was stricken 1991 and sold 7-12-92; *Oilstone* (Y 22) sold 17-12-92; *Oilbird* (Y 25) and *Oilwell* (Y 23) were sold for commercial use on 17-9-98; and *Oilman* (Y 26) was sold for scrap early in 1999.

♦ 1 1600-series fuel oil barge [YON]
Bldr: Appledore Shipbuilders, Appledore (In serv. 1969)

1603(F)

D: 44.8 × 10.2 × . . .

Remarks: 369.1 grt/500 tons cargo deadweight. Based at Portsmouth, operated by SERCO-Denholm. Nonself-propelled. Has two 100-ton/hr cargo pumps, both powered by an 88-bhp Perkins 6-334(M) diesel. There are two 6-kw, 220-v d.c. generators, each powered by an Enfield HO2 Mk. III diesel.

♦ 9 1500-series fuel oil barges [YON]
Bldr: Appledore Shipbuilders, Appledore (In serv. 1965–76)

	Base		Base
1501(F)	Portsmouth	1509(F)	Gibraltar
1502(F)	Faslane	1512(F)	Devonport
1503(F)	Clyde	1514(F)	Portsmouth
1506(F)	Devonport	1515(F)	Devonport
1507(F)	Portsmouth		

1500-series fuel barge 1507(F) Ralph Edwards, 8-03

D: . . . **Dim:** 27.12 × 7.85 × . . . **Cargo:** 250 tons

Remarks: Can carry diesel, oil, or aviation fuel. Nonself-propelled. Have two 100-ton/hr cargo pumps, both powered by an 88-bhp Perkins 6-334(M) diesel. There are two 6-kw, 220-v d.c. generators, each powered by an Enfield HO2 Mk. III diesel. The deckhouse has bunks for four personnel. 1515(F) was formerly used as water barge 1515(W). 1509(F) is naval-operated at Gibraltar; the others are operated by SERCO-Denholm.

♦ 1 Type 82 accommodations and training ship [YPB]
Bldr: Swan Hunter, Wallsend-on-Tyne

	Laid down	L	In serv.
D 23 Bristol	15-11-67	30-6-69	31-3-73

Bristol (D 23) A. A. de Kruijf, 7-05

D: 5,791 tons (7,100 fl—as destroyer) **S:** 28 kts (when operational)
Dim: 154.60 (149.90 wl) × 16.77 × 5.20 **A:** Deleted
M: (Nonoperational) COSAG: 2 A.E.I. geared steam turbines (15,000 shp each), 2 Rolls-Royce Olympus TM1A gas turbines (22,300 shp each); 2 props; 74,600 shp
Boilers: 2 Babcock & Wilcox; 49.2 kg/cm^2, 510° C
Electric: 7,000 kw tot. **Range:** 5,000/18 (when active) **Crew:** . . .

Remarks: Replaced the County-class guided missile destroyer *Kent* (D 12) as Sea Cadet Harbour Training Ship, Portsmouth, recommissioning 22-3-93; the ship is also used to provide accommodations for school children undergoing sail training. The 114-mm Mk 8 gun forward and the antenna for the Type 1022 air early warning radar were removed prior to her assuming her new role, with the latter replaced by antennas from the *Kent;* earlier, the Sea Dart SAM launcher had been removed, and an Ikara ASW missile launcher and the one Limbo ASW mortar had been deleted in 1986 and 1988, respectively. Accommodations for 100 naval cadets were added during 1987 for her role as Cadet Training Ship, in which capacity she served until inactivated 27-6-91. Has about 400 berths for trainees.

♦ 2 Tornado-class torpedo retrievers [YPT]
Bldr: Hall Russell, Aberdeen, Scotland

	Laid down	L	In serv.
A 140 Tornado	2-11-78	24-5-79	15-11-79
A 142 Tormentor	19-3-79	6-11-79	29-4-80

Tormentor (A 142) Bernard Prézelin, 9-99

D: 553 tons light; 660 tons std. (698 fl) **S:** 14 kts
Dim: 47.47 (40.00 pp) × 8.53 × 3.31
Electronics: Radar: 1 Kelvin-Hughes Type 1006 nav.
M: 2 Lister-Blackstone ESL-8-MGR diesels; 2 props; 2,200 bhp **Range:** 3,000/14
Fuel: 110 tons **Crew:** 14 tot.

Remarks: 559 grt/80 dwt. Since 8-7-96, have been Marine Services craft, operated by SERCO-Denholm on the River Clyde.
Hull systems: Stern ramp for weapon recovery. A 140 used in trials 1987 with Qubit TRAC IV B track recording system and Bathymetrics Bathyscan 300 precision side-looking sonar/echo sounder. Are fitted to accept the Fleet Exercise Minelaying System; they are able to lay and recover 20 exercise mines or 16 Versatile Exercise Mines. The system employs two sets of rails mounted on the fantail and adds 30 tons to the displacement when aboard.
Disposals: *Toreador* (A 143) was laid up on the Clyde for disposal in 1995 and sold in 1999, and *Torch* (A 141), laid up at Devonport, was offered for sale in 1998 but withdrawn from sale in 9-98.

♦ 3 torpedo recovery launches [YPT]
Bldr: R. Dunston, Thorne (In serv. 1979)

7868 7869 7870

D: 15 tons **S:** 9 kts **Dim:** 13.8 × 2.98 × 0.76
M: 1 Perkins 6-354 diesel; 1 prop; 104 bhp **Crew:** 4 tot.

Remarks: All based at Greenock. RN-operated.

SERVICE CRAFT *(continued)*

♦ 3 tank cleaning lighters [YRG]

TCL 1901 (ex-1901[TC])
TCL 1905 (ex-1905[TC])
TCL 1907 (ex-1907[TC])

Tank cleaning lighter TCL 1905 A. A. de Kruijf, 9-00

Remarks: Based: TCL 1901 and TCL 1905 at Portsmouth, TCL 1907 at Devonport. Non self-propelled barges, all of the same design, equipped with boilers to provide steam-cleaning of fuel and other shipboard tankage and tanks to hold sludge; no data available. All operated for Marine Services by SERCO-Denholm.

♦ 2 self-propelled lifting lighters [YRS]

Bldr: McTay Marine, Bromborough Dock, Wirral

	L	In serv.
Y 32 Moorhen	10-2-89	26-4-89
Y 33 Moorfowl	21-4-89	30-6-89

Moorhen (Y 32) Martin Mokrus, 6-05

D: 530 tons (fl) **S:** 8 kts **Dim:** 32.25 (30.00 pp) × 11.50 × 2.00
Electronics: Radar: 1 Decca . . . nav.
M: 2 Cummins NT19M diesels; 2 Aquamaster azimuth props; 730 bhp—bow-thruster
Electric: 528 kw (2 Cummins NTA 853 diesels) **Range:** . . . / . . .
Crew: 2 officers, 8 unlicensed, plus 5 divers

Remarks: 530 grt. First two ordered 25-4-88. Y 32 replaced dumb barge-lifting craft 484 at Portsmouth, and Y 33 is at Devonport. Pontoon barge hulls with powerful winches on fantail, open deck to bow spanned by pilothouse/accommodations superstructure.
Disposals: *Cameron* (A 72) was sold in 2004.

♦ 7 250-ton sullage barges [YSRN]

Bldr: D.E. Scarr, Ltd. (In serv. 1969– . . .)

1704(U) 1710(U) 1712(U) 1715(U)
1706(U) 1711(U) 1714(U)

Sullage barge 1715(U) Ralph Edwards, 8-03

Dim: 27.5 × 7.3 × 0.5 light/1.0 loaded

Remarks: 166.63 grt. 1710(U) is based on the Clyde; 1706(U), 1712(U), and 1715(U) are at Portsmouth (last two are "sullage/separator lighters"); 1711(U) and 1714(U) are at Devonport (as "sullage/separator lighters"); and 1704(U), of a different configuration, is Royal Navy–operated at Gibraltar. Nonself-propelled. Sister 1707(U) had been discarded by 2001.

Note: Also in service is sullage barge 1901(U), tonnage rating not available; the craft is based at Portsmouth.

♦ 2 100-ton sullage barges [YSRN]

Bldr: Dunston, Hessle (In serv. 1964–69)

1406(U) 1409(U)

Dim: 23.24 × 6.41 × 0.61 light/1.09 loaded

Remarks: 104.66 grt. Have two liquid-waste cargo tanks. Both are based at Gibraltar. Sisters 1402(U) and 1412(U) had been discarded by 8-00.

♦ 2 Impulse-class large water tractors [YTB]

Bldr: Richard Dunston, Hessle

	L	In serv.
A 344 Impulse	10-12-92	2-4-93
A 345 Impetus	8-2-93	11-6-93

Impetus (A 345) Christopher F. Hockaday, 8-96

D: 492.5 tons light (530 fl) **S:** 12.5 kts (12.75 trials, 12 sust.)
Dim: 32.53 (27.75 pp) × 10.42 × 4.07 **Electronics:** Radar: 1 . . . nav.
M: 2 W.H. Allen 8512, 8-cyl. diesels; 2 Aquamaster 1401 azimuthal props; 3,400 bhp—Jastrum 2-ton bow-thruster
Electric: 740 kw tot (2 × 370-kw Stamford alternators, Cummins KTA-19G2(M), 525-bhp diesels driving
Range: 3,000/10 **Fuel:** 55 tons **Crew:** 6 tot.

Remarks: 319 grt. Originally to have been ordered 1989, but bid process canceled. Ordered 28-2-92 for use at Faslane, Scotland, to move ballistic-missile submarines on and off the ship repair facility ship-lift. Are Marine Services craft operated by SERCO-Denholm.
Hull systems: Have 38.5-ton bollard pull ahead, 36 astern. Both equipped for fire-fighting with a 2,530-liter/min. Angus water monitor and 3.25 tons foam. Also carried are 5 tons oil-spill dispersant and 13 tons fresh water. Have extensive fendering surrounding hulls.

♦ 9 Adept-class large harbor tugs [YTB]

Bldr: Richard Dunston, Hessle

	Laid down	L	In serv.	Based
A 221 Forceful	30-3-84	. . .	29-3-85	Devonport
A 222 Nimble	27-4-84	21-3-85	25-6-85	Faslane
A 223 Powerful	21-6-84	3-6-85	3-10-85	Portsmouth
A 224 Adept	22-7-79	27-8-80	28-10-80	Devonport
A 225 Bustler	28-11-79	20-2-80	15-4-81	Portsmouth
A 226 Capable	5-9-80	2-7-81	11-9-81	Gibraltar
A 227 Careful	15-1-81	12-1-82	12-3-82	Devonport
A 228 Faithful	30-11-84	. . .	13-12-85	Devonport
A 231 Dexterous	18-4-85	25-2-86	24-4-86	Faslane

Dexterous (A 231) Frank Findler, 6-05

SERVICE CRAFT *(continued)*

Nimble (A 222) Martin Mokrus, 6-05

D: 450 tons (fl) **S:** 12.5 kts **Dim:** 38.82 (37.00 pp) × 9.10 × 4.20 (3.40 mean)
Electronics: Radar: 1 Decca . . .
M: 2 Ruston 6 RKCM diesels; 2 Voith-Schneider vertical-cycloidal props; 2,640 bhp
Electric: 294 kw tot. **Fuel:** 49 tons **Crew:** 10 tot.

Remarks: Operated since 8-7-96 as Marine Services craft on contract by SERCO-Denholm, except for A 226, which is operated by the RN and based at Gibraltar. First four ordered 22-2-79. Referred to as "Twin Unit Tractor Tugs" (TUTT). Have 27.5-ton bollard pull. Also used for coastal towing. Pennant numbers had been painted out by mid-1999.

♦ 4 Dog-class large harbor tugs [YTB]
Bldr: Various (In serv. 1962–72)

	Based		Based
A 178 Husky	Clyde	A 201 Spaniel	Clyde
A 182 Saluki	Devonport	A 250 Sheepdog	Portsmouth

Saluki (A 182) Ralph Edwards, 5-04

Sheepdog (A 250) Camil Busquets i Vilanova, 2005

D: 241 tons light (305 fl) **S:** 12 kts **Dim:** 28.65 (25.91 pp) × 7.72 × 3.87 (aft)
Electronics: Radar: 1 Decca . . . nav.
M: 2 Lister-Blackstone ERS-8-MGR diesels; 1 prop; 1,320 bhp
Electric: 40 kw tot. (1 × 40 kw, 220 v d.c.; Lister JK4MA diesel driving)
Range: 2,236/10 **Crew:** 8 tot.

Remarks: Operated since 8-7-96 on contract by SERCO-Denholm. Appearances vary, some having streamlined upper pilothouse structures, others higher pilothouses. Have 18.7-ton bollard pull and two Hamworthy C4 centrifugal salvage pumps capable of moving 200 tons of water for salvage purposes or 100 tons per hour for fire fighting. Pennant numbers had been painted out by spring 1999 but had been restored by summer 2000.
Disposals: *Airedale* (A 102) was sold commercially at Gibraltar, 12-84. *Alsatian* (A 106), *Pointer* (A 188), and *Corgi* (A 330) discarded fall 1993, with the latter for sale at Devonport as of mid-1995, and the other pair sold commercial. *Foxhound* (A 326, ex-*Boxer*) and *Labrador* (A 168) were sold to private operators in early 1996. *Basset* (A 327, ex-*Beagle*) was sold to the port of Portland in mid-1996. *Sealyham* (A 187), *Deerhound* (A 155), and *Elkhound* (A 162) were discarded during 1996. *Mastiff* (A 180) was for sale at Devonport as of 8-00. *Cairn* (A 126) and *Collie* (A 328), converted 1987 as trials craft [YAG] for use at Kyle of Lochalsh, have been retired. *Dalmation* (A 129) and *Setter* (A 189) had been stricken by 2005.

♦ 4 Felicity-class water tractors [YTM]
Bldrs: Richard Dunston, Thorne

	In serv.		In serv.
A 147 Frances	5-80	A 150 Genevieve	29-10-80
A 149 Florence	8-8-80	A 198 Helen	1974

Genevieve (A 150) Camil Busquets i Vilanova, 2005

D: 220 tons (fl) **S:** 10.2 kts **Dim:** 22.25 (20.73 pp) × 6.40 × 2.97 (2.10 hull)
M: 1 Lister-Blackstone ERS-8-MGR diesel; 1 cycliodal prop; 615 bhp
Range: 1,800/8 **Fuel:** 12 tons **Crew:** 4 tot.

Remarks: 138 grt. Marine Services Agency craft operated since 8-7-96 on contract by SERCO-Denholm. Have 5.9- to 6.1-ton bollard pull. Do not have radars. The pennant numbers had been painted out by early 1999, but A 150 was wearing hers as of 7-00 and was painted with black hull with white trim, red lower superstructure, and yellow pilothouse and stack. A 147 and A 149 operate at Devonport; the other two at Portsmouth.
Disposals: Sisters *Georgina* (A 152) and *Gwendoline* (A 196) were sold commercial in mid-1996, the first two to SERCO-Denholm, which operates them on charter to the Royal Navy at Devonport and Portsmouth, respectively. *Felicity* (A 112) was laid up in 1996 and sold commercial in 1998. *Fiona* (A 148) was for sale as of mid-2001.

♦ 3 Triton-class water tractors [YTL]
Bldr: Richard Dunston, Thorne (In serv. 1972–73)

A 170 Kitty
A 172 Lesley
A 199 Myrtle

Norah (A 205)—since retired Maritime Photographic, 3-01

D: 107.5 tons (fl) **S:** 7.75 kts **Dim:** 17.65 (16.76 pp) × 5.26 × 2.8
M: 1 Lister-Blackstone ERS-4-M diesel; 1 Voith-Schneider vertical cycloidal prop; 330 bhp
Crew: 4 tot.

SERVICE CRAFT *(continued)*

Remarks: 50 grt. Marine Services Agency craft operated since 8-7-96 on contract by SERCO-Denholm: A 190, A 170, and A 205 are all at Devonport and the others at Portsmouth. Have 3-ton bollard pull. Do not have radars.
Disposals: Sisters *Irene* (A 181) and *Joyce* (A 193) were placed up for sale summer 1996; *Nancy* (A 202) was sold commercial in mid-1996; *Isabel* (A 183) was for sale as of 9-96; and *Kathleen* (A 166) was sold commercial on 24-9-96. *Mary* (A 175) was for sale at Devonport at the end of 1997; and *Lilah* (A 174) was sold to the Milford Port Authority on 14-2-02. *Joan* (A 190) and *Norah* (A 205) had been retired by 2005.

♦ 4 Challenger 67–class sail-training sloops [YTS]
Bldr: Challenger Enterprises, Plymouth (In serv. 1997)

Endeavour   Challenger   Discoverer   Adventure

Remarks: Ocean racing craft bought 2002–3 to replace five Nicholson 55–class sailing yachts and operated by the Joint Services Adventure Training Centre, Plymouth. Had been built for the 1997 BT Global Challenge race.

♦ 1 Water-class water lighter [YW]
Bldr: Richard Dunston, Hessle (In serv. 6-78)

A 146 Waterman

Waterman (A 146) Leo van Ginderen, 6-05

D: 344 tons (fl) **S:** 11 kts **Dim:** 40.02 (37.50 pp) × 7.50 × 2.44
Electronics: Radar: 1 . . . nav.
M: 1 Lister Blackstone ERS-8-MGR diesel; 1 prop; 600 bhp
Electric: 155 kw tot. **Range:** 1,500/11 **Crew:** 11 tot.

Remarks: Not discarded in 1998 as reported in the last edition. Is still in service on the *Clyde,* operated by SERCO-Denholm. Carries up to 150 tons of water.
Disposals: *Waterfall* (Y 17) was stricken during 1988 and scrapped in 4-96; *Waterside* (Y 20) sold to Ecuador 11-91; *Watershed* (Y 18) was sold for commercial service to a Maltese owner in 7-92; *Waterspout* (Y 19) was sold for scrap in mid-1996; *Watercourse* (Y 30) was placed up for sale in 6-98; and *Waterfowl* (Y 31) was placed up for sale in 10-98 and sold commercial early in 2000.

♦ 4 27-meter water barges [YWN]

1517(W)   1518(W)   1519(W)   1520(W)

Water barge 1518(W)—alongside chartered SERCO-Denholm *Felicity*-class tug *Georgina* Maritime Photographic, 7-98

Remarks: 1518(W) and 1520(W) are at Devonport, the other two at Portsmouth. Cargo capacity: 250 tons. Nonself-propelled. Discarded by mid-2000 was 1510(W) at Devonport (sold commercial during 2001); 1515(W) has been reassigned as fuel barge 1515(F) at Devonport.

Disposal note: *Ham*-class leased training craft *Margherita* (ex-inshore minesweeper *Tresham,* M 2736) was returned to her owner, Vosper Thornycroft, during 2001.

BRITISH ARMY
ROYAL LOGISTIC CORPS

AMPHIBIOUS WARFARE CRAFT

♦ 6 Arromanches-class utility landing craft [WLCU]
Bldr: James & Stone, Brightlingsea

	L	In serv.
L 105 Arromanches (ex-*Agheila,* L 112)	24-7-87	12-6-87
L 107 Andalsnes	16-3-84	22-5-84
L 109 Akyab	20-11-84	21-12-84
L 110 Aachen	25-6-86	26-1-87
L 111 Arezzo	18-11-86	2-3-87
L 113 Audemer	24-6-87	21-8-87

Audemer (L 113) Michael Winter, 6-05

D: 290 tons (fl) **S:** 9.25 kts **Dim:** 33.26 (30.00 pp) × 8.30 × 1.45 loaded
Electronics: Radar: 1 Decca BridgeMaster E 180 nav.
M: 2 Doorman 8 JTCWM diesels; 2 props; 660 bhp **Range:** 900/9 **Fuel:** 17 tons
Crew: 6 tot.

Remarks: Known as Ramped Craft, Logistic (RPL). First two ordered 18-3-80; next three on 31-3-83; and four more in 3-85. L 105 switched name and pennant number with the original *Arromanche* in 1994. Decca BridgeMaster E 180 replacement navigational radars were ordered for the craft in 4-00. Cargo: 96 tons.
Disposals: *Antwerp* (L 106) and *Agheila* (L 105, ex-*Arromanches*) were placed up for sale in 11-94, and *Abbeville* (L 108) was sold at Hong Kong during 1994.

♦ 4 LCVP 4–class landing craft [WLCVP]
Bldr: W. A. Souter & Sons, Cowes

	In serv.		In serv.
LCVP 8402	15-3-85	LCVP 8619	1987
LCVP 8409	18-9-85	LCVP 8620	1987

D: 10 tons (fl) **S:** 20 kts (16 loaded) **Dim:** 13.00 (11.90 pp) × 3.20 × 0.80
A: Provision for 2 single 7.62-mm mg
M: 2 Perkins 76-3544 diesels; 2 props; 440 bhp
Range: 200/12 **Crew:** 3 crew + 35 troops

Remarks: Cargo well 8.80 × 2.13 m, with 5.5-ton capacity. Aluminum construction. Seventeen sisters in R.N. service. Two serve in the Falklands, one in Belize, one in the U.K.

SERVICE CRAFT

♦ 1 Samuel Morley, V.C.–class range safety craft [WYFL]
Bldr: Halmatic, Havant (In serv. 1983)

RSC 8127 Sir William Roe

D: 20.6 tons (23.6 fl) **S:** 22 kts **Dim:** 14.94 (13.41 wl) × 4.65 × 1.30
Electronics: Radar: 1 Decca E 180 BridgeMaster nav.
M: 2 Fiat 828SM diesels; 2 props; 880 bhp **Range:** 320/17 **Crew:** 3 tot.

Remarks: Based at Cyprus. GRP hull design based on commercial Talisman 49 hull. Twelve sisters were transferred to the RMAS on 1-10-88.

♦ 1 general-purpose workboat [WYFL]
Bldr: James & Stone, Brightlingsea

	Laid down	L	In serv.
WB 08 Mill Reef	17-3-86	17-11-86	16-2-87

Mill Reef (WB 08) Derek Fox, 5-04

BRITISH ARMY SERVICE CRAFT *(continued)*

D: 25 tons (fl) **S:** . . . **Dim:** 14.75 × . . . × . . .
Electronics: Radar: 1 Decca E 180 BridgeMaster nav.
M: 2 diesels; 2 props; . . . bhp
Crew: 4 tot.

Remarks: Prototype of design to replace following class. Ordered 6-12-85. Three more planned sisters were not ordered.

♦ **3 general-purpose workboats, Mk II [WYFL]** (In serv. 1966–71)

WB 03 Bream WB 05 Roach WB 06 Perch

Roach (WB 05) Leo van Ginderen, 6-05

D: 19 tons (fl) **S:** 8 kts **Dim:** 14.3 × . . . × . . . **M:** 2 diesels; 2 props; . . . bhp
Crew: 4 tot.

Remarks: Sisters *Barbel* (WB 04) stricken 1987, *Pike* (WB 07) in 1990.

♦ **8 workboats [WYFL]**
Bldr: Anderson, Rigden & Perkins, Whitstable (In serv. 2-3-81; W 208: 2-6-81)

W 201 through W 208 (ex-HL 1 through HL 8)

Mary Brown (W 205) Maritime Photographic, 6-98

D: 8 tons (fl) **S:** 11 kts **Dim:** 11.2 × 3.5 × . . .
M: 1 Perkins T6-354 M diesel; 1 prop; 129 bhp **Crew:** 2 tot.

Remarks: Glass-reinforced-plastic construction, using Halmatic GRP hulls. W 205 is employed as a diving tender. Five sisters were built for the Royal Navy. W 205 is unofficially named *Mary Brown.*

♦ **2 air-cushion vehicles [WYFLA]**
Bldr: Air Vehicles, Cowes

	In serv.
SH 01	11-5-82
SH 02	15-7-82

D: 1 ton (fl) **S:** 34 kts **Dim:** 8.45 × 4.57 × 2.18 (high)
M: 1 diesel; 1 airscrew prop; 1 lift fan; 200 bhp **Crew:** 1 + 11 passengers

BRITISH ARMY ROYAL ENGINEERS

COMBAT SUPPORT BOATS [LCP]

♦ **32 8.8-m combat support boats**
Bldr: Vosper-RTK Marine, Poole (In serv. 11-99 to . . .)

D: 4 tons (fl) **S:** 30+ kts **Dim:** 8.80 × 2.74 × 0.70
M: 2 Yanmar 6-cyl. diesels; 2 Hamilton 274 waterjets; 420 bhp **Range:** . . . / . . .
Crew: 2 tot.

8.8-meter combat support boat Brian Morrison, 10-01

Remarks: Prototype built in response to 9-98 contract tender. Contract for two production prototypes plus two trailers let 6-99. Thirty more (plus option for eight additional) were ordered in 6-00. Replacement design for the following class. Can be used as a pull or push tug.
Hull systems: Catamaran-form, GRP-construction hull. Have 1.66-ton bollard pull. Can operate in Sea State 5. The pilothouse top is removable, and 2 tons of cargo can be carried on deck. Have reflector, but no radar. Can be road-transported.

♦ **. . . Fairey/FBM river crossing boats**

D: 2 tons light (4 fl) **S:** 24 kts (17 loaded) **Dim:** 8.38 (6.98 wl) × 2.49 × 0.66
M: 2 Ford Sabre diesels; 2 Dowty waterjets; 420 bhp
Range: . . . / . . . **Fuel:** 270 liters **Crew:** 2 tot.

Remarks: Aluminum construction craft with twin push-fenders at the bow for maneuvering bridging sections. Design is also widely used by other armies around the world. Can carry a standard 1-ton NATO cargo pallet.

MINISTRY OF DEFENCE

DEFENCE POLICE

Note: Ministry of Defence Police Boats wear a high-visibility yellow and blue checker paint scheme to the sides of the pilothouses. The organization operates the following patrol units:

- *Endeavour, Excaliber, Loyalty*, *Agility*, *Pegasus*, *Watchful*, *Sword*, *Tactful,* and *Dignity* (in serv. 1993–98): 15.5 tons, 13.9 m, 21 kts, 4 crew
- *Omaha* (9313), *Utah* (9414), *Gold* (9315), *Juno* (9316), and *Hawk* (in serv. 1994): 8 tons, 10.4 m, 28 kts, range 300/18, 3 crew

13.90-meter Defence Police launch Watchful Ben Sullivan, 4-05

Also in use are 10.4-m fast motor launch Mk 10 8810, a *Fairey Huntress*–class GRP-hulled VIP launch based at Portsmouth; 10.4-m fast motor launch Mk 3 6547, based at Faslane on the Clyde; Jet Skis AB 8110 and AB 8339 (based on the Clyde); and several Avon Searider 5.4-m RIBs powered by a single Mariner gasoline outboard.

MARITIME AND COAST GUARD AGENCY

Note: The present organization was established in 4-98, combining the Coastguard Agency and the Marine Safety Agency. The organization has four operational regions. Two Cessna 404 and two Sikorsky S-61N helicopters are chartered from Bristow Helicopters for search-and-rescue duties in the English Channel area. Klyne Tugs of Lowestoft operates four towing vessels year-round for the Maritime and Coast Guard Agency. *Anglican Princess* (out of Falmouth), *Anglican Sovereign* (at Shetland and Orkney), *Anglican Monarch* at Dover, and *Anglican Prince* at Stomoway. All are painted with white hulls and a diagonal two-color slash from main deck to waterline with large black letters running across the side reading *Coastguard.* Permanently operated are two 7-m, 150 bhp Orkadian 23–class workboats—one in the Solent and one in the Clyde area—and a number of rigid inflatable boats.

MARITIME AND COAST GUARD AGENCY *(continued)*

Coast Guard S-61N rescue helicopter—painted red and white
Michael Winter, 6-05

On 30-1-03, three Vosper Thornycroft-Halmatic Arctic 22 RIBs were delivered for basing at Holyhead, Hull, and St. Andrews; they are capable of 30 kts on two 90-bhp engines. Also delivered was a 30-kt general-support launch. Four Pacific 32-cabin-equipped RIBs, each with two inboard Yanmar diesels driving waterjets, were delivered by 2004 for use at one Southampton, two at Oban, and one at Cardiff.

SCOTTISH FISHERIES PROTECTION AGENCY
(Department of Agriculture and Fisheries for Scotland)

Scottish Fisheries Patrol Agency (SFPA) ships were painted white in 1998 and gained diagonal blue and yellow hull stripes on either beam forward and the letters *SFPA* on their sides. Aviation assets include one Cessna Titan, three Dornier DO-228-200, and two Cessna Caravan II (all with surveillance radars). About 260 personnel work for the agency. Fisheries protection ships and craft in service include:

- *Sulisker* (1980), *Vigilant* (1982), and *Norna* (1988): 1,177 grt, 18 kts, range 7,000/13, 15 crew

Scottish Fisheries Protection Agency craft Norna
Camil Busquets i Vilanova, 2005

- *Minna* (2003): 855 tons (fl), 47.7m, 14 kts
- *Morven* and *Moidart* (1983): 44 tons, 20 kts, 7 days' endurance, 5 crew
- *Skua* (4-84): 7.5 tons, 24 kts, range 200 n.m., 3 crew

The agency also operates the fisheries research ship *Scotia*. A new 47-m, diesel-electric fisheries patrol ship was ordered during 2-02 from Fegusuon Shipbuilders, Port Glasgow, to replace the *Westra*.

Note: The Cornwall Sea Fisheries Committee took delivery of the 27-m, 32-kt *St. Piran* from Damen Marine, the Netherlands, during 5-00.

H.M. CUSTOMS AND EXCISE MARINE BRANCH

The U.K. Customs and Excise Marine Branch operates the following unarmed patrol units:

- *Seeker* (5-01), *Searcher* (8-01),*Vigilant* (2003), *Valiant* (6-04): 205 tons, 26 kts, range 2,000/12, 17 crew (sisters operate in the Netherlands West Indies Coast Guard and Netherlands Coast Guard)
- *Sentinel* (30-11-94): 172 tons, 30+ kts, range 2,300/12, 17 crew
- *Valiant, Venturous, Vigilant,* and *Vincent* (1988–93): 70 tons, 25 kts, 8 crew
- *Swift, Hunter,* and *Panther* (1993–94): 23.6 tons, 22 kts, range 300/18, 3 crew
- Miscellaneous small launches, including a large number of 4-m Avon Surfrider semi-rigid inflatables.

Customs patrol craft Seeker Ralph Edwards, 6-05

Customs patrol craft Hunter—in Coast Guard colors Frank Findler, 6-05

U.S.A.

United States of America

NAVY

Personnel (as of 11-06): 347,693 total active duty Navy personnel (51,814 officers, 291,452 enlisted and 4,427 midshipmen). Naval Reservists total 131,385, including 70,231 selected (actively drilling) and 61,154 individual (nondrilling). The Department of the Navy employs 175,375 civilians.

The Marine Corps has 179,762 total personnel (18,940 active duty officers and 160,822 active enlisted) along with 39,883 total Marine Corps reserves (3,396 officers, 36,487 enlisted).

The Military Sealift Command (MSC), which manages most auxiliary vessels, has 4,667 civil service mariners, 3,035 contract mariners, 577 Navy Selected Reserves, 600 active Navy, and 980 civil service shore personnel.

Force Levels: As of 6-06, the Navy operated 281 deployable battle force ships, with several hundred more support and special mission ships not counted in the total. 97 auxiliary vessels are managed by the Military Sealift Command along with 23 nondeployable scientific vessels

Bases: The Navy's major U.S. and overseas major commands, bases, and installations are divided into geographical areas as follows:

Norfolk, Virginia, area: Commander-in-Chief U.S. Atlantic Fleet; Commander U.S. 2nd Fleet, Little Creek Naval Amphibious Base; Navy Region Mid-Atlantic, Norfolk; Dam Neck Fleet Combat Training Center Atlantic, Virginia Beach; Northwest Naval Security Group Activity, Chesapeake; Norfolk Naval Shipyard, Portsmouth; Oceana Naval Air Station, Virginia Beach (with Oceana Detachment Norfolk at Chambers Field, Norfolk, formerly Naval Air Station Norfolk); Portsmouth Naval Medical Center; and Yorktown Naval Weapons Station.

Washington, D.C., area: Naval Support Activity (formerly Anacostia Naval Station); Washington Navy Yard; Bethesda National Naval Medical Center; Dahlgren Naval Surface Warfare Center, Virginia; Annapolis Naval Station, Maryland; U.S. Naval Academy, Annapolis; Naval Air Facility DC, Andrews AFB, Maryland; and Patuxent River Naval Air Station, Lexington Park, Maryland.

New England and Northeast area: Navy Region Northeast, Naval Submarine Base, New London, Connecticut (established 3-8-99); Brunswick Naval Air Station, Brunswick, Maine; Portsmouth Naval Shipyard, Maine; Naval Stations, Newport, Rhode Island (est. 30-10-98); Newport Naval Educational Training Center, Rhode Island; New London Naval Submarine Base, Groton, Connecticut; Ballston Spa, Scotia Naval Administrative Unit, Schenectady, New York; Willow Grove Naval Air Station, Joint Reserve Base, Horsham, Pennsylvania; Earle Naval Weapons Station, Colts Neck, New Jersey; and Lakehurst Naval Air Engineering Station, Toms River, New Jersey.

Southeast area: Commander Navy Region Southeast, Naval Air Station, Jacksonville, Florida (est. 2-2-99); Charleston Naval Hospital, Charleston, South Carolina; Beaufort Naval Hospital, Beaufort, South Carolina; Atlanta Naval Air Station, Marietta, Georgia; Kings Bay Naval Submarine Base, St. Marys, Georgia; Naval Air Depot, Cherry Point, North Carolina; Naval Air Depot, Jacksonville, Florida; and Key West Naval Air Facility.

Midwest area: Naval Service Training Command, Great Lakes, Illinois; and Memphis Naval Support Activity, Millington, Tennessee.

Gulf Coast area: Panama City Naval Support Activity; Corry Station, Pensacola, Florida; Pensacola Naval Air Station; Pensacola Naval Hospital; Whiting Field Naval Air Station, Milton, Florida; Meridian Naval Air Station, Mississippi; Gulfport Naval Construction Battalion Center, Gulfport, Mississippi; New Orleans Naval Air Station, New Orleans, Louisiana; Joint Reserve Base, Belle Chasse, Louisiana; New Orleans Naval Support Activity; Fort Worth Naval Air Station and Joint Reserve Base; Ingleside Naval Station, Ingleside, Texas; Corpus Christi Naval Air Station, Texas; and Kingsville Naval Air Station, Texas. In 2004 the Navy relocated U.S. Naval Forces Southern Command from the now-closed Naval Station Roosevelt Roads, Puerto Rico, to Naval Station Mayport, Florida.

West Coast area: Navy Region Northwest, Seattle, Washington; Whidbey Island Naval Air Station, Oak Harbor, Washington; Everett Naval Station, Washington; Bangor Naval Submarine Base, Silverdale, Washington; Bremerton Naval Hospital, Washington; Puget Sound Naval Shipyard, Bremerton, Washington; Naval Station Bremerton, Washington; Fallon Naval Air Station, Nevada; Naval Air Reserve Station Santa Clara, Moffett Field, California; Naval Post Graduate School, Monterey, California; Lemoore Naval Air Station, California; China Lake Naval Air Weapons Station, Ridgecrest, California; Naval Air Station, Pt. Mugu, California; and Port Hueneme Naval Facilities Expeditionary Logistics Center, California.

NAVY *(continued)*

San Diego, California, area: Naval Region Southwest, San Diego, California; U.S. 3rd Fleet; Naval Base San Diego (incorporating Naval Station San Diego, Naval Medical Center San Diego, and the Navy Broadway complex); Naval Base Coronado (North and South Facilities, incorporating the former Naval Air Station North Island, Naval Amphibious Base Coronado, Outlying Field Imperial Beach, and Naval Auxiliary Landing Field San Clemente Island; the Naval Air Station was redesignated a Naval Air Depot on 20-4-01); Naval Base Point Loma (incorporating the former Antisubmarine Warfare Training Center Pacific, Space and Naval Warfare Command Headquarters Facility and Space and Naval Warfare Command Support Center Point Loma, and Navy Consolidated Brig at Marine Corps Air Station Miramar); and El Centro Naval Air Facility, Seeley, California. Fleet Antisubmarine Warfare Command was created at San Diego on 8-4-04.
Hawaiian Islands: Commander-in-Chief, U.S. Pacific Fleet, Pearl Harbor; Navy Region Hawaii, Pearl Harbor; Naval Station Pearl Harbor (subsumed Naval Submarine Base on 9-11-98); Naval Computer and Telecommunications Area Master Station Pacific, Honolulu; and Pearl Harbor Naval Shipyard and Intermediate Maintenance Facility.

Overseas facilities include:

Caribbean area: Naval Station Guantanamo Bay, Cuba (Naval Station Roosevelt Roads, Puerto Rico, closed during 2004).
North Atlantic area: Fleet Air Keflavik Naval Air Station, Keflavik, Iceland; U.S. Naval Activities United Kingdom; Commander, U.S. Naval Forces Europe, London; Naval Station, Rota, Spain.
Mediterranean area: Naval Support Activity, La Maddalena, Sardinia, Italy; U.S. 6th Fleet, Gaeta, Italy; Naval Air Station, Sigonella, Sicily, Italy; Naval Support Activity, Naples, Italy; Commander, Fleet Air Mediterranean, Naples, Italy; and Naval Support Activity, Souda Bay, Crete, Greece.
Indian Ocean area: U.S. Naval Forces Central Command (5th Fleet), Manama, Bahrain; and Naval Support Facility, Diego Garcia.
Western Pacific area: U.S. 7th Fleet, Yokosuka, Japan; U.S. Fleet Activities, Yokosuka; Naval Air Facility and Naval Air Pacific Repair Activity, Atsugi, Japan; Naval Air Facility, Misawa, Japan; U.S. Fleet Activities, Sasebo, Japan; U.S. Fleet Activities, Okinawa, Japan; U.S. Naval Forces, Korea Fleet Activities, Chinhae, South Korea; U.S. Naval Forces Marianas, Guam; and U.S. Naval Logistics Group, Western Pacific, Singapore.

Note: To consolidate administrative functions, in 1999 the Naval Base Norfolk became the Navy Region Mid-Atlantic; the Naval Base Pearl Harbor became the Navy Region Hawaii; the Naval Base San Diego became the Navy Region Southwest; and the Naval Base Seattle became the Navy Region Northwest. There are a large number of smaller facilities both on U.S. territory and overseas.

Naval Aviation: Individual aircraft numbers and characteristics are presented after the aircraft carrier entries that follow. The Navy operates 10 air wings, while Naval Reserve Air Forces operate one Tactical Air Wing, one Patrol/ASW Air Wing, one Helicopter Wing, and one Reserve Logistics Air Wing; the Marine Corps has three active and one Reserve Air Wing.

SHIPBUILDING PROGRAM FISCAL YEAR 2006–11

New Construction:	FY 06	FY 07	FY 08	FY 09	FY 10	FY 11
CVN 21/CVN-78	—	—	1	—	—	—
SSN 774, *Virginia*	1	1	1	1	1	1
CG (X) CG-74	—	—	—	—	—	1
DD-1000, *Zumwalt*	—	2	—	1	1	1
LCS	3	2	3	6	6	6
LHA6	—	1	—	—	1	—
LPD 17, *San Antonio*	1	—	1	—	—	—
Maritime Prepo (Future, aviation and mobile)*	—	—	—	1	1	3
T-AKE 1, *Lewis & Clark*	1	1	1	1	1	1
Total:	6	7	7	10	11	13
Conversions/Upgrades:						
CVN refueling/overhaul	1	—	—	—	1	—
CG Update	—	—	1	2	2	3
SSN/SSBN refuel	1	1	2	1	1	1
LCAC SLEP	6	6	6	6	6	6

* Includes three types, future, mobile, and aviation ship to replace *Wright* (AVB-3) and *Curtiss* (AVB-4).

Note: As is usually the case, the numbers increase in the "out years" but are inevitably revised later.

Marine Corps

The major operational unit is the Marine Expeditionary Force (MEF), which consists of one division, one air wing, and one Force Support Group, for a total of about 50,000 Marines. MEFs typically deploy with 60 days' worth of supplies. There are three standing Marine Expeditionary Force (MEF) divisions (one stationed in Okinawa, two in the United States), each of about 32,000 personnel, and three active air wings. The Fourth Marine division, including their associated air wing and Force Support Group, constitute the Marine reserve cadre and also provide Marines for homeland defense operations in concert with U.S. Northern Command.

The Marine Expeditionary Brigade (MEB) is a smaller operational unit intended to provide a powerful, highly mobile, quick-response force. An MEB consists of a force of between 3,000 and 20,000 Marines with enough supplies to last approximately one month.

The smallest assault unit is the Marine Expeditionary Unit (MEU), consisting of between 1,500 and 3,000 Marines, including a landing team, air squadrons, and support personnel; attached are four tanks, six aircraft, 30 helicopters, and supporting artillery along with a little more than two weeks' worth of supplies.

Bases: Principal facilities at Camp Pendleton, California; Twenty-nine Palms, California; Camp H. M. Smith, Oahu, Hawaii; Camp Lejeune, North Carolina; and Camp Smedley D. Butler, Okinawa. Marine Corps Air Stations (MCAS) are at Beaufort, South Carolina; Cherry Point, North Carolina; Quantico, Virginia; New River, Jacksonville, Florida; Mirimar, San Diego, California; Yuma, Arizona; Kaneohe Bay, Oahu, Hawaii; and Iwakuni, Japan. A Marine Corps Air Station is located at Futenma, Okinawa. Numerous other training, research, communications, etc., facilities exist.

Special Forces

Consisting of 2,450 men, all capable of aerial or seaborne insertion along with 600 Special Warfare Combatant-craft Crewmen; eight SEAL Teams (eight platoons each), two Swimmer Delivery Vehicle Teams, and three Special Boat Squadrons. Additional reserve forces consist of more than 700; eight SEAL Teams (eight platoons each), two Swimmer Delivery Vehicle Teams, and three Special Boat Squadrons. SEALs operate under the joint-services Special Warfare Command. SEAL—Sea, Air, Land.

Naval Construction Division

On 9-8-02 the "Seabee" combat construction organization was altered to include a single Naval Construction Division, headquartered at Little Creek, Virginia (also established on 9-8-02 was the 1st Naval Construction Division Forward [1NCD FWD] at Pearl Harbor). The 22nd Naval Construction Regiment (NCR) was relocated from Little Creek, Virginia, to Gulfport, Mississippi. The 30th NCR is relocating from Pearl Harbor, Hawaii, to Port Hueneme, California, and the two active training regiments, 20th NCR at Gulfport and 31st NCR at Port Hueneme, California, have been renamed 20th Seabee Readiness Group (SRG) and 31st SRG respectively. The 25th NCR is to commission 10-07 at Gulfport, Mississippi.

The Naval Reserve Force

Naval Reserve Force ships have cadre crews of regular naval personnel, with reserve augmentation personnel constituting up to two-thirds of the total crew assigned. Also incorporated in the Naval Reserve program are about 3,000 other units supporting 35 or more programs to augment Regular Navy staffs in wartime.

As of 3-07, the Naval Reserve Force included nine guided-missile frigates, four mine-countermeasures ships, and four minehunters; it also operated around 250 aircraft, including C-130T, C-9, DC-9, and C-40A transports, C-20G VIP transports, C-12B light transports, E-2C AEW aircraft, F-5 combat-training fighters, F/A-18-series fighters, P-3C maritime patrol aircraft, MH-53E mine-countermeasures helicopters, HH-60H combat rescue helicopters, and H-3-series helicopters.

The Military Sealift Command

The Military Sealift Command (MSC), under the joint-services Transportation Command, operates or charters ships in support of the USN and the other armed services. Headed by an active-duty USN flag officer, its ships are manned primarily by civilians, either civil service or contractor mariners. During 2005 the MSC transported some 4,456,790 tons of dry cargo and 5,381,035 long tons of petroleum products, and its Special Mission Ships provided 5,068 sea-days of operations.

WEAPONS AND SYSTEMS

A. MISSILES

♦ Fleet ballistic missiles

Trident-II D-5 (UGM-133A) Bldr: Lockheed Martin

Officially entered operational service 29-3-90 on SSBN 734. Planned inventory is 425. As of 2002 384 missiles had been ordered from Lockheed Martin. Trident D-5 is planned to remain in service until 2042.

First stage weighs 39.15 metric tons, of which 36.9 metric tons is propellant; second stage weighs 11.84 metric tons, of which 11.05 metric tons is propellant; and third stage weighs 2.19 tons, of which 2.03 tons is propellant.

All were to get the new W 88 warhead, but a shortage of nuclear weapons production facilities forced retention of the W 76 warhead on some. A variant with a conventional warhead and employing GPS guidance was reportedly tested on 18-11-93 but did not enter production. The last five Trident-II missiles were purchased in FY 2005 for $715.3 million.

Length: 13.44 m **Diameter:** 2.11 m **Weight:** 53.18 tons at launch
Propulsion: Solid propellant, three stages
Range: 6,000 nautical miles with 122-m circular error probable (CEP)
Payload: Up to eight Mk 5 re-entry vehicles with 100-kiloton W 76 or 300–475-kiloton W88 warheads.

Note: The last Trident-1 C-4 (UGM-96A) SLBMs had been retired from service by 2005.

♦ Surface-to-surface missiles

Tomahawk (BGM-109)
Bldr: Raytheon Systems Co., Tucson, Ariz. (formerly Hughes)

Only the conventionally armed land-attack versions of Tomahawk remain in service for launch by submarines (using torpedo tubes or special vertical launch tubes) or surface ships (using Mk 41 vertical launch cells). During 1993 the first Block III missiles, with better fuzing, 320-kg warhead, 50% more fuel, F107-WR-402 turbojets with 19% more thrust, Mk. 111 booster, global positioning system, and faster missile mission planning entered service; the missiles also featured "time of arrival" control, permitting coordinated simultaneous attacks.

Remaining Block II missiles are being updated to Block IV (Tactical Tomahawk—TACTOM) configuration with a GPS receiver, a new computer, and a satellite data-link. The Block IV has three-meter accuracy at maximum range, improved targeting support, a communications link to the launch platform to permit revised targeting while in flight, improved terminal homing, and a hardened-target destruction-capable warhead.

WEAPONS AND SYSTEMS *(continued)*

The datalink-equipped, 1,600 n.m.–ranged Block IV Tactical Tomahawk variant, able to loiter for upward of two hours over a battlefield before being directed to attack a point target, entered production in mid-2004, with more than 2,300 missiles to be purchased by the end of FY 09. In the future, the low-cost, $575,000 Block IV missile may carry either 16 BAT (Brilliant Anti-Armor), 32 SADARM, or 16 sensor-fuzed munitions; a television camera may later be added to some missiles to act as a battle-damage assessment aid. Tactical Tomahawk is currently launchable only from vertical tubes on submarines operating at periscope depth, but an encapsulated, torpedo tube–launched version for U.K. Royal Navy and U.S. Navy use was expected in operation by 2007.

In 4-99 200 AGM-109B and 424 Block II Tomahawk missiles were ordered for conversion to Block IIIC Tactical Land-Attack Missile (TLAM), the last delivered by Raytheon during 4-02. The updated missiles have improved Digital Scene Matching Area Correlation and either a 454-kg conventional warhead or 166-bomblet BLU-97B warhead (TLAM-D). The deep-penetration version of Tomahawk, using the British Lancer multiwarhead penetrator system, had its successful final test on 5-12-01 and is equipped with a high-temperature incendiary warhead equipped to penetrate some 6 meters (20 ft) of concrete prior to detonation; the missile will cruise at or higher than 25,000 feet, diving to the target; during trials the 500-kg test warhead penetrated a 6-m reinforced concrete target, 10 meters of sand, and then traveled another 800 meters. Future Tomahawks are to be powered by a version of the Williams F-122 turbojet.

Current Navy plans called for the procurement of 2,200 TACTOM missiles.

Data include:

Length: 6.17 m (with booster) **Diameter:** 0.52 m
Weight: 1,542 kg at launch (1.816 kg encapsulated for submarine launch)
Warheads: 454 kg conventional or 166 BLU-97 submunitions (Block III, TLAM-D only)
Propulsion: Solid booster, F-107 (Block III) or F-415 (Block IV) turbojet sustainer
Range: Block III and IV: 900 n.m.; 700 n.m. (TLAM-D only)

Harpoon (RGM-84A/D/F; UGM-84A/B/C/G; AGM-84A/B/C/F)
Bldr: Boeing

An all-weather cruise missile that can be launched by aircraft, surface ships, or submarines. For USN use, 2,006 were procured between FY 82 and FY 91. The submarine-launched, encapsulated UGM-84 version was retired in 1997 as a money-saving measure but is still used by some foreign navies. Many surface ships capable of carrying the RGM-84 missile either carry fewer than the possible total or none at all. The AGM-84 can be carried by P-3C, S-3B, and Air Force B-52 (up to 12 each) aircraft. The U.S. Air Force acquired 85 undelivered Iranian AGM-84 missiles in 8-84.

Length: 4.628 m (RGM-84 ship-launched) or 3.848 m (AGM-84 air-launched)
Diameter: 0.343 m **Wingspan:** 0.914 m
Weight: 681 kg from canister, 680 kg from SAM launcher (with booster), 526 kg air-launched
Warhead: 227 kg
Propulsion: CAE-JA02 turbojet, with a rocket booster added to the ship- and submarine-launched versions
Speed: Mach 0.85 **Range:** "over 67" n.m.
Guidance: Inertial, then active homing on J band in the final trajectory

Block 1 Harpoon missiles had improved seekers and operational software, while Block 1B added a sea-skimming capability with a lower mid-course altitude. Beginning with FY 88 procurement, Block 1C had "Dash-4" seeker and improved guidance. Block 1D missiles (first launch 4-9-91, but none yet ordered by the USN) were designated AGM-84F and have a 0.9-meter longer fuselage to provide sufficient additional fuel to double the range and also have a reattack feature if the missile misses on the first pass; weight was 771 kg. Missiles exported since 1995 are of the A/R/UGM-84M, Block ICR version with software revised to permit reattacks in case of misses, improved ECCM, and a lower flight altitude; none have been procured for the USN. The SLAM and SLAM-ER–series missiles derived from Harpoon are described separately under air-to-surface missiles.

The Boeing A/U/RGM-84L Harpoon Block II variant includes GPS guidance upgrades allowing for antiship operations in crowded littoral regions in addition to a land-attack capability. Successful first sea trials with the Block II were conducted during 6-01. Though the missile was not purchased by the United States, it serves in several foreign navies.

The U.S. Navy has requested FY 07 funding for a proposed Block III variant of the Harpoon, with GPS and retargeting capability via datalink. Current plans call for upgrading some existing USN Block I missiles to Block III standard beginning in FY 2007–8.

Note: The U.S. Marine Corps plans to acquire 45 wheeled HIMAR rocket-launching vehicles to equip two battalions of the 14th Artillery Regiment; using standard MLRS (Multiple Launch Rocket System) launchers, the vehicles are planned to enter service in 2008–9.

♦ Surface-to-air missiles

Standard SM-6 ERAM Bldr: Raytheon Systems Co., Tucson, Ariz.

ERAM = Extended-Range Antiair Missile. Expected to be deployed on future DD(X) and other surface combatants. Sole-source contract given to Raytheon on 10-2-03 for a variant of the Standard family with dual mode active/semiactive radar with initial guidance via the Aegis system and an active radar seeker from the AMRAAM missile for terminal guidance. Will provide increased defense against all types of air threats, including cruise missiles operating over land as well as over water. Expected to complete development by FY 10.

Standard SM-3 LEAP (RIM-161A)
Bldr: Raytheon Systems Co., Tucson, Ariz.

Three-stage antiballistic missile variant of the Standard missile family, intended to counter short- and medium-range missiles in their mid-course phase. The SM-3 program is managed cooperatively by the Navy and the Missile Defense Agency. Carrying a hit-to-kill kinetic warhead, four variants of the SM-3 missile are now in production or development. The SM-3 Block 1A has been in production since 2004 and is deployed in very limited numbers (about 20) aboard between three and six Aegis warships, primarily for testing purposes and limited antimissile defense duties. On 22 June 2006 the SM-3 Block 1A completed its seventh successful intercept test in eight attempts, and succeeded in its first kill against a "separating" target. Future planned variants include the SM-3 Block 1B around 2008, SM-3 Block II by 2012, and the SM 3 Block IIA around 2014.

Standard SM-2 MR Block IIIB (RIM-66C) and IVA (RIM-156A, "Aegis ER") Bldr: Raytheon Systems Co., Tucson, Ariz.

SM-2 Block III, IIIA, and IIIB are the principle surface-to-air missile armament deployed aboard U.S. Navy warships. Block IIIB is a considerably reworked version of Block III for use in Mk 41 vertical launchers on CG-52 and DDG-51 classes; it has a dual-mode radar/infrared seeker; improved radome, guidance, and autopilot; modified dorsal and control fins; and a new shorter but larger-diameter EX-72 booster with thrust vector control. In 7-95 initial contracts were placed for the development of the Missile Homing Improvement Program, which would add an infrared seeker to the Block IIIB's radar homing system.

The Block IV fleet air defense version carries a solid-fuel booster rocket and is capable of extended range (100–200 nm), high altitude, and increased g-turning performance. Modified Block IV missiles have successfully intercepted ballistic-missile test targets in their terminal phase of flight.

Production of Block III and Block IV missiles concluded in 1988 and 2003 respectively, though missile upgrades and upgrade kits continue to enhance missile capability.

Data for the SM-2 Block III include:

Length: 4.72 meters **Diameter:** .34 m
Weight: 708 kg **Range:** 40-90 n.m.
Guidance: Semiactive radar homing (IR in Block IIIB)
Warhead: Radar and contact fuse, blast-fragment warhead.

Standard SM-1 MR (RIM-66B/RIM-67E)
Bldr: Raytheon Systems Co., Tucson, Ariz.

Single-stage missile, replaced Tartar. System comprises a Mk 13 single launcher with a vertical ready-service magazine containing 40 missiles, a computer, an air-search radar, and SPG-51 illumination radars. The missile was retired from USN service at the end of FY 03 but about 2,500–3,000 missiles remain in use by foreign navies.

Data for the SM-1 include:

Length: 4.47 m **Diameter:** 0.34 m **Weight:** 625 kg
Range: 25 n.m **Altitude:** 150–60,000 ft
Guidance: Semiactive homing

ESSM Evolved Sea Sparrow (RIM-162)
Bldr: Raytheon Systems Co., Tucson, Ariz.

Initial 54-month contract let 6-95 to Hughes (now Raytheon) and a consortium of United Defense, Alliant/Hercules, and Norwegian, German, Australian, Canadian, Spanish, Danish, Turkish, and Greek firms for a performance-upgrade version of the RIM-7P missile, with 35- to 50-g maneuverability, increased range, and doubled speed. Uses a 254-mm-diameter motor and has a WAU-17B fragmentation warhead. Evolved Sea Sparrow Missiles (ESSM) are carried in Mk 25 Mod. 0 "Quad Pack" containers in Mk 41 launch vertical launch cells or in single packs in Mk 29 and Mk 48 box launchers.

The first production missile was delivered on 5-9-02. Full rate production approval was given in 2003 with full service entry in 2005.

Length: 3.657 m **Diameter:** 254 mm
Wingspan: 101.6 cm open/63.5 cm folded
Weight: 281.2 kg **Warhead weight:** 38.6 kg **Range:** 8 n.m.

Sea Sparrow (RIM-7-series)
Bldr: Raytheon Systems Co. Tucson, Ariz.

Known initially as the BPDMS (Basic Point Defense Missile System). A lightweight launcher, Mk 29, employing eight folding-fin missiles and the Mk 91 radar fire-control system, is now in use. In Europe this later system, IPDMS (Independent Point Defense Missile System), is also known as NATO Sea Sparrow. The current RIM-7M version uses a blast-fragmentation warhead vice the earlier RIM-7H's expanding rod variety and has a monopulse radar. Latest variant in service is the RIM-7P, which uses the 203-mm-diameter Hercules Mk 58 Mod. 4 rocket motor.

Length: 3.657 m **Diameter:** 0.203 m
Wingspan: 101.6 cm open/63.5 cm folded **Weight:** 231.5 kg
Warhead weight: 38.6 kg **Speed:** Mach 3.5 **Range:** 8 n.m.

SEA RAM Bldr: Raytheon Systems Co., Tucson, Ariz.

SEA RAM is the commercial name for an 11-round launcher for RIM-116A Mod. 1 missiles that also uses the same mounting, Mk 90 Ku-Band search and track radar, surface-mode E/O sensors, and below-decks components as the 20-mm Phalanx CIWS. Instead of operating in self-guided mode, the missile becomes a beam-rider, using the radars within the Phalanx system. Installed on the left side of the mounting are a Pilkington Optronics FLIR detector and a low-light-level t.v. camera. The system is offered for export in cooperation with Germany's RAM-System GmbH, the U.K.'s DML, and Hunting Engineering. The mounting was given a compatibility test aboard British destroyer H.M.S. *York* during 2-01 to 10-01. SEA RAM arms the General Dynamics Flight 0 Littoral Combat Ship variant and may eventually be procured for installation aboard existing *Perry*-class frigates, the first 27 *Arleigh Burke*–class destroyers, and the *San Antonio*–class landing ships.

RAM (Rolling Airframe Missile) (RIM-116A Mod. 0/1)
Bldr: Raytheon Systems Co., Tucson, Ariz.

Developed by General Dynamics (later Hughes Missile Systems and now Raytheon) under a 7-76 agreement by the United States, Denmark, and West Germany. First 30 built under FY 85. Became operational 14-11-92 on *Peleliu* (LHA 5), at which point the system was more than ten years behind schedule. Uses slow spinning for flight stability (hence the name). The missile homes on active radiation from the target until it picks up an infrared target signature and employs the current Stinger seeker in

WEAPONS AND SYSTEMS *(continued)*

conjunction with Sidewinder fuzes, warheads, and rocket motors. The 21-missile Mk 49 launcher installation weighs 4,977 kg above deck, 800 kg below. The U.S. Navy plans to acquire 4,600 total. The Mk 49 launcher has been installed on all LHDs, LHAs, and LSDs and on six DD 963–class destroyers. Unit cost in 1997 was a very expensive $440,000 each, but by FY 01, the price had dropped to $144,000 each. No acquisitions were authorized under the FY 01 Budget, but FY 02 contained 90; 90 were requested under FY 03; 240 requested under FY 04; 86 under FY 05; 90 each under the FY 06 and FY 06 budgets.

The Mod. 1 missile, which completed successful trials in mid-1998, has a laser fuze and an improved, broader-view infrared seeker.

Length: 2.8 m **Diameter:** 127 mm **Weight:** 73.5 kg
Speed: Mach 2+ **Range:** 6 n.m.

Stinger (FIM-92) Bldrs: General Dynamics and Raytheon Systems Co.

The Marine Corps employs the shoulder-launched infrared-homing Stinger with troops, and the Navy procured 585 for shipboard defense. FIM-92A entered service 1981; more than 16,000 have been delivered. Some FIM-92B "Stinger POST" missiles were delivered to the USMC. FIM-92C RMP (Reprogrammed Microprocessor) is the current version.

Length: 1.52 m **Diameter:** 0.07 m **Weight:** 15.1 kg
Warhead: 3 kg (proximity fuze) **Speed:** Mach 2.0

♦ Antisubmarine warfare missiles

ASROC (RUR-5A)
Bldr: Hughes Electronics Div., General Motors (now Raytheon Systems Co.)

Retired from U.S. service in FY 94 and replaced by the Vertical Launch ASROC. Some 12,000 ASROC rounds were procured between 1960 and 1970 and the system is still widely deployed in foreign fleets. All nuclear rounds (used only by the USN) were retired by end FY 89. ASROC was also launched by Mk 26 launchers on five early units of the CG 47 class. Missile is a solid-fueled, unguided rocket with a parachute-retarded Mk 46 torpedo payload. Range is regulated by the combustion time of the rocket motor. Rocket-torpedo separation is timed. Fire control is made up of a computer linked with the sonar.

Length: 4.42 m **Diameter:** 0.324 m **Weight:** 454 kg **Range:** 9,200 m

Vertical-Launch ASROC (RUM-139B) Bldr: Lockheed Martin

Full-scale production began in 3-93 for use with Mk 41 launchers in CG 52 and later *Ticonderoga*-class cruisers and in DDG 51–class destroyers. With booster attached, the weapon is 5.08 m long, 0.358 m in diameter, and weighs about 750 kg. The final 30 were ordered 4-98 and delivered 4-99, for a total of 443 produced for the USN, with no more planned. The relative handful built are cross-decked to deploying ships. VLA has also been purchased by Japan, which has ordered more than 600.

♦ Air-to-surface missiles

Hystrike

The Naval Air Warfare Center Weapons Division, China Lake, California, is developing a Hypersonic Weapons Technology program aimed at introducing the Hystrike land-attack missile around 2012. Some 1,200 missiles would be procured between FY 11 and FY 15 at around $350,000 apiece. Intended to attack hardened targets at ranges of up to 600 n.m., Hystrike would travel at Mach 3.5 to Mach 7 and would be able to penetrate up to 11 m of concrete. The missile could be launched by aircraft, surface ships, and submarines and would replace the Tomahawk land-attack, Harpoon, SLAM, and SLAM-ER missiles.

Note: The Navy withdrew from the Joint Air-to-Surface Strike Missile (JASSM) Program in 2006.

JDAM—Joint Direct Attack Munition
Bldr: Boeing (formerly McDonnell Douglas)

JDAM is a guidance tail kit that converts existing unguided free-fall bombs into accurate, adverse weather "smart" munitions. Current kits are fitted on 2,000-pound BLU-109/MK 84 and 1,000-pound BLU-110/MK 83 bombs to produce a better-than 11-m CEP accuracy. A version for use with Mk 82 500-lb. bombs has also been developed. Contract let 10-95 for initial increment. Planned to acquire 25,496 during 11 years, with the initial 937 conversion kits having begun delivery during 1998 for use on F/A-18-series aircraft. On 25-2-00, 916 were ordered for Navy BLU-109, 2,000-lb. bombs. Procurement of the kits remains high with 6,930 purchased for the Navy in FY 05, 3,400 in FY 06, and 3,400 in FY 07.

JSOW—Joint Stand-Off Weapon (AGM-154A/B/C)
Bldr: Raytheon Systems Co., Lewisville, Texas

Formerly called AIWS (Advanced Interdiction Weapon System), this formerly joint Navy–Air Force program (the Air Force has since withdrawn funding) was originally developed by Texas Instruments. An unpowered, "fire-and-forget" ground-attack weapon to replace Skipper, Walleye, Paveway, and Laser Maverick, JSOW entered limited service late in 1997. Texas Instruments design selected 12-91 and development contract placed 7-92. Guidance is provided by GPS/INS. The Navy AGM-154A version dispenses BLU-97A or -B bomblets. A decision to purchase the AGM-154B version (armed with BLU-108B sensor-fuzed anti-armor submunitions) has been deferred.

In 2005 AGM-154C achieved Initial Operational Capability. AGM-54C uses the British BAe Systems Bomb Royal Ordnance Augmented Charge (BROACH) penetrating warhead and also carries a terminal IR Seeker. Current orders by the Navy included 405 in FY 05, 420 in FY 06, and 397 in FY 07. Operationally, the weapon (carried by F/A-18 and AV-8B aircraft) experienced initial accuracy problems, which were soon fixed.

Length: 4.1 m **Diameter:** 0.330 m **Wingspan:** 2.69 m
Weight: 483 to 681 kg (depending on variant)
Range: high altitude launch: 65 nm; low altitude launch: 15 nm

SLAM-ER (AGM-84K) Bldr: Boeing

The AGM-84K SLAM-ER (Stand-off Land Attack Missile—Expanded Response), authorized by DoD in 2-95 as a replacement for the canceled AGM-137 TSSAM, is a conversion of the original AGM-84E SLAM with long-span folding wings to extend its range beyond 150 n.m. 136 new SLAM-ER missiles have been purchased while some 600 have been converted from AGM-84E configuration. The weapon has a cylindrical warhead with PBX-C-129 explosive and tapered forward end for penetration. Initial low rate of production of SLAM-ER began in 1999 with the conversion of 60 existing SLAM missiles to SLAM-ER configuration. Beginning in 2000, an automatic target acquisition capability was added to the missile, making it the SLAM-ER+. SLAM-ER can be carried by the F/A-18, S-3 Viking, and P-3 Orion aircraft. SLAM-ER can be used against both land and maneuvering ship targets and reportedly has the best CEP of any weapon in Navy inventory.

Length: 4.4 m **Diameter:** 0.343 m **Weight:** 680 kg
Warhead: 227 kg titanium penetrator **Propulsion:** CAE-JA02 turbojet
Speed: Mach 0.85 **Range:** 150+ n.m.

Penguin Mk 2 Mod. 7 (AGM-119B) Bldr: Kongsberg/Northrop-Grumman

Initially tested for the U.S. Navy in 1982–83 as a surface ship-launched weapon, Penguin was procured for launch by SH-60B LAMPS-III helicopters. Has solid-fueled rocket propulsion, programmable inertial mid-course guidance, and infrared terminal homing. Only 193 operational weapons were planned for procurement; total procurement was later reduced to only 106, vastly increasing the unit cost, and only 28 helicopters were modified to carry the missile. First became operational 5-94. In 8-95 Congress expressed a desire for the Navy to request additional missiles for FY 97; an order for six more for delivery by 4-99 was placed with Kongsberg in 7-97 at a very uneconomical total cost of $6.05 million.

Length: 3.00 m **Diameter:** 0.28 m
Wingspan: 1.40 m (0.56 folded) **Weight:** 385 kg
Warhead: Bullpup Mk 19 (120 kg SAP with 50 kg explosive)
Range: 21+ n.m.

Maverick (AGM-65E and AGM-65F)
Bldr: Raytheon Systems Co. (formerly Hughes Missile Systems)

Developed from the Air Force AGM-65D, the AGM-65E is a laser-designated, air-launched missile for the Marine Corps, while the AGM-65F version uses infrared homing and arms Navy F/A-18 aircraft. The AGM 65E carries a 57-kg shaped charge warhead while the AGM 65F is fitted with a 136-kg penetrating warhead. Several thousand have been purchased and remain in service.

Length: 2.49 m **Diameter:** 0.305 m **Wingspan:** 0.72 m
Weight: E: 207 kg; F: 307 kg **Propulsion:** Solid-fuel rocket
Range: 13 n.m.

Harpoon (AGM-84)

See under surface-to-surface missiles.

HARM (AGM-88A/B/C/D/E)
Bldrs: Raytheon (AGM-88E: ATK Missile Systems)

HARM (High-Speed Anti-Radiation Missile) can be employed by the F/A-18 and EA-6B to suppress or destroy ground defenses. Production of the missile began in 1983 and more than 20,000 missiles had been purchased by the time production ended in 1997. Upgraded versions include the AGM-88B Block III, AGM-88C Block IV, and the AGM-88D with a home-on-jam capability.

Length: 4.17 m **Diameter:** 0.253 m **Wingspan:** 1.13 m
Weight: 360 kg **Propulsion:** Solid-propellant, low-smoke rocket
Speed: Mach 2.0+ **Range:** About 80 n.m.

The AGM-88E, also known as the Advanced Anti-Radiation Guided Missile (AARGM), is currently under development. With precision GPS, an active millimeter-wave seeker, and a new wideband passive seeker to the guidance system, the AGM-88E is expected to begin low-rate initial production in 2008.

♦ Anti-armored vehicle missiles

Joint Common Missile Bldr: Lockheed Martin

A notional replacement for current Hellfire, Maverick, and TOW (but not Longbow TOW) anti-armor missiles. Initiated by U.S. Army and joined by Navy and USMC in 8-00. Up to 54,000 could be procured for aviation and ground forces. In 5-04 Lockheed Martin won a four-year $53-million contract for the missile's development and demonstration. Tests of the missile continued through 2005–6. Production could begin as early as FY 09. Will employ a 152-mm-diameter fire-and-forget missile with controllable-thrust rocket propulsion.

TOW-2 (MGM-71) Bldr: Raytheon Systems Co.

Wire-guided, helicopter- or ground-launched antitank weapon that uses optical sight and tube launcher. TOW = Tube-launched, Optically tracked, Wire-guided. More than 400,000 TOWs have been built since 1970 for all customers. TOW-2A detonates reactive armor, then penetrates; 16,000 were in service by 4-88. TOW-2h as not been procured since early 1990s.

Length: 1.174 m **Diameter:** 0.152 m **Wingspan:** 1.14 m
Weight: 18.9 kg ITOW (Improved TOW) weighs 19.1 kg, ITOW-2 weighs 21.5 kg
Warhead: 3.6-kg hollow, shaped-charge **Propulsion:** Solid-propellant rocket
Range: 2.3 n.m. at Mach 1.0

Hellfire/Hellfire II (AGM-114B/K/M) Bldr: Lockheed Martin-Boeing

Antitank missile can also be used to engage helicopters and low/slow-flying aircraft. Has three major variants: Laser-designated (1.625 m, 45.7 kg), RF/IR (Radio-Frequency Infrared), and IRIS (Imaging Infrared). Can be carried by AH-1 and SH-60-series helicopters. All AGM-114B missiles are being phased out by 2009, leaving only the more advanced missiles in service.

Length: 1.727 m or 1.778 m (imaging IR version)
Diameter: 178 mm (span: 0.3262 m)
Weight: 45.7 to 47.88 kg (71 kg in container)
Speed: Mach 1.0+ **Range:** 5+ km

WEAPONS AND SYSTEMS *(continued)*

Under development for the Army and Marines by Lockheed Martin and Boeing is the AGM-114K HOMS (Hellfire Optimized Missile System) with semiactive laser seeker, longer range, and 40% fewer parts.
Characteristics include:

Length: 1.626 m **Diameter:** 178 mm **Weight:** 45 kg **Range:** 0.5 to 9 km

The first of 100 AGM-114M missiles were delivered during 9-00 for use with Navy SH-60B Seahawk and Marine Corps AH-1W SuperCobra helicopters. This 47.6-kg variant is equipped with a 12.5-kg blast-fragmentation warhead and is equipped with a delayed proximity fuze; AGM-114M has a maximum speed of Mach 1.3 and a maximum flight duration of 39 sec., and one round can disable a ship of up to 700 tons displacement.

Note: Also for air-launched use, some 4,000 ADM-141 TALD (Tactical Air-Launched Decoy) glide-missiles in three variants have been acquired: RF for defense saturation, chaff for force-masking, and IR for IR missile training. ITALD (Improved TALD), with turboject propulsion, is in development.

Javelin . . . Bldrs: Texas Instruments and Lockheed Martin

Developmental man-portable fire-and-forget antitank weapon that entered low-rate production in 1994, with full-rate production begun in 5-97. By 2004 some 9,000 missiles had been ordered for use by the U.S. Army and Marine Corps. Used extensively by U.S. forces during operations in Afghanistan and Iraq. Is ready to fire in less than 30 seconds and requires less than 20 seconds to reload. Missile shelf life is 10 years. Uses passive integrated daylight and thermal sight with 4-hour battery.

Length: 1.0812 m (launch tube 1.198 m) **Diameter:** 126.9 mm
Weight: 11.8 kg (22.3 with launch tube and command unit) **Range:** 2,000+ m

Note: Also in service with the Marine Corps are some 750 short-range fire-and-forget Predator assault weapons. Man-portable, the Predator can engage soft or heavily armored targets to a range of 600 meters.

SMAW (Shoulder-Launched Multipurpose Assault Weapon)

Shoulder-Launched Multipurpose Assault Weapon, for U.S. Marine Corps, using Mk 153 Mod. 1 launcher with laser designation sight to fire either Mk 6 Mod. 0 HEAA (High Explosive Anti-Armor) or general-purpose HEDP rocket. Derived from the Israeli B-300 system.

Length: 787 mm stowed, 1,378 mm in firing condition (launcher)
Diameter: 83 mm (rocket)
Weight: Rocket: 6.71 kg HEAA/5.89 kg HEDP/5.89 kg launcher
Range: 500 m (stationary target)

♦ Air-to-air missiles

Sparrow-III (AIM-7F, M, P) Bldr: Raytheon Systems Co.

The AIM-7F entered service in 1976 with a continuous-rod warhead. AIM-7M, the current version, entered service in 1983 with a blast/fragmentation warhead, active fuze, and improved seeker. The AIM-7P variant has a reprogrammable memory. Being phased out of service in favor of the AIM–120 AMRAAM.

Length: 3.65 m **Diameter:** 0.203 m **Weight:** 232 kg
Warhead: 27 kg, proximity fuze **Propulsion:** Solid-fuel rocket
Speed: Mach 2.5 **Range:** 26,000 m **Guidance:** Semi-active homing

Sidewinder (AIM-9L, M, S, X)
Bldrs: Raytheon Systems Co. and Ford Aerospace/Loral

More than 110,000 Sidewinder missiles have been built. The AIM-9L version used an active optical fuze and had a guidance system permitting all-angle attacks. The AIM-9M version supplanted the -9L in production in 1981 and has improved capabilities against countermeasures and against targets seen against warm backgrounds. An AIM-9R with improvements to counter-countermeasures was canceled by Congress during 1992. AIM-9P is an export version for aircraft without internal cooling systems. The AIM-9L is also manufactured by a German/Italian/Norwegian/British consortium. The AIM-9S version weighs 86 kg and has a 10.15-kg warhead with proximity and contact fuzing. The AIM-9M has an 11.35-kg warhead.
Data for the AIM-9L include:

Length: 2.87 m **Diameter:** 0.127 m **Wingspan:** 0.63 m
Weight: 84.4 kg **Warhead:** 9.45-kg fragmentation
Propulsion: solid-fueled rocket **Speed:** Mach 2.5
Range: 22 km **Guidance:** infrared homing

The AIM-9X entered service in 2003 and was in full rate production by 2004. The AIM-9X uses a 127-mm-diameter Sidewinder body and solid rocket engine coupled with thrust vector controls to improve maneuverability and provide high off-bore-sight accuracy. An eventual production total of 5,000 for the Navy during a period of 18 years is expected. Employs operator helmet control.

Disposal note: The last remaining AIM-54 Phoenix air-to-air missiles, carried by the since-retired F-14 Tomcat, were withdrawn from service during 9-04.

AMRAAM (AIM-120A/B/C) Bldr: Raytheon Systems Co.

AMRAAM (Advanced Medium-Range Air-to-Air Missile) was intended to replace the AIM-7 Sparrow in Air Force and naval service. First firings in 1985. Navy goal was 7,249 total, out of 24,320 planned grand total. From FY 89 through FY 00, Congress authorized purchase of 1,553. Sixty-three were approved under FY 01, 57 under FY 02, 76 under FY 03, 42 under FY 04, 37 under FY 05, 85 under FY 06, and 150 were requested under the FY 07 program. Production of the missile will continue past FY 2007. AIM-120B, with a reprogrammable seeker and infrared homing, entered service during 4-95. The AIM-120C version, with clipped wings for internal storage, increased warhead lethality, an improved engine, improved aerodynamic performance, and improved electronic counter-countermeasures (ECCM) capabilities, entered service in 1996. The AIM-120D, undergoing testing on Navy and Air Force aircraft, provides an enhanced navigation capability and other improvements.

Length: 3.65 m **Diameter:** 0.178 m **Weight:** 151.5 kg
Warhead: 22.7 kg **Range:** More than 70 km
Guidance: inertial mid-course, active terminal homing

B. GUNS

155-mm Advanced Gun System

BAe Systems replacement for the 155-mm VGAS (Vertical Gun for Advanced Ships), which never achieved prototype stage. Will have an accuracy within 10 m at maximum range of 100 nm, using GPS. The 155-mm AGS is planned for installation in *Zumwalt* (DDG-1000)-class guided-missile destroyers to provide fire support to forces ashore. AGS is a fully integrated, automatic gun and magazine weapon system that will include two separate guns for each *Zumwalt*-class warship. Each system will be capable of independently firing up to 10 rounds per minute from a fully automated magazine. The AGS program includes development of the GPS guided 155-mm Long-Range Land-Attack Projectile (LRLAP), the first of a family of AGS munitions.
Gun will have trapezoidal external-section, water-cooled barrel 62 calibers long, and a low radar cross-section mounting; initially to fire Army XM982 projectiles or new 260-lb, 88-in-long Extended Range Guided Munitions (ERGM). A projectile planned to enter service would carry 88 M42E1 DPICM bomblets, and that would be followed by variants with 10.9-kg blast fragmentation warheads and a variant with an anti-armor warhead (the Army SADARM—Sense And Destroy Armor—submunition is a candidate for the latter role). The first gun system is scheduled for delivery in FY 2008, to support the first *Zumwalt* destroyers.

155-mm XM777 ultra-lightweight howitzer

U.S. Marine Corps towed or helicopter-deployed weapon, made by BAe Systems RO Defence; first delivered 6-00, with a total of 380 planned to replace the 155-mm M198 in Marine service. Uses 39-cal. barrel manufactured by the U.S. Army's Watervliet Arsenal. Can be towed by a 5-ton 6 × 6 truck or lifted by helicopters or MV-22 Osprey aircraft; two can be accommodated in a C-130 aircraft.

127-mm, Mk 42
Bldr: Northern Ordnance/FMC (now United Defense LP, Armament Systems Division)

No longer in USN active service but remains aboard *Knox*-class frigates in foreign fleets. Single-barrel, dual-purpose gun. Loading is entirely automatic from two ammunition drums in the handling room up to the loading tray by means of a rotating hoist. Each drum contains 20 rounds. The rate of fire can be maintained for only one minute, inasmuch as it is necessary to reload the drums. Firing rate reduced from original 40 rds/min for safety. Most mounts were converted to Mk 42 Mod. 10 configuration with greatly improved reliability.

Length: 54 calibers **Mount weight:** 65.8 tons (Mod. 10: 63.9 tons)
Projectile weight: 32 kg **Muzzle velocity:** 810 m/second
Rate of fire: 20 rds/minute **Arc of elevation:** –5° to +80°
Rate of train: 50°/second **Rate of elevation:** 80°/second
Range: 23,700 m horizontal/14,840 vertical
Fire control: Mk 68 system with SPG-53 radar in most ships
Personnel: 13 men, with 2 in mount

127-mm Mk 45
Bldr: United Defense LP, Armament Systems Division

Single-barrel mount fitted on *Ticonderoga*-class cruisers, *Arleigh Burke*– and since-stricken *Spruance*-class destroyers, as well as in foreign ships. The Mk 45 mount uses the Mk 48 gun with one-piece Mk 19 Mod. 2 or two-piece Mk 19 Mod. 0 barrel. Manufacturer was formerly named Northern Ordnance/FMC. The Mod. 1 version permits rapid switching from one type of ammunition to another and has an electronic vice mechanical fuze-setter.

Length: 54 calibers **Mount weight:** 22.23 tons
Projectile weight: 31.75 kg **Muzzle velocity:** 807.72 m/second
Rate of fire: 16 to 20 rds/minute **Arc of elevation:** –5° to +65°
Range: 23,700 m horizontal/14,840 vertical
Fire control: Mk 86 GFCS with SPQ-9 search radar and SPG-60 tracking radar
Personnel: None on mount; 6 in handling room to reload ammunition drums

The Mk 45 Mod. 4 (previously called the Mk 45 Gun System Technical Improvement Program) is in production with a low-observable, faceted gunmount and a rate of fire of 20 rds/min (10 rds with ERGM—see following). Muzzle velocity is 762 m/sec. with a 45-kg projectile, 914 m/sec. with a 32-kg projectile. A new 62-cal. barrel is fitted, along with a new breech and breech-operating mechanism, modified slide, a new loader drum, and a system that "recognizes" and selects the proper rounds. The gun is aboard DDG 81 and later *Burke*-class DDGs and is being backfitted to CG 52 through 73.
Texas Instruments (now Raytheon, Tucson, Arizona) received a $44-million contract in 10-96 to develop the rocket-assisted EX-171 ERGM (Extended Range Guided Munition) for the Mk 45 gun. As of 2006, however, the technological and financial hurdles required to achieve the hoped-for range of 63 n.m and CEP of 10 to 20 m forced continued delays and eventual cancellation of the program.
An industry team led by Alliant Techsystems successfully tested its competing GPS-guided ANSR (Autonomous Naval Support Round) early in 1-02, with the two test rounds traveling up to 51 n.m.; a range of 54 n.m. was achieved during 6-02. A production version of ANSR would cost less than $20,000 per round and would have a range in excess of 60 n.m. at an initial muzzle velocity of more than 3,400 ft./sec. The round would also be produced in a 155-mm diameter for the larger Advanced Gun System.

76-mm, Mk 75
Bldr: United Defense LP, Armament Systems Division (formerly Northern Ordnance/FMC) and OTO Melara

Single-barrel, license-built version of the OTO Melara Compact, tested in the frigate *Talbot* and used in FFG 7 classes and Coast Guard cutters. Built in the United States, except for FY 85 order to OTO Melara. Northern Ordnance became United Defense LP, Armament Systems Division, in 1994.

Length: 62 calibers **Mount weight:** 6.2 tons
Projectile weight: 6.4 kg **Rate of fire:** 85 rds/minute
Maximum range: 19,200 m horizontal/11,900 m vertical
Fire control: Mk 92 radar system **Personnel:** 4, below deck

WEAPONS AND SYSTEMS *(continued)*

57-mm, Mk 110 (Mk 3 Bofors) Bldr: Bofors Defence

Single-barreled, dual-purpose weapon available in either stealth or convention low radar-reflectivity gunhouse. Being built along with Bofors 3P projectile system for use aboard *Freedom* (LCS-1) class and the Coast Guard *Bertholf* (WMSL-750) and Off-shore Patrol Cutter (WMSM-915) classes.

Length: 70 calibers **Mount weight:** 13,000 kg **Projectile weight:** 6.1–6.5 kg
Rate of fire: 120 rds/min **Maximum range:** 17 km

40-mm L70 Mk 3 AA gun Bldr: Bofors Defence

Selected by the winning design team for use aboard the *Zumwalt* class, with two per ship to be carried. Has a 101-round ready-service magazine and employs a low radar-reflectivity gunhouse.

Length: 70 calibers **Mount weight:** 3,500 kg **Projectile weight:** 2.5 kg
Rate of fire: 330 rds/min **Maximum range:** 12 km

40-mm, Mk 19 Mod. 3 grenade launcher Bldr: Socko Corp.

A lightweight rapid-fire grenade launcher in portable tripod-legged mountings. Found aboard small combatants, auxiliaries, and Coast Guard ships. Range: 2,212 m (1,500 m effective); rate of fire is 300 rds/min, and muzzle velocity is 240 m/sec. The launcher is also employed on the Mk 96 Mod. 0 stabilized mount, co-located with a 25-mm M242 Bushmaster cannon (see following). For use by the Special Forces Command, the Navy ordered 305 Mk 47 40-mm Advanced Lightweight Grenade Launchers (ALGL) from General Dynamics late in 2001; the Mk 47 has a range of 2,000 m.

Note: The General Electric 20-mm and 25-mm Sea Vulcan gatling guns have been sold abroad but have not yet been acquired for the USN; Sea Vulcan 25 uses the GAU-12/U gun (900 or 2,000 rpm) with 500 rds on mount.

35-mm Millennium
Bldrs: Oerlikon Contraves, Zurich, Switzerland, and Lockheed Martin, Akron, Ohio

Intended as a CIWS and capable of firing 1,000 rounds per minute, each round containing 152 subprojectiles to form a cone-shaped firing pattern to destroy low-flying missiles and aircraft and small surface craft. The weapon is said to be lethal against aircraft and helicopters to 3.5 km, cruise missiles to 2 km, and sea-skimming missiles to 1.5 km. Lockheed Martin is providing the fire-control system, and the weapon was tested aboard the trials craft *Sea Slice* in 2002.

30-mm Mk 46 Mod. 0 and Mod. 1 Bldr: General Dynamics

Mod. 0 version is intended for the Expeditionary Fighting Vehicle (EFV, formerly AAAV amphibious assault vehicle) and the Mod. 1 version (without smoke rocket launchers) for fitting aboard the LPD 17 class for defense against smallcraft, helicopters, and light aircraft. Has a maximum range of 6,800 m (5,200 m effective). Mod. 0 mount will have 220 rounds ready-service ammunition, Mod. 1 more than 550. Both mounts have two-axis stabilization. Also being offered with a 40-mm Bushmaster-derivative gun. Has an on-mount laser rangefinder, FLIR, and LLTV fire-control systems and can be fitted with an automatic target tracking system.

Rate of fire: 200 rds/min **Range:** 4,000 yards

25-mm Mk 38 Mod. 1/2 (M 242 Bushmaster)
Bldr: BAE Systems

A "chain gun," using the M242 gun, Mk 88 Mod. 0 mounting, and linked Oerlikon M790 ammunition. For use on major surface combatants, *Cyclone*-class patrol craft, amphibious warfare ships, and Coast Guard ships and craft. From FY 86 through FY 92, Congress authorized procurement of 265 total. 139 were purchased with FY 06 funding, reportedly to be fitted on most ships until the Phalanx CIWS (Block 1B) can be fully fielded. The gun also fires Alliant PGU-32/U semi-armor piercing, high-explosive, incendiary-tracer rounds. The Mk 88 mounting holds 400 rounds of ready-service ammunition and can be reloaded in four minutes, but it is awkward to use due to its low configuration.

Length: 2.74 m overall **Weight:** 109 kg (gun)
Muzzle velocity: 1,100 m/sec. **Rate of fire:** single-shot, 100, or 200 rds/min
Range: 6,598 m (2,469 effective) **Fire control:** Ring sight

Installed in *Cyclone*-class patrol craft, the Mk 96 Mod. 0 stabilized mount carries both a 25-mm M242 Bushmaster gun and a 40-mm Mk 19 grenade launcher; 96 grenades and 400 rds of 25-mm ammunition are carried on the mount, which weighs 1,230 kg without ammunition and 1,430 kg loaded and requires a crew of three. Kollmorgen has built three lightweight Mk 98 stabilized Bushmaster gun mountings, of which two went to the Bahamas and one was used for trials by the U.S. Southern Command (SOCOM). Sixty-seven Mod 2 variants were ordered 9-5-06 for installation aboard DDGs, CGs, and LPDs

20-mm Phalanx, Mk 15 Mod. 0 Block 1, 1A, and 1B CIWS (Close-in Weapon System)
Bldr: General Dynamics (with G.E. gun) or Raytheon (ex-General Electric)

Vulcan/Phalanx "Close-in" system designed to destroy missiles, consisting of a multibarrel, M61A1 20-mm gun co-mounted with two radars, one of which follows the target and the other the projectile stream, using the Mk 90 integrated fire-control system. A computer furnishes necessary corrections for train and elevation so that the two radar returns (target and projectiles) coincide, bringing heavy fire to bear on the target. Only 989 rds were carried in the Block 0 magazine. The first production unit was completed 9-8-79. The improved Block 1 version with 1,550 rounds on mount and a higher rate of fire entered service in late 1988—five years late—and all remaining USN Phalanx mounts have been converted to Block 1. Originally used Mk 149 projectiles with depleted uranium subcaliber penetrators; later, heavier nickel-iron rounds were introduced, and 105-gram nickel-cobalt-tungsten rounds with 50% greater penetration are now being phased in. More than 850 mounts had been produced for 21 nations.

Block 1A Phalanx substituted an improved computer to improve capabilities against rapidly maneuvering targets. Block 1B adds a Pilkington Optronics IR imaging and tracking system to the mount; eleven update kits have been ordered for use on *Oliver Hazard Perry*–class frigates, and more may be procured for amphibious warfare ships and Phalanx-equipped DDG 51–class destroyers. Other modifications to Block 1B include: low-sidelobe modification to the tracking radar; a tunable narrow-band filter added to the search radar; substitution of longer gun barrels (480 mm) on the pneumatic-drive guns; electric controls; and improved, sturdier supports for the gun to reduce dispersion. Raytheon began delivering Block 1B new mounts from a Louisville, Kentucky, facility in 1999, and the first production mount was placed on FFG 50 in 9-00. On 22-10-02 Raytheon received a contract to modify 16 Block 1 mounts to Block 1B configuration, plus four conversion kits for the U.S. Navy with service entry expected in 2007. Data for the Block 1B system include:

Mount weight: 7.25 tons
Rate of fire: 4,500 rds/minute
Maximum range: 3,650 m

12.7-mm GAU-19/A Bldr: General Dynamics Armament Systems

A three-barreled gatling gun with 1,000 or 2,000 r.p.m. firing rate, developed for use aboard patrol and special forces boats. Mount weighs 168.2 kg empty and 260 kg with 800-round ammunition feed. Effective range is more than 1,500 m. Uses Mk 16 Mod. 7 pintle mount, but manufacturer, with Israel's Rafael, is offering the Typhoon stabilized, powered mounting, which weighs 630 kg loaded. Not yet procured for USN.

Note: Browning M2-series 12.7-mm machineguns in single and twin mountings are widely available for installation on USN ships and craft, and smaller 7.62-mm machineguns are used aboard Special Forces boats. Deploying surface combatants are being issued two 7.62-mm Mk 44 gatling minigun mountings each.

C. TORPEDOES

Mk 54 Mod. 0 LHT (Lightweight Hybrid Torpedo)
Bldr: Raytheon NAMS, Keyport, Wash.

The Lightweight Hybrid Torpedo is a next-generation torpedo that combines the Mark 50 search and homing system with the propulsion system of the Mark 46 torpedo for optimized performance in shallow water. 1,000 total are planned with delivery taking place between 2004 and 2011. Employs the Mk 103 warhead and the propulsion system of the Mk 46 torpedo, the sensor from the Mk 50, and the variable-speed control system and software from the Mk 48 Mod. 6 ADCAP; to these are added new digital data distribution, a bottom sensor, a new data processor and software, and a new outer shell. Successful trials with four prototypes were held summer 2001. The weapon is 2.60-m long and 32-cm in diameter and weighs 231 kg.

Mk 50 Barracuda Bldr: Raytheon NAMS, Keyport, Wash.

Formerly known as the ALWT (Advanced Lightweight Torpedo), was conceived as a replacement for the Mk 46 series and was supplied in surface-launched and air-droppable configurations. It is of roughly the same weight as the Mk 46 and of the same dimensions but is deeper-diving (more than 600 m), faster (more than 40 knots), employs lithium fuel, has digital guidance and control systems, and has better homing and counter-countermeasures capabilities. Due to continuing program delays, did not enter service until 1991. Weight: 362 kg; length: 2.93 m. Program was to be terminated under FY 94, with only 1,039 total operational weapons of the originally planned 7,851 procured, but Congress required that 24 more be procured under FY 96, the last year of procurement; the last was delivered in 1999. Upgrade 1, being incorporated as of 1998, improved shallow-water performance.

Mk 48 Mod. 6 and Mod. 7 Bldr: Raytheon, Keyport, Wash.

Two sequential upgrades to existing Mk 48 Mod. 5 ADCAP torpedoes are being undertaken to provide a quieter-running torpedo with upgraded guidance and control. Upgrades to existing inventory began in 1998 and were completed in 2005. Raytheon received an order for 115 modification kits on 22-3-01 for delivery in 2004. In addition, new Ada-based Block IV software began being incorporated starting in FY 01, while conversion to employ the enhanced littoral capability CBASS (Common Broadband Advanced Sonar System) are planned to begin in FY 05. As of fall 2001, Raytheon and the Naval Undersea Warfare Center, Newport, R.I., were developing the Mk 48 Mod. 6AT variant for export, using the same digital beam-forming sonar employed by the Mk 48 Mod. 5 ADCAP and a 295-kg PBXN-5 explosive warhead; the torpedo body also incorporates an internal noise muffler and a skewed-blade shrouded propeller. Dimensions for the Mk 48 Mod. 6AT are 58.6m length with a diameter of 5.3 m. The torpedo weighs 1,572 kg. In 2003 it was announced that the Mk 48 Mod 7 ADCAP was being developed through a collaborative program between the U.S. and Australia. Initial successful trials on the Mod 7 were conducted during 9-04 and it is expected to enter service during 2007.

Mk 48 Mod. 5 ADCAP Bldr: Westinghouse

Mk 48 Mod. 5 program began 1978 to provide weapon with significant performance improvements over the earlier Mk 48 Mod. 4. ADCAP (Advanced Capability) entered service in 1989; 1,427 were authorized for procurement from FY 85 through FY 94. Data for Mk 48 ADCAP include:

Diameter: 533 mm **Length:** 5.84 m **Weight:** 1565 kg
Warhead: 295 kg PBXN-103 **Speed:** more than 28 kts **Range:** 10 n.m.

Mk 48 Mod. 1, Mod. 3–4 Bldrs: Westinghouse and Hughes Helicopter

Mk 48 Mod. 1 entered service 1972. Can be launched from a submarine against a surface target or a submarine, using its own active-passive or acoustic homing system or with a wire-guidance system. The first "Near-Term Update" Mk 48 Mod. 4 torpedo was delivered 12-80. A total of 3,884 Mk 48s was procured through FY 85, plus units for Australia, Canada, and the Netherlands.

Diameter: 0.533 m **Length:** 5.84 m **Weight:** 633 kg
Propulsion: 500-hp Otto-cycle swashplate engine **Speed:** 55 kts
Range: 50 km max. **Depth:** Up to 760 m

WEAPONS AND SYSTEMS *(continued)*

Mk 46 Mod. 1, 2, 5, and 6 NEARTIP

Bldr: Raytheon Systems Co., Mukilteo, Wash. (formerly Hughes Electronics Div., General Motors Telesystems, and previously Honeywell)

Lightweight ASW torpedo using liquid fuel (Otto fuel), and twin, counter-rotating props. Entered service 1963. Active-passive guidance. Launched from Mk 32 ASW torpedo tubes or as payload for the ASROC ASW missile system. Some 25,000 of all versions of Mk 46 have been procured for 26 countries. The torpedo is planned to remain in service through 2015.

The Mk 46 Mod. 1 (surface-launched) and Mod. 2 (air-dropped) have been upgraded to Mod. 6 NEARTIP (Near-Term Improvement Program) status with improved acoustic homing system and countermeasures resistance. Mod. 5 torpedoes are being upgraded to Mod. 5A, with improved sonar and shallow water performance; some 2,700 torpedoes were ultimately updated. The Mk 46 Mod. 4 is the payload for the Captor mine. A Mod. 7 upgrade program is in development, and Mk 46 shallow-water performance and service-life extension upgrades are to supplement further procurement of Mk 50 and Mk 54 torpedoes.

Diameter: 0.324 m **Length:** 2.60 m (4.50 with ASROC booster)
Weight: 232.4 kg **Warhead:** 45.4 kg HE

Seahunter (NT-37E)

Bldr: Raytheon NAMS, Mukilteo, Wash. (formerly Hughes Electronics Div., General Motors Telesystems; formerly Alliant)

Remanufactured and greatly improved Mk 37 homing torpedoes available for export, but not used by USN. Propelled by a 90-hp Otto-fuel motor. The last USN Mk 37–series torpedo was retired 30-9-86. A further improvement, the NT-37F, was ordered by Egypt in 7-91; employing further improvements in guidance and controls, it has a 148-kg HBX warhead. Data for NT-37E include:

Diameter: 0.483 m **Length:** 3.467 m **Weight:** . . .
Warhead: 148 kg HE **Speed:** 35 kts **Range:** 18,000 m

D. MINES

Mk 52 Mod. 1, 2, 3, 5, 6

Air-dropped. All 2.75 m long by 338-mm diameter (830 mm over fins). All carry 270-kg HBX explosive. Mod. 1 is an acoustic mine, weight: 542.5 kg. Mod. 2 is a magnetic-influence version, weight: 568 kg. Mod. 3 is a dual-pressure/magnetic-influence version, weight: 572.5 kg. Mod. 5 is an acoustic/magnetic-influence version, weight: 570.7 kg. Mod. 6 is a pressure/acoustic/magnetic-influence version, weight: 546 kg. All are bottom mines for depths of up to 47 m (Mod. 2: 183 m) and can be carried by USAF B-52H bombers as well as Navy aircraft. Mod. 1 entered service in 1955.

Mk 55 Mod. 2, 3, 5, 6, 7, 11, 12, 13

Air-dropped ASW bottom mines. All 2.89 kg long by .592-m diameter (1.03 m over fins) and carry 577-kg HBX-1 explosive. Versions: Mod. 2: magnetic influence, weight: 989 kg; Mod. 3: pressure/magnetic influence, weight: 994 kg; Mod. 5: acoustic/magnetic influence, weight: 994 kg; Mod. 6: pressure/acoustic/magnetic, weight: 997 kg; Mod. 7: dual-channel magnetic influence, weight: 996 kg. Mod. 11 has a magnetic or magnetic/seismic sensor, Mod. 12 is magnetic, and Mod. 13 is pressure/magnetic. All can be laid in 46-m-deep water, except Mod. 2, 7: 183 m. Can also be laid by surface ships, using portable rails. Entered service 1956. Only Mods 5, 6, and 7 are kept in USN service for emergency use.

Mk 56 Mod. 0

Aircraft-dropped or submarine-launched ASW moored mine. 968 kg. 2.89 m long by 558-mm diameter (1.06 over fins). Total-field magnetic influence exploder. Carries 163-kg HBX-3 explosive. Depth: 365 m. Entered service 1966. Though no longer operational, up to 6,000 remain in inventory for emergency use.

Mk 60 CAPTOR Mod. 1 (enCAPsulated TORpedo)

Submarine-laid or aircraft-dropped. Uses Mk 46 Mod. 4 acoustic-homing torpedo payload. Primarily ASW in function. Development began 1961, with service readiness not declared until 9-79. From FY 80 through FY 86, 1,510 were authorized by Congress. Air-dropped variant weighs 1,075 kg, submarine-launched 932 kg. The torpedo warhead has 43.5 kg PXBN-103 explosive. Length air-launched is 3.68 m, submarine-launched 3.35 m; both are 533 mm in diameter. All Mod. 0 were converted to Mod. 1 to give improved target detection and shallower minimum depth; they have 300-m mooring depth capability. Though no longer considered operational, over 600 remain in storage for emergency use.

Mk 62 DST-36 Quickstrike series (Mods. 0–5)

Aircraft-dropped bottom mine. Converted from 500-lb (227-kg) Mk 82 standard aircraft bomb. Use either TDD Mk 57 magnetic/seismic, TDD Mk 58 magnetic/seismic/pressure, TDD Mk 70 magnetic/seismic, or TDD Mk 71 pressure/magnetic/seismic fuzes. Weight: 261 kg with 87-kg H-6 explosive charge. Length 2.26 m, diameter 384 mm.

Mk 63 DST-40 Quickstrike series (Mods. 0–5)

Aircraft-dropped bottom mine. Converted from 1,000-lb (454-kg) Mk 83 standard aircraft bomb. Uses either TDD Mk 57 magnetic/seismic, TDD Mk 58 magnetic/seismic/pressure, TDD Mk 70 magnetic/seismic, or TDD Mk 71 pressure/magnetic/seismic fuzes. Weight 459 kg, with 204-kg H-6 explosive charge. Length 2,80 m, diameter 572 mm.

Mk 64 DST-41 Quickstrike series (Mods. 0–5)

Aircraft-dropped bottom mine. Converted from 2,000-lb (908-kg) Mk 84 bomb. Uses either TDD Mk 57 magnetic/seismic, TDD Mk 58 magnetic/seismic/pressure, TDD Mk 70 magnetic/seismic, or TDD Mk 71 pressure/magnetic/seismic fuzes. Weight 902 kg, with 429-kg H-6 explosive warhead. Length 3.67 m, diameter 457 mm.

Mk 65 Quickstrike (Mods. 0, 1)

Air-launched bottom mine based on the 2,000-lb (908-kg) Mk 84 bomb. Approved for service 1983. Mod. 0 uses the Mk 57 magnetic/seismic fuze, Mod. 1 the Mk 58 magnetic/seismic/pressure fuze. Weight 1,084 kg, with . . . kg PBX explosive. Length 3.25 m, diameter 531 mm (737 mm across fins).

Note: Quickstrike-series mines being upgraded with the Mk 71 Target-Detecting Device. Procurement began in 2002.

Mk 66

A practice version of CAPTOR.

Notes: The Mk 67 SLMM (Submarine-Launched Mobile Mine) began to be phased out of service in 2000 and the joint U.S./U.K./Australian ISLMM (Improved Submarine-Launched Mobile Mine) program intended to replace it was terminated during 6-00.

Also under development is the aircraft-delivered Naval Mine 2010, sometimes called the Modular Autonomous Undersea Weapon System (MAUWS)

No surface ships are permanently equipped for minelaying except LCU 1641; portable rails have been developed and tested on a number of ship types. Naval aircraft of the S-3 and P-3 types are capable of laying mines, as are some Air Force B-52 bombers. All USN attack submarines, except early units of the SSN 688 class, can lay mines from their torpedo tubes.

E. RADARS

♦ Surface search and navigation

BPS-15, 15A, 15H: X-band. Made by Litton/Sperry Marine. Submarine search, navigational, and fire-control radar. Mounted on telescoping masts. Being updated to BPS-15H with Litton ECDIS-N (Electronic Chart Display and Information System) and Voyage Management System (VMS).

BPS-16(V): X-band. Successor to BPS-15. First of 35 delivered 1990. Being upgraded to BPS-16(V) with Litton ECDIS-N (Electronic Chart Display and Information System) and Voyage Management System (VMS). Used on most SSBNs and four late SSN 688 class. SSN 21 and *Virginia* classes employ the latest variant, BPS-16(V)4, which has clutter suppression features.

SPS-10: C-band, Mods. B through F in service. Made by Raytheon. Primary surface-search set before the introduction of SPS-55. Most have been replaced by SPS-67 in USN service.

SPS-53: X-band. Made by Litton/Sperry Marine. Navigational set replaced by later radars but is still in use abroad.

SPS-55: X-band, slotted waveguide antenna. Made by Cardion. On *Spruance*-class destroyers, FFG 7 frigates, *Avenger*-class minehunters, etc.

SPS-59: X-band. Official designation for the Canadian Marconi LN-66 navigational radar. Most have been replaced by SPS-69, SPS-73, and other later equipments.

SPS-64: X-band or S-band. Made by Raytheon. Range: about 48 n.m.; can automatically track 20 targets. Used by U.S. Coast Guard in (V) 1–4,6–8,10, and 11 versions [(V)4 and (V) 6 are S-band]; U.S. Navy in (V)9, 15, and 18 versions (all X-band); and by U.S. Army in (V)5, 12–14, 16, and 17 versions (all X-band). Commercial trade name is RM 1010, RM 1020, RM 1220, RM 1250, RM 1620, or Raypath plus four-digit number, depending on features. Uses 6-, 9-, or 12-ft. antenna, depending on version. Being replaced by the SPS-73 in Coast Guard service.

SPS-66: X-band. Raytheon 1900 Pathfinder navigational set.

SPS-67: C-band. Made by DRS Technologies, Gaithersburg, Maryland; formerly made by AIL Systems, Inc, div. Eaton Corp. (formerly Norden). A solid-state replacement for the SPS-10, using a similar antenna. Also has an ultra-short pulse mode for navigation. SPS-67(V)1 uses SPS-10 antenna; (V)2 has new antenna with vertical beam-width increased from 17 to 31.5 degrees, two scan rates (15 and 30 r.p.m.), and integrated IFF; (V)3 adds automatic detect and track, gunfire-control interface, motion-compensated digital moving target indicator, and track correlator/processor. More than 125 systems have been built for USN and foreign navies. Lightweight, sturdier (V)4 antenna is in development for the DDG 51–class destroyers and uses a bar-type antenna.

SPS-69: X-band. Raytheon 1900 Pathfinder raster-scan, solid-state replacement for SPS-66, with four different antennas: R20X and R40X in radomes and R21X and R41X slotted-waveguide. Four-kw max. power.

SPS-73: X-band. Japanese Furuno-designed radar made by Hughes Aircraft as successor to the SPS-64. Has a color display. Widely used by the U.S. Coast Guard.

SPS-. . .: DRS/Thales Scout low-probability-of-intercept surface search and navigational radar; being added to CG 52-CG 73 of the *Ticonderoga*-class and is aboard cable layer *Zeus.*

Note: The UPS-3 TDAR (Tactical Defense Alert Radar), a land-based portable set, is available for use aboard amphibious warfare ships. Japanese Furuno 8050D and 904 X-band navigational radars are widely employed on U.S. Navy service craft.

♦ Two-dimensional air-search

SPS-40 series: B-band (400–450 MHz); peak power 130 kw. Beam width 11 degrees in azimuth, 19 degrees in elevation. Made by Lockheed (SPS-40) and Sperry (SPS-40A), Norden (SPS-40B), and Westinghouse (SPS-40E). Range against medium bombers: 150–200 miles. Earlier SPS-40A models with mixed tube and transistor technology were modernized to SPS-40D; all-transistor SPS-40B sets were upgraded to SPS-40C with improved low-flyer detection, higher peak-power, ECCM improvements; SPS-40E is an update to B/C/D models with a solid-state transmitter with very low failure rate.

SPS-49: L-band (851–942 MHz). Made by Raytheon. (V)1 aboard FFG 7–class frigates; (V)2 for New Threat Upgrade (NTU) cruisers; (V)3 for Canadian *Halifax*-class frigates; (V)5 current version with digital pulse-doppler processing; and (V)7 for AEGIS ships. The MPRFU (Medium Pulse Repetition Frequency Upgrade) development was begun in mid-1995 by Raytheon under the sponsorship of the Naval Research Laboratory; new signal processing capabilities are added. The modernized radars are typed SPS-49A(V)1 and are being installed on FFGs, LSD 41/49–class landing ships, the LHD 1 class, and CVN 68, 69, and 76.

WEAPONS AND SYSTEMS *(continued)*

♦ Three-dimensional air-search

SEAPAR: Raytheon-Thales Nederland developmental Self-defense ESSM Active Phased-Array Radar intended to optimize the use of the ESSM version of the Sea Sparrow SAM. An X-band active, electronically scanned radar that will use technology developed for the Thales APAR and Raytheon SPY-3 radars, but in a more compact form. To be capable of horizon search to 30-km ranges and limited volume search at greater ranges; will be able to support four missile engagements simultaneously.

SPS-48C/E: S-band (2900–3100.5 MHz). Made by ITT-Gilfillan. SPS-48C had electronic frequency scanning in elevation; E version has doubled power, armored antenna, reduced side-lobe level, adaptive energy beam management, solid-state transmitter, and three transmitter power modes. SPS-48E radars added to CG 16– and CG 26–class cruisers during the early 1980s have been recycled to ships previously equipped with SPS-48C or SPS-52C sets.

SPY-1: S-band. Aegis system. Made by Lockheed Martin (formerly R.C.A.). Obtaining a directional effect by a steered electronic sweep, it has four fixed phased-array antennas that provide 360-degree coverage. There are 4,096 transmitting and 4,352 receiving elements to the antenna array. Long-range air-search, target-tracking, and missile-guidance. SPY-1B, with reduced side lobes, entered service 1988; SPY-1C developed for possible use on carriers; lighter-weight SPY-1D for DDG 51 program. SPY-1D(V) (formerly SPY-1E), with greater effectiveness against sea-skimming missiles and low-observable targets in cluttered coastal waters, is being introduced on DDG 87. The latest variant, AN/SPY-1D Baseline 7, was operationally certified during 9-05 and is carried aboard USS *Pinckney* (DDG 91). A development contract for a new SPY-1E was issued to Lockheed Martin on 20-2-02, with the prototype delivered by 2006 for use in the sea-based antiballistic missile program. SPY-1F, with 8-ft.-diameter antenna faces and a total of 1,856 transmitter elements, is to be used on Norwegian *Nansen*-class frigates, while SPY-1F(V), with enhanced littoral warfare and antiship missile combat capabilities, and SPY-1K, with a 5-ft. diameter antenna and 912 elements for use on small combatants, are on offer.

SPY-2 VSR: Volume-Search Radar. L (D)-band. A complement to the MFR; development contract not yet let, with Raytheon and Lockheed-Martin competing. Intended to be aboard the DD(X)-class DDG and CVN 77.

SPY-3: Multi-Function Radar (MFR). I/J (X)-band. Development contract for $140.4 million awarded Raytheon on 2-6-99 for a single multipurpose search, low-altitude target designation, target-tracking, and target-illumination radar for use on the DD 21 class and the CVN 77. In effect, it replaces the SPY-1-series Aegis radar and/or TAS Mk 23 and SPQ-9B. May be backfitted into CVN 70 through CVN 76 and installed on the *Zumwalt* class. Full 34,952-lb, $30-million system to use three 14,000-lb, 8-ft. by 6-ft by 2-ft–deep antenna arrays, each with several thousand receiver/transmitters. The land-based test version became operational around 2002.

SPQ-9B: X-band. Made by Northrop Grumman Electronic Systems. Successor to the TAS/Mk 23 system. Multimode, narrow-beam, pulse-doppler radar for detection of sea-skimming missiles at the horizon. Features narrow elevation and azimuth beam-widths; variable air channel pulse widths; fixed surface channel pulse width; very high clutter discrimination improvement; a high scan rate with single-scan detection and track; simultaneous air search, surface search, and beacon tracking; and built-in testing. The transmitter is the same as that used for the F-16 fighter's APG-68 radar. Initial use will be as a stand-alone system on the *San Antonio* class (LPD 17), but is to replace Mk 23 TAS on aircraft carriers. Five (with an update kit for a new, lightweight antenna) were ordered 21-2-01 for LPD 17-20 and CVN 69. Twenty-two are to be fitted aboard *Ticonderoga*-class CGs during modernizations.

TAS/Mk 23: L-band. Made by Hughes Ground Systems Group. Technically a Target Acquisition System, employing a rapidly rotating, stabilized linear-array antenna in conjunction with a UYK-20 computer to counter high- and low-angle aircraft and cruise-missile attacks. Range 20 n.m. on small missiles to 90 n.m. on aircraft. Mod. 1 is on the *Spruance* (DD 963) class, Mod. 2 (with UYA-4 console) on *Sacramento*-class AOE, and Mod. 3 on aircraft carriers and the LHD 1 and LHA 1 classes. Can track 54 targets simultaneously.

♦ Fire-control

Mk 86: SPG-60 and SPQ-9A radars combined into a single system. Made by Lockheed. Versions currently in use include Mod. 3 with Mk 152 computer in *Spruance*-class DD; Mod. 8, with UYK-7 computer in German DDG 2 class; Mod. 9, without the SPG-60 radar, in Aegis cruisers; Mod. 10, an upgrade to Mod. 3 substituting the UYK-7 computer; Mod. 11 (now inactivated), an upgraded Mod. 3 for the LHA 1 class; and Mod. 12, an upgraded Mod. 5.

Mk 90: Technically, the fire-control *system* for the General Dynamics Mk 15 Phalanx CIWS. Uses two radar antennas, one to track the target and one to track the outgoing stream of projectiles.

Mk 92: X-band. Made by Paramax. U.S. Navy adaptation of Dutch Hollandse Signaal Apparaaten (now Thales Nederland) WM-20 series track-while-scan gun/missile fire-control system, itself designated the Mk 94. Used in FFG 7 class and on Coast Guard cutters. Search and fire-control antennas dual-mounted in egg-shaped radome. Combined with a STIR (Separate Target Illumination Radar, a modified SPG-60) antenna in FFG 7 class. Improvement program in FFG 7 ended Phase I in 1984. Phase II CORT (Coherent Receive/Transmit) was intended to further update the system; six sets were authorized under FY 88 (one as a trainer) and first installed on FFG 61 and FFG 36. Further CORT upgrades were canceled. Radar antenna in all versions is the Mk 53 Mod. 0. Mk 92 Mod. 1 is in Coast Guard ships; Mod. 2 is version designed for use with STIR second-channel director in the FFG 7 class; Mod. 5 was the version for use on the Saudi Arabian PCG and PCC classes; and Mod. 6 is the CORT upgrade program version for use with the SYS-2 integrated automatic detection and tracking system.

Mk 95: Used with the Mk 91 fire-control system for the Sea Sparrow SAM system, with either one (Mod. 0) or two (Mod. 1) radar directors per Mk 29 launcher. The radar has separate transmitter and receiver antennas mounted on the same pedestal.

SPG-51B, C, D: Standard MR illuminator-tracker; used with Mk 74 missile fire-control system.

SPG-55A, B: Standard ER illuminator-tracker; used with Mk 76 missile fire-control system.

SPG-60: X-band. Made by Lockheed Martin. Standard MR missile system, four-horn monopulse, pulse-doppler illuminator-tracker for guns in conjunction with Mk 86 GFCS. STIR (Separate Target Illumination Radar) version, used on FFG 7 class, is modified for use with Mk 92 Mod. 2 missile/gun control system. Can track Mach 3.0 targets to 183 km. Has a co-mounted t.v. tracker.

SPG-62: X-band. Made by Raytheon. Standard SM-2 illuminator; used with Aegis system in CG 47 class. Slaved to SPY-1 Aegis system.

SPQ-9: X-band. Made by Lockheed. Track-while-scan special surface search and weapons control for use with Mk 86 GFCS. Antenna mounted in spherical radome. Range: 36 km. Received moving target indicator and "low noise front end" kits starting in 1989.

♦ Air-control radars

SPN-35A: X-band. Made by ITT-Gilfillan. Blind-approach radar, with antenna in large spherical radome. Ship-based version of the TPN-8.

SPN-42: Ka-band ACLS (Automated Carrier Landing System) radar with X-band beacon receiver for aircraft marshaling on LHD 1 and LHA 1 classes.

SPN-43A/B: S-band (3590–3700 MHz). Made by ITT-Gilfillan. The two-dimensional marshalling component of a landing system that also employs the SPN 42 or Textron SPN-46(V) controlling radar. Can also be used as a back-up air-search radar. Range is about 50 n.m. Has replaced SPN-35 installations in carriers by 1996.

SPN-46(V): Ka-band (33.0–33.4 GHz) and X-band. Made by Textron. Low-probability-of-intercept air traffic–control replacement for SPN-42, using the same AS-1347 antenna. Installed in pairs.

F. ELECTRONIC WARFARE COUNTERMEASURES SYSTEMS

Note: This section alphabetically lists systems classified as "countermeasures" by the U.S. Navy, including active and passive electronic systems; mine-countermeasures systems are listed separately at the end of this section.

ADC Mk 1–5, 7–10: Various expendable, submarine-launched decoys, most self-propelled.

APR-39: Litton Applied Technology Division helicopter radar-warning set adapted for use on *Cyclone*-class patrol craft. Commercial version, Triton, has been sold to Egypt.

AR-900: Commercial foreign sales system by ArgoSystems division of Boeing. Offers 360-degree intercept coverage from 2–18 GHz with 2–3-degree accuracy. Can track 500 emitters and library up to 5,000 signals. Argo also offers the CLOAC (Compact Lightweight Omnidirectional Active Countermeasures) system, APECS-II (Advanced Programmable Electronic Countermeasures System), and MAP (Maritime Patrol craft) system, as well as the earlier AR-700 system.

BLQ-10: Lockheed Martin, Syracuse, N.Y. Integrated EW system for the *Virginia*-class (SSN 774) submarine program; may be backfitted to the *Seawolf* class and to some SSN 688 class. First at-sea tests early in FY 00.

Note: The submarine-launched BLQ-11 Long-term Mine Reconnaissance System (LMRS) is discussed in the Mine-Countermeasures section.

BLR-1–10, 13, 15: Radar warning systems for submarines.

BLR-14: BSAWS (Basic Submarine Acoustic Warfare System). Made by Sperry. Used to detect, evade, and counter torpedoes employing the WLR-9A/12 detection systems and the WLR-14 processor. BLR-14 also directs the launching of countermeasures.

BZA: Beach Zone Array, a 45 × 45–m explosive net to clear beach landing zones of antipersonnel mines; deployed via a GPS-navigated glider from a CH-53E helicopter.

COBLU: Cooperative Outboard Logistics Update: An improved version of the SRS-1A system carried on new *Arleigh Burke* Flight IIA destroyers. See also the entry for SSQ-108.

CSA Mk 2: Countermeasures launching system for submarines, employing the Mk 151 launcher. Employed in ballistic missile and SSN 637– and SSN 688–class submarines.

Mk 30: Submarine target simulator, rather than an operational decoy. In service since 1978. Made by Goodyear Aerospace. Torpedo-like device, 6.223 m long by 533 mm in diameter, with an endurance of 30 minutes at 30 kts or up to 4 hrs at 7 kts and capable of operating in depths from 7.6 to 610 m. The Mk 30 can be preprogrammed to perform three-dimensional maneuvers or can be controlled by external acoustic signals. For training runs, is tracked by acoustic or magnetic sensors. Can emit acoustic signals or provide a specific magnetic signature. Only 16 were made, and they are operated at the Barking Sands Underwater Test Range, Hawaii; Atlantic Undersea Test and Evaluation Center (AUTEC), Bahamas; and Atlantic Fleet Warfare Training Facility, St. Croix.

Mk 33/34 RBOC: Rapid-Blooming Off-board Chaff launcher; largely replaced by Mk 36. Mk 33 employed four Mk 135 launchers and was used by frigate-sized and larger ships; Mk 34 employed only two launchers.

Mk 36 SRBOC: "Super-RBOC"—Mod. 1 with two six-tubed mortars for ships less than 140 m length; Mod. 2 with four six-tubed mortars for ships more than 140 m. All use 130-mm Mk 182 chaff-dispensing cartridges, which climb to 244 m; NATO Sea Gnat Mk 241 seduction and Mk 216 distraction rounds; and the Mk 245 Mod. 0 GIANT three-part infrared decoy. Employs the Mk 137 sextuple launcher with tubes fixed at 45-degree or 60-degree elevation. Sippican purchased the Hycor firm that developed and initially manufactured the system, and Hycor was taken over by Raytheon Systems. Several different decoys are in development for launching from the SRBOC system, including the HIRAM-III (Hycor Infrared Anti-Missile) decoy, TORCH floating infrared decoy, CAD radar simulator, ALEX (Automatic Launch of Expendables), and the Sippican-Office of Naval Research Multicloud projectile. Super Chaffstar is the commercial name for the Mk 214 Sea Gnat round. The parachute-equipped Mk 251 Siren active decoy round entered Royal Navy use during 2001. A Launchable-Expendable Acoustic Decoy (LEAD) torpedo decoy round entered service in 10-99; it employs Mk 12 rocket-powered and Mk 15 mortar rounds, both for use with Mk 137 launchers. The Naval Research Laboratory has developed the Multicloud multistage infrared decoy for the Mk 137 launcher to provide a more realistic decoy to incoming seeker systems.

Mk 53 SRBOC: Employs four twin, fixed, vertical launch containers to file Mk 214 and Mk 215 Nulka hovering decoy rockets. The launchers were originally to have been added to the Mk 137 launchers of the Mk 36 SRBOC system but are being installed in a separate group. The first 11 launchers were ordered during 2-99 for use on refitting *Ticonderoga*-class cruisers and *Arleigh Burke*–class destroyers.

WEAPONS AND SYSTEMS *(continued)*

Mk 70 MOSS: Mobile Submarine Simulator—small torpedo-like decoy device for launch by *Ohio*-class SSBNs.

SALAD: Shipboard Automatic Liquid Agent Detection. Detects traces of chemical, biological, and radiological agents. Tests completed 6-98, with eight sets to be ordered initially and 255 ultimately for installation on all surface ships. Production contract not yet placed.

Sea Nymph: Modular submarine SIGINT package; numerical designation not available.

SLA-12: Passive D/F and EW receiver used in conjunction with ULQ-6 and SLQ-22/23/24. Fixed and trainable antenna arrays.

SLA-15: Trainable tracker array for ULQ-6. No longer in USN service.

SLQ-20B: BAE Systems–made programmable shipboard signal processor system; an adjunct to the SLQ-32-series intercept systems. Used aboard CVNs and CG 47–class guided missile cruisers.

SLQ-25 Nixie: Towed noisemaker, made by Sensytech (formerly Northrop Grumman; formerly Aerojet). Employs two winches, each with one towed body, one acting as a spare. Being updated to SLQ-25A with an active component to defeat torpedo influence fuzes. SLQ-25B adds a towed torpedo detection array, a Multisensor Torpedo Recognition and Alertment Processor (MSTRAP) and Launched Expendable Acoustic Decoy (LEAD), the latter to be launched by the Raytheon (ex-*Suippican*, ex-*Hycor*) Mk 137 launchers of the Mk 36 and Mk 50 SRBOC decoy systems.

SLQ-29: The combined WLR-1H/WLR-8/WLR-11 package.

SLQ-32(V)1: Raytheon radar warning (H, I, J bands) for auxiliaries and amphibious ships; most now upgraded to (V)2.

SLQ-32(V)2: Radar warning (B–J bands) for newer destroyers and frigates; replaced WLR-1 where it had been fitted.

SLQ-32A(V)3: Radar warning (B–J bands) and jamming/spoofing (H–J bands) for cruisers and major amphibious ships.

SLQ-32A(V)4: Replacement for SLQ-17 on carriers.

SLQ-32A(V)5: SLQ-32(V)2 with Sidekick active jammer adjunct.

Note: Northrop Grumman (not Raytheon, the usual manufacturer) received a contract on 24-7-02 for four upgraded SLQ-32A(V) sets that would not be delivered until 2007.

SLQ-33: A ship-towed acoustic deception device.

SLQ-34: The Classic Outboard (Organizational Unit Tactical Baseline Operational Area Radio Detection Countermeasures Exploitation) intelligence collection system, with SRD-19 D/F and SLR-16. Carried in 28 ships. Being superceded by the "Combat D/F" system, which will be carried by later units of the DDG 51 class.

Note: Mine-countermeasures associated SLQ-series systems are described in Section J, Mine Countermeasures, which follows.

SLQ-39: Chaff-dispensing buoy, made by Raytheon.

SLQ-41–47: Active expendable EW buoys.

SLQ-49: Air- or surface-launched inflatable decoy, known as "Rubber Duck." U.S. version of U.K. DLF(2). Some 1,650 were procured from Irvin Aerospace, Ltd. Decoys weigh 68 kg each in GRP containers and are deployed from overside launchers. In 1999, the U.S. Navy was evaluating DLF(3), which can create the illusion of a 50,000-m^2 target. A normal complement is 70 buoys per ship in the Royal Navy.

SLQ-50: The Battle-Group Passive Horizon-Extension System (BGPHES), by E-Systems. Employs airborne passive intercept detector and shipboard processing system comprising three UYQ-23 terminals.

SLQ-650: Small ship EW system using SLR-640 intercept and SLQ-630 jammer.

SLR-16: HF SIGINT receiver set using SRD-19 antenna arrays; part of the SSQ-72 Classic Outboard system. Made by Lockheed Martin (formerly Southwestern Research Inst.).

SLR-23: Intercept D/F, J band; works with WLR-1 and SLQ-32. Made by Lockheed Martin (formerly Southwestern Research Inst.).

SLR-24: A towed torpedo detection array. In service since 1995 on the carrier *Nimitz*.

SLR-600: EW intercept system for small ships (2–20 gHz).

SLR-610: Another small-ship EW intercept system (6.5–22 gHz).

SLR-640: Improved SLR-610.

SLT-5, 8: Communications jammers.

SLX-1 MSTRAP: Multi-Sensor Torpedo Recognition and Alertment Processor—Westinghouse processor using existing sonar suites to provide alerting data to countermeasures against antiship torpedoes. Trials were conducted during 1997 aboard the *Arleigh Burke* (DDG 51). In 5-99 14 production sets were ordered from Northrop Grumman Oceanic and Naval Systems for delivery by 3-00.

SLY-2(V) AIEWS: Advanced Integrated Electronic Warfare System. Being developed under a 1998 contract by Lockheed Martin as the successor to the SLQ-32 series. Canceled 15-4-02 due to cost overruns and delays, but may be reinstated, as there is nothing else to replace the obsolete SLQ-32 series. Was to have been installed in the CG 47–class cruisers, DDG 51– and DD-21–class destroyers, the LPD 17 and other amphibious ship classes, and aircraft carriers. Employs COTS components and other existing hardware and software. Formerly designated SLQ-52.

SRD-19: Classic Outboard system's LF/MF/VHF shipboard SIGINT exploitation component, using 24 small deck-edge antennas, whip antennas, and a masthead Adcock-type VHF D/F array; used in conjunction with SLR-16 as part of the SSQ-72 system. Made by Lockheed Martin (formerly by Southwestern Research).

SRS-1: Combat DF Block 0. Less elaborate version of SSQ-72/108 Classic Outboard to detect, process, and target threat signals. Made by Lockheed Martin (formerly Southwestern Research Inst.). SRS-1A adds Automated Digital Acquisition Subsystem to exploit "unconventional and low-probability-of-intercept signals." SRS-1 (Block 0) is in the *Wasp* (LHD 1)-class amphibious ships and the *Arleigh Burke* Flight II (DDG 72) and Flight IIA destroyers. SRS-1A is to be backfitted or fitted in the same ships and three shore stations.

SSQ-72: Classic Outboard Combat D/F suite, with SRD-19 and SLR-16 antennas (the later SSQ-74 is on DD 974). SSQ-108 is a more elaborate version, of which more were acquired.

SSQ-95(V): Active Electronic Buoy (AEB) by Litton/Magnavox. Fits in A-size sonobuoy housing and inflates in water; seawater-activated battery. Weighs 17.2 kg and is 914 mm long.

SSQ-108: Classic Outboard (Organizational Unit Tactical Baseline Operational Area Radio Detection Countermeasures Exploitation System) Combat D/F suite, by Sanders Surveillance Systems; current version of SSQ-72, used by U.S. Navy and Royal Navy. Sanders received a contract to update 35 and U.K. systems with a COBLU (Cooperative Outboard Logistics Update) in 6-00. Operates in the HF, UHF, and VHF bands. COBLU was installed on some CG 47–class and all DDG 51 Batch IIA ships by 2005.

SSTDS: Surface Ship Torpedo Decoy System, an umbrella program encompassing towed and hull-mounted sensors to detect torpedoes and, for highly valuable ships such as aircraft carriers, launchers for modified Mk 46 ASW torpedoes to counter Russian Type 65-80 wake-homing torpedoes; the first 172 production active countermeasures were procured under the FY 93 budget. Phase-I, introduced in 1987, employed the SLQ-25A Nixie. Deliveries of Phase-II, with the SLR-24 detector, began in the mid-1990s. Raytheon received a contract 1-92 to develop the DCLASP (Detection-Classification-Localization Acoustic Signal Processor) in connection with the SSTDS program. Parallel program with U.K. canceled 7-94. U.S. program, with SLR-24 processor and modified Mk 46 torpedoes, did not pass operational evaluation during mid-1994, and a new joint U.K./U.S. development program contract planned to be let in 1-95 was canceled 9-96.

T-Mk 6 Fanfare: Mechanical towed antitorpedo noisemaker. No longer in USN service but still used by foreign fleets.

TRAFS (Torpedo Recognition and Alertment Functional Segment): An adjunct added to eight *Ticonderoga*-class CGs and nine *Spruance*-class DDs by 12-99 that integrates sensors of the SQQ-89 sonar suite to provide a torpedo detection and countermeasures capability. An outgrowth of the Northrop Grumman SLX-1 program.

ULQ-6: Deception repeater/jammer in cruisers, destroyers; largely replaced by SLQ-32(V)3 in high-value ships, but still in use on a few ships transferred abroad.

ULQ-21: Function uncertain. As of 12-00, 371 sets were in use.

Ultrabarricade: A trainable, elevatable decoy launcher, made by Wallop, in the U.K. Initial U.S. installation on PC 14, with several dozen launchers purchased in 2000 and more in the future as a replacement for the SRBOC system. Launcher carries 24 quick-reaction 102-mm rocket decoys in groups of three, plus two tube-launchers, trains through 270 degrees and elevates to 70 degrees. Fires 20–80-meter range seduction, 400–600-m range dump, 800–1,000-m range distraction, and 1,800–12,000-m-range confusion decoys and can also launch illumination rockets, torpedo decoys, and (potentially) small artillery rockets, point-defense missiles, active off-board decoys, and laser and optical obscurants.

URD-9(V): Radar D/F (225–400 MHz).

URD-27: Broadcast frequency D/F device for SIGINT (250 MHz–18 gHz).

WLQ-4E: Sea Nymph ESM system developed by GTE-Sylvania. WLQ-4(V)1 is used by the *Seawolf* class.

WLR-1H(V)7: Obsolescent intercept and analysis system still aboard CVN 65 and CV 67.

WLR-3: Radar warning and signal collection—installed in some surface ships and also in some submarines.

WLR-4: ESM receiver.

WLR-5: Acoustic intercept receiver.

WLR-6: Reconnaissance signal collection system; called Waterboy in submarines. Made by Aitken Industries.

WLR-8: Radar warning system covering 0.5–18 gHz; (V)2 for the SSN 688 class; (V)5 version in *Ohio*-class SSBNs. Surface-ship version canceled 1983, although one (V)3 set was installed in the carrier *Enterprise*. Made by GTE-Sylvania.

WLR-9: Sonar detection system.

WLR-10: Radar warning receiver for submarines; shares telescoping mast array with WLR-8(V)2/5.

WLR-11A: Radar warning/SIGINT system. 7–18 gHz. Uses WLR-1's antenna suite.

WLR-13: Infrared/electro-optical warning receiver.

WSQ-5: Portable ELINT collection system for SSN 688 class; known as Cluster Spectator. Made by Watkins-Johnson.

WSQ-11 Tripwire: An active torpedo-countermeasure antitorpedo torpedo system intended to intercept and destroy attacking torpedoes at ranges up to 5,000 yards. Will be mounted on carriers, large combatants, and major amphibious warfare ships and will use 160-mm launch tubes or modified CSA Mk 2 submarine countermeasures launch tubes. Contract award is expected in 2008 with IOC expected around 2011.

G. SONARS

♦ Bottom arrays:

ADS: The Advanced Deployable System is a rapidly deployable undersea surveillance system under development by Lockheed Martin Federal Systems. Capable of being deployed by small craft operating from amphibious ships or laid by submarines or aircraft in littoral areas. The initial demonstration contract was signed during 4-95 with work on the project continuing throughout 2006–7.

FDS-C: Fixed Distributed Systems-COTS (commercial), being developed from the canceled FDS program. Uses an Underwater Segment (UWS) in development by Lucent; an associated Shore Signal and Information Processing System (SSIPS) is under development by Lockheed Martin. Would employ fixed, bottom-deployed sensor arrays either in deep-ocean areas or across choke points and could also be deployed in strategic shallow-water areas. To use an all-fiber-optic passive hydrophone array. Essentially a successor to the SOSUS system.

SOSUS (Sound Surveillance System): Underwater acoustic detection and monitoring system for tracking of submarines, surface ships, fish, marine mammals, and seismic events. Originally developed in the 1950s and continuously modified and updated since.

♦ On surface ships:

Distant Thunder: BBN Technologies completed trials with four sets of its "Distant Thunder" developmental sonar for the DARPA early in 1998. The system provides a low-frequency, multistatic active sonar for organic rapid area-search and localization of quiet diesel-electric submarines in "acoustically adverse" waters. Trials with 10 upgraded versions in South Korean waters during 1999 were said to be extremely successful.

WEAPONS AND SYSTEMS *(continued)*

LBVDS: Lightweight Broadband Variable-Depth Sonar. Lockheed Martin developmental program for a 1–6-kHz active, towed sonar array originally intended for use with the SQQ-89(V)15 sonar suite on the *Zumwalt* (DD 21) class; intended to improve submarine detection to ranges of 12–15 n.m. in shallow waters.

MFTA: Multi-Function Towed Array. Towed array system for use on DDG 51–class units post-2005 and later on the DD 21 class in conjunction with the SQQ-89(V)15 sonar suite. Array would have high-, medium-, and low-frequency modules, a dual-density tow cable, and the existing tow winch from the SQR-19 system.

SLR-24: A towed linear passive torpedo detection sensor, in service since 1995 aboard the carrier *Nimitz* (CVN 68) as part of the CST Mk 1 torpedo-countermeasures system.

SQQ-14: High-frequency, minehunting, and classification set in variable-depth, retractable-transducer array for mine-countermeasures ships. Essentially combines the 1950s-developed UQS-1 for detection and the U.K.-developed Type 193 sonar for classification. Search mode 80 kHz; 350 kHz for classification. Retractable strut version deployed to 46 m, cable-deployed version (currently in use) to 120 m. Entered service 1960. No longer in USN service, but is still found on ships transferred abroad, and it has been made under license in Italy.

SQQ-28: LAMPS-III helicopter datalink processing system; not a sonar, but employed in ASW.

SQQ-30: Minehunting sonar developed by General Electric for use on mine-countermeasures ships. Essentially a digital, solid-state SQQ-14, using cable-tow transducer deployment to greater depths. Superceded by SQQ-32.

SQQ-32: Raytheon/Thales sonar for later units of the MCM 1 class and for the MSH 1 class. Separate detection and classification transducers lowered through well and towed well below the hull. Uses two UYK-44 computers. Performed extremely well during operations in the Persian Gulf in 1991.

SQQ-89: Suite integrating the SQR-19 towed array, SQS-53B hull-mounted sonar, Mk 116 Underwater Fire Control System, LAMPS-III helicopter, SQQ-28 processor, and UYQ-28 SIMAS (Sonar In-Situ Mode Assessment System) for cruisers, destroyers, and frigates. Trials in DD 980 late 1985. Acoustic Video Processor added under FY 90. Its planned successor, SQQ-89I, has been redesignated SQY-1. The designation SQQ-89 is the result of an administrative error; the system was to have been numbered SQQ-39; there were no SQQ-40 through 88.

The SQQ-89(V)6 baseline system incorporated the USQ-132 Tactical Decision Support System, UYQ-25 Sonar In Situ Mode Assessment System (SIMAS II), USH-XX System Level Recorder, and SQQ-89 Adjunct Processor, with one TAC-3 and one UYQ-65 workstations. Backfits to earlier installations of SQQ-89 include Block I, with a multisensor torpedo warning feature linked to decoy systems; Block II, for shallow water operations, with an echo tracker classifier and reduced false-target generation; Block III, a multistatic upgrade and acoustic processor to provide below-the-layer processing of sonar signals from the active sonar on the helicopter and the SQS-53C sonar; and Block IV, which added a broadband variable-depth sonar capability. DDG 91 and later are to have the SQQ-89(V)15, which will incorporate controls and displays for the WLD-1(V)1 remote minehunting vehicle system. The 100th SQQ-89-series system was installed on DDG 87.

SQR-17: Passive classification device for processing data transmitted from sonobuoys via the now-retired SH-2G SeaSprite LAMPS-I helicopters in Naval Reserve FFG-7 frigates. Uses SKR-4 link receiver, AKT-22 link, ARR-75 sonobuoy receiver, UYS-1 processor. For shipboard use, 97 sets were procured by 1989 (far more than ever would have been needed), plus 16 for Naval Reserve Mobile Inshore Undersea Warfare units.

SQR-18A: TACTAS (Tactical Towed Acoustic Sensor). Built by EDO; 47 sets delivered by 1989; 12 more SQR-18A ordered 6-88 for use on now-deactivated FF 1052 class equipped with SQS-35 VDS; array attached to VDS towed body. Normal cable length is 1,706 m; towed at depths up to 366 m; array is 82.6-mm diameter, 222.5 m long. SQR-18(V)1, with 730-m cable was aboard 35 FF 1052–class ships; it used eight modular hydrophone sections. SQR-18A(V)2 used SQR-19 towing rig for the non-VDS-equipped units of the FF 1052 class and had a 1,524-m tow cable. No longer in use by U.S. Navy.

SQR-19A/B: Improved TACTAS for use on CG 47, DD 963, and FFG 7 classes; deployed through port in stern. 1,707 m cable. Has 16 acoustic reception modules in array: eight VLF, four LF, two MF, two HF. UYQ-21 display. SQR-19A has UYH-3 data storage vice UYH-2. SQR-19B has four UYK-44 computers vice UYK-20; began deliveries 1-91. Most have been stored ashore, due to USN's de-emphasis on ASW, changes in operating areas, and fiscal constraints.

SQS-26: Bow-mounted, low-frequency set, in AXR, BX, and CX versions. Transmits at around 3.5 kHz and receives between 1.5–4.0 kHz. No longer in USN use but is found on *Knox*-class frigates transferred abroad.

SQS-53: SQS-26 with digital computer interface, for use with Mk 116 UWFCS (Underwater Fire Control System) on DD 963, DDG 993, CG 47 classes. The digital SQS-53B (General Electric/Hughes Electronics) has multiple target tracking and classification aids, weapons checkout routines, UYK-44 imbedded computers, UYQ-21 display, UYS-1 signal processor, a 60% reduction in required manning, 2,000-hour mean time between failures, and a 30-minute mean time to repair. SQS-53C has improved active performance, simultaneous active/passive modes, more power, greater bandwidth, UYH-1 mass memory, faster reaction time, etc. SQS-53C Kingfisher/SWAK (Shallow-Water Active Kit) provided a 120° forward-arc mine-avoidance capability at 2.5, 5, 10, and 20 kiloyard range scales; EC-16 (Engineering Change 16) added the same capability to SQS-53A/B ships (DDG 993–996, CG 47–55). EC-84 added the same capability to the DD 963 class. First ten of latest variant, SQS-53D, were ordered 30-12-96.

SQS-56: U.S. Navy variant of the Raytheon 1160B commercial active-passive, hull-mounted, medium-frequency set; used in FFG 7 class. Operates at 5.6, 7.5, and 8.4 kHz. All active units have been or will be equipped with Kingfisher mine-avoidance system covering a 90° forward arc; Engineering Change 10 (EC-10) added SWAK (Shallow-Water Active Kit) with additional display capabilities to the 12 FFGs with the CORT combat system upgrade.

SQS-58: Raytheon. Special set for private R&D trials ship *Sub Sig II;* solid-state MF set, offered for export sale as the DE 1167 system.

SQY-1: Successor system to SQQ-89, with first installations to be in later units of the DDG 51 class. Initially called SQQ-89I and later SQQ-89(V)X. Still in development, it will employ about 50% COTS computers and software (and later 100% COTS equipment) for sonar signal processing, fire control, and training. Both versions will employ Link 16 to link with MH-60R helicopters and their sonar sensors.

UQQ-2 SURTASS: Surveillance Towed-Array Sonar System, for use in the *Stalwart* (T-AGOS 1) class. Tows 1,830-m passive hydrophone array at about 3 knots. Since 1994 a Twin-Line, dual-array version has been employed by *Bold* (T-AGOS 12), and later *Assertive* (T-AGOS 9), to detect small diesel submarines in waters as shallow as 50 m; funding for six more Twin Line arrays were acquired under the FY 00 budget; they are to be cross-decked to ships for operation in littoral waters. Original UQQ-2 arrays are being refurbished to A-180R status with COTS telemetry and 180 acoustic channels.

♦ On submarines

Advanced Mine Detector Sonar (AMDS): A chin-mounted active sonar for the *Los Angeles* class installed for trials in *Asheville* (SSN 758); the configuration includes a large-diameter horizontal array with two protruding transducer domes.

BQG-5A Wide Aperture Array: The BQG-5 passive sonar receiving set was demonstrated aboard *Augusta* (SSN 710) in 1985, is fitted in the *Seawolf* (SSN 21), and was backfitted in one SSN 688I–class unit in 1997. The more affordable BQG-5A was ordered 27-12-95 from Lockheed Martin Federal Systems, working in cooperation with Raytheon, Northrop Grumman, and Litton Industries, and is being fitted on other SSN 688I–series and *Virginia*-class submarines. BQG-5A uses COTS equipment and a repackaged UYQ-70 display console; the first system was delivered in 1999.

BQQ-5: Active-passive system on the SSN 21– and SSN 688–class attack submarines and on *Parche* (SSN 683). Incorporates BQS-11, -12, or -13 spherical bow hydrophone array. BQQ-5C has expanded DIFAR reception. BQQ-5D, with TB-23 long-aperture, thin-line array, operational 1988. BQQ-5E is integrated with the TB-29 thin-line towed passive array. BQQ-5E(V)4, with no active element, is the suite used by later units of the *Ohio*-class.

BQQ-6: Passive-only version of the BQQ-5 system, for earlier units of the SSBN 726 class; has 944 hydrophone transducers mounted on a spherical frame.

BQQ-9: Towed array signal-processing system for BQR-15; made by Rockwell. Is the TASPE (Towed Array Signal Processing Equipment) for the *Ohio* class.

BQQ-10 A-RCI: Acoustic Rapid COTS Insertion sonar suite to update and coordinate existing BSY-1 and BQQ-5 or BQQ-6 sonar equipment in the SSN 688/688I classes. Made by Lockheed Martin, Manassas, Virginia.

BQR-15: Towed array sonar system in *Ohio* class. Uses a 45.7-m-long array of 42 hydrophones towed by a 670-m cable.

BQR-19: Active, short-range, navigational set for SSBNs. Raytheon.

BQR-23: STASS (Submarine Towed Array Sonar System) processor. Current version: BQR-23A.

BQS-13: Raytheon. Active component of the BQQ-5 system; low-frequency transmission (around 3.5 kHz).

BQS-15: Under-ice active set tailored to the requirements of the SSN 688 class.

BQS-20: High frequency, under-ice and mine-avoidance set, used mostly on later SSNs. Part of the BQQ-2, -5, and -6 systems.

BQS-24: MIDAS (MIne Detection and Avoidance Sonar) active set for the SSN-688 SSNs and *Ohio*-class SSBNs.

BSY-1 SUBACS: "Basic" BSY-1 version is suite for SSN 651–773. Uses UYS-1 signal processor and has USH-26 signal recorder and UYK-20A data processor. Passive arrays plus SADS (Submarine Active Detection Sonar, i.e., BQS-24) and towed passive array. IBM is prime contractor. First suite delivered 7-87; SSN 756 and later have full capabilities.

BSY-2: For *Seawolf* class, uses distributed processing and has six ship data displays and 11 consoles. Associated sensors include an external spherical bow array, an LF bow array inside the bow, and active hemispherical array in the lower part of the bow, an HF active array (BQS-24) in the sail, the BQG-5 Wide Aperture Array on the flank, the long TB-12X towed array, and a shorter TB-16D towed array. General Electric is prime contractor.

WLY-1: An acoustic intercept system for the *Virginia* class; used to provide target identification, range, and bearing.

♦ On helicopters

AQS-14: Mine-countermeasures set used by MH-53E helicopters. Being updated to AQS-14A with laser E/O scanner; initial one-year development contract issued to Northrop Grumman during 5-99, with the AQS-14A(V1) officially entering service on 4-10-02 with Helicopter Minesweeping Squadron 14 (HM-14) at Norfolk, Virginia.

AQS-20: Towed mine detection set for the MH-53E to replace AQS-14 and for use by the MH-60S multipurpose helicopter. Made by Raytheon (formerly Westinghouse, with EDO and ARINC). Also to be developed for use as a mine-warning sensor for surface ships, and it will be integrated into the Boeing BLQ-11 Long-term Mine Reconnaissance System (LMRS), along with an airborne laser minehunting system, airborne mine-neutralization system, a shallow-water influence minesweep system, and the Rapid Airborne Mine-Countermeasures System. Planned to enter service in 2007 for use in waters 30–600-ft. deep. An AQS-20X version with a laser mine identification feature is also planned. AQS-20/X is a version intended for tow by the MH-60S helicopter; the volume-search sonar is replaced by an Areté Associates E/O mine identification device.

AQS-22: Raytheon/Thales Undersea Systems-Thales FLASH (Folding Light Acoustic Sonar), initially intended for up to 185 SH-60B and 158 SH-60F helicopters but IOC achieved in 2005 aboard new MH-60R helicopters. Also known as ALFS—Airborne Low-Frequency Sonar.

♦ Sonobuoys

A wide variety are in use, including those listed, which are current production:

SSQ-36	Bathythermograph
SSQ-53D	DIFAR
SSQ-57	Special-Purpose
SSQ-62B	DICASS
SSQ-75	ERAPS
SSQ-77A/B	VLAD
SSQ-86	DLC
SSQ-102	ADAR TSS
SSQ-110	EER (Extended Echo Ranging); drops explosive charges on command to create echoes

Note: DICASS = DIrectional Command-Activated Sonobuoy System; VLAD = Vertical Line-Array DIFAR; ERAPS = Expendable Reliable Acoustic Path Sonobuoy (descends to up to 16,000-ft. depths); ADAR TSS = Air-Deployed Active Receiver Tactical Surveillance Sonar (a bistatic/multistatic sonobuoy that can work with a shipboard sonar acting as its illuminator). SSQ-71 and SSQ-86 are two-way, aircraft/submarine communications buoys.

WEAPONS AND SYSTEMS *(continued)*

H. ELECTRO-OPTICAL SYSTEMS

IRST: Infrared search and track system; made by Lockheed Martin and Raytheon Systems. Provides automatic surveillance, detection, and tracking of potential targets, plus detection of low-altitude antiship missiles. Testing took place between 1999 and 2004 with no production decision yet announced.

Mk 46 Mod. 0: Kollmorgen optronic gun fire-control and surveillance system, mounted on *Arleigh Burke*–class DDGs. Improved Mod. 1 variant is aboard DDG 85 and later.

TISS: Thermal Imaging Sensor System. Boeing, Huntington Beach, California, modular system ordered 10-95. Some 24 were procured for deployment aboard frigates and destroyers attached to the Mid-East 5th Fleet.

I. TACTICAL DATA PROCESSING

ACDS: Advanced Combat Direction System. An outgrowth of the SSDS system and, in effect, the successor to NTDS. Uses satellite and platform-to-platform datalinks and employing COTS components. Used aboard non-Aegis ships, including aircraft carriers and major amphibious warfare ships (LHA, LHD).

Project Akcita: Not an acronym, the name was taken from the Lakota Sioux Indian tribal self-defense force. Intended to provide an integrated air defense system for the CVN 76–class carriers, DD 21 destroyers, and the LPD 17–class landing ships, Akcita will incorporate elements of a multifunction radar, the Evolved Sea Sparrow missile, and the Advanced Integrated Electronic Warfare System (AIEWS), the latter of which will include advanced decoys such as the Australian Nulka. The first unit to have the system is expected to be LPD 22, completing after 2006. The new D-band radar will incorporate monolithic microwave integrated-circuit technology and will be able to track more than 1,000 targets to ranges of 400 km. Akcita will incorporate and supercede the technology of the earlier Ship Self-Defense System.

ULQ-20 BGPHES-ST: Battle Group Passive Horizon Extension System. In development for more than a decade by Navy SPAWAR and Raytheon. Intended to extend battle-group passive threat detection range to 900 n.m. by controlling remote receivers on a deployed aircraft, with data transmitted to the flagship's surface terminal via the Common High Bandwidth Data Link (CHBDL). Interoperable with USAF U-2 reconnaissance aircraft. Was to have been installed in ES-3A shipboard aircraft (now in storage). The sensors are carried in Air Force U-2R aircraft, and the data collected are to be received and analyzed at workstations aboard 23 carriers and LHA/LHD. Trials were conducted 1996 in *John F. Kennedy* (CV 67).

USG-1 and USG-2 CEC (Cooperative Engagement Capability): Intended to link all radar and ESM sensors and all target data within a distributed fleet so that any target can be defended against any attack by any ship within range, regardless of whether the target or the firing ship holds the threat on its own sensors. Uses data from sensors on Aegis-equipped ships, aircraft carriers, and major amphibious warfare ships (including the new LPD 17 class). Link is maintained via a circular Data Distribution System antenna mounted on the principal mast. Development began 1990 by Johns Hopkins University Applied Physics Lab in cooperation with Raytheon and other companies. First ships equipped with USG-1 for trials in 1993–94 with developmental equipment were carrier *Eisenhower* (CVN-69), cruisers *Anzio* (CG 68) and *Cape St. George* (CG 70) and helicopter carrier *Wasp* (LHD 1); also used was a Customs Service P-3 Orion aircraft with APS-38 radar.

In FY 97, two more CGs, a CVN, and one LHA were to be equipped with the AN/USG-2 Common Equipment Set, production version of the CEC; 26 additional units were to have the system by end-FY 01. In 6-98, however, the planned operational test for the production CEC system was delayed two years because of the scope of the systems integration effort. With USG-2, total weight was reduced from original USG-1's 9,000-lb to only 550 lb. As of 12-96, the CEC program envisioned there being some 122 ships with the system as of the end of FY 07, but the number has since been greatly curtailed. Authorization to purchase sets for LPD 18, DDG 84–86, DDG 91–92, CVN 69, and two E-2C Hawkeye aircraft was given on 1-5-00, but plans to install it on the LSD 41 and LHA 1 classes were dropped in 6-00.

Live-fire tests conducted 9-5-00 through 24-5-00 with the *Kennedy* (CV 67) Battlegroup off Puerto Rico were highly successful. A successful technical evaluation (TECHEVAL) from 9-2-01 to 3-3-01 led to an equally successful Operational Evaluation during May and June 2001; the system has demonstrated resistance to jamming.

NTDS (Naval Tactical Data System): Uses USQ-20 digital computers to give an overall picture of a tactical situation—air, surface, and underwater—and enables the commander to employ the means necessary to oppose the enemy. Excellent automatic data transmission systems (Link 11 and Link 14) permit the exchange of tactical information with similarly equipped ships and P-3C Orion and S-3B Viking aircraft carrying the Air Tactical Data System (ATDS) and amphibious landing forces equipped with NTDS. Now used aboard only FFG 7 and LCC 19 classes.

Note: The Tactical Flag Command Center (TFCC) was superceded by the NTCS-A (Naval Tactical Command System-Afloat), which employs COTS DTC, TAC-3, and TAC-4 computers.

All ships are equipped to receive commercial SATCOM (Satellite Communications) messages, although most can send ultra-high-frequency (UHF) messages via satellite and at least 31 can transmit and receive super-high-frequency (SHF) messages. T-AGOS sonar surveillance ships first used the AN/WSC-6-series VHF SATCOM system, which is now widely installed in combatants in the Raytheon WSC-6(V) 4, (V)5, and (V)6 and Harris WSC-6(V)8 (or WSC-9) models. EHF SATCOM employs the USC-38 terminal, which was to be replaced starting in 2001 with a new system from Raytheon.

WSC-8 (Challenge Athena): A program to employ C-band commercial satellite systems to transmit data at very high rates (1,544,000 bits/s). It is used to transmit intelligence data such as imagery and also for shipboard personnel communications with family members at home. It employs a 2.7-m-diameter radome-enclosed dish antenna. First trialed on *George Washington* (CVN 73), it has been widely deployed since then; a datalink system is to be developed to allow CG, DDG, and FFG to link with Challenge Athena equipment on the larger ships.

CHBDL: Common High-Bandwidth Data Link, which permits data from various remote collection platforms to be received and distributed to various shipboard users; the system supports the Advanced Tactical Airborne Reconnaissance System (ATARS) and the Battle Group Passive Horizon Extension System (BGPHES). Successful trials in *John F. Kennedy* (CV 67) resulted in an initial contract in 1-98 for further systems.

ICAN: Integrated Communications and Advanced Network. Being developed for aircraft carrier use by Northrop Grumman to integrate all aircraft carrier internal communications and data transmission systems. First installation was on the carrier *Nimitz* (CVN 68) in 2001, with the system also to be aboard the *Ronald Reagan* (CVN 76), CVN 77, and the refitted *Eisenhower* (CVN 69). Encountered several developmental delays as early as 2002.

IT-21: Information Technology for the 21st Century: A standard "architecture" for data and transmission capacity imposed on shipboard and land information (command, control, communications, and intelligence) facilities to ensure intercommunication. Initially deployed with CVN 65 in late 1998 and aboard CV 67 in 1999, CVN 70 in 2000, all carrier group and amphibious ready groups by 2003, and all shore facilities by 2008. Allows IT-21 ships and facilities to optimize the use of their existing equipment with commercial computing and satellite communications services.

JMICS (Joint Maritime Information Communications System): Used to pass Tomahawk targeting data worldwide. Uses the NTCS-A imagery exploitation work station.

JOTS (Joint Operations Terminal System): A display terminal.

JSIPS (Joint Services Imagery Processing System): System for receiving satellite and other imagery via communications satellites; installed on carriers, all LHA/LHD, and LCC 19 and 20.

NFN (Naval Fires Network): A "network-centric warfare system that provides real-time intelligence correlation, sensor control, target generation, mission planning, and battle-damage assessment capabilities, while also enabling real-time engagement of time-critical targets." Installed on CVN 74 under FY 01 funding and CVN 72 during 2002. Is planned to be fitted aboard LCC 19, LHA 1 and LHA 3, LHD 2, and CV 63 and CV 64, with future plans calling for fitting it to submarines, additional surface ships, and surveillance aircraft.

NTCS-A: An imagery exploitation work station that employs COTS DTC, TAC-3, and TAC-4 computers.

SSDS (Ship Self-Defense System, Mk 1/Mk 2): Hughes Naval and Maritime Systems Program to provide 31 non-Aegis ships with an integrated air-defense system through linking existing sensors and weapons. Trials conducted with *Ashland* (LSD 48) commencing 3-97, using the existing SPS-49 and SPS-67 radars, the SLQ-32 intercept system, the Mk 36 decoy launch system, and the Phalanx and RAM weapons systems; ships equipped with NATO Sea Sparrow and Evolved Sea Sparrow will also have those weapons integrated. Lack of funding has seriously hurt the program, which was originally to have been extended to FFG 7–class frigates and DD 963–class destroyers; current plans call for a slowdown in fleet introduction and reduction of the number of affected ships to the LHD 1–, LSD 41–, and LPD 17–class amphibious warfare ships and to aircraft carriers. *Dwight D. Eisenhower* (CVN 69) and *Wasp* (LHD 1) received the first ACDS (Advanced Combat Defense System) Block 1 variant of the system. No systems were bought with FY 98 funding, but about 3–4 per year were to be acquired from FY 99 on. *Nimitz* (CVN 68) received an SSDS Mk 2 Mod. 0 installation during 2001; installation aboard 22 additional warships is planned by 2011.

J. MINE-COUNTERMEASURES DEVICES

♦ Surface-ship systems:

ALISS: Advanced Lightweight Influence Sweep System, in development. Uses spark-gap transducer arrays and superconducting magnetic technology in combination with lightweight, high-speed towed arrays. If successful, the system would be packaged in modular form for use on LCAC air-cushion landing craft as well as with other mine-countermeasures platforms.

A Mk 4(V): Towed acoustic sweep hammer box; World War II–era development still in use. Streamed from a float and towed about 1,100 m abaft the minesweeper.

A Mk 6(B): Low-frequency acoustic sweep, also of World War II origin. Electrically-driven hammer in a streamlined housing towed about 1,100 m abaft the minesweeper, suspended from a float.

AMNS (Airborne Mine Neutralization System): Initially to have been U.S. version of the German Sea Fox, intended to destroy mines already detected. But on 25-2-03 Raytheon and BAE Systems were selected to provide their Archerfish for trials that will continue into 9-06. Employs a torpedo-shaped vehicle to be towed by an MH-60S helicopter; sonar and video sensors classify the mine, and the vehicle launches self-propelled weapons to destroy the mine.

M Mk 3/4/5(A): Two-electrode magnetic sweep array, of World War II origin. Two-ship version is M Mk 4, and the M Mk 3 is a static sweep used in confined areas, with the minesweeper stationary and the array being towed about by small boats. M Mk 5 can either be deployed diverted by floats to either side of the ship or in a closed-loop mode.

M Mk 6: Electromagnetic sweep in three versions: M Mk 6(a) ("J-sweep") with long sections curving to meet a diverted cable towed also by the sweeper and connected to an Oropesa wire sweep and a kite depressor; M Mk 6(B), a single-ship closed-loop array that uses Oropesa floats to keep the loop sides apart; and M Mk 6(H), a closed-loop sweep with two legs meeting at a diverter line streamed from an Oropesa float.

OASIS (Organic Airborne and Surface Influence Sweep): Planned helicopter-deployed replacement for SPU-1W Magnetic Orange Pipe (q.v.) and the Mk 106 towed sled. Uses an 800-ft tow cable and operates to 100-ft depths. Intended to detect influence mines. To be deployed by MH-60S helicopters beginning in 2008.

Oropesa (O): Wire sweeps in various sizes for sweeping buoyant mines near sea surface. Size 1 is largest; 548-m wire can be towed at up to 8 kts at 9.1–73-m depths. Swept path for double sweep array is 457 m wide.

SLQ-37: A combined array for the MCM 1 class, using an M Mk 5(A) straight-tail magnetic sweep combined with an A Mk 4(V) or A Mk 6(b) acoustic sweep (see below).

SLQ-38: Latest version of Oropesa sweep, can be streamed between two ships. Used on MCM 1 class.

WEAPONS AND SYSTEMS *(continued)*

SLQ-48(V) Mine Neutralization System (MNS): By Hughes Electronics Div., General Motors (formerly Honeywell, then Alliant), an unmanned, tethered remotely operated submersible used to examine and dispose of mines located by the ship's sonar system. Travels at up to 6 kts and has a small, high-definition sonar, an acoustic transponder, and a low-light t.v. camera. Uses MP-1 (Mk 26 Mod. 0) cable cutters and an explosive mine-destruction charge. SLQ-48(V) is powered by two 15-shp electric motors to ranges up to 1,000 m from the ship. The umbilical cable is 1,067 m long. The device (less cable) weighs 1,225 kg and is 3.67 m long by 0.91 m wide. Total system weight is 11.8 metric tons.

MNS II, developed by Hughes Electronics (formerly Alliant), completed prototype trials early in 1996; it had a speed of 8 kts, a new autopilot, fiber-optic cable guidance, and a lower cost operating console, but it was not procured in quantity.

SLQ-53: A Single-Ship Deep Sweep (SSDS), developed from the helicopter-towed AN/37U-1 for the MHC 51 class and possibly later for the MCM 1 class.

SPU-1W MOP (Magnetic Orange Pipe): A magnetized 9.14-m-long, 273-mm-diameter hollow pipe filled with Styrofoam for buoyancy. Weighs 454 kg. One helicopter can tow three in tandem to increase mine sensor's ship-count rate.

Note: Mine-countermeasures divers use the Mk 16 nonferrous, recycling underwater breathing apparatus, PQS-2 hand-held mine-location sonars (50–90 kHz), 40-kHz marker beacons, and Mk 25 ferrous metals ordnance locators, the latter usable in depths of up to 90 meters and having a range of up to 18 m.

WLD-1(V)1/3/4: Remote Minehunting System (RMS), developed by Lockheed Martin Naval Electronics and Surveillance Systems. The first order for only two units, however, was placed with Lockheed Martin on 15-1-02. Eventually, all cruisers, destroyers, frigates, and major amphibious warfare ships are to be able to employ the modular (V)4 full-scale production variant, but the initial recipients are now to be DDG 91 and later units of the *Arleigh Burke* Flight IIA class. The (V)4 version conducted trials from *Pinckney* (DDG 91) during 2003. Rockwell Autonetics developed the (V)1 prototype, known as the RMOP (Remote Minehunting Operational Prototype) when trials began in 1994; the ROV then carried AQS-14 and SeaBat sonars. *Cushing* (DD 985) undertook operational trials with the (V)3 variant early in 1997. Initial deployment is planned for 2007–8 aboard DDG 91. All *Freedom*-class Littoral Combat Ships will also carry the system beginning in 2010.

The 7.5 m long by 1.2 m diameter WLD-1(V)4 weighs 7,300 kg and is powered by 370-bhp Cummins diesel. Maximum speed is 16 kts, while 24-hr patrol speed with AQS-20/R sonar deployed is 12 kts.

♦ Submarine-deployed systems:

BLQ-11 LMRS (Long-term Mine Reconnaissance System): Boeing-developed unmanned submersible that is preprogrammed, torpedo-tube deployed and recovered, with an endurance of 40 hours. The 5-knot BLQ-11 has a 288 n.m. range on its nonrechargeable lithium battery and is able to reconnoiter 650 km^2 during a typical mission. A full outfit would replace eight torpedoes and would include three UUVs, the recovery arm machinery, spare batteries, and control and display modules; it can be operated by four personnel. A more capable reconnaissance and target-detection version is planned to enter service around 2009. One BLQ-11 vehicle can be carried by *Virginia*-class SSNs and several by *Ohio*-class SSGNs. A larger-diameter, longer-endurance version may be developed for the three *Seawolf*-class SSNs and later units of the *Virginia* class. Submarine launch and recovery tests were completed in FY 06. The FY 07 budget included a request for 21 units.

♦ Helicopter-towed or -carried systems:

AMNS (Airborne Mine Neutralization System): German STN Atlas Elektronik mine-disposal system, using a remotely operated, expendable submersible with four propulsors that carries a 1.2-kg shaped-charge warhead. Employed aboard MH-53E helicopters beginning in FY 03 and MH-60S helicopters beginning in 2009.

AES-1 ALMDS (Airborne Laser Mine Detection System): In development to replace the Kaman Magic Lantern system starting in 2008–9 aboard MH-60 helicopters. Employs LIDAR (LIght Detection And Ranging) laser sensor and is a follow-on to the early 1990s ATD-111 project.

LTMRS (Long-term Mine Reconnaissance System): In development for deployment from MH-53E and MH-60S helicopters, it will incorporate (as needed) the AQS-20X dipping sonar, an AES-1 Airborne Laser Mine Detection System (ALMDS), an Advanced Mine Neutralization System (AMNS), a Shallow-Water Influence Minesweep System (SWIMS), and the Rapid Airborne Mine-Countermeasures System (RAMICS).

Magic Lantern: Two or more MH-60S (previously SH-2G) helicopters are equipped with a Kaman-developed laser mine detector system known as Magic Lantern; it is to be replaced by the AES-1 ALMDS.

A Mk2(G) acoustic sweep ("rattle bars"): Towed broadside-on by helicopters at up to 10 kts. Can also be towed by surface ships. Water flow between parallel pipes creates MF to HF banging.

Mk 103: Moored minesweeping system with tow wire, sweep wires with explosive cutters, floats, depressor, and otter pennants. AN/37U-1 variant has controlled depth for use against deeper mines and has been adapted for surface-ship use as the SLQ-53 SSDS.

Mk 104: Acoustic mine-countermeasures system with cavitating disk within a venturi tube. Minimum water depth 9 m. Length 1.24 m, height 889 mm, width 660 mm.

Mk 105: Hydrofoil minesweeping sled, made by EDO. In service since 1970. Towed at 20–25 kts, about 140 m behind helicopter. Has gas-turbine generator to provide electric field for two 183-m-long open-electrode sweep wires streamed from the hydrofoil raft. Minimum useable water depth only 3.6 m. Can be refueled from the helicopter while streamed and can also tow A Mk2(G) or Mk 104 arrays in addition to the electrodes. Sled is deployed from a mother ship. Planned ALQ-166 replacement canceled. The Mk 105 Mod. 4, with improved ease of maintenance, weighs 4,081 kg fully fueled; it is 8.30 m long and was introduced during 2001–2.

Mk 106: Helicopter-towed array incorporating the Mk 105 hydrofoil sled with an Mk 104 acoustic array attached to the end of one of the magnetic electrode tails.

OASIS (Organic Airborne & Surface Influence Sweep): A replacement for the Mk 105 sled, which is too heavy to be towed by the MH-60S helicopter; expected in service by 2008.

RAMACS (Rapid Airborne Mine Clearance System): A helicopter-mounted, laser-targeted, 30-mm Bushmaster gun and fire-control system using supercavitating incendiary shells fired into the water to destroy mines at depths up to 40 ft. IOC expected in 2010.

NUCLEAR-POWERED AIRCRAFT CARRIERS [CVN]

Air Group Composition: Carrier wings in FY 07 generally consist of 22–24 F/A-18E/F (with four used primarily for use in aerial refueling), 22–24 F/A-18C, 4 EA-6B ICAP III, 4 E-2C fixed-wing aircraft, and 6 H-60 series helicopters.

♦ 0 (+ 1 + 2) CVN 21 class

Bldr: Northrop Grumman Newport News (formerly Newport News Shipbuilding), Newport News, Va.

	Laid down	L	In serv.
CVN 78 . . .	2009	. . .	2015
CVN 79 . . .	2013	. . .	2019
CVN 80 . . .	2017	. . .	2023

CVN 78—computer rendering showing F-35, F/A-18, and E-2 aircraft on the flight deck Northrop Grumman, 2006

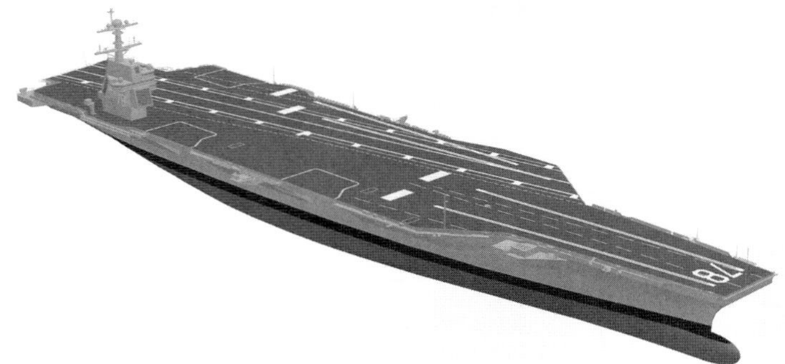

CVN 78—computer rendering Northrop Grumman, 2006

CVN 78—computer rendering U.S. Navy, 2006

D: CVN 78: 102,000 tons (fl); others: 114,000 tons (fl) **S:** 33 kts
Dim: CVN 78: 333 × 41 × 11.8 Others: 336 × 44 × 11.6
Air Group: 24 F/A-18E/F; 20 F-35C; 5 E/A-18G; 4 E-2C/D; 6 H-60-series; 2 C-2A
A: . . . Phalanx block 1B CIWS
Electronics:
Radar: 1/ . . . nav.; 1 Lockheed-Martin SPY-2 volume search; 1 Raytheon SPY-3 MFR (Multi-Function Radar) target detection, tracking, and illumination; . . .
M: Probable: 2 G.E. A4W/A1G pressurized-water reactors (42.3 kg/cm2), 4 sets geared steam turbines; 4 props; 280,000 shp (see Remarks)
Electric: Approx. 64,000 kw tot. hotel services + 8,000 kw emergency
Crew: CVN 78: 2,560–2,700 ship's company + . . . air group; CVN 79: 1,960–2,260 ship's company + . . . air group

NUCLEAR-POWERED AIRCRAFT CARRIERS [CVN] *(continued)*

Remarks: In 12-02 the Navy renamed the CVN(X) program the CVN 21 program, to connote its 21st-century relevance. Initially CVN 78 was to be a totally brand-new design, but in May 1998 it was decided that this was far too expensive and a phased approach began to take shape. The CVN 78 is now envisioned as an enhanced *Nimitz*-class hull design (with a further reduction in operating costs and manpower requirements) while CVN 79 will be larger and based on an entirely new hull design. Funding for CVN 78 is expected in the FY 08 budget and once commissioned will replace *Enterprise* (CVN 65) in service. The name *Gerald R. Ford* has been suggested, though not yet approved, for CVN 78.

CVN 79 is to be ordered in FY 2011 and funding for CVN 80, scheduled to replace *Nimitz* (CVN 68), will follow several years later. It is anticipated that no more than six ships of this class will be built, some to augment the carrier force and some to replace the earlier *Nimitz*-class units.

Beginning in FY 01 Congress provided $21.9 million in advance procurement and design funding for the program and $623.1 million was approved in FY 05 along with $623.1 million in FY 06. $784.1 million was requested in FY 07. Total cost of each carrier is estimated to run $13–$15 billion. The first steel for CVN 78 was cut on 12-8-05. Current plans call for additional units to be funded in the FY 20, FY 24, FY 28, and FY 33 budgets.

Hull systems: The class will likely have a new nuclear propulsion system incorporating a new-design reactor and electric drive. CVN 78 and 79 will employ all-electric auxiliary systems, and carry the Electro-Magnetic Aircraft Launching System (EMALS). CVN 79 will employ a larger hull than CVN 78 and may also carry the Electromagnetic Aircraft Recovery System (EARS), a cableless arrester system. The deck landing area in CVN 79 will be moved farther to port and an 18-degree flight deck with fast fueling and arming stations will be fitted.

♦ 6 (+ 1) Theodore Roosevelt (Improved Nimitz) class

Bldr: Northrop Grumman Newport News (formerly Newport News Shipbuilding), Newport News, Va. (*Atlantic/†Pacific Fleet)

	Laid down	L	In serv.
CVN 71 THEODORE ROOSEVELT*	31-10-81	27-10-84	25-10-86
CVN 72 ABRAHAM LINCOLN†	3-11-84	13-2-88	11-11-89
CVN 73 GEORGE WASHINGTON*	25-8-86	21-7-90	4-7-92
CVN 74 JOHN C. STENNIS†	13-3-91	13-11-93	9-12-95
CVN 75 HARRY S. TRUMAN* (ex-*United States*)	29-11-93	7-9-96	25-7-98
CVN 76 RONALD REAGAN†	12-2-98	4-3-01	12-7-03
CVN 77 GEORGE H. W. BUSH	6-9-03	7-10-06	11-08 (del.)

Abraham Lincoln (CVN 72) U.S. Navy, 3-06

Theodore Roosevelt (CVN 71)—carrying F-14 Tomcats during their final deployment U.S. Navy, 3-06

D: CVN 71: 80,753 tons light (103,658 fl); CVN 72: 81,147 tons light (104,242 fl); CVN 73: 81,083 tons light (104,208 fl); CVN 74: 80,085 tons light (103,020 fl); CVN 75: 78,453 tons light (101.390 fl); CVN 76: 77,607 tons light (98,235 fl); CVN 77: approx. 98,000 tons (fl)

S: 30.9 kts

Dim: 332.85 (CVN 76: 334.67; all but CVN 76: 317.00 wl) × 40.85 (flight deck: 78.33) × 12.50 mean hull

Air Group: 24 F/A-18 E/F; 24 F/A-18A/C; 4 EA-6B; 4 E-2C; 6 SH-60F/HH-60H; 2 C-2A

George Washington (CVN 73) U.S. Navy, 5-06

John C. Stennis (CVN 74) U.S. Navy, 3-06

George Washington (CVN 73) U.S. Navy, 5-06

Ronald Reagan (CVN 76) U.S. Navy 1-06

A: 3 8-round Mk 29 launchers (RIM-7P Sea Sparrow SAM); 4 20-mm Mk 15 Phalanx gatling CIWS; CVN 76 also: 2 21-round RAM Mk 31 SAM syst. (RIM-116A missiles)

Electronics:

Radar: 1 Furuno 900 (CVN 72: Sperry Raster) nav.; 1 SPS-64(V)9 nav.; 1 SPS-67(V)1 surface search; 1 SPS-48E 3-D air search; 1 SPS-49(V)5 (CVN 76/77: SPS-49A(V)1) 2-D air search; all but CVN 76/77: 1 Mk 23 TAS (CVN 76: SPQ-9B) target detection; 2 SPN-46 CCA; 1 SPN-43B air-control; 1 SPN-44 microwave landing aid; 6 Mk 95 Sea Sparrow missile f.c.; 4 Mk 90 Phalanx f.c.

NUCLEAR-POWERED AIRCRAFT CARRIERS [CVN] *(continued)*

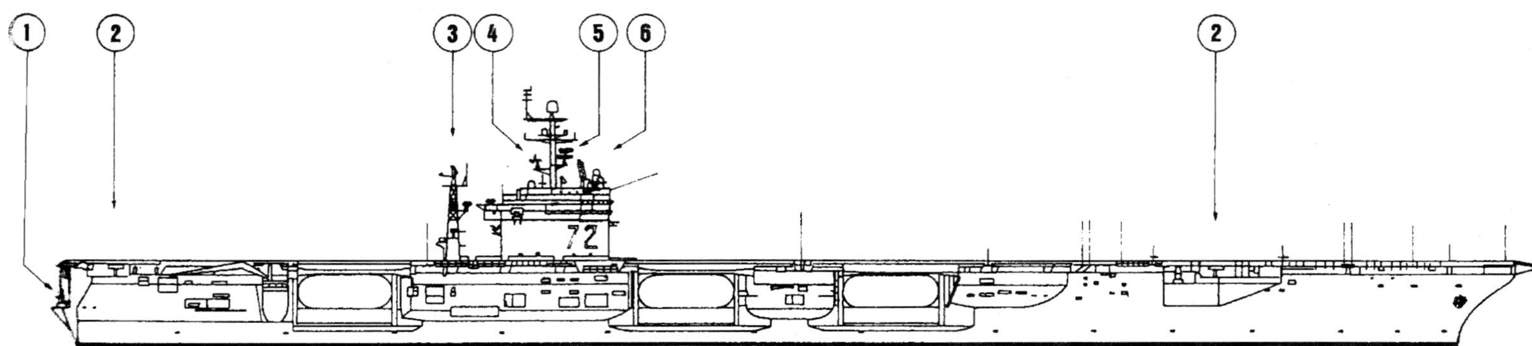

Abraham Lincoln (CVN 72) 1. Mk 15 Phalanx CIWS 2. Mk 29 Sea Sparrow SAM launcher 3. SPS-49 air-search radar 4. SPN-43 air-control radar 5. TAS/Mk 23 target-designation radar 6. SPS-48E 3-D early warning radar Drawing by Jean Moulin, from *Flottes de Combat*

George H. W. Bush—computer rendering U.S. Navy, 2005

TACAN: URN-25
EW: Raytheon SLQ-32(V)4 suite; BAE Systems SLQ-20B signal processor; Mk 36 SRBOC decoy syst. (8 6-round Mk 137 RL); SLQ-25A Nixie SSTDS

M: 2 G.E. A4W/A1G pressurized-water reactors (42.3 kg/cm2), 4 sets geared steam turbines; 4 props; 280,000 shp

Electric: 64,000-kw tot. from turboalternators + 8,000-kw emergency power from 4 diesel sets

Crew: 161–163 officers, 2,932–2,952 enlisted + air wing: 365 officers, 2,500 enlisted air wing + flag staff: 25 officers, 45 enlisted + Marines: 2 officers, 70 enlisted (6,275 tot. accomm.)

Remarks: Authorized: CVN 71 under FY 80, CVN 72 and CVN 73 under FY 83, CVN 74 and CVN 75 under FY 88, and CVN 76 under FY 95. CVN 74 and CVN 75 were ordered 30-6-88 and CVN 76 on 8-12-94. Initial long-lead funding ($832 million) included for CVN 76 was provided under the FY 93 budget, with $1.2 billion more in the FY 94 budget; as of 9-99, however, the ship was $200 million over budget. The ships are expected to serve until 2036, 2039, 2042, 2045, 2047, 2052, and 2058, respectively.

CVN 71, CVN 73, and CVN 75 are homeported at Norfolk, Virginia. CVN 72 is homeported in Everett, Washington, and CVN 74 is homeported at Bremerton, Washington, while CVN 76 is homeported in San Diego. CVN 73 will replace CV 63 in Japan beginning in 2008.

CVN 77 is to have integrated information systems, open-system architecture for computers and combat systems, fiber-optic cabling, and zonal electrical distribution; multifunctional embedded antennas, and composite construction for the island. Concepts and systems are to be employed with a goal of reducing the lifetime operating cost of the ship by about 20% from that of its predecessors and a reduction of 500 crew. The aircraft complement will be significantly reduced from that operating on USN carriers of the 1990s. The first incremental advanced procurement contract for CVN 77 was let on 3-9-98. Congress authorized construction of CVN 77 in the FY 01 budget and provided $4.0537 billion The $3,829,260,045 construction contract was signed on 26-1-01; work on the ship started on 15-3-01. The name was officially assigned on 9-12-02, and the estimated final cost as of 2003 was $11.3 billion, not including aircraft.

Hull systems: Expected to operate for 15 years between refuelings (about 800,000 to 1,000,000 n.m. of steaming). Kevlar armor 63.5 mm thick is fitted over vital spaces, and hull-protection arrangements have been improved over earlier carriers. The two rudders weigh 50 tons each and are 8.84 m high. The distillation plants provide 400,000 gallons of potable water per day. CVN 76 has a prominent, 10.4-m-long bow bulb to the hull, while the island superstructure is one deck lower than in earlier ships and supports two masts; the ship will have improved air-conditioning systems and berthing facilities and some 182,880 m of fiberoptic internal communications cabling. CVN 76 will use 50-person life rafts rather than the current 25-capacity rafts and will carry two rigid-inflatable boats.

Aviation systems: The angled deck is 237.7 m long and is equipped with three arrester wires (four on CVN 71) and a Mk 7 Mod. 3 barrier, as well as four 21.3 × 15.8–m, 47-ton capacity elevators. The hangar has 7.6-m clear height. An aviation payload of some 14,909 tons is carried, including 9,000 tons of aviation fuel and 1,954 tons of aviation ordnance. CVN 71 has four 92.1-m-long C13 Mod. 1 catapults; the others have new, lower-pressure catapults. The arrestor gear system uses 35-mm-diameter cables set 140 mm above the deck at 10.7-m intervals, with the tension on the cables automatically determined by the weight of the landing aircraft. Other data under the *Nimitz* class generally apply. CVN 76 has the three-wire Mk 7 Mod. 4 arrester system, with stronger sheaves and more accessible arrester engines. CVN 76 also has the amidships weapons elevator relocated within the island structure; a larger, two-level, 270°-view flightdeck control position; improved-design, one-piece jet-blast deflectors; and flight deck operations reoriented to the port side of the ship, with simultaneous landings and takeoffs possible from the longer angled-deck extension. CVN 76 can carry 3.4-million gallons of jet fuel.

Combat systems: The combat data systems include NTDS and ACDS, JDTS, POST, and CVIC (Carrier Intelligence Center). Datalinks include Links 4A, 11, and 14. Satellite communications equipment includes SSQ-82, SRR-1, WSC-3 (UHF), WSC-6 (SHF), and USC-38 (EHF). Have SRN-9 and SRN-19 NAVSAT receivers, SMQ-11 weather satellite receiver, WRN-6 GPS receivers. The Sea Sparrow missile systems are supported by three Mk 91 Mod. 1 control systems, each with two Mk 95 radar directors. CVN 71 was fitted with the SLQ-32(V)4 EW system in 1997–98, and the others have been updated. The Joint Services Imagery Processing System-Navy (JSIPS-N) is now fitted to all. CVN 75 has a Sperry Marine Integrated Bridge System, which reduces the number of bridge personnel by more than 80%. CVN 76 will have the Integrated Combat Direction System (ICDS) to coordinate various self-defense systems. Are to receive two Mk 31 RAM missile launchers each. All may eventually be backfitted with the MFR (Multi-Function Radar) and Raytheon VSR (Volume Search Radar) in place of current radars. CVN 71 has received a Telephonics Corp. integrated air-traffic sensor coordination system. All ships of the class will eventually receive the SPQ-9B low-altitude target detection and designation radar in place of the current Mk 23 TAS. CVN 76 is equipped with the SSDS Mk 2 Mod. 1 Ship Self Defense System and has a CEC (Cooperative Engagement Capability) system. During 5-02 it was decided that the ship's radar suite would essentially duplicate that of CVN 76, although it had originally been intended to employ the still-developmental Lockheed Martin SPY-1E or SPY-2 volume search radar and Raytheon SPY-3 target-detection radars, with SPY-1F as a possible fallback for SPY-1E/SPY-2. The planned Lockheed Martin Integrated Communications and Advanced Network (ICAN) system for the ship was canceled during 8-02.

♦ 3 Nimitz class (SCB 102 Type)

Bldr: Northrop Grumman Newport News (formerly Newport News Shipbuilding), Newport News, Va. (*Atlantic Fleet/†Pacific Fleet)

	Laid down	L	In serv.
CVN 68 NIMITZ†	22-6-68	13-5-72	3-5-75
CVN 69 DWIGHT D. EISENHOWER*	15-8-70	11-10-75	18-10-77
CVN 70 CARL VINSON*	11-10-75	15-3-80	13-3-82

Dwight D. Eisenhower (CVN 69) U.S. Navy 4-06

D: CVN 68: 78,280 tons light (101,196 fl); CVN 69: 78,793 tons light (101,713 fl); CVN 70: 78,172 tons light (101.089 fl)

S: 31.5 kts **Dim:** 334.70 (317.00 wl) × 40.85 (flight deck: 77.11, max.: 89.4) × 12.50

Air Group: 24 F/A-18E/F; 24 F/A-18A/C; 4 EA-6B; 4 E-2C; 6 SH-60F/HH-60H; 2 C-2A

NUCLEAR-POWERED AIRCRAFT CARRIERS [CVN] *(continued)*

Dwight D. Eisenhower (CVN 69) U.S. Navy, 4-06

Nimitz (CVN 68) U.S. Navy, 2-06

Carl Vinson (CVN 70) U.S. Navy, 7-05

A: 3 (CVN 68: 2) 8-round Mk 29 launchers (RIM-7P Sea Sparrow SAM); 3 (CVN 68: none; CVN 70: 4) 20-mm Mk 15 Phalanx CIWS; CVN 68 only: 2 21-round RAM Mk 31 SAM syst. (RIM-116A missiles)

Electronics:
Radar: 1 Furuno 900 nav.; 1 SPS-64(V)9 nav.; 1 SPS-67(V)1 surf. search; 1 Mk 23 TAS (CVN 69: SPQ-9B) target detection; 1 SPS-49(V)5 air search; 1 SPS-48E 3-D air search; 1 SPN-44 CCA; 1/SPN-43B air-control; 6 Mk 95 missile f.c., 3 or 4 Mk 90 Phalanx f.c.
TACAN: URN-25
EW: Raytheons SLQ-32(V)4 suite, BAE Systems SLQ-20B signal processor; Mk 36 SRBOC decoy syst. (8 6-round Mk 137 RL); SLQ-25A SSTD

M: 2 G.E. A4W/A1G pressurized-water reactors, 4 sets geared steam turbines; 4 props; 280,000 shp
Electric: 64,000-kw from turboalternators + 8,000-kw emergency power from 4 diesel sets
Endurance: 90 days (limited by provisions)
Crew: 158–160 officers, 2,939–2,963 enlisted + air wing: 365 officers, 2,500 enlisted + Flag staff: 25 officers, 45 enlisted + Marines: 2 officers, 70 enlisted (tot. accomm.: 558–568 officer, 5,046–5,244 enlisted)

Remarks: Authorized: CVN 68 under FY 67, CVN 69 under FY 70, and CVN 70 under FY 74. Originally expected to remain in service until 2025, 2027, and 2032, respectively. CVN 68 began her first $1.2-billion RCOH (Refueling Complex Overhaul) at Newport News SB & DD on 29-5-98, completing 28-6-01; the ship arrived at her new home port, San Diego, on 13-11-01. CVN 69 underwent $404.3-million overhaul 1995 to 1-97 at Newport News Shipbuilding and Dry Dock that did not include nuclear reactor recoring; a three-year recoring overhaul began on 21-5-01 at Newport News with redelivery on 25-3-05. CVN 70 underwent a six-month refit from 7-3-02 to 30-9-02; the ship's three-year refueling and comprehensive overhaul began in 11-05. CVN 68 is homeported in San Diego, California, and CVN 69 is based out of Norfolk, Virginia.
Hull systems: Decks and hull are of extra-strong, high tensile steel to limit the impact of semi-armor-piercing bombs. Apart from the longitudinal bulkheads, there are 23 transverse watertight bulkheads (more than 2,000 hull compartments) and ten firewall bulkheads. Foam devices for firefighting are very well developed, and pumping equipment is excellent, a 15° list being correctable in 20 minutes. *Nimitz*-class ships can withstand three times the severe pounding survived by the *Essex*-class aircraft carriers in 1944–45, and they can take impacts and shock waves in the same proportion. They have been equipped with 65-mm Kevlar armor over vital spaces during refits. Were planned to require only one reactor recoring during their expected 50-year life spans. The evaporators can produce 1,520 tons of fresh water per day. During her 1998–2001 refueling overhaul, CVN 68 had the two upper levels of the island superstructure altered and a new integrated mast/antenna shelter installed.
Aviation systems: The angled part of the flight deck is 237.7 m long and has three Mk 14 arrester wires and a barrier to halt aircraft. There are four side elevators: two forward, one aft of the island to starboard, and one on the stern to port. The four C13 Mod. 1 steam catapults are 94.5 m long. The 15,134 m^3 total aviation magazine spaces can hold 1,954 tons of aviation ordnance, and the total aviation-associated payload is on the order of 15,000 tons; sufficient aviation fuel for 16 days' operations is carried. The hangar has 7.8-m clear height. CVN 69 had the prototype AVCARS (Augmented Visual Carrier Aircraft Recovery System), now fitted to the entire class. CVN 68 conducted trials in late 1997 aimed at increasing the number of F/A-18 strike sorties per day from the normal 125–140 to more than 200; 20 additional pilots and 100 additional maintenance personnel were embarked.
Combat systems: ASCAC (Anti-Submarine Classification and Analysis Center) permits instant sharing of target data between the carrier, its ASW aircraft, and escorting ships. CVN 70 was completed with three Mk 29 launchers for Sea Sparrow, six Mk 95 radar directors for the missiles, and four Mk 15 CIWS (Vulcan/ Phalanx) gatling AA guns. The others have been similarly refitted but still have only three Phalanx CIWS. All Mk 15 CIWS are now protected by "maintenance enclosures." Have three Mk 95 Mod. 1 missile control systems with two Mk 95 radar directors each to control Sea Sparrow missiles. The Mk 23 TAS was added to improve defense against low fliers and cruise missiles and will be replaced by the SPQ-9B, which provides target detection and designation against low-flying threats. SATCOM equipment includes SSQ-82, SRR-1, WSC-3 (UHF), WSC-6 (SHF), and USC-38 (EHF). Have SRN-9 and SRN-19 NAVSAT receivers, SMQ-11 receiver for the TIROS-N ocean weather forecasting satellite, and WRN-6 Global Positioning System receivers. All now have the Joint Services Imagery Processing System-Navy (JSIPS-N). CVN 69 became the first carrier with the ACDS (Aircraft Carrier Defense System) variant of the SSDS (Ship Self-Defense System) weapon and sensor integration package under FY 97 funding. CVN 68 and CVN 69 have had their SPS-49 radars upgraded to SPS-49A(V)1. CVN 68 had the Integrated Combat Direction System (ICDS) added during her 1998–2001 refit to coordinate the various self-defense systems. Are to receive two RAM missile launchers each. The USG-2 Cooperative Engagement Capability system was installed on CVN 69 during 2000–2002; the ship has also received a Telephonics Corp. integrated air-traffic sensor coordination system. From 1995–2000, CVN 68 carried the SLR-24 towed passive linear torpedo detection sensor as part of the prototype CST-1 torpedo-countermeasures system; in its stead, the ship received the Raytheon SSDS (Ship Self-Defense System) Mk 2 Mod. 0 system during 2001. CVN 68 had all Phalanx CIWS and one Mk 29 SAM launcher replaced by two RAM systems during overhaul. Problems with the Lockheed Martin partial Integrated Communications and Advanced Network (ICAN) system added to CVN 68 during overhaul were said to have been resolved during 2002, but the ship's full operational capability had been delayed by several months. CVN 68 also has the SSDS Mk 2 Mod. 1 Ship Self-Defense System.

♦ 1 Enterprise class (SCB 160 type)

Bldr: Northrop Grumman Newport News (formerly Newport News Shipbuilding), Newport News, Va. (Atlantic Fleet)

	Laid down	L	In serv.
CVN 65 Enterprise	4-2-58	24-9-60	25-11-61

D: 75,704 tons light (93,284 fl) **S:** 33.6 kts
Dim: 331.63 (317.00 wl) × 40.54 (flight deck: 78.4) × 11.88 mean hull
Air Group: 24 F/A-18E/F; 24 F/A-18A/C; 4 EA-6B; 4 E-2C; 6 SH-60F/HH-60H; 2 C-2A
A: 3 8-round Mk 29 SAM launchers (RIM-7P Sea Sparrow SAM); 2 21-round RAM Mk 31 SAM syst. (RIM-116A missiles); 3 20-mm Mk 15 Phalanx CIWS gatling AA

NUCLEAR-POWERED AIRCRAFT CARRIERS [CVN] *(continued)*

Enterprise (CVN 65) U.S. Navy, 5-06

Enterprise (CVN 65) U.S. Navy, 11-05

Enterprise (CVN 65) U.S. Navy, 5-06

Electronics:
Radar: 1 Furuno 900 nav.; 1 SPS-64(V)9 nav.; 1 SPS-67(V)1 surf. search; 1 Mk 23 TAS target acquisition; 1 SPS-48E 3-D air search; 1 SPS-49(V)5 air search; 1 SPN-44 microwave landing aid; 1 SPN-43A air-control; 2 SPN-46 CCA; 6 Mk 95 missile f.c.; 3/Mk 90 Phalanx f.c.
TACAN: URN-25
EW: Raytheon SLQ-32(V)4 suite; WLR-1H(V)7 intercept; BAE Systems SLQ-20B signal processor; Mk 36 SRBOC decoy syst. (8 6-round Mk 137 RL); SLQ-25A SSTDS

M: 8 Westinghouse A2W reactors, supplying 32 Foster-Wheeler heat exchangers; 4 sets Westinghouse geared steam turbines; 4 props; 280,000+ shp
Electric: 40,000 kw from turboalternators + 8,000 kw emergency from 4 diesel sets
Crew: 169 officers, 3,149 enlisted + aviation personnel: 358 officers, 2,122 enlisted + flag staff: 25 officers, 45 enlisted + Marines: 2 officers, 70 enlisted

Remarks: Authorized FY 58. Modernized 15-1-79 to 3-82 at Puget Sound NSY, during which the radar and other electronics suites were extensively renovated. Refitted and refueled at builder's 8-1-91 to 27-9-94; an extra six months of repair and upgrade work was required after sea trials, however, delaying availability until 7-7-95. The entire refueling and overhaul cost was more than $3.1 billion. Given $80-million refit by builder from 8-99 to 18-12-99. In May 2003 she completed a one-year, $191-million "Extended Drydock Selected Restricted Availability" at the Naval Shipyard, Portsmouth, Virginia. Currently expected to remain in service until 2013 when she will be replaced by CVN 78. Homeported at Norfolk, Virginia.
Hull systems: Has four rudders vice the two on other U.S. CV/CVNs. When new could make nearly 36 knots; maximum speed is limited primarily by shaft torque. Two of the eight nuclear reactors are now kept nonoperational, limiting maximum speed to around 31 kts.
Aviation systems: There are four C13 Mod. 1 steam catapults and four elevators—one on the port side of the angled deck, three to starboard—two of which are forward of and one abaft the island. Elevators are steel and alloy and weigh 105 tons; 26 m long, 16 m wide, lift 45 tons. The hangar is 7.62 m high and the flight deck has more than 20,000 m^2 area—the largest of any U.S. carrier. Carries 8,500 tons of aviation fuel, which permits up to 12 days of intensive aerial operations without replenishment. Carries fuel to replenish other ships. Retains both bow catapult bridle "horns," although the U.S. Navy no longer operates aircraft that require bridles to launch them.
Combat systems: Has NTDS, ASCAC (Anti-Submarine Classification and Analysis Center) and TFCC (Tactical Flag Communications Center). Link 4A, 11, 14, and 16 are fitted. There are three Mk 91 Mod.1 fire-control systems for the Sea Sparrow missiles, each with two Mk 95 radar directors. Satellite communications equipment includes SSQ-82, SRR-1, WSC-3 (UHF), WSC-6 (SHF), and USC-38 (EHF). Has SRN-9 and SRN-19 NAVSAT receivers, SMQ-11 receiver for the TIROS-N ocean weather forecasting satellite, and WRN-6 GPS receivers.

CONVENTIONALLY POWERED AIRCRAFT CARRIERS [CV]

♦ 1 John F. Kennedy class (SCB 127C type)

Bldr: Northrop Grumman Newport News (formerly Newport News Shipbuilding), Newport News, Va. (Atlantic Fleet)

	Laid down	L	In serv.
CV 67 John F. Kennedy	22-10-64	27-5-67	7-9-68

John F. Kennedy (CV 67) U.S. Navy, 5-05

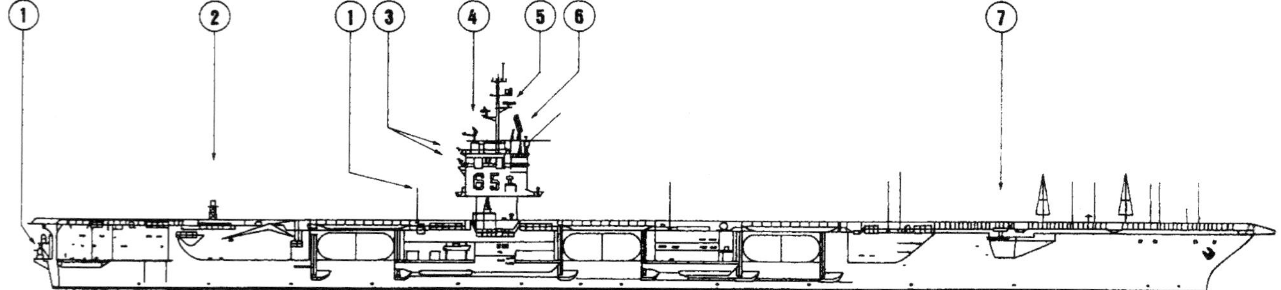

Enterprise (CVN 65) 1. Mk 15 Phalanx CIWS 2. SPN-43A air-control radar 3. SPN-46 landing-aid radars (now side-by-side) 4. SPS-49 air-search radar 5. SPS-67 surface-search radar 6. SPS-48E 3-D early-warning radar 7. Mk 29 Sea Sparrow SAM launcher
Drawing by Jean Moulin, from *Flottes de Combat*

CONVENTIONALLY POWERED AIRCRAFT CARRIERS [CV] *(continued)*

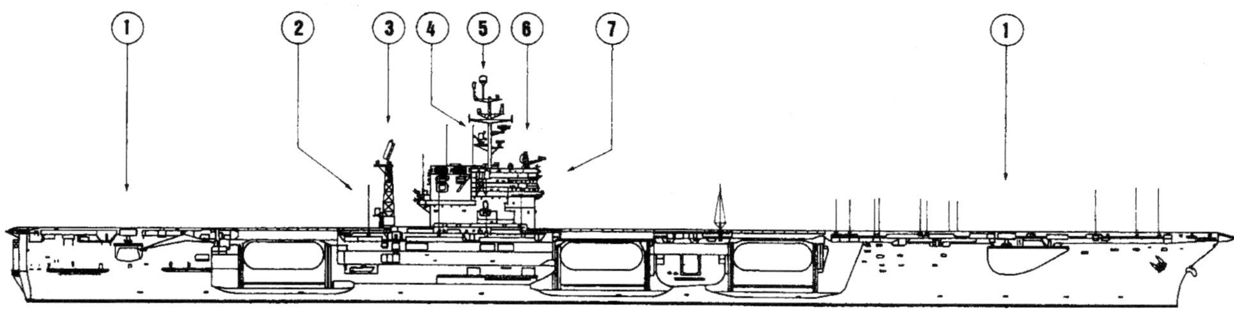

John F. Kennedy (CV 67) 1. Mk 29 launcher for Sea Sparrow SAM 2. SPN-44 landing aid radar 3. SPS-48E 3-D early-warning radar 4. SPN-43A air-control radar 5. WSC-6 satellite communications antenna radome 6. SPS-49 air-search radar 7. Mk 15 Phalanx CIWS (alongside the island) Drawing by Jean Moulin, from *Flottes de Combat*

John F. Kennedy (CV 67) U.S. Navy, 5-05

John F. Kennedy (CV 67) U.S. Navy, 5-05

D: 60,728 tons light (82,655 fl) **S:** 32 kts
Dim: 327.05 (304.54 wl) × 39.62 (flight deck: 81.38, max. 85.95) × 11.28
Air Group: 24 F/A-18E/F; 24 F/A-18A/C; 4 EA-6B; 4 E-2C; 6 SH-60F/HH-60H; 2 C-2A
A: 3 8-round Mk 29 SAM syst. (RIM-7M Sea Sparrow missiles); 3 20-mm Mk 15 Block 1 Phalanx CIWS
Electronics:
Radar: 1 Furuno 900 nav.; 1 Raytheon SPS-64(V)9 nav.; 1 SPS-67(V)1 surf. search; 1 Mk 23 TAS target acquisition; 1 SPS-49(V)5 air search; 1 SPS-48E 3-D air search; 1 SPN-41 microwave landing aid; 1 SPN-43C air-control; SPN-44 microwave landing aid; 2 SPN-46 CCA; 6 Mk 95 missile f.c.; 3 Mk 90 Phalanx f.c.
TACAN: URN-25
EW: Raytheon SLQ-32(V)4 suite; WLR-1H(V)7 intercept; BAE Systems SLQ-20B signal processor; Mk 36 SRBOC decoy syst. (8 6-round Mk 137 RL); SLQ-25A Nixie SSTDS
M: 4 sets G.E. geared steam turbines; 4 props; 280,000 shp
Boilers: 8 Foster-Wheeler; 83.4 kg/cm2, 520° C
Electric: 17,000 kw tot. from turboalternators and emergency diesel sets
Crew: 135 officers, 2,443 enlisted + air group: 329 officers, 1,950 enlisted + flag staff: 25 officers, 45 enlisted + Marines: 2 officers, 70 enlisted (accomm. for 540 officers, 4,818 enlisted)

Remarks: Authorized FY 63. Built with conventional steam propulsion as an economy measure. Distinguishing feature is the stack, which is angled outboard as on some World War II–era Japanese carriers. Was to have received full SLEP modernization 1993–95 but instead had only a 14-month "Complex Overhaul" funded under FY 93. Previously expected to remain in service until 2018, but in 2006 the Navy requested that she be prematurely retired in 2007 to save money. Home port changed from Norfolk to Mayport, Florida, during 1995. Transferred to Naval Reserve Force 1-10-94 to become "operational reserve/training carrier" on completion of overhaul 13-9-95 but was subsequently deployed as if she were a regular Navy carrier. The ship reverted to regular USN status as of 1-10-00. The carrier's material condition had been allowed to decline during the period of its assignment to the Naval Reserve Force.
Aviation systems: Four side elevators, three to starboard (two forward of and one abaft the island) and one on the port quarter. Completely automatic landing system, permitting all-weather operation. Four arrester wires and a barrier on the 227-m angled flight deck. Three 90-m C13 and one 94.5-m C13-1 catapults. The 11,808-m^3 aviation-ordnance magazine can accommodate 1,250 tons of ammunition. Carries 5,919 tons of aviation fuel.
Combat systems: The ship's Combat Direction System Block I failed repeated tests during 1999 and is considered only marginally effective. Satellite communications equipment includes SSQ-82, SRR-1, WSC-3 (UHF), WSC-6(V)4 (SHF), and USC-38(V)4 (EHF). Has SRN-19 and SRN-25 navigational satellite receivers, WRN-6 GPS receiver, and SMQ-11 weather satellite receiver. Is planned to receive two RAM Mk 31 point-defense missile launchers.

♦ 1 Kitty Hawk class (†Pacific Fleet)

	Bldr	Laid down	L	In serv.
CV 63 Kitty Hawk†	New York SB, Camden, NJ	27-12-56	21-5-60	9-4-61

Kitty Hawk (CV 63) U.S. Navy, 7-06

Kitty Hawk (CV 63) U.S. Navy, 5-06

D: 60,933 tons light (81,780 fl) **S:** 33 kts
Dim: 325.83 × 39.62 (flight deck: 76.81; 85.95 max.) × 11.58 mean hull
Air Group: 24 F/A-18E/F; 24 F/A-18A/C; 4 EA-6B; 4 E-2C; 6 SH-60F/HH-60H; 2 C-2A
A: 2 8-round Mk 29 SAM launchers (RIM-7M Sea Sparrow missiles); 2 21-round RAM Mk 31 SAM syst. (RIM-116A missiles); 3 20-mm Mk 15 Phalanx CIWS

CONVENTIONALLY POWERED AIRCRAFT CARRIERS [CV]
(continued)

Kitty Hawk (CV 63) U.S. Navy, 6-06

Electronics:
Radar: 1 Furuno 900 nav.; 1 SPS-64(V)9 nav.; 1 SPS-67(V)1 surf. search; 1 Mk 23 TAS target acquisition; 1 SPS-49(V)5 air search; 1 SPS-48E 3-D air search; 1 SPN-41 microwave landing aid; 1 SPN-43A or C air control; 2 SPN-46 CCA; 6 Mk 95 missile f.c.; 2 or 3 Mk 90 Phalanx f.c.
TACAN: URN-25
EW: Raytheon SLQ-32(V)4 suite; BAE Systems SLQ-20B signal processor; Mk 36 SRBOC decoy syst. (8 6-round Mk 137 RL); SLQ-25A Nixie SSTDS
M: 4 sets Westinghouse geared steam turbines; 4 props; 280,000 shp
Boilers: 8 Foster-Wheeler, 83.4 kg/cm2, 520° C
Electric: 15,000 kw tot. (6 turboalternators, 2 emergency diesel sets)
Range: 4,000/30; 8,000/20 **Fuel:** 7,800 tons
Crew: 147–148 officers, 2,743–2,766 enlisted + air group: 295 officers, 1,815 enlisted + flag staff; 25 officers, 45 enlisted + Marines: 2 officers, 70 enlisted (accomm. for 575–578 officers, 5,046–5,049 enlisted)

Remarks: CV 63 was authorized under FY 56. This class is a great improvement over the *Forrestal* class, on which they were based, and have one significant difference: three elevators on the starboard side, two forward of and one abaft the island, and one to port, abaft the angled flight deck. CV 63 underwent SLEP (Service Life Extension Program) 28-1-88 to 2-8-91 and arrived at Yokosuka, Japan, home port on 11-8-98 to replace *Independence* (CV 62) as the only forward deployed carrier. CV 63 is to be retired in 2008. The ship carried an army special assault helicopter air group during her 10-01 to 12-01 deployment to the Arabian Sea.
Aviation systems: Have four C13 steam catapults. Carry 5,882 tons of aviation fuel. Received new catapult rotary engines, Mk 7 Mod. 3 arrester gear (3 wires), SPN-46 landing-aid radar during SLEP overhauls. During counterterrorism operations in the Arabian Gulf late in 2001, carried eight F/A-18 Hornet fighters, two S-3B refuelers, two C-39B COD transports, and three SH-60 helicopters, plus 20 Special Forces helicopters.
Combat systems: Have three Mk 91 Mod. 1 missile-control systems, each with two radar directors, for the Sea Sparrow SAM system. Have SRN-9 and SRN-19 NAVSAT receivers, SMQ-6 or SMQ-11 receiver for weather forecasting satellite, and WRN-6 GPS receivers. Satellite communications equipment includes SSQ-82, SRR-1, WSC-3 (UHF), WSC-6 (SHF), and USC-38 (EHF). During its SLEP overhauls, CV 63 received SPS-48E and SPS-49(V) upgrade air-search radars, updated NTDS (Naval Tactical Data System), a torpedo decoy system, the WQN-1 Channel-Finder sonar, and upgraded EW equipment; the SYS-2(V)4 sensor data fusion system and the Mk 23 TAS low-altitude radar were added. CV 63 received two RAM missile launchers in place of three Sea Sparrow launchers in a refit at Yokosuka that ended during 8-01.
Disposals: Sister *America* (CV 66) was decommissioned 8-9-96, stricken in 1998, and sunk as a tarket in 2005. *Constellation* (CV 64) decommissioned 6-8-03 and was towed to Bremerton, Washington, for storage on 9-27-03. She was stricken on 2-12-03.

Disposal note: *Forrestal*-class CV *Independence* (CV 62) was decommissioned on 30-9-98 and stricken from the reserve fleet on 8-3-04. Sister *Forrestal* (CV 59) was decommissioned 9-9-93 and stricken 10-9-93. *Saratoga* (CV 60) was decommissioned 20-8-94 and stricken on 30-9-94; she is employed in pier side trials with concepts for the CVN 21 program and has been stored at Newport, Rhode Island, since 7-8-98. *Ranger* (CV 61) was decommissioned on 10-7-93 and was maintained in reserve until stricken on 8-3-04.

NAVAL AND MARINE CORPS AVIATION
U.S. Navy and Marine Corps Active Aircraft Totals
(as of 30-6-06)

♦ 1,010 Fighters

44 F-5 Tiger II:

40	F-5E*	Single-seat adversary training aircraft
4	F-5F	Two-place adversary training aircraft

* including 32 low flight-hour F-5Es repurchased from Switzerland and redesignated F-5N.

16 F-14 Tomcat:

16	F-14D	Super Tomcat; improved systems and engines

F-14s have been withdrawn from operational service.

14 F-16 Fighting Falcon:

10	F-16A	Delivered during 2003 to Naval Strike and Air Warfare Center, Fallon, Nev.; aircraft built for Pakistan but not delivered
4	F-16B	Delivered during 2003 to Naval Strike and Air Warfare Center, Fallon, Nev.; aircraft built for Pakistan but not delivered

936 F/A-18 Hornet:

119	F/A-18A	Initial version, single-seat fighter/attack aircraft
28	F/A-18B	Two-seat combat trainer version
383	F/A-18C	Upgraded F/A-18A, AMRAAM-capable
136	F/A-18D	Two-seat attack version of F/A-18C, for USMC
116	F/A-18E	Super Hornet; single-seat upgrade, new production
150	F/A-18F	Super Hornet; two-seat upgrade, new production
4	NF/A-18A/C/D	Permanently modified for test duties

♦ 153 attack

153 AV-8 Harrier-II:

134	AV-8B/B	Major redesign, improved capability; 74 were updated to AV-8B+ Harrier-II, with APG-65 radar by end 2003
1	NAV-8B	Modified AV-8B for testing
18	TAV-8B	Two-seat trainer; some used for systems evaluations

♦ 111 electronic attack

111 EA-6 Prowler:

111	EA-6B	EW mission; HARM missile-capable

♦ 195 patrol

195 P-3 Orion:

166	P-3C	Improved avionics systems, maritime patrol
16	EP-3E	Electronic reconnaissance ("Aries-II")
12	NP-3D	One converted as Hawkeye 2000 trials aircraft, with rotating radome; others assigned to Naval Weapons Test Squadrons, operating from China Lake and Pt. Mugu, Calif.
1	VP-3A	Executive transport

♦ 40 antisubmarine warfare

40 S-3 Viking:

40	S-3B	S-3A with improved avionics

All remaining S-3s are to be retired by 2009.

♦ 68 airborne early warning

68 E-2 Hawkeye:

67	E-2C	Improved system, several electronics configurations
1	TE-2C	Pilot trainer for E-2C

♦ 16 strategic communications relay

16 E-6 Mercury:

16	E-6B	Modified E-6A TACAMO capable of communicating with all U.S. strategic weapons systems

♦ 266 transports

36 C-2 Greyhound:

36	C-2A	Aircraft carrier logistics support

19 C-9 Skytrain II:

17	C-9B	Militarized commercial DC-9; casualty evacuation and transport; two operated by USMC, others by Naval Reserve; being replaced by the C-40
2	DC-9	Former commercial aircraft

73 C-12 Huron:

4	C-12C	On loan from Army, used at Test Pilot School, Patuxent River NAS
1	RC-12F	Former range-control aircraft, now used as utility transports
1	RC-12M	Range surveillance and clearing
25	TC-12B	Former UC-12B converted for training
21	UC-12B	Passenger logistics
10	UC-12F	Improved UC-12B, newer engines, avionics
10	UC-12M	Utility transports, with improved engines and avionics
1	NC-12B	UC-12B converted for sonobuoy testing

8 C-20 Gulfstream:

3	C-20A/D	Gulfstream III executive transport
5	C-20G	Gulfstream IV cargo/personnel transport

7 C-26 Metro:

7	C-26D	Ex-Air National Guard C-26B light transports refurbished in 1998–99 by Fairchild for liaison use.

12 C-35 Citation:

2	UC-35C	Two Citation Ultra delivered to USMCR as transports in in 2000
10	UC-35D	First Citation Encore delivered mid-2001 to USMC as VIP transport

3 C-37 Gulfstream V:

3	C-37A/B	Replacing VP-3/UP-3 Orions; first unit ordered in 2001

9 C-40A Clipper:

9	C-40A	Boeing 737-700IGW transport, to replace C-9B/DC-9

99 C-130 Hercules:

20	C-130T	Logistics transport, improved over earlier C-130s
1	DC-130A	Drone target launcher and controller; contractor-operated
17	KC-130F	Tactical tanker/cargo transport
21	KC-130J	Latest variant, with increased cargo capacity, 6-bladed props
11	KC-130R	Tactical tanker/transport
28	KC-130T	Improved avionics, tanker capabilities
1	NC-130H	Ex-USCG, with rotating radome; at Patuxent River NAS

NAVAL AND MARINE CORPS AVIATION *(continued)*

♦ 611 trainers and research

23 T-2 Buckeye:

23	T-2C Buckeye	Basic two-seat jet trainer, J85 engines; being phased out of service

48 T-6 Texan II:

48	T-6A	Joint Primary Aircraft Training System (JPATS) propeller trainer, based on Pilatus PC-9; total procurement of 328 is planned. First operational aircraft arrived at Pensacola on 1-11-02.

273 T-34 Mentor:

273	T-34C	Two-seat basic trainer, PT6A-25 turboprop engine

11 T-38 Talon:

11	T-38A/C	Naval Test Pilot School trainer

21 T-39 Sabreliner:

1	T-39D	Utility transport and research; at China Lake, Calif.
6	T-39G	Modified CT-39G; Naval Flight Officer training
14	T-39N	Trainer for Naval Flight Officers

54 T-44 Pegasus:

54	T-44A	Advanced multi-engine trainer

179 T-45 Goshawk:

72	T-45A	Advanced trainer
107	T-45C	Improved avionics

2 U-6 Beaver:

2	U-6A	Naval Test Pilot School trainer; Patuxent River NAS

♦ 46 tilt-rotor assault aircraft

46 V-22 Osprey:

46	MV-22B	Marine Corps transport, production version

♦ 1,256 helicopters

112 H-1 Iroquois/Huey:

21	HH-1N	Search-and-rescue variant
91	UH-1N	Special armed transport, twin-engine T400-CP-400

179 AH-1 Seacobra:

176	AH-1W	Two T-700-GE-401 engines
3	AH-1Z	Planned upgrade with four-bladed rotor, three stores stations, new avionics

26 H-3 Sea King:

11	VH-3D	Assigned to HMX-1, Quantico, Va., for presidential use
1	NVH-3A	VH-3A permanently modified for test duties
14	UH-3H	Utility and rescue; being phased out of service

5 H-6 Cayuse:

5	TH-6B	Naval Test Pilot School helicopter trainer; on loan from Army

221 H-46 Sea Knight:

218	CH-46E	Improved T58-GE-16 engines; all are USMC transports
3	HH-46D	Utility and rescue

37 H-53 Sea Stallion:

37	CH-53D	Marine Corps heavy-lift helicopter

180 H-53E Super Stallion:

148	CH-53E	Marine Corps medium-lift helicopter
32	MH-53E	Navy mine-countermeasures version of CH-53E, larger fuel tanks

122 H-57 Sea Ranger:

45	TH-57B	Basic trainer
77	TH-57C	Advanced instrument trainer

3 H-58 Kiowa:

3	OH-58C	Naval Test Pilot School helicopter trainers; on loan from Army

371 H-60 Seahawk:

38	HH-60H	Combat support strike/rescue variant
11	MH-60R	Upgrade of SH-60B/F to common standard; termed the SH-60R until 25-5-01
89	MH-60S	Fleet combat/logistics support variant; termed the CH-60S until 6-2-01. 237 are planned. Known as the "Knighthawk"
146	SH-60B	Sea-based LAMPS Mk III ASW
3	NSH-60B/F	SH-60s used as trainers at Naval Test Pilot School
72	SH-60F	Carrier-based, dipping sonar
4	UH-60L	Naval Test Pilot School trainer; on loan from Army
8	VH-60N	USMC VIP transport; all assigned to HMX-1, Quantico, Va., for presidential use

Total active inventory: 3,769

Squadron designations: Air squadrons are designated alphanumerically, the letter prefixes for the principal squadron types being:

Navy:	
HC	Helicopter Combat Support (HH-46D, UH-46D, UH-3H)
HCS	Helicopter Combat Search-and-Rescue/Special Warfare Support (HH-60H)
HM	Helicopter Mine Countermeasures (MH-53E)
HS	Helicopter Antisubmarine (SH-60F)
HSC	Helicopter Sea Combat (HH-60H, ex-HCS)
HSM	Helicopter Maritime Strike (MH-60R; ex-HS)
HSL	Light Helicopter Antisubmarine (SH-60B)
HT	Helicopter Training (TH-57)
VAQ	Electronic Attack (EA-6B)
VAW	Carrier Airborne Early Warning (E-2C)
VC	Fleet Composite (utility aircraft)
VF	Fighter (F-14) disestablished 9-06, most converted to VFA
VFA	Strike Fighter (F/A-18)
VFC	Fighter Composite (F/A-18, F-5)
VP	Patrol (P-3)
VPU	Special Projects Patrol (P-3-series)
VQ	Fleet Air Reconnaissance (EP-3), also Strategic Communications (E-6A/B)
VR	Fleet Logistics Support (C-9/DC-9, C-130, UC-12)
VRC	Fleet Logistics Support-COD (Carrier Onboard Delivery) (C-2A)
VS	Sea Control (S-3B)
VT	Training (T-2C, TC-12B, T-34C, T-39G/N, T-44A, T-45A)
VX	Air Test and Evaluation
Marine Corps:	
HMH	Marine Heavy Helicopter (CH-53D/E)
HMLA	Marine Light Attack Helicopter (AH-1W, UH-1N)
HMM	Marine Medium Helicopter (CH-46E)
HMM(T)	Marine Medium Helicopter Training (CH-46E)
HMT	Marine Helicopter Training
HMX	Marine Helicopter (VH-60N, VH-3D, CH-46E, CH-53E)
VMA	Marine Attack (AV-8B)
VMAQ	Marine Electronic Warfare (EA-6B)
VMFA	Marine Fighter-Attack (F/A-18A/C)
VMFA(AW)	Marine Fighter-Attack (All-Weather) (F/A-18B/D/F)
VMGR	Marine Refueler-Transport (KC-130F/J/R/T)
VMGRT	Marine Refueler-Transport Training (KC-130F, KC-130J)
VMM	Marine Medium Tiltrotor (MV-22)
VMM(T)	Marine Medium Tiltrotor (Training) (MV-22)
VMR	Marine Transport Squadron (C-9B)

♦ Marine Corps Aviation

Marine Corps aircraft are procured and "owned" by the Navy and are intended to operate principally from land bases and amphibious-warfare ships, but squadrons of helicopters and attack, reconnaissance, and electronic warfare fixed-wing aircraft can operate from carriers as well. Combat aviation is organized into three active Marine Air Wings (MAWs, with 1st MAW based at Futenma, Okinawa [to be relocated to Guam by 2012]; 2nd MAW at Cherry Point, North Carolina; and 3rd MAW based at Miramar, California) and one reserve wing. In addition, there are four Training Squadrons for fixed-wing aircraft, three for helicopters, and one Base and Command Support Squadron. Unmanned Aerial Vehicle squadrons VMU-1 and VMU-2 were established 15-1-96 at MCAS Cherry Point, North Carolina, and Yuma, Arizona, respectively, to operate RQ-2A/B Predator drone reconnaissance aircraft.

NEW AIRCRAFT PROCUREMENT AUTHORIZATION

	FY 06	FY 07	FY 08	FY 09	FY 10	FY 11
F-35B/C Lightning II (JSF)	—	—	8	32	36	33
F/A-18E/F Hornet	38	30	24	20	22	14
EA-18G Growler	4	12	18	22	20	10
E-2C/D* Hawkeye	2	2	4*	4*	4*	4*
MV-22B Osprey	9	14	19	31	35	37
MH-60S Knighthawk	26	18	20	26	26	26
MH-60R Seahawk	12	25	25	31	32	31
T-45C Goshawk	6	12	—	—	—	—
T-6A Texan-II JPATS	3	21	48	48	48	48
P-8A Multimission (MMA)	—	—	4	—	6	8
C-37	—	—	—	—	—	1
C-40A Clipper	—	—	—	5	1	1
KC-130J Hercules	5	4	4	—	—	—
Broad-Area UAV	—	—	—	—	—	4
VH-71 Kestrel (new presidential helo)	5	—	3	4	3	4
Modernizations:						
UH-1Y & AH-1Z	10	18	19	23	23	23
CH-53	—	—	—	—	2	2
F-5E Tiger II (repurchased from Switzerland for aggressor ops)	9	5	—	—	—	—

NAVAL AIRCRAFT DESIGNATION SYSTEM

In addition to the nickname given to each basic aircraft design (Hornet, Tomcat, Orion, etc.), each basic aircraft type is alphanumerically designated as follows:

1. The letter immediately preceding the hyphen indicates the basic type:

A—attack
B—bomber
C—cargo/transport
E—airborne early warning
F—fighter
H—helicopter
K—tanker, inflight refueling
O—observation
P—patrol
S—antisubmarine
T—training
U—utility
V— VTOL/STOL, vertical or short takeoff
V—and landing
X—research

2. The figure that comes immediately after the hyphen is the design sequence number. When a letter follows this figure, its position in the alphabet indicates that the aircraft is the first, second, third, etc., modification to the original design. Example: F/A-18D = a fighter/attack aircraft, the eighteenth fighter design, the fourth major variant.

NAVAL AIRCRAFT DESIGNATION SYSTEM *(continued)*

3. When a basic aircraft is configured for a function that is not its original mission, a second letter precedes the letter for that mission (see number 1 previously):

A—attack
C—cargo/transport
D—direction or control of drones, aircraft, or missiles
E—special electronic installation
H—search and rescue
K—tanker, inflight, refueling
L—cold weather; for arctic regions
M—multimission or mine countermeasures
Q—drone aircraft
R—reconnaissance
S—antisubmarine
T—trainer
U—utility, general service
V—staff
W—weather, meteorology*

4. A third prefixed letter ahead of an aircraft's designation means:

G—permanently grounded*
J—temporary special test*
N—permanent special test
X—experimental
Y—prototype
Z—planning*

*Not currently used

PRINCIPAL COMBAT AIRCRAFT

♦ F-35B/C Lightning II (Joint Strike Fighter, JSF)
Mfr.: Lockheed Martin Corp., Fort Worth, Texas

Wingspan: F-35B: 10.7 m; F-35C: 13.1 m **Length:** F-35B: 15.6 m; F-35C: 15.7 m
Height: F-35B: 4.6 m; F-35C: 4.7 m
Weight: 13,608 kg empty/27,216 kg max. takeoff **Max. speed:** Mach 1.6+
Engines: 1 Pratt & Whitney F135 or G.E. F136 turbofan (~18,000-kg thrust) wth vectored thrust
Ceiling: 50,000+ ft.
Range with internal fuel: F-35B: 900 n.m.; F-35C: 1,400 n.m.
Internal fuel: F-35B: 5,896 kg; F-35C: 8,618 kg
Armament: Internal: 2 AAMs + 2 ASMs; external: up to 6,804 kg stores on six hard-point positions; 1/25-mm cannon
Avionics: APG-81 Active Electronically Scanned Array (AESA) radar, . . . passive electro-optical/infrared, . . . EW

X-35C Lightning II prototype in U.S. Navy configuration Lockheed Martin, 2006

X-35B Lightning II STOVL variant—note the engine nozzle pointed down for vertical landing Lockheed Martin, 2006

Remarks: The F-35 will be purchased by Navy and Marine Corps aviation in both carrier (F-35C) and STOVL (Short Take-Off/Vertical Landing, F-35B) attack fighter variants. The initial $18,981,928,201 contract was awarded to Lockheed Martin on 26-10-01, with plans calling for F-35A models for the Air Force, F-35C for the Navy, and F-35B for the Marine Corps (and the U.K.); the different variants are to have a 70–90% commonality; the total USN/USMC buy was cut to 680 during 3-02. The designation "F-35" is out of sequence and may have been the result of a slip of the tongue on the part of the Secretary of the Air Force that was not corrected. The Pratt and Whitney F135 engine and the G.E. F136 are to be interchangeable in the aircraft. Officially named the F-35 Lightning II on 7-7-06. First flight of the F-35C is scheduled for 2007.

♦ F/A-18E/F Super Hornet fighter-bombers and E/A-18G Growler EW aircraft
Mfr.: Boeing, St. Louis, Mo.

Wingspan: 13.62 m (9.94 m folded) **Length:** 18.38 m **Height:** 4.88 m
Weight: 13,386 kg light/29,931 kg max. takeoff **Max. speed:** Mach 1.8
Engines: 2 G.E. F414-GE-400 turbofans (9,977-kg thrust each)
Ceiling: 50,000+ ft.
Range: 2,303 n.m. ferry; 665 n.m. radius with 1,814 kg payload
Fuel: 6,558 kg internal, up to 7,429 kg external (3 × 480-gal. tanks)
Armament: 8,050 kg conventional on 11 stores positions; 1/20-mm M61A1 internal cannon
Avionics: APG-73 or APG-79 (AESA) radar, AAS-38 FLIR-pod-capable, ALQ-165 ASPJ EW; E/A-18G only: three ALQ-99 jamming pods

F/A-18E Super Hornet U.S. Navy, 4-06

F/A-18E Super Hornet U.S. Navy, 6-06

F/A-18F Super Hornet—two-seat variant U.S. Navy, 6-06

E/A-18G Growler—test team prototype, fitted with EW jamming pods Boeing, 5-06

PRINCIPAL COMBAT AIRCRAFT *(continued)*

Remarks: E-model is single-seat, F is two-seat and was originally intended to be a trainer variant. Have improved low-observable characteristics over earlier, smaller F/A-18 models.

The planning goal of 1,000 aircraft was cut to 732 in 5-97, to 548 later that year, and to 460 during 3-02, with the last to be ordered under FY 09. The 100th aircraft was delivered on 14-6-02. 42 were ordered in FY 05 for $3 billion, 38 in FY 06 for $2.9 billion and funding for 30 was requested in FY 07.

Prototype (first of seven developmental aircraft) rolled out 9-95. Contract for first production increment awarded 3-6-97 for four F/A-18E and four F/A-18F; first production F/A-18E flew 6-11-98 and was accepted on 18-12-98. The 100th aircraft was delivered on 14-6-02. The first squadron was VFA-122 at Lemoore, California, established 1-10-98. First fleet deployment of the F/A-18E was during the spring of 2002.

Can carry a maximum of eight AIM-7 Sparrow (plus two AIM-9), 12 AIM-9 Sidewinder, or 12 AIM-120 AMRAAM AAM; five 330- or 480-gal. external tanks; 11 Mk 83, 1,000-lb bombs; six AGM-65 Maverick, AGM-154 JSOW, or AGM-88 HARM ASM; or AGM-84H SLAM-ER ASM. Can also carry a centerline aerial refueling store. Combat radius of 665 n.m. would be achieved in Hi-Hi-Hi flight profile with two AIM-9 AAM, four Mk 83 bombs, three 480-gal. external tanks, and two sensor pods. Can land aboard with 4,082-kg armament stores. Total wing area is 46.5 m^2. Deck "spot" area is 23% greater than for earlier F/A-18-series models.

To be added to later aircraft are the Boeing Advanced Targeting Forward-Looking Infrared pod (ATFLIR); Raytheon APG-79 Active Electronically-Scanned Array (AESA) radar in place of the APG-73; the Lockheed Martin ALQ-214 Integrated Defensive Electronic Countermeasures System (IDECM); the capability to employ the AIM-9X missile; and a helmet-mounted cuing system. AESA is being fitted to the 237th and later aircraft. By spring 2003, the Raytheon SHARP (Shared Reconnaissance Pod) was being deployed on F/A-18E/F aircraft of the CVN 68 air group; SHARP is a reconfigurable pod the size of a 330-gallon drop tank that replaces the F-14's TARPS reconnaissance system.

The design is being further developed to produce the EA-18G Growler electronic support successor to the EA-6B, to enter squadron service in 2010. The aircraft has a great deal of commanality with the F/A-18F and would carry three ALQ-99 jamming pods providing the same EW capability as the EA-6B ICAP III system; a total production of 90 are planned. Unit cost of the F/A-18G is approximately $83 million in 2006 dollars. With the electronic warfare pods removed from the stores pylons, the aircraft will have full ground-attack capabilities. Flight testing of the 1st EA-18G began in 9-06.

♦ F/A-18A/B/C/D Hornet fighter-bombers
Mfr.: Boeing-McDonnell Douglas, St. Louis, Mo.

Wingspan: 11.43 m (12.3 with missiles) **Length:** 17.07 m **Height:** 4.67 m
Weight: 10,620 kg empty/25,541 kg max. **Max. speed:** Mach 1.8
Engines: 2 G.E. F404-GE-400 turbofans (6,800-kg thrust each)
Ceiling: 50,000+ ft.
Range: 2,303 n.m. ferry; 410 n.m. radius with 1,814 kg payload
Armament: 5,900-kg conventional or nuclear stores, including up to 4 Harpoon missiles: 2 Sidewinder, 4 Sparrow missiles—1 20-mm M61A1 internal cannon
Avionics: APG-65 (A/B models) or APG-73 (C/D models) radar, AAS-38 FLIR-pod-capable, ALQ-165 ASPJ EW

F/A-18A—assigned to the U.S. Navy's Blue Angels flight demonstration team
U.S. Navy, 5-05

Remarks: Multirole strike fighter. B and D models are two-seat versions. Carry 4,930 kg internal fuel/7,711 kg max. external fuel. F/A-18C/D have APG-73 radar, and 135 earlier aircraft were to have APG-73 backfitted. Uses a microprocessor to control the various weapons systems, depending on combat mode. First USMC squadron operational 7-1-83; first USN during 10-83. F/A-18C/D have AMRAAM and IR Maverick missile capability. F/A-18D for USMC have ATARS tactical reconnaissance pod and are capable of all-weather attack. In 1990–96 130 F/A-18A were retired. Single-seat USMC F/A-18C squadrons began to be integrated aboard carriers beginning 10-94; the shorter-ranged Marine F/A-18D two-seaters will not go aboard carriers. The SHARP reconnaissance pod was developed to permit the F/A-18F to replace TARPS-equipped F-14As beginning around 2003. The last in the series, an F/A-18D for the USMC, was delivered on 25-8-00.

F/A-18C U.S. Navy, 12-05

Marine Corps F/A-18D U.S. Marine Corps, 10-05

Note: The last F-14 Tomcat squadron, VF-31, was retired from service on 30-9-06. A few nonactive F-14s remain in service for test and experimentation duties.

♦ AV-8B Harrier-II V/STOL attack fighters
Mfr.: Boeing-McDonnell Douglas, St. Louis, Mo.

Wingspan: 9.24 m **Length:** 14.10 m (AV-8B+: 14.55) **Height:** 3.53 m
Weight: AV-8B: 8,720 kg max. takeoff in VTOL mode/13,492 kg max. STOL AV-8B+: 6,742 kg empty/14,059-kg max. STOL
Speed: 650 kts max.; 585 kts sea level
Engine: 1 Rolls-Royce Pegasus F402-RR-408 (9,751-kg thrust)
Ceiling: 50,000 ft. **Range:** 2,460 n.m. max. ferry; 100+ n.m. VTOL radius
Armament: 1 25-mm GAU-12/U gatling gun; 2–4 Sidewinder AAM, up to 14/227-kg or 6/454-kg bombs, Maverick, Walleye

AV-8B Harrier II U.S. Navy, 6-05

AB-8B Harrier II+—note longer nosecone housing the APG-65 radar
U.S. Navy, 2-05

PRINCIPAL COMBAT AIRCRAFT *(continued)*

Remarks: 276 were procured for the Marine Corps. Seventeen others were two-seat TAV-8B trainers. First squadron operational 6-85. First of 60 night-capable variant, with FLIR, flew 6-87. Average cost: $21.6 million. One hundred sixty-seventh built and later had the more powerful F402-RR-408 engine; the final 27 had the APG-65 radar added. Can deploy aboard LHA 1– and LHD 1–class amphibious warfare ships. Plans to update 114 of the surviving units to AV-8B Harrier II+ with APG-65 radar and other improved avionics were canceled 3-92 but were reinstated by 5-93 with a new goal of 74 upgraded aircraft; funds to convert the first two production versions were provided under FY 94, and by FY 1997, a steady 12 per year were being modernized, with the last delivered late in 2001.

♦ S-3B Viking shipboard multirole aircraft

Mfr.: Lockheed-California Co., Burbank, Calif.

Wingspan: 20.93 m **Length:** 16.26 m **Height:** 6.94 m
Weight: 12,160 kg empty/23,853 kg max.
Speed: 450 kts max.; 350 kts cruise; 210 kts patrol
Engines: 2 G.E. TF34-GE-400 turbofans (4,210-kg thrust each)
Ceiling: 40,000-ft.
Range: 3,000 n.m. ferry; 1,150 n.m. patrol radius (9-hr, endurance)
Armament: 4 Mk 46 or Mk 50 torpedoes or 4 depth charges or 4 mines or Mk 82 or Mk 83 bombs; 2 Harpoon on underwing stations (see Remarks)
Avionics: APS-137(V)1 radar, ASQ-81(V)1 MAD, ALE-40 ECM, 60 sonobuoys, 90 expendable decoys

S-3B Viking U.S. Navy, 10-05

Remarks: 187 S-3As were built, primarily for use as carrier-deployed ASW aircraft. Beginning in 3-87, 132 were to be updated to S-3B configuration, with APS-137(V)1 synthetic aperture radar, Harpoon ASM launch capability, new auxiliary power unit, ALE-40 countermeasures dispenser, and other updated avionics; last conversion completed 1994. ASW-dedicated aircrew and equipment were being removed from the aircraft as of 1998, and the surviving aircraft are now dedicated to surveillance, photo reconnaissance, and aerial refueling missions. Starting in FY 02, all remaining aircraft are to be retired, with the last leaving service by 2009, although S-3B upgrades were intended to keep the aircraft flying into 2015.

One S-3B was updated to S-3B SSU (Surveillance Systems Upgrade) configuration prior to 2000 and proved so valuable during operations over Afghanistan that conversion of four more was requested. The S-3B SSU carries the APS-137(V)5 radar, with improved range and resolution.

Sixteen S-3As (out of a requirement for 36) were converted to ES-3A Shadow Battle Group Passive Horizon Extension System (BGPHES) ELINT aircraft to replace the retired EA-3B; weight increased to 13,520 kg empty, and 63 antennas fitted, as is the APS-137 inverse synthetic aperture radar. The ALR-76, ALR 81, ALR-82, ALR-92, and ALD-9 electronic support measures systems were installed. The first operational aircraft was delivered to VQ-5 on 22-5-92, but all 16 were withdrawn from service starting 2-99, with most of the aircraft placed in storage with unconverted S-3As in Arizona. US-3A COD (Carrier On-board Delivery) conversions are all now in storage; the one KS-3A tanker prototype was converted to a US-3A in 1984 and subsequently lost. One S-3A is being used for structural life extension update prototype by Lockheed Martin, starting in 1999.

♦ E-2C Hawkeye airborne early-warning and air-control

Mfr.: Northrop-Grumman, Grumman Aerospace Corp., Bethpage, N.Y., and St. Augustine, Fla.

Wingspan: 24.58 m **Length:** 17.60 m **Height:** 5.59 m
Weight: 18,364 kg empty/24,689 kg max. **Wing area:** 65.03 m^2
Speed: 315 kts max.; 260 kts cruise
Engines: 2 Allison T56-A-427 turboprops (5,100 shp each)
Ceiling: 37,000 ft. **Range:** 1,540 n.m. ferry **Endurance** 6 hours
Fuel: 5,625 kg internal **Crew:** 5 **Armament:** None
Avionics: APS-138, APS-139, or APS-145 radar; ESM suite

Remarks: The original APS 125 radar was replaced by APS-138 TRAC-A (Total Radiation Aperture Control Antenna) to reduce side-lobes; it can track upward of 600 air and surface targets within a 250-n.m. radius, while the aircraft controls up to 25 intercepts. The 122nd and 17 later aircraft got later APS-139 radar with improved ECCM, and aircraft delivered since 1992 had the APS-145 radar with overland capability, new IFF, GPS, Link 16, and JTDS (Joint Tactical Information Distribution System). The APS-145 radar increases target detection capability fifteen-fold and covers an area of 6 million square miles. Current plans call for continuing low-rate E-2C production indefinitely and the introduction of an updated E-2D variant, deliveries of which are expected in 2011; the aircraft will employ a Northrop Grumman solid-state, electronically steered UHF radar and will have ballistic missile detection and tracking capabilities. The E-2D is also to have a tactical cockpit, allowing the pilot to function as a fourth mission system operator; a new communications suite; new generators; improved IFF; and an updated mission computer and software.

E-2C Hawkeye U.S. Navy, 4-06

The first Hawkeye-2000 (H-2000) variant of the E-2C, equipped with CEC (Co-operative Engagement Capability) sensor fusion and data distribution equipment, flew on 11-4-98, and 11 of the aircraft had been delivered by 2004. In January 2004 Northrop-Grumman was awarded a contract to produce three Hawkeye 2000 aircraft and five Hawkeye 2000 flight trainers for delivery in 2006. The training version, known as TE-2, is not equipped with the Hawkeye 2000's radar, mission computer, or other prime mission equipment, but the required wiring and hardware fixtures is installed. All aircraft currently on order or programmed will have the CEC feature. All aircraft were fitted with new, eight-bladed, narrow-chord props by 2006, and a new SIRST (Surveillance Infrared Search and Track) sensor is to be added.

♦ EA-6B Prowler combat EW aircraft

Mfr.: Northrop-Grumman, Grumman Aerospace Corp., Calverton, N.Y.

Wingspan: 16.15 m **Length:** 18.11 m **Height:** 4.95 m
Weight: 12,185 kg empty/27,392 kg max. **Speed:** 520 kts max. (410 kts cruise)
Engines: 2 Pratt & Whitney J52-P-409 turbojets (5,442 kg thrust each)
Ceiling: 34,400 ft. **Range:** 2,400 n.m. ferry; 710 n.m. combat radius
Armament: HARM missiles
Avionics: ALQ-149; ALQ-99F jammers; APS-130 radar; etc.

EA-6B Prowler U.S. Navy, 4-06

Remarks: One hundred seventy were delivered between 1-71 and 11-91. Marines have 22. Crew of four. First EA-6B ADVCAP (Advanced Capability) delivered 10-89 with J52-P-409 engines, new slats, improved flaps, ALQ-149 communications intercept/jammer, etc. HARM missile capability was added in 1985. Last nine new EA-6B were procured under FY 89. A program to update 102 earlier aircraft to ADVCAP status was canceled. VAQ-129, Whidbey Island, was established 30-9-95 to provide land-based joint USN/USAF electronic support and crews, VAQ-133 and VAQ-137 were established in 1996, and VAQ-142 and VAQ-128 in 1997. The aircraft are heavily used.

Surviving aircraft are configured in one of two "blocks"—Block 82 and Block 89A. Block 82 aircraft have improved structural, safety, and supportability features, while Block 89A aircraft, of which the prototype conversion was delivered in 8-97, have enhanced computers, ARC-210 radios, and an integral GPS/inertial navigation system; production conversions were to begin delivery in 1999, and all remaining aircraft may ultimately be affected. Further "ICAP III" or Block 89A improvements were funded under FY 99 to retain the aircraft in service through 2015 (although they will probably be retired much sooner); ICAP III aircraft will receive GPS systems, an improved ALQ-99 noise jammer that will be able to direct higher energies at specific threat signals, new radios, and provision for later SATCOM transceiver installation and Link 16. The first of two prototype ICAP III aircraft flew on 16-11-01, and production conversions will become operational in 2005. Plans to convert 18 EA-6B aircraft from Block 82 to Block 89A configuration were terminated in 6-00.

♦ C-2A Greyhound carrier onboard-delivery aircraft

Mfr.: Northrop Grumman, Grumman Aerospace Corp., Bethpage, N.Y.

Wingspan: 24.57 m **Length:** 17.27 m **Height:** 4.85 m
Weight: 14,175 kg empty/24,668 kg max. **Speed:** 343 kts max. (257 kts cruise)
Engines: 2 Allison T56-A-425 turboprops (4,910 shp each)
Ceiling: 33,800 ft. **Range:** 1,490 n.m. at 260 kts

PRINCIPAL COMBAT AIRCRAFT *(continued)*

C-2A Greyhound U.S. Navy, 6-06

Remarks: Variant of the E-2 Hawkeye series with larger-diameter fuselage. Twelve of the original 17 ordered in 1964 remained when a second batch of 39 with uprated engines was ordered in 1983; production ended 1989. Crew of three plus up to 32 passengers or 20 litter patients, rear loading ramp. Payload: 5,535 kg. Usage has been heavier than expected, and only 35 remained in service by 2006. Were to have begun retirement in 2011 but are to be rehabilitated to serve an additional 20 years each.

♦ P-8A Poseidon (Multimission Maritime Aircraft, MMA)

Mfr.: Boeing Aerospace Div., The Boeing Co., Seattle, Wash.

Wingspan: 35.7 m **Length:** 39.4 m **Height:** 12.5 m
Weight: 85,366 kg max.
Speed: 490 kts max
Engines: 2 CFM56 turbofans
Ceiling: 41,000 ft.
Range: 1,200 n.m. patrol radius with 4 hours on station
Armament: Torpedoes, missiles, bombs or mines.
Avionics: APS-115 or APS-137(V) radar; AQS-81(V)1 magnetic anomaly detector; ASQ-114 digital computer; AAS-36 FLIR; 87 sonobuoys

P-8A Poseidon—artist's conception Boeing, 2005

Remarks: Replacement for the P-3C Orion. Two versions of the same airframe are planned: one for maritime patrol and attack, one for surveillance and intelligence collection to replace the EP-3. During 6-04, Boeing was awarded a contract based on a modifed 737-800 airliner. Named P-8A during 4-05. As of 2006, the Navy plans to procure 108 P-8As, with flight testing to begin in 2009 and service entry around 2013.

♦ P-3C Orion maritime surveillance aircraft and variants

Mfr.: Lockheed Martin, Lockheed Aeronautical Systems Co., Burbank, Calif.

Wingspan: 31.13 m **Length:** 36.61 m **Height:** 10.28 m
Weight: 27,892 kg empty/62,994 kg max. (EP-3E: 37,188 kg/64,400 kg)
Speed: 405 kts max (EP-3E: 345 kts).; 209 kts patrol cruise
Engines: 4 Allison T65-A-14 turboprops (4,910 shp each)
Ceiling: 34,000 ft. (EP-3E: 30,000 ft.)
Range: 4,500 n.m. (2,380 n.m. patrol radius/14.5 hrs. endurance)
Armament: 7,700-kg disposable ordnance, including 4 Mk 46 or Mk 50 torpedoes, 4 SLAM, SLAM-ER, or Maverick ASM, 6 908 kg mines, etc.
Avionics: APS-115 or APS-137(V) radar; AQS-81(V)1 magnetic anomaly detector; ASQ-114 digital computer; AAS-36 FLIR; 87 sonobuoys

Remarks: Crew of up to 15. Current plans call for upgrading 68 of the 111 Update II and II.5 P-3Cs to Update III configuration by 2006, for a total of 208; they are to be equipped to track small patrol craft and vehicles ashore. The P-3C Update III is fitted with an A-NEW central operations module built around the ASQ-114 computer, APS-137 ISAR (Inverse Synthetic Aperture Radar), ALR-66(V)5 EW gear, AAS-36 infrared detector, AAR-47 missile-warning system, ALE-47 countermeasures dispensing system, AQS-81 MAD, Boeing UYS-1 acoustic processor, the addition of GPS receivers

P-3C Orion U.S. Navy, 7-04

EP-3E Aries-II U.S. Navy, 9-05

NP-3D Orion—used for testing and research U.S. Navy, 8-05

and ALQ-16 EW equipment, and the capability to carry AGM-65F Maverick and/or AGM-84E SLAM antiship missiles. In a further BMUP (Block Modification Update Program), the aircraft are to receive the ASQ-227 mission computer in place of the ASQ-212, the ALR-66B(V) EW system, the USQ-78B acoustic receiver system, and improved flat-panel display screens. For 221 aircraft, the airframe fatigue life of 38 years may be extended to 48 years in a Service Life Extension Program (SLEP).

A Sustained Readiness Program rehabilitation for 32 aircraft contracted to E-Systems (now Raytheon) in 1994 was canceled in 2-00 with only six aircraft delivered; another seven are to be completed and the equipment purchased for the remainder delivered to the Navy for use on 19 follow-on SRP Aircraft Recovery Program (SARP) aircraft. The Navy requires 146 P-3C aircraft to be updated under the Antisurface Improvement Program (AIP) ASW improvement program but was able to budget only for 58 during the 2001–9 decade. The AIP version, used extensively over Bosnia, Kosovo, and Afghanistan, employs the Advanced Imaging Multispectral Sensor (AIMS) for standoff optical surveillance and targeting and has the ability to launch AGM-84E SLAM and AGM-84H SLAM-ER missiles.

Other variants: The first of 13 P-3C converted to EP-3E "Aries-II" ELINT aircraft for Squadrons VQ-1 and VQ-2 was delivered to VQ-1 on 7-8-90 to replace the earlier EP-3B/E "Aries-I." The EP-3E aircraft have APS-134 Big Look radars, carry 60,000 lbs of fuel for a gross weight of 142,000 lbs, and have crews of seven officers and 17 enlisted. EP-3E aircraft weigh 82,000 lbs empty (142,000 lbs max. takeoff), have an endurance of 12 hrs and a maximum airspeed of 345 kts, and are 30.38 m long. The older EP-3Es will reach retirement age in 2007. A P-3C was converted to EP-3E in 1999–2000 from a P-3C as a replacement for an EP-3E that crashed in 1997. One EP-3E was captured by China after it was severely damaged in a mid-air collision with a Chinese fighter during 4-01, although it was eventually returned to U.S. custody.

♦ E-6A/B Mercury strategic communications aircraft

Mfr.: Boeing Aerospace Div., The Boeing Co., Seattle, Wash.

Wingspan: 45.60 m **Length:** 46.61 m **Height:** 12.93 m
Weight: 78,365 kg empty/155,102 kg max. **Speed:** 530 kts (442 kts cruise)
Engines: 4 CFM Int'l. F108-CF-100 turbofans (9,977 kg thrust each)

PRINCIPAL COMBAT AIRCRAFT *(continued)*

Ceiling: 42,000 ft. cruise **Range:** 6,600 n.m. ferry
Endurance 16.2 hours (72 hours with aerial refueling)
Avionics: VLF communications suite, ALR-68(V)4 ESM, Bendix APS-133 weather radar, Litton LTN-90 inertial nav., OMEGA

E-6B Mercury U.S. Navy, 1998

Remarks: Ordered 29-4-83 to replace EC-130Q TACAMO ("TAke-Charge-And-Move-Out) strategic communications aircraft. First flight 19-2-87; all delivered by end 1991. Nickname changed from "Hermes" in 1992. Operated by VQ-3 from Barber's Point, Oahu, and VQ-4 from Patuxent River, Maryland, until 29-5-92, when both squadrons moved to Tinker AFB, Oklahoma, under Strategic Communications Wing 1. Have an 8,535-m trailing-wire main VLF antenna and a 1,524-m short trailing wire VHF dipole. ECM pod on starboard wingtip. Ten crew, plus eight relief crew. Uses Boeing 707-320B transport airframe. Prototype upgraded E-6B aircraft delivered 16-6-94 by Chrysler Technologies Airborne Systems, Waco, Texas, with enhanced message-handling capabilities, Milstar SATCOMM terminal, 1553B digital databus. Six series E-6B airborne command post conversions ordered 31-1-95 for $95.5 million, with capability to communicate with all U.S. strategic weapons systems command centers on land and sea. All 16 were converted to E-6B by 2003, with the first production conversion handed over on 10-10-97 and the last completed by 9-03. A single Boeing 737 was leased by L-3 Communications during 3-01 for use as a flight trainer for the E-6B.

♦ C-40A Clipper transport
Mfr.: Boeing, Seattle, Wash.

Wingspan: 34.32 m **Length:** 33.63 m **Height:** 12.55 m
Weight: 77,551 kg max. takeoff **Speed:** Mach 0.78 to 0.82
Engines: 2 G.E. CFM56-7 turbofans (24,000 lb thrust each at sea level)
Ceiling: 41,000 ft. **Range:** 3,800 n.m, max.

C-40A Clipper U.S. Navy, 2-04

Remarks: Two Boeing 737-700C airframes were ordered on as C-40A Clippers on 29-8-97, a third in 6-98, and a fourth on 30-7-99 (for delivery 8-01), a fifth in 6-00, and the sixth on 3-1-01. The convertible aircraft can carry up to 121 passengers, or up to eight cargo pallets (17.46 metric tons max.), or a combination of up to three pallets and 70 passengers. They are to replace aging C-9B/DC-9 transports in Naval Reserve service.

♦ MV-22B Osprey tiltrotor assault troop carrier
Mfrs.: The Boeing Co., Vertol Div., Morton, Pa., and Bell Helicopter Textron, Amarillo, Tex.

Wingspan: 14.17 m (25.78 over rotors) **Length:** 17.48 m
Height: 6.73 m (5.28 folded)
Weight: 15,032 kg empty/27,442 kg max. (23,859 for vertical takeoff)
Speed: 340 kts (275 kts cruise)
Engines: 2 Allison T406-AD-400 turboshafts (6,150 shp each sust.)
Ceiling: 32,000 ft.
Range: 1,200 n.m. at 275 kts with 1,814 kg cargo; 2,100 n.m. max. unrefueled ferry
Avionics: AAQ-16 FLIR; AAR-47 missile warning system; APR-39A(V)2 EW

Remarks: 360 total (reduced in 1997 from 473) are planned. The last of 10 developmental aircraft was delivered 9-2-98 and the first production aircraft during 5-99. Navy plans to acquire 48 of the total as HV-22 combat rescue variants, and the U.S. Air Force has ordered 50 CV-22Bs for special operations use, the first of which was completed on 25-7-00. The first five fully operational MV-22Bs were ordered on 28-4-97 for $402 million; they went to Marine squadron VMMT-204, New River, North Carolina. Due to two losses, however, all operational aircraft were grounded during 2001, with flight testing resumed in 4-02. During 2003 the V-22 completed Phase IV shipboard suitability testing aboard USS *Bataan* (LHD 05). Eight MV-22s were ordered in FY 05 at a cost of $1.3 billion. Nine more were ordered in FY 06 and 14 in FY 07.

MV-22 Osprey—taking off from the deck of USS *Wasp* (LHD 1) U.S. Navy, 11-05

MV-22 Osprey—in forward flight mode U.S. Navy, 4-02

Intended to carry 24 troops or 12 litters up to 200 n.m. at about 3,000-ft. altitude. Alternatively, can carry 30 passengers or 9,000 kg of cargo internally or a 4,535-kg external load. Rotor/propeller blade diameter is 11.58 m, giving an overall span of 25.78 m over rotors. Vertical rate of climb is 1,090 ft./min. in vertical mode, and hover ceiling is 14,200 ft. Carries 7,600 liters of fuel internally and has capacity for four auxiliary cabin tanks for another 9,200 liters for ferrying; can be aerial-refueled. General Dynamics received a contract in 4-01 to develop a turret-mounted 12.7-mm GAU-19/A gatling gun for the MV-22B to provide a suppression-fire capability. The Air Force CV-22 Special Forces variant has additional fuel tanks to double the unrefueled range.

♦ SH-60B (LAMPS-III), SH-60F, HH-60H, and MH-60R Seahawk helicopters
Mfr.: Sikorsky Aircraft Div., United Aircraft Corp., Stratford, Conn.

Rotor diameter: 16.36 m **Length:** 19.76 m (15.26 fuselage, 12.47 folded)
Height: 5.23 m
Weight: SH-60B: 6,190 kg empty/9,927 max. takeoff; SH-60F/MH-60R: 10,658 kg max.
Speed: 150 kts (126 cruise)
Engines: 2 T700-GE-401C (1,940 shp max./1,662 shp continuous each)
Range: 150 n.m. mission radius (4 hrs.); 6 hr maximum/678 n.m. ferry range
Armament: 2 Mk 46 or Mk 50 torpedoes (or 1–2 AGM-119B Penguin ASM in some SH-60B or 2 Hellfire ASM); HH-60H: Hellfire missiles and GAU-17, M-240, or M-60D guns
Avionics: SH-60B: APS-124 radar; ASQ-81(V)2 MAD; UYS-1 Proteus sonobuoy processor; 25 A-size sonobuoys; ALQ-142 ESM; Link 11—SH-60F: AQS-13F dipping sonar; no radar or sonobuoy facilities—HH-60: APR-39A(V)2 EW; ALE-47 EW; ALQ-144A EW; SATCOM; FLIR—MH-60R: APS-147 radar; AQS-22 ALFS dipping sonar; UYS-2 sonobuoy processor and sonobuoys

SH-60B Seahawk—LAMPS III ASW version taking on fuel from USS *Ronald Reagan* (CVN 76); note APS-124 radar chin mounted radar and dart-shaped ASQ-81 MAD gear U.S. Navy, 7-06

PRINCIPAL COMBAT AIRCRAFT *(continued)*

SH-60F Seahawk—carrier-borne ASW variant, carries dipping sonar but no chin-mounted radar or MAD gear U.S. Navy, 3-06

HH-60H Seahawk—combat rescue variant U.S. Navy, 7-06

MH-60R—latest variant with radar, dipping sonar, and sonobuoys but no MAD gear U.S. Navy, 4-06

Remarks: The SH-60B, flown by 12 HSL (Light Helicopter Antisubmarine) squadrons, was intended for use aboard frigates and destroyers as part of an ASW suite, with the helicopter linked to the ship by datalink for data processing, sensors displaying on the ship. First flight 12-12-79. Crew of three. Block I update, awarded 12-89, added Mk 50 torpedo capability, Penguin missile capability, 99-channel sonobuoy processor, GPS, and a third weapons station; a total of 171 were to be able to launch AGM-119B Penguin—far more helicopters than there were missiles, but the conversion program was curtailed after 28 had been completed. Block II, which entered service in 1996, added AQS-22 FLASH dipping sonar, substituted a multimode inverse synthetic aperture radar (ISAR), added FLIR, added helo-to-helo datalink capability, and added a targeting capability for ship-launched SLAM missiles and improved countermeasures. Most SH-60Bs now have the more powerful T700-GE-401C engines. For antisurface warfare, 46 SH-60B and 42 HH-60H have been fitted to carry Hellfire missiles, video datalink, a 7.62-mm machinegun, and AAS-44 FLIR.

The first production SH-60F flew on 19-3-87 as a replacement for the carrier-based SH-3 Sea King and differed from the SH-60B in having most of the LAMPS-II equipment deleted and replaced by an AQS-13F dipping sonar. No radar or EW gear is fitted. Last aircraft delivered 1-12-94.

Up to 170 SH-60B and 59 SH-60F were to be converted to MH-60R by 2012, with further conversions to be delivered later for a total of 243. The prototype conversion flew on 22-12-99, and the first of four test conversion aircraft ordered on 16-7-99 flew on 19-7-01. The first five production conversions were ordered during 3-00, with four more approved under FY 01; during 2001, however, the concept was changed to buying all-new MH-60R airframes, starting with six in the FY 04 budget. The designation SH-60R was changed to MH-60R on 25-5-01. MH-60Rs are equipped with an AQS-22 dipping sonar, AYK-14 integrated mission processors, a thermal imager, a laser mine-detection system, APS-147 synthetic aperture radar, passive target classification features added to the ALQ-142 EW system, the UYS-2A acoustic processor, and a new sonobuoy launcher; the MAD gear has been removed to save weight. The MH-60R is able to launch AGM-119 Penguin and AGM-114 Hellfire missiles and Mk 46/50/54 torpedoes and has a door-mounted 7.62-mm mg; the aircraft began to enter squadron service at the end of 2005. Initial production of the MH-60R began with six helicopters purchased in FY 04 at a cost of $385.6 million. Eight were purchased in FY 05, 12 in FY 06, and 25 were requested in FY 07 with eventual total production expected to be 254.

Plans to update 14 HH-60H to MH-60R have been canceled.

♦ MH-60S Knighthawk support helicopters

Mfr.: Sikorsky Aircraft Div., United Aircraft Corp., Stratford, Conn.

MH-60S Knighthawk U.S. Navy, 6-06

Rotor diameter: 16.36 m **Length:** 19.76 m (15.26 fuselage; 15.70 folded)
Height: 4.87 m **Weight:** 6,281 kg empty/10,658 kg max.
Speed: 150 kts (130 cruise)
Engines: 2 T700-GE-401C (1,940 shp max./1,662 shp continuous each)
Range: 620 n.m. (with two 230-gal. external tanks)
Payload: Hellfire missiles; 1 7.62-mm mg; up to 9,000 lbs external cargo; 1 AQS-20(X) towed minehunting sonar; AES-1 Airborne Laser Mine Detection System (ALMDS); Organic Airborne and Surface Influence Sweep (OASIS); SPU-1/W Magnetic Orange Pipe (MOP), Mk 2(g) towed acoustic mine countermeasure.

Remarks: Designation changed from CH-60S to MH-60S on 6-2-01, with the "M" standing for "Multimission;" the aircraft was officially named Seahawk on the same date, the name "Knighthawk" having previously been used unofficially and finally authorized in 3-02. Intended to replace all H-46D and UH-3 utility helicopters, the first of a planned 237 MH-60S Knighthawks entered service in 2001 with HC-3. The YCH-60 demonstrator, converted from an Army UH-60L, first flew on 6-10-97, and two production aircraft were added to the FY 98 budget by Congress; first production conversion flight came on 27-1-00. The first "production" conversion aircraft flew on 27-1-00; 15 were ordered in FY 03 at a cost of $352.5 million. Thirteen were ordered in FY 04, 15 in FY 05, 26 in FY 06, and 18 were requested in FY 07.

Lightweight mine-countermeasures modules will be provided for the MH-60S, theoretically allowing it to replace the MH-53E; the aircraft are also be able to launch Hellfire missiles and will be equipped with an FLIR. Has a crew of four and can carry 13 passengers. Maximum payload is 4,000 lbs internal and 9,000 lbs external (10,000 lbs max. total).

Missions for the aircraft include organic airborne mine countermeasures; fleet combat logistic support; search and rescue; medical evacuation; vertical on-board delivery; special warfare support; humanitarian assistance; and torpedo, UAV, and UUV recovery. They have a rescue hoist, automatic blade fold, and a capacity to carry two standard cargo pallets internally.

Disposal notes: The remaining SH-2G Super SeaSprite LAMPS-I ASW helicopters were retired during FY 01 with the disestablishment of reserve squadrons HSL-94 and HSL-84; the relatively new aircraft were to be transferred to foreign navies.

♦ CH-53E Super Stallion transport and MH-53E Sea Dragon mine-countermeasures helicopters

Mfr: Sikorsky Aircraft Div., United Aircraft Corp., Stratford, Conn.

CH-53E Super Stallion heavy-lift helicopter U.S. Navy, 9-05

Rotor diameter: 24.08 m **Length:** 30.18 m (22.35 fuselage, 18.44 folded)
Height: 8.64 m **Weight:** 15,071 kg empty (MH-53E: 16,482 kg)/33,339 kg max.
Speed: 170 kts (150 cruise)
Engines: 3 G.E.T64-GE-416 turboshafts (4,380 shp max. each/3,695 cont.)
Ceiling: 18,500 ft.
Range: 1,000 n.m. unrefueled ferry; 230 n.m. with 8,630 kg cargo; 50 n.m. with 14,512 kg cargo (MH-53E: 4 hrs. endurance)

PRINCIPAL COMBAT AIRCRAFT *(continued)*

MH-53E Sea Dragon mine-countermeasures helicopter U.S. Navy, 3-06

Remarks: YCH-53E first flew 1-3-74, YMH-53E on 23-12-81. CH-53E can carry 56 fully-equipped troops or up to 14,512 kg cargo. All now operate with the USMC. Crew of three. Seven-bladed main rotor. CH-53E can also be used to tow Mk 105 mine-countermeasures sleds. Both versions are aerial-refuelable. The final two CH-53E were ordered 21-6-95 for delivery by 7-97; one, operated by USMC, is configured to carry presidential vehicles. MH-53E can deploy AQS-14 minehunting sonar, Mk 104 acoustic sled, Mk 105 magnetic sled, one or more Mk 103 mechanical cutter sleds; a 12.7-mm mg is carried for mine disposal. MH-53E has enlarged side sponsons holding 4,478 kg fuel (enough for 4.5 hours) and has a cable winch exerting a 13.6-ton pull; it can also be used to carry 56 troops. Two MH-53E can be accommodated in one C-5B transport. The MH-53E, although relatively new, is to be phased out and replaced by MH-60R/S helicopters with less effective mine-countermeasures modules. As an interim measure, however, four sets of air-towed AQS-14A(V)1 mine-detection sonars are being acquired

The USMC is considering a life-extension program to improve capabilities, reduce maintenance costs, and extend service to 2025 for 111 CH-53Es; the cost would be about $22 million per aircraft, and production updates would start with 15 aircraft in FY 2011. The CH-53X would be re-engined with the Rolls-Royce AE1107C turbo-fan, would receive new composite rotor blades and elastomeric rotor head to increase lift capacity from 7,600 lbs to 28,000 lbs under "hot and high" conditions (and maximum takeoff weight to 35,607 kg), would get a new cargo hook, and would have new cockpit avionics and displays.

♦ CH-53D Sea Stallion transport helicopters

Mfr.: Sikorsky Aircraft Div., United Aircraft Corp., Stratford, Conn.

CH-53D Sea Stallion U.S. Navy, 7-04

Rotor diameter: 22.04 m **Length:** 26.92 (20.48 fuselage) **Height:** 7.59 m
Weight: 10,718-kg empty/19,050-kg max. **Speed:** 170 kts (150 cruise)
Engines: 2 G.E. T64-GE-413 turboshafts (2,925 shp each) **Ceiling:** 21,000 ft.
Range: 886 n.m. ferry; 540 n.m. mission (3.5 hr. endurance)

Remarks: First ordered 8-62 for the Marine Corps. Last of 174 CH-53D versions was delivered 1-72. Can carry 55 combat-equipped troops or 24 stretchers and four attendants or four tons cargo. The 40 remaining in service are now considered to be "medium-lift" helicopters.

♦ UH/HH-46D/CH-46E Sea Knight transport helicopters

Mfr.: The Boeing Co., Vertol Div., Morton, Pa.

Rotor diameter: 15.54 m **Length:** 25.70 m (13.92 fuselage) **Height:** 5.17 m
Weight: 7,048 kg empty/11,023 kg. max. **Speed:** 143 kts max./134 kts cruise
Engines: 2 G.E. T58-GE-16 turboshafts (1,870 shp each, 1,770 sust.)
Ceiling: 14,000 ft. **Range:** 744 n.m. ferry; 206 n.m. mission
Fuel: 2,498 liters max. **Crew:** 2

CH-46E Sea Knight U.S. Navy, 5-05

Remarks: First flight 16-10-62, with 624 procured through 1970. Some 228 CH-46E are operated by 13 Marine Corps regular and reserve squadrons. All CH-46D vertical replenishment models were retired by 2006. CH-46E can accommodate 25 assault troops or 15 stretchers and two attendants. Several HH-46D SAR versions remain in service. Surviving aircraft have been updated with automatic navigation system, armored seats, glass-reinforced plastic rotor blades, and infrared jamming devices.

♦ AH-1W SuperCobra/AH-1Z ground attack helicopters

Mfr.: Bell Helicopter Textron, Inc., Ft. Worth, Texas

AH-1W SuperCobra U.S. Navy, 4-05

AH-1Z—note the four-bladed rotor and the sensor radome above the gunmount Sikorsky, 2001

Rotor diameter: 13.42 m **Length:** 17.47 m (12.93 fuselage) **Height:** 4.17 m
Weight: 4,626 kg empty/6,689 kg max. **Speed:** 180 kts max.
Engines: 2 G.E. T700-GE-410 turboshafts (1,690 shp each)
Ceiling: 10,500 ft. **Range:** 360 n.m. (2 hrs)
Armament: 1/20-mm XM-197 gatling gun, 76/2.75-in. rockets or 2/20-mm miniguns in pods, TOW and Hellfire ASM and/or Sidearm or Sidewinder AAM

Remarks: Improved AH-1T (with T400-CP-400 engines) flew 20-5-76, and 55 production versions were ordered, of which 37 survivors had been converted to AH-1W standard by 1990. Deliveries of new up-engined AH-1W began 27-3-87. Five were transferred from USMC stocks to Turkey in 1991. Although DoD selected the name "Viper" for the AH-1Z, the USMC does not use it.

The AH-1W is to be given a Lockheed Martin infrared sight, color t.v., and laser rangefinder and tracker; an integrated weapons system control, an additional weapons stores pylon to permit carrying up to 16 AGM-114 Hellfire missiles, and four-bladed rotors; the first 18 conversions were funded under FY 98, with the first of 180 production conversions rolled out on 20-11-00. Production conversion onset, however, has been delayed to FY 04, when only 12 UH-1Y/AH-1Z conversions are planned to be requested, with 16 to follow in FY 05, 33 in FY 06, and 41 in FY 07.

♦ UH-1N and HH-1N Iroquois and UH-1Y transport/utility helicopters

Mfr.: Bell Helicopter Textron, Inc., Ft. Worth, Tex.

Rotor diameter: 14.70 m **Length:** 17.47 m (12.93 m fuselage) **Height:** 4.39 m
Weight: 2,517 kg empty/4,763 kg max. **Speed:** 110 kts
Engines: 2 Pratt & Whitney T400-CP-400 turboshafts (1,250 shp max. each)
Ceiling: 15,000 ft. **Range:** 250 n.m. (2 hrs)
Armament: 2/7.62-mm mg, 2 rocket pods (7 × 2.75-in. rockets each)

USMC UH-1N U.S. Marine Corps, 5-05

PRINCIPAL COMBAT AIRCRAFT *(continued)*

Remarks: Normally known as the "Huey." UH-1N is used by the USMC as an armed assault helicopter and the UH-1N and HH-1N by the Navy as utility and rescue helicopters. First UH-1N delivered in 1971. USMC is updating the UH-1N to the UH-1Y with G.E. T700 engines, four-bladed props, and new avionics; the aircraft will be able to carry eight (vice four) troops and will have double the combat radius. The first of two prototype conversion aircraft flew on 20-12-01. Conversion of the two began with nine units in FY 04 and continues with seven in FY 05, 10 in FY 06, and 18 requested in FY 07. One hundred total are to be converted.

Other support and training aircraft include:

- C-12 Huron testing and training transports
- C-20A/D/G Gulfstream III/IV executive and personnel transports
- C-35 Citation VIP transports
- C-37 Gulfstream V transports
- C-130T/KC-130 Hercules transports and tankers
- T-2C Buckeye trainers
- T-6 Texan II trainers
- T-34C Mentor trainers
- T-38 Talon test pilot school trainers
- T-39G Sabreliner trainers
- T-44 Pegasus trainers
- T-45 Goshawk advanced trainers
- F-5E/F Tiger II adversary trainers
- F-16A/B adversary trainers
- TH-57B/C Sea Ranger helicopter trainers
- UH/VH-3 Sea King transport and Presidential helicopters

C-20G Gulfstream-IV U.S. Navy, 4-04

USMC UC-35D Citation Encore U.S. Navy, 2000

C-130T U.S. Navy, 2-04

T-6A Texan II—to replace the T-34C U.S. Navy, 8-03

F-5E Tiger II aggressor aircraft—of VFC-13 U.S. Navy, 1-05

T-44A Pegasus trainer A. D. Baker III, 8-97

VH-3D Sea King—Marine One presidential transport from HMX-1 U.S. Marine Corps, 5-05

T-45C Goshawk trainer U.S. Navy, 4-06

T-34C Mentor trainer—being replaced by the T-6 Texan II U.S. Navy, 5-05

PRINCIPAL COMBAT AIRCRAFT *(continued)*

T-2C Buckeye trainer—this aged aircraft is being phased out of service U.S. Navy, 8-05

NUCLEAR-POWERED BALLISTIC-MISSILE SUBMARINES [SSBN]

Note: Planning will commence around 2010 for a successor to the *Ohio* class, with the design possibly to be based on the smaller *Virginia*-class SSN.

♦ 14 Ohio class (SCB 304 design)

Bldr: General Dynamics Electric Boat Div., Groton, Conn.
(*Atlantic/†Pacific Fleet)

	Program	L	In serv.
SSBN 730 Henry M. Jackson† (ex-*Rhode Island*)	FY 77	15-10-83	6-10-84
SSBN 731 Alabama†	FY 78	19-5-84	20-5-85
SSBN 732 Alaska†	FY 78	12-1-85	25-1-86
SSBN 733 Nevada†	FY 80	14-9-85	16-8-86
SSBN 734 Tennessee*	FY 81	13-12-86	17-12-88
SSBN 735 Pennsylvania†	FY 83	23-4-88	9-9-89
SSBN 736 West Virginia*	FY 84	14-10-89	20-10-90
SSBN 737 Kentucky†	FY 85	11-8-90	13-7-91
SSBN 738 Maryland*	FY 86	10-8-91	13-6-92
SSBN 739 Nebraska†	FY 87	15-8-92	10-7-93
SSBN 740 Rhode Island*	FY 88	17-7-93	9-7-94
SSBN 741 Maine*	FY 89	16-7-94	29-7-95
SSBN 742 Wyoming†	FY 90	15-7-95	13-7-96
SSBN 743 Louisiana†	FY 91	27-7-96	6-9-97

Louisiana (SSBN 743) U.S. Navy, 10-05

Pennsylvania (SSBN 735) U.S. Navy, 7-05

D: 12,500 tons (light); 16,764 tons (surf.)/18,750 tons sub.) **S:** 25 kts (sub.)
Dim: 170.69 × 12.80 × 11.13 (surf.)
A: 24 Trident D-5 strategic ballistic missiles; 4 bow 533-mm Mk 68 TT (Mk 48 or Mk 48 ADCAP torpedoes); Mk 30 decoys

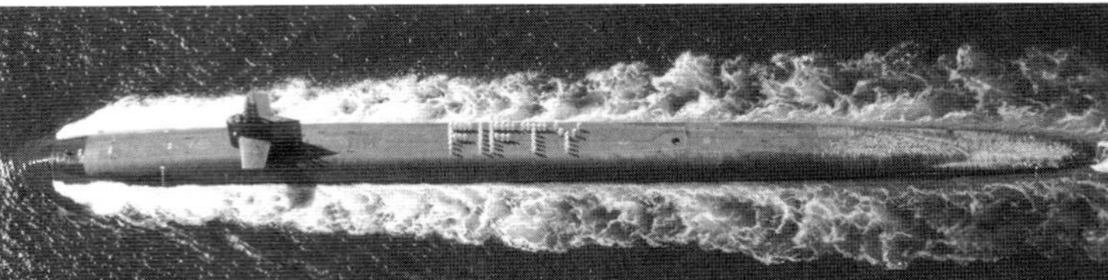

Pennsylvania (SSBN 735)—celebrating its fiftieth sea patrol U.S. Navy, 7-05

Electronics:
Radar: Litton-Sperry BPS-15H (SSBN 741–743: BPS-16(V) nav./surf. search
Sonar: BQQ-5E(V)4 or BQQ-6 passive suite: BQS-13 active; BQS-15 ice-avoidance; BQR-15 towed array with TB-23 thin-line array; BQR-19 active nav.; BQQ-9 TASPE; BQQ-22A (EC-15) sonar receiving set; UQN-4A secure echo-sounder
EW: WLR-8(V)5 suite; WLR-10 radar intercept; SSBN 730–737 only: 8 CSA Mk 1 countermeasures launchers; SSBN 738–743 only: 14 CSA Mk 2 Mod.0/1 countermeasures launchers

M: 1 G.E. S8G natural-circulation pressurized-water reactor; turbo-reduction drive; 1 prop; 35,000 shp
Endurance: 70 days Crew: 15 officers, 148 enlisted (2 crews)

Remarks: As a class, they are currently achieving 92.2% operational availability. Normally, five submarines are on station on patrol, five more are coming or going from patrol stations but still able to launch missiles, and the others are in port or in overhaul. SSBN 726–729 were withdrawn from strategic missile duties during 2002–4 and converted to SSGN configuration (see below). The Trident D-5-equipped submarines are now planned to remain in service for 44 years each.

The fleet is divided between those based at Bangor, Washington, and operate in the Pacific; and those based at Kings Bay, Georgia, for operations in the Atlantic. SSBN 735 and SSBN 737 transferred from Kings Bay to the Bangor, Washington, base during 6-02 and 4-02, SSBN 739 transferred to Bangor during 10-04 with SSBN 741 and 743 following during 9-05; the base has been reconfigured to handle the D-5 missile.

Hull systems: Have a hull-life of 40 years. Able to submerge to 300 m. The reactor plant reportedly does not generate the full rated horsepower in service. Refueling and extensive overhaul began with SSBN 730 in FY 05 and will continue in hull-number order at a rate of one per year through FY 18.

Combat systems: SSBN 730–733 have been retrofitted to carry the D-5 missiles while SSBN 734 and later had Trident D-5 missiles as built. SSBN 734–737 initially carried D-5 missiles with the newer Mk 5/W88, 300 to 450-kiloton variable-yield, re-entry body/warhead; later units initially had the earlier, 100-kiloton Mk 4/W76 combination.

All carry the CCS Mk 2 Mod. 3 combat data system and Mk 98 Mod. 6 or Mod. 7 ballistic missile fire-control and launch system and have two Mk 2 SINS (Ship's Inertial Navigational System) and NAVSAT receivers. The Mk 98 digital computer missile-fire-control system and Mk 118 torpedo-fire-control system are installed. All have one Kollmorgen Type 152 and one Type 82 periscope, with Type 8 replacing the latter. In SSBN 730–737, four 127-mm horizontal countermeasures launch tubes per side are located in the casing below the sail; in SSBN 738, the tubes are 152 mm in diameter and are located four forward of the missile bay and three aft on each side. Early units had BQQ-9 broadband sound processing equipment for their BQR-15 towed arrays; five later units did not receive the equipment and received Rockwell TABIDU (Towed Array Broadband Interim Display Units) during 1994, using COTS components to save considerable cost and complexity. SSBN 734 and 735 tested prototype Lockheed Martin UGM (Universal Gravity Module) passive seabed profilers; the production UGM may be backfitted to all. During 9-94, DoD decided to backfit all but the first four Trident C-4 units with the D-5 missile, later to all but the first six. SSBN 732 began the first modernization at Puget Sound Naval Shipyard in 2000 and was completed during 2-02; SSBN 733 began conversion in 2001, and SSBN 730 and SSBN 731 are to follow.

Note: U.S. Navy nuclear-powered ships, by law, must have crews aboard until the reactor is defueled. Thus, upon deactivation, they are placed in "In Commission, In Reserve" status until they have been stripped of useful materials and the reactor system has been defueled, at which time they are officially decommissioned and stricken.

NUCLEAR-POWERED CRUISE MISSILE SUBMARINES [SSGN]

♦ 4 converted Ohio class

Bldr: General Dynamics, Electric Boat Div., Groton, Conn.
(*Atlantic/†Pacific Fleet)

	Laid down	L	In serv.
SSGN 726 Ohio (ex-SSBN 726)†	10-4-76	7-4-79	11-11-81
SSGN 727 Michigan (ex-SSBN 727)†	4-4-77	26-4-80	11-9-82
SSGN 728 Florida (ex-SSBN 728)*	9-6-77	14-11-81	8-6-83
SSGN 729 Georgia (ex-SSBN 729)*	7-4-79	6-11-82	11-2-84

Ohio (SSGN 726) U.S. Navy, 1-06

NUCLEAR-POWERED CRUISE MISSILE SUBMARINES [SSGN] *(continued)*

Florida (SSGN 728) U.S. Navy, 4-06

D: 16,764 tons (surf.)/18,750 tons sub.) **S:** 25 kts (sub.)
Dim: 170.69 × 12.80 × 11.13 (surf.)
A: 22 vertical-launch tubes (up to 154 Tomahawk Block III or Tactical Tomahawk missiles); 4 bow 533-mm Mk 68 TT (Mk 48 or Mk 48 ADCAP torpedoes, Mk 30 decoys, Unmanned Underwater Vechicles, etc.)
Electronics:
Radar: Litton-Sperry BPS-16(V)4 nav./surf. search
Sonar: BQQ-5E(V)4 passive suite; BQS-13 active, BQS-15 active ice-avoidance; BQR-15 towed array with TB-23 thin-line array; BQR-19 active nav.; BQQ-9 TASPE; BQQ-22A (EC-15) sonar receiving set; UQN-4A secure echo sounder
EW: BLQ-10(V)2 intercept; 4 countermeasures launchers
M: 1 G.E. S8G natural-circulation pressurized-water reactor; turbo-reduction drive; 1 prop; 35,000 shp
Endurance: 70 days
Crew: 140 tot. + 66 (102 in emergencies) SEAL commandos

Remarks: SSBN 726 began refueling and conversion to SSGN at Puget Sound Naval Shipyard on 15-11-02 and was redelivered to the Navy on 17-12-05, re-entering service on 7-2-06. SSBN 727 (at Puget Sound) and SSBN 728 (at Norfolk Naval Shipyard) followed during 2004–5 and re-entered service during 2006. SSBN 729 began conversion in 10-05 at Norfolk Naval Shipyard and is to re-enter service during 2007. All four are expected to serve until 2027–28. Total cost of the conversion program is estimated to be $4 billion, or about $1 billion per submarine. Have two crews for year-round operations.

Hull systems: Have a hull-life of 40 years. Able to submerge to 300 m. During conversion, the existing Trident missile control facilities were replaced by a special operations forces planning compartment, the two forward most ballistic missile tubes were altered for use as nine-man diver-lockout chambers. Two midget submarines or Dry Deck Shelters (or one of each), and a 66-man SEAL force (102 in emergencies) and its equipment can be accommodated. High data-rate SATCOM was fitted, along with a special operations command center.

Combat systems: Carry 22 missile tubes, each capable of carrying seven Tomahawks. Equipped with the CCS Mk 2 Mod. 3 combat data system and two Mk 2 SINS (Ship's Inertial Navigational System) and have navigational satellite receivers. The Mk 98 Mod. 4 digital computer missile-fire-control system and Mk 118 torpedo-fire-control system are installed, with the Mk 98 system modified to handle Tomahawk missiles. During conversion, Kollmorgen Type 18 periscopes were fitted, as were the BLQ-10(V)2 EW system and COTS signal processors. The BLQ-11 Long-term Mine Reconnaissance System will be fitted in the future, and they may be equipped to launch and operate ADM-160A Miniature Air-Launched Decoys and a number of Unmanned Underwater Vechicles (UUVs).

During 2002 a proposed SSGN missile loadout included 21 TLAM IIIC cruise missiles with unitary warheads, five TLAM IIID1 cruise missiles with submunitions; two TLAM IIID2 cruise missiles with nonlethal magnetic pulse and graphite bomb warheads; 28 TTLAM cruise missiles with penetrator warheads; 24 TACMS-U ballistic missiles with 500-lb HE warheads; 24 TACMS-A ballistic missiles with 300 M74 antipersonnel and antimaterial bomblets each; 18 TACMS-P ballistic missiles with Block III Earth Penetrator warheads; 18 TACCMS-L ballistic missiles, each with four GPS-guided miniature autonomous cruise missiles; and four "Search and Attack Specific Shape Targets" (SASST), each capable of attacking such targets as SCUD missiles, tanks, and armored personnel carriers. The TACMS and SASST missiles do not yet exist.

NUCLEAR-POWERED ATTACK SUBMARINES [SSN]

♦ 2 (+ 8 + 20) Virginia class

Bldr: General Dynamics Electric Boat Div., Groton, Conn., and Northrop Grumman Newport News, Newport News, Va.

	Final assembly	Begun	L	In serv.
SSN 774 VIRGINIA	General Dynamics	3-10-97	7-8-03	23-10-04
SSN 775 TEXAS	Northrop Grumman	20-6-00	9-4-05	9-9-06
SSN 776 HAWAII	General Dynamics	26-10-99	17-6-06	3-07 (del.)
SSN 777 NORTH CAROLINA	Northrop Grumman	2-3-01	. . .	6-08 (del.)
SSN 778 NEW HAMPSHIRE	General Dynamics	5-8-02	. . .	2-09 (del.)
SSN 779 NEW MEXICO	Northrop Grumman	14-3-03	. . .	4-10 (del.)
SSN 780 . . .	Northrop Grumman	4-10-04	. . .	4-11 (del.)
SSN 781 . . .	Northrop Grumman	19-4-05	. . .	4-12 (del.)
SSN 782 . . .	General Dynamics	4-8-06	. . .	4-13 (del.)
SSN 783 . . .	Northrop Grumman	3-07	. . .	4-14 (del.)

Virginia (SSN 774)—during sea trials U.S. Navy, 7-04

Virginia (SSN 774)—during sea trials U.S. Navy, 7-04

D: 7,800 tons (sub.) **S:** 25 kts (surf.)/35 kts (sub.) **Dim:** 114.91 × 10.36 × 9.30
A: 12 vertical launch tubes for Tomahawk missiles; 4 533-mm torpedo tubes (38 tot. weapons, including 16 Tomahawk missiles, Mk 48 ADCAP torpedoes, mines, unmanned underwater vehicles, etc.)
Electronics:
Radar: Sperry BPS-16(V)4 ARPA nav./surf. search
Sonar: Lockheed Martin BQQ-10 suite: spherical bow active/passive array; TB-29(A) thin-line towed passive array; TB-16 fat-line towed array; HF active bow and sail mine-avoidance; BQG-5A (WAA) lightweight wide-aperture passive flank array; WLY-1 acoustic intercept; Advanced Deployable System offboard sensor on UAV; BQN-17 secure echo sounder; ACOMMS covert underwater communications
EW: Lockheed Martin BLQ-10(V) intercept; 1 76.2-mm reloadable decoy launcher; 14 152-mm external decoy launchers
E/O: 2 BVS-1 nonpenetrating photonic-imaging masts
M: 1 G-E, S9G pressurized water reactor; 1 pump-jet; approx. 40,000 shp
Crew: 12 officers, 101 enlisted

Remarks: Thirty units are planned. Originally referred to as the "Centurion" class until late 1993 when renamed the NAS (New Attack Submarine); renamed as the New Nuclear-powered Attack Submarine (NSSN) by 1995. Hull numbers return to the traditional sequence, but a plan to return to traditional "fish" names was thwarted by political considerations; SSN 774 was formally named on 23-9-98 and SSN 775 on 13-11-98. Are being authorized at the rate of one per year; a plan to begin ordering two per year under FY 07 was deferred to FY 12 during 11-01. Electric Boat is building the bows and sterns and Newport News the midbodies for the first four boats, a distinct departure from previous U.S. submarine construction practice; the yards will alternate final assembly and outfitting. Later units may be completed with one yard building the entire submarine. The assembly of the initial sections for SSN 774 began on 2-9-99. "Keel-laying" ceremonies were held for SSN 774 on 2-9-02, SSN 775 on 5-5-03, and SSN 777 on 22-5-04.

Hull systems: Test depth: 488 m. The single S9G pressurized water reactor is to have a core expected to last for the 30-year life of the submarines. To be "as quiet at 25 kts as an SSN 688 is alongside the pier," making them clearly superior in noise reduction to all Russian designs. Will have the Sperry WSN-7B ring-laser gyro inertial navigation system. Cost-saving measures include the use of commercial fasteners, spliced cables, combined pumping systems, reverse-osmosis potable water generation, and reduced-volume sound-quieting measures. Exide batteries were ordered for the first four units.

The first eight units will not have an under-ice operational capability. SSN 786 and later units of the class will have a 30-ft. section inserted amidships to accommodate SEAL equipment and up to 50 special forces personnel, as in the *Jimmy Carter* (SSN 23); this would add about 800 tons to the submerged displacement. SSN 777 and later are to have a new mold-in-place anechoic outer hull coating. SSN 782 and later units are planned to have enlarged sails, additional countermeasures and Tomahawk missile capacity, and the equipment necessary to permit under-ice operations. SSN 782 or later may also have a bow conformal sonar array instead of the current spherical array within a flooded bow dome. Submarines of the FY 10 program and later are hoped to employ all-electric drive systems, dispensing with main propulsion turbines; this may result in a complete redesign of the internal arrangements for the submarines and possibly even a new hull form with a fuller form aft.

NUCLEAR-POWERED ATTACK SUBMARINES [SSN] *(continued)*

Combat systems: The combat system design contract was let to a consortium of Lockheed Martin, Raytheon, and Northrop Grumman on 30-9-96, with Raytheon responsible for design of the system to coordinate targeting and torpedo/missile launching and for the sonar system transmitters; it is to have 26 times the signal processing capability and 55 times the data processing capability of the BSY-2 system in the *Seawolf* class. The contract for the first ship-set was issued in 3-97 to Lockheed Martin Federal Systems, for $31.5 million. Two Kollmorgen Model 86 nonpressure hull-penetrating Universal Modular Masts will be fitted; the masts will incorporate ESM arrays, SATCOM antenna, NAVSAT antenna, other communications antennas, and optronic sensors. All will have a new high data-rate, 43-cm-diameter, multiband dish antenna for WSC-6 Milstar and Global Broadcast Service SATCOM connection. All will probably carry Lockheed Martin UGM (Universal Gravity Module) passive bottom profilers as a navigation aid. The navigational/surface-search radar will be supplemented by Litton's ECDIS-N (Electronic Chart Display and Information System) and Voyage Management System (VMS).

SSN 777 and later are to have the CAVES (Conformal Acoustic Velocity Sonar), replacing the current WAA (Wide Aperture Array) passive arrays. All will have high-frequency sail- and chin-mounted active sonar arrays for accurate bottom mapping, object location and tracking, and obstacle avoidance. Units ordered after 2006 are planned to have a conformal rather than spherical bow sonar array; they will also be able to employ offboard sensors.

A special, half-length variant of the Mk 48 ADCAP torpedo employing the seeker from the Mk 46 ASW torpedo may be developed to provide this class with a shallow-water antisubmarine capability; the weapon may be launched from external tubes in later units. A proposed intelligence collection variant may house a large super-high frequency intercept antenna within a "stealth" sail structure. Another variant may be used for mine countermeasures, employing the Submarine Offboard Mine Search System, a remotely piloted submersible launched from a standard 533-mm torpedo tube. The weapons payload in the initial units totals about 86 tons.

Will be equipped with a nine-man lockout chamber and stowage space for SEAL Team Combat Rubber Raiding Craft. The torpedo room will be reconfigurable to give 68 m^3 of stowage space for SEAL equipment and berthing for 40 SEALs. At least the first six of the submarines will be equipped to carry the new 19.8-m Advanced SEAL Delivery System (ASDS); their sails will have provision for a modular Special Forces communications mast.

Fiscal: A full 30-unit program was optimistically estimated to cost $56 billion in FY 98 dollars. The initial $4.2-billion construction contract for SSN 774 was given to Electric Boat as lead yard on 30-9-98. In 8-03 the Navy awarded General Dynamics an $8.7-billion contract for six *Virginia*-class submarines, making it the largest sub procurement contract to date. The final cost of the class per submarine is expected to average more than $2 billion in 2004 dollars.

Note: During 2-99 Newport News received a $47-million contract to design and build a 33.83-m operating scale model of a *Virginia*-class submarine, the *Cutthroat* (LSV-2: Large-Scale Vehicle 2), as a testbed for related technologies and acoustic silencing techniques operated on Lake Pend Orielle, Idaho, at the Acoustic Research Detachment, Bayview. *Cutthroat* has some components manufactured by Electric Boat and was christened on 15-11-00. The craft is propelled by a battery-driven 6,000-shp permanent magnet electric motor.

♦ 3 Seawolf class

Bldr: General Dynamics Electric Boat Div., Groton, Conn. (*Atlantic Fleet/ †Pacific Fleet)

	Begun	L	In serv.
SSN 21 SEAWOLF*/† in mid-07	25-10-89	24-6-95	19-7-97
SSN 22 CONNECTICUT*/† in mid-07	14-9-92	1-9-97	11-12-98
SSN 23 JIMMY CARTER†	12-12-95	5-6-04	19-2-05

Seawolf (SSN 21) U.S. Navy, 1996

Seawolf (SSN 21)—on sea trials General Dynamics, 1998

Jimmy Carter (SSN 23)—note 100-foot hull extension added aft of sail on this unit General Dynamics Electric Boat, 2-05

Jimmy Carter (SSN 23) General Dynamics Electric Boat, 2-05

D: SSN 21, 22: 7,467 tons (surf.)/9,137 tons (sub.); SSN 23: 8,060 (surf.)/12,139 tons sub.
S: 35+ kts (sub.) (SSN 23: 30 kts) **Dim:** 107.60 (SSN 23: 115.8) × 12.80 × 10.95
A: 8 amidships 673-mm TT (50 Tomahawk missiles and/or Mk 48 ADCAP torpedoes, or up to 100 mines)
Electronics:
Radar: 1 Litton-Sperry BPS-16(V)4 ARPA nav./surf. search
Sonar: BQQ-5D suite: WAA (wide-aperture passive array); BQS-24 nav./ice-avoidance; TB-29 towed array; TB-16D towed array—SSN 23 also: 3 BLQ-11 Mine Reconnaissance System UUV
EW: WLQ-4(V)1 suite; BLD-1 D/F; . . . decoy syst.
M: 1 G.E. S6W pressurized-water reactor (200 Mw), . . . drive; 1 pumpjet; 45,500 shp—1 (SSN 23: 2) drop-down azimuthal maneuvering thrusters
Electric: 6,000 kw tot. (2 turbogenerators + auxiliary diesel set)
Crew: 12 officers, 121 enlisted

Remarks: SSN 21 was authorized under FY 89 and ordered 9-1-89. SSN 22 was authorized under FY 91 and ordered on 17-3-92. SSN 23 was authorized under FY 92, although final construction authority was not granted by Congress until FY 96 and funding was not provided until FY 97; the construction order was placed on 29-6-96 (although much of the necessary equipment had already long since been purchased). As of 1999, the total cost of the three-submarine program was estimated at $16 billion, including R&D expenditures.

The hull numbering sequence is unusual and nontraditional, as USN hull numbers are by regulation to be sequential and not reused, yet in theory, the basic SS 21 number dates to 1912. The anomaly apparently came about when "SSN-21" was applied as the project title, indicating "Submarine for the 21st Century." The names *Connecticut* and *Jimmy Carter* are also nontraditional for attack submarines.

Although commissioned in 7-97, SSN 21 did not commence her first operational patrol until 25-6-01. SSN 22's first operational patrol began 1-5-02. SSN 21 and SSN 22 are based at New London, Connecticut, but will transfer to Bangor, Washington in mid-2007, joining SSN 23, there since 2005.

The USN announced on 29-1-99 that SSN 23 was to be longer to incorporate advanced technologies and the capability to carry special warfare forces; under a 10-12-99 contract, the enhanced capabilities added $887 million to the cost of the submarine, delaying her launch by 27 months. The additional 8.2-m section can accommodate 50 SEALs and their equipment, plus displays for remote-controlled mine-hunting submersibles and other remotely operated vehicles, which are stowed in a flush hangar-like section. The 8.3-meter section was added abaft the sail and forward

NUCLEAR-POWERED ATTACK SUBMARINES [SSN] *(continued)*

of the reactor compartment; the pressure hull necks down to a 3-m-diameter section, with the concentric space within the outer hull used for SEAL vehicles and remote-controlled underwater vehicles, including the BLQ-11 mine-reconnaissance vehicle, which is maintained at Bangor, Washington. A 1.52-m-diameter airlock was fitted to allow deploying personnel and submersibles from within the pressure hull, which was reinforced with HY100 high-strength steel in the region of the hull extension. The additional length and weight cost the boat about 1–5 kts in maximum speed. SSN 23 replaces the capabilities in the stricken *Parche* (SSN 683). A further $17.4 million was added to the program on 25-3-03.

SSN 21 was placed out of service during 8-00 due to the discovery of cracking in air flasks needed for the ballast system; the other two boats do not have the problem, due to the use of different materials.

Hull systems: Test depth: 594 m. Design provides significant improvements in speed, quietness, weapons load, sonar processing, etc., over the *Los Angeles* class. Are able to travel at up to 20 kts while silent. Designed for reliability and ease of maintenance, to operate for 15 years before first overhaul. The submarines have smaller length-to-beam ratio than the SSN 688 class to improve maneuverability. Retractable bow planes and six fixed stern fins are fitted. A small wedge at the base of the forward edge of the sail improves hydrodynamic flow. The propeller is of shrouded, pump-jet configuration. Pressure hull constructed of HY120 steel. All three have a drop-down azimuthal maneuvering thruster aft, although SSN 23 has a second one forward. First two have WSN-2 ring-laser gyros, and SSN 23 has the WSN-7B (Sperry Mk 39), which will be backfitted later in the others.

Combat systems: Have Lockheed Martin BSY-2(V) Combat Control System. The Submarine Active Detection System (SADS) with bow-mounted medium-frequency active and high-frequency active sonar capability is fitted. The BQQ-5D passive sonar suite includes three flank arrays per side. The TB-23 thin-line towed array has full-spectrum acoustic processing. The torpedo tubes were originally referred to as being 30 inches in diameter, but liners and other fittings restrict the diameter of weapons and remotely controlled reconnaissance vehicles launched from them to 26.5 inches; the launch system is virtually soundless, but the outer doors cannot be opened when the submarine is traveling at maximum speeds. Up to 12 Tomahawk missiles can be carried in lieu of torpedoes.

♦ 48 Los Angeles/Improved Los Angeles class

Bldr: Northrop Grumman Newport News, Newport News, Va. (NN) or General Dynamics Electric Boat Div., Groton, Conn. (EB) (*Atlantic/†Pacific Fleet)

	Bldr	Laid down	L	In serv.
SSN 688 Los Angeles†	NN	8-1-72	6-4-74	13-11-76
SSN 690 Philadelphia*	EB	12-8-72	19-10-74	25-6-77
SSN 691 Memphis*	NN	23-6-73	3-4-76	17-12-77
SSN 698 Bremerton†	EB	8-5-76	22-7-78	28-3-81
SSN 699 Jacksonville*	EB	21-2-76	18-11-78	16-5-81
SSN 700 Dallas*	EB	9-10-76	28-4-79	18-7-81
SSN 701 La Jolla†	EB	16-10-76	11-8-79	24-10-81
SSN 705 City of Corpus Christi†	EB	4-9-79	25-4-81	8-1-83
SSN 706 Albuquerque*	EB	27-12-79	13-3-82	21-5-83
SSN 708 Minneapolis–Saint Paul*	EB	20-1-81	19-3-83	10-3-84
SSN 709 Hyman G. Rickover*	EB	23-7-81	27-8-83	21-7-84
SSN 710 Augusta*	EB	1-4-82	21-1-84	19-1-85
SSN 711 San Francisco†	NN	26-5-77	27-10-79	24-4-81
SSN 713 Houston†	NN	29-1-79	21-3-81	25-9-82
SSN 714 Norfolk*	NN	1-8-79	31-10-81	21-5-83
SSN 715 Buffalo†	NN	25-1-80	8-5-82	5-11-83
SSN 717 Olympia†	NN	31-3-81	30-4-83	17-11-84
SSN 719 Providence*	EB	30-9-82	4-8-84	27-7-85
SSN 720 Pittsburgh*	EB	15-4-83	8-12-84	23-11-85
SSN 721 Chicago†	NN	5-1-83	13-10-84	27-9-86
SSN 722 Key West*	NN	6-7-83	20-7-85	12-9-87
SSN 723 Oklahoma City*	NN	4-1-84	2-11-85	9-7-88
SSN 724 Louisville*	EB	16-9-84	14-12-85	8-11-86
SSN 725 Helena†	EB	28-3-85	28-6-86	11-7-87
SSN 750 Newport News*	NN	3-3-84	15-3-86	3-6-89
SSN 751 San Juan*	EB	16-8-85	6-12-86	6-8-88
SSN 752 Pasadena†	EB	20-5-86	12-9-87	11-2-89
SSN 753 Albany*	NN	22-4-85	13-6-87	7-4-90
SSN 754 Topeka*	EB	13-5-86	23-1-88	21-10-88
SSN 755 Miami*	EB	24-10-86	12-11-88	30-6-90
SSN 756 Scranton*	NN	29-8-86	3-7-89	26-1-91
SSN 757 Alexandria*	EB	19-6-87	23-6-90	29-6-91
SSN 758 Asheville*	NN	9-1-87	28-10-89	28-9-91
SSN 759 Jefferson City†	NN	21-9-87	17-8-90	28-2-92
SSN 760 Annapolis*	EB	15-6-88	19-5-91	11-4-92
SSN 761 Springfield†	EB	29-1-90	4-1-92	9-1-93
SSN 762 Columbus*	EB	7-1-91	1-8-92	24-7-93
SSN 763 Santa Fe*	EB	9-7-91	12-12-92	9-1-94
SSN 764 Boise* (ex-*Hartford*)	NN	25-8-88	23-3-91	7-11-92
SSN 765 Montpelier*	NN	19-5-89	23-8-91	13-3-93
SSN 766 Charlotte*	NN	17-8-90	3-10-92	16-9-94
SSN 767 Hampton*	NN	2-3-90	3-4-92	6-11-93
SSN 768 Hartford* (ex-*Boise*)	EB	27-4-92	4-12-93	10-12-94
SSN 769 Toledo*	NN	6-5-91	28-8-93	24-2-95
SSN 770 Tucson†	NN	15-8-91	20-3-94	9-9-95
SSN 771 Columbia†	EB	21-4-93	24-9-94	9-10-95
SSN 772 Greenville†	NN	28-2-92	17-9-94	16-2-96
SSN 773 Cheyenne†	NN	6-7-92	16-4-95	13-9-96

Note: SSN 751–SSN 773 are referred to as the Improved Los Angeles class.

D: SSN 688–699: 6,080 tons (surf.)/6,927 tons (sub.); SSN 700–714: 6,130 tons (surf.)/6,977 tons (sub.); SSN 717–718: 6,165 tons (surf.)/7,012 tons (sub.); SSN 719–750: 6,255 tons (surf.)/7,102 tons (sub.); SSN 751–770: 6,300 tons (surf.)/7,147 tons (sub.); SSN 771–773: 6,330 tons (surf.)/7,177 tons (sub.)

Asheville (SSN 758) U.S. Navy, 2-06

Toledo (SSN 769) U.S. Navy, 1-06

City of Corpus Christi (SSN 705) U.S. Navy, 5-06

Louisville (SSN 724) U.S. Navy, 3-05

NUCLEAR-POWERED ATTACK SUBMARINES [SSN] *(continued)*

Asheville (SSN 758) U.S. Navy, 2-06

S: 30+ kts. (sub.) **Dim:** 109.73 × 10.06 × 9.75
A: SSN 719 and later: 12 Mk 36 vertical tubes for Tomahawk missiles; all: 4 533-mm amdiships TT Mk 67 (26 Tomahawk missiles, Mk 48 and Mk 48 ADCAP torpedoes, etc.); SSN 756 and later: mining capability
Electronics:
Radar: 1 BPS-15H or BPS-16(V) nav./surf. search
Sonar: SSN 688–709, 711–750: BQQ-5A(V)1 or BQQ-5C (SSN 717–on: BQQ-5D; SSN 708, 724: BQQ-10 ARCI) suite; BQS-15 under-ice active; BQR-15 towed array with BQR-23 signal processor or TB-16D and TB-23 or TB-29 (10 units) towed arrays; SSN 710, 751–on: BSY-1 suite: same equipment plus BQG-5D WAA flank arrays; SSN 758 only: HF active array (see Remarks)
EW: BRD-7; D/F WLR-8(V)2 intercept; WLR-10 intercept; WLR-9/12 acoustic emmission receiver/processor; WLR-1H intercept; WSQ-5 portable ELINT collection; CSA Mk 1 Mod. 2 acoustic decoy launchers (SSN 760 only: BLQ-10 EW suite)
E/O: SSN 760 only: 1 BVS-1 photonic-imaging non-penetrating mast
M: 1 G.E. S6G pressurized-water reactor, 2 sets geared steam turbines; 1 7-bladed prop (pumpjet in SSN 768–773); 35,000 shp
Crew: 14 officers, 127 enlisted (SSN 724: 15 officers, 149 enlisted)

Remarks: Authorized: SSN 688–690 in FY 70, SSN 691–694 in FY 71, SSN 695–700 in FY 72, SSN 701–705 in FY 73, SSN 706–710 in FY 74, SSN 711–713 in FY 75, SSN 714–715 in FY 76, SSN 716–718 in FY 77, SSN 719 in FY 78, SSN 720 in FY 79, SSN 721–722 in FY 80, SSN 723–724 in FY 81, SSN 725 and 750 in FY 82, SSN 751–752 in FY 83, SSN 753–755 in FY 84, SSN 756–759 in FY 85, SSN 760–763 in FY 86, SSN 764–767 in FY 87, SSN 768–770 in FY 88, SSN 771–772 in FY 89, and SSN 773 in FY 90. Four more (one in FY 90, two in FY 91, one in FY 92) were canceled.

Normally operate on a 24-month cycle, out of which they undertake one six-month deployment. SSN 773 operated for 203 continuous hours at maximum speed during one 36,034 n.m deployment in 1999. SSN 701 was refueled with FY 99 funding, and SSN 705 and 711 were refueled under FY 00, with SSN 705 rehomeported at Guam under SUBRON 15 on completion of recoring 5-8-02 and SSN 711 on 1-9-02, SSN 713 recoring completed in 2004. Funds to refuel SSN 706 ($282.7 million) were approved under FY 01; SSN 713 and SSN 715 under FY 02; SSN 698 and 714 under FY 03; SSN 699 and 717 under FY 04; and SSN 710 under FY 08.

Beginning in 2008 SSN 699 will transfer from Norfolk to Pearl Harbor, SSN 706 will move from Groton to San Diego, and SSN 767 will move from Norfolk to San Diego. Other submarine moves and transfers can also be expected.

SSN 751 and later are described as "Arctic-capable" and are referred to as the "688I" (for "Improved") class. SSN 772 collided with and sank Japanese fisheries training ship *Ehime Maru* (499 grt) off Honolulu on 9-2-01 while surfacing and later that year grounded briefly at Saipan; on 27-1-02, the boat had a minor collision with the *Ogden* (LPD 5). SSN 723 collided with the liquid natural gas carrier *Norman Lady* on 13-11-02 while surfacing near the Straits of Gibraltar, with minor damage to both ships. On 8-1-05 SSN 711 collided with an underground mountain during submerged operations about 350 miles southeast of Guam. One sailor died and 98 crew members suffered injuries. Repairs at Puget Sound Naval Shipyard, expected to complete in 2007, include replacement of the submarine's damaged bow section with that of recently stricken sister SSN 718. On 5-9-05 *Philadelphia* (SSN 690) collided with the Turkish ship *Yasa Aysen* in the Persian Gulf and subsequently underwent repairs at Portsmouth Naval Shipyard.

Hull systems: Maximum operating depth is 450 m. SSN 753 and 754 had partial HY100 steel pressure hull sections to test fabrication procedures for the *Seawolf* class; the others have HY80 steel hulls. Bow is built of glass-reinforced plastic as a streamlined fairing over the spherical BQQ-5A(V)1 sonar array. All have one Fairbanks-Morse 38D8Q diesel generator set and batteries for emergency propulsion. The reactor core was intended to last 10–13 years between refuelings. SSN 751 and later have bow-mounted vice sail-mounted diving planes; most are also equipped with additional anhedral fins at the stern to support towed arrays; these fins are being fitted with 7-celled launchers for 127-mm countermeasures, and the fins have also been added to a few earlier units of the class. SSN 768 and later have improved sound quieting and improved propulsion systems. Several late units (including SSN 773) have shrouded pumpjet propellers, and a few have the propellers themselves connected at the tips by a circular ring to reduce cavitation. Have berths for only 124 personnel, so there is some "hot-bunking." There are two SINS, which are being replaced by the Litton Marine WSSN-7 ring-laser gyro inertial navigation system. SSN 719 and later trim level on the surface, while earlier boats without the vertical missile tubes forward trim up by the bow.

Combat systems: SSN 751 onward have the first-generation BSY-1 (formerly SUBAC—Submarine Advanced Combat System) integrated sonar/weapons-control suite; its development problems slowed delivery of SSN 751–on, and 751–755 were backfitted with their UYK-43 computers after completion. SSN 755 was the first unit with a fully functional BSY-1 system. All carry a UYK-7 general-purpose computer and have WSC-3 UHF SATCOM gear. One Mk 2F optical attack and one Sperry Mk 18 (Mk 15D on early units) multifunction periscope are fitted; later units also have the Sperry Naval Electronic System for Infrared Exploitation (NESSIE), with FLIR, low-light-level t.v., and an EHF SATCOM antenna. The BLD-1 electromagnetic interferometer was added beginning 1985. Mk 113 Mod. 10 torpedo-fire-control system originally installed in SSN 688–699, Mk 117 in later units through SSN 750, and subsequently backfitted into SSN 688–699. Under FY 83, the Mk 117 fire-control system was modified in many to permit launching SUBROC missiles, which were then removed, where carried, in 1989. SSN 719 and later have 12 vertical-launch tubes for Tomahawk cruise missiles, located between the forward end of the pressure hull and the spherical array for the BQQ-5 bow sonar; the arrangement of the tubes differs in SSN 719. SSN 688–717 can carry eight torpedo tube-launched Tomahawk cruise missiles; later units can carry 20 (including the 12 in the vertical launchers). In peacetime, bunks occupy four reload weapon spaces, and four other reload spaces remain empty so that torpedo tubes can be emptied when in port. UGM-84-series Sub-Harpoon missiles were removed during 1996–97.

Also in service with this class is the Northrop Grumman NMRS (Near-term Mine Reconnaissance System) unmanned underwater vehicle, a 533-mm-diameter, 5.23-m-long surveillance drone fitted with AMDS forward-looking and ADS-14-derived side-looking sonar systems and capable of being launched and recovered from the submarine's torpedo tubes; when carried, the system and its associated equipment reduce the torpedo loadout by 6–7 weapons. The NMRS is controlled by 50 n.m. of fiber optic cable and can travel at 4–7 kts for up to 5 hrs; NMRS began limited operations in 1998. The BLQ-11 LMRS (Long-term Mine Reconnaissance System) is being developed by Boeing as a successor to the NMRS and is planned to enter service around 2010; BLQ-11 uses preprogrammed, torpedo-tube deployed and recovered unmanned submersibles with a range of about 70 n.m. and an endurance of 40 hours. The 5-knot BLQ-11 is to have a 288 n.m. range on its nonrechargeable lithium battery and to be able to reconnoiter 650 km^2 during a typical mission. A full outfit would replace eight torpedoes and would include three UUVs, the recovery arm machinery, spare batteries, and control and display modules; it would be operated by four personnel.

Up to ten units of the class have the TB-29 thin-line towed array instead of TB-16D or TB-23, but further procurement was canceled due to excessive production costs; production of the cheaper, smaller, and more effective TB-29A was authorized during 2000. Sonar processing systems were updated to a common software configuration between 1997 and 2005 under the ARCI (Acoustic Rapid COTS Insertion) program using commercial computer equipment. One SSN 751–series ("688I class") boat was said to have received the BQG-5D (WAA) wide-aperture passive side array in a 1997 refit, but all other 688I units began receiving the less-expensive BQG-5A (WAA) starting around 2000.

Trials units: SSN 691 was redesignated as an experimental submarine during 1989 to test composite hull structures, unmanned underwater vehicles, advanced sonars, hull friction reduction, etc., for the SSN 688 and SSN 21 classes but remains combat-capable. During a mid-1990s refit, SSN 691 received a GRP turtleback abaft the sail to accommodate remotely operated vehicles and a towing winch and drum for experimental towed sonar arrays, 4.27-m high by 1.37-m wide vertical surfaces at the ends of the stern stabilizers to accommodate sonar transducer arrays, a 54-mm-diameter towed array dispenser in the port fin (leading to the new winch abaft the sail), supports for the stern stabilizers, new hydraulic systems, fiber-optic databus, and 58 standardized equipment racks to accommodate a wide variety of electronic test gear; the modifications added about 50 tons to the displacement, most of it aft. SSN 691 has also tested a composite material propeller shaft of about half normal weight and, in 1998, the Lockheed Martin Undersea Systems Universal Gravity Module (UGM) passive bottom profiler navigational system. SSN 710 has served as trials boat for the BQG-5D(WAA) Wide Aperture Array passive sonar system since 7-87. SSN 710 and SSN 724 carry prototype AN/BQQ-10 ARCI (Acoustic Rapid COTS Insertion) sonars, which incorporate off-the-shelf computer components, allowing easy introduction of modular upgrades. SSN 773 has been used to develop new flat-screen, interoperative sonar displays based on commercially available equipment.

Early in 1996 SSN 721 operated the Predator Tier II aerial reconnaissance drone to ranges of 100 n.m. and altitudes of up to 20,000 ft. while operating at periscope depths. SSN 758 was used in trials with the Northrop Grumman Sea Ferret reconnaissance drone during 12-96; eventually, Sea Ferret may be launched from within a modified Sub-Harpoon missile canister and controlled by a submerged submarine. Submarine-launched aerial reconnaissance drones are foreseen as useful for covert surveillance, weapons targeting, choke-point interdiction, and battle-damage assessment. During 1-06 SSN 756 successfully demonstrated homing and docking of an Unmanned Underwater Vehicle (UUV). Two UUVs from the AN/BLQ-11 Long-term Mine Reconnaissance System (LMRS) were used during the testing.

SSN 758 is fitted with a developmental Advanced Mine Detection System (AMDS), high-frequency active sonar array with transmitters and receivers in the sail and in a disc-shaped chin sonar dome beneath the hull at the bow. The system is used for target detection, mine avoidance, and bottom navigation.

In 1999, SSN 760 had the BLQ-21 EW suite and BVS-1 photonic mast systems installed for trials. SSN 719, in mid-2000, received the first Submarine High Data-Rate system, using the OE-562/BRC antenna in place of the standard periscope-mounted EHF antenna; the new system provides EHF comms, SHF SATCOM, and Global Broadcast Service receipt capabilities, while also being installed in the EHF On-Hull Antenna, which can be employed while fully submerged.

Special warfare capabilities: Six portable Dry Deck Shelters (DDS) are in use by the USN, all built by Electric Boat Co. DDS-01S ("S" for starboard-side use on twin DDS installations) was completed in 1982 and DDS-02P ("P" for port), -03P, -04S, -05-S, and -06P between 1987 and 1991; displacing some 30 tons when the submarine is submerged, they are 11.58 m long by 2.74 m high and wide and are expected to remain in use for about 40 years each. Each DDS has three pressure sections within the outer GRP fairing: a spherical hyperbaric chamber at the forward end to treat injured divers, a smaller spherical transfer trunk, and a cylindrical hangar with elliptical ends to house a swimmer-delivery vehicle (SDV) or 20 SEALs with four Combat Rubber Raiding Craft (CRRC). The DDS can be transported by trucks or C-5A Galaxy aircraft and requires about one to three days to install and test. The DDS can be carried by *Los Angeles*–class SSNs *Dallas* (SSN 700), *Los Angeles* (SSN 688), *Buffalo* (SSN 715), *Philadelphia* (SSN 690), and *La Jolla* (SSN 701).

SSN 772 completed conversion 3-99 with internal access to the 19.8-m Advanced SEAL Delivery System (ASDS—see description under LSDV) while submerged, and four more of the class were to be similarly fitted.

Disposals: Planned future inactivations through 2025 include FY 07, SSN 708, SSN 709 and 718; FY 10, SSN 688 and 690; FY 11, SSN 691; FY 14, SSN 698, 699, 700, and 711; FY 15, SSN 701, 713; FY 16, SSN 705, 706, and 714; FY 17, SSN 715, 721, 724, and 725; FY 18, SSN 710, 717, and 719; FY 19, SSN 720 and 752; FY 20, SSN 722, 723, and 754; FY 21, SSN 751 and 755; FY 22, SSN 750 and 764; FY 23, SSN 753; FY 24, SSN 756, SSN 757, and SSN 758; FY 25, SSN 759, and SSN 760.

NUCLEAR-POWERED ATTACK SUBMARINES [SSN] *(continued)*

Retirements to date include:

	In Commission /In Reserve	Decomm.	Stricken
SSN 689 *Baton Rouge*	1-11-93	13-1-94	13-2-95
SSN 692 *Omaha*	7-2-95	5-10-95	29-7-96
SSN 693 *Cincinnati*	5-1-95	31-7-95	29-7-96
SSN 694 *Groton*	19-9-96	7-11-97	7-11-97
SSN 695 *Birmingham*	17-4-97	12-97	12-97
SSN 696 *New York City*	19-3-96	30-4-97	30-4-97
SSN 697 *Indianapolis*	2-3-98	22-12-98	22-12-98
SSN 702 *Phoenix*	18-9-97	29-7-98	29-7-98
SSN 703 *Boston*	15-3-99	19-11-99	19-11-99
SSN 704 *Baltimore*	1-10-97	10-7-98	10-7-98
SSN 707 *Portsmouth*	30-9-04	18-8-05	18-8-05
SSN 712 *Atlanta*	1-3-99	1-9-99	1-9-99
SSN 716 *Salt Lake City*	15-1-06	3-11-06	3-11-06
SSN 718 *Honolulu*	1-11-06	2007	2007

Disposal notes: *Sturgeon*-class special operations submarine *Parche* (SSN 683) was placed "in commission, in reserve" on 19-10-04. She was replaced by *Seawolf*-class boat USS *Jimmy Carter* and decommissioned on 18-7-05. *Parche* was the last *Sturgeon*-class boat remaining in service. *Benjamin Franklin*–class special forces transport submarine *Kamehameha* (SSN 642, ex-SSBN 642), after 36 years' service, was placed In Commission In Reserve on 1-10-01 and stricken on 2-4-02; sister *James K. Polk* (SSN 645, ex-SSBN 645) was placed In Commission In Reserve on 16-2-99 and decommissioned and stricken on 8-7-99.

NUCLEAR-POWERED AUXILIARY SUBMARINES [SSAN]

♦ 1 NR-1 class nuclear-powered, deep-diving research submarine

Bldr: General Dynamics Electric Boat Div., Groton, Conn.

	Laid down	L	In serv.
NR-1	10-6-67	25-1-69	27-10-69

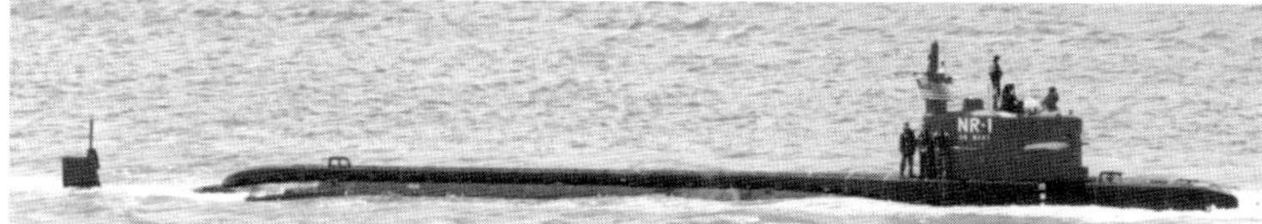

NR-1—with red-painted sail and rudder — Mike Welsford, 6-00

D: 366 tons (surf.)/394 tons (sub.) **S:** 4.5 kts (surf.)/3.5 kts (sub.)
Dim: 44.44 (41.45 wl) × 3.81 (4.83 over stern planes) × 4.60
Electronics:
Radar: Portable nav.
Sonar: DSOAS 3-array active; Klein 4000 side-scan
M: 1 pressurized-water rector, turboelectric drive; 2 3-bladed props; 100 shp—4 7-shp electric thrusters
Endurance: 210 crew days (330 max.) Crew: 3 officers, 8 enlisted, 2 scientists

Remarks: Project approved 18-4-65 and funded under FY 66. Fitted for military and civilian oceanographic missions and for bottom salvage. Now operated by the Naval Submarine Support Group, New London, Connecticut. The chartered *Carolyn Chouest* acts as tender and tows the submarine to and from operating locations. Planned for retirement in 2012 or earlier; planning for a replacement has begun.
Hull systems: Thick HY80 steel cylindrical pressure hull, 29.29 m long. Operating depth is 724 m. Has permanent berths for only four personnel, plus up to three auxiliary berths. Scientific payload is 908 kg. Can remain submerged for up to 30 days. Carries 9,980 kg of lead-shot expendable ballast. The electric main propulsion motors are external to the pressure hull. The four electric thrusters are paired fore and aft in an X-configuration and can maneuver the craft in pitch, roll, elevation, and sideways, delivering 136 kg of thrust each. Two alcohol-filled rubber tires can be lowered to permit the craft to travel on suitable bottoms, and there is a stern anchor to permit hovering or precise depth keeping above a bottom. Has a GPS receiver.
Mission systems: The DSOAS (Deep Submergence Obstacle Avoidance Sonar) system employs three separate high- and low-frequency transducer arrays. The Klein 4000 side-scan sonar replaced an earlier array during 1998. Also fitted are bow- and stern-mounted echo sounders, a VLF sub-bottom profiler, and a 300-kHz doppler own-speed measurer for use within 600 ft. of the bottom. Has a BQN-13 rescue-pinger acoustic beacon. There are three optical viewing ports on the lower edge of the forward end of the pressure hull, and 25 external lights, a low-level light t.v. camera (with zoom), and recording cameras are fitted. No periscope; uses t.v. cameras. Manipulators can pick up objects weighing up to 113 kg from the sea bottom, and a recovery claw can pick up larger objects. A waterjet device can be used to uncover or bury objects on the bottom.

AUXILIARY SUBMARINES [SSA]

Disposal note: *Dolphin*-class research submarine *Dolphin* (AGSS 555) was decommissioned on 8-12-06 following a fire at sea on 22-5-02 while the submarine was acting as a torpedo trials target. She was towed in to port; subsequent repairs costing $40 million were completed in 2005. During 2006, less than a year after repairing the submarine, Navy officials announced that funding cuts would force *Dolphin* to halt operations in 10-06. She is to be sunk as a target in 2007–8.

Note: The various research and rescue submersibles (YSS) are described later under miscellaneous craft. Swimmer delivery vehicles (LSDV) are described at the end of the amphibious warfare ships and craft section.

BATTLESHIPS [BB]

Note: The last remaining *Iowa*-class battleships, *Iowa* (BB 61) and *Wisconsin* (BB served as Mobilization Category B assets until stricken on 17-3-06.

GUIDED-MISSILE CRUISERS [CG]

Note: The Navy returned to discussing a "CG(X)" program in guidance issued during 2002; the design would be an outgrowth of the DD(X) design, as was the *Ticonderoga* class from the *Spruance*-class destroyer, and is expected to provide enhanced anti-missile and air defense capabilities and an integrated electric power system. No firm details have yet been announced.

♦ 22 Ticonderoga class

Bldrs: A: Northrop Grumman Ship Systems, Ingalls Div., Pascagoula, Miss.;
B: General Dynamics Bath Iron Works, Bath, Maine (*Atlantic/†Pacific Fleet)

	Bldr	Laid down	L	In serv.
CG 52 Bunker Hill*	A	11-1-84	11-3-85	20-9-86
CG 53 Mobile Bay†	A	6-6-84	22-8-85	21-2-87
CG 54 Antietam†	A	15-11-84	14-2-86	6-6-87
CG 55 Leyte Gulf*	A	18-3-85	20-6-86	26-9-87
CG 56 San Jacinto*	A	22-7-85	14-11-86	23-1-88
CG 57 Lake Champlain†	A	3-3-86	3-4-87	12-8-88
CG 58 Philippine Sea*	B	8-5-86	25-4-87	18-3-89
CG 59 Princeton†	A	15-10-86	2-10-87	11-2-89
CG 60 Normandy*	B	7-4-87	19-3-88	9-12-89
CG 61 Monterey†	B	19-8-87	22-10-88	16-6-90
CG 62 Chancellorsville†	A	24-6-87	15-7-88	4-11-89
CG 63 Cowpens†	B	23-12-87	11-3-89	9-3-91
CG 64 Gettysburg*	B	17-8-88	22-7-89	22-6-91
CG 65 Chosin (ex-*Shiloh*)†	A	22-7-88	1-9-89	12-1-91
CG 66 Hue City (ex-*Chosin*)*	A	20-2-89	1-6-90	14-9-91
CG 67 Shiloh†	B	1-8-89	14-7-90	18-7-92
CG 68 Anzio*	A	21-8-89	2-11-90	2-5-92
CG 69 Vicksburg (ex-*Port Royal*)*	A	30-5-90	2-8-91	14-11-92
CG 70 Lake Erie†	B	14-3-90	13-7-91	24-7-93
CG 71 Cape St. George*	A	19-11-90	10-1-92	12-6-93
CG 72 Vella Gulf*	A	22-4-91	13-6-92	18-9-93
CG 73 Port Royal†	A	18-10-91	20-11-92	30-4-94

Lake Champlain (CG 57) — U.S. Navy, 2-06

Monterey (CG 61) — U.S. Navy, 4-06

D: 6,997 to 7,242 tons light (9,763 to 10,010 fl)
S: 30+ kts **Dim:** 172.46 (162.36 wl) × 16.76 × 7.46 (10.51 over sonar)
A: 2 Mk 41 Mod. 0 VLS (122 Standard SM-2 MR, Tomahawk, or ASROC missiles); up to 8 Harpoon SSM; 2 single 127-mm 54-cal. Mk 45 Mod. 1 DP (CG 69–73 have Mod. 2); 2 20-mm Mk 15 mod. 12 Block 1 Phalanx gatling CIWS; 2 single 25-mm Mk 38 Bushmaster low-angle; 4 single 12.7-mm mg; 2 triple 324-mm Mk 32 Mod. 14 ASWTT; 1-2 SH-60B LAMPS-III ASW helicopters

GUIDED-MISSILE CRUISERS [CG] *(continued)*

Cowpens (CG 63)—stern view U.S. Navy, 11-05

Chancellorsville (CG 62) U.S. Navy, 12-05

Chosin (CG 65) U.S. Navy, 10-05

Port Royal (CG 73) U.S. Navy, 1-06

Leyte Gulf (CG 55) U.S. Navy, 5-06

Electronics:
Radar: 1 Raytheon SPS-64(V) 9 (CG 72: DRS/Thales Scout) nav.; 1 Cardion SPS-55 surf. search; 1 Raytheon SPS-49(V)6, 7, or 8 air search; 1 Lockheed Martin SPY-1A (CG 59–73: SPY-1B) 3-D air search/f.c.; 4 Raytheon SPG-62 target illumination; 1 Lockheed Martin SPQ-9A gun surface f.c.; 2 General Dynamics Mk 90 Phalanx f.c.
Sonar: CG 52–53: EDO-G.E. SQS-53A bow-mounted LF; CG 54, 55: SQQ-89(V)3 suite (SQS-53A and G.E.-Lockheed Martin SQR-19 towed array); CG 56–67: SQQ-89(V)3 suite (SQS-53B and SQR-19); CG 68–73: SQQ-89(V) . . . suite (SQS-53C and SQR-19)
TACAN: URN-25
IFF: UPX-29 interrogator
EW: Raytheon SLQ-32A(V)3 active/passive; BAE Systems SLQ-20B signal processor; 12 ships: Mk 36 Mod. 18 SRBOC decoy RL syst, (8 6-round Mk 137 RL); 15 ships: Mk 53 Mod. 5 decoy syst. (6 Mk 137 Mod. 4 RL and 4 Mk 137 Mod. 10 Nulka RL); SLQ-25A Nixie towed torpedo decoy syst.; CG 65–73 also: Mk 50 floating decoy syst. (4 Mk 166 launchers for SLQ-49 floating radar reflector buoys)

M: 4 G.E. LM-2500 gas turbines; 2 5-bladed CP props; 100,000 shp max. (86,000 normal)
Electric: 7,500 kw (3 × 2,500-kw Allison 501K gas turbine sets)
Range: 6,000/20 Fuel: 2,000 tons
Crew: 28 officers, 342–359 enlisted

Remarks: Greatly revised version of the *Spruance*-class destroyer, using same hull and propulsion but incorporating the Aegis Mk 7 weapon system (SPY-1-series phased-array radar, four missile illuminator radars, Mk 41 missile-launch system, etc.). Designation changed from DDG to CG on 1-1-80. Named for battles and campaigns.

Authorized: CG 52–53 in FY 82, CG 54–56 in FY 83, CG 57–59 in FY 84, CG 60–62 in FY 85, CG 63–65 in FY 86; CG 66–68 in FY 87, CG 69–73 in FY 88. CG 60–62 were ordered 26-11-84, CG 63 and 64 on 9-1-86, CG 65 on 8-1-86, CG 66–68 on 16-4-87, and CG 69–73 on 25-2-88.

CG 70 was designated a full-time trials ship for the Standard SM-2 Block IVA and SM-3 antiballistic missiles early in 2001 and conducted the first multistage Standard SM-3 launch on 25-1-01, while CG 73 has also been used extensively as a trials ships for the program, both units deploy less frequently as a result.

Problems in mid-1998 with Aegis software updates to CG 66 and CG 69 caused a two-year delay in an effort to integrate all combat systems in the class with the CEC update; CG 61 was delayed three months in deploying in 1998 because of software problems with the Tomahawk land-attack missile system.

Hull systems: The ships have sufficient stability margin to operate at up to 10,200 tons full load—a figure that some of them are approaching. Displacements have grown over time, with the first two having been completed before a rigorous weight-reduction program was instituted. Even so, by 2001 CG 57 displaced 10,100 tons full load, while CG 73, originally listed at 9,613 tons fl, now displaces 9,966 tons. As completed bow

GUIDED-MISSILE CRUISERS [CG] *(continued)*

Monterey (CG 61) U.S. Navy, 4-06

bulwarks were required to keep decks dry, as draft was increased about one meter over that of the original *Spruance* design. Habitability in these ships is cramped. No fin stabilization is fitted. Kevlar armor is incorporated over vital spaces.

CG 61 was modified in 2000 as an Atlantic Fleet "Smart Ship" trials platform for labor- and cost-savings experiments. The ship has tested some 800 different concepts, including the use of off-the-shelf computers, the Sperry Marine integrated bridge, new paints, etc.; similar modifications to CG 53 began during 11-00 and in CG 54 during 2001, all at Pascagoula; modifications cost about $8 million per ship but save $3 million per year each. CG 58 and CG 61 were selected during 8-01 to serve as trials ships for two years for further personnel reductions.

On 26-6-02 CG 65 completed a 232-day overhaul that included incorporation of the *Ticonderoga*-class hull girder modification, a major reinforcement of the hull structure in the area of the forward superstructure that is being performed on all units of the class during overhauls; also being upgraded are the aqueous film-forming foam (AFFF) system and the galleys.

Combat systems: At-sea reload cranes in the VLS launchers have been deleted to permit carrying six more missiles. The Mk 86 Mod. 9 fire-control system for the 127-mm guns provides no AA capability, as no SPG-60 radar is carried. In the earliest ships, the Aegis Mk 7 Mod. 2 system, which used 12 UYK-7 and one UYK-20 computers, employs the four fixed faces of the SPY-1A radar to detect and track up to several hundred targets simultaneously; the four radar illuminators are slaved to the system and can, through time-share switching, serve more than a dozen missiles in the air at once; the Mk 99 missile fire-control system uses four Mk 80 illuminator-directors with SPG-62 radars. The UPX-29 IFF circular antenna array is carried on the mainmast.

The Harpoon missiles, which are launched by the SWG-1 launch-control system, are in an exposed position at the extreme stern. Most ships now carry only four missiles when deployed. All ships have Link 4A, 11, and 14 datalink capability, UQN-4 echo sounders, and WRN-5 and WSC-6 SATCOM terminals. All had the Litton Marine WSN-7 ring-laser gyro inertial navigation system installed during refits, beginning in 2000.

Vertical launch ASROC antisubmarine missiles can be carried in the Mk 41 vertical launchers. All can carry up to 36 Mk 46 ASW torpedoes for their SH-60B helicopters. During 1990s overhauls, the ships had the 127-mm guns upgraded to Mk 45 Mod. 1 and the Phalanx CIWS systems upgraded to Block 1.

During 1999 CG 58, CG 59, and CG 63 became the first of the class to be fitted to launch Nulka hovering decoys from their Mk 137 decoy launchers; the number of Mk 137 launchers for the SRBOC system was been doubled to eight in all (with the system itself now designated Mk 50 vice Mk 36). By 12-99 eight ships of the class had been fitted with TRAFS (Torpedo Recognition and Alertment Functional Segment), a torpedo-detection function added to the SQQ-89 system; seven more of the class had TRAFS by 2003.

Upgrades to the Aegis system software are improving the coordination of combat data. CG 65 has been trials ship for the associated Link 16 TADIL-J (Tactical Distribution Link, Joint) datalink. For the VLS ships, the SWG-3 Tomahawk launch-control system is fitted. CG 56 introduced the SQQ-89(V)3 integrated ASW suite, with SQQ-53B hull-mounted sonar, SQR-19 towed array, and the Mk 116 Mod. 6 ASW fire-control system, although the towed arrays have been removed from the class and stored ashore. CG 65–73 have UYK-43B and UYK-44 computers in place of the heavier UYK-7/UYK-20 combination used in earlier ships; they also have improved UYS-20 data display system and various decision aids and were equipped with the SQS-53C bow sonar and the SQR-17 sonar data processor. The computers have been similarly updated during refits of earlier units.

In 1996 CG 61 became the first VLS ship to receive the Baseline 5 Phase III computer program and equipment upgrade, with Joint Tactical Information Display System (JTIDS, Link 16 Mod. 5), the latest UYK-21 display system, UYK-43 computers in place of UYK-7; CG 59–64 received similar upgrades, except that CG 59 and CG 64 got UYQ-70 displays in place of UYK-21. Twenty-four of the class had the FUSS (Flexible Universal Storage System) magazine modification allowing torpedo magazines to accommodate ordnance for armed helicopter operations,

Modernization: The remaining 22 units of the class will undergo extensive modernization between FY 08 and FY 20. Enhancements include: installation of the Aegis Baseline 7 Phase 1C computer program (allowing for mission expansion and improved open architecture capabilities), Mk 34 gun weapons system including Mk 45 Mod 2 5-inch/62-caliber guns and associated Mk 160 fire-control systems on at least 14 ships, CIWS Block 1B and Evolved Sea Sparrow (ESSM) missile weapon systems, SPQ-9B radar for enhanced detection and engagement of air and surface threats, SQQ-89A(V)15 sonar upgrades in Baseline 3 and 4 units, and the capability to launch both the SM-2 and SM-3 variants of the Standard SAM missile. CG 52 will be the first cruiser to undergo full modernization in FY 08.

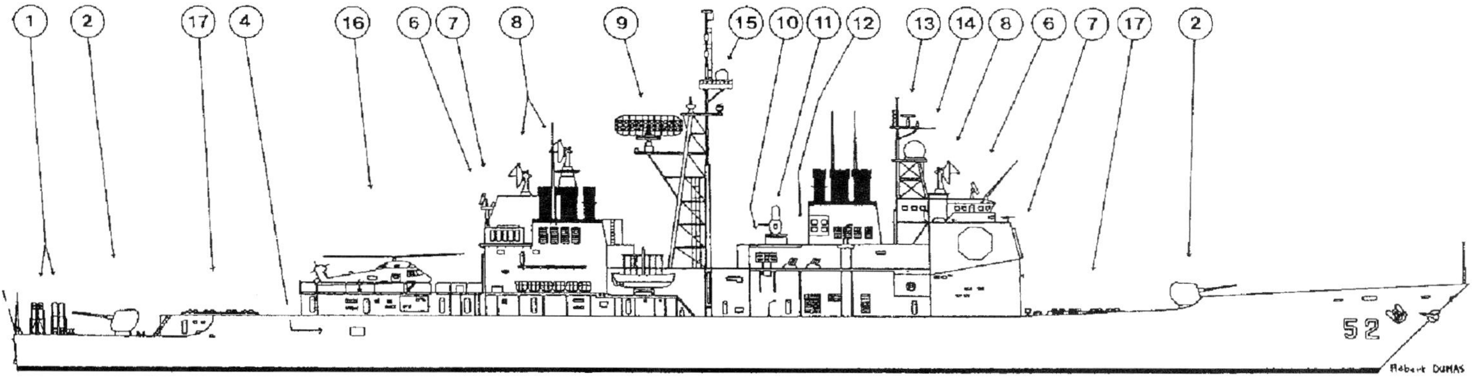

Bunker Hill (CG 52) 1. Harpoon SSM canister-launchers 2. 127-mm Mk 45 DP guns 3. Mk 26 Mod.1 twin-arm guided missile launchers 4. Mk 32 triple ASW TT (behind closed shutters) 5. SH-60B Seahawk LAMPS-III ASW helicopter 6. OE-82 antenna for WSC-3 UHF SATCOM 7. SPY-1A/B 3-D fixed radar antenna arrays 8. SPG-62 radar illuminators 9. SPS-49 2-D air-search radar 10. SLQ-32A(V)3 EW antenna group 11. 20-mm Mk 15 Phalanx CIWS 12. Mk 137 launchers for the Mk 36 SRBOC decoy system 13. SPS-55 surface-search radar 14. SPQ-9A surface gun f.c. radar 15. Antenna for SQQ-28 helicopter datalink, atop IFF interrogator array 16. SH-60B Seahawk LAMPS-III ASW helicopter 17. Mk 41 vertical missile-launch system

Drawings by Robert Dumas from *Flottes de Combat*

GUIDED-MISSILE CRUISERS [CG] *(continued)*

Disposals: *Ticonderoga* (CG 47) was decommissioned 30-9-04, *Yorktown* (CG 48) on 10-12-04, and *Valley Forge* (CG 50) was decommissioned on 30-8-04 and sunk as a target on 2-11-06. *Vincennes* (CG 49) was decommissioned on 30-8-04 and *Thomas S. Gates* (CG 51) on 16-12-05.

GUIDED-MISSILE DESTROYERS [DDG]

♦ 0 (+ 7 + 3) Zumwalt class (DD[X] program)

Bldr: Northrop Grumman and General Dynamics

	Laid down	L	In serv.
DDG 1000 Zumwalt	2009	2011	2012
DDG 1001 . . .	2009	2011	2012
DDG 1002 . . .	. . .	. . .	2017
DDG 1003 . . .	. . .	. . .	2018
DDG 1004 . . .	. . .	. . .	2019

Zumwalt class—computer rendering U.S. Navy, 2006

Zumwalt class—computer rendering Northrop Grumman, 2005

D: 14,564 tons (fl) **S:** 30kts **Dim:** 182.8 × 24.1 × 8.4
A: Mk 57 VLS (80 tubes) for Tomahawk, Standard, ESSM and other missiles; 2 single 155 mm Advanced Gun Systems; 2 57-mm Mk 110 AA; torpedoes; 2 triple 324-mm Mk 32 ASW TT; 1-2 Seahawk sized helicopters; . . . drones/UAVs
Electronics:
Radar: 1 Lockheed-Martin SPY-2 volume search; 1 Raytheon SPY-3 MFR (Multi-Function Radar) target detection, tracking, and illumination; . . .
Sonar: Dual-band bow mounted; multifunction towed array
EW: Mk 36 SRBOC decoy syst.; Nulka decoy syst.; SLQ-25A Nixie towed torpedo decoys; . . .
M: Integrated Power System powered by 2 Rolls Royce MT-30 gas turbines; 2 CP props; 104,930 shp **Electric:** 78 MW **Range:** 4,500/20
Endurance: . . . days **Crew:** 142 tot. (including a 36-person aviation detachment)

Remarks: The DD 21 guided-missile destroyer program was reconstituted as the DD(X) on 1-11-01. Well more than $1 billion in development and design contracts had already been expended when the program was halted. The Department of Defense decided that the DD 21 was too specialized a ship and requested that the new DD(X) be capable of more general-purpose duties and also that it be a smaller ship than the 15,400-ton, 216-m designs offered for DD 21.

A construction contract for the first two ships is expected during FY 07, with the ships to be delivered in 2012, and eight others are planned to be ordered beginning in FY 08. During 3-04 the Navy announced that, at least for the first few ships, Northrop Grumman and General Dynamics will share an equal distribution of work on the project, with system integration to be performed by Raytheon. *Spruance*-class destroyer *Arthur W. Radford* (DD 968) was transferred to Northrop Grumman during FY 03 for rebuild as trials ship for DD(X) propulsion, sensor, and weapon systems, with trials commencing in FY 05 with a civilian crew. The electric propulsion motors are being developed by Kaman Aerospace under a 29-8-02 contract.

Hull systems: Two Rolls Royce MT30 gas turbines vice GE LM2500s will power the ship as part of an Integrated Power System (IPS) to more efficiently distribute power for electrical needs. Expected to be 5,000 tons heavier then DDG 51 class. Heavy investment in "quality of life" improvements with aims to berth all sailors in four-person staterooms. Hull design is of the wave-piercing tumblehome design, which significantly reduces radar cross-section objectives.
Combat systems: To be fitted with Raytheon Mk 57 advanced VLS (80 tubes) and new 155-mm and 57-mm guns. 600 rounds of 155-mm ammunition carried. 155-mm gun is expected to carry the Long-Range Land Attack Projectile (LRLAP) ammunition, said to range 83 n.m.

♦ 23 (+ 12) Arleigh Burke Flight IIA class

Bldrs: General Dynamics Bath Iron Works, Bath, Maine.; Northrop Grumman Ship Systems, Ingalls Div., Pascagoula, Miss. (*Atlantic Fleet/† Pacific Fleet)

	Bldr	Laid down	L	In serv.
DDG 79 Oscar Austin*	Bath	9-10-97	7-11-98	19-8-00
DDG 80 Roosevelt*	Ingalls	15-12-97	10-1-99	14-10-00
DDG 81 Winston S. Churchill*	Bath	7-5-98	17-4-99	10-3-01
DDG 82 Lassen†	Ingalls	24-8-98	15-10-99	21-4-01
DDG 83 Howard†	Bath	9-12-98	20-11-99	20-10-01
DDG 84 Bulkeley*	Ingalls	10-5-99	21-6-00	8-12-01
DDG 85 McCampbell†	Bath	15-7-99	2-7-00	17-8-02
DDG 86 Shoup†	Ingalls	13-12-99	22-11-00	22-6-02
DDG 87 Mason*	Bath	20-1-00	23-6-01	12-4-03
DDG 88 Preble†	Ingalls	22-6-00	1-6-01	9-11-02
DDG 89 Mustin†	Ingalls	15-1-01	12-12-01	26-7-03
DDG 90 Chafee†	Bath	12-4-01	9-11-02	18-10-03
DDG 91 Pinckney†	Ingalls	16-7-01	26-6-02	29-5-04
DDG 92 Momsen†	Bath	25-11-01	19-7-03	28-8-04
DDG 93 Chung-Hoon†	Ingalls	14-1-02	11-12-02	18-9-04
DDG 94 Nitze*	Bath	20-9-02	3-4-04	5-3-05
DDG 95 James E. Williams*	Ingalls	15-7-02	25-6-03	11-12-04
DDG 96 Bainbridge*	Bath	7-5-03	30-10-04	12-11-05
DDG 97 Halsey†	Ingalls	24-2-03	9-1-04	30-7-05
DDG 98 Forrest Sherman*	Ingalls	7-8-03	30-6-04	28-1-06
DDG 99 Farragut*	Bath	30-11-03	9-7-05	10-6-06
DDG 100 Kidd†	Ingalls	29-4-04	12-15-04	12-06 (del.)
DDG 101 Gridley†	Bath	30-7-04	28-12-05	9-06 (del.)
DDG 102 Sampson†	Bath	14-3-05	9-9-06	3-07 (del.)
DDG 103 Truxtun*	Ingalls	11-4-05	18-8-06	1-08 (del.)
DDG 104 Sterett†	Bath	17-11-05	4-07	11-07 (del.)
DDG 105 Dewey†	Ingalls	10-2-06	6-07	11-08 (del.)
DDG 106 Stockdale†	Bath	6-8-06	12-07	7-08 (del.)
DDG 107 Gravely*	Ingalls	2006	. . .	7-09 (del.)
DDG 108 Wayne E. Meyer	Bath	2006	. . .	2-09 (del.)
DDG 109 . . .	Bath	2007	. . .	10-09 (del.)
DDG 110 . . .	Ingalls	2008	. . .	6-10 (del.)
DDG 111 . . .	Bath	2008	. . .	3-10 (del.)
DDG 112 . . .	Bath	2008	. . .	1-11 (del.)

Momsen (DDG 92)—note starboard-side hangar door for WLD-1 Remote Minehunting System U.S. Navy, 4-06

McCampbell (DDG 85) U.S. Navy, 7-06

GUIDED-MISSILE DESTROYERS [DDG] *(continued)*

James E. Williams (DDG 95) U.S. Navy, 11-05

Shoup (DDG 86) U.S. Navy, 4-06

Shoup (DDG 86) U.S. Navy, 4-06

D: DDG 79–84: 9,238 tons (fl); DDG 85–90: 9,300 tons (fl); DDG 91–108: 9,400 tons (fl)
S: 31.6+ kts
Dim: 155.30 (143.56 wl) × 20.27 (18.0 wl) × DDG 79–84: 6.41 hull (9.45 over sonar; 7.62 props); DDG 91–on: 6.68 hull (9.72 over sonar)
A: DDG 79, 80: 2 Mk 41 Mod. 0 vertical-launch groups (1 64-cell, 1 32-cell; 96 Standard SM-2 MR Block IV SAM, VLA ASROC and Tomahawk missiles); 1 127-mm 54-cal. Mk 45 Mod. 1 DP; 2 20-mm Mk 15 Mod. 12 Block I Phalanx gatling CIWS; 2 single 25-mm 75-cal.Mk 38 Mod. 1 Bushmaster guns; 4 single 12.7-mm mg; 2 triple 324-mm Mk 32 Mod. 15 ASW TT (Mk 46 and Mk 50 torpedoes); 2 SH-60R Seahawk helicopters (Penguin and Hellfire missiles, Mk 46 and Mk 50 torpedoes); DDG 81 and later: 2 Mk 41 Mod. 0 vertical-launch groups (1 64-cell, 1 32-cell; 92 Standard SM-2 MR Block IV, LASM, VLA ASROC, and Tomahawk missiles; 24 RIM-162 ESSM Sea Sparrow SAM); 1 127-mm 62-cal. Mk 45 Mod. 4 DP; 2 20-mm Mk 15 Mod. 12 Block IB Phalanx gatling CIWS; 2 single 25-mm 75-cal. Mk 38 Mod. 1 Bushmaster guns; 4 single 12.7-mm mg; 2 triple 324-mm Mk 32 Mod. 15 ASW TT (Mk 46 and Mk 50 torpedoes; Mk 54 on DDG 91 and later); 2 SH-60R Seahawk helicopters (Penguin and Hellfire missiles, Mk 46 and Mk 50 torpedoes) (see Remarks)
Electronics:
Radar: 1 Raytheon SPS-64(V)9 (DDG 87 and later: Decca BridgeMaster E ARPA) nav.; 1 AIL SPS-67(V)3 surf. search; 1 Lockheed Martin SPY-1D(V) 3-D search/weapons control; 3 Raytheon SPG-62 target illumination; 2 Mk 90 Phalanx f.c.
Sonar: DDG 79–90: SQQ-89(V)14 suite: SQS-53C(V)1 hull-mounted, with Kingfisher HF mine-avoidance set, Northrop Grumman SLX-1 Multi-Sensor Torpedo Recognition and Alertment Processor (MSTRAP); DDG 91 and later: SQQ-89(V)15, with same systems plus WLD-1(V)1/3 Remote Minehunting System
TACAN: URN-25
EW: Raytheon SLQ-32A(V)3 active/passive (DDG 85–90: SLQ-32(V) 2 intercept only); Lockheed Martin SRS-1A combat D/F suite (COBLU Phase I on later ships); Mk 36 Mod. 12 SRBOC decoy syst. (4 6-round Mk 137 Mod. 5 RL); DDG 91 and later: Nulka decoy syst. (4 twin Mk 137 Mod. 10 RL); SLQ-25A Nixie towed torpedo decoy (with SSTD Phase I); SLQ-39 active decoy buoy launch system.
E/O: 1 Kollmorgen Mk 46 Mod. 0 (DDG 85 and later: Mod. 1) optronic f.c./surveillance director
M: 4 G.E. LM-2500-30 gas turbines; 2 5-bladed CP props; 105,000 shp (90,000 sust.)
Electric: 7,500 kw tot. (3 Allison 501-K34 gas turbines driving) **Range:** 4,400/20
Fuel: . . . tons
Crew: 32 officers, 348 enlisted (including helicopter detachment: 4 officers, 14 enlisted)

Remarks: Lengthened version of basic *Arleigh Burke* design, with later equipment and hangars added for two helicopters. Funded: DDG 79 in FY 94; DDG 80–82 in FY 95; DDG 83–84 in FY 96; DDG 85–88 in FY 97; DDG 89–92 in FY 98; DDG 93–95 in FY 99; DDG 96–98 in FY 00; DDG 99–101 in FY 01; DDG 102–104 in FY 02; and DDG 105–106 in FY 03. Three (DDG 107–109) under FY 04, and DDG 111–112 under FY 05, bringing the *Burke* series to an end. The FY 03 ships were budgeted at $1.4 billion each.

Under FY 97 Congress authorized advanced procurement for three more under FY 98 and a multiyear, 14-ship procurement for FY 98–01 with Ingalls to build seven ships and Bath Iron Works six; the contracts were signed on 6-3-98, with Ingalls receiving an option contract for two additional units (DDG 98, 100) on 14-12-98. The contracts for DDG 99–101 were given a $998-million increase on 8-12-00, and the option for DDG 102 was taken up on 21-11-01. DDG 102–107 long-lead contracts were placed on 5-6-01. On 17-6-02, however, construction of DDG 102 was transferred to Bath Iron Works, and only one of the class will be assigned each year to Northrop Grumman; in return, Bath will no longer be involved in the LPD 17 program. The DDG 102 was officially recontracted to Bath on 2-8-02. DDG 103–112 were ordered on 13-9-02, with Bath to receive $3.2 billion for six ships and Northrop Grumman to receive $1.9 billion for four; additional $400-million funding contracts for DDG 105 and 106 were issued on 27-12-02.

DDG 80 was named 22-10-96 in honor of both former President Franklin Delano Roosevelt and his wife Eleanor Roosevelt. DDG 81 is named in honor of Sir Winston Churchill; the name was officially changed to add the middle initial on 19-7-99.

DDG 83 and DDG 84 had Baseline 6.1 software and Phalanx CIWS rather than the planned Baseline 6.3 (with no Phalanx but Evolved Sea Sparrow missile) in order to get the ships to the fleet sooner. Ships ordered without Phalanx (DDG 85–90) are receiving it during postcommissioning yard periods. While under construction, DDG 103 suffered a major fire in the command and bridge areas on 20-5-06. Kidd (DDG 100) was damaged in 8-05 by flooding during Hurricane Katrina, delaying completion six months.

Hull systems: Hull lengthened 5 ft. over that of the DDG 51 class, while weight and metacentric height have been reduced through using lighter superstructure scantlings; plating thickness to the lower hull has been increased over three-fourths the hull length amidships; and propellers have improved section to reduce onset of cavitation. In addition, the stern wedge has been extended through the use of a 4-ft fixed flap attached at the lower edge of the transom; the stern wedge and flap add 1.6 kts to the speed over that of the earlier Block I ships, and, with one shaft operating, provide a 28% improvement in range at 20.5 kts on one engine. Do not have fin stabilizers but are equipped with rudder roll-rate reduction. They also have a twisted-section rudder to improve maneuvering efficiency, while Bath Iron Works received a contract during 9-01 to develop a composite-construction version of the new rudder to reduce corrosion. DDG 91 and later have 50 tons of ballast added to port to counter the weight of the hangar, two WLD-1(V)1 minehunting drones and their hoist gear mounted to starboard. Other changes include the addition of five blast-hardened bulkheads to lessen vulnerability, adding a solid-waste-management system, and improving the air-conditioning system. DDG 81 was constructed via a new fabrication technique in which outfitting of hull subsections was undertaken before their integration into major hull sections. The computerized Operational Readiness Test System uses one UYK-44 computer with five OJ-454(V)/UYK display consoles in the weapon-system equipment rooms.

GUIDED-MISSILE DESTROYERS [DDG] *(continued)*

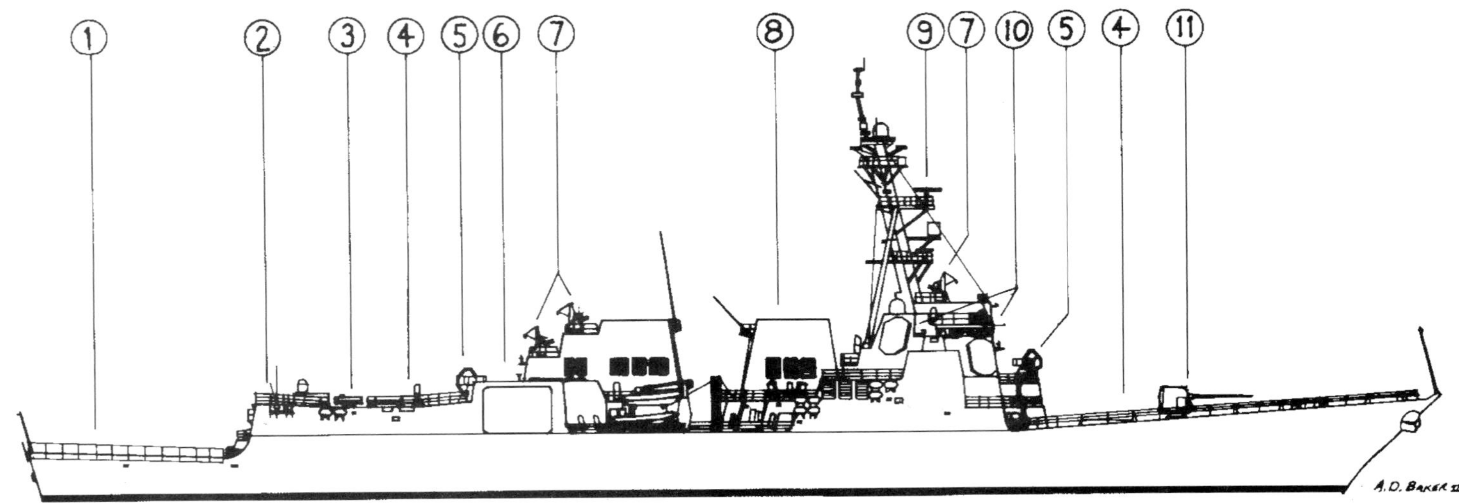

Pinckney (DDG 91) 1. Helicopter deck 2. Twin helicopter hangars 3. Triple Mk 32 Mod. 14 ASW TT 4. Mk 41 Mod. 0 VLS 5. SLY-2 EW syst. 6. Starboard-side hangar for WLD-1(V) Remote Minehunting System 7. SPG-62 target illuminators 8. Decoy launchers 9. SPS-67(V)3 surface-search radar 10. SPY-1D(V) Aegis radar antenna arrays 11. 127-mm 62-cal. Mk 45 Mod. 4 DP gun Drawing by A. D. Baker III

Accommodations have been increased for the air group, and berthing has been provided for four female officers, six female CPOs, and 18 female enlisted. There is no high-pressure air system; auxiliary power units are used to start the generators. A commercial slewing-arm davit handles the 7.3-m rigid inflatable boats. All have the Prairie/Masker air bubbler system to reduce machinery noise radiation below the waterline.

Beginning with DDG 83, they have the "Smart Ship" operational cost-savings features and procedures developed with the cruiser *Yorktown* (CG 48). Systems incorporated include Integrated Condition Assessment System (ICAS) to monitor ship operations; Damage Control System (DCS), with computers, high-speed processors, and touch-screens to monitor ship integrity status; Integrated Bridge System (IBS), which automates bridge and navigational functions, reducing required personnel to as few as two; Standard Monitoring and Control System (SMCS), a computerized propulsion control system; and installation of a fiber-optic local area network (LAN). Units under construction as of 1999 have the Litton Marine WSN-7 ring-laser gyro inertial navigation system, which was to be backfitted in the earlier ships. All earlier ships of the class completed the "Smart Ship" update by the end of 2005.

Aviation systems: Twin hangars aft are served by a RAST (Recovery Assist, Secure and Traverse) system; the aft warping capstan and towing padeye are retractable to keep the helicopter deck clear. Are able to operate Seahawk helicopters in up to State 5 seas. DDG 86 and later were to employ composite-structure helicopter hangars to reduce the ships' radar signatures, while earlier units have composite hangar doors. All ships of this class are to be equipped to carry Northrop Grumman Fire Scout remotely operated, helicopter-type reconnaissance drones equipped with SIGINT, IR, and optical sensors, starting in FY 05.

Combat systems: Have Aegis Weapons System Mk 7 Mod. 11, with the aft pair of SPY-1D antenna panels raised 2.44 m to clear helicopter hangars. Are to incorporate CEC (Cooperative Engagement Capability); USG-2 CEC systems were authorized on 1-5-00 for DDG 84, 85, 86, 91, and 92. DDG 91 will have the SPY-1D(V) radar and Aegis Weapon System Baseline 7.1, incorporating the capability to detect and target theater ballistic missiles, increased target detection and tracking capability, and improved coastal warfare features. The combat systems in all use UYQ-70 displays and a commercial fiber-optic distributed data interface network. Have color large-screen displays in the CIC. The Aegis radar system incorporates a TIP (Track Initiation Processor). DDG 88 was to receive the first Engineering Development Model 4B variant SPY-1E radar, with signal-processing and transmitter changes to improve the radar's capability to detect low-observable targets under clutter conditions. The COBLU (Cooperative Outboard Logistics Update) Phase I variant of the SRS-1A Combat Direction Finding system will be installed on DDG 91 and later ships. All ships of the class have the UPX-29 IFF interrogator/transponder system.

The at-sea reload systems for the VLS groups were eliminated to permit adding three VLS cells per launch group. RIM-9P Evolved Sea Sparrow (ESSM) were to replace the Phalanx installations in DDG 86 and later ships; four missiles will be carried in each of six Mk 41 VLS cells. Phalanx Block 1B CIWS Phalanx mounts, however, were backfitted into DDG 85–86 during 2002 due to delays in the ESSM program and will probably be backfitted through DDG 90–102; DDG 103–113 are to have Phalanx as completed. Harpoon missiles were eliminated to reduce costs, but there is provision to install them later, with the launchers mounted between the stacks; without Harpoon, the ships have no dedicated on-board antiship missile system. DDG 81 was fitted with two 7.62-mm Mk 44 miniguns during a Mideast deployment in early 2003.

DDG 81 and later are able to carry and employ the Tomahawk Land-Attack Standard Missile (LASM) against shore targets. DDG 81 through DDG 95 have stand-alone Tactical Tomahawk Weapons Control Systems, although in later units the missile launch control will be integrated into the overall combat control system.

DDG 81 and later may have the updated 127-mm 62-cal. Mk 45 Mod. 4 gun, with the capability to fire ERGM (Extended-Range Guided Munition) projectiles to 63 n.m. ranges. Mk 45 Mod. 4–equipped ships will carry 232 ERGM rounds and 232 regular rounds of ammunition if the ERGM rounds become available. All but DDG 79 have a faceted, low radar-reflectivity housing for the 127-mm gun. The Mk 46 Mod. 1 optronic director for the 127-mm gun has a laser rangefinder, narrow field-of-view t.v. camera, and (on DDG 82 and later) a thermal imager.

The class does not have a towed-array sonar capability. The SQQ-89(V)10 ASW system, which incorporates the Enhanced Modular Signal Processor (EMSP), uses UYQ-65 displays. The torpedo reload magazine, which can carry up to 40 ASW torpedoes for shipboard and helicopter use, can also accommodate Penguin and Hellfire air-to-ground missiles, Stinger infrared surface-to-air missiles, LAU 68 2.75-in. rockets, and 25-mm gun and 40-mm grenade ammunition.

DDG 91 and later will have the Baseline 7.1 combat system, with a new SPY-1D(V) radar incorporating advanced signal processors; the ships were to have had the canceled SLY-2(V) Advanced Integrated Electronic Warfare System (AIEWS) but will now carry the obsolescent SLQ-32A(V)3. DDG 91 will introduce the WLD-1(V) long-range autonomous mine-countermeasures UUV, with the stowage and handling gear mounted in a hangar on the starboard side; the ships will also carry Tomahawk Block IV cruise missiles.

Note: Design work was completed on a 10,722-ton, lengthened version of the basic *Arleigh Burke* class, the "Flight III," but it was canceled in favor of the *Zumwalt* class; the Flight III, however, could form the basis for continued production of the *Burke* series if the DD(X) is delayed or canceled.

♦ 28 Arleigh Burke class, Flights I and II

Bldrs: General Dynamics Bath Iron Works, Bath, Maine.; and Northrop Grumman Ship Systems, Ingalls Div., Pascagoula, Miss.
(*Atlantic/†Pacific Fleet)

	Bldr	Laid down	L	In serv.
21 Flight I:				
DDG 51 Arleigh Burke*	Bath	6-12-88	16-9-89	4-7-91
DDG 52 Barry (ex-*John Barry*, ex-*Barry*)*	Ingalls	29-2-90	10-5-91	12-12-92
DDG 53 John Paul Jones†	Bath	8-8-90	26-10-91	18-12-93
DDG 54 Curtis Wilbur†	Bath	12-3-91	16-5-92	19-3-94
DDG 55 Stout*	Ingalls	13-9-91	16-10-92	13-8-94
DDG 56 John S. McCain†	Bath	3-9-91	26-9-92	2-7-94
DDG 57 Mitscher*	Ingalls	12-2-92	7-5-93	10-12-94
DDG 58 Laboon*	Bath	23-3-92	20-2-93	18-3-95
DDG 59 Russell†	Ingalls	27-7-92	20-10-93	20-5-95
DDG 60 Paul Hamilton†	Bath	24-8-92	24-7-93	27-5-95
DDG 61 Ramage*	Ingalls	4-1-93	11-2-94	22-7-95
DDG 62 Fitzgerald†	Bath	9-2-93	29-1-94	14-10-95
DDG 63 Stethem†	Ingalls	10-5-93	17-6-94	21-10-95
DDG 64 Carney*	Bath	3-8-93	23-7-94	8-4-96
DDG 65 Benfold†	Ingalls	27-9-93	5-11-94	30-3-96
DDG 66 Gonzalez*	Bath	3-2-94	18-2-95	12-10-96
DDG 67 Cole*	Ingalls	28-2-94	10-2-95	8-6-96
DDG 68 The Sullivans*	Bath	27-7-94	12-8-95	19-4-97
DDG 69 Milius†	Ingalls	8-8-94	1-8-95	23-11-96
DDG 70 Hopper†	Bath	26-2-95	3-2-96	6-9-97
DDG 71 Ross*	Ingalls	10-4-95	23-3-96	28-6-97
7 Flight II:				
DDG 72 Mahan*	Bath	18-6-95	29-6-96	14-2-98
DDG 73 Decatur†	Bath	15-1-96	9-11-96	29-8-98
DDG 74 McFaul*	Ingalls	12-2-96	11-1-97	17-4-98
DDG 75 Donald Cook*	Bath	7-7-96	3-5-97	4-12-98
DDG 76 Higgins*	Bath	17-11-96	4-10-97	24-4-99
DDG 77 O'Kane†	Bath	11-5-97	28-3-98	23-10-99
DDG 78 Porter*	Ingalls	2-12-96	15-10-97	20-3-99

GUIDED-MISSILE DESTROYERS [DDG] *(continued)*

Decatur (DDG 73) U.S. Navy, 7-06

O'Kane (DDG 77) U.S. Navy, 7-06

Donald Cook (DDG 75) U.S. Navy, 1-06

Curtis Wilbur (DDG 54) U.S. Navy, 4-06

D: DDG 51–71: 6,731 tons light (8,850 fl); DDG 72–78: 6,914 tons light (9,033 fl)
S: 31+ kts
Dim: 153.77 (142.03 wl; 135.94 pp) × 20.27 (18.0 wl) × 6.31 (9.35 over sonar; DDG 72–78: 6.60 hull/9.90 over sonar)
A: 2 Mk 41 Mod. 0 vertical-launch groups (1 61-cell, 1 29-cell; 90 Standard SM-2 MR Block III SAM, VLA ASROC and Tomahawk missiles); 4–8 Harpoon SSM; 1 127-mm 54-cal. Mk 45 Mod. 1 DP; 2 20-mm Mk 15 Mod. 12 Phalanx gatling CIWS; 2 single 25-mm 75-cal. Mk 38 Mod. 1 Bushmaster guns; 4 single 12.7-mm mg; 2 triple 324-mm Mk 32 Mod. 15 ASW TT (Mk 46 and Mk 50 torpedoes)

Donald Cook (DDG 75) U.S. Navy, 12-05

Gonzalez (DDG 66) U.S. Navy, 12-05

Russell (DDG 59) U.S. Navy, 3-06

GUIDED-MISSILE DESTROYERS [DDG] *(continued)*

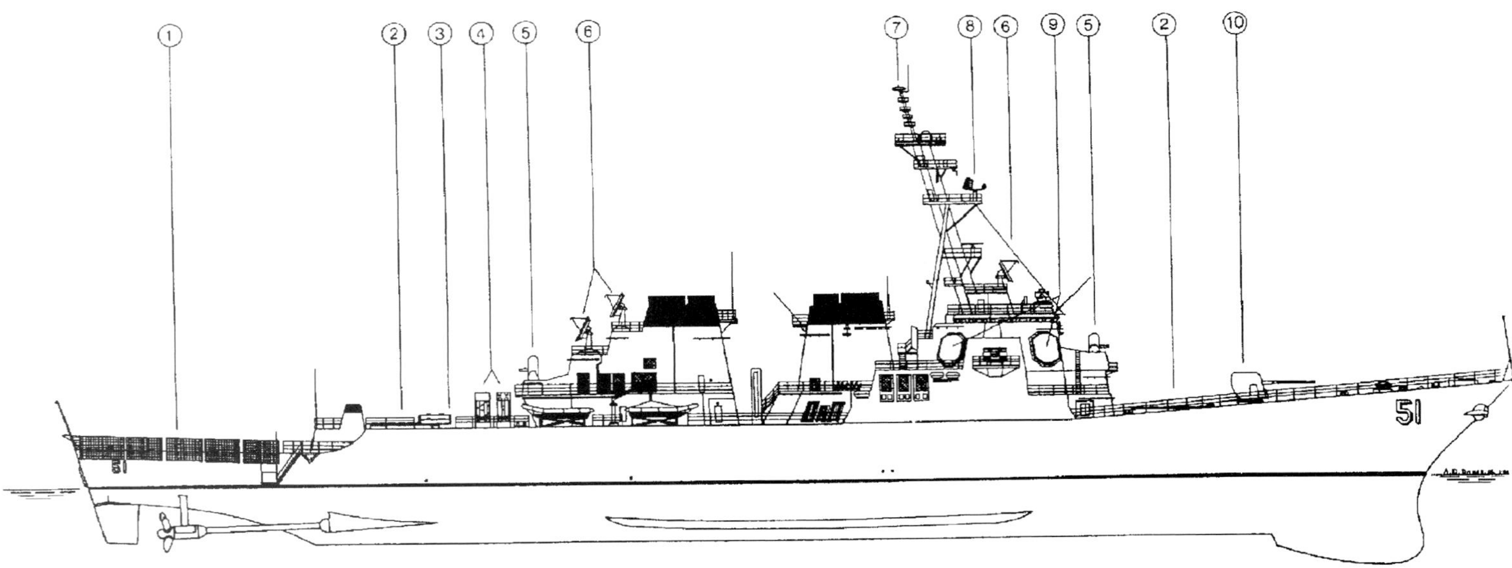

Arleigh Burke (DDG 51) 1. Helicopter deck 2. Mk 41 vertical-launch system 3. Mk 32 triple ASW TT 4. Harpoon antiship missile launch canisters 5. 20-mm Mk 15 Phalanx CIWS 6. SPG-62 radar illuminators 7. URN-25 TACAN 8. SPS-67(V)3 surface-search radar (now a slotted waveguide antenna) 9. SPY-1D Aegis antenna arrays 10. 127-mm Mk 45 DP gun
Drawing by A. D. Baker III

Electronics:

Radar: 1 Raytheon SPS-64(V)9 nav.; 1 AIL SPS-67(V)3surf. search; 1 Lockheed Martin SPY-1D 3-D search/weapons control; 3 Raytheon SPG-62 target illumination; 2 Mk 90 Phalanx f.c.

Sonar: SQQ-89(V)4 suite: SQS-53C(V)1 bow-mounted; Kingfisher mine-avoidance; provision for SQR-19B(V)1 towed array

TACAN: URN-25

EW: Raytheon SLQ-32(V)5 (DDG 68–on: SLQ-32(V)3) active/passive; DDG 72–78 only: Sanders SRS-1A combat D/F; all: Mk 36 Mod. 12 SRBOC decoy syst. (4 6-round Mk 137 RL); SLQ-25A Nixie towed torpedo decoy (with SSTD Phase I); SLQ-39 decoy buoy launch system; DDG 52 also: 4 twin Mk 53 Nulka decoy RL

E/O: Kollmorgen Mk 46 Mod. 0 optronic director

M: 4 G.E. LM-2500-30 gas turbines; 2/5 bladed CP props; 105,000 shp (90,000 sust.)

Electric: 7,500 kw tot. (3 Allison 501-K34 gas turbines driving) **Range:** 4,400/20

Fuel: . . . tons

Crew: 21–22 officers, 315 enlisted (DDG 69: 28 officers, 231 enlisted)

Remarks: Authorized: DDG 51 in FY 85, DDG 52–54 in FY 87 (DDG 54 funded FY 89), DDG 55–58 in FY 89, DDG 59–63 in FY 90, DDG 64–67 in FY 91, DDG 68–72 in FY 92, DDG 73–76 in FY 93, and DDG 77–78 in FY 94. The name for DDG 52 was changed three times—twice in 1989. DDG 70 is named for a woman, Rear Adm. Grace Hopper. DDG 54 became the first of the class to be based overseas, at Yokosuka, Japan, on 30-9-96, followed by DDG 56 on 30-6-97.

DDG 51 was ordered 2-4-85, DDG 52 on 26-5-87, DDG 53 in 8-87. Congress required a third yard to participate in FY 89 construction, but none was selected. Only three were requested for FY 89 in 2-88, but Congress authorized and appropriated funds for three ($2,062,200,000) and authorized the use of unexpended prior-year funds for two more; all five were ordered 13-12-88. DDG 59–63 were ordered 22-2-90, DDG 64–67 were ordered 16-1-91, DDG 68–72 were ordered 8-4-92, and DDG 73–76, authorized and appropriated for $3.25 billion under FY 93, were ordered on 21-1-93. DDG 77–79 were funded at $2.9 billion under FY 94, with DDG 79 being the prototype for the follow-on Flight IIA group described previously.

DDG 66 ran aground 12-11-96 less than a month after commissioning on a charted rock near St. Martin in the Caribbean, damaging the sonar dome, propellers, and shaft struts; repairs by Bath Iron Works were initially expected to cost $56 million but were instead completed during 9-97 for about $10 million.

DDG 67 was heavily damaged by a terrorist attack at Aden, Yemen, on 12-10-00, with 17 killed and 35 injured; the explosion tore a 40 × 40–ft-hole in the ship's sides, flooding the forward generator room and destroying the enlisted messdecks. Repairs were estimated to cost as much as $170 million. Repair contract issued to Ingalls Shipbuilding, Pascagoula, during 1-01, with the ship relaunched on 15-9-01 and all work completed by 2-02.

DDG 60 was in a collision with an Iranian merchant craft on 6-12-02, causing a small hole in the side of the hull.

Hull systems: The ships have steel superstructures and the first comprehensive CBR protection system in a U.S. Navy ship. More than 130 tons of Kevlar or plastic armor are used for vital spaces, including 70 tons around the combat control spaces. In a weight-saving program, DDG 78 and later employed about 50 tons less structural steel than earlier ships. The hull form is unusually broad in relation to length; fin stabilizers are not fitted, but they do have rudder roll-rate reduction. Prairie/Masker air bubbler systems are fitted to the hulls and propellers to reduce machinery noise radiation below the waterline.

The concept of the broad hull was borne out during sea trials for DDG 51, which was able to maintain 30 knots in 35-ft. seas and a 60-knot gale. The ships heel only slightly with full rudder at full speed. Although the hull was configured with a stern wedge to reduce "squatting" at higher speeds and improve fuel endurance, a fixed stern flap is being fitted to the transom below the waterline to further improve fuel efficiency; it had been fitted to DDG 59, DDG 61, and several others by 4-01.

Have automated digital steering system, wherein course is entered and automatically maintained. DDG 64 and later have the Litton Marine WSN-5 ring-laser inertial gyro navigation system, and the Litton Marine WSN-7 ring-laser gyro inertial navigation system is to be backfitted in all during overhauls. Carry two 7.32-m rigid inflatable boats and 15 25-person encapsulated liferafts. The increase in full-load displacements over the originally announced 8,315 tons is primarily the result of adapting void tanks to carry fuel.

Combat systems: Have the Mk 8 Weapon Control system. The Aegis SPY-1D radar has all four faces mounted on the forward superstructure; the system employs five UYK-43B computers, and the Combat Information Center is below the main deck. DDG 69 was the first with Aegis Baseline 5 Phase 3, which incorporated a SPY-1D Track Initiation Processor (which permits the screening of transient detections prior to transition-to-track); X-Windows format Tactical Graphics Capability; and an embedded command and control processor with joint Link 16 capability. WSC-3 UHF SATCOM terminals and Links 11 and 14 are fitted, and during the 1990s, the WSC-6 SHF SATCOM system was added. Commercial satellite communications terminals have also been added to all. The Rockwell USQ-82(V) databus is employed for internal data distribution. DDG 58 and later have improved fire control, extended-range Standard missile employment capability, NTDS Mod. 5, improved displays, and later communications systems.

Block II ships (DDG 72–78) have the Joint Tactical Information Distribution System (JTDS) command and control processor, combat direction finding, the Tactical Information Exchange System (TADIX B), SLQ-32(V)3 active electronics countermeasures, and the capability to launch and control the Aegis Standard Extended Range Missile added.

No helicopter hangar is fitted. The flight deck can accept SH-60B or SH-60F Seahawk helicopters, and the SQQ-28 LAMPS-III datalink/control system is installed. DDG 52 and later have helicopter refueling/rearming facilities, which added 58 tons to the full-load displacement; they can carry nine spare ASW torpedoes for helicopters in a small magazine near the helicopter deck.

The 127-mm gun is controlled by the Mk 34 Mod. 0 Gun Weapon System with Mk 160 Mod. 4 Gun Computing System (which uses radar input data from the SPS-67[V]3 surface-search radar or the SPY-1D Aegis system); the planned Mk 121 Mod. 0 Seafire t.v./laser/infrared director was canceled and replaced by a less-costly system, the Kollmorgen Passive Optical Sight Mk 46 Mod. 0, which is mounted atop an extended deckhouse forward of the forward Mk 99 illuminator; all are being brought up to Mod. 1 standard, with the addition of a laser rangefinder, narrow field-of-view t.v. camera, and a new thermal imager. The gun has a secondary antiaircraft capability and is furnished with 600 rounds of ammunition. The Standard SM-2 MR Block 2 missiles are controlled by the Aegis system, with the Mk 99 missile fire-control system using the three Mk 80 illuminator systems' SPG-62 radars for terminal designation only. The normal deployed load of missiles includes 74 Standard SM-2MR SAMs. Tomahawk launch control is by the SWG-3A system and Harpoon by the SWG-1A(V) system; the Block II ships do not normally to carry the Harpoon missiles, although the racks for two sets of four canister launchers are present.

The SQQ-89(V)4 ASW suite includes the SQS-53C bow-mounted sonar, SQR-19 towed passive sonar array, SQQ-28 helicopter datalink, SIMAS, and the Mk 116 Mod. 7 weapon-control system. Most ships of the class have had the towed hydrophone arrays removed and put into storage. The Mk 116 Mod. 7 ASW fire-control system is carried to handle the launch of shipboard torpedoes and VLS ASROC missiles.

The SLQ-32(V)2 passive-only EW suite in early Flight I units of the class has been upgraded to SLQ-32(V)5 through the addition of "Sidekick" jammers; later Flight I units were completed with Sidekick, while the Flight II ships have the integrated SLQ-32(V)3 intercept and jamming array.

GUIDED-MISSILE DESTROYERS [DDG] *(continued)*

May have one Phalanx mount updated to Block IB electro-optical configuration to deal with smallcraft, mines, and other small targets. Following the attack on the DDG 67 in 10-00, deployed ships are receiving two 25-mm Boeing Mk 88 Bushmaster low-angle guns and four 12.7-mm machineguns. Consideration was being given as of 4-01 to adding two General Dynamics 30-mm Mk 46 gun systems to improve defenses against smallcraft attacks.

Disposal notes: Of the four relatively new and powerful *Kidd*-class guided-missile destroyers, *Kidd* (DDG 993, ex-Iranian *Kouroush*) was decommissioned on 12-3-98, *Callaghan* (DDG 994, ex-*Daryush*) on 31-3-98, *Scott* (DDG 995, ex-*Nader*) on 15-12-98, and *Chandler* (DDG 996, ex-*Andushirvan*) on 24-9-99; they were offered to Taiwan during 1-01 and formally accepted on 2-10-01. Activation and modernization began in 2004 at Detyens SY, Charleston, South Carolina.

DESTROYERS [DD]

Disposal notes: The last remaining *Spruance*-class destroyers were decommissioned during 2005. Disposition of the class is as follows:

	Decomm.	Stricken/Comments
DD 963 *Spruance*	23-3-05	Stricken for disposal on 18-3-05
DD 964 *Paul F. Foster*	14-3-03	Conversion as Self-Defense System Test Ship (redesignated EDD 964 on 16-3-06 under Naval Surface Warfare Center); stricken 6-4-04
DD 965 *Kinkaid*	7-1-03	Sunk as target 14-7-04
DD 966 *Hewitt*	19-7-01	Scrapped 7-11-02
DD 967 *Elliot*	2-12-03	Stricken 6-4-04, sunk as a target on 23-7-05
DD 968 *Arthur W. Radford*	18-3-03	To Northrop Grumman as test ship for *Zumwalt*-class program (6,870 tons light/9,306 fl)
DD 969 *Peterson*	4-10-02	Sunk as target 16-2-04
DD 970 *Caron*	15-10-01	Stricken 5-6-02; sunk prematurely on 4-12-02 during damage-control experiments
DD 971 *David R. Ray*	28-2-02	Stricken 6-11-02, to be scrapped
DD 972 *Oldendorf*	20-6-03	Stricken 6-4-04; sunk as target 22-8-05
DD 973 *John Young*	30-9-02	Stricken 6-11-02; sunk as target 26-4-04
DD 974 *Comte de Grasse*	5-6-98	Stricken 5-6-98; sunk as target 7-6-06
DD 975 *O'Brien*	24-9-04	Sunk as target 9-2-06
DD 976 *Merrill*	26-3-98	Stricken 26-3-98; sunk as target 1-8-03
DD 977 *Briscoe*	2-10-03	Stricken 6-4-04; sunk as target on 7-6-06
DD 978 *Stump*	22-10-04	Stricken 22-10-04; sunk as a target on 7-6-06
DD 979 *Conolly*	18-9-98	Stricken 18-9-98; possible museum
DD 980 *Moosbrugger*	15-12-00	Stricken 25-4-06 for scrapping
DD 981 *John Hancock*	16-10-00	Stricken 25-4-06 for scrapping
DD 982 *Nicholson*	18-12-02	Stricken 6-4-04; sunk as target 30-7-04
DD 983 *John Rodgers*	4-9-98	Stricken 4-9-98; scrapped 2006
DD 984 *Leftwich*	28-3-98	Stricken 28-3-98; sunk as target 1-8-03
DD 985 *Cushing*	21-9-05	Stricken same date for scrapping
DD 986 *Harry W. Hill*	29-5-98	Stricken 29-5-98; sunk as target 15-7-04
DD 987 *O'Bannon*	19-8-05	Stricken same date for scrapping; possible foreign sale
DD 988 *Thorn*	25-8-04	To be sunk as target
DD 989 *Deyo*	6-11-03	Stricken on 6-4-04; sunk as target 25-8-05
DD 990 *Ingersoll*	24-7-98	Stricken 24-7-98; sunk as target 29-7-03
DD 991 *Fife*	28-2-03	Stricken on 6-4-04; sunk as target 25-8-05
DD 992 *Fletcher*	1-10-04	Stricken on 25-8-04; possible foreign transfer
DD 997 *Hayler*	25-8-03	Stricken on 6-4-04; sunk as target 14-11-04

FRIGATES [FF]

Note: The Mk 13 missile launchers on the *Oliver Hazard Perry* class have been removed, thus the class is now listed here, under the [FF] section of the fleet listing though, officially, they remain FFGs.

♦ 30 Oliver Hazard Perry class (SCN 207/2081 type)

(*Atlantic/†Pacific Fleet; 8 Naval Reserve Force ships: FFG 28, 29, 38, 39, 41, 42, 56, 60)

	Bldr	Laid down	L	In serv.
FFG 8 McInerney*	Bath Iron Works	16-1-78	4-11-78	15-12-79
FFG 28 Boone*	Todd, Seattle	27-3-79	16-1-80	15-5-82
FFG 29 Stephen W. Groves*	Bath Iron Works	16-9-80	4-4-81	17-4-82
FFG 32 John L. Hall*	Bath Iron Works	5-1-81	24-7-81	26-6-82
FFG 33 Jarrett†	Todd, San Pedro	11-2-81	17-10-81	2-7-83
FFG 36 Underwood*	Bath Iron Works	3-8-81	6-2-82	29-1-83
FFG 37 Crommelin†	Todd, Seattle	30-5-80	1-7-81	18-6-83
FFG 38 Curts†	Todd, San Pedro	1-7-81	6-3-82	8-10-83
FFG 39 Doyle*	Bath Iron Works	16-11-81	22-5-82	21-5-83
FFG 40 Halyburton*	Todd, Seattle	26-9-80	13-10-81	7-1-84
FFG 41 McCluskey†	Todd, San Pedro	21-10-81	18-9-82	10-12-83
FFG 42 Klakring*	Bath Iron Works	19-2-82	18-9-82	20-8-83
FFG 43 Thach†	Todd, San Pedro	6-2-82	18-12-82	17-3-84
FFG 45 De Wert*	Bath Iron Works	14-6-82	18-12-82	19-11-83
FFG 46 Rentz†	Todd, San Pedro	18-9-82	16-7-83	30-6-84
FFG 47 Nicholas*	Bath Iron Works	27-9-82	23-4-83	10-3-84
FFG 48 Vandegrift†	Todd, Seattle	13-10-81	15-10-82	24-11-84
FFG 49 Robert G. Bradley*	Bath Iron Works	28-12-82	13-8-83	11-8-84
FFG 50 Taylor*	Bath Iron Works	5-5-83	5-11-83	1-12-84
FFG 51 Gary†	Todd, San Pedro	18-12-82	19-11-83	17-11-84
FFG 52 Carr*	Todd, Seattle	26-3-82	26-2-83	27-7-85
FFG 53 Hawes*	Bath Iron Works	22-8-83	17-2-84	9-2-85
FFG 54 Ford†	Todd, San Pedro	16-7-83	23-6-84	29-6-85
FFG 55 Elrod*	Bath Iron Works	14-11-83	12-5-84	6-7-85
FFG 56 Simpson*	Bath Iron Works	27-2-84	31-8-84	9-11-85
FFG 57 Reuben James†	Todd, San Pedro	10-9-83	8-2-85	22-3-86
FFG 58 Samuel B. Roberts*	Bath Iron Works	21-5-84	8-12-84	12-4-86
FFG 59 Kauffman*	Bath Iron Works	8-4-85	29-3-86	21-2-87
FFG 60 Rodney M. Davis*	Todd, San Pedro	8-2-85	11-1-86	9-5-87
FFG 61 Ingraham†	Todd, San Pedro	30-3-87	26-6-88	5-8-89

Underwood (FFG 36)—the Mk 13 launcher has been removed from this class
U.S. Navy, 4-06

John L. Hall (FFG 32) U.S. Navy, 3-06

FRIGATES [FF] *(continued)*

Nicholas (FFG 47) U.S. Navy, 5-06

Carr (FFG 52) U.S. Navy, 1-06

Ford (FFG 54) U.S. Navy, 2005

D: 3,101–3,204 tons light (4,016–4,108 fl) **S:** 29 kts (30.6 trials)
Dim: 138.80 (125.9 wl) × 13.72 × 5.8 (6.7 max.)
A: 1 76-mm 62-cal. Mk 75 DP; 1 20-mm Mk 15 Phalanx Block 1, Block 1A or Block 1B gatling CIWS; 2 single 25-mm 75-cal. Mk 38 Bushmaster low-angle guns; 2 or 4 single 12.7-mm mg; 2 triple 324-mm Mk 32 Mod. 5 or Mod. 17 ASW TT; 1 or 2 SH-60B Seahawk LAMPS-III ASW helicopters
Electronics:
Radar: 1 Cardion SPS-55 surf. search.; 1 Raytheon SPS-49(V)4 or (V)5) air-search; 1 Lockheed-Martin Mk 92 Mod. 2 or Mod. 6 missile/gun f.c.; 1 Lockheed-Martin STIR (SPG-60 Mod.) missile/gun f.c. (see Remarks)
Sonar: SQQ-89(V)2 or (V)9 suite: Raytheon SQS-56 hull-mounted LF; Gould SQR-19(V)2 or SQR-19B(V)2 TACTASS towed array (see Remarks)
TACAN: URN-25
EW: FFG 29, 32, 36, 40, 45–59, 61: Raytheon SLQ-32(V)5 with Sidekick jammer; others: Raytheon SLQ-32(V)2 intercept only; all: Mk 36 SRBOC decoy syst. (2 6-round Mk 137 RL); SLQ-25 Nixie towed acoustic torpedo decoy (SLQ-25A on FFG 36, 47, 51–53, 55, 57–60)
M: 2 G.E. LM-2500 gas turbines; 1 5.5-m diameter CP, 5-bladed prop; 41,000 shp (40,000 sust.)—2/350-shp drop-down electric propulsors
Electric: 3,000 kw tot. **Range:** 4,200/20; 5,000/18
Fuel: 587 tons + 64 tons helicopter fuel
Crew: 17–19 officers, 198 enlisted

Remarks: These ships were originally conceived as low-cost convoy escorts. As older first-line destroyers and frigates were retired without replacement, however, the FFG 7 class has been integrated into the fleet, and numerous updates have been applied to permit it to cope with modern combat conditions. As a result, the fully equipped units displace nearly 700 tons more than the designed displacement, and crews have been greatly enlarged. The soundness of the design has permitted the expansion, and the ships have proven remarkably sturdy. FFG 17, 18, 35, and 44 of this class were built by Todd, Seattle, for Australia, which also built two more in-country. Spain built six, and Taiwan has built eight. Others have been transferred abroad (see following table).

The Standard SM-1 missile system retired from USN service at the end of FY 03, and the existing missile launchers (which launched both the SM-1 and Harpoon ASM) have been replaced with a metal plate covering the area where the Mk 13 was seated. The RAM short-range missile or the hybrid RAM CIWS combination known as SEARAM may be fitted at a future date. In addition, current plans call for a Nulka decoy syst. (4 twin Mk 137 Mod. 10 RL) to be fitted to all active duty frigates.

Hull systems: Displacements have steadily increased, to the detriment of stability. FFG 59 was delivered at 4,100 tons full load, although the class was designed for 3,600 tons and with only 39 tons planned growth margin. The ships are particularly well protected against splinter and fragmentation damage, with 19-mm aluminum-alloy armor over magazine spaces, 16-mm steel over the main engine-control room, and 19-mm Kevlar plastic armor over vital electronics and command spaces. Because of a hull twisting problem, doubler plates have been added over the hull sides amidships just below the main deck.

Speed on one turbine alone is 25 kts. The auxiliary propulsion system uses two retractable, pivoting pods located well forward and can drive the ships at up to 6 kts and can also be used as side-thrusters. Fin stabilizers began to be backfitted in earlier units, beginning with FFG 26 in 1982. Each fin extends 2.36 m and has a mean chord of 2.36 m; they are located 57.9 m abaft the bow perpendicular. At least 21 active units of the class have received the Passive Countermeasures System (PCMS) to reduce radar cross-section.

Aviation systems: Although the ships were intended to operate the LAMPS-III ASW helicopter, FFG 7–35 as completed lacked the equipment necessary to handle them. Beginning with the FY 79 ships (FFG 36 and later), helicopter support equipment was aboard on completion: fin stabilizers, RAST (Recovery Assistance, Securing, and Traversing system—not fitted as completed until FFG 50), and other systems. The RAST system permits helicopter launch and recovery with the ship rolling through 28 degrees and pitching 5 degrees. The equipment was first installed in *McInerney* (FFG 8), which was reconstructed, completing 12-2-81 at Bath Iron Works, to act as LAMPS-III/SH-60B Seahawk helicopter trials ship; the stern was lengthened by 3.16 m by changing the rake of the stern (the extension is slightly lower than the flight deck, to provide clearance for mooring equipment). Of the earlier short-hull ships, FFG 28, 29, 32, and 33 were lengthened and given the RAST system.

Combat systems: The ships had the Mk 13 weapons-direction system. The Mk 92 Mod. 2 fire-control system controls missile and 76-mm gunfire; it uses an STIR (Separate Target Illumination Radar, a modified SPG-60) antenna amidships and a U.S.-built version of the Thales Nederland WM-28 radar forward and can track four separate targets. The CORT (Coherant Receiver/Transmiter) Phase-II upgraded the Mk 92 Mod. 4 weapons-control system to Mod. 6 to improve performance in jamming and clutter; the search radar was upgraded to SPS-49(V)5, and the SYS-2(V)2 integrated

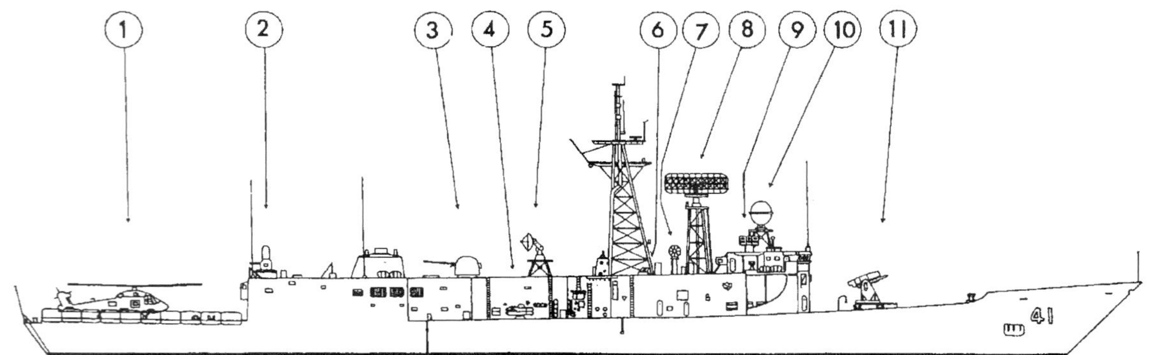

McCluskey (FFG 41) 1. SH-60B Seahawk LAMPS-III ASW helicopter 2. 20-mm Mk 15 Phalanx CIWS 3. 76-mm Mk 75 DP gun 4. Triple Mk 32 ASW TT 5. STIR gun and missile f.c. 6. Mk 137 launchers for the Mk 36 SRBOC decoy system 7. OE-82 antennas (port and starboard) for the WSC-3 UHF SATCOM system. 8. SPS-49 air-search radar 9. SLQ-32(V)2 EW antenna group 10. Mk 92 radar f.c. director 11. Mk 13 Mod. 4 missile launcher *(since removed)* Drawing by Robert Dumas from *Flottes de Combat*

FRIGATES [FF] *(continued)*

action data system was fitted. CORT had been added to FFG 36, 47, 48, 50–55, 57, 59, and 61 by end-1995 when the update program was terminated. Ten other units of the class received the CANDO (Commercial-off-the-shelf Affordable Near-term Deficiency-correcting Ordalts) upgrade to the Mk 92 Mod. 2 fire-control system, incorporating improved clutter rejection in the radars, automatic target track display, and further improvements to the SPS-49(V)4 radar to detect small radar cross-section targets over land and in severe clutter conditions. FFG 47, 48, 50–55, 57, 59, and 61 by 1-99 had the RAIDS (Rapid Antiship Integrated Defense System) modification, which uses a COTS computer to integrate the combat direction system with threat data from the SLQ-32 EW system and the fire-control radar of the CIWS. The SPS-49(V)5 radars are planned to be updated to SPS-49A(V)1 in all surviving ships.

A few ships have been given Furuno-made navigational radars. All have SRR-1 and WSC-3 SATCOM equipment.

The Mk 75 gun is a license-built version of the OTO Melara Compact. Two Mk 24 optical missile and gun target designators (mounted in tubs atop the pilothouse) were not fitted to the ships as completed until FFG 27 but have been backfitted in the earlier ships. The only ship-launched ASW weapons are the Mk 46 or Mk 50 torpedoes in the two triple torpedo tubes; a total of 24 torpedoes can be carried for shipboard and helicopter use. Nineteen of the class have the FUSS (Flexible Universal Storage System) magazine modification allowing torpedo magazines to accommodate ordnance for armed helicopter operations.

The Mk 15 CIWS (Close-In Weapon System) 20-mm Phalanx was backfitted into all by end-1988; the improved Mk 15 Block 1 was backfitted in the 1990s; and the Block 1B, with a surface engagement capability, is to be substituted on 24 surviving units by 2005 (trials with the first mount were conducted on FFG 36 during 2-99; the mount was then transferred to FFG 50 in 9-00).

Two variants of the SQQ-89 sonar system are in service on this class: SQQ-89(V)10 on FFG 37, 50, 51, 52, and 54, with SQR-19B(V)2 towed array sonar; and SQQ-89(V)2 on FFG 28, 29, 32, 33, 36, 38-43, 45–49, 53, 55–59, and 61, with SQR-19(V)2 and the UYQ-25A(V)2 processor. Most ships of the class, however, have had the towed hydrophone arrays removed and put into storage. The antenna for the SRQ-4 helicopter-ship ASW datalink of the LAMPS III system is carried within a radome atop the mainmast. The Kingfisher mine-avoidance modification to the SQS-56 sonar, first installed in FFG 47, is being backfitted as funds permit.

Modernization: Consideration is being given to updating the 24 newest ships and extending their service lives by 10 to 15 years. All would receive hull, engineering, and electrical upgrades and a renewal of their auxiliary equipment; Nulka decoy launchers and an IR surveillance system would be added.

Disposals: The disposition of nonactive units are as follows (NRF = Naval Reserve Force)

	Decomm.	Action	On
FFG 7 *Oliver Hazard Perry*	20-2-97	Stricken	3-5-99
FFG 9 *Wadsworth*	28-6-02	To Poland, but not stricken until 23-7-02	23-7-02
FFG 10 *Duncan*	2-6-95	Stricken; sold to Turkey for spares, 5-4-99	4-9-97
FFG 11 *Clark*	15-3-00	To Poland, donation	15-3-00
FFG 12 *George Philip*	15-3-03	Possible foreign transfer	24-5-04
FFG 13 *Samuel Eliot Morison*	10-4-02	Sale to Turkey; stricken 23-7-02	10-4-02
FFG 14 *Sides*	28-3-03	Possible foreign transfer	2006–7
FFG 15 *Estocin*	4-4-03	Sale to Turkey	4-4-03
FFG 16 *Clifton Sprague*	2-6-95	To Turkey	27-8-97
FFG 19 *John A. Moore**	1-9-00	To Turkey	1-9-00
FFG 20 *Antrim*	8-5-96	To Turkey	27-8-97
FFG 21 *Flatley*	11-5-96	To Turkey	27-8-97
FFG 22 *Fahrion*	31-3-98	Sale to Egypt	31-3-98
FFG 23 *Lewis B. Puller*	18-9-98	Sale to Egypt	18-9-98
FFG 24 *Jack Williams*	13-9-96	To Bahrain	13-9-96
FFG 25 *Copeland*	18-9-96	Sale to Egypt	18-9-96
FFG 26 *Gallery*	14-6-96	To Egypt	26-9-96
FFG 27 *Mahlon S. Tisdale*	27-9-96	Stricken (to Turkey 4-99)	20-2-98
FFG 30 *Reid*	25-9-98	Stricken Sold to Turkey 9-98	25-9-98
FFG 31 *Stark*	7-5-99	Stricken for scrap	7-5-99
FFG 34 *Aubrey Fitch*	12-12-97	Stricken	3-5-99

CORVETTES [FFL]

♦ 0 (+ 2 + 5) Freedom-class Littoral Combat Ships

Bldrs: Lockheed Martin; Marinette Marine Corp, Marinette Wisc.; Bollinger Shipyards, Lockport, La. (In serv. 2007– . . .)

	Bldr	Laid down	L	In serv.
LCS 1 Freedom	Marinette Marine	2-6-05	9-23-06	6-07
LCS 3 . . .	Bollinger Shipyards	2007	2008	1-09

D: 2,840 tons (fl) **S:** 50 kts **Dim:** 115.3 × 17.5 × 3.9

A: 1 21-round Mk 31 SAM launcher (RIM-116A RAM missiles); 1 57-mm Mk 110 AA; 2 12.7-mm mg; 1 MH-60R/S helicopter; . . . UAVs

Electronics:

Radar: 1 EADS-Raytheon TRS-3D/16 3-D search; 1 . . . nav

Sonar: NDS-3070 mine and obstacle avoidance

EW: . . . intercept; 1 Terma DLS Mk II DL-12T 12-round decoy RL

M: CODAG: 2 Fairbanks Morse Colt-Pielstick 16 PA6B STC diesels, 8,700 bhp each; 2 Rolls Royce MT-30 gas turbines, 98,000 shp; 4 waterjets

Range: 3,550/18 Crew: 6 officers and 32 enlisted

Freedom-class Littoral Combat Ship—computer rendering
Lockheed Martin, 2004

Freedom-class Littoral Combat Ship—computer rendering
Lockheed Martin, 2004

Remarks: One outcome of the cancellation of the DD 21–class destroyer on 1-11-01 was initiation of a program to study the possible acquisition of a class of 1,250–2,500-ton "Littoral Combat Ships" (LCS) for use in coastal waters and to combat "asymmetric" threats. In 7-03 the USN selected three possible contractors for the LCS design: Lockheed Martin, General Dynamics, and Raytheon. Northrop Grumman's design was eliminated from the competition in 2003 and the Raytheon design was eliminated in 2004. Two prototype teams (one led by Lockheed Martin and one by General Dynamics) were then contracted to develop "Flight 0" prototypes of their LCS design. The Lockheed Martin design, named the *Freedom* class on 9-5-05, includes a semi-planing ship with a scalable design. It is shorter and heavier but with a shallower draft than its rival. Current plans call for construction of four "Flight 0" ships, two from each final design team. Marinette Marine and Bollinger Shipyards will thus each build one prototype LCS of the *Freedom* class under the Lockheed Martin design. The shipyards will alternate construction once full production begins.

As many as 60 are sought, at a unit cost (not including development) of $300–400 million each.

Modular reconfigurable payloads will be carried as dictated by mission requirements (packages include those for surface warfare, mine warfare, and antisubmarine warfare). Though low observable/stealth capabilities are required of these warships, weapon-system features may preclude optimum stealth design. Each variant must also be able to defend itself; conduct intelligence, surveillance, and reconnaissance operations; and interdict hostile or unknown vessels. The LCS is expected to operate independently in overseas coastal regions and in concert with larger groups including carrier strike and surface action groups. Will be based in San Diego, California.

Will eventually carry the WLD-1(V)1 remote minehunting system and BLQ-11 Long-term Mine Reconnaissance vehicles as well as other unmanned vehicles. Will have USG-2(V) receive-only Cooperative Engagement Capability and Link 16 datalink. Will be able to hangar and support at least one MH-60R helicopter.

♦ 0 (+ 2 + 7) Independence-class Littoral Combat Ships

Bldr: Austal USA, Mobile Ala. (In serv. 2008)

	Bldr	Laid down	L	In serv.
LCS 2 Independence	Austal USA	19-1-06	1-07	11-07
LCS 4 . . .	Austal USA	. . .	. . .	2009

Independence-class Littoral Combat Ship—computer rendering
General Dynamics, 2004

D: 2,675 tons (fl) **S:** 50 kts **Dim:** 127.1 × 30.4 × 4.5

A: 1 21-round Mk 31 SAM launcher (RIM-116A RAM missiles); 1 57-mm 70-cal. Bofors Mk 110 AA; 2 12.7-mm mg; 2 MH-60R/S helicopters; 3 Firescout UAVs

Electronics:

Radar: 1 Ericsson Sea Giraffe AMB 3-D C-band surveillance; 1 . . . nav.

Sonar: . . . mine and obstacle avoidance

EW: 1 EDO ES3601 radar intercept; Mk 36 SRBOC decoy syst. (Mk 137 RL); 2 Nulka . . . decoy syst.

FRIGATES [FF] *(continued)*

Independence-class Littoral Combat Ship—computer rendering
General Dynamics, 2004

M: CODAG: 2 . . . diesels, . . . bhp each; 2 G.E. LM-2500 gas turbines, . . . ; 4 waterjets
Range: 4,300/20 **Crew:** 6 officers and 32 enlisted

Remarks: One outcome of the cancellation of the DD 21-class destroyer on 1-11-01 was initiation of a program to study the possible acquisition of a class of 1,250–2,500-ton "Littoral Combat Ships" (LCS) for use in coastal waters and to combat "asymmetric" threats. In 7-03 the USN selected three possible contractors for the LCS design: Lockheed Martin, General Dynamics, and Raytheon. Northrop Grumman's design was eliminated from the competition in 2003 and the Raytheon design was eliminated in 2004. Two prototype teams (one led by Lockheed Martin and one by General Dynamics) were then contracted to develop "Flight 0" prototypes of their LCS design. The General Dynamics design, named the *Independence* class on 4-4-06, includes a trimaran hull with a scalable design. It is lighter and wider but with a deeper draft than its rival. Current plans call for construction of four "Flight 0" ships, two from each final design team. Austal USA in Mobile, Ala., will build the two prototypes of the LCS *Independence* class under the General Dynamics design.

As many as 60 are sought, at a unit cost (not including development costs) of $300–400 million each.

Modular reconfigurable payloads will be carried as dictated by mission requirements (packages include those for surface warfare, mine warfare and antisubmarine warfare). Though low observable/stealth capabilities are required of these warships, weapon-system features may preclude optimum stealth design. Each variant must also be able to defend itself; conduct intelligence, surveillance, and reconnaissance operations; and interdict hostile or unknown vessels. The LCS is expected to operate independently in overseas coastal regions and in concert with larger groups including carrier strike and surface action groups. To be based in San Diego, California.

RAM system is carried atop the helicopter hangar and 57-mm gun at bow. Fitted with 321-m^2 helicopter hangar able to accommodate two MH-60s and a 1,030-m^2 flight deck capable of landing H-53-size aircraft. An off-board vehicle launch and recovery system is carried aft. Will eventually carry the WLD-1(V)1 remote minehunting system and BLQ-11 Long-term Mine Reconnaissance vehicles as well as other unmanned vehicles. Will have USG-2(V) receive-only Cooperative Engagement Capability and Link 16 datalink. Will be able to hangar and support two MH-60 helicopters.

PATROL CRAFT [PC]

♦ 13 Cyclone Class

Bldr: Bollinger Machine Shop & SY, Lockport, La.
(*Atlantic Fleet/†Pacific Fleet/**on loan and active in Coast Guard service)

	Laid down	L	In serv.
WPC 2 Tempest*/**	30-9-91	4-4-92	21-8-93
PC 3 Hurricane*	20-11-91	6-6-92	15-10-93
WPC 4 Monsoon†/**	15-2-92	6-3-93	22-1-94
PC 5 Typhoon*	15-5-92	3-3-93	12-2-94
PC 6 Scirocco*	20-6-92	29-5-93	11-6-94
PC 7 Squall*	17-2-93	28-8-93	4-7-94
WPC 8 Zephyr†/**	6-3-93	3-12-93	15-10-94
PC 9 Chinook*	16-6-93	6-2-94	26-1-95
PC 10 Firebolt*	17-9-93	10-6-94	10-6-95
PC 11 Whirlwind*	4-3-94	9-9-94	1-7-95
PC 12 Thunderbolt*	9-6-94	2-12-94	7-10-95
WPC 13 Shamal*/**	22-9-94	3-3-95	27-1-96
WPC 14 Tornado*/**	25-8-98	7-6-99	24-6-00

Whirlwind (PC 11)—with original, short stern U.S. Navy, 4-06

Shamal (WPC 13)—lengthened unit in Coast Guard service
U.S. Coast Guard, 10-04

Scirocco (PC 6) U.S. Navy, 4-05

D: 288 tons light; 334 fl (lengthened units: 352 tons light [387 fl])
S: 35 kts (25 cruise)
Dim: 51.62 (48.00 wl; WPC 2, 8, 13, 14: 54.36 overall) × 7.62 × 2.44
A: 1 Stinger point-defense SAM station (6 FIM-92 missiles); 1 25-mm Bushmaster gun/40-mm Mk 19 Mod. 3 grenade launcher in Mk 96 Mod. 0 stabilized mount; WPC 14 also: 1 25-mm Mk 88 Bushmaster Mk 38 Mod. 0 low-angle mount; all: 4 twin and 1 single 12.7-mm M2-HB mg; 2 single 7.62-mm M60D mg; 1 40-mm Mk 19 Mod. 3 grenade launcher; PC 9, 10 also: 2 single 7,62-mm Mk 44 gatling minigun
Electronics:
Radar: 1 Sperry Rascar 3400C X-band nav./surf. search; Sperry Rascar 3400C S-band nav./surf. search
Sonar: Wesmar side-scanning hull-mounted HF
EW: APR-39(V)1 Privateer radar warning; all but WPC 14: 2 Mk 52 Mod. 0 decoy syst. (2 6-round Mk 137 RL); WPC 14 only: 2 Wallop Ultrabarricade decoy syst. (2 26-round RL)
E/O: Marconi Vistar FLIR (WPC 14: Viper optronic gunsight also)
M: 4 Paxman Valenta 16V RP-200 CM diesels; 4 5-bladed (WPC 14: 6-bladed) props; 13,400 bhp
Electric: 310 kw tot. (2 × 155 kw, Caterpillar 3306B DIT Series C diesel sets)
Range: 595/35; 2,500/12 **Fuel:** 40 tons (47,772 liters/12,620 gal.)
Endurance: 10 days
Crew: 5 officers, 23 enlisted + 9 SEAL special forces team (2 officers, 7 enlisted) or 6 Coast Guard law-enforcement detachment

Remarks: Originally to have been a class of 16 intended to replace the 17 over-aged PB Mk-III for use by SEAL Special Boat Squadrons. The craft are able to transport nine-man SEAL teams and their specialized delivery craft or Coast Guard boarding teams for counter-drug inspections, but are considered a bit too large for optimum performance on these missions. Were typed PBC (Patrol Boat, Coastal) until 6-91. All Navy units are assigned to Atlantic Fleet units at Little Creek, Virginia, in Special Boat Squadron Two and wear the same three-tone gray camouflage scheme on the sides.

On 7-11-01 San Diego–based PC 3 and PC 4 and Little Creek, Virginia–based PC 10, PC 11, PC 12, and WPC 13 were assigned to "homeland defense" duties and transferred to Coast Guard operational control under Operation Noble Eagle. They carried Navy crews and also carry a six-strong USCG Tactical Law Enforcement Team for police duties. In 2004–5, WPC 2, 4, 8, 13, and 14 were decommissioned from naval service and transferred to the U.S. Coast Guard under a four-year loan program. Hull numbers for those vessels changed from PC to WPC.

The first seven were authorized under FY 90 and were ordered for $91.3 million on 3-8-90 (along with an option for five more); the next five were authorized under FY 91, with the option picked up on 19-7-91 for $48.7 million. PC 14 was added for $9.2 million by Congress under FY 96, but pressure for a fifteenth under FY 97 ($20 million) was successfully resisted; PC 14 was subsequently ordered 14-8-97 for $23.19 million, more than twice the unit cost of the original units. PC 12 was temporarily transferred to the U.S. Coast Guard on 2-3-98 for a series of trials through 17-7-98.

PC 9 and PC 10 deployed to the Mideast on 18-1-03 to test operational concepts for the planned LCS (Littoral Combat Ship) program and assisted with maritime antiterrorism operations in the Persian Gulf; each craft had two 7.62-mm Mk 44 gatling minigun mountings added. They were joined in the region by PC 5 and PC 6 during 2004.

PATROL CRAFT [PC] *(continued)*

Hull systems: Are about ten times the size of their predecessors but carry about the same payload. Have Vosper fin stabilization system and a stern wedge to improve trim at high speeds. Kevlar armor is fitted to the command space. PC 5 and later employed heavier superstructure plating. Minimum speed is 3 kts. Were to carry two 16-ft SEAL CRRC (Combat Rubber Raiding Craft) and one 6-m rigid inflatable swimmer delivery craft, but on completion carry only the RIB. There is a recessed platform at the stern for swimmer debarking and embarking on the unlengthened units.

Each unit deploying overseas is supported by a shore-based Maintenance Support Team with three 20-ft. vans for spares and repair work. Can refuel at sea, using astern fueling rigs. An active radiated noise cancellation system is to be added.

PC 14 has improved propellers, stern flaps to improve endurance, increased fuel supply, and sound-reduction measures; the hull was also strengthened over that of the earlier units and lengthened to incorporate a ramp at the stern incorporating the Combatant Craft Retrieval System (CCRS) to enable the launch and recovery of Special Warfare boats up to 9.75 m long. WPC 13, WPC 8, and WPC 2 (in that order) have been lengthened and given Combat Craft Retrieval System stern ramps like that on the WPC 14 under a 5-10-99 contract with the builder; the work was started with WPC 13 during 12-99 and was completed on all three by 30-6-00. PC 9 has an earlier horizontal boat launch-and-recovery system employing rails and a hydraulic lift to lower and recover the assault RIB.

Combat systems: The Sperry Vision 2100M combat system employs the navigational radars and the Sperry Voyage Management System integrated navigation and control system as a combat data suite. The craft have a Sperry Marine automated Integrated Bridge System (IBS). Navigation systems include GPS and LORAN receivers. Radio gear includes LST-5C SATCOM/line-of-sight UHF transceiver, A5 Spectra VHF radio, ICM120 Marine Band radio, and RF 5000 HF, VRC-92A VHF, VRC-83(V)2 VHF/UHF transceivers. As of 6-02, were being equipped with commercial SATCOM systems. SAT-2A infrared signaling systems are fitted, and the Marconi Vistar stabilized FLIR sensor with integral low light–level t.v. camera is mounted on the mast. Have IFF transponder but no interrogation capability, although it may be added later. The sonar transducer is retracted within the hull at speeds above 14 kts.

The radar intercept equipment was originally developed for use on helicopters. Each Mk 52 decoy rocket launcher carries 12 ready-service rounds, and 15 more rockets per launcher are carried in adjacent lockers. PC 14 has two 12-round, 102-mm Wallop Ultrabarricade rocket launchers mounted on superstructure platforms for trials; the craft also has an Electronic Chart Display and Information System (ECDIS).

Ammunition supply includes 2,000 rounds 25-mm, 2,000 rounds 12.7-mm, 2,000 rounds 7.62-mm, and 1,000 40-mm grenades. The original Mk 38 gun mounting aft has been replaced with a stabilized Mk 96 mount with combined Viper optronic sight, 25-mm gun, and 40-mm grenade-launcher. Several of the Mk 38 mounts forward have been lost at sea due to wave action, and most have been removed, replaced by a single 12.7-mm mg. Successful trials were conducted in 9-00 with a four-cell Raytheon Stinger Standard Vehicle-Mounted Launcher installed on a Mk 96 gunmount. Coast Guard units do not carry Stinger missiles.

Disposals: *Cyclone* (PC 1) was decommissioned on 28-2-00, stricken on the same date and transferred to the Philippines 6-3-03.

♦ 13 Moose 340C Patrol Catamarans
Bldr: Moose Boats, Nacasio, Calif. (In service 2004–6)

36PB0301 through 36PB036 36PB0401 through 36PB0406
36PB0501

Moose 340C Patrol Catamaran Moose Boats, 2004

D: 7.14 tons **S:** 34+ kts **Dim:** 11.09 (LOA) 8.89 (LWL) × 3.55 × .66
A: 50 cal. and 7.62-mm mg
M: 2 Cummins turbo diesels; propelled by 2 Hamilton 292 Water Jets; 370 hp
Range: 300+ nm **Crew:** 4

Remarks: Aluminum construction, Catamaran hull. Multiple contracts allowed for delivery over a 16-month period with the first unit delivered 7-04. Eight are assigned to stations in Europe and five to bases in the U.S. Cruising speed is approximately 28 kts.

♦ 7 27-ft. Workskiff class
Bldr: Workskiff Inc., . . . (In serv. 2001–2)

27HS0107 through 27HS0110 27HS0113 through 27HS0115

D: . . . tons **S:** . . . kts **Dim:** 8.23 × 2.65 × 1.37 (over props)
A: 2 single 7.62-mm mg
M: 2 Honda gasoline outboard motors; 260 bhp total

27-ft. Inshore Boat–class patrol launch Workskiff, 2004

Electric: 5 kw tot. (1 × 5-kw diesel set)
Range: . . . /. . . **Crew:** 4 tot.

Remarks: Aluminum construction; used for harbor security

♦ 56 34-ft. Dauntless class
Bldr: SeaArk Marine, Monticello, Ark. (In serv. 2002 to . . .)

D: 6.804 tons light **S:** . . . **Dim:** 10.40 × 3.70 × 0.97 (hull)
A: 2 single 7.62-mm mg
M: 2 Cummings turbo diesels; propelled by 2 Hamilton 292 waterjets; 370 hp

Remarks: Ordered 5-02 for the Naval Coastal Warfare Group. No further information available.

♦ 52 2810-V Dauntless class
Bldr: SeaArk Marine, Monticello, Ark. (In serv. 10-01 to . . .)

Dauntless-class patrol boat U.S. Navy, 1-05

D: 4.082 tons light **S:** 42 kts **Dim:** 8.50 × 3.30 × 0.61 (hull)
A: 2 single 7.62-mm M-60 mg **M:** 2 Yamaha gasoline outboards; 2 props; 450 bhp

Remarks: First 14 ordered 7-01; all are assigned to the Pacific Fleet under the designation HSB—Harbor Security Boat–Medium. Aluminum construction. Are equipped with air-conditioning and an a.c. electric power source.

♦ 28 27-ft. Commander RAM Class
Bldr: SeaArk Marine, Monticello, Ark. (In serv. 10-01 to 7-04)

D: 1.542 tons light (3.719 fl) **S:** 35 kts **Dim:** 8.30 × 2.50 × 0.50 (hull)
A: 2 single 7.62-mm M-60 mg **M:** 2 Honda gasoline outboard motors; 260 bhp

Remarks: First six ordered 7-01; for the Atlantic Fleet use under the designation HSB—Harbor Security Boat–Small; another 13 had been ordered by 5-02 and nine more were ordered in 2003. Aluminum construction craft with an air-cushion collar to aid in boarding and shouldering operations. Have air-conditioning and a.c. electric power.

♦ 1 26-ft. 2680 Coastal Runner class
Bldr: Glacier Bay Cats, Monroe, Wash.

26NS0102 (In serv. 2-1-02)

D: 2.38 tons light **S:** 30+ kts **Dim:** 7.92 × 2.59 × 0.56 max.
A: 2 single 7.62-mm M-60 mg **Electronics:** Radar: 1 Furuno . . . nav.
M: 2 Yamaha 150 HP gasoline outboard motors; 300 bhp **Range:** 100/29
Fuel: 180 gallons **Crew:** 2–3 tot.

Remarks: Based at Groton, Connecticut, to escort submarines entering and leaving port. GRP-hulled sport-fishing catamaran design modified with weapons mounts, ammunition stowage, minor structural strengthening, and a heavy-duty fender surrounding the hull. Have GPS and VHF radio. Sister HVA *Escort* is no longer in service.

PATROL CRAFT [PC] *(continued)*

♦ 5 32-ft. Inshore Boat class
Bldr: Willard Marine, Inc., Anaheim, Calif. (In serv. 2001)

32IB0001 through 32B005

32-ft. Inshore Boat–class unit U.S. Navy, 4-06

D: . . . tons **S:** . . . kts **Dim:** 9.75 × . . . × . . . **A:** 3 single 7.62-mm M-60 mg
Electronics: Radar: 1 Furuno . . . nav.
M: 2 Cummins 6BTA5.9-370 diesels; 2 waterjets; . . . bhp **Crew:** 4 tot.

Remarks: Assigned to Naval Coastal Warfare Group One, San Diego, and used for harbor counterterrorism patrol. Additional units are likely to be procured. Design is the builder's Kingston 32 and employs an aluminum hull and superstructure with a rigid inflatable collar. Can be transported in a C-130 transport aircraft.

♦ 2 36-ft. harbor patrol boats
Bldr: Dakota Yacht Industries; . . . 36NS9801: Voyager Marine, Bahrain (In serv. 1998)

36NS9801 M36NS9802

Remarks: Assigned to U.S. Naval Forces, Central Command, Bahrain. GRP-construction craft, powered by two 250-bhp Mercury outboard motors and equipped to mount a 12.7-mm forward.

Note: Also assigned for service in Bahrain are 32HS0101 through 32HS0103, bought locally during 2001 and assigned to Naval Support Activity, Bahrain.

♦ 22 27-ft. Inshore Boat class
Bldr: Tacoma Boat Building, Washington (In serv. 1994)

8MIB9401 through 8MIB9422

27-ft Inshore Boat–class patrol launch Edward McDonnell, 7-04

Remarks: Used as deployable harbor patrol boats. Aluminum-construction craft 8.23-m long, origin unknown. Are assigned to Naval Coastal Warfare Group One, San Diego, and Naval Coastal Warfare Group Two, Little Creek, Virginia. Have a Furuno navigational radar and mounts for two mg. Powered by two diesel-driven waterjets. Boats of this class can be carried on larger ships to provide harbor security support.

♦ 37 24-ft. Harbor Security Boats
Bldr: Peterson Bldrs., Sturgeon Bay, Wisc. (In serv. 29-2-88 to 1990)

From among: 24HS8701–8750 24HS8801–8822

24-ft. Harbor Security Boat U.S. Navy, 2004

D: 2.5 tons (3.8 fl) **S:** 22.5 kts with 4 aboard
Dim: 7.32 × 2.31 × 1.57 (molded depth)
A: 1 or 2 12.7-mm or 7.62-mm M-60 mg
Electronics: Radar: 1 Furuno . . . nav. or none
M: 2 Volvo Penta AQAD 41A diesels with Type 290 outdrives; 165 bhp
Range: . . . / . . . **Crew:** 4 tot.

Remarks: Survivors of 85 built. First 50 ordered 29-7-87; 25 more ordered 9-11-87, and final 10 in 3-88. Aluminum construction. For counterterrorist patrol in sheltered waters. Have 12 V d.c., 50 Amp electrical power. Built to essentially the same design as the 24WB-series Workboats (see under smallcraft).

♦ 4 Raider-class Harbor Security Boats
Bldr: NAPCO International, North Miami, Fla. (In serv. 1986)

Raider-class Harbor Security Boat Paul C. Clift, 5-00

D: 2.0 tons (2.95 fl) **S:** 40 kts **Dim:** 6.81 (6.40 pp) × 2.26 × 0.86
A: 2 single 12.7-mm M2 mg **Electronics:** Radar: None
M: 2 Johnson or Evinrude gasoline outboards; 280 bhp **Range:** 167/40; 222/30
Crew: 3 tot.

Remarks: GRP construction, using Boston Whaler hulls. Class also used by Coast Guard and has been widely exported. Acquired for counterterrorist work. A number of similar craft, outfitted by Boston Whaler itself, are in use for harbor police duties.

♦ 4 3010-V Protector-class Range Security Boats
Bldr: SeaArk Marine, Monticello, Ark. (In serv. 1985–86)

30WB8501 30WB8601
30WB8502 30WB8602

D: . . . tons **S:** . . . kts **Dim:** 9.80 × 3.40 × 0.60
M: 2 Volvo Penta AQAD outdrive diesels; . . . bhp **Crew:** 4 tot. + 7 passengers

Remarks: Acquired for range safety work at the Dahlgren Proving Range, Virginia. Aluminum construction.

♦ 3 ex-Coast Guard Ports and Waterways boats [YFL]
Bldr: Willard Marine, Anaheim, Calif. (In serv. 1977)

32NS9301 32NS9302 34FR7801

D: 7.5 tons light (8.6 fl) **S:** 20.4 kts **Dim:** 10.16 × 3.58 × 0.86
Electronics: Radar: 1 Raytheon SPS-69 nav.
M: 2 Caterpillar 3208 diesels; 2 props; 406 bhp
Range: 190/16.5 Fuel: 0.65 tons Crew: 2–3 tot.

Remarks: GRP construction craft used for local police duties at the Norfolk Naval Base, Norfolk, Virginia. For the Coast Guard, 52 sisters were built.

Boston Whaler Naval Security Boat 05—attached to the submarine base at Gravel Point, San Diego, is typical of the numerous Whalers used for harbor patrol duties George R. Schneider, 6-01

MINE WARFARE SHIPS

Note: In addition to the following ships and craft listed, 32 MH-53E minesweeping helicopters are in service. A limited number of Marine Corps CH-53D helicopters can also be used to tow sweep gear. The entire MH-53E force is to be replaced by MH-60 helicopters by 2010, primarily for reasons of maintenance operating costs. The Navy for many years has also had an extensive Marine Mammal Program using trained dolphins maintained by Explosive Ordnance Disposal Mobile Unit 3, San Diego.

Current plans call for the Navy's Mine Warfare Command to move from its current homeport in Ingleside Texas to San Diego by 2010.

MINE-COUNTERMEASURES SUPPORT SHIP [MCS]

♦ 1 chartered Evolution 10B–class wave-piercing catamaran
Bldr: INCAT, Hobart, Tasmania, Australia

	Laid down	L	In serv.
HSV-X2 Swift (ex-*Incat 061*)	. . .	. . .	12-8-03

Swift (HSV-X2) U.S. Navy, 2-05

Swift (HSV-X2) U.S. Navy, 2-05

Swift (HSV-X2) U.S. Navy, 1-05

D: 1,875 tons (fl) **S:** 47 kts max; 35 kts with 500 tons cargo
Dim: 97.22 (92.00 wl) × 26.60 × 3.43 loaded **Air group:** 2 MH-60S helicopters
A: Provision for: 1 20-mm Phalanx Block 1B CIWS; . . . mg
Electronics:
Radar: 2 Kelvin-Hughes . . . nav. (X and S-band)
E/O: Forward-looking FLIR
M: 4 Ruston Paxman 16RK270 diesels; 4 Lips 120E waterjets; 37,982 bhp
Electric: 1,060 kw tot. (4 × 265 kw, Cummins N14 diesel-driven)
Range: 1,100/35 loaded; 4,000/20
Fuel: 190,080 liters normal/420,476 liters ferry mode
Crew: 100 tot. normal + 102 temporary berths or 250 seated personnel

Remarks: Leased 24-10-02 by Military Sealift Command via Bollinger/Incat U.S.A. and delivered on 15-8-03. Employed as a Mine-Countermeasures Ship (MCS) and based at Ingleside, Texas. Modified commercial vehicle and personnel ferry. On 21-6-02 it was announced that up to $100 million would be expended to lease and operate a commercial Australian wave-piercing catamaran ferry as a replacement for the *Inchon* (MCS 12). The craft, about a tenth the size of the prematurely stricken *Inchon* (MCS 12), would be only a third less expensive to operate and would have only one helicopter landing spot. With a crew of 100, however, it would be able to move more quickly over shorter distances and would be able to operate in shallower waters. The craft will also be available for logistic support transportation duties and will be employed for about half of its operating time in various concepts of using this type of craft for ASW, antipatrol craft, and support to Maritime Prepositioning Ships. Though well suited for low-threat environments, craft of this type are inherently unsuitable for high-intensity combat roles, due to their basic configuration, lack of damage control capability, and lack of protection features.
Hull systems: Capable of maintaining an average speed of 35+ knots loaded with 500 short tons and able to operate at 3–10 kts for 24 hours. Have enclosure for two MH-60S helicopters, one flight deck spot on the 24.7-m-long by 15.24-m-wide deck, and capability to operate CH-46 and UH-1/AH-1 helicopters, but not the standard MH-53E mine-countermeasures helicopter. The stern ramp will be retained and will be capable of deploying up to 63.5-ton loads, including M1 Abrams heavy tanks, onto piers or into the water. Vehicle deck has 380 truck lane-meters 3.1 m wide and 4.35 m clear height. Can carry 267 automobiles. Each hull has a beam of 4.50 m and is subdivided by nine vented watertight bulkheads, each with a transverse bulkhead. One compartment in each hull can be used as a long-range fuel tank. Aluminum construction. Has a Maritime Dynamics automated ride control system, and a hydraulically operated trim tab is mounted on each hull aft. A 10-ton boat crane is fitted. Navigation suite includes two Leica differential GPS, Skipper echo sounder, Lips autopilot, Anschutz gyro, and Transis Navi-Sailor 2400 autochart.

Disposal note: *Iwo Jima*–class mine-countermeasures support ship *Inchon* was to have been retired during FY 05, without replacement, but a fire on 19-10-01 and the cost of repairing ($10 million) and operating ($43 million annually) plus an upcoming overhaul of the ship led to a decision to decommission her; stricken on 24-5-04. She was expended as a target on 5-12-04.

Note: Maritime Applied Physics Corp., Annapolis, Maryland, was awarded a concept design contract for a 2,200-ton HYSWAS (Hydrofoil Small Waterplane Area Ship) mine-countermeasures ship to act as a carrier and deployment ship for autonomous and semiautonomous mine-countermeasures drones. The design is to be based on the HYSWAS prototype craft (see following).

♦ 6 Osprey-class coastal minehunters [MHS]
Bldrs: A: Intermarine U.S.A., Savannah, Ga.; B: Avondale Marine, Gulfport, Miss.

	Bldr	Begun	L	In serv.
MHC 52 Heron	A	7-4-89	21-3-92	6-8-94
MHC 53 Pelican	B	6-5-91	27-2-93	18-11-95
MHC 56 Kingfisher	B	24-3-92	18-6-94	9-8-96
MHC 57 Cormorant	B	8-4-92	21-10-95	5-4-97
MHC 58 Black Hawk	A	12-5-92	27-8-94	11-5-96
MHC 62 Shrike	A	1-8-95	24-5-97	31-5-99

Raven (MHC 61)—retired in early 2007 U.S. Navy, 4-04

Cardinal (MHC 60)—since decommissioned U.S. Navy, 4-03

D: 796–886 tons light (882-973 fl) **S:** 12 kts
Dim: 57.25 (53.10 pp) × 10.95 × 3.35 max. **A:** 2 single 12.7-mm M2 mg
Electronics:
Radar: 1 Raytheon SPS-64(V)9 nav.
Sonar: Raytheon SQQ-32 variable-depth minehunting
M: 2 Isotta-Fraschini ID 36 SS 8V-AM diesels; 2 Voith-Schneider vertical cycloidal props; 1,600 bhp—2 180-shp hydraulic motors for quiet running—1 180-shp bow-thruster
Electric: 900 kw (3 × 300 kw, Isotta-Fraschini ID SS 6V-AM diesels driving)
Range: 2,500/12 **Endurance:** 5 days **Crew:** 5 officers, 46 enlisted

Remarks: Authorized: MHC 51 under FY 86, MHC 52–53 under FY 89, MHC 54–55 under FY 90, MHC 56–57 under FY 91, MC 58–60 under FY 92, MHC 61–62 under FY 93. MHC 51 ordered 20-2-87. Plans to construct a total of 17 were scaled back to 12 in the spring of 1992. MHC 57 transferred to NRF on 11-1-98, MHC 59 on 8-2-98, MHC 60 on 18-10-98, MHC 62 on 1-4-00, and MHC 51 on 1-10-00. All are based at Ingleside, Texas. Current plans call for all remaining units to retire by the end of 2008, with several units expected to transfer to foreign navies.

MINE-COUNTERMEASURES SUPPORT SHIP [MCS] *(continued)*

Hull systems: Displacement grew by 110 tons during final design phase and has continued to rise since completions. Monocoque foam-core GRP hull construction, with the design based on that of the Italian Navy *Lerici* class. Have the SSQ-109 Ship/Machinery Control System and two 400-Hz motor-generator sets. Later units have additional space for provisions and stores. Have berthing space for 15 female crewmembers.
Combat systems: Employ the Alliant SLQ-48(V)2 Mine Neutralization System remote-controlled submersible. Have Paramax SYQ-13 tactical navigation/command and control equipment, which integrates machinery and ship control, the mine-hunting sonar, the mine-neutralization system, inputs from the surface search radar, the precision navigation systems, and various environmental sensors. A new COTS open-architecture system under development by Lockheed Martin may eventually replace the SYQ-13 currently in use. Other navigation equipment includes WRN-6 GPS terminal and Decca URN-30 Hyperfix radio navaid.
The ships have an Indal three-drum winch capable of carrying 1,524 m of sweep cable on the main drum and 595 m each on the other drums to stream and tow the SLQ-53 array.
Disposals: Sisters *Osprey* (MHC 51) and *Robin* (MHC 54) were decommissioned on 15-6-06 with *Oriole* (MHC 55) and *Falcon* (MHC 59) retired on 30-6-06. *Cardinal* (MHC 60) and *Raven* (MHC 61) were decommissioned and stricken in 1-07 for transfer to Egypt.

14 Avenger-class oceangoing minesweeper/minehunters [MHS]
(all in Atlantic Fleet; *Naval Reserve Force)

	Bldr	Laid down	L	In serv.
MCM 1 Avenger	Peterson Bldrs.	3-6-83	15-6-85	12-9-87
MCM 2 Defender*	Marinette Marine	1-12-83	4-4-87	30-9-89
MCM 3 Sentry*	Peterson Bldrs.	8-10-84	20-9-86	2-9-89
MCM 4 Champion*	Marinette Marine	28-6-84	15-4-89	27-7-91
MCM 5 Guardian	Peterson Bldrs.	8-5-85	20-6-87	16-12-89
MCM 6 Devastator	Peterson Bldrs.	9-2-87	11-6-88	6-10-90
MCM 7 Patriot	Marinette Marine	31-3-87	15-5-90	18-10-91
MCM 8 Scout	Peterson Bldrs.	8-6-87	20-5-89	15-12-90
MCM 9 Pioneer	Peterson Bldrs.	5-6-89	25-8-90	7-12-92
MCM 10 Warrior	Peterson Bldrs.	5-9-89	8-12-90	3-4-93
MCM 11 Gladiator*	Peterson Bldrs.	7-5-90	29-6-91	18-9-93
MCM 12 Ardent	Peterson Bldrs.	22-10-90	16-11-91	18-2-94
MCM 13 Dexterous	Peterson Bldrs.	11-3-91	20-6-92	9-6-94
MCM 14 Chief	Peterson Bldrs.	19-8-91	16-12-93	5-11-94

Ardent (MCM 12) U.S. Navy, 7-05

Devastator (MCM 6) U.S. Navy, 5-05

Dexterous (MCM 13) U.S. Navy, 8-04

D: 1,249-1,336 tons light (1,362-1,447 fl) **S:** 13.5 kts
Dim: 68.37 (64.80 wl) × 11.86 × 3.71 (hull)
A: 2 single 12.7-mm M2 mg (MCM 11: 1 25-mm Mk 88 Bushmaster low-angle; 1 7.62-mm gatling mg)
Electronics:
Radar: 1 Raytheon SPS-66(V)9 nav.; 1 Cardion SPS-55 surf. search
Sonar: Raytheon SQQ-32 (MCM 2, MCM 8: SQQ-30) variable-depth minehunting;WQN-1 channel finder
M: MCM 1 and 2: 4 Waukesha L-1616 diesels; 2 CP props; 2,600 bhp; MCM 3–14: 4 Isotta-Fraschini ID 36 SS 6V-AM diesels; 2 CP props; 2,280 bhp; all: 2 200-shp Hansome low-speed motors geared to props; 1 350-shp Omnithruster bow-thruster
Electric: 2,875 kw tot. (1 × 1,750-kw Siemens-Allis-Solar gas turbine sweep generator; 3 × 375 kw, MCM 1, 2: Waukesha (others: Isotta Fraschini ID 36 SS 6V-AM) diesels driving; 451 V 60 Hz. a.c.)
Range: . . . / . . . **Crew:** 6–8 officers, 75 enlisted

Remarks: Authorized: MCM 1 in FY 82, MCM 2 in FY 83, MCM 3–5 in FY 84, MCM 6–9 in FY 85, MCM 10–11 in FY 86, MCM 12–14 in FY 90. MCM 1 was ordered on 29-6-82. MCM 5 and 7 were deployed to Japan in 1994, and their crews are rotated to the U.S. every six months. MCM 12 was homeported at Bahrain on 1-3-00 and MCM 13 on 1-6-00. The others are based at Ingleside, Texas, which is scheduled to close under a 2005 base realignment and closure decision. As a result, the class will be transferred to San Diego by 2010. MCM 3, 6, 8, and 14 were deployed to the Mideast late in 1-03.
Hull systems: The wooden hull employs four glued layers of 127-mm planking over 254-mm × 457-mm frames spaced at 1.07-m intervals. Displacements grew as the class progressed, with later units being about 80 tons heavier. All structural members are built up from thinner materials, using phenol/resorcinal glue. The hull for MCM 1 had to be lengthened by about 1.8 m after construction had begun, due to stability problems, and the ship was also delayed by other design problems and the discovery that the main engines rotated opposite to the gear boxes. The superstructures are constructed of GRP. The ID 36 SS 6V-AM engines are reported to be unreliable, with inadequate cooling, electrical problems, and frequent clutch and bearing failures. The sweep generator provides 5,000 amp, 350 V d.c. power.
Combat systems: Able to sweep deep-moored mines to 180 m as well as to sweep magnetic and acoustic mines. The Mk 116 Mod. 0 Mine Neutralization System (MNS) includes two Alliant (formerly Honeywell) SLQ-48 MNS, a remote-controlled mine-hunting and destruction device 3.8 m long by .9 m high, weighing 1,136 kg; powered by two 15-hp hydraulic motors for 6-kt speeds; it has 1,524 m of control cable. Also aboard are the SLQ-37(V)3 magnetic/acoustic sweep array (incorporating the A Mk-2, A Mk 4[V], and A Mk 6[B] acoustic and M Mk 5, 6, and 7 magnetic arrays), SLQ-38 (Type 0 Size 1) mechanical sweep gear, and two RIBs for mine-disposal divers. Carry the SSN-2(V) PINS (Precision-Integrated Navigation System) and the SYQ-13 navigational/command-and-control system, which employs the Decca URN-30 Hyperfix radio-navaid, WRN-6 GPS terminal, Loran, Motorola MX 610 doppler log, and a WQN-1 Channel-Finder doppler precision sonar; twelve ships of the class received the GEC-Marconi SYQ-15 (Nautis) system vice SYQ-13, beginning in 5-94. A new COTS open-architecture system under development by Lockheed Martin may eventually replace the SYQ-13/15 currently in use. Although the early ships that had SQQ-30 sonars (a digital version of the obsolescent SQQ-14) were to have had them replaced by the end of 1992, that goal was not met until 2000 in MCM 2 and MCM 8. The original 2,500-amp magnetic pulse sweep generators had to be replaced because the Siemens-made sets broke down after 48 hours' use; MagneTek solid-state replacements were first fitted to MCM 9. MHC 53 conducted a four-day trial with the German STN-Atlas Elektronik Seafox C EMNS (Expendable Mine Neutralization System) autonomous mine-destruction vehicle in a demonstration that ended 26-3-01; the system may be purchased via Lockheed Martin for surface ship and MH-53E helicopter employment.

MINESWEEPING BOATS [MSB]

♦ 1 SWATH explosive ordnance disposal boat
Bldr: Swath Ocean Systems, Inc., National City, Calif. (In serv. 5-98)

40MC9601 MHS-1 Swath 1

D: . . . tons **S:** . . . kts **Dim:** 12.19 × 5.49 × . . . **A:** Small arms
Electronics:
Radar: 1 . . . nav.
Sonar: Klein 5500 Multibeam towed side-scan HF; Simrad SM 2000 mine-avoidance HF
M: 2 CAT C-9-503 diesels; 2 props; . . . bhp
Crew: 2 enlisted + 4 Area-Search Detachment enlisted sonar party

Remarks: Name and hull number "MHS-1" are unofficial, while the "MC" in the serial number stands for "mine countermeasures." Can be land-transported and also carried within a C-5A Galaxy transport aircraft, one of which flew the craft to an exercise in Thailand during 4-00, and to the Middle East during 1-02. Is assigned to Explosive Ordnance Disposal Mobile Unit 7 (EODMU 7) at San Diego.

MINESWEEPING BOATS [MSB] *(continued)*

MHS-1 Swath 1 (40MC9601) George R. Schneider, 5-01

MHS-1 Swath 1 (40MC9601) W. Michael Young, 5-99

Hull systems: Aluminum construction. Has been equipped with a davit at the stern to handle a Deep Ocean Engineering Phantom HD 2+2 remotely operated, high-definition sonar submersible used for identifying bottomed objects. Roll is limited to 2° in 3–4-m seas by the automated stabilization system.

Notes: The REMOP (Remote Minehunting Operational Prototype), RMS(V)2 and RMS(V)3 remotely operated mine-countermeasures drone programs are discussed in the Mine-Countermeasures Systems entry at the beginning of the U.S. Navy section.

At least 14 24-ft. RIB craft are used to support mine-countermeasures helicopters, acting as tow craft and for connecting and disconnecting mine-countermeasures sleds. All 14 had completed being re-engined by Saunders Engine Co., Panama City, Florida, by mid-2001. The 2.4-ton (loaded) craft are now powered by a single 260-bhp Cummins BT.59M1 diesel with Konrad 520 outdrive and can achieve 34 kts and a 2,170-lb. bollard pull.

AMPHIBIOUS WARFARE SHIPS AND CRAFT

AMPHIBIOUS WARFARE COMMAND SHIPS [LCC]

♦ 2 Blue Ridge class (SCN 400-65 type) (*Atlantic/†Pacific Fleet)

	Bldr	Laid down	L	In serv.
LCC 19 Blue Ridge†	Philadelphia NSY	27-2-67	4-1-69	14-11-70
LCC 20 Mount Whitney*	Newport News SB & DD	8-1-69	8-1-70	16-1-71

D: LCC 19: 13,038 tons light (19,609 fl); LCC 20: 12,815 tons light (19,729 fl)
S: 21.5 kts
Dim: 193.98 (176.8 wl) × 32.9 (25.0 wl; 54.6 max. extensions) × 8.84 max.
A: 2 single 25-mm 75-cal. Mk 38 Bushmaster low-angle; 2 20-mm Mk 15 Phalanx gatling CIWS; 4 single 12.7-mm mg
Electronics:
Radar: 1 Lockheed Martin SPS-67(V)1 surf.-search; 1 Lockheed SPS-40E air-search (LCC 19 only); 1 SPS-73(V)12 (LCC 20 only); 2 Mk 91 Phalanx f.c.
TACAN: URN-25
EW: Raytheon SLQ-32(V)3 active/passive; Mk 36 SRBOC decoy syst. (4 6-round Mk 137 RL); SLQ-25A SSTD Nixie towed acoustic torpedo decoy
M: 1 set G.E. geared steam turbines; 1 prop; 22,000 shp
Boilers: 2 Foster-Wheeler; 42.3 kg/cm2, 467° C
Range: 13,000/16 **Fuel:** 2,800 tons
Crew: LCC 19: 268 officers, 1,173 enlisted; LCC 20: 161 total navy, 144 MSC civilian (plus flag staff personnel)

Blue Ridge (LCC 19) U.S. Navy, 3-06

Mount Whitney (LCC 20) U.S. Navy, 1-06

Blue Ridge (LCC 19) U.S. Navy, 1-06

Remarks: Authorized: FY 65 and FY 66. Both were originally intended to act as amphibious force flagships, but LCC 19 is now the flagship of the Seventh Fleet and is based at Yokosuka, while LCC 20 became flagship of the Sixth Fleet on 25-2-05 and is based at Gaeta, Italy. Both have recently been unofficially referred to as JCC 19 and 20, with JCC standing for "Joint Command Ship." During 2004 LCC 19 underwent an extended maintenance while in dry dock. During this time *Coronado* (AGF 11) stood in as 7th Fleet Command Ship. LCC 20 transferred to MSC during a 2004 overhaul, but was returned to the active Navy when the refit was completed on 10-12-04. She is now manned by a unique mixed civilian and navy crew commanded by a Navy Captain.

Hull systems: Have the same machinery and basic hull form as the *Iwo Jima*–class LPH. Air-conditioned; fin stabilizers. Kevlar plastic armor has been added. Carry three LCP and two LCVP landing craft, along with one 10-m personnel launch, carried in Welin davits. They have no helicopter hangar, but a landing pad is fitted at the stern; 123,510 gallons of aircraft fuel can be carried.

Combat systems: Satellite communications antennas on after masts differ; equipment includes SSR-1, WSC-3 UHF, WSC-6 SHF, and USC-38 EHF SATCOM systems. Combat data analysis systems include: ACIS (Amphibious Command Information System); NIPS (Naval Intelligence Processing System); NTDS (with Link 4A, 11, and 14), and photographic laboratories and document-publication facilities. Command facilities include a Ship Signals Exploitation Space (SSES), Flag Plot, Landing Force Operations Center (LFOC), Joint Intelligence Center (JIC), Supporting Arms Coordination Center (SACC), Helicopter Logistics Support Group (HLSG), Tactical Air Control Center (TACC), Helicopter Direction Center (HDC), and Helicopter Coordination Section (HCS). Have the SMQ-6 weather satellite receiver and the Joint Services Imagery Processing System–Navy (JSIPS-N).

Planned armament modifications include installing Mk 49 launchers for the RAM point-defense missile fore and aft. LCC 19 received Mk 15 CIWS in 1985 and LCC 20 in 1987, with added stern sponson and bow bulwarks lengthening the ships some 5 m overall. Two twin 76.2-mm DP gunmounts and two octuple Mk 25 BPDMS Sea Sparrow SAM launchers were removed during 1992. The SPS-48 radars have been removed from both vessels.

AMPHIBIOUS WARFARE HELICOPTER CARRIERS [LHD]

♦ 7 (+ 1) Wasp-class helicopter/dock landing ships

Bldr: Ingalls SB, Pascagoula, Miss. (*Atlantic/†Pacific Fleet)

	Laid down	L	In serv.
LHD 1 Wasp*	30-5-85	4-8-87	29-7-89
LHD 2 Essex†	20-3-89	4-1-91	17-10-92
LHD 3 Kearsarge*	6-2-90	26-3-92	25-9-93
LHD 4 Boxer†	8-4-91	13-8-93	11-2-95
LHD 5 Bataan*	22-6-94	15-3-96	20-9-97
LHD 6 Bonhomme Richard†	18-4-95	14-3-97	15-8-98
LHD 7 Iwo Jima*	12-12-97	25-3-00	14-6-01
LHD 8 Makin Island†	16-2-04	15-9-06	3-08

AMPHIBIOUS WARFARE HELICOPTER CARRIERS [LH]
(continued)

Bonhomme Richard (LHD 6) U.S. Navy, 7-06

Kearsarge (LHD 3)—note LCAC exiting the well deck U.S. Navy, 9-05

Bataan (LHD 5) U.S. Navy, 9-05

Essex (LHD 2) U.S. Navy, 2-06

Wasp (LHD 1) U.S. Navy, 11-05

Essex (LHD 2) U.S. Navy, 2-06

Wasp (LHD 1) U.S. Navy, 11-05

D: 27,565–28,295 tons light (40,329–41,133 fl) **S:** 24 kts (22 sust.)
Dim: 257.30 (237.14 wl) × 42.67 (32.31 wl) × 8.53 max. unballasted (LHD 8: 9.1 unballasted)
Air group: Typical: 12 CH-46 helicopters; 4 CH-53E helicopters; 6 AV-8B Harriers; 3 UH-1N helicopters; 4 AH-1W helicopters; carrier mode: 24 AV-8B Harriers and 4–6 SH-60F ASW helicopters
A: 2 8-celled Mk 29 SAM launchers (no reloads; RIM-7P Sea Sparrow missiles); 2 21-round Mk 31 SAM launchers (RIM-116A RAM missiles); 2 20-mm Mk 15 Mod. 13 Phalanx CIWS; 3 single 25-mm 75-cal. Mk 38 Mod. 0 Bushmaster low-angle; 4 single 12.7-mm M2-HB mg
Electronics:
Radar: 1 Raytheon SPS-64(V)9 nav.; 1 Norden SPS-67(V)3 surf.-search; 1 Raytheon SPS-49(V)5 air-search; 1 ITT-Gilfillan SPS-48E 3-D early-warning; 1 Hughes Mk 23 Mod. 3 TAS target designation; 2 Mk 95 f.c. (for Mk 91 f.c.s.); 1 SPN-35A air-control; 1 SPN-43B CCA; 1 SPN-47 precision CCA; 2 Mk 90 Phalanx f.c.
Sonar: WSC-1 Channel Finder mine avoidance (6 transducers)
TACAN: URN-25
EW: SRS-1 Combat D/F syst.; Raytheon SLQ-32(V)3 active/passive; Mk 36 Mod. 12 SRBOC decoy syst. (6 6-round Mk 137 launchers); SLQ-25A Nixie towed acoustic torpedo decoy syst.
M: LHD 1–7: 2 sets Westinghouse geared steam turbines: 2 props; 77,000 shp (70,000 sust.); LHD 8: 2 G.E. LM-2500 gas turbines; 2 props; 72,000 shp; 2 electric low-speed propulsion motors; 10,000 ship (12–13 kts)
Boilers: 2 Combustion Engineering; 49.3 kg/cm^2, 482° C (not in LHD 8)
Electric: LHD 1–7: 14,000 kw (5 × 2,000-kw turboalternators, 2 × 2,000-kw diesel alternator sets)
Range: 9,500/20 **Fuel:** 6,200 tons + plus 1,232 tons JP-5 for aircraft
Crew: 73 officers, 1,009 enlisted + troops: 173 officers, 1,720 enlisted + 200 additional emergency troop accomm.

AMPHIBIOUS WARFARE HELICOPTER CARRIERS [LH] *(continued)*

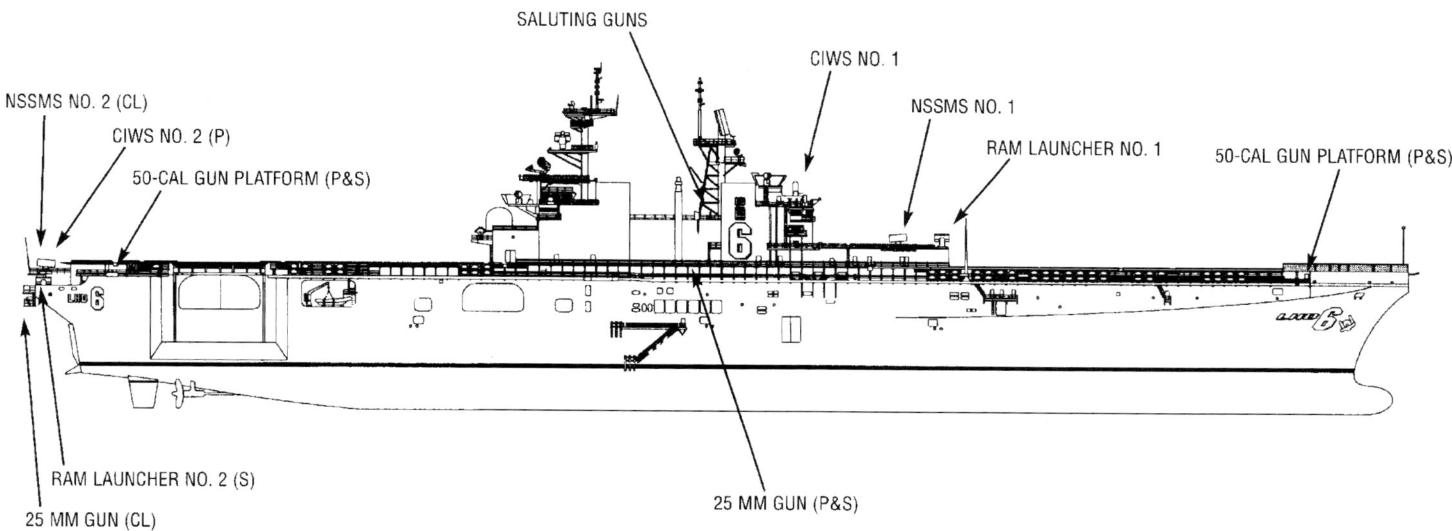

Bonhomme Richard (LHD 6) Northrop Grumman Ingalls

Remarks: Design based on that of the LHA 1 class. Authorized: LHD 1 in FY 84, LHD 2 in FY 86, LHD 3 in FY 88, LHD 4 in FY 89, LHD 5 in FY 91, LHD 6 in FY 93, and LHD 7 (the last steam-powered ship to be built for the U.S. Navy) in FY 96. LHD 8 was inserted in the FY 99 defense budget by Congress, additional funding for construction was provided under FY 00, another $460 million was added by Congress under the FY 01 budget, and final funding was approved under FY 02. LHD 8 will replace LHA 1 in service. LHD 1 was ordered on 28-2-84, LHD 2 on 11-9-85, LHD 3 on 24-11-87, LHD 4 on 3-10-88, LHD 5 on 20-12-91, LHD 6 on 11-12-92, LHD 7 on 28-12-96, and LHD 8 on 19-4-02, the latter for $1.3 billion. Work on LHD 8 began on 22-5-03.

At one point, a total of 11 was planned. LHD 2 has been homeported at Sasebo, Japan, since 26-7-00. During exercises and when not deployed, LHD 7 serves as temporary flagship for Commander, 3rd Fleet.

Hull systems: The ships can take on up to 15,000 tons water ballast to launch landing craft from the floodable stern docking well. Have more than 1,500 hull and superstructure compartments. Differences from the LHA 1 class include use of an LSD/LPD-type lowering stern gate, vice the sectional, rising gate of the LHA; provision for three LCAC in a single-bay, longer (98.1-m), narrower (15.2-m) by 8.5-m high docking well (which can alternatively hold up to six LCM[8], or two LCU landing craft); revised and strengthened aircraft elevators; internal stowage for ship's boats; a bulbous forefoot to the bow; larger-area bilge-keels; a squared-off flight deck forward (made possible by the omission of the 127-mm guns and making the entire deck capable of spotting nine CH-53E helicopters at once); using HY100 steel to construct the stronger flight deck; additional cargo elevators (six 5.4-ton capacity, total: 7.6 × 3.6 m); a lower, narrower, and longer island; a narrower vehicle ramp to the flight deck; and better ballistic protection. In addition to embarked landing craft, the ships carry four LCPLs and two 12.2-m utility boats. They have 2,127 m^2 of vehicle parking space and 3,087 m^3 of dry cargo space. There are four 2,000-gallon/min. turbo-pumps and eight 1,000-gal./min. motor-driven pumps fitted. Hospital facilities include six operating rooms and 578 beds. LHD 4 was selected to test crew-reduction measures in 5-02.

Changes for LHD 8 include gas turbine main propulsion engines, all electric auxiliaries, an advanced machinery control system, water mist fire-protection systems, and new command-and-control and combat systems. The gas turbine plant will provide lower lifetime operating cost despite having a slightly higher fuel consumption than the steam systems used in previous units of the class; electric auxiliary power will drive the ship at up to 13 kts.

Aviation systems: Because of the desire to maximize the number of deck spots, no ski-jump V/STOL ramp was fitted, reducing the potential effectiveness of the Harrier contingent. The hangar has 6.4-m vertical clearance and is 25.9 m wide; it can accommodate 28 CH-46 helicopter equivalents. Have two 34-ton capacity, 15.2 × 13.7–m aircraft elevators, with the stern elevator relocated to starboard from the centerline aft position on the LHA 1 class. In addition to the listed aircraft fuel, about 50 tons of vehicle fuel can be carried.

A typical all-helicopter air group includes 20 CH-46E, 10 CH-53E, six AH-1W, and three UH-1N, while with six AV-8B Harriers aboard, the number of helicopters falls to 14 CH-46E, six CH-53E, six AH-1W, and four UH-1N; up to 28 AV-8B can be carried in the absence of helicopters, while in a mine-countermeasures role, the ships would carry 20 CH-46E and six MH-53E helicopters and six Mk 105 countermeasures sleds. During 2003 LHD 5 and LHD 6 operated off Iraq in the "Harrier carrier" role, each employing 24 AV-8Bs from their flight decks. All are being outfitted to operate the MV-22 Osprey.

Combat systems: Command facilities include an Integrated Tactical Amphibious Warfare Data System, Ship Signals Exploitation Space, Flag Plot, Landing Force Operations Center, Joint Intelligence Center, Supporting Arms Coordination Center, Tactical-Logistical Group, Helicopter Logistics Group, Tactical Air Control Center, Helicopter Direction Center, and Helicopter Coordination Section. LHD 1 was originally fitted with the SPS-52 3-D early warning radar (replaced by SPS-48E) and had the SYS-2(V)3 sensor fusion system for defensive weapons control; later units had SYS-2(V)5. The SPS-48E antennas were mounted higher, atop the foremast, in LHD 5 and later. The USQ-119(V)11 Naval Tactical Command System, Marconi ICS.3 (URC-109) integrated communications system, SMQ-11 weather satellite receiving system, and USQ-82(V) data multiplexing system are fitted. Are to receive the Joint Services Imagery Processing System–Navy (JSIPS-N). Beginning with LHD 1 in 1996–97, all ships of the class have received the SSDS (Ship Self-Defense System) Block 1 integration system for the sensors and weapons to improve response time against antiship missiles; Mk 31 RAM launchers have been mounted at the forward end of the island superstructure and on the starboard quarter, the latter replacing one Phalanx mounting. Two 25-mm guns are mounted to port and one on the starboard side. The SPS-49(V)5 radars are to be upgraded to SPS-49A(V)1. LHD 7 is to have the Sperry integrated bridge system and color electronic chart display. Have USC-1(V), USC-6 (Challenge Athena) UHF, MARISAT MHF, and USC-38(V)1 EHF SATCOM terminals. LHD 8 will not carry the Mk 95 fire control or the SPN-47 precision CCA systems.

♦ 0 (+ 4) LHA(R) amphibious assault ships

Bldr: Northrop Grumman Ship Systems, Pascagoula, Miss. (In serv. 2012– . . .)

	Laid down	L	In serv.
LHA 6 . . .	. . .	. . .	2012
LHA 7 . . .	. . .	. . .	
LHA 8 . . .	. . .	. . .	
LHA 9 . . .	. . .	. . .	

LHA 6—computer rendering Northrop Grumman, 2006

D: 48,775 tons (fl) **S:** 24 kts **Dim:** 280.7 × 45.7 × 7.9

Air group: Options include: 20 F-35B fighters and 4-6 MH-60 helicopters; or 12 MV-22 Osprey, 4 UH-1Y Huey and 4 AH-1Z Supercobra helicopters, 4 CH-53E heavy-lift helicopters, and 6 F-35B strike fighters

A: 2 21-cell RAM SAM syst. (RIM-116 missiles); 1 28-cell RIM-162 ESSM Sea Sparrow SAM syst.; 3 25-mm 75-cal. Mk 38 Bushmaster mounts; 2 20-mm Mk 15 Phalanx gatling CIWS; 7 twin 12.7-mm mg

Electronics:

Radar: 1 3-D early warning; 1 . . . air search; 1 SPS-35N air control; 1 SPN-43B CCA; 2 Mk 90 Phalanx f.c.; 2 Mk 57 Mod. 3 fcs

EW: 1 SRS combat D/F system; Raytheon SLQ-32(V)3 active/passive; Mk 36 Mod. 12 SRBOC decoy syst.; SLQ-25A Nixie towed acoustic torpedo decoy syst.

Tacan: URN-25

M: 2 G.E. LM-2500 gas turbines; 2 props; 72,000 shp; 2 electric low-speed propulsion motors; 10,000 ship (12–13 kts)

Crew: About 1065 total + 1,686 embarked troops

Remarks: Data listed above remain tentative. The first unit of a replacement program for the *Tarawa* class, initially referred to as the LX class and now as the LHA(R) (LHA Replacement) or LHA 6 class, was included in the FY 07 budget request, with the second expected in the FY 10 budget. Only four would be needed, as *Makin Island* (LHD 8) will replace LHA 3. This class represents a further evolution of the previous LHA and LHD designs; optimized for aviation, they will be able to carry and operate up to 24 F-35B Lightning IIs. Planned improvement over the *Tarawa* and *Wasp* classes include an enlarged hangar deck, enhanced aviation maintenance facilities, additional equipment support and stowage space and increased aviation fuel capacity. There are no plans for a well deck.

AMPHIBIOUS WARFARE HELICOPTER CARRIERS [LH]
(continued)

♦ 4 Tarawa-class amphibious assault ships (SCB 410 type)
Bldr: Ingalls SB, Pascagoula, Miss. (*Atlantic/†Pacific Fleet)

	Laid down	L	In serv.
LHA 1 TARAWA†	15-11-71	1-12-73	29-5-76
LHA 2 SAIPAN*	21-7-72	18-7-74	15-10-77
LHA 4 NASSAU*	13-8-73	21-1-78	28-7-79
LHA 5 PELELIU (ex-*Da Nang*)†	12-11-76	25-11-78	3-5-80

Nassau (LHA 4) U.S. Navy, 8-05

Peleliu (LHA 5) U.S. Navy, 1-06

Peleliu (LHA 5) U.S. Navy, 11-05

Saipan (LHA 2)—with LCU approaching from stern U.S. Navy, 6-06

Saipan (LHA 2) U.S. Navy, 5-06

D: 25,884–27,165 tons light (39,438–40,891 fl) **S:** 24 kts (25.3 kts on trials)
Dim: 254.20 (237.14 pp) × 40.23 (32.31 wl) × 8.23 max. unballasted
Air group: Typical: 12 CH-46 helicopters; 4 CH-53E helicopters; 6 AV-8B Harriers; 3 UH-1N helicopters; 4 AH-1W helicopters.; aircraft carrier mode: 20 AV-8B Harriers and 4–6 SH-60F ASW helicopters
A: 2 21-round RAM Mk 31 SAM syst. (RIM-116 missiles); 2 20-mm Mk 15 Phalanx gatling CIWS; 2 single 25-mm 75-cal. Mk 38 Bushmaster low-angle guns; 8 single 12.7-mm M2 mg
Electronics:
Radar: 1 Raytheon SPS-64(V)9 nav.; 1 Norden SPS-67(V)3 surf.-search; 1 Lockheed Martin SPS-40E air-search; 1 ITT-Gilfillan SPS-48E 3-D early-warning; 1 Hughes Mk 23 Mod. 3 TAS target designation; 1 SPN-35A air-control; 1 SPN-43B CCA; 2 Mk 90 Phalanx f.c.
TACAN: URN-25
EW: Raytheon SLQ-32(V)3 active/passive; Mk 36 SRBOC decoy syst.(4 6-round Mk 137 RL); SLQ-25A Nixie SSTD towed acoustic torpedo decoy syst.
M: 2 sets Westinghouse geared steam turbines; 2 props; 77,000 shp (70,000 sust.)—900-hp bow-thruster
Boilers: 2 Combustion Engineering Type V2M-VS; 49.3 kg/cm^2, 482° C
Electric: 14,600 kw (4 × 2,500-kw turboalternators, 2 × 2,000-kw diesel alternator sets; 4 × 150-kw emergency diesel alternator sets)
Range: 10,000/20 **Fuel:** 5,900 tons + 1,200 tons JP-5 for aircraft
Crew: 86–94 officers, 871–979 enlisted + troops: 172 officers, 1,731 enlisted

Remarks: Authorized: LHA 1 in FY 69, LHA 2 in FY 70, and LHA 4 and LHA 5 in FY 71. Were originally to have been a class of nine, with four already on order canceled in 1971. LHA 5 renamed on 15-2-78. The ships are aging more quickly than expected and suffer from thin flight decks, cramped command and berthing spaces, electric power distribution problems, control deficiencies, and obsolete piping systems. They were to have been given a major modernization (SLEP—Service Life-Extension Program), with advanced procurement funding for the first ship to have been requested under the FY 03 budget, but instead they are to be retired from 2011 to 2015 and replaced by LHD 8 and then the planned new LHA(R) class. On 8-5-03, while operating in the Northern Arabian Gulf, LHA 2 suffered an explosion in a trash container, which pierced a bulkhead and wounded 11 Marines.

LHA 1, 4, and 5 are receiving upgrades to keep them in service until at least 2010; LHA 2 was the first to be completed (in 2001) and received a seawater compensation system to improve stability, new radar and combat systems, more-powerful generators, and corrosion-resistant deck coverings.

Hull systems: The boilers were the largest ever installed in U.S. Navy ships; the propulsion plant is highly automated. Are receiving digital computer-controlled propulsion systems to help optimize boiler performance. They have a very complete 352-bed hospital, including four operating rooms; mortuary facilities are fitted. Completely air-conditioned. Planned addition of bulbous bow canceled. Originally had a boat crane and stowage for landing craft on the flight deck abaft the island, now removed.

Aviation systems: Have nine deck landing spots, helicopter elevators to port (20-ton, folding) and aft (40-ton), and a 76-m-long × 23.2-m-broad × 8.1-m-high well deck for up to four LCU 1610 class, or one LCAC, or seven LCM(8) landing craft. The vehicle stowage garage forward of docking well provides 3,134 m^2 of parking space, and the palletized cargo holds total 3,311 m^3.

Combat systems: Communications systems include SRR-1, WSC-3 UHF, WSC-6 SHF, and USC-38 EHF SATCOM receivers, and SMQ-11 weather satellite receiver. As completed, carried two Mk 25 Mod. 1 BPDMS launchers for Sea Sparrow SAMs, controlled by two Mk 71 directors with Mk 115 radars, and three 127-mm DP guns. The Sea Sparrow launchers and the port aft 127-mm gun were removed from all

AMPHIBIOUS WARFARE HELICOPTER CARRIERS [LH]
(continued)

during the early 1990s, and the remaining two gunmounts were deleted during 1997; the associated SPQ-9A surface-fire control radar and SPG-60 AA fire control were removed during 1998–99. Six single 20-mm AA guns have also been removed. All have received two Mk 49, 21-cell RAM point defense missile launchers sited to port atop the pilothouse and to starboard at the aft end of the flight deck and controlled by the SWY-2 weapons control system. LHA 1 completed overhaul 1-95 with RAM launchers, Mk 23 TAS radar, and SPS-48E 3-D radar in place of SPS-52B, a modification now accomplished in all, by using radar sets taken from retired CG 16– and CG 26–class cruisers. The ships of this class are no longer scheduled to receive the SSDS (Ship Self-Defense System) Block 1 update and plans to add the CEC (Cooperative Engagement Capability) were terminated in 6-00. All have had their original WLR-1 EW suites replaced by SLQ-32(V)3 and URN-20 TACANs replaced by URN-25.
Disposals: *Belleau Wood* (LHA 3) was decommissioned on 28-10-03 and sunk as a target on 12-7-06. *Saipan* (LHA 2) is scheduled to be retired in 2007.

AMPHIBIOUS TRANSPORTS, DOCK [LPD]

♦ 2 (+ 7) San Antonio–class dock landing ships
Bldr: Northrop Grumman Avondale, New Orleans, La. (*Atlantic/†Pacific Fleet)

	Laid down	L	In serv.
LPD 17 San Antonio*	9-12-00	12-7-03	14-1-06
LPD 18 New Orleans†	14-10-02	11-12-04	12-06 (del.)
LPD 19 Mesa Verde*	25-2-03	20-11-04	3-07 (del.)
LPD 20 Green Bay†	7-8-03	. . .	3-08 (del.)
LPD 21 New York*	30-8-04	. . .	9-05 (del.)
LPD 22 San Diego†	. . .	. . .	2009
LPD 23 Anchorage†	. . .	. . .	2009
LPD 24 Arlington†	. . .	. . .	2010
LPD 25 Somerset*	. . .	. . .	2011

San Antonio (LPD 17)—the mainmast envelopes the antenna for the SPS-48E radar and the foremast various electronic warfare and IFF antennas U.S. Navy, 4-05

San Antonio (LPD 17) class U.S. Navy, 5-06

San Antonio (LPD 17) class U.S. Navy, 5-06

San Antonio (LPD 17) class Northrop Grumman Ship Systems, 12-05

D: 25,296 tons (fl) **S:** 22 + kts
Dim: 208.48 (200.00 wl) × 32.00 (29.5 wl) × 7.01
A: 2 21-round Mk 31 Mod. 0 RAM SAM launchers (RIM-116A missiles); LPD 18-on: 2 single 30-mm Mk 46 Mod. 1 low-angle guns; LPD 17 only: 3 single 25-mm 75-cal. Mk 38 Mod. 0 Bushmaster low-angle guns; all: 2 single 12.7-mm Mk 26 Mod. 18 mg
Air group: 2 CH-53E or 4 AH/UH-1 or 4 CH-46E helicopters or 2 MV-22B Osprey
Electronics:
Radar: 2 Hughes-Furuno SPS-73 surf.-search; 1 Raytheon SPS-48E 3-D air search; 1 Northrop Grumman SPQ-9B horizon search and target designation
TACAN: . . .
EW: Raytheon SLQ-32A(V)2 intercept; SLA-10B; SLQ-49 floating decoy syst; Mk 36 Mod. 12 SRBOC decoy syst. (4 6-round Mk 137 RL, 4 2-round Mk 53 Nulka hovering decoy RL); SLQ-25A Nixie SSTD towed torpedo decoy syst. (see Remarks)
M: 4 Colt-Pielstick PC2.5 STC 16-cyl., medium-speed diesels; 2 5-bladed Bird-Johnson CP props; 41,600 bhp
Electric: 12,500 kw tot. (5 × 2,500-kw Kato sets, Caterpillar 3608 diesel-driven)
Range: . . . / . . . Fuel: . . . tons + 1,196 m^3 aviation fuel, 38 m^3 vehicle fuel
Crew: 361 tot. (berthing for 30 officers, 392 enlisted) + troops: 66 officers, 639 enlisted + 95 spare

Remarks: Authorized: LPD 17 in FY 96, LPD 18 in FY 99, LPD 19 and 20 in FY 00. Major delays and large cost increases have delayed further authorizations, none were approved under the FY 01 and FY 02 budgets; LPD 21 was approved in FY 03, LPD 22 in FY 04, LPD 23 in FY 05, and LPD 24 in the FY 07 budget. At one time, as many as 46 were planned, this was reduced to 12 and then cut to nine ships in 2005. The class replaces the LKAs, LPDs, LSD 36 class, and *Newport*-class LSTs. Intended to be in service for 40 years. LPD 17, 19, and 25 will be homeported in Norfolk, Virginia, while LPD 18, 20, 22, and 24 will be homeported in San Diego, California. LPD 23 is expected to homeport in Japan. Though LPD 17 was completed in New Orleans, earlier work was begun at Bath, Maine. Fabricated sections were later transferred to New Orleans, La., where work restarted on 19-8-02.

The "winner-take-all" construction contract was awarded 17-12-96 to a consortium of Avondale Shipyards, Bath Iron Works, Hughes, Loral, Sperry Marine, CAE, AT&T, and Intergraph, with every third ship to be built at Bath's facility in Maine and the others in Louisiana. The initial contract provided $641,370,625 for LPD 17 and options to build the next two. LPD 18 was ordered on 18-12-98. LPD 19 was ordered on 22-12-99 (and work began on 16-7-01) and LPD 20 on 30-5-00 (for $477,675, 955), and LPD 21 on 25-11-03 (for $171,050,850). LPD 22 and 23 were ordered on 1-6-06 and LPD 24 was ordered 6-11-06. LPD 17's estimated cost rose to $1.16 billion, while LPD 18 is projected to have a final cost of $781 million, LPD 19 $856 million, and LPD 20 $702 million. Under a 17-6-02 agreement, all units of the class are now to be built by Northrop Grumman, using various resources at its Gulf Coast shipyards; in return, Bath Iron Works is building DDG 102, previously assigned to Northrop Grumman Ingalls. LPD 21 was named on 6-9-02 for the state and the city of New York, in honor of the victims of 11-9-01. Work on LPD 19 at Avondale began on 13-9-02. On 19-12-02, LPD 17 experienced a severe engine room fire during construction.

Hull systems: The docking well is about the size of that on the LPD 4 class and will accommodate two LCAC air-cushion landing craft and 14 EFV amphibious vehicles. The two-part stern gate covers an opening 23.8-m wide by 10.7-m high. There will be two spots for helicopters of up to CH-53E size; three AH-1Z or four CH-46E or one CH-53E or two MV-22 Ospreys are to be accommodated in the hangar. Will also be able to support AV-8B Harrier-II aircraft. Cargo volume is to be 2,323 m^2 of vehicle parking space on three decks, and 708 m^3 of palletized ammunition cargo space. Two cargo ammunition magazines will total 1,007 m^3, and the ships will be able to carry 1,196 m^3 JP-5 cargo fuel and 38 m^3 cargo gasoline. They will have a 100% redundant Shipboard-Wide Area Network (SWAN) to carry internal and external communications and data. Medical facilities include 24 beds, two operating rooms, and space for 100 additional casualties. The hull was designed to reduce the cost of fabrication and is shaped to reduce radar cross-section; the radar cross-section is planned to be only 1% that of the LPD 4 class, and even the 10-ton, 19.8-m reach Allied Systems boat crane incorporates signature-reduction features. The principal radars and communication antennas will be enveloped within two composite material, octagonal "Advanced Enclosed Mast/Sensor" structures to reduce radar signature and required maintenance. To have bow bulb, twin rudders, and no side-thrusters. Will have seven 700-kw air conditioning plants and five 45,000 liter/day reverse osmosis water desalinators. Ten 3,800 l/min firepumps and eight air compressors will be installed. As displacement has grown, expected speed has dropped by 1 kt. Will carry two 7-m and one 11-m RIB-type ship's boats, with stowage provided for two additional special forces RIBs if required. Are the first USN ships designed from the outset to accommodate female crewmembers; the original total crew size has been reduced due to increased automation and the deletion of a number of combat systems. The Sperry Marine Integrated

AMPHIBIOUS TRANSPORTS, DOCK [LPD] *(continued)*

Bridge System (IBS) and CAE's computerized engineering controls system will be installed. Hull of *New York* (LPD 21) contains steel melted and cast from New York City's fallen World Trade Center.

Combat systems: All will have Advanced Combat Direction System (ACDS) Block I, USQ-119C(V)27 Joint Maritime Command Information System (JMCIS), KSQ-1 amphibious assault direction system, SPQ-12(V) radar display distribution system, Mk 2 Ship Self-Defense System (SSDS), and the Integrated Combat Direction System (ICDS) to coordinate various self-defense systems. In addition, LPD 18 and later are planned to receive the USG-2(V) Cooperative Engagement Capability (CEC) system and will have Link 11 and 16, JTIDS, SI communications, ADNS, and TADIX-A capabilities. The KSQ-1 Amphibious Assault Direction system, UPX-29 IFF system, and SPQ-14(V) radar display distribution system will be fitted.

The navigation suite is to include the WSN-7(V)1 inertial system, a digital flux gate magnetic compass, a WRN-6(V)1 GPS receiver, a WQN-1 channel finder mine-avoidance sonar, an SSN-6 digital mapping system, a UQN-4A echo-sounder, and a WQN-2 doppler speed log. Will have a 100% redundant Shipboard-Wide Area Network (SWAN) Asynchronous Transfer Mode–based shipwide fiber-optic data network to carry internal and external communications and data. Are to have HF, UHF, VHF, EHF, and SHF radio communications, including the Challenge Athena SATCOM system.

Originally, all were to have had 16 Mk 41 vertical missile launch cells forward of the superstructure to carry a total of 64 RIM-162 Evolved Sea Sparrow SAMs. The SAM system was initially deleted from the first three and has now been deleted from all, although weight and space provisions remain. Two planned Mk 15 Mod. 12 Phalanx 20-mm CIWS have also been omitted. The General Dynamics 30-mm Mk 46 Mod. 1 stabilized gun in the same armored turret that will be used on the new EFV amphibious armored assault vehicle will be substituted for the 25-mm guns to deal with smallcraft, helicopters, and light aircraft.

The Lockheed Martin SLY-2(V) Advanced Integrated Electronic Warfare System (AIEWS) may replace the current, obsolescent SLQ-32(V)2 system in LPD 22 and later ships. LPD 22 will be the first to have the Project Akcita air-defense sensor and weapon integration system, which is planned to be backfitted later in earlier units; a new D-band radar may replace the SPS-48E.

♦ 8 Austin class (SCB 187B type) (*Atlantic/†Pacific Fleet)

	Bldr	Laid down	L	In serv.
LPD 5 Ogden†	New York NSY	4-2-63	27-6-64	19-6-65
LPD 7 Cleveland†	Ingalls, Pascagoula	30-11-64	7-5-66	21-4-67
LPD 8 Dubuque†	Ingalls, Pascagoula	25-1-65	6-8-66	1-9-67
LPD 9 Denver†	Lockheed SB, Seattle	7-2-64	23-1-65	26-10-68
LPD 10 Juneau†	Lockheed SB, Seattle	23-1-65	12-2-66	12-7-69
LPD 12 Shreveport*	Lockheed SB, Seattle	27-12-65	25-10-66	12-2-70
LPD 13 Nashville*	Lockheed SB, Seattle	14-3-66	7-10-67	14-2-70
LPD 15 Ponce*	Lockheed SB, Seattle	31-10-66	20-5-70	10-7-71

Nashville (LPD 13)—flagship variant — Leo van Ginderen, 9-05

Dubuque (LPD 8) — U.S. Navy, 7-04

D: 8,883–9,962 tons light (16,590–17,479 fl) **S:** 21 kts
Dim: 173.4 × 25.6 (hull) × 7.0–7.2
A: 2 20-mm Mk 15 Phalanx gatling CIWS; 2 single 25-mm 75-cal. Mk 38 Mod. 0 Bushmaster low-angle guns; 8 single 12.7-mm M2 mg

Ogden (LDP 5) — U.S. Navy, 8-05

Dubuque (LPD 8) — U.S. Navy, 7-04

Denver (LPD 9) — U.S. Navy, 5-04

Electronics:
Radar: 1 Raytheon SPS-64(V)9 nav.; 1 Raytheon SPS-10F surf.-search; 1 Lockheed Martin SPS-40E air-search; 2 Mk 90 Phalanx f.c.
TACAN: URN-25
EW: Raytheon SLQ-32(V)1 intercept; Mk 36 SRBOC decoy RL syst. (4 6-round Mk 137 RL); all except LPD 4: SLQ-25A Nixie towed torpedo decoy syst.
M: 2 sets de Laval geared steam turbines; 2 props; 24,000 shp
Boilers: 2 Foster-Wheeler (LPD 5, LPD 12: Babcock & Wilcox), 42.3 kg/cm^2, 467° C
Range: 7,700/20
Crew: 28–29 officers, 361–375 enlisted (+ 60 staff in LPD 7 to LPD 13) + troops: LPD 5, 15: 79 officers, 756 enlisted; others: 69 officers, 812 enlisted)

Remarks: Authorized: three in FY 62, four in FY 63, three in FY 64, two in FY 65; LPD 16, funded and authorized under FY 66, was deferred in favor of the LHA program and canceled entirely during 2-69. Lengthened version of the preceding *Raleigh* (LPD 1) class, combining the capabilities of assault troop transports (LPA) and dock landing ships (LSD). LPD 10 was homeported at Sasebo, Japan, replacing LPD 8 on 28-7-99. LPD 12 grounded 14-2-00 in the Suez Canal, causing propeller and shaft damage that was repaired at Haifa, Israel. LPD 9 collided with the MSC oiler *Yukon* (T-AO 202) on 14-7-00 during refueling operations. All of these ships are in urgent need of replacement. LPD 5 was in a collision with the *Greenville* (SSN 772) on 27-1-02.

Modernization: LPD 7–9, 13 and 15 are planned to receive life-extension overhauls costing about $78 million each to keep them operating up to 2014, the result of the numerous delays in the LPD 17 program. The other ships are to be retired during FY 06 through FY 09. The five rehabilitated ships are to receive increased electrical generating capacity, major boiler repairs, new air-conditioning plants, a new internal communications system, and replacement boat cranes.

Hull systems: As with many older USN classes, displacements vary widely as a result of modifications over the years. Either one LCAC, one LCU plus four LCM(8), or 28 LVT can be carried in the 120.00 × 15.24–m (687 m^2) well deck. One 30-ton and six 4-ton cranes, one 8.15-ton elevator, and two forklifts are carried. Up to six CH-46E helicopters can be carried for brief periods on the 1,394 m^2 flight deck, but the small, telescoping hangar can accommodate only one utility helicopter. LPD 7 to LPD 13 were originally fitted for flagship duty and have one additional superstructure deck. All have 1,379 m^2 vehicle parking space and 1,540 m^3 ammunition stowage, and they can carry 224,500 gallons aviation fuel and 119,000 gallons of vehicle fuel.

AMPHIBIOUS TRANSPORTS, DOCK [LPD] *(continued)*

Combat systems: Command facilities include a CIC, Troop Operations and Logistics Center, and Helicopter Coordination Center; LPD 7–13 also have a Flag Plot, Ship Signals Exploitation Space, and Supporting Arms Coordination Center (some of this equipment had been removed by 1998). All lost their one Mk 56 and two Mk 63 gun fire-control directors in the late 1980s, leaving the 76.2-mm guns locally controlled. Two twin 76.2-mm DP were removed 1977–78 (port fwd, stbd aft), and the remaining mounts in 1992–93. In LPD 5–6 and 15, the SPS-40 radar's antenna is set on a platform well below the apex of the tripod mast, while on the others it is on the masthead platform.

LPD 12 in the Atlantic and LPD 9 in the Pacific were equipped to accommodate and control the Pioneer reconnaissance drone during 11-92 and 1-93; each ship carried five to eight of the drones and was equipped fore and aft with radome-covered tracking and control radars for the Pioneers. Subsequently, the drone equipment was added to LPD 7, 12, 13, and 15.

Disposals: *Coronado* (LPD 11), redesignated as flagship AGF 11, was decommissioned on 25-2-05. *Duluth* (LPD 6) was decommissioned on 28-9-05 to be kept in reserve as a logistical support asset. *Austin* (LPD 4) was retired 27-9-06. *Trenton* (LPD 14) was decommissioned in 1-07 for transfer to India. *Ogden* (LPD 5) and *Shreveport* (LPD 12) are scheduled to decommission in 2007.

DOCK LANDING SHIPS [LSD]

♦ 4 Harpers Ferry class

Bldr: Northrop Grumman Avondale, New Orleans, La.
(*Atlantic Fleet/†Pacific Fleet)

	Laid down	L	In serv.
LSD 49 HARPERS FERRY†	15-4-91	16-1-93	7-1-95
LSD 50 CARTER HALL*	11-11-91	2-10-93	30-9-95
LSD 51 OAK HILL*	21-9-92	11-6-94	8-6-96
LSD 52 PEARL HARBOR†	27-1-95	24-2-96	30-5-98

Carter Hall (LSD 50) U.S. Navy, 2-06

Pearl Harbor (LSD 52) U.S. Navy, 9-05

Harpers Ferry (LSD 49) U.S. Navy, 5-06

D: 11,251–11,604 tons light (16,088–16,601 fl) **S:** 22 kts
Dim: 185.80 (176.80 wl) × 25.60 × 6.04
A: 2 21-round RAM Mk 31 SAM syst. (RIM-116 missiles); 2 20-mm Mk 15 Phalanx gatling CIWS; 2 single 25-mm 75-cal. Mk 38 Mod. 0 Bushmaster low-angle guns; 8 single 12.7-mm M2 mg
Electronics:
Radar: 1 Raytheon SPS-64(V)9 nav.; 1 Norden SPS-67(V)1 surf.-search; 1 Raytheon SPS-49(V)5 air-search; 2 Mk 90 Phalanx f.c.
TACAN: URN-25
EW: Raytheon SLQ-32(V)1 intercept; Mk 36 SRBOC decoy syst. (6 6-round Mk 137 RL); SLQ-25 Nixie towed torpedo decoy system
M: 4 Colt-Pielstick 16 PC2.5V400 diesels; 2 CP props; 41,600 bhp (33,600 sust.)
Electric: 5,200 kw (4 × 1,300-kw Fairbanks-Morse 12D38 1/8 diesel alternator sets)
Range: 8,000/18 **Fuel:** 2,000 tons **Endurance:** 75 days
Crew: 21 officers, 312–313 enlisted + troops: 27 officers, 375 enlisted + 7 officer, 95 enlisted emergency accommodations

Remarks: Authorized: LSD 49 in FY 88, LSD 50 in FY 90, LSD 51 in FY 91, LSD 52 in FY 92. Officially referred to as the "LSD 41 CV (Cargo Variant)" class. Were originally to have been a class of 12, but program terminated 1992 in favor of development of the *San Antonio* class; funds to build LSD 52, approved under FY 92, were rescinded by the first Bush administration, but Congress again appropriated money to build the vessel under FY 93. LSD 49 was ordered on 26-12-89, LSD 50 on 22-12-89, LSD 51 on 27-3-91, and LSD 52 during 10-93. LSD 49's home port was changed to Sasebo, Japan, on 1-9-01, replacing LSD 42.
Hull systems: Modification of LSD 41 design with increased cargo capacity at the expense of a shorter well deck able to accommodate only two CAC, one LCU, or four LCM(8). Carry one 12.2-m utility boat and two LCPL on deck, tended by a single starboard-side 30-ton crane. Cargo space: 1,208 m^2 vehicle parking, 1,133 m^3 cargo volume. Have greater air-conditioning capacity than the LSD 41 class. Flight deck is fixed, as on LSD 41 class, has two landing spots, and is served by an 8-ton cargo elevator.
Combat systems: All ships of the class received the SSDS Block 1 combat system by 2004, beginning with LSD 49 in 1997; the associated Mk 31 RAM SAM launchers were mounted atop the pilothouse and to port, amidships, in all by 1999. Plans to add the CEC (Cooperative Engagement Capability) were terminated in 6-00.

♦ 8 Whidbey Island class (*Atlantic/†Pacific Fleet)

	Bldr	Laid down	L	In serv.
LSD 41 WHIDBEY ISLAND*	Lockheed, Seattle	4-8-81	10-6-83	9-2-85
LSD 42 GERMANTOWN†	Lockheed, Seattle	5-8-82	29-6-84	8-2-86
LSD 43 FORT MCHENRY†	Lockheed, Seattle	10-6-83	1-2-86	8-8-87
LSD 44 GUNSTON HALL*	Avondale	26-5-86	27-6-87	24-2-89
LSD 45 COMSTOCK†	Avondale	27-10-86	16-1-88	3-2-90
LSD 46 TORTUGA*	Avondale	23-3-87	15-9-88	17-11-90
LSD 47 RUSHMORE†	Avondale	9-11-87	6-5-89	1-6-91
LSD 48 ASHLAND*	Avondale	4-4-88	11-11-89	9-5-92

Ashland (LSD 48) U.S. Navy, 9-05

Gunston Hall (LSD 44) U.S. Navy, 7-05

DOCK LANDING SHIPS [LSD] *(continued)*

Fort McHenry (LSD 43) U.S. Navy, 1-05

Tortuga (LSD 46) Leo van Ginderen, 6-05

Tortuga (LSD 46) Leo van Ginderen, 6-05

D: 11,099–11,590 tons light (15,883–16,568 fl) **S:** 22 kts
Dim: 185.80 (176.80 wl) × 25.60 × 6.25 hull
A: 2 21-round RAM Mk 31 SAM syst. (RIM-116 missiles); 2 20-mm Mk 15 Phalanx gatling CIWS; 2 single 25-mm 75-cal. Mk 38 Mod. 0 Bushmaster low-angle guns; 6 single 12.7-mm M2 mg
Electronics:
Radar: 1 . . . nav.; 1 Raytheon SPS-64(V)9 nav.; 1 Norden SPS-67(V) surf.-search; 1 Raytheon SPS-49(V)1 (LSD 45-48: (V)5) air-search; 2 Mk 90 Phalanx f.c.
TACAN: URN-25
EW: Raytheon SLQ-32(V)1 intercept; Mk 36 Mod. 6 SRBOC decoy RL syst. (4 6-round Mk 137 RL); SLQ-25 Nixie towed torpedo decoy syst.
M: 4 Colt-Pielstick 16 PC2.5V400 diesels; 2 5-bladed CP props; 41,600 bhp (33,600 sust.)
Electric: 5,200 kw (4 × 1,300-kw Fairbanks-Morse 12D38 1/8 diesel alternator sets)
Range: 8,000/18 Fuel: 2,000 tons Endurance: 75 days
Crew: 21 officers, 289–299 enlisted + troops: 27 officers, 375 enlisted (including 64 LCAC personnel) + 7 officers, 95 enlisted emergency accomm.

Remarks: The design was originally to have been a near-repeat of the LSD 36 class adapted for diesel propulsion and able to accommodate four LCAC (Air-Cushion Landing Craft). Authorized: LSD 41 in FY 81, LSD 42 in FY 82, LSD 43 in FY 83, LSD 44 in FY 84, LSD 45 and 46 in FY 85, and LSD 47 and 48 in FY 86. In 7-99 LSD 47 began testing systems and concepts intended for use in the LPD 17 class, including new damage-control techniques, a local-area data network, integrated bridge systems, and automated maintenance systems; LSD 47 is also the "Smart Gator" amphibious warfare ship trials platform for "Smart Ship" labor-saving concepts, which were planned to be incorporated in the entire class by 2003; the cost-saving program, however, was canceled during 6-00—on cost grounds. LSD 46 went aground near Morehead City, N.C., on 6 June but was refloated the next day with no significant damage.
Hull systems: The docking well measures 134.0 × 15.24 m clear (1,220 m^2) and floods to 1.8 m fwd/3.0 m aft; the ships can ballast down in 15 minutes and deballast in 30, with a total ballast water capacity of 12,860 tons (and full load displacement of more than 29,000 metric tons when in ballast). The helicopter deck is raised above the docking well (which can accommodate four LCAC, three LCU, 10 LCM(8), or 64 AAVS) to provide all-around ventilation for the gas turbine-engined LCACs. There are two landing spots on the 64.6 × 25.3–m flight deck for up to CH-53E-sized helicopters but no hangar facilities. Forward of the docking well is 1,214 m^2 of vehicle parking space and space for 149 m^3 of palletized cargo. Medical facilities include an operating room and eight beds. Carry 90 tons JP-5 fuel for helicopters. Carry one 15.24-m utility boat, two LCPL Mk 11, and one LCVP on deck, handled by one 20-ton and one 60-ton crane. LSD 44–48 have a collective BW/CW protection system. All have the Inogen Leading Mark optical guidance system for LCAC entry to well deck. LSD 47 was fitted with the Raytheon fiber-optic, closed-loop steering system in 1998 under the "Smart Gator" ship systems improvement developmental program.
Combat systems: Two Mk 49, 21-cell launchers for the RAM missile have been added. In 1999 LSD 44 became the first ship fitted with RAM Mod. 1 (RIM-116A) missiles. LSD 48 received SSDS (Ship Self-Defense System) Block 1 during 9-96 to 1-97 refit, LSD 44 received it during 1997, and LSD 45 had it by 1999; all are to have received SSDS Block 1 by 2004. The SPS-49(V)1 radars are planned to be upgraded to SPS-49A(V)1. Plans to add the CEC (Cooperative Engagement Capability) were terminated in 6-00.

Disposal notes: All three remaining *Anchorage*-class LSDs have been retired. *Pensacola* (LSD 38) was decommissioned and transferred by sale to Taiwan on 30-9-99. LSD 37 retired 4-8-03 and was sunk as a target on 25-4-04 and LSD 39 decommissioned on 25-7-03 and sunk as a target on 12-6-05. *Fort Fisher* (LSD 40) was decommissioned and stricken 27-2-98; offered for sale to Malaysia and to Taiwan during FY 00, the ship was not accepted and remains in MARAD custody awaiting disposal. *Anchorage* LSD 36 was retired 1-10-03 and stricken in 2004 for possible transfer to Taiwan in 2007.

TANK LANDING SHIPS [LST]

♦ **4 Newport class (SCN 405-66 type)** (in *reserve*)
Bldrs: General Dynamics National Steel SB, San Diego, Calif.

	Laid down	L	In serv.	Decomm.
LST 1182 *Fresno*	16-12-67	28-9-68	22-11-69	8-4-93
LST 1187 *Tuscaloosa*	23-11-68	6-9-69	24-10-70	18-2-94
LST 1190 *Boulder*	6-9-69	22-5-70	4-6-71	28-2-94
LST 1191 *Racine*	13-12-69	15-8-70	9-7-71	2-10-93

D: LST 1184: 5,170 tons light (8,770 fl) **S:** 23 kts (20 sust.)
Dim: 159.2 (171.3 over horns) × 21.18 × 5.79 (aft) **A:** None
Electronics: Radar: 1 Raytheon SPS-64(V)9 nav.; 1 Raytheon SPS-10F surf.-search; LST 1184 only: 1 Mk 90 Phalanx f.c.
M: 6 Alco 16-251 diesels; 2 CP props; 16,500 bhp—bow-thruster
Electric: 2,250 kw tot. (3 × 750 kw, Alco 251-E diesels driving; 450 V 60 Hz a.c.)
Range: 14,250/14 Fuel: 1,750 tons
Crew: LST 1184: 12 officers, 219 enlisted + troops: 20 officers, 294 enlisted + 72 emergency accomm.

Remarks: Authorized: one in FY 65, eight in FY 66, 11 in FY 67. Seven more planned under FY 71 were canceled. LST 1182, 1187, 1190, and 1191 are retained in reserve on 180-day recall with Selected Reserve crews of five officers and 45 enlisted assigned full-time. Are to be retained until FY 08.
Hull systems: Can transport 2,000 tons cargo, or, for beaching, 500 tons of cargo on 1,765 m^2 of deck space. There is a 34-m-long, 75-ton-capacity mobile aluminum ramp forward, which is linked to the tank deck by a second from the upper deck. Aft is a 242-m^2 helicopter platform and a stern door for loading and unloading vehicles. Four pontoon causeway sections can be carried on the hull sides. The tank deck, which has a 75-ton-capacity turntable at both ends, can carry 23 AAV7A1 armored personnel carriers or 29 M 48 tanks or 41 2.5-ton trucks, while the upper deck can accept 29 2.5-ton trucks. Normally carry three LCVP and one LCP in Welin davits. Have two 10-ton cranes. Carry 141,600 gallons vehicle fuel.
Combat systems: Mk 63 radar gunfire-control systems removed 1977–78 and the two twin 76.2-mm DP gunmounts during the early 1990s, except from the stricken LST 1195. SLQ-32(V)1 warning EW installation was abandoned. The 76.2-mm guns have been removed.
Disposals: The disposition of the remainder of the class is as follows:

	Decommissioned	Fate:
LST 1179 *Newport*	30-9-92	Transferred to Mexico 23-5-01
LST 1180 *Manitowoc*	30-6-93	Leased Taiwan 14-2-95; sold 2000
LST 1181 *Sumter*	30-9-93	Leased Taiwan 14-7-95; sale FY 02
LST 1183 *Peoria*	28-1-94	Sunk as a target 12-7-04
LST 1184 *Frederick*	5-10-02	Stricken 6-11-02; sold to Mexico on 22-11-02
LST 1185 *Schenectady*	15-12-93	Stricken for disposal on 13-7-01; sunk as a target 2004
LST 1186 *Cayuga*	30-7-94	Leased Brazil, trans. 26-8-94; outright sale FY 02.
LST 1188 *Saginaw*	28-6-94	Sold Australia, trans. 28-8-94
LST 1189 *San Bernardino*	30-9-95	Leased to Chile, trans. 30-9-95; sale FY 99
LST 1192 *Spartanburg County*	16-12-94	Sold Malaysia, trans. 16-12-94
LST 1193 *Fairfax County*	17-8-94	Sold Australia, trans. 27-9-94
LST 1194 *La Moure County*	17-11-00	Aground in Chile 12-9-00; stricken 17-11-00 and sunk as target on 10-7-01
LST 1195 *Barbour County*	30-3-92	Sunk as a target 6-4-04
LST 1196 *Harlan County*	14-4-95	Leased Spain 14-4-95; sale FY 00
LST 1197 *Barnstable County*	29-6-94	Leased Spain, 26-8-94; sale FY 00
LST 1198 *Bristol County*	29-7-94	Donated to Morocco, 16-8-94

LST 1183, leased to Venezuela on 31-12-95 as the *Golfo de Venezuela* (T-81), never left U.S. waters and was repossessed on 31-5-96 when a lease payment was missed.

AMPHIBIOUS CARGO SHIPS [LKA]

♦ 5 Charleston class (SCB 403 type) (all in *reserve*)

Bldr: Northrop Grumman Newport News, Newport News, Va.

	Laid down	L	In serv.	Decomm.
LKA 113 *Charleston*	5-12-66	2-12-67	14-12-68	27-4-92
LKA 114 *Durham*	10-7-67	29-3-68	24-5-69	25-2-94
LKA 115 *Mobile*	15-1-68	19-10-68	29-9-69	21-1-94
LKA 116 *St. Louis*	3-4-68	4-1-69	22-11-69	30-9-93
LKA 117 *El Paso*	22-10-68	17-5-69	17-1-70	21-4-94

Durham (LKA 114)—stored at Pearl Harbor Brian Morrison, 6-00

D: 9,937–10,455 tons light (18,322–19,323 fl) **S:** 20 kts
Dim: 175.26 (167.6 wl) × 24.99 × 7.62 (max.)
A: Removed or inactivated (see Remarks)
Electronics:
Radar: 1 SPS-59 (Canadian Marconi LN-66) nav.; 1 Raytheon SPS-10F surf.-search
EW: Raytheon SLQ-32(V)1 intercept, Mk 36 SRBOC decoy syst. (4 6-round Mk 137 RL); LKA 117 only: fitted for SLQ-25 Nixie towed torpedo decoy syst.
M: 1 set Westinghouse geared steam turbines; 1 prop; 22,000 shp (19,250 sust.)
Boilers: 2 Combustion Engineering; 42.2 kg/cm2, 443° C
Range: 9,600/16 **Fuel:** 2,400 tons
Crew: 22 officers, 334 enlisted + troops: 15 officers, 211 enlisted

Remarks: Authorized: LKA 114, 115 in FY 65, LKA 117 in FY 66. All are being retained as mobilization assets, at 180-day readiness. LKA 113, LKA 115, and LKA 117 are stored at Philadelphia and the other two at Pearl Harbor. LKA 115 and LKA 117 were to be brought to five-day readiness for deployment under Military Sealift Command control during refits at Bethlehem Shipyard, Sparrows Point, Maryland, that began on 12-2-96 for LKA 117 and 26-4-96 for LKA 115; however, when the work was nearly completed, the ships were returned to storage at Philadelphia, with LKA 117 sailing there from Baltimore in one day under her own power with an MSC crew and again placed out of service, on 23-10-96; LKA 115 followed on 1-11-96.
Hull systems: Air-conditioned. Machinery control is automatic. Have a 565-m^2 helicopter platform. Have 2,420 m^3 of cargo capacity, including 4,371 m^2 of vehicle parking space, and 741 m^3 of ammunition stowage. There are one 6-ton and five 2-ton stores elevators. Fittings include two 70-ton heavy-lift derricks, two 40-ton derricks, and eight 15-ton derricks. When active, they normally carried four aluminum LCM(8) Mk 2 and two LCPL landing craft.
Combat systems: Two Mk 56 radar gunfire-control systems and one twin 76.2-mm gunmount removed 1977–78 and another gunmount later in preparation for installation of two 20-mm Mk 15 CIWS. LKA 117 is unique in retaining the two twin 76.2-mm mounts, which are cocooned.

UTILITY LANDING CRAFT, SURFACE-EFFECT [LCUA]

♦ 91 LCAC 1 class

Bldr: Textron, New Orleans, La. (except LCAC 15–23, 34–36, 49–51: Avondale, Gulfport, La.)

LCAC 73—transporting armored vehicles U.S. Navy, 2-06

(*reduced operating status/to be retired in 2007.)

	In serv.		In serv.		In serv.
LCAC 1*	14-12-84	LCAC 32	1-5-91	LCAC 62	31-8-93
LCAC 2	22-2-86	LCAC 33	4-6-91	LCAC 63	30-9-93
LCAC 3*	9-6-86	LCAC 34	31-5-92	LCAC 64	27-10-93
LCAC 4	13-8-86	LCAC 35	31-5-92	LCAC 65	24-11-93
LCAC 5*	26-11-86	LCAC 36	1-5-92	LCAC 66	28-12-93
LCAC 6*	1-12-86	LCAC 37	31-7-91	LCAC 67	25-2-94
LCAC 7	18-3-87	LCAC 38	6-9-91	LCAC 68	25-3-94
LCAC 8	3-6-87	LCAC 39	30-9-91	LCAC 69	29-4-94
LCAC 9	26-6-87	LCAC 40	6-11-91	LCAC 70	5-6-94
LCAC 10	4-9-87	LCAC 41	27-11-91	LCAC 71	21-6-94
LCAC 11*	7-12-87	LCAC 42	12-12-91	LCAC 72	31-7-94
LCAC 12*	23-12-87	LCAC 43	21-2-92	LCAC 73	30-9-94
LCAC 13*	30-9-88	LCAC 44	28-2-92	LCAC 74	10-11-94
LCAC 14	3-11-88	LCAC 45	26-3-92	LCAC 75	6-1-95
LCAC 15	20-9-88	LCAC 46	8-5-92	LCAC 76	14-2-95
LCAC 16	4-11-88	LCAC 47	24-6-92	LCAC 77	29-3-95
LCAC 17	1989	LCAC 48	17-7-92	LCAC 78	23-5-95
LCAC 18*	1989	LCAC 49	16-10-92	LCAC 79	20-7-95
LCAC 19	5-90	LCAC 50	2-93	LCAC 80	23-8-95
LCAC 20	1990	LCAC 51	6-93	LCAC 81	25-10-95
LCAC 21	1990	LCAC 52	2-9-92	LCAC 82	13-12-95
LCAC 22*	11-90	LCAC 53	10-7-92	LCAC 83	29-2-96
LCAC 23	15-6-91	LCAC 54	30-10-92	LCAC 84	25-4-96
LCAC 24	1-3-90	LCAC 55	30-11-92	LCAC 85	25-7-96
LCAC 25	29-6-90	LCAC 56	8-1-93	LCAC 86	26-9-96
LCAC 26	7-90	LCAC 57	26-2-93	LCAC 87	20-11-96
LCAC 27	24-8-90	LCAC 58	31-3-93	LCAC 88	19-2-97
LCAC 28	12-10-90	LCAC 59	30-4-93	LCAC 89	15-4-97
LCAC 29	18-12-90	LCAC 60	4-6-93	LCAC 90	24-10-97
LCAC 30	19-12-90	LCAC 61	30-7-93	LCAC 91	27-3-00
LCAC 31	27-2-91				

LCAC 4 U.S. Navy, 2-06

LCAC—assigned to *Bonhomme Richard* (LHD 6) U.S. Navy, 7-06

D: 87.9–93.4 tons light (166.6 fl; 181.6 overload) **S:** 54 kts (40 when loaded)
Dim: 26.80 (24.69 hull) × 14.33 (13.31 hull) × 0.78 (at rest, loaded)
A: None
Electronics: Radar: 1/Canadian Marconi CMR-91 Seemaster nav.
M: 4 Avco TF40B gas turbines (3,955 shp each; 2 for lift); 2 3.58-m-dia. shrouded airscrews/4 centrifugal, 1.60-m-dia.lift fans; 7,910 shp sust. for propulsion; Mk II variants: see modernization remarks below
Electric: 120 kw tot. (2 × 60-kw Turbomach T-62 gas turbine APU)
Range: 223/48 (light); 200/40 (loaded) **Fuel:** 6.2 tons (7,132 gallons)
Crew: 5 tot. + 24 troops (+ 180 troops or 54 medical litters in personnel module, when fitted)

UTILITY LANDING CRAFT, SURFACE-EFFECT [LCUA]
(continued)

Remarks: Authorized: three in FY 82, three in FY 83, six in FY 84, nine in FY 85, 12 in FY 86, 15 in FY 89, 12 in FY 90, 24 in FY 91, and 12 in FY 92 (of which not all were ordered). Original program was for 108. First unit launched 2-5-84. First 12 ordered from Bell-Halter, numbers 13, 14 ordered 10-85 from Lockheed, with orders for seven other FY 85 units delayed; Avondale bought Lockheed facility and contracts 1-88. On 23-6-92 Avondale was given a contract to produce spare LCAC structures, including "several" complete hull modules, for delivery 1993–94.

LCAC 91 was delivered more than three years late after her use as a prototype for the LCAC SLEP (Service-Life Extension Program). Although the craft were originally said to be intended to last 30 years, they have proven vulnerable to corrosion, and retirements would have been necessitated beginning no later than 2004; thus, a major life-extension program commenced under the FY 01 budget ($15.6 million provided by Congress) with LCAC 25; two more were to follow under FY 02, three under FY 03, four each under FY 04 and FY 05, and six each under FY 06 and FY 07—a rate that will ultimately not sustain retaining the entire inventory goal, which has been reduced to 74 active, with the others maintained in ready reserve. The first three units are to be modernized under a $35-million contract signed on 27-4-01 and the next five (with option for four more) under a $61-million contract signed 10-1-03; in all, 73 units will be modernized.

All 35 Atlantic Fleet units are assigned to Amphibious Craft Unit 4 (ACU 4), Little Creek, Virginia; Pacific Fleet units are assigned to ACU 5, Coronado, California. LCAC 18, 77, and 91 are assigned to the Naval Surface Warfare Center in Florida. LCAC 1, 3, 5–6, 11–13, 18, and 22 are to be retired in FY 07.

Hull systems: Cargo capacity: 60 tons normal/75 overload. Bow ramp is 8.8 m wide, stern ramp 4.6 m. The deck has 168-m^2 parking area and is 204 m long by 8.3 m wide. Are difficult to tow if broken-down. Operator, engineer, navigator, and nine troops travel in starboard side compartment, while deck hand, assistant engineer, loadmaster, and 16 troops travel in port compartments. Navigational equipment includes GPS receiver. Can achieve about 50 kts when loaded and are able to maintain 30 kts loaded in a Sea State 3. The airscrew propellers provide 80% of the thrust and the two swiveling bow ducts the remainder. Can be stopped from full speed in about 460 m. Turning radius at speed is a very unhandy 1,830 m. Can be operated in temperatures from –30° Fahrenheit to +100° Fahrenheit, making them unsuitable for hot desert climates. Can beach on slopes up to 5 deg. and can clear a 1.2-m obstacle. LCAC 91 has Vericor ETF40B gas turbines of 4,745 shp each.

The first four of nine modular Personnel Transport Modules (PTM) acquired 1994–95 were deployed to the Mediterranean in early 1996 for use with LCACs temporarily redesignated MCAC (Multimission Craft, Air Cushion). The PTM can accommodate 145 fully-equipped troops (and 684 ft^3 of stores) or 54 hospital litters plus medical personnel; 180 persons can be accommodated for evacuation duties. The 6,087-kg PTM can be assembled from pieces weighing 75 kg or less by 12 persons in four hours and has integral ventilation, lighting, and communications systems. Disassembled, the PTM fits in a standard 20-ft. cargo container.

Combat systems: Sixteen M58 modular lane-sweeping mine-countermeasures deployment packages (at $40 million each) have been acquired for these craft, permitting them to employ the same towed mine-countermeasures sleds that are used by MH-53E helicopters; the first three were delivered summer 1993. LCAC 66 was used in trials during 1996 with a 30-mm GAU-13 gatling gun in a GPU-5 pod to provide an organic shore fire-suppression capability; if adopted, the LCACs could accommodate two modular installations with a total of four 30-mm gatling guns, 5-inch rocket pods, and Hellfire missiles, while another module could be installed facing aft to cover withdrawal. The radar on these craft is the current version of the Canadian Marconi LN-66.

Modernization: Textron Marine and Land Service is modernizing LCACs with more powerful Vericor ETF40B engines of 4,745 shp each; a new fuel system; new lightweight, longer-wearing skirts, deletion of the keel air bag and its replacement with a "buoyancy box"; upgraded communication and navigation systems; improved data displays; and structural reinforcements. LCAC 2, 4, 7–10, 21 and 25 had been modernized by 6-06. Units that have undergone the Service Life Extension Program are referred to as "LCAC Mk. II." The program is planned to end in 2017 with 73 total updated. The modifications are planned to increase the service life of the craft to 30 years.

UTILITY LANDING CRAFT [LCU]

Note: All utility landing craft (and the remaining LCM(8) LCMs) are administratively assigned either to Assault Craft Unit 1 (ACU-1) and ACU-3 at Coronado, California, or ACU-2 at Little Creek, Virginia, for assignment to larger landing ships as needed.

♦ 35 LCU 1610 class (SCB 149, 149B, and 406 types)

Bldrs: See Remarks (In serv. 6-59 to 12-71, except LCU 1680: 11-10-87, and LCU 1681: 12-11-87)

LCU 1616	LCU 1629–1635	LCU 1653–1666
LCU 1617	LCU 1643–1646	LCU 1680 (135CU8501)
LCU 1619	LCU 1648–1651	LCU 1681 (135CU8502)
LCU 1627		

LCU 1663—loaded with troops — U.S. Navy, 10-05

LCU 1630 — U.S. Navy, 9-05

LCU 1658 — U.S. Navy, 4-06

D: 170 tons (437 fl) (LCU 1680, 1681: 404 tons fl) **S:** 11 kts
Dim: 41.07 × 9.07 × 2.08 **A:** 2/12.7-mm M2 mg
Electronics: Radar: 1 Furuno . . . nav.
M: 4 G.M. 6-71 diesels; 2 Kort-nozzle props; 1,200 bhp (LCU 1680, 1681: 2 G.M. 12V71 TI diesels; 2 Kort-nozzle props; 1,700 bhp)
Range: 1,200/11 **Fuel:** 13 tons
Crew: 10 enlisted (1680, 1681: 2 officers, 12 enlisted)

Remarks: LCU 1616–1619, LCU 1623, LCU 1624 delivered 6-59 to 9-60 by Gunderson Bros., Portland, Ore.; LCU 1621, 1626, 1629, and 1630 delivered 6-60 to 1968 by Southern Shipbuilding, Slidell, La.; LCU 1627, 1628, 1631–1635 built by General Ship & Eng. Wks., East Boston, Mass.; LCU 1643–1645 delivered 8-67 to 1969 by Marinette Marine, Marinette, Wisc.; LCU 1646–1666 delivered 1969–70 by Defoe SB, Bay City, Wisc.; LCU 1667–1670 built by General Ship & Eng. Wks.; LCU 1680, 1681 ordered 10-85 from Moss Point Marine, Escatawpa, Miss., for delivery 9-86 to Naval Reserve Force units; both were laid down 2-4-86, but not delivered until late 1987. Atlantic Fleet units are assigned to Amphibious Craft Unit 2 (ACU 2), Little Creek, Virginia; Pacific Fleet units are assigned to ACU 1 and ACU 3, Coronado, California, except for LCU 1665, assigned to Fleet Activities, Sasebo, Japan, and LCU 1680 and LCU 1681, assigned to Naval Reserve Force training. LCU 1641 acts as an exercise minelayer with a single mine rail over the stern, enlarged pilothouse, and a derrick to port. LCU 1647 is a workboat assigned to the Naval Air Warfare Center, Aircraft Division, from Fort Lauderdale, Florida, and is described on a later page.

Twelve of these extremely useful craft were rehabilitated, beginning with two under FY 87; the others were to have been discarded by the mid-1990s but remain in service. Three others (LCU 1621, 1623, 1628) were converted to ASDV (Auxiliary Swimmer Delivery Vehicle) carriers.

Hull systems: Cargo capacity is 180 tons; cargo space, 36.9 × 7.62 max. (4.5-m-wide bow ramp). Usually unarmed. Up to 400 troops can be accommodated for short periods on deck. Drive-through feature permits marrying bow and stern to other landing craft or causeways. Minor differences as construction progressed. Have kedging anchor starboard side aft to assist in extraction from beaches.

Disposals: LCU 1614 was stricken during 2001. LCU 1613, formerly used as a workboat at Port Hueneme, California, was stricken and sold 1-93. LCU 1652 was scrapped at San Diego in 3-98 through mid-4-98 after grounding on San Clemente Island early in 2-98. Other missing numbers have either been redesignated as yard craft (YFU—see later pages) or transferred to the U.S. Army (LCU 1667–1679). LCU 1624, LCU 1641, and ex-U.S. Army LCU 1466–class unit LCU 1590 were no longer in service as of 2006.

Note: The program to construct 35 new LCUs was cancelled by 2006.

MINOR LANDING CRAFT

Note: Since 2001 there has been a marked increase in the number and types of patrol, boarding, and security craft in naval service. Included in service are the craft listed below, as well as scores of additional small vesssels, jet skis, and RIBs.

MINOR LANDING CRAFT *(continued)*

♦ 54 LCM(8) Mk 2–, 4–, 5– and Mk 6–class aluminum or steel-hulled [LCM]

Bldr: Higgins Industries, New Orleans, La. (In serv. 1953–55; 1985–88; 1991–92)

LCM(8)—from Assault Craft Unit 2 U.S. Navy, 8-05

D: 34 tons light (121 fl) **S:** 9 kts **Dim:** 22.43 × 6.43 × 1.35 fwd./1.47 aft
M: 4 G.M. Detroit Diesel 6-71N or 2 12V-71 diesels; 2 props; 1,080 bhp
Range: 190/9 (loaded) **Crew:** 4–5 tot. enlisted

Remarks: Data listed above are for Mk 2 and Mk 5 classes. Cargo: 60 tons or 150 troops for short distances in 12.8 × 4.3-m open well with 54.6-m^2 space. Some have two G.M. 12V71 diesels. All LCVP Mk 7 class units were retired from service by 2006.

♦ 46 LCPL FY 92, Mk 11, Mk 12, and Mk 13 class [LCP]

Bldrs: Peterson Builders, Sturgeon Bay, Wisc; Watercraft America, Edgewater, Fla.; and Bollinger Boat, Lockport, La. (In serv. 1981–91)

LCPL FY 92 class U.S. Navy, 3-06

LCPL Mk 12–class 36PL8032 George R. Schneider, 10-00

D: 9.8 tons light (13 fl) **S:** 19 kts **Dim:** 10.95 × 3.97 × 1.13
Electronics: Radar: 1/SPS-59 nav. **M:** 1 G.M. 8V71T diesel; 1 prop; 425 bhp
Range: 150/19 **Fuel:** 630 liters **Crew:** 3 tot. + 17 passengers

Remarks: FY 92 units were ordered 26-10-92, have an open cockpit forward rather than the deck found on earlier LCPLs, and are single-skin GRP and vinylester plastic construction . Have 24-V d.c. electrical power. Some units are used as control craft or to carry Explosive Ordnance Disposal swimmers, and can be fitted with a 12.7-mm mg for patrol duties.

♦ 1 steel-hulled LCPL Mk 4 class [LCP]

Remarks: Data similar to LCPLs above. Assigned to a shore facility.

♦ 5 (+ 24) Improved Navy Lighterage System

Bldr: Marinette Marine Corp, Marinette Wisc. (In serv. 2004–5)

D: . . . tons **S:** . . . kts. **Dim:** 24.4 × 7.3 × . . . **M:** 1 . . . waterjet

Improved Navy Lighterage System U.S. Navy, 9-05

Improved Navy Lighterage System—fully deployed during testing U.S. Navy, 9-05

Remarks: Twenty-three unpowered and six powered cargo modules were ordered from Marinette Marine during 2003 to be used to offload vehicles and cargo containers from ships at anchor. The system assembles to form ferries, causeway piers, or ramp roll-off discharge platforms providing delivery of vehicles and critical supplies from ship to shore. Delivery to complete by 2010; expected to serve in Amphibious Construction Battalions and all Maritime Prepositioning Force squadrons.

Disposal notes: All warping tugs were retired from Navy service by 2006.

♦ 20 Mk V Pegasus–class Special Operations Craft [LCW]

Bldr: Trinity-Equitable SY, New Orleans, La. (In serv.: first two: 27-8-95; second pair: 1-96; third pair: 8-96; fourth pair in 1999, others . . .)

From among: 25MPB0001, 25MPB0501, 25MPB9501, 25PB0201 through 25PB0212, 25PB0301 through 25PB0332, 25PB00401 through 25PB0403, 25PN9401

Mk V Special Operations Craft U.S. Navy, 2-03

Special Operations Craft MKVSOC964—note stern ramp Peter Voss, 5-01

MINOR LANDING CRAFT *(continued)*

D: 57 tons (68 fl) **S:** 50+ kts (30 sust.) **Dim:** 24.99 × 5.33 × 1.32
A: 2–4 twin 12.7-mm M2-HB mg; 2 single 7.62-mm M60 mg; 2 single 40-mm Mk 19 Mod. 3 grenade launchers
Electronics: Radar: 1 Furuno . . . . . . nav.
M: 2 MTU 16V396 TE94 diesels; 2 KaMeWa K50S waterjets; 4,570 bhp
Electric: 50 kw tot. (2 × 25-kw diesel sets) **Range:** 500/50; 550/35
Fuel: . . . tons (2,600 gallons) **Crew:** 5 tot. + 16 special forces personnel

Remarks: Two since-discarded prototypes, to two different designs, were ordered 8-93 from Halter Marine for $4.7 million each, including land/air transportation skids. Initial production of two standard units, with an option for 38 additional, was ordered in 9-94; the $11-million contract included one transportation support suite for each craft. Six near-sisters were built for Sri Lanka in 1996–97. Most are assigned to Special Boat Unit 2 (SBU-2) at Little Creek, Virginia, and to SBU-1 at Coronado, California. At least one (numbered 25MPB9501) is assigned to the Naval Surface Warfare Center, Carderock Division Detachment, Norfolk, Virginia.
Hull systems: Aluminum construction. The craft on its transport trailer (with M916A1Ea prime mover vehicle) fits within an Air Force C-5A Galaxy transport. Each boat can launch and retrieve four inflated rubber raiding craft and can also carry a 500-gallon fuel bladder. The open cockpit can be covered by removable hard canopies. All seating is shock mounted. The hull is designed for minimum radar and heat signature. Hull molded depth is 2.36 m. Can tow two 9.14-m rigid inflatable raider boats at 50 kts and can operate in Sea State 3 at 35 kts. A 220 gallon/day potable water generator is fitted.
Combat systems: Communications equipment includes two SATCOM receivers. Have APX-100(V) IFF transponder. Navigation suite includes Magnavox MX200 NAVSAT receiver, GPS receiver, Raytheon echo-sounder, and a chart plotter. Have five weapons mounting positions, each suitable for 40-mm grenade launchers, twin 12.7-mm mg, or 7.62-mm mg. Can also carry Stinger SAMs.

♦ 32 Stinger-class riverine assault craft [LCW]
Bldr: first 14: SeaArk Marine, Monticello, Ark. (In serv.: 7 in 31-7-90, 7 in 1991); others: Swiftships, Inc., Morgan City, La. (In serv. 1994)

Stinger class SeaArk Marine, 1990

D: 7.48 tons (fl) **S:** 38 kts (34.6 sust.) **Dim:** 10.64 × 2.82 × 0.66 (loaded)
A: 2 single 12.7-mm M2 mg; 2 single 7.62-mm M60 mg (see Remarks)
Electronics: Radar: 1 Raytheon SPS-69 Pathfinder nav.
M: 2 Cummins BTA5.9M2 diesels; 1 Hamilton 271 waterjet; 600 bhp
Range: . . . / . . . **Fuel:** 567 liters **Crew:** 4 tot. + 10 troops

Remarks: First seven ordered 5-5-90 as replacements for PBR-type riverine patrol craft for use by Special Boat Units; a second "company" of seven was in service by 6-92. Second contract under FY 92 to Swiftships for 10, followed by an order for eight under FY 93. All are based at Camp Lejeune, North Carolina. Aluminum construction with 3/16-in. plating. Have weapons positions fore and aft that are convertible for twin or single 12.7-mm mg or single Mk 19 40-mm grenade launcher. Can be carried by a C-130 Hercules aircraft.

Note: Plans call for procuring 30 to 40 Special Operations Craft, Riverine (SOC-R) craft to replace the Mini-ATC, Sea Spectre Mk IV, 20 Light Counter Drug Patrol Boats (Boston Whalers), and the five PBRs assigned to SEAL Special Boat Squadrons. The craft were to have a range of 170 n.m. The four Mk 64 Mod. 4 multipurpose weapons mounts would accommodate Mk 19 40-mm grenade launchers, 12.7-mm mg, or 7.62-mm M60 mg, and an additional M60 would be mountable at the bow. Stinger surface-to-air missiles are to be carried. The craft are to accommodate four CRRC (Combat Rubber Raiding Craft), launched or retrieved via a stern ramp while under way. Procurement was to begin under FY 98, but no contracts have been announced to date.

♦ 72 Navy Special Warfare RIB raiding craft [LCW]
Bldr: United States Marine, New Orleans, La. (In serv. 15-11-97 to 2001)

11MRIBAAOO-1 through 11MRIBAAOO-72

D: 8.24 tons (fl) **S:** 45+ kts (33 kts sust.) **Dim:** 10.97 × 3.20 × 0.91 max.
A: 1 or 2 single 12.7-mm mg; 0 or 1 40-mm Mk 19 Mod. 3 grenade launcher; 1 or 2 single 7.62-mm mg
Electronics: 1 Furuno 841 nav.
M: 2 Puckett-Caterpillar 3126 turbocharged diesels; 2 KaMeWa FF280 waterjets; 940 bhp
Range: 200/33 Fuel: 180 gal. Crew: 3 tot. + 8 special forces personnel

Remarks: Development contract placed 6-96 for prototype new generation of 35-ft. rigid inflatable landing craft for use by SEALs. The three prototypes (since retired) began a 170-day competitive trials period on 25-11-96 at MacDill Air Force Base,

11MRIB-series 36-ft. SEAL raiding craft George R. Schneider, 11-06

Tampa Bay, Florida, with a total of 72 production versions procured under the FY 97–00 budgets. The first two production units were delivered to Special Boat Unit 20, Norfolk, Virginia, on 15-11-97.
Hull systems: Have Kevlar-reinforced vinylester deep-vee hull with rigid-inflatable nylon-reinforced neoprene sponsons. As an alternative to personnel, the craft can carry 1.45 metric tons of cargo. Can carry two outboard motors for Combat Rigid Raiding Craft. Navigation equipment includes a Furuno 1600 echo sounder, PSN-11 GPS receiver, and a Ritchie magnetic compass. Payload is 3,200 lbs (1,451 kg). Are not air-droppable. One spare engine for each two boats was delivered as part of the production package.
Combat systems: Standard armament is a 12.7-mm mg forward and either a 40-mm grenade launcher or a second 12.7-mm mg aft; the 7.62-mm mg are usually also carried.

♦ 18 Interim Rigid Inflatable Boats (IRIB) [LCW]
Bldr: Novamarine and Bollinger Machine Ship & SY, Lockport, La. (In serv. 1992–93)

30RB-series

Novamarine Interim Rigid Inflatable Boat George R. Schneider, 8-96

Bollinger Interim Rigid Inflatable Boat 10MRB9307 George R. Schneider, 6-98

24RX-series rigid inflatable Special Operations Craft George R. Schneider, 6-98

D: . . . tons (fl) **S:** 30+ kts **Dim:** 9.14 × 2.74 × 0.61
A: 1 7.62-mm mg or 40-mm Mk 19 Mod. 3 grenade launcher
Electronics: 1 Furuno 1731 nav.
M: 2 Iveco diesels; 2 Parker waterjets; 600 bhp **Range:** . . . / . . .
Crew: 2 tot. + 8 special forces personnel

MINOR LANDING CRAFT *(continued)*

A small SEAL rubber raiding craft of the type carried aboard the Mk V Pegasus class George R. Schneider, 8-99

Remarks: The 1992 order for 18 9-m rigid inflatable raiding craft with Novamarine was canceled when the contractor went bankrupt; a replacement contract with Bollinger Machine Ship and Shipyard in 2-93 produced a prototype that had too little freeboard, and the program was canceled after 16 were built. Have fiberglass gel-coated hulls with Hypalon-coated nylon inflated sponsons and are air-droppable. Can operate in Sea State 4 and survive in Sea State 5. Are equipped with a Ritchie magnetic compass and PSN-11 GPS receiver.

Note: At present, the SEALs employ some 50+ 24-ft. RIBs (in two different models, each capable of transporting four special forces personnel) and 18 10-m RIBs in addition to the classes described previously. In 1-98 Zodiac North America, Stevensville, Maryland, won a contract to supply a large number of its F 470 Rigid Inflatable Boats in part for Special Forces work; the craft are 4.57 m long and are powered by two 35-bhp or one 55-bhp Johnson MARS ASML35D submersible gasoline outboard.

♦ 100 (+ up to 100) Small Unit Riverine Craft (SURC) Program [LCW]
Bldr: Raytheon Naval and Maritime Integrated Systems, Polsboro, Wash. (see Remarks)

D: . . . tons **S:** 30–35 kts loaded **Dim:** 19.97 × 3.86 (over foam collar) × 0.61
A: 1 or 2 12.7-mm and/or 7.62-mm mg
M: 2 Yanmar . . . diesels; 2 Hamilton 292 waterjets; 880 bhp
Crew: 2 + 18 Marines

Remarks: Program begun 1-01 as a replacement for the Marine Rigid Raider Craft and ordered during 5-02. To be capable of lift by a CH-53D helicopter and carriage on its trailer within a C-130 transport (with the foam inflatable collar removed). Will be beachable and will have GPS and Combat Net SATCOM equipment. Construction contract for up to 100 was awarded on 24-7-02, with Safe Boats International, Port Orchard, Washington, providing the boats and Boat Master, Fort Myers, Florida, supplying the trailers. The craft are to be maintained at Camp Lejeune, North Carolina.

♦ 122 Marine Rigid Raider craft [LCW]
Bldr: Boston Whaler, Inc., Rockland, Mass. (In serv. 1988)

Marine Rigid Raider class U.S. DoD, 1998

D: 1.2 tons (fl) **S:** 35 kts **Dim:** 6.81 × 2.26 × 0.46 **A:** 1 7.62-mm mg
M: 2 outboard motors; 140 bhp **Range:** 136/32 **Fuel:** 212 liters
Crew: 1 coxwain, 9–10 assault troops

Remarks: For U.S. Marine Expeditionary Unit (MEU) use. GRP construction, road transportable on special "combat trailer." Replace older Zodiac rigid inflatable craft. Each MEU has 15.

♦ . . . inflatable Combat Rubber Reconnaissance Craft (CRRC) [LCW]
Bldr: . . . (In serv. 1990s)

D: 120 kg empty **S:** . . . kts **Dim:** 4.70 × 1.90 × . . .
M: 2 I-MARS Kort-nozzle gasoline outboards; 70 bhp

Remarks: As of 1-95 407 served the active Marine Corps and another 27 were used by reservists. Intended for riverine, raiding, and reconnaissance duties. I-MARS stands for Improved Military Amphibious Reconnaissance System, and the engines are specially shielded to reduce noise and heat signatures. Cost $10,700 each.

Disposal notes: The remaining three High Speed Boats (HSB) were stricken in 2001 and made available for sale.

♦ 5 PBR (Patrol Boat, Riverine) Mk-II [LCW]
Bldr: Uniflite, Bellingham, Wash. (In serv. 12-81 to 8-83)

D: 8.9 tons (fl) **S:** 24 kts **Dim:** 9.73 × 3.53 × 0.81
A: 1 twin and 1 single 12.7-mm mg; 1 60-mm mortar
Electronics: Radar: 1 Raytheon 1900 Pathfinder (SPS-66) nav.
M: 2 G.M. 6V53N diesels; 2 Jacuzzi water jets; 420 bhp
Range: 150/23 **Crew:** 4 tot.

Remarks: Glass-reinforced plastic hull, plastic armor. Used for Naval Reserve training by Special Boat Unit 22. Three others are museum displays.

Disposal note: Auxiliary Swimmer Delivery Vehicle Carriers *ASDV 1, ASDV 2* and *ASDV 3* were retired between 2003–2006.

SWIMMER DELIVERY VEHICLES [LSDV]

♦ 1 prototype Surface-Planing Wet Submersible (SPWS)
Bldr: Stidd Systems, . . . (In serv. 2002)

D: . . . **S:** 30+ kts surf./6 kts sub. **Dim:** . . . × . . . × . . . **M:** . . .
Range: 165/30 surf.; 18/6 sub. **Crew:** 6 tot.

Remarks: Intended to perform maritime interdiction missions, carrying a six-man SEAL team. Hull planes when surfaced and employs electric propulsion when submerged. The single technology demonstrator was funded by the Special Operations Command.

Note: A "Future Underwater Fighter" concept for launch and recovery from submarines is in development under Project Loki.

♦ 1 (+ . . .) Advanced SEAL Delivery System (ASDS) class
Bldr: Northrop Grumman Oceanic Systems, Annapolis, Md.
(In serv. 24-8-04 to . . .)

ASDS 1

ASDS—aboard USS *Greenville* (SSN 772) U.S. Navy, 7-03

ASDS—aboard USS *Greenville* (SSN 772) U.S. Navy, 7-03

ASDS 1—running in surface trim U.S. DoD, 2001

SWIMMER DELIVERY VEHICLES [LSDV] *(continued)*

D: 55 tons (surf.)/60 tons (sub.) **S:** 8 kts (sub.) **Dim:** 19.81 × 2.44 × . . .
Electronics: Sonar: . . . HF
M: 14 batteries, 1 electric motor; 1 prop—8 electric thrusters.
Range: 125/8 (sub.) **Crew:** 2 tot. + 8 special forces swimmers

Remarks: The prototype new ASDS (Advanced SEAL Delivery System; formerly the ASDV—Advanced SEAL Delivery Vehicle) was ordered from Westinghouse Electric Oceanic Division (now Northrop Grumman Oceanic Systems, Annapolis, Maryland) on 29-9-94, for $69.8 million; the craft was supposed to have been delivered in 8-97, but by 7-02 the program cost had risen to $292 million; the actual final delivery was four years late. By 2006 the entire program was said to have cost more than $625 million. Follow-on craft are expected to cost $58.8 million in 2001 dollars (up from $30 million in 1994). A second craft was planned to be ordered under the FY 03 budget, but Congress cut most of the required funding. Further units may be ordered. The craft are transportable by C-5 and C-17 transport aircraft and are designed to mate via their underside hatch to SSN 688–class submarines, of which the first, *Greenville* (SSN 772), completed testing with the ASDS in mid-2003. Five other SSN 688s, including *Charlotte* (SSN 766), will be able to carry an ASDV, while *Jimmy Carter* (SSN 23) and the first six *Virginia*-class SSNs also have the capability. The first ASDS 1, delivered for trials in 5-00 and accepted on 24-8-01, is operated by SEAL Delivery Team 1 (SDCT-1), Pearl Harbor. However, due to limited battery capacity and other problems, ASDS 1's initial operating availability date was moved to 2006 and request for additional units have been slipped one year each to 2007 and 2009 at the earliest. The crew consists of a submarine officer as pilot and a SEAL as copilot. Though operational requirements call for six units, cost and technical problems (propulsion and radiated noice) will likely limit the purchase to a maximum of three units.
Hull systems: The 14 batteries are carried in individual external titanium cylinders; the batteries are to be replaced with longer-lasting lithium ion batteries. Ballast tanks are fitted within each end of the pressure hull. Top and bottom access hatches are fitted for the swimmer egress trunk amidships. The retractable electric maneuvering thrusters are mounted in an X-configuration fore and aft. The steel pressure hull for the first ASDS was fabricated by Chicago Bridge and Iron, Kankakee, Illinois, which has since closed its facility; the source for future hulls has not been identified; bow and stern fairings are made of composites. Has an automated life-support system and an integrated control and display system. Two folding masts support communications antennas and a non-hull-penetrating electro-optical periscope.

♦ 10 Mk VIII Mod. 1 Swimmer-Delivery Vehicles [LSDV]

SDV Mk VIII U.S. Navy, 2006

Remarks: Used by Navy SEAL special forces. The 6.70-m-long craft can be accommodated in the Dry Deck Shelters carried by SSNs and can carry four swimmers, as well as mines and other weapons. The swimmers are not carried within a dry pressure hull. Ten of the craft began a life-extension refit program at Panama City, Florida, in 1995 and are being equipped with increased range and speed, improved sonar, and improved instrumentation. Three were transferred to the U.K. during 1999, and another has been retired.

AMPHIBIOUS ASSAULT VEHICLES [LAAV]

♦ 3 (+ 10 + 1,000) Expeditionary Fighting Vehicle (EFV)

Bldr: General Dynamics Land Systems, Woodbridge, Va. (In serv. 2010–17)

Weight: 28,712 kg empty; 34,473 kg max. **S:** 20–25 kts afloat, 45 mph ashore
Dim: 9.3 × 3.7 × 2.9 high in afloat mode/3.3 high tracks to turret top
A: 1 30-mm Bushmaster Mk 44 cannon with coaxial 7.62-mm M240 mg
M: 1 MTU MT883 K-523 diesel; twin tracks in land mode (850 bhp max.) or two waterjets (2,800 bhp max.)
Range: 65/20–25 kts afloat; 325 statute miles/45 mph ashore
Fuel: 324 gal. **Crew:** 3 + 17 troops

Expeditionary Fighting Vehicle (EFV) U.S. Marine Corps, 2-06

Remarks: Formerly known as the Advanced Amphibious Assault Vehicle (AAAV). Initial production began in 2006 with first units expected to be fully operational by 2010—a five-year delay over plans announced in 2000; some 1,013 (down from 1,123) total are planned to be procured (including 78 configured as command vehicles), but the total may be reduced to as few as 330, with refurbished AAV7s to fill the remainder of the requirement. General Dynamics design won a contract during 6-96 for three prototypes (one in command configuration) for $200 million. Ten preproduction vehicles were ordered 7-01. An EFV-C command variant is also planned for service entry in 2008. The EFV-C will carry a crew of three plus seven command staff and associated workstations. Dimensions are 9.3 m (10.6 m in water mode) × 3.7 m (3.3 m water mode) × 3.7 m (4.4 water mode).
Hull systems: Afloat, the tracks retract and are covered by plating, while a bow flap is extended and the waterjets are deployed. Can carry 4,150 kg cargo in lieu of troops. Have armor protection against 14-mm mg projectiles and fragments from 155-mm artillery. Full climate control and NBC protection provided. Hull has 27% reserve buoyancy and can recover from a 100-deg. roll. The prototype achieved 37 kts on trials in light condition.
Combat systems: Will carry 215 ready service rounds 30-mm, 600 ready service rounds 7.62-mm ammunition. Gun is fully stabalized allowing for "shoot on the move" operation. Carry thermal sights for night and reduced visabily. The EFV-C command variant will not carry the 30-mm cannon and will have 200 rounds of ready/1200 rounds stowed 7.62 ammunition.

Note: The Marine Corps has 1,311 AAV7-series armored tracked vehicles available for amphibious assault; most are personnel transport (AAVP7A1) variants, though command (AAVC7A1), and recovery (AAVR7A1) variants are also in service. Between 1997 and 2004 680 vehicles (599 AAVP71, 46 AAVC7A1, and 35 AAVR7A1) were updated under the Reliability, Availability, Maintainability Rebuild-to-Standard (RAMS/RS) program. By 10-06 an additional 327 vehicles had received the upgrade, which included a new Cummins VT 903 525-hp engine and modified suspension from the Army's Bradley Fighting Vehicle. The AAVC7 variant is armed with a 12.7-mm mg and Mk 19 40-mm grenade launcher; AAVC7 and AAVR7s are fitted with a 7.62-mm mg. The "AAV7"-series vehicles were first built during the 1980s.

AAVP7A1 U.S. Navy, 6-05

AUXILIARY SHIPS

Note: The Auxiliary section includes regular Navy-subordinated (active and reserve) ships; Navy-chartered ships; research ships operated by private and public research facilities that were built with Navy funding; and ships operated by or long-term chartered by the Military Sealift Command (MSC). MSC-subordinated units, both chartered and Navy "owned," usually have hull numbers prefixed by "T-". The four-digit hull numbers given in parentheses for some ships have been assigned by MSC for administrative purposes and are not true U.S. Navy hull numbers; some long-term chartered units do not have any number assigned at all.

MSC also charters ships for single-voyage deliveries as well as managing the shipment of all military cargo by sea by means of contracts with established U.S.-flag shipping lines. MSC-chartered harbor tugs are listed in the Service Craft section. As of 2006 the Military Sealift Command had 11,177 personnel assigned including 2,173 ashore (195 active duty, 277 reserve, 984 civilians, and 717 contract employees) and 9,576 afloat (399 active duty, 295 reserve, 4,748 civil mariners, and 4,134 contract mariners).

The MSC chartered two AS.330J Puma helicopters and their crews for Mediterranean service from Geo-Seis Helicopters, Fort Collins, Colo. During 2003 the two-aircraft detachment deployed aboard USNS *Spica* and USNS *Saturn*. MSC-subordinated

AUXILIARY SHIPS *(continued)*

military cargo and vehicle prepositioning ships are organized into three Maritime Prepositioning Squadrons (MPS) and one Afloat Prepositioning Squadron (APS): MPS-1, based in the Mediterranean; MPS-2 based at Diego Garcia; MPS-3, based near Saipan while Afloat Prepositioning Squadron 4 (APS-4) works in support of Army prepositioned needs. Maritime Administration (MARAD) Ready Reserve Force (RRF) ships activated for service with prepositioning squadrons remain listed in the Ready Reserve Force section; when they are activated, however, they are administered by MSC rather than MARAD.

♦ 2 (+ 5 + 7) Lewis and Clark–class Dry Cargo/Ammunition Ship [AE]

Bldr: General Dynamics National Steel and Shipbuilding Co. (NASSCO), San Diego, Calif.

	Laid down	L	In serv.
T-AKE 1 Lewis and Clark	22-4-04	21-5-05	20-6-06
T-AKE 2 Sacagawea	7-6-05	24-6-06	2-2-07
T-AKE 3 Alan Shepard	30-1-06	6-12-06	6-07
T-AKE 4 Richard E. Byrd	10-7-06	. . .	10-07
T-AKE 5 Robert E. Peary	30-11-06	. . .	3-08
T-AKE 6 . . .	2007	. . .	8-08
T-AKE 7 . . .	2007	. . .	1-09
T-AKE 8 . . .	2008	. . .	6-09
T-AKE 9 . . .	2008	. . .	10-09
T-AKE 10 . . .	. . .	. . .	2010
T-AKE 11 . . .	. . .	. . .	2012

Lewis and Clark (T-AKE 1) George R. Schneider, 5-06

Lewis and Clark (T-AKE 1) George R. Schneider, 5-06

Sacagawea (T-AKE 2)—under construction at NASSCO George R. Schneider, 3-06

D: 23,852 tons light (40,298 fl) **S:** 20 kts (sust.)
Dim: 210.00 (200.47 pp) × 32.20 × 9.12
A: Provision for one 20-mm Mk 15 Block 1 Phalanx CIWS
Electronics:
Radar: . . .
EW: SLQ-25A(V) Nixie towed torpedo decoy syst.
M: 4 FM/MAN B&W 9L and 8L 48/60 diesels and bow thruster; 1 prop; . . . hp
Electric: 35.7 MW total **Range:** 14,000/20 **Fuel:** 25,000 bbl
Crew: 172 Naval and Civil Service mariners (accomm. for 197 tot.)

Remarks: The Auxiliary Dry Cargo Ship (ACD[X])–class program, first programmed in 1992, was dropped from the FY 95 budget but reinstated in the FY 96 budget; again deleted from the FY 98–03 shipbuilding program in favor of since-canceled life-extension overhauls to Military Sealift Command *Kilauea* (T-AE 26) ammunition ships and *Mars* (T-AFS 1) stores ships, the program was once again revived in the FY 99 budget, and the first was funded under FY 00.

The $406.9-million contract for T-AKE 1 was let on 18-10-01, and T-AKE 2 was simultaneously ordered for $301.6 million; T-AKE 3 (said to cost about $290 million) through T-AKE 10 were funded between 2001 and 2007 with T-AKE 11 through T-AKE 14 to be funded between 2008 and 2011.

The names for the first two were announced 27-10-00, with the class name category stated to be "Explorers." T-AKE 3 was named on 20-1-06. The cargo capacity is rather small for ships of this size and type, which are intended to obtain their cargo fuels from T-AOs in rear areas and then to convey it to ships in a combat zone.

Hull systems: Cargo: 6,675 metric tons (21,181 m^3) dry cargo, 1,716 tons (5,543 m^3) frozen and refrigerated provisions, 3,242 metric tons (23,450 bbl) cargo fuel, and 200 metric tons (52,800 gal) potable water. Will use current underway replenishment systems but will have improved prestaging and inventory management, incorporating some 12,788 m^2 of cargo prestaging space. Replenishment stations will include three stores transfer to port and two to starboard, with a sliding padeye receiving station to starboard; will be able to refuel other ships from one station on each beam and to receive fuel to starboard. Two cargo holds will carry dry stores and munitions, one will carry frozen, chilled, and dry stores, and three specialty cargo and spares holds will be incorporated, as will specialty cargo spaces on the 01 level. There will be three cargo holds; there will be four 4-ton cargo elevators. Four 5-ton cranes will be fitted for cargo loading and unloading alongside a pier or at anchor. Five cargo fuel and two potable water tanks will be incorporated. Will employ computerized inventory, cargo tracking, and planning aids, fiber optics for lighting and interior communications systems, and automation to reduce crew requirement. Hangar space for two MH-60 helicopters is provided.

♦ 5 Kilauea-class ammunition ships [AE] (1 in *reserve*)

Bldrs: T-AE 26: Gen. Dynamics, Quincy, Mass.; others: Northrop Grumman Ship Systems, Ingalls Div., Pascagoula, Miss. (*Atlantic/†Pacific)

	Laid down	L	In serv.
T-AE 26 *Kilauea*	10-3-66	9-8-67	10-8-68
T-AE 32 Flint†	4-8-69	9-11-70	20-11-71
T-AE 33 Shasta†	10-11-69	3-4-71	26-2-72
T-AE 34 Mount Baker*	10-5-70	23-10-71	22-7-72
T-AE 35 Kiska†	4-8-71	11-3-72	16-12-72

Shasta (T-AE 33) Frank Findler, 10-03

Flint (T-AE 32) U.S. Navy, 5-05

D: 10,073 to 10,524 tons light (18,444 to 20,068 fl) T-AE 26: 11,915 tons light (20,169 fl)
S: 20 kts **Dim:** 171.90 (164.59 pp) × 24.69 × 8.50 **A:** Removed
Electronics:
Radar: 1 . . . nav.; 1 Raytheon SPS-10-series surf. search
TACAN: URN-25
M: 3 sets G.E. geared steam turbines; 1 prop; 36,661 shp

AUXILIARY SHIPS *(continued)*

Boilers: 3 Foster-Wheeler; 42.3 kg/cm2, 467° C **Electric:** 3,000 kw tot.
Fuel: 2,612 tons **Crew:** 125 MSC Civil Service mariners + 17 Navy

Remarks: 18,257grt/8,593 dwt. T-AE 26 transferred to MSC 1-10-80, T-AE 32 on 4-8-95, T-AE 35 on 1-8-96, T-AE 34 on 18-12-96, and T-AE 33 on 1-8-97. The U.S. Navy personnel aboard the active units perform ammunition handling and operate the communications systems and helicopters. T-AE 26 was placed in 45-day recall reserve on 12-3-01 and is stored at Port Hueneme, California, with a small caretaker crew.

T-AE 34 completed modifications to MSC standards on 29-4-98 and T-AE 35 on 12-10-98. T-AE 33 was towed from San Diego 20-1-99 for conversion to MSC accommodations standard at Norfolk, Virginia, by Norfolk SB & DD Co. T-AE 33 was in collision with *Guadalupe* (T-AO 200) on 26-2-01, off Pt. Loma, California. *Kilauea* (T-AE 26) was placed in Reduced Operating Status on 12-21-03. To be replaced by the Lewis and Clark class.

Hull systems: Can carry about 6,000 tons of munitions and 2,500 tons cargo fuel. Have a hangar and flight deck for two UH-46D replenishment helicopters. Seven underway replenishment stations are fitted, four to port and three to starboard. Can refuel ships alongside, using the forward, starboard station. Superstructure filled in on starboard side on T-AE 26 to increase accommodations space. The other active units have had only minor alterations to improve accommodations for their civilian crews.

Disposals: *Mount Hood* (TAE 29) was to transfer to MSC on 3-8-98 but was instead decommissioned and stricken on 13-8-99 and transferred to other Maritime Administration on 17-8-99. *Butte* (T-AE 27) was stricken for disposal on 24-5-04, as was *Santa Barbara* (T-AE 28) on 3-8-05.

Flint (T-AE 32) U.S. Navy, 1-05

♦ 2 ex-U.K. Lyness-class combat stores ships [AF]

Bldrs: Swan Hunter & Wigham Richardson, Wallsend-on-Tyne, U.K. (*Atlantic Fleet)

	Laid down	L	In serv.
T-AFS 9 Spica (ex-*Tarbatness*)*	4-66	22-2-67	10-8-67
T-AFS 10 Saturn (ex-*Stromness*)*	10-65	16-9-66	21-3-67

Spica (T-AFS 9) U.S. Navy, 10-04

Saturn (T-AFS 10) U.S. Navy, 8-04

D: 10,205 tons light (16,680 fl) **S:** 19 kts **Dim:** 159.52 (149.35 pp) × 22.0 × 7.92
A: None
Air group: 2 MH-60 or chartered AS.330J Puma helicopters
Electronics:
Radar: 2 . . . nav.
TACAN: URN-25
M: 1 Sulzer 8RD76 diesel; 1 prop; 12,700 bhp
Electric: 3,575 kw tot. (5 × 715-kw diesel alternator sets)
Range: 11,000/19; 27,500/12
Fuel: 1,310 tons heavy oil, 264 tons diesel
Crew: 103 MSC Civil Service mariners + Navy: 44 tot. + 30 Navy helo detachment

Remarks: 12,358 grt/4,744 nrt. T-AFS 9 was leased on 30-9-81 and purchased on 30-9-82. T-AFS 10 was purchased on 13-12-83. T-AFS 10 was modernized under FY 85 with improved helicopter facilities, improved communications, five STREAM transfer stations, an automated data facility, and conversion to use U.S. Navy fuel. T-AFS 9 completed a similar upgrading by 1986. Both are considered very successful, comfortable ships. T-AFS 9 was transferred to Atlantic operations on 13-5-01.

Hull systems: Can support 15,000 personnel at sea for one month. Total cargo volume: 12,234 m^3 (8,313 m^3 dry stores, 3,921 m^3 refrigerated/frozen); this equates to some 3,665 metric tons of cargo, including 2,363 tons of provisions and upward of 40,000 different fleet spare parts items, and an additional 490 tons can be carried on the flight deck and other topside spaces. Have four holds, with 15 levels, 8 stores elevators. Cranes: 1 × 25-ton, 2 × 12.5-ton, 1 × 12-ton, and 2 × 5-ton. The helicopter deck aft is 33.5 × 18.3 m; they carry two MH-60 or chartered Puma helicopter cargo helicopters. Diesel generators were replaced, the cargo-handling and stowage arrangements upgraded, and an underway refueling station added forward, to port, in all three during 1990s refits.

Disposals: Sister *Sirius* (T-AFS 8) was retired on 1-7-05, transferred to the Texas Maritime Academy and renamed *Texas Clipper* III.

♦ 3 Mars-class combat stores ships [AF]

Bldr: General Dynamics National Steel & SB Co. (NASSCO), San Diego, Calif. (*Atlantic/†Pacific)

	Laid down	L	In serv	To MSC
T-AFS 3 Niagara Falls†	22-5-65	25-3-66	29-4-67	23-9-94
T-AFS 5 Concord†	26-3-66	17-12-66	27-11-68	15-10-92
T-AFS 7 San Jose†	8-3-69	13-12-69	23-10-70	15-10-93

San Jose (T-AFS 7) U.S. Navy, 9-06

Niagara Falls (T-AFS 3) U.S. Navy, 1-05

D: 9,574–9,852 tons light (17,098–17,383 fl) **S:** 20 kts
Dim: 177.08 (161.54 pp) × 24.08 × 7.32 **A:** Removed
Electronics:
Radar: 1 Raytheon . . . S-band nav.; 1 Raytheon . . . X-band nav.
TACAN: URN-25
M: 2 sets de Laval (AFS 6: Westinghouse) geared steam turbines; 1 prop; 22,000 shp
Boilers: 3 Babcock & Wilcox; 40.8 kg/cm2, 440° C **Electric:** 4,800 kw tot.
Range: 10,000/20; 18,000/11
Crew: 136 MSC Civil Service mariners + 26 Navy

Remarks: Are to be replaced by the new T-AKE class. T-AFS 5 was transferred to Pacific operations on 13-5-01.

Hull systems: Cargo: 16,597 m^3 total stores volume. They have four M-shaped cargo kingposts with constant-tension equipment; the equipment can transfer cargo from

AUXILIARY SHIPS *(continued)*

the supply ship to the receiving ship in 90 seconds. The five holds (Nos. 1 and 5 for spare parts, 2 for aviation parts, and 3 and 4 for provisions) have only two hatches. Eleven 5.5-ton cargo elevators link the decks; several others feed into the helicopter area. There are four refrigerated cargo compartments, and three for the storage of dried provisions. One boiler is always kept in reserve. Conversion for MSC service entailed adding five cargo elevators, adding permanent ballast to compensate for some 23 tons of topweight removed, greatly upgrading the accommodations (all civilian officers in one-person staterooms and all marines personnel in two-person staterooms), rehabilitating the propulsion plants, and greatly revising the composition and number of different stores types carried for transfer.
Combat systems: SPS-40 air-search radar, Mk 56 fire-control directors, two twin 76.2-mm gunmounts, two 20-mm Mk 15 CIWS, SLQ-32(V)1 intercept equipment, Mk 36 SRBOC decoy launching system, and SLQ-25 Nixie towed torpedo decoy system were removed prior to transfer to MSC. Have platform and hangar for two helicopters.
Disposals: *Sylvania* (AFS 2) was stricken 5-1-95 and stored in the James River 12-9-00 for transfer to MARAD; sold for scrap 28-7-01. The last *Mars*-class combat stores ship in regular Navy service, *White Plains* (AFS 4), was decommissioned 17-4-95, stricken 24-8-95, and sunk as a target on 4-7-02. *Mars* (T-AFS 1) was stricken on 24-05-04 and sunk as a target during 7-06. *San Diego* (T-AFS 6) was stricken 9-8-03 for scrapping.

♦ 1 chartered special warfare submersible support ship [AG]
Bldr: North American Shipbuilding, Larose, La. (In serv. 1997)

C/Commando

C/Commando—with red-orange hull, cream upperworks Ralph Edwards, 9-01

D: 3,773 tons (fl) **S:** 12 kts **Dim:** 67.05 (61.74 pp) × 17.06 × 4.85
M: 2 Caterpillar 3516 DITA 16-cyl. diesels; 2 CP props; 3,420 bhp—bow-thruster
Electric: 900 kw (3 × 300-kw diesel sets)
Crew: 9 contract crew + 34 Navy personnel

Remarks: 2,053 grt/2,206 dwt. Former offshore tug-supply vessel chartered 19-1-00 and again on 1-8-03 from Edison Chouest Offshore LLC, Galliano, Louisiana, for $55.7 million to serve as the support ship for the Naval Special Warfare Command Advanced SEAL Delivery System submersible (ASDS 1). Based at Pearl Harbor since 3-01. Current charter expires on 31-8-08.

♦ 1 Waters-class special mission ship [AG]
Bldr: Northrop Grumman Avondale (formerly Avondale SY), New Orleans, La.

	Laid down	L	In serv.
T-AGS 45 Waters	21-5-91	6-6-92	26-5-93

Waters (T-AGS 45) George R. Schneider, 4-04

D: 7,320 tons light (12,208 fl) **S:** 13.2 kts (12 kts sust.)
Dim: 138.7 (130.6 wl) × 21.0 × 6.40
Electronics:
Radar: 1 Raytheon X-band ARPA nav.; 1 Raytheon S-band ARPA nav.
Sonar: G.E. Seabeam 853E mapping
M: Electric drive: 5 G.M. EMD 16-cyl. diesels, 5 2,500-kw generators, 2 Westinghouse motors; 2 props; 7,400 shp (6,800 sust.)—4/1,200-shp electric tunnel-thrusters
Electric: Ship's service from propulsion generators + 1/365-kw emergency diesel set
Range: 6,500/12 + 30 days on station **Fuel:** 2,000 tons **Endurance:** 60 days
Crew: 32 MSC civil service mariners + 89 technicians

Remarks: Authorized under FY 90 budget. Ordered 4-4-90. Sponsorship for the vessel was transferred to the Director of Strategic Systems Programs during 1-97, and the ship was refitted 4-98 to 10-98 to conduct submarine navigation system testing and ballistic missile flight-test support services; the type-designation and hull number, however, were not changed. Was originally intended to conduct hydrographic and oceanographic surveys in support of the Integrated Undersea Surveillance System and was capable of general oceanographic, bathymetric, and hydrographic survey work. Has a centerline "moonpool" for the launch and recovery of a remotely operated vehicle (ROV). Named for RADM Odale Waters Jr. (1910–86), Oceanographer of the Navy from 1965 through 1970. Under a 5-year, $35-million contract signed on 15-1-03, this ship is operated by DynCorp.

♦ 1 Hayes-class sound trials ship [AG]
Bldr: Todd SY, Seattle, Wash.

	Laid down	L	In serv.
T-AG 195 Hayes (ex-T-AGOR 16)	12-11-69	2-7-70	21-7-71

Hayes (T-AG 195) John Gourley, 3-01

D: 2,329 tons light (4,521 fl) **S:** 12 kts (11 sust.)
Dim: 75.10 (67.06 pp) × 22.86 × 6.68
Electronics:
Radar: 1 Raytheon TM 1650/6X nav.; 1 Raytheon TM 1660/12S nav.
Sonar: TUMS towed sound-measurement array
M: Diesel-electric drive: 3 Caterpillar 3516 diesels (1,410 bhp each), 3 Kato 1,100-kw alternators, 2 Westinghouse motors; 2 props; 2,400 shp—2 165-shp low-speed motors
Electric: 640 kw tot. (2 × 320 kw, Caterpillar 3412 diesels driving)
Range: 6,000/12 **Endurance:** 30 days
Crew: 11 officers, 30 mariners + 33 technicians

Remarks: Conducts sound-measuring acoustic surveys in support of the submarine noise-reduction program. Was not a success in original configuration as an oceanographic research platform, suffering from excessive pitching. Had been laid up since 1982 at Bayonne, N.J., and was transferred from the Oceanographer of the Navy to the Naval Ships Research and Development Center (now Carderock Division, Naval Surface Warfare Center) in 1983 awaiting conversion. Was being converted 8-7-87 to 12-90 by Tacoma Boat, Tacoma, Wash., as sound trials vessel under FY 86 budget to replace *Monob One* (YAG 61); the bankruptcy of the conversion yard in 11-90, however, caused the ship to be towed to the Puget Sound Naval Shipyard, Bremerton, where a new conversion contract was placed on 25-3-91 and the work completed on 19-6-92. Based at Port Canaveral, Florida. Under a 5-year, $35-million contract signed on 15-1-03, this ship is operated by DynCorp.
Hull systems: Catamaran configuration hull, with each hull having 7.3-m beam. Has 371.6 m^2 laboratory space. Re-engined, with original four high-speed diesels driving controllable-pitch props being replaced by a diesel-electric plant with fixed-pitch props that are cavitation-free to 10 kts. New propulsion plant is suspended in a vibration-damping compartment above deck, along with the two diesel generator sets.

Disposal notes: *Raleigh*-class auxiliary command ship *La Salle* (AGF 3) was decommissioned on 27-5-05 and stricken for disposal. *Austin*-class miscellaneous command ship *Coronado* (AGF 11) was decommissioned on 25-2-05, transferred to the Military Sealift Command and placed in reduced operating status prior to decommissioning on 30-9-06.

♦ 1 Impeccable-class SWATH ocean surveillance ship [AGI]
Bldr: Friede-Goldman-Halter, Moss Point, Miss.

	Laid down	L	Del.	In serv.
T-AGOS 23 Impeccable	21-1-96*	25-4-98	13-10-00	23-3-01

*Original keel-laying 15-3-92

D: 2,809 tons light (5,380 fl) **S:** 15 kts (12 sust.)
Dim: 85.80 (70.71 wl) × 29.20 × 7.92
Electronics:
Radar: . . . nav.
Sonar: SQQ-2 SURTASS LFA towed passive array; TB-29A Twinline towed array

AUXILIARY SHIPS *(continued)*

Impeccable (T-AGOS 23) J. & K. Van Raemdonck, 3-01

Impeccable (T-AGOS 23) Leo Dirkx, 9-00

M: 3 G.E. Electromotive Division 12-645F8B diesel generator sets (2,000 kw each), 2 Westinghouse electric motors; 2 5-bladed props; 5,000 shp—2 900-shp Omnithruster JT 1110 omnidirectional jet-thrusters
Electric: Main generators, plus 450-kw diesel emergency set **Range:** 8,000/15
Endurance: 60 days
Crew: 25 civilian contract mariners, 8 contract technicians, 20 Navy

Remarks: Authorized under FY 90 budget. Sister *Integrity* (T-AGOS 24) was authorized under the FY 92 budget but was not ordered. T-AGOS 25 was to have been requested in FY 99 but was dropped from the FY 98 5-year program. Originally, at least six were planned. Enlarged version of T-AGOS 19 SWATH design. A report by the General Accounting Office released 1-93 severely criticized this program on the grounds that the intended WQT-2 active Low-Frequency Array and its mating to a SWATH-type platform had not been sufficiently operationally tested; the WQT-2 suite has not been installed.

T-AGOS 23 was ordered 28-3-91 under FY 90 from Tampa Shipyard Div., American Shipbuilding Co., Tampa, Florida, with option for the two more; work did not begin until 23-3-92 and progressed extremely slowly, stopping entirely during 10-93; the Navy then issued a "cure notice" during 11-93, and after negotiations, a settlement was made and the construction contract canceled. The contract was reassigned during 6-95 to Halter Marine, which employed materials originally ordered and delivered to American Shipbuilding, which had completed about 50 percent of the lower hull structures; most of the structures already completed for the ship were barged to Mississippi. T-AGOS 23 was not formally christened until 1-11-00, 2.5 years after launch. The renewable operating contract went to Maersk Line, Ltd., Norfolk, Virginia, on 16-8-00 and extends into 2007.
Hull systems: The design incorporates measures to improve seakeeping over that of the *Victorious* class. The skew-bladed, fixed-pitch propellers have a diameter of 4.57 m. Two waste-heat distillers provide 4,100 gallons of fresh water per day. Normal mission speed is 3 kts.
Mission systems: Has WSC-3(V)3 and WSC-6(V) SATCOM systems, the latter for datalinking information obtained from the surveillance sonar array. Permission to operate the extremely powerful SQQ-2 Active Towed Array Sonar (ATAS), which is alleged to have caused numerous whale deaths, was not given until 7-02; the system has 18 separate active, low-frequency sonar transducers.

♦ 4 Victorious-class SWATH ocean surveillance ships [AGI]
(1 *in reserve*)
Bldr: McDermott, Inc., Morgan City, La. (*Atlantic/†Pacific)

	Laid down	L	In serv.
T-AGOS 19 VICTORIOUS†	12-4-88	3-5-90	13-8-91
T-AGOS 20 *ABLE*	25-5-89	16-2-91	24-7-92
T-AGOS 21 EFFECTIVE†	15-2-91	26-9-91	15-1-93
T-AGOS 22 LOYAL*	7-10-91	19-9-92	11-7-93

D: 3,100 tons light (3,384 fl) **S:** 16 kts (9.6 sustained with SURTASS deployed)
Dim: 70.71 (58.14 pp) × 28.96 × 7.62
Electronics:
Radar: 2 Raytheon . . . nav.
Sonar: UQQ-2 SURTASS towed passive array; 1 TB-29A towed array (not in T-AGOS 20)
M: 4 Caterpillar-Kato 3512-TA 835-kw diesel generator sets (600 V a.c., 60 Hz; 2 for ship's service); 2 G.E. 750 V dc inductance motors (185 rpm max.); 2 props; 3,200 shp—2 600-hp Omnithruster omnidirectional jet-thrusters
Electric: 1,970 kw tot. (2 × 835-kw main generators, 1 × 300-kw emergency)

Effective (T-AGOS 21) Takatoshi Okano, 2-04

Range: 3,000/9.6 plus . . ./3 **Fuel:** 778 tons **Endurance:** 90 days
Crew: 9 officers, 13 mariner contractor crew + 12 contractor technicians

Remarks: Authorized: T-AGOS 19 in FY 87, T-AGOS 20–22 in FY 89. First ship ordered 31-10-86, the other three on 7-10-88. Operation contracted to Maersk Line, Ltd., Norfolk, Virginia, on 16-8-00, renewed in 2005 and subject to further renewal. *Able* (T-AGOS 20) was placed in Mobilization category B reserve on 8-7-03 but may be reactivated during 2007.
Hull systems: SWATH (Small Waterplane Area, Twin-Hull) hull form, with two submerged pontoons for buoyancy. Horizontal fins between hulls control pitching. Are stable ships, able to operate in higher latitudes in winter than *Stalwart* class, but they are reported to be difficult to handle in high winds. They are able to maintain heading in Sea State 6, however, and have successfully sustained operations at Sea State 9.
Mission systems: The SURTASS array is 2,614 m long and is towed at depths between 152 and 457 meters. Carry same sensor payload as in ASW-dedicated *Stalwart*-class units, including the WSC-6(V)1 satellite communications datalink. Are planned to be backfitted with the Lockheed Martin TB-29A Twinline towed linear passive array and a lightweight, low-power Low Frequency Active (LFA) sonar array.

Disposal note: All 16 *Stalwart*-class ocean surveillance ships have been retired from Navy service as of 2006. Several continue to serve in other governmental agencies including the National Oceanic Atmospheric Administration (NOAA).

♦ 1 chartered undersea surveillance ship [AG]
Bldr: Ulstein Hatlo A/S, Ulsteinvik, Norway (In serv. 1974)

CORY CHOUEST (ex-*Far Clipper*, ex-*Tender Clipper*)

Cory Chouest Mitsuhiro Kadota, 2002

D: Approx. 3,900 tons (fl) **S:** 13.75 kts
Dim: 81.08 (76.21 pp) × 18.04 × 4.32 (5.18 max.)
Electronics:
Radar: 2 . . . nav.
Sonar: SQQ-2 SURTASS LFA (Low-Frequency Active) array
M: 2 Atlas-MaK 6M453AK diesels; 2 CP props; 4,000 bhp
Electric: 2,350 kw tot. (2 × 800 kw, 3 × 250 kw)
Range: 5,940/13.75 **Fuel:** 265 tons
Crew: 16 contract mariners + 41 technicians

Remarks: A 1,597-grt/1,800-dwt former oilfield deck cargo/pipe carrier converted into a diving support, firefighting, and pollution control vessel. Chartered 14-11-91 for 17 months (with two 12-month extension options) from Alpha Marine Services, Galliano, Louisiana, as the primary platform for the development of low-frequency active (LFA) acoustic technology in support of the Space and Naval Warfare Systems Command (SPAWAR); current charter runs through 9-09 for operation by Edison Chouest Offshore.

♦ 1 converted Stalwart-class missile-range tracking ship [AGM]
Bldr: Tacoma Boat, Tacoma, Wash.

	Laid down	L	In serv.
T-AGM 24 INVINCIBLE (ex-T-AGOS 10)	8-11-85	1-11-86	30-1-87

AUXILIARY SHIPS *(continued)*

Invincible (T-AGM 24)—as T-AGOS 10, but in same configuration *Ships of the World, 6-99*

D: 1,459 tons light (2,282 fl) **S:** 11 kts **Dim:** 68.28 (59.13 pp) × 13.11 × 4.60
Electronics: Radar: 2 . . . nav.; 1 Cluster Gemini dual-band tracking and air-search
M: 4 Caterpillar-Kato D-398B 800-bhp diesels, G.E. electric drive; 2 4-bladed props; 2,200 shp (1,600 hp sust.)—550-hp bow-thruster
Electric: 1,500 kVA from main generators, plus 265-kw emergency set
Range: 11,200/11 plus 2,088/3 **Fuel:** 657 tons **Endurance:** 98 days
Crew: 6–8 officers, 11–12 contract crew, 11 technicians

Remarks: Authorized under FY 82 as an ocean submarine tracking ship. Deactivated 6-2-95 and stricken on 9-5-96 but began reactivation on 13-3-98 in support of an Air Force program for monitoring missile tests by North Korea and China; she is painted white, without a hull number visible, and is equipped with a large radome-enclosed radar known as Cluster Gemini. Operation contracted to Maersk Line, Ltd., Norfolk, Virginia, on 16-8-00. The current contract, renewed on 1-10-05 runs through 31-3-13. Reclassified T-AGM 24 on 4-4-00.
Hull systems: Flat-chine hull form without bilge keels. Has passive tank roll stabilization. Up to 518 tons of water ballast can be carried.
Mission systems: Has a new SATCOM antenna radome atop the mainmast and carries a large radome-enclosed air-search radar antenna on the deckhouse abaft the stacks.

♦ 1 Mariner-class missile-tracking ship [AGM]
Bldr: New York Shipbuilding, Camden, N.J.

	L	In serv.
T-AGM 23 Observation Island (ex-AG 154, ex-YAG 57, ex-*Empire State Mariner*)	15-8-53	5-12-53

Observation Island (T-AGM 23) U.S. Navy, 7-06

D: 12,978 tons light (16,076 fl) **S:** 20 kts
Dim: 171.81 (161.09 pp) × 23.16 × 9.14
Electronics:
Radar: 1 Raytheon 1650/9X nav.; 1 Raytheon 1660/12S nav.; 1 SPQ-11 Cobra Judy tracking; 2 . . . tracking
TACAN: URN-25
M: 2 sets G.E. geared steam turbines; 1 prop; 19,251 shp—2 3,000-shp Omnithruster WP 1700 directional pump-jet thrusters
Boilers: 2 Combustion Engineering, 42.3 kg/cm², 467° C **Range:** 17,000/13
Fuel: 2,652 tons
Crew: 66 MSC Civil Service mariners + 34 civilian technicians + . . . USAF personnel (accomm. for 93 officers, 465 enlisted)

Remarks: 14,029 grt/6,322 nrt. Begun as a seven-hold cargo ship. Acquired by the Navy on 10-9-56; used for Polaris and Poseidon missile trials until placed in reserve on 29-9-72. Reclassified T-AGM 23 on 1-5-79. Sponsored by the Ballistic Missile Defense Office in part for strategic arms limitation treaty verification duties; operates mainly in the Pacific. Operated by Maersk Lines Ltd. under a renewable contract. Due to be replaced around 2012 by a new construction missile tracking ship built to a modified Maury-class design.
Hull systems: Painted white. Refitted 10-84 to 3-85 by Northwest Marine, Portland, Ore., with a new foremast, heightened stacks, three new turbogenerator sets, new deckhouses, two new evaporators, and upgraded electronics (including an new X-band tracking radar abaft the stack). A 70-seat movie theater, racquetball and volleyball courts, two gymnasiums, and a sauna are fitted.
Mission systems: Converted between 7-79 and 4-81 to carry the Cobra Judy (SPQ-11) missile-tracking, trainable phased-array radar aft; the trainable antenna weighs 250 tons and has over 12,000 radiating elements. Two parabolic collection antennas are mounted in 9.75-m-diameter geodesic radomes atop the bridge. The twin kingposts forward support four antennas for the WSC-3 UHF SATCOM system as well as the TACAN antenna and the two navigational radar antennas.

Note: The *Pathfinder*-class survey ship *Pathfinder* (T-AGS 60) has been equipped with telemetry/tracking arrays to support ballistic missile tests and is based at Port Canaveral, Florida when required; see below under [AGS] for details.

♦ 1 SWATH oceanographic research ship [AGOR]
Bldr: Atlantic Marine, Inc. (AMI), Jacksonville, Fla.

	Laid down	L	In serv.
AGOR 26 Kilo Moana	9-2-01	17-11-01	31-3-03

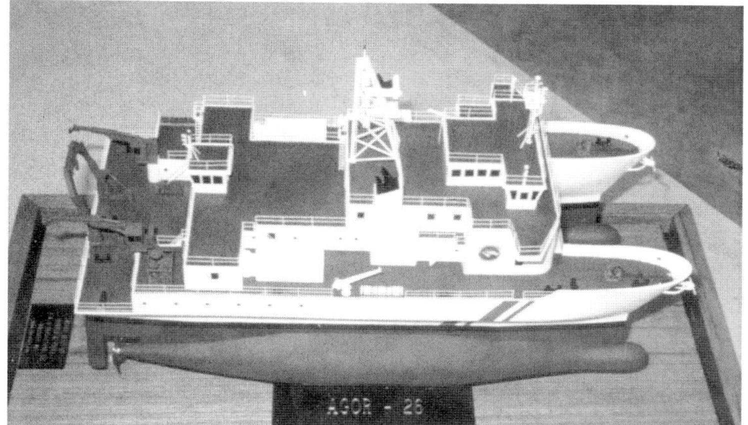

Kilo Moana (AGOR 26)—official model J&D Enterprises, 11-01

D: 1,996 tons light (2,542 fl) **S:** 15 kts (12 sust.)
Dim: 56.57 (52.43 wl) × 26.82 × 7.62
Electronics:
Radar: 1 Raytheon 3-cm Pathfinder nav.; 1 Raytheon 10-cm Pathfinder nav.
Sonar: Simrad EM 120 deepwater multibeam sounder (12 kHz); Simrad EM 1002 shallow water multibeam echo sounder (95 kHz); Simrad EA 500 hydrographic echo sounder (12, 38, and 200 kHz); Simrad HPR 418 acoustic positioning system; Raytheon Model 795 digital depth finder
M: 4 Caterpillar 3508B SCAC diesel generator sets (1,220 bhp each); 2 Westinghouse 1,500-kw electric motors; 2 fixed-pitch props; 4,024 shp—1 Elliot White Gill 40 azimuthal bow thruster (starboard hull)
Range: 10,000/11 **Endurance:** 50 days
Crew: 17 crew, 31 scientists and technicians

Remarks: Added to the FY 97 budget by the Congress. Ordered 27-10-99 for $42.3 million under the UNOLS (University-National Oceanographic Laboratory System) program for bail to the University of Hawaii's School of Ocean and Earth Science and Technology. Lockheed Martin managed the construction program, with Atlantic Marine constructing the ship, and with input from Pacific Marine & Supply, Mitsui Eng. & SB, Syntek, and GTE/BBN. The name means "Oceanographer" in Hawaiian.
Hull systems: Employs a catamaran SWATH (Small Waterplane Area, Twin-Hull) hull form. The mapping sonar functions to 11,000-m depths. Intended primarily to study high sea states and will be fully operational in Sea State 6. There is 4,460 ft² of working space on deck and a 100-ton mission payload can be accommodated. Is equipped with equipment for precise navigation, including station-keeping and track line maneuvering. Can launch and retrieve remotely operated underwater vehicles, scientific instruments, and deep-sea moorings. The lower hulls are 52.12 m long and have fixed stabilizer fins aft and adjustable canard stabilization fins forward. The bow-thruster is to be used to tow up to 9-ton (10,000-lb) arrays at 3 kts in order to avoid fouling the main propellers. Has a dynamic positioning system, integrated bridge; TSS Inc. POS/MV 320 inertial reference unit; POS/MV 30 inertial reference unit, Raytheon STD-20 gyrocompass; Raytheon Raychart 420 Differential GPS; and Inmarsat SATCOM. A 20,000-lb (30-ft. radius)/5,000-lb (40-ft. radius) crane is located aft, to port, and the U-frame stern crane can handle a 20,000-lb weight.

♦ 3 Thomas G. Thompson–class oceanographic research ships [AGOR]
Bldr: Friede-Goldman-Halter, Moss Point, Miss.

	Laid down	L	In serv.
AGOR 23 Thomas G. Thompson (ex-*Ewing*)	29-3-89	27-7-90	8-7-91
AGOR 24 Roger Revelle (ex-*Revelle*)	9-12-93	20-4-95	8-6-96
AGOR 25 Atlantis	16-8-94	1-2-96	15-4-97

D: 2,155 tons light (AGOR 23: 3,051 fl; others: 3,200 fl) **S:** 15 kts
Dim: 83.52 × 16.00 × 5.18 hull
Electronics:
Radar: 2 Raytheon Pathfinder (3cm and 10 cm) nav.
Sonar: AGOR 23: Atlas Elektronik Hydrosweep DS mapping; 2 Raytheon RD-500 depthfinders; 3.5-Khz sub-bottom profiler; 2 12-kHz bottom-profilers; AGOR 24, 25: Seabeam 2112A multibeam mapping system (12 kHz); ODEC deep- and shallow-water bottom profiler (12 and 33 kHz); ODEC sub-bottom profiler (12 TR-109 transducers); RD VM-150-18HP doppler current profiler (150 kHz); 2 Raytheon RD-500 echo sounders
M: 3 Caterpillar 3516 TA diesel generator sets (1,500 kw each), 2 G.E. CD6999 motors; 2 Lips FS-2500-450/1510BO azimuth-thruster props; 6,000 shp—1,117-shp Elliott Gill Model 50 T 35 azimuthal bow-thruster
Electric: 2,395 kw tot. (3 × 715-kw Caterpillar 3508TA diesel sets, 1 × 250-kw Caterpillar 3406TA emergency diesel set)

AUXILIARY SHIPS *(continued)*

Atlantis (AGOR 25) H&L Van Ginderen, 10-00

Roger Revelle (AGOR 24) H&L Van Ginderen, 11-98

Range: 11,300/12 + 30 days on station **Endurance:** 60 days
Crew: 20–22 crew + 37 scientists

Remarks: Authorized: AGOR 23 in FY 88, AGOR 24 in FY 92, and AGOR 25 in FY 94. First ship ordered 10-6-88 to replace AGOR 9, *Thomas G. Thompson,* as part of the UNOLS (University-National Oceanographic Laboratory System); operated by the University of Washington on completion and is entirely civilian-operated. AGOR 24, ordered 13-1-93 (with an option to build two more) was loaned 11-6-96 to the Scripps Institution of Oceanography, La Jolla, California, to replace *Thomas Washington* (AGOR 10); the ship has a dark blue-painted hull. AGOR 25, ordered 17-2-94, was transferred on completion to the Woods Hole Oceanographic Institution in Massachusetts to replace the *Atlantis II*. A fourth unit, *Researcher* (later renamed *Ronald S. Brown*), also ordered 17-2-94, was built for the National Ocean and Atmospheric Administration (NOAA) and was not numbered in the U.S. Navy series (although the ship was incorrectly referred to as "AGOR 26" in some official publications).

Are capable of all-purpose oceanographic research, including chemical and biological oceanography, multidiscipline environmental investigations, ocean engineering, marine acoustics, marine geology, and geophysics. Can also carry out bathymetric, seismic, and magnetometry surveys. AGOR 25 is equipped to support the Navy's research submersible *Alvin* (DSV 2).

Hull systems: Any combination of diesel generators can be employed for 600-v propulsion or 480-v ship's service power. Have Robertson RMP ROBPOS Dynamic Positioning System, accurate to 300 ft. in a 27-kt wind and 11-ft. seas. Other navaids include two Sperry Mk 37 gyros, Mackay 4005 D/F, Morris Tiger Shark Loran-C receiver, Magnavox MX-1107 GPS, Honeywell R/S 906 acoustic positioning system, and ODEC DSN450 dual-axis doppler speed log. Have Telesystems MCS 9120 SATCOM. They are equipped with a seismic survey system using two Price A-300 air compressors for the two towed air/water guns. The conductivity, temperature, and depth-measuring system operates to 11,000-m depths.

Laboratory space totals 372 m^2, and include hydrographic (700 ft^2), wet (235 ft^2), main (1,730 ft^2), bioanalytical (359 ft^2), electronics and computer (820 ft^2), and a staging bay (380 ft^2). Four additional portable lab/accommodations vans can be accommodated on deck. Working space on deck totals 325 m^2. Have a Markey DESH-9-11 double-drum waterfall winch with 10,000 meters of cable; the winch has a 9-ton bollard pull at 2.5 kts for scientific packages. Also have two Markey DESH-5 hydrographic winches. Two 19-ton telescoping boom cranes, two portable foldable one-ton boom cranes, a hydrographic sampling equipment boom, and a stern-mounted equipment A-frame crane are carried.

♦ 2 Melville-class oceanographic research ships (SCB 710 type) [AGOR] Bldr: Defoe SB, Bay City, Mich.

	Laid down	L	In serv.	Modified
AGOR 14 MELVILLE	12-7-67	10-7-68	27-8-69	7-89 to 6-90
AGOR 15 KNORR	9-8-67	21-8-68	14-1-70	11-88 to 1989

Knorr (AGOR 15)—blue hull with white upperworks Douglas A. Cromby, 8-03

Knorr (AGOR 15) Douglas A. Cromby, 8-03

D: 2,670 tons (fl) **S:** 14 kts **Dim:** 85.0 × 14.03 × 4.87
Electronics: Radar: 2 Raytheon ST-series ARPA nav.
M: 4 Caterpillar 3516 diesel generator sets, electric drive; 3 Z-drive props (1 retractable forward); 3,000 shp
Electric: 800 kw tot. (2 × 300 kw, 1 × 200-kw diesel sets) **Range:** 12,000/12
Fuel: 342 tons **Endurance:** 35–40 days **Crew:** 24 crew, 34 scientists

Remarks: 2,100 grt. Operated for the Office of Naval Research, AGOR 14 by Scripps Institution of Oceanography, California, and AGOR 15 by Woods Hole Oceanographic Institution, Massachusetts. Contracts renewed for five years on 28-7-96 and 4-8-96, respectively. The planned AGOR 19 and AGOR 20 of this class were canceled.
Hull systems: Originally had one vertical cycloidal propeller forward and a larger unit aft; these were intended for precise maneuvering but, because a mechanical rather than electric drive was used, proved troublesome. A new 10.36-m midbody was added, and the ships were re-engined, with the original cycloidal props replaced; accommodations were enlarged and the scientific equipment updated. Have six general-purpose labs totaling 341.9-m^2 lab space and 349.7-m^2 deck working space; also have 550-ft^3 storage hold. Two Magnavox 200 GPS receivers, Sperry SRD-301 log, RDI 150 kHz current profiler, and Magnavox MX-2400 Inmarsat SATCOM are fitted. Winches include two Markey DESH-5 hydrographic (10 km cable each), one Northern Line trawl (9 km cable), and one portable Dynacon traction (9 km wire). AGOR 15 has a Sea Beam 2112A (12-kHz) mapping sonar.

Note: A new T-AGS has been inserted into the programmed FY 06 budget; no other information is yet available.

♦ 6 (+ 1) Pathfinder-class hydrographic survey ships [AGS]
Bldr: Friede-Goldman-Halter, Moss Point, Miss.

	Laid down	L	In serv.
T-AGS 60 PATHFINDER	3-8-92	4-10-93	5-12-94
T-AGS 61 SUMNER	18-11-92	19-5-94	30-5-95
T-AGS 62 BOWDITCH	18-8-93	15-10-94	19-7-96
T-AGS 63 HENSON	13-10-95	21-10-96	20-2-98
T-AGS 64 BRUCE C. HEEZEN	19-8-97	25-3-99	13-1-00
T-AGS 65 MARY SEARS	28-7-99	19-10-00	17-12-01

D: 3,019 tons light (4,260 fl; T-AGS 64, 65: 4,772 fl) **S:** 16 kts
Dim: 100.13 (94.49 pp) × 17.68 × 5.79 (hull)
Electronics:
Radar: 2. . . . . . nav.; T-AGS 60 also: 1 Weibel MFTR 2100/43 X-band tracking; 1 . . . C-band tracking, 1 . . . S-band telemetry tracking
Sonar: Simrad EM121A multibeam echo sounder (12 kHz); ODEC Bathy-2000 echo sounder (12/33 kHz); ODEC Bathy 2000 bottom profiler (3 kHz); RD Instruments VM-0150 acoustic doppler current profiler (150 kHz); Sea Beam 2100-series mapping set; DWS towed seismic sub-bottom profiler

AUXILIARY SHIPS *(continued)*

Bowditch (T-AGS 62) U.S. Navy

M: 2 G.E. Electromotive Div. EMD 16-645F7B diesels (3,505 bhp each) with Baylor 855 VUV-372 generators (2,435 kw each), 2 G.E. Electromotive Div. EMD 12-645F76B diesels (2,550 bhp each) with Baylor 855PUV-372 generators (1,822 kw each), 2 G.E. CDF 1944 Model EN14655 motors; 2 4-bladed azimuthal props; 8,000 shp—G.E. CD4773 Model 5CD473NA802C800 electric motor, Lips FS500-234MNR azimuthal, retractable bow thruster; 1,500 shp
Electric: Main alternerator plant, plus 250-kw emergency alternator (G.M. Detroit Diesel 6V92 TA diesel driving)
Range: 12,000/12 + 29 days on station at 3 kts or 12,000/16 **Fuel:** 1,221 tons
Endurance: 70 days **Crew:** 25 ship's company + 27 scientists

Remarks: Authorized: two in FY 90, one in FY 91, one in FY 94, one in FY 96, and one in FY 99. Design essentially an enlarged AGOR 23, with increased space to meet Military Sealift Command accommodations standards and specialized survey equipment. First two ordered 30-1-91; T-AGS 62 ordered 29-5-92, T-AGS 63 on 20-10-94, T-AGS 64 on 15-1-97 for $51.7 million, and T-AGS 65 on 22-12-98 for $53,618,360.00. A modified seventh unit was authorized by Congress in the FY 07 budget. T-AGS 64 was named on 5-6-98 in a nationwide contest for schoolchildren for a deceased USN oceanographer known for work on plate tectonics and sea-floor mapping.

Operated for the Naval Meteorology and Oceanography Command on contract, ships of this class are intended to conduct physical, chemical, and biological oceanography; multidiscipline environmental investigations; ocean engineering and marine acoustics research; coastal hydrographic surveys; marine geology and geophysics research; and bathymetric, gravity, and magnetic surveys in deep ocean and coastal areas. T-AGS 60 has been adapted as a missile-range instrumentation ship and is based at Port Canaveral, Florida; the ship carries the Navy Mobile Instrumentation System, a mobile missile-tracking system incorporating C-band and X-band radars, optical cameras, an S-band multi-object tracking and recording radar, and weather data collection and recording equipment.
Hull systems: Antirolling tanks precision navigation equipment, and on-board data processing equipment are fitted. Are able to launch, operate, and recover remotely operated vehicles. Carry 962 tons ballast water, 32 tons potable water, and 24 tons lube oil. The electric generator plant is integrated to provide power for the propulsion system, ship's service needs, and the laboratories. A portable generator module can be installed on deck to provide power for "silent" operations. Have three multipurpose cranes and five specialized scientific equipment winches. Flow fins have been added forward to reduce bubble interference with the sonar sets.
Mission systems: Laboratory spaces include a 232-m^2 main laboratory, a 16.8-m^2 wet lab, a 32.5-m^2 staging bay contiguous to the 325-m^2 working deck and the wet lab, a 28.2-m^2 dry and biochemical lab, a 5.9-m^2 darkroom, a 7.4-m^2 climate-controlled chamber/salinometer lab, a 7.4-m^2 survey freezer, an 18.6-m^2 electricians' shop, a 22.3-m^2 drafting room, 217.2 m^2 of survey equipment storage, and a 32.5-m^2 library/conference room. The 121-beam mapping sonars are able to cover a swath as wide as 12 nautical miles at a time, and the navigation system can determine a ship's position to within 50 ft. Navigational equipment includes Megapulse Accufix 500N Loran-C receiver, Rockwell-Collins WRN-6(V)1 NAVSTAR global positioning system receiver, Sperry Mk 39 ring-laser gyro, and Simrad/Robertson DPS automatic positioning and course-maintaining propulsor control. A Benthos DS-7000-16, 5- to 50-kHz acoustic positioning system uses Datasonic BFP-312 bottom transponders. Have EG&G G811/813 magnetometer for magnetic field mapping, General Oceanics water sampler, Falmouth ICTD conductivity and temperature depth system to measure water properties to 7,000-m depths, and Sippican expendable sensor launcher and monitor system.

T-AGS 63 carries two 10.36-m inshore survey boats, each equipped with a Simrad EM 1000 multibeam bathymetric system and multibeam survey sonar; the others will be similarly equipped later. All units of the class, and all of their inshore survey boats, have Datasonics SIS-1500 high-resolution side-scan sonar sets.

♦ 1 John McDonnell–class coastal survey ship [AGS]

Bldr: Friede-Goldman-Halter, Moss Point, Miss.

	Laid down	L	In serv.
T-AGS 51 John McDonnell	3-8-89	13-12-90	15-11-91

John McDonnell (T-AGS 51) W. Michael Young, 11-01

D: 1,394 tons light (2,238 fl) **S:** 14 kts (12 sust.) **Dim:** 63.40 × 13.72 × 4.27
Electronics:
Radar: 1 . . . 3 cm nav.; 1 . . . 10 cm nav.
Sonar: Simrad Multibeam hull-mounted (95 kHz); Datasonics SIS-1500 towed side-scan (105 kHz); 2 12-kHz deep-water echo sounders; 2 24-kHz shallow-water echo sounders; 2 200-kHz shallow-water echo sounders
M: 1 G.M. EMD12-645F7B turbocharged, 900-rpm diesel; 1 prop; 2,550 bhp—1 230-bhp Detroit Diesel 6V92N cruising diesel
Electric: 1,200 kw tot. (3 × 350 kw, G.M. 8V92TAB diesel-driven ship's service; 1 × 150 kw, G.M. 6V92N-driven emergency set)
Range: 12,000/12 Crew: 22 crew + 11 survey party

Remarks: Added to FY 87 budget by Congress with nonbinding suggestion that she be converted from existing tuna clippers. Delay in ordering to 10-11-88 occasioned by need to define characteristics. A second pair to replace T-AGS 33 and 34 were to have been included in the FY 94 budget but were dropped.
Hull systems: Intended to collect hydrographic data in waters from 10 to 4,000 m deep. The smaller "son" diesel propels the ship at speeds from 4 to 6 kts. Has roll stabilization tank. Navigation equipment includes GPS and Loran-C receivers, collision avoidance system, dual-axis doppler speed log, and HYSTAR II computerized data collection system. Laboratory space: 700 ft.^{2} deck working space: 1,500 ft.^{2}; and scientific storage space: 2,300 ft^2. Two telescopic, 7-ton max. cranes are fitted. Carries two 10.36 × 2.82 × 0.91-m, 7.4-ton survey launches, equipped with a single 225-bhp diesel for 16 kts. The launches carry a towing winch for a 105-kHz sidescan sonar (range of 600 m, towing speed 12.7 kts) and have two 24-kHz and two 200-kHz echo sounders fitted; the craft have Global Positioning System, a microfix radio navigation system, and can interface with the mother ship's HYSTAR II computerized survey data storage system. There is also a 5.33-m semi-rigid inflatable workboat.

Disposal notes: Sister *Littlehales* (T-AGS 52) was retired during 3-03, transferred to NOAA, and renamed *Thomas Jefferson. Silas Bent*–class survey ship *Wyman* (T-AGS 34) was deactivated on 10-3-97, stricken on 3-5-99, and transferred to MARAD for disposal during 3-01; *Wilkes* (T-AGS 33) was deactivated and transferred by grant to Tunisia on 29-9-95; *Silas Bent* (T-AGS 26) was stricken and transferred to Turkey on 28-10-99; and *Kane* (T-AGS 27) was placed out of service, stricken, and transferred to Turkey on 14-3-01.

♦ 2 Mercy-class hospital ships [AH]

Bldr: General Dynamics National Steel & Shipbuilding Co, (NASSCO), San Diego, Calif.

	L	Conv. start	In serv.
T-AH 19 Mercy (ex-*Worth*)	1976	20-7-84	28-2-87
T-AH 20 Comfort (ex-*Rose City*)	1976	2-4-85	1-12-87

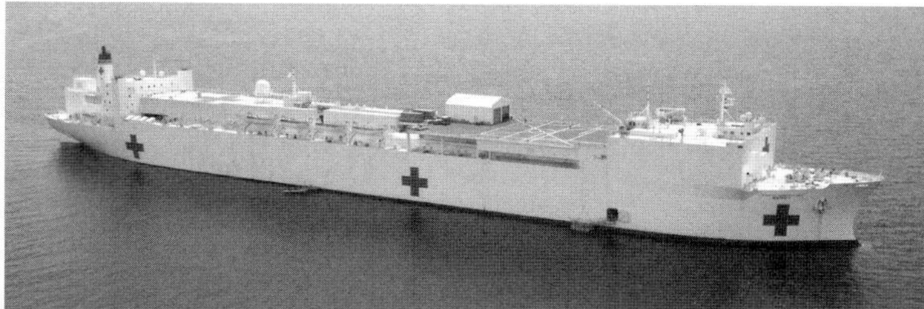

Mercy (T-AH 19) U.S. Navy, 7-06

Comfort (T-AH 20) U.S. Navy, 5-06

D: 24,752 tons light (69,360 fl) **S:** 17.5 kts (16.5 sust.)
Dim: 272.49 (260.61 pp) × 32.23 × 9.98
Electronics:
Radar: 1 . . . nav.; 1 Norden SPS-67 surf. search
TACAN: URN-25
M: 2 sets G.E. geared steam turbines; 1 prop; 24,500 shp **Boilers:** 2 . . .
Electric: 9,250 kw tot. (3 × 2,000-kw diesel, 1 × 1,500-kw diesel, 1 × 1,000-kw turboalternator, 1 × 750-kw emergency diesel set)
Range: 13,420/17.5 **Fuel:** 5,445 tons
Crew: Active: 68 MSC Civil Service mariners, 1,508 Navy staff + 1,000 patients inactive: 12 MSC caretaker crew + Navy Medical Treatment Facility staff: 6 officers, 39 enlisted

Remarks: 54,367 grt/45,480 dwt. Builder contracted 29-6-83 to convert Apex Marine's *San Clemente*–class commercial tanker *Worth* to a hospital ship with FY 83 funds; T-AH 20's conversion ordered from same yard 16-12-83 with FY 84 funds. Were originally 44,875 grt/91,849 dwt. T-AH 19 is maintained in layberth at San Diego, California, and T-AH 20 at Baltimore, Maryland. Both are normally maintained on five-day steaming notice. Carry at least two motor boats know unofficially as "Band Aid 1" and "Band Aid 2."
Hull systems: The entire amidships area was altered to provide a large helicopter deck, accommodations, and boat stowage. Have 12 operating rooms, four X-ray rooms, an 80-bed intensive-care unit, a burn-care facility, a 50-bed reception/triage area, and 1,000 ward beds. Of the 1,508 accommodations for naval personnel, there are 259

AUXILIARY SHIPS *(continued)*

for officers, 31 for chief petty officers, and 530 for enlisted, augmented in emergencies by 372 naval medical support personnel; also aboard would be 14 communications specialists. Freshwater tankage for 1,525 tons is carried, plus two 278-ton/day distilling plants. Much of the displacement is seawater ballast, some of which can be discharged to allow the ships to enter shallow ports and harbors. There are two 7,000-ton/hour ballast pumps.

♦ 8 Watson-class Large Medium-Speed Roll-on Sealift Ships [AK]
Bldr: National Steel and Shipbuilding (NASSCO), San Diego, Calif.

	Laid down	L	In serv.
T-AKR 310 Watson	23-5-96	26-7-97	9-12-99
T-AKR 311 Sisler	15-4-97	28-2-98	1-12-98
T-AKR 312 Dahl	12-11-97	2-10-98	13-7-99
T-AKR 313 Red Cloud	29-6-98	7-8-99	23-5-00
T-AKR 314 Charlton	19-1-99	11-12-99	23-5-00
T-AKR 315 Watkins	30-8-99	28-7-00	2-3-01
T-AKR 316 Pomeroy	23-3-00	10-3-01	14-8-01
T-AKR 317 Soderman	31-10-00	26-4-02	17-9-02

Soderman (T-AKR 317) Edward McDonnell, 3-06

Charlton (T-AKR 314) Ralph Edwards, 3-05

Sisler (T-AKR 311) U.S. Navy, 6-06

D: 36,114 tons (62,700 fl at 10.36-m draft) **S:** 24.9 kts (24 sust.)
Dim: 289.56 (271.28 wl, 275.85 pp) × 32.23 × 12.19 max. (10.36 mean)
Electronics: Radar: . . .
M: 2 G.E. LM-2500-30 gas turbines; 2 7.3-m dia. CP props; 64,000 shp at 95 rpm (59,000 shp sust.)—3,000-shp bow-thruster
Electric: 14,500 kw tot. (5 × 2,500-kw diesel sets, 2,000 kw tot. emergency diesel)
Range: 13,800/24
Crew: 25 civilians (accomm. for: 13 officers, 32 mariners) + military: 2 officers, 48 enlisted + 300 troops

Remarks: Officially referred to as Large Medium-Speed Roll-on Sealift Ships (LMSR). Operated under a 30-7-97 contract by Maersk Line Ltd., they are part of the Brigade Afloat Force, all assigned to Maritime Prepositioning Squadron 2 at Diego Garcia carrying U.S. Army heavy equipment for use in the Middle East and Far East, and all are assigned to APS-4. The initial operating contract was renewed on 8-5-02 for $400 million to operate the ships through 8-07.

T-AKR 310 was ordered 15-9-93 for $269 million, with an option for a further five ships; the ship was delivered on 23-6-98 but did not enter service for another six months. T-AKR 311 and 312 ordered 20-10-94 for $436 million total. T-AKR 313 was ordered 30-1-96, T-AKR 314 on 26-11-96 for $200.25 million, T-AKR 315 in 5-97, T-AKR 316 on 14-11-97, and T-AKR 317 on 28-2-00 (for $230,626,488). T-AKR 317 was added to the FY 00 budget by the Congress in lieu of a planned third Sealift Enhancement Ship for the Marine Corps.

Were originally planned to be 36 kt-capable ships, but costs would have been prohibitive and the strategic advantages minimal. The building yard was purchased by General Dynamics on 8-10-98 but retains its corporate identity.

Hull systems: Have two twin Hägglunds 55-ton capacity twin pedestal cranes (at 29-meters; 35 tons at 40-meters), two side vehicle cargo ports (with modular ramps extendable to 40 m), and a 40-m-long, 7.3-m-wide slewing stern ramp. Are able to carry 13,260 tons military cargo on 35,300 m^2 of parking space, including 58 tanks, 48 other tracked vehicles, and 900 trucks and other wheeled vehicles. The gas turbine main propulsion engines are uprated from the standard version through improved cooling and the use of advanced materials; they employ G.E. double-reduction gearboxes. These are the world's largest gas turbine–powered ships.

♦ 7 Bob Hope–class Large Medium-Speed Roll-on Sealift Ships [AK]
Bldr: Northrop Grumman Avondale, New Orleans, La.

	Laid down	L	In serv.
T-AKR 300 Bob Hope	29-5-95	27-3-97	18-11-98
T-AKR 301 Fisher	15-4-96	21-10-97	24-8-99
T-AKR 302 Seay	24-3-97	25-6-98	28-3-00
T-AKR 303 Mendonca	3-11-97	25-9-99	30-1-00
T-AKR 304 Pililaau	29-6-98	29-1-00	24-7-01
T-AKR 305 Brittin	3-5-99	11-11-00	11-7-02
T-AKR 306 Benavidez	15-12-99	11-8-01	10-9-03

Pililaau (T-AKR 304) George R. Schneider, 9-05

Bob Hope (T-AKR 300) U.S. Navy, 1-04

Benavidez (T-AKR 306) U.S. Navy, 5-03

D: 34,408 tons light (62,096 fl) **S:** 24.9 kts sust.
Dim: 289.56 (271.28 pp) × 32.30 × 11.25 max. **Electronics:** Radar: . . .
M: 4 Colt-Pielstick 10PC4.2V400, 105-rpm diesels; 2 props; 65,160 bhp—2 1,500-shp bow-thrusters
Electric: 5,000 kw (2 × 2,500-kw diesel sets) **Range:** 13,800/24
Crew: 27 tot. contract civilians (accomm. for 95) + 300 troops

Remarks: Officially referred to as Large Medium-Speed Roll-on Sealift Ships (LMSR). First unit was added by Congress to FY 90 shipbuilding request due to concerns that

AUXILIARY SHIPS *(continued)*

the U.S. and its allies lack sufficient sealift assets, military or commercial. First unit ordered 2-9-93 for $265 million from Avondale, with option to build five more. T-AKR 301 and 302 ordered 27-9-94, T-AKR 303 on 27-12-95 (for $206.43 million), T-AKR-304 on 26-11-96 for $211.1 million, T-AKR 305 on 14-11-97 (for $240 million), and T-AKR 306, an FY 99 ship, on18-12-98. Hull numbers AKR 307–309 were reserved for possible future additional orders for units of this class.

Are operated by Maersk Lines Ltd. and Patriot Contracting Services in five-day ready-to-operate condition at U.S. ports. As of of 2006, *Mendonca* (T-AKR 303) was the only unit not in MSC Reduced Operating Status (ROS). T-AKR 301, 304, and 306 are based in Corpus Christi, Texas, T-AKR 300 and 305 are at Violet, Louisiana, and T-AKR-302 and 303 operate out of Baltimore, Maryland. These ships took much longer to build than did the similar but less complex *Watson* class. T-AKR 300 and T-AKR 301 previously activated on 16-10-02 for Mideast service but were returned to standby on 29-12-02. T-AKR 304 was activated on 12-12-03, T-AKR 302 on 18-1-03, and T-AKR 305 on 2-1-03.

Hull systems: Are able to carry 13,260 tons military cargo. In military cargo configuration, have 39,920 m^2 of military vehicle parking space, enough for over 1,000 military vehicles, including tanks. Fitted with a 41-m-long by 7.3-m-wide, 160-ton capacity centerline stern slewing ramp, internal vehicle ramps, side-port vehicle ramps on each beam (with ramps 15.2 m long and 12.2 m wide), and two paired 58-ton capacity (at 29-m radius) electric cranes; when the cranes are operating together, the pairs can lift 112 tons each. There is a modular, portable ramp that can be attached to any of the three sides of the side ramps in lengths of up to 50 m when all four sections are used; it has a vehicle weight capacity of 160 tons and can be used to join the ship to a pier or lighter in up to a State 3 sea.

♦ 3 Shughart-class Large Medium-Speed Roll-on Sealift Ships [AK]

Bldr: Odense Staalskibsværft A/S/Lindo, Denmark (In serv. 1980–81)

	Conversion start	In serv.
T-AKR 295 SHUGHART (ex-*Laura Maersk*)	24-6-94	7-5-96
T-AKR 297 YANO (ex-*Leise Maersk*)	17-5-95	8-2-97
(T-AK 3017) GYSGT FRED W. STOCKHAM (ex-*Soderman,* T-AKR 299, ex-*Lica Maersk*)	12-10-95	18-11-97

Shughart (T-AKR 295) Frank Findler, 10-03

Yano (T-AKR 297) Frank Findler, 11-04

D: 33,971 tons light (55,123 fl) **S:** 24 kts sust.
Dim: 276.43 (269.79 hull, 259.32 pp) × 32.28 × 11.18
Electronics: Radar: 1 Sperry RASCAR-ARPA nav.
M: 2 Burmeister & Wain 12L90-GFCA diesel; 1 6-bladed, 7.51-m-dia. prop; 47,300 bhp (at 97 rpm)—bow and stern CP side-thrusters
Electric: 12,560 kw tot. ship's service + 1,750 kw tot. emergency (3 × 2,500 kw, 3 × . . . kw, 1 × 1,750-kw diesel sets)
Range: 12,200/24 Fuel: 22,600 barrels heavy oil, 659 tons diesel
Crew: T-AKR 295, 297: 13 officers, 32 mariners + Navy: 2 officers, 48 enlisted; T-AK 3017: 13 officers, 32 contract mariners + up to 100 Navy and USMC personnel)

Remarks: 43,325 grt (prior to conversion); deadweight tonnages prior to conversion were around 53,000. Former 3,000 TEU containerships. Contract for $634.9 million let 30-7-93 for long-term lease from Maersk Lines and conversion as military vehicle carriers for Army equipment and supplies by National Steel and Shipbuilding (NASSCO), San Diego. Named for U.S. Army Medal of Honor awardees. Referred to as LMSR (Large Medium-Speed Roll-on/roll-off) ships. Conversion of this class and the *Gordon* class cost $1.06 billion total. During 2000 T-AKR 295 and 297 was reassigned to surge force duties and placed in layup at Norfolk, Virginia; they are operated by American Overseas Marine under a 1-10-05 contract which expires on 10-3-10. T-AKR 297 was activated for Mideast duties on 17-12-02 and T-AKR 295 on 21-1-03. As of 7-06, T-AKR 295 and 297 were back on MSC Reduced Operating Status and berthed at Philadelphia, Pa.

The *Stockham,* reaccepted on 6-7-01 after conversion, now serves as a "Sea Basing" test ship. During a 2004–5 refit, Stockham's flight deck was extended 16.5 m, aviation fueling systems were added, communications upgraded, capabilities to carry two Seahawk helicopters added and the stern ramp reconfigured so that it can be lowered below the water's surface to allow launch and recovery of amphibious vehicles. The ship is now said to operate as an "Afloat Forward Staging Base"; though administrative control remains with MSC, operational control has been assigned to Pacific Command.

Under a 6-1-99 contract, NASSCO converted the former T-AKR 299 into a Marine Corps prepositioning ship; a further contract added $18 million to the work package on 5-5-00, and the work was completed on 1-3-01. For reasons obscure, the *Stockham* has lost her Naval Vessel Registry hull number but has been assigned the unofficial administrative number T-AKR 3017; the name was changed on 16-1-01.

Hull systems: T-AKR 295 and 297 are intended to carry equipment for an Army Armor Task Force, with 58 M1 Abrams tanks, 48 other tracked vehicles, and 900 trucks and other wheeled vehicles. Total cargo parking area 29,356 m^2. They are fitted with a 41-m-long by 7.3-m-wide, 160-ton capacity centerline stern slewing ramp, internal vehicle ramps, side-port vehicle ramps on each beam (with ramps 15.2 m long and 12.2 m wide), and two paired 58-ton capacity (at 29-m radius) electric cranes; when the cranes are operating together, the pairs can lift 112 tons each. Some container cell guides have been retained. There is a modular, portable ramp that can be attached to any of the three sides of the side ramps in lengths of up to 50 m when all four sections are used; it has a vehicle weight capacity of 160 tons and can be used to join the ship to a pier or lighter in up to a State 3 sea. A helicopter platform has been added forward of the pilothouse. Have six vehicle cargo decks. As merchant ships, they were lengthened during 1987 by Hitachi from the original 212.48 m overall (202.01 pp). Fin stabilizers were added during the conversion, and generator capacity was greatly increased. Were equipped with Sperry SRD 331 doppler log, SRD 421/S 2-axis speed logs, Mk 37 Mod. E gyro, ADG 6000 steering control, and GMDSS radio systems during conversions. The conversions came in 808 tons heavier than planned. They have a bulbous bow form.

♦ 2 Gordon-class Large Medium-Speed Roll-on Sealift Ships [AK]

Bldr: A/S Burmeister & Wain's Skibsbyggeri, Copenhagen, Denmark

	L	Conv. start	In serv.
T-AKR 296 GORDON (ex-*Jutlandia*)	1972	15-10-93	23-8-96
T-AKR 298 GILLILAND (ex-*Selandia*)	1973	21-10-93	24-5-97

Gilliland (T-AKR 298)—the helicopter deck is forward of the bridge in this class; note the portable vehicle ramp stowed to starboard of the first pair of cranes
General Dynamics Newport News, 5-97

Gilliland (T-AKR 298) NAVPIC-Holland, 6-98

D: 33,163 tons light (57,000 tons fl) **S:** 24 kts (22 sust.)
Dim: 291.39 (272.65 pp) × 32.24 × 11.00
Electronics: Radar: 1 Sperry RASCAR-ARPA nav.
M: 1 Burmeister & Wain 12K84EF diesel (31,400 bhp), 2 Burmeister & Wain 9K84EF diesels (23,600 bhp each); 3 props; 78,600 bhp—bow CP thruster
Electric: 12,560 kw tot. ship's service + 1,750 kw tot. emergency
Range: 27,000/22
Fuel: 8,486 tons heavy oil, 874 tons diesel
Crew: 13 officers, 32 mariners + Navy: 2 officers, 48 enlisted

Remarks: 54,035 grt (prior to conversion). Former 3,000 TEU container ships. Contract let 30-7-93 for $425.6 million for long-term lease from Maersk/East Asia Co. and conversion as military vehicle carriers by Newport News Shipbuilding & Dry Dock Co. Renamed for U.S. Army Medal of Honor recipients. Delivery dates slipped about eight months. Conversion of this class and the *Shughart* class cost $1.06 billion total. Both were initially assigned to Maritime Prepositioning Squadron 2 at Diego Garcia. During 2001 both were reassigned to Surge Force duties and placed in five-day Reduced Operating Status layup at Norfolk; they are managed by Patriot Contract Services. T-AKR 298 was activated on 9-1-03 for Mideast duties. As of mid-2006 T-AKR 296 was in active service while T-AKR 298 (previously activated on 9-1-03 for Mideast duties) serves on MSC–Reduced Operating Status. T-AKR 296 and 298 are berthed at Newport News, Virginia, and operated by 3PSC, LLC of Cape Canaveral, Fla, under a contract that expires 10-3-10.

AUXILIARY SHIPS *(continued)*

Hull systems: Both were lengthened in 1984 by Hyundai Mipo Dockyard, Ulsan, South Korea. During conversion in U.S.A., were fitted with a 41-m-long by 7.3-m-wide, 160-ton capacity centerline stern slewing ramp, internal vehicle ramps, side-port vehicle ramps on each beam (with ramps 15.2 m long and 12.2 m wide), and two paired 57.5-ton capacity (at 29-m radius) electric cranes. When the cranes are operating together, the pairs can lift 114 tons each at 29-m radius. Some container cell guides have been retained. There is a modular, portable ramp that can be attached to any of the three sides of the side ramps in lengths of to 50 m when all four sections are used; it has a vehicle weight capacity of 160 tons and can be used to join the ship to a pier or lighter in up to a State 3 sea. Fin stabilizers were also added. Have six vehicle cargo decks totaling 30,843 m^2. The ships can be unloaded in 96 hours. The centerline propeller has controllable pitch, while the outboard pair have fixed-pitch propellers. Were equipped with Sperry SRD 331 doppler log, SRD 421/S two-axis speed logs, Mk 37 Mod. E gyro, ADG 6000 steering control, and GMDSS radio systems during conversions.

Note: The *Algol* (SL-7)-class vehicle cargo ships (T-AKR 287 through T-AKR 294) are used for transportation rather than prepositioning; see under [AK].

♦ 1 Wheat-class chartered Maritime Prepositioning Ship [AK]
Bldr: Chernomorskiy Zavod, Mikolayiv, Ukraine (In serv. 1987)

(T-AK 3016) LCpl Roy M. Wheat (ex-*Bazaliya*, ex-*Vladimir Vaslayayev*)

LCpl Roy M. Wheat (T-AK 3016) Edward McDonnell, 2002

D: 50,570 tons (fl) **S:** 26.5 kts (22 sust.)
Dim: 263.10 (239.97 pp) × 30.01 × 10.67
M: 2 Mashproekt-Zorya M-25 reversible gas turbines (18,000 shp each); 2 waste-heat steam turbines (5,300 shp each); 2 fixed-pitch props; 46,000 shp— . . . -shp bow-thruster; 872-shp KaMeWa stern-thruster
Electric: . . . kw tot. (3 × . . . kw Sulzer . . . diesel-driven sets; 2 1815-kw Caterpillar 3516B diesel sets; 1 850-kw Caterpillar 3508B diesel emergency set)
Range: 40,000/26.5 **Fuel:** 8,380 tons
Crew: 25 tot. contract mariners + . . . Navy

Remarks: 32,264 grt. The second conversion unit for the Maritime Prepositioning Force (Enhanced) was authorized in the FY 97 budget; the name was assigned on 1-11-96 in honor of a Marine Vietnam War Medal of Honor recipient. Operates with one of the existing three Maritime Prepositioning Squadrons. Commercially operated and manned, with a small Navy contingent aboard. Contract for $150 million placed 9-4-97 with Ocean Marine Navigation Co., Inc., Annapolis, Maryland, to purchase, convert, operate, and maintain the ship for five years; the ship never having operated, a new contract for $27.1 million was placed on 28-6-01 with Keystone Prepositioning Services, Bala Cynwyd, Pennsylvania, to operate the ship through at least 2008. Built in Ukraine, the ship was registered in Jamaica at time of charter. Converted for MSC service for $134 million by Bender Shipbuilding and Repair, Mobile, Alabama, starting 18-7-97 and delivered on 31-3-02 at a cost of over $200 million, she is attached to Maritime Prepositioning Squadron 3. Due to its origins, the ship is reportedly expensive to operate and difficult to maintain; the conversion has required an inordinate amount of time, and the cost of the conversion more than doubled since the original contract was placed. The unexpected need to remove asbestos (widely used in former Warsaw Pact nation merchant and naval ships) added to the already high cost of the conversion.
Hull systems: Conversion entailed inserting a 35.97-m, mid-body section (built by Tampa SY and by Brown & Root, Houston, Texas) to increase vehicle capacity and installation of a paired cargo crane and a helicopter platform; the section added about .7 meters to the draft and 14,340 tons to the full-load displacement. New Ukrainian-made Zorya M-25 gas turbines were installed during conversion. The three original diesel generator sets had their Sulzer diesel overhauled and new Kato generators provided, while two new 1,815-kw sets (powered by Caterpillar 3516B diesels) and an 850-kw emergency diesel set (powered by a Caterpillar 3508B) were added. A helicopter platform was added aft, and the articulated stern ramp was lengthened and strengthened.

♦ 1 Pitsenbarger-class chartered Maritime Prepositioning Ship [AK]
Bldr: Ch. d'Atlantique, St. Nazaire, France (In serv. 1983)

(T-AK 4638) A1C William H. Pitsenbarger (ex-*Therese Delmas*)

A1C William H. Pitensbarger (T-AK 4638) Edward McDonnell, 2002

D: Approx. 40,000 tons (fl) **S:** 18 kts **Dim:** 189.01 (175.42 pp) × 32.21 × 11.40
Electronics: Radar: 1 . . . nav.
M: 1 Sulzer 7RLB66 7-cyl. slow-speed diesel; 1 prop; 13,800 bhp—1 1,184-shp CP bow-thruster
Electric: 3,000 kw tot. (3 × 1,000-kw Wärtsilä diesel-driven sets; 440-V 50-Hz. a.c.)
Range: 21,600/18 **Fuel:** 2,197.5 tons heavy oil; 297.5 tons diesel
Crew: 20 contract mariners.

Remarks: 30,750 grt/32,709 dwt. Chartered 15-6-01 from RR & VO LLC for $50,913,041.00 for use as a prepositioning ship for Air Force containerized equipment and munitions at Diego Garcia from 11-01 through 11-05. Reflagged U.S.; was previously under Bahamian registry. Renamed for a Vietnam War Medal of Honor recipient and delivered 28-11-01 after a refit at Detyens SY, Charleston, South Carolina. Is operated under contract through at least 2008.
Hull systems: Cargo: Although configured to carry 1,417 TEU when chartered, after conversion carries 885 TEU, of which 135 are in a new "cocoon" above deck; all cargo spaces are dehumidified and air-conditioned. Single-deck container ship with fixed guides and 22 hatches. Has five 40-ton Brissonneau & Lotz cranes.

♦ 2 chartered Maritime Prepositioning Ships [AK]
Bldr: Daewoo Shipbuilding and Heavy Machinery, Ltd., Koje (Carter: Kyung), South Korea

	L
(T-AKR 4496) Ltc John U. D. Page (ex-*Newark Bay*, ex-*Utah*, ex-*Irene D*, ex-*American Utah*)	9-85
(T-AKR 4544) Sgt Edward A. Carter, Jr. (ex-*Sea-Land Oregon*, ex-*OOCL Innovation*, ex-*Nedlloyd Hudson*, ex-*Nebraska*, ex-*Susan C*, ex-*American Nebraska*)	4-85

Ltc John U. D. Page (T-AKR 4496) Edward McDonnell, 5-06

D: 74,500 tons (fl) **S:** 18 kts **Dim:** 289.52 (279.00 pp) × 32.31 × 10.67
Electronics: Radar: 1 . . . nav.
M: 1 Sulzer-Hyundai 9RLB90 low-speed diesel; 1 prop; 28,000 bhp
Electric: *Page:* 3,300 kw (1 diesel generator); *Carter:* 3,300 kw tot. (3 × 1,000 kw, 1 × 300-kw diesel sets)
Range: 37,000/18 **Fuel:** 6,770.5 tons heavy oil, 950 tons diesel
Crew: 22 tot. (contract civilians)

Remarks: *Page:* 57,075 grt/58,869 dwt; *Carter:* 57,075 grt/57,939 dwt. Chartered through 2011 from the operator, Maersk Line, Norfolk, Virginia, to act as containerized U.S. Army ammunition prepositioning ships at Diego Garcia. The *Page* was delivered on 2-3-01 and the *Carter* on 15-6-01. *Carter* suffered four deaths during a serious engine-room fire on 14-7-01 while loading ammunition at Southport, North Carolina.
Hull systems: Carry 2,500 20-ft. containers (2,230 below decks and 270 in four new cocoon structures on the upper deck at the bases of the four new cargo cranes). As commercial container vessels, could carry 4,258 20-ft. containers in 11 holds. There are 36 wing tanks. The main engine is direct reversing. In merchant service, they displaced up to 81,281 tons full load and operated at up to 12.68-m draft.

♦ 1 Sea Wolf–class chartered Maritime Prepositioning Ships [AK]
Bldr: Odense Staalskibsværft A/S, Lindo, Denmark

	In serv.	In MSC
(T-AK 4396) Maj Bernard Fisher (ex-*Sea Fox*, ex-*American Hawaii*, ex-*Sea Fox*)	1985	9-9-99

Sp5 Eric G. Gibson (T-AK 5091)—no longer under charter
Edward McDonnell, 7-04

D: Approx. 44,000 tons (fl) **S:** 18.5 kts **Dim:** 198.86 (186.42 pp) × 32.24 × 10.99
Electronics: Radar: . . .
M: 1 Sulzer 7RTA76 7-cyl. diesel; 1 prop; 23,030 bhp—CP bow and stern thrusters
Electric: 5,550 kw tot. (3 × 1,500 kw, 1 × 1,050-kw diesel sets)
Crew: 25 tot. civilian contract mariners

AUXILIARY SHIPS *(continued)*

Remarks: 34,318 grt/24,500 dwt Ro-Ro and container ship. The *Fisher* was chartered 2-12-98 from Sealift Inc, Oyster Bay, New York, for 59 months; based at Diego Garcia in Maritime Prepositioned Ship Squadron 2 with U.S. Air Force equipment aboard. Renamed for Medal of Honor recipients, with two of the names reused from ships that went off-charter earlier in 1999. Operated by owner under contract through 2009.
Hull systems: Has a quarter stern door and 19.50-m-long by 6.25-m-wide ramp to vehicle deck with 335-m total lane length (about 27 standard trailers). 1,914 TEU container capacity. 200 $ft.^2$ refrigerated cargo space. Nine centerline and 20 wing hatches. Two 40-ton cranes.
Disposals: Sisters *Ltc Calvin P. Titus* (T-AK 5089) and *Sp5 Eric G. Gibson* (T-AK 5091) were deemed surplus and returned to owners Crowley American Transport Inc., in 2003.

♦ 1 MPC Neptun 900–class chartered Maritime Prepositioning Ship [AK]

Bldr: Schiffswerft Neptun GmbH, Rostock, Germany (In serv. 1990)

(T-AK 4729) American Tern (ex-*Kariba*)

American Tern (T-AK 4729) U.S. Navy

D: 17,350 tons **S:** 16 kts **Dim:** 158.9 × 23.2 × 10.1
Electronics: Radar: . . .
M: 1 Selzer 5RTA58 diesel; 1 prop; 10,808 bhp
Electric: 2,956 kw tot. (1 × 1,000-kw, 2 × 712-kw, 1 × 532-kw diesel sets)
Fuel: . . . Crew: 21 tot.

Remarks: Chartered by the MSC 24-12-02 from APL Maritime to replace the *Green Wave* (T-AK 2050) as the primary U.S. Antarctic supply vessel. She conducted her first voyage there during the 2002–3 season. The current contract expires 2010.
Hull systems: Built to Finnish Ice Class 1A specifications. Cargo capacity is 1,033 TEUs. Fitted with four holds and seven hatches, two 40-ton and one 60-ton cranes. Strengthened hull for light ice-breaking capabilities and heavy cargo.

♦ 1 chartered Maritime Prepositioning Ship [AK]

Bldr: Samsung, Koje, South Korea (In serv. 10-84)

(T-AK 4296) Capt Steven L. Bennett (ex-*Sea Pride;* ex-*Martha II,* ex-*TNT Express*)

Capt Steven L. Bennett (T-AK 4296)—note the white-painted sliding cover over the containerized cargo Edward McDonnell, 2-02

D: 59,207 tons (fl) **S:** 18.25 kts **Dim:** 209.40 (200.01 pp) × 30.41 × 11.60
Electronics: Radar: 1 . . . nav. **M:** 1 Sulzer 6RLB76 diesel; 1 prop; 16,320 bhp
Electric: 4,080 kw tot (4 × 1,020-kw diesel sets; 450 V a.c.) **Range:** . . . / . . .
Fuel: 2,857 tons heavy oil **Crew:** 24 tot.

Remarks: 29,223 grt/41,151 dwt. Former bulk cargo vessel with nine holds. Chartered 5-97 for $47.02 million from Ultra Maritime, Inc., division of Sealift, Inc. for operation through 4-01 (and later renewed through 2007) to preposition some 1,922 standard 20-ft. cargo containers of U.S. Air Force munitions in the Mediterranean as part of Maritime Prepositioning Squadron 1. Converted for MSC service at Bender Shipbuilding, Mobile, Alabama, to replace the *American Merlin;* renamed for a U.S. Air Force officer on 1-10-97. Delivered 30-9-98.

♦ 1 1st Lt Harry L. Martin–class chartered Maritime Prepositioning Ship [AK]

Bldr: Bremer Vulkan, Bremen-Vegesack, Germany (In serv. 3-79)

(T-AK 3015) 1st Lt Harry L. Martin (ex-*Tarago,* ex-*NOSAC Cedar,* ex-*CGM Rabelais,* ex-*Rabelais,* ex-*Liliooet*)

D: 51,531 tons (fl) **S:** 21.5 kts **Dim:** 229.85 (210.04 pp) × 32.31 × 10.94
M: 1 Bremer Vulkan-M.A.N. K7-SZ-90/160 diesel; 1 prop; 25,704 bhp
Electric: 5,880 kw tot. (2 × 2,140 kw, 1 × 1,600-kw diesel sets) **Range:** . . . / . . .
Fuel: 4,336 tons heavy oil + 668 tons diesel **Crew:** 24 contract mariners

Remarks: 39,441 grt/34,100 dwt prior to conversion. $110 million was included in FY 95 budget to acquire and convert one Maritime Prepositioning Force (Enhanced) Ship (MPF[E]) for the Marine Corps, but the money was not allocated during FY 95 and the funding authorization was extended into FY 96. The ship was chartered for five years from Tarago Shipholding Corp., Bethesda, Maryland, on 14-2-97 for $145.7 million, $100 million of which was for conversion and refit at Atlantic Drydock, Jacksonville, Florida, with delivery expected in 2-99, but the ship was not delivered until 21-4-00 and entered MSC service on 13-5-00. Cargo cranes were added, the cargo facilities altered, and a helicopter platform installed. Named 14-3-95 in honor of a World War II Marine Medal of Honor recipient. Is attached to Maritime Prepositioning Squadron 1 in the Mediterranean and is operated by its current owner, Keystone Prepositioning Services Inc., under a contract dated from 18-7-05 through 12-09.

1st Lt Harry L. Martin (T-AK 3015) Edward McDonnell, 5-06

Hull systems: The stern quarter vehicle ramp is 48.74 m long by 12 m wide; it has been adapted to permit driving vehicles onto shuttle craft and pontoons. The vehicle cargo space, including the new two-level structure forward, is climate-controlled. Fifteen hydraulically controlled watertight bulkhead doors have been added on the lower four vehicle decks. One 13.4 × 5.5–m and four 14.6 × 5.5–m cargo hatches were added, and the ship can now carry ammunition containers.

♦ 1 TSgt John A. Chapman–class chartered Maritime Prepositioning Ship [AK]

Bldr: Chantiers Shipyard, France (In serv. 1978)

(T-AK 323) TSgt John A. Chapman (ex-*Merlin*)

D: 40,357 tons (fl) **S:** 16 kts **Dim:** 204.2 × 26.5 × 10.5
Electronics: Radar: 1. . . nav.
M: 1 Pielstick diesel; 1 prop; . . . bhp
Range: . . . / . . . **Crew:** 19 contract mariners

Remarks: Operated by Sealift Inc. under a 30-9-02 through 28-8-07 charter. Operated as M/V *Merlin* (T-AK 323) until renamed during 4-05.

Hull systems: Cargo capacity is 143,064 sq. ft. Can carry 1,000 plus 20-ft. TEU cargo containers. In 2003 the ship was fitted with an air-conditioned and dehumidified cocoon storage system similar to that carried aboard the *Steven L. Bennet* (T-AK 4296). Has a vehicle loading ramp at stern.

♦ 5 2nd Lt John P. Bobo–class chartered Maritime Prepositioning Ships [AK]

Bldr: General Dynamics, Quincy, Mass.

	Laid down	L	In serv.
(T-AK 3008) 2nd Lt John P. Bobo	1-7-83	19-1-85	14-2-85
(T-AK 3009) Pfc Dewayne T. Williams	1-9-83	18-5-85	6-6-85
(T-AK 3010) 1st Lt Baldomero Lopez	23-3-84	26-10-85	21-11-85
(T-AK 3011) 1st Lt Jack Lummus	22-6-84	22-2-86	6-3-86
(T-AK 3012) Sgt William R. Button	22-8-84	17-5-86	22-5-86

Sgt William R. Button (T-AK 3012) Edward McDonnell, 4-06

1st Lt Jack Lummus (T-AK 3011) U.S. Marine Corps, 3-04

D: 19,588 tons light (46,111 fl) **S:** 23 kts (18 kts sustained)
Dim: 205.18 (187.32 pp/199.00 wl) × 32.16 × 4.50 light (9.78 max. loaded)
Electronics: Radar: 2 . . . nav.
M: 2 Stork Werkspoor 18TM410V diesels; 1 prop; 26,400 bhp—1,000-shp bow-thruster
Electric: 7,850 kw tot. **Range:** 15,000/18 **Fuel:** 3,080 tons
Crew: 29 contract mariners and 8 Navy (No Navy aboard T-AK 3009 and T-AK 3012)

AUXILIARY SHIPS *(continued)*

Remarks: 44,543 grt/26,523 dwt (22,454 cargo dwt)/14,461 nrt. Maritime Administration C8-M-MA134j design. First two contracted for on 17-8-82, others on 14-1-83. Intended to transport material needed for one Marine Expeditionary Brigade. Are owned by a variety of private holding corporations and are operated on an expected 25-year charter by American Overseas Marine Corp., a subsidiary of General Dynamics, that currently expires by 2011. *Bobo* is in Maritime Prepositioning Squadron One (MPS-1) in the Atlantic; the rest formed MPS-3 in 10-86, operating in the Guam-Saipan area, carrying equipment for the 1st Marine Expeditionary Brigade, Kaneohe Bay, Oahu. The *Williams* was refitted at Newport News SB from 12-2-01 to 7-3-01 and the *Button* from 26-4-01 to 8-5-01.
Hull systems: Cargo: 25,384 tons max. Cargo capacity includes up to 522 standard 20-ft. vans (350 for ammunition, 110 general stores, 30 with fuel drums, and 32 refrigerated), plus 14,000 m^2 of roll-on/roll-off vehicle capacity to carry up to 1,400 vehicles. A 66 long ton capacity, 32-m-long by 4.9-m-wide Navire stern slewing ramp provides access to the six vehicle decks and can either discharge vehicles to a pier or amphibious vehicles of up to 23 tons directly into the water; the stern door is 11 × 4.55 m. The upper deck can stow two LCM(8) landing craft, six unpowered causeway sections, four powered causeway sections, a warping tug, four pipe trailers, and 16 hose reels. The ships carry 5,764.6 m^3 (1,523,000 gallons) of transferable bulk fuel, plus 2,039 55-gallon fuel drums. They can also transport 307 m^3 of potable water. Five 39-ton pedestal cranes are fitted, with two sets being paired, and there is a large helicopter deck at the stern. Unloading rates: all vehicles and cargo at a pier in 12 hrs; all cargo at a pier in three days; all cargo while moored out in five days. There is a four-point mooring system. In addition to listed personnel, have 102 temporary berths for vehicle crews.

♦ 5 Cpl Louis J. Hauge, Jr.–class chartered Maritime Prepositioning Ships [AK]
Bldr: Odense Staalskibsvaerft A/S, Lindo, Denmark

	In serv.	Acq.	In serv.
(T-AK 3000) Cpl Louis J. Hauge, Jr. (ex-*Estelle Maersk*)	10-79	3-1-84	7-9-84
(T-AK 3001) Pfc William B. Baugh (ex-*Eleo Maersk*)	4-79	17-1-83	30-10-84
(T-AK 3002) Pfc James Anderson, Jr. (ex-*Emma Maersk*)	7-79	31-10-83	26-3-85
(T-AK 3003) 1st Lt Alex Bonnyman (ex-*Emelie Maersk*)	1-80	30-1-84	26-9-85
(T-AK 3004) Pvt Franklin J. Phillips (ex-*Pvt F. J. Phillips,* ex-*Pvt Franklin S. Phillips,* ex-*Pvt Harry Fisher,* ex-*Evelyn Maersk*)	4-80	2-4-83	12-9-85

PFC William B. Baugh (T-AK 3001) Edward McDonnell, 5-06

D: 23,414 tons light (49,453 fl) **S:** 21 kts (18.5 sust.)
Dim: 230.25 (215.00 pp) × 27.48 × 5.41 light (10.02 max. loaded)
Electronics: Radar: 2 . . . nav.
M: 1 Sulzer 7RND 76M, 7-cyl. diesel; 1 prop; 16,800 bhp—bow-thruster
Electric: 4,250 kw tot. **Range:** 15,000/18.5 **Fuel:** 1,902 tons
Crew: 25 contract mariners and 7 MSC crew, 30 maintenance crew

Remarks: Operated by former owner, Maersk Lines, on long-term charter. Now owned by several private investment corporations. First three conversions ordered 17-8-82, others on 14-1-83. Were converted by Bethlehem Steel at Sparrows Point, Maryland (*Baugh* and *Bonnyman:* Beaumont, Texas). All five are part of Maritime Prepositioning Ship Squadron 2 at Diego Garcia, with *Phillips,* as flagship, carrying eight-man Navy communications team and equipment for the 7th Marine Expeditionary Brigade, Twenty-Nine Palms, California. *Bonnyman* originally to be named *1st Lt Alexander Bonnyman, Jr.;* changed 4-3-86. Name of *Pvt. Harry Fisher* was belatedly changed during 1991 under a Secretary of the Navy directive signed 27-6-88; "Harry Fisher" was a pseudonym in use by Phillips when he won the Medal of Honor, he having deserted from the Marine Corps earlier under his real name. The charter to operate these ships runs through 2009–2010.
Hull systems: Cargo: 23,000 tons max. Each carries one-fifth of the vehicles, equipment, and supplies to outfit a Marine Expeditionary Brigade. Transport up to 413 containers (280 ammunition, 86 general cargo, 23 drummed fuel, 24 refrigerated), plus providing 11,369 m^2 vehicle cargo space. There are four 30-ton and two 36-ton pedestal cranes, side-loading vehicle ports amidships (with portable 13.7 or 27.4-m ramps), and a 66 long ton capacity, 32-m-long by 4.9-m-wide Navire slewing rampaft, beneath a helicopter deck. There are eight cargo hatches, and three vehicle parking decks. Liquid cargo includes 4,920 m^3 transferable vehicle fuel, 504 m^3 potable water, and 2,252 m^3 of lube oil.

♦ 3 Sgt Matej Kocak–class chartered Maritime Prepositioning Ships [AK]
Bldr: Sun Shpbldg., Chester, Pa. (Converted by National Steel and Shipbuilding, San Diego, Calif.)

	In serv.	Conv. completed
(T-AK 3005) Sgt Matej Kocak (ex-*John B. Waterman*)	14-3-81	5-10-84
(T-AK 3006) Pfc Eugene A. Obregon (ex-*Thomas Heyward*)	1-11-82	15-1-85
(T-AK 3007) Maj Stephen W. Pless (ex-*Charles Carroll*)	14-3-83	1-5-85

Maj Steven W. Pless (T-AK 3007) Marian Wright, 4-02

Sgt Matej Kocak (T-AK 3005) Marian Wright, 4-02

D: 19,588 tons light (51,612 fl) **S:** 20.9 kts (18 kts sustained)
Dim: 250.24 (234.85 pp) × 32.16 × 5.66 light (10.21 max. loaded)
Electronics: Radar: 2 . . . nav.
M: 2 sets G.E. geared steam turbines; 1 6-bladed prop; 32,000 shp
Boilers: 2 Combustion Engineering **Range:** 13,000/20.9
Fuel: 3,450 tons (+ 300 tons diesel)
Crew: 85 crew, 8 Navy, 25 maintenance crew

Remarks: 25,426 grt/22,910 dwt. First two conversions contracted for on 17-8-82, third on 14-1-83, all with Waterman Steamship Co. as operator. Now owned by separate private investment corporations. All operated by Waterman Steamship Corp. in the Mediterranean as Maritime Prepositioning Ship Squadron 1, carrying equipment intended for the 6th Marine Expeditionary Brigade, Camp Lejeune, North Carolina.
Hull systems: Cargo: 25,000 long tons max. Each is intended to transport one-fourth of the vehicles, fuel, supplies, and provisions to support a Marine Expeditionary Brigade. In forward three holds can carry 213 ammunition containers, 150 "Lo/Lo" containers, 10 general cargo containers, 32 drummed fuel containers, and 32 refrigerated containers. Remainder of cargo consists of a large number of vehicles and cargo fuel and water. Lengthened 39.8 m during conversion, and helicopter deck and ramp added. Have paired 50-ton and paired 35-ton portal cranes and retain a 30-ton capacity traveling gantry forward to handle containerized cargo. The articulating stern ramp can support up to 200 tons and is 40.8 m long. There is a 65-ton capacity, 13.6 × 4.4-m internal vehicle elevator.

Disposal notes: Chartered heavy-lift Maritime Prepositioning Ships *American Cormorant* (T-AK 2062, ex-*Ferncarrier,* ex-*Kollbris*) and *Strong Virginian* (T-AKR 9205, ex-*St. Magnus,* ex-*Jolly Indaco,* ex-*St. Magnus*) were returned to owners on 11-9-02 when the Army decided to preposition its floating equipment in Japan rather than at Diego Garcia. *Sagamor* (ex-*Mint Arrow,* ex-*Fas Red Sea II*) was returned to owners, Sealift Inc., on 20-1-05 and replaced in service by M/V *Baffin Strait.*

Prepositioning ship *Green Ridge* (T-AK 9655, ex-*Woerman Mercur,* ex-*Sloman Mercur,* ex-*Carol Mercur,* ex-*Sloman Mercur*) was returned to owners on 30-9-01. Prepositioning roll-on/roll-off cargo ship *Buffalo Soldier* (T-AK 9881, ex-*CGM Monet,* ex-*Monet*) was returned to her owners in 7-01. LASH-type carge barge carriers *Jeb Stuart* (T-AK 9204) and *Green Valley* (T-AK 2049) were discarded early in 2001 and scrapped at Alang, India, starting 7-01; sister *Green Harbour* (T-AK 2064) was sold for scrap in Bangladesh during 4-01. Dock Express–class chartered heavy lift cargo ship *Strong Texan* was returned to its owners during 2002.

♦ 1 Baffin Strait–class chartered prepositioning support ship [AK]
Bldr: Wuhu Shipyard, Wuhu, China (In serv. 7-96)

Baffin Strait (ex-*Steamers Future*)

D: 7,410 tons (fl) **S:** 15.5 kts **Dim:** 100.6 (94.80 pp) × 16.4 × 8.2
Electronics: Radar: . . .
M: 1 Wärtsilä 4-cylinder diesel; 1 CP prop; 3,693 bhp; 1 CP thruster
Electric: 1,500 kw tot. (3 × 500-kw diesel sets) **Range:** . . . / . . .
Crew: 13 tot. contract mariners

Remarks: 4,276 grt/4,599 dwt. A breakbulk/container ship chartered on 10-1-05 from Trans. Atlantic Lines Inc. which also operates the ship. She replaces M/V *Sagamore.* The charter runs until 30-9-09. Carries prepositioned ammunition, rations, and vehicles in support of prepositioning ships at Diego Garcia. Operates between Guam, Singapore, and Diego Garcia.
Hull systems: Has ice-strengthened hull. Has one hold 61.92 m long, served by two 39.4-ton-capacity container cranes mounted to port. Can accommodate 384 total TEU.

♦ 2 Wright-class aviation logistic support ships [AK]
Bldr: Ingalls SB, Pascagoula, Miss.

	In serv.	Converted
T-AVB 3 Wright (ex-*Young America,* ex-*Mormacsun*)	1970	14-12-84 to 14-5-86
T-AVB 4 Curtiss (ex-*Great Republic,* ex-*Mormacsky*)	1969	17-12-85 to 18-8-87

D: 12,409 tons light (23,800 fl) **S:** 23.6 kts
Dim: 183.49 (170.69 pp) × 27.43 × 10.36
Electronics: 2/ . . . nav. **M:** 2 sets G.E. geared steam turbines; 1 prop; 30,000 shp

AUXILIARY SHIPS *(continued)*

Wright (T-AVB 3) George R. Schneider, 9-05

Boilers: 2 Combustion Engineering **Electric:** 3,000 kw tot. (2 × 1,500 kw)
Range: 9,000/23 **Fuel:** 2,781 tons fuel oil + 839 tons diesel
Crew: 11 officers, 22 mariners + 300 Marines

Remarks: 23,255 grt/13,651 dwt. Are Maritime Administration C5-S-78a, Seabridge-type roll-on/roll-off vehicle cargo and container carriers converted by Todd SY, Galveston, Texas, to transport the men and equipment vans of a Marine Intermediate Maintenance Activity in support of aircraft deployed ashore. On 1-10-97 the ships were returned to Maritime Administration custody, which assigned them to the Ready Reserve Force on the same date. T-AVB 3 is in layberth at Baltimore, Maryland, and T-AVB 4 at San Diego, California, with both on five-day recall; they are maintained by (and would be operated by, if activated) American Overseas Marine. During 2003 T-AVB 4 and T-AVB 3 were activated for Mideast duties.

Curtiss (T-AVB 4)—in layup at San Diego W. Michael Young, 6-05

Hull systems: Additional accommodations built on aft and helicopter deck added over former forward holds. Cargo capacity: 34,903 m^3 grain/31,824 m^3 bale, including 170 m^3 refrigerated cargo. In "Intermediate Maintenance Activity" mode carry up to 300 Mobile Maintenance Facility modules and 52 "Access Modules," each the size of a standard 20-ft. cargo container. In "Resupply Mode" (i.e., on subsequent voyages after delivering the aircraft support facility) can carry up to 332 40-ft. containers or 654 20-ft. containers, or 352 vehicles and 14,000 bbl liquid cargo. Have stern ramp and two side doors aft for vehicles. Ten 30-ton, one 70-ton cargo derricks. Six holds, but forward two can only be unloaded by off-ship cranes.

♦ 8 SL-7-class Fast Sealift ships [AK]

	Bldr	In serv.	To Navy	Conv.
T-AKR 287 Algol (ex-*Sea-Land Exchange*)	Rotterdamse DDM, Rotterdam	7-5-73	13-10-81	22-6-84
T-AKR 288 Bellatrix (ex-*Sea-Land Trade*)	Rheinstahl Nordseewerke, Emden	6-4-73	13-10-81	10-9-84
T-AKR 289 Denebola (ex-*Sea-Land Resource*)	Rotterdamse DDM, Rotterdam	4-12-73	27-10-81	10-10-85
T-AKR 290 Pollux (ex-*Sea-Land Market*)	A.G. Weser, Bremen	20-9-73	16-11-81	27-3-86
T-AKR 291 Altair (ex-*Sea-Land Finance*)	Rheinstahl Nordseewerke, Emden	17-9-73	5-1-82	13-11-85
T-AKR 292 Regulus (ex-*Sea-Land Commerce*)	A.G. Weser, Bremen	30-3-73	27-10-81	28-8-85
T-AKR 293 Capella (ex-*Sea-Land McLean*)	Rotterdamse DDM, Rotterdam	4-10-72	16-4-82	30-6-84
T-AKR 294 Antares (ex-*Sea-Land Galloway*)	A.G. Weser, Bremen	27-9-72	16-4-82	12-7-84

Antares (T-AKR 294) Edward McDonnell, 7-04

Denebola (T-AKR 289)—with *Regulus* (T-AKR 292) in the background
Ralph Edwards, 9-04

Algol (T-AKR 287) George R. Schneider, 9-05

D: T-AKR 287, 288, 292: 29,993 tons light (55,588 fl); T-AKR 289, 293: 30,391 tons light (55,560 fl); T-AKR 290, 291: 31,017 tons light (55,425 fl); T-AKR 294: 29,692 tons light (55, 350 fl)
S: 33 kts (30.1 loaded; 25 sust.)
Dim: 288.38 (268.37 pp) × 32.16 × 11.22 max. (T-AKR 287, 288, 292, 294: 11.18)
Electronics: Radar: 2/ . . . nav.
M: 2 sets G.E. MST-19 geared steam turbines; 2 props; 120,000 shp
Boilers: 2 Foster-Wheeler; 61.6 kg/cm^2, 507° C
Electric: 8,000 kw tot. (2 × 3,000-kw, 1 × 1,500-kw, 1 × 500-kw diesel sets)
Range: 14,000/33 light, 12,200/27 loaded **Fuel:** 5,384 tons
Crew: 43 tot. contract mariners (12 tot. layup caretaker crew)

Remarks: 48,525 grt/24,270 dwt (varies). Six acquired under FY 81 and two under FY 82, with the original intent of extensively converting them to serve as T-AKR, Roll-on/Roll-off vehicle cargo ships for the Rapid Deployment Force. Instead, under FY 82 Congress mandated that four be given a "partial" Ro/Ro conversion and the other four be given only a "mini-modification." This was later changed to give all essentially the same modification, T-AKR 287, 288, 293, and 294 under FY 82 and the others under FY 84. The conversions were performed by: T-AKR 287, 288, 292: National Steel, San Diego; T-AKR 289 and 293: Pennsylvania SB, Chester, Pennsylvania; and the others by Avondale SY, Westwego, Louisiana; the latter ships have an additional hinged internal ramp. The ships were given T-AK-series hull numbers when purchased; these were changed to T-AKR without changing the actual numbers assigned, AKR 287 on 19-6-84, AKR 288 on 10-9-84, AKR 293 and 294 on 30-6-84, rest on 1-11-83.

Operated by Maersk Line Ltd. and American Overseas Marine, a division of General Dynamics, since 5-00 with options for renewal; current contracts expire in 2010. Maintained in five-day ready-to-steam status at: T-AKR 287, T-AKR 288, T-AKR 290, and T-AKR 292 at New Orleans, Louisiana; T-AKR 289 at Brooklyn, New York; T-AKR 291 at Norfolk, Virginia; and T-AKR 293 and T-AKR 294 at Jacksonville, Fla. All have caretaker crews. During Operation Desert Shield/Desert Storm in 1990–91, steamed at an average of 27 kts and performed the work of an estimated 116 World War II–era break-bulk ships; seven of the ships carried 11 percent of all the cargo transported to the Mid-East. T-AKR 287 was activated in support of Operation Enduring Freedom on 16-11-02, T-AKR 288 on 27-12-02, T-AKR 290 and T-AKR 294 on 3-1-03, and T-AKR 289 and T-AKR 292 on 16-1-03.

Hull systems: Cargo: 25,500 long tons max. The side vehicle loading ramps are 22.3 m long and 6 m wide and can support 65 long tons. Conversion entailed filling in the amidships portion to produce a five-deck vehicle cargo area and helicopter hangar totaling 12,170 m^2 (can accommodate up to 120 UH-1 helicopters or 183 M-1 tanks). This is topped by a flight deck of 3,252 m^2 with a twin 35-ton crane plumbing two hatches interrupting the forward half. The stern provides 1,719 m^2 of vehicle parking, as well as cargo space for eight "Sea Shed" containerized vehicle stowage or 44 or 46 20-ft. containers; it is served by a twin 50-ton crane. There are vehicle access ramps amidships, port and starboard.

The ships were originally tailored to transport up to 1,086 nonstandard 35-ft. containers (standard cargo containers are either 20 or 40 feet in length); 4,000 containers were purchased along with the first six ships. They proved too expensive to operate for the former merchant owner, and their sophisticated propulsion plants have not been overly reliable in Navy service. Made 35 kts on trials in light condition, 33 kts at 32,600 tons. Fuel tankage originally included 5,384 tons fuel oil, 3,116 tons diesel. Also carry 569 tons potable water and 4,893 tons permanent ballast water. Up to 9,484 tons of saltwater ballast can be carried.

Disposal note: Chartered combination cargo ship *Maersk Constellation* (T-AK 9656) was returned to owner Maersk Lines in 9-01.

♦ 1 chartered Down Range Support Ship [AK]

Bldr: Ira S. Bushey & Sons., New York, NY (In serv. 1958)

Seamark III

D: 550 tons (fl) **S:** . . . kts **Dim:** 45.72 × 15.24 × 2.8
M: 1 Fairbanks-Morse 38D8 diesel; 1 prop; 1,800 bhp

Remarks: Oceangoing tug under charter since 2003 for Down Range Support at the Atlantic Missile Test Range is at Andros Island, the Bahamas, and other Caribbean regional experimental facilities.

AUXILIARY SHIPS *(continued)*

♦ **16 Henry J. Kaiser–class replenishment oilers [AO]** (3 in *reserve*)
Bldr: Northrop Grumman Avondale, Westwego, La. (*Atlantic/†Pacific Fleet)

	Laid down	L	In serv.
T-AO 187 *Henry J. Kaiser*†	22-8-84	5-10-85	19-12-86
T-AO 188 *Joshua Humphreys*	17-12-84	22-2-86	3-4-87
T-AO 189 John Lenthall*	15-7-85	9-8-86	25-6-87
T-AO 190 *Andrew J. Higgins*	21-11-85	17-1-87	22-10-87
T-AO 193 Walter S. Diehl†	7-8-86	2-10-87	13-9-88
T-AO 194 John Ericsson†	15-3-89	21-4-90	19-3-91
T-AO 195 Leroy Grumman*	6-7-87	3-12-88	2-8-89
T-AO 196 Kanawha*	13-7-89	22-9-90	6-12-91
T-AO 197 Pecos†	17-2-88	23-9-89	6-7-90
T-AO 198 Big Horn*	9-10-89	2-2-91	21-5-92
T-AO 199 Tippecanoe†	19-11-90	16-5-92	8-2-93
T-AO 200 Guadalupe†	9-7-90	5-10-91	25-9-92
T-AO 201 Patuxent*	16-10-91	23-7-94	21-6-95
T-AO 202 Yukon†	13-5-91	6-12-93	27-4-94
T-AO 203 Laramie*	10-1-94	6-5-95	7-5-96
T-AO 204 Rappahannock†	29-6-92	14-1-95	7-11-95

Big Horn (T-AO 198) U.S. Navy, 10-05

Yukon (T-AO 202) U.S. Navy, 4-05

Rappahannock (T-AO 204) W. Michael Young, 1-04

D: 9,500 tons light (40,700–42,000 fl) **S:** 20 kts (sust.)
Dim: 206.51 (198.13 pp) × 29.75 × 10.97 max.
A: Provision for 2 20-mm Mk 15 Phalanx gatling CIWS; fitted with 2 single 12.7-mm mg when on deployment
Electronics:
Radar: 2 Raytheon . . . nav.
EW: SLQ-25 towed torpedo decoy syst.

Guadalupe (T-AO 200) U.S. Navy, 1-06

M: 2 Colt-Pielstick 10 PC4.2V 570 diesels; 2 CP props; 32,540 bhp—diesel-electric low-speed drive
Electric: 12,000 kw tot. (2 × 3,500-kw, 2 × 2,500-kw diesel sets)
Range: 6,000/20 **Fuel:** 1,629 tons heavy oil, 165 tons diesel
Crew: 10 officers, 76 MSC Civil Service mariners + 23 Navy (one officer, 22 enlisted)

Remarks: 20,706 grt/28,407 dwt, except T-AO 202–204: 20,706 grt/24,825.5 dwt. Authorized: T-AO 187 in FY 82, T-AO 188 in FY 83, T-AO 189–190 in FY 84, T-AO 191–193 in FY 85, T-AO 194–195 in FY 86, T-AO 196–197 in FY 87, T-AO 198–199 in FY 88, and T-AO 200–204 in FY 89. Design contract let to George Sharp, Inc., 11-7-80. Deliveries were greatly delayed by the bankruptcy of the second-source builder, PennShip, but Avondale's work was also well behind schedule. T-AO 194 and 196 were originally ordered 7-86 from PennShip, but were canceled at the yard's request and reordered 16-6-88 from Avondale. T-AO 198, 200, 202, and 204 were ordered 6-10-88, with T-AO 199, 201, and 203 to have gone to an alternate yard; instead, Avondale bid lowest and won contract 28-3-89, accounting for out-of-sequence construction schedule. Navy had requested only one for FY 89, planned two each year in FY 90 and 91; instead, Congress "bought out" remainder of the program. Have proven very successful in service. Plans to convert three of the class to ammunition ships were dropped. T-AO 202 collided with small civilian cargo ship *Inchcape-14* off Jebel Ali, Dubai, on 27-2-00. T-AO 202 was in collision with the *Denver* (LPD 9) on 13-7-00 near Hawaii; repairs were completed early in 1-01.
Status: T-AO 187 is laid up in Portland, Oregon, in MSC 30-day call-up, reduced operating status. T-AO 188 was placed in reduced operating status in 10-93, with a crew of 25. She was reactivated 1-94 through 16-12-94, placed out of service in reserve on 29-6-96, and again reactivated on 5-12-05; she rejoined the reserve fleet as a mobilization asset on 1-10-06. T-AO 189 was placed in reserve on 11-11-96 but reactivated on 8-2-99. T-AO 190 was placed out of service in reserve on 6-5-96. She was transferred to MARAD the same date and is laid up in the reserve fleet at Suisun Bay.
Hull systems: Cargo: T-AO 187–200: 32 tanks totaling 21,161 m^3, equating to 180,000 bbl liquid (86,400 bbl fuel oil; 54,000 bbl JP-5; 39,600 convertible; plus 327 tons feedwater, 390 tons potable water), plus 534 pallets dry cargo and eight 20-ft. provisions containers. Under a contract modification required by Congress and signed 16-9-92, the final three (T-AO 201, 203, and 204) have double-hull construction, increasing their cost and decreasing their capacity by 17%, with a possible small increase in survivability. The three have a liquid capacity of 29,820 m^3 in 27 tanks (159,500 barrels); some of the double-hull voids, however, have been fitted with valves and piping to permit them to be used for cargo fuel stowage in time of war and restoring most of the lost capacity. All have five alongside liquid transfer stations (three to port) and one solid transfer station per side are fitted; T-AO 194, 197, and 200 have only three replenishment stations in service, due to personnel restrictions. There are eight cargo pumps, with a combined capacity of 5,448 tons/hr. There is a helicopter deck aft but no hangar. The engines for the first two were made by Alstom in France. A CGEE-Alstom integrated auxiliary electric drive system is fitted for low speeds, driving either or both props.
Disposals: The incomplete *Benjamin Isherwood* (T-AO 191) and *Henry Eckford* (T-AO 192) were transferred to MARAD on 15-8-93 for long-term layup in James River, Virginia, with T-AO 191 95.3% complete and T-AO 192 84.0% complete. Both ships were stricken and transferred to the MARAD for disposal on 29-12-97.

♦ **0 (+ 1 + . . .) T-AOE(X) class**

Remarks: The first ship of a replacement combat support ship class was planned for authorization and funding in the FY 09 budget, but was canceled in 2006.

AUXILIARY SHIPS *(continued)*

♦ 4 Supply-class fast combat support ships [AOR]

Bldr: General Dynamics National Steel & Shipbuilding Co. (NASSCO), San Diego, Calif. (*Atlantic Fleet/†Pacific Fleet)

	Laid down	L	In serv.
T-AOE 6 SUPPLY*	24-2-89	6-10-90	26-2-94
T-AOE 7 RAINIER (ex-*Paul Hamilton*)†	31-5-90	28-9-91	21-1-95
T-AOE 8 ARCTIC*	2-12-91	30-10-93	16-9-95
T-AOE 10 BRIDGE†	2-8-94	24-8-96	5-8-98

Supply (T-AOE 6) U.S. Navy, 5-06

Rainier (AOE 7) U.S. Navy, 1-05

Arctic (AOE 8) U.S. Navy, 3-05

D: T-AOE 6: 20,796 tons light (50,858 fl); others: 20,669–20,674 tons light (50,731–50,794 fl)
S: 26 kts **Dim:** 229.73 (222.56 wl) × 32.61 × 11.66 (11.53 mean)
A: T-AOE 6 and 7: none; others: inactivated: 1 8-round Mk 29 SAM launcher (RIM-7P Sea Sparrow missiles); 2 single 25-mm 75-cal. Mk 38 Bushmaster low-angle guns; 2 20-mm Mk 15 Phalanx gatling CIWS; 4 single 12.7-mm M2 mg (see Remarks)
Electronics:
Radar: 1 Raytheon SPS-64(V)9 nav.; 1 Norden SPS-67(V)1 surf. search; AOE 8–10 only: 1 Hughes Mk 23 TAS target designation; 2 Raytheon Mk 95 SAM f.c.; 2 Mk 90 Phalanx f.c. (see Remarks)
TACAN: URN-25
EW: AOE 8–10 only: Raytheon SLQ-32(V)3 active/passive; Mk 36 SRBOC decoy syst. (4 6-round Mk 137 RL); SLQ-25 Nixie towed passive torpedo decoy system (see Remarks)
M: 4 G.E. LM-2500-30 gas turbines; 2/6-bladed fixed-pitch props; 105,000 shp
Electric: 12,500 kw (5 × 2,500-kw Caterpillar 3608, 3,100-bhp diesel-driven sets)
Range: 6,000/22 **Fuel:** 2,654 tons **Crew:** 176 MSC civilian crew, 59 Navy

Remarks: Modified versions of the AOE 1 class with better protective systems and modern propulsion plants. Authorized: AOE 6 in FY 87, AOE 7 in FY 89, AOE 8 in FY 90, AOE 10 in FY 92. AOE 6 ordered 23-1-87, with option to build AOE 7–9. AOE 7 was ordered on 3-11-88, AOE 8 on 6-12-89. AOE 9 (to have been named *Conecuh*) was authorized and funded under FY 91 but the funding was rescinded by the administration and the ship canceled. AOE 10 was authorized and funded under FY 92 and was ordered on 15-1-93. There were originally to have been seven, but no additional units are now planned. The original name for AOE 7 was reassigned to DDG 60. Completions were delayed by engineering and labor problems, and there were considerable cost overruns with the program. Seventeen MSC civilian stewards replaced 24 enlisted food servicemen aboard AOE 6 on 3-3-00 for a year's trial; the ship was transferred to the Military Sealift Command on 13-7-01 as T-AOE 6, while AOE 8 followed on 14-6-02, AOE 7 on 29-8-03; AOE 10 on 24-6-04; the 59-strong Navy contingent on the T-AOE ships includes 31 assigned to the helicopter detachment. T-AOE 6 and AOE 8 are based at Earle, New Jersey, the other two at Bremerton, Washington.
Hull systems: Cargo: 156,000 bbl liquid (30% fuel oil, 40% JP-5, 30% convertible), 500 55-gal drums of fuel oil, 20,000 gal. potable water, and 2,450 tons dry stores (including 1,800 tons ammunition, 400 tons refrigerated provisions, 250 tons other stores, and 800 gas bottles). Have five refueling at sea stations and six solids replenishment-at-sea stations.

There are four 10-ton capacity cargo derricks. The hangar can accommodate two MH-60 utility/vertical replenishment helicopters.
Combat systems: The weapons systems were inactivated in FY 99 to reduce crew requirements by one officer and 40 enlisted personnel; weapons and all sensors other than the navigational radars were removed as part of the transfer to MSC.

Disposal note: *Sacramento*-class fast combat support ships *Sacramento* (AOE 1), *Camden* (AOE 2), *Seattle* (AOE 3), and *Detroit* (AOE 4) were retired during 2005.

♦ 1 T-1-type chartered coastal transport tanker [AOT]

Bldr: Tuzla Gemi Endustrisi, A.S., Tuzla, Turkey (In serv. 1999)

MONTAUK (ex-*Bitten Theresa*)

Montauk—as *Bitten Theresa* Jan Van Den Klooster, 11-00

D: Approx. 7,000 tons (fl) **S:** 13 kts **Dim:** 109.10 (99.60 pp) × 16.00 × 5.69
M: 1 M.A.N.-Burmeister & Wain Alpha 8L28/32 diesel; 1 CP prop; 2,665 bhp—bow-thruster
Range: . . . / . . . **Crew:** . . .

Remarks: 3,457 grt/4,780 dwt. Former Danish chemical tanker chartered 27-11-00 through 8-02 from Sealift Inc. for $10.751 million to transport fuels from Korea to Japan; the contract was later extended through 2006. Cargo: 5,850 m^3 liquid in 12 tanks. The ship replaced the *Valiant* (ex-*Seta*, ex-*Chimorazo*, ex-*Thomona*).

♦ 4 Paul Buck (T5-M-PVT022)–class transport tankers [AOT]

Bldr: American SB, Tampa, Fla.

	Laid down	L	In serv.
T-AOT 1122 PAUL BUCK (ex-*Ocean Champion*)	28-10-84	1-6-85	11-9-85
T-AOT 1123 SAMUEL L. COBB (ex-*Ocean Triumph*)	17-4-85	2-11-85	15-11-85
T-AOT 1124 RICHARD G. MATTHIESEN (ex-*Ocean Spirit*)	13-8-85	15-2-86	18-2-86
T-AOT 1125 LAWRENCE H. GIANELLA (ex-*Ocean Star*)	2-12-85	19-4-86	22-4-86

Richard G. Matthiesen (T-AOT 1124) Michael Young, 4-05

D: 9,000 tons light (39,624 fl) **S:** 16 kts
Dim: 187.45 (179.07 pp) × 27.43 × 10.36
Electronics: Radar: 1/ . . . nav.
M: 1 Mitsubishi- or Ishikawajima-Sulzer 5RTA-76 diesel; 1 prop; 15,300 bhp
Electric: 2,250 kw tot. (3 × 750-kw heavy oil sets) **Range:** 12,000/16
Fuel: 1,422 tons heavy oil, 254 tons diesel
Crew: 9 officers, 15 contract mariners

AUXILIARY SHIPS *(continued)*

Paul Buck (T-AOT 1122) Michael Young, 6-05

Remarks: 21,471 grt (*Buck:* 29,500 dwt; *Matthiesen:* 29,526 dwt; *Cobb:* 32,572 dwt; and *Gianella:* 32,965 dwt). *Paul Buck* was contracted for on 30-9-82, and other three ordered 24-4-83. Some sections of the ships built at Nashville, Tennessee, for later joining to the main body, and the forebodies were subcontracted to Avondale SY. Chartered for five years; renewed. Operated by Ocean Ship Holdings (*Cobb* by Sealift Inc. of New York) for investor-owners. *Lawrence Gianella* acted as a strategic prepositioning ship at Diego Garcia in 1994–95 but is now, like the others, used on worldwide freighting duties. *Matthiesen* was refitted in Greece during 1999. All were bought outright by the U.S. Navy on 15-1-03.
Hull systems: Ice-strengthened hulls. Engines in first two built by Mitsubishi; others by Ishikawajima-Harima Heavy Industries. Cargo: 238,400 bbl (last two: 239,500 bbl). All have three Caterpillar 3/50 diesel generator sets, plus a Nishishiba shaft generator and a G.M. emergency diesel generator. Can make 16 kts at 75% power. Can carry up to 14,675 bbl liquid ballast. *Matthiesen* and *Gianella* have two Modular Fuel Delivery System (MFDS) equipment installations, permitting their use in alongside, underway refueling; they also have an over-the-stern refueling capability.
Disposals: *Gus W. Darnell* (T-AOT 1121) was returned to her owner, Ocean Spirit Inc., Houston, Texas, on 10-9-05.

♦ 1 chartered TSV 101–class Theater Logistics Vessel troop and vehicle transport [AP]

Bldr: Austal Ltd., Fremantle, Australia (In serv. 2001)

HSV 4676 Westpac Express

Westpac Express—at Yokosuka; the bow vehicle ramp is lowered
Mitsuhiro Kadota, 7-01

Westpac Express Austal Ltd., 2001

D: . . . tons **S:** 37 kts (33 sust., loaded)
Dim: 101.00 (88.70 immersed hulls) × 26.65 × 4.20
A: None **Electronics:** Radar: . . .
M: 4 Caterpillar 3618 diesels; 4 KaMeWa 125S11 waterjets; 40,236 bhp
Fuel: 160,000 liters + 240,000 liters in long-range tanks **Crew:** . . . + 970 troops

Remarks: 750 dwt. Chartered for two months starting 3-7-01 and extended since by the 3rd Marine Expeditionary Force, Okinawa, to transport Marine Corps personnel and vehicles between White Beach, Okinawa, and Japanese ports including Yokosuka and Iwakuni; the charter is in effect a trial of the effectiveness of a new Theater Support Vessel concept which, if successful may be expanded to more than ten Westpac Express–type vessels. Retains the builder's blue-and-white paint scheme and carries "Austal.com" on the sides. Charter was transferred to the Military Sealift Command on 30-1-02 having proven extremely useful. "HSV 4676" is the MSC accounting number for the ship, not an official USN hull number, and is not painted on. The current charter runs through 2007.
Hull systems: Wave-piercing, catamaran-hulled design. Can carry up to 550 tons of vehicle cargo in addition to up to 951 Marines. Some 100 HMMWV four-wheeled vehicles or 251 automobiles can be stowed on the mezzanine deck, with four trucks and up to 12 UH-1-sized helicopters on the main deck. The mezzanine deck has 1,190 lane meters of vehicle parking space, with 341 lane meters down the center being high enough to accommodate ten 40-ton trucks, and the vehicle axle load is 15 tons. The entire deck is hoistable in four sections, and there is a bow door for unloading vehicles to a pier. The 7,500-kw diesel engines drive four Reintjes VLJ6831 gearboxes, which in turn drive the four waterjets. The ship may not be suitable for combat, due to a lack of damaged stability and battle damage-control systems.

♦ 2 Samuel Gompers–class destroyer tenders [AR] (in *reserve*)

Bldrs: AD 38, Puget Sound NSY; AD 42: General Dynamics National Steel & Shipbuilding Co. (NASSCO), San Diego, Calif.

	Laid down	L	In serv.	To reserve
AD 38 *Puget Sound*	15-2-65	16-9-66	27-4-68	27-1-96
AD 42 *Acadia*	14-2-78	28-7-79	6-6-81	16-12-94

Acadia (AD 42)—in reserve at Pearl Harbor Brian Morrison, 6-00

D: AD 38: 14,156 tons light (20,830 fl); AD 42: 13,526 tons light (20,473 fl)
S: 20 kts **Dim:** 196.29 × 25.91 × 6.86 **A:** Removed
Electronics:
Radar: 1 Raytheon SPS-64(V)9 nav.; 1 Raytheon SPS-10 surf. search
TACAN: AD 38 only: URN-25
M: 2 sets De Laval geared steam turbines; 1 prop; 20,000 shp
Boilers: 2 Combustion Engineering; 43.6 kg/cm^2, 462° C **Electric:** 12,000 kw tot.
Crew: 43 officers, 578–583 enlisted + repair party: 798 enlisted (accomm.: AD 38: 106 officers, 1,314 enlisted; AD 42: 87 officers, 1,508 enlisted)

Remarks: Maintenance ships for cruisers, destroyers, and frigates. Similar in external appearance to *L. Y. Spear*–class submarine tenders. AD 42 (and later sisters) were considered a separate class (SCB 700 type) and had facilities to carry and overhaul LM-2500 gas turbines, having been tailored to support DD 963–, DDG 993–, and FFG 7–class ships. AD 38 is stored at Pearl Harbor and AD 42 at Philadelphia, Pennsylvania.
Hull systems: Have helo deck aft, but only AD 38 has a hangar. Two 30-ton cranes; two 3.5-ton traveling cranes. Excellent workshops for electronic equipment and surface-to-air missiles. Can carry 60,000 different types of repair parts in 65 storerooms totaling 1,795 m^3.
Combat systems: Originally were planned to carry a Sea Sparrow launcher in AD 41 and later. One 127-mm DP gun removed from AD 38 in 1979; the others never carried the weapon. AD 38 served as 6th Fleet flagship from 7-80 to 4-10-85, having received an extra mast to support a special SATCOM antenna (all had the standard WSC-3 SATCOM installation, with two OE-82 drum-shaped antennas).

Disposal notes: All six of the class were to be retained indefinitely as mobilization assets, but under a 20-2-98 decision, all except *Samuel Gompers* (AD 37) were to be stricken and scrapped, depriving the USN of a potential mobile repair and support capability for surface warships. Stricken 7-4-99, however, were *Samuel Gompers* (AD 37, decommissioned on 27-10-95 and sunk as a target on 22-7-03), *Yellowstone* (AD 41, decommissioned 31-1-96), *Cape Cod* (AD 43, decommissioned 23-9-95), and *Shenandoah* (AD 44, decommissioned 13-9-96).

♦ 1 Zeus-class cable ship [ARC]

Bldr: National Steel and Shipbuilding (NASSCO), San Diego, Calif.

	Laid down	L	In serv.
T-ARC 7 Zeus	1-6-81	9-10-82	19-3-84

Zeus (T-ARC 7) W. Michael Young, 11-04

AUXILIARY SHIPS *(continued)*

Zeus (T-ARC 7) Takatoshi Okano, 4-01

D: 9,110 tons light (14,225 fl) **S:** 15.6 kts **Dim:** 153.2 (138.4 pp) × 22.3 × 7.92
Electronics: Radar: 1 . . . nav.; 1 Thales-DRS Scout surf. search
M: 5 G.M. EMD 20-cyl., 3,600-bhp diesels, electric drive; 2 CP props; 12,500 shp—4 1,200-shp side thrusters (2 forward, 2 aft)
Range: 10,000/15 **Fuel:** 1,816 tons **Electric:** 3,500 kw tot.
Crew: 88 MSC civil service crew + 32 civilian technicians + Navy: 6 enlisted

Remarks: 3,750 dwt. Authorized under FY 79 budget and ordered 17-8-79. Plans to request a second were canceled. After 15 years of primarily Pacific Ocean operations, was transferred to the Atlantic 24-3-97 and refitted at Mobile, Alabama. Operates about 300 days at sea per year. Painted white. Operated by Civil Service mariner crew.
Hull systems: Cable capacity is 1,170 m^3 coiled (about 590 n.m.) plus 1,004 m^3 spare capacity (506 n.m.), and up to 3,117 tons of cable repeaters can be stowed. Can lay 1000 nm of cable in water up to 10 miles deep. Able to conduct acoustic, hydrographic, and bathymetric surveys. The five main engines also provide for the ship's-service generators; there is also a 500-kw emergency generator. Has passive tank roll stabilization.

Note: Five commercial cable ships owned by the British Cable and Wireless Marine were under short-term charter to MSC during mid-2001: *Monarch, Nexus, Seaspread, Sovereign,* and *Sir Eric Sharpe.*

♦ 4 Safeguard-class salvage ships [ARS]
Bldr: Peterson Bldrs., Sturgeon Bay, Wisc. (*Atlantic/†Pacific Fleet)

	Laid down	L	In serv.
ARS 50 Safeguard†	8-11-82	12-11-83	17-8-85
T-ARS 51 Grasp*	30-3-83	21-4-84	14-12-85
ARS 52 Salvor†	16-9-83	28-7-84	14-6-86
T-ARS 53 Grapple*	25-4-84	8-12-84	15-11-86

Salvor (ARS 52) U.S. Navy, 1-06

Safeguard (ARS 50) U.S. Navy, 7-05

D: 2,482–2,633 tons light (3,181–3,317 fl) **S:** 13.5 kts
Dim: 77.72 (73.15 wl) × 15.54 × 5.49 **A:** 2 single 12.7-mm mg
Electronics: Radar: 1 Raytheon SPS-69 nav.; 1 Raytheon SPS-64(V)9 nav.
M: 4 Caterpillar D399, 16-cyl. diesels, geared drive; 2 CP Kort-nozzle props; 4,400 bhp—500-shp electric bow-thruster
Electric: 2,250 kw tot. (3 Caterpillar D399 diesel sets driving; 450 V, 60 Hz a.c.)
Range: 8,000/12 **Crew:** 26 MSC mariners + 4 Navy personnel

Remarks: Authorized: one in FY 81, two in FY 82, one in FY 83. *Safeguard* was ordered during 1981, with an option for four more. One additional unit of this class was planned for request under FY 91 and then deferred to FY 94 but dropped; in FY 91 it was planned to request *two* under FY 96, but by FY 93 the ships had disappeared from the building program. Design developed from ARS 38. Up to 25% of crew can be women. Although these are excellent ships, the USN in general lacks sufficient salvage assets and requires commercial assistance in most major salvage efforts. *Safeguard* has been homeported at Sasebo, Japan, since 16-6-99, *Salvor* is based at Pearl Harbor, and the other two operate from Norfolk, Virginia. *Grasp* and *Grapple* were decommissioned in 2006 and transferred to the Military Sealift Command for further service, they will be followed by *Safeguard* and *Salvor* in 2007.
Hull systems: Have 54-ton open-ocean bollard pull and, using beach extraction gear, are able to exert 360-ton pull. Have 500-hp bow-thruster. 40-ton boom aft, 7.5-ton forward. Are able to dead-lift 150 tons over bow or stern. Cargo hold 596 m^3. Two 914-m-long, 57-mm towing hawsers; able to tow a CVN at 5 kts. Have Mk 12 diving system and are able to support hard-hat divers to 58 m and SCUBA divers; decompression chamber fitted. Four foam firefighting monitors are carried. Can deploy several different types of remotely operated salvage submersibles.

♦ 1 chartered deep-submergence rescue tender [ARS]
Bldr: North American Shipbuilding, Inc., Larose, La. (In serv. 17-3-96)

Kellie Chouest

Kellie Chouest W. Michael Young, 3-05

D: 1,550 tons (fl) **S:** 13 kts **Dim:** 94.48 (88.88 pp) × 15.80 × 4.58
M: 2 G.M. Electromotive Div. EMD 645-E5 16-cyl. diesels; 2 props; 3,900 bhp
Electric: 900 kw tot. (3 × 300-kw diesel sets)
Crew: 13 contract civilians; up to 40 Navy personnel

Remarks: 2,786 grt/2,373 dwt. Edison Chouest Offshore, Galliano, Louisiana, received a $6.7-million contract from MSC on 16-8-94 to build and operate on charter a deep submergence vehicle support ship for Commander, Submarine Force Atlantic. On completion by 1-3-96, ship was to be on a 17-month charter, with options for renewal. The current charter runs from 2004 through 2010. Homeported at San Diego.
Hull systems: During 9-96 the *Kellie Chouest* operated the remote-controlled salvage submersible *Scorpio* and a submarine personnel rescue chamber. Has also been used to deploy a DSRV rescue submersible. There is a submersible lifting platform at the stern to launch and retrieve submersibles. Equipped with four-point mooring system, Robertson dynamic positioning system, ORE Trackpoint II and Nautronix RS-916 tracking systems, and a Racal Pelagos Winfrom integrated navigation system. A 68-ton capacity submersible elevator is used to launch and recover submersibles. Hull painted red-orange and superstructure cream.

♦ 1 chartered deep-submergence support tender [ARS]
Bldr: North American Shipbuilding Co., Galliano, La. (In serv. 1978)

Dolores Chouest

Dolores Chouest Jim Sanderson, 7-03

D: 1,500 tons (fl) **S:** 13 kts **Dim:** 73.2 × 12.20 × 3.64
Electronics: Radar: . . .
M: 2 Caterpillar D399-SCAC diesels; 2 CP props; 2,250 bhp
Fuel: 148.5 tons **Crew:** 7 contract civilians; 32 Navy personnel

Remarks: 199 grt former oilfield supply tug on charter to support the rescue submersible *Mystic* Programs and based at Naval Air Station, North Island, San Diego, California. Hull painted red-orange and superstructure cream. Operated by owner Edison Chouest Offshore, Inc., in support of Commander, Submarine Force Pacific. Charter was renewed in 2004 and runs through 2009. She continues to operate as part of the MSC. There is a lift platform at the stern for launch and recovery of submersibles.

AUXILIARY SHIPS *(continued)*

♦ 1 chartered deep-submergence support tender [ARS]
Bldr: North American Shipbuilding, Inc., Larose, La. (In serv. 1994)

Carolyn Chouest

Carolyn Chouest—with NR-1 and a diving tender alongside at the stern
H&L Van Ginderen, 6-99

D: 1,599 tons (fl) **S:** 12 kts **Dim:** 50.45 × 11.60 × 3.65
M: 2 Caterpillar D399TA diesels; 2 props; 2,440 bhp
Crew: 13 tot. + 40 Navy support personnel

Remarks: 199 grt/450 dwt. Acts as tender to the nuclear-powered submersible NR-1 and is based at Groton, Connecticut. Initial charter contract was let to Edison Chouest Offshore, Galliano, Louisiana, in 6-93. She continues to operate as part of the MSC. *Carolyn Chouest* is a former oilfield tug-supply vessel. Prior to conversion, had two 99-kw diesel-generator sets. Two OE-82 antennas are fitted for the WSC-1(V) UHF SATCOM system. Is painted with red-orange hull and cream upperworks.

♦ 1 chartered submersible tender [ARS]
Bldr: American Marine Corp., New Orleans, La. (In serv. 1972)

Denny Tide (ex-*Research Tide*)

Denny Tide George R. Schneider, 1-00

D: Approx. 2,600 tons (fl) **S:** 10.5 kts **Dim:** 66.15 (61.88 pp) × 17.07 × 4.04
Electronics: Radar: . . .
M: 2 G.M. Electromotive Div. 12-cyl. diesels; 2 CP props; 3,000 bhp—bow and stern thrusters
Electric: 1,350 kw tot. (3 × 450-kw diesel-driven sets) **Range:** . . . / . . .
Fuel: 460.5 tons **Crew:** . . . tot.

Remarks: 497 grt/1,571 dwt. Modified oilfield tug/supply vessel. Has been stationed at Port Hueneme, California, since completion and is for unspecified research purposes. Has a twin hangar aft for probable submersible equipment.

♦ 2 L. Y. Spear–class submarine tenders [AS]
Bldr: Lockheed Shipbuilding, Seattle, Wash. (*Atlantic/†Pacific Fleet)

	Laid down	L	In serv.
AS 39 Emory S. Land*	2-3-76	4-5-77	7-7-79
AS 40 Frank Cable†	2-3-76	14-1-78	5-2-80

D: AS 39: 13,911 tons light (22,978 fl); AS 40: 13,758 tons light (22,826 fl)
S: 20 kts (18 sust.) **Dim:** 196.29 × 25.91 × 8,83 max. **A:** 4 single 12.7-mm mg
Electronics: Radar: 1 Raytheon SPS-64(V)9 nav.; 1 Raytheon SPS-10-series surf. search
M: 1 set de Laval geared steam turbines; 1 prop; 20,000 shp
Boilers: 2 Combustion Engineering; 43.6 kg/cm^2, 462° C **Electric:** 11,000 kw tot.
Crew: AS 39: 83 officers, 1,286 enlisted; AS 40: 81 officers, 1,270 enlisted

Frank Cable (AS 40) U.S. Navy. 4-05

Emory S. Land (AS 39) U.S. Navy, 2-04

Remarks: Able to provide support to up to 12 submarines, with up to four alongside at once; specifically tailored to the needs of the *Los Angeles* class. AS 39 became 6th Fleet/Mediterranean repair ship at La Maddalena, Sardinia, on 24-4-99 and serves surface ships as well as submarines. Current plans call for AS 39 to return to the U.S. in 2008 while AS 40 remains active at Guam.
Hull systems: Have one 30-ton crane and two 5-ton traveling cranes, a total of 53 specialized repair shops, and medical facilities include operating room, 23-bed ward, and dental clinic. Helicopter deck, but no hangar.
Combat systems: Originally planned to fit Mk 15 Phalanx CIWS or Sea Sparrow SAM in later ships. The Mk 67 20-mm guns have been replaced with 12.7-mm machineguns. AS 39 carries 72 vertical-launch Tomahawk missiles, plus a mix of 40 torpedo-tube launched Tomahawk missiles and Mk 48 torpedoes

Disposal notes: The unnamed AS 38 (in FY 69 budget) was canceled 27-3-69. *L. Y. Spear* (AS 36), decommissioned 6-9-96 and was stricken 3-5-99. *Dixon* (AS 37) was decommissioned on 30-9-95, stricken on 18-3-96 and sunk as a target on 21-7-03. *McKee* (AS 41) was decommissioned on 30-9-99 and stricken from the Navy list on 25-4-06.
Simon Lake–class submarine tender *Simon Lake* (AS 33), in reserve since 1999, was striken on 25-4-06 for disposal. Sister *Canopus* (AS 34) was decommissioned 30-11-94, stricken on 3-5-95, and transferred to MARAD for disposal on 1-5-99.

♦ 5 Powhatan-class fleet tugs [ATA] (1 in *reserve*)
Bldr: Marinette Marine, Marinette, Wisc. (*Atlantic/†Pacific)

	Laid down	L	In serv.
T-ATF 168 Catawba†	14-12-77	12-5-79	28-5-80
T-ATF 169 Navajo†	14-12-77	20-12-79	13-6-80
T-ATF 170 *Mohawk*	22-3-79	5-4-80	16-10-80
T-ATF 171 Sioux†	22-3-79	30-10-80	12-5-81
T-ATF 172 Apache*	22-3-79	20-12-80	30-7-81

D: 1,647 tons light (2,260 fl) **S:** 15 kts **Dim:** 73.20 (68.88 pp) × 12.80 × 4.74
Electronics: Radar: 1 Raytheon TM 1660/12S nav.; 1 Raytheon SPS-64(V)9 nav.
M: 2 G.M. EMD 20-645X7 20-cyl. diesels, electric drive; 2 Kort-nozzle CP props; 4,500 shp (3,600 sust.)
Electric: 1,200 kw (3 × 400-kw diesel sets) **Range:** 10,000/13 **Fuel:** 600 tons
Crew: 16 Civil Service Mariners + 4 Navy enlisted communications team

Remarks: 902 grt/613 nrt. Authorized: one in FY 75, three in FY 76, three in FY 78. Modified oilfield tug-supply vessel design built to merchant marine specifications.
Hull systems: Have a 300-hp bow-thruster and one 10-ton electrohydraulic crane. Can carry the Mk 1 Mod. 1, 90-ton deep-diving support module on the stern and can support a 20-man Navy salvage team. Have a 60-ton bollard-pull capacity. Foam firefighting equipment is fitted. Hull has double hard-chine configuration.

AUXILIARY SHIPS *(continued)*

Apache (T-ATF 172) Ralph Edwards, 9-04

Mohawk (T-ATF 170) Takatoshi Okano, 5-04

Disposals: Sister *Powhatan* (T-ATF 166) was deactivated on 1-2-99 and leased to Donjon Marine Co., Hillside, New Jersey, for five years starting 3-99 as standby salvage and towing services tug at New York City. *Narragansett* (ex-T-ATF 167) was deactivated on 18-10-99, transferred to a commercial salvage company, and chartered the same date by MSC but has since been inactive, laid up at Port Hueneme, California; the ship was stricken on 5-6-02 and transferred to the Naval Air Systems Command in 2-8-02 for Pacific fleet operations.

UNCLASSIFIED MISCELLANEOUS SHIPS (IX)

Note: The ships and craft in this section are listed in descending order of IX-series hull number rather than by age. The entries marked with an asterisk (*) are nonself-propelled. The IX category seems to be evolving into a catchall, although most of the craft could have been categorized under one of the USN's existing type designations. Applicable type designations are provided at the ends of the entry header.

♦ 1 missile trials support barge
Bldr: Gunter & Zimmerman, . . . (In serv. 1954)

IX 533 (ex-YD 222)

D: 1,000 tons **S:** 15 kts **Dim:** 43.3 × 18.0 × 1.2

Remarks: Former floating crane stricken on 31-8-00 but reinstated and retyped on 25-6-02 for conversion as a support barge to the SPAWARCOM "Weapon Set-to-Hit Threat Target" (WSTT) program.

♦ 1 chartered fast passenger and vehicle ferry [AP]
Bldr: INCAT, Hobart, Tasmania, Australia

	Laid down	L	In serv.
IX 532 HSV-X1 JOINT VENTURE (ex-*Incat 050,* ex-*TopCat,* ex-*DevilCat*)	19-1-98	7-11-98	21-11-98

Joint Venture (IX 532) U.S. Navy, 5-03

D: 940 tons light (1,668 tons fl) **S:** 52 kts light (37.5 kts fully loaded)
Dim: 96.00 (86.00 hulls) × 26.00 × 3.96 max.

Joint Venture (IX 532) Brian Morrison, 11-04

A: 2 single 7.62-mm Mk 44 gatling guns
Electronics:
Radar: 1 . . . nav.
EW: . . . intercept
M: 4 Caterpillar 3618 diesels; 4 Lips 50D waterjets; 30,000 bhp (at 1,030 rpm)
Electric: 920 kw tot. (4 × 230 kw; 4 Caterpillar 3406B diesels driving; 415 V a.c.)
Range: 1,100/35 (fully loaded; normal fuel)
Fuel: 120 m^3 normal; 490 m^3 max ferry
Crew: 5 officers, 25 enlisted

Remarks: Chartered 21-7-01 by the Army Tank–Automotive and Armament Command (TACOM) on behalf of the Army, Navy, and Coast Guard for West Coast U.S. "Proof of Concept" trials. Assigned Navy number IX 532 on 5-10-01, although she continues to wear the owner's pennant number HSV-X1. Accepted for service on 11-10-01. Is being employed for 18 to 24 months to determine whether such craft can be of use in training and logistic support roles. The contract is being managed by Incat's U.S. partner, Bollinger SY. Long-term Army plans call for acquiring 14 fast ferries of this type. Was initially based at the Naval Amphibious Base, Little Creek, Virginia. Administrative control of the craft was passed to the U.S. Army on 20-3-02 at Rota, Spain, and was returned to the U.S. Navy on 14-11-02 on completion of the ship's overhaul at Bollinger SY, Morgan City, Louisiana. Joint venture was deployed for Operation Iraqi Freedom and took part in combat operations on 20 March 2003, carrying a Marine detachment to guard offshore oil terminals captured by SEALs. During 3-04, she began operating with the U.S. Special Operations Command. She is based at Little Creek, Virginia.
Hull systems: Wave-piercing catamaran design, with 4.50-m beam to each hull. During refit prior to the trials, a launch and recovery system to handle RIB craft up to 11.9 m long was fitted, and a 472-m^2 helicopter platform was added to handle aircraft up to SH-60 and CH-46 size. Cargo deadweight is 800 tons, including the 600 passengers and crew. Has 330 lane meters of vehicle capacity, 2.7-m clear width and 4.3-m clear height. A slewing stern vehicle ramp is fitted that can handle military loads. Has four Reintges VIJ6031 gearboxes to transfer power from the engines to the waterjets, and the engineering plant is highly automated. Normal fuel is carried in four 30 m^3 tanks, while two 170 m^3 tanks in the lower hulls can be employed for fuel when cargo is not carried.

♦ 1 YP 676–class trials craft [YAGE]
Bldrs: Peterson Bldrs., Sturgeon Bay, Wisc.

	Laid down	L	In serv.
IX 531 AFLOAT LAB (ex-YP 679)	18-4-84	11-12-84	6-6-85

D: 172 tons (176 fl) **S:** 13.25 kts (12 kts sust.)
Dim: 32.92 (30.99 pp) × 7.39 × 1.83
Electronics: Radar: 1 SPS-64(V)9 nav.
M: 2 G.M. Detroit Diesel 12V-71N diesels; 2 props; 874 bhp—60-shp bow-thruster
Electric: 100 kw tot. (2 × 50 kw, G.M. Detroit Diesel 3-71 diesels driving)
Range: 1,400/12 **Fuel:** 6,550 gallons **Crew:** 2 officers, 4 enlisted

Remarks: Reclassified from YP 679 on 7-8-01 for use by the Office of Naval Research "in support of various HM&E (Hull, Machinery, and Engineering)–related research and development programs." Two dozen sisters serve as training craft (see under YXT). Was still wearing "679" as of late sighting.
Hull systems: Wooden hull, aluminum superstructure. Made up to 13.3 kts on trials. Has NAVSAT receiver, two echo sounders, Sperry Mk 27 gyrocompass with six repeaters, speed log, anemometer, Sippican expendable bathythermograph system, and a GPS receiver.

♦ 1 YFND 5–class diving tender* [YDTN]
Bldr: Associated SB, Seattle, Wash.

	Laid down	L	In serv.
IX 530 (ex-YFND 5, ex-YFN 268, ex-YF 268)	10-11-40	1-12-40	1-2-41

D: 170 tons (590 fl) **Dim:** 33.53 × 10.66 × 2.13

Remarks: Former dry dock companion craft stricken on 25-6-99 but reinstated as IX 530 on 6-9-00 for use as a diving tender for the Consolidated Divers' Unit, Southwest Regional Maintenance Center, San Diego. Is a rectangular covered barge hull with deckhouse.

Disposal note: Signature reduction trials craft *Sea Shadow* (IX 529) was withdrawn from service and stricken on 22-8-06. The craft and associated support barge (HMB-1) may be converted into museum ships.

♦ 1 YRDH 1–class trials barge* [YAGE]
Bldr: Associated Shipbuilders, Seattle, Wash. (In serv. 1943)

IX 528 (ex-YRDH 1; ex-YR 55)

UNCLASSIFIED MISCELLANEOUS SHIPS (IX) *(continued)*

D: 460 tons (750 fl) **Dim:** 46.02 (45.72 wl) × 10.7 × 1.8

Remarks: Reclassified from a floating dry dock workshop (nonself-propelled) on 7-4-99 for use in support of submarine tests for the Naval Surface Warfare Center, Carderock Div., Bremerton, Washington, Detachment's Southeast Alaska Acoustic Measurement Facility at Ketchikan, Alaska. Three sisters remain typed YRDH. Was originally built as a general-purpose repair barge and has berthing for one officer and 46 enlisted.

♦ 1 YFN 1254–class trials barge* [YAGE]

Bldrs: Steel Style, Inc. (In serv. 1-6-82)

IX 527 (ex-YFN 1259)

D: 174 tons (699 fl) **Dim:** 33.53 (28.65 wl) × 10.67 (9.75 wl) × 2.44

Remarks: Reclassified 7-4-99 for use in submarine tests by the Naval Surface Warfare Center, Carderock Div., Bremerton, Washington, Detachment's Southeast Alaska Acoustic Measurement Facility at Ketchikan, Alaska. Construction was authorized under FY 81 as a covered lighter, nonself-propelled. Rectangular steel barge hull with a small deckhouse.

Note: IX 526 (ex-YRST 1, ex-YDT 11) was reclassified as YR 94 on 3-4-00. Training craft IX 523 (ex-YOG 93), was stricken for disposal on 26-5-05.

♦ 5 AFDB 1–class aerial target service barges* [YGTN]

Bldrs: IX 522: Pacific Bridge Co., Alameda, Calif.; IX 524: Pollock-Stockton Shipbuilding Co., Stockton, Calif.; IX 525: Chicago Bridge Co., Morgan City, La.; IX 534: Navy Shipyard, Pearl Harbor; IX 535: Naval Shipyard, Mare Island (In serv. 1943–44)

IX 522 (ex-AFDB 2, Section D; ex-ABSD 2, Section D; ex-ABD 14)
IX 524 MATSS-1 (ex-AFDB 2, Section F; ex-ABSD 2, Section F; ex-ABD 22)
IX 525 MATSS-2 (ex-AFDB 1, Section C; ex-ABSD 1, Section C, ex-ABD 3)
IX 534 (ex-AFDB 1, Section B; ex-ABSD 1, Section B; ex-ABD 2)
IX 535 (ex-AFDB 2, Section F; ex-ABSD 2, Section H, ex-ABD 10)

IX 524—with UH-3H Sea King helicopter aboard — Nick Galante/ITT, 1997

D: 2,064 tons (fl) **Dim:** 78.03 × 24.38 × 1.52
Electric: 700 kw tot. (2 × 350-kw diesel sets) **Fuel:** 6,400 gallons
Crew: . . .

Remarks: Modules of large sectional floating dry docks that had been in storage at Pearl Harbor. IX 522 was reclassified on 16-8-96 and remain stored at Pearl Harbor. IX 524 was reclassified on 25-4-97 for use at the Pacific Missile Test Range Facility, Kekaha, Kauai, Hawaii, along with IX 525, and used as a support platform for the Mobile Aerial Target Support System (MATSS). IX 524 and IX 525 are based at the Naval Inactive Ship Maintenance Facility, Pearl Harbor, and are towed and tended by a tug when in use; they have been converted as sensor and communications platforms and have crew accommodations. IX 534 and IX 535 were redesignated on 10-10-02 and are based at the Naval Inactive Ship Maintenance Facility, Pearl Harbor; AFDB 2 Section H (ex-ABSD 2, Section F; ex-ABD 10) was to have been reclassified as IX 525 during 1997, but the requirement was canceled and, when reinstated 2-3-98, a different dock section was selected. IX 521 was stricken on 26-4-06.

Hull systems: Previous data apply to IX 524, which has a deck area of 1,765 m^2, with the forward end used as a helicopter platform; 5,500 gallons of JP-5 helo fuel are carried. IX 524 also has launchers for four BQM-74 target drones, a Stabilized High-accuracy Optical Tracking System (SHOTS), a C-band tracking radar with coherent signal processor, and Inmarsat and Vsat SATCOMM links, and a 10-ton capacity deck crane and can carry 23,200 gallons of drinking water and 40,000 gallons of washdown water. Personnel spaces are air conditioned. IX 534 and IX 535 displace 3,350 tons (fl).

Fully assembled with all 10 of their sections, AFDB 1 and 2 were some 282.55 m long by 78 m wide (40.7-m clear width inside dock walls) by 2.74-m draft in light condition; maximum flooded draft was 23.77 m, providing up to 14 m inside draft over the keel blocks. They were intended to support battleships and large aircraft carriers. Each of the 10 sections could be towed separately, and the dock walls could be pivoted to fold flat against the dock floor. Maximum rated lift for all 10 sections together was 90,000 tons.

Disposal notes: *Proteus*-class accommodations hulk *Proteus* (IX 518, ex-AS 19) was transferred to the Maritime Administration for disposal on 24-9-99 and stricken on 13-3-01. Accommodations barge IX 520 (ex-APL 19) was stricken on 13-3-01 and sunk as a target on 13-6-02.

Boat landing float IX 519 was stricken 16-2-02 and has been reclassified as floating equipment.

♦ 1 Stalwart-class ocean training support vessel [YAGE]

	Laid down	L	In serv.
IX 537 PREVAIL (ex-T-AGOS 8)	13-3-85	7-12-85	4-3-86

Prevail (IX 537)—shown here in previous ASW configuration — Takatoshi Okano, 4-01

D: 1,459 tons light (2,262–2,282 fl) **S:** 11 kts
Dim: 68.28 (59.13 pp) × 13.11 × 4.60
Electronics: Radar: 2 . . . nav.
M: 4 Caterpillar-Kato D-398B 800-bhp diesels, G.E. electric drive; 2 4-bladed props; 2,200 shp (1,600 hp sust.)—550-hp bow-thruster
Electric: 1,500 kVA from main generators, plus 265-kw emergency set
Range: 11,200/11 plus 2,088/3 **Fuel:** 657 tons **Endurance:** 98 days
Crew: 6–8 officers, 11–12 MSC contract crew, 11 technicians

Remarks: 1,472–1,486 grt/786 dwt. Authorized in FY 81; recommissioned on 18-11-03 as a training ship. Serves as a dedicated training platform for Atlantic Fleet Carrier Strike Groups, Expeditionary Strike Groups, individual units and submarine on sea trials. Replaces ex-*Gosport* (IX 517).

Disposal notes: *Robert D. Conrad*–class former oceanographic research ship *Gosport* (IX 517) was retired on 19-6-03. She was stricken in 2004 and sunk as a target on 14-11-04

♦ 1 Trident missile firing simulator barge* [YAGN]

Bldr: Seatrain SB Corp., Brooklyn, N.Y. (In serv. 1976)

IX 516 (ex-barge *Matthew*, ex-*Christina F*)

D: 3,122 tons light (3,476 fl) **Dim:** 92.28 × 27.43 × 6.71

Remarks: Former 5,279-grt cargo barge converted to commercial tank barge in 1980. Acquired from Allied Barge Co. and converted by McDermott, Inc., Morgan City, Louisiana, as missile-launch simulation barge for service at the Naval Nuclear Power training facility at Charleston, S.C.

♦ 1 BH 110-type lifting body technology demonstrator craft [YAGEA]

	Bldr	L	In serv.
IX 515 (ex-SES-200, ex-USCG *Dorado*, WSES 1)	Bell-Halter, New Orleans	12-78	9-80

IX 515—prior to major 2003 conversion — Findler & Winter, 9-98

D: 340 tons (fl) **S:** 36 kts **Dim:** 51.0 × 13.1 × 5.63
Electronics: Radar: 2 Decca navigational
M: 2 MTU 16V396 TB 34 diesels; 2 KaMeWa 71562/6II waterjets; 6,960 shp—2 MTU 6V396 TB83 diesels for lift; 1,980 shp
Electric: 140 kw **Range:** . . ./. . . **Fuel:** . . .
Crew: 2 officers, 10 enlisted

Remarks: Relaunched as HYSWAC (Hybrid Small Waterplane Area Craft) in 6-03 by Navatek, Ltd., Pacific Marine, Honolulu, Hawaii. Office of Naval Research funded $18-million effort beginning in 2000. Rework on the vessel has included removal of existing lift system and related components, addition of a 170-ton underwater lifting body with a new propulsion drivetrain. Aft crossfoil was also added for pitch stabilization. Full load displacement for HYSWAC is 270 tons. Originally designed by Bell Aerospace-Textron and built by Halter Marine in a jointly financed effort. Leased 1-80 for one month by U.S. Coast Guard and then again for a longer trials period in 1981. On 29-9-82 the ship came under U.S. Navy control and had accommodations for 14 additional personnel added. Assigned to Carderock Division, Naval Surface Warfare Center, Special Trials Unit, Patuxent River, Maryland. Unofficially named *Jaeger* for European tour 1985–86. Redesignated IX 515 on 11-5-87.

UNCLASSIFIED MISCELLANEOUS SHIPS (IX) *(continued)*

Hull systems: Functions by trapping a fan-generated air bubble between the rigid sidewalls and rubber seals at bow and stern. Two more lift fans added 1984. Original G.M. 8V92 TI lift fan engines replaced 1988. Refitted 4-90 to 2-2-91 with waterjet propulsion by builder; G.M. 16V149 TI diesels (1,600 bhp each) replaced by MTU diesels, with those in turn replaced in 2002 by two MAN B&W Diesel 18VP185 diesels.
Combat systems: In spring 1987, conducted trials with G.E. EX-25, 25-mm gatling gun and in 3-89 with Rockwell Crossbow multi-use stabilized weapons/sensor platform. Used 1997–on as trials ship for the Advanced Lightweight Influence Sweep System (ALISS), which was to use spark-gap transducer arrays and superconducting magnetic technology in combination with lightweight, high-speed towed arrays.

♦ 1 YFU 71–class helicopter training craft [YXT]

Bldr: Pacific Coast Eng. Co., Alameda, Calif.

	Laid down	L	In serv.
IX 514 Bay Lander (ex-HTL-514, ex-YFU 79)	12-67	5-68	7-68

Bay Lander (IX 514) H&L Van Ginderen, 12-94

D: 220 tons (380 fl) **S:** 8 kts **Dim:** 38.1 × 10.97 × 2.30
Electronics: Radar: 1 Decca . . . nav.
M: 4 G.M. Detroit Diesel 6-71 diesels; 2 props: 1,000 bhp
Crew: 1 Navy helicopter control officer, 23 civilian contract mariners

Remarks: Originally built for the U.S. Army. Redesignated an IX on 31-3-86 and completed conversion 28-4-86 to serve as helicopter landing platform training craft at Naval Air Station Pensacola, Florida. HTL = Helicopter Landing Trainer. Operation contracted to Seward Services Inc, Ft. Lauderdale, Florida, on 17-12-99; the ship remains Navy property. From 1985 through 1999 the ship conducted 73,000 Army, Navy, and other government agency helicopter training landings.
Hull systems: Bow ramp welded closed, new superstructure with rudimentary flight-control station and 25.6-m-long, 9.75-m-wide flight deck added.

Disposal note: Satellite navigation system trials craft *Orca* (IX 508) was stricken on 19-6-03. *Benewah*-class barracks ships *Mercer* (IX 502, ex-APB 39, ex-APL 39) and *Nueces* (IX 503, ex-APB 40, ex-APL 40) were reclassified as APL 39 and APL 40, respectively, on 7-3-01; see under [YPL].

♦ 1 sonar test barge [YAGE]

IX 310

IX 310 U.S. Navy, 2000

D: 1,438 (fl) **Dim:** 59.4 × 37.5 × 0.0

Remarks: Built in 1917 as a barge and placed in service as an acoustic trials barge on 1-4-71. Is subordinated to the Naval Undersea Warfare Center Division, Seneca Lake, New York, where the craft is moored with YCF 16 and YFNX 22 (see following). As of 2000, IX 310 consists of two large barges with a bridge joining them. Each barge supports one kingpost for a heavy lift derrick to handle underwater arrays.

Disposal notes: *Elk River* (IX 501, ex-LSMR 501) was stricken on 13-8-99 and sunk as a gunnery target on 24-2-01.

SERVICE CRAFT

Note: Craft are grouped here in the traditional U.S. Navy order, with the universal ship-typing system designations not necessarily in alphabetical order. The entries marked with an asterisk are nonself-propelled.

Disposal note: Former commercial floating drydock AFDB 9 was removed from service during 2003.

♦ 1 small auxiliary floating dock* [YFDL]

Bldr: Chicago Bridge & Iron (In serv. 3-44)

AFDL 6 Dynamic

Dynamic (AFDL 6)—at Little Creek, Va. George R. Schneider, 2-99

Dim: 61.0 × 19.5 **Capacity:** 1,000 tons **Crew:** 1 officer, 23 enlisted

Remarks: Sister *Adept* (AFDL 23) of 1,900-ton capacity was towed from Subic Bay 22-2-92 to Guam, arriving 6-3-92; leased 15-7-94 to Gulf-Copper Ship Repair, Inc., Aransas Pass, Texas, and supports the mine-countermeasures ships at Ingleside, Texas. *Reliance* (AFDL 47) had been reacquired 18-1-81 from Maritime Administration reserve, but was returned 12-8-81; on 15-5-91, the craft was leased to Detyans Shipyard, Mount Pleasant, South Carolina.

Disposal note: The AFDM 3 class medium auxiliary floating dry dock *Resolute* (AFDM 10) was inactivated 7-11-03 and leased commercially 16-12-04.

♦ 2 APL 65–class barracks craft* [YPL]

Bldr: Marinette Marine, Marinette, Wisc.

	L	In serv.
APL 65	30-10-99	12-6-00
APL 66	15-7-00	17-11-00

APL 65—at San Diego W. Michael Young, 4-05

D: 3,162 tons (fl) **Dim:** 82.00 × 21.00 × 1.57

Remarks: Ordered 31-8-98 for $32.5 million. They provide accommodations for ships under repair or overhaul and are capable of being towed at sea. Have berthing for 250 personnel, can provide food services for up to 1,150 each, and have post office, banking, fitness center, barber shop, classroom, laundry, and medical facilities. APL 65 is based at San Diego, APL 66 at Norfolk, Virginia. Hull numbers APL 63 and APL 64 were never assigned.

APL 66—at Annapolis U.S. Navy, 10-03

♦ 2 APL 61–class barracks craft* [YPL]

Bldr: Halter Marine-Gulf Coast Fabrication, Pearlington, Miss.

	Laid down	L	In serv.	Location
APL 61	9-2-96	22-8-96	20-10-97	Norfolk
APL 62	. . .	18-4-97	26-3-98	Pearl Harbor

SERVICE CRAFT *(continued)*

D: 4,680 tons (fl) **Dim:** 109.72 × 28.65 × 1.89

Remarks: Ordered for $50 million in 1995; they have accommodations for 600 personnel, plus dining and locker facilities for 3,020 additional personnel. They are also fitted with office, training, medical, recreation, and other personnel support spaces. Two additional units were authorized but never built.

♦ 2 Benewah-class barracks barges [YPL]

Bldr: Boston Naval Shipyard, Boston, Mass.

	Laid down	L	In serv.
APL 39 Mercer (ex-IX 502, ex-APB 39, ex-APL 39)	25-8-44	17-11-44	19-9-45
APL 40 Nueces (ex-IX 503, ex-APB 40, ex-APL 40)	2-1-45	6-5-45	30-11-45

Nueces (APL 40)—with lighter alongside Ralph Edwards, 10-02

D: 2,189 tons light (3,640 fl) **Dim:** 100.0 × 15.2 × 3.4
M: 2 G.M. 12-267 ATL diesels; 2 props; 1,600 bhp (nonfunctional)
Electric: 500 kw tot.
Crew: Accomm. for 39 officers, 1,295 enlisted

Remarks: Were reclassified from IX 502 and 503 as APL 39 and APL 40, respectively, on 7-3-01. Built on LST 1/542–class landing ship hulls. Recommissioned 1968 for service in Vietnam, they were placed back in reserve during 1969–71 and activated again in 1974 as barracks ships. Propulsion plants were inactivated and eight 40-mm AA removed. Names restored in 1986. Sister *Echols* (IX 504, ex-APB 37) was stricken 22-12-95. APL 39 is at Sasebo, Japan, and APL 40 is assigned to the Naval Ships Repair Facility, Yokosuka, Japan.

♦ 11 APL 2–class barracks craft* [YPL]

	Bldr.	In serv.		Bldr.	In serv.
APL 2	Puget Sound NSY	23-5-45	APL 42	Willamette Iron & Steel, Oregon	30-4-45
APL 4	Everett Pacific Co.	21-9-45			
APL 5	Puget Sound NSY	5-11-45	APL 45	Willamette Iron & Steel, Oregon	28-7-45
APL 15	Nashville Bridge	1-8-44			
APL 18	Tampa SY, Florida	20-9-44	APL 50	Puget Sound Bldg. & Dock, Wash.	2-1-46
APL 29	Tampa SY, Florida	14-5-45			
APL 32	Boston NSY, Mass.	11-1-45	APL 58	Nashville Bridge	16-7-45

APL-4—at San Diego W. Michael Young, 9-05

APL 42—at Mayport Ralph Edwards, 9-04

D: 1,300 tons light (2,580 fl) **Dim:** 79.55 (79.25 wl) × 14.93 × 3.04

Remarks: APL 2–18 are in the Pacific Fleet, the others in the Atlantic. Most can accommodate six officers and 680 to 792 enlisted (APL 18: five officers, 358 enlisted) and have 300-kw generator capacity. APL 45 was officially stricken from the Naval Vessel Registry on 1-11-72 but remains in use in the Atlantic Fleet under her original designation. APL 18 was originally to have been YF 631.
Disposals: APL 31 was stricken for disposal on 1-8-00 and sunk as an artificial reef on 23-7-01. APL 54 was stricken on 9-11-99.

♦ 2 Shippingport-class submarine support docks* [YFDM]

	Bldr	In serv.
ARDM 4 Shippingport	Bethlehem Steel, Sparrows Pt., Md.	27-1-79
ARDM 5 Arco	Todd Pacific, Seattle	27-2-86

Arco (ARDM 5)—note tail fins and covered screw of SSN inside dock
W. Michael Young, 3-05

Arco (ARDM 5) W. Michael Young, 1-05

Dim: 150.0 × 29.3 (29.3 clear width) × 16.6 (max.)
Capacity: 7,800 tons (8,400 emergency)
Crew: ARDM 4: 40 civilians; ARDM 5: 5 officers, 125 enlisted

Remarks: ARDM = Medium Support Dock. Intended to support *Los Angeles*–class submarines. First floating dry docks built for U.S. Navy since World War II. Length of blocks: 118 m. Require shore support. Have two 25-ton cranes. ARDM 5 ordered 13-10-82, laid down 25-7-83, launched 14-12-84. Have accommodations for 12. ARDM 4 based at New London, ARDM 5 at San Diego. General Dynamics Electric Boat Division received a contract during 9-02 to operate ARDM 4 with a civilian crew for one year, with an option for four additional years.
Disposals: Submarine support dock *Oak Ridge* (ARDM 1, ex-ARD 19) was transferred to the U.S. Coast Guard on 7-2-02. Sister *Alamogordo* (ARDM 2, ex-ARD 26) was stricken on 23-11-93 and transferred to the Maritime Administration 21-3-95 for disposal; the dock was transferred to Ecuador on 26-2-01. *Endurance* (ARDM 3, ex-ARD 18) was stricken 31-7-95.

♦ 154 YC open lighters* [YC] (in *reserve*)

Bldrs: Various (see Remarks) (In serv. 5-37 through 27-8-96)

YC 688	YC 1389	YC 1492	YC 1574	YC 1615	YC 1649
YC 746	YC 1391	YC 1494	YC 1575	YC 1619	YC 1650
YC 757	YC 1400	YC 1495	YC 1576	YC 1620	YC 1651
YC 775	YC 1406	YC 1501	YC 1577	YC 1622	YC 1652
YC 783	YC 1407	YC 1510	YC 1578	YC 1623	YC 1653
YC 800	YC 1408	YC 1511	YC 1579	YC 1624	YC 1654
YC 804	YC 1410	YC 1513	YC 1580	YC 1625	YC 1655
YC 821	YC 1417	YC 1524	YC 1583	YC 1626	YC 1656
YC 980	YC 1419	YC 1526	YC 1584	YC 1627	YC 1657
YC 984	YC 1431	YC 1527	YC 1585	YC 1628	YC 1658
YC 1027	YC 1432	YC 1528	YC 1586	YC 1631	YC 1659
YC 1029	YC 1433	YC 1531	YC 1587	YC 1632	YC 1660
YC 1068	YC 1445	YC 1534	YC 1588	YC 1633	YC 1661
YC 1069	YC 1464	YC 1535	YC 1589	*YC 1634*	YC 1662
YC 1070	YC 1469	YC 1536	YC 1590	*YC 1635*	YC 1663
YC 1073	YC 1470	YC 1537	YC 1591	YC 1636	YC 1664
YC 1081	YC 1473	YC 1538	YC 1592	*YC 1637*	YC 1665
YC 1090	YC 1474	*YC 1542*	YC 1593	*YC 1638*	YC 1666
YC 1091	YC 1476	YC 1543	YC 1594	YC 1639	YC 1667
YC 1121	YC 1477	YC 1548	YC 1595	YC 1640	YC 1668
YC 1351	YC 1478	YC 1549	YC 1596	*YC 1641*	YC 1669
YC 1371	YC 1485	*YC 1569*	YC 1598	*YC 1642*	YC 1670
YC 1375	YC 1486	YC 1570	YC 1599	YC 1644	YC 1671
YC 1378	YC 1487	YC 1571	YC 1600	YC 1646	
YC 1380	YC 1490	YC 1572	YC 1601	YC 1647	
YC 1381	YC 1491	YC 1573	YC 1602	YC 1648	
YC 1382					

Remarks: YC 1523 through YC 1527 were delivered 5-81 to 7-81 by Marine Industries; they are of 135 tons light (685 fl). YC 1572 through YC 1602 were delivered 27-2-85 to 23-4-87 by Moss Point Marine, Escatawpa, Mississippi: 250 tons light (660 fl), 33.53 × 9.75 × 1.98 m (max.). YC 1615 through YC 1666 were delivered 1-90

SERVICE CRAFT *(continued)*

YC 1652—carrying two workboats Ralph Edwards, 9-04

YC 1602 Jim Sanderson, 7-03

to 27-8-96 by Orange SB, Orange, Texas: 115 tons light (659 fl), 33.53 × 9.75 × 2.13 m. YC 1583 and 1586 converted 4-86 as cable-reel support barges for the T-AGOS program. YC 1519 became YFNX 40 on 1-2-94. YC 1631 and YC 1633, assigned to the Naval Undersea Warfare Center, Keyport, Washington, as range-support craft with YC 1329 and YC 1470, which have one or more sheds built on deck, are self-propelled, with two 450-bhp G.M. Detroit Diesel 12V-71 outdrive systems providing 7-kt speeds; both have a 125-kw diesel generator, while YC 1470 has 60-kw and 80-kw generators. YC 1594 is employed as a service barge for the nuclear-powered deep-submergence submersible NR-1 at New London, Connecticut. The previously stricken YC 1073 was restored to service on 1-7-98 for use at the Trident submarine facility at Bangor, Washington. YC 1525 was redesignated salvage lighter YLC 2 on 5-6-98. YC 813 and YC 1084 became YFNX 45 and YFNX 46, respectively, on 14-7-98. YC 1321 became YFNX 47 on 22-7-05.
Disposals: YC 1448, YC 1449, and YC 1607 were stricken for disposal on 5-1-01; YC 709, 772, 1076, 1077, 1089, and 1630 were stricken on 13-3-01 and YC 1493 on 19-3-01. YC 1523 was stricken on 30-9-02, YC 1502 on 24-7-03, and YC 728 on 11-12-00. YC 981, 1482, 1484, 1500 and 1523 were all stricken for disposal in 2002, YC 180 and YC 1502 were stricken in 2003. YC 1329, YC 1379, YC 1605, and YC 1606 were stricken on 15-11-05.
Note: In use at Sasebo, Japan, are locally procured barges YC 1 and YC 2, built in 1941, while the 1942-vintage YC 7 is used at Yokosuka; these craft are not on the official Naval Vessel Register, and no data are available.

Disposal note: Car float YCF 16 was stricken in 2005.

♦ 8 YCV 7–class aircraft transportation lighters* [YC]

Bldrs: YCV 10, 11: Naval Base, Pearl Harbor; YCV 16: Bethlehem Steel, San Francisco, Calif.; YCV 19–23: Alabama Shipyard, Mobile, Ala.

	In serv.	Assigned:		In serv.	Assigned to:
YCV 10	21-8-44	Sasebo, Japan	YCV 20	5-89	Yokosuka, Japan
YCV 11	6-10-44	Pearl Harbor, Hi.	YCV 21	3-90	Pearl Harbor, Hi.
YCV 16	29-8-45	Yokosuka, Japan	YCV 22	1-4-91	Sasebo, Japan
YCV 19	4-90	Yokosuka, Japan	YCV 23	2-2-91	Pearl Harbor, Hi.

D: 480 tons light (2,480 fl) **Dim:** 60.96 (54.86 wl loaded) × 19.81 × 2.13 (loaded)

Remarks: All active in Pacific Fleet and used to move aircraft and stored to and from shore facilities to aircraft carriers. YCV 19–21 approved FY 88 and YCV 22 and 23 in FY 90 to replace earlier units; they duplicated the basic characteristics of the World War II–built units.

♦ 1 nuclear reactor transport barge* [YC]

Bldr: American Marine Corp., New Orleans, La. (In serv. 1984)

Barge 40 (ex-ATB 210, ex-*Cheramie Bros.* 107)

D: . . . tons **Dim:** 64.00 × 20.73 × 4.57

Remarks: 2,142 grt. Purchased 1992 from Anderson Tug and Barge, Seward, Alaska, and refitted 1993 by Puget Sound Naval Shipyard to transport 1,000-ton nuclear reactor compartments cut from retired submarines at Bremerton to Hanford, Washington, for burial. Not on navy list.

♦ 1 nuclear reactor transport barge* [YC]

Bldr: Zidell Dismantling, Inc., Tacoma, Wash. (In serv. 1981)

Barge 60 (ex-ZB 1801)

D: . . . tons **Dim:** 70.10 × 18.28 × 4.57

Remarks: 1,775 grt. Modified from commercial salvage barge by Marine Industries Northwest, Tacoma, Washington, in 1996. A sister to the *Edgecumbe* (see following).

Note: The navy owns three other former commercial barges that have no navy list hull numbers; all are assigned to the Puget Sound Naval Shipyard, Bremerton, Washington:

- *Beluga* (In serv. 12-91) 41.45 × 18.28 × 3.96, built by Alabama SY, Mobile, Ala.: 1,774 grt.
- *Edgecumbe* (In serv. 4-78) 70.1 × 18.28 × 4.57, built by Zidell Dismantling, Inc.: 1,775 grt
- *Nestucca* (In serv. 1-69) 70.1 × 16.76 × 4.64, built by Wall SY/M&W Marine Ways, Harvey, La.: 1,612 grt.

♦ 19 YD floating cranes* [YD]

Bldrs: Various (see Remarks)

YD 117	YD 218	YD 248	YD 254	YD 259
YD 189	YD 232	YD 249	YD 255	YD 260
YD 196	YD 246	YD 251	YD 256	YD 261
YD 200	YD 247	YD 252	YD 257	

YD 254 W. Michael Young, 6-05

Remarks: YD 117 was built by Dravo, Wilmington, Delaware (in serv. 1945); YD 189 by Odenbach SB Corp. (in serv. 6-44); YD 196 and YD 232 by Dravo, Pittsburgh, Pennsylvania (in serv. 1-54 and 6-6-53, respectively); YD 200 by Avondale SY, New Orleans (in serv. 4-55); YD 218 by Gunter & Zimmerman (in serv. 6-53); YD 246, YD 248, and YD 254–261 by Halter Marine, Lockport, Mississippi (in serv. 2-91 to 6-94); and YD 247, YD 249–253: Westmont Industries, Los Angeles, California (in serv. 4-91 to 11-91). YD 254–261 were originally ordered 25-7-91 from Alabama SY, Mobile, but the order was transferred to Halter Marine. YD 253 was renamed IX 536.
YD 189, 200, 218, 232, and 245 are ex-U.S. Army Design 264B-class floating cranes: 1,630 tons (fl), 42.67 × 21.34 × 1.91 m, 90–100 tons capacity. YD 117 was built on a 42.67 × 21.3–m barge hull and displaces 1,407 tons light (1,560 fl); YD 247 and YD 249–253 are 2,134 tons (fl), 53.49 × 22.41 × 1.53 m, crew of 12, with 100-ton crane, 150-bhp Caterpillar 3304 diesel maneuvering propulsion; YD 246, YD 248, and YD 254 through YD 261 are 53.34 × 22.86 × 3.96 m molded depth.
Recent disposals: YD 120 and YD 150 were stricken on 13-3-01. YD 222, although stricken on 31-8-00, was retyped IX 533 on 25-6-02. YD 214, 226, 229, 233, and 234 were stricken for disposal on 16-2-02. YD 224 was stricken 14-3-03, YD 225 on 9-6-04, YD 204 on 22-7-04, YD 245 on 27-2-04, YD 237 on 1-10-04, YD 217 on 14-7-05, and YD 243 on 13-7-05. Former Japanese self-propelled floating cranes IX 30–IX 31 were withdrawn from service in 2002 and 2006 respectively.

♦ 2 YDT 17–class diving tenders [YDT]

Bldr: Swiftships, Inc., Morgan City, La.

YDT 17 Neptune (In serv. 25-2-99) YDT 18 Poseidon (In serv. 19-5-99)

Neptune (YDT 17) Skeets Photo Service/Swiftships, 2-99

D: 275 tons (fl) **S:** 20 kts **Dim:** 41.15 (39.93 pp) × 8.23 × 1.83
Electronics:
Radar: 1 Raytheon. . . nav.
Sonar: . . . hull-mounted HF
M: 2 Caterpillar 3508 DITA diesels; 2 Hamilton waterjets; 2,600 bhp—90 shp electric bow-thruster
Electric: 290 kw tot. (2 × 125 kw, Caterpillar 3306 DIT diesel-driven; 1 × 40-kw Caterpillar 3304 DINA diesel-driven emergency)
Range: 540/20 **Fuel:** 2,000 gallons **Crew:** 8 tot. + 7 instructors, 25 trainees

Remarks: Diver training craft ordered 6-97 for $10.5 million to replace the YDT 14 and 15 at the Naval Diving and Salvage Training Center, Panama City, Fla.
Hull systems: Aluminum construction. Capable of operating in Sea State 4 and up to 200 n.m. from land. Have six watertight compartments. Tankage for 4,666 gallons fresh water. Radar and sonar are interfaced with GPS navaids system. Carry a Zodiac Hurricane 472, 4.9-m RIB with 25-bhp outboard. Two diver support cranes are fitted, and there is a large decompression chamber within the main deck superstructure.

Disposal notes: Self-propelled covered lighter [YF] *Keyport* (YF 885), in reserve since 23-8-90, was sold in 2001.

♦ 2 YFB 92–class ferry boats [YFB]

Bldr: Bender SB & Repair, Mobile, Ala. (In serv. 30-1-95)

YFB 92 R. W. Huntington (ex-*Windward*)
YFB 93 William H. Allen (ex-*Leeward*)

SERVICE CRAFT *(continued)*

R. W. Huntington (YFB 92) U.S. Navy, 1998

D: 200 tons (light) **S:** 10 kts **Dim:** 44.50 × 10.97 × 1.68
Electronics: Radar: 1 Furuno 1830 nav.
M: 2 G.M. Detroit Diesel 12V-71 diesels; 2 props; 720 bhp
Electric: 200 kw tot. (2 × 75-kw Kato gen., powered by 2 Detroit Diesel 4-71 diesels; 1 × 50-kw emergency set, Detroit Diesel 4-71 diesel driving)
Range: 1,000/10 **Fuel:** 4,050 gallons **Crew:** 4 tot. + 80 passengers

Remarks: Ordered 11-92 for use at Guantanamo Bay, Cuba. Launched 10-93 and 12-93. In addition to 100 passengers (seating for 40), can carry 15 automobiles or two M1A1 tanks. The propellers are mounted at each end, and the craft are designed to mate with special shore ramps. Renamed 10-95 in honor of Lt. Col. Robert W. Huntington, USMC, who led the first Marines ashore in Cuba on 10-6-1898, and Lt. Cdr. William H. Allen, first commandant of the U.S. Naval Station at Guantanamo Bay, 10-12-1903 to 5-1904.

Disposal note: LCU 1466–class ferry boat YFB 94 (ex-YFB 1504, ex-U.S. Army *Hampton Roads,* LCU 1504) was sold on 28-7-04. Sister YFB 95 (ex-Army *Shenandoah,* LCU 1516) was sold for scrap on 5-1-97.

♦ 6 YFN 1277–class covered lighters* [YC] (2 in *reserve*)
Bldr: Basic Marine, Inc. (In serv. 10-93 to 3-94)

YFN 1278	YFN 1280	YFN 1282
YFN 1279	YFN 1281	YFN 1284

D: 685 tons (fl) **Dim:** 33.5 × 10.7 × 2.4

Remarks: Under FY 90, 12 were to be ordered, with option for 22 additional (YFN 1289–1310) later authorized under FY 91, but only YFN 1277–1284 were ordered. Sister YFN 1283 was reclassified YFNX 25 on 30-10-92. YFN 1278–1279 are assigned to the Naval Intermediate Ships Maintenance Facility, Philadelphia, Pennsylvania, and are inactive; the others are at the Naval Weapons Station, Seal Beach, California. YFN 1277 was stricken from the navy list on 23-1-06.

♦ 12 YFN 1254–class covered lighters* [YC]
Bldrs: YFN 1254–1262: Steel Style, Inc. (In serv. 6-82); YFN 1265–1275: Eastern Marine (In serv. 1-87 to 4-88)

YFN 1258	YFN 1266	YFN 1270
YFN 1261	YFN 1267	YFN 1273
YFN 1262	YFN 1268	YFN 1274
YFN 1265	YFN 1269	YFN 1275

YFN 1254–class covered barge YFN 1267 H&L Van Ginderen, 7-97

D: 174 tons (699 fl) **Dim:** 33.53 (28.65 wl) × 9.14 (wl) × 2.44

Remarks: Rectangular steel barge hulls with a small deckhouse. Authorized under FY 81 (11 actually built), six (three ordered) under FY 85, two under FY 86: were initially said to be 260 tons light (660 fl). YFN 1265–1274 are rated at 144 tons light/694 fl. YFN 1265 delivered 1-87, YFN 1266–1271 in 8-87, and YFN 1273–74 on 18-4-88.

YFN 1258 is assigned to ComSubRon 8; YFN 1261 and YFN 1262 to the Norfolk NSY (YFN 1262 is equipped as an electrical test barge); YFN 1265, YFN 1269, and YFN 1270 to the Yorktown Naval Weapons Station, Virginia; YFN 1266 to ComSubRon 11; YFN 1267 to North Island, San Diego; YFN 1268 to the Naval Ship Repair Facility, Yokosuka, and YFN 1273–1274 to the Naval Station, Everett, Washington. YFN 1271 became YFNX on 16-8-96. YFN 1259 was reclassified as IX 527 on 7-4-99. YFN 1255 was reclassified YFNX 42 on 17-7-95. YFN 1262 is named *Test Barge X-51.* YFN 1275 was stricken on 13-3-01 but was reinstated on 25-6-02 for use as a transport barge at the Norfolk Naval Shipyard.

YFN 1254–class covered barge YFN 1262—converted as Norfolk Naval Shipyard Code 950 Electrical Test Barge Christopher P. Cavas, 7-00

Disposals: YFN 1266 was stricken on 5-1-01 but was reinstated the same date. YFN 1254 and YFN 1257 were stricken on 13-3-01 but returned to service 1-04 for use by Naval Shipyard Portsmouth as a security barrier. YFN 1256 was stricken on 1-10-04. YFN 1272 was stricken on 14-3-03 and reclassified as “floating equipment.” YFN 1239–class covered lighter YFN 1252 was stricken on 26-4-06.

♦ 4 YFN 1196–class covered lighters* [YC]
Bldr: YFN 1203–1204: Gulfport SB Corp., Gulfport, Miss. (In serv. 6-5-54 and 12-10-64); YFN 1217, 1222: Harbor Boat Bldg. (In serv. 2-65 and 6-65)

YFN 1203 YFN 1204 YFN 1217 YFN 1222

D: 144 tons (694 fl) **Dim:** 33.53 × 9.75 × 2.44

Remarks: Rectangular barge hulls with a deckhouse having a peaked roof. YFN 1203, YFN 1204, and YFN 1222 are assigned to Pearl Harbor.

Disposal notes: YFN 1221 was stricken on 5-1-01; YFN 1199 and YFN 1200 on 13-3-01; and YFN 1213 on 24-9-01. YFN 1237 was stricken on 8-7-02.

♦ 1 YFN 1173–class covered lighter* [YC]
Bldr: Richmond Steel Co., Richmond, Va. (In serv. 1964)

YFN 1195

D: 144 tons (694 fl) **Dim:** 33.53 × 10.36 × 2.43

Remarks: Rectangular barge hull with a deckhouse having a peaked roof. YFN 1195 is assigned to the Yorktown Naval Weapons Station, Virginia.
Disposals: Sisters YFN 1173, 1175, 1176, and 1194 were stricken for disposal on 1-10-04. YFN 1172–class covered lighter YFN 1172 was retired by 2006.

♦ 1 YFN 1154–class covered lighters* [YC]
Bldr: Kyle & Co., Stockton, Calif. (In serv. 1952)

YFN 1163

D: 160 tons (590 fl) **Dim:** 33.53 × 10.67 (10.36 wl) × 2.44

Remarks: Rectangular steel barge hulls with a deckhouse. Assigned to Sasebo, Japan. Sister YFN 1156 was stricken for disposal on 22-7-04 along with YFN 1155.

♦ 15 YFN 161–class covered lighters [YC] (3 in *reserve*)
Bldrs: YFN 284: J.K. Welding Co.; YFN 306: Dravo Corp., Wilmington, Del.; YFN 645: Eureka SB Corp.; YFN 652, 797: Bushnell-Lyons; YFN 704 and 934: Bellingham Iron Works, Wash.; YFN 793, 794: American Electric Welding, Md.; YFN 806 and 917: Pointer-William; YFN 958: NSY, Mare Island, Calif.; YFN 968, 973: Gunderson Bros., Portland, Ore. (In serv. 4-41 to 4-45)

YFN 284	YFN 652	YFN 794	*YFN 917*	YFN 968
YFN 306	YFN 704	YFN 797	YFN 934	*YFN 973*
YFN 645	YFN 793	YFN 806	*YFN 958*	YFN 978

YFN 161–class covered barge YFN 652—a typical U.S. Navy World War II–built U.S. Navy barge Christopher P. Cavas, 7-00

D: 160 tons (590 fl) **Dim:** 33.53 × 10.67 (10.36 wl) × 2.43

Remarks: Rectangular barge hulls with a deckhouse having a peaked roof. Most are employed for temporary ammunition storage at naval weapons stations or at naval shipyards. YFN 284, YFN 306 and YFN 794 are at the Naval Inactive Ship Maintenance Facility, Portsmouth, Virginia; YFN 645 is at Portsmouth NSY in Kittery, Maine, and 806 is at Pearl Harbor; YFN 968 at Yokosuka, Japan; YFN 652 at Norfolk NSY; YFN 704 at Sasebo, Japan; YFN 794, 800, and 801 at the Yorktown Weapons Station, Virginia; and YFN 797 at the Naval Nuclear Power Training Unit, Charlestown, South Carolina.

SERVICE CRAFT *(continued)*

Disposals: YFN 276, 278, 691, 694, 803, 901, 956, 962, 964, 980, 981, 983, and 984 were stricken on 13-3-01. YFN 941 was restored to the Navy List on 11-12-98 for use in the Near Term Mine Reconnaissance System development program at the Naval Undersea Warfare Center Div., Keyport, Washington, but was sold on 18-4-02. YFN 656 stricken on 15-4-03.

♦ 1 YFNB 1–class large covered lighter* [YFNB]

Bldrs: Pollock-Stockton, Stockton, Calif. (In serv. 1944)

YFNB 19

D: 831 tons light (2,780 fl) **Dim:** 79.24 × 14.63 × 1.07 light (2.90 loaded)

Remarks: YFNB 31 and 32 retired in 2002; YFNB 30 was reclassified YR 93 on 3-4-00. YFNB 37 was reclassified YRB 30 on 3-4-00. Sister YFNB 4 is on loan to the Maritime Administration as of 2004. YFNB 47 (of separate class) was stricken in 2002 and YFNB 39 in 2005.

♦ 1 YFND 31–class dry-dock companion craft* [YFND] (in *reserve*)

Bldr: Gretna Machine & Iron Works (In serv. 7-65)

YFND 31 (ex-YFNX 34, ex-YFN 1209)

D: 144 tons (694 fl) **Dim:** 33.53 × 9.75 × 2.44

Remarks: Reclassified from YFNX 34 on 1-11-92. Taken out of active service in 1998, she remains in reserve.

♦ 1 YFND 30–class dry-dock companion craft* [YFND]

YFND 30 (ex-YFN 1253)

D: 137 tons (685 fl) **Dim:** 33.53 × 9.75 × 2.44

Remarks: Reclassified from YFN on 1-11-92.

Disposal note: YFND 5–class dry-dock companion craft YFND 29 was retired in 2005 and sold in 2006.

♦ 9 YFNX-series miscellaneous special-purpose lighters* [YAG]

	Bldr	In serv.
YFNX 15 (ex-YNG 22)	Dravo, Pittsburgh, Pa.	6-41
YFNX 22	Island Dock Co., Inc.	6-52
YFNX 30 (ex-*Sea Turtle*, ex-YFN 1186, ex-USAF U-32-1501)	Kyled Co., Stockton, Calif.	3-52
YFNX 39 (ex-YFN 1276)	Eastern Marine	4-88
YFNX 40 (ex-YC 1519)	Diamond Mfgr. Co.	6-77
YFNX 42 SPRUCE BARGE (ex-YFN 1255)	Steel Style, Inc.	6-82
YFNX 43 (ex-YFN 1271)	Eastern Marine	8-87
YFNX 45 (ex-YF 334, ex-YC 813)	Puget Sound Naval SY	31-5-42
YFNX 46 (ex-YC 1084)	Soule Steel, San Francisco, Calif.	1-6-45

Spruce Barge (YFNX 42)—at Norfolk Christopher P. Cavas, 6-00

YFNX 30—configured as a submersible support craft H&L Van Ginderen, 7-97

Remarks: Rectangular barge hulls. All are 33.5 m long and 2.4 m draft, with beam being either 9.8 or 10.4 m. YFNX 15 and 30 are at Portsmouth NSY, Maine; YFNX 22 is assigned to the Naval Undersea Warfare Center and is based at Seneca Lake, New York; YFNX 42 and 43 are based at Norfolk, Virginia; and YFNX 40 is assigned to the Submarine Support Facility, New London, Connecticut. YFNX 39 is based at Ingleside, Texas.

YFNX 39 was reclassified from YFN on 1-11-92. YC 1519 became YFNX 40. YFN 1255 was reclassified YFNX 42 on 17-7-95 and assigned to Submarine Squadron 8 at Norfolk, Virginia. YFNX 45 and YFNX 46 were redesignated on 14-7-98 for use as storage and workshop barges at the Naval Inactive Ship Maintenance Facility, Bremerton, Washington.

YFNX 30 was converted to be the tender to the CURV III tethered, remote-operated submersible and was assigned to the Space and Naval Warfare Systems Center at San Diego until 1998 when she was transferred to the Portsmouth (New Hampshire) Naval Shipyard detachment at San Diego. YFNX 30 displaces 420 tons (fl) on a draft of 1.52 m and is powered by fore and aft Voith Schneider vertical cycloidal propellers for speeds of 5.5 kts ahead or astern, 2 kts sideways, or 1.5 rpm for rotating the hull. Converted from a basic 33.3 × 10–m barge hull, YFNX 30 can berth 24 persons and has a 30-day endurance. Tankage totaling 51,700 gallons can be used either for ballast water or diesel fuel. Two 300-kw and one 60-kw diesel generators are installed.

Disposals: YFNX 35 and YFNX 36 were stricken on 5-1-01 for disposal. YFNX 44 was sold on 17-5-00. YFNX 24 was stricken on 22-7-04, YFNX 20 on 15-11-05, YFNX 37 on 14-2-06.

♦ 1 YFP-series floating power barge* [YFP]

Bldr: Gretna Machine & Ironworks (In serv. 4-65)

YFP 11 (ex-YFN 1207)

D: 144 tons light (694 fl) **Dim:** 33.5 × 9.7 × 2.4

Remarks: Located at Naples, Italy, to support Commander, Service Force, Sixth Fleet Ship Repair Unit, Naples; 2,000 kw total generator capacity.

Disposal notes: Harbor utility craft YFU 81 and YFU 91 were stricken by 2004. All remaining YGN 80–class garbage lighters have been stricken as of 1-04.

♦ 2 YLC salvage lift craft* [YRS]

YLC 1 (ex-YFNX 33, ex-YFN 1192) YLC 2 (ex-YC 1525)

Remarks: YLC 1, completed 6-52 as a covered lighter, became YFNX in 12-74; redesignated a salvage lift craft in 6-86 and is attached to Mobile Diving & Salvage Unit 2, Norfolk, Virginia. Standard Navy 685-ton, 33.5 × 9.8–m barge hull. YLC 2 was redesignated on 5-6-98 and serves Mobile Diving and Salvage Unit One (MOBDIVSALU ONE).

Disposal note: Dredge [YM] YMN 1, completed in 1992, was stricken on 13-3-01.

♦ 1 YNG 1–class gate craft* [YAG]

Bldr: Moore Dry Dock (In serv. 6-41)

YNG 17

D: 110 tons (225 fl) **Dim:** 33.5 × 10.5 × 1.2 **Crew:** 15 tot.

Remarks: Built to tend harbor-defense nets. Based at Pearl Harbor.

♦ 1 YOGN 123–class aviation fuel barge* [YON]

Bldr: Albina Engineering & Machinery, Albina, Ore. (In serv. 6-54)

YOGN 123

D: 434 tons light (2,350 fl) **Dim:** 70.1 × 12.8 × 2.4

Remarks: Based at Fleet Supply Center, Bremerton, Washington. YOGN 126–131 were authorized under FY 91 budget but not ordered.

♦ 5 YOGN 106–class aviation fuel barges* [YON]

Bldr. YOGN 111: Nashville Bridge Co.; others: Albina Engineering and Machinery, Albina, Ore.

	In serv.		In serv.		In serv.
YOGN 111	10-53	YOGN 115	9-52	YOGN 125	6-54
YOGN 114	6-54	YOGN 124	6-53		

D: 245 tons light (1,360 fl—see Remarks) **Dim:** 50.3 × 12.8 × 2.4

Remarks: YOGN 111 based at Norfolk, Virginia; YOGN 114 (displacing 1,776 tons fl) at Fleet Supply Center, Puget Sound; YOGN 115 at Yokosuka, Japan; YOGN 124 at Puget Sound Naval Base, Bremerton; and YOGN 125 at Pearl Harbor. YOGN 113 retired in 2002.

♦ 2 YON 305–class fuel-oil barges* [YON]

Bldr: . . . (In serv. 1-6-52)

YON 305 YON 306

D: 185 tons light (578 fl) **Dim:** 36.58 × 10.06 × 2.44

Remarks: YON 305 is based at Sasebo, Japan; YON 306 at Diego Garcia.

♦ 12 YON 307–class fuel-oil barges* [YON]

Bldrs: YON 307–309: Alabama SY; YON 311–319: Orange SB, Orange, Tex.

	In serv.	Assigned to:		In serv.	Assigned to:
YON 307	1-90	Diego Garcia	YON 314	12-93	Puget Sound NSY
YON 308	12-89	Norfolk, Va.	YON 315	12-93	Puget Sound NSY
YON 309	1-90	Puget Sd NSY	YON 316	1-94	San Diego
YON 311	5-93	Norfolk, Va.	YON 317	1-94	San Diego
YON 312	5-93	Norfolk, Va.	YON 318	12-95	Norfolk, Va.
YON 313	5-93	Norfolk, Va.	YON 319	1-96	Puget Sound NSY

D: 382 tons light (1,806 fl) **Dim:** 56.00 × 10.67 × 3.05

Remarks: Modernized version of YON 245–class design, assigned to various Naval stations, Naval shipyards, and supply depots. YON 307 was stricken 4-9-98 after only eight years' service but was reinstated on the Naval Vessel Register on 3-8-00 for service at Diego Garcia. Unlike the others, YON 318 and YON 319 have no sheer to the hull at the bow end.

SERVICE CRAFT *(continued)*

YON 301–class fuel barge YON 313 A. D. Baker III, 10-00

♦ 15 YON 245–class fuel-oil barges* [YON]

Bldrs: YON 258–274: Gretna Machine & Iron Works; YON 280-283: Marine Power & Equipment; others: Brown-Minn.

	In serv.	Assigned to:		In serv.	Assigned to:
YON 258	17-1-66	Guantanamo Bay	YON 284	12-74	Norfolk, Va.
YON 261	1966	Guantanamo Bay	YON 285	9-75	Yokosuka, Japan
YON 262	5-5-66	Norfolk NSY, Va.	YON 287	1-75	Yokosuka, Japan
YON 272	5-4-68	Diego Garcia	YON 289	10-75	Pearl Harbor, Hi.
YON 273	1-7-68	Pearl Harbor, Hi.	YON 291	10-75	Guam
YON 274	1-7-68	Pearl Harbor, Hi.	YON 293	10-75	Guam
YON 280	3-72	San Diego, Calif.	YON 295	3-76	Little Creek, Va.
YON 281	3-73	Pearl Harbor, Hi.			

YON 245–class fuel barge YON 292—since stricken George R. Schneider, 9-94

D: 250 tons light (1,445 fl) **Dim:** 50.29 × 12.19 × 2.44

Remarks: Hull numbers YON 296–300 were reserved for additional units of this class that were never built. Units built by Brown-Minneapolis were 1 ft. longer and displace 267 tons light (1,506 fl). Several are assigned permanent crews of four enlisted personnel. Sister YON 270 was reassigned as "floating equipment."
Disposals: YON 291 was stricken on 13-12-95 but reinstated on 7-8-01, having in the interim remained in service at Guam. YON 261 was reinstated on the Naval Vessel Register 24 January 2002. YON 286 was stricken on 13-8-99; YON 288, YON 292, YON 301–302 were stricken on 28-3-03; YON 260, YON 282, and YON 283 were stricken in 2005.

♦ 1 YON 245–class fuel-oil barge* [YON]

Bldr: Gunderson Brothers SB, Portland, Ore. (In serv. 6-54)

YON 290

D: 185 tons light (578 fl) **Dim:** 36.58 × 10.06 × 2.44

Remarks: Assigned to Fleet & Industrial Supply Center Detachment, Sasebo, Japan. Acquired from the Army.

♦ 3 YON 89–class fuel-oil barges* [YON]

Bldrs: YON 90, 91: California Steel; YON 98: American Electric Welding

	In serv.	Assigned:		In serv.	Assigned:
YON 90	6-43	Guam	YON 98	12-43	Norfolk, Va.
YON 91	7-43	San Diego, Calif.			

D: 220 tons light (1,270 fl) **Dim:** 50.29 × 10.67 × 2.44

Remarks: Survivors from among a once much larger class, all built during World War II; same hull employed for other liquid-transportation barge types like YOS and YWN. YON 91 has four enlisted personnel assigned. YON 90 was driven ashore at Guam during Typhoon Paka on 16-12-97 and stricken the following month; repaired, she continued to serve as an oily waste reception and storage barge and was reinstated on the Naval Vessel Register on 7-8-01. YON 102 was stricken in 2005.

♦ 5 YOS–series oil-storage barges* [YON]

	Bldr.	In serv.
YOS 24	Maxon Const. Co.	4-46
YOS 33 (ex-YSR 46)	Eureka SB Corp.	6-40
YOS 34 (ex-OB61-2)	. . .	6-65
YOS 36	Alabama SY, Mobile	6-90
YOS 38 (ex-YOGN 26)	American Electric Co.	9-44

Oil-storage barge YOS 36 A. D. Baker III, 10-00

Remarks: All active. YOS 24 is 100 tons light; 24.4 × 10.4 m; YOS 36 (725 tons fl) was requested under FY 87, ordered 29-7-88, and delivered 6-90. Two new YOS were funded under the FY 94 budget but not built. YOS 34 was acquired from the Army in 1979 and is based at Norfolk. YOS 38 was reclassified in 2005 and is assigned to Norfolk NSY.

Disposal note: YOS 17 was stricken on 13-3-01.

Note: The former YOS 34 (ex-Army OB61-2), acquired 1-9-79, has been reclassified as floating property and serves as Former Hull 61-2 at Norfolk Naval Shipyard: 140 tons light; 33.5 3 10.4 m; the hull number YOS 34, however, is still painted on.

♦ 23 YP 676–class patrol craft/training tenders [YXT]

Bldrs: YP 676–682: Peterson Bldrs., Sturgeon Bay, Wisc.; others: Marinette SB, Marinette, Wisc.

	Laid down	L	In serv.		Laid down	L	In serv.
YP 676	7-4-83	9-4-84	14-11-84	YP 690	18-8-86	4-87	10-6-87
YP 677	10-10-83	23-6-84	5-12-84	YP 691	28-10-86	5-87	7-87
YP 680	2-7-84	23-3-85	8-8-85	YP 692	10-12-86	18-6-87	27-7-87
YP 681	29-10-84	1-6-85	30-9-85	YP 694	25-2-87	21-9-87	27-10-87
YP 682	7-1-85	3-8-85	18-11-85	YP 695	24-3-87	26-10-87	1-12-87
YP 683	23-7-85	19-6-86	13-10-86	YP 696	23-4-87	. . .	10-5-88
YP 684	29-8-85	14-8-86	10-12-86	YP 697	26-5-87	1-2-88	26-5-88
YP 685	8-10-85	25-9-86	23-11-86	YP 698	22-6-87	29-3-88	16-6-88
YP 686	23-1-86	25-10-86	12-86	YP 700	22-9-87	12-5-88	21-7-88
YP 687	27-2-86	3-87	7-3-87	YP 701	28-10-87	14-6-88	9-8-88
YP 688	7-4-86	13-3-87	22-5-87	YP 702	10-12-87	19-7-88	2-9-88
YP 689	15-7-86	5-87	10-6-87				

YP 695 U.S. Navy, 5-05

YP 684—leading two sister ships during a Naval Academy training exercise U.S. Navy, 3-06

D: 173 tons (fl) **S:** 13.25 kts (12 kts sust.) **Dim:** 32.92 (30.99 pp) × 7.39 × 1.83
Electronics: Radar: 1 SPS-64(V)9 nav.
M: 2 G.M. Detroit Diesel 12V-71N diesels; 2 props; 874 bhp—60-shp bow-thruster

SERVICE CRAFT *(continued)*

Electric: 100 kw tot. (2 × 50 kw, G.M. Detroit Diesel 3-71 diesels driving)
Range: 1,400/12 **Fuel:** 6,550 gallons
Crew: 4 enlisted + 2 officer instructors and 24 midshipmen (30 berths)

Remarks: Wooden construction boats to replace YP 655 class. YP 676 ordered 15-10-82; YP 677–682 ordered 25-5-83; YP 683–695 ordered 12-6-84; YP 696–702 on 13-9-85. Under FY 88, Congress directed that YP 702 be completed as a prototype inshore minehunter, a conversion neither required nor desired by the Navy, which did not comply; Congress then demanded trials under FY 89, but they do not seem to have been carried out. All assigned to Naval Academy, Annapolis, except YP 697 and 701 at the Naval Undersea Warfare Center, Keyport, Washington (the latter for use as a sound target boat and personnel transport, with a crew of seven and facilities for up to 24 passengers). YP 679, and YP 702 were stricken 20-11-98, but YP 679 was restored to service on 25-6-99 and assigned to the Office of Naval Research for a science and technology demonstration program, while YP 702 was reinstated on the Naval Vessel Register on 3-4-00 and assigned to the Naval Air Station, Pensacola. YP 679 was redesignated IX 531 on 7-8-01 and is subordinated to the Office of Naval Research (ONR).
Hull systems: Aluminum superstructure. Made up to 13.3 kts on trials. Have Magnavox MX 1105 NAVSAT receiver, EPSCO plotter, Kenyon D5300 and Furuno FCV-261 echo sounders, Sperry Mk 27 gyrocompass with six repeaters, speed log, anemometer, Sippican expendable bathythermograph system, Magellan GPS receiver. YP 686 is equipped for oceanographic research and has three small towing and hydrographic winches, four portable davits, and a stern A-frame crane, as well as a dry lab with four IBM computers and a small wet lab. Marinette-built units can be distinguished by their having a single ladder forward to the bridge deck, whereas the Peterson-built craft have two.

Disposal notes: YP 678 was stricken on 20-11-98. YP 693 and YP 699 were stricken on 13-3-01. YP 663 and YP 665 were no longer in service as of 2006. YPD-series floating pile driver *Warf Rat* (YPD 45) was sold during 4-05.

♦ 1 floating workshop* [YR]
Bldr: Everett Pacific Corp. (In serv. 13-2-45)

YR 94 (ex-IX 526, ex-YRST 1, ex-YDT 11, ex-YFNB 12, ex-YFN 723)

D: 700 tons light (2,700 fl) **Dim:** 79.6 × 14.6 × 2.7

Remarks: Former salvage-craft tender (and, before that, diving tender). Reclassified as IX 526 on 26-3-98 for use as an office and work barge at Pearl Harbor but reclassified again on 3-4-00 as a repair barge. Has accommodations for 15 officers and 71 enlisted. Rectangular barge hull with large deckhouse. YRB 30 is very similar in appearance.

♦ 1 YFNB 1–class floating workshop* [YR]
Bldrs: Nashville Bridge Co., Nashville, Tenn.

	Laid down	L	In serv.
YR 93 (ex-YFNB 30, ex-YFN 899)	27-3-45	18-6-45	26-1-46

YR 93 George R. Schneider, 5-01

D: 831 tons light (2,780 fl) **Dim:** 79.24 × 14.63 × 1.07 light (2.90 loaded)

Remarks: Reclassified YR 93 on 3-4-00 and employed in the Pacific Fleet. Same general appearance as YRB 30, YRBM 20, and YRBM 47.

♦ 1 miscellaneous floating workshop* [YR]

	Bldr.	In serv.
YR 83 (ex-YRL 5)	Northeast Boiler & Welding	16-1-43

D: 140 tons light (250 fl) **Dim:** 33.8 × 9.4 × 0.9

Remarks: Stationed at Pearl Harbor. Sister YR 89 (ex-YRR 4, ex-YFN 685), completed in 1937, was stricken on 24-9-01. YR 92 was stricken on 1-10-04.

♦ 1 ex-U.S. Army Design 7011 floating machine shop* [YR]

	Bldr.	In serv.
YR 85 QUALITY (ex-*Army* FMS 87)	Bethlehem Steel, Staten Isl.	6-54

D: 1,160 tons light (1,525 fl) **Dim:** 64.14 (53.62 wl) × 12.19 × 2.36 (max.)
Electric: 400 kw (4 × 100-kw diesel sets) **Fuel:** 140 tons
Crew: 4 officers, 40 enlisted

Remarks: Modified from Army Design 7016 refrigerated stores barge. Has 8.9-ton crane amidships. Workshops include: battery, blacksmith, carpentry, electrical, engine, fuel injector, machine, paint, pipefitting, electronic, refrigeration, sheet metal, shipfitting, and welding. Located at Yokosuka, Japan. Sisters YR 84 and YR 86 were stricken on 1-10-04.

Quality (YR 85)—at Sasebo Takatoshi Okano, 9-00

♦ 5 YR 1–class floating workshops* [YR]

	Bldr.	In serv.
YR 29	Cramp SB, Phila.	24-11-41
YR 63	Mare Isl. NSY	5-2-46
YR 64	Panama Canal Co.	13-5-46
YR 70	Puget Sound B&D	10-2-45
YR 90	Cramp SB	1-42

YR 1–class floating workshop YR 29—with additional deckhouse amidships atop the original superstructure Christopher P. Cavas, 7-97

D: 530 tons light (760 fl) **Dim:** 46.6 (45.7 wl) × 10.7 × 1.8
Crew: 1–4 officers, 40–47 enlisted

Remarks: A once-uniform design, but several now have had additional superstructure added. Are all equipped with machine shops and berthing facilities. YR 90 previously served as YRR 7. YR 70, stricken on 4-4-95, was restored to the Naval Vessel Register on 15-6-00 for use at the Naval Ship Repair Facility, Yokosuka, Japan; the craft is listed at 600 tons light (990 fl) and has a beam of 12.0 m, indicating that it was initially one of a small number equipped as torpedo repair barges and given a bulged hull midbody to improve stability.
Disposals: YR 76 was stricken on 13-3-01 and YR 68 and YR 78 were reclassified YRB 35 and YRB 34 respectively in 2003.

♦ 4 YR 1–class repair and berthing barges* [YPB]

	Bldr.	In serv.
YRB 32 (ex-YR 67)	Pollock-Stockton	15-9-44
YRB 33 (ex-YR 73)	Puget Sound B&D	9-4-45
YRB 34 (ex-YR 68)	Pollock-Stockton	10-11-44
YRB 35 (ex-YR 78)	Puget Sound B&D	19-6-45

YR 1–class repair and berthing barge YRB 35 W. Michael Young, 9-05

D: 530 tons light (760 fl) **Dim:** 46.6 (45.7 wl) × 10.7 × 1.8
Crew: 1–4 officers, 40–47 enlisted

Remarks: First two reclassified on 3-4-00 and are assigned to CINCPACFLT. YRB 34, 35 reclassified 7-03. YRBM 31 was reclassified YRBM 54 in 2005.

♦ 1 YFNB 1–class repair and berthing barge* [YR]
Bldr: Missouri Valley Bridge Co.

	Laid down	L	In serv.
YRB 30 (ex-YFNB 37; ex-YFN 1064)	13-3-45	12-5-45	28-5-45

SERVICE CRAFT *(continued)*

YFNB 1–class repair and berthing barge YRB 30 George R. Schneider, 5-01

D: 700 tons light (2,200 fl) **Dim:** 79.24 × 14.63 × 1.07 light (2.90 loaded)

Remarks: Reclassified YRB 30 on 3-4-00 and employed at San Diego. Same general appearance as YRBM 20 and YRBM 47.

♦ 1 YR 91–class repair, berthing, and messing barge* [YPBN]
Bldr: Halter Marine, Moss Point, Miss. (In serv. 3-93)

YRBM 53 (ex-YR 91)

D: 825 tons (fl) **Dim:** . . . × . . . × . . .

Remarks: Ordered 8-11-91 for service at Pearl Harbor and reclassified YRBM 53 on 3-4-00.

♦ 6 YR 1–class repair, berthing, and messing barges* [YPBN]

	Bldr.	In serv.
YRBM 48 (ex-YR 44)	Cramp SB	22-9-43
YRBM 49 (ex-YR 46)	Cramp SB	26-11-43
YRBM 50 (ex-YR 50)	Mare Isl. NSY	22-9-44
YRBM 51 (ex-YR 60)	Dekon SB	30-9-44
YRBM 52 (ex-YR 77)	Puget Sound B&D	9-6-45
YRBM 54 (ex-YRB 31)	Mare Isl. NSY	15-5-42

YR 1–class repair, berthing, and messing barge YRBM 51—still carrying previous hull number YR 60 W. Michael Young, 9-01

D: 530 tons light (760 fl) **Dim:** 46.6 (45.7 wl) × 10.7 × 1.8
Crew: 1–4 officers, 40–47 enlisted

Remarks: All reclassified on 3-4-00. A once-uniform design, but several now have had additional superstructure added. YRBM 50, based at San Diego, is listed at 600 tons light (990 fl) and has a beam of 12.0 m. Are all equipped with machine shops, berthing facilities, and a galley. YRBM 54 was reclassified on 22-7-05.

♦ 16 YRBM 31–class repair, berthing, and messing barges* [YPBN]
Bldr: Marinette Marine, Marinette, Wisc.

	In serv.		In serv.
YRBM 31	2-81	YRBM 39	8-82
YRBM 32	3-81	YRBM 40	7-82
YRBM 33	6-81	YRBM 41	11-82
YRBM 34	6-81	YRBM 42	11-82
YRBM 35	11-81	YRBM 43	5-83
YRBM 36	11-81	YRBM 44	5-83
YRBM 37	6-82	YRBM 45	6-83
YRBM 38	6-82	YRBM 46	7-83

YRBM 31–class repair, berthing, and messing barge YRBM 39 W. Michael Young, 9-05

D: 603 tons (688 fl) **Dim:** 44.50 × 14.0 × 1.1

Remarks: All YRBMs support ships in overhaul. YRBM 31 class has berthing for 26 officers, 231 enlisted. Are equipped with office, workshop, eating, and recreation spaces, 96-seat training theater, galley, etc. YRBM 33–36, 40–43, and 45 and 46 are in the Atlantic area, the others in the Pacific.

♦ 8 YRBM 23–class repair, berthing, and messing barges* [YPBN]
Bldr: Marinette Marine, Marinette, Wisc.

	In serv.		In serv.
YRBM 23	8-70	YRBM 27	4-71
YRBM 24	8-70	YRBM 28	5-71
YRBM 25	10-70	YRBM 29	6-71
YRBM 26	10-70	YRBM 30	6-71

YRBM 23–class repair, berthing, and messing barge YRBM 26 W. Michael Young, 9-05

D: 498 tons (585 fl) **Dim:** 44.50 × 14.0 × 1.1

Remarks: Have berthing for 26 officers and 231 enlisted. YRBM 23, 24, 27, and 28 are in the Atlantic area, the others in the Pacific. YRBM 23 and YRBM 27 carry the designations YRBML and YRBM(L) 27, reason not known; both are based at Norfolk, Virginia.

♦ 5 YRBM 5–class repair, berthing, and messing barges* [YPBN]
Bldr: Gretna Machine & Iron Works

	In serv.		In serv.
YRBM 8	17-9-62	YRBM 14	10-3-64
YRBM 9	15-12-62	YRBM 15	1-4-64
YRBM 13	28-12-63		

YRBM 5–class repair, berthing, and messing barge YRBM 15 William H. Clarke, 10-00

D: 236 tons light (310 fl) **Dim:** 34.14 (33.53 wl) × 10.97 (10.36 wl) × 0.91

Remarks: Have berthing for 10 officers and 90 enlisted. YRBM 9 and YRBM 15 are based at Norfolk, Virginia.

Disposal notes: Sister YRBM 7 (ex-YFNX 32, reclassified as YRBM 7 on 1-5-92) was stricken 26-10-93; YRBM 10 on 11-12-92; YRBM 11 on 25-11-96; and YRBM 12 on 7-5-98. YRBM 1–class repair, berthing, and messing barge YRBM 3 was stricken on 31-8-00. YRBM 5 and YRBM 6 were both sold during 2001.

♦ 2 YFNB 1–class repair, berthing, and messing barges* [YPBN]
Bldr: YRBM 20: Willamette Iron and Steel, Ore.; YRBM 47: American Bridge, Ambridge, Pa.

	L	In serv.
YRBM 20 (ex-YFNB 26, ex-YFN 751)	23-12-44	9-1-45
YRBM 47 (ex-YFNX 2, ex-YFNB 26, ex-YFN 751)	14-4-45	15-6-45

D: 700 tons light (2,000 fl) **Dim:** 79.55 × 14.63 × 2.74

Remarks: YRBM 20 is based at San Diego and displaces 2,700 tons full load. YRBM 47 is assigned to Submarine Squadron 22 at La Maddalena, Sardinia, and can berth 287 personnel; reclassified from YFNX 2 in 9-78.

SERVICE CRAFT *(continued)*

YRBM 20—at San Diego George R. Schneider, 2-93

♦ 2 YRDH 1–class floating dry-dock workshops, hull* [YFND]

Bldr: Puget Sound NSY

	In serv.
YRDH 6	31-3-44
YRDH 7	15-5-44

D: 460 tons (750-770 fl) **Dim:** 46.6 × 10.7 × 1.8

Remarks: YRDH 6 active at Pearl Harbor. Have berthing for one officer and 46 enlisted. Externally, nearly identical to YRDM series that follows. Sister YRDH 1 (ex-YR 55) became IX 528 on 7-4-99. YRDH 2 was stricken during 2005.

♦ 2 YRDM 1–class floating machinery dry-dock workshops* [YFND]

Bldr: YRDM 5: Norfolk Naval SY; YRDM 7: Puget Sound Boat & Dockyard

YRDM 5 (In serv. 22-4-44) YRDM 7 (In serv. 15-5-44)

YRDM 7—the YRDH 1–class units are nearly identical W. Michael Young, 3-06

D: 490 tons (750 fl) **Dim:** 46.6 × 10.7 × 1.8

Remarks: YRDM 5 is attached to Naval Air Force, Pacific Fleet; YRDM 7 at San Diego. Bow ends are pointed, to improve towing speed.

♦ 2 YRR-11 radiological repair barges* [YRRN]

	Bldr	In serv.
YRR 11 (ex-YRDH 3)	Norfolk NSY	12-43
YRR 14 (ex-YRDM 4)	Norfolk NSY	4-44

YRR 11—note the two additional decks built onto the original YRDH 1–class hull Winter & Findler, 9-97

D: 460 tons light (750 fl)
Dim: 46.63 × 10.97 × 1.83

Remarks: Active in support of submarines, YRR 11 at Puget Sound Naval SY, and YRR 14 at New London, Connecticut. Both have a high-freeboard hull with little superstructure. Have berthing for one officer and 46 enlisted.
Disposals: YRR 9 was reclassified YFNB 47 in 11-83; YRR 4 became YR 89 on 15-8-86. YRR 5 (ex-YRDM 8) was stricken on 7-2-99. YRR 7 was converted at Portsmouth Naval Shipyard and redesignated YR 90 on 1-8-91. YRR 1 and YRR 13 were stricken 19-9-94; YRR 6 (ex-YR 39) and YRR 12 (ex-YRDH 4) were stricken on 31-7-95. YRR 3 (ex-YFN 333) was stricken 25-11-96 but was reclassified as floating equipment on 27-3-97 for further use at Pearl Harbor. YRR 2 (ex-YR 79) was stricken on 1-10-04.

♦ 1 YSD 11–class seaplane wrecking derrick [YD]

Bldr: Pearl Harbor Naval Shipyard

	Laid down	L	In serv.
YSD 74	1-5-43	5-6-43	15-7-44

D: 240 tons (270 fl) **S:** 6 kts **Dim:** 31.70 (30.48 wl) × 9.50 × 1.20
M: 2 Superior diesels; 2 props; 320 bhp **Crew:** 1 officer, 15 enlisted

Remarks: Employed as a self-propelled crane at Naval Intermediate Ships Maintenance Facility, Pearl Harbor. This class was designed to support seaplanes, and the craft were known as "Mary Anns." Has a 10-ton crane.

Disposal notes: The last YSR 30-class sludge barge, YSR 39, was stricken on 11-12-00 and sold on 14-7-05.

Note: Three new large harbor tugs were authorized by Congress in FY 06. They are likely the first members of a new type intended to replace the *Natick* class. No data are yet available.

♦ 18 Natick-class large harbor tugs [YTB]

Bldrs: YTB 763: Southern SB Corp. . . . ; YTB 771: Mobile Ship Repair, Mobile, Ala.; YTB 782–798, 820–836: Marinette Marine Corp., Marinette, Wisc.; YTB 807–812: Peterson Bldrs, Sturgeon Bay, Wisc.

	Laid down	L	In serv.	Based at:
YTB 763 Muskegon	1-2-62	8-8-62	1-4-63	Yokosuka, Japan
YTB 771 Keokuk	5-12-63	21-5-64	23-8-64	Portsmouth, N.H.
YTB 782 Manistee	9-8-65	20-10-65	1-2-66	Yokosuka, Japan
YTB 787 Kittanning	22-12-65	29-3-66	19-5-66	Yokosuka, Japan
YTB 798 Opelika	23-2-68	1-8-68	1-1-69	Yokosuka, Japan
YTB 807 Massapequa	1-10-69	1-5-70	1-11-70	Yokosuka, Japan
YTB 808 Wenatchee	12-69	7-70	12-70	Bremerton, Wash.
YTB 812 Accomac	1-71	6-71	11-71	Bremerton, Wash.
YTB 815 Neodesha	10-5-71	6-10-71	2-1-72	Pearl Harbor, Hi.
YTB 820 Wanamassa	10-72	5-73	7-73	Guantanamo Bay, Cuba
YTB 823 Canonchet	2-73	7-73	9-73	Bremerton, Wash.
YTB 824 Santaquin	3-73	8-73	9-73	Little Creek, Va.
YTB 828 Catahecassa	9-73	5-74	8-74	Bremerton, Wash.
YTB 831 Dekanawida	12-73	9-74	10-74	Norfolk, Va.
YTB 832 Petalesharo	12-73	10-74	11-74	La Maddalena, Sardinia
YTB 834 Negawon	24-7-74	27-3-75	1-5-75	La Maddelena, Sardinia
YTB 835 Skenandoa	9-9-74	3-4-75	10-6-75	Bremerton, Wash.
YTB 836 Pokagon	10-74	4-75	6-75	Bremerton, Wash.

Muskegon (YTB 763) U.S. Navy, 1-05

Opelika (YTB 798) U.S. Navy, 7-04

D: 286 tons (356 fl) **S:** 12.5 kts **Dim:** 33.05 × 9.3 × 4.14
Electronics: Radar: 1/SPS-59 (Canadian Marconi LN-66) or Raytheon SPS-69 nav.
M: 1 Fairbanks-Morse 38D8$^1/_8$ × 12 diesel; 1 prop; 2,000 bhp
Electric: 120 kw tot. **Range:** 2,000/12 **Crew:** 11 tot. (all enlisted)

SERVICE CRAFT *(continued)*

Remarks: All named for Native American tribes. All are active. Two others were built for Saudi Arabia. YTB 836 was overhauled and modified in 1998 with new deck line-handling machinery (a split-drum bowline winch forward, new roller fairleads, new mooring bits, new chocks, etc.); after a one-year evaluation, others were to have been similarly altered. YTB 808 and YTB 823 are operated by civilian crews. YTB 834 was inactivated on 6-11-99, preparatory to disposal, but was reactivated and transferred to La Maddelena, Sardinia, for further use in 11-01.
Disposals: *Edenshaw* (YTB 752) was stricken on 5-5-94 and transferred to the U.S. Coast Guard (and stricken during 2001); *Marin* (YTB 753) was stricken on 14-11-94, *Pontiac* (YTB 756) on 27-11-92, *Oshkosh* (YTB 757) on 25-4-96, *Bogalusa* (YTB 759) on 7-8-96, *Tuscumbia* (YTB 762) on 11-9-95, *Arcata* (YTB 768) on 4-4-95, *Nashua* (YTB 774) on 6-5-94, *Apopka* (YTB 778) on 26-6-96, *Saugus* (YTB 780) on 28-10-97, *Winnemucca* (YTB 785) on 26-12-95, *Tonkawa* (YTB 786) on 7-12-92, *Wapato* (YTB 788) on 25-4-96, *Menomenee* (YTB 790) on 4-9-98, *Natchitoches* (YTB 799) on 13-10-95, *Eufaula* (YTB 800) on 7-12-92, *Palatka* (YTB 801) on 4-4-95, *Cheraw* (YTB 802) on 29-2-96, *Ahuskie* (YTB 804) on 7-3-96, *Ocala* (YTB 805) on 28-10-97, *Hyannis* (YTB 817) on 21-8-97, *Iuka* (YTB 819) on 19-10-95, *Wahtena* (YTB 825) on 28-10-97, *Washtuena* (YTB 826) on 21-8-97, *Chetek* (YTB 827) on 29-2-96, and *Pushmataha* (YTB 830) on 2-10-95. Most stricken units are to be scrapped, but YTB 817 and YTB 826 were transferred to the U.S. Fish and Wildlife Service at Midway Island; YTB 802 and YTB 827 were transferred to the Army Corps of Engineers on 29-2-96; and YTB 759 and YTB 778 were transferred to the Maritime Administration for use at the James River, Virginia, Reserve Fleet anchorage. *Paducah* (YTB 758) and *Antigo* (YTB 792) were stricken on 25-6-99. *Campti* (YTB 816) was placed in reserve on 1-2-99 and stricken on 9-11-99, along with *Nanticoke* (YTB 803), *Agawam* (YTB 809), and *Houma* (YTB 811). *Metacom* (YTB 829) was inactivated on 6-11-99, preparatory to disposal. *Dahlonega* (YTB 702) was placed out of service on 2-2-00, *Marinette* (YTB 791) on 30-6-00, and *Chesaning* (YTB 769) on 9-6-00—all three are to be sold. *Weehawken* (YTB 776), *Mandan* (YTB 794), *Ketchikan* (YTB 795), and *Metacom* (YTB 829) were stricken on 5-1-01; *Dahlonega* (YTB 770), *Nogalesen* (YTB 777), *Piqua* (YTB 793), *Anoka* (YTB 810), and *Tontocany* (YTB 821) on 13-3-01; and *Wapakoneta* (YTB 766) on 16-4-01. YTBs 761, 764, 767, 775, 784, 822, and 833 were retired in 2002. YTBs 783, and 818 were retired in 2003, YTB 779, YTB 796, and YTB 789 in 2004, and YTB 760, YTB 765, and YTB 797 in 2005.

Note: Military Sealift Command–chartered large harbor tugs are listed and described in a separate section at the end of the numbered service craft.

♦ 1 YTL 422–class small harbor tug [YTL]
Bldr: Robert Jacob, City Isl., N.Y. (In serv. 1-3-46)

YTL 602

D: 70 tons light (80 fl) **S:** 8 kts **Dim:** 20.12 (18.90 wl) × 5.49 × 2.44
M: 1 diesel; 375 bhp **Crew:** 4 tot.

Remarks: Active at the Portsmouth Naval Shipyard, YTL 602 is the only Navy Vessel Register survivor of several hundred YTL 422 class tugs; many still serve in foreign navies.

Note: A number of converted LCM(6) landing craft have been converted for use as push-tugs for local use, in place of YTLs; they are listed under workboats, which follows. The commercial tug *Mitchell Herbert,* classified as an "uninspected towing vessel," is on contract to the Naval Submarine Base, Bangor, Washington, and is used for a variety of support duties in the Puget Sound and San Juan Islands areas.

♦ 2 YTT 9–class torpedo trials ships [YPT]
Bldrs: McDermott, Morgan City, La.

	Laid down	L	In serv.
YTT 10 Battle Point	5-10-88	17-8-89	30-11-91
YTT 11 Discovery Bay	3-4-89	22-2-90	30-5-92

Battle Point (YTT 10) McDermott SY, 10-90

D: 1,000 tons light (1,168 fl) **S:** 11 kts sust.
Dim: 56.85 (53.83 pp) × 12.19 × 3.23
A: 2 fixed, underwater 533-mm Mk 59 TT; 1 triple 324-mm Mk 32 Mod. 5 ASW TT
Electronics: Radar: 2 Raytheon SPS-64(V)9 ARPA nav.
M: 1 Cummins KTA-50M diesel; 1 prop; 1,250 bhp—2 electric Z-drive thrusters, 300 shp each—400-shp bow-thruster
Electric: 1,310 kw tot. (3 × 395-kw, Cummins VTA-28 GS/G.C. sets, 1 × 125-kw emergency set)
Range: 1,800/11 **Fuel:** 70 tons **Endurance:** 12 days
Crew: 31 tot. crew + 9 civilian technicians

Remarks: Assigned to the Naval Underwater Warfare Engineering Station, Keyport, Washington, which evidently did not need as many as were ordered on its behalf; only two were ever operational at one time. YTT 10 was ordered on 8-87 and YTT 11 on 31-3-88. Although delivered on date shown, YTT 11 was not activated until 14-4-94. Both are operated on contract by SSI Corporation. YTT 11 has been assigned to the joint NOAA/National Geographic Society Sustainable Sea Expedition five-year study of U.S. coastal waters and carries manned research submersibles; she does not display her hull number.
Hull systems: Working deck aft. Have 7.3-ton capacity electrohydraulic crane to recover torpedoes and to handle sensor arrays and recovery equipment. Also carry smaller, 4.5-ton (to handle recovery vehicles) and 3.5-ton cranes and have four 10-ton vertical traction winches. Can operate on battery power for quiet operations and can maneuver precisely with Z-drive thrusters aft and bow-thruster. Perform tests with Mk 48 ADCAP, Mk 46, and Mk 50 ASW torpedoes. Have extensive telemetry and communications systems, global positioning system, Loran-C, Raytheon RD-500 echo sounder, and WQC-2 underwater telephone.
Dispoals: *Agate Pass* (YTT 12) stricken 13-8-99, never having been made operational; she was transferred to NOAA on 31-1-00. *Cape Flattery* (YTT 9), deactivated on 2-20-96, was stricken 13-8-99 and transferred 26-9-00 to another government agency, which makes the craft available for charter.

♦ 1 YWN 156–class water barge* [YWN]
Bldr: J. Russell Engineering Works (In serv. 6-52)

YWN 156

D: 175 tons light **Dim:** 36.6 × 10.1 × 2.44

Remarks: Based at La Maddalena, Sardinia, in support of Submarine Squadron 22: 175 tons light (. . . fl); 36.6 × 10.1 × 2.44 m.

♦ 3 YWN 71–class water barges* [YWN]

	Bldr.	In serv.
YWN 78	Eureka SB Corp.	13-12-43
YWN 79	Nelson Boiler & Tank	25-4-44
YWN 82	American Pipe, La.	8-1-44

YWN 71–class water barge YWN 78—being moved by commercial tug *Taft Beach* at Norfolk George R. Schneider, 9-99

D: 220 tons light (1,270 fl) **Dim:** 50.3 × 10.7 × 2.4

Remarks: YWN 78 is assigned to the Naval Station, Norfolk, Virginia. YWN 82 is based at Yokosuka, Japan and YWN 79 at Diego Garcia.

Note: YWN 5 is a locally applied, unofficial number given to a 1930-vintage, Japanese-built water barge in use at Sasebo; no data available.

MILITARY SEALIFT COMMAND CHARTERED HARBOR TUGS

In 1995, the Military Sealift Command (MSC) took over management of the contracts for all privately owned harbor tugs on charter to support USN operations as the current contracts expired. Commercial tugs had already been used since the late 1980s to supplement USN tugs or replace them entirely at such bases as Kings Bay, Georgia. Although initially tugs of any and all descriptions were chartered, by 1996 specialized tugs of nearly standardized design were beginning to predominate.

In 12-97 the MSC announced that 40 USN YTBs would be retired and replaced with commercial tugs, starting at Naval Station Pearl Harbor, Naval Activities Guam, and Submarine Base Bangor in 3-98. In addition to the following units listed, in 4-99 Puerto Rico Towing and Barge received a five-year contract to provide two tugs to replace three Navy YTBs at the now closed Roosevelt Roads, Puerto Rico. McAllister Towing & Transportation Co., New York, received a contract in 4-99 to operate a single tug at the Yorktown, Virginia, Naval Weapons Station.

♦ 2 Paul A. Wronowksi–class large tractor harbor tugs [YTB]
Bldr: . . . . (In serv. 1980)

Paul A. Wronowski John P. Wronowski

D: . . . tons **S:** . . . kts **Dim:** 27.4 × . . . × . . . × . . .
M: 2 Cummins . . . diesels; 2 Niigata azimuthal drives; 3,200 bhp

Remarks: *Paul A Wronowski* was leased 2-00 for 17 months, with two 17-month options, from Thames Towing for use at the submarine base, New London, Connecticut. Her lease was renewed in 2004 and is set to expire on 30-9-08. *John P. Wronowski* was leased on 21-4-04 under a lease that runs through 2008.

Disposal note: Chartered KST 35–class large harbor tugs KST 35 and KST 36 were no longer in service as of 2006.

♦ 7 Marci Moran–class tractor large harbor tugs [YTB]
Bldr: Washburn & Doughty, East Boothbay, Me.

	In serv.		In serv.
Marci Moran	9-99	Tracey Moran	4-00
Karen Moran	2-00	Wendy Moran	6-00
Susan Moran	3-00	Kerry Moran	5-10-00
Patricia Moran	2000		

D: Approx. 740 tons (fl) **S:** 13 kts **Dim:** 28.75 × 9.75 × 4.19
Electronics: Radar: 1 Furuno FR 7062/4 nav.
M: 2 G.M. EMD 16-645-E2 diesels; 2 Ulstein 1350H Z-drives with Kort-nozzles; 4,200 bhp—2 Ulstein bow-thrusters
Electric: 100 kw tot. (2 × 50-kw G.M. Detroit Diesel 4-71RC "N" diesel generator sets)
Range: . . . / . . . **Fuel:** 35,000 gallons **Crew:** 3 civilian mariners

MILITARY SEALIFT COMMAND CHARTERED HARBOR TUGS
(continued)

Susan Moran Takatoshi Okano, 4-04

Remarks: 200 grt. All were chartered 1-10-04 from Moran Towing Co., Baltimore, Maryland, to replace 11 USN YTBs at Little Creek and Norfolk, Virginia. Current lease expires 30-9-09

Hull systems: Have two firefighting monitors connected to an Aurora centrifugal pump driven by a Detroit Diesel 8V-71T diesel. Fenders will be fitted along the sides, bow and stern, and chine line, the latter to prevent damage to submarines. Bollard pull is 136 tons aft/45 forward. Navigational equipment includes Furuno GP 35 GPS terminal.

Disposal notes: Punta Lima–class large harbor tugs *Punta Lima* and *Punta Tuna* along with Z-one-class large harbor tug *Z-one* were returned to their respective owners after expiration of their lease.

♦ 6 C-Tractor-series large harbor tugs [YTB]
Bldr: North American SB, Galliano, La. (In serv. 1989–96)

C-Tractor 2 through C-Tractor 5
C-Tractor 10, C-Tractor 13

C-Tractor 10 W. Michael Young, 1-05

D: 265 tons (fl) **S:** 12 kts **Dim:** 32.00 (29.28 pp) × 11.30 (10.05 wl) × 3.96
M: 2 Caterpillar 12-cyl. diesels; 2 Ulstein Z-drive props; 3,960–4,000 bhp
Electric: 300 kw (2 × 150-kw diesel sets) **Crew:** 3 tot.

Remarks: 190 grt. Push-tugs chartered from and operated by Edison Chouest/Alpha Marine Services and, in San Diego, Great Lakes Group. *C-Tractor 2* is stationed at Kings Bay, Georgia; *C-Tractor 3–5* at Mayport, Florida and *C-Tractor 10* at San Diego.

UNNUMBERED NAVY SERVICE CRAFT

In addition to the previous Navy Vessel Registry yard and service craft, thousands of craft are assigned to various ships, commands, and shore stations, including landing craft and small patrol boats. Most of the more significant units are identified by a numbering system that begins with digits signifying the craft's length to the nearest foot (or, in recent years, meter), followed by an alphabetical designator indicating the craft's type, two digits indicating the fiscal year in which the craft was authorized, and subsequent digits indicating *which* craft of that year, i.e., "65PB778" is the eighth 65-ft. patrol boat built under FY 77. Numerous older units, however, are still carried under an earlier numbering system that begins with the letter *C,* and some small craft assigned to Public Works organizations at navy facilities carry numbers in yet another series. *Unofficial* names and hull numbers are in widespread use. The following craft appear in the standard *Combat Fleets* ship-typing system order.

♦ 4 24-ft. Boom Handling Boats [YAG]
Bldr: SeaArk Marine, Monticello, Ark. (In serv. 1980–89)

24BH8901 through 24BH8904

24-ft. Boom Handling Boat A. D. Baker III, 10-01

D: 4.6 tons (fl) **S:** 16.5 kts **Dim:** 23.86 × 2.41 × 0.52
M: 1 G.M. Detroit Diesel 6V-53T diesel; 1 prop; 260 bhp **Range:** . . . / . . .
Fuel: 130 gal. **Crew:** . . . tot.

Remarks: Welded aluminum-construction intended to tow Open Seas Oil Containment Boom, Dunlop Dracone, and Marco Skimmer Boat oil-spill containment devices. Bow and appendages are removable for ease of transportation within a standard 20 × 8 × 8–ft. container. Normally operated in pairs and are stowed ashore when not in use.

♦ 48 DIP-3001-series oil-skimmer launches [YAG]
Bldr: Kvichak Marine Industries, Seattle, Wash. (In serv. 1994–98)

DIP-3001-series oil-skimmer launch—on travel trailer George R. Schneider, 12-97

D: . . . tons **S:** . . . kts **Dim:** 8.53 × 2.44 × . . .
M: 1 Volvo Penta inboard/outboard diesel; 1 prop; . . . bhp

Remarks: Sweeper boats with "jaws" at bow to broaden sweep of collection. Assigned to local Navy Public Works organizations at naval facilities. In 1998 Kvichak also delivered six "Boom Skiffs" for pollution-control work: 5.49 × 2.41 m, aluminum construction.

Notes: The Navy operates numerous other oil-spill sweeping and boom-containment craft with a variety of serial numbers in the 25DP, 26NS, 26WB, 27WB, and 28UB series that were built by Marco Marine, Willard, SeaArk, and JBF Scientific.

21-ft. SeaArk-built Boom Handling Boat—at San Diego; aluminum-construction boat powered by one 150-bhp Johnson outboard George R. Schneider, 12-97

18-ft. Boom-Handling Boat UB-1—assigned to the Norfolk Naval Shipyard Takatoshi Okano, 8-00

UNNUMBERED NAVY SERVICE CRAFT *(continued)*

♦ 4 Ecology Sampling Boats [YAG]
Bldr: Munson Mfg., Edmonds, Wash. (In serv. 1988–. . .)

40NS8901, 40NS9001, 40NS9002, 40NS9101

Ecology Sampling Boat Ecos (40NS8901) George R. Schneider, 2-93

D: 11.3 tons (fl) **S:** 15 kts **Dim:** 12.19 × 3.66 × 0.91
M: 2 Volvo AQAD 40 outdrive diesels; 2 props; . . . bhp **Electric:** 12 kw tot.
Fuel: 100 gallons **Crew:** . . .

Remarks: Built for Naval Ocean Systems Center, San Diego, California. All-aluminum construction, unpainted. Has two 450-kg portable equipment davits and a hydraulic winch. 40NS9001 and 40NS9002 are assigned to Norfolk, Va. 40NS9101 is assigned to Yokosuka, Japan.

♦ 1 former Air Force space booster recovery ship [YAG]
Bldr: Halter Marine, Moss Point, Miss. (L: 27-2-85)

INDEPENDENCE

Independence George R. Schneider, 12-97

D: 1,798 tons (fl) **S:** 13 kts **Dim:** 60.96 (55.47 wl) × 12.19 × 4.11
Electronics: Radar: 1 STN-Atlas Elektronik 8500 nav.; 1 STN-Atlas Elektronik 5500 nav.
M: 2 Cummins KTA 3067-M 16-cyl. diesels; 2 props; 2,500 bhp—2 azimuth thrusters; 1,000 shp—Elliott-White-Gill bow and stern thrusters
Electric: 550 kw tot. (2 × 275-kw sets, Cummins KT 1150-GC diesels)
Range: 7,800/13; 8,500/11 **Fuel:** 99,419 gals. **Endurance:** 30 days
Crew: 13 tot. + 14 scientists/technicians

Remarks: Originally built to recover solid-fuel boosters launched from Vandenberg Air Force Base on the California coast; transferred to the U.S. Navy 1988 and operated for the Naval Facilities Engineering Services Center, Port Hueneme, California, by Western Instrument Corporation. Employed to test underwater sensors and is also available to other government agencies for charter.
Hull systems: Elaborate navigational equipment, including Magnavox MX 4400 GPS (Global Positioning System) receiver, Magnavox 11072 NAVSAT receiver, Robertson dynamic positioning system, two Simrad echo sounders. Has Flume passive-tank stabilization system. Can carry 388 tons deck cargo, including modular laboratories. Has a hyperbaric chamber capable of accommodating seven divers and also a small laboratory. Equipped with a 22-ton crane that telescopes to 19.8-m reach.

♦ 1 sail frigate relic [YAG]
Bldr: Hart's SY, Boston, Mass.

	Laid down	L	In serv.
CONSTITUTION (ex-IX 21)	11-1-1794	21-10-1797	1-10-1798

D: 2,200 tons (fl) **S:** 13 kts (sail) **Dim:** 62.18 (53.34 hull) × 13.26 × 6.86
A: 32 single 24 pdr; 20 single 32-pdr carronade; 2 single 24-pdr bow-chasers
Crew: 2 officers, 45 enlisted (orig.: 450 tot., incl. 55 Marines and 30 "boys")

Remarks: The world's oldest warship in full commission. Wooden construction. First went to sea 22-7-1798. Three masts: 28.7, 31.7, and 24.7 m high. Sail area: 3,968 m^2. Designated IX 21 from 8-12-41 to 1-9-75, and bore name *Old Constitution* from 1917 to 1925. Extensively refitted 1994 to mid-1997, with restoration of the original diagonal internal hull bracing and new rigging, permitting her to be sailed under her own power for the first time since 1886 with an augmented crew of 133 on 21-7-97 from Marblehead, Massachusetts, to Boston. Is on display at the former Charlestown Naval Base, Boston, Massachusetts.

Constitution U.S. Navy, 6-06

♦ 2 Guardian 85-ft.–class trials craft [YAGE]
Bldr: Guardian Marine, Tacoma, Wash. (In serv. 2000, 2003)

25MPB0001 25MPB0501

Guardian 85-ft. class Guardian Marine

D: 105 tons (fl) **S:** 40 kts **Dim:** 25.91 × 7.01 × 1.67
Electronics: 1 Furuno FR-8251 X-band nav.
M: 2 MTU DDC 12V4000 diesels diesels; 2 props; 4,920 bhp
Electric: 64 kw tot. (2 × 32-kw Northern Lights Mod. M984K alternators)
Range: 1,700/ . . . **Endurance:** 7 days **Crew:** . . .

Remarks: GRP-construction, planing-hull "Fast Patrol Craft." 25MPB0001 is assigned as a "test-support platform" to the Naval Surface Warfare Center, Carderock Division, Norfolk Detachment, Little Creek, Virginia.

♦ 1 wave-piercing catamaran trials craft [YAGE]
Bldr: Nichols Bros. Boat Builders, Inc., Freeland, Wash.

	L	In serv.
FSF-1 SEA FIGHTER (ex-X-Craft, IX 534)	5-2-05	31-5-05

D: 1,400 tons (fl) **S:** 50+ kts **Dim:** 79.9 × 21.9 × 3.5
A: 2 12.7-mm mg; 2 H-60 helicopters or 4 UAVs
Electronics: 1 . . . nav.
M: CODOG: 2 MTU 16V 595 diesels (5,850 hp each) and 2 G.E LM2500 gas turbines (33,500 hp each) ; 4 Rolls-Royce 125SII waterjets; . . . bhp
Range: 4000/20 **Crew:** 16 Navy and 10 Coast Guard personnel

Remarks: An experimental high-speed aluminum catamaran, ordered by the Office of Naval Research from Titan Corporation on 25-2-03 for $59.9 million. Construction, begun in 5-03, subcontracted to Nichols Bros. Employed initially for hydrodynamic trials employing various lifting bodies and polymer drag reduction techniques and to test technologies for use in the U.S. Navy's Littoral Combat Ship. Fitted with a "Mission Module Bay" to accommodate more than one mission trials package simultaneously. Mission packages may include mine-countermeasures, ASW, humanitarian support, etc.
Hull systems: Has a helicopter deck with two landing spots and hangar capable of accommodating H-60-series helicopters. The vessel has two decks and a small pilothouse on forward port corner with a cargo deck below for troops and vehicles and a storage capacity of up to 12 cargo containers. Also fitted with a stern ramp for roll-on/roll-off equipment or RIB deployment.

UNNUMBERED NAVY SERVICE CRAFT *(continued)*

Sea Fighter (FSF-1) U.S. Navy, 8-05

Sea Fighter (FSF-1) U.S. Navy, 8-05

Sea Fighter (FSF-1) W. Michael Young, 9-05

♦ 1 Stiletto-class M-hull trials craft

Bldr.: Knight & Carver Yacht Center, San Diego, Calif.

	L	In serv.
Stiletto	30-1-06	1-5-06

Stiletto U.S. Navy, 5-06

D: 183 tons (205 fl) **S:** 50+ knots **Dim:** 24.4 × 12.2 × 0.9
Electronics: Radar: 1 . . . nav.
M: 4 Caterpillar C 32 diesels; 1,650 bhp
Range: 500/50 **Crew:** 3 crew + 12 troops

Navy RIB team entering well deck aboard Stiletto U.S. Navy, 5-06

Remarks: Designed by M Ship Company and built by Knight & Carver Yacht Center of San Diego, California, the project was funded by the U.S. Department of Defense Office of Force Transformation through the Naval Surface Warfare Center, Carderock Division. Total construction cost was $6.0 million plus $4 million for outfitting. The Stiletto began a 2–3-year testing and trials program on 8-5-06. This is the largest carbon-fiber composite ship built in the United States. Unique twin M-shaped hull recaptures the bow wave and uses the energy to create an air cushion providing efficient planing for increased agility, stability, and other benefits in coastal environments. Has a sloped well deck and stern ramp for loading, offloading, and storage of an 11-m RIB. Also capable of launching Unmanned Underwater/Aerial Vehicles (UUV/UAVs). Fitted with "Electronic Keel" maritime data bus to allow for easy weapon, sensor, and mission payload reconfiguration and networking. Manned by operators from the U.S. Special Operations Command. Some reports indicate that she may be numbered M-80.

♦ Small Waterplane Area Ship test craft [YAGE]

Bldr: Pacific Marine & Supply Co., Ltd., Honolulu, Hawaii (L: 11-96)

Sea Slice (ex-*Slice*)

Sea Slice—painted in red, blue, and yellow stripes for recruiting purposes U.S. Navy, 11-05

Sea Slice U.S. Navy, 11-05

D: 183 tons (205 fl) **S:** 31.6 kts (trials) **Dim:** 31.70 × 16.80 × 4.30
Electronics: Radar: 2 Furuno . . . nav.
M: 2 MTU 16V396 TB 94 diesels; 2 2.2-m dia. Lips CP props; 6,850 bhp
Electric: 720 kw tot. (2 × 360-kw Caterpillar 3306 DITA diesel sets)
Range: 400/30; 2,000/22 **Fuel:** . . . tons **Crew:** 2 crew, 4 technicians

Remarks: Jointly funded by the Office of Naval Research ($14.5 million) and Pacific Marine and Supply Company as a prototype commercial inter-island personnel ferry. Intended to test high-speed SWATH (Small Waterplane Area Twin-Hull) design concepts and has a potential payload of 51 tons in up to Sea State 5. No immediate

UNNUMBERED NAVY SERVICE CRAFT *(continued)*

military application is foreseen, but the craft is foreseen as a potential mine-countermeasures or small missile combatant platform. In 1999, $9.5 million was to be used to construct a cargo-barge version of the design to be towed by the *Slice;* the barge may also be evaluated as a missile-launch platform. After losing a fin off Kaua'i during 1999, the craft was placed in reserve, but she was refitted and reactivated 6-01 for a series of demonstration cruises along the Pacific coast, with an Atlantic coast cruise in 2002 and a Great Lakes cruise in 2003; in addition to being operated by Lockheed Martin as a technology demonstrator for the Office of Naval Research, the craft is acting as a recruiting tool and has been painted in a bright silver, blue, red, and yellow paint scheme. The name was changed in 2002.
Hull systems: The Lockheed Martin hull design employs four torpedo-shaped underwater hulls, two per side, with the propellers mounted on the forward pair, which are closer together than the after pair to avoid propeller wake effects. Aluminum-alloy structure. The modular payload deck aft measures 17.37 m long by 16.76 m broad.
Combat system: The 35-mm CIWS and Netfire missile launcher and control system were added for Fleet Battle Experiment Juliet, to take place in the summer of 2002; the Netfire system was used to simulate launching Lockheed Martin "Loitering Attack Munitions," and the ship was also equipped with the Lockheed Martin Silent Sentry radar intercept system and two FLIR Systems Sea Star SAFIRE II devices, each with IR and E/O sensors and laser ranging systems, and a Klein 5000 towed side-looking sonar. Torpedo attacks were to be simulated, and a towed sonar and two remotely controlled mine countermeasures devices will be carried. A lightweight MSP 500 E/O director was fitted to control the gunmount.

♦ 1 Hydrofoil Small Waterplane Area Ship test craft [YAGE]
Bldr: Maritime Applied Physics Corp., Laurel, Md. (L: 7-7-95)

HYSWAS 1 QUEST

Quest (HYSWAS 1) Maritime Applied Physics, 7-95

D: 12 tons (fl) **S:** 37 kts **Dim:** 8.22 × . . . (3.1 over foil) × 2.0 (3.0 hullborne)
M: 2 Cummins . . . diesels; 1 prop; . . .

Remarks: HYSWAS = Hydrofoil Small Waterplane Area Ship. Has a single centerline pylon below the trimaran hull, with two sets of variable-incidence foils mounted on the bulbous foot. Total height is 3.9 m. Trials conducted from Annapolis, Maryland, commencing 7-95. Intended to maintain 35 kts in Sea State 5. The builder received a design feasibility contract for a 1,000-ton mine-countermeasures version of this design during 2001.

♦ 1 acoustic trials support craft [YAGE]
Bldr: Gladding-Hearn SB, Somerset, Mass. (In serv. 7-91)

60NS9001

D: . . . tons **S:** 30 kts **Dim:** 18.28 × 5.79 × 1.82
M: 2 G.M. Detroit Diesel 12 V92TA diesels; 2 props; 1,800 bhp
Electric: 65 kw tot (1 × 45-kw, 1 × 20-kw Onan sets, Cummins diesel-driven)
Range: 1,200/30 **Fuel:** 2,271 liters **Crew:** . . . tot.

Remarks: Aluminum construction, unpainted. Built for use by the Naval Surface Warfare Center, Carderock Detachment, as a towboat; is able to tow a 1.5-ton object at 15 kts.

♦ 1 converted Spruance-class Self-Defense Test Ship [YAGE]
Bldr: Ingalls Shipbuilding, Miss.

	Laid down	L	In serv.
Ex-PAUL F. FOSTER (ex-DD 964)	6-2-73	23-2-74	21-2-76

D: 6,824 tons light (9,282 fl) **S:** 32.5 kts
Dim: 171.68 (161.25 pp) × 16.76 × 7.00 (10.05 over sonar)
A: 1 Mk 41 VLS group (61 Tomahawk SSM and VLA ASROC ASW missiles); 4-8 RGM-84 Harpoon SSM; 1 8-round Mk 29 launcher (24 RIM-7P Sea Sparrow SAM); 2 single 127-mm 54-cal. Mk 45 DP; 2 20-mm Mk 15 Phalanx gatling CIWS; 4 12.7-mm mg; 2 triple 324-mm Mk 32 Mod. 5 ASW TT (18 Mk 46 torpedoes); 1 or 2 SH-60B Sea Hawk LAMPS-III ASW helicopters (see Remarks)

Electronics:
Radar: 1 Raytheon SPS-64(V)9; 1 Cardion SPS-55 surf. search; 1 Lockheed SPS-40E air search; 1 Hughes Mk 23 TAS Mod. 0 target designation; 1 Lockheed SPQ-9A surf. gun f.c.; 1 Lockheed SPG-60 gun f.c.; 1 Mk 95 SAM f.c.; 2 Mk 90 Phalanx f.c. (on mounts)
Sonar: SSQ-89(V)5,6, or 8 Suite: EDO-G.E. SQS-53B/C hull-mounted LF, SQR-19(V)3, SQR-19A(V)3, or SQR-19B(V) TACTAS, WQC-2 and WQC-6 underwater telephones
TACAN: URN-25
EW: SLQ-32(V)3 intercept/jamming;Mk 36 SRBOC decoy syst. (4 6-round Mk 137 RL); SSQ-108 Outboard D/F; SLQ-25A (with SSTD) Nixie towed torpedo decoy; SLQ-49 floating radar reflector bouys
E/O: 2 Boeing TISS Mk 8 Mod. 1 IR imaging
M: 4 G.E. LM-2500 gas turbines; 2 5-bladed CP props; 86,000 shp (80,000 sust.)
Electric: 6,000 kw tot. (3 × 2,000-kw Allison 501-K17 gas turbine-driven sets)
Range: 3,300/30; 6,000/20; 8,000/17 **Fuel:** 1,534 tons + 72 tons aviation fuel
Crew: 24–27 officers, 272–315 enlisted + air group: 8–10 officers, 30 enlisted

Remarks: Decommissioned "special" on 14-3-03; fully decommissioned 27-3-04, stricken 6-4-04, and now designated as "floating equipment." Converted at Port Hueneme, California, as a replacement for the *Decatur* (E 31), re-entering service in 2006. Will test the new Multi-Function Radar and may also have SPS-48E radar installed. Data given are for the ship as a destroyer.

Disposal note: *Decatur*-class self-defense test ship STDS (E 31) was withdrawn from service and was sunk as a target on 21-7-04. Of other former U.S. Navy ships recently employed as targets, ex-*Somers* (DDG 34) was sunk in a SINKEX target on 17-7-00. Ex-*Buchanan* (DDG 14) was sunk as a target on 13-6-00; ex-*Ramsey* (FFG 2) and ex-*Gen. Hugh J. Gaffey* (IX-507, ex-T-AP 121) were sunk on 15-6-00, and ex-*Worden* (CG 18) was sunk on 17-6-00—all as targets during the annual RIMPAC exercise. Sunk as targets during 2001 were ex-*Barbel* (SS 580) on 30-1-01; ex-*Reeves* (CG 24) by Royal Australian Air Force aircraft on 31-5-01; ex-*Lynde McCormick* (DDG 8) on 24-2-01; and ex-*John Paul Jones* (DDG 32, ex-DD 932) on 31-1-01.

Disposal notes: Sea Spectre PB Mk-III trials craft *Navy Prince* (65PB734) and *Plymouth* (65PB777) had been stricken as of 8-02; 65PB777, however, remains active at the Naval Surface Warfare Center, Dahlgren, Virginia.

♦ 2 Asheville-class engineering-trials ships [YAGE]
Bldr: Tacoma Boat, Tacoma, Wash.

	In serv.
165NS761 ATHENA (ex-*Chehalis,* PG 94)	11-8-69
165NS762 ATHENA II (ex-*Grand Rapids,* PG 98)	9-5-70

Athena (165NS761) Dr. Giorgio Arra, 1992

D: 225 tons (250 fl) **S:** 35 kts (13 on diesels)
Dim: 50.14 × 7.28 × 2.9 (3.20 over props)
Electronics: Radar: 2 . . . nav.
M: CODOG: 1 G.E. 7LM-1500-PE 102 LM-1500 gas turbine (12,500 shp), 2 Cummins VT12-875-M diesels (1,450 bhp); 2 CP props
Electric: 260 kw tot. (2 × 100-kw, 1 × 60-kw diesel sets)
Range: 325/37; 2,300/13
Fuel: 50 tons **Crew:** 10 tot. + up to 18 scientific party

Remarks: Operate from Port Lauderdale, Florida, by MAR, Inc., for the Naval Surface Warfare Center, Carderock Division. Have civilian crews and are disarmed. *Athena I* was reclassified as "floating equipment" on 21-8-75 and *Athena II* on 1-10-77. Used in the development of high-speed towed sensors, airborne mine countermeasures, communications systems, and full-scale verifications of propeller designs. *Lauren* was activated in 1990 for trials with the Integrated Warship System Demonstration Program and appears to be involved in signature reduction trials; the ship received the Northrop Grumman Low Observable Multifunction Stack for trials from Panama City, Florida, during 7-01.
Hull systems: Have 366 ft.^{2} of air-conditioned laboratory space and 850 ft.^{2} of working space on the fantail; they have a 10-ton instrumentation payload and both can carry a 14.9-m, portable, glass-reinforced plastic laboratory on the stern, while *Athena I* has a permanent 18.6-m lab added forward. Fuel consumption at 35 knots is 1,000 gal./hr. Navigational equipment included GPS, NAVSAT, and LORAN receivers, echo sounder, and gyrocompass.
Disposals: *Lauren* (165NS763) was retired from service in 2005 and is currently laid up at Philadelphia pending disposal. Two additional units of the class, *Gallup* (PG 85) and *Canon* (PG 90), were transferred to the control of the Naval Ships Research Center, Carderock, Maryland, from the Naval Sea Systems Command, in 7-92 they have since been stricken.

♦ 2 trials support ships [YAGE]
Bldr: McDermott SY, New Iberia, La. (In serv. 1981)

192UB8701 RANGER (ex-*Seacor Ranger,* ex-NUSC *Ranger,* ex-*Sea Level 27*)
192UB8702 NAWC 38 (ex-NADC 38, ex-*Sea Level No. 7*)

UNNUMBERED NAVY SERVICE CRAFT *(continued)*

NAWC 38 (192UB8702) Winter & Findler, 9-01

D: Approx. 1,800 tons (fl) **S:** 12 kts **Dim:** 58.52 × 12.19 × 4.27
A: *Ranger:* 1 bow, submerged 533-mm TT; 1 triple 324-mm Mk 32 ASW TT
Electronics: Radar: NAWC 38: 1 . . . ARPA X-band nav.; 1 . . . ARPA S-band nav.
M: 2 G.M. Electromotive Div. 12-645-E6 diesels; 2 props; 3,000 bhp—300-shp bow tunnel-thruster (G.M. 8V-71 diesel driving)
Electric: 300 kw tot. (2 × 150-kw sets, G.M. 8V-71 diesels driving); NAWC 38 also: 1,200 kw (2 × 600-kw sets, Solar gas turbines driving)
Range: 8,600/12 (NAWC 38: 5,000/10) **Endurance:** NAWC 38: 20–25 days
Crew: NAWC 38: 8 civilian crew + up to 22 scientific party (civil.)

Remarks: 300 grt/1,200 dwt. Converted oilfield tug-supply vessels acquired 1986 and employed as tender for trials services. NAWC 38 is operated for the Naval Air Warfare Center, Aircraft Division, Key West, Florida, as trials craft for littoral warfare technology testing and is equipped with an 79-ton crane (limited to 36 tons at sea), an A-frame gantry at the stern, a 2.9 × 7.9–m centerline moonpool, four-point mooring capability in depths of up to 600 ft., and state-of-the-art navigational systems. *Ranger* is used in support of the AUTEC (Atlantic Undersea Test and Evaluation Center) range at Andros Island, the Bahamas; she is chartered from Seacor/MSO, Inc., which operates her.

Disposal note: Sonobuoy trials craft *Acoustic Pioneer* (180WB8701) was placed up for sale during 7-06.

♦ 1 sonobuoy trials craft [YAGE]
Bldr: Eastern Marine, Inc., Panama City, Fla. (In serv. 12-81)

111NS8801 Acoustic Explorer (ex-*Strong Brio*)

Acoustic Explorer (111NS8801) W. Michael Young, 9-05

D: . . . tons (fl) **S:** . . . kts **Dim:** 38.1 × 9.14 × 1.42
M: 2 diesels; 2 props; . . . bhp

Remarks: Acquired 1988. Assigned to Naval Surface Warfare Center, Crane, Indiana. Has 23 m^2 of laboratory space.

Disposal note: SWATH (Small Waterplane Area, Twin-Hull) research craft *Kaimalino* (SSP 1, 90WB8701), out of service since 1997 and laid up midway through modifications, had been discarded by 2001.

♦ 1 converted LCU 1610–class trials craft [YAGE]
Bldr: Defoe SB, Bay City, Wisc. (In serv. 1969)

LCU 1647 MDSU 2

D: 190 tons (390 normal, 437 fl) **S:** 11 kts **Dim:** 41.07 × 9.07 × 2.08
Electronics: Radar: 1 Raytheon SPS-69 Pathfinder nav.
M: 2 G.M. 12V-71 diesels; 2 Kort-nozzle props; 800 bhp—White-Gill bow and stern thrusters (275-bhp G.M. 6-71 diesel driving forward, 230-bhp G.M. 6V-53 diesel driving aft)
Electric: 110 kw tot (2 × 40-kw, 1 × 30-kw diesel sets)
Range: 1,000/10 **Fuel:** 13 tons **Endurance:** 4-6 days
Crew: 6 tot. + 9 scientific party

Remarks: Cargo capacity is 180 tons; cargo space, 36.9 × 7.62 max. (4.5-m-wide bow ramp). Has a 22.7-ton capacity, 16.8-m reach crane on the port quarter. Can be two-point moored in up to 300 ft. of water. Has A-frame crane, various winches, etc. Navigational suite includes Loran-C and Differential GPS receivers and echo-sounder. Employed since 2003 as workboat, support ship, and diving tender with Mobile Diving and Salvage Unit 2.

♦ 1 former Coast Guard buoy boat trials craft [YAGE]
Bldr: . . . (In serv. . . .)

65NS733 NAWC 03 (ex-USCG 65402)

D: . . . tons **S:** 12 kts **Dim:** 19.81 × 7.92 × 1.83
Electronics: Radar: 1 . . . X-band nav.
M: 2 G.M. 12V-71 TI diesels; 2 props; 1,000 bhp
Electric: 30 kw tot. (1 × 30-kw diesel driving) **Range:** 600/12
Endurance: 1–2 days **Crew:** 6 tot.

Remarks: Former U.S. Coast Guard small buoy tender stricken in 1998 and transferred to the navy for use as a workboat at the Naval Air Warfare Center, Aircraft Division, Key West, Florida. Aluminum construction. Has a dive platform at the stern. Is equipped with Loran-C and portable Differential GPS receivers.

♦ 1 semisubmersible oceanographic research barge [YAGEN]
Bldr: Gunderson Bros., Portland, Ore. (In serv. 6-8-62)

Flip

Flip—in transit configuration George R. Schneider, 4-94

D: 700 tons (fl) **S:** 2–3 kts **Dim:** 109.73 × 8.53 × 3.81
M: 1/60-hp thruster **Crew:** . . .

Remarks: *Flip* is also an acronym for "Floating Instrument Platform." Operated for and by the Scripps Institute of Oceanography of California, although navy-owned. Designed to be towed into position and then "flipped" (hence name) upright to provide vertical enclosed column for water-property research; essentially a long cylinder with a ship-type bow at one end for towing. Refitted at San Diego in 1998.

Disposal note: 36-ft. *Hammerhead*-class diving trials launch *Captain Bart* (36NS9101) were retired from the navy list during 2005.

♦ 8 Mk II Dive Boats [YDT]
Bldr: Peterson Builders, Sturgeon Bay, Wisc. (In serv. 1989–90)

50DW8901 through 50DW8908

Mk II Dive Boat H&L Van Ginderen, 10-00

D: 25.2 tons light (37.6 fl) **S:** 9 kts **Dim:** 15.24 × 4.50 × 0.84
M: 2 G.M. 6V53 diesels; 2 props; 346 bhp **Range:** 220/9 **Fuel:** 418 gallons
Crew: 5 tot. + 5 divers

Remarks: Steel construction. Carry a 5.0 × 3.7 × 2.34–m, 11-ton diving module with compressors and decompression chamber. Can support hard-hat divers to 58 m with Mk 12 diving gear.

♦ 4 65-ft. Explosive Ordnance Disposal Support Craft [YDT]
Bldr: 65SC8801: Swiftships, Inc., Morgan City, La.; others: Oregon Iron Works (In serv. 1989–92)

65SC8801 65SC9101 65SC9102 65SC9201

65SC9102—at San Diego George R. Schneider, 6-96

UNNUMBERED NAVY SERVICE CRAFT *(continued)*

D: 34.51 tons light (41.15 fl) **S:** . . . kts **Dim:** 19.66 × 5.74 × 1.17
Electronics: Radar: 1. . . nav.
M: 2 G.M. Detroit Diesel 8V71N diesels; 2 props; 544 bhp
Range: 324/ . . . **Fuel:** 886 gals. **Crew:** 4 tot.

Remarks: Originally chartered, then purchased outright. Aluminum construction. Have a diver's platform at the stern. Sister 65SC8701 was donated to Florida Atlantic University and renamed *Stephan* during 2002.

Note: For other craft employed as harbor diving tenders, see the following under workboats [YFU].

♦ 5 70-ft. Personnel Boats [YFL]
Bldr: Modutech Marine, Portland, Ore. (In serv.: four in 1970, two in 1990)

70PE8101 TB-13	70PE9001
70PE8102 TB-19	70PE9002
70PE8104 TB-24	

Remarks: Attached to the Naval Station Pearl Harbor and employed in support of transporting tourists to the U.S.S. *Arizona* (BB 39) Memorial. "TB" means "Tourist Boat." Are of GRP construction. Have 2 G.M. 6071 or 6072 HEMH diesels. Sister 70PE8103 TB-21 was retired in 2004.

♦ 1 Chief of Naval Operations Yacht [YFL]
Bldr: Burger Boats, Manitowoc, Wisc. (In serv. 1965)

63CC791 (ex-*Concorde,* ex-*Encore* III, ex-*Still Rovin'* V)

D: Approx. 60 tons (fl) **S:** . . . kts **Dim:** 19.28 × 4.88 × 1.37
M: 2 G.M. Detroit Diesel 8-cyl diesels; 2 props; 360 bhp

Remarks: Seized by counter-drug forces at Miami in 1978 and turned over to the USN. Operates from Washington Navy Yard, Washington, D.C. Aluminum construction.

♦ 1 63-ft. former Air-Sea Rescue Boat [YFL]

C3007

D: 17.7 tons light (29.3 fl) **S:** 28 kts **Dim:** 19.30 × 4.67 × 1.22 max.
Electronics: Radar: 1 . . . nav.
M: 2 Caterpillar 3116-35 diesels; 1 prop; 660 bhp
Range: 450/24 **Fuel:** 1,580 gals. **Crew:** 6 tot.

Remarks: Employed as yacht for CINCPACFLT at Pearl Harbor. Wooden construction craft of World War II–era design and construction. Sister C3148, formerly used as yacht for Commander Naval Forces Marianas at Guam, was placed up for sale in 9-00.

Note: Other personal launches assigned to operational flag officers are usually from among the 40PE-series personnel launches.

♦ 4 13-meter Personnel Boats [YFL]
Bldr: Willard Marine, Anaheim, Calif. (In serv. 1-10-99 to . . .)

13MPE9901 through 13MPE9904

13-meter Personnel Boat 13MPE9904—on skids at San Diego George R. Schneider, 6-00

D: . . . tons **S:** 23 kts **Dim:** 11.2 × . . . × . . . ×
M: 1 Cummins C6BTAS.9280 diesels **Crew:** 3 + 40 passengers

Remarks: GRP construction; intended to serve for 20 years.

♦ 23 40-ft. Personnel Boats Mk 7 [YFL]

40PE, 12MPE and 12MUB series

D: 10 tons light (12.7 fl) **S:** 22.5 kts **Dim:** 12.56 × 3.61 × 1.10
M: 1 Cummins 6BTA5.9-M2 diesel; 1 prop; 214 bhp
Range: . . . / . . . **Fuel:** 150 gals. **Crew:** 3 + 40 passengers

Remarks: GRP-construction with Airex foam core. Intended for VIP and other local transportation. Can be carried aboard ships. 12MUB series were built to metric standards and have greater rake to the bows.

40-ft. Personnel Boat Mk 7—assigned to Commander Submarines Pacific (COMSUBPAC) at Pearl Harbor Brian Morrison, 6-00

♦ 21 33-ft. Personnel Boats Mk 4 [YFL]

33PE and 10MPE series

33-ft. Personnel Boat 33PE8705—at San Diego George R. Schneider, 6-96

D: 5 tons light (8.2 fl) **S:** 10 or 15 kts **Dim:** 10.17 × 3.25 × 0.91
M: 1 . . . G.M. or Cummins diesel; 1 prop; . . . bhp
Range: 150/10 **Fuel:** 100 gals. **Crew:** 3 + 42 passengers

Remarks: GRP-construction craft for shipboard or naval base use. Can be fitted with a portable fabric canopy over the passenger well. Hull has round bilge forward, tapering to flat bottom at stern. 10MPE-series units were built to metric standards.

♦ 2 25-ft. Workskiff launches
Bldr: Workskiff, Inc., Burlington, Wash. (In serv. 9-00)

D: . . . **S:** 38 kts **Dim:** 7.62 × 2.59 × . . .
M: 2 Honda gasoline outboards; 230 bhp

Remarks: Monocoque aluminum hull. Function not available. Were delivered with road trailers.

♦ 425 miscellaneous personnel launches [YFL]

Remarks: Other launch classes of 40-ft. (12.2 m) or less overall length as of 1-01 included:

- 5 26-ft. Personnel Boats (8MPE series; being replaced by 24RB and 7MRB series)
- 20 26-ft. Motor Whaleboats (being retired and replaced by 24RB and 7MRB series)
- 22 26-ft. GRP Inshore Boats (8MIB series)
- 335 24-ft. Rigid Inflatables (24RB and 7MRB—Metric Rigid-inflatable Boat—series)
- 43 miscellaneous craft under 18-ft. long

♦ 1 95-ft. utility boat [YFU]
Bldr: U.S. Coast Guard Yard, Curtis Bay, Md. (In serv. 15-12-53)

95NS8801 951 OLYMPIC VENTURE (ex-*Cape Wash,* WPB 95310)

D: 87 tons (106 fl) **S:** 18 kts **Dim:** 28.96 × 6.1 × 1.55
Electronics: Radar: 1/SPS-64(V)1 nav.
M: 4 Cummins VT-12-M-700 diesels; 2 props; 2,324 bhp
Electric: 40 kw tot. **Range:** 570/20; 1,300/9 **Crew:** 6–8 tot.

Remarks: Unofficial hull number 951 appears on both sides of the bow. Former U.S. Coast Guard "Cape"-class cutter stricken 1-6-87 and transferred to the U.S. Navy for use at the Naval Submarine Base, Bangor, Washington, as a local security patrol craft.

♦ 54 converted LCM(8)-class work and diving boats [YFU]
(In serv. 1953–56, 1969)

D: 59 tons (116 fl) **S:** 9 kts **Dim:** 22.40 × 6.42 × 1.40 (mean)
M: 2 G.M. Detroit Diesel 6-71 diesels; 2 props; 600 bhp

Remarks: Standard U.S. Navy LCM(8) landing craft of different marks adapted for a variety of utility tasks. Twelve are aluminum-hulled Mk 2, 4, and 6 and the remainder are steel-hulled Mod. 1, 3, and 5. Most, if not all, retain their original 74CM-series or C-series landing craft serial numbers. One, used as a liberty launch at La Maddelena, Sardinia, sank on 3-1-01 but was salvaged.

Disposal note: 64-ft. Distribution Box Boat diving tender C12739 was transferred to the city of Long Beach, California, which later sold the craft commercial.

UNNUMBERED NAVY SERVICE CRAFT *(continued)*

74CM6720—a converted LCM(8) landing craft modified as a diving training craft for the Deep Submergence Unit at San Diego W. Michael Young, 12-99

♦ 94 50-ft. Workboats Mk 1, Mk 2 and Mk 3 [YFU]

Bldr: Gulf Copper and Mfgr., Port Arthur, Tex. (in serv. 1994 to 4-95); Marinette Marinette, Marinette, Wisc. (in serv. 1984 to 16-12-85); Oregon Iron Works, Clackamas, Ore. (In serv. 1987–89); and Gulf Copper (in serv. 1994 to . . .)

50WB and 15MWB series

50-ft. Workboat 50WB8708—variant with open cargo well George R. Schneider, 4-00

50-ft. Workboat—variant with cargo well decked over; note push knees at bow H&L Van Ginderen, 3-99

D: 25.6 tons light (42.05 fl) **S:** 9.5 kts loaded **Dim:** 15.3 × 4.4 × 1
M: Mk 1 and 2: 2 G.M. Detroit Diesel 6V71 Mod. 4 diesels; 2 props; 400 bhp; Mk 3: 2 Cummins 6BTA5.9-M2 diesels; 2 props; 440 bhp **Range:** 208/9.5
Fuel: 1,850 liters **Crew:** 3 (Mk 3: 5 tot.)

Remarks: Steel construction. Mk 3 Cargo capacity is 17.5 tons, carried in an 11.6 × 4.6 × 1.6–m deep cargo well forward. Used for general-purpose workboats and as push-tugs. Steel construction. First 28 ordered 2-84, 24 more in 11-84 from Marinette; 50 ordered 12-9-86 from Oregon Iron Works, with 17 more ordered 11-88 (and an option for 64 more, which was not taken up). The 25 ordered 1994 from Gulf Copper were powered by two Cummins 69TA5.9M2 diesels for a total of 450 bhp. Have either an open or covered cargo compartment forward: 11.6 × 4.6 × 1.6 m. Most have been stricken.

♦ 28 converted LCM(6)-class work and diving boats [YFU]

Bldr: Willard Marine, Anaheim, Calif.

15MUB series

D: 24 tons (64 fl) **S:** 10.2 kts **Dim:** 17.07 × 4.37 × 1.22 fwd./1.52 aft
M: 2 Cummins 6BT5.9-180 diesels; 2 props; 330 bhp
Range: 140/10 **Crew:** 4–5 tot.

Remarks: Designed as landing craft and built between 1952 and 1968. Used as push-tugs, waste recovery craft, diving tenders, etc. Mk 2 and Mk 3: 22 tons fl; 15.36 × 4.43 × 1.32. Mk 2 has GRP hull, Mk 3 is built of wood.

LCM(6) C201044—one of several identical converted LCM(6) landing craft converted for use as personnel ferries at La Maddelena, Sardinia, for Submarine Squadron 22; others carry numbers 85 and 87 on the sides of the pilothouse Maurizio Brescia, 6-99

LCM(6)—converted as a divers' workboat, at New London, Conn. Paul C. Clift, 12-98

An LCM(6) converted for use as a tug and hose tender aboard Ready Reserve Force Offshore Petroleum Discharge System (OPDS) tankers; the craft is aboard the *Petersburg* (T-AOT 5075) in this view George R. Schneider, 7-97

♦ 4 50-ft. converted LCM(3) workboats and diving boats [YFU]

50UB series

D: 23.6 tons light (50.8 fl) **S:** 9.5 kts **Dim:** 15.28 × 4.27 × 1.22
M: 2 G.M. 6V71 or 6072A HE diesels; 2 props; 330 bhp
Range: 130/9.5 **Fuel:** 1,730 liters **Crew:** 4 crew + 146 passengers

Remarks: Converted from landing craft. Original cargo well decked over and bow ramp welded shut or deleted entirely.

♦ 2 ex-U.S. Army 45-ft. Design 320 workboat class [YFU]

Bldrs: Various (In serv. 1953)

C5840 C5841

U.S. Army 45-ft. Workboat-class Duke (45WB831)—since stricken Christopher P. Cavas, 7-00

UNNUMBERED NAVY SERVICE CRAFT *(continued)*

D: . . . tons **S:** 9 kts **Dim:** 13.72 × 3.96 × 2.13
M: 1 diesel; 1 prop; 170 bhp

Remarks: Steel construction. Resemble small tugboats. Based at Portsmouth NSY, New Hampshire. One-hundred eighteen were built during World War II and 98 in the early 1950s, originally as tenders to Army dredges; Army Corps of Engineers still operates many units of the class. 45WB831 was built by Roamer Boat Co., Holland, Michigan. 45WB711, 45WB831, and 45WB833 were deleted from the navy list in 2005.

♦ 34 24-ft. Workboat class [YFU]

Bldr: MonArk Marine, Monticello, Ark. (In serv. 1980–86)

24WB 802–808	24WB 851–852, 857
24WB 824–825, 828	24WB 8101, 8311, 8315
24WB 831–834, 836	24WB 8410, 8411, 8413, 8415, 8419, 8422, 8423
24WB 842–844, 846	24WB 8603, 8606, 8607

24-ft. Workboat OP 2—at New London, Conn. Paul C. Clift, 12-98

D: 2.5 tons (3.8 fl) **S:** 22.5 kts with 4 aboard
Dim: 7.32 × 2.31 × 1.57 (molded depth)
M: 2 Volvo Penta AGAD 41A diesels with Type 290 outdrives; 165 bhp
Range: . . . / . . . **Crew:** 4 tot.

Remarks: Aluminum construction. Survivors of 74 built to essentially the same design as the 24-ft. 24HS-series Harbor Security launches (see under patrol boats [PB]). No radar fitted.

♦ 430+ miscellaneous utility boats [YFU]

- 2 41-ft. Sea Mule workboats (41WB series)
- 9 40-ft. Utility Boats (40UB and 12MUB series)
- 6 33-ft. Utility Boats (10MUB series)
- 33 27-ft. Utility Boats (27AP, 27MC, 27NS, 27SC, and 27UB series)
- 74 25-ft. Utility Boats (25MM, 25BW, 25NS, and 25UB series)
- 135 22-ft. Utility Boats (in 22NS, 22SC, 22UB and 22DS series)
- 19 21-ft. Utility Boats
- 13 20-ft. Utility Boats (20UB series)
- 74 19-ft. Utility Boats (19UB series, with most used in oil-spill containment)
- 66 18-ft. Utility Boats (18UB series)
- plus 43 launches under 18-ft. overall

25-ft. utility boat (25MM series)—used in support of the navy's marine mammal programs George R. Schneider, 5-06

♦ 1 inshore survey craft [YGS]

Bldr: . . . (In serv. 2001)

. . . CAVALLUCIO MARINO

D: . . . **S:** 12 kts **Dim:** 10.36 × . . . × . . .
Electronics:
Radar: . . .
Sonar: Multibeam mapping sonar; echo sounder
M: . . . diesels **Crew:** 3 Navy officers, 2–4 civilian technicians

Remarks: Operated by the Navy Fleet Survey Team. GRP craft cost $2 million, exclusive of equipment, and can be transported in a special container to operational area. Based at Ingleside, Texas. The name means "Seahorse" in Italian. Has differential GPS terminal. By end of 2002, had been used to survey Gaeta Bay, Naples, Italy; Apra Harbor, Guam; and waters off Ingleside, Texas.

♦ 1 aerial target-launch craft [YGT]

Bldr: Halter Marine, Moss Point, Miss.

	L	In serv.
ATLS 9701	18-9-97	1-98

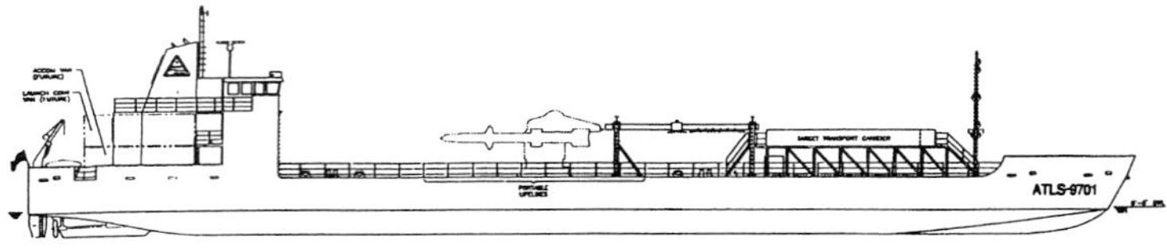

ATLS 9701 U.S. Navy, 1997

D: 857 tons (fl) **S:** 8 kts **Dim:** 80.77 × 7.92 × 1.98
M: 2 . . . diesels; 2 props; 1,342 bhp

Remarks: Ordered late 1995 for the Naval Air Warfare Center, at Point Mugu, California, outside of normal USN ship acquisition process. Is equipped with a Mk 10 twin launcher for Vandal (converted Talos) supersonic targets; reload missiles are carried in a horizontal magazine forward of the launcher. Is later to receive an accommodations module and a rigid-inflatable boat. Most of the hull space is taken up by ballast tanks and voids. Operates from Port Hueneme, California.

♦ 1 large target craft [YGT]

Bldr: Maritime Contractors, Inc., Bellingham, Wash. (In serv. 1994)

MST 9301

MST 9301 U.S. Navy, 1994

D: 850 tons (fl) **S:** 12 kts **Dim:** 80.5 × 7.92 × 1.82
M: 2 Caterpillar 3412 Dita diesels; 2 props; . . . bhp

Remarks: Referred to as the "SST." Operated by the Surface Targets Team, Naval Air Warfare Center, Weapons Division, Point Mugu, California, and based at Port Hueneme. Radio-controlled target. Uses condemned 20-ft. cargo containers stacked to simulate various radar targets.

♦ . . . QST 35A/B/C–class (SEPTAR) target drones [YGT]

(In serv. 1970s to . . .)

D: 13.3 tons light (20.8 fl) **S:** 34 kts **Dim:** 16.68 × 4.15 × 0.70
M: Five Mercury 3-325-622 gasoline engines; 5 props; 1,625 bhp
Range: 160/35 **Fuel:** 2,000 liters **Crew:** 4 tot. (ferrying)

Remarks: Data are for earlier 54-ft. Mk 35 model, now superceded by 56-ft. version with four Mercruiser engines. Can tow target sleds as well as launch aerial target drones. On some, a tall lattice mast supports various target enhancement devices and radio-control antennas. Latest version, now being delivered, is built by Willard Marine under a 1995 contract and uses hull mold from previous builder, Hood Industries. Are currently numbered in the 17MTD series. All are assigned to the Naval Air Warfare Center, Point Mugu, California, which distributes them as needed fleet-wide for exercises; they are based at Port Hueneme, California. An unknown number of QST 33 target drones are also in service.

UNNUMBERED NAVY SERVICE CRAFT *(continued)*

QST 35A–class (SEPTAR) target boat 9301 A. D. Baker III, 6-00

♦ 2 40-ft. Plane Personnel Rescue Boats, Mk. 5 [YH]
Bldr: Willard Marine, Anaheim, Calif. (In serv. 1991)

40PR9001 40PR9002

D: 11.34 tons light (13.15 fl) **S:** . . . kts **Dim:** 12.19 × 3.47 × 1.09
Electronics: Radar: 1 . . . nav.
M: 2 Cummins 6BTA5.9-M2 diesels; 2 props; 486 bhp
Range: . . . / . . . **Fuel:** 500 gals. **Crew:** 3 tot.

Remarks: GRP and vinylester construction. Can carry 4,000 lbs personnel and cargo in addition to crew and are equipped for firefighting. Both are assigned to Jacksonville Naval Air Station.

♦ 1 42-ft. Protector-class air-sea rescue boats [YH]
Bldr: SeaArk Marine, Monticello, Ark. (In serv. 14-10-86)

42PR852

Remarks: Aluminum construction. Based at Bremerton, Wash.

Disposal notes: Sister 42PR854 was stricken in 1995 and placed up for sale on 25-2-99. 42PR851, 42PR853 and 42PR855 were no longer in service as of 2005. 42PR856 was transferred to MARAD for use at Suisun Bay as a tender and is now named *Syrah* (PF 69). 65-ft. air-sea rescue boat AVR 681 (65AR681) was on offer to other government agencies as of 2-00; sister 65AR682 was transferred to Jordan in 1996.

Note: The U.S. Navy also uses a variety of towed targets for gunnery and aerial-attack training purposes. A number of Boeing Canada Technology Barracuda, 7.30 × 2.74–m remote-controlled target boats, powered by a 300-hp diesel for 36 kt maximum speeds or 30 kts for 6 hours were ordered during the early 1990s.

♦ 2 ex-U.S. Air Force 120-ft.-class weapons retrievers [YPT]
Bldr: Swiftships, Inc., Morgan City, La. (In serv. 1988–89)

120MR8804 SL-120 (ex-MR-120-8804)
120NS8801 Seadog (ex-MR-120-8805)

SL-120 (120MR8804)—at Port Hueneme, Calif. George R. Schneider, 7-95

D: 91 tons light (133 fl) **S:** 30 kts (27 sust.)
Dim: 35.78 × 7.51 × 2.06 (max. aft) **Electronics:** Radar: 1/Furuno . . .
M: 4 G.M. Detroit Diesel 16V92 MTA diesels; 4 props; 5,600 bhp **Range:** 600/27
Fuel: 4,920 gallons **Electric:** 50 kw (2 × 25 kw) **Crew:** 10 tot.

Remarks: Intended for location and recovery of practice missiles and can transport 20 tons deck cargo. Transferred from Air Force to U.S. Navy control in 1996. Aluminum construction. *Seadog,* formerly at Wallace Air Base, the Philippines, was relocated to Kadena Air Base, Okinawa. SL-120 operates from Port Hueneme, California, as a range safety craft. Carry 1,100 gallons water for washing down recovered missiles.

♦ 5 TWR 821–class torpedo retrievers [YPT]
Bldr: Peterson Builders, Sturgeon Bay, Wisc.

	Laid down	L	In serv.
120TR821 TWR 821 Swamp Fox	. . .	17-10-84	4-11-85
120TR823 TWR 823 Porpoise	22-8-84	4-5-85	6-12-85
120TR833 TWR 833 . . .	28-5-85	4-4-86	3-7-86
120TR841 TWR 841 . . .	2-8-85	15-8-86	18-10-86
120TR842 TWR 842 Narwhal	23-8-85	22-9-86	24-12-86

D: 174 tons (213 fl) **S:** 16 kts **Dim:** 36.58 × 7.62 × 3.65
Electronics: Radar: 1 Raytheon . . . nav.
M: 2 Caterpillar D 3512 diesels; 2 props; 2,350 bhp **Electric:** 128 kw tot.
Range: 1,700/16 **Fuel:** 28 tons **Endurance:** 7 days
Crew: 1 officer, 14 enlisted

Remarks: First five ordered 8-7-83 for delivery 15-12-84 to 15-3-85; three more ordered 10-83, all for delivery 7-85; two ordered 2-85 for delivery 6-86. Congress halted further procurement in 1985. Stern ramp and electrohydraulic crane aft. Can carry 14 Mk 48 torpedoes. Have 43.7 tons permanent ballast. TWR 833 and TWR 841 have been modified to act as diver-support tenders.

Swamp Fox (TWR 821; 120TR821)—at San Diego W. Michael Young, 1-06

Disposals: TWR 824 and TWR 831 were irreparably damaged during Hurricane Hugo in 1990 at now-closed Roosevelt Roads, Puerto Rico. TWR 822 and TWR 825 were stricken during 1997, and TWR 832 by 2006.

♦ 1 Hugo-class torpedo retriever conversion [YPT]
Bldr: McDermott Shipyards, Inc., New Iberia, La. (In serv. 1982)

180NS8201 Hugo (ex-*Crystal Pelham*)

Hugo (180NS8201) H&L Van Ginderen, 2-99

D: Approx. 1,300 tons (fl) **S:** 12 kts **Dim:** 50.32 × 12.19 × 3.35
M: 2 Caterpillar D399SCAC 16-cyl. diesels; 2 props; 2,250 bhp—bow-thruster
Electric: 270 kw tot. (2 × 135 kw) **Crew:** . . . tot.

Remarks: 298 grt. Former oilfield tug/supply vessel converted by Leevac Shipyard as replacement for TWR 824, lost to the hurricane for which the replacement craft is named. Delivered 3-7-91 after conversion. Attached to NAS Patuxent River.

♦ 1 Hunter-class torpedo retriever conversion [YPT]
Bldr: Quality Shipbldrs, Inc., Moss Point, Moss Point, Miss. (In serv. 1981)

180NS8202 Hunter (ex-*Nola Pelham*)

Hunter (180NS8202) Ralph Edwards, 9-04

UNNUMBERED NAVY SERVICE CRAFT *(continued)*

D: Approx. 1,300 tons (fl) **S:** 12 kts **Dim:** 54.86 × 11.58 × 3.96
M: 2 Caterpillar D399SCAC diesels; 2 props; 2,250 bhp
Electric: 270 kw tot. (2 × 135 kw) **Crew:** . . . tot.

Remarks: 258 grt. Former oilfield tug/supply vessel converted by Leevac Shipyard as replacement for TWR 825. Delivered 3-7-91 after conversion. Based at Key West, Fla.

♦ 1 Rangemaster-class exercise torpedo and decoy service craft [YPT]
Bldr: Steiner Fabricators, Bayou LaBatre, Ala. (In serv. 1981)

110WB8501 RANGEMASTER (ex-*Hull* 108)

D: . . . tons **S:** . . . kts **Dim:** 33.53 × 7.92 × 3.51
M: 1 . . . diesel; 1 prop; . . . bhp

Remarks: 99 grt. Built as a crewboat for the RCA company to support a Navy contract. Purchased 1985 for use in launch and recovery of mobile targets and exercise torpedoes at the AUTEC Range in the Bahamas.

Disposal note: Transporter-class weapons retrievers *Transporter* and *Retriever* were retired in 2004–5.

♦ 2 85-ft. torpedo retrievers [YPT]
Bldr: Tacoma Boat, Tacoma, Wash. (In serv. 1975)

85TR761 (TWR 8) ILIWAI 85TR762 (TWR 7) CHAPARRAL

Chaparral (TWR 7, 85TR762) Brian Morrison, 6-00

D: . . . **S:** 18 kts **Dim:** 25.9 × . . . × . . .
Electronics: Radar: 1/LN-66 nav.
M: 4 G.M. diesels; 2 props; . . . bhp **Crew:** . . .

Remarks: Aluminum construction. 85TR762 was deactivated in 1992 but restored to service in 1997. Both are assigned to Pearl Harbor, Hi.

♦ 1 ex-U.S. Air Force 85-ft. Weapons Retriever class [YPT]
Bldr: Swiftships Inc., Morgan City, La. (In serv. 1967)

85NS681 HM 8

D: 43.5 tons light (54 fl) **S:** 21.7 kts **Dim:** 25.91 × 5.69 × 2.10
M: 2 G.M. Detroit Diesel 16V71N diesels; 2 props; 1,400 bhp
Electric: 40 kw tot. (2 × 20-kw G.M. E5252 ABS diesel sets) **Range:** 800/21.7
Fuel: 10,787 liters **Crew:** 8 tot.

Remarks: Operated from Port Hueneme, California. Numerous sisters were built as patrol boats ("85-ft. Commercial Cruiser Class") under foreign aid programs. Aluminum construction.

Disposal notes: HM 9 (85NS691) went aground and was lost on 21-1-99 at Point Conception, California; TWR 4 (85NS9001; ex-USAF MR-85-1608) was stricken during 1999, and ex-USAF MR-85-1603 had been stricken by 2001.

HM 8 (85NS681) George R. Schneider, 8-01

♦ 2 85-ft. torpedo retrievers [YPT]
Bldr: Sewart Seacraft, Berwick, La. (In serv. 1966)

85TR653 85TR654

D: 61 tons (fl) **S:** 21 kts **Dim:** 25.91 × 5.69 × 1.73
M: 2 G.M. Detroit Diesel 16V71 diesels; 2 props; 1,160 bhp **Range:** 1,000/ . . .
Fuel: 2,400 gals. **Crew:** 8 tot.

Remarks: Aluminum construction. Capable of retrieving and stowing up to eight 1,254-kg practice torpedoes. Sisters 85TR652 and 85TR651 have been stricken.

♦ 2 72-ft. torpedo retrievers Mk 2 [YPT]
Bldr: Tacoma Boat, Wash. (In serv. 1964–65)

72TR645 TRB 32 72TR652 TRB 33

D: 41.2 tons (53 fl) **S:** 18 kts **Dim:** 22.17 × 5.18 × 1.68
Electronics: Radar: 1/Raytheon SPS-69 Pathfinder nav.
M: 2 G. M. Detroit Diesel 12V71 diesels; 2 props; 1,000 bhp
Electric: 22.5 kw tot. (1 × 15-kw, 1 × 7.5-kw diesel sets)
Range: 440/16 **Fuel:** 1,800 gals.
Crew: 5–6 tot.

Remarks: Wooden-hulled craft capable of retrieving and stowing up to 10,884 kg in practice torpedoes or other ordnance. Of sisters, C3211 (TRB 31) was discarded during 1995, 72TR653 in 1996, TRB 37 (C9426) in 1999, and TRB 36 (C4560) during 2001.

♦ 2 65-ft. torpedo retrievers [YPT]
Bldr: . . . (In serv. 10-67)

65TR675 HARRIER 65TR676 PEREGRINE

Harrier (65TR675) Brian Morrison, 6-00

D: 34.8 tons (35.2 fl) **S:** 24 kts **Dim:** 19.80 × 5.25 × 1.14
Electronics: Radar: 1 . . . nav.
M: 2 G.M. Detroit Diesel 12V71 diesels; 2 props; 1,008 bhp (800 sust.)
Range: 280/18 **Electric:** 10 kw **Crew:** 6 tot.

Remarks: Aluminum construction. Can recover up to 5 tons of weapons (three torpedoes). 65TR675 is based at Hawaii, and 65TR676 at Keyport, Washington. Sister 65TR671 was retired in 2005.

♦ 35 SWOB waste-disposal barges [YRGN]
Bldr: Marine Power Equipment Co., Seattle, Wash., and Tacoma Boat Co., Tacoma, Wash. (In serv. 1970s)

SWOB WE01 and SWOB WE10 series

SWOB 21 (WE10-021) Frank Findler, 10-03

D: 105.3 tons light (394.4 fl) **Dim:** 32.84 × 8.43 × 1.80 (0.58 light)

Remarks: SWOB = Ship Waste Oil Barge. Carry liquid wastes from shipboard holding tanks to shore treatment stations. SWOBs 1 through 42 and 56 through 60 were configured as oil-waste barges, while SWOBs 43 through 55 carry sewage to shore processing facilities. Are considered to be "equipment" and are assigned to local Navy Facilities Engineering Command organizations. SWOB 4, 14, 20–22, 39, 40, 45, 49, 50 and 56–59 have been discarded. The "WE" in the serial number indicates SWOB, the next two numbers (01 or 10) the function (human waste or waste-oil collection), and the last three numbers the sequential construction number for the craft (001 through

UNNUMBERED NAVY SERVICE CRAFT *(continued)*

060). Waste-oil barges carry up to 77,000 gallons in four tanks. SWOB nos. 4–10 and 49, and 50 have been retired.

Note: Also in use for waste collection are open-bottom oil/water separator waste oil rafts called "Donuts."

♦ 10 35-ft. salvage workboats [YRS] (5 in *reserve*)

Bldr: SeaArk Marine, Monticello, Ark. (In serv. 1984, except 35WB9001–9003: 1991)

35WB832, 35WB837, 35WB839, 35WB842–845, 35WB9001–9003

Salvage Workboat 35WB845 George R. Schneider, 9-99

D: 6 tons light (9.5 fl) **S:** 11 kts **Dim:** 10.92 × 3.39 × 0.91
M: 2 G.M. Detroit Diesel 4-53N diesels; 2 props; 280 bhp **Range:** 85/11
Fuel: 379 liters **Crew:** 3 tot.

Remarks: One is carried by each *Grapple* (ARS 50)-class salvage ship, while others are assigned to shore stations. All-aluminum construction. Have a 2-ton winch. Bow ramp leads to a 5.2 × 2.3–m cargo well forward.

♦ 2 U.S. Coast Guard Balsam-class salvage training hulks [YRSN]

Bldr: 180NS4401: Marine Iron and SB, Duluth, Minn.; ex-WLB 397: Zenith Dredge Co., Duluth, Minn.

	Laid down	L	In serv.
180NS4401 (ex-*Blackhaw,* WLB 390)	16-4-43	18-6-43	17-2-44
180NS . . . (ex-*Mariposa,* WLB 397)	25-10-43	14-1-44	1-7-44

180NS4401 George R. Schneider, 9-99

D: 697 tons light (1,038 fl) **Dim:** 54.9 (51.8 pp) × 11.3 × 4.0

Remarks: 180NS4401 was stricken from the U.S. Coast Guard 26-2-93 and transferred to the Maritime Administration 31-3-94; reclaimed during 2000 for service with Mobile Diving and Salvage Unit Two at Little Creek, Virginia, as a damage control training hulk in replace the 143NS9201. The machinery and electronics systems have either been removed or are non-operational, and the bulk is intended to be sunk and salvaged repeatedly. *Mariposa* was transferred to the USN on 17-4-00 for use as a non-operational platform for ship-boarding practice and damage-control training and is stationed at Everett, Washington.

♦ 1 (+ . . .) Submarine Rescue Diving and Recompression System (SRDRS)

Bldr: Phoenix International, Largo, Md., and Oceanworks International, Vancouver, Canada (In serv. 2007– . . .)

Remarks: DSRV replacement project comprising a Pressurized Rescue Module (PRM), and a Surface Decompression System (SDS). The PRM, remotely controlled from a topside control console, descends to the submarine, mates with a escape hatch, and can transfer the crew under pressure, if necessary, from the disabled submarine to the SDS. The entire system is designed to be air transported anywhere in the world.

Based on the Australian Remora system and intended to be operated from surface ships. The PRM can mate with rescue hatches, using an articulated skirt, on submarines inclined as much as 60 degrees. The rescue module measures 78.73 long × 47.6 high × 2.43 wide, has a crew of two and can transport 16 sailors per trip to depths of 610.0 meters. The first rescue module entered service in 2006 and the first SDS is scheduled for service entry in 2009.

Pressurized Rescue Module (PRM)—part of the Submarine Rescue Diving and Recompression System (SRDRS) Phoenix International, 2005

♦ 2 DSRV-class deep submergence rescue vehicles [YSS]

(1 in *reserve*) Bldr: Lockheed Missile & Space Co., Sunnyvale, Calif.

	In serv.	Accepted
DSRV 1 MYSTIC	6-8-71	4-11-77
DSRV 2 *AVALON*	28-7-72	1-1-78

Mystic (DSRV 1)—aboard submarine *La Jolla* (SSN 701) U.S. Navy, 4-02

Mystic (DSRV 1)—being loaded aboard a Russian AN-124 Condor cargo aircraft U.S. Navy, 4-04

UNNUMBERED NAVY SERVICE CRAFT *(continued)*

D: 30.5 tons (surf.)/37 tons (sub.) **S:** 4.5 kts (sub.)
Dim: 15.0 × 2.5 × 3.28 (high)
Electronics: Sonar: 1/ . . . obstacle avoidance
M: 1 electric motor; 1 shrouded-pivoting prop; 15 shp
Endurance: 16.4/4.1; 15/1.5 (sub.)
Crew: 4 tot. + 24 rescued personnel

Remarks: A cost overrun of nearly 1,500% prevented the procurement of any more DSRVs. Twelve were originally planned, later reduced to six, and then two. Their size and weight were determined by the possible need to airlift them in an Air Force Lockheed C-141 Starlifter cargo plane. In addition, SSNs have received the equipment necessary to fasten a DSRV to their decks and can transport the DSRV submerged at 15 knots. The SSN then serves as a base for the DSRV. The unofficial names were assigned in 1977. DSRV 1 is based at North Island, San Diego, California, assisted by the chartered tender *Dolores Chouest.* DSRV 2 was inactivated on 31-8-00 and placed in land storage at North Island, San Diego, where she is maintained by Lockheed Martin. Employ support crews of three officers and 17 enlisted personnel in addition to the crew. DSRV 1, which completed a one-year overhaul in 4-00, is to remain in service until 2007. Both are to be replaced by the SRDRS but retained in reserve for emergency use.

Hull systems: The DSRVs were intended to operate at a maximum depth of 1,500 m; stand pressure equal to 2,750 m depth; dive and rise at 30 m a minute; make a maximum speed of 5 knots while submerged; remain submerged for 30 hours at 3 knots; maintain station in a 1-kt current; and operate all machinery even while submerged at a 45° angle. Motor, powered by two 700-am/hr. silver-zinc batteries, turns a regular propulsion propeller and two thrusters, one forward and one aft, which can be positioned to permit a close approach to a sunken object. Hull consists of two HY-140 steel spheres surrounded by a fiberglass outer hull. One received a potassium superoxide (KO) breathing system in 1982, providing 480 man-hours submerged endurance. Have one 1,000-lb capacity manipulation arm and one color and five black-and-white underwater t.v. cameras.

Note: Also available for submarine rescue duties are two McCann/Erickson Submarine Rescue Chambers, SRC 8 (ex-YRC 8) and SRC 21 (ex-YRC 17) completed in 1942 and 1944, respectively at the New York Navy Yard. Survivors of 18 completed 1931–44 and recently outfitted with new lightweight mooring system, the SRCs can be transported in C-5 Galaxy transports. Each can rescue up to eight personnel per cycle from depths up to 260 m.

♦ 1 Alvin-class research submersible [YSS]
Bldr: General Mills, Minneapolis, Minn. (In serv. 6-64)

DSV 2 ALVIN

D: 16 tons **S:** 2 kts **Dim:** 6.9 × 2.4 × . . .
M: Electric motors; 1 prop; 2 thrusters **Crew:** 1 + 2 scientists

Remarks: Operated by civilian Woods Hole Oceanographic Institution on contract to the Navy since 6-71. Sank on 16-10-68, but raised, repaired, and returned to service in 11-72. Single titanium pressure sphere permits descents to 4,500 m. The digital sonar from *Sea Cliff* (DSV 4) was transferred to *Alvin* in 1998.

♦ 3 Log Bronco drydock support tugs [YTL]
Bldr: Modutech, Tacoma, Wash. (In serv. 2001)

D: 12.7 tons (fl) **S:** . . . kts **Dim:** 7.01 × 3.35 × 0.58
M: 1 Cummins 6-cyl C-series diesel; 360-degree hydraulically steerable prop; 255 bhp

Remarks: Employed at Puget Sound Naval Shipyard to position submarines and surface ships in floating dry docks. Have rectangular platform hulls and two push knees at the bow. Can turn in their own lengths. Two delivered 8-01, one later.

♦ 1 specialized push-tug [YTL]
Bldr: Marine Inland Fabricators, Panama City, Fla. (L: 6-96)

36NS9501

D: . . . tons **S:** 7 kts **Dim:** 10.67 × 4.11 × . . .
M: 2 John Deere 6076 AFM diesels; 2 props; 250 bhp
Electric: 20 kw **Crew:** . . .

Remarks: Built for the U.S. Navy Facilities Engineering Service, Port Hueneme, California, for use by a research facility on Lake Pend Oreille, Idaho, to support an acoustic research platform. Has a bollard pull of 4.5 tons.

♦ 21 Navy-44-class sail-training cutters [YTS]
Bldr: Uniflite-Tillotson-Pearson, Inc., Warren, R.I. (In serv. 1987–89)

NA-1 AUDACIOUS	NA-8 FEARLESS	NA-15 FROLIC
NA-2 COURAGEOUS	NA-9 FLIRT	NA-16 RESTLESS
NA-3 INVINCIBLE	NA-10 LIVELY	NA-17 DANDY
NA-4 VALIANT	NA-11 SWIFT	NA-18 DASH
NA-5 ACTIVE	NA-12 VIGILANT	NA-19 BOLD
NA-6 ALERT	NA-13 RESOLUTE	NA-20 CHALLENGER
NA-7 DAUNTLESS	NA-14 INTREPID	NA-21 . . .

D: 14.35 tons (fl) **S:** . . . **Dim:** 13.41 (10.91 wl) × 3.40 × 2.26
Electronics: Radar: 1 Raytheon SPS-66 (1900 Pathfinder) nav.
M: 1 auxiliary diesel; 1 prop; 33 bhp—sail area: 88 m^2 max.
Crew: 8–10 midshipmen

Remarks: All used at the U.S. Naval Academy, Annapolis, Maryland. First eight ordered 3-87, with options for 20 more, only 13 of which were ordered. NA-1 delivered 21-5-87 for extensive trials; NA-2–8 delivered spring 1988. GRP construction. Mast height: 19.66 m above water. Intended to replace Naval Academy's 12 Luders yawls and 18 miscellaneous donated craft used for midshipman training; the older boats in good condition were sent to universities with Naval Reserve Officer Training Centers. Designed by McCurdy and Rhodes, Inc. NA-9 through NA-12 are used by the varsity sailing team. Reputed to be excellent sailors. NA-1 to NA-8 are registered as 44ST8701 through 44ST8708, while NA-9 through NA-20 are 44ST8901 through 44ST8912. Four others were built for the U.S. Coast Guard Academy

Disposal notes: Naval Academy Swan 48–class sloops *Constellation* (48SB721) and *Insurgente* (48SB801) were removed from the Navy small craft listing in 1999 but may remain in use. Sparkman & Stephens 49 sloop *Cinnabar* (49SB 831 14786) was retired from service by 2005. *Pigeon*-class ship-assault training hulk, ex-*Pigeon* (ASR 21), was returned to the Maritime Administration on 4-8-05 for disposal without replacement.

Challenger (NA-20)—and a row of sisters, including *Dandy* (NA-17), at the U.S. Naval Academy George R. Schneider, 9-99

Note: Also in use at the Naval Academy is the sailing yacht *American Promise* (60SB8701), received by donation in 1987. The Naval Academy also employs the following sail training craft: 12 J-24 sloops (numbers and names: 31 *Aegis,* 32 *Harpoon,* 33 *Tomahawk,* 34 *Terrier,* 35 *Phalanx,* 36 *Vampire,* 37 *Goblin,* 38 *Panther,* 39 *Bulldog,* 40 *Madman,* 41 *Tally Ho,* and 42 *Bogie;* their official hull numbers are: 31–40: 24SL8702 through 24SL8711; 41: 24SL8713, and 42: 24SL8712), 20 FJ sloops, 1 J-22 sloop, 24 420 sloops, 100 Laser sloops, six Interclub dinghies, three Tech dinghies, and 60 sailboards (24 Imco, 24 Bermuda, and 12 Funboard). Naval Reserve Officer Training Center facilities at several universities and colleges also possess sail training craft. The Naval Academy also has a large number of oared-powered racing shells and several rigid inflatable speedboats for coaching and rescue duties.

READY RESERVE FORCE
MARITIME ADMINISTRATION

The Ready Reserve Force (RRF), created in 1976, is intended to compensate for the decline of the U.S.-flag merchant marine as a wartime strategic sealift asset. The RRF is maintained within the National Defense Reserve Fleet (NDRF) by the Maritime Administration (MARAD) of the Department of Transportation in 5-, 10-, or 20-day readiness status. RRF ships are activated by a Military Sealift Command request to MARAD and are under the operational control of MSC when active. Selected ships are exercised periodically, and a number are active and operating at any given time in support of U.S. forces worldwide.

Through FY 89, acquisition and maintenance of the RRF ships was funded by the Navy, which retains ownership of former naval units included in the fleet. On 1-10-90 MARAD became responsible for all funding for the RRF, except for some sealift-capability enhancements. Responsibility for acquisition of *additional* ships for the RRF, however, was returned to the Navy in FY 91.

Administrative responsibility for the RRF ships is maintained at NDRF anchorages at Beaumont, Texas; Suisun Bay, California; and in James River, Virginia, but most of the vessels are kept at layberth under management contracts in various ports around the United States in proximity to the shipyards that are under contract to maintain and activate them. In addition to these ships, there are a few older ex-naval or merchant marine militarily useful ships in the NDRF that could be activated given longer notice.

Before inclusion in the Ready Reserve Force, ships have had their navigation, safety, and communications systems updated (including provision of a Marisat SATCOM facility) and are repainted gray, with red, white, and blue stack striping. Certain sealift enhancement features specified by the Military Sealift Command have been added during the acquisition overhauls or during later maintenance overhauls; these include such items as provision to carry "Seashed" or "Flatrack" large-capacity containers, helicopter decks, refueling-at-sea gear, and extra tie-downs.

READY RESERVE FORCE MARITIME ADMINISTRATION
(continued)

New five-year operating contracts for 74 of the RRF ships were announced on 9-5-00: American Overseas Marine Corp (9 ships, $41.4 million); Crowley Liner Services (8 ships, $34.9 million), Interocean Ugland Management (11 ships, $35.4 million), Keystone Shipping (12 ships, $57.2 million), Marine Transport Lines (9 ships. $49.2 million), Mormac Marine (9 ships, $33.9 million), Ocean Duchess (3 ships, $2.6 million), Pacific Gulf Marine (8 ships, $31 million), and Patriot Contract Services (6 ships for $30.8 million); the contractors maintain the ships and provide crews to activated units.

As of 30-6-06, there were 58 ships remaining in the RRF, five of which were active. The four-digit T-series numbers listed in parentheses before the ships' names are administrative numbers assigned by MSC and MARAD and are not U.S. Navy hull numbers. Known as SASDT (Ships and Aircraft Supplemental Data Tables), they are assigned for administrative purposes only; a few long-term chartered units do not have any number assigned at all.

♦ 2 Taabo Italia–class roll-on/roll-off vehicle cargo ships [WAK]
Bldr: Fincantieri, Genoa, Italy (In serv. 1984)

	Acquired	To RRF
(T-AKR 9666) CAPE VINCENT (ex-*Taabo Italia*, ex-*Merzario Italia*)	13-5-93	19-8-94
(T-AKR 9701) CAPE VICTORY (ex-*Merzario Britannia*)	2-4-93	2-9-94

Cape Victory (T-AKR 9701)—alongside *Cape Vincent* (T-AKR 9666) Edward McDonnell, 2004

D: Approx. 27,000 tons (fl) **S:** 16 kts (15.5 sust.)
Dim: 192.62 (172.80 pp) × 26.55 × 8.47
M: 1 GMT-Sulzer 6RNB 66/140 diesel; 1 CP prop; 11,850 bhp
Electric: 4,280 kw tot. (1 × 1,280-kw, 3 × 1,000-kw diesel sets)—bow-thruster
Range: 21,000/16 **Fuel:** 1,840 tons heavy oil, 375 tons diesel **Crew:** . . .

Remarks: 22,423 grt/21,439 dwt. Purchased 12-92 from C.N.M. Compagnia di Navigazione Merzario S.p.A. Both are in layberth at Beaumont, Texas, on five-day recall status. When active, are operated by Keystone Shipping; both previously activated on 17-1-03 for Mideast service. *Cape Vincent* was activated in 2005 for Hurricane Katrina relief efforts.
Hull systems: Hull is 16.10 m molded depth. Have 100,299 ft.^{2} military cargo capacity (2,480 m of vehicle parking lanes). Stern slewing ramp 28 m long by 7.2 m wide. Can carry 1,306 standard 20-ft. cargo containers. Had spar decks added by Bender SB & Repair, Mobile, Alabama, with *Cape Victory* completing modifications in 9-98 and *Cape Vincent* during 11-98; the decks provide additional vehicle parking space topside.

♦ 2 Hual Trader–class roll-on/roll-off vehicle cargo ships [WAK]
Bldr: Stocznia imeni Komuny Paryskiej, Gdynia, Poland

	In serv.	Acquired	In RRF
(T-AKR 9961) CAPE WASHINGTON (ex-*Hual Trader,* ex-*Hoegh Trader*)	1981	7-4-93	5-4-94
(T-AKR 9962) CAPE WRATH (ex-*Hual Transporter*)	1982	14-5-93	3-3-94

Cape Wrath (T-AKR 9962) Frank Findler, 11-04

D: Approx. 47,000 tons (fl) **S:** 17 kts (15.2 sust.)
Dim: 212.61 (195.76 pp) × 32.28 × 11.63
M: 1 Cegielski-Sulzer 6RND 90/155 diesel; 1 CP prop; 17,400 bhp—bow and stern thrusters
Electric: 4,800 kw tot. (5 × 960-kw Sulzer diesel sets)
Range: . . . / . . . **Fuel:** 3,811 tons heavy oil **Crew:** . . .

Remarks: *Cape Washington:* 23,597 grt/32,695 dwt; *Cape Wrath:* 20,563 grt/32,722 dwt. Former automobile carriers purchased 12-92 from Leif Hoegh & Co./Grace Marine, Panama. Both were assigned to the Army Interim Brigade Afloat Force and were based at Saipan carrying prepositioned equipment; they were returned to Ready Reserve Force layup on 27-6-97 and 20-1-97, respectively, with both berthed at Baltimore, Maryland, on five-day recall. Previously reactivated on 24-1-03 for operations in the Mideast.

Hull systems: Hull has 21.60 m molded depth. Originally had 170,762 ft.^{2} military equipment capacity; they could carry 6,000 automobiles or 1,203 20-ft. standard cargo containers, but decks were too weak to support heavy military vehicles. They have had their seven vehicle decks replaced by three stronger decks capable of supporting military vehicles and adding an additional 156,000 ft.^{2} of useful capacity; work on *Cape Washington* began 10-99 and on *Cape Wrath* during 4-00. Ice-strengthened hulls with side doors and 31-m-long by 8-m-wide stern-quarter door/ramps. Clear height in vehicle decks is 6.1 m. Have two 5-ton cranes. Both can carry 789 tons diesel fuel for auxiliary engines.

♦ 1 Finneagle-class roll-on/roll-off vehicle cargo ship [WAK]
Bldr: Kockums AB, Malmö, Sweden (In serv. 20-2-81)

	Acquired	To RRF
(T-AKR 2044) CAPE ORLANDO (ex-*American Eagle,* ex-*Zenit Eagle,* ex-*Finneagle*)	15-4-93	12-9-94

Cape Orlando (T-AKR 2044) Edward McDonnell, 2004

D: 12,500 tons light (32,799 fl) **S:** 22 kts (19.5 kts light)
Dim: 193.63 (180.83 pp) × 28.01 × 3.94 light (9.22 max. loaded)
M: 2 Cegielski-Sulzer 6RND68M diesels; 1 prop; 21,600 bhp
Electric: 4,200 kw (3 × 1,400 kw) **Range:** 7,748/19.5 **Fuel:** 2,833 tons
Crew: 8 officers, 12 mariners

Remarks: 15,632 grt/20,404 dwt. Had been on charter since 22-8-83 from American Automar and operated by Pacific Gulf Marine, Inc., for U.S. to Europe service until purchased 12-92 from the owner, Connecticut National Bank, for the RRF. Renamed 1993. Assigned to West Coast division of RRF and was in layberth at Hunters Point, San Francisco, on five-day recall. Activated on 24-1-03 for duties in the Mideast and remained active until 21-7-06.
Hull systems: Cargo capacity: 18,219 tons max. Versatile design capable of transporting up to 252 standard 20-ft. cargo vans or vehicles, with 10,500 m^2 parking space for the latter. Has 108,157 ft.^{2} military cargo capacity rating. Has two side-by-side 26.8-m-long by 8-m-wide slewing stern ramps, two bow-thrusters. Can carry up to 8,500 tons saltwater ballast. There are five holds and six hatches, and an internal 65-ton capacity cargo elevator is fitted. Cranes include 1 × 25-ton and 1 × 5-ton.

♦ 2 Cape Kennedy–class roll-on/roll-off vehicle cargo ships [WAK]
Bldr: Nippon Kokan, Tsurumi, Japan

	L	Acquired	To RRF
(T-AKR 5082) CAPE KNOX (ex-*Nedlloyd Rouen,* ex-*Rouen*)	10-78	9-95	15-7-96
(T-AKR 5083) CAPE KENNEDY (ex-*Nedlloyd Rosario,* ex-*Rosario*)	1-79	9-95	11-6-96

Cape Knox (T-AKR 5082) Frank Findler, 11-04

D: 36,450 tons (fl) **S:** 19 kts **Dim:** 212.10 (198.81 pp) × 32.29 × 10.72
Electronics: Radar: 2/ . . . nav.
M: 1 Sumitomo-Sulzer 8RND90M diesel; 1 prop; 25,400 bhp—1/CP bow-thruster
Electric: 6,400 kw tot. (4 × 1,600 diesel sets) **Range:** 21,600/19
Fuel: 4,241 tons heavy oil, 330 tons diesel **Crew:** . . . tot.

Remarks: 21,144 grt/29,218 dwt. Acquired 2-95 with FY 95 funding from Nedlloyd Linjen, B.V., Rotterdam. Modified for RRF service at Bender Shipbuilding and Repair, Mobile, Alabama, *Cape Kennedy* beginning 12-95 and *Cape Knox* beginning 1-96. Both are administratively assigned to the Beaumont, Texas, Gulf Coast RRF division and are berthed at New Orleans on five-day recall. Both previously activated on 22-1-03 and again in 2006 for Mideast duty.
Hull systems: Have two vehicle decks with 3,970-m total vehicle lane length and can also be used to carry 1,550 standard 20-ft. containers. Bale cargo capacity rated at 67,290 m^3. Have angled stern door and two ramps.

♦ 3 Barber Tiaf–class roll-on/roll-off vehicle cargo ships [WAK]

	Bldr	To RRF
(T-AKR 5066) CAPE HUDSON (ex-*Barber Tiaf*)	Tangen Vaerft, Kragerø	25-11-86
(T-AKR 5067) CAPE HENRY (ex-*Barber Priam*)	Mitsubishi Heavy Ind., Nagasaki	29-9-86
(T-AKR 5068) CAPE HORN (ex-*Barber Tønsberg*)	Kaldnes Mek. Versted A/S, Tønsberg	15-12-86

READY RESERVE FORCE MARITIME ADMINISTRATION
(continued)

Cape Henry (T-AKR 5067) Werner Globke, 8-01

Cape Horn (T-AKR 5068) Leo Van Ginderen, 1-94

D: 19,091 tons light (51,007 fl) **S:** 21 kts (17 kts sust.)
Dim: 228.50 (211.50 pp) × 32.26 × 4.70 light (10.80 loaded)
M: 1 Burmeister & Wain (*Cape Henry:* Mitsubishi-Sulzer) diesel; 1 prop; 30,700 (*Cape Henry:* 30,150) bhp
Range: 24,317/17 **Fuel:** 3,638 tons
Crew: 9 officers, 18 mariners + 6 Army cargo supervisors

Remarks: Vary slightly in design: *Cape Henry* is 21,747 grt, *Cape Horn* 22,090, and *Cape Hudson* is 21,976 grt. All completed during 1989 and purchased 1-6-86 and overhauled at Norfolk SB & DD before entering RRF. All three previously activated in mid-1994 for use with the Army Interim Prepositioning Force at Diego Garcia; they were to be returned to RRF layup by 30-9-96 but remained active into 1997, with *Cape Hudson* deactivating on 17-7-97 and *Cape Horn* on 3-12-98; *Cape Henry* was reassigned to Operation Joint Guard service on 21-3-97 to support forces in Bosnia. All three are now assigned to the Suisun Bay fleet, with *Cape Henry* in layberth at San Francisco and the other two at Oakland, California; *Cape Horn* was reactivated on 19-3-02 but suffered a fire at sea during 4-02 while en route to Thailand for an exercise; deactivated 13-4-02 for repairs, the ship was reactivated again on 4-7-02 and deactivated on 16-11-02; all three previously activated on 24-1-03 for Mideast duties. *Cape Horn* was activated for service for the Mideast in 2005.
Hull systems: All have one 39-ton crane. The stern ramp is 49.4 m long by 12 m wide and has a capacity of 63.9 long tons. Cargo: 26,742 tons maximum. Can also carry 1,607–1,629 20-ft. containers. There are four internal vehicle cargo decks and a total of 18,287 m^2 of cargo space.

♦ 3 Saudi Riyadh–class roll-on/roll-off vehicle cargo ships [WAK]
Bldr: Kawasaki Heavy Industries, Sakaide, Japan

	In serv.	Acquired	To RRF
(T-AKR 9960) Cape Race (ex-*G and C Admiral,* ex-*Seaspeed America*)	7-77	28-4-93	11-9-94
(T-AKR 9678) Cape Rise (ex-*Saudi Riyadh,* ex-*Seaspeed Arabia*)	2-77	9-8-93	21-11-94
(T-AKR 9679) Cape Ray (ex-*Saudi Makkah,* ex-*Seaspeed Asia*)	4-77	29-4-93	17-12-94

Cape Race (T-AKR 9960) Frank Findler, 11-04

D: Approx, 32,000 tons (fl) **S:** 19.75 kts **Dim:** 197.52 (180.02 pp) × 32.26 × 8.50
M: 2 Kawasaki-M.A.N. 14V 52/55A diesels; 1 CP prop; 28,000 bhp at 430 rpm—bow-and stern-thrusters
Electric: 6,640 kw tot. (2 × 1,920 kw, 2 × 1,400 kw) **Range:** 21,000/18
Fuel: 4,590 tons heavy oil, 278 tons diesel **Crew:** 28 tot.

Remarks: 14,825 grt/22,735 dwt. Purchased 12-92, *Cape Race* from Sunpride, Inc., and the others from the National Shipping Company of Saudi Arabia. They are operated by Keystone Shipping Co., Bala Cynwyd, Pennsylvania, and are maintained at Moon Engineering Co., Portsmouth, Virginia, on five-day recall by 9–10-man skeleton crews. *Cape Rise* and *Cape Race* previously activated on 17-1-03, and *Cape Ray* on 24-1-03 for Mideast duties.
Hull systems: Hull has 19.87-m molded depth. Have 141,685 ft.^{2} rated military cargo space (*Cape Race:* 141,600). Have side doors and stern ramps for vehicle cargo. Can carry 1,315 standard 20-ft. cargo containers. There are four internal vehicle elevators. Have had spar decks added during 1998 to provide additional vehicle stowage, with *Cape Race* completed during 1-99, and *Cape Ray* during 4-99, both by by Bender SB & Repair, Mobile, Alabama, and *Cape Rise* late in 1999 at North Florida Shipyards. The ships can be loaded in as little as 12 hours.

♦ 3 Reichenfels-class roll-on/roll-off vehicle cargo ships [WAK]
Bldr: Howaldtswerke, Kiel (*Cape Taylor:* Sasebo Heavy Industries, Sasebo, Japan) (In serv. 1977)

	Acquired	In RRF
(T-AKR 112) Cape Texas (ex-*Lyra,* ex-*Reichenfels*)	5-2-93	19-8-94
(T-AKR 113) Cape Taylor (ex-*Thekwini,* ex-*ASL Cygnus,* ex-*Cygnus,* ex-*Rabenfels*)	7-4-93	24-7-94
(T-AKR 9711) Cape Trinity (ex-*Santos,* ex-*Canadian Forest,* ex-*Santos,* ex-*Radbod,* ex-*Norefjord,* ex-*Rheinfels*)	24-3-93	15-11-94

Cape Texas (T-AKR 112) U.S. Navy, 2-05

Cape Trinity (T-AKR 9711) Frank Findler, 4-03

D: *Cape Texas:* 9,870 tons light (24,551 tons (fl)); others: 26,455 tons (fl)
S: 20.5 kts (18 kts sust.)
Dim: 191.29 (178.01 pp) × 27.21 × 4.05 light (8.60 max.)
Electronics: Radar: 1 Decca RM 1229 nav.; 1 Decca TM-S 1230 nav.
M: 2 M.A.N. 9L 52/55A heavy-oil diesels; 1 CP prop; 18,980 bhp—2 bow-thrusters
Electric: 3,480 kw tot. (2 × 1,250-kw, 1 × 980-kw diesel sets)
Range: 22,600/16.5 **Fuel:** 2,570 tons heavy oil, 601.5 tons diesel **Crew:** 49 tot.

Remarks: 14,174 grt/15,075 dwt (*Cape Texas:* 12,159 grt/15,074 dwt). Purchased 12-92 from Lykes Brothers. Made about 21.4 kts on trials. *Cape Texas* had operated previously in MSC service as *Lyra.* All three are in layberth at Houston, Texas, on five-day recall. *Cape Trinity* was activated to transport a 500-bed modular field hospital (400 containers and 100 vehicles) to Norway during 3-99. All three were also activated on 22-1-03 in support of Mideast activities.
Hull systems: Hull has 17.60-m molded depth and is ice strengthened; *Cape Texas* is 193.33 m overall, 177.98 m pp. *Cape Trinity* and *Cape Taylor* are rated at 112,700 ft.^{2} military cargo capacity, while *Cape Texas* is rated at 112,761 ft.^{2}. Cargo deadweight is 11,386 tons. Have 4.65 × 4.20–m side vehicle-loading doors port and starboard and a 160–long ton capacity, 10.85-m-long by 22-m-wide stern slewing ramp. Cargo lane length is 3,216 m for vehicles with 2.5-m width, and there is a clear height of 4.2 m between each of the three internal cargo decks. An internal 80-ton cargo elevator is fitted. Bale capacity is 44,400 m^3, and they can carry 340 standard 20-ft. cargo containers or 233 cargo trailers.

♦ 4 Maritime Administration C7-S-95a roll-on/roll-off vehicle cargo ships [WAK]
Bldr: Bath Iron Works, Bath, Me.

	L	In serv.	In RRF
(T-AKR 10) Cape Island (ex-*Mercury,* T-AKR 10; ex-*Illinois*)	7-76	1977	22-11-93
(T-AKR 11) Cape Intrepid (ex-*Jupiter,* T-AKR 11; ex-*Lipscomb Lykes;* ex-*Arizona*)	1-11-75	14-5-76	26-4-86
(T-AKR 5062) Cape Isabel (ex-*Charles Lykes,* ex-*Nevada*)	15-5-76	1977	9-6-86
(T-AKR 5076) Cape Inscription (ex-*Tyson Lykes,* ex-*Maine*)	24-5-75	27-5-76	8-9-87

READY RESERVE FORCE MARITIME ADMINISTRATION *(continued)*

Cape Inscription (T-AKR 5076) Ralph Edwards, 9-04

D: 14,767 tons light (33,900 fl) **S:** 24 kts (23 kts sust.)
Dim: 208.71 (195.07 pp) × 31.09 × 5.16 light (9.78 max. loaded)
Electronics: Radar: 1 Raytheon TM 1650/6X nav.; 1 Raytheon TM 1660/12S nav.
M: 2 sets G.E. geared steam turbines; 2 props; 37,000 shp
Boilers: 2 Babcock & Wilcox; 77.5 kg/cm^2 **Electric:** 4,000 kw tot.
Range: 12,600/23 **Fuel:** 3,465 tons **Crew:** 12 officers, 24 mariners

Remarks: 13,156 grt/19,172 dwt. *Cape Island* was in long-term charter from Lykes Brothers from 14-4-80; later sold to Wilmington Trust Co. and operated in cargo service in Far East with MSC Civil Service crew until transferred to RRF. *Cape Intrepid* and *Cape Island* were renamed from *Jupiter* and *Mercury* in 1993. *Cape Intrepid* and *Cape Island* are in layberth at Tacoma, Washington, *Cape Inscription* and *Cape Isabel* at Long Beach, California; previously activated on 24-1-03 for Mideast operations. *Cape Intrepid* and *Cape Island* are currently in reserve at a layberth at Tacoma, Washington, *Cape Inscription* and *Cape Isabel* are berthed at Long Beach, California; all are on five-day recall notice.
Hull systems: Can carry containers as well as vehicles and 728 tons liquid. Cargo deadweight capacity is 14,876 tons (56,640 m^3 bale, with 16,258 m^2 vehicle cargo space on the four internal vehicle decks). Rated at 153,860 ft.^{2} military cargo space. Two side doors, plus 7.3-m-wide by 24.4-m-long, 100-ton capacity stern quarter ramp. Have one 30-ton capacity crane.

♦ 5 Tombarra-class roll-on/roll-off vehicle cargo ships [WAK]

	Bldr	In serv.	In RRF
(T-AKR 5051) Cape Ducato (ex-*Barranduna*)	Eriksberg M/V, Lindholmen, Sweden	11-9-72	10-12-85
(T-AKR 5052) Cape Douglas (ex-*Lalandia*)	Eriksberg M/V, Lindholmen, Sweden	22-2-73	18-11-85
(T-AKR 5053) Cape Domingo (ex-*Tarago*)	Ch. de France, Dunkerque	11-1-73	28-10-85
(T-AKR 5054) Cape Decision (ex-*Tombarra*)	Eriksberg M/V, Lindholmen, Sweden	30-8-73	10-10-85
(T-AKR 5055) Cape Diamond (ex-*Tricolor*)	Ch. de France, Dunkerque	22-9-72	15-10-85

Cape Decision (T-AKR 5054) Edward McDonnell, 3-06

Cape Douglas (T-AKR 5052) Frank Findler, 11-04

D: 13,140 tons light (34,790 fl) **S:** 22 kts (18 kts sust.)
Dim: 207.40 (193.24 pp) × 29.57 × 4.11 light (10.06 max. loaded)
Electronics: 2 Raytheon . . . nav.
M: French-built: 3 Ch. d'Atlantique-Pielstick diesels; 1 CP prop; 28,890 bhp; Swedish-built: 3 Lindholmen-Pielstick 18 PC2V diesels; 1 CP prop; 27,000 bhp (22,860 sust.)—1,500-hp bow-thruster, 1,000-hp stern-thruster in all
Electric: 6,384 kw (2 × 2,200-kw, 2 × 992-kw diesel sets) **Range:** 19,000/18
Fuel: 3,200 tons heavy oil, 240 tons diesel **Crew:** 9 officers, 18 mariners

Remarks: Tonnages vary: 23,972–24,437 grt/21,299–21,398 dwt. Five-deck vehicle cargo ships purchased 1-85 and "reflagged" (safety features brought into line with U.S. Coast Guard standards) by Bethlehem SY, Sparrows Point, Maryland. *Cape Douglas* was at Diego Garcia with Army Prepositioning Squadron Three (APS-3) until deactivated on 20-5-98; *Cape Decision* was returned to layup at Charleston, South Carolina, on 10-3-97. *Cape Decision* and *Cape Diamond* previously activated on 17-1-03 for Mideast duties, *Cape Douglas* and *Cape Domingo* on 22-3-03, and *Cape Ducato* on 24-1-03. *Cape Decision* was reactivated in 6-06; all five remain in RRF reserve, *Cape Diamond, Cape Domingo, Cape Douglas,* and *Cape Ducato* are at layberth at Charleston, S.C., on a five-day recall notice.
Hull systems: Cargo capacity: 21,650 tons max. The 65-ton-capacity stern ramp is 32 m long by 7 m wide. Can carry 554 20-ft. containers and have 52,863 m^3 bale capacity internal, including 1,784 m^3 refrigerated. Vehicle cargo parking area (including vehicle decks but not weather deck container space): 17,395.4 m^2 (Swedish-built units: 16,802.6 m^2).

Disposal note: Two *Federal Lakes*–class roll-on/roll-off vehicle cargeo ships *Cape Lambert* (T-AKR 5077) and *Cape Lobos* (T-AKR 5078) were downgraded to Maritime reserve status on 31-7-06 and are no longer part of the RRF.

♦ 1 Parralla-class roll-on/roll-off vehicle cargo ship [WAK]
Bldr: Eriksberg M/V, Lindholmen, Sweden

	In serv.	To RRF
(T-AKR 5069) Cape Edmont (ex-*Parralla*)	1972	16-4-87

Cape Edmont (T-AKR 5069) Frank Findler, 5-03

D: 12,256 tons light (32,543 fl) **S:** 20.7 kts (17 kts sust.)
Dim: 199.02 (183.70 pp) × 28.71 × 3.81 light (9.60 max. loaded)
M: 3 Eriksberg-Pielstick 18PC2V 400 diesels; 1 CP prop; 25,920 bhp—bow-thruster
Electric: 5,652 kw tot. (2 × 2,200 kw, 2 × 584 kw, 1 × 84 kw)
Range: 17,000/19; 20,000/17 **Fuel:** 3,250 tons heavy oil, 489 tons diesel
Crew: 32 tot.

Remarks: 12,902 grt/20,303 dwt. Reactivated 24-1-03 for Mideast service. Currently in layberth at Charleston, South Carolina, on five-day recall status.
Hull systems: Container capacity: 309 TEU above decks, 903 below; 13,972 m^2 vehicle parking space. Can carry 317 m^3 liquid cargo (vehicle fuel). Has two 18-ton cranes on one foundation forward. Bale cargo capacity: 50,299 m^3. Cargo deadweight: 17,902 tons. Single stern ramp unfolds to 32 m long, is 6.98 m wide, and can support 220 tons.

♦ 1 Admiral Wm. M. Callaghan–class vehicle cargo ship [WAK]
Bldr: Sun SB & DD Co., Chester, Pa.

	L	In serv.	To RRF
(T-AKR 1001) Admiral Wm. M. Callaghan	17-10-67	12-67	25-6-87

Admiral Wm. M. Callaghan (T-AKR 1001) Don. S. Montgomery, USN, 4-93

D: 13,161 tons light (26,537 fl) **S:** 26 kts (20 kts sustained)
Dim: 211.61 (193.12 pp) × 28.00 × 5.18 light (8.86 max. loaded)
Electronics: Radar: 1 . . . nav.
M: 2 G.E. LM-2500 gas turbines; 2 props; 40,000 shp **Electric:** 1,500 kw tot.
Fuel: 3,939 tons **Range:** 6,000/25; 12,000/20 **Crew:** 10 officers, 18 mariners

Remarks: 24,471 grt/13,500 dwt. Built for U.S. Navy service as the earliest example of the current "Build-and-Charter" concept. Had been on MSC charter from MARAD for 20 years prior to transfer to the RRF. Previously activated for Mideast service 24-1-03. Is currently in reserve at Alameda, California, on five-day recall notice.
Hull systems: Original Pratt & Whitney FT-4 gas turbines replaced 12-77 by LM-2500 engines; used as trials ship for LM-2500 engine life extension and fuel economy improvements. Cargo deadweight: 9,519 tons. Has 12.8-m-long by 4.5-m-wide, 55.8-ton capacity stern ramp and four side-loading ports with 18-m-long by 4.5-m portable ramps. Can carry up to 750 vehicles, on 15,607 m^2 of parking area. Rated at 212 TEU for cargo container carrying. Unusual for a "Ro/Ro" in having full set of cargo derricks: two of 120 tons capacity, six of 25 tons, and ten of 15 tons; flush hatches permit access to 38,515 m^3 of cargo space.

♦ 1 Meteor-class (C4-ST-67a type) vehicle cargo ship [WAK]
Bldr: Puget Sound Bridge & DD

	Laid down	L	In serv.	To RRF
T-AKR 9 Meteor (ex-*Sea Lift;* ex-LSV 9)	19-5-64	17-4-65	25-5-67	3-10-85

D: 9,154 tons light (21,480 fl) **S:** 21.25 kts (20 kts sust.)
Dim: 164.7 × 25.5 × 4.50 light (8.86 max. loaded)

READY RESERVE FORCE MARITIME ADMINISTRATION
(continued)

Meteor (T-AKR 9) Winter & Findler, 9-99

Electronics: Radar: 1 Raytheon TM 1650/6X nav.; 1 Raytheon TM 1660/12S nav.
M: 2 sets geared steam turbines; 2 props; 19,400 shp
Boilers: 2; 52.8 kg/cm^2, 471° C
Range: 10,000/20 **Fuel:** 2,120 tons **Crew:** . . .

Remarks: 16,467 grt/12,326 dwt. Authorized as T-AK 278, completed as T-LSV 9, retyped T-AKR 14-8-69. Renamed 12-9-75. Remains in layberth at Suisun Bay, California, on five-day recall. Transferred to MARAD ownership from Navy during 11-01. Downgraded to maritime reserve status on 31-7-06 but remain on the navy vessel register.
Hull systems: Cargo: 9,030 tons maximum: 26,819 m^3 vehicle parking volume (7,896 m^2 deck space). Has 2 70-ton, 14 15-ton, and 2 10-ton cranes. Has a 13.7-m-long by 5.5-m-wide, 56-ton-capacity straight stern ramp and 13.9-m-long by 4.6-m-wide, 54-ton-capacity portable side vehicle loading ramps. Can carry 12 passengers. The superstructure is set 4 m above the upper deck to permit vehicles to be stowed beneath it.

♦ 1 Maritime Administration C3-ST-14a-type vehicle cargo ship [WAK]
Bldr: Sun SB & DD, Chester, Pa.

	Laid down	L	In serv.	To RRF
T-AKR 7 Comet	15-5-56	31-7-57	27-1-58	15-3-85

Comet (T-AKR 7) Findler & Winter, 10-99

D: 7,605 tons light (18,150 fl) **S:** 19 kts (18 kts sust.)
Dim: 152.1 (141.73 pp) × 23.77 × 4.29 light (8.23 max. loaded)
Electronics: Radar: 1 Raytheon TM 1650/6X nav.; 1 Raytheon TM 1660/12S nav.
M: 2 sets G.E. geared steam turbines; 2 props; 13,200 shp
Boilers: 2 Babcock & Wilcox; 43.3 kg/cm^2, 454° C
Electric: 1,200 kw (2 × 600-kw turboalternators)
Range: 13,000/18 **Fuel:** 2,370 tons **Crew:** 11 officers, 33 mariners

Remarks: 13,792 grt/10,111 dwt. Authorized as T-AK 269, changed to T-LSV 7 on 1-6-63, then to T-AKR 7 on 1-1-69. Deactivated from the Military Sealift Command on 22-4-84, she remained Navy property until transferred to MARAD during 11-01. Activated 15-2-03 for Mideast service; currently in reserve at a layberth at Alameda, California, on five-day recall notice. Downgraded to maritime reserve status on 31-7-06 but remain on the navy vessel register.
Hull systems: Cargo: 8,730 tons or more than 700 military vehicles in holds totaling 19,370 m^3 volume (7,525 m^2 deck space). Has two 60-ton, four 10-ton, and 16 15-ton derricks. The fixed stern ramp has a capacity of 60 long tons and is 9 m long by 5.8 m wide; portable side vehicle ramps of 60-tons capacity can be fitted; they are 12.2 m long by 4.6 m wide. Denny-Brown fin stabilizers are fitted.

♦ 2 Maritime Administration C6-S-MA60d auxiliary crane-ships [WAK]
Bldr: Ingalls SB, Pascagoula, Miss.

	Laid down	L	In serv.	To RRF
T-ACS 9 Green Mountain State (ex-*American Altair*, ex-*Mormacaltair*)	2-12-63	20-8-64	23-6-65	15-3-92
T-ACS 10 Beaver State (ex-*American Draco*, ex-*Mormacdraco*)	19-4-64	14-1-65	28-5-65	6-1-97

Beaver State (T-ACS 10) Winter & Findler, 9-97

D: 11,720 tons light (27,900 fl) **S:** 21 kts
Dim: 98 (193.55 pp) × 22.96 × 10.06
M: 2 sets G.E. geared steam turbines; 1 prop; 19,000 shp
Boilers: 2 Combustion Engineering
Electric: 4,780 kw (2 × 1,640 turboalternators, 2 × 750-kw diesel sets)
Range: 17,000/20 **Fuel:** 4,083 tons **Crew:** 64 + 35 spare berths

Remarks: 16,180 dwt. Conversion authorized FY 88; conversion contract let 27-1-89. Work on T-ACS 9 began 28-2-89 at Norshipco, Norfolk, Virginia, but was slowed by lack of funding. Conversion of T-ACS 10 was begun 26-3-89, also by Norshipco, but was canceled 12-1-90; the work was reassigned to the Charleston Naval Shipyard, Charleston, South Carolina. Both are currently in reserve, part of the MARAD reserve fleet at Suisun Bay, California. For this class, the assigned numbers are actual U.S. Navy hull numbers. Downgraded to maritime reserve status on 31-7-06 but remain on the navy vessel register.
Hull systems: Have three pair 30-ton-capacity, 36.9-m-reach electrohydraulic cranes mounted to starboard.

♦ 2 Maritime Administration C6-S-MA1xb auxiliary crane-ships [WAK]
Bldr: Todd SY, San Pedro, Cal.

	Laid down	L	In serv.	To RRF
T-ACS 7 Diamond State (ex-*President Truman*, ex-*Japan Mail*)	22-11-60	8-8-61	14-4-62	22-2-89
T-ACS 8 Equality State (ex-*American Builder*, ex-*Philippine Mail*, ex-*Santa Rosa*, ex-*President Roosevelt*, ex-*Washington Mail*)	12-5-61	6-1-62	25-7-62	24-5-89

Diamond State (T-ACS 7) George R. Schneider, 9-05

D: 15,138 tons (25,660 fl) **S:** 20 kts **Dim:** 203.61 (192.95 pp) × 23.22 × 10.13
Electronics: Radar: 2 . . . nav.
M: 2 sets G.E. geared steam turbines; 1 prop; 22,000 shp
Boilers: 2 Combustion Engineering **Range:** 14,000/20 **Fuel:** 3,124 tons
Electric: 2,275 kw **Crew:** . . .

Remarks: 16,518 grt/19,871 dwt prior to conversion under FY 86, which was contracted with Tampa SB, Tampa, Florida, 14-9-87. T-ACS 7 is in layberth at Houston, Texas, on five-day recall while T-ACS 8 is at Beaumont, Texas, on 20-day recall notice. Sister *American Banker* was scrapped 11-05. For this class, the assigned numbers are actual U.S. Navy hull numbers. Downgraded to maritime reserve status on 31-7-06 but remain on the navy vessel register.
Hull systems: Resemble *Keystone State* (T-ACS 1), with three pair 30-ton, 36.9-m-reach electrohydraulic cranes mounted to starboard. Were containerships with 625 20-ft. container capacity prior to conversion.

♦ 3 Maritime Administration C5-S-73c auxiliary crane-ships [WAK]
Bldr: Bath Iron Works, Bath, Maine

	In serv.	Converted	To RRF
T-ACS 4 Gopher State (ex-*Export Leader*)	1969	21-10-86 to 22-10-87	10-12-87
T-ACS 5 Flickertail State (ex-*Lightning*)	1970	18-12-86 to 8-2-88	9-2-88
T-ACS 6 Cornhusker State (ex-*Staghound*)	20-6-69	3-87 to 12-4-88	12-4-88

D: 15,060 tons light (25,000 fl) **S:** 20 kts (sust.)
Dim: 185.93 (177.35) × 23.83 × 9.63
Electronics: Radar: 2 . . . nav.
M: 2 sets G.E. geared steam turbines; 1 prop; 17,500 shp
Boilers: 2 Babcock & Wilcox **Range:** 9,340/20 **Fuel:** 3,576 tons
Crew: 11 officers, 41 mariners

Remarks: 17,904 grt/16,709 dwt. All three acquired 11-8-86 from Maritime Administration for conversion by Norshipco, Norfolk. All three activated for Desert Shield/Desert Storm in 8-90; T-ACS 4 and 5 remained active through 5-92. All three are assigned to the James River Fleet, with *Cornhusker State* and *Flickertail State* in layberth at Newport News, Virginia, on five-day recall. T-ACS 4 transferred to the Army Interim Prepositioning fleet 30-9-94, operated for the Army under Military

READY RESERVE FORCE MARITIME ADMINISTRATION
(continued)

Gopher State (T-ACS-4) Marian Wright, 6-03

Cornhusker State (T-ACS 6) Paul C. Clift, 5-00

Sealift Command administration under contract by Inter Ocean Management; she is stationed at Guam and attached to Maritime Prepositioning Squadron 3, carrying Army port facility equipment and vehicles. For this class, the assigned numbers are actual U.S. Navy hull numbers. T-ACS 6 was activated in 11-01 to transport containerized munitions and returned to layberth on 1-5-02; the ship was activated between 18-2-03 and 30-6-03 and again between 4-1-05 and 17-3-05 for Mideast service. All three are currently at Newport News, Virginia, on five-day recall notice (except *Gopher State,* on 10-day recall).
Hull systems: Cargo capacity includes 1,070 standard 20-ft. containers (56 refrigerated). Two pair 30-ton-capacity/36.9-m-reach electrohydraulic cranes mounted on starboard side. Equipped to stow sea shed and standard cargo containers. Can carry three LCM(8) landing craft and two side-loading warping tugs (self-propelled pontoons) and pontoon sections on deck. Bow-thruster added. Two 1,200-kw diesel generators added in after hold during conversion. Have 5,800 tons fixed and portable ballast, 32 lighter mooring fittings added to hull sides.

♦ 3 Maritime Administration C6-S-MA1qd auxiliary crane-ships [WAK]

Bldr: National Steel, San Diego, Calif.

	L	In serv.	Conversion to T-ACS	To RRF
T-ACS 1 Keystone State (ex-*President Harrison*)	2-10-65	1-66	21-3-83 to 7-5-84	1-12-86
T-ACS 2 Gem State (ex-*President Monroe*)	22-5-65	1965	26-9-84 to 31-10-85	31-10-85
T-ACS 3 Grand Canyon State (ex-*President Polk*)	23-1-65	1966	28-10-85 to 27-10-87	12-12-86

Grand Canyon State (T-ACS 3)—alongside *Gem State* (T-ACS 2) Frank Findler, 10-03

Grand Canyon State (T-ACS 3) Findler & Winter, 10-95

D: 16,599 tons light (31,500 fl) **S:** 20.25 kts (19.5 kts sust.)
Dim: 203.82 (192.95 pp) × 23.22 × 5.79 light (10.06 max. loaded)
Electronics: Radar: 2 . . . nav.
M: 2 sets G.E. geared steam turbines; 1 prop; 19,250 shp
Boilers: 2 Foster-Wheeler **Electric:** 4,780 kw tot. **Range:** 13,000/19.5
Fuel: 3,126 tons **Crew:** 14 officers, 50 mariners

Remarks: 16,819 grt/17,729 dwt. Conversion of T-ACS 1 by Bay SB, Sturgeon Bay, Wisconsin, took place under FY 83 funding; ordered 18-3-83. T-ACS 2 (FY 84) converted by Continental Marine, San Francisco. T-ACS 3 under FY 85 converted by Dillingham, San Francisco. T-ACS 1 and T-ACS 3 were both active in 2005. All three are in layberth at Alameda, California, on five-day recall. In this class, the assigned numbers are actual U.S. Navy hull numbers.
Hull systems: Cargo: 10,370 tons max., including 190 20-ft. containers. The original cargo-handling gear was replaced by three sets of twin 30-ton cranes mounted on the starboard side; the four forward most cranes can be ganged together to lift 105 tons. The T-ACS is expected to unload its own container cargo and then unload containers from non-self-sustaining container carriers at the rate of about 300 containers per day; the cranes have a 33-m reach. Additional generator capacity (3,280 kw) was added.

♦ 2 Sea Bee–class, Maritime Administration C8-S-82a cargo-barge carriers [WAK]

Bldr: General Dynamics, Quincy, Mass.

	In serv.	To RRF
(T-AK 5063) Cape May (ex-*Almeria Lykes*)	1972	25-7-86
(T-AK 5065) Cape Mohican (ex-*Tillie Lykes*)	1973	13-9-86

Cape May (T-AK 5063) Ralph Edwards, 9-04

Cape Mohican (T-AK 5065) W. Michael Young, 4-02

D: 18,880 tons light (57,290 fl) **S:** 20.5 kts (19.25 kts sust.)
Dim: 266.39 (219.92 pp) × 32.31 × 5.44 light (11.93 max. loaded)
Electronics: Radar: 2 . . . nav.
M: 2 sets G.E. geared steam turbines; 1 prop; 36,000 shp
Boilers: 2 Babcock & Wilcox
Electric: 4,000 kw (2 × 2,000-kw turbogenerators) **Range:** 14,300/19.5
Fuel: 6,260 tons **Crew:** 12 officers, 26 mariners

Remarks: 21,667 grt/38,410 dwt. All purchased 1-86. *Cape May* is in layberth at Baltimore, Maryland, on five-day recall and *Cape Mohican* at Alameda, California, on five-day recall. Last active in 2005, *Cape Mohican* went aground on South Korean coast on 22-5-01 but, despite severe damage to shafts and engine mountings, was repaired at Sasebo, Japan.
Hull systems: Cargo capacity: 29,780 tons max. The "Sea-Bee" design was intended to carry 38 cargo barges totaling 41,476 m^3 bale capacity and placed in the water via a 2,000-ton-capacity elevator at the stern. Can also accommodate 4,000 bbl (*Cape Mohican:* 11,000 bbl) liquid cargo and 797 tons water. Have 797-ton-capacity passive antirolling tanks. Each has 24 SeaBee barges stored aboard.
Disposal: *Cape Mendocino* (T-AK 5064) was transferred to the MARAD reserve fleet on 1-9-04 and is retained only on "Emergency Sealift" Status.

♦ 2 Maritime Administration C9-S-81d cargo-barge carriers [WAK]

Bldr: Avondale SY, Westwego, La.

	In serv.	To RRF
(T-AK 5070) Cape Flattery (ex-*Delta Norte*)	1973	14-5-87
(T-AK 5073) Cape Farewell (ex-*Delta Mar*)	1973	2-4-87

D: 16,490 tons light (57,082 fl) **S:** 22.75 kts (19.1 kts sust.)
Dim: 272.30 (243.03) × 30.56 × 4.42 light (12.44 max. loaded)
Electronics: Radar: 2 . . . nav.

READY RESERVE FORCE MARITIME ADMINISTRATION
(continued)

Cape Farewell (T-AK 5073)—with a full load of LASH cargo containers H&L Van Ginderen, 2-95

M: 2 sets de Laval geared steam turbines; 1 prop; 32,000 shp
Boilers: 2 Combustion Engineering; 75.7 kg/cm^2
Electric: 4,000 kw (2 × 2,000-kw turbogenerators)
Range: 15,000/19.1 **Fuel:** 5,840 tons **Crew:** 12 officers, 20 mariners

Remarks: 29,508 grt/41,363 dwt. Purchased 1-86, along with *Delta Sud,* which was to have become *Cape Fear* but suffered severe machinery damage during RRF overhaul and was returned to the Maritime Administration for disposal. Both are in layberth at Beaumont, Texas, on 10-day recall.
Hull systems: Cargo: 36,650 tons max. Have 455-ton traveling crane to handle 89 LASH (Lighter Aboard SHip) cargo lighters. Neither is equipped to carry containers. Both had the 89 barges aboard in 1999.

Disposal note: Maritime Administration cargo-barge carriers *Cape Fear* (T-AK 5061) and *Cape Florida* (T-AK 5071) were downgraded to maritime reserve status in 2006. *Cape Nome* (T-AK 1014) was transferred to the MARAD reserve fleet on 1-9-04 and is retained as logistical support assets for cannibalization spares.

♦ 2 Maritime Administration C5-S-75a combination cargo ships [WAK]
Bldr: Newport News SB & DD (In serv. 1968)

	To RRF
(T-AK 2039) Cape Girardeau (ex-*President Adams,* ex-*Alaskan Mail*)	12-4-88
(T-AK 5051) Cape Gibson (ex-*President Jackson,* ex-*Indian Mail*)	1-4-88

Cape Girardeau (T-AK 2039) Frank Findler, 10-03

D: 9,790 tons light (31,995 fl) **S:** 20.75 kts (19.5 sust.)
Dim: 184.41 (177.55 pp) × 25.05 × 9.50 (10.68 max. loaded)
Electronics: Radar: 2 . . . nav.
M: 2 sets G.E. geared steam turbines; 1 prop; 24,000 shp—bow-thruster
Boilers: 2 Babcock & Wilcox **Electric:** 2,500 kw tot. (2 × 1,250 kw)
Range: 23,200/19.5 **Fuel:** 3,668 tons **Crew:** 47 tot.

Remarks: 11,559 grt/18,289 dwt at 9.50-m draft; 15,949 grt/22,564 dwt at 10.68-m draft. Purchased from American President Lines 5-6-87 for $5 million each. Sister *President Taylor* (ex-*Korean Mail*) was acquired at the same time and was to have become *Cape Grieg,* but she remains in the National Defense Reserve Fleet. T-AK 5051 was activated 21-6-02 but returned to the RRF on 23-7-02; the ship was again reactivated later during 2002 in support of Operation Enduring Freedom prior to being laid up during 12-03. She was reactivated during 6-06 for naval training duties. Both are attached to Suisun Bay RRF facility, with T-AK 2039 is currently in layberth at Alameda, California, on five-day recall.
Hull systems: Cargo capacity: 17,832 tons max. Self-sustaining container/break-bulk ships with six holds, seven hatches. Cargo: 409 20-ft. containers/28,830 m^3 bale dry cargo (623 m^3 refrigerated), 17,000 bbl liquid (2,757 m^3), and 22 passengers. Have one 70-ton-, twenty 20-ton-, and four 15-ton-capacity cargo derricks. Both ships are equipped to carry one Modular Cargo Delivery System (MCDS) solid-cargo station on the port side, aft; when the gear is installed, 37 Naval Reservists augment the crew to operate it. Both have a helicopter deck and a broad ramp leading to it from the upper deck on the starboard side.

♦ 1 Maritime Administration C4-S-1u combination cargo ships [WAK]
Bldrs: Cape Jacob, Cape Juby: Newport News SB & DD

	L	In serv.	To RRF
(T-AK 5029) Cape Jacob (ex-*California,* ex-*Santa Rita,* ex-*California*)	28-7-61	1962	15-12-80

Cape John (T-AK 5022)—while still active U.S. Navy, 4-03

D: 9,892 tons light (22,629 fl) **S:** 20.75 kts (19.8 kts sust.)
Dim: 172.22 (161.09 pp) × 23.22 × 4.74 light (9.64 max. loaded)
M: 2 sets G.E. geared steam turbines; 1 prop; 19,250 shp
Boilers: 2 Foster-Wheeler
Electric: 1,500 kw tot. **Range:** 12,600/19.8
Fuel: 3,255 tons **Crew:** 14 off., 30 mariners (see Remarks)

Remarks: GRT normal,12,693 grt max./14,349 dwt. Selected 1986 from ships turned in to the Maritime Administration and stored in the NDRF. Name for *Cape Jacob* was changed 1993. *Cape Jacob* was activated 30-9-98 and assigned on 28-5-99 to the Afloat Prepositioned Ship force at Diego Garcia.
Hull systems: Cargo: 9,875 tons max. in six holds. 22,002 m^3 bale capacity (1,103 m^3 insulated). Can carry up to 200 20-ft. containers and 753 m^3 liquid cargo. Have one 60-ton, ten 20-ton, two 10-ton, and ten 5-ton cargo derricks. *Cape Jacob* underwent modifications at Bender SB & Repair, Mobile, Alabama, commencing 9-92, to carry the Modular Cargo Delivery System (MCDS) stations to allow use as a fleet underway ammunition and stores supply ship. When the MCDS is activated, 37 Naval Reserve Cargo Rig Team (CART) personnel are added to the crew to operate it.

Disposal notes: Sisters *Cape John* (T-AK 5022), *Cape Johnson* (T-AK 5075), and *Cape Juby* (T-AK 5077) were transferred to the MARAD Reserve Fleet on 1-9-04. *Cape John* is held in a “Retention, Break Bulk—Emergency Sealift” Status, *Cape Johnson* has been used as a training platform since 1-3-06, and *Cape Juby* is retained as a logistical support vessel for spare parts.

Maritime Administration C4-S-66a break-bulk cargo ships *Cape Bover* (T-AK 5057) and *Cape Borda* (T-AK 5058) were transferred to the MARAD reserve fleet on 28-4-04 for emergency-only reactivation. Sisters *Cape Breton* (T-AK 5056; ex-*Dolly Turman*) and *Cape Blanco* (T-AK 5060; ex-*Mason Lykes*) were downgraded to the National Defense Reserve Fleet on 19-12-02.

Maritime Administration C4-S-58a break-bulk cargo ships *Cape Alexander* (T-AK 5010) and *Cape Avinoff* (T-AK 5013) were both downgraded to the MARAD Reserve Fleet on 28-4-04 and are held in retention status for emergencies. Sister *Cape Alava* (ex-*Comet,* ex-*African Comet*) was reassigned to the National Defense Reserve Fleet on 1-10-00; she was followed by *Cape Ann* (T-AK 5009; ex-*Mercury;* ex-*African Mercury*) and *Cape Archway* (T-AK 5011; ex-*Neptune;* ex-*African Neptune*) on 19-12-02.

Falcon-class tanker *Mission Capistrano* (T-AOT 5005) was placed in the MARAD Reserve Fleet on 28-4-04.

♦ 2 Chesapeake-class tankers [WAOT]
Bldr: Bethlehem SY, Sparrows Point, Md.

	In serv.	Acquired	To RRF
(T-AOT 5075) Petersburg (ex-*Sinclair Texas,* ex-*Charles Kurz,* ex-*Keystone*)	1963	1-8-91	1-8-94
(T-AOT 5084) Chesapeake (ex-*Hess Voyager*)	1964	20-7-91	20-7-91

Chesapeake (T-AOT 5084) Edward McDonnell, 3-06

Petersburg (T-AOT 5075)—in light condition; note the OPDS barge stowed on an inclined skid to permit its launch to port and the crane installed to handle the five LCM(6) push-tugs John Mortimer, 8-00

D: *Chesapeake:* approx. 65,000 tons (fl); *Petersburg:* 48,993 tons (fl)
S: 15 to 15.5 kts **Dim:** 224.44 (214.89 pp) × 31.22 × 12.13
M: 2 sets Bethlehem geared steam turbines; 1 prop; 15,000 shp
Boilers: 2 . . . **Electric:** 1,200 kw (*Chesapeake*: 1,800 kw)
Range: . . . / . . . **Fuel:** 1,420 tons fuel oil/80 diesel **Crew:** . . .

Remarks: *Chesapeake:* 27,015 grt/50,826 dwt; *Petersburg:* 27,469 grt/50,072 dwt. *Petersburg* acquired 11-1-88. Upgrading to RRF delayed by funding and engineering problems. *Chesapeake* acquired 1989 for conversion as third ship with the Offshore Petroleum Distribution System (see Disposal notes below). As of 1-02, *Chesapeake* was active with Maritime Prepositioning Squadron 2 at Diego Garcia, and *Petersburg* was active with Maritime Prepositioning Squadron 3 at Saipan.

READY RESERVE FORCE MARITIME ADMINISTRATION
(continued)

Hull systems: Cargo volume: *Petersburg:* 61,730 m^3 (25 tanks); *Chesapeake:* 56,146 m^3 (21 tanks). Both have had a 53-metric-ton-capacity crane, platforms for boats, and numerous large hose reels added as part of the OPDS program. Both carry an OPDS utility boat to maneuver the OPDS barge.

Notes: For transportation aboard RRF tankers, six Offshore Petroleum Discharge Systems (OPDS) were procured. The prototype, SALM I, was transferred to the U.S. Virgin Islands for use as a mooring pontoon in 3-01. *American Osprey* had the first production set, consisting of a skid launching system for a 45.7 × 16.5–m barge, four-point mooring system, and hydraulic-powered reels for 6,400 m of 152-mm fuel hose to act as an offshore fuel transfer point to serve beachheads. Also added was a 53-metric-ton-capacity crane and boat stowage on the main deck. *Petersburg* and *Chesapeake* were equipped next, and the fifth and sixth sets, funded under FY 91 and FY 92, were delivered 6-91 and 10-92 by Orange Shipbuilding, Orange, Texas. To act as towboats for the OPDS barges, 15 LCM(6) landing craft were converted and renumbered as utility boats: 56UB775, 779, 7710, 7717, 7719, 784, 785, 789, 7813, 7821, 7841 through 7843, 8601, and 8602.

Disposal notes: *Mount Washington*–class transport tanker *Mount Washington* (T-AOT 5076) was downgraded to the MARAD Reserve Fleet on 30-6-05 for use as a spare parts cannibalization source and logistics support vessel. Sister *Mount Vernon* (ex-*Mount Vernon Victory*), which joined the RRF on 31-3-90, was reassigned to the National Defense Reserve Fleet in early FY 1995 and is berthed at Beaumont, Texas.

Mission Buenaventura–class tanker *Mission Buenaventura* (T-AOT 1012) was downgraded to the MARAD Reserve Fleet on 1-9-04. *American Osprey*–class transport tanker *American Osprey* (T-AOT 5075) was downgraded to the MARAD Reserve Fleet on 1-4-00. She was stripped for disposal during 2005. *Potomac* (T-AOT 181, ex-*Shenandoah;* ex-*Potomac,* T-AO 150) was deactivated on 30-9-92, and downrated from the RRF in 2006. *Alatna*-class small transport tankers *Alatna* (T-AOG 81) and *Chattahoochee* (T-AOG 82) along with *Tonti*-class small transport tanker *Nodaway* (T-AOG 78) were retired for disposal on 30-9-06.

Note: Five former naval ships/merchant ships are operated as school ships for Merchant Marine academies at Vallejo, Cal. (*Golden Bear*), Galveston, Texas (*Texas Clipper III*), Fort Schuyler, New York (*Empire State*, T-AP 1001), Buzzards Bay, Massachusetts (*Enterprise*, T-AP 1004), and Castine, Maine (*State of Maine*). Though not a part of the RRF, they remain on retention status, available for emergency call-up.

Empire State (T-AP 1001) Frank Findler, 6-04

UNITED STATES COAST GUARD

Personnel (as of 11-06): 41,006 active uniformed (including 7,895 officers and 32,111 enlisted) plus 7,219 civilians, 7,911 selective reservists, and 996 USCG cadets.

General: The Revenue Marine, which was created in 1790, became the Coast Guard on 28 January 1915 by an act of Congress. On 1 April 1967 the Coast Guard was transferred from the Department of the Treasury to the Department of Transportation (DoT), and on 1-3-03 it was transferred to the Department of Homeland Security. The act that created the service calls for it to operate in time of crisis under the control of the Navy. In a 1995 reorganization, the Coast Guard was given as its principal responsibilities maritime law enforcement, maritime safety, marine environmental protection, and national security. Since 9-01 its mission has been evolving to include a broader emphasis on homeland security.

Project Deepwater: Begun in 1996, the program to revitalize the USCG cutter and aircraft inventory was won by the Integrated Coast Guard Systems consortium (equal partners Northrop Grumman and Lockheed Martin) on 25-6-02; valued at $11 billion, the contract will be in effect for 20 years and is planned to involve acquisition of ships, fixed-wing aircraft, helicopters, and drone surveillance aircraft, plus the modernization of existing cutters and helicopters; in addition, the USCG's communications, surveillance, and command and control systems are being replaced and upgraded.

Organization: The Coast Guard is divided into two main areas, one for the Pacific and one for the Atlantic. The Coast Guard is further divided into 10 Coast Guard Districts to fulfill its responsibilities along the U.S. coastline (more than 10,000 nautical miles, not including Hawaii).

The Commandant of the Coast Guard, a four-star admiral, heads the organization. Appointed for four years and assisted by a general staff, the commandant reports to the Secretary of Homeland Security.

Commissioned Coast Guard ships have their names preceded by USCGC (United States Coast Guard Cutter). Cutters and patrol craft are white; icebreakers have red hulls; buoy tenders and tugs have black hulls. All ships and craft carry diagonal international orange (with thin white and blue) stripes and the USCG shield on the hull.

Coast Guard aviation: Atlantic bases are at Cape Cod, Massachusetts; Cape May, New Jersey; Elizabeth City, North Carolina; Savannah, Georgia; Miami, Florida; and Borinquen, Puerto Rico. Gulf of Mexico bases are at Clearwater, Florida; Mobile, Alabama; New Orleans, Louisiana; and Houston and Corpus Christi, Texas. Great Lakes Bases are at Chicago, Illinois, and Detroit and Traverse City, Michigan. Pacific Bases are at Port Angeles, Washington; Astoria and North Bend, Oregon; Humboldt Bay, Sacramento, San Francisco, Los Angeles, and San Diego, California; and Barbers Point, Hawaii. Alaska bases are at Sitka and Kodiak. Two VIP transports are kept at Washington, D.C. Aircraft are primarily white in color, but Dolphin and Stingray helicopters are painted orange.

Under Project Deepwater, 36 CASA CN-235 small maritime surveillance aircraft are to be acquired along with 45 Bell Textron VTOL Bell Eagle Eye HV-911 and four RQ-4A Global Hawk UAVs in addition to the upgrading of older (and acquisition of new) HC-130 aircraft and HH-65 helicopters.

Port Security Units (PSUs): There are seven deployable PSUs and one training detachment. PSUs are composed of five active duty and 140 selected reservists and are each equipped with six transportable 25-ft. Boston Whaler patrol launches powered by two 75-bhp outboards each. A PSU can be deployed within 96 hours to provide continual port security services worldwide. PSU 301 is based at Cape Cod, Mass.; PSU 305 at Fort Eustis, Virginia; PSU 307 at St. Petersburg, Florida; PSU 308 at Gulfport, Mississippi; PSU 309 at Port Clinton, Ohio; PSU 311 at Long Beach, California; and PSU 313 at Seattle, Washington. The Training Detachment (TRADET) is at Camp Lejeune, North Carolina.

Established beginning 3-7-02 under the PSU organization are four Maritime Safety and Security Teams (MSST), based at Seattle, Washington, Chesapeake, Virginia, Los Angeles/Long Beach, California, and Houston/Galveston, Texas; these were created to deal with the increased threat after the 11-9-01 attacks on New York and Washington, and six more MSST groups are being formed. Each MSST has 104 personnel (33 reservists) and six armed small Response Boats.

PRINCIPAL U.S. COAST GUARD AIRCRAFT

♦ 2 (+ 34) HC 235A transports
Mfr: EADS-CASA, Seville, Spain

HC 235A maritime patrol aircraft—computer rendering USCG, 2004

Wingspan: 25.8 m **Length:** 21.40 m
Weight: 16,502 max.
Speed: 236 kts cruise
Engines: 2 General Electric CT7-9C3 turboprops turboprops
Operational range: 1,565 nm **Endurance:** 8.7 hours

Remarks: Coast Guard version of the EADS CASA CN 235-300M transport for use in homeland security, search and rescue, law enforcement, drug interdiction, marine environmental protection, military readiness, and international ice patrol, as well as cargo and personnel transport missions. Thirty-six are planned for delivery between 2007 and 2017. Part of Project Deepwater.

♦ 27 HC-130H/J transports
Mfr: Lockheed-Georgia Co., Marietta, Ga.

Wingspan: 40.42 m **Length:** 29.80 m **Height:** 11.66 m
Weight: 35,050 kg empty; 49,780 loaded; 70,300 max.
Speed: 302 kts max.; 287 cruise
Engines: 4 Allison T56-A-15 turboprops; 4,508 shp (4,061 sust.) each
Ceiling: 25,000 ft.
Range: 3,734 n.m. ferry; 2,517 n.m. with max. payload at 5,000 ft.
Fuel: 36,416 liters (10,599 in external tanks)

HC-130H Hercules U.S. Navy, 12-02

PRINCIPAL U.S. COAST GUARD AIRCRAFT *(continued)*

Remarks: Most HC-130Hs have APS-125 radars, while those based at Clearwater, Florida, have APS-137 radars. The four HC-130H-7s, all at Sacramento, California, have FLIR turrets. Two HC-130Hs have side-looking radars for ice-patrol duties. Cabin volume is 128 m^3; length: 12.5 m; width: 3.0 m; height: 2.7 m. Maximum flight time is 17 hours. Twenty-two are operational with five additional units in storage.

♦ 25 HU-25A, 7 HU-25B oil-spill detection, and 9 HU-25C drug intercept Guardian
Mfr.: Dassault Aviation, Vaucresson, France

HU-25A Guardian SAR aircraft USCG

Wingspan: 16.30 m **Length:** 17.15 m **Height:** 5.32 m
Weight: 8,618 kg empty; 9,476 kg loaded; 14,515 kg max.
Speed: 461 kts max.; 150 kts search-speed
Engines: 2 Garrett AiResearch ATF3-6-2C turbofans; 2,512 kg thrust each
Ceiling: 40,000 ft. **Range:** 2,250 n.m. in SAR mode

Remarks: Were initially unsuccessful, not meeting performance specifications. Sixteen of the 25 remaining HU-25A search-and-rescue variants of the design are in storage, along with 4 HU-25B and 1 HU-25C.

The HU-25B has APS-127 radar; APG-65 is carried by the drug-hunting HU-25C. Conversion of nine HU-25As to HU-25B began 1-4-87; they have SLAR (Side-Looking Airborne Radar), an IR/ultraviolet line-scanner, KS-87B aerial camera, and active-gated television camera and are used for detection of oil spills, mapping, and on the International Ice Patrol. Crew of five, including two pilots, surveillance systems operator, and two search crew; can also carry four stretchers. Fifteen HU-25A and C aircraft were upgraded with Wescam 16D FLIR, Telephonics APS-143 synthetic aperture radar (nine aircraft only), and a new integrated workstation under an 18-4-00 contract with California Microwave Systems; the first aircraft redelivered in 2001 and the others at 45–90-day intervals, with the upgraded HU-25As becoming HU-25Ds and the HU-25Cs becoming HU-25C+.

Notes: The HU-25-series aircraft are to be replaced by up to 36 EADS-Casa C-235 maritime patrol aircraft under Project Deepwater.

♦ 42 HH-60J Jayhawk search-and-rescue helicopters
Mfr.: Sikorsky Aircraft Div., United Technologies Corp., Stratford, Conn.

HH-60J Jayhawk USCG, 8-05

Rotor diameter: 16.36 m **Length:** 19.76 m (15.24 fuselage) **Height:** 5.23 m
Weight: 9,435 kg max. **Speed:** 150 kts max.; 140 kts cruise
Engines: 2 G.E. T700-GE-401 turboshafts; 1,723 max. shp each (1,543 sust.)
Range: 700 n.m. (3.5 hrs; 300 n.m. radius with 45 min. on station)

Remarks: First flight 8-8-89. Based at Cape Cod, Traverse City, Elizabeth City, Mobile, San Francisco, and Sitka. One lost at sea in accident on 8-7-97. All have the Bendix RDR-1300C search radar and can carry six rescuees plus the crew of four.

♦ 94 HH-65A/C Dolphin search-and-rescue helicopters
Mfr.: Aerospatiale SNI, Helicopter Div., Marignane, France

Rotor diameter: 11.94 m **Length:** 13.68 m (over rotor) **Height:** 3.99 m
Weight: 2,717 kg empty/4,049 kg max.
Speed: 150 kts max.; 139 kts cruise; 128 kts search mode
Engines: HH-65A 2 Avco-Lycoming LTS 101-750B2 turboshafts; 680 shp each (646 sust.). HH-65C: 2 1,054-shp Turbomeca Arriel 2C2 turboshaft engines
Ceiling: 7,150 ft. **Range:** 400 n.m. max. (3.8 hr mission)

Remarks: Entered service on 19-11-84, with a total of 93 procured, all assembled in Texas; last unit delivered 24-4-89. Were considered underpowered and could not lift full fuel load with crew of four and equipment aboard, but their engines are being increased by 23% in power (to 836 shp) under a $40-million effort begun in 2-00. Carry a crew of two pilots, aircrew/hoist-operator, and up to six passengers. Are based at Cape May, Savannah, Borinquen, Miami, Mobile, Detroit, Chicago, New Orleans,

HH-65A Dolphin—aboard *Healy* (WAGB 20) U.S. Navy, 8-05

Houston, Corpus Christi, Kodiak, Port Angeles, Astoria, North Bend, Humboldt Bay, Los Angeles, San Diego, and Barbers Point. Fourteen of the helicopters are kept in storage. The first prototype of a re-engined version employing two 1,054-shp Turbomeca Arriel 2C2 turboshaft engines took place on 8-10-02. During 3-04 the decision was made to re-engine the entire fleet with these engines, which should completed by 2007. The re-engined models are designated HH-656.

♦ 8 MH-68A Stingray armed tactical helicopters
Mfr.: Augusta Westland, Italy

MH-68A Stingray USCG, 2002

Rotor diameter: 11.0 m **Length:** 13.03 max. over rotors **Height:** 3.5 m
Weight: 1,570 kg empty; 2,850 kg max. takeoff
Speed: 168 kts max., 156 kts cruise
Engines: 2 Pratt & Whitney 206C turboshafts; 670.5 shp each
Ceiling: 20,000 ft. **Range:** 502 n.m. at 5,000 ft.
Endurance: 5 hr max.

Remarks: Selected after trials with two leased A-109 Power light helicopters during 4-00. MH-68A is an A-109E modified for USCG requirements, including fitting an FLIR. All are operated by Helicopter Interdiction Squadron 10 (HITRON-10), Jacksonville, Florida. The first two were delivered in 9-00. Are armed with an M240 machinegun and a 12.7-mm Robar sniping rifle. Used for homeland security and drug-interdiction missions.

Notes: Other aircraft in service include one Grumman Gulfstream I turboprop VIP transport and one Grumman C-20B Gulfstream IV jet VIP transport. The Gulfstream I was acquired 11-01 to replace the grounded USCG VC-4A Gulfstream, and a single C-37A Gulfstream V turbofan VIP transport was ordered during 12-00 for delivery early in 2002 to replace the C-20B Gulfstream IV. The RU-38A surveillance aircraft program was terminated during 2000. The Coast Guard is considering the procurement of the Bell Helicopters HV-609, a commercial variant of the original XV-15 experimental tilt-rotor aircraft, for use in offshore operations; the XV-15 was found to be fully compatible with a standard WMEC flight deck during trials in 1999.

Forty-five Lockheed Martin Eagle Eye drone reconnaissance aircraft are to be acquired under the Deepwater project, with the first to enter service in 2008. The aircraft are to have a range of 750 n.m. and a speed of up to 220 kts. By 2016, the USCG also hopes to acquire four Global Hawk long-range drones.

HIGH-ENDURANCE CUTTERS [WPS]

♦ 0 (+ 2 + 6) National Security Cutter Project
Bldr: Northrop Grumman Ship Systems (In serv. 2007–13)

	Laid down	L	In serv.
WMSL 750 BERTHOLF	29-3-05	11-11-06	2007
WMSL 751 WAESCHE	11-9-06	...	2008
WMSL 752	...	...	...
WMSL 753	...	...	...
WMSL 754	...	...	...
WMSL 755	...	...	...
WMSL 756	...	...	...
WMSL 757	...	...	2013

D: 4,300 tons (fl) **S:** 29 kts **Dim:** 127.4 × 16.46 × 6.42
A: 1 57-mm/70 cal. Mk 110 DP; 1 20-mm Mk 15 Mod. 3 Phalanx CIWS; 4 single 12.7-mm M2 mg; 1-2 helicopters

COAST GUARD HIGH-ENDURANCE CUTTERS [WPS] *(continued)*

National Security Cutter—computer rendering USCG, 2005

Electronics: 1 EADS-Raytheon TRS-3D/16 3-D search; 1 Hughes-Furuno SPS-73 nav.; 1 Lockheed Martin SPQ-9A gun f.c; EW: 1 Raytheon SLQ-32(V)2 intercept; Mk 36 SRBOC decoy syst.
M: CODAG: 2 MTU-Detroit Diesel 20V1163 diesels (9,655 bhp); 1 G.E. LM-2500 gas turbine (30, 565 shp); 2 CP props
Range: 12,000/29 **Crew:** 18 officers, 100 enlisted and up to 30 passengers

Remarks: "Deepwater Capability Replacement Program" initiated 2-98 as a 10-year, $8-billion effort to replace the existing 12 *Hamilton*-class cutters; the contract was awarded on 24-6-02, with work on the first starting during 2004. The first ship is planned to enter service in mid-2007. Some $320 million in developmental funding was approved under the FY 02 budget, and the yearly average acquisition cost during the program is about $523 million. WMSL 750 is to be based at Alameda, Calif. upon completion.
Hull systems: Will have a double helicopter hangar. Can also carry up to four vertical unmanned aerial vehicles. The selected design is a conservatively configured conventional monohull with few, if any, stealth features. A dual stern ramp will be fitted for launch and recovery of RIB rescue and inspection boats. The crew will mostly be accommodated in four-person staterooms, and the ships will have three crew lounges and a fitness center. Deck space and below-decks volume is reserved for insertion of "adaptable mission modules." Will have berthing for up to 148.
Combat systems: Lockheed Martin will perform combat systems integration. The ships will have weight and space allocation for an ASW capability and will be equipped with EW systems. All ships will have a Link 11 capability. A stern ramp will be fitted for RIB deployment and recovery. Will carry at least two small boats.

♦ 12 Hamilton class (378-ft. class)
Bldr: Avondale SY, Westwego, La.

	Laid down	L	In serv.	Based at:
WHEC 715 Hamilton	23-11-65	18-12-65	20-2-67	San Diego, Calif.
WHEC 716 Dallas	7-2-66	1-10-66	1-10-67	Charleston, S.C.
WHEC 717 Mellon	25-7-66	11-2-67	22-12-67	Seattle, Wash.
WHEC 718 Chase	15-10-66	20-5-67	1-3-68	San Diego, Calif.
WHEC 719 Boutwell	12-12-66	17-6-67	14-6-68	Alameda, Calif.
WHEC 720 Sherman	13-2-67	23-9-67	23-8-68	Alameda, Calif.
WHEC 721 Gallatin	17-4-67	18-11-67	20-12-68	Charleston, S.C.
WHEC 722 Morgenthau	17-7-67	10-2-68	14-2-69	Alameda, Calif.
WHEC 723 Rush	23-10-67	16-11-68	3-7-69	Honolulu, Hawaii
WHEC 724 Munro	18-2-70	5-12-70	10-9-71	Kodiak, Alaska
WHEC 725 Jarvis	9-9-70	24-4-71	30-12-71	Honolulu, Hawaii
WHEC 726 Midgett	5-4-71	4-9-71	17-3-72	Seattle, Wash.

Munro (WHEC 724) Frank Findler, 10-03

D: 2,716 tons (3,050 fl) **S:** 29 kts (28.4 postmodernization)
Dim: 115.37 (106.68 pp) × 13.06 × 4.27 (6.2 over sonar)
A: Provision for: up to 8 RGM-84A Harpoon SSM; fitted with: 1 76-mm 62-cal. Mk 75 DP; 1 20-mm Mk 15 CIWS; 2 single 25-mm 87-cal. Mk 88 Bushmaster low-angle guns; 1 HH-65 Dolphin helicopter

Sherman (WHEC 720) U.S. Navy, 5-06

Sherman (WHEC 720) U.S. Navy, 5-06

Rush (WHEC 723) W. Michael Young, 6-05

Electronics:
Radar: 2 Raytheon SPS-64(V)6 nav.; 1 Lockheed SPS-40B air-search; 1 Sperry Mk 92 Mod. 1 f.c.
Sonar: Removed
TACAN: URN-25
EW: WLR-1H(V)5 or (V)7 intercept; WLR-3 intercept; Mk 36 SRBOC decoy syst. (2 6-round Mk 137 RL)
M: CODOG: 2 Fairbanks-Morse 38TD8$^1/_8$, 12-cyl. diesels, 3,500 bhp each; 2 Pratt & Whitney FT4-A6 gas turbines, 18,000 shp each; 2 CP props; 36,000 shp—350-shp retractable bow thruster
Electric: 1,500 kw tot.
Range: 2,400/29; 9,600/19 (gas turbines); 14,000/11 (diesel)
Fuel: 800 tons **Endurance:** 45 days **Crew:** 21 officers, 156 enlisted

Remarks: Named after early Secretaries of the Treasury and Coast Guard heroes. Thirty-six planned, only twelve built. The entire class has received a midlife modernization, eight by Todd SY, Seattle, and WHEC 715, 716, 718, and 721 by Bath Iron Works, Maine; dates as follows:

WHEC 715	10-85 to 15-11-88	WHEC 721	3-90 to 26-1-92
WHEC 716	11-86 to 12-89	WHEC 722	11-11-89 to 12-91
WHEC 717	10-85 to 3-6-89	WHEC 723	7-89 to 9-91
WHEC 718	7-89 to 5-3-91	WHEC 724	12-86 to 11-11-89
WHEC 719	3-3-89 to 4-91	WHEC 725	3-91 to 11-12-92
WHEC 720	14-5-86 to 2-90	WHEC 726	9-90 to 31-3-92

They are planned to serve until replaced by the National Security Cutter Project.
Hull systems: Welded steel hull; aluminum superstructure. Living spaces air-conditioned. Laboratories for weather and oceanographic research. WHEC 716–723 have synchronizing clutches; the final three have synchro-self-shifting (SSS) clutches. WHEC 717, 722, and 725 have rudder roll-stabilization systems. During modernization, the hangars were reactivated and a telescoping section added, and all have Fairey Hydraulics Talon helicopter landing systems. The helicopter platform is 26.82 × 12.20 m. Are equipped with a 6.86-m Zodiac Hurricane 630 rigid inflatable boat with a Volvo Penta outdrive diesel engine; the craft have a GPS receiver and an echo sounder and can carry 11 personnel. WHEC 725 was slightly damaged on 22-12-01 when a commercial dry dock collapsed and sank beneath her at Honolulu, Hawaii.

COAST GUARD HIGH-ENDURANCE CUTTERS [WFF] *(continued)*

Combat systems: Modernizations included: replacing the 127-mm gun and Mk 56 gunfire-control system with a 76-mm Mk 75 (OTO Melara Compact) gun and Mk 92 Mod. 1 radar gunfire-control system, replacing the SPS-29D radar with SPS-40B, and adding one Mk 15 Phalanx CIWS, URN-25 TACAN, and satellite communications gear. All were given the capability to carry Harpoon missiles, but only five ships actually have carried the weapon, and none had it as of 2001. Navigational equipment was updated through the addition of RAYCAS (Raytheon Collision-Avoidance System) and an HP-9020 computer, and secure communications systems were installed. Not carried out were the planned replacement of the WLR-1 EW system with SLQ-32(V)1, addition of the SLQ-25 Nixie towed torpedo decoy system, and adding provision to carry the since-retired LAMPS-I ASW helicopter. The EW system in six of the ships is to be upgraded to WLR-1H(V)7 by Wide Band Systems under a late 2002 contract. The decision was made 7-92 to remove SQS-38 hull-mounted sonar, two sets Mk 32 Mod. 7 ASW torpedo tubes, the Mk 109 underwater fire control system, and SQR-17A(V)1 sonobuoy analyzers. All are now fitted with WSC-3 UHF SATCOM terminals. All had received extensive C4ISR upgrades under the Deepwater program by 2006.

MEDIUM-ENDURANCE CUTTERS [WPS]

♦ 0 (+ 25) Offshore Patrol Cutter Program

Bldr: Northrop Grumman Ship Systems, . . . (In serv. 2012–22)

	In serv.
WMSM 915	2012
WMSM 939	2022

Offshore Patrol Cutter—computer rendering USCG, 2005

D: 3,715 tons (fl) **S:** 25 kts **Dim:** 109.7 × 16.5 × 6.4
A: 1 57-mm Mk 110 DP; 2 12.7-mm mg; 2 helicopters
Electronics: . . .
M: 2 . . . diesels; 2 CP props; . . . **Range:** 9,000/ . . .
Endurance: 45 days **Crew:** 94 total

Remarks: Intended to replace all current WMEC cutters, with the first to enter service around 2012. The design is to be a reduced-sized version of the new National Security Cutter and may prove too slow for most search-and-rescue and counter-drug missions. Will employ "Adaptable Mission Modules" like the larger National Security Cutters.

♦ 13 Famous class (270-ft. class)

Bldrs: WMEC 901–904: Tacoma Boatbuilding, Tacoma, Wash.; WMEC 905–913: Robert E. Derecktor, Middletown, R.I.

	Laid down	L	In serv.	Based at:
WMEC 901 Bear	23-8-79	25-9-80	4-2-83	Portsmouth, Va.
WMEC 902 Tampa	2-4-80	19-3-81	16-3-84	Portsmouth, Va.
WMEC 903 Harriet Lane	15-10-80	6-2-82	20-9-84	Portsmouth, Va.
WMEC 904 Northland	9-4-81	7-5-82	17-12-84	Portsmouth, Va.
WMEC 905 Spencer (ex-*Seneca*)	26-6-82	16-6-84	28-6-86	Boston, Mass.
WMEC 906 Seneca (ex-*Pickering*)	16-9-82	16-6-84	4-5-87	Boston, Mass.
WMEC 907 Escanaba	1-4-83	24-8-85	27-8-87	Boston, Mass.
WMEC 908 Tahoma (ex-*Legare*)	28-6-83	24-8-85	6-4-88	Kittery, Maine
WMEC 909 Campbell (ex-*Argus*)	10-8-84	30-8-86	19-8-88	Kittery, Maine
WMEC 910 Thetis (ex-*Tahoma*)	24-8-84	30-8-86	30-6-89	Key West, Fla.
WMEC 911 Forward (ex-*Erie*)	11-7-86	18-8-87	4-8-90	Portsmouth, Va.
WMEC 912 Legare (ex-*McCulloch*)	11-7-86	18-8-87	4-8-90	Portsmouth, Va.
WMEC 913 Mohawk (ex-*Ewing*)	18-6-87	18-5-88	20-3-90	Key West, Fla.

D: 1,200 tons light (1,780 fl) **S:** 19.5 kts **Dim:** 82.3 (77.7 wl) × 11.58 × 4.11
A: 1 76-mm 62-cal. Mk 75 DP; 2 single 12.7-mm mg; 1 HH-65 Dolphin helicopter
Electronics:
Radar: 1 Raytheon SPS-64(V)1 nav.; 1 Raytheon SPS-64(V)6 nav.; 1 Sperry Mk 92 Mod. 1 f.c.
TACAN: URN-25
EW: Raytheon SLQ-32(V)2 intercept; Mk 36 SRBOC decoy syst. (2 6-round Mk 137 RL)
M: 2 Alco Model 18V-251E, 18-cyl. diesels; 2 Escher-Wyss CP props; 7,200 bhp
Electric: 1,425 kw (3 × 475-kw Kato sets, Caterpillar D398 diesels driving)
Range: 3,850/19.5; 6,370/15; 10,250/12 **Endurance:** 14 days
Crew: 11 officers, 89 enlisted + 16 aircrew

Spencer (WMEC 905) George R. Schneider, 9-05

Spencer (WMEC 905) USCG, 9-05

Tampa (WMEC 902) USN, 11-04

Remarks: Authorized: two in FY 77, two in FY 78, two in FY 79, three in FY 80, one in FY 81, and three in FY 82. Officially styled the "Famous" class because all are named for well-known earlier cutters. The program suffered numerous delays; first ship was to have completed 31-12-80 and WMEC 913 entered active service over three years late. WMEC 905–913 originally ordered from Tacoma Boat in 8-80, but lawsuit caused reassignment to R.E. Derecktor in 17-1-81. Originally intended to be able to act as ASW escorts in wartime, a mission no longer foreseen. Planned to be retired between 2011 and 2020. WMEC 902 was the first to undergo an extensive nine-month overhaul to improve engineering, living quarters, and C4ISR systems under Project Deepwater.
Hull systems: The COMDAC computerized control system on this class has given considerable difficulty. Reportedly are overloaded and very uncomfortable ships in a seaway. Have accommodations for up to 17 officers and 123 enlisted. Have a telescoping helicopter hangar and provision for later installation of fin stabilization. By 2004, all received Sperry Mk 39 Mod. 3A ring-laser gyros in place of the original Mk 29 gyros.

COAST GUARD MEDIUM-ENDURANCE CUTTERS [WPS]
(continued)

Combat systems: No hull-mounted sonar or onboard ASW weapons. Space and weight are reserved for Mk 15 CIWS 20-mm gatling AA gun and two quadruple Harpoon missile-launch canisters, but they are very unlikely ever to have them installed. WSC-3 UHF satellite-communications system is carried. Have six light weapons mounting positions capable of accepting 12.7-mm mg or 40-mm Mk 19 grenade launchers.

♦ 1 U.S. Navy Edenton class
Bldr: Brooke Marine, Lowestoft, U.K.

	Laid down	L	In serv.	Based at:
WMEC 39 Alex Haley (ex-*Edenton,* ATS 1)	1-4-67	15-5-68	23-1-71	Kodiak, Alaska

Alex Haley (WMEC 39) USCG, 5-03

Alex Haley (WMEC 39) George R. Schneider, 10-05

D: 2,650 tons (2,929 fl) **S:** 16 kts **Dim:** 88.0 (80.5 pp) × 15.25 × 4.6
A: 2 single 25-mm 87-cal. Mk 38 Bushmaster low-angle guns; 2 single 12.7-mm M2 mg
Electronics: Radar: 1 Hughes-Furuno SPS-73 nav.; 1 SPS-40 air search
M: 4 Caterpillar 3516 diesels; 2 Escher-Wyss 4-bladed CP props; 6,800 bhp—bow-thruster
Electric: 1,200 kw tot. **Range:** 10,000/13 **Crew:** 7 officers, 92 enlisted

Remarks: Former U.S. Navy salvage and rescue ship decommissioned to reserve 29-3-96, transferred to the Coast Guard on 17-11-97. Converted for use as a cutter at the U.S. Coast Guard Yard, Curtis Bay, Maryland, recommissioning 10-7-99 and fully commissioned on 16-12-99 at her base, Kodiak, Alaska, from where she is employed on fisheries patrol ("Living Marine Resources") and search-and-rescue duties. Sisters *Beaufort* (ATS 2) and *Brunswick* (ATS 3) were transferred to South Korea 12-12-96.
Hull systems: Received new main engines and Caterpillar diesel-driven Onan generator sets during an early 1990s refit and new generators during conversion for USCG service. Most salvage equipment (including the towing winch, cranes, and divers decompression chamber) was removed during conversion. A helicopter platform has been erected over the fantail (additional accommodations may later be added below the helicopter deck, which can accommodate HH-60 and HH-65 aircraft). Carries two RIB inspection craft. Navigational suite includes Sperry Mk 27 gyro, Trimble NT2000 GPS, and Raytheon CRP V850 and SQN-15 echo sounders. During an overhaul completed 2-03, the ship received a telescoping helicopter hangar.

♦ 14 Reliance class (210-ft. class)
Bldrs: A: Todd Shipyards, Houston, Tex.; B: Christy Corp., Sturgeon Bay, Wisc.; C: Coast Guard SY, Curtis Bay, Md.; D: American SB, Lorain, Ohio.

	Bldr	L	In serv.	Based at:
WMEC 615 Reliance	A	25-5-63	20-6-64	New Castle, N.H.
WMEC 616 Diligence	A	20-7-63	26-8-64	Wilmington, N.C.
WMEC 617 Vigilant	A	24-12-63	3-10-64	Cape Canaveral, Fla.
WMEC 618 Active	B	31-7-65	17-9-66	Port Angeles, Wash.
WMEC 619 Confidence	C	8-5-65	19-2-66	Cape Canaveral, Fla.
WMEC 620 Resolute	C	30-4-66	8-12-66	St. Petersburg, Fla.
WMEC 621 Valiant	D	14-1-67	28-10-67	Miami, Fla.
WMEC 623 Steadfast	D	24-6-67	25-9-68	Astoria, Ore.
WMEC 624 Dauntless	D	21-10-67	10-6-68	Galveston, Tx.
WMEC 625 Venturous	D	11-11-67	16-8-68	St. Petersburg, Fla.
WMEC 626 Dependable	D	16-3-68	27-11-68	Portsmouth, Va.
WMEC 627 Vigorous	D	4-5-68	2-5-69	Cape May, N.J.
WMEC 629 Decisive	C	14-12-67	23-8-68	Cape May, N.J.
WMEC 630 Alert	C	19-10-68	4-8-69	Astoria, Ore.

Alert (WMEC 630) George R. Schneider, 5-06

Active (WMEC 618) Frank Findler, 10-03

Steadfast (WMEC 623) W. Michael Young, 3-05

D: 879 tons (1,050 fl) **S:** 18 kts **Dim:** 64.16 (60.96 pp) × 10.36 × 3.25
A: 1 25-mm 87-cal. Mk 38 Bushmaster low-angle gun; 2 single 12.7-mm M2 mg; 1 HH-65 helicopter
Electronics: Radar: 2 Hughes-Furuno SPS-73 nav.
M: 2 Alco 16V-251B diesels; 2 CP props; 5,000 bhp **Electric:** 500 kw tot.
Range: 2,700/18; 6,100/14 **Endurance:** 30 days
Crew: 12 officers, 63 enlisted (accomm.: 12 officers, 72 enlisted)

Remarks: Designed to operate up to 500 miles off the coast. All were modernized by the U.S. Coast Guard Yard, Curtis Bay, Maryland:

WMEC 615	6-4-87 to 1-89	WMEC 623	6-92 to 14-2-94
WMEC 616	7-90 to 12-91	WMEC 624	7-8-93 to 24-2-95
WMEC 617	2-89 to 6-90	WMEC 625	11-2-94 to 27-10-95
WMEC 618	1-10-84 to 12-2-87	WMEC 626	24-2-95 to 15-8-97
WMEC 619	18-10-86 to 6-88	WMEC 627	6-91 to 11-92
WMEC 620	8-94 to 13-9-96	WMEC 629	13-9-96 to 10-10-98
WMEC 621	12-91 to 5-93	WMEC 630	12-92 to 2-9-94

Under Project Deepwater, the surviving ships will be lengthened by 10 ft. through the addition of a stern launch and recovery ramp section for RIB inspection and rescue boats.
Hull systems: During modernization the ships received a new stack, enlarged superstructure, and greater firefighting capability; topweight was reduced, but the helicopter deck was reduced in area. The crews were enlarged to 86 total, provisions

COAST GUARD MEDIUM-ENDURANCE CUTTERS [WPS] *(continued)*

capacities were enlarged, and engine exhausts were rearranged; displacements rose from 930 to more than 1,050 tons. High superstructure permits 360-degree visibility. Can tow a 10,000-ton ship. Air-conditioned. WMEC 615–619 originally had CODAG propulsion, with two 1,500-bhp Cooper-Bessemer FVBM12-T diesels and two Solar Saturn T-100s gas turbines providing an additional 2,000 shp; the gas turbines were soon removed, and the ships were re-engined with Alco 251B engines during the class modernization program. All are now equipped with 6.86-m Zodiac Hurricane 630 rigid inflatable boats with Volvo Penta outdrive diesel engines; the craft have a GPS receiver and an echo sounder and can carry 11 personnel. One 25-ft. Mk V Motor Surf Boat is also carried.

Though planned to be retired beginning in 2011, efforts to extend service life of the class by at least 10 years began in 2005 with nine-month overhauls. All units of the class are expected to modernize by 2015.

Combat systems: The obsolete 76.2-mm 50-cal. gun formerly carried on the forecastle was replaced by the 25-mm Bushmaster chain-gun. The Raytheon SPS-64-series navigational radars have been replaced by two SPS-73 sets, for which there are three displays. By 6-01 the entire class had been fitted with an electronic Integrated Navigation System (INS) employing electronic charts.

Disposals: *Courageous* (WMEC 622) was decommissioned on 27-9-01; *Durable* (WMEC 628) on 20-9-01; WMEC 622 transferred to Sri Lanka on 24-6-04 and WMEC 628 to Colombia on 3-9-03.

♦ 1 U.S. Navy Diver class (213-ft. class)

Bldr: Basalt Rock Co., Napa, Calif.

	Laid down	L	In serv.
WMEC 167 Acushnet (ex-WAGO 167; ex-WAT 167; ex-*Shackle,* ARS 9)	26-11-42	1-4-43	5-2-44

Acushnet (WMEC 167) Chris Sattler, 8-00

D: 1,246 tons (1,746 fl) **S:** 15.5 kts (13 sust.)
Dim: 65.08 (63.09 wl) × 12.50 × 4.57
A: 3/12.7-mm mg **Electronics:** Radar: 2/Raytheon SPS-64(V)1 nav.
M: 4 Cooper-Bessemer GSB-8 diesels, electric drive; 2 props; 3,030 shp
Electric: 460 kw tot. **Range:** 10,000/14.5; 3,700/10.3 **Fuel:** 300 tons
Crew: 7 officers, 65 enlisted

Remarks: Taken over from U.S. Navy in 1946. Based at Ketchikan, Alaska, since 8-98. Expected to serve through 2011.

Disposal notes: Sister *Escape* (WMEC 6) was stricken 29-6-95 and returned to USN 12-7-95 for disposal; *Yocona* (WMEC 168, ex-WAT 168, ex-*Seize,* ARS 26) was stricken 6-6-96 and is currently employed at Pearl Harbor as Navy Afloat Training Group Mid-Pacific's "Visit, Board, Search, and Seizure" (VBSS) training hulk.

♦ 1 Storis class (230-ft. class)

Bldr: Toledo SB, Toledo, Ohio

	Laid down	L	In serv.	Based at:
WMEC 38 Storis (ex-*Eskimo*)	14-7-41	4-4-42	30-9-42	Kodiak, Alaska

Storis (WMEC 38) USCG, 2-02

D: 1,296 tons light (1,916 fl) **S:** 14 kts **Dim:** 70.1 × 13.1 × 4.6
A: 1 25-mm 87-cal. Mk 38 Bushmaster low-angle gun; 4 single 12.7-mm M2 mg
Electronics: Radar: 2 Hughes-Furuno SPS-73 nav.
M: 3 Fairbanks-Morse 38D8$^1/_8$ diesels, electric drive; 1 prop; 1,800 shp
Range: 12,000/14; 22,000/8 **Fuel:** 330 tons **Crew:** 10 officers, 96 enlisted

Storis (WMEC 38) USCG, 2-02

Remarks: Rated as WAG until 1966 and WAGB until 1-7-72, when she was retyped WMEC. Resembles a *Balsam*-class buoy tender, but is larger. Expected to retire in 2007. Has an icebreaker hull, but is no longer considered capable of breaking ice. The obsolete 76.2-mm 50-cal. gun formerly carried on the forecastle was replaced by a 25-mm chain-gun during 1994. Is equipped with 6.86-m Zodiac Hurricane 630 rigid inflatable boats with a 135-bhp Volvo Penta outdrive diesel engine; the craft have a GPS receiver and an echo sounder and can carry 11 personnel and one ton of cargo.

Disposal notes: *Stalwart*-class drug-interdiction cutter *Vindicator* (T-AGOS 3, ex-WMEC 3, ex-T-AGOS 3), transferred to USCG control 20-5-94 and temporarily commissioned for Haiti blockade duties, and decommissioned 19-8-94 and laid up at Curtis Bay, Maryland. Reactivated 1999 after conversion to carry two Fountain Powerboats "Deployable Pursuit Boats." Was to have been operated by Military Sealift Command contractor crew under Coast Guard control and with a 17-strong USCG detachment on counter-narcotics duties. Due to budget problems, the ship was deactivated and returned to the USCG for layup at Curtis Bay on 5-5-01, without having made an operational patrol, and was transferred to the National Oceanographic and Atmospheric Administration (NOAA) during 2001. Sister *Persistent* (WMEC 6, ex-T-AGOS 6) was deactivated from the MSC and transferred 11-10-94 to the USCG and laid up; the ship re-entered service on 28-10-99 (but was then briefly placed in reduced operating condition at Miami, Fla., awaiting operating funds) and was laid up at Curtis Bay in 5-01 and transferred to Maritime Administration custody during 11-01.

PATROL CRAFT [WPC]

Note: Five U.S. Navy *Cyclone*-class patrol craft *Tempest* (PC 2), *Monsoon* (PC 4), *Zephyr* (PC 8), *Shamal* (PC 13), and *Tornado* (PC 14) were decommissioned and transferred to the U.S. Coast Guard in 2004–5 under a four-year loan program. Hull numbers for those vessels have changed from PC to WPC (see U.S. Navy entry under [PC] for data). Sister *Cyclone* (PC 1), transferred to the U.S. Coast Guard on 1-3-00, was stored at Curtis Bay, Maryland, and never reactivated; the ship was transferred to the Philippines on 6-3-03.

Tornado (WPC 14)—five of the class were commissioned into Coast Guard service during 2004. Details on the class can be found in the U.S. Navy patrol craft section USCG, 2004

♦ 0 (+ 58) 140-ft. Fast-Response Cutters (FRC A/B)

Bldr: Bollinger Shipyards, and VT Halter Marine (In serv. 2008–22)

WPC 1101 through WPC 1158

130-ft. Fast Response Cutter (FRC-A design)—computer rendering USCG, 2002

COAST GUARD PATROL CRAFT [WPC] *(continued)*

D: 400 tons (fl) **S:** 32 kts **Dim:** 42.6 × 9.5 × . . .
A: 1 30-mm Mk 46 AA; 2 12.7-mm mg
M: 4 . . . diesels; 2 props; 14,600 bhp **Range:** 4,230/.10 **Crew:** 15 + 4 passengers

Remarks: A component of the Project Deepwater contract of 24-6-02. Intended to replace the current 110-ft. patrol cutters for fishery patrols, law enforcement, maritime security, search and rescue, and national-defense operations. Will be fitted with a stern ramp for the launch and recovery of the crafts' RIB inspection and rescue boats. Each shipyard will build 29 boats. After seakeeping capabilities in the composite hull design were called into question, the program was divided into two variants in 2006. In 11-06 the Coast Guard issued a request for proposals to develop an alternative stop-gap design known as the "B" variant. Current plans call for 12 FRC-B cutters to be built. 46 FRC-A cutters will also be built once problems with the initial hull concept are ironed out. Data listed above refer to the FRC-A variant only.

♦ 1 Guardian 85-ft. class
Bldr: Guardian Marine, Tacoma, Wash. (In serv. 2002)

WPB 85201

WPB 85201—Guardian 85-ft. class Guardian Marine via M. Mazumdar, 2005

D: 105 tons (fl) **S:** 45 kts **Dim:** 25.91 × 7.01 × 1.67 **A:** Small arms
Electronics: 1 Furuno FR-8251 X-band nav.
M: 2 MTU-Detroit Diesel 12V4000 diesels; 2 props; 5,470 bhp
Electric: 64 kw tot. (2 × 32-kw Northern Lights Mod. M984K alternators)
Range: 1,700/13 **Endurance:** 7 days **Crew:** 6 total

Remarks: Ordered 1-3-02 for $4.65 million and is based at Vancouver, Washington. Delivered 6-9-02. The GRP planing hull was molded by ModuTech Marine, Tacoma, Washington. "Fast Patrol Craft" based on builder's 1999 privately funded design, of which one is now operated by the U.S. Navy. Eight others have been built for commercial use, six as tour boats, and two as personnel ferries. Has been seen with small RIB aft and 1–2 MG mounts forward.

♦ 49 Island class (110-ft. class) (†modernized under Project Deepwater/Non-operational as of 11-06)
Bldr: Bollinger Machine Shop & SY, Lockport, La.

	Laid down	L	In serv.	Based at:
WPB 1301 Farallon	. . .	27-8-85	21-2-86	Miami Beach, Fla.
WPB 1302 Manitou†	. . .	9-10-85	28-2-86	Key West, Fla.
WPB 1303 Matagorda†	. . .	15-12-85	25-4-86	Key West, Fla.
WPB 1304 Maui	. . .	13-1-86	9-5-86	Miami Beach, Fla.
WPB 1305 Monhegan†	. . .	15-2-86	16-6-86	Key West, Fla.
WPB 1306 Nunivak†	. . .	15-3-86	4-7-86	Key West, Fla.
WPB 1307 Ocracoke	. . .	12-4-86	4-8-86	San Juan, P.R.
WPB 1308 Vashon†	. . .	10-5-86	15-8-86	Key West, Fla.
WPB 1309 Aquidneck	. . .	14-6-86	26-9-86	Atlantic Beach, N.C.
WPB 1310 Mustang	. . .	11-7-86	29-8-86	Seward, Alaska
WPB 1311 Naushon	. . .	22-8-86	3-10-86	Ketchikan, Alaska
WPB 1312 Sanibel	. . .	3-10-86	14-11-86	Woods Hole, Mass.
WPB 1313 Edisto	. . .	21-11-86	7-1-87	San Diego, Calif.
WPB 1314 Sapelo	. . .	8-1-87	24-2-87	San Juan, P.R.
WPB 1315 Matinicus	. . .	26-2-87	16-4-87	San Juan, P.R.
WPB 1316 Nantucket	. . .	17-4-87	4-6-87	Key West, Fla.
WPB 1317 Attu†	4-5-87	4-12-87	9-5-88	Key West, Fla.
WPB 1318 Baranof	8-6-87	15-1-88	20-5-88	Miami Beach, Fla.
WPB 1319 Chandeleur	13-7-87	19-2-88	8-6-88	Miami Beach, Fla.
WPB 1320 Chincoteague	17-8-87	25-3-88	8-8-88	Key West, Fla.
WPB 1321 Cushing	21-9-87	29-4-88	8-8-88	San Juan, P.R.
WPB 1322 Cuttyhunk	26-10-87	3-6-88	15-10-88	Port Angeles, Wash.
WPB 1323 Drummond	23-11-87	8-7-88	19-10-88	Key West, Fla.
WPB 1324 Key Largo (ex-*Largo*)	1-1-88	12-8-88	24-12-88	Key West, Fla.
WPB 1325 Metomkin†	1-2-88	16-9-88	12-1-89	Key West, Fla.
WPB 1326 Monomoy	21-3-88	21-10-88	16-12-88	Woods Hole, Mass.
WPB 1327 Orcas	25-4-88	25-11-88	14-4-89	Coos Bay, Ore.
WPB 1328 Padre †	30-3-88	6-1-89	24-2-89	Key West, Fla.
WPB 1329 Sitkinak	4-7-88	10-2-89	31-3-89	Miami, Fla.
WPB 1330 Tybee	8-8-88	17-3-89	9-5-89	Woods Hole, Mass.
WPB 1331 Washington	12-9-88	21-4-89	1989	Honolulu, Hawaii
WPB 1332 Wrangell	17-10-88	26-5-89	24-6-89	Portland, Me.
WPB 1333 Adak	25-11-88	30-6-89	17-11-89	Sandy Hook, N.J.
WPB 1334 Liberty	26-12-88	4-8-89	22-9-89	Auke Bay, Alaska
WPB 1335 Anacapa	30-1-89	8-9-89	13-1-90	Petersburg, Alaska
WPB 1336 Kiska	6-3-89	13-10-89	1-12-89*	Hilo, Hawaii
WPB 1337 Assateague	10-4-89	17-11-89	1-1-90*	Honolulu, Hawaii
WPB 1338 Grand Isle	18-6-90	. . .	14-12-90*	Gloucester, Mass.
WPB 1339 Key Biscayne	16-7-90	. . .	27-4-91	St. Petersburg, Fla.
WPB 1340 Jefferson Island	20-8-90	. . .	17-4-91	Portland, Maine
WPB 1341 Kodiak Island	24-9-90	8-2-91	21-6-91	St. Petersburg, Fla.
WPB 1342 Long Island	29-10-90	19-3-91	27-8-91	Valdez, Alaska
WPB 1343 Bainbridge Island	1991	6-9-91	6-12-91*	Highlands, N.J.
WPB 1344 Block Island	14-1-91	. . .	19-7-91*	Atlantic Beach, N.C.
WPB 1345 Staten Island	18-2-91	. . .	23-8-91*	Atlantic Beach, N.C.
WPB 1346 Roanoke Island	25-3-91	. . .	27-9-91*	Homer, Alaska
WPB 1347 Pea Island	29-4-91	. . .	1-11-91*	St. Petersburg, Fla.
WPB 1348 Knight Island	1991	6-9-91	6-12-91*	St. Petersburg, Fla.
WPB 1349 Galveston Island	8-7-91	15-11-91	17-1-92*	Apra Harbor, Guam

* Delivery date vice commissioning date.

Tybee (WPB 1330) George R. Schneider, 4-04

Matagorda (WPB 1303) USCG, 2005

Matagorda (WPB 1303)—modernized and lengthened under Project Deepwater USCG, 2005

D: WPB 1301, 1304, 1309–1317: 117 tons light (165 fl); WPB 1318–1324, 1326, 1327, 1329–1337: 107 tons light (155 fl); WPB 1338–1349: 153 tons (fl); WPB 1302, 1303, 1305, 1306, 1308, 1317, 1325, and 1328: 176 tons (fl)
S: 29.7 kts (WPB 1338–1349: 28 kts); WPB 1302, 1303, 1305, 1306, 1308, 1317, 1325, and 1328: 27.5 kts

COAST GUARD PATROL CRAFT [WPC] *(continued)*

Tybee (WPB 1330) George R. Schneider, 4-04

Dim: 33.53 (37.49 for WPB 1302, 1303, 1305, 1306, 1308, 1317, 1325, and 1328) × 6.40 × 2.23 (max.)
A: 1 25-mm 87-cal. Mk 38 Bushmaster low-angle gun; 2 single 12.7-mm M2 mg
Electronics: Radar: 1 Raytheon SPS-64(V)1 or Hughes-Furuno SPS-73 nav.
M: WPB 1301–37: 2 Alco-Paxman Valenta 16 RP200-1 CM diesels; 2 props; 5,820 bhp (5,760 sust.); WPB 1338–1349: 2 Caterpillar 3516 diesels; 2 props; 5,460 bhp
Electric: 198 kw tot. (2 × 99-kw Caterpillar 3304T diesel-driven sets)
Range: 1,853 n.m. (26 kts × 24 hrs + 13.1 kts × 96 hrs); 3,380/8
Endurance: 5 days **Crew:** 2 officers, 2 CPO, 12 enlisted

Remarks: Fifteen ordered 8-84 from Marine Power & Equipment, Seattle, but award was contested by Bollinger and reassigned; 16th ordered 3-5-85. Sixteen more ordered 11-2-87 under Congressional Coast Defense Augmentation; five more ordered 24-2-87 under Drug Omnibus Act of 1987. WPB 1338–1349, ordered 26-12-89 under FY 90 with Navy funds. The 21 later units have minor improvements, including heavier bow plating, a better anchor, 300 gallon/day water generator added, and C.O.'s cabin relocated. Cost about $6.5 million each.

They were planned to be retired between 2004 and 2012, an unusually short lifespan for this type of craft in USCG service, but instead, under Project Deepwater, eight of class were lengthened during 2004–5 to 37.49 m overall through the addition of a RIB launch and recovery ramp section added at the stern; also upgraded were the crafts' command, control, communications, and search-and-rescue systems. Though initial plans called for all 49 of the class to receive the Project Deepwater modernizations, corrosion and cracks were discovered in several of the lengthened hulls and the effort was halted by 2006. All eight lengthened units were suspended from operations on 30-11-06.

Hull systems: Modified Vosper-Thornycroft design, with increased top hamper. Steel hull, aluminum deck and superstructure. Fin stabilizers fitted. Carry Loran-C and Omega receivers, IFF transponder, and SQN-18 echo sounder. Paxman engines governor-limited to 2,880 bhp each from nominal max. 4,000 bhp. Minimum speed is about 8 kts, making them difficult to employ in SAR and small boat towing. Several ships of the class were used to evaluate a GEC Alstom pulsed clutch that can produce continuous slow speeds down to 2.5 kts. Are now equipped with 5.59-m Zodiac 530 RIBs powered by a 60-bhp outboard engine; the RIBs equipped with a GPS receiver and an echo sounder.

Combat systems: Units through WPB 1337 were initially armed with a 20-mm 70-cal. Mk 67 AA gun, a weapon no longer supported by the U.S. Navy. The 25-mm chain gun had replaced all 20-mm weapons by the end of 1994.

PATROL BOATS [WPB]

The Deepwater contract also included two new Rigid-Hull Inflatable Boat classes, the water-jet powered 11-m, 45-kt capable "Long Range Interceptor," and the 7-m water-jet powered, 33-knot capable "Short-Range Prosecutor." The larger interceptor will have an enclosed pilothouse and will mount at least one 12.7-mm mg.

♦ 65 Marine Protector-class (87-ft-class) Coastal Patrol Boats

Bldr: Bollinger Shipyards, Lockport, La.

	L	Delivered	Comm.	Based at:
WPB 87301 Barracuda	1-9-97	7-4-98	24-4-98	Eureka, Calif.
WPB 87302 Hammerhead	11-5-98	29-7-98	16-10-98	Woods Hole, Mass.
WPB 87303 Mako	29-6-98	9-9-98	11-12-98	Cape May, N.J.
WPB 87304 Marlin	3-8-98	2-12-98	22-1-99	Ft. Myers, Fla.
WPB 87305 Stingray	2-9-98	12-1-99	13-1-99	Mobile, Ala.
WPB 87306 Dorado	7-12-98	23-2-99	23-4-99	Crescent City, Calif.
WPB 87307 Osprey	18-1-99	6-4-99	19-6-99	Port Townsend, Wash.
WPB 87308 Chinook	1-3-99	18-5-99	19-5-99	New London, Conn.
WPB 87309 Albacore	6-4-99	29-6-99	20-8-99	Little Creek, Va.
WPB 87310 Tarpon	18-5-99	10-8-99	22-10-99	Tybee Isl., Ga.
WPB 87311 Cobia	15-6-99	7-9-99	29-10-99	Mobile, Ala.
WPB 87312 Hawksbill	27-7-99	5-10-99	7-1-00	Oceanside, Calif.
WPB 87313 Cormorant	24-8-99	2-11-99	10-12-99	Ft. Pierce, Fla.
WPB 87314 Finback	21-9-99	30-11-99	13-1-00	Cape May, N.J.
WPB 87315 Amberjack	19-10-99	28-12-99	25-1-00	Port Isabel, Tex.
WPB 87316 Kittiwake	16-11-99	25-1-00	30-6-00	Niwiliwilli, Hi.
WPB 87317 Blackfin	14-12-99	22-2-00	4-5-00	Santa Barbara, Calif.
WPB 87318 Bluefin	11-1-00	21-3-00	27-4-00	Ft. Pierce, Fla.
WPB 87319 Yellowfin	8-2-00	18-4-00	12-6-00	Charleston, S.C.
WPB 87320 Manta	8-3-00	17-6-00	31-7-00	Freeport, Tex.
WPB 87321 Coho	4-4-00	13-6-00	13-6-00	Panama City, Fla.
WPB 87322 Kingfisher	5-6-00	11-7-00	11-7-00	Mayport, Fla.
WPB 87323 Seahawk	30-5-00	8-9-00	8-9-00	Clearwater, Fla.
WPB 87324 Steelhead	27-6-00	5-9-00	13-12-00	Port Aransas, Tex.
WPB 87325 Beluga	25-7-00	3-10-00	21-11-00	Little Creek, Va.
WPB 87326 Blacktip	22-8-00	1-11-00	1-2-01	Oxnard, Calif.
WPB 87327 Pelican	18-9-00	29-11-00	8-1-01	Morgan City, La.
WPB 87328 Ridley	17-10-00	27-12-00	23-3-01	Moriches, N.Y.
WPB 87329 Cochito	14-11-00	24-1-01	24-3-01	Little Creek, Va.
WPB 87330 Manowar	13-12-00	20-2-01	31-3-01	Galveston, Tex.
WPB 87331 Moray	16-1-00	20-3-01	4-5-01	Jonesport, Maine
WPB 87332 Razorbill	6-2-00	17-4-01	30-5-01	Gulfport, Miss.
WPB 87333 Adelie	6-3-01	15-5-01	17-8-01	Port Angeles, Wash.
WPB 87334 Gannet	3-4-01	12-6-01	28-7-01	Corpus Christi, Tx.
WPB 87335 Narwhal	1-5-01	10-7-01	2-11-01	Cape Canaveral, Fla.
WPB 87336 Sturgeon	29-5-01	7-8-01	28-9-01	Grand Isle, La.
WPB 87337 Sockeye	26-6-01	4-9-01	14-1-02	Bodega Bay, Calif.
WPB 87338 Ibis	24-7-01	3-10-01	7-12-01	Cape May, N.J.
WPB 87339 Pompano	28-8-01	31-10-01	14-12-01	Gulfport, Miss.
WPB 87340 Halibut	18-9-01	27-11-01	26-4-02	Marina Del Ray, Calif.
WPB 87341 Bonito	16-10-01	20-12-01	20-2-02	Pensacola, Fla.
WPB 87342 Shrike	13-11-01	23-1-02	6-4-02	Cape Canaveral, Fla.
WPB 87343 Tern	11-12-01	20-2-02	20-2-02	San Francisco, Calif.
WPB 87344 Heron	8-1-02	19-3-02	17-5-02	Sabine, Tex.
WPB 87345 Wahoo	5-2-02	16-4-02	9-8-02	Port Angeles, Wash.
WPB 87346 Flyingfish	5-3-02	14-5-02	1-8-02	Boston, Mass.
WPB 87347 Haddock	2-4-02	11-6-02	20-9-02	San Diego, Calif.
WPB 87348 Brant	30-4-02	9-7-02	18-9-02	Corpus Christi, Tx.
WPB 87349 Shearwater	28-5-02	7-8-02	5-10-02	Portsmouth, Va.
WPB 87350 Petrel	25-6-02	3-9-02	28-5-03	San Diego, Calif.
WPB 87352 Sea Lion	15-7-03	23-9-03	18-11-04	Staten Island, N.Y.
WPB 87353 Skipjack	12-8-03	7-10-03	16-12-03	Galveston, Tex.
WPB 87354 Dolphin	9-9-03	4-11-03	13-1-04	Miami, Fla.
WPB 87355 Hawk	7-10-03	16-12-03	7-6-04	St. Petersburg, Fla.
WPB 87356 Sailfish	30-12-03	9-3-04	3-6-04	Sandy Hook, N.J.
WPB 87357 Sawfish	27-1-04	5-4-04	22-5-04	Key West, Fla.
WPB 87358 Swordfish	27-12-04	8-3-05	23-7-05	Port Angeles, Wash.
WPB 87359 Tiger Shark	. . .	5-4-05	11-7-05	Newport, R.I.
WPB 87360 Blue Shark	. . .	30-5-05	16-8-05	Everett, Wash.
WPB 87361 Sea Horse	. . .	31-5-05	7-9-05	Portsmouth, Va.
WPB 87362 Sea Otter	. . .	28-6-05	13-10-05	San Diego, Calif.
WPB 87363 Manatee	. . .	26-7-05	14-10-05	Ingleside, Tex.
WPB 87364 Ahi (ex-*Diamond Back*)	. . .	23-8-05	30-8-05	Honolulu, Hi.
WPB 87365 Pike (ex-*Alligator*)	. . .	20-9-05	20-9-05	San Francisco, Calif.
WPB 87366 Terrapin (ex-*Crocodile*)	. . .	18-8-05	18-10-05	Bellingham, Wash.

Blue Shark (WPB 87360) U.S. Navy, 7-05

Hawksbill (WPB 87312) Frank Findler, 10-03

COAST GUARD PATROL BOATS [WPB] *(continued)*

Pelican (WPB 87327) George R. Schneider, 10-04

D: 91.1 tons (fl) **S:** 27 kts (25 sust.) **Dim:** 26.52 (24.87 pp) × 5.92 × 1.74
A: 2 single 12.7-mm M2 mg **Electronics:** Radar: 1 Hughes-Furuno SPS-73 nav.
M: 2 MTU 8V396 TE94 diesels; 2 5-bladed props; 2,950 bhp (2,680 bhp sust.)
Electric: 120 kw tot. (2 × 60-kw Stamford sets, 2 M.A.N. D 0824 LF01 diesel-driven)
Range: 882/10 **Fuel:** 2,500 gal. **Endurance:** 10 days (5 days' provisions)
Crew: 10 tot. (accomm. for 11 tot.)

Remarks: Originally to have been known as the "Endangered Species" class, with the first to have been named *Condor,* and later the "Marine Species" class, but the name source has been changed to sea creatures (fish and birds). Contract for design and construction of the prototype for $8.9 million was let in 3-96; six more were ordered 15-8-97; hulls 8 and 9 on 4-3-98, and 10 through 22 on 1-11-98, and eight more early in 1999 (with an option for 19 additional). The eighth and later units have design improvements based on tests with WPB 87301. The nonceremonial launches are performed by a crane. Average cost is about $3.5 million. Projected launch and delivery dates and intended bases listed may change. WPB 87351 was ordered for Malta on 30-7-01 and delivered on 15-11-02. During 5-02 it was announced that an additional 13 would be ordered under the "Sea Marshall" program for homeland defense; funding for the first four was approved in the FY 03 budget and five more were requested in FY 04.
Hull systems: Patrol speed is more than 10 kts and minimum speed on one engine is 4 kts. Hull form based on Netherlands builder Damen's STANPAT 2600 design, which was employed on a number of Hong Kong police patrol boats built since 1980. Steel hull construction with Russian-made extruded aluminum panel superstructure. Use a stern ramp to launch and recover a 4.6-m aluminum-construction rigid inflatable Ambar AM 550-CPB inspection/rescue boat in seas up to 2.5-m high; the launch is powered by a 100-bhp Yanmar diesel driving a North American Marine Jet waterjet for 30 kt top speeds. Have integrated pilothouse with radar, echo sounder, GPS receiver, and other sensors linked to a central Sperry Electronic Chart Display & Information System (ECDIS). Tankage for 1,500 liters potable water, with 750 liter/day distillation capacity. Are able to operate safely in water as shallow as two meters and can maneuver at 4 kts. Are considered safe to operate in seas up to 9 m high. Crew have four two-person and one three-person staterooms. A 250 gal./day reverse osmosis water desalinization and purification system is installed, and tanks hold 1,500 liters of potable water.

♦ 44 25-ft. Transportable Port Security Boats
Bldr: Boston Whaler, Edgewater, Fla. (In serv. 1996–99)

25300-series

25-ft. Transportable Port Security Boat Edward McDonnell, 2004

D: 1.622 tons light (3 tons fl) **S:** 40 kts **Dim:** 7.50 × 2.45 × 0.41 (hull)
A: 1 12.7-mm mg; 2 single 7.62-mm M60 mg
Electronics: Radar: 1 Raytheon 2400 or RL70RC nav.
M: 2 Cummins diesel outboards; 380 bhp **Range:** . . . / . . . **Fuel:** 655 liters
Endurance: 5 days **Crew:** 3 or 4 tot. (accomm. for 10)

Remarks: All are of builder's Guardian design. Eleven were in service as of 1998, and another 33 were ordered 7-98 for use as Transportable Port Security Boats by six Port Security Units based at coastal cities in the U.S. Foam-core, unsinkable GRP hull construction. Have night vision device, differential GPS, and encrypted radios. Can carry up to 12 persons. The 33 units ordered in 1998 had the later-model RL70RC radar; the original 11 built had 150-bhp gasoline outboard engines.

AUXILIARIES

♦ 1 Mackinaw-class lake icebreaker [WAGB]
Bldr: Marinette Marine Corp., Marinette, Wisc.

	Laid down	L	Comm.
WLBB 30 Mackinaw	18-12-02	2-4-05	10-6-06

Mackinaw (WLBB 30) USCG, 1-06

D: 3,500 tons (fl) **S:** 15 kts **Dim:** 73.15 × 18.28 × 4.88
Electronics: Radar: . . .
M: Diesel-electric: 3 Caterpillar . . . diesels (4,200 hp each); 2 azimuthal prop pods (9,140 hp)
Crew: 46 tot.

Remarks: In the FY 99 budget, Congress provided $5.3 million toward the design of a replacement for the *Mackinaw* (WAGB 83); the contract was let on 16-10-01 for $82,474,830. The ship, which will be much less powerful than its predecessor, will be able to operate for 185 days of the year and is configured for use as a navigational aids tender during the nonwinter seasons. Intended to be able to break 32-in layered ice at 3 kts and also to be used for law-enforcement, environmental protection, and national security missions. Assistance with hull design is being provided by Kvaerner Masa Marine and Masa-Yards Arctic Technology Center in Finland and Sweden.

Disposal note: The older *Mackinaw*-class lake icebreaker (290-ft. class) *Mackinaw* (WAGB 83) was retired during 6-06 and replaced by WLBB 30.

♦ 1 Healy-class polar icebreaker [WAGB]
Bldr: Avondale Industries, New Orleans, La.

	Laid down	L	Del.	Comm.	Based at:
WAGB 20 Healy	16-9-96	15-11-97	10-11-99	8-00	Seattle, Wash.

Healy (WAGB 20) USCG, 6-05

Healy (WAGB 20) U.S. Navy, 8-05

COAST GUARD AUXILIARIES *(continued)*

D: 17,170 tons (fl) **S:** 17 kts (12.5 kts cruise)
Dim: 128.02 (121.23 pp) × 24.99 × 8.91
A: 2 single 12.7-mm M2 mg; 1 or 2 HH-65A Dolphin helicopters
Electronics:
Radar: 1 . . . nav.; 1. . . surf. search
Sonar: MultiBeam Type 2112 hydrographic mapping set
TACAN: URN-25
M: Diesel-electric: 4 Sulzer-Westinghouse 12 ZA40S medium-speed diesels (10,600-bhp each); 4 8,000-kw, 6,600-volt main alternators, 2 motors; 2 fixed-pitch, 4.88-m-dia. props; 30,000 shp—2000-ship bow-thruster
Electric: 1,500-kw harbor set **Range:** 16,000/12.5; 37,000/9.25
Fuel: 3,400 tons, plus 120 tons aviation fuel **Endurance:** 180 days
Crew: 67 ship's company + 35 scientific party (accomm. for 75 USCG, 50 science party)

Remarks: $274.8 million was authorized and appropriated under the FY 90 navy budget to pay for a new Coast Guard icebreaker; another $62 million was added by Congress under FY 92. Bids requested 13-3-91, but the bidding was canceled 16-3-92 after no yard bid within the available funds. A second round of bidding resulted in a contract signed 16-7-93 for $232 million. A planned second unit was omitted from the FY 92 budget. Named for Michael M. Healy, a pioneering nineteenth-century Revenue Service officer in Alaskan waters.
Hull systems: Capable of breaking 1.4-m ice at 3 kts continuous or 2.4-m ice by backing and ramming. Conventional icebreaker hull not incorporating modern icebreaking technologies. Framing at 15-inch spacing. Has five laboratories totaling 377 m^2, four cranes, LCVP-type landing craft to port. Two 40-ft. equipment vans can be carried in lieu of two of the boats. The engines are mounted on the main deck. Alstom Drives and Controls (formerly Cegelec Projects, Rugby, U.K.), provided engineering and propulsion system integration. All accommodations are in the superstructure, with all cabins having outside ports. Heating by conventional boilers. Has liquid tank-type stabilization system and liquid bow-wash system to lubricate the hull during icebreaking. Fitted with integrated navigations system (electronic charts, autopilot, and GPS) and a dynamic positioning system.

♦ 2 Polar Star–class polar icebreakers (399-ft. class) [WAGB]
Bldr: Lockheed SB, Seattle, Wash.

	Laid down	L	In serv.	Based at:
WAGB 10 POLAR STAR	15-5-72	17-11-73	19-1-76	Seattle, Wash.
WAGB 11 POLAR SEA	27-11-73	24-6-75	23-2-78	Seattle, Wash.

Polar Star (WAGB 10) Chris Sattler, 2-06

Polar Sea (WAGB 11) USCG, 1-02

D: 10,863 tons (13,623 fl) **S:** 15 kts **Dim:** 121.91 (102.78 pp) × 25.45 × 1.14
A: Provision for 2 single 12.7-mm mg; 2 helicopters
Electronics:
Radar: 2 Raytheon SPS-64(V)-series nav.
TACAN: SRN-15
M: CODAG: 6 Alco 16V251 diesels, 3,000 bhp each; 3 Pratt & Whitney FT-4A12 gas turbines, 25,000 shp each, down-rated; electric drive; 3 CP props; 75,000 shp (66,000 shp sust.)
Range: 16,000/18; 28,275/13 **Fuel:** 3,555 tons
Endurance: 38 days at full power; 14 months' provisions
Crew: 14 officers, 128 enlisted + helo detachment of 4 officers, 8 enlisted + up to 30 scientists

Remarks: Scientific facilities upgraded in WAGB 10 in 1990–91 and in WAGB 11 during 1992–93. WAGB 11 reached North Pole in company with Canadian Coast Guard's *Louis S. St. Laurent* on 26-7-94, breaking ice up to 12 ft. thick.
Hull systems: Can break 2-m ice at 3 knots, 6.4-m ice maximum by ramming. Propulsion plant completely cross-connected and automatic. Two 15-ton cranes. Can carry 400 tons general stores (600 m^3). Fuel capacity is 1,345,168 gallons diesel and 45,981 gallons aviation JP-5, while 22,684 gallons lube oil and 26,586 gallons portable water can be accommodated. Carry two Packman-class 34-ft. aluminum landing craft as tenders.

♦ 16 Juniper-class seagoing buoy tenders [WAGL]
Bldr: Marinette Marine Corp., Marinette, Wisc.

	Laid down	L	Del.	In serv.	Based at:
WLB 201 JUNIPER	2-5-94	24-6-95	14-1-96	5-7-96	Newport, R.I.
WLB 202 WILLOW	3-9-95	15-6-96	29-11-96	10-4-97	Newport, R.I.
WLB 203 KUKUI	4-12-96	3-5-97	9-10-97	1-1-98	Honolulu, Hi.
WLB 204 ELM	10-7-97	24-1-98	29-6-98	20-11-98	Atlantic Beach, N.C.
WLB 205 WALNUT	16-2-98	22-8-98	22-2-99	12-7-99	Honolulu, Hi.
WLB 206 SPAR	15-12-99	12-8-00	9-3-01	3-8-01	Kodiak, Alaska
WLB 207 MAPLE	20-3-00	16-12-00	21-6-01	19-10-01	Sitka, Alaska
WLB 208 ASPEN	. . .	21-4-01	28-9-01	12-01	San Francisco, Calif.
WLB 209 SYCAMORE	29-1-01	28-7-01	1-3-02	2-7-02	Cordova, Alaska
WLB 210 CYPRESS	23-4-01	29-10-01	24-6-02	11-10-02	Mobile, Ala.
WLB 211 OAK	30-7-01	26-1-02	17-10-02	7-3-03	Charleston, S.C.
WLB 212 HICKORY	19-11-01	11-5-02	6-3-03	3-7-03	Homer, Alaska
WLB 213 FIR	18-3-02	17-8-02	5-6-03	8-11-03	Astoria, Ore.
WLB 214 HOLLYHOCK (ex-WLB 215)	. . .	25-1-03	15-10-03	30-4-04	Port Huron, Mich.
WLB 215 SEQUOIA (ex-WLB 214)	12-7-02	23-8-03	4-3-04	10-04	Apra Harbor, Guam
WLB 216 ALDER	. . .	2-2-04	2-9-04	10-6-05	Duluth, Minn.

Cypress (WLB 210) George R. Schneider, 9-05

Fir (WLB 213) W. Michael Young, 9-03

D: 2,000 tons (fl) **S:** 15 kts **Dim:** 68.58 (62.79 pp) × 14.02 × 3.96
A: Provision for: 1 25-mm 87-cal. Mk 38 Bushmaster low-angle gun
Electronics: Radar: 2 Decca BridgeMaster E 340 ARPA nav.
M: 2 Caterpillar 3608 TA diesels; 1 4-bladed CP prop; 6,200 bhp—460-shp bow-thruster—550-shp stern-thruster

COAST GUARD AUXILIARIES *(continued)*

Electric: 1,950 kw tot. (2 × 450-kw Caterpillar 3508 diesel sets, 1 × 800-kw reduction gear-driven, 1 × 250-kw Caterpillar 3406 diesel emergency set)
Range: 6,000/12 **Endurance:** 45 days **Crew:** 6 officers, 34 enlisted

Remarks: Intended to perform navigational buoy tender, environmental cleanup, search and rescue, and law enforcement duties. First unit (with option for four more) ordered 28-1-94; second in 7-94. A second pair was authorized under FY 94, with the third unit ordered 1-95 and the fourth and fifth during 3-96. WLB 206 and 207 were ordered 4-9-98, and WLB 208 and 209 were funded in the FY 99 budget (for $72.6 million total) and ordered 12-2-99. WLB 215 and 216 were ordered on 27-11-01. The first five ships are considered the "A" group and the remainder the "B" group, with minor modifications to piping runs, equipment locations, etc. All are named for previous buoy tenders named for trees, except for WLB 206, which commemorates the 10,000 World War II–era USCG women's volunteer group, the SPARs (Semper Paratus Always Ready) and WLB 214, which is named for a herbaceous plant. The builder became a subsidiary of the Manitowoc Marine Group on 20-11-00. Funds to provide 25-mm guns for these ships were requested as a supplement to the FY 03 budget. The hull numbers and intended home ports of WLB 214 and WLB 215 were exchanged on 3-6-02.
Hull systems: Capable of breaking 0.35 m freshwater ice continuously at 3 kts or 1.1 m ice by ramming. A Nautronix ASK 4000 dynamic positioning system and bridge-controlled engines are employed. Navigational aids include Sperry SRD 500 dual-axis speed log and Sperry Mk 27 gyrocompass. Have a 20-ton/18-m reach buoy crane, 2,875-ft.^{2} working deck, and the ability to handle buoys in 8-ft. seas. Deck equipment includes four hydraulic winches and a continuous in-haul chain-handling winch, two anchor winches, and three mooring winches; there is a stern anchor. Capable of towing. Are being equipped with 6.86-m Zodiac Hurricane 630 RIBs powered by a 135-bhp Volvo Penta outdrive engine and equipped with GPS receivers and an echo sounder; the craft can carry 1,122 kg of cargo and 11 personnel.

Disposal notes: Of the *Balsam*-class seagoing buoy tenders, *Acacia* (WLB 406) was decommissioned on 7-6-06. *Evergreen* (WLB 295) was converted to oceanographic research ship and later used as a patrol ship and stricken. *Citrus* (ex-WLB 300) served as a medium-endurance cutter (WMEC 300) from 1979 to 1994, when stricken and later transferred to the Dominican Republic. *Blackthorn* (WLB 391) was rammed and sunk on 28-1-80. *Sagebrush* (WLB 399) was "declared excess" on 26-4-88, and *Mesquite* (WLB 305) went aground 5-12-89 in the Great Lakes and was declared a total loss. *Salvia* (WLB 400) was declared excess on 12-4-91. *Blackhaw* (WLB 390) was declared excess 26-2-93 and cannibalized; the hulk is now used by the Navy as a salvage training device. *Iris* (WLB 296) was declared excess on 20-6-95, *Sorrel* (WLB 296) on 28-6-96 (now operated by the Sea Scouts), *Spar* (WLB 403) on 28-2-97, and *Mallow* (WLB 395) on 24-5-97. *Bittersweet* (WLB 389) was declared excess 18-8-97 and transferred to Estonia on 5-9-97. *Hornbeam* (WLB 394) was declared excess 30-10-98 and stricken 30-9-99. *Basswood* (WLB 388) was stricken on 4-9-98, *Planetree* (WLB 307) on 31-3-99, *Pawpaw* (WLB 308) on 23-7-99, and *Laurel* (WLB 291) on 10-12-99. *Mariposa* (WLB 397) was stricken on 31-3-00 (transferred to the Navy on 17-4-00 for use as a damage-control training platform); *Conifer* (WLB 301) on 21-7-00; *Ironwood* (WLB 297) on 6-10-00; and *Woodrush* (WLB 407) on 28-4-01 (and transferred to Ghana on 4-5-01); *Buttonwood* (WLB 306) on 28-6-01 (donated to the Dominican Republic); and *Sweetbrier* (WLB 401) on 27-8-01 (and transferred to Ghana on 26-10-01). *Sweetgum* (WLB 309) was retired on 15-2-02 and transferred to Panama, and *Madrona* (WLB 302) was stricken on 12-4-02 and was transferred to El Salvador on the same date. *Cowslip* (WLB 277; previously stricken on 23-3-73, sold during 1976, repurchased 19-1-81, and recommissioned 9-11-81) was stricken on 11-12-02 and transferred to Nigeria on 26-1-03. *Sedge* (WLB 402) was decommissioned on 15-11-02 and transferred to Nigeria on 31-12-02. *Bramble* (WLB 392) was decommissioned 22-5-03 and turned into a museum. *Firebush* (WLB 393) was stricken 10-6-03 and transferred to Nigeria. *Sundew* (WLB 404) was authorized for transfer to historical foundation in 2003. *Sassafrass* (WLB 401) was decommissioned 31-10-03 and transferred to Nigeria.

♦ 14 Keeper-class coastal buoy tenders [WAGL]

Bldr: Marinette Marine Corp., Marinette, Wisc.

	Laid down	L	Del.	In serv.	Based at:
WLM 551 Ida Lewis	18-12-94	14-10-95	1-11-96	11-4-97	Newport, R.I.
WLM 552 Katherine Walker	18-1-96	14-9-96	27-6-97	1-11-97	Bayonne, N.J.
WLM 553 Abbie Burgess *(ex-Abigail Burgess)*	12-4-96	5-4-97	19-9-97	31-7-98	Rockland, Maine
WLM 554 Marcus Hanna	31-10-96	23-8-97	26-11-97	19-5-98	S. Portland, Maine
WLM 555 James Rankin	25-4-97	25-4-98	25-4-98	1-5-99	Baltimore, Md.
WLM 556 Joshua Appleby	24-11-97	8-8-98	25-11-98	7-5-99	St. Petersburg, Fla
WLM 557 Frank Drew	9-2-98	5-12-98	17-6-99	5-4-00	Portsmouth, Va.
WLM 558 Anthony Petit	...	30-1-99	1-7-99	18-5-00	Ketchikan, Alaska
WLM 559 Barbara Mabrity	2-5-98	27-3-99	29-7-99	2000	Mobile, Ala.
WLM 560 William Tate	...	8-5-99	16-9-99	3-6-00	Philadelphia, Pa.
WLM 561 Harry Claiborne	...	12-6-99	28-10-99	31-3-00	Galveston, Tex.
WLM 562 Maria Bray	...	28-8-99	6-4-00	26-7-00	Mayport, Fla.
WLM 563 Henry Blake	12-1-99	20-11-99	22-6-00	12-10-00	Seattle, Wash.
WLM 564 George Cobb	...	18-12-99	...	27-10-00	San Pedro, Calif.

D: 845 tons (fl) **S:** 12 kts **Dim:** 53.34 (47.24 pp) × 10.97 × 2.42
Electronics: Radar: 1 Raytheon SPS-64(V)1 or Hughes-Furuno SPS-73 nav.
M: 2 Caterpillar 3508 TA diesels; 2 Ulstein Model 1350H Z-drive azimuth props; 1,998 bhp (1,710 sust.)—400-shp bow-thruster
Electric: 750 kw tot. (3 × 250-kw sets, Caterpillar 3406 DIT diesels driving)
Range: 2,000/10 **Fuel:** 40 tons **Crew:** 1 officer, 17 enlisted + 6 passengers

Harry Claiborne (WLM 561) George R. Schneider, 9-05

George Cobb (WLM 564) W. Michael Young, 1-04

Katherine Walker (WLM 552) Edward McDonnell, 2005

Remarks: Lead ship ordered 22-6-93 for $22 million, with option for 13 more. WLM 552–556 were ordered 1-97 for $73 million total, and WLM 557–564 were ordered during 9-97. Intended to perform aids to navigation maintenance, marine environmental protection, search-and-rescue, national defense and economic exclusion zone patrol, and icebreaking duties. Crew listed is maximum; most currently operate with one officer and 14 enlisted. The builder became a subsidiary of the Manitowoc Marine Group on 20-11-00.
Hull systems: Intended to be able to break 23 mm of freshwater ice at 3 kts and 46 mm of freshwater ice by ramming. Have a 10-ton capacity, 12.8-m reach hydraulic crane forward, with a 3.75-ton auxiliary lift capacity. The ships are also able to operate an oil-skimming and recovery system. Have a hydraulic windlass with two capstans forward, one electric capstan aft, plus hydraulic buoy-hauling winches on the working deck forward. The VOOS (Vessel Of Opportunity System), depot-maintained oil-spill recovery system is employed, with outriggers, floats, containment booms, and Weir skimmer pumps being prepositioned at 12 East Coast, six West Coast, and one Hawaiian port; the equipment can also be employed by available small commercial ships such as trawlers, and the recovered oil is stowed in collapsible barges. Are being equipped with 5.59-m Zodiac 530 rigid-inflatable boats powered by a 60-bhp outboard engine; the craft will be equipped with a GPS receiver and an echo sounder.

Disposal note: The last active *White*-class (133-ft. class) coastal buoy tender, *White Sumac* (WLM 540; ex-YF 416), was stricken on 2-8-02 and transferred to the Dominican Republic.

♦ 9 Katmai Bay–class (140-ft. class) icebreaking seagoing tugs [WATA]

Bldrs: WTGB 107, 109: Bay City Marine, Tacoma, Wash.; others: Tacoma Boatbuilding, Tacoma, Wash.

	Laid down	L	In serv.	Based at:
WTGB 101 Katmai Bay	7-11-77	8-4-78	8-1-79	Sault St. Marie, Mich.
WTGB 102 Bristol Bay	13-2-78	22-7-78	5-4-79	Detroit, Mich.
WTGB 103 Mobile Bay	13-2-78	11-11-78	6-5-79	Sturgeon Bay, Wisc.
WTGB 104 Biscayne Bay	29-8-78	3-2-79	8-12-79	St. Ignace, Mich.
WTGB 105 Neah Bay	6-8-79	2-2-80	18-8-80	Cleveland, Ohio
WTGB 106 Morro Bay	6-8-79	11-7-80	25-1-81	New London, Conn.
WTGB 107 Penobscot Bay	1-7-83	27-7-84	2-1-85	Bayonne, N.J.
WTGB 108 Thunder Bay	20-7-84	15-8-85	4-11-85	Rockland, Maine
WTGB 109 Sturgeon Bay	9-7-86	12-9-87	0-8-88	Bayonne, N.J.

COAST GUARD AUXILIARIES *(continued)*

Penobscot Bay (WTGB 107) Edward McDonnell, 2005

Sturgeon Bay (WTGB 109) USCG, 1-03

D: 662 tons (fl) **S:** 14.7 kts **Dim:** 42.67 (39.62 pp) × 11.43 × 3.66
Electronics: Radar: 1 Raytheon SPS-64(V)1 or Hughes-Furuno SPS-73 nav.
M: 2 Fairbanks-Morse 38D8$^1/_8$ diesels, Westinghouse electric drive; 1 prop; 2,500 shp
Electric: 250 kw tot. (2 × 125 kw) **Range:** 1,800/14.7; 4,000/12 **Fuel:** 71 tons
Crew: 3 officers, 14 enlisted

Remarks: Initially intended to replace the older WYTMs in service. WTGB 109 was ordered on 11-2-86, using Navy funds; at least one more was planned, to be named *Curtis Bay,* but funds were not available. Reclassified from WYTM on 5-2-79. *Morro Bay* (WTGB 106) was laid up on 30-9-98 for lack of operating funds; the ship was refitted at Curtis Bay for reactivation, completing during 1-01, but then again laid up until late in 2001 when she was again reactivated; she was formally recommissioned on 25-11-02 and is based at New London, Connecticut, as a training ship for the Coast Guard Academy and to provide icebreaking services from New York harbor to Maine in the winter, as needed.
Hull systems: Displace 673 tons in fresh water. Can break .51-m ice continuously, or 1.8-m ice by backing and ramming. Have portable bubble-generator system housed in a removable deckhouse on the fantail. Two firefighting monitors atop the pilothouse, which provides near 360-degree viewing. One 2-ton crane handles a 4.9-m plastic workboat. All are now equipped with a 5.59-m Zodiac Hurricane 530 RIB powered by a 60-bhp outboard and equipped with GPS receiver and an echo sounder.
WTGB 102 and 103 operate with 45.72 × 18.29–m aids-to-navigation barges 12001 and 12002, respectively; crewed by seven personnel each, the barges were delivered in 7-91 and 4-92 by Marinette Marine, Marinette, Wisconsin, and are equipped with a 20-ton crane, machine shop, paint locker, bridge/pilothouse, bow-thruster, and indented sterns to permit pushing by another vessel; seven crew.

Disposal note: *Balsam*-class training ship *Gentian* (WIX 290) was decommissioned on 23-6-06.

♦ 1 German Horst Wessel–class sail-training cutter [WAXT]
Bldr: Blohm + Voss, Hamburg, Germany

	L	Based at:
WIX 327 EAGLE (ex-*Horst Wessel*)	13-6-36	New London, Conn.

D: 1,519 tons light (1,816 fl) **S:** 17 kts (10 under power)
Dim: 89.92 (70.41 wl) × 11.92 × 5.18
Electronics: Radar: 1 Raytheon SPS-64(V)1 nav.
M: 1 Caterpillar D-399, V-16 diesel; 1 prop; 1,000 bhp (10 kts); 1,983 m^2 sail area
Electric: 450 kw **Range:** 5,450/7.5 (diesel) **Fuel:** 79 tons
Crew: 19 officers, 46 enlisted, 175 cadets and instructors

Remarks: Training ship at the Coast Guard Academy. Sisters operate in the Portuguese Navy and Russian merchant marine. Has 344 tons fixed ballast. Mast heights: foremast and mainmast: 45.8 m, mizzen: 40.2 m.

Eagle (WIX 327) A. A. de Kruijf, 7-05

Eagle (WIX 327) Martin Mokrus, 6-05

SERVICE CRAFT

♦ 1 Buckthorn-class inland buoy tender [WYGL]
Bldr: Mobile Ship Repair, Mobile, Ala.

	Laid down	L	In serv.	Based at:
WLI 642 BUCKTHORN	1962	. . .	17-7-64	Sault Ste. Marie, Mich.

Buckthorn (WLI 642) Victor M. Baca, 1991

D: 188 tons (196 fl) **S:** 11.9 kts **Dim:** 30.48 (29.26 pp) × 7.32 × 1.42
M: 2 Caterpillar diesels; 2 props; 600 bhp **Range:** 1,300/11.9; 2,000/7.3
Crew: 1 warrant officer, 13 enlisted

Remarks: Bow rectangular at main deck. Has one 5-ton boom.

♦ 2 Bayberry-class (65-ft. class) inland buoy tenders [WYGL]
Bldr: Reliable Welding Works, Olympia, Wash. (L: 2-6-54; In serv. 28-6-54)

	Based at:
WLI 65400 BAYBERRY	Seattle, Wash.
WLI 65401 ELDERBERRY	Petersburg, Alaska

COAST GUARD SERVICE CRAFT *(continued)*

Bayberry (WLI 65400)—note blunt bow form Hartmut Ehlers, 5-99

D: 68 tons (71 fl) **S:** 11.3 kts **Dim:** 19.91 × 5.18 × 1.32
M: 2 G.M. 6-71 diesels; 2 props; 400 bhp
Range: 800/11.3; 1,700/6 **Crew:** 5 tot.

♦ 1 Blackberry-class (65300 class) inland buoy tender [WYGL]

Bldr: Dubuque Boat & Boiler Co., Dubuque, Iowa (In serv. 24-8-46)

WLI 65303 Blackberry

D: 50 tons light (68 fl) **S:** 9 kts **Dim:** 19.81 (19.20 pp) × 5.18 × 1.07
M: 1 G.M. diesel; 1 prop; 220 bhp **Range:** 700/9; 1,500/5 **Crew:** 5 tot.

Remarks: Based at Long Beach, North Carolina. Sister *Chokeberry* (WLI 65304) was retired on 31-7-00.

♦ 1 Cosmos-class (100-ft. class) inland buoy tender [WYGL]

Bldr: Birchfield Boiler Co., Tacoma, Wash.

	Laid down	L	In serv.	Based at:
WLI 313 Bluebell	20-3-44	28-9-44	24-3-45	Portland, Ore.

Bluebell (WLI 313) George R. Schneider, 11-93

D: 153 tons light (178 fl) **S:** 10.5 kts **Dim:** 30.48 (29.26 pp) × 7.49 × 1.62
M: 2 Waukesha diesels; 2 props; 600 bhp **Range:** 1,400/10.5; 2,700/7
Crew: 1 warrant officer, 14 enlisted

Remarks: Four sisters retyped WLIC on 1-10-79, of which *Smilax* (WLIC 315) is still active as an inland construction tender. Carries four 19-ft. (5.8-m) aids-to-navigation skiffs delivered 1993 by Workboats Northwest, Inc., Seattle.

♦ 2 Kankakee-class (75-ft. [F] class) river buoy tenders [WYGL]

Bldr: Avondale Industries, New Orleans, La.

	L	In serv.	Based at:
WLR 75500 Kankakee	8-7-89	1-90	Memphis, Tenn.
WLR 75501 Greenbrier	. . .	12-4-90	Natchez, Miss.

Greenbrier (WLR 75501)—pushing a barge USCG, 2004

D: 136 tons (175 fl) **S:** 12 kts **Dim:** 22.86 (22.25 wl) × 7.32 × 1.53
Electronics: Radar: 1/ . . . nav.
M: 2 Caterpillar 3412-DIT diesels; 2 props; 1,024 bhp
Range: 600/11 **Fuel:** 11 tons **Crew:** 13 tot.

Remarks: Approved under FY 86 budget, to act as push-tugs for Aids-to-Navigation barges 74 and 75, respectively. They were originally employed on the Arkansas River; ordered 3-88. Have six rudders.

♦ 9 Gasconade-class (75-ft. class) river buoy tenders [WYGL]

Bldrs:WLR 75401: St. Louis SB & DD, St. Louis, Mo.; WLR 75402–75405: Maxon Construction Co., Tell City, Ind.; others: Halter Marine, New Orleans, La.

	In serv.	Barge assigned	Based at:
WLR 75401 Gasconade	15-1-64	90013	Omaha, Neb.
WLR 75402 Muskingum	25-3-65	68	Sallisaw, Okla.
WLR 75403 Wyaconda	30-5-65	69	Dubuque, Iowa
WLR 75404 Chippewa	5-10-65	76	Parris Landing, Tenn.
WLR 75405 Cheyenne	3-10-66	99004	St. Louis, Mo.
WLR 75406 Kickapoo	20-5-69	77	Vicksburg, Miss.
WLR 75407 Kanawha	22-9-69	73	Pine Bluff, Ark.
WLR 75408 Patoka	9-2-70	72	Greenville, Miss.
WLR 75409 Chena	27-5-70	71	Hickman, Ky.

Cheyenne (WLR 75405)—pushing 99-ft. construction barge CGB 9904 Victor M. Baca, 1993

D: 127 tons light (141 fl) **S:** 7.6–8.7 kts **Dim:** 22.86 (22.25 pp) × 6.73 × 1.37
M: 2 Caterpillar diesels; 2 props; 600 bhp
Range: 1,600/7.6; 3,100/6.5 **Crew:** 12 tot.

Remarks: Flat-ended, barge-like hulls. WLR 75405 has an associated buoy push-barge, and a slightly larger crew. One one-ton crane. All operate on the Mississippi River and its tributaries. Four new 39.62 × 9.14–m construction barges were ordered for this class in 1985 from Thrift SB & Repair, Sulpher, Louisiana; when the yard went bankrupt, the two incomplete units were completed at USCG Yd., Curtis Bay, Maryland, which delivered CG 72 for use with WLR 75408 and CG 73 for use with WLR 75407 in 4-88.

♦ 6 Ouachita-class (65-ft. class) river buoy tenders [WYGL]

Bldrs: WLR 65501, 65502: Platzer SY, Houston, Tex.; others: Gibbs Corp., Jacksonville, Fla.

	In serv.	Barge assigned	Based at:
WLR 65501 Ouachita	22-7-60	67	Chattanooga, Tenn.
WLR 65502 Cimarron	30-9-60	70	Paris Landing, Tenn.
WLR 65503 Obion	5-1-62	99008	Owensboro, Ky.
WLR 65504 Scioto	27-3-62	99002	Keokuk, Iowa
WLR 65505 Osage	15-5-62	99003	Sewickley, Pa.
WLR 65506 Sangamon	16-6-62	99005	Peoria, Ill.

D: 130 tons light (145 fl) **S:** 10 kts **Dim:** 20.02 × 6.40 × 1.52
M: 2 Caterpillar diesels; 2 props; 600 bhp
Range: 1,700/10.5; 3,500/6 **Crew:** 10 tot.

Remarks: WLR 65504 has a larger crew and an associated push-type buoy barge with a 3-ton crane (barge serial numbers listed previously). All have an on-board 3-ton crane. Operate on the Mississippi River and its tributaries.

♦ 4 Pamlico-class (160-ft. class) inland construction tenders [WYGL]

Bldr: Coast Guard Yard, Curtis Bay, Md.

	Laid down	L	In serv.	Based at:
WLIC 800 Pamlico	1-6-74	13-12-75	11-8-76	New Orleans, La.
WLIC 801 Hudson	6-6-75	29-5-76	14-10-76	Miami Beach, Fla.
WLIC 802 Kennebec	9-1-76	11-12-76	6-4-77	Portsmouth, Va.
WLIC 803 Saginaw	5-7-76	11-6-77	22-9-77	Mobile, Ala.

D: 413 tons light (459 fl) **S:** 11.5 kts **Dim:** 30.48 × 9.14 × 1.17
Electronics: Radar: 1 Raytheon SPS-69 (1900 Pathfinder) nav.
M: 2 Cummins D379, 8-cyl. diesels; 2 props; 1,000 bhp
Range: 1,400/11; 2,200/6.5 **Crew:** 1 officer, 13 enlisted

Remarks: Design combines capabilities of the *Anvil* class and their associated equipment barges. One nine-ton crane. All operate on Atlantic Coast inland waterways.

COAST GUARD SERVICE CRAFT *(continued)*

Pamlico (WLIC 800) George R. Schneider, 9-05

♦ 8 Anvil-class (75-ft. class) inland construction tenders [WYGL]

Bldrs: WLIC 75301–75302: Gibbs SY, Jacksonville, Fla.; WLIC 75303–75305: McDermott Fabricators, Morgan City, La.; WLIC 75306: Sturgeon Bay SB & DD, Sturgeon Bay, Wisc.; others: Dorchester SB, Dorchester, N.J.

	In serv.	Barge assigned	Based at:
WLIC 75301 Anvil	14-5-62	68013	Charleston, S.C.
WLIC 75302 Hammer	20-11-62	68014	Mayport, Fla.
WLIC 75303 Sledge	5-12-62	8400	Baltimore, Md.
WLIC 75304 Mallet	1-2-63	84002	Corpus Christi, Tex.
WLIC 75305 Vise	14-3-63	68012	St. Petersburg, Fla.
WLIC 75306 Clamp	24-11-64	68016	Galveston, Tex.
WLIC 75309 Hatchet	23-6-66	68018	Galveston, Tex.
WLIC 75310 Axe	17-10-66	68020	Morgan City, La.

Axe (WLIC 75310)—pushing construction barge CGB 68020
George R. Schneider, 10-04

D: 129 tons light (145 fl) **S:** 9.1 kts **Dim:** 23,19 (22.26 pp) × 6.83 × 1.37
M: 2 diesels; 2 props; 600 bhp **Range:** 1,000/10 (see Remarks)
Crew: 0 or 1 officer, 9 enlisted

Remarks: All except *Anvil* and *Mallet* have an associated push-type barge with a 9-ton crane; the serial numbers for these are listed previously. WLIC 75306–75310 are 23.2 m overall and can make 9.4 knots. Ranges vary: WLIC 75301 and 75302: 1,300/9; 2,400/5; WLIC 75303–75305: 1,000/9; 2,200/5; others: 1,050/9; 2,500/5.

Disposal note: Sister *Spike* (WLIC 75308) and associated barge were stricken 30-5-86, and *Wedge* (WLIC 75307) has also been stricken.

♦ 1 Cosmos-class (100-ft. class) inland construction tender [WYGL]

Bldr: Dubuque Bopat & Boiler, Dubuque, Iowa

	Laid down	L	In serv.
WLIC 315 Smilax	26-11-43	18-8-44	1-11-44

D: 178 tons (fl) **S:** 10.5 kts **Dim:** 30.48 (29.26 pp) × 7.49 × 1.62
Electronics: Radar: 1 Raytheon SPS-69 (1500 Pathfinder) nav.
M: 2 Waukesha diesels; 2 props; 600 bhp **Range:** 1,400/10.5; 2,700/7
Crew: 1 officer, 14 enlisted

Remarks: Based at Atlantic Beach, North Carolina, since 7-99. Has a 5-ton crane. Is assigned Aids-to-Navigation barge 70018. Sister *Bluebell* (WLI 313) is typed as an inland buoy tender.
Disposals: *Cosmos* (WLIC 293) was stricken in 1985, *Rambler* (WLIC 298) on 3-6-98, and *Primrose* (WLIC 316) on 22-8-99.

Note: In use on inland waterways are 99-ft. (30.2-m), 90-ft. (27.4-m), and 68-ft. (20.7-m) Aids-to-Navigation barges, which are pushed by the various WLR- and WLIC-series tenders and two of the WYTL tugs; for individual units, see the listings under WLR, WLIC, and WYTL.

Disposal notes: Former U.S. Navy large harbor tug [WYTB] *Edenshaw* (50, ex-YTB 752) was stricken and sold commercial during 2001; tug services at the Coast Guard Yard, Curtis Bay, Maryland, are now performed by contract tugs, as needed.

♦ 11 65-ft. class small harbor tugs [WYTM]

	Bldr.	In serv.	Based at:
WYTL 65601 Capstan	Gibbs Corp., Jacksonville, Fla.	19-7-61	Philadelphia, Pa.
WYTL 65602 Chock	Gibbs Corp., Jacksonville, Fla.	12-9-62	Portsmouth, Va.
WYTL 65604 Tackle	Gibbs Corp., Jacksonville, Fla.	1962	Crisfield, Md.
WYTL 65607 Bridle	Barbour Boat, New Bern, N.C.	3-4-63	Southwest Harbor, Maine
WYTL 65608 Pennant	Barbour Boat, New Bern, N.C.	8-63	Boston, Mass.
WYTL 65609 Shackle	Barbour Boat, New Bern, N.C.	7-5-63	South Portland, Maine
WYTL 65610 Hawser	Barbour Boat, New Bern, N.C.	17-1-63	Bayonne, N.J.
WYTL 65611 Line	Barbour Boat, New Bern, N.C.	21-2-63	Bayonne, N.J.
WYTL 65612 Wire	Barbour Boat, New Bern, N.C.	19-3-63	Saugerties, N.Y.
WYTL 65614 Bollard	Western Boatbldg, Tacoma, Wa.	10-4-67	New Haven, Conn.
WYTL 65615 Cleat	Western Boatbldg, Tacoma, Wa.	10-5-67	Philadelphia, Pa.

Chock (WYTL 65602) William H. Clarke, 1-00

D: 62 tons light (72 fl) **S:** 9.8 (first 6: 10.5) kts
Dim: 19.79 (19.08 pp) × 5.82 × 2.74
Electronics: Radar: 1 Raytheon SPS-66A or SPS-69 nav.
M: 1 diesel; 1 prop; 400 bhp (see Remarks)
Range: 850/9.8; 2,700/5.8 (WYTL 65601–65604: 3,600/6.8, 8,900/10.5)
Crew: 10 tot.

Remarks: Can break ice up to 152-mm thick. Six were re-engined during 1993–94 with Caterpillar 3412 diesels of 475 bhp each. The USCG's plans to retire all remaining units before 30-9-00 were thwarted by the Congress, which required them to remain operational, although they are of very little utility except as harbor icebreakers. Aids-to-Navigation barge 31016 is assigned to WYTL 65608.
Disposals: Sister *Bitt* (WYTL 65613) was stricken 10-4-82; *Swivel* (WYTL 65603), *Towline* (WYTL 65605), and *Catenary* (WYTL 65606) on 1-5-95.

SMALL CRAFT

♦ 0 (+ up to 180) Response Boat Medium—RB-M Project

Bldr: Marinette Marine Corporation, Marinette, Wis. (In serv. 2007– . . .)

RB-M Project prototypes—pictured from left to right are those submitted by Ocean Technical Services, Marinette Marine Corp (the winning design), and Textron Marine & Land Systems USCG, 2003

Remarks: Designed to replace the 41-ft. class of Coast Guard utility boats, this new class is known officially as the "Multimission Vessel." The Response Boat Medium (RB-M) Project is being developed as a similar, though larger and more capable, version of the new Defender class small Response Boats. Specifically these vessels will play a key role in homeland security and search and rescue missions.

During 2003, Marinette Marine Corp, Textron Marine & Land Systems, and Ocean Technical Services Inc. each submitted a prototype to the Coast Guard to undergo testing in Portsmouth, Virginia. Of the three, only the Marinette Marine boat was capable of self-righting for survivability. On 23-6-06 the Coast Guard awarded a production contract worth approximately $600 million to Marinette Marine Corporation. Delivery of the first water-jet powered unit is expected in late 2007. Construction is expected to continue at a rate of 30 boats per year for six years.

♦ 3 32-ft. oil-spill control launches [WYAG]

Bldr: Munson Mfgr. Co., Edmonds, Wash.

	In serv.
327001	1986
327032	1991
327100	1987

D: 7.5 tons light (8.6 fl) **S:** 20.4 kts **Dim:** 10.16 × 3.58 × 0.86
Electronics: Radar: 1 Raytheon SPS-69 (1900 Pathfinder) nav.
M: 2 Caterpillar 3208 diesels; 2 props; 406 bhp
Range: 190/16.5 **Fuel:** 0.65 tons **Crew:** 3 tot.

COAST GUARD SMALL CRAFT *(continued)*

Remarks: Former Ports and Waterways boats used for oil-spill control by Strike Team Gulf, Strike Team Atlantic, and Strike Team Pacific. GRP construction. Fifty-two built late 1970s to replace 30-ft. Mk-III class. Have a 90-bhp G.M. 3-53 diesel to drive a 500 gallon/min. fire pump. Four sisters are used by the U.S. Navy at Norfolk, Virginia, while 49 others in the Ports and Waterways Boat category had been retired by 1-01.

♦ 1 50-ft. Passenger Boat [WYFL]
Bldr: Munson Mfgr. Co., Edmonds, Wash. (In serv. 1992)

502001

D: . . . tons **S:** . . . kts **Dim:** 15.24 × 4.97 × . . .
M: 2 G.M. Detroit Diesel . . . diesels; 2 props; 1,300 bhp

Remarks: Operated since 1-95 at Fort Totten, N.Y.

♦ 172 41-ft. Utility Boats [WYFL]
Bldr: USCG Yard, Curtis Bay, Md. (In serv. 1973–82)

41300–41507 series

41-ft. Utility Boat 41424 Takatoshi Okano, 4-04

D: 13–14 tons (fl) **S:** 22–26 kts **Dim:** 12.40 × 4.11 × 1.22
Electronics: Radar: 1/ SPS-69 (Raytheon 1900) nav.
M: 2 Cummins V903M or VT903M diesels; 2 props; 560 or 636 bhp
Range: 300/18 **Fuel:** 1.54 tons **Crew:** 3 tot.

Remarks: Prototype delivered 1971; between 1973–82 some 206 more followed. Are being replaced by 27-ft. Whaler and Safeboat Bayliner RIB rescue craft. Aluminum construction. 41400 has special vanes on the propeller shafts, adding 2.5 kts speed; was to be backfitted to others. Designed weight 12.97 tons, but displacements have increased to almost 14 tons. Have a 250-gal./min. fire pump. Of the total, three are assigned as Aviation Training Boats, and one is in reserve. The class is now being replaced by Bayliner 27-ft. RIBs, but a number of the units inactivated have been brought back into service for antiterrorism defense duties. Onboard radar systems to be replaced by the Sealable Integrated Navigation System. To be phased out during the next decade, these boats will eventually be replaced by the new Response Boat Medium (RB-M) class of patrol boats.

Disposal notes: 38-ft. utility boats 38501 and 38502 were no longer listed as USCG assets as of 1-01. All but three 32-ft. Ports and Waterways Boat–class launches that had been reassigned as oil-spill control craft had been retired by 1-01. 41313, 41328, and 41333 were transferred to NOAA during 2003.

♦ . . . 30-ft. Hurricane RIB Utility Boats [WYFL]
Bldr: American Zodiac, Annapolis, Md. (In serv. 1998–2000)

304430 304431 304435 304437 304440 304444 304450 and others

D: . . . tons **S:** 47 kts **Dim:** 9.14 × 3.04 × 1.00 max.
M: 2 gasoline outboards; 450 bhp **Range:** 85/ . . . **Crew:** . . . tot.

Remarks: Aluminum hulls with rigid-inflatable collars.

♦ 1 28-ft. Protector-class Ports and Waterways Boat [WYFL]
Bldr: SeaArk, Monticello, Ark. (In serv. 1997)

286608

D: 4 tons (fl) **S:** . . . kts **Dim:** 8.53 × 3.91 × 0.61
M: 2 . . . diesels; 2 props; 600 bhp

Remarks: Aluminum construction craft assigned to Valdez, Alaska.

Note: Also in service is 28-ft. Utility Boat 282000, delivered in 1989 by SeaArk and equipped with two OMC 200-bhp gasoline outboards for speeds to 35 kts.

♦ 4 miscellaneous 28-ft. Utility Boats [WYFL]

	In serv.	Bldr	M	S
282000	1989	SeaArk	2 OMC 200-bhp gasoline outboards	35 kts
208500	1987	SeaArk	2 OMC 225-bhp gasoline outboards	40 kts
208501	1988	SeaArk	2 OMC 225-bhp gasoline outboards	40 kts
284397	1997	Safeboats	2 Mercury 200-bhp outboards	48 kts

Remarks: 284397 is builder's American Eagle class and is assigned to Duluth, Minnesota; 208500 is assigned to Baltimore, Maryland.

♦ 200 (+ up to 500) Defender-class (25-foot) Response Boats–Small (RB-S)
Bldr: Safe Boats, Port Orchard, Wash. (In serv. 2003–)

25401 series 25501 series

Defender-class Response Boat 255003 Edward McDonnell, 5-04

D: . . . tons **S:** 40+ kts **Dim:** 7.62 × 2.59 × . . .
A: 2 7.62-mm M60 mg; small arms **Electronics:** 1 Raytheon Raymarine . . . nav.
M: 2 Honda BF225 4-stroke gasoline outboards; 450 bhp **Range:** 175/.35
Fuel: 125 gals. **Crew:** up to 10 tot.

Remarks: Each boat costs approximately $180,000 in 2003 dollars. Up to 700 of these craft may be purchased to replace the nearly 300 nonstandard shore-based boats and provide a standardized platform for new Maritime Safety and Security detachments, with six boats assigned to each unit. Designed to be transportable by road or by C-130 aircraft. The full cabin provides crew protection from the elements and is equipped with a state-of-the-art navigation system, heater, shock mitigating seats, and a communication system capable of communicating with other federal, state, and local homeland security partners. Have echo sounders, WAAS GPS, Raymarine DSC VHF radios, and Motorola secure radio. Have bare aluminum structure with orange polyethylene rigid foam collar; a large pilothouse is fitted. First boats delivered in 2003 with units delivered to the Coast Guard at a minimum of two per week. Can operate efficiently in 30-mph winds and 6-foot seas.

Defender-class Response Boat 255002 Edward McDonnell, 5-04

♦ . . . Boston Whaler 27-ft. Utility Boats [WYFL]
Bldr: Boston Whaler, Edgewater, Fla (In serv. 2003–)

27953 27956 and others

Boston Whaler 27-ft. utility boat 275961 Edward McDonnell, 2005

Remarks: Deliveries began around 2003. Two Mercury outboard engines. No additional data available.

♦ 7 27-ft. Vigilant-class launches [WYFL]
Bldr: Boston Whaler, Edgewater, Fla. (In serv. 1990–2000)

273501–273505 273508 273509

D: 2.27 tons light (4.0 fl) **S:** 34 kts **Dim:** 8.10 × 3.05 × 0.48
Electronics: Radar: 1 Furuno or Raytheon . . . nav.
M: 2 Johnson gasoline outboards; 350 bhp **Range:** . . . / . . .
Fuel: 802 liters **Crew:** 4 tot.

COAST GUARD SMALL CRAFT *(continued)*

27-ft. Vigilant-class 273502 George R. Schneider, 9-99

Remarks: GRP foam-core construction. Employed for harbor patrol duties and replaced 41-ft. Utility Boats in the 7th, 8th, 11th, and 17th Coast Guard Districts. Sisters have been transferred to Romania and Kazakhstan, with USCG training assistance. Can carry up to 12 people. Class prototype 273501 has a smaller pilothouse than the others.

Note: Also in use is SeaArk *Commander*-class Utility Boat 274426, completed 1997 and assigned to Harbor Beach, California; has two 175-bhp Mercury outboards and can reach 42 kts.

♦ 2 26-ft. Utility Boats [WYFL]

Bldr: Ambar (In serv. 1999)

26501 26502

Remarks: Assigned to Gulfport, Mississippi, and Ft. Myers Beach, Florida, respectively. Aluminum hulls have 2.9-m beam, and the craft are powered by two Mercury 150-bhp outboards for 46 kts and 150 n.m. range.

♦ 1 26-ft. Honolulu personnel launch [WYFL]

Bldr: Munson Mfg., Edmonds, Wash. (In serv. early 1990s)

266200

26-ft. Honolulu personnel launch 266200 Victor M. Baca, 3-94

D: 3.2 tons tons (fl) **S:** 25 kts **Dim:** 7.92 × 3.05 × 0.61
M: 1 Volvo AQAD 41 200 diesel, Volvo SP 290 inboard/outboard drive; 200 bhp
Crew: 1 tot.

Remarks: Aluminum construction, 12-passenger launch used to shuttle Coast Guard personnel within the Honolulu, Hawaii, harbor area.

♦ 6 miscellaneous 25-ft. Whaler launches [WYFL]

Bldr: Boston Whaler, Edgewater, Fla. (In serv. 1990s)

D: 1.86 tons light (3.2 fl) **S:** 30+ kts **Dim:** 7.50 × 2.45 × 0.41
Electronics: Radar: 1 Raytheon . . . nav.
M: 2 Johnson gasoline outboards; 300 bhp
Fuel: 534 liters

Remarks: Data apply to *Challenger*-class units 254308 and 254333, completed 1987 and 1990. Also included in this category are *Sentry*-class 252510 (in serv. 1987), *Frontier*-class 252519 (1991), *Vigilant*-class 253503 (1989), and *Outrage*-class 256550 (1990). All are of GRP foam-core construction.

Notes: Other 25-ft. craft in service include: up to five Zodiac Hurricane RIBs; four Mako aluminum-hulled launches (252503, 252522, 252523, and 252524 [in serv. 1987–95]); four SeaArk launches (253504, 254396, 254400, and 254439 [in serv. 1994–2000]); and seven Safe Boat RIBs (256609, 256610, 256000, 256611, 252525, 252526, and 254581 [in serv. 1997–2000]).

25-ft. Vigilant-class launch 253503 H&L Van Ginderen, 3-96

♦ 1 24-ft. V-Commander-class Utility Launch [WYFL]

Bldr: SeaArk, Monticello, Ark. (In serv. 1998)

245564

D: 1.589 tons (light) **S:** 32 kts **Dim:** 7.00 × 2.60 × 0.40
M: 1 Volvo Penta TAMD . . . diesel outdrive; 270 bhp

Remarks: Assigned to Portland, Oregon. Aluminum construction.

Notes: Other 24-ft. launches in service include five Munson-built (247055 for Strike Team Gulf and 247103 for Strike Team Pacific, and 244501–244503 for use on California inland waterways); Avon RIB 242503 (in serv. 1990), based at San Juan, Puerto Rico; and up to 10 Zodiac Hurricane Model 733 RIBs.

♦ . . . 22-ft. Sentry-class launches [WYFL]

Bldr: Boston Whaler, Edgewater, Fla. (In serv. 1990s)

22-ft. Sentry-class launch 220512 Boston Whaler

D: 1.29 tons light (2.5 fl) **S:** 30+ kts **Dim:** 6.80 × 2.30 × 0.36
Electronics: Radar: 1 Raytheon . . . nav.
M: 2 Johnson gasoline outboards; 160 bhp
Fuel: 291 liters

Remarks: GRP foam-core construction. Can carry up to nine persons. Differ from *Guardian* class in having a covered foredeck and a full-width cockpit with windshield.

♦ 38 or more 22-ft. Guardian-class launches [WYFL]

Bldr: Boston Whaler, Edgewater, Fla. (In serv. 1990s)

D: 1.2 tons light (2.3 fl) **S:** 30+ kts **Dim:** 6.80 × 2.30 × 0.36
Electronics: Radar: 1 Raytheon . . . nav.
M: 2 Johnson gasoline outboards; 160 bhp
Fuel: 291 liters

COAST GUARD SMALL CRAFT *(continued)*

22-ft. Guardian-class launch 223506—on trailer Leo Dirkx, 11-99

Remarks: GRP foam-core construction. Can carry up to 11 persons. From 1987 to 6-89, NAPCO International, Hopkins, Minnesota, delivered 24 militarized variants of this design for use by Coast Guard harbor protection personnel; they have since been replaced by larger craft.

♦ 18 21-ft. Commander-class patrol launches [WYFL]

Bldr: SeaArk, Monticello, Ark. (In serv. 2 in 8-91, 2 in 9-91, others: 12-92 to 1994)

21-ft. Commander-class launch 21544—at Savannah, Ga. Leo Dirkx, 5-98

D: 1.362 tons (1.9 fl) **S:** 32 kts **Dim:** 6.40 × 2.60 × 0.44
M: 2 Evinrude gasoline outboards; 200 bhp

Remarks: Aluminum construction, trailer-transportable, deep-vee hulled craft for use on central U.S. inland waters for patrol and search-and-rescue duties. Hulls plane at 18 kts on one engine.

♦ 134 Searider RIB launches [WYFL]

Bldr: Avon, . . . (In serv. 1999–2000)

Remarks: 6-m craft powered by one or two 90-bhp gasoline outboards and intended to be carried aboard larger ships and craft.

♦ 166 21-ft. Hurricane rigid inflatable boats [WYFL]

Bldr: American Zodiac (In serv. 1992–. . .)

21-ft. Hurricane-class RIB 214385—with two Honda outboard motors and Raytheon radar George R. Schneider, 7-01

D: . . . **S:** 35–37 kts **Dim:** 6.40 × . . . × . . .
M: 1 outdrive diesel or 1 or 2 gasoline outboards

Remarks: Acquired to replace Boston Whalers, both as shipboard launches and as utility and rescue launches attached to shore stations. Are radar-equipped. Can be transported by trailers. The initial units were deployed to the Hawaiian Islands in 10-92. Most have a small Raytheon navigational radar.

Notes: Other launches [WYFL] in U.S. Coast Guard service included:

- 23-ft.: 30 Safe Boat aluminum launches for shore stations; one Huskey D-9 airboat (232448, in serv. 2000); . . . RIBs (23475 series)
- 22-ft.: 61 Zodiac Hurricane RIBs with 130-bhp Volvo or Caterpillar inboard/outboard diesels; 18 Ambar-build RIBs for shore stations (in serv. 1998–2000); and up to 29 Boston Whalers of various models
- 21-ft: five Safe Boat RIBs delivered 1997–99 and four Willard RIBs delivered 1996
- 20-ft.: 31 miscellaneous work punts assigned to various ships
- 19-ft.: six miscellaneous aluminum utility boats; 20 Avon RIBs (in serv. 1982–97); and 10 Zodiac Hurricane RIBS (In serv. 1986–2000)
- 18-ft.: 59 miscellaneous RIBs; 47 miscellaneous work punts
- 17-ft.: 87 miscellaneous RIBs; 53 miscellaneous aluminum utility launches
- 15-ft.: 35 miscellaneous Zodiac Hurricane RIBs and aluminum work punts
- 14-ft.: 34 ice skiffs and 39 miscellaneous boats
- 13-ft.: 28 miscellaneous shipboard launches
- 12-ft.: 6 miscellaneous launches
- 10–11-ft.: 14 work punts

♦ 5 Packman-class landing craft [WYFU]

Bldr: William E. Munson Co., Mt. Vernon, Wash. (In serv. 9-01)

D: . . . tons **S:** 40 kts (23 sust.) **Dim:** 10.36 × 3.66 × . . .
Electronics: Radar: 1 only: 1 Furuno . . . nav.
M: 2 Volvo KAD43-DP outdrive diesels; 2 props; 460 bhp **Crew:** 2 tot.

Remarks: Employed as on-board workboats for icebreakers based at Seattle, with one of the five equipped as an arctic survey craft with a crew of six and fitted with a radar, GPS, echo sounder, and an 8-kw generator set. All have a 2.1-m-wide bow door/ramp leading to a 5.5-m vehicle and cargo deck. Aluminum construction.

♦ 3 64-ft. class Buoy-Tending Boats [WYGL]

Bldr: Owen-Short Marine, Bayou La Batre, Ala.

	L	In serv.		L	In serv.
643501	18-6-96	12-12-96	643503	14-2-97	10-4-97
643502	19-11-96	10-1-97			

D: Approx. 130 tons (fl) **S:** 10 kts **Dim:** 19.50 × 7.32 × 1.19
Electronics: Radar: 1 . . . nav.
M: 2 Cummins 6CTA8.3M1 diesels; 2 5-bladed props; 500 bhp
Electric: 100 kw tot. (2 × 50 kw; 2 Cummins 6B5.9MG diesels driving)
Range: . . . / . . . **Crew:** 6 tot.

Remarks: Three ordered 1-96 with option for two more, which was taken up; two left incomplete, however, when the builder went out of business were placed up for sale for commercial use. Have a 2-ton crane and can accommodate up to 13.6 m tons of cargo on deck.

♦ 1 63-ft. Aids-to-Navigation Boat [WYGL] Bldr: . . . (In serv. 1975)

63107

D: Approx. 30 tons (fl) **S:** . . . kts **Dim:** 19.20 × 5.64 × . . .
M: 2 G.M. diesels; 2 props; 800 bhp

Remarks: Transferred from Detroit, Michigan, to Chincoteague, Virginia, during 10-00.

♦ 20 55-ft-class Aids-to-Navigation Boats [WYGL]

Bldr: 55103–55112: Robert E. Derecktor, Mamaroneck, N.Y. (In serv. 1977); others: Coast Guard Yard, Curtis Bay, Md. (In serv. 1980–88)

55103 through 55122

55-ft. Aids-to-Navigation Boat 55115 George R. Schneider, 7-05

D: 28.8 tons (31.25 fl) **S:** 22 kts **Dim:** 17.68 × 5.18 × 1.52
Electronics: Radar: 1 Raytheon SPS-69 (1900 Pathfinder) nav.
M: 2 G.M. Detroit Diesel 12 V71 TI diesels; 2 props; 1,080 bhp
Range: 350/18 **Fuel:** 3,995 liters **Crew:** 4 tot.

Remarks: Aluminum construction. Can carry 4,000 lbs cargo and have a 1,000-lb. crane. 55101 was retired in 2000 and 55102 was sold commercial in 1999.

♦ 26 49-ft. BUSL (Boat, Utility, Stern-Load)-class Aids-to-Navigation Boats [WYGL]

Bldr: Coast Guard Yard, Curtis Bay, Md. (In serv. 9-97 to 11-00)

49401 through 49426

D: . . . tons **S:** 11 kts (10 sust.) **Dim:** 14.9 × 4.82 × . . .
M: 2 Cummins diesels; 2 props; 1,220 bhp **Range:** 200/10 **Crew:** 4 tot.

COAST GUARD SMALL CRAFT *(continued)*

49-ft. BUSL 49418 Ralph Edwards, 3-05

Remarks: Were to have been 40, but program curtailed at 26; initial builder had contract for four but completed only two, which were not delivered. Thirteen more were funded for $18.5 million under FY 95 and were delivered at six-week intervals by the Coast Guard Yard; a second group was ordered later. Have a 2-ton-capacity A-frame crane over the stern and can carry 7.25 tons of stores; can also break 100-mm ice and perform search-and-rescue operations. Aluminum construction.

Disposal notes: All remaining 45-ft. Aids-to-Navigation Boats were to have been retired by the end of 2001. All nine 46-ft. Stern-Loading Buoy Boats had been retired by the end of 2001.

♦ 2 34-ft. Aids-to-Navigation Boats [WYGL]
Bldr: Munson Mfg. Co., Edmonds, Wash.

342500 (In serv. 1987) 344266 (In serv. 1984)

Remarks: Dissimilar craft, but both built of aluminum. 342500 has two Volvo 200-bhp outdrive engines for 28 kts and is based at St. Petersburg, Florida, while 344266 has two 250-bhp Mercury outboards for 37 kts and is based at Portage, Michigan.

♦ 28 23-ft. Trailerable Aids-to-Navigation Boats [WYGL]
Bldr: SeaArk, Monticello, Ark. (In serv. 1991– . . .)

D: 1.27 tons light (3.08 fl) **S:** . . . kts **Dim:** 7.10 × 2.40 × 0.36 (hull)
M: 1 gasoline outboard; 130 bhp

Remarks: Builder's Navigator design. Are used utility boats aboard buoy tenders and, as the older WLBs are retired, as shore-based Aids-to-Navigation service boats.

♦ 90 21-ft. Trailerable Aids-to-Navigation Boats [WYGL]
Bldr: MonArk, Monticello, Ark. (In serv. 1991–92)

21-ft. Trailerable Aids-to-Navigation Boat 21460 George R. Schneider, 7-01

D: 1.59 tons light (3.17 fl) **S:** 28 kts **Dim:** 6.56 × 2.24 × 0.36 (hull)
M: 1 gasoline engine; 1 prop; 228 bhp or Mercruiser/OMC 165 bhp outboard
Range: 100/20 **Crew:** . . . tot.

Remarks: Aluminum construction, design based on builder's 21-V, deep-vee hull design. Can be mounted on a trailer for land transport. Four delivered 11-92, four more during 12-92. Some are painted black, while others have been left in unpainted aluminum, except for the Coast Guard stripes.

Notes: One 19-ft. (5.8-m) skiff was delivered 9-94 by Munson Boats, La Conner, Washington; no details available.

♦ 2 18-ft. class Navigational Aid Skiffs [WYGL]
Bldr: Kvichak Marine Industries, Seattle, Wash. (In serv. 1994)

D: . . . tons (fl) **S:** 35+ kts **Dim:** 5.49 × 2.13 × 0.28
M: 2 OMC gasoline outboard motors; 140 bhp **Crew:** 2 tot.

Remarks: Aluminum hulls with foam flotation. Based at Port Angeles and Kennewick, Washington.

♦ 36 18-ft. Seasled-class Utility Boats [WYGL]
Bldr: Munson Mfg., Edmonds, Wash. (In serv. 1990s)

D: 0.8 tons (fl) **S:** 30 kts **Dim:** 5.49 × 2.29 × 0.30
M: 2 Johnson gasoline outboards; 80 bhp

18-ft. Seasled-class buoy recovery boat Munson, 1993

Remarks: Employed on Mississippi, Ohio, and Missouri Rivers systems as buoy recovery craft. Normally carried aboard river tenders. Aluminum construction. Second order for 20 completed 4-93.

Notes: Also in use are 11 other 18-ft. workboats, built by SeaArk, Workboats, Boston Whaler, Mako, Kann, and Lowe.

♦ 200 47-ft. Motor Life Boat class [WYH]
Bldr: Textron Marine and Land Systems, New Orleans, La.
(In serv. 17-4-98 to 2003)

MLB 47206 through MLB . . .

D: 18.15 tons (fl) **S:** 25 kts (20 sust.)
Dim: 14.61 (13.11 wl) × 4.27 × 1.32 (0.80 hull)
Electronics: Radar: 1 Raytheon 41X nav.
M: 2 G.M. Detroit Diesel 6V92 TA diesels; 2 props; 840 bhp
Range: 220/25; 208/10 **Fuel:** 1,560 liters **Crew:** 4 tot. plus 5 survivors

47-ft. Motor Life Boat MLB 47245 Frank Findler, 10-03

47-ft. Motor Life Boat MLB 47245 George R. Schneider, 5-03

Remarks: Intended to replace the 44-ft. class and to provide significantly greater speed of reaction, with up to 123 to be built. First unit, 47200, was laid down 1-8-89 and delivered on 25-6-90; five preproduction boats were ordered 9-12-91 and completed during 1993, and all six were retired in 1998 and transferred to the U.S. Customs Service and local law-enforcement agencies. Twenty production versions were ordered 11-9-95 and 20 more the following year; 30 were ordered in 1-98, 23 more early in 1999, and the final 24 late that year. During 2000–2001, deliveries were being made every 18 days. The boats are taken by truck to final fitting-out facilities at Astoria, Oregon; Alameda, California; Detroit, Michigan; and Portsmouth, Virginia. Eleven sisters were ordered 1-4-97 for the Canadian Coast Guard from MIL Systems Engineering, Ottawa, and MetalCraft Marine, Kingston, Ontario, and another 20 were ordered during 10-01 from Victoria Shipyards, Victoria, B.C. Final unit delivered 5-03.
Hull systems: Aluminum construction, with deep-vee, self-righting hull form. Trials in heavy seas were highly successful; can maintain 20 kts in 2-ft. seas and tow craft displacing up to 150 tons. Can survive an end-for-end pitch-pole and are capable of operating in 80-kt gales with 9-m swells and 6-m breaking seas. Carry a Motorola MCX1000 VHF radio.

COAST GUARD SMALL CRAFT *(continued)*

♦ 2 Hammerhead 24-class search-and-rescue launches [WYH]
Bldr: Munson Mfg., Edmonds, Wash. (In serv. early 1990s)

D: 2.8 tons (fl) **S:** 45 kts **Dim:** 7.31 × 2.59 × 0.61
M: 2 Evinrude V-6 gasoline outboards

Remarks: Employed at Lake Tahoe, California, search-and-rescue station, operating 7,000 ft. above sea level. Aluminum construction.

♦ 1 Lake Champlain search-and-rescue launch [WYH]
Bldr: SeaArk Boat, Monticello, Ark. (In serv. 1987)

D: . . . **S:** 38 kts **Dim:** 8.69 × 3.56 × 0.56
Electronics: Radar: 1 Furuno . . .nav. **Crew:** 2–3 tot.
M: 2 Volvo AQAD 41/290 outdrive diesels; 2 props; 400 bhp

Remarks: Aluminum construction. Based at Burlington, Vermont. Used for SAR.

Disposal notes: All 44-ft. Motor Life Boats had been retired by the end of 2001. Many have been transferred abroad.

♦ 4 52-ft. Motor Life Boat class [WYH]
Bldr: U.S.C.G. Yard, Curtis Bay, Md.

	In serv.
52312 Victory	29-11-56
52313 Invincible	11-10-60
52314 Triumph II	1-4-61
52315 Intrepid	11-10-61

D: 31.7 tons (35 fl) **S:** 11 kts **Dim:** 15.85 × 4.43 × 1.91
M: 2 G.M. Detroit Diesel 6-71 diesels; 2 props; 340 bhp **Range:** 495/11; 650/ . . .
Crew: 5 + up to 35 rescued personnel

Remarks: Designed for service under extremely heavy sea conditions. All in service on Pacific Northwest coast. Have a 250-gal./min. firefighting and salvage pump. Are to serve to 2012 or later.

Disposal notes: All remaining 30-ft. Surf Rescue Boats were to have been retired by the end of 2001.

♦ 53 Mk V 26-ft. Motor Surf Boats [WYH]
Bldr: Ocean Technical Services, Inc., Harvey, La. (In serv. 5-95 to 3-97)

D: . . . tons (fl) **S:** 18 kts **Dim:** 7.93 × 2.16 × . . .
M: 1 Cummins 4BT3.9M diesel; 1 prop; 130 bhp **Crew:** 3 tot.

Remarks: First 45 ordered spring 1995 for $4.7 million, with option for 10 more. GRP construction, with 1.37-m molded depth. Capable of carrying up to 13 rescuees. Two others have been stricken: 26508 and 26539.

Disposal notes: All remaining 25-ft. Motor Surf Boats have been retired.

♦ 1 LCM(8)-class cable repair craft [WYRC]
72015

D: 34 tons light (121 fl) **S:** 9 kts **Dim:** 22.43 × 6.43 × 1.35 fwd./1.47 aft
M: 4 G.M. Detroit Diesel 6-71N or 2 12V-71 diesels; 2 props; 1,080 bhp
Range: 190/9 (loaded) **Crew:** 4–5 tot.

Remarks: Converted from U.S. Navy LCM(8) landing craft in 1979 and is now stationed at Detroit, Mich., as a telephone- and power-cable layer. New pilothouse and several gooseneck davits added, bow altered. Sister 748281 is assigned to "Detachment Fire and Safety Test"; no other information available.

♦ 1 LCM(6)-class cable repair craft [WYRC]
Bldr: Grafton Boat Co. (In serv. 1969)
560500 (ex-56CM6841)

LCM(6)-class cable repair craft 560500 H&L Van Ginderen, 9-94

D: 50 tons (fl) **S:** 10 kts **Dim:** 17.07 × 4.37 × 1.17
Electronics: Radar: 1 Raytheon SPS-69 (1900 Pathfinder) nav.
M. 2 G.M. Detroit Diesel 6-71 diesels; 2 props; 330 bhp **Range:** 130/10

Remarks: On loan from U.S. Navy. Conversion to cable tender completed 6-86 at USCG Yard, Curtis Bay, Maryland, for service at South Portland, Maine, as a telephone- and power-cable layer. New pilothouse and several gooseneck davits were added, and the bow was altered. Sister 56025 is employed for "Detachment Fire and Safety Test"; no other information available.

♦ 1 ARD 12–class medium-capacity dry dock* [WYFDM]
Bldr: Pacific Bridge, Alameda, Calif. (In serv. 3-44)
Oak Ridge (ex-ARDM 1, ex-ARD 19)

Dim: 163.4 × 24.7 (13.0 clear width) × 2.2 (13.1 sub.) **Capacity:** 8,000 tons
Crew: 5 officers, 174 enlisted (in USN service)

Remarks: Lengthened and capacity increased from 3,500 tons to serve as submarine repair dock. One end is closed, to permit towing. ARDM 1 was transferred from Kings Bay, Georgia, to Groton, Connecticut, arriving 19-5-97. Was deactivated on 10-8-01 and transferred to the U.S. Coast Guard in the spring of 2002 for use at its Curtis Bay yard.

♦ 4 Navy 44-ft.-class sail training craft [WYTS]
Bldr: Uniflite-Tillotson-Pearson, Inc., Warren, R.I. (In serv. 1987–89)

Arctic Tern Blue Goose Shearwater Stormy Petrel

D: 14.35 tons (fl) **S:** . . . **Dim:** 13.41 (10.91 wl) × 3.40 × 2.26
Electronics: Radar: 1 Raytheon SPS-66 nav.
M: 1 auxiliary diesel; 1 prop; 33 bhp—sail area: 88 m^2 **Crew:** 8–10 cadets

Remarks: GRP construction "Luders Yawls." Mast height: 19.66 m above water. Sisters to a series built for the U.S. Naval Academy. They are assigned to the USCG Academy, New London, Connecticut, where also in service are the sloop *Rampage* and sailing craft *Crew 18, Dyer, Eastern 18, Eddystone Light, Fly Junior,* and *Interclub,* and 19 22-ft. (6.7-m) J-22-class, 28 16-ft. (4.9-m), 19 14-ft. (4.3-m), and 27 12-ft. (3.7-m) Laser 13-F sailboats. Also used at the USCG Academy are smallcraft *Steamboat, Tigger,* SISU-30, and CT-64.

U.S. ARMY

The U.S. Army's fleet is divided into landing craft and logistics support craft operated by the Transportation Corps and units operated by the Corps of Engineers (primarily survey craft, dredges, and construction craft). Combat troops also operate large numbers of river-crossing craft.

U.S. ARMY TRANSPORTATION CORPS

Bases: Principal facilities are at Ft. Eustis, Virginia; Southampton, U.K., and Military Ocean Terminal Concord, California (with the latter having been handed over by the U.S. Navy on 22-10-99).

Notes: U.S. Army Transportation Corps ships and craft are classed by design number. They carry alphanumeric serials in the following categories:

BC	Barge, dry cargo, non-self-propelled
BCDK	Barge, decked
BD	Crane, floating
BG	Barge, liquid cargo, non-self-propelled
BK	Barge, dry cargo, non-self-propelled, knock-down
BPL	Pier, barge-type, self-elevating
BR	Barge, refrigerated, non-self-propelled
FB	Ferry
FMS	Repair shop, floating, marine repair, non-self-propelled
HSPC	High-Speed Patrol Craft
J	Work and inspection boat, under 50 ft. (15.24 m) o.a.
LARC	Lighter, Amphibious, Resupply, Cargo
LCM	Landing Craft, Mechanized
LCU	Landing Craft, Utility
LSV	Logistic Support Vessel
LT	Tug, Large, 100 ft. (30.48 m) and over
ST	Tug, Small, under 100 ft. (30.48 m)
T	Freight and supply vessel, small, under 100 ft. (3.48 m)

LOGISTICS SUPPORT SHIPS

♦ 2 modified Gen. Frank S. Besson Jr. class [WLST]
Bldr: VT Halter Marine (formerly Friede Goldman Halter), Moss Point, Escatawpa, Miss.

	Laid down	L	In serv.
LSV-7 SSgt Robert T. Kuroda	8-7-02	21-3-03	2004
LSV-8 MGen Robert Smails	3-03	21-4-04	2005

D: . . . tons **S:** 12 kts (sust.) **Dim:** 95.4 × 18.28 (18.16 wl) × 5.79
M: 2 Caterpillar 3516B diesels; 2 props; 4,520 bhp—540-bhp bow-thruster (1 Caterpillar 3408C diesel driving); 1 300hp electric drive stern-thruster
Electric: 640 kw tot. (2 × 320 kw; 2 Caterpillar 3406C diesels driving); Caterpillar 3304C as emergency generator
Range: 5,500/8kts **Fuel:** 220,000 gals.

Remarks: Three longer variants of the *Gen. Frank S. Besson Jr.* class (dubbed the ELSV—Enhanced Landing Ship Vehicle—by the builder) were requested under the FY 01 through FY 03 budgets, and LSV-7 was ordered from Friede Goldman Halter for $26.9 million on 28-5-01, with an option for two more; after a contract protest, work was allowed to begin after 29-9-01, but was again halted during the yard's transfer of ownership to Vision Technologies, Singapore. The second ship was ordered on 20-12-02, for $43 million. The option for a third ship of the class, to have been numbered LSV-9, was never exercised.
Hull systems: Have a visor-type vertically pivoting bow to allow deployment of the three-piece, 23.16 × 5.49–m articulating bow ramp. A Hatlapa 560 beach-retraction winch and a 16-ft. RIB are carried. 10,500 ft.^{2} deck area can hold 2,000 short tons of equipment, to include approx. two dozen main battle tanks or 50 double-stacked 20-ft. containers.

♦ 6 Gen. Frank S. Besson, Jr. class [WLST]
Bldr: VT Halter Marine (formerly Friede Goldman Halter), Moss Point, Escatawpa, Miss.

	L	In serv.	Based
LSV-1 Gen. Frank S. Besson, Jr.	30-6-87	20-1-88	Ft. Eustis, Va.
LSV-2 CW3 Harold C. Clinger	16-9-87	20-4-88	Ford Isl., Oahu
LSV-3 Gen. Brehon B. Somervell	18-11-87	26-7-88	Tacoma, Wa.
LSV-4 Lt. Gen. William B. Bunker	11-1-88	1-9-88	Ft. Eustis, Va.
LSV-5 MGen. Charles P. Gross	11-7-90	30-4-91	Ford Isl., Oahu
LSV-6 Sp. 4 James A. Loux	7-4-94	5-7-95	Ft. Eustis, Va.

ARMY LOGISTICS SUPPORT SHIPS *(continued)*

Lt. Gen. William B. Bunker (LSV-4) Takatoshi Okano, 4-01

CW3 Harold C. Clinger (LSV-2) Brian Morrison, 6-00

Lt. Gen. William B. Bunker (LSV-4) A. D. Baker III, 6-00

D: 1,612 tons light (4,199 tons fl) **S:** 12 kts trials (11.6 sust.)
Dim: 83.14 (78.03 pp) × 18.28 (18.16 wl) × 1.75 light (3.66 max. loaded)
A: None
Electronics: Radar: 2 Decca BridgeMaster-E ARPA nav. (X-band and S-band)
M: 2 G.M. EMD 16-645-E2 diesels; 2 props; 3,900 bhp—250-shp Schottel bow-thruster
Electric: 599 kw (2 × 250-kw Caterpillar 3406, 1 × 99-kw Caterpillar 3304 diesel sets)
Range: 5,500/12; 8,358/11 **Fuel:** 524 tons **Endurance:** 38 days
Crew: 6 officers, 24 enlisted

Remarks: First four ordered 19-9-86, fifth in 3-90, and sixth in 1993. Design based on Australian roll-on/roll-off, beachable cargo ship *Frances Bay.* Built to commercial specifications. LSV-1 was laid down on 16-1-87. All use rebuilt diesel engines. Two near-sisters were ordered for the Philippines in 1992. LSV-3 was employed by the Washington State Army National Guard until 1995 when transferred to the U.S. Army Reserve program. Two longer variants of the class are listed in previous entry, separately.
Hull systems: Intended to transport 816 to 1,815 metric tons of vehicles or containers on 975-m^2 cargo deck; rated at 48 TEU container capacity. Carry up to 122 tons potable water and 1,631 tons saltwater ballast. Bow and stern ramps of 8.23-m width, with bow being 15.2-m long and stern 4.87 m. There is a 5.18-m-high vehicle cargo space beneath the stern superstructure. LSV-6 can carry a 20-person training classroom made up from four 40-ft. cargo modules. Starting with LSV-4 during 1999, have had their original Raytheon radars replaced with Litton Decca sets, while Litton-Sperry Voyage Management Systems, Litton-Sperry adaptive autopilot, Litton-Sperry Electronic Chart Display, a GPS receiver, and a weather satellite receiving system were added at a cost of about $5 million per ship.

♦ 35 2000 Design utility landing craft [WLCU]

Bldr: LCU-2001–2003: Lockheed SB, Savannah Div., Savannah, Ga.; others: Friede Goldman Halter (formerly Trinity—Moss Point Marine), Escatawpa, Miss. (see Remarks)

	Laid down	L	In serv.
LCU-2001 Runnymede	2-12-86	14-8-87	21-2-90
LCU-2002 Kennesaw Mountain	22-5-87	6-10-87	28-2-90
LCU-2003 Macon	1-10-87	1-2-88	23-3-90
LCU-2004 Aldie	11-4-88	4-89	23-2-90
LCU-2005 Brandy Station	11-9-88	5-89	7-3-90
LCU-2006 Bristoe Station	11-2-89	31-7-89	30-3-90
LCU-2007 Broad Run	11-3-89	28-8-89	4-5-90
LCU-2008 Buena Vista	11-4-89	10-9-89	18-4-90
LCU-2009 Calaboza	22-11-89	9-2-90	13-7-90
LCU-2010 Cedar Run	27-12-89	12-3-90	17-8-90
LCU-2011 Chickahominy	31-1-90	16-4-90	21-9-90
LCU-2012 Chickasaw Bayou	7-3-90	26-5-90	26-10-90
LCU-2013 Churubusco	11-4-90	25-6-90	10-90
LCU-2014 Coamo	16-5-90	28-7-90	4-1-91
LCU-2015 Contreras	20-6-90	3-9-90	8-2-91
LCU-2016 Corinth	25-7-90	10-90	15-3-91
LCU-2017 El Caney	29-8-90	11-90	19-4-91
LCU-2018 Five Forks	3-10-90	17-12-90	24-5-91
LCU-2019 Fort Donelson	7-11-90	1-91	28-6-91
LCU-2020 Fort McHenry	12-12-90	2-91	2-8-91
LCU-2021 Great Bridge	16-1-91	1-4-91	6-9-91
LCU-2022 Harpers Ferry	2-91	5-91	11-10-91
LCU-2023 Hobkirk	27-3-91	6-91	15-11-91
LCU-2024 Hormigueros	1-5-91	15-7-91	20-12-91
LCU-2025 Malvern Hill	5-6-91	8-91	24-1-92
LCU-2026 Matamoros	10-7-91	9-91	28-2-92
LCU-2027 Mechanicsville	8-91	10-91	3-4-92
LCU-2028 Missionary Ridge	18-9-91	11-91	8-5-92
LCU-2029 Molino Del Rey	22-4-91	7-11-91	11-5-92
LCU-2030 Monterrey	27-5-91	5-12-91	15-5-92
LCU-2031 New Orleans	20-6-91	10-1-92	1-6-92
LCU-2032 Palo Alto	15-7-91	6-2-92	9-7-92
LCU-2033 Paulus Hook	15-8-91	5-3-92	18-9-92
LCU-2034 Perryville	15-9-91	2-4-92	4-8-92
LCU-2035 Port Hudson	15-10-91	30-4-92	1-9-92

Missionary Ridge (LCU 2028) M. Mazumdar, 10-02

Churubusco (LCU 2013) Derek Fox, 10-02

D: 672 tons light (1,102 fl) **S:** 11.5 kts
Dim: 53.03 (47.55 pp) × 12.80 × 1.43 (2.60 max. loaded) **A:** None
Electronics: Radar: 1 Raytheon SPS-64(V)2 nav.; 1 Raytheon SPS-64(V) . . . nav.
M: 2 Cummins KTA-50M diesels, 2 Kort-nozzle props; 2,500 bhp—300-shp bow-thruster
Range: 4,500/11.5 (light) **Fuel:** 282 tons **Endurance:** 18 days
Electric: 540 kw (2 × 250 kw, 1 × 40 kw) **Crew:** 2 officers, 11 enlisted

Remarks: First seven ordered 11-6-86, seven more on 31-3-87, three on 22-9-87, five on 26-2-88, one on 30-8-88, and remainder on 11-1-89—all from Thunderbolt Marine, Savannah, Georgia. Two more, to have been named *Sackett's Harbor* and *Sayler's Creek,* were not ordered. Program, including uncompleted first three, transferred to Moss Point when Trinity Marine purchased Thunderbolt Marine from Lockheed; some outfitting was also performed at Moss Point Marine's South Moss Point facility. LCU-2010, -2012, -2015, and -2034 were delivered to Yokohama, Japan, on 25-8-02 for forward layup.
Hull systems: Can carry up to 350 tons beaching cargo, including up to five M1A1 tanks or 24 standard 20-ft. shipping containers. Vehicle/container deck totals 237.8 m^2. Beaching draft forward is 1.22 m. There is a 50-ton kedging winch. Have a MacGregor-Navire 6.56-m-long by 4.48-m-wide bow ramp. Built to commercial, vice military standards. Range can be extended to 10,000 n.m. using voids for fuel.

ARMY LOGISTICS SUPPORT SHIPS *(continued)*

Mechanicsville (LCU 2027)—offloading a vehicle to the beach
Takatoshi Okano, 5-02

♦ **2 LCU 1646–class utility landing craft [WLCU]**
Bldr: General Ship & Engineering Works (In serv. 1976–78)

LCU-1667 MANASSAS LCU-1675 COMMANDO

Commando (LCU-1675) H&L Van Ginderen, 10-00

D: 170 tons light (390 fl) **S:** 11 kts **Dim:** 41.07 × 9.07 × 2.08 (max.)
M: 4 G.M. Detroit Diesel 6-71 diesels; 2 Kort-nozzle props; 1,200 bhp
Electric: 80 kw tot. (2 × 40-kw diesel sets) **Range:** 1,200/11 (light)
Fuel: 13 tons **Crew:** 6 tot.

Remarks: Retain U.S. Navy hull numbers assigned when built. Cargo: 145 tons maximum in 30.48 × 5.49–m cargo deck with ramps at both ends. Have a small navigational radar. LCU 1667 assigned to Kwajalein; LCU 1675 to 558th Transportation Company, Ft. Eustis.

Disposal notes: *San Isidro* (LCU-1670), *Naha* (LCU-1678), and *Chateau-Thierry* (LCU-1679) were placed up for sale at Hythe, U.K., during 8-02. *Catawba Ford* (LCU-1671), *Bush Master* (LCU-1672), *St. Mihiel* (LCU-1674), and *Brandywine* (LCU-1677) were for sale as of 12-02; *Birmingham* (LCU 1676), *Marseilles* (LCU 1669), and *Belleau Wood* (LCU 1668) were no longer in service as of 2003. *Double Eagle* (LCU-1673) was retired in 2004. *Antietam* (LCU 1509) the last of the LCY 1466 class was stricken in 2003.

♦ **29 Modular Causeway Systems [WLCU]**
Bldr: Lake Shore, Inc., Iron Mountain, Mich. (In serv. 1995–96)

D: . . . tons (fl) **S:** 6+ kts **Dim:** 99.98 × 7.32 × 0.91 loaded (0.30 light)
M: 2 . . . diesels; 2 waterjets; . . . bhp

Remarks: Hull made up of air-, rail-, and truck-transportable 20 × 8 ft.–wide by 4-ft.-high modules that can be joined together while afloat in up to Sea State 3. In the full-length, 328-ft. Configuration, the joined units can support 350 tons of cargo. A small modular pilothouse is used for conning.

Army Modular Causeway power unit—at center of three 8-ft. modules
George R. Schneider, 9-99

♦ **71 LCM(8) Mod. 1–class landing craft [WLCM]**
(In serv. 1954–72)

Army LCM(8) LCM-8604 Takatoshi Okano, 8-00

Army LCM(8) LCM-8596—converted into a push-tug and fireboat at Hythe, England
Jim Sanderson, 7-99

D: 58.8 tons light (116 fl) **S:** 9.2 kts (loaded) **Dim:** 22.40 × 6.42 × 1.40 (mean)
Electronics: Radar: LCM 8596, possibly others: 1 Raytheon. . . nav.
M: 2 G.M. Detroit Diesel 6-71 diesels; 2 props; 600 bhp **Range:** 150/9.2 (loaded)
Fuel: 2.4 tons **Crew:** 2–4 tot.

Remarks: Located: at Ft. Eustis, Virginia; Ft. Clayton, Panama; Ft. Belvoir, Virginia (Army Reserve); Kwajalein; Okinawa, in the Azores and in Japan; South Korea; Alaska (National Guard); Florida (Army Reserve); Tacoma, Washington (National Guard); in storage/repair at Charleston, South Carolina; prepositioned on LASH ships; and also at Diego Garcia. A rehabilitation program is under way for all the survivors. LCM 8596 was modernized at Hythe, U.K., in 1999 to function as a push-tug, with bow fenders, a deckhouse in the after half of the tank deck, and an enlarged pilothouse; the bow ramp remains functional. LCM 8265 (ex-Navy C-200779) and LCM 8268 (ex-Navy C200782) were donated to Tunisia during summer 2000.

AUXILIARIES

♦ **1 chartered Evolution 10B–class fast passenger and vehicle ferry [WAP]**
Bldr: INCAT, Hobart, Tasmania, Australia

TSV-1X SPEARHEAD (ex-*Incat 060*)

D: 1,700 tons (fl) **S:** 48 kts; 38 kts with 750 tons cargo
Dim: 97.22 (92.00 wl) × 26.60 × 3.43 loaded
A: Provision for: 2 single 25-mm Mk 38 Bushmaster low-angle; 2 single 12.7-mm mg
Electronics: Radar: 1 . . . nav.
M: 4 Ruston Paxman 20RK270 diesels; 4 Lips 120E waterjets; 37,982 bhp

ARMY AUXILIARIES *(continued)*

Spearhead (TSV-1X) U.S. Navy, 2003

Spearhead (TSV-1X) Brian Morrison, 11-02

Electric: 1,060 kw tot. (4 × 265-kw Cummins N14 diesel sets)
Range: 1,100/35 loaded; 4,000/20 **Fuel:** 190,080 liters/420,476 liters ferry mode
Crew: 31 + up to 900 troops

Remarks: Chartered 9-02 for delivery to INCAT's U.S. partner Bollinger during 11-02 for handover to the Army Tank-Automotive and Armament Command (TACOM) for demonstration and evaluation of the use of larger craft of this type in a variety of troop and vehicle intratheater lift situations. Contract was for one year, with options for one-year extensions. Has a stern loading ramp and can accommodate M1 Abrams heavy tanks. Does not have a helicopter facility. Vehicle deck has 380 truck lane 3.1-m wide and 4.35-m clear height. Can carry 267 automobiles.

Note: On completion of her overhaul at Bollinger Marine, Morgan City, Louisiana, on 14-11-02, operational control of the chartered fast passenger and vehicle ferry *Joint Venture* (HSV-X1) was transferred to the U.S. Navy for further trials.

♦ 6 LT 130 Design Large Diesel Waterway Tugs [WATA]

Bldrs: LT 801–803: Robert E. Derecktor SY, Middletown, R.I.; others: Friede Goldman-Halter Moss Point Marine, Moss Point, Miss.

	Laid down	L	In serv.
LT-801 MGen. Nathanael Greene	25-3-88	4-7-89	6-3-94
LT-802 MGen. Henry Knox	. . .	10-89	7-5-94
LT-803 MGen. Anthony Wayne	11-1-89	2-8-90	7-5-94
LT-804 BGen. Zebulon Pike	. . .	. . .	30-9-94
LT-805 MGen. Winfield Scott	. . .	. . .	30-9-94
LT-806 Col. Seth Warner	. . .	16-12-93	15-11-94

MGen. Anthony Wayne (LT-803) Ben Sullivan, 6-05

D: 924 tons (fl) **S:** 12 kts **Dim:** 39.01 (37.57 pp) × 10.97 × 4.73
A: Provision for 4 single 12.7-mm mg
Electronics: Radar: 2 . . . nav.
M: 2 G.M. EMD 12-645 FM8 diesels; 2 props; 5,100 bhp
Electric: 550 kw (2 × 275 kw) **Range:** 5,000/12 **Fuel:** 224 tons **Crew:** . . .

Remarks: First two ordered from Derecktor on 5-1-88 under FY 87 funding, with option for eight more. Two were ordered 1988, fifth on 22-2-89, and two more in 9-89. Original planned total was 13. The builder defaulted early in 1992, and the contract to finish the ships for which construction was in various stages of completion was awarded to Trinity Industries. LT-801 through -805 had been launched by the Derecktor yard, while LT-806 was transported by barge to Mississippi for launch

Col. Seth Warner (LT-806) A. D. Baker III, 6-00

and outfitting. The names for LT-807 and LT-808, which were never begun, were to have been *SgM. John Champe* and *MGen. Jacob Brown,* respectively. Several have been assigned to the Army Reserve for operation.

PATROL BOATS

♦ 1 36-foot Harbor Security Boat [WPB]

Bldr: Silver Ships (In serv. 2004)

D: . . . **Dim:** 11 × 3.15 × . . .

Remarks: Can be armed with two M60 mg fore and aft. Cruising speed is 32 kts and top speed is 38 kts. Range is 220 km at 32 kts.

SERVICE CRAFT

♦ 3 Decked, enclosed conversion kit barges [WYC] (In serv. 1950s)

BCDK-6204 BCDK-6462 BCDK-6464

D: 175 tons (760 fl) **Dim:** 36.58 × 10.06 × 2.44

Remarks: Employed as spare parts storage barges; are to be retained through 2008.

♦ 5 Deck Cargo Barges, Design 218D/E [WYC]

BK-8415 BK-8469 BK-8472 BK-8477 BK-8479

D: 185 tons (578 fl) **Dim:** 36.58 × 10.06 × 2.59 (loaded)

♦ 2 Nesting Deck Cargo Barges, Design 7001 [WYC]

BK-8327 BK-8336

D: 51 tons (181 fl) **Dim:** 24.69 × 6.70 × 1.45

♦ 8 Deck or Liquid Cargo Barges, Design 231B/C [WYC]

BG-series

D: 185 tons light (763 fl) **Dim:** 36.58 × 10.06 × 2.59

Note: Also in service is BG-1906 of an unknown class.

♦ 33 Miscellaneous BC-series Deck Cargo Barges, Harbor or Ocean Towing [WYC]

Deck Cargo Barge BC-6189 George R. Schneider, 12-92

D: 120 tons (690 fl) **Dim:** 33.53 × 9.75 × 2.34 **Cargo:** 570 tons

Remarks: Most are in storage at Hythe, England.

Disposal notes: Deck cargo barges BC-6101 and BC-6299 (585 tons each) were offered for sale at Hythe, U.K., during 8-02, along with Conversion Kit Enclosure BCDK-6464 and Reverse Osmosis Water Purification Units ROWPU-02 and ROWPU-03, which were mounted on the two barges. Deck barges BC-6156, -6158, -6161, and -6186 were sold at Curtis Bay, Maryland, on 30-10-02. BC-6169, BC-6621, and BC-6606 were for sale as of 12-02.

Notes: In addition to the barges listed previously, there are also 12 Design 455, six Design 456, and three Design 457 assembly barges and 30 portable barge propulsion devices in service. As many as 19 Modular Causeway Systems (consisting of six vehicle cargo discharge platforms, five causeway piers, and eight causeway ferries) were to have been acquired by 1999. All Delong Type A mobile piers had been deleted by the end of 1995.

♦ 4 BD-105-class Barge Derricks [WYD]

Bldr: Bollinger Machine Shop & SY, Lockport, La.

	Laid down	L	In serv.
BD-6801 Keystone State (ex-*Sacketts Harbor*)	6-96	6-97	20-6-98
BD-6802 Saltillo	9-97	6-98	4-99
BD-6803 Springfield	3-98	1-99	3-00
BD-6804 Sausalito	3-99	11-99	11-00

ARMY SERVICE CRAFT *(continued)*

Keystone State (BD-6801) Bollinger Shipyards, 5-98

D: 2,000 tons (fl) **Dim:** 60.96 × 24.38 × 4.37 (loaded)
Electric: 300 kw tot. (1 × 300-kw Kato gen., Cummins 855-G3 diesel driving)
Endurance: 20 days **Crew:** 1 officer or 2 warrant officers, 13 enlisted

Remarks: Intended to work with Military Sealift Command Large Medium-Speed Roll-on/Roll-off ships. First two (with option for four more) ordered for $29 million during 4-97; the options for two more were later exercised, but two others, to have been named *Casablanca* and *Bull Run,* were not ordered. BD-6801 was delivered to the 949th Transportation Co., Brandt U.S. Army Reserve Center, Baltimore, Maryland, BD-6802 to the 73rd Transportation Co., Ft. Eustis, Virginia, and BD-6803 to the 7th Transportation Group, Ft. Eustis. The name for BD-6801 was changed to commemorate 13 Army Reserve soldiers from Greensburg, Pennsylvania, killed in Saudi Arabia in 1991; the name duplicates that of Navy crane ship T-ACS 1.
Hull systems: The crane, built by AmClyde Engineered Products, can lift 115 tons at 18.3-m radius and 50 tons at 53.3-m radius; it is powered by a 1,200-bhp Cummins KTA-38 G2 diesel. The barge hull can also accommodate 453 metric tons of deck cargo, and a galley, mess, recreation space, medical space, and machine shop are fitted. GPS and a VHF radio communications station are also carried.

♦ 2 Design 264B floating cranes [WYD]
Bldr: . . . (In serv. 1950s)

BD-6074 Naples   BD-6701 Big Bethel

D: 1,630 tons (fl) **Dim:** 42.67 × 21.34 × 1.91 **Electric:** 250 kw
Fuel: 40 tons

Remarks: Crane capacity is 89 tons at 24.4-m radius, 75 tons at 31.8-m radius; auxiliary hook can lift 15 tons at 37.3 m. BD-6659 refitted 1989 as prototype for a class-wide refurbishment program. BD-6073 is in storage at Hythe, England, and BD-6072 and 6074 are prepositioned at Diego Garcia; the others are all in active service. *Sicily* (BD-6071) was stricken 1990, *Luzon* (BD-6069) in 6-93, and one other in 1996. The entire class was to have been retired by end-2002, and *Algiers* (BD-6072) and *Pine Ridge* (BD-6073) were placed up for sale during 8-02. *Qui Nhon* (BD 6070), *Prairie Fire* (BD 6660), *Diamond Island* (BD 6661), *Mindanao* (BD 6658), *Big Switch* (BD 6700), and *Wilderness* (BD 6659) were no longer in service as of 2003.

Disposal note: T boat design 2001 inshore transports T 449 and T 600 were no longer in service as of 2003.

♦ 1 Double-ended Harbor Ferry [WYFB]
Bldr: Marinette Marine, Marinette, Wisc. (In serv. 1959)

FB-814

Remarks: 19.81-m ferry used at U.S. Military Academy, West Point.

♦ 2 41-ft. catamaran patrol launches (WYFL)
Bldr: United States Marine, Trinity Marine Group, New Orleans (In serv. 3-92)

HSPC-1   HSPC-2

HSPC-1 and HSPC-2 Trinity Marine, 3-92

D: . . . tons **S:** 45 kts **Dim:** 12.50 × . . . × . . .
M: 2 Ford Merlin turbocharged diesels; 2 Arneson ASD 10 surface outdrives; 800 bhp
Crew: 3 tot. + 8 passengers

Remarks: Employed at Kwajalein Atoll in the Marshall Islands. Have forward-looking infrared sensor, navigational radar, secure communications, and can carry two Zodiac F470 rigid inflatable raiding craft. Hulls constructed of Kevlar fabric over polyvinyl chloride foam cores. HSPC stands for "High-Speed Patrol Craft."

♦ 2 catamaran personnel launches [WYFL]
Bldr: Nichols Bros., Whidbey Island, Wash.

FB-816 Jera (In serv. 2-88)   FB-817 Jelang K (In serv. 1988)

D: 63.7 tons (fl) **S:** 25 kts **Dim:** 23.00 × 8.68 × 1.80
Electronics: Radar: 1/Furuno FCR 1411/6 nav., 1/Furuno 8030D nav.
M: 2 G.M. 16V92 TA diesels; 2 props; 1,920 bhp **Electric:** 100 kw

Remarks: Intended to carry 75 passengers at Kwajalein. Are of the Wavepiercer proprietary design from Australia.

♦ 9 High Speed Patrol launches [WYFL]
Bldr: Livesay Boats, San Diego, Calif. (In serv. 1990s)

J-7850   J-7852 through J-7858   J-7863

Remarks: No data available other than that they are 8.23 m overall and are powered by one outdrive diesel engine. Used as range safety boats at Aberdeen Proving Grounds on Chesapeake Bay, Maryland. Some have locally applied names. 7861 and 7864 were retired by 10-02.

♦ 1 J-boat Design 243B picket boat [WYFL]
Bldr: Lock City Marine (In serv.: 1954)

J-3761

J-3761 William Rau, 1-96

D: 6.7 tons (light) **S:** 15 kts **Dim:** 14.12 × 3.23 × 0.99
M: 2 diesels; 2 props; 400 bhp **Range:** 355/15

Remarks: Steel construction. J-3761 is located at the U.S. Military Academy.

♦ 1 liquid cargo barge [WYON]
Bldr: Conrad Industries Orange SB, Orange, Tex. (In serv. 1996)

BK-9603

Remarks: 59.44 m overall; no other information available.

♦ 1 Design 7011 floating machine shops [WYR]
Bldr: . . .

FMS-789 Vulcan

D: 1,160 tons light (1,525 fl) **Dim:** 64.14 × 12.19 × 2.36 (max.)
Electric: 400 kw (4 × 100 kw) **Fuel:** 140 tons **Crew:** 30 tot.

Remarks: Modified from Design 7016 refrigerated stores barges. Have 8.9-ton crane amidships. Workshops include: battery, blacksmith, carpentry, electrical, engine, fuel injector, machine, paint, pipefitting, electronic, refrigeration, sheet metal, shipfitting, and welding. FMS 789 with the National Guard at Tacoma, Washington. Sisters *Ares* (FMS-788) and *Athena* (FMS 786) were stricken by 2003.

♦ 16 ST-900-class push tugs [WYTB]
Bldr: Conrad Industries Orange SB, Orange, Tex.

	In serv.		In serv.
ST-901 Dorchester Heights	2-9-98	ST-910 Santiago	13-12-01
ST-902 Pelham Point	15-12-99	ST-911 Enduring Freedom (ex-*Vincennes*)	16-5-02
ST-903 Fort Stanwix	21-12-99		
ST-904 Green Springs	21-12-99	ST-912 Fort Moultrie	15-3-02
ST-905 Scholarie	28-3-00	ST-913 . . .	1-03
ST-906 Sag Harbor	28-3-00	ST-914 . . .	3-03
ST-907 Appomattox	24-3-00	ST-915 . . .	2004
ST-908 Sacketts Harbor	20-6-00	ST-916 . . .	10-05
ST-909 Bunker Hill	15-6-01		

D: 109 long tons (light) **S:** 10.5 kts
Dim: 18.19 × 6.90 (6.70 wl) × 2.03
A: 5 5.66-mm M-16 automatic rifles **Electronics:** Radar: 1 Raytheon R40XX nav.
M: 2 Cummins KTA19-M3 diesels; 2 4-bladed Kaplan swivelling-nozzle props; 1,280 bhp
Electric: 110 kw tot. (2 × 55-kw Onan/Admiral MCGGA diesel-driven sets)
Range: 700/10.5 **Fuel:** 3,000 gallons **Crew:** 4 tot. (accomm. for 5)

Remarks: Nine were ordered 6-96 for $30 million to be transported aboard Army-support Military Sealift Command supply ships to move LASH and general cargo barges in harbors and on inland and coastal waterways; delivered at one-month intervals, with three more ordered later. ST-913 and ST-914 were ordered on 12-11-01. Designed by Corning Townsend of C.T. Marine. Are intended to serve for at least 25 years. Two more were ordered fall 2002 for delivery by 10-05. ST-911 was renamed prior to delivery.
Hull systems: Have 16.8-ton bollard pull ahead, 12.2-ton bollard pull astern, and 1.8-ton bollard pull athwartships. Hull molded depth is 2.44 m. Navigation equipment includes a Rockwell GPS receiver. Can turn 360° in their own lengths in 34 sec. and have four rudders.

ARMY SERVICE CRAFT *(continued)*

Dorchester Heights (ST-901)—note the twin push-knees at the bow A. D. Baker III, 6-00

♦ **2 former commercial large harbor tugs [WYTB]**
Bldr: Quality SY, Houma, La.

LT-101 Gulf Condor (In serv. 3-81)
LT-102 Mystic (ex-*Gulf Raven*) (In serv. 4-81)

D: . . . tons **S:** . . . kts **Dim:** 36.88 × 10.36 × 4.24
Electronics: Radar: . . .
M: 2 G.M. Electromotive Div. 12-cyl. diesels; 2 props; 4,200 bhp
Electric: 150 kw tot. (2 × 75-kw diesel sets)
Range: . . . / . . . **Fuel:** 47.9 tons

Remarks: 193 grt. Both employed at Kwajalein and are owned by the Army Transportation Corps.

♦ **4 Design-3006 large harbor tugs [WYTB]**
Bldr: . . . (In serv. mid-1950s)

LT-1974 Champagne-Marne
LT-2076 New Guinea
LT-2085 Anzio
LT-2096 Valley Forge

Champagne-Marne (LT-1974) A. D. Baker III, 6-00

D: 295 tons light (390 fl) **S:** 12.75 kts **Dim:** 32.61 × 8.08 × 3.71 (max.)
M: 1 Fairbanks-Morse (LT-1974, -2085: G.E. EMD 12V-645-E7 diesel); 1 prop; 1,200 bhp (see Remarks)
Electric: 80 kw **Range:** 3,323/12 light **Fuel:** 54 tons
Crew: 16 tot. (accomm. for 20)

Remarks: Bollard pull: 12 tons. Built in two series: LT-1936 through -1977 and LT-2202; and LT-2075 through -2096. LT-2085 is prepositioned at Diego Garcia. All but two were to be retired by 2008, but seven were rehabilitated during 1995–2001 (LT-1973, LT-1974, LT-2081, LT-2085, LT-2090, LT-2092, and LT-2094); they received one 2,350-bhp General Electric EMD 12V-645-E7 diesel and now have a bollard pull of 31.5 tons and a 12.8-kt maximum speed, while the generator plant now totals 330 kw from two Caterpillar 3306-D1 diesel-driven generators, and they can pump 2,000 gallons of firefighting foam per minute. Five of the modernized units were then placed up for sale during 8-02.
Disposals: *Bataan* (LT-2086) and *Kwajalein* (LT-2087) were stricken 2-94 and *Murfreesboro* (LT-1959) in 1995–96. In 8-97, Congress directed the transfer of *Normandy* (LT-1971) and *Salerno* (LT-1953) to the Brownsville Navigational District, Brownsville, Texas. Congress also required the transfer of the *Attleboro* (LT-1977) to a private agency under the FY 99 Defense Authorization Act, but the ship was placed up for sale at Hythe, U.K., during 8-02, along with *Lundy's Lane* (LT-1960), *Shiloh* (LT-1973), *San Sapor* (LT-2081), *Sp.4 Larry G. Dahl* (ST-2090), and *North Africa* (ST-2092). LT-1973, LT-2090, and LT-2092 had recently undergone expensive refurbishments and had been re-engined. *Fredericksburg* (LT-1956), *Gettysburg* (LT-1972), and *Petersburg* (LT-2088) were for sale as of 12-02.

Disposal notes: *Sgt. William W. Seay* (LT 1937) and *Okinawa* (LT 1970) were no longer in service as of 10-03. The last unit of the Design 3004–class 600-bhp medium harbor tug design was sold during 2003.

U.S. ARMY CORPS OF ENGINEERS

The U.S. Army Corps of Engineers operates hundreds of tugs, utility craft, Logistical Amphibious Recovery Craft (LARC), dredges and barges in construction, local transportation, and survey service.

Army Corps of Engineers dredge Wheeler George Schneider, 9-05

Army Corps of Engineers Survey Launch Laborde George Schneider, 9-05

Army Corps of Engineers towboat Goodwin George Schneider, 9-05

Army Corps of Engineers Amphibious LARC 906 Edward McDonnell, 4-05

U.S. ARMY SPACE AND STRATEGIC DEFENSE COMMAND

Note: Headquartered at Redstone Arsenal, Huntsville, Alabama, the Space and Strategic Defense Command operates the missile test and instrumentation range at Kwajalein Atoll in the South Pacific.

♦ **1 Stalwart-class former ocean surveillance ship [WAGM]**
Bldr: Friede Goldman Halter, Moss Point, Miss.

	Laid down	L	In serv.
Worthy (ex-T-AGOS 14)	3-4-86	6-2-88	7-4-89

D: 1,467 tons light (2,258 fl) **S:** 11 kts **Dim:** 68.28 (59.13 pp) × 13.11 × 4.57
Electronics: Radar: 2 Raytheon . . . navigational (S- and X-band)
M: 4 Caterpillar-Kato D-398B 800-bhp diesels, G.E. electric drive; 2/4-bladed props; 2,200 shp (1,600 hp sust.)—550-hp bow-thruster

U.S. ARMY SPACE AND STRATEGIC DEFENSE COMMAND
(continued)

Worthy U.S. Army, 1999

Electric: 1,500 kVA from main generators, plus 250-kw emergency diesel set
Range: 11,200/11 plus 2,088/3 **Fuel:** 657 tons **Endurance:** 98 days
Crew: . . .

Remarks: A former ocean surveillance ship transferred from Military Sealift Command to the U.S. Geological Survey on 30-9-93 and laid up at Redwood City, California, through 6-94; $23.1 million was included in the FY 94 budget to convert her as a research ship to be homeported at Redwood City, California; instead, in 1995, the ship was placed on indefinite loan to the U.S. Army Space and Strategic Defense Command, Redstone Arsenal, Huntsville, Alabama, for use as a missile-range instrumentation ship at Kwajalein Atoll, in the Republic of the Marshall Islands. Operated under contract by Raytheon Range Systems Engineering and used to track and collect telemetry from missiles launched from Vandenberg Air Force Base, California, as platform for the Kwajalein Mobile Range Safety System (KMRSS).
Mission systems: Two 6.70-m-diameter radomes cover the two co-located HELIX command-and-control and telemetry system antennas, and the former SURTASS control room is used as the KMRSS operations center. Three Inmarsat SATCOM antennas are installed forward of the stacks, and there are four GPS receivers. A Mk 51 Optical Acquisition Aid was placed atop the pilothouse.

Note: The U.S. Army also operates several hundred Fairey Marine bridge erection boats.

U.S. DEPARTMENT OF COMMERCE
NATIONAL OCEANIC AND ATMOSPHERIC ADMINISTRATION

Personnel: Approximately 300 commissioned NOAA Corps officers and 400 civilians.

Organization: NOAA operates a fleet of research ships divided into the two categories of Research and Survey. Headquartered in Rockville, Maryland, it has its major maritime facilities at the Atlantic Marine Center in Norfolk, Virginia, and the Pacific Marine Center in Seattle, Washington; minor NOAA maritime facilities exist at Woods Hole, Massachusetts; Pascagoula, Mississippi; Miami, Florida; La Jolla, California; and Honolulu, Hawaii.
Subordinated to NOAA is the National Marine Fisheries Service, which operates an unspecified number of small patrol craft; these display the words "NOAA Enforcement" on the hull sides.

Aviation: NOAA, using about 25 NOAA Corps and 50 civilian personnel, operates two WP-3D Orion, one Gulfstream IV(SP), two DeHavilland DHC-6 Twin Otter, two Shrike Commander 500S, one Turbo Commander 690A, one Cessna Citation-II 550, and two Lake LA-250 Turbo Renegade research aircraft; helicopters include two Bell 212 and one McDonnell Douglas MD-500D. Aviation activities are headquartered at MacDill Air Force Base, Florida.

Note: Hulls and superstructures are white, masts and stacks buff. Hull numbers appear on either side (preceded by "R" for research or "S" for Survey) below the letters "NOAA." The front digit in the three-digit hull number is the NOAA class (i.e., size) number for the ship, determined from the gross tonnage and horsepower.

OCEANOGRAPHIC RESEARCH SHIPS [WAGOR]

♦ 2 (+ 2) FRV-40 class fisheries survey ships
Bldr: Friede Goldman Halter, Moss Point, Escatawpa, Miss.

	Laid down	L	In serv.
R 224 Oscar Dyson	18-4-02*	17-10-03	28-5-05
R 225 Henry B. Bigelow		8-7-05	21-7-06
R . . .	. . .	. . .	. . .
R . . .	. . .	. . .	. . .

*Start of construction

D: . . . tons **S:** 14 kts **Dim:** 64.00 × 14.94 × 8.53
Electronics: Radar: . . .
M: Integrated diesel-electric plant: 2 Caterpillar 3512B DITA diesels (1,824 bhp each), 2 Caterpillar 3508B diesels (1,220 bhp each); 1 Rolls Royce 14-ft. fixed-pitch prop; ASI Robicon bow-thruster

Henry B. Bigelow (R 225) NOAA, 7-05

Oscar Dyson (R 224) NOAA via D. Shirlaw, 2005

Electric: 4,724 kw tot. (2 × 1,360-kw Caterpillar 3512B; 2 × 912-kw Caterpillar 3508B; 1 × 180-kw Caterpillar 3306 backup)
Range: 12,000 / . . . **Endurance:** 40 days
Crew: 20 operating crew with room for 57 total on board.

Remarks: Design process begun 6-93. First unit ordered for $38.3 million on 18-1-01. Initial funding of $39.6 million was requested in the FY 99 budget, and three additional were to be requested, the last in FY 03; instead, the first was authorized under FY 00 but not funded sufficiently to permit construction, while the other three were to be requested under FY 02 through FY 04. Construction start has been delayed by design problems and the builder's financial condition. To be based at Kodiak, Alaska; Woods Hole, Massachusetts; Pascagoula, Mississippi; and Newport, Oregon, respectively.
Mission systems: Will be equipped for fisheries research, hydroacoustic surveys, bottom and pelagic trawling, marine mammal observation, general oceanographic research, and hydrographic survey. Will have a dynamic positioning system, support systems for remotely operated vehicles (ROVs), and several different sonar systems. Will have fish laboratory; wet and dry laboratories; an autosalinometer room; and chemistry, hydrographic, acoustic, and computer laboratories. The integrated propulsion plant allows any or all of the four 600-V a.c. diesel generator sets to provide the necessary power for propulsion and ship systems operation.
A retractable "centerboard" will be fitted for stabilization and instrument-housing purposes.

♦ 1 Thomas G. Thompson class
Bldr: Trinity Marine Halter SY, Moss Point, Miss.

	Laid down	L	In serv.
R 104 Ronald S. Brown (ex-*Researcher*)	21-2-95	30-5-96	19-7-97

Ronald S. Brown (R 104) Werner Globke, 12-04

D: 2,100 tons light (3,250 fl) **S:** 15 kts **Dim:** 83.52 × 16.00 × 5.18
Electronics:
Radar: 2 Sperry RASCAR nav.; Radtec-Enterprise WSR-74C doppler weather-mapping
Sonar: Sea Beam 2112A mapping (12 kHz), Ocean Data sub-bottom profiler (3.5 kHz), Nautronix RS916 acoustic positioning system
M: 3 Caterpillar 3516TA diesels, 3 1,500-kw Kato generators, 2 G.E. electric motors; 2 LIPS azimuth props; 6,000 shp—1,117-shp Elliot White Gill bow-thruster

NOAA OCEANOGRAPHIC RESEARCH SHIPS [WAGOR]
(continued)

Electric: 2,500 kw tot. (3 × 750-kw Kato sets, Caterpillar 3508TA diesels driving; 1 × 250-kw Kato emergency set, Caterpillar 3406TA diesel driving)
Range: 11,300/12 + 30 days on station **Endurance:** 60 days
Crew: 20 crew + 25 scientists (+10 in accomm. vans)

Remarks: 3,180 grt. Ordered 17-2-94 as the fourth unit of the U.S. Navy's *Thomas G. Thompson* (AGOR 23) class but not numbered in the navy series as an AGOR. Work began 15-9-94. Accepted by the Military Sealift Command on 25-4-97 and transferred on the same date to NOAA. R 104 was renamed 30-5-96 in honor of former Secretary of Commerce, killed 3-4-96 in airplane crash in Bosnia. Ran aground in Swanson Bay, British Colombia, on 23-4-00, holing a fuel tank. Homeported at Charleston, South Carolina. During 4-01, conducted the Aerosol Characterization Experiment off the coasts of Japan and Korea, in conjunction with a National Science Foundation C-130 and a Navy Twin Otter light transport.

Capable of all-purpose oceanographic research and, specifically, chemical and biological oceanography, multidiscipline environmental investigations, ocean engineering, marine acoustics, marine geology, and geophysics. Is also capable of carrying out bathymetric and magnetometry surveys. The ship was initially involved in worldwide climate change research.

Hull systems: Has a dynamic positioning system accurate to 300 ft. in a 27-kt wind and 11-ft. seas. Has 372 m^2 of laboratory space and space for four lab/accommodations vans on deck, 325 m^2 working space on deck, stern A-frame and starboard oceanographic gantries, Markey DESH-9-11 double-drum waterfall winch. Navigational equipment includes a DSN-450 doppler speed log, a VN-150-HP acoustic doppler current profiler, Sperry Mk 37 and Mk 39 ring-laser gyrocompasses, Northstar 941X and Ashtech 3DF GPS receivers, and two Raytheon RD-500 echo sounders. Has a Leica MX-2400 Inmarsat-A SATCOMM transceiver. The 18-ft.-diameter radome for the weather-mapping radar is mounted atop the foremast; the radar has a peak power of 250,000 watts and can track, detail, and record storms within 150 n.m. of the ship. A 951-MHz wind-profiling system is to be installed. A 10-m-tall bow-mounted tower supports equipment for the IMET (Improved Meteoroligical) World Ocean Circulation Experiment.

♦ 1 ex-Navy YTT 9–class former torpedo trials ship
Bldr: McDermott, Morgan City, La.

	Laid down	L	In serv.	Base
R 352 NANCY FOSTER (ex-*Agate Pass,* YTT 12)	18-9-89	6-9-90	30-10-92	Charleston, S.C.

Nancy Foster (R 352) NOAA, 2003

D: 1,000 tons light (1,168 fl) **S:** 11 kts sust.
Dim: 56.85 (53.83 pp) × 12.19 × 3.23
Electronics: Radar: 2 Raytheon SPS-64(V)9 ARPA nav.
M: 1 Cummins KTA-50M diesel; 1 prop; 1,250 bhp—2 electric Z-drive thrusters, 300 shp each—400-shp bow-thruster
Electric: 1,310 kw tot. (3 × 395-kw, Cummins VTA-28 GS/G.C. sets, 1 × 125-kw emergency set)
Range: 1,800/11 **Fuel:** 70 tons **Endurance:** 12 days
Crew: 10 (+ up to 15 scientists)

Remarks: Transferred to NOAA on 31-1-00 after never having actively served the USN; was built as a torpedo recovery and trials ship. Conversion to complete 1-03 to replace the *Ferrel* (R 492) to conduct coastal and estuarine seawater circulation studies off the U.S. East Coast and Gulf of Mexico. Sister *Discovery Bay* (YTT 11) was assigned in 2001 to the joint NOAA/National Geographic Society Sustainable Sea Expedition five-year study of U.S. coastal waters and carries manned research submersibles; she does not display her hull number.
Hull systems: Working deck aft. Have 7.3-ton-capacity electrohydraulic crane to recover torpedoes and to handle sensor arrays and recovery equipment. Also carry smaller, 4.5-ton (to handle recovery vehicles) and 3.5-ton cranes and have four 10-ton vertical traction winches. Can operate on battery power for quiet operations and can maneuver precisely with Z-drive thrusters aft and bow-thruster. Has extensive telemetry and communications systems, global positioning system, Loran-C, Raytheon RD-500 echo sounder, and WQC-2 underwater telephone.

♦ 7 ex-U.S. Navy Stalwart-class former ocean surveillance ships
Bldr: Halter Marine, Moss Point, Miss.

	Laid down	L	In serv.
R 333 KA'IMIMOANA (ex-*Titan,* T-AGOS 15)	30-10-86	18-6-88	8-3-89
R 334 HI'IALAKAI (ex-*Vindicator,* T-AGOS 3; ex-WMEC 3; ex-T-AGOS 3)	14-4-83	1-6-84	21-11-84
R 335 OSCAR ELTON SETTE (ex-*Adventurous,* T-AGOS 13)	19-12-85	23-9-87	19-8-88
R 336 GORDON GUNTER (ex-*Relentless,* T-AGOS 18)	22-4-88	12-5-89	12-1-90
R 337 MCARTHUR II (ex-*Indomitable,* T-AGOS 7)	26-1-85	16-7-85	1-12-85
R 338 OKEANOS EXPLORER (ex-*Capable,* T-AGOS 16)	17-10-87	28-10-88	9-6-89
. . . (ex-*Assertive,* T-AGOS 9)	30-7-85	20-6-86	12-9-86

D: 1,652 tons light (2,301 fl) **S:** 11 kts **Dim:** 68.28 (62.1 wl) × 13.10 × 4.57
Electronics:
Radar: 2 . . . navigational
Sonar: . . . sidescan mapping
M: 4 Caterpillar-Kato D-398B 800-bhp diesels, G.E. electric drive; 2/4-bladed props; 2,200 shp (1,600 hp sust.)—550-hp bow-thruster
Electric: 1,500 kVA from main generators, plus 265-kw emergency set
Range: 8,000/10.5 (R 335, 336: 5,500/10.5) **Fuel:** 904 tons **Endurance:** 30 days
Crew: 5 officers, 3 licensed engineers, 13 mariners + 10–15 scientific party

Ka'imimoana (R 333) W. Michael Young, 3-06

Gordon Gunter (R 336) NOAA, 1999

Remarks: R 333: 2,014 grt; others 1,486 grt/786 dwt. Previous data refer specifically to R 333.

R 335 (initially to have been R 331) was transferred to NOAA on 1-6-92 and was delivered to Norfolk, Virginia, with the intent to outfit her as a survey ship. The ship was used for basic training during 1993 and then laid up without modifications. Using FY 01 funding, the ship is undergoing conversion as a fisheries research vessel from 10-01 to 10-02 at Atlantic Dry Dock Corp., Jacksonville, Florida, and was recommissioned at Honolulu on 22-1-03 as replacement for the *Townsend Cromwell* (R 443). The after deck was cleared for use as a long-line fisheries deck, and the ship was equipped with a multibeam echo-sounder and other echo-sounders to permit her use in charting.

R 333, deactivated 33-8-93 from Military Sealift Command, was transferred 11-93 and was converted 5-95 to 3-96 to serve as tender to the Tropic Atmosphere Ocean Buoy Array by Maritime Contractors, Bellingham, Washington; the ship supports the Global Ocean Atmosphere Land System program and is homeported at Honolulu, Hawaii. R 333 has a 950-ft.^{2} laboratory and an oceanographic gallows crane at the stern. An Inmarsat-A SATCOM terminal was added during 1997 for transmittal of research data.

R 336, deactivated 17-3-93 from MSC, was inactive at Norfolk until 1996, when she was towed to Pascagoula, Mississippi; recommissioned as a fisheries research ship on 28-8-98 to replace the *Chapman* (R 446); she is based at Pascagoula. R 336 has a 480-ft.^{2} wet labs, 480-ft.^{2} dry lab, 260-ft.^{2} chemistry/hydrology lab, 170-ft.^{2} computer lab, and 100-ft.^{2} electronics lab. During conversion, a stern trawl ramp and handling gear, and nine deck and oceanographic winches were added.

R 334 was transferred to NOAA on 30-10-01 and sailed for Seattle for conversion into a research diving support ship, with a large hyperbaric chamber for divers and the addition of several small boats. R 334 was renamed in 10-03.

R 337 was transferred to NOAA on 9-12-02 for conversion to a survey ship. Ex-*Assertive* (T-AGOS 9), was deactivated 1-9-03 and transferred to NOAA during 2004 followed by R 338 that same year. A contract to convert R 338 for oceanographic duties was let on 22 August 2005, though during 4-06 she was damaged during a major fire, delaying her entry into service.

♦ 1 Miller Freeman class
Bldr: American Shipbldg., Lorain, Ohio

	L	In serv.	Base
R 223 MILLER FREEMAN	1967	1974	Seattle

D: 1,920 tons (fl) **S:** 14 kts (sust.) **Dim:** 66.0 × 12.5 × 6.1
Electronics: Radar: 1 . . . X-band nav.; 1 . . . S-band nav.
M: 1 G.M. diesel; 1 CP prop; 2,200 bhp—400-shp Schottle rectractable bow-thruster
Electric: 700 kw tot. **Range:** 8,900/12 **Fuel:** 450 tons
Endurance: 41 days
Crew: 7 NOAA officers, 4 licensed officers, 29 mariners, 11 scientists

NOAA OCEANOGRAPHIC RESEARCH SHIPS [WAGOR]
(continued)

Miller Freeman (R 223) Victor M. Baca, 2-01

Remarks: 1,515 grt/680 nrt. Conducts fisheries and living marine resources research. Was to be replaced during 1990s but remained in trawling survey work during 1996–97.
Hull systems: Chemical, wet oceanographic, fish processing, utility labs. Fish-finder sonars, several echo sounders. Has a stern trawl ramp and net-handling gallows. A retractable stabilization centerboard provides mounting positions for oceanographic and acoustic research sensors; when deployed it increases draft to 9.3 m. Inmarsat-B SATCOM terminal added 1997 for automatic transmittal of research data.

♦ 1 Oregon II class
Bldr: Ingalls SB, Pascagoula, Miss.

	L	In serv.	Base
R 332 Oregon II	2-67	8-67	Pascagoula, Miss.

Oregon II (R 332) NOAA, 1987

D: 952 tons **S:** 12 kts (sust.) **Dim:** 51.8 × 10.4 × 4.3
M: 2 Fairbanks-Morse diesels; 1 CP prop; 1,600 bhp **Electric:** 400 kw tot.
Range: 9,500/12 **Fuel:** 255 tons **Endurance:** 30 days
Crew: 6 licensed officers, 10 crew, 11 scientists

Remarks: 703 grt/228 nrt. Conducts fisheries and living marine resource research for the National Marine Fisheries Service in the Gulf of Mexico, Caribbean, and South Atlantic and along the southeast U.S. Atlantic coast. Has two trawls, one hydrographic and one bathythermographic winches, and five laboratories.

♦ 1 Albatross IV class
Bldr: Southern SB, Slidell, Louisiana

	L	In serv.	Base
R 342 Albatross IV	4-62	5-63	Woods Hole, Mass.

Albatross IV (R 342) NOAA, 1987

D: 1,089 tons (fl) **S:** 12 kts (sust.) **Dim:** 57.0 × 10.0 × 4.9
M: 2 Caterpillar diesels; 1 Kort-nozzle CP prop; 1,130 bhp **Electric:** 450 kw tot.
Range: 3,933/10 **Fuel:** 150 tons **Endurance:** 16 days
Crew: 4 NOAA officers, 3 licensed engineers, 13 crew, 14 scientists

Remarks: 1,115 grt/413 nrt. Has conducted fisheries and living marine resources research off the U.S. northeastern Atlantic coast. Inactive 1988 but reactivated under FY 92 budget; to be replaced during the 1990s, but underwent repair period mid-1993. Refitted again 1995–96.

Hull systems: Has wet and dry oceanographic, photographic, biological, plankton, and electronics laboratories, four scientific winches, vertical fish-finding sonar, and deep- and shallow-water echo sounders. There is a 125-hp bow-thruster. Inmarsat-B terminal added 1997 for transmittal of research data.

Disposal note: Fisheries research ship *Townsend Cromwell* (R 443) was retired on 10-10-02.

♦ 1 David Starr Jordan class
Bldr: Christy Corp., Sturgeon Bay, Wisc.

	L	In serv.	Base
R 444 David Starr Jordan	12-64	1-66	San Diego, Calif.

David Starr Jordan (R 444) H&L Van Ginderen, 9-99

D: 993 tons (fl) **S:** 11.5 kts (sust.) **Dim:** 52.1 × 11.2 × 3.8 (4.8 over sonar)
M: 2 White-Superior diesels; 2 CP props; 1,086 bhp **Electric:** 400 kw tot.
Range: 8,560/11.5 **Fuel:** 180 tons **Endurance:** 30 days
Crew: 6 licensed officers, 10 crew, 15 scientists

Remarks: 873 grt/262 nrt. Conducts fisheries and living marine resources research off U.S., Central, and South American Pacific coasts. Physical and biological oceanography, chemical, and photographic labs. Has a retractable fish-finding sonar, a vertical fish-finder, and several echo sounders. Schottel retractable bow-thruster of 200 hp. Has an underwater observation chamber at the bow.

♦ 1 Delaware II class
Bldr: South Portland Engineering Corp., South Portland, Maine

	L	In serv.	Base
R 445 Delaware II	12-67	10-68	Woods Hole, Mass.

Delaware II (R 445) NOAA, 1992

D: 758 tons (fl) **S:** 11.5 kts (sust.) **Dim:** 47.2 × 9.2 × 4.5
M: 1 G.M. diesel; 1 prop; 1,230 bhp **Electric:** 300 kw tot.
Range: 6,600/11.5 **Fuel:** 132 tons **Endurance:** 24 days
Crew: 6 licensed officers, 9 crew, 10 scientists

Remarks: 483 grt/231 nrt. Conducts fisheries and living marine resources research off U.S. Atlantic coast. Two oceanographic labs, fish-finding sonars, stern net ramp. Modernized for an additional 10–12 years' service under FY 94 funding, receiving new oceanographic equipment, additional scientist berthing spaces, and fisheries hydro-acoustic equipment; completed 5-96 at Detyens Shipyard, Mt. Pleasant, South Carolina.

Disposal note: *Ferrel* (R 492) was retired late in 2002 and placed in reserve for transfer to another agency or to a school.

♦ 1 John N. Cobb class
Bldr: Western Boatbldg., Tacoma, Wash.

	L	In serv.	Base
R 552 John N. Cobb	1-50	2-50	Seattle

D: 250 tons (fl) **S:** 9.3 kts (sust.) **Dim:** 28.3 × 7.9 × 3.3
M: 1 Fairbanks-Morse diesel; 1 prop; 325 bhp **Electric:** 60 kw tot.
Range: 2,900/9.3 **Fuel:** 25 tons **Endurance:** 13 days
Crew: 4 licensed officers, 4 crew, 4 scientists

Remarks: 185 grt/78 nrt. Conducts fisheries and living marine resources research off southeastern Alaska and the U.S. Pacific Northwest. Has a single laboratory. Inactivated 1989, but in 1994 was being employed in ocean salmon trawling studies, operating from Juneau, Alaska.

NOAA OCEANOGRAPHIC RESEARCH SHIPS [WAGOR]
(continued)

John N. Cobb (R 552) NOAA

HYDROGRAPHIC SURVEY SHIPS [WAGS]

♦ 1 ex-U.S. Navy John McDonnell–class coastal survey ship
Bldr: Halter Marine, Inc., Moss Point, Miss.

	Laid down	L	In serv.
S 222 Thomas Jefferson (ex-*Littlehales* T-AGS 52)	25-10-89	14-2-92	10-1-93

Thomas Jefferson (S 222) Jim Sanderson, 7-02

D: 2,054 **S:** 14 kts (12 sust.) **Dim:** 63.40 × 13.72 × 4.27
Electronics:
Radar: 1 . . . 3 cm nav.; 1 . . . 10 cm nav.
Sonar: Simrad EM-1002 Multibeam hull-mounted (95 kHz); Klein K 5500 towed side-scan (105 kHz); 2 12-kHz deep-water echo sounders; 2 24-kHz shallow-water echo sounders; 2 200-kHz shallow-water echo sounders
M: 1 G.M. EMD12-645F7B turbocharged, 900 rpm diesel; 1 prop; 2,550 bhp—1 230-bhp Detroit Diesel 6V92N cruising diesel
Electric: 1,200 kw tot. (3 × 350 kw, G.M. 8V92TAB diesel-driven ship's service; 1 × 150 kw, G.M. 6V92N-driven emergency set)
Range: 12,000/12 **Crew:** 19 crew + 11 survey party

Remarks: Transferred to NOAA 3-3-03 to replace the earlier *Whiting* (S 329). Added to FY 87 U.S. Navy shipbuilding budget by Congress with nonbinding suggestion that they should be converted from existing tuna clippers. Delay in ordering to 10-11-88 occasioned by need to define characteristics for the unexpected gifts. Second pair to replace T-AGS 33 and 34 were to have been included in the FY 94 budget but were dropped. Sister *John McDonnell* (T-AGS 51) remains in U.S. Navy (Military Sealift Command) service. Based at Norfolk, Virginia.
Hull systems: Intended to collect hydrographic data in waters from 10 to 4,000 m deep. The smaller "son" diesel propels the ship at speeds from 4 to 6 kts. Has roll stabilization tank. Navigation equipment includes GPS and Loran-C receivers, collision avoidance system, dual-axis doppler speed log and HYSTAR II computerized data-collection system. Laboratory space: 700 ft.^{2}; deck working space: 1,500 ft.^{2}; and scientific storage space: 2,300 ft.^{2} Two telescopic, 7-ton max. cranes are fitted. Carries two 10.36 × 2.82 × 0.91–m, 7.4-ton survey launches, equipped with a single 225-bhp diesel for 16 kts. The launches carry a towing winch for a 105-kHz side-scan sonar (range of 600 m, towing speed 12.7 kts) and have two 24-kHz and two 200-kHz echo sounders fitted; the craft have Global Positioning System, a microfix radio navigation system, and can interface with the mother ship's HYSTAR II computerized survey data storage system. There is also a 5.33-m semi-rigid inflatable workboat.

♦ 2 Mt. Mitchell class
Bldr: Aerojet General SY, Jacksonville, Fla.

	L	In serv.	Base
S 220 Fairweather	. . .	. . .	Ketchikan
S 221 Rainier	15-3-67	2-10-68	Seattle

Rainier (S 221)—with survey launches aboard Victor M. Baca, 1-01

D: 1,800 tons (fl) **S:** 13 kts (sust.) **Dim:** 70.4 × 12.8 × 4.2
M: 2 G.M. diesels; 2 CP props; 2,400 bhp **Electric:** 600 kw tot.
Range: 7,000/13 **Fuel:** 353 tons **Endurance:** 22 days
Crew: 12 NOAA officers, 5 licensed officers, 52 crew, 4 scientists

Remarks: 1,591 grt. Maritime Administration S1-MT-72a design. Sister *Fairweather* (S 220) and *Mt. Mitchell* (S 222), inactivated in 1988 and 9-95, respectively, have been stricken from the NOAA fleet. S 221, inactivated at Seattle in 1995, was reactivated as of 1-99, performing research off the U.S. West Coast. *Fairweather,* however, was refurbished by Cascase General, Inc., of Portland, Oregon, and reactivated during 2-04 for service from Ketchikan, Alaska.

Disposal notes: Survey ship *McArthur* (S 330) was retired 5-03. The smaller *Peirce*-class survey ship *Whiting* (S 329) was also decommissioned 5-03.

♦ 1 Rude class
Bldr: Jakobson SY, Oyster Bay, N.Y.

	L	In serv.	Base
S 590 Rude	17-8-66	3-67	Norfolk

Rude (S 590) 2001

D: 220 tons (fl) **S:** 10 kts (sust.) **Dim:** 27.4 × 6.7 × 2.2
M: 2 Cummins diesels; 2 Kort-nozzle props; 800 bhp **Electric:** 120 kw tot.
Range: 1,000/10 **Fuel:** 12 tons **Endurance:** 3 days
Crew: 3 NOAA officers, 1 licensed officer, 7 crew

Remarks: 150 grt/42 nrt. Sister *Heck* (S 591) was deactivated 30-9-95 for disposal and was sold to Marex Oceanographic Services, Memphis, but S 590 was in refit at end 1995 and now is equipped with the Reson SeaBat 9001S multibeam mapping sonar system. Were designed to work together in making wire drag surveys off U.S. Atlantic and Gulf coasts, but no longer do so. Has side-scan and multibeam bathymetric sonars and computerized data storage and is equipped with a differential GPS receiver. Equipped with two 70-hp hydraulic auxiliary drives, and can support diving teams intended to inspect submerged objects.

Note: *Rude* (S 590) is planned to be replaced by a small SWATH (Small Waterplane Area Twin Hull) ship, for which design studies began during 2002.

SERVICE CRAFT

♦ **1 chartered debris-removal ship [WYAG]**
Bldr: Marco, Seattle, Wash. (In serv. 1977)

OCEAN FURY

D: . . . **S:** . . . kts **Dim:** 37.19 × 8.62 × . . .
M: 1 Caterpillar D-398 diesel; 1 prop; 850 bhp
Crew: 4 + 7 scientists/technicians

Remarks: King-crab fishing vessel chartered 10-01 for several years from Pacific Fishermen, Inc. (a subsidiary of Fury Group, Inc., Edmonds, Washington), for use in clearing debris from along reefs and atolls in the Midway Island–Hawaiian Islands corridor. Was lengthened and widened in 1991.

♦ **3 ex-U.S. Coast Guard 82-ft. Point-class support craft [WYAG]**
Bldr: Coast Guard Yard, Curtis Bay, Md. (*Point Monroe:* J. Martinac SB, Tacoma, Wash.)

	In serv.
POINT GLASS (ex-WPB 82336)	29-8-62
POINT LOBOS (ex-WPB 82366)	29-5-67
POINT MONROE (ex-WPB 82353)	27-12-66

D: 64 tons (66–69 fl) **S:** 23.7 kts (see Remarks) **Dim:** 25.3 × 5.23 × 1.95
Electronics: Radar: 1 Hughes-Furuno SPS-73 nav.
M: 2 Caterpillar 3412 diesels; 2 props; 1,480 bhp
Range: 490/23.7; 1,500/8 **Fuel:** 5.7 tons **Crew:** 8 tot.

Remarks: *Point Glass* was transferred 4-01, *Point Monroe* on 19-8-01, and *Point Lobos* on 13-10-01 on retirement from U.S. Coast Guard, all for service at the Florida Keys National Marine Sanctuary, Key West, Florida. Hull built of mild steel. High-speed diesels controlled from the bridge. Equipped with 4.27-m Avon Searider rigid-inflatable boat powered by a 40-bhp outboard engine; the RIB is equipped with a GPS receiver and an echo sounder. Hull built of mild steel. High-speed diesels controlled from the bridge.

♦ **2 ex-U.S. Army T-boat research craft [WYAG]**
Bldr: Missouri Valley Steel, Leavenworth, Kan. (In serv. 1953)

R 693 SHENAHON (ex-T-465)
R . . . JANE YARN (ex-USN 65WB801, ex-Army T-460)

Shenahon (R 693) George R. Schneider, 7-01

D: 69 tons light (98 fl) **S:** 10 kts **Dim:** 19.96 × 5.38 × 2.00
M: 1 Caterpillar D375 diesel; 1 prop; 270 bhp **Electric:** 42 kw tot.
Range: 700/10 **Fuel:** 3.7 tons **Crew:** 4–6 tot.

Remarks: R 693 was acquired 25-6-65 from the U.S. Army and operates on the Great Lakes from Muskegon, Michigan, for the Great Lakes Environmental Research Laboratory and for the National Weather Service. Appearance similar to craft depicted in Army section. Sister *Virginia Key* (ex-Army T-433), formerly used for training at the NOAA Training Center, Ft. Eustis, Virginia, has been discarded.

♦ **1 small research craft [WYAG]**
Bldr: Equitable SY, New Orleans, La.

LAIDLY (ex- . . .)

D: . . . tons **S:** 18-20 kts **Dim:** 17.98 × . . . 1.06
M: 2 G.M. 12V71 diesels; 2 props; . . . bhp

Remarks: Former oilfield crewboat. Operates from Solomon's Island, Maryland. Also in use are the former shrimp-boat *Gloria Michelle,* on Narragansett Bay, several 30-ft. hydrographic launches, and three 7.92 × 2.74–m aluminum research boats (one powered by a Mercruiser 7.4 inboard/outboard engine and the others by Volvo Penta outdrive diesels) and delivered 8-91 by SeaArk, Monticello, Ark.

♦ **1 Frigatebird-class inshore survey craft [WYGS]**
Bldr: Princess Yachts, Tacoma, Wash.

	In serv.
BAY HYDROGRAPHER (ex-*Frigatebird,* CT 21)	15-10-88

D: 20.4 tons light **S:** 12 kts **Dim:** 17.07 × 5.18 × 1.22
Electronics:
Radar: 1 Raytheon 1220 nav.
Sonar: Dowty Type 3010 towed side-scan array
M: 2 G.M.Detroit Diesel 6-71 diesels; 2 props; 330 bhp
Electric: 15 kw tot. **Range:** 750/12 **Crew:** 9 tot.

Remarks: Prototype for now-canceled program to build COOP (Craft of Opportunity) mine-countermeasures craft for the Naval Reserve force. Glass-reinforced plastic construction. Resembles a small, flush-decked fishing boat. On loan to NOAA as research craft since 1994; *Bay Hydrographer* is based at Norfolk. Sister *Ballena* (ex-*Albatross,* CT 22, renamed to avoid conflict with *Albatross IV,* listed previously) was swamped, ran aground, and was lost on 4-11-00 while serving the Channel Islands National Marine Sanctuary, Santa Barbara, California.

Bay Hydrographer—as *Frigatebird* (CT 21) George R. Schneider, 5-94

Note: U.S. Navy sludge-removal barge YSR 29 was transferred to NOAA 8-85 for use as an underwater habitat support barge. Completed 12-45, the craft displaces 160 tons light (360 fl) and measures 24.4 × 9.8. m. It was re-equipped with a centerline "moonpool." Also operated by NOAA are the 18.8-m Teknicraft Catamaran research ship R/V Shearwater, completed in 5-03 by All American Marine, Bellingham, Washington; a 10.97 × 3.66–m research craft delivered 10-94 by Munson Boats, La Conner, Washington; and a 7.92 × 3.04–m tender completed 8-94 by the same builder.

♦ **3 ex-U.S. Coast Guard 41-ft. Utility Boats [WYFL]**
Bldr: USCG Yard, Curtis Bay, Md. (In serv. 1973–82)

SILIQUA (ex-CG41333)
QUINNAT (ex-CG41328)
MURRELET (ex-CG41313)

Quinnat—former USCG utility boat operated by the NOAA National Marine Fisheries Service George Schneider, 3-04

D: 13–14 tons (fl) **S:** 22–26 kts **Dim:** 12.40 × 4.11 × 1.22
Electronics: Radar: 1/ SPS-69 (Raytheon 1900) nav.
M: 2 Cummins V903M or VT903M diesels; 2 props; 560 or 636 bhp
Range: 300/18 **Fuel:** 1.54 tons **Crew:** 3 tot.

Remarks: Transferred from the Coast Guard during 2003. Operated by NOAA Fisheries Service.

Note: NOAA-subordinated National Marine Fisheries Service operates small patrol boats on fisheries protection service. Among the boats in service are four rigid-inflatable craft delivered by Almar (Aluminum Marine Construction), Tacoma, Washington; from late 1999 to mid-2000; the first two are 8.2-m, 49.7-kt craft powered by twin 225-bhp Evinrude outboards and are based at Homer and Dutch Harbor, Alaska; the third boat is 9.75 × 3.58 m and is based at Sitka; and the fourth is 10.97 × 3.96 m and is based at Kodiak.

U.S. DEPARTMENT OF HOMELAND SECURITY

In addition to serving as the parent agency for the U.S. Coast Guard, the Department of Homeland Security (DHS) also manages the U.S. Immigration and Customs Enforcement (ICE) agency and the U.S. Customs and Border Protection (CBP) agency. ICE and CBP operate over 100 small patrol boats and RIBs at various U.S. ports.

During 2003–4, the U.S. Department of Homeland Security began operating several high-speed harbor security police boats including those numbered 392779 and 329786. They are powered by four 225-hp Mercury outboard engines.

U.S. DEPARTMENT OF HOMELAND SECURITY *(continued)*

U.S. Customs and Border Protection RIB W. Michael Young, 3-05

Department of Homeland Security police boat W. Michael Young, 6-05

URUGUAY

Eastern Republic of Uruguay

Personnel: 5,700 total, including 450 Naval Infantry, 300 Air Arm, and 1,950 Coast Guard (Prefectura Marítima).

Bases: Headquarters and principal base at Punta Lobos, Montevideo; other facilities at La Paloma and Capitán Carlos A. Curbelo Naval Air Station at Laguna la Sauce, Maldonado.

Naval Aviation: Fixed wing: two Jetstream Mk 2, two S-2G Tracker patrol aircraft, and two Beech T-34C trainers. The Escuadrón de Helicópteros operates seven Westland Wessex HC.2 transports, and one Bell 47G-5 trainer; three Westland Wessex Mk. Sixty helicopters are in storage. The ex-Royal Navy Jetstream T.2 aircraft were acquired in 1999 to replace S-2 Tracker aircraft.

Note: Ships' names are formally preceded by ROU (*República Oriental del Uruguay*).

FRIGATES [FF]

♦ 2 French Commandant Riviere class

Bldr: DCAN, Lorient

	Laid down	L	In serv.
1 Uruguay (ex-*Commandant Bourdais*)	4-59	15-4-61	10-3-63
3 Montevideo (ex-*Amiral Charner*)	11-58	12-3-60	14-12-62

D: 1,750 tons (2,070 normal, 2,230 fl) **S:** 26 kts
Dim: 102.70 (98.00 pp) × 11.80 × 4.35 (max.)
A: 2 single 100-mm 55-cal. Model 1963 DP; 2 single 40-mm 70-cal. Bofors L70 AA; 2 triple 550-mm ASW TT (L-3 torpedoes)
Electronics:
Radar: 1 Decca 1226 nav.; 1 Thales DRBV 22A air-search; 1 Thales DRBC 32C f.c.
Sonar: EDO SQS-17 hull-mounted MF search; Thales DUBA 3 HF attack
EW: ARBR 16 intercept
M: 4 SEMT-Pielstick 12PC.1V400 diesels; 2 props; 16,000 bhp
Electric: 1,280 kw tot. **Range:** 2,300/26; 7,500/16.5
Fuel: 210 tons **Endurance:** 45 days
Crew: 9 officers, 150 enlisted

Remarks: *Uruguay* transferred 20-8-90 after striking from French Navy 27-4-90, and *Montevideo* transferred 28-1-91. Both can carry a flag officer and staff; can also carry up to 80 troops. *Uruguay* (1) was placed out of commission 5-00 for a major overhaul.
Combat systems: *Uruguay* was transferred without MM 38 Exocet antiship missiles but received them in 1991–92; the other pair were delivered with missiles aboard. By 2001, however, the missiles had been removed due to shelf-life expiration. The

Montevideo (3) Ignacio Amendolara, 2000

Uruguay (1) and Montevideo (3)—with since-stricken *Artigas* (2)
Ralph Edwards, 5-00

four-barreled 305-mm mortar is no longer operational and is to be removed from both. There is a Sagem DMAA optical secondary gun director atop the bridge; the stabilized, radar-equipped main battery director is aft. All three had two Dagaie decoy rocket launchers removed prior to transfer. The 40-mm AA mounts have been given GRP enclosures.
Disposal: Sister *Artigas* (2, ex-*Victor Schoelcher*) was retired on 27-4-05.

PATROL CRAFT [PC]

♦ 3 Vigilante class

Bldr: CMN, Cherbourg, France

	Laid down	L	In serv.
5 15 de Noviembre	6-12-79	16-10-80	25-3-81
6 25 de Agosto	6-2-80	11-12-80	25-3-81
7 Comodoro Coe	16-5-80	27-1-81	25-3-81

25 de Agosto (6) Ignacio Amendolara, 3-01

D: 166 tons (191 fl) **S:** 28 kts **Dim:** 41.15 (38.00 pp) × 6.80 × 2.50 (1.50 hull)
A: 1 40-mm 70-cal. Bofors AA
Electronics: Radar: 1 Decca TM 1226C nav.; 1 Decca 1229 nav.
M: 2 MTU 12V538 TB91 diesels; 2 props; 5,400 bhp **Range:** 2,400/15
Crew: 5 officers, 23 enlisted

Remarks: Ordered 1978. All commissioned on date of departure under own power from Cherbourg to Montevideo. Considered poor sea boats in conditions off Uruguayan coast and were placed up for sale in mid-1992; no purchasers appeared, however, and the boats remain in service, with the 6 and 7 in major overhaul during 2000–2002. All based at La Paloma.
Combat systems: Have Matra Défense Panda optronic director for the 40-mm gun, which has a GRP weather shield. Twin 20-mm 70-cal. Oerlikon AA planned for installation aft was never mounted. Have HFD/F, with antenna atop mast.

PATROL CRAFT [PC] *(continued)*

♦ 2 ex-U.S. Coast Guard 95-ft Cape class
Bldr: Coast Guard Yard, Curtis Bay, Md.

	In serv.
10 Colonia (ex-*Cape Higgon,* WPB 95302)	14-10-53
11 Río Negro (ex-*Cape Horn,* WPB 95322)	3-9-58

Río Negro (11) Guillermo C. Berger, 4-00

Colonia (10)—outboard the *Paysandú* (12) Ralph Edwards, 5-00

D: 90 tons (106 fl) **S:** 20 kts **Dim:** 28.96 × 6.10 × 1.55
A: 1 12.7-mm M2 mg
Electronics: Radar: 1 Raytheon SPS-64(V)1 nav.
M: 2 G.M. Detroit Diesel 16V149 TI diesels; 2 props; 2,470 bhp
Electric: 60 kw tot. **Range:** 556/20; 1,900/11.5 **Endurance:** 5 days
Crew: 1 officer, 13 enlisted

Remarks: Both transferred 25-1-90, left for Uruguay under own power, and are based at Paysandú. Were re-engined while in USCG service, completing 13-2-81 and 21-1-83, respectively. Have SQN-18 echo sounder, Loran-C, and SATNAV receivers. Unarmed at transfer; had carried 2/12.7-mm mg, 2/40-mm Mk 64 grenade launchers. Despite considerable age, are rugged craft and are being employed on search-and-rescue duties, based at Montevideo.

PATROL BOATS [PB]

♦ 1 U.S. 85-foot Commercial Cruiser
Bldr: Sewart Seacraft, Morgan City, La. (L: 11-68)

12 Paysandú (ex-U.S. 85NS684)

Paysandú (12) Paolo Marsan, 8-99

D: 43.5 tons (54 fl) **S:** 22 kts **Dim:** 25.91 × 5.69 × 2.1
A: 3 single 12.7-mm M2 mg
Electronics: Radar: 1 Raytheon 1500B Pathfinder nav.
M: 2 G.M. 16V71N diesels; 2 props; 1,400 shp **Electric:** 40 kw tot.
Range: 800/21 **Crew:** 8 tot.

Remarks: Built under U.S. Military Assistance Program. Aluminum construction. Based at Montevideo and used for patrolling the Rio de la Plata estuary.

♦ 2 Uruguay 3 class
Bldr: . . ., Buenos Aires (In serv. 2002)

Uruguay 3 Uruguay 4

D: 6 tons (fl) **S:** 32 kts **Dim:** 11.3 × 3.25 × 0.8
A: 3 single 7.62-mm mg
M: 2 Volvo Penta AD 41 diesels; 2 props
Range: 1,500/24 **Crew:** 4 tot.

Remarks: No additional data available.

MINE-COUNTERMEASURES SHIPS

♦ 3 ex-East German Kondor II–class patrol minesweepers [MSC]
Bldr: VEB Peenewerft, Wolgast

	Laid down	L	In serv.
31 Temerario (ex-*Riesa,* 322)	15-5-72	2-10-72	3-2-73
33 Fortuna (ex-*Bernau,* M 2673, ex-343)	28-3-72	3-8-72	1-12-72
34 Audaz (ex-*Eisleben,* M 2671, ex-312)	9-8-72	2-1-73	24-5-73

Audaz (34) Ignacio Amendolara, 10-05

Fortuna (33) Guillermo C. Berger, 8-00

D: 414 tons (479 fl) **S:** 18 kts **Dim:** 56.52 × 7.78 × 2.46
A: 1 40-mm 70-cal. Bofors AA
Electronics: Radar: 1 Raytheon 1900 Pathfinder
M: 2 Russkiy Dizel Type 40-DM diesels; 2 CP Kort-nozzle props; 4,400 bhp
Electric: 625 kw (5 × 125-kw diesel sets)
Range: 2,000/15 **Endurance:** 10 days **Crew:** 6 officers, 25 enlisted

Remarks: Former *Volksmarine* units; 32–34 had served in the *Bundesmarine* briefly after German unification. Transferred 8-11-91 with a five-year supply of spare parts. Left Germany 13-11-91 for Montevideo under their own power, arriving 23-12-91. Sister *Valiente* (32, ex-*Eilenburg,* M 2674, ex-334) was hit by the Panamanian merchant ship *Skyros* on 3-8-00 and sank with eight killed and three personnel missing.
Combat systems: A quadruple SA-5 Grail point-defense SAM launcher and three twin 25-mm Soviet 2M-8 AA were removed prior to transfer; a single 40-mm AA has replaced the forward 25-mm mount. Two minerails remain, but no mines were transferred. The high-frequency, hull-mounted sonar has probably been removed. Although most of the sweep gear was transferred with the ships, they are employed primarily as patrol boats; the MSG-3 magnetic influence sweep array is still carried.

AMPHIBIOUS WARFARE CRAFT

♦ 1 ex-German self-propelled pontoon [LCU]

LD 44 (ex-*Hochtief* 208)

LD 44, at left—with LD 41 Ralph Edwards, 5-00

AMPHIBIOUS WARFARE CRAFT *(continued)*

D: . . . tons **S:** . . . **Dim:** 14.00 × 7.00 × 1.80
M: 2 Caterpillar 3304 diesels; 2 props; 254 bhp **Crew:** 2 tot.

Remarks: Former German construction company self-propelled barge. Has a 10-ton capacity crane and is primarily used as a diving tender.

♦ 1 LD 42-class landing craft [LCM]
Bldr: Dieque Nacional, Montevideo (In serv. 26-7-78)

LD 42

LD 42 Hartmut Ehlers, 4-92

D: 15 tons (31.4 fl) **S:** 9 kts **Dim:** 14.1 × 3.50 × 0.80
M: 2 G.M. Detroit Diesel 6-71 diesels; 2 props; 272 bhp
Range: 580/9 **Crew:** 5 tot.

Remarks: Can carry 10 tons cargo. Refitted 2000–2001 by Servicio de Construcciones y Reparaciones de la Armada (S.C.R.A.), Punta Lobos, Montevideo.

♦ 1 U.S. LCM(6)-class landing craft [LCM]
Bldr: Servicio de Construcciones y Reparaciones de la Armada (S.C.R.A.), Punta Lobos, Montevideo (L: 29-12-89)

LD 41

LD 41 Ralph Edwards, 5-00

D: 24 tons (57 fl) **S:** 10 kts **Dim:** 17.07 × 4.37 × 1.17
M: 2 G.M. Detroit Diesel 4-71 diesels; 2 props; 450 bhp
Range: 130/9 **Crew:** 5 tot.

Remarks: Sister LD 40 was reported stricken in 1997. Cargo: 30 tons.

♦ 2 LD 43–class vehicle and personnel landing craft [LCVP]
Bldr: Servicio de Construcciones y Reparaciones de la Armada (S.C.R.A.), Punta Lobos, Montevideo

	L
LD 45	14-11-79
LD 46	9-8-82

LD 45—with an unidentified small boat alongside Hartmut Ehlers, 12-97

D: 12 tons light (15 fl) **S:** 6 kts **Dim:** 14.1 × 3.5 × 0.80
M: 1 G.M. Detroit Diesel 4-71 diesel; 1 prop; 115 bhp
Range: 580/9 **Crew:** 5 tot.

Remarks: Have a bow ramp and can accommodate light vehicles or cargo totaling about 3 tons. Sister LD 43 was retired in 2002.

AUXILIARIES

♦ 1 ex-German Type 701E frigate supply ship [AOR]

	Bldr	Laid down	L	In serv.
4 GENERAL ARTIGAS (ex-*Freiburg,* A 1413)	Blohm + Voss, Hamburg	1965	15-4-66	27-5-68

D: 3,900 tons (fl) **S:** 17 kts **Dim:** 118.30 × 13.22 × 4.29
A: 1 twin 40-mm 70-cal. Bofors AA
Electronics: Radar: 1 Kelvin-Hughes 14/9 nav.—EW: Thales DR 2000S intercept
M: 2 Maybach MD 874 diesels; 2 CP props; 5,600 bhp
Electric: 1,935 kw tot. **Range:** 3,000/17; 3,200/14 **Crew:** 71–82 tot.

Remarks: Decommissioned from Germany during 11-03 and transferred to Uruguay during 4-05. Converted 1981–84 to support German Type 122 frigates and is equipped with helicopter facilities to permit vertical replenishment, repair facilities for helicopters, and new articulated cranes. Equipped with fin stabilizers.

General Artigas (4) Frank Findler, 4-05

♦ 1 navigational buoy tender [AGL]
Bldr: Servicio de Consrucciones y Reparaciones de la Armada (S.C.R.A.), Punta Lobos, Montevideo (L: 5-2-88)

21 SIRIUS

Sirius (21) Paolo Marsan, 8-99

D: 290 tons (fl) **S:** 11 kts **Dim:** 35.0 × 10.0 × 2.8
M: 2 G.M. Detroit Diesel 12V71 TA diesels; 2 props; 860 bhp
Endurance: 5 days **Crew:** 15 tot.

Remarks: Built with assistance from Damen SY, Hardinxveld, the Netherlands. Electrohydraulic articulated crane forward.

♦ 1 ex-German Helgoland-class (Type 720) survey ship [AGS]
Bldr: Schichau, Bremerhaven

	Laid down	L	In serv.
22 OYARVIDE (ex-*Helgoland,* A 1457)	24-7-64	9-4-65	8-3-66

D: 1,304 tons (1,558 fl) **S:** 16.6 kts **Dim:** 67.91 × 12.74 × 4.60
A: Removed **Electronics:** Radar: 1 Kelvin-Hughes 14/9 nav.
M: 4 MWM 12 RS 18/22-21 AE 1 diesel-generator sets (700 kw each), electric drive; 2 props; 3,300 shp
Electric: 1,065 kVA tot. (4 × 250 kVA, 1 × 65-kVA diesel sets)
Range: 6,400/16 **Crew:** 34 tot.

Remarks: 1,186 grt. Stricken from German Navy 19-12-97 and transferred 1-9-98 after a refit at Neuen Jadewerft, Wilhelmshaven, departing for Uruguay on 7-11-98. Is assigned to the Hydrographic Institute for use as a coastal survey ship but was built as a salvage tug. May be employed as tender to the General Artigas Base in Antarctica. Has high-frequency sonar equipment for salvage work, is equipped for firefighting, and remains equipped with a submersible diver's decompression chamber and hoist system, as well as a full suite of salvage equipment. Ice-strengthened hull permitted use as a harbor icebreaker in German service. Bollard pull: 40 tons. Has GPS receiver.

AUXILIARIES *(continued)*

Oyarvide (22) Ignacio Amendolara, 2-06

♦ **1 Polish Piast–class salvage ship [ARS]**
Bldr: Stocznia Północna, Gdansk (In serv. 29-12-76)

26 VANGUARDIA (ex-*Otto von Guericke,* A 441)

Vanguardia (26) Ignacio Amendolara, 2-06

D: 1,560 tons (1,732 fl) **S:** 16.5 kts **Dim:** 72.6 (67.2 pp) × 12.0 × 4.0
A: None **Electronics:** Radar: 2 TSR-333 nav.
M: 2 Cegielski-Sulzer 6TD48 diesels; 2 CP props; 3,600 bhp
Range: 3,000/12 **Crew:** 16 officers, 44 enlisted

Remarks: Acquired from former East German *Volksmarine* by the newly unified Germany in 10-90. Purchased by Uruguay 10-91, refitted at Neptun-Warnow Werft, Rostock, and sailed for Montevideo in 1-92. Design is a variation of the *Moma*-class navigational aids and survey ship design, adapted for salvage and rescue duties. Has two sisters in the Polish Navy. Carries submersible diver's decompression chamber to port. Can tow and has extensive pump and firefighting facilities.
Combat systems: Armament of two twin 30-mm AK-230 AA mounts and two 25-mm 2M-8 AA mounts were removed, as was the MR-104 Rys' (Drum Tilt) radar director for the 30-mm AA.

♦ **1 ex-German Baltrum-class (Type 722) salvage tug [ATR]**
Bldr: Schichau, Bremerhaven

	Laid down	L	In serv.
23 MALDONADO (ex-*Norderney,* A 1455)	29-5-67	28-2-68	15-10-70

D: 854 tons (1,025 fl) **S:** 13.6 kts **Dim:** 51.78 × 12.11 × 4.20
A: Removed **Electronics:** Radar: 1 Kelvin-Hughes 14/9 nav.
M: 4 MWM TRHS 518 V16-31 AE 16-cyl. diesel generator sets (700 kw each), electric drive; 2 Kort-nozzele shrouded props; 2,400 shp
Electric: 540 kw **Range:** 5,000/10 **Crew:** 31 tot.

Remarks: Was to be stricken from the German Navy on 27-9-02 but was then extended in service until 20-11-02 when transferred to Uruguay to replace the now stricken *Comandante Pedro Campbell* (24). Departed for Uruguay 23-11-02. Bollard pull: 33 tons. Fitted for firefighting. Will be used primarily as an oceanographic research ship. In German service, carried a single 40-mm gun forward, but it was removed during the late 1990s.

Disposal note: U.S. *Auk*-class research ship *Comandante Pedro Campbell* (24; ex-Chickadee, MSF 59) was retired during 11-02.

♦ **1 sail-training ship [AXT]**
Bldr: Soc. Española de Construcción Naval, Matagorda, Cádiz, Spain (In serv. 1930)

20 CAPITÁN MIRANDA (ex-GS 20)

Capitán Miranda (20) A. D. Baker III, 6-00

D: 587 tons (715 fl) **S:** 11 kts (14 sail)
Dim: 54.60 (61.21 over bowsprit/45.00 pp) × 8.40 × 3.60
Electronics: Radar: 1 Decca TM 1226C nav.
M: 1 G.M. diesel; 1 prop; 600 hp—Sail area: 722 m^2.
Fuel: 45 tons **Crew:** 49 tot.

Remarks: Originally built as a hydrographic survey ship. Refitted, re-engined, and rigged as a three-masted schooner for cadet training, recommissioning 1978. Received a further refit during 1993–94 in Spain.

SERVICE CRAFT

♦ **2 diving tenders [YDT]** Bldr: . . ., Germany (In serv. . . .)

D: . . . tons **S:** . . . **Dim:** 7.92 × 2.15 × . . . **M:** 1 gasoline outboard; 130 bhp

Remarks: Also used as diving tenders are the landing craft LD 44 and several Zodiac RIBs.

♦ **1 former East German coastal tug [YTB]**
Bldr: VEB Peenewerft, Wolgast

	Laid down	L	In serv.
27 BANCO ORTIZ (ex-*Zingst,* Y 1695; ex-*Elbe,* A 443)	9-1-58	4-4-59	10-9-59

Banco Ortiz (27) Ignacio Amendolara, 2-06

D: 261 tons (fl) **S:** 10 kts **Dim:** 30.50 × 8.00 (7.50 wl) × 2.50
Electronics: Radar: 1 . . . nav.
M: 1 Buckau-Wolff R6DV 148 diesel; 1 prop; 550 bhp
Range: 1,400/10 **Crew:** 12 tot.

Remarks: Acquired by Germany at unification, 10-90, and used by *Bundesmarine* until transferred to Uruguay 10-91; sailed under own power for Montevideo 13-11-91. Nine-ton bollard pull at 10 kts.

COAST GUARD

(Prefectura Maritima)

The Uruguayan Coast Guard has about 100 officers and 1,800 enlisted personnel. Primarily intended for a shore-based coast watch and port police function, it was integrated into the Uruguayan Navy by the end of 1992. In addition to the units listed below, it has several 4.9-meter outboard-motor-powered semi-rigid inflatable rubber boats.

SERVICE CRAFT

♦ **9 ex-U.S. Coast Guard 44-ft. rescue launches [WYH]**
Bldr: U.S.C.G. Yard, Curtis Bay, Md. (In serv. 31-3-61 to 8-5-73)

ROU 441 through ROU 449

COAST GUARD SERVICE CRAFT *(continued)*

ROU 446 Hartmut Ehlers, 5-00

D: 14.9 tons light (17.7 fl) **S:** 13 kts (11.8 sust.) **Dim:** 13.44 × 3.87 × 1.19
Electronics: Radar: 1 SPS-57 nav.
M: 2 G.M. Detroit Diesel 6V53 diesels; 2 props; 372 bhp
Range: 185/11.8; 200/11 **Fuel:** 1.2 tons **Crew:** 4 tot.

Remarks: Donated and transferred 8-99. "Unsinkable" design. Can carry up to 21 rescued personnel. ROU 444 is ex USCG 44368.

♦ **3 23-meter tug/tenders [WYTL]**
Bldr: Regusci Voulminot, Montevideo (In serv. 1956–57)

ROU 70 (ex-PS 1) ROU 71 (ex-PS 2) ROU 72 (ex-PS 3)

ROU 71—with two Prefectura Maritima RIBs alongside
Ignacio Amendolara, 2-06

D: 90 tons (fl) **S:** 12 kts **Dim:** 22.0 × 5.0 × 1.8
Electronics: Radar: 1 Raytheon . . . nav.
M: 2 G.M. Detroit Diesel diesels; 2 props; 400 bhp **Crew:** 8 tot.

VANUATU

Republic of Vanuatu

MARINE POLICE

Base: Vita, Efate Island

Note: Ship names are preceded by RVS—Republic of Vanuatu Ship.

PATROL CRAFT [WPC]

♦ **1 Australian ASI 315 class**
Bldr: Transfield-ASI, South Coogie, Western Australia

	L	In serv.
Tukoro	20-5-87	13-6-87

Tukoro Chris Sattler, 2005

Tukoro Chris Sattler, 2005

D: 165 tons (fl) **S:** 20 kts **Dim:** 31.50 (28.60 wl) × 8.10 × 2.12 (1.80 hull)
A: 1 12.7-mm mg; 1 7.62-mm mg
Electronics: Radar: 1 Furuno 1011 nav.
M: 2 Caterpillar 3516 diesels; 2 props; 2,820 bhp (2,400 sust.)
Electric: 116 kw tot. **Range:** 2,500/12 **Fuel:** 27.9 tons
Endurance: 8–10 days **Crew:** 3 officers, 15 constables

Remarks: Provided by Australian Defense Cooperation Program and used for customs, fisheries patrol, and general police duties. Ordered 13-9-85. Carries a 5-m aluminum boarding boat. Extensive navigational suite, including Furuno FSN-70 NAVSAT receiver, 525 HF/DF, 120 MF/HFD/F, FE-881 echo sounder, and DS-70 doppler log. The listed armament is normally not carried. Underwent overhaul and modernization during 2004.

VENEZUELA

Bolivarian Republic of Venezuela

Personnel: 18,300 total (including 500 in naval aviation and 7,800 marines)

Bases: The Venezuelan Navy maintains headquarters at Caracas. Primary naval bases are located at Puerto Cabello, Punto Fijo, and Ciudad Bolívar (Orinoco River). The Coast Guard Command headquarters is at La Guaira, Vargas State, with principal stations at La Guira, Maracaibo, Punto Fijo, and Puerto Cabello. Naval air facilities are located at Turiamo, Puerto Hierro, and La Orchila.

Naval Program: Flush with cash as oil prices remained high, Venezuela has ordered four patrol craft and four 102-meter frigates from Spain in addition to two CASA-235 MPA aircraft. The United States has reportedly been working to block the aircraft orders on the grounds that their sale would violate technology transfer laws. Recent reports indicate that the Venezuelan Navy may also be looking to Russia with the expressed interest of purchasing *Amur*-class submarines.

Naval Aviation: Naval aircraft in service include three CASA 212-200 MPA, three CASA 212-400 and two CASA 212-200 Aviocar transports, one de Havilland DHC-7 Dash 7, and one Raytheon B-200 Super King Air transports along with two Cessna Turbo 310Q, a Cessna Turbo 210, and two Cessna Turbo 402B/C for training. Helicopters include eight Agusta Bell 212s equipped with radar and AQS-13 dipping-sonar, seven Bell 412EP for SAR, and one Bell 206B Jet Ranger. The AB-212s can carry two Mk 26 or A-244AS torpedoes, or two SS-12M Marte antiship missiles. The CASA 212-200 MP, AB-212, Bell 212, and Bell 412EPs can be armed with 7.62-mm or 12.7-mm machineguns and 70-mm rocket pods. Venezuelan Air Force Mirage 50EV jet fighters are equipped to launch the AM-39 Exocet antiship missile. As noted above, two CASA-235 MPA aircraft were ordered in 2005.

Venezuelan CASA-212-400 transport José Vargas, FAV Club, 2004

Venezuelan CASA-212-200 maritime patrol aircraft José Vargas, FAV Club, 2004

Venezuelan Agusta-Bell AB-212 José Vargas, FAV Club, 2004

Bell 412EP José Vargas, FAV Club, 2004

Marine Corps: Marine Corps assets include 11 LVT-7-Series tracked amphibian armored vehicles acquired new in 1973 (one LVTC-7 command, nine LVTP-7 personnel carriers, and one LVTR-7 recovery vehicle); 10 German-built TPz-1 Fuchs 6 × 6 armored personnel carriers and 25 Brazilian-built 6 × 6 ENGENSA EE-11 *Urutú;* amphibian armored personnel carrier armed with one 20-mm 90-cal. Oerlikon GAM-BO1 gun or one 12.7-mm. machinegun; and command post and recovery welled amphibian vehicles. Field artillery includes 18 OTO Melara M-56 105-mm howitzers, 120-mm and 40-mm mortars, and AA defense.

Note: All ship names are prefaced by A.R.B.V. (*Armada de la República Bolivariana de Venezuela*). Pennant numbers are now painted in low visibility U.S. Navy style.

ATTACK SUBMARINES [SS]

Note: Media reports in 2006 indicate that the Venezuelan Navy has expressed interest in purchasing three *Amur*-class submarines from Russia as early as 2007.

♦ 2 German Type U209A/1300-Sábalo class

Bldr: Howaldtswerke, Kiel.

	Laid down	L	In serv.
S-31 Sábalo (ex-S-21)	2-5-73	1-7-75	6-8-76
S-32 Caribe (ex-S-22)	1-8-73	6-11-75	11-3-77

Sábalo (S-31) Carlos E. Hernández, 3-00

Caribe (S-32) Carlos E. Hernández, 3-00

D: 1,100 tons (light)/ 1,265 tons. (surf.)/1,265 tons (sub.)
S: 11kts. (surf.) /22 kts (sub.)
Dim: 59.60 × 6,30 × 5.50
A: 8 bow 533-mm bow TT (14 tot. U.S. Mk 37 Mod. 2 and STN Atlas Elektronik SST-4 Mod. 0 wire-guide torpedoes)
Electronics:
Radar: Thomson-CFS Calypso-EW: Thomson-CFS DR-2000 intercept
Sonar: SNT Atlas Elektronik CSU-3 series suite, Thomsom-Sintra DUUX 2 passive ranging
EW: Thales DR-2000 intercept
M: Diesel-electric: 4 MTU MD 12V493 AZ80 GA31L diesels (600 bhp each); 4 405-kw alternators; Siemens electric motors; 5,000 shp. 1 prop; 5,000 shp (4,600 sust.)
Range: 7,500/10 surf.; 11,200/4 (snorkel), 25/20, 445/4 (sub).
Fuel: 108 tons **Endurance:** 50 days **Crew:** 5 officers and 28 enlisted.

Remarks: Ordered 1971; a planned second pair was not ordered. S-32 damaged by fire in 1979 and overhauled at Kiel trough 1981. S-32 was refitted by the builder in 1984. S-31 began refit to West German Navy Type 206A standard by builder in 4-90 and left Germany for Venezuela on 16-11-92; S-32 began a similar refit in 10-92 and was completed and recommisssioned during 1-95. Both to be refitted again during 2004–8 by Diques y Astilleros Nacionales C.A. Dianca shipyards with HWK technical assistance. S-31's refit began 3-04. New electronic equipment is being installed and updated torpedoes will be incorporated. Both boats are expected to remain in active service until 2020–22.
Hull systems: Both boats are six meters larger than other Type U-209s in service. Operating depth: 250 m. Have four 120-cell batteries producing 11,500 amp-hr and weighing 257 tons total. During latest refit, received higher casing and sail and were re-engined.
Combat systems: Originally had H.S.A (now Thales) Mk. 8 Mod. 24 fire-control system. The latest refit includes the installation of the SNT Atlas Elektronik ISUS integrated command, control, and sonar suite and substitution of a Carl Zeiss AS-40 attack periscope for the original AS C1B (the BS 19 search periscope was retained as part of the SERO 40 periscope systems).

FRIGATES [FF]

♦ 4 new construction offshore patrol frigates

Bldr: Navantia, San Fernando, Spain

D: About 2,000 tons (fl) **S:** 27 kts **Dim:** 102 × 14 × 3.75
A: 1 single 76-mm 62-cal. OTO Melara Compact DP; . . . SSMs; . . . CIWS; 1 helicopter

FRIGATES [FF] *(continued)*

Electronics: . . .
M: . . .
Range: 4,000/15 **Fuel:** 350 tons **Crew:** 62 + 8 aviation

Remarks: Ordered 11-05, work began during 5-06. Deliveries are expected between 2008 and 2011. Data listed above are speculative as no additional information is yet available. Strict technology transfer laws preventing the sale of specific weapons technology to Venezuela are said to be causing difficulties in weapons and sensor selection. The class is sometimes referred to as corvettes.

♦ 6 Lupo class

Bldr. CNR, Riva Trigoso (F-23, F-25: Ancona), Italy

	Laid down	L	In serv.
F-21 Mariscal Antonio José de Sucre	4-10-77	28-9-78	14-7-80
F-22 Almirante Luis Brión	26-1-78	22-2-79	7-3-81
F-23 General Rafael Urdaneta	23-1-78	22-3-79	8-8-81
F-24 General Carlos Soublette	26-8-78	4-1-80	4-12-81
F-25 General Bartolomé Salóm	7-11-78	13-1-80	3-4-82
F-26 Almirante José M. García (ex-*General José Félix Rivas*)	21-8-79	4-10-80	30-7-82

Almirante José M. García (F-26) Ralph Edwards, 4-00

D: 2,213 tons (2.525 fl) tons **S:** 35 kts (20.2 on diesel kts.)
Dim: 112.8 (106.0 pp) × 11.98 × 3.84 (hull)
A: 8 Otomat Mk 2 SSM; 1 8-round Albatros SAM systems (8 Aspide missiles); 1 127-mm 54-cal. OTO Melara DP; 2 twin 40-mm 70-cal. OTO Melara Dardo AA; 2 single 12.7-mm mg.; 2 triple 324-mm Mk 32 ASW TT (A-244S torpedoes); 1 AB-212ASW helicopter.
Electronics:
Radar: 1 SMA 3RM-20 nav., 1 Selenia RAN-11/X air/surf. search, 1 Selenia RAN-10S air search, 2/Selenia RAN-10S (F-21, F-22, 1 Elta EL/M-2238 STAR-3D) air search; 2 AESN Orion RTN-10X f.c.; 2 AESN Orion RTN-20X (F-21, F-22, 3 Elta . . .) f.c.
Sonar: Edo 610E hull mounted MF (F-21, F-22, Northrop Grumman 21HS-7 hull-mounted, 7 kHz)
TACAN: SRN-15A
EW: Elisra EWS-NS-9003/9005 intercept/jamming syst.; . . . Electronic Lambda-F D/F-intercept. 2/OTO Melara SCLAR chaff RL (XX × 2)
M: CODOG: 2 Fiat G.E. LM-2500 gas turbines (25,000 shp each). 2 GMT A-230-2M (F-21, F-22: MTU 20V1193-series) diesels (3,900 bhp each; F-21, F-22: 9,900 bhp. each); 2 CP props; 50.000 shp max.
Electric: 3,210 kw tot. (F-21, F-22: MTU 8V396-series diesels driven sets)
Range: 900/35; 1.050/31.7: 5,500/16
Crew: 131 tot. in F-21 and F-22 and 185 tot. in F-23, F-24, F-25, and F-26.

Remarks: Ordered 24-10-75. Near sisters are in service with the Italian and Peruvian navies. The sextet constitutes the Frigate Squadron and is based at Puerto Cabello. Under an 18-12-97 contract, F-21 and F-22 were updated and refitted by Ingalls Shipbuilding, Pascagoula, Mississippi. F-21 and F-22 arrived in the U.S. 10-1-98 to complete their refits in 2-00, although F-21 did not begin postmodernization trials until 25-6-01; Israel's Elbitt preformed the integration of the combat system for the ships. F-21 was recommisssioned in 8-02 and F-22 on 26-11-02. The other four are being modernized in Venezuela with foreign technical assistance. Hull repairs are being performed by Diques y Astilleros Nacionales (Dianca) at Puerto Cabello, and new systems were installed at the Contralmirante Agustin Armario Naval Base. Work was started in 1999 on F-24, in 2000 on F-23, on F-25 in 10-03, and on F-26 in 2004. F-24 began sea trials in 10-03. Fiat Avio Spa. was awarded $24.5 million on 12-98 to refit LM-2500 gas turbines.
Hull systems: Fin stabilizers are fitted. F-21 and F-22 have received upgraded LM-2500 gas turbines, new 2/MTU 20V 1163 diesels engines (of nearly triple the original horsepower), new generator plant and machinery control systems, and hull repairs. The others were overhauled under a 12-98 contract with Fiat Avio, Italy, and the ships have improved air conditioning and reverse-osmosis freshwater generation systems added.
Combat systems: The 127-mm guns and missile fire control is provided by two Elsag NA-10 Mod. 0 systems. The Albatros systems use Aspide missiles, a re-engineered version of NATO Sea Sparrow. Each twin 40-mm Dardo systems antiaircraft mount has an associated RTN-20X radar director. All weapons controlled by an AESN IPN-10 computerized data systems in the unimproved units; in F-21 and F-22, the Israeli Elbit ENTCS 2000 combat information system has been substituted for IPN-10, and all weapons systems have been overhauled under the 1-98 contract, but the obsolescent Otomat missiles are to be retained. Have a fixed nontelescopic hangar. The helicopter performs over-the-horizons targeting for the Otomat missiles as well as ASW duties. The antenna for the TACAN system is mounted on a pole mast atop the forward superstructure.

The Northrop Grumman 21HS-7 sonar is an export version of U.S. Navy's SQS-53C; mine-avoidance capability is incorporated. The DRS Technologies, Canada, SHINCOM (Shipboard Integrated Communications) 2100 system was ordered for the two modernized ships in 1-99. The other four will receive new sonar, but not the new radar and combat data systems, under 3-1-01 contract with DRS Technologies U.S.A.

Mariscal Antonio José de Sucre (F-21)—on postmodernization trials Northrop Grumman Ship Systems, 2002

FRIGATES [FF] *(continued)*

♦ 2 Almirante Clemente class
Bldr: Analog, Laverne

	Laid down	L	In serv.
GC-11 Almirante Clemente (ex-F-11, ex-D-12)	5-5-54	12-12-54	1956
GC-12 General José Trinidad Moran (ex-F-12, ex-D-22)	5-5-54	12-12-54	1956

Almirante Clemente (GC-11) H&L Van Ginderen, 8-99

General José Trinidad Moran (GC-12) French Navy, 1994

D: 1,300 tons (1,500 fl) **S:** 22 kts **Dim:** 97.6 × 10.84 × 2.6
A: 2 single 76-mm 62-cal. OTO Melara Compact DP; 1 twin 40-mm 70-cal. OTO Melara AA; 2 triple 324-mm Whitehead Alexia ILAS-3 ASW TT (6 A-244S torpedoes)
Electronics:
Radar: 1 Decca 1226 nav.; 1 Plissé AWS-2 air/surf. search; 1 AESN Orion RTN-10X f.c.
Sonar: Plissé (now Thales) MS-26 hull-mounted (10 kHz)
M: 2 G.M.T. 16-645E7CA diesels; 2 props; 6,000 bhp
Range: 3,500/15 **Fuel:** 350 tons **Crew:** 12 officers, 150 enlisted

Remarks: Survivors of a class of six: *General José de Austria* was stricken in 1976, *Almirante José Garcia* in 1977, and *General Juan José Flores* and *Almirante Bryon* in 1978. Both were extensively refitted by Camel Laird, Birkenhead, from 1968 to 1975–76 (much delay caused by financial and labor problems). Have operated under the Coast Guard Command since 3-86.
Hull systems: When new, could make 32 kts. Very lightly built, with much use of aluminum alloy. Have Denny-Brown fin stabilizers. Re-engine by CNR, Genoa, Italy, with diesels from 10-84 to 24-7-85.
Combat systems: OTO Melara Compact mounts replaced the original four 102-mm dual-purpose guns. Have Elsag NA-10 GFCS for the 76-mm guns and a lead-computing sight for the 40-mm AA mount.

GUIDED-MISSILE PATROL CRAFT [PTG]

♦ 3 Federación class
Bldr: Vesper Thornycroft, Portsmouth, U.K.

	Laid down	L	In serv.
PC-12 Federación (ex-P-12)	8-73	26-2-74	25-3-75
PC-14 Libertad (ex-P-14)	9-73	5-3-74	12-6-75
PC-16 Victoria (ex-P-16)	3-73	3-9-74	22-9-75

Victoria (PC-16) Carlos E. Hernández, 7-88

D: 150 tons (170 fl) **S:** 31 kts **Dim:** 36.88 (33.53 wl) × 7.16 × 1.80 hull
A: 2 Otomat Mk 2 SSM; 1/30-mm 70-cal. OTO Melara Compact AA; 2 single 12.7-mm M2 mg
M: 2 MTU MD 16V538 TB90 diesels; 1 prop; 7,080 max. bhp (5,900 sust.)
Electronics: Radar: 1 Decca . . . nav.; 1 SMA SPQ-2D surf. search
Electric: 250 kw tot. **Range:** 1,350/16 **Fuel:** 23.5 tons
Crew: 3 officers, 17 enlisted

Remarks: Refitted and modernized 1992–95 by Unidad de Carenado de la Armada, Puerto Cabello. Were re-engined 2000–2002. The 30-mm mount replaced the original Bofors 40-mm mount, and the missile launchers were modified to handle the Otomat Mk 2 SSM. With the *Constitución* class, they constitute the Fleet Command Patrol Squadron and are based at Falcón Naval Base, Punto Fijo.

PATROL CRAFT [PC]

♦ 4 new construction patrol craft
Bldr: Navantia, San Fernando, Spain

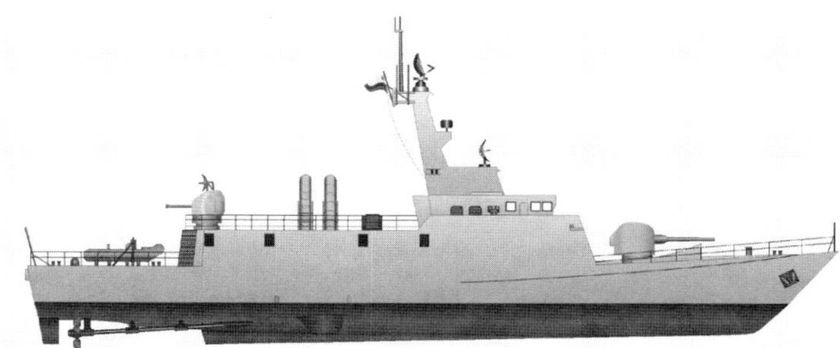

New construction Navantia patrol craft—computer rendering
J. M. Caiella, 2006

D: 1,200 tons (fl) **S:** 25 kts **Dim:** 68 × . . . × . . .
A: . . . SSM; 1 single 76-mm 62-cal. OTO Melara Compact DP; . . . CIWS
Electronics: . . .
M: . . . diesels **Crew:** 45

Remarks: Ordered 11-05, work began during 5-06. Deliveries are expected between 2008 and 2011. Data and computer rendering listed above are speculative. At least one RIB will likely be stowed on deck. Strict technology transfer laws preventing the sale of specific weapons technology to Venezuela are said to be causing difficulties in weapons and sensor selection.

♦ 3 Constitución class
Bldr: Vosper Thornycroft, Portsmouth, U.K.

	Laid down	L	In serv.
PC-11 Constitución	1-73	1-6-73	16-8-74
PC-13 Independencia	2-73	24-7-73	20-9-74
PC-15 Patria	3-73	27-9-73	9-1-75

Constitución (PC-11) Venezuelan Navy, 7-98

D: 150 tons (170 fl) **S:** 31 kts **Dim:** 36.88 (33.53 wl) × 7.16 × 1.80 hull
A: 1 76-mm 62-cal. OTO Melara Compact DP; 2 single 12.7-mm M2 mg
Electronics: Radar: 1 Decca . . . nav.; 1 SMA SPQ-2D surf. search; 1 AESN Orion RTN-10X f.c.
M: 2 MTU MD 16V538 TB90 diesels; 2 props; 7,080 max. bhp (5,900 sust.)
Electric: 250 kw tot. **Range:** 1,350/16 **Fuel:** 23.5 tons
Crew: 3 officers, 17 enlisted

Remarks: The three vessels were refitted and modernized 1992–95 by Unidad de Carenado de la Armada (Navy Yard), in Puerto Cabello and received new engines from 2000 to 2002. A new navigational system will be incorporated during 2004–6. The three craft, together with *Federación*-class PTGs, constitute the Patrol Squadron of Fleet Command and are based at Falcon Naval Base, Punto Fijo. Although they carried the word "Guardacosta" on their side for a period during the 1980s, they were never subordinated to the Coast Guard Command.

PATROL CRAFT [PC] *(continued)*

Hull systems: All equipped with Vosper fin stabilizers. Maximum sustained speed is 12 kts. New Jema 60/400-Hz electricity convector replacing originals in mid-1999.
Combat systems: Have the Elsag NA-10 Mod. 1 f.c.s for radar director for the 76-mm gun.

PATROL BOATS [PB]

Note: In 2006, Venezuela announced its intention to order 39 additional patrol boats from Spanish builder Rodman Polyships. Though no date has been announced for the boats, the order will likely include 30-m, 20-m, and 17-m types.

♦ 12 Gavión-class coastal patrol boats

Bldr: Halter Marine Group, Equitable Shipyards, New Orleans, La.

	In serv.		In serv.
PG-401 Gavión	26-8-99	PG-407 Fardela	2-00
PG-402 Alca	26-8-99	PG-408 Sumarela	2-00
PG-403 Bernacla	26-8-99	PG-409 Negrón	6-00
PG 404 Chamán	26-8-99	PG-410 Pigargo	6-00
PG-405 Cormorán	2-00	PG-411 Pagaza	6-00
PG-406 Colimbo	2-00	PG-412 Serreta	6-00

Alca (PG-402) Halter Marine, 1999

Pagaza (PG-411)—alongside *Chamán* (PG-404) Delso L. López / FAV Club, 7-03

D: 48 tons (fl) **S:** 25 kts **Dim:** 24.30 × 5.44 × 1.75
A: 1 twin 12.7-mm Mk 95 mg; 1 12.7-mm M2 mg
Electronics: Radar: 1 Raytheon R1210 nav.
M: 2 G.M. Detroit Diesel 12V92 TA diesels; 2 props; 2,160 bhp
Electric: 250 kw tot. **Range:** 1,000/15 **Crew:** 2 officers, 8 enlisted

Remarks: Originally to have been ordered in 12-96, but contract was delayed to 24-4-98. Aluminum construction, with components fabricated by other Halter Marine yards. Carry an inspection and rescue dinghy on the fantail. The first four arrived at La Guaira, Venezuela, on 6-10-99. Assigned to Coast Guard Command.

Note: Acquired during 1997 were an unknown number of Rigid Raider rigid inflatable assault boats armed with two 7.62-mm machineguns and powered by two gasoline outboards; a crew of 1 plus 8 troops are carried. The six *Integredad*-class patrol launches have been redesignated as Aids-to-Navigation craft and are now listed under service craft.

♦ 2 U.S. 36-ft. Protector 3612-V–class coastal patrol boats

Bldr: SeaArk Marine, Monticello, Ark.

	In serv.		In serv.
LG-31 Chichiriviche	15-3-94	LG-32 Caruanta	7-3-94

D: 11.1 tons (fl) **S:** . . . kts **Dim:** 11.1 × 4.0 × 0.53 hull
A: 1 7.62-mm mg **Electronics:** Radar: 1 Raytheon . . . nav.
M: 2 . . . diesels; 2 props; . . . bhp **Crew:** 4 tot.

Remarks: Donated by U.S. Aluminum construction. Assigned to Coast Guard Command and based at La Guaria.

♦ 4 U.S. Coast Guard Point-class coastal patrol boats

Bldr: U.S. Coast Guard Yard, Curtis Bay, Md. (PG 32: J. Martinac SB, Tacoma, Wash.)

	In serv.	Transferred
PG-31 Petrel (ex-*Point Knoll,* WPB 82367)	26-6-67	18-10-91
PG-32 Alcatraz (ex-*Point Judith,* WPB 82345)	26-7-66	15-1-92
PG-33 Albatros (ex-*Point Ledge,* WPB 82334)	18-7-62	3-8-98
PG-34 Pelicano (ex-*Point Franklin,* WPB 82350)	14-11-66	3-8-98

Pelicano (PG-34) Carlos E. Hernández, 12-98

D: 64 tons (69 fl) **S:** 23 kts **Dim:** 25.30 × 5.23 × 1.95
A: 1 twin 12.7-mm mg **Electronics:** Radar: 1/Raytheon SPS-64(V)1 nav.
M: 2 Caterpillar 3412 diesels; 2 props; 1,480 bhp
Range: 490/23.7; 1,500/8 **Fuel:** 5.7 tons **Crew:** 1 officer, 9 enlisted

Remarks: Donated for use by the Coast Guard Command in antidrug work. Capable of towing and firefighting. Were re-engined during the early 1990s.

♦ 6 Courage-class fast patrol launches

Bldr: . . . Venezuela

	In serv.		In serv.
LRG-001 Constancia	2-91	LRG-004 Tenacidad	4-93
LRG-002 Perseverancia	12-91	LRG-005 Integridad	1997
LRG-003 Honestidad	12-91	LRG-006 Lealtad	1998

Constancia (LRG-001) Venezuelan Navy, 2-92

Remarks: First two were prototypes of a planned group of 20 delivered 12-91 for use by the Coast Guard Command, but only six were ever delivered. Are 7.5–12.0 m overall. Of "cigarette boat" configuration, with GRP-construction hulls. LRG-005 and -006 are armed with 2 single 7.62-mm mg.

PATROL BOATS [PB] *(continued)*

♦ **7 UFPB-1/1000-class coastal patrol launches**
Bldr: Cougar Marine, Ltd., U.K. (In serv. 1987)

LG-21 Polaris LG-23 Rigel LG-25 Antares LG-27 Altair
LG-22 Sirius LG-24 Aldebaran LG-26 Canopus

Aldebaran (LG-24) Venezuelan Navy, 1998

D: 5 tons (fl) **S:** 50 kts **Dim:** 10.05 (7.92 wl) × 2.60 × 0.78
A: 1/12.7-mm mg **Electronics:** Radar: 1/ . . . nav.
M: 2 diesel outdrives; 400 bhp **Range:** 150/50 **Crew:** 4 tot.

Remarks: GRP construction. All refitted 1998–99 by Unidad de Carenado de la Armada, Puerto Cabello. Assigned to Coast Guard for coastal service.

♦ **. . . 24-ft. RIB raiding launches**
Bldr: Artigiana Batteli, . . . , Italy (In serv. 1997–98)

D: . . . tons **S:** . . . **Dim:** . . . × . . . × . . .
A: 2/7.62-mm mg **Electronics:** 1/ . . . nav.
M: 2 Mercury gasoline outboards; . . . **Crew:** . . . tot.

Remarks: A large number are being procured under 1997 funding for the Navy River Commands, the two Marine Corps River Frontier Commands, and the Coast Guard Command.

♦ **5 or more Caribe/Frontera-class riverine patrol launches**
Bldr: Intermarine C.A., Guatire, Miranda State, Venezuela (In serv. . . .)

D: . . . tons **S:** 39.7 kts **Dim:** 5.00 × 2.10 × 0.20
A: 1 7.62-mm mg
M: 2 gasoline outboards; 130 bhp **Crew:** 6 tot.

Remarks: GRP construction. Assigned to the Marine Corps Frontier River Brigade. Additional units are planned.

♦ **2 or more 7.3-m RIB assault launches**
Bldr: Artigana Battelli, . . . Italy (In serv. 1997)

Remarks: Armed with two 7.62-mm mg and powered by two Mercury outboards. Assigned to the Coast Guard Command.

♦ **5 or more U.S. 22-ft. Guardian-class raider patrol launches**
Bldr: Boston Whaler, Edgewater, Fla. (In serv. 10-97 to . . .)

COFFMU-323, etc.

Three Venezuelan 22-ft. Guardian-class launches—on the Río Orinoco
Javier Nieves/FAV Club, 5-00

22-ft. Guardian-class—with armament aboard Javier Nieves/FAV Club, 5-00

D: 1.2 tons (1.5 fl) **S:** 35 kts **Dim:** 6.81 × 2.30 × 0.36
A: 1 12.7-mm mg; 2 single 7.62-mm mg
Electronics: Radar: 1 Raytheon SPS-66 nav.
M: 2 gasoline outboard motors; 250 bhp
Range: 167/40 **Crew:** 6 tot.

Remarks: Donated by U.S. government for use by the two Marine Corps Frontier River Commands. GRP foam-core hull construction. Additional units are planned.

♦ **8 or more Manapiare-class riverine assault boats**
Bldr: Puerto la Cruz, Venezuela (In serv. 1996– . . .)

Remarks: Aluminum construction. Carry one 7.62-mm machinegun. Powered by two gasoline outboard motors. Are assigned to the Marine Corps River Frontier Brigade.

♦ **9 U.S. 22-ft. Piranha-class river patrol launches**
Bldr: Boston Whaler, Rockland, Mass., and Edgewater, Fla. (In serv.: first two 28-2-94; others 1994 to 10-97)

LCF-101 through LCF-109

D: 1.6 tons light (2 fl) **S:** 39.1 kts **Dim:** 6.81 × 2.26 × 0.36
A: 2 single 12.7-mm mg; 2 single 7.62-mm mg
Electronics: Radar: 1 Raytheon SPS-66 nav.
M: 2 outboard motors; 300 bhp **Range:** 167/39 **Crew:** 4 tot.

Remarks: Donated by U.S. government for use by Navy River Command and two Marine Corps River Frontier Commands. Additional units are planned. Foam-core, unsinkable glass-reinforced plastic construction. All are painted olive drab.

♦ **5 or more Caroní-class riverine patrol launches**
Bldr: . . ., Venezuela (In serv. 1991– . . .)

D: . . . tons **S:** 39.1 kts **Dim:** 4.90 × 1.65 × 0.20
A: 1 7.62-mm mg **M:** 2 gasoline outboards; 130 bhp
Crew: 6 tot.

Remarks: Aluminum construction. Assigned to Marine Corps Frontier River Brigade.

♦ **2 Manaure-class river patrol launches** (In serv. 24-4-73)

PF-21 Manaure PF-22 Mara

Mara (PF-22)—on the Río Orinoco Venezuelan Navy, 7-98

D: 15 tons (fl) **S:** 10 kts **Dim:** 16.5 × 4.3 × 1.3
A: 1 20-mm 70-cal. Oerlikon Mk 10 AA; 1 12.7-mm mg
Electronics: Radar: 1 Raytheon . . . nav. **M:** 2 . . . diesels; 2 props; . . . bhp
Range: 200/10 **Crew:** 8 tot.

Remarks: Resemble a U.S. Navy "Swiftboat" but have narrower beam. Are assigned to the River Squadron River Command.

♦ **2 13.6-ton river patrol launches** (In serv. 24-4-73)

PF-23 Guaicaipuro (ex-PF-11) PF-24 Tamanaco (ex-PF-12)

Remarks: Armed with one 12.7-mm mg. Assigned to the River Squadron/River Command.

♦ **4 Terepaima class**
Bldr: Mercruiser, Miami, Fla. (In serv. 1987)

LA-01 El Amparo PF-31 Terepaima PF-33 Yaracuy PF-34 Sorocaima

Terepaima (PF-31) Venezuelan Navy, 7-88

D: 5 tons (fl) **S:** 35-50 kts **Dim:** 10.60 × 2.90 × 0.75
A: 1 7.62-mm mg **M:** 2 gasoline engines; 2 props; . . . bhp
Range: 200/ . . . **Crew:** 4 tot.

Remarks: LA-01 is used as an ambulance boat. GRP construction. Are assigned to the River Squadron/River Command. *Tiuna* (PF-32) was no longer in service as of 2004. *El Amparo* (LA-01) acts as a sea-ambulance.

PATROL BOATS [PB] *(continued)*

♦ 3 21-ft. Cobia class
Bldr: SeaArk Marine, Monticello, Ark.

COFFMU- . . . (ex-ANMU-81) COFFRI- . . . (ex-PFPJQ-81)
COFFMU- . . . (ex-ANMU 82)

D: 0.5 tons light (1.25 fl) **S:** 30 kts **Dim:** 6.02 × 2.36 × 0.33
A: 1 12.7-mm mg **Electronics:** Radar: 1 Furuno FR 10 nav.
M: 2 Evinrude gasoline outboard motors; 230 bhp **Crew:** 4 tot.

Remarks: Aluminum construction. For river and lake patrol. Equipped with push-knees to act as pusher tugs. Completed 1984 but not delivered until 5-87. The last two are used as yachts. Sisters serve the National Guard.

AMPHIBIOUS WARFARE SHIPS AND CRAFT

♦ 4 Capana-class tank landing ships [LST]
Bldr: Korea-Tacoma SY, Masan, S. Korea

	L	In serv.		L	In serv.
T-61 Capana	25-3-83	21-6-84	T-63 Goajira	. . .	1-11-84
T-62 Esequibo	25-3-83	21-6-84	T-64 Los Llanos	. . .	1-11-84

Esequibo (T-62) Ralph Edwards, 4-00

Goajira (T-63) Leo Dirkx, 5-99

D: 1,800 tons light (4,070 fl) **S:** 15 kts
Dim: 104.0 × 15.4 × 3.0 (4.2 max.)
A: 1 twin 40-mm 70-cal. OTO Melara Dardo AA; 2 single 20-mm 90-cal. Oerlikon GAM-B01 AA
Electronics: Radar: 1 . . . nav.
M: 2 SEMT-Pielstick 16 PA 6V diesels; 2 props; 6,400 bhp (5,600 sust.)
Electric: 750 kw tot. **Range:** 7,500/13
Crew: 13 officers, 104 enlisted + troops: 10 officers, 192 enlisted

Remarks: Ordered 8-82. Improved version of U.S. WW II–era LST design. T-61 and -62 arrived 10-84 in Venezuela, T-63 in 12-84, and T-64 early in 1985; all delivered without armament. T-63 heavily damaged by fire 6-87 and not restored to service until 5-93. Have sisters in the Indonesian Navy. T-62 is employed in commercial cargo transport service between Caracas, Antigua, Grenada, and St. Lucia. The class began overhaul and modernization in 2004.
Hull systems: Cargo: 1,800 tons maximum, 690 beaching load. Have an elevator to the upper deck and a 50-ton tank turntable on the tank deck. Have a helicopter deck aft.
Combat systems: There is an Alenia NA-18 optronic director for the 40-mm mount.

Note: Some $15.9 million was funded during 1997 for purchase of two new utility landing craft of about 45-m length; negotiations began in 1998 with Halter Marine (now Friede Goldman Halter) in the U.S., but the program was canceled.

♦ 2 Margarita-class utility landing craft [LCU]
Bldr: Swiftships, Morgan City, La.

	In serv.		In serv.
T-71 Margarita	20-1-84	T-72 La Orchila	2-4-84

D: 428 tons (fl) **S:** 13 kts
Dim: 39.62 × 10.97 × 1.30 **A:** 2/12.7-mm M2 mg (I × 2)
Electronics: Radar: 1/Raytheon 6410 nav.

Margarita (T-71) Carlos E. Hernández, 11-93

M: 2 G.M. Detroit Diesel 16V149N diesels; 2 props; 1,800 bhp
Electric: 150 kw tot. (2 × 75-kw Delco sets, G.M. 6-71 diesels driving)
Range: 2,500/10 **Fuel:** 64 tons **Crew:** 4 officers, 17 enlisted

Remarks: Aluminum construction. Cargo: vehicles, supplies, up to 108 tons fuel, and 149 tons water. Bow ramp, 15-ton crane on bow. Carry 156 tons ballast. Intended for coastal and riverine use. Both were transferred to the River Command in 1984.

♦ 1 ex-U.S. LCM(8)-series landing craft [LCM] (In serv. 1970s)

LC-21 Curiapo

Curiapo (LC-21) Venezuelan Navy, 4-99

D: 58.8 tons light (116 fl) **S:** 9 kts **Dim:** 22.43 × 6.43 × 1.35 fwd./1.47 aft
A: 1/12.7-mm mg **Electronics:** Radar: 1/ . . nav.
M: 2 G.M. Detroit Diesel 12V-71 diesels; 2 props; 590 bhp
Range: 150/9.2 (loaded) **Crew:** 1 officer, 5 enlisted

Remarks: Steel-hulled former U.S. Army unit donated 4-99 for riverine transport and logistics support service. Carries up to 50 passengers. Cargo: 60 tons or 150 troops for short distances in 12.8 × 4.3–m open well with 54.6-m^2 space. Assigned to the naval River Squadron/River Command.

♦ 1 riverine landing craft [LCVP]
Bldr: . . . (In serv. 1988)

LC-01 Yopito

Yopito (LC-01)—on the Río Orinoco Venezuelan Navy, 7-99

D: 60 tons (fl) **S:** 8 kts **Dim:** 18.00 × 4.60 × 1.50
A: 1 12.7-mm mg **M:** 1 diesel; 1 prop; . . . bhp
Range: 200/8 **Crew:** 1 officer, 3 enlisted

♦ Up to 32 Apure-class riverine assault boats [LCP]
Bldr: San Cristóbal, Venezuela (In serv. mid-1980s to 8-92)

ARV-001 series

D: 500 kg light **S:** 35 kts **Dim:** 5.55 × 2.15 × 0.15
A: 1 7.62-mm mg **M:** 2 gasoline outboards; 130 bhp
Crew: 2 + 6 troops

Remarks: Aluminum construction. Apure-II series were delivered in 8-92. ANFRI-52 was lost through fire on 2-12-88.

AMPHIBIOUS WARFARE SHIPS AND CRAFT *(continued)*

Two Apure/Apure-II-class launches Venezuelan Navy, 2-92

♦ 11 U.S. LVT-7 amphibious armored personnel carriers

LVT-7 amphibious armored personnel carrier—on a travel trailer
Enver Cuervos/FAV Club, 6-03

Remarks: Acquired new from U.S. FMC Corp. in 1973. Tracked vehicles for use by the Venezuelan marines: one LVTC-7 command vehicle, one LVTR-7 recovery vehicle, and nine LVTP-7 personnel carriers. Are being refurbished by the Venezuelan Army Armored Maintenance Center.

Note: Also reported in service are jet ski craft assigned to the Marine Corps Special Operations Command and several other Special Forces launches. The marines also use a considerable number of inflatable rubber assault boats.

AUXILIARIES

♦ 1 multipurpose hydrographic survey ship [AGS]

Bldr: Izar (formerly E.N. Bazán), San Fernando, Spain

	Laid down	L	In serv.
BO-11 Punta Brava	12-88	9-3-90	24-3-91

Punta Brava (BO-11) Carlos E. Hernández, 5-91

D: 1,170 tons (1,250 fl) **S:** 14.6 kts **Dim:** 61.70 (55.60 pp) × 11.90 × 3.46
A: None **Electronics:** Radar: 2 . . . nav.
M: 2 Bazán-M.A.N. 7L 20/27 diesels; 2 props; 2,500 bhp—bow-thruster
Range: 8,000/12.8 **Fuel:** 210 tons
Crew: 6 officers, 8 noncomm. officers, 20 enlisted + 6 scientists

Remarks: Ordered 9-88. Initially assigned to the coast guard, but was transferred 3-94 to the Amphibious and Service Ships Squadron of the Fleet Command, which operates her for the Dirección de Hydrografía y Navegación del la Armada (Navy Hydrographic and Navigation Bureau). Refitted in the U.S. during 2000, with navigational and scientific equipment updated.
Hull systems: Has biological, meteorological, geological, electronic, and oceanographic laboratories in addition to cartographic facilities. Two 8.5-m hydrographic survey launches are carried. Has two Raytheon 6000-m echo sounders.

Disposal note: Refrigerated cargo transport [AK] *Puerto Cabello* (T-44) was stricken mid-2001 and placed up for sale.

♦ 1 Ciudad Bolívar–class replenishment oiler [AOR]

Bldr: Hyundai Heavy Industries SY, Ulsan, South Korea

	Laid down	L	In serv.
T-81 Ciudad Bolívar	8-99	2000	23-9-01

Ciudad Bolívar (T-81) Delso L. López / FAV Club, 7-03

Ciudad Bolívar (T-81) Chris Cavas, 5-02

D: 9,750 tons (fl) **S:** 18.6 kts **Dim:** 137.70 (122.5 pp) × 18.00 × 6.5
A: Provision for: 1 twin 40-mm 70-cal. OTO Melara Fast Forty AA; 2 single 12.7-mm M2 mg
Electronics: Radar: 2 . . . nav.
M: 2 Caterpillar 3616V diesels; 2 CP props; 12,500 bhp
Range: 4,500/15 **Electric:** 725 kw tot.
Crew: 22 officers, 56 enlisted (accomm. for 100 tot.)

Remarks: Ordered early 1999 for $59.8 million. Assigned to the Amphibious and Service Ships Squadron of the Fleet Command.
Hull systems: Cargo: 4,400 tons ship fuel, 100 tons JP-5 aviation fuel, 500 tons potable water, 150 tons munitions, 385 tons dry stores, 8.9 tons frozen provisions, and 8.9 tons refrigerated provisions. Two replenishment stations on each beam, one for liquids and one for solid cargo transfer, the latter using the sliding-stay transfer system; also able to refuel over the stern. Helicopter platform and hangar aft.
Combat systems: The listed armament was still not aboard as of 7-03; the 40-mm gunmount is to have a remote director.

♦ 2 General Miranda-class fleet tugs [ATA]

Bldr: Damen SY, Gorinchem, the Netherlands, and Diques y Astilleros Nacionales, C.A. (DIANCA) Puerto Cabello, Venezuela

	Laid down	L	In serv.
RA-11 General Francisco de Miranda	4-04	2005	2005
RA-12 Manuel Ezequiel Bruzual	. . .	. . .	2006

D: 700 ton. Light **S:** 12.5 kts. **Dim:** 60.10 × 13.60 × 6.0
A: . . . **Electronics:** Radar: 1. . .nav
M: 2 CAT 3606TA diesels; 2 prop.; 5,400 bhp-bow
Electric: . . . **Range:** 7,000 nm./10 kts. **Endurance:** 45 days.
Fuel: . . . **Crew:** 48 tot.

Remarks: Steel construction. Parts built in Holland and shipped to Venezuela where Dianca assembled and completed fitting out. Cargo: 30 tons. Also will be used in logistic, search-and-rescue, buoy tender, and antipollution activities.

Disposal note: Ex-U.S. *Achomawi*-class fleet tug *Contralmirante Miguel Rodriguez* (RA-33) was decommissioned in 2005.

AUXILIARIES *(continued)*

General Francisco de Miranda (RA-11) Dianca via Carlos E. Hernández, 2003

♦ 1 sail-training ship [AXT]

Bldr: Ast. Celeya, Bilbao, Spain

	Laid down	L	In serv.
BE-11 Simón Bolívar	5-6-79	21-9-79	14-8-80

Simón Bolívar (BE-11) A. D. Baker III, 6-00

D: 1,260 tons (fl) **S:** 10.5 kts **Dim:** 82.42 (58.5 pp) × 10.6 × 4.2
M: 1 G.M. Detroit Diesel 12V149T diesel; 1 prop; 875 bhp (750 sust.)
Crew: 17 officers, 76 enlisted + 18 instructors, 84 cadets

Remarks: 934 grt. Ordered 7-78. Sister to Ecuadorian *Guayas.* Three-masted bark; sail area: 1,650 m^2 from a total of 23 sails. Does not have pennant number painted on. Assigned to the Amphibian and Service Ships Squadron of Fleet Command. The Naval Academy, at Meseta de Mamo, also employs several small sail craft, outboard-motor launches, and rigid inflatables for cadet training. BE-11 reportedly underwent refit in 2004–5.

SERVICE CRAFT

Note: In addition to the following craft listed, plans call for the construction of a single vehicle and personnel ferry to support the naval facilities on the Los Monjes Islands in the Golfo de Venezuela.

♦ 2 small VIP yachts [YFL]

La Almiralantaza . . .

Remarks: *La Almiralantaza* is assigned to the Venezuelan Chief of Naval Operations and based at Puerto Cabello. Another VIP craft is based at Capitán de Navío Antonio Díaz Naval Station, La Orchila Island.

♦ 5 BANAR-01-class service launches [YFL]

Banar-01 through Banar-05

D: 12 tons (fl) **S:** 9 kts **Dim:** 10.9 × 3.2 × 1.0
M: 1 G.M. Detroit Diesel 6-71 diesel; 1 props; 225 bhp
Range: 110/9 **Crew:** 3 tot.

Remarks: Former U.S.-built LCVP landing craft rebuilt by Diques y Astilleros Nacionales, C.A. (DIANCA), Puerto Cabello in 1976–77. Are assigned to the Contralmirante Agustin Armario Naval Base, Puerto Cabello. BANAR = BAse Naval ARmario.

♦ 8 or more miscellaneous personnel launches [YFL]

ANGU-01 . . .	ESGLR-01 Zenit
ANGU-07 . . .	ESGLR-114 . . .
EPGMA-01 . . .	LG-0001 Pampatar
EPGMA-07 Bellatrix	LT-01 Turiamo (ex-ANT-01)

Turiamo (LT-01) Venezuelan Navy, 7-99

Pampatar (LG-0001) Carlos E. Hernández, 12-98

Remarks: ANGU-01 (completed 5-80 by Astilleros del Lago, C.A.) and ANGU-07 are assigned to the Capitán de Navío Francisco Javier Gutiérres Naval Station, Puerto Hierro (ANGU = Apostadero Naval GUtiérrez). EPGMA-01 and EPGMA-07 are assigned to the Teniente de Navío Pedro Lucas Uribarri Coast Guard Station, Maracaibo. ESGLR-01 and ESGLR-114 are GRO-construction boats with a single outboard motor each and are assigned to Los Roques Secondary Coast Guard Station for search-and-rescue duties. LG-0001 is a 5.5-m GRP-construction "cigarette boat" assigned to the Pampatar Coast Guard Station, Margarita Island. LT-01 was completed by Navitech Industries, Miami, Florida, in 1983 and is assigned to Teniente de Navío Tomás Vega Naval Station, Turiamo Bay.

♦ 7 miscellaneous riverine service launches [YFL]

COFFRI- . . . Río Atabapo (ex-PFCM-11)
COFFRI- . . . Río Ventuarí (ex-PFCM-21)
COFFRI- . . . Río Orinoco (ex-ANFRI-12)
COFFRI- . . . (ex-ANFRI-13)
COFFRI- . . . Río Temi (ex-ANFRI-11)
COFFRI- . . . (ex-PFCM-12)
COFFRI- . . . Puerto Páez (ex- . . .)

Remarks: All are assigned to General Franz Rizquez Iribarren Marine Corps Frontier River Command. *Río Temi* displaces 10 tons, *Río Orinoco* and *Río Atabapo* 4 tons., ex-PFCM-12 and ex-ANFRI-13 1.5 tons, and *Río Ventuarí* displaces 1.2 tons. *Puerto Páez* was completed by Yamaha Fibra, C.A., San Cristóbal, in 1984, and is assigned to the Capitán de Fragata Tomás Machado Naval Base, Ciudad Bolívar, on the Orinoco river.

♦ 1 navigational aids tender [YGL]

Bldr: Unidad de Carenado de la Armada, Puerto Cabello (In serv. 7-98)

BB-11 Macuro

Macuro (BB-11) Carlos E. Hernández, 3-00

D: 10 tons (fl) **S:** 12 kts **Dim:** 13.00 × 6.85 × . . .
A: 1/20-mm 70-cal. Oerlikon AA—4/12-7-mm mg (I × 4)

SERVICE CRAFT *(continued)*

Electronics: Radar: 1/ . . . nav. **M:** 2 diesels; 2 props. . . . bhp
Range: . . . / . . . **Fuel:** 12 m^3 **Crew:** . . . tot.

Remarks: Steel-construction catamaran laid down 1996. Can carry a standard 20-ft. cargo container with 15 tons cargo, a navigational-aids buoy, or a 23-ton fuel tank. Can also be used to tow targets. Additional units may be built.

♦ 8 Integridad-class aids-to-navigation launches [YGL]

Bldr: Intermarine, Guatire, Venezuela (In serv. 6-96 to 2-3-00)

LSM-001 Punta Macoya (ex-*Integridad,* LGI-101)
LSM-002 Farallón Centinela
LSM-003 Charagato
LSM-004 Bajo Brito
LSM-005 Bajo Araya
LSM-006 Carecare
LSM-007 Vela de Coro
LSM-008 Cayo Macereo

Bajo Araya (LSM-005) Carlos E. Hernández, 8-97

D: 5 tons (fl) **S:** 30 kts **Dim:** 12.70 × 2.74 × . . .
A: 2 single 7.62-mm M60A1 mg **Electronics:** Radar: 1/ . . . nav.
M: 2 diesels; 2 props; 640 bhp **Range:** 520/20
Crew: 1 officer, 4 enlisted

Remarks: GRP construction. Subordinated to the Coast Guard. Originally typed Lancha Interceptora Guardacosta (Coast Guard Interceptor Launch) but were reclassified as Lancha de Señalización Maritima (Aids-to-Navigation Launch) in 1997. First six completed by 1997, with LSM-007 and LSM-008 delivered 2-3-00. The radar has a range of 24 nautical miles; a GPS receiver and HF radios are fitted.

♦ 1 U.S. Coast Guard 21-ft. aids-to-navigation boat [YGL]

Bldr: MonArk, Monticello, Ark. (In serv. late 1980s)

D: 1.59 tons (3.17 fl) **S:** 28 kts **Dim:** 6.56 × 2.24 × 0.36 hull
M: 1 gasoline outboard; 228 bhp **Range:** 100/20 **Crew:** . . . tot.

Remarks: One unit is assigned to the Puerto Cabello Coast Guard Station. Aluminum construction.

♦ 1 hydrographic survey launch [YGS]

Bldr: Diques y Astilleros Nacionales, C.A. (DIANCA), Puerto Cabello (In serv. 8-89)

Maquiritare (ex-F-001, ex-ANFRI-13)

Remarks: 1.5 tons. Built for the Dirección de Geografía y Cartografia de las Fuerzas Armadas, but was transferred to the navy and assigned to the River Command for use in riverine charting.

♦ 2 Gabriela-class hydrographic survey craft [YGS]

Bldr: Abeking & Rasmussen, Lemwerder, Germany

	Laid down	L	In serv.
LH-11 Gabriela (ex-*Península de Araya;* ex-*Gabriela,* LH-01)	10-3-73	29-11-73	5-2-74
LH-12 Lely (ex-*Península de Paraguana;* ex-*Lely,* LH-02)	28-5-73	12-12-73	7-2-74

Gabriela (LH-11) Maritime Photographic, 1-94

D: 90 tons (fl) **S:** 20 kts **Dim:** 27.0 × 5.6 × 1.5
M: 2 MTU diesels; 2 props; 2,300 bhp **Crew:** 1 officer, 9 enlisted

Remarks: Transferred to navy in 9-86 from the Instituto Nacional de Canalizaciones and initially assigned to the River Command and Coast Guard Command, respectively. Now both serve the River Command. Have GPS terminals.

♦ 1 riverine accommodations craft [YPB]

Río Uribante

Remarks: Transferred from the Instituto Nacional de Canalizaciones in 12-93 for use as a mobile floating command post by the River Command on the Río Orinoco. Can accommodate 33 personnel.

♦ 2 salvage, search-and-rescue craft [YRS]

Bldr: . . . (In serv. . . .)

LG-11 Los Taques (ex-LA-11, ex-LA-01, ex- . . .)
LG-12 Los Cayos (ex-LA-12, ex-LA-02, ex-*Puerto Sucre*)

Los Cayos (LG-12) Carlos E. Hernández, 7-88

D: 350 tons (fl) **S:** 8 kts **Dim:** 26.6 × 7.1 × 1.5
A: 2/12.7-mm mg **Electronics:** Radar: 1/Raytheon . . . nav.
M: 1 diesel; 1 prop; 850 bhp **Range:** 8,500/8 **Crew:** 10 tot.

Remarks: Small former fishing trawlers seized and transferred to the navy on 15-5-81 and 9-84, respectively. Are assigned to Coast Guard Command for search and rescue and light salvage duties.

♦ 1 ex-U.S. Cholocco-class medium harbor tug [YTM]

Bldr: Commercial Iron Works, Portland, Ore.

	Laid down	L	In serv.
RP-21 Teniente de Navío Fernando Gómez (ex-R-11, ex-*General José Félix Ribas,* R-13, ex-*Oswegatchie,* YTM 778, ex-YTB 515)	13-8-45	24-10-45	14-12-45

Teniente de Navío Fernando Gómez (RP-21) Carlos E. Hernández, 7-88

D: 250 tons light (345 fl) **S:** 12 kts **Dim:** 30.48 × 7.92 × 2.92
A: 2 single 12.7-mm mg **Electronics:** Radar: 1 . . . nav.
M: 2 Enterprise diesels; 1 prop; 1,270 bhp **Crew:** 14 tot.

Remarks: Transferred from U.S. 4-6-65; had been in reserve from 3-46 to 3-63. Transferred to Coast Guard Command in 1989. Is equipped with oil skimming equipment, including a chemical dispenser on the bow.

NATIONAL GUARD
(*Guardia Nacional*)

Note: The National Guard, Venezuela's fourth armed service organization, has about 30,000 personnel, all volunteers. It has nine Regional Commands, one Air Support Command with about 55 fixed-wing transports and helicopters, one Anti-Drug Command, and one Coastal Vigilance Command with more than 100 patrol boats for customs and internal security duties on the coast and on inland lakes and rivers. Four Enstrom 280FX light helicopters were acquired during 2-02 for training.

National Guard craft display the words "Guardia Nacional" on either side of the hull or superstructure and carry blue-red-blue painted flag on either side of the bow, with the yellow letters "GN" superimposed.

PATROL BOATS [WPB]

♦ 10 54-ft.-class search-and-rescue patrol boats
Bldr: Halter Marine Equitable Shipyards, New Orleans, La.
(In serv. 2-99 to 12-99)

B-9801 Río Orinoco II
B-9802 Río Caroní
B-9803 Río . . .
B-9804 Río . . .
B-9805 Río . . .
B-9806 Río . . .
B-9807 Río . . .
B-9808 Río . . .
B-9809 Río . . .
B-9810 Río . . .

Río Orinoco II (B-9801) Halter Marine, 1999

D: 30 tons (fl) **S:** 36 kts **Dim:** 16.46 × . . . × . . .
A: 2 single 12.7-mm mg **Electronics:** Radar: 1 Raytheon R1210 nav.
M: 2 MTU 12V183 TE93 diesels; 2 props; 2,268 bhp
Range: 750/28 **Crew:** 5 tot.

Remarks: To have been ordered 9-95 for delivery in 1996–97, but contract not placed until 24-4-98. Additional units may be ordered. Aluminum construction. Funded by the Export-Import Bank. First two were to completed 12-98, then two in 3-99, and two in 5-99, 7-99, and 9-99, but program fell behind by about four months. 40-mm Mk 19 grenade launchers can be substituted for the 12.7-mm mgs on the existing mountings.

♦ 5 U.S. 22-ft. Guardian-class raider patrol launches
Bldr: Boston Whaler, Edgewater, Fla. (In serv. 1998)

V- . . . -series

D: 1.5 tons **S:** 35 kts **Dim:** 6.81 × 2.26 × . . .
A: 2 single 12.7-mm mg **Electronics:** Radar: 1 Raytheon SPS-66 nav.
M: 2 gasoline outboards; 250 bhp **Range:** 167/35 **Crew:** 4 tot.

Remarks: Donated by U.S. Government for River Vigilance detachments. Foam-core GRP construction.

♦ 8 35-ft. Raider patrol launches
Bldr: C&W Industrial Fabrication and Marine Equipment Ltd., Canada
(In serv. 6-99)

V-983501 through V-983508 (ex-GN-3501 through GN-3508)

35-ft. Raider patrol launch Guardia Nacional, 9-00

D: . . . tons **S:** . . . kts **Dim:** 10.67 × . . . × . . .
A: 4 single 7.62-mm mg **Electronics:** Radar: 1 . . . nav.
M: 2 gasoline outboards; 350 bhp **Crew:** 6 tot.

Remarks: Ordered 12-96. Intended for riverine service to combat drug trade and insurgencies. Assigned to river detachments and painted olive drab. Have GPS receiver and HF radio. GRP construction.

♦ 25 30-ft. Raider patrol launches
Bldr: C&W Industrial Fabrications and Marine Equipment Ltd., Canada
(In serv. 6-99)

V-983001 through V-983025 (ex-GN-3001 through GN-3025)

D: . . . tons **S:** . . . kts **Dim:** 9.35 × . . . × . . .
A: 4 single 7.62-mm mg **Electronics:** Radar: 1 . . . nav.
M: 2 gasoline outboards; 350 bhp **Crew:** 6 tot.

Remarks: Ordered 12-96. Assigned to Coastal, River, and Lakes Vigilance detachments. GRP construction.

♦ 25 26-ft. Raider patrol launches
Bldr: C&W Industrial Fabrications and Marine Equipment Ltd., Canada
(In serv. 6-99)

V-982601 through V-982625 (ex-GN-2601 through GN-2625)

D: . . . tons **S:** 35-40 kts **Dim:** 7.92 × . . . × . . .
A: 4 single 7.62-mm mg **Electronics:** Radar: 1/ . . . nav.
M: 2 gasoline outboards; 350 bhp **Crew:** 6 tot.

Remarks: Ordered 1997. GRP construction. Have HF radio and a GPS receiver. Assigned to Coastal, River, and Lakes Vigilance detachments. GRP construction.

♦ 20 Precursor-class launches
Bldr: Centro de Mantenimiento Naval, Guanta (In serv. 1996 to . . .)

D: . . . tons **S:** 35 kts **Dim:** 4.8 × 1.6 × 0.9
A: 1 7.62-mm mg **M:** 1 gasoline outboard; 140 bhp
Endurance: 3 hours **Crew:** 1 coxswain + 4 troops

♦ 12 Protector-class
Bldr: SeaArk Workboats, Monticello, Ark.

	Completed		Completed
B-8421 Río Arauca II	2-7-84	B-8427 Río Sarare	4-9-84
B-8422 Río Catatumbo II	2-7-84	B-8428 Río Uribante	4-9-84
B-8423 Río Apure II	1-8-84	B-8429 Río Cinaruco	1-11-84
B-8424 Río Nearo II	1-8-84	B-8430 Río Icabara	1-11-84
B-8425 Río Meta II	30-8-84	B-8431 Río Guarico II	1984
B-8426 Río Portuguesa II	1984	B-8432 Río Yaracuy	1984

Río Sarare (B-8427) H&L Van Ginderen, 2-96

D: 15 tons (fl) **S:** 28 kts **Dim:** 13.03 (12.55 pp) × 4.47 × 1.17
A: 2 single 12.7-mm mg; 2 single 7.62-mm mg
Electronics: Radar: 1 Furuno FR10 nav.
M: 2 G.M. Detroit Diesel 8V92 T diesels; 2 props; 1,100 bhp
Electric: 10.5 kw tot. **Range:** 600/25 **Crew:** 4 tot.

Remarks: Aluminum construction. Not delivered until 5-87. For river and lake patrol. Four of the craft were transferred to the navy's River Command but later returned.

♦ 10 21-ft. Cobia design
Bldr: SeaArk Workboats, Monticello, Ark. (In serv. 5-87)

A-6901 Lago 1
A-6902 Lago 2
A-6903 Lago 3
A-6904 Lago 4
A-7918 Río Cabriales
A-7919 Río Chama
A-7920 Río Caribe
A-7921 Río Tuy
A-7929 Manati
A-8223 Goaigoaza

SeaArk 21-ft. Cobia design SeaArk, 1984

D: 0.5 tons light (1.25 fl) **S:** 30 kts
Dim: 6.02 × 2.36 × 0.33 **A:** 1 12.7-mm mg
Electronics: Radar: 1 Furuno FR 10 nav.
M: 2 Evinrude gasoline outboard motors; 230 bhp
Crew: 4 tot.

Remarks: Aluminum construction. For river and lake patrol. Equipped with push-knees to act as pusher tugs. May have been renumbered with V-series pennants. A-7929 and A-8223 are used as yachts. Sisters serve the navy.

NATIONAL GUARD PATROL BOATS [WPB] *(continued)*

♦ 15 18-ft. chase-boat design
Bldr: SeaArk Workboats, Monticello, Ark. (In serv. 5-87)

SeaArk 18-ft. chase boat SeaArk, 1984

D: 0.5 tons (fl) **S:** 30 kts **Dim:** 5.48 × 2.08 × 0.15
A: 1 12.7-mm mg
M: 1 Evinrude gasoline outboard motor; 140 bhp **Crew:** 4 tot.

Remarks: Completed 11-1-85, but delivery delayed. Aluminum construction.

♦ 12 Punta class
Bldr: Robert E. Derecktor SY, Mamaroneck, N.Y.

A-8201 Punta Barima
A-8202 Punta Mosquito
A-8203 Punta Barima
A-8204 Punta Perret
A-8205 Punta Cardon
A-8206 Punta Playa
A-8207 Punta Macoya
A-8208 Punta Moron
A-8209 Punta Unare
A-8210 Punta Ballena
A-8211 Punta Macuro
A-8212 Punta Mariusa

Punta class—ramped stern version F. Nakajima/Derecktor SY, 1984

D: Approx. 50 tons (fl) **S:** 35 kts **Dim:** 23.44 × 4.88 × 1.70
A: 1/12.7-mm mg **Electronics:** Radar: 1/Furuno . . . nav.
M: 2 MTU 12V183 TE93 diesels; 2 props; 2,268 bhp
Electric: 60 kw tot. **Range:** 1,100/24 **Fuel:** 16,000 liters
Crew: 11 tot. + 40 troops

Remarks: First six ordered 1980, delivered 8-82; second six ordered 1982 for delivery by 10-84, but financing problems delayed arrival until 5-87. A-8201–8203 and A-8207–8209 have a vehicle ramp aft; the others have a small helicopter platform capable of accepting a Bell 206A JetRanger. Aluminum construction. Modernization and re-engining of this class was accomplished at the National Guard Naval Maintenance Center, Guanta, from 1996–98 after most had become nonoperational: armament was reduced to one 12.7-mm machinegun forward; the original General Motors diesels were replaced with a more powerful plant adding about 7 kts to the maximum speed; and a GPS receiver was added. A-8210 was the first to complete, in 8-96.

♦ 20 Italian A-type (Río Orinoco class)
Bldrs: *units: INMA, La Spezia, Italy; others: Diques y Astilleros Nacionales, C.A.(DIANCA), Puerto Cabello (In serv. 1974–76)

A-7414 Río Orinoco*
A-7415 Río Cuyuni
A-7416 Río Ventuari*
A-7417 Río Caparo*
A-7418 Río Tucuyo*
A-7419 Río Venamo*
A-7420 Río Limon*
A-7421 Río San Juan*
A-7422 Río Turbio*
A-7423 Río Torbes*
A-7424 Río Escalante*
A-7425 Río Canaparo
A-7426 Río Yurary
A-7427 Río Caura
A-7628 Río Motatan
A-7629 Río Grita
A-7630 Río Yuruan
A-7631 Río Bocono
A-7632 Río Neveri
A-7633 Río Goigoaza

D: 43 (*48) tons (fl) **S:** 35 kts **Dim:** 23.8 × 4.8 × 1.5
A: 1 12.7-mm mg **Electronics:** Radar: 1 Furuno FR 711 or FR 24 nav.
M: 2 MTU 12V183 TE93 diesels; 2 props; 2,268 bhp
Range: 500–1,000 / . . . **Crew:** 8 to 12 tot.

Remarks: Steel construction. Six sisters have been discarded, and the survivors were in poor condition until a refit program was completed in 1996 at the National Guard Naval Maintenance Center, Guanta. All have been re-engined, increasing their original speed by about 5 kts.
Disposal: *Rio Guanare* (A-7634) had been retired from service by 2006.

♦ 5 French B-type
Bldr: . . . (In serv. 1979)

B-7918 Río Caballes
B-7919 Río Chama
B-7920 Río Caribe
B-7921 Río Tuy
B-7929 Yate Mkanati

D: 45 tons (fl) **S:** 30 kts **Dim:** 21.7 × 4.9 × 1.5
A: 1 12.7-mm mg **Electronics:** Radar: 1 . . . nav.
M: 2 . . . diesels; 2 props; 3,000 bhp **Crew:** 12

Remarks: Twelve were originally delivered, five remain in service; were to be replaced by since-canceled Israeli-built patrol boats.

Notes: Also in use are several rigid inflatable boats, including V-50, V-52, and V-69; these are armed with one 7.62-mm machinegun and were reportedly built by Boston Whaler, entering service in 1997. Locally built, aluminum-hulled launch V-81 is also in use, as well as several imported and locally fabricated RIB launches.

ARMY OF VENEZUELA
(Ejército de Venezuela)

The Venezuelan army has a significant number of aluminum and GRP-hulled boats and rubber inflatable boats for use by engineers, special forces, and other combat units. A series of assault boats with 75-bhp outboard motors was ordered in 1999, and several assault boats were procured in 1996 that can carry 15 troops each. Amphibious vehicles in use by the Army include 101 U.S.-built Dragoon 300–series wheeled vehicles (42 LFV-2 configured as armored cars with one Cockerill Mk III gun, 25 ASV troop carriers, 21 AMV configured to carry an 81-mm mortar, 11 ACV command and communications variants, and two ALV recovery vehicles) and 10 Thyssen-Henschel six-wheeled Fuchs-I armored personnel carriers.

VENEZUELAN AIR FORCE
(Fuerza Aérea Venezolana)

The Venezuelan Air Force has several aluminum and GRP-construction launches and RIB launches based at Mariscal Sucre Air Base, Lago de Valencia, for local patrol, search-and-rescue, and utility duties. No data or total numbers available.

VIETNAM

Socialist Republic of Vietnam

Personnel: Approx. 15,000 total, plus about 27,000 naval infantry.

Bases: Headquarters at Hanoi, with units based at Cam Ranh Bay, Cân Tho, Da Nang, Hue, and Haiphong

Note: Most ship names are not known. The pennant number system works as follows: HQ plus two digits: major combatant; HQ 1XX: seagoing patrol boat; HQ 2XX: harbor patrol craft; HQ 3XX: Soviet- and Russian-supplied seagoing patrol craft classes; HQ 4XX: landing craft; HQ 5XX: amphibious landing ships; HQ 6XX: cargo ships; HQ 7XX: fisheries protection craft; HQ 8XX: mine-warfare units; and HQ 9XX: auxiliaries and service craft. Ships redesignated with BD- (Biên-Dong = East Sea) series pennants are assigned to the Spratly Islands service.

Naval Aviation: Three Soviet Beriev Be-12 Mail antisubmarine patrol amphibians and eight Kamov Ka-28PL Helix-A land-based ASW helicopters. Twelve PZL M-28 Skytruck maritime patrol aircraft (An-28 variants) were ordered from Poland during 2003 with deliveries beginning in 2004. Four PLZ W-3RM Anaconda SAR helcopters were ordered during 2005 with deliveries expected to begin during 2007.

COASTAL SUBMARINES [SSC]

♦ 2 North Korean Sang-o class
Bldr: Bong Dao Bo SY, Singpo (In serv. 1991– . . .)

D: 295 tons surf./325 tons sub. **S:** 7 kts surf./8 kts sub. **Dim:** 34.0 × 3.8 × 3.2
A: 4 bow 533-mm TT (no reloads); 16 mines in external racks
Electronics:
Radar: 1 Furuno . . . nav.
Sonar: probable passive hull array only
M: 1 diesel generator set (probable 300 bhp); 1 shrouded prop; 200 shp
Range: 2,700/8 snorkel **Crew:** 19 tot.

Remarks: Reportedly transferred around mid-1997 in poor condition; as of 12-98 were being refurbished at Cam Ranh Bay naval base. Are probably configured as cited here, rather than being the swimmer infiltration version captured by South Korea. Equipment is primitive, and the units are primarily useful for coast-defense purposes.

FRIGATES [FF]

Remarks: Negotiations were said to have begun with Russia's Northern Project Design Bureau in 1996 for the local construction of a 2,000-ton frigate design called the "KBO 2000." Design work was reported complete in 3-99, at which time the ship was said already to have been ordered. There have been no further reports on any progress on its construction, however, and most recent reports indicate that Vietnam may instead purchase two Indian *Samar*-class patrol ships.

CORVETTES [FFL]

♦ 3 ex-Soviet Petya-II (Project 159A) class

Bldr: Khabarovsk Zavod, Russia

	Laid down	L	In serv.
HQ-13 (ex-SKR-141)	14-4-70	7-8-71	30-9-71
HQ-15 (ex-SKR-130)	11-2-70	5-9-70	20-10-70
HQ-17 (ex-SKR-135)	4-4-72	12-8-72	31-3-73

HQ-17 NAVPIC-Holland, 8-95

HQ-13 Markus Berger, 11-97

D: 938 tons light (1,077 fl) **S:** 29 kts
Dim: 81.80 (78.00 pp) × 9.20 × 2.85 hull (5.85 over sonar)
A: 2 twin 76.2-mm 59-cal. AK-276 DP; 2 quintuple 402-mm ASW TT; 2 12-round RBU-6000 ASW RL; 2 d.c. racks; mines
Electronics:
Radar: 1 Don-2 nav.; 1 Fut-N (Strut Curve) air-search; 1 Fut-B (Hawk Screech) gun f.c.
Sonar: Titan hull-mounted MF search; Vychegda HF attack
EW: 2 Bizan'-4B (Watch Dog) intercept (2-18 gHz)
M: CODAG: 2 M-2 gas turbines (15,000 shp each); 1 Type 61-B3 diesel (6,000 bhp); 3 props (CP on centerline)—2 low-speed maneuvering props (3 kts)
Range: 4,800/10 (diesel); 450/29 (CODAG) **Fuel:** 130 tons **Endurance:** 10 days
Crew: 8 officers, 84 enlisted

Remarks: HQ-13 was transferred during 1983, HQ-15 on 10-5-84, and HQ-17 during 12-84.

♦ 2 ex-Soviet Petya-III (Project 159AE) class

Bldr: Khabarovsk Zavod, Russia

	Laid down	L	In serv.
HQ-09 (ex-SKR-82)	25-9-75	28-4-76	13-7-77
HQ-11 (ex-SKR-96)	27-6-75	25-4-76	29-6-78

HQ-11—rearmed with additional AA weapons in place of ASW ordnance NAVPIC-Holland, 8-95

HQ-09 NAVPIC-Holland, 8-95

D: 960 tons (1,040 fl) **S:** 29 kts
Dim: 81.80 (78.00 pp) × 9.20 × 2.72 hull (5.72 over sonar)
A: HQ 09: 2 twin 76.2-mm 59-cal. AK-276 DP; 1 triple 533-mm TT; 4 16-round RBU-2500 ASW RL; 2 d.c. racks; mines—HQ 11: 2 twin 76.2-mm 59-cal. AK-276 DP; 2 twin 37-mm 63-cal. AA; 2 twin 23-mm ZSU-23 AA; 4 16-round RBU-2500 ASW RL; 2 d.c. racks; mines
Electronics:
Radar: 1 Don-2 nav.; 1 Fut-N (Strut Curve) air-search; 1 Fut-B (Hawk Screech) f.c.
Sonar: Titan hull-mounted MF search; Vychegda HF attack
EW: 2/Bizan'-4B (Watch Dog) intercept (2-18 gHz)
M: CODAG: 2 M-2 gas turbines (15,000 shp each); 1 Type 61-B3 diesel (6,000 bhp); 3 props—2 low-speed maneuvering props (3 kts)
Range: 4,800/10 (diesel); 450/29 (CODAG) **Fuel:** 130 tons
Crew: 8 officers, 84 enlisted

Remarks: HQ-09 and HQ-11 are Petya III export models transferred 21-12-78. By 1995 HQ-11 had had the torpedo tube mount replaced with two 37-mm twin AA mounts and the pair of RBU-2500 ASW rocket launchers forward replaced with two twin 23-mm AA. The ASW rocket launching systems may no longer be functional.

PATROL SHIPS [PS]

♦ 1 ex-U.S. Barnegat-class former seaplane tender

Bldr: Lake Washington SY, Houghton, Washington

	Laid down	L	In serv.
HQ-01 PHAM NGU LAO (ex-*Tham Ngu Lao*, ex-U.S.C.G. *Absecon*, WHEC 374, ex-AVP 23)	23-7-41	8-3-42	28-1-43

D: 1,766 tons (2,800 fl) **S:** 18 kts **Dim:** 94.7 (91.4 wl) × 12.5 × 4.1
A: 1 127-mm 38-cal. Mk 30 DP; 3 single 37-mm 63-cal. AA; 2 twin 25-mm 60-cal. 2M-3M AA; 2 4-round Fasta-4M point-defense SAM syst.
Electronics: Radar: . . .
M: 4 Fairbanks-Morse 38D8$^{1}/_{8}$ × 10 diesels; 2 props; 6,080 bhp
Electric: 600 kw **Range:** 20,000/10 **Fuel:** 26 tons **Crew:** Approx. 200 tot.

Remarks: Transferred to South Vietnam in 1971, having served in the U.S. Coast Guard since 1948. Was equipped with two SS-N-2A Styx missiles on fantail that had been removed from a stricken *Komar*-class missile boat during the late 1970s, but these have probably long since been removed. The close-in defensive suite was augmented, but the 127-mm gun is unlikely to be functional. Has no weapons-control system. Current status uncertain, and the ship may have been discarded.

Disposal note: U.S. *Savage*-class patrol ship *Dai Ky* (HQ-03; ex-*Tran Khan Du;* ex-*Forster,* DER 334) and U.S. *Admirable*-class patrol ship HQ-07 (ex-*Ha Hoi;* ex-*Prowess,* IX 305, ex-MSF 280) had been reduced to hulk status by 1998 but remain afloat as training and accommodations craft.

GUIDED-MISSILE PATROL COMBATANTS [PGG]

♦ 1 (+ 1) BPS 500 class (Russian Project 12418)

Bldr: Ho Chi Minh SY, Ho Chi Minh City (In serv. 1999– . . .)

HQ-381

HQ 381 G. Kuvel via Paolo Marsan, 8-05

D: 517 tons (600 fl) **S:** 32 kts (15 cruise) **Dim:** 62.0 × 11.0 × 2.2 (hull)
A: 8 Kh-35 Uran (SS-N-25 Switchblade) SSM; 1 76.2-mm 59-cal. AK-176 DP; 1 30-mm AK-630 gatling CIWS; 2 single 12.7-mm mg
Electronics:
Radar: 1 . . . nav.; 1 MR-352 Pozitiv-E (Cross Dome) surf./air-search; 1 MR-123E Vympel-E (Bass Tilt) gun f.c.
EW: . . . intercept, 2 16-round PK-16 decoy RL
M: 2 MTU . . . . . . diesels; 2 KaMeWa waterjets; 19,600 bhp (14,400 sust.)
Range: 2,200/14 **Crew:** 28 tot.

GUIDED-MISSILE PATROL COMBATANTS [PGG] *(continued)*

HQ 381 Piet Sinke, 8-05

Remarks: Designed by Severnoye Bureau, St. Petersburg, Russia, which is said to be providing construction assistance. Virtually all components have had to be imported. Design is of about the same size as the *Tarantul* class, but the hull form is wedge-shaped. First unit was planned to be completed during 1997, but did not begin to run trials until 3-99.
Hull: The waterjets have thrust-reversers to permit harbor maneuvering.
Combat systems: Sixteen Kh-35 missiles for the two craft were reportedly delivered in 1999, with another 30–48 ordered later. May also be fitted with the Vikhr-K point-defense SAM system (with 24 missiles) and four ASW torpedo tubes. They may also have had a laser-rangefinder gun director.

♦ 4 Tarantul-I class (Project 1241RE)
Bldr: Volodarskiy SY, Rybinsk (In serv. 1994–2004)

HQ-371 HQ-372 HQ-374 HQ-375

D: 385 tons light (455 fl) **S:** 43 kts
Dim: 56.10 (49.50 pp) × 10.20 (9.40 wl) × 2.14 hull (3.59 props)
A: 4 P-20/21 Rubezh (SS-N-2C Styx) SSM; 1 76.2-mm 59-cal. AK-176 DP; 1 4-round MTU-40S SAM syst. (12 Strela missiles); 2 single 30-mm 65-cal. AK-630 gatling AA
Electronics:
Radar: 1 Kivach-3 nav.; 1 Garpun-E (Plank Shave) targeting; 1 MR-123 Vympel (Bass Tilt) f.c.
EW: 2 16-round PK-16 decoy RL
M: M-15E COGAG plant: 2 DMR-76 cruise gas turbines (4,000 shp each), 2 PR-77 boost gas turbines (12,000 shp each); 2 props; 32,000 shp
Electric: 500 kw tot. (2 × 200-kw, 1 × 100-kw diesel sets)
Range: 760/43; 1,400/13 **Fuel:** 122,634 liters **Endurance:** 10 days
Crew: 7 officers, 32 enlisted

Remarks: Standard export versions, first two delivered together in 10-94, second two in 2004. Negotiations for another pair, ongoing for several years, reportedly resulted in a contract signing during 1-99 for delivery in 2000, indicating that they came from among units completed some years ago but not previously sold, but the contract was not in the end signed, due to Vietnamese funding shortages. Shore-based training simulators for this class were ordered in Russia during 3-01.
Hull systems: Stainless-steel alloy, seven watertight compartment hull with aluminum-alloy superstructure, decks, and internal bulkheads. Very strongly constructed and rugged. Have difficulty maneuvering less than 10 kts due to small size of rudders.
Combat systems: Carry 252 ready-service rounds and another 150 in reserve for the 76.2-mm gun. Weapons system employs digital computers and has many backup features. Normally carry two infrared-homing and two radar-homing antiship missiles. The Garpun-E radar also serves as a passive intercept and targeting system.

GUIDED-MISSILE PATROL CRAFT [PTG]

♦ Up to 8 Soviet Osa-II (Project 205ME) class

HQ-359 HQ-360 HQ-384 HQ-385 HQ- 386 up to 3 others

D: 184 tons (226 normal fl, 245 overload) **S:** 40 (35 sust.) kts
Dim: 38.6 (37.5 wl) × 7.6 (6.3 wl) × 2.0 hull (3.1 props)
A: 4 P-15M/P-20 Rubezh (SS-N-2B/C Styx) SSM; 2 twin 30-mm 65-cal. AK-230 AA
Electronics: Radar: 1 Rangout (Square Tie) surf. search/target-detection; 1 MR-104 Rys' (Drum Tilt) gun f.c.
M: 3 M504 or M-504B diesels; 3 props; 15,000 bhp **Electric:** 400 kw tot.
Range: 500/34; 750/25 **Endurance:** 5 days **Crew:** 4 officers, 24 enlisted

Remarks: Transferred: two in 10-79, two in 9-80, two in 11-80, and two in 2-81. Are probably in only marginal operating condition. The Rangout radar can be used in the passive mode to detect targets.

HYDROFOIL TORPEDO BOATS [PTH]

♦ 3 Turya (Shtorm) class (Project 206M) semi-hydrofoils
Bldrs: Vladivostokskiy Sudostroitel'niy Zavod (Ulis), Vladivostok (In serv. 1984)

HQ-331 HQ-332 HQ-333

D: 215 tons (220 tons normal, 250 fl) **S:** 48 kts (37 sustained)
Dim: 39.6 (37.5 wl) × 7.6 (9.6 over foils; 6.3 wl) × 2.0 (4.0 over foils)
A: 1 twin 57-mm 70-cal. AK-725 AA; 1 twin 25-mm 80-cal. 2M-3M AA; 4 fixed 533-mm OTA-53-206M TT (2 Type 53-56B or 53-56BA and 2 Type 53-65K torpedoes)
Electronics:
Radar: 1 Baklan (Pot Drum) surf. search; 1 MR-103 Bars (Muff Cob) gun f.c.
Sonar: 1 Rat Tail Hormone helicopter-type, dipping
EW: 2 16-round PK-16 decoy RL
M: 3 M504 diesels; 3 props; 15,000 bhp **Range:** 600/37; 1,450/14
Crew: 5 officers, 21 enlisted

Remarks: Two delivered mid-1984; one late in 1984; and two, without torpedo tubes (Project 206ME), in 1-86 (see under [PCH]).
Hull systems: Fixed hydrofoils forward only; stern planes on water surface. Have Osa-II-class hull and propulsion. Intended to be able to maintain 40 kts in Sea State 4 and 35 kts in Sea State 5; the 48-kt calm-water maximum speed listed is probably no longer attainable.
Combat systems: The dipping sonar is housed in a sponson over the starboard quarter. The torpedo tubes can launch both antiship and antisubmarine torpedoes.

TORPEDO BOATS [PT]

♦ 4 Soviet Shershen class (Project 206)

HQ-301 HQ-354 HQ-359 HQ-360

Shershen-class torpedo boat—under refit at Haiphong
G. Kuvel, via Paolo Marsan, 8-00

D: 129 tons light (161 fl) **S:** 41.9 kts
Dim: 34.60 (33.60 wl) × 6.74 (5.60 wl) × 1.72
A: 2 twin 30-mm 65-cal. AK-230 AA; 4 fixed 533-mm TT; mines
Electronics: Radar: 1 Baklan (Pot Drum) surf.-search; 1 MR-104 Rys' (Drum Tilt) gun f.c.
M: 3 M503A diesels; 3 props; 12,000 bhp **Electric:** 84 kw tot. (3 × 28 kw)
Range: 460/42; 600/30; 2,000/14 **Fuel:** 30 tons **Crew:** 2 officers, 20 enlisted

Remarks: Sixteen total were transferred: two in 1973, two (without torpedo tubes) on 16-4-79, two on 12-9-79, two in 8-80, two in 10-80, two in 1981, and four in 6-83. At least 12 have been retired, and one of the units listed has had the torpedo tubes removed and is assigned to the national police force.

HYDROFOIL PATROL CRAFT [PCH]

♦ 2 Turya (Shtorm)-class (Project 206ME) semi-hydrofoils
Bldrs: Vladivostokskiy Sudostroitel'niy Zavod (Ulis), Vladivostok (In serv. 1-86)

HQ-334 HQ-335

D: 215 tons (220 tons normal, 250 fl) **S:** 48 kts (37 sustained)
Dim: 39.6 (37.5 wl) × 7.6 (9.6 over foils; 6.3 wl) × 2.0 (4.0 over foils)
A: 1 twin 57-mm 70-cal. AK-725 AA; 1 twin 25-mm 80-cal. 2M-3M AA
Electronics:
Radar: 1 Baklan (Pot Drum) surf. search; 1 MR-103 Bars (Muff Cob) gun f.c.
EW: 2 16-round PK-16 decoy RL
M: 3 M504 diesels; 3 props; 15,000 bhp **Range:** 600/37; 1,450/14
Endurance: 5 days **Crew:** 5 officers, 21 enlisted

Remarks: Delivered 1-86. May have originally been intended for another customer. Differ from standard torpedo-boat version in lacking torpedo tubes and dipping sonar. Three others, equipped with torpedo tubes, are listed previously under [PTH].
Hull systems: Fixed hydrofoils forward only; stern planes on water surface. Have Osa-II-class hull and propulsion. Intended to be able to maintain 40 kts in Sea State 4 and 35 kts in Sea State 5; the 48-kt calm-water maximum speed listed is probably no longer attainable.

PATROL CRAFT [PC]

♦ 2 Russian Svetlyak class (Project 1041.2) Bldrs: Sudostroitel'noye Obyedineniye "Almaz," Petrovskiy SY, St. Petersburg

	Laid down	L	In serv.
HQ 261 (ex-040)	2001	18-8-02	17-10-02
HQ 262 (ex-041)	2001	18-8-02	17-10-02

D: 328 tons light (365 normal fl, 382 max.) **S:** 32 kts (30 sust.)
Dim: 49.50 (45.00 wl) × 9.20 × 2.14 (hull; 2.50 props)
A: 1 76.2-mm 59-cal. AK-176M DP; 1 30-mm 54-cal. AK-630M gatling AA; 16 SA-14/16 Igla-series shoulder-launched SAMs (see Remarks); 1 or 2 AGS-17 grenade launchers; 1 DP-64 anti-swimmer grenade launcher
Electronics:
Radar: 1 Furuno FR-2150W nav./surf. search, 1 MR-123 Vympel-AM (Bass Tilt) f.c.
EW: Slyabing intercept; MFD/F, 2 16-round PK-16 decoy RL
M: 3 M-520B diesels; 3 props; 15,000 bhp
Electric: 400 kw tot. (1 × 200-kw, 2 × 100-kw diesel sets; 380 V, 50 Hz a.c.)

PATROL CRAFT [PC] *(continued)*

Svetlyak-class (Project 1041.2)—at launch ALMAZ Shipbuilding, 7-02

HQ 262—with old pennant number
Almaz shipbuilding via Mritunjoy Mazumdar & Olga Ignatavitchous, 9-02

Range: 1,600/30; 2,200/13 **Endurance:** 10 days
Crew: 4 officers, 4 warrant officers, 20 enlisted (41 tot. accomm.)

Remarks: The final contract was signed 11-01. Project 1041.2 version does not have ASW equipment. Both left St. Petersburg on a Dutch heavy-lift ship 14-12-02 arriving 1-03. Are planned to serve until at least 2022.
Hull systems: Semi-planing, round-bilge hull with low spray chine forward. Propellers do not project below keel. Steel hull with magnesium/aluminum-alloy superstructure. Can survive with two compartments flooded. Have NBC warfare protection. Engine room coated with vibration-damping material. The pilothouse is equipped with a centerline periscope.
Combat systems: There is an SP-521 Rakurs (Kolonka-2) ringsight backup director for the 30-mm gun, and the 76.2-mm mount can be operated in local control and has an integral electro-optical sighting system. Carry 152 rounds 76-mm (all on-mount) and up to 3,000 rounds 30-mm. The Horizon integrated navigational equipment includes NAVSAT receiver, radio navaid receiver, automatic plot, and echo sounder. An IFF transponder is fitted, but not interrogation equipment. Sources are inconclusive on whether Igla SAMs are carried.

PATROL BOATS [PB]

♦ 4 (+ . . .) Stolkraft 22.4-m design

Bldr: First four: Brisbane Ship Construction, Australia; others: Pacific Asia Industries, Vung Tao, Vietnam (In serv. 3-98 to . . .)

HQ-56 HQ-57 HQ-58 HQ-59

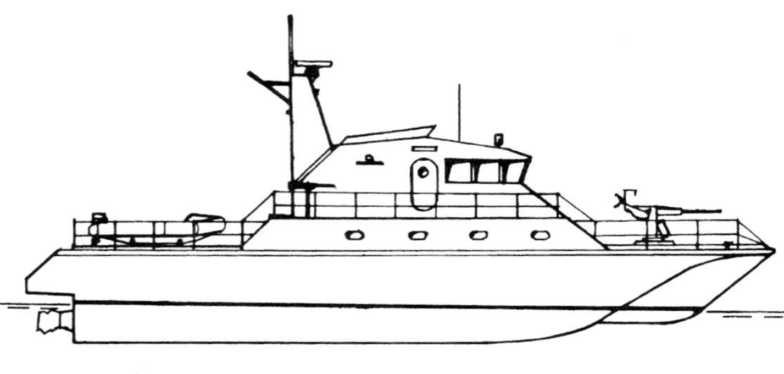

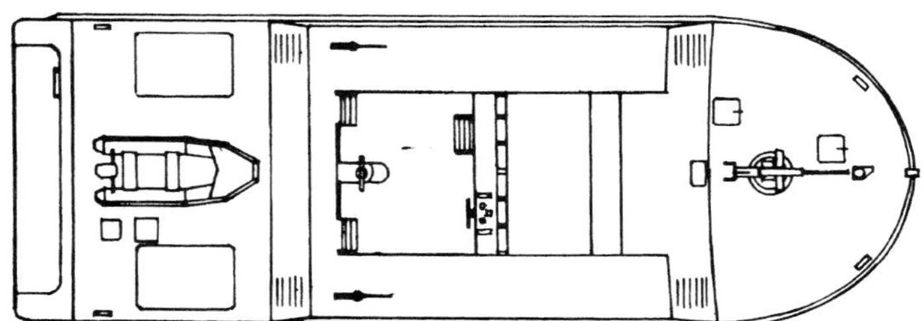

Stolcraft 22.4-m design A. D. Baker III

D: 36 tons (43.3 fl) **S:** 30 kts **Dim:** 22.40 × 7.50 × 1.20
A: 1 20-mm 90-cal Oerlikon AA **Electronics:** Radar: 1 . . . nav.
M: 2 Iveco-FIAT 8061-SRM-25 diesels; 2 Vosper Thornycroft PP waterjets; 1,000 bhp
Range: . . . / . . . **Fuel:** 8,000 liters **Endurance:** 5 days
Crew: 7 total

Remarks: Ordered early 1996 in cooperation between John Lund Marine and Oceanfast of Australia and Pacific Asia Industries of Vietnam for high-speed patrol, interception, rescue, and coordination duties for the Customs Service, though the hull numbers suggest that they have been incorporated into the navy instead. First four were to be completed 3-97 by Oceanfast Marine Group, Henderson, Western Australia, but the craft were instead built by Brisbane Ship Construction; further units were to be built in Vietnam. Use aluminum-construction trimaran hull that employs the Leo Stolk trapped air bubble concept to achieve very high speeds (90 kts in the more powerfully engined Australian prototype) and a stable ride in heavy seas. Can be beached. Were originally to have been equipped with much more powerful diesels.

♦ 4 HQ-37 class

Bldr: VINASHIN, Vietnam (In serv. 1998– . . .)

HQ-37 HQ-55 BP-29-01-01 . . .

HQ-55—a Shershen-class torpedo boat in refit is visible at the left
G. Kuvel, via Paolo Marsan, 8-00

BP-29-01-01—with machineguns fore and aft French Navy, 11-98

D: 38 tons light **S:** 30 kts **Dim:** 29.0 × . . . × . . .
A: 2 twin 14.5-mm 93-cal. mg
Electronics: 1 Lotsiya nav. **M:** 2 Saab Scania DI 14 diesels; 2 props; 2,500 bhp
Range: . . . / . . . **Crew:** 11–14 tot.

Remarks: Design patterned after the Zhuk class that follows, but with simplified hull form and superstructure shape. BP-29-01-01 appears to be assigned to the national police force rather than to the navy.

♦ 11 Soviet Zhuk class (Project 1400M)

T-864 T-874 T-880 T-881 7 others

Zhuk-class T-880 and two sisters French Navy, 11-98

D: 35.9 tons (39.7 fl) **S:** 30 kts
Dim: 23.80 (21.70 wl) × 5.00 (3.80 wl) × 1.00 (hull; 1.90 max.)
A: 2 twin 12.7-mm 60-cal. Utës-Ma mg **Electronics:** Radar: 1 Lotsiya nav.
M: 2 M-401 diesels; 2 props; 2,200 bhp
Electric: 48 kw total (2 × 21-kw, 1 × 6-kw diesel sets
Endurance: 5 days **Range:** 500/13.5 **Crew:** 1 officer, 9 enlisted

Remarks: Transferred: three in 1978, three in 11-80, one in 11-81, one in 5-85, three in 1986, two in 12-89, and two in 1990. Two more were delivered around 1996 from Ukraine. Six have been stricken, and the older survivors are probably in poor condition.
Hull systems: Aluminum-alloy hull. Capable of operating in up to Sea State 4 or 5. Range also reported as 700 n. m. at 28 kts, 1,100 n.m. at 15 kts. The earlier units were Project 1400A, with M50F-4 diesels.
Combat systems: Some carry only one twin machinegun mounting, forward.
Notes: Also in service are the Customs Patrol boat Do Dac Hien 01, River Police patrol boat CA-75-51-09, and unknown patrol boats BP.33.12.01 and BP 33.10.01 which may be assigned to the National Police Force. A few ex-U.S. PBR (Patrol Boat, Riverine) Mk-II-class patrol boats may survive in service from the 290+ captured in 1975.

PATROL BOATS [PB] *(continued)*

Customs Patrol boat Do Dac Hien 01 G. Kuvel, via Paolo Marsan, 8-00

River Police (Canh Sat) patrol boat CA-75-51-09—at Hue G. Kuvel, via Paolo Marsan, 8-00

BP 33.12.01 Jasper van Raemdonck, 11-03

BP 33.10.01 Jasper van Raemdonck, 2003

MINE WARFARE SHIPS AND CRAFT

♦ 2 ex-Soviet Yurka-class (Project 266) fleet minesweepers [MSF]

Bldr: Vladivostokskiy Sudostroitel'niy Zavod (Ulis SY),Vladivostok (In serv. 1961–70)

HQ-851 HQ-885

D: 520 tons normal (560 fl, 619 max.) **S:** 16 kts
Dim: 52.10 (46.00 pp) × 9.60 (9.40 wl) × 2.65 (hull)
A: 2 twin 30-mm 65-cal. AK-230 AA; 2 minerails (10 mines)
Electronics:
Radar: 1 or 2 Don-2 nav.; 1 MR-104 Rys' (Drum Tilt) gun f.c.
Sonar: MG-69 Lan' hull-mounted HF
M: 2 M-503B-3E diesels; 2 CP props; 5,000 bhp
Electric: 500 kw tot. (2 × 200-kw, 1 × 100-kw diesel sets)
Range: 600/16; 1,500/12 **Endurance:** 7 days **Crew:** 5 officers, 41 enlisted

Remarks: Both transferred 12-79 from Soviet Pacific Fleet. Probably have little remaining service life.
Hull systems: Low magnetic signature, aluminum-steel alloy hull, with low magnetic signature machinery. Automatic-controlled degaussing equipment, with local coils around massive equipment. Special measures to reduce acoustic signature. Maximum sweep speed with arrays deployed is 14 kts.
Combat systems: The sonar transducer is mounted in a large dome that can be hoisted within the hull. Intended to sweep mines in 25–150-m depths. A towed television minehunting device is sometimes carried.

♦ 4 Sonya-class (Project 1265E) coastal minesweepers [MSC]

Bldr: Vladivostokskiy Sudostroitel'niy Zavod (Ulis SY),Vladivostok

HQ-861 HQ-862 HQ-863 HQ-864

D: 401 tons (430 fl) **S:** 14 kts **Dim:** 48.80 (46.00 wl) × 10.20 (9.20 wl) × 2.75
A: 1 twin 30-mm 65-cal. AK-230 AA; 1 twin 25-mm 80-cal. 2M-3M AA; 5 mines
Electronics:
Radar: 1 Mius (Spin Trough) nav.
Sonar: MG-89 Serna HF hull-mounted
M: 2 DRA-210-A diesels; 2 3-bladed CP props; 2,000 bhp—2 low-speed thrusters
Electric: 350 kw tot. (3 × 100-kw, 1 × 50-kw diesel sets; 380 V 50 Hz a.c.)
Range: 1,500/10 **Fuel:** 27.1 tons **Endurance:** 10 days
Crew: 5–6 officers, 26 enlisted (45 accomm.)

Remarks: First delivered 16-2-87, second in 2-88, third in 7-89, and fourth in 3-90; all were probably new-construction.
Hull systems: Wooden construction with glass-reinforced plastic hull sheathing. The sweep winch can tow 10 tons at 9 kts.
Combat systems: Carry GKT-2 contact sweep; ST-2, AT-2, and PEMT-2 influence sweeps; and an IT-3 mine detector/exploder. The sonar dome pivots at the after end to retract within the hull.

♦ 2 Soviet Yevgenya-class (Project 1258) inshore minesweepers [MSI]

Bldr: Sudostroitel'noye Obyedineniye "Almaz" (Sredniy Neva), Kolpino

D: 88.5 tons light, 94.5 normal (97.9 fl) **S:** 11 kts
Dim: 26.13 (24.20 wl) × 5.90 (5.10 wl) × 1.38
A: 1 twin 14.5-mm 93-cal. 2M-7 AA; 1 7-round MRG-1 grenade launcher; 4 depth charges (+ 8 emergency stowage)
Electronics:
Radar: 1 Mius (Spin Trough) nav.
Sonar: MG-7 HF dipping
M: 2 Type 3D12 diesels; 2 props; 600 bhp—hydraulic slow-speed drive
Electric: 100 kw tot. (2 × 50-kw diesel sets)
Range: 400/10 **Fuel:** 2.7 tons **Endurance:** 3 days
Crew: 1 officer, 9 enlisted (+ 2–3 mine clearance divers)

Remarks: Delivered to Cam Ranh Bay 11-84. At least one other, delivered in 10-79, has been stricken.
Hull systems: Glass-reinforced plastic hull. Navigational equipment includes Girya-MA gyrocompass and NEL-7 echo-sounder.
Combat systems: Can employ a Neva-1 t.v. minehunting system useful to 30-m depths that dispenses marker buoys to permit later disposal of mines by divers or explosive charges. The sonar is lowered via one of the stern davits. Carry VKT-1 mechanical, AT-2 acoustic, and SEMT-1 solenoid coil sweep gear.

AMPHIBIOUS WARFARE SHIPS

♦ 3 ex-U.S. LST 1- and LST 542-class tank landing ships [LST]

Bldrs: HQ 501: Bethlehem SY, Hingham, Mass.; HQ 502: Jeffersonville Boiler and Mach., Indiana; HQ 503: Chicago Bridge & Iron, Seneca, Ill.

	Laid down	L	In serv.
HQ-501 Tran Khanh Du (ex-*Da Nang*, ex-*Maricopa County*, LST 938)	12-7-44	15-8-44	9-9-44
HQ-502 Qui Nhon (ex-*Bullock County*, LST 509)	7-10-43	23-11-43	8-1-44
HQ-503 Vung Tau (ex-*Coconino County*, LST 603)	10-12-43	15-4-44	15-5-44

Tran Khanh Du (HQ-501) NAVPIC-Holland, 9-95

D: 1,623 tons light (4,080 fl) **S:** 11.6 kts **Dim:** 99.98 × 15.24 × 4.29
A: HQ-501: 2 twin 40-mm 60-cal. Bofors Mk 1 Mod. 2AA; 4 single 40-mm 60-cal. Bofors Mk 3 AA; 4 single 20-mm 70-cal. Oerlikon Mk 10 AA; others: 2 twin 37-mm 63-cal. Type 74 AA
Electronics: Radar: 1 . . .nav.
M: 2 G.M. 12-567A diesels; 2 props; 1,700 bhp
Electric: 300 kw **Range:** 6,000/9 (loaded) **Fuel:** 590 tons
Crew: Approx. 100 tot.

AMPHIBIOUS WARFARE SHIPS *(continued)*

Remarks: Transferred to South Vietnam 12-7-62, 8-4-70, and 4-4-69, respectively. All believed to be operational, although in marginal condition; have been rearmed in part with Soviet-supplied weapons.

♦ 3 ex-Soviet Polnocny-B-class (Project 771) medium landing ships [LSM]
Bldr: Stocznia Polnocna, Gdansk, Poland (In serv. 1968–70)

HQ-511 HQ-512 HQ-513

Polnocny-B-class HQ-511—outboard HQ-513 *Ships of the World,* 1996

D: 558 tons light, 640 tons std. (884 fl) **S:** 18 kts
Dim: 75.00 (70.00 wl) × 9.00 (8.60 wl) × 1.20 fwd/2.40 aft (2.07 mean)
A: 2 twin 30-mm 65-cal. AK-230 AA; 2 18-round 140-mm WM-18 barrage RL (180 rockets)
Electronics: Radar: 1 Mius (Spin Trough); 1 MR-104 Rys' (Drum Tilt) f.c.
M: 2 Type 40DM diesels; 2 props; 4,400 bhp **Range:** 700/18; 2,000/16
Crew: 5 officers, 32 enlisted + 60 to 180 troops

Remarks: Transferred: one in 5-79, one in 11-79, and one in 2-80. Were approaching derelict condition when sighted during 1995–96 but had been refitted by 2000 and remain in commission.
Hull systems: Have a bow door only. Hull has a pronounced "beak" at bow to aid in beaching. Hatches to upper deck are for loading and ventilation only. Cargo: 237 tons max., including six tanks or 180 troops and their equipment; 30 vehicle crew are carried with tank loadout. Vehicle deck is 44.3 m long by 5.3 m wide and 3.6 m high.

Note: Fourteen ex-U.S. LCU 1466–class utility landing craft, 84 U.S. LCM(6), 38 LCM(8), 40 LCVP, and several LCP-type landing craft were abandoned to North Vietnam in 1975; some were probably returned to service and a few may still be operational.

♦ Up to 12 ex-Soviet T4-class (Project 1785) landing craft [LCM]

D: 35 tons light (93 fl) **S:** 10 kts (light) **Dim:** 20.4 × 5.4 × 1.2 max. aft
M: 2 Type 3D-6 diesels; 2 props; 300 bhp
Range: 300/8 **Endurance:** 2 days **Crew:** 2–3 tot.

Remarks: Transferred 1979 and later. Can accommodate up to 50 tons cargo on the 9.5 × 3.9–m vehicle deck.

AUXILIARIES

♦ 1 ex-Russian Dobrynya Nikitich–class icebreaker [AGB]
Bldr: Admiralty SY, St. Petersburg (In serv. 1965)

. . . (ex-*Semen Chelyushkin*)

D: 2,675–2,940 tons (fl) **S:** 14.5 kts (12.0 service)
Dim: 67.70 (62.01 pp) × 18.29 × 6.06
Electronics: Radar: 1 or 2 Don-2 nav.
M: 3 Type 13D100 diesel generator sets; 3/3-bladed props (1 fwd); 5,400 shp
Range: 5,500/12 **Fuel:** 600 tons **Crew:** 39 tot.

Remarks: 2,305 grt/1,092 dwt. Sighted in Vietnamese colors at Da Nang in 6-96 and probably used primarily as a seagoing tug and/or salvage vessel as ice in Vietnam is not generally considered a problem. Former name is tentative; *Semen Chelyushkin,* a Far Eastern unit, is the only unit of the class in that area known to have been stricken.

Note: A former Russian Navy Kamenka-class (Project 870) navigational aids tender, a former Russian Neptun-class mooring buoy tender (Project 706), and the former U.S. Army FS-381-class navigational aids tender *Cuu Long* (ex-*Hoa Giang,* HQ 451, ex-*Ingénieur en Chef Girod,* ex-U.S. Army FS 287), all listed in the previous edition, are now believed to be under civilian subordination.

♦ 1 offshore supply vessel [AK]
Bldr: Halong SY, Vietnam (In serv. 1994)

HQ-966 Truong Sa-01

Truong SA-01 (HQ-966) NAVPIC-Holland, 10-95

D: 1,200 tons **S:** . . . kts **Dim:** 70.6 × 11.8 × . . .
A: 2 twin 25-mm 80-cal. 2M-3M AA **M:** . . . diesels; 1 prop; . . . bhp

Remarks: 1,000 dwt. Intended to support garrisons in the disputed Spratly Islands. Name "Truong Sa" is the Vietnamese name for the Spratly Islands.

♦ 3 offshore supply vessels [AK]
Bldr: . . . (In serv. 1990s)

BD-621 BD-622 BD-632

BD-632 NAVPIC-Holland, 4-99

D: Approx. 1,200 tons (fl) **S:** . . . kts **Dim:** . . . × . . . × . . .
A: 2 single 12.7-mm 79-cal. Mg **M:** 1 . . . diesel; 1 prop; . . . bhp

Remarks: Identical sisters intended for Spratly Islands support missions. Have two cargo holds and a single 1.5-ton capacity crane. First two originally bore pennants HQ-608 and HQ-624; BD stands for *Biển Dong.*

Note: Also in service is the unknown tanker HQ 68.

Navy tanker HQ 68—with unknown small craft alongside
G. Kuvel via Paolo Marsan, 8-05

Note: Various fishing boats have been adapted for offshore supply missions as well.

Note: Russian Iva-class salvage and firefighting tug *Vikhr-2* was transferred to Vietnam in 5-92 and operates as the civilian *Ben Dinh 01.*

♦ 1 ex-Soviet Sorum-class (Project 745.0) oceangoing tug [ATA]
Bldr: Yaroslavl SY, U.S.S.R. (In serv. 1973)

BD-105 (ex- . . .)

BD-105 NAVPIC-Holland, 8-95

D: 1,210 tons (1,656 fl) **S:** 13.8 kts **Dim:** 55.50 × 12.60 × 4.60
Electronics: Radar: 2 Don-2 nav.
M: 2 Type 2D42 (6ChN 30/38) diesels, electric drive; 1 prop; 3,000 shp
Range: 6,200/11 **Fuel:** 322 tons **Endurance:** 40 days
Crew: 35 tot. (civilian + 40 passengers/rescuees)

Remarks: Transferred from Russia by 1995. Operates in support of Spratly Island activities.

♦ 1 Voda (MVT-6)-class (Project 561) water tanker [AWT]
Bldr: Yantar Zavod, Kaliningrad (In serv. 1950s)

BO-82 (Ex-MVT-135?)

AUXILIARIES *(continued)*

BO-82 Kramer, 5-96

D: 982 tons light (2,115 fl) **S:** 12 kts **Dim:** 81.50 × 11.50 × 3.25
Electronics: Radar: 1 Don-2 or Mius (Spin Trough) nav.
M: 2 Type 8DR30/50 diesels; 2 props; 1,600 bhp **Range:** 2,000/9
Endurance: 15 days **Crew:** 38 tot.

Remarks: 1,000 grt. May be the former Russian Pacific Fleet unit MVT-135, which was retired on 31-7-96, but BO-82 was in Vietnam by 5-96. Seventeen were completed, of which several, including the BO-82, were equipped with working decks to permit their use as underway water replenishment ships for deployed steam-powered warships.
Hull systems: Cargo: 700 tons water. Has one 3-ton derrick for hose handling.

SERVICE CRAFT

♦ 2 Nyryat'-2-class (Project 376U) diving tenders [YDT]
Bldr: Yaroslavl Zavod (In serv. 1950s)

D: 50 tons (fl) **S:** 9 kts **Dim:** 21.0 × 3.9 × 1.5
M: 1 Type 3D-6 diesel; 1 prop; 150 bhp
Range: 1,600/8 **Endurance:** 5 days **Crew:** 10 tot.

Remarks: Built during the 1950s. Transferred post-1975. Essentially similar to the PO-2-class patrol craft, except that the hull has bulwarks and there is a small derrick to handle the divers.

♦ Up to 2 ex-U.S. floating dry docks [YFDL] (In serv. 1944)

ex-HQ-9600 (ex-AFDL 13) ex-HQ-9604 (ex-AFDL 22)

Remarks: Ex-HQ 9600 has a capacity of 1,000 tons and is 61.0 × 19.5 m. Ex-HQ 9604 has a capacity of 1,900 tons and is 87.8 × 19.5 m. Both were left behind in 1975.

Note: Also available are two Russian floating dry docks transferred during the 1980s for commercial employment, one with a capacity of 4,500 tons and the other 8,500.

♦ 2 Soviet PO-2-class (Project 376) launches [YFL]
Bldr: Yaroslavl Zavod (In serv. 1950s)

D: 47 tons (fl) **S:** 9 kts **Dim:** 21.0 × 3.9 × 1.4
A: When used as patrol craft: 2 single 12.7-mm 79-cal. mg
Electronics: Radar: 1 Mius (Spin Trough) nav. or none
M: 1 Type 3D-6 diesel; 1 prop; 150 bhp
Range: 1,600/8 **Endurance:** 5 days **Crew:** 6 tot.

Remarks: Transferred 2-80. Utility craft also usable as tugs or, with appropriate equipment, as diving tenders. Two near-sister Nyryat'-2-class diving tenders were also transferred.

♦ 2 ex-U.S. 174-ft.-class gasoline tankers [YO]
Bldr: George Lawley & Sons, Neponset, Mass. (ex-YOG 56: R.T.C. SB, Camden, N.J.)

	Laid down	L	In serv.
ex-HQ-472 (ex-YOG 67)	26-1-45	17-3-45	4-5-45
ex-HQ-475 (ex-YOG 56)	17-5-44	30-9-44	19-2-45

D: 440 tons light (1,390 fl) **S:** 11 kts **Dim:** 53.04 (51.2 pp) × 9.75 × 3.94
A: 2 single 20-mm 70-cal. Oerlikon Mk 10 AA
M: 1 G.M. diesel (ex-YOG 56: Union diesel); 1 prop; 640 bhp (ex-YOG 56: 540 bhp)
Electric: 80 kw **Fuel:** 25 tons **Cargo:** 860 tons **Crew:** 23 tot.

Remarks: Transferred to South Vietnam in 7-67 and 6-72, respectively. Employed in transporting diesel fuel. Remain in service as coastal tankers. Sister ex-HQ 473 (ex-YOG 71) is believed to have been cannibalized to maintain the other two.

♦ 2 ex-Soviet Poluchat-I-class (Project 368) torpedo retrievers [YPT]

D: 84.7 tons (92.8 fl) **S:** 21.6 kts
Dim: 29.60 × 6.10 (5.80 wl) × 1.56 (1.90 props)
A: 2 twin 14.5-mm 93-cal. 2M-7 AA
Electronics: Radar: 1 Mius (Spin Trough) nav.
M: 2 M-50F-4 diesels; 2 props; 2,400 bhp **Electric:** 14 kw tot.
Range: 250/21.6; 550/14 **Crew:** 3 officers, 12 enlisted

Remarks: Transferred 1-90. Can also be employed as patrol boats. Have ramp at stern and crane for recovering exercise torpedoes.

♦ Up to 2 ex-U.S. Cholocco-class medium harbor tugs [YTM]
Bldr: Commercial Iron Wks., Portland, Ore.

	In serv.
ex-HQ-9550 (ex-*Poknoket,* YTM 762; ex-YTB 517)	25-1-46
ex-HQ-9551 (ex-*Hombro,* YTM 769; ex-YTB 508)	7-7-45

Cholocco-class medium harbor tug NAVPIC-Holland, 9-95

D: 260 tons (350 fl) **S:** 11 kts **Dim:** 30.8 × 8.5 × 3.7
A: 2 single 12.7-mm mg **Electronics:** Radar: 2 . . . nav.
M: 2 Enterprise diesels; 1 prop; 1,270 bhp **Crew:** 8 tot.

Remarks: Reclassified YTM from YTB in 1966; transferred to South Vietnam 1971. Sister HQ 9552 (ex-*Nootka,* YTM 771; ex-YTB 506) was lost in 1973 in collision with a barge. One serves at Danang.

♦ Up to 9 ex-U.S. YTL-type small harbor tugs [YTL]

ex-YTL 152	ex-YTL 245	ex-YTL 456
ex-YTL 200	ex-YTL 423	ex-YTL 457
ex-YTL 206	ex-YTL 452	ex-YTL 586

D: 70 tons (80 fl) **S:** 10 kts **Dim:** 20.16 × 5.18 × 2.44
M: 1 Hoover-Owens-Rentschler diesel; 1 prop; 300 bhp
Electric: 40 kw **Fuel:** 7 tons **Crew:** 4 tot.

Remarks: Built 1941–45. Four transferred to South Vietnam in 1955–56, two in 1969, and two in 1971. Quite possibly, any survivors have been turned over to civilian agencies; craft of this description are reported to be operating with CENAC-series alphanumeric pennants.

Note: Former U.S. Navy non-self-propelled harbor craft transferred to South Vietnam that may survive include large covered barges YFNB 18 and YFNB 28; open barges YC 791, YC 797, YC 806, YC 807, YC 1108, YC 1320, YC 1414, and YC 1415; floating cranes HQ-9650 (ex-YD 230) and HQ-9651 (ex-YD 195); repair, berthing, and messing barges HQ-9610 (ex-YRBM 17), HQ-9612 (ex-YRBM 16), HQ-9613 (ex-YRBM 21), and HQ- . . . (ex-YRBM 18); barracks barges HQ-9050 (ex-APL 26) and HQ-9051 (ex-APL 27); repair barges HQ-9601 (ex-YR 24) and HQ-9611 (ex-YR 71); and water barge HQ-9113 (ex-YWN 153). In addition to the ships and craft listed, the Vietnamese Navy undoubtedly employs many smaller craft ("junks") in patrol and logistics duties.

COAST GUARD

Note: Formed in 1998, the Coast Guard does not yet appear to have any craft of its own. To meet a requirement for four to six seagoing patrol craft, Russia's Almaz Central Design Bureau has offered a variant of its Mirazh-class (Project 14310) and the United Kingdom's Vosper Thornycroft, a 34-m version of the *Sentinel,* built for the UK Customs and Excise Service in 1994; the winning design would be built locally in Vietnam.

VIRGIN ISLANDS

British Virgin Islands

ROYAL VIRGIN ISLANDS POLICE FORCE

Base: Road Town, Tortola

PATROL BOATS [WPB]

♦ 1 U.S. 40-ft. Dauntless class
Bldr: SeaArk Marine, Monticello, Ark. (In serv. 1-94)

PB 1

D: 15 tons (fl) **S:** 28 kts **Dim:** 12.19 (11.13 wl) × 3.86 × 0.69 (hull)
A: 2 single 12.7-mm mg; 2 single 7.62-mm mg
Electronics: Radar: 1 Raytheon R40X nav.
M: 2 Caterpillar 3208TA diesels; 2 props; 850 bhp (720 sust.)
Range: 200/30; 400/22 **Fuel:** 250 gallons **Crew:** 5 tot.

Remarks: U.S. Grant-aid. Aluminum construction. C. Raymond Hunt, deep-vee hull design. This unit is not the same boat as the U.S. Customs Service's PB 1, which is similar but has a different propulsion plant.

♦ 1 M 160 class
Bldr: Halmatic, Hamble, U.K. (In serv. 4-7-88)

ST. URSULA

PATROL BOATS [WPB] *(continued)*

St. Ursula P. H. Nargeolet, 1998

D: 17.3 tons (fl) **S:** 27+ knots **Dim:** 15.40 (12.20 pp) × 3.86 × 1.15
A: 1 7.62-mm mg **Electronics:** Radar: 1 Decca 370BT nav.
M: 2 G.M. Detroit Diesel 6V92 TA diesels; 2 props; 1,100 bhp (770 sust.)
Range: 300/20 **Fuel:** 2,700 liters **Crew:** 6 tot.

Remarks: Provided by U.K. government; sisters in several other Caribbean island countries. Glass-reinforced plastic construction. Refitted 1995. Has davits aft for inflatable inspection boat.

♦ **2 Model SR5M Searider dinghies**
Bldr: Avon, U.K. (In serv. 1986)

Remarks: Semi-rigid inflatables with 70-bhp Evinrude outboards; replaced two Sea Eagle RIBs delivered 1980.

YEMEN

YEMEN ARAB REPUBLIC

Personnel: Approx. 1,700 total, plus 500 naval port police.

Bases: Principal bases at Aden and Hodeida, with minor facilities at Al Katib, Mukalla, Perim, and Socotra.

Coastal Defense: Two truck-mounted batteries for SSC-3 Styx-series antiship missiles were supplied by the U.S.S.R. during the 1980s and may still be operational; each truck carries two missiles. On Perim Island, several fixed 100-mm guns in tank turrets are emplaced.

GUIDED MISSILE PATROL CRAFT [PTG]

♦ **1 Tarantul-I class (Project 1241RE)**
Bldr: Volodarskiy SY, Rybinsk (Del.: 7-12-90)

124 (ex-971)

D: 385 tons light (455 fl) **S:** 43 kts
Dim: 56.10 (49.50 pp) × 10.20 (9.40 wl) × 2.14 hull (3.59 props)
A: 4 P-20/P-21 Termit (SS-N-2C Styx) SSM; 1 76.2-mm 59-cal. AK-176 DP; 1 4-round MTU-40S (SA-N-8) SAM syst. (12 Gremlin missiles); 2 single 30-mm 54-cal. AK-630 gatling AA (see Remarks)
Electronics:
Radar: 1 Kivach-3 nav.; 1 Garpun-E (Plank Shave) targeting; 1 MR-123 Vympel (Bass Tilt) gun f.c.
EW: 2 16-round PK-16 decoy RL
M: M-15E COGAG plant: 2 DMR-76 cruise gas turbines (4,000 shp each), 2 PR-77 boost gas turbines (12,000 shp each); 2 props; 32,000 shp
Electric: 500 kw tot. (2 × 200 kw, 1 × 100-kw diesel sets)
Range: 760/43; 1,400/13 **Fuel:** 122,634 liters **Endurance:** 10 days
Crew: 7 officers, 32 enlisted

Remarks: Survivor of two, of which one defected to Oman in mid-July 1994 but was later returned. Standard export version. Sister 125 (ex-976), inoperable as of 1998, had been discarded by 2001, and 124 is in only marginal condition and probably without antiship missiles.
Hull systems: Stainless-steel alloy, seven watertight compartment hull with aluminum-alloy superstructure, decks, and internal bulkheads. Very strongly constructed and rugged. Have difficulty maneuvering below 10 kts due to small size of rudders. The Project 1241RE export version of the Tarantul-I is also stated to have a range of 2,350 n.m. at 12–13 knots (at 34° C) and a maximum speed of 43 kts at 15° C (35 kts at 34° C).
Combat systems: Carry 252 ready-service rounds and another 150 in reserve for the 76.2-mm gun. Weapons system employs digital computers and has many backup features. Normally carried two infrared-homing and two radar-homing antiship missiles, but the Yemini Navy's missile storage and maintenance facility burned out in 1994, and there are probably no missiles available for the craft. The Garpun-E radar also serves as a passive intercept and targeting system.

124—under tow during delivery voyage U.S. Navy, 11-90

♦ **3 Chinese Hounan class (Chinese Project 021)**
Bldr: Jiangnan SY, Shanghai (In serv. 1995)

126 127 128

Hounan class 127 and 128—during delivery voyage 92 Wing Det., RAAF, 5-95

D: 175 tons light, 186.5 normal (205 fl) **S:** 35 kts
Dim: 38.75 × 7.60 × 1.7 (mean)
A: Provision for: 4 C.801 SSM; 1 2-round QW-1 Vanguard point-defense SAM syst.; 2 twin 30-mm 65-cal. Type 69 (AK-230) AA
Electronics: Radar: 1 Type 352C (Square Tie) surf. search/target desig.; 1 Type 347G gun f.c.
M: 3 Type 42-160 (M503A) diesels; 3 props; 12,000 bhp
Electric: 65 kw tot. **Range:** 800/30 **Crew:** 28 tot.

Remarks: Although one was completed by 9-93, the three units transferred to Yemen were not delivered until 5-95. Design is a variation of the Chinese Huangfeng class, itself a variant of the Russian Osa-I, but with two paired launch containers for C.801 rocket-powered antiship missiles located aft and a Type 347G gun fire-control radar added; the superstructure is somewhat wider than in the Huangfeng version. 128 ran aground in 9-97 but has been repaired; at least two, however, are said to be in poor condition. Based at Al Katib.
Hull systems: Soviet-made M503A multi-row radial diesels are difficult to maintain and offer only about 600 hours between overhauls; it is likely that the Chinese-made 42-160 version is even less reliable.
Combat systems: The two-round, manned infrared-homing SAM launcher is mounted amidships, atop the superstructure; the missile is said to be a copy of the Russian SA-18. The antiship missiles may no longer be operational, and the missile tubes had been removed by mid-2002.

Disposal notes: Of eight Osa-II-class guided-missile patrol craft transferred to Yemen from 2-79 to 9-83, five were lost or irreparably damaged during the Yemeni Civil War of 1994 and the three survivors—118, 121, and 122—were retired from service in 2004.

PATROL BOATS [PB]

♦ **10 37-meter patrol boats**
Bldr: Austal Ships, Henderson, Western Australia (In serv. 2005)

P-1022 through P-1031

PATROL BOATS [PB] *(continued)*

P-1022 RAN, 2004

D: 90 tons **S:** 29+ kts **Dim:** 37.5 (32.4 wl) × 7.2 × 2.2
A: 1 twin 25-mm naval gun; 2 single 12.7 mm mg **Electronics:** . . .
M: 2 Caterpillar 3512 diesels; 2 props; **Range:** 1000/25
Fuel: 27,000 liters **Crew:** 19 tot.

Remarks: First unit was launched in 2-04. Intended for coastal patrols around the Gulf of Aden and surrounding waterways. A simplified version of an Australian Customs design, the craft were delivered simultaneously via heavy lift ship in 2005.

♦ 6 CMN 15-60 class
Bldr: CMN, Cherbourg, France (In serv. 1201–1205: 1-8-96; 1206: 1997)

1201 Baklan · 1202 Siyan · 1203 Zuhrab · 1204 Akissan · 1205 Hunaish · 1206 Zakr

Yemeni CMN 15-60–class unit on trials CMN, 1996

D: 12 tons (fl) **S:** 60 kts (55 sust.) **Dim:** 15.50 (12.00 pp) × 3.00 × 0.80
A: 1 12.7-mm mg **Electronics:** Radar: 1 Furuno . . . nav.
M: 2 . . . diesels; 2 Arneson outdrive props; 1,680 bhp
Range: 500/35 **Crew:** 6 tot.

Remarks: Ordered 3-96 at onset of Hanish Islands crisis with Eritrea. Operational deployment of the craft held up through 4-97 by a lack of spares and maintenance support. Referred to by builder as an "ultra-fast interceptor" for police, antismuggling, surveillance, special forces, strike, and liaison duties. Four (with an option for two more) were ordered for Qatar in 1-03.
Hull systems: GRP hull and superstructure. Equipped with GPS receiver, computer-aided navigation system, and HF/VHF/UHF transceivers.

♦ 2 Soviet Zhuk class (Project 1400M)

202 203

Yemeni Zhuk 1981

D: 35.9 tons (39.7 fl) **S:** 30 kts
Dim: 23.80 (21.70 wl) × 5.00 (3.80 wl) × 1.00 (hull; 1.90 max.)
A: 2 twin 12.7-mm 60-cal. Utës-Ma mg
Electronics: Radar: 1 Lotsiya nav.
M: 2 M-401 diesels; 2 props; 2,200 bhp
Electric: 48 kw total (2 × 21-kw, 1 × 6-kw diesel sets)
Range: 500/13.5 **Endurance:** 5 days **Crew:** 1 officer, 9 enlisted

Remarks: Two transferred to former Yemen Arab Republic (North Yemen) in 12-84 and three in 1-87; two transferred to People's Democratic Republic of Yemen (South Yemen) in 2-75. The two survivors are believed to be the former North Yemeni boats; sisters 303 and 404 were discarded around 1997. The twin machineguns are mounted in enclosed gun houses with hemispherical covers. The pair is used for a myriad of duties, including target towing.

MINE-COUNTERMEASURES SHIPS AND CRAFT

♦ 1 Natya-I-class (Project 266ME) minesweeper [MSF]
Bldr: Sudostroitel'noye Obyedineniye "Almaz" (Sredniy Neva), Kolpino (In serv. 3-91)

201 (ex-641)

Yemeni Natya-I-class 201—at Aden Rahn via Werner Globke, 6-02

D: 750 tons std., 804 tons normal (873 fl) **S:** 17.6 kts (16 sust.)
Dim: 61.00 (57.6 wl) × 10.20 × 2.98 hull
A: 2 single 30-mm 54-cal. AK-630M gatling AA; 2 4-round Fasta-4M (SA-N-8) SAM syst. (16 Gremlin missiles); 2 5-round RBU-1200 ASW RL
Electronics:
Radar: 1 Don-2 nav.
Sonar: MG-89 HF hull-mounted (49 kHz)
M: 2 M-503B-3E diesels: 2 shrouded CP props; 5,000 bhp
Electric: 600 kw tot. (3 × 200 kw DGR-200/1500 diesel sets)
Range: 1,800/16; 3,000/12; 5,200/10 **Endurance:** 10–15 days
Crew: 8 officers, 59 enlisted

Remarks: A sister, bearing pennant 634, was delivered to Ethiopia in 1991 and defected to Yemen shortly thereafter; the ship was eventually interned at Djibouti in 1993 and was sold for disposal in 1996. Both were of a new variant with single 30-mm AK-630 gatling guns substituted for the twin 30-mm AK-230 mounts, but without 25-mm guns, fire-control radar, or net trawl facilities. Equipped also to serve as ASW escorts, with the RBU-1200 rocket launchers also used for detonating mines.
Hull systems: Stem cut back sharply below waterline. Low magnetic signature, aluminum-steel alloy hull. Has a DGR-450/1500P diesel-driven degaussing system.
Combat systems: The two SAM launchers are located just abaft the lattice mast. Sweep gear includes SEMP-3 magnetic and MPT-3 mechanical minesweeping arrays. The sonar incorporates a downward-looking, high-frequency, bottomed mine-detection component. Can deploy t.v. minehunting equipment. Has two short minerails.

♦ 5 Soviet Yevgenya-class (Project 1258) inshore minehunter/sweepers [MSI]
Bldr: Sudostroitel'noye Obyedineniye "Almaz" (Sredniy Neva), Kolpino

11 12 15 20 . . .

D: 88.5 tons light, 94.5 normal (97.9 fl) **S:** 11 kts
Dim: 26.13 (24.20 wl) × 5.90 (5.10 wl) × 1.38
A: 1 twin 25-mm 80-cal. 2M-3M AA
Electronics:
Radar: 1 Mius (Spin Trough) nav.
Sonar: MG-7 HF dipping
M: 2 Type 3D12 diesels; 2 props; 600 bhp—hydraulic slow-speed drive
Electric: 100 kw tot. (2 × 50-kw diesel sets)
Range: 400/10 **Fuel:** 2.7 tons **Endurance:** 3 days
Crew: 1 officer, 9 enlisted (+ 2–3 mine-clearance divers)

Remarks: First two delivered to North Yemen 5-82, third in 11-87. The People's Democratic Republic of Yemen (South Yemen) received two in 12-89. Three are based at Aden and two at Al Katib, but as many as three may be nonoperational.
Hull systems: Glass-reinforced plastic hull. Navigational equipment includes Girya-MA gyrocompass, and NEL-7 echo sounder.
Combat systems: Can employ a Neva-1 television minehunting system useful to 30-m depths that dispenses marker buoys to permit later disposal of mines by divers or explosive charges. The sonar is lowered via one of the stern davits. Carry VKT-1 mechanical, AT-2 acoustic, and SEMT-1 solenoid coil sweep gear.

AMPHIBIOUS WARFARE SHIPS AND CRAFT

♦ 1 Polish Project NS-722 medium landing ship [LSM]
Bldr: Stocznia Marynarki Wojennj, Gdynia (In serv. 7-02)

Bilqis

D: 1,363 tons normal (1,410 fl) **S:** 17 kts
Dim: 88.70 (79.00 pp) × 10.00 × 2.40
A: 1 30-mm 54-cal. AK-630M gatling AA; 1 twin 23-mm 87-cal. ZU-23-2 Wrobel-I AA; 2 4-round Fasta-4M (WM-4) launchers for Strela-2M SAMs; 2 single 12.7-mm ZM Turnow mg; 2 20-round 122-mm WM 122/20 artillery rocket launchers

AMPHIBIOUS WARFARE SHIPS AND CRAFT *(continued)*

Bilqis Jaroslaw Malinowski, 2002

Bilqis Jaroslaw Cislak, 5-02

Electronics: Radar: 2 . . . nav. (1 X-band, 1 S-band)
M: 2 Caterpillar 3516B diesels; 2 CP props; 5,200 bhp
Electric: 1,000 kw tot. (4 × 250-kw Caterpillar 3406 B DIT diesels driving)
Range: 2,300/15; 3,600/12 **Endurance:** 30 days **Crew:** 49 tot. + 111 troops

Remarks: Ordered 10-99 but canceled by Poland in 2-00 when the Polish ambassador to Yemen was kidnapped; later reinstated after his release. Is of export version developed for India in the late 1980s but not purchased. Intended for use as a cadet training ship and for disaster relief in addition to amphibious warfare role. Departed Polish waters on 24-5-02 as deck cargo, arriving on 1-8-02 at Aden.
Hull systems: Is able to transport five 42-ton tanks in addition to the troops. Has a flight platform aft for an Agusta-Bell AB-205 or other 4-ton-class helicopter. The weapons control system is named the Sarmat. The listed 30-mm gunmount may not initially be installed. Up to 169 troops can be carried for short periods, and the maximum cargo weight is 290 tons (five 42-ton tanks can be accommodated).

♦ 3 Deba-class (Project NS-717) utility landing craft [LCU]
Bldr: Stocznia Marynarki Wojennej, Gdynia (In serv. 30-6-01)

ABDULKORI (ex-*Thamoud*) HIMYER (ex-*Dhaffar*) SAB'A

Two Yemeni Deba-class landing craft Piet Sinke, 5-01

Deba-class landing craft—aboard heavy-lift ship *Jumbo Vision* for delivery Jaroslaw Cislak, 5-01

D: 238 tons (fl) **S:** 16 kts (15 kts sust.)
Dim: 41.10 (37.00 pp.) × 7.20 (6.60 wl) × 1.68
A: 1 twin 23-mm 87-cal. ZU-23-2 Wrobel-I AA; 2 single 12.7-mm ZM Tarnow mg
Electronics: Radar: 1 SRN-207A nav.
M: 3 Caterpillar 3508B diesels; 3 props; 3,150 bhp
Electric: 300 kw tot. (4 × 75 kw Caterpillar 3304 DIT diesel-alternator sets: 400 V, 50 Hz)
Range: 750/14.5; 1,150/9 **Endurance:** 6 days **Crew:** 10 tot. + 50 troops

Remarks: Order placed during 10-99 to a tropicalized version of a design delivered to the Polish Navy during 1989–90; work began 9-2-00, after a delay caused by the kidnapping of the Polish ambassador to Yemen. Can carry a 37-ton payload.

Note: A utility landing craft capable of transporting tanks was said to be under construction for Yemen at a U.A.E. shipyard as of 4-97; the craft had arrived at Aden by 6-02 and is unarmed; no further information is available.

♦ 2 ex-Soviet Ondatra-class (Project 1176) landing craft [LCM]
(In serv. 1971–79)

13 14

D: 90 tons normal (107.3 fl) **S:** 11.5 kts
Dim: 24.50 × 6.00 × 1.55 **A:** none
Electronics: Radar: 1 Mius (Spin Trough) nav. (portable)
M: 2 Type 3D-12 diesels; 2 props; 600 bhp **Range:** 330/10; 500/5
Endurance: 2 days **Crew:** 6 tot. (enlisted)

Remarks: In all, 29 were built for use aboard Soviet *Ivan Rogov*–class landing ships. Two were transferred to Yemen in 1983. Cargo well is 13.7 × 3.9 m and can accommodate one 40-ton tank or up to 50 tons of general cargo; some 20 troops/vehicle crew can be carried.

SERVICE CRAFT

Notes: A 4,500-ton, Soviet-supplied commercial floating dry dock is available at Aden. The Yemen Department of Maritime Affairs at Aden operates the *Zuqar*, an 18.13 × 5.38 × 1.70–m oil-pollution-control boat delivered late in 1999 by Halmatic, U.K.; the craft is powered by two MTU 12V183 TE 72 diesels (810 bhp each) for a 20.5-kt maximum speed and is fitted with onboard tanks for 6,200 liters of spillage, a spray system, and a 400-m floating containment boom. Navigation equipment includes Raytheon SL70 radar and 620 GPS.

COAST GUARD

A Yemeni Coast Guard has recently begun to take shape and operations started during 2005–, following the 2004 delivery of eight retired U.S. Coast Guard 44-ft craft.

♦ 8 ex-U.S. Coast Guard 44-ft. rescue launches [WYH]
Bldr: U.S.C.G. Yard, Curtis Bay, Md. (In serv. 31-3-61 to 8-5-73)

D: 14.9 tons light (17.7 fl) **S:** 13 kts (11.8 sust.) **Dim:** 13.44 × 3.87 × 1.19
Electronics: Radar: 1 SPS-57 nav.
M: 2 G.M. Detroit Diesel 6V53 diesels; 2 props; 372 bhp
Range: 185/11.8; 200/11 **Fuel:** 1.2 tons **Crew:** 4 tot.

Remarks: Donated and transferred 2004. "Unsinkable" design. Can carry up to 21 rescued personnel.

ZIMBABWE

REPUBLIC OF ZIMBABWE

Bases: Binga and Harare. The following patrol boats are operated along Lake Kariba for patrol, medical assistance, and supply duties.

PATROL BOATS [WPB]

♦ 2 Rodman 46HJ patrol boats
Bldr: Rodman Polyships, Vigo, Spain (In serv. 1999)

D: 12.5 tons (fl) **S:** 30 kts **Dim:** 14 × 3.8 × 0.6
M: 2 Caterpillar 3280 diesels; 2 props; 850 bhp **Crew:** 4
Range: 350/18

Remarks: Used on patrol, medical assistance, and supply duties.

♦ 3 Rodman 38 patrol boats
Bldr: Rodman Polyships, Vigo, Spain (In serv. 1999)

D: 10 tons (fl) **S:** 28 kts **Dim:** 11 × 3.9 × 0.7
M: 2 . . . diesels; 2 props; . . . bhp **Crew:** 4
Range: 300/15

Remarks: Used on patrol, medical assistance, and supply duties.

♦ 5 Rodman 26 patrol boats
Bldr: Rodman Polyships, Vigo, Spain (In serv. 1999)

D: 2.4 tons (fl) **S:** 30 kts **Dim:** 8.1 × 2.7 × 0.7
M: 2 Volvo-Penta . . . diesels; 2 props; . . . bhp **Crew:** 2

Remarks: Used on patrol, medical assistance, and supply duties.

Disposal note: All eight Type B 79 lake patrol boats: *Chipo Chebelgium* (KF 590), *Mudzimundiringe* (KF 591), *Chirovamura* (KF 592), *Vamashayamombe* (KF 593), *Chayamura Varwere* (KF 594), *Chifambisa Nyore* (KF 595), *Chiorora Mvura* (KF 596), and *Chibatanidza Matunhu* (KF 597) have been replaced by the 10 Rodman boats currently in service.

ADDENDA

ALGERIA

In 2006 a contract was signed to upgrade Algeria's two Kilo-class submarines, *Raïs Hadj M'Barek* (012) and *El Hadj Slimane* (013). The modernizations, which are to take place in Russia, will reportedly be completed by 2007 and include upgrades to launch Russian Klub antiship missiles. Media reports also indicate that two additional Kilo-class submarines have been ordered at a cost of roughly $400 million, though no delivery date has yet been announced.

ARGENTINA

Concerns over asbestos use in the two retired French *Ouragan*-class dock landing ships, ex-*Ouragan* and ex-*Ourage,* have delayed their delivery to Argentina and as of February 2007, the ships remain in French waters.

Orage (L 9022)—though transfer was finalized in early 2006, the vessel remains in French waters. Bernard Prézelin, 2003

AUSTRIA

The Austrian Army Danube Flotilla was disestablished on 1 August 2006. All remaining service craft and patrol boats, including *Niederösterreich* (A 604) and *Oberst Brecht* (A 601), have been retired and may be turned into museum ships.

AUSTRALIA

The updated commissioning table for the *Armidale*-class patrol boat program is as follows:

♦ **9 (+ 5) Armidale-class Replacement Patrol Boat project**
Bldr: Austal Ships, Henderson, Western Australia

	In serv.		In serv.
ACPB 83 Armidale	25-6-05	ACPB 90 Broome	2-07
ACPB 84 Larrakia	10-2-06	ACPB 91 Bundaberg	2-07
ACPB 85 Bathurst	10-2-06	ACPB 92 Wollongong	6-07
ACPB 86 Albany	15-7-06	ACPB 93 Childers	5-07
ACPB 87 Pirie	29-7-06	ACPB 94 Launceston	9-07
ACPB 88 Maitland	29-9-06	ACPB 95 Maryborough	. . .
ACPB 89 Ararat	13-11-06	ACPB 96 Glenelg	. . .

All but four remaining *Fremantle*-class patrol craft were decommissioned by 12-06. Units remaining in service as of 2-07 are *Townsville* (FCPB 205), *Launceston* (FCPB 207), *Ipswich* (FCPB 209), and *Gladstone* (FCPB 216).

Underway replenishment oiler *Westralia* (AO-195) was decommissioned on 16-9-06 and has been replaced by the 37,000-ton underway replenishment ship *Sirius.*

BELGIUM

The two retired *Karel Doorman*–class frigates that are being transferred from the Netherlands during 2007–8 will be the ex-*Willem Van Der Zaan* (F 829) and ex-*Karel Doorman* (827). The warships are to be renamed *Louise-Marie* (F 931) and *Leopold I* (F 930) respectively.

BULGARIA

As of 1-07, the Bulgarian Navy was negotiating to purchase the remaining two *Wielingen*-class frigates from Belgium

CANADA

Repairs estimated to cost in excess of 100 million Canadian dollars have delayed service reentry (until 2010) of the submarine *Chicoutimi* (SS 879), which was damaged by a serious onboard fire in October 2004. Two of the four *Victoria*-class submarines, *Cornerbrook* (SS 878) and *Windsor* (SS 877), are now back at sea while *Victoria* (SS 876) undergoes an extended maintenance overhaul prior to a planned 2008 return to service.

In November 2006, the Canadian Navy accepted *Orca*, the first of eight new training craft, into service. Built by Victoria Shipyards, the ship names for all eight of the class—*Orca*, *Raven*, *Grizzly*, *Wolf*, *Renard* (fox), *Caribou*, *Moose*, and *Cougar*—are derived from Canadian "symbolisms based on various aboriginal cultures." The class will serve as replacements for the aging fleet of YAG 300–class wooden-hulled training launches. With an overall length of 33 meters and a displacement of 210 tons, the *Orca* is operated by four sailors along with 16 trainees and carries up to four spare berths. The craft can cruise for up to 660 nautical miles at 15 knots with a maximum endurance of 4 days and have a maximum speed of 18 knots.

Orca (55) Victoria Shipyards via D. Shirlaw, 2006

CHILE

Retired U.K. Type 23 frigate ex-*Norfolk* was transferred to Chile on 22-11-06 and renamed *Almirante Cochrane* (05). The new warship replaces destroyer *Almirante Cochrane* (12, ex-*Antrim*), which was decommissioned in late 2006.

CHINA

In late 2006 China ordered six Pomornik (Zubr)-class (Project 1232.2) air-cushion vehicle landing craft from Almaz Shipbuilders in St. Petersburg, Russia. No estimated delivery date has been announced.

DENMARK

Flyvefisken-class (Stanflex 300) patrol craft *Sværdfisken* (P 556), *Flyvefisken* (P 550), *Hajen* (P 551), and *Lommen* (P 559) were decommissioned by late 2006 as a result of budget cuts finalized in the 2005–9 Defense Plan. They will most likely be transferred to Lithuania.

ECUADOR

Two British *Leander*-class frigates have reportedly been purchased from Chile. The new ships are expected to transfer to Ecuador during 2007–8.

EGYPT

Transfer from the United States of the Osprey-class coastal minehunters *Raven* (MHC 61) and *Cardinal* (60) has been delayed due to engineering and other difficulties.

GERMANY

Type 332 coastal minehunters *Weilheim* (M 1059) and *Frankenthal* (M 1066) were decommissioned from German and transferred to the United Arab Emirates in late June 2006.

GREECE

Service entry for Greece's first Type 214–class submarine, *Papanikolis,* has been delayed after several major problems were uncovered; primary among these were reported flaws in the submarine's air-independent propulsion system. Other problems include an overall lack of stability while surfaced, excessive propeller cavitation, and difficulty with attack periscope vibrations. The defects may cause slippage of planned delivery and operational dates for sister submarines *Pipinos, Matrozos,* and *Katsonis.*

Ex-Dutch *Kortenaer*-class frigates *Kontouriotis* (F 462) and *Adrias* (F 459) had both completed their planned midlife modernizations by 11-06.

INDIA

In January 2007 the U.S. Navy transferred the decommissioned *Austin*-class amphibious transport dock *Trenton* (LPD 14) to the Indian Navy where she has been renamed *Jalashwa* (L 41). Four LCM (8) landing craft were also transferred for use with the ship.

Jalashwa (L 41)—while still in U.S. Navy service U.S. Navy, 2004

In June 2007, India's navy expects to receive the first of twelve MiG-29K and four MiG-29KUB trainer aircraft that were ordered for use aboard the carrier *Vikramaditya.* Up to 40 MiG-29s may eventually be ordered.

Shardul, first of the new class of Tank Landing Ships built at Garden Reach shipbuilders in Calcutta, was commissioned on 4-1-07.

INDONESIA

In October 2006 Indonesia announced its decision to purchase two Amur 950 and four Kilo-class submarines from Russia. The Amur 950 design, which measures roughly 56 meters in length and displaces about 1,300 tons submerged, is a smaller export variant of the Russian Lada class. The selected submarines had been competing against the more capable, albeit more expensive, western European Type 214 and Scorpène-class designs. No details concerning price or expected delivery dates have been made available.

IRAQ

Six retired Italian Coast Guard patrol boats, CP 247, CP 250, CP 2036, CP 2037, CP 2067, and CP 2068, have been transferred to Iraq by 1-07 and renumbered P 701 through P 706. Four new construction Modified Italian *Ubaldo Diciotti*–class patrol craft have also been ordered with delivery planned for 2007–8.

The latest estimates on Iraqi personnel statistics indicate that about 700–800 naval personnel plus 200 Iraqi marines are currently in service. The force is organized into two patrol/assault boat squadrons and one Marine battalion.

KOREA, SOUTH

South Korea's first Type 214 submarine, named *Sohn Won-Il,* was launched on 9-6-06.

Tank landing ships *Unbong* (ex-LST-1010) and *Weebong* (ex-USS *Johnson County,* LST-849) were decommissioned on 28-12-06.

The sixth and final KDX-II class destroyer, *Chae Yaun* (980), was launched on 19-10-06.

LATVIA

The first of five retired Dutch *Alkmaar* (Tripartite)-class coastal minehunters was transferred to Latvia on 18-12-06 and has been renamed *Imanta.*

LITHUANIA

Upon retirement, two U.S. Navy Osprey-class minehunters are expected to transfer to Lithuania during 2007–8. Danish *Flyvefisken*-class (Stanflex 300) patrol craft *Sværdfisken* (P 556), *Flyvefisken* (P 550), *Hajen* (P 551), and *Lommen* (P 559) were decommissioned by late 2006 and will most likely be transferred to Lithuania. Neither deal has yet been finalized.

NEW ZEALAND

Moa-class naval reserve training/mine-warfare craft *Moa* (P 3553) and *Hinau* (P 3556) were decommissioned on 23-1-07. Sisters *Kiwi* (P 3554) and *Wakakura* (P 3555) are to follow later in the year.

OMAN

Three ocean patrol vessels were ordered from Vosper-Thornycroft in 1-07. The 100-meter vessels are expected to enter service between 2010 and 2011. Total program cost is estimated at £400 million.

PAKISTAN

Three new design Marlin-class submarines have been ordered from France. No additional details on the deal have yet been made public. Pakistan has expressed strong interest in purchasing four unmodernized ex-Dutch *Kortenaer*-class frigates from Greece. Broad-beam Leander-class frigate *Shamsher* (F 263) was reportedly decommissioned by 1-07.

PHILIPPINES

The Army has announced plans to acquire between 18 and 30 new short-range fast transport craft that are capable of traveling at 25 knots and can carry 150 troops for operations between islands.

PORTUGAL

Plans to purchase the retired U.S. *Oliver Hazard Perry*–class frigates ex-*George Philip* (FFG 12) and ex-*Sides* (FFG 14) were called off in 2006. Two decommissioned *Karel Doorman*–class frigates will likely be purchased from the Netherlands instead.

RUSSIA

On 10 November 2006 the warship *Stoiky,* the fourth *Steregushchiy*-class (Type 20380) small frigate, was laid down at Severnaya Verf in Saint Petersburg Russia.

On 24-12-06 a test launch of the SS-NX-30 Bulava SLBM failed. It is reportedly the missile's third test failure since September 2006.

Astrakhan, the first Buyan-class patrol craft built for the Russian Federal Border Guard was commissioned on 1-9-06.

SERBIA & MONTENEGRO

With the division of Serbia and Montenegro into separate states, the two nations have agreed to keep only those assets within their borders as of June 2006. Land-locked Serbia has disavowed all ownership of naval and maritime assets, which now below to the newly formed Republic of Montenegro. Though a large portion of Montenegro's inherited fleet will likely be decommissioned and sold off in the near future, the newly formed nation has expressed interest in purchasing two *Minerva*-class corvettes from Italy.

SPAIN

On 27-12-06 *Guardiamarina Barrutia*–class navigational training tender *Guardiamarina Chereuini* (A 85) was renamed *Contramaestre Lamadrid,* keeping the same hull number. Medium harbor tug Y 143 was decommissioned on the same date. Multipurpose workboat Y 541 was commissioned on 5-12-06.

TAIWAN

The U.S. Navy Osprey-class minehunters, *Oriole* (MHC 55) and *Falcon* (MHC 59), are expected to transfer to Taiwan by 2008

TURKEY

Kiliç-class patrol combatant *Zipkin* (P 336) and Aydin-class minehunter *Akçakoca* (M 268) were both launched on 28-9-06. The U.S. Navy *Osprey*-class minehunters *Black Hawk* (MHC 58) and *Shrike* (MHC 62) will likely transfer to Turkey by 2008.

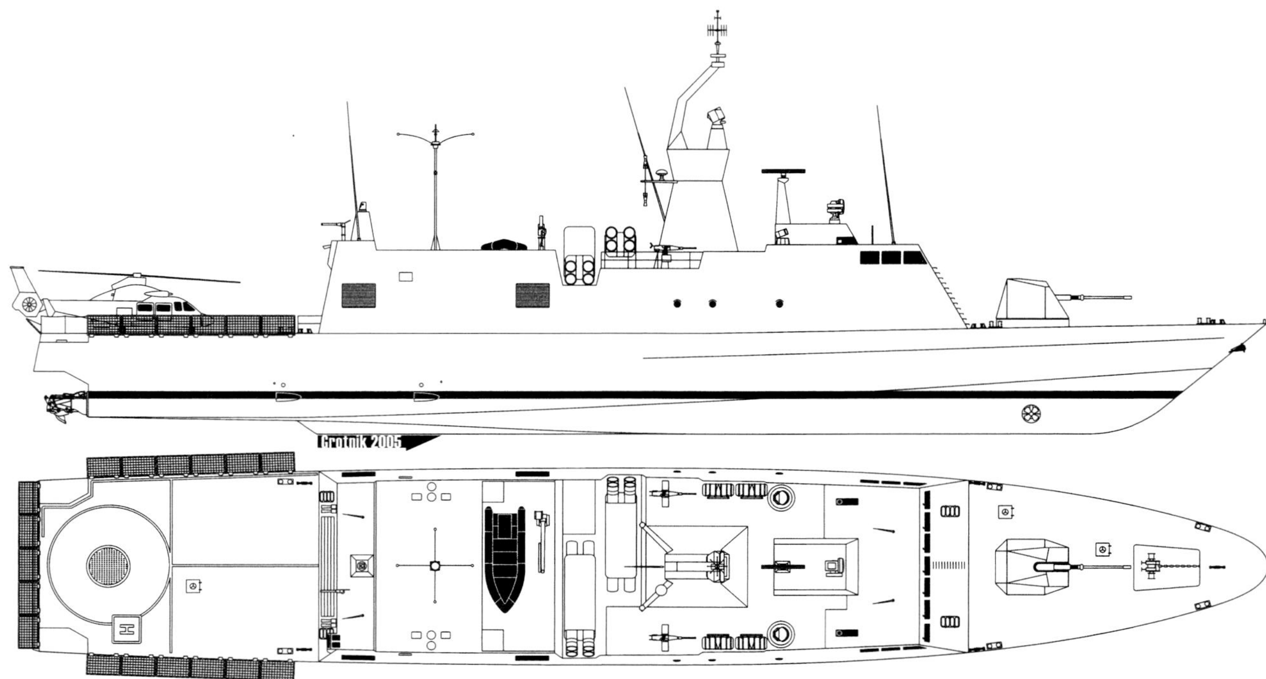

Baynunah class T. Grotnik, 2005

UNITED ARAB EMIRATES

The keel for the first *Baynunah*-class guided-missile patrol combatant was laid down on 6-7-06.

Al Murjan Michael Nitz, 2006

Type 332 coastal minehunters *Weilheim* (M 1059) and *Frankenthal* were decommissioned from Germany and transferred to the United Arab Emirates in late June 2006. They have been named *Al Hasbah* and *Al Murjan* respectively.

UNITED KINGDOM

The second *Daring* (Type 45)-class guided-missile destroyer, HMS *Dauntless* (D 33), was launched on 23-1-07.

Dauntless (D 33)—at launch D. Cullen, 2007

Faced with an estimated £1 billion in defense budgets cuts by 2008, the Ministry of Defence and Royal Navy again face major naval reductions. On the chopping block if the cuts come to fruition are the Type 42 destroyers *Exeter* (D 89) and *Southampton* (D 90), Type 22 frigates *Cumberland* (F 85), *Campbeltown* (F 86), *Chatham* (F 87), *Cornwall* (F 99), South Atlantic/Antarctic patrol ship *Endurance* (A 171), and the replenishment oilers *Brambleleaf* (A 81) and *Oakleaf* (A 111). Additionally, the number of Type 45 destroyers built may be reduced from eight to six.

U.S.A.

CVN 78, lead ship of the CVN 21-class aircraft carriers, was named *Gerald R. Ford* on 17-1-07. *John F. Kennedy* (CV 67) currently suffers from arrester gear corrosion and a host of other problems due to navy neglect and is scheduled to decommission by 30-9-07.

Los Angeles-class submarine *Hyman G. Rickover* (SSN 709) was deactivated from active service on 14-12-07. Sister *Honolulu* (SSN 718) was retired on 1-11-06 and her bow is to be removed and used to repair the damaged submarine *San Francisco* (SSN 711). Research submarine *Dolphin* (AGSS 555), the last diesel-powered submarine operated by the U.S. Navy, was officially decommissioned on 15-1-07.

Arleigh Burke Flight IIA–class destroyer *Gridley* (DDG 101) was delivered on 15-9-06 and commissioned on 16-1-07; sister *Kidd* (DDG 100) was delivered on 18-12-06 and is scheduled to commission on 9-6-07.

The cost of the U.S. Navy's Littoral Combat Ship (LCS) program continues to rise. On 12-1-07 the navy took the drastic step of a 90-day work stoppage on LCS 3 in order to investigate cost escalation.

Current plans call for *Tarawa*-class amphibious assault ship *Saipan* (LHA 3) to decommission on 27-4-07. *San Antonio*-class dock landing ship *New Orleans* (LPD 18) was delivered on 22-12-06 and is scheduled to enter service on 30-3-07; sister *Green Bay* (LPD 20) was launched on 11-8-06.

By 2008 *Osprey*-class minehunters *Oriole* (MHC 55) and *Falcon* (MHC 59) are expected to transfer to Taiwan, *Kingfisher* (MHC 56) and *Cormorant* (MHC 57) to Lithuania, and *Black Hawk* (MHC 58) and *Shrike* (MHC 62) to Turkey. Sisters *Heron* (MHC 52) and *Pelican* (MHC 53) are due to retire on 17-3-07 and possibly transfer to Greece.

Coast Guard icebreaker *Polar Star* (WAGB 10) was placed in a unique caretaker status on 20-6-06 as a maintenance and cost-saving measure. A decision on renovating the ship is expected in 2007. Coast Guard cutter *Storis* (WMEC 38) was decommissioned in 2-07.

VIETNAM

Two Gepard (Project 11661)-class frigates were ordered from Russia on 22-12-06. No estimated delivery dates have yet been announced.

VIRGIN ISLANDS

M 160–class patrol boat *St. Ursula,* in service since 1988, was retired during 12-06 and has been replaced by a new all-aluminum craft of the same name. Data for the new patrol boat appears below:

♦ 1 55-ft. Dauntless class

Bldr: SeaArk Marine, Monticello, Arkansas (In serv. 12-06)

St. Ursula

D: 17.7 tons (fl) **S:** 32 kts **Dim:** 16.76 (15.24 wl) × 1.52 max.
A: . . . **Electronics:** Radar: 1 Furuno . . . nav.
M: 2 Caterpillar C-15 diesels; 2 props; 1,600 bhp
Electric: 16 kw tot. (1 16-kw diesel set)
Crew: 4 tot. **Range:** 300/28 **Fuel:** 800 gallons

INDEX BY SHIPS

All ships are indexed by their full names, e.g., Almirante José Toribo Merino. Abbreviated ranks and titles are indexed as if spelled out.

Aeriell Youngbar

About the Editor

Eric Wertheim is a defense consultant, columnist, and author specializing in naval and maritime issues. He was named editor of the Naval Institute's *Guide to Combat Fleets of the World* in 2002.

As the editor of *Combat Fleets* his duties include tracking, analyzing, and compiling data and photography on every vessel, aircraft, and major weapon system, serving in every naval and paranaval force in the world.

From 1994 through 2004 Mr. Wertheim wrote the bimonthly "Lest We Forget" column on historic U.S. warships for the Naval Institute's *Proceedings* magazine. In 2004 the first of his monthly "Combat Fleets" columns began appearing in *Proceedings,* and his annual review of world navies runs in the March issue of the magazine.

Mr. Wertheim is the co-author (with Norman Polmar) of the books *Chronology of the Cold War at Sea* (1998) and *Dictionary of Military Abbreviations* (1994), both published by the Naval Institute Press. From 1995 to 1996 he worked for Jane's Information Group, publisher of *Jane's Defence Weekly* magazine.

In addition to his naval and maritime writing, Mr. Wertheim works for the defense consulting firm Science Applications International Corporation (SAIC), where he has taken part in numerous studies for the U.S. Air Force, North Atlantic Treaty Organization, and Joint Non-Lethal Weapons Directorate. He currently consults as a communications adviser to several senior defense officials.

Bringing a unique perspective to international naval analysis and writing, Mr. Wertheim is a former Washington, D.C., police officer (Reserve) and graduate of the District of Columbia's Metropolitan Police Academy. Mr. Wertheim was named Reserve Police Officer of the Year in 1997. He holds degrees in political science and history from American University in Washington, D.C.

The Naval Institute Press is the book-publishing arm of the U.S. Naval Institute, a private, nonprofit, membership society for sea service professionals and others who share an interest in naval and maritime affairs. Established in 1873 at the U.S. Naval Academy in Annapolis, Maryland, where its offices remain today, the Naval Institute has members worldwide.

Members of the Naval Institute support the education programs of the society and receive the influential monthly magazine *Proceedings* and discounts on fine nautical prints and on ship and aircraft photos. They also have access to the transcripts of the Institute's Oral History Program and get discounted admission to any of the Institute-sponsored seminars offered around the country. Discounts are also available to the colorful bimonthly magazine *Naval History*.

The Naval Institute's book-publishing program, begun in 1898 with basic guides to naval practices, has broadened its scope to include books of more general interest. Now the Naval Institute Press publishes about seventy titles each year, ranging from how-to books on boating and navigation to battle histories, biographies, ship and aircraft guides, and novels. Institute members receive significant discounts on the Press's more than eight hundred books in print.

Full-time students are eligible for special half-price membership rates. Life memberships are also available.

For a free catalog describing Naval Institute Press books currently available, and for further information about subscribing to *Naval History* magazine or about joining the U.S. Naval Institute, please write to:

Member Services
U.S. Naval Institute
291 Wood Road
Annapolis, MD 21402-5034
Telephone: (800) 233-8764
Fax: (410) 269-7940
Web address: www.navalinstitute.org